7/73

The Dictionary Catalog of the
United States
DEPARTMENT of HOUSING
and
URBAN DEVELOPMENT

Library and Information Division

Washington, D. C.

Volume 16

Strei—United R

G. K. HALL & CO., 70 LINCOLN STREET, BOSTON, MASSACHUSETTS

1972

This publication is printed on permanent/durable acid-free paper.

ISBN 0-8161-1007-7

362.6
S77
Streib, Gordon F
Retirement in American society; impact and process, by Gordon F. Streib and Clement J. Schneider. Ithaca, Cornell University Press, 1971.
316p.

Bibliography: p. 303-310.

1. Old age. 2. Old age - Employment
I. Schneider, Clement J., jt. au. II. Title.

691.11
M17
STRENGTH AND RELATED PROPERTIES OF WOODS GROWN IN THE UNITED STATES.
MARKWARDT, LORRAINE JOSEPH, 1889-
STRENGTH AND RELATED PROPERTIES OF WOODS GROWN IN THE UNITED STATES. BY L.J. MARKWARDT AND T.R.C. WILSON. WASHINGTON, GOVT. PRINT. OFF., 1935.
99P. (U.S. DEPT. OF AGRICULTURE. TECHNICAL BULLETIN NO. 479)

CONTRIBUTION FROM FOREST SERVICE.
LITERATURE CITES : P. 74-77.

1. WOOD. I. WILSON, THOMAS RANDALL CARSON, 1884- , JT. AU.
II. TITLE. (SERIES)

691.32
H15b
Strength of concrete-in compression determined by the Schmidthammer.
Hansen, Henry.
Betongfasthet bestemt ved hjelp av Schmidthammer (Strength of concrete in compression determined by the Schmidthammer) av Henry Hansen og David Togba. Oslo, Norges Byggforskningsinstitutt, 1968.
[3]p. (Oslo. Norges Byggforskningsinstitutt. Saertrykk 154)
Saertrykk fra Betongen idag, nr. 1, 1968.
1. Concrete. 2. Strength of materials.
I. Togba, David, jt. au. II. Oslo. Norges Byggforsknings institutt. III. Title: Strength of concrete in compression determined by the Schmidthammer.

362.6
W34
1971
no. 4
Streib, Gordon F
White House Conference on Aging, Washington, 1971.
Retirement roles and activities; background, by Gordon F. Streib. Issues, by the Technical Committee on Retirement Roles and Activities, with the collaboration of the author. Wash., 1971.
33p. [no. 4]
Cover title: Background and issues; retirement roles and activities.
Bibliography: p. 31-33.
1. Old age. I. Streib, Gordon F.
II. Title.

691.32
I55
STRENGTH AND STABILITY OF CONCRETE MASONRY WALLS.
ILLINOIS. UNIVERSITY. ENGINEERING EXPERIMENT STATION.
STRENGTH AND STABILITY OF CONCRETE MASONRY WALLS; A REPORT ON AN INVESTIGATION... BY FRANK E. RICHART AND OTHERS. URBANA, UNIVERSITY OF ILLINOIS, 1932.
38P. (ITS BULLETIN 251)

UNIVERSITY OF ILLINOIS BULLETIN
V. 29, NO. 89.

1. CONCRETE - RESEARCH.
2. CONCRETE CONSTRUCTION.
(CONTINUED ON NEXT CARD)

690.22
B31
Strength of concrete in high strength revibrated walls.
Bhargava, Jitendra.
Strength of concrete in high strength revibrated walls. Stockholm, National Swedish Institute for Building Research, 1969.
45p. (Stockholm. Statens Institut för Byggnadsforskning. Document no. 6:1969)
Bibliography: p. 35-39.

1. Walls. 2. Concrete construction. 3. Strength of materials. I. Stockholm. Statens Institut för Byggnadsforskning.
II. Title.

691.16
Y17
Strength and creep of laminated plastics.
Yatsenko, V F
Strength and creep of laminated plastics (Prochnost i polzuchest sloistykh plastikov) New Delhi, Published for National Aeronautics and Space Administration and the National Science Foundation by the Indian National Scientific Documentation Centre, 1970.
237p. (TT 67-59014; NASA TT F 461)
Bibliography: p. 229-237.
Naukova Dumka, Kiev, 1966.
Translated from Russian.
1. Plastics. 2. Strength of materials.
(Cont'd on next card)

691.32
I55
ILLINOIS. UNIVERSITY. ENGINEERING EXPERIMENT STATION. STRENGTH AND STABILITY ...1932. (CARD 2)

3. WALLS. I. RICHART, FRANK E.
II. TITLE.

301.158
K88
Strength of ethnic identification and intergenerational mobility aspirations among...
Kuvlesky, William P
Strength of ethnic identification and intergenerational mobility aspirations among Mexican American youth, by William P. Kuvlesky and Victoria M. Patella. College Station, Tex., Texas A. & M. University, 1970.
24p.

Paper presented at the Southwestern Sociological Association meetings, Dallas, March 26-28, 1970.
(Cont'd on next card)

691.16
Y17
Yatsenko, V F   Strength...1970.
(Card 2)

I. Indian National Scientific Documentation Centre, New Delhi. II. U.S. National Aeronautics and Space Administration.
III. U.S. National Science Foundation.
IV. Title.

693.5
B31
Strength and structure of concrete cast in deep forms.
Bhargava, Jitendra.
Strength and structure of concrete cast in deep forms. Stockholm, National Swedish Institute for Building Research, 1969.
27p. (Stockholm. Statens Institut för Byggnadsforskning. Document no. 9:1969)

1. Concrete construction. I. Stockholm. Statens Institut för Byggnadsforskning.
II. Title.

301.158
K88
Kuvlesky, William P   Strength...1970.
(Card 2)

1. Youth. 2. Minority groups.
I. Patella, Victoria M., jt. au.
II. Title: Mexican American Youth.
III. Title.

668.3
P27
The strength and durability of casein glue joints made with preservative-treated wood.
Perkins, Robert H
The strength and durability of casein glue joints made with preservative-treated wood. Lafayette, Ind., Wood Research Laboratory, Purdue University, Agricultural Experiment Station, 1969.
11p. (Purdue University, Wood Research Laboratory. Research bulletin no. 849)
1. Adhesives. 2. Waterproofing. 3. Wood preservation. I. Indiana. Agricultural Experiment Station. (Wood Research Laboratory)
II. Title: Case   in glue joints.
III. Title.

691.421
M17
Strength measurements on stiff fissured Barton Clay from Fawley (Hampshire)
Marsland, A
Strength measurements on stiff fissured Barton Clay from Fawley (Hampshire), by A. Marsland and M.E. Butler. Garston, Eng., Building Research Station, Ministry of Public Building and Works, 1967.
[8]p. (U.K. Building Research Station. Building research current papers. Current paper 30/68)
Reprinted from: Proceedings of the Geotechnical Conference, Oslo, 1967.
1. Clay. 2. Strains and stresses. I. Butler, M.E. II. U.K. Building Research Station.
III. Title.

691.32
T48
The strength of extremely dry and set mature concrete.
Tiusanen, K
The strength of extremely dry and set mature concrete; an experimental study on the effect of vacuum-wetting high-pressure-wetting and oven-drying on the strength of concrete, by K. Tiusanen and S.E. Pihlajavaara. Helsinki, State Institute for Technical Research, 1969.
24p. (Finland. State Institute for Technical Research. Tiedotus, sarja III - Rakennus 139)
1. Concrete. 2. Strength of materials. I. Pihlajavaara, S.E., jt. au.
II. Finland. State Institute for Technical Research. III. Title.

668.3
B27
The strength and durability of thick bluelines.
Bergin, E G
The strength and durability of thick bluelines. Ottawa, Dept. of Fisheries and Forestry, Canadian Forestry Service, 1969.
24p. (Canada. Dept. of Fisheries and Forestry. Canadian Forestry Service publication no. 1260)

1. Adhesives. I. Canada. Dept. of Fisheries and Forestry. II. Title.

691.42
I52
Strength of brick masonry in relation to strength and mix proportion of mortars.
India. National Buildings Organisation.
Report on strength of brick masonry in relation to strength and mix proportion of mortars. New Delhi, National Buildings Organisation and U.N. Regional Housing Centre ECAFE, 1968.
30p.

1. Bricks. 2. Strength of materials. I. United Nations. (Economic Commission for Asia and the Far East) II. Title: Strength of brick masonry in relation to strength and mix proportion of mortars.

690.22
Y64s
Strength of masonry walls under compressive and transverse loads.
Yokel, Felix Y
Strength of masonry walls under compressive and transverse loads, by F.Y. Yokel and others. Wash., National Bureau of Standards, Building Research Div., 1971.
68p. (U.S. National Bureau of Standards. Building science series no. 34)

1. Walls. 2. Strains and stresses.
I. Title.

691.11
F67STREN
STRENGTH AND RELATED PROPERTIES OF WHITE FIR.
U.S. FOREST PRODUCTS LABORATORY, MADISON, WIS.
STRENGTH AND RELATED PROPERTIES OF WHITE FIR, BY C.C. GERHARDS. MADISON, WIS., 1964.
12P. (U.S. FOREST SERVICE RESEARCH PAPER FPL 14)

1. WOOD. I. GERHARDS, C.C.
II. TITLE. III. TITLE: WHITE FIR.

691.32
P34
The strength of concrete.
Philleo, Robert E
The strength of concrete: a statistical view. [Wash.] National Sand and Gravel Association; National Ready Mixed Concrete Association, 1967.
24p. (Stanton Walker lecture series on the materials sciences. Lecture no. 5)

Presented at University of Maryland, College Park, Nov. 16, 1967.

1. Concrete. I. Title.

Strength of materials
xx Building materials

690.015
(485)
S82
R39
1967
Strength of materials.
Acking, Carl-Axel.
For och Konstruktion spännings optiska Studier [Form and structure; photoelasticity studies] av Carl-Axel Acking och Paul Ridemar. Stockholm, Statens Kommitté för Byggnadsforskning, 1967.
175p. (Sweden. Statens Kommitté för Byggnadsforskning. Rapport 39)
1. Building research - Sweden. 2. Strains and stresses. 3. Strength of materials. I. Ridemar, Paul, jt. au. II. Sweden. Statens Kommitté för Byggnadsforskning.

691.16
B27L
STRENGTH OF MATERIALS.
Berndtsson, B   S
Long-term strength of reinforced plastics under static loading. Garston, Eng., Building Research Station, 1971.
27p. (Library communication no. 1646)
Translated from the Swedish.
1. Plastics. 2. Strength of materials. I. U.K. Building Research Station. II. Title. (Series)

690.015
(485)
S82
R20
1968
Strength of materials.
Bring, Christer.
Provningsmetoder för golvmaterial och golvkonstruktioner (Methods of testing flooring materials and flooring constructions) Stockholm, Statens institut för byggnadsforskning, 1968.
141p. (Stockholm. Statens institut för byggnadsforskning. Rapport 20:1968)
Bibliography: p. 111-113.
English summary.
1. Building research - Sweden. 2. Sweden - Building research. 3. Floors and flooring. 4. Strength of materials. I. Stockholm. Statens institut för byggnadsforskning.
(Cont'd on next card)

691.71
A52
Strength of materials.
American Iron and Steel Institute.
Light gage cold-formed steel design manual. [5th ed.] New York, 1962.
127p.
Bibliography: p. 126-127.
Commentary ... ... Commentary, by George Winter. New York, 1962.
71p.
1. Steel - Standards and specifications. 2. Strength of materials. I. Title. II. Winter, George.

690
B27p
Laf.
Strength of materials.
Bersudskiy, V   Ye.
Production of honeycomb constructions, by V. Ye. Bersudskiy and others. Wright-Patterson Air Force Base, Ohio, Foreign Technology Div. 1967.
235p. (U.S. Defense Documentation Center. Defense Supply Agency. [Document] AD 649 422)
Distributed by U.S. Clearinghouse for Federal Scientific and Technical Information.
Translation of Russian text.
1. Building materials. 2. Strength of materials I. U.S. Defense Documentation Center. Defense Supply Agency.
(Cont'd on next card)

690.015
(485)
S82
R2C
1968
Bring, Christer.   Provningsmetoder... 1968.   (Card 2)
II. Title: Methods of testing flooring materials and flooring construction.

691
A52p
STRENGTH OF MATERIALS
American Society for Testing and Materials.
Proceedings, Vol. 1-
Philadelphia, Pa., 19-
v.
Includes reports and technical papers.
SEE SHELF LIST FOR LIBRARY HOLDINGS
1. Building materials. 2. Building research. 3. Strength of materials. 4. Specifications and standards. 5. Materials - Testing.

690
B27p
Bersudskiy, V   Ye.   Production of honeycomb constructions...1967.   (Card 2)
II. U.S. Clearinghouse for Federal Scientific and Technical Information. III. Title. IV. Title: Honeycomb constructions.

693.5
B84c
Strength of materials.
Building Research Advisory Board.
Crack control in concrete masonry unit construction. Report for the Federal Construction Council by Task Group T-43. Washington, National Academy of Sciences, National Research Council, 1964.
36p. (Federal Construction Council. Technical report no. 48)
National Research Council. Publication 1198.
1. Concrete construction. 2. Strength of materials. I. Federal Construction Council.

690
A527
1960
STRENGTH OF MATERIALS.
AMERICAN SOCIETY FOR TESTING AND MATERIALS.
SYMPOSIUM ON METHODS OF TESTING BUILDING CONSTRUCTIONS. SPONSORED BY ASTM COMMITTEE E-6 ON METHODS OF TESTING BUILDING CONSTRUCTION HELD AT WASHINGTON, D.C., NOVEMBER 15, 1960. PHILADELPHIA, 1962.
83P. (ITS SPECIAL TECHNICAL PUBLICATION NO. 312)
1. BUILDING CONSTRUCTION. 2. STRENGTH OF MATERIALS. (SERIES)

690.22
B31
STRENGTH OF MATERIALS.
Bhargava, Jitendra.
Strength of concrete in high strength revibrated walls. Stockholm, National Swedish Institute for Building Research, 1969.
45p. (Stockholm. Statens Institut för Byggnadsforskning. Document no. 6:1969)
Bibliography: p. 35-39.
1. Walls. 2. Concrete construction. 3. Strength of materials. I. Stockholm. Statens Institut för Byggnadsforskning. II. Title.

691.11
C15E
STRENGTH OF MATERIALS.
CANADA. DEPT. OF FORESTRY.
EFFECT OF TOLERANCE ON SELECTION EFFICIENCY OF NONDESTRUCTIVE STRENGTH TEST OF WOOD, BY D.G. MILLER. OTTAWA, 1964.
5P. (FOREST PRODUCTS RESEARCH BRANCH CONTRIBUTION NO. P-43)
1. WOOD. 2. STRENGTH OF MATERIALS. I. MILLER, D.J.

620.1
B17
Strength of materials.
Bassin, Milton G
Statics and strength of materials, by Milton G. Bassin and others. 2d ed. New York, McGraw-Hill, 1969.
463p.
1. Strength of materials. 2. Structural engineering. 3. Civil engineering. I. Title.

620.1
B43
STRENGTH OF MATERIALS.
BIGGS, W   D
THE MECHANICAL BEHAVIOUR OF ENGINEERING MATERIALS. OXFORD, ENG., PERGAMON PRESS, 1965.
146P. (COMMONWEALTH AND INTERNATIONAL LIBRARY OF SCIENCE TECHNOLOGY ENGINEERING AND LIBERAL STUDIES)
1. STRENGTH OF MATERIALS. 2. MATERIALS - TESTING. I. TITLE.

691.110.15
C15N
STRENGTH OF MATERIALS.
CANADA. DEPT. OF FORESTRY.
NON-DESTRUCTIVE TESTING OF CROSS-ARMS FOR STRENGTH, BY D.G. MILLER. OTTAWA, 1963.
18P.
1. WOOD - RESEARCH. 2. STRENGTH OF MATERIALS. I. MILLER, D.G. II. TITLE.

690.248
B18
STRENGTH OF MATERIALS.
BAUM, GUNTEN.
BASIC VALUES ON SINGLE SPAN BEAMS; TABLES FOR CALCULATING CONTINUOUS BEAMS AND FRAME CONSTRUCTIONS INCLUDING PRESTRESSED BEAMS. NEW YORK, SPRINGER-VERLAG, 1966.
113P. TABLES.
1. TRUSSES. 2. STRAINS AND STRESSES. 3. STRENGTH OF MATERIALS. I. TITLE.

629.13
B71
Strength of materials.
Brackett, R   L
Geometric properties of a prestressed segmented spherical shell, by R.L. Brackett and others. Prepared by University of California, Los Angeles, Calif., Wash., National Aeronautics and Space Administration, 1968.
25p. (NASA CR-1231. Issued by originator as report no. 68-23)
1. Aircraft construction. 2. Strength of materials. I. Title. II. California. University. University at Los Angeles. III. U.S. National Aeronautics and Space Administration.

691.11
C15ST
STRENGTH OF MATERIALS.
CANADA. DEPT. OF FORESTRY.
STRENGTHENING RING-CONNECTED TIMBERS WITH STEEL STRAPPING, BY A.P. JESSOME AND D.E. KENNEDY. OTTAWA, QUEEN'S PRINTER, 1960.
6P.
REPRINTED FROM CANADIAN CONSULTING ENGINEER.
1. WOOD. 2. STRENGTH OF MATERIALS. I. JESSOME, A.P. II. KENNEDY, D.E. III. TITLE.

620.1
925
STRENGTH OF MATERIALS.
BELYAYEV, NIKOLAI MIKHAILOVICH.
PROBLEMS IN STRENGTH OF MATERIALS, BY N.M. BELYAYEV. TRANSLATED BY W.U. SIRK. ENGLISH TRANSLATION EDITED BY R. KITCHING. NEW YORK, PERGAMON PRESS, 1966.
531P.
1. STRENGTH OF MATERIALS.

620.1
B72
STRENGTH OF MATERIALS.
BRENEMAN, JOHN W
STRENGTH OF MATERIALS. 3D ED. NEW YORK, MCGRAW-HILL, 1965.
192P.
1. STRENGTH OF MATERIALS. 2. STRAINS AND STRESSES.

623
1034
Laf.
Strength of materials.
Chilver, A   H ed.
Thin-walled structures; a collection of papers on the stability and strength of thin-walled structural members and frames. New York, J. Wiley, 1967.
303p.
1. Structural engineering. 2. Strength of materials. 3. Walls. I. Title.

620.1
C65
NO.12

STRENGTH OF MATERIALS.
COLUMBIA UNIVERSITY. INSTITUTE FOR THE
STUDY OF FATIGUE AND RELIABILITY.
THE ANALYSIS OF STRUCTURAL SAFETY, BY
A.M. FREUDENTHAL AND OTHERS. NEW YORK,
1964.
　　61P. (ITS TECHNICAL REPORT NO. 12)

　　1. STRENGTH OF MATERIALS.
I. FREUDENTHAL, A.M. II. TITLE:
STRUCTURAL SAFETY.

620.1
C65
NO.16

STRENGTH OF MATERIALS.
COLUMBIA UNIVERSITY. INSTITUTE FOR THE
STUDY OF FATIGUE AND RELIABILITY.
ON SECOND ORDER STRAIN ACCUMULATION IN
TORSION FATIGUE, BY MARIA RONAY. NEW
YORK, 1965.
　　51P. (ITS TECHNICAL REPORT NO. 16)

　　1. STRENGTH OF MATERIALS. I. RONAY,
MARIA. II. TITLE: TORSION FATIGUE.

620.1
C65
NO.11

STRENGTH OF MATERIALS.
COLUMBIA UNIVERSITY. INSTITUTE FOR THE
STUDY OF FATIGUE AND RELIABILITY.
SOME DIRECT OBSERVATIONS OF CUMULATIVE
FATIGUE DAMAGE IN METALS BY W.A. WOOD
AND W.H. REIMANN. NEW YORK, 1964.
　　24P. (ITS TECHNICAL REPORT NO. 11)

　　1. STRENGTH OF MATERIALS. I. WOOD,
W.A. II. REIMANN, W.H. III. TITLE:
CUMULATIVE FATIGUE DAMAGE IN METALS.

620.1
C65
NO.3

STRENGTH OF MATERIALS.
COLUMBIA UNIVERSITY. INSTITUTE FOR THE
STUDY OF FATIGUE AND RELIABILITY.
COMPARISON OF FATIGUE MECHANISM IN BCC
IRON AND FCC METALS, BY W.A. WOOD AND
OTHERS. NEW YORK, 1964.
　　511-517P. (ITS TECHNICAL REPORT NO.
3)

　　REPRINTED FROM TRANSACTIONS OF THE
METALLURGICAL SOCIETY OF AIME, V. 230,
APRIL, 1964.

　　1. STRENGTH O F. MATERIALS.
I. WOOD, W.A. II. TITLE.

620.1
C65
NO.9

STRENGTH OF MATERIALS.
COLUMBIA UNIVERSITY. INSTITUTE FOR THE
STUDY OF FATIGUE AND RELIABILITY.
ON STRAIN INCOMPATIBILITY AND GRAIN
BOUNDARY DAMAGE IN FATIGUE, BY MARIA
RONAY. NEW YORK, 1964.
　　28L. (ITS TECHNICAL REPORT NO. 9)

　　1. STRENGTH OF MATERIALS. I. RONAY,
MARIA.

693.55
D25

STRENGTH OF MATERIALS.
Denton, D　R
A dynamic ultimate strength study of
simply supported two-way reinforced
concrete slabs; final report. [Prepared
for] Office of Civil Defense. Vicksburg,
Miss., U.S. Army Engineer Waterways
Experiment Station, Corps of Engineers,
1967.
　　230p. (U S. Waterways Experiment
Station, Vicksburg, Miss. Technical report
no. 1-789)

Summary　　—— ————　　Summary.　　1967
　　　　　　　　　　　　(Cont'd on next card)

620.1
C65
NO.4

STRENGTH OF MATERIALS.
COLUMBIA UNIVERSITY. INSTITUTE FOR THE
STUDY OF FATIGUE AND RELIABILITY.
DEVELOPMENT OF RANDOMIZED LOAD
SEQUENCES WITH TRANSITION PROBABILITIES
BASED ON A MARKOV PROCESS, BY R.A.
HELLER AND M. SHINOZUKA. NEW YORK,
1964.
　　18P. (ITS TECHNICAL REPORT NO. 4)

　　1. STRENGTH OF MATERIALS. I. HELLER,
R.A. II. SHINOZUKA, M.

620.1
C65
NO.1

STRENGTH OF MATERIALS.
COLUMBIA UNIVERSITY. INSTITUTE FOR THE
STUDY OF FATIGUE AND RELIABILITY.
ON UPPER AND LOWER BOUNDS OF THE
PROBABILITY OF FAILURE OF SIMPLE
STRUCTURES UNDER RANDOM EXCITATION, BY
M. SHINOZUKA. NEW YORK, 1963.
　　23L. (ITS TECHNICAL REPORT NO. 1)

　　1. STRENGTH OF MATERIALS.
I. SHINOZUKA, M.

693.55
D25

Denton, D　R　A dynamic ultimate
strength study...,1967.　　(Card 2)

　　17p.

　　1. Concrete, Reinforced. 2. Strength of
materials. I. U.S. Waterways Experiment
Station, Vicksburg, Miss. II. Title.

620.1
C65
NO.15

STRENGTH OF MATERIALS.
COLUMBIA UNIVERSITY. INSTITUTE FOR THE
STUDY OF FATIGUE AND RELIABILITY.
DIFFERENCES IN FATIGUE BEHAVIOR OF
SINGLE COPPER CRYSTALS AND
POLYCRYSTALLINE COPPER AT ELEVATED
TEMPERATURES, BY W.A. WOOD AND H.D.
NINE. NEW YORK, 1965.
　　17P. (ITS TECHNICAL REPORT NO. 15)

　　1. STRENGTH OF MATERIALS. I. WOOD,
W.A. II. NINE, H.D.

620.1
C65
NO.10

STRENGTH OF MATERIALS.
COLUMBIA UNIVERSITY. INSTITUTE FOR THE
STUDY OF FATIGUE AND RELIABILITY.
RANDOM VIBRATION OF A BEAM COLUMN, BY
M. SHINOZUKA. NEW YORK, 1964.
　　28P. (ITS TECHNICAL REPORT NO. 10)

　　1. STRENGTH OF MATERIALS.
I. SHINOZUKA, M.

691.54
D65

STRENGTH OF MATERIALS.
Doleszai, K
Applicability of the autoclave test for
evaluating the magnesia swelling of cements,
by K. Doleszai and L. Szatura. Garston, Eng.,
Building Research Station, 1971.
　　[9]p. (Library communication no. 1613)
Translated from the Hungarian and reprinted
from Epitoanyag, 1970, 22(b), 208-12.

　　1. Cement. 2. Strength of materials.
I. Szatura, L., jt. au. II. U.K. Building
Research Station. III. Title. (Series)

620.1
C65
NO.2

STRENGTH OF MATERIALS.
COLUMBIA UNIVERSITY. INSTITUTE FOR THE
STUDY OF FATIGUE AND RELIABILITY.
FIRST SEMINAR ON FATIGUE AND FATIGUE
DESIGN, BY A.M. FREUDENTHAL AND OTHERS.
NEW YORK, 1963.
　　172P. (ITS TECHNICAL REPORT NO. 2)

　　1. STRENGTH OF MATERIALS.
I. FREUDENTHAL, A.M. II. TITLE:
FATIGUE AND FATIGUE DESIGN.

620.1
C65
NO.6

STRENGTH OF MATERIALS.
COLUMBIA UNIVERSITY. INSTITUTE FOR THE
STUDY OF FATIGUE AND RELIABILITY.
ROOM-TEMPERATURE CREEP IN IRON UNDER
TENSILE STRESS AND SUPERPOSED
ALTERNATING TORSION, BY W.H. REIMANN
AND W.A. WOOD. NEW YORK, 1964.
　　1327-1331P. (ITS TECHNICAL REPORT
NO. 6)

　　REPRINTED FROM TRANSACTIONS OF THE
METALLURGICAL SOCIETY OF AIME, V. 230,
OCTOBER, 1964.
　　1. STRENGTH O F. MATERIALS.
I. REIMANN, W.H. II. WOOD, W.A.

691.110.15
D69

Strength of materials.
Doyle, D　V
Properties of no. 2 dense kiln-
dried southern pine dimension lumber.
Madison, Wis., U.S. Forest Products
Laboratory, 1968.
　　24p. (U.S. Forest Service
research paper FPL 96)

　　1. Wood - Research. 2. Lumber
industry. 3. Strength of materials.
I. U.S. Forest Products Laboratory,
Madison, Wis. II. Title.

620.1
C65
NO.7

STRENGTH OF MATERIALS.
COLUMBIA UNIVERSITY. INSTITUTE FOR THE
STUDY OF FATIGUE AND RELIABILITY.
MECHANISM OF FATIGUE DEFORMATION AT
ELEVATED TEMPERATURES, BY M. RONAY AND
OTHERS. NEW YORK, 1964.
　　24P. (ITS TECHNICAL REPORT NO. 7)

　　1. STRENGTH OF MATERIALS. I. RONAY,
MARIA. II. TITLE.

620.1
C65
NO.13

STRENGTH OF MATERIALS.
COLUMBIA UNIVERSITY. INSTITUTE FOR THE
STUDY OF FATIGUE AND RELIABILITY.
SECOND ORDER EFFECTS IN DISSIPATIVE
SOLIDS, BY MARIA RONAY AND A.M.
FREUDENTHAL. NEW YORK, 1965.
　　88P. (ITS TECHNICAL REPORT NO. 13)

　　1. STRENGTH OF MATERIALS. I. RONAY,
MARIA. II. FREUDENTHAL, A.M.

Strength of materials.
STRENGTH OF MATERIALS
Textbooks
　　Statics and Strength of Materials, J.O. DRAFFIN and W.L.
COLLINS. Ronald Press Co., New York, 1950. 398 p, diagrs,
charts, tables, $6.50.
　　Text for use in technical and architectural courses for
non-engineering students; in statics, coplanar force sys-
tems are treated; chapter is devoted to explanation of
force systems in space; strength of materials portion
covers simple structure elements involving direct stress.
Eng Soc Lib, NY.

112-118　　　　　　　　　　　　　　No. 51--5645
Printed in U.S.A.　　　　　　　　　Engineering Index Service

620.1
C65
NO.14

STRENGTH OF MATERIALS.
COLUMBIA UNIVERSITY. INSTITUTE FOR THE
STUDY OF FATIGUE AND RELIABILITY.
ON GENERAL REPRESENTATION OF A DENSITY
FUNCTION, BY M. SHINOZUKA AND A.
NISHIMURA. NEW YORK, 1965.
　　18P. (ITS TECHNICAL REPORT NO. 14)

　　1. STRENGTH OF MATERIALS.
I. SHINOZUKA, M. II. NISHIMURA, A.

620.1
C65
NO.5

STRENGTH OF MATERIALS.
COLUMBIA UNIVERSITY. INSTITUTE FOR
THE STUDY OF FATIGUE AND RELIABILITY.
SECOND SEMINAR ON FATIGUE AND FATIGUE
DESIGN, BY J. BRANGER. NEW YORK, 1964.
　　92P. (ITS TECHNICAL REPORT NO. 5)

　　1. STRENGTH OF MATERIALS.
I. BRANGER, J. II. TITLE: FATIGUE AND
FATIGUE DESIGN.

620.1
(07)
E24

Strength of materials.
Eckardt, Ottmar W
Strength of materials. New York, Holt,
Rinehart and Winston, 1969.
　　462p.

　　1. Strength of materials - Study and
teaching. I. Title.

691.16
F25
STRENGTH OF MATERIALS.
FELTMAN RESEARCH LABORATORIES,
PICATINNY ARSENAL, N.J.
RESISTANCE OF PLASTICS TO OUTDOOR
EXPOSURE, BY FREDERICK J.H. BLINNE AND
LESTER E. DAY. DOVER, N.J., 1964.
48P. (ITS TECHNICAL REPORT 2102,
ADDENDUM NO. 5)

1. PLASTICS - TESTING. 2. STRENGTH
OF MATERIALS. I. BLINNE, FREDERICK
J.H. II. DAY, LESTER E. III. TITLE.

Strength of materials.

620.1
F45
Filipczynski, Leszek.
Ultrasonic methods of testing materials [by] Prof. Dr.
inz. Leszek Filipczynski, Dr. inz. Zdzislaw Pawlowski and
Dr. inz. Jerzy Wehr; translated [from the Polish] by K. R.
Schlachter and edited by J. Blitz. London, Butterworths,
1966.

Lef.
viii, 280 p. illus. tables, diagrs. 21 cm. 84/-
(B 67-791)
Originally published as Ultradźwiękowe metcdy badania mate-
riałów. Warsaw, Wydawnictwa, 1959.
Bibliography: p. 274-277. 1. Strength of materials.
1. Ultrasonic testing. 2. Pawlowski, Zdzislaw, joint author.
II. Wehr, Jerzy, joint author. III. Title.
jt. su.
TA417.4.F518 620.1127 67-73632
Library of Congress [3]
FKS

Strength of materials.

620.1
F56
Florida. University. Engineering and Industrial Experiment Station.
Thermal buckling of conical shells, by S.Y.
Lu and L.K. Chang [and] Dynamic stability of
heated conical and cylindrical shells, by C.L.
Sun and S.Y. Lu. Gainesville, 1969.
31p. (Its Technical papers no. 424 and
425)
At head of title: Engineering progress at
the University of Florida, Vol. XXIII, no.
1, Jan. 1969.
No. 424 reprinted from AIAA journal,
p. 1877-1822.

(Cont'd on next card)

620.1
F56
Florida. University. Engineering and Industrial Experiment Station. Thermal buckling...1969. (Card 2)

No. 425 reprinted from Developments in
mechanics, Vol. 4, Proceedings of the tenth
Midwestern Mechanics Conference, Aug. 1967,
p. 305-327.

1. Strength of materials. I. Title.
II. Title: Conical shells.

691.328
F87
STRENGTH OF MATERIALS.
FUSS, DAVID S
DYNAMIC COMPRESSION TESTS ON
THIN-SECTION REINFORCED CONCRETE.
PORT HUENEME, 1965.
56P. (U.S. NAVAL CIVIL ENGINEERING
LABORATORY, PORT HUENEME, CALIF.
TECHNICAL REPORT R 406)

1. CONCRETE, REINFORCED.
2. STRENGTH OF MATERIALS. I. TITLE.
II. U.S. NAVAL CIVIL ENGINEERING
LABORATORY, PORT HUENEME, CALIF.

620.1
G17
STRENGTH OF MATERIALS.
Garner, R R
Dynamic properties of materials. Pittsburgh,
Bettis Atomic Power Laboratory, 1969.
56p. (WAPD-TM-753; UC-25)

Bibliography: p. 24-29.

CFSTI. PB 184 724.

1. Strength of materials. 2. Steel.
I. Bettis Atomic Power Laboratory. II. Title.

620.1
G17B
STRENGTH OF MATERIALS.
GARRETT, B R
BROAD APPLICATIONS OF DIFFUSION
BONDING, BY B.R. GARRETT AND OTHERS.
PREPARED BY HEXCEL PRODUCTS, INC. FOR
WESTERN OPERATIONS OFFICE, NATIONAL
AERONAUTICS ANDSPACE ADMINISTRATION.
WASHINGTON, NATIONAL AERONAUTICS AND
SPACE ADMINISTRATION, 1966.
176P. (NASA CONTRACTOR REPORT, NASA
CR-409)

1. STRENGTH OF MATERIALS. 2. METALS.
I. HEXCEL PRODUCTS, INC.
II. U.S. NATIONAL AERONAUTICS AND
(CONTINUED ON NEXT CARD)

620.1
G17B
GARRETT, B R BROAD APPLICATIONS OF
...1966. (CARD 2)

SPACE ADMINISTRATION. III. TITLE:
DIFFUSION BONDING.

691.11
G27
Strength of materials.
Gerhards, C C
Effects of type of testing equipment and
specimen size on toughness of wood. Madison,
Wis., U.S. Dept. of Agriculture, Forest
Service, Forest Products Laboratory, 1968.
12p. (U.S. Forest Service. Research
note FPL 97)

1. Wood. 2. Strength of materials. I. U.S.
Forest Products Laboratory, Madison, Wis.
II. Title.

691
.G61
v.1
Strength of materials.
Goble, G G
Dynamic studies on the bearing capacity of
piles, Vol. 1. Final project report, July
30, 1967, by G.G. Goble and others. Sponsored
by the Ohio Dept. of Highways and the Bureau
of Public Roads. Cleveland, Case Institute
of Technology, 1967.
102p.
Distributed by: Clearinghouse for Federal
Scientific and Technical Information Document PB 177 539.
1. Building materials. 2. Strength of
materials. I. Case Institute of Technology,
Cleveland. II. Title.

691.110.15
G66
Strength of materials.
Goodshall, W D
Effects of vertical dynamic loading on
corrugated fiberboard containers, Madison, Wis.,
U. S. Forest Products Laboratory, 1968.
20p. (U.S. Forest Service research paper
FPL 94)

1. Wood - Research. 2. Strength of materials.
3. Loads. I. U.S. Forest Products Laboratory,
Madison, Wis. II. Title.

620.1
C67
STRENGTH OF MATERIALS.
Gordon, J E
The new science of strong materials.
New York, Walker and Co., 1968.
269p.

Bibliography: p. 262-263.

1. Strength of materials. 2. Strains
and stresses. 3. Building materials.
I. Title.

620.1
G71
Strength of materials.
Granholm, Hjalmar.
Inverkan av stotkraft pa en bropelare.
Goteborg, Scandinavian University Books, 1967.
[191]-202p. (Chalmers University of
Technology, Gothenburg, Sweden. Transactions
no. 318; Avd. Vag-och Vattenbyggnad, Byggnads-
teknik 54. 1967)
Särtryck ur Teknik och Natur.
English summary.
1. Strength of materials. 2. Engineering
research. 3. Structural engineering. I. Chalmers
University of Technology, Gothenburg, Sweden.

691.32
H15b
STRENGTH OF MATERIALS.
Hansen, Henry.
Betongfasthet bestemt ved hjelp av
Schmidthammer (Strength of concrete in com-
pression determined by the Schmidthammer) av
Henry Hansen og David Togba. Oslo, Norges
Byggforskningsinstitutt, 1968.
[3]p. (Oslo. Norges Byggforskningsinstitutt.
Saertrykk 154)
Saertrykk fra Betongen idag, nr. 1, 1968.
1. Concrete. 2. Strength of materials.
I. Togba, David, jt. au. II. Oslo. Norges
Byggforsknings institutt. III. Title:
Strength of concrete in compression
determined by the Schmidthammer.

691.328
H15
Strength of materials.
Hanson, J M
Fatigue tests of reinforcing bars - effect of
deformation pattern, by J.M. Hanson and others.
Skokie, Ill., Portland Cement Association, Research and Development Laboratories, 1968.
13p. (Portland Cement Association. Research
and Development Laboratories. Development Dept.
Bulletin D145)
Bibliography: p. 12-13.
Reprinted from: Journal of the PCA Research
and Development Laboratories, vol. 10, no. 3,
2-13 (Sept. 1968).
1. Concrete, Reinforced. 2. Steel.
3. Strength of materials. I. Portland Cement Asso ciation. II. Title.

620.1
H17
STRENGTH OF MATERIALS.
Harris, Charles Overton.
Strength of materials. 3d ed. Chicago,
American Technical Society, 1971.
231p.

1. Strength of materials. 2. Strains and
stresses. 3. Engineering - Study and teaching.
I. Title.

690.015
(485)
S82
R35
1967
Strength of materials.
Hellers, Bo-Goran.
Eccentrically compressed columns without
tensile strength subjected to uniformly
distributed lateral loads. Stockholm,
Staten Kommitte for Byggnadsforskning,
1967.
56p. (Sweden. Statens Kommitte for
Byggnadsforskning. Rapport 35: 1967)
Bibliography: p. 54-56.
1. Building research - Sweden. 2. Concrete. 3. Strength of materials. 4. Strains and
stresses. I. Sweden. Statens Kommitte for
Byggnadsforskning. II. Title.

691.322
H43a
STRENGTH OF MATERIALS.
Highway Research Board.
Aggregates and concrete durability;
5 reports. Wash., Highway Research Board,
Div. of Engineering, National Research
Council, National Academy of Sciences-
National Academy of Engineering, 1967.
74p. (Highway research record no. 196)
National Research Council. Publication
1527.
1. Concrete aggregates. 2. Strength of
materials. 3. Highways. I. Title.

690.015
(485)
S82
R40
1967
Strength of materials.
Hogberg, Erik.
Mortar bond. Stockholm, Statens Kommitte
for Byggnadsforskning, 1967.
90p. (Sweden. Statens Kommitte for
Byggnadsforskning. Rapport 40: 1967)
Bibliography: p. 88-90.

1. Building research - Sweden. 2. Cement.
3. Strength of materials. I. Sweden.
Statens Kommitte for Byggnadsforskning.
II. Title.

691.328.2
H78
Strength of materials.
Hsu, Thomas T
Torsion of structural concrete uniformly
prestressed rectangular members without web
reinforcement. Skokie, Ill., Portland Cement
Association, Research and Development Laboratories, 1968.
44p. (Portland Cement Association. Research
and Development Laboratories. Development Dept.
bulletin D140)
Reprinted from Journal of the Prestressed
Concrete Institute, April, 1968.
1. Concrete, Prestressed. 2. Strength of
materials. I. Portland Cement Association. II. Title.

691.328
H78
Strength of materials.
Hsu, Thomas T C
Ultimate torque of reinforced rectangular
beams. Skokie, Ill., Portland Cement
Association, Research and Development Labora-
tories, 1968.
485-510p. (Portland Cement Association.
Research and Development Laboratories.
Development Dept. Bulletin D127)
Reprinted from Journal of the Structural
Division, Proceedings of the American Society
of Civil Engineers, Feb., 1968.
1. Concrete, Reinforced. 2. Strength of
materials. I. Portland Cement Association.
II. American Society of Civil Engineers.
III. Title.

658.27
H83
STRENGTH OF MATERIALS.
HUFFINGTON, NORRIS J ED.
BEHAVIOR OF MATERIALS UNDER DYNAMIC LOADING. PAPERS PRESENTED AT A COLLOQUIUM, WINTER ANNUAL MEETING OF THE ASME, CHICAGO, NOV. 9, 1965. NEW YORK, AMERICAN SOCIETY OF MECHANICAL ENGINEERS, 1965.
187P.

1. MATERIALS - TESTING. 2. STRENGTH OF MATERIALS. I. TITLE: DYNAMIC LOADING. II. AMERICAN SOCIETY OF MECHANICAL ENGINEERS.

620.1
J63
STRENGTH OF MATERIALS.
Johnson, Arne I
Strength, safety and economical dimensions of structures. Stockholm, National Swedish Institute for Building Research, 1971.
168p. (Stockholm. Statens Institut för Byggnadsforskning. Document D7:1971)
Bibliography: p. 158-168.

1. Strength of materials. 2. Structural engineering. I. Stockholm. Statens Institut för Byggnadsforskning. II. Title.

691.328
K74U
STRENGTH OF MATERIALS.
KRIZ, LADISLAV B
ULTIMATE STRENGTH OF OVER-REINFORCED BEAMS, BY L.B. KRIZ AND S.L. LEE. SKOKIE, ILL., 1960.
13P. (PORTLAND CEMENT ASSOCIATION. RESEARCH AND DEVELOPMENT LABORATORIES, DEVELOPMENT DEPT. BULLETIN D36)

REPRINTED FROM PROC. PAPER 2502, JOURNAL OF THE ENGINEERING MECHANICS DIVISION, PROCEEDINGS OF THE AMERICAN SOCIETY OF CIVIL ENGINEERS, JUNE 1960.

1. CONCRETE , REINFORCED.
(CONTINUED ON NEXT CARD)

691.11
H85
Strength of materials.
Hunt, Michael O
Derivation of stress grades for structural lumber, by Michael O. Hunt and John F. Senft. Lafayette, Ind., Purdue University, Cooperative Extension Service, Wood Research Laboratory, 1965.
6p. (Purdue University. Wood Research Laboratory. Mimeo F-50).

1. Wood. 2. Strength of materials. 3. Lumber industry. I. Senft, John F., jt. au. II. Purdue University. Wood Research Laboratory. III. Title.

691.110.15
J63
Strength of materials.
Johnson, James W
Bending strength for small joists of Douglas fir treated with fire retardants. Corvallis, Forest Research Laboratory, School of Forestry, Oregon State University, 1967.
12p. (Oregon. Forest Research Laboratory. Report T-23)

1. Wood - Research. 2. Strength of materials. I. Oregon. Forest Research Laboratory. II. Title.

691.323
K74U
KRIZ, LADISLAV B ULTIMATE STRENGTH OF ...1960.   (CARD 2)

2. STRENGTH OF MATERIALS. I. LEE, S.L., JT. AU. II. PORTLAND CEMENT ASSOCIATION.

691.328
H97
pt.C
STRENGTH OF MATERIALS.
Hyttinen, Esko.
On the strength of reinforced concrete slabs. Part C: On the flexural and shearing strength and the deflections of reinforced concrete slabs. Helsinki, State Institute for Technical Research, 1969.
108p. (Finland. State Institute for Technical Research. Julkaisu 138 publication)
Thesis (Doctor of Technology)-Technical University, Otaniemi.
Bibliography: p. 106-108.
1. Concrete, Reinforced. 2. Strength of materials. I. Finland. State Institute for Technical Research. II. Title.

691.116
J63
Strength of materials.
Johnson, James W
Screw-holding abilitiy of particle board and plywood. Corvallis, Forest Research Laboratory, School of Forestry, Oregon State University, 1967.
23p. (Oregon. Forest Research Laboratory. Report T-22)

1. Plywood. 2. Strength of materials. I. Oregon. Forest Research Laboratory. II. Title.

620.1
K83
STRENGTH OF MATERIALS.
Kuhn, Paul.
Residual tensile strength in the presence of through cracks or surface cracks. Wash., National Aeronautics and Space Administration, 1970.
40p. (NASA TN D-5432)

1. Strength of materials. I. U.S. National Aeronautics and Space Administration. II. Title.

691.42
I52
Strength of materials.
India. National Buildings Organisation.
Report on strength of brick masonry in relation to strength and mix proportion of mortars. New Delhi, National Buildings Organisation and U.N. Regional Housing Centre ECAFE, 1968.
30p.

1. Bricks. 2. Strength of materials. I. United Nations. (Economic Commission for Asia and the Far East) II. Title: Strength of brick masonry in relation to strength and mix proportion of mortars.

620.1
K15
Strength of materials.
Kangas, J
Venerin nauls- ja pulttiliitostutkimuksia (Investigations on the strength of nailed and bolted joints of Finnish birch plywood) Helsinki, State Institute for Technical Research, 1966.
64p. (Finland. State Institute for Technical Research. Tiedotus. Serja 3, rekennus 102)
English summary p. 25-27.

1. Strength of materials. 2. Plywood. I. Finland. State Institute for Technical Research.

620.1
L15
STRENGTH OF MATERIALS.
Lancaster Philip Ray.
The mechanics of materials, by P.R. Lancaster and D. Mitchell. New York, McGraw-Hill, 1967.
320p.

1. Strength of materials. I. Mitchell, D., jt. au. II. Title. III. Title: Materials.

690.015
I57
no. 23
Strength of materials.
International Council for Building Research Studies and Documentation.
The concept of probability as applied to the safety of buildings, by R. Levi, Director of Fixed Installations, Societe Nationale des Chemins de Fer Francais (France) Geneva, 1953.
12p. (CIB/23)
At head of title: General Assembly.
(Palais des Nations, Geneva, 25 to 30 June inclusive)

1. Building research. 2. Strength of materials. I. Levi, R.

691.110.15
K69
Strength of materials.
Kozlik, Charles J
Effect of kiln conditions on the strength of Douglas fir and western hemlock. Corvallis, Forest Research Laboratory, School of Forestry, Oregon State University, 1967.
32p. (Oregon. Forest Research Laboratory. Report D-9)

1. Wood - Research. 2. Strength of materials. I. Oregon. Forest Research Laboratory. II. Title.

691.328.2
L26
1964
Strength of materials.
Leonhardt, Fritz.
Prestressed concrete; design and construction. Translated by C. van Amerongen. 2d fully rev. ed. Berlin, Wilhelm Ernst & Son, 1964.
677p.
Bibliography: p. 645-664.

1. Concrete, Prestressed. 2. Concrete construction. 3. Building methods. 4. Strength of materials. I. Title.

691.11
J27
Strength of materials.
Jessome, A P
Strength of selected eastern spruce joists, by A.P. Jessome and K.E. Leach. Ottawa, Dept. of Forestry and Rural Development, 1968.
14p (Canada. Dept. of Forestry and Rural Development. Departmental publication no. 1220)

1. Wood. 2. Strength of materials. I. Leach, K.E., jt. au. II. Canada. Dept. of Forestry and Rural Development. III. Title.

691.328
K74
STRENGTH OF MATERIALS.
KRIZ, LADISLAV B
ULTIMATE STRENGTH CRITERIA FOR REINFORCED CONCRETE. SKOKIE, ILL., 1959.
95-110P. (PORTLAND CEMENT ASSOCIATION. RESEARCH AND DEVELOPMENT LABORATORIES. DEVELOPMENT DEPT. BULLETIN D31)

REPRINTED FROM PROC. PAPER 2095 OF THE JOURNAL OF THE ENGINEERING MECHANICS DIVISION, PROCEEDINGS OF THE AMERICAN SOCIETY OF CIVIL ENGINEERS, JULY, 1959.
(CONTINUED ON NEXT CARD)

620.1
L28
1963
STRENGTH OF MATERIALS.
LEVINSON, IRVING J.
MECHANICS OF MATERIALS. ENGLEWOOD CLIFFS, N.J., PRENTICE-HALL, 1963.
339P.

1. STRENGTH OF MATERIALS. I. TITLE.

690.015
(485)
S82
M22
Strength of materials.
Johnson, Arne I
Strength, safety and economical dimensions of structures. Stockholm, Statens Kommitté för Byggnadsforskning, 1953.
168 p. graphs, tables. (Statens Kommitté för Byggnadsforskning. Meddelanden nr. 22)
References: p. 158-159.

1. Strength of materials. 2. Building materials - Testing. 3. Sweden. Statens Kommitté för Byggnadsforskning. II. Title. III. Title: Economical dimensions of structures.

691.328
K74
KRIZ, LADISLAV B ULTIMATE STRENGTH CRITERIA ...1959.   (CARD 2)
1. CONCRETE, REINFORCED.
2. STRENGTH OF MATERIALS.
I. PORTLAND CEMENT ASSOCIATION.

620.1
L28
STRENGTH OF MATERIALS.
Levinson, Irving J
Mechanics of materials. 2d ed. Englewood Cliffs, N.J., Prentice-Hall, 1970.
338p.

1. Strength of materials. I. Title.

620.1   STRENGTH OF MATERIALS.
L28s   Levinson, Irving J
            Statics and strength of materials. Englewood
        Cliffs, N.J., Prentice-Hall, 1971.
            498p.

            1. Strength of materials. 2. Strains
        and stresses. I. Title.

                    Strength of material.
698   Mateus, Tomás J   E
M17   Bases para o dimensionamento de
        estruturas de Madeira. [Basic elements
        for timber structural design] Lisboa,
        Portugal, Laboratório Nacional de
        Engenharia Civil, 1961.
            306p. (Portugal. Laboratório Nacional
        de Engenharia Civil. Memória no. 179)
            English summary.

            1. Wood. 2. Strength of material. I. Portugal.
        Laboratório Nacional   de Engenharia
        Civil.

691.328 STRENGTH OF MATERIALS.
M62   MOE, JOHANNES.
            SHEARING STRENGTH OF REINFORCED
        CONCRETE SLABS AND FOOTINGS UNDER
        CONCENTRATED LOADS. SKOKIE, ILL.,
        1961.
            135P. (PORTLAND CEMENT ASSOCIATION.
        RESEARCH AND DEVELOPMENT LABORATORIES.
        DEVELOPMENT DEPT. BULLETIN D47)

            1. CEMENT, REINFORCED. 2. STRENGTH
        OF MATERIALS. I. PORTLAND CEMENT
        ASSOCIATION.

            Strength of materials.
691.322 Lewis, R   K
L28t   Tensile splitting tests on structural light-
        weight concrete with "Shalite" aggregate.
        Melbourne, Australia, Commonwealth Scientific
        and Industrial Research Organization, Div. of
        Building Research, 1967.
            15p. (Australia. Commonwealth Scientific
        and Industrial Research Organization, Div. of
        Building Research. Report C3.3.2)

            1. Concrete aggregates. 2. Strength of
        materials. I. Australia. Commonwealth
        Scientific and   Industrial Research
        Organization.   (Div. of Building Re-
        search) II.   Title.

691.542 STRENGTH OF MATERIALS.
M17   Matouschek, F
            The lime saturation value of Portland cement
        clinker relative to the raw material analysis,
        the burning of the clinker, and the mortar
        strengths. Garston, Eng., Building Research
        Station, 1970.
            [27]p. (Library communication no. 1588)
            Translated from the German and reprinted
        from Zement-Kalk-Gips, 1970, 23 (2), 80-87.
            1. Portland cement. 2. Strength of materials.
        I. U.K. Building Research Station. II. Title:
        (Series)

                    Strength of materials.
691.11   Munthe, B   P
M85   Method for evaluating shear properties of
        wood, by B.P. Munthe and R.L. Ethington.
        Madison, Wis., U.S. Dept. of Agriculture,
        Forest Service, Forest Products Laboratory,
        1968.
            8p. (U.S. Forest Service. Research note
        FPL-0195)

            1. Wood. 2. Strength of materials.
        I. Ethington, R.L., jt. au. II. U.S. Forest
        Products Laboratory, Madison, Wis. III. Title.

691.8   STRENGTH OF MATERIALS.
L41   LIBER, THEODORE.
            AN EXPERIMENTAL INVESTIGATION OF
        FRANGIBLE PLATE FRAGMENTATION, SUMMARY,
        BY THEODORE LIBER AND RALPH SARNETT.
        PREPARED FOR OFFICE OF CIVIL DEFENSE.
        CHICAGO, 1966.
            93P. (IITRI PROJECT M6095, FINAL
        REPORT.)

            PREPARED AT THE RESEARCH INSTITUTE OF
        THE ILLINOIS INSTITUTE OF TECHNOLOGY,
        CHICAGO.

            1. PANELS - TESTING. 2. STRENGTH
        (CONTINUED ON NEXT CARD)

691.32   STRENGTH OF MATERIALS.
M17s   Mattison, E   N
            Some tests on the bending strength of
        concrete masonry in running bond, by E.N.
        Mattison and G. Churchward. [Melbourne]
        Commonwealth Scientific and Industrial
        Research Organization, 1969.
            7p. (Australia. Commonwealth
        Scientific and Industrial Research
        Organization. Division of Building
        Research. D.B.R. reprint no. 455)
            Reprinted from: Constructional
        review, Feb.,   1969.
                    (Cont'd on next card)

691.116 Strength of materials.
N47   Niskanen, Erkki.
            On the strength and the elasticity
        characteristics of Finnish structural
        birch plywood. Helsinki, State Institute
        for Technical Research, 1963.
            29p. (Finland. State Institute for
        Technical Research. Publication 81)

        1. Plywood. 2. Strength of materials. 3. Wood-
        using industries. I. Finland. State Institute for
        Technical Research.

691.8   LIBER, THEODORE. AN EXPERIMENTAL
L41   INVESTIGATION ...1966.   (CARD 2)

            OF MATERIALS. I. BARNETT, RALPH L.,
        JT. AU. II. ILLINOIS INSTITUTE OF
        TECHNOLOGY, CHICAGO. RESEARCH INSTITUTE.
        III. TITLE: FRANGIBLE PLATE
        FRAGMENTATION.

691.32   Mattison, E   N   Some tests...
M17s   1969.   (Card 2)

            1. Concrete. 2. Strength of
        materials. I. Churchward, G., jt. au.
        II. Australia. Commonwealth Scientific
        and Industrial Research Organization.
        (Div. of Building Research.) III. Title.

                    Strength of materials.
691.116 Norén, Bengt.
N67s   Svensk furuplywood; hallfasthet och
        tillåtna påkänningar (Swedish pine
        plywood; strength and working stresses)
        Stockholm, Statens råd för Byggnadsforskning,
        1964.
            187p. (Sweden. Statens Kommitté för
        Byggnadsforskning. Handlingar no. 45.
        Transactions)
            English summary.

        1. Plywood. 2. Strength of materials. I. Sweden.
        Statens Kommitté   för Byggnadsforskning.
        (Series)

691.8   STRENGTH OF MATERIALS.
M12r   McNatt, J   Dobbin
            Rail shear test for evaluating edgewise
        shear properties of wood-base panel
        products. Madison, Wis., U.S. Forest
        Products Laboratory, 1969.
            15p. (U.S. Forest Service. Research
        paper FPL 117)

            1. Panels. 2. Strength of materials.
        I. U.S. Forest Products Laboratory, Madison,
        Wis., II. Title.

691.542 STRENGTH OF MATERIALS.
M27   Method for increasing the strength of cement
        formed as a by-product of the manufacture
        of sulphuric acid from calcium sulphate.
        Garston, Eng., Building Research Station,
        1969.
            3p. (U.K. Building Research Station.
        Library communication no. 1509)
            Translated from the German. East German
        patent 63318.

            1. Portland cement. 2. Strength of materi-
        als. I. U.K. Building Research Station.
        (Series)

---

624   STRENGTH OF MATERIALS.
O34   OGIBALOV, P   M
            DYNAMICS AND STRENGTH OF SHELLS,
        TRANSLATED FROM RUSSIAN. JERUSALEM,
        ISRAEL PROGRAM FOR SCIENTIFIC
        TRANSLATION, 1966.
            319P.

            BIBLIOGRAPHY: P.309-316.

            1. STRUCTURAL ENGINEERING - TESTING.
        2. STRENGTH OF MATERIALS. I. TITLE.
        II. TITLE: SHELLS.

620.1   STRENGTH OF MATERIALS.
M15   Mann, Lawrence, Jr.
            Data analysis and correlation with digital
        computers: nondestructive testing (Final
        report), by Lawrence Mann, Jr. and Myron H.
        Young. Baton Rouge, Division of Engineering
        Research, Louisiana State University, 1971.
            75p. (Engineering research bulletin no. 107)
            Sponsored by Advanced Research Projects
        Agency.
            1. Strength of materials. 2. Building materi-
        als - Testing. I. Young, Myron H., jt. au.
        II. Louisiana State University and Agricultural
        and Mechanical   College. Engineering
        Research.   III. Title.

691.11   Strength of materials.
M42   Miettinen, Jorma K
            Mechanical properties of wood-plastic-
        combinates made of four Finnish wood species
        by impregnation with methylmetacrylate or
        polyester and gamma polymerisation, by Jorma K.
        Miettinen and others. Helsinki, State Insti-
        tute for Technical Research, 1968.
            58p. (Finland. State Institute for Technical
        Research. Julkaisu 137 publication)
            Bibliography: p. 56-58.
            1. Wood. 2. Plastics. 3. Strength of materials.
        I. Title. II. Finland. State Institute for
        Technical Research.

691.11   Strength of materials.
O76   Orosz, Ivan.
            Some nondestructive parameters for predic-
        tion of strength of structural lumber.
        Madison, Wis., U.S. Dept. of Agriculture,
        Forest Service, Forest Products Laboratory,
        1968.
            7p. (U.S. Forest Service research paper
        FPL 100)

            1. Wood. 2. Strength of materials. I. U.S.
        Forest Service. Forest Products Laboratory,
        Madison, Wis. II. Title.

690.24   Strength of materials.
M17t   Mertin, K   G
            The tensile strength of bituminous roof-
        ing fabrics. Melbourne, Australia, Common-
        wealth Scientific and Industrial Research
        Organization, 1964.
            24p. (Australia. Commonwealth
        Scientific and Industrial Research
        Organization. Div. of Building Research.
        Technical paper no. 13)

        1. Roofs and roofing. 2. Strength of materials.
        I. Australia. Common-   wealth Scientific
        and Industrial   Research
        Organization. (Div.   of Building Research)

---

620   Strength of materials.
M44   Mikkola, Martti.
            Influence lines of beams on a winkler-type
        elastic foundation, with the effect of the shear
        deformation of the beam taken into account.
        Helsinki, State Institute for Technical Research,
        1967.
            83p. (Finland. State Institute for Technical
        Research. Julkaisu 121, publication)

            1. Engineering. 2. Strength of materials.
        I. Finland. State Institute for Technical Re-
        search. II. Title.

691.6   STRENGTH OF MATERIALS.
O77   OTTO, W   H
            THE EFFECTS OF MOISTURE ON THE
        STRENGTH OF GLASS FIBERS -- A
        LITERATURE REVIEW. SAN DIEGO, CALIF.,
        WHITTAKER CORP., 1965.
            45L.

            SPONSORED BY THE BUREAU OF NAVAL
        WEAPONS AND THE U.S. NAVAL RESEARCH
        LABORATORY.

            1. GLASS. 2. STRENGTH OF MATERIALS.
        I. U.S. NAVAL RESEARCH LABORATORY.
        II. U.S. BUREAU OF NAVAL WEAPONS.

620.1
091

Strength of materials.
Ozaki, Masakazu
A practical method for the analysis of space truss shell structures. Tokyo, Building Research Institute, Ministry of Construction, 1968.
17p. (BRI research paper no. 35)
1. Strength of materials. 2. Building research. I. Title. II. Japan. Building Research Institute.

658.27
P27

STRENGTH OF MATERIALS.
PETERS, ROBERT LOUIS.
MATERIALS DATA NOMOGRAPHS. LONDON, REINHOLD PUB. CORP., 1965.
224P.
1. MATERIALS - TESTING. I. STRENGTH OF MATERIALS. II. TITLE.

690.25
R22

Strength of materials.
Reese, R C
Floor systems by ultimate strength design. Prepared under the direction of the Engineering Practice Committee, Concrete Reinforcing Steel Institute. Chicago, Concrete Reinforcing Steel Institute, 1968.
1v.
Computations for safe load tables by Dr. Elihu Geer.
1. Floors and flooring. 2. Strength of materials. 3. Loads. I. Concrete Reinforcing Steel Institute. II. Title.

Strength of materials.
Parcel, John Ira
Analysis of statically indeterminate structures, by John I. Parcel [and] Robert B. B. Moorman. New York, Wiley [1955].
571p. diagrs., tables.

691.32
P64

Strength of materials.
Poijärvi, Heikki.
Betonin puristuslujuusmäärityksistä erilaisilla keekappaleilla (On the determination of the compressive strength of concrete with various test specimens) by Heikki Poijärvi and Heikki Syrjälä. Helsinki, State Institute for Technical Research, 1965.
41p. (Finland. State Institute for Technical Research. Tiedotus. Sarja - Rakennus (Building 91)
English summary.
(Cont'd on next card)

624.043
R61

STRENGTH OF MATERIALS.
ROARK, RAYMOND JEFFERSON.
FORMULAS FOR STRESS AND STRAIN. 4TH ED. NEW YORK, MCGRAW-HILL, 1965.
432P.
1. STRAIN AND STRESS. 2. STRENGTH OF MATERIALS. I. TITLE.

623
P17

Strength of materials.
Parker, Harry.
Simplified engineering for architects and builders. 4th ed., rev. New York, Wiley, 1967.
Ref. 361p.
1. Structural engineering. 2. Building industry. 3. Strength of materials. 4. Building materials. I. Title.

691.32
P64

Poijarvi, Heikki. Betonnin puristus-lujuusmäärityksistä erilaisilla keekappaleilla...1965 (Card 2)
1. Concrete. 2. Strength of materials. I. Finland. State Institute for Technical Research. II. Title: On the determination of the compressive strength of concrete with various test specimens. III. Syrjala, Heikki, jt. au.

620
R69

STRENGTH OF MATERIALS.
ROYLANCE, T F
ENGINEERING DESIGN. PAPERS GIVEN AT THE UNIVERSITY OF NOTTINGHAM, SEPTEMBER, 1964. EDITED BY T.F. ROYLANCE. OXFORD, PERGAMON PRESS, 1966.
345P.
1. ENGINEERING. 2. AUTOMATION. 3. STRENGTH OF MATERIALS. I. TITLE.

620.1
P17S

STRENGTH OF MATERIALS.
PARKER, HARRY, 1887-
SIMPLIFIED MECHANICS AND STRENGTH OF MATERIALS. 2D ED. NEW YORK, WILEY, 1961.
285P.
1. STRENGTH OF MATERIALS. 2. STRAINS AND STRESSES. I. TITLE.

690.015
(485)
S82
R88

Strength of materials.
Pusch, Roland.
Variationer hos standardlerprovers, hållfasthetsdata (Strength data variations of standard clay samples) Stockholm, Statens råd för Byggnadsforskning, 1963.
16p. (Sweden. Statens Kommitté for Byggnadsforskning. Rapport 88)
English summary.
1. Building research - Sweden. 2. Strength of materials. 3. Clay. I. Sweden. Statens Kommitté för Byggnadsforskning.

621.78
R85

Strength of materials.
Rummler, Donald R
Mechanical properties and column behavior of thin-wall beryllium tubing, by Donald R. Rummler and others. Washington, National Aeronautics and Space Administration, 1968.
76p. (NASA Technical note NASA TN D-4833)
1. Metals. 2. Strains and stresses. 3. Strength of materials. I. U.S. National Aeronautics and Space Administration. II. Title.

620.1
P17

STRENGTH OF MATERIALS.
Pattee, H E
Joining ceramics and graphite to other materials, by H.E. Pattee and others. Prepared under contract for NASA by Battelle Memorial Institute. Wash., Technology Utilization Div., Office of Technology Utilization, National Aeronautics and Space Administration, 1968.
84p. (U.S. National Aeronautics and Space Administration. NASA SP-5052)
Bibliography: p. 81-82.
1. Strength of materials. I. Title. II. U.S. National Aeronautics and Space Administration. III. Battelle Memorial Institute.

691.54
R12

STRENGTH OF MATERIALS.
Rackwitz, R
Variability of concrete cube crushing strength. Garston, Eng., Building Research Station, 1971.
[14]p. (Library communication no. 1634)
Translated from the German.
1. Cement. 2. Strength of materials. I. U.K. Building Research Station. II. Title. (Series)

691.32
R87s

STRENGTH OF MATERIALS.
Rüsch, Hubert.
Statistical analysis of the strength of concrete, by H. Rüsch and others. Garston, Eng., Building Research Station, 1969.
[50]p. (U.K. Building Research Station. Library communication no. 1504)
Translated from the German.
Bibliography: p. 27-28.
1. Concrete. 2. Strength of materials. I. U.K. Building Research Station. II. Title. (Series)

620.1
P24

STRENGTH OF MATERIALS.
Peköz, Teoman B
Torsional flexural buckling of thin-walled sections under eccentric load. With a contribution by N. Celebi. A research project sponsored by the American Iron and Steel Institute. Ithaca, N.Y., Dept. of Structural Engineering, School of Civil Engineering, Cornell University, 1969.
75p. (Cornell engineering research bulletin 69-1)
(Cont'd on next card)

693.55
R22c

Strength of materials.
Reese, R C
Columns by ultimate strength design, including square footings. Prepared under direction of the Engineering Practice Committee, Chicago, Concrete Reinforcing Steel Institute, 1967.
Ref. 1v.
"Computations for safe load table prepared by Computer Center, University of Detroit, under direction of Dr. Elihu Greer."
(Cont'd on next card)

690.015
(485)
S82
R15-
1965

Strength of materials.
Sehlin, Sven.
Diagrams of critical stresses for columns of material without tensile strength. Stockholm, National Swedish Institute for Building Research, 1965.
18p. (Sweden. Statens Kommitté for Byggnadsforskning. Rapport 16-1965)
1. Building research - Sweden. 2. Panels. 3. Strength of materials. I. Sweden. Statens Kommitté for Byggnadsforskning.

620.1
P24

Peköz, Teoman B Torsional flexural...1969. (Card 2)
Bibliography: p. 68-69.
1. Strength of materials. 2. Loads. 3. Steel construction. I. Cornell University. School of Civil Engineering. II. Title.

693.55
R22

Reese, R C Columns by ultimate strength design...1967. (Card 2)
1. Concrete, Reinforced. 2. Loads. 3. Strength of materials. 4. Footings. I. Concrete Reinforcing Steel Institute. II. Title.

620.1
S22

STRENGTH OF MATERIALS.
SEELY, FRED B
RESISTANCE OF MATERIALS, BY FRED B. SEELY AND JAMES O. SMITH. 4TH ED. NEW YORK, WILEY, 1956.
459P.
1. STRENGTH OF MATERIALS. I. SMITH, JAMES O., JT. AU.

Card 1 (691.6 S25):

691.6
S25

STRENGTH OF MATERIALS.
Seminar on the Durability of Insulating
Glass, National Bureau of Standards,
Gaithersburg, Md., 1968.
Proceedings. Edited by Henry E.
Robinson. Sponsored by the American
Society for Testing and Materials,
and others. Wash., Govt. Print. Off.,
1970.
79p. (U.S. National Bureau of
Standards. Building science series 20)

1. Glass. 2. Insulation. 3. Strength
of materials.   (Cont'd on next card)

Card 2 (624 977):

624
977

STRENGTH OF MATERIALS.
STRUCTURAL DESIGN FOR DYNAMIC LOADS, BY
CHARLES H. NORRIS AND OTHERS. NEW
YORK, MCGRAW-HILL, 1959.
453P. ILLUS. (MCGRAW-HILL CIVIL
ENGINEERING SERIES)

COMPILED FROM LECTURE NOTES PREPARED
FOR A SPECIAL TWO-WEEK SUMMER PROGRAM ...
PRESENTED AT THE 1956 SUMMER SESSION OF
THE MASSACHUSETTS INSTITUTE OF TECHNOLOGY.
INCLUDES BIBLIOGRAPHY.

1. STRUCTURAL ENGINEERING.
2. VIBRATION. 3. STRENGTH OF
(CONTINUED ON NEXT CARD)

Card 3 (691.116 F67B):

691.116
F67B

STRENGTH OF MATERIALS.
U.S. FOREST PRODUCTS LABORATORY,
MADISON, WIS.
BENDING STRENGTH AND STIFFNESS OF
PLYWOOD. MADISON, 1964.
26P. (ITS RESEARCH NOTE: FPL 059)

1. PLYWOOD. 2. STRENGTH OF
MATERIALS.

Card 4 (691.6 S25, Card 2):

691.6
S25

Seminar on the Durability of Insulating
Glass...Proceedings...1970. (Card 2)

I. Robinson, Henry E., ed. II. American
Society for Testing and Materials.
III. U.S. National Bureau of Standards.
IV. Title: Durability of insulating
glass.

Card 5 (624 977, Card 2):

624
977

STRUCTURAL DESIGN FOR DYNAMIC LOADS, BY
CHARLES H. NORRIS AND OTHERS. NEW
YORK, MCGRAW-HILL, 1959. 453P. ILLUS.
...(RIES) (CARD 2)

MATERIALS. I. NORRIS, CHARLES HEAD,
1910- II. MASSACHUSETTS INSTITUTE
OF TECHNOLOGY.

Card 6 (691.11 F67C0):

691.11
F67C0

STRENGTH OF MATERIALS.
U.S. FOREST PRODUCTS LABORATORY,
MADISON, WIS.
COMPARISON OF BLOCK SHEAR METHODS FOR
DETERMINING SHEARING STRENGTH OF SOLID
WOOD, BY HOWARD C. HILBRAND. MADISON,
WIS., 1964.
23P. (U.S. FOREST SERVICE RESEARCH
NOTE FPL 030)

1. WOOD. 2. STRENGTH OF MATERIALS.
3. STRAINS AND STRESSES. I. HILBRAND,
HOWARD C. II. TITLE: SHEARING
STRENGTH OF SOLID WOOD.

Card 7 (674 S25):

674
S25

STRENGTH OF MATERIALS.
Senft, John F
Strength of structural lumber under combined
bending and tension loading, by John F. Senft
and Stanley K. Suddarth. Madison, Wis.,
Forest Products Research Society, 1970.
[5]p.
Reprinted from: Forest products journal, vol.
20, no. 7, July, 1970, p. 17-21.
1. Lumber industry. 2. Strength of materials.
I. Suddarth, Stanley K., jt. au. II. Title.

Card 8 (620.1 T45):

620.1
T45

Strength of materials.
Timoshenko, Stephen, 1878- 2d ed.
Strength of materials, by S. Timoshenko ... New York,
D. Van Nostrand company, inc., ~~1930~~. 1940-41.

2 v. illus. diagrs. 24 cm.

~~Paged continuously.~~

CONTENTS.—pt. I. Elementary theory and problems.—pt. II. Advanced theory and problems.

1. Strength of materials.

Library of Congress   TA405.T5   30—16661

[49r37q1]   620.11

Card 9 (677 F67D):

677
F67D

STRENGTH OF MATERIALS.
U.S. FOREST PRODUCTS LABORATORY,
MADISON, WIS.
DERIVATION OF FIBER STRESSES FROM
STRENGTH VALUES OF WOOD POLES, BY L.W.
WOOD AND L.J. MARKWARDT. MADISON, WIS.
1965.
8P. (U.S. FOREST SERVICE RESEARCH
PAPER FPL 39)

1. FIBERS. 2. STRENGTH OF MATERIALS.
3. WOOD. I. MARKWARDT, L.J.

Card 10 (690.237 8451):

690.237
8451

Strength of materials.
Simms, L. G
Loading tests on a three-storey structure.
Garston, Eng., Building Research Station,
Ministry of Technology, 1967.
10p. (U.K. Building Research Station.
Building research current papers. Engineering
papers 44)
Reprinted from: Institute of Structural
Engineers Conference 1966, 19th May.
1. Loads. 2. Steel construction. 3. Strength
of materials. I. U.K. Building Research
Station. II. Title.

Card 11 (691.32 T48):

691.32
T48

STRENGTH OF MATERIALS.
Tiusanen, K
The strength of extremely dry and set
mature concrete; an experimental study on
the effect of vacuum-wetting high-pressure-
wetting and oven-drying on the strength
of concrete, by K. Tiusanen and S.E.
Pihlajavaara. Helsinki, State Institute
for Technical Research, 1969.
24p. (Finland. State Institute for
Technical Research. Tiedotus, sarja
III - Rakennus 139)
1. Concrete. 2. Strength of materials.
I. Pihlajavaara, S.E., jt. au.
II. Finland. State Institute for
Technical Research. III. Title.

Card 12 (691.11 F67EFF):

691.11
F67EFF

STRENGTH OF MATERIALS.
U.S. FOREST PRODUCTS LABORATORY,
MADISON, WIS.
EFFECT OF CONFINING PRESSURE ON THE
COMPRESSION PARALLEL-TO-THE-GRAIN
STRENGTH OF SMALL CLEAR WOOD SPECIMENS,
BY THOMAS LEE WILKINSON. MADISON,
WIS., 1964.
7P. (U.S. FOREST SERVICE RESEARCH
NOTE FPL 057)

1. WOOD. 2. STRENGTH OF MATERIALS.
I. WILKINSON, THOMAS LEE.

Card 13 (674 S72r):

674
S72r

STRENGTH OF MATERIALS.
Stern, Ernest George.
Rigidity of 48" by 40" lumber pallets.
Blacksburg, Virginia Polytechnic Institute,
Research Div., Wood Research and Wood Con-
struction Laboratory, 1969.
pts. (Special reports no. 78,79)
1. Wood-using industries. 2. Lumber indus-
try. 3. Strength of materials. I. Title.
II. Title: Pallets. III. Virginia Polytechnic
Institute. Wood Research and Wood Conserva-
tion Laboratory.

Card 14 (620.1 T86):

620.1
T86

Strength of materials.
Tuomola, T
Koekuutioiden valmistus-, säilytys-ja
koetustaven sekä vesipitoisuuden vaikutus
kevytbetonien lujuusarvoihin (The effect of
the test cube preparing, keeping and testing
procedure and of the cubes water content on
the strength values of light-weight concretes),
av T. Tuomola and S. Rannikko. Helsinki,
State Institute for Technical Research, 1966.
119p. (Finland. State Institute for
Technical Research. Julkaisu 106 publication)
English summary.

(Cont'd on next card)

Card 15 (691.11 F67EFFE):

691.11
F67EFFE

STRENGTH OF MATERIALS.
U.S. FOREST PRODUCTS LABORATORY,
MADISON, WIS.
EFFECT OF SIZE ON BENDING STRENGTH
OF MEMBERS. MADISON, WIS., 1966.
30P. (U.S. FOREST SERVICE RESEARCH
PAPER FPL 56)

1. WOOD. 2. STRENGTH OF MATERIALS.
I. TITLE.

Card 16 (691.328.2 S72):

691.328.2
S72

Strength of materials.
Stevens, R F
Strains in some prestressed concrete struc-
tures, by R.F. Stevens and R.H. Corson. Garston,
Eng., Building Research Station, Ministry of
Technology, 1966.
[10]p. (U.K. Building Research Station.
Building research current papers. Engineering
series 39)
Reprinted from: Conference on Stresses in
Service, arranged by the Institution of Civil
Engineers, March 1966, paper 2, p. 13-22.

(Cont'd on next card)

Card 17 (620.1 T86, Card 2):

620.1
T86

Tuomola, T. Koekuutioiden valmistus-, säilytys-
ja koetustaven sekä vesipitoisuuden vaikutus
kevytbetonien lujuusarvoihin...1966.
(Card 2)

1. Strength of materials. 2. Concrete.
I. Finland. State Institute for Technical
Research. II. Rannikko, S., jt.au.
III. Finland. State Institute for Technical
Research.

Card 18 (668.3 F67e):

668.3
F67e

Strength of materials.
U.S. Forest Products Laboratory, Madison,
Wis.
Effects of adhesive formulation and age on
strength of bonded butt joints, by J.T. Quirk
and others. Madison, 1967.
Laf.   17p. (U.S. Forest Service research note,
FPL-0178)

1. Adhesives. 2. Strength of materials.
3. Building materials. I. Quirk, J.T.
II. Title.

Card 19 (691.328.2 S72, Card 2):

691.328.2
S72

Stevens, R F Strains in some prestressed concrete structures...1966. (Card 2)

1. Concrete, Prestressed. 2. Strength of
materials. I. U.K. Building Research Station.
II. Corson, R.H., jt. au. III. Title.

Card 20 (693.97 U54):

693.97
U54

STRENGTH OF MATERIALS.
U.K. BUILDING RESEARCH STATION.
THE STRENGTH OF ENCASED STANCHIONS,
BY R.F. STEVENS. LONDON, H.M.S.O.,
1965.
38P. (ITS NATIONAL BUILDING STUDIES
RESEARCH PAPER NO. 38)

1. STEEL CONSTRUCTION. 2. STRENGTH
OF MATERIALS. I. STEVENS, R.F.
II. TITLE: ENCASED STANCIONS.

Card 21 (691.16 F67F):

691.16
F67F

STRENGTH OF MATERIALS.
U.S. FOREST PRODUCTS LABORATORY,
MADISON, WIS.
FATIGUE STRENGTH OF PHENOLIC
LAMINATES FROM 1 TO 10 MILLION CYCLES
OF REPEATED LOAD, BY G.H. STEVENS.
MADISON, 1964.
8P. (U.S. FOREST SERVICE. RESEARCH
NOTE FPL 027)

1. PLASTICS - TESTING. 2. STRENGTH
OF MATERIALS. I. STEVENS, GORDON H.
II. TITLE.

Strength of materials.

691.110.15
F67h U.S. Forest Products Laboratory, Madison,
Wis.
Hardness modulus as an alternate measure
of hardness to the standard Janka ball for
wood and wood-base materials, by Wayne G.
Lewis. Madison, Wis., U.S. Dept. of
Agriculture, Forest Service, Forest Products
Laboratory, 1968.
13p. (U.S. Forest Service. Research note
FPL-0189)
Prepared in cooperation with the Univer-
sity of Wisconsin. (Cont'd on next card)

691.11
F671 STRENGTH OF MATERIALS.
U.S. FOREST PRODUCTS LABORATORY,
MADISON, WIS.
SOME STRENGTH AND RELATED PROPERTIES
OF YAGRUMO HENBRA (CECROPIA PELTATA)
FROM PUERTO RICO, BY B.A. BENDTSEN.
MADISON, WIS., 1964.
7P. (U.S. FOREST SERVICE RESEARCH
NOTE FPL 053)

1. WOOD. 2. STRENGTH OF MATERIALS.
I. BENDTSEN, B.A.

690.248
N18 U.S. Naval Civil Engineering Laboratory,
Port Rueneme, Calif.
Dynamic shear strength of reinforced concrete
beams, by William A. Keenan and Richard H.
Seabold. Port Rueneme, Calif., 1965, 1967.
Laf. 2pts. (Its Technical report R 395 and R 502)
U.S. Defense Documentation Center. Defense
Supply Agency [Documents] AD 627 661 and AD
644 823.
Distributed by U.S. Clearinghouse for
Scientific and Technical Information.

(Cont'd on next card)

691.110.15
F67h U.S. Forest Products Laboratory, Madison, Wis.
Hardness modulus as an...1968. (Card 2)

1. Wood - Research. 2. Strength of materials.
I. Lewis, Wayne G. II. Wisconsin. University. III. Title.

691.11
F67STR U.S. FOREST PRODUCTS LABORATORY,
MADISON, WIS.
STRENGTH AND RELATED PROPERTIES OF
MOUNTAIN HEMLOCK. BY ROBERT L.
YOUNGS. MADISON, WIS, 1963.
12P. (U.S. FOREST SERVICE RESEARCH
PAPER FPL 3)

1. WOOD. 2. STRENGTH OF MATERIALS.
I. YOUNGS, ROBERT L. II. TITLE!
MOUNTAIN HEMLOCK.

690.248
N18 U.S. Naval Civil Engineering Laboratory,
Port Rueneme Calif. Dynamic shear
strength of reinforced concrete beams...1967.
(Card 2)

1. Trusses. 2. Strength of materials.
3. Concrete, Reinforced. I. U.S. Defense
Documentation Center. Defense Supply Agency.
II. U.S. Clearinghouse for Federal Scientific
and Technical Information. III. Keenan, William
A. IV. Seabold, Richard H. V. Title.

668.3
F671 Strength of materials.
U.S. Forest Products Laboratory, Madison,
Wis.
Location of failure in adhesive-bonded
butt joints, by J.T. Quirk and others.
Madison, 1967.
Laf. 16p. (U.S. Forest Service research note,
FPL-0177)

1. Adhesives. 2. Strength of materials.
3. Building materials. I. Quirk, J.T.
II. Title.

691.11
F671ST U.S. FOREST PRODUCTS LABORATORY,
MADISON, WIS.
STRENGTH AND RELATED PROPERTIES OF A
RANDOMLY SELECTED SAMPLE OF
SECOND-GROWTH REDWOOD, BY B.A.
BENDTSEN. MADISON, WIS., 1966.
15P. (U.S. FOREST SERVICE RESEARCH
PAPER FPL 53)

1. WOOD. 2. STRENGTH OF MATERIALS.
I. BENDTSEN, B.A. II. TITLE.
III. TITLE: SECOND GROWTH REDWOOD.

690.22
U54 STRENGTH OF MATERIALS.
U.K. Interdepartmental Sub-Committee for
Component Co-Ordination.
Performance requirements for opaque, non
load-bearing partitions. London, 1970.
21p. Technical note no.3)

1. Walls. 2. Panels. 3. Strength of
materials. I Title.

691.110.15
F67n STRENGTH OF MATERIALS.
U.S. Forest Products Laboratory, Madison,
Wis.
Natural decay resistance of fifteen exotic
woods imported for exterior use, by Joe W.
Clark. Madison, Wis., U.S. Dept. of Agricul-
ture, Forest Service, Forest Products Labora-
tory, 1969.
5p. (U.S. Forest Service. Research paper
FPL 103)

1. Wood - Research. 2. Strength of materials. I. Title. II. Clark, Joe W.

691.110.15
F67t Strength of materials.
U.S. Forest Products Laboratory, Madison, Wis.
Tension parallel-to-grain properties of
southern pine dimension lumber, by D.V. Doyle
and L.J. Markwardt. Madison, 1967.
Laf. 36p. (U.S. Forest Service research paper,
FPL 84)

1. Wood - Research. 2. Strength of materials.
I. Doyle, D.V. II. Markwardt, L.J. III. Title.

620.1
U72 STRENGTH OF MATERIALS.
Ur'ev, N B
Characteristics of the mechanism of failure
of glass fibre on formation of new crystals,
by N.B. Ur'ev and others. Garston, Eng.,
Building Research Station, 1968.
[5]p. (Library communication no. 1425)
Translated from the Russian and reprinted
from Doklady Akademii Nauk SSSR, 1967, 177 (6),
1404-6.
1. Strength of materials. I. U.K. Building
Research Station. II. Title: Failure of glass
fibre. III. Title. (Series)

691.11
F67PRO STRENGTH OF MATERIALS.
U.S. FOREST PRODUCTS LABORATORY,
MADISON WIS.
PROPERTIES OF SOUTHERN PINE IN
RELATION TO STRENGTH GRADING OF
DIMENSION LUMBER, BY D.V. DOYLE AND
L.J. MARKWARDT. MADISON, WIS., 1966.
62P. (U.S. FOREST SERVICE.
RESEARCH PAPER FPL 64)

THIS REPORT WAS SPONSORED BY THE
SOUTHERN PINE INSPECTION BUREAU.

1. WOOD. 2. STRENGTH OF
MATERIALS. I. DOYLE, D.V.
(CONTINUED ON NEXT CARD).

658.78
L41 Strength of materials.
U.S. Library of Congress. Science and Tech-
nology Div.
Charles J. Cleary awards for papers on
material sciences. Edited by Lynn E. Catoe.
Washington, Published for Directorate of
Materials and Processes, Aeronautical Systems
Division, Wright-Patterson Air Force Base,
Ohio, 1962.
219p.

(Cont'd on next card)

620.1
U72m STRENGTH OF MATERIALS.
Ur'ev, N B
The mechanism of failure of reinforcing glass
fibre in hardening cement paste, by N.B. Ur'ev
and N.V. Mikhailov. Garston, Eng., Building
Research Station, 1971.
5p. (Library communication no. 1605)
Translated from the Russian and reprinted from
Neorganicheskia Materialy, 1969, 5 (8), 1451-5.

1. Strength of materials. I. Mikhailov, N.V.,
jt. au. II. U.K. Building Research Station.
III. Title. (Series)

691.11
F67PRO U.S. FOREST PRODUCTS LABORATORY,
MADISON WIS. PROPERTIES OF SOUTHERN
...1966. (CARD 2)

II. MARKWARDT, L.J. III. TITLE:
SOUTHERN PINE IN RELATION TO STRENGTH
GRADING. IV. SOUTHERN PINE INSPECTION
BUREAU.

658.78
L41 U.S. Library of Congress. Science and Technology Div...1962. (Card 2)

1. Materials handling. 2. Loads.
3. Strength of materials. I. Cleary, Charles
Joseph, 1891-1945. II. Catoe, Lynn E., ed.
III. U.S. Air Force. (Aeronautical Systems
Division, Directorate of Materials and Pro-
cesses) IV. Title.

624
:69 Strength of materials.
U76 Urquhart, Leonard Church
Civil engineering handbook. 3d ed. New
York, McGraw-Hill, 1950.
x, 1002 p. illus., diagrs., graphs, tables.

Bibliographies at end of chapters.

1.Strength of materials. 2.Trusses. 3.Cement.
4.Concrete construction. 5.Foundations. 6.Steel
construction. 7.Sewerage and sewage disposal.
8.Soils. 9.Water supply. 10.Airports. 11.Highways.
I.Title.

691.11
F67SOM STRENGTH OF MATERIALS.
U.S. FOREST PRODUCTS LABORATORY,
MADISON, WIS.
SOME STRENGTH AND RELATED PROPERTIES
OF GREEN WOOD OF HAWAIIAN EUCALYPTUS
SALIGNA, BY C.C. GERHARDS. MADISON,
WIS., 1963.
8P. (U.S. FOREST SERVICE RESEARCH
NOTE FPL 09)

SUPERSEDED BY RESEARCH PAPER FPL 23,
APRIL 1965.
1. WOOD. 2. STRENGTH OF MATERIALS.
I. GERHARDS, C.C. II. TITLE.

691.8
N18 U.S. Naval Air Engineering Center.
Sandwich constructions and core materials;
general test methods. Military standard.
Philadelphia, Weapons Engineering Standard-
ization Office, Naval Air Engineering Center,
Dept. of the Navy, Dept. of Defense, 1967.
31p. (MIL-STD-401B, 26 Sept. 1967)
Supersedes MIL-STD-401A, 15 June 1956.
1. Panels. 2. Strength of materials.
3. Aircraft construction. 4. Building materials -
Standards and specifications. I. Title.

620.1
V42 STRENGTH OF MATERIALS.
VIERTELS, EPHRAIM.
SIMPLIFIED PROBLEMS IN STRENGTH OF
MATERIALS AND STRUCTURAL DESIGN. NEW
YORK, EDWARD W. SWEETMAN, 1953.
636P.

1. STRENGTH OF MATERIALS.
2. STRUCTURAL ENGINEERING.

620.1
V65
STRENGTH OF MATERIALS.
Volterra, Enrico.
Advanced strength of materials, by Enrico
Volterra and J.H. Gaines. Englewood Cliffs,
N.J., Prentice-Hall, 1971.
522p. (Civil engineering and engineering
mechanics series)

1. Strength of materials. I. Gaines, J.H.,
jt. au. II. Title.

620.1
(016)
L41
Strength of materials - Bibliography.
U.S. Library of Congress. Science and
Technology Division.
Materials research abstracts, a review of
the Air Force materials research and develop-
ment. Edited by Charles D. Thibault.
[Washington] Published for Directorate of
Materials Processes, Aeronautical Systems
Division, Wright-Patterson Air Force Base,
Ohio, 1962.
534p.

1. Strength of materials - Bibl.
I. Thibault, Charles D., ed.
II. U.S. Air Force. III. Title

625.84
071
STRENGTH OF PRESTRESSED CONCRETE
PAVEMENTS.
OSAWA, YUTAKA.
STRENGTH OF PRESTRESSED CONCRETE
PAVEMENTS. SKOKIE, ILL., 1962.
143-164P. (PORTLAND CEMENT
ASSOCIATION. RESEARCH AND DEVELOPMENT
LABORATORIES. DEVELOPMENT DEPT.
BULLETIN D57)

REPRINT FROM PROC. PAPER 3398 OF
JOURNAL OF THE STRUCTURAL DIVISION,
PROCEEDINGS OF THE AMERICAN SOCIETY OF
CIVIL ENGINEERS, OCT. 1962.

1. ROAD CONSTRUCTION.
(CONTINUED ON NEXT CARD)

620.1
V34
Strength of materials.
Whittemore, Herbert L
Strength of houses, application of
engineering principles to structural design,
by Herbert L. Whittemore and others. Washington, National Bureau of Standards, For sale
by the Supt. of Docts., Govt. Print. Off.,
1948.
132p. (U.S. National Bureau of Standards,
Building materials and structures report, BMS
109)

1. Strength of materials. 2. Engineering.
I. U.S. National Bureau of
Standards.

620.1
(016)
N17
STRENGTH OF MATERIALS - BIBLIOGRAPHY.
U.S. NATIONAL BUREAU OF STANDARDS.
NONDESTRUCTIVE EVALUATION OF MATERIALS.
WASHINGTON, 1965.
15P.

1. STRENGTH OF MATERIALS -
BIBLIOGRAPHY. I. TITLE.

625.84
071
OSAWA, YUTAKA. STRENGTH OF PRESTRESSED
...1962. (CARD 2)

2. CONCRETE, PRESTRESSED. I. PORTLAND
CEMENT ASSOCIATION. II. TITLE.

691.16
Y17
STRENGTH OF MATERIALS.
Yatsenko, V F
Strength and creep of laminated plastics
(Prochnost i polzuchest sloistykh plastikov)
New Delhi, Published for National Aeronautics
and Space Administration and the National
Science Foundation by the Indian National
Scientific Documentation Centre, 1970.
237p. (TT 67-59014; NASA TT F 461)
Bibliography: p. 229-237.
Naukova Dumka, Kiev, 1966.
Translated from Russian.
1. Plastics. 2. Strength of materials.

(Cont'd on next card)

620.1
(07)
B51
STRENGTH OF MATERIALS - STUDY AND
TEACHING.
BLACK, PETER.
STRENGTH OF MATERIALS; A COURSE FOR
STUDENTS. OXFORD, NEW YORK, PERGAMON,
1966.
454P.

1. STRENGTH OF MATERIALS - STUDY AND
TEACHING. 2. STRAINS AND STRESSES -
STUDY AND TEACHING.

694.1
I51
Strength of properties and testing method of
finger joints.
Imaizumi, Katsuyoshi.
Strength properties and testing method of fin-
ger joints, by Katsuyoshi Imaizumi and Johannes
Moe. Tokyo, Building Research Institute, Minis-
try of Construction, Japanese Government, 1965.
19p. (Japan. Building Research Institute.
BRI occasional report no. 25)

1. Wood construction. I. Moe, Johannes, jt.
au. II. Japan. Building Research Institute.
III. Title. IV. Title: Finger joints.

691.16
Y17
Yatsenko, V F Strength...1970.
(Card 2)

I. Indian National Scientific Documentation
Centre, New Delhi. II. U.S. National
Aeronautics and Space Administration.
III. U.S. National Science Foundation.
IV. Title.

620.1
(07)
E24
STRENGTH OF MATERIALS - STUDY AND TEACHING.
Eckardt, Ottmar W
Strength of materials. New York, Holt,
Rinehart and Winston, 1969.
462p.

1. Strength of materials - Study and
teaching. I. Title.

691.11
J27
Strength of selected eastern spruce joists...
Jessome, A P
Strength of selected eastern spruce joists,
by A.P. Jessome and K.E. Leach. Ottawa,
Dept. of Forestry and Rural Development, 1968.
14p (Canada. Dept. of Forestry and Rural
Development. Departmental publication no.
1220)

1. Wood. 2. Strength of materials.
I. Leach, K.E., jt. au. II. Canada. Dept. of
Forestry and Rural Development. III. Title.

690.22
Y64
STRENGTH OF MATERIALS.
Yokel, Felix Y
Compressive strength of slender concrete
masonry walls, by Felix Y. Yokel and others.
Wash., 1970.
28p. (U.S. National Bureau of Standards.
Building science series 33)

1. Walls. 2. Strength of materials.
I. U.S. National Bureau of Standards.
II. Title.

620.1
(014)
H15
STRENGTH OF MATERIALS - TESTING.
Hansagi, I
Mining method of determining the strength
of rock in the mass and of classifying rock
(Bergmännisches Verfahren der Gebirgs-
sfestigkeitsbestimmung und der
Gebrigsklassifizierung) Garston, Eng.,
Building Research Station, Ministry of
Public Building and Works, 1968.
6p. (U.K. Building Research Station.
Library communication 1446)
Translated from the German and reprinted
from: Proc. 1st Congress of the
International Society of Rock
(Cont'd on next card)

674
S25
Strength of structural lumber under combined
bending and tension loading.
Senft, John F
Strength of structural lumber under combined
bending and tension loading, by John F. Senft
and Stanley K. Suddarth. Madison, Wis.,
Forest Products Research Society, 1970.
[5]p.
Reprinted from: Forest products journal, vol.
20, no. 7, July, 1970, p. 17-21.
1. Lumber industry. 2. Strength of materials.
I. Suddarth, Stanley K., jt. au. II. Title.

691.7
Z25
STRENGTH OF MATERIALS.
Zender, George W
Compressive properties and column efficiency
of metals reinforced on the surface with bonded
filaments, by George W. Zender and H. Benson
Dexter. Wash., National Aeronautics and Space
Administration., 1968.
45p. (NASA technical note, D-4878)

1. Metals. 2. Strength of materials.
I. Dexter, H. Benson, jt. au. II. U.S.
National Aeronautics and Space Administration.
III. Title.

620.1
(014)
H15
Hansagi, I Mining...1968. (Card 2)

Mechanics, Lisbon. 1966. Vol. I, pp. 179-83.

1. Strength of materials - Testing.
I. U.K. Building Research Station.

690.237.52
:691.71
N17
Strength of tubular steel columns.
U.S. National Bureau of Standards.
Effect of concrete cores on the strength
of tubular steel columns, by D. Watstein and
C. T. Valenti, Jr. Washington, Nov. 1951.
17 p. plates, graphs, tables. (NBS
Report 1276)
Final report, Research project 1950 -
STR-7, Housing and Home Finance Agency.
Project director: D. E. Parsons; Staff
technician: William A. Russell

(over)

620.1
(016)
A52
Lef.
Strength of materials - Bibliography.
American Society for Testing and Materials.
References on fatigue, 1964 (With additional 1963 references) Prepared by Committee E-9 on Fatigue. Philadelphia, 1967.
97p. (ASTM special technical publication
no.9-0)

1. Strength of materials - Bibl. 2. Building materials - Bibl. I. Title: Fatigue.

362.6
N17ST
THE STRENGTH OF OUR YEARS.
NATIONAL COUNCIL ON THE AGING.
THE STRENGTH OF OUR YEARS. NEW YORK,
1964.
20P.

ITS 13TH ANNUAL REPORT; BRIEF SUMMARY
OF THE YEARS ACTIVITIES OF NCOA.

1. OLD AGE. I. TITLE.

691.421
845
The strength of walls built in the labora-
tory...
Simms, L G
The strength of walls built in the
laboratory with some types of clay bricks
and blocks. Garston, Eng., Building
Research Station, Ministry of Technology,
1965.
11p. (U.K. Building Research
Station. Building research current papers.
Engineering series no. 24)
Reprinted from Transactions of the
British Ceramic Society, July 1965, p. 81-
92.

(Continued on
next card)

691.421
S45　Simms, L　G　The strength of walls
built in the laboratory...1965. (Card 2)

1. Clay.　2. Tile construction.
3. Walls.　I. U.K.　Building Research
Station.　II. Title.

352
U71　Strengthening government organizations in
changing communities.
Urban Policy Conference. 5th, University of
Iowa, 1968.
Strengthening government organizations in
changing communities. Proceedings of the Fifth
Annual Urban Policy Conference, Oct. 3-4, 1968.
Iowa City, Institute of Public Affairs, Uni-
versity of Iowa, 1969.
67p.

1. Local government.　I. Iowa.　University.
Institute of Public Affairs.　II. Title.

327
C65　Strengthening the United Nations.
Commission to Study the Organization of Peace.
Strengthening the United Nations. Arthur
N. Holcombe, Chairman. New York, Harper, 1957.
276p.

1. International relations. 2. United Nations.
I. Holcombe, Arthur N　II. Title.

694.183
F67　Strength of wood joints made with nails...
Scholten, John A
Strength of wood joints made with nails,
staples, or screws, by John A. Scholten.
Madison, Wis., 1965.
16p.　(Its Research note FPL-0100)
In cooperation with the University of
Wisconsin.

1. Nails and nailing. 2. Wood. I. Wisconsin.
University. II. U.S. Forest Products Laboratory, Madison, Wis. III. Title.

614
G65　STRENGTHENING HEALTH SERVICES FOR THE
CHRONICALLY ILL AND AGED.
GOLDMANN, FRANZ.
STRENGTHENING HEALTH SERVICES FOR THE
CHRONICALLY ILL AND AGED.　NEW YORK,
COUNCIL OF JEWISH FEDERATIONS AND WELFARE
FUNDS, 1960.
8L.　(CJFWF　GENERAL ASSEMBLY.　PAPER
NO. 29)

DISCUSSION OF COUNCIL OF JEWISH
FEDERATIONS AND WELFARE FUNDS STUDY OF
COORDINATION OF HEALTH SERVICES FOR
PATIENTS WITH LONG-TERM ILLNESS.

1. HEALTH.　2.　OLD AGE.　3. HOUSING
(CONTINUED ON NEXT CARD)

690
H68st　Strengthening urban administration in
IME　developing countries.
no.67　U.S. Dept. of Housing and Urban Development.
Office of International Affairs.
Strengthening urban administration in devel-
oping countries; with emphasis on Latin
America, by PADCO, inc. Prepared for the
Agency for International Development. Wash.,
1971.
62p. (Ideas and methods exchange no.67)
Bibliography: p. 63-65.
1. City planning - Latin America. I. U.S.
Agency for International Development.
II. PADCO, inc　III. Title.

690.015
(485)
S82　Strength, safety and economical dimensions
M22　of structures.
Johnson, Arne I
Strength, safety and economical dimensions
of structures. Stockholm, Statens Kommitté
for Byggnadsforskning, 1953.
168 p.　graphs, tables.　(Statens
Kommitté for Byggnadsforskning.　Meddelanden
nr. 22)
References: p. 158-159.

1. Strength of materials.　2. Building materials - Testing.　I. Sweden. Statens Kommitté
for Byggnadsfor-　skning.　II. Title.
III. Title: Econom-　ical dimensions of structures.

614
G65　GOLDMANN, FRANZ. STRENGTHENING HEALTH
SERVICES ...1960.　(CARD 2)
FOR THE AGED.　I. COUNCIL OF JEWISH
FEDERATIONS AND WELFARE FUNDS.　II. TITLE.

691.54
G74　The strengths of cements reinforced with
glass fibres.
Grimer, F　J
The strengths of cements reinforced
with glass fibres, by F. J. Grimer
and M.A. Ali　Garston, Eng., Building
Research Station, 1969.
[8]p.　(U.K. Building Research
Station. Current paper 40/69)
Reprinted from: Magazine of concrete
research, March, 1969. pp. 23-30.

1. Cement.　2. Concrete, Reinforced.
I. Ali, M.A.　Jt au.　II. U.K. Building
Research sta-　tion. III. Title.

620.1
J63　Strength, safety and economical dimensions...
Johnson, Arne I
Strength, safety and economical dimensions
of structures. Stockholm, National Swedish
Institute for Building Research, 1971.
169p. (Stockholm. Statens Institut för
Byggnadsforskning. Document D7:1971)
Bibliography: p. 158-168.

1. Strength of materials.　2. Structural
engineering. I. Stockholm. Statens Institut
för Byggnadsforskning. II. Title.

352
(746)
C65s　Strengthening local government.
Connecticut. Dept. of Community Affairs.
Strengthening local government. A report on
the progress and potential of the Community
Development Action Plan (CDAP) Program.
Hartford, 1971.
24p.

1. Local government - Conn.　2. Community
development - Conn.　I. Title.　II. Title:
Community Development Action Plan.

614
L21　Stress.
Leary, Michael Edmunds.
Individual stress in the urban
environment　Ithaca, N.Y., Center for
Housing and Environmental Studies, Div.
of Urban Studies, Cornell University, 1968.
97p. (Cornell University. Center for
Housing and Environmental Studies. Theses
in comprehensive health planning)

Bibliography: p. 94-97.
Thesis　(Master of Regional
Planning) -　Cornell University.
(Cont'd on next card)

711.583
J64　Strengthening community services in low-income
neighborhoods.
U.S. Joint Task Force on Health, Education
and Welfare Services and Housing.
Strengthening community services in low-income neighborhoods; a field guide to concerted
services. Washington, For sale by the Supt.
of Doc., Govt. Print. Off., 1967.
17p.

1. Community development - Citizen participation. 2. Social welfare. I. Title.

353
(746)
F22　Strengthening management and budget functions
in the Connecticut State government.
U.S. Federal Technical Assistance Program.
Strengthening management and budget functions
in the Connecticut State government. A briefing
for State executives by the Federal Technical
Assistance Program. [Wash.] 1971.
92p.

1. State government - Conn.　2. State
finance - Conn.　I. Title.

614
L21　Leary, Michael Edmunds.　Individual...
1968.　(Card 2)

1. Health.　I. Cornell University.
Center for Housing and Environmental
Studies. II. Title: Stress. III. Title.

658.3
P81S　STRENGTHENING EMPLOYEE PERFORMANCE
EVALUATION.
PUBLIC PERSONNEL ASSOCIATION.
STRENGTHENING EMPLOYEE PERFORMANCE
EVALUATION, BY ROBERT COOP [AND OTHERS]
CHICAGO [1966?]
46P.　(ITS PERSONNEL REPORT NO. 663)

1. PERSONNEL MANAGEMENT.　I. TITLE.
II. COOP, ROBERT.

VF
33
N17
P39　Strengthening the Congress.
National Planning Association.
Strengthening the Congress, by Robert Heller.
[Washington, Jan. 1945]
41 p.　(Planning pamphlets, no. 39)

1. U.S. Congress. I. Heller, Robert. II. Title.
III. Series.

624
M172　STRESS.
MASSACHUSETTS INSTITUTE OF TECHNOLOGY.
DEPT. OF CIVIL ENGINEERING.
STRESS: A REFERENCE MANUAL, A
PROBLEM-ORIENTED COMPUTER LANGUAGE FOR
STRUCTURAL ENGINEERING, BY STEVEN J.
FENVES AND OTHERS. CAMBRIDGE, 1965.
388P.

1. STRUCTURAL ENGINEERING.
2. AUTOMATION.　I. FENVES, STEVEN JOSEPH.
II. TITLE.

368
C65s
1965
H-H　Strengthening financial condition of
employees' life insurance fund.
U.S. Congress. House. Committee on Post
Office and Civil Service.
Strengthening financial condition of employees' life insurance fund. Hearing before the Subcommittee on Retirement, Insurance,
and Health Benefits of the Committee on Post
Office and Civil Service, House of Representatives, Eighty-ninth Congress, first session on
H.R. 6434. A bill to strengthen the financial
condition of the employees' life insurance
fund... Washington, Govt. Print. Off., 1965.
17p.　　2. Federal civil
1. Insurance.　　I. Title.
service.

658.3
A52ST　STRENGTHENING THE RESEARCH EFFORT.
AMERICAN MANAGEMENT ASSOCIATION.
STRENGTHENING THE RESEARCH EFFORT;
PERSONNEL TOOLS, POTENTIALS. NEW YORK,
1956.
63P.　(RESEARCH AND DEVELOPMENT SERIES
NO. 2)

1. PERSONNEL MANAGEMENT.　2. RESEARCH.
I. TITLE.

624.043
Z42　STRESS ANALYSIS.
ZIENKIEWICZ, O　C　ED.
STRESS ANALYSIS; RECENT DEVELOPMENTS
IN NUMERICAL AND EXPERIMENTAL METHODS.
EDITED BY O. C. ZIENKIEWICZ AND G.S.
HOLISTER. LONDON, NEW YORK, J. WILEY,
1965.
469P.

1. STRAINS AND STRESSES.
I. HOLISTER, G.S., JT. ED. II. TITLE.

691.32
K15

STRESS ANALYSIS OF A UNIVERSAL
CONCRETE TEST SPECIMEN.
KANSAS. STATE UNIVERSITY OF
AGRICULTURE AND APPLIED SCIENCE,
MANHATTAN.
STRESS ANALYSIS OF A UNIVERSAL
CONCRETE TEST SPECIMEN, BY P.G.
KIRMSER AND GEORGE DAILEY. MANHATTAN,
KAN., 1964.
19P. (ITS REPRINT NO. 84)

REPRINTED FROM THE PROCEEDINGS OF THE
RILEM INTERNATIONAL SYMPOSIUM ON THE
EXPERIMENTAL RESEARCH OF FIELD TESTING
OF CONCRETE.

(CONTINUED ON NEXT CARD)

694.1
W17

STRESS GRADE LUMBER.
U.S. WAR PRODUCTION BOARD
(CONSERVATION DIVISION)
NATIONAL EMERGENCY SPECIFICATIONS FOR
THE DESIGN, FABRICATION AND ERECTION OF
STRESS GRADE LUMBER AND ITS FASTENINGS
FOR BUILDERS. DIRECTIVE NO. 29, AUGUST
9, 1943. WASHINGTON, GOVT. PRINT. OFF.,
1943.
63P.

1. WOOD CONSTRUCTION - STANDARDS AND
SPECIFICATIONS. I. TITLE: STRESS
GRADE LUMBER.

691.8
D68

STRESSED SKIN PANEL TEST.
DOUGLAS FIR PLYWOOD ASSOCIATION.
STRESSED SKIN PANEL TEST, BY DONALD H.
DRAWSKY. TACOMA, WASH., 1960.
46L. (ITS LABORATORY REPORT NO. 82)

1. PANELS - TESTING. 2. PLYWOOD.
I. DRAWSKY, DONALD H. II. TITLE.

691.32
K15

KANSAS. STATE UNIVERSITY OF
AGRICULTURE AND APPLIED SCIENCE,
MANHATTAN. STRESS ANALYSIS OF ...
1964. (CARD 2)
1. CONCRETE. I. KIRMSER, P.G.
II. DAILEY, GEORGE. III. TITLE.

691.421
L28

Stress-probe experiments on saturated
normally consolidated clay.
Lewin, P I
Stress-probe experiments on saturated nor-
mally consolidated clay, by P.I. Lewin and
J.B. Burland. Garston, Eng., Building Research
Station, 1970.
56p. (U.K. Building Research Station.
Current paper CP 18/70)
Reprinted from: Geotechnique, 1970, Vol. 20
(1), March pp. 38-56.
1. Clay. 2. Strains and stresses.
I. Burland, J.B., jt. au. II. U.K. Building
Research Station. III. Title.

624.131
C15S

STRESSES AND DEFLECTIONS IN
FOUNDATIONS AND PAVEMENTS.
CALIFORNIA. UNIVERSITY. INSTITUTE OF
TRANSPORTATION AND TRAFFIC
ENGINEERING.
STRESSES AND DEFLECTIONS IN
FOUNDATIONS AND PAVEMENTS. BERKELEY,
1964.
93L.

1. SOILS. 2. FOUNDATIONS (BUILDING)
I. TITLE.

624.131
B27

Laf.

Stress and wave patterns in soils subjected
to dynamic loads.
Bernhard, Rudolf K
Stress and wave patterns in soils subjected to dynamic loads. Hanover, N.H., U.S.
Army Materiel Command, Cold Regions Research & Engineering Laboratory, 1967.
52p. (CRREL Research report 120)

1. Soils. 2. Strains and stresses.
I. U.S. Cold Regions Research and Engineering Laboratory. II. Title.

620.1
S45

Stress-strain behavior of films of four ad-
hesives used with wood...
Simpson, William T
Stress-strain behavior of films of four
adhesives used with wood, by William T.
Simpson and Vernon R. Soper Madison, Wis.,
U.S. Dept. of Agriculture, Forest Service,
Forest Products Laboratory, 1968.
7p. (U.S. Forest Service. Research note
FPL-0198)

1. Strains and stresses. 2. Adhesives.
3. Wood. I. Soper, Vernon R., jt. au.
II. U.S. Forest Products Laboratory,
Madison, Wis. III. Title.

624.131.3
B14

STRESSES AND STRAINS.
BAKER, WARREN J
A STUDY OF PARAMETERS AND METHODS
INVOLVED IN RELATIVE DISPLACEMENT
MEASUREMENTS IN SOIL, BY WARREN J.
BAKER AND ROBERT E. LYNCH.
KIRTLAND AIR FORCE BASE, N.M., AIR
FORCE WEAPONS LABORATORY, 1965.
40P. (U.S. AIR FORCE. WEAPONS
LABORATORY. TECHNICAL REPORT NO.
AFWL TR-65-75)
1. SOILS - TESTING. 2. STRESSES
AND STRAINS. I. LYNCH, ROBERT E.,
JT. AU. I - I. TITLE:
DISPLACEMEN T MEASUREMENTS IN SOIL.

658.564
M17s

STRESS: [Computer program language]
Massachusetts Institute of Technology.
(Dept. of Civil Engineering)
STRESS: [Computer program language] a user's
manual; a problem-oriented computer language
for structural engineering, by Steven J. Fenves
and others. Cambridge, M.I.T. Press, 1967.
55p.

1. Automation. 2. Structural engineering.
I. Fenves, Steven J. II. Title.

624.131.3
S65

STRESS WAVE INTERACTION IN A MODEL
SOIL.
SOLDATE, A M
A THEORETICAL ANALYSIS OF STRESS
WAVE INTERACTION IN A MODEL SOIL -
FURTHER STUDIES. FINAL REPORT,
PREPARED UNDER CONTRACT AF
29(601)-5395 BY SOLDATE, A.M. AND
MIKLOWITZ, J. KIRTLAND AIR FORCE
BASE, N.M., AIR FORCE WEAPONS
LABORATORY, 1964.
73P. (AIR FORCE WEAPONS
LABORATORY TECHNICAL DOCUMENTARY
REPORT NO. WL TDR-64-12)

1. SOILS - TESTING.
(CONTINUED ON NEXT CARD).

624.131
H43s+

STRESSES IN SOILS AND LAYERED
SYSTEMS.
HIGHWAY RESEARCH BOARD.
STRESSES IN SOILS AND LAYERED
SYSTEMS. PRESENTED AT THE 42D ANNUAL
MEETING, JANUARY 7-11, 1963.
WASHINGTON, NATIONAL ACADEMY OF
SCIENCES-NATIONAL RESEARCH COUNCIL,
1963.
180P. (HIGHWAY RESEARCH RECORD NO.
39)

1. SOILS. I. TITLE.

691.7
1620.19
A27

STRESS-CORROSION CRACKING OF
HIGH-STRENGTH ALLOYS.
AEROJET-GENERAL CORPORATION.
STRESS-CORROSION CRACKING OF
HIGH-STRENGTH ALLOYS, A REPORT TO
FRANKFORT ARSENAL. AZUSA, CALIF.,
1964.
1 V. (VARIOUS PAGINGS) (ITS REPORT
NO. 2914, FINAL)

1. CORROSION. 2. METALS.
I. TITLE.

624.131.3
S65

SOLDATE, A M A THEORETICAL
ANALYSIS ...1964. (CARD 2)

2. STRAINS AND STRESSES.
I. MIKLOWITZ, J., JT. AU. II. U.S.
AIR FORCE WEAPONS LABORATORY.
III. TITLE: STRESS WAVE INTERACTION
IN A MODEL SOIL.

388
:308
S78

Strickland, Richard I
Studies of weaving and merging traffic: a
symposium. Weaving practices on one-way
highways, by F. Houston Wynn. Merging
traffic characteristics applied to acceleration lane design, by Stewart M. Gourlay.
A study of merging vehicular traffic movements, by Richard I. Strickland. [n.p.]
Bureau of Highway Traffic, Yale University,
published with funds from Eno Foundation
for Highway Traffic Control, 1948.
130p. (Yale highway traffic series.
Technical report no. 4)

Continued on next card)

624.043
L41

Stress corrosion of high strength steel wires.
Libert, Y
Stress corrosion of high strength steel
wires, by Y. Libert and A. Hache. Garston,
Eng., Building Research Station, 1968.
16p. (U.K. Building Research Station.
Library communication no. 1427)

Translated from the French and reprinted
from VIIIe Colloque de Metallurgie, Cadarache,
1964.
1. Strains and stresses. 2. Concrete,
Prestressed. I. Hache, A., jt. au.
II. U.K. Building Research Station.
III. Title. (Series)

691.421
C17S

STRESS-DEFORMATION AND STRENGTH
CHARACTERISTICS OF COMPACTED CLAYS.
CASAGRANDE, ARTHUR.
SECOND PROGRESS REPORT ON
INVESTIGATION OF STRESS-DEFORMATION
AND STRENGTH CHARACTERISTICS OF
COMPACTED CLAYS, BY A. CASAGRANDE AND
R.C. HIRSCHFELD. CAMBRIDGE, HARVARD
UNIVERSITY, 1962.
122P. (HARVARD SOIL MECHANICS
SERIES NO. 65)

SPONSORED BY THE WATERWAYS
EXPERIMENT STATION IN COOPERATION WITH
HARVARD UNIVERSITY.

(CONTINUED ON NEXT CARD)

388
:308
S78

Studies of weaving and merging traffic: a
symposium...1948. (Card 2)

1. Traffic surveys. 2. Journey to work.
I. Wynn, F. Houston. II. Gourlay, Stewart M.
III. Strickland, Richard I. IV. Yale
University. Bureau of Highway Traffic.

624.131
H43st

Stress distribution in a homogeneous soil.
Highway Research Board.
Stress distribution in a homogeneous soil;
presented at the Twenty-ninth annual meeting,
1949, by Charles R. Foster and S.M. Fergus.
Washington, National Research Council Jan. 1951.
36 p. illus., charts, diagrs. (Its
Research report no. 12-F)

1. Soils. 2. Road construction. I. Title.
II. Foster, Charles R. III. Fergus, S.M.,
jt. author. (Series)

691.421
C17S

CASAGRANDE, ARTHUR. SECOND PROGRESS
REPORT ...1962. (CARD 2)

1. CLAY - TESTING. I. HIRSCHFELD,
R.C., JT. AU. II. U.S. WATERWAYS
EXPERIMENT STATION, VICKSBURG, MISS.
III. TITLE: STRESS-DEFORMATION AND
STRENGTH CHARACTERISTICS OF COMPACTED
CLAYS.

312
C657p

Strickland, Stephen P ed.
U.S. Congress. Senate. Committee on Government
Operations.
Population crisis; hearings before the U.S.
Senate Subcommittee on Foreign Aid Expenditures,
Committee on Government Operations, Wash., D.C.,
1965-1968. Wash., Socio-Dynamics Publication,
1970.
481p. Editor: Stephen P. Strickland.
"A condensation of United States Senate
hearings on the Population crisis."
1. Population. I. Title. II. Strickland,
Stephen P., ed.

697.3
A76EX STRICKLER, J D
U.S. ATOMIC ENERGY COMMISSION.
EXPERIMENTAL EVALUATION OF THE
RADIATION PROTECTION AFFORDED BY
TYPICAL OAK RIDGE HOMES AGAINST
DISTRIBUTED SOURCES, BY T.D. STICKLER
AND J.A. AUZIER. OAK RIDGE, TENN.,
1960.
51P.

AT HEAD OF TITLE: CEX-59-13, CIVIL
EFFECTS EXERCISE.
1. THERMAL RADIATION. 2. CIVILIAN
DEFENSE. I. STRICKLER, J.D.
II. AUZIER, J.A. III. TITLE.

658
B25 STRICTLY BIRDSMANSHIP.
BENSON, BERNARD S
STRICTLY BIRDSMANSHIP; OR, HOW TO LAY
THE EGG THAT KILLS THE GOLDEN GOOSE.
SANTA MONICA, CAL., BENSON-LEHNER CORP.,
1960.
UNPAGED.

1. MANAGEMENT. I. TITLE.

Strikes
xx Building industry - Labor relations
xx Industry
xx Labor relations
sa and xx Trade-unions

711.4
A52ci Strikes.
American federationist.
The cities: people, problems and progress.
Wash., 1965.
24p.

Entire issue: Nov., 1965.

1. City planning. 2. Urban renewal.
3. Labor relations. 4. Strikes.

388
(7471)
B17 Strikes.
Barrington and Co.
The effect of the 1966 [New York City]
transit strike on the travel behavior of
regular transit users. Prepared from a
survey, for the New York City Transit
Authority. [n.p.] 1966.
116p.
U.S. Dept of Housing and Urban Development. Mass Transportation Demonstration
Grant Program.

(Cont'd on next card)

388
(7471)
B17 Barrington and Co. The effect of the 1966
[New York City] transit strike on the
travel behavior of regular transit
users...1966. (Card 2)

1. Transportation - New York (City) 2. Strikes.
3. Traffic surveys - New York (City) 4. Labor
relations - New York (City) I. New York (City)
Transit Authority. II. Title. III. U.S. Dept.
of Housing and Urban Development. Mass Transportation Demonstration Grant Program.

331.892
B74 STRIKES.
Brill, Harry
Why organizers fail: the story of a rent
strike. Berkeley, University of California
Press, 1971.
192p. (California studies in urbanization
and environmental design)

1. Strikes. 2. Poverty. 3. Rents.
I. Title.

Strikes.
LAW
T Bureau of National Affairs, inc. Wash., D.C.
Labor relations reporter: labor relations
expediter. A handbook and guide to law and
practice in the fields of labor-management
relations, collective bargaining, arbitration, and wage, hour, and child labor regulation, with full texts of governing Federal
laws and regulations, Washington, D.C., 1967.
1 v. (Cited as LRX)

1. Labor relations. 2. Federal government - Law
and legislation. 3. Wages and salaries.
4. Strikes. I. Title.

331.892
E74 STRIKES.
Erikson, Erik H
Gandhi's truth; on the origins of militant
nonviolence. New York, W.W. Norton, 1969.
474p.

1. Strikes. 2. Social conditions. 3. Civil
disorders. I. Title.

LAW
T
H685ar STRIKES.
Howlett, Robert G
Arbitration in the public sector. New York,
Matthew Bender & Co., 1969.
231-275p.
Reprinted from: Proceedings of the South-
western Legal Foundation 15th annual Institute
on Labor Law.
1. Labor laws and legislation. 2. Strikes.
I. Southwestern Legal Foundation. Institute
on Labor Law. Proceedings.

331.892
S17 STRIKES.
Saso, Carmen D
Coping with public employee strikes.
Chicago, Public Personnel Association, 1970.
162p.

1. Strikes. 2. Federal civil service.
I. Public Personnel Association. II. Title.

331.892
C65
1967
H-H STRIKES.
U.S. CONGRESS. HOUSE. COMMITTEE
ON EDUCATION AND LABOR.
SITUS PICKETING. HEARINGS BEFORE
THE SPECIAL SUBCOMMITTEE ON LABOR,
NINETIETH CONGRESS, SECOND SESSION, ON
H.R. 100. WASHINGTON, GOVT. PRINT.
OFF., 1967.
379P.

HEARINGS HELD APRIL 3-11, 1967.

1. STRIKES. 2. BUILDING INDUSTRY -
LABOR RELATIONS. I. TITLE.

331.892
C65
1965
H-R STRIKES.
U.S. CONGRESS. HOUSE. COMMITTEE ON
EDUCATION AND LABOR.
SITUS PICKETING. REPORT TO
ACCOMPANY H.R. 10027. WASHINGTON,
GOVT. PRINT. OFF., 1965.
15P. (89TH CONGRESS, 1ST SESSION.
HOUSE OF REPRESENTATIVES. REPORT NO.
1041)

1. STRIKES. 2. BUILDING INDUSTRY -
LABOR RELATIONS. I. TITLE.

331.892
L11 Strikes.
U.S. Bureau of Labor Statistics.
Analysis of work stoppages 1956.
Washington, Govt. Print. Off., June 1956.
35 p. tables, diagrs. (Its Bulletin
no. 1218)

At head of title: 85th Congress, 1st
Session. House Document no. 196.

1. Strikes. 2. Labor relations.

331.892
L11
1958 Strikes.
U.S. Bureau of Labor Statistics.
Analysis of work stoppages 1958, by
Ann James Herlihy and Loretto R. Nolan.
Washington, Govt. Print. Off., 1959.
36p. tables (Its Bulletin no. 1258)

At head of title: 86th Cong. 1st sess.
House, Document no. 176.

1. Strikes. 2. Labor relations. I. Herlihy,
Ann James. II Nolan, Loretto R.

331.892
L11
1959 Strikes.
U.S. Bureau of Labor Statistics.
Analysis of work stoppages 1959, by
Joseph W. Bloch and Loretto R. Nolan.
Washington, Govt. Print. Off., 1960.
60p. tables. (Its Bulletin no. 1278)

At head of title: 86th Cong., 2d sess. House.
Document no. 420.

1. Strikes. 2. Labor relations. I. Bloch,
Joseph W. II. Nolan, Loretto R.

331.892
L11
1961 Strikes.
U.S. Bureau of Labor Statistics.
Analysis of work stoppages, 1961, by
Loretto R. Nolan. Wash., Govt. Print.
Off., 1962.
48p. (Its Bulletin no. 1339)
At head of title: 87th Cong., 2d sess.
House. Document no. 594.

1. Strikes. 2. Labor relations.
I. Nolan, Loretto R.

331.892
L11
1968 STRIKES.
U.S. Bureau of Labor Statistics.
Analysis of work stoppages, 1968, by
Howard N. Fullerton. Wash., Govt. Print.
Off., 1970.
61p. (Its Bulletin no. 1646)

1. Strikes. 2. Labor relations.
I. Fullerton, Howard N. II. Title.

300.15
Y15
v. 4 Strikes.
Warner, William Lloyd, 1898-
The social system of the modern factory. The strike: a
social analysis, by W. Lloyd Warner and J. O. Low. New
Haven, Yale university press; London, G. Cumberlege, Oxford university press, 1947.
xvi, 245 p. tables, diagrs. 24½ cm. (Half-title: Yankee City
series, vol. IV)
1. Social science research. 2. Labor relations-
U.S. 3. Strikes.
3. Strikes and lockouts-Shoe indus-
try-U. S. 3. Industrial relations-U. S. I. Low, Josiah Orne,
1879- joint author. II. Title. III. Ser.

HD5324.W3   331.89288531   47—2640

Library of Congress   [40g²7]

331.892
Z47 STRIKES.
ZISKIND, DAVID.
ONE THOUSAND STRIKES OF GOVERNMENT
EMPLOYEES, BY DAVID ZISKIND, PH. D.
NEW YORK, COLUMBIA UNIVERSITY PRESS,
1940.
279P.

BIBLIOGRAPHY: P. 261-268.

1. STRIKES. 2. FEDERAL CIVIL
SERVICE. I. TITLE.

331.892
(016)
T65 Strikes - Bibliography.
Tompkins, Dorothy C comp.
Strikes by public employees and professional
personnel: a bibliography. Berkeley,
Institute of Governmental Studies, University
of California, 1967.
92p.

1. Strikes - Bibl. 2. Labor relations -
Bibl. I. California. University. Institute
of Governmental Studies. II. Title.

331.892
(016)
T65

Strikes by public employees and professional personnel.
Tompkins, Dorothy C   comp.
Strikes by public employees and professional personnel: a bibliography. Berkeley, Institute of Governmental Studies, University of California, 1967.
92p.

1. Strikes - Bibl. 2. Labor relations - Bibl. I. California. University. Institute of Governmental Studies. II. Title.

693.5
W66s

The strip method for designing slabs.
Wood, R   H
The strip method for designing slabs, by R.H. Wood and G.S.T. Armer. Garston, Eng., Building Research Station, 1970.
53p. (U.K. Building Research Station. Current paper 39/70)

1. Concrete construction. 2. Concrete, Reinforced. I. Armer, G.S.T., jt. au. II. U.K. Building Research Station. III. Title.

697.9
S77
1959

Strock, Clifford, 1900-   ed.
Handbook of air conditioning, heating, and ventilating. Clifford Strock, editor; William B. Foxhall, associate editor. New York, Industrial Press [1959]

1 v. illus. 28 cm.

1. Air conditioning—XXXXXXXXXXXXXXX 2. Heating XXXXXX XXXXXXXXXX 3. Ventilation XXXXXXXXXXXXXXX I. Foxhall, William B., XXX ed.   I. Title

TH7687.S76   697   59—7559

323.4
832

Striner, Herbert E   jt.au.
Sheppard, Harold L
Civil rights, employment and the social status of American Negroes, by H.L. Sheppard and H.E. Striner. Kalamazoo, Mich., W.E. Upjohn Institute for Employment Research, 1966.
85p. (W.E. Upjohn Institute for Employment Research. Studies in employment and unemployment)
Based on a report for U.S. Commission on Civil Rights.

1. Civil rights. 2. Employment - Negroes. I. Upjohn Institute for Employment Research. E., jt.au. II. Striner, Herbert III. Title.

690.015
H45

Strip method for slabs on columns L-shaped plates, etc.
Hillerborg, Arne.
Strip method for slabs on columns L-shaped plates, etc. Translated from Swedish by F. A. Blakey, Division of Building Research. Melbourne, Australia, Commonwealth Scientific and Industrial Research Organization, Division of Building Research, 1964.
29p. (Translation no. 2)

1. Building research. 2. Loads. I. Australia. Commonwealth Scientific and Industrial Research Organization. (Div. of Building Research) II. Title.

697.9
S77
1965

Strock, Clifford
Handbook of air conditioning, heating and ventilating. Clifford Strock [and] Richard Koral, editors. 2d ed. New York, Industrial [c1965]
1472 p. illus. 24 cm.

3c

370
S77

Striner, Herbert E
Continuing education as a national capital investment. Kalamazoo, Mich., W.E. Upjohn Institute for Employment Research, 1971.
118p. (Studies in employment and unemployment)

1. Education. I. Upjohn Institute for Employment Research. II. Title.

VF Neighborhood rehabilitation
DATE OF REQUEST   6/8/53   APR 15 1953   L C. CARD NO.
AUTHOR Stritch, Samuel Cardinal.
TITLE Neighborhood conservation (excerpts from address given at meeting of priests of the Chicago archdiocese on Neighborhood conservation held in Chicago, Nov. 26, 1952)
SERIES Reprint from the Catholic Charities Review, February, 1953, pp. 33-35.
EDITION   PUB. DATE   PAGING 33-35.
PUBLISHER

RECOMMENDED BY   REVIEWED IN   PCP Mar. 30, 1953, p. 6
ORDER RECORD

VF Industrial location
DATE OF REQUEST 10/18/54   L C. CARD NO.
AUTHOR Stroetzel, Donald S.
TITLE Those new jobs in American towns.
SERIES Reprint, Pathfinder, the Town Journal, May, June, July 1954.
EDITION   PUB. DATE 1954   PAGING 6p.
PUBLISHER

RECOMMENDED BY NML   REVIEWED IN   Amr. City 10/54 p.189
ORDER RECORD

331
S77

Striner, Herbert E
1984 and beyond, the world of work. Kalamazoo, Mich., W.E. Upjohn Institute for Employment Research, 1967.
8p.

1. Labor supply. I. Upjohn Institute for Employment Research. II. Title.

628.515
S77

Strobbe, Maurice A   ed.
Understanding environmental pollution. Saint Louis, C.V. Mosby, 1971.
357p.

Bibliography: p. 336-342.

1. Water pollution. 2. Air pollution. 3. Natural resources. I. Title.

658
S77

Stroh, Thomas F
Managing the new generation in business. New York, McGraw-Hill, 1971.
160p.

1. Management. 2. Personnel management. I. Title.

300
S77

Striner, Herbert E
The social sciences and community problems, by H.E. Striner and Henry E. Holmquist. [n.p.] 1958.
21p.

1. Social sciences. 2. Community development. I. Holmquist, Henry E., jt.au.

308
A52
1969

Strobl, Alois K
Problems in city planning for the cartographer and a critical review of cartography. (In American Congress on Surveying and Mapping. Papers from the 29th annual meeting. 1969. p. 137-146)

1. City planning. I. Title.

ANAL.

658
A52r
no.
93

Stroh, Thomas F
The uses of video tape in training and development. New York, American Management Association, 1969.
59p. (American Management Association. AMA research study 93)

1. Management. 2. Films. I. American Management Association. II. Title: Video tape. III. Title.

331
B87

Striner, Herbert E   jt. au.
Burt, Samuel M
Toward greater industry and government involvement in manpower development, by Samuel M. Burt and Herbert E. Striner. Kalamazoo, Mich., W.E. Upjohn Institute for Employment Research, 1968.
21p. (Upjohn Institute for Employment Research. Staff paper)

1. Employment. 2. Education. 3. Labor supply. I. Striner, Herbert E., jt. au. II. Upjohn Institute for Employment Research. III. Title.

651.5
N17P
NO.134+

STROBRIDGE, TRUMAN R
U.S. NATIONAL ARCHIVES AND RECORDS SERVICE.
PRELIMINARY INVENTORY OF THE RECORDS OF THE BUREAU OF PUBLIC ROADS (RECORD GROUP 30) COMPILED BY TRUMAN R. STROBRIDGE. WASHINGTON, 1962. 34P. (ITS PUBLICATION 62-5. PRELIMINARY INVENTORIES. NO. 134)

1. U.S. BUREAU OF PUBLIC ROADS. I. STROBRIDGE, TRUMAN R. COMP.

333.32
S77

Strohbehn, Roger Wallace.
Land ownership in the Great Plains States, 1958. A statistical summary, by Roger W. Strohbehn and Gene Wunderlich. Wash., U.S. Dept. of Agriculture, Agricultural Research Service, 1960.
80p. (U.S. Dept. of Agriculture. Statistical bulletin no. 261)

1. Land tenure. I. Wunderlich, Gene, jt. au. II. U.S. Agricultural Research Service. III. Title.

691.328
A75

The strip method: a new approach to the design of slabs.
Armer, G   S   T
The strip method: a new approach to the design of slabs. Garston Eng., Building Research Station, Ministry of Public Building and Works, 1968.
[6]p. (U.K. Building Research Station. Current paper CP 81/68)
Reprinted from: Concrete, 1968, Vol. 2 (9), September, pp. 358-363.

1. Concrete, Reinforced. I. Title. II. U.K. Building Research Station.

Strock, Clifford   editor of "Heating and Ventilating," is well equipped to write on the subject of heating. He received his B.S. and M.E. degree from Purdue University. He has been connected with the Pennsylvania Railroad and International Heater Company. He is co-author of the Degree-Day Handbook and the Air Conditioning Engineer's Atlas. He is a member of the American Society of Heating and Ventilating Engineers, the American Society of Refrigeration Engineers, and the American Society of Mechanical Engineers.

690.5
551.5
(485)
S77

Strokirk, Evert
Constructional engineer Ernst Sundh builds apartment houses in Avesta with the help of a crane. [Stockholm, Statens Kommitté för Byggnadsforskning? Feb. 1951]
9 1.

Bound with...A survey of winter construction in Sweden by Evert Strokirk. Processed.

1. Winter construction. I. Sweden. Statens Kommitté för Byggnadsforskning.

694.1
UX
Strokirk, Evert.
United Nations. (Economic and Social Council)
Economic Commission for Europe. Timber
Comm.)
Economy in the use of timber for housing
purposes. [New York] March 1951.
16, 10 p. diagrs., tables. (Its
Publication E/ECE/124, E/ECE/TIM/36)

Report by Evert Strokirk, submitted to
the Working Party on More Rational
Utilisation of Wood, July 1950.
1.Wood construction. 2.Building costs.
I.Strokirk,   Evert.

058.7
728.1
1362.6
(794)
A27
STROMME, GEORGE, ED.
ACTIVE RETIREMENT EXECUTIVES
ASSOCIATION.
CALIFORNIA RETIREMENT FACILITIES
REGISTER. GEORGE STROMME, EDITOR.
RESEARCH BY INTERNATIONAL DATA CORP.
LOS ANGELES, 1963.
78P.

1. HOUSING FOR THE AGED - CALIFORNIA
- DIRECTORIES.   I. STROMME, GEORGE, ED.
II. TITLE.

333.71
U71p
Strong, Ann Louise.
U.S. Urban Renewal Administration.
Preserving urban open space, by Ann Louise
Strong. Washington, Govt. Print. Off., 1963.
36p.

1. Open space land. I. Strong, Ann.

690.015
I57
no. 17
Strokirk, E
International Council for Research, Studies
and Documentation.
Scandinavian experience in collaboration
in building research on a sub-regional level,
by M. Jacobsson (Sweden), Director of the
State Committee for Building Research and
E. Strokirk (Sweden), building expert at the
Royal Housing Board. Geneva, 1953.
8p. (CIB/17)
At head of title: General Assembly.
(Palais des Nations, Geneva, 25 to 30
June inclusive)
1. Building research.   I. Jacobsson, M.
I. Strokirk, E.   III. Title.

331
S65
Stromsdorfer, Ernst, W., jt. au.
Somers, Gerald G
A benefit-cost analysis of manpower re-
training, by Gerald G. Somers and Ernst W.
Stromsdorfer. Reproduced from Industrial
Relations Research Association. Proceedings,
1964.   p. 172-185.

1. Employment. 2. Personnel management.
I. Industrial Relations Research Association
Proceedings. II. Stromsdorfer, Ernst. W., jt.
au. III. Title.

651.5
022
Strong, Earl P., jt. au.
Odell, Margaret K
Records management and filing operations,
by Margaret K. Odell and Earl P. Strong.
New Yrok, McGraw Hill, 1947.
342 p. illus.

1.Records management. I.Strong, Earl P.,
jt. au.

690.5
:551.5
(485)
S77
Strokirk, Evert
A survey of winter construction in Sweden.
[Stockholm, Statens Kommittee för Byggnadsforskning? Feb. 1951]
4 l.

Processed.

1.Winter construction. I.Sweden. Statens
Kommittee för Byggnadsforskning.

LAW
T
S776op
Strong, Ann Louise.
Open space for the Penjerdel Region,
1961 working papers for Open Space Conference,
October 18, 1961. Philadelphia, Penjerdel,
1961.
55p.

1. Open space land. I. Pennsylvania-New
Jersey-Delaware-Metropolitan Project Open
Space Conference, 1961.

301.15
S77
Strong, Josiah.
The Twentieth Century city. New York,
Arno Press & The New York Times, 1970, c1898.
186p. (The rise of urban America)

1. Community structure. 2. Social conditions.
I. Title. Series: The rise of urban America)

690.015
(485)
S82
R37
1970
Ström, U   jt. au.
Lindström, B
Kontroll av tillämpade varmebehovsberäkningar
(Investigations of methods used for calcula-
ting heat requirements) av B. Lindström och
U. Ström. Stockholm, 1970.
43p. (Stockholm. Statens Institut för
Byggnadsforskning. Rapport R37:1970)
English summary.
1. Building research - Sweden.
2. Heating. I. Ström, U., jt. au.
II. Stockholm. Statens Institut för
Byggnadsforskning. III. Title: Investigations
of methods used for calculating heat
requirements.

333.71
U71ope
Strong, Ann Louise.
U.S. Urban Renewal Administration.
Open space for urban America, by Ann
Louise Strong for the Urban Renewal
Administration. Wash., For sale by the
Supt. of Doc., Govt. Print. Off., 1965.
154p.
Bibliography: p. 151-154.

1. Open space land. I. Strong, Ann
Louise. II. Title.

658.3
A52r
Strong, Lydia.
American Management Association.
Let's get down to cases, problem
situations for the line supervisor,
by Lydia Strong. New York, 1961.
1v.

1. Personnel management.
I. Strong, Lydia.

690.015
(485)
S82
R53
1968
Strömdahl, Ingvar.
Brandteknisk forskning pa det slackande
brandförsvarets området; förslag till
svenskt (nordiskt) langtidsprogram (Fire
engineering research in the field of fire
fighting; proposal for a Swedish (Nordic)
long-term programme) Stockholm, Statens
Institut för Byggnadsforskning, 1968.
51p. (Stockholm. Statens Institut för
Byggnadsforskning. Rapport 53:1968)
English summary.
1. Building research - Sweden. 2. Sweden -
Building research. 3. Fire prevention - Research. 4. Fire   proof construction;
(Cont'd on next card)

LAW
T
S776op
Strong, Ann Louise.
Open space in the Penjerdel region now or
never. Philadelphia, Pennsylvania, New
Jersey, Delaware Metropolitan Project, 1963.
54p.

1. Open space land. I. Pennsylvania-New
Jersey-Delaware Metropolitan Project.

697.942
T67
Strong-room climate.
Tottle, H   F
Strong-room climate. [n.p.] 1956.
[11] p.

Reprinted from Archivist, 1956. 387-97.

1.Humidity. 2.Archives. I.Title.

690.015
(485)
S82
R53
1968
Strömdahl, Ingvar.   Brandteknisk...1968.
(Card 2)
I. Stockholm. Statens Institut för
Byggnadsforskning. II. Title: Fire
engineering research

333.71
S77
Strong, Ann Louise, ed.
Open space through water resources protection:
an approach applied to the Philadelphia metropolitan area. Proceedings of an Open Space
Conference, sponsored by the Institute for
Urban Studies, University of Pennsylvania, and
held on December 17, 1964. Philadelphia, University of Pennsylvania, Institute for Environmental Studies, 1965.
116p.
1. Open space land. 2. Land use. 3. Water resources. I. Pennsylvania. University. Institute for Environ   mental Studies.
II. Title.

3832-
3837
STRONGSVILLE, OHIO. PLANNING COMMISSION.
COMMUNITY PLANNING: 1. COMPREHENSIVE
PLAN: 2. LAND PLANNING AND SUBDIVISION
REGULATIONS: 3. CAPITAL IMPROVEMENTS: 4.
ZONING ORDINANCE: 5. TECHNICAL
SUPPLEMENT: 6. PROJECT COMPLETION
REPORT. STRONGSVILLE, OHIO, 1968-69.
6 V. (HUD 701 REPORT)

1. MASTER PLAN - STRONGSVILLE, OHIO.
I. HUD 701. STRONGSVILLE, OHIO.

699.81
S77t
Strömdahl, Ingvar.
The Tranas fire tests; field studies of heat
radiation from fires in a timber structure.
Stockholm, Statens Institut for Byggnadsfors-
kning, 1972.
70p. (Document D3:1972)

1. Fire prevention. I. Stockholm. Statens
Institut for Byggnadsforskning. II. Title.

711.4
S77p
Strong, Ann Louise.
Planned urban environments; Sweden, Finland,
Israel, The Netherlands, France. Baltimore,
Johns Hopkins Press, 1971.
406p.

Bibliography: p. 391-396.

1. City planning. I. Title.

711.4
(77131)
C52s
Strongsville, Ohio. Planning Commission.
Cleveland. Regional Planning Commission.
Strongsville 1975; a guide for
community action. Prepared in cooperation
with Strongsville Planning Commission.
Cleveland, 1964.
1v.

U.S. Urban Renewal Adm. UPAP.

1. City planning - Strongsville, Ohio.
I. Strongsville, Ohio. Planning Commission.
II. U.S. URA-UPAP. Strongsville, Ohio.

628.1
G260

STRONTIUM IN NATURAL WATER.
U.S. GEOLOGICAL SURVEY.
OCCURRENCE AND DISTRIBUTION OF
STRONTIUM IN NATURAL WATER, BY MARVIN M.
SKOUGSTAD AND C. ALBERT HORR.
WASHINGTON, GOVT. PRINT. OFF., 1963.
97P. (ITS WATER-SUPPLY PAPER 1496-D)

1. WATER SUPPLY. I. SKOUGSTAD,
MARVIN M. II. HORR, C. ALBERT.
III. TITLE: STRONTIUM IN NATURAL WATER.

624.131
034T

STRUBLE, RICHARD A
OHIO. ENGINEERING EXPERIMENT STATION,
COLUMBUS.
TERRAIN INVESTIGATION TECHNIQUES FOR
HIGHWAY ENGINEERS; FINAL REPORT, BY
OLIN W. MINTZER AND RICHARD A.
STRUBLE. COLUMBUS, OHIO, 1965.
104P.

1. SOILS. 2. SOILS - TESTING.
3. HIGHWAYS. I. MINTZER, OLIN W.
II. STRUBLE, RICHARD A.

VF
690.13
H68

...Structural and insulation requirements for
houses.
U.S. Housing and Home Finance Agency. Office
of the Administrator. Technical Office.
Performance standards; structural and
insulation requirements for houses. Washington, June 1947.
11 p. tables, maps.

1. Insulation. 2. Building standards. I. Title.
II. Title: Structural and insulation requirements
for houses.

355.58
C48ri

Strope, Walmer E
U.S. Office of Civil Defense.
Fire aspects of civil defense.
Evaluation report, by Walmer E. Strope and
John F. Christian. Wash., Govt. Print.
Off., 1964.
10p. (TR-25)

1. Civilian defense. 2. Fire prevention.
3. Thermal radiation. I. Strope, Walmer E.
II. Christian, John F. III. Title.

728.1
1336.18
(74)
S77

STRUCKE, ADELA L
CONSTRUCTION LABOR ON PUBLIC HOUSING
IN THE SOUTH. WASHINGTON, GOVT.
PRINT. OFF., 1952.
10P. (U.S. LABOR STATISTICS
BUREAU. SERIAL NO. R. 2086)
REPRINTED FROM THE MONTHLY LABOR
REVIEW, OCTOBER, 1952.

1. PUBLIC HOUSING - SOUTHERN STATES.
I. HAASE, HENRY E, JT. AU.
II. TITLE.

624.2
B67

Borges, J Ferry.
Structural behaviour and safety criteria.
[Presented at the Seventh Congress of the
International Association for Bridge and
Structural Engineering, Rio de Janeiro,
August, 1964] Lisbon, Portugal, Ministério
das Obras Publicas, Laboratório Nacional de
Engenharia Civil, 1964.
231-240p. (Portugal. Laboratório
Nacional de Engenharia Civil. Technical
paper no. 240)

1. Bridges. 2. Vibra- tion. I. Portugal.
Laboratório Nacional de Engenharia Civil.
II. Title.

VF
711.585
(764)
S77

Strother, Robert S
The sad little story of Wink. Reproduced from the Freeman, October, 1964.
p. 15-20.

1. Urban renewal - Wink, Texas.
I. The Freeman. II. Title.

694.54
I55

Structural analyses and calculations.
Illinois. University. Small Homes Council.
Structural analyses and calculations for (A)
systems of wood framing for dwellings and (B)
1-1/2 story roof truss 2' - 0" O.C., contained in
Housing research paper no. 33 resulting from
Project no. 1-T-118 under contract with the
University of Illinois Small Homes Council and
Housing and Home Finance Agency. [Urbana, Ill.
1953]
112, 48 l. plates.

Project director, James T. Lendrum; staff
technician, Philip Randall.
Processed.

691.328
N67s

Structural behavior of reinforced
concrete beams made with fast-fixlcement.
Nosseir, S B
Structural behavior of reinforced concrete
beams made with fast-fix 1 cement, by
S.B. Nosseir and M.G. Katona. Port Hueneme,
Calif., Naval Civil Engineering Laboratory,
1969.
33p. (Technical report R 614)
Sponsored by Naval Facilities Engineering
Command.
CFSTI. AD 683757.
1. Concrete, Reinforced. 2. Structural
engineering. I. U.S. Naval Civil
Engineering Laboratory. II. Title.

5757

STROUD, OKLA. PLANNING COMMISSION.
A COMPREHENSIVE PLAN. BY COMMUNITY
PLANNING ASSOCIATES. STROUD, OKLA., 1969.
85P. (HUD 701 REPORT)

1. MASTER PLAN - STROUD, OKLA.
I. COMMUNITY PLANNING ASSOCIATES.
II. HUD. 701. STROUD, OKLA.

624
851

STRUCTURAL ANALYSIS.
BLASZKOWIAK, STANISLAW.
ITERATIVE METHODS IN STRUCTURAL ANALYSIS,
BY S. BLASZKOWIAK AND Z. KACZKOWSKI.
TRANSLATED BY A. KACNER AND Z. OLESIAK.
OXFORD, PERGAMON PRESS, 1966.
590P.

REVISED AND ENLARGED FROM THE POLISH
EDITION.
REFERENCES: P.531-536.
1. STRUCTURAL ENGINEERING - RESEARCH.
I. KACZKOWSKI, ZBIGNIEW, JT. AU.
II. TITLE. III. TITLE: STRUCTURAL
ANALYSIS.

624.2
M25

Structural behaviour of the Moat Street flyover.
Menzies, J B
Structural behaviour of the Moat Street
flyover, Coventry. Garston, Eng., Building
Research Station, Ministry of Public Building
and Works, 1968.
967-971p. (U.K. Building Research Station.
Current paper CP 78/68)
Reprinted from: Civil engineering and public
works review, Sept., 1968. pp. 967-971.

1. Bridges. 2. Strains and stresses. 3. Road
construction. I. Title. II. U.K. Building
Research Station.

3960
3961
3962

STROUD, OKLA., PLANNING COMMISSION.
PLANNING: 1, PRELIMINARY ZONING
ORDINANCE; 2, ZONING ORDINANCE AND
SUBDIVISION REGULATIONS; 3, COMPLETION
REPORT. BY COMMUNITY PLANNING ASSOCIATES
AND OTHERS. STROUD, OKLA., 1969.
3 V. (HUD 701 REPORT)

1. CITY PLANNING - STROUD, OKLA.
I. COMMUNITY PLANNING ASSOCIATES.
II. HUD. 701. STROUD, OKLA.

624
B76s

Structural analysis.
Brown, Eric Hugh.
Structural analysis. New York, Wiley, 1967.
v.

1. Structural engineering. I. Title.

690
(492)
B68S

STRUCTURAL BUILDING METHODS.
BOUCENTRUM, ROTTERDAM.
STRUCTURAL BUILDING METHODS.
ROTTERDAM, 1957.
1 V. (VARIOUS PAGINGS) (ITS
PUBLICATION B2.0)

TEXT IN ENGLISH AND DUTCH.

1. BUILDING CONSTRUCTION - NETHERLANDS.
I. TITLE.

711.17
443L
1961

STROUP, ROBERT H
REFLECTIONS ON CONCEPTS FOR IMPACT
RESEARCH, A PAPER PRESENTED AT THE 40TH
ANNUAL MEETING OF THE HIGHWAY RESEARCH
BOARD, WASHINGTON, D.C., JANUARY 13,
1961, BY ROBERT H. STROUP AND LOUIS A.
VARGHA. LEXINGTON, KENT., 1961.
20L.

1. HIGHWAYS. I. VARGHA, ROBERT H.,
JT. AU. II. HIGHWAY RESEARCH BOARD,
MEETING, 40TH, WASHINGTON, D.C. 1961.

624
L18

Structural analysis.
Laursen, Harold I
Structural analysis. New York, McGraw-Hill, 1969.
486p.

1. Structural engineering. I. Title.

Structural characteristics of houses see
Trends in house construction

Strozier, Harry, ed.
Georgia. Laws, statutes, etc.
Code of Georgia annotated, including the Code of
1933 and all laws of general application subsequently
enacted with editorial notes and complete annotations
of the decisions of the Supreme Court and Court of
Appeals of Georgia and of all the federal courts construing Georgia laws. Prepared under the editorial
supervision of Orville A. Park, Harry B. Skillman,
and Harry S. Strozier ... Atlanta, The Harrison
company, 1935-
34v. 24cm.

658.564
P34

STRUCTURAL ANALYSIS SYSTEM.
PHILCO CORP.
STRUCTURAL ANALYSIS SYSTEM; USAGE
REPORT, BY ROBERT J. MELOSH AND
OTHERS. PALO ALTO, CALIF., 1963.
31P.

PREPARED FOR JET PROPULSION
LABORATORY, CALIFORNIA INSTITUTE OF
TECHNOLOGY, PASADENA, CALIFORNIA.

1. AUTOMATION. I. TITLE.
II. MELOSH, ROBERT J.
III. CALIFORNIA INSTITUTE OF
TECHNOLOGY, PASADENA.

691.421
UN

Structural clay products.
United Nations. (Economic Commission for
Asia and the Far East)
Structural clay products. New York,
1967.
30p. ([Document] I7NR/BM/22)
At head of title: Seminar on the
Development of Building Materials, 8-15
January 1968, Bangkok, Thailand.

1. Clay. 2. Bricks. I. Title.

690
1331.86
N17S
STRUCTURAL CLAY PRODUCTS.
U.S. NATIONAL HOUSING AGENCY.
STRUCTURAL CLAY PRODUCTS: BRICKS
AND TILE. WASHINGTON, D.C., NATIONAL
HOUSING AGENCY, 1946.
7L. (ITS PREMIUM PAYMENTS BULLETIN
NO. 1)

1. BUILDING TRADES. 2. WAGE
INCENTIVES. I. TITLE.

693.2
S77b
Structural Clay Products Institute.
Building code requirements for
engineered brick masonry. McLean,
Va., 1969.
36p.

1. Brick construction. 2. Building
codes. I. Title.

690.091.82
S78
STRUCTURAL CLAY PRODUCTS INSTITUTE.
RECOMMENDED BUILDING CODE
REQUIREMENTS FOR ENGINEERED BRICK
MASONRY. WASHINGTON, D.C., 1966.
31P. TABLES.

1. BUILDING CODES - MODEL LAWS
AND ORDINANCES. 2. BRICK
CONSTRUCTION - MODEL LAWS AND
ORDINANCES. I. TITLE: ENGINEERED
BRICK MASONRY. II. TITLE: BRICK
MASONRY.

690.22
P15
STRUCTURAL CLAY PRODUCTS, INC.
PALMER, L A
THE CONSTRUCTION OF WEATHER RESISTANT
MASONRY WALLS. WASHINGTON, STRUCTURAL
CLAY PRODUCTS, INC., 1936.
27P.

1. WALLS. I. STRUCTURAL CLAY
PRODUCTS, INC. II. TITLE: WEATHER
RESISTANT MASONRY WALLS.

355.58
877
Structural Clay Products Institute.
Clay masonry fallout shelters.
Washington, 1960.
16p. diagrs.

Reprinted by: Office of Civil and Defense
Mobilization.

1. Clay. 2. Civilian defense.

693.2
S77r
Structural Clay Products Institute.
Recommended practice for engineered
brick masonry. McLean, Va., 1969.
337p.

Bibliography: p. 329-333.

1. Brick construction. 2. Bricklaying. I. Title.

693.068
1389.6
S77A
STRUCTURAL CLAY PRODUCTS INSTITUTE.
THE ABC OF MODULAR MASONRY. 2D.
ARCHITECTURAL ED. WASHINGTON, 1945.
20P.

1. MODULAR COORDINATION. I. TITLE.

693.2
S77
Structural Clay Products Institute.
Handi-guide on brick and structural tile wall
assemblies. [Washington, 1950?]
144 p. illus., diagrs.

1. Brick construction. 2. Clay.

690.22
S77t
Structural Clay Products Institute.
Technical notes on brick and tile construction.
v.1, no.1, 1950-
v. monthly. notebook.

An up-to-date notebook contains a broken sequence
of volumes and numbers. Old issues are discarded
as they are superseded by new and revised material
on the same subject published in later issues.

SEE SERIAL RECORD.

(over)

VF Walls
DATE OF REQUEST MAY 7 1951
4-30-51
L.C. CARD NO.

AUTHOR
Structural Clay Products Institute

TITLE
Brick and Tile Cavity Walls

SERIES

| EDITION | PUB. DATE 4/50 | PAGING 12p. |

PUBLISHER
2ame   Wash., D.C   1520   18th St. N. W.

RECOMMENDED BY   Mr. Eay | REVIEWED IN

ORDER RECORD

728.
1333
S77
STRUCTURAL CLAY PRODUCTS INSTITUTE.
HOMEBUYER'S HANDBOOK. WASHINGTON,
1964.
1 V.

1. HOME OWNERSHIP. I. TITLE.

693
F71
Structural Clay Products Institute.
Frankl, Lee.
The masonry house; step-by-step construction in tile and
brick [by] Training-Thru-Sight Associates: Lee Frankl, in
cooperation with Structural Clay Products Institute. New
York, Duell, Sloan & Pearce [1950]
124 p. illus. 28 cm. (Basic industrial series)

1. Brick construction.
I. Masonry. 2. Building Brick. 3. Tile construction. I. Train-
ing-Thru-Sight Associates, New York. II. Title. (Series)
III. Structural Clay Products Institute.
TH1199.F7   690   50-8592
Library of Congress   [20]

VF Brick construction
DATE OF REQUEST 11/9/53   1953 C. CARD NO.
DEC 2

AUTHOR
Structural Clay Products Institute.

TITLE
Brick and tile construction details.

SERIES

| EDITION | PUB. DATE 1953 | PAGING 32 p. |

PUBLISHER

RECOMMENDED BY   MZL | REVIEWED IN
Der Merchant 9/53 p. 56

ORDER RECORD

VF Brick construction
DATE OF REQUEST 7/20/52   L.C. CARD NO.
AUG 7 1952

AUTHOR
Structural Clay Products Institute.

TITLE
How to build brick houses that sell with the SCR brick.

SERIES

| EDITION | PUB. DATE [1952?] | PAGING |

PUBLISHER
same

RECOMMENDED BY | REVIEWED IN
NAHB Correlator 7/52 p.106

ORDER RECORD

Acl. Dom. Domeplans   Author (Surname first)   8-10
NOT RUSH
Class No.

Accession No.
Title Modern brick homes:
20 housing and building house plans
Structural Clay Products Inc.

Of Wash., D.C.

Received 2/49
Cost | Edition or Series   Place   Publisher
Charged to | Date 049   Vols.   56 p   List Prop. $.50   Est. Cost
Date of bill | Recommended by
L.C. No. | Address
Reviewed In
Bld St Mo. p. 27,
July 1949.

693.2
P58
1950
Structural Clay Products Institute.
Plummer, Harry Custer, 1897-
Brick and tile engineering; handbook of design. [1st ed.]
Washington, Structural Clay Products Institute, [1950]
vii, 302 p. illus. 24 cm.

"A revised edition of those sections of [Principles of] brick engineering [by the author with L. J. Reardon and [Principles of] tile
engineering [by the author with E. F. Wanner] ... which deal with
unreinforced masonry."
Bibliography: p. 383-387.

1. Brick construction. 2. Building Brick. 3. Tile construction. I. Title.
I. Structural Clay Products Institute.
TA432.P48   693.2   51-905
Library of Congress   [10]

693.2
S77P
STRUCTURAL CLAY PRODUCTS INSTITUTE.
POCKET GUIDE: BRICK AND TILE
CONSTRUCTION. 4TH ED. WASHINGTON, 1959.
129P.

1. BRICK CONSTRUCTION. 2. TILE
CONSTRUCTION. I. TITLE.

693.068
1369.6
877
Structural Clay Products Institute.
Modular dimensioning practices. The
edited papers presented at a symposium for
government architects, engineers and administrators at the National Housing
Center, Washington, D. C., Jan. 12, 1959.
Sponsored by the Structural Clay Products
Institute and the Modular Building Standards Association. Washington, 1959.
32p.

1. Modular coordination.

620
P58
Structural Clay Products Institute, McLean, Va.
Plummer, Harry C
Brick and tile engineering. McLean Va.,
Structural Clay Products Institute, 1962.
466p.
Bibliography: p. 454-459.

1. Engineering. 2. Bricks. 3. Tile.
I. Structural Clay Products Institute, McLean,
Va. II. Title.

693.2
S77PR
STRUCTURAL CLAY PRODUCTS INSTITUTE.
PRINCIPLES OF CLAY MASONRY
CONSTRUCTION. STUDENT'S MANUAL. BY
RAYMOND D. CARAVATY AND HARRY C.
PLUMMER. WASHINGTON, 1960.
113P.

GLOSSARY OF TERMS P. 56-62.

1. BRICKLAYING. 2. CLAY.
I. CARAVATY, RAYMOND D. II. PLUMMER,
HARRY C. III. TITLE: CLAY MASONRY
CONSTRUCTION.

VF Brick construction
DATE OF REQUEST 6/2/53   C. CARD NO.
APR 15 1953

AUTHOR
Structural Clay Products Institute.

TITLE
New brick homes [45 new brick home plans]

SERIES

| EDITION | PUB. DATE c1952 | PAGING 63p. |

PUBLISHER
Washington, DC

RECOMMENDED BY   RLM | REVIEWED IN
Nac. Bldr. 3/53 p.206

ORDER RECORD

691.42 P58 — Structural Clay Products Institute.
Plummer, Harry Custer
Reinforced brick masonry and lateral force design, by Harry C. Plummer and John A. Blume. Wash., Structural Clay Products Institute, 1953. 271p.

Bibliography: p. 262-265.

1. Bricks. 2. Architecture - Designs and plans. I. Blume, John A., jt. au. II. Structural Clay Products Institute. III. Title.

691.8 S77 — Structural Clay Products Research Foundation.
The SCR building panel; its application to vertical building elements, by C. B. Monk, Jr. Geneva, Ill., 1959. 9p. illus., diagrs., tables.

1. Panels. 2. Prefabricated construction. I. Monk, C. B., Jr.

VF 691.4 S77 R7 — Structural Clay Products Research Foundation.
Resistance of structural clay masonry to dynamic forces, a design manual for blast resistance, by C. B. Monk, Jr. Geneva, Ill., 1958.
2c   64p. illus., diagrs. (Its Research report no. 7)

1. Brick construction. 2. Structural engineering. I. Monk, C. B., Jr.

693.2 A55 — Structural Clay Products Institute.
Allen, Malcolm H
A report on the development of prefabricated brick wall panels in Western Europe. McLean, Va. Structural Clay Products Institute, 1968. 81p.
1. Brick construction. 2. Panels. 3. Prefabricated construction - Europe. 4. Europe - Prefabricated construction. I. Structural Clay Products Institute. II. Title: Development of prefabricated brick wall panels in Western Europe.

VF (691.421 (016) S77 — Structural Clay Products Institute.
Technical literature on structural clay products. Washington, 1959. 13p.

1. Clay - Bibliography.

VF 691.4 S77 R2 — Structural Clay Products Research Foundation.
SCR brick wall fire resistance test, by Ohio State University, Engineering Experiment Station, Columbus, Ohio. Chicago, Ill., Structural Clay Products Research Foundation [1952]
6 p. illus., graphs. (Its Research report No. 2)

1.Brick construction - SCR brick. 2.Building materials - Fire resistant. I.Ohio. State University. Engineering Experiment Station.

693.5 S77s — Structural Clay Products Institute.
Structural design of combination tile and concrete slabs, by Guillermo Enciso and Richard La Vigne. Washington, 1960. 24p. diagrs., tables.

1. Concrete construction. 2. Tile construction. I. Enciso, Guillermo. II. La Vigne, Richard.

690.22 S77 1962 — STRUCTURAL CLAY PRODUCTS INSTITUTE.
ULTIMATE COST OF BUILDING WALLS, BY CLAYFORD T. GRIMM AND JAMES G. GROSS. 3D ED. WASHINGTON, 1962.
2c   36P.

1. WALLS. I. GRIMM, CLAYFORD T. II. GROSS, JAMES G., JT. AU.

VF 691.4 S77 R — Structural Clay Products Research Foundation.
Research report No. 1- . Chicago, Ill. 1953 -
v.

1.Brick construction. 2.Tile construction.

Anals. for 1-3, 5

690.22 S77 — Structural Clay Products Institute.
Ultimate cost of building walls, by Clayford T. Grimm and James G. Gross. Washington, 1958. 36p. diagrs., tables.

1. Walls. 2. Building costs. I. Grimm, Clayford T. II. Gross, James G.

(handwritten acquisition card)
Class No. Brick construction
Author (surname first) Structural Clay Products Institute
Title What the prospective home buyer should know about brick and tile construction in homes, chimneys, fireplaces, and gardens
Accession No.
JUN 23 1950
Source phone
JUN 26 1950
Place Wash., D.C. Publisher
Address
Date 1945
H-305 (2-50) HOUSING AND HOME FINANCE AGENCY: Office of the Administrator

---

VF 691.4 S77 R1 — Structural Clay Products Research Foundation.
SCR brick wall tests, by C. B. Monk, Jr. Chicago, Ill., Structural Clay Products Research Foundation, June 1953.
13 p. illus., graphs. (Its Research report no. 1)

1.Brick construction - SCR brick. 2.Building materials - Testing. I.Monk, C B

691.421 S77c — Structural Clay Products Research Foundation.
Clay masonry looks to automation, by C. B. Monk, Jr. New York, F. W. Dodge, 1959. 8p. illus., diagrs.

Reprinted from Architectural record, Oct. 1959.
Bibliography: p. 15-16.

1. Clay. 2. Panels. I. Monk, C. B., Jr.

728.1 I308 W34 — STRUCTURAL CLAY PRODUCTS INSTITUTE.
WHITLOCK, DOUGLAS.
WHITLOCK STATEMENT, BASED ON A MARKET STUDY BY ROBINSON NEWCOMB. WASHINGTON, STRUCTURAL CLAY PRODUCTS INSTITUTE, 1955. 1 V.

INCLUDES PRESS RELEASE OF THE STRUCTURAL CLAY PRODUCTS INSTITUTE AND GRAPHS ISSUED BY ROBINSON NEWCOMB ASSOCIATES.
1. HOUSING MARKET. 2. BRICK INDUSTRY. 3. TITLE. I. NEWCOMB, ROBINSON. II. STRUCTURAL CLAY PRODUCTS INSTITUTE.

VF 691.4 S77 R5 — Structural Clay Products Research Foundation.
Space division in schools, by S. E. Hubbard. Geneva, Ill., June 1956.
18 p. graphs, tables. (Its Research report no. 5)

1.Schools. 2.Tile. 3.Walls. I.Title. II.Hubbard, S E

691.421 S77 — Structural Clay Products Research Foundation.
An interpretation of the engineering significance of the Nevada blast tests on clay masonry, by C. B. Monk, Jr. Geneva, Ill., 1957. 6p.

1. Clay. 2. Protective construction. I. Monk, C. B., Jr.

Structural Clay Products Research Foundation, 1520-18th St., N.W., Washington, D.C.

Robt. B. Taylor appointed Director. (EN-R, p. 56, Feb. 2, 1950) Program to be outlined by Arthur D. Little, Inc., industrial engineers.

Industry-wide long-range research program in the brick and tile industry.

699.85 M65a — Structural Clay Products Research Foundation, Geneva, Ill.
Monk, C B
An analysis for the design of "SCR disaster-proof housing. Geneva, Ill., Structural Clay Products Research Foundation, 1958. 15p.

1. Protective construction. I. Structural Clay Products Research Foundation, Geneva, Ill.

691.421 S77r — Structural Clay Products Research Foundation.
Recent research on insulated clay masonry cavity walls, by C. B. Monk, Jr. Geneva, Ill., 1960. 16p. illus., tables.

Bibliography: p. 15-16.

1. Clay. 2. Walls. 3. Insulation. I. Monk, C. B., Jr.

VF 691.4 S77 R3 — Structural Clay Products Research Foundation.
Comparative costs of low-cost schools, by S. E. Hubbard. Chicago, Ill., Structural Clay Products Research Foundation, Sept. 1954.
19 p. illus., plans, tables. (Its Research report no. 3)

1.Schools. 2.Metal construction. 3.Brick construction - SCR brick. 4.Building costs. I.Title. II.Hubbard, S E

693.5 D18 — STRUCTURAL CONCRETE.
DAVIES, JOHN DUNCAN.
STRUCTURAL CONCRETE. LONDON, PERGAMON PRESS, 1964.
163P. (THE COMMONWEALTH AND INTERNATIONAL LIBRARY. STRUCTURES AND SOLID BODY MECHANICS DIVISION, V. 1)

1. CONCRETE CONSTRUCTION. I. TITLE.

Structural concrete.
691.32
J63   Johnson, R   P
       Structural concrete. London, McGraw-Hill,
       ltd., 1967.
       271p. (European civil engineering series)

       1. Concrete. 2. Structural engineering.
       3. Architecture - Designs and plans.
       I. Title.

624
S77   STRUCTURAL DESIGN FOR DYNAMIC LOADS, BY
      CHARLES H. NORRIS AND OTHERS. NEW
      YORK, MCGRAW-HILL, 1959.
      453P. ILLUS. (MCGRAW-HILL CIVIL
      ENGINEERING SERIES)

      COMPILED FROM LECTURE NOTES PREPARED
      FOR A SPECIAL TWO-WEEK SUMMER PROGRAM ...
      PRESENTED AT THE 1956 SUMMER SESSION OF
      THE MASSACHUSETTS INSTITUTE OF TECHNOLOGY.
      INCLUDES BIBLIOGRAPHY.

      1. STRUCTURAL ENGINEERING.
      2. VIBRATION.   3. STRENGTH OF
                       (CONTINUED ON NEXT CARD)

725.1   Structural engineer.
(41)
M45   Mills, H   E
      Government offices, Horseferry Road, London
      SWI. London, Institution of Structural Engineers,
      1967.
      12p.

      Reprint from: The Structural engineer, Oct.,
      1967.
      1. Public buildings - U.K. 2. Structural
      engineering. 3. Prefabricated construction -
      U.K. I. Institution of Structural Engineers.
      II. Structural engineer. III. Title.

691.322   STRUCTURAL CONCRETE.
S34   SHIDELER, JOSEPH J
      MANUFACTURE AND USE OF LIGHTWEIGHT
      AGGREGATES FOR STRUCTURAL CONCRETE.
      SKOKIE, ILL., 1961.
      14P. (PORTLAND CEMENT ASSOCIATION.
      RESEARCH AND DEVELOPMENT LABORATORIES.
      DEVELOPMENT DEPT. BULLETIN D40)

      1. CONCRETE AGGREGATES.
      I. PORTLAND CEMENT ASSOCIATION.
      II. TITLE: STRUCTURAL CONCRETE.

---

624   STRUCTURAL DESIGN FOR DYNAMIC LOADS, BY
S77   CHARLES H. NORRIS AND OTHERS. NEW
      YORK, MCGRAW-HILL, 1959. 453P. ILLUS.
      ...RIES)   (CARD 2)

      MATERIALS.   I. NORRIS, CHARLES HEAD,
      1910-   II. MASSACHUSETTS INSTITUTE
      OF TECHNOLOGY.

---

690   Structural engineer.
(41)
S72   Stevens, R   F
      Encased stanchions. Garston, Eng.,
      Building Research Station, Ministry of
      Technology, 1965.
      [8]p.   U.K. Building Research Station.
      Building research current papers. Engineer-
      ing series 2=)
      Reprinted from: The Structural engineer,
      Feb., 1965. p. 59-66.

      1. Building construction - U.K. I. U.K.
      Building Research   Station.
      II. Structural   engineer.
      III. Title.

691.322   Structural concrete.
T29   Teychenne, D   C
      Structural concrete made with lightweight
      aggregates. Garston, Eng., Building Research
      Station, Ministry of Public Building and Works,
      1967.
      111-122p. (U.K. Building Research Station.
      Building research current papers. Engineering
      papers 48)
      Reprinted from: Concrete, April 1967.
      1. Concrete aggregates. 2. Concrete
      construction. I. U.K. Building Research
      Station. II. Title.

---

624   STRUCTURAL DESIGN IN ARCHITECTURE.
S15s SALVADORI, MARIO GEORGE.
      STRUCTURAL DESIGN IN ARCHITECTURE, BY
      MARIO SALVADORI AND MATTHYS LEVY, WITH
      EXAMPLE AND PROBLEM SOLUTIONS BY JOHN J.
      FARRELL. ENGLEWOOD CLIFFS, N.J.,
      PRENTICE-HALL, 1967.
      457P.

      1. STRUCTURAL ENGINEERING.   I. LEVY,
      MATTHYS, JT. AU.   II. TITLE.

      Structural engineering
        x Structures, Theory of
        xx Building construction
        xx Engineering

---

624   STRUCTURAL DAMPING.
A52   AMERICAN SOCIETY OF MECHANICAL ENGINEERS.
      APPLIED MECHANICS DIVISION. SHOCK AND
      VIBRATION COMMITTEE.
      STRUCTURAL DAMPING; PAPERS PRESENTED AT
      A COLLOQUIUM ON STRUCTURAL DAMPING HELD AT
      THE ASME ANNUAL MEETING IN ATLANTIC CITY,
      N.J., IN DECEMBER 1959. EDITED BY JEROME
      E. RUZICKA. NEW YORK, 1959.
      165P.

      1. STRUCTURAL ENGINEERING.
      2. VIBRATIONS. I. RUZICKA, JEROME E., ED.
      II. TITLE.

---

690   STRUCTURAL DESIGN OF BUILDINGS.
M12   MCKAIG, THOMAS H
      APPLIED STRUCTURAL DESIGN OF BUILDINGS.
      3D ED. NEW YORK, MCGRAW-HILL, 1965.
      499P.

      1. BUILDING CONSTRUCTION.   I. TITLE.
      II. TITLE: STRUCTURAL DESIGN OF BUILDINGS.

---

624   STRUCTURAL ENGINEERING.
A41   AIAA/ASME Structures, Structural Dynamics and
      Materials Conference, 10th, New Orleans, 1969.
      Collection of technical papers on structures
      and materials. New York, American Society of
      Mechanical Engineers, 1969.
      471p.

      1. Structural engineering. I. American
      Society of Mechanical Engineers. II. Title.
      III. American Institute of Aeronautics and
      Astronautics. IV. Title: Structures and
      materials.

---

624   STRUCTURAL DAMPING IN PERMANENT JOINTS.
K15   KALININ, N   G
      STRUCTURAL DAMPING IN PERMANENT JOINTS,
      BY N.G. KALININ AND YU. A. LEBEDEV.
      WRIGHT-PATTERSON AIR FORCE BASE, OHIO,
      FOREIGN TECHNOLOGY DIVISION, AIR FORCE
      SYSTEMS COMMAND, 1964.
      191P. (FTD-TT-63-755)

      1. STRUCTURAL ENGINEERING.
      2. VIBRATION.   I. LEBEDEV, YU. A.
      II. U.S. WRIGHT-PATTERSON AIR FORCE BASE,
      OHIO. III. TITLE.

---

691   Structural design with fibrous composites.
N17s National Research Council. Materials
      Advisory Board.
      Structural design with fibrous composites.
      Wash., 1968.
      81p. (Its Publication MAB-236)

      CFSTI. AD 682 493.

      Bibliography: p. 75-81.

      1. Building materials. I. Title.

Structural engineering.
629.13
A27   Aerospace Expandable Structures Conference,
      2d, Minnetonka, Minn.
      Transactions. Sponsored by Air Force Aero
      Propulsion Laboratory in cooperation with
      Archer Daniels Midland Company. Wright-
      Patterson Air Force Base, Ohio, Air Force
      Aero Propulsion Laboratory, 1965.
      802p. (U.S. Aero Propulsion Laboratory.
      AFAPL-TR-65-108)

      1. Aircraft construction. 2. Structural
      engineering. I. U.S. Aero Propulsion
      Laboratory.   II. Archer Daniels
      Midland Co.

---

623   Structural design.
M67   Morris, I   E
      Handbook of structural design. New York,
      Reinhold, 1963.
      803p.

      1. Structural engineering. 2. Architecture -
      Designs and plans. I. Title: Structural design.
      II. Title.

691.16   Structural design with plastics.
B25s Benjamin, Bezaleel Solomon.
      Structural design with plastics. New York,
      Van Nostrand Reinhold, 1969.
      259p. (Polymer science and engineering
      series)

      1. Plastics. 2. Structural engineering.
      I. Title.

---

624   STRUCTURAL ENGINEERING.
A55   ALL UNION CONFERENCE ON SHELLS AND PLATES.
      4TH, EREVAN, 1962.
      THEORY OF SHELLS AND PLATES.
      PROCEEDINGS OF THE 4TH ALL-UNION
      CONFERENCE ON SHELLS AND PLATES HELD AT
      EREVAN, OCTOBER 24-31, 1962. EDITED BY
      S.M. DURGARIAN. TRANSLATED FROM THE
      RUSSIAN BY D. LEDERMAN AND A. BAROUCH.
      JERUSALEM, ISRAEL PROGRAM FOR SCIENTIFIC
      TRANSLATIONS, 1966.
      948P.

      AT HEAD OF TITL   E: AKADEMIYA NAUK
      ARMYANSKOI INSTIT   UT MATEMATIKI.
                           (CONTINUED ON NEXT CARD)

---

623   Structural design concepts, some NASA contribu-
824   tions.
      Scipio, L   Albert
      Structural design concepts, some NASA con-
      tributions. Washington, Technology Utilization
      Div., Office of Technology Utilization, National
      Aeronautics and Space Administration, 1967.
Lef. 174p. (NASA Sp-5039)
      Bibliography: p. 121-168.

      1. Structural engineering. 2. Architecture -
      Design. I. U.S. National Aeronautics and Space
      Administration. III. Title.

---

624   STRUCTURAL DYNAMICS.
L45t LIN, YU-KWENG MICHAEL.
      PROBABILISTIC THEORY OF STRUCTURAL
      DYNAMICS. NEW YORK, MCGRAW-HILL, 1967.
      366P.

      BIBLIOGRAPHY: P. 349-359.

      1. STRUCTURAL ENGINEERING.   I. TITLE.
      II. TITLE: STRUCTURAL DYNAMICS.

---

624   ALL UNION CONFERENCE ON SHELLS AND PLATES.
A55   4TH, EREVAN, 1962. THEORY OF SHELLS ...
      1966.   (CARD 2)

      MEKHANIKI;
      PUBLISHED FOR THE NATIONAL AERONAUTICS
      AND SPACE ADMINISTRATION... AND THE
      NATIONAL SCIENCE FOUNDATION.
      1. STRUCTURAL ENGINEERING.   2. STRAINS
      AND STRESSES.   I. DURGARIAN, S.M., ED.
      II. ACADEMY OF SCIENCES OF THE ARMENIAN
      SSR. INSTITUTE OF MATHEMATICS AND
      MECHANICS.   III.   TITLE: SHELLS AND
      PLATES.

691.771
A58us
STRUCTURAL ENGINEERING.
Aluminum Association.
Using aluminum structurally; architectural aluminum report. New York, Aluminum Association; Chicago, Architectural Aluminum Manufacturers Association, 1969.
11p. (Its General information no. 5)

1. Aluminum. 2. Structural engineering. I. Title.

690.4
A54
Structural engineering.
Amirikian, Arsham.
Analysis of rigid frames (an application of slope, deflection) by A. Amirikian ... Washington, U. S. Govt. print. off., 1942.

xiv, 396 p. incl. illus., tables. 23½ cm.

A compilation of a series of 44 articles previously published as technical supplements to the U. S. Bureau of yards and docks News memorandum. *cf.* p. v.

1. Structures—Theory of. I. Title.

TG260.A48   624.171   42—38223

Library of Congress   ₍51r43p1₎

620.1
B17
Structural engineering.
Bassin, Milton G
Statics and strength of materials, by Milton G. Bassin and others. 2d ed. New York, McGraw-Hill, 1969.
463p.

1. Strength of materials. 2. Structural engineering. 3. Civil engineering. I. Title.

623
A51
Structural engineering.
Ambrose, James E.
Building structures primer ₍by₎ James E. Ambrose. New York, Wiley ₍1967₎

vii, 122 p. illus. 26 cm.

Bibliography: p. 119-121.

1. Structural engineering. I. Title.

TA633.A4   624'.1   67-21327

Library of Congress   ₍7₎

FOLIO
711.73
A66
Structural engineering.
Appleyard, Donald.
The view from the road, by Donald Appleyard and others. Cambridge, Mass., published for the Joint Center for Urban Studies of the Massachusetts Institute of Technology and Harvard University, by the M.I.T. Press, 1964.
64p.

1. Highways. 2. Streets. 3. Structural engineering. I. Joint Center for Urban Studies. II. Title.

623
B17
Structural engineering.
Bate, S C C
New designs and research on structural use of concrete. Garston, Eng., Building Research Station, Ministry of Technology, 1966.
[3]p. (U.K. Building Research Station. Building research current papers. Engineering series 36)
Reprinted from Municipal engineering, vol. 143, no. 35, 1966, p. 1739, 41, 43.

1. Structural engineering. 2. Concrete construction. I. U.K. Building Research Station. II. Title.

693.5
A52m
STRUCTURAL ENGINEERING.
American Concrete Institute.
Models for concrete structures. Detroit, 1970.
485p. (ACI publication SP-24)
This symposium was compiled under the sponsorship of ACI Ad Hoc Committee on Structural Models, and contains 17 papers on subjects which emphasize modeling the true inelastic behavior of concrete structures. Seven of these papers were presented at the 64th ACI Annual Convention, Los Angeles, Calif., March 1968.

— (Cont'd on next card)

624
A76
STRUCTURAL ENGINEERING.
ASPLUND, SVEN OLOF.
STRUCTURAL MECHANICS: CLASSICAL AND MATRIX METHODS. ENGLEWOOD CLIFFS, N.J., PRENTICE-HALL, 1966.
474P. (PRENTICE-HALL SERIES IN STRUCTURAL ANALYSIS AND DESIGN)

PRENTICE-HALL INTERNATIONAL SERIES IN THEORETICAL AND APPLIED MECHANICS.

1. STRUCTURAL ENGINEERING. I. TITLE.

624
B17
STRUCTURAL ENGINEERING.
Bate, S C C
Priorities in structural engineering research. Garston, Eng., Building Research Station, 1969.
15-27p. (U.K. Building Research Station. Current paper 12/69)
Reprinted from: Structural engineer, 1969, vol. 47(1), Jan., pp. 15-27.

1. Structural engineering. 2. Engineering research. I. U.K. Building Research Station. II. Title.

693.5
A52m
American Concrete Institute. Models...1970.
(Card 2)

Bibliography: p. 449-487.

1. Concrete construction. 2. Structural engineering. I. Title.

VF
538.56
A87
Structural engineering.
Australia. Commonwealth Scientific and Industrial Research Organization. (Div. of Building Research)
Digital computers and structural engineering, by F. A. Blakey. Victoria, 1961.
[2]p. (Its Reprint no. 193)
Reprinted from Constructional review, vol. 34, no. 7, July, 1961.

1. Automation. 2. Structural engineering. I. Blakey, F. A.

624
B21
STRUCTURAL ENGINEERING.
Beaufait, Fred W
Computer methods of structural analysis, by Fred W. Beaufait and others. Englewood Cliffs, N.J., Prentice-Hall, 1970.
543p. (Computer methods of structural analysis)

1. Structural engineering. 2. Automation. I. Title.

672
A52d
STRUCTURAL ENGINEERING.
American Iron and Steel Institute.
'67 design in steel. New York, 1967.
51p.

1. Steel. 2. Architectural details. 3. Structural engineering. I. Title. II. Title: Design in steel.

690.015
(485)
S82
R54
1968
STRUCTURAL ENGINEERING.
Baehre, Rolf.
Stålstommars måttnoggrannhet; fältmätningar och utvärdering av mätresultaten (Dimensional accuracy of steel frames; field measurements and evaluation of the results)
Stockholm, Statens Institut för Byggnadsforskning, 1968.
47p. (Stockholm. Statens Institut för Byggnadsforskning. Rapport 54:1968)
English summary.
1. Building research — Sweden. 2. Steel construction. 3. Structural engineering. I. Stockholm. Statens
(Cont'd on next card)

691.16
B25s
STRUCTURAL ENGINEERING.
Benjamin, Bezaleel Solomon.
Structural design with plastics. New York, Van Nostrand Reinhold, 1969.
259p. (Polymer science and engineering series)

1. Plastics. 2. Structural engineering. I. Title.

VF
623
A52
Structural engineering.
American Society of Civil Engineers.
Design live loads in buildings, by John W. Dunham. With discussion by D. Lee Narver and others. New York, 1947.
725-744p.

Paper no. 2311.
Reprinted from Transactions, vol. 112, 1947.

1. Structural engineering. I. Dunham, John W.

690.015
(485)
S82
R54
1968
Baehre, Rolf. Stålstommars...1968.
(Card 2)

Institut for Byggnadsforskning. II. Title: Dimensional accuracy of steel frames; field measurements and evaluation of the results.

624
B24
STRUCTURAL ENGINEERING.
BENJAMIN, JACK R
STATICALLY INDETERMINATE STRUCTURES; APPROXIMATE ANALYSIS BY DEFLECTED STRUCTURES AND LATERAL LOAD ANALYSIS. NEW YORK, MCGRAW-HILL, 1959.
350P. (MCGRAW-HILL CIVIL ENGINEERING SERIES)

1. STRUCTURAL ENGINEERING. 2. LOADS.

624
A52
STRUCTURAL ENGINEERING.
AMERICAN SOCIETY OF MECHANICAL ENGINEERS. APPLIED MECHANICS DIVISION. SHOCK AND VIBRATION COMMITTEE.
STRUCTURAL DAMPING; PAPERS PRESENTED AT A COLLOQUIUM ON STRUCTURAL DAMPING HELD AT THE ASME ANNUAL MEETING IN ATLANTIC CITY, N.J., IN DECEMBER 1959, EDITED BY JEROME E. RUZICKA. NEW YORK, 1959.
165P.

1. STRUCTURAL ENGINEERING. 2. VIBRATIONS. I. RUZICKA, JEROME E., ED. II. TITLE.

629.13
B14
STRUCTURAL ENGINEERING.
Baker, E H
Shell analysis manual, by E.H. Baker and others. Prepared by North American Aviation, inc. for Manned Spacecraft Center. Wash., National Aeronautics and Space Administration, 1968.
804p. (NASA contractor report NASA CR-912)
CFSTI. N68-24802.

1. Aircraft construction. 2. Structural engineering. I. North American Aviation. II. U.S. National Aeronautics and Space Administration. III. Title.

693
G27
Structural engineering.
Bergfelt, Allan
Results from deformation measurings in soft clay at dredging and dry-pumping. Göteborg, Scandinavian University Books, 1967.
97p. (Chalmers University of Technology, Gothenburg, Sweden. Transactions no. 317; Avd. Väg-och Vattenbyggnad. Byggnadsteknik 53)

Särtryck ur Teknik och Natur.

1. Building methods. 2. Structural engineering. 3. Clay. I. Chalmers University of Technology, Gothenburg, Sweden.

388
B45

Structural engineering.

Bingham, S H
The Bingham system; a new concept of high-speed "fail-safe" mass transportation; designed, engineered and patented, by S.H. Bingham. New York, 1964.
53p.
1. Transportation. 2. Structural engineering. I. Title. II. Title: High-speed "fail-safe" mass transportation.

620.1
1634.15
B65

STRUCTURAL ENGINEERING.

BOLT, BERANEK AND NEWMAN, INC.
ENERGY DISSIPATION AT STRUCTURAL JOINTS; MECHANISMS AND MAGNITUDES. CAMBRIDGE, MASS., 1964.
131P.

BIBLIOGRAPHY: P.80-82.

1. VIBRATION. 2. STRUCTURAL ENGINEERING. I. TITLE.

624
C15

STRUCTURAL ENGINEERING.

Calcote, Lee R
The analysis of laminated composite structures. New York, Van Nostrand Reinhold Co., 1969.
222p.

1. Structural engineering. I. Title. II. Title: Laminated composite structures.

691.8
B47

Structural engineering.

Bishop, D
Large panel construction. Garston, Eng. Building Research Station, Dept. of Scientific and Industrial Research, 1964. [233-238p.]
Building Research Station. Current papers. Design series 17)
Reprinted from : The Architect and building news, 1964, vol. 225(6), pp. 233-8; (7), pp. 277-280.

1. Panels. 2. Structural engineering. I. U.K. Building Research Station.

538.56
B67

Structural engineering.

Borges, J Ferry.
Computer analysis of structures, Lisboa, Portugal, Laboratório Nacional de Engenharia Civil, 1961.
195-212p. (Portugal. Laboratório Nacional de Engenharia Civil. Technical paper no. 169)
American Society of Civil Engineers. 2nd Conference on Electronic computation, Pittsburgh, 1960.

1. Automation. 2. Structural engineering. I. Portugal. Laboratório Nacional de Engenharia Civil. II. American Society of Civil Engineers. [Proceedings]

694.1
C152

STRUCTURAL ENGINEERING.

CALIFORNIA. UNIVERSITY. INSTITUTE OF ENGINEERING RESEARCH.
ACTION OF TIMBER STRUCTURES SUBJECTED TO LATERAL LOADS. REPORT TO DIVISION OF ARCHITECTURE, STATE DEPARTMENT OF PUBLIC WORKS, SACRAMENTO, CALIFORNIA, BY G.E. TROXELL AND V. BERTERO. BERKELEY, CALIF., 1955.
19P.

1. WOOD CONSTRUCTION. 2. STRUCTURAL ENGINEERING. I. TROXELL, GEORGE EARL. II. BERTERO, V.
III. CALIFORNIA. DEPT. OF PUBLIC (CONTINUED ON NEXT CARD)

690.237
B51

Structural engineering.

Blakey, F A
Construction loads on buildings, by F.A. Blakey and others. [Melbourne] Commonwealth Scientific and Industrial Research Organization [Division of Building Research] 1962.
4p.

Reprinted from Constructional review, Vol. 35, no. 10, page 22, October, 1962.

1. Loads. 2. Structural engineering. I. Australia. Commonwealth Scientific and Industrial Research Organization. (Division of Building Research) II. Title.

623
B67

Structural engineering.

Borrego, John.
Space grid structures. Skeletal frameworks and stressed-skin systems. Cambridge, Mass., MIT Press, 1968.
200p.
Bibliography: p. 198-200.

1. Structural engineering. 2. Architecture - Designs and plans. 3. Prefabricated construction. I. Massachusetts Institute of Technology. II. Title.

624
C17s

STRUCTURAL ENGINEERING.

CARPENTER, JAMES E
STRUCTURAL MODEL TESTING; COMPENSATION FOR TIME EFFECT IN PLASTICS. SKOKIE, ILL., 1963.
47-61P. (PORTLAND CEMENT ASSOCIATION. RESEARCH AND DEVELOPMENT LABORATORIES. DEVELOPMENT DEPT. BULLETIN D60)

REPRINTED FROM THE JOURNAL OF THE PCA RESEARCH AND DEVELOPMENT LABORATORIES, VOL. 5, NO. 7, 1963.

1. STRUCTURAL ENGINEERING. I. PORTLAND CEMENT ASSOCIATION.

693.5
B51

Structural engineering.

Blakey, Frank A
Stripping of formwork for concrete in buildings in relation to structural design, by F.A. Blakey and others. [Melbourne] Commonwealth Scientific and Industrial Research Organization, Div. of Building Research, 1965.
5p. (Australia. Commonwealth Scientific and Industrial Research Organization. Div. of Building Research. D.B.R reprint no. 331)
Reprinted from Civil engineering transactions of the Institution of Engineers, Oct., 1965. p. 92-96.

(Continued on next card)

624
B72

Structural engineering.

Bresler, Boris.
Design of steel structures, by Boris Bresler and others. 2d ed. New York, Wiley, 1968.
820p.

1. Structural engineering. 2. Steel. I. Title.

624
C17

STRUCTURAL ENGINEERING.

CARPENTER, JAMES E
STRUCTURAL MODEL TESTING; TECHNIQUES FOR MODELS OF PLASTIC, BY J.E. CARPENTER, D.D. MAGURA, AND N.W. HANSON. SKOKIE, 1964.
26-47P. (PORTLAND CEMENT ASSOCIATION. RESEARCH AND DEVELOPMENT LABORATORIES. DEVELOPMENT DEPT. BULLETIN D76)
REPRINTED FROM THE JOURNAL OF THE PCA RESEARCH AND DEVELOPMENT LABORATORIES, VOL. 6, NO. 2, 1964.
1. STRUCTURAL ENGINEERING. I. PORTLAND CEMENT ASSOCIATION. II. TITLE. III. MODELS OF PLASTIC.

693.5
B51

Blakey, Frank A Stripping of formwork for concrete in buildings...1965. (Card 2)

1. Concrete construction. 2. Structural engineering. I. Australia. Commonwealth Scientific and Industrial Research Organization. (Div. of Building Research)

624
B76s

STRUCTURAL ENGINEERING.

Brown, Eric Hugh.
Structural analysis. New York, Wiley, 1967.
v.

1. Structural engineering. I. Title.

690
C177

STRUCTURAL ENGINEERING.

CASSIE, W FISHER.
STRUCTURE N BUILDING, BY W. FISHER CASSIE AND J H. NAPPER, WITH A FOREWORD BY W.A. ALLEN. LONDON, ARCHITECTURAL PRESS, 1952.
266P. (MODERN BUILDING CONSTRUCTION SERIES, V. 2

1. BUILDING CONSTRUCTION. 2. STRUCTURAL ENGINEERING. I. NAPPER, J.H., JT. AU. II. TITLE.

621.791
B56

STRUCTURAL ENGINEERING.

BLODGETT, OMER W
DESIGN OF WELDED STRUCTURAL CONNECTIONS, BY OMER W. BLODGETT AND JOHN B. SCALZI. CLEVELAND, JAMES F. LINCOLN ARC WELDING FOUNDATION, 1961.
92P.

1. WELDING. 2. STRUCTURAL ENGINEERING. I. SCALZI, JOHN B., JT. AU.

624
B76

STRUCTURAL ENGINEERING.

BROWNE, J S C
BASIC THEORY OF STRUCTURES. NEW YORK, PERGAMON PRESS, 1966.
243P.

1. STRUCTURAL ENGINEERING. 2. STRAINS AND STRESSES. 3. TRUSSES. I. TITLE.

624
C25

STRUCTURAL ENGINEERING.

CENTRAL HOUSING COMMITTEE.
STRUCTURAL PRACTICES OF FEDERAL HOUSING AGENCIES. FIRST REPORT PREPARED AND SUBMITTED TO THE SUB-COMMITTEE ON DESIGN AND CONSTRUCTION BY THE STRUCTURE REFERENCE GROUP. WASHINGTON, 1937.
40P.

1. STRUCTURAL ENGINEERING. 2. FEDERAL HOUSING PROGRAMS. 3. BUILDING MATERIALS. I. TITLE.

624
B65

STRUCTURAL ENGINEERING.

Bolotin, Vladimir Vasil'evich.
Statistical methods in structural mechanics. Translation by Samuel Aroni. San Francisco, Holden-Day, 1969.
240p. (Holden-Day series in mathematical physics)

Bibliography: p. 223-234.

1. Structural engineering. 2. Statistics. I. Title.

624
B84

STRUCTURAL ENGINEERING.

Building Research Advisory Board. Special Advisory Committee on Full-Scale Testing of New York World's Fair Structures.
Full-scale testing of New York World's Fair structures. Wash., National Academy of Sciences, 1969.
3v.
Contents.-v. I; The Bourbon Street structure.-v. II; The Rathskeller structure.-v. III: The Chimes Tower structure.
1. Structural engineering. 2. New York World's Fair 1964-1965. I. Title.

690.4
C31

Structural engineering.

Chalmers University of Technology, Gothenburg, Sweden.
Influence functions of elastic plates divided in strips, by Gunnar Kärrholm. Goteborg, 1958.
18p. graphs. (Its Transaction no. 201. Avd. Väg- och Vattenbyggnad. Byggnadsteknik. 28)

1. Structural engineering. 2. Metal-work. I. Kärrholm, Gunnar.

510
C31
STRUCTURAL ENGINEERING.
CHAPEL, R E
MATRIX ALGEBRA FOR STRUCTURAL ANALYSIS USING DIGITAL COMPUTER SUBROUTINES, BY R.E. CHAPEL, M.U. AYRES AND J.A. WALLACE. STILLWATER, 1967.
42P. (OKLAHOMA. STATE UNIVERSITY OF AGRICULTURE AND APPLIED SCIENCE, STILLWATER. OFFICE OF ENGINEERING RESEARCH AND ENGINEERING EXPERIMENT STATION. PUBLICATION NO. 150)
1. MATHEMATICS. 2. STRUCTURAL ENGINEERING. 3. AUTOMATION. I. AYRES, M.U., JT. AU. I I. WALLACE, J.A., JT. AU. III. TITLE.

693
I097
Structural engineering.
Cyrus, Nancy Jane.
Accuracy study of finite difference methods, by Nancy Jane Cyrus and Robert E. Fulton. Washington, National Aeronautics and Space Administration, 1968.
29p. (NASA technical note NASA TN D-4372)
1. Building methods. 2. Architecture - Designs and plans. 3. Mathematics. 4. Structural engineering. I. Fulton, Robert E., jt. au. II. U.S. National Aeronautics and Space Administration. III. Title.

624
G15
STRUCTURAL ENGINEERING.
Galambos, Theodore V
Structural members and frames. Englewood Cliffs, N.J., Prentice-Hall, 1968.
373p. (Prentice-Hall series in structural analysis and design)
1. Structural engineering. I. Title.

534.83
C32
STRUCTURAL ENGINEERING.
Cheng, David H
Dynamic response of structural elements exposed to sonic booms, by David H. Cheng and Jacques E. Benveniste. Prepared by City College of New York. Wash., National Aeronautics and Space Administration, 1969.
44p. (NASA CR-1281)
Bibliography: p.18-19.
1. Noise. 2. Structural engineering.
I. Benveniste, Jacques E., jt. au. II. U.S. National Aeronautics and Space Administration. III. New York (City) City College. IV. Title.

711.73
(7531)
D47
Structural engineering.
District of Columbia. Dept. of Highways and Traffic.
North-Central Freeway in the District of Columbia and Montgomery and Prince Georges Counties. [Washington] 1964.
5p.
Joint press release of Dept. of Highways and Traffic and State Roads Commission of Maryland.
(Continued on next card)

693.97
G19
STRUCTURAL ENGINEERING.
GAYLORD, EDWIN H
DESIGN OF STEEL STRUCTURES, INCLUDING APPLICATIONS IN ALUMINUM, BY EDWIN H. GAYLORD AND CHARLES N. GAYLORD. NEW YORK, McGRAW-HILL, 1957.
540P. (McGRAW-HILL CIVIL ENGINEERING SERIES)
1. STEEL CONSTRUCTION. 2. STRUCTURAL ENGINEERING. 3. ALUMINUM. I. GAYLORD, CHARLES N., JT. AU.

623
C34
Structural engineering.
Chilver, A H ed.
Thin-walled structures; a collection of papers on the stability and strength of thin-walled structural members and frames. New York, J. Wiley, 1967.
Lef. 303p.
1. Structural engineering. 2. Strength of materials. 3. Walls. I. Title.

624
E35
Structural engineering.
Egle, D M
An approximate theory for transverse shear deformation and rotary inertia effects in vibrating beams. Wash., National Aeronautics and Space Administration, 1969.
18p. (U.S. National Aeronautics and Space Administration. NASA CR-1317)
CFSTI
Prepared by University of Oklahoma for Langley Research Center, National Aeronautics and Space Administration.
1. Structural engineering. 2. Aircraft construction. I. Oklahoma. University. II. U.S. National Aeronautics and Space Administration. III. Title.

624
G19
Structural engineering.
Gaylord, Edwin H Jr., ed.
Structural engineering handbook, edited by Edwin H. Gaylord, Jr. and Charles N. Gaylord. New York, McGraw-Hill, 1968.
1v.
1. Structural engineering. I. Gaylord, Charles N., jt. ed. II. Title.

629.13
I C66
Structural engineering.
Cooper, Paul A
Effect of shallow meridional curvature on the vibration of nearly cylindrical shells. Wash., National Aeronautics and Space Administration, 1969.
40p. (NASA TN D-5143)
CFSTI.
1. Aircraft construction. 2. Structural engineering. I. Title. II. U.S. National Aeronautics and Space Administration.

691.7
E53
STRUCTURAL ENGINEERING.
ENGINEERING FOUNDATION. COLUMN RESEARCH COUNCIL.
GUIDE TO DESIGN CRITERIA FOR METAL COMPRESSION MEMBERS. EDITED BY BRUCE G. JOHNSON. 2D ED. NEW YORK, WILEY, 1966.
217P.
1. METALS. 2. STRUCTURAL ENGINEERING. I. JOHNSTON, BRUCE GILBERT, ED.

624
G27M
STRUCTURAL ENGINEERING.
GERE, JAMES M
MOMENT DISTRIBUTION. PRINCETON, N.J., VAN NOSTRAND, 1963.
378P. (UNIVERSITY STUDIES IN CIVIL ENGINEERING AND APPLIED MECHANICS)
BIBLIOGRAPHY: P. 247-268.
1. STRUCTURAL ENGINEERING. I. TITLE.

624
C68
STRUCTURAL ENGINEERING.
Cowan, Henry J
Architectural structures; an introduction to structural mechanics. New York, American Elsevier, 1971.
400p. (Elsevier architectural science series)
1. Structural engineering. I. Title.

690
F47t
Structural engineering.
Fischer, Ladislav.
Theory and practice of shell structures. Berlin, Munich, Ernst & Sohn, 1968.
541p.
Translation of Theorie and Praxis der Schalenkonstruktionen.
1. Owner-built houses. 2. Roofs and roofing. 3. Structural engineering. I. Title. II. Title: Shell structures.

624
G27
Structural engineering.
Gerstle, Kurt H
Basic structural design. New York, McGraw-Hill, 1967.
405p.
1. Structural engineering. I. Title.

623
C72c
Structural engineering.
Cressy, L R
Composite construction. London, 1964.
411-422p.
Reprint from the Structural engineer, Dec. 1964.
1. Structural engineering. I. Title.

624
F67
STRUCTURAL ENGINEERING.
FOSTER, E STANTON.
TO INVESTIGATE THE FEASIBILITY AND ADVANTAGE OF STANDARDIZATION, MASS-PRODUCTION AND MARKETING OF A SKELETON FRAME, SUITABLE FOR ONE-STORY, GENERAL PURPOSE BUILDINGS. CONDENSED VERSION. WASH., PUBLIC HOUSING ADMINISTRATION, HOUSING AND HOME FINANCE AGENCY, 1962.
53L.
THESIS (B.S.) - GEORGE WASHINGTON UNIVERSITY.
(CONTINUED ON NEXT CARD)

624
G65
STRUCTURAL ENGINEERING.
GOLDBERG, JOHN E
GENERAL INSTABILITY OF LOW FRAMED BUILDINGS. ZURICH, 1958.
15-36P.
REPRINT FROM THE 18TH VOLUME OF THE PUBLICATIONS OF INTERNATIONAL ASSOCIATION FOR BRIDGE AND STRUCTURAL ENGINEERING.
1. STRUCTURAL ENGINEERING. I. INTERNATIONAL ASSOCIATION FOR BRIDGE AND STRUCTURAL ENGINEERING.

623
C72
Structural engineering.
Creasy, L R
Professional practice and drawing office procedure. London, Institution of Structural Engineers, 1961.
[15]p.
Reprinted from the Structural engineer, Oct. 1961, p. 302-317.
1. Structural engineering.

624
F67
FOSTER, E STANTON. TO INVESTIGATE THE ...1962.
(CARD 2)
1. STRUCTURAL ENGINEERING. 2. BUILDING CONSTRUCTION.

624
G65C
STRUCTURAL ENGINEERING.
GOLDBERG, JOHN EDWARD, 1909-
COMPUTER ANALYSIS OF TALL BUILDING FRAMES FOR WIND AND GENERAL LOADS, BY JOHN E. GOLDBERG AND Z.L. MOH. LAFAYETTE, IND., PURDUE UNIVERSITY, 1963.
30P. (PURDUE UNIVERSITY, LAFAYETTE, IND. ENGINEERING EXPERIMENT STATION. RESEARCH SERIES, 150)
ENGINEERING BULLETIN OF PURDUE UNIVERSITY. V. 47, NO. 3.
BIBLIOGRAPHY: P. 30.
1. STRUCTURAL ENGINEERING
(CONTINUED ON NEXT CARD)

624
G65C
GOLDBERG, JOHN EDWARD, 1909- COMPUTER ANALYSIS ...1963. (CARD 2)

2. BUILDING - WIND STRESSES. I. MOH, Z. L., JT. AU. II. TITLE. (SERIES)

624
H15
HANSON, NORMAN W STRUCTURAL MODEL TESTING. ...1963. (CARD 2)

II. PORTLAND CEMENT ASSOCIATION. III. TITLE.

690.015
(52)
J16L
STRUCTURAL ENGINEERING.
Japan Housing Corp.
Large size structures testing laboratory. Tokyo, 1967.
[6]p.

1. Building research - Japan. 2. Loads. 3. Structural engineering. I. Title.

624
G66
Structural engineering.
Goodman, Louis J
Theory and practice of foundation engineering, by Louis J. Goodman and R.H. Karol. New York, Macmillan, 1968.
433p. (Macmillan series in civil engineering)

1. Structural engineering. 2. Architecture - Designs and plans. 3. Foundations (Building) 4. Civil engineering. I. Karol, R.H., jt. au. II. Title.

623
H15
Structural engineering.
Hansteen, Harald.
Finite element displacement analysis of plate bending based on rectangular elements. Oslo, Norwegian Building Research Institute, 1966.
[13]p. (Oslo. Norwegian Building Research Institute. Reprint 132)
Reprinted from the Proceedings of the Symposium on the Use of Electronic Digital Computers in Structural Engineering, University of Newcastle, July 1966, Working session no. 4, paper no. 14.

1. Structural engineering. I. Oslo. Norges Byggfor- skningsinstitutt.

624.043
A25
STRUCTURAL ENGINEERING.
JENKINS, JOHNSON ANDREW.
ANALYSIS OF LARGE DEFLECTIONS IN STRUCTURES, BY JOHNSON ANDREW JENKINS AND THOMAS BINGHAM SEITZ. WRIGHT-PATTERSON AIR FORCE BASE, OHIO, 1965.
136P.

THESIS (M.S.) - U.S. AIR FORCE INSTITUTE OF TECHNOLOGY.

1. STRAINS AND STRESSES. 2. STRUCTURAL ENGINEERING. I. SEITZ, THOMAS BINGHAM, JT. AU.

620.1
G71
Structural engineering.
Granholm, Hjalmar.
Inverkan av stotkraft pa en bropelare. Goteborg, Scandinavian University Books, 1967.
[191]-202p. (Chalmers University of Technology, Gothenburg, Sweden. Transactions no. 318; Avd. Vag-och Vattenbyggnad, Byggnadsteknik 54. 1967)
Särtryck ur Teknik och Natur.
English summary.

1. Strength of materials. 2. Engineering research. 3. Structural engineering. I. Chalmers University of Technology, Gothenburg, Sweden.

623
H17
Laf.
Structural engineering.
Harris, Charles Overton.
Elementary structural design. [1st ed.] Chicago, American Technical Society, 1951.
163p.

-- Study guide, by Tom C. Plumbridge. Chicago, 1951.
94p.
1. Structural engineering. I. American Technical Society. II. Title.

620.1
J63
STRUCTURAL ENGINEERING.
Johnson, Arne I
Strength, safety and economical dimensions of structures. Stockholm, National Swedish Institute for Building Research, 1971.
168p. (Stockholm. Statens Institut för Byggnadsforskning. Document D7:1971)
Bibliography: p. 158-168.

1. Strength of materials. 2. Structural engineering. I. Stockholm. Statens Institut för Byggnadsforskning. II. Title.

690.015
(485)
S82
1971
R20
STRUCTURAL ENGINEERING.
Granström, Sune.
Byggnaders stabilitet efter katastrofskador. Krafter i elementfogar: modellförsok (Stability of buildings after accidental damage. Forces in element joints: model tests) Stockholm, Statens Institut för Byggnadsforskning, 1971.
31p. (Rapport R20:1971)

1. Structural engineering. I. Stockholm. Statens Institut för Byggnadsforskning. II. Title: Stability of buildings after accidental damage.

625.7
H43pa
Structural engineering.
Highway Research Board.
Pavement design and evaluation, 1963. 9 reports presented at the 43rd annual meeting, January 13-17, 1964. Washington, Highway Research Board of the Div. of Engineering and Industrial Research, National Academy of Sciences, National Research Council, 1964.
153p. (Its Highway research record no. 46)

1. Road construction. 2. Concrete construction. 3. Structural engineering. I. National Research Council. II. Title.

691.32
J63
Structural engineering.
Johnson, R P
Structural concrete. London, McGraw-Hill, ltd., 1967.
271p. (European civil engineering series)

1. Concrete. 2. Structural engineering. 3. Architecture - Designs and plans. I. Title.

FOLIO
711.73
(7531)
J72
Structural engineering.
Greiner (J.E.) Co.
North-Central Freeway, District of Columbia and Montgomery and Prince Georges Counties, Maryland. Engineering feasibility report. Prepared for the D. C. Dept. of Highways and Traffic, and State Roads Commission of Maryland in cooperation with the U.S. Dept. of Commerce, Bureau of Public Roads, Baltimore, 1964.
2 pts. in 1 v.

(Continued on next card)

690.031
H85
N.c.1
Laf.c.2
Long.c.3
Structural engineering.
Hunt, William Dudley, ed.
Creative control of building costs. Edited for the American Institute of Architects. New York, McGraw-Hill, 1967.
239p.

1. Building costs - Estimates. 2. Structural engineering. 3. Building construction - Automation. I. American Institute of Architects. II. Title.

672
J64
Structural engineering.
Joint Committee of the Welding Research Council and the American Society of Civil Engineers.
Commentary on plastic design in steel. New York, 1961.
173p. (ASCE Manuals of engineering practice no. 41)
Bibliography: p. 156-166.
Reprinted 1963.

1. Steel. 2. Structural engineering. I. Title: Plastic design in steel.

FOLIO
711.73
(7531)
G72
Greiner, (J.E.) Co. North-Central Freeway, ...1964. (Card 2)

1. Highways - District of Columbia. 2. Highways - Montgomery Co., Md. 3. Highways - Prince Georges Co., Md. 4. Structural engineering. I. District of Columbia. Dept. of Highways. II. Maryland. State Roads Commission. III. U.S. Bureau of Public Roads. IV. Title.

624.042
I57
Structural engineering.
International Council for Building Research Studies and Documentation
On methods of load calculation. Live loads, technological loads, snow. Three papers prepared for CIB Commission W.23; Basic structural engineering requirements. Rotterdam, 1967.
33p. (CIB report no. 9)
1. Loads. 2. Floors and flooring. 3. Structural engineering. I. Title. II. Title: Methods of load calculation.

624
K15
STRUCTURAL ENGINEERING.
KALININ, N G
STRUCTURAL DAMPING IN PERMANENT JOINTS, BY N.G. KALININ AND YU. A. LEBEDEV. WRIGHT-PATTERSON AIR FORCE BASE, OHIO, FOREIGN TECHNOLOGY DIVISION, AIR FORCE SYSTEMS COMMAND, 1964.
132P. (FTD-TT-63-755)

1. STRUCTURAL ENGINEERING. 2. VIBRATION. I. LEBEDEV, YU. A. II. U.S. WRIGHT-PATTERSON AIR FORCE BASE, OHIO. III. TITLE.

624
H15
STRUCTURAL ENGINEERING.
HANSON, NORMAN W
STRUCTURAL MODEL TESTING; A PROFILE PLOTTER BY N.W. HANSON AND J.E. CARPENTER. SKOKIE, ILL., 1963.
7P. (PORTLAND CEMENT ASSOCIATION. RESEARCH AND DEVELOPMENT LABORATORIES. DEVELOPMENT DEPT. BULLETIN D68)

REPRINTED FROM THE JOURNAL OF THE PCA RESEARCH AND DEVELOPMENT LABORATORIES, VOL. 5, NO. 3, 1963.

1. STRUCTURAL ENGINEERING. I. CARPENTER, J.E., JT. AU. (CONTINUED ON NEXT CARD)

690.248
I84
STRUCTURAL ENGINEERING.
Iwinski, T
Theory of beams; the application of the Laplace transformation method to engineering problems. Translated from the Polish by E.P. Bernat. New York, Pergamon Press, 1958.
85p. (International series of monographs on electronics and instrumentation)

1. Trusses. 2. Structural engineering. 3. Strains and stresses. I. Title. II. Title: Laplace transformation.

624
K54
STRUCTURAL ENGINEERING.
Klingberg, L
Deviations in the horizontal dimensions of structures. Garston, Eng., Building Research Station, 1970.
5p. (U.K. Building Research Station. Library communication 1570)
Translated from the Swedish [and reprinted from] Byggmastaren, 1970, (5), 13-17.

1. Structural engineering. I. U.K. Building Research Station. II. Title. (Series)

690.015
(485)
S 82
R38
1970
STRUCTURAL ENGINEERING.
Klingberg, Lennart.
Måttnoggrannhetsstudier på pelar-balkstomme
(Studies on the dimensional accuracy of a
column and beam framework) Stockholm, 1970.
69p. (Stockholm. Statens Institut för
Byggnadsforskning. Rapport R38:1970)
English summary.
1. Building research – Sweden. 2. Structural
engineering. I. Stockholm. Statens Institut
för Byggnadsforskning. II. Title: Studies on
the dimensional accuracy of a column and beam
framework.

624
L23W
STRUCTURAL ENGINEERING.
LEHIGH UNIVERSITY, BETHLEHEM, PA.
INSTITUTE OF RESEARCH.
WELDED CONTINUOUS FRAMES AND THEIR
COMPONENTS. BETHLEHEM, 1964.
8L.

BIBLIOGRAPHY: P. 7-8.

1. STRUCTURAL ENGINEERING.

VF
690.41
M17
Structural engineering.
Marshall, Walter V.
Architectural mechanics statics. Ann Arbor,
Mich. [Edwards] 1950.
80 p. diagrs.

"Notes for Arch. 29, College of Architecture
and Design." t.-p.

1.Structural engineering. I.Michigan University.
II.Title.

623
K68
Structural engineering.
Kovacs, Austin.
Effect of solar radiation on processed snow
in engineering construction, by Austin Kovacs
and Rene O. Ramseier. Hanover, N.H., U.S.
Army Materiel Command, Cold Regions Research
and Engineering Laboratory, 1968.
23p. (CRREL Technical report 213)
1. Structural engineering. 2. Winter construc-
tion. 3. Foundations (Building) I. Ramseier,
Rene O., jt. au. II. U.S. Army. Cold Regions
Research and Engineering Laboratory, Hanover,
N.H. II. Title.

624
L45
STRUCTURAL ENGINEERING.
Lin, T H
Theory of inelastic structures. New York,
Wiley, 1968.
454p.

1. Structural engineering. I. Title.
II. Title: Inelastic structures.

624
M17
Structural engineering.
Marshall, William Thomas
Solution of problems in structures. 2d ed.
London, Pitman and Sons, ltd (Pitman Paper-
backs), 1967.
441p.

1. Structural engineering. I. Title.

624
K87
STRUCTURAL ENGINEERING.
Kurtz, Max.
Comprehensive structural design guide.
New York, McGraw-Hill, 1969.
320p.

Bibliography: p. 318-320.

1. Structural engineering. I. Title.

624
L48T
STRUCTURAL ENGINEERING.
LIN, YU-KWENG MICHAEL.
PROBABILISTIC THEORY OF STRUCTURAL
DYNAMICS. NEW YORK, MCGRAW-HILL, 1967.
366P.

BIBLIOGRAPHY: P. 349-359.

1. STRUCTURAL ENGINEERING. I. TITLE.
II. TITLE: STRUCTURAL DYNAMICS.

621.78
M17
Structural engineering.
Martin, H L
Effects of low temperatures on the mechanical
properties of structural metals, a report
prepared under contract for NASA by H.L. Martin
and others. Rev. and enl. ed. Wash.,
Technology Utilization Div., Office of
Technology Utilization, National Aeronautics
and Space Administration, 1968.
65p. (NASA SP-5012(01))
1. Metals. 2. Structural engineering.
I. U.S. National Aeronautics and Space
Administration. II. Title.

624
L18
Structural engineering.
Laursen, Harold I
Structural analysis. New York, McGraw-
Hill, 1969.
486p.

1. Structural engineering. I. Title.

624
L54
STRUCTURAL ENGINEERING.
LIVESLEY, R K
MATRIX METHODS OF STRUCTURAL ANALYSIS.
NEW YORK, MACMILLAN, 1964.
265P. (THE COMMONWEALTH AND
INTERNATIONAL LIBRARY OF SCIENCE,
TECHNOLOGY, ENGINEERING AND LIBERAL
STUDIES. STRUCTURES AND SOLID BODY
MECHANICS DIVISION, V. 3)

BIBLIOGRAPHY: P. 259-260.

1. STRUCTURAL ENGINEERING. 2. CIVIL
ENGINEERING. I. TITLE.

624
M171
STRUCTURAL ENGINEERING.
MARTIN, HAROLD CLIFFORD.
INTRODUCTION TO MATRIX METHODS OF
STRUCTURAL ANALYSIS. NEW YORK,
MCGRAW-HILL, 1966.
331P.

BIBLIOGRAPHY: P. 9-10.

1. STRUCTURAL ENGINEERING.

624
L23
STRUCTURAL ENGINEERING.
LEHIGH UNIVERSITY, BETHLEHEM, PA. FRITZ
ENGINEERING LABORATORY.
ANALYSIS OF BEAM-AND-COLUMN
SUBASSEMBLAGES IN PLANAR MULTI-STORY
FRAMES, BY VICTOR LEVI AND OTHERS.
BETHLEHEM, 1964.
103P. (FRITZ ENGINEERING LABORATORY
REPORT NO. 273.11)

BIBLIOGRAPHY: P. 102-103.

1. STRUCTURAL ENGINEERING. I. LEVI,
VICTOR.

693.97
M12
STRUCTURAL ENGINEERING.
McCormac, Jack C
Structural steel design. 2d ed. Scranton,
Pa., Intext Educational Publishers, College Div.
of Intext, 1971.
604p. (Intext series in civil engineering)

1. Steel construction. 2. Structural
engineering. I. Title.

624
M172
STRUCTURAL ENGINEERING.
MASSACHUSETTS INSTITUTE OF TECHNOLOGY.
DEPT. OF CIVIL ENGINEERING.
STRESS: A REFERENCE MANUAL; A
PROBLEM-ORIENTED COMPUTER LANGUAGE FOR
STRUCTURAL ENGINEERING, BY STEVEN J.
FENVES AND OTHERS. CAMBRIDGE, 1965.
388P.

1. STRUCTURAL ENGINEERING.
2. AUTOMATION. I. FENVES, STEVEN JOSEPH.
II. TITLE.

624
L23U
STRUCTURAL ENGINEERING.
LEHIGH UNIVERSITY, BETHLEHEM, PA. FRITZ
ENGINEERING LABORATORY.
THE ULTIMATE STRENGTH OF SINGLE-STORY
FRAMES, BY JOSEPH A. YURA AND THEODORE V.
GALAMBOS. BETHLEHEM, 1964.
38P. (FRITZ ENGINEERING LABORATORY
REPORT NO. 273.18)

BIBLIOGRAPHY: P. 38.

1. STRUCTURAL ENGINEERING. I. YURA,
JOSEPH A. II. GALAMBOS, THEODORE V.

691.32
M12
Structural engineering.
McHenry, Douglas
Toward a generalized treatment of delayed
elasticity in concrete. Skokie, Ill., Portland
Cement Association, Research and Development
Laboratories, 1966.
269-283p. (Portland Cement Association.
Research and Development Laboratories.
Development Dept. Bulletin D 132)
Bibliography: p. 284-286.
Reprint from Publications International
Association for Bridge and Structural Engineer-
ing, Zurich Vol. 26, pp. 269-283. (1966)

(Continued on next card)

658.564
M17s
STRUCTURAL ENGINEERING.
Massachusetts Institute of Technology.
(Dept. of Civil Engineering)
STRESS: [Computer program language] a user's
manual; a problem-oriented computer language
for structural engineering, by Steven J. Fenves
and others. Cambridge, M.I.T. Press, 1967.
55p.

1. Automation. 2. Structural engineering.
I. Fenves, Steven J. II. Title.

693.97
L23S
STRUCTURAL ENGINEERING.
LEHIGH UNIVERSITY, BETHLEHEM, PA.
FRITZ ENGINEERING LABORATORY.
STRUCTURAL STEEL DESIGN, BY LYNN S.
BEEDLE AND OTHERS. NEW YORK, RONALD
PRESS CO., 1964.
829P.

BIBLIOGRAPHY: P. 769-791.

1. STEEL CONSTRUCTION.
2. STRUCTURAL ENGINEERING. I. BEEDLE,
LYNN S. II. TITLE.

691.32
M12
McHenry, Douglas. Toward a generalized...1966.
(Card 2)

1. Concrete. 2. Structural engineering.
I. Portland Cement Association. II. Title.

690.248
M19
Structural engineering.
Mayeda, R
Minimum-weight design of beams for multi-
ple loading, by R. Mayeda and W. Praeger.
Prepared for Office of Naval Research as
Technical rept. no. 8. San Diego, Universi-
ty of California, Dept. of Aerospace and
Mechanical Engineering Sciences, 1967.
21p. (U.S. Defense Documentation Center.
Defense Supply Agency [Document] AD 650 194)
Distributed by U.S. Clearinghouse for
Federal Scientific and Technical Information.

(Continued on next card)

690.248
M19   Mayeda, R   Minimum-weight design of beams
             for multiple loading...1967. (Card 2)

             1. Trusses. 2. Structural engineering.
           3. Loads. I. California. University. II.
           U.S. Defense Documentation Center. Defense
           Supply Agency. III. U.S. Clearinghouse
           for Federal Scientific and Technical Infor-
           mation. IV. Praeger, W., jt. au. V. U.S.
           Office of Naval Research. VI. Title.

Structural engineering.
623
M67   Morris, I   E
             Handbook of structural design. New York,
             Reinhold, 1963.
             803p.

             1. Structural engineering. 2. Architecture -
           Designs and plans. I. Title: Structural design.
           II. Title.

Structural engineering.
693
N28   Newman, Morton.
             Standard structural details for building con-
           struction. New York, McGraw-Hill, 1968.
             361p.

             1. Building methods. 2. Structural engineering.
           3. Architecture - Designs and plans.
           I. Title.

Structural engineering.
551.52
M25   Mellor, Malcolm.
             Ice cap strains and some effects on
           engineering structures, by Malcolm Mellor
           and Sherwood Reed. Hanover, N.H., U.S.
           Army Materiel Command, Cold Regions
           Research and Engineering Laboratory, 1967.
             10p. (CRREL technical rept 202)
             Bibliography: p. 9-10.
             1. Ice. 2. Structural engineering.
           3. Building materials - Climatic effects. 4. Archi-
           tecture and climate. I. Reed, Sherwood, jt. au.
           II. U.S. Army. Cold Regions Research and Engineering
           Laboratory, Hanover,   N.H. III. Title.

Structural engineering.
629.13
M67   Mortimer, Richard W
             MCDIT 21; a computer code for one-dimensional
           elastic wave problems, by Richard W. Mortimer
           and James F. Hoburg. Wash., National Aeronautics
           and Space Administration, 1969.
             29p. (NASA CR-1306)
             Prepared by Drexel Institute of Technology,
           Philadelphia, Pa. for Langley Research Center.
           CFSTI.
             1. Aircraft construction. 2. Structural
           engineering. 3. Automation. I. Title.
           II. Hoburg, James F., jt. au. III. U.S.
           National Aeronau   tics and Space
           Administration.

STRUCTURAL ENGINEERING.
620.1
1634.15   NEWMARK, N   M
N28   COMPUTATION OF DYNAMIC STRUCTURAL
           RESPONSE IN THE RANGE APPROACHING
           FAILURE.   URBANA, ILL., DEPT. OF
           CIVIL ENGINEERING, UNIVERSITY OF
           ILLINOIS, 1952.
             114-129P.

             1. VIBRATION.   2. STRUCTURAL
           ENGINEERING.   3. LOADS.   I. TITLE.

551.52   STRUCTURAL ENGINEERING.
M42   Michel, Bernard.
             Ice pressure on engineering structures.
           Hanover, N.H., Corps of Engineers, U.S. Army
           Cold Regions Research and Engineering Labor-
           atory, 1970.
             71p. (U.S. Army Cold Regions Research and
           Engineering Laboratory. Cold regions science
           and engineering monograph III-B1b)

             Bibliography: p. 67-71.
             1. Ice. 2. Structural engineering. I. U.S.
           Army Cold Regions Research and Engineering
           Laboratory.   II. Title.

Structural engineering.
778
:690.44   Moser, C
M67   Photogrammetric measurements of deformations
           of structures, by C. Moser and W.R. Schriever.
           Ottawa, National Research Council, Jan. 1957.
             20 p.   (Canada. National Research Council.
           Publication NRC 3750)
             "A joint paper of the Divisions of Applied
           Physics and Building Research, presented at the
           RILEM Symposium on the Observation of Structures
           held in Lisbon, Portugal, October 1955."
             Research paper no. 30 of the Division of
           Building Research.

             (over)

STRUCTURAL ENGINEERING.
691.328
N67s   Nosseir, S   B
             Structural behavior of reinforced concrete
           beams made with fast-fix 1 cement, by
           S.B. Nosseir and M.G. Katona. Port Hueneme,
           Calif., Naval Civil Engineering Laboratory,
           1969.
             33p. (Technical report R 614)
             Sponsored by Naval Facilities Engineering
           Command.
             CFSTI. AD 683757.
             1. Concrete, Reinforced. 2. Structural
           engineering.   I. U.S. Naval Civil
           Engineering   Laboratory. II. Title.

Structural engineering.
623
M44   Mikkola, Martti.
             An analysis of physically nonlinear struc-
           tures. Helsinki, State Institute for Tech-
           nical Research, 1966.
             98p. (Finland. State Institute for
           Technical Research. Julksisu 112 publication)
             Thesis - Institute of Technology, Oteniemi.

             1. Structural engineering. I. Finland.
           State Institute for Technical Research.
           II. Title.

Structural engineering.
623
N17   National Forest Products Association.
             The wood-frame house as a structural unit.
           Washington, 1965.
             27p. (Its Technical report no. 5)

             1. Structural engineering. 2. Housing.
           3. Wood. I. Title.

Structural engineering.
624.2
O54   Oliveira, E   R   Arantes E
             Automatização do cálculo de estruturas.
           Lisboa, Ministério das Obras Públicas,
           Laboratório Nacional de Engenharia Civil,
           1964.
             16p. (Portugal. Laboratório Nacional de
           Engenharia Civil. Memória no. 220)
             English summary.
             1. Bridges. 2. Structural engineering.
           I. Portugal. Laboratório Nacional de Engen-
           haria Civil.

Structural engineering.
725.1
(41)   Mills, H   E
M45   Government offices, Horseferry Road, London
           SW1. London, Institution of Structural Engineers,
           1967.
             12p.

             Reprint from: The Structural engineer, Oct.,
           1967.
             1. Public buildings - U.K. 2. Structural
           engineering. 3. Prefabricated construction -
           U.K. I. Institution of Structural Engineers.
           II. Structural engineer. III. Title.

---

624   STRUCTURAL ENGINEERING.
N17   NATIONAL RESEARCH COUNCIL, CANADA.
           DIVISION OF BUILDING RESEARCH.
             SURVEY OF STRUCTURAL RESEARCH FACILITIES
           AND ACTIVITIES AT UNIVERSITIES AND
           RESEARCH ORGANIZATIONS IN CANADA.
           OTTAWA, DIVISION OF BUILDING RESEARCH,
           1965.
             1 V. (VARIOUS PAGINGS) (DBR TECHNICAL
           PAPER NO. 200)

             1. STRUCTURAL ENGINEERING.

Structural engineering.
623
O57   Olszak, W
             Cálculo à retura de estruturas
           heterogéneas artotrópicas [Limit design
           of heterogeneous orthotropic structures]
           por W. Olszak e A. Savczuk. Lisboa,
           Portugal, Laboratório Nacional de
           Engenharia Civil, 1961.
             25p. (Portugal. Laboratório Nacional
           de Engenharia Civil. Memória no. 172)
             English summary.

             1. Structural engineering. I. Savczuk, A., jt. au.
           II. Portugal.   Laboratório Nacional
           de Engenharia Civil.

Structural engineering.
691
M61   Mobay Chemical Co.
             Rigid urethane foam; a new concept in struc-
           tural design. Pittsburgh, 1963.
             18p.

             1. Building materials. 2. Plastics.
           3. Structural engineering. I. Title.

Structural engineering.
691.328
N27   Nervi, Pier Luigi.
             Structures; translated by Guiseppina and
           Mario Salvadori; foreword by Mario Salvadori.
           New York, F. W. Dodge [1956]
             118p. illus.

             1. Structural engineering. 2. Reinforced
           concrete construction. I. Salvadori,
           Giuseppina, tr.

STRUCTURAL ENGINEERING.
720
O77   Otto, Frei, ed.
V.2   Tensile structure; vol. 2: design,
           structure, and calculation of buildings
           of cables, nets, and membranes.
           Cambridge, Mass., M.I.T. Press, 1969.
             171p.

             1. Architecture - Designs and plans.
           2. Structural engineering. I. Title.

Structural engineering.
623
M677   Morris, Glenn Allen.
             A general procedure for the analysis of
           elastic and plastic frameworks, by G.A. Morris
           and S.J. Fenves. A technical report of a re-
           search program sponsored by the Office of
           Naval Research, Dept. of the Navy. Urbana,
           University of Illinois, 1967.
             178p. (Illinois. University. Civil
           engineering studies; structural research
           series no. 325)
             1. Structural engineering. 2. Loads.
           I. Illinois. University. II. Fenves, Steven
           Joseph, jt. au.   III. Title. IV. Title:
           Elastic and plastic frameworks.

693.5   STRUCTURAL ENGINEERING.
N28   Neville, A   M
             Creep of concrete: plain, reinforced and
           prestressed. With chapters 17 to 20 written
           in collaboration with W. Dilger. Amsterdam,
           North-Holland Pub. Co., 1970.
             622p.
             Sole distributors for the U.S.A. and Canada:
           American Elsevier Pub. Co., New York.

             1. Concrete construction. 2. Structural
           engineering. I. Dilger, W., jt. au.
           II. Title.

---

623   Structural engineering.
P17   Parker, Harry.
             Simplified engineering for architects and
           builders. 4th ed., rev. New York, Wiley,
           1967.
Ref.   361p.

             1. Structural engineering. 2. Building
           industry. 3. Strength of materials.
           4. Building materials. I. Title.

624
P17
PARKES, E W
BRACED FRAMEWORKS: AN INTRODUCTION TO THE THEORY OF STRUCTURES. OXFORD, ENG., PERGAMON PRESS, 1965.
198P. (THE COMMONWEALTH AND INTERNATIONAL LIBRARY OF SCIENCE, TECHNOLOGY, ENGINEERING AND LIBERAL STUDIES. STRUCTURES AND SOLID BODY MECHANICS DIVISION)

BIBLIOGRAPHY: P. 193-194.

1. STRUCTURAL ENGINEERING. I. TITLE.

Structural engineering.
623
P67
Portugal. Laboratório Nacional de Engenharia Civil.
A investigacao operacional e o dimensionamento das estruturas [Operational research and structural design] por J. Ferry Borges. Lisboa, 1960. 10p. tables. (Its Memoria no. 147)

English summary.

1. Structural engineering. I. Borges, J. Ferry.

624
R81M
RUBINSTEIN, MOSHE F
MATRIX COMPUTER ANALYSIS OF STRUCTURES. ENGLEWOOD CLIFFS, N.J., PRENTICE-HALL, 1966.
402P. (PRENTICE-HALL INTERNATIONAL SERIES IN ENGINEERING OF THE PHYSICAL SCIENCES)

1. STRUCTURAL ENGINEERING.
2. AUTOMATION. I. TITLE.

623
P27
Peterson, James P
Plastic buckling of plates and shells under biaxial loading. Washington, National Aeronautics and Space Administration, 1968. 32p. (NASA Technical note TN D-4706)

Bibliography: p. 31-32.

1. Structural engineering. 2. Loads. 3. Strains and stresses. I. U.S. National Aeronautics and Space Administration. II. Title.

624
P67
Portugal. Laboratorio Nacional de Engenharia Civil.
A utilizacao de modelos no dimensionamento das estruturas; aplicacaoes diversas, by Manuel Rocha and J. Ferry Borges. Lisboa, 1956.
33p. illus. (Its Memoria no. 92)

English summary.

1. Structural engineering. I. Rocha, Manuel II. Borges, J Ferry.

624
R81
Rubinstein, Moshe F
Structural systems: statics, dynamics and stability. Englewood Cliffs, N.J., Prentice-Hall, 1970.
306p. (Civil engineering and engineering mechanics series)

1. Structural engineering. I. Title.

624
P27
STRUCTURAL ENGINEERING.
Petrovski, J
Dinamicki osobini na povekespratna stanbena zgrada (Cynamic properties of multistory residential building), od J. Petrovski et al. Skopje, Yugoslavia, Institut za Zemjotresno Inzenerstvo i Inzenerska Zeizmologija na Univerzitetot ''Kiril i Metodij!', Laboratorija za Dinamicki Ispicuvanja, 1970.
1v. (Publikacija br. 22)
Bibliography: p. 20-21.
1. Structural engineering. I. Skopje, Yugoslavia. Univerzitet. II. Dynamic properties of multistory residential building.

624
P74
STRUCTURAL ENGINEERING.
Priestley, M J N
Comportamento de estruturas aporticadas sob accão de forcas horizontais – critério de simplificacão, por M.J.N. Priestley e Artur Ravara. Lisboa, Ministério das Obras Públicas, Laboratório Nacional de Engenharia Civil, 1969.
10p. (Portugal. Laboratório Nacional de Engenharia Civil. Memoria no. 342)
English summary.
1. Structural engineering. 2. Loads. I. Ravara, Artur, jt. au. II. Portugal. Laboratório Nacional de Engenharia Civil.

693.5
S13
STRUCTURAL ENGINEERING.
Sahlin, Sven.
Structural masonry. Englewood Cliffs, N.J., Prentice-Hall, 1971.
290p.

1. Concrete construction. 2. Brick construction. 3. Structural engineering. I. Title. II. Title: Masonry.

624
P46
STRUCTURAL ENGINEERING.
Pippard, A J S
The analysis of engineering structures, by A.J.S. Pippard and Sir John Baker. 4th ed. New York, American Elsevier, 1968.
578p.

1. Structural engineering. I. Baker, John, jt. au. II. Title.

620.1
1694.15
P87R
STRUCTURAL ENGINEERING.
PURDUE UNIVERSITY. DIVISION OF ENGINEERING SCIENCES.
RESPONSE OF TALL BUILDINGS TO RANDOM EARTHQUAKES, BY A. CEMAL ERINGE. LAFAYETTE, IND., 1957.
19P. (ITS TECHNICAL REPORT NO. 12)

1. VIBRATION. 2. STRUCTURAL ENGINEERING. 3. EARTHQUAKES. I. ERINGEN, A. CEMAL.

693.97
S15
STRUCTURAL ENGINEERING.
Salmon, Charles G
Steel structures; design and behavior, by Charles G. Salmon and John E. Johnson. Scranton, Pa., Intext Educational Publishers, College Div. of Intext, 1971.
946p. (Intext series in civil engineering)

1. Steel construction. 2. Structural engineering. I. Johnson, John E., jt. au. II. Title.

690.015
(L85)
S82
R21
1968
Structural engineering.
Plem, Erik.
Design of point set structures. Stockholm, National Swedish Institute for Building Research. 1968.
55p. (Report fran byggforskningen 1968:21)

1. Building research – Sweden. 2. Structural engineering. 3. Nails and nailing. 4. Loads. 5. Strains and stresses. I. Stockholm. Statens institut for byggnadsforskning. II. Title.

624
R15
Structural engineering.
Raney, John P
Identification of structural systems by use of near-resonance testing, by John P. Raney and James T. Howlett. Wash., National Aeronautics and Space Administration, 1969.
38p. (NASA TN D-5069)

1. Structural engineering. 2. Air transportation. I. Howlett, James T., jt. au. II. U.S. National Aeronautics and Space Administration. III. Title.

624
S15st
STRUCTURAL ENGINEERING.
Salvadori, Mario.
Statics and strength of structures, by Mario Salvadori and others. Englewood Cliffs, N.J., Prentice-Hall, 1971.
323p. (Prentice-Hall international series in architecture)

1. Structural engineering. I. Title.

693.2
P58R
STRUCTURAL ENGINEERING.
PLUMMER, HARRY CUSTER.
REINFORCED BRICK MASONRY AND LATERAL FORCE DESIGN, BY HARRY C. PLUMMER AND JOHN A. BLUME. 4TH PRINTING. WASHINGTON, STRUCTURAL CLAY PRODUCTS INSTITUTE, 1958.
271P.

BIBLIOGRAPHY: P. 262-265.

1. BRICK CONSTRUCTION. 2. STRUCTURAL ENGINEERING. I. BLUME, JOHN A., JT. AU. II. TITLE.

623
R22
Structural engineering.
Reed, R R
Analysis of structural response with different forms of damping. Washington, National Aeronautics and Space Administration, 1967.
Inf. 48p. (NASA TN D-3861)

1. Structural engineering. 2. Vibration. I. U.S. National Aeronautics and Space Administration. II. Title.

624
S15S
STRUCTURAL ENGINEERING.
SALVADORI, MARIO GEORGE.
STRUCTURAL DESIGN IN ARCHITECTURE, BY MARIO SALVADORI AND MATTHYS LEVY, WITH EXAMPLE AND PROBLEM SOLUTIONS BY JOHN J. FARRELL. ENGLEWOOD CLIFFS, N.J., PRENTICE-HALL, 1967.
457P.

1. STRUCTURAL ENGINEERING. I. LEVY, MATTHYS, JT. AU. II. TITLE.

VF
621.315
P67
Structural engineering.
Portugal. Laboratório Nacional de Engenharia Civil.
Experimental study of towers for high tension lines [by] J. Ferry Borges and J. Arga e Lima. Lisbon, 1956.
14 p. illus. (Its Report no. 86)

Reprinted from the Preliminary Publication of the V Congress of the International Association of Bridge and Structural Engineering.
1. Structural engineering. I. Ferry, Borges, J I. Title: Towers.

624
R63
STRUCTURAL ENGINEERING.
ROGERS, GROVER L
AN INTRODUCTION TO THE DYNAMICS OF FRAMED STRUCTURES. NEW YORK, WILEY, 1959.
355P.

1. STRUCTURAL ENGINEERING. 2. STRAINS AND STRESSES. I. TITLE: DYNAMICS OF FRAMED STRUCTURES.

624
S15
STRUCTURAL ENGINEERING.
SALVADORI, MARIO GEORGE.
STRUCTURE IN ARCHITECTURE, BY MARIO SALVADORI IN COLLABORATION WITH ROBERT HELLER. ENGLEWOOD CLIFFS, N.J., PRENTICE-HALL, 1963.
370P.

1. STRUCTURAL ENGINEERING. 2. ARCHITECTURE. I. HELLER, ROBERT. II. TITLE.

620
S15
Structural engineering
Samuelsson, Alf.
Väg- och vattenbyggar-utbildningen och 'ämnet byggnadsstatik vid "Chalmers" 1829-1967; en historik tillägnad Sven Olof Asplund, av Alf Samuelsson [et al] Göteborg, Scandinavian University Books, 1968.
63p. (Chalmers University of Technology, Gothenburg, Sweden. Transactions no. 323; Avd. Väg- och Vattenbyggnad, Byggnadsteknik 57. 1968)
Bibliography: p. 43-63.
English summary.
1. Civil engineering. 2. Structural engineering I. Chalmers University of Technology, Gothenburg, Sweden.

624
S22e
Structural engineering.
Sechler, Ernest E
Elasticity in engineering. New York, Dover Publications, 1968.
419p.

1. Structural engineering. I. Title.

624
S64
STRUCTURAL ENGINEERING.
Spillers, W R
On the use of examples in structural design, by W.R. Spillers and L.R. Friedland. [n.p., 1969?]
33p.

1. Structural engineering. I. Freidland, L.R., jt. au. II. Title.

629.13
S15
STRUCTURAL ENGINEERING.
San Diego Aircraft Engineering, inc.
Potential structural materials and design concepts for light aircraft. Wash., National Aeronautics and Space Administration, 1969.
135p. (U.S. National Aeronautics and Space Administration. NASA CR-1285)
1. Aircraft construction. 2. Structural engineering. 3. Metals. I. U.S. National Aeronautics and Space Administration. II. Title.

624
S31
STRUCTURAL ENGINEERING.
Shaw, F S
Virtual displacements and analysis of structures. Englewood Cliffs, N.J., Prentice-Hall, 1972.
560p. (Prentice-Hall civil engineering and engineering mechanics series)
Bibliography: p. 550-552.

1. Structural engineering. 2. Strains and stresses. I. Title.

624
S68
STRUCTURAL ENGINEERING.
Spunt, Leonard.
Optimum structural design. Englewood Cliffs, N.J., Prentice-Hall, 1971.
168p. (Prentice-Hall civil engineering and engineering mechanics series)
Bibliography: p. 161-162.

1. Structural engineering. I. Title.

623
S18
Structural engineering.
Savin, G N
Rib-reinforced plates and shells, by G.N. Savin and N.P. Fleishman. Translated from Russian, by A. Barouch. Jerusalem, Published for the National Aeronautics and Space Administration and the National Science Foundation, Washington, by the Israel Program for Scientific Translations, 1967.
Ref.   334p. (NASA TT F-427)
At head of title: Academy of Sciences of the Ukrainian SSR. Institute of Mechanics of the L'vov State University im. Iv. Franko.
Bibliography: p. 318-333.
(Cont'd on next card)

624
S32
STRUCTURAL ENGINEERING.
SHERMER, CARL LOUIS.
FUNDAMENTALS OF STATICALLY INDETERMINATE STRUCTURES. NEW YORK, RONALD, 1957.
264P.

1. STRUCTURAL ENGINEERING. I. TITLE: STATICALLY INDETERMINATE STRUCTURES.

624
S71
STRUCTURAL ENGINEERING.
STANLEY ENGINEERING COMPANY.
COEFFICIENTS FOR ANALYSIS OF FOUR SPAN CONTINUOUS BEAMS OF CONSTANT MOMENT OF INERTIA. EDITED BY RICHARD H. STANLEY. MUSCATINE, IOWA, 1966.
1 v.

1. STRUCTURAL ENGINEERING. 2. STRAINS AND STRESSES. I. STANLEY, RICHARD H., ED. II. TITLE. III. MOMENT OF INERTIA.

623
S18
Savin, G N   Rib-reinforced plates and shells...1967.   (Card 2)

1. Structural engineering. 2. Strains and stresses. I. U.S. National Aeronautics and Space Administration. II. U.S. National Science Foundation. III. Israel Program for Scientific Translations. IV. Title.

629.13
S36
Structural engineering.
Shore, Charles P
Effects of structural damping on flutter of stressed panels. Wash., National Aeronautics and Space Administration, 1969.
32p. (NASA technical note TN D-4990)
Bibliography: p. 23-24.
1. Aircraft construction. 2. Structural engineering. I. Title. II. U.S. National Aeronautics and Space Administration.

623
S72
Structural engineering.
Steffens, R J
Some aspects of structural vibration. Garston, Eng., Building Research Station, Ministry of Technology, 1966.
30p. (U.K. Building Research Station. Building research current papers. Engineering series 37)
Reprinted from Vibration in civil engineering: proceedings of a symposium organized by the British National Section of the International Association for Earthquake Engineering. Bibliography: p. 25-30.
(Cont'd on next card)

624
S24
STRUCTURAL ENGINEERING.
SCIENCE COUNCIL OF JAPAN.
PROCEEDINGS OF THE SYMPOSIUM. PAPERS PRESENTED AT THE ANNUAL SYMPOSIUM ORGANIZED BY THE NATIONAL COMMITTEE FOR BRIDGE AND STRUCTURAL ENGINEERING OF THE SCIENCE COUNCIL OF JAPAN, IN CONJUNCTION WITH THE JAPAN SOCIETY OF CIVIL ENGINEERS AND ARCHITECTURAL INSTITUTE OF JAPAN.
1ST-   TOKYO, JAPAN SOCIETY FOR THE PROMOTION OF SCIENCE, 1955-.
v.
For Library Holdings see main entry
1. STRUCTURAL ENGINEERING. I. JAPAN SOCIETY OF CIVIL ENGINEERING.
(CONTINUED ON NEXT CARD)

624
S45
1962
STRUCTURAL ENGINEERING.
Singelton, Jack
Manual of structural design. 4th ed. Topeka, Kan., H.M. Ives & Sons, 1962.
373p.

1. Structural engineering. 2. Concrete construction. 3. Steel construction. I. Title.

623
S72
Steffens, R.J. Some aspects of structural vibration...1966.   (Card 2)

1. Structural engineering. 2. Vibration. 3. Earthquake resistant construction. I. U.K. Building Research Station. II. Title.

624
S24
SCIENCE COUNCIL OF JAPAN. PROCEEDINGS OF THE ...5.   (CARD 2)

II. ARCHITECTURAL INSTITUTE OF JAPAN. III. JAPAN SOCIETY FOR THE PROMOTION OF SCIENCE.

624
S47
STRUCTURAL ENGINEERING.
Sittig, J
Improved quality brings reduced costs. Garston, Eng., Building Research Station, 1968.
4p. (U.K. Building Research Station. Library communication 1441)
Reprinted and translated from: Bouw, 1966, 39, 1500-1501.

1. Structural engineering. 2. Building costs. I. U.K. Building Research Station. II. Title. (Series)

002
:690
S72
STRUCTURAL ENGINEERING.
Stevens, R F
A study of coding and data co-ordination for the construction industry: structural engineering design, by R.F. Stevens and L. Monument. Garston, Eng., Building Research Station, 1969.
32p. (U.K. Building Research Station. Current paper 5/69)
1. Building documentation. 2. Structural engineering. I. Monument, L., jt. au. II. U.K. Building Research Station. III. Title.

623
S24
Structural engineering.
Scipio, L Albert
Structural design concepts, some NASA contributions. Washington, Technology Utilization Div., Office of Technology Utilization, National Aeronautics and Space Administration, 1967.
Ref.   174p. (NASA SP-5039)
Bibliography: p. 121-168.

1. Structural engineering. 2. Architecture - Design. I. U.S. National Aeronautics and Space Administration. III. Title.

720
S62
STRUCTURAL ENGINEERING.
Spence, William P
Architecture; design, engineering, drawing. Bloomington, Ill., McKnight & McKnight, 1967.
582p.

1. Architecture - Designs and plans. 2. Structural engineering. I. Title.

691.771
S76
STRUCTURAL ENGINEERING.
Stockholm. Statens Institut for Byggnadsforskning.
Aluminiumkonstruktioner; stabilitetsproblem. Forsoksnorm med anvisningar och kommentarer for behandling av stabilitetsproblem. Stockholm, 1970.
226p.

1. Aluminum. 2. Structural engineering.

Structural engineering.

VF
691.4
S77
R7

Structural Clay Products Research Foundation.
Resistance of structural clay masonry to dynamic forces, a design manual for blast resistance, by C. B. Monk, Jr. Geneva, Ill., 1958.
64p. illus., diagrs. (Its Research report no. 7)

1. Brick construction. 2. Structural engineering. I. Monk, C. B., Jr.

624
S95

STRUCTURAL ENGINEERING.
SYMPOSIUM ON THE DESIGN OF HIGH BUILDINGS, UNIVERSITY OF HONG KONG, 1961.
PROCEEDINGS OF A MEETING HELD IN SEPTEMBER 1961 AS PART OF THE GOLDEN JUBILEE CONGRESS OF THE UNIVERSITY OF HONG KONG. EDITED BY SEAN MACKEY. HONG KONG, HONG KONG UNIVERSITY PRESS, 1962. 515P.

1. STRUCTURAL ENGINEERING. 2. BUILDING CONSTRUCTION. I. TITLE: HIGH BUILDINGS.

Structural engineering.

623
T78

Trubert, Marc R   P
Response of elastic structures to statistically correlated multiple random excitations. Gainesville, Fla., University of Florida, Florida Engineering and Industrial Experiment Station, 1963.
15p. (Florida. University. Engineering and Industrial Experiment Station. Technical paper series no. 268)
Engineering progress at the University of Florida, v. 17, no. 8, Aug. 1963.

(Cont'd. on next card)

624
S77

STRUCTURAL ENGINEERING.
STRUCTURAL DESIGN FOR DYNAMIC LOADS, BY CHARLES H. NORRIS AND OTHERS. NEW YORK, MCGRAW-HILL, 1959.
453P. ILLUS. (MCGRAW-HILL CIVIL ENGINEERING SERIES)

COMPILED FROM LECTURE NOTES PREPARED FOR A SPECIAL TWO-WEEK SUMMER PROGRAM ... PRESENTED AT THE 1956 SUMMER SESSION OF THE MASSACHUSETTS INSTITUTE OF TECHNOLOGY. INCLUDES BIBLIOGRAPHY.

1. STRUCTURAL ENGINEERING.
2. VIBRATION. 3 . STRENGTH OF (CONTINUED ON NEXT CARD)

623
T14

Structural engineering.

Takabeya, Fukuhei, 1893-
Multi-story frames; calculation and moment-tables; the methods of Cross, Kani, Takabeya. Berlin, Ernst, 1965.
148p.

1. Structural engineering. 2. Loads.
3. Strains and stresses. I. Title.

623
T78

Trubert, Marc R   P   Response to elastic structures to...(Card 2)

Reprinted from the Journal of Acoustical Society of America, vol. 35, no. 7, July, 1963, p. 1009-1022.

1. Structural engineering. 2. Loads.
I. Florida. University. Engineering and Industrial Experiment Station.

624
S77

STRUCTURAL DESIGN FOR DYNAMIC LOADS, BY CHARLES H. NORRIS AND OTHERS. NEW YORK, MCGRAW-HILL, 1959. 453P. ILLUS. ...RIES)   (CARD 2)

MATERIALS.   I. NORRIS, CHARLES HEAD, 1910-   II. MASSACHUSETTS INSTITUTE OF TECHNOLOGY.

728.3
T15

Laf.

Structural engineering.

Tall buildings; the proceedings of a symposium on tall buildings with particular reference to shear wall structures. Held in the Dept. of Civil Engineering, University of Southampton, April 1966. Edited by A. Coull and B. Stafford Smith. Oxford, N.Y., Symposium Publications Div., Pergamon Press, 1967.
607p.
Sponsored by the University of Southampton and the Civil Engineering Research Association.

(Cont'd on next card)

624
T85

STRUCTURAL ENGINEERING.
Tuma, Jan J
Schaum's outline of theory and problems of structural analysis; with an introduction to transport, flexibility and stiffness matrices and their applications.
New York, McGraw-Hill, 1969.
292p. (Schaum's outline series)

Bibliography: p. 277-283.

1. Structural engineering. I. Title.

693
S82

Structural engineering.

Sudderth, Stanley K
A generalized stiffness analysis of space frames. Lafayette, Ind., Purdue University, Agricultural Experiment Station, 1967.
21p. (Purdue University, Agricultural Experiment Station Research progress report 321)
1. Building methods. 2. Architecture - Designs and plans. 3. Structural engineering. 4. Wood - Research. I. Indiana. Agricultural Experiment Station. II. Title.

728.3
T15

Tall buildings; the proceedings of a symposium on tall buildings with particular reference to shear wall structures...1967.
(Card 2)

1. Architecture - Design. 2. Walls.
3. Structural engineering. 4. Strains and stresses. 5. Buildings - Wind stresses.
I. Coull, A., ed. II. Smith, Bryan Stafford, ed. III. Southampton, Eng. University.
IV. Civil Engineering Research Association.

VF
623
U54e

Structural engineering.

U.K. Building Research Station.
An exhibition of work on structural engineering and soil mechanics. [London] 1955.
36p. illus.

"Selected bibliography:" p. 31-35.

1. Structural engineering. 2. Soils.

691.8
S85

STRUCTURAL ENGINEERING.
Sullins, R T
Manual for structural stability analysis of sandwich plates and shells, by R.T. Sullins and others. Prepared by General Dynamics Corp. Wash., National Aeronautics and Space Administration, 1969.
1v. (U.S. National Aeronautics and Space Administration. NASA CR-1457)

1. Panels. 2. Structural engineering.
I. General Dynamics Corp. II. U.S. National Aeronautics and Space Administration. III. Title.

623
T36

Structural engineering.

Thomas, H   S   H
The measurement of strain in tunnel linings using the vibrating-wire technique. Garston, Eng., Building Research Station, Ministry of Technology, 1966.
8p. (U.K. Building Research Station. Building research current papers. Engineering series 34)
Reprinted from: Strain, 1966, vol. 2(July), p. 16-21.

1. Structural engineering. I. U.K. Building Research   Station. II. Title.
III. Title: Tunnel linings.

624
U54

STRUCTURAL ENGINEERING.
U.K. Dept. of the Environment, Research and Development.
GENESYS; a computer system for structural engineers and others. A report by the Committee on the Application of Computers in the Construction Industry; with a note by the director of the GENESYS Centre. London, 1971.
21p. (R & D paper)

Publication originally prepared under the Ministry of Public Building and Works.
1. Structural engineering. 2. Building industry - Automation. I. U.K. Ministry of Public Building and Works. II. Title.

624
S87

STRUCTURAL ENGINEERING.
SUTHERLAND, HALE.
STRUCTURAL THEORY, BY HALE SUTHERLAND AND HARRY LAKE BOWMAN. 4TH ED. NEW YORK, WILEY, 1950.
394P.

FIRST ED. PUBLISHED IN 1930 UNDER TITLE: AN INTRODUCTION TO STRUCTURAL THEORY AND DESIGN.

1. STRUCTURAL ENGINEERING. I. BOWMAN, HARRY LAKE, JT. AU. II. TITLE.

690.4
T45

Structural engineering.

Timoshenko, S
Theory of structures, by S. Timoshenko and D.H. Young. 1st ed.   New York, McGraw-Hill, c1945.
xiv, 488 p.   diagrs., tables.

1. Structural engineering. I. Young, D   H   , jt. au. II. Title.

690
(41)
U54STU

STRUCTURAL ENGINEERING.
UNITED KINGDOM. DEPT. OF SCIENTIFIC AND INDUSTRIAL RESEARCH.
STRUCTURAL REQUIREMENTS FOR HOUSES, BY F. G. THOMAS. LONDON, H. M. STATIONERY OFF., 1948.
8P. (ITS NATIONAL BUILDING STUDIES SPECIAL REPORT NO. 1)

1. BUILDING CONSTRUCTION - UNITED KINGDOM. 2. STRUCTURAL ENGINEERING. I. THOMAS, F. G. II. TITLE.

690.015
(485)
S82
R24
1966

Structural engineering.

Sweden. Statens Kommitté för Byggnadsforskning.
Helth. Redovisning av konstruktionsberäkningar (Report on structural calculations) Stockholm, 1966.
1 v. (Its Rapport 24:1966)

1. Building research - Sweden.
2. Structural engineering.

624
T68

STRUCTURAL ENGINEERING.
TOWNSEND, CHARLES L
STUDIES AND PROCEDURES FOR THE CONTROL OF CRACKING IN MASS CONCRETE STRUCTURES. DENVER, COLORADO, 1964.
101P. (U.S. BUREAU OF RECLAMATION. TECHNICAL MEMORANDUM NO. 664)

1. STRUCTURAL ENGINEERING. 2. CONCRETE CONSTRUCTION. I. U.S. BUREAU OF RECLAMATION.

624
U54S

STRUCTURAL ENGINEERING.
UNITED KINGDOM. DEPT. OF SCIENTIFIC AND INDUSTRIAL RESEARCH.
A STUDY OF THE VOUSSOIR ARCH, BY A. J. SUTTON PIPPARD AND LETITIA CHITTY. LONDON, H. M. STATIONERY OFF., 1951.
52P. (ITS NATIONAL BUILDING STUDIES RESEARCH PAPER NO. 11)

1. STRUCTURAL ENGINEERING.
I. PIPPARD, A. J. SUTTON. II. CHITTY, LETITIA. III. TITLE: VOUSSOIR ARCH.

VF
623
U54
AE4.2

Structural engineering.
U.S. Army. Corps of Engineers.
Structural design: Concrete construction for buildings (except hydraulic structures). Washington, D.C., Govt. Print. Off., Oct. 1948.
3 p. (Its Engineering manual, military construction. Pt. IV, chap. 2)

1.Structural engineering. 2.Concrete construction. I.Series: Engineering manual for War Department construction.

534.83
N17e

STRUCTURAL ENGINEERING.
U.S. National Bureau of Standards.
The effects of sonic boom and similar impulsive noise on structures. Wash., U.S. Environmental Protection Agency, Office of Noise Abatement and Control, 1971.
19p. (NTID300.12)

1. Noise. 2. Structural engineering. I. U.S. Environmental Protection Agency. II. Title.

624
W15

STRUCTURAL ENGINEERING.
Wang, Chu-Kia.
Matrix methods of structural analysis. 2d ed. Scranton Pa., International Textbook Co., 1970.
406p. (International textbooks in civil engineering)

1. Structural engineering. 2. Civil engineering. I. Title.

VF
623
U54
AE4.1

Structural engineering.
U.S. Army. Corps of Engineers.
Structural design: Load assumptions for buildings. Washington, D.C., Govt. Print. Off., April 1946.
6 p. diagrs. (Its Engineering manual for War Department construction. Pt. IV, chap. 1)

1.Structural engineering. I.Title: Loan assumptions for building. II.Series: Engineering manual for War Department construction.

620.1
163+.15
N18

STRUCTURAL ENGINEERING.
U.S. NAVAL RESEARCH LABORATORY.
CHARACTERISTIC DYNAMIC STRENGTH RATIO AS THE LIMITING PARAMETER IN SHOCK DESIGN, BY H.C. MAYO. WASHINGTON, 1965.
38P. (ITS NRL REPORT 6363)

1. VIBRATION. 2. STRUCTURAL ENGINEERING. I. MAYO, H.C. II. TITLE: SHOCK DESIGN.

624
W15N

STRUCTURAL ENGINEERING.
WANG, PING-CHUN.
NUMERICAL AND MATRIX METHODS IN STRUCTURAL MECHANICS WITH APPLICATIONS TO COMPUTERS. NEW YORK, WILEY, 1966.
426P.

1. STRUCTURAL ENGINEERING. 2. AUTOMATION. I. TITLE.

VF
623
U54
AE4.3

Structural engineering.
U.S. Army. Corps of Engineers.
Structural design: Masonry construction for buildings. Washington, D.C., Govt. Print. Off., Mar. 1946.
6 p. (Its Engineering manual for War Department construction. Pt. IV, chap. 3)

1.Structural engineering. I.Title: Masonry construction for buildings. II.Series: Engineering manual for War Department construction.

624
Y17
1967

STRUCTURAL ENGINEERING
U.S. Yards and Docks Bureau.
Design manual; structural engineering. Washington, 196?.
61 p. diagrs. (Its: NAVDOCKS DM-2)

1. Engineering, Structural. ... I. Title. II. Title: Structural engineering, Design manual.

624
W17

STRUCTURAL ENGINEERING.
WARBURTON, GEOFFREY B
THE DYNAMICAL BEHAVIOR OF STRUCTURES. NEW YORK, MACMILLAN, 1964.
216P. (COMMONWEALTH AND INTERNATIONAL LIBRARY OF SCIENCE, TECHNOLOGY, ENGINEERING AND LIBERAL STUDIES. STRUCTURES AND SOLID BODY MECHANICS DIVISION, V. 5)

BIBLIOGRAPHY: P. 219-211.

1. STRUCTURAL ENGINEERING. 2. STRAINS AND STRESSES. I. TITLE.

VF
623
U54
AE4.4

Structural engineering.
U.S. Army. Corps of Engineers.
Structural design: Structural steel for buildings. Washington, D.C., Govt. Print. Off., Mar. 1946.
6 p. diagrs. (Its Engineering manual for War Department construction. Pt. IV, chap. 4)

1.Structural engineering. 2.Steel construction. I.Series: Engineering manual for War Department construction.

624
V25

STRUCTURAL ENGINEERING.
Venkatraman, B
Structural mechanics with introductions to elasticity and plasticity, by B. Venkatraman and Sharad A. Patel. New York, McGraw-Hill, 1970.
648p.

1. Structural engineering. I. Patel, Sharad A., jt. au. II. Title.

624
W22

STRUCTURAL ENGINEERING.
Weeks, G
Laboratory testing of large structures. Garston, Eng. Building Research Station, 1969.
6p. (U.K. Building Research Station. Current paper 22/69)
To be presented to the RILEM International Symposium on Testing Methodology and Technique of Full-Scale Structures under Static and Dynamic Loads, Bucharest, Sept., 1969.
1. Structural engineering. 2. Loads. I. U.K. Building Research Station. II. Title.

VF
623
U54
AE4.6

Structural engineering.
U. S. Army. Corps of Engineers.
Structural design: Structures other than buildings. Washington, D.C., Govt. Print. Off., Apr. 1946.
2 p. (Its Engineering manual for War Department construction. Pt. IV, chap. 6)

1.Structural engineering. I.Series: Engineering manual for War Department construction.

620.1
V42

STRUCTURAL ENGINEERING.
VIERTELS, EPHRAIM.
SIMPLIFIED PROBLEMS IN STRENGTH OF MATERIALS AND STRUCTURAL DESIGN. NEW YORK, EDWARD W. SWEETMAN, 1953.
636P.

1. STRENGTH OF MATERIALS. 2. STRUCTURAL ENGINEERING.

624
W45

STRUCTURAL ENGINEERING.
Williams, Alan.
The analysis of indeterminate structures. New York, Hart Pub. Co., 1968.
324p.

1. Structural engineering. I. Title.

VF
623
U54
AE4.5

Structural engineering.
U.S. Army. Corps of Engineers.
Structural design: Wood construction for buildings. Washington, D.C., Govt. Print. Off., Mar. 1946.
2 p. (Its Engineering manual for War Department construction. Pt. IV, chap. 5)

1.Structural engineering. 2.Wood construction. II.Series: Engineering manual for War Department construction.

624.043
V51

STRUCTURAL ENGINEERING.
VLASOV, VASILII ZAKHAROVICH.
BEAMS, PLATES AND SHELLS ON ELASTIC FOUNDATIONS, BY V.Z. VLASOV AND N.N. LEONT'EV. TRANSLATED FROM THE RUSSIAN BY A. BAROUCH. JERUSALEM, ISRAEL PROGRAM FOR SCIENTIFIC TRANSLATIONS, 1966.
357P.

PUBLISHED FOR THE NATIONAL AERONAUTICS AND SPACE ADMINISTRATION... AND THE NATIONAL SCIENCE FOUNDATION.
BIBLIOGRAPH Y: P. 347-353.
(CONTINUED ON NEXT CARD)

720
W45s

STRUCTURAL ENGINEERING.
Wilson, Forrest
Structure: the essence of architecture. New York, Van Nostrand Reinhold, 1971.
96p.

1. Architecture. 2. Structural engineering. I. Title.

VF
690.44
F67
D1951
1953

Structural engineering.
U.S. Forest Service. Forest Products Laboratory, Madison, Wis.
Theoretical design of a nailed or bolted joint under lateral load, by Edward W. Kuenzi. Rev. Sept. 1953. Madison, Wis., 1953.
25 p. diagrs., graphs. (Its Report no. D1951)
Processed.
1.Structural engineering. I.Kuenzi, Edward W. II.Title: Nailed or bolted joint under lateral load.

624.043
V51

VLASOV, VASILII ZAKHAROVICH. BEAMS....
1966. (CARD 2)

1. STRAINS AND STRESSES. 2. TRUSSES. 3. STRUCTURAL ENGINEERING. I. TITLE. II. LEONT'EV, N.N.

693.97
W66

STRUCTURAL ENGINEERING.
WOOD, R H
AN ECONOMICAL DESIGN OF RIGID STEEL FRAMES FOR MULTI-STOREY BUILDINGS. LONDON, H.M. STATIONERY OFFICE, 1951. 120P. (U.K. BUILDING RESEARCH STATION. NATIONAL BUILDING STUDIES RESEARCH PAPER NO. 10)

1. STEEL CONSTRUCTION. 2. STRUCTURAL ENGINEERING. I. U.K. BUILDING RESEARCH STATION.

691.328
W66p
STRUCTURAL ENGINEERING.
Wood, R H
A partial failure of limit analysis for slabs, and the consequences for future research. Garston, Eng., Building Research Station, 1970.
[12]p. (U.K. Building Research Station. Current paper 11/70)

Bibliography: p. 89-90.

Reprinted from: The Magazine of concrete
(Cont'd on next card)

691.328
W66p
Wood, R H   A partial...1970.
(Card 2)

research, June, 1969, pp. 79-90.

1. Concrete, Reinforced. 2. Structural engineering. I. U.K. Building Research Station. II. Title.

691.71
W66
Structural engineering.
Wood, R H
Test of a multi-storey rigid steel frame, by R.H. Wood and others. Garston, Eng., Building Research Station, Ministry of Public Building and Works, 1968.
107-119p. (U.K. Building Research Station. Building research current paper 53/68)
Reprinted from: The structural engineer, April, 1968.
1. Steel. 2. Structural engineering.
I. U.K. Building Research Station. II. Title.

621.6
Y58
Structural engineering.
Young, O C
Pipeline design: the relationship between structural theory and laying practice. Garston, Eng., Building Research Station, Ministry of Technology, 1964.
17p. (U.K. Building Research Station. Building research current papers. Engineering series 23)
Reprinted from Public Works and Municipal Services Congress and Exhibition. Final report, 1964, p. 264-73.

1. Pipes. 2. Struc-   tural engineering.
I. U.K. Building Re-   search Station.
III. Title.

624
Z42
Structural engineering.
Ziegler, Hans.
Principles of structural stability. Waltham, Mass., Blaisdell, 1968.
150p. (A Blaisdell book in solid mechanics)
Bibliography: p. 144-147.

1. Structural engineering. I. Title: Structural stability. II. Title.

624
(03)
E52
Structural engineering - Dict.

Encyclopedia of contemporary engineering: structural materials. Wright-Patterson Air Force Base, Ohio, Foreign Technology Division, 1967.
5 pts. (AD 657 256-657 260; FTD-TT-66-22)

Translated from the Russian.

1.Structural engineering - Dict.
I. Wright- Patterson Air Force Base, Ohio

720
K(09)
C65
Structural engineering - History.
Condit, Carl W
American building materials and techniques from the first colonial settlements to the present. Chicago, University of Chicago Press, 1968.
329p. (The Chicago History of American Civilization, Daniel J. Boorstin, editor)
1. Architecture - History. 2. Building industry - History. 3. Building methods. 4. Building materials. 5. Structural engineering - History. 6. Bridges. I. Title.

624
851
STRUCTURAL ENGINEERING - RESEARCH.
BLASZKOWIAK, STANISLAW.
ITERATIVE METHODS IN STRUCTURAL ANALYSIS, BY S. BLASZKOWIAK AND Z. KACZKOWSKI. TRANSLATED BY A. KACNER AND Z. OLESIAK. OXFORD, PERGAMON PRESS, 1966.
590P.

REVISED AND ENLARGED FROM THE POLISH EDITION.
REFERENCES: P. 531-536.
1. STRUCTURAL ENGINEERING - RESEARCH.
I. KACZKOWSKI, ZBIGNIEW, JT. AU.
II. TITLE. III. TITLE: STRUCTURAL ANALYSIS.

690.015
(485)
S82
R25
1969
STRUCTURAL ENGINEERING - RESEARCH.
Stockholm. Statens Institut för Byggnadsforskning.
Byggnadsaerodynamik; revy över aktuella frågeställningar (Building aerodynamics; review of current problems) Stockholm, 1969.
189p. (Its Rapport 25:1969)

English summary.
Collection of papers.

1. Building research - Sweden. 2. Structural engineering - Research. I. Title: Building aerodynamics.

624
J12
PT.1
1965
STRUCTURAL ENGINEERING - STUDY AND TEACHING.
JACKSON, HAROLD THOMAS.
THE DESIGN OF STRUCTURAL MEMBERS, PT. 1, WITH MODEL ANSWERS TO R.I.B.A. INTERMEDIATE EXAMINATION QUESTIONS. 2D ED., REV. AND ENL., LONDON, ARCHITECTURAL PRESS, 1965.
274P.

1. STRUCTURAL ENGINEERING - STUDY AND TEACHING. I. ROYAL INSTITUTE OF BRITISH ARCHITECTS. II. TITLE.

624
J12
PT.2
1962
STRUCTURAL ENGINEERING - STUDY AND TEACHING.
JACKSON, HAROLD THOMAS.
THE DESIGN OF STRUCTURAL MEMBERS, PT. 2, WITH MODEL ANSWERS TO R.I.B.A. FINAL EXAMINATION QUESTIONS. LONDON, ARCHITECTURAL PRESS, 1962.
468P.

1. STRUCTURAL ENGINEERING - STUDY AND TEACHING. I. ROYAL INSTITUTE OF BRITISH ARCHITECTS. II. TITLE.

624
(07)
J64
STRUCTURAL ENGINEERING - STUDY AND TEACHING.
Joiner, J H
Essentials of the theory of structures: revision work for student and graduate engineers. New York, Hart Pub. Co., 1968.
262p.

1. Structural engineering - Study and teaching. I. Title.

624
G72
STRUCTURAL ENGINEERING - TESTING.
GREGORY, MALCOLM S
ELASTIC INSTABILITY: ANALYSIS OF BUCKLING MODES AND LOADS OF FRAMED STRUCTURES. LONDON, SPON, 1967.
354P. (SPON'S CIVIL ENGINEERING SERIES)

1. STRUCTURAL ENGINEERING - TESTING.
I. TITLE. II. TITLE: BUCKLING MODES AND LOADS OF FRAMED STRUCTURES.

624
H67
STRUCTURAL ENGINEERING - TESTING.
HORNE, MICHAEL REX.
THE STABILITY OF FRAMES, BY M.R. HORNE AND W. MERCHANT. 1ST ED. OXFORD, NEW YORK, PERGAMON PRESS, 1965.
179P. (THE COMMONWEALTH AND INTERNATIONAL LIBRARY. STRUCTURES AND SOLID BODY MECHANICS DIVISION)

BIBLIOGRAPHY: P. 155-156.

1. STRUCTURAL ENGINEERING - TESTING.
I. MERCHANT, WILFRED, JT. AU. II. TITLE.

624
L47
STRUCTURAL ENGINEERING - TESTING.
LITLE, WILLIAM A
RELIABILITY OF SHELL BUCKLING PREDICTIONS, BY WILLIAM A. LITLE. CAMBRIDGE, MASS., M.I.T. PRESS, 1964.
VII, 178P. ILLUS. (M.I.T. RESEARCH MONOGRAPH NO. 25)

BIBLIOGRAPHY: P. 173-176.

1. STRUCTURAL ENGINEERING - TESTING.
2. ROOFS AND ROOFING - TESTING.
3. STRAINS AND STRESSES.

624
O34
STRUCTURAL ENGINEERING - TESTING.
OGIBALOV, P M
DYNAMICS AND STRENGTH OF SHELLS. TRANSLATED FROM RUSSIAN. JERUSALEM, ISRAEL PROGRAM FOR SCIENTIFIC TRANSLATION, 1966.
319P.

BIBLIOGRAPHY: P. 309-316.

1. STRUCTURAL ENGINEERING - TESTING.
2. STRENGTH OF MATERIALS. I. TITLE.
II. TITLE: SHELLS.

624
W21
STRUCTURAL ENGINEERING - TESTING.
WEAVER, WILLIAM.
COMPUTER PROGRAMS FOR STRUCTURAL ANALYSIS. PRINCETON, VAN NOSTRAND, 1967.
300P. (A VAN NOSTRAND ENGINEERING PAPERBACK)

1. STRUCTURAL ENGINEERING - TESTING.
2. AUTOMATION. I. TITLE.

624
Y17
1967
Structural engineering, Design manual.
U.S. Yards and Docks Bureau.
Design manual; structural engineering. Washington, 1961.
61 p. diagrs. (Its: NAVDOCKS DM-2)

1. Engineering, Structural. Structural design. I. Title.
II. Title: Structural engineering, Design manual.

624
G19
Structural engineering handbook.
Gaylord, Edwin H Jr., ed.
Structural engineering handbook, edited by Edwin H. Gaylord, Jr. and Charles N. Gaylord. New York, McGraw-Hill, 1968.
1v.

1. Structural engineering. I. Gaylord, Charles N., jt. ed. II. Title.

VF
691
P76
Structural engineering techniques.
Progressive Architecture.
Structural engineering techniques for architects and engineers. 3rd ed. [New York, Reinhold, 1953]
112 p. illus., diagrs., graphs, plans, tables.

"...Structural engineering reports ... selected from past issues of Progressive Architecture".

699.841
S77
STRUCTURAL ENGINEERS ASSOCIATION OF CALIFORNIA.
EARTHQUAKE EFFECT ON BUILDINGS: COSTLY DAMAGE CAN BE REDUCED. SAN FRANCISCO, 1957.
15P.

1. EARTHQUAKE RESISTANT CONSTRUCTION. I. TITLE.

699.841
S77r
Structural Engineers Association of
California.
Recommended lateral force requirements and
commentary. San Francisco, 1968.
100p.
— — Appendix

1. Earthquake resistant construction.
I. Title.

691
(016)
T19
STRUCTURAL LAMINATES LITERATURE SURVEY.
TAYLOR, R   L
STRUCTURAL LAMINATES LITERATURE SURVEY,
BY R.L. TAYLOR AND K.S. PISTER.
WRIGHT-PATTERSON AIR FORCE BASE, OHIO,
AERONAUTICAL RESEARCH LABORATORY, OFFICE
OF AERO-SPACE RESEARCH. U.S. AIR FORCE,
1961.
14P.

1. BUILDING MATERIALS - BIBLIOGRAPHY.
I. PISTER, K.S.   II. U.S. WRIGHT
PATTERSON AIR FORCE BASE, OHIO.
III. TITLE.

624
V25
Structural mechanics with introductions
to elasticity and plasticity.
Venkatraman, B
Structural mechanics with introductions to
elasticity and plasticity, by B. Venkatraman
and Sharad A. Patel. New York, McGraw-Hill,
1970.
648p.

1. Structural engineering. I. Patel,
Sharad A., jt. au. II. Title.

699.841
S77S
STRUCTURAL ENGINEERS ASSOCIATION OF
NORTHERN CALIFORNIA.
SCHOOL CONSTRUCTION UNDER THE FIELD
ACT.   BASED ON THE EXPERIENCE OF THE
PAST TWENTY YEARS OF OPERATION UNDER
THE ACT. SAN FRANCISCO, 1953.
4P.

1. EARTHQUAKE RESISTANT CONSTRUCTION.
2. SCHOOLS - CALIFORNIA.   I. TITLE.

550
T84
Structural landforms.
Twidale, C   R
Structural landforms; landforms associated
with granitic rocks, faults, and folded strata.
Cambridge, Mass., MIT Press, 1971.
247p. (An introduction to systematic geo-
morphology, vol. 5)

Bibliography: p. 219-231.

1. Geology. I. Title.

624
G15
Structural members and frames.
Galambos, Theodore V
Structural members and frames. Englewood
Cliffs, N.J., Prentice-Hall, 1968.
373p. (Prentice-Hall series in structural
analysis and design)

1. Structural engineering. I. Title.

551
(79488)
S77
STRUCTURAL ENGINEERS ASSOCIATION OF
NORTHERN CALIFORNIA.
1952 EARTHQUAKES OF KERN COUNTY
CALIFORNIA.   SAN FRANCISCO, 1955.
113P.

1. EARTHQUAKES - KERN CO., CALIF.

691.322
N27
Structural lightweight-aggregate concrete.
Nesbit, John Kennard.
Structural lightweight-aggregate concrete.
London, Concrete Publications Ltd., 1966.
280p. (Concrete series)
Bibliography: p. 250-4.

1. Concrete aggregates. 2. Concrete construction. I. Title.

624
C17
STRUCTURAL MODEL TESTING.
CARPENTER, JAMES E
STRUCTURAL MODEL TESTING; TECHNIQUES FOR
MODELS OF PLASTIC, BY J.E. CARPENTER, D.D.
MAGURA, AND N.W. HANSON. SKOKIE, 1964.
26-47P. (PORTLAND CEMENT ASSOCATION.
RESEARCH AND DEVELOPMENT LABORATORIES.
DEVELOPMENT DEPT. BULLETIN D76)

REPRINTED FROM THE JOURNAL OF THE PCA
RESEARCH AND DEVELOPMENT LABORATORIES,
VOL. 6, NO. 2, 1964.
1. STRUCTURAL ENGINEERING.   I. PORTLAND
CEMENT ASSOCIATION.   II. TITLE.
III. MODELS OF PLASTIC.

VF
693.55
S77
Structural Engineers Association of
Southern California.
Good practice in engineering design
and construction with reinforced concrete
masonry. [Los Angeles] Jan. 1950.
5 p. (Its Technical bulletin no. 3)

At head of title: Report of special
committee.

1.Reinforced concrete construction.

691.322
P64ra
Structural lightweight aggregate concrete.
Poijärvi, Heikki.
Rakenteellisesta kevytsorabetonista (on
structural lightweight aggregate concrete)
by Heikki Poijärvi and Kunto Ola. Helsinki,
1968.
98p. (Finland. State Institute for Technical
Research. Tiedotus. Sarja 3 - Rakennus
(Building) 128)
English summary.
Bibliography: p. 88-91.
1. Concrete aggregates. I. Finland. State
Institute for Technical Research. II. Title:
Structural light   weight aggregate con-
crete.   III. Ola, Kunto, jt. au.

624
H15
STRUCTURAL MODEL TESTING.
HANSON, NORMAN W
STRUCTURAL MODEL TESTING; A PROFILE
PLOTTER BY N.W. HANSON AND J.E. CARPENTER.
SKOKIE, ILL., 1963.
7P. (PORTLAND CEMENT ASSOCIATION.
RESEARCH AND DEVELOPMENT LABORATORIES.
DEVELOPMENT DEPT. BULLETIN D68)

REPRINTED FROM THE JOURNAL OF THE PCA
RESEARCH AND DEVELOPMENT LABORATORIES,
VOL. 5, NO. 3, 1963.

1. STRUCTURAL ENGINEERING.
I. CARPENTER, J E , JT. AU.
(CONTINUED ON NEXT CARD)

VF
693.5
S77
Structural Engineers Association of Southern
California.
Tilt-up construction. [Los Angeles, Calif.]
Sept. 1950.
[3] p. (Its Technical bulletin no. 2)

At head of title: Report of Special
Committee.

1.Concrete construction. I.Title.

690.091.83
C65r
Structural load testing of a New York City
tenement building.
Construction Research and Development Corp.
Report on the structural load testing of
a New York City tenement building. Prepared
for the United States Dept. of Housing and
Urban Development, Federal Housing Administration. New York, 1968.
100p.
1. Building inspection. 2. Houses - Maintenance and modernization. 3. Loads. I. U.S. Federal
Housing Administration. II. Title: Structural load
testing of a New York City tenement building.

624
H15
HANSON, NORMAN W   STRUCTURAL MODEL TESTING.
...1963.   (CARD 2)

II. PORTLAND CEMENT ASSOCIATION.
III. TITLE.

691.116
A52
...Structural glued laminated lumber.
American Institute of Timber Construction.
Inspection manual for structural glued lami-
nated lumber. 1st ed. Washington, 1955.
23p. illus., diagrs.

"References": p.22-23

693.5
S13
Structural masonry.
Sahlin, Sven.
Structural masonry. Englewood Cliffs, N.J.,
Prentice-Hall, 1971.
290p.

1. Concrete construction. 2. Brick
construction. 3. Structural engineering.
I. Title. II. Title: Masonry.

693.5
M13
STRUCTURAL MODEL TESTING.
MAGURA, DONALD D
STRUCTURAL MODEL TESTING, REINFORCED
AND PRESTRESSED MORTAR BEAMS. SKOKIE,
ILL., 1967.
24P. (PORTLAND CEMENT ASSOCIATION.
RESEARCH AND DEVELOPMENT LABORATORIES.
DEVELOPMENT DEPT. BULLETIN D113)

REPRINTED FROM THE JOURNAL OF THE PCA
RESEARCH AND DEVELOPMENT LABORATORIES,
VOL. 9, NO. 1, 1967.

1. CONCRETE CONSTRUCTION.
I. PORTLAND CEMENT ASSOCIATION.
(CONTINUED ON NEXT CARD)

VF
690.25
F67
Structural investigation of floors for
low-cost housing.
U.S. Forest Service. Forest Products Laborator,
Madison, Wis.
Structural investigation of floors for low-
cost housing, by W. C. Lewis. (In cooperation
with Housing and Home Finance Agency)
Madison, Wis. [June 1949]
49 l./plates, tables.

Typed, not for publication.

1.Floors and flooring. I.Lewis, W. C. II.U.S.
Housing and Home Finance Agency. III.Title.

624
A76
STRUCTURAL MECHANICS.
ASPLUND, SVEN OLOF.
STRUCTURAL MECHANICS; CLASSICAL AND
MATRIX METHODS. ENGLEWOOD CLIFFS, N.J.,
PRENTICE-HALL, 1966.
474P. (PRENTICE-HALL SERIES IN
STRUCTURAL ANALYSIS AND DESIGN)

PRENTICE-HALL INTERNATIONAL SERIES IN
THEORETICAL AND APPLIED MECHANICS.

1. STRUCTURAL ENGINEERING.   I. TITLE.

693.5
M13
MAGURA, DONALD D   STRUCTURAL MODEL
TESTING....1967.   (CARD 2)

II. TITLE.   III. TITLE: MORTAR BEAMS.

693.5
M173s
STRUCTURAL MODEL TESTING.
MATTOCK, ALAN HANSON.
STRUCTURAL MODEL TESTING, THEORY AND
APPLICATIONS. SKOKIE, ILL., 1962.
12-23P. (PORTLAND CEMENT ASSOCIATION.
RESEARCH AND DEVELOPMENT LABORATORIES.
DEVELOPMENT DEPT. BULLETIN D56)

REPRINTED FROM THE JOURNAL OF THE PCA
RESEARCH AND DEVELOPMENT LABORATORIES,
VOL. 4, NO. 3, 1962.

1. CONCRETE CONSTRUCTION.
I. PORTLAND CEMENT ASSOCIATION.
II. TITLE.

VF
691.8
F67s
[Structural performance standards for special
and new wall & floor construction.]
U.S. Forest Service. Forest Products Laboratory,
Madison, Wis.
[Structural performance standards for special
and new wall and floor construction.] Madison,
Wis. [1950]
2 pts. illus., diagrs., graphs, tables.

Pt.1.Behavior of wall facings under impact
load, by Edward W. Kuenzi.-pt.2.House panels
tested for requirements of present and proposed
performance standards, by Edward W. Kuenzi and
R. F. Luxford.
(Continued on next card)

U.S. Forest Service. Forest Products Laboratory
Madison, Wis. [Structural performance
standards ...] [1950] (Card 2)

Final report, Research Project no. O-T-26,
Housing and Home Finance Agency.
Project director, R. F. Luxford; staff
technician, William A. Russell.
Typewritten.

624
C25
STRUCTURAL PRACTICES OF FEDERAL HOUSING
AGENCIES.
CENTRAL HOUSING COMMITTEE.
STRUCTURAL PRACTICES OF FEDERAL HOUSING
AGENCIES. FIRST REPORT PREPARED AND
SUBMITTED TO THE SUB-COMMITTEE ON DESIGN
AND CONSTRUCTION BY THE STRUCTURAL
REFERENCE GROUP. WASHINGTON, 1937.
40P.

1. STRUCTURAL ENGINEERING. 2. FEDERAL
HOUSING PROGRAMS. 3. BUILDING MATERIALS.
I. TITLE.

690.015
H68
T21
Structural properties of light-gage tubular
columns.
U.S. Housing and Home Finance Agency. Office of
the Administrator. Division of Housing
Research.
Structural properties of light-gage tubular
columns. [Washington, Govt. Print. Off., Oct.
1953]
39 p. illus., graphs, tables. (Its
Housing research paper no. 21)

"...Based on laboratory tests performed at the
National Bureau of Standards ... under Research
Project 1950-STR-7 ... Analysis and conclusions
were prepared by Will A. Russell" - p. 1.

691.322
N17
The structural properties of some light-
weight aggregate concrete.
U.S. National Bureau of Standards.
The structural properties of some lightweight
aggregate concrete, by William C. Green and
D. Watstein. Washington, Oct. 1951.
15 p. plates, graphs, tables. (NBS
Report 1166)
"References": p. 14.
Final report, Research project no. 1950-STR-11,
Housing and Home Finance Agency.
Project director: D. E. Parsons; Staff
technician: William A. Russell.
Processed.
(over)

620.1
C65
V9.12
STRUCTURAL SAFETY.
COLUMBIA UNIVERSITY. INSTITUTE FOR THE
STUDY OF FATIGUE AND RELIABILITY.
THE ANALYSIS OF STRUCTURAL SAFETY, BY
A.M. FREUDENTHAL AND OTHERS. NEW YORK,
1964.
61P. (ITS TECHNICAL REPORT NO. 12)

1. STRENGTH OF MATERIALS.
I. FREUDENTHAL, A.M. II. TITLE:
STRUCTURAL SAFETY.

VF
699.83
877
Structural Specialties, Inc.
Hurricane brace method of wood frame
construction. West Palm Beach, Fla. [n.d.]
18 p. illus., plates.

1.Wind resistance. I.Title.

624
Z42
Structural stability.
Ziegler, Hans.
Principles of structural stability.
Waltham, Mass., Blaisdell, 1968.
150p. (A Blaisdell book in solid mechanics)
Bibliography: p. 144-147.

1. Structural engineering. I. Title:
Structural stability. II. Title.

699.81
B87s
Structural steel and fire.
Butcher, E G
Structural steel and fire, by
E. G. Butcher and G.M.E. Cooke.
London, H.M.S.O., 1969.
12p.
At head of title: BCSA Conference
on Steel in Architecture, Nov.
24-26, 1969, Research and development. Session 1, paper 4.
1. Fire prevention. 2. Steel
construction. I. Cooke, G.M.E.,
jt. au. II. Title.

693.97
L23s
STRUCTURAL STEEL DESIGN.
LEHIGH UNIVERSITY, BETHLEHEM, PA.
FRITZ ENGINEERING LABORATORY.
STRUCTURAL STEEL DESIGN, BY LYNN S.
BEEDLE AND OTHERS. NEW YORK, RONALD
PRESS CO., 1964.
829P.

BIBLIOGRAPHY: P. 769-791.

1. STEEL CONSTRUCTION.
2. STRUCTURAL ENGINEERING. I. BEEDLE,
LYNN S. II. TITLE.

693.97
M12
Structural steel design.
McCormac, Jack C
Structural steel design. 2d ed. Scranton,
Pa., Intext Educational Publishers, College Div.
of Intext, 1971.
604p. (Intext series in civil engineering)

1. Steel construction. 2. Structural
engineering. I. Title.

VF
690.015
(94)
I87
31
The structural sufficiency of domestic buildings
Isaacs, David V
The structural sufficiency of domestic
buildings. Sydney, Commonwealth Experimental
Building Station, June 1946.
50 p. diagrs., tables. (Australia.
Commonwealth Experimental Building Station.
Bulletin no. 1)

1.Loads. I.Title. II.Series.

728
:308
M25
Structural surveys of dwelling houses.
Melville, Ian A
Structural surveys of dwelling houses, by
Ian A. Melville and Ian A. Gordon with a
chapter on the legal position of the surveyor
by Peter Scott. Rev. ed. London, Estates
Gazette, 1965.
259p.

1. Architecture, Domestic - Surveys.
2. Surveying. I. Gordon, Ian A., jt. au.
II. Scott, Peter. III. Title.

690.237
M67
Structural synthesis of a stiffened cylinder.
Morrow, William M
Structural synthesis of a stiffened cylinder,
by William M. Morrow II and Lucien A. Schmit,
Jr. Prepared at Case Western Reserve University,
Cleveland, Ohio for Langley Research Center.
Wash., National Aeronautics and Space Adminis-
tration, 1968.
163p. (NASA CR-1217)

1. Loads. I. Case Western Reserve University, Cleveland. II. Schmit, Lucien A.,
jt. au. III. Title.

624
R81
Structural systems.
Rubinstein, Moshe F
Structural systems: statics, dynamics and
stability. Englewood Cliffs, N.J., Prentice-
Hall, 1970.
306p. (Civil engineering and engineering
mechanics series)

1. Structural engineering. I. Title.

690.015
(71)
N17s
Structural test of a house under simulated
wind and snow loads.
National Research Council, Canada. Division
of Building Research.
Structural test of a house under simulated
wind and snow loads, by D. B. Dorey and W. R.
Schriever. Ottawa, 1957.
29-49p. illus. (Its Research paper no.
43)

(Continued on Card 2)

690.015
(71)
N17s
National Research Council, Canada. Division
of Building Research. Structural test...
1957. (Card 2)

"Reprint from American Society for Testing
Materials Symposium on Full Scale Tests on
House Structures, A.S.T.M. Special Technical
Publication No. 210, 1957."

1.Building research - Canada. 2.Loads.
3.Wind resistance. I.Dorey, D B
II.Schriever, W R III.Title.

VF
691.11
F67m
Structural tests of wood interior doors.
U.S. Forest Service. Forest Products Laboratory,
Madison, Wis.
[Miscellaneous special research.] Madison,
Wis [1951-1952]
3 pts. illus., graphs, tables.

Pt.1.Structural tests of wood interior doors,
by Lyman W. Wood.-pt.2.Effect of wetting on
strength and stability of wood and fiberboard
sheathing, by E. C. O. Erickson.-pt.3.Moisture
absorption of fiberboards and wood subjected to
(Continued on next card)

U.S. Forest Service. Forest Products Laboratory,
Madison, Wis. [Miscellaneous special
research.] ... [1951-1952] (Card 2)

soaking or spraying with water, by O. C. E.
Erickson.
Final report, Research Project no. O-T-31,
Housing and Home Finance Agency.
Project director, R. F. Luxford; staff
technician, William A. Russell.
Typewritten.

629.136
M14
Structural tests on an experimental heli-
copter platform.
Mainstone, R J
Structural tests on an experimental heli-
copter platform. Garston, Eng., Building
Research Station, Ministry of Technology,
1966.
65-91p. (U.K. Building Research
Station. Building research current papers.
Engineering series no. 26)
Reprinted from Institution of civil
engineers, Proceedings, Jan., 1966.

1. Heliports. 2. Loads. I. U.K.
Building Research Station.
II. Title.

624
S87
STRUCTURAL THEORY.
SUTHERLAND, HALE.
STRUCTURAL THEORY, BY HALE SUTHERLAND
AND HARRY LAKE BOWMAN. 4TH ED. NEW YORK,
WILEY, 1950.
394P.

FIRST ED. PUBLISHED IN 1930 UNDER TITLE:
AN INTRODUCTION TO STRUCTURAL THEORY AND
DESIGN.

1. STRUCTURAL ENGINEERING. I. BOWMAN,
HARRY LAKE, JT. AU. II. TITLE.

360
S62s
Structure and dynamics of social intervention.
Spencer, Gary.
Structure and dynamics of social intervention:
a comparative study of the reduction of depend-
ency in three low-income housing projects, by
Gary Spencer. Lexington, Mass., Heath Lexington
Books, 1970.
153p. (Northeastern University studies in
rehabilitation no. 9)

Bibliography: p. 151-153.

1. Social service. I. New England Regional
Rehabilitation Research Institute.
II. Northeastern University. III. Title.

666.81
N17
Structure formation in water
suspensions of gypsum.
National Research Council, Canada. Division of
Building Research.
A study of structure formation in water
suspensions of gypsum. (Issledovanie
strukturoobrazovaniia v vodnykh suspenziiakh
gipsa), by V. I. Izmailova and others, tr.
by G. Belkov. Ottawa, 1957.
9 p., diagr. (Its Technical translation
TT-672)
From Doklady Akad. Nauk SSSR. 107 (3):
424-427, 1956. (See Card No. 2)

331
B27s
Structural unemployment in the United States.
Bergmann, Barbara R
Structural unemployment in the United
States. Prepared by Barbara R. Bergmann and
David E. Kaun, the Brookings Institution, for
the U.S. Dept. of Commerce, Economic Develop-
ment Administration. Wash., for sale by the
Supt. of Docs., Govt. Print. Off., 1966.
122p.
1. Labor supply. 2. Employment. I. Kaun,
David E., jt. au. II. U.S. Economic Develop-
ment Administration. III. Brookings Insti-
tution. IV. Title.

720.36
S42
Structure and form in modern architecture.
Siegel, Curt.
Structure and form in modern architecture.
Translated by Thomas E. Burton. New York,
Reinhold, 1962.
308p.

"Originally published in German under
the title Strukturformen, 1961."

1. Architecture, Modern. 2. Architecture
- Design. I. Burton, Thomas E., tr.
II. Title.

666.81
N17
National Research Council, Canada. Division
of Building Research.
A study of structure formation in water
suspensions of gypsum. 1957. (Card No. 2)

References: p. 7

1. Gypsum. I. Izmailova, V. N. II. Belkov,
G , tr. III. Title: Structure formation in
water suspensions of gypsum.

VF
690.013
(41)
G72
CP116
The structural use of precast concrete.
British Standards Institution.
The structural use of precast concrete.
London, Council for Codes of Practice,
British Standards Institution, 1965.
152p. (British standard code of practice
CP 116: 1965)

1. Building standards - U.K. 2. Concrete
construction. I. British Standard Code of
Practice. II. Title.

711.581
F22s
The structure and growth of residential
neighborhoods in American cities.
U.S. Federal Housing Administration.
The structure and growth of residential
neighborhoods in American cities. Washington
[Govt. Print. Off., 1939]
178 p. graphs, maps. (FHA Form no. 2088)

Prepared by Homer Hoyt.

1. Neighborhood surveys. 2. City growth. 3. Land use.
I. Hoyt, Homer. II. Title.

624
S15
STRUCTURE IN ARCHITECTURE.
SALVADORI, MARIO GEORGE.
STRUCTURE IN ARCHITECTURE, BY MARIO
SALVADORI IN COLLABORATION WITH ROBERT
HELLER. ENGLEWOOD CLIFFS, N.J.,
PRENTICE-HALL, 1963.
370P.

1. STRUCTURAL ENGINEERING.
2. ARCHITECTURE. I. HELLER, ROBERT.
II. TITLE.

VF
690.013
(41)
G72
CP112
The structural use of timber in buildings.
U.K. Ministry of Works. Council for Codes of
Practice in Buildings.
General series: The structural use of timber
in buildings (incorporating CP112.100 - Preserva-
tive treatments for timber used in buildings).
London [British Standards Institution] 1952.
83 p. illus., tables. (British standard
code of practice. CP112)
1. Wood construction. 2. Wood-Testing. 3. Wood
preservation. I. Title: The structural use of
timber in buildings. II. Ser.

691.7
P74
Structure and properties of heat-
resistant metals and alloys.
Pridantsev, M V ed.
Structure and properties of heat-
resistant metals and alloys. Jerusalem,
Israel Program for Scientific Translations,
1970.
371p. (NASA TT-F-557; TT 69-55020)
At head of title: Akademiya Nauk SSSR.
Institut Metallurgii imeni A.A. Baikova.
Translated from Russian.
Published pursuant to agreement with
National Aeronautics and Space Administra-
tion and National Science
(Cont'd on next card)

720
K27
STRUCTURE IN ART AND IN SCIENCE.
KEPES, GYORGY.
STRUCTURE IN ART AND IN SCIENCE.
EDITED BY GYORGY KEPES. NEW YORK, GEORGE
BRAZILLER, 1965.
189P. (VISION AND VALUE SERIES)

1. ARCHITECTURE. 2. ARCHITECTURE,
MODERN. I. TITLE.

699.82
M19
Structural waterproofing.
Maxwell-Cook, John C
Structural waterproofing. London,
Butterworths, 1967.
182p.

1. Waterproofing. 2. Moisture condensation. I. Title.

691.7
P74
Pridantsev, M V ed. Structure
and properties...1970. (Card 2)

Foundation.

1. Metals. I. U.S.S.R. Akademiia Nauk
SSSR. Institut Metallurgii imeni A.A.
Baikova. II. U.S. National Aeronautics
and Space Administration. III. Title.

690
C177
STRUCTURE IN BUILDING.
CASSIE, W FISHER.
STRUCTURE IN BUILDING, BY W. FISHER
CASSIE AND J.H. NAPPER. WITH A FOREWORD
BY W.A. ALLEN. LONDON, ARCHITECTURAL
PRESS, 1952.
266P. (MODERN BUILDING CONSTRUCTION
SERIES, V. 2)

1. BUILDING CONSTRUCTION.
2. STRUCTURAL ENGINEERING. I. NAPPER,
J.H., JT. AU. II. TITLE.

720
C67
STRUCTURE AND ARCHITECTURAL DESIGN.
CORKILL, PHILIP A
STRUCTURE AND ARCHITECTURAL DESIGN, BY
PHILIP A. CORKILL, HOMER L. PUDERBAUGH
AND H. KEITH SAWYERS. IOWA CITY,
SERNOLL, 1965.
322P.

BIBLIOGRAPHY: P. 326-328.

1. ARCHITECTURE - DESIGNS AND PLANS.
2. ARCHITECTURAL DETAILS. I. PUDERBAUGH,
HOMER L., JT. AU. II. SAWYERS, H.
KEITH, JT. AU. III. TITLE.

691.421
S27
Structure-formation in aqueous suspensions
of bentonite clay.
Serb-Serbina, N N
Structure-formation in aqueous
suspensions of bentonite clay (Strukturoobrazovanie v vodnykh suspenziyakh
bentonitovykh glin), by N.N.Serb-Serbina
and P.A. Rebinder. Garston, Eng.,
Building Research Station, Ministry of
Public Building and Works, 1968.
8p. (U.K. Building Research
Station. Library Communication 1447)
Translated from the Russian and
reprinted from: Kolloidnyi zhurnal,
1947, 9 (5), 381-91.
1. Clay. (Cont'd on next card)

690.091.82
C41s
The structure of building control.
Cibula, Evelyn.
The structure of building control: an
international comparison. Garston, Eng.,
Building Research Station, 1971.
21p. (U.K. Building Research Station.
Current paper CP 28/71)

1. Building codes. 2. Building standards.
I. U.K. Building Research Station.
II. Title.

624.131
T15
The structure and compression of
cohesionless soils.
Tammirinne, M
Kitkamaalajien rakenne ja kokoonpuristuvuus
(The structure and compression of
cohesionless soils) Helsinki, State
Institute for Technical Research, 1969.
128p. (Finland. State Institute for
Technical Research. Tiedotus. Sarja 3-
Rakennus 136)
English summary.
Bibliography: p. 125-218.
1. Soils. I. Finland. State Institute
for Technical Research. II. Title:
the structure and compression of
cohensionless soils.

691.421
S27
Serb-Serbina, N N Structure...
(Card 2)

I. U.K. Building Research Station.
II. Rebinder, P.A., jt. au.
III. Title: Bentonite clay.
IV. Title.

325
(79494)
M87
The structure of discontent.
Murphy, Raymond J
The structure of discontent: the relationship between social structure, grievance,
and support for the Los Angeles riot, by Raymond J. Murphy and James M. Watson. Los
Angeles, Los Angeles Riot Study, Institute
of Government and Public Affairs, University
of California, 1967.
115p.
1. Minority groups - Los Angeles. 2. Social
conditions - Los Angeles. 3. Social surveys -
Los Angeles. 4. Social welfare - Los Angeles.

(Cont'd on next card)

325
(79494)
M87 Murphy, Raymond J   The structure of discontent...1967.   (Card 2)

5. Race relations. 6. Civil rights.
I. Watson, James M. jt., au. II. California.
University. University at Los Angeles.
Institute of Government and Public Affairs.
(Los Angeles Riot Study) III. Title.

330
(485)
A77 The structure of the Stockholm economy.
Artle, Ronald.
The structure of the Stockholm economy;
toward a framework for projecting metropolitan
community development. ₍American ed₎ Ithaca,
N.Y., Cornell University Press, 1965.
197 p. (Cornell reprints in urban studies)
First published in Stockholm in 1959 under
title: Studies in the structure of the
Stockholm economy.
Bibliography: p. 178-191.

1. Econ. condit. - Stockholm. I. Title.

624
A41 Structures and materials.
AIAA/ASME Structures, Structural Dynamics and
Materials Conference, 10th, New Orleans, 1969.
Collection of technical papers on structures
and materials. New York, American Society of
Mechanical Engineers, 1969.
471p.

1. Structural engineering. I. American
Society of Mechanical Engineers. II. Title.
III. American Institute of Aeronautics and
Astronautics. IV. Title: Structures and
materials.

711.3
(4971)
J27 Structure of influence in local communities.
Jerovsek, Janez.
Structure of influence in local communities.
Ljubljana, Urbanisticni Institut SRS, 1969.
57p.
At head of title: American-Yugoslav Project
in Regional and Urban Planning Studies.

1. Regional planning - Yugoslavia.
2. Community structure. I. Urbanisticni
Institut, Ljubljana. II. American-Yugoslav
Project in Regional and Urban Planning
Studies. III. Title.

388
:308
H25 The structure of urban activity linkages.
Hemmens, George C
The structure of urban activity linkages.
Chapel Hill, Center for Urban and Regional
Studies, Institute for Research in Social
Science, University of North Carolina, 1966.
54p.   (An Urban studies research mono-
graph)

1. Traffic surveys. 2. Journey to work.
I. North Carolina. University. Institute
for Research in Social Science. II. Title.

Structures, Theory of see Structural
engineering

332.72
S34 The structure of the market for multifamily
and nonresidential mortgages.
Shipp, Royal.
The structure of the market for multifamily
and nonresidential mortgages. [Wash.?] [1966?]
49p.

1. Mortgage finance. 2. Investments.
I. Title.

711.5
:347
W45 The structure of urban zoning and its dynamics
in urban planning and development.
Williams, Norman.
The structure of urban zoning and its
dynamics in urban planning and development.
New York, Buttenheim Pub. Corp., 1966.
v.c.1,2 351p.
Laf.c.3

1. Zoning legislation. 2. City planning.
I. Title.

Folio
699.85
A75 Structures to resist the effects of
accidental explosions.
U.S. Armed Services Explosives Safety
Board.
Structures to resist the effects of
accidental explosions. Wash., 1969.
1v. (U.S. Dept. of the Army. Technical
manual TM 5-1300; U.S. Dept. of the Navy.
Publication NAVFAC P-397; U.S. Dept. of
the Air Force. Manual AFM 88-22)
Bibliography: p. B-1 - B-3.
1. Protective construction. I. U.S.
Dept. of the Army. II. U.S. Dept. of the
Navy. III. U.S. Dept. of the Air Force.
IV. U.S.   Dept. of Defense.
V. Title.

330.15
N17o
no.27 The structure of post war prices.
Mills, Frederick Cecil, 1892-
The structure of post war prices.
New York, 1948.
59 p. tables. (National Bureau of
Economic Research. Occasional paper 27).

1. Prices. 2. Inflation. I. Title.
II. National Bureau of Economic Research.
Occasional paper, no. 27.

627.4
(492)
N27s A structure plan for the Southern
Ijsselmeerpolders.
Netherlands. Dept. van Waterstaat.
A structure plan for the Southern
Ijsselmeerpolders. The Hague, 1965.
32p. (Reprint of Rijkswaterstaat
communications nr. 6)

1. Flood control - Netherlands.
I. Title.

388
:331
L16 Structuring the journey to work.
Lapin, Howard S
Structuring the journey to work.
Philadelphia, University of Pennsylvania
Press, 1964.
227p. (Publications in the city planning
series)
Bibliography: p. 216-221.

1. Journey to work. 2. Traffic surveys.
I. Title.

339.3
(41)
M67 The structure of property ownership in Great
Britain.
Morgan, E   Victor.
The structure of property ownership in Great
Britain. Oxford, Clarendon Press, 1960.
207p.

Bibliography: p. 195-202.

1. Income - U.K. 2. Real property - U.K.
3. Finance - U.K. I. Title.

699.85
N17ST STRUCTURE SHIELDING AGAINST FALLOUT
RADIATION.
U.S. NATIONAL BUREAU OF STANDARDS.
STRUCTURE SHIELDING AGAINST FALLOUT
RADIATION. WASHINGTON, 1962.
7L.

1. PROTECTIVE CONSTRUCTION.
2. THERMAL RADIATION. I. TITLE.

940.42
:330
J15 The struggle for survival.
Janeway, Eliot.
The struggle for survival. New York,
Weybright and Talley, 1951.
311p. (Chronicles of America series, vol. 53)

1. World War (1939-1945) - Economic effect.
I. Title.

330
(73)
N17 The structure of the American Economy.
U.S. National Resources Committee.
The structure of the American
Economy. Washington, Govt. Print. Off.,
June 1939. - June 1940.
2 v. charts, map, tables.

Contents.-pt. 1. Basic characteristics;
a report prepared ... under the direction of
Gardiner C. Means. - pt. 2. Toward full
use of resources; a symposium ...

(over)

699.85
N17STR STRUCTURE SHIELDING AGAINST FALLOUT
RADIATION FROM NUCLEAR WEAPONS.
U.S. NATIONAL BUREAU OF STANDARDS.
STRUCTURE SHIELDING AGAINST FALLOUT
RADIATION FROM NUCLEAR WEAPONS, BY L.V.
SPENCER. WASHINGTON, GOVT. PRINT.
OFF., 1962.
134P. (NBS MONOGRAPH 42)

1. PROTECTIVE CONSTRUCTION.
2. THERMAL RADIATION. I. SPENCER, L.V.
II. TITLE.

300
U71 The struggle to bring technology to cities.
Urban Institute.
The struggle to bring technology to cities.
Wash., 1971.
79p.

1. Science and civilization. 2. Metropolitan
areas. 3. Technology. I. Title.

VF
690
L11 Structure of the residential building
industry in 1949.
U. S. Bureau of Labor Statistics.
Structure of the residential building
industry in 1949. Washington, Govt. Print.
Off. [Nov. 1954]
38p. tables. (Its Bulletin no. 1170)

Research Project no. 1-E-107, Housing and
Home Finance Agency.
By Dorothy K. Newman and Adele L. Stucke.
Bibliographical footnotes.

(continued on next card)

720
W45s Structure: the essence of architecture.
Wilson, Forrest.
Structure: the essence of architecture.
New York, Van Nostrand Reinhold, 1971.
96p.

1. Architecture. 2. Structural engineering.
I. Title.

389.6
(016)
S77 Struglia, Erasmus J
Standards and specifications information
sources. A guide to literature and to public
and private agencies concerned with technological uniformities. Detroit, Gale Research,
1965.
187p. (Management information guide 6)
Series editor: Paul Wasserman.

1. Standardization - Bibl. 2. Building societies -
Bibl. 3. Management - Bibl. I. Title. II. Title:
Guide to literature and to public and private agen-
cies concerned with   technological uniform-
ities. III. Wasserman,   Paul, ed. (Series:
Management information   guide 6)

614
(016)
H21
Strunk, Frederick R
Health Information Foundation.
An inventory of social and economic research in health, compiled by Frederick R. Strunk. 1953 ed.   New York, 1953.
180 p.

1.Public health-Bibl. I.Strunk, Frederick R. II.Title. III.Title: Social and economic research in health, An inventory of.

628.1
S77
Struyk, Raymond J
Summary of present practices in evaluation of water resource projects. [Prepared in co-operation with] U.S. Corps of Army Engineers. St. Louis, Institute for Urban and Regional Studies, Washington University, 1967.
40p. (Washington University. Institute for Urban and Regional Studies. Working paper CWR 13)

1. Water resources. 2. Water-supply engineering.

(Cont'd on next card)

333.332
S78
STUART, PATRICIA.
A GUIDE TO PROPERTY REVALUATIONS. STORRS, CONN. INSTITUTE OF PUBLIC HEALTH SERVICE, UNIVERSITY OF CONNECTICUT, 1960.
16P.

1. REAL PROPERTY - VALUATION. 2. APPRAISAL. I. CONNECTICUT. UNIVERSITY. INSTITUTE OF PUBLIC SERVICE. II TITLE.

VP
308
S77
Strunk, Mildred, ed.
The quarter's polls.   *Public Opinion Quarterly*, p. (174)-192, Spring 1950.
Includes housing.

1.Public opinion polls.

628.1
S77
Struyk, Raymond J   Summary of present practices in evaluation...1967. (Card 2)

I. Washington University. St. Louis. Institute for Urban and Regional Studies. II. U.S. Army. Corps of Engineers. III. Title.

711.4
(758231)
A75com
Stuart, Robert C
Community plan for Adamsville and Shallowford Park. [Atlanta] 1956.
[6]p.
U.S. Urban Renewal Administration, Urban Planning Assistance Program.

1. City planning - Atlanta. 2. Neighborhood planning - Atlanta. 3. Parks - Atlanta. I. U.S. Urban Renewal Administration.

VP
332.72
S18p
Strunk, Norman.
Savings Association League of New York State.
Premature to view mortgage interest rates as reaching peaks of summer '57, Strunk says. Atlantic City, 1958.
1p. (Its News)

1. Mortgage interest rates. I. Strunk, Norman.

360
(72951)
C16
STRYKER, SHELDON, JT. AU.
CAPLOW, THEODORE.
THE URBAN AMBIENCE; A STUDY OF SAN JUAN, PUERTO RICO, BY THEODORE CAPLOW, SHELDON STRYKER, AND SAMUEL E. WALLACE. TOTOWA, N.J., BEDMINSTER PRESS, 1964.
243P. (UNIVERSITY OF PUERTO RICO. COLLEGE OF SOCIAL SCIENCES. A SOCIAL SCIENCE RESEARCH CENTER STUDY)

1. SOCIAL CONDITIONS - SAN JUAN, PUERTO RICO. I. STRYKER, SHELDON, JT. AU. II. WALLACE, SAMUEL E., JT. AU. III. TITLE.

711.4
(758231)
A75co
Stuart, Robert C
Atlanta. Metropolitan Planning Commission.
Composite materials for metropolitan Atlanta growth problems report (memorandum) by Burt Sparer and Robert C. Stuart. Atlanta, 1957.
45p. tables.
U.S. Urban Renewal Administration, Urban Planning Assistance Program. (U.R.A. Proj. Ga. I.A.1)

1. City planning - Atlanta. 2. Metropolitan areas - Atlanta. I.U.S. Urban Renewal Administration. II Sparer, Burt. III Stuart, Robert C

652
S76e
Strunk, William Jr.
The elements of style. With revisions, an introduction, and a new chapter on writing, by E. B. White. New York, Macmillan, 1959.
71p.

Copy 2: paperback, 1963.

1. Style manuals. I. White, E. B.

728.1
(438)
S77
STRZELECKI, JAN.
LA QUESTION DE L'HABITATION URBAINE EN POLOGNE; OUVRAGE REDIGE SOUS LA DIRECTION DE JAN STRZELECKI ... GENEVE, SOCIETE DES NATIONS, 1936.
228P. (SERIE DE PUBLICATIONS DE LA SOCIETE DES NATIONS. III. HYGIENE. 1936. III. 1.)

2. HOUSING - POLAND. I. LEAGUE OF NATIONS. II. TITLE: L'HABITATION URBAINE EN POLOGNE.

711.4
(758231)
A75r
Stuart, Robert C
Atlanta. Metropolitan Planning Commission.
Transportation Policy Project. Revised through traffic procedures, by Robert C. Stuart and Richard H. Sears, Jr. Atlanta, 1957.
5p.
U.S. Urban Renewal Administration, Urban Planning Assistance Program. (URA

(Continued on next card)

910
S77
STRUNSKY, SIMEON.
NO MEAN CITY. NEW YORK, DUTTON, 1944.
285P.

1. TRAVEL. 2. SOCIAL CONDITIONS - NEW YORK (CITY) I. TITLE.

711.4
:670
S78
Stuart, Alfred W
Rural industrialization and population growth: the case of Arkansas. Oak Ridge, Tenn., Oak Ridge National Laboratory, 1971.
23p. (ORNL-HUD-4)
Work supported by Dept. of Housing and Urban Development and the U.S. Atomic Energy Commission. Contract no. W-7405-eng-26)
1. Industrial development. 2. Population. I. U.S. Dept. of Housing and Urban Development. II. U.S. Oak Ridge National Laboratory. III. Title.

711.4
(758231)
A75r
Atlanta. Metropolitan Planning Commission.
Transportation Policy...(Card 2)

Proj. Ga. P - 3, I. A. 2)

1. City planning - Atlanta. 2. Transportation - Atlanta. 3 Traffic - Atlanta. I. Stuart, Robert C. II. Sears Richard H., Jr. III. U. S. Urban Renewal Administration. Urban Planning Assistance Program.

336.2
:538.56
S77
Struyk, Raymond J
An analysis of tax structure, public service levels, and regional economic growth. St. Louis, Institute for Urban and Regional Studies, Washington University, 1966.
46p. (Washington University. St. Louis. Institute for Urban and Regional Studies. Working paper CWR 9 and DRA 3)

1. Taxation - Automation. 2. Economic development. I. Washington University, St. Louis. Institute for Urban and Regional Studies. II. Title.

628.1
(768)
S78
Stuart, Leslie B
Comprehensive water and sewer plan, 1970-1990, Upper Cumberland Development District. [Nashville] Tennessee State Planning Commission, 1971.
197p.
U.S. Dept. of Housing and Urban Development. UPAP. HUD project no. Tenn. P-129.
1. Water supply - Tenn. 2. Sewerage and sewage disposal - Tenn. I. Tennessee. State Planning Commission. II. U.S. Dept. of Housing and Urban Development - UPAP. Upper Tenn. III. Title.

382
S78
Stuart, Robert Douglass.
Penetrating the international market, effective overseas distribution. New York, 1965.
176p.

1. Commercial policy. I. American Management Association. II. Title. III. Title: International market.

336.2
S77
Struyk, Raymond J
The size and distribution of the tax base relative to regional economic growth. St. Louis, Institute for Urban and Regional Studies, Washington University [1960]
24p. (Water Resource Investment Project Working paper CWR 3. Design of Regional Accounts Project Working paper DRA 2)
1. Taxation. 2. Economic development. I. Washington University, St. Louis. Institute for Urban and Regional Studies. II. Title.

690
S78
Stuart, Malcolm.
Metric controlling dimensions demonstration building. London, Ministry of Public Building and Works, 1969.
[5]p.
Reprinted from: Industrialised building systems and components, 1969, 6(5) May, p. 38-46.

1. Building industry - U.K. 2. Coordinated components. I. U.K. Ministry of Public Building and Works. II. Title.

382
S78p
Stuart, Robert Douglass.
Purchasing in worldwide operations. New York, American Management Association, International Management Div., 1966.
16p. (American Management Association. Management bulletin 75)

1. Commercial policy. 2. Management. I. American Management Association. II. Title. (Series)

728.1
:336.18
(75931)
S78
STUART, FLA. HOUSING AUTHORITY.
TRANSCRIPT OF THE ORGANIZATION AND ESTABLISHMENT OF THE HOUSING AUTHORITY OF THE CITY OF STUART, FLORIDA. STUART, 1942.
12L.

1. PUBLIC HOUSING - STUART, FLA. 2. STUART, FLA. HOUSING AUTHORITY - HISTORY.

025.4
F67s
The subject approach to information.
Foskett, A C
The subject approach to information. London, Clive Bingley, 1969.
310p.

1. Cataloging. 2. Library science. 3. Documentation. I. Title.

312
(74815)
L15
Stuchell, James.
Lancaster County, Pa. Planning Commission.
The past, present, and future population of Lancaster County, Pennsylvania, by James Stuchell. Lancaster, Pa., 1962.
107p.

1. Population - Lancaster Co., Pa.
I. Stuchell, James.

728.1
:336.18
(75931)
S78
STUART, FLA. HOUSING AUTHORITY - HISTORY.
STUART, FLA. HOUSING AUTHORITY.
TRANSCRIPT OF THE ORGANIZATION AND ESTABLISHMENT OF THE HOUSING AUTHORITY OF THE CITY OF STUART, FLORIDA. STUART, 1942.
12L.

1. PUBLIC HOUSING - STUART, FLA. 2. STUART, FLA. HOUSING AUTHORITY - HISTORY.

Stucco
xx Building materials
xx Plaster and plastering

VF
690
L11
Stucke, Adele L
U. S. Bureau of Labor Statistics.
Structure of the residential building industry in 1949. Washington, Govt. Print. Off. [Nov. 1954]
38p. tables. (Its Bulletin no. 1170)

Research Project no. 1-E-107, Housing and Home Finance Agency.
By Dorothy K. Newman and Adele L. Stucke.
Bibliographical footnotes.

(continued on next card)

72
T19
1948
Stubbins, Hugh A
[Regional qualities in residential design] In Taylor, Walter A., 1948 convention seminars. Washington, D.C. [c1949] p. 87-90.

1. Architecture, Domestic-U.S.

693.627
C31
Stucco.
Chalmers University of Technology, Gothenburg, Sweden.
Puts och lättbetong [Stucco and light-weight concrete] av Hjalmar Granholm. Stockholm, 1956
45 p. illus. (Its Transactions no. 17 [Avd. Väg-och Vattenbyggnad. Byggnadsteknik. 24]

English summary: p. 42-44.

1. Stucco. I. Granholm, Hjalmar.

728.1
:355
S78
STUDEBAKER, IRA JOHN.
THE DESIGN AND PRODUCTION OF AIR FORCE FAMILY HOUSING. AUSTIN, TEX., 1965.
166p.

THESIS (M.A.) - UNIVERSITY OF TEXAS.
BIBLIOGRAPHY: P. 162-165.

1. MILITARY HOUSING. I. TITLE: AIR FORCE FAMILY HOUSING.

720.36
S78
STUBBLEBINE, JO, ED.
THE NORTHWEST ARCHITECTURE OF PIETRO BELLUSCHI. NEW YORK, F.W. DODGE CORPORATION, 1953.
100p.

1. ARCHITECTURE, MODERN. I. BELLUSCHI, PIETRO.

693.627
P67
STUCCO.
PORTLAND CEMENT ASSOCIATION.
PORTLAND CEMENT STUCCO. CHICAGO, 1938.
29p.

1. STUCCO.

Class No. VF: Grants-in-aid.
Author (surname first) Studenski, Paul
Accession No. 00281
Title Federal grants-in-aid.
Ordered
Source pub. Received
Place Chicago Publisher National Tax Assoc.
4/24/50
Date Sept. 29, 1949 Paging 193-214 List Price 1.25 Est. Cost
Edition or Series National Tax Journal.
Purchase Order No. 765-04-50
Date 3/29/50
Recommended by
Reviewed in
L. C. No.
H-305 (3-50) HOUSING AND HOME FINANCE AGENCY: Office of the Administrator

---

728.1
:362.6
S78
Stubbs, Alice C
A small house for the aged or handicapped, by Alice C. Stubbs and Billy R. Stewart. [College Station, Texas] Agricultural and Mechanical College of Texas, Texas Agricultural Extension Service, 1962.
6p. (Study plan 4)

1. Housing for the aged. 2. Housing for the handicapped. I. Stewart, Billy T., jt. au. II. Texas. Agricultural Experiment Station.

690.015
P87r
Stucco.
Ulmer, C Paul
Description and cost analysis of a wood frame and stucco house; House no. 1, Purdue Housing Research Project. Lafayette, Ind. [July-Aug. 1936]
45 p. illus., diagrs., tables. (Purdue Univ. Better Homes in America. Home information, v.1, no.14-15)

In looseleaf binder with Dept. of Housing Research Report and proposal to the Rockefeller Research Foundation.

(Continued on next card)

370
C66s
Student abroad.
The Council on Student Travel.
Student abroad. International programs. New York, 1962.
35p.

1. Educational exchanges. I. Title.

620
H18
1971
Stubbs, Frank W Jr., 1898-1967.
Havers, John A ed.
Handbook of heavy construction. Edited by John A. Havers and Frank W. Stubbs, Jr. 2d ed. New York, McGraw-Hill, 1971.
1v. (McGraw-Hill handbooks)

1. Engineering. I. Stubbs, Frank W. Jr., 1898-1967. II. Title.

693.627
A52
Stucco - Standards and specifications.
American Institute of Architects.
Standard specifications for portland cement stucco and portland cement plastering including requirements for lathing and furring; approved as American Standard by the American Standards Association, Sept. 26, 1946. Wash., 1947.
18p. (A.I.A. file no. 21)
Sponsor organizations: American Institute of Architects and American Society for Testing Materials.

(Cont'd on next card)

VF
728.1
:378
E28
Student accommodations in residential facilities, 1960-61.
U.S. Office of Education.
Student accomodations in residential facilities, 1960-61 and planned for 1965-66, by Leslie F. Robbins. Washington, Div. of Higher Education, Office of Education, U.S. Dept. of Health, Education, and Welfare, 1962.
6p. (College and university physical facilities series. OE-51004-5)

1. Universities and colleges - Housing.
I. Robbins, Leslie F. II. Title.

711.3
(4971)
A52
no.10
Stubbs, Jeffry R
American-Yugoslav Project in Regional and Urban Planning Studies.
The Lowry Model; a mathematical method for forecasting the distribution of population and jobs in an urban region, by Jeffry R. Stubbs and Brian Barber. Ljubljana, 1970.
35p. (Urbanisticni Institut. Spatial policies for regional development; a demonstration study of the Ljubljana region. Technical report no. 10)
1. Regional planning - Yugoslavia. 2. Population. 3. Employment. I. Stubbs, Jeffry R. II. Urbanisticni Institut, Ljubljana. III. Title.

693.627
A52
American Institute of Architects. Standard specifications...1947. (Card 2)

1. Stucco - Standards and specifications. 2. Cement - Standards and specifications. 3. Plaster and plastering - Standards and specifications. I. American Society for Testing Materials. II. Title.

370
C657
1970
S-D
Student aid program.
U.S. Congress. Senate. Committee on Labor and Public Welfare.
Federal and state student aid programs. Prepared for the Subcommittee on Education of the Committee on Labor and Public Welfare, United States Senate. Wash., Govt. Print. Off., 1970.
82p. (91st Cong., 2d sess. Senate. Document no. 91-73)
Bibliography: p. 81-82.
1. Education. I. Title. II. Title: Student aid program.

727.3
M85
Student housing.
Mullins, William.
Student housing: architectural and social aspects, by William Mullins and Phyllis Allen. New York, Praeger, 1971.
248p.

1. Universities and colleges - Buildings. 2. Schools. I. Allen, Phyllis, jt. au. II. Title.

378
E28st
Students and buildings ...
U.S. Office of Education.
Students and buildings; an analysis of selected federal programs for higher education; planning papers of the Office of Program Planning and Evaluation, Office of Education. Washington, Govt. Print. Off., 1968.
72p. (Planning paper 68-2; OE-50054)
1. Universities and colleges. 2. Education. 3. Universities and colleges - Housing. I. Title.

332
C65st
Studies in banking competition and the banking structure.
U.S. Comptroller of the Currency.
Studies in banking competition and the banking structure. Wash., The Administrator of National Banks, U.S. Treasury, 1966.
426p.

Articles reprinted from the National banking review.

1. Banks and banking. 2. Money. I. National banking review. II. Title.

728.1
:378
(016)
C25
Student housing - bibliography.
Central Mortgage and Housing Corp. Library.
Student housing - bibliography. [Ottawa] 1969.
5p.

1. Universities and colleges - Housing - Bibl. I. Title.

333.332
(07)
A52ST
A STUDENT'S DEMONSTRATION APPRAISAL REPORT ON AN APARTMENT HOUSE.
AMERICAN INSTITUTE OF REAL ESTATE APPRAISERS.
A STUDENT'S DEMONSTRATION APPRAISAL REPORT ON AN APARTMENT HOUSE. PREPARED BY VISUAL AIDS TECHNICAL COMMITTEE FOR THE EDUCATION COMMITTEE. CHICAGO, 1966.
56P.

1. APPRAISAL - STUDY AND TEACHING. 2. APARTMENT HOUSES. I. TITLE.

Studies in Business and Economics.
Maryland. University. Bureau of Business and Economic Research.
Studies in Business and Economics, v. 1- no. 4-
College Park, Md. 1948-

For full information see Periodical Kardex file.

1. Economic research. I. Title.

728.1
:378
C15A/
Student housing cost study.
California. University. (University Residential Building System Project)
Student housing cost study. Berkeley, Calif., 1967.
125p. (URBS publication 3)
Consultant: Building Systems Development, inc.
1. Universities and colleges - Housing. 2. Building costs - Estimates. 3. Architecture - Designs and plans. I. Title: University Residential Building System. II. Title.

333.332
(07)
A52S
A STUDENT'S DEMONSTRATION APPRAISAL REPORT ON A SINGLE-FAMILY RESIDENCE.
AMERICAN INSTITUTE OF REAL ESTATE APPRAISERS.
A STUDENT'S DEMONSTRATION APPRAISAL REPORT ON A SINGLE-FAMILY RESIDENCE. PREPARED FOR THE EDUCATION COMMITTEE BY THE VISUAL AIDS TECHNICAL COMMITTEE. CHICAGO, 1964.
38P.

1. APPRAISAL - STUDY AND TEACHING. 2. FAMILY INCOME AND EXPENDITURE - HOUSING. I. TITLE. II. TITLE: A SINGLE-FAMILY RESIDENCE.

711.585
(77434)
W19
Studies in change and renewal in an urban community.
Wayne State University, Detroit.
Studies in change and renewal in an urban community. Co-directors: E. P. Wolf and Charles N. Lebeaux. Detroit, 1965.
2 v.

Prepared for the Mayor's Committee for Community Renewal in Detroit.
U.S. Urban Renewal Adm. CRP.

(Continued on next card!)

323.4
S87
Student Nonviolent Coordinating Committee.
Sutherland, Elizabeth, ed.
Letters from Mississippi. New York, New American Library, 1965.
214p.

A Signet book.

1. Civil rights. 2. Negroes. 3. Minority groups - Miss. 4. Student Nonviolent Coordinating Committee. I. Title.

378
E28stu
Students enrolled for advanced degrees.
U.S. Office of Education.
Students enrolled for advanced degrees. Part A. Summary data, Part B. Institutional data, Fall, 19
Washington, U.S. Dept. of Health, Education, and Welfare, Office of Education, National Center for Educational Statistics, 1969-

v.
Report 1966/67: by Marjorie O. Chandler.
For Library holdings see main entry.
1. Universities and colleges. 2. Education - Statistics. I. Chandler, Marjorie O. II. Title.

711.585
(77434)
W19
Wayne State University, Detroit. Studies ... (Card 2)

1. Urban renewal - Detroit. 2. Relocation - Detroit. 3. Minority groups - Detroit. 4. Social conditions - Detroit. 5. Race relations. 6. Detroit. Community Renewal Program. I. Detroit. Mayor's Committee for Community Renewal. II. U.S. URA-CRP. Detroit. III. Title.

323.4
Z45
Student Nonviolent Coordinating Committee.
Zinn, Howard.
SNCC (Student Nonviolent Coordinating Committee): the new abolitionists. Boston, Beacon Press, 1965.
286p.

1. Civil rights. 2. Negroes. I. Title: Student Nonviolent Coordinating Committee.

720
(07)
F71
Students, What's bugging them?
Fraser, Jack.
Students: what's bugging them? Wash., American Institute of Architects, [1969?]
10p.

1. Architecture - Study and teaching. I. American Institute of Architects. II. Title.

690.22
C65
Studies in composite construction.
Colbourne, J R
Studies in composite construction: an elastic analysis of wall-beam structures. Garston, Eng., Building Research Station, 1969.
11p. (U.K. Building Research Station. Current paper CP15/69)

1. Walls. I. U.K. Building Research Station. II. Title.

658.3
H68tr
Student planners.
U.S. Housing and Home Finance Agency. Office of the Administrator. Div. of Personnel.
Training program for student planners. Washington, 1959.
5p.
Training program.

1. Personnel management. 2. Nursing homes - Study and teaching. 3. Urban renewal - Study and teaching. I. Title: Student planners.

333.33
(07)
L85
A student's workbook for real estate principles.
Lundberg, Edna A
A student's workbook for real estate principles. Prepared under staff direction of the Pasadena City Junior College District and the California Dept. of Real Estate. Rev. Sacramento, California, Dept. of Real Estate, 1969.
338p.
1. Real estate business - Study and teaching. I. Title.

330
A52s
Studies in economic stabilization.
Ando, Albert, ed.
Studies in economic stabilization, ed. by Albert Ando and others. Wash., Brookings Institution, 1968.
299p. (Brookings Institution. Studies of government finance)

Bibliography: p. 288-294.
1. Economic policy. 2. Taxation. I. Brookings Institution. II. Title.

370.015
Z11
Student-teacher population growth model...
Zabrowski, Edward K
Student-teacher population growth model; working papers, by Edward K. Zabrowski and others. Washington, U.S. Dept. of Health, Education and Welfare, National Center for Educational Statistics, 1968.
110p. (U.S. Office of Education. OE-10055)
Bibliography: p. 107-110.
1. Education. 2. Schools. 3. Population. I. U.S. National Center for Educational Statistics. II. Title.

614
S23
Studies for health system planning.
Schultz, George Park, ed.
Studies for health system planning; a collection of student papers. Seattle, Dept. of Urban Planning, University of Washington, 1969.
181p. (Washington. University. Dept. of Urban Planning. Urban planning development series no. 6)
1. Health. I. Washington (State) University. Dept. of Urban Planning. II. Title.

551
M12
Studies in gathering earthquake damage statistics.
McClure, Frank E
Studies in gathering earthquake damage statistics [n.p.] Frank E. McClure and David L. Messinger, Consulting Structural Engineers, 1967.
1v.
Consultant: Studies of earthquake risk, ESSA [Environmental Science Services Administration] — Coast and Geodetic Survey.
Bibliography: p. 6-31 - 6-32.
1. Earthquakes. I. U.S. Environmental Science Services Administration. II. U.S. Coast and Geodetic Survey. III. Title.

711.73
H43s
Studies in highway administration.
U.S. Highway Research Board.
Studies in highway administration.
Washington, 1958.
50p. (Its Bulletin 200)

Presented at the thirty-seventh annual
meeting, January 6-10, 1958.
Highway Research Board publication 626.

1. Highways. I. Title.

551
(083.41)
C61
Studies in seismicity and earthquake damage
statistics, 1969.
U.S. Coast and Geodetic Survey.
Studies in seismicity and earthquake damage
statistics, 1969; summary and recommendations.
A report prepared for Dept. of Housing and
Urban Development, Office of Economic and
Market Analysis, 1969.
3v. (Incl. appx A, B)

1. Earthquakes - Statistics. I. U.S. Dept.
of Housing and Urban Development. II. Title.

331
C65ST
1960
S-R
STUDIES IN UNEMPLOYMENT...
U.S. CONGRESS. SENATE. SPECIAL
COMMITTEE ON UNEMPLOYMENT PROBLEMS.
STUDIES IN UNEMPLOYMENT... PURSUANT
TO S. RES. 196... WASHINGTON, GOVT.
PRINT. OFF., 1960.
432P.
AT HEAD OF TITLE: 86TH CONGRESS, 2D
SESSION. COMMITTEE PRINT.

1. EMPLOYMENT. I. TITLE.

33(73)
C65
Studies in income and wealth.
Conference on research in income and wealth.
Studies in income and wealth ... by the Conference on re-
search in national income and wealth. New York, National
bureau of economic research, 1937-
v. diagrs. 24 cm.

For full information see shelf list card.

2. Econ. condit.-U.S.
1. Income. 2. Wealth.—3. U. S.—Econ. condit.—1918-
1. National bureau of economic research. II. Title.

HC106.3.C714   330.973   38—2909

Library of Congress   [52r44k²]

301
M12
Studies in social movements.
McLaughlin, Barry, ed.
Studies in social movements; a social
psychological perspective. New York, Free
Press, 1969.
497p.

1. Sociology. I. Title. II. Title: Social
movements.

025.3
L41ST
STUDIES OF DESCRIPTIVE CATALOGING.
U.S. LIBRARY OF CONGRESS. PROCESSING
DEPT.
STUDIES OF DESCRIPTIVE CATALOGING; A
REPORT TO THE LIBRARIAN OF CONGRESS BY
THE DIRECTOR OF THE PROCESSING
DEPARTMENT. WASHINGTON, GOVT. PRINT.
OFF., 1946.
48P.

1. CATALOGING. I. TITLE.

712
J25

Laf.
Studies in landscape design.
Jellicoe, Geoffrey Alan, 1900-
Studies in landscape design. London, New York, Oxford
University Press, 1960.
xvi,   illus., plates. 24 cm.
2 v.

1. Landscape architecture. I. Title.

SB476.J4   712   60-1523

Library of Congress   [5]

360
K13s
Studies in social policy and planning.
Kahn, Alfred J
Studies in social policy and planning.
New York, Russell Sage Foundation, 1969.
326p.

Companion volume to Theory and practice of
Social planning.

1. Social conditions. 2. Social welfare.
II. Title.

690.015
(485)
S82
1971
R28
Studies of dimensional accuracy in prefab
buildings with flexible joints.
Klingberg, Lennart.
Mätnoggrannhetsstudier på elementhus
med flexibel fogutformning (Studies of
dimensional accuracy in prefab buildings
with flexible joints) Stockholm, Statens
Institut för Byggnadsforskning, 1971.
65p. (Rapport R28:1971)
English summary.
1. Prefabricated construction - Sweden.
I. Stockholm. Statens Institut for Byggnadsforskning. II. Title: Studies of dimensional
accuracy in prefab buildings with flexible
joints.

647.1
N282
STUDIES IN LIVING COSTS IN LARGE AND
SMALL COMMUNITIES.
NEW YORK (STATE) DEPARTMENT OF LABOR.
STUDIES IN LIVING COSTS IN LARGE AND
SMALL COMMUNITIES. NEW YORK, 1947.
69P.

1. COST AND STANDARD OF LIVING.
I. TITLE.

640
C17
Studies in the demand for consumer household
equipment...
Carman, James A
Studies in the demand for consumer household
equipment, with contributions by Frederick
Manzara and John D. Kaczor. Berkeley, Calif.,
Research Program in Marketing, Graduate School
of Business Administration, University of
California, Institute of Business and Economic
Research, 1965.
131p. (California. University. Institute
of Business and Economic Research. Special
publications)
Bibliography: p. 125-131.

(Cont'd on next card)

534.83
L68
Studies of helicopter rotor noise.
Lowson, M V
Studies of helicopter rotor noise; final
report, by M.V. Lowson and J.B. Ollerhead.
Huntsville, Ala., Wyle Laboratories, 1969.
161p. (U.S. Army Aviation Materiel
Laboratories technical report 68-60; Wyle
research staff report WR 68-9)
CFSTI AD 684 394.
Bibliography: p. 83-86.
1. Noise. 2. Air transportation.
I. Ollerhead, J.B., jt. au. II. Wyle
Laboratories. III. U.S. Army. Aviation
Materiel Lab-   oratories. IV. Title:
Helicopter   rotor noise. V. Title.

711.333
(747)
J65
Studies in regional development.
Jones, Barclay G
Studies in regional development: a factor
analysis approach to sub-regional defini-
tion in Chenango, Delaware, and Otsego
Counties, by Barclay G. Jones and William
W. Goldsmith. Ithaca, N.Y., Div. of Urban
Studies, Center for Housing and Environ-
mental Studies, Cornell University, 1965.
83p.

1. County planning - New York (State) I. Goldsmith,
William W., jt. au. II. Cornell University.
Center for Housing and   Environmental Studies.
II. Title.

640
C17
Carman, James A   Studies in the demand...
1965.   (Card 2)

1. Household equipment. 2. Market surveys.
I. California. University. Institute of
Business and Economic Research. II. Title.

534.83
(016)
E24
Studies of random noise.
Eckstein, Herbert P
Studies of random noise: an annotated
bibliography; [originated by] Redstone Sci-
entific Information Center, Redstone Arsenal,
Alabama. Processed for U.S. Defense Doc-
umentation Center, Defense Supply Agency.
[Wash.?] U.S. Bureau of Standards, Institute
for Applied Technology, 1966.
44p.
Distributed by U.S. Clearinghouse for
Federal Scientific and Technical Information.

(Cont'd on next card)

711.333
(747)
J65s
Studies in regional development.
Jones, Barclay G
Studies in regional development: popula-
tion, activities, and incomes in Chenango,
Delaware, and Otsego Counties, by Barclay G.
Jones and John T. Lang. Ithaca, N.Y.,
Center for Housing and Environmental Studies,
Division of Urban Studies, Cornell Univer-
sity, 1965.
134p.

1. County planning - New York (State)
I. Lang, John T., jt. au. II. Cornell
University.   Center for Housing and
Environmental   Studies. Division of
Urban Studies.   III. Title.

330
G65
Studies in the national balance sheet of the
United States.
Goldsmith, Raymond W
Studies in the national balance sheet of
the United States, by R.W. Goldsmith and
Robert E. Lipsey. A study by the National
Bureau of Economic Research. [n.p.] Princeton
University Press, 1963.
2 v. (National Bureau of Economic
Research. Studies in capital formation
and financing)

1. Economic research. 2. Finance. I. Title.
II. Title: National   balance sheet of
the United   States.
III. Lipsey,   Robert E., jt. au.
IV. National Bureau   of Economic Research.

534.83
(016)
E24
Eckstein, Herbert P   Studies of random
noise: an annotated bibliography...(Card2)

1. Noise-Bibliography. I. U.S. Clear-
inghouse for Federal Scientific and Tech-
nical Information. II. U.S. Defense
Documentation Center for Scientific and
Technical Information. III. U.S. Redstone
Arsenal. IV. Title.

551
E58
Studies in seismicity and earthquake damage
statistics.
U.S. Environmental Science Services
Administration.
Studies in seismicity and earthquake damage
statistics. A report prepared for Dept. of
Housing and Urban Development, Office of Pro-
gram Policy, Studies of natural disasters.
[Wash.] U.S. Dept. of Commerce, Environmental
Science Services Administration, Coast &
Geodetic Survey, [1968?]
2pts.
1. Earthquakes. I. Title. II. U.S. Dept.
of Housing and Urban Development.

711.13
M45
Studies in the structure of the urban
economy.
Mills, Edwin S
Studies in the structure of the urban
economy. Baltimore, Published for Resources
for the Future by Johns Hopkins Press, 1972.
151p.
Bibliography: p. 143-145.

1. Decentralization. 2. City growth.
I. Resources for the Future. II. Title.
III. Title: Urban economy.

627.4
G26
no.772
Studies of relations of rainfall and run-off
in the United States.
U.S. Geological Survey.
Studies of relations of rainfall and run-off
in the United States, by W. G. Hoyt and others.
Washington, Govt. Print. Off., 1936.
301 p. illus., graphs, tables. (Its
Water-supply paper 772)

"References": p. 283-294.

1. Flood control. I. Hoyt, W. G. II. Title.
III. Title: Rainfall and run-off in the United
States.

690.015
(485)
882
R27-1965

Studies of the building and community planning process.
Sweden. Statens Kommitté för Byggnadsforskning.
Studies of the building and community planning process. Stockholm, National Swedish Institute for Building Research, 1965.
51p. (Its Report 27-1965)

1. Building research - Sweden. 2. City planning - Sweden. I. Title.

691.542
G87
Gutt, W

Studies of the role of calcium sulphate in the manufacture of portland cement clinker.
Studies of the role of calcium sulphate in the manufacture of portland cement clinker, by W. Gutt and M.A. Smith. Garston, Eng., Building Research Station, Ministry of Public Building and Works, 1968.
489-509p. (U.K. Building Research Station. Current papers CP 89/68)
Bibliography: p. 508-509.
Reprinted from: Transactions of the British Ceramic Society, Oct., 1968, pp. 487-509.
1. Portland cement. I. Title. II. Smith, M.A., jt. au. III. U.K. Building Research Station.

388
:308
S78

Studies of weaving and merging traffic: a symposium. Weaving practices on one-way highways, by F. Houston Wynn. Merging traffic characteristics applied to acceleration lane design, by Stewart M. Gourlay. A study of merging vehicular traffic movements, by Richard I. Strickland. [n.p.] Bureau of Highway Traffic, Yale University, published with funds from Eno Foundation for Highway Traffic Control, 1948.
130p. (Yale highway traffic series. Technical report no. 4)

Continued on next card)

388
:308
S78

Studies of weaving and merging traffic: a symposium...1948. (Card 2)

1. Traffic surveys. 2. Journey to work. I. Wynn, F. Houston. II. Gourlay, Stewart M. III. Strickland, Richard I. IV. Yale University. Bureau of Highway Traffic.

628.515
072s

Studies on effects of watershed practices on streams.
Oregon. State University, Corvallis. School of Forestry.
Studies on effects of watershed practices on streams. [Prepared] for the Environmental Protection Agency. [Wash.] Govt. Print. Off., 1971.
173p. (Water pollution control research series)

1. Water pollution. I. U.S. Environmental Protection Agency. II. Title.

728.1
(798)
W44

Studies on housing for Alaska natives.
Wik, Dennis R
Studies on housing for Alaska natives, by Dennis R. Wik and others. Edited by John L. S. Hickey. Anchorage, Alaska, U.S. Dept. of Health, Education and Welfare, Public Health Service, Environmental Sanitation Section, Arctic Health Research Center, 1965.
127p. (Environmental health series. Arctic health)
Public health service publication, no. 999-AH-1.

(Continued on next card)

728.1
(798)
W44

Wik, Dennis R Studies on housing for Alaska natives...1965 (Card 2)

1. Housing - Alaska. 2. Family living requirements. I. Hickey, John L. S., ed. II. U.S. Public Health Service. (Arctic Health Research Center) III. Title.

691
V15

Studies on solutions of cellulose.
Valtasaari, Lea.
Studies on solutions of cellulose. Helsinki, State Institute for Technical Research, 1967.
13p. (Finland. State Institute for Technical Research. Julkaisu 125 publication)
Bibliography: p. 12-13.

1. Building materials. I. Finland. State Institute for Technical Research. II. Title.

690.015
(485)
S 82
R38
1970

Studies on the dimensional accuracy of a column and beam framework.
Klingberg, Lennart.
Måttnoggrannhetsstudier på pelar-balkstomme (Studies on the dimensional accuracy of a column and beam framework) Stockholm, 1970.
69p. (Stockholm. Statens Institut för Byggnadsforskning. Rapport R38:1970)
English summary.
1. Building research - Sweden. 2. Structural engineering. I. Stockholm. Statens Institut för Byggnadsforskning. II. Title: Studies on the dimensional accuracy of a column and beam framework.

385.
(7437)
C65

Studies on the economic impact of railway abandonment and service discontinuance.
U.S. Dept. of Commerce. (Transportation Research)
Studies on the economic impact of railway abandonment and service discontinuance.
[Sect. 1] Implications of railway abandonments (a general survey), by W.B. Saunders Co. [Sect. 2] The economic impact of the discontinuance of the Rutland Railway (condensed version) by Boston University, Bureau of Business Research. Wash., For sale by the Supt. of Doc., Govt. Print. Off., 1965.
1 v. (PB 167 640)

(Cont'd on next card)

385.
(7437)
C65

U.S. Dept. of Commerce. (Transportation Research) Studies on the economic impact of railway abandonment and service discontinuance...1965. (Card 2)

Distributed by U.S. Clearinghouse for Federal Scientific and Technical Information.

1. Railroads - Rutland, Vt. 2. Transportation - Economic effect. I. Saunders (W.B.) & Co. Implications of railway abandonment. II. Boston University. Bureau of Business Research. The economic impact of the discontinuance of the Rutland Railway. III. U.S. Clearinghouse for Federal Scientific and Technical Information. IV. Title.

628.2
L23

Studies on the situation height of manhole covers and catch basins on street pavements.
Lehtinen, Eero.
Kadun ajorata ja kaivonkannet (Studies on the situation height of manhole covers and catch basins on street pavements) (Helsinki, Suomen teknillinen korkeakoulu?)1969.
7p.
English summary.

Eripainos Maarakennus ja kuljetus-lehdesta nio 3/1969.
1. Sewers. 2. Streets. I. Helsinki. Suomen teknillinen korkeakoulu. II. Title: Studies on the situation height of manhole covers and catch basins on street pavements.

690.015
(485)
S 82
R25
1970

Studies, planning and design in the building process.
Eliasson, Göran.
Utredning och projektering i byggprocessen (Studies, planning and design in the building process) Stockholm, 1970.
254p. (Stockholm. Statens Institut för Byggnadsforskning. Rapport R25:1970)
English summary.
Bibliography: p. 226-254.
1. Building research - Sweden. 2. Architecture - Designs and plans. I. Stockholm. Statens Institut för Byggnadsforskning. II. Title: Studies, planning and design in the building process.

728.1
:362.6
I57s

Study about housing the elderly.
International Federation for Housing and Planning. (International Standing Committee for Social Housing.
Study about housing the elderly. Paris, Secretariat du Comite Permanent, Confederation Francaise pour l'Habitation it l'Urbanisme, [1969?]
1v.

1. Housing for the aged. I. Title.

058.7
:378
UN

Study abroad; international handbook, fellowships, scholarships, educational exchange.
United Nations Educational, Scientific and Cultural Organization.
Study abroad; international handbook, fellowships, scholarships, educational exchange. 10th ed. Paris, 1958.
779p.

English, French, and Spanish.

1. Universities and colleges - Directories. 2. Educational exchange. I. Title.

058.7
:378
UN
1960

Study abroad.
United Nations Educational, Scientific and Cultural Organization.
Study abroad; international handbook, fellowships, scholarships, educational exchange. 12th ed. Paris, 1960.
766p.

English, French and Spanish.

1. Universities and colleges - Directories. 2. Educational exchanges. I. Title.

628.515
N87s

Study and experiments in waste water reclamation by reverse osmosis.
Nusbaum, I
Study and experiments in waste water reclamation by reverse osmosis, by I. Nusbaum and others. For the Federal Water Quality Administration, Dept. of the Interior. San Diego, Calif., Gulf General Atomic, inc., 1970.
116p. (U.S. Federal Water Quality Administration. Water pollution control research series 17040-05 70)
1. Water pollution. I. Gulf General Atomic, inc. II. U.S. Federal Water Quality Administration. III. Title.

628.1
H25

Study and interpretation of the chemical characteristics of natural water.
Hem, John D
Study and interpretation of the chemical characteristics of natural water; a review of chemical, geologic, and hydrologic principles and processes that control the composition of natural water, with methods for studying and interpreting chemical analyses. 2d. ed. Wash., Govt. Print. Off., 1970.
363p. (U.S. Geological Survey. Geological survey water-supply paper 1473)
Bibliography: p 338-358.

1. Water resources. I. U.S. Geological Survey. II. Title.

728.1
C653
H

Study and investigation of housing.
U.S. Congress. Joint Committee on Housing.
Study and investigation of housing. Hearings before the Joint Committee on Housing (established pursuant to H. Con. Res. 104, 80th Congress). 80th Cong., 1st sess. Proceedings [held Sept. 10, 1947 to Jan. 28, 1948] Washington [Govt. Print. Off., 1948.
6 pts.

(Continued on next card)

U.S. Congress. Joint Committee on Housing. Study and investigation of housing ... 1948. (Card 2)

Contents.-[Introd.]Preliminary discussion at Washington.-Pt.1.Pittsburgh, Pa; Cleveland, Ohio; Detroit, Mich.; Indianapolis, Ind.; St. Louis, Mo.; Cincinnati, Ohio; Columbus, Ohio; Chicago, Ill.; Milwaukee, Wis.-Pt.2.Miami, Fla.; Jacksonville, Fla.; Atlanta, Ga.; Birmingham, Ala.; Little Rock, Ark.; Dallas, Tex.; San Antonio, Tex.; Houston, Tex.; Baton Rouge, La.; New Orleans, La.; Memphis, Tenn.-Pt.3.Boston, Mass.; (Continued on next card)

U.S. Congress. Joint Committee on Housing. Study and investigation of housing ... 1948. (Card 3)

Contents continued.
New York, N.Y.; Newark, N.J.; Hartford, Conn.; Philadelphia, Pa.-Pt.4.San Diego, Calif.; Los Angeles, Calif.; San Francisco, Calif.; Portland, Oreg.; Seattle, Wash.; Tacoma, Wash.; Honolulu, Territory of Hawaii.-Pt.5.Washington, D.C.: The need for housing, costs and supply of building materials, building codes and zoning laws, administration and operation of existing federal housing laws, organization and operations of (Continued on next card)

U.S. Congress. Joint Committee on Housing.
Study and investigation of housing ... 1948.
(Card 4)
    Contents continued.
federal, state, and municipal government agencies concerned with housing; private and government housing finance, and other phases of the field of housing.

627.4
(758)
F79
U.S. Study Commission. Southeast River Basins.
Fry, Albert S
Flood plain management for the Southeast River Basins. Atlanta, U.S. Study Commission, Southeast River Basins, 1962.
38p.

1. Flood control - Georgia.
I. U.S. Study Commission.
Southeast River Basins.

628.1
(795)
072s
Study design.
Oregon Coastal Planning Group.
Study design. Prepared for the Oregon Coastal Conservation and Development Commission. San Francisco, 1972.
79p.

Bibliography: p. 74-79.

1. Water resources - Or. I. Oregon. Coastal Conservation and Development Commission. II. Title.

621.32
F47
Study and measurements of the luminance distribution of flourescent lamps.
Fischer, D
Study and measurements of the luminance distribution of fluorescent lamps. Garston, Eng., Building Research Station, 1971.
[11]p. (Library communication no. 1607)
Translated from the German, by P.A. Ross.

1. Lighting. I. U.K. Building Research Station. II. Title. (Series)

339.5
S77
U.S. Study Commission. Southeast River Basins.
Plan for development of the land and water resources of the Southeast River Basins, 1960, 1975, 2000. Atlanta, 1963.
1v.

Appendix -- --- Appendix 1-13; 11v.

Contents:- no.1. Savannah basin.- no.2. Ogeechee basin.- no.3. Altamaha basin.-
(Cont'd on next card)

Study design for a comprehensive development plan for the seven-county Kansas City Metropolitan Region.
711.3
(77841)
K15
Kansas City, Metropolitan Planning Commission.
Study design for a comprehensive development plan for the seven-county Kansas City Metropolitan Region. Kansas City, Mo., 1967.
131p.
U.S. Dept. of Housing and Urban Development.
1. Metropolitan area planning - Kansas City, Mo. I. U.S. HUD-UPAP. Kansas City, Mo. II. Title.

711.585.1
A17
A study and provision of technical assistance through simulation for more effective citizen participation in...
ABT Associates
A study and provision of technical assistance through simulation for more effective citizen participation in the Model Cities Program. Report on tasks I and II: game development. Submitted to: Model Cities Administration, United States Dept. of Housing and Urban Development. Cambridge, Mass., 1970.
88p.
Contract no. H-1295.
1. Model cities 2. Community development
(Cont'd on next card)

339.5
S77
U.S. Study Commission. Southeast River Basins. Plan for development of the...
(Card 2)
no.4. Satilla-St. Marys basins.- no.5. Suwannee basin.- no.6. Ochlockonee basins.- no.7. Apalachicola-Chattahoochee-Flint basins.- no.8. Choctawhatchee-Perdido basins.- no.9. Economics.- nos. 10-11 in 1v. no.10. Hydrology, no.11 Engineering and cost.- nos. 12-13 in 1v. no.12. Planning.- no.13. History and organization of the Commission.
(Cont'd on next card)

711.3
(41)
S78
STUDY CONFERENCE ON THE COUNTRYSIDE IN 1970. LONDON. 1963.
PROCEEDINGS OF THE STUDY CONFERENCE HELD AT FISHMONGERS' HALL, LONDON, 4-5 NOVEMBER 1963. LONDON, H.M. STAT. OFF., 1964.
286P.

1. REGIONAL PLANNING - U.K. 2. OPEN SPACE LAND - U.K. I. TITLE: THE COUNTRYSIDE IN 1970.

711.585.1
A17
ABT Associates. A study...1970. (Card 2)

- Citizen participation. I. U.S. Dept. of Housing and Urban Development. Model Cities Administration. II. Title.

339.5
S77
U.S. Study Commission. Southeast River Basins. Plans for development of the...
(Card 3)

1. Natural resources. 2. Open space land. 3. Water resources. 4. Master plan - Southeastern states. I. Title.

388
(77434)
D27s
Study design for comprehensive transportation and land use programs for the Detroit region.
Detroit Metropolitan Area Regional Planning Commission.
Study design for comprehensive transportation and land use programs for the Detroit region. Developed in cooperation with Michigan State Highway Department [and others] Detroit, 1964.
97p.
U.S. Urban Renewal Adm. UPAP.

1. Transportation - Detroit. 2. Land use - Detroit. I. Title. II. U.S. URA-UPAP. Detroit.

711.585.1
C65s
A study and provision of technical assistance through simulation for more effective citizen participation in...
CONSAD Research Corp.
A study and provision of technical assistance through simulation for more effective citizen participation in the Model Cities Program. Final report. Prepared for U.S. Dept. of Housing and Urban Development, Contracts and Agreements Div. Pittsburgh, 1971.
32p.
1. Model cities. 2. Community development - Citizen participation. I. U.S. Dept. of Housing and Urban Development. II. Title.

628.1
(764)
S78
U.S. Study Commission - Texas.
The report of the U.S. Study Commission - Texas, pts. 1-
A report to the President and to the Congress, by the United States Study Commission on the Neches, Trinity, Brazos, Colorado, Guadalupe, San Antonio, Nueces, and San Jacinto River Basins, and intervening areas. Houston, Texas, 19
pts.
At head of title: Cong., sess. House. Document no. pt. 1-
1. Water-supply - Texas 2. Land use - Texas. 3. Economic development - Texas. I. U.S. Congress.

LAW
U.S.
Study draft of a new Federal criminal code.
U.S. National Commission on Reform of Federal Criminal Laws.
Study draft of a new Federal criminal code (Title 18, United State Code) Wash., Govt. Print. Off., 1970.
344p.

1. Criminal law. I. Title.

711.583
C51
Suburban land conversion in the United States.
Clawson, Marion.
Suburban land conversion in the United States: an economic and governmental process. Baltimore, Published for Resources for the Future by the Johns Hopkins Press, 1971.
406p.

1. Suburbs. I. Resources for the Future. II. Title.

5249
STUDY COMMISSION OF THE PHILADELPHIA METROPOLITAN AREA.
PHYSICAL AND GOVERNMENTAL ORGANIZATION FOR REGIONAL SEWAGE FACILITIES. BY FELS INSTITUTE OF LOCAL AND STATE GOVERNMENT, UNIVERSITY OF PENNSYLVANIA. PHILADELPHIA, 1960.
56P. (HUD 701 REPORT)

1. SEWERAGE AND SEWAGE DISPOSAL - PHILADELPHIA. I. PENNSYLVANIA. UNIVERSITY. FELS INSTITUTE OF LOCAL & STATE GOVERNMENT. II. HUD. 701. PHILADELPHIA.

728.1
:336.18
(7471)
R13
Study Group of New York Housing and Neighborhood Improvement.
Rafsky, William L
Publicly assisted housing. [Prepared for the] Study Group of New York Housing and Neighborhood Improvement, E.J. Logue, Chairman. New York, Institute of Public Administration, 1966.
12p.

1. Public housing - New York (City) 2. Housing projects - New York (City) 3. Mortgage finance - New York (City) 4. Building costs - New York (City) I. Study Group of New York Housing and Neighborhood Improvement. II. Lindsay, John V. III. Institute of Public Administration. IV. Title.

711.585.1
P51
A study and reports on issues and projects of national interest to Model Cities for technical assistance.
Planning Research Corp.
A study and reports on issues and projects of national interest to Model Cities for technical assistance. Proposal prepared for the Department of Housing and Urban Development. Los Angeles, 1970.
1v. (Its Technical proposal Q-10478)

1. Model cities. I. Title. II. U.S. Dept. of Housing and Urban Development.

362.6
C34
Study Committee on the Aged.
Child (John) and Company, Honolulu.
A study of Oahu's aged, by John Child and Co., Robert C. Schmitt, research analyst, for the Study Committee on the Aged, Oahu Health Council, and Honolulu Council of Social Agencies. Honolulu, 1953.
35, [41] p. illus., maps, tables.

Bibliographical footnotes.

1. Old age - Oahu. I. Schmitt, Robert C II. Study Committee on the Aged.

Study group on the 1970 Census and Vital and Health Statistics.
614
(083.41)
N17ni
U.S. National Center for Health Statistics.
The 1970 census and vital and health statistics; a study group report of the Public Health Conference on Records and Statistics. A study of the plans for the 1970 Census of Population being developed by the Bureau of the Census; their relation to vital and health statistics; and recommendations for ways to incorporate census data in state and national statistical programs. Wash., U.S.
(Cont'd on next card)

614
(083.41)
N17ni
U.S. National Center for Health
Statistics. The 1970...1969. (Card 2)

Dept. of Health, Education, and Welfare,
Public Health Service, 1969.
14p. (Its Vital and health statistics,
series 4, no. 10)

U.S. Public Health Service. Publication
no. 1,000-series 4, no. 10.

1. Health - Statistics. 2. Census - 1970
(Cont'd on next card)

614
(083.41)
N17ni
U.S. National Center for Health
Statistics. The 1970...1969. (Card 3)

I. Study group on the 1970 Census and
Vital and Health Statistics. II. U.S.
Public Health Service. III. Title.

Study guide for how to plan a house.

728.3
(07)
B17
Battenburg, R W
Study guide for how to plan a house.
Based on the textbook, How to plan a house,
by G. Townsend and J.R. Dalzell. [Chicago]
American Technical Society, 1962.
60p.

1. House plans - Study and teaching.
2. Architecture, Domestic - Design.
I. Dalzell, J.   Ralph. II. Title.
III. American   Technical Society.

649.1
N17
A study in child care.
U.S. National Center for Educational Communica-
tion.
A study in child care. Sponsored by the Office
of Economic Opportunity. Wash., 1971.
3v. in 12 pts. (Day care programs reprint
series)
Contents.-v. 1. Findings, coordinated by S.J.
Fitzsimmons and M.P. Rowe.-v. 2-A. Center case
studies. [no. 1] A Rolls-Royce of day care:
Amalgamated Day Care Center, Chicago, Ill., by
B. O'Farrell. [no. 2] Hey, Georgie, get yourself
together: AVCO Day Care Center, Boston, Mass.,
by P. Bergstein. [no. 3] Life is good,
(Cont'd on next card)

649.1
N17
U.S. National Center for Educational Communica-
tion. A study in child care...1971. (Card 2)

right? Right: 5th City Pre-School, Chicago, Ill.,
by B. O'Farrell. [no. 4] Children as kids:
Georgetown Day Care Center, Washington, D.C., by
B. O'Farrell. [no. 5] Like being at home: Greeley
Parent Child Center, Greeley, Colo., by R.R.
Ruopp. [no. 6] Good vibes: Haight-Ashbury Child-
ren's Center, San Francisco, Calif., by L. Elbow.
[no. 7] They understand: The Children's Center,
Syracuse University, Syracuse, N.Y., by B.
O'Farrell. [no. 8]   All kinds of love -- in
(Cont'd on next card)

649.1
N17
U.S. National Center for Educational Communica-
tion. A study in child care...1971. (Card 3)

a Chinese restaurant: West 80th Street Day Care
Center, New York, N.Y., by M. Rowe.-v. 2-B.
System case studies. [no. 1] They brag on a
child to make him feel good: Kentucky Child
Welfare Research Foundation, Inc., Rural Child
Care Project, Frankfort, Ky., by K. Rosenthal.
[no. 2] Someplace secure: Neighborhood Centers
Day Care Association, Houston, Tex., by K.
Rosenthal.-v. 3.   Cost and quality issues
for operators.   (Cont'd on next card)

649.1
N17
U.S. National Center for Educational Communica-
tion. A study in child care...1971. (Card 4)

1. Day nurseries. 2. Children. I. Title.
II. Title: Child care.

388
C67
Study in new systems of urban transport-
ation.
Cornell Aeronautical Laboratory.
Bi-modal urban transtportation system study.
Prepared for the U.S. Dept. of Housing and
Urban Development. Buffalo, 1968.
2v. (Its CAL v.1 report no. VJ-2431-v-2)
On cover: Study in new systems of urban
transportation.
1. Transportation. I. U.S. Dept. of Hous-
ing and Urban Development. II. Title.
III. Title: Study in new systems of urban
transportation.

388
S71fu
Study in new systems of urban transporta-
tion.
Stanford Research Institute.
Future Urban Transportation systems:
impacts on urban life and form. Final report
I, by Clark Henderson and others. Final
report II, by Robert A. Burco and David A.
Curry. Prepared for Urban Transportation
Administration, Dept. of Housing and Urban
Development, Wash., D.C., Menlo Park, Claif.,
1968.
2v.
On cover: Study in new systems of urban
transportation.
1. Transporta   tion. 2. Journey to
work.   (Cont'd on next card)

388
S71fu
Stanford Research Institute.   Future
Urban Transportation systems...1968.
(Card 2)

3. Transportation - Automation. I. Henderson,
Calrk. II. Burco, Robert A. III. Curry,
David A. IV. U.S. Dept. of Housing and
Urban Development. V. Title. VI. Title:
Study in new systems of urban transportation.

388
B17m
Study in new systems of urban transportation.
Battelle Memorial Institute. Columbus Lab-
oratories.
Monographs on potential RD & D projects
summary report. Prepared for New Systems
Study Project, Urban Transportation Admini-
stration, Dept. of Housing and Urban Develop-
ment, Columbus, Ohio, 1968.
1v.
On cover: Study in new systems of urban
transportation.
Project staff - Kaj L. Nielsen, manager.

(Cont'd on next card)

388
B17m
Battelle Memorial Inttitute. Columbus
Laboratories.   Monographs...1968.
(Card 2)

1. Transportation. 2. Transportation -
Automation. I. U.S. Dept. of Housing and
Urban Development. II. Nielsen, Kaj L.
III. Title. IV. Title: Study in new systems
of urban transportation.

388
G25m
Study in new systems of urban transportation.
General Motors Corp.
New systems implementation study, final
study. Prepared for the U.S. Dept. of Housing
and Urban Development, Urban Transportation
Administration, by E.T. Canty and others.
[Detroit] 1968.
3v. (Its Research publication GMR-710B)
Contents: v.1. Summary and conclusions.-
v.2. Planning and evaluation methods.-v.3.
Case studies.
On cover: Study in new systems of Urban
Transportation.
1. Transporta   tion. 2. Transporta-
tion - Research.   3. Transportation -
Automation.   (Cont'd on next card)

388
G25m
General Motors Corp.   New systems...1968.
(Card 2)

I. Canty, E.T. II. U.S. Dept. of Housing
and Urban Development.
III. Title. IV. Title: Study in new
systems of urban transportation.

388
M42sp
Midwest Research Institute.
Special transportation requirements in
small cities and towns, final report, by
Bruce W. Macy and others. Prepared for the
U.S. Dept. of Housing and Urban Development.
[Kansas City, Mo.] 1968.
87p.
On cover: Study in new systems of urban
transportation.
1. Transportation - Automation. I. U.S. Dept. of Housing and
Urban Development. II. Macy, Bruce W.
III. Title.
(Cont'd on next card)

388
M42sp
Midwest Research Institute.   Special
transportation requirements...1968.
(Card 2)

IV. Title: Study in new systems of urban
transportation. V. Title: Transportation
requirements in small cities and towns.

388
P21
Peat, Marwick, Livingston & Co., New York.
Projection of urban personal transportation
demand. Prepared for the U.S. Dept. of Housing
and Urban Development. New York, 1968.
72p.
At head of title: Study in new systems of
urban transportation.
1. Transportation. 2. Journey to work.
3. Transportation - Automation. I. U.S. Dept.
of Housing and Urban Development. II. Title.
III. Title: Study in new systems of urban
transportation.

388
G25st
Study in new systems of urban transportation.
General Electric Co. Transportation Systems
Div.
A study of command control systems for
urban transportation. Prepared for Urban
Transportation Administration, Dept. of
Housing and Urban Development, Wash. D.C.,
Erie, Pa., Transportation Equipment Projects
and Marketing Operation, General Electric Co.,
Transportation Systems Div., 1968.
360p.
H.W. Merritt, Director.
On cover: Study in new systems of urban
transportation.
(Cont'd on next card)

388
G25st
General Electric Co. Transportation Systems
Div.   A study of command and control
systems...1968. (Card 2)

1. Transportation. 2. Transportation -
Automation. I Merritt, H.W. II. U.S. Dept.
of Housing and Urban Development. III. Title.
IV. Title: Study in new systems of urban
transportation.

388
W27s
Study in new systems of urban transportation.
Westinghouse Air Brake Co.
Study of evolutionary urban transportation.
Organizations participating: Westinghouse Air
Brake and others. Prepared for the U.S. Dept.
of Housing and Urban Development. [Pittsburgh]
1968.
v.   (v.1. v.2. Appendices 1, 2, and 3.
[and] v.3. Appendix 4)
At head of title: Study in new systems of
urban transportation.
1. Transportation. 2. Transportation - Automation. 3. Jour   ney to work. 4. Transportation - Sta   tistics.
(Cont'd on next card)

388
W27s
Westinghouse Air Brake Co.   Study of
evolutionary urban transportation...1968.
(Card 2)

I. U.S. Dept. of Housing and Urban Development. II. Title. III. Title: Study in new
systems of urban transportation.

388
O25s   Study in new systems of urban transportation.
General Research Corp.
Systems analysis of urban transportation.
Prepared for the U.S. Dept. of Housing and
Urban Development. Santa Barbara, Calif., 1968.
4v.   (H-777)
On cover: Study in new systems of urban
transportation.
Contents: v.1. Summary. v.2. Cases for study.-
v.3. Network flow analyses.- v.4. Supporting
analyses.
1. Transportation. 2. Transportation - Re-
search. 3. Journey to work. 4. Transportation -
Automation. I. U. S. Dept. of Housing
and Urban Develop-ment.
(Cont'd on next card)

388
O25s   General Research Corp.   Systems analysis...
1968.   (Card 2)

II. Title. III. Title: Study in new systems
of urban transportation.

388
B17u   Study in new systems of urban transportation.
Battelle Memorial Institute. Columbus
Laboratories.
Urban goods: movement demand, by David
N. Goss and others; final report. Prepared
for New Systems Study Project, Urban Trans-
portation Administration, Dept. of Housing
and Urban Development, Wash., D.C., Colum-
bus, Ohio, Battelle Memorial Institute,
Columbus Laboratories, 1967.
232p.
On cover: Study in new systems of urban
transportation.

388
B17u   Battelle Memorial Institute. Columbus
Laboratories. Urban goods... 1967.
(Card 2)
1. Transportation. 2. Transportation
- Automation. I. U.S. Dept. o f Housing
and Urban Development. II. Goss, David N.
III. Title. IV. Title: Study in new systems
of urban transportation.

699.844   A study; insulating houses from aircraft
B65   noise.
Bolt Beranek and Newman, inc, Los Angeles.
A study; insulating houses from aircraft
noise; developed under the Technical Studies
Program of the Dept. of Housing and Urban
Development, Federal Housing Administration.
Washington, For sale by the Supt. of Doc.,
Govt. Print. Off., 1967.
[78]p.

1. Soundproofing. 2. Noise. 3. Insulating
materials. I. U.S. Federal Housing Adm. Technical Studies Program. II. Title. III. Title:
Aircraft noise.

LAW   A STUDY OF ADMINISTRATIVE LAW.
T   NEVADA. LEGISLATIVE COUNSEL BUREAU.
N28lst   A STUDY OF ADMINISTRATIVE LAW;
ADMINISTRATIVE RULE MAKING; THE CONDUCT OF
ADMINISTRATIVE HEARINGS, AND THE JUDICIAL
REVIEW THEREOF. CARSON CITY, 1958.
55P. (ITS BULLETIN NO. 37)

1. ADMINISTRATIVE PROCEDURE. I. TITLE.
II. TITLE: ADMINISTRATIVE RULE MAKING.
III. TITLE: THE CONDUCT OF ADMINISTRATIVE
HEARINGS.

VF
697.353   A study of a ceiling panel heating system.
N17   U.S. National Bureau of Standards.
A study of a ceiling panel heating system, by
O. N. McDorman, Minoru Fujii [and] P. R. Achenbach.
[Washington] Apr. 1954.
11 l./plates, tables.

Final report, Research Project no. 1-T-124,
Housing and Home Finance Agency.
Project director, R. S. Dill; staff technician,
Robert Thulman.
Processed.

728.1   STUDY OF HOUSING AND URBAN AFFAIRS.
C65STU   U.S. CONGRESS. SENATE. COMMITTEE ON
1968   RULES AND ADMINISTRATION.
S-R   STUDY OF HOUSING AND URBAN AFFAIRS.
NO.986   REPORT TO ACCOMPANY S. RES. 206.
WASHINGTON, GOVT. PRINT. OFF., 1968.
4P. (90TH CONGRESS, 2D SESSION.
SENATE. REPORT NO. 986)

1. FEDERAL HOUSING PROGRAMS.
I. TITLE.

711.417   A study of a prototype floating community.
T74   Triton Foundation.
A study of a prototype floating community.
Prepared for the Dept. of Housing and Urban
Development. Cambridge, Mass., 1968.
1v.
Cover title: Triton City: a prototype
floating community.
U.S. Dept. of Housing and Urban Development.
Urban Planning Research and Demonstration
Project. (Mass. PD-6)
CFSTI PB180051.
Bibliography: p. A-104 - A-105.

(Cont'd on next card)

711.417   Triton Foundation.   A study...1968.
T74   (Card 2)

1. New towns. 2. Harbors. I. Title.
II. Title: Triton City: a prototype floating
community. III. Title: Floating community.
IV. U.S. HUD—UPRDP.

711.73   A study of a truck terminal under a freeway.
(79494)   Claire, William H
C51   A study of a truck terminal under a freeway.
[Los Angeles] Institute of Traffic Engineers,
Committee on Geometric Design Standards of
Truck Terminal Facilities, 1952.
29p.

1. Highways - Los Angeles. 2. Community
facilities - Los Angeles. I. Institute of
Traffic   Engineers, Los Angeles.
II. Title.

658   THE STUDY OF ADMINISTRATION.
(07)   OREGON. UNIVERSITY. SCHOOL OF BUSINESS
O67   ADMINISTRATION.
THE STUDY OF ADMINISTRATION, BY E.S.
WENGERT AND OTHERS. EUGENE, 1961.
149P.

1. MANAGEMENT - STUDY AND TEACHING.
2. PUBLIC ADMINISTRATION - STUDY AND
TEACHING. I. WENGERT, EGBERT S.
II. TITLE.

697.8   A study of air pollution in Townsend, Three
(786)   Forks, the Gallatin Valley and West
M65   Yellowstone.
Montana. State Dept. of Health. (Div. of
Air Pollution Control and Industrial Hygiene)
A study of air pollution in Townsend, Three
Forks, the Gallatin Valley and West Yellowstone,
November, 1967 - November, 1968. Helena, [1969]
40p.

1. Air pollution - Mont. I. Title.

384   Study of aircraft in short haul transportation
N17s   systems.
U.S. National Aeronautics and Space
Administration.
Study of aircraft in short haul transportation
systems. Prepared by the Boeing Company,
Renton, Wash., for Ames Research Center. Wash-
ington, For sale by Clearinghouse for Federal
Scientific and Technical Information,
Springfield, Va., 1968.
Ref.   68p. (NASA CR-986)
1. Air transportation. 2. Aircraft con-
struction. I. Boeing Co., Renton, Wash.
II. U.S. Clearinghouse for Federal Scientific
and Technical In-formation. III. Title.

728.1   A STUDY OF APPROPRIATE MAXIMUM
(77434)   INCOME LIMITS.
D27S   DETROIT. HOUSING COMMISSION.
A STUDY OF APPROPRIATE MAXIMUM
INCOME LIMITS FOR ADMISSION TO AND
CONTINUED OCCUPANCY IN LOW-RENT
HOUSING. DETROIT, 1947.
16L.

1. HOUSING - DETROIT. 2. LOW
INCOME HOUSING - DETROIT. I. TITLE.

720   The study of architectural history.
(09)   Allsopp, Bruce.
A55s   The study of architectural history. New York,
Praeger, 1970.
128p.

1. Architecture - History. I. Title.

332   Study of banking and currency matters.
C657s   U.S. Congress. Senate. Committee on Rules
1968   and Administration.
S-R   Study of banking and currency matters.
Report to accompany S. Res. 209. Washington,
1968.
4p. (90th Cong., 2d sess. Senate. Report
no. 988)

1. Banks and banking. 2. Finance.
I. Title.

331.2   Study of beginning salary offers.
C65stu   College Placement Council. (Salary Survey
Committee)
Study of beginning salary offers.
Bethlehem, Pa., 1967.
20p.

1. Wages and salaries. 2. Universities
and colleges - Surveys. I. Title.

333.7   A study of blighted vacant land.
C34   Chicago. Plan Commission.
A study of blighted vacant land. Prepared
for the Chicago Land Clearance Commission.
Chicago, 1950.
93p.

1. Vacant land. 2. Slums - Chicago.
I. Chicago. Land Clearance Commission.
II. Title.

333.7   A study of blighted vacant land.
C34   Chicago. Plan Commission.
1951   A study of blighted vacant land.
Prepared for the Chicago Land Clearance
Commission. 2d ed. Chicago, 1951.
32p.

1. Vacant land. 2. Slums - Chicago.
I. Chicago. Land Clearance Commission.
II. Title.

711.13   A STUDY OF CERTAIN OF THE EFFECTS OF
B67   DECENTRALIZATION ON BOSTON.
BOSTON. FINANCE COMMISSION.
A STUDY OF CERTAIN OF THE EFFECTS OF
DECENTRALIZATION ON BOSTON AND SOME
NEIGHBORING CITIES AND TOWNS. BOSTON,
1941.
23P.

1. DECENTRALIZATION. 2. POPULATION
SHIFTS - BOSTON. 3. METROPOLITAN
AREAS - BOSTON. I. TITLE.

624.131 M47	A study of chemical stabilization of soils. Mississippi. State University. Engineering and Industrial Research Station. A study of chemical stabilization of soils. Report no. 2. Termination report. State College, Miss., 1966. 51p. Conducted by Mississippi State University for the Mississippi State Highway Dept. in cooperation with U.S. Dept. of Commerce. (Cont'd on next card)

690 (41) G45	Gilchrist, A A study of coding...1969. (Card 2) 3. Building industry - Automation. I. U.K. Building Research Station. II. Gaster, Kathleen, jt. au. III. Title.

69 B84 1953	Study of conservation in building construction. Building Research Advisory Board. Study of conservation in building construction. Part II - second year. Implementation of the 1952 recommendations. Performed by the Building Research Advisory Board under contract DPA-5 between the Defense Production Administration (Office of Defense Mobilization, successor) and the National Academy of Sciences. Final report, June 30, 1953. Washington, June 1953. 28, 179 1. tables. Processed.

624.131 M47	Mississippi. State University. Engineering and Industrial Research Station. A study...1966. (Card 2) 1. Soils. I. Mississippi. State Highway Dept. II. Title: Chemical stabilization of soils. III. Title.

690 (41) N25	A study of coding and data co-ordination for the construction industry: instructions. Nelson, J I'a A study of coding and data co-ordination for the construction industry: instructions to operatives. Garston, Eng., Building Research Station, 1969. 30p. (U.K. Building Research Station. Current paper 10/69) 1. Building industry - U.K. 2. U.K. - Building industry. 3. Building industry - Automation. I. U.K. Building Research Station. II. Title.

647.1 C657	STUDY OF CONSUMER EXPENDITURES, INCOMES, AND SAVINGS) CONFERENCE ON CONSUMPTION AND SAVING, UNIVERSITY OF PENNSYLVANIA, 1959. PROCEEDINGS. EDITED BY IRWIN FRIEND AND ROBERT JONES. PHILADELPHIA, UNIVERSITY OF PENNSYLVANIA, 1960. 2 V. (STUDY OF CONSUMER EXPENDITURES, INCOMES, AND SAVINGS) 1. FAMILY INCOME AND EXPENDITURE - CONGRESSES. 2. BUYING - CONGRESSES. I. FRIEND, IRWIN, ED. II. JONES, ROBERT, ED. (SERIES: STUDY OF CONSUMER EXPENDITURES, INCOMES, AND SAVINGS)

720 H65	A study of coding and data co-ordination for the construction industry: *architecture design* Honey, C R A study of coding and data co-ordination for the construction industry: architectural design. Garston, Eng., Building Research Station, Ministry of Public Building and Works, 1969. 29p. (U.K. Building Research Station. Current paper 4/69) 1. Architecture - Designs and plans. 2. Building documentation. 3. Building construction - U.K. 4. U.K. - Building construction. I. U.K. Building Research Station. II. Title.

002 :690 F67	A study of coding and data co-ordination for the construction industry: *mechanical* Foster, A G A study of coding and data co-ordination for the construction industry: mechanical engineering services, by A.G. Foster and others. Garston, Eng., Building Research Station, Ministry of Public Building and Works, 1969. 81p. (U.K. Building Research Station. Current paper 6/69) 1. Building documentation. 2. Building industry. 3. Architecture - Designs and plans. 4. Civil engineering. I. U.K. Building Research Station. II. Title.

69 M17s	A study of costs and organization in thirteen construction firms. Massachusetts Institute of Technology. A study of costs and organization in thirteen construction firms by F. E. Balderston. Cambridge, Mass., May 1953. 1 v.(various pagings) plates, tables. Final report, Research Project no. O-T-85, Housing and Home Finance Agency. Project director, W. Rubert MacLaurin; staff technician, Philip A. Randall. Processed.

002 :690 B74	A study of coding and data co-ordination for the construction industry: *Contractors* Britten, John R A study of coding and data co-ordination for the construction industry: contractors' management. Garston, Eng., Building Research Station, 1969. 46p. (U.K. Building Research Station. Current paper 9/69) 1. Building documentation. 2. Building industry - U.K. 3. U.K. - Building industry. 4. Contractors (Building industry) I. U.K. Building Research Station. II. Title.

002 :690 S72	A study of coding and data co-ordination for the construction industry. Stevens, R F A study of coding and data co-ordination for the construction industry: structural engineering design, by R.F. Stevens and L. Monument. Garston, Eng., Building Research Station, 1969. 32p. (U.K. Building Research Station. Current paper 5/69) 1. Building documentation. 2. Structural engineering. I. Monument, L., jt. au. II. U.K. Building Research Station. III. Title.

649 C652c v.1	A study of courage and fear. Coles, Robert. Children of crisis; a study of courage and fear. New York, Delta, 1968. 401p. (Children of crisis, v. 1) 1. Children. 2. Psychology. 3. Race relations. I. Title: A study of courage and fear. (Series: Children of crisis, v. 1)

002 :690 B74	A study of coding and data co-ordination for the construction industry: contractors' management. Britten, John R A study of coding and data co-ordination for the construction industry: contractors' management. Garston, Eng., Building Research Station, 1969. 46p. (U.K. Building Research Station. Current paper 9/69) 1. Building documentation. 2. Building industry - U.K. 3. U.K. - Building industry. 4. Contractors (Building industry) I. U.K. Building Research Station. II. Title.

388 G25st	A study of command and control systems... General Electric Co. Transportation Systems Div. A study of command control systems for urban transportation. Prepared for Urban Transportation Administration, Dept. of Housing and Urban Development, Wash. D.C., Erie, Pa., Transportation Equipment Projects and Marketing Operation, General Electric Co., Transportation Systems Div., 1968. 360p. H.W. Merritt, Director. On cover: Study in new systems of urban transportation. (Cont'd on next card)

690.512.2 N87	A study of decision rules for site control: guidance for foremen when programmes change. Nuttall, J F A study of decision rules for site control: guidance for foremen when programmes change. Garston, Eng., Building Research Station, Ministry of Technology, 1965. [3]p. (U.K. Building Research Station. Building research current papers. Construction series 19) Reprinted from: Builder, Aug., 1965, p. 407-9. 1. Site planning. I. U.K. Building Research Station. II. Title.

690 (41) J63	A study of coding and data co-ordination for the construction industry: electrical design. Johnston, H P A study of coding and data co-ordination for the construction industry: electrical design and contracting. Garston, Eng., Building Research Station, Ministry of Public Building and Works, 1969. 70p. (U.K. Building Research Station. Current paper 7/69) 1. Building industry - U.K. 2. U.K. - Building industry. 3. Building industry - Automation. 4. Electrical wiring. I. U.K. Building Research Station. II. Title.

388 G25st	General Electric Co. Transportation Systems Div. A study of command and control systems...1968. (Card 2) 1. Transportation. 2. Transportation - Automation. I. Merritt, H.W. II. U.S. Dept. of Housing and Urban Development. III. Title. IV. Title: Study in new systems of urban transportation.

VF 690.21 S68	Study of design criteria for floating or structural concrete slab floors laid on grade Southwest Research Institute. Housing Research Foundation. Study of design criteria for floating or structural concrete slab floors laid on grade. San Antonio, Tex., Feb. 1952. 4 1. HHFA research project no. OT-22, at Southwest Research Institute, C W. Smith, project director; William A. Russell, staff technician. Processed.

690 (41) G45	A study of coding and data co-ordination for the construction industry: information. Gilchrist, A A study of coding and data co-ordination for the construction industry: information systems relating to the construction industry, by A. Gilchrist and Kathleen Gaster. Garston, Eng., Building Research Station, Ministry of Public Works, 1969. 65p. (U.K. Building Research Station. Current paper 11/69) Bibliography: p. 57-64. 1. Building industry - U.K. 2. U.K. - Building industry. (Cont'd on next card)

362 (7447) H67	A study of community needs for short-term general hospital facilities in the Greater Milwaukee area. Hospital Area Planning Committee, Milwaukee. A study of community needs for short-term general hospital facilities in the Greater Milwaukee area. A summary report. Milwaukee, 1964. 40p. 1. Hospitals - Milwaukee. I. Title.

690.015 (485) S82 R19- 1965	Study of dimensions re equipment in housing for old persons. Sweden. Statens Kommitté for Byggnadsforskning. Study of dimensions re equipment in housing for old persons. Stockholm, 1965. [57]p. (Its Rapport 19-1965) 1. Building research - Sweden. 2. Housing for the aged - Sweden. 3. Household equipment - Sweden. 4. Building methods - Sweden. I. Title.

360
S11

Study of discrimination against persons born out of wedlock

Saario, Vieno Voitto.
Study of discrimination against persons born out of wedlock. New York, Sub-Commission on Prevention of Discrimination and Protection of Minorities, United Nations, 1967.
227p. (United Nations [Document] E/CN.4/Sub. 2/265/Rev.1)
United Nations Publication. Sales no.: E. 68.XIV.3.
1. Social conditions. 2. Family. I. United Nations. II. Title.

720
P74

A study of education for environmental design.

Princeton University.
A study of education for environmental design. Sponsored by the American Institute of Architects. Final report. Co—directors: Robert L. Geddes and Bernard P. Spring. Princeton, N.J., 1967.
61p.

1. Architecture - Designs and plans. 2. Architecture - Study and teaching. I. American Institute of Architects. II. Geddes, Robert L. III. Spring, Bernard L. IV. Title.

727
1(713541)
T67

Study of educational facilities.

Toronto. School Board.
Study of educational facilities. SEF T1-Introduction to the first SEF building system. SEF T2. Specifications for the first SEF building system. Toronto, 1968.
2v. (loose-leaf)

1. Schools - Toronto. 2. Building construction - Toronto. 3. Building methods. 4. Building costs - Toronto. I. Title.

370
K15

A study of educational values in contrasting rural communities of low-income areas.

Kansas. Agricultural Experiment Station.
A study of educational values in contrasting rural communities of low-income areas; final report, by Joan Sistrunk and others. [Wash.] U.S. Office of Education, Bureau of Research, 1967.
68p.
Bibliography: p. 58-68.
1. Education. I. Title. II. Sistrunk, Joan.

331
(083.41)
C48s
1967

Study of employment of women in the Federal government, 1967.

U.S. Civil Service Commission. Bureau of Management Services.
Study of employment of women in the Federal government, 1967. Prepared for the Federal Women's Program. Wash., Govt. Print. Off., 1968.
235p. (Its MS 62-3)
1. Employment - Statistics. 2. Federal government. I. U.S. Federal Women's Program. II. Title. III. Title: Women in the Federal government.

331
C48s

Study of employment of women in the Federal Government.

U.S. Civil Service Commission. (Bureau of Management Services)
Study of employment of women in the Federal Government, 1968. Prepared for the Federal Women's Program. Wash., 1969.
237p. (U.S. Civil Service Commission. Bureau of Management Services SM 62-04)

1. Employment. 2. Minority groups. I. Title: Women. II. Title.

331
C48s
1970

Study of employment of women in the Federal government.

U.S. Civil Service Commission.
Study of employment of women in the Federal government, 1970. Prepared for the Federal Women's Program. Wash., 1971.
236p. (SM 62-06)

1. Women. 2. Employment. I. U.S. Federal Women's Program. II. Title.

333
A17

The study of energy fuel mineral resources.

ABT Associates, Cambridge, Mass.
The study of energy fuel mineral resources. [Prepared] for Public Land Law Review Commission. Cambridge, Mass., 1969.
3v.

Bibliography: p. E-31 - E-35.

1. Public lands. 2. Power resources. 3. Land use. I. U.S. Public Land Law Review Commission. II. Title.

628.3
(759)
S18

A study of estuarine pollution problems on a small unpolluted estuary and a small polluted estuary in Florida.

Seville, Thorndike.
A study of estuarine pollution problems on a small unpolluted estuary and a small polluted estuary in Florida. Gainsville, Florida Engineering and Industrial Experiment Station, College of Engineering, University of Florida, 1966.
202p. (Florida. University. Engineering and Industrial Experiment Station. Bulletin series no. 125)
Engineering progress at the University of Florida. Aug. 1966.

(Cont'd on next card)

628.3
(759)
S18

Seville, Thorndike. A study of estuarine pollution problems on a small unpolluted estuary and a small polluted estuary in Florida...1966.   (Card 2)

1. Sewerage and sewage disposal - Florida. 2. Water pollution - Florida. 3. Sanitation - Florida. I. Florida. University. Engineering and Industrial Experiment Station. II. Title.

388
W27s

Study of evolutionary urban transportation.

Westinghouse Air Brake Co.
Study of evolutionary urban transportation. Organizations participating: Westinghouse Air Brake and others. Prepared for the U.S. Dept. of Housing and Urban Development. [Pittsburgh] 1968.
v. (v.1. v.2. Appendices 1, 2, and 3. [and] v.3. Appendix 4)
At head of title: Study in new systems of urban transportation.

1. Transportation. 2. Transportation - Automation. 3. Journey to work. 4. Transportation - Statistics.
(Cont'd on next card)

388
W27s

Westinghouse Air Brake Co. Study of evolutionary urban transportation...1968.   (Card 2)

I. U.S. Dept. of Housing and Urban Development. II. Title. III. Title: Study in new systems of urban transportation.

647.1
(764)
071

A STUDY OF FAMILY INCOMES IN ORANGE, TEXAS.

ORANGE, TEXAS. HOUSING AUTHORITY.
A STUDY OF FAMILY INCOMES IN ORANGE, TEXAS, ORANGE, TEXAS, 1948.
17P.
IN COOPERATION WITH PUBLIC HOUSING ADMINISTRATION. FORT WORTH, TEXAS.

1. FAMILY INCOME AND EXPENDITURE - ORANGE, TEXAS. 2. HOUSING - ORANGE, TEXAS. I. TITLE.

628.515
1(747)
S97

A study of fat and oil pollution of New York State waters...

Syracuse University Research Corp.
A study of fat and oil pollution of New York State waters, by Gunter Zweig and others. Prepared for New York State Dept. of Health. Syracuse, N.Y. 1967.
90p. (Its Research report no. 16)

1. Water pollution - New York (State) I. Zweig, Gunter. II. New York (State) Dept. of Health. III. Title.

351.7
:332
C65s
1964

A study of Federal credit programs.

U.S. Congress. House. Committee on Banking and Currency.
A study of Federal credit programs. Subcommittee on Domestic Finance, Committee on Banking and Currency, House of Representatives, Eighty-eighth Congress, second session. Washington, Govt. Print. Off., 1964.
2 v.
Arnold H. Diamond (HHFA) senior economist of the Committee's staff has been responsible for project.

(Continued on next card)

351.7
:332
C65s
1964

U.S. Congress. House. Committee on Banking and Currency. A study of Federal credit programs...1964.   (Card 2)

1. Federal government. 2. Credit. 3. Money. I. Title. II. Title: Federal credit programs. III. Diamond, Arnold H.

361
C65S
1965
H=R
NO.632

STUDY OF FEDERAL FINANCIAL ASSISTANCE TO NATURAL DISASTER VICTIMS.

U.S. CONGRESS. HOUSE. COMMITTEE ON BANKING AND CURRENCY.
STUDY OF FEDERAL FINANCIAL ASSISTANCE TO NATURAL DISASTER VICTIMS. REPORT TO ACCOMPANY S. 408. WASHINGTON, GOVT. PRINT. OFF., 1965.
13P. (89TH CONGRESS, 1ST SESSION. HOUSE OF REPRESENTATIVES. REPORT NO. 632)

1. DISASTER SERVICES. I. TITLE.

361
C65S
1965
S=R

STUDY OF FEDERAL FINANCIAL ASSISTANCE TO VICTIMS OF FLOOD.

U.S. CONGRESS. SENATE. COMMITTEE ON BANKING AND CURRENCY.
STUDY OF FEDERAL FINANCIAL ASSISTANCE TO VICTIMS OF FLOOD, EARTHQUAKE, AND OTHER DISASTERS. REPORT TO ACCOMPANY S. 408. WASHINGTON, GOVT. PRINT. OFF., 1965.
6P. (89TH CONGRESS, 1ST SESSION. SENATE. REPORT NO. 11)

1. DISASTER SERVICES. I. TITLE.

728.1
C65STU
1964
S=R
NO.836

STUDY OF FEDERAL HOUSING PROGRAMS.

U.S. CONGRESS. SENATE. COMMITTEE ON RULES AND ADMINISTRATION.
STUDY OF FEDERAL HOUSING PROGRAMS. REPORT TO ACCOMPANY S. RES. 257. WASHINGTON, GOVT. PRINT. OFF., 1964.
4P. (88TH CONGRESS, 2D SESSION. SENATE. REPORT NO. 836)

1. FEDERAL HOUSING PROGRAMS. I. TITLE.

728.1
C65STU
1965
S=R
NO9

STUDY OF FEDERAL HOUSING PROGRAMS.

U.S. CONGRESS. SENATE. COMMITTEE ON BANKING AND CURRENCY.
STUDY OF FEDERAL HOUSING PROGRAMS. REPORT TO ACCOMPANY S. RES. 15. WASHINGTON, GOVT. PRINT. OFF., 1965.
3P. (89TH CONGRESS, 1ST SESSION. SENATE. REPORT NO. 9)

1. FEDERAL HOUSING PROGRAMS. I. TITLE.

728.1
C65
1965
S=R
NO.15

STUDY OF FEDERAL HOUSING PROGRAMS.

U.S. CONGRESS. SENATE. COMMITTEE ON RULES AND ADMINISTRATION.
STUDY OF FEDERAL HOUSING PROGRAMS. REPORT TO ACCOMPANY S. RES. 15. WASHINGTON, GOVT. PRINT. OFF., 1965.
4P. (89TH CONGRESS, 1ST SESSION. SENATE. REPORT NO. 15)

1. FEDERAL HOUSING PROGRAMS. I. TITLE.

728.1
C65STU
1967
S-R
NO.5
STUDY OF FEDERAL HOUSING PROGRAMS.
U.S. CONGRESS. SENATE. COMMITTEE ON
BANKING AND CURRENCY.
STUDY OF FEDERAL HOUSING PROGRAMS.
REPORT TO ACCOMPANY S. RES. 46.
WASHINGTON, GOVT. PRINT. OFF., 1967.
3P. (90TH CONGRESS, 1ST SESSION.
SENATE. REPORT NO. 5)

1. FEDERAL HOUSING PROGRAMS.
I. TITLE.

VF
699.81
868
Study of home fire hazards and methods of control.
Southwest Research Institute. Fire Technology Division.
Study of home fire hazards and methods of control. [San Antonio, Texas] June 1952.
1 v.(various pagings) plates, form, tables
"Literature survey": p. A-1 - A-2.
Final report, Research Project no. 1-T-131, Housing and Home Finance Agency.
Project director, Charles W. Vickery; staff technician, Jefferson Brooks.
Processed.

331.252
815
A STUDY OF INDUSTRIAL RETIREMENT PLANS.
BANKERS TRUST COMPANY, NEW YORK.
A STUDY OF INDUSTRIAL RETIREMENT PLANS, INCLUDING ANALYSES OF COMPLETE PROGRAMS RECENTLY ADOPTED OR REVISED.
NEW YORK, BANKERS TRUST CO.,
V.
SUBTITLE VARIES.
For Library holdings see main entry
1. PENSIONS. 2. OLD AGE.
I. TITLE. II. TITLE: INDUSTRIAL RETIREMENT PLANS.

728.1
C65STU
1966
S-R
NO.940
STUDY OF FEDERAL HOUSING PROGRAMS.
U.S. CONGRESS. SENATE. COMMITTEE ON
BANKING AND CURRENCY.
STUDY OF FEDERAL HOUSING PROGRAMS.
REPORT TO ACCOMPANY S. RES. 172.
WASHINGTON, GOVT. PRINT. OFF., 1966.
3P. (89TH CONGRESS, 2D SESSION.
SENATE. REPORT NO. 940)

1. FEDERAL HOUSING PROGRAMS.
I. TITLE.

VF
728.1
:711
P26
A study of housing and town and country planning in the United States and Puerto Rico.
People's Homesite and Housing Corporation, Manila.
A study of housing and town and country planning in the United States and Puerto Rico [by Sim. F. Garcia] [Manila, Oct. 1952]
58 l. tables.
Work performed under a UN fellowship.
Processed.

728.1
(73:347)
C65st
1963
S-H
Study of international housing.
U.S. Congress. Senate. Committee on Banking and Currency.
Study of international housing. Hearings before a subcommittee of the Committee on Banking and Currency of the United States Senate, Eighty-eighth Congress, first session on a compendium of papers prepared for the study of international housing. Washington, Govt. Print. Off., 1963.
232p.

U.S. Hous and Home Finance Agency, p. 34-35.
(Cont'd. on next card)

728.1
C65STU
1966
S-R
NO.960
STUDY OF FEDERAL HOUSING PROGRAMS.
U.S. CONGRESS. SENATE. COMMITTEE ON
RULES AND ADMINISTRATION.
STUDY OF FEDERAL HOUSING PROGRAMS.
REPORT TO ACCOMPANY S. RES. 172.
WASHINGTON, GOVT. PRINT. OFF., 1966.
4P. (89TH CONGRESS, 2D SESSION.
SENATE. REPORT NO. 960)

1. FEDERAL HOUSING PROGRAMS.
I. TITLE.

728.1
C65STU
1967
S-R
NO.41
STUDY OF HOUSING AND URBAN AFFAIRS.
U.S. CONGRESS. SENATE. COMMITTEE ON
RULES AND ADMINISTRATION.
STUDY OF HOUSING AND URBAN AFFAIRS.
REPORT TO ACCOMPANY S. RES. 46.
WASHINGTON, GOVT. PRINT. OFF., 1967.
4P. (90TH CONGRESS, 1ST SESSION.
SENATE. REPORT NO. 41)

1. FEDERAL HOUSING PROGRAMS.
I. TITLE.

728.1
(73:347)
C65st
1963
S-H
U.S. Congress. Senate. Committee on Banking and Currency. Study of of international housing...(Card 2)

Hearings held April 22-25, 1963.

1. Housing legislation. I. Title.

362.6
F22s
Study of FHA-assisted nursing homes.
U.S. Federal Housing Administration.
Study of FHA-assisted nursing homes. Washington, U.S. Dept. of Housing and Urban Development, Federal Housing Administration, 1966.
32p. (U.S. Dept. of Housing and Urban Development. HUD TS-4)

1. Nursing homes. 2. Grants-in-aid.
3. Old age. I. Title.

728.1
F15
Study of housing and urban development in the United States.
Feng, Ailu-hua.
Final report on the study of housing and urban development in the United States. [Taipei] Taiwan, Republic of China, Taiwan Public Works Bureau, Provincial Government of Taiwan, 1967.
Long. 67p.
c.1,2 1. Housing. 2. City growth. 3. Mortgage finance. 4. Urban renewal. I. Taiwan. Public Works Bureau. II. Title. III. Title: Study of housing and urban development in the United States

---

388
(768551)
M27
Study of interstate highway interchange area development for Metropolitan.
Metropolitan Government of Nashville and Davidson County. Metropolitan Planning Commission.
Study of interstate highway interchange area development for Metropolitan Nashville and Davidson County, Tennessee. Nashville, 1965.
43p.

1. Transportation - Nashville. 2. Transportation - Davidson Co., Tenn. 3. Zoning - Nashville metropolitan area.
4. Highways - Economic effect.
I. Title.

628.3
B14
A study of flow reduction and treatment of waste water from households.
Bailey, James R
A study of flow reduction and treatment of waste water from households, by James R. Bailey and others. For the Federal Water Quality Administration. Groton, Conn., General Dynamics Electrical Boat Div., 1969.
154p. (U.S. Federal Water Quality Administration. Water pollution control research series 11050FKE 12/69)
Bibliography: p. 118-130.
1. Sewerage and sewage disposal. I. General Dynamics. II. U.S. Federal Water Quality Administration. III. Title.

728.1
:325
(756622)
L21
A study of housing decisions by Negro home owners and Negro renters.
Leaman, Samuel Hardy.
A study of housing decisions by Negro home owners and Negro renters. Chapel Hill, University of North Carolina, Dept. of City and Regional Planning, 1967.
136p.
Bibliography: p. 132 - 136.
Thesis (M.A. in Regional Planning) - University of North Carolina.
1. Minority groups - Housing - Greensboro, N.C. I. North Carolina. University. Dept. of City and Regional Planning. II. Title.

690.091.82
(774)
P81
A study of local building codes and their administration in the southeast Michigan six-county region.
Public Administration Service.
A study of local building codes and their administration in the southeast Michigan six-county region. Detroit, Metropolitan Fund, inc., 1966.
41p.
Cover title: Regional building codes.

1. Building codes - Michigan.
I. Metropolitan Fund, inc. II. Title.
III. Title: Regional building codes.

333.33
(79482)
D18
A study of Fresno multiple listing service estimates of residential prices.
Davis, Irving F
A study of Fresno multiple listing service estimates of residential prices. Fresno, Calif., Fresno State College, Bureau of Business Research and Service, 196
115p. (Fresno State College. Bureau of Business Research and Service. Study no. 17)
Bibliography: p. 114-115.
1. Real property - Fresno Co., Calif.
2. Real property - Valuation. 3. Residential areas. I. California. State College, Fresno. Bureau of Business Research and Service. II. Title.

388
G78
Study of hydrofoil seacraft.
Grumman Aircraft Engineering Corp.
Study of hydrofoil seacraft. Phase I Technical report for U.S. Dept. of Commerce, Maritime Administration. Prepared in fulfillment of the requirements of Contract no. MA-1730 by Grumman Aircraft Engineering Corp. Bethpage, New York, and its affiliate Dynamic Development Inc., Babylon, New York. Bethpage, New York, 1958.
2v. (PB 161759)
Distributed by U.S. Dept. of Commerce, (Office of Technical Services)

(Cont'd on next card)

711.4
:670
B15s
A study of local leadership in community economic planning.
Banas, Paul A
A study of local leadership in community economic planning, by Paul A. Banas and others. Prepared for U.S. Economic Development Administration. McLean, Va., Human Sciences Research, inc., 1968.
1v. (HSR-RR-66/12-AB)
CFSTI. PB 178 932.
1. Community development - Citizen participation. 2. Economic planning.
I. Human Sciences Research, inc. II. Title.

352.1
(758)
G26
A study of Georgia municipal salaries, wages and fringe benefits.
Georgia Municipal Association.
A study of Georgia municipal salaries, wages and fringe benefits. Atlanta, 1966.
pts. (pt. 2)

1. Municipal finance - Georgia.
2. Wages and salaries. I. Title.

388
G78
Grumman Aircraft Engineering Corp.
Study of hydrofoil seacraft.
(Card 2)

1. Transportation. I. U.S. Dept. of Commerce, (Office of Technical Services)
II. U.S. Maritime Administration.
III. Title. IV. Title: Hydrofoil seacraft.

728.1
G71
A study of low-cost housing.
Gray, George Herbert
Housing and citizenship; a study of low-cost housing. With a foreword by C. E. A. Winslow. New York, Reinhold, 1946.
254 p. illus., diagrs., plans.

Bibliography: p. 244-246.

388
:308
I57

Study of major urban activity circulation...
International Research and Technology Corp.
Study of major urban activity circulation systems and their impact on congested areas. Final report. Wash., 1971.
1v. (IRT-205-R)
Prepared for U.S. Dept. of Housing and Urban Development under Contract H-1067.

1. Traffic surveys. I. U.S. Dept. of Housing and Urban Development. II. Title.

630
:331
C65
1967
S-R

STUDY OF MIGRATORY LABOR.
U.S. CONGRESS. SENATE. COMMITTEE ON RULES AND ADMINISTRATION.
STUDY OF MIGRATORY LABOR; REPORT TO ACCOMPANY S. RES. 44. WASHINGTON, GOVT. PRINT. OFF., 1967.
7P. (90TH CONGRESS, 1ST SESSION. SENATE. REPORT NO. 51)
AT HEAD OF TITLE: CALENDAR NO. 54.

1. AGRICULTURAL LABORERS. I. TITLE.

331
C48

Study of minority group employment in the Federal Government.
U.S. Civil Service Commission.
Study of minority group employment in the Federal Government. Wash., Govt. Print. Off., 1965.
193p.

1. Employment - Negroes. 2. Federal government. 3. Employment. I. Title. II. Title: Minority group employment in the Federal Government.

020
:538.56
B66

Study of mechanization in DOD libraries and information centers.
Booz, Allen Applied Research, inc.
Study of mechanization in DOD libraries and information centers. Bethesda, Md., 1966.
1v. (U.S. Defense Documentation Center. Defense Supply Agency. AD 640 100. BAARINC report no. 914-1-1)
Distributed by: U.S. Clearinghouse for Federal Scientific and Technical Information.

1. Library science - Automation. 2. Libraries. I. Title.

630
:331
C65
1963
S-R
NO.43

STUDY OF MIGRATORY LABOR.
U.S. CONGRESS. SENATE. COMMITTEE ON RULES AND ADMINISTRATION.
STUDY OF MIGRATORY LABOR; REPORT TO ACCOMPANY S. RES. 22. WASHINGTON, GOVT. PRINT. OFF., 1963.
7P. (88TH CONGRESS, 1ST SESSION. SENATE. REPORT NO. 43)
AT HEAD OF TITLE: CALENDAR NO. 42.

1. AGRICULTURAL LABORERS. I. TITLE.

331
C48st

Study of minority group employment in the Federal government.
U.S. Civil Service Commission.
Study of minority group employment in the Federal government. Wash., 1969.
644p. (SM 70-69B)

1. Employment - Minority groups. 2. Federal civil service. I. Title.

628.3
M12s

A study of methods of preventing failure of septic-tank percolat'... system...
McGauhey, P H
A study of methods of preventing failure of septic-tank percolation systems, by P.H. McGauhey and J.H. Winneberger. Prepared for the Dept. of Housing and Urban Development, Federal Housing Administration, Technical Studies Program. Berkeley, Calif., Sanitary Engineering Research Laboratory, College of Engineering and School of Public Health, University of California, 1967.
30p.
1. Septic tanks. I. Winneberger, J.H., jt. au.
(Continued on next card)

630
:331
C65
1964
S-R

STUDY OF MIGRATORY LABOR.
U.S. CONGRESS. SENATE. COMMITTEE ON RULES AND ADMINISTRATION.
STUDY OF MIGRATORY LABOR; REPORT TO ACCOMPANY S. RES. 290. WASHINGTON, GOVT. PRINT. OFF., 1964.
5P. (88TH CONGRESS, 2D SESSION. SENATE. REPORT NO. 878)

1. AGRICULTURAL LABORERS. I. TITLE.

728.69
C65s

A study of mobile home parks, spaces ...
Connett, Russell R
A study of mobile home parks, spaces, and residents in Humboldt County, 1966, by Russel R. Connett, and others. Arcata, Calif., Division of Business, Humboldt State College, 1966.
67p.
Bibliography: p. 66-67.

1. Mobile homes. I. California. Humboldt State College, Arcata. II. Title.

628.3
M12s

McGauhey, P H
A study...1967. (Card 2)

II. California. University. Sanitary Engineering Research Laboratory. III. U.S. Federal Housing Administration. Technical Studies Program. IV. Title.

630
:331
C65
1962
S-R

STUDY OF MIGRATORY LABOR.
U.S. CONGRESS. SENATE. COMMITTEE ON RULES AND ADMINISTRATION.
STUDY OF MIGRATORY LABOR; REPORT TO ACCOMPANY S. RES. 273. WASHINGTON, GOVT. PRINT. OFF., 1962.
13P. (87TH CONGRESS, 2D SESSION. SENATE. REPORT NO. 1159)
AT HEAD OF TITLE: CALENDAR NO. 1138.

1. AGRICULTURAL LABORERS. I. TITLE.

332.72
C65st
1967

A study of mortgage credit.
U.S. Congress. Senate. Committee on Banking and Currency.
A study of mortgage credit. Prepared by Subcommittee on Housing and Urban Affairs for the Committee on Banking and Currency, United States Senate. Wash., For sale by the Supt. of Doc., Govt. Print. Off., 1967.
467p.
At head of title: 90th Cong., 1st sess.
U.S. Dept. of Housing and Urban Development, p. 41-116.

1. Mortgage finance. 2. U.S. Dept. of Housing and Urban Development. I. Title.

388
(7472)
M12

A study of metropolitan New York transportation.
Madigan-Hyland, inc.
A study of metropolitan New York transportation. Prepared for Triborough Bridge and Tunnel Authority. New York, Triborough Bridge and Tunnel Authority, 1967.
33p.

1. Transportation - New York (City) metropolitan area. I. Triborough Bridge and Tunnel Authority. II. Title.

630
:331
C65
1966
S-R

STUDY OF MIGRATORY LABOR.
U.S. CONGRESS. SENATE. COMMITTEE ON RULES AND ADMINISTRATION.
STUDY OF MIGRATORY LABOR; REPORT TO ACCOMPANY S. RES. 188. WASHINGTON, GOVT. PRINT. OFF., 1966.
6P. (89TH CONGRESS, 2D SESSION. SENATE. REPORT NO. 991)
AT HEAD OF TITLE: CALENDAR NO. 963.

1. AGRICULTURAL LABORERS. I. TITLE.

332.72
C65st
1958

Study of mortgage credit.
U.S. Congress. Senate. Committee on Banking and Currency.
Study of mortgage credit. Does the decade 1961-70 pose problems in private housing and mortgage markets which require Federal legislation by 1960? Washington, Govt. Print. Off., 1958.
397p. graphs, tables.
85th Cong., 2d sess.

1. Mortgage finance. I. Title. 2. Mortgage credit.

630
:331
C65
1968
S-R

STUDY OF MIGRATORY LABOR.
U.S. CONGRESS. SENATE. COMMITTEE ON LABOR AND PUBLIC WELFARE.
STUDY OF MIGRATORY LABOR; REPORT TO ACCOMPANY S. RES. 222. WASHINGTON, GOVT. PRINT. OFF., 1968.
5P. (90TH CONGRESS, 2D SESSION. SENATE. REPORT NO. 967)
AT HEAD OF TITLE: CALENDAR NO. 977.

1. AGRICULTURAL LABORERS. I. TITLE. II. TITLE: MIGRATORY LABOR.

630
:331
C65
1960
S-R
NO.1088

STUDY OF MIGRATORY LABOR...
U.S. CONGRESS. SENATE. COMMITTEE ON RULES AND ADMINISTRATION.
STUDY OF MIGRATORY LABOR... REPORT TO ACCOMPANY S. RES. 267. WASHINGTON, GOVT. PRINT. OFF., 1960.
4P. (86TH CONGRESS, 2D SESSION. SENATE. REPORT NO. 1088)

1. AGRICULTURAL LABORERS. I. TITLE.

332.72
C65st
1961

Study of mortgage credit.
U.S. Congress. Senate. Committee on Banking and Currency.
Study of mortgage credit. Does the decade 1961-70 pose problems in private housing and mortgage markets which require Federal legislation? Recommendations of Federal agencies. Committee on Banking and Currency, Subcommittee on Housing, United States Senate. Washington, Govt. Print. Off., 1961.
255p.
At head of title: 87th Cong., 1st sess.

1. Mortgage finance. 2. Mortgage credit. I. Title.

630
:331
C65
1961
S-R
NO.66

STUDY OF MIGRATORY LABOR...
U.S. CONGRESS. SENATE. COMMITTEE ON RULES AND ADMINISTRATION.
STUDY OF MIGRATORY LABOR... REPORT TO ACCOMPANY S. RES. 86. WASHINGTON, GOVT. PRINT. OFF., 1961.
4P. (87TH CONGRESS, 1ST SESSION. SENATE. REPORT NO. 66)

1. AGRICULTURAL LABORERS. I. TITLE.

630
:331
W47

A study of migratory workers in cucumber harvesting.
Wisconsin. University.
A study of migratory workers in cucumber harvesting; Waushara County, Wisconsin. [Madison] 1964.
88p.

1. Agricultural laborers. I. Title.

332.72
C65
1959
S-H

Study of mortgage credit.
U.S. Congress. Senate. Committee on Banking and Currency.
Study of mortgage credit. Hearings before a subcommittee of the Committee on Banking and Currency, United States Senate, Eighty-sixth Congress, first session on a study of the question: Does the decade 1961-70 pose problems in private housing and mortgage markets which require federal legislation

(Continued on next card)

332.72
C65
1959
S-H

U.S. Congress. Senate. Committee on Banking and Currency. Study of ... (Card 2)

by 1960? Washington, Govt. Print. Off.,
1959.
397p. diagrs., tables.

Hearings held May 14-29, 1959.

1. Mortgage finance.   I. Title.

614.8
:711.73
H82

A study of pedestrian fatalities in
Wayne County, Michigan.
Huelke, Donald F
A study of pedestrian fatalities in
Wayne County, Michigan, by Donald F.
Huelke and Rollin A. Davis. Ann Arbor,
Mich., Highway Safety Research Institute,
University of Michigan, 1969.
52p. (HSRI report no. Bio-9)

Bibliography: p. 21-22.
1. Traffic safety. I. Davis, Rollin A.,
jt. au. II. Michigan. University.
Highway Safety   Research Institute.
III. Title: Pedestrian fatalities.
IV. Title.

621.32
H18

Study of psychological glare in interiors.
Haubner, P
Study of psychological glare in interiors,
by P. Haubner and H. Johanni. Garston, Eng.,
Building Research Station, 1970.
[13]p. (Library communication no. 1584)
Translated from the German and reprinted
from Lichttechnik, 1970, 22 (6), 304-6; (7)
345-7.

1. Lighting. I. Johanni, H., jt. au.
II. U.K. Building Research Station. III. Title:
Glare. IV. Title.

628.1
(758)
G26

A study of municipal water and sewer utility
rates and practices in Georgia.
Georgia Municipal Association.
A study of municipal water and sewer
utility rates and practices in Georgia.
[Part] 1. Cities above 10,000 population.
Atlanta, 1965, 1966
2 pts.
Part 3. Cities under 5,000 population.

1. Water-supply - Georgia. 2. Sewerage
and sewage disposal - Georgia. 3. Public
utilities - Georgia. I. Title.

711.583
(77434)
M27

A study of personal and community information
service in the Southeast Michigan Six-
County Region.
Metropolitan Fund, inc.
A study of personal and community information service in the Southeast Michigan
Six-County Region. Three documents relating
to the involvement of citizens of the region
in the resolution of regional problems. A
research project. Detroit, 1966.
41p.

1. Community development - Citizen
participation - Detroit. 2. Metropolitan
area planning - Detroit. I. Title.

727
(78883)
D25s

A study of pupil population ...

Denver. Public Schools.
A study of pupil population, school
boundaries, pupil transportation,
school buildings. Report. Denver, 1962.
42p.

1. Schools - Denver. 2. School
management and organization. I. Title.

725.83
W34

A study of neighborhood center programs in ...
White, Arthur.
A study of neighborhood center programs
in rural community action agencies.
New York, Daniel Yankelovich, 1969.
106p.

Prepared for the Office of Economic
Opportunity.
CFSTI. PB 183024.

1. Community centers. 2. Rural
planning. I. Yankelovich (Daniel) inc.
II. Title.

320
M12

The study of political parties.
McDonald, Neil A
The study of political parties. New York,
Random House, 1955.
97p. (Studies in political science, 26)
Bibliography: [p.95] - 97.

1. Political science. I. Title.

333.33
(79493)
S 23

A study of real estate research and
education needs in the Long Beach...
Schultz, Raymond G
A study of real estate research and
education needs in the Long Beach
California region. Long Beach, School
of Business Administration, California State College at Long Beach, 1969.
86p.

1. Real estate business - Long Beach,
Calif. I. California. State College,
Long Beach. School of Business Adminis-
tration. II. Title.

628.3
M22

A study of nitrification and denitrification.
Mechalas, B J
A study of nitrification and denitrification,
by B.J. Mechalas and others. [Prepared] for
the Federal Water Quality Administration.
El Monte, Calif., Envirogenics, 1970.
90p. (Water pollution control research
series 17010 DRD 07/70)

1. Sewerage and sewage disposal. 2. Water
pollution. I. Envirogenics Co. II. Title.
III. U.S. Federal Water Quality Administration.

628.515
O65s

A study of pollution-water...
U.S. Congress. Senate. Committee on
Public Works.
A study of pollution-water; staff
report to the Committee on Public Works,
United States Senate. Washington, Govt.
Print. Off., 1963.
100p.
At head of title: 88th Cong., 1st sess.

1. Water pollution. I. Title.

312.1
(74461)
D78

Study of residential mobility within an
urban ghetto.
D.S.W., inc.
Study of residential mobility within an
urban ghetto. New York, 1968.
29p.

1. Population shifts - Boston. 2. Minority
groups - Housing - Boston. I. Title.

331
(41)
J21

Study of operative skills: a guide to the
first report.
Jeanes, R E
Study of operative skills: a guide to
the first report. Garston, Eng., Building
Research Station, Ministry of Technology,
1966.
6p.   (U.K. Building Research Station.
Building research current paper. Construction series 30)

1. Labor supply - U.K. 2. Building
industry - U.K. I. U.K. Building Research Station. II. Title.

312
H18s

The study of population.
Hauser, Philip M   ed.
The study of population: an inventory and
appraisal, edited by Philip M. Hauser and Otis
Dudley Duncan. Chicago, University of Chicago
Press, 1959.
864p.

1. Population. I. Duncan, Otis Dudley,
jt. ed. II. Title.

628.1
L45

A study of residential water use.

Linaweaver, F P
A study of residential water use. A
report prepared for the Technical Studies
Program of the Federal Housing Administration, Dept. of Housing and Urban Development, by F.P. Linaweaver and others.
Baltimore, Dept. of Environmental Engineering Science, Johns Hopkins University, For
sale by the Supt. of Documents, Govt.
Print. Off., 1967.
79p.   (U.S. Department of Housing and
Urban Development. TS-12)

(Cont'd on next card)

VF
301.15
(762)
M47

A study of organized communities in Mississippi
Mississippi. State College. The Social Science
Research Center.
A study of organized communities in
Mississippi, by A. Alexander Fanelli and Raymond
Payne.   State College, Miss., June 1953.
79 p.   graphs, map, tables. (Its
Community studies no. 1)

Processed.

1.Community organization. I.Fanelli, A. Alexander.
II.Payne, Raymond. III.Title.

647.1
L11stu

A study of prices charged in food stores
located in low and higher income areas of
six large cities.
U.S. Bureau of Labor Statistics.
A study of prices charged in food stores
located in low and higher income areas of
six large cities. Prepared for the National
Commission on Food Marketing. Washington,
1966.
28p.

1. Cost and standard of living. 2. Family
income and expenditure. 3. Prices. I. U.S.
National Commission on Food Marketing.
II. Title.

628.1
L45

Linaweaver, F.P. A study of residential water
use...1967.   (Card 2)

1. Water-supply. I. U.S. Federal Housing
Administration. Technical Studies Program.
II. Title.

333
N67s

Study of outer continental shelf lands...
Nossaman, Waters, Scott, Krueger & Riordan.
Study of outer continental shelf lands of
the United States. Prepared under contract
with Public Land Law Review Commission. Los
Angeles, 1968.
2v.
Summary -- --- Summary. 1968.
77p.
1. Public lands. 2. Natural resources.
3. Water resources. I. U.S. Public Land
Law Review Commission. II. Title: Continental
shelf lands of the United States.

690.072
M45

A study of problems of manpower utilization
in the construction industry.
Mills, D Q
A study of problems of manpower utilization
in the construction industry: intermittency
of employment, unemployment and labor short-
ages. Wash., Manpower Administration, U.S.
Dept. of Labor, 1969.
113p.

1. Building construction - Labor
requirements. I. U.S. Manpower
Administration. II. Title.

628.1
R63

A study of resource use in urbanizing
watersheds.
Rogers, Peter.
A study of resource use in urbanizing watersheds, by Peter Rogers and Carl Steinitz.
Washington, Office, Chief of Engineers, Dept.
of the Army, 1970.
1v. (Plan formulation and evaluation studies
environmental analysis. Contract report no. 2)
Prepared under contract no. DACW 33-68-DC-0151
Harvard University, Graduate School of Design,
Dept. of Landscape Architecture, Research Office.
1. Water resources. 2. Man - Influence of
environment. 3. Drainage. I. Steinitz, Carl,
jt. au. II. U.S. Army. Corps of Engineer.
III. Title.

020
G26

A study of resources and major subject holdings
available in U.S. Federal Libraries.
George Washington University, Washington, D.C.
Biological Sciences Communication Project.
A study of resources and major subject holdings
available in U.S. Federal Libraries, maintaining
extensive or unique collections of research
materials, by Mildred Benton and others. Final
report. [Sponsored by U.S. Federal Library Committee Task Force on Acquisition of Library
Materials and Correlation of Federal Library
Resources] Wash., 1970.
670p.
Preliminary edition.

(Cont'd on next card)

628.44
(774)
O 14

Study of solid waste refuse disposal in the
southeast Michigan six-county region.
Oakes, Donald.
Study of solid waste refuse disposal in the
southeast Michigan six-county region. Detroit,
Metropolitan Fund, inc., 1966.
13p.
Cover title: Regional refuse disposal.

1. Refuse and refuse disposal - Michigan.
I. Metropolitan Fund, inc. II. Title.
III. Title: Regional refuse disposal.

388
1308
M22

McConcochie, W   R   Study of
terminal transfer facilities in conjunction
with urban freeways...1967.   (Card 2)

4. Urban renewal. I. DeLeuw, Cather & Co.,
Chicago. II. Minnesota. Dept. of Highways.
III. U.S. Bureau of Public Roads. IV. U.S.
Clearinghouse for Federal Scientific and
Technical Information. V. Title.

020
G26

George Washington University, Washington, D.C.
Biological Sciences Communication Project.
A study of resources...1970.   (Card 2)

Prepared under contract with the U.S. Office
of Education, Dept. of Health, Education, and
Welfare.
1. Library science. 2. Libraries. I. Benton,
Mildred. II. U.S. Federal Library Committee.
Task Force on Acquisition of Library Materials
and Correlation of Federal Library Resources.
III. U.S. Office of Education. IV. Title.

711.73
1336
(758)
G26

A study of State Highway Department expenditure
trends in Georgia, 1955-1963.
Georgia Municipal Association.
A study of State Highway Department ex-
penditure trends in Georgia, 1955-1963.
Atlanta, 1965.
118p.
Preliminary draft reviewed by Georgia
State Highway Dept.

1. Highways - Finance - Georgia.
I. Title. II. Georgia. State Highway Dept.

330
(75)
G17

A study of the ability of Tennessee Appalachian
Counties to pay for projects partially funded by
Federal grants.
Garriott, William C
A study of the ability of Tennessee
Appalachian Counties to pay for projects
partially funded by Federal grants, for
the Tennessee Appalachian Staff of the Office
of Urban and Federal Affairs, State of
Tennessee. [Nashville] 1967.
49p.
On cover: Resource Development Internship
project.
Bibliography: p. 45-47.

1. Economic   development - Appalachian region.   (Cont'd on next card)

647.1
N27s

A STUDY OF RESPONSE ERRORS IN
EXPENDITURES DATA FROM HOUSEHOLD
NETER, JOHN.
A STUDY OF RESPONSE ERRORS IN
EXPENDITURES DATA FROM HOUSEHOLD SURVEYS,
BY JOHN NETER AND JOSEPH WAKSBERG.
MINNEAPOLIS, 1964.
18-55P. (MINNESOTA. UNIVERSITY.
REPRINT SERIES, 5)

REPRINTED FROM THE JOURNAL OF THE
AMERICAN STATISTICAL ASSOCIATION, MARCH
1964, V. 59.

1. FAMILY INCOME AND EXPENDITURE.
2. SURVEY METHODS. I. TITLE.
(CONTINUED ON NEXT CARD)

355.58
H15

Study of tactical movement concepts and procedures for civil defense planning.
Hamberg, W A
Study of tactical movement concepts and
procedures for civil defense planning, by W.
A. Hamberg and others. Prepared under contract
for Director of Research, Office of Civil Defense,
Dept. of Defense. Silver Spring, Md., Operations Research, Inc., 1963.
206p. (Technical report 210)

1. Civilian defense. I. U.S. Office of
Civil Defense. II. Operations Research, inc.
III. Title.

330
(75)
G17

Garriott, William C   A study...1967.
   (card 2)

2. Local government - Appalachian
region. 3. Grants-in-aid. I. Tennessee.
Office of Urban and Federal Affairs.
II. Title.

647.1
N27s

NETER, JOHN. A STUDY OF ...1964.(CARD 2)

II. WAKSBERG, JOSEPH, JT. AU.
III. MINNESOTA. UNIVERSITY. GRADUATE
SCHOOL OF BUSINESS ADMINISTRATION.

600
N17s

A study of technology assessment.
National Academy of Engineering. Committee
on Public Engineering Policy.
A study of technology assessment. Wash.,
Committee on Science and Astronautics, U.S.
House of Representatives, 1969.
208p.
Committee print.

1. Technology. I. U.S. Congress. House.
Committee on Science and Astronautics.
II. Title.

388
G48

A study of the applicability of air-pad
support for urban transportation vehicles.
Givens, W R
A study of the applicability of air-pad
support for urban transportation vehicles.
Columbus, Ohio, Battelle Memorial Institute,
Columbus Laboratories, 1967.
9p. (Battelle Memorial Institute.
Columbus Laboratories. Monograph no. 19)
Prepared for New Systems Study Project,
Urban Transportation Administration, Dept. of
Housing and Urban Development.
U.S. Mass Transportation Demonstration
Grant Program.   Contract no. H-778.
   (Cont'd on next card)

325
L28s

A study of slum culture.
Lewis, Oscar.
A study of slum culture; backgrounds for
la vida. With the assistance of Douglas
Butterworth. New York, Random House, 1968.
240p.

Bibliography: p. 227-229.

1. Spanish-Americans. 2. Poor - New York
(City) I. Butterworth, Douglas, jt. au.
II. Title.

691.322
823

A study of tenacity of aggregates in surface
treatments.
Schweyer, H E
A study of tenacity of aggregates in sur-
face treatments, by H. E. Schweyer and
William Gertner, Jr. Gainesville, Florida
University, Engineering and Industrial
Experiment Station, 1962.
19p. (Florida. University. Engineer-
ing and Industrial Experiment Station.
Technical paper no. 342)
Engineering progress at the University of
Florida, vol. XX, no. 2, Feb., 1966.
Reprinted from Highway research record,

(Continued on   next card)

388
G48

Givens, W R   A study of
the...1967.   (Card 2)

1. Transportation. 2. Journey to work.
3. Air transportation. I. Battelle
Memorial Institute. Columbus
Laboratories. II. U.S. Dept. of Housing
and Urban Development. Urban
Transportation Administration. III. U.S.
Mass Transportation Demonstration Grant
Program. IV. Title.

728.1
J12

A study of small community needs as related to
Federal housing and community development...
Jacobs Co.
A study of small community needs as related
to Federal housing and community development
assistance. Chicago, 1970.
2v.
Prepared for the Dept. of Housing and Urban
Development. Contract H-1074.

1. Federal housing programs. 2. Community
development. I. U.S. Dept. of Housing and
Urban Development. II. Title.

691.322
823

Schweyer, H E   A study of tenacity
of aggregates in surface...1962. (Card 2)

no. 104 on Surface treatments, bituminous mixtures and pavements, from the 44th annual
meeting, Jan. 11-15, 1965. p. 18-35.

1. Concrete aggregates. 2. Road construc-
tion. I. Gertner, William, jt. au.
II. Florida. University. Engineering and
Industrial Experiment Station. III. Title.

388
H19s

A study of the applicability of the linear
electric motors to urban transportation.
Hazard, H R
A study of the applicability of the
linear electric motors to urban
transportation. Columbus, Ohio, Battelle
Memorial Institute, Columbus Laboratories,
1967.
12p. (Battelle Memorial Institute.
Columbus Laboratories. Monograph no. 17)
Prepared for New Systems Study Project,
Urban Transportation Administration, Dept.
of Housing and Urban Development.
   (Cont'd on next card)

628.44
R15

A study of solid waste collection systems
comparing one-man with multi-man crews.
Ralph Stone and Co.
A study of solid waste collection systems
comparing one-man with multi-man crews; final
report. Wash., U.S. Bureau of Solid Waste
Management, 1969.
175p. (U.S. Public Health Service publication no. 1892; Report (SW-9c))
Bibliography: p. 153-158.
1. Refuse and refuse disposal. I. U.S.
Bureau of Solid Waste Management. II. Title.

388
1308
M22

Study of terminal transfer facilities.
McConcochie, W R
Study of terminal transfer facilities in
conjunction with urban freeways, for
Minnesota Dept. of Highways and Bureau of
Public Roads. Chicago, DeLeuw, Cather and
Co., 1967.
54p.
U.S. Clearinghouse for Federal Scientific
and Technical Information   document PB
175 759.

1. Traffic surveys. 2. Transportation.
3. Highways.
   (Cont'd on next card)

388
H19s

Hazard, H R   A study of
the...1967.   (Card 2)

U.S. Mass Transportation Demonstration
Grant Program. Contract no. H-778.
1. Transportation. 2. Journey to work.
3. Electricity. 4. Engineering. I. Battelle
Memorial Institute. (Columbus Laboratories)
II. U.S. Dept. of Housing and Urban
Development. Urban Transportation
Administration. III. U.S. Mass
Transportation Demonstration Grant Program.
IV. Title.

625.84
R63
A study of the behavior of reinforced concrete beams subjected to repeated loads.
Rogers, William A
A study of the behavior of reinforced concrete beams subjected to repeated loads. Final report. Lafayette, Ind., Purdue University, 1967.
133p. (Purdue University. Joint Highway Research Project. No. 30)
Bibliography: p. 891-99.
1. Road construction. 2. Concrete, Reinforced. I. Purdue University. Joint Highway Research Project. II. Title.

330
W34s
v. 1
Study of the effects of... the 1967 amendments to the Economic opportunity act.
White, Arthur.
Study of the effects of Sections 210 and 211 of the 1967 amendments to the Economic opportunity act as required under Section 233(C) of the amendments. Vol. I, summary and conclusions. New York, Daniel Yankelovich, inc., 1969.
61p.
CFSTI PB 183 182.
1. Economic development. 2. Social welfare. 3. U.S. Office of Economic Opportunity. I. Title.

330
M27s
A study of the nation-wide regional econometric model.
Mera, Koichi.
A study of the nation-wide regional econometric model: comments and survey of model building for regional economies. Cambridge, Mass., 1969.
14p. (Harvard University. Program on Regional and Urban Economics. Discussion paper no. 55)
Bibliography: p. 16-17
1. Economic planning. 2. Economic research. I. Harvard University. Program on Regional and Urban Economics. II. Title.

333.33
(794)
W45
A study of the causes of employment turnover of real estate licensees in California.
Wilson, John E
A study of the causes of employment turnover of real estate licensees in California; causes of activity and inactivity of real estate licensees and brokers after employment turnover, by John E. Wilson and S. Thomas Cleveland. Sacramento, Calif., Center for Business Research, Sacramento State College, 1969.
68p.
1. Real estate business - Calif. I. Cleveland, S. Thomas, jt. au.
(Cont'd on next card).

711.73
(761781)
M66
A study of the expected economic and social impact of interstate highways ...
Moore, Charles Thomas.
A study of the expected economic and social impact of interstate highways in the industrial and commercial trading area of Birmingham, Alabama, the first phase, by C.T. Moore and others. University, Alabama Highway Research Project, Dept. of Marketing, School of Commerce and Business Administration, University of Alabama, 1964.
132p.

(Cont'd on next card)

725.83
A17
A study of the Neighborhood Center Pilot Program.
ABT Associates, inc.
A study of the Neighborhood Center Pilot Program. Prepared for the Executive Office of the President, Bureau of the Budget. Cambridge, Mass., 1969.
4v.
Contents.-v. 1: Summary and recommendations.-v. 2: The neighborhood service programs.-v. 3: A model for neighborhood service programs.-v. 4: Federal support.
1. Community centers. 2. U.S. Neighborhood Center Pilot Program. 3. Poor. I. Title.

333.33
(794)
W45
Wilson, John E   A study...1969.
(Card 2)

II. California. State College, Sacramento. Center for Business Research. III. Title. IV. Title: Real estate licenses in California.

711.73
(761781)
M66
Moore, Charles Thomas. A study of the expected economic and social impact of interstate highways in the industrial and commercial trading area...1964.
(Card 2)

1. Highways - Economic effect - Birmingham, Ala. 2. Highways - Social effect. I. Alabama. University. II. Alabama. Highway Dept. III. Title.

728.1
:325
(76638)
K56
A study of the nonwhite population distribution and housing characteristics in ...
Knowles, Laurie.
A study of the nonwhite population distribution and housing characteristics in Oklahoma City, Oklahoma, 1940-1960. Norman, Okla., 1965.
111p.
Thesis-Oklahoma University (Regional and City Planning)
Bibliography: p. 108-111.
1. Minority groups - Housing - Oklahoma City. 2. Population - Oklahoma City. 3. Negroes. I. Title.

VF
728.1
:336.18
(7526)
B15s
A study of the characteristics of white applicants for public housing.
Baltimore, Md. Housing Authority.
A study of the characteristics of white applicants for public housing in Baltimore, Maryland, 1952. Baltimore, Md., Sept. 1953.
23 l. graphs, tables.
Study planned and report written by Sara Shuman Hartman, Assistant Director, Research and Statistics Division.
Processed.
1. Public housing projects-Tenants. 2. Housing for the aged. I. Hartman, Sara Shuman. II. Title. III. Title: Characteristics of white applicants for public housing.

386
(795)
C67
A study of the feasibility of developing small boat harbors in six Oregon counties.
Cornell, Howland, Hayes & Merryfield.
A study of the feasibility of developing small boat harbors in six Oregon counties. [Prepared for] U.S. Dept. of Commerce, Area Redevelopment Administration. Washington, Govt. Print. Off., 1965.
61p.
1. Harbors - Oregon. I. U.S. Area Redevelopment Administration. II. Title.

711.4
(778)
V17
A study of the planning provision of the small constitution charter cities...
Varenhorst, Glenn E
A study of the planning provisions of the smaller constitutional charter cities in Missouri. Columbia, Dept. of Regional and Community Affairs, School of Social and Community Services, University of Missouri, 1972.
93p.
Bibliography: p. 91-93.
1. City planning - Mo. I. Missouri. University. II. Title.

690
(07)
C15
A study of the curriculum in building construction at institutions of higher learning throughout the United States.
Caldwell, Wofford T
A study of the curriculum in building construction at institutions of higher learning throughout the United States. Tallahassee, Florida State University, Graduate School, 1964.
41p.
Thesis (Building Construction) - Florida State University.
Bibliography: p. 38-41.
1. Building industry - Study and teaching. I. Florida State University, Tallahassee. II. Title.

301
P72r
Study of the inner city.
Presbyterian Church in the United States of America.
Report of Special Committee of Board of National Missions of the Presbyterian Church in the U.S.A., on study of the inner city. New York, 1960.
42p.
1. Church and social problems. 2. Metropolitan areas. I. Title: Study of the inner city.

711.3
C65a
Intro.
A study of the potential for America's cities.
Chamber of Commerce of the United States of America. Task Force on Economic Growth and Opportunity.
A study of the potential for America's cities. Washington, 1966.
[11]p.
Cover title.
1. City growth. 2. City planning. I. Title.

333
P81s
Study of the development, management, and use of water resources on the public lands
U.S. Public Land Law Review Commission.
Study of the development, management, and use of water resources on the public lands. Prepared for the Public Land Law Review Commission. [Wash.] 1969.
2v.
1. Public lands. 2. Water resources. 3. Land use. I. Title.

388
:331
M67s
A study of the journey to work by central business district workers.
Morrall, J F
A study of the journey to work by central business district workers, by J.F. Morrall, and B.G. Hutchinson. [n.p.] [1969?]
99-114p.
1. Journey to work. 2. Transportation. 3. Business districts. I. Hutchinson, B.G., jt. au. II. Title.

301.158
:308
R66
A study of the problems, attitudes and aspirations of rural youth.
Roper (Elmer) and Associates.
A study of the problems, attitudes and aspirations of rural youth. Prepared for Rockefeller Brothers Fund. [n.p.] 1963.
176p.
1. Youth - Surveys. I. Rockefeller Brothers Fund. II. Title. III. Title: Rural youth.

330
(79473)
S15
pt.1
A study of the economy of Santa Clara County, California.
Santa Clara County, Calif. Planning Dept.
A study of the economy of Santa Clara County, California. Part 1. San Jose, Calif., 1967.
36p.
1. Economic conditions - Santa Clara Co., Calif. I. Title.

352
(774)
V27
A study of the legal powers of Michigan local governments comparing cities, townships, charter townships and villages.
VerBurg, Kenneth.
A study of the legal powers of Michigan local governments comparing cities, townships, charter townships and villages. Rev. East Lansing, Mich., Institute for Community Development and Services, Continuing Education Service, Michigan State University, 1969.
37p.
1. Local government - Mich. I. Michigan. State University. Institute for Community Development and Services. II. Title. III. Title: Legal powers of Michigan local governments.

362.6
C65de
A study of the problems of the aged and aging.
U.S. Congress. Senate. Special Committee on Aging.
Developments in aging, 1959 to 1963. A report of the Special Committee on Aging, United States Senate, together with supplemental and minority views pursuant to S. Res. 33, Feb. 13, 1961, and S. Res. 238, Feb. 7, 1962, resolutions authorizing a study of the problems of the aged and aging. Washington, 1963.
224p. (88th Cong., 1st sess. Senate. Report no. 8)
1. Old age. 2. Housing for the aged. 3. Nursing homes. I. Title: A study of the problems of the aged and aging. II. Title.

333.334
L45
A study of the problems of abandoned housing.
Linton, Mields and Coston.
A study of the problems of abandoned housing. Washington, 1971.
301p.
Bibliography: Appx C. p. 1-24.
U.S. Dept. of Housing and Urban Development. Low-income Housing Demonstration Grant.

(Cont'd on next card)

630
Uni
A study of the social and economic implications of the large scale introduction...
United Nations Research Institute for Social Development.
A study of the social and economic implications of the large scale introduction of high-yielding varieties of foodgrain; a selection of readings; an Institute staff study, by Antonio Barreto. Geneva, 1971.
173p. (Report no. 71.6)

1. Agriculture. I. Barreto, Antonio. II. Title.

388
(77841)
G45
v.2
Study of transit service.
Gilman (W.C.) and Co.
Study of transit service; Greater Kansas City Metropolitan area. Volume II: Conclusions and recommendations. Prepared for Metropolitan Planning Commission, Kansas City Region. New York, 1966.
1v.
U.S. Dept. of Housing and Urban Development. UPAP.
U.S. Urban Renewal Adm. UPAP.
1. Transportation - Kansas City, Mo. I. Kansas City, Mo. Metropolitan Planning Commission. II. Title. III. U.S. HUD-UPAP. Kansas City, Mo.

333.334
L45
A study of the problems of abandoned housing.
Linton, Mields and Coston. A study...
(Card 2)

1. Abandoned buildings - St. Louis.
2. Abandoned buildings - Chicago.
3. Abandoned buildings - New Orleans.
4. Abandoned buildings - Oakland, Calif.
I. U.S. HUD. Low-income Housing Demonstration Grant. II. Title.
III. Title: Abandoned housing.

388
W17st
A study of the social, economic and environmental impact of highway transportation ...
Washington (State) State University, Pullman.
A study of the social, economic and environmental impact of highway transportation facilities on urban communities. Prepared for Washington State Dept. of Highways in cooperation with the U.S. Bureau of Public Roads...Pullman, Highway Research Section, Engineering Research Div., Washington State University, 1968.
208p.

(Cont'd on next card)

VF
711.729
(753)
D22
A study of transit fringe parking usage.
Deen, Thomas B
A study of transit fringe parking usage. Wash., Alan M. Voorhees and Associates, inc., 1965.
40p.

1. Parking - District of Columbia. 2. Journey to work. I. Voorhees (Alan M.) and Associates, inc., Washington, D.C. II. Title.

352
L18
A study of the role, organization and intergovernmental relationships of the Mid-America Council of Governments.
Lawrence-Leiter and Co.
A study of the role, organization and intergovernmental relationships of the Mid-America Council of Governments. Prepared for the Mid-America Council of Governments. Kansas City, Mo., 1969.
112p.

1. Intergovernmental relations. 2. Local government. 3. Mid-America Council of Governments. I. Title.

388
W17st
Washington (State) State University, Pullman. A study...1968. (Card 2)

1. Transportation - Economic effect. 2. Highways. I. Washington (State) Dept. of Highways. II. Title.

388
P65
The study of transportation requirement.
Polenske, Karen R
The study of transportation requirement using national and multiregional input-output techniques. Cambridge, Harvard Economic Research Project, 1967.
71p.
Prepared for the Secretary of Transportation under contract.
Distributed by U.S. Clearinghouse for Federal Scientific and Technical Information as document PB 174 742
1. Transportation - Economic effect. 2. Industry - Statistics. I. Harvard Economic Research Project. (Cont'd on next card)

332.72
S78
Study of the Savings and Loan Industry.
Submitted to the Federal Home Loan Bank Board. Washington, Govt. Print. Off., 1970.
4v.
Directed by Irwin Friend, University of Pennsylvania, Wharton School of Finance and Commerce.
c.1
40.66
1. Savings and loan associations. I. Friend, Irwin. II. U.S. Federal Home Loan Bank Board. III. Pennsylvania. University. Wharton School of Finance and Commerce.

690.022
C15
A study of the structural problems of the housebuilding industry.
California. University. Bureau of Business and Economic Research.
A study of the structural problems of the housebuilding industry in the San Francisco-Oakland metropolitan area, by Sherman J. Maisel, assisted by Jack D. Rogers. Berkeley, Calif., Aug. 1951.
1 v.(various pagings) forms, tables.
Research Project no. O-E-50, Housing and Home Finance Agency.
Project director, Sherman J. Maisel; staff technician, E. Everett Ashley.
Bibliographical footnotes.
Processed.

388
P65
Polenske, Karen R The study of transportation requirement...1967. (Card 2)

II. U.S. Dept. of Transportation. III. U.S. Clearinghouse for Federal Scientific and Technical Information. IV. Title.

332.72
F74
Summary
Study of the savings and loan industry.
Friend, Irwin.
Study of the savings and loan industry; summary and recommendations. Wash., Federal Home Loan Bank Board, 1969.
79p.

1. Savings and loan associations. I. U.S. Federal Home Loan Bank Board. II. Title.

711.74
(764)
H68s
A study of thoroughfare development in the southeast area ...
Houston, Texas. City Planning Commission.
A study of thoroughfare development in the southeast area of Metropolitan Houston and Harris County. Houston, 1963.
13p.

1. Streets - Houston, Tex. 2. Highways - Houston, Tex. 3. Transportation - Houston, Tex. 4. Journey to work. I. Title.

370
(773)
I55s
A study of urban education.
Illinois. School Problems Commission.
A study of urban education. A report by the Urban Studies Sub-Committee of the Tenth School Problems Commission, State of Illinois [Springfield] 1969.
59p.

Bibliography: p. 56-59.

1. Education - Ill. I. Title.

711.583
H68com
no.4
A study of the Seattle Unicenter.
U.S. Dept. of Housing and Urban Development.
A study of the Seattle Unicenter. [Prepared by Booz-Allen and Hamilton] Wash., 1972.
108p. (Community development evaluation series no. 4)

1. Community development. 2. Labor supply - Seattle. 3. Intergovernmental relations. I. Booz-Allen and Hamilton. II. Title. (Series: Community development evaluation series no. 4)

690.24
G72s
A study of the variables involved in the saturating of roofing felts.
Greenfield, Sidney H
A study of the variables involved in the saturating of roofing felts. Wash., Building Research Div., Institute for Applied Technology, National Bureau of Standards, 1969.
16p. (U.S. Institute for Applied Technology. Building Research Div. Building science series 19)
1. Roofs and roofing. 2. Building materials - Climatic effects.
(Cont'd on next card)

728.1
(72951)
C67
Study of urban housing in Latin America;
Cornell University. Center for Housing and Environmental Studies.
Study of urban housing in Latin America; preliminary report on San Juan Pilot Study. [Ithaca, N.Y.] 1967.
213p.

1. Housing - San Juan, P.R. I. Title.

621.39
B67s
A study of the single emergency telephone number.
Bordner, Kenneth R
A study of the single emergency telephone number, by Kenneth R. Bordner and J. Spenser Huston. Philadelphia, Franklin Institute Research Laboratories, 1970.
28p.

1. Communication systems. 2. Disaster services. 3. Municipal services. I. Huston, J. Spenser, jt. au. II. Franklin Institute Research Laboratories. III. Title.

690.24
G72s
Greenfield, Sidney H study...1969. (Card 2)

I. U.S. Institute for Applied Technology. Building Research Div. II. Title.

711.400.15
H18s
The study of urbanization.
Hauser, Philip Morris, 1909- ed.
The study of urbanization, edited by Philip M. Hauser and Leo F. Schnore. New York, Wiley, 1965.
554p.

1. City planning - Research. 2. City growth. 3. Sociology, Urban. 4. Economic development. I. Schnore, Leo Francis, 1927- jt. ed. II. Title.

621.32 C62s

A study of user preferences for fluorescent lamp colours for daytime and night-time lighting.
Cockram, A H
A study of user preferences for fluorescent lamp colours for daytime and night-time lighting, by A.H. Cockram and others. Garston, Eng., Building Research Station, 1971.
[8]p. (Current paper no. 13/71)

Reprinted from: Lighting research and technology, vol. 2, no. 4, 1970, pp. 249-256.

1. Lighting. I. U.K. Building Research Station. II. Title.

---

388 (79495) P56

A study to determine improvements to the San Bernardino municipal transit system.
Plotkin (H.M.) and Associates.
A study to determine improvements to the San Bernardino municipal transit system for increasing employment opportunities to residents of depressed areas. Prepared for the City of San Bernardino. San Bernardino, Calif., 1968.
88p.
U.S. Mass Transportation Demonstration Grant Program.
Bibliography: p. 84-85.
1. Transportation - San Bernardino, Calif. 2. Journey to work. 3. Employment - San Bernardino, Calif.
(Cont'd on next card)

---

330 (7443) L67

Sturbridge, Mass. Planning Board.
Lord (E.H.)- Wood Associates.
Town of Sturbridge, Massachusetts: basic studies report. Prepared for Sturbridge Planning Board. Hartford, 1964.
59p.
U.S. Urban Renewal Adm. UPAP.

1. Economic base studies - Sturbridge, Mass. I. Sturbridge, Mass. Planning Board. II. U.S. URA-UPAP. Sturbridge, Mass.

---

333 P81st

Study of withdrawals and reservations of public domain lands.
U.S. Public Land Law Review Commission.
Study of withdrawals and reservations of public domain lands. Wash., [1969?]
2v.

1. Public lands. 2. Land use. I. Title.

---

388 (79495) P56

Plotkin (H.M.) and Associates.   A study... 1968.   (Card 2)

I. Title. II. U.S. Mass Transportation Demonstration Grant Program. San Bernardino, Calif.

711.4 (7443) S78

Sturbridge, Mass. Planning Board.
Lord (E.H.)-Wood Associates.
Town of Sturbridge, Massachusetts, comprehensive plan report. Prepared for Sturbridge Planning Board. Hartford, 1965.
46p.
U.S. Urban Renewal Adm. UPAP.

1. Master plan - Sturbridge, Mass. I. Sturbridge, Mass. Planning Board. II. U.S. URA-UPAP. Sturbridge, Mass.

711.73 (711) B74

A study on highway planning.
British Columbia. Technical Committee for Metropolitan Planning.
A study on highway planning. Part 1. Surveys for the metropolitan area of the lower mainland of British Columbia. Part 2. Freeways with rapid transit for metropolitan Vancouver, British Columbia. Vancouver, B.C., 1959.
pts.

1. Highways - British Columbia. 2. Metropolitan area planning - British Columbia. I. Title.

339.3 (742) B68

A study to identify low income areas in New Hampshire.
Bowring, James R
A study to identify low income areas in New Hampshire; background data, by James R. Bowring and Kenneth A. Taylor. Durham, University of New Hampshire, Dept. of Resource Economics, 1965.
59p. (University of New Hampshire, Dept. of Resource Economics. Resource economics research mimeo. no. 36)
1. Income - New Hampshire. 2. Economic conditions - New Hampshire. I. Taylor, Kenneth A., jt. au. II. New Hampshire. University. III. Title.

---

650 :325 S78

Sturdivant, Frederick D
Business and the Mexican-American community. [n.p.] 1969.
[8]p.

Reprinted from California management review, 1969, p. 73-80.

1. Business - Minority groups. I. California management review. II. Title: Mexican-American community. III. Title.

693.5 N14

Study on load-deflection characteristics of prestressed concrete structures.
Nakano, Kiyoshi.
Study on load-deflection characteristics of prestressed concrete structures. Tokyo, Building Research Institute, Ministry of Construction, Japanese Government, 1965.
33p. (Japan. Building Research Institute. BRI occasional report no. 24)

1. Concrete construction. 2. Concrete, Prestressed. I. U.K. Building Research Station. II. Title.

728.1 :308 UNs 1964

Study tour of the United States of America.
United Nations. (Economic Commission for Europe. Committee on Housing, Building and Planning)
Study tour of the United States of America, June 6-18, 1964. [New York] 1964.
38p. (United Nations. [Document] HOU/118)
Summary of final "Round Up" prepared by the U.S. Housing and Home Finance Agency.

1. Housing market. I. U.S. Housing and Home Finance Agency. II. Title.

LAW T S787TR

STURGES, WESLEY A
A TREATISE ON COMMERCIAL ARBITRATIONS AND AWARDS. KANSAS CITY, MO., VERNON LAW BOOK, 1930.
1082P.

1. COMMERCIAL LAW. 2. AWARDS. I. TITLE: COMMERCIAL ARBITRATIONS.

---

388 D19

Study on new systems of urban transportation.
Day and Zimmerman, inc., Philadelphia.
Potential near term improvements in urban transportation. Prepared for U.S. Department of Housing and Urban Development. [Philadelphia] 1968.
304p.
On cover: Study in new systems of urban transportation.
1. Transportation. 2. Eminent domain. 3. Transportation - Automation. I. U.S. Dept. of Housing and Urban Development. II. Title. III. Title: Study on new systems of urban transportation.

---

308 W17

Studying your community.
Warren, Roland Leslie.
Studying your community. New York, Free Press, 1965.
385p. (A Free Press paperback)
Originally supported and published by Russell Sage Foundation.
List of Agencies: Governmental, Washington, D.C. p. 363-369.

1. Social surveys. 2. Social surveys - Citizen participation. 3. City planning. 4. Housing. 5. Community development. I. Russell Sage Foundation. II. Title.

333.33 B76

STURGESS, ALBERT HENLEY, JT. AU.
BROWN, ROBERT KEVIN.
REAL ESTATE PRIMER, BY ROBERT K. BROWN AND A.H. STURGESS, SR. ENGLEWOOD CLIFFS, N.J., PRENTICE-HALL, 1966.
249P.

1. REAL ESTATE BUSINESS. I. STURGESS, ALBERT HENLEY, JT. AU. II. TITLE.

699.844 K83

A study on the collective noise source.
Kuga, Shinichi.
A study on the collective noise source. [Tokyo] Building Research Institute, Ministry of Construction, 1968.
42p. (Japan. Building Research Institute. Research paper no. 30)

1. Architectural acoustics. I. Japan. Building Research Institute. II. Title.

691.421 S78

STULL, RAY T
LOW-COST GLAZES FOR STRUCTURAL CLAY PRODUCTS, BY RAY STULL AND PAUL V. JOHNSON. WASHINGTON, U.S. NATIONAL BUREAU OF STANDARDS, 1942.
20P.

1. CLAY. I. U.S. NATIONAL BUREAU OF STANDARDS. II. JOHNSON, PAUL V., JT. AU. III. TITLE: GLAZES FOR STRUCTURAL CLAY PRODUCTS.

Ref. 720 (03) S78

Sturgis, Russell.
A dictionary of architecture and building: biographical, historical and descriptive. New York, Macmillan, 1902.
3 v. illus.

Republished by Gale Research Company, 1966.
Bibliography: v. 3, columns 1141-1212.

(Continued on next card)

---

674 S15

Study on the utilization of forest products in construction.
Salokangas, Raimo.
Puun käyttö rakennusalalla (Study on the utilization of forest products in construction) by Raimo Salokangas et al. Helsinki, State Institute for Technical Research, 1970.
83p. (Finland. State Institute for Technical Research. Tiedotus. Sarja III - Rakennus 146)
English summary.

1. Lumber industry. I. Finland. State Institute for Technical Research. II. Title: Study on the utilization of forest products in construction.

---

300 S78

Stulman, Julius
Fields within fields within fields; man, mankind, the universe; the methodology of the creative process. Illustrated and designed by Don Stacy. New York, The World Institute, 1968.
33p.
On cover: Singular system organization synthesis metamorphosis.
vol. 1, no. 1, Spring 1968, and vol. 1, No. 2, 1968
1. Social sciences. 2. Social conditions. I. Title.

Ref. 720 (03) S78

Sturgis, Russell.
A dictionary of architecture and building: ....   (Card 2)

1. Architecture - Dictionaries. 2. Architecture - History - Dictionaries. 3. Building construction - Dictionaries. 4. Architecture - Biography. I. Title.

ml/jb

711.14
(769885)
878
Sturgis, Ky. City Planning Commission.
Existing land-use analysis, City
of Sturgis, Kentucky. Sturgis, [1960?]
7p.
Prepared with the assistance of the
Division of Planning and Zoning, Kentucky
Dept. of Economic Development.
U.S. Urban Renewal Adm. UPAP.
1. Land use - Sturgis, Ky. I. U.S.
URA-UPAP. Sturgis, Ky.

691.54
S68C
STUTTERHEIM, NIKO.
SOUTH AFRICAN COUNCIL FOR SCIENTIFIC
AND INDUSTRIAL RESEARCH.
CEMENT FROM BLASTFURNACE SLAG, BY N.
STUTTERHEIM. PRETORIA, 1964.
3P. (CSIR REFERENCE NO. R BOU 108)

REPRINTED FROM THE 1963/64 SOUTH
AFRICAN REVIEW.

1. CEMENT. I. STUTTERHEIM, NIKO.

711.4
(437)
878
Štván, Jaromír.
Urbanization and urban pattern.
Prague, Research Institute for Building and
Architecture VUVA, Dept. for Physical Planning,
Brno, 1967.
1v.
Bibliography: p. 3-28, appendix.

1. City growth - Czechslovakia. 2. City
planning - Czechslovakia. I. Prague. Research Intitute for Building and Architecture. II. Title.

711.4
(769885)
878
Sturgis, Ky. Planning Commission.
Kentucky. Dept. of Commerce. Div. of
Planning and Zoning.
General plan, Sturgis, Kentucky.
[Prepared for Sturgis Planning Commission]
[Frankfort, Ky?] 1965.
96p.
U.S. Urban Renewal Adm. UPAP.

1. Master plan - Sturgis, Ky.
I. Sturgis, Ky. Planning Commission.
II. U.S. URA-UPAP. Sturgis, Ky.

728
:551.5
I77d
Stutterheim, N.
Israel Institute of Technology. (Building
Research Station)
Deterioration of concrete in hot dry regions due to excessive shrinkage of aggregates. Deterioration de beton dans les
regions chaudes et seches causee par le
retrait excessif des agregats, by N. Stutterheim. Haifa, Israel, 1960.
16p. illus., diagrs.

International Symposium on Concrete and Reinforced
Concrete in Hot Countries, 17-19 July 1960.
1. Architecture and   climate. 2. Concrete
aggregates.   I. Stutterheim, N.

720
(09)
M12
Style and society; architectural ideology in
Britain, 1835-1914.
MacLeod, Robert.
Style and society; architectural ideology in
Britain, 1835-1914. London, Royal Institute
of British Architects, 1971.
144p.

1. Architecture - History. 2. Architecture -
U.K. I. Royal Institute of British Architects.
II. Title.

VF
711.4
(77419)
S78
Sturgis, Mich. Plan Board.
An area plan for Sturgis, Mich.; prepared
by Sturgis Plan Board and Scott Bagby, City
Planning Consultant. [Sturgis, Mich., Feb.
1955]
58 p. plans.

1.Master plan - Sturgis, Mich. I.Bagby, Scott.

691.542
S68
Stutterheim, Niko.
South African Council for Scientific and In-
dustrial Research. National Building
Research Institute.
Properties and uses of high-magnesia port-
land slag cement concretes, by Niko Stutter-
heim. Pretoria, 1960.
[19]p. illus., diagrs., tables.

Reprinted from Journal of the American Concrete
Institute, April 1960; Proceedings v. 56, p. 1027-
1045.

1. Portland cement. I. Stutterheim, Niko.

LAW
T
D671C0
STYLE MANUAL.
DORIS, LILLIAN
CORPORATE SECRETARY'S MANUAL AND
GUIDE. REV. ED., BY LILLIAN DORIS AND
EDITH J. FRIEDMAN, COMPLETELY REVISED
BY HOWARD HILTON SPELLMAN. NEW YORK,
PRENTICE-HALL, 1952.
1520P.

1. CORPORATIONS. 2. STYLE MANUAL.
I. FRIEDMAN, EDITH J. II. SPELLMAN,
HOWARD HILTON. III. TITLE.

LAW
S
(Ariz.)
Sturm, Albert L
Recent trends in State constitutional
revision. An address prepared for delivery
on October 12, 1964 on revision of Arizona's
Constitution. Sponsored by the Arizona
Academy, Grand Canyon, Ariz., October 12-14,
1964. Tempe, Ariz., Bureau of Government
Research, Arizona State University, 1965.
16p. (Arizona State University. Bureau
of Government Research. Public affairs
series no. 11)

1. Constitutional   law - Ariz. 2. Constitution, State.   I. Arizona. University.
Bureau of Government   Research. II. Title.

690
(43)
S78
Stuttgart. Institut für Technische Physik.
Veröffentlichungen.
Stuttgart,
v.

For complete information see shelflist.

1. Building methods. 2. Building materials - Germany.

652
G68a
1967
Style manual (abridged).
U.S. Government Printing Office.
Style manual (abridged) Issued by the
Public Printer, under authority of section
51 of an act of Congress approved January 12,
1895. Rev. Washington, 1967.
286p.

1. Style manuals. 2. Printing and publishing. I. Title.

388
t331
S78
Sturt, Alan R
The relationship between distance and
commuting to central London, 1951-1961.
London, London School of Economics and
Political Science, Graduate Geography Dept.,
1968.
12p. (London School of Economics and
Political Science. Graduate School of Economics and Political Science. Discussion
paper no. 25)
1. Journey to work. 2. Transportation - U.K.
3. U.K. - Transportation. I. London School of
Economics and Political Science. Graduate
School of   Geography. II. Title.

711
(016)
C65
no.173
Stutz, Frederick P
Research on intra-urban social travel:
introduction and bibliography. San Diego,
San Diego State College, Dept. of Geography,
1971.
12p. (Council of Planning Librarians.
Exchange bibliography no. 173)

1. Planning - Bibl. 2. Traffic surveys -
Bibl. I. California. State College, San
Diego. II. Title: Intra-urban social travel.
(Series: Council of Planning Librarians.
Exchange bibliography no. 173)

Style manuals
x Writing
aa Letter-writing
aa Report writing

325.3
(016)
S54
STURTEVANT, WILLIAM C , COMP.
SMITHSONIAN INSTITUTION. BUREAU OF
AMERICAN ETHNOLOGY.
SELECTED REFERENCES ON INDIANS.
COMPILED BY WILLIAM C. STURTEVANT.
WASHINGTON, 1958-59.
2PTS.
CONTENTS.- PT. 1 SELECTED REFERENCES
ON FEDERAL INDIAN POLICY AND
ADMINISTRATION. 1959.- PT. 2. SELECTED
REFERENCES ON PRESENT-DAY CONDITIONS
AMONG U.S. INDIANS. 1958.
1. INDIANS - BIBLIOGRAPHY.
I. STURTEVANT, WILLIAM C., COMP.
II. TITLE.

711.585
R611
STUYVESANT TOWN.
ROBERTS, ROSEMOND G
3000 FAMILIES MOVE TO MAKE WAY FOR
STUYVESANT TOWN, A STORY OF TENANT
RELOCATION BUREAU, INC. NEW YORK,
JAMES FELT & CO., 1946.
23P.

1. SLUM CLEARANCE. 2. URBAN
RENEWAL. I. TITLE: STUYVESANT TOWN.
II. TITLE.

652
A52
Style manuals.
Anderson, Ruth I
130 basic typing jobs, by Ruth I. Anderson
and Leonard J. Porter. Englewood Cliffs, N. J.,
Prentice-Hall, 1960.
31p.

1. Letter writing. 2. Style manuals.
I. Porter, Leonard J., jt. su.

Stutterheim, N
690.015
(68)
S68b
South African Council for Scientific and Industrial Research. National Building Research Institute.
Building research and the municipal engineer, by N. Stutterheim. Pretoria, 1960.
15p.

Reprinted from the Institution of Municipal Engineers Annual journal, vol. 1, no. 13, January
1960.

1. Building research - Union of South Africa.
I. Stutterheim, N.

711.585
(7471)
N282
STUYVESANT TOWN CORPORATION.
NEW YORK (STATE) SUPREME COURT.
STUYVESANT TOWN CORPORATION'S
REDEVELOPMENT PROJECT; OPINION OF
THE N.Y. SUPREME COURT IN PRATT VS LA
GUARDIA ET AL. DECIDED ON MARCH 17,
1944. NATIONAL HOUSING AGENCY, OFFICE
OF THE GENERAL COUNSEL, 1944.
6L.

1. URBAN RENEWAL - NEW YORK (CITY)
2. MINORITY GROUPS - HOUSING.
I. STUYVESANT TOWN CORPORATION.
II. TITLE.

Style manuals.
R
029
C15
Campbell, William Giles.
A form book for thesis writing. Boston,
Houghton Mifflin, 1939.
1v. diagrs., tables.

1. Style manuals. 2. Theses.

Ref.
652
C34
1969
Style manuals.
Chicago. University.
A manual of style. 12th ed., rev. Chicago,
University of Chicago Press, 1969.
546p.
Bibliography: p. 513-520.

1. Style manuals. I. Title.

652
T14
1964
Style manuals.
Teintor, Sarah Auguste.
The secretary's handbook; a manual of
correct usage, by Sarah Auguste Teintor
and Kate M. Monro. 8th ed., completely rev.
New York, Macmillian, 1964.
559p.

1. Letter-writing. 2. Style manuals.
I. Monro, Kate M., jt. au. II. Title.

R
652
G68
Style manuals.
U.S. Government Printing Office.
Style manual, 1939, 1945, 1953. Rev.
Washington, Govt. Print. Off., 1939-
v.
Library keeps latest ed., only.
For complete information see shelflist.

1. Style manuals.

1949 - 00209 (00487, 00210 missing 3/13/57)
1953 - 7 c - (Keep 1 only when superseded unless
accessioned)

652
C34
1949
STYLE MANUALS.
Chicago. University. University Press.
A manual of style, containing typographical and
other rules for authors, printers, and publishers
recommended by the University of Chicago Press,
together with specimens of type. 11th ed.
Chicago, 1949.
534 p. illus.

1. Style manuals. I. Title.

jm

R
029
T87
Style manuals.
Turabian, Kate L
A manual for writers of term papers, theses
and dissertations. Rev. Chicago, U. of
Chicago Press, 1958.
82p. tables.

1. Style manuals. 2. Theses. I. Title.

652
G68a
Style manuals.
U.S. Government Printing Office.
Style manual (abridged). Rev. Washing-
ton, Govt. Print. Off., 1959.
280p.

1. Style manuals.

651.4
L17
1959
Style manuals.
Larsen, Lenna Andrea, 1894-
Reference manual for office employees,
by Lenna A. Larsen and Apollonia M. Koebele.
4th ed. Cincinnati, South-western Pub. Co.,
1959.
150p.

Previous editions published under title:
Stenographer's reference manual.

1. Office management. 2. Style manuals.
3. Letter writing. I. Koebele,
Apollonia M., jt. au. II. Title.

029
T87
1960
STYLE MANUALS.
TURABIAN, KATE L
A MANUAL FOR WRITERS OF TERM PAPERS,
THESES AND DISSERTATIONS. CHICAGO,
UNIVERSITY OF CHICAGO PRESS, 1960.
110P. (A PHOENIX BOOKS PAPERBACK
SERIES)

1. STYLE MANUALS. I. TITLE.

652
G68
Suppl.
Style manuals.
U.S. Government Printing Office.
Word division. 5th ed. Washington,
1954.
124.

Supplement to Government Printing Office
Style manual.

1. Style manuals.

R
652
N28
Style manuals.
New York times.
The New York times style book for writers
and editors. Edited and revised by Lewis
Jordan. New York, McGraw-Hill, 1962.
124p.

1. Style manuals. 2. Printing and publishing. 3. Copying processes. 4. Report writing.
I. Jordan, Lewis. II. Title.

Ref.
029
T87
1967
Style manuals.
Turabian, Kate L
A manual for writers of term papers, theses,
and dissertations. 3d ed rev. Chicago,
University of Chicago Press, 1967.
164p. (Phoenix books)

1. Style manuals. 2. Theses. I. Title.

652
G68
1962
Suppl.
Style manuals.
U.S. Government Printing Office.
Word division. 6th ed. Washington, 1962.
190p.

Supplement to Government Printing Office
style manual.

1. Style manuals. I. Title.

424
062
STYLE MANUALS.
OPDYCKE, JOHN B
MARK MY WORD; A GUIDE TO MODERN USAGE
AND EXPRESSION. NEW YORK, HARPER, 1949.
687P.

1. ENGLISH LANGUAGE. 2. STYLE MANUALS.

652
A47
Style manuals.
U.S. Air Force.
Preparing and processing written
communications. Washington, 1965.
55p. (Air Force manual no. 10-1)
At head of title: Air Force manual:
written communications.

1. Letter writing. 2. Style manuals.
3. Management - Study and teaching.
I. Title: Written communications.

070.44
N17
Style manuals.
U.S. National Archives and Records Service.
Federal Register handbook on document
drafting. Washington, General Services
Administration, National Archives and Record
Services, Office of the Federal Register,
1966.
63p.

1. Report writing. 2. Style manuals.
3. Office procedures. I. Title.

652
S44
STYLE MANUALS
SKILLIN, MARJORIE E
WORDS INTO TYPE, A GUIDE IN THE
PREPARATION OF MANUSCRIPTS FOR WRITERS,
EDITORS, PROOFREADERS AND PRINTERS. BASED
ON STUDIES BY MARJORIE E. SKILLIN, ROBERT
M. GAY, AND OTHER AUTHORITIES. NEW REV.
ED. NEW YORK, APPLETON-CENTURY-CROFTS,
1964.
596P.

1. STYLE MANUALS. I. GAY,
ROBERT M., JT. AU. II. TITLE.

R
655.03
V65
Style manuals.
U.S. Government Printing Office.
Manual of foreign languages for the use of librarians,
bibliographers, research workers, editors, translators, and
printers, by George F. von Ostermann. 4th ed., rev. and
enl. New York, Central Book Co., 1952.
414 p. illus. 24 cm.
First published in 1934 under title: Foreign languages for the use
of printers and translators.

1. Printing, Practical—Style-manuals. I. Von Ostermann, George
Frederick, 1873- ed. II. Title.

Z253.U581 1952   655.25   52-2409

Library of Congress   [53x10]

020.44
C65
Style manuals.
U.S. Committee on Scientific and Technical
Information.
Guidelines to format standards for scientific
and technical reports prepared by or for the
Federal Government. Wash., 1968.
16p.
CFSTI PB 180 600.

1. Report writing. 2. Style manuals.
I. Title.

652
S76e
Style manuals.
Strunk, William Jr.
The elements of style. With revisions,
an introduction, and a new chapter on
writing, by E. B. White. New York,
Macmillan, 1959.
71p.

1. Style manuals. I. White, E. B.

652
G68a
1967
Style manuals.
U.S. Government Printing Office.
Style manual (abridged) Issued by the
Public Printer, under authority of section
51 of an act of Congress approved January 12,
1895. Rev. Washington, 1967.
286p.

1. Style manuals. 2. Printing and publishing. I. Title.

728.1
:362.6
(74811)
N17
The style of life in urban, high-rise low-
rent buildings for the independent
elderly.
Nash, George.
The style of life in urban, high-rise low-
rent buildings for the independent elderly, by
George Nash and Patricia Nash. Philadelphia,
Philadelphia Geriatric Center and Columbia
University Bureau of Applied Social Research,
1968.
40p.

1. Housing for the aged - Philadelphia.
2. Old age - Social service. I. Nash, Patricia. II. Philadelphia Geriatric Center.
III. Columbia University. Bureau of
Applied Research. IV. Title.

711.4
(016)
C15c

Styles, Frederick G , comp.
California. University. Dept. of City and Regional Planning.
The concept of the ideal urban form; a selected bibliography of recent theorists of urban form, comp. by Frederick G. Styles. Rev. [Berkeley] 1958.
18p.

1. City planning - Bibliographies.
2. Regional planning - Bibliographies.
I. Styles, Frederick G , comp.

VF
711.73
A15

Subdivision.
Abner, Carl E
Report on the costs of developing roads in subdivisions. [Louisville, Ky.] June 1954.
8 p. tables.

Prepared for the Louisville and Jefferson County Planning and Zoning Commission.

1. Subdivisions. 2. Road construction.
I. Louisville and Jefferson Co., Ky. Planning and Zoning Commission. II. Title: Costs of developing roads i subdivisions.

711.333
(74921)
B27L

SUBDIVISION.
BERGEN CO., N.J. COUNTY PLANNING BOARD.
LAND SUBDIVISION, BERGEN COUNTY. HACKENSACK, 1939.
25P.

1. COUNTY PLANNING - BERGEN CO., N.J.
2. SUBDIVISION. I. TITLE.

920
C51w

STYRON, WILLIAM. THE CONFESSIONS OF NAT TURNER.
Clarke, John Henrik, ed.
William Styron's Nat Turner; ten black writers respond. Boston, Beacon Press, 1968.
120p.
Appendix (p. [93]-117): The text of the Confessions of Nat Turner.

1. Styron, William. The confessions of Nat Turner. I. Turner, Nat, 1800? - 1831. The confessions of Nat Turner. II. Title.

VF
T
A5207p

Subdivision.
Anderson, Robert M
Planning, zoning and subdivision: a summary of statutory law in the 50 states, by Robert M. Anderson and Bruce B. Roswig. Albany, New York State Federation of Official Planning Organizations, 1966.
231p.

1. Planning - New York (State) 2. Zoning - New York (State) 3. Subdivision, 4. Planning - Legislation. I. Roswig, Bruce B., jt. au. II. New York State Federation of Official Planning Organizations. III. Title.

711.14
B27

SUBDIVISION.
Bestor, George C
The challenge of residential land planning. Chicago, Mobile Homes Manufacturers Association, 1967.
[66]p.
Reprinted and distributed by Mobile Homes Manufacturers Association from the Journal of the Urban Planning and Development Division, Proceedings of the American Society of Civil Engineers, vol. 93, no. UP2, June 1967, p. 27-92.
(Cont'd on next card)

693.97
L23

THE SUBASSEMBLAGE METHOD OF DESIGNING UNBRACED MULTI-STORY FRAMES.
LEHIGH UNIVERSITY, BETHLEHEM, PA. FRITZ ENGINEERING LABORATORY.
THE SUBASSEMBLAGE METHOD OF DESIGNING UNBRACED MULTI-STORY FRAMES, BY J. HARTLEY DANIELS AND LE-WU LU. BETHLEHEM, 1966.
97P. (FRITZ ENGINEERING LABORATORY REPORT NO. 273.37)

1. STEEL CONSTRUCTION. I. DANIELS, J. HARTLEY. II. LU, LE-WU. III. TITLE.

333.38
A74c

Subdivision.
Arkansas. University. City Planning Division.
A guide for subdividers, Clarksville. [Prepared for Clarksville City Planning Commission] [Fayetteville, Ark.] 1959.
1v. diagrs.
U.S. Urban Renewal Administration, Urban Planning Assistance Program.

1. Subdivision. I. Clarksville, Ark. City Planning Commission. II. U.S. URA-UPAP. Clarksville, Ark.

711.14
B27

Bestor, George C The challenge...1967.
(Card 2)

Proc. paper 5264.

1. Land use. 2. Subdivision. 3. Zoning. I. American Society of Civil Engineers. Proceedings. II. Mobile Homes Manufacturers Association. III. Title.

625.84
C65P

SUBBASES FOR CONCRETE PAVEMENTS.
COLLEY, B E
PERFORMANCE OF SUBBASES FOR CONCRETE PAVEMENTS UNDER REPETITIVE LOADING, BY B.E. COLLEY AND J.W. NOWLEN. SKOKIE, ILL., 1958.
32-58P. (PORTLAND CEMENT ASSOCIATION. RESEARCH AND DEVELOPMENT LABORATORIES. DEVELOPMENT DEPT. BULLETIN D23)

REPRINT FROM BULLETIN 202 OF THE HIGHWAY RESEARCH BOARD, 1958.

1. ROAD CONSTRUCTION.
(CONTINUED ON NEXT CARD)

333.38
A74d

Subdivision
Arkansas. University. City Planning Division.
A guide for subdividers, Dardanelle. [Prepared for] Dardanelle City Planning Commission. [Fayetteville, Ark.] 1959.
1v. diagrs.
U.S. Urban Renewal Administration, Urban Planning Assistance Program.

1. Subdivision I. Dardanelle, Ark. City Planning Commission. II. U.S. URA-UPAP. Dardanelle, Ark.

333.38
C151

SUBDIVISION.
CALIFORNIA. UNIVERSITY (LOS ANGELES) GRADUATE SCHOOL OF BUSINESS ADMINISTRATION.
THE REMOTE SUBDIVISION; ECONOMIC AND LEGAL ASPECTS OF LAND SALES PROMOTION. SUMMARY OF RESEARCH REPORTS BY CLAUDE E. ELIAS, JR. AND WILLIAM D. WARREN. LOS ANGELES, UNIVERSITY OF CALIFORNIA, REAL ESTATE RESEARCH PROGRAM, GRADUATE SCHOOL OF BUSINESS ADMINISTRATION, DIVISION OF RESEARCH, 1963.
21P. (ITS PAMPHLET NO. 2)
1. SUBDIVISION. I. TITLE. II. ELIAS, CLAUDE E., JR.

625.84
C65P

COLLEY, B E PERFORMANCE OF SUBBASES ...1958. (CARD 2)

I. PORTLAND CEMENT ASSOCIATION. II. TITLE: SUBBASES FOR CONCRETE PAVEMENTS. III. TITLE: CONCRETE PAVEMENTS.

333.38
A74m

Subdivision.
Arkansas. University. City Planning Division.
A guide for subdividers, Morrilton. [Prepared for Morrilton City Planning Commission] [Fayetteville, Ark.] 1959.
1v. diagrs.
U.S. Urban Renewal Administration, Urban Planning Assistance Program.

1. Subdivision. I. Morrilton, Ark. City Planning Commission. II. U.S. URA-UPAP. Morrilton, Ark.

VF
711.583
C25 Can.

Land Subdivision.
Central Mortgage and Housing Corporation.
Housing design. Ottawa, 1952-1953.
2 pts. graphs, maps, plans, tables.
"Previously appeared as a supplement to the Journal of the Royal Architectural Institute of Canada and as a supplement to the Community Planning Review" - cover.
1. Community planning. 2. Housing projects. 3. Land subdivision. 4. Architecture, domestic- Design. I. Title.

Sub-contractors register
see
Contractors register

333.38
A74

Subdivision.
Arkansas. University. City Planning Division.
A guide for subdividers, Russellville. [Prepared for Russellville City Planning Commission] [Fayetteville, Ark.] 1959.
1v. diagrs.
U.S. Urban Renewal Administration, Urban Planning Assistance Program.

1. Subdivision. I. Russellville, Ark. City Planning Commission. II. U.S. URA-UPAP. Russellville, Ark.

333.38
C47

SUBDIVISION.
CITY HOUSING CORPORATION.
SUNNYSIDE GARDENS; A HOME COMMUNITY. NEW YORK, 1930.
16P.

1. SUBDIVISION. I. TITLE.

Subdivision
  x   Land subdivision
  xx   City growth
  xx   City planning
  xx   Real estate business
  xx   Real property
  sa   Suburbs

711.4
:333.38
(768865)
A73

Subdivision.
Athens, Tenn. Regional Planning Commission.
Subdivision standards for the Athens, Tennessee, planning region [proposed] Assisted by the Tennessee State Planning Commission, East Tennessee Office. Athens, 1956.
24p. maps.
Urban Renewal Administration, Urban Planning Assistance Program.

1. City planning - Athens, Tenn. 2. Subdivision. I. Tennessee. State Planning Commission. II. U.S. Urban Renewal Administration.

711.5
(781)
C65

Subdivision.
Community Studies, inc.
Zoning and subdivision study. Prepared for Johnson-Wyandotte [Kan.] Regional Planning Commission. Kansas City, Mo., 1960.
245p.

U.S. Urban Renewal Adm. UPAP.

1. Zoning - Johnson—Wyandotte, Kan. 2. Subdivision. I. Johnson-Wyandotte (Kan.) Regional Planning Commission. II. U.S. URA-UPAP. Johnson - Wyandotte, Kan.

333.38
C67
c.3
Subdivision, .
Cornick, Philip H
Premature subdivision and its consequences;
a study made for the State Planning Council of
New York of the premature subdivision for urban
purposes of outlying lands in selected
metropolitan areas of New York State. New York,
Institute of Public Administration, Columbia
University, 1938.
xxi, 346 p.

Bibliography: p. 328-330
"Authorized reprint of the official report."

333.33
(794)
C15p
no.2
Elias, Claude E   The remote subdivision
and legal aspects of land sales...(Card 2)

1. Real property - California.
2. Subdivision. I. Warren, William D. jt. au.
II. California. University. University at
Los Angeles. Real Estate Research Program.

333.38
F47R
SUBDIVISION.
FISHER, ERNEST MCKINLEY.
REAL ESTATE SUBDIVIDING ACTIVITY AND
POPULATIONX GROWTH IN NINE URBAN AREAS.
ANN ARBOR, 1928.
61P. (MICHIGAN. UNIVERSITY. BUREAU
OF BUSINESS RESEARCH. MICHIGAN
BUSINESS STUDIES. V. 1, NO. 9)

1. SUBDIVISION.   2. CITY GROWTH.
(SERIES)

333.38
C67
Subdivision.
Cornick, Philip H
A report to the State Planning Council of New
York on the problems created by the premature
subdivision of urban lands in selected
metropolitan districts in the state of New York.
Albany, N.Y., Division of State Planning, Feb.,
1938.
xxi, 346 p.

Bibliography: p. 328-330.

1.Subdivision,   2.Tax delinquent land.
I.New York. State Planning Council.

333.38
E54
Subdivision.
Elias, C   Edward, Jr.
The unanchored subdivision: a preliminary
study of development practices and their
impact on California investors. Los Angeles,
Real Estate Research Program, Graduate School
of Business Administration, University of
California, 1962.
[152]p.
Partial contents:-Legal problems in the
interstate sale of promotional subdivision
land, by W.D. Warren. (Cont'd. on next card)

VF
711.4
(759)
F56
Subdivision.
Florida. University. Engineering and Industrial
Experiment Station.
Community planning and development. Proceedings
of the 7th Florida Municipal and Public Health
Engineering Conference, March 9-10, 1954, spon-
sored by the Florida State Board of Health and
Civil Engineering Department. Gainesville,
Fla., 1954.
56p. (Its Bulletin series no. 66)
1. City planning - Florida. 2. Community de-
velopment - Florida. 3. Subdivision. (Series)

333.38
C76
SUBDIVISION.
CROSSLEY, ALAN.
SUBDIVISION PLANNING. OTTAWA,
COMMUNITY PLANNING ASSOCIATION OF
CANADA, 1955.
8P.

TEXT IN ENGLISH AND FRENCH.
REPRINTED FROM COMMUNITY PLANNING
REVIEW. V. 5, NO. 3, 1955.

1. SUBDIVISION.   I. COMMUNITY
PLANNING ASSOCIATION OF CANADA.

333.38
E54
Elias, C   Edward, Jr.   The unanchored
subdivision: a preliminary study...(Card 2)

1. Subdivision. 2. Real estate business -
California. I. Warren, William D. Legal
problems in the interstate sale of promotional
subdivision land. II. California. University.
University at Los Angeles. (Real Estate
Research Program)

LAW
T
H177ca
Subdivision.
Hastings law journal.
California land use controls. San
Francisco, University, Hastings College of the
Law, 1962.
414p.

Entire issue, Feb., 1962.

1. Land use - California. 2. Subdivision.
3. Zoning - Calif. I. Title.

333.38
D25
Subdivision.
Delaware County, Pa. Planning Commission.
Subdivision in Delaware county 1951-1955.
Media, 1956.
7p. tables, charts. (Its Information
bulletin no. 10)

1. Subdivision.

711.6
F14
SUBDIVISION DESIGN.
Fairfax Co., Va. Planning Commission.
Residential subdivision design
along major arterial streets and
highways. Fairfax, 1969.
29p.

1. Subdivision design. I. Title.

VF
728.1
:940.42
I57
Subdivision.
International Union, United Automobile, Aircraft
and Agricultural Implement Workers of America
(UAW-CIO).
Homes for workers in planned communities thru
collective action.   Detroit, c1943.
62 p.   illus., plans.

1.Housing-Wartime. 2.Subdivision. I.Title.

333.38
D25
1951/58
Subdivision.
Delaware County, Pa. Planning Commission.
Subdivision in Delaware County,
1951-1958. Media, Pa., 1959.
11p. diagrs., tables. (Its Information bulletin no. 12)

1. Subdivision.

711.74
(75529)
F14
Subdivision.
Fairfax County, Va. Dept. of Public
Works. Div. of Streets, Drainage and
Subdivision Design.
Design and construction standards.
Fairfax, Va., 1963.
88p.

1. Streets - Fairfax Co., Va. 2. Streets -
Standards and specifications. 3. Subdivision. I. Title.

728.1
:308
K14
SUBDIVISION.
Kaiser, Edward John.
Toward a model of residential developer
locational behavior. Chapel Hill, Center for
Urban and Regional Studies, University of
North Carolina, 1966.
291p. (Environmental policies and urban
development thesis series no. 4)
Thesis (Doctor of Philosophy) - University
of North Carolina
Bibliography: p 284-291.
1. Housing market. 2. Subdivision. I. North
Carolina. University. II. Title. (Series:
Environmental policies and urban development
thesis series no. 4)

333.38
D71
SUBDIVISION.
DRAKE, WALTER M
SUBDIVISION SITE SELECTION TO
MANUFACTURED LOTS IN SOUTHERN
CALIFORNIA. BLOOMINGTON, IND., 1962.
36P.

1. SUBDIVISION.

333.38
F47
Subdivision.
Fisher, Ernest M
Land subdividing and the rate of utilization;
a study of the relationship between the rate at
which urban sites are created and the rate at
which they are absorbed into use with particular
reference to the Grand Rapids metropolitan region,
by Ernest M. Fisher and Raymond F. Smith.   Ann
Arbor, Mich., Univ. of Michigan, Bureau of
Business Research, 1932.
80 p.   graphs, tables.   (Michigan.
University. Bureau of Business Research. Michigan
business studies, v. 4 no. 5)

VF
711.417
(75284)
K27
Subdivision.
Kettler Brothers, inc.
Montgomery village. Washington, 1966.
[24]p.

1. New towns - Montgomery County, Md.
2. Subdivision. I. Title.

333.33
(794)
C15p
no.2
Subdivision.
Elias, Claude E
The remote subdivision; economic and
legal aspects of land sales promotion.
Summary of research reports by Claude E.
Elias, Jr. and William D. Warren. Los
Angeles, Real Estate Research Program,
Graduate School of Business Administration,
Division of Research, University of Cali-
fornia, 1963.
21p. (Real Estate Research Program,
University of California, Los Angeles.
Pamphlet no. 2)   (Cont'd. on next card)

333.38
F47S
SUBDIVISION,
FISHER, ERNEST M
SPECULATION IN SUBURBAN LANDS.   1933.
P. 152-162.

REPRINTED FROM AMERICAN ECONOMIC
REVIEW, SUPPLEMENT, V. 23, NO. 1, MARCH
1933.

1. SUBDIVISION.   2. SUBURBS.
I. TITLE.

333.38
K45
SUBDIVISION.
Kinney, Paul
Planned unit development in Orange County.
A joint study of California State College at
Fullerton and the Orange County Planning Dept.
Fullerton, Calif., 1968.
48p.

1. Subdivision. 2. Housing market - Orange
Co., Calif. I. California. State College,
Fullerton. II. Orange County, Calif. Planning
Dept. III. Title.

711.4
(764)
V42
no.8

Subdivision.
Koch & Fowler and Grefe.
Victoria comprehensive plan: subdivision manual. [Prepared for Texas State Department of Health and Victoria City Planning Commission] [Dallas, 1961?]
16p. (Its Comprehensive plan [report] 8)
U.S. Urban Renewal Adm. UPAP.

1. Master plan - Victoria, Tex. 2. Subdivision. I. Victoria, Tex. City Planning Commission. II. U.S. URA-UPAP. Victoria, Tex.

333.38
M21

SUBDIVISION.
MEADVILLE HOUSING CORPORATION. HILLCREST. MEADVILLE, PA., 1936.
24P.

1. SUBDIVISION. I. TITLE.

333.38
N671

SUBDIVISION.
NORTH CAROLINA. UNIVERSITY. INSTITUTE FOR RESEARCH IN SOCIAL SCIENCE. LOCATION DECISION FACTORS IN A PRODUCER MODEL OF RESIDENTIAL DEVELOPMENT, BY EDWARD J. KAISER. CHAPEL HILL, CENTER FOR URBAN AND REGIONAL STUDIES, INSTITUTE FOR RESEARCH IN SOCIAL SCIENCE, UNIVERSITY OF NORTH CAROLINA, 1966.
27L.

1. SUBDIVISION. 2. SITE SELECTION. I. KAISER, EDWARD J.

333.38
K67

Subdivision.
Kostka, V Joseph
Planning residential subdivisions.
[Winnipeg, 1954]
127 p. illus., diagrs., plans.
Bibliography: p. 127.
Sponsored by the Appraisal Institute of Canada.

1. Subdivision. 2. Site selection. 3. Landscape architecture. I. Appraisal Institute of Canada. II. Title.

728.1
(44)
M27

Subdivision.
Mercadel, G
Rapport methodologique sur l'elaboration d'un modele de localisation des logements neufs dans une agglomeration, por G. Mercadel and others. Puteaux, Centre d'Etudes et de Recherches sur l'Amenagement Urbain, 1967.
3v.
At head of title: Ministere de l'Equipement. Service Technique Central d'Amenagement et d'Urbanisme.

1. Housing - France. 2. Subdivision. 3. France - Housing.

(Cont'd on next card)

333.38
N67

Subdivision.
North Carolina. University. Water Research Institute.
Lake-oriented subdivisions in North Carolina: decision factors and policy implications for urban growth patterns. Raleigh, 1967.
2pts. (Its Report no. 9-10)
Contents: pt. 1. Developer decisions by Raymond J. Burby.-pt.2.Consumer decisions, by Newton W. Andrus.

1. Subdivision. 2. City planning - N.C. 3. Water resources - N.C. I. Burby, Raymond J. II. Andrus, Newton W. III. Title.

352.5
L21a

Subdivision.
League of California Cities.
Annexation and subdivision charge survey.
[Berkeley, Calif.] 1960.
28p.

1. Annexation - California. 2. Subdivision.

728.1
(44)
M27

Mercadel, G. Rapport....1967 (Card 2)

I. Centre d'Etudes et de Recherches sur l'Amenagement Urbain. II. Title.

711.33
(758)
N67

Subdivision.
Northam, Ray M
Functional regions of Georgia: their delimitation and nature, by Ray M. Northam and others. Athens, Ga., Published by Dept. of Geography and the Institute of Community and Area Development, University of Georgia, 1963.
34p. (Georgia. University. Institute of Community and Area Development. Publication no. 10)
1. State planning - Georgia. 2. Subdivision. I. Georgia. University. Institute of Community and Area Development.

711.4
(79494)
L67p
1964

Subdivision.
Los Angeles. City Planning Dept.
Planning report; procedures. Los Angeles, 1964.
[48]p.

1. City planning - Los Angeles. 2. Zoning - Los Angeles. 3. Subdivision.

333.38
M67

Subdivision.
Morrow Planning Associates.
Sample form for subdivider's agreement. Prepared for the Holmdel Planning Board. [Ridgewood, N.J.] 1958.
1v.
U.S. Urban Renewal Adm. UPAP.

1. Subdivision. I. Holmdel, N.J. Planning Board. II. U.S. URA-UPAP. Holmdel, N.J.

VF
712.41
031

Subdivision.
Ogburn, Charlton, Jr.
The battle to save the trees. Detached from Saturday Evening Post, Jan. 28, 1961. p. 28, 29, 68-70.

1. Trees. 2. Subdivision. I. Saturday Evening Post.

333.38
L67

Subdivision.
Los Angeles County, Calif. Regional Planning Commission.
Penalties of excess subdividing, by Charles D. Clark. [Los Angeles] 1934.
14p.
Reprinted from City planning, April 1934.

1. Subdivision. I. Clark, Charles D.

333.38
N17

SUBDIVISION.
NATIONAL GOLF FOUNDATION, INC.
PLANNING AND BUILDING THE GOLF COURSE. CHICAGO, 1959.
28P.

1. SUBDIVISION. 2. RECREATION. I. TITLE: GOLF COURSE.

VF
352.6
057

Subdivision.
Ontario. Dept. of Planning and Development. Community Planning Branch.
The installation of municipal services in new subdivisions. Toronto, 1954.
12,5,13 l.
Supplements to its Ontario Planning, June - July and Aug. - Sept. 1954.

1. Municipal services. 2. Subdivision. I. Title.

336.211
M12

Subdivision.
Mace, Ruth L
Do single-family homes pay their way? A comparative analysis of costs and revenues for public services, by Ruth L. Mace and Warren J. Wicker. Wash., Urban Land Institute, 1968.
47p. (Urban Land Institute. Research monograph 15)

1. Real property - Taxation. 2. Municipal services. 3. Subdivision. I. Wicker, Warren J., jt. au. II. Urban Land Institute. III. Title. (Series)

333.38
(749)
N28L

Subdivision.
New Jersey. State Planning Board.
Land subdivision in New Jersey, its extent, quality, and regulation. Trenton, 1938.
74p.

1. Subdivision. 2. State planning - N.J. I. Title.

333.332
(795)
072R

SUBDIVISION.
OREGON. STATE HIGHWAY DEPARTMENT. RESIDENTIAL SUBDIVISIONS ALONG SUBURBAN FREEWAYS GREATER PORTLAND AREA. SALEM, APRIL 1961.
32P. (LEGAL AND RIGHT OF WAY DIVISION. EDUCATIONAL REPORT NO. 3)
AT HEAD OF TITLE: VALUE TREND STUDIES.

1. REAL PROPERTY - VALUATION - OREGON. 2. SUBDIVISION. 3. HIGHWAYS - OREGON. I. TITLE. II. TITLE: VALUE STUDIES. (CONTINUED ON NEXT CARD)

333.38
M12

Subdivision
McMichael, Stanley L 1879-
Real estate subdivisions. New York, Prentice-Hall, 1949.
vi, 393 p. illus., maps, forms, plans. 24 cm. (Prentice-Hall real estate series)

"Deals largely with problems associated with the acquisition, development and sale of subdivision land": Foreword.

1. Land subdivision. 2. Cities and towns - Planning. City planning.

HD257.M14   333.33   49-6713*
Library of Congress   [20]

333.38
N28N

SUBDIVISION.
NEW CONCEPTS OF LAND SUBDIVISION USING PLANORAMA 3-DIMENSIONAL SCALE MODELS (SLIDES) WASHINGTON NATIONAL ASSOCIATION OF HOME BUILDERS, 1968.
34 COLOR SLIDES, 20P.

1. SUBDIVISION. I. NATIONAL ASSOCIATION OF HOME BUILDERS. II. TITLE: PLANORAMA.

350
(79549)
P67

Subdivision.
Portland, Or. Metropolitan Study Commission.
The metropolitan borough: what is it? A report submitted to the Portland Metropolitan Study Commission by Orbel Etter, Commission Counsel. [Portland] 1966.
23p.

1. Public administration - Portland, Or. 2. Subdivision. 3. Metropolitan government - Portland, Or. I. Title.

333.38
R26
Subdivision.
Reps, John W
Control of urban land subdivision, by John W. Reps and Jerry L. Smith. Ithaca, N.Y., Center for Housing and Environmental Studies, Div. of Urban Studies, Cornell University, 1963.
[21]p. (Cornell University. Center for Housing and Environmental Studies. Div. of Urban Studies. Article 3, reprints)
Reprinted from Syracuse law review, Spring, 1963, p. 405-425.

(Cont'd on next card)

728.1
:308
S 76
SUBDIVISION.
Stollenwerk, Donald Albert.
Cost factors in the choice of subdivision locations by residential developers. Chapel Hill, Center for Urban and Regional Studies, University of North Carolina, 1964.
90p. (North Carolina. University. Center for Urban and Regional Studies. Environmental policies and urban development thesis series no. 2)
Thesis (Master of Regional Planning - University of North Carolina.
Bibliography: p. 87-90.

(Cont'd on next card)

333.38
T74
pt.3
Subdivision.
Tri-County Regional Planning Commission, Lansing, Mich.
Guiding land subdividing. Part 3. Residential standards. Lansing, 1964.
42p.

1. Subdivision. 2. Residential areas.

333.38
R26
Reps, John W. Control of urban land subdivision...1963. (Card 2)

1. Subdivision. I. Smith, Jerry L., jt. au. II. Cornell University. Center for Housing and Environmental Studies. Div. of Urban Studies. III. Title.

728.1
:308
S 76
Stollenwerk, Donald Albert. Cost factors...1964. (Card 2)

1. Housing market. 2. Subdivision. I. North Carolina. University. Center for Urban and Regional Studies. II. Title. (Series: Environmental policies and urban development series no. 2)

VF
333.38
T85
1949
Subdivision.
Tulare County, Calif. Planning Commission.
Community subdivision practices, Tulare County, California. Tulare Co., Calif., July 1949.
8 p.

333.38
R87
SUBDIVISION.
RUTH, HERMAN D
WESTBOROUGH HOMES; A GENERAL PLAN FOR COMMUNITY DEVELOPMENT FOR WESTBOROUGH HOMES, SAN MATEO COUNTY, CALIFORNIA. SANSALITO, CALIF., SASAKI, WALKER & ASSOCIATES, 1962.
58P.

1. SUBDIVISION. I. TITLE.

333.38
S81
SUBDIVISION.
SUBURBAN MARYLAND BUILDERS ASSOCIATION.
LAND DEVELOPMENT REPORT AND SCHEDULE.
SILVER SPRING, MD., 1964.
2L. 2 CHARTS IN POCKET.

1. SUBDIVISION. I. TITLE.

333.38
F22
SUBDIVISION.
U.S. FEDERAL HOUSING ADMINISTRATION. LAND PLANNING DIVISION.
BETTER SUBDIVISIONS MEAN BETTER LOANS.
WASHINGTON, N.D.
1 V.

1. SUBDIVISION.

711.14
S54
SUBDIVISION.
SMITH, FORREST P
HELP FOR THE HOME BUILDER IN DEVELOPING LAND; A SUGGESTED PLAN FOR FHA-INSURED LOANS FOR LAND DEVELOPMENT. COLUMBUS, OHIO HOME BUILDERS ASSOCIATION, 1955.
2P.

ARTICLE IN OHIO BUILDER, JUNE 1955.
FORREST P. SMITH IS DIRECTOR, COLUMBUS OFFICE, FEDERAL HOUSING ADMINISTRATION.
1. LAND USE.
2. SUBDIVISIO N.

333.38
S85
SUBDIVISION.
SUNNYSIDE GARDENS COMMUNITY ASSOCIATION.
ECONOMIC SURVEY OF HOMEOWNERS IN SUNNYSIDE GARDENS, LONG ISLAND CITY, N.Y. NEW YORK, 1933.
P.23-30.

1. SUBDIVISION.

LAW
T
U711L
Subdivision
Urban Land Institute.
Legal principles and forms for homes associations. An advance chapter and appendix from the Home Association Study. Washington, 1963.
73p.
"Material is subject to revision."

1. Real covenants. 2. Subdivision. I. Title. II. Title: Homes associations.

333.38
S66
Subdivision.
Spokane County, Wash. Planning Commission.
Subdivision activity 1950-1957; a detailed analysis of subdivision activity. Supplement no.
Spokane,
v.
For complete information see shelflist.

1. Subdivision.

711.583
T25
Subdivision.
Tennessee. State Planning Commission.
Subdivision improvement costs: who pays for what; a summary of existing practices, comp. by Anna Sternheimer. Nashville, 1958.
95p. tables.

1. Community development. 2. Community facilities. 3. Subdivision. I. Sternheimer, Anna, comp.

711.6
V63
Subdivision.
Vogel, Joshua H
Design of subdivisions. Seattle, Bureau of Governmental Research and Services, University of Washington, in cooperation with Association of Washington Cities, 1965.
108p. (Washington (State) University. Bureau of Governmental Research and Services. Report no. 157)

1. Subdivision design. 2. Subdivision. I. Washington (State) University. Bureau of Governmental Research and Services.

333.38
S71
Subdivision.
Stamford, Conn. Planning Board.
Residential subdivision activity, 1950 thru 1960, Stamford, Connecticut. Stamford, 1961.
12p.
One of a series of reports concerning the planning program prepared by the Stamford Planning Board.
Cover title.

1. Subdivision.

333.38
T29
Subdivision.
Texas. Engineering Experiment Station.
A case for south living, by Robert F. White. College Station, Tex., 1960.
11p. diagrs. (Its Reprint 102)

Reprinted from the Autumn 1959 issue of Landscape architecture.

1. Subdivision. I. White, Robert F.

333.38
W17
SUBDIVISION.
WASHINGTON. UNIVERSITY. COLLEGE OF ARCHITECTURE AND URBAN PLANNING.
LOCATIONAL FACTORS INVOLVED IN SUBURBAN LAND DEVELOPMENT. PREPARED FOR THE WEYERHAEUSER COMPANY BY M.R. WOLFE, AND OTHERS. SEATTLE, 1961.
1 V.

1. SUBDIVISION. 2. SUBURBS - SEATTLE. I. WOLFE, M.R. II. WEYERHAEUSER CO.

333.38
S71b
Subdivision.
Stanislaus Cities-County Advance Planning Staff.
Basic steps in subdivision development for the communities of the Stanislaus urban region; procedures and techniques to assure better communities by means of good land planning. Modesto, Calif., 1959.
19p. diagrs. (Its Guide series no. 6)
U.S. Urban Renewal Administration, Urban Planning Assistance Program.

1. Subdivision. I. U.S. Urban Renewal Administration. Urban Planning Assistance Program.

333.38
T32
Subdivision.
Theobald, A D
Financial aspects of subdivision development. Chicago, Institute for Economic Research, 1930.
88p. (Institute for Economic Research. Studies in land economics. Research monograph no. 3)

1. Subdivision. I. Institute for Economic Research. II. Title.

333.38
W24
SUBDIVISION.
Weiss, Shirley F
Residential developer decisions; a focused view of the urban growth process, by Shirley F. Weiss and others. Chapel Hill, N.C., Center for Urban and Regional Studies, Institute for Research in Social Science, University of North Carolina, 1966.
94p. (An Urban studies research monograph)
1. Subdivision. 2. City growth - Greensboro, N.C. I. North Carolina. University. Institute for Research in Social Science. Center for Urban and Regional Studies.
II. Title.

333.38
W34

Subdivision.

Whitten, Robert Harvey, 1873-
    A research into the economics of land subdivision, with particular reference to a complete neighborhood unit for low or medium cost housing, by Robert Whitten ... Prepared under the joint auspices of the School of citizenship and public affairs of Syracuse university and the Regional plan of New York and its environs. [Syracuse, N. Y., Printed by the School of citizenship and public affairs of Syracuse university] 1927.
    xi, 72 p. double pl., plans (part fold.) 20½^{cm}.

1. Cities and towns—Planning. 2. Cities and towns—U. S. 3. Housing—New York (State). 4. New York (City)—Public works. I. Syracuse university. School of citizenship and public affairs. II. Regional plan of New York and its environs. III. Title. IV. Title: Neighborhood unit for low or medium cost housing.

(Continued on next card)

Library of Congress   NA9105.W5

[48h1]

711.14
S235

SUBDIVISION - PLANNING.
SCHREIBER, WILLIAM L
HILLSIDE DEVELOPMENT; GOVERNMENTAL CONTROLS - PRIVATE DEVELOPERS POLICY.
BERKELEY, CALIF., ASSOCIATED HOME BUILDERS OF GREATER EASTBAY, INC., N.D.
21P. ILLUS.

1. LAND USE. 2. SUBDIVISION - PLANNING. I. TITLE. II. ASSOCIATED HOME BUILDERS OF GREATER EASTBAY.

711.14
A77

SUBDIVISION DESIGN.
ASSOCIATED HOME BUILDERS OF GREATER EASTBAY, INC.
THE PRESERVATION OF SCENIC VIEWS.
BERKELEY, CALIFORNIA, 1964.
14L.

1. LAND USE. 2. SUBDIVISION DESIGN. I. TITLE.

333.38
(016)
P72

SUBDIVISION - BIBLIOGRAPHY.
PRESIDENT'S CONFERENCE ON HOME BUILDING AND HOME OWNERSHIP.
BIBLIOGRAPHY ON LAND SUBDIVISION AND RELATED SUBJECTS. N.P., 1931?
73L.

1. SUBDIVISION - BIBLIOGRAPHY.

FOLIO
333.38
!711
(79454)
L4b

SUBDIVISION - PLANNING - SACRAMENTO, CALIF.
LINDSEY AND COMPANY.
EL DORADO HILLS. BROCHURE PREPARED BY VICTOR GRUEN ASSOCIATES.
SACRAMENTO, CAL., 1963.
12P.

1. SUBDIVISION - PLANNING - SACRAMENTO, CALIF. I. TITLE.

712
B51

Subdivision design.

Blake, Peter.
    God's own junkyard; the planned deterioration of America's landscape. New York, Holt, Rinehart and Winston, 1963.
    143p.

1. Landscape architecture. 2. Subdivision design. 3. Site planning. I. Title.

333.38
(7946)
R47

Subdivision - Bibliography.

Risse, Edward M
    Subdivision control; observations and a bibliography [preliminary] by Edward M. Risse and Ronald W. Williamson. [Prepared] for Land Use Seminar, University of California, School of Law. Berkeley, Spring, 1965. [n.p.] 1965.
    43p.

1. Subdivision regulation - San Francisco Bay area. 2. Subdivision - Bibl.
I. Williamson, Ronald W., jt. au.
II. Title.

333.38
B71

SUBDIVISION - SOCIAL ASPECTS.
BRACEY, HOWARD E
NEIGHBOURS; SUBDIVISION LIFE IN ENGLAND AND THE UNITED STATES. BATON ROUGE, LOUISIANA STATE UNIVERSITY PRESS, 1964.
208P.

1. SUBDIVISION - SOCIAL ASPECTS.
2. SOCIAL CONDITIONS. I. TITLE.
II. TITLE: SUBDIVISION LIFE IN ENGLAND AND THE UNITED STATES.

VF
711.6
C15
1959

Subdivision design.

Canada. Central Mortgage and Housing Corporation.
    Federal-Provincial Housing and Land Assembly. Ottawa. 1959.
    folder

"CMHC 941."

1. Subdivision design. I. Title.

711.583
(751)
D65

SUBDIVISION - DELAWARE.
DOLAN, PAUL.
BROOKSIDE; A STUDY OF A SUBURBAN REAL ESTATE DEVELOPMENT IN DELAWARE, BY PAUL DOLAN AND ALBERT H. DUNN.
NEWARK, DEL., BUREAU OF ECONOMIC AND BUSINESS RESEARCH, UNIVERSITY OF DELAWARE, SPRING 1959.
40P. TABLES.

1. SUBURBS - DELAWARE.
2. SUBDIVISION - DELAWARE. I. TITLE.

VF
333.38
N28

Subdivision control.

New York. Dept. of Commerce. Bureau of Planning.
    Subdivision control: a step toward better communities; a manual of subdivision regulation for municipal officials, subdivision developers, builders and planning boards. Albany, 1946.
    35 p. illus.

"List of references": p. 35.

1. Subdivision regulation. I. Title.

711.6
C15

Subdivision design.

Canada. Central Mortgage and Housing Corporation.
    Federal - provincial projects. [Ottawa] 1954.
    5 p.

"CMHC 941"

1. Subdivision design. 2. Rental housing - Canada. I. Title.

333.38
(7471)
N28F

SUBDIVISION - NEW YORK (CITY)
NEW YORK LIFE INSURANCE COMPANY.
FRESH MEADOWS. NEW YORK, 1950.
31P.

1. SUBDIVISION - NEW YORK (CITY)

333.38
(7946)
R47

Subdivision control; observations and a bibliography [preliminary]

Risse, Edward M
    Subdivision control; observations and a bibliography [preliminary] by Edward M. Risse and Ronald W. Williamson. [Prepared] for Land Use Seminar, University of California, School of Law. Berkeley, Spring, 1965. [n.p.] 1965.
    43p.

1. Subdivision regulation - San Francisco Bay area. 2. Subdivision - Bibl.
I. Williamson, Ronald W., jt. au.
II. Title.

728.3
C25

SUBDIVISION DESIGN.
CENTRAL MORTGAGE AND HOUSING CORPORATION.
PRINCIPLES OF SMALL HOUSE GROUPING.
OTTAWA, N.D.
55P.

1. HOUSE PLANS. 2. SITE PLANNING.
3. SUBDIVISION DESIGN. I. TITLE.

333.38
!711
(71)
C76

SUBDIVISION - PLANNING.
CROSSLEY, ALAN.
SUBDIVISION PLANNING. [OTTAWA]
COMMUNITY PLANNING ASSOCIATION OF CANADA, 1955.
8P.
TEXT IN ENGLISH AND FRENCH.
REPRINTED FROM COMMUNITY PLANNING REVIEW, V. 5, NO. 3, 1955.

1. SUBDIVISION - PLANNING. I. TITLE.
II. COMMUNITY PLANNING ASSOCIATION OF CANADA.

Subdivision design
    x Land planning
    sa and xx Site planning

711.581
(77311)
C34B

SUBDIVISION DESIGN.
CHICAGO. PLAN COMMISSION.
BUILDING NEW NEIGHBORHOODS;
SUBDIVISION DESIGN AND STANDARDS...
CHICAGO, 1943.
44P.

1. NEIGHBORHOOD PLANNING - CHICAGO.
2. SUBDIVISION DESIGN. I. TITLE.

FILM
333.38
!711
N28

SUBDIVISION - PLANNING.
NEW CONCEPTS OF LAND SUBDIVISION USING PLANORAMA 3-DIMENSIONAL SCALE MODELS (SLIDES) WASHINGTON, NATIONAL ASSOCIATION OF HOME BUILDERS, 1963.
34 COLOR SLIDES, 20P.

1. SUBDIVISION - PLANNING.
2. SUBDIVISION REGULATION.
I. NATIONAL ASSOCIATION OF HOME BUILDERS.

711.6
A52C

SUBDIVISION DESIGN.
AMERICAN SOCIETY OF PLANNING OFFICIALS.
CLUSTER SUBDIVISIONS. CHICAGO, 1960.
35P. (ITS PLANNING ADVISORY SERVICE.
INFORMATION REPORT NO. 135)

1. SUBDIVISION DESIGN. I. TITLE.

711.14
C64

Subdivision design.

Coke, James G
    Fragmentation in land-use planning and control, by James G. Coke and John J. Gargan. Prepared for the National Commission on Urban Problems. Wash., Govt. Print. Off., 1969.
    91p. (U.S. National Commission on Urban Problems. Research report no. 18)
    Paul H. Douglas, chairman.
    1. Land use. 2. Subdivision design. I. Gargan, John J., jt. au. II. U.S. National Commission on Urban Problems. III. Title. (Series: U.S. National Commission on Urban Problems. Research report no. 18)

711.4
(74787)
C67

SUBDIVISION DESIGN.
CORNELL UNIVERSITY. COLLEGE OF
ARCHITECTURE.
A COMMUNITY DEVELOPMENT, CAMPUS
HEIGHTS. ITHACA, 1956.
1 v. (unpaged)

1. CITY PLANNING - OSWEGO, N.Y.
2. SUBDIVISION DESIGN. I. TITLE.

711.729
(77311)
H92

Subdivision design.
Hyde Park-Kenwood Community Conference.
(Committee on Community Reference)
Suggestions for designing urban
parking lots. Chicago, 1961.
14p.

1. Parking - Chicago. 2. Subdivision
design.

711.6
N17
1958

Subdivision design.
National Association of Home Builders. (Land
Planning Committee)
Home builders manual for land development.
2d rev. ed. Washington, 1958.
264p. illus.

Editors: Max S. Wehrly and M. Ross McKeever
of the Urban Land Institute.

1. Subdivision design. I. Urban Land Institute. II. Title.

728.1
N176b
no.36

SUBDIVISION DESIGN.
Edwards, Gordon.
Land assembly: problems & techniques.
Submitted to: National Commission on Urban
Problems. [n.p.] 1968.
204p. (Background paper [no. 36] for
U.S. National Commission on Urban Problems)
Draft.

1. Housing 2. Land use. 3. Subdivision
design. 4. City growth. I. U.S. National
Commission on Urban Problems. Background paper
no. 36. II. Title.

VF
711.6
I57

Subdivision design.
International Federation for Housing
and Town Planning, 21st Congress,
Lisbon, 1952.
Relation between dwelling type and
and plan and layout of the residential
quarter; general report by K. H. Brunner.
Oporto, Imprensa Portuguesa, Sept. 1952.
24 p.

Summaries in French and Portugese.

(over)

711.6
N17l

SUBDIVISION DESIGN.
National Association of Home Builders.
Land development manual. Rev. Washington.
1969.
376p.

1. Subdivision design. I. Title.

712.21
F25

SUBDIVISION DESIGN.
FELDMAN, HARRY H
PARK AND RECREATION LAND REQUIREMENTS
IN NEW SUBDIVISIONS AND RE-PLATTINGS.
2D ED. REV. WHEELING, W. VA., AMERICAN
INSTITUTE OF PARK EXECUTIVES, 1964.
36P. (AMERICAN INSTITUTE OF PARK
EXECUTIVES, INC. MANAGEMENT AID
BULLETIN NO. 18)

1. PARKS. 2. RECREATION.
3. SUBDIVISION DESIGN. I. AMERICAN
INSTITUTE OF PARK EXECUTIVES.
II. TITLE.

711.6
K17

Subdivision design.
Katz, Robert D
Design of the housing site; a critique of
American practice. Urbana, Ill., Small
Homes Council— Building Research Council,
University of Illinois, 1966.
223p.
U.S. Dept. of Housing and Urban Development. Demonstration Grant Program.

1. Site planning. 2. Subdivision design.
I. Illinois. University. Small Homes
Council. II. Title. III. U.S. Dept. of
Housing and Urban Development.
Demonstration Grant Program.

711.6
N17n

Subdivision design.
National Committee on Housing.
Neighborhood design and control, an
analysis of the problems of planned subdivisions, by Henry S. Churchill and
Roslyn Ittleson. New York, 1944.
39p.

1. Subdivision design. 2. Subdivision regulation.
I. Churchill, Henry S. II. Ittleson, Roslyn.

711.6
G17

SUBDIVISION DESIGN.
Gardner, C D
The planned unit development handbook; a
complete guide to planning, processing, and
developing the successful P.U.D., including
a set of pre-approved documents and forms
for P.U.D. processing. [Prepared by C.D.
Gardner. Berkeley] Associated Home Builders
of the Greater Eastbay [1970]
1v.
Cover title.
1. Subdivision design. 2. Housing.
I. Associated Home Builders of the Greater
Eastbay. II. Title.

711.581
K67

SUBDIVISION DESIGN.
KOSTKA, V JOSEPH.
NEIGHBORHOOD PLANNING. SPONSORED BY
THE APPRAISAL INSTITUTE OF CANADA.
WINNIPEG, 1957.
142P.

1. NEIGHBORHOOD PLANNING.
2. SUBDIVISION DESIGN. I. APPRAISAL
INSTITUTE OF CANADA.

VF
711.6
N172

Subdivision design.
National Housing Association.
Triumphing over the gridiron plan, by
Lawrence Veiller. New York, Dec. 1918.
[10] p. plans (Its Publication no. 52)

Reprinted from Architectural Record, July
1918.

1. Subdivision design. I. Veiller, Lawrence. II. Title.

LAW
T
H117Law

Subdivision design.
Haar, Charles M ed.
Law and land; Anglo-American planning
practice. Cambridge, Mass., Harvard University Press and the Massachusetts Institute of Technology Press, 1964.
290p. (Joint Center for Urban Studies.
Publication.)
Partial contents:-Land planning and land
ownership.-The making and effect of the
land plan.-The individual and the machinery
of planning. (Cont'd. on next card)

VF
333.38
M87

Subdivision design.
Murray, J Wray.
Subdivision development and financing.
[Chicago, Mortgage Bankers Association of
America] 1954.
47 p.

Bibliography: p. 46-47.

1954 Certificate of Merit Award, Mortgage
Bankers Association of America and School of
Commerce, Northwestern University.

1. Construction loans. 2. Subdivision design.

711.4
[(43)]
N67

Subdivision design.
North Rhine-Westphalia. Ministerium für
Landesplanung, Wohnungsbau und Öffentliche
Arbeiten.
Neuzeitliche Siedlungs-und Wohnformen;
Beispiele aus dem Städtebauprogramm des Landes
Nordrhein-Westfalen. Text und Zeichnungen:
Heinz Müller. München, Verwaltungs-Verlag-
BmbH., [1969?]
204p.
1. City planning - Germany. 2. Germany -
City planning. 3. Subdivision design.
4. Regional planning - Germany. 5. Germany -
Regional planning. 6. Architecture,
Domestic - Designs and plans. 7. Site
planning. 8. Apartment houses - Plans.
9. House Plans. I. Müller, Heinz.

LAW
T
H117Law

Haar, Charles M ed. Law and land ...
(Card 2)

-Regulation and taking property under planning laws.

1. Land use. 2. City planning. 3. Land
titles. 4. Subdivision design. 5. Eminent
domain. I. Joint Center for Urban Studies.
II. Title.

711.6
N17
1953

Subdivision design.
National Association of Home Builders. Land
Planning Committee.
Home builders manual for land development.
Rev. ed. [Washington, c1953]
274 p. diagrs., plans, tables.
Albert Balch, Chairman.
Editors, Max S. Wehrly and J. Ross McKeever.

1. Subdivision design. I. Urban Land Institute.
II. Title. III. Wehrly, Max S. IV. McKeever, J. Ross.

Folio
711.6
O76

Subdivision design.
Oross (E. Eugene) Associates.
The design for a community development in
Marlboro Township, Monmouth County, New
Jersey, by E. Eugene Oross Associates and
Thomas J. Michalski. Presented in October
1962, to Robilt Incorporated, Lakewood,
N.J. [n.p.] 1962.
[23]p.

1. Subdivision design. 2. Community
development - Marlboro, N.J. 3. Open
space land. I. Michalski,
Thomas J., jt. su.

720.2
H63

Subdivision design.
Hoffmann, Hubert.
Row houses and cluster houses; an international survey. New York, Frederick A.
Praeger, 1967.
175p. (Books that matter)

1. Architecture - Design. 2. Apartment
houses. 3. Subdivision design. 4. Housing
surveys. I. Title. II. Title: Cluster
houses.

711.6
N17

Subdivision design.
National Association of Home Builders. Land
Planning Committee.
Home builders manual for land development.
[Washington, D.C., c1950]
156 p. diagrs., plans, tables.

Cover title.
David D. Bohannon, Chairman.
"Collection of Land Planning Service bulletins
appearing in NAHB Correlator, 1947-49, organized
and edited by Urban Land Institute."-Foreword.
1. Subdivision design. I. Urban Land Institute.
II. Title.

711.6
P67

Subdivision design.
Posada, Reinaldo.
Apuntes sobre agrupaciones de vivienda.
Bogota, Centro Interamericano de Vivienda
y Planeamiento, 1963.
122p. (Planeamiento resúmenes de clase)

Bibliography: p. [117]-122.

1. Subdivision design. 2. Open space
land. 3. Site planning. 4. Housing -
Latin America.
I. Inter-American Housing
and Planning Center.

728.1
:061.3
P72
1931
v.1
Subdivision design.
President's Conference on Home Building and Home Ownership, Washington, 1931.
Planning for residential districts. Reports of the committees ... ed. by John M. Gries and James Ford. Washington [c1932]
227 p. illus. (Its Final reports of committees, 1)
Includes bibliographies.
1.Neighborhood planning. 2.Zoning. 3.Subdivision design. 4.Landscape architecture. I.Title.

VF
711.6
C65
Subdivision design.
U.S. Congress. Joint Committee on Washington Metropolitan Problems.
Land planning considerations in the Washington Metropolitan Area. Staff study [by Charles W. Eliot] for the Joint Committee on Washington metropolitan problems, Congress of the United States, Washington. Govt. Print. Off., 1958.
12p.
85th Cong., 2d sess.
(Continued on next card)

711.6
F22S
SUBDIVISION DESIGN.
U.S. FEDERAL HOUSING ADMINISTRATION.
SUCCESSFUL SUBDIVISIONS: PRINCIPLES OF PLANNING FOR ECONOMY AND PROTECTION AGAINST NEIGHBORHOOD BLIGHT. WASHINGTON, GOVT. PRINT. OFF., 1940.
28P. (ITS LAND PLANNING BULLETIN NO. 1)
COVER SUBTITLE: PLANNED AS NEIGHBORHOODS FOR PROFITABLE INVESTMENT AND APPEAL TO HOME OWNERS.
FOREWORD BY STEWART MCDONALD.
1. SUBDIVISION DESIGN. I. TITLE. II. SERIES.

333.38
(46)
S27
Subdivision design.
Serrano Guirado, Enrique.
Planificación territorial política del suelo y administración local. Madrid, Secretaría General Tecnica, Ministerio de la Vivienda, 1963.
97p. (Spain. Ministerio de la Vivienda. Conferencias y discursos 12)
1. Subdivision regulation - Spain. 2. Subdivision design. 3. City planning administration.
I. Spain. Ministerio de la Vivienda.

VF
711.6
C65
Subdivision design.
U.S. Congress. Joint Committee on Washington Metropolitan Problems. Land ... (Card 2)
1. Subdivision design. 2. Metropolitan area planning - District of Columbia.
I. Eliot, Charles W.

LAW
T
F222
H68su
Subdivision design.
U.S. Federal Housing Administration.
Suggested legal documents for planned-unit developments. Wash., Federal Housing Administration, Veterans Administration, 1965.
20p. (FHA form 1400, VA form 26-8200, rev. 1965)
1. Subdivision design. 2. Veterans' guaranteed loans. I. U.S. Veterans Administration. II. Title.

VF
711.6
S62
Subdivision design.
Spence-Sales, Harold
How to subdivide for housing developments. Ottawa, Community Planning Association of Canada, 1950.
36 p. maps, table.
On cover: A handbook on the layout of housing developments.
1.Subdivision design. 2.Site selection. I.Title.

VF
728.1
:940.42
E52
Subdivision design.
U.S. Office for Emergency Management. Division of Defense Housing Coordination
Summary of planning standards for defense housing projects. [Washington] Jan. 1941.
15 L.
1. Building standards - Wartime.
2. Subdivision design.

VF
711.6
H68
Subdivision design.
U.S. Housing Authority.
Design of low-rent housing projects; planning the site. [Washington, Govt. Print. Off., 1939]
84 p. illus.
1.Site planning. 2.Subdivision design. 3.Housing projects. I.Title.

711.74
T71
Subdivision design.
Traffic engineering.
Tentative standards for subdivision streets. Wash., Institute of Traffic Engineers, 1964.
16p.
A reprint from Traffic engineering, September, 1964, by Barton-Aschman Associates.
1. Streets. 2. Traffic. 3. Subdivision design. I. Barton-Aschman Associates.

711.6
F22
Subdivision design.
U.S. Federal Housing Administration.
Planned-unit development with a homes association. Washington, For sale by the Supt. of Documents, Govt. Print. Off., 1963.
64p. (Its Land planning bulletin no. 6)
1. Subdivision design. I. Title.
(Series)

711.6
U54
Subdivision design.
United States Savings and Loan League.
What the savings and loan association needs to know about land planning. [Chicago?1956]
32 p. illus., diagrs.
1.Subdivision design. 2.Neighborhood planning.
I.Title: Land planning.

711.15
(41)
U54
Subdivision design.
U.K. Ministry of Housing and Local Government.
The density of residential areas. London, H. M. Stationery Off., 1952.
71 p. illus., graphs, tables(part fold.)
1.Population density. 2.Housing-U.K. 3.Subdivision design. I.Title.

711.6
F22
1964
SUBDIVISION DESIGN.
U.S. FEDERAL HOUSING ADMINISTRATION.
PLANNED-UNIT DEVELOPMENT WITH A HOMES ASSOCIATION. REV. WASHINGTON, GOVT. PRINT. OFF., 1964.
64P. (ITS LAND PLANNING BULLETIN NO. 6; FHA NO. 1097)
TEXTUAL REVISION ONLY: P.38, PARAGRAPH 6.21, UNDERLINED SENTENCE, THE DESIGN MUST BE AT A LAND-USE INTENSITY... IS ONLY BASIC CHANGE: FROM 1963 ED.
1. SUBDIVISION DESIGN. I. TITLE.

VF
728.1
(41)
W65
Subdivision design.
Womersley, J L
Housing costs today, with a foreword by Harold Macmillan and a review by J. H. Forshaw. London, Municipal Journal, 1952.
53 p. illus., plans.
1.Building costs-U.K. 2.Family living requirements 3.Prefabricated construction-U.K. 4.Subdivision design. I.Title.

711.4
(41)
U54
Subdivision design.
U.K. Ministry of Housing and Local Government.
Design in town and village. London, H. M. Stationery Off., 1953.
120 p. illus.
Contents.-pt.1.The English village, by Thomas Sharp.-pt.2.The design of residential areas, by Frederick Gibberd.-pt.3.Design in city centres, by W. G. Holford.
1.City planning-U.K. 2.Neighborhood planning-U.K. 3.Subdivision design. I.Sharp, Thomas. II.Gibberd, Frederick. III.Holford, William Graham. IV.Title.

711.6
F22
1970
SUBDIVISION DESIGN.
U.S. Federal Housing Administration.
Planned-unit development, with a homes association. Rev. [Wash.] 1970.
64p. (Its Land planning bulletin 6; HUD 81-F)
Formerly FHA 1097.
1. Subdivision design. 2. Landscape architecture. 3. Housing - Associations. I. Title.

711.6
W39
Subdivision design.
Whyte, William H
Cluster development. Foreword by Laurence S. Rockefeller. New York, American Conservation Association, 1964.
130p.
1. Subdivision design. 2. Housing. 3. Open space land. 4. Site planning. I. American Conservation Association. II. Title.

69
(41)
G72
1949
Suppl.3
Subdivision design.
U.K. Ministry of Housing and Local Government.
Houses 1953; third supplement to the Housing manual, 1949. London, H.M. Stationery Off., 1953.
64 p. illus., plans.
1.Architecture, Domestic-Design. 2.Subdivision design. I.Title. II.Title: The housing manual, 1949.

69
F22
TB no.7
1938
Subdivision design.
U.S. Federal Housing Administration.
Planning profitable neighborhoods. Washington [1938]
35 p. illus., diagrs. (Its Technical bulletin no. 7)
1.Subdivision design. I.Title. II.Series.

712
W66
Subdivision design.
Wood, Samuel E
The phantom cities of California, by Samuel E. Wood and Alfred E. Heller. Sacramento, Calif., California Tomorrow, 1963.
66p.
1. Landscape architecture. 2. Subdivision design. 3. Municipal government. I. Heller, Alfred E., jt. au. II. Title.

711.6
V63
Subdivision design.
Vogel, Joshua H
Design of subdivisions. Seattle, Bureau of Governmental Research and Services, University of Washington, in co-operation with Association of Washington Cities, 1965.
108p. (Washington (State) University. Bureau of Governmental Research and Services. Report no. 157)

1. Subdivision design. 2. Subdivision. I. Washington (State) University. Bureau of Governmental Research and Services.

711.4
(78142)
W42s
Subdivision improvements.
Wichita, Kan. Board of City Commissioners.
Subdivision improvements. Requirements made of subdevelopers in Wichita and fifteen Midwestern cities. Wichita, 1957.
17p. tables.

1. Capital improvement programs - Wichita, Kan. 2. Subdivision regulation - Wichita, Kan. I. Title.

333.38
A52L
SUBDIVISION REGULATION.
AMERICAN SOCIETY OF PLANNING OFFICIALS.
LAND DEVELOPMENT ORDINANCES: GRADING; CURB CUTS AND DRIVEWAYS; STREET TREES. CHICAGO, THE SOCIETY, MAY 1956.
35P. (ITS PLANNING ADVISORY SERVICE INFORMATION BULLETIN NO. 86)

1. SUBDIVISION REGULATION. 2. SITE PLANNING. I. TITLE.

711.14
(016)
N17
Subdivision design - Bibliography.
National Housing Center. Library.
Land development; including special sections on cluster development and golf course (country club) subdivisions. Washington, 1964.
17p. (Reference list no. 68)

1. Land use - Bibl. 2. Recreation - Bibl. 3. Subdivision design - Bibl.

333.38
B71
SUBDIVISION LIFE IN ENGLAND AND THE UNITED STATES.
BRACEY, HOWARD E
NEIGHBOURS; SUBDIVISION LIFE IN ENGLAND AND THE UNITED STATES. BATON ROUGE, LOUISIANA STATE UNIVERSITY PRESS, 1964.
208P.

1. SUBDIVISION - SOCIAL ASPECTS. 2. SOCIAL CONDITIONS. I. TITLE. II. TITLE: SUBDIVISION LIFE IN ENGLAND AND THE UNITED STATES.

333.38
A52
Subdivision regulation.
American Society of Planning Officials.
A model state subdivision control law, granting power and authority to municipal corporations and counties to regulate the subdivision of land. Chicago, Mar. 1947.
48 l.

Processed.

1. Subdivision regulation. I. Title.

711.6
(74461)
M17
SUBDIVISION DESIGN - BOSTON METROPOLITAN AREA.
MASSACHUSETTS. DEPT. OF COMMERCE.
THE EFFECTS OF LARGE LOT SIZE ON RESIDENTIAL DEVELOPMENT. WASHINGTON, URBAN LAND INSTITUTE, 1958.
52P. (TECHNICAL BULLETIN NO. 32)

A STUDY BY MASSACHUSETTS DEPT. OF COMMERCE AND THE M.I.T. URBAN AND REGIONAL STUDIES SECTION.

1. SUBDIVISION DESIGN - BOSTON METROPOLITAN AREA. 2. SITE PLANNING - BOSTON METROPOLITAN AREA. I. TITLE. (SERIES: URBAN LAND (CONTINUED ON NEXT CARD)

333.38
(794)
C15su
1969
Subdivision manual.
California. Dept. of Real Estate.
Subdivision manual; an explanation of subdivision planning and development, processing and controls, with excerpts from pertinent statutes. 5th ed. [Sacramento] 1969.
140p.

1. Subdivision regulation - Calif. I. Title.

711.5
A52p
Subdivision regulation.
American Society of Planning Officials.
Problems of zoning and land-use regulation. Prepared for the consideration of the National Commission on Urban Problems. Washington, D.C., Govt. Print. Off., 1968.
80p. (U.S. National Commission on Urban Problems. Research report no. 2)
Study directed by Dennis O'Harrow. Chairman, National Commission on Urban Problems, Paul H. Douglas.

1. Zoning. 2. Land use. 3. Subdivision regulation. I. U.S. National Commission on Urban Problems. (Cont'd on next card)

711.6
(74461)
M17
MASSACHUSETTS. DEPT. OF COMMERCE.
THE EFFECTS ... 1958. (CARD 2)
INSTITUTE. TECHNICAL BULLETIN NO. 32)

333.38
(794)
C15su
1956
SUBDIVISION MANUAL.
CALIFORNIA. DIVISION OF REAL ESTATE.
SUBDIVISION MANUAL; AN EXPLANATION OF THE REAL ESTATE COMMISSIONER'S JURISDICTION AND REQUIREMENT IN THE DEVELOPMENT OF NEW SUBDIVISION. SACRAMENTO, CALIFORNIA STATE PRINTING OFFICE, 1956.
45P.

1. SUBDIVISION REGULATION - CALIFORNIA. I. TITLE.

711.5
A52p
American Society of Planning Officials.
Problems of zoning and land-use...1968. (Card 2)
I. II. O'Harrow, Dennis. III. Douglas, Paul H. IV. Title. (Series: U.S. National Commission on Urban Problems. Research report no.2)

728
:333
P66
SUBDIVISION DESIGN - CALIF.
Pope, Joseph C
Home owners associations in planned unit developments: an evaluation of their current problems and future feasibility. Berkeley, Calif., Associated Home Builders of the Greater Eastbay, 1971.
83p.
Bibliography: p. 80-83.
1. Home ownership. 2. Subdivision design - Calif. I. Associated Home Builders of the Greater Eastbay. II. Title: Planned unit developments. III. Title.

333.38
(794)
C15su
1959
SUBDIVISION MANUAL.
CALIFORNIA. LEGISLATURE. SENATE. INTERIM COMMITTEE ON SUBDIVISION DEVELOPMENT AND PLANNING.
SUBDIVISION MANUAL. SACRAMENTO, SENATE OF THE STATE OF CALIFORNIA, 1959.
116P.

1. SUBDIVISION REGULATION - CALIF. I. TITLE.

711.5
A52re
SUBDIVISION REGULATION.
American Society of Planning Officials.
Regulatory devices; papers presented at the regulatory devices short course held at the 1969 ASPO National Planning Conference. Short course Chairman: Frederick H. Bair, Jr. Editor: Virginia Curtis. Chicago, 1969.
68p.

1. Zoning. 2. Subdivision regulation. I. Curtis, Virginia, ed. II. Title.

728.1
:325
M66
Subdivision development.
Monchow, Helen C
The use of deed restrictions in subdivision development. Chicago, Institute for Research in Land Economics and Public Utilities, 1928.
84 p. (Studies in land economics. Research monograph, no. 1)

1. Deed restrictions. 2. Real property. 3. City planning. I. Institute for Research in Land Economics and Public Utilities. II. Title. III. Title: Subdivision development.

333.38
(711)
(71)
C76
SUBDIVISION PLANNING.
CROSSLEY, ALAN.
SUBDIVISION PLANNING. OTTAWA, COMMUNITY PLANNING ASSOCIATION OF CANADA, 1955.
8P.
TEXT IN ENGLISH AND FRENCH.
REPRINTED FROM COMMUNITY PLANNING REVIEW, V. 5, NO. 3, 1955.

1. SUBDIVISION - PLANNING. I. TITLE. II. COMMUNITY PLANNING ASSOCIATION OF CANADA.

711.5
B15
Subdivision regulation.
Balk, Alfred.
The easy chair: invitation to bribery. How a recipe for America the Beautiful turned out - in many communities - to be a license for chaos and corruption. Reproduced from Harper's magazine, Oct. 1966. p. 18, 20, 23-24.

1. Zoning. 2. Subdivision regulation. 3. Land use. I. Harper's magazine. II. Title.

332.72
F22su
SUBDIVISION DEVELOPMENT.
U.S. FEDERAL HOUSING ADMINISTRATION.
SUBDIVISION DEVELOPMENT. STANDARDS FOR THE INSURANCE OF MORTGAGES ON PROPERTIES LOCATED IN UNDEVELOPED SUBDIVISIONS, TITLE II OF THE NATIONAL HOUSING ACT. WASHINGTON, GOVT. PRINT. OFF., 1935-39.
5 NOS. (ITS CIRCULAR NO. 5)

1. MORTGAGE FINANCE. I. TITLE.

Subdivision regulation (geographic subdivision)
xx Zoning legislation

711.4
H17
v.7
Subdivision regulation.
Bassett, Edward Murray, 1863–
Model laws for planning cities, counties, and states, including zoning, subdivision regulation, and protection of official map, by Edward M. Bassett, Frank B. Williams, Alfred Bettman and Robert Whitten. Cambridge, Harvard university press, 1935.
viii, 137 p. 25cm. (Half-title: Harvard city planning studies. VII)
1. City planning. 2. Zoning-Legislation. 3. Cities and towns-Housing. 4. Cities and towns-Planning-Zone system. 5. Cities and towns-U. S. I. Williams, Frank Backus, 1864– II. Bettman, Alfred, 1873– III. Whitten, Robert Harvey, 1873– IV. Title. V. Ser. 3. Subdivision regulation.
35—27004
Library of Congress NA9108.R27
———— Copr 2.
Copyright A 79060 [38u1-] 711

LAW
T
B287La
1956
Subdivision regulation.
Beuscher, J H   ed.
Land use controls: cases and materials.
Madison, Wis., The College Typing Co.,
[1956?]
1v. (various pagings)

Cover title: Materials on land use
controls.

1. Subdivision regulation. 2. Zoning legislation.
3. Deed restrictions. I. Title.
4. Land use.

LAW
T
H671La
Subdivision regulations.
Horack, Frank B , jr.
Land use controls, supplementary materials
on real property, by Frank E. Horack, Jr. and
Val Nolan, Jr. St. Paul, Minn., West Pub-
lishing Co., 1955.
240p. (American casebook series)

1. Zoning legislation. 2. Subdivision regulations. I. Nolan, Val, jr. II. Title.

711.17
N171
Subdivision regulation.
National Association of Home Builders.
(Governmental Affairs Div.)
The Interstate land sales full disclosure
act; legislative report. Wash. 1968.
13p. (LR 90-24; Aug. 19, 1968)

1. Land acquisition. 2. Subdivision
regulation. I. Title.

LAW
T
B287La
1964
Subdivision regulation.
Beuscher, J H ed.
Land use controls-cases and materials.
3d ed. Madison, Wis., College Printing and
Typing Co., 1964.
577p.

1. Subdivision regulation. 2. Zoning
legislation. 3. Deed restrictions.
4. Land use. I. Title.

333.38
I57
SUBDIVISION REGULATION.
INTERNATIONAL CITY MANAGERS'
ASSOCIATION.
MUNICIPAL REGULATION OF SUBDIVISIONS.
CHICAGO, THE ASSOCIATION, AUGUST 1956.
11P. (ITS MANAGEMENT INFORMATION
SERVICE, REPORT 151)

BIBLIOGRAPHY: P.10

1. SUBDIVISION REGULATION. I. TITLE.

711.5
N171
Subdivision regulation.
National Association of Home Builders.
Land use and development; review of model
zoning and subdivision codes. Washington
[1968?]
12p.

1. Zoning. 2. Subdivision regulation.
3. Land use. I. Title.

LAW
T
C158s
Subdivision regulation.
Campbell, Ernest H
Surveys, subdivision and platting, and bound-
aries. Washington State laws and judicial de-
cisions, by Ernest H. Campbell and Joshua H.
Vogel. Seattle, Bureau of Governmental Research
and Services, University of Washington, 1965.
215p. (Washington. University. Bureau of
Governmental Research and Services. Report no.
156; Revision of report no. 137)

Bibliography: p. 214-215.

Continued on next
card)

333.38
J25
SUBDIVISION REGULATION.
JENNINGS, FLOYD M
REGULATING SUBDIVISIONS: THE CONTROL
OF PLATS, SUBDIVISIONS OR DEDICATIONS,
BY FLOYD M. JENNINGS AND ERNEST H.
CAMPBELL, ASSOCIATION OF WASHINGTON
CITIES, IN COOPERATION WITH THE
UNIVERSITY OF WASHINGTON, BUREAU OF
GOVERNMENTAL RESEARCH AND SERVICES.
SEATTLE, 1954.
41P. (INFORMATION BULLETIN NO. 167)

1. SUBDIVISION REGULATION.
2. SUBDIVISION REGULATION -
WASHINGTON (S   TATE) I. ASSOCIATION
(CONTINUED ON NEXT CARD)

711.6
M17n
Subdivision regulation.
National Committee on Housing.
Neighborhood design and control, an
analysis of the problems of planned sub-
divisions, by Henry S. Churchill and
Roslyn Ittleson. New York, 1944.
39p.

1. Subdivision design. 2. Subdivision regulation.
I. Churchill, Henry S. II. Ittleson, Roslyn.

LAW
T
C158s
Campbell, Ernest H   Surveys...(Card 2)

1. Subdivision regulation. 2. Site planning.
I. Vogel, Joshua H., jt. au. II. Washington
(State) University. Bureau of Governmental
Research and   Services. III. Title.

333.38
J25
JENNINGS, FLOYD M REGULATING
SUBDIVISIONS....1954.   (CARD 2)

OF WASHINGTON CITIES. II. WASHINGTON
(STATE) UNIVERSITY. GOVERNMENTAL
RESEARCH & SERVICES.

VF
333.38
N28
1954
Subdivision regulation.
New York. Dept. of Commerce.
Control of land subdivision; a manual of
subdivision regulation for municipal officials,
subdivision developers, builders and planning
boards. [Albany, 1954.]
44p.   illus.

VF
711.4
(772)
:06
C65
Subdivision regulation.
Community Planning Institute, Turkey Run State
Park.
Summary of proceedings,3- annual Community
Planning Institute, sponsored by Indiana Economic
Council. Indianapolis, Ind., Indiana Economic
Council, 1949-
v.
For full information see shelf list card.
Processed.
1. City planning-Ind. 2. Zoning. 3. Subdivision regu-
lation. 4. Annexation. I. Indiana. Economic Council.
Analytics: Ashton, R. C.; Middleton, P. E.
5. City planning-Congr   es.

333.38 (73)
L18
Subdivision regulation.
Lautner, Harold William.
Subdivision regulations; an analysis of land
subdivision control practices, by Harold W. Lautner
...Chicago, Public administration service, 1941.
xvii, 346 p. incl. tables, diagrs.

Bibliography: p. 300-313, 343-346.

1. City planning. 2. Subdivision regulations-U.S.

VF
333.38
N28
Subdivision regulation.
New York. Dept. of Commerce. Bureau of Planning.
Subdivision control: a step toward better
communities; a manual of subdivision regulation
for municipal officials, subdivision developers,
builders and planning boards. Albany, 1946.
35 p.   illus.

"List of references": p. 35.

1. Subdivision regulation. I. Title.

711.4
(746)
C65
Subdivision regulation
Connecticut. *Development Commission.*
Planning aids for community development; presenting a
factual guide ... for the assistance of local planning and
zoning commissions in the accomplishment of their work.
[Hartford, 1950?]
1 v. (loose-leaf) illus., maps. 29 cm.
Cover title.
Includes bibliographical references.

For full tracing see main entry.
1. Cities and towns—Planning—Connecticut. 2. Zoning—Connecticut.

NA9125.C6A53   711   50-62774
Library of Congress   [2]

711.4
M15
Subdivision regulation.
Mandelker, Daniel R
Controlling planned residential develop-
ments. Chicago, American Society of
Planning Officials, 1966.
66p.
Bibliography: p. 63-66.

1. Residential areas. 2. Zoning.
3. Subdivision regulation. I. American
Society of Planning Officials. II. Title.
III. Title: Planned residential developments.

FILM
333.38
:711
N28
SUBDIVISION REGULATION.
NEW CONCEPTS OF LAND SUBDIVISION USING
PLANORAMA 3-DIMENSIONAL SCALE MODELS
(SLIDES) WASHINGTON, NATIONAL
ASSOCIATION OF HOME BUILDERS, 1963.
34 COLOR SLIDES, 20P.

1. SUBDIVISION - PLANNING.
2. SUBDIVISION REGULATION.
I. NATIONAL ASSOCIATION OF HOME
BUILDERS.

LAW
T
H117La
1971
SUBDIVISION REGULATION.
Haar, Charles M
Land-use planning; a casebook on the use
misuse, and re-use of urban land. Boston,
Little Brown, 1971.
788p. (Law school casebook series)

1. Land use. 2. City planning. 3. Subdivision regulation. 4. Zoning. I. Title.

333.38
M678
SUBDIVISION REGULATION.
MOTT, SEWARD H
SUBDIVISION REGULATIONS AND
PROTECTIVE COVENANTS, THEIR APPLICATION
TO LAND DEVELOPMENT, BY SEWARD H. MOTT
AND MAX S. WEHRLY. WASHINGTON, URBAN
LAND INSTITUTE, 1947.
8P. (TECHNICAL BULLETIN NO. 8)

1. SUBDIVISION REGULATION. 2. DEED
RESTRICTIONS. I. WEHRLY, MAX S., JT.
AU. II. TITLE: PROTECTIVE COVENANTS.
(SERIES: URBAN LAND INSTITUTE.
TECHNICAL BULLETIN NO. 8)

333.38
O45
Subdivision regulation.
Oklahoma. University. Institute of Community
Development.
Standards and regulations for the subdivision
of land, by Lee Rodgers. [Prepared for] the
Oklahoma Dept. of Commerce and Industry.
[Norman, Okla.] 1959.
35p.

U.S. Urban Renewal Adm. UPAP.

1. Subdivision regulation. I. Rodgers,
Lee. II. U.S. URA-UPAP.

333.38
(795)
O7cL
SUBDIVISION REGULATION.
OREGON. REAL ESTATE DEPT.
LAND DEVELOPER'S GUIDE. WILLIAM E.
HEALY, EDITOR. SALEM, OR., 1963.
36P.

INCLUDES LEGISLATION.

1. SUBDIVISION REGULATION.
I. HEALY, WILLIAM E., ED. II. TITLE.

VF
333.38
H68
1960
Subdivision regulation.
U.S. Housing and Home Finance Agency. Div.
of Housing Research.
Suggested land subdivision regulations.
Rev. Washington, Govt. Print. Off., 1960.
68p. illus., diagrs.

Bibliography: p. 63-64.

1. Subdivision regulation.

333.38
W74
Subdivision regulation.
Wright, Henry.
Some principles relating to the economics
of land subdivision; paper and discussion at
the meeting of the American City Planning
Institute, held at Briarcliff Manor, New York,
November 1, 1929. New York (City) American
City Planning Institute, 1930.
20p. (American City Planning Institute
Paper no. I, Series of 1930)

1. Subdivision regulation. I. American City Planning
Institute, New York, 1929.

728.1
N176b
no.2
Subdivision regulation.
Raymond & May Associates.
Land development decisions in suburban
areas; three case studies of planning and
zoning decisions in the New York suburbs.
White Plains, N.Y., 1968.
1v. (Background paper [no.2] for U.S.
National Commission on Urban Problems)

1. Housing. 2. Subdivision regulation.
3. Suburbs. I. U.S. National Commission
on Urban Problems. II. Title.

333.38
H68
1962
Subdivision regulation.
U.S. Housing and Home Finance Agency.
(Office of the Administrator) Div. of
Housing Research.
Suggested land subdivision regulations.
Rev. Washington, 1962.
68p.

Bibliography: p. 63-64.

1. Subdivision regulation.

333.38
Y21
SUBDIVISION REGULATION.
Yearwood, Richard M
Land subdivision regulation: policy and
legal considerations for urban planning.
New York, Praeger, 1971.
315p. (Praeger special studies in U.S.
economic and social development)
Bibliography: p. 295-315.

1. Subdivision regulation. I. Title.

333.38
P47
Subdivision regulation.
Pittsburgh. University. (Institute of Local
Government)
Proceedings [of] Local Government Conference
on Subdivision Control, May 16, 17, 1957.
[Pittsburgh] 1957.
82p. "General references": p. 70-78.

1.Subdivision regulation. 2.Local government.

VF
728.1
:355.1
H68c
no. 2
Subdivision regulation.
U.S. National Housing Agency.
Building sites for veterans housing;
setting up the action program, sites for
1946 building. Washington, May-Sept. 1946.
2 pts. (Its Community action bulletin
no. 2 & 2A)
Bulletin 2A called: Subdivision control
and building sites; pp. 1-8, 51 also published
as Bulletin 7.

1.Site selection. 2.Subdivision regulation.
I.Title. (Series)

LAW
T
Y645La
Yokley, E C
The law of subdivisions. [Charlottesville,
Va.] Michie Co., 1963.
492p.

Table of cases: p. [403]-440.

1. Subdivision regulation. I. Title.

VF
333.38
S68
Subdivision regulation.
Southern Association of State Planning and
Development Agencies.
A guide to subdivision regulation. [n.p.]
1953.
37 p. illus.

1.Subdivision regulation. I.Title.

VF
333.38
N17
Subdivision regulation.
U.S. National Housing Agency.
A check list for the review of local
subdivision controls. Washington, Jan. 1947.
43 p. (Its NHA Technical series no. 1)

1. Subdivision regulation.

333.38
(76131)
A11
Subdivision regulation - Abbeville, Ala.
Abbeville, Ala. City Planning Commission.
Abbeville, Alabama; land subdivision regu-
lations and manual. [In cooperation with]
Alabama State Planning and Industrial De-
velopment Board. Abbeville, 1957.
1v. diagrs.

U.S. Urban Renewal Administration, Urban
Planning Assistance Program.

(Continued on next
card)

VF
333.38
A28
1936
Subdivision regulation.
U.S. Advisory Committee on City Planning and
Zoning.
Model subdivision regulations; a guide for
local planning commissions in the preparation of
local regulations governing the subdivision of
land. Washington, National Resources Committee,
Dec. 1936.
26 p.

Mimeographed.

1.Subdivision regulation. I.U.S. National
Resources Committee.

VF
333.38
N17c
Subdivision regulation.
U.S. National Housing Agency. (Office
of the Administrator. Office of the
General Counsel)
Comparative analysis of the principal
provisions of state subdivision control
laws relating to housing and urban development. Washington, 1945.
[2]p.

1. Subdivision regulation. I. Title.

333.38
(76131)
A11
Abbeville, Ala. City Planning Commission. Abbeville, ... (Card 2)

1. Subdivision regulation - Abbeville,
Ala. I. Alabama. State Planning and
Industrial Development Board. II. U.S.
Urban Renewal Administration. Urban
Planning Assistance Program.

VF
333.38
H68
Subdivision regulation.
U.S. Housing and Home Finance Agency. (Office of
the Administrator) Division of Housing
Research.
Suggested land subdivision regulations.
Washington, Govt. Print. Off., Feb. 1952.
65 p. illus., plans.
Prepared by the Division of Housing Research
and the Community Planning Branch of the Division
of Slum Clearance and Urban Redevelopment, and the
Land Planning Section, Federal Housing
Administration.
Bibliography: p. 62.

VF
728.1
:355.1
H68c
no. 7
Subdivision regulation.
U.S. National Housing Agency.
Subdivision control and veterans housing.
Washington, Nov. 1946.
12 p. (Its community action bulletin
no. 7)
Bibliography: p. 12
Identical with bulletin 2A, p. 1-8, 51.

1.Subdivision regulation. (Series)

333.38
(77349)
A14
Subdivision regulation - Abingdon, Ill.
Abingdon, Ill. Ordinances, etc.
Zoning and subdivision ordinance, Abing-
don, Illinois. Abingdon [1959?]
22p.

U.S. Urban Renewal Administration, Urban Planning
Assistance Program.

1. Subdivision regulation - Abingdon, Ill. 2. Zoning legislation - Abingdon, Ill. I. U.S. Urban Renewal Administration, Urban Planning Assistance
Program. Abingdon, Ill.

VF
333.38
H68
1957
Subdivision regulation.
U.S. Housing and Home Finance Agency. (Of-
fice of the Administrator) Div. of
Housing Research.
Suggested land subdivision regulations.
Rev. Washington, Govt. Print. Off., 1957.
64p. illus., diagrs.

Bibliography: p. 61-62.

1. Subdivision regulation.

VF
711.14
W39
Subdivision regulation.
Whyte, William H , Jr.
A plan to save vanishing U.S. countryside;
an expert observer tells how to protect our
open spaces and halt the land-killing dis-
ease of urban sprawl. Detached from Life,
Aug. 17, 1959. p. 88-100.

1. Land use. 2. Subdivision regulation.

333.38
(7441)
A21
Subdivision regulation - Adams, Mass.
Adams, Mass. Ordinances, etc.
Rules and regulations governing the sub-
division of land, Adams, Massachusetts.
[Adams, Mass., 1950?]
9p.

U.S. Urban Renewal Adm. UPAP.

1. Subdivision regulation - Adams, Mass.
I. U.S. URA-UPAP Adams, Mass.

Subdivision regulation - Addison, Ala.

333.38
(76174)
A22
Addison, Ala. Town Planning Commission.
Addison, Alabama: subdivision regulations.
[Prepared in cooperation with] Alabama
State Planning and Industrial Development
Board. Addison, 1963.
39p.

U.S. Urban Renewal Adm. UPAP.

1. Subdivision regulation - Addison,
Ala. I. U.S. URA-UPAP. Addison, Ala.

Subdivision regulation - Albany, Or.

711.14
(79535)
072
Oregon. University. Bureau of Municipal
Research and Service.
Land use in the Albany Planning area. Pre-
pared for the Albany City Planning Commission.
Eugene, Or. 1959?
1v. tables.
U.S. Urban Renewal Administration, Urban
Planning Assistance Program.

1. Land use - Albany, Or. 2. Subdivision
regulation - Albany, Or. I. Albany, Or. City
Planning Commission. II. U.S. Urban Renewal
Administration. Urban Planning Assistance Program. Albany, Or.

78
SUBDIVISION REGULATION - ALPINE CO.,
CALIF.
ALPINE CO., CALIF. PLANNING COMMISSION.
PROPOSED LAND DIVISION ORDINANCE.
MARKLEEVILLE, CALIF., 1968.
24P. (HUD 701 REPORT)

1. SUBDIVISION REGULATION - ALPINE CO.,
CALIF. I. HUD. 701. ALPINE CO., CALIF.

385
SUBDIVISION REGULATION - ADEL, GA.
ADEL, GA. PLANNING COMMISSION.
SUBDIVISION REGULATIONS. PREPARED UNDER
CONTRACT WITH THE STATE PLANNING BUREAU BY
COASTAL PLAIN AREA PLANNING AND
DEVELOPMENT COMMISSION. ATLANTA, 1969.
18L. (HUD 701 REPORT)

1. SUBDIVISION REGULATION - ADEL, GA.
I. COASTAL PLAIN AREA PLANNING AND
DEVELOPMENT COMMISSION. II. HUD. 701.
ADEL, GA.

2172
SUBDIVISION REGULATION - ALDA, NEB.
ALDA, NEB. BOARD OF TRUSTEES.
FORM OF SUBDIVISION REGULATIONS. BY
HENNINGSON, DURHAM AND RICHARDSON. ALDA,
NEB., 1970.
1 V. (HUD 701 REPORT)

1. SUBDIVISION REGULATION - ALDA, NEB.
I. HENNINGSON, DURHAM AND RICHARDSON.
II. HUD. 701. ALDA, NEB.

810
SUBDIVISION REGULATION - ALTA, IOWA.
ALTA, IOWA. TOWN COUNCIL.
PROPOSED SUBDIVISION ORDINANCE. DES
MOINES, ANDERSON ENGINEERING CO., N.D.
13P. (HUD 701 REPORT)

1. SUBDIVISION REGULATION - ALTA, IOWA.
I. ANDERSON ENGINEERING CO. II. HUD.
701. ALTA, IOWA.

2
SUBDIVISION REGULATION - ALABASTER, ALA.
ALABASTER, ALA. PLANNING COMMISSION.
SUBDIVISION REGULATIONS. ALABASTER, ALA.,
1970.
27P. (HUD 701 REPORT)

1. SUBDIVISION REGULATION - ALABASTER, ALA.
I. HUD. 701. ALABASTER, ALA.

Subdivision regulation - Algonquin, Ill.

333.38
(77322)
K45
Kincaid (Evert) and Associates.
Proposed subdivision regulations,
Algonquin, Illinois. Chicago, 1958.
28p.

U. S. Urban Renewal Administration,
Urban Planning Assistance Program.

1. Subdivision regulation - Algonquin,
Ill. I. Algonquin, Ill. Ordinances,
etc. II. U.S. URA-UPAP. Algonquin,
Ill.

815
SUBDIVISION REGULATION - ALTA, IOWA.
ALTA, IOWA. TOWN COUNCIL.
ZONING AND SUBDIVISION ORDINANCES.
ALTA, IOWA, 1970.
1 V. (HUD 701 REPORT)

1. ZONING - ALTA, IOWA. 2. SUBDIVISION
REGULATION - ALTA, IOWA. I. HUD. 701.
ALTA, IOWA.

Subdivision regulation - Alabaster, Ala.

333.38
(76179)
A51
Alabaster, Ala. Town Planning Commission.
Alabaster, Alabama: land subdivision
regulations and manual. [In cooperation with]
Alabama State Planning and Industrial Development Board. Alabaster, 1957.
1v. diagrs.

U.S. Urban Renewal Administration, Urban
Planning Assistance Program.

(Continued on next card)

Subdivision regulation - Aliceville, Ala.

333.38
(76185)
A54
Aliceville, Ala. City Planning Commission.
Aliceville, Alabama: land subdivision regulations and manual. [In cooperation with]
Alabama State Planning and Industrial Development Board. Aliceville, 1958.
23p. diagrs.

U.S. Urban Renewal Administration, Urban Planning
Assistance Program.

1. Subdivision regulation - Aliceville, Ala. I. U.S.
URA-UPAP. Aliceville, Ala.

Subdivision regulation - Altoona, Ala.

333.38
(76167)
A57
Altoona, Ala. Town Planning Commission.
Altoona, Alabama: subdivision regu-
lations. [Prepared in cooperation with]
Alabama State Planning and Industrial
Development Board. Altoona, 1963.
39p.

U.S. Urban Renewal Adm. UPAP.

1. Subdivision regulation - Altoona,
Ala. I. U.S. URA-UPAP. Altoona, Ala.

333.38
(76179)
A51
Alabaster, Ala. Town Planning Commission.
Alabaster, Alabama: land ...(Card 2)

1. Subdivision regulation - Alabaster, Ala.
I. Alabama. State Planning and Industrial
Development Board. II. U.S. Urban Renewal
Administration. Urban Planning Assistance
Program.

Subdivision regulation - Allegheny Co., Pa.

333.38
(74885)
H45
Hill (Carroll V.) & Associates.
Model subdivision regulations,
Northwest Allegheny Regional Planning
Association. Pittsburgh, [1962?]
26p.

U.S. Urban Renewal Adm. UPAP.

1. Subdivision regulation - Allegheny Co., Pa.
2. Northwest Allegheny Regional Planning
Association. I. U.S. URA-UPAP. Allegheny
Co., Pa.

Subdivision regulation - Altoona metropolitan
area.

333.38
(74875)
B51
Blair Regional Planning Commission.
A plan for land subdivision regulations.
[In cooperation with] Clifton E. Rodgers
and Associates. Altoona, Pa., 1958.
1v.

U.S. Urban Renewal Administration, Urban Planning
Assistance Program.

1. Subdivision regulation - Altoona metropolitan
area. I. Rodgers (Clifton E.) and Associates.
II. U.S. URA-UPAP. Altoona metropolitan area.

Subdivision regulation - Alamo, Ga.

333.38
(758835)
G26
Georgia. Dept of Commerce.
Suggested subdivision regulations for
Alamo, Georgia. Prepared for the Alamo
Planning Commission. Atlanta, 1959.
16p.

U.S. Urban Renewal Administration, Urban Planning
Assistance Program.
1. Subdivision regulation - Alamo, Ga. I. Alamo,
Ga. Planning Commission. II. U.S. URA-UPAP.
Alamo, Ga.

Subdivision regulation - Allendale, N.J.

711.4
(74921)
A55m
no. 7
Community Planning Associates.
Borough of Allendale: subdivision
review. West Trenton, N.J., 1959.
4p. (Borough of Allendale
master plan studies memo. no. 7)

U.S. Urban Renewal Adm. UPAP.

1. Master plan - Allendale, N.J.
2. Subdivision regulation - Allendale, N.J.
I. U.S. URA-UPAP. Allendale, N.J.

1770
SUBDIVISION REGULATION - AMCHIR, N.Y.
AMCHIR, N.Y. PLANNING BOARD.
PROPOSED SUBDIVISION REGULATIONS.
AMCHIR, N.Y., 1967.
29L. (HUD 701 REPORT)

1. SUBDIVISION REGULATION - AMCHIR, N.Y.
I. HUD. 701. AMCHIR, N.Y.

Subdivision regulation - Albany, Or.

333.38
(79535)
A51
Albany, Or. Ordinances, etc.
An ordinance providing subdivision
standards and procedures. Ordinance
no. 2718. Albany, 1956.
11p.

1. Subdivision regulation - Albany, Or.

Subdivision regulation - Alpine, N.J.

333.38
(74921)
A56
Alpine, N.J. Ordinances, etc.
Proposed revisions to subdivision
ordinance, Borough of Alpine. [Alpine,
1960]
4p.

U.S. Urban Renewal Adm. UPAP.

1. Subdivision regulation - Alpine, N.J.
I. U.S. URA-UPAP. Alpine, N.J.

Subdivision regulation - Americus, Ga.

333.38
(75891)
H45
Hill and Adley Associates.
Proposed subdivision regulations for
Americus, Georgia. Prepared for Americus-
Sumter County Planning Commission, under
contract with the Georgia Dept. of Commerce.
Atlanta, 1959.
24p.

U.S. Urban Renewal Adm. UPAP.

1. Subdivision regulation - Americus, Ga. I. Americus-
Sumter County (Ga.) Planning Commission. II. U.S.
URA-UPAP. Americus, Ga.

Subdivision regulation - Anadarko, Okla.

333.38
(76641)
045
Oklahoma. University. Institute of Community Development.
An ordinance for the regulation of land subdivision, Anadarko, Oklahoma. Proposed. Norman, Okla., 1957.

U.S. Urban Renewal Administration, Urban Planning Assistance Program.

1. Subdivision regulation - Anadarko, Okla. I. U.S. URA-UPAP. Anadarko, Ok

---

711.4
(791)
A52
SUBDIVISION REGULATION - ARIZONA.
American Institute of Planners. Desert Southwest Chapter.
Proposed Arizona enabling legislation for municipal planning, zoning and subdivision regulation. [n.p.] 1968.
1v.

1. City planning - Arizona. 2. Zoning legislation - Arizona. 3. Subdivision regulation - Arizona. I. Title.

Subdivision regulation - Ashland, Ala.

333.38
(76158)
A73
Ashland, Ala. Town Planning Commission.
Ashland, Alabama: land subdivision regulations and manual. [In cooperation with] Alabama State Planning and Industrial Development Board. Ashland, 1959.
23p. diagrs.

U.S. Urban Renewal Administration, Urban Planning Assistance Program.

1. Subdivision regulation - Ashland, Ala. I. U.S. URA-UPAP. Ashland, Ala.

Subdivision regulation - Andover, Conn.

333.38
(7464)
Y17
Yarwood & Block, inc.
Subdivision regulations, Andover, Connecticut. Proposed revision. Simsbury, Conn., 1960.
12p.

[Prepared for] Andover Planning and Zoning Commission.
U.S. Urban Renewal Adm. UPAP.

1. Subdivision regulation - Andover, Conn. I. Andover, Conn. Planning and Zoning Commission.
II. U.S. URA-UPAP. Andover, Conn.

333.38
(767)
A74
Subdivision regulations - Arkansas.
Arkansas. University. City Planning Division.
A guide for subdivision regulations, by William S. Bonner. [Fayetteville, Ark.] 1957
12p. (Its Publication no. 209)

1. Subdivision regulation - Arkansas.
I. Bonner, William S

15
SUBDIVISION REGULATION - ASHLAND, ALA.
ASHLAND, ALA. TOWN PLANNING COMMISSION.
SUBDIVISION REGULATIONS. ASHLAND, ALA.,
1970.
34P. (HUD 701 REPORT)

1. SUBDIVISION REGULATION - ASHLAND, ALA.
I. HUD. 701. ASHLAND, ALA.

Subdivision regulation - Andover, N.J.

333.38
(74976)
C65
Community Planning Associates.
Subdivision ordinance review. Memorandum to Andover [N.J.] Township Planning Board. [West Trenton, N.J.] 1959.
2p.
U.S. Urban Renewal Adm. UPAP.

1. Subdivision regulation - Andover, N.J.
I. Andover, N.J. Township Planning Board.
II. U.S. URA-UPAP. Andover, N.J.

Subdivision regulation - Arlington, Or.

333.38
(79567)
A75
Arlington, Or. Ordinances, etc.
An ordinance providing subdivision standards and procedures. Arlington, Or., 1959.
9p.

U.S. Urban Renewal Administration, Urban Planning Assistance Program.

1. Subdivision regulation - Arlington, Or.
I. U.S. URA-UPAP. Arlington, Or.

Subdivision regulation - Ashland, Ill.

333.38
(773465)
A73
Ashland, Ill Plan Commission.
Suggested subdivision ordinance, Ashland, Illinois, by Gregory Bassett. Urbana, Ill. 1960.
15p.

U.S. Urban Renewal Adm. UPAP.

1. Subdivision regulation - Ashland, Ill. I. Bassett, Gregory. II. U.S. URA-UPAP. Ashland, Ill.

1502
SUBDIVISION REGULATION - ANNE ARUNDEL
CO., MD.
ANNE ARUNDEL CO., MD. OFFICE OF PLANNING AND ZONING.
PROPOSED SUBDIVISION REGULATIONS.
MARCOU, O'LEARY AND ASSOCIATES.
ANNAPOLIS, MD., 1967.
63L. (HUD 701 REPORT)

1. SUBDIVISION REGULATION - ANNE ARUNDEL CO., MD. I. MARCOU, O'LEARY AND ASSOCIATES. II. HUD. 701. ANNE ARUNDEL CO., MD.

Subdivision regulation - Arlington Heights, Il

333.38
(77311)
K45p
Kincaid (Evert) and Associates.
Proposed subdivision regulations, Arlington Heights, Illinois. [Prepared for Village Plan Commission] Rev. Chicago, 1958.
59p.
U.S. Urban Renewal Administration, Urban Planning Assistance Program.

1. Subdivision regulation - Arlington Heights Ill. I. Arlington Heights, Ill. Village Plan Commission. II. U.S. Urban Renewal Administration. Urban Planning Assistance Program. Arlington Heights, Ill.

Subdivision regulation - Athens, Ala.

333.38
(76198)
A73
Athens, Ala. City Planning Commission.
Athens, Alabama: land subdivision regulations and manual. [In cooperation with] Alabama State Planning and Industrial Development Board. Athens, 1959.
1v. diagrs.

U.S. Urban Renewal Administration, Urban Planning Assistance Program.

1. Subdivision regulation - Athens, Ala. I. U.S. URA-UPAP. Athens, Alabama.

333.38
(76393)
M17
Subdivision regulation - Arcadia, La.
Martin (Dan S.) and Associates.
Subdivision regulations, Arcadia, Louisiana. Prepared for the Arcadia Planning Commission. New Orleans, 1959.
17p.

U.S. Urban Renewal Administration, Urban Planning Assistance Program.

1. Subdivision regulation - Arcadia, La. I. Arcadia, La. Planning Commission. II. U.S. URA-UPAP. Arcadia, La.

1432
SUBDIVISION REGULATION - ARMADA, MICH.
ARMADA, MICH. VILLAGE PLANNING COMMISSION.
SUBDIVISION REGULATIONS FOR THE PLATTING OF LAND IN THE VILLAGE OF ARMADA, MICHIGAN. PREPARED BY DEVELOPMENT PLANNING COMPANY. PONTIAC, MICH., 1966.
36L. (HUD 701 REPORT)

1. SUBDIVISION REGULATION - ARMADA, MICH. I. DEVELOPMENT PLANNING CO., PONTIAC, MICH. II. HUD. 701. ARMADA, MICH.

Subdivision regulation - Atlanta, Ga.

711.4
(758725)
818s
Savannah, Ga. Metropolitan Planning Commission.
Subdivision regulations, City of Savannah and Chatham County. First rough draft, prepared for the purpose of discussion by the Subdivision Development Committee. A part of the master plan for the City of Savannah and Chatham County. [Tentative ed.] Savannah, 1956.
42p.
U.S. Urban Renewal Administration,
(Continued on next card)

5360
SUBDIVISION REGULATION - ARCADIA, N.Y.
ARCADIA, N.Y. PLANNING COMMISSION.
PROPOSED SUBDIVISION REGULATIONS (A DRAFT FOR DISCUSSION AND REVIEW).
SYRACUSE, N.Y., 1964.
47L. (HUD 701 REPORT)

1. SUBDIVISION REGULATION - ARCADIA, N.Y. I. HUD. 701. ARCADIA, N.Y.

386
SUBDIVISION REGULATION - ASHBURN, GA.
ASHBURN, GA. PLANNING COMMISSION.
SUBDIVISION REGULATIONS. PREPARED UNDER CONTRACT WITH THE STATE PLANNING BUREAU, BY COASTAL PLAIN AREA PLANNING AND DEVELOPMENT COMMISSION. ATLANTA, 1969.
28P. (HUD 701 REPORT)

1. SUBDIVISION REGULATION - ASHBURN, GA. I. COASTAL PLAIN AREA PLANNING AND DEVELOPMENT COMMISSION. II. HUD. 701. ASHBURN, GA.

711.4
(758725)
818s
Savannah, Ga. Metropolitan Planning Commission. Subdivision ... (Card 2)

Urban Planning Assistance Program.

1. Master plan - Savannah, Ga. 2. Master plan - Chatham Co., Ga. 3. Subdivision regulation - Chatham Co., Ga. 4. Subdivision regulation - Atlanta, Ga. I. U.S. Urban Renewal Administration. Urban Planning Assistance Program.

Subdivision regulation - Ariton, Ala.

333.38
(76133)
A74
Ariton, Ala. Town Planning Commission.
Ariton, Alabama: subdivision regulations. [Prepared for] Alabama State Planning and Industrial Development Board. Ariton, 1960.
36p.

U.S. Urban Renewal Adm. UPAP.

1. Subdivision regulation - Ariton, Ala. I. U.S. URA-UPAP. Ariton, Ala.

Subdivision regulation - Ashford, Ala.

333.38
(761295)
A73
Ashford, Ala. Town Planning Commission.
Ashford, Alabama: subdivision regulations. [Prepared for] Alabama State Planning and Industrial Development Board. Ashford, 1960.
36p.

U.S. Urban Renewal Adm. UPAP.

1. Subdivision regulation - Ashford, Ala. I. U.S. URA-UPAP. Ashford, Ala.

333.38
(7418)
B51
Subdivision regulation - Auburn, Me.
Blackwell, John T
Subdivision regulations for the City of Auburn. Boston, 1958.
32p.

U.S. Urban Renewal Administration, Urban Planning Assistance Program.

1. Subdivision regulation - Auburn, Me. I. U.S. Urban Renewal Administration. Urban Planning Assistance Program.

Subdivision regulation - Auburn, Wash.

333.38
(79777)
A81
Auburn, Wash. Ordinances, etc.
Subdivision ordinance for the City of Auburn, Washington, by George Schuler and others. [Auburn] 1960.
22p.

U.S. Urban Renewal Adm. UPAP.

1. Subdivision regulation - Auburn, Wash. I. Schuler, George. II. U.S. URA-UPAP. Auburn, Wash.

711.3
(7526)
B15
no.8
Subdivision regulation - Baltimore.

Baltimore Regional Planning Council.
Zoning and subdivision laws in the Baltimore region. Baltimore, Maryland State Planning Dept., 1963.
103p. (Its Technical rept. no. 8)

U.S. Urban Renewal Adm. UPAP.

1. Metropolitan area planning - Baltimore. 2. Zoning legislation - Baltimore. 3. Subdivision regulation - Baltimore.
I. U.S. URA-UPAP. Baltimore.

711.4
(76122)
B68
Bayou La Batre, Ala. Town Planning Commission. Bayou La Batre, Alabama: land subdivision . . . (Card 2)

1. City planning - Bayou La Batre, Ala.
2. Subdivision regulations - Bayou La Batre, Ala. I. Alabama. State Planning and Industrial Development Board. II. U.S. Urban Renewal Administration.

SUBDIVISION REGULATION - AU SABLE, MICH.

2996
OSCODA-AU SABLE REGIONAL PLANNING COMMISSION.
PROPOSED SUBDIVISION REGULATIONS; AN ORDINANCE FOR THE PLATTING OF LAND, AU SABLE TOWNSHIP, IOSCO COUNTY, MICHIGAN. BY VILICAN-LEMAN AND ASSOCIATES, INC. SOUTHFIELD, MICH., 1964.
29P. (HUD 701 REPORT)

1. SUBDIVISION REGULATION - AU SABLE, MICH. I. VILICAN-LEMAN AND ASSOCIATES. II. HUD. 701. AU SABLE, MICH.

333.38
(769125)
B17
Subdivision regulation - Barbourville, Ky.

Barbourville, Ky. City Planning Commission.
Subdivision regulations, City of Barbourville, Kentucky. Barbourville, [1960?]
19p.
Prepared with the assistance of the Dept. of Economic Development, Div. of Planning and Zoning, East Kentucky Office.
U.S. Urban Renewal Adm. UPAP.

1. Subdivision regulation - Barbourville, Ky. I. U.S. URA-UPAP. Barbourville, Ky.

333.38
(79543)
B21
Subdivision regulation - Beaverton, Or.

Beaverton, Or. Ordinances, etc.
An ordinance providing subdivision standards and procedures. Proposed subdivision regulations for Beaverton. [Eugene, Or.] 1958.
16p.
"Preliminary draft."
U.S. Urban Renewal Adm. UPAP.

1. Subdivision regulation - Beaverton, Or. I. U.S. URA-UPAP. Beaverton, Or.

821
SUBDIVISION REGULATION - AVOCA, IOWA.
AVOCA, IOWA. TOWN COUNCIL.
PROPOSED SUBDIVISION ORDINANCE. BY ANDERSON ENGINEERING CO. AVOCA, IOWA, 1968.
24P. (HUD 701 REPORT)

1. SUBDIVISION REGULATION - AVOCA, IOWA. I. ANDERSON ENGINEERING CO. II. HUD. 701. AVOCA, IOWA.

333.38
(74877)
B17
Subdivision regulation - Barnesboro, Pa.

Barnesboro, Pa. Ordinances, etc.
Proposed subdivision code for Barnesboro, Pennsylvania. Pittsburgh, Planning Consultants, 1961.
12p.

U.S. Urban Renewal Adm. UPAP.

1. Subdivision regulation Barnesboro, Pa. I. Planning Consultants, Pittsburgh, Pa. II. U.S. URA-UPAP. Barnesboro, Pa.

711.14
(79543)
072
Subdivision regulation - Beaverton, Or.

Oregon. University. Bureau of Municipal Research and Service.
Some suggested standards relating to the dedication of land for public use as a condition of subdivision approval, City of Beaverton, Oregon. Eugene, Or., 1958.
4p.

U.S. Urban Renewal Adm. UPAP.

1. Land use - Beaverton, Or. 2. Subdivision regulation - Beaverton, Or. I. U.S. URA-UPAP. Beaverton, Or.

822
SUBDIVISION REGULATION - AVOCA, IOWA.
AVOCA, IOWA. TOWN COUNCIL.
SUBDIVISION ORDINANCE. BY ANDERSON ENGINEERING CO. AVOCA, IOWA, 1969.
24P. (HUD 701 REPORT)

1. SUBDIVISION REGULATION - AVOCA, IOWA. I. ANDERSON ENGINEERING CO. II. HUD. 701. AVOCA, IOWA.

VF
333.38
(763181)
B17
Subdivision regulation - Baton Rouge, La.

Baton Rouge, La. City-Parish Planning Commission.
City-Parish subdivision ordinance, adopted April 27, 1955. Baton Rouge, 1958.
15p.

U.S. Urban Renewal Adm. UPAP.

1. Subdivision regulation - Baton Rouge, La. I. U.S. URA-UPAP. Baton Rouge, La.

333.38
(79543)
072
Subdivision regulation - Beaverton, Or.

Oregon. University. Bureau of Municipal Research and Service.
Subdivision procedures, City of Beaverton. Eugene, Or., 1957.
7p.

U.S. Urban Renewal Administration, Urban Planning Assistance Program.

1. Subdivision regulation - Beaverton, Or. I. U.S. URA-UPAP. Beaverton, Or.

457
SUBDIVISION REGULATION - BACON CO., GA.
ALMA-BACON CO., GA. PLANNING COMMISSION.
PROPOSED SUBDIVISION REGULATIONS, BACON COUNTY, GEORGIA. PREPARED UNDER CONTRACT WITH THE STATE PLANNING BUREAU OF THE STATE OF GEORGIA BY THE SLASH PINE AREA PLANNING AND DEVELOPMENT COMMISSION. WAYCROSS, GA., 1969.
32L. (HUD 701 REPORT)

1. SUBDIVISION REGULATION - BACON CO., GA. I. SLASH PINE AREA PLANNING & DEVELOPMENT COMMISSION. II. HUD. 701. BACON CO., GA.

468
SUBDIVISION REGULATION - BAXLEY, GA.
BAXLEY-APPLING COUNTY PLANNING COMMISSION.
BAXLEY, GEORGIA, COMPREHENSIVE PLAN SUBDIVISION REGULATIONS. PREPARED UNDER CONTRACT WITH THE STATE PLANNING BUREAU BY ALTAMAHA AREA PLANNING AND DEVELOPMENT COMMISSION. ATLANTA, STATE PLANNING BUREAU, 1969.
35L. (HUD 701 REPORT)

1. SUBDIVISION REGULATION - BAXLEY, GA. I. ALTAMAHA AREA PLANNING AND DEVELOPMENT COMMISSION. II. HUD. 701. BAXLEY, GA.

711.5
(74871)
:347)
RG2
Subdivision regulation - Bedford, Pa.

Rodgers (Clifton E.) and Associates.
Bedford, 1958: zoning ordinance and subdivision regulations. Harrisburg, Pa. 1958.
1v. map.

U.S. Urban Renewal Administration, Urban Planning Assistance Program.

1. Zoning legislation - Bedford, Pa. 2. Subdivision regulation - Bedford, Pa. I. U.S. URA-UPAP. Bedford, Pa.

2942
SUBDIVISION REGULATION - BALDWIN, MICH.
BALDWIN, MICH. PLANNING COMMISSION.
SUBDIVISION ORDINANCE, BALDWIN TOWNSHIP, IOSCO CO., MICHIGAN. BALDWIN, MICH., 1968.
12L. (HUD 701 REPORT)

1. SUBDIVISION REGULATION - BALDWIN, MICH. I. HUD. 701. BALDWIN, MICH.

333.38
(76121)
B19
Subdivision regulation - Bay Minette, Ala.

Bay Minette, Alabama. City Planning Commission.
Bay Minette, Alabama; subdivision regulations. [Prepared in cooperation with] Alabama State Planning and Industrial Development Board, Bay Minette, Ala., 1963.
39p.

U.S. Urban Renewal Adm. UPAP.

1. Subdivision regulation - Bay Minette, Ala. I. U.S. URA-UPAP. Bay Minette, Ala.

2929
SUBDIVISION REGULATION - BELDING, MICH.
BELDING, MICH. PLANNING COMMISSION.
PROPOSED SUBDIVISION REGULATIONS ORDINANCE; AN ORDINANCE FOR THE PLATTING OF LAND, CITY OF BELDING, IONIA COUNTY, MICHIGAN. STANDARDS BY: VILICAN-LEMAN AND ASSOCIATES, INC. SOUTHFIELD, MICH., 1968.
45L. (HUD 701 REPORT)

1. SUBDIVISION REGULATION - BELDING, MICH. I. VILICAN-LEMAN AND ASSOCIATES. II. HUD. 701. BELDING, MICH.

333.38
(79493)
B15
Subdivision regulation - Baldwin Park, Calif.

Baldwin Park, Calif. Ordinances, etc.
Subdivision ordinance of the City of Baldwin Park. [Preliminary] Baldwin Park, Calif. [1961?]
[26]p.

U.S. Urban Renewal Adm. UPAP.

1. Subdivision regulation - Baldwin Park, Calif. I. U.S. URA-UPAP. Baldwin Park, Calif.

711.4
(76122)
B68
Subdivision regulations - Bayou La Batre, Alabama.

Bayou La Batre, Ala. Town Planning Commission.
Bayou La Batre, Alabama: land subdivision regulations and manual. [In cooperation with Alabama State Planning and Industrial Development Board] Bayou La Batre, 1957.
29p. diagrs.

U.S. Urban Renewal Administration, Urban Planning Assistance Program.
(Continued on next card)

333.38
(79469)
P12
Subdivision regulation - Belmont, Calif.

Pacific Planning and Research.
Proposed subdivision ordinance; first draft, Belmont, California, Feb. 15, 1959. Palo Alto, Calif., 1959.
35p.

1. Subdivision regulation - Belmont, Calif. 2. Land use - Belmont, Calif.

4135   SUBDIVISION REGULATION - BERNVILLE, PA.
BERNVILLE, PA. PLANNING COMMISSION.
LAND SUBDIVISION REGULATIONS.
BERNVILLE, PA., 1966.
1 V. (HUD 701 REPORT)

1. SUBDIVISION REGULATION - BERNVILLE,
PA. I. HUD. 701. BERNVILLE, PA.

333.38   Subdivision regulation - Blountsville, Ala.
(76172) Blountsville, Ala. Town Planning Commission.
B56   Blountsville, Alabama: land subdivision
regulations and manual. [In cooperation with]
Alabama State Planning and Industrial Development Board. Blountsville, 1958.
1v. diagrs.

U.S. Renewal Administration, Urban
Planning Assistance Program.

(Continued on next card)

333.38   Subdivision regulation - Boswell, Pa.
(74944) Planning Consultants, Pittsburgh.
P51   Proposed subdivision code for Boswell,
Pennsylvania. Pittsburgh, 1961.
10p.

U.S. Urban Renewal Adm. UPAP.

1. Subdivision regulation - Boswell, Pa.
I. Boswell, Pa. Ordinances, etc. II. U.S. URA-UPAP.
Boswell, Pa.

Subdivision regulation - Bibliography.
333.38
(016)   California. Dept. of Finance.
C15   Subdivision regulations for hillsides: an
inventory of provisions in California subdivision ordinances and a basis for research.
[Sacramento, Calif.] 1960.
32p. (Its Bibliography no. 2)

1. Subdivision regulation - Bibliography.

333.38   Bloutsville, Ala. Town Planning Commission.
(76172) Blountsville, Alabama: land ...(Card 2)
356

1. Subdivision regulation - Blountsville,
Ala. I. Alabama. State Planning and In-
dustrial Development Board. II. U.S. Urban
Renewal Administration. Urban Planning
Assistance Program.

4784   SUBDIVISION REGULATION - BRANCH, PA.
BRANCH, PA. PLANNING COMMISSION.
SUBDIVISION REGULATIONS. BRANCH, PA.,
1963.
1 V. (HUD 701 REPORT)

1. SUBDIVISION REGULATION - BRANCH, PA.
I. HUD. 701. BRANCH, PA.

VF   Subdivision regulation - Bibliographies.
333.38
(016)   U.S. Housing and Home Finance Agency. Office
H68   of the Administrator. Library Reference
Service.
Subdivision regulations; suggested
references. [Washington] July 1948.
2 L.

1. Subdivision regulation - Bibliographies.

SUBDIVISION REGULATION - BOILING
SPRINGS, N.C.
3038   BOILING SPRINGS, N.C. PLANNING BOARD.
SUBDIVISION REGULATIONS. BY THE STATE
OF NORTH CAROLINA, DEPARTMENT OF LOCAL
AFFAIRS. BOILING SPRINGS, N.C., 1970.
27P. (HUD 701 REPORT)

1. SUBDIVISION REGULATION - BOILING
SPRINGS, N.C. I. NORTH CAROLINA. DEPT.
OF LOCAL AFFAIRS. II. HUD. 701.
BOILING SPRINGS, N.C.

Subdivision regulation - Brandenburg, Ky.
333.38
(76985) Brandenburg, Ky. City Planning Commission.
B71   Subdivision regulations, City of
Brandenburg, Ky. [Brandenburg, 1960?]
15p.
Prepared with the assistance of the
Division of Planning and Zoning, Kentucky
Dept. of Economic Development.
U.S. Urban Renewal Adm. UPAP.

1. Subdivision regulation - Brandenburg, Ky. I. U.S.
URA-UPAP. Brandenburg, Ky.

Subdivision regulation - Billerica, Mass.
333.38
(7444) Billerica, Mass. Planning Board.
B45   Rules and regulations governing the
subdivision of land in Billerica,
Massachusetts. Rev. Billerica, 1958.
34p.

U.S. Urban Renewal Adm. UPAP.

1. Subdivision regulation - Billerica,
Mass. I. U.S. URA-UPAP. Billerica, Mass.

1650   SUBDIVISION REGULATION - BOLIVAR, MO.
BOLIVAR, MO. PLANNING COMMISSION.
ZONING AND SUBDIVISION REGULATIONS.
PREPARED BY BUCHER AND WILLIS. BOLIVAR,
1969.
136P. (HUD 701 REPORT)

1. ZONING - BOLIVAR, MO.
2. SUBDIVISION REGULATION - BOLIVAR, MO.
I. BUCHER AND WILLIS. II. HUD. 701.
BOLIVAR, MO.

SUBDIVISION REGULATION - BRANTLEY CO.,
GEORGIA.
389   BRANTLEY CO., GA. PLANNING COMMISSION.
PROPOSED SUBDIVISION REGULATIONS,
BRANTLEY COUNTY, GEORGIA. PREPARED UNDER
CONTRACT WITH THE STATE PLANNING BUREAU OF
THE STATE OF GEORGIA, BY THE SLASH PINE
AREA PLANNING & DEVELOPMENT COMMISSION.
ATLANTA, STATE PLANNING BUREAU, 1969.
27L. (HUD 701 REPORT)

1. SUBDIVISION REGULATION - BRANTLEY
CO., GEORGIA. I. SLASH PINE AREA
PLANNING & DEVELOPMENT COMMISSION.
II. HUD. 701. BRANTLEY CO., GA.

1868   SUBDIVISION REGULATION - BILOXI, MISS.
BILOXI, MISS. CITY PLAN COMMISSION.
PROPOSED SUBDIVISION REGULATIONS. BY
PLANNING SERVICES, INC. BILOXI, MISS.,
1963.
35P. (HUD 701 REPORT)

1. SUBDIVISION REGULATION - BILOXI,
MISS. I. PLANNING SERVICES, INC.
II. HUD. 701. BILOXI, MISS.

333.38   Subdivision regulation - Bolivar, Tenn.
(76828) Bolivar, Tenn. Municipal Regional Planning
B65   Commission.
Subdivision regulations for Bolivar, Tennessee planning region. With the assistance of the Tennessee State Planning Commission, West Tennessee Office. Bolivar,
1957.
38p. diagrs., maps.

U.S. Urban Renewal Administration, Urban
(Continued on next card)

Subdivision regulation - Brilliant, Ala.
333.38
(76189) Brilliant, Ala. Town Planning Commission.
B74   Brilliant, Alabama: subdivision regulations. [Prepared in cooperation with]
Alabama State Planning and Industrial
Development Board. Brilliant, [1961]
36p.

U.S. Urban Renewal Adm. UPAP.

1. Subdivision regulation - Brilliant,
Ala. I. U.S. URA-UPAP.
Brilliant, Ala.

SUBDIVISION REGULATIONS -
BIRMINGHAM, ALA.
333.38   BIRMINGHAM, ALA. PLANNING COMMISSION.
(761781) SUBDIVISION REGULATIONS.
B47   BIRMINGHAM, ALA., 1962.
39P.

1. SUBDIVISION REGULATIONS -
BIRMINGHAM, ALA.

333.38   Bolivar, Tenn. Municipal Regional Planning
(76828) Commission. Subdivision ... (Card 2)
B65
Planning Assistance Program.

1. Subdivision regulation - Bolivar,
Tenn. I. Tennessee. State Planning
Commission. II. U.S. Urban Renewal Ad-
ministration. Urban Planning Assistance
Program.

Subdivision regulation - Bristow, Okla.
333.38
(76684) Bristow, Okla. Ordinances, etc.
B74   An ordinance for the regulation of land
subdivision for the City of Bristow, Oklahoma. Bristow, [1960?]
16p.

U.S. Urban Renewal Administration, Urban Planning Assistance Program.

1. Subdivision regulation - Bristow, Okla.
I. U.S. URA-UPAP. Bristow, Okla.

333.38   SUBDIVISION REGULATION - BISHOP, CALIF.
(79487) Hahn, Wise and Associates, inc.
H13   City of Bishop (Calif.); subdivision
ordinance. In cooperation with Koebig and
Koebig. San Carlos, Calif., 1963.
26p.

1. Subdivision regulation - Bishop, Calif.
I. Koebig and Koebig. II. Title.

711.5   Subdivision regulation - Booneville, Ark.
(76737   Arkansas. University. City Planning Div.
:347)   A guide for the administration of a
A51   zoning ordinance and subdivision and land
development regulations. Prepared for the
Booneville Planning Commission. Fayetteville, 1963.
1v.
U.S. Urban Renewal Adm. UPAP.
1. Zoning legislation - Booneville, Ark.
2. Subdivision regulation - Booneville, Ark.
I. Booneville, Ark.   Planning Commission.
II. U.S. URA-UPAP.   Booneville, Ark.

Subdivision regulation - Brockway, Pa.
333.38
(74862) Rodgers (Clifton E.) & Associates.
R62   Land subdivision regulations, Borough of
Brockway, Jefferson County, Pa. [n.p.]
1962.
[24]p.

U.S. Urban Renewal Adm. UPAP.

1. Subdivision regulation - Brockway,
Pa. I. Brockway, Pa. Ordinances, etc.
II. U.S. URA-UPAP. Brockway, Pa.

SUBDIVISION REGULATION - BROWN DEER,
4894   WIS.
4895   BROWN DEER, WIS. PLANNING COMMISSION.
       URBAN PLANNING: 1, PROPOSED
       SUBDIVISION CODE; 2, PROPOSED OFFICIAL
       MAP DETAILS. PREPARED BY CARL L.
       GARDNER AND ASSOCIATES, INC. CHICAGO,
       1965.
       2 V. (HUD 701 REPORT)

       1. SUBDIVISION REGULATION - BROWN DEER,
       WIS. I. GARDNER (CARL L.) AND
       ASSOCIATES. II. HUD. 701. BROWN DEER,
       WIS.

1058   SUBDIVISION REGULATION - BULLITT CO., KY.
       BULLITT CO., KY. PLANNING COMMISSION.
       SUBDIVISION REGULATIONS. BY JAMES R.
       AHART AND ASSOCIATES, INC. DAYTON, OHIO,
       1970.
       40P. (HUD 701 REPORT)

       1. SUBDIVISION REGULATION - BULLITT CO.,
       KY. II. AHART (JAMES R.) AND
       ASSOCIATES. II. HUD. 701. BULLITT
       CO., KY.

VF   Subdivision regulations - California.
333.38
(794) California. Legislature. Senate. Interim
C15   Committee on Subdivision Development and
1950   Planning.
           Second partial report of the Senate
       Interim Committee on Subdivision Development
       and Planning. Sacramento, 1955.
           55p.

           Senate Resolution No. 160, 1955.

           1. Subdivision regulations - California.

333.38   SUBDIVISION REGULATION - BROWNSVILLE, PA.
(74884) Beckman, Swenson & Associates.
B22   Proposed subdivision and land development
       ordinance, Brownsville Borough, Fayette
       County, Pennsylvania. Pittsburgh, [1970?]
           15p.

           1. Subdivision regulation - Brownsville,
       Pa. 2. Land use - Brownsville, Pa.

333.38   Subdivision regulation - Burgettstown, Pa.
(74882) Burgettstown, Pa. Ordinances, etc.
B87   Land subdivision regulations.
       Burgettstown, [1961?]
           1v.

           U.S. Urban Renewal Adm. UPAP.

           1. Subdivision regulation - Burgettstown,
       Pa. I. U.S. URA-UPAP. Burgettstown, Pa.

333.38   SUBDIVISION REGULATION - CALIF.
(794) CALIFORNIA. LEGISLATURE. SENATE.
C15SU INTERIM COMMITTEE ON SUBDIVISION
1959   DEVELOPMENT AND PLANNING.
       SUBDIVISION MANUAL. SACRAMENTO,
       SENATE OF THE STATE OF CALIFORNIA, 1959.
       116P.

       1. SUBDIVISION REGULATION - CALIF.
       I. TITLE.

333.38   Subdivision regulation - Brundidge, Ala.
(76135) Brundidge, Ala. City Planning Commission.
B78   Brundidge, Alabama: land subdivision regu-
       lations and manual. [In cooperation with]
       Alabama State Planning and Industrial De-
       velopment Board. Brundidge, 1957.
           1v. diagrs.

           U.S. Urban Renewal Administration, Urban
       Planning Assistance Program.

           (Continued on next card)

333.38   Subdivision regulation - Burlington, Wash.
(79772) Graham (John) and Co.
G71b   Proposed subdivision ordinance, City of
       Burlington, Washington. [In cooperation
       with] Dept. of Commerce and Economic De-
       velopment, State of Washington. Seattle,
       1960.
           17p.

           U.S. Urban Renewal Adm. UPAP.
           1. Subdivision regulation - Burlington,
       Wash. I. U.S. URA-UPAP. Burlington, Wash.

333.38   Subdivision regulation - California.
(794) California. Div. of Real Estate.
C15su   Subdivision manual, an explanation of
1960   subdivision planning and development, proces-
       sing and controls, with excerpts from per-
       tinent statutes. Rev. Sacramento, 1960.
           98p.

           1. Subdivision regulation - California.

333.38   Brundidge, Ala. City Planning Commission.
(76135)   Brundidge, Alabama: land ... (Card 2)
B78

           1. Subdivision regulation - Brundidge,
       Ala. I. Alabama. State Planning and In-
       dustrial Development Board. II. U.S. Urban
       Renewal Administration. Urban Planning
       Assistance Program.

333.38   Subdivision regulation - Butler, Ala.
(76137) Butler, Ala. Town Planning Commission.
B87   Butler, Alabama: land subdivision regu-
       lations and manual. [In cooperation with]
       Alabama State Planning and Industrial De-
       velopment Board. Butler, 1958.
           1v. diagrs.

           U.S. Urban Renewal Administration, Urban
       Planning Assistance Program.

           (Continued on next card)

333.38   Subdivision regulation - California.
(794) California. Division of Real Estate.
C15su   Subdivision manual; an explanation of
1962   subdivision planning and development, pro-
       cessing and controls, with excerpts from
       pertinent statutes. 3d ed. Sacramento,
       1962.
           102p.

           1. Subdivision regulation - California.

333.38   Subdivision regulation - Buckley, Wash.
(79778) Buckley, Wash. Ordinances, etc.
B82   Subdivision ordinance for the City of
       Buckley. [Buckley, 1959?]
           20p.

           U.S. Urban Renewal Adm. UPAP.

           1. Subdivision regulation - Buckley, Wash.
       I. U.S. URA-UPAP. Buckley, Wash.

333.38   Butler, Ala. Town Planning Commission.
(76137)   Butler, Alabama: land sub- ...(Card 2)
B87

           1. Subdivision regulation - Butler, Ala.
       I. Alabama. State Planning; and Industrial
       Development Board. II. U.S. Urban Re-
       newal Administration. Urban Planning
       Assistance Program.

333.38   Subdivision regulation - California.
(794) California. Division of Real Estate.
C15su   Subdivision manual: an explanation of
1966   subdivision planning and development, pro-
       cessing and controls, with excerts from
       pertinent statutes. 4th ed. Sacramento,
       1966.
           138p.

           1. Subdivision regulation - California.

333.38   Subdivision regulation - Buckley, Wash.
(79778) July Town Planners.
J85   Proposed subdivision regulations for the
       Town of Buckley [Wash.] 1960. [n.p.] 1960.
           20p.
           Prepared under general supervision of
       Washington State Dept. of Commerce and
       Economic Development.
           U.S. Urban Renewal Adm. UPAP.

           1. Subdivision regulation - Buckley, Wash.
       I. U.S. URA-UPAP. Buckley, Wash.

333.38   Subdivision regulation - Butler, Pa.
(74891) Butler, Pa. Ordinances, etc.
B87   Land subdivision regulations of the City
       of Butler, Butler County, Pennsylvania.
       Proposed. [Butler] 1958.
           20p.

           U.S. Urban Renewal Adm. UPAP.

           1. Subdivision regulation - Butler, Pa.
       I. U.S. URA-UPAP. Butler, Pa.

333.38   SUBDIVISION REGULATION - CALIFORNIA.
(794) CALIFORNIA. DIVISION OF REAL ESTATE.
C15SU SUBDIVISION MANUAL: AN EXPLANATION OF
1956   THE REAL ESTATE COMMISSIONER'S
       JURISDICTION AND REQUIREMENT IN THE
       DEVELOPMENT OF NEW SUBDIVISION.
       SACRAMENTO, CALIFORNIA STATE PRINTING
       OFFICE, 1956.
           45P.

           1. SUBDIVISION REGULATION -
       CALIFORNIA. I. TITLE.

333.38   Subdivision regulation - Buena Vista, Ga.
(75848) Georgia. Dept. of Commerce.
G26   Suggested subdivision regulations for
       Buena Vista, Georgia and adjoining areas of
       Marion County. Prepared for the Buena
       Vista-Marion County Planning Commission.
       Atlanta, 1959.
           16p.

       U.S. Urban Renewal Administration, Urban Planning
       Assistance Program.

       1. Subdivision regulation - Buena Vista, Ga.
       I. Buena Vista-Marion County Planning Commission.
       II. U.S. URA-UPAP. Buena Vista, Ga.

6067   SUBDIVISION REGULATION - CALERA, ALA.
       CALERA, ALA. TOWN PLANNING COMMISSION.
       SUBDIVISION REGULATIONS. CALERA, 1970.
       27P. (HUD 701 REPORT)

       1. SUBDIVISION REGULATION - CALERA, ALA.
       I. HUD. 701. CALERA, ALA.

333.38   Subdivision regulation - California.
(794)
C15su California. Division of Real Estate.
           Subdivision manual: an explanation
       of the Real Estate Commissioner's juris-
       diction and requirements in the develop-
       ment of new subdivisions. [Sacramento,
       1957]
           45 p.

           D. D. Watson, Real Estate Commissioner.

           1. Subdivision regulation - California.

333.38
(794)
C15au
1969
SUBDIVISION REGULATION - CALIF.
California. Dept. of Real Estate.
  Subdivision manual; an explanation of subdivision planning and development, processing and controls, with excerpts from pertinent statutes. 5th ed. [Sacramento] 1969.
  140p.

  1. Subdivision regulation - Calif. I. Title

Subdivision regulation - Canton, Conn.

333.38
(7462)
S72
Stelling (A. Carl) Associates.
  Town of Canton subdivision regulations. Prepared for Town of Canton Planning Commission. West Hartford, Conn., 1957?
  1v.

  U.S. Urban Renewal Administration, Urban Planning Assistance Program.
  1. Subdivision regulation - Canton, Conn. I. Canton, Conn. Planning Commission. II. U.S. Urban Renewal Administration. Urban Planning Assistance Program.

333.38
(74882)
C17
Carroll, Pa. Planning Commission. Recommendations for land subdivision ...
                                      (Card 2)

  U.S. Urban Renewal Adm. UPAP.

  1. Subdivision regulation - Carroll, Pa. I. Community Planning Services. II. U.S. URA-UPAP. Carroll, Pa.

VF
333.38
(794)
C15a
Subdivision regulation - California.

California. (State) Real Estate Commissioner.
  Subdivision control in California; report to Senate Finance Committee, by D.D. Watson, State Real Estate Commissioner. [Sacramento?] 1953.
  46p.
  Report prepared by the Real Estate Research Program, Bureau of Business and Economic Research University of California.
  Reprinted from the Senate Journal of March 11, 1953.
  1. Subdivision regulation - Calif. I. California. University. Bureau of Business and Economic Research.

VF
333.38
(7447)
C15
Subdivision regulation - Canton, Mass.

Canton, Mass. Ordinances, etc.
  Rules and regulations governing the subdivision of land. Canton, Massachusetts. (Adopted under the Subdivision Control Law, Sections 81-GG inclusive, Chapter 41, G.L.) Canton, Mass., [1958?]
  1v.

  U.S. Urban Renewal Administration, Urban Planning Assistance Program.
  1. Subdivision regulation - Canton, Mass. I. U.S. Urban Renewal Administration. Urban Planning Assistance Program.

2191
SUBDIVISION REGULATION - CASS CO., NEB.
CASS CO., NEB. PLANNING COMMISSION.
  SUBDIVISION REGULATIONS. PLATTSMOUTH, NEB., 1967.
  22P. (HUD 701 REPORT)

  1. SUBDIVISION REGULATION - CASS CO., NEB. I. HUD. 701. CASS CO., NEB.

VF
333.38
(794)
C15
Subdivision regulation - Calif.

California. Senate. Interim Committee on Subdivision Development and Planning.
  Partial report to the legislature. [Sacramento, California State Print. Off., 1955]
  64 p.

333.38
(76176)
C17
Subdivision regulation - Carbon Hill, Ala.
Carbon Hill, Ala. City Planning Commission.
  Carbon Hill, Alabama: land subdivision regulations and manual, adopted February 25, 1958. [In cooperation with] Alabama State Planning and Industrial Development Board. Carbon Hill, 1958.
  1v. diagrs., tables.
  U.S. Urban Renewal Administration, Urban Planning Assistance Program.
  1. Subdivision regulation - Carbon Hill, Ala. Ala. State Planning and Industrial Development Board. II. U.S. Urban Renewal Administration. Urban Planning Assistance Program.

711.4
(74827)
C17s
Subdivision regulation - Catasauqua, Pa.
Candeub, Cabot and Associates.
  Borough of Catasauqua, Pennsylvania, master plan report. Subdivision ordinance. [Prepared for Catasauqua Borough Planning Commission. Scranton, Pa., 1962.
  28p.

  U.S. Urban Renewal Adm. UPAP.

  1. Master plan - Catasauqua, Pa. 2. Subdivision regulation - Catasauqua, Pa. I. Catasauqua, Pa. Planning Commission. II. U.S. URA-UPAP. Catasauqua, Pa.

333.38
(794)
C18
1961
Subdivision regulation - California.
Civil Engineers and Land Surveyors Association of California.
  Subdivision ordinance recommended to cities for consideration, by Harold A. Barnett. Draft. 4th ed. Los Angeles, 1961.
  31p.

  1. Subdivision regulation - California. I. Barnett, Harold A.

5700
SUBDIVISION REGULATION - CARBONDALE, ILL.
CARBONDALE, ILL. PLANNING COMMISSION.
  SUBDIVISION CONTROL ORDINANCE. CARBONDALE, ILL., 1962.
  26P. (HUD 701 REPORT)

  1. SUBDIVISION REGULATION - CARBONDALE, ILL. I. HUD. 701. CARBONDALE, ILL.

333.38
(77439)
V45
Subdivision regulation - Center Line, Mich.
Vilican-Leman & Associates.
  Proposed subdivision regulations; an ordinance for the platting of land, City of Center Line, Macomb County, Michigan. Prepared for Center Line Planning Commission. Southfield, Mich., 1964.
  21p.
  U.S. Urban Renewal Adm. UPAP.

  1. Subdivision regulation - Center Line, Mich. I. Center Line, Mich. Planning Commission. II. U.S. URA-UPAP. Center Line, Mich.

711.3
(74765)
C15
Subdivision regulation - Camillus, N.Y.
Camillus, N.Y. Town Planning Board.
  Rules and regulations for the subdivision of land, the Town of Camillus, New York, by Arthur Reed. Syracuse, N.Y., 1959.
  21p.

  U.S. Urban Renewal Adm. UPAP.

  1. Master plan - Camillus, N.Y. 2. Subdivision regulation - Camillus, N.Y. I. Reed, Arthur. II. U.S. URA-UPAP. Camillus, N.Y.

333.38
(7444)
C17
Subdivision regulation - Carlisle, Mass.
Carlisle, Mass. Planning Board.
  Proposed rules and regulations governing the subdivision of land in Carlisle, Massachusetts, [by] Allen Benjamin. Wayland, Mass., 1959.
  [16]p.

  U.S. Urban Renewal Adm. UPAP.

  1. Subdivision regulation - Carlisle, Mass. I. Benjamin, Allen. II. U.S. URA-UPAP. Carlisle, Mass.

333.38
(76983)
C25
Subdivision regulation - Central City, Ky.
Central City, Ky. City Planning and Zoning Commission.
  Subdivision regulations, City of Central City, Kentucky. With assistance by Kentucky Dept. of Economic Development. Central City, 1958.
  18p.
  U.S. Urban Renewal Administration, Urban Planning Assistance Program.
  1. Subdivision regulation - Central City, Ky. I. U.S. URA-UPAP. Central City, Ky.

333.38
(76153)
C15
Subdivision regulation - Camp Hill, Ala.
Camp Hill, Ala. Town Planning Commission.
  Camp Hill, Alabama: subdivision regulations. [Prepared in cooperation with] Alabama State Planning and Industrial Development Board. Camp Hill, 1961.
  36p.
  U.S. Urban Renewal Adm. UPAP.

  1. Subdivision regulation - Camp Hill, Ala. I. U.S. URA-UPAP. Camp Hill, Ala.

333.38
(74886)
C17
Subdivision regulation - Carnegie, Pa.
Carnegie, Pa. Ordinances, etc.
  Land subdivision regulations. [Carnegie 1958?]

  U.S. Urban Renewal Administration, Urban Planning Assistance Program.

  1. Subdivision regulation - Carnegie, Pa. I. U.S. URA-UPAP. Carnegie, Pa.

333.38
(74767)
C25
Subdivision regulation - Central Square, N.Y.
Central Square, N.Y. Village Planning Commission.
  Subdivision regulations, by Joseph H. Katulski. Central Square, [1959]
  22p.

  U.S. Urban Renewal Adm. UPAP.

  1. Subdivision regulation - Central Square, N.Y. I. Katulski, Joseph H. II. U.S. URA-UPAP. Central Square, N.Y.

333.38
(74882)
C15
Subdivision regulation - Canonsburg, Pa.
Canonsburg, Pa. Ordinances, etc.
  Land subdivision regulations. Canonsburg, 1959.
  1v.

  U.S. Urban Renewal Adm. UPAP.

  1. Subdivision regulation - Canonsburg, Pa. I. U.S. URA-UPAP. Canonsburg, Pa.

333.38
(74882)
C17
Subdivision regulation - Carroll, Pa.
Carroll, Pa. Planning Commission.
  Recommendations for land subdivision regulations, Carroll Township, Washington County, Pa. [Carroll?] 1962.
  [22]p.

  Community Services, inc., Monroeville, Pa., consultants.

  Prepared in cooperation with Pennsylvania Dept. of Commerce, Bureau of Community Development.
  (Cont'd. on next card)

333.38
(76165)
C25
Subdivision regulation - Centre, Ala.
Centre, Ala. City Planning Commission.
  Centre, Alabama: land subdivision regulations and manual. [In cooperation with] Alabama State Planning and Industrial Development Board. Centre, 1959.
  23p. diagrs.

  U.S. Urban Renewal Administration, Urban Planning Assistance Program.

  1. Subdivision regulation - Centre, Ala. I. U.S. URA-UPAP. Centre, Ala.

711.5
(74844
:347)
C31

Chambersburg, Pa. Planning and Zoning
Commission.
Codes and ordinances study, 1959, by
Jack M. Kendree, planning consultant.
[n.p.] [1960?]
13p.

U.S. Urban Renewal Adm. UPAP.

1. Zoning legislation - Chambersburg, Pa.
2. Subdivision regulation - Chambersburg, Pa.
I. Kendree, Jack M. II. U.S. URA-UPAP.
Chambersburg, Pa.

711.4
(758724)
C31

Chatham County-Savannah Metropolitan Planning
Commission. Land subdivision...(Card 2)

55p.

U.S. Urban Renewal Administration, Urban
Planning Assistance Program.

1. Subdivision regulation - Chatham Co.,
Ga. 2. Subdivision regulation - Savannah,
Ga. I. U.S. Urban Renewal Administration.
Urban Planning Assistance Program.

Subdivision regulation - Cherokee, Ala.

333.38
(761915)
C32

Cherokee, Ala. Town Planning Commission.
Cherokee, Alabama: land subdivision regulations and manual. [In cooperation with]
Alabama State Planning and Industrial Development Board. Cherokee, 1959.
23p. diagrs.

U.S. Urban Renewal Administration, Urban Planning
Assistance Program.

1. Subdivision regulation - Cherokee, Ala. I. U.S.
URA-UPAP. Cherokee, Ala.

Subdivision regulation - Charleroi, Pa.

333.38
(74882)
C31

Charleroi, Pa. Planning Commission.
Recommendations for land subdivision
regulations. Charleroi, 1962.
[23]p.

Community Planning Services, inc.,
Monroeville, Pa.

Prepared in cooperation with
Pennsylvania Dept. of Commerce, Bureau of
Community Development.
(Cont'd. on next
card)

Subdivision regulation - Chatham Co., Ga.

333.38
(758724)
C31s

Chatham County-Savannah Metropolitan Planning
Commission.
Special report of the committee appointed
to study residential minimum lot sizes, net
dwelling density, building coverage and
utility easements. [Tentative ed.] Savannah,
1957.
33p. diagrs., tables.

U.S. Urban Renewal Administration, Urban
Planning Assistance Program.

(Continued on next card)

Subdivision regulation - Chester, N.J.

333.38
(74974)
C65re

Community Planning Associates.
A review of the land subdivision ordinance
of Chester Township, Morris County, New
Jersey. Prepared for the Township Planning
Board. West Trenton, N.J., 1960.
4p.

U.S. Urban Renewal Adm. UPAP.

1. Subdivision regulation - Chester, N.J. I. Chester,
N.J. Township Planning Board. II. U.S. URA-UPAP.
Chester, N.J.

333.38
(74882)
C31

Charleroi, Pa. Planning Commission.
Recommendations for land ... (Card 2)

U.S. Urban Renewal Adm. UPAP.

1. Subdivision regulation - Charleroi,
Pa. I. Community Planning Services.
II. U.S. URA-UPAP. Charleroi, Pa.

333.38
(758724)
C31s

Chatham County-Savannah Metropolitan Planning
Commission. Special report...(Card 2)

1. Subdivision regulation - Chatham Co.,
Ga. 2. Subdivision regulation - Savannah,
Ga. I. U.S. Urban Renewal Administration.
Urban Planning Assistance Program.

Subdivision regulation - Chesterfield, N.J.

333.38
(74961)
C32

Community Planning Associates.
A review of the Chesterfield subdivision
ordinance. Prepared for the Chesterfield
Township Planning Board. Financed by
appropriation of the State of New Jersey
and by local funds. West Trenton, N.J.,
1959.
3p.

U.S. Urban Renewal Adm. UPAP.

1. Subdivision regulation - Chesterfield, N.J.
I. Chesterfield, N.J. Township Plan-
ning Board. II. U.S. URA-UPAP.
Chesterfield, N.J.

333.38
(74813)
C32

SUBDIVISION REGULATION - CHARLESTOWN, PA.
Charlestown, Pa. Board of Supervisors.
Land subdivision regulations of
Charlestown township. Board of Super-
visors Charlestown Township, Chester
County, Pennsylvania. Devon, Pa., ANRO
Printing and Letter Service, [1967?]
20p.

1. Subdivision regulation - Charlestown,
Pa. 2. Streets - Charlestown, Pa.
I. Title.

711.4
(758725)
818s

Savannah, Ga. Metropolitan Planning Commission.
Subdivision regulations, City of Savannah
and Chatham County. First rough draft, prepared for the purpose of discussion by the
Subdivision Development Committee. A part
of the master plan for the City of Savannah
and Chatham County. [Tentative ed.]
Savannah, 1956.
42p.
U.S. Urban Renewal Administration,
(Continued on next card)

Subdivision regulation - Chillicothe, Ill.

333.38
(77352)
S27m

Scruggs and Hammond.
Maps, plans and subdivision code of
Chillicothe, Illinois and contiguous area.
Prepared for the Planning Commission of
Chillicothe, Illinois and Illinois State
Housing Board. Peoria, Ill., 1960.
20p.

U.S. Urban Renewal Administration,
Urban Planning Assistance Program.

1. Subdivision regulation - Chillicothe, Ill.
I. Chillicothe, Ill. Planning Commission.
II. U.S. URA-UPAP. Chillicothe, Ill.

Subdivision regulation - Charleston, W.
Va.

333.38
(75438)
C31

Charleston, W. Va. Municipal Planning
Commission.
Subdivision regulations, Charleston,
West Virginia and environs as adopted by
ordinance of the City Council, City of
Charleston, W. Va. Charleston, 1964.
32p.

1. Subdivision regulation - Charleston,
W. Va.

711.4
(758725)
818s

Savannah, Ga. Metropolitan Planning Commission. Subdivision ... (Card 2)

Urban Planning Assistance Program.

1. Master plan - Savannah, Ga. 2. Master
plan - Chatham Co., Ga. 3. Subdivision
regulation - Chatham Co., Ga. 4. Subdivision regulation - Atlanta, Ga. I. U.S.
Urban Renewal Administration. Urban Planning Assistance Program.

Subdivision regulation - Citronelle, Ala.

333.38
(76122)
C47

Citronelle, Ala. Town Planning Commission.
Citronelle, Alabama: land subdivision
regulations and manual. [In cooperation
with] Alabama State Planning and Industrial Development Board. Citronelle,
1958.
1v. diagrs.

U.S. Urban Renewal Administration, Urban
Planning Assistance Program.

(Continued on next
card)

Subdivision regulation - Chatham Co., Ga.

711.4
(758725)
818
no. 4

Chatham County-Savannah Metropolitan Planning Commission.
Draft of proposed subdivision regulations
for the Chatham County-Savannah Metropolitan
Planning District. Savannah, 1957.
2 pts. plans. (Savannah, Ga. Metropolitan
Planning Commission. Master plan report
no. 4, pts. 1 and 2)
(Continued on next card)

1298

SUBDIVISION REGULATION - CHATHAM, MASS.
CHATHAM, MASS. PLANNING BOARD.
COMPREHENSIVE PLAN STUDY: CHAPTER 5,
LEGAL AND FISCAL IMPLEMENTATION PROGRAMS,
SECTION 16: SUBDIVISION REGULATIONS.
CHATHAM, 1966.
30L. (HUD 701 REPORT)

1. SUBDIVISION REGULATION - CHATHAM,
MASS. I. HUD. 701. CHATHAM, MASS.

333.38
(76122)
C47

Citronelle, Ala. Town Planning Commission.
Citronelle, Alabama: land subdivision
regulations ... 1958. (Card 2)

1. Subdivision regulation - Citronelle,
Ala. I. Alabama. State Planning and
Industrial Development Board. II. U.S.
Urban Renewal Administration. Urban
Planning Assistance Program.

Subdivision regulation - Chatham Co., Ga.

711.4
(758724)
C31

Chatham County-Savannah Metropolitan Planning
Commission.
Land-subdivision regulations, Chatham County
-Savannah Metropolitan Planning District.
Second rough draft prepared for the purpose of
discussion by the Metropolitan Planning Commis-
sion's Subdivision Development Committee. A
part of the master plan for the Chatham County-
Savannah Metropolitan Planning District. [Tenta-
tive ed.] Savannah, 1956.

(Continued on next card)

3547

SUBDIVISION REGULATION - CHELSEA, MICH.
CHELSEA, MICH. VILLAGE PLANNING
COMMISSION.
PROPOSED SUBDIVISION REGULATIONS FOR
THE VILLAGE OF CHELSEA, WASHTENAW COUNTY,
MICHIGAN. PREPARED BY PARKINS, ROGERS &
ASSOCIATES, INC. DETROIT, 1969.
23P. (HUD 701 REPORT)

1. SUBDIVISION REGULATION - CHELSEA,
MICH. I. PARKINS, ROGERS AND ASSOCIATES.
II. HUD. 701. CHELSEA, MICH.

Subdivision regulation - Clanton, Ala.

333.38
(76181)
C51

Clanton, Ala. City Planning Commission.
Clanton, Alabama: subdivision regulations.
[In cooperation with] Alabama State Planning
and Industrial Development Board. Clanton,
[1961?]
36p.

U.S. Urban Renewal Adm. UPAP.

1. Subdivision regulation - Clanton, Ala.
I. U.S. URA-UPAP. Clanton, Ala.

Subdivision regulation - Claremont, Calif.

333.38
(79493)
C51   Claremont, Calif. Ordinances, etc.
        An ordinance regulating the division and
        subdivision of land in the City of Clare-
        mont... Fifth revision. Claremont, 1959.
        40p.

U.S. Urban Renewal Administration, Urban Planning
Assistance Program.

1. Subdivision regulation - Claremont, Calif.
I. U.S. URA-UPAP. Claremont, Calif.

1877   SUBDIVISION REGULATION - CLINTON, MISS.
         CLINTON, MISS. CITY PLANNING BOARD.
         CLINTON SUBDIVISION REGULATIONS. BY
         BIGGS, WEIR, NEAL, AND CHASTAIN,
         ARCHITECTS. CLINTON, MISS., 1969.
         34P. (HUD 701 REPORT)

         1. SUBDIVISION REGULATION - CLINTON,
         MISS. I. BIGGS, WEIR, NEAL, AND
         CHASTAIN, ARCHITECTS. II. HUD. 701.
         CLINTON, MISS.

Subdivision regulation - Colchester, Conn.

333.38
(7465)
C65   Colchester, Conn. Ordinances, etc.
        Subdivision regulations of the Town of
        Colchester. Colchester, Conn., 1957.
        7p.

        U.S. Urban Renewal Administration, Urban
        Planning Assistance Program.

        1. Subdivision regulation - Colchester,
        Conn. I. U.S. Urban Renewal Administra-
        tion. Urban Planning Assistance Program.

6371   SUBDIVISION REGULATION - CLARK CO., NEV.
         CLARK CO., NEV. PLANNING BOARD.
         SUBDIVISION ORDINANCE. BY EISNER,
         STEWART AND ASSOCIATES. CARSON CITY,
         1966.
         60L. (HUD 701 REPORT)

         1. SUBDIVISION REGULATION - CLARK CO.,
         NEV. I. EISNER, STEWART AND ASSOCIATES.
         II. HUD. 701. CLARK CO., NEV.

Subdivision regulation - Clinton, N.J.

333.38
(74791)
N28   New Jersey. Dept. of Conservation and Eco-
        nomic Development. (Div. of Planning and
        Development)
        Land subdivision ordinance of the Town of
        Clinton. Suggested changes and additions.
        Trenton, 1958.
        11p.
        "Rough draft."
        U.S. Urban Renewal Administration, Urban
        Planning Assistance Program.
        1. Subdivision regulation - Clinton, N.J.
        II. U.S. Urban   Renewal Administration.
        Urban Planning   Assistance Program.

Subdivision regulation - Collinsville, Ala.

333.38
76166)
C65   Collinsville, Ala. Town Planning
        Commission.
        Collinsville, Alabama: subdivision regu-
        lations. [Prepared in cooperation with]
        Alabama State Planning and Industrial
        Development Board. Collinsville, 1961.
        36p.
        U.S. Urban Renewal Adm. UPAP.

        1. Subdivision regulation - Collinsville,
        Ala. I. U.S.   URA-UPAP.
        Collinsville,   Ala.

Subdivision regulation - Clark Co., Ohio.

333.38
(77149)
C51   Clark County-Springfield Regional Planning
        Commission.
        Subdivision regulations for Clark County,
        Ohio. Springfield, Ohio, 1957.
        44p.

"Preliminary draught."
U.S. Urban Renewal Administration, Urban Planning
Assistance Program.

1. Subdivision regulation - Clark Co., Ohio.
I. U.S. Urban Renewal Administration. Urban
Planning Assistance   Program. Clark Co.,
Ohio.

333.38   Subdivision regulation - Clinton, Tenn.
(76873)   Clinton, Tenn. Regional Planning Commis-
C54   sion.
           Subdivision standards of the Clinton,
           Tennessee planning region. Assisted by
           the Tennessee State Planning Commission,
           East Tennessee Office. Clinton, 1957.
           46p. diagrs., maps.

           U.S. Urban Renewal Administration,
           Urban Planning Assistance Program.

           (Continued on next card)

Subdivision regulation - Columbia, Ala.

333.38
(761295)
C65   Columbia, Ala. Town Planning Commission.
        Columbia, Alabama: subdivision regulations.
        [In cooperation with] Alabama State Planning
        and Industrial Development Board. Columbia,
        1960.
        36p.
        U.S. Urban Renewal Adm. UPAP.

        1. Subdivision regulation - Columbia, Ala.
        I. U.S. URA-UPAP. Columbia, Ala.

333.38   SUBDIVISION REGULATION - CLARKSON, N.Y.
(74788)   Monroe Co., N.Y. Planning Council.
M65   Proposed revised land subdivision regulations,
1970   Town of Clarkson, Monroe County, New York.
           Prepared for the Town Planning Board.
           Monroe, 1970.
           58p.

           1. Subdivision regulation - Clarkson, N.Y.

333.38   Clinton, Tenn. Regional Planning Commis-
(76873)   sion. Subdivision ... (Card 2)
C54

           1. Subdivision regulation - Clinton,
           Tenn. I. Tennessee. State Planning
           Commission. II. U.S. Urban Renewal Ad-
           ministration. Urban Planning Assistance
           Program.

Subdivision regulation - Columbiana, Ala.

333.38   Columbiana, Ala. Town Planning Commission.
(76179)   Columbiana, Alabama: land subdivision
C65   regulations and manual. [In cooperation
           with] Alabama State Planning and Industrial
           Development Board. Columbiana, 1958.
           1v. diagrs.

           U.S. Urban Renewal Administration, Urban
           Planning Assistance Program.
           1. Subdivision regulation - Columbiana,
           Ala. I. Alabama. State Planning and Indus-
           trial Develop-   ment Board. II. U.S.
           Urban Renewal   Administration. Urban
           Planning Assist-   ance Program.

Subdivision regulation - Cleveland, Okla.

333.38
(76626)
O45   Oklahoma. University. Institute of
        Community Development.
        An ordinance for the regulation of land
        subdivision, Cleveland, Oklahoma. Proposed.
        Norman, Okla., 1957.
        17p.

        U. S. Urban Renewal Administration, Urban
        Planning Assistance Program.

        1. Subdivision regulation - Cleveland, Okla. I. U. S.
        URA-UPAP. Cleveland, Okla.

Subdivision regulation - Closter, N.J.

333.38
(74921)
C56   Community Planning Associates.
        Review of land subdivision ordinance.
        Memorandum to Borough of Closter Plan-
        ning Board. [West Trenton, N.J.] 1959.
        3p.

        U.S. Urban Renewal Adm. UPAP.

        1. Subdivision regulation - Closter, N.J.
        I. Closter, N.J. Planning Board. II. U.S.
        URA-UPAP. Closter, N.J.

Subdivision regulation - Colusa, Calif.

VF
333.38
(79433)
C65   Colusa, Calif. Ordinances, etc.
        City of Colusa: ordinance no. 184.
        An ordinance establishing regulation for
        division and subdivision of land. Colusa,
        1962.
        [15]p.

        U.S. Urban Renewal Adm. UPAP.

        1. Subdivision regulation - Colusa, Calif.
        I. U.S. URA-UPAP.   Colusa, Calif.

Subdivision regulation - Cleveland, Tenn.

333.38   Cleveland, Tenn. Planning Commission.
(76887)   Proposed subdivision regulations, Cleve-
C58   land, Tennessee. Technical assistance by
           Southeast Tennessee Office, Tennessee State
           Planning Commission. Cleveland, 1959.
           18p.

           U.S. Urban Renewal Administration, Urban
           Planning Assistance Program.

           (Continued on next card)

2982   SUBDIVISION REGULATION - CLYDE - MICH.
         CLYDE, MICH. TOWNSHIP PLANNING
         COMMISSION.
         SUBDIVISION REGULATIONS FOR THE
         TOWNSHIP OF CLYDE, ST. CLAIR COUNTY,
         MICHIGAN. BY PARKINS, ROGERS &
         ASSOCIATES, INC. DETROIT 1966.
         20L. (HUD 701 REPORT)

2983   -- ---- PLAT SUBMITTAL PROCEDURES.
         SUPPLEMENT. DETROIT, 1966.
         5, 2L. (HUD 701 REPORT)

         1. SUBDIVISION REGULATION - CLYDE -
         MICH. I. PARKINS, ROGERS &
                         (CONTINUED ON NEXT CARD)

333.38   SUBDIVISION REGULATION - COMMERCE,
1448   MICH.
FOLIO   COMMERCE, MICH. PLANNING COMMISSION.
           PROPOSED SUBDIVISION REGULATIONS.
           PREPARED BY DRIKER ASSOCIATES, INC.
           BIRMINGHAM, MICH., 1969.
           28L. (HUD 701 REPORT)

           1. SUBDIVISION REGULATION - COMMERCE,
           MICH. I. DRIKER ASSOCIATES. II. HUD.
           701. COMMERCE, MICH.

333.38   Cleveland, Tenn. Planning Commission. Pro-
(76887)   posed subdivision ... 1959 (Card 2)
C58

           1. Subdivision regulation - Cleveland,
           Tenn. I. U. S. Urban Renewal Administra-
           tion. Urban Planning Assistance Program.

2982   CLYDE, MICH. TOWNSHIP PLANNING
         COMMISSION. SUBDIVISION REGULATIONS
         FOR ....1966.   (CARD 2)

         ASSOCIATES. II. HUD. 701. CLYDE, MICH.

Subdivision regulation - Conn.

VF
333.38   Connecticut. Development Commission.
(746)   An approach to the regulation of sub-
C65   divisions. [Hartford] 1961.
           5p.

           1. Subdivision regulation - Conn.

333.38
(76367)
T25

SUBDIVISION REGULATION - COOKEVILLE, TENN.
Tennessee. State Planning Commission.
Proposed subdivision regulations for Cookeville, Tenn. Nashville, Tennessee State Planning Commission, Middle Tennessee Office, 1969.
23p.

U.S. Dept. of Housing and Urban Development. UPAP. HUD project no. Tenn. P-97.
1. Subdivision regulation - Cookeville, Tenn. I.   U.S. HUD-UPAP. Cookeville,   Tenn. II. Title.

Subdivision regulation - Coventry, R. I.

333.38
(7454)
C68

Coventry, R.I. Planning Board.
Coventry, Rhode Island. Regulations governing the subdivision of land. Coventry [1957?]
"Draft"   1v.   diagrs.
U.S. Urban Renewal Administration, Urban Planning Assistance Program.
1. Subdivision regulation - Coventry, R.I. I. U.S. URA-UPAP, Coventry, R. I.

4136

SUBDIVISION REGULATION - CUMRU, PA.
CUMRU, PA. PLANNING COMMISSION.
LAND SUBDIVISION REGULATIONS. CUMRU, PA., 1966.
55P. (HUD 701 REPORT)

1. SUBDIVISION REGULATION - CUMRU, PA. I. HUD. 701. CUMRU, PA.

333.38
(79523)
072p

Subdivision regulation - Coquille, Or.
Oregon. University. Bureau of Municipal Research and Service.
Proposed subdivision ordinance for Coquille, Oregon. Prepared for the Coquille City Planning Commission. Eugene, Or., 1959.
18p.

"Draft"
U. S. Urban Renewal Administration, Urban Planning Assistance Program.

1. Subdivision regulation - Coquille, Or. I. Coquille, Or. City Planning Commission. II. U. S. URA-UPAP. Coquille, Or.

333.38
(7454)
R36

Subdivision regulation - Coventry, R.I.
Rhode Island. Development Council.
Subdivision ordinance. Prepared for Coventry Planning Board. Providence, 1957.
5p. (Coventry worksheet no. 7A)

U.S. Urban Renewal Administration, Urban Planning Assistance Program.

1. Subdivision regulation - Coventry, R.I. I. Coventry, R.I. Planning Board. II. U.S. URA-UPAP. Coventry, R.I.

333.38
(76941)
C95

Subdivision regulation - Cynthiana, Ky.
Cynthiana, Ky. City Planning and Zoning Commission.
Subdivision regulations, city of Cynthiana, Kentucky. With assistance of the Kentucky Dept. of Economic Development. Cynthiana, 1958.
1v.
U.S. Urban Renewal Administration, Urban Planning Assistance Program.
1. Subdivision regulation - Cynthiana, Ky. I. U.S. URA-UPAP. Cynthiana,   Ky.

333.38
(769125)
C67

Subdivision regulation - Corbin, Ky.
Corbin, Ky. City Planning Commission.
Subdivision regulations, City of Corbin, Kentucky. [Corbin, 1960?]
18p.
Prepared with the assistance of the Division of Planning and Zoning.
U.S. Urban Renewal Adm. UPAP.

1. Subdivision regulation - Corbin, Ky. I. U.S. URA-UPAP. Corbin, Ky.

333.38
(74891)
H45

Subdivision regulation - Cranberry, Pa.
Hill (Carroll V.) & Associates.
Review of existing subdivision regulations for Cranberry Township, Butler County, and suggestions for possible amendments. Columbus, Ohio and Pittsburgh, [1963?]
17p.

U.S. Urban Renewal Adm. UPAP.

1. Subdivision regulation - Cranberry, Pa.   I. U.S. URA-UPAP.   Cranberry, Pa.

333.38
(79496)
C96

Subdivision regulation - Cypress, Calif.
Cypress, Calif. Ordinances, etc.
Proposed amendments to Cypress subdivision ordinance no. 77. Cypress, 1963.
1 v.

U.S. Urban Renewal Adm. UPAP.

1. Subdivision regulation - Cypress, Calif. I. U.S. URA-UPAP. Cypress, Calif.

333.38
(76176)
C67

Subdivision regulation - Cordova, Ala.
Cordova, Ala. City Planning Commission.
Cordova, Alabama: land subdivision regulations and manual. [In cooperation with] Alabama State Planning and Industrial Development Board. Cordova, 1957.
1v. diagrs.

U.S. Urban Renewal Administration, Urban Planning Assistance Program.
1. Subdivision regulation - Cordova, Ala. I. Alabama . State Planning and Industrial Development Board. II. U.S. Urban Renewal Administration. Urban Planning Assistance Program.

124

SUBDIVISION REGULATION - CROSSVILLE, ALA.
CROSSVILLE, ALA. TOWN PLANNING COMMISSION.
SUBDIVISION REGULATIONS. CROSSVILLE, ALA., 1969.
35P. (HUD 701 REPORT)

1. SUBDIVISION REGULATION - CROSSVILLE, ALA. I. HUD. 701. CROSSVILLE, ALA.

333.38
(76153)
D12

Subdivision regulation - Dadeville, Ala.
Dadeville, Ala. City Planning Commission.
Dadeville, Alabama: subdivision regulations. [Prepared in cooperation with] Alabama State Planning and Industrial Development Board. Dadeville, 1961.
36p.

U.S. Urban Renewal Adm. UPAP.

1. Subdivision regulation - Dadeville, Ala. I. U.S. URA-UPAP. Dadeville, Ala.

333.38
(798)
A51c

Subdivision regulation - Cordova, Alaska.
Alaska. State Housing Authority.
Subdivision control ordinance, City of Cordova. Cordova, [1963?]
14p.

U.S. Urban Renewal Adm. UPAP.

1. Subdivision regulation - Cordova, Alaska. I. U.S. URA-UPAP. Cordova, Alaska.

333.38
(758265)
H45

Subdivision regulation - Cummings, Ga.
Hill and Adley Associates.
Proposed subdivision regulations for the City of Cumming, Georgia. [Prepared for] Cumming-Forsyth County Planning Commission. [Atlanta, Ga., 1959]
14p.

U.S. Urban Renewal Administration, Urban Planning Assistance Program.

1. Subdivision regulation - Cummings, Ga. I. Cumming-Forsyth County Planning Commission. II. U.S. URA-UPAP. Cumming, Ga.

333.38
(76133)
D15

Subdivision regulation - Daleville, Ala.
Daleville, Ala. Town Planning Commission.
Daleville, Alabama: subdivision regulations. [Prepared for] Alabama State Planning and Industrial Development Board. Daleville, 1960.
36p.

U.S. Urban Renewal Adm. UPAP.

1. Subdivision regulation - Daleville, Ala. I. U.S. URA-UPAP. Daleville, Ala.

333.38
(795341)
072p

Subdivision regulation - Corvallis, Or.
Oregon. University. Bureau of Municipal Research and Service.
Proposed subdivision ordinance for Corvallis, Oregon. Prepared for the Corvallis City Planning Commission. Eugene, Or., 1959.
15p.

"Preliminary draft."
U. S. Urban Renewal Administration, Urban Planning Assistance Program.

1. Subdivision regulation - Corvallis, Or. I. Corvallis, Or. City Planning Commission. II. U. S. URA-UPAP. Corvallis, Or.

333.38
(74885)
C71

Subdivision regulation - Crafton, Pa.
Crafton, Pa. Ordinances, etc.
Proposed subdivision code for Crafton, Pennsylvania. Crafton, 1961.
10p.

Planning Consultants, Pittsburgh, Pa.
U.S. Urban Renewal Adm. UPAP.

1. Subdivision regulation - Crafton, Pa. I. Planning Consultants, Pittsburgh. II. U.S. URA-UPAP. Crafton, Pa.

333.38
(79538)
072

Subdivision regulation - Dallas, Or.
Oregon. University. Bureau of Municipal Research and Service.
Subdivision control. Memorandum prepared for Dallas City Planning Commission. Eugene, Or., 1959.
1v. maps, tables.

U.S. Urban Renewal Administration, Urban Planning Assistance Program.

1. Subdivision regulation - Dallas, Or. I. Dallas, Or. City Planning Commission. II. U.S. URA-UPAP. Dallas, Or.

333.38
(795341)
072

Subdivision regulation - Corvallis, Or.
Oregon. University. Bureau of Municipal Research and Service.
Subdivision control. Memorandum to Corvallis City Planning Commission. Eugene, Or., 1959.
18p.

U.S. Urban Renewal Administration, Urban Planning Assistance Program.

1. Subdivision regulation - Corvallis, Or. I. Corvallis, Or. City Planning Commission. II. U.S. URA-UPAP. Corvallis, Or.

333.38
(774842)
P25

Subdivision regulation - Cumberland, Pa.
Pennsylvania. University. Government Consulting Service.
Land subdivision control ordinance, Cumberland Township, Adams County, Pennsylvania. [n.p.] 1960.
23p.

U.S. Urban Renewal Adm. UPAP.

1. Subdivision regulation - Cumberland, Pa. I. Cumberland, Pa. Ordinances, etc. II. U.S. URA-UPAP. Cumberland,   Pa.

5447

SUBDIVISION REGULATION - DALTON, MASS.
DALTON, MASS. PLANNING BOARD.
PROPOSED REVISED RULES AND REGULATIONS GOVERNING THE SUBDIVISION OF LAND. BY CHARLES M. EVANS AND ASSOCIATES. DALTON, 1961.
21L. (HUD 701 REPORT)

1. SUBDIVISION REGULATION - DALTON, MASS. I. EVANS (CHARLES M.) AND ASSOCIATES. II. HUD. 701. DALTON, MASS.

Subdivision regulation - Danville, Pa.

333.38
(74839) Rodgers (Clifton E.) and Associates.
R62　　Proposed land subdivision regulations,
Danville Borough Planning Commission.
Presented for review by the Planning Commission of the Borough of Danville. Harrisburg, Pa., 1958.
1v.
U.S. Urban Renewal Adm. UPAP.

1. Subdivision regulation - Danville, Pa. I. Danville,
Pa. Planning Commission. II. U.S. URA-UPAP.
Danville, Pa.

Subdivision regulation - Demarest, N.J.

333.38
(74921) Morrow Planning Associates.
M67　　Proposed revisions to the subdivision
ordinance of the Borough of Demarest, New
Jersey. Ridgewood, N.J., 1959.
3p.

U.S. Urban Renewal Adm. UPAP.

1. Subdivision regulation - Demarest,
N.J. I. U.S. URA-UPAP. Demarest,
N.J.

141　SUBDIVISION REGULATION - DETROIT, ALA.
DETROIT, ALA. TOWN PLANNING COMMISSION.
SUBDIVISION REGULATIONS, BY ALABAMA
STATE PLANNING AND INDUSTRIAL DEVELOPMENT
BOARD. DETROIT, ALA., 1969.
35P. (HUD 701 REPORT)

1. SUBDIVISION REGULATION - DETROIT, ALA.
I. ALABAMA. STATE PLANNING &
INDUSTRIAL DEVELOPMENT BOARD. II. HUD.
701. DETROIT, ALA.

3551　SUBDIVISION REGULATION - DAVISON, MICH.
DAVISON-RICHFIELD REGIONAL PLANNING
COMMISSION.
SUBDIVISION ORDINANCE, DAVISON,
MICHIGAN. DAVISON, MICH., CA. 1969.
12L. (HUD 701 REPORT)

1. SUBDIVISION REGULATION - DAVISON,
MICH. I. HUD. 701. DAVISON, MICH.

Subdivision regulation - Denton, Tex.

333.38
(764) Denton, Tex. Planning and Zoning Commission.
D25　　Proposed subdivision rules and regulations
for the city of Denton, Texas. [n.p.] 1959.
22p.
Planning consultants: Freese and Nichols
and Caldwell and Caldwell.
Prepared through the cooperation of the
Texas State Dept. of Health.
U.S. Urban Renewal Adm. UPAP.

1. Subdivision regulation - Denton, Tex. I. Caldwell
and Caldwell. II. U.S. URA-UPAP. Denton, Tex.

Subdivision regulation - Dolton, Ill.

333.38
(7731) Kincaid (Evert) and Associates.
K45　　Suggested technical recommendations for
subdivision regulations for the village of
Dolton, Illinois. Prepared for Village Plan
Commission. Chicago, 1958.
43p.

U.S. Urban Renewal Administration, Urban
Planning Assistance Program.

1. Subdivision regulation - Dolton, Ill. I. Dolton,
Ill. Plan Commission. II. U.S. URA-UPAP.
Dolton, Ill.

3552　SUBDIVISION REGULATION - DAVISON
TOWNSHIP, MICH.
DAVISON TOWNSHIP, MICH. PLANNING
COMMISSION.
SUBDIVISION ORDINANCE, DAVISON
TOWNSHIP, GENESEE COUNTY, MICHIGAN.
DAVISON TOWNSHIP, CA. 1969.
12L. (HUD 701 REPORT)

1. SUBDIVISION REGULATION - DAVISON
TOWNSHIP, MICH. I. HUD. 701. DAVISON
TOWNSHIP, MICH.

333.38
(78883) SUBDIVISION REGULATION - DENVER.
D25　DENVER. PLANNING OFFICE.
SUBDIVISION CONTROL; PLANNING OFFICE
SUBDIVISION REGULATIONS; DEPARTMENT OF
PUBLIC WORKS SUBDIVISION REGULATIONS.
DENVER, 1964.
1 V.

1. SUBDIVISION REGULATION - DENVER.

2197　SUBDIVISION REGULATION - DONIPHAN, NEB.
DONIPHAN, NEB. BOARD OF TRUSTEES.
FORM OF SUBDIVISION REGULATIONS. BY
HENNINGSON, DURHAM AND RICHARDSON.
DONIPHAN, NEB. 1970.
1 V. (HUD 701 REPORT)

1. SUBDIVISION REGULATION - DONIPHAN,
NEB. I. HENNINGSON, DURHAM AND
RICHARDSON. I. HUD. 701. DONIPHAN,
NEB.

1067　SUBDIVISION REGULATION - DAYTON, KY.
DAYTON, KY. PLANNING AND ZONING BOARD.
SUBDIVISION REGULATIONS, CITY OF
DAYTON, COMMONWEALTH OF KENTUCKY.
PREPARED BY NORTHERN KENTUCKY AREA
PLANNING COMMISSION. NEWPORT, KY., 1969.
1 V. (HUD 701 REPORT)

1. SUBDIVISION REGULATION - DAYTON, KY.
I. NORTHERN KENTUCKY AREA PLANNING
COMMISSION. II. HUD. 701. DAYTON, KY.

711.4
(78883) Subdivision regulation - Denver.
D25　Inter-County Regional Planning Commission,
no.25A　Denver.
Selected features of land development
policies in the Denver metropolitan area.
Denver, 1965.
72p. (Its Master plan report 25A)

U.S. Urban Renewal Adm. UPAP.

1. Master plan - Denver. 2. Subdivision
regulation - Denver. I. Title. II. Title:
Land development policies. III. U.S. URA-
UPAP. Denver.

Subdivision regulation - Dora, Ala.

333.38
(76176) Dora, Ala. Town Planning Commission.
D67　　Dora, Alabama: land subdivision regulations and manual. [In cooperation with] Alabama State Planning and Industrial Development Board. Dora, 1958.
1v. diagrs.

U.S. Urban Renewal Administration, Urban
Planning Assistance Program.

(Continued on next card)

333.38
(76883) Subdivision regulation - Dayton, Tenn.
D19　Dayton, Tenn. Municipal Planning Commission.
Subdivision standards for the Dayton planning region. Dayton, 1958.
1v. map.

U.S. Urban Renewal Administration, Urban
Planning Assistance Program.

1. Subdivision regulation - Dayton, Tenn.
I. U.S. Urban Renewal Administration. Urban
Planning Assistance Program.

333.38
(7467) Derby, Conn. Planning Commission.
D27　　City of Derby, New Haven County, Connecticut, subdivision regulations. [In cooperation with] Connecticut Development Commission.
Rev. New York, 1958.
50p.

Theodore T. McCrosky, Consulting Engineer;
Harry S. Weinroth, Senior Planner.
U.S. Urban Renewal Administration, Urban
Planning Assistance Program.
(Continued on next
card)

333.38
(76176) Dora, Ala. Town Planning Commission. Dora,
D67　　Alabama: land subdivision ... (Card 2)

1. Subdivision regulation - Dora, Ala.
I. Alabama. State Planning and Industrial
Development Board. II. U.S. Urban Renewal
Administration. Urban Planning Assistance
Program.

4897　SUBDIVISION REGULATION - DAYTON, WIS.
DAYTON, WIS. PLANNING COMMISSION.
DEVELOPMENT PLAN REPORT: LAND
SUBDIVISION REGULATIONS. PREPARED BY
GREEN ENGINEERING CO., INC. MITTLETON,
WIS., 1965.
20L. (HUD 701 REPORT)

1. SUBDIVISION REGULATION - DAYTON, WIS.
I. GREEN ENGINEERING CO. II. HUD.
701. DAYTON, WIS.

333.38
(7467) Derby, Conn. Planning Commission.　City
D27　　of Derby, New Haven ... (Card 2)

1. Subdivision regulation - Derby, Conn.
I. Connecticut. Development Commission.
II. U.S. Urban Renewal Administration.
Urban Planning Assistance Program.

Subdivision regulation - Douglas, Alaska.

333.38
(798) Bloch (Ivan) and Associates.
B56p　Proposed subdivision ordinance for the
City of Douglas, Alaska, by Harlan Nelson. Portland, Or., 1959.
17p.
U.S. Urban Renewal Administration, Urban Planning Assistance Program.

1. Subdivision regulation - Douglas, Alaska.
I. Nelson, Harlan. II. Douglas, Alaska. Ordinances, etc. III. U.S. URA-UPAP. Douglas,
Alaska.

Subdivision regulation - Delran, N.J.

333.38
(74961) New Jersey. Dept. of Conservation and Economic Development. (Div. of Planning and
N28　　Development)
Land subdivision ordinance of the Township
of Delran. Suggested changes and additions.
Trenton, 1958.
11p.
"Rough draft."
U.S. Urban Renewal Administration, Urban
Planning Assistance Program.
1. Subdivision regulation - Delran, N. J.
I. U.S. Urban　　Renewal Administration.
Urban Planning　　Assistance Program.

333.38
(77434) Subdivision regulation - Detroit metropolitan
M42　area.
Michigan. Planning Commission.
A study of subdivision development in
the Detroit metropolitan area. Lansing,
Mich., 1939.
38p.

1. Subdivision regulation - Detroit
metropolitan area.

Subdivision regulation - Downington, Pa.

333.38
(74813) Downington, Pa. Ordinances, etc.
D68　　The land subdivision ordinance of
Downington, Pennsylvania, by Jack M.
Kendree. Recommended revisions and
additions. Philadelphia, [1959?]
[6]p.

U.S. Urban Renewal Adm. UPAP.

1. Subdivision regulation - Downington,
Pa. I. Kendree, Jack M. II. U.S. URA-
UPAP.　　Downington, Pa.

338.33
(77677)
D85
SUBDIVISION REGULATION - DULUTH.
DULUTH. CITY PLANNING DEPARTMENT.
LAND PLATTING IN DULUTH, 1856-1939.
DULUTH, 1940.
70P.
SURVEY MADE WITH ASSISTANCE OF WPA
OFFICIAL PROJECT 65-71-6891, WORK
PROJECT 2453.

1. SUBDIVISION REGULATION - DULUTH.
I. TITLE.

Subdivision regulation - Dumas, Ark.

333.38
(76785)
A74
Arkansas. University. City Planning
Division.
Administrative procedures and design
guide for subdivision development,
Dumas, Arkansas. Prepared for the Dumas
Planning Commission. Fayetteville, Ark.,
1962.
1v.

U.S. Urban Renewal Adm. UPAP.

1. Subdivision regulation - Dumas, Ark.
I. Dumas, Ark. Planning
Commission. II. U.S. URA-
UPAP. Dumas, Ark.

Subdivision regulation - Dunlevy, Pa.

333.38
(74882)
D85
Dunlevy, Pa. Planning Commission.
Recommendations for land subdivision
regulations. [Dunlevy] 1962.
[23]p.

Pennsylvania Dept. of Commerce,
Bureau of Community Development.

Community Planning Services, inc.,
Monroeville, Pa., consultants.

U.S. Urban Renewal Adm. UPAP.

(Cont.d on next card)

333.38
(74882)
D85
Dunlevy, Pa. Planning Commission. Rec-
ommendations for land subdivision ...
(Card 2)

1. Subdivision regulation - Dunlevy, Pa.
I. Community Planning Services. II. U.S.
URA-UPAP. Dunlevy, Pa.

Subdivision regulation - Durango, Colo.

333.38
(78829)
H17
Harman, O'Donnell and Henninger, Associates.
Subdivision regulations, City of Durango.
Prepared for Colorado State Planning Divi-
sion. Denver, [1958]
14p.

U.S. Urban Renewal Administration, Urban
Planning Assistance Program.

1. Subdivision regulation - Durango, Colo.
I. Colorado. State Planning Division.
II. U.S. Urban Renewal Administration.
Planning Assistance Program.

Subdivision regulation - Duxbury, Mass.

711.5
(7448
:347)
D87
Duxbury, Mass. Planning Board.
Zoning and subdivision regulations, Duxbury.
Prepared for the Duxbury Planning Board, and
the Massachusetts Department of Commerce by
James L. Harris. Cambridge, Mass., 1959.
1v.

U.S. Urban Renewal Administration, Urban Planning
Assistance Program.

1. Zoning legislation - Duxbury, Mass. 2. Subdivision regulation - Duxbury, Mass. I. Harris, James L.
II. U.S. URA-UPAP. Duxbury, Mass.

333.38
(76815)
D92
Subdivision regulation - Dyersburg, Tenn.
Dyersburg, Tenn. Regional Planning Commission.
Subdivision regulations, Dyersburg, Tennessee.
[With the assistance of the Tennessee State Plan-
ning Commission, West Tennessee Office] Dyers-
burg, 1956.
41p. maps, tables.

U.S. Urban Renewal Administration, Urban
Planning Assistance Program.

1. Subdivision regulation - Dyersburg, Tenn.
I. Tennessee. State Planning Commission. II.
U.S. Urban Renewal Administration. Urban
Planning Assistance Program.

Subdivision regulation - East Aurora, N. Y.

711.4
(74796)
E17
no. 4
addend.
Tryon and Schwartz and Associates.
Proposed subdivision regulations, Village
of East Aurora, N.Y. Buffalo, N. Y., 1959.
24p. (East Aurora, N.Y. Village Planning Commission. Master plan rept. no. 4,
addendum)

Addendum to proposed development plan.
U.S. Urban Renewal Administration, Urban
Planning Assistance Program.

1. Master plan - East Aurora, N.Y. 2. Subdivision
regulation - East Aurora, N. Y. I. East Aurora,
N.Y. Village Planning Commission. II. U.S.
URA-UPAP.

711.4
(761265)
E18
East Brewton, Ala. City Planning Commission.
Land subdivision regulations and manual. In
cooperation with Alabama State Planning Board.
East Brewton, 1952.
27p. plans.

1. Subdivision regulation - East Brewton,
Ala. 2. City planning - East Brewton, Ala.
I. Alabama. State Planning Board.

Subdivision regulation - East Brunswixk, N.J

333.38
(74941)
N28
New Jersey. Dept. of Conservation and Eco-
nomic Development. (Div. of Planning and
Development)
Land subdivision ordinance of the township
of East Brunswick. Suggested changes and
additions. Trenton, 1958.
12p.
"Rough draft."
U.S. Urban Renewal Administration, Urban
Planning Assistance Program.

1. Subdivision regulation - East Brunswick,
N.J. I. U.S. Urban Renewal Administration.
Urban Plan- ning Assistance Program.

Subdivision regulation - East Hanover, N.J.

333.38
(74974)
C65s
Community Planning Associates.
Subdivision ordinance review. Memorandum
to East Hanover [N.J.] Planning Board.
[West Trenton, N.J.] 1959.
2p.

U.S. Urban Renewal Adm. UPAP.

1. Subdivision regulation - East Hanover,
N.J. I. East Hanover, N.J. Planning Board.
II. U.S. URA-UPAP. East Hanover, N.J.

Subdivision regulation - East Peoria,
Ill.

1805
EAST PEORIA, ILL. CITY PLAN COMMISSION.
PROPOSED SUBDIVISION ORDINANCE. BY
HARLAND BARTHOLOMEW AND ASSOCIATES. EAST
PEORIA, ILL., 1968.
46P. (HUD 701 REPORT)

1. SUBDIVISION REGULATION - EAST
PEORIA, ILL. I. BARTHOLOMEW (HARLAND)
AND ASSOCIATES. II. HUD. 701. EAST
PEORIA, ILL.

Subdivision regulation - East Windsor, Conn.

VF
333.38
(7462)
P22
Pedersen and Tilney.
Subdivision regulations for the Town of
East Windsor, Connecticut. Prepared for
Planning and Zoning Commission of East
Windsor. [New Haven, 1957?]
8p.

U.S. Urban Renewal Administration, Urban Planning Assistance Program.

1. Subdivision regulation - East Windsor, Conn.
I. East Windsor, Conn. Planning and Zoning Commission. II. U.S. URA- UPAP.

SUBDIVISION REGULATION - EATON RAPIDS,
MICH.

3574
EATON RAPIDS, MICH. CITY PLANNING
COMMISSION.
PROPOSED SUBDIVISION REGULATIONS FOR
THE CITY OF EATON RAPIDS, EATON COUNTY,
MICHIGAN. BY PARKINS, ROGERS AND
ASSOCIATES, INC. DETROIT, 1969.
24L. (HUD 701 REPORT)

1. SUBDIVISION REGULATION - EATON
RAPIDS, MICH. I. PARKINS, ROGERS AND
ASSOCIATES. II. HUD. 701. EATON
RAPIDS, MICH.

Subdivision regulation - Eatonville, Wash.

333.38
(79778)
P42
Pierce County, Wash. Planning Commission.
Proposed Eatonville subdivision ordinance.
Prepared for the Eatonville Planning Commission and the Town Council. [Tacoma]
1959.
20p.

U.S. Urban Renewal Adm. UPAP.

1. Subdivision regulation - Eatonville, Wash.
I. Eatonville, Wash. Planning Commission.
II. U.S. URA-UPAP. Eatonville,
Wash.

Subdivision regulation - Ebensburg, Pa.

333.38
(74877)
E12
Ebensburg, Pa. Borough Planning
Commission.
Recommended land subdivision
regulations. Borough of Ebensburg,
Cambria County, Pennsylvania.
Ebensburg, 1962.
19p.

U.S. Urban Renewal Adm. UPAP.

1. Subdivision regulation - Ebensburg,
Pa. I. U.S. URA-UPAP. Ebensburg, Pa.

Subdivision regulation - Economy, Pa.

333.38
(74892)
R62
Rodgers (Clifton E.) and Associates.
Land subdivision regulations, Borough
of Economy. [Beaver Falls, Pa., 1963?]
[24]p.

U.S. Urban Renewal Adm. UPAP.

1. Subdivision regulation - Economy,
Pa. I. Economy, Pa. Ordinances, etc.
II. U.S. URA-UPAP. Economy, Pa.

SUBDIVISION REGULATION - EDEN, N.C.

3056
EDEN, N.C. PLANNING BOARD.
SUBDIVISION REGULATIONS. BY STATE OF
NORTH CAROLINA, DEPARTMENT OF LOCAL
AFFAIRS. EDEN, N.C., 1969.
30P. (HUD 701 REPORT)

1. SUBDIVISION REGULATION - EDEN, N.C.
I. NORTH CAROLINA. DEPT. OF LOCAL
AFFAIRS. II. HUD. 701. EDEN, N.C.

Subdivision regulation - Eden, N.Y.

333.38
(74796)
T79
Tryon and Schwartz and Associates.
Proposed subdivision regulations, Town
of Eden, N.Y. Prepared for Town Planning
Board. Buffalo, 1958.
26p.

Addendum to proposed development plan.
U.S. Urban Renewal Administration, Urban
Planning Assistance Program.

1. Subdivision regulation - Eden, N.Y. I. Eden,
N.Y. Town Planning Board. II. U.S. URA-UPAP.
Eden, N.Y.

Subdivision regulation - Elba, Ala.

333.38
(76134)
E51
Elba, Ala. City Planning Commission.
Elba, Alabama: land subdivision regulations and manual. [In cooperation with
the Alabama State Planning and Industrial
Development Board] Elba, 1955.
29p. diagrs.

U. S. Urban Renewal Administration,
Urban Planning Assistance Program.

1. Subdivision regulation - Elba, Ala. I. U.S.
URA-UPAP. Elba, Ala.

Subdivision regulation - Elizabethtown, Ky.

333.38
(769845)
E54
Elizabethtown, Ky. City Planning and
Zoning Commission.
Subdivision regulations, City of Elizabethtown, Kentucky. With assistance of
the Division of Planning and Zoning, Kentucky Dept. of Economic Development.
Elizabethtown, 1957.
19p.

U.S. Urban Renewal Administration, Urban

(Continued on next card)

333.38
(769845)
E54   Elizabethtown, Ky. City Planning and
Zoning Commission. Subdivision regulation, ... (Card 2)

Planning Assistance Program.

1. Subdivision regulation - Elizabethtown, Ky. I. Kentucky. Dept. of Economic Development. II. U.S. Urban Renewal Administration. Urban Planning
Assistance Program.

333.38
(74921)
R19p   Raymond and May Associates.
Proposed amendments of regulations for
Residence District no. 5. Memorandum no. 32
to Planning Board, City of Englewood, New
Jersey. [n.p.] 1959.
2p.

U.S. Urban Renewal Adm. UPAP.

1. Subdivision regulation - Englewood, N.J.
I. Englewood, N.J. Planning Board. II. U.S.
URA-UPAP. Englewood, N.J.

Subdivision regulation - Englewood, N.J.

Subdivision regulation - Fallsburgh, N.Y.

333.38
(74735)
817
1963   Sergent-Webster-Crenshaw & Folley.
Proposed subdivision regulations, town
of Fallsburgh, Sullivan County, New York.
Rev. Prepared in cooperation with the
Sullivan Co., N.Y. Planning Board.
Syracuse, N.Y., 1963.
34p.
U.S. Urban Renewal Adm. UPAP.

1. Subdivision regulation - Fallsburgh, N.Y.
2. County planning - Sullivan Co., N.Y.
I. Sullivan County, N.Y. Planning Board.
II. U.S. URA-   UPAP. Sullivan
County, N.Y.

SUBDIVISION REGULATION - ELKHORN CITY,
KY.
1404   PIKE CO., KY. PLANNING COMMISSION.
SUBDIVISION REGULATIONS. BY MICHAEL
BAKER, JR., INC. ELKHORN, KY., 1969.
49L. (HUD 701 REPORT)

1. SUBDIVISION REGULATION - ELKHORN
CITY, KY. 2. SUBDIVISION REGULATION -
PIKE CO., KY. I. BAKER (MICHAEL, JR.)
INC. II. HUD. 701. ELKHORN CITY, KY.
III. HUD. 701. PIKE CO., KY.

Subdivision regulation - Entiat, Wash.

333.38
(79759)
C32   Chelan County, Wash. Joint Planning Office.
Proposed subdivision regulation ordinance
for the Town of Entiat, Washington. [Prepared
for] State Dept. of Commerce and Economic Development. Wenatchee, Wash., [1958]
16p.

U.S. Urban Renewal Administration, Urban Planning
Assistance Program.

1. Subdivision regulation - Entiat, Wash. I. U.S.
URA-UPAP. Entiat, Wash.

SUBDIVISION REGULATION - FARMINGTON,
WIS.
5306   FARMINGTON, WIS. PLANNING COMMISSION.
LAND SUBDIVISION REGULATIONS. PREPARED
BY GREEN ENGINEERING CO., INC.
MIDDLETON, WIS., 1965.
2CP. (HUD 701 REPORT)

1. SUBDIVISION REGULATION - FARMINGTON,
WIS. I. GREEN ENGINEERING CO.
II. HUD. 701. FARMINGTON, WIS.

Subdivision regulation - Ellwood City, Pa.

333.38
(74892)
E55   Ellwood City, Pa. Ordinances, etc.
Proposed subdivision ordinance for
the Borough of Ellwood City, Pennsylvania.
Ellwood City, [1960?]
36p.

U.S. Urban Renewal Adm. UPAP.

1. Subdivision regulation - Ellwood City,
Pa. I. U.S. URA-UPAP. Ellwood City, Pa.

Subdivision regulation - Enumclaw, Wash.

333.38
(79777)
E58   Enumclaw, Wash. Ordinances, etc.
Proposed subdivision ordinance for the
City of Enumclaw, Washington, by J. David
Jensen and Harlan Nelson. Seattle, 1959.
20p.

U.S. Urban Renewal Adm. UPAP.

1. Subdivision regulation - Enumclaw, Wash.
I. Jensen, J. David. II. Nelson, Harlan.
III. U.S. URA-   UPAP. Enumclaw,
Wash.

SUBDIVISION REGULATION - FARMINGTON,
MICH.
3587   FARMINGTON, MICH. PLANNING COMMISSION.
PROPOSED SUBDIVISION REGULATIONS
ORDINANCE, FARMINGTON TOWNSHIP. PREPARED
BY VILICAN-LEMAN AND ASSOCIATES, INC.
SOUTHFIELD, MICH., 1968.
26L. (HUD 701 REPORT)

1. SUBDIVISION REGULATION - FARMINGTON,
MICH. I. VILICAN-LEMAN AND ASSOCIATES.
II. HUD. 701. FARMINGTON, MICH.

Subdivision regulation - Emerson, N. J.

711.5
(74921
:347)
S11   Saalbach, Carl F
Data for implementing the master plan of the
Borough of Emerson. A basis for an official
map, a revision to the subdivision ordinance,
a new zoning ordinance, offered for consideration by borough officials and citizens, and
legal review by the Borough attorney. Prepared
for the Borough of Emerson, Bergen County, New
Jersey. Emerson, N. J., 1957.
28p. map, tables.

Planning proposals for Emerson, N. J.

(Continued on next card)

---

216   SUBDIVISION REGULATION - EUTAW, ALA.
EUTAW, ALA. CITY PLANNING COMMISSION.
SUBDIVISION REGULATIONS, BY ROBERT S.
BATEMAN AND ASSOCIATES, INC. EUTAW, ALA.,
1968.
47P. (HUD 701 REPORT)

1. SUBDIVISION REGULATION - EUTAW, ALA.
I. BATEMAN (ROBERT S.) AND ASSOCIATES,
INC. II. HUD. 701. EUTAW, ALA.

Subdivision regulation - Fayette, Ala.

333.38
(76187)
F19   Fayette, Ala. City Planning Commission.
Fayette, Alabama: land subdivision regu-
lations and manual. [In cooperation with]
Alabama State Planning and Industrial De-
velopment Board. Fayette, 1957.
1v. diagrs.
U.S. Urban Renewal Administration, Urban
Planning Assistance Program.

1. Subdivision regulation - Fayette, Ala.
I. Alabama. State Planning and Industrial
Development   Board. II. U.S. Urban
Renewal Admin-   istration. Urban Plan-
ning Assistance   Program.

711.5
(74921
:347)
811   Saalbach, Carl F
Data for implementing
the master plan ... 1957. (Card 2)

Master plan project.
U.S. Urban Renewal Administration, Urban
Planning Assistance Program.

1. Zoning legislation - Emerson, N. J.
2. Subdivision regulation - Emerson, N. J.
I. Emerson, N.J. Planning Board. II. U.S.
Urban Renewal Administration. Urban Planning Assistance Program.

Subdivision regulation - Evesham, N. J.

333.38
(74961)
E82   Evesham, N. J. Ordinances, etc.
The land subdivision ordinance of Evesham Township, recommended revisions
and additions, by Jack M. Kendree. Philadelphia, 1959.
6p.
U.S. Urban Renewal Administration, Urban Planning
Assistance Program.
1. Subdivision regulation - Evesham, N. J.
I. Kendree, Jack M. II. U.S. URA-UPAP. Evesham,
N. J.

Subdivision regulation - Fayetteville, Ark.

333.38
(76714)
A74s   Arkansas. University. City Planning
Div.
A subdivision and development guide.
Prepared for City Planning Commission,
Fayetteville, Arkansas. Fayetteville,
1961.
1v.
"Draft copy."
U.S. Urban Renewal Adm. UPAP.

1. Subdivision regulation - Fayetteville, Ark.
I. Fayetteville, Ark.   Planning
Commission. I. U.S.   URA-UPAP.
Fayetteville, Ark.

Subdivision regulation - Emmaus, Pa.

333.38
(74827)
E55   Emmaus, Pa. Planning Commission.
Land subdivision rules and regulations
for the Borough of Emmaus, Pennsylvania,
by Russell VanNest Black. Emmaus,
[1957?]
12p.
U.S. Urban Renewal Administration, Urban Planning
Assistance Program.

1. Subdivision regulation - Emmaus, Pa. I. Black,
Russell VanNest II. U.S. URA-UPAP. Emmaus,
Pa.

Subdivision regulation - Fairfield, Alabama.

711.4
(76178)
F14l   Fairfield, Ala. City Planning Commission.
Fairfield, Alabama: land subdivision regulations and manual. [In cooperation with
Alabama State Planning and Industrial Development Board] Fairfield, 1957.
21p.

U.S. Urban Renewal Administration, Urban

(Continued on next card)

Subdivision regulation - Fayetteville, Ark.

333.38
(76714)
F19   Fayetteville, Ark. Planning Commission.
Subdivision regulations, Fayetteville,
Arkansas. Fayetteville, Ark., 1959.
14p.

U.S. Urban Renewal Administration,
Urban Planning Assistance Program.

1. Subdivision regulation - Fayetteville,
Ark. I. U.S. URA-UPAP. Fayetteville, Ark.

Subdivision regulation - Emporium, Pa.

333.38
(74866)
E56   Emporium, Pa. Ordinances, etc.
Proposed land subdivision regulations
of the Borough of Emporium, Cameron
County, Pennsylvania. [n.p.] 1960.
16p.

U.S. Urban Renewal Adm. UPAP.

1. Subdivision regulation - Emporium, Pa.
I. U.S. URA-UPAP. Emporium, Pa.

711.4
(76178)
F14l   Fairfield, Ala. City Planning Commission.
Fairfield, Alabama: land ... (Card 2)

Planning Assistance Program.

1. City planning - Fairfield, Ala. 2. Subdivision regulation - Fairfield, Ala. I.
Alabama. State Planning and Industrial Development Board. II. U.S. Urban Renewal
Administration.

SUBDIVISION REGULATION - FLAT ROCK,
MICH.
3590   FLAT ROCK, MICH. PLANNING COMMISSION.
PLANNING PROGRAM: 9, PROPOSED
SUBDIVISION REGULATIONS, FLAT ROCK,
MICH., CA. 1969.
26L. (HUD 701 REPORT)

1. SUBDIVISION REGULATION - FLAT ROCK,
MICH. I. HUD. 701. FLAT ROCK, MICH.

Subdivision regulation - Florence, Ky.

333.38
(76936)
F56
Florence, Ky. City Planning Commission.
Subdivision regulations, City of Florence, Kentucky. [Florence, 1960?]
20p.
Prepared with the assistance of the Division of Planning and Zoning, Kentucky Dept. of Economic Development.
U.S. Urban Renewal Adm. UPAP.

1. Subdivision regulation - Florence, Ky.
I. U.S. URA-UPAP. Florence, Ky.

Subdivision regulation - Fort Collins, Colo.

333.38
(78868)
F67
Fort Collins, Colo. Planning and Zoning Board.
Subdivision regulations, City of Fort Collins, Colorado, by Harold Beier. Prepared for the Colorado State Planning Div. Fort Collins, 1958.
51p.
U.S. Urban Renewal Adm. UPAP.

1. Subdivision regulation - Fort Collins, Colo. I. Beier, Harold. II. U.S. URA-UPAP. Fort Collins, Colo.

Subdivision regulation - Franklin, Tenn.

333.38
(76856)
F71
Franklin, Tenn. Municipal Planning Commission.
Subdivision regulations for Franklin, Tennessee. Assisted by Tennessee State Planning Commission, Middle Tennessee Office. Franklin, 1957.
30p. diagrs., maps. (MTO Publication no. 57-21)

U.S. Urban Renewal Administration.
(Continued on next card)

Subdivision regulation - Foley, Ala.

333.38
(76121)
F65
Foley, Ala. City Planning Commission.
Foley, Alabama: land subdivision regulations and manual. [In cooperation with] Alabama State Planning and Industrial Development Board. Foley, 1959.
23p. diagrs.

U.S. Urban Renewal Administration, Urban Planning Assistance Program.

1. Subdivision regulation - Foley, Ala. I. U.S. URA-UPAP. Foley, Ala.

---

355   SUBDIVISION REGULATION - FORT LUPTON, COLO.
FORT LUPTON, COLO. PLANNING COMMISSION.
FORT LUPTON ZONING AND SUBDIVISION REGULATIONS, BY NELSON, HALEY, PATTERSON AND QUIRK. DENVER, COLORADO STATE PLANNING OFFICE, 1969.
65L. (HUD 701 REPORT)

1. ZONING LEGISLATION - FORT LUPTON, COLO. 2. SUBDIVISION REGULATION - FORT LUPTON, COLO. I. NELSON, HALEY, PATTERSON, AND QUIRK, INC. II. HUD. 701. FORT LUPTON, COLO.

333.38
(76856)
F71
Franklin, Tenn. Municipal Planning Commission. Subdivision ... (Card 2)

Urban Planning Assistance Program.

1. Subdivision regulation - Franklin, Tenn. I. Tennessee. State Planning Commission. II. U.S. Urban Renewal Administration. Urban Planning Assistance Program.

Subdivision regulation - Folsom, Calif.

VF
333.38
(79453)
F65
Folsom, Calif. Ordinances, etc.
An ordinance of the City of Folsom establishing regulations for the division and subdivision of land. Folsom. [1962?]
13p.

U.S. Urban Renewal Adm. UPAP.

1. Subdivision regulation - Folsom, Calif. I. U.S. URA-UPAP. Folsom, Calif.

Subdivision regulation - Foster, Pa.

333.38
(74834)
T79
Tryon and Schwertz & Associates.
Subdivision regulations, Township of Foster, Pennsylvania. Preliminary report. [Prepared in cooperation with] Harland Bartholomew and Associates. [n.p., 1963?]
19p.
U.S. Urban Renewal Adm. UPAP.

1. Subdivision regulation - Foster, Pa. I. Foster, Pa. Ordinances, etc. II. Bartholomew (Harland) and Associates. III. U.S. URA-UPAP. Foster, Pa.

Subdivision regulation - Franklin Co., Ohio.

711.333
(77156)
F71
no. 12
Franklin County, Ohio. Regional Planning Commission.
Subdivision regulations for Franklin County, Ohio: standards, specifications and requirements for construction of improvements; health requirements. Columbus, Ohio. 1956.
34p. (Master plan report no. 12)

U.S. Urban Renewal Adm. UPAP.

1. Master plan - Franklin Co., Ohio. 2. Subdivision regulation - Franklin Co., Ohio. I. U.S. URA-UPAP. Franklin Co., Ohio.

333.38
(76767)
A74
Subdivision regulation - Fordyce, Ark.
Arkansas. University. City Planning Division.
Fordyce, Arkansas: subdivision regulations; subdivision design standards for Fordyce, Arkansas; general zoning regulations. [Fayetteville, Ark.] 1958.
[2]v. maps.

v. 2; 18 maps.

U.S. Urban Renewal Administration, Urban Planning Assistance Program.
1. Subdivision regulation - Fordyce, Ark. I. U.S. URA-UPAP. Fordyce, Ark.

---

568   SUBDIVISION REGULATION - FOX LAKE, ILL.
FOX LAKE, ILL. ORDINANCES, ETC.
SUBDIVISION REGULATIONS, PASSED FEBRUARY 3, 1969. FOX LAKE, ILL., 1969.
37P. (HUD 701 REPORT)

1. SUBDIVISION REGULATION - FOX LAKE, ILL. I. HUD. 701. FOX LAKE, ILL.

Subdivision regulation - Franklin Lakes, N.J.

711.4
(74921)
F71s
Community Planning Associates.
Borough of Franklin Lakes master plan studies; subdivision review. Memorandum #12 [to Franklin Lakes Planning Board] West Trenton, N.J., 1959.
3p.

U.S. Urban Renewal Adm. UPAP.

1. Master plan - Franklin Lakes, N.J. 2. Subdivision regulation - Franklin Lakes, N.J. I. Franklin Lakes, N.J. Planning Board. II. U.S. URA-UPAP. Franklin Lakes, N.J.

Subdivision regulation - Forrest City, Ark.

711.74
(76791)
A74
Arkansas. University. City Planning Division.
Forrest City, Arkansas; major street plan; land use plan, Forrest City; subdivision regulations, Forrest City; zoning ordinance, Forrest City. Fayetteville, Ark. 1959.
2v. maps.
v. 2; 12 maps.
U.S. Urban Renewal Administration, Urban Planning Assistance Program.
(Continued on next card)

Subdivision regulation - Foxborough, Mass.

333.38
(7447)
K17
Kargman, Mitchell and Sargent.
Subdivision regulations for the Town of Foxborough, Massachusetts. Prepared for Foxborough Planning Board and Massachusetts Dept. of Commerce. Suggested revision. Cambridge, Mass., [1959?]
13p.
U.S. Urban Renewal Adm. UPAP.

1. Subdivision regulation - Foxborough, Mass. I. Foxborough, Mass. Planning Board. II. U.S. URA-UPAP. Foxborough, Mass.

Subdivision regulation - Fulton, Ky.

333.38
(76999)
F85
Fulton, Ky. City Planning and Zoning Commission.
Subdivision regulations, City of Fulton, Kentucky. With assistance of the Kentucky Dept. of Economic Development. Fulton, 1958.
1v.

U.S. Urban Renewal Administration, Urban Planning Assistance Program.
1. Subdivision regulation - Fulton, Ky. I. U.S. URA-UPAP. Fulton, Ky.

711.74
(76791)
A74
Arkansas. University. City Planning Division. Forrest City, ... (Card 2)

1. Street planning - Forrest City, Ark. 2. Land use - Forrest City, Ark. 3. Subdivision regulation - Forrest City, Ark. 4. Zoning legislation - Forrest City, Ark. I. U.S. Urban Renewal Administration. Urban Planning Assistance Program.

Subdivision regulation - Franklin, Ky.

333.38
(769735)
F71
Franklin, Ky. City Planning and Zoning Commission.
Subdivision regulations, City of Franklin, Kentucky. Franklin, [1960?]
15p.
Prepared with the assistance of the Division of Planning and Zoning, Kentucky Dept. of Economic Development.
U.S. Urban Renewal Adm. UPAP.

1. Subdivision regulation - Franklin, Ky. I. U.S. URA-UPAP. Franklin, Ky.

---

574   SUBDIVISION REGULATION - FULTON CO., ILL.
FULTON CO., ILL. PLANNING COMMISSION.
PROPOSED LAND SUBDIVISION REGULATIONS FOR FULTON CO., ILL. BY HARLAND BARTHOLOMEW AND ASSOCIATES. LEWISTOWN, ILL., 1969.
16P. (HUD 701 REPORT)

1. SUBDIVISION REGULATION - FULTON CO., ILL. I. BARTHOLOMEW (HARLAND) AND ASSOCIATES. II. HUD. 701. FULTON CO., ILL.

4201   SUBDIVISION REGULATION - FOREST, MICH.
FOREST, MICH. TOWNSHIP PLANNING COMMISSION.
SUBDIVISION REGULATIONS FOR THE PLATTING OF LAND IN FOREST TOWNSHIP, MICHIGAN. PREPARED BY DRIKER ASSOCIATES, INC. BIRMINGHAM, MICH., 1967.
33L. (HUD 701 REPORT)

1. SUBDIVISION REGULATION - FOREST, MICH. I. DRIKER ASSOCIATES. II. HUD. 701. FOREST, MICH.

Subdivision regulation - Franklin (Gloucester Co.) N.J.

333.38
(74981)
C651
Community Planning Associates.
General plan, Franklin Township, Gloucester County, N.J. 1. Suggested subdivision standards. 2. A basis for a zoning ordinance. Prepared for Franklin Planning Board. West Trenton, N.J., 1959.
50p. maps, tables.
U.S. Urban Renewal Adm. UPAP.

1. Subdivision regulation - Franklin (Gloucester Co.) N.J. 2. Zoning - Franklin (Gloucester Co.) N.J. I. Franklin (Gloucester Co.) N.J. Planning Board. II. U.S. URA-UPAP. Franklin (Gloucester Co.) N.J.

Subdivision regulation - Gardendale, Ala.

333.38
(76187)
G17
Gardendale, Ala. City Planning Commission.
Gardendale, Alabama: land subdivision regulations and manual. [In cooperation with] Alabama State Planning and Industrial Development Board. Gardendale, 1958.
1v. diagrs.

U.S. Urban Renewal Administration, Urban Planning Assistance Program.

1. Subdivision regulation - Gardendale, Ala. I. Alabama. State Planning and Industrial Development Board. II. U.S. Urban Renewal Administration. Urban Planning Assistance Program.

333.38
(76741)
A74
Subdivision regulation - Garland Co., Ark.
Arkansas. University. City Planning
Div.
Recommended subdivision regulations.
Prepared for Garland County Regional
Planning Commission. Fayetteville, Ark.,
1962.
[18]p.

U.S. Urban Renewal Adm. UPAP.

1. Subdivision regulation-Garland Co., Ark.
I. Garland County Ark. Regional Planning
Commission. II. U.S. URA-UPAP. Garland Co.,
Ark.

333.38
(76972)
G51
Subdivision regulation - Glasgow, Ky.
Glasgow, Ky. City Planning and Zoning
Commission.
Subdivision regulations for the City of
Glasgow, Kentucky. With assistance of the
Kentucky Dept. of Economic Development.
Glasgow, 1958.
1v.

U.S. Urban Renewal Administration, Urban Planning
Assistance Program.

1. Subdivision regulation - Glasgow, Ky. I. U.S.
URA-UPAP. Glasgow, Ky.

4236
SUBDIVISION REGULATION - GRATIOT CO.,
MICH.
GRATIOT CO., MICH. PLANNING COMMISSION.
MODEL LOCAL GOVERNMENT SUBDIVISION
REGULATION ORDINANCE RECOMMENDED. BY
WILLIAMS AND WORKS. GRAND RAPIDS, 1968.
14L. (HUD 701 REPORT)

1. SUBDIVISION REGULATION - GRATIOT
CO., MICH. I WILLIAMS AND WORKS.
II. HUD. 701. GRATIOT CO., MICH.

711.5
(74786
:347)
G25
Subdivision regulation - Geneva, N. Y.
Geneva, N. Y. Ordinances, etc.
Zoning and subdivision recommendations, by
Floyd F. Walkley. Prepared under contract
with the New York State Dept. of Commerce.
Pittsford, N. Y., 1958.
1v. map.

U.S. Urban Renewal Administration, Urban Planning
Assistance Program.

1. Zoning legislation - Geneva, N.Y. 2. Subdivision
regulation - Geneva, N. Y. I. Walkley, Floyd F.
II. U.S. URA-UPAP. Geneva, N. Y.

333.38
(79753)
N25
Subdivision regulation - Goldendale, Wash.
Nelson (Harlan) and Associates.
Proposed subdivision ordinance for the
City of Goldendale, Washington. Oswego,
Or., 1959.
17p.

U.S. Urban Renewal Adm. UPAP.

1. Subdivision regulation - Goldendale,
Wash. I. U.S. URA-UPAP. Goldendale,
Wash.

711.4
(76178)
G71
Subdivision regulations - Graysville, Alabama.
Graysville, Ala. City Planning Commission.
Graysville, Alabama: land subdivision regu-
lations and manual. [In cooperation with
Alabama State Planning and Industrial Develop-
ment Board] Graysville, 1956.
1v. diagrs. charts.

U.S. Urban Renewal Administration, Urban

(Continued on next card)

333.38
(758)
A21
SUBDIVISION REGULATION - GA.
Adams, L Clifford.
Land subdivision regulation in Georgia.
Prepared by Georgia Municipal Association
in cooperation with Graduate School of
City Planning, Georgia Institute of
Technology and The Georgia Power Company.
[Atlanta] Georgia Municipal Association, 1961.
90p.

1. Subdivision regulation - Ga.
I. Georgia Municipal Association.
II. Georgia Institute of Technology.
Graduate school of City Planning.
III. Title.

333.38
(76159)
G66
Subdivision regulation - Goodwater, Ala.
Goodwater, Ala. Town Planning Commission.
Goodwater, Alabama: land subdivision regu-
lations and manual. [In cooperation with]
Alabama State Planning and Industrial De-
velopment Board. Goodwater, 1957.
23p. diagrs.

U.S. Urban Renewal Administration, Urban Planning
Assistance Program.

1. Subdivision regulation - Goodwater, Ala. I. U.S.
URA-UPAP. Goodwater, Ala.

711.4
(76178)
G71
Graysville, Ala. City Planning Commission.
Graysville, Alabama: land . . . (Card 2)

Planning Assistance Program.

1. City planning - Graysville, Ala. 2. Sub-
division regulations - Graysville, Ala.
I. Alabama. State Planning and Industrial
Development Board. II. U.S. Urban Renewal
Administration.

333.38
(76137)
G26
Subdivision regulation - Georgiana, Ala.
Georgiana, Ala. Town Planning Commission.
Georgiana, Alabama: land subdivision reg-
ulations and manual. [In cooperation with]
Alabama State Planning and Industrial De-
velopment Board. Georgiana, Ala., 1959.
23p. diagrs.

U.S. Urban Renewal Administration, Urban Planning
Assistance Program.

1. Subdivision regulation - Georgiana, Ala.
I. U.S. URA-UPAP. Georgiana, Ala.

333.38
(76185)
G67
Subdivision regulation - Gordo, Ala.
Gordo, Ala. Town Planning Commission.
Gordo, Alabama: subdivision regulations.
[Prepared for] Alabama State Planning and
Industrial Development Board. Gordo, 1960.
36p.

U.S. Urban Renewal Adm. UPAP.

1. Subdivision regulation - Gordo, Ala.
I. U.S. URA-UPAP. Gordo, Ala.

333.38
(74883)
H45
SUBDIVISION REGULATION - GREENE CO., PA.
Hill (Carroll V) & Associates.
Suggested model subdivision regulations for
townships of the second class. Waynesburg, Pa.
Greene County Planning Commission, [1964?]
39p.

1. Subdivision regulation - Greene Co., Pa.
I. Greene Co., Pa. Planning Commission.
II. Title.

333.38
(77383)
G47
Subdivision regulation - Girard, Ill.
Girard, Ill. Plan Commission.
Suggested subdivision ordinance, Girard,
Illinois, by Gregory Bassett. Girard,
1960.
15p.

U.S. Urban Renewal Administration,
Urban Planning Assistance Program.

1. Subdivision regulation - Girard, Ill. I. Bassett,
Gregory. II. U.S. URA-UPAP. Girard, Ill.

333.38
(74794)
T79
Subdivision regulation - Gowanda, N.Y.
Tryon and Schwartz and Associates.
Proposed subdivision regulations, Village
of Gowanda, N.Y. Prepared for Village Planning Board. Buffalo, 1958.
24p.

Addendum to proposed development plan.
U.S. Urban Renewal Administration, Urban
Planning Assistance Program.

1. Subdivision regulation - Gowanda, N.Y. I. Gowanda,
N.Y. Village Planning Board. II. U.S. URA-UPAP.
Gowanda, N.Y.

333.38
(756622)
G72
Subdivision regulation - Greensboro, N.C.
Greensboro, N.C. Ordinances, etc.
Subdivision regulations, city of
Greensboro, North Carolina. Greensboro,
N.C., 1955.
[8]p.

1. Subdivision regulation - Greensboro,
N.C.

4224
SUBDIVISION REGULATION - GLADSTONE,
MICH.
GLADSTONE, MICH. PLANNING COMMISSION.
SUBDIVISION REGULATION ORDINANCE.
PREPARED BY WILLIAMS AND WORKS. GRAND
RAPIDS, 1968.
12L. (HUD 701 REPORT)

1. SUBDIVISION REGULATION - GLADSTONE,
MICH. I. WILLIAMS AND WORKS. II. HUD.
701. GLADSTONE, MICH.

333.38
(76331)
M17s
Subdivision regulation - Gramercy, La.
Martin (Dan S.) and Associates.
Subdivision regulations, Gramercy,
Louisiana. Prepared for the Gramercy
Planning Commission. New Orleans, 1959.
17p.

U.S. Urban Renewal Administration, Urban
Planning Assistance Program.

1. Subdivision regulation - Gramercy, La. I. Gramercy, La. Planning Commission. II. U.S. URA-
UPAP. Gramercy, La.

711.5
(74881
:347)
G72r
Subdivision regulation - Greensburg, Pa.
Greater Westmoreland (Pa.) Regional
Planning Commission.
Review of zoning and subdivision controls
for Greensburg, Pennsylvania. Greensburg,
Pa., 1961.
[8] p.

U.S. Urban Renewal Adm. UPAP.

1. Zoning legislation - Greensburg, Pa.
2. Subdivision regulation - Greensburg, Pa.
I. U.S. URA-UPAP. Greensburg, Pa.

333.38
(79541)
G72
Subdivision regulation - Gladstone, Or.
Oregon. University. Bureau of Municipal
Research and Service.
Review of the Gladstone subdivision ordi-
nance. Memorandum to Gladstone City Plan-
ning Commission. Eugene, Or., 1960.
5p.

U.S. Urban Renewal Administration, Urban Planning
Assistance Program.

1. Subdivision regulation - Gladstone, Or. I.
Gladstone, Or. City Planning Commission. II. U.S.
URA-UPAP. Gladstone, Or.

9906
SUBDIVISION REGULATION - GRANDVIEW, MO.
GRANDVIEW, MO. PLANNING COMMISSION.
SUBDIVISION ORDINANCE. PREPARED BY
HARE AND HARE, INC. GRANDVIEW, MO., 1968.
12L. (HUD 701 REPORT)

1. SUBDIVISION REGULATION - GRANDVIEW,
MO. I. HARE AND HARE, INC. II. HUD.
701. GRANDVIEW, MO.

333.38
(74881)
G72
Subdivision regulation - Greensburg, Pa.
Greensburg, Pa. City Planning Commission.
Rules and regulations for the sub-
division of land Greensburg, [1963?]
9p.

U.S. Urban Renewal Adm. UPAP.

1. Subdivision regulation -
Greensburg, Pa. I. U.S. URA-UPAP.
Greensburg, Pa.

Subdivision regulation - Greenville, Ala.

333.38
(76137)
G72   Greenville, Ala. City Planning
        Commission.
          Greenville, Alabama: subdivision regu-
        lations. [Prepared in cooperation with]
        Alabama State Planning and Industrial
        Development Board. Greenville, 1963.
        39p.
          U.S. Urban Renewal Adm. UPAP.

        1. Subdivision regulation - Greenville,
        Ala. I. U.S.   URA-UPAP. Green-
        ville, Ala.

Subdivision regulation - Guin, Ala.

333.38
(76189)
G84   Guin, Ala. Town Planning Commission.
          Guin, Alabama; subdivision regulation.
        [Prepared in cooperation with] Alabama
        State Planning and Industrial Development
        Board. Guin, 1961.
        36p.
          U.S. Urban Renewal Adm. UPAP.

        1. Subdivision regulation - Guin,
        Ala. I. U.S.   URA-UPAP. Guin,
        Ala.

SUBDIVISION REGULATION - HANCOCK CO.,
KY.

1073   HANCOCK CO., KY. PLANNING COMMISSION.
          HANCOCK COUNTY SUBDIVISION REGULATIONS.
        BY R.W. BOOKER AND ASSOCIATES, INC.
        HAWESVILLE, KY., 1970.
        54L. (HUD 701 REPORT)

        1. SUBDIVISION REGULATION - HANCOCK
        CO., KY. I. BOOKER (R.W.) AND
        ASSOCIATES. II. HUD. 701. HANCOCK
        CO., KY.

Subdivision regulation - Greenville, Ill.

333.38
(77387)
G72   Greenville, Ill. Plan Commission.
          Subdivision ordinance, City of Green-
        ville, Illinois. Greenville, 1957.
        22p.

        1. Subdivision regulation - Greenville, Ill.

Subdivision regulation - Hackleburg, Ala.

333.38
(76189)
H12   Hackleburg, Ala. Town Planning Commission.
          Hackleburg, Alabama: subdivision regu-
        lations. [Prepared in cooperation with]
        Alabama State Planning and Industrial
        Development Board. Hackleburg, 1961.
        36p.
          U.S. Urban Renewal Adm. UPAP.

        1. Subdivision regulation - Hackleburg,
        Ala. I. U.S.   URA-UPAP.
        Hackleburg,   Ala.

Subdivision regulation - Hanover, N. H.

VF   Hanover, N. H. Town Planning Board.
333.38   Proposed subdivision regulations, Town
(7423) of Hanover, New Hampshire. Detached from
H15   the Hanover Gazette, Dec. 6, 1956.

        1. Subdivision regulation - Hanover,
        N. H.

Subdivision regulation - Greenville, Ky.

333.38
(76983)
G72   Greenville, Ky. City Planning and Zoning
        Commission.
          Subdivision regulations of Greenville,
        Kentucky. With assistance of the Kentucky
        Dept. of Economic Development. Greenville,
        [1958?]
        1v.
          U.S. Urban Renewal Administration, Urban Planning
        Assistance Program.
        1. Subdivision regulation - Greenville, Ky. I. U.S.
        URA-UPAP. Greenville, Ky.

Subdivision regulation - Hahira, Ga.

333.38
(758864)
P45   Pill and Adley Associates.
          Subdivision regulations for the City of
        Hahira, Georgia. Proposed. Prepared under
        contract with Georgia Dept. of Commerce.
        [Atlanta, Ga., 1959?]
        13p.

          U.S. Urban Renewal Administration,
        Urban Planning Assistance Program.

        1. Subdivision regulation - Hahira, Ga. I. U.S.
        URA-UPAP. Hahira, Ga.

Subdivision regulation - Harlan, Iowa.

711.4
(77748)
H17   Daly (Leo A.) Co.
no.5   Zoning and subdivisions; a study report
        element of the Harlan, Iowa comprehensive
        plan. Presented to the City Planning
        Commission of Harlan, Iowa. Prepared for
        the Iowa Development Commission. [n.p.]
        1964.
        1v.   (Its Comprehensive plan series
        5)
          U.S. Urban Renewal Adm. UPAP.

                        (Continued on
                        next card)

SUBDIVISION REGULATION - GREENVILLE,
N.Y.

2492   GREENVILLE, N.Y. PLANNING BOARD.
          PROPOSED SUBDIVISION REGULATIONS. BY
        RAYMOND AND MAY ASSOCIATES. GREENVILLE,
        N.Y., 1967.
        30L. (HUD 701 REPORT)

        1. SUBDIVISION REGULATION - GREENVILLE,
        N.Y. I. RAYMOND AND MAY ASSOCIATES.
        II. HUD. 701. GREENVILLE, N.Y.

SUBDIVISION REGULATION - HALL CO., NEB.

2825   HALL CO., NEB. REGIONAL PLANNING
        COMMISSION.
          FORM OF SUBDIVISION REGULATIONS. BY
        HENNINGSON, DURHAM AND RICHARDSON. GRAND
        ISLAND, NEB., 1970.
        1 V. (HUD 701 REPORT)

        1. SUBDIVISION REGULATION - HALL CO.,
        NEB. I. HENNINGSON, DURHAM AND
        RICHARDSON. II. HUD. 701. HALL CO.,
        NEB.

711.4
(77748)
H17   Daly (Leo A.) Co. Zoning and subdivisions;
no.5   a study report element of the Harlan,
        Iowa comprehensive plan...1964   (Card 2)

        1. Master plan - Harlan, Iowa. 2. Zoning
        legislation - Harlan, Iowa. 3. Subdivision
        regulation - Harlan, Iowa. I. Harlan, Iowa.
        City Planning Commission. II. U.S. URA-
        UPAP. Harlan, Iowa.

Subdivision regulation - Greenville, Pa.

333.38
(74895)
K56   Knowles (Morris) Inc.
          Borough of Greenville, Mercer County,
        Pennsylvania: land subdivision ordinance.
        [Prepared for Greenville Planning Commis-
        sion] Easton, Pa., 1957.

          U.S. Urban Renewal Administration, Urban Planning
        Assistance Program.

        1. Subdivision regulation - Greenville, Pa. I. Green-
        ville, Pa. Planning and Zoning Commission. II. U.S.
        URA-UPAP. Greenville,   Pa.

Subdivision regulation - Hamilton, Ala.

333.38
(76189)
H15   Hamilton, Ala. Town Planning Commission.
          Hamilton, Alabama; subdivision regu-
        lations. [Prepared in cooperation with]
        Alabama State Planning and Industrial
        Development Board. Hamilton, 1961.
        36p.
          U.S. Urban Renewal Adm. UPAP.

        1. Subdivision regulation - Hamilton,
        Ala. I. U.S. URA-UPAP. Hamilton, Ala.

Subdivision regulation - Harrisburg, Pa.

333.38
(74818)
R23   Regional Planning Commission of Greater
        Harrisburg.
          Land subdivision regulations, 1958.
        Harrisburg, Pa., 1958.
        1v.
          U.S. Urban Renewal Administration, Urban
        Planning Assistance Program.

        1. Subdivision regulation - Harrisburg,
        Pa. I. U.S. Urban Renewal Administration.
        Urban Planning Assistance Program.

Subdivision regulation - Gretna, La.

333.38
(76338)
P15   Palmer and Baker Engineers.
          Gretna, Louisiana: subdivision regulations.
        New Orleans, 1961.
        31p.
          Prepared in cooperation with the Louisiana
        Dept. of Public Works.
          U.S. Urban Renewal Adm. UPAP.

        1. Subdivision regulation - Gretna, La.
        I. U.S. URA-UPAP. Gretna, La.

Subdivision regulation - Hamilton, N.Y.

333.38
(74764)
H15   Hamilton, N.Y. Village Planning Commission.
          Subdivision regulations, Village of Hamil-
        ton, New York.
        15p.

          U.S. Urban Renewal Administration, Urban Planning
        Assistance Program.

        1. Subdivision regulation - Hamilton, N.Y. I. U.S.
        URA-UPAP. Hamilton, N.Y.

Subdivision regulation - Hartford, Vt.

333.38
(74365)
H17   Hartford, Vt. Ordinances, etc.
          Town of Hartford, Vermont subdivision
        regulations. Hartford, [1959?]
        1v.
          U.S. Urban Renewal Administration, Urban
        Planning Assistance Program.

        1. Subdivision regulation - Hartford, Vt.
        I. U.S. Urban Renewal Administration.
        Urban Planning Assistance Program.

Subdivision regulation - Guadalupe, Calif.

333.38
(79491)
G81   Guadalupe, Calif. Ordinances, etc.
          Proposed subdivision regulations,
        City of Guadalupe. Guadalupe, 1959.
        [32]p.

          U.S. Urban Renewal Adm. UPAP.

        1. Subdivision regulation -
        Guadalupe, Calif. I. U.S. URA-UPAP.
        Guadalupe, Calif.

Subdivision regulation - Hanceville, Ala.

333.38
(76173)
H15   Hanceville, Ala. Town Planning Commission.
          Hanceville, Alabama: subdivision regula-
        tions. [Prepared for] Alabama State Plan-
        ning and Industrial Development Board.
        Hanceville, 1960.
        36p.
          U.S. Urban Renewal Adm. UPAP.

        1. Subdivision regulation - Hanceville,
        Ala. I. U.S. URA-UPAP. Hanceville, Ala.

SUBDIVISION REGULATION - HARWICH, MASS.

5453   HARWICH, MASS. PLANNING BOARD.
          TOWN OF HARWICH, MASSACHUSETTS;
        PROPOSED REVISED LAND SUBDIVISION
        REGULATIONS. BY METCALF AND EDDY.
        HARWICH, 1966.
        33L. (HUD 701 REPORT)

        1. SUBDIVISION REGULATION - HARWICH,
        MASS. I. METCALF AND EDDY. II. HUD.
        701. HARWICH, MASS.

1736   SUBDIVISION REGULATION - HAWARDEN, IOWA.
HAWARDEN, IOWA. PLAN COMMISSION.
PROPOSED SUBDIVISION REGULATIONS.
HAWARDEN, IOWA, CA. 1969.
11L. (HUD 701 REPORT)

1. SUBDIVISION REGULATION - HAWARDEN,
IOWA. I. HUD. 701. HAWARDEN, IOWA.

5362   SUBDIVISION REGULATION - HIGHLANDS, N.Y.
HIGHLANDS, N.Y. PLANNING COMMISSION.
SUBDIVISION REGULATIONS OF THE
HIGHLANDS-HIGHLAND FALLS COMMUNITY, NEW
YORK. NEW YORK, 1967.
38L. (HUD 701 REPORT)

1. SUBDIVISION REGULATION - HIGHLANDS,
N.Y. I. HUD. 701. HIGHLANDS, N.Y.

Subdivision regulation - Holly Springs, Miss.

711.4
(76288) Urban Consultant Associates.
H65s   Subdivision regulations; a part of the
comprehensive city plan for Holly Springs,
Mississippi. In cooperation with the City
of Holly Springs, Mississippi and the
Holly Springs City Planning Commission.
Montgomery, Ala., 1960.
15p.
U.S. Urban Renewal Adm. UPAP.
1. Master plan - Holly Springs, Miss. 2. Subdivision
regulation - Holly Springs, Miss. I. Holly Springs,
Miss. City Planning   Commission.
II. U.S. URA-UPAP.   Holly Springs, Miss.

333.38   Subdivision regulation - Headland, Ala.
(76131)
E21   Headland, Ala. City Planning Commission.
Headland, Alabama: land subdivision regulations and manual. [In cooperation with]
Alabama State Planning and Industrial Development Board. Headland, 1957.
23p. diagrs.

U.S. Urban Renewal Administration, Urban Planning
Assistance Program.

1. Subdivision regulation - Headland, Ala. I. U.S.
URA-UPAP. Headland,   Ala.

333.38   Subdivision regulation - Highspire, Pa.
(74818)
R23   Regional Planning Commission of
1963   Greater Harrisburg.
Land subdivision regulations, Borough of
Highspire, Dauphin County, Pa. [Prepared
for] Borough of Highspire Planning
Commission. [n.p. 1963?]
28p.

U.S. Urban Renewal Adm. UPAP.

1. Subdivision regulation - Highspire, Pa.
I. Highspire, Pa.   Planning Commission.
II. U.S. URA-UPAP.   Highspire, Pa.

333.38   Subdivision regulation - Holmdel, N.J.
(74946)
M67   Morrow Planning Associates.
Proposed subdivision ordinance, Township of Holmdel, New Jersey. Prepared for
the Holmdel Planning Board. [Ridgewood,
N.J.] 1958.
48p.

U.S. Urban Renewal Adm. UPAP.

1. Subdivision regulation - Holmdel,
N.J. I. Holmdel, N.J. Planning Board.
II. U.S. URA-UPAP. Holmdel,
N.J.

Subdivision regulation - Healdton, Okla.

333.38
(76658) Oklahoma. University. Institute of Com-
045   munity Development.
An ordinance for the regulation of land
subdivision, Healdton, Oklahoma. Proposed.
Prepared for the Healdton City Council and
Planning Commission. Norman, Okla., 1958.
17p.

U.S. Urban Renewal Administration, Urban Planning
Assistance Program.

1. Subdivision regulation - Healdton, Okla. I.
Healdton, Okla. City Planning Commission.   II.
U.S. URA-UPAP.   Healdton, Okla.

333.38   Subdivision regulation - Hobson City, Ala.
(76163)
H61   Hobson City, Ala. Town Planning Commission.
Hobson City, Alabama: land subdivision
regulations and manual. [In cooperation with]
Alabama State Planning and Industrial Development Board. Hobson City, 1958.
23p. diagrs.

U.S. Urban Renewal Administration, Urban Planning
Assistance Program.

1. Subdivision regulation - Hobson City, Ala.
I. U.S. URA-UPAP.   Hobson City, Ala.

Subdivision regulation - Homer, La.

333.38
(76394) Martin (Dan S.) and Associates.
M17   Subdivision regulations, Homer, Louisiana.
Prepared for the Homer Planning Commission.
New Orleans, 1959.
17p.   diagrs.

U.S. Urban Renewal Administration,
Urban Planning Assistance Program.

1. Subdivision regulation - Homer, La.
I. Homer, La. Planning Commission.
II. U.S. URA-UPAP. Homer, La.

Subdivision regulation - Heber Springs, Ark.

333.38
(767285) Arkansas. University. City Planning
A74   Division.
Subdivision regulations, Cleburne County,
Heber Springs, Arkansas. Prepared for
Cleburne County, Heber Springs Planning
Commission. Fayetteville, Ark., 1962.
8p.

U.S. Urban Renewal Adm. UPAP.

1. Subdivision regulation - Heber Springs, Ark.
I. Heber Springs,   Ark. Planning
Commission.   II. U.S. URA-UPAP.
Heber Springs,   Ark.

333.38   Subdivision regulation - Hohenwald, Tenn.
(76843)
H63   Hohenwald, Tenn. Municipal Planning Commission.
Subdivision regulations, effective January
15, 1957. Hohenwald, Tenn., 1957.
8p. diagrs. (MTC Publication no. 57-4)

1. Subdivision regulation - Hohenwald,
Tenn.

---

722.   SUBDIVISION REGULATION - HOMERVILLE, GA.
HOMERVILLE - CLINCH COUNTY PLANNING
COMMISSION.
PROPOSED LAND SUBDIVISION REGULATIONS,
CITY OF HOMERVILLE CLINCH COUNTY,
GEORGIA. PREPARED UNDER CONTRACT WITH THE
STATE PLANNING BUREAU OF THE STATE OF
GEORGIA, BY THE SLASH PINE AREA PLANNING
AND DEVELOPMENT COMMISSION. ATLANTA, 1969.
24L. (HUD 701 REPORT)

1. SUBDIVISION REGULATION - HOMERVILLE,
GA. I. SLASH PINE AREA PLANNING AND
DEVELOPMENT COMMISSION. II. HUD.
701. HOMERVILLE, GA.

333.38   Subdivision regulation - Henderson, Ky.
(769871)
H25   Henderson, Ky. Ordinances, etc.
Proposed subdivision regulations of
Henderson, Kentucky. Henderson, 1957.
18p. forms.

1. Subdivision regulation - Henderson,
Ky. I. U.S. Urban Renewal Administration. Urban Planning Assistance Program.

333.38   Subdivision regulation - Holbrook, Mass.
(7447)
H65   Holbrook, Mass. Ordinances, etc.
Holbrook subdivision regulations.
Holbrook, 1960.
[2]p.

U.S. Urban Renewal Adm. UPAP.

1. Subdivision regulation - Holbrook, Mass.
I. U.S. URA-UPAP. Holbrook, Mass.

Subdivision regulation - Homewood, Ill.

333.38
(7731) Gardner (Carl L.) and Associates.
G17   Proposed subdivision regulations, Homewood
Illinois. [Prepared for the Rezoning Commission of the Village of Homewood, Illinois]
Chicago, 1958.
32p.

U.S. Urban Renewal Administration, Urban Planning
Assistance Program.

1. Subdivision regulation - Homewood, Ill.
I. Homewood, Ill. Rezoning Commission.
II. U.S. URA-UPAP.   Homewood, Ill.

Subdivision regulation - Hickory, Pa.

333.38
(74882) Shenango Valley Regional Planning
832   Commission.
Hickory Township subdivision regulations, Mercer County, Penna. Harrisburg,
Rev. June 1960.
40p.

U.S. Urban Renewal Adm. UPAP.

1. Subdivision regulation - Hickory, Pa.
I. U.S. URA-UPAP. Hickory, Pa.

5439   SUBDIVISION REGULATION - HOLBROOK, MASS.
HOLBROOK, MASS. PLANNING BOARD.
LAND SUBDIVISION RULES AND REGULATIONS,
REV. JAN. 1965. BY ATWOOD AND BLACKWELL,
PLANNERS. BOSTON, 1965.
16L. (HUD 701 REPORT)

1. SUBDIVISION REGULATION - HOLBROOK,
MASS. I. ATWOOD AND BLACKWELL, PLANNERS.
II. HUD. 701. HOLBROOK, MASS.

---

591   SUBDIVISION REGULATION - HOOPESTON, ILL.
HOOPESTON, ILL. CITY PLAN COMMISSION.
ANALYSIS OF THE SUBDIVISION ORDINANCE,
BY TEC-SEARCH, INC. HOOPESTON, ILL., 1970.
5P. (HUD 701 REPORT)

1. SUBDIVISION REGULATION - HOOPESTON,
ILL. I. TEC-SEARCH, INC. II. HUD.
701. HOOPESTON, ILL.

Subdivision regulation - Highlands, N.J.

711.4
(74946) Community Planning Associates.
H43m   Master plan, Borough of Highlands,
Monmouth County, N.J. 1. Suggested
subdivision standards. 2. A basis for
a zoning ordinance. [West Trenton,
N.J. 1959?]
[38]p.

U.S. Urban Renewal Adm. UPAP.

1. Master plan - Highlands, N.J. 2. Zoning
legislation - Highlands, N.J. 3. Subdivision
regulation - Highlands, N.J. I. U.S. URA-UPAP.
Highlands, N.J.

5364   SUBDIVISION REGULATION - HOLLEY, N.Y.
HOLLEY, N.Y. PLANNING BOARD.
SUBDIVISION REPORT. PREPARED BY
CANDEUB, FLEISSIG AND ASSOCIATES. NEW
YORK, 1968.
31L. (HUD 701 REPORT)

1. SUBDIVISION REGULATION - HOLLEY, N.Y.
I. CANDEUB, FLEISSIG AND ASSOCIATES.
II. HUD. 701. HOLLEY, N.Y.

333.38   Subdivision regulation - Hope, Ark.
(76754)
A74   Arkansas. University. City Planning
Div.
Development guide for the Hope City
Planning Commission. Fayetteville, Ark.,
1962.
1v.

U.S. Urban Renewal Adm. UPAP.

1. Subdivision regulation - Hope, Ark.
I. Hope, Ark. Planning Commission.
II. U.S. URA- UPAP. Hope, Ark.

333.38
(76754)
A74s

Subdivision regulation - Hope, Ark.
Arkansas. University. City Planning Division.
Subdivision regulations, Hope, Arkansas. Prepared for the Hope Planning Commission. Fayetteville, 1961.
16p.

U.S. Urban Renewal Adm. UPAP.

1. Subdivision regulation - Hope, Ark. I. Hope, Ark. Planning Commission. II. U.S. URA—UPAP. Hope, Ark.

333.38
(74733)
C51

Subdivision regulation - Hyde Park, N.Y.
Clark (Frederick P.) and Associates.
Review of subdivision regulations and procedures, town of Hyde Park, N.Y. Prepared for Hyde Park, N.Y. Town Planning Board and New York State Dept. of Commerce. Rye, N.Y., 1960.
18p.

U.S. Urban Renewal Adm. UPAP.

1. Subdivision regulation - Hyde Park, N.Y. I. Hyde Park, N.Y. Town Planning Board. II. U.S. URA-UPAP. Hyde Park, N.Y.

333.38
(77346)
K45
1959

Subdivision regulation - Jacksonville, Ill.
Kincaid (Evert) and Associates.
Suggested requirements for establishing subdivision regulations for Jacksonville, Illinois. Prepared for the Jacksonville Plan Commission. Chicago, 1959.
26p.

U.S. Urban Renewal Adm. UPAP.

1. Subdivision regulation - Jacksonville, Ill. I. Jacksonville, Ill. Plan Commission. II. U.S. URA-UPAP. Jacksonville, Ill.

333.38
(74783)
T79

Subdivision regulation - Hornell, N.Y.
Tryon and Schwartz and Associates.
Proposed subdivision regulations, City of Hornell, New York. Prepared for City Planning Board. Buffalo, 1958.
24p.

Addendum to proposed development plan.
U.S. Urban Renewal Administration, Urban Planning Assistance Program.

1. Subdivision regulation - Hornell, N.Y. I. Hornell, N.Y. City Planning Board. II. U.S. URA-UPAP. Hornell, N.Y.

333.38
(772)
H21

Subdivision regulation - Indiana.
Head, W J
County subdivision control: model ordinance with discussion. Lafayette, Ind., Purdue University, Engineering Experiment Station in cooperation with the County Commissioners of Indiana, 1962.
46p. (County highway series no. 3)
Purdue University. Engineering Experiment Station. Engineering bulletin.
On cover: Highway Extension and Research Project for Indiana Counties. (HERPIC)
(Cont'd. on next card)

333.38
(77346)
K45
1960

Subdivision regulation - Jacksonville, Ill.
Kincaid (Evert) and Associates.
Suggested requirements for establishing subdivision regulations for Jacksonville, Illinois. Prepared for the Jacksonville Plan Commission. Rev. Chicago, 1960.
26p.

U.S. Urban Renewal Adm. UPAP.

1. Subdivision regulation - Jacksonville, Ill. I. Jacksonville, Ill. Plan Commission. II. U.S. URA- UPAP. Jacksonville, Ill.

333.38
(74882)
H68

Subdivision regulation - Houston, Pa.
Houston, Pa. Ordinances, etc.
Land subdivision regulations. [Houston, 1961?]
[16]p.

Clifton Rodgers, planning consultant.
U.S. Urban Renewal Adm. UPAP.

1. Subdivision regulation - Houston, Pa. I. Rodgers, Clifton. II. U.S. URA-UPAP. Houston, Pa.

333.38
(772)
H21

Head, W J County subdivision control... (Card 2)

1. Subdivision regulation - Indiana. 2. Highways - Indiana. I. Purdue University. Engineering Experiment Station. II. Highway Extension and Research Project for Indiana Counties.

711.4
(76176)
J17 1a

Subdivision regulation - Jasper, Alabama
Jasper, Ala. City Planning Commission.
Jasper, Alabama: land subdivision regulations and manual. [In cooperation with Alabama State Planning and Industrial Development Board] Jasper, 1955.
29p. diagrs.

U.S. Urban Renewal Administration, Urban
(Continued on next card)

333.38
(764)
H68

Subdivision regulation - Houston, Tex.
Houston, Tex. City Planning Commission.
Land subdivision, 1940-1946. Houston, 1946.
19p.

1. Subdivision regulation - Houston, Tex.

711.4
(764)
I78p

Subdivision regulation - Irving, Tex.
Leipziger-Pearce (Hugo) and Associates.
Public utilities, proposed subdivision regulations, comprehensive development plan, Irving, Texas. Prepared through the cooperation of the Texas State Dept. of Health. Houston, Tex., 1960.
[52]p.
Cover title.
U.S. Urban Renewal Adm. UPAP.

1. Master plan - Irving, Tex. 2. Public utilities - Irving, Tex. 3. Subdivision regulation - Irving, Tex. I. U.S. URA- UPAP. Irving, Tex.

711.4
(76176)
J17 1a

Jasper, Ala. City Planning Commission. Jasper, Alabama: land ... (Card 2)

Planning Assistance Program.

1. Master plan - Jasper, Ala. 2. Subdivision regulation - Jasper, Ala. I. Alabama. State Planning and Industrial Development Board. II. U.S. Urban Renewal Administration.

333.38
(76228)
H82

Subdivision regulation - Hueytown, Ala.
Hueytown, Ala. City Planning Commission.
Hueytown, Alabama: subdivision regulation. [Prepared in cooperation with] Alabama State Planning and Industrial Development Board. Hueytown, 1961.
36p.
U.S. Urban Renewal Adm. UPAP.

1. Subdivision regulation - Hueytown, Ala. I. U.S. URA-UPAP. Hueytown, Ala.

333.38
(74881)
B14

Subdivision regulation - Irwin, Pa.
Baker (Michael) inc.
Rules and regulations for the subdivision of land, Borough of Irwin, Westmoreland County, Pennsylvania. Prepared for the Irwin Borough Planning Commission. Rochester, Pa., [1962?]
29p.

1. Subdivision regulation - Irwin, Pa. I. Irwin, Pa. Planning Commission.

333.38
(74881)
B22

Subdivision regulation - Jeanette, Pa.
Beckman, Mueller and Cotter.
Proposed subdivision code for Jeanette, Pennsylvania. Pittsburgh, 1961.
10p.

U.S. Urban Renewal Adm. UPAP.

1. Subdivision regulation - Jeanette, Pa. I. Jeanette, Pa. Ordinances, etc. II. U.S. URA- UPAP. Jeanette, Pa.

333.38
(76823)
H85

Subdivision regulation - Humboldt, Tenn.
Humboldt, Tenn. Municipal-Regional Planning Commission.
Subdivision regulations, Humboldt, Tennessee. Humboldt, 1958.
42p. diagrs., maps.
U.S. Urban Renewal Administration, Urban Planning Assistance Program.

1. Subdivision regulation - Humboldt, Tenn. I. U.S. Urban Renewal Administration. Urban Planning Assistance Program.

1082

SUBDIVISION REGULATION - JACKSON, KY.
JACKSON-BREATHITT COUNTY PLANNING COMMISSION.
SUBDIVISION REGULATIONS OF THE CITY OF JACKSON, KENTUCKY. BY KENTUCKY PROGRAM DEVELOPMENT OFFICE, DIVISION OF PLANNING. CORBIN, KY., 1969.
55P. (HUD 701 REPORT)

1. SUBDIVISION REGULATION - JACKSON, KY. I. KENTUCKY. PROGRAM DEVELOPMENT OFFICE. DIVISION OF PLANNING. II. HUD 701. JACKSON, KY.

729

SUBDIVISION REGULATION - JEFFERSON, GA.
JACKSON CO., GA. PLANNING COMMISSION.
SUBDIVISION REGULATIONS, JEFFERSON, GEORGIA. ATHENS, GA., NORTHEAST GEORGIA AREA PLANNING AND DEVELOPMENT COMMISSION, 1970.
44L. (HUD 701 REPORT)

1. SUBDIVISION REGULATION - JEFFERSON, GA. I. NORTHEAST GEORGIA AREA PLANNING AND DEVELOPMENT COMMISSION. II. HUD 701. JEFFERSON, GA.

711.5
(77352)
T74

Subdivision regulation - Illinois.
Tri-County Regional Planning Commission, Peoria, Ill.
A digest of the zoning and subdivision study for Peoria, Woodford and Tazewell counties. An interim report. Peoria, 1956.
15p.

1. Zoning - Illinois. 2. Subdivision regulation - Illinois.

333.38
(78866)
J12

Subdivision regulation - Jackson Co., Colo.
Jackson Co., Colo. Ordinances, etc.
Subdivision resolution. [Walden] [1969?]
10p.

1. Subdivision regulation - Jackson Co., Colo.

333.38
(77867)
J23

Subdivision regulation - Jefferson Co., Mo.
Jefferson County, Mo. Planning and Zoning Commission.
Subdivision regulations for Jefferson County, Missouri. Hillsboro, Mo., 1964.
53p.

1. Subdivision regulation - Jefferson Co., Mo.

736   SUBDIVISION REGULATION - JESUP, GA.
JESUP - WAYNE COUNTY PLANNING COMMISSION.
JESUP, GEORGIA, COMPREHENSIVE PLAN,
SUBDIVISION REGULATIONS. PREPARED UNDER
CONTRACT WITH THE STATE PLANNING BUREAU,
BY MAYES, SUDDERTH AND ETHEREDGE, INC.
ATLANTA, STATE PLANNING BUREAU, 1969.
26L. (HUD 701 REPORT)

1. SUBDIVISION REGULATION - JESUP, GA.
I. MAYES, SUDDERTH AND ETHEREDGE, INC.
II. HUD. 701. JESUP, GA.

Subdivision regulation - Kelso, Wash.
333.38
(79788) Clark-Coleman and Associates.
C51   Subdivision ordinance; a draft proposal
for the City of Kelso, Washington. [Seattle]
1959.
21p.

U.S. Urban Renewal Adm. UPAP.

1. Subdivision regulation - Kelso, Wash.
I. Kelso, Wash. Ordinances, etc. II. U.S.
URA-UPAP. Kelso, Wash.

Subdivision regulation - Kodiak, Alaska.
333.38
(798)   Alaska. State Housing Authority.
A51   Subdivision control ordinance, City of
Kodiak, Alaska. [Kodiak, 1963?]
14p.

U.S. Urban Renewal Adm. UPAP.

1. Subdivision regulation - Kodiak,
Alaska. I. U.S. URA-UPAP. Kodiak, Alaska.

711.5   SUBDIVISION REGULATION - JONES CO., GA.
(758567 Middle Georgia Area Planning Commission.
:347   The comprehensive land development resolution
M42   for the unincorporated area of Jones County;
zoning and subdivision regulations. Atlanta,
State Planning Bureau, 1970.
84p.
U.S. Dept. of Housing and Urban Development.
UPAP. UPA Ga. P-149(C)

1. Zoning legislation - Jones Co., Ga.
2. Subdivision regulation - Jones Co., Ga.
I. Jones Co., Ga. Board of Commissioners.
II. U.S. HUD-UPAP. Jones Co., Ga.

Subdivision regulation - Kenai, Alaska.
333.38
(798)   Alaska. State Housing Authority.
A51k   Subdivision control ordinance, City of
Kenai, Alaska. Kenai, 1962.
153-163p.

U.S. Urban Renewal Adm. UPAP.

1. Subdivision regulation - Kenai,
Alaska. I. U.S. URA-UPAP. Kenai,
Alaska.

Subdivision regulation - Lacon, Ill.
333.38
(773515) Scruggs and Hammond.
827   Maps, plates and subdivision code of
Lacon, Illinois and contiguous area. Prepared for the Planning Commission of Lacon,
Illinois and Illinois State Housing Board.
Peoria, Ill., [1960]
20p.

U.S. Urban Renewal Administration,
Urban Planning Assistance Program.

1. Subdivision regulation - Lacon, Ill. I. Lacon,
Ill. Planning Commission. II. U.S. URA-UPAP.
Lacon, Ill.

Subdivision regulation - Josephine Co., Or.
333.38
(79525) Josephine County, Or. Ordinances, etc.
J67   Subdivision regulation for Josephine
County. Proposed by the Josephine County
Planning Commission. Grants Pass, Or.,
1958.
28p.

U.S. Urban Renewal Administration, Urban Planning
Assistance Program.

1. Subdivision regulation - Josephine Co., Or.
I. Josephine County, Or. Planning Commission.
II. U.S. URA-UPAP. Josephine Co., Or.

Subdivision regulation - Kenner, La.
333.38 Martin (Dan S.) and Associates.
(76338)   Subdivision regulations, Kenner, Louis-
M17   iana. A report to the Planning Commission.
New Orleans, 1957.
17p.
U.S. Urban Renewal Administration, Urban
Planning Assistance Program.

1. Subdivision regulation - Kenner, La.
I. Kenner, La. Planning Commission. II. U.S.
Urban Renewal Administration. Urban Planning
Assistance Program. Kenner, La.

Subdivision regulation - Lafourche,
Parish, La.
711.4
(76339) Carter-Horan and Chapin.
C17   Zoning and subdivision regulations:
Phase VII of the comprehensive plan, lower
Lafourche regional planning area. Baton
Rouge, La., [1960]
1v. maps.

U.S. Urban Renewal Adm. UPAP.

1. Master plan - Lafourche Parish, La. 2. Zoning
legislation - Golden Meadow, La. 3. Subdivision
regulation - Lafourche Parish, La. I. U.S. URA-UPAP.
Lafourche Parish, La.

Subdivision regulation - Juneau, Alaska.
333.38
(798)   Bloch (Ivan) and Associates.
B56   Proposed subdivision ordinance for the City
of Juneau, Alaska. Portland, Or., 1959
17p.

U.S. Urban Renewal Administration, Urban Planning
Assistance Program.

1. Subdivision regulation - Juneau, Alaska.
I. Nelson, Harlan. II. U.S. URA-UPAP. Juneau,
Alaska.

Subdivision regulation - Kewanee, Ill.
333.38
(77338) Kincaid (Evert) and Associates.
K45   Suggested requirements for establishing
subdivision regulations for Kewanee, Illinois. Prepared for the Kewanee Plan Commission. Chicago, 1959.
27p.

U.S. Urban Renewal Administration, Urban Planning
Assistance Program.

1. Subdivision regulation - Kewanee, Ill. I. Kewanee, Ill. Plan Commission. II. U.S. URA-
UPAP. Kewanee, Ill.

711.5   SUBDIVISION REGULATION - LAKE CITY, S.C.
(75784
:347)   Carter, Sydney.
C17   Recommended comprehensive zoning ordinance
and subdivision regulations. Prepared under
contract with the Community Planning
Division, State Planning and Grants
Division, State of South Carolina. Prepared
for Lake City Planning and Zoning
Commission. Lake City, South Carolina.
Augusta, Ga., 1970.
23p.
U.S. Dept. of Housing and Urban Development. Comprehensive Planning
(Cont'd on next card)

Subdivision regulation - Kansas City, Mo.
333.38
(77841) American Public Works Association.
A52   Kansas City Metropolitan Chapter.
Regulations for the residential subdivision of land. [Kansas City?] 1966.
13p.

1. Subdivision regulation - Kansas
City, Mo. I. Title.

Subdivision regulation - Killingly, Conn.
333.38
(74645) Stelling (A. Carl) Associates.
872   Town of Killingly subdivision regulations.
[Prepared for] Planning Commission, Killingly,
Connecticut. [Hartford] 1957.
1v. tables.
U.S. Urban Renewal Administration, Urban
Planning Assistance Program.
1. Subdivision regulation - Killingly, Conn.
I. Killingly, Conn. Planning Commission.
II. U.S. Urban Renewal Administration.
Urban Planning Assistance Program.

711.5
(75784
:347)   Carter, Sydney. Recommended...1970.
C17   (Card 2)

Grant Program. HUD project no. S.C. P-32.

1. Zoning legislation - Lake City, S.C.
2. Subdivision regulation - Lake City, S.C.
I. Lake City, S.C. Planning and Zoning
Commission. II. U.S. HUD-Comprehensive
Planning Grant Program. Lake City, S.C.

Subdivision regulation - Kansas City, Mo.
333.38
(781391) Kansas City, Mo. City Plan Commission.
K15   Subdivision regulations. Kansas City,
Mo., 1954.
11p.

1. Subdivision regulation - Kansas City,
Mo.

Subdivision regulation - Klamath Co., Or.
333.38
(79591) Oregon. University. Bureau of Municipal
072   Research and Service.
Proposed subdivision regulation for Klamath County. Prepared for the Klamath
County Planning Commission. Eugene, Or.,
1959.
15p.

U.S. Urban Renewal Administration, Urban Planning
Assistance Program.
1. Subdivision regulation - Klamath Co., Or.
I. Klamath Co., Or. Planning Commission.
II. U.S. URA-UPAP. Klamath Co., Or.

Subdivision regulation - La Habra, Calif.
333.38
(79496) La Habra, Calif. Ordinances, etc.
L11   [Ordinances] La Habra, [1963?]
1v.
U.S. Urban Renewal Adm. UPAP.

1. Subdivision regulation - La
Habra, Calif. I. U.S. URA-UPAP. La Habra,
Calif.

Subdivision regulation - Keene, N.H.
333.38
(74729) Keene, N.H. City Planning Board.
K22   Proposed land subdivision regulations
(revised) Keene, New Hampshire. Keene,
1960.
1v. diagrs.
U.S. Urban Renewal Administration, Urban Planning
Assistance Program.

1. Subdivision regulation - Keene, N.H. I. U.S.
URA-UPAP. Keene, N.H.

Subdivision regulation - Kleberg, Tex.
711.4
(764)   Hollin, Robert W
K52   Kleberg, Dallas County, Texas: thoroughfares,
no. 1   land use, zoning, subdivision control. Prepared
for the city of Kleberg, Texas [in cooperation
with] Homer A. Hunter and Associates. Dallas,
1959.
2 v. (Comprehensive city plan report no. 1)
v. 2 Maps and plates.
U.S. Urban Renewal Adm. UPAP.
1. Master plan - Kleberg, Tex. 2. Streets - Kleberg,
Tex. 3. Land use - Kleberg, Tex. 4. Zoning - Kleberg,
Tex. 5. Subdivision regulation - Kleberg,
Tex. I. Hunter (Homer A.) Associates. II. U.S.
URA-UPAP. Kleberg, Tex.

---

351   SUBDIVISION REGULATION - LA JUNTA, COLO.
LA JUNTA, COLO. CITY PLANNING COMMISSION.
SUBDIVISION REGULATIONS FOR LA JUNTA,
COLORADO, BY WILSON AND COMPANY. DENVER,
COLORADO STATE PLANNING OFFICE, 1969.
18L. (HUD 701 REPORT)

1. SUBDIVISION REGULATION - LA JUNTA,
COLO. I. WILSON AND COMPANY. II. HUD.
701. LA JUNTA, COLO.

Subdivision regulation - La Marque, Tex.

711.4
(764)
L15z

La Marque, Texas. City Planning Commission.
Master plan for La Marque, Texas: zoning,
land subdivision control. Prepared through
the cooperation of the Texas State Dept. of
Health. Houston, Tex., 1959.
25p. (Interim report, phases 3 and 4)
Planning consultants: Caldwell and Caldwell
and Chas. R. Haile Associates.
U.S. Urban Renewal Adm. UPAP.

1. Master plan - La Marque, Tex. 2. Zoning - La
Marque, Tex. 3. Subdivision regulation - La Marque,
Tex. I. Caldwell and   Caldwell. II. U.S.
URA-UPAP. La Marque,   Tex.

Subdivision regulation - La Marque, Tex.

333.38
(764)
L15

La Marque, Tex. City Planning Commission.
Subdivision rules and regulations, City
of La Marque, Texas. Houston, Tex., 1959
20p.
Planning consultants: Caldwell and Caldwell
and Chas. R. Haile Associates.
U.S. Urban Renewal Adm. UPAP.

1. Subdivision regulation - La Marque, Tex.
I. Caldwell and Caldwell. II. U.S. URA-UPAP.
La Marque, Tex.

711.4
(76156)
L15£

Subdivision regulation - Lanett, Ala.
Lanett, Ala. City Planning Commission.
Lanett, Alabama: land subdivision regula-
tions and manual. [In cooperation with Alabama
State Planning and Industrial Development Board]
Lanett, 1956.
12p.

U.S. Urban Renewal Administration, Program
of Urban Planning Assistance.

1. Master plan - Lanett, Ala. 2. Subdivision
regulation - Lanett, Ala. I. Alabama State
Planning and Industrial Development Board.
II. U.S. Urban   Renewal Administration.

338.38
(74978)
M12

Subdivision regulation - Lapatcong, N.J.
McCrosky, Theodore T
Lopatcong Township, Warren County,
New Jersey: proposed subdivision ordinance.
Prepared for the Planning Board. Prelimi-
nary draft. New York, 1958.
46p.

U.S. Urban Renewal Adm. UPAP.

1. Subdivision regulation - Lapatcong, N.J.
I. Lopatcong, N.J. Planning Board. II. U.S.
URA-UPAP.   Lopatcong, N.J.

Subdivision regulation - Lawnside, N. J.

333.38
(74987)
L18

Lawnside, N. J. Ordinances, etc.
Borough of Lawnside land subdivision or-
dinance. Lawnside, 1957.
20p.
U.S. Urban Renewal Administration,
Urban Planning Assistance Program.

1. Subdivision regulation - Lawnside,
N. J. I. U.S. Urban Renewal Administration. Urban Planning Assistance Program.

333.38
(76192)
T74

Subdivision regulation - Lawrence, Co., Ala.
Tri-County (Ala.) Regional Planning
Commission.
Tri-County Region, Alabama: subdivision
regulations and manual. [Prepared in
cooperation with] Alabama State Planning
and Industrial Development Board. [n.p.]
1961.
40p.
U.S. Urban Renewal Adm. UPAP.

1. Subdivision regulation - Lawrence Co., Ala.
2. Subdivision regulation - Limestone Co., Ala.
3. Subdivision regula- tion -
Morgan Co., Ala.   I. U.S. URA-UPAP.
Alabama.

333.38
(76946)
L18

Subdivision regulation - Lawrenceburg, Ky.
Lawrenceburg, Ky. Ordinances, etc.
Proposed subdivision regulations of Lawrenceburg, Kentucky. Lawrenceburg, 1957.
17p. forms

U.S. Urban Renewal Administration, Urban
Planning Assistance Program.

1. Subdivision regulation - Lawrenceburg,
Ky. I. U.S. Urban Renewal Administration,
Urban Planning Assistance Program.

Subdivision regulation - Lawrenceburg, Tenn.

333.38
(76842)
L18

Lawrenceburg, Tenn. Regional Planning
Commission.
Proposed subdivision regulations,
Lawrenceburg, 1958.
[18]p. diagrs.

U.S. Urban Renewal Administration,
Urban Planning Assistance Program.

1. Subdivision regulation - Lawrenceburg, Tenn. I. U.S. Urban Renewal Administration. Urban Planning Assistance Program.

333.38
(77376)
K45

Subdivision regulation - Lawrenceville, Ill.
Kincaid (Evert) and Associates.
Subdivision regulations, Lawrenceville,
Illinois. Chicago, 1957.
28p.

U. S. Urban Renewal Administration, Urban
Planning Assistance Program.

1. Subdivision regulation - Lawrenceville,
Ill. I. Lawrenceville, Ill. Ordinances,
etc. II. U. S.   URA-UPAP. Lawrenceville,
Ill.

333.38
(76951)
L21

Subdivision regulation - Lebanon, Ky.
Lebanon, Ky. City Planning and Zoning
Commission.
Subdivision regulations, City of Lebanon,
Kentucky. With assistance of the Kentucky
Dept. of Economic Development. Lebanon,
1958.
19p.
U.S. Urban Renewal Administration, Urban
Planning Assistance Program.
1. Subdivision regulation - Lebanon, Ky.
I. U.S. Urban Renewal Administration. Urban
Planning Assistance Program. Lebanon, Ky.

333.38
(74819)
R62p

Subdivision regulation - Lebanon Co., Pa.
Rodgers (Clifton E.) and Associates.
A plan for county subdivision regulations,
Lebanon County, Pennsylvania. Prepared for
the Regional Planning Commission of Lebanon
County. Harrisburg, Pa., 1957.
1v. diagrs.

U.S. Urban Renewal Administration, Urban
Planning Assistance Program.

(Continued on next card)

333.38
(74819)
R62p

Rodgers (Clifton E.) and Associates.
A plan for county subdivision ...(Card 2)

1. Subdivision regulation - Lebanon Co.,
Pa. I. Lebanon Co., Pa. Regional Plan-
ning Commission. II. U.S. Urban Renewal
Administration. Urban Planning Assistance
Program.

333.38
(74819)
R62

Subdivision regulation - Lebanon Co. Pa.
Rodgers (Clifton E.) and Associates.
Prototype land subdivision regulations.
Presented for review by the planning commissions of the member municipalities and the
Committee on Land Subdivision Regulations of
the Regional Planning Commission. Harrisburg, 1957.
1v.

U.S. Urban Renewal Administration, Urban
Planning Assistance Program.

(Continued on next
card)

333.38
(74819)
R62

Rodgers (Clifton E.) and Associates. Prototype land subdivision ...(Card 2)

1. Subdivision regulation - Lebanon Co.
Pa. I. Lebanon Co., Pa. Regional Plan-
ning Commission. II. U.S. Urban Renewal
Administration. Urban Planning Assistance
Program.

Subdivision regulation - Leeds, Ala.

333.38
(76178)
L22

Leeds, Ala. City Planning Commission.
Leeds, Alabama: subdivision regulations.
[Prepared in cooperation with the]
Alabama State Planning and Industrial
Development Board. [Leeds] 1961.
36p.

U.S. Urban Renewal Adm. UPAP.

1. Subdivision regulation - Leeds, Ala.
I. U.S. URA-   UPAP. Leeds, Ala.

333.38
(76192)
T74

Subdivision regulation - Limestone Co., Ala.
Tri-County (Ala.) Regional Planning
Commission.
Tri-County Region, Alabama: subdivision
regulations and manual. [Prepared in
cooperation with] Alabama State Planning
and Industrial Development Board. [n.p.]
1961.
40p.
U.S. Urban Renewal Adm. UPAP.

1. Subdivision regulation - Lawrence Co., Ala.
2. Subdivision regulation - Limestone Co., Ala.
3. Subdivision regula- tion -
Morgan Co., Ala.   I. U.S. URA-UPAP.
Alabama.

Subdivision regulation - Lincoln Park, N.J.

333.38
(74974)
C65

Community Planning Associates.
Review of land subdivision ordinance.
Memorandum to Borough of Lincoln Park
Planning Board. [West Trenton, N.J.]
1959.
[2]p.

U.S. Urban Renewal Adm. UPAP.

1. Subdivision regulation - Lincoln Park, N.J.
I. Lincoln Park, N.J.   Planning Board.
II. U.S. URA-UPAP.   Lincoln Park, N.J.

333.38
(76158)
L45

Subdivision regulation - Lineville, Ala.
Lineville, Ala. Town Planning Commission.
Lineville, Alabama: subdivision regu-
lations. [Prepared in cooperation with]
Alabama State Planning and Industrial
Development Board. Lineville, 1963.
39p.

U.S. Urban Renewal Adm. UPAP.

1. Subdivision regulation - Lineville,
Ala. I. U.S. URA-UPAP. Lineville, Ala.

333.38
(74815)
L47

Subdivision regulation - Lititz, Pa.
Lititz, Pa. Ordinances, etc.
Revision of the subdivision ordinance,
the Borough of Lititz, Lancaster County.
Preliminary draft. Lititz, 1958.
14p.

U.S. Urban Renewal Adm. UPAP.

1. Subdivision regulation - Lititz, Pa.
I. U.S. URA-UPAP. Lititz, Pa.

333.38
(74761)
L57

Subdivision regulation - Little Falls, N.Y.
Little Falls, N.Y. City Planning Board.
Subdivision regulations, Little Falls, New
York. Little Falls, 1958.
15p.

Russell D. Bailey, Planning Consultant.

U.S. Urban Renewal Administration, Urban
Planning Assistance Program.

1. Subdivision regulation - Little Falls, N.Y.
I. Bailey, Russell D. II. U.S. URA-UPAP. Little
Falls, N.Y.

333.38
(78882)
L47

Subdivision regulation - Littleton, Colo.
Littleton, Colo. City Planning Commission.
A procedure for the administration of
subdivision regulations, Littleton, Colo-
rado. Littleton, 1958.
14p.
[Prepared by] Development Planning
Associates.
U.S. Urban Renewal Adm. UPAP.

1. Subdivision regulation - Littleton,
Colo. I. Development Planning Associates.
II. U.S. URA-UPAP. Littleton, Colo.

333.38
(76141)
L48

Subdivision regulation - Livingston, Ala.

Livingston, Ala. Town Planning Commission.
Livingston, Alabama: subdivision regulations. [Prepared in cooperation with] Alabama State Planning and Industrial Development Board. Livingston, 1963.
39p.

U.S. Urban Renewal Adm. UPAP.

1. Subdivision regulation - Livingston, Ala.   I. U.S. URA-UPAP.   Livingston, Ala.

VF
333.38
(74978)
L66

Subdivision regulation - Lopatcong, N.J.

Lopatcong, N.J. Ordinances, etc.
Land subdivision ordinance, Township of Lopatcong, Warren County, N.J. Lopatcong, 1959.
folder.

U.S. Urban Renewal Adm. UPAP.

1. Subdivision regulation - Lopatcong, N.J.
I. U.S. URA-UPAP. Lopatcong, N.J.

333.38
(764)
C18

Subdivision regulation - McAllen, Tex.

Caudill, Rowlett and Scott.
Subdivision regulations for the City of McAllen. Prepared under contract for the Texas State Dept. of Health. [Houston, Tex., 1960?]
29p.

U.S. Urban Renewal Adm. UPAP.

1. Subdivision regulation - McAllen, Tex.
I. U.S. URA-UPAP. McAllen, Tex.

333.38
(77324)
G17

Subdivision regulation - Lombard, Ill.

Gardner (Carl L.) and Associates.
Proposed subdivision ordinance, Village of Lombard, Illinois. Chicago, 1959.
24p.

U.S. Urban Renewal Administration, Urban Planning Assistance Program.

1. Subdivision regulation - Lombard, Ill. I. U.S. URA-UPAP. Lombard, Ill. II. Lombard, Ill. Ordinances, etc.

333.38
(75528)
L68

Subdivision regulation - Loudoun Co., Va.

Loudoun County, Va. Ordinances, etc.
Subdivision ordinance of Loudoun County, Virginia. Effective April 1, 1957 with amendments effective March 8, 1960. Leesburg, Va. 1960.
19p.

1. Subdivision regulation - Loudoun Co., Va.

333.38
(74885)
M12
1957

Subdivision regulation - McCandless, Pa.

McCandless, Pa. Township Zoning and Planning Commission.
Draft of revised land subdivision regulations of McCandless Township, recommended by the McCandless Township Zoning and Planning Commission. McCandless, Pa., 1957.
26p.

U.S. Urban Renewal Administration, Urban Planning Assistance Program.

1. Subdivision regulation - McCandless, Pa. I. U.S. Urban Renewal Administration. Urban Planning Assistance Program.

352.1
(79491)
L65

Subdivision regulation - Lompoc, Calif.

Lompoc, Calif. Ordinances, etc.
Subdivision ordinance. Lompoc, Calif. [1962?]
35p.

U.S. Urban Renewal Adm. UPAP.

1. Subdivision regulation - Lompoc, Calif. I. U.S. URA-UPAP. Lompoc, Calif.

333.38
(75528)
L68
June
1962

Subdivision regulation - Loudoun Co., Va.

Loudoun County, Va. Ordinances, etc.
Subdivision ordinance of Loudoun County, Virginia. Effective April 1, 1957, with amendments effective July 11, 1959, March 8, 1960, May 16, 1961, and June 7, 1962. Leesburg, Va., 1960.
19p.

1. Subdivision regulation - Loudoun Co., Va.

VF
333.38
(74885)
M12
1954

Subdivision regulation - McCandless, Pa.

McCandless, Pa. Ordinances, etc.
McCandless Township planning ordinance. McCandless, Pa. 1954.
15p.
U.S. Urban Renewal Administration, Urban Planning Assistance Program.

1. Subdivision regulation - McCandless, Pa. I. U.S. Urban Renewal Administration. Urban Planning Assistance Program.

1878

SUBDIVISION REGULATION - LONG BEACH, MISS.

LONG BEACH, MISS. CITY PLANNING COMMISSION.
SUBDIVISION REGULATIONS, BY ROBERT S. BATEMAN AND ASSOCIATES. LONG BEACH, MISS., 1964.
21P. (HUD 701 REPORT)

1. SUBDIVISION REGULATION - LONG BEACH, MISS. I. BATEMAN (ROBERT S.) AND ASSOCIATES. II. HUD. 701. LONG BEACH, MISS.

333.38
(76321)
M17

Subdivision regulation - Lutcher, La.

Martin (Dan S.) and Associates.
Subdivision regulations, Lutcher, Louisiana. Prepared for the Lutcher Planning Commission. New Orleans, 1959.
17p.

U.S. Urban Renewal Administration. Urban Planning Assistance Program.

1. Subdivision regulation - Lutcher, La. I. Lutcher, La. Planning Commission. II. U.S. URA-UPAP. Lutcher, La.

333.38
(76785)
A74m

Subdivision regulation - McGehee, Ark.

Arkansas. University. City Planning Div.
Administrative procedures and a design guide for subdivision development, McGehee, Ark. [Fayetteville] 1962.
1v. (Doc. no. 3D-2)

U.S. Urban Renewal Adm. UPAP.

1. Subdivision regulation - McGehee, Ark. I. McGehee, Arkansas. Planning Commission. II. U.S. URA-UPAP. McGehee, Arkansas.

711.5
(76778
:347)
A74a

Subdivision regulation - Lonoke, Ark.

Arkansas. University. City Planning Div.
Administrative guide for the zoning ordinance and subdivision regulations, Lonoke, Arkansas. Prepared for Lonoke Planning Commission. Fayetteville, Ark., 1962.
[28]p. (Document 1D-1)

U.S. Urban Renewal Adm. UPAP.

(Cont'd on next card)

333.38
(76136)
L88

Subdivision regulation - Luverne, Ala.

Luverne, Ala. City Planning Commission.
Luverne, Alabama: land subdivision regulations and manual. [In cooperation with] Alabama State Planning and Industrial Development Board. Luverne, 1957.
23p. diagrs.

U.S. Urban Renewal Administration, Urban Planning Assistance Program.

1. Subdivision regulation - Luverne, Ala. I. U.S. URA-UPAP. Luverne, Ala.

1910

SUBDIVISION REGULATION - MACON, MO.

MACON, MO. PLANNING COMMISSION.
SUBDIVISION CONTROL REPORT AND SUGGESTED SPECIFICATIONS, A PART OF THE COMPREHENSIVE MASTER PLAN. PREPARED BY GENERAL PLANNING AND RESOURCE CONSULTANTS. MACON, 1964.
27P. (HUD 701 REPORT)

1. SUBDIVISION REGULATION - MACON, MO. I. GENERAL PLANNING AND RESOURCE CONSULTANTS. I. HUD. 701. MACON, MO.

711.5
(76778
:347)
A74a

Subdivision regulation - Lonoke, Ark.

Arkansas. University. City Planning Div.
Administrative guide...(Card 2)

1. Zoning legislation - Lonoke, Ark.
2. Subdivision regulation - Lonoke, Ark. I. Lonoke, Ark. City Planning Commission. II. U.S. URA-UPAP. Lonoke, Ark.

333.38
(76174)
L95

Subdivision regulation - Lynn, Ala.

Lynn, Ala. Town Planning Commission.
Lynn, Alabama: subdivision regulations. [Prepared in cooperation with] Alabama State Planning and Industrial Development Board. Lynn, 1963.
39p.

U.S. Urban Renewal Adm. UPAP.

1. Subdivision regulation - Lynn, Ala.
I. U.S. URA-UPAP. Lynn, Ala.

333.38
(76197)
M12

Subdivision regulation - Madison, Ala.

Madison, Ala. Town Planning Commission.
Madison, Alabama: subdivision regulations. [Prepared in cooperation with] Alabama State Planning and Industrial Development Board. Madison, 1961.
36p.

U.S. Urban Renewal Adm. UPAP.

1. Subdivision regulation - Madison, Ala. I. U.S. URA-UPAP. Madison, Ala.

333.38
(76778)
A74

Subdivision regulation - Lonoke, Ark.

Arkansas. University. City Planning Div.
Proposed subdivision regulations for the City of Lonoke, Arkansas. Prepared for Lonoke Planning Commission. Fayetteville, Ark., 1962.
11p.

U.S. Urban Renewal Adm. UPAP.

1. Subdivision regulation - Lonoke, Ark. I. Lonoke, Ark. City Planning Commission. II. U.S. URA-UPAP. Lonoke, Ark.

333.38
(766751)
O45

Subdivision regulation - McAlester, Okla.

Oklahoma. University. Institute of Community Development
An ordinance for the regulation of land subdivision, McAlester, Oklahoma (proposed) Prepared for the McAlester City Council and Planning Commission. [Norman, Okla.] 1958.
17p.

U.S. Urban Renewal Adm. UPAP.

1. Subdivision regulation - McAlester, Okla. I. McAlester, Okla. Planning Commission. II. U.S. URA-UPAP. McAlester, Okla.

1002

SUBDIVISION REGULATION - MADISON, GA.

MORGAN CO., GA. PLANNING COMMISSION.
LAND SUBDIVISION REGULATIONS, MADISON, GEORGIA. BY NORTHEAST GEORGIA AREA PLANNING COMMISSION. ATHENS, GA., 1970.
38L. (HUD 701 REPORT)

1. SUBDIVISION REGULATION - MADISON, GA. I. NORTHEAST GEORGIA AREA PLANNING COMMISSION. II. HUD. 701. MADISON, GA.

333.38
(77584)
M12
Subdivision regulation - Madison, Wis.
Madison, Wis. City Plan Commission.
Land subdivision, City of Madison, Wisconsin. Madison, 1960.
46p. illus., diagrs., maps.

1. Subdivision regulation - Madison, Wis.

333.38
(74815)
M15
Subdivision regulation - Manheim, Pa.
Knowles (Morris) Inc.
Land subdivision ordinance, Township of Manheim, Lancaster County, Pennsylvania. Pittsburgh, 1958.
1v.
U.S. Urban Renewal Administration, Urban Planning Assistance Program.

1. Subdivision regulation - Manheim, Pa.
I. U.S. Urban Renewal Administration. Urban Planning Assistance Program.

2536
SUBDIVISION REGULATION - MARION, N.Y.
MARION, N.Y. PLANNING BOARD.
LAND SUBDIVISION REGULATIONS. BY
HERBERT H. SMITH ASSOCIATES. MARION,
N.Y., 1967.
25P. (HUD 701 REPORT)

1. SUBDIVISION REGULATION - MARION, N.Y.
I. SMITH (HERBERT H.) ASSOCIATES.
II. HUD. 701. MARION, N.Y.

333.38
(77584:347)
M12
Subdivision regulation - Madison. Wis.
Madison, Wis. Ordinances, etc.
Subdivision regulations, Madison, Wis.
Madison, 1957.
28 p.

Ivan A. Nestingen, Mayor.

1. Subdivision regulation - Madison, Wis.

711.5
(79455
:347)
W45
Subdivision regulation - Manteca, Calif.
Williams, Sydney.
Zoning and subdivision ordinance recommendations. [Prepared for Manteca City Planning Commission] San Francisco, 1962.
6p.
U.S. Urban Renewal Adm. UPAP.

1. Zoning legislation - Manteca, Calif.
2. Subdivision regulation - Manteca, Calif.
I. Manteca, Calif. Planning Commission.
II. U.S. URA- UPAP. Manteca, Calif.

1615
SUBDIVISION REGULATION - MARLBOROUGH,
MASS.
MARLBOROUGH, MASS. PLANNING BOARD.
RULES AND REGULATIONS FOR THE
SUBDIVISION OF LAND. MARLBOROUGH, 1966.
16L. (HUD 701 REPORT)

1. SUBDIVISION REGULATION -
MARLBOROUGH, MASS. I. HUD. 701.
MARLBOROUGH, MASS.

333.38
(76742)
A74
Subdivision regulation - Malvern, Ark.
Arkansas. University. City Planning Division.
Subdivision regulations, design standards for Malvern, Arkansas. Fayetteville, Ark. 1958.
8p.
U.S. Urban Renewal Administration, Urban Planning Assistance Program.

1. Subdivision regulation - Malvern, Ark. I. U.S. URA-UPAP. Malvern, Ark.

333.38
(74981)
C65
Subdivision regulation - Mantua, N. J.
Community Planning Associates.
Mantua Township general plan. Subdivision ordinance review and zoning ordinance. [West Trenton, N. J. 1958?]
44p.

U.S. Urban Renewal Administration, Urban Planning Assistance Program.

1. Subdivision regulation - Mantua, N. J.
2. Zoning legislation - Mantua, N. J. I. Mantua, N. J. Ordinances, etc. II. U.S. URA-UPAP. Mantua, N. J.

333.38
(75284)
M17
Subdivision regulation - Maryland—Washington Regional District.
Maryland. Maryland-National Capital Park and Planning Commission.
Subdivision regulations for the Maryland-Washington Regional District within Montgomery County. Silver Spring, Md. [1968?]
43p.

1. Subdivision regulation - Maryland-Washington Regional District. 2. Subdivision regulation - Montgomery Co., Md.
I. Title.

VP
333.38
(7428)
M15
Subdivision regulation - Manchester, N.H.
Manchester, N.H. City Planning Board.
Subdivision regulations, city of Manchester, New Hampshire. Manchester, 1965.
[4]p.

1 Subdivision regulation - Manchester, N.H.

333.38
(74961)
P25
Mar.1958
Subdivision regulation - Maple Shade, N.J.
Pennsylvania. University. Fels Institute of Local and State Government. (Government Consulting Service)
Recommended amendments to the land subdivision ordinance of the Township of Maple Shade. Memorandum to Maple Shade Township Planning Board. Philadelphia, 1958.
9p.

U.S. Urban Renewal Adm. UPAP.

1. Subdivision regulation - Maple Shade, N.J. I. Maple Shade, N.J. Planning Board. II. U.S. URA-UPAP. Maple Shade, N.J.

333.38
(79435)
M17
Subdivision regulation - Marysville, Calif.
Marysville, Calif. Ordinances, etc.
Ordinance 704. Marysville, [1963?]
27p.

U.S. Urban Renewal Adm. UPAP.

1. Subdivision regulation - Marysville, Calif. I. U.S. URA-UPAP. Marysville, Calif.

333.38
(74948)
C65
Subdivision regulation - Manchester, N.J.
Community Planning Associates.
Recommended changes to the Manchester Township subdivision ordinance. Prepared for the Township Planning Board. [West Trenton, N.J.] 1958.
5p.
U.S. Urban Renewal Adm. UPAP.

1. Subdivision regulation - Manchester, N.J.
I. Manchester, N.J. Planning Board.
II. U.S. URA-UPAP. Manchester, N.J.

333.38
(74961)
P25
Apr.1958
Subdivision regulation - Maple Shade, N.J.
Pennsylvania. University. Fels Institute of Local and State Government. (Government Consulting Service)
Recommended amendments to the land subdivision ordinance of the Township of Maple Shade. Memorandum to Maple Shade Township Planning Board. Rev. Philadelphia, 1958.
10p.
U.S. Urban Renewal Adm. UPAP.
1. Subdivision regulation - Maple Shade, N.J.
I. Maple Shade, N.J. Planning Board. II. U.S. URA-UPAP. Maple Shade, N.J.

333.38
(768885)
M17
Subdivision regulation - Maryville, Tenn.
Maryville, Tenn. Municipal Planning Commission.
Subdivision standards for Maryville, Tennessee. Maryville, 1958.
26p. diagrs.

U.S. Urban Renewal Administration, Urban Planning Assistance Program.

1. Subdivision regulation - Maryville, Tenn. I. U.S. Urban Renewal Administration. Urban Planning Assistance Program.

5367
SUBDIVISION REGULATION - MANCHESTER,
N.Y.
MANCHESTER, N.Y. PLANNING BOARD.
PROPOSED SUBDIVISION REGULATIONS.
PREPARED BY CANDEUB, CABOT AND
ASSOCIATES. NIAGARA FALLS, N.Y., 1966.
30P. (HUD 701 REPORT)

1. SUBDIVISION REGULATION - MANCHESTER,
N.Y. I. CANDEUB, CABOT AND ASSOCIATES.
II. HUD. 701. MANCHESTER, N.Y.

157
SUBDIVISION REGULATION - MARIANNA, ARK.
MARIANNA, ARK. CITY PLANNING COMMISSION.
ZONING ORDINANCE AND SUBDIVISION
REGULATIONS, MARIANNA, ARKANSAS, PREPARED
BY ELLERS AND REAVES, INC.,
FANNING-OAKLEY. MEMPHIS, 1969.
2PTS. IN 1 V. (HUD 701 REPORT)

1. ZONING LEGISLATION - MARIANNA, ARK.
2. SUBDIVISION REGULATION - MARIANNA, ARK.
I. ELLERS, REAVES, FANNING AND OAKLEY,
INC. II. HUD. 701. MARIANNA, ARK.

LAW
8
Subdivision regulation - Mass.
Massachusetts. Dept. of Commerce.
Municipal planning and subdivision control legislation including 1962 amendments. Boston, Mass. Dept. of Commerce, Div. of Planning, 1962.
33p.

1. City planning legislation - Mass.
2. Subdivision regulation - Mass. I. Title.

333.38
(76312)
M17s
Subdivision regulation - Mandeville, La.
Martin (Dan S.) and Associates.
Subdivision regulations, Mandeville, Louisiana. [Prepared for Mandeville Planning Commission] [New Orleans] 1959.
17p.
U.S. Urban Renewal Adm. UPAP.

1. Subdivision regulation - Mandeville, La. I. Mandeville, La. Planning Commission. II. U.S. URA-UPAP. Mandeville, La.

333.38
(76189)
M17
Subdivision regulation - Marion, Ala.
Marion, Ala. City Planning Commission.
Marion, Alabama: subdivision regulations. [Prepared in cooperation with] Alabama State Planning and Industrial Development Board. Marion, 1961.
36p.
U.S. Urban Renewal Adm. UPAP.

1. Subdivision regulation - Marion, Ala.
I. U.S. URA- UPAP.
Marion, Ala.

333.38
(744)
M17
Subdivision regulation - Massachusetts.
Massachusetts. Dept. of Commerce. (Div. of Planning)
Suggested rules and regulations governing the subdivision of land. Boston, 1963.
19p.

1. Subdivision regulation - Massachusetts.
I. Title.

Subdivision regulation - Matteson, Ill.

711.5
(7731   Tec-Search. (Planning Div.)
:347)   Matteson planning program. Evanston,
T22   Ill., 1960-61.
     8 nos. in 1 v. (Technical report 60-
13-T5-T10)
     Contents:-Technical report T5: Zoning
workshop guide. Review of existing ordinance.
-no.T6: Proposed comprehensive amendment to
the Matteson Zoning Ordinances (3 pts.:
preliminary 2 pts.-no.T7: Proposed
comprehensive amendment to the Matteson

                (Continued on next card)

711.5
(7731   Tec-Search. (Planning Div.) Matteson
:347)   planning program. (Card 2)
T22

     subdivision regulations (2 pts.: preliminary,
final)-no.T8: Population and economic bases.-
no.T9: Community facilities.-no.T10: Public
improvements program.
     U.S. Urban Renewal Adm. UPAP.
1. Zoning legislation - Matteson, Ill. 2. Subdivision
regulation - Matteson, Ill. 3. Community facilities -
Matteson, Ill. I. Matteson, Ill. Plan Commission.
II. U.S. Urban Renewal   Adm. UPAP.

1091   SUBDIVISION REGULATION - MAYFIELD, KY.
     MAYFIELD, KY. PLANNING COMMISSION.
     SUBDIVISION REGULATIONS, MAYFIELD,
     KENTUCKY. MAYFIELD, KY., 1969.
     32L. (HUD 701 REPORT)

     1. SUBDIVISION REGULATION - MAYFIELD,
     KY. I. HUD. 701. MAYFIELD, KY.

333.38   Subdivision regulation - Meadville, Pa.
(74897) Knowles (Morris) inc.
K56   City of Meadville, Crawford County,
Pennsylvania: land subdivison regulations.
[Prepared for] Meadville City Planning [and
Zoning] Commission. Easton, Pa., 1958.
     1v.

     U.S. Urban Renewal Adm. UPAP.

1. Subdivision regulation - Meadville, Pa.
I. Meadville, Pa. City Planning and Zoning Com-
mission. II. U.S.   URA-UPAP.
Meadville, Pa.

333.38   Subdivision regulation - Medford, Or.
(79527) Medford, Or. Ordinances, etc.
M22   An ordinance adopting subdivision
regulations. Medford, Or., 1959.
     15p.
     "Ordinance no. 7235."

     U.S. Urban Renewal Administration, Urban
Planning Assistance Program.

1. Subdivision regulation - Medford, Or. I. U.S.
URA-UPAP. Medford, Or.

333.38   Subdivision regulation - Mendham, N.J.
(74974) Morrow Planning Associates.
M67   Proposed subdivision ordinance of the
Township of Mendham, New Jersey. Ridgewood, N.J., 1958.
     19p.

     U.S. Urban Renewal Adm. UPAP.

     1. Subdivision regulation - Mendham, N.J.
I. U.S. URA-UPAP. Mendham, N.J.

333.38   Subdivision regulation - Menomonee Falls,
(77593)   Wis.
S97   Syracuse, Lee.
     Mandatory dedication of open space in
residential development; report and survey;
land use and development department.
[Washington] [National Association of Home
Builders] [1968]
     [19]p.

     1. Subdivision regulation - Menomonee
Falls, Wis. 2. Schools - Menomonee Falls, Wis.
3. Land use - Menomonee Falls, Wis. 4. Open space
land. I. National Association of Home Builders. II.
Title.

333.38   Subdivision regulation - Mercer Co., Pa.
(74895) Mercer County, Pa. Planning Commission.
M27   Subdivision regulations, Mercer County,
Pa. [n.p. 1958]
     15p.

     U.S. Urban Renewal Administration, Urban
Planning Assistance Program.

1. Subdivision regulation - Mercer Co., Pa. I. U.S.
URA-UPAP. Mercer Co., Pa.

711.4   Subdivision regulation - Meriden, Conn.
(7467) Candeub and Fleissig.
M27   Regulatory controls and capital improve-
no.7   ments program. Submitted to the Meriden
City Planning Commission. Newark, N.J.,
1960.
     15, 10p. (Meriden, Conn. Master plan
report no. 7)

     1. Master plan - Meriden, Conn. 2. Zon-
ing - Meriden, Conn. 3. Subdivision regulation - Meriden, Conn. 4. Capital improvement
programs -   Meriden, Conn. I. Meriden, Conn.   City Planning Commission.

     Subdivision regulation - Metter, Ga.
333.38
(75877) Urban Consultant Associates.
U71   Metter, Georgia: subdivision
regulations. Prepared under contract with the Georgia Department
of Commerce. Metter, [1960?]
     15p.

     U.S. Urban Renewal Adm. UPAP.

     1. Subdivision regulation - Metter,
Ga. I. U.S. URA-UPAP. Metter, Ga.

333.38   SUBDIVISION REGULATION - MICHIGAN.
(774)   Michigan. Bureau of Local Government Serv-
M42   ices.
     A model guide for an ordinance regulating
subdivision of land under authority of the
State Subdivision control act of 1967, Act
288, Public acts of 1967, effective Jan. 1,
1968. Lansing, Local Property Services Div.,
Bureau of Local Government Services, Dept. of
Treasury, 1968.
     45p.
     1. Subdivision regulation - Michigan.
I. Title.

333.38   Subdivision regulation - Middlesex, N.J
(74941) New Jersey. Dept. of Conservation and
N28m   Economic Development. (Div. of Planning and Development)
     Land subdivision ordinance of the Borough
of Middlesex. Suggested changes and
additions. [Trenton] 1959.
     14p.

     U.S. Urban Renewal Adm. UPAP.
1. Subdivision regulation - Middlesex, N.J. I. U.S.
URA-UPAP. Middlesex,   N.J.

     Subdivision regulation - Middletown, N.J.
333.38
(74946) Community Planning Associates.
C65   Suggested amendments to the land subdivision ordinance of the Township of
Middletown, Monmouth County, New Jersey.
West Trenton, N.J., [1960?]
     4p.

     U.S. Urban Renewal Adm. UPAP.

     1. Subdivision regulation - Middletown,
N.J. I. U.S. URA-UPAP. Middletown, N.J.

     Subdivision regulation - Middletown, Pa.
333.38
(74814) Middletown, Pa. Planning and Zoning
M42   Commission.
     Proposed land subdivision regulations,
Borough of Middletown. Middletown, 1960.
     22p.

     Clifton E. Rodgers and Associates,
planning consultants.
     Prepared in cooperation with
Pennsylvania Dept. of Commerce,
Bureau of Community Development.
          (Cont'd. on next card)

333.38   Middletown, Pa. Planning and Zoning
(74814) Commission. Proposed land subdivision
M42   regulations ...   (Card 2)

     U.S. Urban Renewal Adm. UPAP.

     1. Subdivision regulation - Middletown,
Pa. I. Rodgers (Clifton E.) and Associates.
II. U.S. URA-UPAP. Middletown, Pa.

     Subdivision regulation - Midland, Pa.
333.38
(74892) Knowles (Morris) Inc.
K56   The Borough of Midland, Beaver County,
Pennsylvania: land subdivision ordinance and
land subdivision regulations. Prepared [for]
Bureau of Community Development, Pennsylvania
Dept. of Commerce and the Midland Borough
Planning and Zoning Commission. Easton, Pa.,
1960.
     1v. ([Midland, Pa.] report no. 4)
     U.S. Urban Renewal Adm. UPAP.
1. Subdivision regulation - Midland, Pa. I. Midland,
Pa. Planning and   Zoning Commission.
II. U.S. URA-UPAP.   Midland, Pa.

711.4   Subdivision regulation - Midland City, Ala.
(76133) Midland City, Ala. City Planning Commission.
M42   Midland City, Alabama: land subdivision
regulations and manual. [In cooperation with
Alabama State Planning and Industrial Development Board] Midland City, 1957.
     29p.

     U.S. Urban Renewal Administration, Urban

          (Continued on next card)

711.4   Midland City, Ala. City Planning Commission.
(76133) Midland City, Alabama: land ... (Card 2)
M42

     Planning Assistance Program.

     1. Master plan - Midland City, Ala. 2. Sub-
division regulation - Midland City, Ala.
I. Alabama. State Planning and Industrial Development Board. II. U.S. Urban Renewal
Administration.

     Subdivision regulation - Millersville, Pa.
333.38   Millersville, Pa. Ordinances, etc.
(74815)   Millersville Borough Ordinance no. 87, regu-
M47   lating the sub-division and platting of land,
and making applicable to the Borough all provisions and penalties of the Borough Code relating to or incident to land subdivision.
Millersville, Pa., 1958.
     1v.

     U.S. Urban Renewal Administration, Urban
Planning Assistance Program.

     1. Subdivision regulation - Millersville,
Pa. I. U.S.   Urban Renewal Administration. Urban   Planning Assistance

---

211   SUBDIVISION REGULATION - MILLPORT, ALA.
     MILLPORT, ALA. TOWN PLANNING COMMISSION.
     SUBDIVISION REGULATIONS, BY ALABAMA
     STATE PLANNING AND INDUSTRIAL DEVELOPMENT
     BOARD. MILLPORT, ALA., 1969.
     35P. (HUD 701 REPORT)

     1. SUBDIVISION REGULATION - MILLPORT,
ALA. I. ALABAMA. STATE PLANNING &
INDUSTRIAL DEVELOPMENT BOARD. II. HUD.
701. MILLPORT, ALA.

333.38   Subdivision regulation - Milltown, N.J.
(74941) Community Planning Associates.
C65   A review of the Milltown subdivision
ordinance. Prepared for the Milltown
Borough Planning Board. West Trenton,
N.J., 1959.
     3p.

     U.S. Urban Renewal Adm. UPAP.

     1. Subdivision regulation - Milltown, N.J.
I. Milltown, N.J. Planning Board. II. U.S.
URA-UPAP. Milltown, N.J.

333.38
(76396)
M17
Martin (Dan S.) and Associates.
   Subdivision regulations, Minden planning
region, Louisiana. Prepared for the Minden
Regional Planning Commission. [New Orleans]
1959.
   17p.

   U.S. Urban Renewal Adm. UPAP.

   1. Subdivision regulation - Minden, La.
I. Minden, La. Regional Planning Commission. II. U.S. URA-UPAP. Minden, La.

Subdivision regulation - Minneapolis-St. Paul.

333.38
(77657)
M45
Minneapolis-St. Paul Metropolitan Planning
Commission.
   Guide to subdivision control. St. Paul,
1960.
   17p. (Its Local planning bulletin no. 2)

   1. Subdivision regulation - Minneapolis-
St. Paul.

333.38
(74881)
C65
Subdivision regulation - Monessen, Pa.
Community Planning Services.
   Subdivision regulations of the City
of Monessen. Monroeville, Pa., 1957.
   1v.

   U.S. Urban Renewal Administration,
Urban Planning Assistance Program.

   1. Subdivision regulation - Monessen, Pa.
I. U.S. URA-UPAP. Monessen, Pa.

Subdivision regulation - Monroe, Ga.

333.38
(75821)
M65
Monroe, Ga. Planning Commission.
   Draft of proposed subdivision regulations
for Monroe, Georgia, by Sydney Carter. Rev.
Prepared under contract with Georgia Dept.
of Commerce. Augusta, Ga., 1960.
   19p.

   U.S. Urban Renewal Adm. UPAP.

   1. Subdivision regulation - Monroe, Ga.
I. U.S. URA-UPAP. Monroe, Ga.

Subdivision regulation - Monroe, La.

333.38
(763871)
M65
Monroe, La. Ordinances, etc.
   Outline and index of subdivision regulations for the City of Monroe and that part
of Ouachita Parish in the parish planning
area. Monroe, La., 1960.
   1v.

   U.S. Urban Renewal Adm. UPAP.

   1. Subdivision regulation - Monroe, La.
I. U.S. URA-UPAP. Monroe, La.

Subdivision regulation - Monterey, Calif.

333.38
(79476)
M65
1961
Monterey, Calif. Ordinances, etc.
   Monterey, California: proposed subdivision
ordinance. San Francisco, Sydney Williams,
1961.
   31p.

   U.S. Urban Renewal Adm. UPAP.

   1. Subdivision regulation - Monterey,
Calif. I. Williams, Sydney. II. U.S.
URA-UPAP. Monterey, Calif.

333.38
(79476)
M65
1962
Subdivision regulation - Monterey, Calif.
Monterey, Calif. Ordinances, etc.
   Proposed subdivision ordinance,
Monterey, Calif. Revised draft.
Monterey, 1962.
   31p.

   U.S. Urban Renewal Adm. UPAP.

   1. Subdivision regulation -
Monterey, Calif. I. U.S. URA-UPAP.
Monterey, Calif.

Subdivision regulation - Montgomery Co., Md.

333.38
(75284)
M17
Maryland. Maryland-National Capital Park
and Planning Commission.
   Subdivision regulations for the Maryland-
Washington Regional District within Montgomery County. Silver Spring, Md. [1968?]
   43p.

   1. Subdivision regulation - Maryland-
Washington Regional District. 2. Subdivi-
sion regulation - Montgomery Co., Md.
I. Title.

Subdivision regulation - Monticello, Ark.

333.38
(767825)
A74
Arkansas. University. City Planning
Div.
   Administrative procedures and design
guide for subdivision development,
Monticello, Ark. Prepared for Monticello
Planning Commission. [Fayetteville, Ark.]
1962.
   1v.

   U.S. Urban Renewal Adm. UPAP.

   1. Subdivision regulation - Monticello,
Ark. I. Monticello, Ark.
Planning Commission.
II. U.S. URA-UPAP. Monticello,
Ark.

333.38
(74735)
M65
Subdivision regulation - Monticello, N.Y.
Monticello, N.Y. Planning Board.
   Requirements for the approval of subdivi-
sion plans in the Village of Monticello.
Draft land subdivision rules and
regulations recommended by Russell VanNest
Black. Monticello, N.Y., [1959?]
   14p.

   U.S. Urban Renewal Administration, Urban
Planning Assistance Program.

   1. Subdivision regulation - Monticello, N.Y. I. Black,
Russell VanNest. II. U.S. URA-UPAP.
Monticello, N.Y.

Subdivision regulation - Morgan Co., Ala.

333.38
(76192)
T74
Tri-County (Ala.) Regional Planning
Commission.
   Tri-County Region, Alabama: subdivision
regulations and manual. [Prepared in
cooperation with] Alabama State Planning
and Industrial Development Board. [n.p.]
1961.
   40p.

   U.S. Urban Renewal Adm. UPAP.

   1. Subdivision regulation - Lawrence Co., Ala.
2. Subdivision regulation - Limestone Co., Ala.
3. Subdivision regula-   tion -
Morgan Co., Ala.   I. U.S. URA-UPAP.
Alabama.

Subdivision regulation - Morristown, Tenn.

333.38
(76892)
M67
Morristown, Tenn. Regional Planning Commission.
   Subdivision standards for Morristown, Tennessee, and surrounding area. Assisted by Tennessee State Planning Commission. Morristown,
1956.
   18p. diagrs., maps.

   U.S. Urban Renewal Administration, Urban
Planning Assistance Program.

   1. Subdivision regulation - Morristown, Tenn.
I. Tennessee. State Planning Commission. II.
U.S. Urban Renewal Administration. Urban Plan-
ning Assistance   Program.

Subdivision regulation - Moulton, Ala.

711.4
(76192)
M68La
Moulton, Ala. Town Planning Commission.
   Moulton, Alabama: land subdivision regulations and manual. [In cooperation with Alabama State Planning and Industrial Development
Board] Moulton, 1955.
   29p. diagrs.

   U.S. Urban Renewal Administration, Urban
Planning Assistance Program.

   1. Master plan - Moulton, Ala. 2. Subdivi-
sion regulation - Moulton, Ala. I. Alabama.
State Planning and Industrial Development Board.
U.S. Urban Renewal Administration.

333.38
(758975)
868
SUBDIVISION REGULATION - MOULTRIE, GA.
Southwest Georgia Planning and Development
Commission.
   Recommended subdivision regulations; City of
Moultrie, Ga. Atlanta, State Planning Bureau,
1969.
   18p.
   Preparation of document financed in part
through comprehensive planning grant from
the Dept. of Housing and Urban Development.
HUD project no. Ga. P-149.
   1. Subdivision regulation - Moultrie, Ga.
I. Title. II.   U.S. Dept. of Housing
and Urban Development.

Subdivision regulation - Moundville, Ala.

333.38
(76143)
M68
Moundville, Ala. Town Planning Commission.
   Moundville, Alabama: land subdivision regulations and manual. [In cooperation with]
Alabama State Planning and Industrial Development Board. Moundville, 1959.
   23p. diagrs.

   U.S. Urban Renewal Administration, Urban Planning Assistance Program.

   1. Subdivision regulation - Moundville, Ala.
I. U.S. URA-UPAP. Moundville, Ala.

2559
SUBDIVISION REGULATION - MOUNT HOPE,
N.Y.
MOUNT HOPE, N.Y. PLANNING BOARD.
   SUBDIVISION REGULATIONS. BY RAYMOND
AND MAY ASSOCIATES. MIDDLETOWN, N.Y.,
1967.
   31L. (HUD 701 REPORT)

   1. SUBDIVISION REGULATION - MOUNT HOPE,
N.Y. I. RAYMOND AND MAY ASSOCIATES.
II. HUD. 701. MOUNT HOPE, N.Y.

Subdivision regulation - Mt. Laurel, N.J.

711.14
(74961)
M681
Mt. Laurel, N.J. Planning Board.
   Land development recommendations.
Part I. Subdivision ordinance recommendations. Part II. Zoning ordinance recommendations. [Mt. Laurel, N.J.] 1958.
   32p.

   U.S. Urban Renewal Adm. UPAP.

   1. Land use - Mt. Laurel, N.J. 2. Subdivision
regulation - Mt. Laurel, N.J. 3. Zoning legislation -
Mt. Laurel, N.J. I.   U.S. URA-UPAP.
Mt. Laurel, N.J.

Subdivision regulation - Mount Shasta, Calif.

VF
333.38
(79421)
M68
Mount Shasta, Calif. Ordinances, etc.
   Subdivision ordinance, an ordinance
providing for the subdividing of land
within the City of Mt. Shasta. Mount
Shasta, Calif., 1959.
   11p.

   Ordinance no. 178.
   U.S. Urban Renewal Adm. UPAP.

   1. Subdivision regulation - Mount Shasta, Calif.
I. U.S. URA-UPAP. Mount Shasta, Calif.

VF
333.38
(77234)
M68
SUBDIVISION REGULATION - MT. VERNON, IND.
Mount Vernon, Ind. City Plan Commission.
   Supplementary technical recommendations
for the proposed subdivision ordinance.
Mount Vernon, Ind., [1965?]
   10p.

   1. Subdivision regulation - Mt. Vernon, Ind.
I. Title.

Subdivision regulation - Mount Vernon, Wash.

333.38
(79772)
G71
Graham (John) and Company.
   Proposed subdivision ordinance, City
of Mount Vernon, Washington. [Prepared
for] Dept. of Commerce and Economic Development, State of Washington. Seattle,
1961.
   17p.

   U.S. Urban Renewal Adm. UPAP.

   1. Subdivision regulation - Mount Vernon, Wash.
I. Mount Vernon, Wash. Ordinances, etc. II. U.S.
URA-UPAP. Mount   Vernon, Wash.

Subdivision regulation - Mountain Home, Ark.

333.38
(76721)
A74
Arkansas. University. City Planning
Div.
   Subdivision regulations: Mountain
Home, Arkansas. Prepared for City
Planning Commission, Mountain Home,
Arkansas. Payetteville, 1961.
   [7]p.

   U.S. Urban Renewal Adm. UPAP.

   1. Subdivision regulation - Mountain Home, Ark.
I. Mountain Home, Ark. City Planning Commission.
II. U.S. URA-UPAP.   Mountain Home,
Ark.

163　SUBDIVISION REGULATION ● MULBERRY, ARK.
MULBERRY, ARK. PLANNING COMMISSION.
IMPLEMENTING MEASURES FOR MULBERRY
ARKANSAS. FORT SMITH, ARK., ARKHOMA
REGIONAL PLANNING COMMISSION, 1970.
3 PTS. IN 1 V. (HUD 701 REPORT)

CONTENTS.● PT.1. CAPITAL IMPROVEMENTS
PROGRAM.● PT.2. ZONING ORDINANCE.● PT.3.
SUBDIVISION REGULATIONS.

1. CAPITAL IMPROVEMENT PROGRAMS ●
MULBERRY, ARK.　2. ZONING LEGISLATION ●
MULBERRY, ARK.　3. SUBDIVISION
REGULATION ● MULB　ERRY, ARK.
(CONTINUED ON NEXT CARD)

163　MULBERRY, ARK. PLANNING COMMISSION.
IMPLEMENTING MEASURES ●●●1970. (CARD 2)

I. ARKHOMA REGIONAL PLANNING COMMISSION.
II. HUD. 701. MULBERRY, ARK.

5369　SUBDIVISION REGULATION ● MURRAY, N.Y.
MURRAY, N.Y. PLANNING BOARD.
SUBDIVISION REPORT. PREPARED BY
CANDEUB, FLEISSIG AND ASSOCIATES.
NIAGARA FALLS, N.Y., 1968.
31L. (HUD 701 REPORT)

1. SUBDIVISION REGULATION ● MURRAY, N.Y.
I. CANDEUB, FLEISSIG AND ASSOCIATES.
II. HUD. 701. MURRAY, N.Y.

Subdivision regulation - Nashville, Ga.

333.38
(75886)　Hill and Adley Associates.
H45　Proposed subdivision regulations for
the City of Nashville, Georgia. Atlanta,
[1960?]
14p.

Prepared under contract with the Georgia
Dept. of Commerce.
U.S. Urban Renewal Adm. UPAP.

1. Subdivision regulation - Nashville, Ga. I. U.S.
URA-UPAP. Nashville,　Ga.

Subdivision regulation - Nashville.

333.38
(76855)　Nashville. City Planning Commission.
N17　Evaluation of subdivision regulation in
Nashville and Davidson County. Staff memorandum. [In cooperation with] Davidson
County Planning Commission. [Nashville]
1961.
1v.
U.S. Urban Renewal Adm. UPAP.

1. Subdivision regulation - Nashville.
I. U.S. URA-　UPAP. Nashville.

3008　SUBDIVISION REGULATION ● NEBRASKA.
NEBRASKA. DEPT. OF ECONOMIC DEVELOPMENT.
STANDARD FORM OF RECOMMENDED
SUBDIVISION REGULATION PROVISIONS.
LINCOLN, NEB., 1969.
32P. (HUD 701 REPORT)

1. SUBDIVISION REGULATION ● NEBRASKA.
I. HUD. 701. NEBRASKA.

Subdivision regulation - Needham, Mass.

333.38
(7447)　Needham, Mass. Ordinances, etc.
N22　Needham subdivision regulations, by John T.
Blackwell. Boston, Mass., 1960.
23p.

U.S. Urban Renewal Adm. UPAP.

1. Subdivision regulation - Needham, Mass.
I. Blackwell, John T. II. U.S. URA-UPAP.
Needham, Mass.

Subdivision regulation - New Brockton, Ala

333.38
(76134)　New Brockton, Ala. Town Planning
N28　Commission.
New Brockton, Alabama: subdivision regu-
lations. [Prepared in cooperation with]
Alabama State Planning and Industrial
Development Board. New Brockton, 1961.
36p.
U.S. Urban Renewal Adm. UPAP.

1. Subdivision regulation - New Brockton, Ala. I. U.S. URA-UPAP. New Brockton, Ala.

SUBDIVISION REGULATION - NEW CASTLE,
DEL.
6393　NEW CASTLE, DEL. PLANNING COMMISSION.
OUTLINE OF SUGGESTED SUBDIVISION AND
LAND DEVELOPMENT REGULATIONS; SUPPLEMENT
2 TO PLANS INTO ACTION. NEW CASTLE, 1965.
19L. (HUD 701 REPORT)

1. SUBDIVISION REGULATION ● NEW CASTLE,
DEL. I. HUD. 701. NEW CASTLE, DEL.

Subdivision regulation - New Castle Co.,
Del.
333.38
(7511)　New Castle County, Del. Regional Plan-
N28　ning Commission.
Rules and regulations; guide for real
estate developments and land subdivisions
filing of plats. Wilmington, Del., 1942.
26p.

1. Subdivision regulation - New Castle
Co., Del.

Subdivision regulation - New Eagle, Pa.

333.38
(74882)　New Eagle, Pa. Planning Commission.
N28　Recommendations for land subdivision
regulations. New Eagle, 1962.
1 v.

Prepared in cooperation with Pennsylvania
Dept. of Commerce, Bureau of Community
Development.

Community Planning Services, inc.
Monroeville, Pa., consultants.
(Cont'd. on next card)

333.38
(74882)　New Eagle, Pa. Planning Commission.
N28　Recommendations for land subdivision
regulations ... (Card 2)
U.S. Urban Renewal Adm. UPAP.

1. Subdivision regulation - New Eagle, Pa.
I. Community Planning Services. II. U.S. URA-
UPAP. New Eagle, Pa.

Subdivision regulation - New Jersey.
333.38
(749)　New Jersey. Dept. of Conservation and
N28　Economic Development. (Division of
Planning and Development)
A guide for the preparation of
municipal land subdivision control
ordinances for use in accordance with
the powers conferred upon municipalities
having planning boards by Chapter 433 of
the laws of 1953 of the State of New
Jersey. Trenton, 1956.
11 p.

1. Subdivision regulation - New Jersey.

Subdivision regulation - New Johnsonville,
Tennessee.
333.38
(76837)　New Johnsonville, Tenn. Regional Plan-
N28　ning Commission.
Proposed subdivision regulations, New
Johnsonville, Tennessee. Assisted by the
Tennessee State Planning Commission, Middle
Tennessee Office. New Johnsonville, 1957.
18p. forms, map. (MTO publication
no. 57-24)

U.S. Urban Renewal Administration, Urban
(Continued on next card)

333.38
(76837)　New Johnsonville, Tenn. Regional Planning
N28　Commission. Proposed ... (Card 2)

Planning Assistance Program.

1. Subdivision regulation - New Johnsonville, Tenn. I. Tennessee. State Planning Commission. II. U.S. Urban Renewal
Administration. Urban Planning Assistance
Program.

Subdivision regulation - New Orleans.
333.38
(76335)　New Orleans. City Planning Commission.
N28　Regulations governing the subdivision
of land in New Orleans, Louisiana.
Officially adopted by the City Planning
Commission of New Orleans at a meeting
held on February 2, 1950, effective
May 6, 1950. 3rd ed. New Orleans, 1962.
28p.

1. Subdivision regulation - New Orleans.

Subdivision regulation - New York (City)

711.5
(7471)　Makielski, S　J
M14　The politics of zoning; the New York
experience. New York, Columbia University
Press, 1966.
241p. (Metropolitan politics series
no. 4)

Bibliography: p. [229]-233.

1. Zoning - New York (City) 2. Subdivision regulation - New York (City)
3. Land use -　New York (City)
I. Title.　(Series: Metropolitan
politics　series no. 4)

Subdivision regulation - New York (State)
333.38
(747)　New York (State) Dept. of Commerce.
N28　Control of land subdivision; a manual of
1963　subdivision regulations for municipal
officials, subdivision developers, builders
and planning boards. Rev. Albany, N.Y.,
New York State Dept. of Commerce, Bureau
of Planning, 1963.
48p.

1. Subdivision regulation - New York
(State) 2. Residential areas.

Subdivision regulation - New York (State)
333.38
(747)　New York (State) Office of Planning Coor-
N28　dination.
1967　Control of land subdivision, a manual of
subdivision regulations for municipal
officials, subdivision developers and planning
boards. Albany, 1967.
63p.

1. Subdivision regulation - New York
(State) 2. Residential areas. I. Title.

Subdivision regulation - New York (State)
333.38
(747)　New York (State) Office of Planning Coordina-
N28　tion.
1968　Control of land subdivision; a manual of
subdivision regulations for municipal officials, subdivision developers and planning
boards. Albany, 1968.
63p.

1. Subdivision regulation - New York (State)
I. Title.

Subdivision regulation - Newberg, Or.
333.38
(79539)　Oregon. University. Bureau of Municipal
O72　Research and Service.
Newberg proposed subdivision ordinance;
list of proposed revisions to preliminary
draft. Eugene, Or., 1959.
4p.

U.S. Urban Renewal Administration, Urban Planning
Assistance Program.

1. Subdivision regulation - Newberg, Or. I. U.S.
URA-UPAP. Newberg, Or.

Subdivision regulation - Newberg, Or.

333.38
(79539)
072p

Oregon. University. Bureau of Municipal
Research and Service.
Proposed subdivision ordinance for
Newburg, Oregon. Prepared for the Newberg
City Planning Commission. Eugene, Or.
1959.
16p.

"Preliminary draft."
U. S. Urban Renewal Administration,
Urban Planning Assistance Program.

I. Subdivision regulation - Newberg, Or.
I. Newberg, Or. City Planning Commission.
II. U. S. URA-UPAP. Newberg, Or.

Subdivision regulation - Newberg, Or.

333.38
(79539)
072pr

Oregon. University. Bureau of Municipal
Research and Service.
Proposed subdivision ordinance for Newberg,
Oregon. Prepared for the Newberg City Planning Commission. [Eugene, Or.] 1959.
18p.

U.S. Urban Renewal Adm. UPAP.

1. Subdivision regulation - Newberg, Or. I. Newberg,
Or. City Planning Commission. II. U.S. URA-UPAP.
Newberg, Or.

Subdivision regulation - Newbern, Tenn.

333.38
(76815)
N28

Newbern, Tenn. Municipal-Regional Planning Commission.
Subdivision regulations, Newbern, Tennessee. With the assistance of the Tennessee
State Planning Commission, West Tennessee
Office. Newbern, 1958.
35p. diagrs., map.

U.S. Urban Renewal Administration, Urban
Planning Assistance Program.

1. Subdivision regulation - Newbern, Tenn.
I. U.S. Urban Renewal Administration. Urban
Planning   Assistance Program.

1357   SUBDIVISION REGULATION - NEWELL, IOWA.
NEWELL, IOWA. PLANNING COMMISSION.
PROPOSED SUBDIVISION ORDINANCE. BY
ANDERSON ENGINEERING CO. NEWELL, IOWA,
CA. 1970.
14P. (HUD 701 REPORT)

1. SUBDIVISION REGULATION - NEWELL,
IOWA. I. ANDERSON ENGINEERING CO.
II. HUD. 701. NEWELL, IOWA.

Subdivision regulation - Newport, Or.

333.38
(79533)
072

Oregon. University. Bureau of Municipal
Research and Service.
Proposed subdivision ordinance for Newport, Oregon. Prepared for the Newport
City Planning Commission. Preliminary
draft. [Eugene, Or.] 1960.
18p.

U.S. Urban Renewal Adm. UPAP.

1. Subdivision regulation - Newport, Or. I. Newport,
Or. City Planning   Commission. II. U.S.
URA-UPAP. Newport, Or.

333.38
(768895)
N28

Subdivision regulation - Newport, Tenn.
Newport, Tenn. Regional Planning Commission.
Policies on land subdivision. [Assisted by Tennessee State Planning Commission, East Tennessee Office]
Newport, 1959.
28p. diagrs.

U.S. Urban Renewal Administration, Urban Planning Assistance Program.

1. Subdivision regulation - Newport, Tenn. I. U.S.
URA-UPAP. Newport, Tenn.

333.38
(76133)
N28

Subdivision regulation - Newton, Ala.
Newton, Ala. Town Planning Commission.
Newton, Alabama: land subdivision regulations and manual. [In cooperation with]
Alabama State Planning and Industrial Development Board. Newton, 1959.
23p. diagrs.

U.S. Urban Renewal Administration, Urban Planning Assistance Program.

1. Subdivision regulation - Newton, Ala. I. U.S.
URA-UPAP. Newton, Ala.

Subdivision regulation - Newton, N.J.

333.38
(74976)
N28pro

New Jersey. Dept. of Conservation and
Economic Development. (Div. of Planning
and Development)
Proposed land subdivision ordinance provisions for the Town of Newton, New Jersey.
Rough draft. [Trenton] 1960.
37p.
U.S. Urban Renewal Adm. UPAP.

1. Subdivision regulation - Newton, N.J. I. U.S.
URA-UPAP. Newton, N.J.

Subdivision regulation - Newton, N.J.

333.38
(74976)
N28pr

New Jersey. Dept. of Conservation and
Economic Development. (Div. of Planning
and Development)
Proposed subdivision in southeastern part
of town. Memorandum to Newton Planning
Board. [Trenton] 1958.
3p.
U.S. Urban Renewal Adm. UPAP.

1. Subdivision regulation - Newton, N.J. I. Newton,
N.J. Planning Board. II. U.S. URA-UPAP. Newton,
N.J.

333.38
(74976)
N28p

New Jersey. Dept. of Conservation and
Economic Development. (Div. of
Planning and Development)
Proposed subdivision of Noillim Inc.
Memorandum to Newton Planning Board.
[Trenton] 1958.
3p.
U.S. Urban Renewal Adm. UPAP.

1. Subdivision regulation - Newton, N.J.
I. Newton, N.J. Planning Board. II. U.S.
URA-UPAP. Newton, N.J.

Subdivision regulation - Newton, N.J.

333.38
(74976)
N28

New Jersey. Dept. of Conservation and
Economic Development. (Div. of Planning
and Development)
Sample for section 800 design standards,
proposed land subdivision ordinance for the
Town of Newton, New Jersey. Rough draft.
[Trenton] 1960.
13p.
Final draft to be prepared by Town Engineer
or other duly authorized engineer, and
included in the Land subdivision ordinance.
U.S. Urban   Renewal Adm. UPAP.
1. Subdivision regu   lation - Newton,
N.J. I. U.S. URA-   UPAP. Newton, N.J.

---

804   SUBDIVISION REGULATION - NOME, ALASKA.
NOME, ALASKA. CITY COUNCIL.
SUBDIVISION CONTROL REGULATIONS. BY
ALASKA CONSULTANTS. NOME, 1968.
19P. (HUD 701 REPORT)

1. SUBDIVISION REGULATION - NOME, ALASKA.
I. ALASKA CONSULTANTS. II. HUD. 701.
NOME, ALASKA.

---

436   SUBDIVISION REGULATIONS - NORCO, CALIF.
NORCO, CALIF. PLANNING COMMISSION.
PROPOSED SUBDIVISION ORDINANCE. BY
WILSEY AND HAM. NORCO, CALIF., 1969.
41P. (HUD 701 REPORT)

1. SUBDIVISION REGULATIONS - NORCO,
CALIF. I. WILSEY AND HAM. II. HUD.
701. NORCO, CALIF.

333.38
(76873)
N67

Subdivision regulation - Norris, Tenn.
Norris, Tenn. Municipal Planning Commission.
Proposed subdivision standards, Norris,
Tennessee. Prepared by East Tennessee
Office, Tennessee State Planning Commission. Norris, 1957.
19p.

U.S. Urban Renewal Administration, Urban
Planning Assistance Program.

(Continued on next card)

333.38
(76873)
N67

Norris, Tenn. Municipal Planning Commission. Proposed subdivision ... (Card 2)

1. Subdivision regulation - Norris, Tenn.
I. Tennessee. State Planning Commission.
II. U.S. Urban Renewal Administration.
Urban Planning Assistance Program.

333.38
(79523)
072

Subdivision regulation - North Bend, Or.
Oregon. University. Bureau of Municipal
Research and Service.
Subdivision regulations for North Bend,
Oregon. Prepared for the North Bend City
Planning Commission. Eugene, Or., 1959.
16p.

U.S. Urban Renewal Administration, Urban Planning Assistance Program.

1. Subdivision regulation - North Bend, Or. I.
North Bend, Or. City Planning Commission. II.
U.S. URA-UPAP. North   Bend, Or.

711
:308
(756)
N67

Subdivision regulation - North Carolina.
North Carolina. Dept. of Conservation and
Development. (Div. of Community planning)
Local development policies: a survey of
current practices in North Carolina.
[Raleigh, N.C.] 1967.
39p.

1. Community development - N.C.
2. Subdivision regulation - N.C.   I. Title.

333.38
(756)
S74

SUBDIVISION REGULATION - NORTH CAROLINA.
Stipe, Robert E
An introduction to subdivision regulations
in North Carolina. Chapel Hill, Institute of
Government, University of North Carolina, 1965.
20p.

1. Subdivision regulation - N.C. I. North
Carolina. University. Institute of
Government.

333.38
(77352)
S27

Subdivision regulation - North Chillicothe, Ill
Scruggs and Hammond.
Maps, plans and subdivision code of North
Chillicothe, Illinois and contiguous area.
Prepared for the Planning Commission of North
Chillicothe, Illinois and Illinois State Housing Board. Peoria, Ill., [1960]
20p.

U.S. Urban Renewal Administration,
Urban Planning Assistance Program.

1. Subdivision regulation - North Chillicothe, Ill.
I. North Chillicothe, Ill. Planning Commission.
II. U.S. URA-UPAP.   North Chillicothe,
Ill.

333.38
(7459)
N67

Subdivision regulation - North Kingstown, R.I.
North Kingstown, R.I. Planning Commission.
Subdivision regulations, Town of North
Kingstown, R.I. North Kingstown, [1958]
13p. diagrs.

U.S. Urban Renewal Administration, Urban
Planning Assistance Program.

1. Subdivision regulation - North Kingstown, R.I. I. U.S. Urban Renewal Administration. Urban Planning Assistance Program.
North Kingstown, R. I.

333.38
(7451)
N67S
1957

SUBDIVISION REGULATION - NORTH
SMITHFIELD, R.I.
NORTH SMITHFIELD, R.I. PLANNING BOARD.
SUBDIVISION REGULATIONS. NORTH
SMITHFIELD, R.I., 1957.
10L.

1. SUBDIVISION REGULATION - NORTH
SMITHFIELD, R.I.

Subdivision regulation - North Smithfield, R.I.

333.38 (7451) North Smithfield, R.I. Planning Board.
N67s   Subdivision regulations, North Smithfield,
R.I. North Smithfield, 1958.
7p.

U.S. Urban Renewal Adm. UPAP.

1. Subdivision regulation - North Smithfield,
R.I. I. U.S. URA-UPAP. North Smithfield, R.I.

Subdivision regulation- Oldmans, N.J.

333.38 (74991) New Jersey. Dept. of Conservation and Eco-
N28   nomic Development. (Div. of Planning and
Development)
Land subdivision ordinance of Oldmans Township. Suggested changes and additions. Trenton, 1958.
11p.

U.S. Urban Renewal Administration, Urban
Planning Assistance Program.

1. Subdivision regulation - Oldmans, N. J.
I. U.S. Urban Renewal Administration. Urban
Planning   Assistance Program.

Subdivision regulation - Orting, Wash.

333.38 (79778) [Orting, Wash. Ordinances, etc.]
078p   Proposed subdivision regulations for
the Town of Orting 1960. [Orting] 1960.
20p.

Prepared under general supervision of
Washington State Dept. of Commerce and
Economic Development.

1. Subdivision regulation - Orting, Wash.
I. U.S. URA-UPAP. Orting, Wash.

Subdivision regulation - North Smithfield,
R.I.

333.38 (7451) Rhode Island. Development Council.
R36   Subdivision ordinance, North Smithfield.
Providence, 1958.
5p.   (Its Community Assistance Program.
North Smithfield Worksheet no. 4)

U.S. Urban Renewal Adm. UPAP.

1. Subdivision regulation - North
Smithfield, R.I. I. U.S. URA-UPAP.
North Smithfield, R.I.

Subdivision regulation - Omak, Wash.

333.38 (79728) Bloch (Ivan) and Associates.
B56   Proposed subdivision ordinance for the
City of Omak, Washington. Portland, Or.,
1959.
20p.

U.S. Urban Renewal Adm. UPAP.

1. Subdivision regulation - Omak, Wash.
I. U.S. URA-UPAP. Omak, Wash.

Subdivision regulation - Orting, Wash.

333.38 (79778) Orting, Wash. Ordinances, etc.
078   Subdivision ordinance for the City
of Orting, Wash. [Orting, 1959?]
20p.

U.S. Urban Renewal Adm. UPAP.

1. Subdivision regulation - Orting, Wash.
I. U.S. URA-UPAP. Orting, Wash.

711.4 (74669)   Subdivision regulation - Norwalk, Conn.
N67   Norwalk, Conn. City Planning Commission.
Subdivisions land development in Norwalk,
1949-1957, master plan report. Norwalk,
1957.
20 p. maps.

1. Master plan - Norwalk, Conn.
2. Subdivision regulation - Norwalk, Conn.

333.38 (76172)   Subdivision regulation - Oneonta, Ala.
052   Oneonta, Ala. City Planning Commission.
Oneonta, Alabama: subdivision regulations. [Prepared in cooperation with]
Alabama State Planning and Industrial
Development Board. Oneonta, 1963.
39p.

U.S. Urban Renewal Adm. UPAP.

1. Subdivision regulation - Oneonta,
Ala. I. U.S. URA-UPAP. Oneonta, Ala.

1383   SUBDIVISION REGULATION - OSCEOLA, IOWA.
OSCEOLA, IOWA. PLANNING AND ZONING
COMMISSION.
SUBDIVISION REGULATIONS REPORT. BY
STANLEY CONSULTANTS. OSCEOLA, IOWA, CA.
1969.
32L. (HUD 701 REPORT)

1. SUBDIVISION REGULATION - OSCEOLA,
IOWA. I. STANLEY CONSULTANTS.
II. HUD. 701. OSCEOLA, IOWA.

5909   SUBDIVISION REGULATION - O'FALLON, MO.
5910   O'FALLON, MO. CITY PLANNING COMMISSION.
PROPOSED ZONING ORDINANCE; PROPOSED
SUBDIVISION ORDINANCE. BY HARE & HARE.
KANSAS CITY, MO., 1966.
2 V. (HUD 701 REPORT)

1. ZONING LEGISLATION - O'FALLON, MO.
2. SUBDIVISION REGULATION - O'FALLON, MO.
I. HARE AND HARE. II. HUD. 701.
O'FALLON.

Subdivision regulation - Ontario.

333.38 (713)   Ontario. Dept. of Planning and Development.
057   (Community Planning Branch)
Subdivision approval manual; a manual of
procedure relating to the approval of plans of
subdivision under the Planning act, 1955.
Toronto, 1958.
44p.

1. Subdivision regulation - Ontario.

Subdivision regulation - Ossining, N.Y.

333.38 (74727) Ossining, N.Y. Ordinances, etc.
077   Village of Ossining, N.Y.: proposed
subdivision regulations of 1958, by
Theodore T. McCrosky. New York, 1958.
23p.

U.S. Urban Renewal Adm. UPAP.

1. Subdivision regulation - Ossining, N.Y.
I. McCrosky, Theodore T. II. U.S. URA-UPAP.
Ossining, N.Y.

5911   SUBDIVISION REGULATION - O'FALLON, MO.
5912   O'FALLON, MO. CITY PLANNING COMMISSION.
ZONING ORDINANCE; SUBDIVISION
ORDINANCE. O'FALLON, MO., 1967.
2 V. (HUD 701 REPORT)

1. ZONING LEGISLATION - O'FALLON, MO.
2. SUBDIVISION REGULATION - O'FALLON, MO.
I. HUD. 701. O'FALLON, MO.

333.38 (795)   Subdivision regulation - Oregon.
072f   Oregon. University. Bureau of Municipal
Research and Service.
File notes on subdivision improvement requirements. Eugene, Or., 1959.
2p.

U.S. Urban Renewal Administration, Urban Planning
Assistance Program.

1. Subdivision regulation - Oregon. I. U.S. URA-
UPAP. Oregon.

Subdivision regulation - Oswego, Or.

333.38 (79541) Oregon. University. Bureau of Municipal
072p   Research and Service.
Proposed subdivision ordinance for
Oswego [Oregon]. [Eugene, Or.] 1957.
26p.

"Revised draft."
U.S. Urban Renewal Adm. UPAP.

1. Subdivision regulation - Oswego, Or.
I. U.S. URA-UPAP. Oswego, Or.

711.5 (792:347)   Subdivision regulation - Ogden City, Utah
032   Ogden City, Utah. City Planning Commission.
A guide for zoning and subdividing in
Ogden City, Utah. Ogden City, 1956.
[12] p. illus., maps.

1. Zoning legislation - Ogden City, Utah.
2. Subdivision regulation - Ogden City, Utah.

333.38 (795)   Subdivision regulation - Oregon.
072   Oregon. University. Bureau of Municipal
Research and Service.
Some suggested standards relating to the
dedication of land for public use as a
condition of subdivision approval. Eugene,
Or., 1959.
4p.

U.S. Urban Renewal Administration, Urban
Planning Assistance Program.

1. Subdivision regulation - Oregon. I. U.S. URA-UPAP.
Oregon.

4376   SUBDIVISION REGULATION - OWOSSO, MICH.
MID-COUNTY REGIONAL PLANNING COMMISSION,
OWOSSO, MICH.
A REPORT ON SUBDIVISION REGULATIONS; A
GUIDE FOR SUBDIVISION ORDINANCES. BY
VILICAN-LEMAN AND ASSOCIATES, INC.
SOUTHFIELD, MICH., 1967.
27, A-3L. (HUD 701 REPORT)

1. SUBDIVISION REGULATION - SHIAWASSEE
CO., MICH. 2. SUBDIVISION REGULATION -
OWOSSO, MICH. I. VILICAN-LEMAN AND
ASSOCIATES. II. HUD. 701. SHIAWASSEE,
MICH. III. HUD. 701. OWOSSO, MICH.

Subdivision regulation - Chatchee, Ala.

333.38 (76163) Chatchee, Ala. Town Planning Commission.
031   Chatchee, Alabama: subdivision regulations. [Prepared in cooperation with]
Alabama State Planning and Industrial
Development Board. Chatchee, 1961.
36p.

U.S. Urban Renewal Adm. UPAP.

1. Subdivision regulation - Chatchee,
Ala. I. U.S. URA-UPAP. Chatchee, Ala.

VF 711.4 (795:347) Oregon. University. Bureau of Municipal
072   Subdivision regulation - Oregon.
Research and Service.
A suggested ordinance for establishing a
city planning commission. [Eugene, Ore.]
June 1956.
18 L.

1. City planning legislation - Model
laws and ordinances. 2. City planning
legislation - Oregon. 3. Zoning legislation -
Oregon.   4. Subdivision regulation-
Oregon.

Subdivision regulation - Oxford, Ala.

333.38 (76163) Oxford, Ala. City Planning Commission.
093   Oxford, Alabama; subdivision regulations.
[Prepared in cooperation with] Alabama
State Planning and Industrial Development
Board. Oxford, 1961.
36p.

U.S. Urban Renewal Adm. UPAP.

1. Subdivision regulation - Oxford, Ala.
I. U.S. URA-UPAP. Oxford, Ala.

Subdivision regulation - Oxford, N.J.

333.38
(74978) New Jersey. Dept. of Conservation and
N23   Economic Development. (Div. of Planning
and Development)
    Suggested land subdivision ordinance for
the Township of Oxford, New Jersey. [Pre-
pared for the Oxford Planning Board]
Trenton, 1953.
    24p.

    U.S.   Urban Renewal Adm.   UPAP.

1. Subdivision regulation - Oxford, N.J.   I. Oxford,
N.J. Planning Board. II. U.S. URA-UPAP. Oxford,
N.J.

SUBDIVISION REGULATION - PENNSYLVANIA.

333.38
(748)   BLAIR REGIONAL PLANNING COMMISSION.
851   LAND SUBDIVISION REGULATIONS; BLAIR
REGION, PENNSYLVANIA. PREPARED BY
BLAIR REGIONAL PLANNING COMMISSION AND
CLIFTON E. RODGERS AND ASSOCIATES.
ALTOONA, PA., 1958.
    1 V. (VARIOUS PAGINGS)

    1. SUBDIVISION REGULATION -
PENNSYLVANIA. I. TITLE.

Subdivision regulation - Piedmont, Ala.

333.38
(76163) Piedmont, Ala. City Planning Commission.
P42   Piedmont, Alabama: subdivision regu-
lations. [Prepared in cooperation with]
Alabama State Planning and Industrial
Development Board. Piedmont, 1961.
    36p.

    U.S.   Urban Renewal Adm.   UPAP.

    1. Subdivision regulation -
Piedmont, Ala. I. U.S. URA-UPAP.
Piedmont,   Ala.

Subdivision regulation - Ozark, Ala.

333.38
(76133) Ozark, Ala. City Planning Commission.
O91   Ozark, Alabama: land subdivision regulations and manual. [In cooperation with]
Alabama State Planning and Industrial Development Board. Ozark, 1959.
    23p.   diagrs.

U.S.   Urban Renewal Administration, Urban Planning
Assistance Program.

1. Subdivision regulation - Ozark, Ala.   I. U.S.
URA-UPAP. Ozark, Ala.

Subdivision regulation - Penn, Pa.

333.38
(74891) Penn, Pa. Ordinances, etc.
P25   Land subdivision regulations of Penn
Township, Butler County, Pennsylvania.
[Monroeville, Pa., 1960?]
    19p.

    U.S.   Urban Renewal Adm.   UPAP.

    1. Subdivision regulation - Penn, Pa.
I. U.S. URA-UPAP. Penn, Pa.

Subdivision regulation - Piggott, Ark.

333.38
(767995) Arkansas. University. City Planning
A74   Div.
    Administrative guide, subdivision
regulations. Prepared for City Planning
Commission, Piggott, Ark. Fayetteville,
Ark., 1963.
    13p.

    U.S.   Urban Renewal Adm.   UPAP.

1. Subdivision regulation - Piggott, Ark.
I. Piggott, Ark. City Planning Commission.
II. U.S. URA-UPAP.   Piggott, Ark.

Subdivision regulation - Palm Springs, Calif.

711.5
(79497 Eisner (Simon) and Associates.
:347)   Critical analysis, zoning ordinance
E17   and subdivision ordinance, City of Palm
Springs. South Pasadena, 1959.
    29p.

    U.S.   Urban Renewal Adm.   UPAP.

    1. Zoning legislation - Palm Springs,
Calif. 2. Subdivision regulation -
Palm Springs, Calif. I. U.S. URA-UPAP.
Palm Springs, Calif.

Subdivision regulation - Pennsylvania.

711.3
(748)   Pennsylvania. University. Fels Institute
P25   of Local and State Government.
    Planning measures and controls in South-
eastern Pennsylvania. Part 1: Planning activity. Part 2: Subdivision control. Part 3:
Zoning. Prepared for Pennsylvania Dept. of
Commerce and Study Commission of the Philadelphia metropolitan area. Philadelphia, 1960.
    3 pts. map, tables.

U.S.   Urban Renewal Administration, Urban Planning
Assistance Program.

                (Continued on next
                    card)

SUBDIVISION REGULATION - PIKE CO., KY.

1404   PIKE CO., KY. PLANNING COMMISSION.
    SUBDIVISION REGULATIONS. BY MICHAEL
BAKER, JR., INC. ELKHORN, KY., 1969.
    49L. (HUD 701 REPORT)

    1. SUBDIVISION REGULATION - ELKHORN
CITY, KY. 2. SUBDIVISION REGULATION -
PIKE CO., KY. I. BAKER (MICHAEL, JR.)
INC. II. HUD. 701. ELKHORN CITY, KY.
III. HUD. 701. PIKE CO., KY.

Subdivision regulation - Paramount, Calif.

333.38
(79493) Whitnall, Gordon.
W34   Subdivision ordinance for the City
of Paramount, California, by Gordon
Whitnall and Brysis N. Whitnall. Los
Angeles, [1960?]
    21p.

    U.S.   Urban Renewal Adm.   UPAP.

    1. Subdivision regulation - Paramount,
Calif. I. Whitnall, Brysis N., jt. au.
II. U.S. URA-UPAP. Paramount, Calif.

711.3
(748)   Pennsylvania. University. Fels Institute
P25   of Local and State Government. Planning
measures and ... 1960. (Card 2)

    1. Regional planning - Pennsylvania. 2. Metropoli-
tan areas - Philadelphia. 3. Subdivision regulation - Pennsylvania. 4. Zoning - Pennsylvania.
I. U.S. URA-UPAP. Pennsylvania.

Subdivision regulation - Pikeville, Ky.

333.38
(76923) Pikeville, Ky. City Planning Commission.
P44   Subdivision regulations, City of Pikeville,
Kentucky. Pikeville, [1960?]
    19p.
    [In cooperation with] the Kentucky Dept.
of Economic Development.
    U.S.   Urban Renewal Adm.   UPAP.

    1. Subdivision regulation - Pikeville,
Ky. I. U.S. URA-UPAP. Pikeville, Ky.

SUBDIVISION REGULATION - PARKERS
PRAIRIE, MINN.

5391   PARKERS PRAIRIE, MINN. PLANNING
COMMISSION.
    PROPOSED SUBDIVISION CONTROLS ORDINANCE.
BY COMMUNITY PLANNING AND DESIGN
ASSOCIATES, INC. MINNEAPOLIS, 1968.
    12L. (HUD 701 REPORT)

    1. SUBDIVISION REGULATION - PARKERS
PRAIRIE, MINN. I. COMMUNITY PLANNING
AND DESIGN ASSOCIATES. II. HUD. 701.
PARKERS PRAIRIE, MINN.

Subdivision regulation - Pequannock, N.J.

333.38
(74974) Community Planning Associates.
C65r   A review of the land subdivision ordinance
of the Township of Pequannock, Morris County,
New Jersey. Prepared for the Pequannock Town-
ship Planning Board. [West Trenton, N.J.]
1960.
    6p.
    [Prepared in cooperation with] New Jersey
Expanded State and Regional Planning Program.
    U.S.   Urban Renewal Adm.   UPAP.
1. Subdivision regulation - Pequannock, N.J.
I. Pequannock, N.J.   Township Planning
Board. II. U.S. URA-   UPAP. Pequannock,
N.J.

Subdivision regulation - Pismo Beach, Calif.

333.38
(79478) Whipple, Murphy, Pearson and Associates.
W34   Report and recommendations on the
subdivision regulations of the City of
Pismo Beach. Pismo Beach, Calif., 1962.
    10p.

    U.S.   Urban Renewal Adm.   UPAP.

    1. Subdivision regulation - Pismo
Beach, Calif. I. U.S. URA-UPAP.
Pismo Beach, Calif.

Subdivision regulation - Parrish, Ala.

333.38
(76176) Parrish, Ala. Town Planning Commission.
P17   Parrish, Alabama: subdivision regu-
lations. [Prepared in cooperation with]
Alabama State Planning and Industrial
Development Board. Parrish, 1961.
    36p.
    U.S.   Urban Renewal Adm.   UPAP.

    1. Subdivision regulation - Parrish,
Ala. I. U.S. URA-UPAP. Parrish, Ala.

Subdivision regulations - Perryopolis, Pa.

333.38
(74884) Perryopolis, Pa. Ordinances, etc.
P27   Land subdivision regulations. Perryopolis, [1958]
    1v.

U.S.   Urban Renewal Administration, Urban Planning Assistance Program.

    1. Subdivision regulations - Perryopolis, Pa.
I. U.S. URA-UPAP. Perryopolis, Pa.

Subdivision regulation - Pittsburgh.

333.38
(74886) Pittsburgh. Dept. of City Planning.
P47   Subdivision regulations and standards
1963   for the City of Pittsburgh, Pa.
Pittsburgh, 1963.
    23p.

    1. Subdivision regulation - Pittsburgh.

Subdivision regulation - Pascagoula, Miss.

711.4
(76212) Bateman (Robert S.) and Associates.
P17s   Subdivision regulations (a part of the comprehensive city plan) for Pascagoula,
Mississippi. In cooperation with the City
of Pascagoula and the Pascagoula City Planning Commission. Prepared for the Mississippi Agricultural and Industrial Board.
Mobile, Ala., 1959.
    26p.
    U.S.   Urban Renewal Adm.   UPAP.
1. Master plan - Pascagoula, Miss. 2. Subdivision
regulation - Pascagoula,   Miss. I. Pascagoula,
Miss. City Planning   Commission. II. U.S.
URA-UPAP. Pascagoula,   Miss.

Subdivision regulation - Philadelphia.

333.38
(74811) Philadelphia. City Planning Commission.
P34   Philadelphia subdivision ordinance,
effective June 4, 1954. Philadelphia,
1954.
    26p. diagrs.

    1. Subdivision regulation - Philadelphia.

Subdivision regulation - Pittsburgh.

333.38
(74886) Pittsburgh. Dept. of City Planning.
P47   Subdivision regulations and standards
1964   for the City of Pittsburgh, Pa. Part II.
pt.2   Improvement subdivision regulations
(for large-scale unified developments)
Pittsburgh, 1964.
    20p.

    1. Subdivision regulation -
Pittsburgh.

711.4
(74832)
P47
no.8

Subdivision regulation - Pittston, Pa.
Candeub & Associates.
Master plan, Pittston, Pennsylvania.
Report no. 8. Subdivision ordinance.
Submitted to Pittston City Planning
Commission. Scranton, Pa., 1960.
23p.
U.S. Urban Renewal Adm. UPAP.

1. Master plan - Pittston, Pa.
2. Subdivision regulation - Pittston, Pa.
I. U.S. URA-UPAP. Pittston, Pa.

333.38
(764)
F68

Subdivision regulation - Post, Tex.
Fowler and Grafe, inc.
Post administrative regulations.
[Prepared in cooperation with the] Texas
State Dept. of Health and Post City
Planning Commission. Dallas, 1964.
41p.

U.S. Urban Renewal Adm. UPAP.

1. Subdivision regulation - Post, Tex.
2. Zoning - Post, Tex. I. Post, Tex.
City Planning Commission.
II. U.S. URA-UPAP.
Post, Tex.

333.38
(769815)
P74

Subdivision regulation - Princeton, Ky.
Princeton, Ky. City Planning and Zoning
Commission.
Subdivision regulations, city of Princeton,
Kentucky. With assistance of the Kentucky
Dept. of Economic Development. Princeton,
1958.
1v.

U.S. Urban Renewal Administration, Urban
Planning Assistance Program.
1. Subdivision regulation - Princeton, Ky.
I. U.S. Urban Renewal Administration. Urban
Planning Assistance Program.
Princeton, Ky.

VF
333.38
(79441)
E52

Subdivision regulation - Placerville, Calif.
El Dorado County, Calif. Planning
Dept.
Subdivision ordinance, City of
Placerville, State of California.
Draft for study only. [n.p.] 1963.
40p.

U.S. Urban Renewal Adm. UPAP.

1. Subdivision regulation - Placerville, Calif. I. U.S. URA-UPAP.
Placerville, Calif.

333.38
(74812)
P25

Subdivision regulation - Pottstown, Pa.
Pennsylvania. University. Fels Institute
of Local and State Government. (Govern-
ment Consulting Service)
Proposed land subdivision control ordinance,
Pottstown Borough, Montgomery County, Penn-
sylvania. Prepared for review by the Borough
Council and the Borough Planning Commission.
[Philadelphia] 1958.
20p.

U.S. Urban Renewal Adm. UPAP.
1. Subdivision regulation - Pottstown, Pa.
I. Pottstown, Pa. Planning Commission.
II. U.S. URA-UPAP. Pottstown, Pa.

1408

SUBDIVISION REGULATION - PRINCETON, KY.
PRINCETON, KY. PLANNING COMMISSION.
SUBDIVISION REGULATIONS. BY JAMES R.
AHART AND ASSOCIATES, INC. DAYTON, OHIO,
1970.
34P. (HUD 701 REPORT)

1. SUBDIVISION REGULATION - PRINCETON,
KY. I. AHART (JAMES R.) AND
ASSOCIATES. II. HUD. 701. PRINCETON,
KY.

333.38
(74754)
S17

Subdivision regulation - Plattsburgh, N.Y.
Sargent-Webster-Crenshaw & Folley.
Proposed subdivision regulations, town
of Plattsburgh, Clinton County, New York.
(A draft for discussion and review)
[Prepared for New York State Department
of Commerce] Syracuse, N.Y., 1965.
46p.
U.S. Urban Renewal Adm. UPAP.

1. Subdivision regulation - Plattsburgh,
N.Y. I. U.S. URA-UPAP. Plattsburgh,
N.Y.

333.38
(74733)
P68

Subdivision regulation - Poughkeepsie, N.Y.
Poughkeepsie, N. Y. Town Planning Board.
Land subdivision regulations. Poughkeepsie, N.Y., 1955.
23p.

Adopted June 13, 1940; revised Nov. 29,
1945, June 16, 1955. Effective July 25,
1955.

1. Subdivision regulation - Poughkeepsie, N. Y.

333.38
(74893)
H45

Subdivision regulation - Pulaski, Pa.
Hill (Carroll V.) and Associates.
Proposed land subdivision regulations,
Pulaski Township, Lawrence County, Pa.
Prepared for the Township Board of
Supervisors and the Township Planning
Commission. Dayton, Ohio [1960?]
25p.

U.S. Urban Renewal Adm. UPAP.

1. Subdivision regulation - Pulaski, Pa.
I. U.S. URA- UPAP. Pulaski, Pa.

711.4
(76178)
P52

Subdivision regulation - Pleasant Grove, Ala.
Pleasant Grove, Ala. City Planning Commission.
Pleasant Grove, Alabama: land subdivision
regulations and manual. [In cooperation with
Alabama State Planning and Industrial Development Board] Pleasant Grove, 1956.
29p.

U.S. Urban Renewal Administration, Urban
(Continued on next page)

333.38
(76752)
A74

Subdivision regulation - Prescott, Ark.
Arkansas. University. City Planning Div.
Subdivision regulations, Prescott,
Arkansas. Prepared for the Prescott
Planning Commission. Fayetteville, Ark.,
1961.
16p.

U.S. Urban Renewal Adm. UPAP.
1. Subdivision regulation - Prescott, Ark.
I. Prescott, Ark. Planning Commission.
II. U.S. URA-UPAP. Prescott, Ark.

711.333
(76773)
P85g
no. 4

Subdivision regulation - Pulaski Co., Ark.
Pulaski County, Ark. Metropolitan Area Planning Commission
A guide to standards for subdivision in the
metropolitan area. Little Rock, Ark., 1956.
59p. diagrs. Its Guide report no. 4)

U.S. Urban Renewal Administration, Urban
Planning Assistance Program.

1. County planning - Pulaski Co., Ark.
2. Subdivision regulation - Pulaski Co.,
Ark. I. U.S. Urban Renewal Administration.

711.4
(76178)
P52

Pleasant Grove, Ala. City Planning Commission.
Pleasant Grove, Alabama: land... (Card 2)

Planning Assistance Program.

1. Master plan - Pleasant Grove, Ala. 2. Subdivision regulation - Pleasant Grove, Ala.
I. Alabama. State Planning and Industrial Development Board. II. U.S. Urban Renewal
Administration.

333.38
(7411)
A72

Subdivision regulation - Presque Isle, Me.
Architects Collaborative.
Proposed subdivision control ordinance for
the City of Presque Isle, Maine. Cambridge,
Mass., 1957.
9p.
U.S. Urban Renewal Administration, Urban
Planning Assistance Program.

1. Subdivision regulation - Presque Isle, Me.
I. Presque Isle, Me. Ordinances, etc. II. U.S.
Urban Renewal Administration Urban Planning
Assistance Pro- gram.

711.333
(76773)
P85g
no. 5

Subdivision regulation - Pulaski Co., Ark.
Pulaski County, Ark. Metropolitan Area Plan-
ning Commission.
A guide to uniform codes and ordinances.
Little Rock, Ark., 1957.
190p. tables. (Its Guide report no. 5)
U.S. Urban Renewal Administration, Urban
Planning Assistance Program.

1. County planning - Pulaski Co., Ark. 2.
Housing codes - Pulaski Co., Ark. 3. Subdivi-
sion regulation - Pulaski Co., Ark. 5. Zoning
- Pulaski Co., Ark. I. Title. II. U.S. Urban
Renewal Administration.

333.38
(79465)
P12

Subdivision regulation - Pleasanton, Calif.
Pacific Planning and Research.
Pleasanton, California proposed subdivision
ordinance. First draft. Palo Alto, Calif.,
1958.
44p.

U.S. Urban Renewal Adm. UPAP.

1. Subdivision regulation - Pleasanton,
Calif. I. U.S. URA-UPAP. Pleasanton,
Calif.

333.38
(76122)
P74

Subdivision regulation - Prichard, Ala.
Prichard, Ala. City Planning Commission.
Prichard, Alabama: land subdivision regulations and manual. [In cooperation with]
Alabama State Planning and Industrial Development Board. Prichard, 1957.
23p.

U.S. Urban Renewal Administration, Urban
Planning Assistance Program.

1. Subdivision regulation - Prichard, Ala.
I. U.S. Urban Renewal Administration. Urban
Planning Assistance Program. Prichard, Ala.

333.38
(74645)
P87

Subdivision regulation - Putnam, Conn.
Putnam, Conn. Ordinances, etc.
Subdivision regulations for the Town and
City of Putnam, Connecticut. Zoning ordi-
nance, City of Putnam, Windham County,
Connecticut. Putnam, 1956.
79p.

U.S. Urban Renewal Administration, Urban Planning
Assistance Program.

1. Subdivision regulation - Putnam, Conn. 2. Zoning legislation - Putnam, Conn. I. U.S. URA-
UPAP. Putnam, Conn.

1392

SUBDIVISION REGULATION - PLYMOUTH, IOWA.
PLYMOUTH, IOWA. PLANNING COMMISSION.
PROPOSED SUBDIVISION REGULATIONS. BY
WALLACE, HOLLAND, KASTLER AND SCHMITZ.
PLYMOUTH, IOWA.
19P. (HUD 701 REPORT)

1. SUBDIVISION REGULATION - PLYMOUTH,
IOWA. I. WALLACE, KASTLER, HOLLAND, AND
SCHMITZ. II. HUD. 701. PLYMOUTH, IOWA.

711.5
(75251)
P74

SUBDIVISION REGULATION - PRINCE GEORGE'S CO.,
MD.
Prince George's County, Md. Planning Board.
A proposal for comprehensive design regula-
tions. Riverdale, Md., Prince George's
County Planning Board of the Maryland-
National Capital Park and Planning Commission,
1970.
80p.

1. Zoning - Prince George's Co., Md.
2. Subdivision regulation - Prince George's
Co., Md. I. Title.

333.38
(79778)
P89

Subdivision regulation - Puyallup, Wash.
[Puyallup, Wash. Ordinances, etc.]
Subdivision ordinance for the City of
Puyallup. [Puyallup, 1958?]
20p.

U.S. Urban Renewal Adm. UPAP.

1. Subdivision regulation - Puyallup,
Wash. I. U.S. URA-UPAP. Puyallup, Wash.

1012   SUBDIVISION REGULATION - QUITMAN, GA.
QUITMAN, GA. PLANNING COMMISSION.
SUBDIVISION REGULATIONS, QUITMAN,
GEORGIA. PREPARED BY COASTAL PLAIN AREA
PLANNING AND DEVELOPMENT COMMISSION.
ATLANTA, GA., STATE PLANNING BUREAU, 1969.
28L. (HUD 701 REPORT)

    1. SUBDIVISION REGULATION - QUITMAN, GA.
I. COASTAL PLAIN AREA PLANNING AND
DEVELOPMENT COMMISSION. II. HUD. 701.
QUITMAN, GA.

333.38
(76185)   Reform, Ala. Town Planning Commission.
R23   Reform, Alabama: subdivision regulations.
[In cooperation with] Alabama State Planning
and Industrial Development Board. Reform,
1960.
    36p.

    U.S. Urban Renewal Adm. UPAP.

    1. Subdivision regulation - Reform, Ala.
I. U.S. URA-UPAP. Reform, Ala.

Subdivision regulation - Reform, Ala.

VF
711.4
(77331)
R65   Rockford and Winnebago Co., Ill. City-County
1954   Planning Commission. The comprehensive
plan. 1954-   (card 2)

    1. Master plan - Rockford, Ill. 2. Housing
codes - Rockford, Ill. 3. Subdivision
regulation-Rockford, Ill.

1409   SUBDIVISION REGULATION - RADCLIFF, KY.
RADCLIFF, KY. PLANNING COMMISSION.
SUBDIVISION REGULATIONS, CITY OF
RADCLIFF, KENTUCKY. PREPARED BY SCRUGGS
AND HAMMOND, INC. LEXINGTON, KY., 1970.
27L. (HUD 701 REPORT)

    1. SUBDIVISION REGULATION - RADCLIFF,
KY. I. SCRUGGS AND HAMMOND, INC.
II. HUD. 701. RADCLIFF, KY.

3617   SUBDIVISION REGULATION - REIDSVILLE,
N.C.
REIDSVILLE, N.C. PLANNING BOARD.
SUBDIVISION REGULATIONS, BY STATE OF
NORTH CAROLINA, DEPARTMENT OF
CONSERVATION AND DEVELOPMENT.
REIDSVILLE, N.C., 1968.
13P. (HUD 701 REPORT)

    1. SUBDIVISION REGULATION - REIDSVILLE,
N.C. I. NORTH CAROLINA. DEPT. OF
CONSERVATION AND DEVELOPMENT. II. HUD.
701. REIDSVILLE, N.C.

333.38   Subdivision regulation - Rocky Hill, Conn.
(7462)   Rocky Hill, Conn. Planning and Zoning
R62   Commission.
    Town of Rocky Hill, Connecticut: subdivi-
sion regulations. Rocky Hill, [1960]
    17p.

    Planning consultants: S. Spielvogel &
Associates.
    U.S. Urban Renewal Adm. UPAP.

1. Subdivision regulation - Rocky Hill, Conn.
I. Spielvogel (S.) and Associates. II. U.S. URA-
UPAP. Rocky Hill, Conn.

    Subdivision regulation - Randolph, N.J.
333.38
(74974) Community Planning Associates.
C65rev   A review of the land subdivision ordinance
of Randolph Township, Morris County, New
Jersey. Prepared for the Township Planning
Board. West Trenton, N.J., 1960.
    5p.
    New Jersey Expanded State and Regional
Planning Program.
    U.S. Urban Renewal Adm. UPAP.

1. Subdivision regulation - Randolph, N.J.
I. Randolph, N.J.   Township Planning
Board. II. U.S. URA-   )   UPAP. Randolph,
N.J.

333.38   Subdivision regulation - Richmond, Calif.
(79463)   Richmond, Calif. City Council.
R42   Subdivision ordinance. Richmond, Calif.
1956
    55 p.

    1. Subdivision regulation - Richmond,
Calif.

333.38   Subdivision regulation - Rogers, Ark.
(76713) Arkansas. University. City Planning
A74a   Div.
    An administrative guide for the Rogers
Planning Commission. Fayetteville, Ark.,
1962.
    [20]p.   (Administrative guide
4D-3)

    1. Subdivision regulation - Rogers, Ark.
I. Rogers, Ark. City Planning Commission.
II. U.S. URA-   UPAP. Rogers, Ark.

    Subdivision regulation - Red Bay, Ala.
333.38
(76199)   Red Bay, Ala. Town Planning Commission.
R22   Red Bay, Alabama; subdivision regulations. [Prepared in cooperation with]
Alabama State Planning and Industrial
Development Board. Red Bay, 1963.
    39p.

    U.S. Urban Renewal Adm. UPAP.

    1. Subdivision regulation - Red Bay,
Ala. I. U.S. URA-UPAP. Red Bay, Ala.

333.38   Subdivision regulation - Ridgely, Tenn.
(76812) Ridgely, Tenn. Municipal-Regional Plan-
R42   ning Commission.
    Subdivision regulations, Ridgely, Ten-
nessee. With the assistance of the Tennessee State Planning Commission, West Tennessee Office. Ridgely, 1957.
    30p. diagrs., maps.
    U.S. Urban Renewal Administration, Urban
Planning Assistance Program.

    (Continued on next card)

333.38   Subdivision regulation - Rogers, Ark.
(76713) Arkansas. University. City Planning
A74   Division.
    Subdivision regulations, Rogers,
Arkansas. Prepared for the Rogers
Planning Commission. Fayetteville, Ark.,
1961.
    16p.

    U.S. Urban Renewal Adm. UPAP.

1. Subdivision regulation - Rogers, Ark.
I. Rogers, Ark.   Planning
Commission.   II. U.S. URA-UPAP.
Rogers, Ark.

    Subdivision regulation - Red Lion, Pa.
333.38
(74841)   Red Lion, Pa. Zoning and Planning
R22   Commission.
    Rules and regulations for the subdivision
of land, Borough of Red Lion Pennsylvania,
by Richard H. Young. First draft. Red
Lion, 1959.
    16p.
    U.S. Urban Renewal Adm. UPAP.

1. Subdivision regulation - Red Lion, Pa. I. Young,
Richard H. II. U.S. URA-UPAP. Red Lion, Pa.

333.38   Ridgely, Tenn. Municipal-Regional Planning
(76812)   Commission. Subdivision ... (Card 2)
R42

    1. Subdivision regulation - Ridgely, Tenn.
I. Tennessee. State Planning Commission.
II. U.S. Urban Renewal Administration.
Urban Planning Assistance Program.

    Subdivision regulation - Rogersville, Tenn.
333.38 Rogersville, Tenn. Regional Planning Com-
(76895)   mission.
R63   Subdivision regulations for the Rogersville,
Tennessee planning region as adopted by the
Rogersville Regional Planning Commission on
July 29, 1958. Rogersville, 1958.
    46p. diagrs., maps.

    U.S. Urban Renewal Administration, Urban
Planning Assistance Program.

    1. Subdivision regulation - Rogersville,
Tenn. I. U.S. Urban Renewal Administration.
Urban Planning   Assistance Program.

333.38   Subdivision regulation - Red Lion, Pa.
(74841)
Y67   York County, Pa. Planning Commission.
    Proposed subdivision regulations for
Red Lion Borough. York, Pa., 1963.
    1 v.
    First draft.
    U.S. Urban Renewal Adm. UPAP.

    1. Subdivision regulation - Red Lion,
Pa.

    Subdivision regulation - Ringwood, N. J.
333.38 New Jersey. Dept. of Conservation and
(74923)   Economic Development. (Div. of Planning
N28   and Development)
    Land subdivision ordinance of the Borough
of Ringwood. Suggested changes and additions. Trenton. 1958.
    11p.
    "Rough draft."
    U.S. Urban Renewal Administration,   n
Urban Planning Assistance Program.
    1. Subdivision regulation - Ringwood, N.J.
I. U.S. Urban Renewal Administration.
Urban Planning   Assistance Program.

2265   SUBDIVISION REGULATION - ROMEO, MICH.
ROMEO, MICH. VILLAGE PLANNING COMMISSION.
SUBDIVISION REGULATIONS FOR THE
PLATTING OF LAND IN THE VILLAGE OF ROMEO,
MICHIGAN. PREPARED BY DEVELOPMENT
PLANNING COMPANY, PONTIAC, MICHIGAN.
PONTIAC, MICH., 1966.
36L. (HUD 701 REPORT)

    1. SUBDIVISION REGULATION - ROMEO, MICH.
I. DEVELOPMENT PLANNING CO., PONTIAC,
MICH. II. HUD. 701. ROMEO, MICH.

3616   SUBDIVISION REGULATION - RED SPRINGS,
N.C.
RED SPRINGS, N.C. PLANNING BOARD.
SUBDIVISION REGULATIONS, BY STATE OF
NORTH CAROLINA, DEPARTMENT OF LOCAL
AFFAIRS. RED SPRINGS, N.C., 1970.
35P. (HUD 701 REPORT)

    1. SUBDIVISION REGULATION - RED
SPRINGS, N.C. I. NORTH CAROLINA. DEPT.
OF LOCAL AFFAIRS. II. HUD. 701. RED
SPRINGS, N.C.

VF
711.4
(77331)   Subdivision regulation-Rockford, Ill.
R65   Rockford and Winnebago Co., Ill. City-County
1954   Planning Commission.
    The comprehensive plan; reports no.

    Rockford, Ill., 1954-
       v.
    Contents.-no. 1A: Planning prospectus, 1954.

    no. 3E: A land subdivision guide.-

    no. 4B1 & 4B1a: ousing code, City of
Rockford.
         (see card 2)

    Subdivision regulation - Rosenberg, Tex.
711.4
(764)   Rosenberg, Tex. City Planning Commission.
R67z   City plan for Rosenberg, Texas; zoning,
land subdivision control. Rosenberg, 1959.
    22p. (Interim report phase 2)
    U.S. Urban Renewal Adm. UPAP.

    1. City planning - Rosenberg, Tex.
2. Zoning - Rosenberg, Tex. 3. Subdivision
regulation - Rosenberg, Tex. I. U.S. URA-
UPAP. Rosenberg,   Tex.

333.38 Subdivision regulation - Rosenberg, Tex.
(764)
R67　Rosenberg, Tex. City Planning Commission.
　　Proposed subdivision rules and regulations
　　City of Rosenberg, Texas. Houston, Tex., 1959.
　　21p.
　　　Planning consultants: Caldwell and Caldwell
　　and S. A. Russell.
　　　U.S. Urban Renewal Adm.

　　　1. Subdivision regulation - Rosenberg, Tex.
　　I. Caldwell and Caldwell. II. U.S. URA-UPAP.
　　Rosenberg, Tex.

333.38 Subdivision regulation - Roseville, Calif.
(79438)
R67　Roseville, Calif. Planning Commission.
　　Proposed subdivision ordinance, City of
　　Roseville. Rev. study draft no. 4. Rose-
　　ville, 1959.
　　17p.

　　　Master plan project, City of Roseville.

　　　U.S. Urban Renewal Administration, Urban
　　Planning Assistance Program.

　　1. Subdivision regulation - Roseville, Calif. I. U.S.
　　URA-UPAP. Roseville, Cal.

1021　SUBDIVISION REGULATION - ROSWELL, GA.
　　ROSWELL, GA. ZONING AND PLANNING BOARD.
　　RECOMMENDED SUBDIVISION ORDINANCE. BY
　　KIDD-WRIGHT ASSOCIATES, INC. ATLANTA,
　　1970.
　　25L. (HUD 701 REPORT)

　　　1. SUBDIVISION REGULATION - ROSWELL, GA.
　　I. KIDD-WRIGHT ASSOCIATES, INC.
　　II. HUD. 701. ROSWELL, GA.

VF
333.38 Subdivision regulation - Roxbury, N.J.
(74974)
R69　Roxbury, N.J. Ordinances, etc.
　　Suggested changes to the land subdivision
　　ordinance of the Township of Roxbury, New
　　Jersey. [Roxbury] 1959.
　　2p.

　　　U.S. Urban Renewal Adm. UPAP.

　　　1. Subdivision regulation - Roxbury, N.J.
　　I. U.S. URA-UPAP. Roxbury, N.J.

Subdivision regulation - Ruidoso, N.M.
333.38
(789)　Bartholomew (Harland) and Associates.
B17p　Proposed land subdivision regulations,
　　Village of Ruidoso, New Mexico. For Village
　　Planning and Zoning Commission. Rev. St.
　　Louis, 1959.
　　1v.
　　　U.S. Urban Renewal Adm. UPAP.

　　1. Subdivision regulation - Ruidoso, N.M. I. Ruidoso,
　　N.M. Planning and Zoning Commission. II. U.S. URA-
　　UPAP. Ruidoso, N.M.

333.38 Subdivision regulation - Russellville, Ky.
(76976)
R87　Russellville, Ky. City Planning and
　　Zoning Commission.
　　Subdivision regulations of Russellville,
　　Kentucky. With assistance of the Kentucky
　　Dept. of Economic Development. Russell-
　　ville, [1958?]
　　1v.

　　U.S. Urban Renewal Administration, Urban
　　Planning Assistance Program.

　　1. Subdivision regulation - Russellville, Ky. I. U.S.
　　URA-UPAP. Russellville, Ky.

4811　SUBDIVISION REGULATION - SAGINAW, MICH.
　　SAGINAW, MICH. TOWNSHIP PLANNING
　　COMMISSION.
　　SUBDIVISION ORDINANCE. SAGINAW, MICH.,
　　CA. 1967.
　　15L. (HUD 701 REPORT)

　　　1. SUBDIVISION REGULATION - SAGINAW,
　　MICH. I. HUD. 701. SAGINAW, MICH.

711.333
(76333)
P51　Planning Services, New Orleans.
no.4　The comprehensive plan, St. Charles
　　Parish, Louisiana. [Report no. 4] Sub-
　　division regulations. Prepared for St.
　　Charles Parish Planning Commission in co-
　　operation with DeLaurel, inc. New Orleans,
　　1965.
　　32p.
　　　Prepared for the Louisiana Dept. of Pub-
　　lic Works.
　　　U.S. Urban Renewal Adm. UPAP.

　　　　　(Cont'd on next card)

711.333 Planning Services, New Orleans. The com-
(76333) prehensive plan, St. Charles Parish,
P51　Louisiana...1965.　(Card 2)
no.4

　　　1. County planning - St. Charles Parish,
　　La. 2. Master plan - St. Charles Parish,
　　La. 3. Subdivision regulation - St.
　　Charles Parish, La. I. DeLaurel Engi-
　　neers, inc. II. St. Charles Parish, La.
　　Planning Commission. III. U.S. URA-UPAP.
　　St. Charles Parish, La.

Subdivision regulation - St. Helens, Or.
333.38
(79547) Oregon. University. Bureau of Municipal
072　Research and Service.
　　Proposed subdivision ordinance for St.
　　Helens, Oregon. Preliminary draft. Prepared
　　for the St. Helens City Planning Commission.
　　[Eugene, Or.], 1959.
　　18p.

　　　U.S. Urban Renewal Administration, Urban
　　Planning Assistance Program.
　　1. Subdivision regulation - St. Helens, Or.
　　I. St. Helens, Or. City Planning Commission.
　　II. U.S. Urban Renewal Administration. Urban
　　Planning　　　Assistance Program.

Subdivision regulation - St. Helens, Or.
333.38
(79547) Oregon. University. Bureau of Municipal
072r　Research and Service.
　　The regulation of land subdivision, St.
　　Helens and vicinity. [Eugene, Or.] 1959.
　　7p. maps.

　　　U.S. Urban Renewal Administration, Urban
　　Planning Assistance Program.
　　1. Subdivision regulation - St. Helens,
　　Or. I. U.S. Urban Renewal Administration.
　　Urban Planning Assistance Program.

1554　SUBDIVISION REGULATION - ST. LEO, MINN.
　　ST. LEO, MINN. VILLAGE PLANNING
　　COMMISSION.
　　SUBDIVISION CONTROLS ORDINANCE.
　　COMMUNITY PLANNING AND DESIGN ASSOCIATES,
　　INC. ST. LEO, MINN., 1969.
　　12L. (HUD 701 REPORT)

　　　1. SUBDIVISION REGULATION - ST. LEO,
　　MINN. I. COMMUNITY PLANNING AND DESIGN
　　ASSOCIATES. II. HUD. 701. ST. LEO,
　　MINN.

333.38 Subdivison regulation - Salem, Mass.
(7445)
B51　Blair and Stein Associates.
　　Subdivision regulations, Salem, Mass.
　　Prepared in cooperation with the Salem
　　Planning Board and the Mass. Dept. of
　　Commerce. Providence, 1962.
　　24p.

　　　U.S. Urban Renewal Adm. UPAP.

　　　1. Subdivision regulation - Salem,
　　Mass. I. Salem, Mass. Planning Board.
　　II. U.S. URA-　　UPAP. Salem,
　　　　　　　　　Mass.

Subdivision regulation - Samson, Ala.
333.38
(76129) Samson, Ala. City Planning Commission.
S15　Samson, Alabama: land subdivision regu-
　　lations and manual. [In cooperation with]
　　Alabama State Planning and Industrial De-
　　velopment Board. Samson, 1957.
　　23p. diagrs.
　　　U.S. Urban Renewal Administration, Urban
　　Planning Assistance Program.

　　　1. Subdivision regulation - Samson, Ala.
　　I. U.S. Urban Renewal Administration.
　　Urban Planning　　　Assistance Program.

Subdivision regulation - San Bruno, Calif.
333.38
(79469)
815p　San Bruno, Calif. Ordinances, etc.
　　A plan line ordinance. An ordinance
　　adopting a precise streets and highway
　　plan for the City of San Bruno; establish-
　　ing regulations for the application and
　　enforcement thereof; establishing official
　　plan lines on certain streets and highways
　　... San Bruno, [1962?]
　　7p.

　　　U.S. Urban Renewal Adm. UPAP.
　　1. Subdivision regu-　　lation - San Bruno,
　　Calif. I. U.S.　　URA-UPAP. San Bruno,
　　Calif.

Subdivision regulation - San Francisco Bay
333.38　area.
(7946) Risse, Edward M
R47　Subdivision control; observations and a
　　bibliography [preliminary] by Edward M.
　　Risse and Ronald W. Williamson. [Prepared]
　　for Land Use Seminar, University of Cali-
　　fornia, School of Law. Berkeley, Spring,
　　1965. [n.p.] 1965.
　　43p.

　　　1. Subdivision regulation - San Francis-
　　co Bay area. 2. Subdivision - Bibl.
　　I. Williamson　　Ronald W., jt. au.
　　II. Title.

Subdivision regulation - San Mateo County,
333.38　Calif.
(79469)
815　San Mateo County, Calif. Planning
　　Commission.
　　The subdivision of land in San Mateo
　　County, California. San Mateo County,
　　Calif., 1932.
　　78p.

　　　I. Subdivision regulation - San Mateo
　　County, Calif.

Subdivision regulation - Santa Clara, Calif.
333.38
(79473) American Society of Planning Officials.
A52　Subdivision improvement policies, City
　　of Santa Clara. Chicago, 1959.
　　1v. tables.

Planning and Advisory Service special report.

　　1. Subdivision regulation - Santa Clara, Calif.

SUBDIVISION REGULATION - SANTA CLARA
333.38　CO., CALIF.
815　SANTA CLARA COUNTY, CALIF. PLANNING
　　COMMISSION.
　　HILLSIDE SUBDIVISION STANDARDS. SAN
　　JOSE, CALIF., 1961.
　　8L. (ITS RESOLUTION NO. 6082)

　　　1. SUBDIVISION REGULATION - SANTA
　　CLARA CO., CALIF. I. TITLE.

Subdivision regulation - Sarasota Co., Fla.
333.38
(75961) Sarasota County, Fla. Planning Commission.
817　Subdivision regulations for Sarasota
　　County, Florida. [Sarasota] Fla., 1960.
　　36p.

　　　1. Subdivision regulation - Sarasota
　　Co., Fla.

Subdivision regulation - Saratoga Co.,
333.38　N.Y.
(74748) Saratoga County, N.Y. County Planning
817　Board.
　　Subdivision regulations; a model.
　　[Ballston Spa, N.Y.] 1963.
　　1v.

　　　1. Subdivision regulation - Saratoga Co.,
　　N.Y.

Subdivision regulation - Satsuma, Ala.

333.38
(76122)
S17

Satsuma, Ala. Town Planning Commission.
Satsuma, Alabama: subdivision regu-
lations. [Prepared in cooperation with]
Alabama State Planning and Industrial
Development Board. Satsuma, 1963.
36p.

U.S. Urban Renewal Adm. UPAP.

1. Subdivision regulation - Satsuma,
Ala. I. U.S. URA-UPAP. Satsuma, Ala.

Subdivision regulation - Scottsboro, Ala.

333.38
(76195)
S26

Scottsboro, Ala. City Planning Commission.
Scottsboro, Alabama: subdivision regu-
lations. [Prepared in cooperation with]
Alabama State Planning and Industrial
Development Board. Scottsboro, 1961.
36p.

U.S. Urban Renewal Adm. UPAP.

1. Subdivision regulation - Scottsboro,
Ala. I. U.S. URA-UPAP. Scottsboro, Ala.

Subdivision regulation - Shawnee, Okla.

333.38
(76636)
O45

Oklahoma. University. Institute of Community Developments.
An ordinance for the regulation of land
subdivision, Shawnee, Oklahoma. Proposed.
Norman, Okla., 1957.
17p.

U.S. Urban Renewal Administration, Urban Planning
Assistance Program.

1. Subdivision regulation - Shawnee, Okla. I. U.S.
URA-UPAP. Shawnee, Okla.

Subdivision regulation - Sausalito, Calif.

333.38
(79462)
S18

Sausalito, Calif. Ordinances, etc.
Sausalito, California: proposed subdivision ordinance. [Sausalito] 1958.
37p.

U.S. Urban Renewal Adm. UPAP.

1. Subdivision regulation - Sausalito,
Calif. I. U.S. URA-UPAP. Sausalito,
Calif.

Subdivision regulation - Seaside, Calif.

333.38
(79476)
S21

Seaside, Calif. Ordinances, etc.
Seaside subdivision ordinance. Seaside,
Calif., [1957?]
43p.

U.S. Urban Renewal Administration, Urban Planning
Assistance Program.

1. Subdivision regulation - Seaside, Calif. I. U.S.
URA-UPAP. Seaside, Calif.

Subdivision regulation - Shelbyville, Tenn.

333.38
(76858)
832

Shelbyville, Tenn. Regional Planning Commission.
Subdivision regulations for the Shelbyville planning region. Assisted by the Tennessee State Planning Commission, Middle
Tennessee Office, Shelbyville, 1957.
18p. diagrs., maps. (MTO Publication
57-11)
1. Subdivision regulation - Shelbyville,
Tenn. I. Tennessee. State Planning Commission. II. U.S. Urban Renewal Administration. Urban Planning Assistance
Program.

Subdivision regulations - Savannah, Ga.

711.4
(758724)
C31

Chatham County-Savannah Metropolitan Planning
Commission.
Land-subdivision regulations, Chatham County
-Savannah Metropolitan Planning District.
Second rough draft prepared for the purpose of
discussion by the Metropolitan Planning Commis-
sion's Subdivision Development Committee. A
part of the master plan for the Chatham County -
Savannah Metropolitan Planning District. [Tenta-
tive ed.] Savannah, 1956.

(Continued on next card)

Subdivision regulation - Seaside, Or.

333.38
(79546)
O72

Oregon. University. Bureau of Municipal
Research and Service.
Subdivision control. Memorandum to
Seaside City Planning Commission. Eugene,
Or., [1958?]
3p.

U.S. Urban Renewal Adm. UPAP.

1. Subdivision regulation - Seaside, Or. I. Seaside,
Or. City Planning Commission.
II. U.S. URA-UPAP. Seaside, Or.

SUBDIVISION REGULATION - SHIAWASSEE
CO., MICH.
MID-COUNTY REGIONAL PLANNING COMMISSION,
OWOSSO, MICH.
A REPORT ON SUBDIVISION REGULATIONS; A
GUIDE FOR SUBDIVISION ORDINANCES. BY
VILICAN-LEMAN AND ASSOCIATES, INC.
SOUTHFIELD, MICH., 1967.
27, A-3L. (HUD 701 REPORT)

4376

1. SUBDIVISION REGULATION - SHIAWASSEE
CO., MICH. 2. SUBDIVISION REGULATION -
OWOSSO, MICH. I. VILICAN-LEMAN AND
ASSOCIATES. II. HUD 701. SHIAWASSEE,
MICH. III. HUD 701. OWOSSO, MICH.

711.4
(758724)
C31

Chatham County-Savannah Metropolitan Planning
Commission. Land subdivision...(Card 2)
55p.

U.S. Urban Renewal Administration, Urban
Planning Assistance Program.

1. Subdivision regulation - Chatham Co.,
Ga. 2. Subdivision regulation - Savannah,
Ga. I. U.S. Urban Renewal Administration.
Urban Planning Assistance Program.

Subdivision regulation - Shamong, N.J.

333.38
(74961)
N28s

New Jersey. Dept. of Conservation and
Economic Development. (Div. of Planning
and Development)
Land subdivision ordinance of the Township
of Shamong. Suggested changes and additions.
[Trenton] 1959.
14p.

U.S. Urban Renewal Adm. UPAP.

1. Subdivision regulation - Shamong, N.J.
I. U.S. URA-UPAP. Shamong, N.J.

Subdivision regulation - Sitka, Alaska.

333.38
(798)
A51s

Alaska. State Housing Authority.
Subdivision control ordinance, City of
Sitka, Alaska. Sitka, 1960.
14p.

U.S. Urban Renewal Adm. UPAP.

1. Subdivision regulation - Sitka,
Alaska. I. U.S. URA-UPAP. Sitka,
Alaska.

Subdivision regulation - Savannah, Ga.

333.38
(758724)
C31s

Chatham County-Savannah Metropolitan Planning
Commission.
Special report of the committee appointed
to study residential minimum lot sizes, net
dwelling density, building coverage and
utility easements. [Tentative ed.] Savannah,
1957.
33p. diagrs., tables.

U.S. Urban Renewal Administration, Urban
Planning Assistance Program.

(Continued on next card)

SUBDIVISION REGULATION - SENATOBIA,
MISS.
SENATOBIA, MISS. CITY PLANNING
COMMISSION.
SUBDIVISION REGULATIONS. SENATOBIA,
MISS., 1970.
65P. (HUD 701 REPORT)

1885

1. SUBDIVISION REGULATION - SENATOBIA,
MISS. I. HUD 701. SENATOBIA, MISS.

Subdivision regulation - Slidell, La.

333.38
(76312)
M17

Martin (Dan S.) and Associates.
Subdivision regulations, Slidell,
Louisiana. Prepared for the Slidell
Planning Commission. [New Orleans] 1959.
17p.

U.S. Urban Renewal Adm. UPAP.

1. Subdivision regulation - Slidell, La.
I. Slidell, La. Planning Commission.
II. U.S. URA-UPAP. Slidell, La.

Subdivision regulation - Savannah, Ga.

333.38
(758724)
C31s

Chatham County-Savannah Metropolitan Planning
Commission. Special report...(Card 2)

1. Subdivision regulation - Chatham Co.,
Ga. 2. Subdivision regulation - Savannah,
Ga. I. U.S. Urban Renewal Administration.
Urban Planning Assistance Program.

Subdivision regulation - Sharon, Tenn.

333.38
(76824)
S31

Sharon, Tenn. Municipal-Regional Planning
Commission.
Subdivision regulations for Sharon, Tennessee planning region. With the assistance
of the Tennessee State Planning Commission,
West Tennessee Office. Sharon, 1957.
30p. maps.

U.S. Urban Renewal Administration, Urban
Planning Assistance Program.

(Continued on next card)

Subdivision regulation - Sloatsburg, N.Y.

711.4
(74728)
S56

Brown and Blauvelt.
Sloatsburg, New York: master plan, zoning
ordinance, subdivision regulations, by Harry A.
Anthony. Submitted to the Dept. of Commerce
of the State of New York and to the Sloatsburg Planning Board. New York, 1958.
168p. maps, tables.

U.S. Urban Renewal Administration, Urban Planning
Assistance Program.
1. Master plan - Sloatsburg, N.Y. 2. Zoning legisla-
tion - Sloatsburg, N.Y. 3. Subdivision regulation -
Sloatsburg, N.Y. I. Anthony, Harry A. II.
Sloatsburg, N.Y. Plan-   ning Board. III. U.S.
URA-UPAP. Sloatsburg, N.Y.

SUBDIVISION REGULATION - SCHUYLKILL
HAVEN, PA.
SCHUYLKILL HAVEN, PA. PLANNING
COMMISSION.
RULES AND REGULATIONS TO GOVERN THE
SUBDIVISION OF LAND. SCHUYLKILL HAVEN,
PA., 1959.
14P. (HUD 701 REPORT)

4776

1. SUBDIVISION REGULATION - SCHUYLKILL
HAVEN, PA. I. HUD 701. SCHUYLKILL
HAVEN, PA.

333.38
(76824)
S31

Sharon, Tenn. Municipal-Regional Planning
Commission. Subdivision ... (Card 2)

1. Subdivision regulation - Sharon, Tenn.
I. Tennessee State Planning Commission.
II. U.S. Urban Renewal Administration.
Urban Planning Assistance Program.

Subdivision regulation - Slocomb, Ala.

333.38
(76129)
S56

Slocomb, Ala. Town Planning Commission.
Slocomb, Alabama: land subdivision regulations and manual. [In cooperation with]
Alabama State Planning and Industrial Development Board. Slocomb, 1958.
23p. diagrs.

U.S. Urban Renewal Administration, Urban
Planning Assistance Program.

1. Subdivision regulation - Slocomb,
Ala. I. U.S. Urban Renewal Administration.
Urban Planning Assistance Program.
Slocomb, Ala.

Subdivision regulation - Smithfield, R.I.

333.38
(7451)
S54

Smithfield, R.I. Ordinances, etc.
Subdivision regulations for the Town of
Smithfield. Smithfield, 1956.
11p. diagrs.

"Draft."

U.S. Urban Renewal Administration, Urban
Planning Assistance Program.

1. Subdivision regulation - Smithfield,
R. I. I. U.S. Urban Renewal Administration. Urban Planning Assistance Program.

3119   SUBDIVISION REGULATION - SOUTH GLENS
FALLS, N.Y.
SOUTH GLENS FALLS, N.Y. PLANNING BOARD.
PROPOSED SUBDIVISION REGULATION
STANDARDS. BY CANDEUB, FLEISSIG, ADLEY
AND ASSOCIATES. SOUTH GLENS FALLS, N.Y.,
1965.
65L. (HUD 701 REPORT)

1. SUBDIVISION REGULATION - SOUTH GLENS
FALLS, N.Y. I. CANDEUB, FLEISSIG, ADLEY
AND ASSOCIATES. II. HUD. 701. SOUTH
GLENS FALLS, N.Y.

Subdivision regulation - Sprague, Conn.

333.38
(7465)
S67

Sprague, Conn. Planning and Zoning Commission.
Subdivision regulations for the Town of
Sprague, Connecticut. Sprague, 1959.
18p.

U.S. Urban Renewal Administration, Urban
Planning Assistance Program.

1. Subdivision regulation - Sprague, Conn.
I. U.S. Urban Renewal Administration. Urban
Planning Assistance Program.

Subdivision regulation - Smithville, Tenn.

333.38
(76853)
S54

Smithville, Tenn. Planning Commission.
Subdivision standards. Prepared by the Tennessee State Planning Commission, Middle
Tennessee State Office. Smithville, 1958.
1v. (MTO Publication no. 58-24)

U.S. Urban Renewal Administration, Urban
Planning Assistance Program.

1. Subdivision regulation - Smithville, Tenn.
I. Tennessee. State Planning Commission.
II. U.S. Urban Renewal Administration. Urban
Planning Assistance Program.

Subdivision regulation - South
Jacksonville, Ill.

333.38
(77346)
K45s

Kincaid (Evert) and Associates.
Suggested requirements for establishing
subdivision regulations for South Jacksonville, Illinois. Prepared for the South
Jacksonville Plan Commission. Chicago, 1959.
26p.

U.S. Urban Renewal Adm. UPAP.

1. Subdivision regulation - South Jacksonville, Ill.
I. South Jacksonville, Ill. Plan Commission.
II. U.S. URA-UPAP.   South
Jacksonville, Ill.

Subdivision regulation - Springdale, Ark.

333.38
(76714)
A74

Arkansas. University. City Planning Div.
Subdivision regulations, Springdale,
Arkansas. Ordinance no. 514. Prepared
for Springdale Planning Commission.
Fayetteville, Ark., 1961.
12p.

U.S. Urban Renewal Adm. UPAP.

1. Subdivision regulation - Springdale, Ark.
I. Springdale, Ark. City Planning Commission.
II. U.S. URA-UPAP.   Springdale, Ark.

Subdivision regulation - Snowden, Pa.

333.38
(74885)
S56

Snowden, Pa. Ordinances, etc.
Proposed land subdivision regulation
of Snowden Township, Allegheny County,
Pennsylvania. [Snowden, 1964?]
18p.

U.S. Urban Renewal Adm. UPAP.

1. Subdivision regulation - Snowden, Pa.
I. U.S. URA-UPAP. Snowden, Pa.

Subdivision regulation - South Kingstown, R.I.

333.38
(7459)
R36s

Rhode Island. Development Council.
Subdivision ordinances. (The following are
copies of the two ordinances passed by the
South Kingstown Town Council to implement the
Subdivision regulations) [Prepared for the
South Kingstown Planning Board] Providence,
1957.
[3]p. (South Kingstown worksheet no. 16)
U.S. Urban Renewal Administration, Urban
Planning Assistance Program.
(Continued on next
card)

Subdivision regulation - Springhill, La.

333.38
(76396)
M17s

Martin (Dan S. and Associates.
Subdivision regulations, Springhill,
Louisiana. Prepared for the Springhill
Planning Commission. [New Orleans] 1959.
17p.

U.S. Urban Renewal Adm. UPAP.

1. Subdivision regulation - Springhill, La.
I. Springhill, La. Planning Commission.
II. U.S. URA-UPAP. Springhill, La.

Subdivision regulation - Snyder, Pa.

333.38
(74862)
R62l

Rodgers (Clifton E.) & Associates.
Land subdivision regulations, Township of
Snyder, Jefferson County, Pennsylvania.
[n.p.] 1961.
24 p.
U.S. Urban Renewal Adm. UPAP.

1. Subdivision regulation - Snyder,
Pa. I. Snyder, Pa. Ordinances, etc.
II. U.S. URA-UPAP. Snyder, Pa.

333.38
(7459)
R36s

Rhode Island. Development Council. Subdivision ordinances. ... 1957. (Card 2)

1. Subdivision regulation - South Kings-
town, R. I. I. South Kingstown, R. I.
Planning Board. II. U.S. Urban Renewal
Administration. Urban Planning Assistance
Program. South Kingstown, R. I.

1423   SUBDIVISION REGULATION - STANFORD, KY.
STANFORD, KY. PLANNING COMMISSION.
STANFORD SUBDIVISION REGULATIONS. BY
R.W. BOOKER AND ASSOCIATES, INC.
STANFORD, 1969.
25L. (HUD 701 REPORT)

1. SUBDIVISION REGULATION - STANFORD,
KY. I. BOOKER (R.W.) AND ASSOCIATES.
II. HUD. 701. STANFORD, KY.

Subdivision regulation - South Amboy, N.J.

333.38
(74941)
C17

Carr, H Thomas.
Land subdivision ordinance, City of
South Amboy, New Jersey. [Perth Amboy,
N.J.] 1959.
1v.

U.S. Urban Renewal Adm. UPAP.

1. Subdivision regulation - South Amboy,
N.J. I. U.S. URA-UPAP. South Amboy, N.J.

Subdivision regulation - South Kingstown, R.I.

333.38
(7459)
S68

South Kingstown, R.I. Planning Board.
Subdivision regulations, Town of South
Kingstown, R.I. 1957.
15p.
U.S. Urban Renewal Administration, Urban
Planning Assistance Program.

1. Subdivision regulation - South Kingstown,
R.I. I. U.S. Urban Renewal Administration.
Urban Planning Assistance Program. South
Kingstown, R. I.

Subdivision regulation - Stanislaus Co.,
Calif.

333.38
(79457)
S71

Stanislaus Cities-County Advance Planning
Staff.
Model subdivision ordinance; a guide for
better communities. Modesto, Calif., 1959.
67p. diagrs., tables. (Its Guide series
report no. 3)

U.S. Urban Renewal Administration, Urban
Planning Assistance Program.

1. Subdivision regulation - Stanislaus Co., Calif. I.
U.S. URA-UPAP. Stanislaus Co., Calif.

Subdivision regulation - South Daytona,
Fla.

333.38
(75921)
B67

Bostwick, inc.
An ordinance of the City Council of
the City of South Daytona, Florida for
subdivision regulation. Prepared with
the assistance of the Florida Development Commission.
26p.
U.S. Urban Renewal Adm. UPAP.

1. Subdivision regulation - South Daytona, Fla.
I. South Daytona, Fla. Ordinances, etc.
II. U.S. URA-UPAP. South Daytona,
Fla.

Subdivision regulation - Spain.

333.38
(46)
S27

Serrano Guirado, Enrique.
Planificación territorial política del
suelo y administración local. Madrid,
Secretaría General Tecnica, Ministerio de
la Vivienda, 1963.
97p. (Spain. Ministerio de la Vivienda.
Conferencias y discursos 12)

1. Subdivision regulation - Spain. 2. Subdivision
design. 3. City planning administration.
I. Spain. Ministerio de la Vivienda.

1524   SUBDIVISION REGULATION - STEARNS CO.,
MINN.
STEARNS CO., MINN. PLANNING COMMISSION.
SUBDIVISION REGULATIONS. PREPARED BY
CONSULTING SERVICES CORPORATION. ST.
CLOUD, MINN., 1970.
21P. (HUD 701 REPORT)

1. SUBDIVISION REGULATION - STEARNS
CO., MINN. I. HUD. 701. STEARNS CO.,
MINN.

1847   SUBDIVISION REGULATION - SOUTH ELGIN,
ILL.
SOUTH ELGIN, ILL. PLAN COMMISSION.
A REPORT ON A SUBDIVISION REGULATIONS
ORDINANCE. BY TEC-SEARCH, INC. SOUTH
ELGIN, ILL., 1968.
47P. (HUD 701 REPORT)

1. SUBDIVISION REGULATION - SOUTH
ELGIN, ILL. I. TEC-SEARCH, INC.
II. HUD. 701. SOUTH ELGIN, ILL.

5758   SUBDIVISION REGULATION - SPENCER, OKLA.
SPENCER, OKLA. PLANNING COMMISSION.
STANDARDS AND REGULATIONS FOR THE
SUBDIVISION OF LAND FOR THE TOWN OF
SPENCER, OKLAHOMA. SPENCER, OKLA., 1967.
32P. (HUD 701 REPORT)

1. SUBDIVISION REGULATION - SPENCER,
OKLA. I. HUD. 701. SPENCER, OKLA.

1848   SUBDIVISION REGULATION - STEPHENSON
CO., ILL.
STEPHENSON CO., ILL. PLAN COMMISSION.
SUBDIVISION REGULATIONS. BY WM. S.
LAWRENCE AND ASSOCIATES. FREEPORT, ILL.,
1968.
1 V. (HUD 701 REPORT)

1. SUBDIVISION REGULATION - STEPHENSON
CO., ILL. I. LAWRENCE (WM. S.) AND
ASSOCIATES. I. HUD. 701. STEPHENSON
CO., ILL.

1842   SUBDIVISION REGULATION - STERLING, ILL.
STERLING, ILL. PLAN COMMISSION.
SUGGESTED STANDARDS FOR THE DEVELOPMENT
OF SUBDIVISIONS. BY WM. S. LAWRENCE AND
ASSOCIATES. STERLING, ILL., 1969.
35P. (HUD 701 REPORT)

1. SUBDIVISION REGULATION - STERLING,
ILL. I. LAWRENCE (WM. S.) AND
ASSOCIATES. II. HUD. 701. STERLING,
ILL.

333.38
(79529)
072p
Subdivision regulation - Sutherlin, Or.
Oregon. University. Bureau of Municipal
Research and Service.
Proposed subdivision regulations for
Sutherlin, Oregon. Preliminary draft.
Prepared for the Sutherlin City Planning
Commission. [Eugene, Or.] 1958.
13p.

U.S. Urban Renewal Adm. UPAP.

1. Subdivision regulation - Sutherlin, Or.
I. Sutherlin, Or. City Planning Commission.
II. U.S. URA-   UPAP.
Sutherlin, Or.

711.4
(76178)
T17
Subdivision regulation - Tarrant City, Ala.
Tarrant City, Ala. City Planning Commission.
Tarrant City, Alabama: land subdivision regu-
lations and manual. [In cooperation with Alabama
State Planning and Industrial Development Board]
Tarrant City, 1957.
29p. illus., diagrs., maps.

U.S. Urban Renewal Administration, Urban
Planning Assistance Program.

1. City planning - Tarrant City, Ala. 2. Subdivision regulation - Tarrant City, Ala. I. Alabama. State Planning and Industrial Development
Board. II. U.S.   Urban Renewal Administration.

333.38
(76195)
S72
Subdivision regulations - Stevenson, Ala.
Stevenson, Ala. Town Planning Commission.
Stevenson, Alabama; subdivision regu-
lations. [Prepared in cooperation with]
Alabama State Planning and Industrial
Development Board. Stevenson, 1963.
39p.
U.S. Urban Renewal Adm. UPAP.

1. Subdivision regulation - Stevenson,
Ala. I. U.S.   URA-UPAP. Stevenson,
Ala.

333.38
(79529)
072
Subdivision regulation - Sutherlin, Or.
Oregon. University. Bureau of Municipal
Research and Service.
Proposed subdivision regulations.
Memorandum to Sutherlin City Planning
Commission. Eugene, Or., 1958.
3p.

U.S. Urban Renewal Adm. UPAP.

1. Subdivision regulation - Sutherlin, Or.
I. Sutherlin, Or. City Planning Commission.
II. U.S. URA-UPAP.   Sutherlin, Or.

---

62   SUBDIVISION REGULATION - TELLER, ALASKA.
TELLER, ALASKA. CITY COUNCIL.
SUBDIVISION CONTROL REGULATIONS. BY
ALASKA CONSULTANTS. DRAFT. TELLER, 1968.
9P. (HUD 701 REPORT)

1. SUBDIVISION REGULATION - TELLER,
ALASKA. I. ALASKA CONSULTANTS. II. HUD.
701. TELLER, ALASKA.

333.38
(764)
S76
SUBDIVISION REGULATION - STOCKDALE,
TEX.
Stockdale, Tex. Ordinances, etc.
Proposed subdivision regulations -
Stockdale, Tex....Stockdale, [1970?]
16p.

1. Subdivision regulation - Stockdale,
Tex.

333.38
(74814)
S81
SUBDIVISION REGULATION - SWARTHMORE, PA.
Swarthmore, Pa. Planning Commission.
Subdivision regulations. Swarthmore,
Pa., 1968.
29p.

1. Subdivision regulation - Swarthmore,
Pa.

---

31   SUBDIVISION REGULATION - TEMPE, ARIZ.
TEMPE, ARIZ. PLANNING AND ZONING
COMMISSION.
SUBDIVISION ORDINANCE. PREPARED BY VAN
CLEVE ASSOCIATES. DRAFT. TEMPE, 1968.
1 V. (HUD 701 REPORT)

1. SUBDIVISION REGULATION - TEMPE, ARIZ.
I. VAN CLEVE ASSOCIATES. II. HUD. 701.
TEMPE, ARIZ.

333.38
(76186)
S85
Subdivision regulation - Sulligent, Ala.
Sulligent, Ala. Town Planning Commission.
Sulligent, Alabama; subdivision regulations.
[In cooperation with] Alabama State Planning
and Industrial Development Board. Sulligent,
1960.
36p.
U.S. Urban Renewal Adm. UPAP.
1. Subdivision regulation - Sulligent, Ala.
I. U.S. URA-UPAP. Sulligent, Ala.

690.015
(485)
S82
R17
1968
Subdivision regulation - Sweden
Ryman, Nils E
Hur fyra bostadsområden planerats (How four
dwelling areas were planned) Stockholm,
Statens institut för byggnadsforskning, 1968.
242p. (Stockholm. Statens institut för
byggnadsforskning. Rapport 17:1968)
English summary.
1. Building research - Sweden. 2. Sweden -
Building research. 3. Subdivision regulation - Sweden. 4. Sweden - Subdivision regulation. I. Stockholm. Statens institut för
byggnadsforskning. II. Title: How four
dwelling areas we   re planned.

333.38
(768)
T25s
Subdivision regulation - Tennessee.
Tennessee. State Planning Commission.
Subdivision regulations, a model set
of standards for Tennessee communities.
Nashville, 1953.
18p. diagrs. (Its Publication no. 248)

1. Subdivision regulation - Tennessee.

333.38
(76176)
S85
Subdivision regulation - Sumiton, Ala.
Sumiton, Ala. Town Planning Commission.
Sumiton, Alabama: land subdivision regula-
tions and manual. [In cooperation with]
Alabama State Planning and Industrial Develop-
ment Board. Sumiton, 1958.
23p. diagrs.
U.S. Urban Renewal Administration, Urban
Planning Assistance Program.
1. Subdivision regulation - Sumiton, Ala.
I. U.S. Urban Renewal Administration. Urban
Planning Assistance Program. Sumiton, Ala.

333.38
(77847)
S 82
SUBDIVISION REGULATION - SWEET SPRINGS,
MO.
Sweet Springs, Mo. Ordinances,
etc.
Subdivision ordinance. Sweet Springs,
[1969?]
15p.

U.S. Dept. of Housing and Urban
Development. UPAP.

1. Subdivision regulation - Sweet
Springs, Mo. I. U.S. HUD-UPAP.
Sweet Springs, Mo.

333.38
(768)
T25
Subdivision regulation - Tennessee.
Tennessee. State Planning Commission.
Subdivision standards for use by Tennessee
local planning commissions as a guide to
adoption of a set of standards for their
community. Nashville, 1959.
20p. diagrs. (Its Publication no. 298)
U.S. Urban Renewal Adm. UPAP.

1. Subdivision regulation - Tennessee.
I. Urban Renewal Administration. Urban
Planning Assistance Program. Tennessee.

2229   SUBDIVISION REGULATION - SUMPTER, MICH.
SUMPTER, MICH. TOWNSHIP PLANNING
COMMISSION.
SUBDIVISION REGULATIONS ORDINANCE.
PREPARED BY VILICAN-LEMAN AND ASSOCIATES,
INC. SOUTHFIELD, MICH., 1969.
30L. (HUD 701 REPORT)

2230   -- --- SUPPLEMENTARY MATERIAL.
FOLIO   1 ENVELOPE.

1. SUBDIVISION REGULATION - SUMPTER,
MICH. I. VILICAN-LEMAN AND ASSOCIATES.
II. HUD. 701. SUMPTER, MICH.

333.38
(76888)
S82
Subdivision regulation - Sweetwater, Tenn.
Sweetwater, Tenn. Regional Planning Commis-
sion.
Subdivision standards for the Sweetwater,
Tennessee planning region. Sweetwater,
1958.
28p. diagrs.
U.S. Urban Renewal Administration, Urban
Planning Assistance Program.
1. Subdivision regulation - Sweetwater,
Tenn. I. U.S. Urban Renewal Administra-
tion. Urban Planning Assistance Program.
Sweetwater,   Tenn.

711.4
(7444)
T28
appendix
Subdivision regulation - Tewksbury, Mass.
Technical Planning Associates, New Haven, Conn.
Master plan report, including capital
budget, subdivision regulations, zoning
by-law. Prepared for Tewksbury Planning
Board and Massachusetts Department of
Commerce. New Haven, 1958.
1v. diagrs., maps, tables.

U.S. Urban Renewal Administration, Urban
Planning Assistance Program.

1. Master plan - Tewksbury, Mass. 2. Zoning legislation-
Tewksbury, Mass. 3.   Subdivision regulation -
Tewksbury, Mass. I.   Tewksbury, Mass. Planning
Board. II. U.S. URA-UPAP. Tewksbury, Mass.

4518   SUBDIVISION REGULATION - SUMTER CO.,
S.C.
SUMTER CO., S.C. PLANNING BOARD.
SUBDIVISION REGULATIONS. SUMTER, 1969.
34P. (HUD 701 REPORT)

1. SUBDIVISION REGULATION - SUMTER CO.,
S.C. I. HUD. 701. SUMTER CO., S.C.

711.4
(76161)
S95
Subdivision regulation - Sylacauga, Ala.
Sylacauga, Ala. City Planning Commission.
Sylacauga, Alabama: land subdivision regu-
lations and manual. [In cooperation with
Alabama State Planning and Industrial Develop-
ment Board] Sylacauga, 1957.
28p. maps.

U.S. Urban Renewal Administration, Urban
Planning Assistance Program.

1. City planning - Sylacauga, Ala. 2. Subdivision regulation - Sylacauga, Ala. I. Alabama. State Planning and Industrial Development Board. II.   U.S. Urban Renewal
Administration.

711.4
(764)
T29z
Subdivision regulation - Texas City, Tex.
Texas City, Tex. City Planning Commission.
Master plan report for Texas City: zoning,
land subdivision control. [Prepared through
the cooperation of the Texas State Dept. of
Health] Houston, Tex., 1959.
36p. (Interim report, stage 2)
Planning consultants: Caldwell and Caldwell
and Chas. R. Haile Associates.
U.S. Urban Renewal Adm. UPAP.

1. Master plan - Texas City, Tex. 2. Zoning - Texas
City, Tex. 3. Subdivision regulation - Texas City,
Tex. I. U.S. URA-   UPAP. Texas City,
Tex. II. Caldwell and   Caldwell.

Subdivision regulation - Texas City, Tex.

333.38
(764) Texas City, Tex. City Planning Commission.
T29 Subdivision rules and regulations, City of
Texas City, Texas. With the cooperation of
the Texas State Dept. of Health. Houston,
Tex., 1959.
16p.

Planning consultants: Chas. R. Haile
Associates, Inc. and Caldwell and Caldwell.
U.S. Urban Renewal Adm. UPAP.
1. Subdivision regulation - Texas City,
Tex. I. U.S. URA-UPAP. Texas City, Tex.
II. Caldwell and   Caldwell.

Subdivision regulation - Titusville, Pa.

333.38
(74897) Titusville, Pa. Ordinances, etc.
T47 Land subdivision regulations.
[Titusville, 1958]
[15]p.

U.S. Urban Renewal Adm. UPAP.

1. Subdivision regulation - Titusville,
Pa. I. U.S. URA-UPAP. Titusville, Pa.

Subdivision regulation - Trumann, Ark.

333.38
(76796) Arkansas. University. City Planning
A74 Div.
Subdivision regulations, Trumann,
Arkansas. Ordinance no. 152. Prepared
for City Planning Commission, Trumann,
Arkansas. Fayetteville, Ark., 1963.
[12]p.

U.S. Urban Renewal Adm. UPAP.

1. Subdivision regulation - Trumann, Ark.
I. Trumann, Ark.   City Planning
Commission. II. U.S.   URA-UPAP. Trumann,
Ark.

Subdivision regulation - Thibodaux, La.

333.38
(76339) Martin (Dan S.) and Associates.
M17 Subdivision regulations, Thibodaux planning region, Louisiana. Prepared for the
Thibodaux Regional Planning Commission.
[New Orleans] 1959.
20p.

U.S. Urban Renewal Administration, Urban Planning
Assistance Program.

1. Subdivision regulation - Thibodaux, La. I.
Thibodaux, La. Regional Planning Commission.
II. U.S. URA-UPAP.   Thibodaux, La.

Subdivision regulation - Tiverton, R.I.

333.38
(7456) Rhode Island. Development Council.
R36 Subdivision regulations, Tiverton, Rhode
Island. [In cooperation with] Tiverton Plan-
ning Board. Final draft. Providence, 1958.
8p. (Its Community Assistance Program.
Tiverton worksheet no. 15)
U.S. Urban Renewal Adm. UPAP.

1. Subdivision regulation - Tiverton, R.I.
I. Tiverton, R.I. Planning Board. II. U.S.
URA-UPAP. Tiverton, R.I.

Subdivision regulation - Trumann, Ark.

333.38
(76796) Arkansas. University. City Planning Div.
A74a Administrative guide, subdivision
regulations. Prepared for City Planning
Commission, Trumann, Arkansas.
Fayetteville, Ark., 1963.
12p. (Document no. 3D-3)

U.S. Urban Renewal Adm. UPAP.

1. Subdivision regulation - Trumann, Ark. I. Trumann, Ark. City Planning Commission. II. U.S.
URA-UPAP. Trumann,   Ark.

Subdivision regulation - Thomasville, Ala.

711.4
(761245) Thomasville, Alabama. City Planning Com-
T36a mission.
Thomasville, Alabama: land subdivision
regulations and manual. [In cooperation
with Alabama State Planning and Industrial
Development Board] Thomasville, 1956.
29p. diagrs.

U.S. Urban Renewal Administration, Urban

(Continued on next card)

Subdivision regulation - Toccoa, Ga.

352.1
(75813) Bartholomew (Harland) and Associates.
B17 Public improvements and administration
of the comprehensive plan. [Prepared for]
Toccoa-Stephens County Joint Planning
Commission [Under contract with Georgia
Dept. of Commerce] Atlanta, 1959.
1v. tables.

U.S. Urban Renewal Administration,
Urban Planning Assistance Program.

1. Capital improvement programs - Toccoa, Ga.
2. Subdivision regulation - Toccoa, Ga. I. Toccoa-
Stephens County Joint   Planning Commission.
II. U.S. URA-UPAP.   Toccoa, Ga.

Subdivision regulation - Trussville, Ala.

333.38
(76178) Trussville, Ala. City Planning Commission.
T78 Trussville, Alabama: land subdivision regulations. [In cooperation with] Alabama
State Planning and Industrial Development
Board. Trussville, 1959.
10p.

U.S. Urban Renewal Administration, Urban Planning
Assistance Program.

1. Subdivision regulation - Trussville, Ala. I. U.S.
URA-UPAP. Trussville,   Ala.

711.4
(761245) Thomasville, Alabama. City Planning Com-
T36a mission. Thomasville, ... (Card 2)

Planning assistance Program.

1. City planning - Thomasville, Ala. 2.
Subdivision regulation - Thomasville, Ala.
I. Alabama. State Planning and Industrial
Development Board. II. U.S. Urban Renewal
Administration. Urban Planning Assistance
Program.

Subdivision regulation - Toledo, Or.

333.38
(79533) Oregon. University. Bureau of Municipal
T65 Research and Service.
Proposed subdivision ordinance for Toledo,
Oregon. Prepared for the Toledo City Plan-
ning Commission. Preliminary draft. [Eugene,
Or.] 1960.
13p.

U.S. Urban Renewal Adm. UPAP.
1. Subdivision regulation - Toledo, Or. I. Toledo,
Or. City Planning Commission. II. U.S. URA-UPAP.
Toledo, Or.

Subdivision regulation - Tulia, Tex.

711.4
(764) Koch & Fowler and Grafe, inc.
T85 Tulia administrative regulations. [Pre-
no.6 pared for Texas State Department of Health
and Tulia City Planning Commission] Dallas,
1961.
62 p. (Its Comprehensive plan report 6)

U.S. Urban Renewal Adm. UPAP.

1. Master plan - Tulia, Tex. 2. Subdivision regulation - Tulia, Tex. 3. Zoning
legislation - Tulia, Tex. I. Tulia, Tex.
City Planning   Commission. II. U.S.
URA-UPAP.   Tulia, Tex.

SUBDIVISION REGULATION - THOMASVILLE, GA.

333.38
(758981) Southwest Georgia Planning and Development
S68 Commission.
Recommended subdivision regulations;
City of Thomasville, Ga. Atlanta, State
Planning Bureau, 1970.
13p.
U.S. Dept. of Housing and Urban Devel-
opment. Comprehensive Planning Grant
Program. HUD project no. Ga. P-149.
1. Subdivision regulation - Thomasville,
Ga. I. U.S. HUD-Comprehensive Planning
Grant Program.   Thomasville, Ga.
II. Title.

Subdivision regulation - Totowa, N.J.

333.38
(74923) Morrow Planning Associates.
M67 Proposed subdivision ordinance of the
Borough of Totowa, New Jersey. Ridgewood,
N.J., 1959.
19p.

U.S. Urban Renewal Adm. UPAP.

1. Subdivision regulation - Totowa, N.J.
I. U.S. URA-UPAP. Totowa, N.J.

Subdivision regulation - Two Rivers, Wis.

333.38
(77567) [Schellie (Kenneth L.) and Associates]
S23 Platting. Indianapolis, 1960.
19p.

At head of title: Chapter 15.
U.S. Urban Renewal Adm. UPAP.

1. Subdivision regulation - Two Rivers,
Wis. I. U.S. URA-UPAP. Two Rivers, Wis.

Subdivision regulation - Thomson, Ga.

333.38
(75863) Thomson, Ga. Planning Commission.
T36 Draft of proposed subdivision regu-
lations for Thomson, Georgia, by Sydney
Carter. Prepared under contract with
Georgia Dept. of Commerce. Rev. Augusta,
Ga., 1960.
19p.

U.S. Urban Renewal Adm. UPAP.

1. Subdivision regulation - Thomson, Ga.
I. U.S. URA-UPAP. Thomson, Ga.

2162 SUBDIVISION REGULATION - TRENTON, MO.
TRENTON, MO. CITY PLANNING COMMISSION.
PROPOSED SUBDIVISION REGULATIONS, BY
HARE AND HARE. TRENTON, MO., 1970.
12P. (HUD 701 REPORT)

1. SUBDIVISION REGULATION - TRENTON, MO.
I. HARE AND HARE. II. HUD. 701.
TRENTON, MO.

Subdivision regulation - Union Springs, Ala.

333.38
(76148) Union Springs, Ala. City Planning Commission.
U54 Union Springs, Alabama: subdivision regulations. [Prepared for] Alabama State Planning
and Industrial Development Board. Union
Springs, 1960.
36p.

U.S. Urban Renewal Adm. UPAP.

1. Subdivision regulation - Union Springs,
Ala. I. U.S. URA-UPAP. Union Springs, Ala.

1033 SUBDIVISION REGULATION - TIFTON, GA.
TIFTON, GA. PLANNING COMMISSION.
SUBDIVISION REGULATIONS FOR TIFTON,
GEORGIA. BY COASTAL PLAIN AREA PLANNING
AND DEVELOPMENT COMMISSION. TIFTON, GA.,
1970.
33L. (HUD 701 REPORT)

1. SUBDIVISION REGULATION - TIFTON, GA.
I. COASTAL PLAIN AREA PLANNING AND
DEVELOPMENT COMMISSION. II. HUD. 701.
TIFTON, GA.

Subdivision regulation - Trenton, Tenn.

333.38
(76823) Trenton, Tenn. Municipal-Regional Planning
T72 Commission.
Subdivision regulations, Trenton, Tennessee. [Assisted by the Tennessee State Planning Commission, West Tennessee Office]
Trenton, 1959.
40p. diagrs.

U.S. Urban Renewal Administration, Urban
Planning Assistance Program.
1. Subdivision regulation - Trenton, Tenn.
I. U.S. URA-UP   Trenton, Tenn.

---

235 SUBDIVISION REGULATION - UNIONTOWN, ALA.
UNIONTOWN, ALA. PLANNING COMMISSION.
SUBDIVISION REGULATIONS, BY ALABAMA
DEVELOPMENT OFFICE. UNIONTOWN, ALA., 1970.
30P. (HUD 701 REPORT)

1. SUBDIVISION REGULATION - UNIONTOWN,
ALA. I. ALABAMA. DEVELOPMENT OFFICE.
II. HUD. 701. UNIONTOWN, ALA.

Subdivision regulation - Uniontown, Ala.

333.38
(76144)
U54
Uniontown, Ala. Town Planning Commission.
Uniontown, Alabama: land subdivision regulations and manual. [In cooperation with] Alabama State Planning and Industrial Development Board. Uniontown, 1958.
23p. diagrs.

U.S. Urban Renewal Administration, Urban Planning Assistance Program.

1. Subdivision regulation - Uniontown, Ala. I. U.S. URA-UPAP. Uniontown, Ala.

Subdivision regulation - Versailles, Ky.

333.38
(769465)
V27
Versailles, Ky. Ordinance, etc.
Subdivision regulations of Versailles, Kentucky, adopted February 5, 1957.
Versailles, 1957.
15p.

U.S. Urban Renewal Administration, Urban Planning Assistance Program.

1. Subdivision regulation - Versailles, Ky. I. U.S. Urban Renewal Administration. Urban Planning Assistance Program.

Subdivision regulation - Wall, N.J.

333.38
(74946)
N28
New Jersey. Dept. of Conservation and Economic Development. (Div. of Planning and Development)
Land subdivision ordinance of the Township of Wall. Suggested changes and additions. [Trenton] 1959.
25p.

U.S. Urban Renewal Adm. UPAP.

1. Subdivision regulation - Wall, N.J. I. U.S. URA-UPAP. Wall, N.J.

Subdivision regulation - Uniontown, Pa.

333.38
(74844)
U54
Uniontown, Pa. Ordinances, etc.
Uniontown, Pa.: sub-division ordinance.
Uniontown, 1957.
24p. diagrs.

U.S. Urban Renewal Administration, Urban Planning Assistance Program.

1. Subdivision regulation - Uniontown, Pa. I. U.S. URA-UPAP. Uniontown, Pa.

Subdivision regulation - Victor, N.Y.

333.38
(74786)
V42
Victor, N. Y. Town Planning Board.
Rules and regulations for the subdivision of land. Victor, 1959.
19p.

U.S. Urban Renewal Adm. UPAP.

1. Subdivision regulation - Victor, N. Y. I. U.S. URA-UPAP. Victor, N. Y.

Subdivision regulation - Walpole, Mass.

333.38
(7447)
W15
Walpole, Mass. Planning Board.
Proposed rules and regulations governing the subdivision of land in Walpole, Massachusetts, by Allen Benjamin. Wayland, Mass., 1956.
25p.

U.S. Urban Renewal Administration, Urban Planning Assistance Program.

1. Subdivision regulation - Walpole, Mass. I. I. Benjamin, Allen. II. U.S. URA-UPAP. Walpole, Mass.

1035 SUBDIVISION REGULATION - UPSON CO., GA. THOMASTON - UPSON COUNTY PLANNING COMMISSION.
PROPOSED SUBDIVISION REGULATIONS FOR UPSON COUNTY. BY ADLEY ASSOCIATES, INC., FOR THE CHATTAHOOCHEE - FLINT AREA PLANNING AND DEVELOPMENT COMMISSION. LAGRANGE, GA., 1970.
45L. (HUD 701 REPORT)

1. SUBDIVISION REGULATION - UPSON CO., GA. I. ADLEY ASSOCIATES, INC. II. HUD. 701. UPSON CO., GA.

Subdivision regulation - Virden, Ill.

333.38
(77383)
V47
Virden, Ill. Plan Commission.
Suggested subdivision ordinance, by Gregory Bassett. Urbana, Ill., 1960.
15p.

U.S. Urban Renewal Adm. UPAP.

1. Subdivision regulation - Virden, Ill. I. Bassett, Gregory. II. U.S. URA-UPAP. Virden, Ill.

1045 SUBDIVISION REGULATION - WARNER ROBINS, GA.
WARNER ROBINS, GA. PLANNING COMMISSION.
RECOMMENDED SUBDIVISION REGULATIONS (REVISIONS). BY ERIC HILL ASSOCIATES, INC. WARNER ROBINS, GA., 1969.
26L. (HUD 701 REPORT)

1. SUBDIVISION REGULATION - WARNER ROBINS, GA. I. HILL (ERIC) ASSOCIATES. II. HUD. 701. WARNER ROBINS, GA.

Subdivision regulation - Valley Head, Ala.

333.38
(76166)
V15
Valley Head, Ala. Town Planning Commission.
Valley Head, Alabama: land subdivision regulations and manual. [In cooperation with] Alabama State Planning and Industrial Development Board. Valley Head, 1959.
23p. diagrs.

U.S. Urban Renewal Administration, Urban Planning Assistance Program.

1. Subdivision regulation - Valley Head, Ala. I. U.S. URA-UPAP. Valley Head, Ala.

711.4
(755:347)
V47
Subdivision regulation - Virginia.
Virginia. Dept. of Conservation and Development. Division of Planning and Economic Development. Planning legislation, Virginia. Richmond, Va., Sept. 1952.
84 p.

Processed.

1. City planning legislation-Va. 2. County planning legislation-Va. 3. Subdivision regulation-Va. 4. Zoning legislation-Va.

Subdivision regulation - Warner Robins, Ga.

333.38
(758515)
H45
Hill and Adley Associates.
Subdivision regulations for Warner Robins, Georgia. Prepared for the Warner Robins Planning Commission. Warner Robins, 1959.
21p.

For discussion purposes only.

U.S. Urban Renewal Administration, Urban Planning Assistance Program.

1. Subdivision regulation - Warner Robins, Ga. I. Warner Robins, Ga. Planning Commission. II. U.S. URA-UPAP. Warner Robins, Ga.

333.38
(76735)
A74
Subdivision regulation - Van Buren, Ark.
Arkansas. University. City Planning Division.
Subdivision regulations, Van Buren, Arkansas. Proposed for the Van Buren Planning Commission. Fayetteville, Ark., 1961.
16p.

Preliminary draft for discussion only.

1. Subdivision regulation - Van Buren, Ark.

333.38
(755)
V47
Subdivision regulation - Virginia.
Virginia. Division of Planning and Economic Development.
Suggestions for regulating subdivisions. Richmond, Va. [1955?]
33p.

1. Subdivision regulation - Virginia.

Subdivision regulation - Warren, N.J.

333.38
(74944)
C65
Community Planning Associates.
A review of the Warren Township, subdivision ordinance. Prepared for the Warren Township Planning Board. West Trenton, N.J., 1959.
6p.
New Jersey Expanded State and Regional Planning Program.
U.S. Urban Renewal Adm. UPAP.

1. Subdivision regulation - Warren, N.J. I. Warren, N.J. Township Planning Board. II. U.S. URA-UPAP. Warren, N.J.

VF
333.38
(77433)
P17
Subdivision regulation - Van Buren, Mich.
Perkins, Rogers & Associates.
Subdivision regulations, township of Van Buren, Wayne County, Michigan. Detroit [1965?]
27p.

U.S. Urban Renewal Adm. UPAP.

1. Subdivision regulation - Van Buren, Mich. I. U.S. URA-UPAP. Van Buren, Mich.

Subdivision regulation - Wadley, Ala.

333.38
(76157)
W12
Wadley, Ala. Town Planning Commission.
Land subdivision regulations and manual. [In cooperation with] Alabama State Planning and Industrial Development Board. Wadley, 1958.
1v. diagrs.

U.S. Urban Renewal Administration, Urban Planning Assistance Program.

1. Subdivision regulation - Wadley, Ala. I. U.S. URA-UPAP. Wadley, Ala.

1048 SUBDIVISION REGULATION - WARRENTON, GA.
WARRENTON-WARREN COUNTY PLANNING COMMISSION.
WARRENTON SUBDIVISION REGULATIONS. BY CENTRAL SAVANNAH RIVER AREA PLANNING AND DEVELOPMENT COMMISSION. WARRENTON, GA., 1970.
24P. (HUD 701 REPORT)

1. SUBDIVISION REGULATION - WARRENTON, GA. I. CENTRAL SAVANNAH RIVER AREA PLANNING & DEVELOPMENT COMMISSION. II. HUD. 701. WARRENTON, GA.

Subdivision regulation - Vernon, Ala.

333.38
(76186)
V27
Vernon, Ala. Town Planning Commission.
Vernon, Alabama: subdivision regulations. [Prepared for] Alabama State Planning and Industrial Development Board. Vernon, 1960.
36p.

U.S. Urban Renewal Adm. UPAP.

1. Subdivision regulation - Vernon, Ala. I. U.S. URA-UPAP. Vernon, Ala.

2619 SUBDIVISION REGULATION - WALL, N.J.
WALL, N.J. PLANNING BOARD.
BASIS FOR A REVISED LAND SUBDIVISION ORDINANCE, TOWNSHIP OF WALL, APRIL 1969. PREPARED BY THE MONMOUTH COUNTY PLANNING BOARD. WALL, 1969.
53L. (HUD 701 REPORT)

1. SUBDIVISION REGULATION - WALL, N.J. I. MONMOUTH CO., N.J. PLANNING BOARD. II. HUD. 701. WALL, N.J.

Subdivision regulation - Warrior, Ala.

333.38
(76178)
W17
Warrior, Ala. City Planning Commission.
Warrior, Alabama: subdivision regulations. [Prepared in cooperation with] Alabama State Planning and Industrial Development Board. Warrior, 1963.
39p.

U.S. Urban Renewal Adm. UPAP.

1. Subdivision regulation - Warrior, Ala. I. U.S. URA-UPAP. Warrior, Ala.

333.38
(797)
D17

Subdivision regulation - Washington (State)

Derbyshire, Ralph R
Regional codes and ordinance study; a
survey of subdivision ordinances in the
central Puget Sound region. Prepared in
cooperation with the Washington State Dept.
of Commerce and Economic Development.
Seattle, Puget Sound Governmental Conference,
Puget Sound Regional Planning Council, 1967.
50p.
U.S. Dept. of Housing and Urban Development. UPAP.

1. Subdivision regula-   tion - Washington
(State) I. Puget   Sound Regional Planning
Council.   II. U.S. HUD-UPAP.
Washington (State)

333.38
(74881)
W17

SUBDIVISION REGULATION - WASHINGTON, PA.

Washington, Pa. Ordinances, etc.
Washington township land subdivision
regulations. Philadelphia, Kendree
and Shepherd Planning Consultants, [1962?]
59p.

1. Subdivision regulation - Washington,
Pa. I. Kendree and Shepherd Planning
Consultants. II. Title.

333.38
(77364)
K45

Subdivision regulation - Watseka, Ill.

Kincaid (Everett) and Associates.
Subdivision regulations for the City
of Watseka, Illinois. Chicago, 1959?
31p.

U.S. Urban Renewal Administration, Urban Planning Assistance Program.

1. Subdivision regulation - Watseka, Ill.
I. U.S. URA-UPAP. Watseka, Ill.

333.38
J25

SUBDIVISION REGULATION - WASHINGTON
(STATE)

JENNINGS, FLOYD M
REGULATING SUBDIVISIONS: THE CONTROL
OF PLATS, SUBDIVISIONS OR DEDICATIONS,
BY FLOYD M. JENNINGS AND ERNEST H.
CAMPBELL, ASSOCIATION OF WASHINGTON
CITIES, IN COOPERATION WITH THE
UNIVERSITY OF WASHINGTON, BUREAU OF
GOVERNMENTAL RESEARCH AND SERVICES.
SEATTLE, 1954.
41P. (INFORMATION BULLETIN NO. 167)

1. SUBDIVISION REGULATION.
2. SUBDIVISION REGULATION -
WASHINGTON (S TATE) I. ASSOCIATION
(CONTINUED ON NEXT CARD)

711.333
(74882)
W17
no.3

Subdivision regulation - Washington Co.,
Pa.

Hill (Carroll V.) and Associates.
Major thoroughfares and subdivision controls, Greater Washington Region, Pennsylvania. [Prepared for] Regional Planning
Commission of Greater Washington, Pennsylvania. Dayton, Ohio, 1959.
23p. (Comprehensive plan report no. 3)
U.S. Urban Renewal Adm. UPAP.

1. Master plan - Washington Co., Pa. 2. Highways -
Washington Co., Pa. 3. Subdivision regulation - Wash-
ington Co., Pa.   I. Greater Washington(Pa.
Planning Commission.   II. U.S. URA-
UPAP. Washington Co.,   Pa.

5358

SUBDIVISION REGULATION - WAUPACA, WIS.

WAUPACA, WIS. PLANNING COMMISSION.
LAND SUBDIVISION REGULATIONS. PREPARED
BY GREEN ENGINEERING CO., INC.
MIDDLETON, WIS. 1965.
20L. (HUD 701 REPORT)

1. SUBDIVISION REGULATION - WAUPACA,
WIS. I. GREEN ENGINEERING CO.
II. HUD 701. WAUPACA, WIS.

333.38
J25

JENNINGS, FLOYD M REGULATING
SUBDIVISIONS....1954.   (CARD 2)

OF WASHINGTON CITIES. II. WASHINGTON
(STATE) UNIVERSITY. GOVERNMENTAL
RESEARCH & SERVICES.

333.38
(74882)
H45

Subdivision regulation - Washington Co.
Pa.

Hill (Carroll V.) and Associates.
Proposed subdivision regulations.
[Prepared for] Regional Planning Commission of Greater Washington, Pennsylvania. Dayton, Ohio, [1959?]
26p.

U.S. Urban Renewal Adm. UPAP.

1. Subdivision regulation - Washington Co. Pa.
I. Greater Washington, (Pa.) Regional Planning
Commission.   II. U.S. URA-
UPAP. Wash-   ington Co., Pa.

333.38
(76837)
W18

Subdivision regulation - Waverly, Tenn.

Waverly, Tenn. Regional Planning Commission.
Subdivision regulations, effective Jan. 3,
1957. Waverly, Tenn., 1957.
8p. diagrs., maps. (MTO Publication
no. 57-2)

"Assisted by the Tennessee State Planning Commission."

1. Subdivision regulation - Waverly, Tenn.
I. Tennessee. State Planning Commission.

333.38
(797)
V63

Subdivision regulations - Washington.

Vogel, Joshua Holmes, 1889-
Surveys, subdivision and platting, and boundaries. Wash-
ington State laws and judicial decisions. Information for
city engineers, surveyors, civil engineers, and attorneys, by
Joshua H. Vogel, Ernest Howard Campbell ,and, Wilbur
K. Wilson. Seattle, Bureau of Governmental Research and
Services, University of Washington, 1949.
184 p. maps, diagrs. 21 cm. ([Washington (State) University.
Bureau of Governmental Research and Services, Report no. 96)
"Selected bibliography": p. 183-134.
I. Subdivision regulations Wash. 2. Boundaries (Es-
tate) - Washington (State) i. Title. [Series]
JA37.W3 no. 96   526.98   A 50-9132
Washington (State)   Univ. Library
for Library of Congress   [2]†

333.38
(74827)
K56

Subdivision regulation - Washington Township
Pa.

Knowles (Morris) inc.
Draft of proposed land subdivision
regulations, Washington Township, Lehigh
County, Pennsylvania. Pittsburgh [1964?]
28p.

1. Subdivision regulation - Washington
Township, Pa.

711.5
(7444
:347)
W19

Subdivision regulation - Wayland, Mass.

Wayland, Mass. Planning Board.
Zoning and subdivision regulations,
Wayland [Mass.] by James L. Harris.
Cambridge, Mass., [1959]
1v.

U.S. Urban Renewal Adm. UPAP.

1. Zoning legislation.- Wayland, Mass.
2. Subdivision regulation - Wayland, Mass.
I. Harris, James L. II. U.S. URA-UPAP.
Wayland, Mass.

Vogel, Joshua Holmes   Surveys, subdivision
and platting, and boundaries ... 1949 (Card 2)

———Supplement. Seattle, Bureau of
Governmental Research and Services, Univ. of
Washington, Sept. 1951.
9 p. ([Washington (State) University.
Bureau of Governmental Research and Services]
Report no. 96, suppl.)

333.38
(77435)
W17s

Subdivision regulation - Washtenaw Co.,
Mich.

Washtenaw County, Mich. Metropolitan
Planning Commission.
A subdivision guide for preparing
plats in township areas of Washtenaw
County. Ann Arbor, Mich., 1963.
63p.

1. Subdivision regulation - Washtenaw
Co., Mich. 2. County planning -
Washtenaw Co., Mich.

333.38
(74883)
W19

Subdivision regulation - Waynesburg, Pa.

Waynesburg, Pa. Ordinances, etc.
Proposed subdivision ordinance for
the Borough of Waynesburg, Pennsylvania.
[Waynesburg, 1963?]
36p.

U.S. Urban Renewal Adm. UPAP.

1. Subdivision regulation - Waynesburg,
Pa. I. U.S. URA-UPAP. Waynesburg, Pa.

333.38
(797)
V63
1958

SUBDIVISION REGULATION - WASHINGTON.

VOGEL, JOSHUA H
SURVEYS, SUBDIVISIONS AND PLATTING,
AND BOUNDARIES; WASHINGTON STATE LAWS
AND JUDICIAL DECISIONS. BY JOSHUA H.
VOGEL AND OTHERS. SEATTLE, UNIVERSITY
OF WASHINGTON PRESS, 1958.
175P.

1. SUBDIVISION REGULATION -
WASHINGTON.

333.38
(77435)
W17
1953

Subdivision regulation - Washtenaw Co., Mich.

Washtenaw County, Mich. Planning Commission.
A guide for the subdivision of land in
unincorporated areas of Washtenaw County,
Mich., suggestions, recommendations and
requirements for land platting. [Prepared]
in cooperation with these agencies: Washtenaw
Co. Drain Commissioner, Health Dept. [and]
Road Commission. Rev. Ann Arbor, Mich.,
1953.
38p.

1. Subdivision regulation - Washtenaw Co., Mich.
I. Washtenaw Co.,   Mich. Road Commission.

333.38
(77324)
G17p

Subdivision regulation - West Chicago, Ill.

Gardner (Carl L.) and Associates.
Proposed subdivision regulations, West
Chicago. Chicago, 1959.
24p.

U.S. Urban Renewal Administration, Urban Planning
Assistance Program.

1. Subdivision regulation - West Chicago, Ill.
I. West Chicago, Ill. Ordinances, etc.
II. U.S. Urban Renewal Administration. Urban
Planning Assistance Program. West Chicago, Ill.

333.38
(74882)
R62

Subdivision regulation - Washington, Pa.

Rodgers (Clifton E.) & Associates.
Land subdivision regulation, Township of
Washington, Pennsylvania. [n.p.] 1961.
[16]p.

U.S. Urban Renewal Adm. UPAP.

1. Subdivision regulation - Washington,
Pa. I. Washington, Pa. Ordinances, etc.
I. U.S. URA-UPAP. Washington, Pa.

711.4
(76282)
W17s

Subdivision regulation - Water Valley, Miss.

Urban Consultant Associates.
Subdivision regulations, a part of the comprehensive city plan of Water Valley, Mississippi. [In cooperation with] Water Valley City
Planning Commission. Prepared for the Mississippi Agricultural and Industrial Board.
Montgomery, Ala., [1960]
15p.
U.S. Urban Renewal Adm. UPAP.
1. Master plan - Water Valley, Miss. 2. Subdivision
regulation - Water Valley, Miss. I. Water Valley,
Miss. City Planning   Commission. II. U.S.
URA-UPAP. Water   Valley, Miss.

333.38
(76387)
M17

Subdivision regulation - West Monroe, La.

Martin (Dan S.) and Associates.
Subdivision regulations, West Monroe,
Louisiana. Prepared for the West Monroe
Planning Commission. [New Orleans] 1959.
17p.

U.S. Urban Renewal Adm. UPAP.

1. Subdivision regulation - West Monroe,
La. I. West Monroe, La. Planning Commission.
II. U.S. URA-UPAP. West Monroe, La.

Subdivision regulation - West Point, Miss.

711.4
(762945)
W27s

Urban Consultant Associates.
   Subdivision regulations, a part of the comprehensive city plan for West Point, Mississippi. In cooperation with the City of West Point, Mississippi. Prepared for the Mississippi Agricultural and Industrial Board. Montgomery, Ala., 1960.
   15p.
   U.S. Urban Renewal Adm. UPAP.

1. Master plan - West Point, Miss. 2. Subdivision regulation - West Point, Miss. I. West Point, Miss. City Planning Com-   mission. II. U.S. URA-UPAP. West   Point, Miss.

Subdivision regulation - Westwood, Mass.

711.14
(7447)
W27

Westwood, Mass. Ordinances, etc.
   Proposed rules and regulations governing the subdivision of land in the town of Westwood, Massachusetts, by Allen Benjamin. [Westwood] 1960.
   19p.

"Preliminary draft."

1. Subdivision regulation - Westwood, Mass. I. Benjamin, Allen.

Subdivision regulation - Wichita, Kan.

711.4
(78142)
W42s

Wichita, Kan. Board of City Commissioners.
   Subdivision improvements. Requirements made of subdevelopers in Wichita and fifteen Midwestern cities. Wichita, 1957.
   17p. tables.

1.Capital improvement programs - Wichita, Kan. 2.Subdivision regulation - Wichita, Kan. I.Title.

Subdivision regulation - West Stockbridge, Mass.

333.38
(7441)
C15

Candeub and Fleissig.
   Proposed subdivision regulations, Town of West Stockbridge, Massachusetts. Prepared for the Town of West Stockbridge, Massachusetts under contract with the Dept. of Commerce of the Commonwealth of Massachusetts. Newark, N.J., 1960.
   10p.
   U.S. Urban Renewal Adm. UPAP.

1. Subdivision regulation - West Stockbridge, Mass.I. U.S. URA-UPAP. West Stockbridge, Mass.

Subdivision regulation - Wharton, N.J.

333.38
(74974)
N28L

New Jersey. Dept. of Conservation and Economic Development. (Div. of Planning and Development)
   Land subdivision ordinance of the Borough of Wharton. Suggested changes and additions. [Trenton] 1959.
   15p.

   U.S. Urban Renewal Adm. UPAP.

1. Subdivision regulation - Wharton, N.J. I. U.S. URA-   UPAP. Wharton, N.J.

Subdivision regulation - Wichita, Kan.

333.38
(78142)
W42

Wichita, Kan. City Planning Commission.
   Subdivision rules and recommendations for the Wichita area. Wichita, 1947.
   15p.

1. Subdivision regulation - Wichita, Kan.

Subdivision regulation - Westchester Co., N.Y.

333.71
(74727)
W27

Westchester County, N.Y. Dept. of Planning.
   Municipal subdivision regulations, reservation of recreational and open spaces. White Plains, N.Y., 1959.
   6p.

1. Open space land - Westchester Co., N.Y. 2. Subdivision regulation - Westchester Co., N.Y.

Subdivision regulation - Wheatland, Pa.

333.38
(74895)
S32

Shenango Valley Regional Planning Commission.
   Subdivision regulations, Borough of Wheatland, Mercer County, Pennsylvania. Sharon, Pa. 1959
   1v.

   U.S. Urban Renewal Adm. UPAP.

1. Subdivision regulation - Wheatland, Pa. I. U.S. URA-UPAP. Wheatland, Pa.

Subdivision regulation - Wilsonville, Ala.

333.38
(76179)
W45

Wilsonville, Ala. Town Planning Commission.
   Wilsonville, Alabama: land subdivision regulations and manual. [In cooperation with] Alabama State Planning and Industrial Development Board. Wilsonville, 1957.
   23p. diagrs.

U.S. Urban Renewal Administration, Urban Planning Assistance Program.

1. Subdivision regulation - Wilsonville, Ala. I. U.S. URA-UPAP. Wilsonville, Ala.

Subdivision regulation - Westerly, R.I.

333.38
(7459)
R36d

Rhode Island. Development Council.
   Development in rural areas. Subdivision regulations (ordinance) [Prepared for Westerly Planning Board] Providence, 1957.
   3p. (Westerly worksheet no. 8A)

   U.S. Urban Renewal Administration, Urban Planning Assistance Program.

1. Subdivision regulation - Westerly, R.I. 2. Rural planning. I. Westerly, R.I. Planning Board. II. U.S. Urban Renewal Administration. Urban Planning Assistance Program. Westerly,   R. I.

Subdivision regulation - White Pine, Tenn.

333.38
(768924)
W34

White Pine, Tenn. Regional Planning Commission.
   Subdivision standards for White Pine, Tennessee and surrounding area. Assisted by Tennessee State Planning Commission, East Tennessee Office. White Pine, 1957.
   22p.
   U.S. Urban Renewal Administration, Urban Planning Assistance Program.

(Continued on next card)

SUBDIVISION REGULATION - WILLIAMSTON, N.C.

5770

WILLIAMSTON, N.C. PLANNING COMMISSION.
PROPOSED SUBDIVISION REGULATIONS.
WILLIAMSTON, N.C., 1968.
34P. (HUD 701 REPORT)

1. SUBDIVISION REGULATION - WILLIAMSTON, N.C. I. HUD. 701. WILLIAMSTON, N.C.

Subdivision regulation - Westerly, R.I.

333.38
(7459)
R36dr

Rhode Island. Development Council.
   Draft subdivision regulations. [Prepared for Westerly Planning Board. Providence] 1958.
   1v.

   U.S. Urban Renewal Administration, Urban Planning Assistance Program.

1. Subdivision regulation - Westerly, R.I. I. Westerly, R.I. Planning Board. II. U.S. Urban Renewal Administration. Urban Planning Assistance Program. Westerly, R. I.

Subdivision regulation - White Pine, Tenn.

333.38
(768924)
W34

White Pine, Tenn. Regional Planning Commission. Subdivision ... (Card 2)

1. Subdivision regulation - White Pine, Tenn. I. Tennessee. State Planning Commission. II. U.S. Urban Renewal Administration, Urban Planning Assistance Program.

Subdivision regulation - Wilton, Ala.

333.38
(76179)
W451

Wilton, Ala. Town Planning Commission.
   Wilton, Alabama: land subdivision regulations and manual. [In cooperation with] Alabama State Planning and Industrial Development Board. Wilton, 1957.
   23p. diagrs.

U.S. Urban Renewal Administration, Urban Planning Assistance Program.

1. Subdivision regulation - Wilton, Ala. I. U.S. URA-UPAP. Wilton, Ala.

Subdivision regulation - Westerly, R.I.

333.38
(7459)
R36

Rhode Island. Development Council.
   Subdivision regulations (development in rural areas study). [Prepared for Westerly Planning Board] Providence, 1957.
   14p. (Westerly worksheet no. 13)

   U.S. Urban Renewal Administration, Urban Planning Assistance Program.

1. Subdivision regulation - Westerly, R.I. I. Westerly, R.I. Planning Board. II. U.S. URA-UPAP. Westerly, R.I.

Subdivision regulation - Wichita, Kan.

333.38
(78186)
W42

Wichita-Sedgwick County, Kan. Metropolitan Area Planning Dept.
   Area development standards. Wichita, 1961.
   44p. (Report no. 61-7)

   U.S. Urban Renewal Adm. UPAP.

1. Subdivision regulation - Wichita, Kan. I. U.S. URA-UPAP. Wichita, Kan.

Subdivision regulation - Windber, Pa.

333.38
(74879)
B14

Baker (Michael, Jr.) inc.
   Rules and regulations for the subdivision of land, Borough of Windber, Somerset County, Pennsylvania. Rochester, Pa., 1959.
   15p.

   U.S. Urban Renewal Adm. UPAP.

1. Subdivision regulation - Windber, Pa. I. U.S. URA-UPAP. Windber, Pa.

SUBDIVISION REGULATION - WESTON, CONN.

279

WESTON, CONN. TOWN PLANNING AND ZONING COMMISSION.
PROPOSED LAND SUBDIVISION REGULATIONS.
FREDERICK P. CLARK ASSOCIATES. WESTON, 2969.
36L. (HUD 701 REPORT)

1. SUBDIVISION REGULATION - WESTON, CONN. I. CLARK (FREDERICK P.) ASSOCIATES. II. HUD. 701. WESTON, CONN.

Subdivision regulation - Wichita, Kan.

333.38
(78186)
W42l

Wichita-Sedgwick County, Kan. Metropolitan Area Planning Dept.
   Lot and parcel development standards. Wichita, 1961.
   72p. (Report no. 61-6)

   U.S. Urban Renewal Adm. UPAP.

1. Subdivision regulation - Wichita, Kan. I. U.S. URA-UPAP. Wichita, Kan.

Subdivision regulation - Winfield, Ala.

VF
333.38
(76189)
W45

Winfield, Ala. City Planning Commission.
   Land subdivision regulations and manual. [In cooperation with] Alabama State Planning and Industrial Development Board. Winfield, 1957.
   1v. diagrs.

U.S. Urban Renewal Administration, Urban Planning Assistance Program.

1. Subdivision regulation - Winfield, Ala. I. U.S. URA-UPAP. Winfield, Al.

243 SUBDIVISION REGULATION - WINFIELD, ALA.
WINFIELD, ALA. CITY PLANNING COMMISSION.
SUBDIVISION REGULATIONS, BY TOWN
PLANNING ASSOCIATES. WINFIELD, ALA., 1970.
1 V. (HUD 701 REPORT)

   1. SUBDIVISION REGULATION - WINFIELD,
ALA. I. TOWN PLANNING ASSOCIATES.
II. HUD. 701. WINFIELD, ALA.

5762 SUBDIVISION REGULATION - WOODLAWN, OHIO.
WOODLAWN, OHIO. PLANNING COMMISSION.
SUBDIVISION REGULATIONS. WOODLAWN,
OHIO, 1969.
22P. (HUD 701 REPORT)

   1. SUBDIVISION REGULATION - WOODLAWN,
OHIO. I. HUD. 701. WOODLAWN, OHIO.

Subdivision regulations for the Maryland Washinton..

333.38
(75284)
M17
   Maryland. Maryland-National Capital Park
and Planning Commission.
   Subdivision regulations for the Maryland-
Washington Regional District within Montgomery County. Silver Spring, Md. [1968?]
43p.

   1. Subdivision regulation - Maryland-
Washington Regional District. 2. Subdivi-
sion regulation - Montgomery Co., Md.
I. Title.

5321 SUBDIVISION REGULATION - WISCONSIN.
NORTHEASTERN WISCONSIN REGIONAL PLANNING
COMMISSION.
MODEL SUBDIVISION ORDINANCE. APPLETON,
WIS., 1968.
30P. (HUD 701 REPORT)

   1. SUBDIVISION REGULATION - WISCONSIN.
I. HUD. 701. WISCONSIN.

1717 SUBDIVISION REGULATION - WORTH CO.,
IOWA.
WORTH CO., IOWA. BOARD OF SUPERVISORS.
SUBDIVISION REGULATIONS. BY WALLACE
HOLLAND KASTLER AND SCHMITZ. NORTHWOOD,
IOWA, CA. 1970.
18P. (HUD 701 REPORT)

   1. SUBDIVISION REGULATION - WORTH CO.,
IOWA. I. WALLACE, HOLLAND, KASTLER AND
SCHMITZ. II. HUD. 701. WORTH CO.,
IOWA.

Sub-employment in the slums of Boston.

331
(74461)
L11
   U.S. Dept. of Labor.
   Sub-employment in the slums of Boston.
A survey. [Washington] 1966.
[9]p.

   1. Employment - Boston. 2. Slums-
Boston. I. Title.

333.38
(775)
W472
SUBDIVISION REGULATION - WISCONSIN.
WISCONSIN. DIRECTOR OF REGIONAL
PLANNING.
WISCONSIN PLATTING STATUTE (AS
REVISED 1955) AND RULES AND REGULATIONS
(AFFECTING PLATTING) OF THE STATE BOARD
OF HEALTH AND THE STATE HIGHWAY
COMMISSION, WITH COMMENTS BY STATE
DIRECTOR OF REGIONAL PLANNING.
MADISON, WIS., OCT. 1, 1956.
39P.

   1. SUBDIVISION REGULATION - WISCONSIN.

1534 SUBDIVISION REGULATION - YELLOW
MEDICINE CO., MINN.
YELLOW MEDICINE CO., MINN. PLANNING
ADVISORY COMMISSION.
PROPOSED SUBDIVISION REGULATIONS LAW.
N.P., 1968.
15L. (HUD 701 REPORT)

   1. SUBDIVISION REGULATION - YELLOW
MEDICINE CO., MINN. I. HUD. 701.
YELLOW MEDICINE CO., MINN.

Sub-employment in the slums of Cleveland.

331
(77132)
L11
   U.S. Dept. of Labor.
   Sub-employment in the slums of Cleveland.
A survey. [Washington] 1965.
[8]p.

   1. Employment - Cleveland. 2. Slums -
Cleveland. I. Title.

VF
333.38
(775)
W471
Subdivision regulation - Wisconsin.

Wisconsin. Legislative Council.
   Report, Volume IV: Conclusions and
recommendations of the judiciary committee,
on the subdivision and platting of land;
submitted to the governor and the legislature.
[Madison] January 1955.
43 p.

   1. Subdivision regulation - Wisconsin.

711.4
(76141)
Y67l
Aug.
1956
Subdivision regulation - York, Ala.

York, Ala. City Planning Commission.
   York, Alabama: land subdivision regulations
and manual. [In cooperation with Alabama
State Planning and Industrial Development
Board] York, 1956.
29p. diagrs.

   U.S. Urban Renewal Administration,

(Continued on next card)

331
(79494)
L11
Sub-employment in the slums of Los
Angeles.
   U.S. Dept. of Labor.
   Sub-employment in the slums of Los
Angeles. A survey. [Washington, 1966?]
[8]p.

   1. Employment - Los Angeles.
2. Slums - Los Angeles. I. Title.

333.38
(775)
W47
Subdivision regulation - Wisconsin.

Wisconsin. University. Law School.
   Subdivision control in Wisconsin, by Marygold
S. Melli. Madison, Wis., Mar. 1953.
v, 108 p. forms, maps, tables. (Its
Research report no. 1)

   On cover: Law in action.
   Bibliography: p. 107-108.
   Processed.

   1. Subdivision regulation-Wisconsin. I. Melli,
Marygold S.

711.4
(76141)
Y67l
Aug.
1956
York, Ala. City Planning Commission. York,
   Alabama: land subdivision...(Card 2)

Urban Planning Assistance Program.

   1. City planning - York, Ala. 2. Sub-
division regulation - York, Ala. I. Ala-
bama. State Planning and Industrial
Development Board. II. U.S. Urban
Renewal Administration. Urban Planning
Assistance Program.

331
(76335)
L11
Sub-employment in the slums of New
Orleans.
   U.S. Dept. of Labor.
   Sub-employment in the slums of New
Orleans. A survey. [Washington, 1966?]
[8]p.

   1. Employment - New Orleans.
2. Slums - New Orleans. I. Title.

2778 SUBDIVISION REGULATION - WIXOM, MICH.
WIXOM, MICH. PLANNING COMMISSION.
SUBDIVISION REGULATIONS ORDINANCE.
PREPARED BY VILICAN-LEMAN & ASSOCIATES,
INC. SOUTHFIELD, MICH., 1966.
1 V. (HUD 701 REPORT)

   1. SUBDIVISION REGULATION - WIXOM, MICH.
I. VILICAN-LEMAN & ASSOCIATES.
II. HUD. 701. WIXOM, MICH.

711.4
(76141)
Y67l
Dec.
1956
Subdivision regulation - York, Ala.

York, Ala. City Planning Commission.
   York, Alabama: land subdivision regulations
and manual. [In cooperation with Alabama
State Planning and Industrial Development
Board] York, 1956.
29p. diagrs.

   U.S. Urban Renewal Administration,

(Continued on next card)

331
(7472)
L11
Sub-employment in the slums of New York.
   U.S. Dept. of Labor.
   Sub-employment in the slums of New York.
A survey. [Washington] 1966.
[12]p.

   1. Employment - New York metropolitan
area. 2. Slums - New York metropolitan
area. I. Title.

5436 SUBDIVISION REGULATION - WOBURN, MASS.
WOBURN, MASS. PLANNING BOARD.
PROPOSED REVISED LAND SUBDIVISION
REGULATIONS. BY METCALF AND EDDY,
ENGINEERS. BOSTON, 1967.
A-48 P. (HUD 701 REPORT)

   1. SUBDIVISION REGULATION - WOBURN,
MASS. I. METCALF AND EDDY. II. HUD.
701. WOBURN, MASS.

711.4
(76141)
Y67l
Dec.
1956
York, Ala. City Planning Commission. York,
   Alabama: land subdivision...(Card 2)

Urban Planning Assistance Program.

   1. City planning - York, Ala. 2. Sub-
division regulation - York, Ala. I. Ala-
bama. State Planning and Industrial
Development Board. II. U.S. Urban Renewal
Administration. Urban Planning Assistance
Program.

331
(79466)
L11
Sub-employment in the slums of Oakland,
Calif.
   U.S. Dept. of Labor.
   Sub-employment in the slums of
Oakland. A survey. [Washington] 1966.
[7]p.

   1. Employment - Oakland, Calif.
2. Slums - Oakland, Calif. I. Title.

Sub-employment in the slums of Philadelphia

331
(74811) U.S. Dept. of Labor.
L11   Sub-employment in the slums of
        Philadelphia. A survey. [Washington
        1966?]
        [9]p.

        1. Employment - Philadelphia.
        2. Slums - Philadelphia. I. Title.

651.5   Subject filing.
N17su   U.S. National Archives and Records Service.
        (Office of Records Management)
        Subject filing. [Wash.] 1966.
        40n. (Records management handbook; managing
        current files FPMR 11.3)

        1. Records management. I. Title.

SUBJECT HEADINGS WITH LOCAL
        SUB-DIVISION.
025.3   U.S. LIBRARY OF CONGRESS. CATALOG
L41SU   DIVISION.
1935   SUBJECT HEADINGS WITH LOCAL
        SUB-DIVISION, COMPILED BY MARY WILSON
        MACNAIR. 5TH ED. WASHINGTON, GOVT.
        PRINT. OFF., 1935.
        36P.

        1. CATALOGING. I. TITLE.
        II. MACNAIR, MARY WILSON.

Sub-employment in the slums of St Louis.

331
(79866) U.S. Dept. of Labor.
L11   Sub-employment in the slums of St. Louis.
        A survey. [Washington, 1966?]
        [8]p.

        1. Employment - St. Louis. 2. Slums -
St. Louis. I. Title.

---

050   Subject guide to periodical indexes and
K84   review indexes.
        Kujoth, Jean Spealman.
        Subject guide to periodical indexes and
        review indexes. Metuchen, N.J., Scarecrow
        Press, 1969.
        129p.

        1. Periodicals. I. Title. II. Title:
Periodical indexes.

The subject is race;

325
R67   Rose, Peter I
        The subject is race; traditional ideologies
        and the teaching of race relations. New
        York, Oxford University Press, 1968.
        181p.
        Bibliography: p. 170-178.

        1. Minority groups. 2. Race relations.
I. Title.

Sub-employment in the slums of San Antonio.

331
(764)   U.S. Dept. of Labor.
L11   Sub-employment in the slums of San
        Antonio. A survey. [Washington, 1966?]
        [4]p.

        1. Employment - San Antonio. 2. Slums -
San Antonio. I. Title.

SUBJECT HEADINGS FOR THE INFORMATION
        FILE.
025.3   BALL, MIRIAM OGDEN, COMP.
B15S   SUBJECT HEADINGS FOR THE INFORMATION
1951   FILE, COMPILED BY MIRIAM OGDEN BALL ...
        7TH ED. NEW YORK, H.W. WILSON, 1951.
        166P.
        BASED ON A LIST OF SUBJECT HEADINGS
USED IN THE PUBLIC LIBRARY OF NEWARK,
NEW JERSEY.

        1. CATALOGING. I. TITLE.

Sublett, Charles William, 1906-   joint ed.
Colorado. *Laws, statutes, etc.*
        1935 Colorado statutes annotated, with cumulative pocket
        part service, containing all the laws of Colorado of a general
        and permanent nature completely annotated by the editorial
        staff of the publisher under the direction of A. Hewson Michie
        assisted by Chas. W. Sublett and R. R. Rusmisel under the
        general supervision of the Legislative statutory commission ...
        Denver, Col., The Bradford-Robinson printing company
        [1936-]
        6 v. 26½ cm.
        Vol. 1 published in 1937.
                                    (Continued on next card)
                                                    36—18037
                                    [44r38i1]

Sub-employment in the slums of San
        Francisco.
331
(79461) U.S. Dept. of Labor.
L11   Sub-employment in the slums of San
        Francisco. A survey. [Washington] 1965.
        [8]p.

        1. Employment - San Francisco.
        2. Slums - San Francisco. 3. Employment -
Survey methods. I. Title.

Subject headings see Cataloging

Sublett, Charles William, 1906-   joint ed.
Colorado. *Laws, statutes, etc.*   1935 Colorado statutes
        annotated ... [1936-] (Card 2)
        Six volumes in one; each volume having special t.-p. and separate
pagination.
        Lists of statutes and reports consulted, at beginning of each volume.

        I. Michie, Addinell Hewson, 1897- ed. II. Sublett, Charles Wil-
liam, 1906-   joint ed. III. Rusmisel, Roy Raymond, 1909-   joint
ed. IV. Lee, Samuel Lile, 1908-   joint ed. V. Colorado. Legislative
statutory commission. VI. Title.
                                                    36—18037
Library of Congress   [44e1]

---

500   SUBJECT CATEGORY LIST.
(03)   U.S. COMMITTEE ON SCIENTIFIC AND
C65   TECHNICAL INFORMATION.
1964   COSATI SUBJECT CATEGORY LIST. 1ST ED.
        WASHINGTON, FEDERAL COUNCIL FOR SCIENCE
        AND TECHNOLOGY, 1964.
        55P.

        1. SCIENCE - DICTIONARIES.
        2. TECHNOLOGY - DICTIONARIES. I. TITLE.
        II. TITLE: SUBJECT CATEGORY LIST.

Subject headings used in catalog of the HHFA
        Library.
025.3   U.S. Housing and Home Finance Agency.
H68   Office of the Administrator. Library.
        Subject headings used in catalog of the
        HHFA Library. Washington, 1962.
        148p.

        1. Cataloging. I. Title.

624.131 SUBMARINE SLOPE FAILURES.
T27V   TERZAGHI, KARL.
        VARIETIES OF SUBMARINE SLOPE
        FAILURES. CAMBRIDGE, HARVARD
        UNIVERSITY, DIVISION OF ENGINEERING
        AND APPLIED PHYSICS, 1956.
        16P. (HARVARD SOIL MECHANICS SERIES
        NO. 52)

        REPRINTED FROM PUBLICATION NO. 25 OF
THE NORWEGIAN GEOTECHNICAL INSTITUTE
AND ORIGINALLY PUBLISHED IN THE
PROCEEDINGS OF THE EIGHTH TEXAS
CONFERENCE ON SOIL MECHANICS AND
FOUNDATION ENGINEERING, SEPTEMBER
                        (CONTINUED ON NEXT CARD)

---

500   SUBJECT CATEGORY LIST.
(03)   U.S. COMMITTEE ON SCIENTIFIC AND
C65   TECHNICAL INFORMATION.
1965   COSATI SUBJECT CATEGORY LIST
        (DOD-MODIFIED). WASHINGTON, DEFENSE
        DOCUMENTATION CENTER, DEFENSE SUPPLY
        AGENCY, 1965.
        69P.

        1. SCIENCE - DICTIONARIES.
        2. TECHNOLOGY - DICTIONARIES. I. TITLE.
        II. TITLE: SUBJECT CATEGORY LIST.

Subject headings used in the dictionary
        catalogs of the Library of Congress.
025.3   U.S. Library of Congress. Subject
L41   Cataloging Division.
        Subject headings used in the dictionary
        catalogs of the Library of Congress, ed. by
        Marguerite V. Quattlebaum. 6th ed. Washington,
        1957.
        1357p.
        Supplements. For complete information see
shelflist.
        1. Cataloging. I. Quattlebaum, Marguerite V
II. Title.

624.131 TERZAGHI, KARL. VARIETIES OF
T27V   SUBMARINE ...1956.   (CARD 2)

        1956.

        1. SOILS. I. TITLE: SUBMARINE
SLOPE FAILURES.

SUBJECT FILE MANUALS: THE WHY AND HOW
651.5   OF THEIR DEVELOPMENT. WASHINGTON,
B21   BEACH, TERRY
        SUBJECT FILE MANUALS: THE WHY AND HOW
        OF THEIR DEVELOPMENT. WASHINGTON, THE
        AMERICAN ARCHIVIST, 1952. 105-126P.
        REPRINTED FROM THE AMERICAN ARCHIVIST,
        VOL. 15, NO. 2, APRIL, 1952.

        1. RECORDS MANAGEMENT. I. TITLE.

Subject headings used in the dictionary
        catalogs of the Library of Congress.
025.3   U.S. Library of Congress. Subject Catalog-
L41   ing Div.
1966   Subject headings used in the dictionary
        catalogs of the Library of Congress, ed. by
        Marguerite V. Quattlebaum. 7th ed.
        Washington, Govt. Print. Off., 1966.
        1432p.

        Files in Cataloging Section.
        Supplements. For holdings see shelflist.

        1. Cataloging. 2. Library science.
        I. Quattle   baum, Marguerite V.,
ed.   II. Title.

Submission of agency accounting systems for GAO
        approval.
657   U.S. Congress. House. Committee on Govern-
0657   ment Operations.
1968   Submission of agency accounting systems for
H-R   GAO approval. Twenty second report by the
        Committee on Government Operations. Washington,
        Govt. Print. Off., 1968.
        19p. (90th Cong., 2d sess. House. Report
no. 1159)

        1. Accounting. 2. Federal government.
I. Title.

657
C657
1966
H-H

SUBMISSIONS OF AGENCY ACCOUNTING
SYSTEMS FOR GAO APPROVAL - 1966.
U.S. CONGRESS. HOUSE. COMMITTEE ON
GOVERNMENT OPERATIONS.
SUBMISSIONS OF AGENCY ACCOUNTING
SYSTEMS FOR GAO APPROVAL - 1966.
HEARINGS BEFORE A SUBCOMMITTEE,
EIGHTY-NINTH CONGRESS, SECOND SESSION.
WASHINGTON, GOVT. PRINT. OFF., 1966.
78P.

HEARING HELD SEPTEMBER 19, 1966.

1. ACCOUNTING.   I. TITLE.

657
C657
1965
H-H

SUBMISSIONS OF AGENCY ACCOUNTING
SYSTEMS FOR GAO APPROVAL.
U.S. CONGRESS. HOUSE. COMMITTEE ON
GOVERNMENT OPERATIONS.
SUBMISSIONS OF AGENCY ACCOUNTING
SYSTEMS FOR GAO APPROVAL. HEARINGS
BEFORE A SUBCOMMITTEE, EIGHTY-EIGHTH
CONGRESS, SECOND SESSION. WASHINGTON,
GOVT. PRINT. OFF., 1965.
75P.

HEARINGS HELD JULY 2 AND 28, 1964.

1. ACCOUNTING.   I. U.S. HOUSING AND
HOME FINANCE AGENCY.   II. TITLE.

657
C657
1965
H-R

SUBMISSIONS OF AGENCY ACCOUNTING
SYSTEMS FOR GAO APPROVAL.
U.S. CONGRESS. HOUSE. COMMITTEE ON
GOVERNMENT OPERATIONS.
SUBMISSIONS OF AGENCY ACCOUNTING
SYSTEMS FOR GAO APPROVAL. THIRD REPORT
BASED ON A STUDY BY THE EXECUTIVE AND
LEGISLATIVE REORGANIZATION SUBCOMMITTEE.
WASHINGTON, GOVT. PRINT. OFF., 1965.
32P. (89TH CONGRESS, 1ST SESSION.
HOUSE. REPORT NO. 179)

1. ACCOUNTING.   I. TITLE.

353
Z45su
1970

Subnational politics.
Zimmerman, Joseph F   ed.
Subnational politics; readings in State and
local government. 2d ed. New York, Holt,
Rinehart and Winston, 1970.
446p.

First ed. published in 1964 under title:
Readings in State and local government.

1. Intergovernmental relations. 2. State
government. 3. Local government. I. Title.

360
D72

Subramanian, Muthu, jt. au.
Drewnowski, Jan.
Studies in the methodology of social planning,
by Jan Drewnowski and Muthu Subramanian with the
cooperation of Claude Richard-Proust. Geneva,
United Nations Research Institute for Social
Development, 1970.
127p. (United Nations Research Institute for
Social Development. Report no. 70.5)

1. Social conditions. 2. Automation - Social
effect. I. Subramanian, Muthu, jt. au.
II. United Nations Research Institute for Social
Development. III.   Title: Social planning.

LAW
T
M241su

Subsequent arrests...
McKay, Henry D   ed.
Subsequent arrests, convictions and commit-
ments among former juvenile delinquents.
[Report] submitted to the President's Commission on Law Enforcement and Administration
of Justice. [Wasington, D.C.] 1967.
124p.

1. Juvenile delinquency. 2. Law
enforcement. I. U.S. President's Commission
on Law Enforcement and Administration of
Justice. II. Title.

Subsidized housing see Public housing

711.583
(74811)
M45

The subsidized noose.
Miller, Kenneth.
The subsidized noose: the role of
Pennsylvania State government in suburban
housing opportunities. Philadelphia, Housing
Association of Delaware Valley, 1971.
1v.

1. Suburbs - Philadelphia. 2. Low-income
housing - Philadelphia. 3. Minority groups -
Housing - Philadelphia. I. Housing Association of Delaware Valley. II. Title.

336.18
L41s
1965

Subsidy and subsidy-effect programs of the
U.S. Government.
U.S. Library of Congress. Legislative
Reference Service.
Subsidy and subsidy-effect programs of the
U.S. Government. Materials prepared for the
Joint Economic Committee, Congress of the
United States. Washington, Govt. Print.
Off., 1965.
85p.

At head of title: 89th Cong., 1st sess.

1. Grants-in-   aid. I. U.S.
Congress.   Joint Economic
Committee.   II. Title.

336.18
L41s
1960

Subsidy and subsidylike programs of the
U.S. Government.
U.S. Library of Congress. Legislative
Reference Service.
Subsidy and subsidylike programs of the
U.S. Government. Materials prepared for the
Joint Economic Committee, Congress of the
United States. Washington, Govt. Print.
Off., 1960.
80p.

At head of title: 86th Cong., 2d sess.

1. Grants- in-   aid. I. U.S.
Congress.   Joint Economic
Committee.   II. Title.

VF
711.1
A77

Subsistence homesteads.
Association for Planning and Regional Reconstruction.
Land settlement in ten countries; prepared
by G. Rosenberg. [London] Jan. 1947.
27 p. (Its Review A3)

Bibliographies.

1. Subsistence homesteads. I. Rosenberg, G. II. Title.

711.1
I57

SUBSISTENCE HOMESTEADS.
INTERNATIONAL HOUSING ASSOCIATION.
UMSIEDLUNG. SUBSISTENCE HOMESTEADS.
COLONISATION INTÉRIEURE. INTERNATIONAL
HOUSING CONGRESS, PRAHA 1935. FRANKFURT
A. MAIN, INTERNATIONALER VERBAND FÜR
WOHNUNGSWESEN, 1935.
112P.

GERMAN, ENGLISH AND FRENCH.

1. SUBSISTENCE HOMESTEADS.

711.1
K82

SUBSISTENCE HOMESTEADS.
KUPPERS, GUSTAV ADOLF, 1891-
GESAMTDARSTELLUNG DES DEUTSCHEN
SIEDLUNGSWESENS IN ALLEN FORMEN UND
SPIELARTEN. BERLIN, DIE
GRUND-STUCKS-WARTE, 1933.
132P. (HIS DEUTSCHE SIEDLUNG, IDEE
UND WIRKLICHKEIT, V. 1)

BENUTZTE LITERATUR: P. 113-123.

1. SUBSISTENCE HOMESTEADS.
2. POPULATION SHIFTS - GERMANY.
I. TITLE: DEUTSCHE SIEDLUNG.

711.1
M82

Subsistance homesteads.
Münster. Universitat. Institut fur
Siedlungs- und Wohnungswesen.
Tätigkeitsbericht,
Sonderdruck nr.
Munster i. W.,
v.

For complete information see shelflist.

1. Subsistance homesteads.

711.1
A37

Subsistence homesteads.
U.S. Bureau of Agricultural Economics.
A place on earth: a critical appraisal of
subsistence homesteads. Editors: Russell
Lord [and] Paul H. Johnstone. Wash., 1942.
202p.

1. Subsistence homesteads. I. Lord,
Russell, ed. II. Johnstone, Paul H., ed.
III. Title.

690
H68
IME
no.63

Subsistence homesteads.
U.S. Dept. of Housing and Urban Develop-
ment.
Squatter settlements; the problem and the
opportunity. Prepared for the Agency for
International Development, by Charles Abrams.
Wash, 1966.
48p. (Its Ideas and methods exchange
no. 63- 302, Urban planning)
Bibliography: p. 45-48.

1. Building industry. 2. Subsistence
homesteads. I. U.S. Agency for international   Development.
II. Abrams,   Charles. III. Title.

VF
711.1
L11

Subsistence homesteads.
U.S. Bureau of Labor Statistics.
Housing under the resettlement
administration, Monthly Labor Review,
June 1937. Washington, Govt. Print. Off.,
1937.
14 p. illus. (Its Serial no. R576)

1. Subsistence homesteads. 2. U.S. Resettlement Administration.

711.1
L15

SUBSISTENCE HOMESTEADS.
U.S. BUREAU OF LAND MANAGEMENT.
HOMESTEADING, PAST AND PRESENT.
[WASHINGTON, 1959]
19P.

1. SUBSISTENCE HOMESTEADS.   I. TITLE.

711.1
N17

Subsistence homesteads.
U.S. National Park Service.
Prospector, cowhand, and sodbuster. Historic
places associated with the mining, ranching,
and farming frontiers in the Trans-Mississippi
West. Washington, U.S. Dept. of the Interior,
National Park Service, For sale by Supt. of
Doc., Govt. Print. Off., 1967.
320p. (The National survey of historic
sites and buildings. vol. 11)
Robert G. Ferris, series editor.

(Cont'd on next card)

711.1
N17

U.S. National Park Service. Prospector,
cowhand, and sodbuster...1967.
(Card 2)

1. Subsistence homesteads. 2. Natural
resources. 3. Architecture - Conservation and
restoration. 4. Site selection. I. Title.
II. Title: Historic places associated with the
mining, ranching and farming frontiers.

711.1
R27

SUBSISTENCE HOMESTEADS.
U.S. RESETTLEMENT ADMINISTRATION.
INTERIM REPORT. WASHINGTON, GOVT.
PRINT. OFF., 1936.
34P.

1. SUBSISTENCE HOMESTEADS.

711.1
S81
SUBSISTENCE HOMESTEADS.
U.S. DIVISION OF SUBSISTENCE HOUSING.
A HOMESTEAD AND HOPE. WASHINGTON,
GOVT. PRINT. OFF., 1935.
24P.

1. SUBSISTENCE HOMESTEADS.   I. TITLE.

SUBSTANDARD DWELLINGS (definition)
structures needing major repairs or unfit for
use or those lacking heating, lighting or private
bathroom facilities, or containing over 1.5 persons
per room and an extra family of two or more persons
(or either if renting for less than forty dollars
per month)

Chicago Land Use Survey of 1939.

711.33
C68su
Sub-state district systems.
Council of State Governments.
Sub-state district...   (Card 2)

1. State planning. I. National Governors'
Conference. (Committee on Executive Manage-
ment and Fiscal Affairs. Advisory Task
Force) II. U.S. HUD-CPRDP. III. Title.

711.1
W13
SUBSISTENCE HOMESTEADS.
WAGER, PAUL W
ONE FOOT ON THE SOIL; A STUDY OF
SUBSISTENCE HOMESTEADS IN ALABAMA.
TUSCALOOSA, BUREAU OF PUBLIC
ADMINISTRATION, UNIVERSITY OF ALABAMA,
230P.

1. SUBSISTENCE HOMESTEADS.   I. TITLE.

728.1
(767731)
L47
SUBSTANDARD HOUSING.
LITTLE ROCK, ARK. HOUSING AUTHORITY.
LITTLE ROCK'S SUBSTANDARD HOUSING;
A SUMMARY. LITTLE ROCK, ARK., 1952.
21P.

1. HOUSING - LITTLE ROCK, ARK.
I. TITLE: SUBSTANDARD HOUSING.

628.44
I57
Subsurface disposal of industrial wastes.
Interstate Oil Compact Commission.
Subsurface disposal of industrial wastes; a
study conducted by Research Committee, Interstate Oil Compact Commission. Oklahoma City,
1968.
109p.

1. Refuse and refuse disposal. I. Title.

711.1
W42
SUBSISTENCE HOMESTEADS.
WIENER SIEDLUNGSGESELLSCHAFT.
AUSTRIA IS HELPING HER UNEMPLOYED TO
HELP THEMSELVES. VIENNA, 1935.
32P.

TEXT IN ENGLISH AND GERMAN.

1. SUBSISTENCE HOMESTEADS.
2. EMPLOYMENT.   I. TITLE.

VF
728.1
(083.6)
H17
Substandard urban housing in United
States:
Hartman, George W   and John C   Hook.
Substandard urban housing in United
States: A quantitative analysis. Economic
geography, p. 95-114, April 1956.
graphs, maps, tables.

Reprint.

Bibliographical footnotes.

628.2
H43
Subsurface drainage.
Highway Research Board.
Subsurface drainage. Presented at the
thirtieth annual meeting, 1951. Wash.,
Highway Research Board, Div. of Engineering
and Industrial Research, National Research
Council, 1951.
20p.   (Its Bulletin no. 45)

1. Drainage. I. Title.

711.1
(016)
H15
SUBSISTENCE HOMESTEADS - BIBLIOGRAPHY.
HANNAY, ANNIE M   , COMP.
LAND SETTLEMENT; A LIST OF REFERENCES.
WASHINGTON, 1944.
167P. (U.S. DEPT. OF AGRICULTURE.
LIBRARY. LIBRARY LIST NO. 9)
PARTIALLY SUPPLEMENTS THE
BIBLIOGRAPHY ON LAND SETTLEMENT AND THE
BIBLIOGRAPHY ON LAND UTILIZATION, ISSUED
BY THE U.S. DEPT. OF AGRICULTURE IN
1934 AND 1938... RESPECTIVELY.
1. SUBSISTENCE HOMESTEADS -
BIBLIOGRAPHY.   2. LAND USE -
BIBLIOGRAPHY.   I. U.S. DEPT. OF
AGRICULTURE - LIBRARY. II. TITLE.

331.2
C65SU
1945
S-H
SUBSTANDARD WAGES.
U.S. CONGRESS. SENATE. COMMITTEE ON
EDUCATION AND LABOR.
SUBSTANDARD WAGES.   HEARINGS BEFORE A
SUBCOMMITTEE, SEVENTY-EIGHTH CONGRESS,
SECOND SESSION, PURSUANT TO S. CON. RES.
48, A RESOLUTION DETERMINING THAT A
STRAIGHT TIME HOURLY RATE OF 65 CENTS IS
THE MINIMUM BELOW WHICH THE NATIONAL WAR
LABOR BOARD SHALL CONSIDER ANY WAGE
SUBSTANDARD ... WASHINGTON, GOVT. PRINT.
OFF., 1945-
1 V.

CONTENTS.- PT .1. HEARINGS, NOV.
(CONTINUED ON NEXT CARD)

628.2
H43s
Subsurface drainage.
Highway Research Board.
Symposium on Subsurface Drainage; 7 reports.
Wash., Highway Research Board, Div. of Engi-
neering, National Research Council, National
Academy of Sciences, National Academy of
Engineering, 1967.
102p. (Its Highway research record no.
203)
Papers presented to the Symposium on Sub-
surface Drainage - Memorial to E.S. Barber,
Highway Research Board annual meeting, Jan.,
1967.
National Research Council. Publica-
tion 1534.
1. Drainage.   2. Soils. I. Title: Subsurface drainage.

711.1
(016)
A37
SUBSISTENCE HOMESTEADS - BIBLIOGRAPHY.
U.S. DEPT. OF AGRICULTURE.
BIBLIOGRAPHY ON LAND SETTLEMENT, WITH
PARTICULAR REFE..ENCE ON SMALL HOLDINGS
AND SUBSISTENCE HOMESTEADS, COMPILED BY
LOUISE O. BERCAW AND OTHERS - UNDER THE
DIRECTION OF MARY G. LACY. WASHINGTON,
GOVT. PRINT. OFF., 1934.
492P. (ITS MISCELLANEOUS PUBLICATION
NO. 172)

1. SUBSISTENCE HOMESTEADS -
BIBLIOGRAPHY.   I. BERCAW, LOUISE O.,
COMP. II. TITLE.

331.2
C65SU
1945
S-H
U.S. CONGRESS. SENATE. COMMITTEE ON
EDUCATION AND LABOR. SUBSTANDARD
WAGES....1945.   (CARD 2)

17-18, 1944.

1. WAGES AND SALARIES.   2. COST AND
STANDARD OF LIVING.   I. TITLE.

624.131
A75su
Subsurface investigations; soils.
U.S. Army. (Corps of Engineers)
Subsurface investigations; soils. Wash.,
1954.
17p. (Part DCXVIII, Chap. 3, March 1954;
EM 1110-2-1803)

At head of title: Engineering manual; civil
works construction.

1. Soils. I. Title.

711.1
S81
U.S. DIVISION OF SUBSISTENCE HOUSING.
A HOMESTEAD AND HOPE. WASHINGTON,
GOVT. PRINT. OFF., 1935.
24P.

1. SUBSISTENCE HOMESTEADS.   I. TITLE.

332.72
G25
Substantial benefits available...
U.S. General Accounting Office.
Substantial benefits available through earlier
collection of mortgage insurance premiums,
Federal Housing Administration, Dept. of Housing
and Urban Development; report to the Congress
by the Comptroller General of the United States.
Washington, 1968.
14p.

1. Mortgage finance. 2. U.S. Federal
Housing Administration. I. Title.

628.3
K44
Subsurface sewage disposal.
Kiker, John E   , Jr.
Subsurface sewage disposal. Gainesville,
Fla., Florida Engineering and Industrial
Experiment Station, December 1948.
72 p. illus., diagrs., tables. (Florida
Engineering and Industrial Experiment Station.
Bulletin no. 23)
"References": p. 68.

1. Sewerage and sewage disposal. 2. Septic tanks.
I. Florida. University. Engineering and Industrial
Experiment Station. II. Title.

658.3
C655
THE SUBSTANCE OF SUPERVISORY TRAINING.
CONNECTICUT. UNIVERSITY. SCHOOL OF
BUSINESS ADMINISTRATION.
THE SUBSTANCE OF SUPERVISORY TRAINING,
BY SIEGMAR F. BLAMBERG. STORRS, CONN.,
1961.
1 V. (VARIOUS PAGINGS) (ITS BULLETIN
NO. 10)

1. PERSONNEL MANAGEMENT.
I. BLAMBERG, SIEGMAR F.   II. TITLE.

711.33
C68su
Sub-state district systems.
Council of State Governments.
Sub-state district systems. A report
prepared for the National Governors' Con-
ference, Committee on Executive Management
and Fiscal Affairs, Advisory Task Force.
Lexington, Ky., 1971.
44p. (RM-468)
U.S. Dept. of Housing and Urban Development.
Comprehensive Planning Research and Demon-
stration Program.
NTIS PB 206 253.

(Cont'd on next card)

711.15
K82
SUBSURFACE TUNNEL ROAD EASEMENTS.
KUEHNLE, WALTER R
CASE STUDIES IN AIR RIGHTS AND
SUBSURFACE TUNNEL ROAD EASEMENTS, BY
WALTER R. KUEHNLE AND OTHERS.
CHICAGO, AMERICAN INSTITUTE OF REAL
ESTATE APPRAISERS, 1965.
39P.
PREPARED FOR EDUCATION PROGRAM,
AMERICAN INSTITUTE OF REAL ESTATE
APPRAISERS, 1964 CONVENTION, LOS
ANGELES.

1. AIR RIGHTS.   2. APPRAISAL.
I. AMERICAN INSTITUTE OF REAL ESTATE
(CONTINUED ON NEXT CARD)

711.15
K82
KUEHNLE, WALTER R CASE STUDIES IN ...
1965.   (CARD 2)

APPRAISERS.   II. TITLE.
III. TITLE: SUBSURFACE TUNNEL ROAD
EASEMENTS.

Class No.
Old codes
Suburbs ... on ...
official meeting of **Conference**
Accession No.

JUN 19 1950
Source
HHS
Received
JUN 28 1950
Cost

Purchase Order No.

Date

L. C. No.

Author (surname first) *Suburban Building Officials*
Title *Suburban building regulations for residences*

Place *Chicago 3, Ill.* Publisher *same*
Address *79 W. Monroe St. Room 1018*

Date *1949*   Pages   List Price   Est. Cost *gratis*

Edition or Series

Recommended by

Reviewed in *Ind. Civic Council Jan 1950*

H-305 (2-50)   HOUSING AND HOME FINANCE AGENCY: Office of the Administrator   16—61162-1 GPO

711.552
(74921)
F14
Suburban downtown in transition, a problem
in business change in Bergen County, N. J.
Fairleigh Dickinson University. Insti-
tute of Research.
Suburban downtown in transition, a
problem in business change in Bergen
County, New Jersey, by Samuel Pratt and
Lois Pratt. Rutherford, N. J., 1958.
113p. maps, tables.

1. Business districts - Bergen Co., N. J.
2. Shopping centers. I. Pratt, Samuel.
II. Pratt, Lois. III. Title.

VF
728
(94)
L15
Sub-tropical housing.
Langer, Karl
Sub-tropical housing. Brisbane, Australia,
Univ. of Queensland, May 1944.
12 p. diagrs., plans. (University of
Queensland. Faculty of Engineering. Papers, v. 1,
no. 7)

1. Architecture, Domestic-Australia. I. Queensland.
University. II. Title.

711.583
D51
THE SUBURBAN COMMUNITY.
DOBRINER, WILLIAM MANN, ED.
THE SUBURBAN COMMUNITY. NEW YORK,
PUTNAM, 1958.
416P.

1. SUBURBS.   I. TITLE.

VF
711.583
(747)
N28
Suburban growth in the New York area.
New York State Commerce Review, p. 11-17,
Nov. 1948.

1. Suburbs-New York, N.Y. 2. Population shifts-New York, N.Y.

SUBURB   (definition)

An outlying part of a city; a smaller place adjacent
to a city; the residential region or districts on the
outskirts of any city or large community.

(N.Y.S. Commerce Review, p. 8, May 1950)

711.14
(713541)
A25
SUBURBAN DESIGN.
Adler, Gerald M
Land planning by administrative regula-
tion; the policies of the Ontario
Municipal Board. Toronto, University of
Toronto Press, 1971.
246p.

1. Land use - Toronto. 2. Suburban
design. I. Ontario. Municipal Board.
II. Title.

728.3
P65FIFT
SUBURBAN HOMES.
POLLMAN, RICHARD B
50 SUBURBAN HOMES EDITION. DETROIT,
HOME PLANNERS, INC., 1963.
48P. (DESIGNS FOR CONVENIENT
LIVING, BOOK NO. 45)

1. ARCHITECTURE, DOMESTIC - DESIGNS
AND PLANS. I. TITLE: SUBURBAN HOMES.

SUBURB: (definition)

...a population center "which is under the town to
which it is attached". It has no independent life in
the sense that a city has, and when it achieves such
independence and insofar as it achieves it, it ceases
to be a suburb.

(Dahir, Communities for better living, p. 106)

711.4
(79467)
H17
Suburban development as a stochastic process.
Harris, Curtis C
Suburban development as a stochastic
process. Berkeley, Calif., Center for Real
Estate and Urban Economics, Institute of
Urban and Regional Development, University
of California, 1966.
87p. (Center for Real Estate and
Urban Economics, Institute of Urban and
Regional Development. University of
California, Berkeley. Technical report
no. 1)

(Continued on   next card)

711.583
(485)
C17
Suburban housing in Sweden.
Carrier, Michael
Suburban housing in Sweden, by Michael
Carrier, ARIBA [Associate of the Royal Insti-
tute of British Architecture] [n.p.] 1965.
[3]p.
Reprinted from OAP, Nov. 1965, p. 1570-
1572.

1. Suburbs - Sweden. 2. City planning -
Sweden. I. Title.

711.4
:670
S81o
c.1 E.0.
Suburban Action Institute.
Open or closed suburbs: corporate location
and the urban crisis. White Plains, N.Y.,
[1971?]
34p.
Contents.-Corporate location and the urban
crisis, by William H. Brown.-Plant location:
a corporate social responsibility, by Samuel
C. Jackson, Assistant Secretary for Metropolitan
Planning and Development.-Corporate relocation
to restrictive suburbs, by John H. Powell, Jr.
1. Industrial location. 2. Employment -

(Cont'd on next card)

711.4
(79467)
H17
Harris, Curtis C   Suburban development
as a stochastic process...1966. (Card 2)

1. City growth - Berkeley, Calif.
2. Suburbs - Berkeley, Calif. 3. Land use -
Berkeley, Calif. I. California. University.
Institute of Urban and Regional Development.
II. Title.

711.583
G26
Suburban idyll; tree, sunlight, traffic ...
George Washington University Magazine.
Suburban idyll: tree, sunlight, traffic
fumes. Wash , Office of Public Relations,
George Washington University, 1969.
36p.

Entire issue, Winter, 1969-70.

1. Suburbs. I. Title.

711.4
:670
S81o
Suburban Action Institute. Open or...1971?.
(Card 2)

Minority groups. 3. Minority groups -
Housing. I. Title. II. Brown, William H.
Corporate location and the urban crisis.
III. Jackson, Samuel C. Plant location:
a corporate social responsibility.

711.33
(7511)
C76
Suburban development in metropolitan northern
Delaware.
Crosswhite, William M
Suburban development in metropolitan
northern Delaware, by William M. Crosswhite
and Gerald F. Vaughn. Newark, Del.,
Agricultural Experiment Station, Cooperative
Extension Service, University of Delaware,
1966.
26p. (Delaware. Agricultural Experi-
ment Station. Cooperative bulletin no. 3)

1. State planning - Delaware. 2. Population - Delaware. 3. Suburbs.
I. Vaughn,   Gerald F. jt.au.
II. Delaware.   Agricultural Experiment. Station.   III. Title.

711.583
C65S
1965
H=H
SUBURBAN LAND DEVELOPMENT
CORPORATION.
U.S. CONGRESS. HOUSE. COMMITTEE ON
AGRICULTURE.
SUBURBAN LAND DEVELOPMENT
CORPORATION. HEARINGS BEFORE THE
SUBCOMMITTEE ON CONSERVATION AND
CREDIT. EIGHTY-NINETH CONGRESS, FIRST
SESSION, ON H.R. 7500. WASHINGTON,
GOVT. PRINT. OFF., 1965.
46P.

HEARINGS HELD JUNE 1 AND 23, 1965.
1. SUBURBS. 2. LAND USE.
I. TITLE.

711.583
N28s
The suburban apartment boom;
Neutze, Max.
The suburban apartment boom; case study of
a land use problem. Resources for the Future.
Distributed by Johns Hopkins Press. Wash.,
1968.
170p.

1. Apartment houses. 2. Suburbs. 3. Land
use. I. Resources for the Future. II. Title.

711.583
(485)
P17
The suburban development process in a large
Swedish city.
Pass, David.
Vallingby and Farsta: from idea to reality;
the suburban development process in a large
Swedish city. [Stockholm] Rikets Allmänna
Kartverk, 1969.
494p.
On cover: National Swedish building
research.
Bibliography: p. 475-494.
1. Suburbs - Sweden. I. Sweden. Rikets
Allmänna Kartverk. II. Title. III. Title:
The suburban development process in a large
Swedish city.

333.38
S81
SUBURBAN MARYLAND BUILDERS ASSOCIATION.
LAND DEVELOPMENT REPORT AND SCHEDULE.
SILVER SPRING, MD., 1964.
2L. 2 CHARTS IN POCKET.

1. SUBDIVISION. I. TITLE.

690
(752)
S61
Suburban Maryland Builders Association.
The Suburban Maryland Builders Association, ninth anniversary. Silver Spring, 1963.
37p.

1. Building industry - Maryland. 2. Housing - Associations.

711.417
C65s
U.S. Congress. House. Committee on Banking and Currency...1949.
(Card 2)

Hearings held March 18 and 24, 1949.

1. Garden cities. 2. Greenbelt, Md. I. Title.

744
S61
Suburban Washington library film service.
Suburban Washington Library Film Service.
Suburban Washington library film service. [n.p.] 1969.
309p. (Its Catalog 70-71)

1. Films. 2. Libraries - District of Columbia metropolitan area. I. Title.

388
(7731)
G72
A suburban mayor looks at rapid transit....
Greisdorf, Myron.
A suburban mayor looks at rapid transit; address before Institute for Rapid Transit, third Annual Meeting, Washington, D.C., May 14. [n.p.] 1964.
6p.

1. Transportation - Skokie, Ill. 2. Journey to work. I. Institute for Rapid Transit. Meeting, Washington, 1964. II. Title.

728.1
(771
1308)
T74
SUBURBAN RESIDENTIAL DEVELOPMENTS. TRI-COUNTY REGIONAL PLANNING COMMISSION (MEDINA, SUMMIT, PORTAGE COUNTIES, OHIO)
A SURVEY OF ANALYSIS OF THE PHYSICAL-ECONOMIC CHARACTERISTICS OF SELECTED RECENT SUBURBAN RESIDENTIAL DEVELOPMENTS AND THE SOCIO-ECONOMIC CHARACTERISTICS OF THEIR INHABITANTS. AKRON, OHIO, 1965. 103P. (ITS REGIONAL PLANNING STUDY NO. 34)

1. HOUSING MARKET - OHIO. I. U.S. URA-UPAP. OHIO. II. TITLE. SUBURBAN RESIDENTIAL DEVELOPMENTS.

058.7
(05)
A75
Suburban Washington union periodical list.
Arlington County, Va. Dept. of Libraries.
Suburban Washington union periodical list. Arlington, 1971.
180p.

1. Periodicals - Directories. I. Title.

728.1
(74461)
I57
The suburban noose.
Interfaith Housing Corp.
The suburban noose: a story of nonprofit housing development for the modest-income family in metropolitan Boston. [Boston] 1969.
43p.
U.S. Dept. of Housing and Urban Development. Low-Income Housing Demonstration Grant Program. (Mass. LIHD-4)

1. Low-income housing - Boston. 2. Non-profit housing organizations. 3. Suburbs - Boston. I. U.S. HUD-Low-Income Housing Demonstration Grant Program. Boston. II. Title.

711.552.1
(016)
M92
1970
Suburban shopping centers.
Myers, Robert H
Suburban shopping centers. Rev. Wash., Small Business Administration, 1970.
11p. (Small business bibliography no. 27)

Bibliography: p. 7-11.

1. Shopping centers - Bibl. I. U.S. Small Business Administration. II. Title.

711.583
(79549)
T37
The suburban zone of metropolitan Portland, Oregon.
Throop, Vincent M
The suburban zone of metropolitan Portland, Oregon. Chicago, Univ. of Chicago, 1948.
244p.
Thesis: University of Chicago.

1. Suburbs - Portland, Or. I. Chicago. University. II. Title.

711.4
G662
SUBURBAN PLANNING.
GOODALL, MERRILL, ED.
SUBURBAN PLANNING; THREE STUDIES. CLAREMONT, CALIF., CLAREMONT ADMINISTRATIVE STUDIES, 1962.
63P.

CONTENTS.- PT.1. THE CLAREMONT PLANNING COMMISSION, BY ENID HART DOUGLASS.- PT.2. THE ELECTION CASE BY FRANK J. TYSEN.- PT.3. RECREATION PLANNING, BY DAVID STERN.

1. CITY PLANNING. I. TITLE. II. DOUGLASS, ENID HART.
(CONTINUED ON NEXT CARD)

711.583
(71354)
C51
The suburban society.
Clark, S D
The suburban society. [Toronto, Can.?] University of Toronto Press, 1966.
233p.

1. Suburbs - Toronto. 2. Sociology, Urban. I. Title.

711.5
1347
B11
SUBURBAN ZONING AND THE APARTMENT BOOM.
BABCOCK, RICHARD F
SUBURBAN ZONING AND THE APARTMENT BOOM, BY RICHARD F. BABCOCK AND FRED P. BOSSELMAN. WASHINGTON, NATIONAL ASSOCIATION OF HOME BUILDERS, 1963.
1040-1091P.

ON COVER: THE COMPENDIUM OF MULTI-FAMILY HOUSING.
REPRINTED FROM THE UNIVERSITY OF PENNSYLVANIA LAW REVIEW, V. 3, NO. 8, JUNE 1963.

1. ZONING. 2. APARTMENT HOUSES.
(CONTINUED ON NEXT CARD)

711.4
G662
GOODALL, MERRILL, ED. SUBURBAN PLANNING ...1962.
(CARD 2)

III. TYSEN, FRANK J. IV. STERN, DAVID.

VF - Shopping center

DATE OF REQUEST 10/16/53   L. C. CARD NO.

AUTHOR

TITLE The suburban store.

SERIES Reprint, Jewelers Circ, Aug. 1953, p. 122-33.

EDITION   PUB. DATE   PAGING
PUBLISHER

RECOMMENDED BY   REVIEWED IN LJ 9/12/53 p. 20

ORDER RECORD

711.5
1347
B11
BABCOCK, RICHARD F SUBURBAN ZONING AND ...1963.
(CARD 2)

I. BOSSELMAN, FRED P II. NATIONAL ASSOCIATION OF HOME BUILDERS. III. TITLE.

711.583
(791)
M12
Suburban problem solving.
McGaw, Dickinson L
Suburban problem solving: an information system for Tempe, Arizona. Tempe, Institute of Public Administration, Arizona State University, 1971.
135p. (Papers in public administration, no. 20)
1. Suburbs - Tempe, Ariz. 2. City planning - Tempe, Ariz. I. Arizona. State University, Tempe. Institute of Public Administration. II. Title.

711.583
D68
The suburban trend.
Douglass, Harlan Paul.
The suburban trend. New York, Arno Press and the New York Times, 1970, 1925.
340p. (The rise of urban America)

Bibliography: p. 335-340.

1. Suburbs. 2. City growth. I. Title.
(Series: The rise of urban America)

VF
353
(74744)
F74
"Suburbanitis" in Schenectady County.
Friedman, Albert L
"Suburbanitis" in Schenectady County. [Schenectady, N. Y., Schenectady Real Estate Board, Inc., 1956]
[42] p.

"The following series of articles appeared in the schenectady (sic.) Union-Star in 1955" ...

711.417
C65s
Suburban resettlement projects.
U.S. Congress. House. Committee on Banking and Currency.
Suburban resettlement projects. Hearings before the Committee on Banking and Currency, House of Representatives, Eighty-first Congress, first session on H.R. 2440 a bill to authorize the Public Housing Commissioner to sell the suburban resettlement projects known as Greenbelt, Md.; Greendale, Wis.: and Greenhills, Ohio, without regard to provisions of law requiring competitive bidding or public advertising. Wash., Govt. Print. Off., 1949.
60p.
(Cont'd on next card)

744
S61
Suburban Washington Library Film Service.
Suburban Washington library film service. [n.p.] 1969.
309p. (Its Catalog 70-71)

1. Films. 2. Libraries - District of Columbia metropolitan area. I. Title.

388
(74797)
N67
Suburbanization of industry.
Notess, Charles B
Suburbanization of industry, residential segregation, and access to employment opportunities; preliminary report, by Charles B. Notess and Robert E. Paaswell. Buffalo, Dept. of Civil Engineering, State University of New York at Buffalo, 1969.
1v.
Cover title: The mobility of inner city residents; a preliminary report.
Sponsor: New York State Science and Technology Foundation.
(Cont'd on next card)

388
(74797)
N67

Notess, Charles B   Suburbanization of
industry...1969.   (Card 2)

1. Transportation - Buffalo. 2. Journey
to work. 3. Employment - Minority groups.
I. Paaswell, Robert E., jt. au. II. New York
(State) University, Buffalo. Dept. of Civil
Engineering. III. New York (State) Science
and Technology Foundation. IV. Title.

711.3
H68
no. 68-4

Suburbia and urbia.
U.S. Dept. of Housing and Urban Development.
Suburbia and urbia: community diversity in
the Birmingham metropolitan area, by Jerome
P. Pickard. Wash., 1968.
29p. (Its Background paper 68-4)

1. Metropolitan areas. 2. Metropolitan
areas - Birmingham, Ala. 3. Employment -
Birmingham, Ala. I. Pickard, Jerome P.
II. Title.

711.58:
W66

Suburbia, its people and their politics.
Wood, Robert Coldwell.
Suburbia, its people and their politics.
Boston, Houghton, 1958.
340p.

1. Suburbs. 2. Metropolitan areas.
3. Local government. I. Title.

711.4
:67
827

Suburbanization of manufacturing activity
within standard metropolitan areas.
Scripps Foundation for Research in Population
Problems.
Suburbanization of manufacturing activity
within standard metropolitan areas, by Evelyn
M. Kitagawa and Donald J. Bogue. [Oxford,
Ohio] Scripps Foundation for Research in
Population Problems, Miami Univ., and Population
Research and Training Center, Univ. of Chicago.
[1955]
162 p.   (Its Studies in population
distribution, no. 9).

711.3
H68
no. 68-MI-R

Suburbia and urbia.
U.S. Dept. of Housing and Urban Development.
Suburbia and urbia: community diversity
in the South Bend, Ind., metropolitan area,
by James F. Miller. Wash., 1968.
18p. (Its Background paper 68-MI-R)
1. Metropolitan areas. 2. Metropolitan
areas - South Bend, Ind. 3. Family income
and expenditure - South Bend, Ind.
I. Miller, James F. II. Title.

VF
711.583
(753)
S85

Suburbia 1960.
Sunday Star.
Suburbia 1960. Washington, 1959.
[5] pts. in folder.

Contents: Arlington booming as metro
center; county planning expansion of its
modern services, by Paul Hope. Sept. 13,
1959, p. A-15. Fairfax is fastest growing
area, by Mary Lou Werner and Jack Kelso.
Sept. 27, 1959, p. A-21. Past, present
meet in Alexandria; old city keeps much of
its ancient charm but new problems have
followed postwar growth, by John Barron.
Oct. 11, 1959, p. B-6. Montgomery
sees pros-   perity; county attracts
(Continued on next card)

711.4
:67
827

Scripps Foundation for Research in Population
Problems.   Suburbanization of manufacturing ...
[1955]   (Card 2)

"Research and studies forming the basis for
this monograph were performed pursuant to a
contract with the Office of the Administrator,
Housing and Home Finance Agency (project no.
0-U-66) ..." - cf. p. iii.

711.3
H68
no.68-3

Suburbia and urbia.
U.S. Dept. of Housing and Urban Development.
Suburbia and urbia: "homogenized" communities
and geographic diversity in the San Bernardino-
Riverside-Ontario SMSA, by Jerome P. Pickard.
Wash., 1968.
31p. (Its Background paper 68-3)

1. Metropolitan areas. 2. Metropolitan areas
- San Bernardino Co., Calif. 3. Community
development - San Bernardino Co., Calif.
I. Pickard, Jerome P. II. Title.

VF
711.583
(753)
S85

Sunday Star.
Suburbia 1960. ... 1959. (Card 2)

new developments, by Anne H. Christmas.
Sept. 20, 1959, p. B-7.

1. Suburbs - District of Columbia. 2. Metropolitan
areas - District of Columbia. I. Title.

711.4
:67
827s

Suburbanization of service industries within
standard metropolitan areas
Scripps Foundation for Research in Population
Problems.
Suburbanization of service industries
within standard metropolitan areas, by Raymond
P. Cuzzort.   [Oxford, Ohio] Scripps Foundation
for Research in Population Problems, Miami
Univ., and Population Research and Training
Center, Univ. of Chicago [1955]
71 p.   graphs, maps, tables.   (Its
Studies in population distribution, no. 10)
"Research and studies forming the basis for
this monograph were performed pursuant to a con-
tract with the Office of the Administrator, Housing and Home Finance Agency (project no. 0-U-66)..
- cf. p. iv.

711.3
H68
No. 68-8

Suburbia and urbia: median ages of major
suburbs in U.S. metropolitan areas (1965)
U.S. Dept. of Housing and Urban Development.
Suburbia and urbia: median ages of major
suburbs in U.S. metropolitan areas (1965) by
Jerome P. Pickard and James M. Schneider.
Wash., 1968.
[43] p.   (Its Background paper 68-8)

1. Metropolitan areas. 2. Suburbs.
I. Pickard, Jerome P. II. Schneider, James M.
III. Title.

Suburbs (geographic subdivision)
xx   City planning
xx   Subdivision
sa   Municipal services
sa and xx Annexation
sa and xx City growth
sa and xx Fringe areas
sa and xx Garden cities
sa and xx Metropolitan area planning
sa and xx Metropolitan areas
sa and xx New towns
sa and xx Satellite cities

711.3
H68
no.
68-1

Suburbia and urbia.
U.S. Dept. of Housing and Urban Development.
Suburbia and urbia: a study in contrast and
diversity among community types in the
Chicago metropolitan area, by Jerome P.
Pickard. [Washington] 1968.
25p. (Background paper 68-1)

1. Metropolitan areas. 2. Metropolitan
areas - Chicago. 3. Housing - Chicago.
I. Pickard, Jerome P. II. Title.

711.3
H68
No. 68-7

Suburbia and urbia: suburban functions.
U.S. Dept. of Housing and Urban Development.
Suburbia and urbia: suburban functions: an
analysis of major suburbs in U.S. metropolitan areas (1963/65) by Jerome P. Pickard.
Wash. 1968.
[30] p. (Its Background paper 68-7)

1. Metropolitan areas. 2. Suburbs.
3. City growth. I. Pickard, Jerome P.
II. Title.

711.583
B27

SUBURBS.
BERGER, BENNETT M
THE MYTH OF SUBURBIA. URBANA,
UNIVERSITY OF ILLINOIS, 1959.
21P.

1. SUBURBS. 2. HOUSING - SOCIAL
ASPECTS. I. TITLE.

711.3
H68
no. 68-5

Suburbia and urbia: community diversity in
the Kansas City metropolitan area.
U.S. Dept. of Housing and Urban Development.
Suburbia and urbia: community diversity in
the Kansas City metropolitan area, by Jerome
P. Pickard. Wash., 1968.
32p. (Its Background paper 68-5)

1. Metropolitan areas. 2. Metropolitan areas -
Kansas City, Mo. 3. Suburbs. I. Pickard,
Jerome P. II. Title.

711.3
H68
no. 68-6

Suburbia and urbia.
U.S. Dept. of Housing and Urban Development.
Suburbia and urbia: urbanized area and
plateau communities in the Johnstown, Pa.
metropolitan area, by Jerome P. Pickard.
Wash. 1968.
28p. (Its Background paper 68-6)
1. Metropolitan areas - Johnstown, Pa.
2. Community development - Johnstown, Pa.
I. Pickard, Jerome P. II. Title.

VF
728.3
B27

Suburbs.
Better Homes and Gardens.
The new house next door; a report ... on
the new homes families are building, furnishing,
and equipping today for their own occupancy.
Des Moines, Iowa, Meredith, c1950.
66 p.   illus. diagrs.

"This study is the third in a series made by
Better Homes and Gardens with the cooperation of
the F.W. Dodge Corporation." - p.5.

1. Architecture, Domestic-Surveys. 2. Owner-built
houses (contractor). 3. Basements. 4. Suburbs.
I. Dodge (F.W.) Corporation. II. Title.

711.3
H68
no. 68-2

Suburbia and urbia.
U.S. Dept. of Housing and Urban Development.
Suburbia and urbia: community diversity in
the Newark metropolitan area, by Jerome P.
Pickard. [Washington] 1968.
22p. (Its Background paper 68-2)

1. Metropolitan areas. 2. Metropolitan
areas - Newark. I. Pickard, Jerome P.
II. Title.

711.583
G65

Suburbia: civic denial; a portrait in urban
civilization.
Goldston, Robert.
Suburbia: civic denial; a portrait in urban
civilization. Illustrated by Donald Carrick.
New York, Macmillan, 1970.
184p.

1. Suburbs. 2. Metropolitan area planning.
3. Land use. I. Title.

711.3
B47

SUBURBS.
Birch, David L
The future of American cities - and suburbs.
New York, MGIC Investment Corp., 1971.
[4]p.
The MGIC newsletter, May, 1971.

1. City growth. 2. Suburbs. I. Mortgage
Guarantee Insurance Corp. II. MGIC
newsletter. III. Title.

Suburbs.

711.583
C17   Carver, Humphrey.
        Cities in suburbs. [Toronto] University
        of Toronto Press, 1962.
        120p.

        1. Suburbs.   2. Metropolitan areas.
        I. Title.

Suburbs.

711.583
C66e   Cooke, Alistair.
        The eagle in the square. Mr. Alistair
        Cooke gives the RIBA annual discourse.
        Reproduced from the Builder, May 26, 1961.
        p. 988-989.

        1. Suburbs.   2. City growth.   I. Royal
        Institute of British Architects.

711.585   SUBURBS.
D617   DOBRINER, WILLIAM M
        CLASS IN SUBURBIA. ENGLEWOOD
        CLIFFS, N.J., PRENTICE-HALL, 1963.
        166P.

        1. SUBURBS.   2. HOUSING - SOCIAL
        ASPECTS. I. TITLE.

Suburbs.

353
C34   Chinitz, Benjamin, ed.
        City and suburb; the economics of
        metropolitan growth. Englewood Cliffs,
        N.J., Prentice-Hall, 1964.
        181p.   (Modern economic issues)

        Bibliography: p. 179-181.

        1. Metropolitan areas.   2. Transportation -
        Metropolitan areas.   3. Sociology, Urban.
        4. Suburbs. I. Title.

Suburbs.

352
068   Coulter, Philip B
        Politics of metropolitan areas: selected
        readings. New York, Crowell 1967.
        497p.
        Bibliography: p. 479-497.
        Partial contents: Suburban decision-making
        [and] Suburban no-party politics, by Robert C.
        Wood, Under Secretary of U.S. Dept. of Hous-
        ing and Urban Development.

        (Cont'd on next card)

Suburbs.

711.583
D51   DOBRINER, WILLIAM MANN, ED.
        THE SUBURBAN COMMUNITY. NEW YORK,
        PUTNAM, 1958.
        416P.

        1. SUBURBS.   I. TITLE.

711.583   SUBURBS.
C51   Clawson, Marion.
        Suburban land conversion in the United
        States: an economic and governmental process.
        Baltimore, Published for Resources for the
        Future by the Johns Hopkins Press, 1971.
        406p.

        1. Suburbs. I. Resources for the Future.
        II. Title.

352
068   Coulter, Philip B. Politics of metropolitan
        areas: selected readings...1967.
                            (Card 2)

        1. Local government.   2. Metropolitan
        government.   3. Intergovernmental relations.
        4. Suburbs.   5. Minority groups.   6. Democracy.
        I. Wood, Robert Coldwell. Suburban decision-
        making. II. Wood, Robert Coldwell. Suburban
        no-party politics. III. Title.

711.583   SUBURBS.
D68   Douglass, Harlan Paul.
        The suburban trend. New York, Arno Press
        and the New York Times, 1970, 1925.
        340p. (The rise of urban America)

        Bibliography: p. 335-340.

        1. Suburbs.   2. City growth.   I. Title.
        (Series: The rise of urban America)

728
:392   Suburbs.
C52   Clements (Mark) Research, inc.
        Upper level suburbia series of studies,
        conducted for House & Garden. New York,
        1960.
        33p. (House & Garden research report
        no. 2613)

        1. Family living requirements. 2. Suburbs.
        I. House & Garden. II. Title.

711.33   Suburbs.
(7511)
C76   Crosswhite, William M
        Suburban development in metropolitan
        northern Delaware, by William M. Crosswhite
        and Gerald F. Veughn. Newark, Del.,
        Agricultural Experiment Station, Cooperative
        Extension Service, University of Delaware,
        1966.
        26p.   (Delaware. Agricultural Experi-
        ment Station. Cooperative bulletin no. 3)

        1. State planning - Delaware. 2. Popula-
        tion - Delaware. 3. Suburbs.
        I. Veughn,   Gerald F. jt.au.
        II. Delaware,   Agricultural Experi-
        ment. Station.   III. Title.

711.583   Suburbs.
E71   Erber, Ernest.
        Suburbia, a passing phenomenon?
        An address delivered to the students
        of the College of Business Administration
        at Fairleigh Dickinson University, Rutherford,
        New Jersey, March 9, 1961.
        21p.

        1 Suburbs.

711.583   SUBURBS.
C645   COMMONWEALTH CONFERENCE, UNIVERSITY OF
        OREGON, 1942.
        THE RURAL-URBAN FRINGE, PROCEEDINGS,
        APRIL 16-17, 1942. EUGENE, UNIVERSITY
        OF OREGON, 1942.
        80P.

        1. SUBURBS.   2. LAND USE - OREGON.
        I. TITLE.

711.581   Suburbs.
C85   Cunningham, James V
        The resurgent neighborhood. Notre Dame,
        Ind., Fides Publishers, 1965.
        224p.

        1. Neighborhood planning. 2. City
        planning - Social aspects. 4. Social
        conditions. 5. Suburbs. I. Title.

711.4   Suburbs.
F15   Faltermayer, Edmund K
        Redoing America: a nationwide report on how
        to make our cities and suburbs livable. New
        York, Harper & Row, 1968.
        242p.
        Bibliography: p. 228-234.

              1. City planning. 2. Metropolitan areas.
        3. Suburbs. 4. Air pollution. 5. Water pollution.
        6. Climate and health. 7. Metropolitan government.
        I. Title. II. Title: How to make our cities and
        suburbs livable.

711.583
C65g   Suburbs.
        Connecticut. University. Institute of Public
        Service.
        Growing suburbs and town finance; a study
        of the effect of suburban growth on property tax
        expenditures in four Connecticut towns [by]
        Beldon H. Schaffer. Storrs, Conn., Nov. 1954.
        vi, 291.   tables.
        Processed.

        1. Suburbs. 2. Municipal services. 3. Survey
        methods. I. Schaffer, Beldon H. II. Title.

711.4   Suburbs.
D13
        Dahir, James, 1904-
        Communities for better living; citizen achievement in
        organization, design and development. [1st ed.] New York,
        Harper [1950]
        xiv, 321 p. illus., plans. 22 cm.
        Bibliography: p. 288-311.
        Individual local groups and organizations are
        discussed.
        For full tracing see main entry card.

        1. Cities and towns-Planning. 2. Community organization
        3. U.S.A.

        NA9030.D3   711   50-7171
        Library of Congress   [50h10]

333.38'   SUBURBS.
F47S   FISHER, ERNEST M
        SPECULATION IN SUBURBAN LANDS.   1933.
        P. 152-162.

        REPRINTED FROM AMERICAN ECONOMIC
        REVIEW, SUPPLEMENT, V. 23, NO. 1, MARCH
        1933.

        1. SUBDIVISION.   2. SUBURBS.
        I. TITLE.

711.583
C65   Suburbs.
        Connecticut. University. Institute of Public
        Service.
        Small homes and community growth; a study
        of the small low cost home -- community asset
        or liability [by] Beldon H. Schaffer. Storrs,
        Conn. [Sept. 1954]
        vi, 20 l.   tables.
        Processed.

        1. Suburbs. 2. Municipal services. 3. Survey
        methods. I. Schaffer, Beldon H. II. Title.
        III. Title: The   low cost home, com-
        munity asset or liability.

388
D15   Danielson, Michael N
        Federal metropolitan politics and the
        commuter crisis. New York, Columbia
        University Press, 1965.
        244p. (Metropolitan political
        series no. 2)

        1. Transportation. 2. Metropolitan area planning.
        3. Intergovernmental relations. 4. Suburbs.
        5. Journey to work. 6 U.S. Housing and Home
        Finance Agency.   I. Title.

Suburbs.

711.583
G15   Gans, Herbert J
        The white exodus to suburbia steps up.
        Reproduced from the New York Times magazine,
        January 7, 1968. p. 25, 88-89, 92 and [94]

        1. Suburbs. 2. City growth. 3. Minority
        groups. I. New York Times magazine. II. Title.

711.583
G26

SUBURBS.
George Washington University Magazine.
Suburban idyll: tree, sunlight, traffic
fumes. Wash., Office of Public Relations,
George Washington University, 1969.
36p.

Entire issue, Winter, 1969-70.

1. Suburbs. I. Title.

360
L21

Suburbs.
League of Women Voters of the United States.
Will the suburbs house their poor? [n.p.]
1965.
20p.

1. Social welfare. 2. Suburbs.
3. Housing statistics. I. Title.

711.583
N287

SUBURBS.
NEWSWEEK.
THE NEW AMERICA: SUBURBIA - EXURBIA
- URBIA. NEW YORK, NEWSWEEK, 1957.
1 v.

REPRINT FROM NEWSWEEK MAGAZINE:
APRIL 1, JUNE 3, AND SEPT. 2, 1957.

1. SUBURBS. 2. CITY GROWTH.
I. TITLE: THE NEW AMERICA: SUBURBIA
- EXURBIA - URBIA.

658.83
G26

Suburbs.
Georgia. State College of Business Administration. Bureau of Business and Economic
Research.
Marketing implications of interurban development, by Stephen Paranka. Atlanta, 1958.
39p. tables. (Its Research paper series
no. 11)

1. Marketing. 2. Suburbs. I. Paranka,
Stephen.

649
L67

SUBURBS.
LOTH, DAVID.
CRIME IN THE SUBURBS. NEW YORK, MORROW,
1967.
266P.

1. JUVENILE DELINQUENCY. 2. SUBURBS.
I. TITLE.

VF
728.1
:325
O12

Suburbs.
Oberdorfer, Don.
Will Negroes crack the suburbs? by Don
Oberdorfer and Milton MacKaye. Armed with
Kennedy's mandate, Robert Weaver plans to
free Negroes from the city ghettos. In
Saturday Evening Post, Dec. 22-29, 1962.
p. 71-73.

1. Minority groups - Housing. 2. Suburbs.
I. MacKaye, Milton, jt. au.

711.583
G65

SUBURBS.
Goldston, Robert.
Suburbia: civic denial; a portrait in urban
civilization. Illustrated by Donald Carrick.
New York, Macmillan, 1970.
184p.

1. Suburbs. 2. Metropolitan area planning.
3. Land use. I. Title.

339.5
N17s
1967

Suburbs.
National Conference on Soil, Water, and
Suburbia, Washington, D.C., 1967.
Soil, water, and suburbia. A report of
the proceedings of the Conference, sponsor-
ed by the U.S. Dept. of Agriculture and the
U.S. Dept. of Housing and Urban Development,
June 15-16, 1967. Washington, For sale by
the Supt. of Docs., Govt. Print. Off.,
1968.
160p.
Chairman: Robert C. Wood, Under Secretary,
Dept. of Housing and Urban Development.

(Continued on next card)

728.1
N176b
no.2

Suburbs.
Raymond & May Associates.
Land development decisions in suburban
areas; three case studies of planning and
zoning decisions in the New York suburbs.
White Plains, N.Y., 1968.
1v. (Background paper [no.2] for U.S.
National Commission on Urban Problems)

1. Housing. 2. Subdivision regulation.
3. Suburbs. I. U.S. National Commission
on Urban Problems. II. Title.

301.15
G72

Suburbs.
Green, Constance McLaughlin.
The rise of urban America. New York,
Harper & Row, 1965.
208p.

1. City growth. 2. Suburbs. 3. Negroes.
4. Race relations. 5. Sociology, Urban.
I. Title.

399.5
N17s
1967

National Conference on Soil, Water, and
Suburbia, Washington, D.C., 1967.
Soil, water, and suburbia... (Card 2)

Partial contents: Federal-State-Local
partnership in suburban development, by
R. C. Weaver, Secretary, Dept. of Housing
and Urban Development.-The suburban land
resource and its use, by Philip J. Maloney,
Deputy Commissioner, Mortgage Credit and
Federal Housing, U.S. Dept. of Housing and
Urban Development. Community action:
achieving the livable suburb, by
H. Ralph Taylor, Assistant Secretary,
(Continued on next card)

711.5
R19

Suburbs.
Raymond and May Associates.
Zoning controversies in the suburbs; three
case studies. Prepared for the consideration
of the National Commission on Urban Problems.
Wash., Govt. Print. Off., 1968.
82p. (U.S. National Commission on Urban
Problems. Research report no.11)
Paul H. Douglas, chairman.

1. Zoning. 2. Land use. 3. Suburbs.
I. Douglas, Paul H. II. U.S. National Commission on Urban Problems. III. Title.

711.4
G78

Suburbs.
Gruen, Victor, 1903-
The heart of our cities; the urban
crisis: diagnosis and cure. New York,
Simon and Schuster, 1964.
368p.

Bibliography: p. 348-351.

1. City planning. 2. Suburbs.
3. Transportation. 4. Journey to work.
5. Traffic. 6. Shopping centers. I. Title.

339.5
N17s
1967

National Conference on Soil, Water, and
Suburbia, Washington, D.C. 1967.
Soil, water, and suburbia... (Card 3)

U.S. Dept. of Housing and Urban Development.

1. Soils. 2. Water-supply. 3. Suburbs.
4. Community development. I. Weaver,
Robert Clifton. Federal-State-Local partnership in suburban development. II. Maloney,
Philip J. The suburban land resource and
its use. III. Taylor, H. Ralph. Community
action:

(Continued on next card)

VF
711.583
(O4)
S23

Suburbs.
Schnore, Leo F
The functions of metropolitan suburbs.
American Journal of Sociology, p. 453-458.
Mar. 1956. tables.
Reprint.
Contains bibliographical footnotes.
"Paper read at the annual meeting of the
Regional Science Association, New York City
Dec. 30, 1955."

352.5
(774)
J15

SUBURBS.
JANS, RALPH T
. THE URBAN FRINGE PROBLEM: SOLUTIONS
UNDER MICHIGAN LAW. ANN ARBOR, MICH.,
BUREAU OF GOVERNMENT, INSTITUTE OF
PUBLIC ADMINISTRATION, UNIVERSITY OF
MICHIGAN, 1957.
57P. (MICHIGAN PAMPHLETS NO. 26)

1. FRINGE AREAS - MICHIGAN.
2. SUBURBS. I. MICHIGAN. UNIVERSITY.
INSTITUTE OF PUBLIC ADMINISTRATION.
II. TITLE.

339.5
N17s
1967

National Conference on Soil, Water, and
Suburbia, Washington, D.C. 1967.
Soil, water, and suburbia...(Card 4)

achieving the livable suburb. IV. U.S.
Dept. of Agriculture. V. U.S. Dept. of
Housing and Urban Development. VI. Wood,
Robert C. VII. Title.

301.15
S235

Suburbs.
Schnore, Leo Francis, 1927-
The urban scene; human ecology and
demography. New York, Free Press, 1965.
374p.

1. City growth. 2. Metropolitan areas.
3. Sociology, Urban. 4. Satellite cities.
5. Suburbs. 6. Population shifts. I. Title.

728.1
L66

Suburbs.
Look magazine.
How we live; up in the city, down on the
farm, out in the suburbs, homes packed with
pride, prejudice and love. Des Moines,
Iowa, 1964.
74p. (Entire issue, January 14, 1964)

1. Housing. 2. Housing - Social aspects.
3. Suburbs. 4. Farm housing.

711.583
N28s

Suburbs.
Neutze, Max.
The suburban apartment boom; case study of
a land use problem. Resources for the Future.
Distributed by Johns Hopkins Press. Wash.,
1968.
170p.

1. Apartment houses. 2. Suburbs. 3. Land
use. I. Resources for the Future. II. Title.

300.15
S27c

Suburbs.
Scripps Foundation for Research in Population
Problems.
Comparative population and urban research
via multiple regression and covariance analysis;
a methodological experiment, with an illustrative
application to the study of factors in the growth
and suburbanization of metropolitan population,
by Donald J. Bogue and Dorothy L. Harris.
Oxford, Ohio, Scripps Foundation for Research in
Population Problems, Miami Univ., and Population
Research and Training Center, Univ. of Chicago,
1954.

(continued on next card)

Scripps Foundation for Research in Population
   Problems. Comparative population...1954
   (card 2)

   vii, 75 p.   maps, graphs, tables.   (Its
Studies in population distribution, no. 8)

1. Population. 2. City growth. 3. Suburbs.
4. Research. I. Bogue, Donald J. II. Hariss,
Dorothy L. III. Miami University. IV. Chicago.
University. Population Research and Training
Center. V. Title.   VI. Series.

VF
711.583   Time Magazine.
T45   Suburbia U.S.A. Detached from Time
   Magazine, June 20, 1960. p. 14-18.

   Cover title: One-third of a nation:
U.S. Surbia, 1960.

1. Suburbs.

711.3   SUBURBS.
H68   U.S. Dept. of Housing and Urban Development.
No. 68-7   Suburbia and urbia: suburban functions: an
analysis of major suburbs in U.S. metropolitan areas (1963/65) by Jerome P. Pickard.
Wash., 1968.
   [30]p. (Its Background paper 68-7)

1. Metropolitan areas. 2. Suburbs.
3. City growth. I. Pickard, Jerome P.
II. Title.

711.583   SUBURBS.
S61   Sobin, Dennis P
   The future of the American suburbs;
survival or extinction? Port Washington,
N.Y., National University Publications, 1971.
152p. (National University Publications.
Series in American studies)

   Bibliography: p. 139-144.

1. Suburbs. I. Title.

   Suburbs.
352
A28me   U.S. Advisory Commission on Intergovernmental Relations.
   Metropolitan social and economic dis-
parities: implications for intergovernmental
relations in central cities and suburbs.
Washington, Govt. Print. Off., 1965.
   253p. (A-25)

1. Intergovernmental relations. 2. Metropolitan areas. 3. Suburbs. 4. Sociology,
Urban.

VF
711.583   Suburbs.
N17   U.S. National Housing Agency. Office of the
1944   Administrator. Urban Development Division.
Special report on the post-war suburban
push. [Washington] Oct. 1944.
   31 p.

   Processed.

1.Suburbs. I.Title: The post-war suburban push.

   Suburbs.
301.36
S77   Strauss, Anselm L   ed.
   The American City; a sourcebook of urban
imagery. Chicago, Aldine, 1968.
   530p.
   Contents:-no.1. Images and perspectives.
2. Contrasting conceptions of the same city.-
3. The frontier and the city.-4. City destiny.-
5. Early versions of the rural-urban dialogue.-
6. Perils of the great city.-7. Success and the
perilous city.-8.Poverty and its solutions.-
9. Democracy, politics, and municipal reform.-
10. Order and disorder in the city.-11. Sociol-
ogists study social   worlds.-12. The city
without human   purpose.-13. Rural
           (Continued on next card)

   Suburbs.
630
A37   U.S. Dept. of Agriculture.
1963   A place to live; the yearbook of agriculture, 1963. Washington, For sale by the
Supt. of Documents, Govt. Print. Off., 1963.
   584.

1. Agriculture. 2. Housing. 3. Farm
housing. 4. Land use. 5. Intergovernmental
relations. 6. City planning. 7. Recreation.
8. Suburbs. I. Title. II. Title: Yearbook
of agriculture,   1963.

711.583   SUBURBS.
P72   U.S. President's Task Force on Suburban
v.1   Problems.
   Final report. [v.1.] Wash., 1968.
   406p.
   Contents: Chap.1. Suburbia: its profile and
problems. chap. 2. The Federal role in
suburbia. chap. 3. Policies and programs:
task force recommendations.

1. Suburbs. 2. City growth. 3. Community
facilities.

301.36
S77   Strauss, Anselm L   ed.
   The American City;...1968.   (Card 2)

   amenities and urban attributes.- 14. Suburbia.
-15. Visitors: fun and esthetics.-16. City
planning.-17.-Urban imagery and urban theory.

   1. Sociology, Urban. 2. Metropolitan areas.
3. Suburbs. 4. City planning - Social aspects.
5. Church and social problems. 6. Metropolitan
government. 7. Recreation. I. Title.
II. Title: A sourcebook of urban imagery.

711.583   SUBURBS. U.S. CONGRESS. HOUSE. COMMITTEE ON
C65S   AGRICULTURE.
1965   SUBURBAN LAND DEVELOPMENT
H-H   CORPORATION. HEARINGS BEFORE THE
SUBCOMMITTEE ON CONSERVATION AND
CREDIT, EIGHTY-NINETH CONGRESS, FIRST
SESSION, ON H.R. 7500. WASHINGTON,
GOVT. PRINT. OFF., 1965.
   46P.

   HEARINGS HELD JUNE 1 AND 23, 1965.
   1. SUBURBS. 2. LAND USE.
   I. TITLE.

711.583   SUBURBS.
P72   U.S. President's Task Force on Suburban
v.3   Problems.
   Final report [v.3] Urban development bank.
Wash., 1968.
   103p.

   1. Suburbs. 2. Banks and banking.
I. Title: Urban development bank.

LAW
T   Suburbs.
   Symposium: Apartments in Suburbia:
Local Responsibility and Judicial
Restraint, Northwestern University,
School of Law, 1964.
   The battle for apartments in benign
suburbia: a case of judicial lethargy.
In Northwestern University law review.
July-August 1964, vol. 59, no. 3,
p. 344-432.   (Cont'd. on next card)

711.585   Suburbs.
H68be   U.S. Housing and Home Finance Agency.
   Beauty in the urban environment. How
Federal urban and housing aids can make
cities and suburbs more attractive. Washington, Govt. Print. Off., 1965.
   8p.

1. City planning. 2. Metropolitan area
planning. 3. Suburbs. 4. Housing. I. Title.

711.583   SUBURBS.
P72   U.S. President's Task Force on Suburban
v.4   Problems.
   Final report: [v.4] policy and program
papers. Wash., 1968.
   232p.
   Contents: Relieving local government fiscal
burdens, by Arnold Diamond, Asst. Director,
Office of Economic and Market Analysis, Dept.
of Housing and Urban Development.-Suburban
mobility: present trends and future transportation requirements, by Leon M. Cole,
Director, Office of Metropolitan Development,
Dept. of Housing and Urban Development.
         (Cont'd on next card)

LAW
T   Symposium: Apartments in Suburbia:
Local Responsibility and Judicial
Restraint, Northwestern University,
School of Law, 1964.   The battle for
apartments in benign suburbia ... (Card 2)
   Contents: Aesthetic control of land use:
a house built upon the sand?-Flexible land use
control: herein of the special use.-The legal
significance of cost considerations in the
regulation of apartments by suburbs.
1. Apartment houses - Congresses. 2. Apartment houses
- Social effect.   3. Land use.
4. Suburbs.   I. Apartments in
Suburbia, Local   Responsibility and
Judicial Restraint,   Symposium.

711.3   SUBURBS.
H68   U.S. Dept. of Housing and Urban Development.
no. 68-5   Suburbia and urbia: community diversity in
the Kansas City metropolitan area, by Jerome
P. Pickard. Wash., 1968.
   32p. (Its Background paper 68-5)

   1. Metropolitan areas. 2. Metropolitan areas -
Kansas City, Mo. 3. Suburbs. I. Pickard,
Jerome P. II. Title.

711.583
P72   U.S. President's Task Force on Suburban
v.4   Problems. Final report...1968.   (Card 2)

   1. Suburbs. I. Diamond, Arnold. Relieving
local government fiscal burdens. II. Cole,
Leon M. Suburban mobility: present trends and
future transportation requirements.
III. Title: Policy and program papers, Final
report.

711.417   SUBURBS.
T19   Taylor, Graham Romeyn.
   Satellite cities; a study of industrial
suburbs. New York, Arno Press and The
New York Times, 1970, °1915.
   333p. (The rise of urban America. National
Municipal League series)

   1. Satellite cities. 2. Suburbs.
I. National Municipal League. II. Title.
(Series: The rise of urban America)

711.3   SUBURBS.
H68   U.S. Dept. of Housing and Urban Development.
No. 68-8   Suburbia and urbia: median ages of major
suburbs in U.S. metropolitan areas (1965) by
Jerome P. Pickard and James M. Schneider.
Wash., 1968.
   [43]p. (Its Background paper 68-8)

   1. Metropolitan areas. 2. Suburbs.
I. Pickard, Jerome P. II. Schneider, James M.
III. Title.

711.583   SUBURBS.
P72   U.S. President's Task Force on Suburban
v.5   Problems.
   Final report: [v.5] statistical papers.Wash.,
1968.
   286p.
   Contents.-Metropolitan systems of the USA,
1950-1967, by Constance Perin, Office of Metropolitan Development, Dept. of Housing and Urban
Development.-Suburban functions: an analysis of
major suburbs in U.S. metropolitan areas (1963/
65), by Jerome P. Pickard, Dept. of Housing and
Urban Development.-Median ages of major suburbs
in U.S. metropolitan areas (1963/65), by
         (Cont'd on next card)

711.583
P72
v.5

U.S. President's Task Force on Suburban Problems. Final report...[1968] (Card 2)

Jerome P. Pickard, Dept. of Housing and Urban Development.-Median ages of major suburbs in U.S. metropolitan areas (1965), by Jerome P. Pickard.-Housing and land: some contrasts between the city and the suburb, by William Sorrentino, Office of Metropolitan Development, Dept. of Housing and Urban Development.-Poverty, socioeconomic status, occupational structure, and educational attainment in metropolitan areas, by ⌒Constance Perin.-attitudes of suburbanites, (Cont'd on next card)

711.583
P72
v.5

U.S. President's Task Force on Suburban Problems. Final report...[1968] (Card 3)

by Mary A. Behrman, Office of Metropolitan Development, Dept. of Housing and Urban Development.

1. Suburbs. I. Perin, Constance. Metropolitan systems of the USA, 1950-1967. II. Pickard, Jerome P. Suburban functions: an analysis of major suburbs in U.S. metropolitan areas (1963/65) III. Pickard, Jerome P. Median ages of ⌒major suburbs in U.S. met- (Cont'd on next card)

711.583
P72
v.5

U.S. President's Task Force on Suburban Problems. Final report...[1968] (Card 4)

ropolitan areas (1965) IV. Sorrentino, William. Housing and land; some contrasts between the city and the suburb. V. Perin, Constance. Poverty, socioeconomic status, occupational structure, and educational attainment in metropolitan areas. VI. Behrman, Mary A. Attitudes of suburbanites.

711.583
P72
v.6

SUBURBS.
U.S. President's Task Force on Suburban Problems.
Final report, statistical papers: [v.6.] Profile of the suburbs. Wash., 1968.
106p.

1. Suburbs. 2. Population density.
I. Title: Profile of the suburbs.

711.583
P72
v.7

SUBURBS.
U.S. President's Task Force on Suburban Problems.
Final report. [v.7] Statistical papers. Case studies of seven metropolitan areas. Wash., 1968.
282p.
Contents:-The Birmingham metropolitan area, by J.P. Pickard. Director, Office of the Deputy, Under Secretary, U.S. Dept. of Housing and Urban Development. Chicago metropolitan area, Kansas City metropolitan area. Newark metropolitan area. San Bernardino-Riverside-Ontario SMSA.
(Cont'd on next card)

711.583
P72
v.7

U.S. President's Task Force on Suburban Problems. Final report...1968. (Card 2)

South Bend, Indiana metropolitan area, by James P. Miller. Urban Planner, Office of Metropolitan Development. Dept. of Housing and Urban Development.

1. Suburbs. 2. Metropolitan areas.
I. Pickard, Jerome P. Case studies of seven metropolitan areas. II. Miller, James P. The South Bend, Indiana metropolitan area.

VF
711.4
W21c

Suburbs.
Weaver, Robert Clifton.
The city and its suburbs. Reproduced from New city; man in metropolis: a Christian response. Mar. 1, 1964.
p. 4-6.

1. City planning - Social aspects.
2. Suburbs. 3. Metropolitan areas.

352
(74811)
W45

Suburbs.
Williams, Oliver P
Suburban differences and metropolitan policies: a Philadelphia story, by Oliver P. Williams and others. Philadelphia, Univ. of Pennsylvania Press, 1965.
263p.

1. Metropolitan government - Philadelphia. 2. Suburbs. 3. Building costs - Philadelphia metropolitan area.

711.583
W66

Suburbs.
Wood, Robert Coldwell.
Suburbia, its people and their politics. Boston, Houghton, 1958.
340p.

1. Suburbs. 2. Metropolitan areas.
3. Local government. I. Title.

VF
711.583
W74

Suburbs.
Wright, Charles Alan
Are suburbs necessary. Minnesota Law Review, p. 341-355, Mar. 1951.

VF
711.13
Z22

Suburbs.
Zeckendorf, William
Fluid suburbia. Detached from Yale Review, Autumn, 1958.
p. 27-40.

1. Decentralization. 2. Suburbs. 3. City growth. I. Yale Review.

711.4
(79467)
H17

Suburbs - Berkeley, Calif.
Harris, Curtis C
Suburban development as a stochastic process. Berkeley, Calif., Center for Real Estate and Urban Economics, Institute of Urban and Regional Development, University of California, 1966.
87p. (Center for Real Estate and Urban Economics, Institute of Urban and Regional Development. University of California, Berkeley. Technical report no. 1)

(Continued on next card)

711.4
(79467)
H17

Harris, Curtis C Suburban development as a stochastic process...1966. (Card 2)

1. City growth - Berkeley, Calif.
2. Suburbs - Berkeley, Calif. 3. Land use - Berkeley, Calif. I. California. University. Institute of Urban and Regional Development. II. Title.

711
(016)
C65
no.180

SUBURBS - BIBLIOGRAPHY.
Klain, Ambrose.
Zoning in suburbia: keep it, reject it or replace it? Middletown, Pa., Pennsylvania State University, 1971.
17p. (Council of Planning Librarians. Exchange bibliography no. 180)

1. Planning - Bibl. 2. Zoning - Bibl.
3. Suburbs - Bibl. I. Pennsylvania. State University, Middletown. II. Title.
(Series: Council of Planning Librarians. Exchange bibliography no. 180)

728.1
(74461)
I57

SUBURBS - BOSTON.
Interfaith Housing Corp.
The suburban noose: a story of nonprofit housing development for the modest-income family in metropolitan Boston. [Boston] 1969.
43p.
U.S. Dept. of Housing and Urban Development. Low-Income Housing Demonstration Grant Program. (Mass. LIHD-4)

1. Low-income housing - Boston. 2. Nonprofit housing organizations. 3. Suburbs - Boston. I. U.S. HUD-Low-Income Housing Demonstration Grant Program. II. Title.

711.583
(74461)
W17

Suburbs - Boston.
Warner, Sam Bass.
Streetcar suburbs the process of growth in Boston, 1870-1900. Cambridge, Harvard University Press, 1962.
xxi, 208 p. illus., maps, tables. 25 cm. (Publications of the Joint Center for Urban Studies)
"Bibliographical note": p. [187]-191. Bibliographical references included in "Notes" (p. [193]-203)

1. Suburbs - Boston. 2. City growth - Boston.

1. Boston—Suburbs and environs. I. Title. (Series: Joint Center for Urban Studies. Publications)

HN80.B7W3   301.362   62-17228 rev

Library of Congress   [63r3]

360
(74461)
W66

SUBURBS - BOSTON.
Woods, Robert A.
The zone of emergence; observations of the lower middle and upper working class communities of Boston, 1905-1914, by Robert A. Woods and Albert J. Kennedy. Abridged and edited with a preface by Sam Bass Warner, Jr. 2d. ed. Cambridge, Mass., M.I.T. Press, 1969.
219p.
1. Social conditions - Boston. 2. Suburbs - Boston. I. Kennedy, Albert J., jt. au. II. Warner, Sam Bass, Jr., ed. III. Title.

711.583
(77132)
S23

SUBURBS - CLEVELAND.
SCHAUFFLER, MARY.
THE SUBURBS OF CLEVELAND, A FIELD STUDY OF THE METROPOLITAN DISTRICT OUTSIDE THE ADMINISTRATIVE AREA OF THE CITY. CHICAGO, 1945.
1 V. (VARIOUS PAGINGS)

PART OF THESIS - UNIVERSITY OF CHICAGO, DEPT. OF SOCIOLOGY, JUNE, 1941.

1. SUBURBS - CLEVELAND.

352
(7731)
R14

SUBURBS - COOK COUNTY, ILL.
RAKOVE, MILTON.
THE CHANGING PATTERNS OF SUBURBAN POLITICS IN COOK COUNTY, ILLINOIS. CHICAGO, LOYOLA UNIVERSITY, CENTER FOR RESEARCH IN URBAN GOVERNMENT, 1965.
34P. (CRUG OCCASIONAL STUDIES NO. 1)

1. MUNICIPAL GOVERNMENT - COOK COUNTY, ILL. 2. SUBURBS - COOK COUNTY, ILL. I. LOYOLA UNIVERSITY, CHICAGO. CENTER FOR RESEARCH IN URBAN GOVERNMENT. II. TITLE.

728.1
:325
(77173)
G78

SUBURBS - DAYTON, OHIO.
Gruen, Nina Jaffe.
Low and moderate income housing in the suburbs; an analysis for the Dayton, Ohio region, by Nina Jaffe Gruen and Claude Gruen. Foreward by William L.C. Wheaton. New York, Praeger, 1972.
234p. (Praeger special studies in U.S. economic and social development)
Bibliography: p. 227-234.
Preparation of report financed in part through urban planning grant contract
(Cont'd on next card)

728.1
:325
(77173)
G78

Gruen, Nina Jaffe. Low and...1972. (Card 2)

between Dept. of Housing and Urban Development and Miami Valley Regional Planning Commission, Dayton, Ohio.
1. Minority groups - Housing - Dayton, Ohio 2. Suburbs - Dayton, Ohio. 3. Low-income housing - Dayton, Ohio. 4. Moderate income housing - Dayton, Ohio. I. Gruen, Claude, jt au. II. Title. III. U.S. Dept. of Housing and Urban Development. IV. Miami Valley Regional Planning Commission.

711.583
(751)
D65
SUBURBS - DELAWARE.
DOLAN, PAUL.
  BROOKSIDE; A STUDY OF A SUBURBAN REAL ESTATE DEVELOPMENT IN DELAWARE, BY PAUL DOLAN AND ALBERT H. DUNN. NEWARK, DEL., BUREAU OF ECONOMIC AND BUSINESS RESEARCH, UNIVERSITY OF DELAWARE, SPRING 1959.
  40P. TABLES.

  1. SUBURBS - DELAWARE.
  2. SUBDIVISION - DELAWARE. I. TITLE.

352.5
(756622)
E77
Suburbs - Greensboro, N.C.
Esser, George H   Jr.
  Greensboro suburban analysis, by George H. Esser, Jr. [with] Ruth L. Mace and Dave McCallum. Chapel Hill, N. C., Institute of Government, University of North Carolina, 1956.
  197 p.   plans, tables.

  1.Suburbs - Greensboro, N. C. 2.Annexation - Greensboro, N. C. 3.Municipal services. I.Mace, Ruth (Lovens) II.Title.

711.417
(74961)
G15
Suburbs - Philadelphia.
Gans, Herbert J
  The Levittowners; ways of life and politics in a new suburban community. New York, Pantheon Books, 1966.
  474p.
  Bibliography: p. 452-462.

  1. Planned communities - Levittown, N.J. 2. Suburbs - Philadelphia. 3. Community development - Levittown, N.J. 4. Minority groups - Levittown, N.J. 5. Church and social problems. 6. Sociology. I. Title.

VF
711.583
(753)
S85
Suburbs - District of Columbia.
Sunday Star.
  Suburbia 1960. Washington, 1959.
  [5]pts. in folder.
  Contents:-Arlington booming as metro center; county planning expansion of its modern services, by Paul Hope. Sept. 13, 1959, p. A-18.-Fairfax is fastest growing area, by Mary Lou Werner and Jack Kelso. Sept. 27, 1959, p. A-21.-Past, present meet in Alexandria; old city keeps much of its ancient charm but new problems have followed postwar growth, by John Barron. Oct. 11,   1959, p. B-6.-Montgomery sees prosperity; county attracts
      (Continued on next card)

352.5
(756622)
N67
Suburbs - Greensboro, N.C.
North Carolina. University. Institute of Government.
  Are new residential areas a tax liability? A report to the Greensboro City Council concerning the financial impact of annexing subdivisions, by George H. Esser, Jr. Rev. Chapel Hill, N.C., 1956.
  30 p. tables, diagrs.

      (see card 2)

711.583
(74811)
M45
SUBURBS - PHILADELPHIA.
Miller, Kenneth.
  The subsidized noose: the role of Pennsylvania State government in suburban housing opportunities. Philadelphia, Housing Association of Delaware Valley, 1971.
  1v.

  1. Suburbs - Philadelphia. 2. Low-income housing - Philadelphia. 3. Minority groups - Housing - Philadelphia. I. Housing Association of Delaware Valley. II. Title.

VF
711.583
(753)
S85
Sunday Star.
  Suburbia 1960. ... 1959. (Card 2)
  new developments, by Anne H. Christmas. Sept. 20, 1959, p. B-7.

  1. Suburbs - District of Columbia. 2. Metropolitan areas - District of Columbia. I. Title.

711.583
(75825)
H45
Suburbs - Marietta, Ga.
Hill and Adley Associates.
  Marietta (Ga.) a suburban analysis study. Atlanta, 1959.
  57p.

  1. Suburbs - Marietta, Ga.
  2. Annexation - Marietta, Ga.

711.583
(74811)
G45
Suburbs - Philadelphia metropolitan area.
Gilbert, Charles E
  Governing the suburbs. Bloomington, Indiana University Press, 1967.
  364p.
  Bibliography: p. 338-356.
  1. Suburbs - Philadelphia metropolitan area. 2. Metropolitan area planning - Philadelphia. 3. County planning - Bucks Co., Pa. 4. County planning - Montgomery Co., Pa. 5. Local government - Philadelphia. 6. County planning - Delaware Co., Pa. 7. Taxation - Philadelphia. I. Title.

711.583
(753)
N17
Suburbs - District of Columbia.
U.S. National Capital Regional Planning Council.
  Community center development, based on the year 2000 policies plan for the Washington metropolitan area. A manual, including a prototype design. Washington, 1963.
  54p.

  1. Community development - District of Columbia. 2. Retail trade. 3. Metropolitan area planning - District of Columbia. 4. Suburbs-   District of Columbia.

711.583
(74725)
Z72
SUBURBS - NASSAU CO., N.Y.
Zschock, Dieter K   ed.
  Economic aspects of suburban growth; studies of the Nassau-Suffolk planning region. Stony Brook, Economic Research Bureau, State University of New York At Stony Brook, 1969.
  163p.

  1. Suburbs - Nassau Co., N.Y. 2. Suburbs - Suffolk Co., N.Y. 3. City growth - Nassau Co., N.Y. 4. City growth - Suffolk Co., N.Y. I. Title.

VF
711.4
(74886)
B21
Suburbs - Pittsburgh.
Beachler, Edwin H
  Growing pains in the suburbs; the story of metropolitan Pittsburgh's building boom. Pittsburgh. Pittsburgh Press, 1951.
  36p. illus.
  A collection of 16 articles reprinted from The Pittsburgh Press.

  1. City growth - Pittsburgh metropolitan area. 2. Suburbs - Pittsburgh.

725.83
(75529)
V66
Suburbs - District of Columbia.
Voorhees (Alan M.) and Associates.
  Fairfax Center; a proposal for a year 2000 plan suburban center. [Washington] 1962.
  14p.
  "Prepared for the National Capitol Regional Planning Council."
  1. Community centers - Fairfax Co., Va. 2. Community centers - District of Columbia metropolitan area. 3. Suburbs - District of Columbia. I. U.S. National Capital Regional Planning Council.

711.3
(7471)
S23
Suburbs - New York (City)
Schlivek, Louis B
  Man in metropolis. A book about the people and prospects of a metropolitan region. Garden City, N.Y., Doubleday, 1965.
  432p.
  Bibliography: p. 419-423.

  1. Metropolitan areas - New York (City) 2. City planning - New York (City) metropolitan area. 3. Suburbs - New York (City) 4. City growth - New York (City) 5. City planning - Social   aspects. I. Title.

711.583
(79549)
T37
Suburbs - Portland, Or.
Throop, Vincent M
  The suburban zone of metropolitan Portland, Oregon. Chicago, Univ. of Chicago, 1948.
  244p.
  Thesis: University of Chicago.

  1. Suburbs - Portland, Or. I. Chicago. University. II. Title.

711.583
(471)
V86
SUBURBS - FINLAND.
Vuokola, Aimo.
  Helsingin maalaiskunta Helsinge (Helsinki rural commune) by Aimo Vuokola and Ari Yrjänä. Helsinki, Söderström, 1968.
  1v.

  Finnish, English.

  1. Suburbs - Finland. I. Yrjana, Ari, jt. au. II. Title: Helsinki rural commune.

VF
711.583
(747)
N28
SUBURBS - NEW YORK, N.Y.
  Suburban growth in the New York area. New York State Commerce Review, p. 11-17, Nov. 1948.

  1. Suburbs-New York, N.Y. 2. Population shifts-New York, N.Y.

711.583
(74965)
S72
SUBURBS - PRINCETON, N.J.
Sternlieb, George.
  The affluent suburb: Princeton, by George Sternlieb and others. New Brunswick, N.J., Transaction Books, 1971.
  259p.

  1. Suburbs - Princeton, N.J. I. Title.

388
(7531)
M87
SUBWAYS.
Murin, William J
  Mass transit policy planning: an incremental approach. Lexington, Mass., Heath Lexington Books, 1971.
  123p. (Studies in social and economic process)

  Bibliography: p. 105-112.

  1. Transportation - District of Columbia metropolitan area. 2. Subways. 3. Journey to work. I. Title.

VF
711.4
(74811)
C47g
Suburbs - Philadelphia.
Citizens' Council on City Planning, Philadelphia.
  Governmental problems, city and suburban, by Richardson Dilworth and others. Philadelphia, 1959.
  9p. (Its Report no. 73)

  1. City planning - Philadelphia. 2. Suburbs - Philadelphia. I. Dilworth, Richardson.

352
(79454)
L17
Suburbs - Sacramento, Calif.
Larsen, Christian L
  Growth and government in Secramento, by Christian L. Larsen and others. Bloomington, Ind., Indiana University Press, 1965.
  238p. (Metropolitan action studies no. 4)

  1. Metropolitan areas - Sacramento, Calif. 2. Metropolitan government - Sacramento, Calif. 3. Suburbs - Sacramento, Calif. I. Title. (Series: Metropolitan section studies   no. 4)

711.583
(79461)
S81

SUBURBS - SAN FRANCISCO.
The Suburbs of San Francisco. Photographs by Michael Bry. San Francisco, Chronicle Books, 1969.
181p.

Contents.-Marin County, by William Chapin.-Peninsula, by Alvin D. Hyman.-East Bay, by Jonathan Carroll.

1. Suburbs - San Francisco.

711.583
(74725)
Z72

SUBURBS - SUFFOLK CO., N.Y.
Zschock, Dieter K   ed.
Economic aspects of suburban growth; studies of the Nassau-Suffolk planning region. Stony Brook, Economic Research Bureau, State University of New York At Stony Brook, 1969.
163p.

1. Suburbs - Nassau Co., N.Y. 2. Suburbs - Suffolk Co., N.Y. 3. City growth - Nassau Co., N.Y. 4. City growth - Suffolk Co., N.Y. I. Title.

355.58
157C

SUBVERSIVE HOSTILE ACTS.
U.S. INTERDEPARTMENTAL ADVISORY COMMITTEE ON SUBVERSIVE ACTIVITIES. CODE FOR PROTECTION OF FEDERAL BUILDINGS AND THEIR CONTENTS FROM SUBVERSIVE HOSTILE ACTS. WASHINGTON, U.S. GOVT. PRINT. OFF., 1942.
39P.

1. CIVIL DEFENSE. I. TITLE: SUBVERSIVE HOSTILE ACTS.

VF
353
(74744)
F74

Suburbs - Schenectady, N. Y.
Friedman, Albert L
"Suburbanitis" in Schenectady County. [Schenectady, N. Y., Schenectady Real Estate Board, Inc.,] 1956]
[42] p.

"The following series of articles appeared in the schenectady (sic.) Union-Star in 1955" ...

711.583
(485)
C17

SUBURBS - SWEDEN.
Carrier, Michael
Suburban housing in Sweden, by Michael Carrier, ARIBA [Associate of the Royal Institute of British Architecture] [n.p.] 1965.
[3]p.
Reprinted from OAP, Nov. 1965, p. 1570-1572.

1. Suburbs - Sweden. 2. City planning - Sweden. I. Title.

388
(79461)
S15m

Subway stations.
San Francisco Planning and Urban Renewal Association.
Market Street subway stations, a SPUR report,
San Francisco,
v. (Its report no.

For complete information see main card.
1. Transportation - San Francisco.
2. Journey to work. I. Title: Subway stations.

333.38
W17

SUBURBS - SEATTLE.
WASHINGTON. UNIVERSITY. COLLEGE OF ARCHITECTURE AND URBAN PLANNING. LOCATIONAL FACTORS INVOLVED IN SUBURBAN LAND DEVELOPMENT. PREPARED FOR THE WEYERHAEUSER COMPANY BY M.R. WOLFE, AND OTHERS. SEATTLE, 1961.
1 V.

1. SUBDIVISION. 2. SUBURBS - SEATTLE. I. WOLFE, M.R. II. WEYERHAEUSER CO.

711.583
(485)
P17

SUBURBS - SWEDEN.
Pass, David.
Vallingby and Farsta: from idea to reality; the suburban development process in a large Swedish city. [Stockholm] Rikets Allmänna Kartverk, 1969.
494p.
On cover: National Swedish building research.
Bibliography: p. 475-494.
1. Suburbs - Sweden. I. Sweden. Rikets Allmänna Kartverk. II. Title. III. Title: The suburban development process in a large Swedish city.

Subways ~~~~~~~~

FOLIO
711.583
(46)
861e

Suburbs - Spain.
Spain. Instituto Nacional de la Vivienda.
Entrevías. Transformación urbanística de un suburbio de Madrid. Madrid, 1965.
1 v.

1. Suburbs - Spain. 2. City planning - Spain. 3. Universities and colleges - Housing. 4. Housing - Spain.

711.583
(791)
M12

SUBURBS - TEMPE, ARIZ.
McGaw, Dickinson L
Suburban problem solving: an information system for Tempe, Arizona. Tempe, Institute of Public Administration, Arizona State University, 1971.
135p. (Papers in public administration, no. 20)
1. Suburbs - Tempe, Ariz. 2. City planning - Tempe, Ariz. I. Arizona. State University, Tempe. Institute of Public Administration. II. Title.

388
S76b

SUBWAYS.
Stone, Tabor R
Beyond the automobile: reshaping the transportation environment. Englewood Cliffs, N.J., Prentice-Hall, 1971.
148p. (A Spectrum book)

1. Transportation. 2. Journey to work. 3. Subways. I. Title.

VF
728.1
(46)
861u
Spanish

Suburbs - Spain.
Spain. Ministerio de la Vivienda.
Urbanismo y vivienda; tratamiento de zonas suburbanas en Madrid. Madrid, 1963.
[12]p.

Text in Spanish.

1. Housing - Spain. 2. Suburbs - Spain.

711.583
(71354)
C51

Suburbs - Toronto.
Clark, S D
The suburban society. [Toronto, Can.?] University of Toronto Press, 1966.
233p.

1. Suburbs - Toronto. 2. Sociology, Urban. I. Title.

388.1
C65RAI

SUBWAYS.
U.S. CONGRESS. HOUSE. COMMITTEE ON THE DISTRICT OF COLUMBIA.
RAIL RAPID TRANSIT FOR THE NATIONAL CAPITAL REGION. REPORT TOGETHER WITH MINORITY VIEWS TO ACCOMPANY H.R. 4822. WASHINGTON, GOVT. PRINT. OFF., 1965.
79P. (89TH CONGRESS, 1ST SESSION. HOUSE. REPORT 536)

1. SUBWAYS.

VF
728.1
(46)
861u

Suburbs - Spain.
Spain. Ministerio de la Vivienda.
Urbanismo y vivienda; treatment of suburban zones in Madrid. Madrid, 1963.
[12]p.

Text in English.

1. Housing - Spain. 2. Suburbs - Spain.

728.1
(41)
H15

Suburbs - U.K.
Hampstead Garden Suburb Trust. (U.K.)
The Hampstead Garden Suburb: its achievements and significance. [London, 1936]
24p.

1. Housing - U.K. 2. Suburbs - U.K. I. Title.

388.1
C65RAP

SUBWAYS.
U.S. CONGRESS. HOUSE. COMMITTEE ON THE DISTRICT OF COLUMBIA.
RAPID RAIL TRANSIT FOR THE NATION'S CAPITAL. HEARINGS BEFORE SUBCOMMITTEE NO. 5, 89TH CONGRESS, 1ST SESSION, ON H.R. 4822. WASHINGTON, GOVT. PRINT. OFF., 1965.
316P.

1. SUBWAYS. I. TITLE.

711.3
(797371)
S66

Suburbs - Spokane, Wash.
Spokane, Wash. City Plan Commission.
Spokane metropolitan area study; a plan of action to help further the proper development of Spokane's suburbs both within and bordering the city's limits. Spokane, 1959.
102p. maps, tables. (Spokane metropolitan area study report no. 1; Report no. 8, City plan series I)

1. Metropolitan areas - Spokane, Wash. 2. Suburbs - Spokane, Wash.

711.583
(79461)
S81

The Suburbs of San Francisco. Photographs by Michael Bry. San Francisco, Chronicle Books, 1969.
181p.

Contents.-Marin County, by William Chapin.-Peninsula, by Alvin D. Hyman.-East Bay, by Jonathan Carroll.

1. Suburbs - San Francisco.

388.1
C65R

SUBWAYS.
U.S. CONGRESS. SENATE. COMMITTEE ON THE DISTRICT OF COLUMBIA.
RAIL RAPID TRANSIT FOR THE NATIONAL CAPITAL REGION. HEARINGS, 89TH CONGRESS, 1ST SESSION, ON H.R. 4822 AND S. 1117. WASHINGTON, GOVT. PRINT. OFF., 1965.
287P.

HEARINGS HELD JULY 20-23, 1965.

1. SUBWAYS. I. TITLE.

388.1
C65RA
SUBWAYS.
U.S. CONGRESS. SENATE. COMMITTEE ON
THE DISTRICT OF COLUMBIA.
RAIL RAPID TRANSIT FOR THE NATIONAL
CAPITAL REGION. REPORT TO ACCOMPANY
H.R. 4822. WASHINGTON, GOVT. PRINT.
OFF., 1965.
55P. (89TH CONGRESS, 1ST SESSION.
SENATE. REPORT 637)

1. SUBWAYS. I. TITLE.

808.5
H23
The successful speaker's planning guide.
Hegarty, Edward J
The successful speaker's planning guide.
New York, McGraw-Hill, 1970.
275p.

1. Public speaking. I. Title.

330
(662)
871
The Sudan, Middle East Bridge to Africa.
U.S. Dept. of State. (Public Services
Div.)
Background: the Sudan Middle East bridge
to Africa. Washington, Govt. Print. Off.,
1958.
20p. illus. (Its Near and Middle Eastern
series 28)

1. Economic conditions - Sudan. 2. Technical assistance programs - Sudan. I. Title.
The Sudan, Middle East bridge to Africa.

388
(43)
H15s
SUBWAYS - GERMANY.
Hamburg. Baubehörde.
Schnellbahnbau in Hamburg. Hamburg,
Baubehörde, Amt fur Ingenieurwesen,
1969.
81p. (Hamburger Schriften zum Bau-,
Wohnungs- und Siedlungswesen. Heft
49/1969)

1. Transportation - Germany. 2.
Journey to work. 3. Railroads -
Germany. 4. Subways - Germany. I.
Title.

711.6
F22S
SUCCESSFUL SUBDIVISIONS.
U.S. FEDERAL HOUSING ADMINISTRATION.
SUCCESSFUL SUBDIVISIONS; PRINCIPLES
OF PLANNING FOR ECONOMY AND PROTECTION
AGAINST NEIGHBORHOOD BLIGHT.
WASHINGTON, GOVT. PRINT. OFF., 1940.
28P. (ITS LAND PLANNING BULLETIN NO.
1)
COVER SUBTITLE: PLANNED AS
NEIGHBORHOODS FOR PROFITABLE INVESTMENT
AND APPEAL TO HOME OWNERS.
FOREWORD BY STEWART MCDONALD.
1. SUBDIVISION DESIGN. I. TITLE.
II. SERIES.

690.091.82
(713)
S82
Sudbury, Can. Council.
Bylaw no. 2017 regulating the erection and
to provide for the safety of building in the
city of Sudbury, Ontario, passed April 17, 1939.
[Sudbury, 1939?]
128 p. tables.

1. Building codes-Canada.

333.33
(749)
N28S
SUCCESS PATTERNS IN THE REAL ESTATE
BUSINESS IN THE STATE OF NEW JERSEY.
NEW JERSEY. DEPT. OF CONSERVATION AND
ECONOMIC DEVELOPMENT.
SUCCESS PATTERNS IN THE REAL ESTATE
BUSINESS IN THE STATE OF NEW JERSEY.
PREPARED BY RIDER COLLEGE, UNDER A
SMALL BUSINESS ADMINISTRATION GRANT
AWARDED TO THE NEW JERSEY DEPARTMENT OF
CONSERVATION AND ECONOMIC DEVELOPMENT.
NEW JERSEY, 1963?
75P.
1. REAL ESTATE BUSINESS - NEW JERSEY.
I. U.S. SMALL BUSINESS ADMINISTRATION.
II. TITLE.

658.3
G27
Successful supervision; a guide for
training supervisors.
Gerletti, John D
Successful supervision; a guide for
training supervisors, by John D. Gerletti
and Frank B. Black. Dubuque, Iowa, W. C.
Brown Co., 1956.
66 p.

Bibliography: p. 56-66.

1. Personnel management. 2. Public administration. I. Title. II. Black, Frank B., jt. au.

711.4
(7444)
S82
Sudbury, Mass. Planning Board.
Downe, Charles E
Master plan study [Sudbury, Mass.]
[Prepared for] Planning Board, Sudbury,
Massachusetts. West Newton, Mass., 1962.
232p.
Prepared for Massachusetts Department of
Commerce, and the Town of Sudbury.
U.S. Urban Renewal Adm. UPAP.

1. Master plan - Sudbury, Mass. I. Sudbury,
Mass. Planning Board. II. U.S. URA-UPAP.
Sudbury, Mass.

690
H68S
SUCCESSFUL BUILDER IDEAS.
HOUSE AND HOME.
SUCCESSFUL BUILDER IDEAS; THE BEST OF
HOUSE AND HOME FOR DESIGN, CONSTRUCTION,
MANAGEMENT [AND] SALES. NEW YORK CITY
[1967?]
127P.

1. BUILDING INDUSTRY. I. TITLE.

658.3
V15
The successful supervisor in government and
business.
Van Dersal, William R
The successful supervisor in government
and business. New York, Harper & Brothers,
1962.
192p.

Books and journals: p. 180-188.

1. Personnel management. I. Title.

711.3
(744)
S82
Sudbury Valley Commission, Sudbury, Mass.
Report of the Sudbury Valley Commission
relative to the Sudbury River and its
environs, under Chapter 34, Resolves
of 1949. Boston, 1950.
142p. maps.

At head of title: House. No. 2351.

1. Regional planning - Massachusetts.
I. Massachusetts. General Court. House.

658
075
The successful computer system...
Orlicky, Joseph.
The successful computer system; its planning,
development, and management in a business
enterprise. New York, McGraw-Hill, 1969.
238p.

1. Management - Automation. 2. Automation.
3. Business. I. Title.

070.44
H42
SUCCESSFUL TECHNICAL WRITING.
HICKS, TYLER G
SUCCESSFUL TECHNICAL WRITING;
TECHNICAL ARTICLES, PAPERS, REPORTS,
INSTRUCTION AND TRAINING MANUALS, AND
BOOKS. NEW YORK, MCGRAW-HILL, 1959.
294P.

1. REPORT WRITING. 2. ENGLISH
LANGUAGE. I. TITLE.

693
S82d
Suddarth, Stanley K
A detailed study of a W truss made with
metal gusset plates. Lafayette, Ind., Purdue
University, Agricultural Experiment Station,
1963.
16p. (Purdue University, Agricultural
Experiment Station, Research progress report
50)

1. Building methods. 2. Wood. I. Indiana.
Agricultural Experiment Station. II. Title.

658.3
(07)
Z25
Successful conference and discussion
techniques.
Zelko, Harold P
Successful conference and discussion
techniques. New York, McGraw-Hill, 1957.
264p. illus.

1. Personnel management - Study and teaching.
I. Title. II. Title: Discussion techniques.

Ref.
808.5
P76s
The successful toastmaster;
Prochnow, Herbert Victor.
The successful toastmaster; a treasure
chest of introductions, epigrams, humor, and
quotations, by Herbert V. Prochnow, and
Herbert V. Prochnow, Jr. New York, Harper
& Row, 1966.
502p.

2. Quotations. I. Prochnow, Herbert
Victor, Jr., jt. au. II. Title.
1. Public speaking.

658.564
S82
SUDDARTH, STANLEY K
A DIGITAL COMPUTER PROGRAM FOR
ANALYSIS OF MEMBER STRESSES IN
SYMMETRIC W TRUSSES, BY STANLEY K.
SUDDARTH AND OTHERS. LAFAYETTE, IND.,
AGRICULTURAL EXPERIMENT STATION, 1964.
23P. (WOOD RESEARCH LABORATORY
RESEARCH BULLETIN NO. 783)

1. AUTOMATION. 2. TRUSSES.

658
H17SU
SUCCESSFUL PATTERNS FOR EXECUTIVE
ACTION.
HARVARD BUSINESS REVIEW.
SUCCESSFUL PATTERNS FOR EXECUTIVE
ACTION. NEW YORK, HARPER, 1958.
107P.

ARTICLES PREVIOUSLY APPEARED IN THE
HARVARD BUSINESS REVIEW.

1. MANAGEMENT. I. TITLE.

300.15
S82e
Suchman, Edward A
Evaluative research; principles and practices
in public service and social action programs.
New York, Russell Sage Foundation, 1967.
186p.

1. Social science research. I. Russell Sage
Foundation. II. Title.

690.248
152d
Suddarth, Stanley K
Indiana. Agricultural Experiment Station.
(Wood Research Laboratory)
Determination of member stresses in
wood trusses with rigid joints, by Stanley
K. Suddarth. Lafayette, 1961.
15p. (Its Research bulletin no. 714)

1. Trusses. I. Suddarth, Stanley K.

691.110.15
S82 Suddarth, S K
Future importance of computers in wood engineering, by S.K. Suddarth and F.E. Goodrick. Madison, Wis., Forest Products Research Society, 1966.
6p.

Reprinted from Forest Products Journal. v. 17, no. 6.

1. Wood - Research. 2. Engineering - Research. 3. Automation. I. Goodrick, F.E., jt. au. II. Title.

674
S25 Suddarth, Stanley K   jt. au.
Senft, John F
Strength of structural lumber under combined bending and tension loading, by John F. Senft and Stanley K. Suddarth. Madison, Wis., Forest Products Research Society, 1970.
[5]p.
Reprinted from: Forest products journal, vol. 20, no. 7, July, 1970. p. 17-21.
1. Lumber industry. 2. Strength of materials. I. Suddarth, Stanley K., jt. au. II. Title.

355.58
(71)
S83 SUFFIELD EXPER MENTAL STATION, RALSTON, ALTA. CAN.
MODEL STUDIES OF BLAST EFFECTS, PTS. 1-8. RALSTON, ALTA., CAN., 1959-61.
9V. (ITS SUFFIELD TECHNICAL PAPERS)
Lib has
1-2 typeing
3-8
1. CIVILIAN DEFENSE - CANADA. 2. PROTECTIVE CONSTRUCTION.   I. TITLE.

693
S82 Suddarth, Stanley K
A generalized stiffness analysis of space frames. Lafayette, Ind., Purdue University, Agricultural Experiment Station, 1967.
21p. (Purdue University, Agricultural Experiment Station Research progress report 321)
1. Building methods. 2. Architecture - Designs and plans. 3. Structural engineering. 4. Wood - Research. I. Indiana. Agricultural Experiment Station. II. Title.

711.585
(713)
S82 Sudbury, Can. Planning Board.
A study for urban renewal in Sudbury, Ontario. Prepared for the City Council by Sudbury Planning Board and Project Planning Associates. Sudbury, Ont., 1963.
45p.

1. Urban renewal - Canada. 2. Neighborhood rehabilitation - Canada. I. Project Planning Associates, Toronto.

72
(42)
C32 Suffolk building.
Chesterton, Maurice
Suffolk building, some critical considerations [Ipswich] East Suffolk County Council, 1949.
48 p.   illus.

1. Architecture-U.K. 2.Architecture, Domestic-U.K. I.Title.

VF
694.183
I52ho Indiana. Agricultural Experiment Station.
How to select hardwood lumber for structural gluing; a guide for builders, lumber dealers, and small sawmill operators, in the selection of 2x4, 2x6, and 2x8 hardwood lumber, by Stanley K. Suddarth. Lafayette, Ind., 1957.
9p. illus., diagrs. (Purdue University. Agricultural Extension Service. Extension circular 440)

(See Card No. 2)

360
M17s Suicide.
Maris, Ronald W
Social forces in urban suicide. Homewood, Ill., Dorsey Press, 1969.
214p. (The Dorsey series in anthropology and sociology)

Bibliography: p. 199-206.

1. Social conditions. I. Title. II. Title: suicide.

628.3
(747245)
S83 Suffolk County, N.Y. Dept. of Health.
Report on need and feasibility for public sewage disposal facilities in Western Suffolk, by John M. Flynn and Charles G. Lind. Riverhead, N.Y., Suffolk County Center, 1962.
67p.

1. Sewerage and sewage disposal - Suffolk County, N.Y. 2. Water-supply - Suffolk County, N.Y. I. Flynn, John M. II. Lind, Charles G.

VF
694.183
I52ho Indiana. Agricultural Experiment Station.
How to select hardwood lumber for structural gluing ... 1957.   (Card No. 2)

1.Nails and nailing. 2.Wood construction. I.Suddarth, Stanley K   II.Title. III.Series: Purdue University. Agricultural Extension Service. Extension circular 440.

614
N17su Suicide in the United States, 1950-1964.
U.S. National Center for Health Statistics.
Suicide in the United States, 1950-1964. A study of suicide statistics showing trends for 1950-64 and differences by age, sex, color, marital status, and geographic area for selected periods. Washington, U.S. Dept. of Health, Education, and Welfare, 1967.
34p. (U.S. Public Health Service. Vital and health statistics. Series 20, no. 5)
U.S. Public Health Service. Publication no. 1000, series 20, no. 5.
1 Health. 2. Medical research. I. U.S. Public Health Service. II. Title.

711.14
(747245)
S83 Suffolk County, N.Y. Dept. of Planning.
Existing land use; residential, commercial, institutional, open space, by Lee E. Koppelman. Hauppauge, N.Y., 1962.
42p.

1. Land use - Suffolk Co., N.Y. I. Koppelman, Lee E.

694.1
P27 Suddarth, Stanley K
Percival, Donald H
Investigation of the mechanical characteristics of truss plates on fire-retardant-treated wood, by Donald H. Percival and Stanley K. Suddarth. [n.p.] Forest Products Research Society, 1971.
7p. (Illinois. University. Small Homes Council-Building Research Council. Technical note no. 6)
1. Wood construction. I. Suddarth, Stanley K. II. Illinois. University. Small Homes Council-Building Research Council. III. Title.

728.1
:325
S82e Sudman, Seymour.
The extent and characteristics of racially integrated housing in the United States, by Seymour Sudman and others. Chicago, University of Chicago, 1969.
[43] p.
Reprinted from: Journal of business of the University of Chicago, Jan., 1969, p. 50-92.

1. Minority groups - Housing. I. Title.

711.333
(747245) Suffolk County, N.Y. Dept. of Planning.
S83p A plan for open space in Suffolk County.
vol.2 Hauppauge, N.Y. 1964.
121p. (Its comprehensive plan series vol. 2)

Lee Edward Koppelman, Director of Planning.
1. Master plan - Suffolk Co., N.Y. 2. County planning - Suffolk Co., N.Y. 3. Open space land. I. Koppelman, Lee Edward.

694.183
I52na Suddarth, Stanley K
Indiana. Agricultural Experiment Station. (Wood Research Laboratory)
Nail popping, a result of wood shrinkage, by Stanley K. Suddarth and Hugh D. Angleton. Lafayette, Ind., 1956.
41p. (Its Bulletin 633)

1. Nails and nailing. I. Suddarth, Stanley K. II. Angleton, Hugh D.

728.1
:325
S82 Sudman, Seymour.
Social psychological factors in intergroup housing; results of pilot test, by S. Sudman and Norman Bradburn. Chicago, National Opinion Research Center, 1966.
159p. (Report no. 111-A)
Summary -- --- Summary. Chicago, 1966. [12]p.
1. Minority groups - Housing. 2. Race relations. I. Bradburn, Norman, jt. au. II. National Opinion Research Center, Chicago. III. Title.

330
(747245)
S83 Suffolk County, N.Y. Planning Commission.
Economic base, Suffolk, a growing County in a growing market, by Lee E. Koppelman, director of planning. Hauppauge, L.I., N.Y., 1962.
109p.
"Draft copy."

1. Economic base studies - Suffolk Co., N.Y. I. Koppelman, Lee E.

693.002.22
I52 Suddarth, Stanley K
Indiana. Agricultural Experiment Station. (Wood Research Laboratory)
Prefabricated, demountable panels for pole buildings, by Stanley K. Suddarth and Robert H. Perkins. Lafayette, Ind., 1959.
16p. illus., diagrs. (Its Research bulletin no. 683)

1. Prefabricated construction. 2. Panels. I. Suddarth, Stanley K. II. Perkins, Robert H.

610.1
B76 Suffet, Frederick, jt. au.
Brotman, Richard.
Delinquency prevention report; the drug problem, by Richard Brotman and Frederick Suffet. [Wash.] U.S. Youth Development and Delinquency Prevention Administration, 1970.
8p. (Delinquency prevention reporter)

1. Drugs. 2. Juvenile delinquency. I. Suffet, Frederick, jt. au. II. U.S. Youth Prevention and Delinquency Prevention Administration. III. Title. IV. Title: The drug problem.

711.333
(747245)
S83n Suffolk County, N.Y. Planning Commission.
Need and feasibility for mapping program in Suffolk County, by Lee E. Kopplman. Hauppauge, L.I., N.Y., 1964.
39p.

1. County planning - Suffolk Co., N.Y. 2. Maps and mapping - Suffolk Co., N.Y. I. Koppelman, Lee E.

711.333
(747245)
S83   Suffolk County, N. Y. Planning Board.
Progress report, 1954 -   [Patchogue
(etc.) N. Y.] 1954 -
   v. maps.

For complete information see shelflist card.

    1. County planning - Suffolk Co., N. Y.

352
(747245) Suffolk County, N.Y. Planning Commission.
S83   Report on local government analysis.
[New York] 1962.
80p.

    1. Local government - Suffolk County,
N.Y.

712.21
(747245) Suffolk County, N.Y. Planning Commission.
S83   Report on need and feasibility for county
park facilities in Suffolk County. New York,
1962.
23p.

    1. Parks - Suffolk Co., N.Y.

628.1   Suffolk Co., N.Y. Water Authority.
(747245)
S67   Soren, Julian.
Results of subsurface exploration in
the mid-island area of Western Suffolk
County, Long Island, New York. With a
section on potential development of
groundwater in the mid-island area, by
Philip Cohen. Prepared by U.S. Geolog-
ical Survey in cooperation with Suffolk
County Legislature, Suffolk County Water
Authority. Riverhead, N.Y., Suffolk
County Water Authority, 1971.
60p. (Long Island water resources
       (Cont'd on next card)

628.1
(747245) Soren, Julian. Results of...1971.
S67   (Card 2)

bulletin no. 1)
Bibliography: p. 40-41.

    1. Water resources - Suffolk Co., N.Y.
I. Suffolk Co., N.Y. Water Authority.
II. Cohen, Philip. III. Title.

Sugar-cane **see**   Bagasse

711.4   Sugar Creek, Mo. City Planning Commission.
(77841)   Runnells and Winholtz.
S83   The comprehensive plan, Sugar Creek,
Missouri. [Prepared for Sugar Creek City
Plan Commission] Kansas City, Mo., 1964.
86p.
Prepared for Missouri Division of Com-
merce and Industrial Development.
U.S. Urban Renewal Adm. UPAP.

    1. Master plan - Sugar Creek, Mo.
I. Sugar Creek, Mo. City Planning Com-
mission. II. U.S. URA-UPAP. Sugar
Creek, Mo.

629.136
H45a   A suggested action program for the relief
of airfield congestion at selected airports.
Million, L N
A suggested action program for the relief
of airfield congestion at selected airports,
by L.N. Million and others. Wash. Dept. of
Transportation, Federal Aviation Administration,
1969.
189p.

    1. Airports. 2. Air transportation.
I. U.S. Federal Aviation Administration.
II. Title.

712.21
(77311)   Suggested goals in park and recre-
           ation planning.
C34   Chicago. Park District.
Suggested goals in park and recreation planning. Published jointly with
Chicago Recreation Commission. Chicago,
1959.
42p.

    1. Parks - Chicago. 2. Recreation -
Chicago. I. Chicago. Recreation
Commission. II. Title.

690.22   Suggested guide specifications for stainless
            steel components in curtain walls.
D92   Dyer, Ben H
Suggested guide specifications for stainless
steel components in curtain walls. New York,
International Nickel Company, inc. in cooper-
ation with Committee of Stainless Steel
Producers, American Iron and Steel Institute,
1968.
19p.
    1. Walls - Standards and specifications.
I. International Nickel Company, inc.
II. American Iron And Steel Institute.
III. Title.

690.281   Suggested guide specifications for stainless
            steel swinging doors and frames.
D92   Dyer, Ben H
Suggested guide specifications for stainless
steel swinging doors and frames. New York,
International Nickel Company, inc. in cooperation with Committee of Stainless Steel
Producers, American Iron and Steel Institute,
1968.
14p.
    1. Doors - Standards and specifications.
2. Steel. I. International Nickel Company,
inc. II. American Iron and Steel Institute.
III. Title.

---

370   Suggested guidelines for the evaluation and future
E28su   planning of projects under Title I of Elementary
U.S. Office of Education. Secondary Edu. Act.
Suggested guidelines for the evaluation
and future planning of projects under Title
I of the Elementary Secondary Education Act.
Submitted by Robert Chamberlain, Chairman of
Community Advisory Committee, James Kernen,
Consultant in Continuing Education [and]
Harry Butler, Supervisor of ESEA Title I.
[n.p., n.d.]
9p.

    1. Education. 2. Education - Legis-
lation. I.   Chamberlain, Robert.
II. Title.   III. Title: Elementary secondary   education act.

VF
333.38   Suggested land subdivision regulations.
H68   U.S. Housing and Home Finance Agency. Office of
the Administrator. Division of Housing
Research.
Suggested land subdivision regulations.
Washington, Govt. Print. Off., Feb. 1952.
65 p.   illus., plans.
Prepared by the Division of Housing Research
and the Community Planning Branch of the Division
of Slum Clearance and Urban Redevelopment, and the
Land Planning Section, Federal Housing
Administration.
Bibliography: p. 61-62.

LAW
T   Suggested legal documents for planned-unit
F222   developments.
H68su   U.S. Federal Housing Administration.
Suggested legal documents for planned-unit
developments. Wash., Federal Housing Administration, Veterans Administration, 1965.
20p.   (FHA form 1400, VA form 26-8200,
rev. 1965)

    1. Subdivision design. 2. Veterans' guaran-
teed loans. I. U.S. Veterans Administration.
II. Title.

355.58
O652s   Suggested long-range policy toward new construction for the national shelter program.
Condit, Richard I
Suggested long-range policy toward new
construction for the national shelter program. Prepared for: Office of Civil Defense,
Dept. of Defense and Urban Renewal Administration, Housing and Home Finance Agency. Menlo
Park, Calif., Stanford Research Institute, 1962.
1v. (Technical report no. I-5. S.R.I. project no. IM-4075)
    1. Civilian defense. 2. Protective construc-
tion. I. U.S. Office of Civil Defense. II. U.S
Urban Renewal Administration. III. Stanford Research Insti-   tute. IV. Title.

658
S51   SUGGESTED MANAGEMENT GUIDES.
U.S. SMALL BUSINESS ADMINISTRATION.
SUGGESTED MANAGEMENT GUIDES; A PRACTICAL
GUIDE FOR LARGE COMPANIES AND OTHERS WHO
ARE INTERESTED IN HELPING THE SMALL
BUSINESSMAN IMPROVE HIS MANAGMENT SKILLS,
BY H. EARL SANGSTON. WASHINGTON, GOVT.
PRINT. OFF., 1962.
308P.

    1. INDUSTRIAL MANAGEMENT.   I. SANGSTON,
H. EARL.   II. TITLE.

333.38   Suggested model subdivision regulations for
(74883)   townships of the second class.
H45   Hill (Carroll V.) & Associates.
Suggested model subdivision regulations for
townships of the second class. Waynesburg, Pa.
Greene County Planning Commission, [1964?]
39p.

    1. Subdivision regulation - Greene Co., Pa.
I. Greene Co., Pa. Planning Commission.
II. Title.

728.69   SUGGESTED MODEL ORDINANCE REGULATING
H62   MOBILE HOME PARKS.
1960   HODES, BARNET.
SUGGESTED MODEL ORDINANCE REGULATING
MOBILE HOME PARKS.   3D REVISION.
CHICAGO, MOBILE HOMES MANUFACTURERS
ASSOCIATION, 1960.
8P.

    1. MOBILE HOMES.   I. TITLE.

VF
362.6   Suggested ordinance on existing buildings...
A52sug   American Insurance Association.
Suggested ordinance on existing buildings
used or converted for use as nursing and
convalescent homes, and residential-custodial
care facilities. New York, 1969.
16p.

    1. Nursing homes. I. Title.

629.136   Suggested outline for the preparation of
F11   urban (metropolitan) area airport studies.
U.S. Federal Aviation Agency.
Suggested outline for the preparation of
urban (metropolitan) area airport studies.
Wash., 1959.
7p.   (Planning series, item no. 1)

    1. Airports. I. Title.

711.585   SUGGESTED PLAN FOR NEIGHBORHOOD
(757271)   RECLAMATION AND REDEVELOPMENT.
G72   GREENVILLE, S.C. REAL ESTATE BOARD.
SUGGESTED PLAN FOR NEIGHBORHOOD
RECLAMATION AND REDEVELOPMENT.
GREENVILLE, S.C., 1953.
6L.

    1. NEIGHBORHOOD REHABILITATION -
GREENVILLE, S.C.   I. TITLE.

711.585
(792)
U71
A suggested program for the conservation and rehabilitation of urban communities in Utah County.
Utah County, Utah. Planning Commission.
A suggested program for the conservation and rehabilitation of urban communities in Utah County. [Provo] 1968.
15p.
U.S. Dept. of Housing and Urban Development. UPAP.
1. Neighborhood rehabilitation - Utah County, Utah. I. Title. II. Title: Conservation and rehabilitation of urban communities in Utah County. III. U.S. HUD-UPAP. Utah Co., Utah.

Suggestion systems
x Employee suggestions
xx Personnel management

058.7
:658.3
N17
Suggestion systems.
National Association of Suggestion Systems.
Membership list and by-laws.
1957, 58-
Chicago.
v.
For complete information see shelf list.
1. Suggestion systems.

651.4
(016)
I57
Suggested readings for the Interior Department secretarial staff.
U.S. Dept. of the Interior. Library.
Suggested readings for the Interior Department secretarial staff. Compiled by Elise Karen Brandt. Wash., 1967.
8p.
1. Office management - Bibl. 2. Office procedures - Bibl. I. Brandt, Elise Karen, comp. I. Title.

658.3
B87p
no.76
Suggestion systems.
Bureau of National Affairs, Washington, D.C.
Upward communications. Washington, 1964.
29p. (Its Personnel policies forum survey no. 76)
1. Personnel management. 2. Labor relations. 3. Suggestion systems. I. Title.

658.3
N17o
Suggestion systems.
National Association of Suggestion Systems.
(Cleveland Chapter)
The objectives of a suggestion system. Chicago, 1958.
33p.
1. Suggestion systems.

650.015
F67s
1950
Suggested research problems.
U.S. Bureau of Foreign and Domestic Commerce. Office of Industry and Commerce.
Suggested research problems: business - economics. 6th ed. Washington, U.S. Dept. of Commerce, 1950.
116 p. (U.S. Bureau of Foreign and Domestic Commerce. Domestic commerce series no. 24)
Edited by Lyle C. Bryant.
Processed.

658.3
C194U
SUGGESTION SYSTEMS.
CALIFORNIA. STATE MERIT AWARD BOARD.
USING EMPLOYEE SUGGESTIONS TO IMPROVE OUR STATE GOVERNMENT. SACRAMENTO, 1958.
26P.
1. SUGGESTION SYSTEMS. I. TITLE.

658.3
N17so
Suggestion systems.
National Association of Suggestion Systems.
Some questions and answers prepared by Advisory Service Committee. [Chicago, 1963]
31p.
1. Suggestion systems.

333.38
(744)
M17
Suggested rules and regulations governing the subdivision of land.
Massachusetts. Dept. of Commerce. (Div. of Planning)
Suggested rules and regulations governing the subdivision of land. Boston, 1963.
19p.
1. Subdivision regulation - Massachusetts. I. Title.

658.3
N17a
Suggestion systems.
National Association of Suggestion Systems.
(Philadelphia Chapter)
Administration of a suggestion plan. Chicago, 1957.
54p. charts.
1. Suggestion systems.

658.3
N17st
Suggestion systems
National Association of Suggestion Systems.
Statistical report, 1956-
Chicago, 1957-
v. annual
For further information see shelf list.
1. Suggestion systems.

711
(016)
C65
no. 154
Suggested series of movies for a course in urban planning.
Klain, Ambrose.
Suggested series of movies for a course in urban planning. Middletown, Pennsylvania State University, 1970.
6p. (Council of Planning Librarians. Exchange bibliography no. 154)
1. Planning - Bibl. 2. Films - Bibl. I. Pennsylvania. State University. II. Title. (Series: Council of Planning Librarians. Exchange bibliography no. 154)

658.3
N17an
Suggestion systems.
National Association of Suggestion Systems. (New York City Chapter)
Anonymous, partially, and fully identified suggestion plans. Chicago, 1961.
1v.
1. Suggestion systems.

658.3
N17s
Suggestion systems.
National Association of Suggestion Systems.
(Pittsburgh Chapter)
Suggestion boxes. Chicago, 1957.
28p. illus.
1. Suggestion systems.

LAW
T
C684s
Suggested State legislation...
Council of State Governments.
Suggested State legislation,
Chicago, 19
v.
For complete information see main card.
1. Legislation. 2. Legislative bodies. 3. State planning legislation. I. Title: State legislation. II. Title.

658.3
N17e
Suggestion systems.
National Association of Suggestion Systems.
(New York City Chapter)
Eligibility of suggesters. Chicago, 1959.
20p. charts.
1. Suggestion systems.

352
821
Suggestion systems.
Scandlyn, Sammie Lynn, comp.
101 winning ways to better municipal relations. Washington, National League of Cities, 1967.
36p.
1. Municipal government. 2. Suggestion systems. 3. Municipal services. I. National League of Cities, Washington, D.C. II. Title.

LAW
T
S728su
Suggested zoning by-law of the town of See-Konk.
Stewart, Pearson H
Suggested zoning by-law of the Town of See-Konk, by Pearson H. Stewart and Morton B. Braun. Prepared for Seekonk Planning Board. Seekonk, Mass., 1956.
1v. map.
Draft no. 3, December 1956.
1. Zoning legislation - Seekonk, Mass. I. Braun, Morton B., jt. au. II. Title.

LAW
T
N17
A778Le
Suggestion systems.
National Association of Suggestion Systems.
(Chicago Chapter)
Legal aspects and implications of suggestion plans. Chicago, 1960.
1v.
1. Suggestion systems. I. Title.

658.3
S23
SUGGESTION SYSTEMS.
SCHINAGL, MARY S
HISTORY OF EFFICIENCY RATINGS IN THE FEDERAL GOVERNMENT. NEW YORK, BOOKMAN ASSOCIATES, 1966.
147P.
BIBLIOGRAPHICAL NOTES: P.101-136.
1. SUGGESTION SYSTEMS. I. TITLE: EFFICIENCY RATINGS.

658.3
C48GU   SUGGESTION SYSTEMS.
U.S. CIVIL SERVICE COMMISSION.
A GUIDE FOR USING SUGGESTIONS AWARDS
TO IMPROVE GOVERNMENT OPERATIONS.
WASHINGTON, THE COMMISSION, 1955.
25P.

    1. SUGGESTION SYSTEMS. ~~I. TITLE.~~
2. FEDERAL CIVIL SERVICE .

658.3
C4d   Suggestion systems.
U.S. Civil Service Commission.
A guide to promotion and publicity for an
effective incentive awards program. Washington,
Govt. Print. Off., 1958.
57p. illus.

    1.Suggestion systems.

658.3
B681   Suggestion systems.
U.S. Housing and Home Finance Agency.
Ideas, performance and you; incentive
awards handbook. Washington, 1963.
12p.

    1. Suggestion systems. 2. Personnel manage-
ment. I. Title.

658.3
:770
N17   Suggestions systems - Films.
National Association of Suggestion Systems.
Mass film library listing. Chicago,
[1964?]
[11]p.

    1. Suggestions systems - Films.
2. Films - Bibl. 3. National Association
of Suggestion Systems - Films.

711.3
(75)
E26s   Suggestions for planning and zoning in
Appalachia.
U.S. Economic Research Service.
Suggestions for planning and zoning in
Appalachia. Wash., U.S. Dept. of Agriculture,
Economic Research Service, 1967.
52p. (ERS-330)

    1. Regional planning - Appalachian region.
2. Zoning - Appalachian region. I. Title.

331.252
N172   SUGGESTIONS FOR RESEARCH IN THE
ECONOMICS OF PENSIONS.
NATIONAL BUREAU OF ECONOMIC RESEARCH.
SUGGESTIONS FOR RESEARCH IN THE
ECONOMICS OF PENSIONS; REPORT OF AN
EXPLORATORY SURVEY OF THE ECONOMIC
ASPECTS OF ORGANIZED PROVISION FOR THE
AGED AND SURVIVING DEPENDENTS. NEW
YORK, 1957.
51P.

    1. PENSION. I. TITLE.

VF
690
F67   Suggestions of improved service of exterior
paint on FHA-insured houses.
U.S. Forest Service. Forest Products Laboratory,
Madison, Wis.
[Frame dwelling construction practices]
Madison, Wis. [1952?]
8 v. illus. tables.

    Contents:-pt.1. Current housing construction
practices in the Central, Lake and Northeastern
States, by L. O. Anderson, O.C. Heyer, L.V.
Teesdale.-pt. 2.Current housing construction
practices in West Coast states, by L.V. Teesdale,
W.G. Youngquist.-pt.3.Current housing practices

VF
690
F67   U.S. Forest Service. Forest Products Laboratory,
Madison, Wis. [Frame dwelling construction
practices] [1952?] (Card 2)

in the Southeastern and Southern states, by O.C.
Heyer, T.B. Heebink.-pt.4. A survey of exterior
painting on low cost houses, by F.L. Browne.-
pt.5. A survey of exterior painting on recently
built houses in southern Arizona, by F.L.Browne.-
pt.6.Cause of paint peeling on wood siding of
houses in Seattle, by Laurence V. Teesdale.-
pt.7.Suggestions for improved service of exterior

VF
690
F67   U.S. Forest Service. Forest Products Laboratory,
Madison, Wis. [Frame dwelling construction
practices] [1952?] (Card 3)

paint on FHA-insured houses, by F. L. Browne.-
pt.8. Heavy snows and cold weather may cause
roof leaks, by L. V. Teesdale.

    Final report, Research project O-T-24.
Housing and Home Finance Agency. Project
director: R. F. Luxford, Staff technician:
William A. Russell.
Typewritten.

VF
690
F67   U.S. Forest Service. Forest Products Laboratory,
Madison, Wis. [Frame dwelling construction
practices] [1952?] (Card 4)

    1.Building methods. 2.Paints and painting.
3.Winter construction. 4.Housing research
contracts. I.Luxford, R.F. II.Russell, Wm. A. III. U.S.
Housing and Home Finance Agency, Office of the Adminis-
trator, Division of Housing Research. IV.Title.
V.Anderson, L.O. VI.Heyer, O.C. VII.Teesdale, L.V.
VIII.Youngquist,W. G. IX.Heebink, T.B. X.Browne, F.L.
XI.Title:Current housing construction practices.
(Over)

332.721
(746)
C65S   SUGGESTIONS TO THE HOME BUYER.
CONNECTICUT. STATE HOUSING AUTHORITY.
SUGGESTIONS TO THE HOME BUYER, HOME
OWNERSHIP PROGRAM OF THE STATE OF
CONNECTICUT. HARTFORD, 1949.
16P.

    1. DIRECT LOANS FOR HOUSING -
CONNECTICUT. 2. HOME OWNERSHIP -
CONNECTICUT. I. TITLE. II. TITLE:
HOME OWNERSHIP PROGRAM OF THE STATE OF
CONNECTICUT.

325.3
I52s   Suicide among the American Indians.
U.S. Indian Health Service.
Suicide among the American Indians; two
workshops: Aberdeen, South Dakota, Sept. 1967;
Lewistown, Montana, November 1967. [Bethesda,
Md.] 1969.
37p. (U.S. Public Health Service
publication no. 1903)

    1. Indians. 2. Health. I. Title.

711.3
(75251)
M17   SUITLAND-DISTRICT HEIGHTS.
MARYLAND-NATIONAL CAPITAL PARK AND
PLANNING COMMISSION.
SUITLAND-DISTRICT HEIGHTS, PLANNING
AREA 17, PRELIMINARY PLAN.... SILVER
SPRING, MD., 1965.
36P.

    IN POCKET: 8 FOLDED MAPS.

    1. REGIONAL PLANNING - PRINCE
GEORGES CO., MD. 2. LAND USE -
PRINCE GEORGES CO., MD. 3. ZONING -
PRINCE GEORGE S CO., MD. I. TITLE.

332
C65i
1964   Suits, Daniel Burbridge, 1918-
Commission on Money and Credit.
Impacts of monetary policy. A series
of research studies prepared for the
Commission on Money and Credit by
Daniel B. Suits and others. Englewood
Cliffs, N.J., Prentice-Hall, 1964.
688 p.
"Especially prepared for the Com-
mission on money and credit as part of
its ... Money and credit: their in-
fluence on jobs, prices, and growth."
(Cont'd next card)

332
C65i
1964   Commission on Money and Credit. Impacts
of monetary policy...1964. (Card 2)

    1. Finance. I. Suits, Daniel Burbridge,
1918- II. Title.

333.33
(7471)
S84   SUKLOFF, HYMAN.
SMALL PROPERTY OWNER'S LEGAL GUIDE.
NEW YORK, ARCO, 1965.
112P.

    1. REAL PROPERTY - NEW YORK (CITY)
I. TITLE.

691.32
E53   SULFATE-RESISTANT CONCRETE.
ENGLAND, O LYNN.
SULFATE-RESISTANT CONCRETE:
LITERATURE REVIEW. VICKSBURG, MISS.,
U.S. ARMY ENGINEERING WATERWAYS
EXPERIMENT STATION, 1961.
23P. (U.S. WATERWAYS EXPERIMENT
STATION. TECHNICAL REPORT NO. 6-569,
REPORT 1)

    1. CONCRETE. I. U.S.
WATERWAYS EXPERIMENT STATION,
VICKSBURG, MISS. II. TITLE.

330
(747)
S97E   SULFRIN, SIDNEY C
SYRACUSE UNIVERSITY. BUSINESS RESEARCH
CENTER.
THE ECONOMIC STATUS OF UPSTATE NEW
YORK AT MID-CENTURY, WITH SPECIAL
REFERENCE TO DISTRESSED COMMUNITIES AND
THEIR ADJUSTMENTS, BY SIDNEY C. SUFRIN
AND OTHERS. A REPORT TO THE NEW YORK
STATE TEMPORARY STATE COMMISSION ON
ECONOMIC EXPANSION. SYRACUSE, N.Y.,
1960.
149L.

    1. ECONOMIC CONDITIONS - NEW YORK
(STATE) I. NEW YORK (STATE)
(CONTINUED ON NEXT CARD)

330
(747)
S97E   SYRACUSE UNIVERSITY. BUSINESS RESEARCH
CENTER. THE ECONOMIC STATUS ...1960.
(CARD 2)

TEMPORARY STATE COMMISSION ON ECONOMIC
EXPANSION. II. SULFRIN, SIDNEY C.
III. TITLE.

697.8
H62   Sulfur dioxide.
Hochheiser, Seymour.
Methods of measuring and monitoring atmosph-
eric sulfur dioxide. Cincinnati, U.S. Robert
A. Taft Sanitary Engineering Center, 1964.
48p. (U.S. Public Health Service. Publi-
cation no. 999-AP-6; Environmental health
series, air pollution)
CFSTI. PB 168 865.

    1. Air pollution. I. U.S. Robert A. Taft
Sanitary Engineering Center. II. Title.
III. Title: Sulfur dioxide.

697.8
N174co   Sulfur oxide.
U.S. National Air Pollution Control
Administration.
Control techniques for sulfur oxide air
pollutants. Wash., 1969.
1v.
Bibliography: p. 6-15 - 6-23.

    1. Air pollution. I. Title: Sulfur
oxide. II. Title.

388
N671   Sulkin, M.A.
        North American Rockwell Corp.
            Implementation requirements for four ad-
        vanced urban transportation systems. Final
        report by Transportation System Technology,
        M.A. Sulkin, Program Manager. Los Angeles,
        1968.
            211p. (NA-68-807)
            Prepared for the U.S. Dept. of Housing
        and Urban Development. Contract H-779,
        Phase II.
        U.S. Mass Transportation Demonstration
        Grant Program.
        CFSTI.   PB 183 039.
                        (Cont'd on next card)

388
N671   North American Rockwell Corp. Implemen-
        tation...1968.   (Card 2)

            1. Transportation. 2. Journey to work.
        I. Sulkin, M.A. II. U.S. Dept. of
        Housing and Urban Development. III. U.S.
        Mass Transportation Demonstration Grant
        Program. IV. Title.

378
S85   Sulkin, Sidney.
            Complete planning for college. Rev. New York,
        Harper & Row, 1968.
            324p.

            1. Universities and colleges. 2. Education.
        I. Title.

396
S85   Sullerot, Evelyne.
            Woman, society and change. New York, World
        University Library, 1971.
            256p.

            Translated from the French by Margaret
        Scotford Archer.
            Bibliography: p. 249-250.

            1. Women. I. Title.

711.4
(76186) Sulligent, Ala. Town Planning Commission.
S85   Sulligent, Alabama: community facilities
        plan. [Prepared in cooperation with]
        Alabama State Planning and Industrial
        Development Board. Sulligent, 1962.
            28p.
        U.S. Urban Renewal Adm. UPAP.

            1. Master plan - Sulligent, Ala.
        2. Community facilities - Sulligent, Ala.
        I. U.S. URA-   UPAP. Sulligent,
        Ala.

711.14
(76186) Sulligent, Ala. Town Planning Commission.
S85   Sulligent, Alabama: long range land use
        plan. [In cooperation with] Alabama State
        Planning and Industrial Development Board.
        Sulligent, 1960.
            44p.
        U.S. Urban Renewal Adm. UPAP.

            1. Land use - Sulligent, Ala. I. U.S.
        URA-UPAP. Sulligent, Ala.

711.4
(76186) Sulligent, Ala. Town Planning Commission.
S85   Sulligent, Alabama: major thoroughfare
        plan. [Prepared in cooperation with]
        Alabama State Planning and Industrial
        Development Board. Sulligent, 1961.
            [48]p.
        U.S. Urban Renewal Adm. UPAP.

            1. Master plan - Sulligent, Ala.
        2. Streets -   Sulligent, Ala.
        I. U.S.   URA-UPAP. Sulligent,
        Ala.

352.1
(76186) Sulligent, Ala. Town Planning Commission.
S85   Sulligent, Alabama; public improvements
        program. [Prepared in cooperation with]
        Alabama State Planning and Industrial
        Development Board. Sulligent, 1962.
            20p.

        U.S. Urban Renewal Adm. UPAP.

            1. Capital improvement programs -
        Sulligent, Ala.   I. U.S. URA-UPAP.
        Sulligent,   Ala.

333.38
(76186) Sulligent, Ala. Town Planning Commission.
S85   Sulligent, Alabama: subdivision regulations.
        [In cooperation with] Alabama State Planning
        and Industrial Development Board. Sulligent,
        1960.
            36p.

        U.S. Urban Renewal Adm. UPAP.

            1. Subdivision regulation - Sulligent, Ala.
        I. U.S. URA-UPAP. Sulligent, Ala.

711.5
(76187 Sulligent, Ala. Town Planning Commission.
:347)   Sulligent Alabama: zoning ordinance. [In
S85   cooperation with] Alabama State Planning and
        Industrial Development Board. Sulligent, 1960.
            21p.

        U.S. Urban Renewal Adm. UPAP.

            1. Zoning legislation - Sulligent, Ala.
        I. U.S. URA-UPAP. Sulligent, Ala.

691.8
S85   Sullins, R   T
            Manual for structural stability analysis of
        sandwich plates and shells, by R.T. Sullins
        and others. Prepared by General Dynamics Corp.
        Wash., National Aeronautics and Space Adminis-
        tration, 1969.
            1v. (U.S. National Aeronautics and Space
        Administration. NASA CR-1457)

            1. Panels. 2. Structural engineering.
        I. General Dynamics Corp. II. U.S. National
        Aeronautics and Space Administration.
        III. Title.

002
M24   Sullivan, Dennis J   jt. au.
        Meister, David.
            Evaluation of user reactions to a prototype
        on-line information retrieval system, by David
        Meister and Dennis J. Sullivan. Prepared by
        Bunker-Ramo Corp., Canoga Park, Calif. for
        National Aeronautics and Space Administration.
        Alexandria, Va., U.S. Clearinghouse for Federal
        Scientific and Technical Information, 1967.
            58p.
            1. Documentation. 2. Automation. 3. Library
        science - Automation. I. Sullivan, Dennis J.,
        jt. au. II. Bunker-   Ramo Corp., Conoga
        Park, Calif.
                        (Cont'd on next card)

002
M24   Meister, David.   Evaluation of user
        reactions...1967.   (Card 2)

            III. U.S. National Aeronautics and Space
        Administration. IV. Title.

331
S85   Sullivan, David.
            Labor's role in the war on poverty. Wash.,
        U.S. Dept. of Labor, Manpower Administration,
        1967.
            34p.
        At head of title: Seminar on Manpower Policy
        and Program, Apr. 1967.

            1. Labor relations. 2. Public assistance.
        I. U.S. Dept. of Labor. II. Title.
        III. Title: Seminar on Manpower Policy and
        Program, 1967.

334.1
(7471) Sullivan, Donald G
S85   Cooperative housing and community develop-
        ment; a comparative evaluation of three
        housing projects in East Harlem. New York,
        Praeger, 1971.
            217p. (Praeger special studies in U.S.
        economic and social development)
            Bibliography: p. 207-217.
            1. Cooperative housing - New York (City)
        2. Community development - New York (City)
        3. Housing surveys - New York (City)
        I. Title.

Fl.-Va.-Norfolk
DATE OF REQUEST 8/5/54   L.C. CARD NO.

AUTHOR
SULLIVAN, FRANK
TITLE Norfolk clears slum areas in huge program.

SERIES Reprint, The Commonwealth, Feb. 1954.

EDITION   PUB. DATE   PAGING
PUBLISHER

RECOMMENDED BY   REVIEWED IN
MWL   HB Newsltr 6/30/54 p. 4
                    ORDER RECORD

VF
711.585 Sullivan, Frank.
(75552)   The Norfolk urban redevelopment program.
S85   [Norfolk] 196C
            [5]p.   illus.

            Reprinted from the Commonwealth, the
        magazine of Virginia, Nov. 1960.

            1. Urban renewal - Norfolk, Va.
        2. Neighborhood rehabilitation - Norfolk,
        Va.

628.3   Sullivan, Gerald M
R61st   U.S. Robert A. Taft Sanitary Engineering
        Center.
            A study of serial distribution for soil
        absorption systems, by Gerald M. Sullivan
        and others. Field investigations by W. F.
        Smith and A. J. Muhich. Random sampling
        experiment by Harold A. Thomas Jr. and
        Allan B. Edwards. Report to the Federal
        Housing Administration. Cincinnati, 1959.
            32p.   diagrs., tables.
        1. Septic tanks. 2. Soils. I. Sullivan, Gerald M.
        II. U.S. Federal Housing Administration. III. Title:
        Serial distribution for   soil absorption systems.

628.1   SULLIVAN, GERALD M
(791)   U.S. ROBERT A   TAFT SANITARY
R61   ENGINEERING CENTER, CINCINNATI.
        DOMESTIC WATER USE IN PHOENIX,
        ARIZONA; FINAL REPORT TO THE FEDERAL
        HOUSING ADMINISTRATION, BY GERALD M.
        SULLIVAN AND OTHERS. CINCINNATI, 1959.
            20L.

            1. WATER SUPPLY - PHOENIX, ARIZ.
        I. SULLIVAN, GERALD M. II. U.S.
        FEDERAL HOUSING ADMINISTRATION.
        III. TITLE.

325
(74811) Sullivan, Leon H
S85   Build, brother, build. Philadelphia, Macrae
        Smith, 1969.
            192p.

            1. Negroes - Philadelphia. 2. Community
        development - Citizen participation.
        I. Title.

728.1
S85   Sullivan, Leonor K
            Address by Democratic Congresswoman
        from Missouri, before the 34th annual
        meeting of the National Housing Conference,
        March 15, 1965. [n.p.], 1965.
            10p.

            1. Federal housing programs. I. National
        Housing Conference, 34th, Wash., D. C., 1965.

920
K18

SULLIVAN, LOUIS.
    Kaufman, Mervyn.
      Father of skyscrapers; a biography of Louis
Sullivan. Boston, Little, Brown, 1969.
    171p.

      1. Sullivan, Louis.. 2. Architecture.
I. Title.

711.333
(74735)
S85c

Sullivan County, N.Y. Planning Board.
    New York University. Graduate School of
Public Administration.
      The comprehensive master plan for Sullivan
County, New York. Prepared in cooperation
with the Sullivan County Planning Board.
New York, 1962.
    125p.
    U.S. Urban Renewal Adm. UPAP.

      1. Master plan - Sullivan Co., N.Y.
2. County planning - Sullivan Co., N.Y.
I. Sullivan County, N.Y. Planning Board.
II. U.S. URA-   UPAP. Sullivan Co.,
N.Y.

4788-
4796

SULLIVAN CO., PA. PLANNING COMMISSION.
COMPREHENSIVE PLAN....1969.   (CARD 2)

      1. MASTER PLAN - SULLIVAN CO., PA.
I. NORTHERN TIER REGIONAL PLANNING
COMMISSION. II. HUD. 701. SULLIVAN
CO., PA.

720
W74g
1971

SULLIVAN, LOUIS.
    Wright, Frank Lloyd, 1869-1959.
      Genius and the mobocracy. Enl.ed. New York,
Horizon Press, 1971.
    247p.

      1. Architecture. 2. Sullivan, Louis.
I. Title.

711.333
(74735)
S85c
vol.1

Sullivan County, N.Y. Planning Board.
    New York University. Graduate School
of Public Administration.
      A comprehensive plan for Sullivan County.
Basic studies and surveys Vol. 1. Prepared
in cooperation with the Sullivan Co.
Planning Board. New York, 1961.
    164p.
    U.S. Urban Renewal Adm. UPAP.

      1. Master plan - Sullivan Co., N.Y.
2. County planning - Sullivan Co., N.Y.
I. Sullivan County, N.Y. Planning Board.
II. U.S.   URA-UPAP. Sullivan
Co., N.Y.

5203
5204
5205
5206

SULLIVAN CO., PA. PLANNING COMMISSION.
PLANNING: 1, DEVELOPMENT AIDS PROGRAM;
2, THE HISTORICAL DEVELOPMENT; 3,
PHYSICAL FEATURES AND NATURAL RESOURCES;
4, EXISTING LAND USE. BY NORTHERN TIER
REGIONAL PLANNING COMMISSION. LAPORTE,
PA., 1969.
    4 V. (HUD 701 REPORT)

      1. COUNTY PLANNING - SULLIVAN CO., PA.
I. NORTHERN TIER REGIONAL PLANNING
COMMISSION. II. HUD. 701. SULLIVAN,
PA.

920
1720
B87

SULLIVAN, LOUIS HENRY, 1856-1924.
BUSH-BROWN, ALBERT.
    LOUIS SULLIVAN. NEW YORK, G.
BRAZILLER, 1960.
    128P. (THE MASTERS OF WORLD
ARCHITECTURE SERIES)

      SELECTED BIBLIOGRAPHY OF BOOKS AND
ARTICLES WRITTEN BY LOUIS SULLIVAN : P.
120. SELECTED BIBLIOGRAPHY ON LOUIS
SULLIVAN : P. 121-122.

      1. ARCHITECTS. 2. SULLIVAN, LOUIS
HENRY, 1856-1924 .

339.5
(74735)
G26

Sullivan Co., N.Y. Planning Board.
    Geotechnics and Resources inc., New York.
      The natural resources of Sullivan County,
New York. A general and preliminary study
for the Sullivan County Planning Board and
the New York State Dept. of Commerce.
Under subcontract to New York University.
New York, 1961.
    1 v.
    U.S. Urban Renewal Adm. UPAP.

         (Cont'd on next card)

4779
4780

SULLIVAN CO., PA. PLANNING COMMISSION.
SOIL SURVEY: 1, SOIL SURVEY MAPS OF
DEVELOPING AREAS; 2, SOIL SURVEY
INTERPRETATIONS FOR DEVELOPING AREAS. BY
UNITED STATES SOIL CONSERVATION SERVICE.
LAPORTE, PA., 1968.
    2 V. (HUD 701 REPORT)

      1. SOIL SURVEYS - SULLIVAN CO., PA.
I. U.S. SOIL CONSERVATION SERVICE.
II. HUD. 701. SULLIVAN CO., PA.

VF
691.421
W15

Sullivan, R R jt.au.
    Welton, J D
      Felted ceramics, by J.D. Welton and R.R.
Sullivan. Presented at the 67th Annual
Meeting of the American Ceramic Society in
Philadelphia, May 3, 1965 (Society
Symposium 2, no. 5-82-65) [Philadelphia?]
American Ceramic Society, 1966.
    586-589p.
    Reprinted from the American Ceramic
Society bulletin, June 7, 1966.

1. Clay. 2. Tile construction. I. Sullivan, R.R.,
jt. au. II. American   Ceramic Society.
67th Meeting,   Philadelphia, 1966.
III. Title.

339.5
(74735)
G26

    Geotechnics and Resources inc. New York.
      The natural resources of Sullivan County,
New York...1961.   (Card 2)

      1. Natural resources - Sullivan Co., N.Y.
2. Water resources - Sullivan Co., N.Y.
I. Sullivan Co., N.Y. Planning Board.
II. New York University. Graduate School
of Public Administration. III. U.S. URA-
UPAP. Sullivan Co., N.Y.

324
K15k

Sullivant, Charles A
    Kansas. University. Governmental Research
Center.
      Kansas votes, gubernatorial elections,
1859-1956, by Clarence J. Hein and Charles A.
Sullivant. Lawrence, Kan., 1958.
    103p. tables.

      1. Elections. 2. State government - Kansas.
I. Hein, Clarence J. II. Sullivant, Charles
A.

LAW
S

Sullivan, Raymond R
    California. Legislature. Assembly. Interim
Committee on Revenue and Taxation.
      Taxation of property in California; a major
tax study. Part 5. A report for the California Legislature Assembly Interim Committee
on Revenue and Taxation, Dec. 1934, by David
R. Doerr and Raymond R. Sullivan, with special sections by Harold M. Somers and others.
[Sacramento] Calif., 1964.
    361p.   (Its v. 4, no. 12)

1. Real property - Tax-   ation. 2. Taxation -
California. I. Doerr,   David R.
II. Sullivan, Raymond   R. II. Title.

711.5
(74735)
1347
R19

Sullivan County, N.Y. Planning Board
    Raymond & May Associates.
      Proposed zoning ordinance, village of
Liberty, Sullivan County New York. Prepared in cooperation with the Sullivan
County, N.Y. Planning Board. New York,
1965.
    70p.
    U.S. Urban Renewal Adm. UPAP.

1. Zoning legislation - Liberty, N.Y. 2. County
planning - Sullivan Co., N.Y. I. Sullivan County,
N.Y. Planning Board. II. U.S. URA-UPAP. Liberty,
N.Y.

324
K15

Sullivant, Charles A
    Kansas. University. Governmental Research
Center.
      Kansas votes, national elections,
1859-1956, by June G. Cabe and Charles A.
Sullivant. Lawrence, Kan., 1956.
    215p. tables.

      1.Elections. I.Cabe, June G II.Sullivant,
Charles A III.Title.

711.4
(77862)
S85

Sullivan, Mo. City Planning Commission.
    Bartholomew (Harland) and Associates.
      A report upon the comprehensive plan for
Sullivan, Missouri. Prepared for the City
Planning Commission, Sullivan, Mo.
St. Louis, 1964.
    65p.
    Prepared for Missouri Division of Commerce
and Industrial Development.
    U.S. Urban Renewal Adm. UPAP.

      1. Master plan - Sullivan, Mo.
I. Sullivan, Mo. City Planning Commission.
II. U.S.   URA-UPAP.
Sullivan,   Mo.

333.38
(74735)
S17
1963

Sullivan County, N.Y. Planning Board.
    Sargent-Webster-Crenshaw & Folley.
      Proposed subdivision regulations, town
of Fallsburgh, Sullivan County, New York.
Rev. Prepared in cooperation with the
Sullivan Co., N.Y. Planning Board.
Syracuse, N.Y., 1963.
    34p.
    U.S. Urban Renewal Adm. UPAP.

      1. Subdivision regulation - Fallsburgh, N.Y.
2. County planning - Sullivan Co., N.Y.
I. Sullivan County, N.Y. Planning Board.
II. U.S. URA-   UPAP. Sullivan
County, N.Y.

628.1
(781)
K15k

Sullivant, Charles A
    Kansas. University. Governmental Research
Center.
      The Kansas watershed district, by Charles A.
Sullivant. Lawrence, Kan., 1960.
    29p. maps. (Its Citizen's pamphlet
no. 27)

      1. Water resources - Kansas. I. Sullivant, Charles
A. (Series)

3125
3126
3127

SULLIVAN, N.Y. PLANNING BOARD.
    A COMPREHENSIVE MASTER PLAN: 1, BASIC
STUDIES, TOWN AND VILLAGE; 2,
COMPREHENSIVE PLAN, TOWN AND VILLAGE; 3,
PROPOSED ZONING REGULATION, TOWN.
CHITTENANGO, N.Y., 1970.
    3 V. (HUD 701 REPORT)

      1. MASTER PLAN - SULLIVAN, N.Y.
2. MASTER PLAN - CHITTENANGO, N.Y.
I. HUD. 701. CHITTENANGO, N.Y.

4788-
4796

SULLIVAN CO., PA. PLANNING COMMISSION.
COMPREHENSIVE PLAN: 1, POPULATION; 2,
COMMUNITY FACILITIES STUDY; 3, ECONOMIC
BASE STUDY; 4, DEVELOPMENT OF
ALTERNATIVES AND ESTABLISHMENT OF
POLITICS, STANDARDS AND OBJECTIVES; 5,
HOUSING; 6, FISCAL AND GOVERNMENTAL
STRUCTURE; 7, TRANSPORTATION STUDY; 8,
RELATED STUDY OF AN AREAWIDE SCOPE; 9,
EXTERNAL INFLUENCE FACTORS STUDY. BY
NORTHERN TIER REGIONAL PLANNING
COMMISSION. LAPORTE, PA., 1969.
    9 V. (HUD 701 REPORT)

      (CONTINUED ON NEXT CARD)

LAW
I

Sulphur oxide.
    Japan. Laws, statutes, etc.
      Air pollution control law (1968)
(ambient air quality standard for
sulphur oxide) (emission standard)
(Tokyo) 1969.
    50p.

      1. Air pollution - Japan - Law and
legislation. I. Title: Sulphur oxide.
II. Title.

697.8
N175
Sulphur oxides.
U.S. National Industrial Pollution Control Council.
Air pollution by sulfur oxides. Staff report. Wash., 1971.
24p.

1. Air pollution. I. Title. II. Title: Sulphur oxides.

690.091.82
S25
Sumichrast, Michael, jt. au.
Seldin Maury.
Urban development planning; a construction data approach (developing a perpetual inventory) Address on data processing and econometric modeling, at the American Real Estate and Urban Economics Association, New York City, by Maury Seldin and Michael Sumichrast. [n.p.] 1969.
14p.
1. Building permits. 2. Housing market. 3. Housing statistics. I. Sumichrast, Michael, jt. au. II. Title.

628.44
L23
Summaries of solid waste research and training grants - 19 0.
Lefke, Louis W
Summaries of solid waste research and training grants - 19 0, by Louis W. Lefke and others. [Wash.] U.S. Environmental Protection Agency, Solid Waste Management Office, 1971.
134p. (SW-5r 2)

1. Refuse and refuse disposal. I. U.S. Environmental Protection Agency. II. Title.

690.596
S85
Sumichrast, Michael.
Demolition and other factors in housing replacement demand, by Michael Sumichrast and Norman Farquhar. Wash., Homebuilding Press of the National Association of Home Builders, 1967.
98p.
Bibliography: p. 95-96.
1. Demolition. 2. Housing market. I. Farquhar, Norman, jt. au. II. National Association of Home Builders. III. Title.

711.4
(76176)
S85
Sumiton, Ala. Town Planning Commission.
Sumiton, Alabama: comprehensive town plan. Land use plan, major street plan, community facilities plan, public utilities plan, public works program. [In cooperation with] Alabama State Planning and Industrial Development Board. Sumiton, 1958.
1v. diagrs., maps, tables.
U.S. Urban Renewal Administration, Urban Planning Assistance Program.
1. Master plan - Sumiton, Ala. I. U.S. Urban Renewal Administration. Urban Planning As-   sistance Program.

649
H21s
U.S. Dept. of Health, Education and Welfare. Office of Juvenile Delinquency and Youth Development.
Summaries of training projects. Training projects being supported under the Juvenile delinquency and youth offenses control act (Public law 87-274 as amended by Public law 88-368) Administered by the Office of Juvenile Delinquency and Youth Development in cooperation with the President's Committee on Juvenile Delinquency and Youth Crime. Washington, Govt. Print. Off., 1965.
167p.   (Continued on next card)

728.1
:308
N17ho
Sumichrast, Michael.
National Association of Home Builders.
Housing vacancy rates; how useful are they for market analysis? Paper by Michael Sumichrast. [Washington] 1963.
Lef. [26]p. (Its Technical paper no.1)
At head of title: Economic news notes: special report.

1. Vacancy surveys. 2. Housing market analysis. I. Sumichrast, Michael. II. Title.

333.38
(76176)
S85
Sumiton, Ala. Town Planning Commission.
Sumiton, Alabama: land subdivision regulations and manual. [In cooperation with] Alabama State Planning and Industrial Development Board. Sumiton, 1958.
23p. diagrs.
U.S. Urban Renewal Administration, Urban Planning Assistance Program.
1. Subdivision regulation - Sumiton, Ala. I. U.S. Urban Renewal Administration. Urban Planning Assistance Program. Sumiton, Ala.

649
H21s
U.S. Dept. of Health, Education and Welfare. Office of Juvenile Delinquency and Youth Development. Summaries of training ...
(Card 2)

1. Juvenile delinquency. 2. Youth. I. U.S. President's Committee on Juvenile Delinquency and Youth Crime. II. Title.

728.1
:308
M15
Sumichrast, Michael.
Manheim, Uriel.
How to do housing market research; a handbook for local home builders associations. Prepared in cooperation with the NAHB Economics and Policy Staff. Edited by Michael Sumichrast. Washington, National Association of Home Builders, 1963.
185p.

1. Housing market. 2. Building industry. I. Sumichrast, Michael. II. National Association of Home Builders. III. Title: Handbook for local home builders associations.

711.5
(76176
:347)
S85
Sumiton, Ala. Town Planning Commission.
Sumiton, Alabama: zoning ordinance. [In cooperation with] Alabama State Planning and Industrial Development Board. Sumiton, 1958.
1v. map, tables.
U.S. Urban Renewal Administration, Urban Planning Assistance Program.
1. Zoning legislation - Sumiton, Ala. I. U.S. Urban Renewal Administration. Urban Planning Assistance Program. Sumiton, Ala.

628.1
W17s
A summary analysis of nineteen tests of proposed evaluation procedures on selected water and...
U.S. Water Resources Council. (Special Task Force)
A summary analysis of nineteen tests of proposed evaluation procedures on selected water and land resources projects. Wash., 1970.
1v.

1. Water resources. 2. Land use. I. Title.

728.1
:308
S85
Sumichrast, Michael.
Opportunities for American builders abroad. Prepared for International Housing Committee. Washington, National Association of Home Builders of the United States, 1964.
29p.

1. Housing market. 2. Building industry. I. National Association of Home Builders of the United States. II. Title.

VF
711.585
H68
Summaries of local redevelopment programs.
U.S. Housing and Home Finance Agency. Office of the Administrator. Division of Slum Clearance and Urban Redevelopment.
Summaries of local redevelopment programs.
Series 1 -   Dec. 1950 -
Washington, 1950 -
pts.

For full information see shelf list card.
1. Urban redevelopment. I. Title. II. Title: Local redevelopment summaries.

312
1963
C25m
v.1
Summary and subject statistics.
U.S. Bureau of the Census.
Census of manufacturers, 1963. Vol. 1: Summary and subject statistics. Wash., For sale by the Supt. of Doc., Govt. Print. Off., 1966.
1v.

1. Census - Manufacturers - 1963. I. Title: Summary and subject statistics.

690
S85
Sumichrast, Michael.
Profile of the builder and his industry, by Michael Sumichrast and Sara A. Frankel. Wash., National Association of Home Builders, 1970.
222p.

1. Building industry. 2. Housing market. I. Frankel, Sara A., jt. au. II. National Association of Home Builders. III. Title.

VF
711.585
(73:347)
H68
3c
Summaries of slum clearance and public housing decisions.
U.S. Housing and Home Finance Agency. Office of the Administrator. Division of Law.
Summaries of slum clearance and public housing decisions. [Washington, D.C.], Oct. 1949.
157 p.
Processed.
Cover title.
1. Urban redevelopment-U.S.-Legislation. 2. Public housing-U.S.-Legislation. I. Title. II. Title: Slum clearance and public housing decisions.

312
1967
C25m
v.1

312
1967
C25m
MC67
(1)-
Summary and subject statistics.
U.S. Bureau of the Census.
Census of manufactures, 1967. Vol. 1: Summary and subject statistics. Wash., Govt. Print. Off., 1970.
v.

— --- Preprints. (Its Summary and subject series MC67(1)-1-12)
v.

(Cont'd on next card)

690.091.82
H65u
Sumichrast, Michael
Homer Hoyt Institute.
The uniform building permit reporting system: a demonstration in the Washington, D.C. SMSA. The final report of a Homer Hoyt Institute project conducted under the direction of Michael Sumichrast and Maury Seldin. Wash., 1970.
135p.
Prepared under contract H-1020 for the Dept. of Housing and Urban Development.
1. Building permits. I. Sumichrast, Michael. II. Seldin, Maury. III. U.S. Dept. of   Housing and Urban Development. IV. Title.

628.440.15
B72
Summaries of solid waste intramural research and development projects.
Breidenbach, Andrew W
Summaries of solid waste intramural research and development projects. [Wash.] U.S. Environmental Protection Agency, Solid Waste Management Office, 1971.
24p. (SW-14r)

1. Refuse and refuse disposal - Research. I. U.S. Environmental Protection Agency. II. Title.

312
1967
C25m
v.1

312
1967
C25m
MC67
(S)-
U.S. Bureau of the Census. Census of manufactures, 1967...1970.   (Card 2)

— --- Preprints. (Its Special report series MC67 (S)-1-8)
v.

1. Census - Manufacturers - 1967. I. Title: Summary and subject statistics.

336
(753)
D47s
Summary budget review for the City of
Washington, D.C.
District of Columbia.
Summary budget review for the City of
Washington, D.C., fiscal year, 19 .

Wash., 19

v.

For Library holdings see main entry.

1. Budget - District of Columbia. I. Title.

658
S85
Summary of binary arithmetic and related
number systems. [n.p.1970?]
[6]p.
Xeroxed copy: p. 7-12.

1. Management. 2. Automation.
I. Title: Binary arithmetic and related
number systems. II. Title: Number
systems.

VF
336
C25
G-GF
Summary of Governmental finances.
U. S. Bureau of the Census.
Summary of governmental finances.

Washington, 1952-
v. (Its Governmental finances in
the United States, G-GF series.)

For full information see shelflist card.
see also its Governmental debt in 1950-52.
Vols. for 1959- have series: G-GR no.1

1.Finance. I.Title. II.Title: Governmental
finances, summary.

534.83
E58s
Summary, conclusions and recommendations from
report to the President and Congress on noise.
U.S. Environmental Protection Agency.
Summary, conclusions and recommendations
from report to the President and Congress on
noise. Wash., 1971.
13p. (NRC500.1)

1. Noise. I. Title.

352.1
C25
no.1
Summary of city government finances.
U.S. Bureau of the Census.
Summary of city government finances in 194?-

Washington, 194?-
v. (Its City finances, G-CF series,
no. 1)

For full information see shelf list card.

336
H68s
Summary of HUD budget.
U.S. Dept. of Housing and Urban Development.
Summary of the HUD budget, 197?-173;

Washington, 1972-
/ v.

For Library holdings see main entry.

1. Budget. 2. U.S. Dept. of Housing and
Urban Development - Appropriations and
expenditures. I. Title.

362.6
A52SU
SUMMARY OF A SURVEY OF NURSING HOMES.
AMERICAN NURSING HOME ASSOCIATION.
SUMMARY OF A SURVEY OF NURSING HOMES,
1958-1959. A STUDY BY THE AMERICAN
NURSING HOME ASSOCIATION AND THE
AMERICAN MEDICAL ASSOCIATION, COUNCIL ON
MEDICAL SERVICE. CHICAGO, AMERICAN
MEDICAL ASSO., COUNCIL ON MEDICAL
SERVICE, 1960?
5P.
THIS IS ONLY AN INQUIRY INTO MEDICAL
CARE FACILITIES OF NURSING HOMES, NOT A
STATISTICAL INVENTORY TYPE SURVEY AS
THAT OF AUG. 28 , 1957.

(CONTINUED ON NEXT CARD)

353
(794)
C15s
Summary of Council activities and accom-
plishments.
California. Intergovernmental Council on
Urban Growth.
Summary of Council activities and accom-
plishments. [n.p.] 1967.
5p.

1. Metropolitan government - California.
2. Intergovernmental relations - California.
I. Title.

VF
720.2
H68
A summary of historic preservation aids
available through programs of the
U.S. Dept. of Housing and Urban Development.
A summary of historic preservation aids
available through programs of the Dept. of
Housing and Urban Development. Washington,
1966.
5p.

1. Architecture - Conservation and
restoration. I. Title.

362.6
A52SU
AMERICAN NURSING HOME ASSOCIATION.
SUMMARY OF A ...1960 (CARD 2
1. NURSING HOMES. 2. NURSING HOMES -
SURVEYS. I. TITLE. II. TITLE:
SURVEY OF NURSING HOMES, 1958-1959.
III. AMERICAN MEDICAL ASSOCIATION.
COUNCIL ON MEDICAL SERVICE.

352.6
E24
SUMMARY OF ECONOMIC ASPECTS.
EDISON ELECTRIC INSTITUTE.
SUMMARY OF ECONOMIC ASPECTS, SINGLE
COMPLETE ELECTRIC SERVICE COMPARED WITH
DUAL ELECTRIC AND GAS SERVICE FOR
MULTIPLE HOUSING. NEW YORK, 1959.
12P.

1. PUBLIC UTILITIES. I. TITLE.

728.1
1336.18
(7471)
N280o
no.6
Summary of Housing and Redevelopment Board
program as of June 30, 1962.
New York (City) Housing and Redevelopment
Board. (Bureau of Planning and Program
Research)
Summary of Housing and Redevelopment Board
program as of June 30, 1962. Prepared by
Rhoda Radisch. New York, 1962.
[4]p. (Its Occasional memo no. 6)

1. Public housing - New York (City)
2. Public housing projects. I. Radisch,
Rhoda. II. Title.

332
C65SUM
SUMMARY OF ACTIVITIES.
U.S. CONGRESS. SENATE. COMMITTEE ON
BANKING AND CURRENCY.
SUMMARY OF ACTIVITIES: REPORT.
WASHINGTON, GOVT. PRINT. OFF., 1956.
42P. (84TH CONGRESS, 2D SESSION.
SENATE. REPORT NO. 2828)

1. FINANCE. 2. HOUSING LEGISLATION.
I. TITLE.

627.4
R67
Summary of floods in the United States during 1963.
Rostvedt, J   O
Summary of floods in the United States during
1963; floods of 1963 in the United States.
Prepared in cooperation with Federal, State,
and local agencies. Wash., Govt. Print. Off.,
1968.
120p. (Geological survey water-supply
paper 1830-B)
Bibliography: p. H115-H116.

1. Floods. I. Title. II. U.S. Geological
Survey.

988
(79TTT1)
D25
Summary
Summary of interim report to the Puget
Sound Governmental Conference...
De Leuw, Cather and Company.
Summary of interim report to the Puget
Sound Governmental Conference on feasi-
bility of rapid transit operation within
the Seattle area. San Francisco, 1965.
[4]p.

U.S. Urban Renewal Adm. UPAP.

1. Transportation - Seattle.
I. Puget Sound Governmental Conference.
II. Title. III. U.S. URA-UPAP. Seattle.

728.1
H681s
Summary of activities in State using aids
available through programs of the Housing and
Home Finance Agency, Office of the Adminis-
U.S. Housing and Home Finance Agency. trator.
Office of the Administrator.
Summary of activities in [State] using
aids available through programs of the
Housing and Home Finance Agency, Office
of the Administrator. Washington, [1961-
v.
Cover title: Housing and community
development; cover title on some, lacking.
For complete information see main card or
shelflist.
1. Federal housing   programs. I. Title.

627.4
R67
1964
Summary of floods in the United States during
1964.
Rostvedt, J   O
Summary of floods in the United States during
1964, by J.O. Rostvedt and others. Prepared
in cooperation with Federal, State and local
agencies. Wash., Govt. Print. Off., 1970.
124p. (U.S. Geological Survey water-supply
paper 1840-C)
Bibliography: p. 116-117.

1. Floods. I. U.S. Geological Survey.
II. Title.

LAW
US
Summary of legislation of interest to the Housing and Home
Finance Agency, enacted during the 88th Congress.
U.S. Housing and Home Finance Agency.
Summary of legislation of interest
to the Housing and Home Finance Agency,
enacted during the 88th Congress.
[Washington] 1964.
17p.

1. Housing legislation.
I. U.S. Congress. II. Title.

LAW
T
Summary of bills of interest in the field of aging.
U.S. Dept of Health Education and Welfare.
(Special Staff on Aging)
Summary of bills of interest in the field of
aging introduced up to February 27, 1959, 1st
session, 86th Congress. A brief summary of 486
bills of interest in the field of aging classified according to subject matter prepared by
the Special Staff on Aging, Department of Health,
Education and Welfare. Washington, 1959.
31p.

1. Old age. I. Title.

VF
728.1
:336.18
(43)
W13
Summary of German law ...
Wagner, Bernard.
Summary of German law, concerning
housing expenditure subsidy
(Wohngeldgesetz: April 1, 1965) Wash.,
Office of International Housing, Dept. of
Housing and Urban Development, 1965.
5p.

1. Public housing - Germany. I. U.S.
Dept. of Housing and Urban Development.
Office of International Housing.
II. Title.

352.6
C657s
Summary of Legislative activities and
accomplishments of the Committee on Public...
U.S. Congress. Senate. Committee on Public
Works.
Summary of Legislative activities and
accomplishments of the Committee on Public
Works, United States Senate for the Ninety-
first Congress. Wash., Govt. Print. Off.,
1971.
98p.
At head of title: 92d Cong., 1st sess.
Committee print.
Serial no. 92-18.
1. U.S. Congress. Senate. Committee on
Public Works. 2. Community facilities.
I. Title.

728.1
(73
:347)
S18
SUMMARY OF NATIONAL HOUSING ACT.
SAVINGS BANKS TRUST COMPANY.
SUMMARY OF NATIONAL HOUSING ACT, TITLE
II, SECTIONS 203 AND 207; TITLE VI,
SECTIONS 603 AND 608, AND RULES AND
REGULATIONS THEREUNDER AS AMENDED TO
DATE. NEW YORK, 1947.
1 V. (LOOSE-LEAF)

1. HOUSING LEGISLATION.   I. TITLE.
II. TITLE: NATIONAL HOUSING ACT.

352
(778)
M47s
Summary of program and recommendations.
Missouri. Governor's Advisory Council on
Local Government Law.
Summary of program and recommendations.
Jefferson City, [1969?]
13p.

U.S. Dept. of Housing and Urban Development. UPRDP.

1. Local government - Mo. I. Title.
II. U.S. HUD-UPRDP. Mo.

VF
728.1
:362.6
(746)
C65s
Summary of state-assisted elderly
housing developments.
Connecticut. Public Works Dept. Housing Div.
Summary of state-assisted elderly
housing developments, 19

Hartford, 19

v.
For Library holdings see main entry.

1. Housing for the aged - Conn.
I. Title.

362.6
:347
(747)
N28
A summary of 19 New York State legislation
affecting the aging.
New York (State) Office for the Aging.
A summary of 19 New York State legislation
affecting the aging. Albany, 19

v
For Library holdings see main entry.
1. Old age - Law and legislation - New York.
I. Title.

336.2
L41s
Summary of proposals for tax reform and
tax incentives in the 90th Congress.
U.S. Library of Congress. Legislative
Reference Service.
Summary of proposals for tax reform and
tax incentives in the 90th Congress, by
George J. Leibowitz. Wash., 1968.
29p. (S-123)

1. Taxation. I. Leibowitz, George J.
II. Title: Proposals for tax reform.
III. Title.

353
C25
no.1
Summary of state government finances.
U.S. Bureau of the Census.
Summary of state government finances in 1947-

Washington, 1950-
v. (Its state finances, G-SF series,
no. 1)

For full information see shelf list card.

325
(73
:347)
A52
SUMMARY OF 1962 AND 1963 STATE
ANTI-DISCRIMINATION LAWS.
AMERICAN JEWISH CONGRESS. COMMISSION ON
LAW AND SOCIAL ACTION.
SUMMARY OF 1962 AND 1963 STATE
ANTI-DISCRIMINATION LAWS.   NEW YORK,
1964.
27P.

1. MINORITY GROUPS - LAWS AND
LEGISLATION.   2. MINORITY GROUPS -
HOUSING - LAWS AND LEGISLATION.
I. TITLE.

339.5
Z45
Summary of rate schedules of natural gas
pipeline companies.
Zinder (H.) and Associates.
Summary of rate schedules of natural
gas pipeline companies as filed with the
Federal Power Commission. 30th ed.
Wash., 1969.
83p.

1. Power resources. 2. Public utilities.
I. Title: Rate schedules of natural gas
pipeline companies. II. Title.

347
(744)
M17
A summary of the comprehensive criminal justice
plan for crime prevention and control.
Massachusetts. Committee on Law Enforcement
and Administration of Criminal Justice.
A summary of the comprehensive criminal
justice plan for crime prevention and control.
[Boston, 1970]
106p.

1. Law enforcement - Mass. I. Title.

534.83
E58su
Summary of noise programs in the Federal
government.
U.S. Environmental Protection Agency.
(Office of Noise Abatement and Control)
Summary of noise programs in the Federal
government. Wash., 1971.
1v. (NTID 300.10)

1. Noise. I. Title.

333.33
(748)
W67
SUMMARY OF REAL ESTATE ACTIVITY IN
PITTSBURGH.
U.S. WORK PROJECTS ADMINISTRATION.
PENNSYLVANIA.
SUMMARY OF REAL ESTATE ACTIVITY IN
PITTSBURGH AND ALLEGHENY COUNTY IN THE
SECOND QUARTER OF 1937. PREPARED...
UNDER THE SUPERVISION OF THE BUREAU OF
BUSINESS RESEARCH, UNIVERSITY OF
PITTSBURGH. PITTSBURGH, 1937.
23L. (SERIES 2, NO. 2)
1. REAL ESTATE BUSINESS - PITTSBURGH.
2. REAL ESTATE BUSINESS - ALLEGHENY
CO., PA. I. TITLE. II. PITTSBURGH.
UNIVERSITY BUREAU OF BUSINESS
RESEARCH.

VF
728.1
H68s
A summary of the evolution of housing activities
in the Federal government.
U.S. Housing and Home Finance Agency. Office of
the Administrator.
A summary of the evolution of housing activities
in the Federal Government. Housing and Home Finance
Agency: Office of the Administrator, Home Loan Bank
Board; Federal Housing Administration, Public Housing
Administration, National Housing Council.   Washing-
ton, D.C., Dec. 1950 [i. e. 1951]
23 p.

(Continued on next card)

628.1
S77
Summary of present practices in evaluation.
Struyk, Raymond J
Summary of present practices in evaluation
of water resource projects. [Prepared in co-
operation with] U.S. Corps of Army Engineers.
St. Louis, Institute for Urban and Regional
Studies, Washington University, 1967.
40p. (Washington University. Institute for
Urban and Regional Studies. Working paper
CWR 13)

1. Water resources. 2. Water-supply engineering.

(Cont'd on next card)

628.44
N28s
Summary of research on effects of solid waste
planning grants.
New York (State) Legislature. Joint Committee on Metropolitan and Regional Area
Study.
Summary of research on effects of solid
waste planning grants on metropolitan solution
to waste disposal collection and treatment
problems; submitted by Robert Wieboldt.
Albany, 1966.
7p.
1. Refuse and refuse disposal. 2. Grants-in-
aid. I. Wieboldt, Robert. II. Title.
III. Title: Effects of solid waste planning
grants on metro-   politan solution to
solid waste dis-   posal collection and
treatment prob-   lems.

U.S. Housing and Home Finance Agency. Office of the
Administrator.   A summary of the evolution of
housing activities in the Federal Government...
1950.   (Card 2)

1. Housing. 2. U.S. Housing and Home Finance Agency.
3. U.S. Home Loan Bank Board. 4. U.S. Federal
Housing Administration. 5. U.S. Public Housing
Administration. 6. U.S. National Housing Council.
I. Title.

628.1
S77
Struyk, Raymond J   Summary of present
practices in evaluation...1967. (Card 2)

I. Washington University. St. Louis. Institute for Urban and Regional Studies.
II. U.S. Army. Corps of Engineers. III. Title.

628.1
:308
D25
Summary of reservoir sediment deposition surveys made in the United States through 1965.
Dendy, F E comp.
Summary of reservoir sediment deposition
surveys made in the United States through 1965,
comp. by F.E. Dendy and W.A. Champion. Wash.,
Agricultural Research Service, United States
Dept. of Agriculture, 1969.
64p. (U.S. Dept. of Agriculture. Miscellaneous publication no. 1143)

1. Water resources - Surveys. 2. Soils -
Surveys. I. Champion, W.A., jt. comp.
II. U.S. Agricultural Research Service.
III. Title.

VF
711.4
C16
Summary of the housing act of 1949. In Caplow,
Theodore, City planning.   Minneapolis, Minn.,
c1950. p. 211-216.

Contents.-National housing goals and policies.-
Slum clearance.-Low-rent public housing.-Housing
research.-Farm housing.

[Reprinted from U.S. Housing and Home Finance
Agency, A handbook of information on provisions of
the housing act of 1949, July 1949?]
1. Housing act of   1949.

Summary of proceedings.

LAW
T Conference on United States Government.
Research & Development Contracts. George
Washington University, Wash. D.C., 1962.
Summary of proceedings. Sponsored by the
National Law Center of the George Washington
University in cooperation with Federal Publi-
cations. Washington, D.C., George Washington
University and Federal Publications, 1962.
76p.
1. Federal contracts - Congresses. I. George
Washington University. National Law Center.
II. Title.

362
R23
Summary of RSRI health system
planning studies, 1963-1969.
Regional Science Research Institute,
Philadelphia.
Summary of RSRI health system planning
studies, 1963-1969. Philadelphia, 1969.
19p.

1. Hospitals. I. Title.

728.1
H68su
1959
Summary of the Housing act of 1959.
U.S. Housing and Home Finance Agency.
Office of the Administrator. Office of
the General Counsel.
Summary of the Housing act of 1959.
Washington, [1959]
14p. (Public law 86-372, 73 stat. 654.
86th Cong., (S. 2654) approved Sept. 23, 1959)

1. Housing legislation. I. Title.

728.1
E68su
Summary of the Housing act of 1961.
U.S. Housing and Home Finance Agency.
Office of the Administrator. Office
of the General Counsel.
Summary of the Housing act of 1961.
Washington, 1961.
35p. (Public law 87-70, 75 stat. 149.
87th Cong. (S. 1922) approved June 30, 1961)

1. Housing legislation. I. Title.

728.1
(73:347)
H68su
A summary of the main provisions, "The Housing
and urban development act of 1965."
U.S. Housing and Home Finance Agency.
Office of the Administrator.
A summary of the main provisions,
"The Housing and urban development act
of 1965." Public law 89-117, approved
August 10, 1965. Wash., 1965.
6p.

1. Housing legislation. I. Title.

728.1
(492)
N27su
Summary of the Physical planning act of the
new Housing act.
Netherlands. Ministry of Housing and
Building.
Summary of the Physical planning act of
the new Housing act. The Hague, 1962.
12p.

1. Housing - Netherlands. 2. Netherlands -
Housing. 3. Building industry - Netherlands.
4. Netherlands - Building industry.
I. Title.

711.4
(492)
N27s
Summary of the second memorandum on physical
planning.
Netherlands. Ministry of Housing and Physical
Planning.
Summary of the second memorandum on physical
planning. The Hague, Ministry of Housing and
Physical Planning, Information Service, 1967.
10p.

1. City planning - Netherlands. I. Netherlands
Ministry of Housing and Physical Planning.
II. Title.

711.585
:347
H68
Summary of the Urban Renewal Program:
incorporating changes resulting from...
U.S. Dept. of Housing and Urban
Development.
Summary of the Urban Renewal Program:
incorporating changes resulting from the
Housing and urban development act of 1965.
Wash., 1965.
15p.

1. Urban renewal legislation. I. Title.

711.585
:347
H68
1966
Summary of the Urban Renewal Program.
U.S. Dept. of Housing and Urban Development.
Summary of the Urban Renewal Program:
incorporating changes resulting from the
Demonstration cities and metropolitan act of
1966. Washington, Govt. Print. Off., 1966.
9p. (HUD IP-26)

1. Urban renewal legislation. I. Title.

388
H68s
A summary of Urban transportation demonstration
projects.
U.S. Dept. of Housing and Urban Development.
A summary of Urban transportation demonstra-
tion projects. Washington, 1967.
63p.

1. Transportation. 2. Management.
3. Grants-in-aid. I. Title. II. Title:
Urban transportation demonstration projects.

628.1
(774)
M42s
A summary of water and related land
resources in Michigan.
Michigan. Water Resources Commission.
A summary of water and related land
resources in Michigan. Lansing, 1966.
76p.

U.S. Dept. of Housing and Urban Development. UPAP.

1. Water resources - Michigan. 2. Land use
- Michigan. I. Title. II. U.S. HUD-UPAP.
Mich.

711.4
(758996)
S68
Summary plan report.
Southwest Georgia Planning and Development
Commission.
Summary plan report, City of Donalsonville,
Georgia. Atlanta, State Planning Bureau,
1970.
30p.
On Cover: Comprehensive Development Plan.
U.S. Dept. of Housing and Urban
Development Comprehensive Planning Grant
Program. Ga. P-149.
1. City planning - Donalsonville, Ga.
2. Master plan - Donalsonville, Ga. I. U.S.
HUD-Comprehensive Planning Grant
Program. Donalsonville, Ga.
II. Title.

711.4
(758975)
M68
Summary plan report; Moultrie, Ga.
Southwest Georgia Planning and Development
Commission.
Summary plan report; Moultrie, Ga. Atlanta,
State Planning Bureau, 1970.
15p.
Cover title: Comprehensive development plan;
City of Moultrie.
Preparation of document financed in part
through comprehensive planning grant from Dept.
of Housing and Urban Development. HUD project
no. Ga. P-149.
1. Master plan - Moultrie, Ga. I. Title.
II. U.S. Dept. of Housing and Urban
Development.

002
073
1971
Summary record of the 14th meeting held in
Paris on 18th, 19th and 20th November, 1970.
Organisation for Economic Co-operation and
Development.
Summary record of the 14th meeting held in
Paris on 18th, 19th and 20th November, 1970.
Paris, Directorate for Scientific Affairs,
Scientific and Technical Information Policy
Group, Organisation for Economic Co-operation
and Development, 1971.
15p.

1. Documentation. 2. Scientific research.
I. Title.

711.4
(764)
L17
Summary
Summary report.
Caudill, Rowlett, Scott.
Summary report; prepared for the people
of Laredo and Webb County, Texas. [Pre-
pared in cooperation with the] Laredo City
Planning Commission. Houston, Tex., 1964.
213p.
U.S. Urban Renewal Adm. UPAP.
1. Master plan - Laredo, Tex. 2. Master
plan - Webb Co., Tex. 3. County planning -
Webb Co., Tex. I. Laredo, Tex. City Planning
Commission. II. U.S. URA-UPAP. Laredo, Tex.
III. U.S. URA-UPAP. Webb Co., Tex.
IV. Title.

333.65
H68
Summary report of the Housing Administration
and Management Workshop.
U.S. Dept. of Housing and Urban Development.
Div. of International Affairs.
Summary report of the Housing Administration
and Management Workshop (Spanish Section)
Sept. 9 - Oct. 21, 1966. Presented for the
Agency for International Development. Wash.,
1966.
44p.

1. Housing management. I. U.S. Agency
for International Development. II. Title.

378
(083.41)
E28s
Summary report on bachelor's and higher
degrees...
U.S. Office of Education.
Summary report on bachelor's and
higher degrees, conferred during the
year 19
Washington, 19
v.
19 Prepared by
the Higher Education Surveys Branch,
National Center for Educational Statistics.
For complete information see main card.
1. Universities and colleges - Statistics.
2. Education - Statistics.
I. Title.

388
(748)
P25s
Summary; state of the region.
Penn-Jersey Transportation Study, Philadelphia.
Summary; state of the region. Philadelphia
[1967]
[7] p.

1. Transportation - Pennsylvania. 2.
Transportation - New Jersey. I. Title.

658
N28p
SUMMER, CHARLES EDGAR, JT. AU.
NEWMAN, WILLIAM HERMAN, 1909-
THE PROCESS OF MANAGEMENT: CONCEPTS,
BEHAVIOR, AND PRACTICE BY WILLIAM H.
NEWMAN AND CHARLES E. SUMMER, JR.
ENGLEWOOD CLIFFS, N.J., PRENTICE-HALL,
1961.
675P.

1. INDUSTRIAL MANAGEMENT.
2. PERSONNEL MANAGEMENT. I. SUMMER,
CHARLES EDGAR, JT. AU. II. TITLE.

697.8
S85
Summer, W
Odour pollution of air; causes and control.
Cleveland, CRC Press, 1971.
310p.

1. Air pollution. I. Title.

VF
690.015
P42
R2
Summer comfort factors.
Mackey, C O
Summer comfort factors as influenced by
thermal properties of building materials, by
C. O. Mackey and L. T. Wright. John B. Pierce
Foundation [c1943]
27 p. tables. (John B. Pierce
Foundation. Research study 2)

1. Insulation. 2. Building materials. I. Wright, L.T.
II. Title. III John B. Pierce Foundation.

378
(083.41)
E28hi
Summer enrollment in higher education.
U.S. Office of Education.
Higher education; summer enrollment in
higher education, 19
Wash., 19
v. (OE-
On cover: National Center for Educational
Statistics.
For Library holdings see main entry.
1. Universities and colleges - Statistics.
I. Title: Summer enrollment in higher
education. II. Title.

333
(471)
K64
Summer house sites.
Koivikko, Pentti.
Kesämökkitonttien hinnat Helsingin
ympäristössä keväällä 1965; ekonometrinen
poikkileikkausanalyysi (Prices of summer house
sites near Helsinki in the spring, an econometric analysis) Helsinki, State Institute
for Technical Research, 1968.
67p. (Finland. State Institute for Technical Research Tiedotus. Sarja 3 - Rakennus 130)
English summary.
1. Land economics - Finland. 2. Finland -
Land economics. 3. Family income and expenditure - Housing - Finland.
(Cont'd on next card)

333
(471)
K64
Koivikko, Pentti. Kesämökkitonttien...
1968. (Card 2)
4. Finland - Family income and expenditure -
Housing. I. Finland. State Institute for
Technical Research. II. Title: Prices of
summer house sites near Helsinki. III. Title:
Summer house sites.

712.25
(7471)
C05

Summer in New York.

Community Council of Greater New York.
Summer in New York, 1965; analysis of summer programs carried out with anti-poverty funds, under the auspices of the New York City Council Against Poverty and the Economic Opportunity Committee. New York, Economic Opportunity Committee, 1965.
64p.

1. Recreation - New York (City) 2. Youth.
3. Community centers - New York (City)
4. Social service. I. New York (City) Economic Opportunity Committee. II. Title.

336
C657su

Summer review of the 1969 budget.

U.S. Congress. Joint Economic Committee.
Summer review of the 1969 budget. Hearing before the Joint Economic Committee, Congress of the United States, Ninetieth Congress, second session. Wash., Govt. Print. Off., 1968.
57p.
Hearing held Sept. 12, 1968.

1. Budget. 2. U.S. Appropriations and expenditures. I. Title.

720
S85v

Summerson, John.
Victorian architecture; four studies in evaluation. New York, Columbia University Press, 1970.
131p. (Bampton lectures in America no. 19)

Delivered at Columbia University: 1968.

1. Architecture. I. Title.

360
(7471)
N28s

Summer in our city, New York City.

New York (City) Office of the Mayor.
Summer in our city, New York City: 1967 and 1968. Report to Mayor John V. Lindsay. New York, 1968.
45p.

Barry Gottehrer, chairman, Urban Action Task Force.
1. Social conditions - New York (City)
2. Employment - New York (City) 3. Recreation - New York (City) 4. Youth. I. Title.

500
H58
1966
Summary

Summer Study on Science and Urban Development. Woods Hole, Mass. 1966.
U.S. Dept. of Housing and Urban Development.
Summer Study on Science and Urban Development, held at the National Academy of Science Summer Study Center, Woods Hole, Mass., June, 1966. Summary reports and recommendations. Sponsored by the Department of Housing and Urban Development and the Office of Science and Technology, Executive Office of the President. Washington, 1966.
Kit. (7 pieces)
Contents: [no.1] Transportation Panel.-
(Cont'd on next card)

658.564
C17M

SUMMITT, ROGER K   , JT. AU.
CARROLL, KENNETH D
MACHINE APPLICATIONS TO TECHNICAL INFORMATION CENTER OPERATIONS, BY KENNETH D. CARROLL AND ROGER K. SUMMITT. SUNNYVALE, CALIF., LOCKHEED MISSILES & SPACE COMPANY, 1962.
24P. (AD401227)

1. AUTOMATION. I. LOCKHEED MISSILES AND SPACE CO. II. SUMMITT, ROGER K., JT. AU. III. TITLE.

658
(07)
S85

Summer Institute in Executive Development for Federal Administrators, University of Wisconsin, 1963.
Summer Institute in Executive Development for Federal Administrators, [Madison]
v.   annual.

For complete information see shelflist.

1. Management - Study and teaching.
2. Public administration - Study and teaching.
3. Federal civil   service.

500
H68
1966
Summary

U.S. Dept. of Housing and Urban Development. Summer Study on Science and Urban Development...1966   (Card 2)

[no.2]Health Services Panel.-[no.3]Environmental Engineering Panel.-[no.4] Rehabilitation Panel report.-[no.5] New Housing Panel.-[no.6] Transcript of summary report of Summer Study on Science and Urban Development.-[no.7] Working papers of the Summer Study on Science and Urban Development.

(Cont'd on next card)

002
S85

Summit, Roger K
Remote information retrieval facility. Wash., National Aeronautics and Space Administration, 1969.
44p. (U.S. National Aeronautics and Space Administration. NASA CR-1318)
Prepared by Lockheed Aircraft Corp. for National Aeronautics and Space Administration. CFSTI.
1. Documentation. 2. Automation. I. Lockheed Aircraft Corp. II. U.S. National Aeronautics and Space Administration. III. Title.

711
S85

Summer Institute of Government. 33d, Seattle, 1968.
Quality environment: a shared responsibility; proceedings of the thirty-third annual Summer Institute of Government, 1968. Seattle, University of Washington Press, 1969.
61p. (Washington (State) University. Bureau of Governmental Research and Services. Report no. 169)
Sponsored by Bureau of Governmental Research and Services, University of Washington, Seattle and others.
(Cont'd on next card)

500
H68
1966
Summary

U.S. Dept. of Housing and Urban Development. Summer Study on Science and Urban Development...1966   (Card 3)

1. Science. 2. City planning. 3. Housing. 4. Mortgage finance. 5. Urban renewal. 6. Transportation. I. Summer Study on Science and Urban Development. Woods Hole, Mass., 1966. II. U.S. Office of Science and Technology.

4797
4798
4799

SUMMIT, PA. PLANNING COMMISSION.
COMPREHENSIVE PLAN: 1, GENERAL DEVELOPMENT PLAN; 2, CAPITAL IMPROVEMENTS PROGRAM; 3, SUBDIVISION REGULATIONS. SUMMIT, PA., 1966.
3 V. (HUD 701 REPORT)

1. MASTER PLAN - SUMMIT, PA. I. HUD 701. SUMMIT, PA.

711
S85

Summer Institute of Government. 33d, Seattle, 1968.   Quality environment...1969.
(Card 2)

1. Planning - Citizen participation. 2. Man - Influence of environment. I. Washington (State) University. Bureau of Governmental Research and Services. II. Title. (Series)

551.49
N28
no. 80

Summers, W   K
New Mexico. Institute of Mining and Technology.
A preliminary report on New Mexico's geothermal energy resources, by W.K. Summers. Socorro, N.M., 1965.
41 p. (Its: Circular 80)
Bibliography: p. 32-36.

1. Hydrology. 2. Power resources. I. Summers, W.K. II. Title: New Mexico's geothermal energy resources.

711.333
(78845)
H82

Summit Co., Colo. Planning Commission.
Huddleston, Sam L
Summit County, Colorado: the master plan. [Prepared for] Summit County Planning Commission. Denver, 1963.
95p.
Prepared in cooperation with Colorado State Planning Division.
U.S. Urban Renewal Adm. UPAP.

1. County planning - Summit Co., Colo.
2. Master plan - Summit Co., Colo. I. Summit Co., Colo. Planning Commission. II. U.S. URA-UPAP.   Summit Co., Colo.

744
(016)
M62s

Summer movies.

Modern Talking Picture Service, inc.
Summer movies, Washington, D.C., 1967.
9p.

1. Films - Bibl. I. Title.

720
S85

Summerson, John Newenham, 1904-
The classical language of architecture. Cambridge, M.I.T. Press, 1963.
63p.

Bibliography: p. 53-56.

1. Architecture. I. Title.

6354

SUMMIT CO., UTAH. CITIZENS' COUNCIL.
GOALS AND POLICIES TO GUIDE FUTURE GROWTH. N.P. 1965.
20P. (HUD 701 REPORT)

1. COUNTY PLANNING - SUMMIT CO., UTAH. I. HUD 701. SUMMIT CO., UTAH.

301.158
S14

Summer 1968 Youth Opportunity Program. St. Louis, Mo. City Plan Commission.
Summer 1968 Youth Opportunity Program: work project report. St. Louis, 1969.
119p.
U.S. Dept. of Housing and Urban Development. CRP.
Program grant no. Mo. R-66 (CR)

1. Youth. 2. Employment - St. Louis, Mo.
3. Education - St. Louis, Mo. I. Title: Youth Opportunity Program. II. Title. III. U.S. HUD-CRP. St. Louis, Mo.

City pl. - England - London

JAN 15 1951   L. C. CARD NO.

AUTHOR
Summerson, John.
TITLE The nature of London (The Plans for London, 1) (Copy of a talk broadcast in the B.B.C. Third Programme, 18th March. 1950)
SERIES

EDITION   PUB. DATE 1950   PAGING   6
PUBLISHER
British Broadcasting Corp.

RECOMMENDED BY   REVIEWED IN
                                 Min.ofT.&C.P. 7-8/50 pg.14
ORDER RECORD

6357

SUMMIT CO., UTAH. PLANNING COMMISSION.
MASTER PLAN, 1965-1980. BY PLANNING AND RESEARCH ASSOCIATES. N.P. 1965.
43P. (HUD 701 REPORT)

------- SUPPLEMENTARY MATERIAL IN ENVELOPE.

1. COUNTY PLANNING - SUMMIT CO., UTAH. I. PLANNING AND RESEARCH ASSOCIATES. II. HUD. 701. SUMMIT CO., UTAH.

6355   SUMMIT CO., UTAH. PLANNING COMMISSION.
PRELIMINARY MASTER PLAN. N.P., 1966.
1 V. (HUD 701 REPORT)

1. COUNTY PLANNING - SUMMIT CO., UTAH.
I. HUD. 701. SUMMIT CO., UTAH.

1700   SUMNER, IOWA. PLANNING AND ZONING
COMMISSION.
COMPREHENSIVE COMMUNITY PLAN;
PRELIMINARY REPORT. V. 8, CENTRAL
BUSINESS DISTRICT. SUMNER, IOWA, CA.
1969.
1 V. (HUD 701 REPORT)

1. MASTER PLAN - SUMNER, IOWA.
I. HUD. 701. SUMNER, IOWA.

4985   SUMTER CO., S.C. PLANNING BOARD.
PROJECT COMPLETION REPORT. PREPARED BY
THE COMMUNITY PLANNING DIVISION, STATE
PLANNING AND GRANTS DIVISION, OFFICE OF
THE GOVERNOR. COLUMBIA, 1970.
6L. (HUD 701 REPORT)

1. COUNTY PLANNING - SUMTER CO., S.C.
I. SOUTH CAROLINA. STATE PLANNING AND
GRANTS DIV. II. HUD. 701. SUMTER CO.,
S.C.

711.5
(74899
:347)
S85
   Summit, Pa. Ordinances, etc.
Proposed zoning ordinance, Summit
township, Erie County, Pa. Summit, 1957.
26p.

1. Zoning legislation - Summit, Pa.
I. Title.

1393-
1399
   SUMNER, IOWA. PLANNING AND ZONING
COMMISSION.
COMPREHENSIVE PLAN; PRELIMINARY
REPORT: 1, INTRODUCTION; 2, EXISTING
LAND USE; 3, ECONOMIC ENVIRONMENT; 4,
FUTURE LAND USE; 5, ZONING; 6,
SUBDIVISION CONTROL; 7, COMMUNITY
FACILITIES. SUMNER, IOWA, CA. 1969.
8 V. (HUD 701 REPORT)

1. MASTER PLAN - SUMNER, IOWA.
I. HUD. 701. SUMNER, IOWA.

4516-
4517
   SUMTER, S.C. PLANNING COMMISSION.
URBAN PLANNING. 1. STUDY OF
COMMERCIAL AREAS IN THE SUMTER URBAN
AREA. 2. NEIGHBORHOOD ANALYSIS.
SUMTER, 1968.
75P. (HUD 701 REPORT)

1. CITY PLANNING - SUMTER, S.C.
I. HUD. 701. SUMTER, S.C.

4979   SUMMIT CO., UTAH. PLANNING COMMISSION.
ZONING ORDINANCE. COALVILLE, 1968.
19L. (HUD 701 REPORT)

1. ZONING - SUMMIT CO., UTAH. I. HUD.
701. SUMMIT CO., UTAH.

2229   SUMPTER, MICH. TOWNSHIP PLANNING
COMMISSION.
SUBDIVISION REGULATIONS ORDINANCE.
PREPARED BY VILICAN-LEMAN AND ASSOCIATES,
INC. SOUTHFIELD, MICH., 1969.
30L. (HUD 701 REPORT)

2230
FOLIO
   -------- SUPPLEMENTARY MATERIAL.
1 ENVELOPE.

1. SUBDIVISION REGULATION - SUMPTER,
MICH. I. VILICAN-LEMAN AND ASSOCIATES.
II. HUD. 701. SUMPTER, MICH.

4520   SUMTER CO., S.C. PLANNING BOARD.
PUBLIC IMPROVEMENTS PROGRAM AND CAPITAL
IMPROVEMENTS BUDGET. BY RUST URBAN
PLANNING GROUP, RUST ENGINEERING CO.,
BIRMINGHAM, ALA. SUMTER, 1970.
45P. (HUD 701 REPORT)

1. COUNTY PLANNING - SUMTER CO., S.C.
I. RUST ENGINEERING CO., BIRMINGHAM, ALA.
II. HUD. 701. SUMTER CO., S.C.

5233
5234
5235
5236
   SUMMIT HILL, PA. PLANNING COMMISSION.
COMPREHENSIVE PLAN: 1, COMPREHENSIVE
PLAN; 2, CAPITAL IMPROVEMENTS PROGRAM; 3,
SUBDIVISION REGULATIONS; 4, PROPOSED
ZONING ORDINANCE. BY CANDEUB, CABOT AND
ASSOCIATES. SUMMIT HILL, PA., 1966.
4 V. (HUD 701 REPORT)

1. MASTER PLAN - SUMMIT HILL, PA.
I. CANDEUB, CABOT AND ASSOCIATES.
II. HUD. 701. SUMMIT HILL, PA.

2234
2235
   SUMPTER, MICH. TOWNSHIP PLANNING
COMMISSION.
TECHNICAL MEMORANDUM: 4, COMMUNITY
FACILITIES AND RECREATION PLAN; 5,
ECONOMIC DEVELOPMENT STUDY. BY
VILICAN-LEMAN AND ASSOCIATES, INC.
SOUTHFIELD, MICH., 1969.
2 V. (HUD 701 REPORT)

1. CITY PLANNING - SUMPTER, MICH.
I. VILICAN-LEMAN AND ASSOCIATES.
II. HUD. 701. SUMPTER, MICH.

4518   SUMTER CO., S.C. PLANNING BOARD.
SUBDIVISION REGULATIONS. SUMTER, 1969.
34P. (HUD 701 REPORT)

1. SUBDIVISION REGULATION - SUMTER CO.,
S.C. I. HUD. 701. SUMTER CO., S.C.

920
D65
   SUMNER, CHARLES.
Donald, David.
Charles Sumner and the rights of man.
New York, Knopf, 1970.
595p.

1. Sumner, Charles. 2. Civil rights.
3. History.

2232
2233
   SUMPTER, MICH. TOWNSHIP PLANNING
COMMISSION.
TECHNICAL MEMORANDUM: 1, EXISTING LAND
USE SURVEY AND ANALYSIS; 2, HOUSING
CONDITION ANALYSIS. BY VILICAN-LEMAN AND
ASSOCIATES, INC. SOUTHFIELD, MICH., 1968.
2 V. (HUD 701 REPORT)

1. LAND USE - SUMPTER, MICH.
2. HOUSING - SUMPTER, MICH.
I. VILICAN-LEMAN AND ASSOCIATES.
II. HUD. 701. SUMPTER, MICH.

4521   SUMTER CO., S.C. PLANNING BOARD.
A SURVEY AND ANALYSES OF LAND USES. BY
RUST ENGINEERING CO., BIRMINGHAM, ALA.
SUMTER, 1970.
47P. (HUD 701 REPORT)

1. COUNTY PLANNING - SUMTER CO., S.C.
I. RUST ENGINEERING CO., BIRMINGHAM, ALA.
II. HUD. 701. SUMTER CO., S.C.

728.1
:336.18
(776579)
M45H
   SUMNER FIELD HOMES.
MINNEAPOLIS. CITY PLANNING
COMMISSION.
HISTORY OF THE SUMNER FIELD HOMES,
FEDERAL HOUSING PROJECT.
MINNEAPOLIS, 1936.
35L.

1. PUBLIC HOUSING - MINNEAPOLIS.
I. TITLE: SUMNER FIELD HOMES.

712
S85
   Sumter, S.C. City Planning Commission.
Community appearance plan. Sumter, [1966?]
36p.

1. Landscape architecture. I. Title.

697.133
S85
   Sun, C T
Thermodynamic foundation of finite
elastic locking medium. Ames, Engineering
Research Institute, Iowa State University,
1968.
58p. (Iowa. State University of Science
and Technology, Ames. Engineering Research
Institute. Engineering research report
70)
Bibliography: p. 57-58.
1. Heat transmission. I. Iowa. State
University of Science and Technology, Ames.
Engineering Research Institute. II.
Title.

1701   SUMNER, IOWA. PLANNING AND ZONING
COMMISSION.
COMPREHENSIVE COMMUNITY PLAN. BY
POWERS-WILLIS AND ASSOCIATES. SUMNER,
IOWA, 1969.
279P. (HUD 701 REPORT)

1. MASTER PLAN - SUMNER, IOWA.
I. POWERS-WILLIS AND ASSOCIATES.
II. HUD. 701. SUMNER, IOWA.

333.71
(757691)
S85
   Sumter, S.C. City Planning Commission.
Open space acquisition plan. Sumter,
[1966?]
11p.

1. Open space land - Sumter, S.C. 2. Land
acquisition. I. Title.

711.552
(756621)
H43
   Sun, John T
High Point, N. C. City Planning Dept.
High Point CBD, a preliminary core
study, by John T. Sun. High Point,
1959.
1v. maps, tables.

1. Business districts - High Point, N.C.
I. Sun, John T.

VF
728
:551.5
B15s
Sun data for the building designer.
Ballantyne, E R
Sun data for the building designer.
Melbourne, Australia, Commonwealth Scientific and Industrial Research Organization, Div. of Building Research, 1964.
4p. (Australia. Commonwealth Scientific and Industrial Research Organization. Div. of Building Research. D.B.R. reprint no. 309)
CIB, no. 4, 1964.

1. Architecture and climate. 2. Solar radiation. I. Australia. Commonwealth Scientific and Industrial Research Organization. (Div. of Building Research) II. Title.

5353

SUN PRAIRIE, WIS. PLANNING COMMISSION. CAPITAL IMPROVEMENTS PROGRAM 1969-1973. PREPARED BY MIDWEST PLANNING AND RESEARCH, INC. MADISON, WIS., 1968. 20L. (HUD 701 REPORT)

1. CAPITAL IMPROVEMENT PROGRAMS - SUN PRAIRIE, WIS. I. MIDWEST PLANNING AND RESEARCH, INC. II. HUD. 701. SUN PRAIRIE, WIS.

5348
5349
5350
5351
5352

SUN PRAIRIE, WIS. PLANNING COMMISSION. COMPREHENSIVE CITY PLAN: 1, PLANNING ADMINISTRATION; 2, SURVEY AND ANALYSIS; 3, COMPREHENSIVE PLAN; 4, SUBDIVISION REGULATION; 5, ZONING REGULATIONS. PREPARED BY MIDWEST PLANNING AND RESEARCH, INC. MADISON, WIS., 1967-68. 5 V. (HUD 701 REPORT)

1. CITY PLANNING - SUN PRAIRIE, WIS. I. MIDWEST PLANNING AND RESEARCH, INC. II. HUD. 701. SUN PRAIRIE, WIS.

728
:551.5
D15
Sun protection
Danz, Ernst
Sun protection, an international architectural survey. New York, Praeger, 1967.
149p.

1. Architecture and climate. 2. Engineering. 3. Solar radiation. I. Title.

711.14
(74275)
N28
Sunapee, N.H. Planning Board.
New Hampshire. State Planning and Development Commission.
Land use report, Sunapee, New Hampshire, a report to the Sunapee Planning Board. [Concord] 1958.
5p.
U.S. Urban Renewal Administration, Urban Planning Assistance Program.

1. Land use - Sunapee, N. H. I. Sunapee, N.H. Planning Board. II. U.S. Urban Renewal Administration. Urban Planning Assistance Program.

711.4
(74275)
S85
Sunapee, N.H. Planning Board.
New Hampshire. State Planning and Development Commission.
A plan for the improvement of Sunapee Harbor. Preliminary study on: conservation and rehabilitation, traffic circulation and parking. A report to Sunapee Planning Board by Elliot G. Hansen. /Concord, N. H./ 1958.
7p.
U.S. Urban Renewal Administration.

(Continued on next card)

711.4
(74275)
S85
New Hampshire. State Planning and Development Commission. A plan...(Card 2)

1. City planning - Sunapee Harbor, N.H. 2. Traffic - Sunapee Harbor, N. H. I. Hansen, Elliot G. II. Sunapee, N.H. Planning Board. III. U.S. Urban Renewal Administration.

711.5
(74275
:347)
S85
Sunapee, N.H. Planning Board.
Proposed zoning ordinance for the Town of Sunapee, New Hampshire. In cooperation with New Hampshire State Planning and Development Commission. Sunapee, N.H. 1958?
6p.
U.S. Urban Renewal Administration, Urban Planning Assistance Program.
1. Zoning legislation - Sunapee, N.H. I. New Hampshire. State Planning and Development Commission. II. U.S. Urban Renewal Administration. Urban Planning Assistance Program.

VF
33
(77245)
I52
Sundal, A. Philip
Indiana. Economic Council.
Economic survey of the Terre Haute area. Indianapolis, Ind., July 1951-May 1952.
2 pts. graphs, tables. (Its Bulletin no. 14, 15)
Contents.-pt.1.General direction of the survey, by A. Philip Sundal.-pt.2.Analysis of industrial activity;

1.Terre Haute, Ind.-Econ. condit. I.Sundal, A. Philip. II.Series.

Sunday Bulletin, Philadelphia.
The road ahead.

see

Philadelphia. City Representative.
The road ahead.

711.4
(78883)
S85
Sunday Denver Post.
Denver, a progress report of the greater Denver area. Denver, 1957.
3v. illus.

Supplement to Empire, the Magazine of the Denver Post, Voice of the Rocky Mountain Empire.

1. City growth - Denver. I. Title.

325.2
C47
Sunday in the park, on July 13, 1969.
Citizens Interracial Committee of San Diego Co., San Diego, Calif.
Sunday in the park, on July 13, 1969. San Diego, Calif. San Diego, 1969.
128p.

Bibliography: p. 127-128.

1. Race relations. 2. Civil disorders. 3. Parks - San Diego, Calif. I. Title.

624.2
S85
Sunday Star.
Beauty and a bridge; the Ponte Vecchio, to cross Washington Channel in line of 10th Street. Washington, 1966.
19-25p. (Section W)

Issue of October 30, 1966.

1. Bridges. 2. Natural resources - District of Columbia. 3. Landscape architecture. I. Title: Ponte Vecchio. II. Title.

711.552
(753)
S85
Sunday Star.
F Street, shoppers' mecca. Tomorrow's F Street, looking west from 13th Street. Washington, 1966.
35-51p. (Section W)

Issue of October 30, 1966.

1. Business districts - District of Columbia. I. Title.

711.3
(7531)
D47
The Sunday Star. METRO. City of tomorrow. (Detached from the Sunday Star, Washington, Oct. 6, 13, 20, 27, Nov. 3, 10, 17, 24, 1957)
8 pts. illus.

Contents: -[pt I] New urban problem needs new answers, Oct. 6.-[pt.II] Washington area ponders its future, Oct. 13.-[pt. 3] Congestion forces new transit approach, Oct. 20.-[pt. 4] Potomac is key to future water supply, Oct. 27.-[pt.5] Human problems call for regional attack, Nov. 3.-
(See Card No. 2)

711.3
(7531)
D47
The Sunday Star. METRO. 1957. (Card No. 2)
-[pt.6] Area lacks unity in control of pollution, Nov. 10. -[pt. 7] Area seeks ways to keep open spaces, Nov. 17. -[pt. 8] Regional action wins wide acceptance, Nov. 24.

1.Metropolitan area planning - District of Columbia metropolitan area. 2.City planning - District of Columbia. 3.Urban renewal - District of Columbia. 4.Transportation - District of Columbia metropolitan area. 5.Regional planning
(See Card No. 3)

711.3
(7531)
D47
The Sunday Star. METRO. 1957. (Card No. 3)
- District of Columbia metropolitan area.
6.Water pollution - District of Columbia metropolitan area. 7.Water supply - District of Columbia metropolitan area. I.Title.

VF
711.3
(7531)
S85
Sunday Star.
The new Washington; an era of renaissance. Washington, the Sunday Star, September 17, 1961, Section W.
[20]p.

1. Metropolitan area planning - District of Columbia. 2. Transportation - District of Columbia.

388
(753)
S85
Sunday Star.
Preview of 1970; the subway station to be built under 8th and G Streets N.W. by 1970. Washington, 1966.
27-33p. (Section W)

Issue of October 30, 1966.

1. Transportation - District of Columbia. 2. Journey to work. I. Title.

VF
711.583
(753)
S85
Sunday Star.
Suburbia 1960. Washington, 1959.
[5]pts. in folder.

Contents:-Arlington booming as metro center; county planning expansion of its modern services, by Paul Hope. Sept. 13, 1959, p. A-18.-Fairfax is fastest growing area, by Mary Lou Werner and Jack Kelso. Sept. 27, 1959, p. A-21.-Past, present meet in Alexandria; old city keeps much of its ancient charm but new problems have followed postwar growth, by John Barron. Oct. 11, 1959, p. B-6.-Montgomery sees prosperity; county attracts
(Continued on next card)

VF
711.583
(753)
S85
Sunday Star.
Suburbia 1960. ... 1959. (Card 2)

new developments, by Anne H. Christmas. Sept. 20, 1959, p. B-7.

1. Suburbs - District of Columbia. 2. Metropolitan areas - District of Columbia. I. Title.

VF
388
(7531)
S85
The Sunday Star.
Subway and road needs for 1980 outlined in survey, by George Beveridge. [With] Summary of mass transit program for Capital area. Washington, July 12, 1959.
clippings. illus.

1. Transportation - District of Columbia Metropolitan Area.   I. Beveridge, George.

711.4
(753)
S85
Sunday Star.
Washington today... tomorrow. Change and the city. National Square, looking north from 15th and E Streets N.W. Washington, 1966.
17p.   (Section W)

Issue of October 30, 1966.

1. City planning - District of Columbia. I. Title.

728
A52B
SUNDBERG, ELMER W.
AMERICAN TECHNICAL SOCIETY.
BUILDING TRADES BLUEPRINT READING, BY ELMER W. SUNDBERG. PART 1 - FUNDAMENTALS. 4TH ED. CHICAGO, 1967. 136P.

1. ARCHITECTURE, DOMESTIC - DESIGNS AND PLANS.   2. BUILDING CONSTRUCTION - STUDY AND TEACHING.   I. TITLE.   II. SUNDBERG, ELMER W.

728.1
(78882)
A87
Sundell, Richard H
Aurora, Colo. Planning Dept.
Analysis of housing conditions, Aurora, Colorado, by R. H. Sundell. Research and surveys report. Prepared for the Colorado State Planning Div. [Denver, 1953?]
3p.

U.S. Urban Renewal Adm. UPAP.

1. Housing - Aurora, Colo. I. Sundell, R.H. II. U.S. URA-UPAP. Aurora, Colo.

711.14
(78882)
C65
Sundell, Richard H
Colorado. State Planning Div.
Land classification study for City of Aurora, Colorado, by R. H. Sundell. [Denver, 1958?]
18p.

U.S. Urban Renewal Adm. UPAP.

1. Land use - Aurora, Colo. I. Sundell, R.H. II. U.S. URA-UPAP. Aurora, Colo.

712.21
(78882)
A87
Sundell, Richard H
Aurora, Colo. Planning Dept.
Preliminary parks and recreation report, by R. H. Sundell. Prepared for the Colorado State Planning Div. [Denver, 1958?]
52p.

U.S. Urban Renewal Adm. UPAP.

1. Parks - Aurora, Colo. 2. Recreation - Aurora, Colo. I. Sundell, R.H. II. U.S. URA-UPAP. Aurora, Colo.

711.4
(78882)
A87
Sundell, Richard H
Aurora, Colo. Planning Dept.
Research and surveys: comprehensive plan, section 2, by R. H. Sundell. Denver, 1958.
1v.

U.S. Urban Renewal Adm. UPAP.

1. Master plan - Aurora, Colo. I. Sundell, R.H. II. U.S. URA-UPAP. Aurora, Colo.

711.4
(78882)
A87
Sect. 3
Sundell, Richard H
Aurora, Colo. Planning Dept.
Traffic and transportation: comprehensive plan, section 3, by Richard H. Sundell. Denver, 1959.
11p.

U.S. Urban Renewal Adm. UPAP.

1. Master plan - Aurora, Colo. 2. Traffic - Aurora, Colo. 3. Transportation - Aurora, Colo. I. Sundell, Richard H. II. U.S. URA-UPAP. Aurora, Colo.

728.1
:325
Y15
Sunderhauf, Milo B   jt. au.
Yankauer, Marian P
Housing: equal opportunity to choose where one shall live, by Marian P. Yankauer and Milo B. Sunderhauf. In Journal of Negro education, vol. 32, no. 4, Fall, 1963. Yearbook no. 32. p. 402-414.

1. Minority groups - Housing. I. Sunderhauf, Milo B., jt. au. II. Journal of Negro education.   III. Title.

332.72
S85
SUNDHEIM, JOSEPH HOFFMAN, 1878-
LAW OF BUILDING AND LOAN ASSOCIATIONS. 3D ED. CHICAGO, CALLAGHAN, 1933. 448P.

1. SAVINGS AND LOAN ASSOCIATIONS - LAW AND LEGISLATION.

540
S85
Sundquist, J
Versuche zur Synthese von einigen thermisch stabilen hetero-aromatischen Linearpolymeren. Helsinki, State Institute for Technical Research, 1971.
22p. (Finland. State Institute for Technical Research. Julkaisi 166 publication)

1. Chemistry. I. Finland. State Institute for Technical Research. II. Title.

VF
940.42
(42)
A52
Sundquist, James L
American Municipal Association.
The British defense program and local government, compiled from British documents and periodicals by Don K. Price and James L. Sundquist. Chicago, Public Administration Service, 1940.
55 p.   (Public Administration Service. Publication no. 69)

Housing: p. 37-41.

1.National defense. 2.Civilian defense. 3.Housing-U.K. I.Price, Don K. II.Sundquist, James L. III. Public Administration Service. IV.Title.

353
S85
Sundquist, James L
Making Federalism work; a study of program coordination at the community level, by James L. Sundquist, with the collaboration of David W. Davis. Wash., Brookings Institution, 1969.
293p.
Partial contents.-Model cities as a coordinating structure.
1. Intergovernmental relations. 2. Federal government. 3. Model cities. 4. Grants-in-aid. I. Davis, David W., jt. au. II. Brookings Institution. III.   Title.

362.5
P27
no.2
Sundquist, James L   ed.
On fighting poverty, perspectives from experience. Edited by James L. Sundquist with the assistance of Corinne Saposs Schelling. New York, Basic Books, 1969.
256p. (Perspectives on poverty, 2)
American Academy of Arts and Sciences Library.
Based on papers presented at a continuing seminar of the American Academy of Arts and Sciences on problems of race and poverty during the academic year 1966-67.
1. Poverty. 2. Social service.
I. Sundquist, James L., ed. II. American Academy of Arts and Sciences, Boston. Library. (Series: Perspectives on poverty, 2)

320
S85
Sundquist, James L
Politics and policy; the Eisenhower, Kennedy, and Johnson years. Wash., Brookings Institution, 1968.
560p.

1. Political science. 2. Federal government. 3. Economic policy. I. Brookings Institution. II. Title.

711.4
(44)
S82
Sundreau, Pierre
Giraudoux et l'esprit de l'urbanisme. Paris, Imprimerie E. Pigelet, 1960.
15p.

Extrait de La Revue Des Deux Mondes du 1er janvier 1960.

1. City planning - France.

694.183
S85
SUNLEY, J   G
SIGNIFICANCE OF BASIC AND APPLIED RESEARCH ON MECHANICAL FASTENERS FOR RESIDENTIAL CONSTRUCTION IN THE UNITED KINGDOM. BUILDING RESEARCH INSTITUTE CONFERENCE, NOVEMBER 19-21, 1963. WASHINGTON, BRI, 1963.
12P.

1. NAILS AND NAILING.   I. BUILDING RESEARCH INSTITUTE.

674
U54T
SUNLEY, J   G
U.K. DEPT. OF SCIENTIFIC AND INDUSTRIAL RESEARCH.
TESTING OF STRUCTURAL TIMBERS, POLES AND PIT-PROPS, BY J.G. SUNLEY. LONDON, H.M. STAT. OFF., 1963.
4P. (ITS FOREST PRODUCTS RESEARCH SPECIAL REPORT NO. 19)

1. LUMBER INDUSTRY.   I. SUNLEY, J.G.
II. TITLE: STRUCTURE TIMBER.

696.92
R42
Sunlight and buildings.
Richards, S   J
Sunlight and buildings. Paper presented at the annual Congress of the South African National Committee on Illumination at Benononi, May, 1967. Pretoria, South African Council for Scientific and Industrial Research, National Building Research Institute, 1967.
[5]p. (C.S.I.R. reference no. R/Bou 233)
Reprinted from S.A. Architectural record, Dec., 1967.

1. Daylight. 2. Windows. I. South African Council for Scientific and Industrial Research. National Building Research Institute. II. Title.

728.2
(7471)
N17
SUN-LIGHTED TENEMENTS.
NATIONAL HOUSING ASSOCIATION.
SUN-LIGHTED TENEMENTS; THIRTY-FIVE YEARS EXPERIENCE AS AN OWNER, BY ALFRED T. WHITE. NEW YORK, 1912.
20P. (ITS PUBLICATIONS, 12)

1. APARTMENT HOUSES - NEW YORK (CITY)
I. TITLE.   II. NATIONAL HOUSING ASSOCIATION.

696.92
K78
THE SUNLIGHTING RULE.
KRUGER, A   J
THE SUNLIGHTING RULE; A SIMPLE APPLICATION FOR PREDICTING THE SUNLIGHTING AND THE DAYLIGHTING FROM THE DRAWING. ROTTERDAM, RESEARCH INSTITUTE FOR PUBLIC HEALTH ENGINEERING T.N.O., 1959.
15-22P.

1. DAYLIGHT.   I. TITLE.

333.38
C47

SUNNYSIDE GARDENS.
CITY HOUSING CORPORATION.
SUNNYSIDE GARDENS, A HOME COMMUNITY.
NEW YORK, 1930.
16p.

1. SUBDIVISION.   I. TITLE.

712
S85s
2c

Sunset Books.
    Sunset garden and patio building book, by
the editors of Sunset Books and Sunset Magazine.
New ed. Menlo Park, Calif., Lane Books, 1970.
96p.

1. Landscape architecture. 2. Terraces.
3. Fences. I. Title: Garden and patio building
book.

674
L44s

Suomalaisten rima.
    Liiri, Osmo.
    Suomalaisten rima - ja sälelevyjen
lujuusominaisuuksista (Strength properties
of Finnish blockboards and laminboards I)
by Osmo Liiri et al, and Antti Kivisto.
Helsinki, State Institute for Technical
Research, 1967.
    48p. (Finland Institute for Technical
Research. Tiedotus. Sarja 1 - PUU (Wood)
40)
    English summary.
    1. Lumber industry. I. Kivisto, Antti, jt. au
II. Finland. State Institute for Technical
Research. III. Title.

333.38
S85

SUNNYSIDE GARDENS COMMUNITY ASSOCIATION.
ECONOMIC SURVEY OF HOMEOWNERS IN
SUNNYSIDE GARDENS, LONG ISLAND CITY,
N.Y. NEW YORK, 1933.
P.23-30.

1. SUBDIVISION.

728.1
:325
F72

Sunshine, Morris H   jt. au.
Freeman, Linton C
    Patterns of residential segregation, by
Linton C. Freeman and Morris H. Sunshine.
Cambridge, Mass., Schenkman, 1970.
[159]p.
    Bibliography: p. 85-87.

1. Minority groups - Housing. I. Sunshine,
Morris H., jt. au. II. Title.

388
S86

Suomen Arkkitehtiliiton Asemakaava- ja
Standardisoimislaitos.
    Liikenne, moottoriajoneuvojen melun
torjuminen (Traffic, prevention of motor
traffic noise) Helsinki, 1968.
11p.

1. Traffic. 2. Noise.

727
(791)
P45s

Sunnyside school district no. 12.
    Pima County, Ariz. Planning Dept.
    Sunnyside school district no. 12; elemen-
tary school location study. Tucson, Ariz.
1967.
11p.

1. Schools - Tucson, Ariz. 2. School
management and organization. I. Title.

VF
728.1
:362.6
(77157)
C65s

Sunshine Terrace.
    Columbus, Ohio. Metropolitan Housing
Authority.
    Sunshine Terrace. [Columbus, Ohio] 1964.
16p.

1. Housing for the aged - Columbus, Ohio.
2. Old age. I. Title.

693.068
:389.6
(471)
S86

Suomen Arkkitehtiliitto Standardisoimislaitos.
    Moduulijärjestely, soveltamisperusteita.
Helsinki, 1966.
15p. (Its Rakennusteollisuuden
moduulijarjestely RT 038.96)

1. Modular coordination - Finland.

711.4
(79473)
S85

Sunnyvale, Calif. City Planning
Commission.
Sunnyvale, Calif. City Planning Dept.
    General plan for Sunnyvale. Adopted by the
City Planning Commission, 11 September 1957.
Adopted by the City Council, 8 October 1957.
Sunnyvale, 1957.
44p. maps tables.

Prepared jointly with the Planning Commission.

1. Master plan - Sunnyvale, Calif. I. Sunnyvale, Calif. City Planning Commission.

728.2
(471)
S86

Suokko, Seppo.
    Asuinkerrostalojen taloudellinen käyttöaika
(Economic life of apartment houses) Helsinki,
State Institute for Technical Research, 1970.
64p. (Finland. State Institute for
Technical Research. Tiedotus. Sarja 3 -
Rakennus 152)
    English summary.
    Bibliography: p. 56-58.
    1. Apartment houses - Finland.
2. Depreciation and obsolescence (Buildings)
I. Finland. State Institute for Technical
Research. II. Title: Economic life of
apartment houses.

690.022
(471)
S86
2c.

Suomen Betoniteollisuuden Keskusjärjestön.
    BES; tutkimus avoimen elementti- järjestelmän
kehittämiseksi. [Helsinki, 1969?]
89p.
    English summary.

1. Prefabricated construction - Finland.
2. Concrete construction.

711.4
(79473)
S85

Sunnyvale, Calif. City Planning Dept.
    General plan for Sunnyvale. Adopted by the
City Planning Commission, 11 September 1957.
Adopted by the City Council, 8 October 1957.
Sunnyvale, 1957.
44p. maps tables.

Prepared jointly with the Planning Commission.

1. Master plan - Sunnyvale, Calif. I. Sunnyvale, Calif. City Planning Commission.

728.1
:308
(471)
S86

Suokko, Seppo.
    Kerrostalohuoneistojen hinnat Helsingissä
v. 1966-1969 (The prices of multistorey-house
dwellings in Helsinki in 1966...1969)
Helsinki, State Institute for Technical
Research, 1970.
62p. (Finland. State Institute for Technical
Research. Tiedotus. Sarja 3 - Rakennus 142)
    Finnish and English.
    Bibliography: p. 52-53.
    1. Housing market - Finland. 2. Family
income and expenditure - Housing - Finland.
I. Finland. State Institute for Technical
Research. II. Title: The prices of
multistorey house dwellings in Helsinki.

728.1
S86

Suomen Siviili- ja Asevelvollisuusinvaliidien
Liitto.
    Ohjeita liikuntaesteiden poistamiseksi.
Helsinki, 1965.
61p.

English summary.

1. Housing for the handicapped. 2. Handicapped. I. Title.

643.52
S85

Sunset Books.
    Planning and remodeling bathrooms, by the
editors of Sunset Books and Sunset Magazine.
Menlo Park, Calif., Lane Books, 1970.
80p.

1. Bathrooms. I. Title.

728.3
:333
S86

Suokko, Seppo.
    Marknadspriser på nya radhuslägenheter i
Helsingfors, Esbo och Grankulla 1967
(Price of new terrace houses in
Helsinki, Espoo and Kauniainen in 1967)
Helsinki, State Institute for Technical
Research, 1969.
44p. (Finland. State Institute for
Technical Research. Julkaisu 151)
    English summary.
    Bibliography: p. 41-42.
                    (Cont'd on next card)

658.8
A52s
1957

Super market land, an analysis of super
market sales.
American Weekly
    Super market land, an analysis of super
market sales as currently revealed and pin-
pointed by the American Weekly Marketing
Guide. New York, 1957.
31p. diagrs.

1. Retail trade. I. Title.

325.3
S85
c.1 E.O.

Sunset Books.
    Southwest Indian country; Arizona, New Mexico,
Southern Utah and Colorado, by the editors of
Sunset Books and Sunset Magazine. Menlo Park,
Calif., Lane Books, 1970.
79p.

1. Indians. I. Title.

728.3
:333
S86

Suokko, Seppo. Marknadspriser på...1969.
                    (Card 2)

1. Houses - Sales price. 2. Housing
market - Finland. I. Finland. State
Institute for Technical Research.
II. Title: Price of new terrace
houses in Helsinki.

658.8
A52s
1958

Super market land, 1958.
American Weekly. (Marketing Div.)
    Super market land, 1958. Report supple-
menting Super market land (1957). New
York, 1958.
6p. tables.

1. Retail trade. I. Title.

658.8
A52
Super market land, U.S.A.

American Weekly. (Marketing Div.)
Super market land, U.S.A. County list, indicating blue ground and other counties; total number of super markets, January 1958, number opened during 1957. New York, 1958.
21p. tables.
With this is issued: Map of Super market land, U.S.A., showing blue ground of sales, metropolitan market areas, supermarket counties, and key cities.

1. Retail stores. I. Title.

Supt. of Documents.

see

U.S. Government Printing Office.

388
(7531)
D47
Superail transit system for mass transportation, Washington, D.C. to Dulles International Airport.

D.C. Transit System, inc., Washington, D.C.
Proposal for a demonstration model of a controlled high-speed Superail transit system for mass transportation, Washington, D.C., to Dulles International Airport. In collaboration with S. H. Bingham. [Washington] 1962.
83p.

1. Transportation - District of Columbia metropolitan area. 2. Railroads. I. Bingham, Sidney H.
II. Title: Superail transit system for mass transportation, Washington, D.C. to Dulles International Airport.

711.4
K25
The supercity.

Kern, Robert Russ.
The supercity; a planned physical equipment for city life, by Robert R. Kern ... Washington, D. C., 1924.
4 p. l., 7-349 p. diagrs. 21ᶜᵐ.

1. City planning. 2. Cities and towns - Planning. 3. Cities and towns - Civic improvement. I. Title.

Library of Congress   HT151.K4   24-25881

———— Copy 2.
Copyright A 807569   [29.1]

Superior, Wisconsin.

VF

Housing-U.S.-Wisconsin-Superior.

LAW
Ref.
Supergrade and research-scientific positions in various Federal agencies.

U.S. Congress. House. Committee on Post Office and Civil Service.
Supergrade and research-scientific positions in various Federal agencies. Hearings before the Committee on Post Office and Civil Service. House of Representatives, Eighty-sixth Congress, first session on S. 1845 and H.R. 8479, bills to provide for the establishment of rates of basic compensation for certain positions in the Patent Office, in the Dept. of Commerce and for other purposes.   Washington, Govt. Print. Off., 1959.   1959.
60p.

1. Federal civil service. I. Title.

Film
Superfluous people: 60-minute film.
Produced by Columbia Broadcasting System. Distributed by, Washington, Bureau of Family Services, Dept. of Health, Education, and Welfare. New York, CBS Television Network Recording Operations [1962?]
16mm. 2000 ft. sound. 60 min. b/w.
Emmie award 1962/63.

1. Films. 2. Relocation - Films.
3. Urban renewal films. I. CBS Television Network Recording Operations. II. U.S. Dept. of Health, Education, and Welfare. Bureau of Family Services.

728.1
1336.18
(77512)
S86
SUPERIOR, WIS. HOUSING AUTHORITY.
REPORT. 1949/40, 1947/48, 1932/50
SUPERIOR,
3v. ANNUAL.

REPORT FOR 1949 50 ALSO CONTAINS A 12-YEAR SUMMARY OF THE AUTHORITY'S ACTIVITIES.

1. PUBLIC HOUSING - SUPERIOR, WIS.

2862.
2865
SUPERIOR, NEB. PLANNING COMMISSION.
COMPREHENSIVE PLAN: 1. COMPREHENSIVE PLAN; 2. CAPITAL IMPROVEMENTS PROGRAM; 2. PROPOSED SUBDIVISION REGULATIONS ORDINANCE; 4. PROPOSED ZONING ORDINANCE.
SUPERIOR, NEB., 1969.
4 V. (HUD 701 REPORT)

1. MASTER PLAN - SUPERIOR, NEB.
I. HUD. 701. SUPERIOR, NEB.

331.2
C658UP
SUPERGRADE AND SCIENTIFIC RESEARCH AND DEVELOPMENT POSITIONS.
U.S. CONGRESS. SENATE. COMMITTEE ON POST OFFICE AND CIVIL SERVICE.
SUPERGRADE AND SCIENTIFIC RESEARCH AND DEVELOPMENT POSITIONS FOR THE DEPARTMENT OF DEFENSE; REPORT TO ACCOMPANY H.R. 6059. WASHINGTON, GOVT. PRINT. OFF., 1959.
8P. (86TH CONGRESS, 1ST SESSION. SENATE. REPORT NO. 882)

1. FEDERAL GOVERNMENT - SALARIES.
2. FEDERAL CIVIL SERVICE. I. TITLE.

DATE OF REQUEST 7/17/51   JUL 23 1951   L.C. CARD NO.

AUTHOR
Superior City Planning Commission

TITLE
Study of federal housing sites

SERIES

EDITION   PUB. DATE 5/31/51   PAGING 34pp

PUBLISHER
Processed.
Map

RECOMMENDED BY   REVIEWED IN
RLM   RL, 7/2, p/5

ORDER RECORD

534.83
B65noi
U.S. Office of Supersonic Transport Development.

Bolt, Beranek and Newman.
Noise exposure forecast contours for expected 1985 and 1990 operations at seven U.S. airports. Submitted to Office of Supersonic Transport Development, Dept. of Transportation. [n.p.] 1971.
87p. (Report 2076)
CFSTI. AD 722 365.

1. Noise. 2. Airports. I. U.S. Office of Supersonic Transport Development.
II. Title.

351.1
C657s
1968
S-R
Supergrades...
U.S. Congress. Senate. Committee on Post Office and Civil Service.
Supergrades; report to accompany S. 3672. Washington, Govt. Print. Off., 1968.
14p. (90th Cong., 2d sess. Senate. Report no. 1306)

1. Federal civil service. I. Title.

VF
333.33
N17su
Superior equipment of the realtor.
National Association of Real Estate Boards.
Superior equipment of the realtor. Chicago [1965?]
10p.

1. Real estate business. I. Title.

384
M12s
Supersonic transport operating practices during simulated operations in future air traffic control system environments.
McLaughlin, Milton D
Supersonic transport operating practices during simulated operations in future air traffic control system environments, by Milton D. McLaughlin and Richard H. Sawyer. Wash., National Aeronautics and Space Administration, 1969.
63p. (NASA Technical note TN D-5018)

1. Air transportation. I. Title. II. Sawyer, Richard H., jt. au. III. U.S. National Aeronautics and Space Administration.

331.2
C65SUPE
SUPERGRADES IN THE FEDERAL GOVERNMENT.
U.S. CONGRESS. HOUSE. COMMITTEE ON POST OFFICE AND CIVIL SERVICE.
SUPERGRADES IN THE FEDERAL GOVERNMENT. HEARINGS, EIGHTY-SIXTH CONGRESS, SECOND SESSION ON H.R. 10114 AND H.R. 10849... WASHINGTON, GOVT. PRINT. OFF., 1960.
23P.

HEARING HELD JUNE 24, 1960.

1. FEDERAL GOVERNMENT - SALARIES.
I. TITLE.

351.1
C486
SUPERIOR PERFORMANCE AWARDS.
U.S. CIVIL SERVICE COMMISSION.
A GUIDE FOR USING SUPERIOR PERFORMANCE AWARDS TO IMPROVE GOVERNMENT OPERATIONS.
WASHINGTON, 1958.
28P.

1. PERSONNEL MANAGEMENT. I. TITLE.

1. FEDERAL CIVIL SERVICE. I. TITLE: SUPERIOR PERFORMANCE AWARDS.

025
F19
SUPERVISING LIBRARY PERSONNEL.
FAY, ADRA M
SUPERVISING LIBRARY PERSONNEL.
CHICAGO, AMERICAN LIBRARY ASSOCIATION, 1950.
23P.

ISSUED IN 1949 BY THE MINNEAPOLIS PUBLIC LIBRARY UNDER THE TITLE SUPERVISION, A MANUAL.

1. LIBRARY ADMINISTRATION. I. TITLE.

711.73
L21
Superhighway.
Leavitt, Helen.
Superhighway: superhoax. Garden City, N.Y., Doubleday, 1970.
324p.

Bibliography: p. 305-310.

1. Highways. I. Title.

VF
658.8
886
Supermarkets. The New Englander, Sept. 1956, p. 11, 26-31. illus.

Clipping.

1. Retail stores.

658.3
E81
Supervising R & D personnel.
Evans, C George.
Supervising R & D personnel. New York, American Management Association, 1969.
142p.

1. Personnel management. 2. Scientific research. I. American Management Association. II. Title.

658.3
C48r
Supervising troubled employees.
U.S. Civil Service Commission. (Bureau of Policies and Standards)
Recognizing and supervising troubled employees. A guide for supervisors and others who counsel troubled employees. Wash., Govt. Print. Off., 1967.
15p. (Its Personnel management series no. 18)

1. Personnel management. 2. Federal civil service. I. Title. II. Title: Supervising troubled employees.

658.3
F22S
SUPERVISOR TRAINING PROGRAM.
U.S. FEDERAL PUBLIC HOUSING AUTHORITY. PERSONNEL DIVISION.
SUPERVISOR TRAINING PROGRAM.
CONFERENCES NO. 1-5. WASHINGTON, 1943.
1 V.

1. PERSONNEL MANAGEMENT.   I. TITLE.

352
(774)
S86p
Supervisors Inter-County Committee, Detroit. Meeting.
Proceedings of
Combined six County Boards of Supervisors. Detroit.
v.   annual.

For complete information see shelflist.

1. Metropolitan area planning - Michigan.
2. Metropolitan   government - Michigan

351.1
(016)
C48SU
SUPERVISION.
U.S. CIVIL SERVICE COMMISSION. LIBRARY.
SUPERVISION; A SELECTED LIST OF REFERENCES. WASHINGTON, 1945.
34P.

1. FEDERAL CIVIL SERVICE - BIBLIOGRAPHY. 2. PERSONNEL ADMINISTRATION - BIBLIOGRAPHY. I. TITLE.

658.3
H29
THE SUPERVISOR'S BASIC MANAGEMENT GUIDE.
HEYEL, CARL, 1908-
THE SUPERVISOR'S BASIC MANAGEMENT GUIDE; AN A-Z MANUAL ON SUPERVISORY EFFECTIVENESS. NEW YORK, MCGRAW-HILL [1965]
496P.

1. PERSONNEL MANAGEMENT.   I. TITLE.

352
(774)
S86
Supervisors Inter-County Committee, Detroit.
Report 1962-65

Detroit
4 v.   annual

For complete information see shelflist.

1. Metropolitan government - Mich.
2. Metropolitan area planning - Mich.

690.015
F22
R54
Supervision and inspection of federal construction.
Federal Construction Council.
Supervision and inspection of federal construction. Prepared by Task Group T-50 of the Federal Construction Council, Building Research Advisory Board, Division of Engineering, National Research Council. Wash., National Academy of Sciences, National Research Council, 1968.
57p. (Its Technical report no. 54)
National Research Council. Publication no. 1609.
1. Building construction. 2. Federal government. 3. Building   construction - Standards and   specifications. I. Title.

658.3
H15s
Supervisors guide to human relations.
Hannaford, Earle S
Supervisors guide to human relations. Chicago, National Safety Council, 1967.
341p.

Bibliography: p. 333-335.

1. Personnel management. I. National Safety Council. II. Title.

628.3
(774)
N17r
Supervisors Inter-County Committee, Detroit.
National Sanitation Foundation.
Report on metropolitan environmental study: sewerage and drainage problems and administrative affairs. Six-County metropolitan area, Southeastern Michigan. Prepared for the Supervisors Inter-County Committee. Ann Arbor, Mich., 1964.
147p.

Cover title: Southeastern Michigan sewerage and drainage study.

(Continued on   next card)

658.3
L17
Supervision, The techniques of.
Lateiner, Alfred R
The techniques of supervision.   New London, Connecticut, National Foremen's Institute [1954].
207p.

658.3
F15
SUPERVISORS IN ACTION.
FAMULARO, JOSEPH J
SUPERVISORS IN ACTION; DEVELOPING YOUR SKILLS IN MANAGING PEOPLE. DRAWINGS BY A.S.H. ASSOCIATES. NEW YORK, MCGRAW-HILL, 1961.
238P.

1. PERSONNEL MANAGEMENT.   I. TITLE.

628.3
(774)
N17r
National Sanitation Foundation. Report on metropolitan environmental study...1964
(Card 2)

1. Sewerage and sewage disposal - Mich.
2. Drainage. I. Supervisors Inter-County Committee, Detroit. II. Title: Southeastern Michigan sewerage and drainage study.

658.3
P343
1958
THE SUPERVISION OF PERSONNEL.
PFIFFNER, JOHN M
THE SUPERVISION OF PERSONNEL; HUMAN RELATIONS IN THE MANAGEMENT OF MEN. 2D ED. ENGLEWOOD CLIFFS, N.J., PRENTICE-HALL, 1958.
500P.

1. PERSONNEL MANAGEMENT.   I. TITLE.

352.6
(774)
S86
Supervisors Inter-County Committee, Detroit.
Detroit metropolitan area "planned" public works. Detroit, 1961.
1v.

1. Community facilities - Detroit metropolitan area. 2. Metropolitan areas - Detroit.

628.3
(774)
N17
Supervisors Inter-County Committee, Detroit.
National Sanitation Foundation.
A report on sewage disposal problems; six county metropolitan area, Southeastern Michigan. Prepared for the Supervisors Inter-County Committee. Ann Arbor, Mich., 1964.
61p.
Cover title: Southeastern Michigan sewerage and drainage study

1. Sewerage and sewage disposal - Mich. 2. Drainage.   I. Supervisors Inter-County Committee, Detroit. II. Title: Southeastern Michigan Sewerage and   drainage study.

658.3
A75S
SUPERVISOR DEVELOPMENT PROGRAM.
U.S. DEPT. OF THE ARMY.
SUPERVISOR DEVELOPMENT PROGRAM, BASIC COURSE, WITHIN-GRADE INCREASES AND EMPLOYEE PRODUCTIVITY. WASHINGTON, GOVT. PRINT. OFF., 1964.
39P.

1. PERSONNEL MANAGEMENT.   I. TITLE.

352.6
(774)
S86
1963
Supervisors Inter-County Committee, Detroit.
The Detroit metropolitan area "Planned" public works program. 3d ed. Detroit, 1963.
1v.

1. Community facilities - Detroit metropolitan area.   2. Metropolitan areas - Detroit.

VF
711.3
(774)
S86s
Supervisors Inter-County Committee, Detroit.
Supervisors Inter-County Committee: what it is, how it works its accomplishments. Detroit, 1963.
30p.

1. Metropolitan area planning - Michigan. 2. Metropolitan areas - Detroit. 3. Community facilities - Detroit metropolitan area.

658.3
A75SU
SUPERVISOR SELECTION.
U.S. DEPT. OF THE ARMY.
SUPERVISOR SELECTION; CHOOSING TOMORROW'S MANAGERS. WASHINGTON, GOVT. PRINT. OFF., 1958.
42P.

1. PERSONNEL MANAGEMENT.   I. TITLE.

352.6
(774)
S86
1964
Supervisors Inter-County Committee, Detroit.
The Detroit metropolitan area "Planned" public works program. 4th ed. Detroit, 1964.
1 v.

1. Community facilities - Detroit metropolitan area. 2. Metropolitan areas - Detroit. I. Title.

628.1
(774)
N17
Supervisors Inter-County Committee, Detroit.
National Sanitation Foundation.
The water supply for the six-county metropolitan area, Southeastern Michigan. Prepared for the Supervisors Inter-County Committee. Detroit, 1957.
72p.

1. Water-supply - Mich. I. Supervisors Inter-County Committee, Detroit. II. Title.

614.8
N17s
Supervisors safety manual.
National Safety Council.
Supervisors safety manual.
3d ed. Chicago, 1970.
341p.

Bibliography: p. 336-337.

1. Accidents. I. Title.

U. S. *Congress. Senate. Committee on Post Office and Civil Service.* Supervisory selection in the Federal Government ... 1952. (Card 2)

iii, 41 p. 24 cm. (82d Cong. 2d sess. Senate. Report no. 2100)

1. Personnel management. 2. Civil service—U. S. I. Title. (Series: U. S. 82d Cong. 2d sess. 1952. Senate. Report no. 2100)

JK765.A5 1952d   *351.3 351.1   52-61533

Library of Congress   (2)

351.7
:8
C65
1970
Suppl.
S-H
Supplemental appropriations for fiscal year 1970.
U.S. Congress. Senate. Committee on Appropriations.
Supplemental appropriations for fiscal year 1970. Hearings before the Committee on Appropriations, United States Senate, Ninety-first Congress, second session on H.R. 17399, an act making supplemental appropriations for the fiscal year ending June 30, 1971 and for other purposes. Wash., Govt. Print. Off., 1970.
1642p.
1. U.S. Executive departments - Appropriations and expenditures. I. Title.

658.3
C48IN
SUPERVISORY CASE STUDIES.
U.S. CIVIL SERVICE COMMISSION.
INDEX OF SUPERVISORY CASE STUDIES; AND A REVIEW OF THE CASE METHOD.
WASHINGTON, 1958.
23P. (PERSONNEL METHODS SERIES, NO. 8)

1. PERSONNEL MANAGEMENT. I. TITLE; SUPERVISORY CASE STUDIES.

658.3
(07)
F22
SUPERVISORY TRAINING COURSE.
U.S. FEDERAL HOUSING ADMINISTRATION.
SUPERVISORY TRAINING COURSE.
WASHINGTON, PERSONNEL DIVISION, FEDERAL HOUSING ADMINISTRATION, 1961
6 PARTS IN 22 VOLS. (ITS CONFERENCE OUTLINE, 1-21)

CONTENTS.- PT. I, SUPERVISOR'S JOB.-PT. II, PERSONNEL MANAGEMENT.- PT. III, EMPLOYEE DEVELOPMENT.- PT. IV, JOB MANAGEMENT.- PT. V, SELF-DEVELOPMENT.-PT. VI, SUPPL. TO BASIC COURSE.-UNNUMBERED VOL. I INSTRUCTION FOR CONFERENCE LEADER.
(CONTINUED ON NEXT CARD)

351.7
:8
C65
1969
Suppl.
H-CR
Supplemental appropriations for the fiscal year ending June 30, 1969...
U.S. Congress. House. Committee of Conference.
Supplemental appropriations for the fiscal year ending June 30, 1969; conference report to accompany H.R. 20300. Washington, Govt. Print. Off., 1968.
11p. (90th Cong., 2d sess. House. Report no. 1972)
1. U.S. Executive departments - Appropriations and expenditures. 2. U.S. Dept. of Housing and Urban Development - Appropriations and ex penditures. I. Title.

658.3
P67
SUPERVISORY DEVELOPMENT CONFERENCE GUIDE.
U.S. POST OFFICE DEPARTMENT.
SUPERVISORY DEVELOPMENT CONFERENCE GUIDE. WASHINGTON, GOVT. PRINT. OFF., 1959.
67P. (ITS PERSONNEL HANDBOOK, SERIES P-9)

1. PERSONNEL MANAGEMENT. I. TITLE.

658.3
(07)
F22
U.S. FEDERAL HOUSING ADMINISTRATION.
SUPERVISORY TRAINING COURSE....1961
(CARD 2)
1. PERSONNEL MANAGEMENT - STUDY AND TEACHING. I. TITLE.

351.7
:8
C65
1969
Suppl.
S-R
Supplemental appropriation bill, 1969;
U.S. Congress. Senate. Committee on Appropriations.
Supplemental appropriation bill, 1969; report to accompany H.R. 20300. Washington, Govt. Print. Off., 1968.
33p. (90th Cong., 2d sess. Senate. Report no. 1667)
1. U.S. Executive departments - Appropriations and expenditures. 2. U.S. Dept. of Housing and Urban Development - Appropriations and expenditures. I. Title.

658.3
V27S
SUPERVISORY DEVELOPMENT CONFERENCE SERIES.
U.S. VETERANS ADMINISTRATION.
SUPERVISORY DEVELOPMENT CONFERENCE SERIES. WASHINGTON, VETERANS ADMINISTRATION, 1959.
3 V.

1. PERSONNEL MANAGEMENT. I. TITLE.

332.72
S86
Supplee, Andrew R
FHA financing for sales housing, section 203(b); a hypothetical case. Wash., Builders Services Div., National Association of Home Builders, 1970.
68p.
1. Mortgage finance. 2. Home ownership. 3. U.S. Federal Housing Administration. I. National Association of Home Builders. Builders Services Div. II. Title.

360
N17re
Suppl.
Supplemental studies for the National...
U.S. National Advisory Commission on Civil Disorders.
Supplemental studies for the National Advisory Commission on Civil Disorders. Three studies conducted at the University of Michigan Survey Research Center, the Johns Hopkins University, and Columbia University, Bureau of Applied Social Research. Wash., 1968.
243p.
Contents.-Racial attitudes in fifteen American cities, by Angus Campbell and Howard Schuman.- Between White and Black; the faces of American institutions in the (Cont'd on next card)

658.3
(07)
M42S
SUPERVISORY LEADERSHIP DEVELOPMENT.
MICHIGAN. CIVIL SERVICE COMMISSION.
SUPERVISORY LEADERSHIP DEVELOPMENT.
AN INSTRUCTION SOURCE BOOK TO BE USED IN THE DEVELOPMENT OF FIRST-LINE SUPERVISORS IN THE PUBLIC SERVICE.
LANSING, MICH., 1956-1959.
56P.

1. PERSONNEL MANAGEMENT - STUDY AND TEACHING. I. TITLE.

332.72
S86f
Supplee, Andrew R
FHA financing for sales housing, section 235; a hypothetical case. Wash., Builders Services Div., National Association of Home Builders, 1970.
46p.
1. Mortgage finance. 2. Home ownership. 3. U.S. Federal Housing Administration. I. National Association of Home Builders. Builders Services Div. II. Title.

360
N17re
Suppl.
U.S. National Advisory Commission on Civil Disorders. Supplemental studies...1968. (Card 2)

ghetto, by Peter H. Rossi and others.-Who riots? A study of participation in the 1967 riots, by Robert M. Fogelson and Robert B. Hill.
1. Civil disorders. 2. Social conditions. 3. Minority groups. 4. Race relations. 5. Sociology, Urban. I. Title. II. Campbell, Angus. Racial attitudes in fifteen American cities.
(Cont'd on next card)

352
S32
Supervisory methods in municipal administration.
Sherwood, Frank P
Supervisory methods in municipal administration, by Frank P. Sherwood and Wallace H. Best. Chicago, International City Managers' Association, 1958.
302p. (Municipal management series)
Bibliography: p. 285-292.
1. Municipal government. I. Best, Wallace H., jt. au. II. International City Managers' Association. III. Title.

341.1
:338
P72S
SUPPLEMENT TO MESSAGE RELATIVE TO FOREIGN AID.
U.S. PRESIDENT, 1963-1969 (JOHNSON)
SUPPLEMENT TO MESSAGE RELATIVE TO FOREIGN AID. COMMUNICATION FROM THE PRESIDENT OF THE UNITED STATES...
WASHINGTON, GOVT. PRINT. OFF., 1965.
3P. (89TH CONGRESS, 1ST SESSION. HOUSE OF REPRESENTATIVES. DOCUMENT NO. 161)

1. TECHNICAL ASSISTANCE PROGRAMS. 2. U.S. PRESIDENT - MESSAGES. I. TITLE.

360
N17re
Suppl.
U.S. National Advisory Commission on Civil Disorders. Supplemental studies...1968. (Card 3)

III. Rossi, Peter H. Between White and Black; the faces of American institutions in the ghetto. IV. Fogelson, Robert M. Who riots? a study of participation in the 1967 riots. V. Schuman, Howard, jt. au. VI. Berk, Richard A., jt. au. VII. Hill, Robert B., jt. au.

351.1
C65
no.2100
Supervisory selection in the Federal Government
U. S. *Congress. Senate. Committee on Post Office and Civil Service.*
Supervisory selection in the Federal Government; a report with conclusions and recommendations made as a result of the investigation into the personnel needs and practices of the various governmental agencies being conducted by the Subcommittee on Federal Manpower Policies pursuant to Senate Resolution 53, as amended by Senate Resolutions 206 and 288, with the purpose of formulating policies for the most effective utilization of civilian personnel during the period of the national emergency. Washington, U. S. Govt. Print. Off., 1952.

(Continued on next card)
52-61533
(2)

351.7
:8
C65
1969
Suppl.
H-H
Supplemental appropriation bill, 1969.
U.S. Congress. House. Committee on Appropriations.
Supplemental appropriation bill, 1969. Hearings before Subcommittees of the Committee on Appropriations, House of Representatives, Ninetieth Congress, second session. Wash., Govt. Print. Off., 1969.
375p.
1. U.S. Executive departments - Appropriations and expenditures. 2. U.S. Dept. of Housing and Urban Development - Appropriations and expenditures. I. Title.

388
B69
Supplemental studies of urban transportation systems analysis.
Boys, J A
Supplemental studies of urban transportation systems analysis, by J.A. Boys and others. Conducted under contract with the Office of the Secretary, Dept. of Housing and Urban Development. Santa Barbara, Calif., General Research Corp., 1968.
162p. (CR-777-2)
Bibliography: p. 161-162.
HUD contract no. H-777.
1. Transportation. 2. Journey to work. I. Title. II. Title: Urban transportation systems analysis. III. General Research Corp. IV. U.S. Dept. of Housing and Urban Develop ment.

628.515
W96
Supplementary aeration of lagoons in rigorous climate areas.
Wyoming. University. Dept. of Civil Engineering.
Supplementary aeration of lagoons in rigorous climate areas, by Robert L. Champlin [Prepared] for the Environmental Protection Agency. Wash., Govt. Print. Off., 1971. 73p. (Water pollution control research series)

1. Water pollution. I. Champlin, Robert L. II. U.S. Environmental Protection Agency. III. Title.

658
(016)
S86S
U.S. BUREAU OF SUPPLIES AND ACCOUNTS (NAVY DEPT.) LIBRARY.
THE SPECIALIST AND THE GENERALIST, A WORKING BIBLIOGRAPHY. WASHINGTON, 1961. 10P.

1. MANAGEMENT - BIBLIOGRAPHY.
I. TITLE.

711.585
1572
INTERNATIONAL HOUSING ASSOCIATION. BESEITIGUNG VON ...1935. (CARD 2)

I. TITLE. II. TITLE: SUPPRESSION DE QUARTIERS MISÉRAUX.

VF
590.015
F22
747s
Supplementary field investigation of underground heat distribution systems.
Federal Construction Council.
Supplementary field investigation of underground heat distribution systems. Prepared by Task Group T-54 of the Federal Construction Council, Building Research Advisory Board, Div. of Engineering, National Research Council as a service of the National Academy of Sciences for Air Force [and others] Washington, National Academy of Sciences, National Research Council, 1966. 25p. (Its technical report no. 475)
National Research Council. Publication no. 1481.

(Continued on next card)

728.1
W24
Supply conditions for low-cost housing production.
Weiner, Neil S
Supply conditions for low-cost housing production. Arlington, Va., Institute for Defense Analyses, Program Analysis Div., 1968.
115p. (Institute for Defense Analyses. Program Analysis Div. Study S-323)

Conducted for Dept. of Housing and Urban Development.
HUD contract no. H-931.

(Cont'd on next card)

330
(52)
886
Supreme Commander for the Allied Powers. (LC)
(Natural Resources Section)
The Japanese village in transition, by Arthur F. Raper and others. Tokyo, 1950. 272p. (Its Report no. 136)

1. Economic development - Japan. 2. Agriculture - Japan I. Raper, Arthur F II. Title.

VF
690.015
F22
R47s
Federal Construction Council. Supplementary field...1966. (Card 2)

1. Heating. 2. Pipes. 3. Insulation. I. Title.

728.1
W24
Weiner, Neil S Supply...1968. (Card 2)

1. Low-income housing. 2. Construction costs. 3. Housing market. I. U.S. Dept. of Housing and Urban Development. II. Institute for Defense Analyses. III. Title.

U.S. Supreme court.

Alaska federal reports; cases argued and determined in the United States Circuit and District courts of California and Oregon, District courts of Washington, District courts of Alaska, Circuit courts of appeals, as well as decisions of the Supreme court of the United States in cases arising in Alaska ... 1869-[1937] St. Paul, Minn., West publishing co., 1938.
5 v. 23½ cm.
This work is issued as a supplement to Alaska reports, making available all reported cases arising in Alaska since its purchase in 1867. cf. Explanation.

(Continued on next card)
38—23343
[51g1]

332
F45s
1966
Supplementary high rate bond values.
Financial Publishing Co.
Supplementary high rate bond values, showing net returns on bonds and other redeemable securities paying interest semiannually. Boston, 1966.
160p. (Its Publication no. 21)

1. Bond yield tables. I. Title.

VF
691
(71)
C15
A
Supply of building materials in Canada.
Canada. Dept. of Reconstruction and Supply.
Supply of building materials in Canada, outlook 1947
Ottawa, 1947
v. tables.
Title varies: 1947, Production of basic and building materials in Canada; 1951, Supply of basic and building materials in Canada.
Discontinued after 1953 issuance.

1. Building materials-Canada. I. Title.

U.S. Supreme court.

Alaska federal reports ... 1938. (Card 2)
"Alaska federal reports, volumes 1-5, will be supplemented in future through Alaska reports, volume 9 and following. This means that future volumes of Alaska reports will contain not only the cases of the Alaska District court, but also those cases adjudicated in the Circuit court of appeals, 9th circuit, and of the United States Supreme court arising in Alaska."—p. iv.

1. Law reports, digests, etc.—Alaska. 2. Law reports, digests, etc.—U. S. I. Alaska (Ter.) Courts. II. U. S. District court. Alaska (Ter.) III. U. S. Courts. IV. U. S. Supreme court. V. West publishing co., St. Paul. VI. Title: Alaska reports.

38—23343

Library of Congress [51g1]

VF
333.38
(77234)
M68
Supplementary technical recommendations for the proposed subdivision ordinance.
Mount Vernon, Ind. City Plan Commission.
Supplementary technical recommendations for the proposed subdivision ordinance. Mount Vernon, Ind., [1965?]
10p.

1. Subdivision regulation - Mt. Vernon, Ind. I. Title.

690.015
(485)
S82
R9
1970
The supply of energy to buildings.
Stockholm. Statens Institut för Byggnadsforskning.
Byggnaders energiförsörjning; data för jämförande kostnadsberäkningar av samarbetsgruppen för byggnaders energiförsörjning (The supply of energy to buildings; data for comparative cost calculations by the joint working group for the supply of energy to buildings) Stockholm, 1970.
37p. (Its Rapport R9:1970)
English summary.
1. Building research - Sweden. 2. Heating. I. Title: The supply of energy to buildings.

U.S. Supreme court.
U. S. *District court. Alaska (Ter.)*
Alaska reports. v.
Cases argued and determined in the District courts of Alaska as well as U. S. Circuit court of appeals and Supreme court of the United States in cases arising in Alaska ... May 17, 1884- St. Paul, Minn., West publishing co., 1903-
v. 23½". For Additions or Holdings
Subtitle varies: v. 1, Containing the unpublished decisions of the District courts of the territory of Alaska ...
v. 2-7, Containing the decisions of the district judges of Alaska territory ...

(Continued on next card)
3-28601 rev
[r47c2]

325.3
C65S
1961
S-R
SUPPLEMENTING AND AMENDING THE ACT OF JUNE 30.
U.S. CONGRESS. SENATE. COMMITTEE ON INTERIOR AND INSULAR AFFAIRS.
SUPPLEMENTING AND AMENDING THE ACT OF JUNE 30, 1948, RELATING TO THE FORT HALL INDIAN IRRIGATION PROJECT... REPORT TO ACCOMPANY S. 1294. WASHINGTON, GOVT. PRINT. OFF., 1961.
10P. (87TH CONGRESS, 1ST SESSION. SENATE. REPORT NO. 135)

1. INDIANS. 2. IRRIGATION. I. TITLE. II. TITLE: THE FORT HALL INDIAN IRRIGATION PROJECT.

332.72
M17s
Support for the mortgage market.
Martin, Preston.
Support for the mortgage market: advances policy and FHLMC policy. Wash., Federal Home Loan Bank Board, 1970.
22p.
Federal Home Loan Bank Board news, Nov. 10, 1970.
Presented to the 78th annual convention, United States Savings and Loan League...San Francisco, Calif.
1. U.S. Federal Home Loan Bank Board. 2. Mortgage finance. I. Title.

U.S. Supreme court.
U. S. *District court. Alaska (Ter.)* Alaska reports ...
1903- (Card 2)
v. 8- Cases argued and determined in the District courts of Alaska as well as U. S. Circuit court of appeals and Supreme court of the United States in cases arising in Alaska ... (varies slightly)
Editor: v. 1-8, James Wickersham.
Alaska federal reports (5 v.) 1869-1937 are supplementary to v. 1-8.

1. Law reports, digests, etc.—U. S. 2. Law reports, digests, etc.—Alaska. I. U. S. Circuit court of appeals (9th circuit) II. U. S. Supreme court. III. Wickersham, James, 1857-1939, ed. IV. West publishing co., St. Paul. V. Title.

3-28601 rev

Library of Congress [r47c2]

658
(016)
S86
U.S. BUREAU OF SUPPLIES AND ACCOUNTS (NAVY DEPT.) LIBRARY.
BIBLIOGRAPHY FOR THE MANAGEMENT ANALYST. WASHINGTON, GOVT. PRINT. OFF., 1961.
144P. (NAVSANDA PUBLICATION 405)

1. MANAGEMENT - BIBLIOGRAPHY.
2. OFFICE MANAGEMENT - BIBLIOGRAPHY.
3. AUTOMATION - BIBLIOGRAPHY.

711.585
1572
SUPPRESSION DE QUARTIERS MISÉRAUX.
INTERNATIONAL HOUSING ASSOCIATION.
BESEITIGUNG VON ELENDSVIERTELN UND VERFALLSWOHNUNGEN. SLUM CLEARANCE AND RECONDITIONING OF INSANITARY DWELLINGS. STUTTGART, J. HOFFMANN, 1935.
2 V. IN 1.

GERMAN, ENGLISH AND FRENCH IN PARALLEL COLUMNS.
CONTENTS.- V.1. TEXT.- V.2. PLANE.

1. SLUM CLEARANCE.
2. NEIGHBORHOOD REHABILITATION.
(CONTINUED ON NEXT CARD).

U.S. Supreme court.
Digest of United States Supreme court reports, annotated with case annotations, dissenting and separate opinions since 1900, collateral references, covering 1-332 (p369) U S, 1-91 L Ed, 1-67 S Ct...
Rochester, N.Y., The Lawyers co-operative publishing company, 1948-51.
17v. 25cm.

U.S. Supreme court digest annotated.
Digest of United States Supreme court reports, annotated with case annotations, dissenting and separate opinions since 1900, collateral references, covering 1-332 (p369) U S, 1-91 L Ed, 1-67 S Ct...
Rochester, N.Y., The Lawyers co-operative publishing co mpany, 1948-51.
17v. 25cm.

U.S. Supreme court.
Shepard's United States citations; statutes – department reports ... [1943] (Card 2)
—— Supplement 1943-1947. 5th ed. New York, Frank Shepard Co. [1947]
1015 p. 26cm.

Supreme court reporter.
Federal digest, 1754–date ... covering Supreme Court of the United States, United States Court of Appeals for the District of Columbia, United States Circuit Courts of Appeals, United States Court of Customs and Patent Appeals, District Courts of the United States, United States Court of Claims, as well as all other federal courts from the earliest times to date. St.Paul, West publishing co., 1940–
72v. 26½cm.

U.S. Supreme court.
Federal digest, 1754–date ... covering Supreme Court of the United States, United States Court of Appeals for the District of Columbia, United States Circuit Courts of Appeals, United States Court of Customs and Patent Appeals, District Courts of the United States, United States Court of Claims, as well as all other federal courts from the earliest times to date. St. Paul, West publishing co., 1940–
72v. 26½cm.

LAW
T
J124SU

U.S. SUPREME COURT.
JACKSON, ROBERT H
THE SUPREME COURT IN THE AMERICAN SYSTEM OF GOVERNMENT. CAMBRIDGE, HARVARD UNIVERSITY PRESS, 1957.
92P.

1. U.S. SUPREME COURT.

Suranyi-Unger, Theodore, Jr.
500.15   U.S. National Science Foundation.
(016)   Bibliography on the economic and social
M17b   implications of scientific research and development. A selected and annotated edition, by Theodore Suranyi-Unger, Jr. and Elizabeth Harris. Washington, 1959.
53p. (Its NSF 59-41)

1. Scientific research - Bibliography.
I. Suranyi-Unger, Theodore, Jr. II. Harris, Elizabeth.

U.S. Supreme court.
Federal rules of civil procedure and New title 28, U. S. Code, Judiciary and Judicial Procedure, with combined index. 1951 Rev. ed. St. Paul, Minn., West publishing co. [c1951]
xviii, 522 p. 25½cm.

I. U.S. Laws, statutes, etc.

LAW
T
R612JU

U.S. SUPREME COURT.
ROBERTSON, REYNOLDS
JURISDICTION OF THE SUPREME COURT OF THE UNITED STATES, BY REYNOLDS ROBERTSON AND FRANCIS R. KIRKHAM. ST. PAUL, WEST PUBL. CO., 1936.
1048P.

1. U.S. SUPREME COURT. I. KIRKHAM, FRANCIS R. II. TITLE.

VF
690
S87   Surety Association of America.
Construction: the bonded contract is the owner's protection. New York, 1950.
c.2.   21p. illus.

1. Building construction. 2. Contract documents.

LAW
U.S.

U.S. Supreme Court.
Joseph Lee Jones and Barbara Jo Jones, petitioners, v. Alfred H. Mayer Co., a corporation, Alfred Realty Co., a corporation, Paddock Country Club, inc., a corporation, Alfred H. Mayer, an individual, and an officer of the above corporations, respondents. On writ of certiorari to the United States Court of Appeals for the Eighth Circuit. Brief amici curiae and appendix for National Committee Against Discrimination in Housing, National Associa tion for the Advancement of Colored People.

2c

(Cont'd on next card)

LAW
T
S727SU

U.S. SUPREME COURT.
STERN, ROBERT L 1908–
SUPREME COURT PRACTICE; JURISDICTION, PROCEDURE, ARGUING AND BRIEFING TECHNIQUES, FORMS, STATUTES, RULES FOR PRACTICE IN THE SUPREME COURT OF THE UNITED STATES, BY ROBERT L. STERN AND EUGENE GRESSMAN. 2D ED. WASHINGTON, BUREAU OF NATIONAL AFFAIRS, 1954.
585P.

1. U.S. SUPREME COURT.
I. GRESSMAN, EUGENE, 1917– , JT. AU.

332.6
887   Surety Association of America.
Bonds of suretyship. New York, 1959.
44p.

1. Bond yields. I. Title.

LAW
U.S.

U.S. Supreme Court.   Joseph Lee Jones...
1968.   (Card 2)

Anti-defamation of B'nai B'rith and the American Jewish Congress.
New York, Bar Press, 1968.
103p. (October term, 1967, no. 645)

1. Civil rights. 2. Minority groups - Housing. 3. U.S. Laws, statutes, etc. 4. Housing - Social aspects. I. National Committee Against Discrimination in Housing. II. Anti-defa mation League of B'nai B'rith. III. Title.

920
C65t

U.S. SUPREME COURT.
U.S. Congress.
Tributes to the Honorable Earl Warren, Chief Justice of the United States to commemorate the occasion of his retirement from the Supreme Court, June 23, 1969. Delivered in the House of Representatives of the United States Senate. Wash., Govt. Print. Off., 1970.
136p.
At head of title: 91st Cong., 2d sess. House. Document no. 348.

1. Warren, Earl, 1891– 2. U.S. Supreme Court. I. Title.

690
S87
1960

SURETY ASSOCIATION OF AMERICA.
CONSTRUCTION, THE BONDED CONTRACT IS THE OWNER'S PROTECTION. NEW YORK, 1960.
27P.

1. BUILDING CONSTRUCTION. I. TITLE.
2. Suretyship and guaranty.

U.S. Supreme court.
Shepard's United States citations, cases; a compilation of citations to United States Supreme Court cases ... 5th ed., Case ed., 1943. New York, Frank Shepard Co. [1943]
3547 p. 26 cm.
"Compiled by the publisher's editorial staff."
Kept up to date by cumulative supplements.
—— Supplement 1943–1947. 5th ed. New York, Frank Shepard Co. [1947]
1015 p.
1. Annotations and citations (Law)—U. S. I. U. S. Supreme Court. II. Shepard (The Frank) Company, New York.

43-11485 rev*

Library of Congress   [r49k2]

728.1
:325
C51

U.S. Supreme Court.
U. S. *Dept. of Justice.*
Prejudice and property, an historic brief against racial covenants, submitted to the Supreme Court by Tom C. Clark, Attorney General of the U. S. and Philip B. Perlman, Solicitor General of the U. S. Washington, Public Affairs Press [1948]
104 p. 21 cm.
Bibliography: p. 86–104.
1. Real covenants—U. S. I. Clark, Thomas Campbell, 1889– II. Perlman, Philip Benjamin, 1890– III. U. S. Supreme Court. IV. Title. v. Title: Racial covenants. 2.Minority groups=Hsg.

48—6853*

Library of Congress   [48o7†]

VF
690
S87
1964   Surety Association of America.
Construction: the bonded contract is the owner's protection. New York, 1964.
27p.

1. Building construction. 2. Contract documents.

U.S. Supreme court.
Shepard's United States citations; statutes—department reports; a compilation of citations to United States Constitution, United States code, United States Statutes at large and United States Supreme court rules ... 5th ed., Statute and department reports ed. [1943] New York, The Frank Shepard company [1943]
913 p. 26 cm.
"Compiled by the publisher's editorial staff."—p. [14]
"The complete work ... consists of this bound volume and the cumulative supplement."—Pref.
1. Annotations and citations (Law)—U. S. 2. Law reports, digests, etc.—U. S. I. U. S. Supreme court. II. Shepard, The Frank, company, New York.

43—11484

Library of Congress   (Continued on next card)

U.S. Supreme Court - Directories.
LAW
U.S. *Dept. of Justice.*
Register, Dept. of Justice and the Courts of the United States, ed.
19

Washington, 19
v.
For complete information see main card.

1. U.S. Dept. of Justice - Direct. 2. U.S. Courts - Direct. 3. U.S. Supreme Court - Direct.

332
S87

Surety Association of America.
Rate manual of all classes of fidelity, forgery and surety bonds. New York, 19 –
2c.   1v. (loose-leaf)

1. Bond yield tables. 2. Insurance. I. Title.

368
B12 SURETY ASSOCIATION OF AMERICA.
BACKMAN, JULES.
  SURETY RATE-MAKING; A STUDY OF THE
ECONOMICS OF SURETYSHIP. NEW YORK, THE
SURETY ASSOCIATION OF AMERICA, 1948.
492P. TABLES.

  1. INSURANCE. 2. SURETYSHIP AND
GUARANTY. I. SURETY ASSOCIATION OF
AMERICA.

Suretyship and guaranty. (Law)

728.3
S87 SURFACE COMBUSTION CORPORATION, TOLEDO.
  LET'S PLAN A PEACETIME HOME. A GUIDE
TO HOME PLANNING BY MARY DAVIS GILLIES
AND OTHERS. TOLEDO, 1945.
  11P.

  1. HOUSE PLANS. I. GILLIES, MARY
DAVIS.

LAW
T
C656
H68s
  Surety bonds for Federal employees.
  U.S. Congress. House. Committee on Post
  Office and Civil Service.
    Surety bonds for Federal employees. Hearing
  before the Subcommittee on Manpower and Civil
  Service, Ninety-second Congress, second
  session on H.R. 13150, a bill to provide that
  the Federal Government shall assume the risks
  of its fidelity losses, and for other purposes.
  Wash., Govt. Print. Off., 1972.
    93p.
    Hearing held February 29, 1972.
    1. Suretyship and guarantee. 2. Federal
  civil service.   I. Title.

LAW
T
C656
H68s
  SURETYSHIP AND GUARANTEE.
  U.S. Congress. House. Committee on Post
  Office and Civil Service.
    Surety bonds for Federal employees. Hearing
  before the Subcommittee on Manpower and Civil
  Service, Ninety-second Congress, second
  session on H.R. 13150, a bill to provide that
  the Federal Government shall assume the risks
  of its fidelity losses, and for other purposes.
  Wash., Govt. Print. Off., 1972.
    93p.
    Hearing held February 29, 1972.
    1. Suretyship and guarantee. 2. Federal
  civil service.   I. Title.

628.515
M45s
  Surface discharge of heated water.
  Minnesota. University. St. Anthony Falls
  Hydraulic Laboratory.
    Surface discharge of heated water, by
  H. Stefan and others. [Prepared] for the
  Office of Research and Monitoring, Environ-
  mental Protection Agency. Wash., Govt.
  Print. Off., 1971.
    1v. (Water pollution control research
  series)
    1. Water pollution. I. Stefan, H.
  II. U.S. Environmental Protection Agency.
  III. Title.

368
N67
  Surety bonds for officials and employees of
  North Carolina cities and towns under 5,000.
  North Carolina League of Municipalities.
    Surety bonds for officials and employees
  of North Carolina cities and towns under
  5,000, by Jim Burgess. Raleigh, 1961.
    19p. (Its Report no. 107)

    1. Insurance. I. Burgess, Jim.
  II. Title.

2645
  SURF CITY, N.J. PLANNING BOARD.
  A COMPREHENSIVE DEVELOPMENT PLAN,
BOROUGH OF SURF CITY, 1970, OCEAN COUNTY,
NEW JERSEY. BY E. EUGENE OROSS
ASSOCIATES. SURF CITY, 1970.
  25P. (HUD 701 REPORT)

  1. CITY PLANNING - SURF CITY, N.J.
I. OROSS (E. EUGENE) ASSOCIATES.
II. HUD 701 SURF CITY, N.J.

691.110.15
F67s Surface flammability of various wood-base.
  U.S. Forest Service. Forest Products Labora-
  tory, Madison, Wis.
    Surface flammability of various wood-base
  building material. Madison, Wis., 1968.
    12p. (Its research note FPL-0186)
    "Revision of...report no. 2140, under the
  same title originally written in 1959 by H.D.
  Bruce and L.E. Downs."
    1. Wood - Research. 2. Building materials,
  Fireproof. I. Bruce, H.D. II. Title.

333.33
R24 SURETY FEDERAL SAVINGS AND LOAN
      ASSOCIATION.
  REID, GARE B   , JR.
    FINANCING OF TRADE-IN HOUSING.
PREPARED FOR GRADUATE SCHOOL OF SAVINGS
AND LOAN, INDIANA UNIVERSITY. DETROIT,
SURETY FEDERAL SAVINGS AND LOAN
ASSOCIATION, 1961.
  36P.

  1. TRADE-IN HOUSES. 2. MORTGAGE
FINANCE - MICHIGAN. I. SURETY FEDERAL
SAVINGS AND LOAN ASSOCIATION.
II. TITLE.

362.5
S87 Surface, Bill.
  The hollow. New York, Coward-McCann, 1971.
    190p.

  1. Poverty. I. Title.

339.5
I57s Surface mining and our environment.
  U.S. Dept. of the Interior.
    Surface mining and our environment. A
  special report to the Nation. Washington,
  1967.
    124p.

    1. Natural resources. 2. Open space land.
  3. Drainage. I. Title.

368
B12 SURETYSHIP AND GUARANTY.
BACKMAN, JULES.
  SURETY RATE-MAKING; A STUDY OF THE
ECONOMICS OF SURETYSHIP. NEW YORK, THE
SURETY ASSOCIATION OF AMERICA, 1948.
492P. TABLES.

  1. INSURANCE. 2. SURETYSHIP AND
GUARANTY. I. SURETY ASSOCIATION OF
AMERICA.

691
A75f Surface bond materials.
  U.S. Army. (Corps of Engineers. Ohio River
  Div.)
    Feasibility study of masonry systems utiliz-
  ing surface-bond materials by S.J. Hubberd.
  Cincinnati, 1966.
    76p. (Technical rept. no. 4-43)

    1. Building materials. 2. Cement.
  3. Glass. 4. Fibers. I. Hubberd, S.J.
  II. Title. III. Title: Surface bond materials.

690.015
(485)
S82
1971
R26
  Surface temperatures and heat losses at
  concrete floor slabs in external walls.
  Adamson, Bo.
    Yttemperaturer och varmeforluster vid
  batongbjalklag i fasadvagg (Surface temperatures and heat losses at concrete floor
  slabs in external walls. Heat insulation or
  heating cable?) Stockholm, Statens Institut
  for Byggnadsforskning, 1971.
    76p. (Rapport R26:1971)
    English summary.
    1. Insulating materials. 2. Concrete.
  3. Walls. I. Stockholm. Statens Institut
  for Byggnadsforskning. II. Title: Surface
  temperatures and heat losses at concrete
  floor slabs in   external walls.

LAW
T
S72 Suretyship and guaranty.
Stearns, Arthur Adelbert.
  The law of suretyship, covering personal surety-
ship, commercial guarantees, corporate and compensat-
ed suretyship, defenses of the surety, suretyship as
related to bonds to secure private obligations,
official and judicial bonds, surety companies, by
James L. Elder. 5th ed. Cincinnati, W. H. Anderson
Co., 1951.
  720p.

  1. Suretyship and guaranty. I. Title.

691.110.15
F67su
  SURFACE CHARACTERISTICS OF WOOD
  AS THEY AFFECT DURABILITY
  U.S. FOREST PRODUCTS LABORATORY,
  MADISON, WIS.
  SURFACE CHARACTERISTICS OF WOOD.
AS THEY AFFECT DURABILITY OF
FINISHES. BY HAROLD TARKOW AND
OTHERS. MADISON, WIS., 1966.
  60P. (U.S. FOREST SERVICE. FPL
RESEARCH PAPER NO. 57)

  BIBLIOGRAPHY: P.59-60.

  1. WOOD - RESEARCH. 2. WOOD
PRESERVATI ON. I. TARKOW,
HAROLD. II. TITLE.

614.8
I711.73
C65s
1957
H-H
  SURFACE TRANSPORTATION.
  U.S. CONGRESS. HOUSE. COMMITTEE ON
  INTERSTATE AND FOREIGN COMMERCE.
    SURFACE TRANSPORTATION; SAFETY
  LEGISLATION HEARINGS, EIGHTY-FIFTH
  CONGRESS, FIRST SESSION ON BILLS TO
  PROVIDE FOR GREATER SAFETY IN SURFACE
  TRANSPORTATION. WASHINGTON, GOVT.
  PRINT. OFF., 1957.
    241P.

    HEARINGS HELD MARCH 28, 29 AND APRIL
  1, AND 12, 1957.

    1. TRAFFIC   SAFETY. I. TITLE.

690
S87
1960
  SURETYSHIP AND GUARANTY.
  Surety Association of America.
    Construction, the bonded contract is
  the owner's protection. New York, 1960.
    27 p.

    1. Building construction. 2. Suretyship
  and guaranty.

691.42
T18 Surface colouring of bricks.
  Tauber, A
    Surface colouring of bricks and other
  structural clay products, by A. Tauber and E.
  R. Schmidt. Pretoria, South African Council
  for Scientific and Industrial Research,
  National Building Research Institute, 1967.
    [3]p. (C.S.I.R. reference no. R/Bou 238)
    Reprinted from Claycraft and structural
  ceramics, Dec., 1967.
    1. Bricks. 2. Clay. I. Schmidt, E.R., jt.
  au. II. Claycraft and structural ceramics.
  III. Canada.   Dept. of Forestry and
  Rural Development. IV. Title.

VF
690.013
(41)
G72
CP303
  Surface water and subsoil drainage.
  United Kingdom. Ministry of Works. Council for
  Codes of Practice for Buildings.
    General series: Surface water and subsoil
  drainage. London [British Standards Institution]
  1952.
    15 p. (British standard code of practice.
  CP 303, 1952)

    1.Drainage. 2.Building standards-U.K. I.Title.
  II.Series.

628.1
(7531)
M27su
Surface water bodies.
Metropolitan Washington Council of Governments.
Surface water bodies. Washington, Metropolitan Council of Governments, 1968?.
map.

1. Water resources - Maps - District of Columbia metropolitan area. 2. Maps and mapping - District of Columbia metropolitan area. I. Title.

368
L11
SUMMER
1959
SURGICAL AND MEDICAL BENEFITS.
U.S. BUREAU OF LABOR STATISTICS.
HEALTH AND INSURANCE PLANS UNDER COLLECTIVE BARGAINING; SURGICAL AND MEDICAL BENEFITS, LATE SUMMER 1959.
WASHINGTON, 1960.
39P. (ITS BULLETIN NO. 1280)

1. INSURANCE. I. TITLE.
II. TITLE: SURGICAL AND MEDICAL BENEFITS.

666.81
A87m
Surkevicius, H
Australia. Commonwealth Scientific and Industrial Research Organization. (Div. of Building Research)
Mechanism of the retardation of the set of gypsum plaster, by M. J. Ridge and H. Surkevicius. Melbourne, 1960.
[18]p. illus., diagrs. (Its Reprint no. 169)

Reprinted from the Australian Journal of applied science, vol. 11, no. 3, 1960. p. 385-398.
1. Gypsum. 2. Plaster and plastering. I. Ridge, M. J.
II. Surkevicius, H.

627.4
(749)
R87
Surface water control in New Jersey...
Rutgers University, New Brunswick, N.J. Bureau of Government Research.
Surface water control in New Jersey; drainage, flood control and related policies in an urban state, by Stephen A. Decter. Final report to the New Jersey Joint Committee on Drainage. New Brunswick, 1967.
2pts.

1. Flood control - New Jersey. 2. Water-supply - New Jersey. I. Decter, Stephen A. II. Title.

691.11
1620.197
C155
SURGING.
CANADA. DEPT. OF FORESTRY.
SURGING; ITS CAUSE AND CONTROL IN WOOD PRESERVATION, BY W.M. CONNERS. OTTAWA, 1964.
8P. (ITS PUBLICATION NO. 1062)

1. WOOD PRESERVATION. I. CONNERS, W.M. II. TITLE.

666.81
R42
pt. 1
Ridge, M   J
Variations in the kinetics of setting of calcined gypsum. 1. Effects of retarders and accelerators, by M. J. Ridge and H. Surkevicius. Melbourne, 1961.
420-427p. (Australia, Commonwealth Scientific and Industrial Research Organization. D.B.R. Reprint no. 208)
Reprinted from the Journal of applied chemistry, Nov. 11, 1961.
1. Gypsum. I. Surkevicius, H. II. Australia. Commonwealth Scientific and Industrial Research Organization. (Div. of Building Research)

628.1
(747)
E74
no. 2
Surface water in the Erie-Niagara Basin, New York.
Harding, W   E
Surface water in the Erie-Niagara Basin, New York, by W.E. Harding and B.K. Gilbert. With a chapter on storage required to maintain flows, by R.M. Beall. Albany, N.Y., Conservation Dept., Water Resources Commission, 1968.
118p. (Erie-Niagara Basin Regional Water Resources Planning Board. Planning report ENB-2)
Prepared by U.S. Dept. of the Interior Geological Survey in cooperation with the New York State Conservation Dept., Div. of Water Resources.
(Cont'd on next card)

711.4
M125
SURGING CITIES.
MCCROSKY, THEODORE TREMAIN.
SURGING CITIES; A SECONDARY SCHOOL TEXTBOOK IN TWO PARTS, BY THEODORE T. MCCROSKY, CHARLES A. BLESSING AND J. ROSS MCKEEVER. BOSTON, GREATER BOSTON DEVELOPMENT COMMITTEE, 1948.
287P.

1. CITY PLANNING. 2. CITY PLANNING - BOSTON METROPOLITAN AREA. I. BLESSING, CHARLES A., JT. AU. II. MCKEEVER, J. ROSS., JT. AU. III. TITLE.

666.81
A87st
Surkevicius, H
Australia. Commonwealth Scientific and Industrial Research Organization. (Div. of Building Research)
Stabilization of the set of gypsum plaster., by M. J. Ridge and H. Surkevicius. Melbourne, 1960.
9p. (Its Report F1-4)

1. Gypsum. 2. Plaster and plastering. I. Ridge, M. J. II. Surkevicius, H.

628.1
(747)
E74
no. 2
Harding, W   E   Surface water...1968.
(Card 2)

Bibliography: p. 104-105.
1. Water resources - New York (State)
I. New York (State) Conservation Dept.
II. Beall, R.M. III. Gilbert, B.K., jt. au.
IV. Title. (Series: Erie-Niagara Basin Regional Water Resources Planning Board. Planning report ENB-2)

699.844
S87
SURI, R   L   ,1910-
ACOUSTICS, DESIGN AND PRACTICE. NEW YORK, ASIA PUB. HOUSE, 1966-
1v.

CONTENTS.- V.1 GENERAL ACOUSTICS; CHOICE OF ABSORBERS; NOISE AND VIBRATION AND THEIR CONTROL.

Library has v.1 only

1. ARCHITECTURAL ACOUSTICS. I. TITLE.

666.81
A87va
Surkevicius, H
Australia. Commonwealth Scientific and Industrial Research Organization. (Div. of Building Research)
Variations in the response of gypsum plaster to the action of retarders, by M. J. Ridge and H. Surkevicius. Melbourne, 1961.
4p. (Its Report F1-5)
1. Gypsum. 2. Plaster and plastering. I. Ridge, M. J. II. Surkevicius, H.

628.1
(746)
M27
Surface water supplies available in Southeastern Connecticut.
Metcalf and Eddy.
Report to Eastern Connecticut Industrial Fresh Water Development Commission upon surface water supplies available in Southeastern Connecticut. Boston, 1962.
92p.

1. Water-supply - Connecticut. I. Connecticut. Eastern Connecticut Industrial Fresh Water Development Commission. II. Title: Surface water supplies available in Southeastern Connecticut.

VF
666.81
A87de
Surkevicius, H
Australia. Commonwealth Scientific and Industrial Research Organization. (Div. of Building Research)
Determination of chlorides in gypsum and gypsum products, by H. Surkevicius. [Victoria] 1961.
[2]p. (Its Reprint no. 200)
Authorized reprint from the copyrighted Materials research and standards, vol. 1, no. 8, August 1961, published by the American Society for Testing Materials.

1. Gypsum. I. Surkevicius, H.

360
(768)
T25
Surla, Leo T
Tennessee. State Planning Commission.
The incidence of poverty; social and economic conditions in Tennessee, by Jerry J. Williams and Leo T. Surla. Nashville, State Planning Office, Tennessee State Planning Commission, 1965.
36p.
U.S. Urban Renewal Adm. UPAP.

1. Social conditions - Tennessee. 2. Economic conditions - Tennessee. I. Williams, Jerry J. II. Surla, Leo T. III. Title. IV. U.S. URA-UPAP.

628.1
G26CO
SURFACE WATERS OF THE UNITED STATES.
U.S. GEOLOGICAL SURVEY.
COMPILATION OF RECORDS OF SURFACE WATERS OF THE UNITED STATES, OCT. 1950 TO SEPT. 1960. PT. 10. THE GREAT BASIN. WASHINGTON, GOVT. PRINT. OFF., 1963.
318P. (ITS WATER-SUPPLY PAPER 1734)

1. WATER SUPPLY. I. TITLE: SURFACE WATERS OF THE UNITED STATES.

VF
666.81
R421
Surkevicius, H
Ridge, M   J
Influence of some conditions of calcination on the reactivity of calcium sulphate hemihydrate, by M.J. Ridge and H. Surkevicius. Melbourne, Australia, Commonwealth Scientific and Industrial Research Organization, Division of Building Research, 1962.
[8]p. (Australia. Commonwealth Scientific and Industrial Organization. Division of Building Research. D.B.R. reprint no. 234)
(Cont'd. on next card)

351.7
:8
C65
1946
SUPPL.
H-H
PT.1
SURPLUS APPROPRIATION RESCISSION BILL, 1946.
U.S. CONGRESS. HOUSE. COMMITTEE ON APPROPRIATIONS.
FIRST SUPPLEMENTAL SURPLUS APPROPRIATION RESCISSION BILL, 1946. HEARINGS BEFORE THE SUBCOMMITTEE... SEVENTY-NINTH CONGRESS, FIRST SESSION. WASHINGTON, GOVT. PRINT. OFF., 1945-
v.
For Library holdings see main entry
CONTENTS.- PT.1. DEPARTMENTS AND CIVIL AGENCIES.

1. U.S. EXECUTIVE DEPARTMENTS - APPROPRIATIONS AND EXPENDITURES.
(CONTINUED ON NEXT CARD)

628.44
S87
U.S. Surgeon General's Conference on Solid Waste Management for Metropolitan Washington.
Proceedings; Surgeon General's Conference on Solid Waste Management for Metropolitan Washington, July 19-20, 1967. Edited by Leo Weaver. Cincinnati, U.S. Dept. of Health, Education, and Welfare, Public Health Service, National Center for Urban and Industrial Health, 1967.
194p. (U.S. Public Health Service. Publication no. 1729)
1. Refuse and refuse disposal. I. Weaver, Leo, ed. II. U.S. Public Health Service.

VF
666.81
R421
Ridge, M   J   Influence of some conditions on the reactivity of calcium sulphate...1962. (Card 2)

Reprinted from the Journal of applied chemistry, 1962, vol. 12, p. 425-432.

1. Gypsum. I. Surkevicius, H. II. Australia. Commonwealth Scientific and Industrial Research Organization. (Div. of Building Research)

351.7
:8
C65
1946
SUPPL.
H-H
PT.1
U.S. CONGRESS. HOUSE. COMMITTEE ON APPROPRIATIONS. FIRST SUPPLEMENTAL SURPLUS ...1945- (CARD 2)

2. RECONSTRUCTION. I. TITLE: SURPLUS APPROPRIATION RESCISSION BILL, 1946.

333.33
C65d
1970
H-H
Surplus Federal property.
U.S. Congress. House. Committee on Government Operations.
Disposal of surplus Federal property for park and recreational purposes. Hearing before a subcommittee of the Committee on Government Operations, House of Representatives, Ninety-first Congress, second session on H.R. 15870, to amend the land and water conservation fund act of 1965, as amended, and for other purposes. Wash., Govt. Print. Off., 1970.
50p.
Hearing held June 9, 1970.

(Cont'd on next card)

333.33
C65d
1970
H-H
U.S. Congress. House. Committee on Government Operations. Disposal...1970. (Card 2)

1. Real property. 2. Parks. 3. Recreation. I. Title. II. Title: Surplus Federal property.

330
C65POS
1944
S-H
SURPLUS GOVERNMENT PORPERTY AND PLANTS.
U.S. CONGRESS. SENATE. SPECIAL COMMITTEE ON POST-WAR ECONOMIC POLICY AND PLANNING.
POST-WAR ECONOMIC POLICY AND PLANNING. JOINT HEARINGS BEFORE THE SPECIAL COMMITTEES ON POST-WAR ECONOMIC POLICY AND PLANNING, CONGRESS OF THE UNITED STATES, SEVENTY-EIGHTH CONGRESS, SECOND SESSION, PURSUANT TO S. RES. 102 AND H. RES. 408... WASHINGTON, GOVT. PRINT. OFF., 1944-
1V.

CONTENTS.- P T.1 DISPOSAL OF
(CONTINUED ON NEXT CARD)

330
C65POS
1944
S-H
U.S. CONGRESS. SENATE. SPECIAL COMMITTEE ON POST-WAR ECONOMIC POLICY AND PLANNING. POST-WAR ECONOMIC POLICY ...1944- (CARD 2)

SURPLUS GOVERNMENT PROPERTY AND PLANTS. JUNE 16 AND 20, 1944.

1. ECONOMIC POLICY. 2. RECONSTRUCTION. I. U.S. CONGRESS. HOUSE. SPECIAL COMMITTEE ON POST-WAR ECONOMIC POLICY AND PLANNING. II. TITLE. III. TITLE: DISPOSAL OF SURPLUS GOVERNMENT PROPERTY AND
(CONTINUED ON NEXT CARD)

330
C65POS
1944
S-H
U.S. CONGRESS. SENATE. SPECIAL COMMITTEE ON POST-WAR ECONOMIC POLICY AND PLANNING. POST-WAR ECONOMIC POLICY ...1944- (CARD 3)

PLANTS. IV. TITLE: SURPLUS GOVERNMENT PROPERTY AND PLANTS.

728.1
:355.1
F22SU
SURPLUS HOUSING FOR VETERANS.
U.S. FEDERAL PUBLIC HOUSING AUTHORITY.
SURPLUS HOUSING FOR VETERANS; HOW THE FEDERAL GOVERNMENT IS RE-USING SURPLUS HOUSING TO MEET THIS EMERGENCY NEED. WASHINGTON, U.S. GOVT. PRINT. OFF., 1946.
FOLDER.

1. VETERANS' HOUSING. I. TITLE.

333
H68s
Surplus land for community development program.
U.S. Dept. of Housing and Urban Development.
Surplus land for community development program.
Action program guidelines. Wash., 1968.
6p.

1. Public lands. 2. Land use. I. Title.

333
H68su
Surplus land for community development program.
U.S. Dept. of Housing and Urban Development.
Surplus land for community development program (SLCD) Summary program description. Wash., 1969.
3p.

1. Public lands. 2. Land use. I. Title.

351
H66
1955
Rept.15A
Surplus property.
U. S. Commission on organization of the Executive Branch of the Government, 1953-1955.
Report on use and disposal of Federal surplus property, prepared ... by the Task Force on Use and Disposal of Federal Surplus Property, February 1955. [Washington, Govt. Print. Off., 1955.]
259 p.

1.Real property. I.Hoover Commission reports.
II.Title:Surplus property.

351
H66
1955
Rept.15
Surplus property.
U. S. Commission on Organization of the Executive Branch of the Government, 1953-1955.
Use and disposal of Federal surplus property; a report to the Congress, April 1955. [Washington, Govt. Print. Off., 1955.]
96 p.

Cover title: Surplus property.

Also issued as 84th Congress, 1st session, House document no. 141.

333.65
C657
1958
S-R
NO.1284
SURPLUS PROPERTY.
U.S. CONGRESS. SENATE. COMMITTEE ON GOVERNMENT OPERATIONS.
ADVERTISED AND NEGOTIATED DISPOSALS OF SURPLUS PROPERTY. REPORT... TO ACCOMPANY S. 2224, A BILL AMENDING THE FEDERAL PROPERTY AND ADMINISTRATIVE SERVICES ACT OF 1949, AS AMENDED... WASHINGTON, GOVT. PRINT. OFF., 1958.
16P. (85TH CONGRESS, 2D SESSION. SENATE. REPORT NO. 1284)

1. PROPERTY MANAGEMENT.
I. TITLE. I. TITLE: DISPOSALS.
(CONTINUED ON NEXT CARD)

333.65
C657
1958
S-R
NO.1284
U.S. CONGRESS. SENATE. COMMITTEE ON GOVERNMENT OPERATIONS. ADVERTISED AND ...1958... (CARD. 2)
OF SURPLUS PROPERTY. I. TITLE: SURPLUS PROPERTY. II. TITLE: FEDERAL PROPERTY AND ADMINISTRATIVE SERVICES ACT OF 1949.

333.33
C65T
1946
H-H
SURPLUS PROPERTY ACT.
U.S. CONGRESS. HOUSE. COMMITTEE ON EXPENDITURES IN THE EXECUTIVE DEPARTMENTS.
TO AMEND THE SURPLUS PROPERTY ACT. HEARINGS BEFORE THE COMMITTEE ON EXPENDITURES IN THE EXECUTIVE DEPARTMENTS, HOUSE OF REPRESENTATIVES, SEVENTY-NINTH CONGRESS, SECOND SESSION, ON H.R. 5329, H.R. 5517, H.R. 4432, AND OTHERS RELATING TO THE DISPOSITION OF SURPLUS PROPERTY. FEBRUARY 14, 15, 19, 20, 21, 27, MARCH 1, 5, 6, 7, 8, 12, AND 13, 19 46... WASHINGTON, GOVT. PRINT. OFF., 1946.
(CONTINUED ON NEXT CARD)

333.33
C65T
1946
H-H
U.S. CONGRESS. HOUSE. COMMITTEE ON EXPENDITURES IN THE EXECUTIVE DEPARTMENTS. TO AMEND THE ...1946. (CARD 2)

533P.

CARTER MANASCO, CHAIRMAN.

1. REAL PROPERTY. I. TITLE: SURPLUS PROPERTY ACT.

333.65
C657
1958
H-R
NO.1920
SURPLUS PROPERTY DISPOSALS.
U.S. CONGRESS. HOUSE. COMMITTEE ON GOVERNMENT OPERATIONS.
AMENDING SECTION 207 OF THE FEDERAL PROPERTY AND ADMINISTRATIVE SERVICES ACT OF 1949 SO AS TO MODIFY AND IMPROVE THE PROCEDURE FOR SUBMISSION TO THE ATTORNEY GENERAL OF CERTAIN PROPOSED SURPLUS PROPERTY DISPOSALS FOR HIS ADVICE AS TO WHETHER SUCH DISPOSALS WOULD BE INCONSISTENT WITH THE ANTITRUST LAWS. REPORT TO ACCOMPANY S. 2752. WASHINGTON, GOVT. PRINT. OFF., 1958.
15P. (85TH CONGRESS, 1ST
(CONTINUED ON NEXT CARD)

333.65
C657
1958
H-R
NO.1920
U.S. CONGRESS. HOUSE. COMMITTEE ON GOVERNMENT OPERATIONS. AMENDING SECTION ...1958. (CARD 2)
SESSION. HOUSE OF REPRESENTATIVES. REPORT NO. 1920)

1. PROPERTY MANAGEMENT. 2. FINANCE - LAW AND LEGISLATION. I. TITLE: FEDERAL PROPERTY AND ADMINISTRATIVE SERVICES ACT OF 1949. II. TITLE: SURPLUS PROPERTY DISPOSALS.

333.65
C657
1958
S-R
NO.1277
SURPLUS PROPERTY DISPOSALS.
U.S. CONGRESS. SENATE. COMMITTEE ON GOVERNMENT OPERATIONS.
AMENDING SECTION 207 OF THE FEDERAL PROPERTY AND ADMINISTRATIVE SERVICES ACT OF 1949 SO AS TO MODIFY AND IMPROVE THE PROCEDURE FOR SUBMISSION TO THE ATTORNEY GENERAL OF CERTAIN PROPOSED SURPLUS PROPERTY DISPOSALS FOR HIS ADVICE AS TO WHETHER SUCH DISPOSALS WOULD BE INCONSISTENT WITH THE ANTITRUST LAWS. REPORT TO ACCOMPANY S. 2752. WASHINGTON, GOVT. PRINT. OFF., 1958.
16P. (85TH CONGRESS, 2D SESSION.
(CONTINUED ON NEXT CARD)

333.65
C657
1958
S-R
NO.1277
U.S. CONGRESS. SENATE. COMMITTEE ON GOVERNMENT OPERATIONS. AMENDING SECTION ...1958. (CARD 2)
SENATE. REPORT NO. 1277)

1. PROPERTY MANAGEMENT. 2. FINANCE - LAW AND LEGISLATION. I. TITLE: FEDERAL PROPERTY AND ADMINISTRATIVE SERVICES ACT OF 1949. II. TITLE: SURPLUS PROPERTY DISPOSALS.

711.333
(41)
S87
SURREY FEDERATION OF LABOUR PARTIES (PLANNING SUB-COMMITTEE)
A TOWN AND COUNTRY PLAN FOR SURREY. NEW MALDEN, 1943.
24P.

1. COUNTY PLANNING - U.K. - SURREY.

362.6
:308
A52
SURVEY...
AMERICAN NURSING HOME ASSOCIATION.
SURVEY... OF AVAILABLE NURSING AND CONVALESENT HOMES AS OF AUGUST 28, 1957. WASHINGTON, 1957.
3L.

1. NURSING HOMES - SURVEYS.
2. NURSING HOMES - STATISTICS.
I. TITLE.

370
:308
A52
A survey and analysis of earned doctorates, 1916-1966.
American University, Washington, D.C.
A survey and analysis of earned doctorates, 1916-1966, by Lois E. Torrence. Washington, 1969.
114p.

1. Education - Surveys. 2. Universities and colleges. 3. Employment - Surveys.
I. Torrence, Lois E. II. Title.

728.2
(74812)
G76
SURVEY AND ANALYSIS OF NEW APARTMENT
      CONSTRUCTION.
GROSSMAN, HOWARD J
      SURVEY AND ANALYSIS OF NEW APARTMENT
CONSTRUCTION IN A SUBURBAN COUNTY.
NORRISTOWN, PA., MONTGOMERY CO.
PLANNING COMMISSION, 1965.
      65P.

      1. APARTMENT HOUSES - MONTGOMERY
CO., PA.   I. MONTGOMERY CO., PA.
PLANNING COMMISSION.   II. TITLE.

Survey methods
      x   Community survey manuals
      sa Architecture, Domestic - Surveys
      sa Building construction - Surveys
      sa City planning - Surveys
      sa Employment - Surveys
      sa Heating surveys
      sa Housing market analysis
      sa Housing surveys
      sa Industrial surveys
      sa Land use surveys
      sa Local government - Surveys
      sa Metro-   politan area surveys

(Cont'd)

711.3
(4971)
A52
no.7
SURVEY METHODS.
American-Yugoslav Project in Regional and
      Urban Planning Studies.
      Methodology for a survey of environmental
preferences, by Jay Moor. Ljubljana, 1970.
      31p. (Urbanisticni Institut. Spatial
policies for regional development; a demon-
stration study of the Ljubljana region.
Technical report no. 7)
      1. Regional planning - Yugoslavia. 2. City
planning - Yugoslavia. 3. Survey methods.
I. Moor, Jay. II. Urbanisticni Institut,
Ljubljana. III. Title. IV. Title:
Environmental   preferences.

351.7
C65s
Survey and study of administrative organization,
procedure, and practice in the federal agencies
by the Committee on Government Operations.
U.S. Congress. House. Committee on Government Operations.
      Survey and study of administrative organiza-
tion, procedure, and practice in the federal
agencies by the Committee on Government Operations. Agency response to questionnaire.
Washington, Govt. Print. Off., 1957.
      11 pts. in 14 v.

Contents.-pt. 1-Dept. of Agriculture. -pt.2 Dept.
of Commerce.-pt. 3. Dept. of Defense.-pt. 4. Dept.
of Health, Education and Welfare.-pt. 5. Dept. of

      [Continued on next card]

Survey methods   (Card 2)
      sa Neighborhood surveys
      sa Parking - Surveys
      sa Public utilities - Surveys
      sa Regional planning - Surveys
      sa Relocation - Surveys
      sa Rental housing - Surveys
      sa Social surveys
      sa Traffic surveys
      sa Trailers and trailer courts - Surveys
      sa Universities and colleges - Surveys
      sa Urban renewal - Surveys
      sa Vacancy   surveys
      sa and xx Public opinion polls

728.1
:308
C15
SURVEY METHODS.
California. University. Center for Real
      Estate and Urban Economics.
      A comparison of two techniques for obtaining
housing vacancy and turnover data. [Berkeley]
1968.
      22p.

HUD contract no. H-819.

      1. Vacancy surveys. 2. Survey methods.
I. U.S. Dept. of Housing and Urban Development.   II. Title.

351.7
C65s
U.S. Congress. House. Committee on Govern-
ment Operations. Survey...1957. (Card 2)

the Interior.-pt. 6. Dept. of Justice.-pt. 7.Dept.
of Labor.-pt. 8. Post Office Dept.-pt. 9. Dept. of
State.-pt. 10. Dept. of the Treasury.-pt. 11 (A-D)-
Independent agencies.

      1. U.S.   Executive departments.   I. Title

658.8
A53
Survey methods
Alfred Politz Research, Inc.
      Survey of U.S markets, 1956, a national
survey ... sponsored by Look Magazine.   [New
York, 1956]
      1 v.   (unpaged)

1.Market surveys. 2.Survey methods. 3.Household
equipment. 4.Housing surveys. I.Look magazine.

728
:392
F15
v.1
Survey methods.
Callender, John Hancock
      Introduction to studies of family living.
New York, John B. Pierce Foundation, Dec. 1943.
      22 p. (Family living as the basis for
dwelling design, 1)
      The John B. Pierce Foundation, Research
study 4.
      1.Family living requirements. 2.Survey methods.
I.John B. Pierce Foundation. II.Title. III.Series.

VF
643.3
:648
W45
Survey before plan.

      2. Willis, E. M. The hub of the house. 1946.

308
A52
SURVEY METHODS.
American Congress on Surveying and Mapping.
Papers from   annual meeting.

Wash., 19

      v.
For Library holdings see main entry.

      1. Survey methods. 2. Maps and mapping.

711.585
(77193)
C15m
Survey methods.
Candeub, Fleissig, Adley and Associates.
      Martins Ferry, Ohio, Community Improve-
ment Program. Manual for field surveys.
[n.p.] 1965.
      11p.

      1. Workable program - Martins Ferry, Ohio.
2. Survey methods. 3. Land use - Martins
Ferry, Ohio. 4. Community development -
Martins Ferry, Ohio.

325.2
S87
Survey graphic.
      Segregation; color pattern from the past -
our struggle to wipe it out. Twelfth calling
America number. New York, Survey Associates,
1947.
      128p.
      Entire issue: Jan., 1947.

      1. Race relations. I. Title.

658
A52me
Survey methods.
American Management Association.
      Measuring and evaluating public relations
activities. [New York]
1968.
      30p. (AMA management bulletin no. 110)

      1. Management. 2. Public administration.
3. Social science research. 4. Survey methods.
I. Title. (Series)

VF
308
C31
1933
Survey methods.
Chamber of Commerce of the United States. Con-
struction and Civic Development Department.
      Outline for a "master" community survey.
Washington, D.C. [1933]
      53 p.   forms, tables.

Mimeographed.

1.Survey methods.

711.3
S17
Survey manual for comprehensive urban planning
Saroff, Jerome R
      Survey manual for comprehensive urban plan-
ning; the use of opinion surveys and sampling
techniques in the planning process, by Jerome
R. Saroff and Alberta Z. Levitan. College,
Alaska, Institute of Social, Economic, and
Government Research, 1969.
      143p. (SEG report no. 19)
      U.S. Dept. of Housing and Urban Development.
UPAP.
      Bibliography: p. 139-143.

      1. Metropolitan   area planning - Citizen
participation.

      (Cont'd on next card)

728.1
:613.5
(308)
A52
SURVEY METHODS.
AMERICAN   PUBLIC HEALTH ASSOCIATION.
      A NEW METHOD FOR MEASURING THE
QUALITY OF URBAN HOUSING; A TECHNIC OF
THE COMMITTEE ON THE HYGIENE OF
HOUSING. NEW YORK, 1943.
      729-740P.

      ADAPTED FROM A PAPER PRESENTED FOR
THE COMMITTEE BY ALLAN A. TWICHELL,
TECHNICAL SECRETARY, AT THE 71ST ANNUAL
MEETING OF THE AMERICAN PUBLIC HEALTH
ASSOCIATION, ST. LOUIS, MO., OCT. 28,
1942.
      REPRINTED FR OM AMERICAN JOURNAL OF
            (CONTINUED ON NEXT CARD)

311
C31h
SURVEY METHODS.
Chakravarti, I   M
      Handbook of methods of applied
statistics, by I.M. Chakravarti, R.G.
Laha and J. Roy. New York, Wiley, 1967.
      2 v.
      1. Statistics. 2. Sampling (Statistics)
3. Survey methods. I. Title.

711.3
S17
Saroff, Jerome R   Survey manual...1969.
                              (Card 2)

2. Public opinion polls. 3. Survey methods.
4. Metropolitan area planning - Providence.
5. Master plan. I. Levitan, Alberta Z., jt. au.
II. Alaska. University. Institute of Social,
Economic and Government Research. III. U.S.
HUD-UPAP. IV. Title.

728.1
:613.5
(308)
A52
AMERICAN PUBLIC HEALTH ASSOCIATION. A
      NEW METHOD ...1943.   (CARD 2)

PUBLIC HEALTH, V. 33, NO. 6, JUNE 1943.

      1. HOUSING AND HEALTH. 2. SURVEY
METHODS.   I. AMERICAN JOURNAL OF
PUBLIC HEALTH.

647.1
C34
1947
Survey methods.
Chicago, Ill. Housing Authority.
      What is a low income family? An analysis
of incomes of urban families of various types.
Chicago, 1947.
      24 p.   graphs.

      Prepared by John M. Ducey, Director of
Planning, with the assistance of Harry Schaffner
and Shirley Hillmer.

      1.Family income and expenditure. 2.Survey methods.
3.Tenant selection. I.Ducey, John M. II.Title.

711.583
C65g
Survey methods.
Connecticut. University. Institute of Public Service.
Growing suburbs and town finance; a study of the effect of suburban growth on property tax expenditures in four Connecticut towns [by] Beldon H. Schaffer. Storrs, Conn., Nov. 1954.
vi, 291. tables.
Processed.

1. Suburbs. 2. Municipal services. 3. Survey methods. I. Schaffer, Beldon H. II. Title.

308
:728.1
D25
Survey methods.
Denver. University. Bureau of Business and Social Research.
Manual for conducting and implementing local housing market surveys. Denver, Colo., Aug. 1952.
155, 31 l. illus., forms, graphs, maps, tables.

Final report, Research Project no. 0-E-70 and 1-E-91, Housing and Home Finance Agency.
Project director, F. L. Carmichael; staff technician, Ernest Jurkat.
Processed.

308
I52
Survey methods.
India. Secretariat.
Technical records of sample design, instructions to field workers and list of sample villages and urban blocks, comp. by Hari Bhajan Choudhury and Birendra Mohan Das Gupta. Delhi, Manager of Publications, 1960.
337p. tables. (Indian Statistical Institute. National sample survey no. 27)

1. Survey methods. I. Indian Statistical Institute. II. Chaudhury, Hari Bhajan, comp. III. Das Gupta, Birendra Mohan, comp.

711.583
C65
Survey methods.
Connecticut. University. Institute of Public Service.
Small homes and community growth; a study of the small low cost home -- community asset or liability [by] Beldon H. Schaffer. Storrs, Conn. [Sept. 1954]
vi, 20 l. tables.
Processed.

1. Suburbs. 2. Municipal services. 3. Survey methods. I. Schaffer, Beldon H. II. Title. III. Title: The ... low cost home, community asset or liability.

728.1
:308
D47
SURVEY METHODS.
DISTRICT OF COLUMBIA REDEVELOPMENT AGENCY.
GENERAL FIELD INSTRUCTION TO SURVEY STAFF [MAKING SURVEY OF HOUSES AND HOUSEHOLDS IN THE DISTRICT OF COLUMBIA] WASHINGTON, 1957.
28P. (RLA-S-2)
SAMPLE SURVEY FORM ATTACHED.

1. HOUSING SURVEYS. 2. HOUSING SURVEYS - DISTRICT OF COLUMBIA METROPOLITAN AREA. 3. SURVEY METHODS.

VF
647.1
I57c
Survey methods.
International Labour Office.
Cost-of-living statistics; methods and techniques for the post-war period: report prepared for the sixth International Conference of Labour Statisticians (Montreal, 4-12 August 1947). Geneva, 1947.
56 p. (Its Studies and reports, new series, no. 7, pt. 2)
Bibliographical footnotes.
1. Family income and expenditure. 2. Cost and standard of living. 3. Survey methods. I. International Conference of Labour Statisticians, 6th, 1947. II. Title.

VF
308
C66
Survey methods.
Cook County, Ill. Housing Authority.
Scoring community desirability. Chicago, Ill., Feb. 9, 1949.
17 p. tables. (Its Housing information service.)

Mimeographed.

308
E72
SURVEY METHODS.
Erdos, Paul L
Professional mail surveys, by Paul L. Erdos with the assistance of Arthur J. Morgan. New York, McGraw-Hill, 1970.
289p.

Bibliography: p. 276-277.

1. Survey methods. 2. Postal service. I. Morgan, Arthur J., jt. au. II. Title.

VF
647.1
I57
Survey methods.
International Labour Office.
Methods of family living studies. Geneva, 1949.
63 p.

Prepared for the Seventh International Conference of Labour Statisticians, Geneva, Sept. 1949.
Bibliographical footnotes.
1. Family income and expenditure. 2. Family income and expenditure-Housing. 3. Survey methods. I. Title: Family living studies.

308
:728.1
C66
Survey methods.
Coordinating Committee of the Central Statistical Board and the Works Progress Administration.
Technique for a real property survey; prepared jointly by ... and the Division of Economics and Statistics, Federal Housing Administration. Washington, July 1935.
v.
Contents. - pt. 1. Survey procedure.

(over)

R
352
068
Survey methods.
Government Affairs Foundation.
Metropolitan surveys: a digest. Chicago, Public Administration Service, 1958.
256p. maps, tables.

1. Metropolitan areas. 2. Survey methods. I. Title.

VF
308
(769)
K25
no.7
Survey methods.
Kentucky. University. Bureau of Community Service.
Preparing a community profile: the methodology of a social reconnaissance. Lexington, Ky., May 1952.
18 l. (Kentucky community series no. 7)

Processed.

1. Survey methods. I. Title. II. Series.

308
:728.1
(41)
C68
Survey methods.
Council for Research on Housing Construction
Housing standards and statistics; the second report of the Council. London, P.S. King, 1935.
79 p.
Bibliography: p. 73-74.

1. Housing surveys - U.K. 2. Survey methods.

311.2
(07)
H15
Survey methods.
Hansen, Morris H
Sample survey methods and theory, by Morris H. Hansen, William N. Hurwitz and William G. Madow. New York, Wiley, 1966.
2v. (Wiley series in probability and mathematical statistics)

1. Sampling (Statistics) - Study and teaching. 2. Survey methods. I. Hurwitz, William N., jt. au. II. Madow, William G. jt. au. III. Title.

728.1
:336.18
(79494)
L67r
Survey methods.
Los Angeles, Calif. Housing Authority.
A report on a survey of home conditions at Ramona Gardens. Los Angeles, Oct. 1942.
56 p.

1. Public housing - Los Angeles, Calif. 2. Survey methods. 3. Family living requirements.

VF
728.1
C87
Survey methods.
Curtis Publishing Co., Philadelphia, Pa.
Urban housing survey. Philadelphia, Pa., c1945.
71 p. illus., tables.

"Interviews conducted August 1944; information compiled and published as of June 1945."

1. Housing surveys. 2. Survey methods. 3. Home ownership. I. Title.

308
H182
SURVEY METHODS.
HAUCK, MATHEW
SURVEY RELIABILITY AND INTERVIEWER COMPETENCE, BY MATHEW HAUCK AND STANLEY STEINKAMP. URBANA, ILLINOIS, BUREAU OF ECONOMIC AND BUSINESS RESEARCH, UNIVERSITY OF ILLINOIS, 1964.
112P. (INTER-UNIVERSITY COMMITTEE FOR RESEARCH ON CONSUMER BEHAVIOR. CONSUMER SAVING PROJECT. STUDIES IN CONSUMER SAVINGS, NO. 4)

1. SURVEY METHODS. I. STEINKAMP, STANLEY, JT. AU. II. ILLINOIS. UNIVERSITY. BUREAU OF (CONTINUED ON NEXT CARD)

778.35
L82
SURVEY METHODS.
LUEDER, DONALD R
AERIAL PHOTOGRAPHIC INTERPRETATION: PRINCIPLES AND APPLICATIONS. NEW YORK, MCGRAW-HILL, 1959.
462P. (MCGRAW-HILL CIVIL ENGINEERING SERIES)

INCLUDES BIBLIOGRAPHY.

1. AERIAL PHOTOGRAPHY. 2. SURVEY METHODS. II. TITLE: PHOTOGRAPHIC INTERPRETATION.

308
:728.1
D25
Prelim.
Survey methods.
Denver. University. Bureau of Business and Social Research.
Manual for conducting and implementing a local survey of vacancy and intensity of use of dwelling units. Denver, Colo., August 1951.
119 p. plates, forms, maps, tables.

Prepared under Research Project no. 0-E-70 and 1-E-91, Housing and Home Finance Agency.
Project director: F.L. Carmichael; staff technician, Ernest Jurkat.

Typewritten.

308
H182
HAUCK, MATHEW. SURVEY RELIABILITY AND ... 1964. (CARD 2)

ECONOMIC AND BUSINESS RESEARCH. III. TITLE. IV. TITLE: INTERVIEWER COMPETENCE.

VF
308
M43
Survey methods.
Michigan. Department of Economic Development. Area Development Division.
A personal opinion of my home town. [Lansing, Mich., 1951?]
18 p. diagrs., forms.

Cover title.
C. Dwight Wood, chief.
Processed.

1. Survey methods. I. Title.

VF
308
M42

Survey methods.
Michigan. University. Survey Research Center.
   Four Americans talk about their cities; illustrative interviews from the study of cities.   Ann Arbor, Mich., Oct. 1947.
   32 l.   (Its Study no. 15)
   Cover title.
   "...Part of a study of four large American cities conducted...by the Center in Oct. and Nov. 1947."
   Mimeographed.

1.Social surveys. 2.Survey methods. I.Title.

628.3
(74763)
N28

Survey methods.
   Newsweek.
   The Utica story; a 1966 research report. [Washington] 1966.
   62p.

1. Sewerage and sewage disposal - Utica, N.Y. 2. Sampling (Statistics) 3. Public opinion polls. 4. Survey methods. I. Title.

VF
308
T29

Survey methods.
Texas. University. Bureau of Business Research.
   An economic survey method for small areas [by] Alfred G. Dale. Austin, Texas, 1955.
   47 p.

Bibliography: p. 42-47.

VF
308
:M47

Survey methods.
Mississippi. University. Bureau of Business Research.
   A manual for community surveys.   University, Miss., 1947.
   50 p.   (Its Short study series. No. 3)

Bibliography: p. 45-50.

1.Survey methods. I.Series.

308
P17

Survey methods.
Parten, Mildred Bernice, 1902-
   Surveys, polls, and samples; practical procedures. New York, Harper [1950]
   xii, 624 p. 22 cm. (Harper's social science series)
   Bibliography: p. 537-602.

1. Social surveys. 2. Public opinion polls. I. Title.
3.Survey methods. 4.Sampling.
HN29.P3   307.2   50-6574
Library of Congress   [80]

VF
308
:312
T28

Survey methods.
Texas. University. Bureau of Research in the Social Sciences.
   The use of city directories in the study of urban populations: a methodological note.   Austin, Texas, Jan. 8, 1942.
   29 p. forms.   (Texas. University. Publication no. 4202)

   Method used in study made by the University, Population mobility in Austin, Tex.

1.Survey methods. I.City directories.

VF
308
:388
N17

Survey methods.
National Research Council. Highway Research Board.
   Origin and destination surveys; methods and costs. Presented at the thirty-second annual meeting, January 13-16, 1953. Washington, 1953.
   v, 65 p. illus., graphs, tables.
(Highway Research Board. Bulletin 76)

1.Survey methods. I.Title.

311.2
R14

SURVEY METHODS.
Raj, Des.
   The design of sample surveys. New York, McGraw-Hill, 1972.
   390p. (McGraw-Hill series in probability and statistics)

1. Sampling (Statistics) 2. Survey methods. I. Title.

308
:728.1
(71)
T67

Survey methods.
Toronto. University. School of Social Work.
   An experimental study of local housing conditions and needs; a report, by Albert Rose. [Ottawa, Central Mortgage and Housing Corporation, 1955.]
   150 p. forms, map, tables.

   Cover title: Local housing conditions and needs.

Bibliography: p. 144-150.

647.1
N27

SURVEY METHODS.
NETER, JOHN.
CONDITIONING EFFECTS FROM REPEATED HOUSEHOLD INTERVIEWS, BY JOHN NETER AND JOSEPH WAKSBERG. MINNEAPOLIS, 1964.
51-56P. (MINNESOTA. UNIVERSITY. REPRINT SERIES, 7)

REPRINTED FROM JOURNAL OF MARKETING, V. 28, NO. 2, APRIL 1964.

1. FAMILY INCOME AND EXPENDITURE.
2. SURVEY METHODS. I. TITLE.
II. WAKSBERG, J OSEPH, JT. AU.
III. MINNESOTA. UNIVERSITY.
   (CONTINUED ON NEXT CARD)

308
R27

Survey methods.
   Research methods in social relations, with especial reference to prejudice [by] Marie Jahoda, Morton Deutsch, and Stuart W. Cook. [Contributing authors: Isidor Chein, and others] New York, Dryden Press [1951]
   2 v. (x, 759 p.) 22 cm.
   "Published for the Society for the Psychological Study of Social Issues."
   Bibliography: v. 1, p. [301]-406, repeated in v. 2, p. [727]-742.
   Contents.—pt. 1. Basic processes.—pt. 2. Selected techniques.

   1. Social science research. I. Jahoda, Marie. II. Society for the Psychological Study of Social Issues.

H62.R45   307.2   51-12509
Library of Congress   [20]

711.3
(05)
T68

Survey methods.
   Town and Country Planning Technical Broadsheet, no.1-24. [Edinburgh, Dept. of Health for Scotland, June 1948-Sept. 1949].
   24 pts. in 1.

1.Regional planning-Period. 2.Survey methods.
3.Maps and mapping.

647.1
N27

NETER, JOHN. CONDITIONING EFFECTS FROM
...1964.   (CARD 2)

GRADUATE SCHOOL OF BUSINESS ADMINISTRATION.

711.3
S17

Survey methods.
Saroff, Jerome R
   Survey manual for comprehensive urban planning; the use of opinion surveys and sampling techniques in the planning process, by Jerome R. Saroff and Alberta Z. Levitan. College, Alaska, Institute of Social, Economic, and Government Research, 1969.
   143p. (SEG report no. 19)
   U.S. Dept. of Housing and Urban Development. UPAP.
   Bibliography: p. 139-143.

   1. Metropolitan   area planning - Citizen participation.

   (Cont'd on next card)

308
B82

SURVEY METHODS.
U.S. Bureau of the Budget.
   Household survey manual. [Wash.] 1969.
   237p.

1. Survey methods. 2. Housing surveys.
3. Census - Population. I. Title.

647.1
N27S

SURVEY METHODS.
NETER, JOHN.
A STUDY OF RESPONSE ERRORS IN EXPENDITURES DATA FROM HOUSEHOLD SURVEYS, BY JOHN NETER AND JOSEPH WAKSBERG. MINNEAPOLIS, 1964.
18-55P. (MINNESOTA. UNIVERSITY. REPRINT SERIES, 5)

REPRINTED FROM THE JOURNAL OF THE AMERICAN STATISTICAL ASSOCIATION, MARCH 1964, V. 59.

1. FAMILY INC OME AND EXPENDITURE.
2. SURVEY METHO DS. I. TITLE.
   (CONTINUED ON NEXT CARD)

711.3
S17

Saroff, Jerome R   Survey manual...1969.
   (Card 2)

2. Public opinion polls. 3. Survey methods.
4. Metropolitan area planning - Providence.
5. Master plan. I. Levitan, Alberta Z., jt. au.
II. Alaska. University. Institute of Social, Economic and Government Research. III. U.S. HUD-UPAP. IV. Title.

312
C25t
no.24

SURVEY METHODS.
U.S. Bureau of the Census.
   The annual survey of manufactures: a report on methodology, by Jack L. Ogus and Donald F. Clark. Wash., 1971.
   107p. (Its Technical paper no. 24)

   1. Census - Manufacturers. 2. Survey methods. I. Ogus, Jack L. II. Clark, Donald F., jt. au. III. Title.

647.1
N27S

NETER, JOHN. A STUDY OF ...1964.(CARD 2)

II. WAKSBERG, JOSEPH, JT. AU.
III. MINNESOTA. UNIVERSITY. GRADUATE SCHOOL OF BUSINESS ADMINISTRATION.

308
S95

SURVEYS METHODS.
Symposium on the Foundations of Survey Sampling, University of North Carolina, 1968.
   New developments in survey sampling. Norman L. Johnson, editor and Harry Smith, Jr., editor. New York, Wiley-Interscience, 1969.
   732p.
   Sponsored by the Departments of Biostatistics and Statistics, University of North Carolina, Chapel Hill.
   1. Survey methods. 2. Sampling (Statistics) I. Johnson, Norman L., ed. II. Smith, Harry, Jr., jt. ed. III. North Carolina. University. IV. Title.

308
C25

Survey methods.
U.S. Bureau of the Census.
   Manual of enumerator's instructions for the District of Columbia income survey, February 1948. [Washington, 1948?]
   50 p. forms, tables.

   Manual prepared for survey of income in D.C., requested by National Capital Park and Planning Commission for purpose of carrying out the provisions of the D.C. Redevelopment Act of 1945. Processed.
1.Survey methods. 2.Income. I.U.S. National Capital Park and Planning Commission. II.District of Columbia income survey, February 1948.

```
333.33    SURVEY METHODS.
C25       U.S. CENTRAL STATISTICAL BOARD.
          TECHNIQUE FOR A REAL ESTATE ACTIVITY
          SURVEY. PREPARED JOINTLY BY
          COORDINATING COMMITTEE OF THE CENTRAL
          STATISTICAL BOARD AND THE WORKS
          PROGRESS ADMINISTRATION, AND THE
          DIVISION OF ECONOMICS AND STATISTICS,
          FEDERAL HOUSING AUMINISTRATION.
          WASHINGTON, 1937.
          V.
          1. REAL PROPERTY.  2. SURVEY METHODS.
          I. TITLE.  II. U.S. FEDERAL HOUSING ADM
INISTRATION. III.            U.S. WORKS PR
OGRESS ADMINISTRATIC
```

```
728.1     SURVEY METHODS.
1308      U.S. FEDERAL PUBLIC HOUSING AUTHORITY
F22D      (DIVISION OF RURAL HOUSING)
          DRAFT OF INSTRUCTIONS TO SUPERVISORS,
          SURVEY OF RURAL HOUSING NEEDS, 1942.
          ← WASHINGTON, 1942.
          6L.

          1. HOUSING SURVEYS.  2. SURVEY
METHODS.  I. TITLE: RURAL HOUSING
NEEDS.
```

```
690.015   Survey methods
H68       U.S. National Housing Agency. Office of the
T4        Administrator. Technical Office.
          Selected references on family living require-
ments and public acceptance factors relating to
housing design.  Washington, D.C., Apr. 1947.
          6, [13] l.  (U S. Housing and Home Finance
Agency. Office of the Administrator. Technical
Office. Technical paper no. 4)

          Reissued by U.S. Housing and Home Finance Agency.
Processed.

          (Continued on next card)
```

```
332.72    SURVEY METHODS.
F22TE     U.S. FEDERAL HOUSING ADMINISTRATION.
          TECHNIQUE FOR A MORTGAGE EXPERIENCE
          STUDY.  WASHINGTON, DIVISION OF
          ECONOMICS AND STATISTICS, FEDERAL
          HOUSING ADMINISTRATION, 1937.
          67X.

          1. MORTGAGE FINANCE.  2. SURVEY
METHODS.  I. TITLE.
```

```
VF
647.1     Survey methods.
F22m      U.S. Federal Reserve System. Board of Governors.
          Methods of the survey of consumer finances.
          [Washington, 1950]
          15 p.

          Reprinted from the Federal Reserve Bulletin,
July 1950.
          "Prepared by the staff of the Survey Research
Center, University of Michigan ... by George
Katona, Program Director, Leslie Kish ... John B.
Lansing ... and James K. Dent."
```

```
614       SURVEY METHODS.
P81MET    U.S. PUBLIC HEALTH SERVICE.
          METHODOLOGICAL ASPECTS OF A HEARING
          ABILITY INTERVIEW SURVEY.  WASHINGTON,
          GOVT. PRINT. OFF., 1965.
          19P.  (ITS PUBLICATION NO. 1000,
          SERIES 2, NO. 12)
          AT HEAD OF TITLE: VITAL AND HEALTH
          STATISTICS; DATA EVALUATION AND METHODS
          RESEARCH; NATIONAL CENTER FOR HEALTH
          STATISTICS.

          1. SAMPLING (STATISTICS)  2. HEARING.
          3. SURVEY METHODS.  I. TITLE.
```

```
VF
308       Survey methods.
:728.1    U.S. Federal Housing Administration. Division of
F22       Economics and Statistics.
1938      Local residential occupancy-vacancy surveys;
          a suggested procedure.  Washington, May 1938.
          63 l.  forms.

          Prepared by James S. Taylor, Howard G.
Brunsman, Lee Amann, Margaret Kane and others.-p.1.
Processed.

          1.Vacancy surveys. 2.Survey methods. I.Taylor,
James S. II.Title.
```

```
VF
308       Survey methods.
F67       U.S. Bureau of Foreign and Domestic Commerce.
1944      An outline for making surveys, especially
          adaptable in evaluating the industrial and
          commercial status of a community or region and
          potentialities for improving its position in
          both the industrial and consumer market.
          Washington, D.C., U.S. Govt. Print. Off., 1944.
          vi, 45 p.  (Its Economic series.  No. 34)

          "Sources of related material": p. 44-45.
          Prepared in the Special Studies Unit, Division
of Small Business.
          1.Survey methods.      I.Series.
```

```
308       SURVEY METHODS.
W67       U.S. WORK PROJECTS ADMINISTRATION.
NO.9      DIVISION OF PROFESSIONAL AND SERVICE
SUPPL.    PROJECTS.
          LOW INCOME HOUSING AREA SURVEY,
          SUPPLEMENT; A CIRCULAR PRESENTING THE
          TECHNIQUE FOR THE PREPARATION OF
          SUMMARY TABLES TO BE DERIVED FROM THE
          BASE TABLES PREPARED ON HOUSING
          PROJECTS UTILIZING THE LOW INCOME
          HOUSING AREA SURVEY.  WASHINGTON, 1940.
          18L.  (ITS TECHNICAL SERIES.
          RESEARCH, STATISTICAL, AND SURVEY
          PROJECT CIRCULAR NO. 9)
                        (CONTINUED ON NEXT CARD)
```

```
VF
308       Survey methods.
:728.1    U.S. Federal Housing Administration. Division of
F22       Research and Statistics.
          A procedure for postal vacancy surveys,
          prepared by Fielding L. Huesmann.  [Washington,
1941]
          14 l.  forms.

          Processed.

          1.Vacancy surveys. 2.Survey methods. I.Huesmann,
Fielding L. II.Title.
```

```
308       Survey methods.
:728.1    U. S. Housing and Home Finance Agency.
H68       Office of the Administrator.  Division
          of Housing Research.
          How to make and interpret locational studies
          of the housing market, by Maurice R. Brewster
          and William A. Flinn and Ernest H. Jurkat.
          Washington, Govt. Print. Off., 1955.
          vii, 66 p.  forms, graphs, maps, tables.
          (PB111653)

          Published by U. S. Department of Commerce,
Office of Technical Services.
```

```
308       U.S. WORK PROJECTS ADMINISTRATION.
W67       DIVISION OF PROFESSIONAL AND SERVICE
NO.9      PROJECTS. LOW INCOME HOUSING ...1940.
SUPPL.                                   (CARD 2)
          1. SURVEY METHODS.  2. LOW INCOME
HOUSING - SURVEYS.  I. TITLE.
```

```
728.1     SURVEY METHODS.
1308      U.S. FEDERAL HOUSING ADMINISTRATION.
F22T      (DIVISION OF ECONOMICS AND STATISTICS)
          TECHNIQUE FOR A RESURVEY OF HOUSING.
          WASHINGTON, 1939.
          142 l.

          1. HOUSING SURVEYS.  2. SURVEY METHODS.
          I. TITLE.
```

```
          U. S. Housing and Home Finance Agency.
          Office of the Administrator.  Division
          of Housing Research.  How to make and...
          1955. (Card 2)

          A report based largely upon a study by the
State Engineering Experiment Station, Georgia
Institute of Technology (HHFA Research Project
0-E-69).

          1.  Housing market analysis. 2.  Housing surveys.
3.  Survey methods. 4.  Housing research contracts.
I.  Brewster, Maurice   II.  Flinn, Wm. A. III.
Jurkat, Ernest H.  IV.  Georgia. State Engin
eering Experiment   Station. V.  U. S. Office
of Technical Services. VI. Title. VII. Title:
```

```
308       SURVEY METHODS.
W67       U.S. WORKS PROGRESS ADMINISTRATION.
NO.1      DIVISION OF SOCIAL RESEARCH.
          COMPILATION OF PROPERTY IDENTIFICATION
          MAPS; SUGGESTIONS ON TECHNIQUES FOR THE
          PREPARATION OF PROPERTY MAPS, ASSIGNMENT
          OF PROPERTY IDENTIFICATION NUMBERS, AND
          CROSS INDEXING TO AN OWNERSHIP CARD FILE.
          WASHINGTON, 1938.
          29P.  (ITS TECHNICAL SERIES.
          RESEARCH, STATISTICAL, AND SURVEY PROJECT
          CIRCULAR NO. 1)
          1. SURVEY METHODS.  2. REAL PROPERTY -
MAPS.  I. TITLE.  II. TITLE:
PROPERTY IDENTIFICATION MAPS.
```

```
332.72    SURVEY METHODS.
F22TE     U.S. FEDERAL HOUSING ADMINISTRATION.
NOV.1937  DIVISION OF ECONOMICS AND
          STATISTICS.
          TECHNIQUE FOR A MORTGAGE EXPERIENCE
          STUDY, NOVEMBER 1, 1937.  [N.P.] 1937.
          25L.

          1. MORTGAGE FINANCE.  2. SURVEY
METHODS.  I. TITLE.
```

```
728.1     SURVEY METHODS.
1335.63   U.S. HOUSING AUTHORITY.
H68T      TECHNIQUE FOR A SURVEY OF LOW-RENT
          HOUSING NEEDS. WASHINGTON, 1940.
          140L.

          1. RENTAL HOUSING - SURVEYS.
          2. SURVEY METHODS.  I. TITLE.
```

```
308       SURVEY METHODS.
W67       U.S. WORKS PROGRESS ADMINISTRATION.
NO.2      DIVISION OF SOCIAL RESEARCH.
          INDEX OF DEEDS, MORTGAGES, AND OTHER
          ENCUMBRANCES; SUGGESTIONS ON TECHNIQUES
          FOR THE PREPARATION OF AN INDEX OF DEEDS,
          MORTGAGES, AND OTHER ENCUMBRANCES BY
          PROPERTY LOCATION. WASHINGTON, 1938.
          23P.  (ITS TECHNICAL SERIES.
          RESEARCH, STATISTICAL, AND SURVEY PROJECT
          CIRCULAR NO. 2)
          1. SURVEY METHODS.  2. REAL PROPERTY -
SURVEYS.  I. TITLE.  II. TITLE: DEEDS,
MORTGAGES, AND OTHER ENCUMBERANCES.
```

```
728.1     SURVEY METHODS.
1308      U.S. FEDERAL PUBLIC HOUSING AUTHORITY
F22DR     (DIVISION OF RURAL HOUSING)
          DRAFT OF INSTRUCTIONS TO ENUMERATORS;
          SURVEY OF RURAL HOUSING NEEDS, 1942.
          WASHINGTON, 1942.
          14L.

          1. HOUSING SURVEYS.  2. SURVEY
METHODS.  I. TITLE: RURAL HOUSING
NEEDS.
```

```
647.1     Survey methods.
(862)
L11       U.S. Bureau of Labor Statistics.
          Foreign and international labor information;
          methods used in a survey of family income,
          expenditures, and living costs, Panama City,
          1952. [Washington] 1955.
          44p. tables.

          1.Family income and expenditure - Panama.
2.Survey methods.
```

```
308       SURVEY METHODS.
W67       U.S. WORKS PROGRESS ADMINISTRATION.
NO.9      (DIVISION OF SOCIAL RESEARCH)
          LOW INCOME HOUSING AREA SURVEY; A
          CIRCULAR PRESENTING THE TECHNIQUE FOR
          SECURING AND TABULATING DATA ON
          COMPOSITION, INCOME, AND EXPENDITURES FOR
          HOUSEHOLD FACILITIES, OF FAMILIES LIVING
          IN DWELLING UNITS FOUND TO BE SUBSTANDARD
          ON THE BASIS OF DATA CONCURRENTLY
          GATHERED IN A REAL PROPERTY SURVEY.
          WASHINGTON, 1939.
          247L.  (ITS TECHNICAL SERIES.
          RESEARCH, STATISTICAL, AND SURVEY
          PROJECT CIRCULAR NO. 9)
                        (CONTINUED ON NEXT CARD)
```

308
W67
NO.9
U.S. WORKS PROGRESS ADMINISTRATION.
(DIVISION OF SOCIAL RESEARCH) LOW
INCOME HOUSING ...1939.   (CARD 2)
  1. SURVEY METHODS.   2. LOW INCOME
HOUSING - SURVEYS.   I. TITLE.

308
W67
NO.5
SURVEY METHODS.
U.S. WORKS PROGRESS ADMINISTRATION
(DIVISION OF SOCIAL RESEARCH)
REAL ESTATE ACTIVITY SURVEYS; TRENDS OF
DEEDS AND MORTGAGES RECORDED IN A LONG
TERM PERIOD; A CIRCULAR PRESENTING THE
TECHNIQUE FOR TRANSCRIBING, TABULATING,
AND SUMMARIZING DATA OBTAINED FROM DEED
AND MORTGAGE TRANSCRIPTIONS FOR A LONG
TERM PERIOD. WASHINGTON, 1938.
  65L. (ITS: TECHNICAL SERIES.
RESEARCH, STATISTICAL, AND SURVEY PROJECT
CIRCULAR NO. 5)
  1. SURVEY METHODS.   2. REAL ESTATE
BUSINESS - SURVEYS.   I. TITLE.

Survey methods

see also

Architecture, Domestic - Surveys.
City planning - Surveys.
Housing surveys.
Public utilities - Surveys.
Public opinion polls
Social surveys
Housing market analysis.
Churches
Mortgage finance
Real property
Rental housing

728.1
:308
W67
SURVEY METHODS.
U.S. WORKS PROGRESS ADMINISTRATION.
DIV. OF SOCIAL RESEARCH.
LOW INCOME HOUSING AREAS SURVEY, A
CIRCULAR PRESENTING THE TECHNIQUE FOR
SECURING AND TABULATING DATA ON
COMPOSITION, INCOME, AND EXPENDITURES
FOR HOUSEHOLD FACILITIES, OF FAMILIES
LIVING IN DWELLING UNITS FOUND TO BE
SUBSTANDARD ON THE BASIS OF DATA
CONCURRENTLY GATHERED IN A REAL PROPERTY
SURVEY. WASHINGTON, 1939.
  247P. (W.P.A. TECHNICAL SERIES.
RESEARCH, STATISTICAL, AND SURVEY
PROJECT CIRCULAR NO. 9)
    (CONTINUED ON NEXT CARD)

333.33
:308
W67
SURVEY METHODS.
U.S. WORKS PROGRESS ADMINISTRATION.
DIV. OF SOCIAL RESEARCH.
TECHNIQUE FOR A REAL PROPERTY SURVEY,
TABULATION INSTRUCTIONS FOR DWELLING
SURVEY. WASHINGTON, 1938.
  1 V. (W.P.A. TECHNICAL SERIES.
RESEARCH, STATISTICAL, AND SURVEY
PROJECT CIRCULAR NO. 6)

  1. REAL PROPERTY - SURVEYS.
2. HOUSING SURVEYS.   3. SURVEY METHODS.
I. TITLE.

VF
711.585
:308
(753)
A52
Survey of a proposed redevelopment area.
American University. Bureau of Social Science
Research.
  Survey of a proposed redevelopment area.
Washington, Feb. 1953.
  107 L.   xiii p.   forms, tables, maps.

  Final report, Research project no. 6-U-81,
Housing and Home Finance Agency.
  Project director: Robert M. Bower; Staff
Technician: E. Everett Ashley.

  Processed.

728.1
:308
W67
U.S. WORKS PROGRESS ADMINISTRATION.
DIV. OF SOCIAL RESEARCH. LOW INCOME
HOUSING ...1939.   (CARD 2)
  1. LOW-INCOME HOUSING - SURVEYS.
2. HOUSING SURVEYS.   3. SURVEY METHODS.

308
W24
SURVEY METHODS.
Weiss, Carol H
  An introduction to sample surveys for
government managers, by Carol H. Weiss and
Harry P. Hatry. Wash., Urban Institute, 1970.
  45p. ([Working paper no. 108-65])

  1. Survey methods.   I. Urban Institute.
II. Hatry, Harry P., jt. au.   III. Title.

628.515
D95
A survey of alternate methods for cooling
condenser discharge water.
Dynatech R/D Co.
  A survey of alternate methods for cooling
condenser discharge water; large-scale heat
rejection equipment. [Prepared] for Water
Quality Office, Environmental Protection
Agency. Cambridge, Mass., 1969.
  127p. (Water pollution control research
series)

  1. Water pollution. I. U.S. Environmental
Protection Agency. II. Title.

308
W67
NO.10
SURVEY METHODS.
U.S. WORKS PROGRESS ADMINISTRATION.
(DIVISION OF RESEARCH)
  AN OUTLINE OF SURVEYS IN THE FIELD OF
REAL PROPERTY AND HOUSING; A CIRCULAR
OFFERING SUGGESTIONS FOR A COORDINATED
PROGRAM OF SURVEYS IN THE FIELD OF REAL
PROPERTY AND HOUSING. WASHINGTON, 1939.
  13L. (ITS TECHNICAL SERIES.
RESEARCH, STATISTICAL, AND SURVEY
PROJECT CIRCULAR NO. 10)

  1. SURVEY METHODS.   2. REAL PROPERTY
- SURVEYS.   3.   HOUSING SURVEYS.
I. TITLE.

VF
728.1
:613.5
W45
Survey methods.
Wilner, Daniel M
  How does the quality of housing affect
health and family adjustment? American
Journal of Public Health, p. 736-744, June
1956.
  "References": p. 744.
  Reprint.

  1. Housing and health.   2. Survey methods.

628.515
D95sur
A survey of alternate methods for cooling
condenser discharge water.
Dynatech R/D Co.
  A survey of alternate methods for cooling
condenser discharge water; total community
considerations in the utilization of
rejected heat. [Wash.] Environmental
Protection Agency, 1970.
  57p. (Water pollution control research
series)

  1. Water pollution. I. U.S. Environmental Protection Agency. II. Title.

308
W67
NO.3
SURVEY METHODS.
U.S. WORKS PROGRESS ADMINISTRATION.
DIVISION OF SOCIAL RESEARCH.
  REAL ESTATE ACTIVITY SURVEYS; A
LIMITED SURVEY OF DEEDS AND MORTGAGES
RECORDED IN A RECENT PERIOD; A CIRCULAR
PRESENTING THE TECHNIQUE FOR
TRANSCRIBING, TABULATING, AND SUMMARIZING
DATA OBTAINED FROM DEED AND MORTGAGE
TRANSCRIPTIONS FOR A RECENT PERIOD.
WASHINGTON, 1938.
  103L. (ITS TECHNICAL SERIES.
RESEARCH, STATISTICAL, AND SURVEY PROJECT
CIRCULAR NO. 3)

    (CONTINUED ON NEXT CARD)

711.585
W66
Survey methods.
Woodbury, Coleman, ed.
  Urban redevelopment: problems and practices,
by Charles S. Ascher [and others]. Chicago,
University of Chicago Press [1953]
  xvi, 525 p.   illus., map.

  "This volume and its companion, The future of
cities and urban redevelopment, are the chief
products of the Urban Redevelopment Study."
  Includes bibliographies.
    (Continued on next card)

628.515
D95a
A survey of alternate methods for cooling
condenser discharge water operating...
Dynatech R/D Co.
  A survey of alternate methods for cooling
condenser discharge water operating character-
istics and design criteria. [Prepared] for the
Water Quality Office, Environmental Protection
Agency. Cambridge, Mass., 1970.
  94p. (Water pollution control research
series)
  Bibliography: p. 84-94.

  1. Water pollution. I. U.S. Environmental
Protection Agency. II. Title.

308
W67
NO.3
U.S. WORKS PROGRESS ADMINISTRATION.
DIVISION OF SOCIAL RESEARCH. REAL
ESTATE ACTIVITY ...1938.   (CARD 2)
  1. SURVEY METHODS.   2. REAL ESTATE
BUSINESS - SURVEYS.   I. TITLE.

Woodbury, Coleman, ed.   Urban redevelopment ...
  [1953]   (Card 2)

  Contents.-Measuring the quality of housing in
planning for urban redevelopment, Allan A.
Twichell.-Urban densities and their costs: an
exploration into the economics of population
densities and urban patterns, William H. Ludlow.-
Private covenants in urban redevelopment, Charles
S. Ascher.-Urban redevelopment short of clearance:
rehabilitation, reconditioning, conservation and
code enforcement, in local programs, William L.
    (Continued on next card)

628.515
D95su
A survey of alternate methods for cooling
condenser discharge water system...
Dynatech R/D Co.
  a survey of alternate methods for cooling
condenser discharge water system, selection,
design, and optimization. [Prepared] for the
Water Quality Office, Environmental Protection
Agency. Cambridge, Mass., 1971.
  108p. (Water pollution control research
series)

  1. Water pollution. I. U.S. Environmental
Protection Agency. II. Title.

308
W67
NO.7
SURVEY METHODS.
U.S. WORKS PROGRESS ADMINISTRATION.
(DIVISION OF SOCIAL RESEARCH)
  REAL ESTATE ACTIVITY SURVEYS; INTENSIVE
ANALYSIS OF DEEDS AND MORTGAGES RECORDED
IN A RECENT PERIOD. WASHINGTON, SEPT.
V.1-2 1938.
v.2   2 V. (W.P.A. TECHNICAL SERIES.
RESEARCH STATISTICAL AND SURVEY PROJECT
CIRCULAR NO. 7, V. 1-2)

  1. SURVEY METHODS.   2. REAL PROPERTY -
SURVEYS.   3. MORTGAGE FINANCE - SURVEYS.
I. TITLE.

Woodbury, Coleman, ed.   Urban redevelopment ...
  [1953]   (Card 3)

Slayton.-Relocation of families displaced in urban
redevelopment: experience in Chicago, Jack Meltzer
[and] Sheilah Orloff.-Eminent domain in acquiring
subdivision and open land in redevelopment
programs: a question of public use, Ira S. Robbins
and Marian Perry Yankauer.

658.1
:308
S87
SURVEY OF AMERICAN LISTED CORPORATIONS.
U.S. SECURITIES AND EXCHANGE COMMISSION.
SURVEY OF AMERICAN LISTED CORPORATIONS.
REPORTED INFORMATION. REGISTRANTS
UNDER THE SECURITIES AND EXCHANGE ACT OF
1934, AT JUNE 30, 1939. NEW YORK, 1939.
  2 V.

  CONTENTS.- V.1. SELECTED MANUFACTURING
GROUPS.- V.2. SELECTED INDUSTRY GROUPS.

  1. CORPORATIONS - SURVEYS.
2. MANUFACTURERS - SURVEYS.
3. INDUSTRIAL SURVEYS.   I. TITLE.

VF
728.2
:690.591.003   A survey of apartment dwelling operating
P22   experience in large American cities.
U.S. Federal Housing Administration. Division
of Economics and Statistics.
A survey of apartment dwelling operating
experience in large American cities.   Washington,
Govt. Print. Off., 1940.
138 p.   illus., graphs, tables.

690.091.82
S97   Syracuse. University.   Survey of building
and housing regulation systems... 1951-52.
(card 2)

Syracuse, N.Y., White Plains, N.Y.
*Library lacks
Final report, Research project 1-R-96,
Housing and Home Finance Agency.
Project director: Spencer D. Parratt; staff
technician: Gilbert Barnhart.

690.091.82
S97a   _____ Analysis of selected questions
from a sample of the building regulations
questionnaire.   1952.

333.33   PIEROVICH, ANDREW L A SURVEY OF ...
(794)   1963.   (CARD 2)
P42
CLAIFORNIA. I. BAIN, HARRY O., JT.
AU. II. CALIFORNIA. UNIVERSITY.
CENTER FOR REAL ESTATE AND URBAN
ECONOMICS. III. TITLE.

720.2   Survey of architectural history in Cambridge.
C15   Cambridge, Mass. Historical Commission.
Survey of architectural history in
Cambridge. Cambridge, Mass., 1965.
101p. (Its Report no. 1)

Bibliography: p. 98-100.

1. Architecture - Conservation and
restoration. 2. Architecture - Cambridge,
Mass. I. Title.

690.091.82
S97   Syracuse. University.   Survey of building and
housing regulations systems... 1951-52.
(card 3)

1. Housing law enforcement. 2. Building
code administration. 3.Housing research contracts. 4. Heating codes. 5. Plumbing codes.
6. Electrical codes. 7. Building codes - Albuquerque, N.M. 8. Building codes-Cambridge,
Mass. 9. Building codes-Cleveland,Ohio. 10.
Building codes-Detroit, Mich. 11.Building codes
-East Chicago, Ind. 12. Building codes-Kansas
City,Mo. 13. Building codes-Los Angeles Co.,
Calif. 14. Building codes-Minot,N.D.
15. Building   codes-Nashville,Tenn.

Survey of changes in family finances...
647.1
:G68   U.S. Board of Governors of the Federal
Reserve System.
Survey of changes in family finances, by
Dorothy S. Projector and others. Wash., 1968.
321p. (Federal Reserve technical papers)

1. Family income and expenditure.
2. Market surveys. I. Title. II. Projector,
Dorothy S.

---

020   A survey of automated activities in the
P17   libraries of the United States.
Patrinostro, Frank S   comp.
A survey of automated activities in the
libraries of the United States   Compiled by
Frank S. Patrinostro. Edited and indexed by
Nancy P. Sanders. Tempe, Ariz., LARC Assn., 197.
v.   (World survey series)

For Library holdings see main entry.

1. Library science – Automation.
I. Sanders, Nancy P., ed. II. Title.
III. Library Automation Research and Consulting
Association.

690.091.82
S97   Syracuse. University.   Survey of building and
housing regulations systems... 1951-52.
(card 4)

16. Building codes-Portland,Ore. 17.Building
codes-Salt Lake City, Utah. 18.Building codes-
San Mateo Co.,Calif. 19.Building codes-Syracuse,N.Y. 20.Building codes-White Plains,N.Y.
21.Housing codes-Albuquerque,N.M. 22.Housing
codes-East Chicago,Ind. 23.Housing codes-Kansas City,Mo. 24.Housing codes-Los Angeles Co.,
Calif. 25.Housing codes-Nashville,Tenn. 26.
Housing codes-Portland,Ore. 27.Housing codes-
Salt Lake City, Utah. 28.Housing codes-Syracuse,N.Y.   I Parratt,Spencer D.
II.Barnhart,Gilbert   III.H.H.F.A. O.A. Div.of
Hsg.Res.   IV.Title.

332.72   SURVEY OF COMPTROLLER'S DIVISION.
:308   WOLF MANAGEMENT ENGINEERING CO.,
W65S   CHICAGO.
SURVEY OF COMPTROLLER'S DIVISION,
FEDERAL HOUSING ADMINISTRATION REPORT
AND RECOMMENDATIONS ON METHODS AND
PROCEDURES. CHICAGO, 1956.
268 .

1. U.S. FEDERAL HOUSING
ADMINISTRATION. COMPTROLLER'S DIVISION
. SURVEYS. 2. GOVERNMENTAL RESEARCH .
CONTRACTS AND SPECIFICATIONS.
I. TITLE.

---

020   A survey of automated activities in the
P17s   libraries of the U.S. and Canada.
Patrinostro, Frank S   comp.
A survey of automated activities in the
libraries of the U.S. and Canada, comp. by
Frank S. Patrinostro and Debra New. 2d ed.
Costa Mesa, Calif., LARC Publications Office,
1971.
1v.

1. Library science - Automation. I. New,
Debra, jt. comp. II. Library Automation
Research and Consulting Association.
III. Title.

Survey of building capacities and pupil
727   membership.
(78883)   Denver. Public Schools.
D25   Survey of building capacities and pupil
membership. [Denver] 1963.
10p.

1. Schools - Denver. I. Title.

332.72   SURVEY OF COMPTROLLER'S DIVISION OF
:308   FEDERAL HOUSING ADMINISTRATION.
W65   WOLF MANAGEMENT ENGINEERING CO.,
CHICAGO.
SURVEY OF COMPTROLLER'S DIVISION OF
FEDERAL HOUSING ADMINISTRATION; REPORT
AND RECOMMENDATIONS. CHICAGO, 1956.
134 ℓ.

1. U.S. FEDERAL HOUSING
ADMINISTRATION. COMPTROLLER'S DIVISION
. SURVEYS. 2. GOVERNMENTAL RESEARCH .
CONTRACTS AND SPECIFICATIONS.
I. TITLE.

691.018.44   Survey of available information on the toxi-
D83   city of the combustion and thermal...
Dufour, R   E
Survey of available information on the toxicity of the combustion and thermal decomposition
products of certain building materials under
fire conditions. Chicago, Underwriters' Laboratories, inc., 1963.
Lef.   66p. (Underwriters' Laboratories, Research
bulletin no. 53)
Bibliography: p. 53-66.
1. Building materials - Fire resistance.
2. Fire prevention. I. Underwriters' Laboratories, inc. II. Title.

Survey of business and industry in
331   San Francisco.
(79461)   San Francisco. Chamber of Commerce.
S15   1969 survey of business and industry in
1969   San Francisco, Calif.; completed Sept.
1969 for the concentrated employment
program of the Economic Opportunity Council
of San Francisco. San Francisco, 1969.
25p.
1. Employment - San Francisco. 2.
Economic conditions - San Francisco.
I. Title: Survey of business and industry
in San Francisco.

334.1   A survey of condominium housing activity in
E55   selected United States metropolitan market
areas.
Elliot (Bill) and Associates.
A survey of condominium housing activity
in selected United States metropolitan market
areas. Hackensack, N.J., 1970.
[25]p.

1. Cooperative housing. 2. Housing market.
I. Title.

621.39   Survey of broadcast journalism.
A53   The Alfred I. Dupont-Columbia University survey
1969/70   of broadcast journalism, 1969-1970. Year
of challenge, year of crisis. Ed. by Marvin
Barrett. New York, Grosset & Dunlap, 1970.
156p.

1. Communication systems. I. Barrett,
Marvin, ed. II. Dupont, Alfred I.
III. Columbia University. IV. Title: Survey
of broadcast journalism.

Survey of buying power.
R
711.729   Sales management; survey of buying
S15   power

New York, Sales Management, inc.
v.   annual.

For complete information see shelflist.

1. Retail trade. 2. Family income
and expenditure. I. Title: Survey of
buying power.

VF
351.712   Survey of construction plans of state and
C25   local governments.
U.S. Bureau of the Census.
Survey of construction plans of state and
local governments.   Washington, April 4, 1955.
12p.   tables.

Sponsored by U.S. Council of Economic Advisers
and Housing and Home Finance Agency; prepared
pursuant to Section 702 of the Housing Act of 1954.

690.091.82   Survey of building and housing regulation
S97   systems.
Syracuse. University.
Survey of building and housing regulation
systems; a study of the administration of
building and housing regulation systems in
seventeen cities.   Syracuse, N.Y., 1951-52.
pts.
Reports deal with the following cities:
Albuquerque, N.M., Baltimore, Md., Cambridge,
Mass., Charlotte, N.C., Cleveland, Ohio, Detroit,
Mich., East Chicago, Ind., Kansas City, Mo.,
Los Angeles Co., Calif., Milwaukee, Wis., Minot,
N.D., Nashville, Tenn., Portland, Ore., Salt
Lake City, Utah,   San Mateo Co., Calif.,

333.33   A SURVEY OF CALIFORNIA'S REAL ESTATE
(794)   INDUSTRY.
P42   PIEROVICH, ANDREW L
A SURVEY OF CALIFORNIA'S REAL ESTATE
INDUSTRY, ITS CHARACTERISTICS AND
INFORMATION SOURCES, BY ANDREW L.
PIEROVICH AND HARRY O. BAIN. BERKELEY
CALIF., 1963.
73P.
A SPECIAL REPORT FOR THE CENTER FOR
REAL ESTATE AND URBAN ECONOMICS,
INSTITUTE OF URBAN AND REGIONAL
DEVELOPMENT, UNIVERSITY OF CALIFORNIA,
BERKELEY.

1. REAL ESTATE BUSINESS .
(CONTINUED ON NEXT CARD)

647.1   Survey of consumer expenditures...
L116s   U.S. Bureau of Labor Statistics.
Survey of consumer expenditures;
field editing manual. Washington,
1961.
54p.

1. Family income and expenditure.
I. Title.

647.1
L116

Survey of consumer expenditures...
U.S. Bureau of Labor Statistics.
Survey of consumer expenditures;
interviewers' collection manual.
Washington, 1961.
[181]p.

1. Family income and expenditure.
I. Title.

VF
647.1
F22

Survey of consumer finances.
U.S. Federal Reserve System. Board of Governors.
Survey of consumer finances.
Washington [Govt. Print. Off.]
v.

For full information see shelf list card.
First survey made in 1946 (for 1945) by the
Bureau of Agricultural Economics.

330
F68S

SURVEY OF CURRENT BUSINESS.
U.S. BUREAU OF FOREIGN AND DOMESTIC
COMMERCE.
SURVEY OF CURRENT BUSINESS. V. 1-
AUG. 1, 1921-   WASHINGTON,
GOVT. PRINT. OFF.
V. MONTHLY.
For Library holdings see main entry
--- --- SUPPLEMENT. 1931-
WASHINGTON, GOVT. PRINT. OFF.
V.
ANNUAL, 1931-32; BIENNIAL, 1936-

1. ECONOMIC CONDITIONS. I. TITLE.

VF
647.1
L11st

Survey of consumer expenditures in 1950.
U.S. Bureau of Labor Statistics.
Statistical tables of data from
survey of consumer expenditures in 1950
to be prepared by the Bureau of Labor
Statistics of the U.S. Department of
Labor for the study of consumer income,
expenditures and savings by the Wharton
School of Finance and Commerce, University
of Pennsylvania. Rev. Washington, 1955.
13p.

1.Family income and expenditure. I.Title:
Survey of consumer expenditures in 1950.

691.32
T29s

A survey of crushed stone sands for concrete.
Teychenne, D C
A survey of crushed stone sands for concrete.
Garston, Eng., Ministry of Public Building and
Works, Building Research Station, 1968.
5p. (Building Research Station. Current
paper 11)
Reprinted from: British Granite and Whin-
stone Federation Journal, 1967, p. 53-60.

1. Concrete. I. U.K. Building Research
Station. II. Title.

339.3
B87
1958

Survey of current business.
U.S. Office of Business Economics.
U.S. income and output. Washington,
1958.
241p. diagrs., tables.

A supplement to the Survey of current
business.

1. National income. I. Title: Survey of
current business.

VF
647.1
L11su

Survey of consumer expenditures in 1950.
U.S. Bureau of Labor Statistics.
Survey of consumer expenditures in 1950:
summary of family characteristics, expenditures, income and savings, by income class.
Washington, Dept. of Labor [1957]
[7] p.

1.Family income and expenditures. I.Title.

647.1
S87
1960
1961
1962
1963
1964
1967

SURVEY OF CONSUMER FINANCES, 1960-69,
ANN ARBOR, INSTITUTE FOR
SOCIAL RESEARCH, SURVEY RESEARCH
CENTER, UNIVERSITY OF MICHIGAN, 1961-
6 V. ANNUAL.
TITLE VARIES.

1. FAMILY INCOME AND EXPENDITURE.
2. INSTALLMENT FINANCE. I. MICHIGAN.
UNIVERSITY. SURVEY RESEARCH CENTER.

339.3
F671

Survey of current business.
U.S. Office of Business Economics.
Income distribution in the United States,
by size, 1944-1950. Washington, Govt. Print.
Off., 1953.
86p.
On cover: A supplement to the Survey of
current business.
"The report was written by George Jaszi and
Selma F. Goldsmith." - cf. p. v.
1. National income. 2. Family income and expenditure.
I. Jaszi, George. II. Goldsmith, Selma F. III. Survey
of current business.   IV. Title.

647.1
L11i

Survey of consumer expenditures 1960-61.
U.S. Bureau of Labor Statistics.
The impact of rising prices on younger
and older consumers. Washington, 1963.
[28]p. (BLS rept. no. 238-2)

At head of title: Survey of consumer
expenditures, 1960-61.

1. Family income and expenditure. I. Title:
Survey of consumer expenditures 1960-61.

332.748
C87

Survey of current business.
Cutler, Frederick.
U.S. direct investments abroad, 1966. Part
1: balance of payments data. Wash., U.S.
Dept. of Commerce, Office of Business Economics, 1966.
239p. (OBE-SUP71-01)

A supplement to the Survey of current business.

1. Foreign exchange. I. Survey of current
business. II. U.S. Office of Business
Economics. III. Title.

339.3
(798)
B87

SURVEY OF CURRENT BUSINESS.
U.S. OFFICE OF BUSINESS ECONOMICS.
INCOME IN ALASKA. WASHINGTON, GOVT.
PRINT. OFF., 1960.
35P.
ISSUED AS A SUPPLEMENT TO THE SURVEY
OF CURRENT BUSINESS.

1. INCOME - ALASKA. I. SURVEY OF
CURRENT BUSINESS.

658.83
M42C

SURVEY OF CONSUMER FINANCES.
MICHIGAN. UNIVERSITY. SURVEY RESEARCH
CENTER.
CORRESPONDENCE BETWEEN FEDERAL
HOUSING ADMINISTRATION LIBRARY, BOARD
OF GOVERNORS OF THE FEDERAL RESERVE
SYSTEM, AND THE SURVEY RESEARCH CENTER,
UNIVERSITY OF MICHIGAN, RELATIVE TO THE
TRANSFER OF RESPONSIBILITY FOR THE
SURVEY OF CONSUMER FINANCES FROM THE
BOARD OF GOVERNORS TO THE SURVEY
RESEARCH CENTER... ANN ARBOR, MICH.,
WASHINGTON, 1960.
FOLDER.
(CONTINUED ON NEXT CARD)

339.3
S23

Survey of current business.
Schwartz, Charles F
Personal income by states, since 1929, by
Charles F. Schwartz and Robert E. Graham.
Washington, U.S. Dept. of Commerce, Office
of Business Economics, 1956.
229p.
A supplement to the Survey of current
business.

1. Income. I. Graham, Robert E., jt. au.
II. U.S. Office of Business Economics.
III. Title: Survey of current
business.   IV. Title.

VF
339.3
(969)
B87

Survey of Current Business.
U.S. Office of Business Economics.
Income of Hawaii, by Charles F. Schwartz.
Washington, Govt. Print. Off., 1953.
73 p. graphs, tables.

On cover: A supplement to the Survey of Current
Business.

1.Income. I.Schwartz, Charles F. II.Survey of
Current Business. III.Title: Hawaii, Income of.

658.83
M42C

MICHIGAN. UNIVERSITY. SURVEY RESEARCH
CENTER. CORRESPONDENCE BETWEEN
FEDERAL ...1960. (CARD 2)
1. MARKET SURVEYS. I. U.S. FEDERAL
HOUSING ADMINISTRATION. LIBRARY.
II. U.S. BOARD OF GOVERNORS OF THE
FEDERAL RESERVE SYSTEM. III. TITLE:
SURVEY OF CONSUMER FINANCES.

332.748
F67

Survey of Current Business.
U.S. Bureau of Foreign and Domestic Commerce.
Office of Business Economics.
Balance of payments of the United States,
1949-1951. Washington, Govt. Print. Off.,
1952.
165 p. graphs, tables.

On cover: A supplement to the Survey of
Current Business.

1.Economic conditions. I.Survey of Current
Business. II.Title.

339.3
F67
1954

Survey of Current Business.
U.S. Office of Business Economics.
National income, 1954, prepared by the
National Income Division. Washington, Govt.
Print. Off., 1954.
249p. graphs, tables.

A supplement to the Survey of Current
Business.

VF
647.1
F22m

Survey of consumer finances.
U.S. Federal Reserve System. Board of Governors.
Methods of the survey of consumer finances.
[Washington, 1950]
15 p.
Reprinted from the Federal Reserve Bulletin,
July 1950.
"Prepared by the staff of the Survey Research
Center, University of Michigan ... by George
Katona, Program Director, Leslie Kish ... John B.
Lansing ... and James K. Dent."

33
B87

Survey of Current Business.
U.S. Bureau of Foreign and Domestic Commerce.
Office of Business Economics.
Foreign aid by the United States Government,
1940-1951. Washington, Govt. Print. Off., 1952.
118 p. illus., graphs, tables.

On cover: A supplement to the Survey of
Current Business.

1.Economic development. I.Survey of Current
Business. II.Title.

339.3
F67

Survey of Current Business.
U.S. Bureau of Foreign and Domestic Commerce.
Office of Business Economics.
National income and product of the United
States, 1929-1950, prepared by the National Income
Division. Washington, Govt. Print. Off., 1951.
216 p. graphs, tables.
Cover title: National income, 1951 edition, a
supplement to the Survey of Current Business.

1.National income. I.Survey of Current Business.

33(73)
F62
1951
Survey of Current Business.
U.S. Bureau of Foreign and Domestic Commerce.
Office of Business Economics.
Regional trends in the United States economy.
Washington, Govt. Print. Off., 1951.
121 p.   graphs, tables.
On cover: A supplement to the Survey of Current Business.
Prepared by Charles A. R. Wardwell, Chief, Current Business Analysis Division.
1.Econ. condit.-U.S. I.Wardwell, Charles A. R.
II.Survey of Current Business. III.Title.

33
083.41 U.S. Bureau of Foreign and Domestic Commerce.
F67 Office of Business Economics.
Statistical supplement to the Survey of Current Business.
Washington, Govt. Print. Off.,
v.
Title varies: 1951 ed., Business statistics.
For full information see shelf list card.

628.3
S64
Survey of desalting processes for use in waste water treatment.
Spiewak, I
Survey of desalting processes for use in waste water treatment. Oak Ridge, Tenn., Oak Ridge National Laboratory, 1971.
31p. (ORNL-HUD-21)
Work supported by the Dept. of Housing and Urban Development and the U.S. Atomic Energy Commission. Contract no. W-7405-eng-26.
1. Sewerage and sewage disposal. I. U.S. Oak Ridge National Laboratory. II. U.S. Dept. of Housing and Urban Development. III. Title.

728.1
I333.63
N17S
SURVEY OF DEVELOPMENTS FINANCED UNDER FHA-221-D-3. WASHINGTON,
NATIONAL ASSOCIATION OF HOUSING AND REDEVELOPMENT OFFICIALS.
SURVEY OF DEVELOPMENTS FINANCED UNDER FHA-221-D-3. WASHINGTON, 1969.
14L.
1. RENTAL HOUSING. 2. RENTAL HOUSING -SURVEYS. 3. U.S. FEDERAL HOUSING ADMINISTRATION. I. TITLE.

352.1
M85s
no.1965f
Survey of EDP procedures and systems.
Municipal Finance Officers Association of the United States and Canada.
(Committee on Data Processing)
Survey of EDP procedures and systems.
Chicago, 1965.
8p. (Special bulletin 1965 f.)
In ring binder 352.1 M85s.
1. Automation. I. Title.

388
G25su
Survey of electronic command and control systems.
General Electric Co. (Transportation Systems Div.)
Survey of electronic command and control systems. Prepared for Urban Transportation Administration, U.S. Dept. of Housing and Urban Development, Washington, D.C. Erie, Pa., Transportation Equipment Projects and Marketing Operation, General Electric Co., Transportation Systems Div., 1967.
1v.
1. Transportation. 2. Journey to work. 3. Transportation - Automation. I. U.S. Dept. of Housing and Urban Development. II. Title.

---

desk
(Mrs. Landis) Survey of European research on building.
U.S. Housing and Home Finance Agency. Office of the Administrator. International Housing Activities.
Survey of European research on building.
[Washington, 1950]
99 p.   charts.
HHFA use only.
Includes bibliographies.
Contents.-Summary and recommendations.-Belgium, by Winters Haydock.-Denmark, by Robert E. McCabe.-France, by Donald Laidig.
(Continued on next card)

U.S. Housing and Home Finance Agency. Office of the Administrator. International Housing Activities. Survey of European research on building...1950. (Card 2)
(Contents cont'd)
Great Britain, by Robert E. McCabe.-Holland, by Winters Haydock.-Sweden, by Winters Haydock.
Typed

002
I690
B12
Survey of existing abstracting and indexing tools.
Baer, Karl A
Survey of existing abstracting and indexing tools, by Librarian, National Housing Center. Washington, 1960.
4p.
Delivered at Symposium on Building Information Problems sponsored by Office of Documentation, NAS-NRC, at Cleveland, Ohio, June 9, 1960.
1. Building documentation - Congresses. 2. Building industry - Bibliography. I. National Housing Center. Library. II. Symposium on Building Information Problems, Cleveland, 1960. III. National Research Council. IV. Title.

VF
690
F67
Survey of exterior painting on low-cost houses.
U.S. Forest Service. Forest Products Laboratory, Madison, Wis.
[Frame dwelling construction practices]
Madison, Wis. [1952?]
8 v.   illus. tables.
Contents:-pt.1. Current housing construction practices in the Central, Lake and Northeastern States, by L. O. Anderson, O.C. Heyer, L.V. Teesdale.-pt.2.Current housing construction practices in West Coast states, by L.V. Teesdale, W.G. Youngquist.-pt.3.Current housing practices

---

VF
690
F67
U.S. Forest Service. Forest Products Laboratory, Madison, Wis. [Frame dwelling construction practices] [1952?] (Card 2)
in the Southeastern and Southern states, by O.C. Heyer, T.B. Heebink.-pt.4. A survey of exterior painting on low cost houses, by F.L. Browne.-pt.5. A survey of exterior painting on recently built houses in southern Arizona, by F.L.Browne.-pt.6.Cause of paint peeling on wood siding of houses in Seattle, by Laurence V. Teesdale.-pt.7.Suggestions for improved service of exterior

---

VF
690
F67
U.S. Forest Service. Forest Products Laboratory, Madison, Wis. [Frame dwelling construction practices] [1952?] (Card 3)
paint on FHA-insured houses, by F. L. Browne.-pt.8. Heavy snows and cold weather may cause roof leaks, by L. V. Teesdale.
Final report, Research project O-T-24.
Housing and Home Finance Agency. Project director: R. F. Luxford, Staff technician: William A. Russell.
Typewritten.

VF
690
F67
U.S. Forest Service. Forest Products Laboratory, Madison, Wis. [Frame dwelling construction practices] [1952?] (Card 4)
1.Building methods. 2.Paints and painting. 3.Winter construction. 4.Housing research contracts. I.Luxford, R.F. II.Russell, Wm. A. III. U.S. Housing and Home Finance Agency, Office of the Administrator, Division of Housing Research. IV.Title. V.Anderson, L.O. VI.Heyer, O.C. VII.Teesdale, L.V. VIII.Youngquist,W. G. IX.Heebink, T.B. X.Browne, F.L. XI.Title:Current housing construction practices.
(Over)

388
P15
A survey of factors which affect transportation cost.
Pan American Union.
A survey of factors which affect transportation cost. Prepared in the Dept. of Economic Affairs of the Pan American Union, General Secretariat, Organization of American States. Wash., 1964.
76p.
1. Transportation. I. Title.

312.1
P81
SURVEY OF FAMILIES MOVING FROM LOW-RENT HOUSING.
U.S. PUBLIC HOUSING ADMINISTRATION. MOBILITY AND MOTIVATIONS; SURVEY OF FAMILIES MOVING FROM LOW-RENT HOUSING.
WASHINGTON, 1958.
66L.
1. POPULATION SHIFTS. 2. PUBLIC HOUSING. I. TITLE. II. TITLE: SURVEY OF FAMILIES MOVING FROM LOW-RENT HOUSING.

728.1
I336.18
(758231)
P81
SURVEY OF FAMILIES MOVING FROM LOW-RENT HOUSING.
U.S. PUBLIC HOUSING ADMINISTRATION. SURVEY OF FAMILIES MOVING FROM LOW-RENT HOUSING. MOBILITY AND MOTIVATIONS. CITY REPORT, ATLANTA, GA. WASHINGTON, 1958.
1 V.
1. PUBLIC HOUSING - ATLANTA. 2. POPULATION SHIFTS - ATLANTA. I. TITLE. II. TITLE: MOBILITY AND MOTIVATIONS.

728.1
I336.18
(7526)
P81
SURVEY OF FAMILIES MOVING FROM LOW-RENT HOUSING.
U.S. PUBLIC HOUSING ADMINISTRATION. SURVEY OF FAMILIES MOVING FROM LOW-RENT HOUSING. MOBILITY AND MOTIVATIONS. CITY REPORT, BALTIMORE, MD. WASHINGTON, 1958.
1 V.
1. PUBLIC HOUSING - BALTIMORE. 2. POPULATION SHIFTS - BALTIMORE. I. TITLE. II. TITLE: MOBILITY AND MOTIVATIONS.

728.1
I336.18
(74797)
P81
SURVEY OF FAMILIES MOVING FROM LOW-RENT HOUSING.
U.S. PUBLIC HOUSING ADMINISTRATION. SURVEY OF FAMILIES MOVING FROM LOW-RENT HOUSING. MOBILITY AND MOTIVATIONS. CITY REPORT, BUFFALO. WASHINGTON, 1958.
1 V.
1. PUBLIC HOUSING - BUFFALO. 2. POPULATION SHIFTS - BUFFALO. I. TITLE. II. TITLE: MOBILITY AND MOTIVATIONS.

728.1
I336.18
(7463)
P81
SURVEY OF FAMILIES MOVING FROM LOW-RENT HOUSING.
U.S. PUBLIC HOUSING ADMINISTRATION. SURVEY OF FAMILIES MOVING FROM LOW-RENT HOUSING. MOBILITY AND MOTIVATIONS. CITY REPORT, HARTFORD, CONN. WASHINGTON, 1958.
1 V.
1. PUBLIC HOUSING - HARTFORD. 2. POPULATION SHIFTS - HARTFORD. I. TITLE. II. TITLE: MOBILITY AND MOTIVATIONS.

728.1
I336.18
(763335)
P81
SURVEY OF FAMILIES MOVING FROM LOW-RENT HOUSING.
U.S. PUBLIC HOUSING ADMINISTRATION. SURVEY OF FAMILIES MOVING FROM LOW-RENT HOUSING. MOBILITY AND MOTIVATIONS. CITY REPORT, NEW ORLEANS, LOUISIANA. WASHINGTON, 1958.
1 V.
1. PUBLIC HOUSING - NEW ORLEANS. 2. POPULATION SHIFTS - NEW ORLEANS. I. TITLE. II. TITLE: MOBILITY AND MOTIVATIONS.

728.1
I336.18
(77352)
P81
SURVEY OF FAMILIES MOVING FROM LOW-RENT HOUSING.
U.S. PUBLIC HOUSING ADMINISTRATION. SURVEY OF FAMILIES MOVING FROM LOW-RENT HOUSING. MOBILITY AND MOTIVATIONS. CITY REPORT, PEORIA, ILL. WASHINGTON, 1958.
1 V.
1. PUBLIC HOUSING - PEORIA, ILL. 2. POPULATION SHIFTS - PEORIA, ILL. I. TITLE. II. TITLE: MOBILITY AND MOTIVATIONS.

728.1
:336.18
(79454)
P81

SURVEY OF FAMILIES MOVING FROM
LOW-RENT HOUSING.
U.S. PUBLIC HOUSING ADMINISTRATION.
SURVEY OF FAMILIES MOVING FROM
LOW-RENT HOUSING. MOBILITY AND
MOTIVATIONS. CITY REPORT, SACRAMENTO,
CALIF. WASHINGTON, 1958.
1 V.

1. PUBLIC HOUSING - SACRAMENTO,
CALIF. 2. POPULATION SHIFTS -
SACRAMENTO, CALIF. I. TITLE.
II. TITLE: MOBILITY AND MOTIVATIONS.

362.6
H68su

Survey of FHA-assisted nursing homes.
U.S. Dept. of Housing and Urban
Development.
Survey of FHA-assisted nursing homes.
Wash., Govt. Print. Off., 1969.
47p. (HUD-64-F)

1. Nursing homes. 2. U.S. Federal
Housing Administration. I. Title.

728.1
(63)
A32

A survey of housing in Ethiopia with special
emphasis on the capital city of Addis Abeba
U.S. Agency for International Development.
(The Housing Survey Team)
A survey of housing in Ethiopia with
special emphasis on the capital city of
Addis Ababa. Addis Ababa, 1965.
104p.

1. Housing - Ethiopia.
2. Housing statistics - Ethiopia.
3. Housing surveys - Ethiopia. I. Title.

728.1
:336.18
(77866)
P81

SURVEY OF FAMILIES MOVING FROM
LOW-RENT HOUSING.
U.S. PUBLIC HOUSING ADMINISTRATION.
SURVEY OF FAMILIES MOVING FROM
LOW-RENT HOUSING. MOBILITY AND
MOTIVATIONS. CITY REPORT, ST. LOUIS,
MO. WASHINGTON, 1958.
1 V.

1. PUBLIC HOUSING - ST. LOUIS.
2. POPULATION SHIFTS - ST. LOUIS.
I. TITLE. II. TITLE: MOBILITY AND
MOTIVATIONS.

339.3
P76

Survey of financial characteristics of
consumers.
Projector, Dorothy S
Survey of financial characteristics of
consumers, by Dorothy S. Projector and
Gertrude S. Weiss, in collaboration with
others. Washington, Board of Governors
of the Federal Reserve System, 1966.
116p.

1. Income. 2. Family income and
expenditure. 3. Cost and standard of living. I. Weiss, Gertrude S., jt. au.
II. U.S.   Board of Governors
of the   Federal Reserve
System.   III. Title.

LC

A survey of housing in urban San Antonio.
Research and Planning Council, San Antonio.
A survey of housing in urban San Antonio.
San Antonio, 1957.
58 l. maps. (part col.) diagrs. (2 fold in
pocket) tables.

HD 7304 S27 R4

1. Housing - San Antonio. I. Title.

728.1
:336.18
(797771)
P81

SURVEY OF FAMILIES MOVING FROM
LOW-RENT HOUSING.
U.S. PUBLIC HOUSING ADMINISTRATION.
SURVEY OF FAMILIES MOVING FROM
LOW-RENT HOUSING. MOBILITY AND
MOTIVATIONS. CITY REPORT, SEATTLE,
WASH. WASHINGTON, 1958.
1 V.

1. PUBLIC HOUSING - SEATTLE.
2. POPULATION SHIFTS - SEATTLE.
I. TITLE. II. TITLE: MOBILITY AND
MOTIVATIONS.

551.5
B45

Survey of frozen precipitation in urban
areas as related to climatic conditions.
Bilello, Michael A
Survey of frozen precipitation in urban
areas as related to climatic conditions.
Hanover, N. H., U. S. Army Material Command,
Cold Regions Research & Engineering Laboratory,
1967.
30p. (U.S. Army. Cold Regions Research and
Engineering Laboratory Technical Report 162)

1. Climatology. 2. Weather. I. U.S.
Army Cold Regions Research and Engineering
Laboratory, Hanover, N.H. II. Title.
III. Title: Frozen precipitation
in urban areas.

728.1
:308
(74725)
N28

Survey of housing need and demand, town of
Islip, New York.
New York (State) Div. of Housing and
Community Renewal.
Survey of housing need and demand, town
of Islip, New York. New York, 1963.
20p.

1. Housing surveys - Islip, N.Y.
2. Housing market - Islip, N.Y. I. Title.

728.6
A37SU

SURVEY OF FARM HOUSING AND OTHER FARM
BUILDINGS.
U.S. BUREAU OF AGRICULTURAL ECONOMICS.
SURVEY OF FARM HOUSING AND OTHER FARM
BUILDINGS, 1950. WASHINGTON, 1950.
KIT (9 PIECES)

CONTAINS INTERVIEWER INSTRUCTIONS,
TRAINING GUIDE, AND FORMS OF REPORTS
USED IN THE SURVEY.

1. FARM BUILDINGS. 2. HOUSING
SURVEYS. I. TITLE.

332.72
(73:347)
P26

Survey of housing.
Peoples Gas Light and Coke Co. Community
Relations Section.
Survey of housing financed under Section
221 (d)(3) of the National housing act of
1961. Chicago, 1964.
1v.

1. Mortgage finance. 2. Low-income
housing. 3. Minority groups - Housing.
4. Family income and expenditure -Housing.
I. Title. II. Title: National Housing
Act of 1961.

728.1
:308
(747245)
N28s

Survey of housing need and demand, town
of Oyster Bay, New York.
New York (State) Div. of Housing and
Community Renewal.
Survey of housing need and demand,
town of Oyster Bay, New York. New York,
1964.
[13]p.

1. Housing surveys - Oyster Bay, N.Y.
2. Housing market - Oyster Bay, N.Y.
I. Title.

332.3
(016)
S51s

A survey of Federal government publications
of interest to small business.
U.S. Small Business Administration.
A survey of Federal government publications
of interest to small business, compiled by
Elizabeth M. Heidbreder. Wash., Govt. Print.
Off., 1962.
63p.

1. Small business - Bibl. 2. Federal
government - Publications. I. Heidbreder,
Elizabeth M., comp. II. Title.

728.1
:308
(74932)
N29

SURVEY OF HOUSING CONDITIONS IN
NEWARK, N.J.
NEWARK, N.J. HOUSING AUTHORITY.
SURVEY OF HOUSING CONDITIONS IN
NEWARK, N.J. EMPLOYMENT DATA AND
TRENDS. NEWARK, N.J. 1940.
16P.
PREPARED FOR NATIONAL DEFENSE
COUNCIL.

1. HOUSING SURVEYS - NEWARK, N.J.
2. DEFENSE HOUSING. I. TITLE.

058.7
:728.100.15
B84
1952
Prelim.

A survey of housing research.
Building Research Advisory Board.
A survey of housing research.
[Washington, National Academy of Sciences -
National Research Council] April 1952.
1 v. (unpaged) forms, tables.

Final report. Research Project No. O-T-59.
Housing and Home Finance Agency.
Project director: William H. Scheick;
Staff technician: Eugene A. Tilleux.
Processed.

332.3
(016)
S51s
1969

A survey of Federal government publications
of interest to small business.
U.S. Small Business Administration.
A survey of Federal government publications
of interest to small business, compiled by
Elizabeth G. Janezeck. 3d ed. Wash., Govt.
Print. Off., 1969.
85p.

1. Small business - Bibl. 2. Federal government - Publications. I. Janezeck, Elizabeth
G., comp. II. Title.

728.1
:362.6
(74946)
P81

Survey of housing characteristics of old age
and survivors insurance beneficiaries,
Monmouth County, New Jersey.
U.S. Public Housing Administration.
(Program Planning Div.)
Survey of housing characteristics of old
age and survivors insurance beneficiaries,
Monmouth County, New Jersey, [Washington]
1962.
4p. tables.

1. Housing for the aged - Monmouth Co.,
N.J. 2. Old age. 3. Social security -
Monmouth Co., N.J. I. Title.

728.1
:336.18
N175SU

SURVEY OF LHA OPERATIONS.
NATIONAL ASSOCIATION OF HOUSING AND
REDEVELOPMENT OFFICIALS (SOUTHWEST
REGIONAL COUNCIL)
SURVEY OF LHA OPERATIONS.
OPERATIONAL POLICIES AND PRACTICES OF
LOCAL HOUSING AUTHORITIES IN THE
SOUTHWEST. N.P., 1954.
19L.

1. LOCAL HOUSING AUTHORITIES.
I. TITLE.

370
L47

A survey of Federal programs in higher
education; summary describing the programs...
Little, James Kenneth, 1906-
A survey of Federal programs in higher
education; summary describing the programs,
participating institutions, and the effects of
the programs on the institutions. Washington,
U.S. Dept. of Health, Education, and Welfare,
Office of Education; for sale by the Supt. of
Documents, Govt. Print. Off., 1962.
56p. (U.S. Office of Education.
Bulletin, 1963, no. 5)
OE-50033.
Bibliography: p. 52-56.

1. Education. 2. Uni-   versities and colleges.
I. U.S. Office of Edu-   cation. II. Title.

728.1
:362.6
(41)
H65

A survey of housing for old people.
Hole, W V
A survey of housing for old people, by W.
V. Hole and P. G. Allen. Garston, Eng.,
Building Research Station, Dept. of
Scientific and Industrial Research [1965?]
[20]p. (U.K. Building Research
Station. Building research current papers.
Design series 33)
Reprinted from: The Architects' Journal,
1962, vol. 135, p. 1017-24, 1026. 1964,
vol. 139 (2) p. 75-82.

1. Housing for the   aged - U.K. 2.
Old age. I. Allen, P.   G., jt. au. II.
U.K. Building Research   Station. III. Title.

Folio
728.1
:333.63
(74885)
A55

A survey of low-rent housing needs in
Duquesne.
Allegheny County, Pa. Housing Authority.
A survey of low-rent housing needs in
Duquesne, Pa. WPA project 27993, sponsored
by the Allegheny County Housing Authority.
Pittsburgh, 1941.
1 v. maps, tables.

1. Rental housing - Duquesne, Pa. I. Title.

Survey of manufactures.

670
(755)
V47
Virginia. Dept. of Labor and Industry.
Survey of manufactures. [Richmond]
v. annual.

For complete information see shelflist.

1. Manufacturers - Virginia.
I. Title.

331.7
(016)
I21
A survey of literature related to selected
nonprofessional occupations.
Idaho. State Occupational Research Unit.
A survey of literature related to selected
nonprofessional occupations. Moscow, State
Occupational Research Unit, College of Educa-
tion, University of Idaho, 1966.
34p.
Research performed pursuant to contract with
U.S. Dept. of Health, Education, and Welfare.

1. Occupations - Bibl. 2. Employment - Bibl.
I. Title.

362.6
A52SU
AMERICAN NURSING HOME ASSOCIATION.
SUMMARY OF A ...1960   (CARD 2)
1. NURSING HOMES. 2. NURSING HOMES -
SURVEYS. I. TITLE. II. TITLE:
SURVEY OF NURSING HOMES, 1958-1959.
III. AMERICAN MEDICAL ASSOCIATION.
COUNCIL ON MEDICAL SERVICE.

690.08
H68
A survey of minority construction
contractors.
U.S. Dept. of Housing and Urban Development.
A survey of minority construction contractors. Wash., Office of the Assistant Secretary for Equal Opportunity, Dept. of Housing
and Urban Development, 1971.
32p.

1. Contractors. 2. Employment - Minority
groups. I. Title.

647.1
(74771)
N28
Survey of low-rent and middle-income hous-
ing need and demand, Ithaca, New York.
New York (State) Div. of Housing and
Community Renewal.
Survey of low-rent and middle-income hous-
ing need and demand, Ithaca, New York.
New York, 1963.
35p.

1. Family income and expenditure - Hous-
ing - Ithaca, N.Y. 2. Rental housing -
Ithaca, N.Y.   3. Housing market -
Ithaca, N.Y.   I. Title.

712.25
087ni
Survey of outdoor Recreation activities.
U.S. Bureau of Outdoor Recreation.
The 1970 survey of outdoor recreation
activities; preliminary report, [Wash.] 1972.
105p.

1. Recreation. I. Title: Survey of outdoor
Recreation activities.

711.585.1
(794)
S22
Survey of model cities applications in
Northern California.
Sedway/Cooke.
Survey of model cities applications in
Northern California. Berkeley, University
of California Extension, Continuing Educa-
tion in Environmental Design, 1968.
61p.

1. Model cities - California.
I. California. University. II. Title.

658.564
F79s
Survey of management information systems
and their languages.
Fry, J
Survey of management information systems
and their languages, by J. Fry and J. Gosden.
[n.p.] Mitre Corp., 1968.
25p. (MTP-313)

Research sponsored by Defense Communication
Agency.

Bibliography: p. 24-25.

1. Automation. 2. Management. I. Gosden,
J., jt. au.   II. Mitre Corp.
III. Title.

711
(016)
C65
no. 62
A survey of planning information in
standard reference books.
Baerwald, Diane A
A survey of planning information in
standard reference books. [n.p.] Victor
Gruen Foundation for Environmental Planning,
1968.
34p. (Council of Planning Librarians.
Exchange bibliography no. 62)

1. Planning - Bibl. 2. City planning -
Bibl. I. Gruen (Victor) Foundation for
Environmental Planning. II. Title.
(Series: Council of Planning Librarians.
Exchange bib-   liography no. 62)

VF
728.3
:333
F22
Survey of new home sales.
Federal Reserve Bank of Philadelphia.
Survey of new home sales, [by] Federal Reserve
Bank of Philadelphia, Home Builders' Association of
Philadelphia and Suburbs, Society of Residential
Appraisers, Philadelphia Chapter, [and] Market
Survey.   Philadelphia, July 14, 1950.
2 [7] l.   tables.

Explanatory press release, July 7, 1950,
attached.

(Continued on next card)

728.1
:308
(74743)
N28SU
SURVEY OF MIDDLE-INCOME AND LOW-RENT
HOUSING NEEDS AND DEMAND IN ALBANY,
NEW YORK (STATE) DIVISION OF HOUSING
AND COMMUNITY RENEWAL.
SURVEY OF MIDDLE-INCOME AND LOW-RENT
HOUSING NEEDS AND DEMAND IN ALBANY,
NEW YORK. NEW YORK, 1962.
50P.

1. HOUSING MARKET - ALBANY.
2. HOUSING - ALBANY. I. TITLE.

691.16
B15
Survey of plastics sandwich construction.
Baldanza, Nicholas T
Survey of plastics sandwich construction.
Dover, N.J., Plastics Technical Evaluation
Center, Picatinny Arsenal, 1968.
93p. (PLASTEC report 34)

CFSTI. AD 673 713.

1. Plastics. 2. Panels. I. U.S. Plastics
Technical Evaluation Center. II. Title.

728.1
(7471)
A77
Federal Reserve Bank of Philadelphia.   Survey of
new home sales...July 14, 1950.   (Card 2)

"The first time this information has been
published by the Bank in this form"
Mimeographed.

1.Houses-Sales price. I.Home Builders' Associa-
tion of Philadelphia and Suburbs. II.Society of
Residential Appraisers, Philadelphia Chapter.
III.Market Survey. IV.Title.

728.1
(7471)
A77
A SURVEY OF MIDDLE-INCOME FAMILIES
SEEKING NEW HOUSING.
ASSOCIATION OF MIDDLE INCOME HOUSING.
A SURVEY OF MIDDLE-INCOME FAMILIES
SEEKING NEW HOUSING. NEW YORK, 1962
3L.

1. HOUSING - NEW YORK (CITY)
I. TITLE.

690.015
(485)
S82
1971
R16
Survey of premises as a basis for physical
planning.
Granfelt, Bertel.
Uppmätning av lokaler som underlag för
fysisk planering (Survey of premises as a
basis for physical planning) Stockholm,
Statens Institut för Byggnadsforskning, 1971.
97p. (Rapport R16:1971)
English summary.

1. City planning - Sweden. I. Stockholm.
Statens Institut för Byggnadsforskning.
II. Title: Survey of premises as a basis
for physical pla-   ning.

R
058.7
728.100.15
B84
1952
A survey of housing research in the United
States.
Building Research Advisory Board.
A survey of housing research in the United
States.   Washington [Govt. Print. Off.] Nov.
1952.
723 p.

"Housing research."
Study carried out under contract with HHFA.

331
P25s
Survey of non-white employees in state
government in Pennsylvania.
Pennsylvania. Human Relations Commission.
Sixth survey of non-white employees in state
government in Pennsylvania. Harrisburg, 1969.
11p.

1. Employment - Minority groups. I. Title:
Survey of non-white employees in state
government in Pennsylvania.

VF
690.37
U54
1950
Survey of problems of low cost rural housing
in tropical areas.
United Nations. Secretariat. Department of
Social Affairs.
Survey of problems of low cost rural housing
in tropical areas; a preliminary report with
special reference to the Caribbean area. New
York, N.Y., Nov. 1950.
93 p. (UN General ST/SOA/2 17 Nov. 1950)
Bibliography: p 71-93.
1.Housing in the tropics. 2.Building materials-
Tropics. I.Title. II.Title: Low cost rural
housing in tropical areas.

728.1
:308
N17s
A survey of international housing
activities...
National Association of Home Builders.
A survey of international housing activities of international organizations, U.S.
Government agencies, manufacturers, investors,
builders. Washington, 1965.
69p.

1. Housing surveys. 2. Housing market.
I. Title.

362.6
A52SU
SURVEY OF NURSING HOMES, 1958-1959.
AMERICAN NURSING HOME ASSOCIATION.
SUMMARY OF A SURVEY OF NURSING HOMES,
1958-1959. A STUDY BY THE AMERICAN
NURSING HOME ASSOCIATION AND THE
AMERICAN MEDICAL ASSOCIATION, COUNCIL ON
MEDICAL SERVICE. CHICAGO, AMERICAN
MEDICAL ASSO., COUNCIL ON MEDICAL
SERVICE, 1960?
5P.
THIS IS ONLY AN INQUIRY INTO MEDICAL
CARE FACILITIES OF NURSING HOMES, NOT A
STATISTICAL INVENTORY TYPE SURVEY AS
THAT OF AUG. 28 , 1957.

(CONTINUED ON NEXT CARD)

690.072
F67
A survey of progress in house building.
Forbes, W S
A survey of progress in house building.
Garston, Eng., Building Research Station,
1969.
88-91p. (U.K. Building Research Station.
Current paper 25/69)
Reprinted from: Building technology and
management, Apr., 1969, pp. 88-91.

1. Building construction - Labor requirements. I. U.K. Building Research Station.
II. Title.

658
G25s

Survey of progress in implementing the planning-programming-budgeting system in Executive agencies.
U.S. General Accounting Office.
Survey of progress in implementing the planning-programming-budgeting system in Executive agencies. Report to the Congress by the Comptroller General of the United States. Wash., 1969.
103p.

1. Management. 2. Budget. 3. Public administration. I. Title: Planning-programming-budgeting system. II. Title.

711
(016)
C65
no.
138

Survey of recent housing studies.
Toizer, Alfred.
Survey of recent housing studies: an annotated guide. Philadelphia, City Planning Commission, 1970.
39p. (Council of Planning Librarians. Exchange bibliography no. 138)

1. Planning - Bibl. 2. Federal housing programs - Bibl. 3. Housing - Philadelphia Bibl. I. Philadelphia. City Planning Commission. II. Title. (Series: Council of Planning Librarians. Exchange Bibliography no. 138)

728.1
(016)
P34

Survey of recent housing studies.
Philadelphia. City Planning Commission.
Survey of recent housing studies; an annotated guide. Philadelphia, 1970.
36p.

1. Housing - Bibliography. 2. Housing market - Bibliography. I. Title

---

728.1
:308
(68)
S68

A survey of rent-paying capacity of urban natives in South Africa.
South African Council for Scientific and Industrial Research.
A survey of rent-paying capacity of urban natives in South Africa. Report of the Committee on Socio-Economic Surveys for Bantu Housing Research. Pretoria, 1960.
123p. diagrs., tables.

1. Housing surveys - Union of South Africa. 2. Family income and expenditure - Housing - Union of South Africa.   I. Title.

690.015
(41)
U54s

Survey of research and development for the construction industry.
U.K. Ministry of Public Building and Works.
Survey of research and development for the construction industry. London, H.M.S.O., 1968.
177p. (U.K. Ministry of Public Building and Works. Directorate of Research and Information. R & D bulletin no. SFB Aa2)
1. Building research - U.K. 2. U.K. - Building research. 3. Building industry - U.K. 4. U.K. - Building industry. I. Title.

333.332
B11s

Survey of residential land pricing methods.
Babcock (Frederick M.) and Co.
Survey of residential land pricing methods. Washington, [1961]
103p.
Prepared under contract no. 561-OA-61 with Urban Renewal Administration.

1. Real property - Valuation. 2. Real property - Surveys. 3. Appraisal. I. U.S. Urban Renewal Administration. II. Title.

728.1
(77595)
168

Survey of residents in homes purchased from Northside Citizens' Neighborhood Conserva...
U.S. Dept. of Housing and Urban Development.
Survey of residents in homes purchased from Northside Citizens' Neighborhood Conservation Corporation. Wash., [1970]
52p.
U.S. Dept. of Housing and Urban Development. Low-Income Housing Demonstration Program.

1. Low-income housing - Milwaukee. 2. Housing surveys - Milwaukee. I. Northside Citizens' Neighborhood Conservation Corporation. II. Title. III. U.S. HUD-Low-income Housing Demonstration Pro gram. Milwaukee.

691.7
:620.19
A73

A survey of salt deposits in compressors of flight gas turbine engines.
Ashbrook, Richard L
A survey of salt deposits in compressors of flight gas turbine engines. Wash., National Aeronautics and Space Administration, 1969.
23p. (NASA Technical note TN D-4999)

1. Corrosion. 2. Strains and stresses. I. U.S. National Aeronautics and Space Administration. II. Title.

339.5
(7946)
A75

Survey of San Francisco Bay and tributaries.
U.S. Army. Corps of Engineers, San Francisco.
Technical report on barriers; a part of the comprehensive survey of San Francisco Bay and tributaries, California. San Francisco, 1963.
293p.

1. Natural resources - San Francisco Bay Area.   I. Title: Survey of San Francisco Bay and tributaries.

323.4
C65s

Survey of school desegregation in the Southern and border States, 1965-66.
U.S. Commission on Civil Rights.
Survey of school desegregation in the Southern and border States, 1965-66. Wash., Govt. Print. Off., 1966.
70p.

1. Civil rights. 2. Schools. 3. Education - Negroes. I. Title.

728.1
1362.6
(77418)
A55

SURVEY OF SENIOR CITIZENS IN KALAMAZOO.
ALLEN, WILLIAM D
SURVEY OF SENIOR CITIZENS IN KALAMAZOO, A STUDY SPONSORED BY THE KALAMAZOO COMMITTEE ON AGING OF THE COUNCIL OF SOCIAL AGENCIES OF KALAMAZOO. PREPARED BY WILLIAM D. ALLEN AND SAMUEL V. BENNETT. KALAMAZOO, WESTERN MICHIGAN UNIVERSITY, 1961
58P.
1. HOUSING FOR THE AGED - KALAMAZOO, MICH. 2. OLD AGE - KALAMAZOO, MICH. I. KALAMAZOO COMMITTEE ON AGING. II. BENNETT, SAMUEL V. III. TITLE.

534.83
P68s

A survey of sonic boom experiments.
Powers, John O
A survey of sonic boom experiments, by John O. Powers and Domenic J. Maglieri. [Wash.] Federal Aviation Administration: National Aeronautics and Space Administration, 1968.
46p.
Prepared for the 1968 Aviation and Space Conference of the American Society of Mechanical Engineers, June 16-19, 1968, Beverly Hills, Calif.
1. Noise. 2. Air Transportation. I. Maglieri, Domenic J., jt. au. II. U.S. Federal Aviation Administration. III. Title.

058.7
r026
S87

Survey of special libraries serving the Federal Government, 1965. Compiled by Frank L. Schick, Director, School of Library and Information Science, University of Wisconsin, Milwaukee, in cooperation with the Federal Library Committee, Paul Howard, Executive Secretary and the National Center of Educational Statistics, U.S. Office of Education. Milwaukee, 1967.
25p.
1. Libraries - Direct. 2. Federal government. I. Schick, Frank L., comp. II. Wisconsin. University. School of Library and Information Scien ce)
(Cont'd on next card)

058.7
r026
S87

Survey of special libraries serving Federal Government...1967. (Card 2)

III. Federal Library Committee, Wash., D.C. IV. U.S. National Center of Educational Statistics.

026
S23

Survey of special libraries serving the Federal government.
Schick, Frank L
Survey of special libraries serving the Federal government. Prepared by Frank L. Schick with the assistance of Paul Howard, in cooperation with the National Center for Educational Statistics. Washington, U.S. Dept. of Health, Education, and Welfare, Office of Education, for sale by the Supt. of Docs., Govt. Print. Off., 1968.
108p. (OE-15067)

1. Libraries. 2. Federal government. 3. Wages and salaries. I. Howard, Paul, jt. au. II. U.S. National Center for Educational Statistics. III. U.S. Office of Education. IV. Title.

711.400.15
A52su

A survey of spending on urban-regional research by selected public bodies in Canada in 1965-66.
Anderson, Bruce.
A survey of spending on urban-regional research by selected public bodies in Canada in 1965-66. Ottawa, Canadian Council on Urban and Regional Research, 1968.
14p.
1. City planning - Research. 2. City planning - Canada. I. Canadian Council of Urban and Regional Research. II. Title.

69
:331.86
N17

A survey of technical education in the building industry.
National Federation of Building Trades Employers.
A survey of technical education in the building industry. London [Sept. 1951]
81 p.

1. Building trades - Study and teaching. I. Title.

388
:308
M17

Survey of technology for high speed ground transport.
Massachusetts Institute of Technology.
Survey of technology for high speed ground transport. Part 1 [of the Northeast Corridor Transportation Project] Prepared for the United States Dept. of Commerce. Cambridge, Mass., 1965.
271p. (PB 168 648)
Distributed by Clearinghouse for Federal Scientific and Technical Information.

1. Traffic surveys. 2. Transportation. 3. Journey to work. I. Northeast Corridor Transportation Project. II. Title.

728.1
N176b
no.28

Survey of the administration of construction codes in selected metropolitan areas.
Williams, Lawrence A
Survey of the administration of construction codes in selected metropolitan areas, by Lawrence A. Williams and others, Washington, National League of Cities, 1968.
125p. (Background paper [no.28] for U.S. National Commission on Urban Problems. Prepared under contract no. H-912 for U.S. Dept. of Housing and Urban Development.
1. Housing. 2. Building codes. 3. Building inspection. I. U.S. National Commission on Urban Problems II. Title. III. National League of Cities.

347
M17

A survey of the comprehensive civil justice plan for crime prevention and control.
Massachusetts. Committee on Law Enforcement and Administration of Justice.
A survey of the comprehensive civil justice plan for crime prevention and control. Boston, [1969?]
106p.

1. Law enforcement. I. Title.

LAW
T
S547

SURVEY OF THE LAW OF PROPERTY.
SMITH, CHESTER H
SURVEY OF THE LAW OF PROPERTY, BY CHESTER H. SMITH AND RALPH E. BOYER. 2D ED. ST. PAUL, WEST PUB. CO., 1971.
510P.

1. REAL PROPERTY. I. BOYER RALPH E., JT. AU. II. TITLE.

728.69
S87

A SURVEY OF THE MOBILE HOME CONSUMER.
CHICAGO, TRAILER TOPICS MAGAZINE,
1959.

34P.

SUMMARY OF QUESTIONNAIRE PREPARED AND
CODED BY C.M. EDWARDS, DIRECTOR,
MICHIGAN STATE UNIVERSITY MOBILE HOMES
EDUCATION PROGRAM.

1. MOBILE HOMES. I. EDWARDS, C.M.
II. MICHIGAN. STATE UNIVERSITY.
MOBILE HOMES EDUCATION PROGRAM.
(CONTINUED ON NEXT CARD)

728.69
S87

A SURVEY OF THE MOBILE HOME CONSUMER.
CHICAGO, TRAILER TOPICS MAGAZINE,
1959. .... (CARD 2)

III. TRAILER TOPICS MAGAZINE.
IV. TITLE: THE MOBILE HOME CONSUMER.

VF
332.72
F56

Florida. University. Bureau of Economic and
Business Research. [Survey of the
mortgage market ...] [1952] (Card 2)

Final report, Research contract no. O-F-63,
Housing and Home Finance Agency.

Project director: George B. Hurff; Staff
technician: Henry Schechter.

Processed.

VF
332.72
F56

Survey of the mortgage market of Jacksonville,
Florida.
Florida. University. Bureau of Economic and
Business Research.
[Survey of the mortgage market of Jackson-
ville, Florida.] [Gainesville, Fla., 1952]
2 pts. graphs, tables.

Contents.-pt. 1. Closing costs and settlement
payments in the Jacksonville, Florida mortgage
market, February 15-August 15, 1950.-pt. 2.
Facility of residential mortgage financing,
Jacksonville, Florida, first six months of 1950.

Folio
711.33
I57

A survey of the present status.
Institute on State Programming for the
70's.
A survey of the present status, effectiveness, and acceptance of planning and
advanced programming in State government.
Composite report. [n.p.] 1967.
87p.
U.S. Dept. of Housing and Urban Development. UPAP.
Information incorporated in report is
also available on punched cards and this
file of punched cards is maintained by the
Office of ADP Systems Management
and Operations. Contact Library Director
for use of punched cards.
(Cont'd on next card)

Folio
711.33
I57

Institute on State Programming for the
70's. A survey...1967. (Card 2)

1. State planning - Automation.
2. State planning - Statistics. I. Title.
II. U.S. HUD-UPAP.

538.56
A17

Survey of the state of the art: social, political, and economic models and simulations.
ABT Associates, Cambridge, Mass.
Survey of the state of the art: social,
political, and economic models and simulations.
Summary volume. Prepared for the [U.S.]
National Commission on Technology, Automation,
and Economic Progress, Wash. D.C. Cambridge,
1965.
18p.

1. Automation. 2. Governmental research.
I. U.S. National Commission on Technology,
Automation and Economic Progress. II. Title.

658.3
H58

Survey of training needs report.
U.S. Housing and Home Finance Agency. Office
of the Administrator. Personnel Division.
Survey of training needs report. Washington,
1958.
20p.

1. Personnel management. I. Title.

658.3
H58
Sept.
1965

Survey of training needs report.
U.S. Housing and Home Finance Agency.
Office of the Administrator. Personnel
Division.
Survey of training needs report.
Washington, 1965.
[26]p.

1. Personnel management. 2. Housing -
Study and teaching. I. Title.

355.58
B62

A survey of underground utility tunnel
practice.
Boegly, W J Jr.
A survey of underground utility tunnel
practice, by W.J. Boegly, Jr. and W.L.
Griffith. Oak Ridge, Tenn., Oak Ridge
National Laboratory operated by Union
Carbide Corporation for the U.S. Atomic
Energy Commission, 1967.
115p. (ORNL-TM-1714)
Bibliography: p. 109-110.
1. Civilian defense. 2. Public utilities.
I. Griffith, W.L., jt. au. II. U.S. National Labora-
tory, Oak Ridge, Tenn. III. Union Carbide Corp.
V. Title.

650.015
F67

Survey of university business and economic
research projects.
U.S. Bureau of Foreign and Domestic Commerce.
Office of Industry and Commerce.
Survey of university business and economic
research projects,
Washington,
v.
For full information see shelf list card.

Title varies: Survey of university business
research projects, 1943-1944.
Processed.

362.6
(77427)
L15

SURVEY OF UNLICENSED NURSING HOMES
IN THE LANSING AREA.
LANSING, MICHIGAN. COMMUNITY SERVICES
COUNCIL.
SURVEY OF UNLICENSED NURSING HOMES
IN THE LANSING AREA. LANSING, 1962.
31P.

1. NURSING HOMES - LANSING, MICH.
I. TITLE.

711.74
I57s

A survey of urban arterial design standards.
Institute for Municipal Engineering.
A survey of urban arterial design standards.
[Final report of the IME Committee on Streets
and Traffic] Chicago, American Public Works
Association, 1969.
91p.

Mary Ann Zimmerman, Principal investigator.

Bibliography: p. 90-91.

1. Streets. I. Automotive Safety Foundation.
II. Title. III. Title: Urban arterial
design standards.

711.4
F56s

Survey of urban information and technical
service needs in Florida.
Florida. Bureau of Planning.
Survey of urban information and technical
service needs in Florida. [Tallahassee, Fla.]
Bureau of Planning, Dept. of Administration,
1969.
67p.
Preparation of report financed in part
through an Urban information and technical
assistance grant from the Dept. of Housing and
Urban Development.
1. City planning - Automation. 2. Local
government - Florida. 3. State government -
Florida. I. U.S. Dept. of Housing and
Urban Development. II. Title.

711.14
(77311)
C34v
1963

Survey of vacant land in the City of
Chicago, 1963.
Chicago. Dept. of City Planning.
Survey of vacant land in the City of
Chicago, 1963. Chicago, 1964.
91p. (Its land use study series no. 2)

"This report provides essential bench-
mark data on the supply of vacant land."

1. Land use - Chicago. 2. Land use -
Surveys. I. Title. II. Title: Vacant
land in the City of Chicago.

658.511
M42

Survey of working conditions.
Michigan. University. Survey Research
Center.
Survey of working conditions. Final
report on univariate and bivariate tables.
Wash., U.S. Dept. of Labor, Employment
Standards Div., 1971.
484p.
Bibliography: p. 485-486.

1. Job analysis. I. U.S. Dept. of
Labor. (Employment Standards Administration) II. Title.

312
C25
HVet

Survey of World War II veterans and dwelling
unit vacancy and occupancy ...
U.S. Bureau of the Census.
Survey of World War II veterans and dwelling
unit vacancy and occupancy in ... [109 selected
localities] Washington, 1946-1947.
114 pts. graphs, tables. (Its HVet)
Survey made at the request of the National
Housing Agency.
Loose-leaf binder.
1. Census-Housing. 2. Housing surveys. I. U.S.
National Housing Agency. II. Title.

711.585
(5694)
I57s

Survey old town - Ashkeson (Migdal)
Institute for Planning and Development,
Tel Aviv.
Survey old town - Ashkeson (Migdal) Pre-
pared for the Physical Planning Div. of the
Ministry of Housing. Tel Aviv, 1967.
24p.
Presented to the Authority for Clearance
and Rebuilding of Rehabilitation Areas.

1. Urban renewal - Israel. I. Title.
II. Israel. Ministry of Housing.

691
I55

Survey on construction materials demonstration
and training center.
Illinois Institute of Technology. Armour Research Foundation.
Survey on construction materials demonstration and training center. Final report to
Technical Cooperation Administration, Dept.
of State. Chicago, 1951.
245p. illus., maps, tables.

1. Building materials. I. Title. II. U.S. Technical Cooperation Administration.

500
UN

Survey on the main trends of inquiry in
the field of the natrual sciences.
United Nations. (Economic and Social
Council)
Survey on the main trends of inquiry in
the field of the natural sciences, the
dissemination of scientific knowledge and
the application of such knowledge for
peaceful ends, by Pierre Auger. New
York, 1960.
445p. (UNESCO/NS/ES/19)

1. Thirtieth session, agenda item 3 (e). 2. Science.
I. Auger, Pierre. II. Title.

711.33
I57

A survey of the present status, effectiveness,
and acceptance of planning and advanced...
Institute on State Programming for the 70's.
A survey of the present status, effectiveness,
and acceptance of planning and advanced programming in state government. State report.
Chapel Hill, 1967-

v.

For Library holdings see main entry.
One volume for each of the 50 states.

1. State planning - Automation. 2. State
planning - Surveys. I. Title.

331
A77
SURVEY ON EMPLOYEE TURNOVER.
ASSOCIATION OF CASUALTY AND SURETY
COMPANIES. DEPT. OF RESEARCH.
SURVEY ON EMPLOYEE TURNOVER. NEW YORK
[1961]
19L.

1. EMPLOYMENT. I. TITLE.

301.15
(016)
F72
Survey research on comparative social change.
Frey, Frederick W   ed.
Survey research on comparative social change:
a bibliography. With the assistance of the
Staff of the Human Factors in Modernization
Project, Center for International Studies,
M.I.T. Cambridge, Mass., M.I.T. Press, 1969.
1v.
1. Social change - Bibl. 2. Social science
research - Bibl. I. Massachusetts Institute
of Technology. Center for International
Studies. II. Title.

526
P25
SURVEYING.
Penman, A   D   M
Measuring movements of engineering structures,
by A.D.M. Penman and J.A. Charles. Garston,
Eng., Building Research Station, 1971.
16p. (U.K. Building Research Station.
Current paper CP 32/71)
Reprinted from: Proceedings of the 13th
International Congress of Surveyors, Wiesbaden,
1971, Commission 6, Paper 605,4.
1. Surveying. I. Charles, J.A., jt. au.
II. U.K. Building Research Station.
III. Title.

VF
320
F72
A survey on the problem areas affecting
freedom.
Freedom House, New York.
A survey on the problem areas affecting
freedom, New York, 1964.
30p.
At head of title: Perspectives on
freedom: 1964.

1. Democracy. 2. Civil rights.
I. Title.

711.585.1
(74934)
E17s
Survey results and base line data, 19
East Orange, N.J. Model Cities Program.
Survey results and base line data, 19
19 . East Orange, N.J., 19
v.

For Library holdings see main entry.

1. Model cities - East Orange, N.J.
I. Title.

333.332
U54
Surveying.
U.K. Ministry of Labour and National
Service.
Surveying. London, H.M. Stat. Off.,
1958.
55p. illus., diagrs. (Choice of
careers 87)

1. Appraisal. I. Title.

330
(77311)
C342
A SURVEY PORTRAYING THE RESOURCES OF
THE CHICAGO INDUSTRIAL AREAS FOR
CHICAGO ASSOCIATION OF COMMERCE AND
INDUSTRY.
A SURVEY PORTRAYING THE RESOURCES OF
THE CHICAGO INDUSTRIAL AREAS FOR
BUSINESS EXECUTIVES AND ENGINEERS
INTERESTED IN PLANT ESTABLISHMENT.
CHICAGO, 1946
1 V. (LOOSE-LEAF)

1. ECONOMIC BASE STUDIES - CHICAGO.
I. TITLE.

526
A52
SURVEYING.
AMERICAN SOCIETY OF CIVIL ENGINEERS.
TECHNICAL PROCEDURE FOR CITY SURVEYS.
COMPILED BY THE COMMITTEE ON CITY SURVEYS.
ADOPTED JANUARY 15, 1934. NEW YORK, 1934.
125P. (ITS MANUALS FOR ENGINEERING
PRACTICE, NO. 10)

1. SURVEYING. I. TITLE: CITY SURVEYS.

Surveying
   x   Land surveying
   xx   Engineering

308
H182
SURVEY RELIABILITY AND INTERVIEWER
COMPETENCE.
HAUCK, MATHEW.
SURVEY RELIABILITY AND INTERVIEWER
COMPETENCE, BY MATHEW HAUCK AND STANLEY
STEINKAMP. URBANA, ILLINOIS, BUREAU OF
ECONOMIC AND BUSINESS RESEARCH,
UNIVERSITY OF ILLINOIS, 1964.
112P. (INTER-UNIVERSITY COMMITTEE FOR
RESEARCH ON CONSUMER BEHAVIOR. CONSUMER
SAVING PROJECT. STUDIES IN CONSUMER
SAVINGS, NO. 4)

1. SURVEY METHODS. I. STEINKAMP,
STANLEY, JT. AU.
II. ILLINOIS. UNIVERSITY. BUREAU OF
(CONTINUED ON NEXT CARD.)

LAW
T
C5162t
Surveying.
Clark, Frank Emerson.
A treatise on the law of surveying and
boundaries. 3d ed., by John S. Grimes.
Indianapolis, Bobbs-Merrill, 1959.
1031p.

1. Surveying. I. Grimes, John S. II. Title.
III. Title: The law of surveying and boundaries.

620
D25
Surveying.
De Leeuw, A
The profession of the land in western
Europe. Gold medal paper 1964. London, The
Furnival Press, 1964.
29p.
At head of title: The Brussels Conference
of Surveyors, 1964.

1. Surveying. I. Brussels Conference of
Surveyors, 1964. II. Title.

308
H182
HAUCK, MATHEW. SURVEY RELIABILITY AND ...
1964.   (CARD 2)

ECONOMIC AND BUSINESS RESEARCH.
III. TITLE. IV. TITLE: INTERVIEWER
COMPETENCE.

526
H15
SURVEYING.
Hamburg. Baubehörde.
125 Jahre hamburgische Stadt- und Katasterver-
messung. Eine Stadt wird vermessen. Hamburg,
1970.
84p. (Hamburger Schriften zum Bau-, Wohnungs-
und Siedlungswesen, Heft 51)

1. Surveying.

526
H65
SURVEYING.
Honey, F   C
A further experiment in mechanisation,
by F.C. Honey and A.W. Gynn. London,
Royal Institution of Chartered Surveyors,
[1968?]
[3]p.

1. Surveying. I. Gynn, A.W., jt. au.
II. Royal Institution of Chartered
Surveyors. III. Title.

728.1
:333.63
(747)
N28s
Survey report on rental housing.
New York (State) Div. of Housing and
Community Renewal.
Survey report on rental housing. New
York, 1965.
93p.

1. Rental housing - New York (State)
I. Title.

526
H43
SURVEYING.
HIGHWAY RESEARCH BOARD.
ELECTRONIC SURVEYING, 1960 DEVELOPMENTS.
PRESENTED AT THE 39TH ANNUAL MEETING,
JANUARY 11-15, 1960. WASHINGTON, 1960.
31P. (ITS BULLETIN 258)

1. SURVEYING. I. TITLE.

728
:308
M25
Surveying.
Melville, Ian A
Structural surveys of dwelling houses, by
Ian A. Melville and Ian A. Gordon with a
chapter on the legal position of the surveyor
by Peter Scott. Rev. ed. London, Estates
Gazette, 1965.
259p.

1. Architecture, Domestic - Surveys.
2. Surveying. I. Gordon, Ian A., jt. au.
II. Scott, Peter. III. Title.

Survey Research Center

see

Michigan. University. Survey Research Center.

711.6
P17
SURVEYING.
PARKER, HARRY.
SIMPLIFIED SITE ENGINEERING FOR
ARCHITECTS AND BUILDERS, BY HARRY PARKER
AND JOHN W. MACGUIRE. NEW YORK, WILEY,
1954.
250P.

1. SITE PLANNING. 2. SURVEYING.
I. MACGUIRE, JOHN W., JT. AU.
II. TITLE.

526
N28
SURVEYING.
New Mexico. State Board of Registration
for Professional Engineers and Land
Surveyors.
Report, 1969
Santa Fe, 19

v. annual.

For Library holdings see main entry.

1. Surveying. 2. Engineering.

526
P15

SURVEYING.
Pan American Institute of Geography and History.
Canadian Section.
Surveying and mapping of urban areas (discussion of basic technical and organizational problems) Papers presented at the North American Symposium on Urban Surveying and Mapping, Mexico City, 13-17 January 1969. [n.p.] 1969.
52p.

1. Surveying. 2. Maps and mapping.
3. Photogrammetry. I. North American Symposium on Urban Surveying and Mapping, Mexico City, 1969. II. Title.

728.6
B87S

SURVEYING STRUCTURAL LEVEL AND CONDITION OF FARMHOUSES.
BURROUGHS, ROY J
SURVEYING STRUCTURAL LEVEL AND CONDITION OF FARMHOUSES. WASHINGTON, 1952.
33-43P.

(IN AGRICULTURAL ECONOMICS RESEARCH, V. 4, NO. 2, APR. 1952)
CONCERNS PART H OF THE U.S. BUREAU OF AGRICULTURAL ECONOMICS SURVEY OF FARM HOUSING AND OTHER FARM BUILDINGS, 1950.

1. FARM BUILD-INGS. 2. HOUSING SURVEYS. I. U .S. BUREAU OF
(CONTINUED ON NEXT CARD)

LAW
T
C158s

Surveys, subdivision and platting, and boundaries
Campbell, Ernest H
Surveys, subdivision and platting, and boundaries. Washington State laws and judicial decisions, by Ernest H. Campbell and Joshua H. Vogel. Seattle, Bureau of Governmental Research and Services, University of Washington, 1965.
215p. (Washington. University. Bureau of Governmental Research and Services. Report no. 156; Revision of report no. 137)

Bibliography: p. 214-215.

Continued on next card)

526
A75

SURVEYING.
U.S. Army.
Elements of surveying. Wash., 1971.
1v. (Its TM 5-232)

1. Surveying. I. Title.

728.6
B87S

BURROUGHS, ROY J SURVEYING STRUCTURAL LEVEL ...1952. (CARD 2)

AGRICULTURAL ECONOMICS.
II. AGRICULTURAL ECONOMICS RESEARCH.
III. TITLE.

LAW
T
C158s

Campbell, Ernest H Surveys...(Card 2)

1. Subdivision regulation. 2. Site planning.
I. Vogel, Joshua H. jt. au. II. Washington (State) University. Bureau of Governmental Research and Services. III. Title.

333
G25M

SURVEYING.
U.S. GENERAL LAND OFFICE.
MANUAL OF INSTRUCTIONS FOR THE SURVEY OF THE PUBLIC LANDS OF THE UNITED STATES. 1930. PREPARED AND PUBLISHED UNDER THE DIRECTION OF THE COMMISSIONER OF THE GENERAL LAND OFFICE. REPRINT 1934. WASHINGTON, GOVT. PRINT. OFF., 1934.
530P.

1. PUBLIC LANDS. 2. SURVEYING.

362.6
S87

Surveys and Research Corp., Washington, D.C.
Guide for State surveys on aging; a manual to aid States and communities in program planning for their growing population of older citizens, to assist in preparations for participation in the 1961 White House Conference on Aging. With adaptations for community use. Wash., U.S. Dept. of Health, Education, and Welfare, Staff for the White House Conference on Aging, 1959.
110p.

1. Old age. I. Title. II. U.S. Dept. of Health, Education, and Welfare.

333.38
(797)
V63

Surveys, subdivision and platting, and boundaries.
Vogel, Joshua Holmes, 1889-
Surveys, subdivision and platting, and boundaries. Washington State laws and judicial decisions. Information for city engineers, surveyors, civil engineers, and attorneys, by Joshua H. Vogel, Ernest Howard Campbell [and] Wilbur K. Wilson. Seattle, Bureau of Governmental Research and Services, University of Washington, 1949.
134 p. maps, diagrs. 21 cm. (Washington (State) University. Bureau of Governmental Research and Services, Report no. 96)
"Selected bibliography" : p. 133-134.
1. Subdivision regulation—Wash. 2. Boundaries (Estates)—Washington (State) I. Title. II. Series (Continued on next card)
JA37.W3 no. 96 526.98 A 50-9132
Washington (State) Univ. Library
for Library of Congress [2,†]

526
C65
1960/61

SURVEYING -- CONGRESSES.
CONFERENCE ON LAND SURVEYING. PURDUE UNIVERSITY.
PROCEEDINGS.
LAFAYETTE, IND., PURDUE UNIVERSITY.

V. (PURDUE UNIVERSITY. LAFAYETTE, IND. ENGINEERING EXTENSION DEPT. EXTENSION DEPT. NO.
For Library holdings see main entry
ISSUED AS ENGINEERING BULLETIN OF PURDUE UNIVERSITY.
CONFERENCES SPONSORED BY THE PURDUE UNIVERSITY SC HOOL OF CIVIL ENGINEERING, ITS DIVISION OF ADULT (CONTINUED ON NEXT CARD)

362.6
S87m

Surveys & Research Corp., Washington, D.C.
Market study of the nursing home industry.
Washington, 1969.
65p.

1. Nursing homes. 2. Old age. 3. Hospitals.
4. Housing for the aged. I. Title. II. Title: The nursing home industry.

Vogel, Joshua Holmes Surveys, subdivision and platting, and boundaries ... 1949 (Card 2)

----Supplement. Seattle, Bureau of Governmental Research and Services, Univ. of Washington, Sept. 1951.
9 p. ([Washington (State) University. Bureau of Governmental Research and Services] Report no. 96, suppl.)

526
C65
1960/61

CONFERENCE ON LAND SURVEYING. PURDUE UNIVERSITY. PROCEEDINGS.... (CARD 2)

EDUCATION AND THE INDIANA SOCIETY OF PROFESSIONAL LAND SURVEYORS.

1. SURVEYING -- CONGRESSES. (SERIES)

388
S87

Surveys & Research Corp., Washington, D.C.
The role of transportation in area development and redevelopment. Draft report. Wash., 1962.
51p.
Bibliography: p. i-viii.

1. Transportation. 2. Journey to work.
3. Highways. I. Title.

355.58
A52s

Survival and recovery; industrial preparedness in the nuclear age.
American Management Association.
Survival and recovery; industrial preparedness in the nuclear age. New York, 1962.
36p. (AMA management bulletin no. 15)

1. Atomic bomb.
2. Civilian defense. I. Title.
(Series)

526
P15

Surveying and mapping of urban areas.
Pan American Institute of Geography and History.
Canadian Section.
Surveying and mapping of urban areas (discussion of basic technical and organizational problems) Papers presented at the North American Symposium on Urban Surveying and Mapping, Mexico City, 13-17 January 1969. [n.p.] 1969.
52p.

1. Surveying. 2. Maps and mapping.
3. Photogrammetry. I. North American Symposium on Urban Surveying and Mapping, Mexico City, 1969. II. Title.

690.5
:551.5
W45

Surveys of winter working practices in Scotland.
Wilson, P H
Surveys of winter working practices in Scotland. Garston, Eng., Building Research Station, Ministry of Technology, 1965.
5p. (U.K. Building Research Station. Building research current papers. Construction series 20)

1. Winter construction. 2. Labor productivity. I. U.K. Building Research Station. II. Title.

355.58
(747)
N2b

SURVIVAL IN A NUCLEAR ATTACK.
NEW YORK (STATE) COMMITTEE ON FALLOUT PROTECTION.
SURVIVAL IN A NUCLEAR ATTACK; PLAN FOR PROTECTION FROM RADIOACTIVE FALLOUT. REPORT TO GOV. NELSON A. ROCKEFELLER. ALBANY, 1960.
66P.

1. CIVILIAN DEFENSE. 2. ATOMIC BOMB.
I. TITLE. II. TITLE: RADIOACTIVE FALLOUT.

VF
691
H68s

Surveying materials used in house construction.
U.S. Housing and Home Finance Agency. Office of the Administrator. Division of Housing Research.
Surveying materials used in house construction. Washington, D.C., July 1951.
10 p.

"For immediate release, July 18, 1951".
"This article on results of the HHFA Materials Use Survey will appear in the forthcoming first issue of Housing Research, a new quarterly publication of the agency".
Processed.
(Continued on next card)

308
P17

Surveys, polls, and samples.
Parten, Mildred Bernice, 1902-
Surveys, polls, and samples; practical procedures. New York, Harper [1950]
xii, 624 p. (Harper's social science series)

Bibliography: p. 537-602.

1. Social surveys. 2. Public opinion polls. 3. Survey methods. 4. Sampling. I. Title.

355.56
(778664)
F22

SURVIVAL IN PUBLIC SHELTERS.
U.S. FEDERAL CIVIL DEFENSE ADMINISTRATION.
SURVIVAL IN PUBLIC SHELTERS; A PAPER BASED ON A TECHNICAL STUDY OF HYPOTHETICAL NUCLEAR ATTACK ON THE METROPOLITAN AREA OF ST. LOUIS. WASHINGTON, GOVT. PRINT. OFF., 1957.
41P.

1. CIVILIAN DEFENSE -- ST. LOUIS.
2. ATOMIC BOMB. I. TITLE.

330
H17s   Harrer, J George.
Survival or fulfillment. An address given at the California Institute of Technology Conference on the Next Ninety Years, March 7, 1967. New York, Rockefeller Foundation, 1967.
15p.

1. Social conditions. 2. International relations. I. Rockefeller Foundation, New York. II. Title.

332.3
C65su   U.S. Congress. Senate. Committee on Finance.
Suspensions of investment credit and accelerated depreciation. Hearings before the Committee on Finance, United States Senate, Eighty-ninth Congress, second session on H.R. 17607, an act to suspend the investment credit and the allowance of accelerated depreciation in the case of certain real property. Wash., Govt. Print. Off., 1966.
474p.
Hearing held Oct. 3-6, 1966.

1. Credit.   2. Investments.
3. Real pro-   perty. I. Title.

VF
33(73)
C655   The sustaining economic forces ahead.
U. S. *Congress. Joint Committee on the Economic Report.*
The sustaining economic forces ahead; materials prepared for the Joint Committee on the Economic Report by the Committee staff. Washington, U. S. Govt. Print. Off., 1952.
viii, 70 p. diagrs., tables. 24 cm.

At head of title: 82d Cong., 2d sess. Joint committee print.

1. U. S.—Econ. condit.—1945-   I. Title.

HC106.5.A532 195~   330.973   52-63221

Library of Congress   [3]

355.58
(759)
F56   SURVIVAL PLAN.
FLORIDA. CENTRAL FLORIDA CIVIL DEFENSE OPERATIONAL AREA.
PRELIMINARY OPERATIONAL SURVIVAL PLAN. 1958. N.P., 1958.
1 V. (VARIOUS PAGINGS)

1. CIVILIAN DEFENSE - FLORIDA.
I. TITLE: SURVIVAL PLAN.

332.3
C65S
1966
S-R   SUSPENSIONS OF INVESTMENT CREDIT AND ACCELERATED DEPRECIATION.
U.S. CONGRESS. SENATE. COMMITTEE ON FINANCE.
SUSPENSIONS OF INVESTMENT CREDIT AND ACCELERATED DEPRECIATION. REPORT...TO ACCOMPANY H.R. 17607... WASHINGTON, GOVT. PRINT. OFF., 1966.
45P. (89TH CONGRESS, 2D SESSION. SENATE. REPORT NO. 1724)

1. CREDIT.   2. REAL PROPERTY.
3. INVESTMENTS.   I. TITLE.

331
(669)
L11   Suter, Ann C
U.S. Bureau of Labor Statistics.
Labor in Nigeria, by Ann C. Suter and others. [Prepared] in cooperation with Agency for International Development. Washington, Govt. Print. Off., 1963.
45. (Report no. 261)

1. Employment - Nigeria. 2. Wages and salaries. 3. Labor relations - Nigeria. I. Suter, Ann C. II. U.S. Agency for International Development.

355.58
(759)
F56P   SURVIVAL PLAN.
FLORIDA. NORTHEAST FLORIDA CIVIL DEFENSE OPERATIONAL AREA.
PRELIMINARY OPERATIONAL SURVIVAL PLAN. 1958. N.P., 1958.
1 V. (VARIOUS PAGINGS)

1. CIVILIAN DEFENSE - FLORIDA.
I. TITLE: SURVIVAL PLAN.

5207-
5219   SUSQUEHANNA CO., PA. PLANNING COMMISSION.
COMPREHENSIVE PLAN: 1, POPULATION; 2, PUBLIC FACILITIES STUDY; 3, HISTORICAL DEVELOPMENT; 4, DEVELOPMENT POLICIES, STANDARDS AND OBJECTIVES; 5, HOUSING; 6, PHYSICAL FEATURES AND NATURAL RESOURCES; 7, DEVELOPMENT AIDS PROGRAM; 8, EXTERNAL INFLUENCE FACTORS STUDY; 9, AN INVENTORY OF EXISTING LAND USE; 10, TRANSPORTATION STUDY; 11, FISCAL AND GOVERNMENTAL STRUCTURE; 12, ECONOMIC BASE STUDY; 13, RELATED STUDIES   OF AN AREA-WIDE SCOPE. BY NORT HERN TIER REGIONAL
(CONTINUED ON NEXT CARD)

690.091.82
:613.5
N17h   Sutermeister, Oscar. Inadequacies and inconsistencies in the definition of substandard housing.
U.S. National Commission on Urban Problems.
Housing code standards: three critical studies. Wash., Govt. Print. Off., 1969.
108p. (Research report no. 19)
Contents.-The development, objective, and adequacy of current housing code standards, by E.W. Mood.-Administrative provisions of housing codes, by B. Lieberman.-Inadequacies and inconsistencies in the definition of substandard housing, by O. Sutermeister.
1. Housing codes. 2. Housing - Standards. 3. U.S. Dept.   of Housing and Urban Development.
(Cont'd on next card)

300
T69   Surviving the future.
Toynbee, Arnold.
Surviving the future. New York, Oxford University Press, 1971.
164p.

1. Science and civilization. 2. Social conditions. I. Title.

5207-
5219   SUSQUEHANNA CO., PA. PLANNING COMMISSION. COMPREHENSIVE PLAN.... 1969.   (CARD 2)

PLANNING COMMISSION. MONTROSE, PA., 1969.
13 V. (HUD 701 REPORT)

1. MASTER PLAN - SUSQUEHANNA CO., PA. I. NORTHERN TIER REGIONAL PLANNING COMMISSION.   II. HUD. 701. SUSQUEHANNA CO., PA.

690.091.82
:613.5
N17h   U.S. National Commission on Urban Problems.
Housing code standards...1969. (Card 2)

I. Mood, Eric W. The development, objective, and adequacy of current housing code standards. II. Lieberman, Barnet. Administrative provisions of housing codes.
III. Sutermeister, Oscar. Inadequacies and inconsistencies in the definition of substandard housing. IV. Title.

351.1
C65s
1970
H-H   Survivor annuities.
U.S. Congress. House. Committee on Post Office and Civil Service.
Survivor annuities. Hearings before the Subcommittee on Retirement, Insurance, and Health Benefits of the Committee on Post Office and Civil Service, House of Representatives, Ninety-first Congress, second session on H.R. 3661 and related bills, a bill to amend chapter 83, title 5, United States Code, to eliminate the reduction in the annuities of employees or members who elected reduced annuities in order to provide a survivor annuity if predeceased by the person
(Cont'd on next card)

LAW
T
157usu   Susquehanna River Basin Compact.
Interstate Advisory Committee on the Susquehanna River Basin.
Susquehanna River Basin Compact. Draft, June, 1966. Harrisburg, Pa., 1966.
53p.
"Created by action of the states of New York, Pennsylvania, and Maryland...with the cooperation of the U.S. Dept. of Housing and Urban Development and others."

1. Regional planning - Susquehanna River Basin.
2. Water resources - Susquehanna River Basin.
3. Land use - Susque-   hanna River Basin.
I. U.S. Dept. of   Housing and Urban Development.   II. Title.

711.417
(75529)
S87   Sutermeister, Oscar.
A neighborhood plan for the development of proposed neighborhood C-17 B, Fairfax County, Virginia. [Prepared in cooperation with] members and representatives of the Ravenwood Park Civic Association. Bethesda, Md., 1959.
17p.

Cover title: A planned community; Ravenwood, Buffalo Hill, Ravenwood Park, Sleepy Hollow Manor, Fairfax County.
(Continued on next card)

351.1
C65s
1970
H-H   U.S. Congress. House. Committee on Post Office and Civil Service. Survivor...1970.
(Card 2)

named as survivor and permit a retired employee or member to designate a new spouse as survivor if predeceased by the person named as survivor at the time of retirement. Wash., Govt. Print. Off., 1970.
74p.
Hearings held June 10 - Aug. 4, 1970.
1. Federal civil   service. 2. Old age. I. Title.

628.1
C65su
1970
H-H   Susquehanna River Basin compact.
U.S. Congress. House. Committee on the Judiciary.
Susquehanna River Basin compact. Hearings before Subcommittee no. 3 of the Committee on the Judiciary, House of Representatives, Ninety-first Congress, second session on H.J. Res. 380, H.J. Res. 381, H.J. Res. 382, H.J. Res. 543 and H.J. Res. 609 consenting to the Susquehanna River Basin Compact... Wash., Govt. Print. Off., 1970.
203p.
Hearings held June 4-Sept. 30, 1970.
1. Water resou   rces. 2. Intergovernmental relations. I. Ti   tle.

711.417
(75529)
S87   Sutermeister, Oscar. A neighborhood ...
(Card 2)

1. Planned communities - Fairfax Co., Va.
I. Ravenwood Park Civic Association.

332.3
C653SU   SUSPENSIONS OF INVESTMENT CREDIT AND ACCELERATED DEPRECIATION.
U.S. CONGRESS. CONFERENCE COMMITTEES, 1966.
SUSPENSIONS OF INVESTMENT CREDIT AND ACCELERATED DEPRECIATION. CONFERENCE REPORT TO ACCOMPANY H.R. 17607. WASHINGTON, GOVT. PRINT. OFF., 1966.
11P. (89TH CONGRESS, 2D SESSION. HOUSE. REPORT NO. 2308)

1. CREDIT.   2. REAL PROPERTY.
3. INVESTMENTS.   I. TITLE.

3700   SUSSNA (STEPHEN) ASSOCIATES.
DELRAN, N.J. PLANNING BOARD.
MASTER PLAN REPORT, DELRAN TOWNSHIP, BURLINGTON COUNTY, NEW JERSEY. BY STEPHEN SUSSNA ASSOCIATES. DELRAN, 1969.
106P. (HUD 701 REPORT)

1. CITY PLANNING - DELRAN, N.J.
I. SUSSNA (STEPHEN) ASSOCIATES.
II. HUD. 701. DELRAN, N.J.

Sutermeister, Oscar, jt. au.

VF
711.5
(753)
D47
Prelim.
no. 6   Lewis, Harold M
Off-street parking and loading, by Harold M. Lewis and Oscar Sutermeister. Wash., Washington Zoning Revision Office, 1956.
70p. (Rezoning study of the District of Columbia. Preliminary report no. 6)

1. Zoning - District of Columbia.
2. Parking - District of Columbia.
I. District of Columbia. Zoning Revision Office.   II. Sutermeister, Oscar, jt. au.   III. Title.

711.55
(755)
N67
SUTERMEISTER, OSCAR.
NORTHERN VIRGINIA REGIONAL PLANNING AND
ECONOMIC DEVELOPMENT COMMISSION.
PROBLEMS OF COMMERCIAL LAND USE
PLANNING IN THE NORTHERN VIRGINIA
REGION; A REPORT BY OSCAR SUTERMEISTER.
ARLINGTON, VA., 1962.
117P.

1. BUSINESS DISTRICTS - VIRGINIA.
2. CITY PLANNING - VIRGINIA. I. SUTERMEISTER, OSCAR. II. TITLE:
COMMERCIAL LAND USE.

LAW
T
S873st
Sutherland, Jabez Gridley, 1825-1902.
Statutes and statutory construction, by J. G. Sutherland.
3d ed., by Frank E. Horack, Jr. ... Chicago, Callaghan and
company, 1943.

3 v. 24½ cm.

On cover: Sutherland Statutory construction.

v.2 c.2

1. Statutes—U. S. 2. Legislation—U. S. 3. Law—U. S.—Interpretation and construction. I. Horack, Frank Edward, 1907— ed.
II. Title.

43—9449

Library of Congress

711.74
(79529)
S87
Sutherlin, Or. City Planning Commission.
A plan for arterial streets in Sutherlin,
Oregon. In cooperation with the Bureau of
Municipal Research and Service, University
of Oregon. Sutherlin, 1958.
15p.

U.S. Urban Renewal Adm. UPAP.

1. Street planning - Sutherlin, Or. I. Oregon.
University. Bureau of Municipal Research and Service. II. U.S.
URA-UPAP.
Sutherlin, Or.

355.58
S87
Sutermeister, Oscar
Reduction of vulnerability in the
Milwaukee area; an exploratory study,
submitted to City of Milwaukee Civil Defense
Administration and Milwaukee Metropolitan
Civil Defense Commission. Milwaukee, 1954.
viii, 74 p. maps.

Bibliographical footnotes.

1. Civilian defense. I. Milwaukee, Wis. Civil
Defense Administration. II. Milwaukee Metropolitan
Civil Defense Comm. III. Title.

331
S87
Sutherland, Robert L
Puede cambiar un adulto. Factores clave
en las relaciones del trabajo en la industria.
2d ed. San Jose, Costa Rica, Escuela Superior de Administracion Publica America Central.
1964.
10p. (San Jose, Costa Rica. Escuela Superior de Administracion Publica America
Central. Aspectos humanos de la administracion
no. 125)
ESAPAC/EXT/002/1000/64.
1. Labor relations. 2. Sociology. 3. Education.
I. San Jose, Costa Rica. Escuela Superior de
Administracion Publica America Central.

333.38
(79529)
072
Sutherlin, Or. City Planning Commission.
Oregon. University. Bureau of Municipal
Research and Service.
Proposed subdivision regulations.
Memorandum to Sutherlin City Planning
Commission. Eugene, Or., 1958.
3p.

U.S. Urban Renewal Adm. UPAP.

1. Subdivision regulation - Sutherlin, Or.
I. Sutherlin, Or. City Planning Commission.
II. U.S. URA-UPAP.
Sutherlin, Or.

711.3
(016)
S87
SUTERMEISTER, OSCAR, COMP.
READING LISTS IN REGIONAL PLANNING:
FINE ARTS S7C ASSIGNED READINGS. 1940
HARVARD SUMMER SCHOOL. CAMBRIDGE,
MASS., HARVARD UNIVERSITY, DEPT. OF FINE
ARTS, 1941.
30L.

1. REGIONAL PLANNING - BIBLIOGRAPHY.
I. HARVARD UNIVERSITY. DEPT. OF FINE
ARTS.

721.25
D68
SUTHERLAND, WILLARD C , JT. AU.
DOUGLASS, PAUL F ED.
RECREATION IN THE AGE OF AUTOMATION.
EDITED BY PAUL F. DOUGLASS, JOHN L.
HUTCHINSON, WILLARD C. SUTHERLAND.
PHILADELPHIA, 1957.
208P. (THE ANNALS OF THE AMERICAN
ACADEMY OF POLITICAL AND SOCIAL
SCIENCE, V. 313).

1. RECREATION. 2. AUTOMATION.
I. HUTCHINSON, JOHN L., JT. AU.
II. SUTHERLAND, WILLARD C., JT. AU.
III. AMERICAN ACADEMY OF POLITICAL
AND SOCIAL SCIENCE.

333.38
(79529)
072p
Sutherlin, Or. City Planning Commission.
Oregon. University. Bureau of Municipal
Research and Service.
Proposed subdivision regulations for
Sutherlin, Oregon. Preliminary draft.
Prepared for the Sutherlin City Planning
Commission. [Eugene, Or.] 1958.
13p.

U.S. Urban Renewal Adm. UPAP.

1. Subdivision regulation - Sutherlin, Or.
I. Sutherlin, Or. City Planning Commission.
II. U.S. URA-UPAP.
Sutherlin, Or.

323.4
S87
Sutherland, Elizabeth, ed.
Letters from Mississippi. New York, New
American Library, 1965.
214p.

C.I.E.O.

A Signet book.

1. Civil rights. 2. Negroes. 3. Minority
groups - Miss. 4. Student Nonviolent Coordinating Committee. I. Title.

LAW
T
C176ar
Sutherland, William A jt.au.
Carrington, Paul.
Articles of partnership for law firms, by
Paul Carrington and William A. Sutherland.
Prepared for the American Bar Association,
Standing Committee on Economics of Law Practice.
[St. Paul] West Publishing Co., 1961.
102p. (American Bar Association. Economics
of law practice series. Pamphlet no. 6)

1. Lawyers. I. Sutherland, William A., jt. au.
II. American Bar Association
(Standing Committee on
Economics of Law Practice)
III. Title.

370
E283
SUTTER, ROBERT.
EDUCATIONAL FACILITIES LABORATORIES.
SCHOOL SCHEDULING BY COMPUTER: THE
STORY OF GASP. REPORT BY JUDITH MURPHY.
CENTER SECTION BY ROBERT SUTTER. NEW
YORK, 1964.
46P.

1. SCHOOLS. 2. AUTOMATION.
I. MURPHY, JUDITH. II. SUTTER, ROBERT.
III. TITLE.

691.328
S87
SUTHERLAND, HALE.
INTRODUCTION TO REINFORCED CONCRETE
DESIGN BY HALE SUTHERLAND AND OTHERS.
2D ED. BASED ON 1ST ED. BY HALE
SUTHERLAND AND WALTER W. CLIFFORD.
NEW YORK, WILEY, 1953.
559P.

1. CONCRETE, REINFORCED.

534.83
S32
Sutherland, W W jt. au.
Shepherd, L J
Relative annoyance and loudness judgments
of various simulated sonic boom waveforms, by
L.J. Shepherd and W.W. Sutherland. Washington,
National Aeronautics and Space Administration,
1968.
52p. (NASA CR-1192)
Prepared by Lockheed-California Co., Burbank,
Calif. for Langley Research Center, National
Aeronautics and Space Administration.
1. Noise. 2. Air transportation. I. U.S
National Aeronautics and Space Administration.
II. Lockheed-California Co. III. Sutherland, W.W., jt. au. IV. Title.

728.1
1336.18
(79434)
S87
SUTTER COUNTY, CALIF. HOUSING
AUTHORITY.
ANNUAL REPORT, 2d - 1952/53 -
YUBA CITY, 1953
1V.

1. PUBLIC HOUSING - SUTTER COUNTY,
CALIF.

624
S87
SUTHERLAND, HALE.
STRUCTURAL THEORY, BY HALE SUTHERLAND
AND HARRY LAKE BOWMAN. 4TH ED. NEW YORK,
WILEY, 1950.
394P.

FIRST ED. PUBLISHED IN 1938 UNDER TITLE:
AN INTRODUCTION TO STRUCTURAL THEORY AND
DESIGN.

1. STRUCTURAL ENGINEERING. I. BOWMAN,
HARRY LAKE, JT. AU. II. TITLE.

Sutherlin, Oreg.

VF
Housing-U.S.-Oreg.

711.4
(79434)
Y81
Sutter Co., Calif. Planning Commission
Yuba City, Calif. Planning Commission.
Master plan report, City of Yuba City,
County of Sutter, California. Rev. and
supplemented. [In cooperation with] the
Planning Commission of Sutter County.
Yuba City, 1959.
30p. maps, tables.

U. S. Urban Renewal Administration,
Urban Planning Assistance Program.

1. Master plan - Yuba City, Calif. I. Sutter
Co., Calif. Planning Commission. II. U. S.
URA-UPAP. Yuba City, Calif.

Sutherland, Ian R

331
L11f
U.S. Bureau of Labor Statistics.
Factory jobs: employment outlook for
workers in jobs requiring little or no
experience or specialized training, by
Ian R. Sutherland. Washington, Govt.
Print. Off., 1961.
26p. (Its Bulletin no. 1288)
"Prepared in cooperation with the
Veterans Administration."
At head of title: 87th Cong., 1st sess.
House. Document no. 51.

1. Employment. I. Sutherland, Ian R.

711.14
(79529)
072
Sutherlin, Or. City Planning Commission.
Oregon. University. Bureau of Municipal
Research and Service.
Land use in Sutherlin. Memorandum to
Sutherlin City Planning Commission.
Eugene, Or., 1958.
5p.

U.S. Urban Renewal Adm. UPAP.

1. Land use - Sutherlin, Or. I. Sutherlin, Or.
City Planning Commission. II. U.S. URA-UPAP.
Sutherlin, Or.

301.36
S87
Suttles, Gerald D
The social order of the slum; ethnicity and
territory in the inner city. Preface by
Morris Janowitz. Chicago, University of
Chicago Press, 1968.
243p. (Studies of urban society)
Bibliography: p. 235-238.
1. Sociology, Urban. 2. Slums - Chicago.
3. Minority groups - Chicago. 4. Youth.
I. Title.

VF
690.015
(41)
U54t
no.3

Sutton, A. G.
U.K. Ministry of Works.
The importance of thermal insulation
in building, by A. G. Sutton. London,
H.M. Stationery Off., 1957.
11 p. (Its Technical notes no. 3)

1. Insulation. I. Sutton, A. G.
II. Title: Thermal insulation in
building. (Series)

690.25
S82

Svendsen, Sven D
Avretting av betonggulv med PVAc-mørtler
Oslo, 1962.
9p. (Oslo. Norges
Byggforskningsinstitutt. Saertrykk nr. 70)

Saertrykk av BYGG nr. 7, 1962.

1. Concrete floors. I. Oslo. Norges
Byggforskningsinstitutt.

Svendsen, Sven D   jt. au.

690.22
B47n

Birkeland, Øivind.
Norwegian test methods for rain penetration
through masonry walls, by Øivind Birkeland
and Sven D. Svendsen. [Philadelphia]
American Society for Testing and Materials,
1962.
15p. (Oslo. Norges Byggforskningsinstitutt,
Reprint no. 80)

Reprint from Symposium on Masonry Testing,
Special technical publication no. 320.

(Cont'd. on next card)

DATE OF REQUEST 1/9/52   L.C. CARD NO.

Heat pumps JAN 22 195

AUTHOR
Sutton, George E.

TITLE
The heat pump - a gold mine?

SERIES
Leaflet 30.

EDITION   PUB. DATE 8/51   PAGING

PUBLISHER
Univ. of Florida
Gainesville, Fla.

RECOMMENDED BY
Thulman   REVIEWED IN
g. Div. Record. 10/51 p. 7.

ORDER RECORD

691.55
S82

Svendsen, Sven D
Bomskader ved puss (Defects in plastering)
Oslo, Norges Byggforskningsinstitutt, 1966.
7p. (Oslo. Norges Byggforskningsinstitutt. Saertrykk 136)
Saertrykk fra Murmesteren, nr. 9 og
10/1966.

1. Plaster and plastering. I. Oslo.
Norges Byggforskningsinstitutt.

690.22
B47n

Birkeland, Øivind.   Norwegian test ...
(Card 2)

1. Walls. I. Svendsen, Sven D., jt. au.
II. American Society for Testing and
Materials. III. Oslo. Norges Byggforskningsinstitutt. IV. Title: Rain penetration through masonry walls.

VF
711.4
:67
/697.9
W24

Sutton, George E
Weil, Joseph
Research for the industrial expansion of
Florida, by Joseph Weil; [and] Roof spray - a low
cost approach to summer comfort, by George E.
Sutton. Journal, Florida Engineering Society,
13 p., April 1953. illus., graphs.

Reprint; issued as Florida Engineering and
Industrial Experiment Station, Leaflet no. 41 [and]
no. 42.
1.Industrial location-Fla. 2.Air conditioning.
I.Sutton, George E. II.Title: Research for the
industrial expansion Florida. III.Title: Roof
spray. IV.Series: lorida. University.
Engineering and Industrial Experiment Station.
Leaflets

699.82
S82

SVENDSEN, SVEN D
DRIVING RAIN; EXPERIMENTAL RESEARCH
ON THE RESISTANCE OF EXTERNAL WALLS
AGAINST RAIN PENETRAATION. OSLO, 1954.
19L.

AT HEAD OF TITLE: NORWEGIAN BUILDING
RESEARCH INSTITUTE.
REFERENCES: P. 18-19.

1. WATERPROOFING. 2. WALLS.
I. OSLO. NORGES BYGGFORSKNINGS
INSTITUTT. I. I. TITLE.

691.54
S82n

Svendsen, Sven D
Nye murmørteltyper. Oslo, Norges
Byggforskningsinstitutt, 1966.
6p. (Oslo. Norges Byggforsknings-
institutt. Saertrykk 96)
Saertrykk av Tegl, nr. 2/1964.

2c

1. Cement. 2. Brick construction. I. Oslo.
Norges Byggforskningsinstitutt.

711.4
O55

Sutton, S B ed.
Olmsted, Frederick Law, 1822-1903.
Civilizing American cities; a selection of
Frederick Law Olmsted's writings on city
landscapes, ed. by S.B. Sutton. Cambridge,
Mass., MIT Press, 1971.
310p.

1. City planning. 2. Landscape architecture.
I. Sutton, S.B., ed. II. Title.

690.5
:551.5
S82

Svendsen, Sven D
Litt om vintermuring. Oslo, Norges
Byggforskningsinstitutt, 1966.
17p. (Oslo. Norges Byggforskningsinstitutt. Saertrykk 122)
Saertrykk fra Murmesteren, nr. 1 og
2/1966.

2c

1. Winter construction. 2. Walls.
I. Oslo. Norges Byggforskningsinstitutt.

691.55
O75s

Svendsen, Sven D.
Oslo. Norges Byggforskningsinstitutt.
Skader pa puss, arsaker og botemidler, av
Sven D. Svendsen. Oslo, 1961.
17p. (Its Saertrykk nr. 57)

Saertrykk av BYGG, nr. 5-6, 1961.

1. Plaster and plastering. I. Svendsen,
Sven D.

627.4
S87

Sutton, Walter G
Control of flood plain use. Presented
at the Seminar on River Basin Planning,
Corps of Engineers, U.S. Army, Fort Belvoir,
27-31 May 1963. [Washington] 1963.
[15]p.

1. Flood control. I. Seminar on River
Basin Planning, Corps of Engineers, Fort
Belvoir, 1963. II. U.S. Army.
Corps of Engineers.

691.42
S82

Svendsen, Sven D
Maling og slemming av teglsteinsfasader
(Painting and thin coating of brick masonry)
Oslo, Norges Byggforskningsinstitutt, 1966.
5p. (Oslo. Norges Byggforsknings-
institutt Saertrykk 128)
Saertrykk fra Murmesteren, nr. 4/1966.

1. Bricks. 2. Paints and painting.
I. Oslo. Norges Byggforskningsinstitutt.

691.54
S82

Svendsen, Sven D
Undersøkelser av slemmestad murcement.
Oslo, Norges Byggforskningsinstitutt, 1966.
11p. (Oslo. Norges Byggforsknings-
institutt. Saertrykk 123)
Saertrykk fra Betongtekniske publikasjoner,
Januar 1966.

1c

1. Cement. I. Oslo. Norges Byggforskningsinstitutt.

627.4
S87P

SUTTON, WALTER G
PLANNING FOR OPTIMUM ECONOMIC USE OF
FLOOD PLAINS. WASHINGTON, DEPT. OF THE
ARMY, 1963.
17P.

PRESENTED BY THE ENVIRONMENTAL
ENGINEERING CONFERENCE, AMERICAN SOCIETY
OF CIVIL ENGINEERS, ATLANTA, GEORGIA,
FEBRUARY 25-28, 1963.

1. FLOOD CONTROL. 2. LAND USE.
3. SOILS. I. TITLE. I. TITLE:
FLOOD PLAINS.

691.54
S82m

Svendsen, Sven D
Murcement. Oslo, Norges Byggforskningsinstitutt, 1965.
6p. (Oslo. Norges Byggforskningsinstitutt. Saertrykk 114)
Saertrykk fra Betongen Idag, nr. 4/1965/

2c

1. Cement. I. Oslo. Norges
Byggforskningsinstitutt.

645.04
S82

Svenner, Elsa.
Boligens oppbevaringsplasser (Storage place
in dwellings) Oslo, Norges Byggforskningsinstitutt, 1966.
8p. (Oslo. Norges Byggforskningsinstitutt. Saertrykk 137)
Saertrykk fra Bygg nr. 10/1966.

2c

1. Household storage. I. Oslo. Norges
Byggforskningsinstitutt.

693.5
(485)
S88

Suu, V
Tolerance measurements in precast concrete
construction at Norrköping. Garston, Eng.,
Building Research Station, 1971.
[9]p. (Library communication no. 1621)
Translated from the Swedish.

1. Concrete construction - Sweden.
I. U.K. Building Research Station.
II. Title. (Series)

VF
690.282
O75n

Svendsen, Sven D
Oslo. Norges Byggforskningsinstitutt.
Norwegian test methods for wind and rain
penetration through windows, by Sven D.
Svendsen and Robert Wigen. Trondheim, 1958.
10 p. diagrs. (Its Reprint no. 39)

Reprint from the Symposium on Testing Window
Assemblies, Special Technical publication no. 251,
published by the American Society for Testing
Materials.

1. Windows. I. Svendsen, Sven D. II. Wigen,
Robert.

728.1
:333.63
(481)
S82

Svenner, Elsa.
Hvordan møblerer leieboerne sine
leiligheter? Oslo, Norges Byggforskningsinstitutt, 1965.
9p. (Oslo. Norges Byggforskningsinstitutt. Saertrykk 116)
Saertrykk fra Bygg nr. 10/1964.

2c

1. Rental housing - Norway. 2. Interior
decoration. I. Oslo. Norges Byggforskningsinstitutt.

728.1
S82

Svennar, Elsa.
Tetthet i boligområder (Density of residential areas) Oslo, Norges Byggforskningsinstitutt, 1970.
55p. (Oslo. Norges Byggforskningsinstitutt. Rapport 50)
English summary.
1. Housing - Social aspects. 2. Space considerations. 3. Land use - Norway. 4. Housing projects - Norway. I. Oslo. Norges Byggforskningsinstitutt. II. Title: Density of residential areas.

711.417
(485)
S82va

Svenska Bostäder.
Vällingby. Stockholm, 1966.
16p.

In English.

1. New towns - Sweden.

728.1
(485)
S82P

SVENSKA VANFÖREVARDENS CENTRALKOMMITTÉ.
THE PHYSICALLY HANDICAPPED HOUSEWIFE.
NEW YORK, INTERNATIONAL SOCIETY FOR THE WELFARE OF CRIPPLES, 1959.
68P. ILLUS. (ITS PUBLICATION SERIES, NO. 6)

TRANSLATION OF HANDIKAPPAD HUSMODER.

1. HOUSING FOR THE HANDICAPPED - SWEDEN. I. INTERNATIONAL SOCIETY FOR THE WELFARE OF CRIPPLES. II. TITLE.

711.58
(481)
S82

Svennar, Elsa.
Tetthet i boligområder (Density of residential areas) Oslo, Norges Byggforskningsinstitutt, 1970.
[3]p. (Saertrykk 190)
Saertrykk fra Byggekunst nr. 2 1970.

1. Residential areas - Norway.
2. Population density. I. Oslo. Norges Byggnadsforskningsinstitutt. II. Title: Density of residential areas.

Svenska Bostadskreditkassan.

see

Swedish Housing Credit Fund.

728.1
(485)
J63

SVENSSON, WALDEMAR.
JOHANSSON, ALF.
SWEDISH HOUSING POLICY, BY ALF JOHANSSON AND WALDEMAR SVENSSON.
STOCKHOLM, ROYAL SWEDISH COMMISSION - NEW YORK WORLD'S FAIR, 1939.
47P.

REPRINTED FROM THE MAY 1938 ISSUE OF THE ANNALS OF THE AMERICAN ACADEMY OF POLITICAL AND SOCIAL SCIENCES.
CONTENTS.- JOHANSSON, ALF. SOCIAL HOUSING POLICY IN SWEDEN.- SVENSSON, WALDEMAR. HOME OWNERSHIP IN SWEDEN.

(CONTINUED ON NEXT CARD)

691
(485)
S82

Svensk Byggtjänst.
Svensk byggkatalog
Stockholm,
v. illus., diagrs., tables.

For full information see shelf list card.

1.Building materials-Sweden. 2.Building codes-Sweden.

058.7
: 690
(485)
S 82

Svenska Byggnadsentreprenörföreningen.
Medlemmar, 1970;
Stockholm, 19
/ v.
For Library holdings see main entry.

1. Building industry - Sweden - Direct.

728.1
(485)
J63

JOHANSSON, ALF. SWEDISH HOUSING POLICY.
...1939. (CARD 2)
1. HOUSING - SWEDEN. 2. HOME OWNERSHIP - SWEDEN. I. SVENSSON, WALDEMAR. II. TITLE.

72
(485)
S82n

Svenska Arkitekters Riksförbund.
New Swedish architecture. [Stockholm?, A. Börtzells, 1939?]
136 p. illus., plans.

Swedish and English.
Swedish title: Ny Svensk arkitektur.

1.Architecture-Sweden. 2.Architecture, Domestic-Sweden. I.Title.

728.1
(485)
S82s

Svenska Byggnadsentreprenörföreningen.
Swedish housing policy. Stockholm, 1957.
[5]p.

1.Housing - Sweden.

Sveriges officiella statistik. Byggnadsverksamhet och bostadsförhållanden.

see

Sweden. Bostadsstyrelsen.

72
(485)
S82

Svenska Arkitekters Riksförbund.
Ten lectures on Swedish architecture.
[Stockholm, Victor Petterson, 1949]
116 p. plates.
Contents.-New Swedish architecture, Nils Ahrbom.-Development of population and social reform in Sweden, Alva Myrdal.-Town-planning problems in Sweden to-day, Sune Lindström.-Recent Swedish town plans, Harald Mjöberg.-Town-planning in Stockholm. Some statistics, Erland von Hofsten.-Town-planning in Stockholm. Housing and traffic, Sven Markelius.-

(Continued on next card)

728.1
(485)
M42

Svenska institutet för kulturell utbyte med...
Michanek, Ernst.'
Housing standard and housing construction in Sweden; some facts and views. Compiled by Ernst Michanek. Stockholm, Swedish Institute for Cultural Relations with Foreign Countries, 1962.
31p.
1. Housing - Sweden. 2. Sweden - Housing. 3. Building industry - Sweden. 4. Sweden - Building industry. I. Svenska institutet för kulturell utbyte med utlandet, Stockholm. II. Title.

711.4
(47)
S82

Svetlichnyi, B
Soviet town planning today. Reproduced from Problems of economics, vol. 3, no. 8, Dec. 1960. p. 29-36.

Translation of original which appeared in Voprosy Ekonomiki, no. 7, 1960.

1. City planning - U.S.S.R.

Svenska Arkitekters Riksförbund. Ten lectures on Swedish architecture...1949. (Card 2)

Contents cont'd.: A Swedish housing investigation, Sten Lindegren.-Housing and furnishing problems, Lena Larsson.-What is HSB, and how does it work?, Sven Wallander.-Architectural activities in the Swedish co-operative movement, Eskil Sundahl.

1.Architecture-Sweden. 2.Architecture, Domestic-Sweden. 3.City planning-Sweden. 4.Family living requirements. I.Ahrbom, Nils. II.Larsson, Lena. III.Markelius, Sven. IV.Myrdal, Alva.

362.6
M42o

Svenska institutet för kulturelt utbyte med utlandet, Stockholm.
Michanek, Ernst.
Old age in Sweden. Stockholm, Swedish Institute for Cultural Relations with Foreign Countries, 1962.
38p.

1. Old age. 2. Social welfare - Sweden. 3. Sweden - Social welfare. I. Svenska institutet för kulturelt utbyte med utlandet, Stockholm.

VF
711.4
S84

Sviridoff, Mitchell
Planning and participation. New York, Ford Foundation, 1969.
15p. (SR/37)
Address delivered before the American Institute of Planners.

1. City planning - Citizen participation. I. Ford Foundation. II. Title.

711.4
(485)
S82s

Svenska Bostäder.
Skärholmen: the big community centre of the motor-car age. Stockholm, 1968.
4p.

1. City planning - Sweden. 2. Community centers - Sweden. I. Title.

693.002.22
(485)
S82

Svenska Trähus.
Monteringsfärdiga Svenska Trähus; förslagstyper till mindre och större enfamiljshus, flerfamiljshus, sportstugor och specialhus. Stockholm [n.d.]
1 v. (loose-leaf) plans.

1.Prefabricated construction-Sweden. I.Title.

658
S59

SWACKHAMER, GENE L , JT. AU.
SNYDER, JAMES G
MANAGEMENT PLANNING AND CONTROL SYSTEMS, BY JAMES C. SNYDER AND GENE L. SWACKHAMER. LAFAYETTE, 1966.
32P. (INDIANA. AGRICULTURAL EXPERIMENT STATION, LAFAYETTE. RESEARCH BULLETIN NO. 809)

1. OPERATIONS RESEARCH. 2. MANAGEMENT. 3. SYSTEMS ANALYSIS. I. SWACKHAMER, GENE L. JT. AU. II. INDIANA. AGRICULTURAL EXPERIMENT STATION, LAFAYETTE. III. TITLE.

728.1
:325
(7471)
S81
Svados, Harvey.
When black and white live together, in Rochdale Village, New York City. New York, 1966.
6p.

Reprinted by United Housing Foundation from New York Times magazine, Nov. 13, 1966.

1. Minority groups - Housing - New York (City) 2. Race relations. I. Title.

728.1
:362.6
S81F
SWAIM, WILLIAM T   JR.
FINANCIAL ARRANGEMENTS AT VARIOUS HOMES FOR THE AGING. DILLSBURG, PRESBYTERIAN HOMES OF CENTRAL PENNSYLVANIA, 1959.
9P.

1. HOUSING FOR THE AGED.   2. HOUSING - STANDARDS AND SPECIFICATIONS. I. TITLE.   II. PRESBYTERIAN HOMES OF CENTRAL PENNSYLVANIA, DILLSBURG, PA.

711.14
(797)
P17
Parker, Merwin W. Swamp, marsh and bog areas in the central Puget Sound region.
(Card 2)

1. Land use - Washington (State)
2. Open space land. I. Puget Sound Governmental Conference. II. Puget Sound Regional Planning Council. III. U.S. HUD-UPAP. Washington (State) IV. Title.

628.1
(774)
S81
Swager, W   L
Alternative long-range water use plans for the Tri-County Region, Michigan. A technical-economic report to Tri-County Regional Planning Commission, by W. L. Swager and others Columbus, Ohio, Battelle Memorial Institute, 1963.
184p.
Bibliography: p. 167-169.
U.S. Urban Renewal Adm. UPAP.

(Continued on next card)

362.6
S81T
SWAIM, WILLIAM T
TWO DOZEN TRADITIONAL MISTAKES MADE BY WOMEN'S BOARDS OF HOMES FOR THE AGING. DILLSBURG, PRESBYTERIAN HOME OF CENTRAL PENNSYLVANIA, 1963.
7P. (TOPIC NO. 20, 1963 SHORT COURSE...)

1. OLD AGE.   I. TITLE. II. PRESBYTERIAN HOMES OF CENTRAL PENNSYLVANIA.

33
(73)
F22
P6
Swan, Eliot J.
U.S. Federal Reserve System. Board of Governors. Housing, social security, and public works. Washington, June 1946.
94 p. (Its Postwar economic studies, no. 6)

Contents.-Housing needs and the housing market, Ramsey Wood.-Economic aspects of social security, Eliot J. Swan.-Public works and services in the postwar economy, Walter F. Stettner.

628.1
(774)
S81
Swager, W   L   Alternative... (Card 2)

1. Water resources - Mich. 2. Water-supply engineering. I. Tri-County Regional Planning Commission, Clinton, Eaton, Ingham County, Mich. II. Battelle Memorial Institute. III. U.S. URA-UPAP. Michigan.

VF-Hsg for the aged
DATE OF REQUEST 10/1/53   OCT 27 1953   L.C. CARD NO.

AUTHOR Swaim, W. T., Jr.

TITLE A treat - not a retreat: new concepts in group living for older adults.

SERIES Reprint, Currents..., Summer 1953, p. 7-13.

EDITION   PUB. DATE   PAGING

PUBLISHER Pa. Citizens Assoc. for Health and Welfare, 1 N. 13th St., Phila. 7, Pa.

RECOMMENDED BY   NWL   REVIEWED IN   LJS 8/22/53 p. 16

ORDER RECORD

332.72
S81
SWAN, HERBERT S
CAN MORTGAGE INVESTMENTS NEW HOUSING AND SOUND CITY PLANNING BE COMBINED TO REVITALIZE MATURE NEIGHBORHOODS. THE HOUSING SURVEY AS A BUSINESS TOOL. NEW YORK, 1945.
8P.

1. MORTGAGE FINANCE.   2. URBAN RENEWAL.

388
(7531)
S81
Swaim, Stephen C
Transit for the 70s; why public transit is dying in Washington; a strategy for revitalization. An Agenda for the 70s special report, by Stephen C. Swaim and Tom Kelly. Wash., Washington Center for Metropolitan Studies, 1972.
43p.

1. Transportation - District of Columbia metropolitan area. 2. Journey to work. I. Kelly, Tom, jt. au. II. Washington Center for Metropolitan Studies.   III. Title.

658
:538.56
881
Swaine, H   R
A proposal for control of local service subsidies. Data published in American aviation, vol. 28, May 1965, p. 50-51. Santa Monica, Calif., Rand Corp., 1965.
24p. (Rand Corp. Paper)(P-3184)

1. Management - Automation. 2. Federal contracts. 3. Air transportation. I. American aviation. II. Rand Corp. III. Title.

728.1
(7471)
S81

3c.

Swan, Herbert Siegfried, 1888-
The housing market in New York city, by Herbert S. Swan ... A study made for the Institute of public administration. New York, N. Y., Reinhold publishing corporation, 1944.
2 p. l., vi, 204 p. diagrs. 23 cm.
Reproduced from type-written copy.
Bibliographical foot-notes.

1. Housing market-New York, N.Y. I. Housing - New York (City). 2. Building trades - New York (City). I. Institute of public administration, New York. II. Title.

Library of Congress   HD7304.N5S83   44-4374
[48k2]   331.833

728.1
:362.6
S81
SWAIM, WILLIAM T   JR.
ADVANTAGES OF A SMALL CENTRAL SITE FOR A HOME FOR THE AGING. DILLSBURG, PA., OFFICE OF THE EXECUTIVE SECRETARY, PRESBYTERIAN HOMES OF CENTRAL PENNSYLVANIA, 1958.
11L.

1. HOUSING FOR THE AGED. I. PRESBYTERIAN HOMES OF CENTRAL PENNSYLVANIA, DILLSBURGH, PA.

1023
SWAINSBORO, GA. PLANNING COMMISSION. COMPLETION REPORT, URBAN PLANNING ASSISTANCE PROGRAM, PROJECT GEORGIA NO. P-86. PREPARED BY STATE PLANNING AND PROGRAMMING BUREAU, STATE OF GEORGIA. ATLANTA, 1970.
5L. (HUD 701 REPORT)

1. CITY PLANNING - SWAINSBORO, GA. I. GEORGIA. STATE PLANNING AND PROGRAMMING BUREAU. II. HUD. 701. SWAINSBORO, GA.

711.4
:670
S81
SWAN, HERBERT S
SELLING A CITY TO INDUSTRY. ATTRACTION AND DEVELOPMENT OF MANUFACTURES. NEW YORK, 1939.
21P.

1. INDUSTRIAL LOCATION.   2. COMMUNITY DEVELOPMENT. I. TITLE. II. TITLE: ATTRACTION AND DEVELOPMENT OF MANUFACTURERS.

728.1
:362.6
S81A
SWAIM,   WILLIAM T
APARTMENTS FOR THE AGING. DILLSBURG, PA., PRESBYTERIAN HOMES OF CENTRAL PENNSYLVANIA, 1959.
13L.

1. HOUSING FOR THE AGED.

658.564
S81
Swallow, Kenneth P
Elements of computer programming, by Kenneth P. Swallow and Wilson T. Price. 2d ed. New York, Holt, Rinehart and Winston, 1970.
456p.

1. Automation. I. Prince, Wilson T., jt. au. II. Title. III. Title: Computer programming.

VF
711.17
S81
Swan, Herbert S
Theory and practice in building lines under eminent domain. New York, National Municipal League, 1931.
557-566p.
Supplement to the National Municipal Review, Sept., 1931, vol. XX, no. 9.

1. Eminent domain. 2. Architectural control. I. National Municipal League.

025.3
S81
1963
Swain, Olive, comp.
Notes used on catalog cards; a list of examples. 2d ed. Chicago, American Library Association, 1963.
82p.

1. Cataloging. I. American Library Association. II. Title.

711.4
(797)
P17
Swamp, marsh and bog areas in the central Puget Sound region. Vol. 2. Natural open spaces.
Parker, Merwin W
Swamp, marsh and bog areas in the central Puget Sound region. Vol. 2. Natural open spaces. Seattle Puget Sound Governmental Conference, Puget Sound Regional Planning Council, 1964.
24p. (Project Open Space. Report no. 11)
Prepared in cooperation with Washington State Dept. of Commerce and Economic Development.
U.S. Dept. of Housing and Urban Development.
(Cont'd on ext card)

711.4
:670
(771391)
S81
Swan, Herbert S
Youngstown offers industry opportunity; an interpretation of basic economic factors which attract and support local industry. Youngstown, Ohio, New Industries Committee, Greater Youngstown Area Foundation, [1963?]
96p.

1. Industrial location - Youngstown, Ohio. 2. Occupations - Youngstown, Ohio.

625.7
H43r
Swanberg, John H   , jt. author.
Highway Research Board.
    Resealing joints and cracks in concrete pavement (Minnesota); presented at the Thirty-first annual meeting, January 1952, by J.C. Robbers and John H. Svanberg. Washington, National Research Council, 1952.
    19 p. illus., chart. (Its Bulletin no. 63)

    1. Road construction. I. Title. II. Robbers, J.C. III. Swanberg, John H., jt. author. (Series)

353
(79737)
S66
Swanson, K   T   W
Spokane Co., Wash. Planning Commission.
    Governmental units in Spokane County; a description of the organization, function, and responsibility of the units of government, prepared by K.T.W. Swanson. Spokane, Wash., Nov. 1955.
    81 L.   Charts, tables.

    1. County government - Spokane Co., Wash. I. Swanson, K   T   W   II. Title.

333.38
(74814)
S81
Swarthmore, Pa. Planning Commission.
    Subdivision regulations. Swarthmore, Pa., 1968.
    29p.

    1. Subdivision regulation - Swarthmore, Pa.

325
(7471)
H17
Swanson, Bert E   jt. au.
Harris, Louis.
    Black-Jewish relations in New York City, by Louis Harris and Bert E. Swanson. New York, Praeger, 1970.
    234p. (Praeger special studies in U.S. economic and social development)

    1. Minority groups - New York (City) I. Swanson, Bert E., jt. au. II. Title.

711.400.15
S81
Swanson, Leland M   ed.
    The cybernetic approach to urban analysis. Edited by Leland M. Swanson and Glenn O. Johnson. Los Angeles, Graduate Program in City and Regional Planning, University of Southern California, 1964.
    207p.
    Bibliography: p. 201-203.
    1. City planning - Research. 2. Automation. I. Johnson, Glenn O., jt. ed. II. Los Angeles. University of Southern California. Graduate Program in City   and Regional Planning. III. Title.

027
L41p
Swartz, Roderick G
Library Buildings Institute, Chicago, 1963.
    Problems in planning library facilities; consultants, architects, plans, and critiques. Proceedings. Sponsored by the Library Administration Div., American Library Association. Edited by William A. Katz and Roderick G. Swartz. Chicago, American Library Association, 1964.
    208p.   (Cont'd. on next card)

301.15
S81
Swanson, Bert E
    The concern for community in urban America. New York, Odyssey Press, 1970.
    179p.

    Bibliography: p. 169-175.

    1. Community structure. I. Title.

711.14
(747)
N28
Swanson, Roger A
New York (State) Office of Planning Coordination.
    The land use and natural resource inventory of New York State, by Roger A. Swanson. Albany, 1969.
    20p.
    U.S. Dept. of Housing and Urban Development. Urban Planning Assistance Program.

    1. Land use - New York (State) 2. Natural resources - New York (State) I. Swanson, Roger A. II.   U.S. HUD-UPAP. New York (State)   III. Title.

027
L41p
Library Buildings Institute, Chicago, 1963.
    Problems in planning library facilities ...
    (Card 2)

    1. Libraries. 2. Architecture - Congresses. I. Katz, William A., ed. II. Swartz, Roderick, G., jt. ed. III. American Library Association. Library Administration Div. IV. Title.

352
A33
Swanson, Bert E   jt. au.
Agger, Robert E
    The rulers and the ruled political power and impotence in American communities, by Robert E. Agger, Daniel Goldrich and Bert E. Swanson. New York, Wiley, 1964.
    789p.

    Bibliography: p. 776-779.

    1. Local government. I. Goldrich, Daniel, jt. au. II. Swanson, Bert E., jt. au. III. Title.

658.564
(016)
A47
SWANSON, ROWENA W
U.S. AIR FORCE. OFFICE OF SCIENTIFIC RESEARCH.
    CYBERNETICS IN EUROPE AND THE U.S.S.R. - ACTIVITIES, PLANS, AND IMPRESSIONS, BY ROWENA W. SWANSON. WASHINGTON, 1966.
    43P.
    - Bibliography
    1. AUTOMATION. I. SWANSON, ROWENA W. II. TITLE.

330
(6834)
S81
Swaziland. Government Information Services.
    A handbook to the Kingdom of Swaziland. Mbabane, 1968.
    126p.
    Bibliography: p. 124.

    1. Economic conditions - Swaziland. I. Title.

630
(7462)
C65
Swansen, C L W
Connecticut. Agricultural Experiment Station.
    Soils and land use, Hartford County, Connecticut; an area of specialized agriculture and rapid suburbanization, by Alexander Ritchie, jr. and C. L. W. Swansen. New Haven, 1957.
    35p. tables. (Its Bulletin 606)

    1. Agriculture - Hartford Co., Conn. 2. Soils. I. Ritchie, Alexander, jr. II. Swansen, C L W

002
S81
Swanson, Rowena.
    Documentation activities in the United States of America. Wash., Air Force Office of Scientific Research, Office of Aerospace Research, United States Air Force, 1963.
    25p. (U.S. Defense Documentation Center. Defense Supply Agency. [Document] AD 613 374; AFOSR-5445)
    Distributed by U.S. Clearinghouse for Federal Scientific and Technical Information
    Bibliography: p. 12-25.
    1. Documentation. 2. Library science - Automation - Bibl. I. U.S. Air Force. (Office of Aerospace Research) II. Title.

Sweat equity *see* Owner-built houses

711.4
:670
(758741)
G26
Swanson, Ernst W
Georgia. State Engineering Experiment Station.
    A petroleum refinery for Brunswick, Georgia; a feasibility analysis, by Ernest W. Swanson and others. Atlanta, 1958.
    103p. maps, tables.

    U.S. Urban Renewal Adm. UPAP.

    1. Industrial location - Brunswick, Ga. 2. Petroleum industry and trade. I. Swanson, Ernst W. II. U.S. URA-UPAP.   Brunswick, Ga.

002
S811
Swanson, Rowena Weiss.
    Information; an exploitable commodity. Arlington, Va., Air Force Office of Scientific Research, Office of Aerospace Research, United States Air Force, 1968.
    65p. (AFOSR 68-0652)
    Bibliography: p. 62-64.
    CFSTI AD 677 197.
    Paper prepared for presentation at the fourth National Congress on Data Processing, Jerusalem, 8 and 9 April, 1968.
    1. Documentation. I. Title. II. U.S. Air Force.   Office of Scientific Research.

330
(485)
C34
1936
SWEDEN.
CHILDS, MARQUIS WILLIAM.
    SWEDEN, THE MIDDLE WAY, BY MARQUIS W. CHILDS. NEW HAVEN, YALE UNIVERSITY PRESS, 1936.
    171P.

    1. ECONOMIC POLICY - SWEDEN. 2. COOPERATIVE HOUSING - SWEDEN. I. TITLE.

VF
336.211
(794)
S81
Swanson, John E
    Cooperative administration of property taxes in Los Angeles County [by] J. E. Swanson, W. R. Bigger and W. W. Crouch. Los Angeles, 1949.
    63 p. 28 cm. (Studies in local government, no. 12)
    Bibliography: p. [59]-63.

    Real property.
    1. Taxation—Los Angeles Co., Calif. I. Title. (Series: California. University. University at Los Angeles. Bureau of Governmental Research. Studies in local government, no. 12)

    JS45.C3 no. 12   352.1   49-45478*
    Library of Congress   [3]

LAW
T
Swanstrom Roy.
    The United States Senate 1787-1801. A dissertation on the first fourteen years of the upper legislative body. Washington, Govt. Print. Off., 1962.
    325p.
    At head of title: 87th Cong., 1st sess., 1962. Senate. Document no. 64.
    Thesis - University of California.

    1. U.S. Congress. Senate.

720
(485)
S21
Sweden - Architecture.
Scarlat, Alexander.
    Introduction à l'architecture en Suède. [Stockholm, Sweden Information Centre, 1962]
    8p.
    At head of title: Connaissance de la Suède.

    1. Architecture - Sweden. 2. Sweden - Architecture. I. Swedish Information and Documentation Center.

VF
914.89
(016)
H22

Sweden - Bibl.
Hedin, Naboth, comp.
Guide to information about Sweden. New York, American Swedish News Exchange, 1947.
61 p.

"Housing": p. 31.

1. Sweden - Bibl. 2. Housing - Sweden - Bibl.

690.015
(485)
S82
R32
1968

Sweden - Building research.
Baehre, Rolf.
Theoretische und experimentelle Untersuchungen über die Bemessungsgrundlagen für Tragwerke aus elastoplastischem Material. Stockholm, Statens institut för byggnadsforskning, 1968.
18p. (Stockholm. Statens institut för byggnadsforskning. Rapport 32:1968)
1. Building research - Sweden. 2. Sweden - Building research. 3. Aluminum. 4. Loads. I. Stockholm. Statens institut för byggnadsforskning.

690.015
(485)
S82
R13
1969

Christiansson, Gerth. Plan...1969.
(Card 2)
2. Sweden - Building research. 3. Master plan - Sweden. 4. Sweden - Master plan. I. Title: Plan and reality in two expanding centres of industry; a study of master planning. II. Stockholm. Statens Institut för Byggnadsforskning.

690.031
(485)
S15

Sweden - Building costs.
Salaj, Branko.
Bostadsproduktionens prisutveckling [Residential construction prices in Sweden, 1950-65] Stockholm, Almquist & Wiksell, 1968.
196p.
Bibliography: p. 194-196.
English summary.

1. Building costs - Sweden. 2. Sweden - Building costs. I. Title: Residential construction prices in Sweden, 1950-65.

690.015
(485)
S82
R20
1968

Sweden - Building research.
Bring, Christer.
Provningsmetoder för golvmaterial och golvkonstruktioner (Methods of testing flooring materials and flooring constructions) Stockholm, Statens institut för byggnadsforskning, 1968.
141p. (Stockholm. Statens institut för byggnadsforskning. Rapport 20:1968)
Bibliography: p. 111-113.
English summary.
1. Building research - Sweden. 2. Sweden - Building research. 3. Floors and flooring. 4. Strength of materials. I. Stockholm. Statens institut för byggnadsforskning.
(Cont'd on next card)

690.015
(485)
S82
R21
1969

SWEDEN - BUILDING RESEARCH.
Franzen, Birger.
Kontorsrummet 2 - en klimatstudie i nio kontorshus (Offices 2 - a study of climate in nine office blocks) Stockholm, Statens Institut för Byggnadsforskning, 1969.
71p. (Stockholm. Statens Institut för Byggnadsforskning. Rapport 21:1969)
English summary.
1. Building research - Sweden. 2. Sweden - Building research. 3. Heating. 4. Office buildings. 5. Air conditioning. I. Title: Offices 2 - a study of climate in nine office blocks. II. Stockholm. Statens Institut för Byggnadsforskning.

728.1
(485)
M42

Sweden - Building industry.
Michanek, Ernst.
Housing standard and housing construction in Sweden; some facts and views. Compiled by Ernst Michanek. Stockholm, Swedish Institute for Cultural Relations with Foreign Countries, 1962.
31p.
1. Housing - Sweden. 2. Sweden - Housing. 3. Building industry - Sweden. 4. Sweden - Building industry. I. Svenska institutet for kulturell utbyte med utlandet, Stockholm. II. Title.

690.015
(485)
S82
R20
1968

Bring, Christer. Provningsmetoder...
1968. (Card 2)
II. Title: Methods of testing flooring materials and flooring construction.

690.015
(485)
S82
R48
1968

Sweden - Building research.
Hansen, Flemming.
Deformation, sättning och skador hos långa hus. (Deformation, setting and damages in long buildings), av Flemming Hansen och Åke Holmberg. Stockholm, Statens institut för byggnadsforskning, 1968.
7p. (Stockholm. Statens institut för byggnadsforskning. Rapport 48:1968)
1. Building research - Sweden. 2. Sweden - Building research. 3. Building maintenance. I. Holmberg, Åke, jt. au. II. Stockholm. Statens institut för byggnadsforskning. III. Title: Deformation, setting and damages in long buildings.

690.015
(485)
S82
R15
1969

SWEDEN - BUILDING RESEARCH.
Andersson, Sven Åke.
Husbyggandet åren 1960-1964. Arbetskraftsåtgång och byggnadskostnader enligt arbetsmarknadsstyrelsens byggnadsinventeringar (Building 1960-1964. Labour consumption and building costs according to the building inventories of the National Swedish Labour Market Board) Stockholm, Statens Institut för Byggnadsforskning, 1969.
50p. (Stockholm. Statens Institut för Byggnadsforskning. Rapport 15:1969)
English summary.
(Cont'd on next card)

690.015
(485)
S82
R35
1968

Sweden - Building research.
Campanello, Louis.
Stadsförnyelse ur internationell synvinkel (Urban renewal from international points of view) Stockholm, Statens institut för byggnadsforskning, 1968.
50p. (Stockholm. Statens institut för byggnadsforskning. Rapport 35:1968)
Bibliography: p. 41-44.
English summary.
1. Building research - Sweden. 2. Sweden - Building research. 3. Urban renewal. 4. Land acquisition. I. Stockholm. Statens institut för byggnads forskning. II. Title: Urban renewal from international points of view.

690.015
(485)
S82
R27
1968

Sweden - Building research.
Hellström, Gunnar.
Tillåten last på långa stödpålar av betong inom Östra Nordstaden, Göteborg (Allowable load on long end-bearing concrete piles in Östra Nordstaden, Gothenburg) Stockholm, Statens institut för byggnadsforskning, 1968.
112p. (Stockholm. Statens institut för byggnadsforskning. Rapport 27:1968)
English summary.
1. Building research - Sweden. 2. Sweden - Building research. 3. Concrete construction. 4. Steel construction. I. Stockholm. Statens institut för byggnadsforskning. II. Title: Allowable load on long end-bearing concrete piles.
(Cont'd on next card)

690.015
(485)
S82
R15
1969

Andersson, Sven Åke. Husbyggandet...1969
(Card 2)
1. Building research - Sweden. 2. Sweden - Building research. 3. Building construction - Labor requirements. 4. Building costs - Sweden. 5. Sweden - Building costs. I. Title: Building 1960-1964. Labour consumption and building costs according to the building inventories of the National Swedish Labour Market Board. II. Title: Labor consumption and building costs according to the building inventories of the National Swedish Labour Market Board. III. Sweden.
(Cont'd on next card)

690.015
(485)
S82
R16
1968

Sweden - Building research.
Carlestam, Gösta.
Studier av utomhusaktiviteter med automatisk kamera (Investigation of outdoor activities with an automatic camera) Stockholm, Statens institut för byggnadsforskning, 1968.
88p. (Stockholm. Statens institut för byggnadsforskning. Rapport 16:1968)
Bibliography: p. 62-64.
English summary.
1. Building research - Sweden. 2. Sweden - Building research. 3. City planning - Sweden. 4. Sweden - City planning. I. Stockholm. Statens institut för byggnadsforskning.
(Cont'd on next card)

690.015
(485)
S82
R27
1968

Hellström, Gunnar. Tillåten...1968.
(Card 2)
piles in Östra Nordstaden, Gothenburg.

690.015
(485)
S82
R15
1969

Andersson, Sven Åke. Husbyggandet...1969
(Card 3)
Arbetsmarknadsstyrelsen. IV. Stockholm. Statens institut för Byggnadsforskning.

690.015
(485)
S82
R16
1968

Carlestam, Gösta. Studier...1968
(Card 2)
II. Title: Investigation of outdoor activities with an automatic camera.

690.015
(485)
S82
R30
1968

Sweden - Building research.
Johansson, Arne.
Avvikelser i armeringsstängernas läge (Deviations in position of reinforcing bars), av Arne Johansson och Birger Warris. Stockholm, Statens institut för byggnadsforskning, 1968.
20p. (Stockholm. Statens institut för byggnadsforskning. Rapport 30:1968)
1. Building research - Sweden. 2. Sweden - Building research. 3. Concrete construction. I. Warris, Birger, jt. au. II. Stockholm. Statens institut för byggnadsforskning. III. Title: Deviations in position of reinforcing bars.

690.015
(485)
S82
R31
1968

SWEDEN - BUILDING RESEARCH.
Baehre, Rolf.
Theoretische Untersuchungen zum Tragverhalten von Druckstaben aus elastoplastischem Material. Stockholm, Statens Institut för Byggnadsforskning, 1968.
36p. (Stockholm. Statens institut for Byggnadsforskning. Rapport 31:1968)
1. Building research - Sweden. 2. Sweden - Building research. 3. Aluminum. I. Stockholm. Statens Institut for Byggnadsforskning.

690.015
(485)
S82
R13
1969

SWEDEN - BUILDING RESEARCH.
Christiansson, Gerth.
Plan och verklighet i Två expanderande industriorter; en studie i generalplanering (Plan and reality in two expanding centres of industry; a study of master planning) Stockholm, Statens Institut för Byggnadsforskning, 1969.
174p. (Stockholm. Statens Institut för Byggnadsforskning. Rapport 13:1969)
English summary.
Bibliography: p. 173-174.

1. Building research - Sweden.
(Cont'd on next card)

690.015
(485)
S82
R14
1969

SWEDEN - BUILDING RESEARCH.
Johansson, Germund.
Tillämpning av plasticitetsteori inom stålbyggnadstekniken (Plastic design of steel structures) Stockholm, Statens Institut för Byggnadsforskning, 1969.
100p. (Stockholm. Statens Institut för Byggnadsforskning. Rapport 14:1969)
English summary.
[A literature review]
1. Building research - Sweden. 2. Sweden - Building research. 3. Steel construction. 4. Stresses and strains.
(Cont'd on next card)

690.015
(485)
S82
R14
1969
  Johansson, Germund. Tillämpning...1969.
                   (Card 2)
    I. Title: Plastic design of steel structures.
II. Stockholm. Statens Institut för
Byggnadsforskning.

690.015
(485)
S82
R34
1968
  Pettersson, Ove.   Pågående...1968.
                   (Card 2)
    I. Ödeen, Kai, jt. au. II. Stockholm.
Statens institut för byggnadsforskning.
III. Title: Fire engineering research in
Sweden - in progress and under planning.

690.015
(485)
S82
R53
1968
      Sweden - Building research.
  Strömdahl, Ingvar.
    Brandteknisk forskning på det släckande
brandförsvarets områden; förslag till
svenskt (nordiskt) långtidsprogram (Fire
engineering research in the field of fire
fighting; proposal for a Swedish (Nordic)
long-term programme) Stockholm, Statens
Institut för Byggnadsforskning, 1968.
    51p. (Stockholm. Statens Institut för
Byggnadsforskning. Rapport 53:1968)
    English summary.
    1. Building research - Sweden. 2. Sweden -
Building research. 3. Fire prevention - Research. 4. Fire proof construction.
             (Cont'd on next card)

690.015
(485)
S82
R14
1968
     Sweden - Building research.
  Kimbré, Siv.
    Boendestudier i Kiruna, Luleå och Sundsvall
(User studies in Kiruna, Luleå and Sundsvall)
Stockholm, Statens institut för byggnadsfor-
skning, 1968.
    136p. (Stockholm. Statens institut för
byggnadsforskning. Rapport 14:1968)
    Bibliography: p. 127-128.
    English summary.
    1. Building research - Sweden. 2. Sweden -
Building research. 3. Housing - Social aspects.
4. Housing market - Sweden. 5. Sweden -
Housing market. I. Stockholm. Statens
institut för byggnadsforskning.
II.Title: User studies in Kiruna, Luleå
and Sundsvall.

690.015
(485)
S82
R39
1968
    SWEDEN-BUILDING RESEARCH.
  Pusch, Roland.
    Markförstärkning genom urgravning och
återfyllning med mera bärigt material; en
metod att begränsa sättningarna hos
byggnadsverk grundlagda på lager av lös lera
(Improvement of bearing and settling properties of subsoils by excavation and refill-
ing with coarse soil material: a method of
limited settling of structures founded on
layers of soft clay) Stockholm, Statens
Institut för Byggnadsforskning, 1968.
    56p. (Stockholm. Statens Institut
för Byggnads- forskning. Rapport 39:
1968)
        (Cont'd on next card)

690.015
(485)
S82
R53
1968
  Strömdahl, Ingvar.   Brandteknisk...1968.
                 (Card 2)
    I. Stockholm. Statens Institut för
Byggnadsforskning. II. Title: Fire
engineering research

690.015
(485)
S82
R47
1968
     Sweden - Building research.
  Larsson, Olov.
    Beräkning av rökkanaler - en litteratur-
granskning (Calculations on flues - a review
of existing literature) Stockholm, Statens
institut för byggnadsforskning, 1968.
    15p. (Stockholm. Statens institut för
byggnadsforskning. Rapport 47:1968)
    1. Building research - Sweden. 2. Sweden -
Building research. 3. Chimneys - Bibl.
I. Stockholm. Statens institut för byggnadsforskning. II. Title: Calculations on flues,
a review of existing literature.

690.015
(485)
S82
R39
1968
  Pusch, Roland. Markförstärkning genom
...1968.   (Card 2)
    English summary.
    Bibliography: p. 54-55.
    1. Building research - Sweden. 2. Sweden -
Building research. 3. Soils. 4. Found-
ations (Building) I. Stockholm. Statens
Institut för Byggnadsforskning. II. Title:
Improvement of bearing and settling
properties of subsoils.

690.015
(485)
S82
R56
1968
    SWEDEN - BUILDING RESEARCH.
  Talme, Oskar A.
    Clay sensitivity and chemical stabilization.
Stockholm, Statens Institut för Byggnads-
forskning, 1968.
    192p. (Stockholm. Statens Institut för
Byggnadsforskning. Rapport 56:1968)
    Bibliography: p. 187-192.
    1. Building research - Sweden. 2. Sweden -
Building research. 3. Clay. I. Title.
II. Stockholm. Statens Institut för
Byggnadsforskning.

690.015
(485)
S82
R33
1968
     Sweden - Building research.
  Mandorff, Sven.
    Värmeförbrukning i skolor (Heat consumption
recorded in schools). Stockholm, Statens
institut för byggnadsforskning, 1968.
    66p. (Stockholm. Statens institut för
byggnadsforskning. Rapport 33:1968)
    English summary.
    1. Building research - Sweden. 2. Sweden -
Building research. 3. Heating. 4. Ventilation.
I. Stockholm. Statens institut för
byggnadsforskning. II. Title: Heat consumption recorded in schools.

690.015
(485)
S82
R28
1968
     Sweden - Building research.
  Pusch, Roland.
    A technique for investigation of clay micro-
structure. Stockholm, Statens institut för
byggnadsforskning, 1968.
    963-986p. (Stockholm. Statens institut för
byggnadsforskning. Rapport 28:1968)
    Bibliography: p. 984-985.
    Reprinted from J. Microscopie (1967), 963-
986.
    1. Building research - Sweden. 2. Sweden -
Building research. 3. Clay. 4. Soils.
I. Stockholm. Statens institut för
byggnadsforskning. II. Title.

690.015
(485)
S82
R46
1968
     Sweden - Building research.
  Thiberg, Sven.
    The determination of dimensions by full-
scale laboratory tests. Stockholm, National
Swedish Institute for Building Research, 1968.
    86p. (Stockholm. Statens institut för
byggnadsforskning. Rapport 46:1968)
    Bibliography: p. 81-86.
    1. Building research - Sweden. 2. Sweden -
Building research. I. Stockholm. Statens
institut för byggnadsforskning. II. Title.

690.015
(485)
S82
R22
1968
     Sweden - Building research.
  Norén, Bengt.
    Nailed joints - their strength and rigidity
under short-term and long-term loading.
Stockholm, National Swedish Institute for
Building Research, 1968.
    80p. (Stockholm. Statens institut för
byggnadsforskning. Rapport 22:1968)
    Bibliography: p. 78-80.
    1. Building research - Sweden. 2. Sweden -
Building research. 3. Nails and nailing.
4. Loads. I. Stockholm. Statens institut
för byggnadsforskning.

690.015
(485)
S82
R17
1968
     Sweden - Building research.
  Ryman, Nils E
    Hur fyra bostadsområden planerats (How four
dwelling areas were planned) Stockholm,
Statens institut för byggnadsforskning, 1968.
    242p. (Stockholm. Statens institut för
byggnadsforskning. Rapport 17:1968)
    English summary.
    1. Building research - Sweden. 2. Sweden -
Building research. 3. Subdivision regulation - Sweden. 4. Sweden - Subdivision regulation. I. Stockholm. Statens institut for
byggnadsforskning. II. Title: How four
dwelling areas were planned.

690.015
(485)
S82
R50
1968
     Sweden - Building research.
  Thiberg, Sven.
    Samhällsplanering för rörelsehindrade
- boende i invalidbostäder (Town planning
for the disabled - special housing)
Stockholm, Statens Institut för Byggnads-
forskning, 1968.
    35p. (Stockholm. Statens Institut för
Byggnadsforskning. Rapport 50:1968)
    English summary.
    1. Building research - Sweden. 2. Sweden -
Building research. 3. Housing for the
handicapped. I. Stockholm. Statens
Institut för Byggnadsforskning.
II. Title: Town planning for the
disabled - special housing.

690.015
(485)
S82
R45
1968
     Sweden - Building research.
  Nylund, Per Olof.
    Rörelser hos fasadelement av betong.
Stockholm, Statens institut för byggnadsfor-
skning, 1968.
    8p. (Stockholm. Statens institut för
byggnadsforskning. Rapport 45:1968)
    English summary.
    1. Building research - Sweden. 2. Sweden -
Building research. 3. Concrete. I. Stockholm.
Statens institut för byggnadsforskning.

690.015
(485)
S82
R37
1968
     Sweden - Building research.
  Stockholm. Statens institut för
byggnadsforskning. (Committee on Housing,
Building and Planning)
    Måttsamordning inom byggbranschen - aktuell
utveckling i ECE-länder (Dimensional co-
ordination in building - current trends in
ECE countries) Stockholm, 1968.
    50p. (Its Rapport 37:1968)
    Report on an inquiry undertaken by the
Committee on Housing, Building and Planning.
    1. Building research - Sweden. 2. Sweden -
Building research. 3. Modular coordination -
Europe. 4. Europe - Modular coordination. I. Title: Dimensional co-ordination
in building current trends in ECE countrie

690.015
(485)
S82
R41
1968
     Sweden - Building research.
  Walldén, Marja.
    Aktivitetsfält, del 1: den geografiska
fördelningen av aktiviteter utanför bostaden.
Litteratur- och metodstudier. (Fields of
activity, part 1; the geographical distribution of activities outside the dwelling.
Studies of literature and methods) Stockholm,
Statens Institut för Byggnadsforskning, 1968.
    109p. (Stockholm. Statens Institut för
Byggnadsforskning. Rapport 41:1968)
    English summary.
    Bibliography: p. 85-87.
    1. Building research - Sweden.
2. Sweden - Building research.
3. City planning.
           (Cont'd on next card)

690.015
(485)
S82
R34
1968
     Sweden - Building research.
  Pettersson, Ove.
    Pågående och planerad byggnadsteknisk
brandforskning i Sverige (Fire engineering research in Sweden - in progress and under planning), av Ove Pettersson och Kai Ödeen.
Stockholm, Statens institut för byggnadsforskning, 1968.
    52p. (Stockholm. Statens institut för
byggnadsforskning. Rapport 34:1968)
    Bibliography: p. 49-50.
    English summary.
    1. Building research - Sweden. 2. Sweden -
Building research.   3. Fireproof construction.   4. Engineering research.
      (Cont'd on next card)

690.015
(485)
S82
R10
1968
     Sweden - Building research.
  Stockholm. Statens Institut för
Byggnadsforskning.
    Ritningsplanering: el redovisnings-tekniska
anvisningar, del 3 (Planning of drawings:
electrical technical directions, part 3)
Stockholm, 1968.
    37p. (Its Rapport fran Byggnadsforskning
1968:10)
    At head of title: EL-Gruppen.
    1. Building research - Sweden. 2. Sweden -
Building research. 3. Electric wiring.

690.015
(485)
S82
R41
1968
  Walldén, Marja.   Aktivitetsfält...1968.
                 (Card 2)
    4. Sweden - City planning.
I. Stockholm. Statens Institut för
Byggnadsforskning. II. Title: Fields of
activity, part 1.

Sweden - Building research.

690.015
(485)
S82
R26
1968

Wåstlund, Holger.
Industriområden i region, general-och detaljplanering (Industrial estates in comprehensive and detail planning) Stockholm, Statens institut för byggnadsforskning, 1968.
88p. (Stockholm. Statens institut för byggnadsforskning. Rapport 26:1968)
Bibliography: p. 87-88.
English summary.
1. Building research - Sweden. 2. Sweden - Building research. 3. Industrial location - Sweden. 4. Sweden - Industrial location.
I. Stockholm. Statens institut för byggnadsforsk ning.
(Cont'd on next card)

690.015
(485)
S82
R26
1968

Wåstlund, Holger.   Industriområden...1968.
(Card 2)

II. Title: Industrial estates in comprehensive and detail planning.

690.015
(485)
S82
R29
1968

Westelius, Orvar.
Trafikrörelsers sammansättning - en undersökning i Uppsala 1965 (Travel - pattern within an urban area). Stockholm, Statens institut för byggnadsforskning, 1968.
74p. (Stockholm. Statens institut för byggnadsforskning. Rapport 29:1968)
English summary.
1. Building research - Sweden. 2. Sweden - Building research. 3. Traffic - Sweden. 4. Sweden - Traffic. I. Stockholm. Statens institut för byggnadsforskning. II. Title: Travel-pattern within an urban area.

690.015
(485)
S82
R22
1969

SWEDEN - BUILDING RESEARCH.
Westerberg, Bo.
Utmattning av betong och armerad betong; en littertaröversikt (Fatigue of plain and reinforced concrete; a review of literature) Stockholm, Statens Institut för Byggnadsforskning, 1969.
66p. (Stockholm. Statens Institut för Byggnadsforskning. Rapport 22:1969)
English summary.
1. Building research - Sweden. 2. Sweden - Building research. 3. Concrete - Bibl. 4. Concrete, Reinforced - Bibl.
(Cont'd on next card)

690.015
(485)
S82
R22
1969

Westerberg, Bo.   Utmattning...1969.
(Card 2)

I. Title: Fatigue of plain and reinforced concrete: a review of literature.
II. Stockholm. Statens Institut för Byggnadsforskning.

690.015
(485)
S82
R2
1969

Wittrock, Jan.
Säsongutjämnat byggande - en internationell översikt (Construction without seasonal fluctuations - an international review) Stockholm, Statens Institut för Byggnadsforskning, 1969.
134p. (Stockholm. Statens Institut för Byggnadsforskning. Rapport 2:1969)
English summary.
1. Building research - Sweden. 2. Sweden - Building research. 4. Weather. I. Stockholm. Statens Institut för Byggnadsforskning. II. Title: Construction without seasonal fluctuations - an international review.

711.552
(485)
S21

Sweden - Business districts.

Scarlat, Alexander.
La renovation du centre de Stockholm, Hötorget, courte description. Stockholm, Information Centre Sweden, [1965?]
4p.
At head of title: Connaissance de la Suede.

1. Business districts - Sweden. 2. Sweden - Business districts. I. Swedish Information and Documentation Center.

690.015
(485)
S82
R16
1968

Sweden - City planning.

Carlestam, Gösta.
Studier av utomhusaktiviteter med automatisk kamera (Investigation of outdoor activities with an automatic camera) Stockholm, Statens institut för byggnadsforskning, 1968.
88p. (Stockholm. Statens institut för byggnadsforskning. Rapport 16:1968)
Bibliography: p. 62-64.
English summary.
1. Building research - Sweden. 2. Sweden - Building research. 3. City planning - Sweden. 4. Sweden - City planning.
I. Stockholm. Statens institut för byggnadsforskn ing.
(Cont'd on next card)

690.015
(485)
S82
R16
1968

Carlestam, Gösta.   Studier...1968.
(Card 2)

II. Title: Investigation of outdoor activities with an automatic camera.

690.015
(485)
S82
R41
1968

Sweden - City planning.

Wallden, Marja.
Aktivitesfält, del 1: den geografiska fördelningen av aktiviteter utanför bostaden. Litteratur- och metodstudier. (Fields of activity, part 1; the geographical distribution of activities outside the dwelling. Studies of literature and methods) Stockholm, Statens Institut för Byggnadsforskning, 1968.
109p. (Stockholm. Statens Institut för Byggnadsforskning. Rapport 41:1968)
English summary.
Bibliography: p. 85-87.
1. Building research - Sweden. 2. Sweden - Building research. 3. City planning - Sweden.
(Cont'd on next card)

690.015
(485)
S82
R41
1968

Wallden, Marja.   Aktivitesfält...1968.
(Card 2)

4. Sweden - City planning.
I. Stockholm. Statens Institut for Byggnadsforskning. II. Title: Fields of activity, part 1.

725.83
(485)
S82

Sweden - Community centers.

Swedish Information and Documentation Center. Farsta Centre. Stockholm, [1961?]
[4]p.
At head of title: Meet Sweden.

1. Community centers - Sweden. 2. Sweden - Community centers. I. Title.

VF
352.6
(485)
S21

Sweden - Community facilities.

Scarlat, Alexander.
Social and cultural facilities in new urban districts in Sweden. Stockholm, Information Centre Sweden, [1965?]
19p.
At head of title: Meet Sweden.

1. Community facilities - Sweden. 2. Sweden - Community facilities. I. Title. II. Swedish Information and Documentation Center.

330
(485)
S76

Sweden - Economic conditions.

Stockholms Enskilda Bank.
Some data about Sweden, 1967-68.
Stockholm, 1967.
117p.

1. Economic conditions - Sweden. 2. Population - Sweden. 3. Sweden - Economic conditions. 4. Sweden - Population. I. Title.

728.1
(485)
M42

Sweden - Housing.

Michanek, Ernst.
Housing standard and housing construction in Sweden; some facts and views. Compiled by Ernst Michanek. Stockholm, Swedish Institute for Cultural Relations with Foreign Countries, 1962.
31p.
1. Housing - Sweden. 2. Sweden - Housing. 3. Building industry - Sweden. 4. Sweden - Building industry. I. Svenska institutet for kulturell utbyte med utlandet, Stockholm. II. Title.

728.1
(485)
E57

Sweden - Housing for the aged.

Eltz, Sylvia.
Housing for the aged and the disabled in Sweden. Stockholm, Swedish Institute for Cultural Relations with Foreign Countries, 1963.
23p.

1. Housing for the aged - Sweden. 2. Housing for the handicapped. 3. Sweden - Housing for the aged. I. Title.

728.1
:362.6
(485)
S82

Sweden - Housing for the aged.

Sweden. National Housing Board.
Housing for the elderly citizens in Sweden. [Stockholm] 1963.
1v.

1. Housing for the aged - Sweden. 2. Sweden - Housing for the aged. I. Title.

690.015
(485)
S82
R14
1968

Sweden - Housing market.

Kimbre, Siv.
Boendestudier i Kiruna, Luleå och Sundsvall (User studies in Kiruna, Luleå and Sundsvall) Stockholm, Statens institut för byggnadsforskning, 1968.
136p. (Stockholm. Statens institut för byggnadsforskning. Rapport 14:1968)
Bibliography: p. 127-128.
English summary.
1. Building research - Sweden. 2. Sweden - Building research. 3. Housing - Social aspects. 4. Housing market - Sweden. 5. Sweden - Housing market. I. Stockholm. Statens institut för byggnadsforskning. II. Title: User studies in Kiruna, Luleå and Sundsvall.

690.015
(485)
S82
R26
1968

Sweden - Industrial location.

Wåstlund, Holger.
Industriområden i region, general-och detaljplanering (Industrial estates in comprehensive and detail planning) Stockholm, Statens institut för byggnadsforskning, 1968.
88p. (Stockholm. Statens institut för byggnadsforskning. Rapport 26:1968)
Bibliography: p. 87-88.
English summary.
1. Building research - Sweden. 2. Sweden - Building research. 3. Industrial location - Sweden. 4. Sweden - Industrial location.
I. Stockholm. Statens institut för byggnadsforsk ning.
(Cont'd on next card)

690.015
(485)
S82
R26
1968

Wåstlund, Holger.   Industriområden...1968.
(Card 2)

II. Title: Industrial estates in comprehensive and detail planning.

690.015
(485)
S82
R13
1969

SWEDEN - MASTER PLAN.
Christiansson, Gerth.
Plan och verklighet i Två expanderande industriorter; en studie i generalplanering (Plan and reality in two expanding centres of industry; a study of master planning) Stockholm, Statens Institut for Byggnadsforskning, 1969.
174p. (Stockholm. Statens Institut för Byggnadsforskning. Rapport 13:1969)
English summary.
Bibliography: p. 173-174.
1. Building research - Sweden.
(Cont'd on next card)

690.015
(485)
S82
R13
1969

Christiansson, Gerth.   Plan...1969.
                              (Card 2)
2. Sweden - Building research. 3. Master
plan - Sweden. 4. Sweden - Master plan.
I. Title: Plan and reality in two expanding
centres of industry; a study of master
planning. II. Stockholm. Statens Institut för
Byggnadsforskning.

711.552.1
(485)
S82

Sweden - Shopping centers.
Swedish Information and Documentation
Center.
   Skarholmen. Stockholm, [1967?]
[8]p.

   On cover: Meet Sweden.

   1. Shopping centers - Sweden.
   2. Sweden - Shopping centers. I. Title.

690.015
(485)
S82
R15
1969

Andersson, Sven Åke.   Husbyggandet...1969
                              (Card 2)
   1. Building research - Sweden. 2. Sweden -
Building research. 3. Building construction -
Labor requirements. 4. Building costs -
Sweden. 5. Sweden - Building costs. I. Title:
Building 1960-1964. Labour consumption and
building costs according to the building
inventories of the National Swedish Labour
Market Board II. Title: Labor consumption
and building costs according to the building
inventories of   the National Swedish
Labour Mar   ket Board. III. Sweden.
              (Cont'd on next card)

352
(485)
C15

Sweden - Municipal government.
Calmfors, Hans.
   Urban government for Greater Stockholm,
by Hans Calmfors and others. New York,
Published in cooperation with the Institute
of Public Administration, Frederick A. Praeger
1968.
   178p. (Praeger special studies in international politics and public affairs. Institute of Public Administration. The International urban studies no.4)
   1. Municipal government - Sweden. 2. Public
administration - Sweden. 3. Sweden - Public
administration.   4. Sweden - Municipal
government. I.   Institute of Public
Administration.   New York. II. Title.

331.252
(485)
S82v

Sweden - Social security.
Swedish Information and Documentation
Center.
   La vieillesse; l'assurance-maladie en
Suede. Stockholm, 1965.
   4p.
   At head of title: Connaissance de la
Suede.

   1. Social security - Sweden. 2. Sweden -
Social security. 3. Old age. 4. Insurance.

690.015
(485)
S82
R15
1969

Andersson, Sven Åke.   Husbyggandet...1969
                              (Card 3)
Arbetsmarknadsstyrelsen. IV. Stockholm.
Statens Institut för Byggnadsforskning.

VF
352
(485)
S 82

SWEDEN - MUNICIPAL GOVERNMENT.
Swedish Information and Documentation
Center.
   Administration locale et remembrement
des communes en Suede. Stockholm,
Information Centre Sweden, [1965?]
[4]p.

   At head of title: Connaissance de la
Suede.

   1. Municipal government - Sweden.
   2. Sweden -   Municipal government.

362.6
M42o

Sweden - Social welfare.
Michanek, Ernst.
   Old age in Sweden. Stockholm, Swedish
Institute for Cultural Relations with Foreign
Countries, 1962.
   38p.

   1. Old age. 2. Social welfare - Sweden.
3. Sweden - Social welfare. I. Svenska
institutet for kulturelt utbyte med utlandet,
Stockholm.

614
(485)
H62

SWEDEN. BESTYRELSEN FÖR SVERIGES
DELTAGANDE I NEW YORK-UTSTÄLLNINGEN
HÖJER, JOHAN AXEL, 1890-
   SOME ASPECTS OF SWEDISH SOCIAL WELFARE,
BY A. HÖJER, T. JERNEMAN AND O.R.
WANGSON. NEW YORK, THE ROYAL SWEDISH
COMMISSION - NEW YORK WORLD'S FAIR, 1939.
102P.

   PRINTED IN SWEDEN.
   REPRINTED ... FROM THE MAY, 1938
ISSUE OF THE ANNALS OF THE AMERICAN
ACADEMY OF POLITICAL AND SOCIAL
SCIENCES.
   CONTENTS... PUBLIC HEALTH AND
MEDICAL CARE, BY AXEL HÖJER...
                 (CONTINUED ON NEXT CARD)

312
(485)
M97

Sweden - Population.
Myrdal, Alva.
   Nation and family; the Swedish experiment
in democratic family and population policy.
Cambridge, Mass., M.I.T. Press, 1968.
   441p.

   Bibliography: p. 427-436.

   1. Population - Sweden. 2. Sweden -
Population. 3. Family. I. Title.

690.015
(485)
S82
R17
1968

Sweden - Subdivision regulation.
Ryman, Nils E
   Hur frya bostadsområden planerats (How four
dwelling areas were planned) Stockholm,
Statens institut for byggnadsforskning, 1968.
   242p. (Stockholm. Statens institut för
byggnadsforskning. Rapport 17:1968)
   English summary.
   1. Building research - Sweden. 2. Sweden -
Building research. 3. Subdivision regulation - Sweden. 4. Sweden - Subdivision regulation. I. Stockholm. Statens institut for
byggnadsforskning. II. Title: How four
dwelling areas we   re planned.

614
(485)
H62

HÖJER, JOHAN AXEL, 1890-   SOME ASPECTS
OF ...1939.   (CARD 2)
MATERNAL AND CHILD WELFARE, BY O.R.
WANGSON... SOCIAL INSURANCE IN SWEDEN, BY
TOR JERNEMAN

   1. HEALTH - SWEDEN.   2. SOCIAL
SECURITY - SWEDEN.   I. JERNEMAN, TOR
GUNNAR, 1894-   II. WANGSON, OTTO
ROBERT, 1893-   III. SWEDEN.
BESTYRELSEN FÖR SVERIGES DELTAGANDE I
NEW YORK-UTSTÄLLNINGEN, 1939.

330
(485)
S76

Sweden - Population.
Stockholms Enskilda Bank.
   Some data about Sweden, 1967-68.
Stockholm, 1967.
   117p.

   1. Economic conditions - Sweden.
2. Population - Sweden. 3. Sweden - Economic
conditions. 4. Sweden - Population.
I. Title.

690.015
(485)
S82
R29
1968

Sweden - Traffic.
Westelius, Orvar.
   Trafikrörelsers sammansättning - en
undersökning i Uppsala 1965 (Travel - pattern
within an urban area). Stockholm, Statens
institut för byggnadsforskning, 1968.
   74p. (Stockholm. Statens institut för
byggnadsforskning. Rapport 29:1968)
   English summary.
   1. Building research - Sweden. 2. Sweden -
Building research. 3. Traffic - Sweden.
4. Sweden - Traffic. I. Stockholm. Statens
institut för byggnadsforskning. II. Title:
Travel-pattern   within an urban area.

FOL10
728.1
(485
1347)
S82
1962/63

SWEDEN. BOSTADSSTYRELSEN.
ANVISNINGAR. STOCKHOLM, 1962-63.
1 V. (LOOSE-LEAF)

   1. HOUSING LEGISLATION - SWEDEN.

352
(485)
C15

Sweden - Public administration.
Calmfors, Hans.
   Urban government for Greater Stockholm,
by Hans Calmfors and others. New York,
Published in cooperation with the Institute
of Public Administration, Frederick A. Praeger
1968.
   178p. (Praeger special studies in international politics and public affairs. Institute of Public Administration. The International urban studies no.4)
   1. Municipal government - Sweden. 2. Public
administration - Sweden. 3. Sweden - Public
administration.   4. Sweden - Municipal
government. I.   Institute of Public
Administration.   New York. II. Title.

331
(485)
S82

Sweden. Arbetsmarknadsstyrelsen.
   Arbetsmarknadsutbildning 1969 (Training
for labour market, reasons 1969) Stockholm,
1971.
   54p. (Arbetsmarknadsstatistik. (Labour
market statistics) nr 3B, 1971; Årgång 19)

   1. Labor supply - Sweden.   2. Employment -
Sweden.

VF
728.1
(485)
S82

Sweden. (Kungl.) Bostadsstyrelsen.
   Arsberattelse, 1951/52-1953/54-
Stockholm, Sweden, K. L. Beckmans Boktryckeri,
1955-
   v. (Its Skrifter)

   1. Housing - Sweden.

658.8
((485))
S21

Sweden - Retail stores.
Scarlat, Alexander.
   Swedish collective centers for retail trade.
[Stockholm, Information Centre Sweden] 1964.
6p.
   At head of title: Meet Sweden.

   1. Retail stores - Sweden. 2. Sweden -
Retail stores. 3. Retail trade. I. Title.
II. Swedish Information Documentation
Center.

690.015
(485)
S82
R15
1969

Sweden. Arbetsmarknadsstyrelsen.
Andersson, Sven Ake
   Husbyggandet åren 1960-1964. Arbetskraft-
sätgång och byggnadskostnader enligt
arbetsmarknadsstyrelsens byggnadsinventeringar (Building 1960-1964. Labour consumption
and building costs according to the building
inventories of the National Swedish Labour
Market Board) Stockholm, Statens Institut för
Byggnadsforskning, 1969.
   50p. (Stockholm. Statens Institut för
Byggnadsforskning. Rapport 15:1969)
   English   summary.
                 (Cont'd on next card)

690
(485)
S82b

Sweden. Bostadsstyrelsen.
   Bostadsbyggandet, 1963-55; 56-58, 59/60, 161-6,
Stockholm, Boktr. P. A. Norstedt,
1969- in 2p 14v. annual. tables. (Sweden.
Statistiska Centralbyran. Sveriges
Officiella statistik. Byggnadsverksamhet
och bostadsförhallanden)

   For complete information see shelflist.

                 (See Card No. 2)

690
(485)
S82b

Sweden. Bostadsstyrelsen.
    Bostadsbyggandet. (Card No. 2)

    English summary.

    1.Building industry - Sweden. 2.Housing -
Sweden. (Series)

690
(485)
S 82by

Sweden. Byggbranschens Fortbildningsråd.
    Byggbranschens kurskatalog; kurser och
konferenser för byggfacket våren 1971.
Stockholm, 1971.
    16p. (Publikation 7)

    1. Building construction - Sweden.

614.8
:711.73
S82

Sweden. National Board of Urban Planning.
    Principles for urban planning with respect
to road safety; the SCAFT guidelines 1968.
In collaboration with the National Road
Administration. Stockholm, 1968.
    34p. (Sweden. Statens Planverk. Publica-
tion no. 5 (English))

    1. Traffic safety. I. Title.

728.1
(485)
S82po

Sweden. Bostadsstyrelsens.
    God bostad; forslag den 15 April 1970.
Stockholm, 1970.
    1v.

    1. Housing - Sweden.

693.068
:389.6
(485)
B27

Sweden. Byggstandardiseringen.
Bergvall, Lennart.
    Byggstandardiseringens modulutredning, av
Lennart Bergvall and Erik Dahlberg. [Stockholm]
Sveriges Industriforbund [1946]
    89 p.   diagrs.

Suppl. --------Byggstandardiseringen's report on modular
coordination...Tr. by Constance Bruzelius.
[Stockholm] Federation of Swedish Industries[1946?]
    79 l.

    Processed.

(Continued on next card)

711.4
(485)
S82t

Sweden. National Board of Urban Planning.
    Towards new planning and building legislation
in Sweden. Stockholm, 1968.
    12p. (Its Statens planverk information in
English no. 1)

    1. City planning - Sweden. 2. Building
industry - Sweden. I. Title.

728.1
(485)
S82g

Sweden. Bostadsstyrelsen.
    God bostad i dag och i morgon. Stockholm,
1964.
    65p.

    1. Housing - Sweden.

Bergvall, Lennart. Byggstandardiseringens
    modulutredning...[1946] (Card 2)

    "Translation should be studied together with
the original Swedish edition, as the illustrations
and diagrams therein are necessary for understanding the text.".

    1.Modular coordination-Sweden. I.Dahlberg, Erik,
jt.au. II.Bruzelius, Constance, tr. III.Sweden.
Byggstandardiseringen.

728.1
(485)
S82c

Sweden. National Housing Board.
    Current trends and policies in the field of
housing, building and planning. Stockholm,
1969-70;

    For Library holdings see main entry.

    1. Housing - Sweden. 2. Building industry -
Sweden. 3. City planning - Sweden. I. Title.

711.417
(485)
S82

Sweden. Bostadsstyrelsen.
    Skärholmen. [Stockholm, Bostadsstyrelsen?]
1968.
    32p.
    Produktion: AB Svenska Bostäder

    1. New towns - Sweden. I. Title.

336
(485)
S82

Sweden. Finansdepartementet.
    The Swedish budget, 1969/70 ; 70/71

a summary published by the Ministry of Finance.
Stockholm, 19
    2 v.
    For Library holdings see main entry.

    1. Finance - Sweden. 2. Budget - Sweden.
I. Title.

728.1
:362.6
(485)
S82

Sweden. National Housing Board.
    Housing for the elderly citizens in
Sweden. [Stockholm] 1963.
    1v.

    1. Housing for the aged - Sweden.
2. Sweden - Housing for the aged. I. Title.

728.1
(083.41
:485)
S82

Sweden. Bostadsstyrelsen.
    Uppgifter om bostader, hushall och boendef-
orhallanden aren 1960 och 1965 i lanen och
storstadsomradena. Stockholm, 1968.
    56p. (Sweden. Bostadsstyrelsen. Planerings-
byran. Statistik/utredningar/ information
nr. 1968:18)

    1. Housing statistics - Sweden.

728.1
:333.63
S82

SWEDEN. JUSTITIEDEPARTEMENTET.
    BETÄNKANDE MED FÖRSLAG TILL
REFORMERAD HYRESLAGSTIFTNING...
STOCKHOLM, KUNGL. BOKTRYCKERIET, 1938.
    277P. (STATENS OFFENTLIGA
UTREDNINGAR 1938:22)

    1. RENTAL HOUSING - SWEDEN.

Sweden. National Board of Housing.

728.1
(485)
T67

Toronto. Metropolitan Housing Authority.
    Housing in Sweden. [Prepared in
cooperation with] Ontario Association of
Housing Authorities, and the National
Board of Housing, Sweden. Toronto, 1962.
    39p.

    1. Housing - Sweden. 2. Housing -
Netherlands. 3. Housing - Denmark.
I. Sweden. National Board of Housing.
II. Ontario   Association of
Housing   Authorities.

711.417
(485)
S82v

Sweden. Bostadsstyrelsen.
    Vällingby [Stockholm, Bostadsstyrelsen?]
1966.
    20p.
    Produktion: AB Svenska Bostäder.

    1. New towns - Sweden. I. Title.

690.091.82
(485)
S82

SWEDEN. KUNGL. BYGGNADSSTYRELSEN.
    ANVISNINGAR TILL BYGGNADSTADGAN.
STOCKHOLM, 1960.
    303P. (BABS 1960)

    1. BUILDING CODES - SWEDEN.

Sweden. National Swedish Committee for
    Building Research

        see

Sweden. Statens Nämnd för Byggnadsforskning.

690
(485)
S82by
1970

Sweden. Byggbranschens Fortbildningsrad.
    Byggbranschens kurskatalog; kursen och
konferenser for byggfacket hosten.
Stockholm, 1970.
    15p. (Publikation 6)

    1. Building construction - Sweden.

Sweden. Labour Market Board.

        see

Sweden. Arbetsmarknadsstyrelsen.

711.583
(485)
P17

Sweden. Rikets Allmänna Kartverk.
Pass, David.
    Vallingby and Farsta: from idea to reality;
the suburban development process in a large
Swedish city. [Stockholm] Rikets Allmänna
Kartverk, 1969.
    494p.
    On cover: National Swedish building
research.
    Bibliography: p. 475-494.
    1. Suburbs - Sweden. I. Sweden. Rikets
Allmänna Kartverk. II. Title. III. Title:
The suburban development process in a large
Swedish city.

728.1
(485)
H15

Sweden.   Royal Housing Board.

Hald, Arthur, ed.
Swedish housing. Published by the Swedish Institute, the Royal Housing Board, the National Association of Swedish Architects, and the Swedish Society of Arts and Crafts. Edited by Arthur Hald, Per Holm and Gotthard Johansson. Translation by Burnett Anderson. [Stockholm, Swedish Institute, distributed by Forum, 1949]

64 p. illus., plans. 21 cm.
For full tracing see main entry card.
1. Housing - Sweden. 2. Cities and towns - Planning - Sweden. 3. Architecture, Domestic - Sweden. I. Svenska institutet för kulturellt utbyte med utlandet, Stockholm.

HD7350.A3H3   331.833   50-14937

Library of Congress   [2]

36
(485)
S82
2c

Sweden.   Royal Social Board.
Social work and legislation in Sweden.
2d rev. English ed.   Stockholm, Tryckeriaktie-bolaget Tiden, 1938.
352 p.   illus., tables.

"New Sweden tercentenary publications."
Housing: p. 284-307.
New rev. ed. published in 1952 under title Social Sweden.
1.Social welfare-Sweden. 2.Housing-Sweden.

690.015
(485)
882
R34
1967

Sweden. Statens Kommitté för Byggnadsforskning.
An attempt to measure objectively the quality of air. Stockholm, 1967.
42p.   (Its Rapport 34:1967)

1. Building research - Sweden. 2. Ventilation. I. Title.

Sweden.   Royal Ministry for Foreign Affairs.

see

Sweden. Utrikesdepartementet.

728.1
(4)
J63

SWEDEN. SOCIAL DEPARTEMENTET.
STATENS OFFENTLIGA UTREDNINGAR.
JOHANSSON, ALF.
METHODS AND RESULTS OF HOUSING POLICY IN FOREIGN COUNTRIES.   TRANSLATED BY BURTON G. YOUNG.   STOCKHOLM, 1935.
145-175P.   (SWEDEN.
SOCIALDEPARTEMENTET.   STATENS OFFENTLIGA UTREDNINGAR, 1935: 2. BILAGA 5)

1. HOUSING - EUROPE.   I. SWEDEN.
SOCIAL DEPARTEMENTET. STATENS OFFENTLIGA UTREDNINGAR, 1935: 2.
II. TITLE.

690.015
(485)
882
R2
1967

Sweden. Statens Kommitté för Byggnadsforskning.
Elmroth, Arne.
Analys av icke stationära värmeströmsförhållanden för ett plant tak med RC-nätverksmetod (Analysis of non-steady-state heat flow for a flat roof by an RC-network method) av Arne Elmroth och Ingemar Hoglund. Stockholm, 1967.
15p.   (Sweden. Statens Kommitté för Byggnadsforskning. Rapport 2:1967)
Särtryck ur tidskriften Byggmästaren 11: 1966.
English summary.

(Cont'd on next card)

360
(485)
S82
1928

SWEDEN. ROYAL SOCIAL BOARD.
SOCIAL WORK AND LEGISLATION IN SWEDEN.
SURVEY PUB. BY ORDER OF THE SWEDISH GOVERNMENT. STOCKHOLM, NORSTEDT, 1928.
289P.

ISSUED ALSO IN SWEDISH.

1. SOCIAL WELFARE - SWEDEN.
2. HOUSING - SWEDEN.   I. TITLE.

Sweden.   Social Welfare Board.

Name changed in 1952 from Sweden. Royal Social Board.

690.015
(485)
S82
R2
1967

Elmroth, Arne. Analys av icke stationära värmeströmsförhållanden för ett tak med RC-nätverksmetod...1967. (Card 2)

1. Building research - Sweden. 2. Heat transmission. 3. Roofs and roofing. I. Hoglund, Ingemar, jt. su. II. Sweden. Statens Kommitté för Byggnadsforskning.

360
(485)
S82
SWEDISH

SWEDEN. ROYAL SOCIAL BOARD.
SOCIALLAGSTIFTNING OCH SOCIALT ARBETE I SVERIGE. STOCKHOLM, TIDENS FÖRLAG, 1932.
288P.

ENGLISH EDITION HAS TITLE: SOCIAL WORK AND LEGISLATION IN SWEDEN.

1. SOCIAL WELFARE - SWEDEN.
2. HOUSING - SWEDEN.   I. TITLE.

36
(485)
S82
1952

Sweden. Social Welfare Board.
Social Sweden. [Stockholm, 1952]
462 p.   illus., chart (fold.), map.
New revision of Social work and legislation in Sweden, published by the Royal Social Board in 1938.
"Swedish housing policy": p. 325-347.
1.Social welfare-Sweden. 2.Housing-Sweden.

690.015
(485)
882
R20
1965

Sweden. Statens Kommitté for Byggnadsforskning.
Anatomy for planners 1; list of literature. Stockholm, 1965.
124p.   (Its Rapport no. 20, 1965)

1. Building research - Sweden. 2. Family living requirements - Bibl. I. Title.

Ref. pubs - Sweden
DATE OF REQUEST 12/23/52   L. C. CARD NO.

Sweden.
AUTHOR Royal Institute of Technology. Swedish Cement and Concrete Research Institute, Stockholm.
TITLE Stable concrete mixes.

SERIES Bulletin 14.

EDITION   PUB. DATE 1951   PAGING 32 p.
PUBLISHER
same Stockholm.

RECOMMENDED BY | REVIEWED IN
                               R 12/11/52 p.85
              ORDER RECORD

Sweden.   Socialstyrelsen

see

Sweden.   Royal Social Board.

690.015
(485)
S82
R53

Sweden. Statens Kommitté för Byggnadsforskning.
Andamålsenliga handlingar för byggnadskonstruktioner; rekommendationer. [Selected documents for use in conjunction with building design; recommendations. Separate drawings] Stockholm, 1959.
1v. diagrs. (Its Rapport 53)

-- Ritningsbilaga. Drawings. Stockholm, 1959.

1. Archi-   tecture.

VF
728.1
(48)
N25

Sweden. Ministry of Social Affairs.
Nelson, George R   ed.
Freedom and welfare; social patterns in the northern countries of Europe: Chapter V, Housing. [Copenhagen] 1954.
48 p.   illus.

Sponsored by the Ministries of Social Affairs of Denmark, Finland, Iceland, Norway, Sweden. Reprint.

Sweden. Statens Institut för Byggnadsforskning.

see also

Stockholm. Statens Institut för Byggnadsforskning.

Sweden. Statens Kommitte for Byggnadsforskning.

690.015
(485)
S82
R89

Rasmussen, Poul H
Anvisningar för provning av oljeeldade villapannor enligt svensk standard SIS 57 42 01 (Directions for testing of oil-fired domestic boilers in accordance with Swedish standard SIS 57 42 01) Stockholm, Statens råd för Byggnadsforskning, 1963.
61p. (Sweden. Statens Kommitté för Byggnadsforskning. Rapport 89)
English summary.

1. Building research - Sweden. 2. Boilers. I. Sweden.   Statens Kommitté för Byggnadsforskning.

Sweden.   Royal Social Board.

Name changed in 1952 to Sweden. Social Welfare Board.

690.15
:551.5
(485)
S77

Sweden. Statens Kommitté för Byggnadsforskning.
Naslund, Bertil
Additional costs of winter work on housing construction. [Stockholm, Statens Kommitté för Byggnadsforskning? Feb. 1951?]
9 l.   graphs

Bound with...A survey of winter construction in Sweden by Evert Strokirk.
Processed.

690.015
(485)
S82
R82

Sweden. Statens Kommitté för Byggnadsforskning.
A-gruppen. Ändamålsenliga arkitekthandlingar; Redovisning av trappor. Riktlinjer avseende trappor och räcken [Illustration of staircases on architectural drawings. Directions for staircases and railings] Stockholm, 1962.
19p. (Its Rapport no. 82)

Cover-title.

1. Stairs.

690.015
(485) Sweden. Statens Kommitté för
S82   Byggnadsforskning.
R110   A-gruppen halth. Måttsättning.
Redovisningstekniska anvisningar, del 2.
Stockholm, 1964.
31p.   (Its Rapport 110)

1. Building standards - Sweden.

690.015
(485) Sweden. Statens Kommitté för Byggnadsforsk-
S82   ning.
R50   Arbetskraftåtgang vid traditionella byggen
och monteringsbyggen [Labor requirements for
traditional building versus unit construc-
tion] av Hans G. Rahm och Gunnar Thunblad.
Stockholm, 1959.
94p. diagrs., tables.   (Its Rapport 50)

English summary.

1. Building construction - Labor requirements.   I.   Rahm, Hans G. II.
Thunblad, Gunnar.

690.015
(485) Sweden. Statens Kommitté för Byggnadsfors-
S82   kning.
R38   Barnfamiljer i höghus och trevanings
låghus i Vällingby; sociologisk undersökning.
[Families with children in multi-storied
flats and three-story buildings at Vallingby:
a sociological investigation] av Edmund
Dahlstrom. Stockholm, 1957.
80p. tables.   (Its Rapport 38)

1. Family living requirements. 2. Housing -
Social aspects. 3. Apartment houses.
I. Dahlstrom, Edmund.

690.015
(485) Sweden. Statens Kommitté for Byggnads-
382   forskning.
R114   A-gruppen halth. Redigering, revidering,
registrering redovisningstekniska anvisningar,
del 3. Stockholm, 1965.
24p.   (Its Rapport 114)

1. Building standards - Sweden.

Sweden. Statens Kommitté för
Byggnadsforskning.
690.015
(485)   Jernström, Sven.
S82   Arbetskraftåtgang vid traditionella byggen
R87   och monteringsbyggen (Utredning 2)
(Labour consumption for traditional building
versus assembly building) av Sven Jernström,
och Gunnar Thunblad. Stockholm, Statens råd
för Byggnadsforskning, 1962.
16p.   (Sweden. Statens Kommitté för
Byggnadsforskning. Rapport 87)

English summary.   (Continued on next card)

690.015
(485) Sweden. Statens Kommitte' för
S82   Byggnadsforskning.
R22   Barntillsyn, I. Behov av daghemsplatser
1967   fram til 1975 [Child supervision, 1. Need
for places in day nurseries up till 1975]
Stockholm, 1967.
83p.   (Its Rapport 22:1967)

1. Building research - Sweden.
2. Social welfare - Sweden. 3. Children.

690.015
(485) Sweden. Statens Kommitté för Byggnadsfors-
S82   kning.
R21   A-gruppen halth. Redovisningsexempel till
1966 redovisningstekniska anvisningar, del 1-4.
Stockholm, 1966.
155p.   (Rapport 21:1966)

1. Building standards - Sweden.

690.015
(485)   Jernstrom, Sven.   Arbetskraftatgang
S82   vid traditionella byggen...1962.   (Card 2)
R87

1. Building research - Sweden.
2. Building   construction - Labor
requirements. I. Thunblad, Gunnar, jt. au.
II. Sweden.   Statens Kommitte
for   Byggnadsforskning.

690.015
(485) Sweden. Statens Kommitté för Byggnadsforsk-
S82   ning.
R25   Barntillsyn II, litteraturinventering. Child
1967 supervision II, list of literature. Stockholm,
1967.
56p.   (Its Rapport 25:1967)

1. Building research - Sweden. 2. Children -
Bibl. I. Title: Child supervision.

690.015
(485) Sweden. Statens Kommitté för Byggnads-
S82   forskning.
R20   A-gruppen halth. Ritningsplanering,
1966 redovisningstekniska anvisningar, del 4.
(Building. Planning of drawings technical
directions, part 4) Stockholm. 1966.
53p.   (Its Rapport 20:1966)

1. Building research - Sweden.
2. Building standards - Sweden.
3. Building industry - Sweden.

Sweden. Statens Kommitté for Byggnadsforskning.
690.015
(485) Wirdenius, Hans.
S82   Arbetsledares uppgifter inom
R85   husbyggnadsindustrin. [Functions of
supervisors in the building industry]
av Hans Wirdenius och Sterner Lönnsjo.
Stockholm, Statens råd for Byggnadsforskning,
1962.
95p.   (Sweden. Kommitté för Byggnadsforskning. Rapport 85)

1. Personnel management. 2. Building
industry - Sweden. I. Lönnsjo, Sterner,
jt. au.   II. Sweden. Statens
Kommitté för   Byggnadsforskning.

693.5
H65   Holmberg, Åke.
Behaviour of load-bearing sandwich-type
structures, by Åke Holmberg and Erik Plem.
Stockholm, Statens Institut för
Byggnadsforskning, 1965.
95p.   (Sweden. Statens Kommitté for
Byggnadsforskning. Handlingar nr.49
Transactions)

1. Concrete construction. 2. Loads.
3. Panels. I. Plem, Erik, jt. au. II. Sweden. Statens   Kommitté for
Byggnadsforsk-   ning. (Series)

690.015
(485) Sweden. Statens Kommitté for Byggnads-
S82   forskning.
R109   A-gruppen halth. Ritteknik. Redovisningstekniska anvisningar, del. 1. Stockholm, 1964.
31p.   (Its Rapport 109)

1. Building standards - Sweden.

Sweden. Statens Kommitté för Byggnadsforskning
690.015
(485)   Jacobsson, Mejse
S82   Arbetsteknik vid egentliga byggnadsarbeten
M17   för bostadshus. Organization and working
methods in dwelling house construction. With
a summary in English. Stockholm, Statens
Kommitté för Byggnadsforskning, 1970.
243 p.   tables.   (Sverige. Statens
Kommitté för Byggnadsforskning. Meddelanden,
nr. 17)

Bibliography: p. 167-168.

Sweden. Statens Kommitté för
Byggnadsforskning.
690.015
(485) Sahlin, Sven.
S82   Beräkning av bärförmågan hos elementväggar
R76   och murade väggar. (Calculation of the
bearing capacity of prefabricated wall
elements and brick masonry walls.) Stockholm,
Statens råd for Byggnadsforskning, 1962.
37p.   (Sweden. Statens Kommitté för
Byggnadsforskning. Rapport 76)

1. Walls. I. Sweden. Statens Kommitté
för Byggnadsforskning.

Sweden. Statens Kommitté for Byggnadskorak-
ning.
690.015
(485) Anders, Berg.
382   A-gruppen redovisning av stenarbeten.
R84   Riktlinjer avseende invandiga och utvandiga
naturstensarbeten. [Illustration of stone
surfacing on architectural drawings. Directions for internal and external natural
stone surfacings] av Berg Anders and others.
Stockholm, Statens råd for Byggnadsforskning,
1962.
18p.   (Sweden. Statens Kommitté för
Byggnadsforskning. Rapport 84)

(Cont'd. on next card)

690.015
(485) Sweden. Statens Kommitte for
S82   Byggnadsforskning.
R8-1965   Automatisk databehandling av
bulleranalyser. Stockholm, Statens
Institut for Byggnadsforskning, 1965.
[37]p.   (Sweden. Statens Kommitté
för Byggnadsforskning. Rapport 8-1965)

1. Building research - Sweden.
2. Automation. I. Sweden. Statens
Kommitté för Byggnadsforskning.

Sweden. Statens Kommitté för
Byggnadsforskning.
690.015
(485) Christianssen, Tore.
S82   Beräkning av luftinblasningssystem för
R1   konstant statiskt tryck samt datamaskin-
1967 programmering av beräkningsmetoden (Formulation of an air injection system with constant static pressure. Computer programming
of the method) av Tore Christianssen och
Ingmar Enegorg. Stockholm, 1967.
16p.   (Sweden. Statens Kommitté för
Byggnadsforskning. Rapport 1:1967)
Reviderat och kompletterat särtryck ur
tidskriften VVS 11:1965 och 4:1966.

(Cont'd on next card)

690.015
(485) Anders, Berg.   A-gruppen redovisning av
S82   stenarbeten...1962 (Card 2)
R84

1. Building research - Sweden.
2. Architectural drawing. I. Sweden. Statens
Kommitté för   Byggnadskorskning.

690.015
(485) Sweden. Statens Kommitté för Byggnadsfors-
S82   kning.
R36   Bad-och campingplatser (Bathing and camping
1966 sites) Stockholm, 1966.
32p.   (Its Rapport 36:1966)

1. Building research - Sweden.
2. Recreation - Sweden.

690.015
(485) Christianssen, Tore. Beräkning av luftin-
S82   blasningssystem för konstant statiskt tryck
R1   samt datamaskinprogrammering av beräknings-
1967   metoden...1967.   (Card 2)

1. Building research - Sweden. 2. Air
conditioning. 3. Automation. I. Sweden.
Statens Kommitté för Byggnadsforskning.
II. Eneborg, Ingmar, jt.au.

Sweden. Statens Kommitté för Byggnadsforskning.

690.015
(485)
S82
R83
Eriksson, Folke.
Bestämning av formrivningstider, av Folke Eriksson [med flera] [Determination of time the form removal] Stockholm, Statens råd för Byggnadsforskning, 1962.
44p. (Sweden. Statens Kommitté för Byggnadsforskning. Rapport 83)
At head of title: Byggforskningen.

1. Building research - Sweden. 2. Building construction. I. Sweden. Statens Kommitté för Byggnadsforskning.

690.015
(485)
S82
R55
Sweden. Statens Kommitté för Byggnadsforskning.
Bostadens matt [Area of domestic rooms av John Sjöström. Stockholm, 1959.
44p. diagrs., tables. (Its Rapport 55)

1. Space considerations. I. Sjöström, John.

690.015
(485)
S82
R25
Sweden. Statens Kommitté för Byggnadsforskning.
Building research in Sweden; a brief survey. Stockholm, 1952.
41 l. (Its Rapporter nr. 25)

Processed.

1. Building research-Sweden. I. Title.

690.015
(485)
S82
R29
1967
Sweden. Statens Kommitté för Byggnadsforskning.
Betongelement för husbyggnad (Precast concrete units in housing production) Stockholm, 1967.
47p. (Its Rapport 29:1967)

1. Building research — Sweden. 2. Concrete construction. 3. Prefabricated construction - Sweden. I. Title: Precast concrete units in housing production.

551.5
:614
S82
Sweden. Statens Kommitté för Byggnadsforskning.
Bostadsklimatet i murverkshus och betonghus; två års jämförande studier av temperatur-, fukt- och ventilationsforhållanden. Indoor climate in brick and concrete houses; 2-year comparative studies of temperature, moisture, and ventilation, av Hans E. Ronge. Stockholm, 1961.
59p. (Its Handlingar nr. 38)
English summary.
1. Climate and health. I. Ronge, Hans E. (Series)

690.015
B56
Sweden. Statens Kommitté för Byggnadsforskning.
Blomgren, Boris
Building research in Sweden; a brief survey, by Boris Blomgren and Sten Rosenström. [Stockholm, Statens Kommitté för Byggnadsforskning] Jan. 1949.
26 l.

1. Building research-Sweden. I. Rosenström, Sten jt. au. II. Sweden. Statens Kommitté för Byggnadsforskning.

690.015
(485)
S82
R14
1967
Sweden. Statens Kommitté för Byggnadsforskning.
Betongpumpar och betongkanoner. (Concrete pumps and concrete guns) Stockholm, 1967.
56p. (Its Rapport 14:1967)
Summary in English.
Bibliography: p. 24-25.

1. Building research - Sweden. 2. Concrete. I. Title: Concrete pumps and concrete guns.

690.015
(485)
S82
R77
Sweden. Statens Kommitté for Byggnadsforskning.
Erikson, Bengt E
Bostadsventilation. Fältundersökningar av bostadsventilationens funktion och ventilationsskanalers täthet. (Ventilation of dwellings. Field investigation of the function of dwelling ventilation and the tightness of ventilation ducts) Stockholm, Statens institut för byggnadsforskning, 1962.
57p. (Sweden. Statens Kommitté för Byggnadsforskning. Rapport 77)
1. Building research - Sweden. 2. Ventilation. I. Sweden. Statens Kommitté för Byggnadsforskning.

690.015
(485)
S82b
Sweden. Statens Kommitte for Byggnadsforskning.
Byggforskningen. Stockholm, 1966.
47p.

1. Building research - Sweden. 2. Building industry - Sweden.

2C

690.015
(485)
S82
R17
1966
Sweden. Statens Kommitté för Byggnadsforskning
Fröroth, Ake.
Betongvarubranschens struktur, av Ake Fröroth och Kjell Bodvik (Structure of the concrete products industry) Stockholm, Stetens Institut för Byggnadsforskning, 1966.
56p. (Sweden. Statens Kommitté för Byggnadsforskning. Rapport 17: 1966)
English summary.

1. Building research - Sweden. 2. Concrete. I. Bodvik, Kjell, jt. au. II. Sweden. Statens Kommitté för Byggnadsforskning.

690.015
(485)
S82
R28
1967
Sweden. Statens Kommitté för Byggnadsforskning.
Building and planning in developing countries; a partially annotated bibliography. Stockholm, 1967.
71p. (Its Rapport 28:1967)

1. Building research - Sweden. 2. Building construction - Bibl. 3. Planning - Bibl. 4. Underdeveloped countries. I. Title.

690.015
(485)
S82
R32
1967
Sweden. Statens Kommitté för Byggnadsforskning.
Byggindustrialisering; föredrag och diskussionsinlägg vid konferens på tekniska mässan i Stockholm 1967. [Industrialization of building. Lectures and discussion from a conference held at the Stockholm Technical Fair, 1967] Stockholm, 1967.
73p. (Its Rapport 32:1967)

2C

1. Prefabricated construction - Sweden. I. Title: Industrialization of building.

VF
711.6
S82
Sweden. Statens Kommitté för Byggnadsforskning.
Bilar på tomtmark. Stockholm, 1963.
[6]p. (Its Blad 1963:1)

1. Site planning. 2. Traffic safety.

690.015
(485)
S82
R8
1967
Sweden. Statens Kommitté för Byggnadsforskning.
Building climatology, list of literature.
Pt. II: Air. Stockholm, 1967.
81p. (Its Report 8:1967)

1. Building research - Sweden. 2. Architecture and climate - Bibl. 3. Air pollution. I. Title.

690.015
(485)
S82
R3
1966
Sweden. Statens Kommitté för Byggnadsforskning.
Byggmaterial: elva uppsatser (Building materials: eleven essays) Stockholm, 1966.
56p. (Its Rapport 3, 1966)
Särtryck ur Teknisk tidskrift 4:1965 och 3:1966.

1. Building research - Sweden. 2. Building materials - Sweden.

690.015
(485)
S82
R100
Sweden. Statens Kommitté för Byggnadsforskning.
Holm, Lennart.
Bostad och sol; undersökningar av soltillgängens betydelse för lufthygien, inomhusklimat och trivsel. Dwelling and sun; investigations on the influence of the access to sunshine on the hygiene of the air, the climate indoors and the well-being at home, by Lennart Holm and others. Stockholm, Statens råd för Byggnadsforskning, 1964.
76p. (Sweden. Statens Kommitté för Byggnadsforskning. Rapport 100)
(Cont'd. on next card)

690.015
(485)
S82
R7
1966
Sweden. Statens Kommitté for Byggnadsforskning.
Building climatology. Part 1. Odor. Stockholm, 1966.
64p. (Report 7: 1966)

1. Building research - Sweden. 2. Air pollution. 3. Ventilation. I. Title.

690.015
(485)
S82
M1
Sweden. Statens Kommitté för Byggnadsforskning.
Tengvik, Nils
Byggnadsforskningen i Sverige; en sammanställning. Stockholm, Statens Kommitté för Byggnadsforskning, 1945.
234 p. (Sverige. Statens Kommitté för Byggnadsforskning. Meddelanden, nr. 1)

1. Building research-Sweden. I. Sverige. Statens Kommitté för Byggnadsforskning.

690.015
(485)
S82
R100
Holm, Lennart.   Bostad och sol ...
(Card 2)

1. Building research - Sweden.
2. Daylight. 3. Architecture and climate. I. Sweden. Statens Kommitté för Byggnadsforskning.

690.015
(485)
S82
R33
1967
Sweden. Statens Kommitté för Byggnadsforskning.
Building climatology. Part III. Heat. Stockholm, 1967.
80p. (Rapport 33: 1967)

1. Architecture and climate. 2. Heating. I. Title.

690.015
(485)
S82
M20
Sweden. Statens Kommitté för Byggnadsforskning
Tengvik, Nils
Byggnadsmaterial från jord-och stenindustrien: produktion, kvalitet, distribution och prissättning. Building materials from the clay and stone industry: production, quality, distribution and pricing. Summary in English. Stockholm, Statens Kommitté för Byggnadsforskning, 1952.
61 p. graphs. (Sweden. Statens Kommitté för Byggnadsforskning. Meddelanden, nr. 20)

Bibliography: p. 42-45.

690.015
(485)
S82
R4
.966

Sweden. Statens Kommitté för Byggnadsfor-skning.
Jonson, Jen-Åke.
Byggnadsmaterialförsörjningen i Västerbottens och Norrbottens län (Supply building materials in the counties of Västerbotten and Norrbotten) Stockholm, Statens Institut för Byggnadsforskning, 1966.
126p. (Sweden. Statens Kommitté för Byggnadsforskning. Rapport 4, 1966)
English summary.
1. Building research - Sweden. 2. Building materials - Sweden. I. Sweden. Statens Kommitté för Byggnadsforskning.

691.421
P87

Sweden. Statens Kommitté for Byggnadsforskning.
Pusch, Roland.
Clay particles, their size, shape and arrangement in relation to some important physical properties of clays. [Stockholm] Statens råd för byggnadsforskning, 1962.
150p. (Sweden. Statens Kommitté for Byggnadsforskning. Handlingar no. 40, transactions)
1. Clay. I. Sweden. Statens Kommitté for Byggnadsforskning. (Series)

690.015
(485)
S82
R16-
1965

Sweden. Statens Kommitté för Byggnadsfor-skning.
Sehlin, Sven.
Diagrams of critical stresses for columns of material without tensile strength. Stockholm, National Swedish Institute for Building Research, 1965.
18p. (Sweden. Statens Kommitté för Byggnadsforskning. Rapport 16-1965)
1. Building research - Sweden. 2. Panels. 3. Strength of materials. I. Sweden. Statens Kommitté för Byggnadsforskning.

690.015
(485)
S82
M4

Sweden. Statens Kommitté för Byggnadsforskning
Dickson, Harald
Byggnadskostnader och byggnadsmaterial-marknader; studier rörande utvecklingen i Sverige. Stockholm, Statens Kommitté för Byggnadsforskning, 1946.
80 p. graphs, tables. (Sverige. Statens Kommitté för Byggnadsforskning. Meddelanden, nr. 4)
1.Building costs-Sweden. 2.Building materials-Sweden. I.Sverige. Statens Kommitté för Byggnadsforskning.

690.015
(485)
S82
M25

Sweden. Statens Kommitté för Byggnadsforsk-ning.
Pleijel, Gunnar
The computation of natural radiation in architecture and town planning. [Stockholm] Statens Nämnd för Byggnadsforskning [1954]
155 p. diagrs., graphs, tables.
(Statens Nämnd för Byggnadsforskning. Meddelande 25)
Bibliography: p. 139-143.
1. Solar radiation. I. Sweden. Statens Kommitté för Byggnadsforskning. II. Title. III. Title: Natural radiation in architecture and town planning.

690.015
(485)
S82
R35
1967

Sweden. Statens Kommitté for Byggnadsforskning.
Hellers, Bo-Goran.
Eccentrically compressed columns without tensile strength subjected to uniformly distributed lateral loads. Stockholm, Staten Kommitte för Byggnadsforskning, 1967.
56p. (Sweden. Statens Kommitté for Byggnadsforskning. Rapport 35: 1967)
Bibliography: p. 54-56.
1. Building research - Sweden. 2. Con-crete. 3. Strength of materials. 4. Strains and stresses. I. Sweden. Statens Kommitté for Byggnadsforskning. II. Title.

690.015
(485)
J12

Sweden. Statens Kommitté för Byggnadsforskning.
Jacobsson, Mejse.
Byggnadsproduktionen, problem och forsknings-behov (The building production, problems and valuable researches) Stockholm, Statens råd för Byggnadsforskning, 1963.
143p. (Sweden. Statens Kommitté för Byggnadsforskning. Programskrift nr. 1)
English summary.
1. Building research - Sweden. I. Sweden. Statens Kommitté för Byggnadsforskning. 2. Building Industry - Sweden.

690.015
(485)
S82
H19
1967

Sweden. Statens Kommitté för Byggnadsforskning.
Nordbeck, Stig.
Computer cartography point in polygon pro-grams, by Stig Nordbeck and Bengt Rystedt. Stockholm, National Swedish Institute for Building Research, 1967.
34p. (Rapport fran byggnadsforskningen, 6/67) Reprinted from Nordisk Tidskrift for Informationsbehandling, Bind 7, Hefte 1., 1967.
Simultaneously published in Lund studies in geography. Ser. C. General and Mathematical geography, no. 7.
(Cont'd on next card).

690.015
(485)
S82
R21-
1965

Sweden. Statens Kommitté för Byggnadsforskning.
Larsson, Olov.
Dimensionering av panneffekten i små och medelstore varmeanläggninger ett dis-kussionsinlägg (Aspects on the dimensioning of boiling effect in small and medium-sized heating plants) Stockholm, Statens Institut för Byggnadsforskning, 1965.
31p. (Sweden. Statens Kommitté för Byggnadsforskning. Rapport 21-1965)
1. Building research - Sweden. 2. Heating. 3. Boilers. I. Sweden. Statens Kommitté for Byggnadsforskning.

690.015
(485)
S82
D11

Sweden. Statens Kommitté för Byggnadsforskning
Danielsson, Hilmer J
Byggnadssätt och byggnadskostnader in Stockholm 1883-1939, Hilmer J. Danielsson [och] Mejse Jacobsson. Stockholm, Statens Kommitté för Byggnadsforskning, 1948.
100 p. illus., tables. (Sverige. Statens Kommitté för Byggnadsforskning. Meddelanden, nr. 11)
English summary attached.

690.015
(485)
S82
H19
1967

Nordbeck, Stig. Computer cartography point in polygon programs...1967. (Card 2)
1. Building research - Sweden. 2. Automation. I. Rystedt, Bengt, jt. au. II. Sweden. Statens Kommitté för Byggnadsforskning. III. Title.

690.015
(485)
S82
R57

Sweden. Statens Kommitté för Byggnads-forskning.
Dimensionering av traditionella valvformar [Dimensioning of traditional form works for floor slabs] av Gunnar Backsell och Yngve Hammarlund. Stockholm, 1959.
1v. diagrs., tables. (Its Rapport 57)
1. Floors and flooring. I. Backsell, Gunnar. II. Hammarlund, Yngve.

690.015
(485)
S82
L18

Sweden. Statens Kommitté för Byggnadsforskning.
Kreuger, Harry
Byggnadsteknisk ljusekonomi. Economics of interior lighting with special reference to building constructions. With a summary in English. Stockholm, Statens Kommitté för Byggnadsforskning, 1950.
117 p. (Sverige. Statens Kommitté för Byggnadsforskning. Meddelanden, nr. 18)
Bibliography: p. 112-113.

690.5
:551.5
(485)
S77

Sweden. Statens Kommitté för Byggnadsforskning.
Strokirk, Evert
Constructional engineer Ernst Sundh builds apartment houses in Avesta with the help of a crane. [Stockholm, Statens Kommitté för Byggnadsforskning? Feb. 1951]
9 l.
Bound with...A survey of winter construction in Sweden by Evert Strokirk. Processed.

690.015
(485)
S82
R90

Sweden. Statens Kommitté för Byggnadsfor-skning.
Backsell, Gunnar.
Dimensioneringstabeller för traditionella valvformar (Tables for the dimensioning of traditional form works for floor slabs) av Gunnar Backsell och Yngve Hammarlund. Stockholm, Sweden, Statens Kommitté för Byggnadsforskning, 1963.
[27]p. (Sweden. Statens Kommitté för Byggnadsforskning. Rapport no. 90)
English summary.
1. Building research - Sweden. 2. Floors and flooring. I. Sweden. Statens Kommitté for Byggnadsforskning.

690.015
(485)
S82
R91

Sweden. Statens Kommitté för Byggnadsforskning
Eneborg, Ingmar.
Centraliserad uppvärmning av småhusområden (District heating for areas comprising one-family houses) Stockholm, Statens Kommitté för Byggnadsforskning, 1963.
40p. (Sweden. Statens Kommitté för Byggnadsforskning. Rapport no. 91)
English summary: p. 28-29.
1. Building research - Sweden. 2. Heating, Central. I. Sweden. Statens Kommitté för Byggnadsforskning.

690.015
(485)
S82
R95

Sweden. Statens Kommitté för Byggnads-forskning.
Bring, Christer.
Data om golv; material, egenskaper, krav läggning, ekonomi (Data on floors; material, properties, demands, laying, economy) Stockholm, Statens råd för Byggnadsforskning, 1963.
152p. (Sweden. Statens Kommitté för Byggnadsforskning. Rapport 95)
English summary.
1. Building research - Sweden. 2. Floors and flooring. I. Sweden. Statens Kommitté för Byggnadsforskning.

690.015
(485)
S82
R15
1966

Sweden. Statens Kommitté för Byggnadsforskning.
Backsell, Gunnar.
Dimensioneringstabeller för traditionella valvformer (Tables for the dimensioning of traditional formworks for floor slabs) av Gunnar Backsell and others. Stockholm. Statens råd for Byggnadsforskning. 1966.
28p. (Sweden. Statens Kommitté för Byggnadsforskning. Rapport 15:1966)
1. Building research - Sweden. 2. Floors and flooring. I. Sweden. Statens Kommitté för Byggnadsforskning.

690.015
(485)
S82
R?-1955

Sweden. Statens Kommitté för Byggnads-forskning.
Centralkapprummet i högstadieskolor. Stockholm, 1965.
37p. (Its Rapport 3-1965)
1. Building research - Sweden. 2. Schools - Sweden.

690.015
(485)
S82
R34
1966

Sweden. Statens Kommitté för Byggnadsfor-skning.
Sehlin, Sven.
Design methods for walls with special reference to the load-carrying capacity. Stockholm, Statens Institut för Byggnadsforskning, 1966.
28p. (Sweden. Statens Kommitté för Byggnadsforskning. Rapport 34:1966)
1. Building research - Sweden. 2. Walls. I. Sweden. Statens Kommitté for Byggnadsforskning. II. Title.

690.015
(485)
S82
R65

Sweden. Statens Kommitté för Byggnadsforskning
Distributionsvägar och distributionskostnader för byggnadsmaterial, en metodstudie med exempel från vvs-branschen, [Roads and costs for the distribution of building materials, a study of methods illustrated by some examples from the fields of heating, water, and sanitation] av Per Holm. Stockholm, 1960.
65p. tables. (Its Rapport 65)
1. Building materials. I. Holm, Per.

690.015 (485) S82 R97
Sweden. Statens Kommitté för Byggnadsforskning.
Larsson, Olov.
Driftekonomi och driftproblem I medelstora oljeeldade värmeanläggniger (Operational economy and problems in medium-sized oil-fired heating plants) Stockholm, Statens råd for Byggnadsforskning, 1963.
52p. (Sweden. Statens Kommitté för Byggnadsforskning. Rapport 97)
English summary.
1. Building research - Sweden. 2. Heat transmission. I. Sweden. Statens Kommitté för Byggnadsforskning.

690.015 (485) S82 R12 1966
Sweden. Statens Kommitté för Byggnadsforskning.
Backsell, Gunnar.
Experimental investigations into deformations resulting from stresses perpendicular to grain in Swedish whitewood and redwood in respect of the dimensioning of concrete formwork. Stockholm, National Swedish Council for Building Research., 1966.
113p. (Sweden. Statens Kommitté för Byggnadsforskning. Rapport 12:1966)
1. Building research - Sweden. 2. Concrete construction. I. Sweden. Statens Kommitté för Byggnadsforskning.

333.332 (485) S82
Sweden. Statens Kommitté för Byggnadsforskning.
Fastighetspriser i Nyköping. Stockholm, 1966.
[6]p. (Its Blad 31, 1966)
1. Real property - Valuation - Sweden. 2. Real estate business - Sweden.

690.015 (485) S82 R42- 1966
Sweden. Statens Kommitté för Byggnadsforskning.
Hansen, Torben C
Effect of wind on creep and drying shrinkage of hardened cement mortar and concrete. Stockholm. 1966.
19p. (Sweden. Statens Kommitté för Byggnadsforskning. Rapport 42:1966)
Reprinted from Materials research and standards, vol. 6, no. 1.
1. Building research - Sweden. 2. Cement. 3. Concrete. 4. Architecture and climate. I. Sweden. Statens Kommittee för Byggnadsforskning.

690.015 (485) S82 R14 1966
Sweden. Statens Kommitté för Byggnadsforskning.
Exploateringsanläggningar - från översiktlig kostnadsbedömning till kostnadsanalys (Site exploitation works - from general estimates of cost to cost analysis) Stockholm, Statens Institut för Byggnadsforskning, 1966.
59p. (Its rapport 14:1966)
English summary.
1. Building research - Sweden. 2. Building costs - Sweden.

690.015 (485) S82 R18 1966
Sweden. Statens Kommitté för Byggnadsforskning.
Fire tests with plastic tubes carried out at the Research Station in Studsvik, Spring 1963. Stockholm, 1966.
35p. (Its Rapport 18:1966)
1. Building research - Sweden. 2. Plastics. 3. Fire protection (Municipal) I. Title.

690.015 (485) S82 R18 1967
Sweden. Statens Kommitté för Byggnadsforskning.
Larsson, Olov.
Eldning med inhemska bränslen [Firing of furnaces with domestic fuels] Stockholm, 1967.
12p. (Sweden. Statens Kommitté för Byggnadsforskning. Rapport 18:1967)
Sertryck ur tidskriften VVS 4:1967.
1. Building research - Sweden. 2. Furnaces. 3. Fuel. I. Sweden. Statens Kommitté för Byggnadsforskning.

690.015 (485) S82 R16
Sweden. Statens Kommitté för Byggnadsforskning.
Andersson, Börje
Färger för målning av trä utomhus. Exterior house paints. Av Börje Andersson och Paul Nylén. Stockholm, Statens Kommitté för Byggnadsforskning, 1950.
91 p. illus., tables. (Sverige. Statens Kommittée för Byggnadsforskning. Meddelanden, nr. 16)
English summary: p. 60-61.
Bibliography: p. 62-63.

690.015 (485) S82 R49
Sweden. Statens Kommitté för Byggnadsforskning.
Flerfamiljshusens biutrymmen, förvarings behov och relativ ekonomi. [Non-living space in multi-family houses] Stockholm, 1959.
1v. diagrs., tables. (Its Rapport no. 49)
1. Space considerations.

693.002.22 (485) S82e
Sweden. Statens Kommitté för Byggnadsforskning.
Elemenbyggda enfamiljhus i Göteborg [Unit constructed one-family houses in Goteborg], av Erik Friberger. Stockholm, 1958.
84p. illus., diagrs., tables. (Its Handlingar nr. 33)
English summary.
1. Prefabricated construction - Sweden. 2. Housing - Sweden. I. Friberger, Erik. (Series)

690.015 (485) S82 R10 1966
Sweden. Statens Kommitté för Byggnadsforskning.
Carlegrim, Erik.
Fastighetsmarknad 1957-1963. Fastighetsmarknadens omfattning, struktur och prisutveckling för villafastigheter och fritidsfastigheter i tolv län (Real estate market 1957-1963. The extent, structure and price development of the real estate market for villas and holiday-house properties in twelve counties) Stockholm, Statens Institut för Byggnadsforskning, 1966.
277p. (Sweden. Statens Kommitté för Byggnadsforskning. Rapport 10:1966)
English summary.
(Cont'd on next card)

690.015 (485) S82 R79
Sweden. Statens Kommitté för Byggnadsforskning.
Fog, Hans.
Flerfamiljshusens markutrymmen. [Clearing land for multi-family housing.] [Stockholm] Statens råd för Byggnadsforskning, 1960.
60p. (Sweden. Statens Kommitté för Byggnadsforskning. Rapport 79)
1. Building research - Sweden. 2. Apartment houses - Sweden. I. Sweden. Statens Kommitté för Byggnadsforskning.

690.015 (485) S82 R107
Sweden. Statens Kommitté för Byggnadsforskning.
Sahlin, Sven.
Elementvaggar inbyggda mellan bjalklag; spanningar, deformationer, kraftexcentriciteter ochbärformäga (Wall panels built in between floors; stresses, deformations, eccentricity of forces, and load bearing capacity) av Sven Sahlin och Sven Jansson. Stockholm, Sweden, Statens råd för Byggnadsforskning, 1964.
[124] p. (Sweden. Statens Kommitté för Byggnadsforskning. Rapport 107)
(Cont'd on next card)

690.015 (485) S82 R10 1966
Carlegrim. Erik. Fastighetsmarknad 1957-1963...1966. (Card 2)
1. Building research - Sweden. 2. Real estate business - Sweden. I. Sweden. Statens Kommitté för Byggnadsforskning.

690.015 (485) S82 R32 1966
Sweden. Statens Kommitté för Byggnadsforskning.
Flexibla lägenheter: en intervjuundersökning i "experimenthuset" i Järnbrott, Göteborg (Flexible flats; an investigation in an experimental block of flats in Järnbrott, Gothenburg) Stockholm 1966.
81p. (Its Rapport 32:1966)
1. Building research - Sweden. 2. Space considerations. 3. Housing - Sweden.

690.015 (485) S82 R107
Sahlin, Sven. Elementvaggar... (Card 2)
English summary.
1. Building research - Sweden. 2. Panels. 3. Walls. I. Jansson, Sven, jt. au. II. Sweden. Statens Kommitté för Byggnadsforskning.

690.015 (485) S82 R45 1966
Sweden. Statens Kommitté för Byggnadsforskning.
Fastighetsmarknad i Nyköping 1930-1964, samt mindre undersökningar i Märsta, Gävle, Hässelby, Brännkyrka, Solns, Djurö, Norre Öland och Stockholms skärgård (The real estate market in Nyköping 1930-1964, together with smaller, special investigations in Märsta, Gevle, Hässelby, Brännkyrka, Solns, Djurö, North Öland and the Stockholm archipelago) Stockholm, 1966.
79p. (Sweden. Statens Kommitté för Byggnadsforskning. Rapport 45:1966)
Sertryck ur SOU 1966:24 "Markfragen 11", bilaga 5.
(Cont'd on next card)

690.015 (485) S82 R39 1967
Sweden. Statens Kommitté för Byggnadsforskning.
Acking, Carl-Axel.
For och Konstruktion spännings optiska Studier. [Form and structure; photoelasticity studies] au Carl-Axel Acking och Paul Ridemar. Stockholm, Statens Kommitté for Byggnadsforskning, 1967.
175p. (Sweden. Statens Kommitté för Byggnadsforskning. Rapport 39)
1. Building research - Sweden. 2. Strains and stresses. 3. Strength of materials. I. Ridemar, Paul, jt. au. II. Sweden. Statens Kommitté för Byggnadsforskning.

690.015 (485) S82 R41 1966
Sweden. Statens Kommitté för Byggnadsforskning.
El-gruppen. Redovisning av elcentraler riktlinjer för redovisningen (Electric distribution board guiding principles for reports) Stockholm, 1966.
12p. (Its Rapport 41:1966)
1. Building research - Sweden. 2. Electric wiring.

690.015 (485) S82 R45 1966
Sweden. Statens Kommitté för Byggnadsforskning. Fastighetsmarknad i Nyköping 1930-1964...1966. (Card 2)
1. Building research - Sweden. 2. Real estate business - Sweden.

690.015 (485) S82 R40
Sweden. Statens Kommitté för Byggnadsforskning.
Förbrukningen av rör och rördelar i bostadshus av Thure Nilvall och Per Holm. Stockholm, 1957.
48 p. tables. (Its Rapport no. 40)
1. Building construction - Sweden. 2. Pipes. I. Nilvall, Thure. II. Holm, Per (Series)

Sweden. Statens Kommitté för
Byggnadsforskning.

690.015
(485)
S82
R101

Tynelius, Sven.
Förnyelse av det äldre villabestandet;
en modellundersökning i eskilstuna
(Modernization of old detached houses; a
pattern survey) Stockholm, Statens rad
for Byggnadsforskning, 1964.
36p. (Sweden. Statens Kommitté för
Byggnadsforskning. Rapport no. 101)
English summary.
1. Building research - Sweden. 2. Houses -
Maintenance and modernization. I. Sweden. Statens
Kommitté för   Byggnadsforskning.

690.015
(485)
S82
R30-1965

Sweden. Statens Kommitté för Byggnadsforskning.
Halth armering riktlinjer för ritning
och specificering. Stockholm, 1965.
17p. (Its Rapport 30-1965)

1. Building research - Sweden.
2. Concrete, Reinforced.

Sweden. Statens Kommittée för Byggnadsforshning.
Handlingar. Transactions.

691.116
N67s

no.
45

Norén, Bengt. Svensk furuplywood-
hållfasthet och tillåtna påkänningar
(Swedish pine plywood; strength and
working stresses) 1964.

538.56
N67

Sweden. Statens Kommitté för Byggnadsforskning.
Nordbeck, Stig.
Framställning av kartor med hjälp av
siffermaskiner (Production of maps with the
help of digital computers) Stockholm,
Statens rad för Byggnadsforskning, 1964.
117p. (Sweden. Statens Kommitté för
Byggnadsforskning, Handlingar 44, Transactions)

1. Automation. 2. Maps and mapping. I. Sweden.
Statens Kommitté för   Byggnadsforskning.
(Series)

690.19
:624.131
S82

691.55
:693.625
S82

Sweden. Statens Komitté för Byggnadsforskning.
Handlingar.

No. 28 Bergfelt, Allan. - Investigation of
corrosion risks in clay. 1957.

No. 29 Saretok, Vitold. - Puts och putsning, ett
kritakt litteraturstudium [plaster and
plastering] 1957

Sweden. Statens Kommitté för Byggnadsforshning.
Handlingar. Transactions.

691.328.2
L67

624.131
P87
643.5

693.5
H65

no.
47

no.
48

no.
49

Lorentsen, Mogens. Shear and bond in
prestressed concrete beams without
sheer reinforcement. 1964.

Pusch, Roland. On the structure of
clay sediments. 1964.

Holmberg, Åke. Behaviour of load-bearing
sandwich-type structures. 1965.

690.015
(485)
S82
R108

Sweden. Statens Kommitte for Byggnadsforskning.
Hellsten, Göran.
Fran stadsplan till inflyttning; bygg-
processens förlopp i 30 produktionsexempel
[From town plan to moving-in, 30 case
studies] av Göran Hellsten och Yngve
Palm. Stockholm, Sweden, Statens rad för
Byggnadsforskning, 1964.
57p. (Sweden. Statens Kommitte for
Byggnadsforskning. Rapport 108)
English summary.
1. Building research - Sweden. 2. Housing
projects -   Sweden. I. Sweden.
Statens   Kommitté for Bygg-
nadsforskning.

624.138
S82

624.138
S82v

690.21
S82

693.00222
(485)
S82a

Sweden. Statens Komitté för Byggnadsforskning.
Handlingar.
No. 30 Ingberk, K. - Soil stabilisation by
injection. 1957.

No. 31 Wenner, Carl-Gosta - Thermal conductivity
of soils.

No. 32 Ericsson, Hans. - Houses with out basements with special reference to
foundations.

No. 33 Friberger, Erik. Elementbyggda
enfamiljhus i Göteborg. Unit con-
struct; one-family houses in
Gothenburg. 1958.

690.015
(485)
S82
R31
1966

Sweden. Statens Kommitte för Byggnads-
forskning.
Nuder, Ants.
Hisser och trappor i kontorshus (Lifts
and staircases in office buildings) by
Ants Nuder and Bengt Johansson. Stockholm,
1966.
12p. (Sweden. Statens Kommitte för
Byggnadsforskning. Rapport 31:1966)
English summary.

1. Building research - Sweden. 2. Eleva-
tors. 2. Industrial buildings. 3. Stairs.
I. Johnsson, Bengt, jt. au. II. Sweden.
Statens   Kommitté för
Byggnads-   forskning.

690.015
(485)
S82
R30
1966

Sweden. Statens Kommitté för Byggnadsfor-
skning.
Tynelius, Sven.
Fri sikt i gathörn (Clear view at street
corners), av Sven Tynelius and Carl-Olof
Berglund. Stockholm, Statens Institut för
Byggnadsforskning, 1966.
99p. (Sweden. Statens Kommitté för
Byggnadsforskning. Rapport 30: 1966)
English summary.

1. Building research - Sweden.
2. Traffic safety. I. Berglund, Carl-
Olof, jt.au. II. Sweden. Statens Kommitté
för Byggnadsfor-   skning.

697.3
S82

690.22
S82

690.22
:73.82
S82

Sweden. Statens Kommitté för Byggnadsforskning.
Handlingar.

no.
34

no.
35

no.
36

Enoborg, Ingmar. Stora eller sma varme-
centraler. Large or small central heating plants. 1959.

Sahlin, Sven. Structural interaction of
walls and floor slabs. 1959.

Brown, Gosta. Yttervaggs värmeisolerings-
formaga. Thermal resistance of exterior
walls with particular emphasis on multi-
storied apartment houses. 1959.

690.015
(485)
S82
R48

Sweden. Statens Kommitté för Byggnadsforskning.
Höghus och laghus i smastadsmiljö, av
Lillemor Landström. Stockholm, 1958.
93p. tables. (Its Rapport no. 48)

1. Family living requirements. 2. Housing -
Sweden - Social aspects. 3. Apartment houses.
I. Landström, Lillemor.

690.015
(485)
S82
R112

Sweden. Statens Kommitte for Byggnadsforskning.
Bring, Christer.
Friktion och halkning (Friction
and slipping) Stockholm, Sweden,
Statens rad for Byggnadsforskning,
1964.
152p. (Sweden. Statens Kommitté
for Byggnadsforskning. Rapport 112)
English summary.
1. Building research - Sweden. 2. Accidents.
3. Floors and flooring. I. Sweden. Statens
Kommitté for Byggnadsforskning.

690.24
S82

551.5
:614
S82

Sweden. Statens Kommitté for Byggnadsforskning.
Handlingar.

no.
37

no.
38

Noren, Bengt. Takstolar av trä. Small
timber roof trusses and their design.
1959.

Ronge, Hans E. Bostadsklimatet i
murverkshus och betonghus. 1961.

690.22
H63

Sweden. Statens Kommitté for Byggnadsforsknin
Hoglund, Ingemar.
Hogisolerande yttervaggars värmemostand
(Thermal resistance of highly insulated outer
walls) Stockholm, Sweden, Statens rad för
Byggnadsforskning, 1962.
193p. (Sweden. Statens Kommitté för
Byggnadsforskning. Handlingar nr. 41,
transactions)
English summary.

1. Walls. 2. Insulating materials. I. Sweden.
Statens   Kommitte för   Byggnadsforskning.
(Series)

690.015
(485)
S82
R44
1966

Sweden. Statens Kommitté for Byggnadsfor-
skning.
Victorin, Gunnar.
Fuktmätningar i trähus (Moisture measure-
ments in timber houses) Stockholm, Statens
Institut för Byggnadsforskning, 1966.
51p. (Sweden. Statens Kommitté för
Byggnadsforskning. Rapport 44:1966)

1. Building research - Sweden.
2. Moisture condensation. I. Sweden.
Statens Kommitté for Byggnadsforskning.

691.421
P87

690.22
H63

Sweden. Statens Kommitté for Byggnadsforskning.
Handlingar.

no.
40

no.
41

Pusch, Roland. Clay particles their
size, shape and arrangement in
relation to some important physical
properties of clays. 1962.

Höglund, Ingemar. Thermal resistance
of highly insulated outer walls.
1962.

690.21
S82

Sweden. Statens Kommitté för Byggnadsforskning.
Hus utan kallare grundlaggningsmetoder.
Houses without basements with special reference to
foundations, av Hans Ericsson. Stockholm, 1958.
137p. (Its Handlingar no. 32.)
English summary.

1. Foundations. I. Ericsson, Hans. (Series)

690.015
(485)
S82
R85
English

Sweden. Statens Kommitté för Byggnadsforskning.
Wirdenius, Hans.
Functions of supervisors in the building
industry, by Hans Wirdenius and Sterner
Lönnsjö. Translated from the Swedish by
H.Q. panel. Stockholm, State Council for
Building Research, 1962.
93p. (Sweden. Building Research Council.
Report 85. U.K. Ministry of Public Building
and Works. Library. Translation no. 216)

1. Personnel management. 2. Building industry -
Sweden. I. Lonnsjo, Sterner, jt. au. II. Sweden. Statens
Kommitté för Byggnads-   forskning.

697.133
H63

538.56
N67

Sweden. Statens Kommittée för Byggnadsforshning.
Handlingar. Transactions.

no.
43

no.
44

Hoglund, Ingemar. Värmeförluster I
smahus, resultat från två försökshus.
(Heat losses in small houses, results
of experiments in two houses) 1963.

Nordbeck, Stig.
Framställlning av kartor med hjälp av
siffermaskiner (production of maps
with the help of digital computers)
1964.

690.015
(485)
S82
R41

Sweden. Statens Kommitté för Byggnadsforskning.
Icke traditionella yttervaggar i hyreshus
[nonconventional exterior walls in multi-storied
flats] av Folke Hagman. Stockholm, 1957.
124p. illus. (Its Rapport 41)

Attached: English summary, 13p.

1. Building research - Sweden. 2. Walls.
I. Hagman, Folke. (Series)

690.015 (485) S82 R106
Sweden. Statens Kommitté för Byggnadsforskning.
Höglund, Ingemar.
Inre konvektion i byggnadskonstruktioner-negra studier speciellt av isolering med mineralull, av Ingemar Höglund och Tore Hansson. Stockholm, Statens råd för Byggnadsforskning, 1964.
40p. (Sweden. Statens Kommitté för Byggnadsforskning. Rapport 106)

1. Building research - Sweden. 2. Heating. 3. Insulation. I. Sweden. Statens Kommitté för Byggnadsforskning. II. Hansson, Tore, jt. au.

690.015 (485) S82 R117
Sweden. Statens Kommitté för Byggnads-forskning.
Klassrummet för låg- och mellenstadiet (The class-room for elementary schools) Stockholm, 1965.
155p. (Its Rapport no. 117)

1. Building research - Sweden. 2. Schools - Sweden. I. Title: The class-room for elementary schools.

690.015 (485) S82 R60
Sweden. Statens Kommitté för Byggnads-forskning.
Korrosionsrisken vid användning av kalciumklorid i betong [Risk of corrosion due to use of calcium as admixture to concrete] av Sven G. Bergström och Hans E. Holst. Stockholm, 1960.
21p. illus., tables. (Its Rapport 60)

1. Corrosion. I. Bergström, Sven G. II. Holst, Hans E.

690.015 (485) S82 R47
Sweden. Statens Kommitte för Byggnadsforskning.
Injekteringens inverkan pa en förspänd balks statiska verkningssätt. [Effect of injection on static structural action of prestressed concrete beams] av Mogens Lorentsen. Stockholm, 1958.
[132]p. illus., diagrs. (Its Rapport no. 47)

1. Concrete, Prestressed. I. Lorentsen, Mogens.

690.015 (485) S82 R59
Sweden. Statens Kommitte för Byggnads-forskning.
Klassrummets dagerbelysning. Tva modellstudier. [Daylight illumination of classrooms. Two studies with models] Stockholm, 1960.
38p. diagrs. (Its Rapport 59)

1. Schools - Sweden. 2. Daylight.

690.015 (485) S82 R102
Sweden. Statens Kommitté för Byggnadsforsk-ning.
Lindquist, N
Kostnader för stadsplaneanläggningar för höga och låge hus; en undersökning av Hagsätra och Västertorp (Costs for town planning operations, such as site preparations, utility system, and sewer installation; an investigation of the Hagsätra and Västertorp developments) Stockholm, Statens råd för Byggnadsforsk-ning, 1963. (Cont'd. on next card)

690.015 (485) S82 R78
Sweden. Statens Kommitté för Byggnadsforskning.
Mandorff, Sven.
Inreglering av värmesystem (Adjustment of hot-water heating pipe systems) Stockholm, Statens råd for byggnadsforskning, 1962.
61p. (Sweden. Statens Kommitté for Byggnadsforskning. Rapport 78)

1. Heating, Central. 2. Heating, Hot-water. I. Sweden. Statens Kommitté for Byggnadsforskning.

690.015 (485) S82 R67
Sweden. Statens Kommitte för Byggnadsforskning.
Klimatfysiologiska laboratoriet i Uppsala 1949-1959; beskrivning av anläggning och mätutrustning, av Börje Löfstedt och Hans Ronge. [Laboratory for climatic physiology, Uppsala, 1949-1959. Description of installation and measuring equipment] Stockholm, 1961.
61p. (Its Rapport 67)

1. Climatology. I. Löfstedt, Börje. II. Ronge, Hans.

690.015 (485) S82 R102
Lindquist, N Kostnader for stadsplanean-läggingar for höga och låge hus ...
62p. (Sweden. Statens Kommitté för Byggnadsforskning. Rapport no. 102)
English summary.
1. Building research - Sweden. 2. Capital improvement programs - Sweden. 3. Building costs - Sweden. I. Sweden. Statens Kommitté för Byggnadsforskning.

690.015 (485) S82 R13 1966
Sweden. Statens Kommitté för Byggnadsforskning
Carlsson, Axel.
Inventering av byggskador (Inventory of defects and damages to buildings) Stockholm, Statens Institut for Byggnadsforskning, 1966.
27p. (Sweden. Statens Kommitté för Byggnadsforskning. Rapport 13:1966)
English summary.

1. Building research - Sweden. 2. Building maintenance. I. Sweden. Statens Kommitté för Byggnadsforskning.

690.015 (485) S82 R30 1967
Sweden. Statens Kommitte för Byggnadsforskning.
Klimatmätningar i skolor. Measurements of climate in schools. Stockholm, 1967.
87p. (Its Rapport 30: 1967)
Concluding remarks in English.

1. Building research - Sweden. 2. Schools. 3. Climate and health. I. Title: Measurements of climate in schools.

690.015 (485) S82 R73
Sweden. Statens Kommitté för Byggnadsforskning.
Kostnadsberäkning inom byggnadsindustrin av Arbetsgruppen för enhetliga redovisningsmetoder inom byggnadsindustrin. (Normal accounts schedule for the building industry) Stockholm, 1962.
85p. (Its Rapport 73)

1. Building costs - Estimates.

690.015 (485) S82 R42 1967
Sweden. Statens Kommitte for Byggnadsforskning.
Inventering av stomsystem för elementbyggda flerfamiljshus (Inventory of industrialized building systems for system-built blocks of flats) Stockholm, Statens Institut for Byggnadsforskning, 1967.
115p. (Rapport 42:1967)
English summary.
1. Building research - Sweden. 2. Pre-fabricated construction - Sweden.

690.015 (485) S82 R52
Sweden. Statens Kommitte för Byggnads-forskning.
Kontoplan för fastighetsförvaltningar, med anvisningar. Stockholm, 1959.
43p. (Its Rapport 52)

1. Accounting. 2. Real property.

690.015 (485) S82 R105
Sweden Statens Kommitté för Byggnadsforskning.
Ericsson Alvar.
Läggning och sättning av keramiska plattor; en sammanställning av nyare undersökningar (Tile fixing; a summary of recent investigations) Stockholm, Statens råd för Byggnadsforskning, 1964.
39p. (Sweden. Statens Kommitté för Byggnadsforskning. Rapport no. 105)
English summary.
1. Building research - Sweden. 2. Tile construction. I. Sweden. Statens Kommitté för Byggnadsforskning.

690.015 (485) S82 R46
Sweden. Statens Kommitté för Byggnadsfor-skning.
Kalk-och kalkcementbruk invändig puts på betong, av Gerhard Hinderson. Stockholm, 1958.
42p. illus., tables. (Its Rapport 46)

1. Building materials - Lime. I. Hinderson, Gerhard.

690.015 (485) S82 R26 1967
Sweden. Statens Kommitté för Byggnadsforskning.
Kontorshus. Litteraturinventering. (Office buildings. List of literature) Stockholm, 1967.
1v. (Its Rapport 26:1967)

1. Building research - Sweden. 2. Office buildings - Bibl. I. Title: Office buildings. List of literature.

690.015 (485) S82 R19 1966
Sweden. Statens Kommitté för Byggnadsfor-skning.
Lågtemperaturkorrosion i värmepannor-symposieenferenden med diskussionsinlägg (Low temperature corrosion in central heating furnaces - Symposium with reports and discussions) Stockholm, 1966.
77p. (Its Rapport 19:1966)

1. Building research - Sweden. 2. Corrosion. 3. Heating, Central.

025.4 S82
Sweden. Statens Kommitté för Byggnadsforskning.
Klassifikation inom byggbranschen problem och forskningsbehov (Building classification, problems and research requirements) Stockholm, 1964.
47p. (Its Programskrift no. 3)

English summary.

1. Cataloging. 2. Building documentation. I. Title: Building classification, problems and research requirements.

690.015 (485) S82 R104
Sweden. Statens Kommitté för Byggnadsforskning.
Engvall, Ulf.
Koordinatangivningsmetoder för samhälls-planeringen (Methods of determining coordinates for community planning) av Ulf Engvall och Erik Larsson. Stockholm, Statens råd for Byggnadsforskning, 1964.
62p. (Sweden. Statens Kommitté för Byggnadsforskning. Rapport 104)
English summary: p. 18.
1. Building research - Sweden. 2. City planning. 3. Automation. I. Larsson, Erik, jt. au. II. Sweden. Statens Kommitté för Byggnadsforskning.

690.015 (485) S82 R31 1967
Sweden. Statens Kommitté för Byggnadsforsk-ning.
Lärare bedömer klassrumsklimatet, en enkätundersökning. Teachers opinions of class-room climate, a questionnaire survey. Stockholm, 1967.
52p. (Its Rapport 31:1967)
English summary.

1. Building research - Sweden. 2. Schools - Sweden. 3. Climate and health. I. Title: Teachers opinions of classroom climate.

690.015
(485) Sweden. Statens Kommitte för Byggnads-
S82L   forskning.
       List of publications, 1964/65,68; 1948.66;

     Stockholm, 1965-1969
     3 v.

     For complete information see main card.
     Contents: A short presentation of the
     National Swedish Institute for Building
     Research (Litteratur fran Byggforskningen)
     Literature from the Building Research.
1949/1968 has tab. Publ. from: (Cont'd on next card)

690.015
(485)
S82   Sweden. Statens Kommitte för
R69   Byggnadsforskning.
     Markförstärkning genom elektro-osmos och
     elektrokemisk behandling, [Soil stabilisation
     by electro-osmosis and by electro-chemical
     treatment.] av Roland Pusch. Stockholm, 1961.
     25p. (Its Rapport 69)

     English summary.

     1. Soils. I. Pusch, Roland.

690.015
(485) Sweden. Statens Kommitte' för
S82   Byggnadsforskning.
R11   Mekaniska hjälpmedel vid gruppbygge av
1967   småhus [Mechanical aids in the mass production
     of one-family houses] Stockholm, 1967.
     104p. (Its Rapport 11:1967)
     English summary.

     1. Building research - Sweden. 2. Archi-
     tecture, Domestic - Sweden. 3. Building
     methods.

690.015
(485) Sweden. Statens Kommitte för Byggnads-
S82L   forskning. List of publications...19
               (Card 2)

     1. Building research - Sweden.
     2. Sweden. Statens Kommitte for
     Byggnadsforskning-Publications.

624.138
S82   Sweden. Statens Kommitté för Byggnadsforskning.
     Markstabilisering genom injektering.
     [Soil stabilisation by injection] av Kjell
     Ingberk and others. Stockholm, 1957.
     110 p., illus., diagrs. (Its Handlingar
     nr. 30, transactions)

     English summary.

     1. Soils. I. Ingberk, K

690.015 Sweden. Statens Kommitte för Byggnadsforskning
(485) Hogberg, Erik.
S82   Morter bond. Stockholm, Statens Kommitté
R40   for Byggnadsforskning, 1967.
1967   90p. (Sweden. Statens Kommitte for
     Byggnadsforskning. Rapport 40: 1967)
     Bibliography: p. 88-90.

     1. Building research - Sweden. 2. Cement.
     3. Strength of materials. I. Sweden.
     Statens Kommitté för Byggnadsforskning.
     II. Title.

     Sweden. Statens Kommitté för Byggnadsforsk-
690.015   ning.
(485) Kihlman, Tor.
S82   Ljudtransmission genom springor (Sound
R93   transmission through slits) Stockholm,
     Statens Kommitte for Byggnadsforskning, 1963.
     [61]p. (Sweden. Statens Kommitté för
     Byggnadsforskning. Rapport no. 93)

     1. Building research-Sweden.
     2. Soundproofing. 3. Architectural
     accoustics.   I. Sweden.
     Statens   Kommitté
     for   Byggnadsfor-
     skning.

     Sweden. Statens Kommittee för Byggnadsforskning.
697.133
A21 Adamson, Bo.
     Marktemperaturer under hus utan källare
     (Soil temperatures under houses without
     basement) av Bo Adamson and others.
     Stockholm, Statens råd för Byggnadsforskning,
     1964.
     64p. (Sweden. Statens råd för
     Byggnadsforskning. Handlingar nr. 46.
     Transactions)
     English summary.
1. Heat transmission. 2. Basementless houses.
3. Foundations (Buildings) I. Sweden. Statens
Kommitte for Byggnads-   forskning. II. Title:
Soil temperature   under houses
without basement.

690.015
(485)   Sweden. Statens Kommitté för Byggnads-
S82n   forskning.
     The National Swedish Institute for
     Building Research. Stockholm, 1966.
     47p.

     1. Building research - Sweden.
     2. Sweden. Statens Kommitté för Byggnads-
     forskning.

690.015
S82   Sweden. Statens Kommitté för Byggnads-
R63   forskning.
     Lokala motstand i korsrörsforbindningar.
     Uppvärmningssystem med enrors huvudledning.
     Oversättningar av tva rapporter fran USSR.
     [Local resistance in cross-pipes, heating
     system with one tube's main pipe. Trans-
     lations of two reports from USSR] Stock-
     holm, 1960.
     1v. diagrs. (Its Rapport nr. 63)

     1. Pipes. 2. Heating.

690.015
(485)   Sweden. Statens Kommitté für Byggnads-
S82   forskning.
R37   Material och konstruktioner i gruppbyggda
1967   smahus. Material and construction in houses
     built in groups. Stockholm, 1967.
     35p. (Its Rapport 37)

     1. Building research - Sweden. 2. Building
     materials - Sweden. 3. Building methods.

     Sweden. Statens Kommitté för Byggnadsfor-
690.015   skning.
(485) Thiberg, Sven.
S82   Non-institutional housing for the elderly.
R5   Stockholm, 1967.
1967   36p. (Sweden. Statens Kommitté för
     Byggnadsforskning. Rapport 5:1967)
2 c.

     1. Building research - Sweden. 2. Hous-
     ing for the aged - Sweden. I. Sweden.
     Statens Kommitté för Byggnadsforskning.

     Sweden. Statens Kommitté för
690.015   Byggnadsforskning.
(485) Brendt, Ove.
S82   Luftljudsisolering hos vägger:
R13-   sammenställning av mätresultat (Airborne
1965   sound insulation of walls: a collection of
     measurement results) av Ove Brendt och Sven
     Aberg. Stockholm, Statens Institut för
     Byggnadsforskning, 1965.
     78p. (Sweden. Statens Kommitté för
     Byggnadsforskning. Rapport 13-1965)
     English summary.

1. Building research - Sweden. 2. Soundproofing.
3. Walls. I. Aberg,   Sven, jt. au.
II. Sweden. Statens   Kommitté för
Byggnadsforskning.

690.015
(485) Sweden. Statens Kommitté för Byggnadsforsk-
S82   ning.
R54   Mattnoggrannhet och toleranser vid monterings-
     byggeri [Measurement accuracy and tolerances
     at prefabricated buildings] av Ingemar Nyquist.
     Stockholm, 1959.
     47p. illus., diagrs. (Its Rapport 54)

     1. Prefabricated construction - Sweden.
     I. Nyquist, Ingemar.

690.015
S82   (485) Sweden. Statens Kommitté för Byggnadsforskning.
R74   Normalkontoplan for byggnadsindustrin av
     Arbetsgruppen för enhetliga redovisningsmetoder
     inom byggnadsindustrin. Stockholm, 1962.
     89p. (Its Rapport 74)

     1. Accounting. 2. Credit.

     Sweden. Statens Kommitté för Byggnadsfor-
690.015   skning.
(485) Ingemansson, Stig.
S82   Luft- och stegljudsisolering; en sammen-
R1   fattning av de viktigaste teorierna och deras
1966   tillämpning (Airborne and impact sound insula-
     tion; a brief account of the most important
     theories and their application) Stockholm,
     Statens Institut for Byggnadsforskning, 1966.
     49p. (Sweden. Statens Kommitté för
     Byggnadsforskning. Rapport 1, 1966)
     English summary.

     1. Building research - Sweden. 2. Sound-
     proofing.   I. Sweden. Statens
     Kommitte för   Byggnadsforskning.

690.015
(485) Sweden. Statens Kommitté för Byggnadsforskning.
S82   Meddelanden. Nr. 1 -
M   Stockholm, 1945 -
       v.

     For full information see shelf list card.

     1. Building research-Sweden.
     analyzed.

624.131 Sweden. Statens Kommitte for Byggnadsforskning
P87 Pusch, Roland.
     On the structure of clay sediments.
     Stockholm, Statens rad för Byggnadsforskning,
     1964.
     60p. (Sweden. Statens Kommitte for
     Byggnadsforskning. Handlingar no. 48,
     transactions)

     1. Soils. 2. Clay. I. Sweden. Statens
     Kommitte för Byggnadsforskning. (Series)

     Sweden. Statens Kommitté för Byggnadsfor-
690.015   skning.
(485) Brendt, Ove.
S82   Luft- och stegljudsisolering hos bjälklag;
R14-   sammenställning av mätresultat (Airborne end
1965   impact sound insulation of floors; a
     collection of measurement results) av Ove
     Brendt och Sven Aberg. Stockholm, Statens
     Institut for Byggnadsforskning, 1965.
     285p. (Sweden. Statens Kommitté för
     Byggnadsforskning. Rapport 14-1965)

1. Building research - Sweden. 2. Soundproofing.
3. Floors and flooring. I. Aberg, Sven, jt.
au. II. Sweden.   Statens Kommitté
for Byggnadsforskning.

690.015   Sweden. Statens Kommitté för
(485)   Byggnadsforskning.
S82 Friberger, Erik
M2   Mekaniserad bostadsproduktion; en- och
     tvåvåningshus. Stockholm, Statens Kommitté
     för Byggnadsforskning, 1945.
     51 p. illus. (Sverige. Statens Kommitté
     för Byggnadsforskning. Meddelanden, nr. 2)

     English summary: p. 49-51.

1. Prefabricated construction-Sweden. I.Sverige.
Statens Kommitté för Byggnadsforskning.

     Sweden. Statens Kommitté för Byggnadsfor-
690.015   skning.
(485) Thiberg, Sven.
S82   Orientation and floor-level; a study in
R35   preferences of dwellers in point-blocks, by
1966   Sven Thiberg and Surya Kant Misra. Stockholm,
     National Swedish Institute for Building
     Research, 1966.
     19p. (Sweden. National Swedish
     Institute for Building Research. Report
     35:1966)

     1. Building research - Sweden. 2. Archi-
     tecture, Domestic - Design. 3. Family
     living require-   ments. I. Misra, Surya
     Kant, jt.au.   II. Sweden. Statens
     Kommitté för   Byggnadsforskning.

Sweden. Statens Kommitté för Byggnadsforskning.

690.015
(485)
S82
R80
Lindskoug, Nils-Eric.
Östbergaprojektet—en redogörelse för HSB:s försöksbebyggelse. (The Östberga Project; a report on HSB's/i.e. The National Association of Tenants, Savings and Building Societies, experimental building scheme) Stockholm, Statens råd för byggnadsforskning, 1962.
220p. (Sweden. Statens Kommitté for Byggnadsforskning. Rapport 80)

1. Savings and loan associations. I. National Association of Tenants. II. Sweden. Statens Kommitté for Byggnadsforskning.

690.015
(485)
S82
R16
1966
Sweden. Statens Kommitté för Byggnadsforskning.
Persson, Bengt O
Polyesterbetong i västtyskland (Polyester concrete in West Germany) Stockholm, Statens Institut för Byggnadsforskning, 1966.
8p. (Sweden. Statens Kommitté för Byggnadsforskning. Rapport 16 1966)
Särtryck ur tidskriften Byggmästaren 12:1965.
English summary.

1. Building research - Sweden. 2. Concrete. I. Sweden. Statens Kommitté för Byggnadsforskning.

690.015
(485)
S82
M23
Sweden. Statens Kommitté för Byggnadsforskning.
Ahrbom, Nils
Radhuset, dess planläggning och ekonomi. [Stockholm] Statens Nämnd för Byggnadsforskning [1953]
235 p. graphs, plans(part fold.), tables. (Statens Nämnd för Byggnadsforskning. Meddelanden nr. 23)

1. Architecture, Domestic-Design. 2.Housing-Sweden. I.Sweden. Statens Kommitté för Byggnadsforskning. II.Title: Row houses, their planning and economy.

690.015
(485)
S82
R2
1966
Sweden. Statens Kommitté för Byggnadsforskning.
Larsson, Olov.
Pannrum I småhus dimensioneringsstudier (Boiler rooms in small houses: studies of dimensions) av Olov Larsson och Torsten Norell. Stockholm, Statens Institut för Byggnadsforskning, 1966.
23p. (Sweden. Statens Kommitté för Byggnadsforskning. Rapport 2: 1966)
English summary.

1. Building research - Sweden. 2. Room sizes. 3. Space considerations. 4. Heating, Central. I. Norell, Torsten, jt. au. II. Sweden. Statens Kommitté för Byggnadsforskning.

VF
690.24
A87
Sweden. Statens Kommitté för Byggnadsforskning.
Australia. Commonwealth Scientific and Industrial Research Organization.
The problem of flat roofs; paper by Frederik Schutz. From: Report no. 16 of conference on 22nd Nov. 1948, Swedish State Committee for Building Research. [Melbourne, 1952]
66 p. diagrs. ([Translation no.] 1260)
Bibliography: p. 9-19.
Processed.
1.Roofs and roofing. I.Schutz, Frederik. II.Sweden. Statens Kommitté för Byggnadsforskning. III.Title: Flat roofs. The problem of.

690.015
(485)
S82
R
Sweden. Statens Kommitté för Byggnadsforskning.
Rapporter, nr. (analyzed)
Stockholm
v. illus.

For complete information see shelflist card.

1. Building research-Sweden.

R16

690.015
(485)
S82
R103
Sweden. Statens Kommitté för Byggnadsforskning.
Borgelin, Gunnar.
Parkeringsvanor inom citykärnor (Parking habits in town centres) Stockholm, Statens råd för Byggnadsforskning, 1963.
165p. (Sweden. Statens Kommitté för Byggnadsforskning. Rapport no. 103)

1. Parking - Sweden. I. Sweden. Statens Kommitté för Byggnadsforskning.

690.015
(485)
S82
R13
1967
Sweden. Statens Kommitté för Byggnadsforskning.
Busk, Gunnar.
Provbelastning av grundplattor på sprängstensmassor [Load-bearing tests of load-bearing plates on rock-fills] Stockholm, 1967.
72p. (Sweden. Statens Kommitté för Byggnadsforskning. Rapport 13:1967)
English summary.

1. Building research - Sweden. 2. Footings. 3. Foundations (Building) I. Sweden. Statens Kommitté för Byggnadsforskning.

690.015
(485)
S82
R33-1965
Sweden. Statens Kommitté för Byggnadsforskning.
Rationellt skolbyggande; åtta anföranden vid skolbyggnadskonferensen på Teknorama den 26 April 1965. (Rationalization in school building) Stockholm, 1965.
56p. (Its Rapport 33-1965)

1. Building research - Sweden. 2. Schools - Sweden.

690.015
(485)
S82
R1-1965
Sweden. Statens Kommitté för Byggnadsforskning.
Planeringsunderlag för lamellhus. Stockholm, 1965.
45p. (Its Rapport 1-1965)

1. Building research - Sweden. 2. Apartment houses - Sweden.

690.015
(485)
S82
R25
1966
Sweden. Statens Kommitté för Byggnadsforskning.
Hellström, Gunnar.
Provbelastning av långa stödpålar av betong (Test loading of long combined end-bearing and friction precast concrete piles) Stockholm, 1966.
11p. (Sweden. Statens Kommitté för Byggnadsforskning. Rapport 25:1966)
English summary.

1. Building research - Sweden. 2. Concrete, Prestressed. 3. Loads. I. Sweden. Statens Kommitté för Byggnadsforskning.

690.015
(485)
S82
R113
Sweden. Statens Kommitté för Byggnadsforskning.
Redovisning av inredningsenheter; riktlinjer avseende inredningsenheter, möbler och fast inredning. Stockholm, 1964.
22p. (Its Rapport no. 113)
At head of title: Chalmers Tekniska Högskola, Sektionen för Arkitektur, Institutionen för Formlära. Utarbetad i samråd med A-gruppen.

1. Building research - Sweden. 2. Architectural drawing. 3. Interior decoration.

690.015
(485)
S82
R61
Sweden. Statens Kommitté för Byggnadsforskning.
Plantyper i friliggande enfamiljshus 1950, 1954, 1957. [Types of plans of detached one-family houses built in 1950, 1954, and 1957] Stockholm, 1960.
62p. diagrs. (Its Rapport 61)

English summary.

1. House plans. 2. Housing - Sweden.

691.55
:693.625
S82
Sweden. Statens Kommitté för Byggnadsforskning.
Puts och putsning, ett kritiskt litteraturstudium [plaster and plastering], av Vitold Saretok. Stockholm, 1957.
161 p. illus., charts. (Its Handlingar nr 29, transactions)
English summary.

Published also in English by Building Research Station as BRS Library Communications no. 791. (See Card No. 2)

690.5
:551.5
(485)
S77
Sweden. Statens Kommitté för Byggnadsforskning.
Regulations valid in Sweden concerning the execution of certain works under winter conditions. [Stockholm, 1951?]
2 l.

Bound with.. A survey of winter construction in Sweden, by Evert Strokirk.
Processed.

1.Winter construction.

690.015
(485)
S82
M21
Sweden. Statens Kommitté för Byggnadsforskning.
Larsson, Göran
Plywood som konstruktions-material, by Göran Larsson and Georg Wästlund. [Stockholm] Statens Kommitté för Byggnadsforskning [1953]
127 p. illus., graphs, tables. (Sverige. Statens Kommitté för Byggnadsforskning. Meddelanden, nr. 21)
Bibliography: p. 45-48 and 118-120.
English summaries.
1.Plywood. I.Wästlund, Georg. II.Sweden. Statens Kommitté för Byggnadsforskning.

691.55
:693.625
S82
Sweden. Statens Kommitté för Byggnadsforskning.
Puts och putsning, ett kritiskt litteraturstudium. 1957. (Card No. 2)

1.Plaster and plastering. 2.Building construction - Sweden - Bibliographies. I.Saretok, Vitold.

690.015
(485)
S82
R111
Sweden. Statens Kommitté för Byggnadsforskning.
Petersson, Tage.
Rektangulära och T-formade betongbalkars skjuvhållfasthet en jämförelse. Stockholm, Sweden, Statens råd för Byggnadsforskning, 1964.
140p. (Sweden. Statens Kommitté för Byggnadsforskning. Rapport 111)

English summary.

1. Building research - Sweden. 2. Loads. I. Sweden. Statens Kommitté för Byggnadsforskning.

690.5
:551.5
(485)
S77
Sweden. Statens Kommitté för Byggnadsforskning.
Bernhard, H
PM on estimating winter compensation for state-financed multi-family houses. [Stockholm, Statens Kommitté för Byggnadsforskning? Feb. 1951]
4 l.

Bound with...A survey of winter construction in Sweden, by Evert Strokirk.
Processed.

690.015
(485)
S82
R27
1967
Sweden. Statens Kommitté för Byggnadsforskning.
Quality of dwellings and housing areas; published in agreement with the United Nations. Stockholm, 1967.
149p. (Sweden. Statens Kommitté for Byggnadsforskning. Rapport 27)
1. Housing - Sweden. 2. Housing - Social aspects. 3. Housing and health. I. United Nations. II. Title.

690.015
(485)
S82
R43
1966
Sweden. Statens Kommitté för Byggnadsforskning.
Halvorsen, Ulf A
Reparation av betonggolv. Stockholm, 1966.
12p. (Sweden. Statens Kommitté för Byggnadsforskning. Rapport 43:1966)
Eftertryck ur skriften Prosjektering og utførelse av betonggulv, utgiven av Den Norske Ingeniørforening, januari 1966.

1. Building research - Sweden. 2. Concrete floors. I. Sweden. Statens Kommitté för Byggnadsforskning.

690.015
(485)
:016)
S82
Sweden. Statens Kommitté för Byggnadsforskning.
Reports in English from Byggforskningen,
the Swedish Building Research, 1965-1967.
Literature from the National Swedish
Institute for Building Research. Stockholm,
1968.
1v.

1. Building research - Sweden.
2. Building research - Bibl.

690.015
(485)
S82
R51
Sweden. Statens Kommitte for Byggnadsforskning.
Rumsuppvärmning med små varmluftsmängder
[A model study on room heating with small
amounts of hot air] av Börje E. Löfstedt
och Hans E Ronge. Stockholm, 1959.
39p. (Its Rapport 51)

English summary.

1. Heating - Sweden. I. Löfstedt, Borje E.
II. Ronge, Hans E.

690.015
(485)
S82
R92
Sweden. Statens Kommitté för Bygnadsfors-
kning. Skolbyggnadens plantyp...(Card 2)

52p. (Sweden. Statens Kommitté for
Byggnadsforskning. Rapport 92)

1. Building research - Sweden.
2. Schools - Sweden.

690.015
(485)
S82
R23
1967
Sweden. Statens Kommittee för
Byggnadsforskning.
Holmström, Ingmar.
Restaurering av gamla byggnader ur främst
teknisk och antikverisk synvinkel [Restora-
tion of old buildings-mainly from the techni-
cal and antiquarian point of view] av Ingmar
Holmström och Iwar Anderson. Stockholm, 1967.
59p. (Sweden. Statens Kommitte' för
Byggnadsforskning. Rapport 23:1967)
English summaries.
Särtryck ur tidskriften byggmästaren
12:1966 och 1:1967.

(Cont'd on next card)

VF
727.1
(485)
W13
Sweden. Statens Kommitte for Byggnadsforskning.
Wahlström, Olle.
The school building: layout and cost.
Stockholm, Statens Kommitté för Byggnadsforskning, 1963.
[5]p.

1. Schools - Sweden. I. Sweden. Statens
Kommitté for Byggnadsforskning.

690.015
(485)
S82
R81
Sweden. Statens Kommitte for Byggnadsfor-
skning.
Hulteberg, Maurits.
Skolbyggnader i USA av Mauritz Hulteberg
och Olle Wåhlström. (School building in U.S.A.)
Stockholm, Statens råd for byggnadsforskning,
1962.
48p. (Sweden. Statens Kommitté för
Byggnadsforskning. Rapport 81)

1. Schools - Sweden. I. Wåhlström, Olle,
jt. au. II. Sweden. Statens Kommitté för
Byggnadsforskning.

690.015
(485)
S82
R23
1967
Holmström, Ingmar. Restaurering av gamla
byggnader ur främst teknisk och antikverisk
synvinkel...1967. (Card 2)

1. Building research - Sweden. 2. Architecture -
Conservation and restoration. I. Anderson, Iwar,
jt. au. II. Sweden. Statens Kommitté för
Byggnadsforskning.

691.328.2
L67
Sweden. Statens Kommitte for Byggnadsforskning.
Lorentsen, Mogens.
Shear and bond in prestressed concrete beams
without shear reinforcement. Stockholm, Sta
Kommitte for Byggnadsforskning, 1964.
195p. (Sweden. Statens Kommitte for
Byggnadsforskning. Handlinger nr. 47, Trans-
actions)

1. Concrete, Prestressed. I. Title.
II. Sweden. Statens Kommitte for Byggnadsforskning
(Series)

690.015
(485)
S82
R20
1967
Sweden. Statens Kommitté för Byggnadsforskning.
Skolgruppen AB. Skolprojekt, generell
projekteringsplan (Type plan for projection of school construction) Stockholm,
1967.
84p. (Its Rapport no. R-20, 1967)
Bibliography: p. 73-84.

1. Building research - Sweden.
2. Schools - Sweden. 3. Architecture -
Sweden.

690.015
(485)
S82
R72
Sweden. Statens Kommitté för Byggnads-
forskning.
Müller, Henrik.
Rörelsehindrades stadsbygdsmiljö - en studie
från Högdalen. [City suburb and environment
for disabled persons - a study of Högdalen]
Stockholm, Statens råd for Byggnadsforskning,
1961.
40p. (Sweden. Statens Kommittee för
Byggnadsforskning. Rapport 72)
English summary: p. 39-40.

1. Housing for the handicapped. I. Sweden. Statens
Kommitté för Byggnadsforskning.

690.15
:551.5
(485)
S77
Sweden. Statens Kommitté för
Byggnadsforskning.
Blomgren, Boris
Simplified foundation methods for houses.
[Stockholm, Statens Kommitté för Byggnadsforskning,
Feb. 1951]
8 l.

Bound with...A survey of winter construction
in Sweden by Evert Strokirk.
Processed.

690.015
(485)
S82
R58
Sweden. Statens Kommitte för Byggnadsforskning.
Skolpaviljonger. Skolpaviljonger till
skola av Blb-typ Klassrunspaviljonger.
[School pavilions. Pavilions for schools of
type Blb. Pavilions for classrooms] Stockholm, 1960.
19p. diagrs. (Its Rapport 58)

1. Schools.

690.015
(485)
S82
R15
1967
Sweden. Statens Kommitte för
Byggnadsforskning.
Rumsmått i byggnadsproduktionen-tre studier
[Room dimensions in housing production; three
studies] Stockholm, 1967.
143p. (Its Rapport 15:1967)
English summary.

1. Building research - Sweden. 2. Architecture, Domestic. 3. Room sizes.

690.015
(485)
S82
R56
Sweden. Statens Kommitté för Byggnadsforskning.
Skolbyggnadens plantyp och kostnad 1. Ett
lokalprogram för mellan- och högstadieskola
studerat i 10 alternativa planlösningssystem.
[Plans and costs of a school building I.
Building plans for an intermediate and advanced school. Study of ten alternative solu-
tions] Stockholm, 1959.
50p. diagrs., tables. (Its Rapport nr. 56)

1. Schools - Sweden.

690.015
(485)
S82
R64
Sweden. Statens Kommitte för Byggnadsforskning.
Skolplanering i Orebro län. School
planning in Orebro County. Utredningar
utförda inom Orebro läns landstings
regionplanekontor under ledning, av
Bo Fredzell. Stockholm, 1960.
104p. maps, tables. (Its Rapport 64)

1. Schools - Sweden. I. Fredzell, Bo.

690.015
(485)
S82
R41
1967
Sweden. Statens Kommitte for
Byggnadsforskning.
Rullstoler i Sverige 1962-1964.

Stockholm, 1967.
76p. (Its Rapport 41:1967)

1. Public health - Sweden. I. Title: Wheel
chairs in Sweden 1962-1964.

690.015
(485)
S82
R71
Sweden. Statens Kommitte for Byggnadsforskning.
Skolbyggnadens plantyp och kostnad 2.
Ett lokalprogram för lag- och mellan-
stadieskola studerat i 13 alternativa
planlösningssystem. [Plans and costs of
a school building. 2. Building plans for
a junior stage and a middle stage school
[of the nine years' compulsory school]
Study of thirteen alternative solutions]
Stockholm, 1961.
58p. (Its   Rapport 71)

1. Schools -   Sweden.

690.015
(485)
S82
R96
Sweden. Statens Kommitté för
Byggnadsforskning.
Algers, Börje.
Småhusbyggande i storstadsregion;
produktionsförhållandena i stockholmstrakten
[Building of small houses in Greater Stock-
holm] Stockholm, Statens rad för Byggnads-
forskning, 1963.
120p. (Sweden. Statens Kommitté
för Byggnadsforskning. Rapport 96)

English summary.
(Cont'd. on next card)

690.015
(485)
S82
R51
suppl.
Sweden. Statens Kommitté för Byggnadsforskning.
[Rumsuppvärmning med små varmluftsmängder
[Komplement till rapport nr 51. A model
study on room heating with small amounts of
hot air] av Börje E. Löfstedt och Hans E.
Ronge. Stockholm, 1959.
[10]p. (Särtryck nr. 9, 1959)

English summary.
1. Heating - Sweden. I. Löfstedt, Börje E.
II. Ronge, Hans E.

690.015
(485)
S82
R92
Sweden. Statens Kommitté för Byggnadsforskning.
Skolbyggnadens plantyp och kostnad 3.
Ett lokalprogram för en högstadie- och
gymnasieskola studerat i 8 alternativa
planlosningssystem (Plans and costs of
a school building 3. Building plans for
an upper department and a senior secondary
school. Study of 8 alternative solutions)
Stockholm. Statens råd för Byggnadsforskning, 1962.

(Cont'd. on next card)

690.015
(485)
S82
R96
Algers, Börje.   Småhusbyggande i
storstadsregion ...   (Card 2)

1. Building research - Sweden.
2. Housing - Sweden. 3. Building industry -
Sweden. I. Sweden. Statens Kommitten for
Byggnadsforskning.

690.21
S82s

Sweden. Statens Kommitté för
Byggnadsforskning.
Småhusgrunder problem och forsknings-
behov. (Foundations of small houses:
problems and research requirements)
Stockholm, 1964.
36p. (Its Programskrift no. 2)

English summary.

1. Foundations (Building) 2. Architecture -
Sweden. 3. Housing - Sweden.

690.015
(485)
S82
R11
1966

Sweden. Statens Kommitte för Byggnadsforskning. Brown, Gösta.
Solvärme genom fönster och solskydd
(Solar heat through windows and solar shad-
ing devices) Stockholm, Statens Institut
för Byggnadsforskning, 1966.
29p. (Sweden. Statens Kommitté för
Byggnadsforskning. Rapport 11:1966)
Särtryck ur tidskriften VVS6:1965 och 2:
1966.
English summary.

1. Building research - Sweden.
2. Heating. Solar. I. Sweden.
Statens Kommitte för
Byggnadsfor-   skning.

690.015
(485)
S82
R115

Sweden. Statens Kommitte for
Byggnadsforskning. Berglund, Dag Torsten.
Störningar i köksavloppssystem. (Obstruc-
tions in waste-pipe systems in kitchens)
Stockholm, Statens råd för Byggnadsforskning,
1964.
164p. (Sweden. Statens Kommitte for
Byggnadsforskning. Rapport 115)

English summary.

1. Building research - Sweden. 2. Kitchens.
3. Pipes. I. Sweden. Statens Kommitte for
Byggnadsforskning.

690
(485)
S82s

Sweden. Statens Kommitté för Byggnadsforskning.
Smaskrift,
Stockholm,
v. illus., diagrs.

For complete information see shelflist.

1. Building construction - Sweden.

690.15
:551.5
(485)
S77

Sweden. Statens Kommitté för
Byggnadsforskning.
Ericson, Sture
Some practical measures in winter building.
[Stockholm, Statens Kommitté för Byggnadsforskning?
Feb. 1951]
2 p.

Bound with...A survey of winter construction
in Sweden by Evert Strokirk.
Processed.

690.015
(485)
S82
M22

Sweden. Statens Kommitté för Byggnadsforskning.
Johnson, Arne I
Strength, safety and economical dimensions
of structures. Stockholm, Statens Kommitté
for Byggnadsforskning, 1953.
168 p. graphs, tables. (Statens
Kommitté for Byggnadsforskning. Meddelanden
nr. 22)
References: p. 158-159.

1. Strength of materials. 2. Building materials - Testing. I. Sweden. Statens Kommitté
for Byggnadsfor-   skning. II. Title.
III. Title: Econom-   ical dimensions of structures.

690
(485)
S82s

Sweden. Statens Kommittee för Byggnadsforskning.
Smaskrift.

no. 12. Betonggolv Direkt Pa Mark. av
Hans Ericsson och Nils Holmqvist.
1957.

no. 13. Armering av betongkonstruktioner.
1958.

no. 14. Murning av bärande väggar. 1958.

(continued on next card)

690.015
(485)
S82
R7
1967

Sweden. Statens Kommitté för Byggnadsforskning.
Kihlman, Tor.
Sound radiation into a rectangular room.
Applications to airborne sound transmission in
buildings. Stockholm, Sweden, Statens Kommitté
for Byggnadsforskning, 1967.
[11]-20p. (Sweden. Statens Kommitté för
Byggnadsforskning. Rapport 7/67)
Reprinted from Acustica, vol. 18, no. 1.
Summary in English, German, and French.
1. Building research - Sweden. 2. Sound-
proofing. 3. Insulation. I. Sweden. Statens
Kommitte for Byggnadsforskning. II. Title.

690.22
S82

Sweden. Statens Kommitté för Byggnadsforskning.
Structural intersection of walls and floor
slabs; effect of deformation of joints on
load-carrying capacity of brick masonry
walls, light-weight cellular concrete element walls, and iron-reinforced concrete
frames, by Sven Sahlin. Stockholm, 1959.
215p. illus., diagrs., tables. (Its
Handlingar nr. 35)

1. Walls. I. Sahlin, Sven. (Series)

690
(485)
S82s

Sweden. Statens Kommittee för Byggnadsforskning.   (card 2)
Smaskrift,

no. 15. Spik-och bultförband i träkonstruktioner. 1958.

no. 16. Byggnadskranar. av
Hans E. Holst. 1959.

no. 17. Byggnadshissar. 1960.

no. 18. Inläggningsfardigt armeringsstal.
en   kostnadsstudie.
1960.   (Continued on next card)

690.015
(485)
S82
R38
1967

Sweden. Statens Kommitte für
Byggnadsforskning.
Stadsplaners genomförande [The implementation
of the detailed development plans] Stockholm
1967.
96p. (Its Rapport 38)

1. City planning - Sweden.

690.015
(485)
S82
R33
1966

Sweden. Statens Kommitte för Byggnadsforskning.
Structure, activities and new development
of the Swedish building industry. Stockholm,
1966.
43p. (Its Rapport 33:1966)

1. Building research - Sweden.
2. Building industry - Sweden.

690.015
(485)
S82
R5
1968

Sweden. Statens Kommitté för Byggnadsforskning.
The social environment and its effect on
the design of the dwelling and its immediate
surroundings. Stockholm, 1967.
237p. (Sweden. Statens Kommitté för
Byggnadsforskning. Report 5: 1968)
1. Architecture - Designs and plans.
2. Housing - Social effect. 3. Man -
Influence of environment. I. Title.

690.015
(485)
S82
R26
1966

Sweden. Statens Kommitté för Byggnadsforskning.
Ohlin, Jan.
Statistisk beräkning av toleranser för
summemått (Statistical calculation of sum-
tolerances) Stockholm, Statens Institute
för Byggnadsforskning, 1966.
23p. (Sweden. Statens Kommitté för
Byggnadsforskning. Rapport 26:1966)
English summary.

1. Building research - Sweden. 2. Coordinated components. 3. Prefabricated construction. I. Sweden. Statens Kommitté
för Byggnadsfor-   skning.

690.015
(485)
S82
R27-1965

Sweden. Statens Kommitté för Byggnadsforskning.
Studies of the building and community
planning process. Stockholm, National
Swedish Institute for Building Research,
1965.
51p. (Its Report 27-1965)

1. Building research - Sweden. 2. City
planning - Sweden. I. Title.

690.015
(485)
S82
R75

Sweden. Statens Kommitté för Byggnadsforskning.
Brown, Gösta.
Solar position at various hours, dates and
latitudes, ta les. Solens läge på himlen vid
olika klockslag, årstider och latituder,
tabeller, by Gösta Brown and Teuvo Tuominen.
Stockholm, Statens Råd för Byggnadsforskning,
1962.
44p. (Sweden. Statens Kommitté för
Byggnadsforskning. Rapport 75)

1. Solar radiation. I. Sweden. Statens Kommitté
för Byggnadsforskning. II. Tuominen, Teuvo,
jt. au.

690.015
(485)
S82
R36
1967

Sweden. Statens Kommitté för Byggnadsforskning.
Nilsson, Stig.
Stobesvar incm bostadsomraden (soot nuisance
in residential areas) Stockholm, Statens Kom-
mitte for Byggnadsforskning, 1967.
11p. (Sweden. Statens Kommitte for
Byggnadsforskning. Rapport 36: 1967)
Särtryck ur tidskriften VVA 8 och 9: 1967
1. Air pollution - Sweden. 2. Fuel.
I. Sweden. Statens Kommitté för
Byggnadsforskning. II. Title: Soot nuisance
in residential areas.

690.015
(485)
S82
R19-
1965

Sweden. Statens Kommitté för
Byggnadsforskning.
Study of dimensions re equipment in
housing for old persons. Stockholm, 1965.
[57]p. (Its Rapport 19-1965)

1. Building research - Sweden.
2. Housing for the aged - Sweden.
3. Household equipment. 4. Building
methods - Sweden. I. Title.

690.015
(485)
S82
R94

Sweden. Statens Kommitté för Byggnadsforskning.
Pleijel, Gunnar.
Solinstrålning genom fönster i norra,
mellersta och södra Sverige. [Sun
radiation through windows in northern,
central and southern Sweden] Stockholm,
Statens råd för byggnadsforskning, 1963.
97p. (Sweden. Statens Kommitté
for Byggnadsforskning. Rapport no. 94)

1. Building research - Sweden. 2. Solar
radiation. I. Sweden. Statens Kommitté
för Byggnads-   forskning.

697.3
S82

Sweden. Statens Kommitte för Byggnadsforskning.
Stora eller sma värmecentraler (Large or
small heating plants) av Ingmar
Eneborg. Stockholm, 1959.
124p. diagrs., tables. (Its Handlingar
nr. 34)
English summary: p. 110.

1. Heating, central. I. Eneborg, Ingmar.
(Series)

690.5
:551.5
(485)
S77

Sweden. Statens Kommitté för
Byggnadsforskning.
Strokirk, Evert
A survey of winter construction in Sweden.
[Stockholm, Statens Kommitté för Byggnads-
forskning? Feb. 1951]
4 l.

Processed.

691.116
N67s

Sweden. Statens Kommitté för Byggnadsforskning.
Norén, Bengt.
Svensk furuplywood; hållfasthet och tillåtna påkänningar (Swedish pine plywood; strength and working stresses) Stockholm, Statens råd för Byggnadsforskning, 1964.
187p. (Sweden. Statens Kommitté för Byggnadsforskning. Handlingar no. 45. Transactions)
English summary.
1. Plywood. 2. Strength of materials. I. Sweden. Statens Kommitté för Byggnadsforskning. (Series)

690.015
(485)
S82
F62

Sweden. Statens Kommitté för Byggnadsforskning.
Takterrasser, tätskikt och skyddsbeläggning. (Flat roofs. Waterproofing layers and protective coverings) av Rune Hanson. Stockholm, 1960.
75p. illus., diagrs. (Its Rapport 62)
1. Roofs and roofing. 2. Waterproofing. I. Hanson, Rune.

690.015
(485)
S82
R22
1966

Sweden. Statens Kommitté för Byggnadsforskning.
U-gruppen. Entreprenadupphandling (Tendering procedure) Stockholm, 1966.
44p. (Its Report 22:1966)
1. Building research - Sweden. 2. Building standards - Sweden.

690.015
(485)
S82
R14

Sweden. Statens Kommitté för Byggnadsforskning.
Rosenström, Sten, ed.
Svensk husbyggnadsteknisk litteratur; sammandrag från åren 1944-1948. Stockholm, Statens Kommitté för Byggnadsforskning, 1949.
147 p. (Sverige. Statens Kommitté för Byggnadsforskning. Meddelanden, nr. 14)
1.Building construction-Bibl. I.Sverige. Statens Kommitté för Byggnadsforskning.

690.015
(485)
S82
R27
1966

Sweden. Statens Kommitté för Byggnadsforskning.
Hansen, Torben C
Temperature change effect on behavior of cement paste, mortar, and concrete under load, by Torben C. Hansen and Leif Eriksson. Stockholm, 1966.
[16]p. (Sweden. Statens Kommitté för Byggnadsforskning. Rapport 27:1966)
Reprinted from Journal of the American Concrete Institute, Apr. 1966, p. 489-504.
1. Building research - Sweden. 2. Architecture and climate. 3. Concrete, Reinforced. I. Eriksson, Leif, jt.au. II. Sweden. Statens Kommitté för Byggnadsforskning.

690.015
(485)
S82
R2-1965

Sweden. Statens Kommitté för Byggnadsforskning.
Underhåll av bostadsfastigheter. Oversettning ur ECE-rapporten:(Cost, repetition, maintenance, related aspects of building prices) Stockholm, 1965.
72p. (Its Rapport R2-1965)
Issued also in English as U.N. Document ST/ECE/HOU/7.
1. Building research - Sweden. 2. Building costs - Europe. 3. Building maintenence - Europe. 4. Building materials - Europe. I. United Nations. Cost, repetition, maintenance... [U.N. Document] ST/ECE/HOU/7)

690.015
(485)
S82
R44

Sweden. Statens Komitté för Byggnadsforskning.
Svetsade fackverk och några därmed sammanhängande materialproblem [Investigation of welded frame structures] av Sture Sabelström. Stockholm, 1958.
51p. (Its Rapport 44)
1. Building research - Sweden. 2. Steel construction. I. Sabelström, Sture.

VF
690.015
(485)
H65

Sweden. Statens Kommitté för Byggnadsforskning.
Holm, Lennart.
Three planning essentials: make it serviceable, make it durable, make it buildable. Stockholm, Statens Kommitté för Byggnadsforskning, [1963?]
[4]p.
1. Building research - Sweden. I. Sweden. Statens Kommitté för Byggnadsforskning.

690.015
(485)
S82
M24

Sweden. Statens Kommitté för Byggnadsforskning.
Bildmark, Knut
Underhållskostnader för hyresfastigheter i Stockholm. (Maintenance cost for apartment houses in Stockholm.) [Stockholm] Statens Nämnd för Byggnadsforskning [1954]
299 p. illus., graphs, plans, tables. (Statens Nämnd för Byggnadsforskning. Meddelande 24)
In collaboration with G.A. Mårdh.
1. Building maintence. 2. Apartment houses-operating costs. I. Mårdh, G.A. II. Sweden. Statens Kommitté för Byggnadsforskning. III. Title: Maintenance costs for apartment houses in Stockholm.

690.015
(485)
S82
R28
1966

Sweden. Statens Kommitté för Byggnadsforskning.
TA-gruppen.Måttsättning för t-ritninger, redovisningstekniska anvisningar, del 2 (Landscape architecture. Measurements and scaling of drawings, technical directions, part 2) Stockholm, 1966.
27p. (Its Rapport 28:1966)
1. Building research - Sweden. 2. Architectural drawing. 3. Landscape architecture.

690.015
(485)
S82
R23-
1965

Sweden. Statens Kommitté för Byggnadsforskning.
Jensson, Ingvar.
Timber joints. Stockholm, National Swedish Institute for Building Research, 1965.
1v. (Sweden. Statens Kommitté för Byggnadsforskning. Rapport 23-65)
1. Building research-Sweden. 2. Nails and nailing - Bibl. I. Title. II. Sweden. Statens Kommitté för Byggnadsforskning.

620.19
:624.131
S82

Sweden. Statens Kommitté för Byggnadsforskning.
Undersökning av korrosionsrisker i lera. Investigation of corrosion risks in clay, av Allan Bergfelt. Stockholm, 1957.
63 p. illus., tables, diagrs. (Its Handlingar nr 28 - transactions)
English summary.
1.Corrosion. 2.Soils. I.Bergfelt, Allan.

690.015
(485)
S82
R6
1966

Sweden. Statens Kommitté för Byggndsforskning.
TA-gruppen, rittteknik för t-ritninger. Redovisningstekniska anvisninger, del 1. (Landscape architecture. Technics of drawing technical directions) Part 1. Stockholm, 1966.
32p. (Its Rapport 6: 1966)
1. Building research - Sweden. 2. Architectural drawing. 3. Landscape architecture.

VF
711.4
S82

Sweden. Statens Kommitté för Byggnadsforskning.
Trafikolyckor i bostadsomreden. Stockholm, 1963.
[4]p. (Its Blad 1963:12)
1. Residential areas. 2. Traffic safety.

711.4
(485)
S82u

Sweden. Statens Kommitté för Byggnadsforskning.
Urbanisering och ytor. Stockholm, 1966.
[4]p. (Its Blad 36, 1966)
1. City planning - Sweden.

690.015
(485)
S82
R45

Sweden. Statens Kommitté för Byggnadsforskning.
Tätheten hos rörfogar i avloppsledningar, av Lave Niklasson. Stockholm, 1958.
88p. illus., tables. (Its Rapport 45)
English summary.
1.Plumbing.

690.15
:551.5
(485)
S77

Sweden. Statens Kommitté för Byggnadsforskning.
Röhfors, H
The treatment of concrete at winter construction. [Stockholm, Statens Kommitté för Byggnadsforskning? Feb. 1951?]
3 l.
Bound with...A survey of winter construction in Sweden by Evert Strokirk.
Processed.

690.015
(485)
S82
R42

Sweden. Statens Kommitté för Byggnadsforskning.
Utomhusfärger för trä (exterior house paints), av Börje Andersson och Paul Nylén. Stockholm, 1957.
84p. tables, charts. (Its Rapport no. 42)
1.Paints and painting. I.Andersson, Börje.

690.24
S82

Sweden. Statens Kommitté för Byggnadsforskning.
Takstolar av trä [small timber roof trusses and their design] av Bengt Norén. Stockholm, 1959.
129p. illus., diagrs., tables. (Its Handlingar nr. 37)
English summary: p. 113-115.
1. Roofs and roofing. I. Norén, Bengt. (Series)

690.015
(485)
S82
R23
1966

Sweden. Statens Kommitté för Byggnadsforskning.
U-Gruppen. Entreprenadbeskrivning (Bill of quantities) Stockholm, 1966.
1 v. (Sweden. Statens Kommitté för Byggnadsforskning. Rapport 23:1966)
1. Building research - Sweden. 2. Building standards - Sweden.

690.015
(485)
S82
R37
1966

Sweden. Statens Kommitté för Byggnadsforskning.
Val av hustyp, L Ett års stadsplaner (Choice of types of buildings, I.One year's town plans) Stockholm, 1966.
69p. (Its Rapport 37:1966)
English summary.
1. Building research - Sweden. 2. City planning - Sweden.

690.015
(485)
S82
R38
1966

Sweden. Statens Kommitté för Byggnadsforskning.
Val av hustyp, II. Hus och mark i 21 planexempel (Choice of types of buildings, II. Housing and land in 21 plan examples) Stockholm, Statens Institut för Byggnadsforskning 1966.
199p. (Its Rapport 38:1966)
English summary.

1. Building research - Sweden. 2. City planning - Sweden. 3. Site planning.

690.015
(485)
S82
R70

Sweden. Statens Kommitté för Byggnadsforskning.
Värmecentraler för bostadsområden. Föredrag och diskussioner vid Svenska Teknologföreningens konferens i Stockholm den 3-4 oktober 1960. [Central heating plants for housing areas. Lectures and discussions at a conference held in Stockholm, 1960, by the Swedish Association of Engineers and Architects.) Stockholm, 1961.
154p. (Its Rapport 70)

1. Heating, Central.

.690.015
(485)
S82
R9
1966

Sweden. Statens Kommitte för Byggnadsforskning.
Wollander, Sven.
Vi kan bygga fler och bättre bostäder till lägre kostnader med mindre arbetskraft (We can build more and better dwellings cheaper and with fewer workers) Stockholm, Institut for Byggnadsforskning, 1966.
7p. (Sweden. Statens Komitte for Byggnadsforskning. Report 9: 1966)
English summary.

1. Building research - Sweden. 2. Building methods. 3. Building costs - Sweden. I. Sweden. Statens Kommitte för Byggnadsforskning.

690.015
(485)
S82
R39
1966

Sweden. Statens Kommitté för Byggnadsforskning.
Val av hustyp, III, Huset och dess planegenskaper (Choice of types of buildings, III, Housing and the characteristics of its plans) Stockholm, 1966.
117p. (Its Rapport 39:1966)
English summary.

1. Building research - Sweden. 2. Architectural details. 3. Architecture, Domestic - Design.

697.326
C17

Carlsson, Sten.
Värmeförluster från kulvertledningar (Heat losses from underground heating mains) by Sten Carlsson and Ingmar Eneborg. Stockholm, Sweden, Statens råd för Byggnadsforskning, 1952.
101p. (Sweden. Statens Kommitté för Byggnadsforskning. Handlingar nr 42, Transactions)
English summary.

1. Heating, Central. 2. Heating research. 3. Culverts. I. Eneborg, Ingmar, jt. au. I. Sweden. Statens Kommitté för Byggnads- forskning. (Series)

690.015
(485)
S82
R21
1967

Sweden. Statens Kommitte för Byggnadsforskning
Bring, Christer.
Vidhäftning mellan härdnat betongunderlag och pågjutet golvskikt (Adhesion of concrete floor topping to hardened base concrete) Stockholm, Statens Institut for Byggnadsforskning, 1967.
112p. (Sweden. Statens Kommitte för Byggnadsforskning. Rapport 21:67)

1. Building industry. 2. Concrete floors. I. Sweden. Statens Kommitte för Byggnadsforskning. II. Title: Adhesion of concrete floor topping.

690.015
(485)
S82
R40
1966

Sweden. Statens Kommitté för Byggnadsforskning.
Eriksson, Einar.
Val av hustyp, IV, Ekonomiska synpunkter en litteraturgenomgång (Choice of types of buildings, IV, Economic aspects. A review of publications) Stockholm, 1966.
99p. (Sweden. Statens Kommitté för Byggnadsforskning. Rapport 40:1966)
English summary.
Bibliography: p. 97-99.

1. Building research - Sweden. 2. Architecture, Domestic - Design. 3. Building costs - Sweden. I. Sweden. Statens Kommitté för Byggnadsforskning.

697.133
H63

Sweden. Statens Kommitté för Byggnadsforskning.
Höglund, Ingemar.
Värmeförluster I småhus, resultat från två försökshus (Heat losses in small houses, results of experiments in two houses) Stockholm, Statens råd för Byggnadsforskning 1963.
128p. (Sweden. Statens Kommitté för Byggnadsforskning. Handlingar nr. 43. Transactions)
English summary.

1. Heat transmission. I. Sweden. Statens Kommitté för Byggnadsforskning. II. Title: Heat losses in small houses. (Series)

690.015
(485)
S82
R3
1967

Sweden. Statens Kommitté för Byggnadsforskning.
Nylund, Per-Olof.
Vindtäthet hos flerskiktväggar (Windproofing in multi-layer walls) Stockholm, 1967.
8p. (Sweden. Statens Kommitté för Byggnadsforskning. Rapport 3:1967)
Eftertryck ur tidskriften Byggmästaren 11:1966.
English summary.

1. Building research - Sweden. 2. Insulation. 3. Walls. 4. Wind resistance. I. Sweden. Statens Kommitté för Byggnadsforskning.

690.015
(485)
S82
R116

Sweden. Statens Kommitté för Byggnadsforskning.
Val av skolort och skoltomt. Regional och kommunal skolplanering. (The choice of a school site; regional and municipal planning of schools) Stockholm, Statens råd för Byggnadsforskning, 1965.
63p. (Rapport nr. 116)
English summary.

1. Building research - Sweden. 2. Site selection. 3. Schools - Sweden. I. Title: The choice of a school site.

624.138
S82v

Sweden. Statens Kommitté för Byggnadsforskning.
Värmeledningstal hos olika jordarter. Thermal conductivity of soils, av Erik Saare och Carl-Goste Wenner. Stockholm, 1957.
196p. graphs, tables. (Its Handlingar no. 31)
English summary.

1. Soils. I. Saare, Erik. II. Wenner, Carl-Gosta. (Series)

690.015
(485)
S82
R86

Sweden. Statens Kommitté för Byggnadsforskning
Eriksson, Folke.
Vinterbygge, merkostnader i landets olika zoner (Building construction in vinter, additional costs in various zones of Sweden) av Folke Eriksson och Jan-Åke Jonson Stockholm, Statens råd för Byggnadsforskning, 1962.
10p. (Sweden. Statens Kommitté för Byggnadsforskning. Rapport 86)
English summary.

(Cont'd. on next card)

690.015
(485)
S82
R66

Sweden. Statens kommitte för byggnadsforskning.
Värdeminskning hos flerfamiljshus [Depreciation on multi-family blocks of flats] utarbetad av värdeminsknings-gruppen inom Statens nämnd för byggnadsforskning. Stockholm, 1961.
[75]p. (Its Rapport 66)

1. Depreciation and obsolescence.

690.015
(485)
S82
R15-
1965

Sweden. Statens Kommitté för Byggnadsforskning.
Lyng, Odd.
Värmetransport genom fönster: litteraturstudie med bibliografi (Heat transfer through windows: a literature study with bibliography) Stockholm, Statens Institut för Byggnadsforskning, 1965.
82p. (Sweden. Statens Kommitté för Byggnadsforskning. Rapport 15-1965)
Bibliography: p. 66-80.
English summary.

1. Building research - Sweden. 2. Heat transmission. I. Sweden. Statens Kommitté för Byggnadsforskning.

690.015
(485)
S82
R86

Eriksson, Folke. Vinterbygge, merkostnader i landets olika zoner...1962. (Card 2)

1. Building research - Sweden. 2. Building construction - Sweden. I. Jonson, Jan-Åke, jt. au. II. Sweden. Statens Kommitté för Byggnadsforskning.

690.015
(485)
S82
R5
1966

Sweden. Statens Kommitté för Byggnadsforskning.
Vårdrum för somatisk vårdavdelning dimensioneringsstudier för Enskededalens sjukhus (Wards for somatic diseases. Studies of dimensions for the Enskededalen Hospital) Stockholm, 1966.
41p. (Its Rapport 5, 1966)
English summary.

1. Building research - Sweden. 2. Hospitals - Sweden.

690.015
(485)
S82
M15

Sweden. Statens Kommitté för Byggnadsforskning
Rydberg, John
Ventilationens storlek i bostäder. The rate of ventilation in dwellings. Av John Rydberg och Åke Arnell. Stockholm, Statens Kommitté för Byggnadsforskning, 1949.
82 p. tables. (Sverige. Statens Kommitté för Byggnadsforskning. Meddelanden, nr. 15)

English summary: p. 54-56.
Bibliography: p. 53.

690.015
(485)
S82n

Sweden. Statens Kommitté för Byggnadsforskning.
The National Swedish Institute for Building Research. Stockholm, 1966.
47p.

1. Building research - Sweden. 2. Sweden. Statens Kommitté för Byggnadsforskning.

690.015
(485)
S82
R88

Sweden. Statens Kommitté för Byggnadsforskning.
Pusch, Roland.
Variationer hos standardlerprovers, hållfasthetsdata (Strength data variations of standard clay samples) Stockholm, Statens råd för Byggnadsforskning, 1963.
16p. (Sweden. Statens Kommitté för Byggnadsforskning. Rapport 88)
English summary.

1. Building research - Sweden. 2. Strength of materials. 3. Clay. I. Sweden. Statens Kommitté för Byggnadsforskning.

690.015
(485)
S82 v.

Sweden. Statens (Kommitté) för Byggnadsforskning.
Verksamhetsberättelse, 1953/54 - Stockholm, 1954-
v.
For complete information see shelflist card. annual report.

1. Building research - Sweden.

690.015
(485)
S82 L

Sweden. Statens Kommitté for Byggnadsforskning. List of publications...19
(Card 2)

1. Building research - Sweden. 2. Sweden. Statens Kommitte for Byggnadsforskning-Publications.

690.015
(485)
S82
R43
     Sweden. Statens Kommitté för
     Byggnadsforskning.
     Vinterbygge några arbetsmetoder och
     hjälpanordningar, av Hans A. Vinberg.
     Stockholm, 1957.
     64p. illus., charts, tables. (Its
Rapport no. 43)

     1.Winter construction. I.Vinberg, Hans A

698
S82
     Sweden. Statens Råd för Byggnads-
     forskning.
     Byggmålning: problem och forskningsbehov
     (Housepainting: problems and research
     requirement) Utredning av Byggforsknings-
     rådets programgrupp for målningsforskning.
     Stockholm, 1969.
     95p. (Its Programskrift 9)
     English summary.
     Bibliography: p. 71-90.
     1. Paints and painting. I. Title:
Housepainting - problems and research
requirement.

2c

693.97
S82
     Sweden. Statens Råd för Byggnadsforskning.
     Stålbyggnad; utveckling och forskningsbehov.
     Stockholm, 1970.
     160p. (Its Programskrift 11)

     Bibliography: p. 150-154.

     1. Steel construction.

690.015
(485)
S82
R29-
1965
     Sweden. Statens Kommitté for Byggnads-
     forskning.
     VVS-gruppen, ritteknik och måttsättning
     för VVS-ritningar. Redovisningstekniska
     anvisningar, del 1. [Stockholm] 1965.
     [43]p. (Its Rapport no 29-65)

     1. Building research - Sweden. 2. Venti-
lation.

690.022
S82
     Sweden. Statens Rad för
     Byggnadsforskning.
     Elementbyggnad: problem och
     forskningsbehov (Prefabrication in
     building: problems and research requirement)
     Stockholm, 1969.
     124p. (Its Programskrift nr. 10)

     Bibliography: p. 98-123.
     1. Prefabricated construction. 2. Build-
ing research. I. Title: Prefabrication in
building: problems and research
requirement.

690.015
(485)
S82s
     Sweden. Statens Råd för Byggnadsforskning.
     The Swedish Council for Building Research.
     Stockholm, 1970.
     [9]p.

     1. Building research - Sweden. I. Title.

690.22
:728.2
S82
     Sweden. Statens Kommitté för Byggnadsfor-
     skning.
     Ytterväggars värmeisoleringsförmaga,
     främst i flervanings bostadshus (Thermal
     resistance of exterior walls with particular
     emphasis on multi-storied apartment houses)
     av Gösta Brown. Stockholm, 1959.
     174p. illus., diagrs., tables. (Its
     Handlingar nr. 36)

     English summary: p. 152.

     1. Walls. 2. Apartment houses. I. Brown,
Gösta. (Series)

690.022
(485)
011
     Sweden. Statens Råd för Byggnadsforskning.
     Gabrielson, Inger.
     40 sätt att bygga småhus, av Inger
     Gabrielson och Carl-Ivar Ringmar. Stockholm,
     Statens Råd for Byggnadsforskning, 1970.
     80p.

     Bibliography: p. 76-77.

     1. Prefabricated construction - Sweden.
I. Ringmar, Carl-Ivar, jt. au. II. Sweden.
Statens Råd för Byggnadsforskning.

2c

690.015
(485)
S82u
     Sweden. Statens Råd för Byggnadsforskning.
     Utredning och projektering -
     metodforskning och metodutveckling; en
     översikt av forskningsbehov och förslag
     till åtgärder. [Stockholm] 1969.
     48p. (Its Programskrift 7)

     Bibliography: p. 41-48.

     1. Building research - Sweden.

690.015
(485)
S82L
     Sweden. Statens Kommitte for Byggnads-
     forskning-Publications.
     Sweden. Statens Kommitte for Byggnads-
     forskning.
     List of publications,

     Stockholm, 19
     v.

     For complete information see main card.
     Contents: A short presentation of the
National Swedish Institute for Building
Research (Litteratur fran byggforskningen)
Literature from the Building Research.
(Cont'd on next card)

699.82
A21
     Sweden. Statens Rad for Byggnadsforskning.
     Adamson, Bo.
     Fukt; byggnadstekniska fuktproblem, av Bo
     Adamson et al. Stockholm, Statens Rad for
     Byggnadsforsknning, 1970.
     132p. (Programskrift 12)

     Bibliography: p. 123-127.

     1. Moisture condensation. I. Sweden.
Statens Rad for Byggnadsforskning.

2c

300.15
(485)
S82
     Sweden. Statens Råd för Samhällforskning.
     20 års samhällsforskning; socialvetens-
     kaplig forskning; rättsvetenskaplig forskning;
     psykologisk och pedagogisk forskning.
     Statens Råd för Samhällsforskning, 1948-1968.
     Stockholm, P.A. Norstedt & Söners Förlag,
     1969.
     300p.

     1. Social science research - Sweden.

     Sweden. Statens Nämnd för Byggnadsforskning,

     see

     Sweden. Statens Kommitté för Byggnadsforskning.

669
S82
     Sweden. Statens Råd för Byggnadsforskning.
     Metallbeslag och armatur; lämpliga ytbelagg-
     ningar. Stockholm, 1970.
     37p. (Korrosion 5; Smaskrift nr. 30)

     1. Metal-work. 2. Corrosion.

VF
711.4
(485)
S82
     Sweden. Statens Reproduktionsanstalt.
     Stockholm City. Centre de Stockholm.
     Stockholmer zentrum. Stockholm, 1959.
     18p. illus., maps.

     In Swedish, English, French and German.

     1. City planning - Sweden.

712.25
(485)
S76
     Sweden. Statens Naturvårdsverk.
     Stockholm. Statens Institut för Byggnadsfor-
     skning.
     Planering för friluftsliv. Stockholm, Statens
     Naturvårdsverk; Statens Institut för
     Byggnadsforskning, 1971.
     154p.

     Bibliography: p. 147-152.

     1. Recreation - Sweden. 2. Open space land -
Sweden. I. Sweden. Statens Naturvårdsverk.

691.16
S82
     Sweden. Statens Råd för Byggnadsforskning.
     Plast inom byggnadstekniken. Utveckling
     och forskningsbehov. Stockholm, 1971.
     176p. (Programskrift 13)

     Bibliography: p. 165-170.

     1. Plastics.

2c.

690
(485
:083.41)
S82
     Sweden. Statistiska Centralbyran.
     Statistiska meddelanden; bostadsbyggandet
     under..., 19

     Stockholm, 19
     v.
     For Library holdings see main entry.

     1. Building construction - Sweden -
Statistics.

69
(485)
S82
     Sweden. Statens Offentliga Utredningar.
     Byggnadsindustrien i Sverige; utredning och
     betänkande avgivet av 1934 ars byggnads industri-
     saffuniga. Stockholm, Iduns Tryckeri, 1938.
     3 v. tables. (Its 1938: 3, 4, 10)

     Contents.-v.1.Allmän översikt och
     förslag.-v.2.Arbersgivares ochlöntagares inkomster.
     v.3.Arberslöshetens omfattning och växlinger.

     1.Building industry-Sweden.

711
(485)
S82
     Sweden. Statens Rad för Byggnadsforskning.
     Samhälls planerings forskning, en
     problemanalys. Stockholm, 1971.
     64p. (Programskrift 14)

     1. Planning - Sweden. 2. Building
industry - Sweden.

72
(485)
S54
     Sweden builds.
     Smith, G E Kidder
     Sweden builds; its modern architecture and
     land policy, background, development and
     contribution. New York, Stockholm, Bonnier
     [1950]
     279 p. illus., plans.
     Bibliography: p. 275-278.
     Published in cooperation with the Swedish
Institute, Stockholm.
     1.Architecture-Sweden. 2.Architecture, Domestic-
Sweden. I.Swedish Institute. II.Title.

728.1
(485)
S45

Sweden plans for better housing.
Silk, Leonard Solomon, 1918-
Sweden plans for better housing. Durham, N. C., Duke Univ. Press, 1948.
xiv, 149 p. illus., maps. 24 cm. (Duke University publications)
"An earlier ... version of this study was accepted as ... the author's doctoral dissertation at Duke University."
Bibliography: p. 142-145.

1. Housing—Sweden.   I. Title.   II. Ser.

HD7350.A3S5   331.833   48-8682*

Library of Congress   ₁₅₁

362.6
A52s

Swedish Chamber of Commerce of the United States.
American Swedish Monthly.
Sweden salutes Seattle. Stockholm, Swedish Chamber of Commerce of the United States, inc., 1962.
70p.
Partial contents.-The old age home is not a dumping ground: a place to live, not a place to die, by Robert J. Nelson.-We must help our elderly to live out their lives in dignity and happiness, by Bo Boustedt.
Entire issue: May, 1962.
1. Old age. 2. Housing for the aged - Sweden.   I. Nelson, Robert J.
The old age home   is not a dumping
(Cont'd on next card)

728.1
:308
(485)
L85

Swedish housing market.
Lundevall, Owe
Swedish housing market. Stockholm, Hyresgästernas Förlags, 1957.
70p.

1. Housing market - Sweden. I. Title.

362.6
A52s

Sweden salutes Seattle.
American Swedish Monthly.
Sweden salutes Seattle. Stockholm, Swedish Chamber of Commerce of the United States, inc., 1962.
70p.
Partial contents.-The old age home is not a dumping ground: a place to live, not a place to die, by Robert J. Nelson.-We must help our elderly to live out their lives in dignity and happiness, by Bo Boustedt.
Entire issue: May, 1962.
1. Old age. 2. Housing for the aged - Sweden.   I. Nelson, Robert J.
The old age home   is not a dumping
(Cont'd on next card)

362.6
A52s

American Swedish Monthly.   Sweden salutes...
1962.   (Card 2)

ground: a place to live, not a place to die.
II. Boustedt, Bo. We must help our elderly to live out their lives in dignity and happiness. III. Swedish Chamber of Commerce of the United States. IV. Title.

728.1
(485)
J63

SWEDISH HOUSING POLICY.
JOHANSSON, ALF.
SWEDISH HOUSING POLICY, BY ALF JOHANSSON AND WALDEMAR SVENSSON. STOCKHOLM, ROYAL SWEDISH COMMISSION - NEW YORK WORLD'S FAIR, 1939.
47P.

REPRINTED FROM THE MAY 1938 ISSUE OF THE ANNALS OF THE AMERICAN ACADEMY OF POLITICAL AND SOCIAL SCIENCES.
CONTENTS.- JOHANSSON, ALF. SOCIAL HOUSING POLICY IN SWEDEN.- SVENSSON, WALDEMAR. HOME - OWNERSHIP IN SWEDEN.

(CONTINUED ON NEXT CARD)

362.6
A52s

American Swedish Monthly.   Sweden salutes...
1962.   (Card 2)

ground: a place to live, not a place to die.
II. Boustedt, Bo. We must help our elderly to live out their lives in dignity and happiness. III. Swedish Chamber of Commerce of the United States. IV. Title.

658.8
((485)
S21

Swedish collective centers for retail trade.
Scarlat, Alexander.
Swedish collective centers for retail trade. [Stockholm, Information Centre Sweden] 1964.
6p.
At head of title: Meet Sweden.
1. Retail stores - Sweden. 2. Sweden - Retail stores. 3. Retail trade. I. Title. II. Swedish Information Documentation Center.

728.1
(485)
J63

JOHANSSON, A. F. SWEDISH HOUSING POLICY.
...1939.   (CARD 2)
1. HOUSING - SWEDEN. 2. HOME OWNERSHIP - SWEDEN. I. SVENSSON, WALDEMAR. II. TITLE.

330
(485)
C34

Sweden, the middle way.
Childs, Marquis W
Sweden; the middle way. Rev. and enl. ed. New Haven, Yale University Press, 1938.
184p.

1. Economic policy - Sweden. 2. Co-operative housing - Sweden.   I. Title.

72(485)
K66

Swedish cooperative union and wholesale society' architects' office.
Kooperativa Forbundets Arkitektkontor.
Swedish cooperative union and wholesale society's architects' office. Stockholm, Kooperativa Forbundets Bokforlag, 1949.
2 v.   diagrs., plates (part col.)

Contents.-v. 1. 1935-1949 non-housing designs.-v. 2. Housing 1925-1949.

1.Cooperative housing-Sweden. 2.Architecture, domestic-Sweden. 3.Architecture-Sweden. I.Title. 4.Space considerations.

Swedish Industries' Building Study Group.

see

Industrins Byggutredning

Swedish Building Centre, Stockholm.
see
Stockholm. Svensk Byggtjänst.

690.015
(485)
S82s

The Swedish Council for Building Research.
Sweden. Statens Råd för Byggnadsforskning.
The Swedish Council for Building Research. Stockholm, 1970.
[9]p.

1. Building research - Sweden. I. Title.

VF
352
(485)
S 82

Swedish Information and Documentation Center.
Administration locale et remembrement des communes en Suede. Stockholm, Information Centre Sweden, [1965?]
[4]p.

At head of title: Connaissance de la Suede.

1. Municipal government - Sweden.
2. Sweden -   Municipal government.

690.091.82
(485)
E77

Swedish building standards 67.
Essunger, Gunnar.
Swedish building standards 67. Garston, Eng., Building Research Station, 1968.
10p. (Library communication no. 1429)
Translated from the Swedish and reprinted from Byggmastaren, 1968, 47 (March), 4-10.

1. Building standards - Sweden.
I. U.K. Building Research Station.
II. Title. (Series)

690.015
(485
:016)
S 76s

Swedish documentation on building.
Stockholm. Statens Institut for Byggnadsforskning.
Svensk byggdokumentation; utredning av Byggforskningsradets Dokumentationskommitte [Swedish documentation on building; an investigation made by the Documentation Committee of the National Swedish Council for Building Research] Stockholm, Statens Rad for Byggnadsforskning, 1966.
97p. (Its Programskrift 4)
1. Building research - Sweden - Bibl.
2. Building documentation. I. Title:
Swedish documentation on building.

658.8
S82

Swedish Information and Documentation Center.
Commercial distribution in Sweden no. 3.
Published by the Swedish Retail and Wholesale Research Institute in co-operation with the Swedish Co-operative Union and the Information Centre, Sweden. Stockholm, 1968.
15p.
At head of title: Meet Sweden.

1. Retail trade. I. Title.

336
(485)
S 82

The Swedish budget.
Sweden. Finansdepartementet.
The Swedish budget, 19

a summary published by the Ministry of Finance. Stockholm, 19
v.
For Library holdings see main entry.

1. Finance - Sweden. 2. Budget - Sweden.
I. Title.

VF
332.72
(485)
S82

Swedish Housing Credit Fund.
Om billiga egnahemslan-just nu [Cheap own home loans at present] Stockholm, 1935.
12p. (Special report no. 44)

1. Mortgage finance - Sweden.

VF
711.3
(485)
S21

Swedish Information and Documentation Center.
Scarlat, Alexander.
Le développement de l'urbanisme en Suede. Stockholm, Information Centre Sweden, [1965?]
[7]p.

At head of title: Connaissance de la Suede.

1. City growth - Sweden. I. Swedish Information and Documentation Center.

VF
658.8
(485)
S21d
Swedish Information and Documentation Center.
  Scarlat, Alexander.
    La distribution commerciale en Suede. Stockholm, Information Centre Sweden, 1969.
      7p.

    At head of title: Connaissance de la Suede.

      1. Retail stores - Sweden. 2. Retail trade. I. Swedish Information and Documen-   tation Center.

VF
352.6
(485)
S21
Swedish Information and Documentation Center.
  Scarlat, Alexander.
    Social and cultural facilities in new urban districts in Sweden. Stockholm, Information Centre Sweden, [1965?]
      19p.
    At head of title: Meet Sweden.

      1. Community facilities - Sweden. 2. Sweden - Community facilities. I. Title. II. Swedish Information and Documentation Center.

72
(485)
S54
Swedish Institute.
  Smith, G E Kidder
    Sweden builds; its modern architecture and land policy, background, development and contribution. New York, Stockholm, Bonnier [1950]
      279 p.   illus., plans.

    Bibliography: p. 275-278.
    Published in cooperation with the Swedish Institute, Stockholm.

    1.Architecture-Sweden. 2.Architecture, Domestic-Sweden. I.Swedish Institute. II.Title.

VF
352.6
(485)
S21
Swedish Information and Documentation Center.
  Scarlat, Alexander.
    L'equipement socio-culturel des ensembles d'habitations en Suede. Stockholm, Information Centre Sweden, [1965?]
      [18]p.

    At head of title: Connaissance de la Suede.

      1. Community facilities - Sweden. I. Swedish Information and Documentation Center.

658.8
((485)
S21
Swedish Information Documentation Center.
  Scarlat, Alexander.
    Swedish collective centers for retail trade. [Stockholm, Information Centre Sweden] 1964.
      6p.
    At head of title: Meet Sweden.

      1. Retail stores - Sweden. 2. Sweden - Retail stores. 3. Retail trade. I. Title. II. Swedish Information Documentation Center.

728.1
(485)
H15
Swedish Institute.
  Hald, Arthur, ed.
    Swedish housing. Published by the Swedish Institute, the Royal Housing Board, the National Association of Swedish Architects, and the Swedish Society of Arts and Crafts. Edited by Arthur Hald, Per Holm and Gotthard Johansson. Translation by Burnett Anderson. [Stockholm, Swedish Institute, distributed by Forum, 1949]
      64 p. illus., plans. 21 cm.
    For full tracing see main entry card.
      1. Housing - Sweden. 2. Cities and towns - Planning - Sweden. 3. Architecture, Domestic - Sweden. 4. Svenska institutet för kulturellt utbyte med utlandet, Stockholm.

    HD7350.A3H3   331.833   50-14937

    Library of Congress   [2]

VF
658.8
(485)
S21m
Swedish Information and Documentation Center.
  Scarlat, Alexander.
    Les magasins collectifs de commercants independants en Suede. Stockholm, Information Centre Sweden, [1969?]
      [8]p.

    At head of title: Connaissance de la Suede.

      1. Retail stores - Sweden. 2. Retail trade. I. Swedish Information and Documentation Center.

331.252
(485)
S82v
Swedish Information and Documentation Center.
    La vieillesse; l'assurance-maladie en Suede. Stockholm, 1965.
      4p.
    At head of title: Connaissance de la Suede.

      1. Social security - Sweden. 2. Sweden - Social security. 3. Old age. 4. Insurance.

728.1
(485)
S82sv
Swedish Institute.
    Swedish housing, by Per Holm. Stockholm, 1957.
      96p.

      1. Housing - Sweden. 2. Architecture, Domestic - Sweden. 3. City planning - Sweden. I. Holm, Per.

725.83
(485)
S82
Swedish Information and Documentation Center.
    Farsta Centre. Stockholm, [1961?]
      [4]p.
    At head of title: Meet Sweden.

      1. Community centers - Sweden. 2. Sweden - Community centers. I. Title.

711.4
(485)
A77
Swedish Institute.
  Åström, Kell.
    City planning in Sweden. [Stockholm] Swedish Institute for Cultural Relations with Foreign Countries, [1967]
      159p.

      1. City planning - Sweden. I. Swedish Institute. II. Title.

711.552
(485)
S82
Swedish Institute.
    Swedish planning of town centres. Stockholm, [1963?]
      53p.

      1. Business districts - Sweden. 2. City planning - Sweden. I. Title.

720
(485)
S21
Swedish Information and Documentation Center.
  Scarlat, Alexander.
    Introduction à l'architecture en Suede. [Stockholm, Sweden Information Centre, 1962]
      8p.
    At head of title: Connaissance de la Suede.

      1. Architecture - Sweden. 2. Sweden - Architecture. I. Swedish Information and Documentation Center.

331.252
(485)
S82
Swedish Institute.
    Social benefits in Sweden. Stockholm, EJ. Brolins Boktr AB, 1959.
      56p.

      1. Social security - Sweden.

Swedish Institute for Cultural Relations with Foreign Countries.
    see Svenska institutet for kulturelt utbyte med utlandet, Stockholm.

711.552
(485)
S21
Swedish Information and Documentation Center.
  Scarlat, Alexander.
    La renovation du centre de Stockholm, Hotorget, courte description. Stockholm, Information Centre Sweden, [1965?]
      4p.
    At head of title: Connaissance de la Suede.

      1. Business districts - Sweden. 2. Sweden - Business districts. I. Swedish Information and Documentation Center.

360
(485)
S82s
Swedish Institute.
    Social benefits in Sweden in the normal course of life. [Stockholm] 1968.
      68p.

    Sponsored by the Swedish Institute and others.

      1. Social service - Sweden. I. Title.

030.8
(397)
N62
1962
Swedish language - Dictionaries - English.
  Noejd, Ruben.
    McKay's modern English-Swedish and Swedish English dictionary, by R. Nöjd and others. New York, David McKay Co., 1962.
      220p.

      1. Swedish language - Dictionaries - English. 2. English language - Dictionaries - Swedish. I. Title.

711.552.1
(485)
S82
Swedish Information and Documentation Center.
    Skarholmen. Stockholm, [1967?]
      [8]p.

    On cover: Meet Sweden.

      1. Shopping centers - Sweden. 2. Sweden - Shopping centers. I. Title.

36
(485)
H62
Swedish Institute.
  Höjer, Karl J
    Social welfare in Sweden.   [Stockholm] The Swedish Institute [1949]
      154 p.   illus.

    Bibliographies: p. 143-151.
    Housing: p. 64-76.

    1.Social welfare-Sweden. 2.Housing-Sweden. I.Swedish Institute.

030.8=397
N62
Swedish language - Dictionary - English.
  Nöjd, Ruben
    Engelsk-Svensk ordbok av Ruben Nöjd. Svensk-Engelsk ordbok av Astrid Tornberg och Margareta Angström. Stockholm, Bonnier [1947-1948]
      viii, 248, iv, 220 p.

    English-Swedish and Swedish-English.

    1.Swedish language-Dict.-English.

711.552
(485)
S82
Swedish planning of town centres.
Swedish Institute.
    Swedish planning of town centres.
Stockholm, [1963?]
    53p.

    1. Business districts - Sweden. 2. City
planning - Sweden. I. Title.

693.002.22
(485)
S82s
Swedish Timber House Export Association.
    STEX houses. Stockholm, 1949.
    1v.   illus.

    1. Wood construction - Sweden.

371.4
S82
SWEENEY, MARY AGNES, 1901-
    TODAY'S HANDBOOK FOR LIBRARIANS.
READY REFERENCE DATA WITH LISTS OF
SOURCES OF INFORMATION ABOUT INDUSTRIAL
EMPLOYMENT AND TRAINING OPPORTUNITIES,
OPPORTUNITIES IN THE ARMED SERVICES AND
THE QUALIFICATIONS THEY DEMAND,
REHABILITATION, AND OTHER SOCIAL AND
EMOTIONAL PROBLEMS INVOLVING INDIVIDUAL
READJUSTMENT AND GUIDANCE. BY MARY A.
SWEENEY ... CHICAGO, AMERICAN LIBRARY
ASSOCIATION, 1944.
    99P.

                    (CONTINUED ON NEXT CARD)

711.552.1
(485)
S76
Swedish shopping centres.
Stockholm. Chamber of Commerce.
    Swedish shopping centres; experiments
and achievements. Stockholm, [1965]
    36p.

    1. Shopping centers - Sweden. I. Title.

VF
728.1
:362.6
(775)
W47h
Sweeney, Clara G
Wisconsin. Agricultural Experiment Station.
    Housing rural aged people in Wisconsin, by
May L. Cowles and Clara G. Sweeney. Madison,
1959.
    20p. diagrs. (Its Bulletin 536)

1. Housing for the aged - Wisconsin.   I. Cowles,
May L. II. Sweeney, Clara G.

371.4
S82
SWEENEY, MARY AGNES, 1901- TODAY'S
HANDBOOK ...1944.   (CARD 2)

    REPRODUCED FROM TYPE-WRITTEN COPY.

    1. VOCATIONAL GUIDANCE.
2. OCCUPATIONS. 3. VOCATIONAL GUIDANCE
- BIBLIOGRAPHY. I. AMERICAN LIBRARY
ASSOCIATION. II. TITLE.

728.1
(485)
H15
Swedish Society of Arts and Crafts.
Hald, Arthur, ed.
    Swedish housing. Published by the Swedish In-
stitute, the Royal Housing Board, the National
Association of Swedish Architects, and the Swedish
Society of Arts and Crafts. Edited by Arthur Hald,
Per Holm and Gotthard Johansson. Translation by
Burnett Anderson. [Stockholm, Swedish Institute,
distributed by Forum, 1949]
    64 p. illus., plans.

    For full tracing see main entry card.

VF 728.1
:362.6
(775)
W47
Sweeney, Clara G
Wisconsin. University. College of Agriculture. (Extension Service)
    Meeting housing needs of older people
in rural areas, by May L. Cowles and
Clara G. Sweeney. Madison, 1957.
    8p. diagrs. (Its Circular 545)

    1. Housing for the aged - Wisconsin.
I. Cowles, May L. II. Sweeney, Clara G.

350
A52a
Sweeney, Stephen B   ed.
American Society for Public Administration.
    Achieving excellence in public service.
A symposium. Edited by Stephen B. Sweeney
and James C. Charlesworth. Philadelphia,
1963.
    209p.

    1. Public administration. 2. Management.
3. Federal government. I. Sweeney, Stephen
B., ed. II. Charlesworth, James C., ed.
III. Title.

690.015
(485)
S82
R12
1969
Swedish Society of Civil Engineers.
    SVRs Plananvisningskommitté. Rekommenda-
tioner för tekniska och ekonomiska utredningar
vid upprättande av planforslag. Del 2: Vatten-
och avloppsförhållanden (Planning Committee of
the Swedish Society of Civil Engineers. Recommendations for technical and economic surveys
for town and regional planning. Part 2: Water
supply and sewerage conditions) Stockholm,
Statens Institut för Byggnadsforskning,
1969.
    89p. (Stock   holm. Statens Institut för
Byggnadsfor   skning. Rapport 12:1969)
English   summary.
                (Cont'd on next card)

720
S82
Sweeney, James Johnson.
    Antoni Gaudi, by James Johnson Sweeney and
Josep Lluis Sert. Rev. ed. New York, Praeger,
1970.
    191p.

    Bibliography: p. 187-191.

    1. Architecture. 2. Gaudi, Antoni.
I. Sert, Josep Lluis, jt. au.

300.15
S82
Sweeney, Stephen B   ed.
    Governing urban society: new scientific
approaches by S.B. Sweeney and James C.
Charlesworth. Philadelphia, American
Academy of Political and Social Science,
1967.
    254p. (American Academy of Political
and Social Science. Monograph 7)
    Cosponsors: Fels Institute of Local and
State Government and the American Society
for Public Administration.

                    (Cont'd on next card)

690.015
(485)
S82
R12
1969
Swedish Society of Civil Engineers.   SVRs.
..1969.   (Card 2)

    Bibliography: p. 85-89.

    1. Building research - Sweden. 2. Water-
supply. 3. Sewerage and sewage disposal.
I. Title: Recommendations for technical and
economic surveys for town and regional planning. II. Title: Water supply and sewerage
conditions. III. Stockholm. Statens Institut
för Byggnads   forskning.

338
A52
Sweeney, Joseph.
American Embassy, Stockholm.
    Labor-operated enterprises in the
Swedish building industry, by Joseph
Sweeney. Stockholm, 1956.
    10p. (American Embassy, Stockholm.
Foreign service dispatch no. 536, 1956)

    1. Labor productivity. I. Sweeney, Joseph.
(Series: American Embassy, Stockholm. Foreign
service dispatch no. 536, 1956)

300.15
S82
Sweeney, Stephen B   Governing urban
society: new scientific approaches...
1967.   (Card 2)

    Contents: Government and the intellectual:
the necessary alliance for effective action
to meet urban needs, by R.C. Wood. Defining
and implementing the urban observatories
concept, by H. Ralph Taylor.

VF
693.068
:389.6
S82
Swedish Standards Association. Building Dept.
    Committee on Module System.
    Practical applications of the module system.
Stockholm [1952?]
    12, 11 l.   diagrs., graphs, tables.

    English and French.
    Processed.

    1. Modular coordination - Sweden.

711.400.15
W27
Sweeney, Joseph L. Technical
    specifications for a computer-generated
    mapping system.
West Haven, Conn. Redevelopment Agency.
    Limited urban observatory, West Haven.
Final report. Prepared by the West Haven
Redevelopment Agency and others. West Haven,
1969.
    1v.
    Contents.-Stage I - General specifications
for the West Haven limited urban observatory,
by W.L. Clarke.-Stage II - Technical specifications for a computer-generated mapping
system for the West Haven limited urban observatory, by   J.L. Sweeney and W.L.
Clarke.   (Cont'd on next card)

300.15
S82
Sweeney, Stephen B. Governing urban society:
    new scientific approaches...1967. (Card 3)

    1. Social science research. 2. City plan-
ning. 3. Public administration.
I. Charlesworth, James C. jt. ed.
II. American Academy of Political and Social
Science. III. Wood, Robert Coldwell. Govern-
ment and the intellectual... IV. Taylor, H.
Ralph. Defining and implementing the urban
observatories concept. V. Title.

Swedish State Committee for Building Research

        see

Sweden. Statens Kommitté för Byggnadsvorakning.

711.400.15
W27
West Haven, Conn. Redevelopment Agency.
    Limited urban...1969.   (Card 2)

    1. City planning - Research. 2. Urban
renewal - West Haven, Conn. I. Clarke,
William L. General specifications for the
West Haven limited urban observatory.
II. Sweeney, Joseph L. Technical specifications for a computer-generated mapping
system. III. Title.

352
S82
Sweeney, Stephen B   ed.
    Metropolitan analysis; important elements
of study and action, ed. by Stephen B. Sweeney
and George S. Blair. Philadelphia, University of Pennsylvania Press, 1958.
    189p.

    1. Metropolitan government. 2. Metropolitan
areas. I. Blair, George S., jt. ed.

Class No. | Author (surname first) Sweet, C. B., Pres.
Title Statement in Evening Star
4/5/50 — (low cost homes...)
Accession No.
Ordered 6 1950
MAY 1 6 1950
Source
Received MAY 1 8 1950
Place Wash, D.C. Publisher National Retail
Address Lumber Dealers' Assn
Date 1950 Paging 1p. List Price Est. Cost
Purchase Order No. Edition or Series
Date Recommended by
L.C. No. Reviewed in
H-305 (2-50) HOUSING AND HOME FINANCE AGENCY: Office of the Administrator 10—61167-1 GPO

674
A37
Sweet, C V
U.S. Dept. of Agriculture.
Selection of lumber for farm and home build-
ing, by C. V. Sweet and R.P.A. Johnson.
Washington, 1936.
45p. illus., diagrs. (Farmers' bulletin
no. 1756)

1. Lumber industry. 2. Farmhouses. I. Sweet,
C. V. II. Johnson, R.P.A.

Sweet, Cyrus B
Speeches.

See speeches collection.

628.1
B17e
Sweet, David C
Battelle Memorial Institute.
The economic and social importance of
estuaries. David C. Sweet, Project Director.
Wash., U.S. Environmental Protection Agency,
1971.
1v. (Estuarine pollution study series - 2)

1. Water resources. I. Sweet, David C.
II. U.S. Environmental Protection Agency.
III. Title.

332.3
(8)
M12
Sweet, Morris L
Madden, Carl H ed.
Exporting to Latin America; problems and
opportunities for U.S. small business
Prepared by Lehigh University under the
Small Business Administration Management
Research Grant Program. Edited by Carl H.
Madden and Morris L. Sweet. Washington,
Small Business Administration, 1963.
215p. (Small Business management.
research
Bibliography: p. 191-195.
(Cont'd. on next card)

332.3
(8)
M12
Madden, Carl H ed. Exporting
to Latin America; problems in ... (Card 2)

1. Small business - Latin America.
2. Commercial policy - Latin America.
I. Sweet, Morris L. II. Lehigh University,
Bethlehem, Pa. III. U.S. Small Business
Administration. IV. Title.

711.585
(7471)
N28
Sweet, Morris L
New York (City) Housing and Redevelopment
Board. (Bureau of Planning and Program
Research)
A large-scale residential rehabilitation
program for New York City, by Morris L.
Sweet and William Pincus. New York, 1967.
46p. (HRB rept. no. 14)

1. Neighborhood rehabilitation - New
York (City) I. Sweet, Morris L.
II. Pincus, William. III. Title.

VF
352
(71354l)
S82
Sweet, Morris L
Modernizing metropolitan government.
Toronto's experience.
32-42p.

[Reprinted] from the Business and Government Review, University of Missouri,
September-October 1963.

1. Metropolitan government - Toronto.

728.1
:336.18
(7471)
N28oc
no.10
Sweet, Morris L
New York (City) Housing and Redevelopment
Board. (Bureau of Planning and Program
Research)
New legislation to rehabilitate the down-
town business area? Prepared by Morris L.
Sweet and others. New York, 1963.
7p. (Its Occasional memo no. 10)
1. Public housing - New York (City)
2. Business districts - New York (City)
I. Sweet, Morris L. II. Title.

VF
711.4
:670
S82
Sweet, Morris L
State and local government loans for industrial development. New York, Florham Park
Press, [1967?]
5p.

Reprinted from the Journal of business,
Seton Hall University.

1. Industrial development. I. Journal of
business. II. Title.

711.74
(79535)
S82
Sweet Home, Or. City Planning Commission.
A plan for arterial streets for Sweet
Home, Oregon. In cooperation with the
Bureau of Municipal Research and Service,
University of Oregon. Sweet Home, 1958.
26p.

U.S. Urban Renewal Adm. UPAP.

1. Street planning - Sweet Home, Or.
I. Oregon. University. Bureau of Municipal
Research and Ser- vice. I. U.S.
URA-UPAP. Sweet Home,
Or.

711.4
(79535)
072
Sweet Home, Or. City Planning Commission.
Oregon. University. Bureau of Municipal
Research and Service.
A review of Sweet Home regulatory ordinances
related to community planning. [Prepared for]
Sweet Home City Planning Commission. Eugene,
Or., 1959.
15p. maps.
U.S. Urban Renewal Administration, Urban
Planning Assistance Program.

1. City planning - Sweet Home, Or. I. Sweet Home, Or.
City Planning Commission. II. U.S. URA-UPAP. Sweet
Home, Or.

312
(79535)
072
Sweet Home, Or. City Planning Commission.
Oregon. University. Bureau of Municipal
Research and Service.
Sweet Home's population and economic re-
sources. Prepared for the Sweet Home City
Planning Commission. Eugene, Or., 1959.
40p. maps, tables.
U.S. Urban Renewal Administration, Urban Planning
Assistance Program.

1. Population - Sweet Home, Or. 2. Natural re-
sources - Sweet Home, Or. I. Sweet Home, Or.
City Planning Commis- sion. II. U.S.
URA-UPAP. Sweet Home Orr

1979
SWEET SPRINGS, MO. CITY PLANNING
COMMISSION.
COMPREHENSIVE PLAN, BY HARE AND HARE,
INC. SWEET SPRINGS, MO., 1969.
65P. (HUD 701 REPORT)

1. MASTER PLAN - SWEET SPRINGS, MO.
I. HARE AND HARE. II. HUD. 701. SWEET
SPRINGS, MO.

333.38
(77847)
S 82
Sweet Springs, Mo. Ordinances,
etc.
Subdivision ordinance. Sweet Springs,
[1969?]
15p.

U.S. Dept. of Housing and Urban
Development. UPAP.

1. Subdivision regulation - Sweet
Springs, Mo. I. U.S. HUD-UPAP.
Sweet Springs, Mo.

711.5
(77847
:347)
S82
Sweet Springs, Mo. Ordinances, etc.
Zoning ordinance. Sweet Springs,
[1969?]
1v.
U.S. Dept. of Housing and Urban
Development. UPAP.

1. Zoning legislation - Sweet Springs,
Mo. I. U.S. HUD-UPAP. Sweet Springs,
Mo.

R
058.7
:691
S82l
Sweet's Catalog Service.
Light construction file; a file of manufacturer's catalogs compiled for the use of
designers and builders of houses and other light
structures. New York, F. W. Dodge.
v.

For complete information see shelf list.
Keep latest edition only.

1. Building materials - Catalogs. I. Dodge
(F W) corp. II. Title.

Sweet's Catalog Service

see also

McGraw-Hill Information Systems Co. Sweet's
Construction Div.

Sweet's Construction Div.

see

McGraw-Hill Information Systems Co. Sweet's
Construction Div.

312
(74461)
S82
Sweetser, L
The population of Greater Boston projected
to 1970. Boston, Greater Boston Economic
Study Committee, Associates of the Committee
for Economic Development, 1959.
16p. (Greater Boston Economic Study
Committee. Economic base report no. 2)

1. Population - Boston. 2. Population
forecasting. 3. Economic base studies -
Boston. I. Greater Boston Economic Study
Committee.

711.14
(76888)
S82
Sweetwater, Tenn. Regional Planning Commis-
sion.
Land use analysis, Sweetwater, Tennessee.
[Prepared for the Sweetwater Regional Plan-
ning Commission, by the East Tennessee State
Planning Commission, East Tennessee Office]
Sweetwater, 1959.
24p. maps.
U.S. Urban Renewal Administration, Urban
Planning Assistance Program.

(Continued on next card)

711.14
(76888)
S82
Sweetwater, Tenn. Regional Planning Commission. Land use... 1959. (Card 2)

1. Land use - Sweetwater, Tenn. I. Tennessee. State Planning Commission. II. U.S. Urban Renewal Administration. Urban Planning Assistance Program. Sweetwater, Tenn.

691.11
L68s
no.11
Swelling behavior in corewood and mature-wood of southern pine.
Louisiana. Agricultural Experiment Station.
Swelling behavior in corewood and mature-wood of southern pine. Agricultural Experiment Station Research Release. Baton Rouge, La., Agricultural Experiment Station, Louisiana State University & A & M College, School of Forestry & Wildlife Management, 1968.
5p. (LSU Wood utilization note no. 11)

1. Wood. I. Title.

691.54
N177D
NATIONAL RESEARCH COUNCIL, CANADA. DIVISION OF BUILDING RESEARCH. DETECTION OF ...1960. (CARD 2)

PUBLICATION NO. 266, 1959.

1. CEMENT. I. SWENSON, E.G. II. AMERICAN SOCIETY FOR TESTING MATERIALS.

711.74
(76888)
S82
Sweetwater, Tenn. Regional Planning Commission.
Major road plan for the Sweetwater, Tennessee planning region. Prepared by Tennessee State Planning Commission, East Tennessee Office. Sweetwater, 1958.
5p. maps.

U.S. Urban Renewal Administration, Urban Planning Assistance Program.

(Continued on next card)

690.015
(485)
S82
1971
R35
Swelling shale in the Ostersund area.
Jangdal, Curt-Erik.
Skiffersvallningen i östersundsområdet (Swelling shale in the Ostersund area)
Stockholm, Statens Institut för Byggnadsforskning, 1971.
116p. (Rapport R35:1971)
English summary.
1. Foundations (Building) I. Stockholm. Statens Institut för Byggnadsforskning.
II. Title: Swelling shale in the Ostersund area.

691.54
N177K
SWENSON, E G
NATIONAL RESEARCH COUNCIL, CANADA. DIVISION OF BUILDING RESEARCH.
KINGSTON STUDY OF CEMENT-AGGREGATE REACTION, BY E.G. SWENSON AND R.F. LEGGET. OTTAWA, 1960.
9P. (ITS TECHNICAL PAPER NO. 103)

REPRINTED FROM CANADIAN CONSULTING ENGINEER, V. 2, NO. 8, AUGUST 1960, P.38-46.

1. CEMENT. 2. CONCRETE. I. SWENSON, E. G.

711.74
(76888)
S82
Sweetwater, Tenn. Regional Planning Commission. Major road... 1958. (Card 2)

1. Highways - Sweetwater, Tenn. I. Tennessee. State Planning Commission. II. U.S. Urban Renewal Administration. Urban Planning Assistance Program. Sweetwater, Tenn.

691.32
N17
Swenson, E. (Series)
National Research Council, Canada. Division of Building Research.
Methods for rating concrete waterproofing materials, by F. Kocataskin and E. G. Swenson. Ottawa, 1958.
67-72p. illus. (Its Research paper no. 58)
Reprinted from A.S.T.M. Bulletin no. 229, April 1958.
NRC no. 4625.

1. Concrete. 2. Waterproofing. I. Kocataskin, F. II. Swenson, E (Series)

691.32
N17S
SWENSON, E G
NATIONAL RESEARCH COUNCIL, CANADA. DIVISION OF BUILDING RESEARCH.
SOME FUNDAMENTAL ASPECTS RELATIVE TO THE DESTRUCTION OF CONCRETE BY FREEZING AND THAWING, BY E.G. SWENSON. OTTAWA, 1953.
35-41L. ITS TECHNICAL NOTE NO. 148)

REPRINTED FROM PROCEEDINGS OF THE SECOND MEETING ON CONCRETE AND CEMENT RESEARCH IN CANADA, OCT. 9-10, 1952.

1. CONCRETE. 2. CLIMATE. I. SWENSON, E.G.

4484
4485
SWEETWATER, TENN. REGIONAL PLANNING COMMISSION.
PLANNING: 1, COMPREHENSIVE PLAN; 2, ANNUAL REPORT. SWEETWATER, TENN., 1969.
2 V. (HUD 701 REPORT)

1. MASTER PLAN - SWEETWATER, TENN. I. HUD. 701. SWEETWATER, TENN.

691.322
S82AD
SWENSON, E G
ADMIXTURES IN CONCRETE. OTTAWA, JUNE 1964.
23L. (NATIONAL RESEARCH COUNCIL, CANADA. DIVISION OF BUILDING RESEARCH. TECHNICAL PAPER NO. 181)

1. CONCRETE AGGREGATES. 2. CONCRETE. I. TITLE. (SERIES)

693.547.3
(71)
N171
Swenson, E G
National Research Council, Canada. Division of Building Research.
Weather in relation to winter concreting, by E. G. Swenson. Ottawa, Canada, Feb. 1957.
48 p. (Its Technical paper no. 46)

Reprinted form Rilem Symposium: Winter concreting. Copenhagen, February 1956.
Bibliography: p. 36-37.
1. Concrete construction - Canada.
I. Swenson, E G II. Title.

333.38
(76888)
S82
Sweetwater, Tenn. Regional Planning Commission.
Subdivision standards for the Sweetwater, Tennessee planning region. Sweetwater, 1958.
28p. diagrs.

U.S. Urban Renewal Administration, Urban Planning Assistance Program.
1. Subdivision regulation - Sweetwater, Tenn. I. U.S. Urban Renewal Administration. Urban Planning Assistance Program. Sweetwater, Tenn.

691.322
N17c
Swenson, E G
National Research Council, Canada. Division of Building Research.
Cement, aggregate reaction in concrete of a Canadian bridge, by E. G. Swenson. Ottawa, 1958.
1043-1056p. (Its Research paper no. 59)
Reprinted from Proceedings of the American Society for Testing Materials, vol. 57, 1957.

1. Concrete aggregates. 2. Bridges. I. Swenson, E G (Series)

693.547.3
N17
Swenson, E G
National Research Council, Canada. Division of Building Research.
Winter concreting trends in Europe, by E. G. Swenson. Ottawa, 1957.
369-384p. (Its Technical paper no 48)
"Reprinted from the Journal of the American concrete Institute v. 29, no. 5, Nov. 1957."

1. Concrete construction. 2. Winter construction. I. Swenson, E G (Series)

VF
711.585
(77434)
S82
3c.
Sweinhart, James
What Detroit's slums cost its taxpayers. Detroit, Mich., The Detroit News, 1946.
30 p. illus., graphs, maps. (Detroit News reprints.)

Cover title.
Articles appeared in The Detroit News from Nov. 26 to Dec. 1, 1945.

1.Slums-Detroit, Mich. 2.Slums-Economic effect. 3.Slums-Social effect. I.The Detroit News. II.Title

---

691.322
S82C
SWENSON, E G
CHARACTERISTICS OF KINGSTON CARBONATE ROCK REACTION, BY E.G. SWENSON AND J.E. GILLOTT. OTTAWA, 1961.
18-31P. (NATIONAL RESEARCH COUNCIL, CANADA. DIVISION OF BUILDING RESEARCH. RESEARCH PAPER NO. 130)

REPRINTED FROM HIGHWAY RESEARCH BOARD BULLETIN NO. 275, 1960.
1. CONCRETE AGGREGATES. I. GILLOTT, J E, JT. AU. II. TITLE. (SERIES)

628.1
G26P
SWENSON, H A
U.S. GEOLOGICAL SURVEY.
A PRIMER ON WATER QUALITY, BY H.S. SWENSON AND H.L. BALDWIN. WASHINGTON, GOVT. PRINT. OFF., 1965.
27P.

1. WATER SUPPLY. I. SWENSON, H.A. II. BALDWIN, H.L. III. TITLE: WATER QUALITY.

628.1
A52
Sweitzer, Robert J
American Concrete Pressure Pipe Association.
Basic water works manual, by Robert J. Sweitzer and others. Chicago, 1958.
181p. illus.

1. Water-supply. I. Sweitzer, Robert J.

691.54
N177D
SWENSON, E G
NATIONAL RESEARCH COUNCIL, CANADA. DIVISION OF BUILDING RESEARCH.
DETECTION OF LIGNOSULFONATE RETARDER IN CEMENT SUSPENSIONS AND PASTES, BY E.G. SWENSON AND T. THORVALDSON. OTTAWA, 1960.
P. 159-169. (ITS RESEARCH PAPER NO. 187)

REPRINTED FROM AMERICAN SOCIETY FOR TESTING MATERIALS, SYMPOSIUM ON EFFECT OF WATER-REDUCING AND SET-RETARDING ADMIXTURES ON PROPERTIES OF CONCRETE, SPECIAL TECHNICAL
(CONTINUED ON NEXT CARD)

634.9
S82
Swenson, Norman P
Federal forestry policies; effects on regional employment and income in Southwest Oregon.
St. Louis, Institute for Urban and Regional Studies, Washington University, 1968.
56p. (U.S. Economic Development Administration. Working paper EDA 7)
1. Forests and forestry. I. Washington University, St. Louis. Institute for Urban and Regional Studies. II. U.S. Economic Development Administration. III. Title.

712.25
882 Swenson, Norman P
    Recreation visits and retail trade outside
of standard metropolitan statistical areas.
St. Louis, Institute for Urban and Regional
Studies, Washington University, 1966.
    12p.   ([Water Resource Investment Project]
Working paper CWR 11)

    1. Recreation. 2. Retail trade - Statistics.
I. Washington University. Institute for
Urban and Regional Studies. II. Title.

711.585
(77311)
S82   Swenson, William.
    The continuing colloquium on University
of Chicago demonstration projects in
Woodlawn. Aspects of a major university's
commitment to an inner-city ghetto.
Report of a summer study grant (Contract
H-979) for the Dept. of Housing and Urban
Development. Chicago, Center for Urban
Studies, University of Chicago, 1968.
    138p.
    U.S. Dept. of Housing and Urban Develop-
ment. Demonst   ration Grant Program.
    1. Neighbor   hood rehabilitation -
Chicago.
            (Cont'd on next card)

711.585
(77311)
S82   Swenson, William.   The continuing
        colloquium...1968.   (Card 2)

    2. Community development - Citizen partic-
ipation. I. Title. II. Title: Colloquium
on University of Chicago Demonstration
Projects in Woodlawn. III. U.S. HUD-
Demonstration Grant Program. IV. Chicago.
University. Center for Urban Studies.

332
(100)
S82   Swerling, Boris C
    Current issues in commodity policy.
Princeton, N.J., Princeton University,
International Finance Section, Dept. of
Economics, 1962.
    41p.   (Princeton University. International
Finance Section, Essays in international
finance no. 38)

    1. Finance.   I. Princeton University.

333.33
S25r   Swesnik, Richard H   jt. au.
    Seldin, Maury.
    Real estate investment strategy, by Maury
Seldin and Richard H. Swesnik. New York,
Wiley-Interscience, 1970.
    248p.
    Bibliography: p. 233-238.

    1. Real estate business. 2. Investments.
I. Swesnik, Richard H., jt. au. II. Title.

Swett, William R   jt. au.

658
S31   Shaw, Richard H
    Manpower utilization in production control,
by Richard H. Shaw and William R. Swett.
New York, American Management Association,
Manufacturing Division, 1964.
    20p. (American Management Association.
AMA management bulletin no. 40)

    1. Management. I. Swett, William R., jt.
au. II. American   Management Association.
III. Title.   (Series)

728
(438)
S84   Swiechowski, Zygmunt.
    Architektura na slasku do polowy.
xiii wieku, Warszawa, Budownictwo i
Architektura, 1955.
    436p. illus. (Pomniki architektury
Polskiej zesz. 2)

    1. Architecture, Domestic - Poland.

728.1
(41)
S84   Swift, Stewart.
    Housing administration; a practical
handbook for the use of public health
officials and others interested in
housing. London, Butterworth, 1935.
    432p. tables.

    1. Housing - U.K.

728.1
(41)
S84   SWIFT, STEWART.
1938   HOUSING ADMINISTRATION; A PRACTICAL
HANDBOOK FOR THE USE OF PUBLIC HEALTH
OFFICIALS, STUDENTS, AND OTHERS
INTERESTED IN HOUSING. SECOND EDITION
BY THE AUTHOR. LONDON, BUTTERWORTH,
1938.
    484P.

    1. HOUSING - U.K.

538.56
S84   Swigert, Paul.
    Compute; a time-sharing desk calculator pro-
gram. Wash., National Aeronautics and Space
Administration, 1968.
    20p. (NASA Technical note TN D-4917)

    1. Automation. I. U.S. National Aeronautics
and Space Administration. II. Title.

658.564
C15   Swigert, Paul   jt. au.
    Canright, R   Bruce, Jr.
    Implementation and structure of COMPUTE, a
time-sharing calculator program, by R. Bruce
Canright, Jr. and Paul Swigert. Cleveland,
Lewis Research Center, National Aeronautics
and Space Administration, 1969.
    89p. (NASA Technical note TN D-5350)

    1. Automation. I. Swigert, Paul, jt. au.
II. U.S. Lewis Research Center, Cleveland.
III. Title.

658.564
S18I   SWIHART, STANLEY J
    AN INPUT SYSTEM FOR AUTOMATED
LIBRARY INDEXING AND INFORMATION
RETRIEVAL INCLUDING PREPARATION OF
CATALOG CARDS, BY STANLEY J. SWIHART
AND ELIZABETH BODIE. LIVERMORE,
CALIF., SANDIA CORPORATION LIVERMORE
LABORATORY, 1963.
    20L. (SANDIA CORPORATION REPRINT
SCR-317)

    1. AUTOMATION. 2. LIBRARY SCIENCE.
I. TITLE.   II. SANDIA CORP.

712.25
(41)
U54   Swimming bath costs with some notes on design.
1965   U.K. Ministry of Housing and Local
Government.
    Swimming bath costs with some notes on
design. London, H.M. Stat. Off., 1965.
    12p.   (Its Design bulletin 9)

    1. Recreation - U.K. I. Title.

697.4
S54s   Swimming pool heaters.
    Smith (A.O.) Corp.
    Swimming pool heaters. Kanakee, Ill.,
1968.
    8p.

    1. Heating, Hot water. 2. Recreation.
I. Title.

Swimming pools   *see*   Recreation

Swimming pools.

712.25
(41)
U54   U.K. Ministry of Housing and Local Government.
    Swimming pools. London, H.M. Stat. Off.,
1962.
    16p.   (Design bulletin 4)

    1. Recreation - U.K. I. Title.

712.25
F22   SWIMMING POOLS.
    U.S. FEDERAL HOUSING ADMINISTRATION.
MINIMUM PROPERTY STANDARDS FOR
SEMI-PRIVATE SWIMMING POOLS.
WASHINGTON, 1962.
    15P. (ITS FHA NO. 550)

    1. RECREATION. I. TITLE: SWIMMING
POOLS.

712.25
C68   Swimming pools; a guide to their planning.
    Council for National Cooperation in Aquatics.
    Swimming pools; a guide to their planning,
design and operation. Edited by M. Alexander
Gabrielsen. Fort Lauderdale, Fla., Hoffman
Publications, 1969.
    224p.

    1. Recreation. I. Gabrielsen, M. Alexander,
ed. II. Title.

361
S84   SWINNEY, OLIVE WALKER.
    STUDY OF PUBLIC HOUSING RENT POLICIES OF
PUBLIC WELFARE AGENCIES. PREPARED ... FOR
JUNE 19-20, 1958 MEETING, NAHRO
MANAGEMENT COMMITTEE. CHICAGO, NATIONAL
ASSOCIATION OF HOUSING AND REDEVELOPMENT
OFFICIALS, 1958.
    1 V.

    1. PUBLIC ASSISTANCE. 2. PUBLIC
HOUSING PROJECTS - RENTS. I. NATIONAL
ASSOCIATION OF HOUSING AND REDEVELOPMENT
OFFICIALS.

691.322
S84   SWINZOW, G   K
    PRELIMINARY INVESTIGATIONS OF
PERMACRETE. HANOVER, N.H., 1965.
    19P. (CRREL TECHNICAL REPORT 127)

    1. CONCRETE AGGREGATES. 2. FROZEN
GROUND. I. U.S. ARMY. COLD REGIONS
RESEARCH AND ENGINEERING LABORATORY,
HANOVER, N.H.

728.6
S83   SWIRE, FLORENCE M
    HOUSING IN RURAL AMERICA.
UNIVERSITY, LA., 1939.
    449-457P.
    (IN RURAL SOCIOLOGY, V. 4, NO. 4, DEC.
1939)
    CONTAINS THE MAJOR POINTS IN THE
WRITER'S MASTER'S THESIS, RURAL HOUSING
IN THE UNITED STATES...COLUMBIA
UNIVERSITY.

    1. FARM HOUSING. I. RURAL SOCIOLOGY.
II. TITLE.

310
(494)
S 84
Swiss Credit Bank.
Guide statistique Suisse (Swiss statistical abstract. Zurich, 1969.
93p.

Bibliography: p. 92-93.

1. Statistics - Switzerland.
I. Title: Swiss statistical abstract.

711
(494)
:016)
I57
Switzerland - Regional planning-Bibliography.
Institut für Orts-, Regional - und Landesplanung an der Eth.
Berichte   Kurzfassungen. Zurich,

v.

For Library holdings see main entry.

1. Planning - Switzerland - Bibl. 2. Regional planning - Switzerland - Bibl. 3. Switzerland - Planning - Bibl. 4. Switzerland - Regional planning - Bibl.

690
(494
:083.41)
884
1958/59
Switzerland. Delegierte für Arbeitsbeschaffung.
Bautätigkeit 1958 und Bauvorhaben 1959 in der Schweiz. Activité dans l'industrie du batiment en 1958 et constructions projetees pour 1959 en Suisse. [Activity in the construction industry during 1958 and projected construction for 1959 in Switzerland] Berne, 1959.
75p. tables. (American Embassy, Bern. Foreign service dispatch no. 38, 1959, encl no.1)

(Continued on next card)

310
(494)
S 84
Swiss statistical abstract.
Swiss Credit Bank.
Guide statistique Suisse (Swiss statistical abstract. Zurich, 1969.
93p.

Bibliography: p. 92-93.

1. Statistics - Switzerland.
I. Title: Swiss statistical abstract.

VF
728.1
(494)
884
Switzerland. Commission fédérale du contrôle des prix.
L'encouragement à la construction de logements économiques. Berne, Switz., 1956.
37 p.

Enclosure no. 1 to despatch no. 586, 2/27/57, American Embassy, Bern.

1.Housing - Switzerland.

690
(494
:083.41)
884
1958/59
Switzerland. Delegierte für Arbeitsbeschaffung. Bautätigkeit ... (Card 2)
Attached American Embassy, Bern. Foreign service dispatch no. 38, 1959.

1. Building construction - Statistics - Switzerland. (Series: American Embassy, Bern. Foreign service dispatch no. 38, 1959, encl. no. 1)

AUTHOR
Switzer, J. F. Q.
TITLE
A land agent's bookshelf; VI. Town and country planning. A bibliography.
SERIES Reprint, J. Land Agents' Soc., 1951, vol. 50, Oct., 439-442;
EDITION   PUB. DATE   PAGING

PUBLISHER
P. Collins, Hampton House, The Avenue, Twickenham, Middlesex, England.
RECOMMENDED BY   REVIEWED IN
                      AL #77 p. 14p
ORDER RECORD

728.1
(494)
884m
Switzerland. Commission Fédérale pour la Construction de Logements.
Le marche locatif et la politique en matière de logements. Berne, Switzerland, 1963.
59p.
Edite par la Feuille Officielle suisse du Commerce, Berne.
72 supplement de La Vie économique, publié par le Département Fédéral de l'Economie Publique.

1. Housing - Switzerland. 2. Housing market -   Switzerland.

Switzerland. Délegue aux Possibilites de Travail.

see

Switzerland. Delegierte für Arbeitsbeschaffung.

VF
690.031
S84
Switzer, J F Q
The life of buildings in an expanding economy. Reproduced from the Chartered surveyor, p. 70-77.

At head of title: Gold medal paper 1963.

1. Building costs. 2. Real property - Valuation. I. Title. II. Chartered surveyor.

728.1
:362.6
(494)
884
Switzerland. Commission fédérale pour la construction de logements.
Wohnungsbau für ältere Alleinstehend und Ehepaare. [Housing for elderly single people and married couples] Bern, 1960.
11p. (Its Bulletin no. 3)

Attached: Translation from the German by Charles Baumgardner.

1. Housing for the aged - Switzerland.
I. Baumgardner, Charles,   trans.

Switzerland. Delgato per le Occasioni di Lavoro.

see

Switzerland. Delegierte für Arbeitsbeschaffung.

728.1
S84
Switzer, Mary E
The new housing act and the disabled, by Mary E. Switzer and others. Wash., Vocational Rehabilitation Administration, 1964.
37-40p.

In: Rehabilitation record, Sept.-Oct., 1964.

1. Housing for the handicapped.
I. Rehabilitation record. II. Title.

Switzerland. Il Delegato per le Occasioni di Lavoro

see

Switzerland. Delegierte für Arbeitsbeschaffung

Switzerland. Eidgenoessische Wohnbaukommission.

see

Switzerland. Commission fédérale pour la construction de logements.

Switzerland.
see also
Zurich.
Beratungsgruppe --
Institut für Ort, Regional

690
(494
:083.41)
884
1957/58
Switzerland. Delegierte für Arbeitsbeschaffung.
Bautätigkeit, 1957 und Bauvorhaben 1958 in der Schweiz. Activité dans l'industrie du batiment en 1957 et constructions projetees pour 1958 en Suisse. [Activity in the construction industry during 1957 and projected construction for 1958 in Switzerland] Berne, 1958.
77p. tables. (American Embassy, Bern.

(Continued on next card)

711.417
(494)
S84
Switzerland. Fachgruppe Bauplanung der Studiengruppe "Neue Stadt"
Projekt einer studienstadt im Raume Otelfingen im Furttal, Kt. Zuerich. Zurich, 1958.
1v.

1. New towns - Switzerland. I. Title.

711
(494
:016)
I57
Switzerland - Planning - Bibliography.
Institut für Orts-, Regional - und Landesplanung an der Eth.
Berichte   Kurzfassungen. Zurich,

v.

For Library holdings see main entry.

1. Planning - Switzerland - Bibl. 2. Regional planning - Switzerland - Bibl. 3. Switzerland - Planning - Bibl. 4. Switzerland - Regional planning - Bibl.

690
(494
:083.41)
884
1957/58
Switzerland. Delegierte für Arbeitsbeschaffung. Bautätigkeit, ... (Card 2)
Foreign service dispatch no. 27, 1958, encl. no. 1)

Attached. American Embassy, Bern. Foreign service dispatch no. 38, 1958.
1. Building construction - Statistics - Switzerland. (Series: American Embassy, Bern. Foreign service dispatch no. 27, 1958,   encl. no. 1)

534.83
S84
Switzerland. Justiz- und Polizeidepartement.
La lutte centre le bruit en Suisse. Rapport de la Commission fédérale d'experts au Conseil fédéral. [Berne, 1963]
339p.
At head of title: Département fédéral de justice et police.

1. Noise. I. Switzerland. Bundesrat.

34.:
(494) Switzerland. Office cantonal vaudois
S85   du logement.
       La famille et le logement; enquête
sociale. Avec le concours de la Commission
de l'habitat de l'Union internationale des
architectes (UIA) et de l'USAL (Union suisse
pour l'amélioration du logement) Lausanne,
1960.
       68p.
       Tiré à part de la revue Habitation,
numéros de novembre et décembre 1960.
       1. Coopera-   tive housing -
Switzerland.

728.1
(494) Switzerland. Preiskontrollkommission.
S84f   Die Förderung des sozialen Wohnungsbaues.
Bericht der Eidgenossischen Preiskontroll-
kommission. Bern, Eidg. Volkswirtschafts-
department, 1956.
       37p. (Sonderheft 63 der Volkswirtschaft)
       1. Housing - Switzerland. (Series:
Switzerland. Volkswirtschaftsdepartment.
Die Volkswirtschaft ... Sonderheft 63)

628.1
(494) Switzerland. Dept. des Travaux Publics.
S 84   Carte des zones de protection des eaux.
Geneve, 1966.
       Map.
       1. Water resources - Switzerland.

728.1
(494) Switzerland. Volkswirtschaftsdepartment.
S84f   Die Volkswirtschaft ... Sonderheft 63.
       Switzerland. Preiskontrollkommission.
       Die Förderung des sozialen Wohnungsbaues.
Bericht der Eidgenossischen Preiskontroll-
kommission. Bern, Eidg. Volkswirtschafts-
department, 1956.
       37p. (Sonderheft 63 der Volkswirtschaft)
       1. Housing - Switzerland. (Series:
Switzerland. Volkswirtschaftsdepartment.
Die Volkswirtschaft ... Sonderheft 63)

Switzerland. Volkswirtschaftsdepartement.
       Preiskontrollkommission.
              see
Switzerland. Preiskontrollkommission.

336
S86   Swoboda, Alexander K
       The Euro-dollar market: an interpretation.
Princeton, N.J., International Finance Section,
Dept. of Economics, Princeton University, 1968.
       47p. (Princeton University. International
Finance Section. Essays in international
finance no. 64)
       1. Finance. 2. Money. 3. Foreign exchange.
I. Princeton University. (International Finance
Section) II. Title.

Folio Sycamore, Ill. Plan Commission.
711.4   Lawrence (Wm. S.) and Associates.
(77328)   A comprehensive plan for Sycamore, Illinois.
S92   Prepared for the City of Sycamore Plan Commis-
sion... Chicago, 1969.
       128p.
       U.S. Dept. of Housing and Urban Development.
UPAP. Ill. P-175.
       1. Master plan - Sycamore, Ill.
I. Sycamore, Ill. Plan Commission. II. Title.
III. U.S. HUD-UPAP. Sycamore, Ill.

711.585
(71)
S95   Sydney, N.B
       Sydney, Canada; the development of the
city. Montreal, 1960.
       67p.
       1. Urban renewal - Sydney, N.B.

690.031 Sydney. University. Dept. of Architectural
L82   Science.
       Lucas, John G
       Building contracts; documentation at tender
stage. Sydney, Dept. of Architectural Science,
University of Sydney, 1970.
       6-19p. (General report GR-2)
       1. Building costs - Estimates. 2. Building
construction - Contracts and specifications.
I. Sydney. University. Dept. of Architectural
Science. II. Title.

690.022 Sydney. University. Dept. of Architectural
C68   Science.
       Cowan, Henry J
       Building systems: forms-factors-functions.
Sydney, Dept. of Architectural Science,
University of Sydney, 1970.
       [8]p. (General report GR-3)
       Bibliography: p. 41-42.
       Building forum, June 1970, p. 35-42.
       1. Prefabricated construction. 2. Building
methods. I. Sydney. University. Dept. of
Architectural Science. II. Title.

690.26   Sydney. University. Dept. of Architectur-
F67   al Science.
       Forwood, Bruce S
       Computer simulated lift design-analysis,
by Bruce S. Forwood and John S. Gero.
Sydney, Australia, Dept. of Architectural
Science, University of Sydney, 1970.
       20p.
       At head of title: Computer report CR9, 1970.
       4. Elevators. I. Gero, John S., jt. au.
II. Sydney. University. Dept. of Architec-
tural Science. III. Title.

---

720   Sydney. University. Dept. of Architectural
G27   Science.
       Gero, John S
       Computers and the architecture student.
Sydney, Australia, University of Sydney, Dept.
of Architectural Science, 1970.
       4p. (Computer report CR4, 1970)
       Reprinted from: RAIA News, April 1970,
pp. 49-52.
       1. Architecture - Automation. I. Sydney.
University. Dept. of Architectural Science.
II. Title.

---

720   Sydney. University. Dept. of Architectural
G27c   Science.
       Gero, John S
       Computers in architectural science. Sydney,
Australia, University of Sydney, Dept. of
Architectural Science, 1970.
       [6]p. (Computer report CR6, 1970)
       Reprinted from: Architectural science
review, March, 1970, p. 11-16.
       1. Architecture. I. Architectural science
review. II. Sydney. University. Dept. of
Architectural Science. III. Title.

---

720   Sydney. University. Dept. of Architectural
(016)   Science.
G27   Gero, John S
       A selective bibliography of computers in
architecture, by John S. Gero and Maurice
Brown. Sydney, Australia, University of
Sydney, Dept. of Architectural Science, 1970.
       9p. (Computer report CR5, 1970)
       1. Architecture - Automation - Bibl.
I. Brown, Maurice, jt. au. II. Sydney.
University. Dept. of Architectural Science.
III. Title: Computers in architecture.

711.585
(94)   Sydney. University. Planning Research Center.
892   Urban redevelopment in inner city areas;
ways and means of achievement. Sydney, Edwards
and Shaw, 1966.
       47p.
       Edited by John Roseth.
       1. Urban renewal - Australia. 2. City plan-
ning - Australia - Research. I. Title.

Sydney's green belt.
333.71
C85   Cumberland County, Australia. County
       Council.
       Sydney's green belt. Sydney, 1963.
       10p.
       1. Open space land. I. Title.

Sykes, Allen, jt. au.
332.6
M27f   Merrett, A J
       The finance and analysis of capital
projects, by A.J. Merrett and Allen Sykes.
New York, Wiley, 1963.
       544p.
       1. Investments. 2. Finance. 3. Economics.
I. Sykes, Allen, jt. au. II. Title.

332.72   SYKES, ALLEN, JT. AU.
(41)   MERRETT, A J
M27   HOUSING FINANCE AND DEVELOPMENT; AN
ANALYSIS OF A PROGRAMME FOR REFORM, BY
A.J. MERRETT AND ALLEN SYKES. LONDON,
LONGMANS, 1965.
       127P.
       1. MORTGAGE FINANCE - U.K.
2. HOUSING - U.K. I. SYKES, ALLEN,
JT. AU. II. TITLE.

360
S94   Sykes, Gresham M
       Social problems in America. Glenview, Ill.,
Scott, Foresman and Co., 1971.
       334p. (Scott, Foresman series in institutions
and modern social problems)
       1. Social conditions. I. Title.

352.6
(76161) Sylacauga, Ala. City Planning Commission.
S95   Sylacauga, Alabama: community facilities
plan. Parks and playgrounds, schools, public buildings. [In cooperation with] Alabama State Planning and Industrial Development Board. Sylacauga, 1959.
       38p. maps.
       U.S. Urban Renewal Administration, Urban Planning
Assistance Program.
       1. Community facilities - Sylacauga, Ala. I. U.S.
URA-UPAP. Sylacauga,   Ala.

711.4
(76161) Sylacauga, Ala. City Planning Commission.
S95   Sylacauga, Alabama: land subdivision regulations and manual. [In cooperation with
Alabama State Planning and Industrial Development Board] Sylacauga, 1957.
       28p. maps.
       U.S. Urban Renewal Administration, Urban
Planning Assistance Program.
       1. City planning - Sylacauga, Ala. 2. Sub-
division regulation - Sylacauga, Ala. I. Alabama. State Planning and Industrial Development Board. II   U.S. Urban Renewal
Administration

711.14
(76161)
S95

Sylacauga, Ala. City Planning Commission.
Sylacauga, Alabama: long range land use plan. Population, economy, analysis of residential neighborhoods, neighborhood facilities, transportation, future land uses. [In cooperation with] Alabama State Planning and Industrial Development Board. Sylacauga, 1957.
1v. diagrs., maps, tables.
U.S. Urban Renewal Administration, Urban

(Continued on next card)

711.14
(76161) Sylacauga, Ala. City Planning Commission.
S95   Sylacauga, Alabama: long... 1957. (Card 2)

Planning Assistance Program.

1. Land use - Sylacauga, Ala. I. U.S. Urban Renewal Administration. Urban Planning Assistance Program. Sylacauga, Ala.

711.74
(76161) Sylacauga, Ala. City Planning Commission.
S95   Sylacauga, Alabama: major street plan. [In cooperation with] Alabama State Planning and Industrial Development Board. Sylacauga, 1959.
24p. maps, tables.

U.S. Urban Renewal Administration, Urban Planning Assistance Program.

1. Street planning - Sylacauga, Ala. I. U.S. URA-UPAP. Sylacauga, Ala.

351.712
(76161) Sylacauga, Ala. City Planning Commission.
S95   Sylacauga, Alabama: public works program. [In cooperation with] Alabama State Planning and Industrial Development Board. Sylacauga, 1959.
28p. illus., maps, tables.

U.S. Urban Renewal Administration, Urban Planning Assistance Program.

1. Public works - Sylacauga, Ala. I. U.S. URA-UPAP. Sylacauga, Ala

---

711.5
(76161
:345) Sylacauga, Ala. City Planning Commission.
S95   Sylacauga, Alabama: zoning ordinance. [In cooperation with] Alabama State Planning and Industrial Development Board. Sylacauga, 1958.
20p. map, tables.

U.S. Urban Renewal Administration, Urban Planning Assistance Program.

1. Zoning legislation - Sylacauga, Ala. I. U.S. Urban Renewal Administration. Urban Planning Assistance Program. Sylacauga, Ala.

362.6
M423 A SYLLABUS AND ANNOTATED BIBLIOGRAPHY. MICHIGAN. UNIVERSITY. INSTITUTE FOR SOCIAL GERONTOLOGY.
A SYLLABUS AND ANNOTATED BIBLIOGRAPHY. EDITED BY IRVING L. WEBBER. ANN ARBOR, 1959.
5 V. (SERIES OF SYLLABI IN SOCIAL GERONTOLOGY)

CONTENTS.- V.1, THE ECONOMICS OF AN AGING POPULATION.- V.2, THE PSYCHOLOGY OF AGING AND THE AGED.- V.3, THE SOCIOLOGY OF AGING AND THE AGED.- V.4, SOCIAL WELFARE AND THE AGED. (NOT IN LIBRARY)- V.5, INTERDISCIPLINARY
(CONTINUED ON NEXT CARD)

362.6
M423 MICHIGAN. UNIVERSITY. INSTITUTE FOR SOCIAL GERONTOLOGY. A SYLLABUS AND ...
1959. (CARD 2)

COURSE IN SOCIAL GERONTOLOGY.

1. OLD AGE - BIBLIOGRAPHY. I. WEBBER, IRVING L., ED. II. TITLE.

Sylvania recreation area management plan.
712.23
.F67 U.S. Forest Service.
Sylvania recreation area management plan. Ottawa National Forest. [Wash.] U.S. Dept. of Agriculture, Forest Service, 1963.
45p.

1. National parks and reserves. 2. Recreation. 3. Open space land. I. Title. II. Ottawa National Forest.

Symbology, the use of symbols in visual communications.
744
V47 Visual Communications Conference. 4th, New
1959 York, 1959.
Symbology, the use of symbols in visual communications. A report on the fourth Communications Conference of the Art Directors Club of New York. Elwood Whitney, editor. New York, Hastings House, 1960.
192p. (Communication arts books)

1. Visual aids - Congresses. 2. Communication systems. 3. Art. I. Whitney, Elwood. II. Title.

Symbols used in the National union catalog of the Library of Congress.
018
L41s U.S. Library of Congress. Processing Dept.
Symbols used in the National union catalog of the Library of Congress. 9th rev. ed. Washington, 1965.
214 p.

1. Library catalogs. I. Title: National Union Catalog of the Library of Congress. II. Title.
rdz

693.5
?690.24 ... Symmetric cylindrical shells.
U54 United Kingdom. Building Research Station.
Analysis of symmetric cylindrical shells; its application to civil engineering design, by John McNamee. London, H.M. Stat. Off., 1955.
84 p.

Bibliographies.

1. Concrete construction. 2. Roofs and roofing. I. McNamee, John. I. Title: Symmetric cylindrical shells.

Symmes, Roderick O. How to marshal Federal agency programs to help urban information systems.
711.4
U71urba Urban and Regional Information Systems Association.
Urban and regional information systems: Federal activities and specialized systems. Papers from the sixth annual conference of the Urban and Regional Information Systems Association, September 5-7, 1968, Clayton, Missouri, edited by John E. Rickert. Akron, Ohio, Kent State University, 1969.
277p.
Partial contents.-How to marshal Federal agency programs to help urban information
(Cont'd on next card)

711.4
U71urba Urban and Regional Information Systems Association. Urban...1969. (Card 2)

systems, by R.O. Symmes, Director, Data Systems Development, Dept. of Housing and Urban Development, p. 18-21.

1. City planning - Automation. I. Rickert, John E., ed. II. Symmes, Roderick O. How to marshal Federal agency programs to help urban information systems. III. Title: Urban information systems. IV. Title.

658
S95 Symonds, Curtis W
A design for business intelligence. New York, American Management Association, 1971.
168p.

1. Management. I. American Management Association. II. Title.

VF
725.822.91
S95 Symons, Farrell G H
Municipal auditoriums. Chicago, Public Administration Service [c1950]
78 p. tables.

1. Auditoriums. I. Public Administration Service. II. Title.

628.1
S95 Symons, George E
pt.1 Water works practices; operation, maintenance, management. Chicago, Water and Sewage Works, [1951?]
[34]p.
Reprinted from Water and sewage works.

1. Water-supply.
2. Water pollution.

628.1
S95 Symons, George E
pt.2 Water works practices. Part II [of a series on the Water works practices] Chicago, Scranton Pub. Co., 1963.
33p.
Reprinted from Water and sewage works magazine.

1. Water-supply. 2. Sewerage and sewage disposal.

628.1
W17w Symons, James M., comp.
Water quality behavior in reservoirs; a compilation of published research papers. Compiled by James M. Symons. Cincinnati, Ohio, Consumer Protection and Environmental Health Service, Environmental Control Administration, Bureau of Water Hygiene, 1969.
616p.

Public Health Service Publication no. 1930.
1. Water-supply. I. Symons, James M., comp. II. U.S. Consumer Protection and Environmental Health Service.

388
S23 Symons, John G Jr., jt. au.
Schneider, Jerry B
Locating ambulance dispatch centers in an urban region: a man-computer interactive problem - solving approach, by Jerry B. Schneider and John G. Symons, Jr. Philadelphia, Regional Science Research Institute, 1971.
40p. (RSRI discussion paper series: no. 49)

1. Transportation. 2. Health. I. Regional Science Research Institute, Philadelphia. II. Symons, John G., Jr., jt. au. III. Title.

614
S23r Symons, John G Jr., jt. au.
Schneider, Jerry B
Regional health facility system planning: an access opportunity approach, by Jerry B. Schneider and John G. Symons, Jr. Philadelphia, Regional Science Research Institute, 1971.
77p.

1. Health. I. Symons, John G., Jr., jt. au. II. Regional Science Research Institute, Philadelphia. III. Title.

LAW
T Symposium: Apartments in Suburbia: Local Responsibility and Judicial Restraint, Northwestern University, School of Law, 1964.
The battle for apartments in benign suburbia a case of judicial lethargy. In Northwestern University law review. July-August 1964, vol. 59, no. 3, p. 344-432.
(Cont'd on next card)

LAW
T

Symposium: Apartments in Suburbia:
Local Responsibility and Judicial
Restraint, Northwestern University,
School of Law, 1964.   The battle for
apartments in benign suburbia ... (Card 2)

Contents: Aesthetic control of land use:
a house built upon the sand?--Flexible land use
control: herein of the special use.--The legal
significance of cost considerations in the
regulation of apartments by suburbs.
1. Apartment houses - Congresses. 2. Apartment houses
- Social effect.   3. Land use.
4. Suburbs.   I. Apartments in
Suburbia, Local   Responsibility and
Judicial Restraint,   Symposium.

691.7
1620.19
S95

SYMPOSIUM ON ATMOSPHERIC CORROSION OF
NON-FERROUS METALS, ATLANTIC CITY,
1955.
     SYMPOSIUM ON ATMOSPHERIC CORROSION
OF NON-FERROUS METALS, PAPERS AND
REPORT PRESENTED AT THE FIFTY-EIGHTH
ANNUAL MEETING, AMERICAN SOCIETY FOR
TESTING MATERIALS. PHILADELPHIA,
AMERICAN SOCIETY FOR TESTING
MATERIALS, 1955, C1956.
158P. (ASTM SPECIAL TECHNICAL
PUBLICATION NO. 175)

     1. CORROSIO   N. I. AMERICAN
           (CONTINUED ON NEXT CARD)

002
:690
P27

Pettengill, George E   Users' needs and library
needs for building ... 1960. (Card 2)

1. Building documentation - Congresses. 2. Architec-
ture. I. American Institute of Architects. Library.
II. National Research Council. III. Symposium of
Building Information Problems, Cleveland, 1960.
IV. Title.

385
S95

Symposium International sur l'Emploi de la
Cybernétique dans les Chemins de Fer. 2d,
Montreal, 1967.
     Mémoires. Paris, l'Union Internationale
des Chemins de Fer et par les Chemins de Fer
Nationaux du Canada, 1967.
298p.

     1. Railroads. I. International Railroad
Union. II. Canadian National Railways.

691.7
1620.19
S95

SYMPOSIUM ON ATMOSPHERIC CORROSION OF
NON-FERROUS METALS, ATLANTIC CITY,
1955. SYMPOSIUM ON ATMOSPHERIC ...
1956.   (CARD 2)

SOCIETY FOR TESTING MATERIALS.
II. TITLE: ATMOSPHERIC CORROSION OF
NON-FERROUS METALS.

002
:690
F72

Symposium on Building Information Problems,
Cleveland, 1960.
Freeman, Elsa g
     Users needs and library needs in the
housing and planning fields, by Librarian,
U.S. Housing and Home Finance Agency, Office
of the Administrator, Library, Washington,
D.C. Washington, National Academy of Sciences
National Research Council, 1960.
     6p.
     Paper delivered at Symposium on Building
Information Problems, sponsored by Office of
Documentation, NAS-NRC, Cleveland, Ohio, 9
June, 1960.
     (Continued on next card)

711.4
S95a

Symposium on America's Private Construction
Industry and the Future American City,
Riverside, Calif., 1966.
     America's private construction industry and
the future American city. Edited proceedings
of a symposium on the subject sponsored by
American Cement Corporation and Urban
America, inc., held at Riverside, Calif. in
January of 1966. Edited by Harold F. Wise.
[n.p.] American Cement Corp., 1966.
155p.
     1. City growth. 2. Building industry.
3. Urban renew-   al. 4. New towns.
         (Cont'd on next card)

002
:690
S95

Symposium on Building, Housing, and Planning
Information, 2d, San Francisco, 1961.
     Proceedings, at 1961 Convention, Special
Libraries Association. [Washington, National
Housing Center] 1961.
37p.
     Symposium sponsored by Office of
Documentation, NAS-NRC.
     1. Building documentation - Congresses.
I. Special Libraries Association. II. National
Research Council.

002
:690
F72

Freeman, Elsa g   Users needs and library
needs ... 1960. (Card 2)

1. Building documentation - Congresses. 2. Housing.
3. Planning. I. Symposium on Building Information
Problems, Cleveland, 1960. II. U.S. Housing and Home
Finance Agency. Office of the Administrator. Library,
III. National Research   Council. IV. Title.

711.4
S95a

Symposium on America's Private Construction
Industry and the Future American City,
Riverside, Calif., 1966. America's...1966.
(Card 2)

I. Urban America, inc. II. Wise, Harold F.,
ed. III. American Cement Corp. IV. Title.

002
:690
B11

Symposium on Building Information Problems,
Cleveland, 1960.
Babb, Janice B
     Herbert U. Nelson Library and Information
Service, by Librarian, National Association
of Real Estate Boards. [Washington, National
Academy of Sciences, National Research
Council, 1960]
     3p.
     Paper delivered at the Symposium on
Building Information Problems, sponsored by
the Office of Documentation, NAS-NRC,
Cleveland, Ohio, 9 June 1960.

     (Continued on next card)

323.4
R29

A symposium on civil rights.
Rezazadeh, Reza, ed.
     A symposium on civil rights. Wisconsin
State University, Platteville, Forum on
Public Affairs. Unit one. Platteville,
Wisconsin State University, 1964.
51p. (Wisconsin. State University.
General bulletin vol. 1, no. 1)

     1. Civil rights. I. Wisconsin. State
University. Platteville. Forum on Public
Affairs. Unit one. II. Title.

711.4
F66

Symposium on America's Private Construction
Industry and the Future American City, Los
Angeles, 1966.
Foote, Nelson N
     Soul and system of the city. Paper presented
to Symposium on America's Private Construction
Industry and the Future American City, Los
Angeles, Calif., January 6, 1966. [n.p.] 1966.
22p.
     1. City planning. 2. Planned communities.
3. Building industry. I. Symposium on America's
Private Construction Industry and the Future
American City, Los Angeles, 1966. II. Title.

002
:690
B11

Babb, Janice B   Herbert U. Nelson Library
... 1960. (Card 2)

1. Building documentation - Congresses. 2. Real estate
business. I. National Association of Real Estate Boards
Library. II. Symposium on Building Information
Problems, Cleveland, 1960. III. National Research
Council. IV. Title.

301.15
S95

Symposium on Communities of Tomorrow, Washington, 1967.
     National growth and its distribution. Sym-
posium on Communities of Tomorrow, Dec. 11 and
12, 1967. Sponsored by United States Dept.
of Commerce; Dept. of Health, Education and
Welfare; Dept. of Labor; Dept. of Housing and
Urban Development; and Dept. of Transportation,
with the cooperation of the Community Resources
Institute. Wash., Govt. Print. Off., 1968.
     Partial contents - Address by Robert C.
Weaver.

     (Continued on next card)

LAW
T
A845o

Symposium on Anti-Discrimination legislation,
Freedom of Choice, and Property Rights in
Housing.
Avins, Alfred, ed.
     Open occupancy vs. forced housing under the
fourteenth amendment; a Symposium on Anti-
Discrimination Legislation, Freedom of Choice,
and Property Rights in Housing. New York, Book-
mailer, 1963.
316p.
     Foreword signed by Norman P. Mason.
     Also issued in Chicago-Kent Law Review,
v. 40, no. 1, April 1963.
         (Cont'd on next card)

002
:690
B12

Symposium on Building Information Problems,
Cleveland, 1960.
Baer, Karl A
     Survey of existing abstracting and in-
dexing tools, by Librarian, National Housing
Center. Washington, 1960.
     4p.
     Delivered at Symposium on Building Information Prob-
lems sponsored by Office of Documentation, NAS-NRC, at
Cleveland, Ohio, June 9, 1960.

     1. Building documentation - Congresses. 2. Building
industry - Bibliography. I. National Housing Center.
Library. II. Symposium on Building Information Problems, Cleveland, 1960.   III. National Research
Council. IV. Title.

301.15
S95

Symposium on Communities of Tomorrow, Washington, 1967. National growth...1968. (Card 2)

     1. City growth. 2. Population. I. Weaver,
Robert C. II. U.S. Dept. of Agriculture.
III. Community Resources Institute. IV. Title:
Communities of tomorrow. V. Title.

trans-
cript   1967. Transcript of proceedings. 2 v.

LAW
T
A845o

Avins, Alfred, ed. Open occupancy vs. forced
housing under the fourteenth amendment...
        (Card 2)

     1. Minority groups - Housing.
2. Housing legislation. 3. Symposium on Anti-
Discrimination legislation, Freedom of Choice,
and Property Rights in Housing. I. Title.

002
:690
P27

Symposium of Building Information Problems,
Cleveland, 1960.
Pettengill, George E
     Users' needs and library needs for building
information from the standpoint of the archi-
tectural library, by Librarian, the American
Institute of Architects. [Washington, Na-
tional Academy of Sciences, National Research
Council, 1960]
     6p.

     Paper delivered at the Symposium on Building Infor-
mation Problems, sponsored by Office of Documentation, NAS-NRC, Cleveland, Ohio, 9 June 1960.

        (Continued on next card)

658.564
S95C

SYMPOSIUM ON COMPUTER-CENTERED DATA
BASED SYSTEMS. 2D, SANTA MONICA,
CALIF., 1965.
     PROCEEDINGS. EDITED BY C. BAUM AND
L. GORSUCH. SANTA MONICA, CALIF.,
1965.
     1 V. (SYSTEM DEVELOPMENT CORP.
TECHNICAL MEMORANDUM SERIES TM-2624/
100/00)

     1. AUTOMATION. I. BAUM, CLAUDE, ED.
II. GORSUCH, L., ED.

625.7
H43sy
SYMPOSIUM ON CONSTRUCTION
TOLERANCES-STRUCTURES.
HIGHWAY RESEARCH BOARD.
SYMPOSIUM ON CONSTRUCTION
TOLERANCES-STRUCTURES, 7 REPORTS.
PRESENTED AT THE 43D ANNUAL MEETING,
JANUARY 13-17, 1964. WASHINGTON,
NATIONAL ACADEMY OF SCIENCES-NATIONAL
RESEARCH COUNCIL, 1965.
29P. ILLUS. (ITS HIGHWAY RESEARCH
RECORD NO. 85)

NAS-NRC PUBLICATION 1301.

1. ROAD CONSTRUCTION. I. TITLE.

728
:551.5
V15
Symposium on Environmental Physics as Applied
to Buildings in the Tropics, New Delhi, 1969.
Van Straaten, J   F
The sun and the design of buildings for
tropical climates, by J.F. Van Straaten and
others. Pretoria, National Building Research
Institute, South African Council for Scientif-
ic and Industrial Research, 1970.
8p. (South African Council for Scientific
and Industrial Research. National Building
Research Institute. C.S.I.R. reference no.
R/BOU 275)
Presented at the Symposium on Environmental
Physics as applied   to Buildings in the
Tropics, New Delhi, Feb. 1969.
(Cont'd on next card)

LAW
T
N28
L183s
2 C
Symposium on housing and home finance.
New York law forum.
Symposium on housing and home finance. New
York, 1964.
459—653p.

Issue of December 1964.
Contents:Part 1. Introduction, Robert C.
Weaver.-Housing our low-income population:
Federal and local powers and potentials, by
J. Burstein.-The development of new middle
income housing in New York, by E. J. Morris.-
Free choice in housing, by Robert A. Sauer.-

(Continued on
next card)

628.515
S95
Symposium on Direct Tracer Measurement of the
Reaeration Capacity of Streams and Estuaries,
1970.
Proceedings. Cosponsors: Environmental
Protection Agency and the Georgia Institute
of Technology, School of Civil Engineering.
Wash., Govt. Print. Off., 1972.
194p. (Water pollution control research
series)

1. Water pollution. I. U.S. Environmental
Protection Agency. II. Georgia. Institute of
Technology. (School of Civil Engineer-
ing)

728
:551.5
V15
Van Straaten, J   F   The sun and the
design...1970.   (card 2)

1. Architecture and climate. I. South
African Council for Scientific and Industrial
Research. Building Research Institute.
II. Symposium on Environmental Physics as
Applied to Buildings in the Tropics, New Delhi,
1969.

LAW
T
N28
L183s
New York law forum. Symposium ... (Card 2)
The college housing loan program, by Judah J.
Harris and Nick M. Nibi.

1. Federal housing programs. 2. Mortgage finance.
3. Universities and colleges - Housing. I. Title.
II. Burstein, Joseph. Housing our low-income
population: Federal and local powers and potentials. III. Morris, Eugene J. The development
of new middle income housing in New York.
IV. Sauer, Robert A. Free choice in housing.

(Continued on
next card)

699.841
S95
Symposium on Earthquake Engineering. 3d,
Roorkee, India, 1966.
Proceedings and discussions. Held under the
auspices of the School of Research and Train-
ing in Earthquake Engineering, University of
Roorkee, 4-6 November, 1966. New Delhi, Sahu
Cement Service, 1966.
2pts.

1. Earthquake resistant construction.
2. Civil engineering. I. Sahu Cement Service.
II. Roorkee,   India. University.

624.131
S95
SYMPOSIUM ON EXPANSIVE CLAYS, 1957-58,
JOHANNESBURG, SOUTH AFRICAN
INSTITUTION OF CIVIL ENGINEERS, 1958.
68P.

REPRINTED FROM TRANSACTIONS OF THE
SOUTH AFRICAN INSTITUTION OF CIVIL
ENGINEERS, SEPTEMBER AND DECEMBER 1957
AND JUNE 1958.

1. SOILS. I. SOUTH AFRICAN
INSTITUTION OF CIVIL ENGINEERS.
II. TITLE: E XPANSIVE CLAYS.

LAW
T
N28
L183s
New York law forum. Symposium ... (Card 3)

V. Harris, Judah J. The college housing loan
program. VI. Weaver, Robert C.

330
S95p
Symposium on Economic Growth, Washington, D.C.,
1963.
Proceedings. [Washington? c1963]
139 p.
Sponsored by the American Bankers Association.

1. Economic policy. I. American Bankers
Association.

699.81
S95f
Symposium on Fire Test Performance, Denver,
1969.
Fire test performance; a symposium presented
at the winter meeting, American Society for
testing and materials, Denver, Colo., 2-7 Feb.
1969. Philadelphia, American Society for
Testing and Materials, 1970.
243p. (ASTM special technical publication
464)
Sponsored by ASTM Committee E-5 on Fire
Tests of Materials and Construction.
1. Fire prevention. I. American Society
for Testing and   Materials. II. Title.
(Series)

LAW
T
Symposium on housing and home finance.
Part 2.
New York law forum.
Symposium on housing and home finance. Part
2. New York, 1965.
185p.

Entire issue of Spring, 1965.

Partial contents:-The Housing act of 1964:
urban renewal, by Melvin Stein.-Housing for
senior citizens, by Sidney Spector.-Expand-
ing relocation responsibilities of local
renewal agencies, by Herbert M. Franklin.-
Relocation pay-   ments in urban
renewal: more   just compensation,
(Continued on   next card)

699.81
S95
Symposium on Effects of Environmental and
Complex Load History on Fatigue Life,
Atlanta, 1968.
Effects of environment and complex load
history on fatigue life; a symposium.
Philadelphia, American Society for Testing
and Materials, 1970.
328p. (ASTM special technical publication
462)
Presented at the fall meeting, American
Society for Testing and Materials, 29 Sept.
- 4 Oct. 1968. Sponsored by Committee E-9
on Fatigue.
1. Fire prevention. I. American Society
for Testing and Materials. II. Title.

353
P22
Symposium on Federal Taxation, Washington, 1965.
Pechman, Joseph A
Financing state and local government.
Washington, Brookings Institution, 1965.
71-84p. (Brookings Institution. Studies of
government finance. Reprint 103)
Reprinted from the Proceedings of a Symposium
on Federal Taxation sponsored by the American
Bankers Association.
1. State finance. 2. Local government.
3. Intergovernmental relations. I. Brookings
Institution. I. Symposium on Federal Taxation,
Washington, 1965. Proceedings. II. Title.

LAW
T
New York law forum. Symposium on housing and
home finance. Part 2....1965. (Card 2)

by D. E. Pinsky -The planning stage agreement
as a land disposal technique, by R. P. Selya.

1. Federal housing programs. 2. Mortgage finance.
3. Housing for the aged. 4. Urban renewal.
5. Relocation. I. Stein, Melvin. The Housing
act of 1964: urban renewal. II. Spector,
Sidney. Housing for senior citizens.
III. Franklin,   Herbert M. Ex-
pending reloca-   tion responsibilities of local re-   newal agencies.
IV. Title.

620.015
895p
1963
Symposium on Engineering for Major Scientific
Programs. Georgia Institute of Technology,
1963.
Proceedings of the Symposium on Engineering
for Major Scientific Programs, Georgia
Institute of Technology, February 5-6, 1963.
Supported by the National Science Foundation.
[Atlanta] Georgia Institute of Technology,
1963.
198n.
On cover: 75th Anniversary Symposium.
1. Engineering   research - Congresses.
I. Georgia Institute   of Technology.

691.32
S95
SYMPOSIUM ON FLY-ASH IN CONCRETE,
WASHINGTON, 1964.
FIVE REPORTS PRESENTED AT THE 43D
ANNUAL MEETING, JANUARY 13-17,
1964. WASHINGTON, HIGHWAY RESEARCH
BOARD, 1965.
44P. (NATIONAL RESEARCH COUNCIL.
PUBLICATION 1257)

HIGHWAY RESEARCH RECORD NO. 73.

1. CONCRETE.
2. HIGHWAYS.

332.72
(54)
S95
Symposium on Housing Finance, New Delhi, 1965.
Selected papers from Symposium on Housing
Finance (held in New Delhi on 1-3 Feb. 1965)
New Delhi, National Buildings Organisation
and U.N. Regional Housing Centre (ESCAFE) 1966.
18p.
1. Mortgage finance - India. I. India.
National Buildings Organization. II. United
Nations. (Economic Commission for Asia and the
the Far East. Regional Housing Center. New
Delhi)

620.015
S95
Symposium on Engineering Research. 1st, University of
Minnesota, 1949.
Proceedings of the Symposium on Engineering Research
held at Center for Continuation Study, University of Min-
nesota, March 14-15-16, 1949. Edited by C. E. Lund.
[Minneapolis, 1949]
ix, 114 p. 23 cm. (Minnesota. University. Institute of Tech-
nology. Bulletin no. 20)
Bulletin of the University of Minnesota, v. 52, no. 34.
"Sponsored by the Institute of Technology and the Minnesota
Branch of American Society for Engineering Education in cooperation
with local industries."
1. Engineering research. 2. Research, Industrial.   I. Lund,
Clarence Edward, ed.   II. (Series) Analytics: Furnas,
C. C., Waterman, A. T.   A 50-175
Minnesota. Univ. Libr.
for Library of Congress   [3]

728.1
I54
Symposium on Housing, Durham, N.C., 1967.
Ink, Dwight A
The Department of Housing and Urban Development - building a new federal department.
Durham, N.C., Duke University, School of Law,
1967.
383p.
Reprinted from the Symposium on Housing:
Part II. Published as the Summer, 1967 issue
of Law and contemporary problems, Duke University School of Law, Durham, N.C.
1. U.S. Dept. of Housing and Urban Development. I. Symposium on Housing, Durham, N.C.,
1967. II. Law and   Contemporary Problems.
III. Title.

624.131
S95i
SYMPOSIUM ON INSTRUMENTATION AND
APPARATUS FOR SOIL AND ROCK,
LAFAYETTE, IND., 1965.
INSTRUMENTS AND APPARATUS FOR SOIL
AND ROCK MECHANICS: A SYMPOSIUM
PRESENTED AT THE SIXTH-EIGHTH ANNUAL
MEETING, AMERICAN SOCIETY FOR
TESTING AND MATERIALS, LAFAYETTE,
IND., JUNE 13-18, 1965.
PHILADELPHIA, 1965.
169P. (AMERICAN SOCIETY FOR
TESTING AND MATERIALS. SPECIAL
TECHNICAL PUBLICATION NO. 392)

(CONTINUED ON NEXT CARD)

624.131.3
S95I
SYMPOSIUM ON INSTRUMENTATION AND
APPARATUS FOR SOIL AND ROCK,
LAFAYETTE, IND., 1965.
INSTRUMENTS AND ...1965.   (CARD 2)

SPONSORED BY COMMITTEE D-18 ON
SOIL AND ROCK FOR ENGINEERING
PURPOSES.

1. SOILS - TESTING.   I. AMERICAN
SOCIETY FOR TESTING AND MATERIALS.
II. TITLE.   III. SERIES.

331
S95
Symposium on Manpower and Private
Resources, Wash., 1968.
Proceedings. Conducted by the Inter-
national Manpower Institute under
sponsorship of the Agency for Interna-
tional Development [and] U.S. Dept. of
Labor. [Wash.] International Manpower
Institute, 1968.
138p.
At head of title: U.S. Dept. of Labor.
Manpower Administration, International
Manpower Institute.
(Cont'd on next card)

691.110.15
S95
1965
SYMPOSIUM ON NON-DESTRUCTIVE
TESTING OF WOOD, SPOKANE, WASH.,
1965. PROCEEDINGS OF THE ...1965.
(CARD 2)

UNIVERSITY, PULLMAN. RESEARCH
DIVISION.

684.131.3
S95
SYMPOSIUM ON LABORATORY SHEAR
TESTING OF SOILS, OTTAWA, 1963.
LABORATORY SHEAR TESTING OF SOILS;
A SYMPOSIUM. PHILADELPHIA, 1964.
505P. (AMERICAN SOCIETY FOR
TESTING AND MATERIALS. SPECIAL
TECHNICAL PUBLICATION NO. 361)

SPONSORED BY THE NATIONAL
RESEARCH COUNCIL OF CANADA AND THE
AMERICAN SOCIETY FOR TESTING AND
MATERIALS.

1. SOILS   - TESTING.
(CONTINUED ON NEXT CARD)

331
S95
Symposium on Manpower and Private Resources.
Proceedings...1968.   (Card 2)

1. Labor supply. 2. Employment. 3.
Economic development. I. U.S. Dept.
of Labor. Manpower Administration.

697.8
A52S
SYMPOSIUM ON ODOR.
AMERICAN SOCIETY FOR TESTING MATERIALS.
SYMPOSIUM ON ODOR.   PRESENTED AT THE
57TH ANNUAL MEETING, ASTM, CHICAGO, JUNE
15, 1954. PHILADELPHIA, 1954.
81P. (ASTM SPECIAL TECHNICAL
PUBLICATION NO. 164)

1. AIR POLLUTION.   I. TITLE.
II. TITLE: ODOR.

624.131.3
S95
SYMPOSIUM ON LABORATORY SHEAR
TESTING OF SOILS, OTTAWA, 1963.
LABORATORY SHEAR ...1964. (CARD 2)

I. NATIONAL RESEARCH COUNCIL,
CANADA. (SERIES)

658.564
S95
SYMPOSIUM ON MATERIALS INFORMATION
RETRIEVAL, DAYTON, OHIO, 1962.
PROCEEDINGS.   DAYTON, OHIO, 1963.
159P.

AF. PROJECT 7381, TASK NO. 738103.
SECOND COPY IS PREPRINT EDITION.

2c.

1. AUTOMATION.   I. TITLE:
MATERIALS INFORMATION RETRIEVAL.

370
S95
SYMPOSIUM ON OPTICAL CHARACTER
RECOGNITION. WASHINGTON, 1962.
OPTICAL CHARACTER RECOGNITION;
PROCEEDINGS. EDITED BY GEORGE L.
FISCHER, JR. AND OTHERS. WASHINGTON,
SPARTAN BOOKS, 1962.
412P.

HELD ... UNDER THE JOINT SPONSORSHIP OF
THE OFFICE OF NAVAL RESEARCH AND THE
RESEARCH INFORMATION CENTER OF THE
NATIONAL BUREAU OF STANDARDS.

1. EDUCATION.   I. FISCHER, GEORGE
(CONTINUED ON NEXT CARD)

333
S95
1961
Symposium on Land Economics Research,
Lincoln, Neb., 1961.
Land economics research; papers presented
at a symposium held at Lincoln, Nebraska,
June 16-23, 1961, under the joint sponsorship of Farm Foundation [and] Resources for
the Future, inc. Edited by Joseph Ackerman,
Marion Clawson, and Marshall Harris. Washington, Resources for the Future; distributed by Johns Hopkins Press, Baltimore,
1962.
3 c.   270p.

1. Land economics.   I. Ackerman, Joseph, ed.
II. Farm Foundation,   Chicago.
III. Resources for the   Future.

697.8
S95
1969
Symposium on Multiple-source Urban Diffusion
Models, Chapel Hill, N.C., 1969.
Proceedings. Sponsors: National Air Pollution
Control Administration and North Carolina Consor-
tium on Air Pollution. Research Triangle Park,
N.C., U.S. Environmental Protection Agency, Air
Pollution Control Office, 1970.
1v. (Publication no. AP-86)
Editor: Arthur C. Stern
1. Air pollution. I. Stern, Arthur C., ed.
II. U.S. Air Pollution Control Office.

370
S95
SYMPOSIUM ON OPTICAL CHARACTER
RECOGNITION. WASHINGTON, 1962.   OPTICAL
CHARACTER ...1962.   (CARD 2)

L., ED.   II. U.S. OFFICE OF NAVAL
RESEARCH.   III. U.S. NATIONAL BUREAU OF
STANDARDS RESEARCH INFORMATION CENTER.
IV. TITLE.

728.1
(8)
S95
1962
Symposium on Latin American Housing, New
York, 1962.
Housing in Latin America. Sponsored
by the Chase Manhattan Bank. New York,
1962.
[28]p.

1. Housing - Latin America. I. Chase
Manhattan Bank, New York.

691.110.15
S95P
SYMPOSIUM ON NEEDS FOR
NON-DESTRUCTIVE TESTING IN THE
FOREST PRODUCTS INDUSTRIES,
MADISON, WIS., 1964.
PROCEEDINGS. MADISON, WIS.,
FOREST PRODUCTS RESEARCH
LABORATORY, 1965.
96P. (U.S. FOREST SERVICE
RESEARCH NOTE FPL-080)

1. WOOD - RESEARCH.   I. U.S.
FOREST PRODUCTS RESEARCH
LABORATORY   , MADISON, WIS.

691.338
S95
1967
Symposium on Particleboard, 1st, Pullman,
Wash., 1967.
Proceedings. Edited by Thomas M. Maloney.
Sponsored by Wood Technology Section, Engi-
neering Research Div., Washington State
University and Technical Extension Service,
Washington State University. Pullman,
Washington State University, 1967.
474p.
1. Wallboard. I. Maloney, Thomas M., ed.
II. Washington (State) State University,
Pullman. III. Title: Particleboard.

027
W45
Symposium on Library Functions in the
Changing Metropolis, Dedham, Mass., 1963.
Wilson library bulletin.
Dialogue in Dedham? [Mass.] A report on
the Symposium on Library Functions in the
Changing Metropolis, Dedham, Mass., 1963.
In Wilson library bulletin vol. 38, no. 1,
Sept. 1963. p. 50-64.

1. Libraries - Congresses. 2. Library
science. I. Symposium on Library Functions in
the Changing Metropolis, Dedham, Mass., 1963.

691.110.15
S9ZZ5
1963
SYMPOSIUM ON NONDESTRUCTIVE TESTING
OF WOOD, MADISON, WIS., 1963.
PROCEEDINGS.   SPONSORED JOINTLY
BY THE NATIONAL LUMBER
MANUFACTURERS ASSOCIATION AND THE
FOREST PRODUCTS LABORATORY.
MADISON, WIS., FOREST PRODUCTS
LABORATORY, 1964.
56P. (U.S. FOREST SERVICE
RESEARCH NOTE FPL-0401)
1. WOOD - RESEARCH.   I. NATIONAL
LUMBER MANUFACTURERS ASSOCIATION.
II. U.S. FOREST PRODUCTS
LABORATORY   , MADISON, WIS.

691.338
S95
Symposium on Particleboard. 2d, Washington
State University, 1968.
Proceedings. Edited by Thomas M. Maloney.
Sponsored by Wood Technology Section, Engineer-
ing Research Division and Technical Extension
Service. Pullman, Washington State University,
1968.
397p.
1. Wallboard. I. Maloney, Thomas M., ed.
II. Washington (State) State University,
Pullman. III. Title: Particleboard.

500.15
A47
Symposium on Long-Range Forecasting and
planning. Colorado Springs. 1966, Proceedings.
U.S. Air Force. (Office of Aerospace Research)
Long-range forecasting and planning; a sym-
posium held at the U.S. Air Force Academy,
Colorado, 16-17 August, 1966. Colorado
Springs? 1967.
200p.
Distributed by U.S. Clearinghouse for Federal
Scientific and Technical Information.
1. Governmental research. I. Title.
II. Symposium on Long-Range Forecasting and
Planning. Colorado Springs. 1966, Proceedings.

691.110.15
S95
1965
SYMPOSIUM ON NON-DESTRUCTIVE
TESTING OF WOOD, SPOKANE, WASH.,
1965.
PROCEEDINGS OF THE SECOND
SYMPOSIUM. EDITED BY WILLIAM L.
GALLIGAN. SPONSORED BY WASHINGTON
STATE UNIVERSITY, SUPPORTED BY THE
NATIONAL SCIENCE FOUNDATION.
SPOKANE, 1965.
543P.

1. WOOD - RESEARCH.
I. GALLIGAN, WILLIAM L., ED.
II. WASHINGTON (STATE) STATE
(CONTINUED ON NEXT CARD)

002
S95
Symposium on Photography in Information Storage
and Retrieval, Washington, 1965.
1965 symposium on photography in information
storage and retrieval. Advance printing of
invited papers and summaries, Washington, D.C.,
October 21-23, 1965. Washington, Society of
Photographic Scientists and Engineers, 1965.
98p.
Co-sponsor - Army Research Office, Office of
the Chief of Research and Development, Dept. of
the Army.
1. Documentation. 2. Library science -
Automation. I.   Society of Photographic
Scientists and Eng ineers. II. U.S. Army.

339.5
895
1967
Symposium on Power Systems for Electric Vehicles, New York, 1967.
Extended abstracts. [Prepared] under the joint sponsorship of the U.S. Dept. of Health, Education and Welfare, Columbia University, [and] Polytechnic Institute of Brooklyn, New York, Law School, Columbia University, 1967.
1 v.
Partial contents: The electric car, by K.W.C. Jeremy.
Henry, B. Linford, Chairman.

(Cont'd on next card)

339.5
895
1967
Symposium on Power Systems for Electric Vehicles...1967.

1. Power resources. 2. Fuel. 3. Transportation. I. U.S. Dept. of Health, Education and Welfare. II. Columbia University. Law School. III. Polytechnic Institute, Brooklyn.

690.24
S95
SYMPOSIUM ON RECENT RESEARCH ON BITUMINOUS MATERIALS, ATLANTIC CITY, 1963.
RECENT RESEARCH ON BITUMINOUS MATERIALS. A SYMPOSIUM PRESENTED AT THE SIXTY-SIXTH ANNUAL MEETING, AMERICAN SOCIETY FOR TESTING AND MATERIALS, ATLANTIC CITY, N.J., JUNE 26, 1963. PHILADELPHIA, AMERICAN SOCIETY FOR TESTING AND MATERIALS, 1964.
111P. (ASTM SPECIAL TECHNICAL PUBLICATION NO. 347)

SPONSORED BY   ASTM COMMITTEE D-8 ON
(CONTINUED ON NEXT CARD)

690.24
S95
SYMPOSIUM ON RECENT RESEARCH ON BITUMINOUS MATERIALS, ATLANTIC CITY, 1963. RECENT RESEARCH ON ...1964.
(CARD 2)

BITUMINOUS AND OTHER ORGANIC MATERIALS FOR ROOFING, WATERPROOFING, AND RELATED BUILDING OR INDUSTRIAL USES.
1. ROOFS AND ROOFING.
2. WATERPROOFING. 3. BUILDING MATERIALS. I. TITLE: BITUMINOUS MATERIALS. (SERIES: AMERICAN SOCIETY FOR TESTING AND MATERIALS. SPECIAL TECHNICAL PUBLICATION NO. 347)

690.21
S95
1968
Symposium on R and D in Rapid Excavation, Sacramento, Calif., 1968.
Proceedings. 2nd ed. Sacramento, State College, 1969.
1v.
Sponsored by School of Engineering, Sacramento State College in cooperation with the Committee on Rapid Excavation, National Academy of Engineering.
Howard L. Hartman, ed.
1. Foundations (Building) I. National Academy of Engineering.
(Cont'd on next card)

690.21
S95
1968
Symposium on R and D in Rapid Excavation, Sacramento, Calif., 1968. Proceedings... 1969.
(Card 2)

II. California. State College, Sacramento.
III. Hartman, Howard L., ed.

691.328
A526
SYMPOSIUM ON REINFORCED CONCRETE COLUMNS.
AMERICAN CONCRETE INSTITUTE.
SYMPOSIUM ON REINFORCED CONCRETE COLUMNS. DETROIT, 1966.
377P. (ITS PUBLICATION SP-13)

A SYMPOSIUM OF 14 PAPERS ON VARIOUS ASPECTS OF MASS CONCRETE WATERFRONT STRUCTURES AND CONCRETE WATER HOLDING STRUCTURES, AND CONCRETE CONSTRUCTION IN AQUEOUS ENVIRONMENTS PRESENTED AT THE 15TH FALL MEETING OF THE AMERICAN CONCRETE INSTITUTE, SEATTLE, WASH., SEPT. 28-29, 1962.
INCLUDES BIBLIOGRAPHIES.
(CONTINUED ON NEXT CARD)

693.55
895
Symposium on reinforced concrete in India today, New Delhi, Nov. 11-13, 1953.
Proceedings ... edited and compiled by N. K. Patwardhan.   Bulletin of the Central Building Research Institute, August 1956.
134 p.

1. Reinforced concrete construction. I. Patwardhan, N K., ed. II. India. Central Building Research Institute.

301.15
N28
Symposium on Research and the Community, Sterling Forest, N.Y., 1961.
New York (State) Dept. of Commerce.
Research and the community. Albany, 1962.
87p.
"Program of the Symposium on Research and the Community."

1. Community development. 2. Scientific research. I. Symposium on Research and the Community, Sterling Forest, N.Y., 1961.

691.16
S95R
SYMPOSIUM ON RESINOGRAPHY OF CELLULAR PLASTICS.
RESINOGRAPHY OF CELLULAR PLASTICS. A SYMPOSIUM PRESENTED AT THE SIXTY-NINTH ANNUAL MEETING, AMERICAN SOCIETY FOR TESTING AND MATERIALS, ATLANTIC CITY, N.J., JUNE 26 -JULY 1, 1966. PHILADELPHIA, 1967.
95P. (AMERICAN SOCIETY FOR TESTING AND MATERIALS. SPECIAL TECHNICAL PUBLICATION NO. 414)
1. PLASTICS. I. AMERICAN SOCIETY FOR TESTING AND MATERIALS.
II. TITLE. (SERIES)

362.6
A745
SYMPOSIUM ON RETIREMENT AND THE AGING, ARIZONA. STATE COLLEGE, TEMPE.
SYMPOSIUM ON RETIREMENT AND THE AGING. APRIL 13 AND 14, 1956. TEMPE, ARIZ., THE COLLEGE, 1956.
61L.

BIBLIOGRAPHY: P.51-54.

1. OLD AGE. 2. OLD AGE - ARIZONA. I. TITLE.

728.1
:362.6
895
1962
Symposium on Specialized Needs in Housing, Washington, D.C., 1962.
A two-day conference held at the National Housing Center, Washington, D.C., July 12-13, 1962. Sponsored by the National Housing Center and the National Association of Home Builders. Washington, National Association of Home Builders of the United States, 1962.
14p.

1. Housing for the aged - Congresses.
2. Nursing homes. I. National Housing Center.

658.564
S956
SYMPOSIUM ON STATISTICAL ASSOCIATION METHODS FOR MECHANIZED DOCUMENTATION, WASHINGTON, D.C., 1964.
STATISTICAL ASSOCIATION METHODS FOR MECHANIZED DOCUMENTATION, SYMPOSIUM PROCEEDINGS, WASHINGTON, 1964. EDITED BY MARY E. STEVENS AND OTHERS. WASHINGTON, GOVT. PRINT. OFF., 1965.
261P. (NATIONAL BUREAU OF STANDARDS. MISCELLANEOUS PUBLICATION 269)

1. AUTOMATION. I. STEVENS, MARY ELIZABETH, ED. II. TITLE.

694.183
M12
Symposium on Structural Properties of Wood, Seattle, 1965.
McGowan, W
A nailed plate connector for glued-laminated timbers. Philadelphia, American Society for Testing and Materials, 1966.
509-535p.
Presented at the Symposium on Structural Properties of Wood, Seattle, 1965.
Reprinted from Journal of Materials, Sept., 1966.
1. Nails and nailing. 2. Wood construction.
I. American Society for Testing and Materials.
II. Journal of materials. III. Symposium on Structural Properties of Wood, Seattle, 1965.
IV. Title.

699.85
S95
SYMPOSIUM ON SURVIVAL SHELTERS, MIAMI BEACH, FLA, 1962.
PAPERS PRESENTED AT THE SYMPOSIUM ON SURVIVAL SHELTERS BY THE ASHRAE TASK GROUP ON SURVIVAL SHELTERS DURING THE 69TH ANNUAL MEETING OF THE AMERICAN SOCIETY OF HEATING, REFRIGERATING AND AIR-CONDITIONING ENGINEERS. NEW YORK, AMERICAN SOCIETY OF HEATING, REFRIGERATING AND AIR-CONDITIONING ENGINEERS, 1963.
200P.

1. PROTECTIVE CONSTRUCTION.
(CONTINUED ON NEXT CARD).

699.85
S95
SYMPOSIUM ON SURVIVAL SHELTERS, MIAMI BEACH, FLA, 1962. PAPERS PRESENTED AT ...1963.
(CARD 2)

2. ATOMIC BOMB. I. AMERICAN SOCIETY OF HEATING, REFRIGERATING AND AIR-CONDITIONING.

300
S95
Symposium on Systems Analysis for Social Problems, National Bureau of Standards, Gaithersburg, Md., 1969.
Proceedings. Ed. by Alfred Blumenstein and others. Wash. Washington Operations Research Council, 1970.
331p.

1. Social sciences. 2. Systems analysis.
I. Washington Operations Research Council.
II. Blumenstein, Alfred, ed.

690
(415)
S95
Symposium on Technical Documentation for the Building Industry, Dublin, 1967.
Technical documentation for the building industry, sponsored by An Foras Forbartha Teoranta, the National Institute for Physical Planning and Construction Research. Edited by: Pierce T. Pigott and Lindsay N. Johnston. Dublin, National Institute for Physical Planning and Construction Research, 1967.
306p.
A project for the Government of Ireland assisted by the United Nations Special Fund and the United Nations.
(Cont'd on next card)

690
(415)
S95
Symposium on Technical Documentation for the Building Industry, Dublin, 1967. Technical...1967.
(Card 2)

1. Building industry - Ireland.
2. Building documentation. I. Pigott, Pierce T., ed. II. Ireland (Eire) National Institute for Physical Planning and Construction Research.
III. United Nations. IV. Title.

672
U54
1967
Symposium on the Behaviour of Structural Steel in Fire, Herts, 1967.
U.K. Ministry of Technology and Fire Officers' Committee Joint Fire Research Organization.
Behaviour of structural steel in fire.
Proceedings of the symposium held at the Fire Research Station, Herts on 24th January, 1967.
London, H.M.S.O., 1968.
135p. (Its Symposium no. 2)

1. Steel. 2. Building materials. Fire proof.
I. Symposium on the Behaviour of Structural Steel in Fire, Herts, 1967. II. Title.

624
S95
SYMPOSIUM ON THE DESIGN OF HIGH BUILDINGS, UNIVERSITY OF HONG KONG, 1961.
PROCEEDINGS OF A MEETING HELD IN SEPTEMBER 1961 AS PART OF THE GOLDEN JUBILEE CONGRESS OF THE UNIVERSITY OF HONG KONG. EDITED BY SEAN MACKEY. HONG KONG, HONG KONG UNIVERSITY PRESS, 1962. 515P.

1. STRUCTURAL ENGINEERING. 2. BUILDING CONSTRUCTION. I. TITLE: HIGH BUILDINGS.

697.8
A74
Symposium on the Development of Air Quality
Standards, Santa Barbara, Calif., 1969.
Atkisson, Arthur, ed.
Development of air quality standards, ed. by
Arthur Atkisson and Richard S. Gaines.
Riverside, Calif., Environmental Resources, inc.,
Columbus, Ohio, C.E. Merrill, 1970.
220p.
A symposium held under the auspices of:
National Air Conservation Commission and others
Oct. 23-25, 1969, Santa Barbara, Calif.
1. Air pollution. I. Gaines, Richard S.,
jt. ed. II. Environmental Resources, inc.
III. Symposium on the Development of Air Quality
Standards, Santa Barbara, Calif., 1969.
IV. Title. V. Tit   le: Air quality standards.

330
S95
1966
Symposium on the Role of Economic Models in
Policy Formulation, Washington, D.C., 1966.
Policymakers and model builders, cases and
concepts; papers. Vincent P. Rock, editor.
Introd. by Wasily Leontief. New York, Gordon
and Breach, 1969.
639p.
Sponsored by National Resource Evaluation
Center Office of Emergency Planning of the
Executive Office of the President, and the
Dept. of Housing and Urban Development.
Bibliography: p. 631-639.
1. Economic policy. I. Rock, Vincent P.,
ed. II. U.S.   National Resource Evaluation
Center III.   U.S. Dept. of Housing and
Urban Develop   ment. IV. Title.

691.11
A527
SYMPOSIUM ON TIMBER.
AMERICAN SOCIETY FOR TESTING MATERIALS.
SYMPOSIUM ON TIMBER. PRESENTED AT
THE FOURTH PACIFIC AREA NATIONAL
MEETING, LOS ANGELES, CALIF. OCTOBER
2, 1962. PHILADELPHIA, 1964.
103P. (ITS SPECIAL TECHNICAL
PUBLICATION NO. 353)

1. WOOD. I. TITLE.

336
395
Symposium on the Federal Budget in a Dynamic
Economy, Washington, 1968.
Proceedings, April 2, 1968. New York,
American Bankers Association, 1968.
159p.
1. Budget. 2. U.S. Appropriations and
expenditures. 3. Economic policy. I. Title:
Federal budget in a dynamic economy.
II. American Bankers Association.

360
S95
Symposium on the Urban Crisis: selections from
the 1968 Department of Housing and Urban
Development summer study in urban affairs.
Berkeley, Calif., Center for Planning and
Development Research, University of Califor-
nia, 1968.
464p.
1. Social conditions. 2. City planning.
I. U.S. Dept. of Housing and Urban Development.
Summer study in urban affairs. II. California.
University. Center for Planning and Development
Research. III.   Title: Urban crisis.

634.9
895
1959
Symposium on Timber and Allied Products.
New Delhi, 1959.
Proceedings. Edited by G.C. Mathur.
New Delhi, India, National Buildings
Organisation, Ministry of Works, Housing and
Supply, 1961.
452p.

1. Forests and forestry. 2. Building
materials -   India. I. Mathur,
G.C., ed.

308
S95
Symposium on the Foundations of Survey Sampling,
University of North Carolina, 1968.
New developments in survey sampling. Norman
L. Johnson, editor and Harry Smith, Jr., editor.
New York, Wiley-Interscience, 1969.
732p.
Sponsored by the Departments of Biostatistics
and Statistics, University of North Carolina,
Chapel Hill.
1. Survey methods. 2. Sampling (Statistics)
I. Johnson, Norman L., ed. II. Smith, Harry, Jr.,
jt. ed. III. North Carolina. University.
IV. Title.

690
S95p
1970
Symposium on the Use of Computers for
Environmental Engineering Related to
Buildings.
Proceedings. 1st-   1970-
Washington, Govt. Print. Off., 1971-
v. (Building science series 39-
Editor: 1970-   by T. Kusuda.
1970-   sponsored by the National Bureau
of Standards and others.
1. Building industry - Automation. I. Kusuda,
T   ed. II. U.S. National Bureau of
Standards.

711.585
S95
Symposium on Urban Renewal, Hartford, Conn.
1960.
The responsibility of private industry in
urban renewal. Summary of National Redevelopment Symposium. Hartford, 1960.
kit (19 pieces)

1. Urban renewal - Congresses. I. Title: Private industry in urban renewal.

624.131
A52
1950
Symposium on the identification and classification of soils; presented at the fifty-
third annual meeting, American Society for
Testing Materials, Atlantic City, N.J., June
29, 1950.   Philadelphia, American Society
for Testing Materials [c1951]
91 p.   tables.   (A.S.T.M. Special technical
publication no. 113)
Includes bibliographies.
George W. McAlpin, chairman.
(Continued on next card)

301.015
E17
Symposium on the use of official statistics
for thesis topics in the field of sociology
Eastern Sociological Society.
Symposium on the use of official statistics
for thesis topics in the field of sociology;
report of a panel discussion. New York,
Milbank Memorial Fund, 1965.
p. 7-41.
Reprinted from The Milbank Memorial Fund
Quarterly, January 1965, p. 7-41.
1. Sociology - Research. 2. Stat. I. Title.

711.585
P.68sy
Symposium on urban renewal conservation and
reconditioning.
U.S. Housing and Home Finance Agency.
Office of the Administrator. Office
of International Housing.
Symposium on urban renewal conservation
and reconditioning; for use of Housing
Committee, United Nations Economic Com-
mission for Europe, by Garrett B.
Ratcliff. Washington, 1960.
13p.
1. Urban renewal. I. Ratcliff, Garett B.
II. Title.

Symposium on the identification and classification
of soils ... [c1951]   (Card 2)

1.Soils. I.McAlpin, George W. II.Series: American
Society for Testing Materials. Special technical
publications.

691.320.15
A528
1949
SYMPOSIUM ON USE OF POZZOLANIC
MATERIALS IN MORTARS AND CONCRETES.
AMERICAN SOCIETY FOR TESTING
MATERIALS.
SYMPOSIUM ON USE OF POZZOLANIC
MATERIALS IN MORTARS AND CONCRETES.
PRESENTED AT THE FIRST PACIFIC AREA
NATIONAL MEETING, SAN FRANCISCO,
CALIF., OCT. 10-14, 1949.
PHILADELPHIA, 1950.
203P. (ITS SPECIAL TECHNICAL
PUBLICATION NO. 99)
1. CONCRETE - RESEARCH.
I. TITLE. II. TITLE: POZZOLANIC
MATERIALS. (SERIES)

388
D18
Symposium on Urban Survival and Traffic,
University of Durham, England, 1961
Davis, Harmer E
Some aspects of urban transportation planning,
by Harmer E. Davis and W. Norman Kennedy.
[Berkeley, Calif.] Institute of Transportation
and Traffic Engineering, University of Calif-
ornia, 1961.
10p.
A paper prepared for presentation at the
Symposium on Urban Survival and Traffic, King's
College, University of Durham, England, April
10-14, 1961.
1. Transportation.-   I. Kennedy, W.
Norman, jt. au.   II. Symposium on
Urban Survival and   Traffic, University
of Durham, England, 1961.

301.15
M19m
Symposium on the Impact of Urbanization on
Man's Environment, Onaway, Mich., 1970.
May, Richard, Jr.
Major trends in world urbanization and their
environmental implications; Symposium on the
Impact of Urbanization on Man's Environment,
Onaway, Mich., 14-20 June 1970. Working paper
no. 1, Agenda item 1. New York, United
Nations, 1970.
54p.
Sponsored by the United Nations in co-
operation with the International Trade Union
of the United Automobile, Aerospace and
Agricultural Implement Workers of America.
(Cont'd on next card)

691.16
895
Symposium on the Weatherability of Plastic
Materials, Gaithersburg, Md., 1967.
Weatherability of plastic materials. Symposi-
um held at National Bureau of Standards,
Gaithersburg, Maryland, February 8-9, 1967.
Editor: Muss R. Kemal. New York, Interscience
Publishers, 1967.
306p. (Applied polymer symposia no. 4)
"Sponsored by National Bureau of Standards
and Manufacturing Chemists' Association"
Includes bibliographies.
(Cont'd on next card)

388
895
Symposium: Urban Traffic Congestion. Virginia
Law Review, p. 831-872, Nov. 1950; p. 989-1055,
Dec. 1950.
Reprint.
1.Traffic. 2.Parking. I.Title: Urban Traffic
Congestion.

301.15
M19m
May, Richard, Jr. Major...1970. (Card 2)
Bibliography: p. 53-54.
1. City growth. I. Symposium on the Impact
of Urbanization on Man's Environment, Onaway,
Mich., 1970. II. United Automobile,
Aerospace and Agricultural Implement Workers
of America. III. Title. IV. Title: Impact
of Urbanization on man's environment.
V. United Nations.

691.16
895
Symposium on the Weatherability of Plastic
Materials.   Weatherability of plastic
materials...1967.   (Card 2)
1. Plastics. 2. Insulation
I. Kemal, Muss R., ed. II. U.S.
National Bureau of Standards. III. Manufacturing Chemists' Association. IV. Title.

030.8
R62
The synonym finder.
Rodale, J   I   ed.
The synonym finder. Edward J. Fluck
associate editor. Collaborators, Gordon
Marshall Pitts and others. Emmaus, Pa.,
Rodale Books, 1961.
1388p.
1. English language - Dictionaries.
I. Fluck, Edward   J., ed. II. Title.

628.44
S95

Synectics Corp.
A system for industrial waste treatment
RD&D project priority assignment. /Prepared/
for the Environmental Protection Agency.
Allison Park, Pa., 1971.
91p. (Water pollution control research
series)

1. Refuse and refuse disposal. I. U.S.
Environmental Protection Agency. II. Title.

728.2
897

Syracuse, Lee A
Arguments for apartment zoning. Washington,
National Association of Home Builders, Home
Building Press, 1968.
58p. (National Association of Home Builders.
Information bulletin no. 1)
Bibliography: p. [59-60]
1. Apartment houses. 2. Zoning. 3. Family
living requirements. 4. Family income and
expenditure - Housing. I. National Association
of Home Builders. II. Title.

Folio
711.4
(74765)
S97g

Syracuse, N.Y. Dept. of City Planning.
A general plan, Syracuse, New York.
Syracuse, 1955.
78p.

1. Master plan - Syracuse, N.Y.

Synonyms see English language - Synonyms

711.5
S97

Syracuse, Lee A
How to get apartment zoning; a guide to
argument presentation at the public hearing.
Wash., National Association of Home Builders,
1969.
44p. (National Association of Home
Builders. Information bulletin no. 4)

1. Zoning. 2. Apartment houses.
I. National Association of Home Builders.
II. Title.

711.552
(74765)
S97

SYRACUSE, N.Y. CITY PLANNING
COMMISSION.
THE CENTRAL DISTRICT. SYRACUSE,
N.Y., SYRACUSE-ONONDAGA POST-WAR
PLANNING COUNCIL, 1944.

1. BUSINESS DISTRICTS - SYRACUSE,
N.Y. I. SYRACUSE-ONONDAGA POST-WAR
PLANNING COUNCIL.

Synonyms and related words.

Ref.
030.8
F85f

Funk & Wagnalls modern guide to synonyms and
related words. List of antonyms, copious cross-
references, a complete and legible index.
Edited by S.I. Hayakawa. New York, 1968.
726p.

1. English language - Synonyms. 2. English
language - Dictionaries. I. Hayakawa, S.I.,
ed. II. Title: Modern guide to synonyms and
related words. III. Title: Synonyms and
related words.

333.38
(77593)
S97

Syracuse, Lee.
Mandatory dedication of open space in
residential development; report and survey;
land use and development department.
[Washington] [National Association of Home
Builders] [1968]
[19]p.

1. Subdivision regulation - Menomonee
Falls, Wis. 2. Schools - Menomonee Falls, Wis.
3. Land use - Menomonee Falls, Wis. 4. Open space
land. I. National Association of Home Builders. II.
Title.

VF
728.1
:336.18
B87

Syracuse, N.Y. City Planning Commission.
Bureau of Municipal Research, Syracuse, N.Y.
Report on new residential construction near
two public housing projects [submitted to the
Syracuse City Planning Commission] Syracuse,
N.Y. [Aug. 1955]
5 L. / charts

A synopsis of the planning legislation in
seven countries.

LAW
T
1573s

International Federation for Housing and
Planning.
A synopsis of the planning legislation
in seven countries, by Stephan Ronart.
Amsterdam, [1957?]
130p.

1. Planning - Legislation. I. Ronart, Stephan.
II. Title.

711.4
S97

Syracuse, Lee A.
Shaping urban design, by Lee A. Syracuse,
and John M. King. Washington, Task Force on
Economic Growth and Opportunity, Chamber of
Commerce of the United States, [1967?]
53p.

1. City planning. 2. City growth.
3. Urban renewal. I. King, John M., jt. au.
II. Chamber of Commerce of the United
States. Task Force on Economic Growth and
Opportunity. III. Title IV. Title: Urban
design.

FOLIO
711.585
(74765)
897c

Syracuse, N.Y. Dept. of City Planning.
A community renewal program, 1964-
1980; a long-range renewal program.
Syracuse, N.Y., 1964.
123p.

U.S. Urban Renewal Adm. CRP.

1. Urban renewal - Syracuse, N.Y.
I. U.S. URA-CRP. Syracuse, N.Y.

628.44
S95

Synectics Corp.
A system for industrial waste treatment
RD&D project priority assignment. [Prepared]
for the Environmental Protection Agency.
Allison Park, Pa., 1971.
91p. (Water pollution control research
series)

1. Refuse and refuse disposal. I. U.S.
Environmental Protection Agency. II. Title.

647.1
S97

Syracuse, Lee A
The single family home; a financial asset
to the community. Wash., Home Building Press,
1968.
47p. (National Association of Home
Builders. Information bulletin no. 3)

1. Family income and expenditure - Housing.
2. Municipal services. 3. Municipal finance.
I. National Association of Home Builders.
II. Title.

312
(74765)
E26

Syracuse, N.Y. Dept. of City Planning.
Economic Consultants Organization, inc.
Population characteristics, 1960-1980,
Syracuse, New York. A special report for
the Dept. of City Planning, Syracuse, N.Y.
Syracuse, N.Y., 1965.
53p. Its Special report 1)

1. Population - Syracuse, N.Y.
2. Master plan - Syracuse, N.Y.
I. Syracuse, N.Y. Dept. of City Planning.
II. Title.

628.515
S61

SYNTHETIC DETERGENTS IN PERSPECTIVE.
SOAP AND DETERGENT ASSOCIATION.
SYNTHETIC DETERGENTS IN PERSPECTIVE;
THEIR RELATIONSHIP TO SEWAGE DISPOSAL
AND SAFE WATER SUPPLIES. NEW YORK,
1962.
39P.

BIBLIOGRAPHY: P. 32-33.

1. WATER POLLUTION. I. TITLE.
II. TITLE: DETERGENTS IN PERSPECTIVE.

Syracuse, N. Y.

VF
Housing-U.S.-N.Y.
Land use-N.Y.
Population-U.S.-New York State.

711.4
(74765)
897

Syracuse, N. Y. Dept. of City Planning.
Report. 1953, 55, 58, 63
Syracuse, 1956
4v. annual.
Issued 1953, 55, 58 published by City Plann
For complete information see shelf list.
Dept of City Planning. Created 1938
1. City planning - Syracuse, N.Y.

628.515
(016)
P81f
1962

SYNTHETIC DETERGENTS IN WATER AND
WASTE.
U.S. PUBLIC HEALTH SERVICE. DIVISION
OF WATER SUPPLY AND POLLUTION
CONTROL.
BIBLIOGRAPHY ON SYNTHETIC DETERGENTS
IN WATER AND WASTE INCLUDING
ANALYTICAL METHODS AND PHYSIOLOGICAL
EFFECTS. CINCINNATI, 1962.
53P.

1. WATER POLLUTION - BIBLIOGRAPHY.
I. TITLE: SYNTHETIC DETERGENTS IN
WATER AND WASTE.

Syracuse, N.Y. Bureau of Municipal Research.

see

Bureau of Municipal Research, Syracuse, N.Y.

712.41
S97

Syracuse, N.Y. Dept. of City Planning.
Trees in the city. Syracuse, N.Y.,
1960.
7p. (Its Planning information bulletin, vol. 2, no. 1. April-May 1960)

1. Trees.

Class No. *(?)file*
Accession No.
Ordered 4/19/50
Source 1tr
Received APR 28 1950
Cost
Purchase Order No.
Date
L. C. No.

Author (surname first) Syracuse, New York Civil Development Committee.
Title Report on community organization and progress.
Place Syracuse, N.Y. Publisher Syracuse-Onondaga county Civil development committee.
Address
Date 1949 Paging 8, 4 List Price Est. Cost gratis
Edition or Series
Recommended by
Reviewed in Joint Reference Library, 4/3/50

H-305 (2-50) HOUSING AND HOME FINANCE AGENCY: Office of the Administrator 16—61187-1 GPO

Class No.
Accession No.
Ordered MAY 5 1950
Received MAY 10 1950
Cost
Purchase Order No.
Date
L. C. No.

Author (surname first) Council of Social Agencies of Syracuse and Onondaga County
Title Some facts about the current housing shortage in Syracuse, N.Y.
Place Syracuse 2, N.Y. Publisher (same as author)
Address 615-622 Law Bldg.
Date Oct '49 Paging List Price Est. Cost gratis
Edition or Series
Recommended by
Reviewed in Housing and related research in state N.Y. 10/49 thru 11/49.

H-305 (2-50) HOUSING AND HOME FINANCE AGENCY: Office of the Administrator 16—61187-1 GPO

711.333
(747)
S61

Syracuse Governmental Research Bureau. A profile of central New York: the five central New York counties...[1966]

1. County planning - New York (State)
2. City planning - New York (State)
I. Spaulding, Richard C. II. Metropolitan Development Association of Syracuse and Onondaga County. III. Title.

711.14
(74765)
S97

SYRACUSE, N.Y. HOUSING AUTHORITY.
GENERAL LAND USE, CITY OF SYRACUSE.
SYRACUSE, 1937.
1 V.

BOUND IN AT END: SECTION 5.3 OF
BUILDING CODE OF THE CITY OF SYRACUSE,
N.Y., 1930. 5L.

1. LAND USE - SYRACUSE, N.Y.
2. BUILDING CODES - SYRACUSE, N.Y.

711.585.1
(74765)
S97

Syracuse, N.Y. Office of the Mayor
Application to the Department of Housing and Urban Development for a grant to plan a comprehensive city demonstration program.
Syracuse, N.Y., 1967.
1v.
Selected to receive the first HUD
Model Cities Program planning grants.
1. Model cities - Syracuse, N.Y.
I. U.S. HUD - Model Cities Program first planning grants.

711.3
(74765)
S97

Syracuse Governmental Research Bureau, inc.
A profile of Onondaga County. An interim document containing an outline of the major characteristics of Onondaga County together with the factors to be considered in the planning of a modern metropolitan area. In short, this is a report making possible future action toward a Syracuse metropolitan area. Prepared for the Metropolitan Development Association of Syracuse and Onondaga County, [Syracuse, N.Y.] 1961.
75p.

1. Metropolitan area planning - Onondaga
Co., N.Y. I. Metro- politan Development
Association of Syracuse and Onondaga County.
[N.Y.]

712.25
(74765)
S97

SYRACUSE, N.Y. HOUSING AUTHORITY.
OUTDOOR RECREATIONAL FACILITIES.
SYRACUSE, 1937.
59L.

1. RECREATION - SYRACUSE, N.Y.

690.091.82
(74765)
S97

SYRACUSE. ORDINANCES, ETC.
THE BUILDING CODE OF THE CITY OF
SYRACUSE, N.Y., AS AMENDED TO
JANUARY 1, 1913. SYRACUSE, DEHLER,
1913.
182P.

1. BUILDING CODES - SYRACUSE, N.Y.

728.1
(74765
S97G

SYRACUSE HOUSING AUTHORITY.
GENERAL REPORT, AUGUST 1937.
SYRACUSE, N.Y., 1937.
1 V. (VARIOUS PAGINGS)

1. HOUSING - SYRACUSE, N.Y.

728.1
:336.18
(74765)
S97
1939
1940
1941
1942
1943
1944
1945

1948
1949

SYRACUSE, N.Y. HOUSING AUTHORITY.
REPORT, 1939-45, 1948-49, 1955-56
SYRACUSE.
6 V. ANNUAL.

1. PUBLIC HOUSING - SYRACUSE, N.Y.

1955/56

690.091.82
1613.5
(74765)
S97

SYRACUSE, N.Y. ORDINANCES, ETC.
HOUSING CODE OF THE CITY OF
SYRACUSE. CHAPTER 27 OF THE
REVISED GENERAL ORDINANCES...
ADOPTED JUNE 1, 1963. SYRACUSE,
N.Y., 1963.
45P.

1. HOUSING CODES - SYRACUSE, N.Y.

728.1
(74765)
S97H

SYRACUSE HOUSING AUTHORITY.
HELPING FAMILIES TO ASSUME
RESPONSIBILITY, BY BEATRICE MCKIBBIN.
SYRACUSE, NEW YORK, 1963.
14P.

1. HOUSING - SYRACUSE, N.Y.
2. PUBLIC HOUSING - SYRACUSE, N.Y.
3. SOCIAL WELFARE - SYRACUSE, N.Y.
I. MCKIBBIN, BEATRICE. II. TITLE.

711.585
(74765)
H16

SYRACUSE, N.Y. HOUSING AUTHORITY.
HAMLIN, TALBOT FAULKNER, 1889-
A REVIEW AND REPORT ON PIONEER HOMES,
A HOUSING DEVELOPMENT OF THE SYRACUSE
HOUSING AUTHORITY. WASHINGTON,
FEDERAL PUBLIC HOUSING AUTHORITY, 1944.
22L.

1. SLUMS - SYRACUSE, N.Y.
2. PUBLIC HOUSING - SYRACUSE, N.Y.
I. SYRACUSE, N.Y. HOUSING AUTHORITY.
II. U.S. FEDERAL PUBLIC HOUSING
AUTHORITY. III. TITLE: PIONEER
HOMES.

711.585
(74765)
S97

Syracuse, N.Y. Dept. of Urban Improvement.
Report
Syracuse,
v.   annual.
For complete information see shelf list.

1. Urban renewal - Syracuse, N.Y.

312
(74765)
S97
1936

SYRACUSE HOUSING AUTHORITY.
SYRACUSE POPULATION ACCORDING TO THE
UNITED STATES CENSUS TRACTS REVISED
IN 1936. ANALYZED ON THE BASIS OF
CENSUS TRACTS REVISED IN 1936.
SYRACUSE, 1937.
119L.

1. CENSUS - SYRACUSE, N.Y.
I. TITLE.

711.585
(74765)
S97S

SYRACUSE, N.Y. HOUSING AUTHORITY.
SOME ASPECTS OF THE REAL ESTATE
SITUATION RELATED TO LOW-RENTAL
HOUSING. SYRACUSE, 1937.
14L.

1. SLUMS - SYRACUSE, N.Y.

711.585
(74765)
C34

Syracuse, N.Y. Dept. of Urban Improvement.
Chiles, William M
Sponsorships; an aid to relocation.
Syracuse, N.Y., Dept. of Urban Improvement, 1962.
16p.

1. Relocation - Syracuse, N.Y.
I. Syracuse, N.Y. Dept. of Urban Improvement.

728.1
(74765)
S97

SYRACUSE HOUSING AUTHORITY.
SYRACUSE POPULATION CHARACTERISTICS
AND TRENDS. SYRACUSE, N.Y., 1937.
1 V. (VARIOUS PAGINGS)

2. HOUSING - SYRACUSE, N.Y.
2. POPULATION - SYRACUSE, N.Y.
I. TITLE.

728.1
:336.18
(74765)
S97R
1938
1939

SYRACUSE, N.Y. HOUSING AUTHORITY.
WOMEN'S HOUSING COMMITTEE.
REPORT, 1938-39
SYRACUSE.
1V.

1. PUBLIC HOUSING - SYRACUSE, N.Y.

711.333
(747)
S61

Syracuse Governmental Research Bureau.
A profile of central New York: the five central New York counties of Cayuga, Cortland, Madison, Onondaga and Oswego, including the cities of Auburn, Cortland, Fulton, Oneida, Oswego, and Syracuse. [Prepared by] Richard C. Spaulding and others.
Syracuse Governmental Research Bureau, inc. and the Metropolitan Development Association of Syracuse and Onondaga County. [1966]
84p.

(Cont'd on next card)

2419
2420
2421

SYRACUSE-ONONDAGA COUNTY PLANNING AGENCY.
CENTRAL NEW YORK REGION; PHASE II,
ANALYSIS: A SERIES OF TECHNICAL MEMOS:
1, FREIGHT MOVEMENT; 2, MASS
TRANSPORTATION; 3, WATER RELATED
ENVIRONMENTAL SERVICES. SYRACUSE,
CENTRAL NEW YORK REGIONAL PLANNING AND
DEVELOPMENT BOARD, 1970.
3 V. (HUD 701 REPORT)

1. REGIONAL PLANNING - SYRACUSE, N.Y.
I. HUD. 701 SYRACUSE, N.Y.

388
(74765)
S97

Syracuse-Onondaga County Planning Agency.
Job accessibility: a study of factors
inhibiting employment. Syracuse, N.Y., 1969.
30p.
U.S. Mass Transportation Demonstration Grant
Program.

1. Transportation - Syracuse, N.Y.
2. Employment - Syracuse, N.Y. I. Title.
II. U.S. Mass Transportation Demonstration
Grant Program.

VF
690.091.82
H68a
Prelim.

Syracuse. University.
U.S. Housing and Home Finance Agency. Office of
the Administrator. Division of Housing
Research.
Administrative procedures for enforcement of
building regulations. [Washington] July 1953.
106 p. tables.

Bibliographical footnotes.
"Tentative issuance"
"Material for this study was prepared by Syracuse University under a research contract" - pref.
Processed.
1. Housing law enforcement. 2. Building codes.
3. Zoning legislation 4. Housing research contracts. I. Syracuse University. II. Title.

VF
690.091.82
H68s

Syracuse University.
U.S. Housing and Home Finance Agency. Office of
the Administrator. Division of Housing
Research.
State legislation relating to building
regulation. [Washington] Nov. 1953.
78 p.
Research Contract No. 1-R-97, with Syracuse
Univ.

Tentative issuance.
Processed
Project director: Spencer D. Parratt.
Staff Technician: Gilbert Barnhart.

3128
3129
3130
3131
S97

SYRACUSE-ONONDAGA CO., N.Y. PLANNING
AGENCY.
SYRACUSE METROPOLITAN AREA
COMPREHENSIVE PLAN: 1, COMPONENTS OF AN
OPEN SPACE SYSTEM; 2, HISTORIC AND
ARCHITECTURAL SURVEY; 3, INFORMATION
SYSTEM DESIGN; 4, PUBLIC FACILITIES AND
SERVICES INVENTORY. SYRACUSE, N.Y., 1969.
4 V. (HUD 701 REPORT)

1. METROPOLITAN AREA PLANNING -
SYRACUSE, N.Y. I. HUD. 701. SYRACUSE,
N.Y.

628.515
S97

Syracuse University.
Benefits of water quality enhancement.
[Prepared] for the Environmental Protection
Agency. Syracuse, 1970.
201p. (Water pollution control research
series)

1. Water pollution. I. U.S. Environmental
Protection Agency. II. Title.

690.091.82
S97

Syracuse University.
Survey of building and housing regulation
systems; a study of the administration of
building and housing regulation systems in
seventeen cities. Syracuse, N.Y., 1951-52.
14 pts.
Reports deal with the following cities:
Albuquerque, N.M., Baltimore, Md., Cambridge,
Mass., Charlotte, N.C., Cleveland, Ohio, Detroit,
Mich., East Chicago, Ind., Kansas City, Mo.,
Los Angeles Co., Calif., Milwaukee, Wis., Minot,
N.D., Nashville, Tenn., Portland, Ore., Salt
Lake City, Utah, San Mateo Co., Calif.,

711.552
(74765)
S97

SYRACUSE-ONONDAGA POST-WAR PLANNING
COUNCIL.
SYRACUSE, N.Y. CITY PLANNING
COMMISSION.
THE CENTRAL DISTRICT, SYRACUSE,
N.Y. SYRACUSE-ONONDAGA POST-WAR
PLANNING COUNCIL, 1944.

1. BUSINESS DISTRICTS - SYRACUSE,
N.Y. I. SYRACUSE-ONONDAGA POST-WAR
PLANNING COUNCIL.

628.1
S97

Syracuse University.
Carbon column operation in waste water treatment. Prepared for the Water Quality Office,
Environmental Protection Agency. Syracuse, N.Y.,
1970.
71p. (Water pollution control research series)
Bibliography: p. 51-54.

1. Water-supply. I. U.S. Environmental
Protection Agency. II. Title.

690.091.82
897

Syracuse University. Survey of building
and housing regulation systems... 1951-52.
(card 2)

Syracuse, N.Y., White Plains, N.Y.
Library cards
Final report, Research project 1-R-96,
Housing and Home Finance Agency.
Project director: Spencer D. Parratt; staff
technician: Gilbert Barnhart.

690.091.82
897a

Analysis of selected questions
from a sample of the building regulations
questionnaire. 1952.

711.3
(74765)
S97R

SYRACUSE-ONONDAGA POST-WAR PLANNING
COUNCIL.
THE REPORT TO THE CITIZENS OF THE
CITY OF SYRACUSE AND ONONDAGA COUNTY.
SYRACUSE, N.Y., 1945.
154P.

COVER TITLE: THE POST-WAR REPORT,
1945.
BIBLIOGRAPHY: P. 153-154.

1. REGIONAL PLANNING - ONONDAGA CO.,
N.Y. 2. CITY PLANNING - SYRACUSE,
N.Y.

728
.333
H63

Syracuse University.
Hoffman, Bernard Benjamin.
Forced home ownership; a study of a hypothesis which claims that involuntary ownership,
blighted neighborhoods and inordinate property
taxation are associated with elderly and single
owners in older suburbia and the rural-urban
fringe. Syracuse, N.Y., Syracuse University,
1967.
142p.
1. Home ownership. 2. Slums - Economic effect.
3. Social conditions. I. Syracuse University.
II. Title.

690.091.82
897

Syracuse University. Survey of building and
housing regulations systems... 1951-52.
(card 3)

1. Housing law enforcement. 2. Building
code administration. 3. Housing research contracts. 4. Heating codes. 5. Plumbing codes.
6. Electrical codes. 7. Building codes - Albuquerque, N.M. 8. Building codes-Cambridge,
Mass. 9. Building codes-Cleveland, Ohio. 10.
Building codes-Detroit, Mich. 11. Building codes
-East Chicago, Ind. 12. Building codes-Kansas
City, Mo. 13. Building codes-Los Angeles Co.,
Calif. 14. Building codes-Minot, N.D.
15. Building codes-Nashville, Tenn.

728.1
(74765)
S97

SYRACUSE POPULATION CHARACTERISTICS
AND TRENDS.
SYRACUSE HOUSING AUTHORITY.
SYRACUSE POPULATION CHARACTERISTICS
AND TRENDS. SYRACUSE, N.Y., 1937.
1 V. (VARIOUS PAGINGS)

2. HOUSING - SYRACUSE, N.Y.
2. POPULATION - SYRACUSE, N.Y.
I. TITLE.

690.091.82
:659.11
897

Syracuse University.
Public relations for the building official,
by William P. Ehling. Syracuse, N. Y.,
1951-52.
169 L.
Part of final report, Research contract no.
1-R-97, Housing and Home Finance Agency.
Project director: Spencer D. Parratt;
Staff technician: Gilbert Barnhart.

Processed.

690.091.82
897

Syracuse University. Survey of building and
housing regulations systems... 1951-52.
(card 4)
16. Building codes-Portland, Ore. 17. Building
codes-Salt Lake City, Utah. 18. Building codes-
San Mateo Co., Calif. 19. Building codes-Syracuse, N.Y. 20. Building codes-White Plains, N.Y.
21. Housing codes-Albuquerque, N.M. 22. Housing
codes-East Chicago, Ind. 23. Housing codes-Kansas City, Mo. 24. Housing codes-Los Angeles Co.,
Calif. 25. Housing codes-Nashville, Tenn. 26.
Housing codes-Portland, Ore. 27. Housing codes-
Salt Lake City, Utah. 28. Housing codes-Syracuse, N.Y. I. Parratt, Spencer D.
II. Barnhart, Gilbert III. H.H.F.A. O.A. Div. of
Hsg. Res. IV. Title.

VF
332.72
(74765)
897

Syracuse Savings Bank.
Let's take the mystery out of mortgages.
Syracuse, N. Y. [1958]
12p.

1. Mortgage finance - Syracuse, N. Y.
2. Mortgage finance - Savings-banks.

U.S. Housing and Home Finance Agency. Office of
the Administrator. Division of Housing
Research. A report on administrative
procedures... Apr. 1954. (Card 2)

"Material for this report was prepared by
Syracuse University under a research contract"-
Foreword.

1. Housing law enforcement. 2. Building codes.
3. Housing research contracts. I. Barnhart, Gilbert
R. II. American Society of Building Officials.
III. Syracuse University IV. Title. V. Title:
Administrative procedures for enforcement of
building regulations.

330
(747)
S97E

SYRACUSE UNIVERSITY. BUSINESS RESEARCH
CENTER.
THE ECONOMIC STATUS OF UPSTATE NEW
YORK AT MID-CENTURY; WITH SPECIAL
REFERENCE TO DISTRESSED COMMUNITIES AND
THEIR ADJUSTMENTS, BY SIDNEY C. SUFRIN
AND OTHERS. A REPORT TO THE NEW YORK
STATE TEMPORARY STATE COMMISSION ON
ECONOMIC EXPANSION. SYRACUSE, N.Y.,
1960.
149L.

1. ECONOMIC CONDITIONS - NEW YORK
[STATE] I. NEW YORK (STATE)
(CONTINUED ON NEXT CARD)

352
M17m

Syracuse Seminar on Metropolitan Research,
Syracuse University, 1959.
Martin, Roscoe C
The metropolis and its problems, by
Roscoe C. Martin and Douglas Price. A
report occasioned by the first Syracuse
Seminar on Metropolitan Research, Aug. 31-
Sept. 9, 1959. Syracuse, Maxwell Graduate
School of Citizenship and Public Affairs,
1960.
39p.
1. Metropolitan areas. I. Price, Douglas, jt. au.
II. Syracuse. University. Maxwell Graduate School
of Citizenship and Public Affairs.
III. Syracuse Seminar on Metropolitan
Research, Syracuse University, 1959.

VF
690.091.82
H68a
Apr.
1954

Syracuse University
U.S. Housing and Home Finance Agency. Office of
the Administrator. Division of Housing
Research.
A report on administrative procedures for
enforcement of building regulations, by Gilbert R.
Barnhart ... in collaboration with the American
Society of Building Officials. Washington
[Govt. Print. Off.] Apr. 1954.
53 p. tables.

Bibliographical footnotes.

(Continued on next card)

330
(747)
S97E

SYRACUSE UNIVERSITY. BUSINESS RESEARCH
CENTER. THE ECONOMIC STATUS ...1960.
(CARD 2)

TEMPORARY STATE COMMISSION ON ECONOMIC
EXPANSION. II. SUFRIN, SIDNEY C.
III. TITLE.

Syracuse University. Business Research Center.
Marketing series.

711.552.1
897   no. 3 Neff, Edgar R   . Planned shopping
                centers.

711.552.1
897   Syracuse, University. Business Research
            Center.
        Planned shopping centers vs. neighborhood
        shopping areas: a study of the impact of
        the Shoppingtown and Nottingham centers on
        the Westcott Street neighborhood area in
        Syracuse, New York, by Edgar R. Neff, with
        a foreward by Alfred W. Swinyard. Syracuse,
        N. Y., 1957.
            17 p. illus. (Its Marketing series no. 3)

            1. Shopping centers. I. Neff, Edgar R.
        II. Title.

        Syracuse University. Business Research Center.
388
K17   Harmon, George M   ed.
        Tomorrow's transportation systems. Proceed-
        ings of the 17th annual Transportation Con-
        ference and Salzberg Memorial Lecture of
        Syracuse University's College of Business
        Administration and College of Engineering.
        Syracuse, N.Y., Syracuse University, Business
        Research Center, 1965.
            71p.   (Salzberg lecture series no. 17)

            1. Transportation. I. Syracuse University,
        Business Research Center. II. Title.
        (Series; Salzberg   lecture series no. 17)

301.15
(016)   SYRACUSE   UNIVERSITY. CENTER FOR
897   OVERSEAS OPERATIONS AND RESEARCH.
            A WORLD OF CITIES: A CROSS-CULTURAL
        URBAN BIBLIOGRAPHY, EDITED BY ROBERT
        LORENZ AND OTHERS. SYRACUSE, NEW YORK,
        SYRACUSE UNIVERSITY, MAXWELL GRADUATE
        SCHOOL OF CITIZENSHIP AND PUBLIC
        AFFAIRS, CENTER FOR OVERSEAS OPERATIONS
        AND RESEARCH, 1964.
            150P. (PUBLICATION NO. 12)

            PREPARED FOR THE CROSS CULTURAL
        PROJECT)

                            (CONTINUED ON NEXT CARD)

301.15 SYRACUSE UNIVERSITY. CENTER FOR
(016)   OVERSEAS OPERATIONS AND RESEARCH.   A
897   WORLD ...1964.   (CARD 2)
            1. CITY GROWTH - BIBLIOGRAPHY.
        I. LORENZ, ROBERT, ED.   II. TITLE.

        Syracuse, University. College of Business
711.585   Administration.
B56   Bloom, Max P
        Valuation problems and urban redevelopment;
        a talk to the Society of Residential Appraisers,
        by associate professor, Syracuse University,
        College of Business Administration, [n.p.] 1961.
            15p.

            1. Urban renewal - Addresses. 2. Real
        property - Valuation. I. Syracuse. University.
        College of Business Administration.

        Syracuse, University. College of Business Administra-
            tion. Business Research Center.
                        see
        Syracuse, University. Business Research Center.

728.1
107)   SYRACUSE UNIVERSITY. COLLEGE OF HOME
S97   ECONOMICS.
            HOUSING IN THE HOME ECONOMICS
        CURRICULUM.   A UNIT OF STUDY DESIGNED
        TO FACILITATE USE OF HOUSING MATERIAL IN
        HOME ECONOMICS COURSES. SYRACUSE, N.Y.,
        SYRACUSE UNIV., 1941.
            12L.

            1. HOUSING - STUDY AND TEACHING.
        I. TITLE.

        Syracuse, University, Graduate Economics Seminar.
            Publications.
VF
691332 no. Lutin, D.L. Government control of residential
L87   5   construction as an anti-cyclical device.
                1951.

362.6
S97   SYRACUSE UNIVERSITY. INSTITUTE ON
            SOCIAL AND HEALTH NEEDS.
            TOWARD BETTER SOCIAL WORK SERVICES FOR
        THE AGING. SYRACUSE, N.Y., SCHOOL OF
        SOCIAL WORK, SYRACUSE UNIVERSITY, 1960.
            62P.

            1. OLD AGE - SOCIAL SERVICE.

711.4
B47   Syracuse University. Maxwell Graduate
            School of Citizenship and Public Affairs.
        Bishop, Donald G
            Community planning in a democracy; analysis of the
        problem by Donald G. Bishop [and] Wallace E. Lamb, teach-
        ing aids by Emily B. Smith [and] Edith E. Starratt. Wash-
        ington, Pub. for the Maxwell Graduate School of Citizen-
        ship and Public Affairs, Syracuse Univ. by the National
        Council for the Social Studies, 1948.
            x, 110 p. illus. 23 cm. (Community study series, no. 3. Resource
        units for secondary-school teachers)

            The National Council for the Social Studies. Bulletin no. 21.
        Bibliography: p. 103-109.

                            (Continued on next card)
                                            48-10322°
                            [12]

        Bishop, Donald G   Community planning in a
            democracy ... 1948. (Card 2)
            "Films": p. 110.

            1. City planning-Study and teaching.
        2. Cities and towns-Planning.   I. Lamb, Wallace Emerson,
        1905-   joint author. II. Syracuse University. Maxwell Graduate
        School of Citizenship and Public Affairs. III. Title. IV. (Series
        V. Series: National Council for the Social Studies. Bulletin no. 21)

            NA9030.B55   711   48-10322°

        Library of Congress   [12]

658.3
897   Syracuse, University. Maxwell Graduate
            School of Citizenship and Public Affairs.
            Leadership and the vigorous mind; advice
        to young public administrators. Syracuse,
        N.Y. [1960]
            27p.

            1. Personnel management.

352
M17m   Syracuse, University. Maxwell Graduate School
            of Citizenship and Public Affairs.
        Martin, Roscoe C
            The metropolis and its problems, by
        Roscoe C. Martin and Douglas Price. A
        report occasioned by the first Syracuse
        Seminar on Metropolitan Research, Aug. 31-
        Sept. 9, 1959. Syracuse, Maxwell Graduate
        School of Citizenship and Public Affairs,
        1960.
            39p.

            1. Metropolitan areas. I. Price, Douglas, jt. au.
        II. Syracuse. University. Maxwell Graduate School
        of Citizenship and   Public Affairs.
        III. Syracuse Seminar   on Metropolitan
        Research, Syracuse   University, 1959.

352
897   Syracuse University. Maxwell Graduate School
1961   of Citizenship and Public Affairs.
            Metropolitan issues: social, governmental,
        fiscal. Background papers for the Third Annual
        Faculty Seminar on Metropolitan Research, ed.
        by Guthrie S. Birkhead and others. Syracuse,
        1962.
            84p.

            1. Metropolitan areas. 2. Metropolitan
        government. I. Birkhead, Guthrie S., ed.

300
S97   Syracuse University. Maxwell Graduate School
            of Citizenship and Public Affairs.
            Report, 1967/68,
        Syracuse, N.Y.
            /v.   annual.

            For complete information see main card.

            1. Social sciences.

378
897   Syracuse, University. Maxwell Graduate School
            of Citizenship and Public Affairs.
            Twenty-fifth anniversary, 1924-1949. [Syracuse,
        N. Y., 1949]
            136 p. illus.

            1.Syracuse. University. Maxwell Graduate
        School of Citizenship and Public Affairs.

        Syracuse, University. Maxwell Graduate
            School of Citizenship and Public Affairs.

378
897   Syracuse. University. Maxwell Graduate School
            of Citizenship and Public Affairs.
            Twenty-fifth anniversary, 1924-1949. [Syracuse,
        N. Y., 1949]
            136 p. illus.

            1.Syracuse. University. Maxwell Graduate
        School of Citizenship and Public Affairs.

        Syracuse University. Maxwell Graduate School
            of Citizenship and Public Affairs.
352   Scott, Stanley.
826   Two notes on metropolitan research, by
        Stanley Scott and others. Resulting from
        the second annual Faculty Seminar on Metro-
        politan Research, August 28-September 7,
        1960. [Syracuse] Maxwell Graduate School of
        Citizenship and Public Affairs, 1961.
            30p.

            1. Metropolitan areas. 2. Metropolitan
        government. I. Syracuse University. Maxwell
        Graduate   School of Citizen-
        ship and Public Affairs.

VF   Syracuse, N.Y. A Maxwell Graduate School of
300.15   Citizenship and Public Affairs.
H81   Hubbert, Erin
            Opportunities for Federally sponsored social
        science research [by] Erin Hubbert [and] Herbert
        H. Rosenberg.   [Washington] Syracuse Univ.,
        Maxwell Graduate School of Citizenship and Public
        Affairs, Washington Research Office, Dec. 1951.
            52 p.

            Cover date: Nov. 1951.
            Bibliography: p. 49-52.

        Syracuse University. New York State College of
            Forestry. Technical publications.
691.11
H69   no.27 rev. Hoyle, R. J. Wood-using industries of
                New York; a 1946 census including
                comparisons with surveys of 1912, 1919
                and 1926. c.949.

362.5
F24
Syracuse University. Rehabilitation Counselor Education Program.
Feinberg, Lawrence B
Rehabilitation and poverty: bridging the gap, by Lawrence B. Feinberg and Julius S. Cohen. Syracuse, N.Y., Rehabilitation Counselor Education Program, Div. of Special Education and Rehabilitation, School of Education, Syracuse University, 1969.
76p.

1. Poverty. 2. Vocational guidance. I. Cohen, Julius S., jt. au. II. Syracuse University. Rehabilitation Counselor Education Program. III. Title.

360
W45
Syracuse, University. Youth Development Center.
Willie, Charles V
The effect of social service upon rental-paying patterns of low-income problem families, by C.V. Willie and others. Syracuse, N.Y., Youth Development Center, Syracuse University, 1961.
19p.

1. Social welfare. 2. Public housing. I. Syracuse. University. Youth Development Center. II. Title.

691.338
S97
Syska, Arthur D
Exploratory investigation of fire-retardant treatments for particleboard. Madison, Wis., U.S. Forest Products Laboratory, 1969.
19p. (U.S. Forest Service. Research note FPL-0201)

Bibliography: p. 18-19.

1. Wallboard. 2. Building materials, Fireproof. I. U.S. Forest Products Laboratory, Madison, Wis. II. Title: Particleboard. III. Title.

371.4
F24
Syracuse University. Rehabilitation Counselor Education Program.
Feinberg, Lawrence B
Rehabilitation in the inner city, by Lawrence B. Feinberg and R. William English. Syracuse, N.Y., Rehabilitation Counselor Education Program, Div. of Special Education and Rehabilitation, School of Education, Syracuse University, 1970.
119p.
Bibliography: p. 111-112.
1. Vocational guidance. I. English, R. William, jt. au. II. Syracuse University. Rehabilitation Counselor Education Program. III. Title.

628.515
(016)
S97
SYRACUSE UNIVERSITY RESEARCH CORPORATION.
BIBLIOGRAPHY ON ORGANIC PESTICIDE PUBLICATIONS HAVING RELEVANCE TO PUBLIC HEALTH AND WATER POLLUTION PROBLEMS. PREPARED FOR NEW YORK STATE DEPT. OF HEALTH. SYRACUSE, NEW YORK, 1963.
122P. (ITS RESEARCH REPORT NO. 10, PT. II)

1. WATER POLLUTION - BIBLIOGRAPHY.

690.022
I(41)
C31
System building in Britain.
Chan, W W L
System building in Britain. [Blacksburg, Va., Virginia Polytechnic Institute, 1968?]
[20]p.
Bibliography: p. 19-20.

1. Prefabricated construction - U.K. 2. U.K. - Prefabricated construction. 3. Building methods. I. Virginia Polytechnic Institute. II. Title.

720
(74765)
S97
Syracuse University. School of Architecture.
Architecture worth saving in Onondaga County. New York, New York State Council on the Arts, 1964.
201p.

1. Architecture - Onondaga County, N.Y. 2. Architecture - Conservation and restoration. 3. Depreciation and obsolescence (Buildings) I. New York (State) State Council on the Arts. II. Title.

628.515
(74787)
S97
SYRACUSE UNIVERSITY RESEARCH CORPORATION.
EVALUATION OF THE EXTENT AND NATURE OF PESTICIDE AND DETERGENT INVOLVEMENT IN SURFACE WATERS OF A SELECTED WATERSHED, PREPARED FOR NEW YORK STATE DEPT. OF HEALTH. SYRACUSE, N.Y., 1963.
74P. (ITS RESEARCH REPORT NO. 10, PT. I)

1. WATER POLLUTION - WAYNE CO., N.Y.

690
H65
System building: sponsorship and disciplines.
Honey, C R
System building: sponsorship and disciplines. Garston, Eng., Building Research Station, Ministry of Technology, 1966.
11p. (U.K. Building Research Station. Building research current papers. Design series 52)
Reprinted from: Architectural review, June, September 1966. p. 48-6; 241-8.

1. Building industry. 2. Architectural details. 3. Building methods. I. U.K. Building Research Station. II. Title.

711.4
G74p
Syracuse University. School of Architecture.
Grimm, Sergei N
Physical urban planning; system of general concepts and principal features. Syracuse, N.Y., the School of Architecture, Syracuse University, 1961.
87p.

1. City planning. 2. City planning - Citizen participation. I. Syracuse. University. School of Architecture. II. Title.

628.515
I(747)
S97
Syracuse University Research Corp.
A study of fat and oil pollution of New York State waters, by Gunter Zweig and others. Prepared for New York State Dept. of Health. Syracuse, N.Y. 1967.
90p. (Its Research report no. 16)

1. Water pollution - New York (State) I. Zweig, Gunter. II. New York (State) Dept. of Health. III. Title.

693.002.22
I572
System building 2.
Interbuild.
System building 2. London, 1964.
119p.

1. Prefabricated construction. 2. Building methods. I. Title.

690.22
S97
SYRACUSE UNIVERSITY. SCHOOL OF ARCHITECTURE.
A STUDY OF EXTERIOR WALL CONSTRUCTION FOR PUBLIC HOUSING BUILDINGS, BY ROBERT S. VAN KEUREN AND D. KENNETH SARGENT. FINAL REPORT, DECEMBER 31, 1958. SYRACUSE, 1958. SYRACUSE, 1958.
1 V.

SPONSORED BY STATE OF NEW YORK, DIVISION OF HOUSING.

1. WALLS. I. VAN KEUREN, ROBERT S. II. SARGENT, D. KENNETH.

330
(569)
N97
Syria.
Nyrop, Richard F
Area handbook for Syria, by Richard F. Nyrop and others. Wash., Govt. Print. Off., 1971.
357p.
Bibliography: p. 311-344.
One of a series of handbooks prepared by Foreign Area Studies (FAS) of The American University.
1. Economic conditions - Syria. I. American University, Washington, D.C. Foreign Area Studies. II. Title: Syria. III. Title.

331
C65sy
The system can work.
U.S. Commission on Civil Rights.
The system can work (a case study in contract compliance) Wash., 1971.
[28]p. (Clearinghouse publication no. 29)

1. Employment - Minority groups. I. Title.

711.552
(74763)
S97
Syracuse, University. School of Architecture.
Urban planning for the central area of Utica, New York. Part I: Background data. Part II: Central area designs. Syracuse, N.Y., Syracuse University, Graduate Program in Regional Planning of the School of Architecture, 1968.
2 pts.
1. Business districts - Utica, N.Y. I. Title.

691.32
P64
Syrjälä, Heikki, jt. au.
Poijärvi, Heikki.
Betonin puristuslujuusmäärityksistä erilaisilla keekappaleilla (On the determination of the compressive strength of concrete with various test specimens) by Heikki Poijärvi and Heikki Syrjälä. Helsinki, State Institute for Technical Research, 1965.
41p. (Finland. State Institute for Technical Research. Tiedotus. Sarja - Rakennus (Building 91))
English summary.

(Cont'd on next card)

691.54
G87
The system CaO-2CaO.SiO2-CaF2.
Gutt, W
The system CaO-2CaO.SiO2-CaF2, by W. Gutt and G.J. Osborne. [Garston, Eng.] Building Research Station, 1970.
[5]p. (U.K. Building Research Station. Current paper 27/70)
Reprinted from Transactions of the British Ceramic Society, May 1970. p. 125-129.
1. Cement. I. Osborne, G.J., jt. au. II. U.K. Building Research Station. III. Title.

333.38
W34
Syracuse university. School of citizenship and public affairs.
Whitten, Robert Harvey, 1873-
A research into the economics of land subdivision, with particular reference to a complete neighborhood unit for low or medium cost housing, by Robert Whitten ... Prepared under the joint auspices of the School of citizenship and public affairs of Syracuse university and the Regional plan of New York and its environs. [Syracuse, N.Y., Printed by the School of citizenship and public affairs of Syracuse university] 1927.
xi, 72 p. double pl. plans (part fold.) 20½ᵐ.
1. Cities and towns - Planning. 2. Cities and towns - U.S. 3. Housing - New York (State) 4. New York (City) - Public works. I. Syracuse university. School of citizenship and public affairs. II. Regional plan of New York and its environs. III. Title. IV. Title: Neighborhood unit for low or medium cost housing.
(Continued on next card)
Library of Congress   NA9105.W5
                           [43h1]

691.32
P64
Poijarvi, Heikki. Betonnin puristus-lujuusmäärityksistä erilaisilla keekappaleilla...1965   (Card 2)

1. Concrete. 2. Strength of materials. I. Finland. State Institute for Technical Research. II. Title: On the determination of the compressive strength of concrete with various test specimens. III. Syrjälä, Heikki, jt. au.

711.73
I57
System considerations for urban freeways.
Institute of Traffic Engineers.
System considerations for urban freeways; an informational report. Wash., 1967.
48p.

1. Highways. 2. Transportation. I. Title.

System Design Concepts, Inc.
Model Cities Transportation Project.

SEE

U.S. HUD. Model Cities Program. Model Cities
Transportation Project.

658.564
S97CO   SYSTEM DEVELOPMENT CORP.
COSTS ASPECTS OF COMPUTER
PROGRAMMING FOR COMMAND AND CONTROL,
BY LEONARD FARR AND BURT NANUS. SANTA
MONICA, CALIF., 1964.
26P. (AD 430259 SP-1372/000/01)

1. AUTOMATION. I. TITLE.
II. FARR, LEONARD. III. NANUS, BURT.

020
417   System Development Corp.
Markuson, Barbara Evans.
Guidelines for library automation; a handbook
for Federal and other libraries, by Barbara
Evans Markuson and others. Santa Monica, Calif.
System Development Corp., 1972.
401p.
Bibliography: p. 389-401.

1. Library science - Automation. I. System
Development Corp. II. Title.

711.73
(74932)
S97   System Design Concepts, inc.
A proposal for the joint development of the
Route 75 corridor in the city of Newark, N.J.
[n.p.] 1969.
1v.

1. Highways - Newark, N.J. I. Title.

538.56
S97d   System Development Corp.
Department of Housing and Urban Develop-
ment.data systems study. Final report.
Fall Church, Va., 1967.
1v. (Its Technical memo TN series TM-
WD-(L)-267/700/01)

1. Automation. 2. Management - Automation. 3. Public administration.
4. U.S. Dept. of Housing and Urban
Development.

658.564
B27h   System Development Corp.
Bernstein, M   I
Hand-printed input for on-line systems, by
M.I. Bernstein and H.L. Howell. Prepared by
System Development Corp. Wash., National
Aeronautics and Space Administration, 1969.
108p. (NASA CR-1284)
CFSTI.
Bibliography: p. 17-18.

1. Automation. I. Howell, H.L., jt. au.
II. U.S. National Aeronautics and Space
Administration. III. System Development Corp.
IV. Title.

658.564
W17   System design concepts.
Watson, Richard W
Timesharing system design concepts. New
York, McGraw-Hill, 1970.
270p. (McGraw-Hill computer science series)

Bibliography: p. 254-259.

1. Automation. I. Title. II. Title: System
design concepts.

658.564
S97F   SYSTEM DEVELOPMENT CORP.
FACTORS THAT AFFECT THE COST OF
COMPUTER PROGRAMMING. SANTA MONICA,
CALIF., 1964.
2 V. (ELECTRONIC SYSTEMS DIVISION,
AIR FORCE SYSTEMS COMMAND.
ESD-TM-1447-000-02; ESD-TDR-64-448)

1. AUTOMATION. I. U.S. AIR FORCE.
SYSTEMS COMMAND. II. TITLE.

002
897   System Development Corp., Santa Monica, Calif.
The information center: some selected examples,
by Emory H. Holmes. Santa Monica, 1964.
33p. (U.S. Defense Documentation Center.
Defense Supply Agency. [Document] AD 606 174)
Distributed by U.S. Clearinghouse for Federal
Scientific and Technical Information as SP-1702.
Bibliography: p. 31-32.

1. Documentation. 2. Library science -
Automation. I. Holmes, Emory H. II. Title.

658.564
L12   SYSTEM DESIGN FOR COMPUTER
APPLICATIONS.
LADEN, H   N
SYSTEM DESIGN FOR COMPUTER
APPLICATIONS, BY H.N. LADEN AND T.R.
GILDERSLEEVE. NEW YORK, WILEY, 1963.
330P.

1. AUTOMATION. I. GILDERSLEEVE,
T.R., JT. AU. II. TITLE.

330
K15   System Development Corp., Santa Monica, Calif.
Kamrany, Nake M
Economic development planning and informa-
tion systems: a discussion and bibliography.
Santa Monica, Calif., System Development Corp.,
1966.
90p. (U.S. Defense Documentation Center.
Defense Supply Agency. Document AD 628 213)
Distributed by U.S. Clearinghouse for
Federal Scientific and Technical Information.

1. Economic development. 2. Automation.
3. Economic development - Bibl. I. System Develop-

(Continued on next card)

388
(7946)
K28   Kevany, Michael J
An information system for urban trans-
portation planning; the BATSC [Bay Area
Transportation Study Commission] approach.
Santa Monica, Calif., 1968.
56p. (System Development Corp. Tech-
nical memo TM-3920/000/01)
U.S. Dept. of Housing and Urban
Development, Contract California PD-1.
Bibliography: p. 55-56

(Cont'd on next card)

658.564
N176S   SYSTEM DESIGN OF DIGITAL COMPUTERS.
U.S. NATIONAL BUREAU OF STANDARDS.
SYSTEM DESIGN OF DIGITAL COMPUTERS
AT THE NATIONAL BUREAU OF STANDARDS:
METHODS FOR HIGH-SPEED ADDITION AND
MULTIPLICATION. WASHINGTON, GOVT.
PRINT. OFF., 1958.
22P. (NBS CIRCULAR 591)

1. AUTOMATION. I. TITLE.

330
K15   Kamrany, Nake M   System Development
Corp., Santa Monica, Calif. Economic...1966.
(Card 2)

ment Corp., Santa Monica, Calif. II. U.S.
Defense Supply Agency. III. U.S. Clearing-
house for Federal Scientific and Technical
Iformation. IV. Title.

388
(7946)
K28   Kevany, Michael J   An information...1968
(Card 2)

1. Transportation - San Francisco Bay
area. I. Bay Area Transportation Study
Commission. II. U.S. Dept. of Housing and
Urban Development. III. System Development Corp. IV. Title.

658.564
S97C   SYSTEM DEVELOPMENT CORP.
COMPUTER PROGRAMMER SELECTION AND
TRAINING IN SYSTEM DEVELOPMENT
CORPORATION, BY DALLIS PERRY AND
GORDON CANTLEY. SANTA MONICA, CALIF.,
1965.
62P. (ITS TECHNICAL MEMORANDUM
2234, AD 612 956)

1. AUTOMATION. 2. AUTOMATION -
STUDY AND TEACHING. I. TITLE.
II. PERRY, DALLIS. III. CANTLEY,
GORDON.

538.56
897   System Development Corp.
Electronic data processing systems for
state and local governments. Santa Monica,
Calif., 1964.
28p.
SDC magazine. vol. 7, Nov. 1964.
American Society for Public Administration.
Reprint service.

2c

1. Automation. 2. State government.
3. Local government. I. Title. II. American
Society for Public   Administration.
Reprint service.

360
J23   System Development Corp., Santa Monica, Calif
Jeffers, Camille.
Living poor; a participant observer study of
priorities and choices. With an introduction
by Hylan Lewis. Ann Arbor, Mich., Ann Arbor
Publishers, 1967.
N.c.1 123p.
Long.c.2,3

1. Social conditions. 2. Public housing -
Social effect. 3. Family income and expenditure.
4. Family living requirements. I. Title.

538.56
897c   System Development Corp.
[The Corporation] Falls Church, Va.
[1965?]
17p.

1. Automation. 2. System Development
Corp.

711.4
S97g   System Development Corp.
A geographic base file for urban
data systems. Santa Monica, Calif.,
1969.
[24]p.

2c

1. City planning - Automation.
I. Title.

658
:538.56
N25   System Development Corporation.
Nelson, E   A
Management handbook for the estimation of
computer programming costs, Santa Monica
Calif., System Development Corp., 1967.
141p. (U.S. Defense Documentation
Center, Defense Supply Agency, Document
AD 648 750; U.S. Air Force. Systems
Command. Technical Memo. TM 3225/000/
01)
Distributed by U.S. Clearinghouse for
Federal Scientific and Technical Infor-
mation.
1. Manage- ment - Automation.
2. Accounting. I. U.S.   Air Force. Systems
Command. II. System Development Corp. III. Title.

658
K13

SYSTEM DEVELOPMENT CORPORATION.
KAGDIS, J
THE MODELING OF MANAGEMENT CONTROL, BY
J. KAGDIS AND M.R. LACKNER. SANTA
MONICA, CALIFORNIA, SYSTEM DEVELOPMENT
CORPORATION, 1963.
16P. (AD 430304)

1. MANAGEMENT. 2. AUTOMATION.
I. LACKNER, M.R., JT. AU. II. SYSTEM
DEVELOPMENT CORPORATION. III. TITLE.

538.56
F22r

U.S. Federal Council for Science and
Technology. Committee on Scientific and
Technical Information. Recommendations
for national document handling...1965.
(Card 2)

-- ---Appendix A: a background study.
Santa Monica, Calif., System Development
Corp., 1965.
2v.

1. Automation. 2. Documentation. 3. Library
science. I. System Development Corp.,
Santa Monica, Calif. II. Title.

394
L67s

System Development Corp., Santa Monica,
Calif.
Los Angeles Airways, Inc.
Skylounge air operations study. [Final
report. Prepared for System Development
Corp.] Los Angeles, [1967]
1v.
Cover title.
U.S. Mass Transportation Demonstration
Grant Program. Subcontract no.: 67-60.
1. Air transportation. 2. Heliports.
I. System Development Corp., Santa Monica,
Calif. II. Title: Skylounge Project.
III. U.S. Mass Transportation Demonstration
Grant Program. IV. Title.

002
C17

System Development Corp., Santa Monica, Calif.
Carter, Launor F
National document-handling systems for science
and technology, by L.F. Carter and others [of]
System Development Corp., Santa Monica Calif.
New York, John Wiley, 1967.
344p. (Information sciences series)
Bibliography: p. 335-344.

1. Documentation. 2. Indexing. 3. Automation. 4. Library science. I. System Development Corp., Santa Monica, Calif. II. Title.

020
#538.56
C17

System Development Corp.
Carter, Launor F
Research and Technology Division report,
System Development Corp., by L. F. Carter
and others. Santa Monica, Calif., System
Development Corp., 1965.
155p. (Technical memorandum TM ser.
530/008/00, U.S. Defense Documentation
Center, Defense Supply Agency. Document
AD 612 614)
1. Library science - Automation.
2. Documentation. I. System Development
Corp.

384
A47s

System development Corp.
AirportTransit.
Skylounge ground operations study.
[Final report for Skylounge project,
November 1, 1966-July 27, 1967. Prepared
for System Development Corporation] Los
Angeles, 1967.
157p.
Cover title.
U.S. Mass Transportation Demonstration
Grant Program. Subcontract no.:
67-59.
(Cont'd on next card)

658.562
S97

SYSTEM DEVELOPMENT CORP.
NEW FRONTIERS OF QUALITY CONTROL, BY
PAUL PEACH. SANTA MONICA, CALIF.,
1965.
12P. (AD 613 260)

1. QUALITY CONTROL. 2. AUTOMATION.
I. PEACH, PAUL. II. TITLE.

538.56
S97r

System Development Corp.
Research directorate report. C. Baum,
editor. Santa Monica, Calif., 1962.
171p. (TM-530-005-00)

1. Automation. I. Baum, C., ed.

384
A47s

AirportTransit. Skylounge...1967.
(Card 2)

1. Air transportation. 2. Transpor-
tation - Finance. I. System Development
Corp. II. U.S. Mass Transportation
Demonstration Grant Program. III. Title:
Skylounge project. IV. Title.

711.33
(788)
T67

System Development Corp.
Totschek, Robert A
Outline of proposed planning guide for
the Inter-County Regional Planning Commission. Santa Monica, Calif., System
Development Corp., 1967.
47p. (System Development Corp. Technical
memo, TM-3483/000/00)

1. State planning - Colorado. 2. County
planning - Colorado. I. Inter-County
Regional Planning Commission, Denver. II.
System Development Corp. III. Title.

020
#538.56
B67

System Development Corporation, Santa Monica,
Calif.
Borko, Harold.
Research in document classification and
file organization. Santa Monica, Calif.,
System Development Corporation, 1964.
12p. (System Development Corporation
SP-1423)
U.S. Defense Documentation Center for
Scientific and Technical Information;
Document AD425531.
1. Library science - Automation.
2. Documentation. I. System Development
Corporation, Santa Monica, Calif. II. Title.

384
B82

System Development Corp.
Budd Co. (Railway Div.)
Skylounge ground transporter study.
[Prepared for System Development Corporation
under a subcontract for the Los Angeles
Dept. of Airports] Philadelphia, 1967.
2v.
Cover title.
U.S. Mass Transportation Demonstration
Grant Program. Contract no.: 67-57.
1. Air transportation. 2. Aircraft
construction. 3. Heliports. I. System
Development Corp. II. Los Angeles. Dept. of
Airports. III. Title: Skylounge pro-
ject. IV. U.S. Mass Transportation
Demonstration Grant Program.

301
F15

System Development Corp.
Fenwick, Charles.
The place of engineering analysis in handling
social problems. Santa Monica, Calif., System
Development Corp., 1966.
8p. (System Development Corp. SP-2650)
Paper presented at the Los Angeles Council
meeting of the Institute of Electrical and
Electronics Engineers, on November 29, 1966.
1. Sociology. 2. Automation. I. System Develop-
ment Corp. II. Institute of Electrical and
Electronics Engineers. III. Title.

658.564
W24

SYSTEM DEVELOPMENT CORPORATION.
WEINWURM, GEORGE F
RESEARCH IN THE MANAGEMENT OF
COMPUTER PROGRAMMING. SANTA MONICA,
CAL., SYSTEM DEVELOPMENT CORPORATION,
1965.
11P. (AD NO. 615 117)

1. AUTOMATION. I. SYSTEM
DEVELOPMENT CORPORATION. II. TITLE.

384
S97

System Development Corp.
The Skylounge system, analysis and design,
technical and economic feasibility study.
Sponsored by the U.S. Dept. of Housing and
Urban Development and the Los Angeles, Dept.
of Airports. Los Angeles, 1969.
120p.
Cover title: Skylounge project final
report.
U.S. Mass Transportation Demonstration
Grant Program.
1. Air transportation. 2. Aircraft con-
struction. I. Los Angeles. Dept. of
(Cont'd on next card)

025
S97

System Development Corp.
Planning for on-the-job training of library
personnel, by Everett M. Wallace and others.
Santa Monica, Calif., System Development
Corp., 1968.
28p. (TM-3762/000/01)

1. Library administration. 2. Library
science. I. Wallace, Everett M. II. Title.

323.25
H27r

System Development Corp.
Herrmann, William W
Riot prevention and control: operations
research response. Santa Monica, Calif.,
System Development Corp., 1968.
23p. (SP-3116)

Paper presented at the second National
Symposium on Law Enforcement Science and
Technology, conducted by the Law Enforcement
Science Technology Center, IIT Research
Institute, on April 17, 1968.
1. Civil disorders. I. System Development
Corp. II. Title.

384
S97

System Development Corp. The Skylounge
...1969. (Card 2)

Airports. II. U.S. Mass Transportation
Demonstration Grant Program. III. Title:
Skylounge Project. IV. Title.

538.56
F22r

System Development Corp., Santa Monica, Calif.
U.S. Federal Council for Science and
Technology. Committee on Scientific and
Technical Information.
Recommendations for national document
handling systems in science and technology.
Wash., U.S. Dept. of Commerce, National
Bureau of Standards, Institute for Applied
Technology, 1965.
18p. (PB 168 267, AD 624 560)
Distributed by: Clearinghouse for Federal
Scientific and Technical Information.

(Continued on
next card)

658.564
(016)
S97

SYSTEM DEVELOPMENT CORPORATION.
SDC DOCUMENTS APPLICABLE TO STATE
AND LOCAL GOVERNMENT PROBLEMS.
COMPILED BY HERBERT M. ISSACS. SANTA
MONICA, CALIFORNIA, 1964.
8P. (AD 606181)

1. AUTOMATION -- BIBLIOGRAPHY.
I. ISSACS, HERBERT M. II. TITLE.

384
S97s

System Development Corporation.
Skylounge system final report, summary.
A technical and economic feasibility study.
Sponsored by the U.S. Dept. of Housing and
Urban Development and the Los Angeles Dept.
of Airports. Conducted by System Develop-
ment Corp., and others. [Los Angeles] 1969.
23p.
U.S. Mass Transportation Demonstration
Grant Program.
1. Air transportation. 2. Heliports.
3. Aircraft construction. I. Los Angeles.
Dept. of Airports. II. U.S. Mass
Transportation Demonstration Grant
Program. III. Title: Skylounge
Project. IV. Title.

538.56
A55

System Development Corp., Santa Monica, Calif.
Almendinger, Vladimir V
Span reference manual; span: introduction and general description. Santa Monica, Calif., System Development Corp., 1963.
17p. (System Development Corp. Technical memorandum (TM series) TM-1563/000/00)
Document was produced by SDC in performance of U.S. Government contracts.
1. Automation. 2. Federal contracts. I. System Development Corp., Santa Monica, Calif.
II. Title.

711.4
S 97u
pt.1-4

System Development Corp.
Urban and regional information systems: support for planning in metropolitan areas. Wash., Govt. Print. Off., 1968.
4 pts. in 1v. (HUD M/MP-71)
U.S. Dept. of Housing and Urban Development. Urban Planning Research and Demonstration Project.
Part 1 also published separately as Technical memo TM-(L)-3595/000/00 by Joel M. Kibbee and others. Santa Monica, Calif., System Development Corp., 1968. 222p.

(Cont'd on next card)

690.015
(485)
S82
R18
1969

Thiberg, Sven. Beskrivnings-...1969.
(Card 2)
2. Building documentation.
3. Architecture, Domestic - Designs and plans. I. Stockholm. Statens Institut för Byggnadsforskning. II. Title: System for description and evaluation of features of housing and urban areas.

020
S97

System Development Corp.
A system study of abstracting and indexing. Detroit, Management Information Services, [1967?]
228p.
Bibliography: p. 207-228.
1. Abstracting. 2. Indexing. I. Title.

711.4
S 97u
pt.1-4

System Development Corp. Urban...1968.
(Card 2)
1. City planning - Automation.
2. Regional planning - Automation.
3. Metropolitan area planning - Automation.
I. Kibbee, Joel M. II. Title. III. U.S. HUD-UPRDP.

628.44
S95

A system for industrial waste treatment. Synectics Corp.
A system for industrial waste treatment RD&D project priority assignment. [Prepared] for the Environmental Protection Agency. Allison Park, Pa., 1971.
91p. (Water pollution control research series)
1. Refuse and refuse disposal. I. U.S. Environmental Protection Agency. II. Title.

347
H27

Lav.

System Development Corp., Santa Monica, Calif.
Herrmann, William W
The systems approach in crime prevention and control. Santa Monica, Calif., System Development Corp. 1967.
19p. (U.S. Defense Documentation Center. Defense Supply Agency. [Document] AD 648 758)
Distributed by U.S. Clearinghouse for Federal Scientific and Technical Information.
1. Law enforcement. 2. Municipal services. I. System Development Corp., Santa Monica, Calif. II. U.S. Defense Documentation Center. Defense Supply Agency. III. U.S. Clearinghouse for Federal Scientific and Technical Information. IV. Title. Title: Crime prevention and control.

711.3
K41u

System Development Corp.
Kibbee, Joel M
Urban and regional information systems: the role of the Dept. of Housing and Urban Development, by Joel M. Kibbee and others. Santa Monica, Calif., System Development Corp., 1968.
74p. (System Development Corp. TM-(L)-3595/003/00)
HUD contract no. Calif. PD-2.
U.S. Dept. of Housing and Urban Development. UPAP.
Bibliography: p. 73-74.
1. Metropolitan area planning - Automation. 2. Regional planning - Automation. I. System Development Corp. II. Title. III. U.S. HUD-UPAP.

360
(7531)
M27

A system for inventorying social services available in the Washington metropolitan area.
Metropolitan Washington Council of Governments.
A system for inventorying social services available in the Washington metropolitan area. Wash., 1968.
8p.
U.S. Dept. of Housing and Urban Development. UPAP.
HUD project no. D.C. P-3.
1. Social welfare - District of Columbia metropolitan area. I. U.S. HUD-UPAP. District of Columbia metropolitan area. II. Title.

711.015
A22

SYSTEM DEVELOPMENT CORPORATION.
ADELSON, MARVIN.
TOWARD A FUTURE FOR PLANNING. SANTA MONICA, CALIF., SYSTEM DEVELOPMENT CORPORATION, 1966.
17P. ON 5L.
1. PLANNING - RESEARCH.
2. AUTOMATION. I. SYSTEM DEVELOPMENT CORPORATION. II. TITLE.

538.56
897u

System Development Corp.
Users guide for a manual PERT (Program Evaluation and Review Technique) operation. Santa Monica, Calif., 1962.
31p.
Reprint, note, an internal working paper.
1. Automation. I. Title: PERT (Program Evaluation and Review Technique)

711.585
R32

A SYSTEM FOR URBAN REDEVELOPMENT WITHOUT SUBSIDY.
RHEINSTEIN, ALFRED.
A SYSTEM FOR URBAN REDEVELOPMENT WITHOUT SUBSIDY. NEW YORK, [N.D.]
15P.
1. URBAN RENEWAL. I. TITLE.

711.4
(538.56
A55

System Development Corp., Santa Monica, Calif.
Almendinger, Vladimir V
Urban and regional information systems: on the threshold of a technology, by Vladimir V. Almendinger and others. Santa Monica, Calif., System Development Corp., 1966.
17p. (System Development Corp. Technical memorandum (TM series) TM 3288/000/00)
Document was supported in part by funds from the U.S. Dept. of Housing and Urban Development.
1. City planning - Automation. I. System Development Corp., Santa Monica, Calif. II. U.S. Dept. of Housing and Urban Development. III. Title.

538.56
897c

System Development Corp.
System Development Corp.
[The Corporation] Falls Church, Va. [1965?]
17p.
1. Automation. 2. System Development Corp.

658.564
R811

System life cycle.
Rubin, Martin L
Introduction to the system life cycle. Thomas Harrell, technical editor. Princeton, N.J., Brandon Systems Press, 1970.
227p. (Handbook of data processing management, vol. 1)
Partial contents.-Appx B-Automated system and program documentation, by Peter Zuckerman and Roger C. Dickenson.
1. Automation. I. Zuckerman, Peter. II. Dickenson, Roger C. III. Title. IV. Title: System life cycle. (Series: Handbook of data processing management, vol. 1)

711.4
(016)
A55

System Development Corporation.
Almendinger, Vladimir V
Urban and regional information systems: a selected bibliography, by Vladimir V. Almendinger and Robert A. Totschek. Santa Monica, Calif., System Development Corp., 1968.
128p. (System Development Corporation. Technical memorandum (TM series) TM-L-3595/001/00)
1. City planning - Bibl. I. Totschek, Robert A., jt. au. II. System Development Corporation. III. Title.

301.15
897

System Development Corp. Magazine.
Urban systems. Santa Monica, Calif., 1966. Entire issue SDC System Development Corp. Magazine. Summer 1966.
1. City growth. 2. Automation. 3. City planning - Automation. 4. Sociology, Urban. I. Title.

658.564
Z82

System life cycle standards.
Zuckerman, Peter.
System life cycle standards - forms method. Princeton, N.J., Grandon/Systems Press, 1970.
235p. (Handbook of data processing management, vol. 3)
1. Automation. 2. Systems analysis. I. Title. II. Title: Handbook of data processing management.

352
K41

System Development Corporation.
Kibbee, Joel M
Urban and regional information systems: selected case studies, by Joel M. Kibbee and others. Santa Monica, Calif., System Development Corp., 1968.
100p. (System Development Corp. TM-(L)-3595/004/00)
HUD Contract Calif. PD-2.
1. Local government - Automation. 2. City planning - Automation. I. System Development Corp. II. U.S. Dept. of Housing and Urban Development. III. Title.

690.015
(485)
S82
R18
1969

System for description and evaluation of features of housing and urban areas.
Thiberg, Sven.
Beskrivnings- och värderingssystem för bostads- och stadsdelsegenskaper (System for description and evaluation of features of housing and urban areas) Stockholm, Statens Institut for Byggnadsforskning, 1969.
54p. (Stockholm. Statens Institut för Byggnadsforskning. Rapport 18:1969)
English summary.
1. Building research - Sweden.
(Cont'd on next card)

658.564
R81

System life cycle standards.
Rubin, Martin L
System life cycle standards. Princeton, N.J., Brandon/Systems Press, 1970.
319p. (Handbook of data processing management, vol. 2)
1. Automation. 2. Systems analysis. I. Title. (Series)

690.015
(485)
S82
1971
R19

A system of describing and classifying
information relating to the landscape.
Moller, Sven G
   System att beskriva och klassificera
information om landskapet (A system of
describing and classifying information
relating to the landscape) Stockholm,
Statens Institut för Byggnadsforskning,
1971.
   56p. (Rapport R19: 1971)
   English summary.
   1. Land use - Sweden. 2. Landscape
architecture. 3. Photogrammetry. I. Stockholm. Statens Institut för Byggnadsforskning
II. Title: A system of describing and
classifying information relating to
the landscape.

728
(41)
B78

A systematic procedure for recording English
vernacular architecture.
Brunskill, R W
   A systematic procedure for recording
English vernacular architecture. Reprinted
from the Transactions of the Ancient Monuments
Society, vol. 13, 1965-1966. p43-126.

   1. Architecture, Domestic - U.K.
I. Title.

651.4
M17o

Systemation, inc.
Matthies, Leslie H
   Office layout; the house where your system
lives. Colorado Springs, Colo., Systemation,
inc., 1971.
   14p.

   1. Office management. 2. Space considerations.
I. Systemation, inc. II. Title.

301.15
M17s

A system of linked models for forecasting
urban residential growth.
Massie, Ronald Wayne.
   A system of linked models for forecasting
urban residential growth. Chapel Hill, University of North Carolina, 1969.
   99p. (North Carolina. University. Center
for Urban and Regional Studies. Environmental
policies and urban development thesis series
no. 13)
   Thesis (Master of Regional Planning) -
University of North Carolina.
   Bibliography: p. 96-99.
   1. City growth. 2. City planning - Research.
3. Housing market. I. North Carolina.
University. II. Title.

360
R48

Systematic thinking for social action.
Rivlin, Alice M
   Systematic thinking for social action.
H. Rowan Gaither Lectures, delivered January
1970, at the University of California, Berkeley,
under the sponsorship of the Graduate School
of Business Administration and the Center for
Research in Management Science. Wash.,
Brookings Institution, 1971.
   150p. (The H. Rowan Gaither Lectures in
Systems Science)
   1. Social welfare. I. Brookings Institution.
II. Title.

658
M17p

Systemation, inc.
Matthies, Leslie H
   Policy as a systems tool. Produced under
direction of the Foundation for Administrative Research, Colorado Springs, Colo.,
Colorado Springs, Colo., Systemation, inc.,
1968.
   109p. (Its Subject no. 2)
   From the Systemation letter.
   1. Management. 2. Systems analysis. I. Title.
II. Foundation for Administrative Research,
Colorado Springs, Colo. III. Systemation,
inc. IV. Systemation letter.

352.6
B62

System requirements for underground utility
installation.
Boegly, W J
   System requirements for underground utility
installation, by W.J. Boegly, Jr. and others.
Oak Ridge, Tenn., Oak Ridge National Laboratory,
1971.
   98p. (ORNL-HUD-19; UC-41-health and safety)
   Bibliography: p. 86-89.
   Work supported by Dept. of Housing and Urban
Development and U.S. Atomic Energy Commission
under interagency agreement no. IAA-H-2-69,
AEC 40-155A-68.
   1. Public utilities. I. U.S. Oak Ridge
National Laboratory. II. U.S. Dept. of Housing
and Urban Development. III. Title.

658
B18

SYSTEMATIC WORK SIMPLIFICATION.
BAUMBACK, CLIFFORD M
   SYSTEMATIC WORK SIMPLIFICATION.
NORMAN, OKLA., BUREAU OF BUSINESS
RESEARCH, COLLEGE OF BUSINESS
ADMINISTRATION, UNIVERSITY OF OKLAHOMA,
1960.
   57P. (UNIVERSITY OF OKLAHOMA STUDIES IN
BUSINESS AND ECONOMICS NO. 29; INDUSTRIAL
MANAGEMENT SERIES NO. 2)

   1. MANAGEMENT. 2. SPACE CONSIDERATIONS.
I. TITLE.

658.4
M17

Systemation.
Matthies, Leslie H
   The quest for systems principles. Colorado
Springs, Systemation, 1970.
   110p. (Subject no. 17)

   From the Systemation letter.

   1. Systems analysis. I. Systemation.
II. Title.

020
S97

A system study of abstracting and
indexing.
System Development Corp.
   A system study of abstracting and
indexing. Detroit, Management Information
Services, [1967?]
   228p.

   Bibliography: p. 207-228.

   1. Abstracting. 2. Indexing. I. Title.

658.4
M17b

Systemation, inc.
Matthies, Leslie H
   Basic systems techniques. From the Systemation letter. Produced under direction of
the Foundation for Administrative Research.
Colorado Springs, Systemation, inc., 1968.
   109p. (Subject no. 16)

   1. Systems analysis. I. Systemation, inc.
II. Foundation for Administrative Research.
III. Title.

651.5
M17

SYSTEMATION, INC.
MATTHIES, LESLIE H
   RECORDS; THE SYSTEMS MEMORY OF
ACTION; FROM THE SYSTEMATION LETTER.
TULSA, OKLA., SYSTEMATION, INC., 1966.
   110P. (SUBJECT NO. 7)

   PRODUCED UNDER THE DIRECTION OF THE
FOUNDATION FOR ADMINISTRATIVE RESEARCH.

   1. RECORDS MANAGEMENT. 2. INDEXING.
I. SYSTEMATION, INC. II. FOUNDATION
FOR ADMINISTRATIVE RESEARCH. III. TITLE.

510
C15

SYSTEM THEORY.
CALIFORNIA. UNIVERSITY. ELECTRONICS
RESEARCH LABORATORY.
   NOTES ON SYSTEM THEORY. BERKELEY,
CALIF., 1961-62.
   2V. (ITS SERIES, NO. 60, ISSUE NO.
408, 426)
   1. MATHEMATICS. I. TITLE: SYSTEM
THEORY.

651.4
M17f

Systemation, inc.
Matthies, Leslie H
   Forms design; applied principles. From
the Systemation letter. Colorado Springs,
Colo., Systemation, inc., 1969.
   109p. (Systemation, inc. Subject no. 5)

   Published under direction of the Foundation
for Administrative Research.

   1. Office procedures. I. Systemation, inc.
II. Title.

331.86
M17

Systemation, inc.
Matthies, Leslie H
   Techniques for on-the-job learning.
Colorado Springs, Colo., Systemation, inc.,
[1969?]
   9p.

   1. Apprenticeship. 2. Occupations.
I. Title: On-the-job learning. II. Systemation, inc. III. Title.

658.564
B76s

System/360 job control language.
Brown, Gary Devard.
   System/360 job control language. New York,
Wiley, 1970.
   292p.

   Bibliography: p. 283-284.

   1. Automation. I. Title. II. Title: Job
control language.

658
M17man

Systemation, inc.
Matthies, Leslie H
   Management systems; the pictorial view of
the system. Colorado Springs, Colo.,
Systemation, inc., 1970.
   124p. (Systemation, inc. Subject no. 14)
   For the Systemation letter.

   1. Management. I. Systemation, inc.
II. Title.

658
M17d

Systemation letter.
Matthies, Leslie H
   Data analysis; applied principles.
Produced under direction of the Foundation
for Administrative Research, Colorado
Springs, Colo., Colorado Springs,
Systemation, 1969.
   108p. (Subject no. 5)

   From the Systemation letter.

   1. Management - Automation. 2. Systems
analysis. 3. Automation.
   (Cont'd on next card)

020
R13

Systematic analysis of university libraries.
Raffel, Jeffrey A
   Systematic analysis of university libraries:
an application of cost-benefit analysis to the
M.I.T. libraries, by Jeffrey A. Raffel and
Robert Shishko. Cambridge, Mass., M.I.T. Press,
1969.
   107p.
   Bibliography: p. 103-104.
   1. Library science. 2. Universities and
colleges. I. Shishko, Robert, jt. au.
II. Title.

658
M17ma

Systemation, inc.
Matthies, Leslie H
   Management techniques through systems.
From the Systemation letter. Colorado
Springs, Colo., 1969.
   107p.

   1. Management. I. Systemation, inc.
II. Title.

658
M17d

Matthies, Leslie H Data...1969. (Card 2)

   I. Foundation for Administrative Research,
Colorado Springs, Colo. II. Systemation
letter. III. Title.

658
M17p

Systemation letter.
Matthies, Leslie H
  Policy as a systems tool. Produced under
direction of the Foundation for Administrative Research, Colorado Springs, Colo.,
Colorado Springs, Colo., Systemation, inc.,
1968.
  109p. (Its Subject no. 2)
  From the Systemation letter.
  1. Management. 2. Systems analysis. I. Title.
II. Foundation for Administrative Research,
Colorado Springs, Colo. III. Systemation,
inc. IV. Systemation letter.

711.400.15
A52o

SYSTEMS ANALYSIS.
Anderson, James.
  On general systems theory and the concept of
entropy in urban geography. London, London
School of Economics and Political Science,
1969.
  17p. (London School of Economics and Political Science. Graduate School of Geography.
Discussion paper no. 31)
  Bibliography: p. 15-17.
  1. City planning - Research. 2. Systems
analysis. I. London School of Economics and
Political Science. Graduate School of Geography.   II. Title. III. Title:
General   systems theory.

658
C15

Systems analysis.
Cantor, Jerry.
  Profit-oriented manufacturing systems.
New York, American Management Association, 1969.
  139p.

  1. Industrial management. 2. Systems analysis.
3. Automation. I. American Management
Association. II. Title.

658.511
M17

Systemation, inc.
Matthies, Leslie H
  Work methods for improved systems.
From the Systemation letter. Colorado
Springs, Colo., 1969.
  100p. (Systemation, inc. Subject no. 8)

  1. Job analysis. I. Systemation, inc.
II. Title.

658.83
A52c

SYSTEMS ANALYSIS.
Andrews, Howard F
  Central place theory and the consumer's
action space. London, London School of
Economics and Political Science, 1969.
  8p. (London School of Economics and Polit-
ical Science. Graduate School of Geography.
Discussion paper no. 30)
  1. Marketing. 2. Systems analysis.
I. London School of Economics and Political
Science. Graduate School of Geography.
II. Title.

658.564
C31

SYSTEMS ANALYSIS.
CHAPIN, NED.
  AN INTRODUCTION TO AUTOMATIC
COMPUTERS. 2D ED. PRINCETON, N.J.,
VAN NOSTRAND, 1963.
  503P. (VAN NOSTRAND SERIES IN
BUSINESS ADMINISTRATION AND ECONOMICS)

  1. AUTOMATION. 2. SYSTEMS ANALYSIS.
I. TITLE: AUTOMATIC COMPUTERS.

323.25
S97

Systemetrics.
  Analysis of twenty civil disorders relevent
to thirteen particular activities of interest
to HUD. Wash., U.S. Dept. of Housing and Urban
Development, [1969?]
  2pts.
  Report includes information developed from
research activities under Phase II of Contract
H-918 with the Dept. of Housing and Urban
Development, Office of Research and Technology.
  1. Civil disorders. I. U.S. Dept. of Housing
and Urban Development. II. Title.

658
B221

SYSTEMS ANALYSIS.
BECKER, JOSEPH.
  INFORMATION STORAGE AND RETRIEVAL:
TOOLS, ELEMENTS, THEORIES, BY JOSEPH
BECKER AND ROBERT M. HAYES. NEW YORK,
JOHN WILEY, 1963.
  448P.

  BIBLIOGRAPHY: P.427-430.

  1. AUTOMATION. 2. SYSTEMS ANALYSIS.
I. TITLE. II. HAYES, ROBERT M., JT. AU.

020
C31

SYSTEMS ANALYSIS.
Chapman, Edward A
  Library systems analysis guidelines, by Edward
A. Chapman and others. New York, Wiley-Inter-
science, 1970.
  226p.

  Bibliography: p. 208-222.

  1. Library science. 2. Systems analysis.
I. Title.

330
S97

Systemetrics.
  A framework for Federal policies and programs
covering urban problems. Wash., 1969.
  256p.

  CFSTI. PB 182 455.

  1. Economic development. 2. Intergovernmental
relations. 3. Metropolitan areas. I. Title.

350
B51

SYSTEMS ANALYSIS.
Black, Guy.
  The application of systems analysis to government operations. New York, Praeger, 1968.
  186p. (Praeger special studies in U.S.
economic and social development)

  1. Public administration. 2. Systems
analysis. I. Title.

658.4
C38s

Systems analysis.
Churchman, Charles West.
  The systems approach. New York, Delacorte
Press, 1968.
  243p.
  Bibliography: p. 239-243.

  1. Systems analysis. 2. Management.
I. Title.

.1
.16)
05
.91

Systemic planning.
Catanese, Anthony James.
  Systemic planning: an annotated bibliography
and literature guide. [Atlanta] Georgia
Institute of Technology, 1969.
  13p. (Council of Planning Librarians.
Exchange bibliography no. 91)

  1. Planning - Bibl. I. Georgia Institute
of Technology. II. Title. (Series: Council
of Planning Librarians. Exchange bibliography no. 91)

352
B51d

Systems analysis.
Black, Guy.
  The decentralization of urban government:
a systems approach. Wash., Program of Policy
Studies in Science and Technology, The George
Washington University, 1968.
  30p. (George Washington University.
Program of Policy Studies in Science and
Technology. Staff discussion paper 102)
  1. Municipal government. 2. Metropolitan
government. 3. Systems analysis. I. Title.
II. George Washington University. Program
of Policy Studies in Science and Technology.

658
C52

SYSTEMS ANALYSIS.
Cleland, David I   comp.
  Systems, organizations, analysis, management:
a book of readings, by David L. Cleland and
William R. King. New York, McGraw-Hill, 1969.
  383p. (McGraw-Hill series in management)

  1. Operations research. 2. Systems analysis.
I. King, William R., 1907- jt. comp.
II. Title.

711
C17

Systemic planning: theory and application.
Catanese, Anthony James.
  Systemic planning: theory and application,
by Anthony James Catanese and Alan Walter
Steiss. Lexington, Mass., D.C. Heath, 1970.
  376p. (Studies in social and economic
process)

  Bibliography: p. 361-370.

  1. Planning. 2. City planning. I. Steiss,
Alan Walter, jt. au. II. Title.

658
B58

SYSTEMS ANALYSIS.
BLUMSTEIN, ALFRED.
  THE CHOICE OF ANALYTICAL TECHNIQUES IN
COST-EFFECTIVENESS ANALYSIS. ARLINGTON,
VA., 1965.
  14L. (INSTITUTE FOR DEFENSE ANALYSES.
RESEARCH PAPER P-206)

  1. OPERATIONS RESEARCH. 2. ACCOUNTING.
3. SYSTEMS ANALYSIS. I. INSTITUTE FOR
DEFENSE ANALYSES. II. TITLE: COST-
EFFECTIVENESS ANALYSIS.

658.4
C67

SYSTEMS ANALYSIS.
CORRIGAN, ROBERT E
  WHY SYSTEM ENGINEERING, BY ROBERT E.
CORRIGAN AND ROGER A. KAUFMAN. WITH
THE TECHNICAL ASSISTANCE OF HAROLD A.
BAUER. PALO ALTO, FEARON, 1966.
  71P.

  GLOSSARY OF TERMS: P.69-71.

  1. SYSTEMS ANALYSIS. I. KAUFMAN,
ROGER A., JT. AU. II. TITLE.

727.1
G74

Systems; an approach to school construction.
Griffin, C W
  Systems; an approach to school construction.
New York, Educational Facilities Laboratories,
1971.
  96p.

  1. Schools. I. Educational Facilities
Laboratories. II. Title.

301
B82

SYSTEMS ANALYSIS.
Buckley, Walter.
  Sociology and modern systems theory.
Englewood Cliffs, N.J., Prentice-Hall,
1967.
  227p. (Prentice-Hall sociology series)

  Bibliography: p. 209-221.

  1. Sociology. 2. Systems analysis.
I. Title.

658.4
D25

SYSTEMS ANALYSIS.
De Neufville, Richard.
  Systems analysis for engineers and managers,
by Richard de Neufville and Joseph H. Stafford.
New York, McGraw-Hill, 1971.
  353p.

  1. Systems analysis. 2. Engineering.
3. Management. I. Stafford, Joseph H., jt. au.
II. Title.

320
E17
SYSTEMS ANALYSIS.
Easton, David.
A systems analysis of political life.
New York, Wiley, 1965.
507p.

1. Political science. 2. Systems analysis.
I. Title.

658.564
M17P
SYSTEMS ANALYSIS.
MARTIN, JAMES THOMAS.
PROGRAMMING REAL-TIME COMPUTER
SYSTEMS, BY JAMES MARTIN. ENGLEWOOD
CLIFFS, N.J., PRENTICE-HALL, 1965.
386P. (PRENTICE-HALL SERIES IN
AUTOMATIC COMPUTATION)

1. AUTOMATION. 2. MANAGEMENT.
3. SYSTEMS ANALYSIS. I. TITLE.

658
867
1962
SYSTEMS ANALYSIS.
OPTNER, STANFORD L
SYSTEMS ANALYSIS FOR BUSINESS
MANAGEMENT. ENGLEWOOD CLIFFS, N.J.,
PRENTICE-HALL, C1960, 1962.
276P.

BIBLIOGRAPHY: P.269-270.

1. MANAGEMENT. 2. SYSTEMS ANALYSIS.

658
E53
SYSTEMS ANALYSIS.
English, J   Morley, ed.
Cost effectiveness; the economic eval-
uation of engineered systems. New York,
John Wiley & Sons, 1968.
301p. (California. University. Engineer-
ing and physical sciences extension series)
Bibliography: p. 255-260.

1. Management. 2. Systems analysis.
3. Accounting. I. Title.

658.4
M17b
SYSTEMS ANALYSIS.
Matthies, Leslie H
Basic systems techniques. From the System-
ation letter. Produced under direction of
the Foundation for Administrative Research.
Colorado Springs, Systemation, inc., 1968.
109p. (Subject no. 16)

1. Systems analysis. I. Systemation, inc.
II. Foundation for Administrative Research.
III. Title.

658
067
SYSTEMS ANALYSIS.
Optner, Stanford L
Systems analysis for business management.
2d ed. Englewood Cliffs, N.J., Prentice-Hall,
1968.
277p.

Bibliography: p. 263-272.

1. Management. 2. Systems analysis.
I. Title.

690
1045
Systems analysis.
Gill, Paul G
Systems management techniques for builders
and contractors. New York, McGraw-Hill, 1968.
210p.
Bibliography: p. 201-204.

1. Building industry. 2. Systems analysis.
I. Title.

658
M17d
SYSTEMS ANALYSIS.
Matthies, Leslie H
Data analysis; applied principles.
Produced under direction of the Foundation
for Administrative Research, Colorado
Springs, Colo., Colorado Springs,
Systemation, 1969.
108p. (Subject no. 5)

From the Systemation letter.

1. Management - Automation. 2. Systems
analysis. 3.   Automation.
(Cont'd on next card)

355.58
Q81
SYSTEMS ANALYSIS.
QUADE, EDWARD S
ANALYSIS FOR MILITARY DECISIONS.
EDITED BY E.S. QUADE. SANTA MONICA,
RAND CORPORATION, 1964.
382P.

1. NATIONAL DEFENSE. 2. SYSTEMS
ANALYSIS. I. TITLE.

658
G72
Systems analysis.
Greenwood, Frank.
Managing the systems analysis function.
New York, American Management Association,
1968.
137p.

1. Management. 2. Automation. 3. Systems
analysis. I. American Management Association.
II. Title.

658
M17d
Matthies, Leslie H Data...1969. (Card 2)

I. Foundation for Administrative Research,
Colorado Springs, Colo. II. Systemation
letter. III. Title.

301.15
R15
SYSTEMS ANALYSIS.
Ramo, Simon.
Century of mismatch. New York, David McKay,
1970.
204p.

1. Man - Influence of environment.
2. Systems analysis. I. Title.

519
H17a
Systems analysis.
Hare, Van Court, Jr.
Systems analysis: a diagnostic
approach. New York, Harcourt, Brace
& World, 1967.
544p. (The Harbrace series in
business and economics)

Bibliography: p. 519-533.

1. Systems analysis. 2. Management.
3. Automation. I. Title.

658
M17p
Systems analysis.
Matthies, Leslie H
Policy as a systems tool. Produced under
direction of the Foundation for Administra-
tive Research, Colorado Springs, Colo.,
Colorado Springs, Colo., Systemation, inc.,
1968.
109p. (Its Subject no. 2)
From the Systemation letter.
1. Management. 2. Systems analysis. I. Title.
II. Foundation for Administrative Research,
Colorado Springs, Colo. III. Systemation,
inc. IV. Systemation letter.

300.15
R15c
SYSTEMS ANALYSIS.
Ramo, Simon.
Cure for chaos; fresh solutions to social
problems through systems approach. New York,
David McKay Co., 1969.
116p.

1. Social science research. 2. Systems
analysis. I. Title.

711.4
M12u
SYSTEMS ANALYSIS.
McLoughlin, J   Brian
Urban and regional planning; a systems
approach. New York, Praeger, 1969.
331p.
Bibliography: p. 313-324.

1. City planning. 2. Regional
planning. 3. Systems analysis.
I. Title.

658.4
M17
SYSTEMS ANALYSIS.
Matthies, Leslie H
The quest for systems principles. Colorado
Springs, Systemation, 1970.
110p. (Subject no. 17)

From the Systemation letter.

1. Systems analysis. I. Systemation.
II. Title.

658
R15S
SYSTEMS ANALYSIS.
RAND CORPORATION.
SYSTEMS ANALYSIS TECHNIQUES FOR
PLANNING-PROGRAMMING-BUDGETING, BY E.S.
QUADE. SANTA MONICA, CALIF., 1966.
31P.

1. MANAGEMENT. 2. SYSTEMS ANALYSIS.
I. TITLE. II. QUADE, E.S.

658.564
M25
SYSTEMS ANALYSIS.
MCMILLAN, CLAUDE.
SYSTEMS ANALYSIS; A COMPUTER
APPROACH TO DECISION MODELS, BY CLAUDE
MCMILLAN AND RICHARD F. GONZALEZ.
HOMEWOOD, ILL. IRWIN, 1965.
336P. (IRWIN SERIES IN QUANTITATIVE
ANALYSIS FOR BUSINESS)

1. AUTOMATION. I. GONZALEZ,
RICHARD F., JT. AU. II. TITLE.
III. TITLE: A COMPUTER APPROACH TO
DECISION MODELS.

658
M67
SYSTEMS ANALYSIS.
Morton, Michael S   Scott.
Management decision systems; computer-based
support for decision making. Boston, Div. of
Research, Graduate School of Business Adminis-
tration, Harvard University, 1971.
216p.

Bibliography: p. 211-216.

1. Management - Automation. 2. Systems
analysis. I. Harvard University. Graduate
School of Business Administration. II. Title.

658
R42
SYSTEMS ANALYSIS.
RICHARDS, MAX DE VOE.
MANAGEMENT DECISION MAKING, BY MAX D.
RICHARDS AND PAUL S. GREENLAW. HOMEWOOD,
ILL., R.D. IRWIN, 1966.
564P. ILLUS. (THE IRWIN SERIES IN
MANAGEMENT)

1. MANAGEMENT. 2. SYSTEMS ANALYSIS.
I. GREENLAW, PAUL STEPHEN, JT. AU.
II. TITLE.

658.564
R81ad
SYSTEMS ANALYSIS.
Rubin, Martin L   ed.
Advanced technology - systems concepts.
Martin L. Rubin, editor; Thomas Harrell,
technical editor. Princeton, N.J., Auerbach,
1971.
362p. (Handbook of data processing manage-
ment, vol. 5)

1. Automation. 2. Systems analysis.
I. Harrell, Thomas, jt. ed. II. Title.
(Series: Handbook of data processing management,
vol. 5)

352
(746)
W24
SYSTEMS ANALYSIS.
Weiner, Myron E
Systems analysis and municipal government.
[Storrs] Municipal Information Technology
Program, Institute of Public Service, Univer-
sity of Connecticut, 1969.
31p.

1. Municipal government - Conn. 2. Systems
analysis. I. Connecticut. University.
Municipal Information Technology Program.
II. Title.

336
(03)
G25
Systems analysis and planning, programming,
budgeting.
U.S. General Accounting Office.
Glossary for systems analysis and planning,
programming, budgeting. Washington, 1969.
72p.

1. Budget - Dict. I. Title. II. Title:
Systems analysis and planning, programming,
budgeting.

658.564
R81
SYSTEMS ANALYSIS.
Rubin, Martin L
System life cycle standards. Princeton,
N.J., Brandon/Systems Press, 1970.
319p. (Handbook of data processing
management, vol. 2)

1. Automation. 2. Systems analysis.
I. Title. (Series)

658.4
W34
SYSTEMS ANALYSIS.
Whitehead, Clay Thomas.
Uses and limitations of systems analysis.
Santa Monica, Calif., Rand Corp., 1967.
182p. (Rand Corp. P-3683)

Partial contents.-Behavioral theories of
decision-making.

1. Systems analysis. 2. Management.
3. U.S. Dept. of Defense. 4. National
defense. 5. Social science research.
I. Rand Corp. II. Title: Decision-
making... III. Title.

355.58
S97
Systems analysis and policy planning:
applications in defense. Edited by
E.S. Quade and W.I. Boucher. New York,
American Elsevier Pub. Co., 1968.
453p.

Bibliography: p. 430-439.

1. National defense. 2. Systems analysis.
I. Quade, Edward S., ed. II. Boucher,
W.I., ed.

658.4
R82
SYSTEMS ANALYSIS.
Rudwick, Bernard H
Systems analysis for effective planning;
principles and cases. New York, Wiley,
1969.
469p. (Wiley series on systems engineering and analysis)

1. Systems analysis. 2. Management.
I. Title.

658.564
Z82
SYSTEMS ANALYSIS.
Zuckerman, Peter.
System life cycle standards - forms
method. Princeton, N.J., Grandon/Systems
Press, 1970.
235p. (Handbook of data processing
management, vol. 3)

1. Automation. 2. Systems analysis.
I. Title. II. Title: Handbook of data
processing management.

388
S97
Systems Analysis and Research Corp.
Cost-based freight rates: desirability and
feasibility. Prepared for the Under Secre-
tary for Transportation, U.S. Department of
Commerce, Wash, D.C. Cambridge, Mass., 1966.
1v.
Distributed by U.S. Clearinghouse for
Federal Scientific and Technical Information
as Document PB 173 209.
1. Transportation. 2. Railroads. I. U.S.
Dept. of Commerce. II. Title.

711.4
S54s
SYSTEMS ANALYSIS.
Smith, Robert G
The systems approach and the urban dilemma.
Wash., George Washington University, 1968.
45p. (George Washington University.
Program of Policy Studies in Science and
Technology. Staff discussion paper 101)

CFSTI. PB 183 869.

1. City planning. 2. Urban renewal.
3. Systems analysis. I. George Washington
University. Program of Policy Studies in
Science and Technology. II. Title.

658
(016)
R65
SYSTEMS ANALYSIS - BIBLIOGRAPHY.
RONAYNE, MAURICE F   ED.
AN ANNOTATED BIBLIOGRAPHY FOR THE
SYSTEMS PROFESSIONAL, EDITED BY MAURICE
F. RONAYNE, WITH ASSISTANCE FROM A.
RICHARD DELUCA, N. LOUIS SENSNSIEB AND
RICHARD W. REYNOLDS. [DETROIT ?
SYSTEMS AND PROCEDURES ASSOCIATION, 1962]
353P.

1. INDUSTRIAL MANAGEMENT -
BIBLIOGRAPHY. 2. SYSTEMS ANALYSIS -
BIBLIOGRAPHY. I. TITLE.

388
(744)
M17m
Suppl.
no.3
Systems Analysis and Research Corp.
Supplementary statistics and analysis
relating to the Demonstration Project.
Prepared under the direction of Joseph
F. Maloney for the Mass Transportation
Commission, Commonwealth of Massachusetts.
Boston, 1964.
234p.
Supplement no. 3 to Mass transportation
in Mass.

(Cont'd. on next card)

658
S59
SYSTEMS ANALYSIS.
SNYDER, JAMES G
MANAGEMENT PLANNING AND CONTROL SYSTEMS,
BY JAMES C. SNYDER AND GENE L.
SWACKHAMER. LAFAYETTE, 1966.
32P. (INDIANA. AGRICULTURAL EXPERIMENT
STATION, LAFAYETTE. RESEARCH BULLETIN NO.
809)

1. OPERATIONS RESEARCH. 2. MANAGEMENT.
3. SYSTEMS ANALYSIS. I. SWACKHAMER,
GENE L., JT. AU. II. INDIANA.
AGRICULTURAL EXPERIMENT STATION, LAFAYETTE.
III. TITLE.

Systems analysis ...

658
H17s
Hare, Van Court
Systems analysis: a diagnostic approach.
New York, Harcourt, Brace, & World, 1967.
544p. (The Harbrace series in business
and economics)

Bibliography: p. 519-533.

1. Management. 2. Automation. I. Title.

388
(744)
M17m
Suppl.
no.3
Systems Analysis and Research Corp.
Supplementary statistics and analysis
relating to the Demonstration Project ...
(Card 2)

U.S. Housing and Home Finance Agency.
Mass Transportation Demonstration Grant
Program.
1. Transportation - Mass. 2. Transportation -
Finance. I. Maloney, Joseph F. II. Massachusetts.
Mass Transportation Commission. ... III. U.S.
Housing and Home
Finance Agency. Mass Transportation
Demonstration Grant Program.

300
S95
SYSTEMS ANALYSIS.
Symposium on Systems Analysis for Social Problems,
National Bureau of Standards, Gaithersburg, Md.,
1969.
Proceedings. Ed. by Alfred Blumenstein and
others. Wash., Washington Operations Research
Council, 1970.
331p.

1. Social sciences. 2. Systems analysis.
I. Washington Operations Research Council.
II. Blumenstein, Alfred, ed.

519
H17s
Systems analysis: a diagnostic approach.
Hare, Van Court, Jr.
Systems analysis: a diagnostic
approach. New York, Harcourt, Brace
& World, 1967.
544p. (The Harbrace series in
business and economics)

Bibliography: p. 519-533.

1. Systems analysis. 2. Management.
3. Automation. I. Title.

388
(016)
S97
Systems Analysis and Research Corp.
Trans-ocean transportation of high val-
ue packaged cargo. Bibliography. Prepared
for the Under Secretary for Transportation,
U.S. Dept. of Commerce, Wash., D.C.
Cambridge, Mass., 1966.
64p.
Distributed by U.S. Clearinghouse for
Federal Scientific and Technical Informa-
tion. as Document PB 173 007.
1. Transportation - Bibl. I. U.S.
Commerce. II. Title.

355.58
S97
SYSTEMS ANALYSIS.
Systems analysis and policy planning;
applications in defense. Edited by
E.S. Quade and W.I. Boucher. New York,
American Elsevier Pub. Co., 1968.
453p.

Bibliography: p. 430-439.

1. National defense. 2. Systems analysis.
I. Quade, Edward S., ed. II. Boucher,
W.I., ed.

352
(746)
W24
Systems analysis and municipal government.
Weiner, Myron E
Systems analysis and municipal government.
[Storrs] Municipal Information Technology
Program, Institute of Public Service, Univer-
sity of Connecticut, 1969.
31p.

1. Municipal government - Conn. 2. Systems
analysis. I. Connecticut. University.
Municipal Information Technology Program.
II. Title.

658
823s
Systems analysis and the political process.
Schlesinger, James R
Systems analysis and the political process.
Santa Monica, Calif., Rand Corp., 1967.
31p. (Rand Corp. Paper 3464)

1. Management. 2. Federal government.
I. Rand Corp. II. Title.

538.56
06/s

Systems analysis as a planning tool.
Optner (Stanford L.) and Associates.
Systems analysis as a planning tool,
by Stanford L. Optner. [n.p.] 1960.
7p.

"Presented to Annual Conference, American
Institute of Planners, Philadelphia, 1960."

1. Automation. 2. City planning.
I. American Institute of Planners. II. Title.

658
538.56
F67

Systems analysis as an aid in air
transportation.
Fort, Donald M
Systems analysis as an aid in air
transportation planning. Santa Monica,
Calif., Rand Corp., 1966.
42p. [Rand Corp. Paper] P3293-1
Presented at a National Transportation
Symposium in San Francisco on May 5, 1966.

1. Management - Automation. 2. Air
transportation. I. Rand Corp. II. Title.

650
C54

Systems analysis for business data processing.
Clifton, H D
Systems analysis for business data processing. Princeton, N.J., Auerbach Pub., 1970.
244p.

1. Business - Automation. I. Title.

658
067

Systems analysis for business management.
Optner, Stanford L
Systems analysis for business management.
2d ed. Englewood Cliffs, N.J., Prentice-Hall,
1968.
277p.

Bibliography: p. 263-272.

1. Management. 2. Systems analysis.
I. Title.

658.4
R82

Systems analysis for effective planning.
Rudwick, Bernard H
Systems analysis for effective planning;
principles and cases. New York, Wiley,
1969.
469p. (Wiley series on systems engineering and analysis)

1. Systems analysis. 2. Management.
I. Title.

658.4
D25

Systems analysis for engineers and managers.
De Neufville, Richard.
Systems analysis for engineers and managers,
by Richard de Neufville and Joseph H. Stafford.
New York, McGraw-Hill, 1971.
353p.

1. Systems analysis. 2. Engineering.
3. Management. I. Stafford, Joseph H., jt. au.
II. Title.

628.515
E58sy

Systems analysis for water quality manage-
ment: survey and abstracts.
Enviro Control, inc.
Systems analysis for water quality manage-
ment: survey and abstracts. [Wash.] Water
Quality Office, Environmental Protection
Agency, 1971.
1v.

1. Water pollution. I. U.S. Environmental
Protection Agency. II. Title.

711.4
L65s

Systems analysis in the USAC cities.
Long Island University, Brooklyn.
Systems analysis in the USAC cities, by
Kenneth L. Kraemer and others. Wash., Dept.
of Housing and Urban Development [1972]
1v.
Prepared for Urban Information Systems Inter
Agency Committee.
Bibliography: p. E-1 - E-18.
NTIS. PB 208 505.
1. City planning. I. Kraemer, Kenneth L.
II. U.S. Dept. of Housing and Urban Develop-
ment. III.   U.S. Urban Information
Systems Inter-   Agency Committee. IV.Title.

628.1
D25

Systems analysis in water resources planning.
DeLucia, Russell J
Systems analysis in water resources
planning. Prepared for National Water
Commission by Meta Systems, inc. Cambridge,
Mass., 1971.
393p.
NTIS. PB 204 274.

1. Water resources. I. U.S. National
Water Commission. II. Meta Systems, inc.
III. Title.

711.400.15
S72

A systems analysis model of urbanization
and change.
Steinitz, Carl.
A systems analysis model of urbanization
and change; an experiment in interdisciplinary education, by Carl Steinitz and
Peter Rogers. Cambridge, Mass., MIT Press,
1970.
78p. (MIT report no. 20)

1. City planning - Research. 2. City
growth. I. Rogers, Peter, jt. au. II. Title.

690.031
U71

A systems analysis of housing development
cost information.
Urban Systems Research & Engineering.
A systems analysis of housing development
cost information: policy implications.
Boston, 1969.
1v.

1. Building costs. I. Title.

320
E17

A systems analysis of political life.
Easton, David.
A systems analysis of political life.
New York, Wiley, 1965.
507p.

1. Political science. 2. Systems analysis.
I. Title.

628.44
M67

Systems analysis of regional solid waste
handling.
Morse, Norman.
Systems analysis of regional solid waste
handling, by Norman Morse and Edwin W. Roth.
[Wash.] Bureau of Solid Waste Management, 1970.
1v. (U.S. Public Health Service publication
no. 2065)
Report (SW-15c) prepared by Cornell Aeronau-
tical Laboratory, inc. for the Bureau of Solid
Waste Management.
1. Refuse and refuse disposal. I. Roth,
Edwin W., jt. au. II. Cornell Aeronautical
Laboratory. III. U.S. Bureau of Solid
Waste Management. IV. Title.

384
M17

A systems analysis of short haul air transportation.
Massachusetts Institute of Technology.
A systems analysis of short haul air transportation. Part 3. [of High speed ground trans-
port] Prepared for the U.S. Dept. of Commerce.
Distributed by the U.S. Clearinghouse for Federal
Scientific and Technical Information. Cambridge,
Mass., 1965.
1 v. (PB 169 521 M.I.T. Flight Transportation Laboratory. Technical rept. 65-1)
1. Air transportation. 2. Building costs.
I. U.S. Clearinghouse for Federal Scientific
and Technical   Information.
II. Title.

388
(7531)
V66

A systems analysis of transit routes
and schedules.
Voorhees (Alan M.) and Associates.
A systems analysis of transit routes
and schedules. Prepared for Washington
Metropolitan Area Transit Commission.
McLean, Va., 1969.
101p.
U.S. Mass Transportation Demonstration
Grant Program.
1. Transportation - District of Columbia
metropolitan area. 2. Journey to work.
I. Washington Metropolitan Area Transit
Commission.   (Cont'd on next card)

388
(7531)
V66

Voorhees (Alan M.) and Associates,
inc. A systems...1969. (Card 2)

II. U.S. Mass Transportation Demonstration
Grant Program. District of Columbia
metropolitan area. III. Title.

388
025s

Systems analysis of urban transportation.
General Research Corp.
Systems analysis of urban transportation.
Prepared for the U.S. Dept. of Housing and
Urban Development. Santa Barbara, Calif., 1968.
4v. (H-77)
On cover: Study in new systems of urban
transportation.
Contents: v.1. Summary. v.2. Cases for study.--
v.3. Network flow analyses.-- v.4. Supporting
analyses.
1. Transportation. 2. Transportation - Re-
search. 3. Journey to work. 4. Transportation -
Automation. I. J.   S. Dept. of Housing
and Urban Develop-   ment.
(Cont'd on next card)

388
025s

General Research Corp.   Systems analysis...
1968.   (Card 2)

II. Title. III. Title: Study in new systems
of urban transportation.

385
(74)
S97

Systems Analysis Research Corp.
Feasibility of high-speed rail service;
a report prepared for the New England
Regional Commission by Systems Analysis
Research Corporation and Thomas K. Dyer,
inc. [n.p.] New England Regional
Commission, 1969.
96p.

1. Railroads - New England. 2. Journey
to work. I. Dyer (Thomas K.) inc. II. New
England Re-   gional Commission.
III. Title.

658
R15s

SYSTEMS ANALYSIS TECHNIQUES FOR
PLANNING-PROGRAMMING-BUDGETING.
RAND CORPORATION.
SYSTEMS ANALYSIS TECHNIQUES FOR
PLANNING-PROGRAMMING-BUDGETING, BY E.S.
QUADE. SANTA MONICA, CALIF., 1966.
31P.

1. MANAGEMENT. 2. SYSTEMS ANALYSIS.
I. TITLE. I. QUADE, E.S.

651.4
L19

SYSTEMS AND PROCEDURES.
LAZZARO, VICTOR.
SYSTEMS AND PROCEDURES; A HANDBOOK OF
BUSINESS AND INDUSTRY, EDITED BY VICTOR
LAZZARO. CONTRIBUTORS: WILLIAM H.
BRUSH, AND OTHERS. ENGLEWOOD CLIFFS,
N.J., PRENTICE-HALL, 1959.
464P.

1. OFFICE MANAGEMENT. 2. OFFICE
PROCEDURES. I. TITLE.

651.4
157S
SYSTEMS AND PROCEDURES.
U.S. INTERNAL REVENUE SERVICE (DATA PROCESSING SYSTEMS DIVISION)
SYSTEMS AND PROCEDURES; A NOTEBOOK FOR THE SYSTEMS MAN. 2D ED. WASHINGTON, 1963.
42P. (U.S. INTERNAL REVENUE SERVICE PUBLICATION NO. 460 (2-63))

1. OFFICE PROCEDURES. 2. AUTOMATION. I. TITLE.

728.1
(4)
S23
Systems and significance of individual subsidization of accommodation costs in European countries.
Schwarz, Günter.
Systems and significance of individual subsidization of accommodation costs in European countries. Translated from the German by John Marin. Bonn, Domus-Verlag Gmbh, 1966.
73p. (Institute for Town Planning, Housing, and Building Societies series vol. 8)
Title of the German original: System und Bedeutung individueller Zuschüsse zu den Wohnkosten in europäischen Ländern.

1. Housing - Europe. 2. Rental housing.
3. Low income housing Europe. I. Marin, John, tr. II. Title.

658.3
A52s
American Management Association.
The systems approach to personnel management. New York, 1965.
24p. (Its AMA management bulletin no. 62)

1. Personnel management. 2. Management. I. Title.(Series)

VF
658.7
:658
897
Systems and Procedures Association.
(Washington Chapter)
The Association. Cleveland, 1964.
[26]p.

1. Management - Direct.

658.4
C38s
Churchman, Charles West.
The systems approach. New York, Delacorte Press, 1968.
243p.
Bibliography: p. 239-243.

1. Systems analysis. 2. Management. I. Title.

690
(485)
N16
1970
A systems approach to the Swedish building industry.
Napier, Ian A
A systems approach to the Swedish building industry. Stockholm, National Swedish Institute for Building Research, 1970.
188p. (Stockholm. Statens Institut för Byggnadsforskning [document] D9:1970)
Bibliography: p. 183-188.

1. Building industry - Sweden. I. Stockholm. Statens Institut for Byggnadsforskning. II. Title.

658
897
1964
Systems and Procedures Association.
Ideas for management. Papers and case histories presented at the 1964 International Systems Meeting. Cleveland, 1964.
376p.
Contains papers delivered at the 17th International Systems Meeting, held in Philadelphia Oct. 12-14, 1964.

1. Management - Congresses. I. International Systems Meeting. 17th, Philadelphia, 1964. II. Title.

711.4
S54s
Smith, Robert G
The systems approach and the urban dilemma. Wash., George Washington University, 1968.
45p. (George Washington University. Program of Policy Studies in Science and Technology. Staff discussion paper 101)

CFSTI. PB 183 869.

1. City planning. 2. Urban renewal.
3. Systems analysis. I. George Washington University. Program of Policy Studies in Science and Technology. II. Title.

711.4
N17sy
Systems approaches to the city.
National Academy of Engineering.
Systems approaches to the city; a challenge to the University. Summary proceedings of the workshop sponsored by the National Academy of Engineering and the National Science Foundation, Oct. 23 and 24, 1969. Wash., 1970.
68p.

1. City planning. 2. Urban renewal.
3. Universities and colleges - Research services to neighboring communities. I. National Science Foundation. II. Title.

347
H27

Laf.
The systems approach in crime prevention and control.
Herrmann, William W
The systems approach in crime prevention and control. Santa Monica, Calif., System Development Corp. 1967.
19p. (U.S. Defense Documentation Center. Defense Supply Agency. [Document] AD 648 758)
Distributed by U.S. Clearinghouse for Federal Scientific and Technical Information.
1. Law enforcement. 2. Municipal services.
I. System Development Corp., Santa Monica, Calif.
II. U.S. Defense Documentation Center. Defense Supply Agency. III. U.S. Clearinghouse for Federal Scientific and Technical Information.
IV. Title. Title: Crime prevention and control.

658
(016)
897
Systems and Procedures Association.
Publications. Cleveland, [1964?]
[10]p.

1. Management - Bibl.
2. Systems and Procedures Association - Publications.

388
L15d
Systems Associates.
Lampert, Seymour.
Developing area transportation study. Program formulation. Long Beach, Calif., Systems Associates, 1968.
139p.
CFSTI. AD 673 432.

1. Transportation. 2. Journey to work. I. Systems Associates. II. Title.

658
(016)
897
Systems and Procedures Association - Publications
Systems and Procedures Association.
Publications. Cleveland, [1964?]
[10]p.

1. Management - Bibl.
2. Systems and Procedures Association - Publications.

711
(016)
C65
no. 49
The systems approach in urban administration planning.
Kraemer, Kenneth L
The systems approach in urban administration planning, management and operations, by Kenneth L. Kraemer and Ralph J. Lewis. Irvine, Calif., Graduate School of Administration, University of California, 1968.
60p. (Council of Planning Librarians. Exchange bibliography no. 49)
1. Planning - Bibl. 2. Municipal government - Bibl. 3. City planning - Automation.
I. Lewis, Ralph J., jt. au. II. Title.
(Series: Council of Planning Librarians. Exchange bibliography no. 49)

690.022
S23
Systems building.
Schmid, Thomas.
Systems building; an international survey of methods, by Thomas Schmid and Carlo Testa. New York, Praeger, 1969.
239p.

1. Prefabricated construction.
2. Building methods. I. Testa, Carlo, jt. au. II. Title.

Ref.
658
(016)
M67
Systems & procedures, including office management.
Morrill, Chester.
Systems & procedures, including office management; information sources; a guide to literature and bodies concerned with the systems and procedures aspects of organization and management, including office management, whether in business, industry, or government. Detroit, Gale Research Co., 1967.
375p. (Management information guide no. 12)
1. Management - Bibl. 2. Automation - Bibl. 3. Business - Bibl. 4. Office management - Bibl. I. Title.
II. Gale Research. Co.

720
H15s
Systems approach to architecture.
Handler, A Benjamin.
Systems approach to architecture. New York, American Elsevier, 1970.
184p. (Elsevier architectural science series)

1. Architecture. I. Title.

658
A52sy
Systems contracting...
American Management Association.
Systems contracting; a streamlined purchasing technique with companywide implications. New York, 1965.
39p. (AMA management bulletin no. 63)

1. Management. 2. Contract documents. I. Title. (Series)

651.4
T38
SYSTEMS AND PROCEDURES RESPONSIBILITY.
THURSTON, PHILIP H
SYSTEMS AND PROCEDURES RESPONSIBILITY; AN ADMINISTRATIVE VIEW OF THE DIVISION OF RESPONSIBILITY BETWEEN OPERATING PEOPLE AND SPECIALISTS FOR SYSTEMS AND PROCEDURE WORK. BOSTON, DIVISION OF RESEARCH, GRADUATE SCHOOL OF BUSINESS ADMINISTRATION, HARVARD UNIVERSITY, 1959.
110P.

1. OFFICE MANAGEMENT. 2. OFFICE PROCEDURES. I. TITLE.

711.4
(774)
M42s
A SYSTEMS APPROACH TO COMMUNITIES.
MICHIGAN. STATE UNIVERSITY. INSTITUTE FOR COMMUNITY DEVELOPMENT AND SERVICES.
A SYSTEMS APPROACH TO COMMUNITIES, COMMUNITY CENTERS, AND PLANNING AREAS, BY STEWART MARQUIS. EXCERPTED FROM A SERIES OF PAPERS ON THE SPATIAL PATTERNS OF DEVELOPMENT IN THE LANSING REGION, PREPARED FOR THE LANSING TRI-COUNTY REGIONAL PLANNING COMMISSION. EAST LANSING, MICH., 1963.
67P.
1. CITY PLANNING - MICHIGAN.
2. REGIONAL PLANNING - MICHIGAN.
I. MARQUIS, STEWART. II. TITLE.

658
B65
Systems contracting: a new purchasing technique.
Bolton, Ralph A
Systems contracting; a new purchasing technique. New York, American Management Association, 1966.
125p.

1. Buying. 2. Management. 3. Automation. I. American Management Association. II. Title.

657
(016)
D65

DonVito, P   A
Systems cost analysis.
Annotated bibliography on systems cost
analysis. Santa Monica, Calif., Rand Corp.,
1966.
65p.   (Rand Corporation. Memorandum RM-
4848-PR)
"Sponsored by the United Air Force under
Project Rand-Contract no. AF 49 (638)-1700."

1. Accounting - Bibl. I. Title.
II. Title: Systems cost
analysis.

620
A87f

Au, Tung.
Systems engineering — *probabilistic models.*
Fundamentals of systems engineering -
probabilistic models, by Tung Au and others.
Reading, Mass., Addison-Wesley, 1968.
1v.
On cover: Dept. of Civil Engineering,
Carnegie Institute of Technology, Carnegie-
Mellon University.
1. Engineering. 2. Operations research.
I. Carnegie Institute of Technology.
II. Title: Systems engineering. III. Title.

696.9
N17.

SYSTEMS OF ELECTRICAL UNITS.
U.S. NATIONAL BUREAU OF STANDARDS.
SYSTEMS OF ELECTRICAL UNITS, BY
FRANCIS B. SILSBEE. WASHINGTON, GOVT.
PRINT. OFF., 1962.
42P. (ITS MONOGRAPH 56)
REPRINTED FROM THE JOURNAL OF RESEARCH
OF THE NATIONAL BUREAU OF STANDARDS -C.
ENGINEERING AND INSTRUMENTATION, V. 66C,
NO. 2, APRIL-JUNE 1962.

1. ELECTRIC APPARATUS AND APPLIANCES.
I. SILSBEE, FRANCIS B.   II. TITLE.

657
(016)
D65
1967

Don Vito, P   A
Systems cost analysis.
Annotated bibliography on systems cost
analysis. Prepared for U.S. Air Force Project Rand. Santa Monica, Calif., Rand
Corporation, 1967.
80p.   (Rand Corp. Memorandum. RM-4848-
1-PR)

1. Accounting - Bibl. 2. Automation -
Bibl. 3. Budget - Bibl. I. U.S. Air
Force, Project Rand. II. Rand Corp.
III. Title: Systems cost analysis.

378
N17sy

U.S. National Science Foundation.
Systems for measuring and reporting the
resources.
Systems for measuring and reporting the
resources and activities of colleges and
universities. Washington, Govt. Print. Off.,
1967.
444p.   (NSF 67-15)
Bibliography: p. 425-435.
Sponsored by: the National Science Foundation and the National Institutes of Health.
1. Universities and colleges. 2. School
management and organization. 3. Education -
Finance. I. U.S. National Institutes of Health.
II. Title. III.   Title: Resources and
activities of   colleges and universities.

LAW
T
S255sy

Sellin, Thorsten
Systems of reporting crimes known to the
police in selected foreign countries.
Systems of reporting crimes known to the
police in selected foreign countries. Report
submitted to the President's Commission on Law
Enforcement and Administration of Justice.
[Washington, D.C] 1967.
60p.

1. Law enforcement. 2. Law enforcement -
Europe. I. U.S. President's Commission on
Law Enforcement and Administration of Justice.
II. Title.

711.585.1
S97

Systems Discipline, inc.
Recommendations for training in auditing
and evaluating a city demonstration agency
information system. New York, 1971.
46p.
Submitted to Dept. of Housing and Urban
Development. HUD Model Cities contract
H-1329.
1. Model cities. I. U.S. HUD-Model
Cities Program. II. Title.

711.4
R81

Rubel, John H
Systems in cities; and Urban America.
Systems in cities; an Urban America.
report on business in urban development.
Wash., Urban America, 1967.
20p.
The paper upon which this booklet is based
was delivered at Urban America's Washington
symposium "The Troubled Environment" in
December, 1965.
1. City growth. 2. City planning.
I. Urban America, inc. II. Title.

658
C52

Cleland, David I   comp.
Systems, organizations, analysis, management.
Systems, organizations, analysis, management;
a book of readings, by David L. Cleland and
William R. King. New York, McGraw-Hill, 1969.
383p. (McGraw-Hill series in management)

1. Operations research. 2. Systems analysis.
I. King, William R., 1907-   jt. comp.
II. Title.

711.4
C65s

Consulting engineer.
Systems engineering as applied to five major
social problems of our time.
Systems engineering as applied to five major
social problems of our time. Saint Joseph,
Mich., R.W. Roe, 1968.
352p.
Contents:-Where did it come from? Where will
it go? by W. Edward Cushen.-Systems teams,
Joseph Schofer and Gyan Agarwal.-Systems
techniques, by Tibor Fabian.-Systems tools,
by R. Machol.-A way to save our cities, by
Robert F. Kennedy.-A systems concept for
urban renewal,by Dalton-Dalton Associates.-
Untangling urban   transportation, by Alan
                           (Continued on next card)

658
:538.56
S97

Systems Management Services.
Automated management control system
description. Arlington, Texas, Systems
Management Services, Ling-Temco-Vought,
inc., [1967?]
1 v.

1. Management - Automation. 2. Automation. I. Title.

330
(611)
S97

Systems Research Corp.
Area handbook for the Republic of Tunisia,
by Howard C. Reese and others. Prepared for
the American University [Foreign Area Studies]
Wash., Govt. Print. Off., 1970.
415p.
2c.   Bibliography: p. 381-401.

1. Economic conditions - Tunisia. I. Reese,
Howard C. II. American University, Foreign
Area Studies. III. Title. IV. Title: Tunisia.

711.4
C65s

Consulting engineer. Systems engineering...
1968.   (Card 2)

S. Boyd.-Metropolitan area transportation,
by Gibbs & Hill, inc.-Water, water, every-
where, by Stewart L. Udall.-Water pollution
abatement, by Bernard Johnson Engineers,
inc.-Our basic right to breathe, by Edmund
S. Muskie.- Metropolitan air pollution control
by Rust Engineering Co. and Applied Scienc Div.
Litton Industries.-We need a rural renaissance, by Winthrop Rockefeller.- The
                  Continued on next card)

690
G45

Gill, Paul G
Systems management techniques for builders.
Systems management techniques for builders
and contractors. New York, McGraw-Hill, 1968.
210p.
Bibliography: p. 201-204.

1. Building industry. 2. Systems analysis.
I. Title.

658.564
S97N

SYSTEMS RESEARCH LABORATORIES, INC.
A NEW APPROACH TO COMPUTER
STRUCTURES. BY JOHN C.K. KIM, LARRY
E. IRWIN, AND ELIZABETH B. MAIER.
GRIFFISS AIR FORCE BASE, N.Y.,
INFORMATION PROCESSING BRANCH, ROME
AIR DEVELOPMENT CENTER, RESEARCH AND
TECHNOLOGY DIVISION, AIR FORCE SYSTEMS
COMMAND, 1964.
82P. (AD 607363. TECHNICAL
DOCUMENTARY REPORT NO. RADC-TDR-64-135)
1. AUTOMATION. I. KIM, JOHN C.K.
II. U.S. GRIFFISS AIR FORCE BASE,
ROME, N.Y.   III. TITLE.

711.4
C65s

Consulting engineer. Systems engineering...
1968.   (Card 3)

route to rural redevelopment, by Daniel, Mann,
Johnson, & Mendenhall.-Urge labor law reform,
by Edgar A. Poe.-Housing shortage to stimulate
building demand, by Ralph S. Torgerson.-NYACE
explains "Dropping" of Metcalf & Eddy by
Stanley Cohen.-CEC-AIA visit Capitol Hill, by
Stanley Cohen.-
Entire issue: March 1968.
1. Social conditions. 2. Sociology, Urban.
3. Man - Influ   ence of environment.
I. Title.

658
(07)
M17

Matthies, Leslie H
The systems manual.
The systems manual; from the systemation
letter. Produced under direction of the
Foundation for Administrative Research.
Colorado Springs, Systemation, inc. 1967.
125p. (Subject no. 6)
1. Management - Study and teaching.
2. Office management - Study and teaching.
I. Title.

352
(7531)
S97

Systems Science Corp.
A regional law enforcement systems design.
A study prepared for Metropolitan
Washington Council of Governments.
Bloomingsale, Ind., 1966.
174p.
Keps2c   U.S. Urban Renewal Adm. UPAP.

1. Municipal services - District of
Columbia metropolitan area. 2. Automation.
I. Metropolitan Washington Council of
Governments. II. Title. III. Title: Law
enforcement   systems design.
IV. U.S. JBA-   UPAP. District of
Columbia metro-   politan area.

658
C32

Chestnut, Harold.
Systems engineering methods.
Systems engineering methods. New York, Wiley,
1967.
392p. (Wiley series on systems engineering
and analysis)

Bibliography: p. 379-382.

1. Management. 2. Engineering.
I. Title.

690.091.82
C41

Cibula, Evelyn.
Systems of building control.
Systems of building control. Garston,
Eng., Building Research Station, 1970.
[7]p. (U.K. Building Research Station.
Current paper CP 31/70)

1. Building codes. I. U.K. Building
Research Station. II. Title.

330
S97s

Systems simulation for regional analysis; an
application to River-Basin planning by H.R.
Hamilton and others. Cambridge, Mass.,
M.I.T. Press [1968, c1969]
407p.
An outgrowth of a series of research
programs dealing with the economic growth
of the Susquehanna River Basin, conducted by
Battelle Memorial Institute, Columbus
Laboratories
1. Economic planning. I. Hamilton, Henry
R., 1932-   II. Battelle Memorial Institute
(Columbus Laboratories)

658.564
F222
A SYSTEMS STUDY COVERING AN
INTEGRATED INFORMATION SYSTEM.
U.S. FEDERAL HOUSING ADMINISTRATION.
A SYSTEMS STUDY COVERING AN
INTEGRATED INFORMATION SYSTEM TO
CONTROL HOME MORTGAGE INSURANCE
OPERATIONS AND OTHER APPLICATIONS.
WASHINGTON, 1960.
88P.

1. AUTOMATION. 2. MORTGAGE FINANCE.
I. TITLE.

690.022
C657
Szczepanski, Charles Z
U.S. Congress. Joint Economic Committee.
Industrialized housing. Materials compiled
and prepared for the Subcommittee on Urban
Affairs of the Joint Economic Committee,
Congress of the United States. Wash., Govt.
Print. Off., 1969.
257p.
At head of title: 91st Cong., 1st sess.,
Joint Committee Print.
Partial contents.–Industrialized building –
a comparative analysis of European experience,
by Philip F. Patman, E. Jay Howenstine, Charles
Z. Szczepanski, Jack R. Warner, staff of
Dept. of Hous ing and Urban Develop-
ment, Div. of International Affairs.
(Cont'd on next card)

693.1
S92
Research Correlation Conference. 2d, Washington,
D.C., 1950. Fire resistance...1951.
(Card 3)

Davison.–Costs of exterior non-load-bearing walls,
J.P.H. Perry.–The viewpoint of the code official,
Emil J. Szendy.–Fire hazards and fire protection,
James K. McElroy.–Proposed restrictions for
exterior non-load-bearing walls with respect to
fire safety, John W. Dunham.–The sandwich-type
spandrel wall, Nolan D. Mitchell.

388
(81)
L18
A systems study of transportation...
Lave, Roy E Jr.
A systems study of transportation in North-
east Brazil, by Roy E. Lave, Jr. and Donald
W. Kyle. Stanford, Calif., Institute in
Engineering-Economic Systems, Stanford Univer-
sity, 1966.
82p. (Stanford University. Institute in
Engineering-Economic Systems. DPS-1)
Bibliography: p. 76-82.
1. Transportation - Brazil. 2. Railroads -
Brazil. 3. Highways - Brazil. I. Kyle, Donald
W., jt. au. II. Stanford University.
III. Title.

690.022.22
C657
U.S. Congress. Joint Economic Committee.
Industrialized housing...1969. (Card 2)

1. Prefabricated construction. 2. Low-income
housing. I. Title. II. Patman, Philip F.
III. Howenstine, E. Jay. IV. Szczepanski,
Charles Z. V. Warner, Jack R. VI. U.S. Dept.
of Housing and Urban Development, Div. of
International Affairs.

693.1
S92
Szerelmey, Limited
The cause and cure of damp and decay in
masonry. [9th ed.] London, 1955.
47 p.

I. Title. II. Title: Masonry, The cause
and cure of damp and decay in.

026
:658.564
F22
Systems study. Phase I - general proposal
consolidation and automation of HUD
libraries.
U.S. Federal Housing Administration.
Systems study. Phase I - general proposal
consolidation and automation of HUD libraries.
By Nancy L. Ayer. Wash., Data Processing
Methods Section, Comptroller's Div., Federal
Housing Administration, 1966.
8p.

1. Libraries - Automation. 2. Housing docu-
mentation. 3. Building documentation. 4. U.S.
Dept. of Housing and Urban Development.
Library. I. Ayer, Nancy L.
II. Title.

330
S92
Sze, T W
New criterion for urban economic planning.
A final technical r port. Pittsburgh, University
of Pittsburgh, Dept. of Electrical Engineering,
1971.
70p.
Research supported by a grant to University of
Pittsburgh from the Dept. of Housing and Urban
Development, Urban Mass Transportation Adminis-
tration, Project No. PENN-R11-8-69.
1. Economic planning. I. Pittsburgh. Univer-
sity. Dept. of Ele ctrical Engineering.
II. U.S. Dept. of Housing and Urban Develop-
ment. III. Title.

VF
69
S95
Szmak, G
Causes retarding residence construction. In-
formal address - November 18, 1937, Washington,
D.C., before the Chamber of Commerce of the United
States, Conference on Residential Construction.
[Washington, D.C., Chamber of Commerce of the
United States?, 1937]
4 l.

Processed.

1. Building industry. I. Title.

301.15
C31s
Systems technology applied to social and
community problems.
Chartrand, Robert L
Systems technology applied to social and
community problems. New York, Spartan Books,
1971.
478p.
Originally prepared for the Subcommittee on
Employment, Manpower, and Poverty of the
Committee on Labor and Public Welfare of the
United States Senate.
Bibliography: p. 443-468.
1. Man - Influence of environment.
2. Technology. I. U.S. Congress. Senate.
Committee on Labo r and Public Welfare.
II. Title.

334.1
S92
Szego, G C
Cost-reducing condominium systems for low-
cost homes. Arlington, Va., Institute for
Defense Analyses, Program Analysis Div., 1968.
131p. (Institute for Defense Analyses.
Program Analysis Div. Study S-325)
[Conducted for] Dept. of Housing and Urban
Development.
HUD contract no. H-931.
1. Cooperative housing. 2. Low-income
housing. 3. Home ownership. I. U.S. Dept.
of Housing and Urban Development. II. Insti-
tute for Defense Analyses. III. Title.
IV. Title: Condo minium systems for low-
cost homes.

325
S98
Szwed, John F. ed.
Black America. New York, Basic Books, 1970.
303p.

1. Negroes. I. Title.

711.4
C31s
A systems view of planning.
Chadwick, George.
A systems view of planning; towards and theory
of the urban and regional planning process.
Oxford, Pergamon Press, 1971.
390p.

1. City planning. 2. Regional planning.
I. Title.

Szendy, Emil J

Technical Director
New York State Building Code Commission
1740 Broadway
New York 19, N.Y.   4/51

332.72
S99
1962
Szymczak, Matt S
Financial structures and policies in the
United States before the ninth Congress of the
International Union of Building Societies
and Savings Associations. Washington, Inter-
national Union of Building Societies and
Savings Associations, 1962.
16p.
Prepared in cooperation with C. J. Devine
and Co.
1. Savings and loan associations. 2. Building
societies. I. International Union of Building
Societies and Savings Associations.
9th Congress, Washingto D.C., 1962.
II. Devine (C. J.) and Co.

352
(7471)
S91
Szanton, Peter L
Working with a city government; Rand's
experience in New York. New York, New
York City Rand Institute, 1970.
5p. (Rand Corp. RM-6236)

1. Municipal government - New York (City)
I. New York City Rand Institute.
II. Rand Corp. III. Title.

VF
699.81
R27
Szendy, Emil J.
Research Correlation Conference. 2d, Washington,
D.C., 1950.
Fire resistance of non-load-bearing exterior
walls, National Academy of Sciences, Nov. 21, 1950.
Washington, Building Research Advisory Board, Div.
of Engineering and Industrial Research, National
Research Council, Feb. 1951.
60 p. illus., diagrs. (Research Advisory
Board. Research Conference report no. 2)

(Continued on next card)

TIAA-CREF (Teachers Insurance and Annuity
Association - College Retirement Equities
Fund)
Report

see

Teachers Insurance and Annuity Association
Report

691.54
D65
Szatura, L jt. au.
Doleszai, K
Applicability of the autoclave test for
evaluating the magnesia swelling of cements,
by K. Doleszai and L. Szatura. Garston, Eng.,
Building Research Station, 1971.
[9]p. (Library communication no. 1613)
Translated from the Hungarian and reprinted
from Epitoanyag, 1970, 22(b), 204-12.
1. Cement. 2. Strength of materials.
I. Szatura, L., jt. au. II. U.K. Building
Research Station. III. Title. (Series)

Research Correlation Conference. 2d, Washington,
D.C., 1950. Fire resistance...1951.
(Card 2)

Bibliography: p. 58-60, prepared by Clement
R. Brown and Fred L. Mayer of the Science
Division, Library of Congress.
Partial contents.–The background of requirements for fire resistance of exterior non-
load-bearing walls, George N. Thompson.–The wall -
what do we want?, J. Walter Severinghaus.–The
viewpoint of the research director, Robert L.

(Continued on next card)

025
C65
TICA 3, third Conference on Technical...
Conference on Technical Information Center
Administration, 3d, Philadelphia, 1966.
TICA 3, third Conference on Technical
Information Center Administration, Philadelphia,
Pa., Aug. 29-Sept. 1, 1966, edited by Arthur
W. Elias. New York, Spartan Books, 1967.
135p. (Drexel Institute of Technology.
Drexel information science series, vol. 4)

1. Library administration. 2. Library science
Automation. I. Drexel Institute of Technology.
II. Elias, Arthur W., ed. III. Title.

690
(492)
T56   T. N. O. for the building world. The Hague
       [1960?]
       61p.

       1. Building construction - Netherlands.
       I. Nederlandse Central Organisatie voor
       Toegepast Natuurvetenschappelyk Onderzoel.

330
(63)   TWA's services to Ethiopia.
N17   National Planning Association.
       TWA's services to Ethiopia, by Theodore Geiger.
       Washington, 1959.
       80p. illus. (Eighth case study on United
       States business performance abroad)

       1. Economic conditions - Ethiopia. I. Geiger,
Theodore. II. Title.

312
(774437)
T11   Tableman, Betty
       Intra-community migration in the Flint
metropolitan district. [Ann Arbor, Mich.]
Institute for Human Adjustment. University of
Michigan, Sept. 1948.
       viii, 75 l.

       A Social Science Research Project.
       Bibliography: 2 leaves at the end.
       Processed.
       1.Population shifts-Flint, Mich. I.Michigan.
Univ. Institute for Human Adjustment.

TRED

SEE

Committee on Taxation, Resources and Economic
Development

711.585.1
(77311)   T.W.O.'s [The Woodlawn Organization]
C48   model cities plan.
       U.S. Commission on Civil Rights.
       T.W.O.'s [The Woodlawn Organization]
model cities plan, by Beryl A. Radin.
Wash., Govt. Print. Off., 1969.
       28p. (Its Clearinghouse publication,
urban series no. 2)

       1. Model cities - Chicago. I. Radin,
Beryl A. II. Title.

311.2
N17   Tables describing small-sample properties
         of the mean.
       U.S. National Bureau of Standards.
       Tables describing small-sample properties
of the mean, median, standard deviation, and
other statistics in sampling from various
distributions. Washington, Govt. Print. Off.,
1963.
       14 p. (Its: Technical note 191)

       1. Sampling (statistics) I. Title.

TRW Systems Group (Thompson Ramo Woolridge)
   x Thompson Ramo Woolridge)

388
:331
T11   Taafe, Edward J
       The peripheral journey to work; a
geographic consideration, by Edward
J. Taaffe and others. [Evanston, Ill.]
Published for the Transportation Center
at Northwestern University, by Northwestern
University Press, 1963.
       125p.

       1. Journey to work. 2. Traffic surveys.
I. Northwestern University. Transportation
Center.   II. Title.

333.332
E55   TABLES FOR REAL ESTATE APPRAISING
1959   AND FINANCING.
       ELLWOOD, L   W
       ELLWOOD TABLES FOR REAL ESTATE
APPRAISING AND FINANCING. RIDGEWOOD,
N.J., 1959.
       330P.

       1. REAL PROPERTY - VALUATION.
2. APPRAISAL.   3. AMORTIZATION TABLES.
I. AMERICAN INSTITUTE OF REAL ESTATE
APPRAISERS. II. TITLE: TABLES FOR
REAL ESTATE APPRAISING AND FINANCING.

711.3
(754)   TRW (Thompson Ramo Wooldridge) Systems
427   Group.
       West Virginia. Dept. of Commerce.
       The rural cities program; an urban
alternative for the nation by the State of
West Virginia. [Dept. of Commerce] with
TRW [Thompson Ramo Wooldridge] Systems
Group. Charleston 1967.
       50p.

       1. Rural planning - W. Va. 2. Community
development - W. Va. I. TRW (Thompson
Ramo Wooldridge) Systems Group. II. Title.

370
T11   Taba, Hilda.
       Intergroup education in public schools.
Experimental programs sponsored by the project
in intergroup education in cooperating schools:
theory, practice, and in-service education, by
Hilda Taba and others. Washington, American
Council on Education, 1952.
       337p.

       1. Education. 2. Minority groups.
3. Community development - Citizen participation. I. American Council on Education.
II. Title.

333.332
E55   Tables for real estate appraising and
           financing.
       Ellwood, L   W
       Ellwood tables for real estate appraising
and financing. 2d ed. Chicago, American
Institute of Real Estate Appraisers, 1967.
       398p.

Suppl.   -- ---Supplement. Chicago, 1969. 60p.

       1. Real property - Valuation. 2. Appraisal.
3. Amortization tables. I. American Institute
of Real Estate Appraisers. II. Title: Tables
for real estate appraising and financing.

VF
711.3
T25   TVA as a symbol of resource development.
       Tennessee Valley Authority. Technical Library.
       TVA as a symbol of resource development in
many countries; a digest and selected bibliography
of information. Knoxville, Tenn., Jan. 1952.
       55 p.   illus.
       "To provide some concept of the scope and
magnitude of foreign projects or plans which have
been influenced by the TVA example" - Foreword.
       Includes bibliographies.
       Processed.
       1.Regional planning. 2.Water resources. I.Title.

691.54
V54   Tabakova, N   jt. au.
       V'lkov, V
       The effect of P205 on clinker formation and
the quality of the cement, by V. V'lkov and
N. Tabakova. Garston, Eng., Building Research
Station, 1971.
       [11]p. (Library communication no. 1602)
       Bibliography: p. 5-6.
       Translated from the Bulgarian and reprinted
from Stroitelni materiali i silikatna promish-
lenost, 1967, 8 (9), 6-10.
       1. Cement. I. Tabakova, N., jt. au.
II. U.K. Building Research Station.
III. Title.   (Series)

333.332
E55   Tables for real estate appraising and
1970   financing.
       Ellwood, L   W
       Ellwood tables for real estate appraising
and financing. 3d ed. Chicago, American
Institute of Real Estate Appraisers, 1970.
       2pts.

       1. Real property - Valuation. 2. Appraisal.
3. Amortization tables. I. American Institute
of Real Estate Appraisers. II. Title:
Tables for real estate appraising and
financing.

728.69
T25T   TVA DEMOUNTABLE COTTAGES.
       TENNESSEE VALLEY AUTHORITY.
       TVA DEMOUNTABLE COTTAGES.
       KNOXVILLE, TENN., 1941.
       6L.

       1. DEMOUNTABLE HOUSES. I. TITLE.

325
T11   Tabb, William K
       The political economy of the black ghetto.
New York, Norton, 1970.
       152p.

       1. Negroes. 2. Economic conditions.
I. Title.

311
P21   Tables for statisticians and biometric-
           ians.
       Pearson, Karl, Editor.
       Tables for statisticians and biometric-
ians. London, England, Cambridge University Press, 1930.
       2v.
       Part 1 (1930) 3d edition. lxxxiii,
143 pp., tables.
       Part 2 (1931) 1st edition. ccl, 262 pp.,
tables.
       1. Statistics. 2. Title.

VF
627
B52   TVA Tennessee River history.
       Blee, C   E
       TVA Tennessee River history. Based
on the paper: Development of the
Tennessee River waterway, by Chief
engineer, Tennessee Valley Authority,
before the American Society of Civil
Engineers, Centennial meeting in Chicago,
Illinois, Sept. 12, 1952. [Chicago?]
1959.
       [8]p.

1. Tennessee Valley   Authority.
I. Title.

551
A51   A TABLE OF ALASKAN EARTHQUAKES.
       ALASKA. UNIVERSITY. GEOPHYSICAL
INSTITUTE.
       A TABLE OF ALASKAN EARTHQUAKES, BY T.
NEIL DAVIS AND CAROL ECHOLS. COLLEGE,
ALASKA, 1962.
       1 V.

       1. EARTHQUAKES. I. DAVIS, T   NEIL.
II. ECHOLS, CAROL.   III. TITLE.

690.015
(485)   Tables for the dimensioning of traditional
S 82   formworks for floor slabs.
R15   Backsell, Gunnar.
1970   Dimensioneringstabeller för traditionella
valvformar (Tables for the dimensioning of
traditional formworks for floor slabs) av
Gunnar Backsell and others. Stockholm,
1970.
       34p. (Stockholm, Statens Institut för
Byggnadsforskning. Rapport R15:1970)
       English summary.
       1. Building research - Sweden. 2. Floors
and flooring I. Stockholm. Statens Institut
för Byggnads forskning. II. Title: Tables
for the dimensioning of traditional
formworks for floor slabs.

311
(016)
G72
Tables in mathematical statistics.
Greenwood, Joseph Arthur, 1927-
Guide to tables in mathematical statistics by J. Arthur Greenwood and H.O. Hartley. Princeton, N.J., Princeton University Press, 1962.
1014 p.

1. Statistics - Bibl. 2. Automation. I. Title. II. Title: Tables in mathematical statistics. III. Hartley, H.O., jt. au.

510
N17
Tables of the exponential function ex.
U.S. National Bureau of Standards.
Tables of the exponential function e^x. 4th ed. Wash., Govt. Print. Off., 1961. 537p. (Its Applied mathematics series, 14) Prepared by National Bureau of Standards Computation Laboratory.
Supersedes MT2.

1. Mathematics. I. Title: Exponential function e^x. II. Title.

312.1
(54)
I52t
1969
Tables with notes on internal migration.
India. Secretariat.
Tables with notes on internal migration (rural) by H.B. Chaudhury. New Delhi, 1969. 24p. (Indian Statistical Institute. National sample survey no. 128)
At head of title: the National sample survey, fourteenth found: July 1958 - June 1959.

1. Population shifts - India. I. Chaudhury, H.B. II. Indian Statistical Institute. III. Title.

332.725
F22ta
Tables of factors for use in determining the unearned charge on FHA Title 1 property...
U.S. Federal Housing Administration.
Tables of factors for use in determining the unearned charge on FHA Title 1 property improvement loans prepared or refinanced. Wash., U.S. Dept. of Housing and Urban Development, Federal Housing Administration, 1968.
30p. (FHA no. 1355)
1. Property improvement loans. 2. Mortgage loan servicing. I. Title.

311
:658
.564
L42
Tables of the hypergeometric probability distribution.
Lieberman, Gerald J
Tables of the hypergeometric probability distribution by Gerald J. Lieberman and Donald B. Owen. Stanford, Calif., Stanford University Press, 1961.
726 p. (Stanford studies in mathematics and statistics, 3)
Includes bibliography.
1. Statistics. 2. Mathematics. I. Title. II. Owen, Donald B.

711.4
:670
(54)
I52
1964
Tables with notes on the annual survey of industries, 1964, sample sector.
India. Secretariat.
Tables with notes on the annual survey of industries, 1964, sample sector: summary results, by U.N. Banerji and others. New Delhi, 1969. 131p. (Indian Statistical Institute. National sample survey no. 132)

1. Industrial location - India. I. Banerji, U.N. II. Indian Statistical Institute. III. Title.

020
:538.56
N17
Tables of four letter computer codes used in library retrieval program.
U.S. Naval Ordnance Laboratory.
Tables of four letter computer codes used in library retrieval program, by Eva Liberman and Hoyt L. Stevens. White Oak, Md., 1962. 676p. (U.S. Defense Documentation Center. Defense Supply Agency. Document AD 277 676)

1. Library science - Automation. 2. Documentation. I. Liberman, Eva. II. Stevens, Hoyt L. III. Title.

338
(73)
L111ta
Tables of working life.
U.S. Bureau of Labor Statistics.
Tables of working life; Length of working life for men. Washington, Govt. Print. Off., 1950. 74 p., graphs, tables. (Its: Bulletin, No. 1001).

1. Labor productivity. I. Title: Length of working life for men. II. Title.

711.4
:670
(54)
I52
1965
Tables with notes on the annual survey of...
India. Secretariat.
Tables with notes on the annual survey of industries, 1965, sample sector: summary results, by U.N. Bannerji and others. New Delhi, 1970. 178p. (Indian Statistical Institute. National sample survey no. 161)

1. Industrial location - India. I. Banerji, U.N. II. Indian Statistical Institute. III. Title.

VF 9.
694.3
:690.013
F22
1946
TABLES OF MAXIMUM ALLOWABLE SPANS FOR WOOD FLOOR JOISTS.
U.S. FEDERAL HOUSING ADMINISTRATION.
TABLES OF MAXIMUM ALLOWABLE SPANS FOR WOOD FLOOR JOISTS, CEILING JOISTS, RAFTERS IN RESIDENTIAL CONSTRUCTION. REV. MAY 1946. WASHINGTON, 1946. 42P.

1. WOOD CONSTRUCTION. 2. WOOD CONSTRUCTION - CONTRACTS AND SPECIFICATIONS. 3. ROOFS AND ROOFING. I. TITLE.

331
(54)
I52e
1970
Tables with notes on employment and ...
India. Secretariat.
Tables with notes on employment and unemployment in rural areas, by Debkumar Dutta-Mazunder. Delhi, Manager of Publications, 1970. 127p. (Indian Statistical Institute. National sample survey no. 173)
At head of title: The National sample survey, 19th round: July 1964 - June 1965.

1. Employment - India. I. Indian Statistical Institute. II. Title.

711.437
(54)
I52t
Tables with notes on villages and towns in India: some results.
India. Secretariat.
Tables with notes on villages and towns in India: some results, by Jagadish Chandra Das and others. Delhi, Manager of Publications, 1970. 58p. (Indian Statistical Institute. National sample survey no. 167)

Nineteenth round: July 1964-June 1965.
1. Villages - India. 2. Rural planning - India. I. Indian Statistical Institute. II. Das, Jagadish Chandra. III. Title.

VF
694.3
:690.013
F22
1949
TABLES OF MAXIMUM ALLOWABLE SPANS FOR WOOD FLOOR JOISTS.
U.S. FEDERAL HOUSING ADMINISTRATION.
TABLES OF MAXIMUM ALLOWABLE SPANS FOR WOOD FLOOR JOISTS, CEILING JOISTS, RAFTERS IN RESIDENTIAL CONSTRUCTION. REV. DEC. 1949. WASHINGTON, 1949. 54P.

1. WOOD CONSTRUCTION. 2. WOOD CONSTRUCTION - CONTRACTS AND SPECIFICATIONS. 3. ROOFS AND ROOFING. I. TITLE.

728.1
(54)
I52ta
Table with notes on housing condition.
India. Secretariat.
Table with notes on housing condition, by B.R. Panesar and others. Delhi, Manager of Publications, 1970. 84p. (Indian Statistical Institute. National sample survey no. 170)

Eighteenth round: February 1963-January 1964.
1. Housing - India. 2. Housing statistics - India. I. Indian Statistical Institute. II. Panesar, B.R. III. Title.

725.23
T11
Tabor, Philip.
Pedestrian circulation in offices. Cambridge, Eng., University of Cambridge, School of Architecture, 1969. 70p. (Cambridge, Eng. Center for Land Use and Built Form Studies. Working paper 17)
Bibliography: p.66-70.
1. Office buildings. 2. Space considerations. I. Cambridge, Eng. University. Centre for Land Use and Built Form Studies. II. Title.

VF
694.3
:690.013
F22
1950
Tables of maximum allowable spans for wood floor joists, ceiling joists, rafters.
U.S. Federal Housing Administration.
Tables of maximum allowable spans for wood floor joists, ceiling joists, rafters, in residential construction. Rev. Dec. 1949. FHA-2550. [Washington, 1949] vii, 54 p.

1. Wood construction-Contracts and specifications. 2. Wood construction-Tables, calculations, etc. 3. Roofs and roofing. I. Title.

332
(54)
I52t
Tables with notes on indebtedness of scheduled tribe households.
India. Secretariat.
Tables with notes on indebtedness of scheduled tribe households, by Jagadish Chandra Das and P.C. Kundu. New Delhi, Manager of Publications, 1969. 57p. (Indian Statistical Institute. National sample survey no. 143)
At head of title: The National sample survey, eighteenth round: Feb. 1963 - Jan. 1964.
1. Finance - India. I. Das, Jagadish Chandra. II. Indian Statistical Institute. III. Title.

311.26
U54
Tabular presentation.
U.S. Bureau of the Census.
Manual of tabular presentation; an outline of theory and practice in the presentation of statistical data in tables for publication, prepared by Bruce L. Jenkinson. Washington, U.S. Govt. Print. Off., 1949. xiv, 266 p.

1. Statistics-Charts, tables, etc. 2. Statistical presentation. I. Jenkinson, Bruce Le Roy, 1906- II. Title: Tabular presentation.

311.2
A57
Tables of probabilities for use in stop-or-go sampling.
U.S. Air Force.
Tables of probabilities for use in stop-or-go sampling. Issued by Department of the Air Force Comptroller, Auditor General. Washington, Govt. Print. Off., 1961. 1 v.

1. Sampling (Stat) I. Title. II. Title: Probabilities for use in stop-or-go sampling.

711.437
(54)
I52
Tables with notes on Indian villages.
India. Secretariat.
Tables with notes on Indian villages; some important results, by D. Pant and others. Delhi, Manager of Publications, 1970. 65p. (Indian Statistical Institute. National sample survey no. 172)

Eighteenth round February 1963-January 1964.

1. Villages - India. I. Pant, D. II. Indian Statistical Institute. III. Title.

311
L68
TABULATING EQUIPMENT AND ARMY MEDICAL STATISTICS.
LOVE, ALBERT G
TABULATING EQUIPMENT AND ARMY MEDICAL STATISTICS, BY ALBERT G. LOVE, EUGENE L. HAMILTON AND IDA LEVIN HELLMAN. WASHINGTON, GOVT. PRINT. OFF., 1958. 202 P.

1. STATISTICS. I. TITLE. II. HAMILTON, EUGENE L., JT. AU. III. HELLMAN, IDA LEVIN, JT. AU. IV. TITLE: MEDICAL STATISTICS.

690.24
K69
Tabunshchikov, Yu   A   jt. au.
Kozhinov, I   A
Analytical study of the thermal resistance
of ventilated cavity roofs, by I.A. Kozhinov
and Yu. A. Tabunshchikov. Garston, Eng.,
Building Research Station, 1971.
[5]p. (Library communication no. 1629)
Translated from the Russian.

1. Roofs and roofing. 2. Ventilation.
I. Tabunshchikov, Yu. A., jt. au. II. U.K.
Building Research Station. III. Title.
(Series)

711.4
(797781
:016)
T12
Tacoma. [City Planning Commission]
A listing of studies, plans, programs
and ordinances involved in the planning
process. Tacoma, 1965.
7p.

1. City planning - Tacoma - Bibl.
2. Urban renewal - Tacoma - Bibl.

711.535.1
(797731)
T12
U.S. HUD. Model Cities Program. Tacoma.

1970c.2   1. First year action program, 1970.
1971   2. Technical Assistance Project, Final
              report, 1971.
1971a   3. First year action program. Program
              package. 2 pts.

691
(493)
C62
Tack, F   A   M   jt.au.
Cockx, A
Review of the structure, activities and
new developments in the building industry,
by A. Cockx and F.A.M. Tack. [n.p.] 1961.
30p.   (National monograph - Belgium)

1. Building industry - Belgium.
2. Housing - Belgium. I. Tack, F.A.M, jt.au.
II. Title.

DATE OF REQUEST Tacoma MAR 1 9 1951
March 8, 1951   L. C. CARD NO.

AUTHOR
Tacoma, Washington. Housing Authority.

TITLE
Public housing in Tacoma.

SERIES

EDITION | PUB. DATE 1950 | PAGING unpaged

PUBLISHER
same

RECOMMENDED BY | REVIEWED IN
                        WL 12/23/50 pg.4
              ORDER RECORD

712.25
(797781)
T12
Tacoma. City Planning Commission.
A recommended study program for waterfront
areas of Tacoma, Washington, including
policy recommendations for Ruston Way--
Bayside Drive Area. Tacoma, Wash., 1964.
15p.

1. Recreation - Tacoma. 2. Natural
resources - Tacoma. I. Title: Waterfront
areas of Tacoma.

691
H99
The tack coat of asphalt surfacings...
Hyyppä, J   M   I
The tack coat of asphalt surfacings, and
sealing of joints. Helsinki, State Institute
for Technical Research, 1968.
54p. (Finland. State Institute for Technical
Research. Tiedotus. Sarja 3 - Rakennus 116)

1. Building materials. 2. Road construction.
I. Finland. State Institute for Technical
Research. II. Title.

DATE OF REQUEST 6/26/52   1952   L. C. CARD NO.

AUTHOR
Tacoma, Wash. City Planning Commission.

TITLE
Parks - play areas - schools. A part of the Tacoma
master plan.

SERIES

EDITION | PUB. DATE 1952 | PAGING 60 p.

PUBLISHER
same

RECOMMENDED BY | REVIEWED IN
                        IPO Newsltr 6/52 p. 43
              ORDER RECORD

711.4
(797781)
T12r
Tacoma. City Planning Commission.
Report, 19

Tacoma, 19
v.   annual.

For complete information see main card.

1. City planning - Tacoma.

Tacoma, Wash.

VF
Land use-Wash.
~~Traffic, transit & highways-Wash.~~

352.6
(797781)
T12
Tacoma, Washington. City Planning
Commission.
Capital improvement program.
Tacoma,
v.   annual.

For complete information see shelflist.

1. Capital improvement programs -
Tacoma, Wash.

711.585
(797781)
T12r
Tacoma. City Planning Commission.
A review of progress under the
workable program for community improvement. Tacoma, Wash., 1965.
26p.

Submitted to U.S. Housing and
Home Finance Agency Feb. 23, 1965.

1. Workable program - Tacoma.
I. U.S. Housing and Home Finance Agency.

VF
312
(797781)
T12
Tacoma.
Population trends and projections
1900-1985. Rev. (Tentative)
Tacoma, Wash., 1964.
3p.

1. Population - Tacoma.

Tacoma. City Planning Commission.

725.822.91
E26
Economic Research Associates.
Feasibility of a civic auditorium in
Tacoma, Washington. Prepared for the City
of Tacoma. Los Angeles, 1964.
1v.

1. Auditoriums. 2. Public buildings -
Tacoma. I. Tacoma. City Planning Commission.
II. Title.

711.552
(797781)
T12
pt. 3
Tacoma, Wash. City Planning Commission.
Tacoma central business district
studies. Part 3, CBD frame. Tacoma, 1962.
60p.

1. Business districts - Tacoma.

711.552
(797781)
T12
pt. 2
Tacoma. City Planning Commission.
The Broadway mall. Tacoma central
business district studies part II. Tacoma,
1961.
69p.

1. Business districts - Tacoma.

711.14
(797781)
T12
Tacoma. City Planning Commission.
The generalized land use plan; a part
of the comprehensive plan for Tacoma,
Wash. Adopted by the Tacoma City Planning
Commission on March 15, 1960 and recom-
mended to the City Council for adoption.
Tacoma, 1960.
16p.

1. Land use - Tacoma. 2. Master plan - Tacoma.

711.552
(797781)
T12
pt.4
Tacoma, Wash. City Planning Commission.
Tacoma central business district
studies. Part 4. The central business
district, comprehensive land use and
development plan. A part of the comprehensive plan for Tacoma, Washington.
Tacoma, Wash., 1963.
94p.
Cover title: The CBD plan.
1. Business districts - Tacoma, Wash. 2. Land
use - Tacoma, Wash.   3. Master plan -
Tacoma, Wash.

711.552
(797781)
T12
pt.1
Tacoma, Wash. City Planning Commission.
The central core. Central business
district studies, pt. 1. Tacoma,
Washington, 1959.
94p.

1. Business districts - Tacoma, Wash.

711.4
(797781)
T12
Tacoma, Wash. City Planning Commission.
Preliminary report: major thoroughfares.
Tacoma, 1955.
16 p. maps, diagrs.

1. Traffic - Tacoma, Wash. 2. Community
development - Tacoma, Wash.

711.585
(797781)
R62
Tacoma. City Planning Commission.
Rockrise and Watson.
Planning and design objectives for the
new Tacoma urban renewal project.
[Prepared in cooperation with] Office
of Urban Renewal and Tacoma City Plan
Commission. San Francisco, 1963.
1v.

1. Urban renewal - Tacoma. 2. Tacoma.
City Planning Commission. 3. Tacoma.
Office of Urban Renewal.

330
(797781)
T12
TACOMA. CITY PLANNING COMMISSION.
WHAT TACOMA HAS TO OFFER; THE
ECONOMY OF THE CITY AND ITS REGION.
A PART OF THE MASTER PLAN. TACOMA,
WASH., 1948.
41P.

1. ECONOMIC CONDITIONS - TACOMA.
2. ECONOMIC CONDITIONS - WASHINGTON
(STATE)   3. MASTER PLAN - TACOMA.
I. TITLE.

711.4
(797781)
T120
TACOMA, WASH. PLANNING COMMISSION.
OUTLINE OF A MASTER PLAN FOR TACOMA;
A PRELIMINARY REPORT ... TACOMA,
WASH., CITY PLANNING COMMISSION, 1947.
9L.

1. MASTER PLAN - TACOMA, WASH.

711.585
(797781)
T12
Tacoma. Office of Urban Renewal.
Urban renewal plan for New Tacoma
urban renewal area. Rev. Tacoma, 1965.
/21/p.

1. Urban renewal - Tacoma.

Tacoma. City planning Commission.
see also Tacoma. Planning Dept.

711.4
(797781)
T12S
TACOMA, WASH. PLANNING COMMISSION.
SITE, HISTORY, POPULATION; A
PRELIMINARY REPORT. A PART OF THE
TACOMA MASTER PLAN. TACOMA, 1948.
45P.

1. CITY PLANNING - TACOMA, WASH.
2. MASTER PLAN - TACOMA, WASH.

711.585
(797781)
R62
Tacoma. Office of Urban Renewal.
Rockrise and Watson.
Planning and design objectives for the
new Tacoma urban renewal project.
/Prepared in cooperation with/ Office
of Urban Renewal and Tacoma City Plan
Commission. San Francisco, 1963.
1v.

1. Urban renewal - Tacoma. 2. Tacoma.
City Planning Commission. 3. Tacoma.
Office of Urban Renewal.

728.1
:336.18
(797781)
T12
1942
1943-2 c
1949/50
1950/55
TACOMA. HOUSING AUTHORITY.
REPORT. 1942, 1943, 1949/50, 1950/55
TACOMA.
v. ANNUAL.

SOME REPORTS HAVE INDIVIDUAL TITLES.

1. PUBLIC HOUSING - TACOMA.

Tacoma. Planning Dept.
see also Tacoma. City Planning Commission.

388
(797781)
G45
Tacoma Transit Company.
Gilman (W.C.) and Co.
Tacoma Transit Company; review of service
earnings and property. Jan. 28, 1949.
New York, 1949.
72p.

1. Transportation - Tacoma. I. Title.

711.585.1
(797781)
T12
1968
Tacoma. Office of the Mayor.
Application to the Department of Housing
and Urban Development for a grant to plan
a comprehensive city demonstration program.
Tacoma, 1968.
1v.
Selected to receive a HUD Model Cities
Program planning grant.
1. Model cities - Tacoma. I. U.S.
HUD-Model Cities Program.

388
:308
(797781)
W17
Tacoma. Dept. of Public Works.
Washington (State) Dept. of Highways.
Origin and destination traffic survey,
Tacoma, Wash., 1948-1949. Olympia, Wash.,
[1950?]
54p.
Conducted by the State of Washington Dept.
of Highways in cooperation with Dept. of
Commerce, Bureau of Public Roads and the City
of Tacoma Dept. of Public Works.
1. Traffic surveys - Tacoma, Wash. 2. Journey to work. I. Tacoma. Dept. of Public
Works. II.   Title.

538.56
T12
Taconic Foundation.
Urbandoc: a report on computerized
documentation and information retrieval in
the literature of urban planning and
renewal. A project ... with the cooperation
of: The American Institute of Planners,
New York Chapter, The City Planning and
Housing Library, a unit of the Municipal
Reference Library, The New York Public
Library and others. New York, Institute of
Public Administration, 1964.
24p.   (Cont'd on next card)

711.4
(797781)
T12?
TACOMA. MAYOR'S RESEARCH COMMITTEE
ON URBAN PROBLEMS.
TACOMA, THE CITY WE BUILD. 2D ED.
TACOMA, 1944.
147P.

1. CITY PLANNING - TACOMA.
2. ECONOMIC CONDITIONS - TACOMA.

711.585.1
(797781)
T12
1967
Tacoma. Office of the Mayor.
Application to the Dept. of Housing and
Urban Development for a grant to plan a
comprehensive city demonstration program.
Tacoma, 1967.
1v.
Selected to receive HUD Model Cities
Program planning grant.

1. Model cities - Tacoma. I. U.S. HUD.
Model Cities Program.

538.56
T12
Taconic Foundation.   Urbandoc ... (Card 2)

1. Automation. 2. City planning.
3. Urban renewal. 4. Library science. I
I. Sessions, Vivian S. II. New York (City)
Municipal Reference Library. (City Planning
and Housing) III. Institute of Public
Administration, New York. IV. Title.

690.091.82
(797781)
T12
TACOMA, WASH. ORDINANCES, ETC.
BUILDING CODE. TACOMA, WASH.,
1966.
49P. (ORDINANCE NO. 18377)

1. BUILDING CODES - TACOMA, WASH.

711.14
(797781)
R21
Tacoma, Wash. Dept. of Urban Renewal.
Real Estate Research Corp.
Land utilization and marketability
study, New Tacoma Project, Tacoma, Washington. Prepared for Office of Urban
Renewal, Tacoma, Washington. Tacoma,
1963.
81p.

1. Land use - Tacoma, Wash.
2. Land economics - Tacoma, Wash.
I. Tacoma, Wash. Dept. of Urban Renewal.

325
T12C
TAEUBER, ALMA F   , JT. AU.
TAEUBER, KARL ERNEST.
THE CHANGING CHARACTER OF NEGRO
MIGRATION, BY KARL E. TAEUBER AND ALMA
F. TAEUBER. [CHICAGO, 1965]
429-441P.
REPRINTED FROM: THE AMERICAN JOURNAL
OF SOCIOLOGY, JANUARY 1965.

1. NEGROES. 2. MINORITY GROUPS.
3. POPULATION SHIFTS. I. TAEUBER, ALMA
F., JT. AU.   II. TITLE.

711.14
(797781)
T12L
TACOMA. PLANNING COMMISSION.
LAND USE AND ZONING; A PART OF THE
TACOMA MASTER PLAN. TACOMA, 1949.
25P.

1. LAND USE - TACOMA. 2. ZONING -
TACOMA. 3. MASTER PLAN - TACOMA.

388
(797781)
854
Tacoma. Office of Urban Renewal.
Smith (Wilbur) and Associates.
New Tacoma project; traffic planning
study. Prepared for City of Tacoma,
Office of Urban Renewal. San Francisco,
1963.
51p.

1. Traffic - Tacoma. 2. Parking - Tacoma.
I. Tacoma. Office of Urban Renewal.

325
T12
Taeuber, Alma F   jt. au.
Taeuber, Karl E
Negroes in cities; residential segregation
and neighborhood change, by Karl E. Taeuber
and Alma F. Taeuber. Chicago, Aldine, 1965.
284p.   (Population research and training
center monographs)
Bibliography: p. 276-277.

1. Negroes. 2. Minority groups - Housing.
3. Race relations. 4. Social conditions.
I. Taeuber, Alma F., jt. au. II. Title.

312
T12

Taeuber, Conrad.
The changing population of the United States, by Conrad Taeuber and Irene B. Taeuber, for the Social Science Research Council, in cooperation with the U.S. Department of Commerce, Bureau of the Census. New York, Wiley, 1958.
357p. charts, maps, tables.

1.Population. I.Taeuber, Irene B jt. au. II.U.S. Bureau of the Census.

312
T12p

Taeuber, Conrad, jt. au.
Taeuber, Irene B
People of the United States in the 20th Century; a census monograph, by Irene B. Taeuber and Conrad Taeuber. Prepared in cooperation with the Social Science Research Council. Wash. U.S. Dept. of Commerce, Bureau of the Census, 1971.
1046p.

1. Census - Population. I. Social Science Research Council. II. Taeuber, Conrad, jt. au. III. U.S. Bureau of the Census. IV. Title.

312.1
T12

Taeuber, Conrad.
A research memorandum on internal migration resulting from the war effort, by Conrad Taeuber and Irene Barnes Taeuber. New York, Social Science Research Council, 1942.
36 p.
1. Population shifts. I. Taeuber, Irene Barnes. II. Social Science Council. II. Title: Internal migration resulting from the war effort.

312.1
L48

Taeuber, Conrad, jt. au.
Lively, C E
Rural migration in the United States, by C. E. Lively and Conrad Taeuber. Washington, Works Progress Administration, Division of Research, 1939.
192p. (U.S. Works Progress Administration. Research monograph XIX)

1. Population shifts. 2. Housing for migrant workers. I. Taeuber, Conrad, jt. au. II. U.S. Works Progress Administration.

312
T12

Taeuber, Irene B jt. au.
Taeuber, Conrad.
The changing population of the United States, by Conrad Taeuber and Irene B. Taeuber, for the Social Science Research Council, in cooperation with the U.S. Department of Commerce, Bureau of the Census. New York, Wiley, 1958.
357p. charts, maps, tables.

1.Population. I.Taeuber, Irene B jt. au. II.U.S. Bureau of the Census.

312
T12p

Taeuber, Irene B
People of the United States in the 20th Century; a census monograph, by Irene B. Taeuber and Conrad Taeuber. Prepared in cooperation with the Social Science Research Council. Wash. U.S. Dept. of Commerce, Bureau of the Census, 1971.
1046p.

1. Census - Population. I. Social Science Research Council. II. Taeuber, Conrad, jt. au. III. U.S. Bureau of the Census. IV. Title.

312.1
T12

Taeuber, Irene Barnes, jt. au.
Taeuber, Conrad.
A research memorandum on internal migration resulting from the war effort, by Conrad Taeuber and Irene Barnes Taeuber. Social Science Research Council, 1942.
36 p.
1. Population shifts - U.S. I. Taeuber, Irene Barnes. II. Social Science Council. II. Title: Internal migration resulting from the war effort.

325
T12C

TAEUBER, KARL ERNEST.
THE CHANGING CHARACTER OF NEGRO MIGRATION, BY KARL E. TAEUBER AND ALMA F. TAEUBER. [CHICAGO, 1965]
429-441P.
REPRINTED FROM: THE AMERICAN JOURNAL OF SOCIOLOGY, JANUARY 1965.

1. NEGROES. 2. MINORITY GROUPS. 3. POPULATION SHIFTS. I. TAEUBER, ALMA F., JT. AU. II. TITLE.

312.1
T12C

TAEUBER, KARL E
COHORT POPULATION REDISTRIBUTION AND THE URBAN HIERARCHY. NEW YORK, 1965.
450-462P.

REPRINTED FROM THE MILBANK MEMORIAL FUND QUARTERLY, V. 48, NO. 4, 1965.

1. POPULATION SHIFTS. I. TITLE.

312
(77311)
C34l
1960

Taeuber, Karl E jt. ed.
Kitagawa, Evelyn M ed.
Local community fact book, Chicago metropolitan area, 1960. Edited by Evelyn M. Kitagawa and Karl E. Taeuber. Chicago, Chicago Community Inventory, University of Chicago, 1963.
345p. (Community Renewal Program Study)
U.S. Urban Renewal Adm. CRP.

1. Urban renewal - Chicago. 2. Metropolitan areas - Chicago. 3. Population - Chicago metropolitan area. I. Taeuber, Karl E., jt. ed.
(Cont'd on next card)

312
(77311)
C34l
1960

Kitagawa, Evelyn M ed. Local community fact book, Chicago metropolitan ...
(Card 2)

II. Chicago. Community Renewal Program. III. Title. IV. U.S. URA-CRP. Chicago. V. Chicago. University. Chicago Community Inventory.

312.1
T12m

Taeuber, Karl E
Migration in the United States; an analysis of residence histories, by Karl E. Taeuber and others. [Wash.] Health Services and Mental Health Administration, 1968.
151p. (Public health monograph no. 77)
U.S. Public Health Service publication no. 1575.
1. Population shifts. I. U.S. Health Services and Mental Health Administration. II. Title.

325
T12

2c

Taeuber, Karl E
Negroes in cities; residential segregation and neighborhood change, by Karl E. Taeuber and Alma F. Taeuber. Chicago, Aldine, 1965.
284p. (Population research and training center monographs)
Bibliography: p. 276-277.

1. Negroes. 2. Minority groups - Housing. 3. Race relations. 4. Social conditions. I. Taeuber, Alma F., jt. au. II. Title.

728.1
:325
T12

TAEUBER, KARL E
RESIDENTIAL SEGREGATION. NEW YORK, SCIENTIFIC AMERICAN, INC., 1965.
12-19P.

CLIPPED FROM SCIENTIFIC AMERICAN, V. 213, NO. 2, AUGUST 1965.

1. MINORITY GROUPS - HOUSING. I. TITLE. II. SCIENTIFIC AMERICAN.

628.515
(016)
P81
1957

Taft, Robert A.
U.S. Public Health Service.
Handbook of selected biological references on water pollution control, sewage treatment, water treatment, by William Marcus Ingram and Robert A. Taft. Rev. 1957. Washington, Govt. Print. Off., 1957.
95p. illus. (Its Publication no. 214; Public health bibliography series no. 8)

(See Card no. 2)

628.515
(016)
P81
1957

U.S. Public Health Service. Handbook of selected biological references on water pollution control, etc. (Card no. 2)

1. Water pollution - Bibliographies.
2. Sewerage and sewage disposal - Bibliographies. I. Ingram, William Marcus. II. Taft, Robert A.

728.1
:1336.18
C342

TAFT-ELLENDER-WAGNER-BILL.
CHICAGO. UNIVERSITY. ROUND TABLE. THE POLITICS OF HOUSING; A RADIO DISCUSSION BY RAYMOND SMITH AND LOUIS WIRTH...IN COOPERATION WITH THE NATIONAL BROADCASTING COMPANY. CHICAGO, 1948.
29P. (ITS NO. 539)

A RADIO DISCUSSION...INCLUDING A SUPPLEMENT ON POST-WAR HOUSING: THE TAFT-ELLENDER-WAGNER BILL AND THE PRESENT HOUSING SITUATION.

1. PUBLIC HOUSING. 2. SOCIAL
(CONTINUED ON NEXT CARD)

728.1
:1336.18
C342

CHICAGO. UNIVERSITY. ROUND TABLE. THE POLITICS OF ...1948. (CARD 2)

WELFARE - LAW AND LEGISLATION. 3. TAFT-ELLENDER-WAGNER-BILL. I. SMITH, RAYMOND. II. WIRTH, LOUIS. III. TITLE.

728.1
:1336.18
J65

TAFT-ELLENDER-WAGNER HOUSING BILL.
JONES, HARRY WILMER.
STATEMENT OF CONCLUSIONS WITH RESPECT TO THE YIELD INSURANCE AND TENANT ELIGIBILITY FOR PUBLIC HOUSING PROVISIONS OF THE TAFT-ELLENDER-WAGNER HOUSING BILL. NEW YORK, COLUMBIA UNIVERSITY, 1948.
17L.

1. PUBLIC HOUSING. 2. TENANT SELECTION. 3. TAFT-ELLENDER-WAGNER HOUSING BILL. I. TITLE.

728.1
(73
:347)
C65
1948
S-R
NO.140
PT.2

TAFT-ELLENDER-WAGNER BILL.
U.S. CONGRESS. SENATE. COMMITTEE ON BANKING AND CURRENCY.
HOUSING ACT; SUPPLEMENTAL REPORT TO ACCOMPANY S. 866. WASHINGTON, GOVT. PRINT. OFF., 1948.
44P. (80TH CONGRESS, 2D SESSION. SENATE. REPORT NO. 140, PART 2)

1. TAFT-ELLENDER-WAGNER BILL.

352
T13

Tager, Jack.
The intellectual as urban reformer; Brand Whitlock and the progressive movement. Cleveland, Case Western Reserve University, 1968.
198p.
Bibliography: p. 183-192.

1. Municipal government. 2. Political science. 3. Whitlock, Brand. I. Case Western Reserve University. II. Title.

301.15
T13
Tager, Jack ed.
The urban vision; selected interpretations of the modern American city, ed. by Jack Tager and Park Dixon Goist. Homewood, Ill., Dorsey Press, 1970.
310p. (The Dorsey series in American history)
Partial contents.-A narrative of the rise of the industrial city.-pt.1. The challenge of the city, 1890-1915.-pt.2. Urbanism as a way of life, 1915-1945.-pt.3. An urban nation, 1945-1965.-Metropolis: suburb and core.- Megalopolis: crisis and challenge.
1. City growth. 2. Metropolitan areas. I. Goist, Park Dixon, jt. ed. II. Title.

657.47
:69
B78
Taggart, H F
Brummet, R L
Record keeping for the small home builder, prepared by R.L. Brummet and D.A. Thomas, under the supervision of H.F. Taggart. Washington, Housing and Home Finance Agency, Office of the Administrator, Division of Housing Research, January 1952.
85 p. + full size forms in separate envelope. forms(part fold.), tables.

(Continued on next card)

652
T14
1964
Teintor, Sarah Augusta.
The secretary's handbook; a manual of correct usage, by Sarah Augusta Teintor and Kate M. Monro. 8th ed., completely rev. New York, Macmillian, 1964.
559p.

1. Letter-writing. 2. Style manuals. I. Monro, Kate M., jt. au. II. Title.

621.3
T13
TAGG, GEORGE FRANK.
EARTH RESISTANCES. NEW YORK, PITMAN PUB. CORP., 1964.
258P.

1. ELECTRICITY. 2. SOILS. I. TITLE.

Brummet, R L Record keeping for the small home builder...1952. (Card 2)
HHFA research project no. O-E-52 at University of Michigan School of Business Administration; Max Lipowitz, staff technician.
1.Contractors-Accounting. I.Thomas, D.A., jt. au. II.Taggart, H.F. III.Michigan. University. School of Business Administration. IV.U.S. Housing and Home Finance Agency. Office of the Administrator. Division of Housing Research. V.Title.

LAW
T
T148eq
Taiwan. Land Bank. (Research Dept.)
The equalization of urban land rights act. [n.p.] 1968.
33p.

1. Land use - Taiwan. I. Title: Urban land rights act. II. Title.

728.1
T13
Taggart, Robert, III.
Low-income housing: a critique of Federal aid. Baltimore, Johns Hopkins Press, 1970.
146p. (Policy studies in employment and welfare no. 8)

1. Low income housing. 2. Federal housing programs. 3. Public housing. I. Title.

VF
711.4
(764)
F67t
Taggart, M W ed.
Fort Worth, Tex. Chamber of Commerce.
Tomorrow's greater Fort Worth. Edited by M.W. Taggart. Fort Worth, Tex., 1956.
58p.

Entire issue vol. 32, no. 3, March 1956.

1. City planning - Fort Worth, Tex. I. Taggart, M.W., ed.

308
(529)
R16
Taiwan. National Taiwan University, Taipei.
Raper, Arthur F
Urban and industrial Taiwan, crowded and resourceful, by Arthur F. Raper [and others] Taipei, Taiwan, China, Foreign Operations Administration, Mutual Security Mission to China, September 1954.
vii, 370 p. illus., graphs, tables, maps.

At head of title: Foreign Operations Administration, Mutual Security Mission to China and National Taiwan University.

331
L28s
Taggart, Robert III, jt. au.
Levitan, Sar A
Social experimentation and manpower policy: the rhetoric and the reality, by Sar A. Levitan and Robert Taggart III. Baltimore, Johns Hopkins Press, 1971.
111p. (Policy studies in employment and welfare, no. 9)

1. Employment. 2. Labor supply. I. Title. II. Taggart, Robert III, jt. au.

658
B23
Tagiuri, Renato.
Behavioral science concepts in case analysis; the relationship of ideas to management action by Renato Tagiuri and others. Boston, Division of Research, Graduate School of Business Administration, Harvard University, 1968.
147p.

1. Management. 2. Operations research. I. Tagiuri, Renato.

711.417
(529) Taiwan. (Provincial Government) Public
T14 Works Bureau.
Chung Hsing Village, a new community in central Taiwan, Republic of China. Taipei, Taiwan, 1961.
62p.

1. Planned communities - Taiwan.

658.564
B27t
Tagged arithmetic.
Bettinger, Paula J
Tagged arithmetic, by Paula J. Bettinger and others, Lewis Research Center. Wash., National Aeronautics and Space Administration, 1969.
18p. (NASA TN D-5370)

CFSTI.

1. Automation. I. U.S. National Aeronautics and Space Administration. II. Title.

711.4
(76688)
O45
Tahlequah, Okla. City Planning Commission.
Oklahoma. University. Institute of Community Development.
A plan for development, Tahlequah, Oklahoma, Prepared for the Oklahoma Dept. of Commerce and Industry [and the Tahlequah City Planning Commission] Norman, Okla., 1960.
60p.
U.S. Urban Renewal Adm. UPAP.

1. City planning - Tahlequah, Okla. I. Tahlequah, Okla. City Planning Commission. II. U.S. URA- UPAP. Tahlequah, Okla.

728.1
:355
(529)
T14
Taiwan. (Provincial Government) Public Works Bureau.
A housing project for military dependents, Republic of China. Taipei, 1960.
16p. illus.

1. Military housing - Taiwan.

657.47
:690
M42
Taggert, Herbert F.
Michigan. University. School of Business Administration.
[Cost accounting systems for home builders] prepared by R. L. Brummet and D. A. Thomas. Washington, Dec. 1951 - Feb. 1952.
2 pts. forms, tables.

Contents.-part 1. Record keeping for the small home builder.-part 2. Accounting procedures for home builders.

VF
728.1
:362.6
(747)
N28a
Taietz, Philip.
New York (State) Agricultural Experiment Station.
Administrative practices and personal adjustment in homes for the aged, by Philip Taietz. Ithaca, N. Y., 1953.
39p. tables. (Its Bulletin 899)

1. Housing for the aged - New York (State) I. Taietz, Philip.

728.1
:336.18
(529)
T14
Taiwan. (Provincial Government) Public Works Bureau.
Hailung new district, Hualien: low-cost housing, public road, water works, drainage and sewerage projects. [n.p.] 1960.
[16]p.

1. Public housing - Taiwan. 2. Public works - Taiwan. I. Title: Low-cost housing.

657.47
:690
M42
Michigan. University. School of Business Administration. [Cost accounting systems for home builders] (Card 2)
Final report, Research project no. O-E-52, Housing and Home Finance Agency.
Project director: Herbert F. Taggert; Staff technician: George Kinzie.

Processed.

652
T14
Taintor, Sarah Augusta.
The secretary's handbook; a manual of correct usage, by Sarah Augusta Taintor and Kate M. Monro. 7th ed., completely rev. New York, Macmillan Co., 1949.
xiv, 578 p. illus. 20 cm.
Includes bibliographies.

1. Secretaries-Private. 2. Letter-writing. I. Monro, Kate M., joint author. II. Title.
HF5547.T25 1949   651.74   49-2409*
Library of Congress   [491*10]

728.1
(529)
T14
Taiwan. Public Works Bureau.
Demonstration housing project in Taipei, Taiwan, Republic of China. Taipei, 1961.
42p.

1960 edition has color illustrated cover, identical text.

1. Housing projects - Taiwan.

VP
728.3
(529)
T14
Taiwan (Provincial Government) Dept. of Social Affairs.
Model housing project at Lungchin. [Taipei, Taiwan?] 1964.
[16]p.

1. Model houses - Taiwan. I. Title.

628.1
(969)
T14
Takasaki, K J
Water resources of Windward Oahu, Hawaii, by K.J. Takasaki and others. Wash., Govt. Print. Off., 1969.
119p. (Geological Survey water-supply paper 1894)
Prepared in cooperation with the State of Hawaii, Dept. of Land and Natural Resources, Div. of Water and Land Development.
Bibliography: p. 114-115.
1. Water resources - Hawaii. I. U.S. Geological Survey. II. Hawaii. Dept. of Land and Nat ural Resources. III. Title.

362.6
D12
Takos, Michael
Dade County, Fla. Dept. of Public Health.
A study of welfare clients residing in institutions for the aged in Dade County, Florida, by Michael J. Takos and others. [Miami, Fla. 1960?]
23p. tables.

1. Old age. I. Takos, Michael J.

728.1
F15
Taiwan. Public Works Bureau.
Fang, Kai-Che.
Final report on the study of housing and urban development in the United States. [Taipei] Taiwan, Republic of China, Taiwan Public Works Bureau, Provincial Government of Taiwan, 1967.
Long. 67p.
c.1,2 1. Housing. 2. City growth. 3. Mortgage finance. 4. Urban renewal. I. Taiwan. Public Works Bureau. II. Title. III. Title: Study of housing and urban development in the United States

---

699.81
I47
Takata, Arthur N.
IIT Research Institute, Chicago.
Development and application of a complete fire-spread model, by Arthur N. Takata and Frederick Salzberg. Final report. Chicago, IIT Research Institute, Technology Center, 1968.
4v. (U.S. Naval Radiological Defense Laboratory. NRDL-TRC-68-36)
Prepared for Office of Civil Defense.
1. Fire prevention. 2. Atomic bomb. I. Takata, Arthur N. II. Salzberg, Frederick. III. U.S. Naval Radiological Defense Laboratory. IV. Title.

352
(7468)
T15
Talbot, Allan R
The Mayor's game. Richard Lee of New Haven and the politics of change. 1st ed. New York, Harper & Row, 1967.
270p.

1. Municipal government - New Haven. 2. Lee, Richard Charles. 3. City planning - New Haven. 4. Urban renewal - New Haven. 5. Political science. I. Title.

728.6
(529)
T14
Taiwan. Public Works Bureau.
Housing design for farmers. [Taipei, Taiwan,] Republic of China, 1962.
52p.

1. Farm housing - Taiwan. 2. House plans. I. Title.

699.81
W17
Takata, A.N., jt. au.
Waterman, T E
Laboratory study of ignition of host materials by firebrands. Final technical report. Prepared by T.E. Waterman and A.N. Takata for Office of Civil Defense. Chicago, Engineering Mechanics Div., IIT Research Institute, 1969.
48p.
1. Fire prevention. I. Takata, A.N., jt au. II. Illinois Institute of Technology. Research Institute. III. U.S. Office of Civil Defense. IV. Title.

352
(7468)
T15
1970
Talbot, Allan R
The mayor's game; Richard Lee of New Haven and the politics of change. New York, Praeger, 1970.
274p. (Praeger university series)

1. Municipal government - New Haven. 2. Lee, Richard. 3. City planning - New Haven. 4. Urban renewal - New Haven. I. Title.

623
T14
Takabeya, Fukuhei, 1893-
Multi-story frames; calculation and moment-tables; the methods of Cross, Kani, Takabeya. Berlin, Ernst, 1965.
148p.

1. Structural engineering. 2. Loads. 3. Strains and stresses. I. Title.

699.81
T14
Takata, Arthur N
Mathematical modeling of fire defenses. Final technical report. Prepared for Office of Civil Defense. Chicago, Engineering Mechanics Div., IIT Research Institute, 1969-70.
2 pts.
1. Fire protection. I. Illinois Institute of Technology. Research Institute. II. Title.

339.5
(914)
T15
Talbot, Lee M
Renewable natural resources in the Philippines; status, problems and recommendations; South East Asia Project general report on the Philippines, by Lee M. Talbot and Martha H. Talbot. Manila, 1964.
1v.
Bibliography: p. XI-1 - XI-7.
South East Asia Project (SEAP) of the International Commission on National Parks; International Union for Conservation of Nature and Natural Resources.
(Cont'd on next card)

624.131
A759G
TAKAGI, SHUNSUKE.
U.S. ARMY. COLD REGIONS RESEARCH AND ENGINEERING LABORATORY, HANOVER, N.H. GEOMETRIC INTERPRETATION OF THE THREE-DIMENSIONAL YIELD CRITERION OF SOILS, BY SHUNSUKE TAKAGI. HANOVER, N.H., 1965.
8P. (ITS RESEARCH REPORT 164)

1. SOILS. I. TAKAGI, SHUNSUKE.

699.81
T14p
Takata, Arthur N
Power density rating for fire in urban areas. Final technical report. Prepared for Office of Civil Defense. Chicago, Engineering Mechanics Div., IIT Research Institute, 1969.
83p.

1. Fire prevention. I. Illinois Institute of Technology. Research Institute. II. U.S. Office of Civil Defense. III. Title.

339.5
(914)
T15
Talbot, Lee M   Renewable...1964.   (Card 2)

1. Natural resources - Philippines.
I. Talbot, Martha H., jt. au. II. International Commission on National Parks. III. International Union for Conservation of Nature and Natural Resources.

624.131
A759P
TAKAGI, SHUNSUKE.
U.S. ARMY. COLD REGIONS RESEARCH AND ENGINEERING LABORATORY, HANOVER, N.H. PLANE PLASTIC DEFORMATION OF SOILS, BY SHUNSUKE TAKAGI. HANOVER, N.H., 1966.
42P. (ITS RESEARCH REPORT 87)

1. SOILS. 2. STRAINS AND STRESSES. I. TAKAGI, SHUNSUKE.

690
(52)
T14
Takenaka Komuten, Osaka.
Takenaka of Japan. Osaka, [1972]
151p.

1. Building industry - Japan.
2. Architecture - Japan.

339.5
(914)
T15
Talbot, Martha H   jt. au.
Talbot, Lee M
Renewable natural resources in the Philippines; status, problems and recommendations; South East Asia Project (SEAP) general report on the Philippines, by Lee M. Talbot and Martha H. Talbot. Manila, 1964.
1v.
Bibliography: p. XI-1 - XI-7.
South East Asia Project (SEAP) of the International Commission on National Parks; International Union for Conservation of Nature and Natural Resources.
(Cont'd on next card)

624.131
A759PR
TAKAGI, SHUNSUKE.
U.S. ARMY COLD REGIONS RESEARCH AND ENGINEERING LABORATORY, HANOVER, N.H. PRINCIPLES OF FROST HEAVING, BY SHUNSUKE TAKAGI. HANOVER, N.H., 1966.
35P. (ITS RESEARCH REPORT NO. 140)

1. SOILS. 2. FROZEN GROUND.
I. TAKAGI, SHUNSUKE. II. TITLE; FROST HEAVING.

030.8=956
K 25
Takenobu, Yoshitaro, ed.
Kenkyusha's new Japanese-English dictionary. American ed., Cambridge, Mass., Harvard Univ. Press, 1942.
iv, 2280 p.

1. Japanese language-Dict.-English. I.Title.

339.5
(914)
T15
Talbot, Lee M   Renewable...1964.   (Card 2)

1. Natural resources - Philippines.
I. Talbot, Martha H., jt. au. II. International Commission on National Parks. III. International Union for Conservation of Nature and Natural Resources.

690.282
T15

Talbott, John W
   Frameless glazing system for framed wood buildings and wood foundations for economy housing. Pullman, Washington State University, Technical Extension Service, 1967.
   13p. (Washington (State) University. College of Engineering. Research Div. Bulletin 307)
   Paper presented at the Economy Housing Seminar, Lincoln, Nebraska, 1967.

(Cont'd on next card)

VF
711.4
:67
L56

A tale of too many cities.

Lloyd, George W
   A tale of too many cities. [Detroit, the Detroit Edison Company, n.d.]
[30] p.

1. Industrial location. I. Title.

728.3
T15

Laf.

Tall buildings; the proceedings of a symposium on tall buildings with particular reference to shear wall structures. Held in the Dept. of Civil Engineering, University of Southampton, April 1966. Edited by A. Coull and B. Stafford Smith. Oxford, N.Y., Symposium Publications Div., Pergamon Press, 1967.
   607p.
   Sponsored by the University of Southampton and the Civil Engineering Research Association.

(Cont'd on next card)

690.282
T15

Talbott, John W   Frameless...
        1967.   (Card 2)

   1. Windows. 2. Foundations (Building) 3. Wood construction. I. Washington (State) University. (College of Engineering) II. Title.

711.4
(77594)
P27

Taliesin Associated Architects.

Peters, William Wesley.
   Schematic master plan for the city of Madison, Wisconsin. Madison, Monona Basin Project. 1967.
   89p.
   Bibliography: p. 87-89.

   1. Master plan - Madison, Wis. I. Taliesin Associated Architects. II. Frank Lloyd Wright Foundation, Taliesin, Wis. III. Title.

728.3
T15

Tall buildings; the proceedings of a symposium on tall buildings with particular reference to shear wall structures...1967.
        (Card 2)

   1. Architecture - Design. 2. Walls. 3. Structural engineering. 4. Strains and stresses. 5. Buildings - Wind stresses. I. Coull, A., ed. II. Smith, Bryan Stafford, ed. III. Southampton, Eng. University. IV. Civil Engineering Research Association.

690.25
T15

2C.

TALBOTT, JOHN W
   LOW-PROFILE WOOD FLOOR SYSTEMS, BY JOHN W. TALBOTT. PULLMAN, DIVISION OF INDUSTRIAL RESEARCH, WASHINGTON STATE UNIVERSITY, 1963.
   76L. (WASHINGTON STATE INSTITUTE OF TECHNOLOGY. BULLETIN 277)

   PREPARED FROM A STUDY SPONSORED BY NATIONAL LUMBER MANUFACTURERS ASSOCIATION.
   BIBLIOGRAPHY: LEAVES 55-64.

   1. FLOORS AND FLOORING.
      (CONTINUED ON NEXT CARD)

711.5
A37

Talks on rural zoning.

U.S. Agricultural Research Service.
   Talks on rural zoning. Washington, Agricultural Research Service, Farm Economic Research Division, U.S. Dept. of Agriculture, 1960.
   95p.
   A series of talks on rural zoning made by Erling D. Solberg.

   1. Rural zoning. I. Solberg, Erling D. II. Title.

711.4
(76161)
T15

Talladega, Ala. City Planning Commission.
   Talladega, Alabama: community facilities plan: parks and playgrounds, schools, public buildings. [In cooperation with Alabama State Planning and Industrial Development Board] Talladega, 1956.
   43p. charts, diagrs.

   U.S. Urban Renewal Administration, Urban Planning Assistance Program.

(Continued on next card)

690.25
T15

TALBOTT, JOHN W LOW-PROFILE WOOD FLOOR
   ...1963.   (CARD 2)

   I. WASHINGTON (STATE) STATE UNIVERSITY, PULLMAN. INSTITUTE OF TECHNOLOGY. II. NATIONAL LUMBER MANUFACTURERS ASSOCIATION. III. TITLE: WOOD FLOOR SYSTEMS.

699.81
I57p

TALL BUILDINGS.
International Conference on Firesafety in High-Rise Buildings, Wash., 1971.
   Proceedings: reconvened Conference on Firesafety in High-Rise Buildings Oct. 5, 1971. Wash., General Services Administration, Public Buildings Service, 1971.
   1v.

   1. Fire prevention. 2. Tall buildings. I. U.S. Public Buildings Service.

711.4
(76161)
T15

Talladega, Ala. City Planning Commission.
   Talladega, Alabama: community ... (Card 2)

   1. Master plan - Talladega, Ala. 2. Community facilities - Talladega, Ala. I. Alabama. State Planning and Industrial Development Board. II. U.S. Urban Renewal Administration.

690.015
T15

Talbott, John W
   Performance of experimental houses embodying some new concepts in floor, foundation, and heating systems. Pullman, Wash., Washington State University, College of Engineering, Research Div., Technical Extension Service, 1969.
   48p. (Washington (State) University. College of Engineering. Research Div. Bulletin 311)

   1. Experimental houses. 2. Floors and flooring.   (Cont'd on next card)

699.841
H47

TALL BUILDINGS -- JAPAN.
Tall buildings.
Hisada, Toshihiko.
   Earthquake response of tall buildings, by Toshihiko Hisada and others. Tokyo, Building Research Institute, 1964.
   2pts. (BRI occasional report no. 18, 20)

   1. Earthquake resistant construction. 2. Earthquakes - Japan. I. Japan. Building Research Institute. II. Title. 3. Tall buildings - Japan.

711.4
(76161)
T15m

Talladega, Ala. City Planning Commission.
   Talladega, Alabama: major street plan. [In cooperation with Alabama State Planning and Industrial Development Board] Talladega 1956.
   15p. diagrs., charts.

   U.S. Urban Renewal Administration, Urban Planning Assistance Program.
   1. Master plan - Talladega, Ala. 2. Street planning - Talladega, Ala. I. Alabama. State Planning and Industrial Development Board. II. U.S. Urban Renewal Administration. Urban Planning Assistance Program.

690.015
T15

Talbott, John W   Performance...1969.
        (Card 2)

   3. Foundations (Building). 4. Heating. I. Washington (State) University. College of Engineering. II. Title.

551
(469)
B67

TALL BUILDINGS - PORTUGAL.
Borges, J. Perry
   Behaviour of tall buildings during the Caracas earthquake of 1967, by J. Perry Borges and others. Lisboa, Portugal, Laboratorio Nacional de Engenharia Civil, 1970.
   14p. (Memoria no. 347)
   English and Portuguese summary.

   1. Earthquakes - Portugal. 2. Tall Buildings - Portugal. I. Portugal. Laboratorio Nacional de Engenharia Civil. I. Title: Caracas earthquake of 1967.

711.4
(76161)
T15p

Talladega, Ala. City Planning Commission.
   Talladega, Alabama: public works program. [In cooperation with Alabama State Planning and Industrial Development Board] Talladega, 1957.
   [18]p.

   U.S. Urban Renewal Administration, Urban Planning Assistance Program.
   1. Master plan - Talladega, Ala. 2. Public works - Talladega, Ala. 3. Capital improvement programs - Talladega, Ala. I. Alabama. State Planning and Industrial Development Board. II. U.S. Urban Renewal Administration.

711.3
N17t

A tale of five cities.
National Broadcasting Co.
   A tale of five cities; a photographic essay of life in the 1970's showing the quality of urban life. [New York, 1970?]
   12p.

   1. Metropolitan areas. 2. City growth. I. Title.

720.112
(79461)
B78

TALL BUILDINGS - SAN FRANCISCO.
Brugmann, Bruce, ed.
   The ultimate highrise: San Francisco's mad rush toward the sky, edited by Bruce Brugmann and Greggar Sletteland. San Francisco, San Francisco Bay Guardian Books, 1971.
   255p.

   1. Tall buildings - San Francisco. 2. Apartment houses - San Francisco. I. Sletteland, Greggar, jt. ed. II. Title.

711.4
(759881)
T15

Tallahassee, Fla. City Planning Board.
Tallahassee, Fla. Planning Department.
   A comprehensive plan for future development, Tallahassee, Florida. [Prepared for Tallahassee] City Planning Board. Tallahassee, 1963.
   4 pts.
   U.S. Urban Renewal Adm. UPAP.

   1. Master plan - Tallahassee, Fla. I. Tallahassee, Fla. City Planning Board. II. U.S. URA-UPAP. Tallahassee, Fla.

711.4
(759881)
T15

Tallahassee, Fla. Planning Department.
A comprehensive plan for future development, Tallahassee, Florida. [Prepared for Tallahassee] City Planning Board. Tallahassee, 1963.
4 pts.
U.S. Urban Renewal Adm. UPAP.

1. Master plan - Tallahassee, Fla.
I. Tallahassee, Fla. City Planning Board.
II. U.S. URA-UPAP. Tallahassee, Fla.

301.36
T15

Talmage, T DeWitt.
Evils of the cities; a series of practical and popular discourses delivered in the Brooklyn Tabernacle. Chicago, Rhodes & McClure, 1891.
397p.

1. Sociology, Urban. 2. Social conditions.

332
M651

TAMAGNA, FRANK M
MONETARY MANAGEMENT, [A SERIES OF RESEARCH STUDIES] PREPARED FOR THE COMMISSION ON MONEY AND CREDIT. [BY] FRANK M. TAMAGNA [AND OTHERS] ENGLEWOOD CLIFFS, N.J., PRENTICE HALL [1963]
472P.

1. FINANCE. I. TAMAGNA, FRANK M.
II. COMMISSION ON MONEY AND CREDIT.

693.5
T15

TALLAMY (BERTRAM D.) ASSOCIATES, WASHINGTON, D.C.
EVALUATION OF METHODS OF REPLACEMENT OF DETERIORATED CONCRETE IN STRUCTURES. WASHINGTON, HIGHWAY RESEARCH BOARD OF THE DIVISION OF ENGINEERING AND INDUSTRIAL RESEARCH, NATIONAL ACADEMY OF SCIENCES-NATIONAL RESEARCH COUNCIL, 1964.
56P. (NATIONAL COOPERATIVE HIGHWAY RESEARCH PROGRAM. REPORT 1)

NAS-NRC PUBLICATION 1200.
BIBLIOGRAPHY: P.52-53.

(CONTINUED ON NEXT CARD)

711.585
(77311)
T15

Talman Federal Savings and Loan Association.
Talmanac visits a neighbor, Hyde Park-Kenwood, by Emil J. Seliga. Chicago, 1960?
30p. illus.

1. Neighborhood rehabilitation - Chicago. 2. Hyde Park Kenwood area. I. Seliga, Emil J.

VF
711.4
F67
Illus.

Tamburi, Orfeo, illus.
Fortune.
The streets of the city, illustrated by Orfeo Tamburi. Clipping from Fortune. Sept. 1957, p. 127-134.

1. Streets. 2. Architecture, Domestic.
I. Tamburi, Orfeo, illus.

693.5
T15

TALLAMY (BERTRAM D.) ASSOCIATES, WASHINGTON, D.C. EVALUATION OF METHODS ...1964. (CARD 2)

1. CONCRETE CONSTRUCTION.
2. HIGHWAYS. 3. BRIDGES. I. NATIONAL COOPERATIVE HIGHWAY RESEARCH PROGRAM. II. TITLE: DETERIORATED CONCRETE IN STRUCTURES.

728.1
:336.18
(7471)
N28m

Talmas, David, jt. au.
New York (City) Housing and Redevelopment Board. (Planning and Program Research Division)
Mitchell-Lama housing; rents, room counts and development costs. Prepared by Louis Winnick and David Talmas. New York, 1961.
11p. (Its Report no. 3)

1. State aided housing programs - New York (City) 2. Public housing projects.
I. Winnick, Louis. II. Talmas, David, jt. au.
III. Title. (Series)

711.3
A52f

Tamiment Institute.
American Academy of Arts and Sciences.
The future metropolis. Middletown, Conn., Wesleyan Univ. Press, 1960.
216p. see also 711.3 F62
In cooperation with Tamiment Institute.
Daedalus, Journal of the American Academy of Arts and Sciences, Winter 1961.
Issued as vol. 90, no. 1 of the Proceedings of the American Academy of Arts and Sciences.
Guest editors: Lloyd Rodwin and Kevin Lynch.
Contents:-A world of cities, by Kevin Lynch and Lloyd Rodwin.- The social system, by Oscar Handlin.- the economics and finances

(Continued on next card)

1024

TALLAPOOSA, GA. PLANNING COMMISSION.
TALLAPOOSA CENTRAL BUSINESS DISTRICT STUDY. BY COOSA VALLEY AREA PLANNING AND DEVELOPMENT COMMISSION. ROME, GA., 1970.
48L. (HUD 701 REPORT)

1. BUSINESS DISTRICTS - TALLAPOOSA, GA.
I. COOSA VALLEY AREA PLANNING AND DEVELOPMENT COMMISSION. II. HUD. 701.
TALLAPOOSA, GA.

728.1
:336.18
(7471)
N28oc
no.7

Talmas, David.
New York (City) Housing and Redevelopment Board. (Bureau of Planning and Program Research)
Time series analysis of project development costs of the Mitchell-Lama Program. Prepared by David Talmas. New York, 1963.
5p. (Its Occasional memo no. 7)
1. Public housing - New York (City)
2. Public housing projects. 3. State aided housing programs - New York (City) I. Talmas, David. II. Title.

711.3
A52f

American Academy of Arts and Sciences.
The future metropolis...1960. (Card 2)

of the large metropolis, by Raymond Vernon.-The influence of technology on urban forms, by Asron Fleisher.-The political implications of metropolitan growth, by Edward C. Banfield.-The pattern of the metropolis, by Kevin Lynch.-On social communication and the metropolis, by Karl W. Deutsch.-The changing uses of the city, by John Dyckman.-Metropolitan policy for developing areas, by Lloyd Rodwin.-Notes on expression and communication in the

(Continued on next card)

VF
728.1
:362.6
H681h

Talle, Henry O
U.S. Housing and Home Finance Agency.
The Housing and Home Finance Agency and its role in the field of housing for the aged, submitted by Henry O. Talle, Assistant Administrator to the Subcommittee on Problems of the Aged and the Aging, Senate Committee on Labor and Public Welfare, July 30, 1959. [Washington] 1959.
27p. tables.

see also 362.6 C65f; VF 728.1:362.6 H681t.
1. Housing for the aged. I. Talle, Henry O.

690.015
(485)
S82
R56
1968

Talme, Oskar A
Clay sensitivity and chemical stabilization. Stockholm, Statens Institut för Byggnads-forskning, 1968.
192p. (Stockholm. Statens Institut för Byggnadsforskning. Rapport 56:1968)
Bibliography: p. 187-192.
1. Building research - Sweden. 2. Sweden - Building research. 3. Clay. I. Title.
II. Stockholm. Statens Institut för Byggnadsforskning.

711.3
A52f

American Academy of Arts and Sciences.
The future metropolis...1960. (Card 3)

cityscape, by George Kepes.-The American intellectual versus the American city, by Morton and Lucia White.-Utopian traditions and the planning of cities, by Martin Meyerson.
Also published as The future metropolis, edited by Lloyd Rodwin. New York, George Braziler, 1961. 263p.
1. Metropolitan areas. 2. City planning.
3. City growth. I. Daedalus. II. Title.
III. Tamiment Institute. IV. Rodwin, Lloyd, ed. V. Lynch, Kevin, ed.

VF
728.1
:362.6
H681t

Talle, Henry O
U.S. Housing and Home Finance Agency.
Testimony of Henry O. Talle, Assistant Administrator, Housing and Home Finance Agency before the Subcommittee on Problems of the Aged and Aging, Senate Committee on Labor and Public Welfare, July 30, 1959. [Washington] 1959.
4p.

see also 362.6 C65f; VF 728.1:362.6 H681h.
1. Housing for the aged. I. Talle, Henry O.

690.015
(485)
B82
R46
1966

Talme, Oskar A
Secondary changes in the strength of clay layers and the origin of sensitive clays, by Oskar A. Talme and others. Stockholm, 1966.
138p. (Sweden. Statens Kommitté för Byggnadsforskning. Rapport 46:1966)
Bibliography: p. 135-138.

1. Building research - Sweden. 2. Soils.
3. Clay.

711.4
E52t

Taming megalopolis, ed.
Eldredge, Hanford Wentworth.
Taming megalopolis. Vol. 1. What it is and what could be. Vol. 2. How to manage an urbanized world. Garden City, N.J., Doubleday, 1967.
2v. (Anchor books)
Partial contents: the contributions of political science to the study of urbanism, by Robert C. Wood Under Secretary of the Dept. of Housing and Urban Development. Vol. 1, ch. 5.
1. City planning. 2. Metropolitan area planning. 3. City planning as a profession.

(Cont'd on next card)

360
L42t

Tally's corner.
Liebow, Elliot.
Tally's corner; a study of Negro street-corner men. Foreword by Hylan Lewis. Boston, Little, Brown, 1967.
260p.
Bibliography: p.257-260.

1. Social conditions. 2. Negroes.
3. Family living requirements. 4. Family.
I. Title.

388
(77311)
T15

Talvitie, Antti Petri.
An econometric model for downtown work trips: Chicago, Chicago Area Transportation Study, 1971.
123p.

1. Transportation - Chicago. 2. Traffic surveys - Chicago. I. Chicago Area Transportation Study. II. Title.

711.4
E52t

Eldredge, Hanford Wentworth, ed. Taming megalopolis...1967. (Card 2)

4. New towns - Europe. 5. Urban renewal - Social effect. 6. Automation. 7. Housing.
8. Social welfare. I. Wood, Robert Coldwell. The contributions of political science to the study of urbanism. II. Title.

Tammirinne, M   jt. au.

624.131
K67
  Korhonen, K   H
    Maa - ja kalliopera rekennuspohjana pein-
talojen pohjatutkimukset. (Soil and bedrock
as foundation materials; site exploration for
small houses) by K. H. Korhonen and M. Tammirinne. Helsinki, State Institute for Technical
Research, 1967.
    149p. (Finland. State Institute for Techni-
cal Research. Tiedotus. Sarja 3 - Rakennus
(Building) 120)

    1. Soils. 2. Foundations (Building)
I. Finland. State Institute for Technical Research. II. Tammirinne, M., jt. au.

728.1
:336.18
(759651)
T15I
    TAMPA, FLA. HOUSING AUTHORITY.
      INFORMATION ABOUT PONCE DE LEON
COURTS. TAMPA, N.D.
    6P.

    1. PUBLIC HOUSING - TAMPA, FLA.

690.091.82
(759651)
T15
    TAMPA, FLA. ORDINANCES, ETC.
      COMPILED BUILDING CODE OF THE
CITY OF TAMPA, FLORIDA, 1962.
TAMPA, 1962.
    396P.

    1. BUILDING CODES - TAMPA, FLA.

624.131
T15
  Tammirinne, M
    Kitkamaalajien rakenne ja kokoonpuristuvuus
(The structure and compression of
cohesionless soils) Helsinki, State
Institute for Technical Research, 1969.
    128p. (Finland. State Institute for
Technical Research. Tiedotus. Sarja 3-
Rakennus 136)
    English summary.
    Bibliography: p. 125-218.
    1. Soils. I. Finland. State Institute
for Technical   Research. II. Title:
the structure   and compression of
cohensionless   soils.

690.091.82
(759651)
T15G
    TAMPA, FLA. ORDINANCES, ETC.
      GAS CODE, 1964. CHAPTER 17 OF
THE CITY OF TAMPA CODE - GAS
FITTERS, PIPING AND APPLICANCES.
TAMPA, FLA., 1964.
    58P.

    1. BUILDING CODES - TAMPA, FLA.
I. TITLE: GAS CODE.

624.131
T15t
  Tammirinne, Markku.
    Tiiveyden vaikutus kitkamaalajien Lujuusomin-
aisuuksiin (Effect of density on the strength
properties of cohesionless soils) Helsinki,
State Institute for Technical Resaearch, 1970.
    48p. (Finland. State Institute for Technical
Research. Tiedotus. Sarja 3 - Rakennus 144)

    English summary.
    Bibliography: p. 46-48.
    1. Soils. I. Finland. State Institute for
Technical Research. II. Title: Effect of
density on the   strength properties of
cohesionless soils.

728.1
:336.18
(759651)
T15R
    TAMPA, FLA. HOUSING AUTHORITY.
      REPORT, 1940-66
TAMPA.
    17 V. ANNUAL.

    SOME REPORTS HAVE INDIVIDUAL TITLES.

    1. PUBLIC HOUSING - TAMPA, FLA.

[handwritten marginal notes: 1940, 1941, 1943/44, 1944/45-66, 1945/46, 1946/47, 1948/49, 1951/52-66, 1952/53-66, 1953/54, 1956/57-66, 1957/58, 1958/59, 1965/66]

690.091.82
(759651)
T15M
    TAMPA, FLA. ORDINANCES, ETC.
      MECHANICAL CODE. CHAPTER 13A OF
THE CITY OF TAMPA CODE. TAMPA,
FLA., 1966.
    1 V.

    1. BUILDING CODES - TAMPA, FLA.
I. TITLE.

690.21
T15
  Tammirinne, Markku.
    Silttimaalajille perustetun rakennuksen
painuminen (Settlement of a building founded
on silty soil) Helsinki, State Institute for
Technical Research, 1970.
    45p. (Finland. State Institute for Techni-
cal Research. Tiedotus. Sarja 3 - Rakennus
145)
    English summary.
    Bibliography: p. 44-45.
    1. Foundations (Building) 2. Soils.
I. Finland. State Institute for Technical
Research. II. Title: Settlement of a
building founded   on silty soil.

728.1
:308
(759651)
T15
    TAMPA, FLA. HOUSING AUTHORITY.
      REPORT OF REAL PROPERTY SURVEY AND
LOW INCOME HOUSING AREA SURVEY,
TAMPA, FLORIDA. WORK PROJECTS
ADMINISTRATION. SPONSORED BY CITY OF
TAMPA, FLORIDA AND THE HOUSING
AUTHORITY OF THE CITY OF TAMPA,
FLORIDA. TAMPA, CITY PLANNING AND
ZONING COMMISSION, 1940.
    58P.
    1. HOUSING SURVEYS - TAMPA, FLA.
I. TITLE: REAL PROPERTY SURVEY.
II. TITLE: LOW INCOME HOUSING
AREA SURVEY.

690.091.82
:613.5
(759651)
T15
    TAMPA, FLA. ORDINANCES, ETC.
      MINIMUM HOUSING STANDARDS CODE.
AMENDED THROUGH 1963. TAMPA, FLA.,
1963.
    1 P.

    1. HOUSING CODES - TAMPA, FLA.

Tampa, Fla.

VF
Housing-U.S.-Fla.

696.1
:690.091.82
(759651)
T15
    TAMPA, FLA. ORDINANCES, ETC.
      PLUMBING CODE. CHAPTER 27 OF
THE CITY OF TAMPA CODE. TAMPA,
FLA., 1963.
    127P.

    1. PLUMBING CODES - TAMPA, FLA.

711.585.1
(759651)
T15t
  Tampa, Fla. City Demonstration Agency.
    Tampa Model Cities Program. Citizens
statement. Tampa, [1969?]
    1v.
    U.S. Dept. of Housing and Urban
Development. Model Cities Program.

    1. Model cities - Tampa, Fla.
I. U.S. HUD-Model Cities Program.

711.585.1
(759651)
T15
  Tampa, Fla. Office of the Mayor.
    Application to the Department of Housing
and Urban Development for a grant to plan a
comprehensive city demonstration program.
Tampa, Fla., 1967.
    1v.
    Selected to receive the first HUD Model
Cities Program planning grants.

    1. Model cities - Tampa, Fla. I. U.S. HUD
Model Cities Program first planning grants.

516
    TAMPA BAY, FLA. REGIONAL PLANNING COUNCIL.
      HOUSING AND THE ENVIRONMENT: A REGIONAL
PROSPECTIVE. ST. PETERSBURG, FLA., 1970.
78P. (HUD 701 REPORT)

    1. HOUSING - TAMPA BAY, FLA. I. HUD.
701. TAMPA BAY, FLA.

728.1
:336.18
(759651)
T15
    TAMPA, FLA. HOUSING AUTHORITY.
      GOOD AND BAD HOUSING; A REPORT OF
RECENT SURVEYS OF THE HOUSING
AUTHORITY OF THE CITY OF TAMPA.
TAMPA, 1951.
    17P.

    1. PUBLIC HOUSING - TAMPA, FLA.

621.18
T15
    TAMPA, FLA. ORDINANCES, ETC.
      BOILER CODE. CHAPTER 8 OF THE CITY
OF TAMPA CODE. TAMPA, FLA., 1964.
    27, 12P.

    1. BOILERS - STANDARDS AND
SPECIFICATIONS. 2. AIR POLLUTION.

513
    TAMPA BAY, FLA. REGIONAL PLANNING COUNCIL.
      MASS TRANSIT CONCEPTS OF THE TAMPA BAY
REGION. ST. PETERSBURG, FLA., 1970.
76P. (HUD 701 REPORT)

    1. TRANSPORTATION - TAMPA BAY, FLA.
I. HUD. 701. TAMPA BAY, FLA.

514

TAMPA BAY, FLA. REGIONAL PLANNING COUNCIL.
MASS TRANSIT IN THE TAMPA BAY REGION,
SUMMARY REPORT. ST. PETERSBURG, FLA.,
1970.
9P. (HUD 701 REPORT)

1. TRANSPORTATION - TAMPA BAY, FLA.
I. HUD. 701. TAMPA BAY, FLA.

515

TAMPA BAY, FLA. REGIONAL PLANNING COUNCIL.
URBAN MANPOWER; A STUDY OF THE TAMPA
BAY REGION. ST. PETERSBURG, FLA., 1969.
112P. (HUD 701 REPORT)

1. LABOR SUPPLY - TAMPA BAY, FLA.
I. HUD. 701. TAMPA BAY, FLA.

Tanganyika

see also

Tanzania

(The United Republic of Tanzania formed Oct. 29, 1964,
by combination of Tanganyika and Zanzibar.)

388
(759651)
T15

Tampa Bay Regional Planning Council.
Mass transit in the Tampa Bay region;
summary report. St. Petersburg, Fla., [1970]
folder.
U.S. Dept. of Housing and Urban Development. UPAP.

1. Transportation - Tampa, Fla. 2. Journey
to work. I. Title. II. U.S. HUD-UPAP.
Tampa, Fla.

517

TAMPA BAY, FLA. REGIONAL PLANNING COUNCIL.
WATER RESOURCES IN THE TAMPA BAY REGION,
BY BRILEY, WILD AND ASSOCIATES. ST.
PETERSBURG, FLA., 1970.
193P. (HUD 701 REPORT)

1. WATER RESOURCES - TAMPA BAY, FLA.
I. BRILEY, WILD AND ASSOCIATES. II. HUD.
701. TAMPA BAY, FLA.

330
(678)
T15

Tanganyika.
Tanganyika; five-year plan for economic
and social development, July 64 - Je 69

Dar-Es-Salaam, Government Printer,
v.
Contents:
vol. 2. The Programmes.
1. Economic development - Tanganyika. 2. Social
conditions - Tanganyika. 3. Economic development -
Zanzibar. 4. Social   conditions -
Zanzibar.

519

TAMPA BAY, FLA. REGIONAL PLANNING COUNCIL.
PUBLIC FORUMS IN THE TAMPA BAY REGION.
ST. PETERSBURG, FLA., 1970.
22P. (HUD 701 REPORT)

1. PLANNING - CITIZEN PARTICIPATION.
I. HUD. 701. TAMPA BAY, FLA.

614
(798
1083,41)
A17T

TANANA HOSPITAL SERVICE UNIT.
U.S. ARCTIC HEALTH RESEARCH CENTER,
ANCHORAGE, ALASKA.
TANANA HOSPITAL SERVICE UNIT;
BASELINE AND SERVICE STATISTICS.
ANCHORAGE, ALASKA, ARCTIC HEALTH
CENTER, 1958.
1 V.

1. HEALTH - ALASKA - STATISTICS.
2. HOSPITALS - TANANA, ALASKA.
I TITLE.

967.8
U54
1948

Tanganyika.
United Nations. (Trusteeship Council.)
United Nations Visiting Mission to East Africa
report on Tanganyika and related documents.
Lake Success, New York [1948]
315 p.   tables.   (T/218 & T/218/Add.1,
T/333, T/376, 13 Nov. 1948)
Trusteeship Council Official records Fourth
session, suppl. no. 3
French and English.
1. Tanganyika.

711.4
(759651)
T15

Tampa Bay (Fla.) Regional Planning Council.
Report, 1969.

Tampa, 1970-

v. annual.

For Library holdings see main entry.

1. City planning - Tampa Bay Region.

378
T15

Tanck, James.
College volunteers; a guide to action:
helping students to help others. Wash.,
National Program for Voluntary Action, 1969.
73p.

1. Universities and colleges. 2.
Social service. I. National Program for
Voluntary Action. II. Title.

720
(52)
T15

Tange, Kenzo.
Architecture and urban design, 1946-1969.
Edited by Udo Kultermann. New York, Praeger,
1970.
304p.

Bibliography: p. 302-303.

1. Architecture - Japan. I. Kultermann, Udo,
ed.

6299

TAMPA BAY REGIONAL PLANNING COUNCIL.
STUDY DESIGN; A STRATEGY FOR THE TAMPA
BAY REGION. TAMPA, FLA., 1969.
FOLDER. (HUD 701 REPORT)

1. PLANNING - TAMPA BAY, FLA. I. HUD.
701. TAMPA BAY, FLA.

712
T15

TANDY, CLIFFORD R   V   , ED.
LANDSCAPE AND HUMAN LIFE; THE IMPACT OF
LANDSCAPE ARCHITECTURE UPON HUMAN
ACTIVITIES. AMSTERDAM, DJAMBATAN, 1966.
132P.

RECORD OF THE 9TH CONGRESS OF THE
INTERNATIONAL FEDERATION OF LANDSCAPE
ARCHITECTS HELD IN JAPAN IN 1964.

1. LANDSCAPE ARCHITECTURE.
2. LANDSCAPE ARCHITECTURE - JAPAN.
3. MAN - INFLUENC E OF ENVIRONMENT.
I. CONGRESS OF TH E INTERNATIONAL
(CONTINUED ON NEXT CARD)

920
t720
B69

TANGE, KENZO, 1913-
BOYD, ROBIN.
KENZO TANGE. NEW YORK, G. BRAZILLER,
1962.
125P. (MAKERS OF CONTEMPORARY
ARCHITECTURE)

CREATION IN PRESENT-DAY ARCHITECTURE
AND THE JAPANESE TRADITION BY KENZO
TANGE. REPRINTED IN ABRIDGED FORM FROM
THE MAGAZINE SHINKENCHIKU (THE JAPAN
ARCHITECT) JUNE 1956 : P. 113-117.

1. ARCHITECTS.
2. TANGE, KENZO , 1913-. I. TITLE.

511

TAMPA BAY, FLA. REGIONAL PLANNING COUNCIL.
TAMPA BAY MASS TRANSIT; PLANNING FOR
TOMORROW. ST. PETERSBURG, FLA., 1970.
106P. (HUD 701 REPORT)

1. TRANSPORTATION - TAMPA BAY, FLA.
I. HUD. 701. TAMPA BAY, FLA.

712
T15

TANDY, CLIFFORD R   V   , ED.
LANDSCAPE AND ...1966.   (CARD 2)

FEDERATION OF LANDSCAPE ARCHITECTS, TOKYO,
1964. II. TITLE.

351.81
C15
NO.43

TANGENTIAL OFF-RAMPS ON FREEWAYS.
CALIFORNIA. UNIVERSITY AT
LOS ANGELES. INSTITUTE OF
TRANSPORTATION AND TRAFFIC
ENGINEERING.
TANGENTIAL OFF-RAMPS ON FREEWAYS;
FINAL REPORT, BY SLADE HULBERT. LOS
ANGELES, CALIF., INSTITUTE OF
TRANSPORTATION AND TRAFFIC ENGINEERING,
DEPARTMENT OF ENGINEERING, DECEMBER,
1965.
8P. ILLUS. (ITS RESEARCH REPORT 43)
1. TRAFFIC REGULATIONS. 2. TRAFFIC
SAFETY. I. TITLE. II. HULBERT,
SLADE.

512

TAMPA BAY, FLA. REGIONAL PLANNING COUNCIL.
TAMPA BAY MASS TRANSIT; PLANNING FOR
TOMORROW; SUMMARY REPORT. ST. PETERSBURG,
FLA., 1970.
25P. (HUD 701 REPORT)

1. TRANSPORTATION - TAMPA BAY, FLA.
I. HUD. 701. TAMPA BAY, FLA.

691.110.15
T15

Tang, Walter K
Effect of inorganic salts on pyrolysis of
wood, cellulose, and lignin determined by
differential thermal analysis, by Walter K.
Tang and Herbert W. Eickner. Madison, Wis.,
U.S. Dept. of Agriculture, Forest Service,
Forest Products Laboratory, 1967.
30p. (U.S. Forest Service Research paper
FPL 82)
1. Wood - Research. 2. Building materials.
I. Eickner, Herbert W., jt. au. II. U.S.
Forest Products Laboratory, Madison, Wis.
III. Title.

301.15
T15

Tangum, Richard Roland.
A conceptual information system for
environmental analysis. Blacksburg, Va.,
Virginia Polytechnic Institute, 1969.
79p.
Thesis (Master of Architecture in
Environmental Systems) - Virginia
Polytechnic Institute.

Bibliography: p. 75-79.

1. Man - Influence of environment.
2. City   planning. I. Virginia
(Cont'd on next card)

301.15
T15 Tangum, Richard Roland. A conceptual...
  1969.   (Card 2)

  Polytechnic Institute, Blacksburg.
  II. Title: Environmental analysis.
  III. Title.

VF
325
(7471) Tannenbaum, Dora.
T15   The Puerto Rican migration; a report by
  Dora Tannenbaum, Sara McCaulley and H. Daniel
  Carpenter. [New York] Hudson Guild Neighborhood House, Colony House and The Grand Street
  Settlement, 1955.
  13 p. illus.

  1.Minority groups - New York, N. Y. 2.Population
  shifts. I.Hudson Guild Neighborhood House. II.
  Title.

Tanzania
 see also
Tanganyika; Zanzibar

  (The United Republic of Tanzania formed Oct. 29, 1964,
  by combination of Tanganyika and Zanzibar.)

711.3
(742) TANI, SULI J
N28G NEW HAMPSHIRE. STATE PLANNING AND
  DEVELOPMENT COMMISSION.
  THE GREAT BAY PLAN; A REPORT TO THE
  1945 LEGISLATURE BY THE NEW HAMPSHIRE
  STATE PLANNING AND DEVELOPMENT
  COMMISSION. PREPARED UNDER THE
  SUPERVISION OF THORSTEN V. KALIJARVI,
  BY ARNOLD PERRETON, SULI J. TANI AND
  THE COMMISSION'S STAFF. CONCORD, 1945.
  59P.

  1. REGIONAL PLANNING - NEW HAMPSHIRE.
  I. PERRETON, ARNOLD. II. TANI, SULI
  J. III. TITLE.

341.1
:338 Tannenwald, Theodore, Jr.
T15 The new foreign aid legislation. In
  U.S. Dept. of State News letter, no. 6,
  October 1961. p. 3-4.

  1. Technical assistance programs.
  2. Economic development.

332.72
(60) Tanzania. Ministry of Commerce and
A37r Cooperatives.
1967 African Conference on the Mobilization of
  Local Savings. 5th, University College, Dar
  es Salaam, Tanzania, 1967.
  Report. Sponsored by the Ministry of
  Commerce and Cooperation of the Republic of
  Tanzania and the World Extension Dept. CUNA
  International inc. Madison, Wis., CUNA
  International, 1967.
  178p.
  1. Savings and loan associations - Africa.
  I. Tanzania. Ministry of Commerce and
  Cooperatives. II. CUNA International.

711.14
(969) Tanimura, Clinton T
H18 Hawaii. University. Legislative Reference
  Bureau.
  A study of large land owners in Hawaii,
  by Clinton T. Tanimura and Robert M. Kamins.
  Honolulu, 1957.
  28 p. maps, tables. (Its Report no. 2)

  1.Land use - Hawaii. I.Tanimura, Clinton T
  II.Kamins, Robert M III.Title: Land owners in
  Hawaii.

691.32
N67 Tanner, James T
  North Carolina. State College. Dept. of
  Engineering Research.
  The use of fly ash as a pozzolan in dense
  and light-weight concrete, by James T.
  Tanner and Wilfred M. Kenan. Raleigh, N. C.,
  1958.
  26p. illus., tables. (Its Bulletin no. 69)

  1. Building materials. 2. Concrete construction. I. Tanner, James T II. Kenan,
  Wilfred M

330
(678) Tanzania. Ministry of Economic Affairs
T15p and Development.
  The people's plan for progress; a
  popular version of the second Five Year
  Plan for economic and social development,
  1969-1974. Dar es Salaam, Ministry of
  Economic Affairs and Development Planning,
  1969.
  64p.
  1. Economic planning - Tanzania.
  I. Title.

697.4
S54t Tank type heaters;
  Smith (A.O.) Corp.
  Tank type heaters; installation data.
  Kankee, Ill., 1968.
  12p.

  1. Heating, Hot water. I. Title.

LAW
T
T155G TANNEY, JOSEPH P
  GOVERNMENT CONTRACT LAW AND
  ADMINISTRATION. CHICAGO, CALLAGHAN,
  1930.
  234P.

  1. FEDERAL CONTRACTS. I. TITLE.

711
(678) Tanzania. Ministry of Lands, Housing and
T15 Urban Development.
  Second five year plan pamphlet. Dar
  es Salaam, 1969.
  16p.

  1. Planning - Tanzania. I. Title.

370
E28pro Tankard, George G., Jr., jt. au.
  U.S. Office of Education.
  Property accounting for local and state
  school systems. Compiled in the Office of
  Education by Paul L. Reason and George G.
  Tankard, Jr. Wash. 1966.
  194p. (Its State educational records and
  reports series: handbook III. Bulletin no.
  22, 1959. OE-21019)

  1. School management and organization.
  2. Accounting. I. Reason, Paul L.
  II. Tankard, George G., Jr., jt. au.
  III. Title.

628.1
(752) Tennien, Francis Xavier, 1933-
T15 Water and sewer supply decisions: a case
  study of the Washington Suburban Sanitary
  Commission. Ann Arbor, Mich., University
  Microfilms, 1965.
  209p.

  Thesis. University of Virginia.

  1. Water-supply - Md. 2. Sewerage and
  sewage disposal - Md. I. Washington Suburban
  Sanitary Commission.
  II. Title.

VF
728.1
T15 Tanzer, Lester.
  The housing lobby. Its tactics point
  up growing sophistication of big pressure
  groups. Detached from the Wall Street
  Journal, Friday, April 3, 1959, p. 1, 16.

  1. Federal housing programs. I. Title.

370
E28pup Tankard, George G., Jr., jt. au.
  U.S. Office of Education.
  Pupil accounting for local and state
  school systems. Compiled in the Office
  of Education by John F. Putnam and George
  G. Tankard, Jr. [Wash.] 1964.
  133p. (Its State educational records and
  reports series: handbook V. Bulletin no.
  39, 1964. OE-23035)

  1. School management and organization.
  2. Accounting. I. Putnam, John F.
  II. Tankard, George G., Jr., jt. au.
  III. Title.

FF - International - Community development

DATE OF REQUEST 6/8/55 L. C. CARD NO.

AUTHOR Tannous, Afif I.

TITLE Assumptions and implications of community development
in underdeveloped countries, summary of remarks of
 assistant to administrator, technical assis-
SERIES Seminar at Chapel Hill, N.C.,   tance.
 Dec. 27-29, 1954.

EDITION PUB. DATE [1954] PAGING 11p.

PUBLISHER

RECOMMENDED BY   REVIEWED IN
   HHFA Catalog, 4/55, p.61.
  ORDER RECORD

4013
 TAOS, N.M. TOWN PLANNING COMMISSION.
 COMPREHENSIVE TOWN PLAN. TAOS, 1963.
 81P. (HUD 701 REPORT)

  1. CITY PLANNING - TAOS, N.M. I. HUD
 701. TAOS, N.M.

728.1
(5694) Tanne, David.
I77 Israel. Ministry of Labour. Housing Division.
  Housing in Israel. Extracts from an
  article by David Tanne for the "Economic
  Quarterly." [n.p.,] 1957]
  23p. tables.

  1.Housing - Israel. I.Tanne, David.

996.7
T15 Tansill, William Raymond, 1916 -
  Guam and its administration. Washington,
  Library of Congress, June 1951.
  140 p. (U.S. Library of Congress.
  Legislative Reference Service. Public affairs
  bulletin no. 95)

  Bibliographical footnotes.

  1.Guam. I.Series.

711.3
H24 Tapanainen, Veikko, jt. au.
  Heiskanen, Ossi.
  Uusjakotoimitusten rationalisoinnista
  (Uber die rationalisierung von flurbereinigungs-
  verfahren) [by] Ossi Heiskanen and Veikko
  Tapanainen. Helsinki, State Insitute for
  Technical Research, 1970.
  93p. (Finland. State Institute for Tech-
  nical Research. Tiedotus. Sarja 3 - Rakennus
  156)
  German summary.
  Bibliography: p. 67-68.
  1. Rural planning. I. Finland. State
  Institute for Technical Research.
  II. Tapanainen, Veikko, jt. au.

538.56
V47t
Tape preparation progress for marathon digital computer systems.
Visapaa, Asko.
Tape preparation programs for mathatron digital computer systems. Helsinki, State Institute for Technical Research, 1967.
123p. (Finland. State Institute for Technical Research. Julkaisu 120, publication)

1. Automation. I. Finland. State Institute for Technical Research. II. Title.

658.564
U54o
TAPES.
United States of America Standards Institute.
USA standard one-inch perforated paper tape for information interchange. Sponsor: Business Equipment Manufacturers Association. New York, 1967.
6p.
At head of title: USAS X3.18-1967.

1. Automation. 2. Tapes. I. Business Equipment Manufacturers Association. II. Title.

332.72
T16
TAPPER, CLARENCE A
REAL ESTATE FORECLOSURE PROCEDURE IN THE STATE OF INDIANA. HAMMOND, INDIANA. CALUMET FEDERAL SAVINGS AND LOAN, 1960?
31L.

THESIS PREPARED FOR THE GRADUATE SCHOOL OF SAVINGS AND LOAN, AMERICAN SAVINGS AND LOAN INSTITUTE, CHICAGO, ILL.
1. MORTGAGE FORECLOSURE - PROCEDURE. I. AMERICAN SAVINGS AND LOAN INSTITUTE. I. I. TITLE.

711.585
R22
Tape
Tape.
Reeves Soundcraft Corp.
Meeting of the U.R.A. Planned Conference, February 10, 1958. Side 1. U.R.A. Conference, Reel no. 2, date: February 10, 1958. Side 2, no. title and date. New York, [n.d.]
1 reel. (Soundcraft plus (50% extra playing time) magnetic recording tape. Type PL-18)
Mylar base. Dupont polyester film, one fourth inch x 1800 ft.

1. U.S. Urban Renewal Conference. Meeting. 1958-   2. Tapes

658.564
U54t
TAPES.
United States of America Standards Institute.
USA standard perforated tape code for information interchange. Sponsor: Business Equipment Manufacturers Association. New York, 1965.
7p.
At head of title: USAS X3.6-1965.

1. Automation. 2. Tapes. I. Business Equipment Manufacturers Association. II. Title.

691.71
A52
Tariff.
American Iron and Steel Institute.
The steel import problem. New York, 1967.
77p.

1. Steel. 2. Steel industry. 3. Tariff. I. Title.

920
T16
Taper, Bernard.
[Charles Abrams]; a lover of cities. [n.p.] 1967.
[24]p.

Detached from: The New Yorker, Feb. 4, 11, 1967.

1. Abrams, Charles. I. New Yorker. II. Title.

658.654
U54d
TAPES.
United States of America Standards Institute.
USA standard recorded magnetic tape for information interchange (800 CPI, MRZI) Sponsor: Business Equipment Manufacturers Association. New York, 1967.
16p.

1. Automation. 2. Tapes. I. Business Equipment Manufacturers Association. II. Title.

388
&538.56
B17
Annex
Tariff.
Battelle Memorial Institute.
Feasibility of computer storage and retrieval of freight tariff information - Phase I. Columbus, Ohio, 1966.
54p.
... ...Technical annex. 1966. 282p.

1. Transportation - Automation. 2. Tariff. I. U.S. Dept. of Commerce. II. Title.

333.33
(79461)
S15
TAPER, BERNARD.
SAN FRANCISCO. HOUSING AUTHORITY. 1939 REAL PROPERTY SURVEY, SAN FRANCISCO CALIF. A REPORT ON WORK PROJECTS ADMINISTRATION PROJECT 665-08-3-173. SAN FRANCISCO, 1940-41. 3 V.
For Library holdings see main entry
VOL. 3 IS A DIGEST OF THE REPORT BY BERNARD TAPER.

1. REAL PROPERTY - SAN FRANCISCO. 2. HOUSING - SAN FRANCISCO. I. TAPER, BERNARD.

658.564
U54a
TAPES.
United States of America Standards Institute.
USA standard take-up reels for one-inch perforated tape for information interchange. Sponsor: Business Equipment Manufacturers Association. New York, 1967.
12p.
At head of title: USAS X3.20-1967.

1. Automation. 2. Tapes. I. Business Equipment Manufacturers Association. II. Title.

381
C65n
Tariff.
Committee for Economic Development.
A new trade policy for the United States; a statement on national policy by the Research and Policy Committee of the Committee for Economic Development. [New York] 1962.
35p.

1. Commercial policy. 2. Tariff.

728.1
D28
Tape
TAPES.
Developments in moderate and low income housing, by Charles L. Edson and others. Casette 1 and 2. (Tapes) Stamford, Conn., Condyne, 1971.
tapes. (Casette 1 (01-008-1 and Casette 2 (01-008-2) (includes 2 scripts & 1 letter)
Condyne law-tapes licensed by the Practising Law Institute.
Contents casette 1: Overview of 1971 housing legislation by Charles L. Edson.- Taxes and Federally assisted housing, by Bruce S. Lane.- Accountant's role in Federally assisted
(Cont'd on next card)

744
(016)
C25
Tapes - Bibliography.
Center for the Study of Democratic Institutions.
Tapes: 176 tapes for broadcast and discussion, offered to radio stations, discussion groups, classrooms, etc. Santa Barbara, Calif., 1967.
36p.

1. Tapes - Bibl. 2. Visual aids. I. Title.

381
C65NE
TARIFF.
COMMITTEE FOR ECONOMIC DEVELOPMENT. A NEW TRADE POLICY FOR THE UNITED STATES. A STATEMENT ON NATIONAL POLICY BY THE RESEARCH AND POLICY COMMITTEE OF THE COMMITTEE FOR ECONOMIC DEVELOPMENT. NEW YORK, 1962.
48p.

1. COMMERCIAL POLICY. 2. TARIFF. I. TITLE.

728.1
D28
Tape
TAPES.
Developments in moderate and low income housing...1971.   (Card 2)

housing, by Frank J. Grey.-Casette 2. Sections 235 and 236, by Eugene J. Morris.- State housing problems, by Arthur Abba Goldberg.- Management of Federally assisted housing, by William R. Bruce.
1. Moderate-income housing - Tapes.- 2. Low income housing - Tapes. 3. Tapes. I. Condyne, Stamford, Conn. II. Practising Law Institute. III. Edson, Charles L.

R
728.1
:744
H68
1967
Tapes - Bibliography.
U.S. Dept. of Housing and Urban Development. Library.
Films, filmstrips, slides, and audio tapes on housing and community development; a selected bibliography. Rev. Wash., Govt. Print. Off., 1967.
38p.   (HUD MP-29)

1. Housing films. 2. Community development - Films.   3. Films - Bibl. 4. Tapes - Bibl.   5. Visual aids - Bibl. I. Title.

388
N17na
TARIFF.
National Motor Freight Traffic Association.
National motor freight classification; classes and rules applying on freight traffic covered by this classification as such tariffs may provide.
Wash., American Trucking Asso., 19-
v.
For Library holdings see main entry.
Supple-   ments.
(Cont'd on next card)

658.564
U54n
TAPES.
United States of America Standards Institute.
USA standard eleven-sixteenths inch perforated tape. Sponsor: Business Equipment Manufacturers Association. New York, 1967.
7p.
At head of title: X3.19-1967.

1. Automation. 2. Tapes. I. Business Equipment Manufacturers Association. II. Title.

744
(016)
C25
Tapes: 176 tapes for broadcast and discussion, offered to radio stations, discussion groups, classrooms, etc.
Center for the Study of Democratic Institutions.
Tapes: 176 tapes for broadcast and discussion, offered to radio stations, discussion groups, classrooms, etc. Santa Barbara, Calif., 1967.
36p.

1. Tapes - Bibl. 2. Visual aids. I. Title.

388
N17na
National Motor Freight Traffic Association.
National ..19-   (Card 2)

Wash. 19
v.

1. Transportation. 2. Tariff. I. American Trucking Association. II. Title.

336.2
T17   U.S. Tariff Commission.
    Report.

      Washington, Govt. Print. Off.,
        v.   annual.

      Report year ends June 30.
      Issued in the Congressional series as a
  House document.

      For complete information see shelf list.

        1. Tariff.

711.333
(75234)   Terrant, Julian.
T17   Comprehensive master plan, Queen Anne's
    County, Maryland, 1965. [Prepared for]
    County Planning and Zoning Commission,
    Centreville, Maryland. Richmond, 1965.
      73p.

      U.S. Urban Renewal Adm. UPAP.

      1. County planning - Queen Anne's Co.,
  Md. 2. Master plan - Queen Anne's Co.,
  Md.   I. Centreville, Md.
  County   Planning and Zoning
  Commission.   II. U.S. URA-UPAP.
  Queen Anne's   Co., Md.

711.14
(76178)   Tarrant City, Ala. City Planning Commission.
T17   Tarrant City, Alabama: long range land use
    plan. [In cooperation with] Alabama State
    Planning and Industrial Development Board.
    Tarrant City, 1957.
      1v. diagrs., maps, tables.

      U.S. Urban Renewal Administration,
  Urban Planning Assistance Program.

      1. Land use - Tarrant City, Ala. I. U.S.
  URA-UPAP. Tarrant City, Ala.

336.2
T17   U.S. Tariff Commission.
    Report.

      Washington, Govt. Print. Off.,
        v.   annual.

      Report year ends June 30.
      Issued in the Congressional series as a
  House document.

      For complete information see shelf list.

        1. Tariff.

711.552
(756561)   Tarrant, Julian.
T17   A downtown development plan, Durham,
  North Carolina. A final report to the
  Downtown Association and the Durham City
  Council. Richmond, 1960.
      39p.

      1. Business districts - Durham, N.C.
  I. Durham, N.C. City Council.

711.74
(76178)   Tarrant City, Ala. City Planning Commis-
T17   sion.
      Tarrant City, Alabama: major street plan.
    [In cooperation with] Alabama State Planning
    and Industrial Development Board. Tarrant
    City, 1959.
      24p. maps, tables.

      U.S. Urban Renewal Administration, Urban Planning
  Assistance Program.

      1. Street planning - Tarrant City, Ala. I. U.S.
  URA-UPAP. Tarrant   City, Ala.

691:110.15
F67SU   TARKOW, HAROLD.
    U.S. FOREST PRODUCTS LABORATORY,
    MADISON, WIS.
      SURFACE CHARACTERISTICS OF WOOD
    AS THEY AFFECT DURABILITY OF
    FINISHES, BY HAROLD TARKOW AND
    OTHERS. MADISON, WIS., 1966.
      60P. (U.S. FOREST SERVICE FPL
    RESEARCH PAPER NO. 57)

      BIBLIOGRAPHY: P.59-60.

      1. WOOD - RESEARCH. 2. WOOD
  PRESERVATION. I. TARKOW,
  HAROLD.   II. TITLE.

711.4
(755786)
T17   Tarrant, Julian.
      Master plan of recreation areas and facilities
  Radford, Va.; a report to the City Planning
  Commission. [Richmond, Va.] 1956.
      27 p. plans, tables.

  1.Master plan - Radford, Va.
  2.Recreation - Radford, Va. I.Radford, Va.
  City Planning Commission.

351.712
(76178)   Tarrant City, Ala. City Planning Commis-
T17   sion.
      Tarrant City, Alabama: public works pro-
    gram. [In cooperation with] Alabama State
    Planning and Industrial Development Board.
    Tarrant City, 1959.
      19p. illus., maps, tables.

  U.S. Urban Renewal Administration, Urban Planning
  Assistance Program.

      1. Public works - Tarrant City, Ala. I. U.S. URA-
  UPAP. Tarrant City,   Ala.

691.771
U54   TARLETON, R D   , JT. AU.
    U.K. DEPT. OF SCIENTIFIC AND
    INDUSTRIAL RESEARCH.
      EFFECT OF EMBEDDING ALUMINUM AND
    ALUMINUM ALLOYS IN BUILDING MATERIALS,
    BY F.E. JONES AND R.D. TARLETON.
    LONDON, H.M. STAT. OFF., 1963.
      62P. (ITS NATIONAL BUILDING
    STUDIES, RESEARCH PAPER NO. 36)

      1. ALUMINUM. I. JONES, F.E.
  II. TARLETON, R.D., JT. AU.

711.4
(75938)   Tarrant, Julian.
M41   Miami, Fla. City Planning and Zoning Board.
      The Miami long range plan. Miami, Fla.,
  Mar. 1955 -
      v.
  For complete information see shelflist card.
    Contents-pt.1. Proposed generalized land
  use plan.-pt. 2. Report on tentative plan
  for trafficways, prepared by Julian Tarrant,
  consultant.

      1.Master plan - Miami, Fla. 2.Highways -
  Miami, Fla. 3.Land use - Miami, Fla. I.
  Tarrant, Julian.

711.5
(76178:   Tarrant City, Ala. City Planning Commission.
.:347)   Tarrant City, Alabama: zoning ordinance.
T17   [In cooperation with] Alabama State Planning
    and Industrial Development Board. Tarrant
    City, 1958.
      20p. map.
      U.S. Urban Renewal Adm. UPAP.

      1. Zoning legislation - Tarrant City, Ala.
  I. U.S. Urban Renewal Administration. Urban
  Planning Assistance Program. Tarrant City,
  Ala.

691.7   Tarleton, R   D
:620.19   Everett, L H
E82   Recognition of corrosion hazards to
  metals in building, by L. H. Everett and
  R. D. J. Tarleton. Garston, Eng., Building
  Research Station, Ministry of Technology,
  1967.
      [4] p. (U.K. Building Research Station
  current papers. Design series 62)
      Reprinted from British Corrosion Journal,
  1967, vol.2 (March) pp. 61-64.

N.c.1
Laf.c.2

      (Cont'd on next card)

711.4
(755294)
T17   Tarrant and Alten, Consulting City Planners,
2c.   Associated.
      Master plan report, no. 1-
  [Richmond, Va.], May 1954-
      v.
  For complete information see shelflist card.
  Prepared for the Falls Church, Va. City
  Planning Commission.
      Contents.-No. 1, Background for planning.

      No. 3, Transportation

  1.Master plan-Falls Church, Va. I.Falls Church, Va.
  City Planning Commission.

920
T17   Tarry, Ellen.
      The third door; the autobiography of an
  American Negro woman. New York, Guild Press,
  1966.
      374p.

C.; E.O.

      1. Tarry, Ellen. 2. Negroes. I. Title.

691.7   Everett, L H   Recognition of corrosion
:620.19   hazards to metals in building...(Card 2)
E82

      1. Corrosion. 2. Metal construction.
  I. Tarleton, R. D. J., jt. au. II. U.K.
  Building Research Station. III. Title.

352.6
(76178)   Tarrant City, Ala. City Planning Commis-
T17   sion.
      Tarrant City, Alabama: community facilities
    plan. Parks and playgrounds, schools, public
    buildings. [In cooperation with] Alabama
    State Planning and Industrial Development
    Board. Tarrant City, 1959.
      29p.

  U.S. Urban Renewal Administration, Urban Planning
  Assistance Program.
      1. Community facilities - Tarrant City, Ala. I.
  U.S. URA-UPAP. Tarrant City, Ala.

920
T17   TARRY, ELLEN.
    Tarry, Ellen.
      The third door; the autobiography of an
  American Negro woman. New York, Guild Press,
  1966.
      374p.

      1. Tarry, Ellen. 2. Negroes. I. Title.

690.591
E12   TARPLEY, DONALD GREENE, JT. AU.
    EBERLEIN, HAROLD DONALDSON.
      REMODELLING AND ADAPTING THE SMALL
    HOUSE, BY HAROLD DONALDSON EBERLEIN
    AND DONALD GREEN TARPLEY; WITH 127
    ILLUSTRATIONS AND PLANS.
    PHILADELPHIA, LIPPINCOTT, 1933.
      163P. (LIPPINCOTT'S HOME-MAKER
    SERIES)

      FIRST EDITION.
    1. HOUSES - MAINTENANCE AND
  MODERNIZATION. 2. ARCHITECTURE,
  DOMESTIC. I. TARPLEY, DONALD
  GREENE, JT. AU. II. TITLE.

711.4
(76178)   Tarrant City, Ala. City Planning Commission.
T17   Tarrant City, Alabama: land subdivision regu-
    lations and manual. [In cooperation with Alabama
    State Planning and Industrial Development Board]
    Tarrant City, 1957.
      29p. illus., diagrs., maps.
    U.S. Urban Renewal Administration, Urban
  Planning Assistance Program.

      1. City planning - Tarrant City, Ala. 2. Sub-
  division regulation - Tarrant City, Ala. I. Alabama. State Planning and Industrial Development
  Board. II. U.S.   Urban Renewal Administration.

VF
614   Tarshis, Barry.
T17   The cockroach, a new suspect in the
  spread of infectious hepatitis. [Baltimore]
  Williams and Wilkins Co., 1962.
      [7]p.
      Reprinted from American Journal of tropical
  medicine and hygiene. Vol. 11, no. 5, p. 705-
  711.

      1. Public health. I. Title.

312
045

Tarver, James D
Oklahoma State University of Agriculture and
Applied Science.
A component method of estimating and projecting state and subdivisional populations,
by James D. Tarver. Stillwater, Okla., 1959.
43p. tables. (Its Miscellaneous publication MP-54)

1. Population forecasting.   I. Tarver, James D.

S

Task, a magazine for architects and planners.
No.   Cambridge, Mass.
       v.   irregular.

For full information see periodical kardex file.

1. Architecture—Period. 2. Housing—Period.
3. City planning—Period.

728.1
H85h

U.S. Task Force on Housing the American
Family.
Humphrey, Hubert Horatio, 1911–
Housing the American family; a statement of
Vice President Hubert H. Humphrey. [Wash.]
Task Force on Housing the American Family,
[1968?]
6p.

1. Federal housing programs. I. U.S. Task
Force on Housing the American Family.
II. Title.

312
045IB

TARVER, JAMES D
OKLAHOMA. AGRICULTURAL EXPERIMENT
STATION.
IBM 650 PROGRAM INSTRUCTIONS FOR
ESTIMATING THE CURRENT POPULATION OF
SUBDIVISION OF THE UNITED STATES BY
BUREAU OF THE CENSUS: METHOD II AND THE
VITAL RATES METHOD, BY JAMES D. TARVER
AND JEANIE HILL. STILLWATER, OKLA.,
1960.
131P.
1. POPULATION FORECASTING.
2. AUTOMATION.   I. TARVER, JAMES D.
II. HILL, JEANIE E.   III. TITLE.

551
T17

U.S. Task Force on Earthquake Hazard Reduction.
In the interest of earthquake safety. Findings
and conclusions by members of the Task Force on
Earthquake Hazard Reduction, Office of Science
and Technology, Executive Office of the President.
Berkeley, Institute of Governmental Studies,
University of California, 1971.
22p.

1. Earthquakes. I. California. University.
Institute of Governmental Studies. II. Title.

728.1
T17h

U.S. Task Force on Housing   the American
Family.
Housing the American family; Housing Task
Force report to Vice President Hubert H.
Humphrey. [Wash., 1968?]
21p.

1. Low-income housing. 2. Middle-income
housing. I. Title.

312
0451

Tarver, James D
Oklahoma. Agricultural Experiment Station.
IBM 650 program instructions for making
state, county, and city population projections by the component method, by James D.
Tarver and Jeanie Hill. Stillwater, Okla.
1960.
40p. diagrs. (Processed series P-353)

1. Population forecasting. I. Tarver, James D.
II. Hill, Jeanie.

614
T17s

U.S. Task Force on Environmental Health
and Related Problems.
A strategy for a livable environment. A
report to the Secretary of Health, Education
and Welfare. Washington, For sale by the
Supt. of Documents, Govt. Print. Off., 1967.
90p.
Add. copy, AIP/Ewald notebooks (711.4 A52ne no.25
1. Public health. 2. Climate and health.
3. Air pollution. 4. Water pollution.
I. U.S. Dept. of Health, Education, and
Welfare. II. Title.

353
T17

U.S. Task Force on Planning Assistance.
A Federal planning assistance strategy;
recommendations to improve the management and
effectiveness of Federal planning assistance
programs. [Wash.] 1969.
65p.

For administrative use only.

1. Intergovernmental relations. I. Title.

312.1
(758)
T17

Tarver, James D
Migration in Georgia. Athens, Ga.,
University of Georgia, College of Agriculture
Experiment Stations, 1968.
62p. (Georgia. Agricultural Experiment
Station. Research report, 26)

1. Population shifts – Georgia. I. Georgia.
Agricultural Experiment Station. II. Title.

627.4
T17

U.S. Task Force on Federal Flood Control
Policy.
A unified national program for managing
flood losses. Communication from the President
of the United States transmitting a report by
the Task Force on Federal Flood Control Policy.
Wash., Govt. Print. Off., 1966.
47p.
Published in the Congressional series as 89th
Cong., 2d sess., House Document no 465.
Referred to the Committee on Public Works,
Aug. 10, 1966.
(Cont'd on next card)

301.15
T17

U.S. Task Force on Research Planning in
Environmental Health Service.
Man's health and the environment; some
research needs. Wash., 1970.
258p.

Bibliography: p. 241-243.

1. Man – Influence of environment. 2. Health.
I. Title.

312
(758)
T17

Tarver, James D
Population trends of Georgia towns and
cities, by James D. Tarver and others.
Athens, University of Georgia, College of
Agriculture Experiment Stations, 1969.
66p. (Georgia. Agriculture Experiment
Stations. Research report 43)
Bibliography: p. 40-42.
1. Population – Ga. I. Georgia.
Agriculture Experiment Stations. II. Title.

627.4
T17

U.S. Task Force on Federal Flood Control
Policy. A unified national program...1966.
(Card 2)

1. Flood control. 2. Flood insurance.
I. U.S. Congress. House. Committee on Public
Works.

331
T17

Task Force on State and Local Government Labor
Relations.
Report. Chicago, Public Personnel Association
on behalf of the 1967 Executive Committee of the
National Governors' Conference [1967]
101p.

Bibliography: p. 91-101.
— —— Supplement. Chicago. 1968-(70
Suppl.   For Library holdings see main entry.
1. Labor relations. 2. State government.
3. Local government. I. Public Personnel
Association. II. National Governors'
Conference. Executive Committee.

312
(766)
045

Tarver, James D
Oklahoma. Agricultural Experiment Station.
Projections of the population of Oklahoma
to 1970, by James D. Tarver. [Stillwater]
1960.
47p. (Its Bulletin B-545)

1. Population – Oklahoma. I. Tarver,
James D.

U.S. Task Force on Health.

see

U.S. Dept. of Health, Education, and
Welfare. Task Force on Health.

Task Force on Urban Education.

see

National Education Association. Task Force on
Urban Education.

691
T15

Tarzwell, C M
The resistance of construction materials to
penetration by rats, by C.M. Tarzwell and
others. Washington, U.S. Dept. of Health,
Education and Welfare, Public Health Service,
1953.
16p. (U.S. Public Health Service. Public
Health monograph no. 11. Public Health publication no. 277)

1. Building materials. 2. Rodents. I. U.S.
Public Health Service. II. Title.

U.S. Task Force on Historical and Comparative
Perspectives.

see

U.S. National Commission on the Causes and
Prevention of Violence. Task Force on Historical
and Comparative Perspectives.

LAW
P727cc

Task Force report: corrections.
U.S. President's Commission on Law Enforcement
and Administration of Justice.
Task Force report: corrections. Washington,
Govt. Print. Off., 1967.
222p.

1. Law enforcement. I. Title. II. Title:
Corrections.

LAW Task force report: crime and its impact.
T U.S. President's Commission on Law Enforcement
P727cr and Administration of Justice.
Task force report: crime and its impact, an
assessment. Washington, Govt. Print. Off., 1967.
220p.

1. Law enforcement. 2. Vandalism. I. Title.
II. Title: Crime and its impact.

LAW Task force report: the police.
T U.S. President's Commission on Law Enforcement
P727po and Administration of Justice.
Task force report: the police. Washington,
Govt. Print. Off., 1967.
239p.

1. Law enforcement. 2. Intergovernmental
relations. I. Title. II. Title: the police.

690.22 Tasker, H E
A87 Australia. Commonwealth Experimental
Building Station.
Rationalized traditional timber wall
framing, by C. P. Sorensen and H. E.
Tasker. Sidney, 1959.
26p. illus., tables. (Its Tech-
nical study no. 40)

1. Walls. 2. Wood construction. I. Sorensen, C. P.
II. Tasker, H. E.

LAW Task force report: drunkenness; annotations.
T U.S. President's Commission on Law Enforcement
P727d and Administration of Justice.
Task force report: drunkenness; annotations,
consultants' papers, and related materials.
Washington, Govt. Print. Off., 1967.
131p.

1. Law enforcement. 2. Public health. I. Title.
II. Title: Drunkenness.

---

658 Task Force reports on organization.
H68t U.S. Dept. of Housing and Urban Development.
Task Force reports on organization.
Washington, 1966.
4 v.
On spine: Organization Task Force reports.
Contents:-Bk.1 Metropolitan development.
Renewal and housing assistance.-Bk.2. Dept.
field structure. Metropolitan desks.- Bk.3.
General services. Financial management.
Audit consolidation.-Bk.4. Management analysis.
Personnel management. Employee development
program. Merit promotion program.-

(Cond't on next card)

VF
690.015
(94)
A87
D13
Tasker, H E
Report on simulated wind pressure tests
carried out on four full-size test walls.
Sydney, Australia, Commonwealth Experimental
Building Station, April 1947.
13 / 31 1. (Australia. Commonwealth
Experimental Building Station. Duplicated
document no. 13)

Processed.

1.Wind resistance.

LAW Task force report: juvenile delinquency and
T youth crime.
U.S. President's Commission on Law Enforcement
and Administration of Justice.
Task force report: juvenile delinquency and
youth crime. Report on juvenile justice and
consultants' papers. Washington, Govt. Print.
Off., 1967.
428p.

1. Law enforcement. 2. Juvenile delinquency.
3. Youth. I. Title. II. Title: Juvenile
delinquency and youth crime.

---

658 U.S. Dept. of Housing and Urban Development.
H68t Task Force report on organization. 1966.
(Card 2)

1. Management. 2. Personnel management.
3. U.S. Dept. of Housing and Urban Development - Reorganization. I. Title.

690.237 Tasker, H E
T17 Shear in flat-plate construction under
uniform loading, by H.E. Tasker and K.J.
Wyatt. Sydney, Commonwealth Experimental
Building Station, Dept. of Works, 1963.
31p. (Australia. Commonwealth Experimental Building Station. Special report
no. 23)

1. Loads. 2. Building construction.
I. Wyatt, K. I. Australia.
Commonwealth Experimental
Building Station.

LAW Task force report: narcotics and drug abuse.
T U.S. President's Commission on Law Enforcement
and Administration of Justice.
Task force report: narcotics and drug abuse;
annotations and consultants' papers. Washington,
Govt. Print. Off., 1967.
158p.

1. Law enforcement. 2. Municipal services.
I. Title. II. Title: Narcotics and drug abuse.

336.18 U.S. Task Group on Administrative Simplifica-
T17 tion of Planning Assistance Programs.
Federal assistance simplification; an interim
report by the Task Group on Administrative
Simplification of Planning Assistance Programs.
Prepared under the direction of the Federal
Assistance Review. [Wash.] 1970.
2C. 14p.

1. Grants-in-aid. I. Title. II. Title:
Planning assistance programs.

---

330 Tasks of monetary policy.
M14 Maisel, Sherman J
Tasks of monetary policy. Remarks of
Sherman J. Maisel, member, Board of
Governors of the Federal Reserve System,
at the 22nd annual Conference of the Finan-
cial Analysts Federation, St. Louis, Mo.,
May 12, 1969. [n.p.] 1969.
8p.

1. Economic policy. 2. Money.
I. Title.

LAW Task force report: organized crime, annotations.
T U.S. President's Commission on Law Enforcement
and Administration of Justice.
Task force report: organized crime; annotations
and consultants' papers. Washington, Govt. Print.
Off., 1967.
126p.

1. Law enforcement. 2. Municipal services.
I. Title. II. Title: Organized crime.

341.1 The task of development.
:338 U.S. Agency for International Development.
A32t The task of development. Proposed program
fiscal year 1969. Wash., [1968?]
36p.

1. Technical assistance programs.
2. Economic development. I. Title.

---

658 Tasso, Charles A ., jt. au.
A52r Reichenbach, Robert R
no.92 Organizing for data processing, by Robert
R. Reichenbach and Charles A. Tasso. New
York, American Management Association,
1968.
159p. (American Management Association.
AMA research study 92)

1. Management. 2. Automation. I. Tasso,
Charles A., jt. au. II. American Management Association. III. Title.

LAW Task force report: science and technology.
T U.S. President's Commission on Law Enforcement
P727s and Administration of Justice.
Task force report: science and technology, by
the Institute for Defense Analyses, to the
President's Commission on Law Enforcement and
Administration of Justice. Wash., Govt. Print.
Off., 1967.
228p.
1. Law enforcement. 2. Science. I. Institute
for Defense Analyses. II. Title.

693.2 Tasker, H E
A87 Australia. Dept. of Works.
Cracking in brick and block masonry, by
C. P. Sorensen and H. E. Tasker. Sydney,
Dept. of Works, Commonwealth Experimental
Building Station, 1965.
53p. (It's Technical study no. 43)

1. Brick construction. I. Sorensen,
C. P. II. Tasker, H. E. III. Title.

621.397 Tate, Charles.
T17 Cable television in the cities; community
control, public access, and minority ownership. Wash., Urban Institute, 1971.
184p.

Bibliography: p. 180-184.

1. Television. I. Urban Institute.
II. Title.

LAW Task force report: the courts.
T U.S. President's Commission on Law Enforcement
P727co and Administration of Justice.
Task force report: the courts. Washington,
Govt. Print. Off., 1967.
178p.

1. Law enforcement. I. Title. II. Title: The
courts.

690.21 Tasker, H E
T17 Pier-and-beam footings for single-storey
domestic construction, by H.E. Tasker and
C.P. Sorensen. Sydney, Dept. of Works,
Commonwealth Experimental Building Station,
1962.
25p. (Australia. Commonwealth Experimental Building Station. Technical study no.
42)

1. Foundations (Building). I. Sorensen,
C.P., jt. au. II. Australia.
Commonwealth Experimental
Building Station.

339.3 TATE, JANET HANSEN, JT. AU.
876 BROWN, BONNAR.
INCOME TRENDS IN THE UNITED STATES
THROUGH 1975, BY BONNAR BROWN AND JANET
HANSEN TATE. MENLO PARK, CALIF.,
STANFORD RESEARCH INSTITUTE, 1957.
125P.

1. INCOME. I. TATE, JANET HANSEN, JT.
AU. II. TITLE. III. STANFORD RESEARCH
INSTITUTE.

728.1
T17C TATLOCK, MARY.
A CONSIDERATION OF CLIENT'S HOUSING IN
THE CHELSEA-LOWELL DISTRICT OF THE
CHARITY ORGANIZATION SOCIETY, BY MARY
TATLOCK AND OTHERS. CHELSEA, MASS.,
1935.
46L.

1. LOW INCOME HOUSING. 2. SOCIAL
CONDITIONS.

336
T18 TAUBENHAUS, LEON J
PERFORMANCE REPORTING AND PROGRAM
2c. BUDGETING: TOOLS FOR PROGRAM EVALUATION,
BY LEON J. TAUBENHAUS, ROBERT H. HAMLIN,
AND ROBERT C. WOOD. NEW YORK, AMERICAN
PUBLIC HEALTH ASSOCIATION, 1957.
P.432-438.

REPRINTED FROM AMERICAN JOURNAL OF
PUBLIC HEALTH, V. 47, NO. 4, APRIL 1957.
1. BUDGET. 2. PUBLIC HEALTH.
I. HAMLIN, ROBERT H. II. WOOD, ROBERT C.
III. AMERICAN JO URNAL OF PUBLIC HEALTH.
IV. TITLE.

691.421
T181 Tauber, E   Investigation of the
...1969.   (Card 2)

1. Clay. I. Hill, R.K., jt. au.
II. Australia. Commonwealth
Scientific and Industrial Research
Organization. Division of Building
Research. III. Title.

691.32
P670 TATMAN, PHIL J
PORTLAND CEMENT ASSOCIATION.
OUTDOOR CONCRETE EXPOSURE TEST PLOT
AT SKOKIE, BY PHIL J. TATMAN AND ROBERT
LANDGREN. SKOKIE, ILL., 1966.
30-41P. (ITS RESEARCH DEPT. BULLETIN
NO. 202)

REPRINTED FROM THE JOURNAL OF THE PCA
RESEARCH AND DEVELOPMENT LABORATORIES,
V. 8, NO. 2, MAY 1966.

1. CONCRETE. I. TATMAN, PHIL J.
II. LANDGREN, ROBERT. ~~III. TITLE~~

698
T18 Tauber, A
The production of ceramic colours from
baddeleyite from Phalaborwa, South Africa, by
A. Tauber and E.R. Schmidt. Pretoria, National
Building Research Institute, Council for
Scientific and Industrial Research, 1970.
8p. (National Building Research Institute
bulletin, 60; CSIR research report 291, pp. 1-8)
1. Paints and painting. 2. Color.
3. Natural resources - South Africa.
I. South African Council for Scientific and
Industrial Research. National Building
Research Institute. II. Schmidt, E.R., jt. au.
III. Title.

5450
TAUNTON, MASS. PLANNING BOARD.
A GENERAL DESIGN FOR COMPREHENSIVE
DEVELOPMENT OF THE MILL RIVER PARKWAY,
1966. BY COMMUNITY PLANNING SERVICES, A
DIVISION OF WHITMAN AND HOWARD. TAUNTON,
1966.
1 V. (HUD 701 REPORT)

1. TRANSPORTATION - TAUNTON, MASS.
I. WHITMAN AND HOWARD. COMMUNITY
PLANNING SERVICES. II. HUD. 701.
TAUNTON, MASS.

621.39
T18 Taub, Herbert.
Principles of communication systems, by
Herbert Taub and Donald L. Schilling.
New York, McGraw-Hill, 1971.
514p. (McGraw-Hill electrical and electronic
engineering series)

1. Communication systems. I. Schilling,
Donald L., jt. au. II. Title.

691.42
T18 Tauber, A
Surface colouring of bricks and other
structural clay products, by A. Tauber and E.
R. Schmidt. Pretoria, South African Council
for Scientific and Industrial Research,
National Building Research Institute, 1967.
[3]p. (C.S.I.R. reference no. R/Bou 238)
Reprinted from Claycraft and structural
ceramics, Dec., 1967.

1. Bricks. 2. Clay. I. Schmidt, E.R., jt.
au. II. Claycraft and structural ceramics.
III. Canada.   Dept. of Forestry and
Rural Development.   IV. Title.

658.564
T18 TAUBE, MORTIMER.
COMPUTERS AND COMMON SENSE; THE MYTH
OF THINKING MACHINES. NEW YORK,
COLUMBIA UNIVERSITY PRESS, 1963.
136P. (MCGRAW-HILL PAPER BACKS)

1. AUTOMATION. I. TITLE.
II. TITLE: THE MYTH OF THINKING
MACHINES.

668.3
T18 Tauber, E
Ceramic pattern and case-mould making with
epoxy resins. Melbourne, Australia, Commonwealth Scientific and Industrial Research
Organization, 1963.
[2]p. (Australia. Commonwealth Scientific
and Industrial Research Organization. Div. of
Building Research. D.B.R. reprint no. 248)

Reprinted from Australian National clay,
vol 4, no. 6, April 1963. p. 26-27.

(Cont'd. on next card)

5437
TAUNTON, MASS. PLANNING BOARD.
INDUSTRIAL PLANNING STUDY REPORT, 1966.
BY COMMUNITY PLANNING SERVICES, DIVISION
OF WHITMAN AND HOWARD, ENGINEERS.
TAUNTON, 1966.
117P. (HUD 701 REPORT)

1. INDUSTRIAL DEVELOPMENT - TAUNTON,
MASS. I. WHITMAN AND HOWARD. PLANNING
SERVICES. II. HUD. 701. TAUNTON, MASS.

VF
500.15
T18 Taube, Mortimer.
New tools for the control and use of research
materials. [Philadelphia, Pa., American
Philosophical Society, 1949]
248-252 p.

Preprinted from Proceedings of the American
Philosophical Society, v. 93, no. 3, June 1949.

1. Research. 2. Scientific research.

668.3
T18 Tauber, E   Ceramic pattern and case-
mould making...   (Card 2)

1. Adhesives. I. Australia. Commonwealth
Scientific and Industrial Research Organi-
zation. (Div. of Building Research)
II. Title.

691.421
T18 Tauber, E
Some new ceramic finishes and cladding
materials. Melbourne, Div. of Building
Research, Commonwealth Scientific and Indus-
trial Research Organization, 1967.
2p. (Australia. Commonwealth Scientific
and Industrial Research Organization, Div.
of Building Research. Reprint no. 394)
Reprinted from Proceedings of the third
Australian Building Research Congress, 1967.
1. Clay. 2. Tile. 3. Building materials.
I. Australia. Commonwealth Scientific and
Industrial Re   search Organization.
(Div. of Buildi   ng Research)
(Cont'd on next card)

551.5
T18 Taubenfeld, Howard J
Weather modification: law, controls, operations. A survey of responses to questionnaires
of the Special Commission on Weather Modification of the National Science Foundation by
States, research and experimental organizations, commercial operators, and Federal
agencies. Report to the Special Commission on
Weather Modification, National Science
Foundation. [Wash.] National Science
Foundation [1966?]
73p. (National Science Foundation.
NSF 66-7)   (Continued on
next card)

691.322
T18 Tauber, E
Coloured stone for exposed aggregate panels,
by E. Tauber and M.J. Murray. Melbourne,
Australia Div. of Building Research, Common-
wealth Scientific and Industrial Research
Organization, 1968.
5p. (Australia. Commonwealth Scientific
and Industrial Research Organization. Div. of
Building Research. DBR Reprint no. 441)
Reprinted from: Constructional review, Vol.
41, no. 7, page 24, July 1968.
1. Concrete aggregates. 2. Panels. I. Title.
II. Murray, M.J.,   jt. au. III. Australia.
Commonwealth Scie   ntific and Industrial
Research Organiza   tion. (Div. of Building
Research)

691.421
T18 Tauber, E   Some new ceramic finishes...
1967.   (Card 2)

II. Australian Building Research Congress,
3d, 1967. III. Title.

551.5
T18 Taubenfeld, Howard J   Weather modification:
law, controls, operations...[1966?]
(Card 2)

1. Weather. 2. Climate. I. U.S. National
Science Foundation. (Special Commission on
Weather Modification) II. Title.

691.421
T181 Tauber, E
Investigation of the drying process of
clays and ceramic bodies with a
barelattograph, by E. Tauber and R.K. Hill.
Melbourne Commonwealth Scientific and
Industrial Research Organization, 1969.
7p. (Australia. Commonwealth Scientific
and Industrial Research Organization.
Division of Building Research. Reprint
no. 452)
Reprinted from: Journal of the
Australian   Ceramic Society, May,
1969, p. 1-8.
(Cont'd on next card)

018
T18 Tauber, Maurice Falcolm, 1908-   comp.
Book catalogs; compiled, by Maurice F. Tauber and
Hilda Feinberg. Metuchen, N. J., Scarecrow Press, 1971.
572 p. illus, facsims. 22 cm.
Bibliography: p. 521-539.

1. Library catalogs.
1. Catalogs, Book—Addresses, essays, lectures.   I. Feinberg,
Hilda, joint comp. II. Title.

Z695.87.T39   023.3
ISBN 0-8108-0372-0   72-149994
Library of Congress   71 [30-5]   MARC

658.564
K25
TAULBEE, ORRIN E. JT. ED.
KENT, ALLEN.
ELECTRONIC INFORMATION HANDLING,
EDITED BY ALLEN KENT AND ORRIN E.
TAULBEE. WASHINGTON, SPARTAN BOOKS,
1965.
355P. (THE KNOWLEDGE AVAILABILITY
SYSTEMS SERIES)

PAPERS PRESENTED AT A NATIONAL
CONFERENCE CO-SPONSORED BY THE
UNIVERSITY OF PITTSBURGH, GOODYEAR
AEROSPACE CORPORATION, AND WESTERN
MICHIGAN UNIVERSITY, OCTOBER 7-9,
1964.
(CONTINUED ON NEXT CARD)

658.564
K25
KENT, ALLEN. ELECTRONIC INFORMATION
HANDLING....1965. (CARD 2)

1. AUTOMATION. I. TAULBEE, ORRIN
E., JT. ED. II. TITLE.

728.1
¦336.18
(74485)
T18
(Library Inst.
1951
TAUNTON, MASS. HOUSING AUTHORITY.
REPORT, 1951-
TAUNTON.
/ V. ANNUAL.

1. PUBLIC HOUSING - TAUNTON, MASS.

728
¦333
T18
TAUSCHER, ARTHUR.
100 QUESTIONS BEFORE BUYING YOUR HOME,
BY ARTHUR TAUSCHER. NEW YORK, HOME
INSPECTION CONSULTANTS, 1958.
8P.

1. HOME OWNERSHIP.

658
A52r
no.77
Taussig, John N
EDP applications for the manufacturing
function. New York, American Management
Association, 1966.
55p. (American Management Association.
AMA research study 77)

1. Automation. 2. Management.
3. Manufacturers. I. American Management
Association. II. Title.

658
A52r
no.82
Taussig, John N
Expense account control. New York,
American Management Association, 1967.
64p. (American Management Association.
AMA research study no. 82)

1. Management. 2. Accounting.
3. Credit. 4. Money. I. American Management Association. II. Title.

026
P67
Tavares, Joao F Cansado.
Portugal. Laboratorio Nacional de Engenharia
Civil.
A Seccao de Documentacao do Laboratorio Na-
cional de Engenharia Civil, por Joao F. Cansado
Tavares. Lisboa, 1958.
13p. illus., diagrs. (Its Memoria no. 132)
English summary.

1. Libraries - Portugal. 2. Documentation.
I. Tavares, Joao F. Cansado.

301.15
C65p
Tax, Sol, ed.
Community Service Workshop, Chicago, 1966-67.
The people vs. the system; a dialogue in
urban conflict. Proceedings of the Community
Service Workshop funded under Title I of the
Higher education act of 1965 and held at the
University of Chicago, Oct. 1966-June 1967.
Edited by Sol Tax. Chicago, Acme Press, 1968.
515p.
Contents.-pt.I: Politics and the welfare
system.-pt.II: Dominant issues in urban edu-
cation.-pt.III: Major developments in the field
of housing.-pt.IV: Youth and the community.-pt.
V: The city and   the community - a
confrontation   (suggested courses of
action).-Federal   housing programs.
(Cont'd on next card)

301.15
C65p
Community Service Workshop, Chicago, 1966-67.
The people...1968.   (Card 2)

opportunities for innovation, by Joseph
Burstein, General Counsel, Housing Assistance
Administration, Dept. of Housing and Urban
Development.-New directions in urban housing,
by Joseph Burstein, General Counsel, Housing
Assistance Administration, Dept. of Housing
and Urban Development.-Model cities; citizen
participation and politics, by Archie Hardwicke,
Citizen participation Advisor, Model Cities
Staff, Dept. of Housing and Urban Develop-
ment, Region IV and David McMullin,
(Cont'd on next card)

301.15
C65p
Community Service Workshop, Chicago, 1966-67.
The people...1968.   (Card 3)

Community Services Officer, Dept. of Housing
and Urban Development, Region IV.

1. City growth. 2. Housing. 3. Urban renewal.
4. Model cities. I. Tax, Sol, ed. II. Title.
III. Burstein, Joseph. Federal housing programs: opportunities for innovation.
IV. Burstein, Joseph. New directions in urban
housing. V. Hardwicke, Archie. Model cities;
citizen participation and politics. VI. McMullin,
David. Model   cities; citizen participation and poli   tics.

336.2
C657T
1966
H-R
NB.1323
TAX ADJUSTMENT ACT OF 1966.
U.S. CONGRESS. CONFERENCE
COMMITTEES, 1966.
TAX ADJUSTMENT ACT OF 1966.
CONFERENCE REPORT TO ACCOMPANY H.R.
12752. WASHINGTON, GOVT. PRINT. OFF.,
1966.
13P. (89TH CONGRESS, 2D SESSION.
HOUSE. REPORT NO. 1323)

1. TAXATION. 2. INCOME TAX.
I. TITLE.

336.2
C657T
1966
H-R
NB.1285
TAX ADJUSTMENT ACT OF 1966.
U.S. CONGRESS. HOUSE. COMMITTEE ON
WAYS AND MEANS.
TAX ADJUSTMENT ACT OF 1966. REPORT
TO ACCOMPANY H.R. 12752. WASHINGTON,
GOVT. PRINT. OFF., 1966.
54P. (89TH CONGRESS, 2D SESSION.
HOUSE. REPORT NO. 1285)

1. TAXATION. 2. INCOME TAX.
I. TITLE.

336.2
C657T
1966
S-H
TAX ADJUSTMENT ACT OF 1966.
U.S. CONGRESS. SENATE. COMMITTEE ON
FINANCE.
TAX ADJUSTMENT ACT OF 1966. HEARINGS,
EIGHTY-NINTH CONGRESS, SECOND SESSION ON
H.R. 12752. WASHINGTON, GOVT. PRINT.
OFF., 1966.
246P.

HEARINGS HELD FEBRUARY 25 - MARCH 1,
1966.

1. TAXATION. 2. INCOME TAX.
I. TITLE.

336.2
C657t
1968
H-R
Tax adjustment act of 1968.
U.S. Congress. House. Committee on Ways
and Means.
Tax adjustment act of 1968. Report to
accompany H.R. 15414. Washington, 1968.
14p. (90th Cong., 2d sess. House. Report
no. 1104)

1. Taxation. 2. Communication systems.
3. Transportation. I. Title.

336.2
C657t
1968
S-R
Tax adjustment act of 1968.
U.S. Congress. Senate. Committee on
Finance.
Tax adjustment act of 1968; report to
accompany H.R. 15414. Wash., Govt. Print.
Off., 1968.
19p. (90th Cong., 2d sess. Senate.
Report no. 1014)

1. Taxation. I. Title.

334.1
H13
Laf.
The tax advantages of cooperatives and con-
dominiums.
Hagendorf, Stanley.
The tax advantages of cooperatives and
condominiums. New York, Alexander Hamilton
Institute, 1967.
15p.
At head of title: Taxes interpreted, by Howard
A. Rumpf.

1. Cooperative housing - Taxation. I. Rumpf,
Howard A. Taxes interpreted. II. Alexander
Hamilton Institute, New York. III. Title.

352.1
C72t
Tax and investment opportunities with municipal
bonds.
Crestol, Jack.
Tax and investment opportunities with municipal bonds. New York, Moody's Investors Service,
1970.
20p.

1. Municipal bonds. 2. Taxation.
I. Moody's Investors Service. II. Title.

336.211
A75
Tax aspects of real estate transactions.
Atlas, Martin.
Tax aspects of real estate transac-
tions. Rev. ed.-annotated. Wash., BNA
inc., a division of the Bureau of
National Affairs, 1959.
238p.

1. Real property - Taxation.
I. Bureau of National Affairs.
II. Title.

336.211
A75
1971
Tax aspects of real estate transactions.
Atlas, Martin, 1914-
Tax aspects of real estate transaction Rev.
with the assistance of Orton W. Boyd. 5th ed.
rev. and annotated. Washington, BNA inc., 197
394p.

1. Real property - Taxation. I. Boyd, Orton
Wells, 1895- ed. II. Title.

697.8
W45
Tax assistance and environmental pollution.
Wilson, Douglas B
Tax assistance and environmental pollution.
Princeton, N.J., Tax Institute of America, 1970.

11p.

Tax policy, July-Aug., 1970.

1. Air pollution. 2. Water pollution.
3. Taxation. I. Tax Institute of America.
II. Title.

334.1
C65t
Tax breaks in co-op housing.
Commerce Clearing House.
Tax breaks in co-op housing. New York,
1967.
31p. (Its Federal tax guide reports.
SD-730)

1. Cooperative housing. 2. Real property -
Taxation. I. Title.

336.2
S71 · Tax changes and modernization in the textile industry.
Stanback, Thomas M
Tax changes and modernization in the textile industry. New York, National Bureau of Economic Research, distributed by Columbia University Press, 1969.
119p. (Fiscal study no. 13)

1. Taxation. 2. Tax incentives. 3. Industry.
I. Title. II. National Bureau of Economic Research.

336.211
.19t · Tax credits.
Tax Foundation, inc.
Tax credits; past experience and current issues. New York, 1969.
35p. (Its Research publication 21 (New series)

1. Tax incentives. I. Title.

333.38
C67 · Tax delinquent land.
Cornick, Philip H
A report to the State Planning Council of New York on the problems created by the premature subdivision of urban lands in selected metropolitan districts in the state of New York. Albany, N.Y., Division of State Planning, Feb., 1938.
xxi, 346 p.

Bibliography: p. 328-330.

1.Subdivision. 2.Tax delinquent land.
I.New York. State Planning Council.

336.2
C653t · Tax changes for shortrun stabilization.
U.S. Congress. Joint Economic Committee.
Tax changes for shortrun stabilization. Hearings before the Subcommittee on Fiscal Policy of the Joint Economic Committee, Congress of the United States, Eighty-ninth Congress, second session. Washington, Govt. Print. Off., 1966.
313p.

Hearings held Mar. 16-30, 1966.

1. Taxation. 2. Income tax.
I. Title.

336.211
(77311)
C34 · TAX DELINQUENCY AND HOUSING IN CHICAGO.
CHICAGO. HOUSING AUTHORITY.
TAX DELINQUENCY AND HOUSING IN CHICAGO. CHICAGO, 1942.
14P.

1. REAL PROPERTY - TAXATION - CHICAGO. I. TITLE.

336.211
H45 · Tax delinquent land.
Hillhouse, Albert Miller, 1903-
Tax-reverted properties in urban areas, by A. M. Hillhouse ... and Carl H. Chatters ... Chicago, Public administration service, 1942.
viii, 183 p. incl. illus. (map, plan) diagr., forms. 23½ cm.
Bibliographical foot-notes.

1. Land—Taxation—U. S. 2. Municipal finance—U. S. 3. Real property—U. S. I. Chatters, Carl Hallack, 1898- joint author. II. Public administration service, Chicago. III. Title.

Library of Congress   HJ4182.D4H5   42—50326
[49f2]   336.1

336.2
C653t
suppl. · Tax changes for shortrun stabilization.
U.S. Congress. Joint Economic Committee.
Tax changes for shortrun stabilization. A report of the Subcommittee on Fiscal Policy of the Joint Economic Committee, Congress of the United States together with supplementary and dissenting individual views. Washington, Govt. Print. Off., 1966.
23p.

At head of title: 89th Cong., 2d sess.

1. Taxation. 2. Income tax.
I. Title.

336.211
N17t · Tax delinquency and rural land-use adjustment
National Resources Planning Board.
Tax delinquency and rural land-use adjustment, by the Subcommittee on Tax Delinquency of the Land Committee, N.R.P.B. Washington [Govt. Print. Off.] 1942.
190 p. charts, tables. (Its Technical paper no. 8)

1.Tax delinquent land. 2.Land use. I.Title.

336.211
L13 · TAX DELINQUENT LAND.
LAGERMAN, JOHN A
THE PLIGHT OF AMERICAN CITIES; A STUDY OF PROBLEMS CONTRIBUTING TO TAX FORFEITURE, TAX DELINQUENCY AND DEPRECIATION OF BUSINESS REAL ESTATE VALUES IN SAINT PAUL WITH SUGGESTIONS FOR PROBABLE REMEDIES; A REPORT PREPARED BY JOHN A. LAGERMAN AND OTHERS, MEMBERS OF A COMMITTEE APPOINTED BY MAYOR JOHN J. MCDONOUGH. ST. PAUL, 1941.
359-370P.

REPRINTED FROM MINNESOTA
(CONTINUED ON NEXT CARD)

336.2
C653te · Tax consequences of contributions to needy older relatives.
U.S. Congress. Senate. Special Committee on Aging.
Tax consequences of contributions to needy older relatives. Hearing before the Special Committee on Aging, United States Senate, Eighty-ninth Congress, second session. Wash., For sale by Supt. of Doc., Govt. Print. Off., 1966.
82p.

Hearing held June 15, 1966.

1. Taxation. 2. Old age. I. Title.

336.211
A52 · Tax delinquent land.
American Society of Planning Officials.
A program for the use of tax-abandoned lands. Chicago, 1942.
38p.

1. Tax delinquent land. 2. Vacant land.

336.211
L13 · LAGERMAN, JOHN A   THE PLIGHT OF ...
1941.   (CARD 2)

MUNICIPALITIES, SEPT. 1941.

1. TAX DELINQUENT LAND. 2. REAL PROPERTY - VALUATION. I. TITLE.

336.2
C65TA
1966
S-R · TAX CONSEQUENCES OF CONTRIBUTIONS TO NEEDY OLDER RELATIVES.
U.S. CONGRESS. SENATE. SPECIAL COMMITTEE ON AGING.
TAX CONSEQUENCES OF CONTRIBUTIONS TO NEEDY OLDER RELATIVES. REPORT TOGETHER WITH MINORITY VIEWS. WASHINGTON, GOVT. PRINT. OFF., 1966.
31P. (89TH CONGRESS, 2D SESSION. SENATE. REPORT NO. 1721)

1. TAXATION. 2. OLD AGE. I. TITLE.

711.4
C652
1940 · Tax delinquent land.
Conference on Planning Problems and Administration, Chicago, 1940.
Proceedings. Chicago, Ill., American Society of Planning Officials, Jan. 1940.
85 p.

1.City planning administration. 2.Zoning. 3.City planning - Congresses. 4.Master plan. 5.Tax delinquent land. I.American Society of Planning Officials.

336.2
L45
1965 · Tax delinquent land.
Lindholm, Richard W ed.
Property taxation, U.S.A. Proceedings of a symposium sponsored by the Committee on Taxation, Resources and Economic Development (TRED) at the University of Wisconsin, Milwaukee, 1965. Madison, University of Wisconsin Press, 1967.
315p.

N.c.1,
2
Laf.c.3

1. Taxation. 2. Personal property - Taxation. 3. Real property - Taxation. 4. Tax delinquent land. I. Title.

336.2
S23 · Tax considerations in organizing foreign operations.
Seghers, Paul D
Tax considerations in organizing foreign operations. New York, American Management Association, Finance Div., 1967.
16p. (American Management Association. AMA management bulletin no. 108)

1. Taxation. 2. Commercial policy. I. American Management Association. II. Title. (Series)

336.211
C66 · Tax delinquent land.
Cook County, Ill. Housing Authority.
Dead land, a report to the Illinois State Housing Board. Chicago, 1949.
90p. illus. (Housing information service)

A study of chronic tax delinquency and abandonment with a program for the development of encumbered urban vacant land.

1. Tax delinquent land.

336.211
N17t · Tax delinquent land.
National Resources Planning Board.
Tax delinquency and rural land-use adjustment, by the Subcommittee on Tax Delinquency of the Land Committee, N.R.P.B. Washington [Govt. Print. Off.] 1942.
190 p. charts, tables. (Its Technical paper no. 8)

1.Tax delinquent land. 2.Land use. I.Title.

336.2
M19t · A tax credit for certain educational expenses.
Maxwell, James Achley, 1897-
A tax credit for certain educational expenses, by James A. Maxwell and Bernard L. Weinstein. Wash., Govt. Print. Off., 1971.
58p.

1. Taxation. 2. Education - Finance.
I. U.S. President's Commission on School Finance. II. Weinstein, Bernard L., jt. au. III. Title.

333.38
C67
c.3 · Tax delinquent land.
Cornick, Philip H
Premature subdivision and its consequences; a study made for the State Planning Council of New York of the premature subdivision for urban purposes of outlying lands in selected metropolitan areas of New York State. New York, Institute of Public Administration, Columbia University, 1938.
xxi, 346 p.

Bibliography: p.328-330
"Authorized reprint of the official report."

711.14
(795)
G722 · TAX DELINQUENT LAND.
OREGON. STATE PLANNING BOARD.
MANAGEMENT OF TAX REVERTED LANDS IN OREGON, BY ARTHUR DAMSCHEN ... IN COLLABORATION WITH V.B. STANBERY. SALEM, 1938.
95P.

PREPARED AS A REPORT ON PROJECTS O.P. 465-94-3-83 AND APN 165-94-6063 UNDER AUSPICES OF THE WORKS PROGRESS ADMINISTRATION.

1. LAND USE - OREGON. 2. TAX DELINQUENT LAND. I. DAMSCHEN,
(CONTINUED ON NEXT CARD)

711.14
(795)
9722
OREGON. STATE PLANNING BOARD.
MANAGEMENT OF ...1938.   (CARD 2)

ARTHUR.   II. STANBERY, V.B.
III. TITLE.   IV. TITLE: TAX REVERTED
LAND.

Tax exemption

see

Tax incentives

336.2
T19a
1967
Tax Foundation, inc., New York.
Allocating tax burdens and government
benefits by income class, [1961 and 1965]
New York, 1967.
2c   12p.   (Its Government finance brief
no. 8)

1. Income tax. 2. National income.
I. Title.

711.4
(77132)
R23
P13
Tax delinquent land.
Wheaton, William L
Tax delinquent lands in Cuyahoga County.
Cleveland, Regional Association of Cleveland,
Oct. 1941.
48 p.   map, tables.   (Regional Association
of Cleveland. Publication no. 13)

Mimeographed.

728.1
711.585
(7471)
N28
Tax exempt housing projects.
New York, N. Y. Comptroller.
Report to the Board of Estimate on
Title I Slum clearance projects and tax
exempt housing projects [by] Lawrence E.
Gerosa, Comptroller.   New York, May 9, 1956.
6, 45, 3 p.   tables.

Processed.

1. Urban redevelopment - New York, N. Y. 2. Housing
projects - New York, N. Y. 3. Tax incentives. I. Gerosa,
Lawrence E. II. New York, N.Y. Board of Estimate.
III. Title: Tax exempt housing projects. IV. Title:
Title I Slum Clearance Projects.

336.2
T19a
Tax Foundation.
Allocation of the tax burden by income
class, by George Bishop. New York, 1960.
24p.   tables. (Its Project note no. 45)

1. Income tax. I. Bishop, George.

336.211
(016)
A37
Tax delinquent land - Bibliography.
U.S. Bureau of Agricultural Economics.
Tax delinquency on rural real estate,
1928-1941; selected references compiled
by Helen E. Hennefrund under the direction
of Margaret T. Olcott, Librarian.   Washington,
Jan. 1942.
314 p.   (Its Agricultural economics
bibliography no. 94)

1. Tax delinquent land - Bibl. I. Hennefrund,
Helen E   comp.   (Series)

336.211
(747)
C87
Tax exemption of educational property in
New York.
Curtiss, W   David.
Tax exemption of educational property in
New York. Ithaca, N.Y., Center for Housing
and Environmental Studies, Division of Urban
Studies, Cornell University, 1967.
18p. (Cornell University. Center for
Housing and Environmental Studies. Article
20 reprints)
Reprinted from Cornell University Law
quarterly, Spring, 1967.

1. Real property - Taxation - New York
(State) 2. Schools. 3. Universities
and colleges.
(Cont'd on next card)

336.2
(016)
T19
no. 5
Tax Foundation.
Bibliography on Federal tax revision.
New York, 1960.
12p.   (Its Research bibliography no. 5)

1. Taxation - Bibliography.

332.3
:336.2
C65
Tax depreciation allowances on capital
equipment.
U.S. Congress. Senate. Select Committee
on Small Business.
Tax depreciation allowances on capital
equipment. Report of the Select Committee
on Small Business, United States Senate on
the effects of current federal tax depreciation policies on small business together with
supplemental views. Washington, Govt. Print.
Off., 1960.
16p.   (86th Cong., 2d sess. Senate.
Report no. 1017)

1. Small   business - Taxation.
I. Title.

336.211
(747)
C87
Curtiss, W   David.   Tax exemption...
1967.   (Card 2)

I. Cornell University. Center for Housing
and Environmental Studies. (Div. of Urban
Studies) II. Title.

DATE OF REQUEST 6/2/54   CARD NO.
                APR 7 1954
AUTHOR
    Tax Foundation.
TITLE
    Budgeting--civic guide to economy in municipal
    government.
SERIES

EDITION	PUB. DATE	PAGING
PUBLISHER

RECOMMENDED BY   REVIEWED IN
    Greer
            ORDER RECORD

336.2
(94)
W66
Tax executive.
Woodruff, A   M
Property taxes and land use patterns in
Australia and New Zealand, by A.M. Woodruff
and L.L. Ecker-Racz. Wash., Tax Executives
Institute, 1965.
16-63p.

Reprinted from the Tax executive, Oct.
1965.

1. Taxation - Australia. 2. Taxation - New
Zealand. 3. Real   property - Taxation.
4. Real estate   business. I. Ecker-
Racz, L.L., jt. au.   II. Tax executive.
III. Title.

336.2
C65taxe
1970
S-H
Tax exemptions for charitable organizations
affecting poverty programs.
U.S. Congress. Senate. Committee on Labor
and Public Welfare.
Tax exemptions for charitable organizations
affecting poverty programs. Hearings
before the Subcommittee on Employment,
Manpower, and Poverty of the Committee on
Labor and Public Welfare, United States Senate,
Ninety-first Congress, second session...
Wash., Govt. Print. Off., 1970.
539p.
Hearings held Nov. 16-17, 1970.
1. Taxation. 2. Poverty. 3. Foundations,
Charitable and   educational. I. Title.

336.2
T19c
Tax Foundation.
City income tax. New York, 1967.
8p. (Its Government finance brief no.
11)
2c
1. Income tax. I. Title.

378
C65ta
Tax-exempt foundations and charitable trusts:
their impact on the economy.
U.S. Congress. House. Select Committee
on Small Business.
Tax-exempt foundations and charitable
trusts: their impact on our economy.
Chairman's report. Washington, Govt.
Print. Off., 1962.
135p. (87th Cong. House. Committee
print)

1. Foundations, Charitable and educational.
2. Taxation.   I. Title.

333.33
A52t
Tax factors in real estate operations.
Anderson, Paul E
Tax factors in real estate operations. 3d ed.
Englewood Cliffs, N.J., Prentice-Hall, 1969-
1v. (loose-leaf)

1. Real estate business. 2. Taxation.
3. Real property. I. Title.

336.2
(016)
T19
no. 2
Tax Foundation.
Comparative analysis of state tax burdens.
New York, 1959.
6p. (Its Research bibliography no. 2)

1. Taxation - Bibliography. 2. State finance -
Bibliography.

378
C65ta
1963
Tax-exempt foundations and charitable trusts:
their impact on our economy.
U.S. Congress. House. Select Committee
on Small Business.
Tax-exempt foundations and charitable
trusts: their impact on our economy. 2d
installment. Subcommittee Chairman's report
to Subcommittee no. 1, Select Committee on
Small Business, House of Representatives.
Washington, Govt. Print. Off., 1963.
405p. (88th Cong. House. Committee
print)

1. Foundations, Charitable and educational.
2. Taxation.   I. Title.

332.72
:368
C65
1959
S-H
TAX FORMULA FOR LIFE INSURANCE
COMPANIES.
U.S. CONGRESS. SENATE. COMMITTEE ON
FINANCE.
TAX FORMULA FOR LIFE INSURANCE
COMPANIES. HEARINGS... EIGHTY-SIXTH
CONGRESS, FIRST SESSION, ON H.R.
4245... MARCH 3, 4, 5, 17, 18, 19,
1959. WASHINGTON, 1959.
704P.

1. LIFE INSURANCE COMPANIES -
TAXATION. I. TITLE.

336
T19co
Tax Foundation.
Congressional control of Federal
expenditures. New York, 1965.
7p. (Government finance brief no. 1,
new series)

1. Budget. 2. Finance. I. Title.

336
T19con Tax Foundation.
    Congressional expenditure limitations:
an evaluation. New York, 1969.
      14p. (Its Government finance brief no.
17)

      1. Budget. I. Title.

355.1
T19 Tax Foundation.
    Federal benefits for veterans, by
Vincent Finneran. New York, 1960.
      36p. tables. (Its Project note
no. 47)

1. Veterans.
2. Veterans' guaranteed loans. I. Title.
II. Finneran, Vincent.

336.18
H17 Tax Foundation, inc.
    Harriss, C   Lowell.
    Federal revenue sharing: a new appraisal.
New York, Tax Foundation, inc., 1969.
      27p. (Tax Foundation, inc. Government
finance brief no. 16)

      1. Grants-in-aid. I. Tax Foundation, inc.
II. Title.

336
T19c Tax Foundation.
    Controlling Federal expenditures. New
York, 1963.
2c   48p. (Its Project note no. 51)

      1. Finance. I. Title.

336
T19fe Tax Foundation.
    The Federal budget for fiscal year 1973
future implications. New York, 1972
      v. (Government finance brief)

2c   For Library holdings see main entry.

      1. Budget. I. Title.

336.2
(016)
T19 Tax Foundation.
no.9   Federal tax revision. New York, 1963.
      16p. (Its Research bibliography no. 9)

2c

      1. Taxation - Bibl.

VF
332.3
T19 The Tax Foundation, Inc.
    Controlling government corporations.
New York, August 1955.
      43 p. (Its Project note no. 37)

    1.Government corporations. I.Title.

351.1
T19 Tax Foundation.
    Federal civilian employment, pay, and benefits.
New York, 1969.
      36p. (Its Research publication no. 20
2c (new series))

      1. Federal civil service. 2. Federal
government - Salaries. 3. Employment -
Statistics. I. Title.

336
T19f Tax Foundation.
    Federal trust funds: budgetary and other
implications. New York, 1970.
2c.   36p. (Its Research publication no. 25 (new
series)

      1. Budget. I. Title.

336.2
T19coo Tax Foundation.
    The corporation income tax; an examination
of its role in the Federal tax system. New
York, 1968.
      76p. (Its Research publication no. 19
(New series))

      1. Taxation. 2. Business. I. Title.

331.2
T19
Suppl. Tax Foundation, inc.
1970 Federal civilian employment, pay, and
benefits; supplement. New York, 1970.
      9p.

2c   1. Federal government - Salaries.
2. Federal civil service. I. Title.

353
T19 Tax Foundation, Inc.
    The financial challenge to the states;
an analysis of state fiscal developments,
1946-1957. New York, 1958.
      47p. tables. (Its Project note no. 43)

      1.State finance. 2.Intergovernmental
relations.

336.2
T19cu Tax Foundation.
    Current problems and issues in State
taxation of interstate commerce. 1. The
background. 2. The changes proposed. 3. The
debate on proposed changes. New York, 1966.
      12p. (Its Government finance brief no.
3 (New series))

      1. Taxation. 2. State finance. I. Title.

336.2
T19f Tax Foundation.
    Federal fiscal issues. New York,
1961.
2c   54p.

      1. Taxation. 2. Finance.

336.2
(016)
T19 Tax Foundation.
no. 3 Financing municipal government. New York,
1959.
      13p. (Its Research bibliography no. 3)

    1. Taxation - Bibliography. 2. Municipal finance -
Bibliography.

336.2
T19e Tax Foundation.
    Economic aspects of the social security
tax. New York, 1966.
      63p. (Its Research publication no. 5.
(New series))
2c

      1. Taxation. 2. Social security.
I. Title.

336.2
T19fe Tax Foundation, inc.
    Federal non-income taxes; an
examination of selected revenue
sources. New York, 1965.
      70p.
2c

      1. Taxation. 2. Finance. I. Title.

353
T19f Tax Foundation, inc.
Brief Fiscal outlook for state and local government to 1975, by Elsie M. Watters. New York,
1966.
2c 7) 11p. (Its Government finance brief no.

      1. State finance. 2. State government.
3. Local government - Finance. 4. Taxation.
I. Watters, Elsie M. II. Title.

336
T19 Tax Foundation.
    Facts and figures on Government finance.
      9 v.
      Keep latest edition only.

    1.Finance. I.Title.

339.3
T19 Tax Foundation, inc.
    Federal revenue sharing with the States.
New York, 1967.
2c   20p. (Its Government finance brief
no. 9)

      1. National income. 2. Grants-in-aid.
3. Intergovernmental relations. 4. Taxation.
I. Title.

353
T19f Tax Foundation, inc.
    Fiscal outlook for state and local govern-
ment to 1975. New York, 1966.
      128p. (Its Research publication no. 6
(New series))

2c   1. State finance. 2. State government.
3. Local government - Finance. 4. Taxation.
I. Title.

336
T193   Tax Foundation.
     Growth of Federal domestic spending
     programs 1947-1963. New York, 1962.
     47p. (Its Project note no. 49)

     Expenditures for Housing: p. 40-42.

     1. Finance. I. Title: Federal domestic
     spending programs.

697.8
T19   Tax Foundation.
     Pollution control; perspectives on the
     government role. New York, 1971.
     46p.

     1. Air pollution. 2. Water pollution.
     I. Title.

331.252
T19s   Tax Foundation.
     State and local employee pension systems.
     New York, 1969.
     64p.

     1. Pensions. I. Title.

351
T19   Tax Foundation, inc., New York.
     Growth trends of new Federal programs,
     1955-1968. New York, 1967.
Laf.   30p. (Its Research publication no. 10, new
     series)

     1. Federal government. 2. Budget. 3. Grants-
     in-aid. I. Title. II. Title: Federal programs:
     1955-1968.

353
T19P   TAX FOUNDATION.
     POSTWAR TREND IN STATE DEBT. A
     STATE-BY-STATE ANALYSIS. NEW YORK, 1950.
     26p. (PROJECT NOTE NO. 27)

     1. STATE FINANCE. I. TITLE.

336.2
T19s   Tax Foundation.
     State and local sales taxes; a summary.
     New York, 1970.
     15p.

     1. Taxation. 2. State finance.
     3. Municipal finance. I. Title.

       Tax Foundation.
353
H17   Harriss, C   Lowell.
     Handbook of state and local government
     finance. New York, Tax Foundation, 1966.
     64p.

     1. State finance. 2. State government.
     3. Taxation. I. Tax Foundation.
     II. Title.

336.2
T19p   Tax Foundation.
     Proceedings of a conference on
     national defense and taxation. New
     York, 1961.
     79p.

     1. Taxation. 2. National defense.

353
T19s   Tax Foundation.
     State expenditure controls; an
     evaluation. New York, 1965.
     11p. (Government finance brief no.
     2, new series)

     1. State finance. 2. State government.

331.252
T19   Tax Foundation, inc., New York.
     Issues in future financing of social
     security. New York, 1967.
     52p. (Research publication no. 11
     (new series))

     1. Social security. 2. Insurance.
     I. Title. II. Title: Financing of social
     security.

361
T19   Tax Foundation.
     Public assistance   a survey of selected
     aspects of state programs. New York, 1960.
     64p. tables. (Its Project note no. 46)

     1. Public assistance.

336.2
(016)
T19   Tax Foundation.
no. 1   Tax and other financial inducements to
     industrial location. New York, 1960.
     3p. (Its Research bibliography no. 1)

     1. Taxation - Bibliography. 2. Industrial
     location - Bibliography.

614
T19   Tax Foundation.
     Medicaid: state programs after two years.
     New York, 1968.
     72p.

     1. Public health. 2. Old age. 3. Social
     welfare. I. Title.

379
T19   Tax Foundation.
     Public financing of higher education. New
     York, 1966.
     50p.

     1. Education - Finance. 2. Universities
     and colleges. I. Title.

336.211
T19t   Tax Foundation, inc.
     Tax credits; past experience and current
     issues. New York, 1969.
     35p. (Its Research publication 21
     (New series)

     1. Tax incentives. I. Title.

336
T19n   Tax Foundation.
     The new Federal budget concept; an explana-
     tion and evaluation. New York, 1968.
     12p. (Its Government finance brief no.
     14)

     1. Budget. I. Title.

360
T19   Tax Foundation, inc.
     Public welfare programs: issues, problems,
     and proposals. New York, 1969.
     14p. (Its Government finance brief no. 15)

     1. Social welfare. I. Title.

382
T19   Tax Foundation, inc.
     Tax harmonization in Europe and U.S.
     business. New York, 1968.
     32p. (Its Research publication no. 16
     (new series))

     1. Commercial policy. 2. Taxation -
     Europe. 3. Foreign exchange. I. Title

VF
33
T19   Tax Foundation, Inc.
     Our foreign aid programs.   New York, c1953.
     36 p.   graphs, tables. (Its Project
     note no. 34)

     On cover: A survey of U.S. international
     assistance programs, 1941-1952.

     1. Economic development. I. Title: Foreign aid
     programs. II. Title: International assistance
     programs, 1941-1952.

LAW
T
T193r   Tax Foundation, New York.
     Reconstructing the Federal Tax system;
     a guide to the issues. New York, 1963.
     54p.

     1. Taxation. I. Title. II. Title:
     Federal tax system.

VF State finance

DATE OF REQUEST 4/23/53	APR 24 1953	L. C. CARD NO.

AUTHOR
   Tax Foundation (New York, N. Y.)

TITLE   Trends in State Expenditures, 1940-1951. An
   analysis of state spending during and after World
   War II.

SERIES   Project note No. 30

EDITION	PUB. DATE 1952	PAGING 30p.

PUBLISHER

RECOMMENDED BY	REVIEWED IN

ORDER RECORD

388
T19
Tax Foundation.
Urban mass transportation in perspective.
New York, 1968.
48p. (Its Research publication no. 14
(new series))

1. Transportation. 2. Journey to work.
I. Title.

VF
336.211 District of Columbia. Dept. of General
(753)   Administration. (Finance Office)
D47   Real estate taxes, urban renewal and
          slums. [Washington] 1960.
          7p.

1. Real property - Taxation - District of
Columbia. 2. Tax incentives.

Tax Incentives.
336.2
S71   Stanback, Thomas M
      Tax changes and modernization in the textile
      industry. New York, National Bureau of Eco-
      nomic Research, distributed by Columbia Uni-
      versity Press, 1969.
      119p. (Fiscal study no. 13)

1. Taxation. 2 Tax incentives. 3. Industry.
I. Title. II. National Bureau of Economic
Research.

353
(969)
T19c   Tax Foundation of Hawaii.
1969   A compendium of governmental finances in
         Hawaii, 1949-1968. Honolulu, 1969.
         78p.

.1. State finance - Hawaii. 2. Municipal
finance - Hawaii. 3. County finance -
Hawaii. I. Title.

Tax incentives.
336.211
F72   Freedman, Abraham L
        Tax exemption of housing projects; an
      address before the Advisory Committee of the
      Philadelphia Housing Authority on December 7,
      1939. [Philadelphia, Philadelphia Housing
      Authority, 1939]
      9 p.

1. Tax incentives.

TAX INCENTIVES.
336.211 Tax Foundation, inc.
         Tax credits; past experience and current
         issues New York, 1969.
         35p. (Its Research publication 21
         (New series)

1. Tax incentives. I. Title.

353
(969)
T19   Tax Foundation of Hawaii.
        Government in Hawaii; a handbook of
      financial statistics, 1969.

      Honolulu, 19
        v.
      For Library holdings see main entry.
      1. State finance - Hawaii. 2. Municipal
finance - Hawaii. 3. County finance -
Hawaii. 4. Taxation - Hawaii. I. Title.

330.15 TAX INCENTIVES.
N178   LENT, GEORGE E
NO.47   THE OWNERSHIP OF TAX EXEMPT
        SECURITIES, 1913-1953. NEW YORK, 1955.
        140 P. (NATIONAL BUREAU OF ECONOMIC
        RESEARCH. OCCASIONAL PAPER 47)

1. SECURITIES. 2. TAX INCENTIVES.
I. TITLE. II. NATIONAL BUREAU OF
ECONOMIC RESEARCH. OCCASIONAL PAPER,
NO. 47.

VF
336.211 Tax incentives.
C65   U. S. Congress. Joint Committee on Housing.
         Effects of taxation upon housing. Report of a subcommit-
       tee of the Joint Committee on Housing, Congress of the
       United States, pursuant to H. Con. Res. 104, 80th Congress.
       Washington, U. S. Govt. Print. Off., 1948.
       v, 29 p. 23 cm.
       At head of title: 80th Cong., 2d sess. Joint committee print.

1. Housing—U. S. 2. Land—Taxation—U. S. 3. Income tax—U. S.
4. Taxation, Exemption from—U. S.

HD7293.A5 1948t   331.833   49-46827*

Library of Congress   [8]

382
T19   Tax harmonization in Europe and U.S. business.
      Tax Foundation, inc.
        Tax harmonization in Europe and U.S.
      business. New York, 1968.
      32p. (Its Research publication no. 16
      (new series))

1. Commercial policy. 2. Taxation -
Europe. 3. Foreign exchange. I. Title

Tax incentives.
728.1   New York, N. Y. Comptroller.
711.585   Report to the Board of Estimate on
(7471) Title I Slum clearance projects and tax
N28   exempt housing projects [by] Lawrence E.
        Gerosa, Comptroller.   New York, May 9, 1956.
        6, 45, 3 p.   tables.

        Processed.

1. Urban redevelopment - New York, N. Y. 2. Housing
projects - New York, N. Y. 3. Tax incentives. I. Gerosa,
Lawrence E. II. New York, N.Y. Board of Estimate.
III. Title: Tax exempt housing projects. IV. Title:
Title I Slum Clearance Projects.

Tax incentives.
336.211
C65t   U.S. Congress. Senate. Committee on
       Finance.
         Tax incentives to encourage housing in
       urban poverty areas. Hearings before the
       Committee on Finance, United States Senate,
       Ninetieth Congress, first session on S.
       2100 to encourage and assist private enter-
       prise to provide adequate housing in urban
       poverty areas for low-income persons.
       Wash., Govt. Print. Off., 1967.
       478p.
         Hearings held Sept. 14-16, 1967.
         1. Tax incen-   tives. 2. Urban renewal.

         (Cont'd on next card)

Tax incentives

see also

Real property - Taxation

Tax incentives.
VF
336.211 New York (City) Housing and Redevelopment
N28   Board.
           Differential tax exemption; a means for
         providing relocation housing for low-income
         families in Mitchell-Lama apartments. New
         York, 1961.
         3p. (The West Side urban renewal plan)

1. Tax incentives. 2. State aided housing
programs - New York (City) I. Title:
Mitchell-Lama apartments.

336.211
C65t   U.S. Congress. Senate. Committee on Finance.
       Tax incentives to encourage housing...1967.
                                      (Card 2)

3. Low-income housing. 4. Family income and
expenditure - Housing. I. Title. II. Title:
Housing in urban poverty areas.

362.6   TAX INCENTIVES.
A52F   AMERICAN ASSOCIATION OF HOMES FOR THE
1963   AGING.
          FOCUS NO. 1; NATIONAL AND REGIONAL
        ISSUES FACING NON-PROFIT INSTITUTIONS
        SERVING OLDER PEOPLE. NEW YORK, 1963.
        23P.

        CO-SPONSORED BY THE CALIFORNIA
        ASSOCIATION OF HOMES FOR THE AGING.

        1. NURSING HOMES. 2. TAX INCENTIVES.
        I. TITLE. II. TITLE: NATIONAL AND
        REGIONAL ISSUES FACING NON-PROFIT
        INSTITUTIONS SE RVING OLDER PEOPLE.
                      (CONTINUED ON NEXT CARD)

Tax incentives.
336.211 Pennsylvania Economy League, (Eastern Div.)
(74811)   The problem of tax-exempt property in
P25   Philadelphia. [Prepared in cooperation
         with] Pennsylvania Bureau of Municipal
         Research. Philadelphia, 1966.
         48p. (Report no. 1. Governmental
         property)
           Prepared from financial assistance of
         Thomas Skelton Harrison Foundation.

1. Real property - Taxation - Philadelphia. 2. Tax incentives. I. Pennsylvania.   Bureau of Municipal
Research.   II. Title.

TAX INCENTIVES.
336.211 U.S. HOUSING AUTHORITY.
H68   NEED AND JUSTIFICATION FOR TAX
         EXEMPTION OF PUBLIC HOUSING PROJECTS.
         WASHINGTON, 193-.
         15L.

1. TAX INCENTIVES. I. TITLE.

362.6   AMERICAN ASSOCIATION OF HOMES FOR THE
A52F   AGING. FOCUS NO. 1....1963.   (CARD 2)
1963

III. CALIFORNIA ASSOCIATION OF HOMES FOR
THE AGING.

728.1   TAX INCENTIVES.
1336.18 SHIELDS AND CO.
S34   OBLIGATIONS OF LOCAL HOUSING
         AUTHORITIES; A QUESTIONNAIRE. NEW
         YORK, 1943.
         12P.
           RELATES TO LOCAL HOUSING AUTHORITY
         BONDS ISSUED UNDER UNITED STATES
         HOUSING ACT OF 1937.

1. LOCAL HOUSING AUTHORITIES.
2. MUNICIPAL BONDS. 3. TAX
INCENTIVES.   I. HOUSING ACT OF 1937.
II. TITLE.

Tax incentives.
LAW
T   U.S. Internal Revenue Service.
      Organizations described in Section 170(c)
    of the Internal Revenue Code of 1954.
    Cumulative list, revised to December 31, 1964.
    Wash., Govt. Print. Off., 1965.
    429p. (Its Publication no. 78
    (rev. 12-64)

-- --- Supplement no.
    Wash., 19
      v.

    1. Taxation.   2. Tax incentives.
    I. Title.

336.2
F76
Tax incentives and capital spending.
Fromm, Gary, ed.
Tax incentives and capital spending.
Papers presented at a conference of experts
held on November 3, 1967. Wash., Brookings
Institution, 1971.
301p. (Studies of government finance)

Bibliography: p. 280-296.

1. Taxation. 2. Finance. I. Brookings
Institution. II. Title.

697.8
L41
Tax incentives for investment in water and
air pollution control facilities.
U.S. Library of Congress. Legislative
Reference Service.
Tax incentives for investment in water and
air pollution control facilities: analysis
of bills introduced in 1st session of the
90th Congress, by Harold A. Kohnen. Wash.,
1968.
53p. (E-273; HG 4625 U.S.F.)

1. Air pollution. 2. Water pollution.
3. Taxation. I. Kohnen, Harold A. II. Title.

336.211
C65t
Tax incentives to encourage housing.
U.S. Congress. Senate. Committee on
Finance.
Tax incentives to encourage housing in
urban poverty areas. Hearings before the
Committee on Finance, United States Senate,
Ninetieth Congress, first session on S.
2100 to encourage and assist private enter-
prise to provide adequate housing in urban
poverty areas for low-income persons.
Wash., Govt. Print. Off., 1967.
478p.
Hearings held Sept. 14-16, 1967.
1. Tax incen-   tives. 2. Urban renewal.
(Cont'd on next card)

336.211
C65t
U.S. Congress. Senate. Committee on Finance.
Tax incentives to encourage housing...1967.
(Card 2)

3. Low-income housing. 4. Family income and
expenditure - Housing. I. Title. II. Title:
Housing in urban poverty areas.

336.2
(54)
N17
Laf.
Tax incidence on housing.
National Council of Applied Economic Research,
New Delhi.
Tax incidence on housing. New Delhi, 1967.
66p.

1. Real property - Taxation - India.
2. Low-income housing - India. I. Title.

Tax Institute, Incorporated. Name changed
in 1963.

Now   Tax Institute of America.

Interfile

336.2
T19A
1963
Tax Institute of America.
Alternatives to present federal taxes,
by Dan Throop Smith and others. Symposium
conducted by the Tax Institute of America,Oct.,1963
Princeton, N.J., 1964.
257p.

1. Taxation. I. Smith, Dan Throop.
II. Title.

711.4
:670
W15
Tax Institute.
Walker, Mabel.
Business enterprise and the city. Princeton,
N.J., Tax Institute, 1958.
144p.

1. Industrial location. 2. Office buildings.
I. Tax Institute. II. Title.

336.2
B87
Tax Institute of America.
Business taxes in state and local governments.
Symposium conducted by the Tax Institute
of America; November 5-6, 1970. Lexington,
Mass., D.C. Heath, 1972.
176p. (Lexington books)

1. Taxation. 2. State finance. 3. Local
government - Finance. I. Tax Institute of
America.

LAW
T
T192C
TAX INSTITUTE OF AMERICA.
CERTIFICATE OF INCORPORATION BYLAWS
TAX-EXEMPT RULING. PRINCETON, N.J.,
1963.
15P.

1. TAXATION.

336.2
T19CUR
TAX INSTITUTE.
CURBING INFLATION THROUGH TAXATION,
BY MARRINER S. ECCLES, ALVIN H.
HANSEN, HOMER HOYT AND OTHERS...
SYMPOSIUM CONDUCTED BY... FEBRUARY 7-8,
1944. NEW YORK, TAX INSTITUTE, INC.,
C1944.
261P.

1. TAXATION. 2. INFLATION.
I. ECCLES, MARRINER S. II. TITLE.

336.2
T194
Tax Institute, Princeton, N. J.
Depreciation and taxes, by E. Cary Brown
and others. Princeton, 1958.
238p. (Series on The impact of taxation on management responsibility)

"Symposium conducted by the Tax Institute,
November 20-21, 1958."

1. Taxation. I. Title.

LAW
T
T194D
TAX INSTITUTE, PRINCETON, N.J.
A DYNAMIC ORGANIZATION MAKING AN
IMPORTANT CONTRIBUTION TO THE NATION.
PRINCETON, N.J., 1961.
12P.

1. TAXATION.

LAW
T
T194EF
TAX INSTITUTE, PRINCETON, N.J.
THE EFFECT OF TAX POLICY ON EXECUTIVE
AND WORKER COMPENSATION. PRINCETON,
N.J., 1958.
80P. (THE IMPACT OF TAXATION ON
MANAGEMENT RESPONSIBILITY)

1. TAXATION. 2. INCOME.

353
F22
Tax Institute of America.
Federal-State-local fiscal relationships.
[Papers and discussions] by C. Lowell Harriss
[and others] Princeton, N.J., Tax Institute
of America, 1968.
502p.
Symposium conducted by the Tax Institute of
America, Nov. 29 - Dec. 1, 1967.
Partial contents:-Strengthening local govern-
ment through state action: the dynamics of Fed-
eralism, by Norman Beckman, Director, Office of
Intergovernmental Relations and Planning Assist-
ance, U.S. Dept. of Housing and Urban Develop-
ment.
(Cont'd on next card)

353
F22
Federal-State-local fiscal...1968.   (Card 2)

1. Intergovernmental relations. 2. Grants-in-
aid. 3. State finance. 4. Municipal finance.
5. County finance. I. Tax Institute of America.
II. Beckman, Norman. Strengthening local government through state action.

336.211
(41)
T19
TAX INSTITUTE OF AMERICA.
SHOULD THE UNITED STATES ADOPT THE
BRITISH SYSTEM OF ASSESSING REALTY.
NEW YORK, 1944.
31P. (ITS FORUM PAMPHLET 2)

1. REAL PROPERTY - TAXATION - U.K.
2. REAL PROPERTY - VALUATION - U.K.
I. TITLE.

336
F22s
Tax Institute of America.
Federal-State-local fiscal relationships.
Symposium conducted by the Tax Institute of
America, Nov. 29 - Dec. 1, 1967.
Princeton, N.J., Tax Institute of America,
1968.
502p.
Partial contents:-Strengthening local gov-
ernment through State action: the dynamics of
Federalism, by Norman Beckman, Director,
Office of Intergovernmental Relations and
Planning Assistance, U.S. Dept. of Housing
and Urban Development.
(Cont'd on next card)

336
F22s
Federal-State-local fiscal...1968.   (Card 2)

1. Finance. 2. Grants-in-aid. 3. Intergovernmental relations. I. Tax Institute of
America. II. Beckman, Norman. Strengthening
local government.

711.73
:330
082
Tax Institute, Princeton, N. J.
Owen, Wilfred.
Financing highways, by Wilfred Owen
and others. Princeton, N. J., Tax Institute,
1957.
217 p.

"Symposium conducted by the Tax Institute,
November 8-9, 1956, Princeton."

1. Highways - Finance. I. Tax Institute,
Princeton, N. J.

352.1
T19
1955
Tax Institute, Princeton, N.J.
Financing metropolitan government, by Carl H.
Chatters and others. Symposium conducted by
the Tax Institute, November 18-19, 1954.
Princeton, N.J., 1955.
295p.

1. Municipal finance. 2. Taxation.
3. Metropolitan government. I. Chatters,
Carl H. II. Title.

336
T194   TAX INSTITUTE.
          FINANCING THE WAR, BY ROBERT WARREN,
HOMER JONES, FRANK E. SEIDMAN, AND
OTHERS. SYMPOSIUM CONDUCTED BY THE TAX
INSTITUTE, DECEMBER 1-2, 1941,
PHILADELPHIA. PHILADELPHIA, TAX
INSTITUTE, 1942.
          357P.

          BIBLIOGRAPHY: P.344-352.

          1. FINANCE. 2. WORLD WAR, 1939-1945 -
ECONOMIC EFFECT.
I. WARREN, ROBERT BEACH.   II. TITLE.

336.2
T19ta Tax Institute, Princeton, N.J.
          The Tax Institute, a dynamic organization
making an important contribution to the
nation. Princeton, N.J., 1960.
          12p. illus.

          1. Taxation.

          Tax overlapping in the United States.
LAW
T   U.S. Advisory Commission on Intergovernmental
A284t   Relations.
1961   Tax overlapping in the United States. An
information report. Washington, 1961.
          136p.   (M-11)

          1. Taxation. 2. State finance. I. Title.

339.5   Tax Institute of America.
S54   Smith, Dan Throop.
          Improvement in the quality of the environment:
costs and benefits. Princeton, N.J., Tax Institute of America, 1970.
          11p.
          Tax policy, March-April, 1970.

          1. Natural resources. 2. Air pollution.
3. Water pollution. 4. Refuse and refuse
disposal. I. Tax Institute of America.
II. Title.

          Tax Institute.
          Tax Institute bookshelf.

          SEE KARDEX

          Tax overlapping in the United States.
LAW
T   U.S Advisory Commission on Intergovernmental
A284ta   Relations.
          Tax overlapping in the United States. An
information report. Washington, 1964.
          235p.   (M-23)
Suppl.-- --- Supplement to Report M-23.
Washington, D.C., 1966.
          66p.

          1. Taxation. 2. State finance. I. Title.

LAW   Tax Institute, Princeton, N. J.
T   Income tax differentials, by Dan Throop
T1941 Smith and others. Princeton, 1958.
          258p.

          "Symposium conducted by the Tax Insti-
tute, November 21-22, 1957."

          1. Taxation. I. Smith, Dan Throop.
I. Title.

T194;

336.2
T19ta Tax Institute, Princeton, N.J.
1964   The Tax Institute of America; a dynamic
organization making an important contribution to the Nation. Princeton, N.J.,
1964.
          12p.

          1. Taxation.

711.535   Tax policies and urban renewal.
(7471) Citizens' Housing and Planning Council
C47t   of New York. (Special Committee on
          Tax Policies)
          Tax policies and urban renewal in New
York City; a report on a tax study, with
recommendations. New York, 1960.
          19p. tables.

          1. Urban renewal - New York (City) 2. Real estate
business - Taxation - New York (City)   I. Title.

336.2
T19m   Tax Institute, Princeton, N.J.
          Management's stake in tax
administration. Princeton, 1961.
          260p.   (Series on The impact of
taxation on Management responsibility)

          "Symposium conducted by the Tax
Institute, September 29-30, 1960."

          1. Taxation.   2. Management.
I. Title.

336.2
(8)   Tax Institute of America.
T19   Tax policy on United States investment in
1962   Latin America, by William Sprague Barnes and
others. Symposium conducted by the Tax
Institute of America, October 25-26, 1962.
Princeton, N.J., 1963.
          275p.

          1. Taxation - Latin America. I. Barnes,
William Sprague.   II. Title.

711.3
T19   TAX POLICY (PERIODICAL)
          THE DISINTEGRATION OF AMERICAN CITIES.
NEW YORK, TAX INSTITUTE, 1947.
          12P.

          ISSUE OF JUNE-JULY 1947, V. 14, NOS.
6-7.

          1. METROPOLITAN AREAS.   2. CITY
GROWTH - HISTORY.

336.211
T19   Tax Institute of America.
          The property tax: problems and potentials,
by Alfred G. Buehler and others. Symposium
conducted by the Tax Institute of America,
November 2-4, 1966. Princeton, 1967.
Ref.   494p.
          Bibliography: p. 461-485.

          1. Real property - Taxation. 2. Personal
property - Taxation. 3. Taxation. I. Buehler,
Alfred G. II. Title.

336.2
T19t   Tax Institute, Princeton, N.J.
          Taxation and operations abroad, by Russell
Baker and others. Princeton, 1960.
          308p. (Series on the Impact of taxation on
management responsibility)
          "Symposium conducted by the Tax Institute
December 3-4, 1959."

          1. Taxation.   I. Baker, Russell.

728.1   Tax policy and urban redevelopment.
N176b Beck, Morris.
no. 11   Tax policy and urban redevelopment: an
evaluation of Federal, State and local incentives for investment in urban real
estate. Newark, N.J., Rutgers, the State
University 1966.
          18p. (Background paper [no. 11] for U.S.
HUD 8-66 and U.S. National Commission on
Urban Problems)

          1. Housing. 2. Real property Taxation.
3. Urban   renewal. I. Rutgers
                 (Cont'd on next card)

336.2
T19r   Tax Institute, Princeton, N.J.
          Reappraisal of business taxation, by
Harold M. Groves and others. Symposium
conducted by the Tax Institute, December 7-8,
1961. Princeton, 1962.
          242p.

          1. Taxation. I. Groves, Harold M.
II. Title.

336
T19t   Tax Institute, Princeton, N. J.
          Total government expenditures in 1956, by
Jeanne-Louise Haviland. Princeton, 1958.
          7p. May 1958.

          Tax policy. Vol. XX5, no. 5, May 1958.

          1. Finance - U.S. I. Haviland, Jeanne-
Louise.

728.1
N176b Beck, Morris. Tax...1966.   (Card 2)
no. 11
          University, New Brunswick, N.J. II. U.S.
National Commission on Urban Problems.
III. U.S. Dept. of Housing and Urban
Development. IV. Title.

697.8   Tax Institute of America.
W45   Wilson, Douglas B
          Tax assistance and environmental pollution.
Princeton, N.J., Tax Institute of America, 1970.
          11p.

          Tax policy, July-Aug., 1970.

          1. Air pollution. 2. Water pollution.
3. Taxation. I. Tax Institute of America.
II. Title.

336.211   Tax Institute of America.
W15   Walker, Mabel.
          What's ahead in property taxation? Princeton,
N.J., Tax Institute of America, 1970.
          10p.
          Tax policy, May-June, 1970.

          1. Real property - Taxation. 2. Personal
property - Taxation. I. Tax Institute of
America. II. Title.

336.211
T194   TAX POLICY LEAGUE, INC., NEW YORK.
          PROPERTY TAXES, SYMPOSIUM, CONDUCTED
IN DECEMBER 27-29, 1939, PHILADELPHIA,
PA. NEW YORK, 1940.
          288P.

          BIBLIOGRAPHY: P. 275-283.

          1. TAXATION. 1. REAL PROPERTY -
TAXATION. I. WOODWORTH, LEO DAY.
II. MUELLER, PAUL M.   I. TITLE.

Tax Policy League

see

Tax Institute.

336.2
C657
1969
S-R

Tax reform act of 1969.
U.S. Congress. Senate. Committee on Finance.
Tax reform act of 1969. Report of the Committee on Finance, United States Senate to accompany H.R. 13270, together with separate and individual views. Washington, Govt. Print. Off., 1969.
352p. (91st Congress. 1st session. Senate. Report no. 91-552)

1. Taxation. 2. Finance. I. Title.

336.211
H45

Tax-reverted properties in urban areas.
Hillhouse, Albert Miller, 1903-
Tax-reverted properties in urban areas, by A. M. Hillhouse ... and Carl H. Chatters ... Chicago, Public administration service, 1942.
viii, 183 p. incl. illus. (map, plan) diagr., forms. 23½ cm.
Bibliographical foot-notes.

1. Land—Taxation—U. S. 2. Municipal finance—U. S. 3. Real property—U. S.   I. Chatters, Carl Hallack, 1898-   joint author.   II. Public administration service, Chicago.   III. Title.

Library of Congress   HJ4182.D4H5
                                          42—50326
     ⌐49f2⌐   336.1

336.2
(8)
T19
1962

Tax policy on United States investment in Latin America.
Tax Institute of America.
Tax policy on United States investment in Latin America, by William Sprague Barnes and others. Symposium conducted by the Tax Institute of America, October 25-26, 1962. Princeton, N.J., 1963.
275p.

1. Taxation - Latin America. I. Barnes, William Sprague. II. Title.

336.2
C657ta
1969
H-H

Tax reform proposals contained in the message from the President of April 21, 1969.
U.S. Congress. House. Committee on Ways and Means.
Tax reform proposals contained in the message from the President of April 21, 1969 and presented by representatives of the Treasury Dept. to the Committee on Ways and Means at public hearings on the subject of tax reform on Tuesday, April 22, 1969. Wash., Govt. Print. Off., 1969.
310p.
At head of title: 91st Cong., 1st sess. Committee print.
1. Taxation. I. Title.

728.1
:061.3
N17c
1962

TAX SAVING IDEAS FOR THE HOME BUILDER AND LAND DEVELOPER.
NATIONAL ASSOCIATION OF HOME BUILDERS OF THE UNITED STATES.
TAX SAVING IDEAS FOR THE HOME BUILDER AND LAND DEVELOPER. PROCEEDINGS OF THE TAX PANEL SESSION OF THE 19TH ANNUAL CONVENTION AND EXPOSITION OF THE NATIONAL ASSOCIATION OF HOME BUILDERS OF THE UNITED STATES. CHICAGO, 1962.
45L.

1. HOUSING - CONGRESSES.
2. TAXATION. 3. REAL PROPERTY - TAXATION. I. TITLE.

336.2
C65taxp

Tax proposals contained in the President's economic policy.
U.S. Congress. House. Committee on Ways and Means.
Tax proposals contained in the President's economic policy. Hearings.
Washington, Govt. Print. Off., 1971.

Hearings held: Sept. 8-17, 1971.

1. Taxation. 2. Economic policy. I. Title.

336.2
C657
1969
H-H

Tax reform, 1969.
U.S. Congress. House. Committee on Ways and Means.
Tax reform, 1969. Hearings before the Committee on Ways and Means, House of Representatives, Ninety-first Congress, first session, on the subject of tax reform. Wash., Govt. Print. Off., 1969.
15pts.
----Appx. pt.1, appx.1.
Hearings held Feb. 18-April 24, 1969.

1. Taxation. I. Title.

VF
728
:333
N17t

Tax savings for home buyers.
National Association of Home Builders.
Tax savings for home buyers. Washington, [1958]
folder.

1. Home ownership. I. Title.

336.2
(755)
A87

Tax rates in Virginia cities and urban counties.
Austin, Robert J
Tax rates in Virginia cities and urban counties. Charlottesville, Virginia, Municipal League and Institute of Government, University of Virginia, 1967.
56p. (Virginia Municipal League and Institute of Government, University of Virginia joint report no. 24)
1. Taxation - Virginia. 2. Personal property - Taxation. 3. Real property - Taxation - Virginia. I. Virginia Municipal League. II. Virginia. University. Institute of Government. III. Title.

336.2
T72

Tax reform studies and proposals.
U.S. Treasury Dept.
Tax reform studies and proposals. Joint publication: Committee on Ways and Means of the U.S. House of Representatives and Committee on Finance of the U.S. Senate. Wash., Govt. Print. Off., 1969.
4pts.
At head of title: 91st Cong., 1st sess. Committee Print.
1. Taxation. I. U.S. Congress. House. Committee on Ways and Means. II. U.S. Congress. Senate. Committee on Finance. III. Title.

728.1
:061.3
N17c
1965

Tax saving techniques for the home builder and land developer.
National Association of Home Builders of the United States.
Tax saving techniques for the home builder and land developer. Proceedings of the NAHB tax panel. Wash., 1965.
36p.
Twenty-second annual convention and exposition.

1. Housing - Congresses. 2. Taxation. 3. Real property - Taxation. 4. Leases. 5. Land use. I. Title.

336.2
C65taxr
1970
H-H

Tax recommendations of the President.
U.S. Congress. House. Committee on Ways and Means.
Tax recommendations of the President. Hearings before the Committee on Ways and Means, House of Representatives, Ninety-first Congress, second session on the subject of the tax recommendations of the President. Wash., Govt. Print. Off., 1970.
544p.
Hearings held Sept. 9 - 17, 1970.
1. Taxation. I. Title.

336.2
(797)
W17

Tax reform to meet the challenge of growth.
Washington (State) University. Bureau of Governmental Research and Services.
Tax reform to meet the challenge of growth. Proceedings of the thirty-second annual Summer Institute of Government, 1967. Seattle, 1967.
55p. (Its Report no. 166)

1. Taxation - Washington (State) 2. City growth - Washington (State) I. Washington (State) University. Summer Institute of Government. II. Title.

336.2
(75)
G15

The tax structure of the Southern States.
Galambos, Eva.
The tax structure of the Southern States: an analysis. Atlanta, Southern Regional Council, inc., 1969.
18p. (Southern Regional Council. Resources Development Center. Publication no. 1)

1. Taxation - Southeastern states. I. Southern Regional Council. II. Title.

336.2
C657
1969
H-R

Tax reform act of 1969.
U.S. Congress. Committee of Conference.
Tax reform act of 1969. Conference report to accompany H.R. 13270. Washington, Govt. Print. Off., 1969.
346p. (91st Cong., 1st sess. Report no. 91-782)

1. Taxation. I. Title.

711.14
(795)
8722

TAX REVERTED LAND.
OREGON. STATE PLANNING BOARD.
MANAGEMENT OF TAX REVERTED LANDS IN OREGON, BY ARTHUR DAMSCHEN ... IN COLLABORATION WITH V.B. STANBERY. SALEM, 1938.
95P.

PREPARED AS A REPORT ON PROJECTS O.P. 465-94-3-83 AND APN 165-94-6063 UNDER AUSPICES OF THE WORKS PROGRESS ADMINISTRATION.

1. LAND USE - OREGON. 2. TAX DELINQUENT LAN... I. DAMSCHEN,
(CONTINUED ON NEXT CARD)

VF
336.211
B58

Tax subsidies for rental housing.
Blum, Walter J
Tax subsidies for rental housing, by Walter J. Blum and Norman Bursler. The University of Chicago Law Review, v.15, no. 2, winter 1948, p. 255-281.

Bibliography footnotes.

336.2
C657
1969
S-H

Tax reform act of 1969.
U.S. Congress. Senate. Committee on Finance.
Tax reform act of 1969. Hearing before the Committee on Finance, United States Senate, Ninety-first Congress, first session, on H.R. 13270 to reform the income tax laws. Wash., Govt. Print. Off., 1969.
pts.

1. Taxation. I. Title.

711.14
(795)
8722

OREGON. STATE PLANNING BOARD.
MANAGEMENT OF ...1938.   (CARD 2)

ARTHUR. II. STANBERY, V.B. III. TITLE. IV. TITLE: TAX REVERTED LAND.

336.2
T19

Tax systems, a reference book of legislative and statistical information for all of the United States and for numerous other countries and jurisdictions. 12th ed. New York, Commerce Clearing House, 1950.
482p. tables.

1. Taxation. I. Commerce Clearing House. II. New York (State) Tax Commission.

Folio
336.2
T19
Tax systems; a yearbook of legislative and statistical information including all the states of
the United States and certain Canadian and
foreign data. 1st- ed; 1930- Chicago,
Commerce clearing house, inc. [1930-
3v. 1940 1943 1948
Prepared by the Research Foundation under the
sponsorship of the New York State Tax Commission,
1930-1942.
Prepared by the Tax Research Department of Commerce Clearing House, 1946-
1. Taxation.   I. New York (State) Tax
Commission.   II.   Commerce Clearing House.
Tax Research. Dept.

333.33
A52t
TAXATION.
Anderson, Paul E
Tax factors in real estate operations. 3d ed.
Englewood Cliffs, N.J., Prentice-Hall, 1969-
1v. (loose-leaf)

1. Real estate business. 2. Taxation.
3. Real property. I. Title.

336.2
B82
Buchanan, James M
Fiscal choice through time: a case for
indirect taxation by James M. Buchanan and
Francesco Forte Wash., Brookings Institution,
1964.
144-157p.   (Brookings Institution.
Studies of government finance. Reprint no. 81)
Reprinted from the National tax journal, June
1964.

1. Taxation. 2. Finance. I. Brookings
Institution. II. Forte, Francesco, jt. au.
III. Title.

Tax treatment of earnings of cooperatives.

334
C65
U.S. Congress. House. Committee on Ways and
Means.
Tax treatment of earnings of cooperatives. Hearings before the Committee on Ways and Means, House
of Representatives, Eighty-sixth Congress, second
session on the subject of tax treatment of earnings of cooperatives. Washington, Govt. Print.
Off., 1960.
439p. diagrs., maps, tables.
Hearings held Feb. 1-5, 1960.
1. Cooperatives.   2. Taxation. I. Title.

330
A52s
TAXATION.
Ando, Albert, ed.
Studies in economic stabilization, ed. by
Albert Ando and others. Wash., Brookings
Institution, 1968.
299p. (Brookings Institution. Studies of
government finance)

Bibliography: p. 288-294.
1. Economic policy. 2. Taxation.
I. Brookings Institution. II. Title.

336
B823
1940
TAXATION.
BUEHLER, ALFRED G
PUBLIC FINANCE.   2D ED.   NEW YORK,
MCGRAW-HILL, 1940.
846P.

1. FINANCE.   2. TAXATION.

Taxation

see also

Income tax
Real property - Taxation
Tax delinquent land
Tax incentives

332.6
B17
Taxation.
Barlow, Robin.
Economic behavior of the affluent, by
Robin Barlow and others. Wash., Brookings
Institution, 1966.
285p.   (Brookings Institution. Studies
of government finance)

1. Investments. 2. Family income and
expenditure. 3. Taxation. I. Title.

336.2
B87
TAXATION.
Business taxes in state and local governments.
Symposium conducted by the Tax Institute
of America; November 5-6, 1970. Lexington,
Mass., D.C. Heath, 1972.
176p. (Lexington books)

1. Taxation. 2. State finance. 3. Local
government - Finance. I. Tax Institute of
America.

336.2
A522
TAXATION.
AMERICAN FEDERATION OF LABOR AND
CONGRESS OF INDUSTRIAL ORGANIZATON.
RESEARCH DEPT.
FEDERAL TAXES; A HANDBOOK ON PROBLEMS
AND SOLUTIONS. WASHINGTON, AMERICAN
FEDERATION OF LABOR AND CONGRESS OF
INDUSTRIAL ORGANIZATION, 1960.
118P. (AFL-CIO PUBLICATION NO. 108)

1. TAXATION.   I. TITLE.

LAW
T
B477fe
1971

Suppl.
TAXATION.
Bittker, Boris I
Federal income taxation of corporations and
shareholders, by Boris I. Bittker and James
S. Eustice. 3d ed. Boston, Warren, Gorham &
Lamont, 1971.
1v.
-- --- Supplement. no.1-   1972-
v.
1. Corporations. 2. Taxation. 3. Income
tax. I. Eustice, James S., jt. au. II. Title.

388
C31b
Taxation.
Chamber of Commerce of the United States.
(Transportation and Communication Dept.)
Business views on local transit; an
analysis of how 1, 129 Chambers of Commerce
view the need for a federal subsidy program.
Washington, 1963.
13p.

1. Transportation. 2. Taxation.
3. Grants-in-aid.

336.2
A52
Taxation.
American Municipal Association.
Municipal exemptions from Federal excise
taxes. A League Syndicate article, by
Wilber E. Smith. Washington, 1957.
9p.

1. Taxation. I. Smith, Wilber E.

336.2
B71
TAXATION
Brabson, George Dana.
Federal taxation; basic principles and procedures. 2d ed.
Cincinnati, F. C. Rosselot Co. [1965]
xiv, 348 p.   26 cm.

1. Taxation.--Income tax. 2. Income tax.
I. Title.
336.294
Library of Congress   65-3713
[1]

VF
336.2
C31
Taxation.
Champion, George.
Taxes and the government debt: a plan for
the 'sixties. An address before the State
Bank Division, American Bankers Association
Convention, San Francisco, October 16, 1961.
13p.

1. Taxation. I. American Bankers
Association Convention, San Francisco,
1961.

VF
352.1
A52
(Federal) taxation.
American Management Association.
Tax exemptions and liabilities of municipalities; a compilation showing federal taxes from
which municipalities are exempt and for which
they are liable with particular emphasis on
excise taxes, by Randy H. Hamilton. Chicago,
April 1954.
8 p.   (Its Publication BJM)

1. Municipal finance. 2. Federal taxation.
I. Hamilton, Randy H

336
B72
Taxation.
Break, George F
Intergovernmental fiscal relations in the
United States. A background paper prepared
for a conference of experts held November 18-
19, 1965, together with a summary of the con-
ference discussion. Washington, Brookings
Institution, 1967.
273p.   (Studies of government finance)

1. Finance. 2. Taxation. 3. Grants-in-aid.
4. Intergovernmental relations. I. Brookings
Institution. II. Title.

LAW
T
C342f
Taxation - Congresses.
Chicago. University. Law School.
Federal Tax Conference [Papers]

Chicago, Commerce Clearing House,
v.   annual.

Reprinted from Taxes, the tax magazine.

1. Taxation - Congresses. I. Commerce
Clearing House. II. Title.

336.2
A52s
Taxation.
Anderson, Lynn F
State-local fiscal effort, a measurement.
Austin, Tex., Institute of Public Affairs,
University of Texas, 1960.
6p.

Public affairs comment, vol. VI, no. 6,
Nov., 1960.

1. Taxation. I. Texas. University. Institute
of Public Affairs.

336.2
B82E
TAXATION.
BUCHANAN, JAMES M
THE ECONOMICS OF EARMARKED TAXES.
WASHINGTON, THE BROOKINGS INSTITUTION,
1963.
P. 457-469.

REPRINTED FROM THE JOURNAL OF
POLITICAL ECONOMY, DECEMBER 1963.

1. TAXATION.   2. ECONOMICS.
I. BROOKINGS INSTITUTION.   II. TITLE.

LAW
T
C665TA
TAXATION.
COOLEY, THOMAS M
THE LAW OF TAXATION. 4TH ED. BY
CLARK A. NICHOLS. CHICAGO, CALLAGHAN,
1924.
4 V.

1. TAXATION.   I. NICHOLS, CLARK A.,
ED.

Taxation.

336.2
C65n   Commerce Clearing House.
New depreciation rules with explanation.
Chicago, 1962.
56p.

1. Depreciation and obsolescence.
2. Taxation.

Taxation.

336.2
C65re   Committee for Economic Development.
Reducing tax rates for production and
growth; a statement on national policy
by the Research and Policy Committee.
New York, 1962.
56p.

1. Taxation. 2. Economic development.

333
E17r   TAXATION
EBS Management Consultants. inc.
Revenue sharing and payments in lieu of
taxes on the public land. Prepared for
Public Land Law Review Commission.
Wash., 1968.
4v.

1. Public lands. 2. Taxation.
3. Payment in lieu of taxes. I. U.S.
Public Land Law Review Commission.
II. Title.

Taxation.

336.2
C655s   Commerce Clearing House.
State tax handbook,

Washington, 19

v.

For complete information see main card.

1. Taxation. 2. State finance. I. Title.

336.2
C65   Taxation.
Committee for Economic Development.
Tax reduction and tax reform - when and how;
a statement on national policy by the Research
and Policy Committee. New York, 1957.
40 p. illus., tables.

1. Taxation.

336.2
E97   TAXATION.
Extractive resources and taxation; [proceedings
of a symposium sponsored by the Committee
on Taxation, Resources, and Economic De-
velopment (TRED) at the University of
Wisconsin-Milwaukee, 1964] Ed. by Mason
Gaffney. Madison, University of Wisconsin
Press, 1967.
450p.
1. Taxation. 2. Natural resources.
I. Gaffney, Mason, ed. II. Committee on
Taxation, Resources, and Economic Development.

Taxation.

336.2
C65u   Commerce Clearing House.
US master tax guide, 19

Washington, 19
v.

For complete information see main card.

1. Taxation. 2. Income tax. 3. Personal
property - Taxation. 4. Real property -
Taxation. I. Title.

Taxation.

336
C655t   Committee for Economic Development.
(Research and Policy Committee)
Taxes and the budget: a program for
prosperity in a free economy; a statement
on national policy. New York, 1947.
77p. graphs, tables.

1.Budget - U.S. 2.Taxation.

Taxation.

336.2
F22   Federal Reserve Bank of Philadelphia.
Tax cut: price of prosperity? Philadelphia,
1963.
9p. (Series for economic education)

1. Taxation.

336.2
C65be   Taxation.
Committee for Economic Development.
A better balance in Federal taxes on
business. A statement on national policy
by the Research and Policy Committee of the
Committee for Economic Development. New
York, 1966.
37p.

1. Taxation. 2. National income.
I. Title.

336.2
C65tax   Taxation.
Committee for Economic Development.
Taxes and trade: 20 years of CED policy.
Report of the Twentieth anniversary meeting,
Washington, D.C., May 9, 1963. [Addresses]
New York, 1963.
53p.

Excerpts from the address by President
John F. Kennedy, printed in this volume.

1. Taxation. I. Title.

728.1
1355
F22S   TAXATION.
FEDERATION OF TAX ADMINISTRATORS.
STATE AND LOCAL TAX STATUS OF MILITARY
HOUSING PROGRAMS. CHICAGO, 1956.
10L. (RM 342)

1. MILITARY HOUSING. 2. TAXATION.

VF
336.2
C65b   Taxation.
Committee for Economic Development.
Big budgets and tax reform. An address by
Howard C. Petersen before the 51st annual
Conference on Taxation of the National Tax
Association, Philadelphia, October 28, 1958.
New York, 1958.
15p.

1. Taxation. 2. Budget. I. Peterson,
Howard C

336.2
C655   Taxation.
Committee on Federal Tax Policy.
Financing America's future: taxes, economic
stability and growth. New York, 1963.
64p.

1. Taxation. 2. Economic development.

336.2
F67   TAXATION.
FOREIGN TAX POLICIES AND ECONOMIC
GROWTH, A CONFERENCE REPORT OF THE
NATIONAL BUREAU OF ECONOMIC RESEARCH
AND THE BROOKINGS INSTITUTION. NEW
YORK, NATIONAL BUREAU OF ECONOMIC
RESEARCH; DISTRIBUTED BY COLUMBIA
UNIVERSITY PRESS, 1966.
482P.

1. TAXATION. 2. ECONOMIC DEVELOPMENT.
I. NATIONAL BUREAU OF ECONOMIC RESEARCH.
II. BROOKINGS INSTITUTION.

Taxation.

336.2
C65e   Committee for Economic Development.
Essays in Federal taxation, by Herbert
Stein and Joseph A. Pechman. [Requested
by the Committee on Ways and Means, House of
Representatives] New York, 1959.
82p. tables.

Reprinted from the Tax Revision Compendium.

1. Taxation. I. Stein, Herbert. II. Pechman,
Joseph A.

336.2
C653   Taxation.
Conference on Economic Progress.
Taxes and the public interest. Tax policies
to: promote maximum employment, production
and economic growth, help meet our great
national priorities, advance economic and
social justice, balance the budget, at
maximum prosperity levels. Washington, 1963.
86p.

1. Taxation. 2. Economic policy.

LAW
T   Taxation.
Fremont-Smith, Marion R
Foundations of government; State and
Federal law and supervision. New York,
Russell Sage Foundation, 1965.
564p.

List of cases: p. 535-539.

1. Foundations, Charitable and educational.
2. Federal government. 3. Taxation. I. U.S.
Internal Revenue Service. II. Russell Sage
Foundation. III. Title.

Taxation.

336.2
C65g   Committee for Economic Development.
Growth and taxes, steps for 1961; a statement on national policy by the Research and
Policy Committee of the Committee for Economic Development. New York, 1961.
38p.

1. Taxation. 2. Economic development.

352.1
C72t   TAXATION.
Crestol, Jack.
Tax and investment opportunities with municipal bonds. New York, Moody's Investors Service,
1970.
20p.

1. Municipal bonds. 2. Taxation.
I. Moody's Investors Service. II. Title.

336.2
F76   TAXATION.
Fromm, Gary, ed.
Tax incentives and capital spending.
Papers presented at a conference of experts
held on November 3, 1967. Wash., Brookings
Institution, 1971.
301p. (Studies of government finance)

Bibliography: p. 280-296.

1. Taxation. 2. Finance. I. Brookings
Institution. II. Title.

360
G72

TAXATION.
Green, Christopher.
Negative taxes and the poverty problem; a background paper prepared for a conference of experts held June 8-9, 1966, together with a summary of the conference discussion. Washington, Brookings Institution, 1967.
210p. (Studies of government finance)
Bibliography: p. 197-202.

1. Social welfare. 2. Family income and expenditure. 3. Taxation. I. Brookings Institution, Washington, D.C. II. Title.

336.18
H43

TAXATION.
Highlights of revenue sharing; reform, renewal for the 70's. [n.p., 1971?]
30p.

1. Grants-in-aid. 2. Municipal finance.
3. State finance. 4. Taxation.

336.2
J25

TAXATION.
JENSEN, JENS PETER.
PROPERTY TAXATION IN THE UNITED STATES. CHICAGO, UNIVERSITY OF CHICAGO PRESS, 1931.
532P.

BIBLIOGRAPHY P. 493-515.

1. TAXATION. I. TITLE.

336.2
G76

Taxation.
Groves, Harold M.
Postwar taxation and economic progress. New York, McGraw-Hill, 1946.
432 p. charts, tables.

At head of title: Committee for Economic Development. Research Study.

352.1
H45r

Taxation.
Hillhouse, Albert Miller.
Revenue estimating by cities, by Albert Miller Hillhouse and S. Kenneth Howard. Chicago, Municipal Finance Officers Association of the United States and Canada, 1965.
16p.
Bibliography: p. 15-16.

1. Municipal finance. 2. Taxation.
I. Howard, S. Kenneth, jt. au. II. Municipal Finance Officers Association of the United States and Canada. III. Title.

336.2
J63

TAXATION.
Johnson, Harry L, ed.
State and local tax problems. Knoxville, University of Tennessee Press, 1969.
190p.

1. Taxation. 2. State finance.
3. Municipal finance. I. Title.

336.2
G76P

TAXATION.
GROVES, HAROLD M
PRODUCTION, JOBS AND TAXES. POSTWAR REVISION OF THE FEDERAL TAX SYSTEM TO HELP ACHIEVE HIGHER PRODUCTION AND MORE JOBS. NEW YORK, MCGRAW HILL, 1944.
116P. (COMMITTEE FOR ECONOMIC DEVELOPMENT RESEARCH STUDY)

1. TAXATION. I. COMMITTEE FOR ECONOMIC DEVELOPMENT. II. TITLE.

352.1
H45

Taxation.
Hillhouse, Albert Miller
Where cities get their money: Supplements 1947, 1949, 1951, 1956,
Chicago, Municipal Finance Officers' Association of the United States and Canada, 1947-
v.
Title: 1951- Municipal nonproperty taxes.

1949 suppl. by Miner B. Phillipps; 1956 suppl., pt. 1: The shifting revenue pattern, by Harold F. Alderfer; pt. 2. Municipal nonproperty tax developments, by Robert L. Funk.

[over]

339.3
K25t

TAXATION.
Kelly, L A
Income maintenance, tax savings and the incentive to work. Kingston, Ont., Industrial Relations Centre, Queen's University, 1970.
18p. (Research series no. 13)

Bibliography: p. 17-18.

1. Income. 2. Taxation. I. Kingston, Ont. Queen's University. Industrial Relations Centre. II. Title.

352.1
G78

Taxation.
Grunloh, James J
Alternate measures of fiscal capacity. [Prepared] under a grant from the Committee on Urban Economics, Resources for the Future, Inc. St. Louis, Institute for Urban and Regional Studies, Washington University, 1967.
19p. (Washington University. Institute for Urban and Regional Studies. Working paper DRA 6)

1. Municipal finance. 2. Taxation.
3. Grants-in-aid. I. Resources for the Future. II. Washington (State) University Institute for Urban and Regional Studies.

352
H45

Taxation.
Hindman, Jo
Blame metro, when urban renewal strikes! When laws oppress. Caldwell, Idaho, Caxton Printers, 1966.
175p.

1. Intergovernmental relations. 2. Public administration. 3. Urban renewal. 4. Metropolitan government. 5. Taxation. I. Title.

336.2
K59

TAXATION.
Keyserling, Leon H
Taxation of whom and for what; "tax reform" versus tax reform. Wash., Conference on Economic Progress, 1969.
65p.

1. Taxation. I. Conference on Economic Progress. II. Title.

353
H17

Taxation.
Harriss, C Lowell.
Handbook of state and local government finance. New York, Tax Foundation, 1966.
64p.

1. State finance. 2. State government.
3. Taxation. I. Tax Foundation.
II. Title.

336.2
H65a

TAXATION.
Holland, Daniel M ed.
The assessment of land value. Madison, Published for the Committee on Taxation, Resources and Economic Development by the University of Wisconsin Press, 1970.
292p. (TRED publication no. 5)
Proceedings of a symposium sponsored by the Committee on Taxation, Resources and Economic Development (TRED) at the University of Wisconsin, Milwaukee, 1969.
1. Taxation. 2. Real property - Taxation.
I. Committee on Taxation, Resources and Economic Development. II. Title: Land value. III. Title.

336.2
K45

Taxation.
Kimmel, Lewis H
Governmental costs and tax levels, by Lewis H. Kimmel [and] Mildred Maroney. Washington, Brookings Institution, c1948.
153 p. tables.

1. Taxation. I. Maroney, Mildred. II. Brookings Institution. III. Title.

330
:355.8
H17f

(Federal) taxation.
Hart, Albert G
Financing defense; federal tax and expenditure policies [by] Albert G. Hart [and] E. Cary Brown, assisted by H. F. Rasmussen; with policy recommendations by the Committee on Economic Stabilization.
161 p.

1. Economic policy. 2. National defense. 3. Federal taxation. I. Brown, E Cary, jt. author. II. Twentieth Century Fund. Committee on Economic Stabilization. III. Title.

336
H681

TAXATION.
HOWARD, MAYNE S
PRINCIPLES OF PUBLIC FINANCE. CHICAGO, COMMERCE CLEARING HOUSE, INC., 1940.
438P.

1. FINANCE. 2. TAXATION.

336.2
K45T

TAXATION.
KIMMEL, LEWIS H
TAXES AND ECONOMIC INCENTIVES. WASHINGTON, THE BROOKINGS INSTITUTION, 1950.
217P.

1. TAXATION. I. TITLE.

LAW
T
H277op

Taxation.
Herring, Frances W ed.
Open space and the law, by Roger W. Findley and others. Berkeley, Calif., Institute of Governmental Studies, University of California, 1965.
160p.

1. Open space land - Legislation. 2. Taxation. I. Findley, Roger W. II. California. University. Institute of Governmental Studies. III. Title.

333.332
I57

TAXATION.
International Association of Assessing Officers.
State assessment districts. Chicago, 1969.
11p. (Its Monograph no. 3)

1. Appraisal. 2. Real property - Valuation.
3. Taxation. I. Title.

336.2
L23

Taxation.
Legler, John B
The responsiveness of state tax revenue to economic growth, by John B. Legler and Perry Shapiro. St. Louis, Institute for Urban and Regional Studies, Washington University, 1967.
21p. (Resources for the Future. Committee on Urban Economics. Working paper DRA 8)
1. Taxation. 2. Cost and standard of living. I. Shapiro, Perry, jt. au. II. Resources for the Future. III. Washington University, St. Louis. Institute for Urban and Regional Studies. IV. Title.

Taxation.

336
L28
   Lewis, Wilfred, Jr.
     Federal fiscal policy in the postwar
recessions. Washington, Brookings
Institution, 1962.
     311p. (Brookings Institution. Studies
of government finance)

     1. Finance. 2. Taxation. I. Brookings
Institution. II. Title.

Taxation.

LAW
T
   Montgomery, Robert H
     Montgomery's federal taxes. 36th ed.
Ed. by Philip Bardes and others. New
York, Ronald Press, 1955.
     1v.

     1. Taxation. I. Bardes, Philip, ed.

LAW   Taxation.
T
N17   National Association of Home Builders.
A772r   Real estate investment trusts (amendments
to internal revenue code) by Leonard L.
Silverstein and Burton C. Wood.
   Tax report. Washington, 1960.
     5p.

     1. Taxation. 2. Real property - Legislation.
I. Silverstein, Leonard L. II. Wood, Burton C.
III. Title.

336.2   Taxation.
L45
1965   Lindholm, Richard W   ed.
     Property taxation, U.S.A. Proceedings of a
symposium sponsored by the Committee on Taxation, Resources and Economic Development
(TRED) at the University of Wisconsin, Milwaukee, 1965. Madison, University of Wiscon-
N.c.1, sin Press, 1967.
2   315p.
L&f.c.3
     1. Taxation. 2. Personal property - Taxation.
3. Real property - Taxation. 4. Tax delinquent
land. I. Title.

336.2   Taxation.
M67
   Moryadas, Virginia.
     Property taxation and metropolitan area open
space, by Virginia Moryadas and Royal Shipp.
Wash., Urban Land Institute, 1968.
     76p.
     Supplements The present and potential role
of state and local taxation in the preservation
or development of open space land in urban
fringe areas, by John E. Rickert.
     Prepared for the U.S. Dept. of Housing and
Urban Development.
     1. Taxation. 2. Real property - Taxation.
3. Open space land. I. Urban Land Institute.
II. Rickert, John E. III. Title. IV. U.S.
Dept. of Housing and Urban Development.

333.332   Taxation.
N17r   National Association of Home Builders.
     Residential development, a financial
asset to the community, by Robert C.
Ledermann. An evaluation of surveys and
reports on the impact of new homes on a
community's cost-revenue structure.
Washington, 1960.
     12p.

     1. Real property - Valuation.
2. Taxation. I. Ledermann, Robert C.

Taxation.

331
M12
   McKean, Eugene C
     The taxable wage base in unemployment
insurance financing. Kalamazoo, Mich., W. E.
Upjohn Institute for Community Research, 1965.
     96p. (W. E. Upjohn Institute for
Employment Research. Unemployment insurance
monograph)

     1. Employment. 2. Taxation. I. Upjohn
Institute for Employment Research. II. Title:
Unemployment insurance financing.

---

330   TAXATION.
(73)
M68   Moulton, Harold Glenn, 1883-
     Capital expansion, employment, and economic
stability, by Harold G. Moulton and others.
Washington, The Brookings institution, 1940.
     413 p. (The Institute of Economics of the
Brookings Institution. Publication no. 82).
     1. Economic policy. 2. Econ. condit.
3. Finance. 4. Investments. 5. Taxation.
I. Title. II. Brookings Institution, Washington, D.C. Institute of Economics. Publication no. 82.

728.1   TAXATION.
:061.3 NATIONAL ASSOCIATION OF HOME BUILDERS
N17C   OF THE UNITED STATES.
1962   TAX SAVING IDEAS FOR THE HOME BUILDER
     AND LAND DEVELOPER. PROCEEDINGS [OF
THE TAX PANEL SESSION] OF THE 19TH
ANNUAL CONVENTION AND EXPOSITION OF THE
NATIONAL ASSOCIATION OF HOME BUILDERS
OF THE UNITED STATES. CHICAGO, 1962.
     45L.

     1. HOUSING - CONGRESSES.
2. TAXATION. 3. REAL PROPERTY -
TAXATION. I. TITLE.

LAW   Taxation.
T
M152ma Mandelker, Daniel R
     Managing our urban environment: cases, text,
and problems. Indianapolis, Bobbs-Merrill,
1966.
     1003p. (Contemporary legal education
series)

     1. Law - Cases. 2. Annexation. 3. Eminent
domain. 4. Housing codes. 5. Housing law
enforcement. 6. Zoning. 7. Taxation.
I. Title. II. Title (Series: Contemporary
legal education series)

---

336   Taxation.
M87
   Musgrave, Richard A   ed.
     Essays in fiscal federalism. Washington,
Brookings Institution, 1965.
     301p. (Studies of government finance)

     1. Finance. 2. National income.
3. Taxation. 4. Intergovernmental relations.
I. Brookings Institution. II. Title.

728.1   Taxation.
:061.3
N17c   National Association of Home Builders of
1965   the United States.
     Tax saving techniques for the home
builder and land developer. Proceedings
of the NAHB tax panel. Wash., 1965.
     36p.
     Twenty-second annual convention and
exposition.

     1. Housing - Congresses. 2. Taxation.
3. Real property - Taxation. 4. Leases.
5. Land use. I. Title.

336.2   TAXATION.
M19t
   Maxwell, James Achley, 1897-
     A tax credit for certain educational ex-
penses, by James A. Maxwell and Bernard L.
Weinstein. Wash., Govt. Print. Off., 1971.
     58p.

     1. Taxation. 2. Education - Finance.
I. U.S. President's Commission on School
Finance. II. Weinstein, Bernard L., jt. au.
III. Title.

---

336   Taxation.
M87t
   Musgrave, Richard A
     The theory of public finance; a study in
public economy. New York, McGraw-Hill, 1959.
     628p.

     1. Finance. 2. Taxation. 3. Money.
4. Investments. 5. Monopolies. I. Title.

338.53   Taxation.
N17
   National Association of Manufacturers.
     Inflation; the silent tax. New York, 1967.
     30p.
     Proceedings of a special feature session,
72nd Congress of American Industry, New York,
New York, Dec. 8, 1967.

     1. Inflation. 2. Budget. 3. Taxation.
I. Title.

336.2   Taxation.
M19
   Maxwell, James A
     Tax credits and intergovernmental fiscal
relations. Washington, Brookings Institution,
1962.
     202p.

     1. Taxation. 2. Credit. 3. Intergovern-
mental relations. I. Brookings Institution,
Washington, D.C.

---

379   Taxation.
M87
   Mushkin, Selma J
     Local school expenditures; 1970 projections,
by Selma J. Mushkin and Eugene P. McLoone.
Chicago, Council of State Governments in
cooperation with the National Association of
Counties [and others] 1965.
     84p. (Council of State Governments.
Research memorandum 382)

     1. Education - Finance. 2. Education -
Statistics. 3. Taxation. I. McLoone,
Eugene P., jt. au. II. Council of State
Governments. III. Title.

336.2   Taxation.
N17g
   National Association of Tax Administrators.
     Guide for assessment-sales ratio studies.
Report of the Committee on Sales Ratio
Data. Chicago, Federation of Tax Adminis-
trators, 1954.
     69p.
     Bibliography: p. 61-69.

     1. Taxation. 2. Real property - Valuation.
I. Federation of Tax Administrators.
II. Title. III. Title: Assessment-sales
ratio studies.

VF   Taxation.
711.585 Memphis. Housing Authority.
(768191)   Costs vs benefits. Railroad Avenue
M25c   Project; a case history in urban renewal.
Memphis [1964?]
     folder.

     1. Urban renewal - Memphis.
2. Taxation - Memphis.

336.2   Taxation.
M87
   Mushkin, Selma J
     Project '70; projecting the State-local
sector, by Selma J. Mushkin and Gabrielle C.
Lupo. Washington, George Washington
University, State-Local Finances Project, 1966.
     51p.

     1. Taxation. 2. Intergovernmental relations.
I. Lupo, Gabrielle C., jt. au. II. George
Washington University. State-Local Finances
Project. III. Title.

---

336   TAXATION.
N17pu
   National Bureau of Economic Research.
     Public expenditures and taxation. Economic
research: retrospect and prospect. Fiftieth
anniversary colloquium IV. New York, National
Bureau of Economic Research; distributed by
Columbia University Press, 1972.
     74p. (National Bureau of Economic Research
general series96)

     1. Finance. 2. Taxation. I. Title.

LAW
T
917
IS28TA

TAXATION.
NATIONAL INDUSTRIAL CONFERENCE BOARD,
INC.
THE TAXATION OF BANKS. NEW YORK,
1934.
148P.

1. TAXATION.   2. BANKS AND BANKING.

336.2
O77   Ott, David J   Federal tax treatment of
state and local...1963.   (Card 2)

1. Taxation.   2. Finance.
I. Meltzer,   Allan H., jt. au.
II. Brookings
Institution.

336.2
P25f   Pennell, John S
Federal income taxation of partners and
partnerships, by John S. Pennell and John
C. O'Byrne. Philadelphia, Joint Committee
on Continuing Legal Education of the American
Law Institute and the American Bar Association, 1970.
355p.
1. Taxation. I. O'Byrne, John C., jt. au.
II. Joint Committee on Continuing Legal
Education of the American Law Institute
and the American Bar Association. III. Title.

330
N1746 Nation's business.
Boardwalks to barbecue pits: look what your
Federal taxes buy. Nation's business editors,
in on-the-scene check of public works spending,
find amazing tangle of costly local projects
financed by U.S. taxpayers. In Nation's
business, Oct. 1963. p. 34-37, 112-118, 122-
124.

1. Taxation. 2. Community facilities.
I. Title.

336.2
P18   TAXATION.
Paul, Randolph E
Taxation in the United States. Boston,
Little, Brown, 1954.
830p.

1. Taxation. I. Title.

353
(748)
P25a

Taxation.
Pennsylvania. Dept. of Internal Affairs.
An analysis of local tax collection costs
in Pennsylvania (second issue) by Richard F.
Schier and Eric A. Vadelund. Harrisburg,
Pa., 1958.
36p.

1. State finance - Pennsylvania. 2.
Taxation. I. Schier, Richard F II. Vadelund,
Eric A

330
N1746 Nation's business.
How Washington would control your city; this
example shows how power grows. In Nation's
business, Oct. 1963. p. 34-37, 112-118,
122-124.

1. Taxation. 2. Community facilities.
I. Title.

336.2
P22f   Taxation.
Pechman, Joseph A
Federal tax policy. Washington,
Brookings Institution, 1966.
321p.   (Studies of government
finance)

1. Taxation. I. Brookings Institution.
II. Title.

331.252
P25
1964

Taxation.
Pensions and profit sharing, by Herman C.
Riegel and others. 3d ed. Washington, BNA,
inc., 1964.
283p.

1. Pension funds. 2. Social security. 3. Taxation. 4. Life insurance. I. Riegel, Herman C.
II. Bureau of National Affairs, Washington.

336.211
N27   Taxation.
Netzer, Dick.
Economics of the property tax. Wash.,
Brookings Institution, 1966.
326p.   (Studies of government finance)

1. Real property - Taxation. 2. Taxation.
3. Economic policy. I. Brookings
Institution, Washington, D.C.

336.2
P22   Taxation.
Pechman, Joseph A
Individual income tax provisions of the
Revenue act of 1964. Washington, Brookings
Institution, 1965.
247-272p.   (Brookings Institution.
Studies of government finance. Reprint 96)
Reprinted from the Journal of finance,
May 1965.

1. Taxation. 2. Income tax.
3. Real property - Taxation. I. Brookings
Institution.   II. Title.

336
P27   Taxation.
Perloff, Harvey S   ed.
Revenue sharing and the city. Edited by
Harvey S. Perloff and Richard P Nathan.
Papers and the discussion by Walter W. Heller
and others. Based on a conference sponsored
by the Committee on Urban Economics of
Resources for the Future, inc. [Baltimore]
Published for Resources for the Future, inc.
by the Johns Hopkins Press, 1968.
112p.

1. Finance. 2. Federal government. 3.
Intergovernmental relations. 4. Taxation.

336.211
N271   Netzer, Dick.
Impact of the property tax; effect on
housing, urban land use, local government,
finance. Prepared for the consideration of
the National Commission on Urban Problems.
Washington, D.C., Govt. Print. Off., 1968.
82p. (National Commission on Urban Problems.
Research report no.1)
Chairman, National Commission on Urban Prob-
lems, Paul H. Douglas.
1. Real property - Taxation. 2. Taxation.
I. Douglas, Paul H. II. Title. (Series:
National   Commission on Urban
Problems.   Research report no.1)

336.2
P22f
1971

TAXATION.
Pechman, Joseph A
Federal tax policy. rev. ed. Wash.,
Brookings Institution, 1971.
344p. (Studies of government finance)

Bibliography: p. 320-332.

1. Taxation. I. Brookings Institution.
II. Title.

336
P27   Perloff, Harvey S   ed. Revenue sharing
and the city...1968.   (Card 2)

I. Nathan, Richard P., jt. au. II. Heller,
Walter W. III. Resources for the Future, inc.
IV. Title.

336.211
N271
Joint
Committee
Print

TAXATION.
Netzer, Dick.
Impact of the property tax: effect on hous-
ing, urban land use, local government finance.
Prepared for the consideration of the National
Commission on Urban Problems. Wash., Govt.
Print. Off., 1968.
48p.
At head of title: 90th Cong., 2d sess.
Cover title: Impact of the property tax: its
economic implications for urban problems.

1. Real property - Taxation. 2. Taxation.
I. U.S. National Commission on Urban
Problems.   II. Title.

336.2
P22r   TAXATION.
Pechman, Joseph A
The rich, the poor, and the taxes they pay.
Wash., Brookings Institution, 1969.
[22]p. (Brookings Institution reprint
no. 168)
Reprinted from: the Public interest,
no. 17 (fall 1969), pp. 21-43.

1. Taxation. I. Brookings Institution.
II. Title.

336.18
P34   TAXATION.
Philip, Kjeld.
Intergovernmental fiscal relations; Federal,
state and local finances. Copenhagen, Institute of Economics and History, 1954.
171p.
Bibliography: p. 163-171.
1. Grants-in-aid. 2. Intergovernmental
relations. 3. Taxation. I. Title.

336.2
O77   Ott, David J
Federal tax treatment of state and local
securities, by David J. Ott and Allan H.
Meltzer. Washington, Brookings Institution,
1963.
146p. (Brookings Institution. Studies of
Government finance)

"A background paper prepared for
conference of experts held Jan. 25-26
together with a summary of the conference
discussion."

(Continued on next card)

352.1
P25

Taxation.
Pelletier, Lawrence Lee.   Hollowell
Financing local government. Brunswick, Me., 1948.
190 p. 23 cm. (Bowdoin College. Municipal research series, no.
12) Maine Municipal Association. Handbook
series, no.6)

For the Maine Municipal Association.

1. Municipal finance—U. S. 2. Taxation—U. S. I. Title.
III Series) II.Maine Municipal Association.
HJ9145.P4   352.1   49-3622*
Library of Congress   (7)

336.2
P42   Taxation.
Pickard, Jerome P
Changing urban land uses as affected by
taxation; a conference summary report.
Washington, D.C., Urban Land Institute, 1962.
105p. (Urban Land Institute. Research
monograph 6)

1. Taxation. 2. Land use. I. Urban Land
Institute.   (Series)
3. Real property - Taxation.

336.2
P42t
    Taxation.
Pickard, Jerome P
    Taxation and land use in metropolitan and urban America. Washington, Urban Land Institute, 1966.
    40p.   (Urban Land Institute. Research monograph no. 12)

    1. Taxation. 2. Land use. 3. Real property - Taxation. I. Urban Land Institute.

336.2
R21
    Taxation.
Research Institute of America.
    Tax guide for homeowners. New York, 1962.
    40p.   (Its Planning report, 1962)

    1. Taxation. 2. Real property - Taxation.

353
S15
N.c.1,2
Laf.c.3
    Taxation.
Sanford, Terry.
    Storm over the states. New York, McGraw-Hill, 1967.
    218p.

    1. State government. 2. Federal government. 3. Intergovernmental relations. 4. Taxation. 5. Political science. I. Title.

336.2
P66
    Taxation.
Poole, Richard W
    State-local taxes and industrial location; a logical frame of reference. Durant, Okla., Technology Use Studies Center, Southeastern State College, 1965.
    9p. (Oklahoma. Southeastern State College. Technology Use Studies Center. Bulletin 3)

    1. Taxation. 2. Industrial location. I. Oklahoma. Southeastern State College, Durant. II. Title.

336.2
R42
    Taxation.
Richman, Raymond.
    Effects of a development project on the revenues of state and local governments. St. Louis, Institute for Urban and Regional Studies, Washington University, 1966.
    48p. (Water Resource Investment Project. Working paper CWR 6)

    1. Taxation. 2. State government. 3. Intergovernmental relations. 4. Water resources. I. Washington University. Institute for Urban and Regional Studies. II. Title.

LAW
T
    Taxation.
Schwartz, William.
    Future interests and estate planning. Cincinnati, W. H. Anderson, 1965.
    512p.

    1. Real estate business. 2. Taxation. 3. Life insurance. I. Title.

336.2
P72f
    TAXATION.
Prentice-Hall, inc.
    Federal tax handbook. Englewood Cliffs, N.J., 1972.
    629p.

    1. Taxation. I. Title.

336.2
R65
    TAXATION.
THE ROLE OF DIRECT AND INDIRECT TAXES IN THE FEDERAL RESERVE SYSTEM. A CONFERENCE REPORT OF THE BUREAU OF ECONOMIC RESEARCH AND THE BROOKINGS INSTITUTION. PRINCETON, N.J., PRINCETON UNIVERSITY PRESS, 1964.
    321P.

    1. TAXATION. I. NATIONAL BUREAU OF ECONOMIC RESEARCH. II. BROOKINGS INSTITUTION. III. TITLE: FEDERAL RESERVE SYSTEM.

336.2
S23
    TAXATION.
Seghers, Paul D
    Tax considerations in organizing foreign operations. New York, American Management Association, Finance Div., 1967.
    16p. (American Management Association. AMA management bulletin no. 108)

    1. Taxation. 2. Commercial policy. I. American Management Association. II. Title. (Series)

LAW
T
P725gu
    Taxation.
Prentice-Hall, inc.
    Guide to successful legal research; including catalog of publications on taxes and government regulations. 5th ed. Englewood Cliffs, N.J., 1959.
    61p.

    1. Taxation. I. Title.

336.2
R81
    Taxation.
Rubloff, Arthur.
    Let's tax our slums to death. Detached from Congressional Record, vol. 107, no. 2, Jan. 4, 1961. p. A29-A30.

    Reprinted from Look Magazine.

    1. Taxation. 2. Slum clearance. I. Look Magazine.

336
S25
    TAXATION.
SELIGMAN, EDWIN ROBERT ANDERSON, 1861-1939. STUDIES IN PUBLIC FINANCE, BY EDWIN R.A. SELIGMAN. NEW YORK, MACMILLAN, 1925.
    302P.

    1. FINANCE. 2. TAXATION.

360
R15
    Taxation.
Randolph (A. Philip) Institute, New York.
    A "Freedom Budget" for all Americans. Budgeting our resources, 1966-1975 to achieve "freedom from want." New York, 1966.
    84p.

    1. Social welfare. 2. Social security. 3. Public assistance. 4. Taxation. I. Title.

VF
336.2
R81p
    Taxation.
Rubloff, Arthur.
    A property tax program to encourage private development downtown [an address at the] National Downtown Services and National Retail Merchants Association Workshop, October 13-14, 1964. [n.p.] 1964.
    12p.

    1. Taxation. 2. Real property - Taxation. 3. Business districts. I. National Downtown Services and National Retail Merchants Association Workshop, 1964.

336.2
S54
    Taxation.
Slitor, Richard E
    The Federal income tax in relation to housing. Prepared for the consideration of the National Commission on Urban Problems. Washington, D.C., For sale by the Supt. of Docs., Govt. Print. Off., 1968.
    162p. (U.S. National Commission on Urban Problems. Research report no. 5)
    Paul H. Douglas, chairman.
    1. Taxation. 2. Income tax. 3. Mortgage finance. I. Douglas, Paul H. II. U.S. National Commission on Urban Problems. III. Title.

352.1
R23
    Taxation.
Regional and Urban Planning Implementation, inc.
    Special assessments. Cambridge, Mass., 1965.
    41p.
    Bibliography: p. 40-41.

    1. Municipal finance. 2. Municipal services. 3. Taxation. 4. Metropolitan area planning - Latin America.

336.2
S12
    Taxation.
Sacks, Seymour.
    Metropolitan area finances. Washington, Brookings Institution, 1964.
    411-430p. (Brookings Institution. Reprint 84)
    Reprinted from the 1963 Proceedings of the 56th annual Conference on Taxation of National Tax Association, October 1964.

    1. Taxation. 2. Municipal finance. 3. State finance. I. Title. II. Brookings Institution.

336.2
S71
    Taxation.
Stanback, Thomas M
    Tax changes and modernization in the textile industry. New York, National Bureau of Economic Research, distributed by Columbia University Press, 1969.
    119p. (Fiscal study no. 13)

    1. Taxation. 2. Tax incentives. 3. Industry. I. Title. II. National Bureau of Economic Research.

352.1
R23u
    Taxation.
Regional and Urban Planning Implementation, inc.
    User charges in government finance. Cambridge, Mass., 1965.
    [111]p.

    1. Municipal finance. 2. Municipal services. 3. Taxation. 4. Metropolitan area planning - Latin America. I. Title.

336.2
S15
    TAXATION.
Sandman, Cal M
    An information file for a municipal income tax system. [Louisville] 1969.
    49p.

    Bibliography: p. 47-49.

    1. Income tax. 2. Taxation. I. Title.

330
S72
    Taxation.
Stein, Herbert.
    The fiscal revolution in America. Chicago, University of Chicago Press, 1969.
    526p. (Chicago. University. Graduate School of Business. Studies in business and society)

    1. Economic policy. 2. Finance. 3. Taxation. 4. Budget. I. Title.

301
P81
no.461

TAXATION.
Stewart, Maxwell S
Money for our cities: revenue sharing the answer? New York, Public Affairs Committee, 1971.
24p.   (Public affairs pamphlet no. 461)

1. Municipal finance. 2. Grants-in-aid.
3. Taxation. I. Title. (Series)

Taxation.

336.2
T19fe
Tax Foundation, inc.
Federal non-income taxes; an examination of selected revenue sources. New York, 1965.
70p.

1. Taxation. 2. Finance. I. Title.

336.2
T19CUR

TAXATION.
TAX INSTITUTE.
CURBING INFLATION THROUGH TAXATION, BY MARRINER S. ECCLES, ALVIN H. HANSEN, HOMER HOYT AND OTHERS... SYMPOSIUM CONDUCTED BY... FEBRUARY 7-8, 1944. NEW YORK, TAX INSTITUTE, INC., C1944.
261P.

1. TAXATION. 2. INFLATION.
I. ECCLES, MARRINER S. II. TITLE.

Taxation.

336.2
S77
Struyk, Raymond J
The size and distribution of the tax base relative to regional economic growth. St. Louis, Institute for Urban and Regional Studies, Washington University [1960]
24p. (Water Resource Investment Project Working paper CWR 3. Design of Regional Accounts Project Working paper DRA 2)
1. Taxation. 2. Economic development.
I. Washington University, St. Louis. Institute for Urban and Regional Studies. II. Title.

Taxation.

339.3
T19
Tax Foundation, inc.
Federal revenue sharing with the States. New York, 1967.
20p.   (Its Government finance brief no. 9)

1. National income. 2. Grants-in-aid.
3. Intergovernmental relations. 4. Taxation.
I. Title.

Taxation.

336.2
T19d
Tax Institute, Princeton, N. J.
Depreciation and taxes, by E. Cary Brown and others. Princeton, 1958.
238p.   Series on The impact of taxation on management responsibility

"Symposium conducted by the Tax Institute, November 20-21, 1958."

1. Taxation. I. Title.

Taxation.

336.2
T19co
Tax Foundation.
The corporation income tax; an examination of its role in the Federal tax system. New York, 1968.
76p. (Its Research publication no. 19 (New series))

1. Taxation. 2. Business. I. Title.

Taxation.

353
T19f
Brief
Tax Foundation, inc.
Fiscal outlook for state and local government to 1975, by Elsie M. Watters. New York, 1966.
11p.   (Its Government finance brief no. 7)

1. State finance. 2. State government.
3. Local government - Finance. 4. Taxation.
I. Watters, Elsie M. II. Title.

LAW
T
T194D

TAXATION.
TAX INSTITUTE, PRINCETON, N.J.
A DYNAMIC ORGANIZATION MAKING AN IMPORTANT CONTRIBUTION TO THE NATION. PRINCETON, N.J., 1961.
12P.

1. TAXATION.

Taxation.

336.2
T19cu
Tax Foundation.
Current problems and issues in State taxation of interstate commerce. 1. The background. 2. The changes proposed. 3. The debate on proposed changes. New York, 1966.
12p.   (Its Government finance brief no. 3 (New series))

1. Taxation. 2. State finance. I. Title.

Taxation.

353
T19f
Tax Foundation, inc.
Fiscal outlook for state and local government to 1975. New York, 1966.
128p.   (Its Research publication no. 6 (New series))

1. State finance. 2. State government.
3. Local government - Finance. 4. Taxation.
I. Title.

LAW
T
T194EF

TAXATION.
TAX INSTITUTE, PRINCETON, N.J.
THE EFFECT OF TAX POLICY ON EXECUTIVE AND WORKER COMPENSATION. PRINCETON, N.J., 1958.
80P. (THE IMPACT OF TAXATION ON MANAGEMENT RESPONSIBILITY)

1. TAXATION. 2. INCOME.

336.2
T19s

TAXATION.
Tax Foundation.
State and local sales taxes; a summary. New York, 1970.
15p.

1. Taxation. 2. State finance.
3. Municipal finance. I. Title.

Taxation.

336.2
T19p
Tax Foundation.
Proceedings of a conference on national defense and taxation. New York, 1961.
79p.

1. Taxation. 2. National defense.

Taxation.

352.1
T19
1955
Tax Institute, Princeton, N.J.
Financing metropolitan government, by Carl H. Chatters and others. Symposium conducted by the Tax Institute, November 18-19, 1954. Princeton, N.J., 1955.
295p.

1. Municipal finance. 2. Taxation.
3. Metropolitan government. I. Chatters, Carl H. II. Title.

Taxation.

336.2
T19a
1963
Tax Institute of America.
Alternatives to present federal taxes, by Dan Throop Smith and others. Symposium conducted by the Tax Institute of America, Oct., 1963 Princeton, N.J., 1964.
257p.

1. Taxation. I. Smith, Dan Throop.
II. Title.

Taxation.

LAW
T
T193r
Tax Foundation, New York.
Reconstructing the Federal tax system; a guide to the issues. New York, 1963.
54p.

1. Taxation. I. Title. II. Title: Federal tax system.

Taxation.

LAW
T
T194i
Tax Institute, Princeton, N. J.
Income tax differentials, by Dan Throop Smith and others. Princeton, 1958.
258p.

"Symposium conducted by the Tax Institute, November 21-22, 1957."

1. Taxation. I. Smith, Dan Throop.
I. Title.

Taxation.

336.2
T19e
Tax Foundation.
Economic aspects of the social security tax. New York, 1966.
63p. (Its Research publication no. 5. (New series))

1. Taxation. 2. Social security.
I. Title.

LAW
T
T192C

TAXATION.
TAX INSTITUTE OF AMERICA.
CERTIFICATE OF INCORPORATION BYLAWS TAX-EXEMPT RULING. PRINCETON, N.J., 1963.
15P.

1. TAXATION.

Taxation.

336.211
T19
Tax Institute of America.
The property tax; problems and potentials, by Alfred G. Buehler and others. Symposium conducted by the Tax Institute of America, November 2-4, 1966. Princeton, 1967.
494p.
Bibliography: p. 461-485.

1. Real property - Taxation. 2. Personal property - Taxation. 3. Taxation. I. Buehler, Alfred G. II. Title.

Taxation.

336.2
T19r Tax Institute, Princeton, N.J.
Reappraisal of business taxation, by
Harold M. Groves and others. Symposium
conducted by the Tax Institute, December 7-8,
1961. Princeton, 1962.
242p.

1. Taxation. I. Groves, Harold M.
II. Title.

Taxation.

336.2
T19f Tax Foundation.
Federal fiscal issues. New York,
1961.
54p.

1. Taxation. 2. Finance.

Taxation.

336.2
T19m Tax Institute, Princeton, N.J.
Management's stake in tax
administration. Princeton, 1961.
260p. (Series on The impact of
taxation on Management responsibility)

"Symposium conducted by the Tax
Institute, September 29-30, 1960."

1. Taxation. 2. Management.
I. Title.

336.2 Taxation.
T19ta Tax Institute, Princeton, N.J.
The Tax Institute, a dynamic organization
making an important contribution to the
nation. Princeton, N.J., 1960.
12p. illus.

1. Taxation.

Taxation.
336.2
T19ta Tax Institute, Princeton, N.J.
1964 The Tax Institute of America; a dynamic
organization making an important contribution to the Nation. Princeton, N.J.,
1964.
12p.

1. Taxation.

Taxation.
336.2
T19t Tax Institute, Princeton, N.J.
Taxation and operations abroad, by Russell
Baker and others. Princeton, 1960.
308p. (Series on the Impact of taxation on
management responsibility)

"Symposium conducted by the Tax Institute
December 3-4, 1959."

1. Taxation. I. Baker, Russell.

336.2 Taxation.
T19 Tax systems, a reference book of legislative and statistical information for
all of the United States and for numerous
other countries and jurisdictions. 12th
ed. New York, Commerce Clearing House,
1950.
482p. tables.

1. Taxation. I. Commerce Clearing House.
II. New York (State) Tax Commission.

TAXATION.

Folio Tax systems; a yearbook of legislative and statis-
336.2 tical information including all the states of
T19 the United States and certain Canadian and
foreign data. 1st- ed; 1930- Chicago,
Commerce clearing house, inc. [1930-
v.
Prepared by the Research Foundation under the
sponsorship of the New York State Tax Commission,
1930-1942. For Library holdings see main card
Prepared by the Tax Research Department of Commerce Clearing House, 1946-

1. Taxation. I. New York (State) Tax
Commission. II. Commerce Clearing House.
Tax Research Dept.

336.2 Taxation.
T36
Thomson, John Cameron.
Taxation for growth, based on a statement
on national policy issued by the Research
and Policy Committee of the Committee for
Economic Development. New York, Committee for
Economic Development, 1957.
20 p. illus.

1. Taxation. I. Committee for Economic
Development. II. Title.

Taxation.
VP
336.2 Tulsa, Okla. Chamber of Commerce.
T85 1966 survey of comparative tax rates of
141 American cities. Final report. Tulsa,
Okla., Dept. of Business Research, Chamber
of Commerce, 1966.
17p.

1. Taxation. 2. Municipal finance.
I. Title.

Taxation.
657
T87 Ture, Norman B
Accelerated depreciation in the United
States, 1954-60. New York, National Bureau
of Economic Research; distributed by
Columbia University Press, 1967.
238p. (National Bureau of Economic
Research. Fiscal studies 9)

1. Accounting. 2. Taxation. 3. Business.
I. National Bureau of Economic Research.
II. Title.

Taxation.
336.2
T82 TWENTIETH CENTURY FUND.
FACING THE TAX PROBLEM. A SURVEY OF
TAXATION IN THE UNITED STATES AND A
PROGRAM FOR THE FUTURE. NEW YORK, 1937.
606P.

1. TAXATION. I. TITLE.

(Federal) taxation.
332.6
:336.2 United Nations. (Dept. of Economic Affairs.)
U54 United States income taxation of private
United States investment in Latin America.
(A description of the United States system and
some of its limitations.) New York, Jan. 1953.
viii, 80 p. graphs, tables (part fold. in
back) (ST/ECA/18)

1. Federal taxation. 2. Investments. I. Title: Income
taxation of private United States investment in
Latin America.

TAXATION.
336.2
A28c U.S. Advisory Commission on Intergovernmental Relations.
The commuter and the municipal income
tax; a background paper. Wash., 1970.
32p.

Bibliography: p. 21-32.

1. Income tax. 2. Municipal finance.
3. Taxation. I. Title.

Taxation.
336.2
A28 U.S. Advisory Commission on Intergovernmental Relations.
Coordination of State and Federal
inheritance, estate, and gift taxes;
a commission report. Washington,
1961.
134p. diagrs., tables.

1. Taxation. 2. Intergovernmental
relations.

Taxation.
336.2
A28in U.S. Advisory Commission on Intergovernmental
Relations.
The intergovernmental aspects of documentary
taxes. A Commission report. Washington, 1964.
29p. (A-23)

1. Taxation. 2. Intergovernmental
relations.

Taxation.
336.2
A28i U.S. Advisory Commission on Intergovernmental Relations.
Intergovernmental cooperation in tax
administration; some principles and possibilities; a Commission report. [Wash-
ington] 1961.
20p.

1. Taxation. 2. Intergovernmental
relations.

Taxation.
336.2
A28l U.S. Advisory Commission on Intergovernmental
Relations.
Local nonproperty taxes and the coordinating
role of the state; a commission report.
[Washington] 1961.
68p.

1. Taxation. 2. Intergovernmental relations.

Taxation.
336.2
A28m U.S. Advisory Commission on Intergovernmental
Relations.
Measures of state and local fiscal capacity
and tax effort. Washington, 1962.
150p. (A staff report. M-16)

1. Taxation. 2. Intergovernmental
relations.

TAXATION.
353
A28m U.S. Advisory Commission on Intergovernmental
Relations.
Measuring the fiscal capacity and effort
of State and local areas. Wash., 1971.
209p. (M-58)

Bibliography: p. 98-99.

1. State finance. 2. Municipal finance.
3. Taxation. I. Title.

Taxation.
336.2
A28r U.S. Advisory Commission on Intergovernmental Relations.
The role of the states in strengthening
the property tax. Washington, For sale by
the Supt. of Documents, Govt. Print. Off.,
1963.
v.

1. Taxation. 2. Personal property -
Taxation. 3. Real property - Taxation.
4. Intergovernmental relations.

353
A28so
TAXATION.
U.S. Advisory Commission on Intergovernmental Relations.
Sources of increased state tax collections: economic growth vs. political choice; an information report. Wash., 1968.
19p. (M-41)

1. State finance. 2. Taxation. I. Title.

Taxation.

336.2
A72
U.S. Area Redevelopment Administration.
Tax incentives to promote investment in redevelopment areas, by Edwin W. Hanczaryk. [Washington] Dept. of Commerce, Area Redevelopment Administration, Office of Planning and Research, 1963.
23p. (Staff study no. 10)

1. Taxation. 2. Economic development. I. Hanczaryk, Edwin, W.

Taxation.

VF
352
C25
G-SS
no.46
U.S. Bureau of the Census.
Tax revenue of state and local governments in calendar 1962. Washington, 1963.
14p. (Its State and local government special studies no. 46; G-SS-no. 46)

1. Taxation. (Series)

336.2
A28st
Taxation.
U.S. Advisory Commission on Intergovernmental Relations.
State and local taxes; significant features, 1968. Wash., For sale by the Supt. of Docs., Govt. Print. Off., Wash., 1968.
212p. (M-37)

At head of title: An information report.

1. Taxation. 2. State government. 3. Local government. I. Title.

Taxation.

VF
336.2
C25
G-SF
1961
no.4
U.S. Bureau of the Census.
Detail of state tax collections in 1961. Wash., For sale by the Bureau of the Census, 1961.
30p. (G-SF61-no. 4)

1. Taxation. I. Title.

336.2
065te
Taxation.
U.S. Dept. of Commerce.
Technological innovation: its environment and management [by the] Panel on Invention and Innovation. Washington, For sale by the Supt. of Documents, Govt. Print. Off., 1967.
83p.

1. Taxation. 2. Economic development. 3. Finance. I. Title.

Taxation.

LAW
T
A284tax
U.S. Advisory Commission on Intergovernmental Relations.
State constitutional and statutory restrictions on local taxing powers. A Commission report. Washington, D.C., 1962.
122p. (A-14)

1. Taxation. 2. Intergovernmental relations. 3. State finance. I. Title.

Taxation.

VF
336.2
C25
G-SF
1962
no.4
U.S. Bureau of the Census.
Detail of state tax collections in 1962. Washington, 1962.
30p. (G-SF62-no. 4)

1. Taxation.

336.2
C657T
1966
H-R
N8.1323
TAXATION.
U.S. CONGRESS. CONFERENCE COMMITTEES, 1966.
TAX ADJUSTMENT ACT OF 1966.
CONFERENCE REPORT TO ACCOMPANY H.R. 12752. WASHINGTON, GOVT. PRINT. OFF., 1966.
13P. (89TH CONGRESS, 2D SESSION. HOUSE. REPORT NO. 1323)

1. TAXATION. 2. INCOME TAX. I. TITLE.

336.2
A28s
Taxation.
U.S. Advisory Commission on Intergovernmental Relations.
State-local taxation and industrial location. A Commission report. Wash., 1967.
114p.
"A-30."

1. Taxation. 2. Industrial location. 3. Intergovernmental relations. I. Title.

312
1959
C25
Agric.
v.5
pt.4
Taxation.
U.S. Bureau of the Census.
Farm mortgage debt and farm taxes (a cooperative report) Special reports. Washington, Govt. Print. Off., 1962.
87p.
At head of title: United States census of agriculture: 1959. Final report, vol. 5, part 4, Special reports.

1. Census - Agriculture - 1959. 2. Taxation. 3. Farm mortgages. I. U.S. Economic Research Service.

336.2
C656T
1959
H-R
NO.587
TAXATION.
U.S. CONGRESS. CONFERENCE COMMITTEES, 1959.
TAX RATE EXTENSION ACT OF 1959, CONFERENCE REPORT TO ACCOMPANY H.R. 7523. WASHINGTON, GOVT. PRINT. OFF., 1959.
5P. (86TH CONGRESS, 1ST SESSION. HOUSE. REPORT NO. 587)

1. TAXATION.

Taxation.

LAW
T
A28lt
1961
U.S. Advisory Commission on Intergovernmental Relations.
Tax overlapping in the United States. An information report. Washington, 1961.
136p. (M-11)

1. Taxation. 2. State finance. I. Title.

Taxation.

VF
352
C25
CGA
no.5
U.S. Bureau of the Census.
Property tax assessments in the United States. Washington, 1957.
39 p. tables. (Its Census of governments advance releases no. 5)

1. Taxation. 2. Real property - Taxation. I. Title. (Series)

336.2
C65R
1962
H-R
NO.2508
TAXATION.
U.S. CONGRESS. CONFERENCE COMMITTEES, 1962.
REVENUE ACT OF 1962. CONFERENCE REPORT TO ACCOMPANY H.R. 10650. WASHINGTON, GOVT. PRINT. OFF., 1962.
48P. (87TH CONGRESS, 2D SESSION. HOUSE. REPORT NO. 2508)

1. TAXATION.

Taxation.

LAW
T
A28lt
1964
U.S Advisory Commission on Intergovernmental Relations.
Tax overlapping in the United States. An information report. Washington, 1964.
235p. (M-23)
Suppl.--- Supplement to Report M-23. Washington, D.C., 1966.
66p.

1. Taxation. 2. State finance. I. Title.

Taxation.

VF
352
C25
GC
P4
U.S. Bureau of the Census.
Property tax assessments in the United States. Washington, 1962.
15p. (Its Census of governments. 1962. Preliminary report no. 4; GC-P4)

1. Taxation. 2. Real property - Taxation. I. Title.

336.2
C656T
1962
H-R
NO.1935
TAXATION.
U.S. CONGRESS. CONFERENCE COMMITTEES, 1962.
TAX RATE EXTENSION ACT OF 1962. CONFERENCE REPORT TO ACCOMPANY H.R. 11879. WASHINGTON, GOVT. PRINT. OFF., 1962.
7P. (87TH CONGRESS, 2D SESSION. HOUSE. REPORT NO. 1935)

1. TAXATION.

336.2
A37
Taxation.
U.S. Dept. of Agriculture. Economic Research Service.
State action relating to taxation of farmland on the rural-urban fringe, by Peter House. Washington, 1961.
23p. (ERS-13)

1. Taxation. 2. Fringe areas. I. House, Peter.

Taxation.

VF
352
C25
G-SS
no.47
U.S. Bureau of the Census.
Property taxation in 1962. Washington, 1963.
19p. (Its State and local government special studies no. 47; G-SS no. 47)

1. Taxation. 2. Real property - Taxation. (Series)

336.2
C65R
1964
H-R
TAXATION.
U.S. CONGRESS. CONFERENCE COMMITTEES, 1964.
REVENUE ACT OF 1964. CONFERENCE REPORT TO ACCOMPANY H.R. 8363. WASHINGTON, GOVT. PRINT. OFF., 1964.
56P. (88TH CONGRESS, 2D SESSION. HOUSE. REPORT NO. 1149)

1. TAXATION.

336.2
C65EX
1965
H=R
NO.525
TAXATION.
U.S. CONGRESS. CONFERENCE COMMITTEES,
1965.
EXCISE TAX REDUCTION ACT OF 1965.
CONFERENCE REPORT TO ACCOMPANY H.R.
8371. WASHINGTON, GOVT. PRINT. OFF.,
1965.
12P. (89TH CONGRESS, 1ST SESSION.
HOUSE. REPORT NO. 525)

1. TAXATION. I. TITLE.

336.2
C65EX
1965
H=R
NO.433
TAXATION.
U.S. CONGRESS. HOUSE. COMMITTEE ON
WAYS AND MEANS.
EXCISE TAX REDUCTION ACT OF 1965.
REPORT. TO ACCOMPANY H.R. 8371.
WASHINGTON, GOVT. PRINT. OFF., 1965.
41P. (89TH CONGRESS, 1ST SESSION.
HOUSE. REPORT NO. 433)

1. TAXATION. I. TITLE.

336.2
C65IN
1959
H=R
NO.1170
TAXATION.
U.S. CONGRESS. HOUSE. COMMITTEE ON
WAYS AND MEANS.
INCOME TAX TREATMENT OF CERTAIN
DEALERS' RESERVES. REPORT TO ACCOMPANY
H.R. 8684. WASHINGTON, GOVT. PRINT.
OFF., 1959.
14P. (86TH CONGRESS, 1ST SESSION.
HOUSE. REPORT NO. 1170)

1. TAXATION. I. TITLE.

336.2
C657r
1968
H-CP
Taxation.
U.S. Congress. House. Committee of
Conference.
Revenue and expenditure control act of
1968; conference report to accompany H.R.
15414. Wash., Govt. Print. Off., 1968.
50p. (90th Congress, 2d sess. Report
no. 1533)

1. Taxation. 2. U.S. Executive
departments – Appropriations and expenditures. I. Title.

336.2
C65EX
1957
H=R
TAXATION.
U.S. CONGRESS. HOUSE. COMMITTEE ON
WAYS AND MEANS.
EXCISE TAX TECHNICAL CHANGES ACT OF
1957. REPORT. TO ACCOMPANY H.R. 7125,
A BILL TO MAKE TECHNICAL CHANGES IN THE
FEDERAL EXCISE TAX LAWS AND FOR OTHER
PURPOSES. WASHINGTON, GOVT. PRINT.
OFF., 1957.
212P. (85TH CONGRESS, 1ST SESSION.
HOUSE. REPORT NO. 481)

1. TAXATION. I. TITLE.

336.2
C65p
Taxation.
U.S. Congress. House. Committee on
Ways and Means.
President's 1961 tax recommendations.
Hearings before the Committee on Ways
and Means, House of Representatives,
Eighty-seventh Congress, first session
on the tax recommendations of the President
contained in his message transmitted to
the Congress, April 20, 1961. Washington,
Govt. Print. Off., 1961.
4 v.
Hearings held May 3-5, 8-11, 1961.
1. Taxation. I. U.S. President,
1961- (Kennedy)

336.2
C657r
1968
CCP
Taxation.
U.S. Congress. Committee of Conference.
Revenue and expenditure control act of
1968; explanation of the bill H.R. 15414 as
agreed to in conference. Wash., Govt.
Print. Off., 1968.
30p.

1. Taxation. 2. U.S. Executive departments
– Appropriations and expenditures.
I. Title.

336.2
C65ext
1971
H-H
TAXATION.
U.S. Congress. House. Committee on Ways and
Means.
Extension of interest equalization tax.
Hearing before the Committee on Ways and Means,
House of Representatives, Ninety-second Con-
gress, first session on administration proposal
to extend the interest equalization tax act.
Wash., Govt. Print. Off., 1971.
51p.
Hearing held Feb. 22, 1971.

1. Taxation. 2. Interest rates. 3. Foreign
exchange. I. Title.

336.2
C65p
1963
Taxation.
U.S. Congress. House. Committee on Ways
and Means.
President's 1963 tax message. Hearings
before the Committee on Ways and Means,
House of Representatives, Eighty-eighth
Congress, first session on the tax recommen-
dations of the President contained in his
message to the Congress, Jan. 24, 1963.
Washington, Govt. Print. Off., 1963-
pts.
Hearings held Feb.-March 1963.
1. Taxation. I. Title.
II. U.S. President, 1961- (Kennedy)

336.2
C657
1969
H-R
TAXATION.
U.S. Congress. Committee of Conference.
Tax reform act of 1969. Conference
report to accompany H.R. 13270.
Washington, Govt. Print. Off., 1969.
346p. (91st Cong., 1st sess. Report
no. 91-782)

1. Taxation. I. Title.

336.2
C65FEDE
1966
H=R
TAXATION.
U.S. CONGRESS. HOUSE. COMMITTEE ON
WAYS AND MEANS.
FEDERAL TAX LIEN ACT OF 1966.
REPORT. TO ACCOMPANY H.R. 11256, A
BILL TO AMEND THE INTERNAL REVENUE
CODE OF 1954 WITH RESPECT TO THE
PRIORITY AND EFFECT OF FEDERAL TAX
LEINS AND LEVIES. WASHINGTON, GOVT.
PRINT. OFF., 1966.
123P. (89TH CONGRESS, 2D SESSION.
HOUSE. REPORT NO. 1884)

1. TAXATION. I. TITLE.

336.2
C657p
1967
H-H
Taxation.
U.S. Congress. House. Committee on Ways
and Means.
President's 1967 surtax proposal: continuation of hearing to receive further administration proposal concerning expenditure
cuts—November 1967. Hearings before the
Committee on Ways and Means, House of
Representatives, Ninetieth Congress, first
session on...Wash., Govt. Print. Off.,
1967.
200p.
Hearings held: Nov. 29-30, 1967.
1. Taxation. I. U.S. President,
1963- (Johnson) II. Title.

336.2
C65s
1964
H-R
Taxation.
U.S. Congress. House. Committee on the
Judiciary.
State taxation of interstate commerce.
Report of the Special Subcommittee on State
Taxation of Interstate Commerce of the
Committee on the Judiciary, House of
Representatives, pursuant to Public law
86-272, as amended. Washington, Govt. Print.
Off., 1964.
2v. (88th Cong., 2d sess. House. Rept.
no. 1480)
Contents:-pt.   1. General
information.-   pt. 2. Income taxes.
1. Taxation.   2. State finance.
3. Commercial   policy.

336.2
C65GE
1958
H-H
TAXATION.
U.S. CONGRESS. HOUSE. COMMITTEE ON
WAYS AND MEANS.
GENERAL REVENUE REVISION, HEARINGS,
EIGHTY-FIFTH CONGRESS, SECOND SESSION.
WASHINGTON, GOVT. PRINT. OFF., 1958.
3PTS.

1. TAXATION.

336.2
C657PRE
1967
H-H
TAXATION.
U.S. CONGRESS. HOUSE. COMMITTEE ON
WAYS AND MEANS.
PRESIDENT'S 1967 TAX PROPOSALS.
HEARING, NINETIETH CONGRESS, FIRST
SESSION. WASHINGTON, GOVT. PRINT.
OFF., 1967.
2PTS.

1. TAXATION. 2. INCOME TAX.
I. TITLE.

333
C65
1947
H=R
TAXATION.
U.S. CONGRESS. HOUSE. COMMITTEE ON
PUBLIC LANDS.
STUDY OF THE PROBLEMS IN CONNECTION
WITH PUBLIC LANDS OF THE UNITED STATES,
THE TAX PROBLEMS CONNECTED WITH THE
ACQUISITION OF SUCH LANDS AND BURDEN UPON
LOCAL UNITS BY REASON OF THE USE OF LARGE
TRACTS OF PUBLIC LANDS FOR PUBLIC USE,
ETC., AS PROVIDED BY H.R. NO. 96,
SEVENTY-NINTH CONGRESS, FIRST SESSION.
WASHINGTON, GOVT. PRINT. OFF., 1947.
21P. (80TH CONGRESS, 1ST SESSION.
HOUSE. REPORT N O. 5)
1. PUBLIC LANDS. 2. TAXATION.

336.2
C65IN
1959
H=R
NO.982
TAXATION.
U.S. CONGRESS. HOUSE. COMMITTEE ON
WAYS AND MEANS.
INCOME TAX EXEMPTION FOR CERTAIN
NONPROFIT ORGANIZATIONS ORGANIZED
AFTER AUG. 31, 1951, AND BEFORE SEPT.
1, 1957. REPORT TO ACCOMPANY H.R.
6155. WASHINGTON, GOVT. PRINT. OFF.,
1959.
3P. (86TH CONGRESS, 1ST SESSION.
HOUSE. REPORT NO. 982)

1. TAXATION. I. TITLE.

336.2
C657pl
1967
H-H
Taxation.
U.S. Congress. House. Committee on Ways
and Means.
President's surtax proposal; continuation
of hearing—January 1968. Hearings before
the Committee on Ways and Means, House of
Representatives, Ninetieth Congress, second
session on President's 1967 surtax proposal:
continuation of hearing. Wash., Govt. Print.
Off., 1968.
166p.
Hearings held: Jan. 22-23, 1968.
1. Taxation. I. U.S. President, 1964-
(Johnson) II. Title.

336.2
C65A
1959
H=H
TAXATION.
U.S. CONGRESS. HOUSE. COMMITTEE ON
WAYS AND MEANS.
ADVISORY GROUP RECOMMENDATIONS ON
SUBCHAPTERS C, J, AND K OF THE INTERNAL
REVENUE CODE. HEARINGS BEFORE THE
COMMITTEE ON WAYS AND MEANS, HOUSE OF
REPRESENTATIVES, EIGHTY-SIXTH CONGRESS,
FIRST SESSION. WASHINGTON, GOVT. PRINT.
OFF., 1959.
1044P.

HEARING HELD FEB. 24-MAR. 5, 1959.
1. TAXATION.
I. TITLE.

336.2
C65IN
1967
H=R
TAXATION.
U.S. CONGRESS. HOUSE. COMMITTEE ON
WAYS AND MEANS.
INCOME TAX TREATMENT OF CASUALTY
LOSSES ATTRIBUTABLE TO MAJOR DISASTERS.
REPORT TO ACCOMPANY H.R. 6097.
WASHINGTON, GOVT. PRINT. OFF., 1967.
6P. (90TH CONGRESS, 1ST SESSION.
HOUSE. REPORT NO. 104)

1. TAXATION. 2. INCOME TAX.
I. TITLE.

336.2
C657PR
1967
H=H
TAXATION.
U.S. CONGRESS. HOUSE. COMMITTEE ON
WAYS AND MEANS.
PRESIDENT'S TAX MESSAGE. WASHINGTON,
GOVT. PRINT. OFF., 1961.
295P.

1. TAXATION. 2. U.S. PRESIDENT,
1961- (KENNEDY)

336.2
C656P
1966
H-H

TAXATION.
U.S. CONGRESS. HOUSE. COMMITTEE ON
WAYS AND MEANS.
PRIORITY OF FEDERAL TAX LIENS AND
LEVIES. HEARINGS, EIGHTY-NINTH
CONGRESS, SECOND SESSION ON H.R. 11256
AND H.R. 11290. WASHINGTON, GOVT.
PRINT. OFF., 1966.
242P.

1. TAXATION. I. TITLE: LIENS AND
LEVIES.

336.2
C656T
1962
NO.1738

TAXATION.
U.S. CONGRESS. HOUSE. COMMITTEE ON
WAYS AND MEANS.
TAX RATE EXTENSION ACT OF 1962.
REPORT TO ACCOMPANY H.R. 11879.
WASHINGTON, GOVT. PRINT. OFF., 1962.
27P. (87TH CONGRESS, 2D SESSION.
HOUSE. REPORT NO. 1738)

1. TAXATION.

334
C65

Taxation.
U.S. Congress. House. Committee on Ways and
Means.
Tax treatment of earnings of cooperatives. Hearings before the Committee on Ways and Means, House
of Representatives, Eighty-sixth Congress, second
session on the subject of tax treatment of earnings of cooperatives. Washington, Govt. Print.
Off., 1960.
439p. diagrs., maps, tables.
Hearings held Feb. 1-5, 1960.
1. Cooperatives. 2. Taxation. I. Title.

336.2
C65R
1962
H-R
NO.1447

TAXATION.
U.S. CONGRESS. HOUSE. COMMITTEE ON
WAYS AND MEANS.
REVENUE ACT OF 1962. REPORT, TO
ACCOMPANY H.R. 10650. WASHINGTON,
GOVT. PRINT. OFF., 1962.
207P. (87TH CONGRESS, 2D SESSION.
HOUSE. REPORT NO. 1447)

1. TAXATION. 2. DEPRECIATION AND
OBSOLESCENCE. I. TITLE.

336.2
C656T
1963
H-R

TAXATION.
U.S. CONGRESS. HOUSE. COMMITTEE ON
WAYS AND MEANS.
TAX RATE EXTENSION ACT OF 1963.
REPORT TO ACCOMPANY H.R. 6755.
WASHINGTON, GOVT. PRINT. OFF., 1963.
18P. (88TH CONGRESS, 1ST SESSION.
HOUSE. REPORT NO. 370)

1. TAXATION.

332.72
1368
C65
1958
H-R

TAXATION.
U.S. CONGRESS. HOUSE. COMMITTEE ON
WAYS AND MEANS.
TAXATION OF LIFE INSURANCE COMPANIES.
REPORT TO ACCOMPANY H.R. 10021.
WASHINGTON, 1958.
4P. (85TH CONGRESS, 2D SESSION.
HOUSE. REPORT NO. 1296)

1. LIFE INSURANCE COMPANIES -
TAXATION. 2. TAXATION.

336.2
C657T
1966
H-R
NO.1285

TAXATION.
U.S. CONGRESS. HOUSE. COMMITTEE ON
WAYS AND MEANS.
TAX ADJUSTMENT ACT OF 1966. REPORT
TO ACCOMPANY H.R. 12752. WASHINGTON,
GOVT. PRINT. OFF., 1966.
54P. (89TH CONGRESS, 2D SESSION.
HOUSE. REPORT NO. 1285)

1. TAXATION. 2. INCOME TAX.
I. TITLE.

336.2
C65taxr
1970
H-H

TAXATION.
U.S. Congress. House. Committee on Ways and
Means.
Tax recommendations of the President. Hearings before the Committee on Ways and Means,
House of Representatives, Ninety-first Congress,
second session on the subject of the tax
recommendations of the President. Wash.,
Govt. Print. Off., 1970.
544p.
Hearings held Sept. 9 - 17, 1970.
1. Taxation. I. Title.

336.2
C65ta

Taxation.
U.S. Congress. House. Committee on Ways
and Means.
Taxation of mutual savings banks and savings
and loan associations. Hearings before the
Committee on Ways and Means, House of Representatives, Eighty-seventh Congress, first
session on Treasury Department report on
taxation of mutual savings banks and savings
and loan associations. Washington, Govt. Print.
Off., 1961.
425p.
Hearings held Aug. 9-10, 1961. 2. Savings and
1. Taxation.
loan associations.

336.2
C657t
1968
H-R

Taxation.
U.S. Congress. House. Committee on Ways
and Means.
Tax adjustment act of 1968. Report to
accompany H.R. 15414. Washington, 1968.
14p. (90th Cong., 2d sess. House. Report
no. 1104)

1. Taxation. 2. Communication systems.
3. Transportation. I. Title.

336.2
C657
1969
H-H

TAXATION.
U.S. Congress. House. Committee on Ways
and Means.
Tax reform, 1969. Hearings before the
Committee on Ways and Means, House of
Representatives, Ninety-first Congress,
first session, on the subject of tax
reform. Wash., Govt. Print. Off., 1969.
15pts.
-----Appx. pt.1, appx.1.
Hearings held Feb. 18-April 24, 1969.

1. Taxation. I. Title.

378
C65ta

Taxation.
U.S. Congress. House. Select Committee
on Small Business.
Tax-exempt foundations and charitable
trusts: their impact on our economy.
Chairman's report. Washington, Govt.
Print. Off., 1962.
135p. (87th Cong. House. Committee
print)

1. Foundations, Charitable and educational.
2. Taxation. I. Title.

336.2
C65taxp

TAXATION.
U.S. Congress. House. Committee on Ways
and Means.
Tax proposals contained in the President's
economic policy. Hearings.
Washington, Govt. Print. Off., 1971.

Hearings held: Sept. 8-17, 1971.

1. Taxation. 2. Economic policy. I. Title.

336.2
C657ta
1969
H-H

TAXATION.
U.S. Congress. House. Committee on Ways and
Means.
Tax reform proposals contained in the message from the President of April 21, 1969 and
presented by representatives of the Treasury
Dept. to the Committee on Ways and Means at
public hearings on the subject of tax reform
on Tuesday, April 22, 1969. Wash., Govt.
Print. Off., 1969.
310p.
At head of title: 91st Cong., 1st sess.
Committee print.
1. Taxation. I. Title.

378
C65ta
1963

Taxation.
U.S. Congress House. Select Committee
on Small Business.
Tax-exempt foundations and charitable
trusts: their impact on our economy. 2d
installment. Subcommittee Chairman's report
to Subcommittee no. 1, Select Committee on
Small Business House of Representatives.
Washington, Govt. Print. Off., 1963.
405p. (88th Cong. House. Committee
print)
1. Foundations, Charitable and educational.
2. Taxation. I. Title.

336.2
C656T
1959
H-R
NO.436

TAXATION.
U.S. CONGRESS. HOUSE. COMMITTEE ON
WAYS AND MEANS.
TAX RATE EXTENSION ACT OF 1959.
REPORT TO ACCOMPANY H.R. 7523.
WASHINGTON, GOVT. PRINT. OFF., JUNE 4,
1959.
13P. (86TH CONGRESS, 1ST SESSION.
HOUSE. REPORT NO. 436)

1. TAXATION.

336.2
C657TAX
1959

TAXATION.
U.S. CONGRESS. HOUSE. COMMITTEE ON
WAYS AND MEANS.
TAX REVISION COMPENDIUM.
COMPENDIUM OF PAPERS ON BROADENING THE
TAX BASE, SUBMITTED BY PANELISTS
INVITED TO APPEAR IN CONNECTION WITH
THE PANEL DISCUSSIONS ON THE SAME
SUBJECT, TO BE CONDUCTED BY THE
COMMITTEE ON WAYS AND MEANS BEGINNING
NOVEMBER 16, 1959. WASHINGTON, GOVT.
PRINT. OFF., 1959.
3 V.

86TH CONGRESS.
(CONTINUED ON NEXT CARD)

336.2
C65
1952

TAXATION.
U.S. CONGRESS. JOINT COMMITTEE ON THE
ECONOMIC REPORT.
FEDERAL TAX CHANGES, AND ESTIMATED
REVENUE LOSSES UNDER PRESENT LAW.
MATERIALS, PREPARED FOR THE COMMITTEE
... BY THE COMMITTEE STAFF. WASHINGTON,
GOVT. PRINT. OFF., 1952.
8P.
AT HEAD OF TITLE: 82D CONGRESS, 2D
SESSION. JOINT COMMITTEE PRINT.

1. TAXATION. 2. TITLE.

336.2
C656T
1961
H-R

TAXATION.
U.S. CONGRESS. HOUSE. COMMITTEE ON
WAYS AND MEANS.
TAX RATE EXTENSION ACT OF 1961.
REPORT TO ACCOMPANY H.R. 7446.
WASHINGTON, GOVT. PRINT. OFF., 1961.
16P. (87TH CONGRESS, 1ST SESSION.
HOUSE. REPORT NO. 450)

1. TAXATION.

336.2
C657TAX
1959

U.S. CONGRESS. HOUSE. COMMITTEE ON
WAYS AND MEANS. TAX REVISION
COMPENDIUM....1959. (CARD 2)
1. TAXATION.

658.1
C65T

TAXATION.
U.S. CONGRESS. JOINT COMMITTEE ON THE
ECONOMIC REPORT.
TAXATION OF CORPORATE SURPLUS
ACCUMULATIONS. THE APPLICATION OF
EFFECT, REAL AND FEARED, OF SECTION 102
OF THE INTERNAL REVENUE CODE.
WASHINGTON, 1952.
260P.
AT HEAD OF TITLE: 82D CONGRESS, 2D
SESSION. JOINT COMMITTEE PRINT.

1. CORPORATIONS. 2. TAXATION.
I. TITLE.

336.2
C65f
U.S. Congress. Joint Economic Committee.
The Federal revenue system: facts and problems, 1959. Materials assembled by the Committee staff. Washington, Govt. Print. Off., 1959.
266p. tables.

86th Congress, 1st session.

1. Taxation. I. Title.

336.2
C65EX.
1965
S-R
TAXATION.
U.S. CONGRESS. SENATE. COMMITTEE ON FINANCE.
EXCISE TAX REDUCTION ACT OF 1965. REPORT TO ACCOMPANY H.R. 8371. WASHINGTON, GOVT. PRINT. OFF., 1965.
62P. (89TH CONGRESS, 1ST SESSION. SENATE. REPORT NO. 324)

1. TAXATION. I. TITLE.

336.2
065r
1963
S-H
Taxation.
U.S. Congress. Senate. Committee on Finance.
Revenue act of 1963. Hearings before the Committee on Finance, United States Senate, Eighty-eighth Congress, first session on H.R. 8363, an act to amend the Internal Revenue Code of 1954 to reduce individual and corporate income taxes, to make certain structural changes with respect to the income tax, and for other purposes. Washington, Govt. Print. Off., 1963.
pts.

1. Taxation. 2. Income tax.

336.2
C65F
1961
TAXATION.
U.S. CONGRESS. JOINT ECONOMIC COMMITTEE.
THE FEDERAL REVENUE SYSTEM: FACTS AND PROBLEMS, 1961. WASHINGTON, GOVT. PRINT. OFF. 1961.
290P. (87TH CONGRESS, 1ST SESSION. JOINT COMMITTEE PRINT)

1. TAXATION. I. TITLE.

336.2
C65EX.
1958
S-R
TAXATION.
U.S. CONGRESS. SENATE. COMMITTEE ON FINANCE.
EXCISE TAX TECHNICAL CHANGES ACT OF 1958. REPORT TO ACCOMPANY H.R. 7125. WASHINGTON, GOVT. PRINT. OFF., 1958.
217P. (85TH CONGRESS, 2D SESSION. SENATE. REPORT NO. 2090)

1. TAXATION.

336.2
C65R
1964
S-R
TAXATION.
U.S. CONGRESS. SENATE. COMMITTEE ON FINANCE.
REVENUE ACT OF 1964. REPORT TO ACCOMPANY H.R. 8363. WASHINGTON, GOVT. PRINT. OFF., 1964.
2PTS. (88TH CONGRESS, 2D SESSION. SENATE. REPORT NO. 830)

1. TAXATION.

VF
336.2
C65fe
Taxation.
U.S. Congress. Joint Committee on the Economic Report.
Federal tax policy for economic growth and stability. Report of the Joint Committee on the Economic Report to the Congress of the United States. Washington, Govt. Print. Off., 1956.
16p. (84th Cong., 2d sess. Senate. Report no. 1310)
1. Taxation. 2. Economic development.

336.2
C65FEDE
1966
S-R
TAXATION.
U.S. CONGRESS. SENATE. COMMITTEE ON FINANCE.
FEDERAL TAX LIEN ACT OF 1966. REPORT TO ACCOMPANY H.R. 11256. WASHINGTON, GOVT. PRINT. OFF., 1966.
36P. (89TH CONGRESS, 2D SESSION. SENATE. REPORT NO. 1708).

1. TAXATION. I. TITLE.

336.2
C65r
1971
S-H
TAXATION.
U.S. Congress. Senate. Committee on Finance.
The Revenue act of 1971. Hearings Ninety-second Congress, first session on H.R. 10947, an act to provide a job development investment credit, to reduce individual income taxes, to reduce certain excise taxes, and for other purposes. Wash., Govt. Print. Off., 1971.

1. Taxation. I. Title.

336.2
065fed
Taxation.
U.S. Congress. Joint Economic Committee.
The Federal tax system: facts and problems 1964. Materials assembled by the Committee staff of the Joint Economic Committee, Congress of the United States. Washington, Govt. Print. Off., 1964.
321p.

At head of title: 88th Cong., 2d sess.

1. Taxation. I. Title.

336.2
C65IN
1960
S-R
NO.1034
TAXATION.
U.S. CONGRESS. SENATE. COMMITTEE ON FINANCE.
INCOME TAX EXEMPTION FOR CERTAIN NONPROFIT ORGANIZATIONS ORGANIZED AFTER AUG. 31, 1951, AND BEFORE SEPT. 1, 1957. REPORT TO ACCOMPANY H.R. 6155. WASHINGTON, GOVT. PRINT. OFF., 1960.
4P. (86TH CONGRESS, 2D SESSION. SENATE. REPORT NO. 1034)

1. TAXATION. I. TITLE.

336.2
C657T
1966
S-H
TAXATION.
U.S. CONGRESS. SENATE. COMMITTEE ON FINANCE.
TAX ADJUSTMENT ACT OF 1966. HEARINGS, EIGHTY-NINTH CONGRESS, SECOND SESSION ON H.R. 12752. WASHINGTON, GOVT. PRINT. OFF., 1966.
246P.

HEARINGS HELD FEBRUARY 25 - MARCH 1, 1966.

1. TAXATION. 2. INCOME TAX. I. TITLE.

336.2
C657L
TAXATION.
U.S. Congress. Joint Economic Committee.
Long-term economic implications of current tax and spending proposals. Hearings before the Subcommittee on Fiscal Policy...Ninety-second Congress, first session. Wash., Govt. Print. Off., 1971.
220p.
Hearings held May 5-24, 1971.

1. Taxation. 2. U.S. Appropriations and expenditures. I. Title.

332.3
C657RE
1967
S-H
TAXATION.
U.S. CONGRESS. SENATE. COMMITTEE ON FINANCE.
RESTORATION OF INVESTMENT CREDIT AND ACCELERATED DEPRECIATION.
HEARINGS...ON H.R. 6950... WASHINGTON, GOVT. PRINT. OFF., 1967.
140P.
HEARINGS HELD: MARCH 20 AND 21, 1967.

1. ECONOMIC CONDITIONS. 2. TAXATION. 3. DEPRECIATION AND OBSOLESCENCE. 4. REAL PROPERTY. I. TITLE.

336.2
C65ft
1968
S-R
Taxation.
U.S. Congress. Senate. Committee on Finance.
Tax adjustment act of 1968; report to accompany H.R. 15414. Wash., Govt. Print. Off., 1968.
19p. (90th Cong., 2d sess. Senate. Report no. 1014)

1. Taxation. I. Title.

336.2
C653t
Taxation.
U.S. Congress. Joint Economic Committee.
Tax changes for shortrun stabilization. Hearings before the Subcommittee on Fiscal Policy of the Joint Economic Committee, Congress of the United States, Eighty-ninth Congress, second session. Washington, Govt. Print. Off., 1966.
313p.

Hearings held Mar. 16-30, 1966.

1. Taxation. 2. Income tax. I. Title.

336.2
C65R
1962
S-H
TAXATION.
U.S. CONGRESS. SENATE. COMMITTEE ON FINANCE.
REVENUE ACT OF 1962, HEARINGS, EIGHTY-SEVENTH CONGRESS, SECOND SESSION ON H.R. 10650. WASHINGTON, GOVT. PRINT. OFF., 1962.
12PTS.

1. TAXATION. 2. DEPRECIATION AND OBSOLESENCE. I. TITLE.

336.2
C656T
1959
S-R
TAXATION.
U.S. CONGRESS. SENATE. COMMITTEE ON FINANCE.
TAX RATE EXTENSION ACT OF 1959. REPORT TO ACCOMPANY H.R. 7523. WASHINGTON, GOVT. PRINT. OFF., 1959.
4P. (86TH CONGRESS, 1ST SESSION. SENATE. REPORT NO. 427)

1. TAXATION.

336.2
C653t
suppl.
Taxation.
U.S. Congress. Joint Economic Committee.
Tax changes for shortrun stabilization. A report of the Subcommittee on Fiscal Policy of the Joint Economic Committee, Congress of the United States together with supplementary and dissenting individual views. Washington, Govt. Print. Off., 1966.
23p.

At head of title: 89th Cong., 2d sess.

1. Taxation. 2. Income tax. I. Title.

336.2
C65r
1962
S-R
Taxation.
U.S. Congress. Senate. Committee on Finance.
Revenue act of 1962. Report of the Committee on Finance, United States Senate to accompany H.R. 10650 a bill to amend the internal revenue code of 1954 to provide a credit for investment in certain depreciable property, to eliminate certain defects and inequities, and for other purposes, together with individual, additional, dissenting, supplemental and minority views. Washington, Govt. Print. Off., 1962.
425p. (87th Cong., 2d sess. Senate. Report no. 1881)

1. Taxation.

336.2
C656T
1962
S-H
TAXATION.
U.S. CONGRESS. SENATE. COMMITTEE ON FINANCE.
TAX RATE EXTENSION ACT OF 1962. HEARINGS... ON H.R. 11879, EIGHTY-SEVENTH CONGRESS, SECOND SESSION. WASHINGTON, GOVT. PRINT. OFF., 1962.
40P.

HEARINGS HELD JUNE 13, 1962.

1. TAXATION.

336.2
C656T
1962
S-H
NO.1604

TAXATION.
U.S. CONGRESS. SENATE. COMMITTEE ON FINANCE.
TAX RATE EXTENSION ACT OF 1962.
REPORT TO ACCOMPANY H.R. 11879.
WASHINGTON, GOVT. PRINT. OFF., JUNE 18, 1962.
26P. (87TH CONGRESS, 2D SESSION.
SENATE. REPORT NO. 1604)

1. TAXATION.

336.18
C651
1969
S-H

U.S. Congress. Senate. Committee on Government Operations. Intergovernmental revenue...1970.   (Card 3)

under specified conditions. Wash., Govt. Print. Off., 1970.
379p.

Hearings held Sept. 22-Feb. 19, 1970.

1. Grants-in-aid. 2. Intergovernmental relations.   3. Taxation.
I. Title.

336.2
E26

U.S. Economic Research Service.
Farm real estate taxes; recent trends and developments. Washington, U.S. Dept. of Agriculture, 196.
17p. (RET-1)

1. Taxation. 2. Real property - Taxation.
I. Title.

336.2
C656T
1962
S-R
NO.1616

TAXATION.
U.S. CONGRESS. SENATE. COMMITTEE ON FINANCE.
TAX RATE EXTENSION ACT OF 1962.
REPORT TO ACCOMPANY H.R. 11879.
WASHINGTON, GOVT. PRINT. OFF., 1962.
26P. (87TH CONGRESS, 2D SESSION.
SENATE. REPORT NO. 1616)

1. TAXATION.

336.2
C65taxa
1970
S-H

TAXATION.
U.S. Congress. Senate. Committee on Labor and Public Welfare.
Tax exemptions for charitable organizations affecting poverty programs. Hearings before the Subcommittee on Employment, Manpower, and Poverty of the Committee on Labor and Public Welfare, United States Senate, Ninety-first Congress, second session...
Wash., Govt. Print. Off., 1970.
539p.
Hearings held Nov. 16-17, 1970.
1. Taxation. 2. Poverty. 3. Foundations, Charitable and   ducational. I. Title.

379
E28n

Taxation.
U.S. Office of Education.
Nonproperty taxation for schools; possibilities for local application, by Albert L. Alford. Washington, For sale by the Supt. of Documents, Govt. Print. Off., 1963.
144p. (Its Bulletin 1964, no. 4)

"OE-22021"

1. Education - Finance 2. Taxation. I. Alford, Albert L. II. Title.

336.2
C656T
1963
S-H

TAXATION.
U.S. CONGRESS. SENATE. COMMITTEE ON FINANCE.
TAX RATE EXTENSION ACT OF 1963.
REPORT TO ACCOMPANY H.R. 6755.
WASHINGTON, GOVT. PRINT. OFF., 1963.
14P. (88TH CONGRESS, 1ST SESSION.
SENATE. REPORT NO. 281)

1. TAXATION.

336.2
C65t

(Federal) taxation.
U.S. Congress. Senate. Committee on Small Business.
Tax problems of small business. Hearings before the Select Committee on Small Business, U.S. Senate, Eighty-fifth Congress, First session on the impact of Federal taxation on small business. Part 1. Washington, Govt. Print. Off., 1957.
600p.

1. Federal taxation.

336.2
F22M

TAXATION.
U.S. FEDERAL PUBLIC HOUSING AUTHORITY. (MANAGEMENT STANDARDS DIVISION)
MEETING OF REGIONAL TAX ANALYSTS, NOVEMBER 27, 28, AND 29, 1944 ...
SUMMARY REPORT. WASHINGTON, 1944.
7P.

1. TAXATION. I. TITLE: REGIONAL TAX ANALYSTS.

336.2
C657
1969
S-H

TAXATION.
U.S. Congress. Senate. Committee on Finance.
Tax reform act of 1969. Hearing before the Committee on Finance, United States Senate, Ninety-first Congress, first session, on H.R. 13270 to reform the income tax laws. Wash., Govt. Print. Off., 1969.
pts.

1. Taxation. I. Title.

336.2
C653ta

Taxation.
U.S. Congress. Senate. Special Committee on Aging.
Tax consequences of contributions to needy older relatives. Hearing before the Special Committee on Aging, United States Senate, Eighty-ninth Congress, second session. Wash., For sale by Supt. of Doc., Govt. Print. Off., 1966.
82p.

Hearing held June 15, 1966.

1. Taxation.   2. Old age. I. Title.

353
H68
1966

Taxation.
U.S. Dept. of Housing and Urban Development.
Urban development intergovernmental awards program. Entries, 1966, Washington, 1966.
5v.
Contents: [v.] Air pollution control. Annexation and consolidation.—Beautification.—Codes.—Coordinating agency activities.—Day care centers.—Education.—Hospitals and medical care facilities.—v.2. Industrial development.—Municipal services planning.—Police.—Purchasing.—Refuse collection and disposal.

(Cont'd on next card)

336.2
C657
1969
S-R

TAXATION.
U.S. Congress. Senate. Committee on Finance.
Tax reform act of 1969. Report of the Committee on Finance, United States Senate to accompany H.R. 13270, together with separate and individual views. Washington, Govt. Print. Off., 1969.
352p. (91st Congress. 1st session. Senate. Report no. 91-552)

1. Taxation. 2. Finance. I. Title.

336.2
C6TA
1966
S-H

TAXATION.
U.S. CONGRESS. SENATE. SPECIAL COMMITTEE ON AGING.
TAX CONSEQUENCES OF CONTRIBUTIONS TO NEEDY OLDER RELATIVES. REPORT TOGETHER WITH MINORITY VIEWS. WASHINGTON, GOVT. PRINT. OFF., 1966.
31P. (89TH CONGRESS, 2D SESSION. SENATE. REPORT NO. 1721)

1. TAXATION. 2. OLD AGE. I. TITLE.

353
H68
1966

U.S. Dept. of Housing and Urban Development.
Urban development intergovernmental awards program entries.   (Card 2)

-v.3. Relocation and housing. Systems engineering.—Taxation and bond issues.—Transportation.—Water supply and sewage disposal.—v.4. Omnibus activities and solutions.—v.5. Philadelphia, intergovernmental award program, 1966.

(Cont'd on next card)

336.18
C651
1969
S-H

TAXATION.
U.S. Congress. Senate. Committee on Government Operations.
Intergovernmental revenue act of 1969 and related legislation. Hearings before the Subcommittee on Intergovernmental Relations of the Committee on Government Operations, United States Senate, Ninety-first Congress on S. 2483, to establish a system of general support grants to State and local governments; to allow partial Federal income tax credit for State and local income tax payments; to authorize Federal collection of State income   taxes; to enlarge the
(Cont'd on next card)

336.2
C656T
1939
S-H

TAXATION.
U.S. CONGRESS. SENATE. SPECIAL COMMITTEE ON TAXATION OF GOVERNMENTAL SECURITIES AND SALARIES.
TAXATION OF GOVERNMENTAL SECURITIES AND SALARIES. HEARINGS, SEVENTY-SIXTH CONGRESS, 1ST SESSION, PURSUANT TO S. RES. 303 (75TH CONGRESS) WASHINGTON, GOVT. PRINT. OFF., 1939.
745P.

1. TAXATION. I. TITLE.

.353
H68
1966

U.S. Dept. of Housing and Urban Development.
Urban development intergovernmental awards program entries.   (Card 3)

1. Intergovernmental relations. 2. Local government. 3. Municipal services. 4. City planning. 5. Industrial districts. 6. Taxation. I. Title. II. Title: Awards program entries.

336.18
C651
1969
S-H

U.S. Congress. Senate. Committee on Government Operations. Intergovernmental revenue...1970.   (Card 2)

Federal estate tax credit for State death tax payments; and to permit States or local taxing authorities to tax property located in Federal areas and S. 2048, to permit States or other duly constituted taxing authorities to subject persons to liability for payment of property taxes on property located in Federal areas within such States
(Cont'd on next card)

336.2
E2oe

TAXATION.
U.S. Economic Research Service.
The effects of taxes and public financing programs on local industrial development; a survey of the literature, by Thomas F. Stinson. Wash., U.S. Dept. of Agriculture, Economic Research Service, 1968.
24p. (Agricultural economic report no. 133)
Bibliography: p. 22-24.

1. Tax-   ation. 2. Industrial location.   I. Stinson, Thomas F. II. Title.

LAW
T
I572c

Taxation.
U.S. Internal Revenue Service.
Cumulative list, revised to Organizations described in Section 170(c) of the Internal Revenue Code of 1954. Wash.,

(Its Publication no. 78 (rev.)

Suppl. -- ---Supplement. Wash.,
v.

1. Taxation.   I. Title.

336.2
I57d
Taxation.
U.S. Internal Revenue Service.
Depreciation; guidelines and rules.
Washington, 1962.
56p. (Its Publication no. 456 (7-62))

1. Depreciation and obsolescence.
2. Taxation.

336.18
L41fe
TAXATION.
U.S. Library of Congress. Legislative
Reference Service.
Federal revenue sharing: background informa-
tion and comparison of the various proposals
introduced during the 91st Congress, 1st
session, by Maureen McBreen. Wash., 1970.
73p. (70-43 E)

1. Grants-in-aid. 2. Taxation. 3. Intergovernmental relations. I. McBreen, Maureen.
II. Title. III. Title: Revenue sharing.

336.2
P81
TAXATION.
U.S. Bureau of Public Roads.
Road-user and property taxes on
selected motor vehicles, 1970, by
Laurence L. Liston and Robert W.
Sherrer. [Wash., 1970]
66p.

1. Taxation. 2. Highways - Finance.
3. Personal property - Taxation.
I. Liston, Laurence L. II. Sherrer,
Robert W. III. Title.

336.2
I57H
TAXATION.
U.S. INTERNAL REVENUE SERVICE.
HOW THE FEDERAL INCOME TAX APPLIES TO
CONDEMNATION OF PRIVATE PROPERTY FOR
PRIVATE USE. WASHINGTON, GOVT. PRINT.
OFF., 1962.
17P.

1. TAXATION. I. TITLE.

336.2
L41
Taxation.
U.S. Library of Congress. Legislative
Reference Service.
Federal revenues and expenditures in the
several states; averages for the fiscal
years, 1959-61, by I.M. Labovitz.
Washington, 1964.
97p. (EJ 8 US D)

1. Taxation. 2. Income tax. 3. Intergovernmental relations. 4. National
income. I. Labovitz, I.M. II. Title.

690.591
T72
TAXATION.
U.S. Dept. of the Treasury.
Asset depreciation range (ADR) system.
[Wash.] 1971.
98p.

1. Depreciation and obsolescence (Buildings)
2. Taxation. 3. Industry. I. Title.

LAW
T
Taxation.
U.S. Internal Revenue Service.
Organizations described in Section 170(c)
of the Internal Revenue Code of 1954.
Cumulative list, revised to December 31, 1964.
Wash., Govt. Print. Off., 1965.
429p. (Its Publication no. 78
(rev. 12-64)

-- --- Supplement no.
Wash., 19
v.

1. Taxation. 2. Tax incentives.
I. Title.

336.2
L41s
TAXATION.
U.S. Library of Congress. Legislative
Reference Service.
Summary of proposals for tax reform and
tax incentives in the 90th Congress, by
George J. Leibowitz. Wash., 1968.
29p. (S-123)

1. Taxation. I. Leibowitz, George J.
II. Title: Proposals for tax reform.
III. Title.

336.2
T72I
TAXATION.
U.S. TREASURY DEPT. COMMITTEE ON
INTERGOVERNMENTAL FISCAL RELATIONS.
INTERGOVERNMENTAL FISCAL RELATIONS.
WASHINGTON, 1943.
6 V.

1. TAXATION. I. TITLE.

336.2
I57t
Taxation.
U.S. Internal Revenue Service.
Tax guide for small business. Individ-
ual corporations, partnerships, income,
excise, and employment taxes. 1959 ed.
Washington, Govt. Print. Off., 1958.
125p. tables. (Its Publication no. 334)

1. Taxation. 2. Small business.

697.8
L41
TAXATION.
U.S. Library of Congress. Legislative
Reference Service.
Tax incentives for investment in water and
air pollution control facilities: analysis
of bills introduced in 1st session of the
90th Congress, by Harold A. Kohnen. Wash.,
1968.
53p. (E-273; HG 4625 U.S.F.)

1. Air pollution. 2. Water pollution.
3. Taxation. I. Kohnen, Harold A. II. Title.

336.2
T72
Taxation.
U.S. Treasury Dept.
Tax reform studies and proposals. Joint
publication; Committee on Ways and Means of the
U.S. House of Representatives and Committee on
Finance of the U.S. Senate. Wash., Govt. Print.
Off., 1969.
4pts.
At head of title: 91st Cong., 1st sess.
Committee Print.
1. Taxation. I. U.S. Congress. House.
Committee on Ways and Means. II. U.S. Congress.
Senate. Committee on Finance. III. Title.

336.2
J87
TAXATION.
U.S. DEPARTMENT OF JUSTICE.
TAXATION OF GOVERNMENT BONDHOLDERS AND
EMPLOYEES. THE IMMUNITY RULE AND THE
SIXTEENTH AMENDMENT. A STUDY MADE BY
THE DEPARTMENT OF JUSTICE. WASHINGTON,
GOVT. PRINT. OFF., 1938.
219P.

1. TAXATION. I. TITLE.

332.3
P72
TAXATION.
U.S. President, 1963- (Johnson)
Restoration of investment tax credit.
Message from the President of the United
States... Washington, Govt. Print. Off.,
1967.
4 p. (U.S. 90th Congress, 1st session.
House doc. 81)

1. Credit. 2. Taxation. I. Title. II.
Title: Investment tax credit.

336.2
U54
Taxation.
United States Savings and Loan League.
A comparison of the tax status of com-
mercial banks and savings and loan asso-
ciations. Chicago, 1961.
[14]p. diagrs.

1. Taxation. 2. Banks and banking.
3. Savings and loan associations.

VF
351
L41
Taxation.
U.S. Library of Congress. Legislative Reference Service.
Adverse effects of the expanding activities of
the National Government on the private economy
and federal system: the case for free enterprise
and local self-government. Washington, 1957.
9 pts. (various pagings)

Contents: -Federal credit agencies. -Electric
power. -Reclamation. -Agriculture. -Housing.
(Continued on next card)

336.2
P72
Taxation.
U.S. President, 1961- (Kennedy)
Revision of our tax structure. Message
from the President of the United States,
transmitting recommendations relative to a
revision of our tax structure. Washington,
Govt. Print. Off., 1963.
24p.
At head of title: 88th Cong., 1st sess.
House. Document no. 43.
1. Taxation. 2. U.S. President -
Messages.

711.14
W23
TAXATION.
WEHRLY, MAX S.
URBAN LAND USE AND PROPERTY TAXATION,
BY MAX S. WEHRLY AND J. ROSS
MCKEEVER. WASHINGTON, URBAN LAND
INSTITUTE, 1952.
28P. (TECHNICAL BULLETIN NO. 18)

1. LAND USE. 2. TAXATION.
I. MCKEEVER, J. ROSS, JT. AU.
II. TITLE. (SERIES: URBAN LAND
INSTITUTE. TECHNICAL BULLETIN NO. 18)

VF
351
L41
U.S. Library of Congress. Legislative Reference Service. Adverse effects...(Card 2)

Taxation. -Foreign aid. -Grants-in-aid.
-Education.

1. Federal government. 2. Finance. 3. Housing. 4. Taxation. 5. Public housing. 6. Grants-
in-aid.

336.2
P72b
TAXATION.
U.S. President's Task Force on Business
Taxation.
Business taxation. The report. Washington,
1970.
82p.

1. Taxation. I. Title.

351
W24
Taxation.
Weidenbaum, Murray L
Federal resources and urban needs.
Prepared for Washington University Conference
on Planning for the Quality of Urban Life.
St. Louis, Dept. Of Economics, Washington
University, 1965.
38p. (Washington University, St. Louis
Dept. of Economics. Working paper 6507)

1. Federal government. 2. Taxation.
3. Grants-in-aid. I. Washington University,
St. Louis. Dept. of Economics. II. Title.

711.4
:670
W43

TAXATION.
Wightman, James W
The impact of state and local fiscal policy on redevelopment areas in the Northeast. Boston, Federal Reserve Bank of Boston, 1967.
207p. (Research report to the Federal Reserve Bank of Boston no. 40)
Sponsored by the New England Economic Research Foundation and financed jointly by the Area Redevelopment Administration and the Federal Reserve Bank of Boston.
Bibliography: p. 196-207.
1. Industrial districts - Redevelopment. 2. Taxation. I. Federal Reserve Bank of Boston. II. Title.

LAW
T
W347h

Taxation.
White, Melvin
Horizontal inequality in the Federal income tax treatment of homeowners and tenants, by Melvin and Anne White. Wash., Brookings Institution, 1966.
225-259p. (Brookings Institution. Studies of government finance. Reprint no. 114)
Reprinted from the National tax journal, Sept. 1965.

1. Taxation. 2. Finance. 3. Real property - Taxation. I. White, Anne, jt. au. II. Brookings Institution. III. Title.

697.8
W45

TAXATION.
Wilson, Douglas B
Tax assistance and environmental pollution. Princeton, N.J., Tax Institute of America, 1970.

11p.

Tax policy, July-Aug., 1970.

1. Air pollution. 2. Water pollution. 3. Taxation. I. Tax Institute of America. II. Title.

LAW
T

Taxation.
Wolf, Karl E
State and local taxation. Washington, George Washington University, Government Contracts Program, 1962.
54p. (George Washington University. Government Contract Program. Government contracts monograph no. 5)

1. Taxation. I. George Washington University. Government Contracts Program. II. Title.

352.1
W74

TAXATION.
Wright, Edward T ed.
Sources of municipal revenue. Springfield, Ill., Charles C. Thomas, 1971.
108p.

1. Municipal finance. 2. Taxation. 3. Grants-in-aid. I. Title.

353
(767)
A74f

Taxation - Arkansas.
Arkansas. Budget and Accounting Div.
Financial report, 19

Little Rock, Ark., 19

v. biennial

For Library holdings see main entry.

1. State finance - Arkansas. 2. Taxation - Arkansas.

353
(767)
A74

Taxation - Arkansas.
Arkansas. State Comptroller.
A report on finance and taxation in Arkansas for state, counties, municipalities, and school districts including a description of Arkansas taxes. [Little Rock] 1966.
252p.

1. State finance - Arkansas. 2. Taxation - Arkansas. I. Title.

336.2
(767)
A74

Taxation - Arkansas.
Arkansas. University. Industrial Research and Extension Center.
Taxes and government services in Arkansas; ... preliminary report on the relative burden of state and local taxes and the relative level of public services in Arkansas; prepared for the Arkansas Industrial Development Commission. Fayetteville, Ark. June 1956.
1 v.

1. Taxation - Arkansas. 2. Municipal services - Arkansas. 3. Public health - Ark. 4. Public assistance - Ark. I. Arkansas Industrial Development Commission.

336.2
(755295)
B79

Taxation - Arlington Co., Va.
Bryant, Lyle C
The Arlington story: real estate assessment reform as a factor in the self-renewal of cities. [A paper presented during the national convention of the American Society of Planning Officials at Philadelphia, April 18, 1966] [Wash., 1966?]
21-34p.

1. Taxation - Arlington Co., Va. 2. Real estate business - Arlington Co., Va. I. American Society of Planning Officials, Philadelphia, 1966. II. Title.

711.4
(758231)
A75fin

Taxation - Atlanta.
Buehler, Alfred G
Financing public services and improvements in Atlanta. Atlanta, 1957.
248p. charts, tables.

U.S. Urban Renewal Administration, Urban Planning Assistance Program.

1. City planning - Atlanta. 2. Municipal finance - Atlanta. 3. Taxation - Atlanta. I. U.S. Urban Renewal Administration.

711.4
(758231)
A75fin
summary

Taxation - Atlanta.
Buehler, Alfred G
Financing public services and improvements in Atlanta. A summary report. Atlanta, 1957.
51p. charts, tables.

U.S. Urban Renewal Administration, Urban Planning Assistance Program.

1. City planning - Atlanta. 2. Municipal finance - Atlanta. 3. Taxation - Atlanta. I. U.S. Urban Renewal Administration.

336.2
(94)
W66

Taxation - Australia.
Woodruff, A M
Property taxes and land use patterns in Australia and New Zealand, by A.M. Woodruff and L.L. Ecker-Racz. Wash., Tax Executives Institute, 1965.
16-63p.

Reprinted from the Tax executive, Oct. 1965.

1. Taxation - Australia. 2. Taxation - New Zealand. 3. Real property - Taxation. 4. Real estate business. I. Ecker-Racz, L.L., jt. au. II. Tax executive. III. Title.

336.2
:538.56
S77

Taxation - Automation.
Struyk, Raymond J
An analysis of tax structure, public service levels, and regional economic growth. St. Louis, Institute for Urban and Regional Studies, Washington University, 1966.
46p. (Washington University, St. Louis. Institute for Urban and Regional Studies. Working paper CWR 9 and DRA 3)

1. Taxation - Automation. 2. Economic development. I. Washington University, St. Louis. Institute for Urban and Regional Studies. II. Title.

336.2
(016)
B27

TAXATION = BIBLIOGRAPHY.
BERKMAN, HERMAN GERALD.
BIBLIOGRAPHY ON SPECIAL ASSESSMENTS. CHICAGO, AMERICAN SOCIETY OF PLANNING OFFICIALS, 1941.
25P.

1. TAXATION = BIBLIOGRAPHY. I. AMERICAN SOCIETY OF PLANNING OFFICIALS.

336.2
(016)
N28

TAXATION = BIBLIOGRAPHY.
NEWCOMER, MABEL, COMP.
SELECTED BIBLIOGRAPHY ON INTERGOVERNMENTAL FISCAL RELATIONS. PREPARED...FOR THE STUDY OF INTERGOVERNMENTAL FISCAL RELATIONS, AND SUBMITTED BY THE COMMITTEE ON INTERGOVERNMENTAL FISCAL RELATIONS TO THE TREASURY DEPT., OCT. 12, 1942. WASHINGTON, U.S. TREASURY DEPT. N.D. 83P.

1. TAXATION = BIBLIOGRAPHY.

336.2
(016)
T19
no. 5

Taxation - Bibliography.
Tax Foundation.
Bibliography on Federal tax revision. New York, 1960.
12p. (Its Research bibliography no. 5)

1. Taxation - Bibliography.

336.2
(016)
T19
no. 2

Taxation - Bibliography.
Tax Foundation.
Comparative analysis of state tax burdens. New York, 1959.
6p. (Its Research bibliography no. 2)

1. Taxation - Bibliography. 2. State finance - Bibliography.

336.2
(016)
T19
no.9

Taxation - Bibliography.
Tax Foundation.
Federal tax revision. New York, 1963.
16p. (Its Research bibliography no. 9)

1. Taxation - Bibl.

336.2
(016)
T19
no. 3

Taxation - Bibliography.
Tax Foundation.
Financing municipal government. New York, 1959.
13p. (Its Research bibliography no. 3)

1. Taxation - Bibliography. 2. Municipal finance - Bibliography.

336.2
(016)
T19
no. 1

Taxation - Bibliography.
Tax Foundation.
Tax and other financial inducements to industrial location. New York, 1960.
3p. (Its Research bibliography no. 1)

1. Taxation - Bibliography. 2. Industrial location - Bibliography.

353
(016)
T65S

TAXATION = BIBLIOGRAPHY.
TOMPKINS, DOROTHY C
STATE AND LOCAL FINANCE AND TAXATION: A BIBLIOGRAPHY OF MATERIALS PUBLISHED 1941-1946. BERKELEY, BUREAU OF PUBLIC ADMINISTRATION, UNIVERSITY OF CALIFORNIA, 1946.
97P. (CALIFORNIA. UNIVERSITY. BUREAU OF PUBLIC ADMINISTRATION. POSTWAR BIBLIOGRAPHIES NO. 2)

SELECTION FROM THE FINANCE SECTION OF THE BUREAU OF PUBLIC ADMINISTRATION'S CATALOG.

(CONTINUED ON NEXT CARD)

353
(016)
T65S

TOMPKINS, DOROTHY C STATE AND LOCAL ...
1946.   (CARD 2)

1. STATE FINANCE - BIBLIOGRAPHY.
2. LOCAL GOVERNMENT - FINANCE -
BIBLIOGRAPHY.   3. TAXATION -
BIBLIOGRAPHY.   I. CALIFORNIA.
UNIVERSITY. BUREAU OF PUBLIC
ADMINISTRATION.

VF
336.2
(74461)
B67

Taxation - Boston.
Boston Municipal Research Bureau.
Higher and still higher. Boston, 1958.
7p.

1. Taxation - Boston.

VF
336.2
(794)
C15.6
pt. 1

Taxation - Calif.

California. Legislature. Senate. Interim
Committee on State and Local Taxation.
Local government finance in California,
1940-1953. Part 1. Sacramento, 1955.
140p. tables.

1. Taxation - Calif. 2. State finance -
Calif.

336.2
(016)
I57

TAXATION - BIBLIOGRAPHY.
U.S. INTERNAL REVENUE SERVICE.
PUBLICATIONS CATALOG. WASHINGTON,
GOVT. PRINT. OFF., 1965.
33P.

1. TAXATION - BIBLIOGRAPHY.   I. TITLE.

336.2
(74461)
O52

Taxation - Boston.
Oldman, Oliver.
Assessment-sales ratios under the Boston
property tax, by Oliver Goldman and Henry
Aaron. Reproduced from the National tax
journal, March 1965, p. 36-49.

1. Taxation - Boston. 2. Real property -
Taxation - Boston. I. Aaron, Henry, jt. au.
II. National tax journal. III. Title.

336.2
(794)
C15E

TAXATION - CALIFORNIA.
CALIFORNIA. UNIVERSITY. INSTITUTE OF
TRANSPORTATION AND TRAFFIC ENGINEERING.
ECONOMIC CONSIDERATIONS IN THE
GEOGRAPHIC DISTRIBUTION OF HIGHWAY USER
TAX REVENUES, BY RICHARD R. CARLL AND
TILLO E. KUHN. BERKELEY, 1962.
91P. (ITS RESEARCH REPORT NO. 33)

1. TAXATION - CALIFORNIA.   I. CARLL,
RICHARD R.   II. KUHN, TILLO E., JT. AU.

333.71
(016)
U71
1965

Taxation - Bibliography.
Urban Land Institute.
Open space land, planning and taxation: a
selected bibliography; by John E. Rickert
and Jerome P. Pickard. Prepared by Urban
Land Institute for the Urban Renewal
Administration, Housing and Home Finance
Agency. Washington, For sale by the Supt.
of Doc., Govt. Print. Off., 1965.
58p.

(Continued on next card)

336.211
B21

Taxation - California.
Beaton, Charles R
The effect of the property tax on manufacturing location, by Charles R. Beaton and
Young P. Joun. A real estate education
and Research fund project. Fullerton,
California State College, Div. of Real
Estate, 1968.
54p.
Study is the result of a research project
financed through the Div. of Real Estate of
the State of Calif.
1. Taxation - California. 2. Industrial
location - Calif.   I. Joun, Young P.
jt. au. II. California   State College, Fuller
Div. of Real Estate.   III. Title.

VF
336.2
(794)
C15

Taxation - California.

California Taxpayers' Association.
Property tax levies; California
local governments, 1953-54 through 1956-57.
Los Angeles, 1957.
9 p. (Its Association report no. 9,
1957 series)

1. Taxation - California. I. Title.

333.71
(016)
U71
1965

Urban Land Institute. Open space land,
planning and taxation...1965. (Card 2)

"First product of the work on the study
of the present and potential role of State
and local taxation in the preservation and
development of open-space land in urban areas
under contract with the Housing and Home
Finance Agency.
1. Open space land - Bibl. 2. Planning - Bibl.
3. Taxation - Bibl. I. Pickard, Jerome P., jt. au.
II. Rickert, John E.   III. U.S. Urban
Renewal Administration

TAXATION - CALIFORNIA - LAW.
California. Laws, statutes, etc.
... Revenue and taxation code annotated of the
state of California. Adopted May 16, 1939, with
amendments up to and including those of the second
extraordinary session of the Legislature, 1952...
Annotated and indexed by the publisher's editorial
staff. San Francisco, Bancroft-Whitney company, 1952.
3v. 23½cm. (Deering's California codes)

VF
690.591
C15

Taxation - Cambridge, Mass.

Cambridge, Mass. Board of Assessors.
Home maintenance does not increase your
taxes. [Cambridge, 1959]
folder. (Neighborhood conservation information bulletin: Taxes)

1. Houses - Maintenance and modernization.
2. Taxation - Cambridge, Mass.

333.71
(016)
U71
1967

Taxation - Bibliography.
Urban Land Institute.
Open space land planning and taxation; a
selected bibliography by John E. Rickert with
the collaboration of Jerome P. Pickard. Pre-
pared for the U.S. Dept. of Housing and Urban
Development. Rev. Washington, for sale by the
Supt. of Documents, Govt. Print. Off., 1967.
54p. (U.S. Dept. of Housing and Urban
Development. HUD MP-34/rev. 1967)

1. Open space land - Bibl. 2. Taxation -
Bibl. I. U.S. Dept. of Housing and Urban
Development.   II. Rickert, John E.
III. Pickard,   Jerome P. IV. Title.

TAXATION - CALIFORNIA - LAW.
California. Laws, statutes, etc.
... Revenue and taxation code of the state of California.
Adopted May 16, 1939. With amendments up to and including
those of the fifty-fifth
Legislature. Compiled by the publisher's editorial staff. San
Francisco, Bancroft-Whitney company, 1944.
xv, 816 p. 23½cm. (Deering's California codes)

1. Taxation—California—Law.   I. Bancroft-Whitney company,
San Francisco.

Library of Congress   HJ3268.A3 1944   45-8598
    [5]   336.2

336.2
(71)
F52

TAXATION - CANADA.
FLEMING, DONALD M
BUDGET SPEECH DELIVERED BY DONALD M.
FLEMING, MINISTER OF FINANCE, MEMBER FOR
EGLINTON IN THE HOUSE OF COMMONS, JUNE
20, 1961. OTTAWA, QUEEN'S PRINTER, 1961.
166P.

1. TAXATION - CANADA.   I. TITLE.

336.2
(016)
V15

Taxation - Bibliographies.

Van Wagner, Doris A
Tax-exempt securities: a bibliography.
Washington, 1957.
16 p.

1. Taxation - Bibliographies.
2. Investments.

LAW
S

Taxation - California.
California. Legislature. Assembly. Interim
Committee on Revenue and Taxation.
Taxation of property in California; a major
tax study. Part 5. A report for the California Legislature Assembly Interim Committee
on Revenue and Taxation, Dec. 1964, by David
R. Doerr and Raymond R. Sullivan, with special sections by Harold M. Somers and others.
[Sacramento] Calif., 1964.
361p. (Its v. 4, no. 12)

1. Real property - Tax-   ation. 2. Taxation -
California. I. Doerr,   David R.
II. Sullivan, Raymond   R. II. Title.

VF
336.2
(75791)
C31

Taxation - Charleston County, S. C.
Charleston County, S. C. Planning Board.
(Citizens Advisory Committee)
Tax assessment and capital improvements
containing recommendations for tax assessment
procedures and capital improvement programming. Charleston, S. C., 1957.
10 p.

Paul A. Belknap, Chairman.

1. Taxation - Charleston County, S. C.
2. Capital improvement programs - Charleston
County, S. C.

711.4
(74923)
B56m
no. 4

Taxation - Bloomingdale, N.J.
Candeub (Isadore) and Associates.
Tax base of Bloomingdale, New Jersey.
Report to the Bloomingdale Planning Board.
Newark, N.J., 1959.
2p. (Bloomingdale master plan memo-
randum no. 4)
U.S. Urban Renewal Adm. UPAP.

1. Master plan - Bloomingdale, N.J. 2. Taxation -
Bloomingdale, N.J. I. Bloomingdale, N.J. Planning
Board. II. U.S. URA-UPAP. Bloomingdale, N.J.

336.2
(794)
C15r
pt. 7

Taxation - California
California. Legislature. Senate. Interim
Committee on State and Local Taxation.
Fiscal problems of urban growth in California. Report, part seven. Sacramento,
1953.
253p. illus., maps, tables.

1. Taxation - California.

336.2
I57ta

Taxation - Charts, tables, etc.
U.S. Internal Revenue Service.
Tables for applying revenue procedure
62-21. Washington, Govt. Print. Off.,
1962.
20p. (Its publication no. 457 (8-62))

1. Taxation - Charts, tables, etc.

330
C341n
Taxation - Chicago.
Chicago Area Transportation Study.
Forecasting economic activity: income and taxes, by Irving Hoch. Chicago [1958]
47p. tables.

"In cooperation with U.S. Bureau of Public Roads."

1. Economic forecasting. 2. Taxation - Chicago. 3. Income - Chicago. I. Hoch, Irving.

711.585
(77434)
D27u
Taxation - Detroit.
[Detroit. Housing Commission.]
Urban renewal and tax revenue: Detroit's success story. Detroit, 1964.
18p.

1. Urban renewal - Detroit.
2. Taxation - Detroit.

336.2
[(480)
K14
Taxation - Finland.
Kaksonen, V
Tilastomatemaattisten menetelmien käytöstä erässä arvioimis - ja suunnittelutehtävissä (The use of statistics in some taxation and planning problems) by V. Kaksonen et V. Tervola. Helsinki, State Institute for Technical Research, 196?
98p. (Finland. State Institute for Technical Research. Tiedotus. Sarja 3 - Rakennus (Building) 11?)
1. Taxation - Finland. 2. Economic conditions - Finland - Statistics. I. Finland. State Institute for Technical Research. II. Tervola.

336.2
(77132)
C47
Taxation - Cleveland.
Citizens League of Greater Cleveland.
Greater Cleveland's tax problems: time for decisions. Cleveland, [1966?]
27p.

1. Taxation - Cleveland. I. Title.

336.2
(77434)
D27
TAXATION - DETROIT.
Detroit. City Plan Commission.
Social purpose taxation; a policy proposal. Detroit, 1971.
138p.
Preparation of document financed through a grant from the Dept. of Housing and Urban Development under the provisions of Section 104 of the Demonstration Cities and Metropolitan Development Act of 1966.
1. Taxation - Detroit. 2. Municipal finance. - Detroit. I. U.S. Dept. of Housing and Urban Development. II. Title.

336.2
(759)
F56
Taxation - Florida.
Florida. Development Commission. (Industrial Services Division)
Florida state taxes as they affect business and industry. Tallahassee, 1958.
23p. tables. (Its Business information leaflet no. 2)

1. Taxation - Florida.

336
(861)
C65
TAXATION - COLOMBIA.
Colombia. Departamento de Contraloria.
Informe financiero, 19
Bogota, 19
v.
Report prepared by various divisions of the department.
Issued by the dept. under a variant name: Contraloria General de la Republica.
For Library holdings see main entry.
1. Finance - Colombia. 2. Taxation - Colombia.

333.71
(7531)
M29
Taxation - District of Columbia metropolitan area.
Meyers, Carol S
Taxation and development; the use of tax policies for preserving open space and improving development patterns in the bi-county region. Prepared for the Maryland-National Capital Park and Planning Commission. Wash., Washington Center for Metropolitan Studies, 1968.
82p. (Washington Center for Metropolitan Studies. Working paper no. 4)
Bibliography: p. 77-82.
1. Open space land - District of Columbia metropolitan area.
(Cont'd on next card)

336.2
(759)
F56f
Taxation - Florida.
Florida. Development Commission.
Florida taxes. Tallahassee, 1966.
26p.

1. Taxation - Florida.

711.33
(.46)
C65st
Taxation - Conn.
Connecticut. Commission to Study the Necessity and Feasibility of Metropolitan Government.
The State's biggest business: local and regional problems. [Hartford] 1967.
59p.

1. State planning - Conn. 2. Metropolitan government - Conn. 3. Intergovernmental relations - Conn. 4. Taxation - Conn. I. Title.

352.1
(77389)
R15
Taxation - East St. Louis, Ill.
Ranney, David C
A fiscal crisis in East St. Louis, Illinois. Edwardsville, Ill., Southern Illinois University, Public Administration and Metropolitan Affairs Program, 1967.
96p. (Public policy background study. Report no. PP 4)

1. Municipal finance - East St. Louis, Ill. 2. Taxation - East St. Louis, Ill. I. Illinois, Southern University, Edwardsville. Public Administration and Metropolitan Affairs Program.
II. Title.

336.2
(759)
F56f
1968
Taxation - Florida.
Florida. Development Commission.
Florida taxes. Tallahassee, 1968.
36p.

1. Taxation - Florida. I. Title.

VF
352
(75938)
M41
Taxation - Dade Co., Fla.
Miami-Dade County, Fla. Chamber of Commerce.
Local government in Dade County. A short course. Miami, Government Research Council, Miami-Dade County Chamber of Commerce, 1965.
19p.

1. Local government - Dade Co., Fla.
2. Taxation - Dade Co., Fla. I. Title.
3. Metropolitan government - Miami-Dade Co., Fla.

382
T19
Taxation - Europe.
Tax Foundation, inc.
Tax harmonization in Europe and U.S. business. New York, 1968.
32p. (Its Research publication no. 16 (new series))

1. Commercial policy. 2. Taxation - Europe. 3. Foreign exchange. I. Title

---

336.2
(7942)
G74
Taxation - Fresno County, Calif.
Griffenhagen, Kroeger, Inc.
Effects of tax exemption for improvements and/or personality. A study for the Assembly Interim Sub-Committee on Tax Exemption, California legislature.
[San Francisco] 1962.
123p.
Vernon Kilpatrick, chairman.

1. Taxation - Fresno County, Calif.

VF
33(755666)
V17
Taxation - Danville, Va.
Virginia. University. *Bureau of Population and Economic Research.*
Economic summary of Danville, Virginia. [Charlottesville] 1947.
38, 46 l. diagrs., tables. 29 cm.

"Preliminary report on business and occupation taxation in the city of Danville, Virginia, prepared by the Bureau of Public Administration, University of Virginia": 66 leaves at end.

1. Danville, Va.—Econ. condit. 2. Danville, Va.—Population. 3. Pittsylvania Co., Va.—Econ. condit. 4. Pittsylvania Co., Va.—Population. 5. Taxation—Danville, Va. I. Virginia. University. Bureau of Public Administration.

A 50-9442

Virginia. State Library for Library of Congress [1]

336.2
(75529)
H68
Taxation - Fairfax Co., Va.
House, Peter.
Farm taxes on the rural urban fringe. A base study of Fairfax County, Virginia. Washington, U.S. Dept. of Agriculture, Farm Production Economics Division, Economic Research Service, 1963.
12p. [[U.S. Economic Research Service] ERS-102]

1. Taxation - Fairfax Co., Va.
2. Fringe areas - Fairfax Co., Va. I. Title. II. U.S. Economic Research Service.

VF
33
(758)
B76
c.1
Georgia - Taxation.
Brooks, Robert P
Georgia in 1950; a survey of financial and economic conditions. Athens, Ga., Univ. of Georgia, Sept. 1950.
33 p. map, tables. [[Georgia. University] Institute for the study of Georgia problems. Monograph no. 8]
Bulletin of the University of Georgia, v. 51, no. 7a.
Bibliographical footnotes.
1. Georgia-Econ. condit. 2. Georgia-Taxation. I. Title. II. Series.

336.211
(77473)
D19
v.1
Taxation - Dayton, Ohio.
Dayton, Ohio. Tax Study Advisory Committee.
Taxation and urban blight; a case study of greater Dayton. Vol 1. Prepared in cooperation with Management Services Associates. Dayton, Ohio, 1962.
30p.
Prepared for Lincoln Foundation of Cleveland.

1. Real property - Taxation - Dayton, Ohio. 2. Taxation - Dayton, Ohio.
3. Slums - Dayton, Ohio. I. Management Services Associates, New York.
II. Lincoln Foundation of Cleveland.

Taxation - Federal
see
~~Federal~~ Taxation.

353
(758)
G26c
TAXATION - GA.
Georgia. Tax Revision Committee.
Comparison of State revenue systems. Atlanta, 1948.
227p.

William M. Lester, Director, Tax Revision Committee.

1. State finance - Ga. 2. Taxation - Ga. I. Lester, William M. II. Title.

336.2
(746)
C16
Taxation - Hartford.
Capitol Region Planning Agency, East
Hartford, Conn.
Municipal taxation and regional develop-
ment in the Capitol region. East Hartford,
Conn., 1963.
26p.

U.S. Urban Renewal Adm. UPAP.

1. Taxation - Hartford. 2. Metropolitan area
planning - Hartford.   I. U.S. URA-UPAP.
Connecticut.

336.2
(772)
M67
TAXATION - INDIANA.
Mott, Charles F
Financing local government in Indiana: a study
of property tax rate limits and alternative local
nonproperty revenue sources, by Charles F. Mott
and James R. Ukockis. Indianapolis, Institute of
Public Administration, Indiana University, 1966.
85p.
Bibliography: p. 86-89.
1. Taxation - Indiana. 2. Local government -
Finance. I. Ukockis, James R., jt. au. II.
Indiana. University. Institute of Public Adminis-
tration. III. Indiana. Commission State Tax and
Financing Policy.   IV. Title.

336.2
(763)
R67
Taxation - Louisiana.
Ross, William D
Louisiana's industrial tax exemption program.
Baton Rouge, La., Division of Research, College
of Commerce, Louisiana State University, 1953.
87p. (Louisiana. State University. Div.
of Research. Louisiana business bulletin,
vol. 15, no. 2)

1. Taxation - Louisiana. I. Louisiana.
State University. (Div. of Research)

336.2
(969)
L67
Taxation - Hawaii.
Los Angeles. Bureau of Municipal Research.
Economic implications of the Hawaiian tax
system. Part of an economic base study of
the Island of Oahu in collaboration with the
Oahu Planning Associates, contractors with
the Honolulu Planning Commission. Participating with Charles B. Bennet and Associates of Los Angeles. Los Angeles, 1959.
48p. illus., maps.

1. Taxation - Hawaii. 2. Economic base studies -
Hawaii. I. Bennett (Charles B.) and Associates.
II. Honolulu, H.I.   City Planning Com-
mission.

VF
336.2
(777)
I68
Taxation - Iowa.
Iowa. Tax Commission.
Your tax dollars 1956-1957, where they came
from, who paid them, where the money goes.
Property levies, special tax collections and
allocations 1956-1957. Des Moines, 1958.
[17]p.

1. Taxation - Iowa.

336.2
(77386)
C62
Taxation - Madison Co., Ill.
Cohen, Leo
Intra-county tax uniformity in Madison
and St. Clair Counties, Illinois.
Edwardsville, Ill., Public Administration
and Metropolitan Affairs Program, Southern
Illinois University, 1965.
65p. (Illinois. Southern Illinois
University, Edwardsville. Public Admin-
istration and Metropolitan Affairs Program.
Research and information mono-
graphs)

(Continued   on next card)

336.211
(969)
M44
TAXATION - HAWAII.
Miklius, Walter.
Taxation of urban land: nonconforming use
residential properties, by Walter Miklius
with consulting services of Manuel Gottlieb.
Honolulu, Economic Research Center, Univer-
sity of Hawaii, 1968.
51p.
1. Real property - Taxation - Hawaii.
2. Taxation - Hawaii. 3. Land use - Hawaii.
I. Gottlieb, Manuel, jt. au. II. Hawaii.
University. Economic Research Center.
III. Title.

336.2
(7292)
H65
Taxation - Jamaica.
Holland, Daniel M
The taxation of unimproved value in
Jamaica. Supported by Regional and Urban
Planning Implementation, inc., under a con-
tract from AID. [n.p.] 1966.
98p.

1. Taxation - Jamaica. 2. Economic conditions - Jamaica. I. U.S. Agency for
International Development.

336.2
(77386)
C62
Cohen, Leo. Intra-county tax uniformity
in Madison and St. Clair Counties,
Illinois...1965.   (Card 2)

1. Taxation - Madison Co., Ill. 2. Taxation - St. Clair Co., Ill. I. Illinois.
Southern Illinois University, Edwardsville. Public Administration and Metropolitan Affairs Program

---

353
(969)
T19
TAXATION - HAWAII.
Tax Foundation of Hawaii.
Government in Hawaii; a handbook of
financial statistics, 19

Honolulu, 19

v.
For Library holdings see main entry.
1. State finance - Hawaii. 2. Municipal
finance - Hawaii. 3. County finance -
Hawaii. 4. Taxation - Hawaii. I. Title.

LAW
S
(Kan.)
.266
Taxation - Kansas.
McDonald, James T
Decisions of the 1966 budget and special
sessions of the Kansas Legislature. Lawrence, Kansas University, Governmental
Research Center, 1966.
130p. (Kansas. University. Governmental Research Center. Citizen's pamphlet series no. 38)

1. State government - Kansas. 2. State finance -
Kansas. 3. Taxation - Kansas. 4. Legislation -
Kansas. I. Kansas. University. Governmental
Research Center.   II. Kansas. Laws,
statutes, etc.   III. Kansas. Leg-
islature. IV. Title.   (Series)

336.2
(77386)
C63
Taxation - Madison, Co., Illinois.
Cohen, Leo.
Property tax equity and tax reform in
Illinois: Madison County case study.
Edwardsville, Ill., Public Administration
and Metropolitan Affairs Program, Southern
Illinois University, 1968.
27p. (Illinois. Southern Illinois Uni-
versity, Edwardsville. Public Administration
and Metropolitan Affairs Program. Research
and information monograph: Report no. RI-7)
Bibliography: p. 28-29.
1. Taxation - Madison, Co., Ill. I. Illi-
nois. Southern Illinois University, Edwardsville.
Public Administration and Metropolitan Affairs
Program. II. Title.

353
(773)
I55
Taxation - Illinois.
Illinois. Dept. of Revenue.
Report,

Springfield,
v. annual.

Report year ends June 30.
For complete information see main card.

1. State finance - Illinois.
2. Taxation - Illinois.

336.2
(8)
R72
Taxation - Latin America.
Regional and Urban Planning and Implementa-
tion, inc.
An evaluation of self-assessment under a
property tax. [n.p.] 1966.
77p.
Discussion of scheme suggested by Arnold
Harberger.

1. Taxation - Latin America. 2. Real property - Latin America. I. Harberger, Arnold.

336.2
(741)
M14
Taxation - Maine.
Maine. Legislative Research Committee.
Public revenues and the economy of Maine,
by John F. Sly. First report. Augusta,
Me., 1960.
55p. tables. (Publication no. 100-1)

1. Taxation - Maine. I. Sly, John F.

336.2
(54)
I52
Taxation - India.
India. Parliament.
The finance bill, 1959— (As intro-
duced in Lok Sabha) New Delhi, 1959—
v

For complete information see shelflist.

1. Taxation - India.

336.2
(8)
T19
1962
Taxation - Latin America.
Tax Institute of America.
Tax policy on United States investment in
Latin America, by William Sprague Barnes and
others. Symposium conducted by the Tax
Institute of America, October 25-26, 1962.
Princeton, N.J., 1963.
275p.

1. Taxation - Latin America. I. Barnes,
William Sprague.   II. Title.

336.2
(752)
M17
TAXATION - MARYLAND.
Maryland. Legislative Council. Committee
on Taxation and Fiscal Matters.
Report, 19

Annapolis, 19
v. annual.
For Library holdings see main entry.

1. Taxation - Md. 2. State finance -
Md.

336.2
(773)
C63
Taxation - Ill.
Cohen, Leo.
Alternative tax programs and economic
growth. [Springfield, Ill.] State of
Illinois. Dept. of Business and Economic
Development, 1967.
53p.
U.S. Urban Renewal Adm. UPAP.

1. Taxation - Ill. 2. Economic develop-
ment - Ill. 3. Industrial location - Ill.
4. Economic policy. 5. Economic planning -
Ill. I. Illinois. Dept. of Business and
Economic Develop ment. II. U.S. URA -
UPAP. Illinois.   III. Title.

336.211
H85
1924
TAXATION - LAW AND LEGISLATION.
HUNTINGTON, CHARLES WHITE.
ENCLAVES OF ECONOMIC RENT FOR THE
YEAR 1924; BEING A COMPENDIUM OF THE
LEGAL DOCUMENTS INVOLVED, TOGETHER
WITH A HISTORICAL DESCRIPTION. 5TH
ANNUAL VOLUME. HARVARD, MASS., FISKE
WARREN, 1925.
249P.

1. REAL PROPERTY - TAXATION.
2. TAXATION - LAW AND LEGISLATION.
I. TITLE. II. TITLE: ECONOMIC RENT.

VF
362.6
M17m
Taxation - Maryland.
Maryland. State Commission on the Aging.
Maryland tax relief legislation for low-
income elderly home-owners; how it works, who
benefits, effect on rate. Baltimore, 1962.
folder.

1. Old age. 2. Taxation - Maryland.

352.1
(752)
M17

Taxation - Maryland.
Maryland. State Fiscal Research Bureau.
Local government finances in Maryland;
report, 1952/53, 1955/56-
5th, 8th-
to the Governor and General Assembly of
Maryland. Baltimore, 1954-
v. tables.

1. Municipal finance - Maryland. 2. Taxation - Maryland.

352.5
(752)
E26

Taxation - Maryland.
U.S. Economic Research Service.
Differential assessment of farmland near
cities. Experience in Maryland through 1965.
Washington, Govt. Print. Off., 1967.
39p. (ERS no. 358)

1. Fringe areas - Maryland. 2. Land use -
Maryland. 4. Real property - Maryland.
5. Agriculture - Maryland. 6. Taxation - Maryland. I. Title.

333.332
G27

Taxation - Massachusetts.
Gere, Edwin A   ed.
Assessment administration in Massachusetts. Proceedings of the ninth annual
School for Massachusetts Assessors, August
18-21, 1964. Sponsored by Bureau of
Government Research, Massachusetts Dept.
of Corporations and Taxation [and]
Association of Massachusetts Assessors.
Amherst, Mass., Bureau of Government
Research, University of Massachusetts,
1964.
82p.

(Continued on
next card)

333.332
G27

Gere, Edwin A   ed. Assessment administration in Massachusetts...(Card 2)

1. Real property - Valuation.
2. Appraisal. 3. Taxation - Massachusetts.
I. Massachusetts. University. Bureau of
Government Research.

336.2
(744)
M17

TAXATION - MASSACHUSETTS.
MASSACHUSETTS. SPECIAL COMMISSION ON
REAL ESTATE TAXATION AND RELATED
MATTERS.
REPORT. MARCH 15, 1945. BOSTON,
WRIGHT & POTTER PRINTING CO., 1945.
348P. (MASSACHUSETTS. GENERAL COURT,
1945. HOUSE. DOC. 1800)

1. TAXATION - MASSACHUSETTS. 2. REAL
PROPERTY - MASSACHUSETTS.
3. MASSACHUSETTS - ECONOMIC CONDITIONS.

728.1
(725)
F45

Taxation - Mexico City.
Financing urban development in Mexico City;
a case study of property tax, land use,
housing and urban planning, by Oliver Oldman
and others. Cambridge, Harvard University
Press, 1967.
356p.
Translation of laws: p. [247]-345.
Bibliography: p. 244-246.

1. Housing - Mexico City. 2. Land use -
Mexico City. 3. Taxation - Mexico City.
I. Oldman, Oliver Stanford.

336.2
(774)
C54

Taxation - Michigan.
Cline, Denzel C
Michigan tax reform, by Denzel C. Cline and
Milton C. Taylor. East Lansing, Institute
for Community Development and Services, A Continuing Education Service of Michigan State
University, 1966.
98p.

1. Taxation - Michigan. 2. Income tax.
I. Taylor, Milton C., jt. au. II. Michigan.
State University. Institute for Community
Development and Services. III. Title.

711.3
(774)
S64

Taxation - Mich.
Sokolow, Alvin D
Governmental response to urbanization:
three townships on the rural-urban gradient.
East Lansing, Mich., Economic Research
Services, United States Dept. of Agriculture
in cooperation with Institute for Community
Development and Service, Michigan State
University, 1968.
58p. (U.S. Economic Research Service.
Agriculture economic report no. 132)
Bibliography: p. 58-[60]

1. City   growth - Mich.

(Cont'd on next card)

711.3
(774)
S64

Sokolow, Alvin D   Governmental response.
...1968.

2. Taxation - Mich. 3. Municipal finance -
Mich. I. Michigan. State University, East
Lansing. Institute for Community Development and Service. II. U.S. Economic
Research Service. III. Title.

336.2
(774)
U64

Taxation - Michigan.
Upjohn Institute for Employment Research.
Taxation and industrial location in
Michigan, by Harvey E. Brazer. Kalamazoo,
Mich., 1959.
305-327p.

"A reprint of Appendix Chapter B of a
book entitled The Michigan economy: its
potentials and its problems."

1. Taxation - Michigan. 2. Industrial location -
Michigan. I. Title: The Michigan
economy: its potentials and its problems.

336.2
(774)
U64
1960

TAXATION - MICHIGAN.
UPJOHN INSTITUTE FOR EMPLOYMENT RESEARCH.
TAXES AND ECONOMIC GROWTH IN MICHIGAN;
A STUDY UNDERTAKEN AT THE REQUEST OF THE
COMMITTEE ON MICHIGAN'S ECONOMIC FUTURE.
PAUL W. MCCRACKEN, EDITOR; WITH
CONTRIBUTIONS BY THEODORE A. ANDERSEN
AND OTHERS. KALAMAZOO, MICH., 1960.
167P.

1. TAXATION - MICHIGAN. 2. ECONOMIC
DEVELOPMENT - MICHIGAN. I. TITLE.

336.2
(77594)
M45

Taxation - Milwaukee Co., Wis.
Milwaukee. Metropolitan Study
Commission.
Taxation and revenue distribution
in Milwaukee County. Final recommendations. [Milwaukee] 1961.
11p.

1. Taxation - Milwaukee Co., Wis.

336.2
(77657)
L47

Taxation - Minneapolis-St. Paul.
metropolitan area.
Litterer, Oscar F
Twin Cities metropolitan tax study.
Minneapolis, Upper Midwest Research and
Development Council, 1966.
166p.

1. Taxation - Minneapolis-St. Paul
metropolitan area. I. Upper Midwest
Research and Development Council.
II. Title.

VF
336.2
(786)
L28

Taxation - Montana.
Lewis, Gordon D
A possible approach to forest land
taxation. Missoula, Montana Forest and
Conservation Experiment Station, School
of Forestry, 1962.
15p. (Montana. State University of
Forestry. School Bulletin no. 22)

1. Taxation - Montana. 2. Forests and
forestry.

711.4
:670
(747245)
M17

Taxation - Nassau Co., N.Y.
Nassau County, N.Y. Planning Commission.
Industrial land and taxation: a
supplement to "Industry in Nassau County."
Mineola, N.Y., 1965.
24p.

1. Industrial location - Nassau Co.,
N.Y. 2. Taxation - Nassau Co., N.Y.

336.2
(782)
R62

Taxation - Nebraska.
Roesler, Theodore W
Allocating highway user taxes in Nebraska;
a statistical study of the present methods
and of several proposals for change. [Lincoln]
Neb., Bureau of Business Research, College of
Business Administration, Univ. of Nebraska,
1963.
101p. (Nebraska. University. College
of Business Administration. Business research bulletin no. 67)

1. Taxation - Nebraska. 2. State finance - Nebraska.
3. Highways - Nebraska. I. Nebraska. University. College of   Business Administration.

VF
336.2
(793)
N28

Taxation - Nevada.
Nevada. Tax Commission.
Instructions to county assessors. Bulletin.
Carson City.
Nos.
For complete information see shelf list.

1. Taxation - Nevada.

336.2
(742)
N28

Taxation - N.H.
New Hampshire. State Planning and Development
Commission.
New Hampshire initial town property survey
report 1957, by Charles L. Crangle and Paul
Hendrick. Concord, N.H. 1959.
94p. tables.

In conjunction with the New Hampshire Economic Growth Survey Committee.
1. Taxation - N.H. 2. Real property - Valuation. I. Crangle, Charles L. II. Hendrick,
Paul.

336.2
(749)
M45

Taxation - New Jersey.
Miller, William
Revenue-cost ratios of rural townships with
changing land uses. A report of a study for
the Rural Advisory Council, New Jersey Dept.
of Agriculture. Trenton, 1963.
92p.

1. Taxation - New Jersey. 2. Land use -
New Jersey. 3. Rural planning - New Jersey.
I. New Jersey. Rural Advisory
Council.   II. Title.

336.211
(749)
N28

Taxation - New Jersey.
New Jersey. Legislature. Senate. Committee
on Revision and Amendment of Laws.
Public hearing on Senate concurrent resolution no. 4, proposing to amend Article VIII,
Section 1, of the Constitution of the State
of New Jersey, by adding a new paragraph to
be numbered 4, to provide tax exemption on
the dwelling house owned by a citizen and
resident of the State of the age of 65 or more
years, and Senate concurrent resolution no.
6, proposing to amend Article IV, Section III,
paragraph I, of the Constitution of the State
of New Jersey, to   apportion the members

(Continued on next
card)

336.211
(749)
N28

Taxation - New Jersey.
New Jersey. Legislature. Senate. Committee
on Revision and Amendment of Laws.   Public
hearing ... 1960.   (Card 2)

of the General Assembly by the method of calculation known as equal proportions. Trenton,
1960.
10p.

1. Taxation - New Jersey.

336.2
(749)
N28

TAXATION - NEW JERSEY.
New Jersey. Dept. of the Treasury.
(Div. of Taxation)
Report, 19-
Trenton, N.J., 19-
v. annual

For Library holdings see main entry.

1. Taxation - New Jersey.

333.332
(7471)
N28
1942/43

TAXATION - NEW YORK CITY.
NEW YORK (CITY) TAX DEPT.
TENTATIVE LAND VALUE MAPS OF THE
CITY OF NEW YORK FOR THE FISCAL YEAR
JULY 1, 1942-JUNE 30, 1943. NEW YORK,
1942.
182P.

1. REAL PROPERTY - VALUATION - NEW
YORK CITY. 2. TAXATION - NEW YORK
CITY. I. TITLE.

336.2
(756)
N57

Taxation - North Carolina.
North Carolina. Tax Study Commission.
Report of the Tax Study Commission of
the State of North Carolina. Raleigh, N.C.,
1966.
179p.

1. Taxation - North Carolina.
2. Income tax. 3. State finance - North
Carolina.

336.2
(789)
N28

Taxation - New Mexico.
New Mexico. Economic Development Commission.
New Mexico, a favorable tax climate for
industry. In conjunction with the Taxpayers'
Association of New Mexico. Santa Fe, [1958]
[4]p.

1. Taxation - New Mexico. 2. Industrial
location - New Mexico. I. Taxpayers' Association of New Mexico.

333.332
(7471)
N28
1935

TAXATION - NEW YORK CITY.
NEW YORK (CITY) DEPT. OF TAXES AND
ASSESSMENTS.
TENTATIVE LAND VALUE MAPS OF THE
CITY OF NEW YORK FOR 1935. NEW YORK,
1934.
172P.

1. REAL PROPERTY - VALUATION - NEW
YORK CITY. 2. TAXATION - NEW YORK
CITY. I. TITLE.

336.2
(771)
B68

TAXATION - OHIO.
Bowman, John H
Report on local government tax revision in
Ohio to the State of Ohio, by John H. Bowman
and others. Columbus, Ohio, Battelle
Memorial Institute, Columbus Laboratories,
1968.
100p.

1. Taxation - Ohio. 2. Local government -
Ohio. I. Battelle Memorial Institute.
Columbus Laboratories.

336.2
(789)
N28

Taxation - New Mexico.
New Mexico. Economic Development Commis-
sion.
The tax climate. In conjunction with the
Taxpayers Association of New Mexico. Santa
Fe, N. M., 1958.
3p. tables.

1. Taxation - New Mexico. I. Taxpayers'
Association of New Mexico.

336.2
(747)
N28

TAXATION - NEW YORK (State)
NEW YORK (STATE) STATE TAX COMMISSION.
ANNUAL REPORT, 1915-
ALBANY, 1916-
V.

ISSUED IN THE SERIES OF DOCUMENTS OF
THE LEGISLATURE.

1. TAXATION - NEW YORK (STATE)

352.1
(771)
O34a

Taxation - Ohio.
Ohio. Legislative Service Commission.
Analysis of Ohio general fund operations,
1947 to 1958. Columbus, 1959.
11p. tables.

This information bulletin is a revised
version of Chapter I of Staff research report no. 32, State finances and tax resources in Ohio. (352.1(771)O34)

1. State finance - Ohio. 2. Taxation -
Ohio.

336.2
(7471)
C47

Taxation - New York (City)
Citizens Budget Commission, New York.
Real estate tax exemption in New York
City; a design for reform. New York, 1967.
66p.

1. Taxation - New York (City)
2. Real property - New York (City)
I. Title.

352.1
(7471)
N28b

Taxation - New York (City)
New York (City) Temporary Commission on
City Finances.
Better financing for New York City. Final
report. Including the first, second, and
third reports and additional materials. New
York, 1966.
251p.

1. Municipal finance - New York (City)
2. Taxation - New York (City) I. Title.

352.1
(771)
O34

Taxation - Ohio.
Ohio. Legislative Service Commission.
State finances and tax resources in Ohio.
Columbus, 1959.
36p. tables. (Its Staff research report
no. 32)

Revised version of Chapter I, titled:
Analysis of Ohio general fund operations,
1947 to 1958. (352.1(771)O34a)

1. State finance - Ohio. 2. Taxation -
Ohio.

336.211
(7471)
C47

TAXATION - NEW YORK (CITY)
CITIZENS' HOUSING COUNCIL OF NEW YORK.
LOCAL TAXATION AND HOUSING.
MAJORITY REPORT OF TAXATION COMMITTEE
OF THE CITIZENS' HOUSING COUNCIL. NEW
YORK, 1939.
72P.

1. REAL PROPERTY - TAXATION - NEW
YORK (CITY) 2. TAXATION - NEW YORK
(CITY)

352.1
(7471)
N28b2

Taxation - New York (City)
New York (City) Temporary Commission on
City Finances.
Blueprint for fiscal improvement: recom-
mendations for strengthening municipal
development, services, and management in
New York City. Third report. New York,
1966.
89p.
Also included in Its Final report.

1. Municipal finance - New York (City)
2. Taxation - New York (City) 3. Municipal govern-   ment - New York (City)
I. Title.

VF
336.2
(771)
O34e

Taxation - Ohio.
Ohio. Dept. of Taxation.
Local government fund. Amounts distributed
to Ohio cities from county local government
funds by county budget commissions, calendar
years 1955 —1957. Columbus, 1958.
3p. tables.

1. Taxation - Ohio.

336.2
(7471)
E26

Taxation - New York (City)
Economic Development Council of New York
City.
An analysis of the impact of taxes on jobs
in New York City. New York, 1966.
16p. (Its Economic Development Council. Policy study no.1)

1. Taxation - New York (City) 2. Municipal finance - New York (City) 3. Employment - New York (City) 4. Municipal
services - New York (City) I. Title.

333.332
N28

TAXATION - NEW YORK (STATE)
NEW YORK (STATE) CONFERENCE OF MAYORS
AND OTHER MUNICIPAL OFFICIALS.
SCIENTIFIC METHODS AND RULES FOR
ASSESSING LAND AND IMPROVEMENTS.
ALBANY, 1931.
41P. (NEW YORK (STATE) BUREAU OF
TRAINING AND RESEARCH. PUBLICATION,
NO. 2)

1. APPRAISAL. 2. TAXATION - NEW
YORK (STATE) I. TITLE.

VF
336.2
(771)
O34

Taxation - Ohio.
Ohio. Dept. of Taxation. (Div. of Research
and Statistics)
Local government fund: total amount of the
Ohio local government fund, source of fund
monies, and distribution made therefrom by the
county budget commissions, by county, calendar
year 1957. Columbus, Ohio, 1958.
2p. tables.

1. Taxation - Ohio.

711.4
:670
(7471)
L47

Taxation - New York (City)
Little (Arthur D.) inc.
A program to meet New York City's indus-
trial problems. Report to New York City
Planning Commission. New York, 1964.
97p.

1. Industrial location - New York (City)
2. Relocation - New York (City) 3. Taxation - New York (City) I. New York (City)
City Planning Commission. II. Title.

336.2
(94)
W66

Taxation - New Zealand.
Woodruff, A M
Property taxes and land use patterns in
Australia and New Zealand, by A.M. Woodruff
and L.L. Ecker-Racz. Wash., Tax Executives
Institute, 1965.
16-63p.

Reprinted from the Tax executive, Oct.
1965.

1. Taxation - Australia. 2. Taxation - New
Zealand. 3. Real   property - Taxation.
4. Real estate   business. I. Ecker-
Racz, L.L., jt. au.   II. Tax executive.
III. Title.

336.211
(771)
O34

Taxation - Ohio.
Ohio. Dept. of Taxation.
Property taxes: intangible personal:
amount of taxes levied on property having
a state situs, by type of holder and form
of property, annually, calendar years 1948-1957.
Columbus, Ohio, 1957.
1p.

1.Taxation - Ohio. 2. Real property -
Taxation.

336.2
(771)
034r

TAXATION - OHIO.
Ohio. Dept. of Taxation.
Report, 19

Columbus, 19

v. annual.

For Library holdings see main entry.

1. Taxation - Ohio.

336.2
(862)
J64
1964

Taxation - Panama.

Joint Tax Program of the Organization of
American States and the Inter-American
Development Bank.
Fiscal survey of Panama; problems and pro-
posals for reform. Report of the Fiscal
Mission of the Joint Tax Program of the
Organization of American States and Inter-
American Development Bank. Baltimore, Johns
Hopkins Press, 1964.
212p.
At head of title: Joint tax program,
OSA/IDB.
1. Taxation - Panama.   2. Economic develop-
ment - Panama.   I. Inter-American
Development Bank.   II. Title.

TAXATION - REAL PROPERTY

see

REAL PROPERTY - TAXATION

352.1
(766861)
T85l

Taxation - Oklahoma.
Tulsa, Okla. Metropolitan Area Planning
Commission.
Legal basis of revenue for local govern-
ment. A supplement to 1975 metropolitan
Tulsa public financial capacity. Tulsa,
1961.
1v.

1. Municipal finance - Tulsa, Okla.
2. Taxation - Oklahoma. 3. Metropolitan
areas - Tulsa, Okla. I. Title.

336.2
(748)
P25

Taxation - Pennsylvania.
Pennsylvania. Dept. of Internal Affairs.
Local taxation in Pennsylvania's urbanized
area boroughs, 1956, by J. Martin Kelly, Jr.
Harrisburg, Pa., 1958.
34p. tables.

1. Taxation - Pennsylvania. I. Kelly, J
Martin, Jr.

711.015
A52

Taxation - Research.
American Institute of Planners.
Planning research,   Washington, 19

v.

For complete information see main card.

1. Planning-Research. 2. Taxation -
Research. 3. Automation. 4. City planning - Automation.

VF
336.2
(795)
O72

Taxation - Oregon.
Oregon. University. Bureau of Municipal
Research and Service.
Memorandum on trends in the assessed
value of taxable property in Oregon, 1950-
1956. Eugene, Or., 1957.
14 p., tables.

1.Taxation - Oregon. 2.Real property -
Taxation - Oregon. I.Title: Trends in
the assessed value of taxable property in
Oregon.

LAW
S
(Pa.)

Taxation - Pennsylvania.
Schier, Richard F
The legislative and judicial development
of act 481: 1947-1959. Harrisburg, Pa.,
Dept. of Internal Affairs, 1960.
84p.

1. State finance - Pennsylvania.
2. Taxation - Pennsylvania. I. Pennsylvania.
Dept. of Internal Affairs. II. Title.

352.1
(745)
R36

TAXATION - RHODE ISLAND.
Rhode Island. Dept. of Community Affairs.
State report on local government finances
and tax equalization, 19

Providence, 1

v. annual.
For Library holdings see main entry.
1. Municipal finance - Rhode Island.
2. Real property - Taxation - Rhode Island.
3. Taxation - Rhode Island. I. Title.

336.2
(795)
O72p

Taxation - Oregon.
Oregon. University. Bureau of Municipal
Research and Service.
Property tax levies in Oregon cities for
the fiscal year 1958-   In cooperation with
the League of Oregon Cities. Eugene, Or.
1958-
v.   tables. (Its Information bulletin
no. 110)
For complete information see shelflist.

1. Taxation - Oregon. I. Title.
II. League of Oregon Cities.

711.583
(74811)
G45

Taxation - Philadelphia.
Gilbert, Charles E
Governing the suburbs. Bloomington,
Indiana University Press, 1967.
364p.
Bibliography: p. 338-356.
1. Suburbs - Philadelphia metropolitan
area. 2. Metropolitan area planning -
Philadelphia. 3. County planning - Bucks
Co., Pa. 4. County planning - Montgomery
Co., Pa. 5. Local government - Philadelphia.
6. County planning - Delaware Co., Pa.
7. Taxation - Philadelphia. I. Title.

353
(745)
R36

Taxation - Rhode Island.
Rhode Island Public Expenditure Council.
Public spending: spending, up or down?
Providence, R.I., 1960.
40p. tables.

1. Finance - Rhode Island. 2. Taxation - Rhode
Island.

336.2
(795)
O72r

Taxation - Oregon.
Oregon. University. Bureau of Municipal
Research and Service.
Revenue sources of Oregon counties for the
fiscal year 1958-59. Prepared for the
Legislative Interim Committee on Education
and the Legislative Interim Committee on
Taxation. Eugene, Or., 1960.
19p.   tables. (Its Information bulletin
no. 118)

1. Taxation - Oregon.

VF
336.2
(79549)
P67

Taxation - Portland, Or.
Portland, Or. Development Commission.
The tax story of the South Auditorium,
Urban Renewal Project. Portland, Or., 1963.
15p.

1. Taxation - Portland, Or. 2. Urban
renewal - Portland, Or.

336.2
(77386)
C62

Taxation - St. Clair Co., Ill.
Cohen, Leo.
Intra-county tax uniformity in Madison
and St. Clair Counties, Illinois.
Edwardsville, Ill., Public Administration
and Metropolitan Affairs Program, Southern
Illinois University, 1965.
65p.   (Illinois. Southern Illinois
University, Edwardsville. Public Administration and Metropolitan Affairs Program. Research and information monographs)

(Continued   on next card)

336.2
(795)
O72r
1963/64

Taxation - Oregon.
Oregon. University. Bureau of Municipal
Research and Service.
Revenue sources of Oregon counties for
the fiscal year 1963-64. Eugene, Or.,
1965.
21p.   (Its Information bulletin no.
147)

1. Taxation - Oregon.

VF
330
N17
P105

Taxation - Puerto Rico.
National Planning Association.
A tax program to encourage Puerto Rico's
economic growth, by Charles F. Phillips, and
a statement by the NPA Puerto Rican Committee.
Washington, 1958.
38p. (Its Planning pamphlet no. 105)

1. Taxation - Puerto Rico. 2. Economic
development - Puerto Rico. I. Phillips,
Charles F. (Series)

336.2
(77386)
C62

Cohen, Leo. Intra-county tax uniformity
in Madison and St. Clair Counties,
Illinois...1965.   (Card 2)

1. Taxation - Madison Co., Ill. 2. Taxation - St. Clair Co., Ill. I. Illinois.
Southern Illinois University, Edwardsville. Public Administration and Metropolitan Affairs Program

---

728.1
(549)
P14i

Taxation - Pakistan.
Pakistan. Planning Commission.
(Physical Planning and Housing Section)
Incentives for housing. Karachi, Trade
and Industry House, 1964.
33p.   (Study no. P.P. & H.9)

1. Housing - Pakistan. 2. Taxation -
Pakistan. I. Title.

VF
336.2
(7295)
P82

Taxation - Puerto Rico.
Puerto Rico. Dept. of the Treasury. (Office
of Economic and Financial Research)
What you should know about taxes in Puerto
Rico. San Juan, 1958.
77p. charts, tables.

1. Taxation - Puerto Rico.

336.2
(757)
A85

TAXATION - SOUTH CAROLINA.
AULL, G   H
THE PROBABLE ECONOMIC EFFECTS OF A
HOMESTEAD EXEMPTION ACT ON PUBLIC
REVENUES IN SOUTH CAROLINA. CLEMSON,
S.C., 1939.
30P. (SOUTH CAROLINA. AGRICULTURAL
EXPERIMENT STATION. BULLETIN 323)

1. TAXATION - SOUTH CAROLINA.
2. HOME OWNERSHIP.   I. SOUTH CAROLINA.
AGRICULTURAL EXPERIMENT STATION.

VF
711.4
:67
(783)
P17

Taxation - South Dakota.
Patterson, Robert Foster.
Industrial development in South Dakota with special reference to the tax climate for business and industry. Vermillion, Business Research Bureau, School of Business Administration, University of South Dakota, 1950.
24 p. 23 cm. (South Dakota. University. School of Business Administration. Business Research Bureau; Bulletin no. 24)

1. Industrial location-S.D.
4. South Dakota—Indus. 2. Taxation—South Dakota. 1. Title.
II Series.
HF5006.S6 no. 24   338   50-63371
Library of Congress   (2)

336.2
(783)
S68

Taxation - South Dakota
South Dakota. Citizens Tax Study Committee.
Report of South Dakota Citizens Tax Study Committee, appointed by Gov. Ralph Herseth. Pierre, S.D., 1959.
167p.

1. Taxation - South Dakota.

336.2
(75)
G15

TAXATION - SOUTHEASTERN STATES.
Galambos, Eva.
The tax structure of the Southern States: an analysis. Atlanta, Southern Regional Council, inc., 1969.
18p. (Southern Regional Council. Resources Development Center. Publication no. 1)

1. Taxation - Southeastern states.
I. Southern Regional Council.
II. Title.

VF
336.2
(485)
S41
no.3

Taxation - Sweden.
Skattebetalarnas Förening, Stockholm.
A key to Swedish taxes, by Lars Akselsson. Stockholm, 1954.
24p. (Its Meddelanden nr. 3)

1. Taxation - Sweden. I. Akelsson, Lars.

Taxation - Tennessee.

353
(768)
N17

Nashville. City Planning Commission.
Fact book on State-local fiscal relations; presenting information concerning where taxes were collected and the amounts of funds allocated to Tennessee cities, counties and special school districts during 1957-1958. [In cooperation with] Davidson County Planning Commission. Nashville, 1959.
465p.
U.S. Urban Renewal Adm. UPAP.
1. State finance - Tennessee. 2. Inter-governmental relations - Tennessee.. 3. Taxation - Tennessee. I. Davidson Co., Tenn. Planning Commission. II. U.S.   URA-UPAP. Tennessee.

336.211
(764)
T29t

Taxation - Texas.
Texas. State Tax Study Commission.
Taxation in Texas; our property taxes: a research staff study. Austin, 1958.
26p. illus., tables. (Its Report no. 6)

1. Real property - Taxation - Texas.
2. Taxation - Texas.

711.4
(79569)
B56

Taxation - Umatilla, Or.
Bloch (Ivan) and Associates.
Umatilla, Oregon planning studies. Part I. Economic study. Part II. Abstract of taxes. Part III. Suggestions for a comprehensive community planning and development program. By Harlan Nelson. Portland, Or., 1959.
29p.

U.S. Urban Renewal Adm. UPAP.

1. City planning - Umatilla, Or. 2. Taxation - Umatilla, Or.   I. U.S. URA-UPAP. Umatilla, Or.

336.2
S34

TAXATION - U.K.
SHIRRAS, GEORGE FINDLAY, 1885-
THE BURDEN OF BRITISH TAXATION, BY G. FINDLAY SHIRRAS AND L. ROSTAS. CAMBRIDGE, ENG., THE UNIVERSITY PRESS, 1942.
240P. (HALF-TITLE: THE NATIONAL INSTITUTE OF ECONOMIC AND SOCIAL RESEARCH. ECONOMIC AND SOCIAL STUDIES. II)

1. TAXATION - U.K.   I. ROSTAS, LASZIO, JT. AU.   II. TITLE.

VF
352.1
(41)
U54

Taxation - U.K.
United Kingdom. Ministry of Housing and Local Government.
Rates and rateable values in England and Wales, 1955-56. London, H.M. Stat. Off., 1956.

——— Supplement, showing rateable values and number of hereditaments in the new valuation lists ... 1st April 1956.
Enclosures 5 & 6 to dispatch 2012, 2/14/57, American Embassy, London.
For complete information see shelflist card.
1. Municipal finance - U. K. 2. Taxation - U. K. I. Title.

VF
352.1
(41)
E51

Taxation - United Kingdom.
U.S. Embassy. United Kingdom.
Proposed changes in local government financial system -- as requisite to strengthening the local government system. London, 1957.
16 L. (Its Despatch 2012, Feb. 14, 1957)

Enclosures no. 1 and 3 attached; for no.5 and 6 see:

U.K. Ministry of Housing and Local

(See Card No.2)

VF
352.1
(41)
E51

U.S. Embassy. United Kingdom.
Proposed changes in local government... (Card No. 2)

Government. Rates and rateable values ... 1955/56 (≠ suppl.) VF 352.1 (41) U54.

1. Municipal finance - United Kingdom.
2. Taxation - United Kingdom.

4964

TAXATION - UTAH.
UTAH. UNIVERSITY. DEPT. OF ECONOMICS.
REVENUE PROJECTIONS FOR THE STATE OF UTAH AND THE BASIC UNDERLYING ECONOMIC FACTORS. SALT LAKE CITY, 1969.
34L. (HUD 701 REPORT)

1. TAXATION - UTAH.   I. HUD. 701. UTAH.

336.2
(755)
A87

Taxation - Virginia.
Austin, Robert J
Tax rates in Virginia cities and urban counties. Charlottesville, Virginia, Municipal League and Institute of Government, University of Virginia, 1967.
56p. (Virginia Municipal League and Institute of Government, University of Virginia joint report no. 24)
1. Taxation - Virginia. 2. Personal property - Taxation. 3. Real property - Taxation - Virginia. I. Virginia Municipal League. II. Virginia. University. Institute of Government. III. Title.

Taxation - Virginia.
Bain, Chester W
Tax rates in Virginia cities; a compilation of tax rates and service charges levied by Virginia cities. Richmond, League of Virginia Municipalities, 1950.
v, 22 l. (League of Virginia Municipalities and Bureau of Public Administration, University of Virginia. Joint report no. 4)

o.p.10/51

51-21853

336.2
(755)
L21
1953

Taxation - Virginia.
League of Virginia Municipalities.
Tax rates in Virginia cities, by Betty Blakey. Richmond, 1953.
21p. tables. (League of Virginia Municipalities and Bureau of Public Administration, U. of Virginia. Joint report no. 6)

1. Taxation - Virginia. I. Blakey, Betty. II. Virginia. University. Bureau of Public Administration.

336.2
(755)
L21
1958

Taxation - Virginia.
League of Virginia Municipalities.
Tax rates on Virginia cities, by Walter Stenehem. Richmond, 1958.
25p. tables. (League of Virginia Municipalities and Bureau of Public Administration, U. of Virginia. Joint report no. 11)

1. Taxation - Virginia. I. Stenehem, Walter. II. Virginia. University. Bureau of Public Administration.

336.2
(755:73)
M24

Federal taxation - Va.
McKinney, George Wesley, Jr.
Federal taxing and spending in Virginia, a quantitative study. Prepared for Committee on Public Finance. [Richmond, Va.] The Advisory Committee on the Virginia Economy, June 1950.
57 l. tables.

Bibliographical footnotes.
Processed.
Abridgment of doctoral dissertation, University of Virginia.

(Continued on next card)

McKinney, George Wesley, Jr. Federal taxing and spending in Virginia...June 1950. (Card 2)

1. Federal taxation-Va. I. Virginia. Advisory Committee on the Virginia Economy. II. Title.

336.2
(755)
V47

Taxation - Virginia.
Virginia. Commission on State and Local Revenues and Expenditures and Related Matters.
State and local revenues and expenditures. Report of the Commission ... to the Governor and the General Assembly of Virginia. Richmond, 1957.
43p.

Senate document no. 12.

1. Taxation - Virginia. 2. State finance - Virginia.

336.2
(797)
B42

Taxation - Washington (State)
Biesen, Chester.
The Washington city; its greatness is at stake: the case for local sales tax sharing. [Seattle, Association of Washington Cities, 1965?]
172p.

1. Taxation - Washington (State) 2. State government - Washington (State) 3. City growth. 4. Intergovernmental relations - Washington (State) I. Association of Washington Cities. II. Title.

336.2
(797)
W17p
1966

TAXATION - WASH. (STATE)
Washington (State) Tax Advisory Council.
Proposals for changes in Washington's tax structure. Olympia, 1966.
133p.

1. Taxation - Wash. (State) I. Title.

336.2
(797)
W17pr
1968

TAXATION - WASH. (STATE)
Washington (State) Tax Advisory Council.
Proposals for changes in Washington's tax structure. Second report of the Tax Advisory Council of the State of Washington. Olympia, 1968.
79p.

1. Taxation - Wash. (State) I. Title.

336.2
T36

Taxation for growth.
Thomson, John Cameron.
Taxation for growth, based on a statement on national policy issued by the Research and Policy Committee of the Committee for Economic Development. New York, Committee for Economic Development, 1957.
20 p. illus.

1. Taxation. I. Committee for Economic Development. II. Title.

332.72
1368
C65
1956
S-R

TAXATION OF INSURANCE COMPANY INCOME.
U.S. CONGRESS. SENATE. COMMITTEE ON FINANCE.
TAXATION OF INSURANCE COMPANY INCOME. REPORT TO ACCOMPANY H.R. 7201. WASHINGTON, 1956.
38P. (84TH CONGRESS, 2D SESSION. SENATE. REPORT NO. 1571)

1. LIFE INSURANCE COMPANIES - TAXATION. 1. TITLE.

336.2
(797)
W17

Taxation - Washington (State)
Washington (State) University. Bureau of Governmental Research and Services.
Tax reform to meet the challenge of growth. Proceedings of the thirty-second annual Summer Institute of Government, 1967. Seattle, 1967.
55p. (Its Report no. 166)

1. Taxation - Washington (State) 2. City growth - Washington (State) I. Washington (State) University. Summer Institute of Government. II. Title.

336.2
P18

Taxation in the United States.
Paul, Randolph E
Taxation in the United States. Boston, Little, Brown, 1954.
830p.

1. Taxation. I. Title.

728.69
(777)
I68

TAXATION OF MOBILE HOMES.
IOWA LEGISLATIVE RESEARCH BUREAU.
TAXATION OF MOBILE HOMES. (DES MOINES, IOWA) 1957.
11L. (ITS BULLETIN NO. 21)

1. MOBILE HOMES - IOWA. I. TITLE.

332
(71)
M27

Taxation - Winnipeg, Can.
Metropolitan Corporation of Greater Winnipeg.
Current revenue and expenditure estimates of the Metropolitan Corporation of Greater Winnipeg for the year ending 31st December, 1965. Winnipeg, Can., 1965.
v.

For complete information see main card.

1. Municipal finance - Winnipeg, Can.
2. Taxation - Winnipeg, Can.

658.1
C65T

TAXATION OF CORPORATE SURPLUS ACCUMULATIONS.
U.S. CONGRESS. JOINT COMMITTEE ON THE ECONOMIC REPORT.
TAXATION OF CORPORATE SURPLUS ACCUMULATIONS. THE APPLICATION OF EFFECT, REAL AND FEARED, OF SECTION 102 OF THE INTERNAL REVENUE CODE. WASHINGTON, 1952.
260P.
AT HEAD OF TITLE: 82D CONGRESS, 2D SESSION. JOINT COMMITTEE PRINT.

1. CORPORATIONS. 2. TAXATION. I. TITLE.

VF
728.69
336.2
M42

The taxation of mobile homes.
Michigan. State College. Bureau of Business Research.
The taxation of mobile homes, by Richard D. Duke [and] Avery A. Haak. [East Lansing, Mich., 1955?]
38 p. tables.

Sponsored by Michigan Trailer Parks Association.

1. Trailers. I. Duke, Richard D. II. Haak, Avery A. III. Michigan Trailer Parks Association. IV. Title.

336.2
(775)
W47

Taxation - Wisconsin.
Wisconsin. Legislature. Committee on Revenue Sources.
Report to the 1957 Wisconsin Legislature, v. 1-
Madison, 1956-
v. illus.

For complete information see shelflist.

1. Taxation - Wisconsin.

336.2
C656T
1939
S-H

TAXATION OF GOVERNMENTAL SECURITIES AND SALARIES.
U.S. CONGRESS. SENATE. SPECIAL COMMITTEE ON TAXATION OF GOVERNMENTAL SECURITIES AND SALARIES.
TAXATION OF GOVERNMENTAL SECURITIES AND SALARIES. HEARINGS, SEVENTY-SIXTH CONGRESS, 1ST SESSION, PURSUANT TO S. RES. 303 (75TH CONGRESS) WASHINGTON, GOVT. PRINT. OFF., 1939.
745P.

1. TAXATION. I. TITLE.

LAW
S

Taxation of property in California...
California. Legislature. Assembly. Interim Committee on Revenue and Taxation.
Taxation of property in California; a major tax study. Part 5. A report for the California Legislature Assembly Interim Committee on Revenue and Taxation, Dec. 1954, by David R. Doerr and Raymond R. Sullivan, with special sections by Harold M. Somers and others. [Sacramento] Calif., 1964.
361p. (Its v. 4, no. 12)

1. Real property - Taxation - California. I. Doerr, David R. II. Sullivan, Raymond R. II. Title.

VF
336.2
(787)
W96

Taxation - Wyoming.
Wyoming Taxpayers Association.
Budget Times-News. Cheyenne, Wyo., 1958.
26p. tables. (Its Report no. 231)

1. Taxation - Wyoming. 2. Local Government - Wyoming - Finance.

728.69
034

Taxation of house trailers in Ohio and other states.
Ohio. Dept. of Taxation.
Taxation of house trailers in Ohio and other states. Columbus, Ohio, 1958.
18p.

1. Trailers and trailer courts - Taxation. I. Title.

336.2
J87

TAXATION OF GOVERNMENT BONDHOLDERS AND EMPLOYEES.
U.S. DEPARTMENT OF JUSTICE.
TAXATION OF GOVERNMENT BONDHOLDERS AND EMPLOYEES. THE IMMUNITY RULE AND THE SIXTEENTH AMENDMENT. A STUDY MADE BY THE DEPARTMENT OF JUSTICE. WASHINGTON, GOVT. PRINT. OFF., 1938.
219P.

1. TAXATION. I. TITLE.

333.71
(7531)
M29

Taxation and development; the use of tax policies for preserving open space.
Meyers, Carol S
Taxation and development; the use of tax policies for preserving open space and improving development patterns in the bi-county region. Prepared for the Maryland-National Capital Park and Planning Commission. Wash., Washington Center for Metropolitan Studies, 1968.
82p. (Washington Center for Metropolitan Studies. Working paper no. 4)
Bibliography: p. 77-82.
1. Open space land - District of Columbia metropolitan area.

(Cont'd on next card)

332.72
:368
C65
1958
H-H

TAXATION OF INCOME OF LIFE INSURANCE COMPANIES.
U.S. CONGRESS. HOUSE. COMMITTEE ON WAYS AND MEANS.
TAXATION OF INCOME OF LIFE INSURANCE COMPANIES. HEARINGS BEFORE THE SUBCOMMITTEE ON INTERNAL REVENUE TAXATION... EIGHTY-FIFTH CONGRESS, SECOND SESSION, NOVEMBER 17, 18, 19, AND 20, 1958. WASHINGTON, 1958.
482P.

1. LIFE INSURANCE COMPANIES - TAXATION. I. TITLE.

336.211
(969)
M44

Taxation of urban land.
Miklius, Walter.
Taxation of urban land: nonconforming use residential properties, by Walter Miklius with consulting services of Manuel Gottlieb. Honolulu, Economic Research Center, University of Hawaii, 1968.
51p.
1. Real property - Taxation - Hawaii.
2. Taxation - Hawaii. 3. Land use - Hawaii. I. Gottlieb, Manuel, jt. au. II. Hawaii. University. Economic Research Center. III. Title.

333.71
(7531)
M29

Meyers, Carol S Taxation...1968.

(Card 2)

2. Taxation - District of Columbia metropolitan area. I. Maryland. Maryland-National Capital Park and Planning Commission. II. Washington Center for Metropolitan Studies. III. Title.

332.72
:368
C65
1955
H-R

TAXATION OF INSURANCE COMPANY INCOME.
U.S. CONGRESS. HOUSE. COMMITTEE ON WAYS AND MEANS.
TAXATION OF INSURANCE COMPANY INCOME, REPORT TO ACCOMPANY H.R. 7201. WASHINGTON, 1955.
38P. (84TH CONGRESS, 1ST SESSION. HOUSE. REPORT NO. 1098)

1. LIFE INSURANCE COMPANIES - TAXATION. I. TITLE.

336.2
K29

Taxation of whom and for what.
Keyserling, Leon H
Taxation of whom and for what; "tax reform" versus tax reform. Wash., Conference on Economic Progress, 1969.
65p.

1. Taxation. I. Conference on Economic Progress. II. Title.

336.2
(774)
U64
1960　　TAXES AND ECONOMIC GROWTH IN MICHIGAN.
UPJOHN INSTITUTE FOR EMPLOYMENT RESEARCH.
TAXES AND ECONOMIC GROWTH IN MICHIGAN;
A STUDY UNDERTAKEN AT THE REQUEST OF THE
COMMITTEE ON MICHIGAN'S ECONOMIC FUTURE.
PAUL W. MCCRACKEN, EDITOR; WITH
CONTRIBUTIONS BY THEODORE A. ANDERSEN
AND OTHERS. KALAMAZOO, MICH., 1960.
167P.

1. TAXATION - MICHIGAN. 2. ECONOMIC
DEVELOPMENT - MICHIGAN. I. TITLE.

388
(74886)
R17　　Rattien, Stephen.　　The Pittsburgh...1971.
(Card 2)

I. Duckett, E. Joseph, jt. au. II. Pittsburgh.
University. Environmental Health Program.
III. U.S. Dept. of Housing and Urban Develop-
ment. IV. Title. V. Title: Taxicab study 1970.

325.3
T19　　Taylor, Benjamin J　　Indian...1969.
(Card 2)

3. Labor supply - Western states. I. O'Connor,
Dennis J., jt. au. II. Arizona. State
University, Tempe. Bureau of Business and
Economic Research. III. Title.

336.2
K45T　　TAXES AND ECONOMIC INCENTIVES.
KIMMEL, LEWIS H
TAXES AND ECONOMIC INCENTIVES.
WASHINGTON, THE BROOKINGS INSTITUTION,
1950.
217P.

1. TAXATION. I. TITLE.

336.2
(789)
N28　　Taxpayers' Association of New Mexico.
New Mexico. Economic Development Commission.
New Mexico, a favorable tax climate for
industry. In conjunction with the Taxpayers'
Association of New Mexico. Santa Fe, [1958]
[4]p.

1. Taxation - New Mexico. 2. Industrial
location - New Mexico. I. Taxpayers' Association of New Mexico.

624.131
:308
(74824)
S64　　Taylor, David C
U.S. Soil Conservation Service.
Soil survey of Pike County, Pennsylvania, by
David C. Taylor. In cooperation with Pennsylvania
State University, College of Agriculture and
Agricultural Experiment Station and Pennsylvania
Dept. of Agriculture. Wash., 1969.
Bibliography: p. 82-83.
83p.
1. Soil surveys - Pike County, Pa.
I. Taylor, David C. II. Title.

336.2
C65tax　　Taxes and trade: 20 years of CED policy.
Committee for Economic Development.
Taxes and trade: 20 years of CED policy.
Report of the Twentieth anniversary meeting,
Washington, D.C., May 9, 1963. [Addresses]
New York, 1963.
53p.

Excerpts from the address by President
John F. Kennedy, printed in this volume.

1. Taxation. I. Title.

VF
352
(016)
M17　　A taxpayer's library.
Massachusetts Federation of Taxpayers Associations,
Inc.
A taxpayer's library; books and pamphlets
helpful in studying city and town government in
Massachusetts. Boston, May 1948.
iii, 28 p.

Processed.

1.Municipal government-Bibl. 2.Municipal
government-Mass.-Bibl. 3.Citizen participation
in government-Bibl. 4.City manager government-

(Continued on next card)

624.131
T19　　TAYLOR, DONALD WOOD.
FUNDAMENTALS OF SOIL MECHANICS. NEW
YORK, WILEY, 1955.
700P.

1. SOILS.

333.33
H24　　Taxes and urban housing.
Heilbrun, James.
Real estate taxes and urban housing.
New York, Columbia University Press, 1966.
195p.

1. Real estate business. 2. Real
property - Taxation. 3. Housing market.
I. Title. II. Title: Taxes and urban
housing.

Massachusetts Federation of Taxpayers Associations,
Inc. A taypayer's library ... 1948 (Card 2)

Bibl. 5.Municipal finance-Bibl. 6.Parking-Bibl.
7.Traffic-Bibl. 8.Building codes-Bibl. 9.Building
inspection-Bibl. 10City planning-Bibl. 11.Severage
and sewage disposal-Bibl. 12.Schools-Bibl.
I.Title.

711(41)
A77t　　Taylor, E　　G　　R
Climate in relation to planning. In AFFR
Town and Country planning textbook. London
[1950] p. 14-24.

1.Climate-Gt. Brit. 2.Planning and climate.

711.585
(749)
G25　　Taxes, housing, and urban renewal.
Genung, George R　　Jr.
Taxes, housing, and urban renewal. Wash.,
National Association of Housing and Redevelop-
ment Officials, 1969.
22p.
NAHRO publication no. N532
1. Urban renewal - New Jersey. 2. Real pro-
perty - Taxation - New Jersey. 3. State aided
housing programs - New Jersey. I. National
Association of Housing and Redevelopment
Officials. II. Title.

711.4
(759881)
T17　　Taylor, A　　D
Florida Capitol Center; a report on the
proposed development; prepared for the State
of Florida through Board of Commissioners
of State Institution and Florida State
Improvement Commission, by A. D. Taylor [and]
Herbert L. Flint. [Tallahassee, Fla.] 1947.
93 p. illus. plans.

1.City planning - Tallahassee, Fla. I.Flint,
Herbert L　Jt. Au. II.Florida. State
Improvement Commis-　sion. III.Florida. Board
of Commissioners of　State Institutions.

711(41)
A77t　　Taylor, E　　G　　R
Distribution of population and industry. In
AFFR Town and Country planning textbook. London
[1950] p. 25-40.

1.Population-Gt. Brit. 2.Industrial location-Gt. Br.

388
(7472)
T74　　Taxi survey.
Tri-State Transportation Commission.
(Connecticut-New Jersey-New York)
Findings of the taxi survey. New York,
1968.
12p. (Its Technical bulletin, vol. IV,
no. 3, April, 1968)

1. Transportation - New York
metropolitan area. 2. Traffic surveys -
New York metropolitan area. I. Title:
Taxi survey.

712.21
(77131)
T19　　TAYLOR, A　　D
FOREST HILL PARK; A REPORT ON THE
PROPOSED LANDSCAPE DEVELOPMENT
PREPARED FOR THE CITY OF CLEVELAND
HEIGHTS,
OHIO AND THE CITY OF EAST CLEVELAND,
OHIO. CLEVELAND, 1938.
104P.

1. PARKS - CUYAHOGA CO., OHIO.
I. TITLE.

728.1
R87　　TAYLOR, EUGENE J　　, JT. AU.
RUSK, HOWARD A
LIVING WITH A DISABILITY, BY HOWARD A.
RUSK AND EUGENE J. TAYLOR, IN
COLLABORATION WITH MURIEL ZIMMERMAN AND
JULIA JUDSON. 1ST ED. GARDEN CITY,
N.Y., BLAKISTON CO., 1953.
207P.

1. HOUSING FOR THE HANDICAPPED.
I. TAYLOR, EUGENE J., JT. AU.
II. TITLE.

388
(74886)
R17　　Taxicab study 1970.
Rattien, Stephen.
The Pittsburgh taxicab study; 1970; final
report, by Stephen Rattien and E. Joseph
Duckett. Pittsburgh, Environmental Health
Program, Graduate School of Public Health,
University of Pittsburgh, 1971.
195p.
Bibliography: p. 151-195.
Research supported by a grant from the Dept.
of Housing and Urban Development, Project no.
PENN-R11-8-69.

1. Transportati　on - Pittsburgh.
(Cont'd on next card)

325.3
T19　　Taylor, Benjamin J
Indian manpower resources in the Southwest:
a pilot study, by Benjamin J. Taylor and Dennis
J. O'Connor. Tempe, Arizona State University,
Bureau of Business and Economic Research,
1969.
374p.
Chapters 2-6, also published separately as
Occasional paper no. 3-7 of the Bureau of
Business and Economic Research, Arizona State
University.
1. Indians. 2. Employment - Minority groups.
(Cont'd on next card)

624.131
:308
(746)
T19　　Taylor, F　　B
Soil survey of Bexar County, Texas, by
F.B. Taylor and others. Wash., U.S.
Soil Conservation Service; in cooperation
with Texas Agricultural Experiment
Station, 1966.
126p. (Series 1962, no. 12)

1. Soil surveys - Bexar Co., Tex.
I. U.S. Soil Conservation Service.
II. Title.

```
63      Taylor, Florence
:331
T36   Thomas, Howard E
        Migrant farm labor in Colorado; a study of
      migratory families. Report prepared by Howard
      E. Thomas and Florence Taylor.   New York,
      National Child Labor Committee, Nov. 1951.
        116 l.    tables.

        Prepared for the Colorado Survey Committee
      on Migrant Labor.
        "How the migrants live:" p. 35-47.
        Mimeographed.
```

```
339.5
N17s    National Conference on Soil, Water, and
1967     Suburbia, Washington, D.C. 1967.
         Soil, water, and suburbia...(Card 4)

      achieving the livable suburb. IV. U.S.
      Dept. of Agriculture. V. U.S. Dept. of
      Housing and Urban Development. VI. Wood,
      Robert C. VII. Title.
```

```
728
(07)    Harvard University. Graduate School of
H17      Design...1966.              (Card 2)
pt.2

        1. Architectures - Study and teaching.
      2. Architecture, Domestic. I. Title.
      II. Taylor, H. Ralph. III. Urban Design
      Conference, 10th, 1966.
```

```
658     TAYLOR, FREDERICK WINSLOW, 1856-1915.
T19P      THE PRINCIPLES OF SCIENTIFIC MANAGEMENT,
        BY FREDERICK WINSLOW TAYLOR ... NEW YORK,
        HARPER, 1915.
          144P.

          1. INDUSTRIAL MANAGEMENT.   2. LABOR
        RELATIONS.
```

```
300.15   Taylor, H. Ralph. Defining and implementing
S82      the urban observatories concept.
       Sweeney, Stephen B
         Governing urban society: new scientific
       approaches by S.B. Sweeney and James C.
       Charlesworth. Philadelphia, American
       Academy of Political and Social Science,
       1967.
         25p.    (American Academy of Political
       and Social Science. Monograph 7)
         Cosponsors: Fels Institute of Local and
       State Government and the American Society
       for Public Administration.

                           (Cont'd on next card)
```

```
711.585.1
T19      Taylor, H    Ralph.
           Model cities? A total, unified attack
         on slum area problems offers hope of rapid
2c.      changes. In Agenda, March 1967. p. 8-11.

           At head of title: Cities and their pro-
         blems.
           Author is Assistant Secretary for Demon-
         strations and Intergovernmental Relations.

           1. Model cities. 2. Urban renewal -
         Social effect. 3. Slums. 4. Neighborhood
         rehabilita-              tion. I. Title:
         Cities and          their problems.
```

```
336     Taylor, Graeme M      jt. au.
H45   Hinrichs, Harley H
        Program budgeting and benefit-cost analysis;
      cases, text and readings, by Harley H. Hinrichs
      and Graeme M. Taylor. Pacific Palisades,
      Calif., Goodyear Pub. Co., 1969.
        420p.
        Bibliography: p. 379-420.

        1. Budget. 2. Management. 3. Public admin-
      istration. I. Taylor, Graeme M., jt. au.
      II. Title.
```

```
300.15
S82    Sweeney, Stephen B      Governing urban
     society: new scientific approaches...
     1967.                      (Card 2)

       Contents: Government and the intellectual:
     the necessary alliance for effective action
     to meet urban needs, by R.C. Wood. Defining
     and implementing the urban observatories
     concept, by H. Ralph Taylor.
```

```
711.585  Taylor, H    Ralph.
N17m   National Association of Housing and Redevelop-
       ment Officials.
         The model cities program a HUD-NAHRO dia-
       logue. Questions and answers on demonstration
       cities: summary of a discussion between
       H. Ralph Taylor, Asst. Secretary for Demonstra-
       tions and Intergovernmental Relations, Dept.
       of Housing and Urban Renewal and members
       of NAHRO 9th National Work-
       shop on Urban Renewal, Nov. 21, 1966, in
       New Haven, Conn. Washington, 1967.
         8p.

                           (Cont'd on next card)
```

```
711.417
T19     Taylor, Graham Romeyn.
          Satellite cities; a study of industrial
        suburbs. New York, Arno Press and The
        New York Times, 1970, c1915.
          333p. (The rise of urban America. National
        Municipal League series)

          1. Satellite cities. 2. Suburbs.
        I. National Municipal League. II. Title.
        (Series: The rise of urban America)
```

```
300.15
S82    Sweeney, Stephen B. Governing urban society:
       new scientific approaches...1967. (Card 3)

         1. Social science research. 2. City plan-
       ning. 3. Public administration.
       I. Charlesworth, James C.   jt. ed.
       II. American Academy of Political and Social
       Science.  III. Wood, Robert Coldwell. Govern-
       ment and the intellectual... IV. Taylor, H.
       Ralph. Defining and implementing the urban
       observatories   concept. V. Title.
```

```
711.585  National Association of Housing and Redevelop-
N17m     ment Officials. The model cities program a
         HUD-NAHRO dialogue...1967.       (Card 2)

           1. Urban renewal. 2. Intergovernmental
         relations. I. Taylor, H. Ralph. II. National
         Workshop on Urban Renewal, New Haven, 1966.
         III. Title. IV. U.S. Dept. of Housing and
         Urban Development.
```

```
       Taylor, H    Ralph.    Community action:
339.5     achieving  the livable suburb.
N17s   National Conference on Soil, Water, and
1967     Suburbia, Washington, D.C. 1967.
         Soil, water, and suburbia. A report of
       the proceedings of the Conference, sponsored
       by the U.S. Dept. of Agriculture and the
       U.S. Dept. of Housing and Urban Development,
       June 15-16, 1967. Washington, For sale by
       the Supt. of Docs. Govt. Print. Off.,
       1968.
         160p.
         Chairman: Robert C. Wood, Under Secretary,
       Dept. of Housing and Urban Development.

                           (Continued on next card)
```

```
711.400.15  Taylor, H Ralph. Defining and implement-
P25        ing the urban observatories concept.
1966    Pennsylvania. University. Fels Institute of
        Local and State Government.
          Urban observatories: an approach to a nation-
        wide program of urban research. Proceedings
        of the 1966 Colloquium of Fels Institute of
        Local and State Government, University of
        Pennsylvania, Philadelphia, Pennsylvania,
        September 2, 1966. Philadelphia, 1966.
          54p.
          "Father of the urban observatory concept
        is Dr. Robert C. Wood, Under Secretary of the
        Dept. of Housing and Urban Development."

                           (Cont'd on next card)
```

```
Taylor, H        Ralph.
Speeches.




See speeches collection.
```

```
399.5
N17s    National Conference on Soil, Water, and
1967     Suburbia, Washington, D.C., 1967.
         Soil, water, and suburbia... (Card 2)

         Partial contents: Federal—State-Local
       partnership in suburban development, by
       R. C. Weaver, Secretary, Dept. of Housing
       and Urban Development.—The suburban land
       resource and its use, by Philip J. Maloney,
       Deputy Commissioner, Mortgage Credit and
       Federal Housing, U.S. Dept. of Housing and
       Urban Development. Community action:
       acheiving the        livable suburb, by
       H. Ralph Taylor,      Assistant Secretary.
               (Continued on next card)
```

```
711.400.15
P25     Pennsylvania. University. Fels Institute of
1966     Local and State Government. Urban observa-
         tories...1966.                (Card 3)

           1. City planning - Research. 2. Univer-
         sities and colleges - Research facilities.
         3. Local government - Research. 4. Community
         development - Citizen participation. I. Wood,
         Robert C. II. Taylor, H. Ralph. Defining
         and implementing the urban observatories con-
         cept. III. National Urban Library (Proposed)
         IV. Title.
```

```
728.1     Taylor H    Ralph.
H68repo  U.S. Dept. of Housing and Urban Develop-
         ment.
           A report on the past, present and future
         of the U.S. Department of Housing and Urban
         Development. Presented at the annual con-
         vention of the National Housing Conference,
         Washington, D.C., April 9, 1967, by Secre-
         tary Robert C. Weaver, Under Secretary
         Robert C. Wood, Assistant Secretary Philip
         N. Brownstein, Assistant Secretary Charles
         M. Haar, Assistant Secretary H. Ralph
         Taylor, Assistant Secretary Dwight A. Ink,
         General Counsel    Thomas V. McGrath.
         Wash., 1967.
         [35]p.            (Cont'd on next card)
```

```
339.5
N17s    National Conference on Soil, Water, and
1967     Suburbia, Washington, D.C. 1967.
         Soil, water, and suburbia... (Card 3)

       U.S. Dept. of Housing and Urban Development.

         1. Soils. 2. Water-supply. 3. Suburbs.
       4. Community development. I. Weaver,
       Robert Clifton. Federal-State-Local part-
       nership in suburban development. II. Maloney,
       Philip J. The suburban land resource and
       its use. III. Taylor, H. Ralph. Community
       action:
                           (Continued on next card)
```

```
728     Taylor, H    Ralph.
(07)    Harvard University. Graduate School of
H17      Design.
pt.2     Education and environment. Part II. The
         design of education for design. Urban
         Design Conference, Tenth June 1966.
         [Cambridge, Mass.] 1966.
           35p.
           Partial contents: Keynote address, by H.
         Ralph Taylor, Asst. Secretary for Demon-
         strations and Intergovernmental Relations,
         U.S. Department of Housing and Urban Develop-
         ment.

                           (Cont'd on next card)
```

```
728.1    U.S. Dept. of Housing and Urban Develop-
H68repo  ment. A report on the past, present and
         future of the U.S. Department of Housing
         and Urban Development...1967. (Card 2)

           1. U.S. Dept. of Housing and Urban
         Development. I. Weaver, Robert Clifton.
         II. Wood, Robert Coldwell. III. Brownstein,
         Philip Nathan. IV. Haar, Charles Monroe.
         V. Hummel, Don. VI. Taylor, H. Ralph.
         VII. Ink, Dwight Albert. VIII. McGrath,
         Thomas V.
```

728.1
C653no   Taylor, H   Ralph.
U.S. Congress. Senate. Committee on
Banking and Currency.
Nominations of Bernard L. Boutin, Don
Hummel, H. Ralph Taylor, and Francis M.
Wheat. Hearing before the Committee on
Banking and Currency, United States Senate,
Eighty-ninth Congress, second session on the
nominations of Bernard L. Boutin, to be Ad-
ministrator of the Small Business Adminis-
tration; Don Hummel and H. Ralph Taylor, to
be Assistant Secretaries of the Department
of Housing and   Urban Development;

(Continued on   next card)

728.1
C653no   U.S. Congress. Senate. Committee on Banking and Currency. Nominations of Bernard
L. Boutin, Don Hummel, H. Ralph Taylor,
and Francis M. Wheat...1966.   (Card 2)
and Francis M. Wheat, to be a member of the
Securities and Exchange Commission.
Washington, Govt. Print. Off., 1966.
25p.

1. Boutin, Bernard L. 2. Hummel, Don.
3. Taylor, H.   Ralph. 4. Wheat,
Francis M.   5. U.S. Dept. of
Housing and   Urban Development.
I. Title.

690.591
N17r   Taylor, Harold.
National Association of Housing and Redevelop-
ment Officials.
Rehabilitation operational guide and training
manual. Prepared for the Urban Renewal Agency,
City of Toledo, Ohio by Harold Taylor and
Marian Wojciechowski. Wash., 1971.
140p. (NAHRO publication no. N547)

1. Houses - Maintenance and modernization.
2. Housing law enforcement. I. Toledo. Urban
Renewal Agency. II. Taylor, Harold.
III. Wojciechowski, Marian, jt. au. IV. Title.

331.2
T36   TAYLOR, HAROLD C , JT. AU.
THOLE, HENRY C
ARE WAGES HIGH IN DETROIT   BY HENRY
C. THOLE AND HAROLD C. TAYLOR.
KALAMAZOO, W.E. UPJOHN INSTITUTE FOR
EMPLOYMENT RESEARCH, 1963.
86P. (STUDIES OF THE MICHIGAN ECONOMY)

1. WAGES AND SALARIES.   I. TAYLOR,
HAROLD C. JT. AU.   II. UPJOHN
INSTITUTE FOR EMPLOYMENT RESEARCH.
III. TITLE.

352.6
(77417)
M12   Taylor, Harold C , jt. au.
McKean, Eugene C
Paying for public facilities in Kalamazoo
County, by Eugene C. McKean and Harold C.
Taylor. Kalamazoo, Mich., W.E. Upjohn
Institute for Community Research, 1968.
40p.

1. Community facilities - Kalamazoo Co.,
Mich. I. Upjohn Institute for Employment
Research. II. Taylor, Harold C., jt. au.
III. Title.

312
(77417)
T19   Taylor, Harold C
The population of Kalamazoo County, Michigan;
estimates as of July 1, 1956 and forecasts to
1975. Kalamazoo, Mich., W.E. Upjohn Institute
for Community Research, Sept. 1956.
22 p.

1. Population - Kalamazoo Co., Mich. I. W.E.
Upjohn Institute for Community Research.

351.712
W28   Taylor, Harold C
W. E. Upjohn Institute for Community Research.
Public works and employment from the
local government point of view [by] Eugene C.
McKean and Harold C. Taylor. Chicago, Public
Administration Service, 1955.
274 p. illus.

Bibliography: p. 257-266.

1. Building cycles. 2. Employment. I. McKean,
Eugene C. II. Taylor, Harold C. III. Public
Administration Service, IV. Title.

711.73
:330
H15   Taylor, Harold H., jt. au.
Hallberg, M   C
Econometric analysis of properties
severed by interstate highways by M.C.
Hallberg and Harold H. Taylor. University
Park, Institute for Research on Land and
Water Resources, Pennsylvania State
University, 1969.
29p. (Pennsylvania. State University.
Institute for Research on Land and Water
Resources. Research publication no. 59)
1. Highways - Economic effect. I. Taylor,
Harold H., jt. au. II. Pennsylvania. State
University.   Institute for Research on
Land and Water   Resources. III. Title.

LAW
T
T1951a   Taylor, Irwin M
Law of insurance. New York, Oceana Publica-
tions [c1955] 1965.
96p. (Legal almanac series, no. 37)

1. Insurance. I. Title.

658
T19   TAYLOR, JACK W
HOW TO SELECT AND DEVELOP LEADERS. NEW
YORK, MCGRAW-HILL, 1962.
262P.

1. MANAGEMENT.   2. PERSONNEL MANAGEMENT.
I. TITLE.

711.552.1
S68   Taylor, James D
South Dakota. University. Business Research
Bureau.
The effect on retail of outlying shopping
districts, by James D. Taylor. Vermillion,
S. D., 1961.
24p. (Its Bulletin no. 72)

1. Shopping centers. 2. Retail trade.
I. Taylor, James D.   (Series)

658.8
T19   Taylor, J   D
Retail store hours in South Dakota.
Vermillion, S.D., South Dakota State
University, School of Business, Business
Research Bureau, 1962.
84p. (South Dakota. University.
Business Research Bureau. Bulletin no. 77)

1. Retail trade.   (Series)

VF
727
E28   Taylor, James L
U.S. Office of Education.
Designing elementary classrooms; an approach
to the problem of classroom design in relation to
the school child and program, prepared by James L.
Taylor, Jack D. Herrington ... [Washington,
Govt. Print. Off., 1953]
viii, 55 p. illus., tables. (Its Special
publication no. 1)

Selected references: p. 50-52.

1. Schools. I. Taylor, James L. II. Herrington, Jack
D. III. Title.

727.1
T19   Taylor, James L
Functional schools for young children, by
James L. Taylor and others. Washington,
Dept. of Health, Education, and Welfare,
Office of Education, 1961.
81p. (U.S. Office of Education. Special
publication no. 8)
"Selected bibliography": p. 71-75.

1. Schools. I. Title. II. U.S. Office
of Education.

VF
727.1
E28g   Taylor, James L.
U.S. Office of Education.
Good and bad school plants in the United
States as revealed by a nationwide school
facilities survey. Prepared by James L. Taylor
and James Woofter. [Washington, Govt. Print.
Off., 1954]
77 p. illus. (Its Special publication
no. 2)

1. Schools. I. Taylor, James L. II. Woofter, James.

727.1
E28p   Taylor, James L
U.S. Office of Education.
Planning and designing the multipurpose
room in elementary schools, its meaning,
characteristics, and uses as reflected in
survey reports from all States, Hawaii, and
Alaska, by James L. Taylor. Washington,
1957.
48p. illus., plans. (Its Special publication no. 3)

1. Schools. I. Taylor, James L.

640
E28   Taylor, James L.
U.S. Office of Education.
Planning functional facilities for home
economics education, by James L. Taylor and
Johnie Christian. Wash., 1965.
48 p. (U.S. Office of Education. OE-83015;
Special publication no. 12)
Bibliography: p. 47-48.

1. Home economics. I. Taylor, James L.
II. U.S. Office of Education. III. Title.

VF
727.1
E28sch   Taylor, James L
U.S. Office of Education.
School sites, selection, development,
and utilization, by James L. Taylor. Washington, 1958.
91p. illus., tables. (Its Special publication no. 7)

1. Schools. I. Taylor, James L

VF
727.1
E28   Taylor, James L
U. S. Office of Education.
The secondary school plant, an approach for
planning functional facilities, by James L.
Taylor. Washington, Govt. Print. Off., 1956.
60p. illus. (Its Special publication no.5)

1. Schools. I. Taylor, James L

728
:333
G742   TAYLOR, JAMES S
GRIES, JOHN M
HOW TO OWN YOUR HOME; A HANDBOOK FOR
PROSPECTIVE HOME OWNERS. PREPARED BY
JOHN M. GRIES AND JAMES S. TAYLOR.
WASHINGTON, GOVT. PRINT. OFF., 1925.
28P.

1. HOME OWNERSHIP.   I. TAYLOR, JAMES S.
II. TITLE.

728
:333
G742
1931   TAYLOR, JAMES S
GRIES, JOHN M
HOW TO OWN YOUR HOME; A HANDBOOK FOR
PROSPECTIVE HOME OWNERS. PREPARED BY
JOHN M. GRIES AND JAMES S. TAYLOR. 2D
ED. WASHINGTON, GOVT. PRINT. OFF., 1931.
26P. (BUILDING AND HOUSING
PUBLICATION, BH17)

1. HOME OWNERSHIP.   I. TAYLOR, JAMES S.
II. TITLE.

308
:728.1
T22
1938
Taylor, James S
U.S. Federal Housing Administration. Division of Economics and Statistics.
Local residential occupancy-vacancy surveys; a suggested procedure. Washington, May 1938.
63 l. forms.

Prepared by James S. Taylor, Howard G. Brunsman, Lee Amann, Margaret Kane and others.-p.l. Processed.

1.Vacancy surveys. 2.Survey methods. I.Taylor, James S. II.Title.

728.1
T19
TAYLOR, JAMES S
THE ROLE OF GOVERNMENT IN HOUSING.
WASHINGTON, FEDERAL HOUSING ADMINISTRATION, 1936.
15P.

1. FEDERAL HOUSING PROGRAMS.
2. HOUSING. I. TITLE.

690
C653S
TAYLOR, JAMES S
CONFERENCE ON UNEMPLOYMENT, WASHINGTON, D.C., 1921. COMMITTEE ON SEASONAL OPERATION IN THE CONSTRUCTION INDUSTRIES.
SEASONAL OPERATION IN THE CONSTRUCTION INDUSTRIES, THE FACTS AND REMEDIES; REPORT AND RECOMMENDATIONS OF A COMMITTEE OF THE PRESIDENT'S CONFERENCE ON UNEMPLOYMENT, WITH A FOREWORD BY HERBERT HOOVER. 1ST ED. NEW YORK [ETC] MCGRAW-HILL BOOK COMPANY, ONC., 1924.
213P.

1. BUILDING INDUSTRY.
(CONTINUED ON NEXT CARD)

690
C653S
CONFERENCE ON UNEMPLOYMENT, WASHINGTON, D.C., 1921. COMMITTEE ON SEASONAL OPERATION IN THE CONSTRUCTION INDUSTRIES. SEASONAL OPERATION IN ... 1924.   (CARD 2)

2. EMPLOYMENT. I. PRESIDENT'S CONFERENCE ON UNEMPLOYMENT. II. TITLE. III. GRIES, JOHN M. IV. TAYLOR, JAMES S.

Taylor, James S
Speeches.

See speeches collection.

LAW
T
Taylor, John.
Construction construed and constitutions vindicated. New York, Da Capo Press, 1970.
344p.

An unabridged republication of the 1820 ed.

1. Constitutional law. 2. Constitutions, State. I. Title.

720
T19m
Taylor, John R
Model building for architects and engineers.
New York, McGraw-Hill, 1971.
152p.

1. Architecture - Designs and plans.
I. Title.

339.3
(742)
B68
Taylor, Kenneth A., jt. au.
Bowring, James R
A study to identify low income areas in New Hampshire; background data, by James R. Bowring and Kenneth A. Taylor. Durham, University of New Hampshire, Dept. of Resource Economics, 1965.
59p. (University of New Hampshire, Dept. of Resource Economics. Resource economics research mimeo. no. 36)
1. Income - New Hampshire. 2. Economic conditions - New Hampshire. I. Taylor, Kenneth A., jt. au. II. New Hampshire. University. III. Title.

624.131
Y65
TAYLOR, L O, JT. AU.
YONG, RAYMOND.
A TECHNIQUE FOR MEASUREMENT OF SWELLING PRESSURES OF MONTMORILLONITE UNDER DEPRESSED TEMPERATURES, BY RAYMOND YONG AND L.O. TAYLOR. OTTAWA, DIRECTORATE OF PHYSICAL RESEARCH, DEFENSE RESEARCH BOARD, 1961.
32L. (REPORT NO. D. PHYS. R. (G) MISC. 7)

PART 2 OF SOME SHEARING CHARACTERISTICS OF FROZEN SOIL.
1. FROZEN GROUND. 2. SOILS - TESTING. I. TAYLOR, L.O., JT. AU.

352.1
(774)
T19
TAYLOR, MILTON C
LOCAL INCOME TAXES AS A SOURCE OF REVENUE FOR MICHIGAN COMMUNITIES. EAST LANSING, MICHIGAN, INSTITUTE FOR COMMUNITY DEVELOPMENT AND SERVICES, MICHIGAN STATE UNIVERSITY, 1961.
27P. (INSTITUTE FOR COMMUNITY DEVELOPMENT AND SERVICES. CONTINUING EDUCATION SERVICE MICHIGAN STATE UNIVERSITY. GENERAL BULLETIN NO. 6)

1. MUNICIPAL FINANCE - MICHIGAN.
2. INCOME TAX.
I. TITLE. II. MICHIGAN. STATE
(CONTINUED ON NEXT CARD)

352.1
(774)
T19
TAYLOR, MILTON C LOCAL INCOME TAXES ... 1961.   (CARD 2)

UNIVERSITY. INSTITUTE FOR COMMUNITY DEVELOPMENT AND SERVICES.

336.2
(774)
C54
Taylor, Milton C   jt. au.
Cline, Denzel C
Michigan tax reform, by Denzel C. Cline and Milton C. Taylor. East Lansing, Institute for Community Development and Services, A Continuing Education Service of Michigan State University, 1966.
98p.

1.Taxation - Michigan. 2. Income tax. I. Taylor, Milton C., jt. au. II. Michigan. State University. Institute for Community Development and Services. III. Title.

711.73
:330
(746)
T19
Taylor, Paul N
The Connecticut turnpike and labor market relationships, Storrs, Conn., Agricultural Experiment Station, in cooperation with the Connecticut State Highway Department and Bureau of Public Roads, U.S. Dept. of Commerce, 1962.
15p. (Storrs Agricultural Experiment Station. Progress report 47)
1. Highways - Connecticut - Economic effect. I. Connecticut. Agricultural Experiment Station, Storrs.

711.73
:330
(746)
C65
Taylor, Paul.
Connecticut. Agricultural Experiment Station, Storrs.
New manufacturing and the Connecticut turnpike, by Paul Taylor. Storrs, Conn., [1960?]
16p.

"The economic and social effects of the Connecticut Turnpike on Eastern Connecticut."

1. Highways - Conn - Economic effect.
I. Taylor, Paul

301.15
(54)
T19
Taylor, Paul S
Community development. [Washington, International Cooperation Administration, 1958?]
15p.

1. Community development - India. I. U.S. International Cooperation Administration.

693.55
T19
Taylor, R
Some fatigue tests on reinforced concrete beams. Garston, Eng., Building Research Station, Dept. of Scientific and Industrial Research, 1964.
[8]p. (U.K. Building Research Station. Building research current papers. Engineering series 16)

2c

Reprinted from: Magazine of concrete research, vol. 16(46) 1964. p. 3-8.

1. Concrete, Reinforced. I. U.K. Building Research Station.

691.32
T19
Taylor, R
Some shear tests on reinforced concrete beams with stirrups. Garston, Eng., Building Research Station, Ministry of Public Building and Works, 1967.
10p. (U.K. Building Research Station. Building research current papers. Engineering series 47)

1. Concrete, Reinforced. 2. Building methods. I. U.K. Building Research Station. II. Title.

691
(016)
T19
TAYLOR, R L
STRUCTURAL LAMINATES LITERATURE SURVEY, BY R.L. TAYLOR AND K.S. PISTER. WRIGHT-PATTERSON A R FORCE BASE, OHIO, AERONAUTICAL RESEARCH LABORATORY, OFFICE OF AERO-SPACE RESEARCH. U.S. AIR FORCE, 1961.
14P.

1. BUILDING MATERIALS - BIBLIOGRAPHY.
I. PISTER, K.S. II. U.S. WRIGHT PATTERSON AIR FORCE BASE, OHIO.
III. TITLE.

378
A77u
Taylor, R Robb, ed.
Association of Urban Universities.
University and community. Proceedings of a conference, April 25-26, 1963, under the auspices of the Association of Urban Universities and the Johnson Foundation. R. Robb Taylor, editor. Milwaukee, 1963.
147p.

1. Universities and colleges. I. Johnson Foundation, Racine, Wis. II. Taylor, R. Robb, ed. III. Title.

LC
Taylor, Rattray.
The social basis of town planning. In Architects' year book 4. London, Paul Elek [1952] p. 27-32.

1.City planning.I.Title.

744
T19
Taylor, Richard.
A basic course in graphic design. London, Studio Vista, 1971.
96p.

1. Visual aids. I. Title. II. Title: Graphic design.

699
T19
Taylor, Robert.
Materials & labor estimator for the entire building industry. Compiled and edited by Robert Taylor. New York, William Dogan Annual Publications Associates, 1967.
Laf. 366p.

1. Building industry. 2. Building materials. 3. Building construction - Labor requirements. I. Title.

711.4
T19
Taylor, Thomas Griffith, 1880–
Urban geography; a study of site, evolution, pattern and classification in villages, towns and cities. New York, Dutton [1949]
xv, 430 p. illus., maps. 23 cm. [Dutton advanced geographies]
Bibliography: p. [425]–434.

y planning.
1. Cities and towns.   I. Title.

HT151.T36 1949r   323.35
Library of Congress   [20]   49–10022*

323.4
T19
Taylor, William L
Hanging together: equality in an urban nation. New York, Simon and Schuster, 1971.
348p.

c.1,E.0   Bibliography: p. 323–330.

1. Civil rights. I. Title.

388
(79494)
T19c
Taylor, S   Sam.
Centropolis transportation 1980, Los Angeles vista. An address by Los Angeles City Traffic Engineer. Presented at the 38th Annual Meeting of the Downtown Businessmen's Association, Los Angeles, Calif., June 27, 1962. Los Angeles, Dept. of Traffic, 1962.
27p.
1. Transportation - Los Angeles. I. Downtown Businessmen's Association, Los Angeles.   38th Meeting. 1962.   II. Los Angeles.   Dept. of Traffic.

020
E56
Taylor, Vernie L   comp.
Enoch Pratt Free Library.
Library language; a list for new staff members. Compiled by Vernie L. Taylor. Baltimore, 1963.
32p.

1. Library science. I. Taylor, Vernie L., comp. II. Title.

2700–
2704
TAYLOR, MICH. PLANNING COMMISSION. MASTER PLAN STUDY: 1. LAND USE AND RENEWAL CLASSIFICATION INVENTORY; 2. RESIDENTIAL NEIGHBORHOOD PLAN; 3. RECREATION AND COMMUNITY FACILITIES; 4. NEIGHBORHOOD ANALYSIS; 5. PROJECT COMPLETION REPORT; BY STATE OF MICHIGAN, DEPARTMENT OF COMMERCE, COMMUNITY PLANNING DIVISION. PREPARED BY VILICAN-LEMAN AND ASSOCIATES, INC. SOUTHFIELD, MICH., 1968–69.
5 V. (HUD 701 REPORT)

1. MASTER PLAN - TAYLOR, MICH.
(CONTINUED ON NEXT CARD)

388
(79494)
T19
Taylor, S   Sam.
Minutes, not miles. An address by Los Angeles City Traffic Engineer. Presented to Los Angeles Chamber of Commerce (Construction Industry's Div.) Sept. 12, 1962. Los Angeles, Dept. of Traffic, 1962.
11p.

1. Transportation - Los Angeles. 2. Journey to work. I. Los Angeles. Dept. of   Traffic.

VF=O Ref=
DATE OF REQUEST 1/22/54   L. C. CARD NO.
                   FEB 1 1954
AUTHOR
Taylor, Walter A
TITLE
[Report on Architectural education]
SERIES
Higher Education (U.S. Dept. of H.E.W.)
EDITION | PUB. DATE Oct. 1953 | PAGING 17-27
PUBLISHER
AIA
RECOMMENDED BY   REVIEWED IN
M.L   Arch 1/54 p. 167
                   ORDER RECORD

2700–
2704
TAYLOR, MICH. PLANNING COMMISSION. MASTER PLAN......8–69.   (CARD 2)

I. VILICAN-LEMAN AND ASSOCIATES. II. MICHIGAN. DEPT. OF COMMERCE. COMMUNITY PLANNING DIV. III. HUD '701' TAYLOR, MICH.

388
(79494)
T19n
Taylor, S   Sam.
New attacks on traffic tangles. An address by Los Angeles City Traffic Engineer. Los Angeles, Dept. of Traffic, 1962.
26p.

1. Traffic - Los Angeles. 2. Journey to work. I. Los Angeles. Dept. of Traffic.

625.7
T19
TAYLOR, W   H
STABILIZING ORGANIC FILLS WITH LIME IN LOUISIANA. WASHINGTON, AMERICAN ROAD BUILDERS' ASSOCIATION, 1957.
11P. (TECHNICAL BULLETIN NO. 233)

1. ROAD CONSTRUCTION. I. AMERICAN ROAD BUILDERS' ASSOCIATION. II. TITLE.

711.4
(76935)
T19
Taylor Mill, Ky. Planning and Zoning Commission.
Northern Kentucky Area Planning Commission. Master (comprehensive) plan for city of Taylor Mill, State of Kentucky. Prepared for city of Taylor Mill Planning and Zoning Commission, Newport, Ky., 1965.
91p.
U.S. Urban Renewal Adm. UPAP.

1. Master plan - Taylor Mill, Ky. I. Taylor Mill, Ky. Planning and Zoning Commission. II. U.S. URA-UPAP. Taylor Mill, Ky.

UK - New towns
DATE OF REQUEST 2/13/55   L. C. CARD NO.
AUTHOR
Taylor, Stephen.
TITLE
New towns for a new society [appraisal of the fourteen new towns initiated under the Labor govt.).
SERIES Reprint, Socialist Commentary, Ag '54, 18:211-13.
EDITION | PUB. DATE Ag. '54 | PAGING
PUBLISHER
RECOMMENDED BY   REVIEWED IN
M.L   AIB, 12/4/54, p.14.
                   ORDER RECORD

72
T19
1948
Taylor, Walter A
1948 convention seminars; addresses and discussions on aesthetics, urban planning, dwellings, retail business buildings, modular design. Washington, D.C., American Institute of Architects, Department of Education and Research, c1949
161 p.

Processed.
Brief biiographical notes on participants in the seminars.

(Continued on next card)

693.002.22
(41)
T19
Taylor Woodrow-Anglian.
Industrialized building. Ealing, Eng., 1968.
[12]p.
SfB (2) Gf2.

1. Prefabricated construction - U.K. 2. U.K. - Prefabricated construction. I. Title. II. Larsen and Nielsen, Copenhagen.

DATE OF REQUEST 1/29/52   L. C. CARD NO. 51-37501
Cement
                   FEB 11 1952
AUTHOR
Taylor, Thomas Geer
TITLE
Determination of the air content of mortars by the pressure method.
SERIES Portland Cement Assoc. Research Lab. Bulletin 27.
EDITION | PUB. DATE 1949 | PAGING 12 p.
PUBLISHER
Portland Cement Assoc.
RECOMMENDED BY   REVIEWED IN
                   ORDER RECORD

Taylor, Walter A.   1948 convention seminars...
1949   (Card 2)

1.Architecture-Congresses. 2.City planning. 3.Architecture, Domestic. 4.Modular coordination. I.American Institute of Architects. Dept. of Education and Research.
Analytics: Roterus, V.; Wirth, L.; Mitchell,R.B.; Kent, T.J.; Winslow, C.-E.A.; Sargent, D.K.; Stubbins, H.A.; Kamphoefner, H.L.; Belluschi, P.; Ketchum, M.; McCandless, S.; Yost, L.M.

058.7
:351
T19
Taylor's encyclopedia of Government officials, Federal and State. v. 1- ;   1967/68-69 /70 ;
Dallas, Political Research, Inc. 1948-69
2 v. illus., maps ports. 31 cm.
Part of the illustrative matter is col.
c.1 ref.   For Library holdings see main entry.
Suppl.   Supplement. v. 1-   1967/68-
Dallas, Political Research, Inc. See Kardex
v. 31 cm.
1. Federal government. Direct.   JK6.T362
1. Official and employees. I.Political Research, Inc., Dallas
Direct. I.Title.   Encyclopedia of government
JK6.T36   officials, federal   and state.
officials, federal   353.00025   Ref. 67-22269
                   .55
                   T19

Taylor, Thomas Geer.
Determination of the air content of mortars by the pressure method. [Chicago] 1949.
12 p. 23 cm. (Portland Cement Association [Chicago] Research Laboratories. Bulletin 27)
Cover title.
"Authorized reprint from ... ASTM Bulletin, no. 155, December, 1948."
"References": p. 12.

1. Mortar—Testing.   (Series)

TA439.P83 no. 27   620.135   51-37501
Library of Congress   [1]
          7904^   December 1951

691.32
T19C
TAYLOR, WALTER HAROLD.
CONCRETE TECHNOLOGY AND PRACTICE. NEW YORK, AMERICAN ELSEVIER PUB. CO., 1965.
639P.

2C.   1. CONCRETE.   I. TITLE.

Taylorsville, Ky.

VF
Econcondit.-Ky.

DATE OF REQUEST 9/24/52   L. C. CARD NO.
OCT 8, 1952

[Taylorsville-Spencer Co., Ky. Development Assoc.]
TITLE
Economic and industrial survey of Taylorsville, Ky.

SERIES

EDITION   PUB. DATE July 1952   PAGING 9 p.
PUBLISHER

RECOMMENDED BY   REVIEWED IN
GPO Newsltr 9/52 p.72
ORDER RECORD

711.585
(755521)
M14
Tazewell, William L.
The making of the new Norfolk.
Reprinted herein is a series of five
articles on the "new spirit" in Norfolk,
by staff writer William L. Tazewell,
which appeared July 23-27, 1961 in the
Virginian-Pilot. Norfolk, Va.
[Virginian-Pilot?] [1967?]
Kit   (18 pieces)

Partial contents: -The record speaks
best for renewal in Norfolk, by John I.
Brooks.-
(Continued on next card)

711.585
(755521)
M14
The making of the new Norfolk...[1967?]
(Card 2)

Norfolk's urban renewal program, nation's
first saved business area from economic
strangulation, by Frank Sullivan.

1. Urban renewal - Norfolk, Va.
I. Tazewell, William L.

301.15
(755521)
T19
Tazwell, William L
The making of the new Norfolk.
[Norfolk, Va., 1962?]
folder.
Reprinted ... series of five articles
on the "New Spirit" ... which appeared
Jan 23-27 in The Virginia Pilot.

1. City growth - Norfolk, Va.

4486
TAZEWELL-NEW TAZEWELL, TENN. REGIONAL
PLANNING COMMISSION.
CODES AND CODES ENFORCEMENT. TAZEWELL,
TENN., 1969.
1 V. (HUD 701 REPORT)

1. HOUSING CODES - TAZEWELL, TENN.
I. HUD. 701. TAZEWELL-NEW TAZEWELL,
TENN.

4487
4488
TAZEWELL-NEW TAZEWELL, TENN. REGIONAL
PLANNING COMMISSION.
TAZEWELL, ZONING CODE; NEW TAZEWELL,
ZONING CODE. TAZEWELL, TENN., 1970.
2 V. (HUD 701 REPORT)

1. ZONING - TAZEWELL, TENN. 2. ZONING
- NEW TAZEWELL, TENN. I. HUD. 701.
TAZEWELL, TENN. II. HUD. 701. NEW
TAZEWELL, TENN.

614
L11
Teach them to lift.
U.S. Bureau of Labor Standards.
Teach them to lift. Rev. [Wash.] 1970.
31p. (Its Bulletin 110)

1. Health. 2. Occupation. 3. Accidents.
I. Title.

720
(07)
T21
1962
Teacher Seminar of the American Institute of
Architects and the Association of Collegiate
Schools of Architecture, Cranbrook Academy
of Art, Bloomfield Hills, Mich., 1962.
The architect and the city. Papers from
the AIA-ACSA Teacher Seminar, Cranbrook Academy of
Art, June 11-12, 1962. Cambridge, Mass.,
M.I.T. Press, 1966.
172p.

1. Architecture - Study and teaching.
2. Architects. I. Whiffen, Marcus, ed.
II. American   Institute of Architects.   III. Title.

720
(07)
T21
1963
Teacher Seminar of the American Institute of
Architects and the Association of Collegiate
Schools of Architecture, Cranbrook Academy
of Art, Bloomfield Hills, Mich., 1963.
The teaching of architecture. Papers from
the 1963 AIA-ACSA Teacher Seminar edited by
Marcus Whiffen with an introduction by Harold
Bush-Brown. Washington, Office of Educa-
tional Programs, The American Institute of
Architects for the AIA-ACSA Teacher Seminar
1964.
147p.
(Cont'd on next card)

720
(07)
T21
1963
Teacher Seminar of the American Institute of
Architects and the Association of Colle-
giate Schools of Architecture...1963.
(Card 2)

1. Architecture - Study and teaching.
2. Architects. I. Whiffen, Marcus, ed.
II. American Institute of Architects.
III. Association of Collegiate School of
Architecture. IV. Title.

374
R48
Teachers for our big city schools.
Rivlin, Harry N
Teachers for our big city schools.
New York, Anti-Defamation League of
B'nai B'rith, 1964.
31p.

1. Education. 2. Schools. I. Title.

370
F85
Teachers for tomorrow.
The Fund for the Advancement of Education.
Teachers for tomorrow. New York, 1956.
72p. illus., diagrs., graphs. (Its
Bulletin no. 2)

1.Education. I.Title.

368
T21
Teachers Insurance and Annuity Association.
Report, 19-68
New York, Teachers Insurance and Annuity
Association - College Retirement Equities
Fund, 19-69.
/ v. annual

Suppl.   ----- Investment supplement to the...
report, 19-68
New York, 19-69
/ v. annual
(Cont'd on next card)

368
T21
Teachers...Association.
Report ... 19-69.   (Card 2)

For Library holdings see main entry.

1. Insurance. 2. Old age.

---

690. 015
(485)
882
R31
1967
Teachers opinions of classroom climate.
Sweden. Statens Kommitté for Byggnadsforskning.
Lärare bedömer klassrumsklimatet, en
enkätundersökning. Teachers opinions of class-
room climate, a questionnaire survey.
Stockholm, 1967.
52p. (Its Rapport 31 1967)
English summary.

1. Building research - Sweden. 2. Schools -
Sweden. 3. Climate and health.
I. Title: Teachers opinions of classroom
climate.

728.69
M61t
Teaching aids.
Mobile Homes Manufacturers Association.
Teaching aids; mobile home planning
for schools...4-H...F.H.A. Clubs...
extension. Chicago, [1970]
kit (16 pieces)
Partial contents.-Mobile home industry
bibliography; June, 1963 through June,
1969.-Careers for men in the mobile
home industry.-Careers for women in the mobile
home industry.-Selected publications
(with order form) Mobile Homes Manufacturers   Association.

1. Mobile   homes. I. Title.

370
S76
TEACHING BY MACHINE.
STOLUROW, LAWRENCE M
TEACHING BY MACHINE. WASHINGTON, GOVT.
PRINT. OFF., 1961.
173P.

ISSUED BY U.S. DEPT. OF HEALTH,
EDUCATION, AND WELFARE, OFFICE OF
EDUCATION.

1. VISUAL AIDS. I. TITLE.

339.5
F67
Teaching conservation through outdoor education
areas.
U.S. Forest Service.
Teaching conservation through outdoor
education areas. Wash., Govt. Print. Off.,
1968.
23p.

1. Natural resources. I. Title.

701
(07)
S52
TEACHING DESIGN AND FORM.
SNEUM, GUNNAR.
TEACHING DESIGN AND FORM. NEW YORK,
REINHOLD PUB. CORP., 1965.
125P.

1. ART - STUDY AND TEACHING. I. TITLE.

643.3
887
TEACHING KITCHEN PLANNING.
NUTLER, ELSIE ROSS.
TEACHING KITCHEN PLANNING. URBANA,
ILL. UNIVERSITY OF ILLINOIS, SMALL
HOMES COUNCIL, 1955.
40P.

1. KITCHENS. I. ILLINOIS.
UNIVERSITY. SMALL HOMES COUNCIL.
BUILDING RESEARCH COUNCIL. II. TITLE.

370
(016)
F79
TEACHING MACHINES.
FRY, EDWARD B
TEACHING MACHINES: AN ANNOTATED
BIBLIOGRAPHY, BY EDWARD B. FRY, GLENN
L. BRYAN, AND JOSEPH W. RIGNEY.
WASHINGTON, NATIONAL EDUCATION
ASSOCIATION, DEPARTMENT OF AUDIOVISUAL
INSTRUCTION, 1960.
8CP.

AUDIO VISUAL COMMUNICATION REVIEW, V.
8, NO. 2, SUPPLEMENT 1.

1. VISUAL AIDS - BIBLIOGRAPHY.
I. NATIONAL EDUCATION ASSOCIATION.
(CONTINUED ON NEXT CARD)

370
(016)
F79

FRY, EDWARD B TEACHING MACHINES....1960.
(CARD 2)

AUDIOVISUAL INSTRUCTION DEPARTMENT.
II. AUDIO VISUAL COMMUNICATION REVIEW.
III. TITLE.

657
T21
v.1

Teaching Systems Corp. An auditor's approach
to statistical sampling...1967. (Card 2)

1. Accounting. 2. Sampling (Statistics)
3. Statistics - Study and teaching.
I. American Institute of Certified Public
Accountants.

711.4
(74921)
T21t

Teaneck, N.J. Planning Board.

Smith (Herbert H.) Associates.
Teaneck, general development plan.
[In cooperation with the] Planning
Board. West Trenton, N.J., 1962.
1v.

U.S. Urban Renewal Adm. UPAP.

1. Master plan - Teaneck, N.J.
I. Teaneck, N.J. Planning Board.
II. U.S. URA-UPAP. Teaneck, N.J.

370
(016)
T21

TEACHING MACHINES AND PROGRAMED
LEARNING.
TEACHING MATERIALS CORPORATION.
TEACHING MACHINES AND PROGRAMED
LEARNING, A BIBLIOGRAPHY. COMPILED BY
INA CAMPBELL. NEW YORK, 1962.
27P. (ITS TMC-SR-3)

1. EDUCATION - AUTOMATION -
BIBLIOGRAPHY. I. CAMPBELL, INA, COMP.
II. TITLE.

705
1670
T21

TEAGUE, WALTER DORWIN.
DESIGN THIS DAY; THE TECHNIQUE OF ORDER
IN THE MACHINE AGE. NEW YORK, HARCOURT,
BRACE, 1940.
291P.

1. DESIGN, INDUSTRIAL.
2. ARCHITECTURE. I. TITLE.

VF
711.4
(74921)
T21

Teaneck, N.J. Township Planning Board.

Smith (Herbert H.) Associates.
General development plan for the
development of land use and community
facilities, summary report. Prepared for
the Township Planning Board, Teaneck, N.J.
Teaneck, N.J., 1963.
Folder.
U.S. Urban Renewal Adm. UPAP.

1. Master plan - Teaneck, N.J. 2. Land
use - Teaneck, N.J. I. Teaneck, N.J.
Township Plann' Board. II. U.S. URA-
UPAP. Teaneck, N.J.

370
(016)
T21

TEACHING MATERIALS CORPORATION.
TEACHING MACHINES AND PROGRAMED
LEARNING. A BIBLIOGRAPHY. COMPILED BY
INA CAMPBELL. NEW YORK, 1962.
27P. (ITS TMC-SR-3)

1. EDUCATION - AUTOMATION -
BIBLIOGRAPHY. I. CAMPBELL, INA, COMP.
II. TITLE.

720
T21

TEAGUE, WALTER DORWIN.
DESIGN THIS DAY; THE TECHNOLOGY OF ORDER
IN THE MACHINE AGE. LONDON, STUDIO
PUBLICATIONS, 1949.
237P, 128P.

1. ARCHITECTURE. I. TITLE.

728.1
(862)
T21

Teare, Wallace G
A housing program for the Panama Canal.
[n.p.] 1945.
84p. plans.

Prepared through arrangements with the
National Housing Agency and Federal Public
Housing Authority.

1.Housing - Panama Canal Zone. 2.House
plans - Panama Canal Zone.

720
(07)
T21
1963

The teaching of architecture .
Teacher Seminar of the American Institute of
Architects and the Association of Collegiate
Schools of Architecture, Cranbrook Academy
of Art, Bloomfield Hills, Mich., 1963.
The teaching of architecture. Papers from
the 1963 AIA-ACSA Teacher Seminar edited by
Marcus Whiffen with an introduction by Harold
Bush-Brown. Washington, Office of Educa-
tional Programs, The American Institute of
Architects for the AIA-ACSA Teacher Seminar
1964.
147p.

(Cont'd on next card)

728
R28

Teague, Walter D
Revere Quality House Institute.
Revere's part in better living. [1-25]
New York [n.d.]
25 pts. illus.

728
:333
T21

Tebbel, Robert.
The slum makers. New York, The
Dial Press, 1963.
190p.

3c.

1. Home ownership. 2. Housing
market. 3. Mortgage finance. I. Title.

720
(07)
T21
1963

Teacher Seminar of the American Institute of
Architects and the Association of Colle-
giate Schools of Architecture...1963.
(Card 2)

1. Architecture - Study and teaching.
2. Architects. I. Whiffen, Marcus, ed.
II. American Institute of Architects.
III. Association of Collegiate Schools of
Architecture. IV. Title.

VF
332.72
C65
1952
HR2501

Teague Committee.
U.S. Congress. House. Select Committee to
Investigate Educational, Training, and Loan
Guaranty Programs Under GI Bill.
Veterans' Loan Guaranty Program. Eighty-
second Cong., second sess., created pursuant to
H. Res. 93. Washington, Govt. Print. Off.,
1952.
161 p. ([U.S.] 82d Cong., 2d sess. [1952]
House. Report no. 2501)
Olin E. Teague, chairman.
1.Veterans guaranteed loans. 2.Investigation of
house construction.

325
T21

Tebbel, John.
South by southwest; the Mexican-American and
his heritage, by John Tebbel and Ramon Eduardo
Ruiz. Illustrated by Earl Thollander. Garden
City, N.Y., Doubleday & Co., 1969.
122p.

c.1, E.O.

1. Minority groups. I. Ruiz, Ramon Eduardo,
jt. au. II. Title. III. Title: Mexican-
American and his heritage.

370
N17p
no.30

Teaching resources for low-achieving mathematics classes.
Travers, Kenneth J
Teaching resources for low-achieving
mathematics classes, by Kenneth J. Travers
and others. Wash., U.S. Dept. of Health,
Education and Welfare, Office of Education,
National Center for Educational Communication,
1972.
34p. (Putting research into educational
practice. Report no.30)
Bibliography: p. 19-34.
1. Education. 2. Mathematics - Study and
teaching. I. U. S. National Center for
Educational   Communication. II. Title.

353
F45

Teamwork among governments in the Penjerdel
region.
Fine, Philip.
Teamwork among governments in the Penjerdel
region. Philadelphia, Penjerdel, Pennsylvania-
New Jersey-Delaware Metropolitan Project, Inc.,
1962.
24p.

1. Intergovernmental relations.
I. Pennsylvania- New Jersey-Delaware
Metropolitan Project. II. Title.

690.015
(5694
:016)
I77r

Technion Research and Development Foundation,
Haifa.
Israel Institute of Technology.
Research report, v.

Haifa, Israel, Technion Research and Development
Foundation, 19
v.
For Library holdings see main entry.
v.6. Civil engineering.[and] Building research
station.

1. Building research - Israel - Bibl.
I. Technion Research and Development Foundation,
Haifa.

657
T21
v.1

Teaching Systems Corp.
An auditor's approach to statistical sampling. Vol. 1. An introduction to statistical
concepts and estimation of dollar values.
Programed for the American Institute of Certified Public Accountants. New York, American
Institute of Certified Public Accountants,
1967.
60p.
657 -- --- Supplementary section. New York, 1967.
T21 68p.
Suppl

(Cont'd on next card)

711.583
C65T

TEAMWORK IN COMMUNITY SERVICES.
U.S. OFFICE OF COMMUNITY WAR SERVICES.
TEAMWORK IN COMMUNITY SERVICES,
1941-1946; A DEMONSTRATION IN FEDERAL,
STATE AND LOCAL COOPERATION.
WASHINGTON, FEDERAL SECURITY AGENCY,
OFFICE OF COMMUNITY WAR SERVICES, 1946.

1. COMMUNITY DEVELOPMENT - CITIZEN
PARTICIPATION. I. TITLE.

020
W24

Technical-abstracting fundamentals.
Weil, B H
Technical-abstracting fundamentals, by B.H.
Weil and others. Presented before the
American Documentation Institute. [Washington?
1963?]
2 pts.
Reprinted from Journal of chemical documenta-
tion, April, 1963, p. 86-89, 125-132.

1. Abstracting. 2. Documentation.
I. American Documentation Institute.
II. Journal of chemical documentation.
III. Title.

711.3
P85

Technical advisory committees.
Pulaski County, Ark. Metropolitan Area Planning
Commission.
Technical advisory committees. Little Rock,
Ark., [1956]
[3]p.

U.S. Urban Renewal Administration, Urban
Planning Assistance Program.

1. Metropolitan area planning. I. U.S. Urban
Renewal Administration. II. Title.

VF
341.1
:338
C15

Technical assistance for underdeveloped areas.
Calderwood, James D
Technical assistance for underdeveloped areas,
by James D. Calderwood and Laurence De Rycke.
[n.p.] Jan. 1954.
41 l.
Bibliographical footnotes.
Processed.
1. Technical assistance programs. I. De Rycke,
Laurence. II. Title.

341.1
:338
A52
Mar.
1950

Technical assistance programs.
American Academy of Political and Social Science.
Aiding underdeveloped areas abroad, ed. by
Halford L. Hoskins. Philadelphia, 1950.
259 p. (Its Annals, v. 268)

1. Technical assistance programs. I. Hoskins,
Halford L., ed. II. Title.

Technical Advisory Corporation.

711.4
S67

Springfield, Mass. Planning Board.
A city plan for Springfield, Mass.; Technical
Advisory Corporation, Consulting Engineers;
Frederick Law Olmsted, Special Advisor.
Springfield, Mass., 1923.
212 p. illus., charts plans (4 in envelope)

1. Master plan - Springfield, Mass. I.
Technical Advisory Corporation.

341.1
:338
(59)
824

Technical assistance in Vietnam.
Scigliano, Robert.
Technical assistance in Vietnam; the Michigan State University experience, by Robert
Scigliano and Guy H. Fox. New York, Praeger,
1965.
78p. (Praeger special studies in international economics and development)
Bibliography: p. 73-78.
1. Technical assistance programs - Vietnam.
2. Economic development - Vietnam. I. Fox, Guy
H., jt. au. II. Michigan. State University.
III. Title.

341.1
:338
A52

Technical assistance programs.
American Assembly.
International stability and progress:
United States interests and instruments.
Final ed. New York, American Assembly,
Graduate School of Business, Columbia
University, 1957.
184 p.
Partial contents: Final report of the
Eleventh American Assembly.
1. Technical assistance programs. 2. Economic
development. 3. Economic conditions - Asia.
I. Title.

.384
M12

Technical and economic evaluation of
aircraft.
McDonnell Aircraft Corp.
Technical and economic evaluation of air-
craft for intercity short-haul transportation.
Final report. Prepared for Federal Aviation
Agency, Aircraft Development Service. St.
Louis, 1966.
3v. (Its Report E390; FAA ADS-74, I)

1. Air transportation. I. U.S. Federal
Aviation Agency. II. Title.

728.1
:061.3
A51

Technical assistance programs.
Albert Farwell Bemis Foundation.
Housing and economic development; the report
of a conference sponsored at the Massachusetts
Institute of Technology...on April 30 and May 1
and 2, 1953. Edited by Burnham Kelly. [Cam-
bridge, Mass., School of Architecture and Planning,
Massachusetts Institute of Technology] Jan. 1955
161 p.

Processed.

Partial contents. - The economist's view of
the role of   housing, Max F.
(continued on next card)

341.1
:338
A52
July 1950

Technical assistance programs.
American Academy of Political and Social Science, *Phila-
delphia*.
Formulating a point four program. Edited by Ernest
Minor Patterson. Philadelphia, 1950.
vii, 211 p. 24 cm. (*Its Annals*, v. 270)

1. Technical assistance programs.
2. Industrialization.   I. Patterson, Ernest Minor, 1879-   ed.
II. Title. (Series)

H1.A4 vol. 270   338.91   50-13380
------- Copy 2.   HC59.A785
Library of Congress   [25]

388
1075

Technical and managerial capabilities.
Orlando, Martin.
Technical and managerial capabilities.
A summary. New York, Martin-Marietta, Corp.
[1967?]
11p. (Martin-Marietta Corp. OR 3630)

1. Transportation. 2. Transportation - Automation. 3. Journey to work. I. Martin-
Marietta Corp. II. Title.

Albert Farwell Bemis Foundation. Housing and
economic...1955 (card 2)

Milliken. - Possibilities of international
financing of housing, Leo Grebler. - The dilem-
mas of housing, Paul A. Samuelson. - The case for
regional planning and urban dispersal, Catherine
Bauer. - The importance of housing and planning
in Latin America, Anatole A. Solow. - Importance
of Physical Planning in economic development,
Ernest Weissmann. - Measuring housing needs in
underdeveloped countries, Lloyd Rodvin. - Land

(continued on next card)

VF
330
N17
P124

Technical assistance programs.
Asher, Robert E
International development and the U.S.
national interest, by Robert E. Asher with
an NPA joint statement. Wash., National
Planning Association, 1967.
32p. (National Planning Association.
Planning pamphlet no. 124)

1. International relations. 2. Technical
assistance programs. I. National Planning
Association. II. Title. (Series)

332.72
(60)
UN

Technical and social problems of urbaniza-
tion with emphasis on financing of
housing.
United Nations. (Economic Commission for
Africa)
Report on the Regional Meeting on Technical
and Social Problems of Urbanization with
Emphasis on Financing of Housing, Addis Ababa,
8-23 Jan. 1969. [New York] 1969.
64p.
At head of title: Economic Commission for
Africa and German Foundation for Developing
Countries.
DOK 465 A-F 1/69.
1. Mortgage   finance - Africa.
2. City grow   th - Africa.
(Cont'd on next card)

Albert Farwell Bemis Foundation. Housing and
economic...1955 (card 3)

Policies and their effect on development poss-
ibilities, Charles Abrams. - Housing in a village
of India, Robert E. Alexander. - Design, José Luis
Sert. - Housing experience of the Standard Oil
Company, K.H. Quick. - A study of permanent housing
in overseas mining development, David M. Hansen. -
Redevelopment in El Salvador, George A. Dudley. -
Operational and statistical research in building,
J. Bronowski. - The role of the U.S. Government,

301.15
UNre

Technical assistance programs.
Asian Seminar on Planning and Administration
of National Community Development Programmes,
Bangkok, 1961.
Report; organized by the United Nations in
cooperation with the Government of Thailand.
New York, United Nations, 1962.
153p. (ST/TAO/SER.C/54 ST/SOA/SER.T/3)

1. Community development - Congresses.
2. Technical assistance programs. I. United
Nations.

332.72
(60)
UN

United Nations. (Economic Commission for
Africa)   Report...1969.   (Card 2)

I. Title: Technical and social problems of
urbanization with emphasis on financing of
housing.

Albert Farwell Bemis Foundation. Housing and
economic...1955 (card 4)

Jacob L. Crane. - Opportunities for training,
Howard T. Fisher.
1. Housing-Congresses. 2. Economic Planning.
3. Technical assistance Programs. 4. Under-
developed countries. I. Kelly, Burnham. II. Grebler,
Leo. III. Bauer, Catherine IV. Solow, Anatole A.
V. Weissmann, Ernest. VI. Rodvin, Lloyd. VII.
Abrams, Charles. VIII. Sert, José Luis. IX. Dudley,
George A. X. Crane, Jacob L. XI. Fisher, Howard T.
XII. Title.

330
B17

TECHNICAL ASSISTANCE PROGRAMS.
Baranson, Jack.
Industrial technologies for developing coun-
tries. Introduction by Walter A. Chudson.
New York, Frederick A. Praeger, 1969.
168p. (Praeger special studies in inter-
national economics and development)
Bibliography: p. 145-168.

1. Economic development. 2. Technical assistance programs. 3. Underdeveloped countries.
I. Title.

332.72
E26L

Technical appraisal of the 1960 sample survey
estimates of farm debt
U.S. Economic Research Service.
Technical appraisal of the 1960 sample
survey estimates of farm debt, by Fred L.
Garlock and Philip T. Allen. Washington,
Farm Production Economics Div., Economic
Research Service, U.S. Dept. of Agriculture,
1964.
28p. (Its ERS 167)

1. Farm mortgages. 2. Agriculture.
I. Garlock, Fred L. II. Allen, Philip T.
III. Title.

341.1
:338
A55

TECHNICAL ASSISTANCE PROGRAMS.
Alliance for Progress.
1970 year-end review of the Alliance for
Progress. Wash., 1970.
52p.

1. Technical assistance programs.
2. Economic development.

728.1
:341.1
:388
B87

Technical assistance programs.
Burroughs, Roy J
Orientation in housing economics,
finance, and market analysis. Revised.
[Washington] Housing and Home Finance Agency,
International Housing Service, May 1956-
4 pts. in 2v.

For complete information see shelflist.

Contains bibliographies.

728.1
:341.1 Burroughs, Roy J., Orientation in housing
:388   economics ... May 1956. (Card 2)
B87
         Contents. - pt. 1. Significance of housing
       in economic development. - pt. 2. What to
       learn of legal and financial structure. - pt. 3.
       Summary description of housing finance in the
       United States. - pt. 4. Housing market analysis.

       1.Technical assistance programs. 2.Housing market
       analysis. 3.Federal housing programs. 4.Mortgage finance
       5.Housing. I.U.S. Housing and Home Finance Agency. Office
       of the Administrator. International Housing Service.
       II.Title.

341.1   Technical assistance programs.
:338   Congressional Quarterly Service, Washington,
065e\   D.C.
         Evolution of foreign aid, 1945-1965. A
       comprehensive chronology of foreign aid
       legislation, highlighting major aid poli-
       cies, programs, congressional debates and
       Government aid agencies. Washington, 1965.
       46p.

         1. Technical assistance programs.
         2. International relations. I. Title.

VF   Technical assistance programs.
728
:333   Home ownership for export.
H65   First Federal Savings of Chicago, F-F saver,
       p. 11-13, Sept. 1956. illus.

         1. Home ownership. 2. Technical assistance
       programs.

VF   Technical assistance programs.
341.1
:338   Calderwood, James D
C15   Technical assistance for underdeveloped areas,
       by James D. Calderwood and Laurence De Rycke.
       [n.p.] Jan. 1954.
         41 l.
         Bibliographical footnotes.
         Processed.

         1.Technical assistance programs. I.De Rycke,
       Laurence. II.Title.

341.1   Technical assistance programs.
:338   Delaware Conference on World Economic Development,
D25   2d, April 10-11, 1950, Newark, Delaware.
1950   Papers and discussions.   Newark, Del., Univ.
       of Delaware Press [c1951]
         114 p.
         Sponsored by the Institute for Inter-American
       Study and Research, Univ. of Delaware.

         1.Technical assistance programs. I.Delaware.
       University. Institute for Inter-American Study and
       Research.

VF   Technical assistance programs.
312   Hugh Moore Fund.
H83   The population bomb. New York, [1960?]
       [20]p.

       Cover title.

         1. Population. 2. Technical assistance programs.

---

338   TECHNICAL ASSISTANCE PROGRAMS.
C65pa Commission on International Development.
       Partners in development. New York,
       Praeger, 1969.
         399p. (Praeger paperbacks)

         Lester B. Pearson, Chairman.

         1. Business cycles. 2. Economic
       development. 3. Technical assistance
       programs. 4. Underdeveloped countries.
       I. Pearson, Lester B. II. Title.

341.1   Technical assistance programs.
:338   Espy, Willard R
E76   Bold new program.   New York, Bantam Books
       [1950]
         278 p.

         Bibliography: p. 265-271.

       1.Technical assistance programs. I.Title.

711.4   Technical assistance programs.
H85   Humphrey, Hubert Horatio, 1911-
         Remarks, Vice President, [at] Urban
       Development Seminar, Washington, D.C.,
       September 15, 1965. Sponsored by Housing
       and Home Finance Agency, and Agency for
       International Development. [Washington?]
       1965.
         8p.

         1. City growth. 2. Technical assistance
       programs. I. Urban Development Seminar,
       Washington, D.C.,   1965.

---

330   TECHNICAL ASSISTANCE PROGRAMS.
C65as Committee for Economic Development. (Research
       and Policy Committee)
         Assisting development in low-income countries:
       priorities for U.S. Government policy. A state-
       ment of National policy by the Research and
       Policy Committee of the Committee for Economic
       Development. New York, 1969.
         81p.

         1. Economic development. 2. Technical
       assistance programs. 3. Underdeveloped
       countries.   I. Title.

            Technical assistance programs.
334.1
F68   Foundation for Cooperative Housing, Wash., D.C.
         A program of assistance for cooperative
       housing in less developed countries. Prepared
       by the Foundation for Cooperative Housing for
       the Agency for International Development.
       Wash., 1962.
         1 v.

         1. Cooperative housing. 2. Underdeveloped
       countries. 3. Technical assistance programs.
       I. U.S. Agency for International Development.
       II. Title.

---

332   Technical assistance programs.
I57r   International Basic Economy Corp.
         Report,
       New York,
         v. illus., tables. annual.

       For complete information see shelflist.

         1. Finance. 2. Technical assistance programs.

VF   Technical assistance programs.
341.1
:338   Condliffe, J   B
C65   Point four and the world economy.   New York,
       N.Y., Foreign Policy Association, c1950.
         62 p.   charts.   (Headline series, no.79)

         Bibliography: p. 62.
         Contents.-Point Four: Economic development, by
       J.B.Condliffe.-Brazil: A case study, by Harold H.
       Hutcheson.   assistance programs-Brazil.
       1.Technical assistance programs. 2.Technical
       I.Hutcheson, Harold H. II.Ser.

---

320   Technical assistance programs.
G66   Goodfriend, Arthur.
         The only war we seek. With a foreword by
       Chester Bowles. [New York] Published for
       Americans for Democratic Action, by Farrar,
       Straus and Young, 1951.
         128p.

         1. Democracy. 2; Technical assistance
       programs. I. Americans for Democratic Action,
       Washington, D.C.

341.1   Technical assistance programs.
:338   International Cooperation Center of Hawaii.
I57h   Hawaii, U.S.A.; resources for technical
       assistance. Honolulu, 1958.
       [149]p. illus.

         1. Technical assistance programs. 2. Muni-
       cipal services - Hawaii. I. Title.

355.58   Technical assistance programs.
C65f   Conference on Foreign Aspects of U.S. National
         Security, Washington, D. C., 1958.
         Foreign aspects of U.S. national security.
       Conference report and proceedings. Washington,
       Committee for International Economic Growth,
       1958.
         120p. illus.

         1. National defense. 2. Technical assist-
       ance programs.

---

330   Technical assistance programs.
H15d   Hambidge, Gove, 1890-   ed.
         Dynamics of development: an international
       development reader. Foreword by Teodoro
       Moscoso. Introd. by Paul G. Hoffman. New
       York, Praeger, 1964.
         401p.   (Books that matter)

         Bibliography: p. 373-376.

         1. Economic development. 2. Technical
       assistance programs. I. Title.

728.1   Technical assistance programs.
I57e   International Labour Office.
         Economic and social aspects of workers'
       housing in non-metropolitan territories, with
       special reference to responsibilities for its
       provision.   Geneva, 1953.
         128 p.   (CNT/3/II)

         At head of title: Committee of Experts on
       Social Policy in Non-Metropolitan Territories,
       Third session, Lisbon, 7-19 December 1953, Second
       item on the agenda.
                          (Continued on next card)

            Technical assistance programs.
711.3
C65pr Conference on International Rural
1964   Development, Washington, 1964.
         Proceedings. Jointly sponsored by Agency
       for International Development, U.S. Department
       of Agriculture, Association of State
       Universities and Land-Grant Colleges.
       Washington, 1964.
         185p.
       1. Rural planning - Congresses. 2. Agriculture -
       Congresses. 3. Technical assistance programs.
       I. U.S. Agency for International Development.
       II. U.S. Dept. of   Agriculture.

341.1   Technical assistance programs.
:338   Hoffman, Michael L
H63   Development needs the business man. [Wash-
       ington, D.C.]   1963.
         12p.

         Reprinted from Lloyds bank review, April,
       1963.
         1. Technical assistance programs. 2. Under-
       developed countries. I. Lloyds bank review.

         International Labour Office.   Economic and
            social aspects ... 1953.   (Card 2)

         Bibliographical footnotes.
         Processed.

         1.Housing-Africa. 2.Housing-British West Indies.
       3.Technical assistance programs. 4.Public housing.
       I.Title. II.Title: Workers' housing in non-
       metropolitan territories.

341.1
:338
J12

Technical assistance programs.
Jackson, Sir Robert Gillman Allen.
The case for an International Development
Authority; with an introduction, by Harlan
Cleveland. Syracuse, Syracuse Univ. Press,
[1959]
70p.

Bibliography: p. 69-70.

1. Technical assistance programs. I. Cleveland,
Harlan, ed.

341.1
:338
N17

Technical assistance programs.
National Conference on International Economic
and Social Development, First, 1952.
World neighbors working together for peace
and plenty; report of the first National
Conference on International Economic and Social
Development, Washington, D. C., April 7-8-9,
1952. [Washington, 1952]
198 p. illus.

1.Technical assistance programs. I.Title.

VF
341.1
:338
P81
no.7

Technical assistance programs.
Public Affairs Institute
Foreign aid and our economy, by Seymour E.
Harris. Washington [1950]
75 p. graphs, maps, tables. (Bold new
programs series, no. 7)
Bibliography: p. 72-[76]
"The series was made possible through funds
granted ... by the Foundation for World
Government." - p.[2]
1.Technical assistance programs. 2.Economic
conditions. I.Harris, Seymour E. II.Foundation
for World Government. III.Title. IV.Series.

330
J18

Technical assistance programs.
Javits, Benjamin A
The Peace by Investment Corporation, to
build people-to-people economic relations,
by Benjamin A. Javits and Leon H. Keyserling. Washington, International Committee
for Peace by Investment, 1961.
63p.
1. Underdeveloped countries. 2. Technical
assistance programs. I. Keyserling, Leon H.
II. Title.

VF
330
N17p

Technical assistance programs.
National Conference on International Economic
and Social Development, Fifth, 1958.
Partnership for plenty; a report on the Fifth
National Conference... ed. by David C, Williams.
Washington, 1958.
39p.

1. Economic development. 2. Technical assistance programs. I. Williams, David C. ed.

VF
341.1
:338
P81
no.3

Technical assistance programs.
Public Affairs Institute.
Groundwork for action, by Morris Llewellyn
Cooke with Calvin J. Nichols, Dorothy Detzer and
Peter G. Franck. Washington [1950]
96 p. illus. (Bold new program series,
no. 3)
"The series was made possible through funds
granted ... by the Foundation for World
Government." - p.[2]
1.Technical assistance programs. 2.Economic
planning. I.Cooke, Morris Llewellyn. II.Nichols,
Calvin J. III.Detzer, Dorothy. IV.Franck, Peter G.
V.Foundation for World Government. VI.Series.

341.1
:338
K67

Technical assistance programs.
Kotschnig, Walter M
Social action: an instrument of foreign
policy. Speech delivered at the 85th Annual
Forum, National Conference on Social Welfare.
Chicago, May 1958. [Washington, Office of
International Economic and Social Affairs]
1958.
17p.

1.Technical assistance programs. 2.Under-
developed countries. I. U.S. Dept. of State.

388
082s

Technical assistance programs.
Owen, Wilfred.
Strategy for mobility. Washington,
Brookings Institution, Transport Research
Program, 1964.
249p.
Bibliography: p. 229-236.

1. Transportation. 2. Technical
assistance programs. 3. Economic development. I. Brookings
Institution. II. Title.

VF
341.1
:338
P81
no.6

Technical assistance programs.
Public Affairs Institute
Helping people help themselves, by Wallace J.
Campbell and Richard Y. Giles [and The adjustment
of industry, by Willard Z. Park] Washington
[1950]
71 p. (Bold new program series, no. 6)
"The series was made possible through funds
granted ... by the Foundation for World
Government." - p.[2]

VF
341.1
:338
L17

Technical assistance programs.
Lasswell, Harold
Psychological aspects of foreign aid and
development programs. Washington, Department
of State, Foreign Service Institute, 1949.
17 p.

Speech delivered at New State Building, May 5
1949.

1.Technical assistance programs. I.U.S. Dept.
of State. Foreign Service Institute.

341.1
:338
P15

Technical assistance programs.
Pan American Union, Washington, D.C.
The record of Punta del Este (Alianza
Para el Progreso). Washington, 1962?
40p.
"This booklet is a record of official doc-
uments establishing the Alliance for Progress.
These documents emanate from a Special
Meeting of the Inter-American Economic and
Social Council at the Ministerial level. This
Meeting was held in Punta de Este, Uruguay from
Aug. 3-17, 1961."
1. Technical assistance programs. 2. Inter-
national relations. I. Inter-American
Economic and Social Council. Punta
de Este, 1961.

VF
341.1
:338
P81
no.5

Technical assistance programs.
Public Affairs Institute.
People, food, machines, by Stephen Raushenbush.
Washington [1950]
80 p. illus., graphs, tables. (Bold new
program series, no. 5)
"The series was made possible through funds
granted ... by the Foundation for World
Government." - p.[2]
1.Technical assistance programs. 2.Population.
I.Raushenbush, Stephen. II.Foundation for World
Government. III.Title. IV.Series.

341.1
:338
M2

Technical assistance programs.
Maddison, Angus.
Foreign skills and technical assistance
in economic development. Paris, Development
Centre of the Organization for Economic
Cooperation and Development, 1965.
104p. (Development Centre Studies)

1. Technical assistance programs.
2. Economic development. 3. Labor supply.
4. Education. I. Organization for Economic
Cooperation and Development. Development
Centre. II. Title.

341.1
P15r

Technical assistance programs.
Pan American Union.
Revised proposed program and budget for
the economic and social activities for the
fiscal year ending June 30, 1962; submitted
by the Secretary General. Washington, 1961.
95p. (OEA/Ser.D/II.1-1962 (English),
Add. 27 March 1961)

Original in Spanish.

1. International organizations. 2. Technical
assistance programs.

VF
341.1
:338
P81
no.1

Technical assistance programs.
Public Affairs Institute.
A policy and program for success, by Dewey
Anderson and Stephen Raushenbush. Washington
[1950]
76 p. illus. (Bold new program series,
no. 1)
"The series was made possible through funds
granted ... by the Foundation for World Government" - p.[2]
1.Technical assistance programs. I.Anderson,
Dewey. II.Raushenbush, Stephen. III.Foundation
for World Government. IV.Series.

341.1
:338
M44

Technical assistance programs.
Mikesell, Raymond F
Public foreign capital for private
enterprise in developing countries.
Princeton, N.J., Princeton University, International Finance Section, Dept. of Economics,
1966.
29p. (Princeton University. International Finance Section. Essays in international finance no. 52)

1. Technical assistance programs.
2. Foreign exchange. 3. International relations.
I. Princeton University (International Finance
Section) II. Title.

341.1
:338
P45

Technical assistance programs.
Pincus, John.
Economic aid and international cost sharing.
A report prepared for the Office of the Assistant
Secretary of Defense, International Security
Affairs. Santa Monica, Calif., Rand Corp., 1965
221p. [Rand Corp. Paper](R-431-ISA)
Bibliography: p. 194-201.

1. Technical assistance programs. 2. Inter-
national relations. 3. Economic development.
I. U.S. Dept. of Defense. II. Rand Corp.
III. Title.

VF
341.1
:338
P81
no.2

Technical assistance programs.
Public Affairs Institute.
Two-thirds of the world; problems of a new
approach to the peoples of Asia, Africa, and
Latin America, by Harold R. Isaacs. Washington
[1950]
64 p. maps. (Bold new program series,
no. 2)
"The series was made possible through funds
granted ... by the Foundation for World Government" - p.[2]
1.Technical assistance programs. I.Isaacs, Harold
R. II.Foundation for World Government. III.Title.
IV.Series.

341.1
:338
M67

Technical assistance programs.
Moscoso, Teodoro.
The Alliance for Progress; its program and
goals. Wash., U.S. Dept. of State, Agency
for International Development, 1961.
[16]p.

1. Technical assistance programs.
2. Economic development. I. U.S. Agency
for International Development. II. Title.

VF
341.1
:338
P81
no.4

Technical assistance programs.
Public Affairs Institute.
Engineers of world plenty, by James Rorty.
Washington [1950]
71 p. illus. (Bold new program series,
no. 4)
"The series was made possible through funds
granted ... by the Foundation for World
Government." - p.[2]
1.Technical assistance programs. I.Rorty, James.
II.Foundation for World Government. III.Title.
IV.Series.

VF

VF
341.1
:338
P81
no. 8

Technical assistance program.
Public Affairs Institute
Where is the money coming from? by Morris S.
Rosenthal. Washington [1950]
58 p. (Its Bold new program series, no. 8)

Series made possible through funds granted by
the Foundation for World Government.

1. Technical assistance program. 2. Economic
development. I. Rosenthal, Morris S. II.
Foundation for World Government. (Series)

341.1
P83

Technical assistance programs.

Puerto Rico. Planning Board.
A program of technical assistance to economically underdeveloped countries. Puerto Rico's participation. Rev. [San Juan] 1950.
48 p.

1.Technical assistance programs.
2.Underdeveloped countries.

339.5
T24

Teitelbaum, Perry D
Energy...1963.   (Card 2)

development (Washington: U.S. Government Printing Office, 1963)

1. Power resources. 2. Atomic energy.
3. Underdeveloped countries. 4. Technical assistance programs. I. Resources for the Future, inc. II. Title.

341.1
:338
UNp

Technical assistance programs.
United Nations. (Technical Assistance Programs)
Public administration aspects of community development programmes. New York, 1959.
107p. (ST/TAC/M/14)

1. Technical assistance programs.
2. Public administration.

VF
341.1
:338
(7295)
P82

Technical assistance programs.
Puerto Rico. Planning Board. (Office of Technical Cooperation.)
Puerto Rico: training ground for technical cooperation. San Juan [1953]
99 p. illus., tables.
"... Essentially a catalogue of the fields of training offered under the Technical Cooperation Program in Puerto Rico and of the training agencies of the Commonwealth Government" - p. 1.

1.Technical assistance programs. 2.Education.

341.13
U54
C

Technical assistance programs.
United Nations.
Catalogue of economic and social projects. Lake Success, N.Y.
v. (Its Publications)

For full information see shelf list card.

1.City planning-Research. 2.Economic research.
3.Housing research. 4.Population. I.Title.

301.15
UNr

Technical assistance programs.
United Nations. (Economic Commission for Africa)
Report on the workshop on planning and administration of national programmes of community development, Addis Ababa, Ethiopia, 14 - 25 September 1959. New York, 1959.
1v. (E/CN.14/24; E/CN.14/A.C.1/6)

1. Community development. 2. Technical assistance programs.

341.1
:338
R62

Technical assistance programs.
Rockefeller Foundation.
Report, 1956, 57- New York, 1957, 1958- illus. annual.

For complete information see shelf list.

1. Technical assistance programs.

301.15
UNco
1963

Technical assistance programs.
United Nations. (Dept. of Economic and Social Affairs)
Community development and national development. Report by an ad hoc Group of Experts appointed by the Secretary-General of the United Nations. New York, 1963.
78p. (United Nations. [Document] E/CN.5/379/Rev.1)

1. Community development. 2. Economic development. 3. Technical assistance programs.

341.1
:338
U54t

Technical assistance programs.
United Nations.
Technical assistance for economic development; plan for an expanded co-operative programme through the United Nations and the specialized agencies. Report prepared by the Secretary-General in consultation with the executive heads of the interested agencies through the Administrative Committee on Co-ordination pursuant to resolution 180 (VIII) of the Economic and Social Council. Lake Success, N.Y., May 1949.
viii, 328 p. tables. (UN Publications. Sales no.:1949.11.B.1)
Errata sheet inside front cover.

1.Technical assistance programs.

341.1
:338
S31

Technical assistance programs.
Sharp, Walter R.
International technical assistance, programs and organization. Chicago, Public Administration Service, 1952.
146 p.

Bibliography: p. 129-131
Processed.

1. Technical assistance programs. I. Public Administration Service.

5/53

301.15
UNc

Technical assistance programs.
United Nations, (Economic and Social Council)
Community development and related services. [New York] 1956.
23p.

"Twentieth report of the Administrative Committee on Co-ordination to the Economic and Social Council; Annex III."

1. Community development. 2. Technical assistance programs.

341.1
:338
UNu

Technical assistance programs.
United Nations, (Economic and Social Council)
United States of America: report of experience in the field of social development of potential assistance to under-developed countries. Information furnished in response to Resolution 731 C (XXVII) of the Economic and Social Council. New York 1960.
226p.

Bibliography: p. I-IX.

1. Technical assistance programs. 2. Under-developed countries.

728.1
S54f

Technical assistance programs.
Smigel, Stanley E
Financing problems of housing programs in developing countries. [Views expressed at the] annual meeting of the American Statistical Association, Los Angeles, California, August 17, 1966. Washington, 1966.
45p.
Author is International Economic Advisor in the U.S. Dept. of Housing and Urban Development.

1. Federal housing programs. 2. Technical assistance programs. 3. Building costs. I. American Statistical Association, Annual Meeting, Los Angeles, 1966. II. U.S. Dept. of Housing and Urban Development. III. Title.

341.1
:338
UN

Technical assistance programs.
United Nations. (Economic and Social Council)
Consideration of the establishment of an economic commission for Africa; certain questions related to the establishment and development of regional economic commissions. [Geneva] 1958.
1 v. (E/3052)

1.Technical assistance programs.

VF
341.1
:338
A28

Technical assistance programs.
U.S. Advisory Commission on Educational Exchange.
Trading ideas with the world; international educational and technical exchange. Washington, Govt. Print. Off., 1949.
88 p. /map. illus., charts, graphs, tables.

Dept. of State publication 3551, International information and cultural series 7.

1.Technical assistance programs. I.Title.

341.1
:338
T15

Technical assistance programs.
Tannenwald, Theodore, Jr.
The new foreign aid legislation. In U.S. Dept. of State News letter, no. 6, October 1961. p. 3-4.

1. Technical assistance programs.
2. Economic development.

341.1
:338
U54f

Technical assistance programs.
United Nations. (Secretariat. Technical Assistance Administration.)
Formulation and economic appraisal of development projects ... lectures delivered at the Asian Centre on Agricultural and Allied Projects, Lahore, Pakistan, Oct. - Dec. 1950. [Lahore?] Technical Assistance Administration Training Institute on Economic Appraisal of Development Projects [1951]
2 v.

VF
658.3
A32

Technical assistance programs.
U.S. Agency for International Development.
The A.I.D. participant training program; how it works. Washington, D.C., 1962.
8p.

1. Personnel management - Study and teaching. 2. Technical assistance programs.

339.5
T24

Technical assistance programs.
Teitelbaum, Perry D
Energy cost comparisons; theoretical and practical problems in comparing nuclear and conventional energy costs, with particular reference to less developed areas. Washington, Resources for the Future, inc., 1963.
222p. (Resources for the Future, inc. Reprint number 38)
Reprinted from Science, technology, and development - United States papers prepared for the United Nations Conference on the Application of Science and Technology for the Benefit of the Less Developed Areas. Vol. I, Natural resources - Energy, water, and river basin
(Continued on next card)

341.1
:338
U54
1949

Technical assistance programs.
United Nations. (Secretariat. Department of Economic Affairs.)
Methods of financing economic development in under-developed countries. Lake Success, N.Y., 1949.
vii, 163 p. (UN publications sales no.: 1949.II.B.4)

1.Technical assistance programs.

658.3
A32a

Technical assistance programs.
U.S. Agency for International Development.
A.I.D. participant training program. The transfer and use of development skills. An evaluation study of U.S. technical training programs for participants from underdeveloped areas. Washington, U.S. Dept. of State, Agency for International Development, 1966.
286p.
Bibliography: p.284-286.
1. Personnel management - Study and teaching.
2. Technical assistance programs. 3. Underdeveloped countries. I. Title.

Technical assistance program.

341.1
:338
A32a
U.S. Agency for International Development.
Alliance for Progress, an American partnership. Washington, 1963.
32p.

1. Technical assistance program.
2. Economic development. I. Title.

Technical assistance programs.

VF
341.1
:338
A32
U.S. Agency for International Development.
The story of A.I.D. Washington
[1962?]
[32]p.

1. Technical assistance programs.

351
H66
1955
Rept.10A
Technical assistance programs.
U. S. Commission on Organization of the Executive Branch of the Government, 1953-1955
Report on overseas economic operations, prepared ... by the Task Force on Overseas Economic Operations, June 1955. [Washington, Govt. Print. Off., 1955.]
854 p. graphs, tables.

1. International relations. 2. Technical assistance programs. I. Hoover Commission reports. II. Title: Overseas economic operations.

341.1
:338
A32f
Technical assistance programs.
U.S. Agency for International Development.
The Foreign Assistance Program: annual report to the Congress, 19

Washington, 19
v.
Issued in the Congressional series as House documents.
For complete information see main card.

1. Technical assistance programs. 2. International relations. I. Title.

341.1
:338
A32t
Technical assistance programs.
U.S. Agency for International Development.
The task of development. Proposed program fiscal year 1969. Wash., [1968?]
36p.

1. Technical assistance programs.
2. Economic development. I. Title.

341.1
:338
C652
TECHNICAL ASSISTANCE PROGRAMS.
U.S. CONGRESS. CONFERENCE COMMITTEES,
1960.
MUTUAL SECURITY ACT OF 1960...
CONFERENCE REPORT TO ACCOMPANY H.R.
11510... WASHINGTON, GOVT. PRINT. OFF.,
1960.
21P. (86TH CONGRESS, 2D SESSION.
HOUSE. REPORT NO. :593)

1. TECHNICAL ASSISTANCE PROGRAMS.
2. INTERNATIONAL RELATIONS. I. TITLE.

341.1
:338
A321
Technical assistance programs.
U.S. Agency for International Development.
Implementation of the Humphrey amendment to the Foreign assistance act of 1961. Third annual report to the Congress (fiscal year 1964) Washington, Govt. Print. Off., 1964.
75p. (88th Cong., 2d sess. Senate. Document no. 111)

1. Technical assistance programs. I. U.S. Congress. Senate. II. Title: Humphrey amendment to the Foreign assistance act of 1961.

341.1
:338
I57ta
Technical assistance programs.
U.S. Agency for International Development.
A task to share. A.I.D. participant training program for foreign nationals. Washington, D.C., Dept. of State, Agency for International Development, International Training Division [1962?]
18p.

1. Technical assistance programs. I. U.S. Dept. of State.

341.1
:338
C653F
1961
H-R
TECHNICAL ASSISTANCE PROGRAMS.
U.S. CONGRESS. CONFERENCE COMMITTEES,
1961.
FOREIGN ASSISTANCE ACT OF 1961.
CONFERENCE REPORT TO ACCOMPANY S. 1983.
WASHINGTON, GOVT. PRINT. OFF., 1961.
74P. (87TH CONGRESS, 2D SESSION.
HOUSE. REPORT NO. 1088)

1. TECHNICAL ASSISTANCE PROGRAMS.
2. U.S. AGENCY FOR INTERNATIONAL DEVELOPMENT. I. TITLE.

341.1
:338
A32p
1968
Technical assistance programs.
U.S. Agency for International Development.
Proposed foreign aid program fy 1968.
Summary presentation to the Congress. Washington, Govt. Print. Off., 1967.
297p.

1. Technical assistance program. 2. Economic development. I. Title.

658.3
A32
1962
Technical assistance programs.
U.S. Agency for International Development.
Training for development. AID participant training for social and economic development of cooperating countries. Washington, D.C., 1962.
31p.

1. Personnel management - Study and teaching.
2. Technical assistance programs.

341.4
:338
C65
1962
H-R
TECHNICAL ASSISTANCE PROGRAMS.
U.S. CONGRESS. CONFERENCE COMMITTEES,
1962.
FOREIGN ASSISTANCE ACT OF 1962.
CONFERENCE REPORT TO ACCOMPANY S. 2996.
WASHINGTON, GOVT. PRINT. OFF., 1962.
21P. (87TH CONGRESS, 2D SESSION.
HOUSE OF REPRESENTATIVES. REPORT NO.
2008)

1. TECHNICAL ASSISTANCE PROGRAMS.
I. TITLE.

341.1
:338
A32S
TECHNICAL ASSISTANCE PROGRAMS.
U.S. AGENCY FOR INTERNATIONAL DEVELOPMENT.
SECTION-BY-SECTION ANALYSIS OF THE PROPOSED FOREIGN ASSISTANCE ACT OF 1965, TO AMEND FURTHER THE FOREIGN ASSISTANCE ACT OF 1961. WASHINGTON, GOVT. PRINT. OFF., 1965.
14P. (89TH CONGRESS, 1ST SESSION. COMMITTEE PRINT)

PREPARED FOR THE COMMITTEE ON FOREIGN AFFAIRS, HOUSE OF REPRESENTATIVES.

1. TECHNICAL ASSISTANCE PROGRAMS.
(CONTINUED ON NEXT CARD)

341.1
:338
A32u
Technical assistance programs.
U.S. Agency for International Development.
U.S. foreign assistance and assistance from international organizations, obligations and loan authorizations, July 1, 1945-June 30, 1961. Rev. Washington, 1962.
130p.

1. Technical assistance programs.

341.1
:338
C653F
1963
H-R
NO.1087
TECHNICAL ASSISTANCE PROGRAMS.
U.S. CONGRESS. CONFERENCE COMMITTEES, 1963.
FOREIGN AID AND RELATED AGENCIES.
CONFERENCE REPORT TO ACCOMPANY H.R.
9499. WASHINGTON, GOVT. PRINT. OFF.,
1963.
6P. (88TH CONGRESS, 1ST SESSION.
HOUSE OF REPRESENTATIVES. REPORT NO.
1087)

1. TECHNICAL ASSISTANCE PROGRAMS.
I. TITLE.

341.1
:338
A32S
U.S. AGENCY FOR INTERNATIONAL DEVELOPMENT. SECTION-BY-SECTION ANALYSIS ...1965. (CARD 2)

I. TITLE: FOREIGN ASSISTANCE ACT OF 1965. II. U.S. CONGRESS. HOUSE. COMMITTEE ON FOREIGN AFFAIRS.

341.1
:338
A32v
Technical assistance programs.
U.S. Agency for International Development.
(Communications Resources Div.)
Village technology handbook. Washington, 1964.
2v. (Its C-11-12)

1. Technical assistance programs.
2. Water-supply. 3. Tools. I. Title.
II. Title: Technology handbook.

341.1
:338
C653F
1963
H-R
TECHNICAL ASSISTANCE PROGRAMS.
U.S. CONGRESS. CONFERENCE COMMITTEES, 1963.
FOREIGN ASSISTANCE ACT OF 1963. H.R.
7885. CONFERENCE REPORT ... TO AMEND FURTHER THE FOREIGN AID ASSISTANCE ACT OF 1961. WASHINGTON, GOVT. PRINT. OFF., 1963.
32P. (88TH CONGRESS, 1ST SESSION.
HOUSE. REPORT. 1006)

1. TECHNICAL ASSISTANCE PROGRAMS.
I. TITLE.

330
A32
Technical assistance programs.
U.S. Agency for International Development.
Specific risk investment guaranty handbook. Rev. ed. Washington, D.C., 1966.
54p.

1. Economic development. 2. Technical assistance programs. 3. Insurance. 4. Investments. 5. Foreign relations. I. Title.

351
H66
1955
Rept.10
Technical assistance programs.
U. S. Commission on Organization of the Executive Branch of the Government, 1953-1955
Overseas economic operations; a report to the Congress, June 1955. [Washington, Govt. Print. Off., 1955.]
75 p.

1. International relations. 2. Technical assistance programs. I. Hoover Commission reports. II. Title.

341.1
:338
C653F
1964
H-R
NO.1091
TECHNICAL ASSISTANCE PROGRAMS.
U.S. CONGRESS. CONFERENCE COMMITTEES, 1964.
FOREIGN AID AND RELATED AGENCIES APPROPRIATION BILL, 1964. CONFERENCE REPORT TO ACCOMPANY H.R. 9499.
WASHINGTON, GOVT. PRINT. OFF., 1963.
4P. (88TH CONGRESS, 1ST SESSION.
HOUSE OF REPRESENTATIVES. REPORT NO.
1091)

1. TECHNICAL ASSISTANCE PROGRAMS.
I. TITLE.

341.1
:338
C653F
1964
H-R

TECHNICAL ASSISTANCE PROGRAMS.
U.S. CONGRESS. CONFERENCE COMMITTEES,
1964.
FOREIGN ASSISTANCE ACT OF 1964;
CONFERENCE REPORT TO ACCOMPANY H.R.
11380. WASHINGTON, GOVT. PRINT. OFF.,
1964.
18P. (88TH CONGRESS, 2D SESSION.
HOUSE OF REPRESENTATIVES. REPORT NO.
1925)

1. TECHNICAL ASSISTANCE PROGRAMS.
I. TITLE.

341.1
:338
C65F
1965
H-R

TECHNICAL ASSISTANCE PROGRAMS.
U.S. CONGRESS. HOUSE. COMMITTEE ON
APPROPRIATIONS.
FOREIGN ASSISTANCE AND RELATED
AGENCIES APPROPRIATION BILL, 1965.
REPORT TO ACCOMPANY H.R. 11812.
WASHINGTON, GOVT. PRINT. OFF., 1964.
31P. (88TH CONGRESS, 2D SESSION.
HOUSE OF REPRESENTATIVES. REPORT NO.
1518)

1. TECHNICAL ASSISTANCE PROGRAMS.
I. TITLE.

Technical assistance programs.

341.1
C65f

U.S. Congress. House. Committee on
Appropriations.
Foreign operations appropriations for
1962. Hearings before the subcommittee
of the Committee on Appropriations, House
of Representatives, Eighty-seventh Congress,
first session. Washington, Govt. Print.
Off., 1961.
pts.

1. Technical assistance programs. I. Title.

341.1
:338
C653F
1965
H-R

TECHNICAL ASSISTANCE PROGRAMS.
U.S. CONGRESS. CONFERENCE COMMITTEES,
1965.
FOREIGN ASSISTANCE ACT OF 1965;
CONFERENCE REPORT ON H.R. 7750.
WASHINGTON, GOVT. PRINT. OFF., 1965.
26P. (89TH CONGRESS, 1ST SESSION.
HOUSE. REPORT NO. 811)

1. TECHNICAL ASSISTANCE PROGRAMS.
I. TITLE.

341.1
:338
C65F
1966
H-R

TECHNICAL ASSISTANCE PROGRAMS.
U.S. CONGRESS. HOUSE. COMMITTEE ON
APPROPRIATIONS.
FOREIGN ASSISTANCE AND RELATED
AGENCIES APPROPRIATION BILL, 1966.
REPORT TO ACCOMPANY H.R. 10871.
WASHINGTON, GOVT. PRINT. OFF., 1965.
39P. (89TH CONGRESS, 1ST SESSION.
HOUSE OF REPRESENTATIVES. REPORT NO.
955)

1. TECHNICAL ASSISTANCE PROGRAMS.
I. TITLE.

Technical assistance programs.

327
C65f
1963
H-H

U.S. Congress. House. Committee on
Appropriations.
Foreign operations appropriations for 1963.
Hearings before a subcommittee of the Committee
on Appropriations, House of Representatives,
Eighty-seventh Congress, second session.
Washington, Govt. Print. Off., 1962.
pts.

1. International relations.
2. Technical assistance program.
I. Title.

341.1
:338
C65FO
1966
4-R

TECHNICAL ASSISTANCE PROGRAMS.
U.S. CONGRESS. CONFERENCE COMMITTEES,
1965.
FOREIGN ASSISTANCE APPROPRIATIONS FOR
1966; CONFERENCE REPORT TO ACCOMPANY
H.R. 10871. WASHINGTON, GOVT. PRINT.
OFF., 1965.
4P. (89TH CONGRESS, 1ST SESSION.
HOUSE OF REPRESENTATIVES. REPORT NO.
1103)

1. TECHNICAL ASSISTANCE PROGRAMS.
I. TITLE.

341.1
:338
C65F
1967
H-R

TECHNICAL ASSISTANCE PROGRAMS.
U.S. CONGRESS. HOUSE. COMMITTEE ON
APPROPRIATIONS.
FOREIGN ASSISTANCE AND RELATED
AGENCIES APPROPRIATION BILL, 1967.
REPORT TO ACCOMPANY H.R. 17788.
WASHINGTON, GOVT. PRINT. OFF., 1966.
38P. (89TH CONGRESS, 2D SESSION.
HOUSE OF REPRESENTATIVES. REPORT NO.
2045)

1. TECHNICAL ASSISTANCE PROGRAMS.
I. TITLE.

Technical assistance programs.

327
C65f
1964
H-H

U.S. Congress. House. Committee on
Appropriations.
Foreign operations appropriations for
1964. Hearings before a subcommittee of the
Committee on Appropriations, House of
Representatives, Eighty-eighth Congress,
first session. Washington, Govt. Print.
Off., 1963.
pts.

1. International relations. 2. Technical
assistance programs. I. Title.

341.1
:338
C653F
1966
H-R

TECHNICAL ASSISTANCE PROGRAMS.
U.S. CONGRESS. CONFERENCE COMMITTEES,
1966.
FOREIGN ASSISTANCE ACT OF 1966;
CONFERENCE REPORT ON H.R. 15750, TO
AMEND FURTHER THE FOREIGN ASSISTANCE ACT
OF 1961, AS AMENDED, AND FOR OTHER
PURPOSES. WASHINGTON, GOVT. PRINT.
OFF., 1966.
30P. (89TH CONGRESS, 2D SESSION.
HOUSE. REPORT NO. 1927)

1. TECHNICAL ASSISTANCE PROGRAMS.
2. HOUSING - LATIN AMERICA.
I. TITLE.

341.1
:338
C65F
1965
S-H

TECHNICAL ASSISTANCE PROGRAMS.
U.S. CONGRESS. SENATE. COMMITTEE ON
APPROPRIATIONS.
FOREIGN ASSISTANCE AND RELATED
AGENCIES APPROPRIATIONS FOR 1965;
HEARINGS, EIGHTY-EIGHTH CONGRESS, SECOND
SESSION, ON H.R. 11812, AN ACT MAKING
APPROPRIATIONS FOR... THE FISCAL YEAR
ENDING JUNE 30, 1965. WASHINGTON, GOVT.
PRINT. OFF., 1964.
697P.

1. TECHNICAL ASSISTANCE PROGRAMS.
I. TITLE.

Technical assistance programs.

327
C65f
1965
H-H

U.S. Congress. House. Committee on
Appropriations.
Foreign operations appropriations for
1965. Hearings before a subcommittee of
the Committee on Appropriations, House of
Representatives, Eighty-eighth Congress,

Washington, Govt. Print. Off., 1964.
2 pts.

1. International relations. 2. Technical
assistance programs. I. Title.

341.1
:338
C65FO
1967
H-R

TECHNICAL ASSISTANCE PROGRAMS.
U.S. CONGRESS. CONFERENCE COMMITTEES,
1966.
FOREIGN ASSISTANCE AND RELATED
AGENCIES APPROPRIATION BILL, 1967.
CONFERENCE REPORT TO ACCOMPANY H.R.
17788. WASHINGTON, GOVT. PRINT. OFF.,
1966.
4P. (89TH CONGRESS, 2D SESSION.
HOUSE OF REPRESENTATIVES. REPORT NO.
2203)

1. TECHNICAL ASSISTANCE PROGRAMS.
I. TITLE.

Technical assistance programs.

341.1
:338
C65f
1966
H-H

U.S. Congress. House. Committee on
Appropriations.
Foreign assistance and related agencies
appropriations for 1966. Hearings before a
subcommittee of the Committee on Appropriations, House of Representatives, Eighty-
ninth Congress, first session. Washington,
Govt. Print. Off., 1965.
1719p.

1. Technical assistance programs.
2. Underdeveloped countries.

341.1
:338
C65mu

Technical assistance programs.

U.S. Congress. House. Committee on Appropriations.
Mutual security appropriations for 1959.
Hearings before the subcommittee of the Committee on Appropriations, House of Representatives, Eighty-fifth Congress, second
session. Washington, Govt. Print. Off.,
1958.
1566p. tables.

1. Technical assistance programs. 2. National defense. 3. U.S. - Appropriations
and expenditures.

VF
341.1
:338
C65m

Technical assistance programs.

U.S. Congress. House.
Mutual security act of 1959. Conference
report to accompany H.R. 7500. Washington,
Govt. Print. Off., 1959.
37p. (86th Cong., 1st sess. House. Report no. 695)

1. Technical assistance programs. 2. Economic development.

341.1
:338
C65F
1967
H-H

TECHNICAL ASSISTANCE PROGRAMS.
U.S. CONGRESS. HOUSE. COMMITTEE ON
APPROPRIATIONS.
FOREIGN ASSISTANCE AND RELATED
AGENCIES APPROPRIATIONS FOR 1967;
HEARINGS... EIGHTY-NINTH CONGRESS,
SECOND SESSION BEFORE... SUBCOMMITTEE ON
FOREIGN OPERATIONS AND RELATED AGENCIES
APPROPRIATIONS... WASHINGTON, GOVT.
PRINT. OFF., 1966.
2V.

1. TECHNICAL ASSISTANCE PROGRAMS.
I. TITLE.

341.1
:338
C65A
1956
H-H

TECHNICAL ASSISTANCE PROGRAMS.
U.S. CONGRESS. HOUSE. COMMITTEE ON
BANKING AND CURRENCY.
AREA ASSISTANCE ACT OF 1956.
HEARINGS...EIGHTY-FOURTH CONGRESS,
SECOND SESSION, ON H.R. 8555.
WASHINGTON, GOVT. PRINT. OFF., 1956.
392P.

HEARINGS HELD APR. 12, 13, 18, 19,
23-26, 1956.

1. TECHNICAL ASSISTANCE PROGRAMS.
2. ECONOMIC DEVELOPMENT. I. TITLE.

341.1
:338
C65f
1964
H-R

Technical assistance programs.

U.S. Congress. House. Committee on
Appropriations.
Foreign aid and related agencies appropria-
tion bill, 1964. Report. Washington, Govt.
Print. Off., 1964.
67p. (88th Cong. 1st sess. House.
Report no. 1040)

1. Technical assistance programs.
I. Title.

341.1
:338
C65f
1972
H-H

TECHNICAL ASSISTANCE PROGRAMS.
U.S. Congress. House. Committee on
Appropriations.
Foreign assistance and related agencies
appropriations for 1972. Hearings before a
Subcommittee of the Committee on Appropriations,
House of Representatives, Ninety-second Congress,
first session. Washington, Govt. Print. Off.,
1971.
pts.

1. Technical assistance programs.
2. Underdeveloped countries. I. Title.

341.1
:338
C653B

TECHNICAL ASSISTANCE PROGRAMS.
U.S. CONGRESS. HOUSE. COMMITTEE ON
FOREIGN AFFAIRS.
BACKGROUND MATERIAL, FOREIGN
ASSISTANCE ACT, FISCAL YEAR 1966.
WASHINGTON, GOVT. PRINT. OFF., 1965.
39P.
AT HEAD OF TITLE: 89TH CONGRESS, 1ST
SESSION. COMMITTEE PRINT.
COMPILED BY THE AGENCY FOR
INTERNATIONAL DEVELOPMENT.
1. TECHNICAL ASSISTANCE PROGRAMS.
I. U.S. AGENCY FOR INTERNATIONAL
DEVELOPMENT. II. TITLE: FOREIGN
ASSISTANCE ACT, 1966. III. TITLE.

341.1
:338
C653
1962
H-H

TECHNICAL ASSISTANCE PROGRAMS.
U.S. CONGRESS. HOUSE. COMMITTEE ON
FOREIGN AFFAIRS.
FOREIGN ASSISTANCE ACT OF 1962.
HEARINGS... EIGHTY-SEVENTH CONGRESS, 2D
SESSION, ON A DRAFT BILL TO AMEND
FURTHER THE FOREIGN ASSISTANCE ACT OF
1961, AS AMENDED, AND FOR OTHER
PURPOSES. WASHINGTON, GOVT. PRINT.
OFF., 1962.
6PTS. (1131P.)
For library holdings see main entry
HEARINGS HELD MAR. 14-APR. 18, 1962.
1. TECHNICAL ASSISTANCE PROGRAMS.
I. TITLE.

341.1
:338
C653
1966
H-H

TECHNICAL ASSISTANCE PROGRAMS.
U.S. CONGRESS. HOUSE. COMMITTEE ON
FOREIGN AFFAIRS.
FOREIGN ASSISTANCE ACT OF 1966.
HEARINGS... EIGHTY-NINTH CONGRESS,
SECOND SESSION ON H.R. 12449...AND H.R.
12450.... WASHINGTON, GOVT. PRINT. OFF.,
1966.
7pts.
1. TECHNICAL ASSISTANCE PROGRAMS.
2. U.S. AGENCY FOR INTERNATIONAL
DEVELOPMENT. I. TITLE.

355.58
C65m

Technical assistance programs.
U.S. Congress. House. Committee on
Foreign Affairs.
Mutual Security Act of 1958. Report of
the Committee on Foreign Affairs on H.R.
12181 to amend further the Mutual Security
Act of 1954, as amended, and for other
purposes, May 7, 1958. Washington, Govt.
Print. Off., 1958.
124p. diagrs., maps. (85th Cong., 2d
sess., House report no. 1696)

1. National defense. 2. Technical assistance programs.

341.1
:338
C653
1962
H-R

TECHNICAL ASSISTANCE PROGRAMS.
U.S. CONGRESS. HOUSE. COMMITTEE ON
FOREIGN AFFAIRS.
FOREIGN ASSISTANCE ACT OF 1962.
REPORT...ON H.R. 11921 TO AMEND FURTHER
AND FOREIGN ASSISTANCE ACT OF 1961, AS
AMENDED, AND FOR OTHER PURPOSES.
WASHINGTON, GOVT. PRINT. OFF., 1962.
95P. (87TH CONGRESS, 2D SESSION.
HOUSE. REPORT NO. 1788)

1. TECHNICAL ASSISTANCE PROGRAMS.
2. HOUSING -- LATIN AMERICA. I. TITLE.

341.1
:338
C653
1966
H-R

TECHNICAL ASSISTANCE PROGRAMS.
U.S. CONGRESS. HOUSE. COMMITTEE ON
FOREIGN AFFAIRS.
FOREIGN ASSISTANCE ACT OF 1966.
REPORT... ON H.R. 15750 TO AMEND
FURTHER THE FOREIGN ASSISTANCE ACT OF
1961. WASHINGTON, GOVT. PRINT. OFF.,
1966.
91P. (89TH CONGRESS, 2D SESSION.
HOUSE. REPORT NO. 1651)

1. TECHNICAL ASSISTANCE PROGRAMS.
I. TITLE.

341.1
:338
C65m
H-H
1960

Technical assistance programs.
U.S. Congress. House. Committee on Foreign
Affairs.
Mutual security act of 1960. Hearings before the Committee on Foreign Affairs, House
of Representatives, Eighty-sixth Congress,
second session on draft legislation to amend
further the Mutual Security Act of 1954, as
amended, and for other purposes. Washington,
Govt. Print. Off.,
pts.

For complete information see shelf list.

1. Technical assistance programs. I. Title.

341.1
:338
C65
1963
H-H

Technical assistance programs.
U.S. Congress. House. Committee on
Foreign Affairs.
Foreign assistance act of 1963. Hearings
before the Committee on Foreign Affairs,
House of Representative, Eighty-eight Congress,
first session of H.R. 5490. To amend further
the Foreign assistance act of 1961, as amended,
and for other purposes. Part 1- Washington,
Govt. Print. Off., 1963.
pts.

Hearings held April 5-10, 1963-

1. Technical assistance programs.

341.1
:338
C653
1967
H-H

TECHNICAL ASSISTANCE PROGRAMS.
U.S. CONGRESS. HOUSE. COMMITTEE ON
FOREIGN AFFAIRS.
FOREIGN ASSISTANCE ACT OF 1967.
HEARINGS... NINTIETH CONGRESS, FIRST
SESSION, ON H.R. 7099 AND H.R.
12048.... WASHINGTON, GOVT. PRINT. OFF.,
1967.
1413P.
HEARINGS HELD APR. 4-JUNE 8, 1967.
INCLUDES PARTS I-VI AND INDEX.

1. TECHNICAL ASSISTANCE PROGRAMS.
2. U.S. AGENCY FOR INTERNATIONAL
DEVELOPMENT. I. TITLE.

341.1
:338
C653re

Technical assistance programs.
U.S. Congress. House. Committee on Foreign
Affairs.
Report of the Special Study Mission to Asia,
Western Pacific, Middle East, Southern Europe
and North Africa of the Committee on Foreign
Affairs pursuant to H. Res. 113, a resolution
authorizing the Committee on Foreign Affairs
to conduct thorough studies and investigations
of all matters coming within the jurisdiction
of such committee. Washington, Govt. Print.
Off., 1960.
84p. diagrs., tables. (86th Cong., 2d
sess. House Re-   port no. 1386)
1. Technical assistance programs.

341.1
:338
C653
1963
H-R

TECHNICAL ASSISTANCE PROGRAMS.
U.S. CONGRESS. HOUSE. COMMITTEE ON
FOREIGN AFFAIRS.
FOREIGN ASSISTANCE ACT OF 1963.
REPORT ON H.R. 7885, TO AMEND FURTHER
THE FOREIGN ASSISTANCE ACT OF 1961...
WASHINGTON, GOVT. PRINT. OFF., 1963.
140P.

1. TECHNICAL ASSISTANCE PROGRAMS.
I. U.S. AGENCY FOR INTERNATIONAL
DEVELOPMENT. II. TITLE.

341.1
:338
C653
1964
H-R

TECHNICAL ASSISTANCE PROGRAMS.
U.S. CONGRESS. HOUSE. COMMITTEE ON
FOREIGN AFFAIRS.
FOREIGN ASSISTANCE ACT OF 1964.
REPORT...ON H.R. 11380 TO AMEND FURTHER
THE FOREIGN ASSISTANCE ACT OF 1961.
WASHINGTON, GOVT. PRINT. OFF., 1964.
75P. (88TH CONGRESS, 2D SESSION.
HOUSE OF REPRESENTATIVES. REPORT NO.
1443)

1. TECHNICAL ASSISTANCE PROGRAMS.
I. TITLE.

341.1
:338
C653r

Technical assistance programs.

U.S. Congress. House. Committee on
Foreign Affairs.
Report on foreign policy and mutual
security ... submitted pursuant to H.Res. 29
(85th Cong.). Washington, Govt. Print. Off.,
1957.
367 p.

85th Congress, 1st session, House report
no. 551. Union Calendar no. 181.

1. Technical assistance programs.

341.1
:338
C653
1964
H-H

TECHNICAL ASSISTANCE PROGRAMS.
U.S. CONGRESS. HOUSE. COMMITTEE ON
FOREIGN AFFAIRS.
FOREIGN ASSISTANCE ACT OF 1964.
HEARINGS, EIGHTY-EIGHTH CONGRESS, SECOND
SESSION, ON H.R. 10502, TO AMEND
FURTHER THE FOREIGN ASSISTANCE ACT OF
1961.
826P.
HEARINGS HELD MARCH 23 - MAY 6, 1964.

1. TECHNICAL ASSISTANCE PROGRAMS.
I. TITLE.

341.1
:338
C653
1967
H-R

TECHNICAL ASSISTANCE PROGRAMS.
U.S. CONGRESS. HOUSE. COMMITTEE ON
FOREIGN AFFAIRS.
FOREIGN ASSISTANCE ACT OF 1967.
REPORT... TOGETHER WITH MINORITY VIEWS
AND ADDITIONAL VIEWS ON H.R. 12048....
WASHINGTON, GOVT. PRINT. OFF., 1967.
137P. (90TH CONGRESS, 1ST SESSION.
HOUSE. REPORT NO. 551)

1. TECHNICAL ASSISTANCE PROGRAMS.
II. TITLE.

332
C65s

Technical assistance programs.
U.S. Congress. House. Committee on
Foreign Affairs.
Staff memorandum on international lend-
ing agencies. Washington, Govt. Print.
Off., 1959.
143p. tables.

1. Banks and banking. 2. Technical
assistance programs. I. Title: International lending agencies.

341.1
:338
C653
1965
H-H

TECHNICAL ASSISTANCE PROGRAMS.
U.S. CONGRESS. HOUSE. COMMITTEE ON
FOREIGN AFFAIRS.
FOREIGN ASSISTANCE ACT OF 1965.
HEARINGS... EIGHTY-NINTH CONGRESS, FIRST
SESSION. WASHINGTON, GOVT. PRINT. OFF.,
1965.
9 V. (1372P.)
HEARINGS HELD FEB. 4-APR. 7, 1965.
PART 9: APPENDIX AND INDEX.

1. TECHNICAL ASSISTANCE PROGRAMS.
I. TITLE.

327
C657

Technical assistance programs.
U.S. Congress. House. Committee on
Foreign Affairs.
Foreign assistance act of 1968;
report of the Committee on Foreign
Affairs together with minority, additional, and supplemental views on H.R.
15263 to amend further the Foreign
assistance act of 1961, as amended, and
for other purposes. Washington, Govt.
Print. Office, 1968.
61p. (90th Cong., 2d sess. House.
Report no. 1587)

1. Inter-   national relations.
2. Technical   assistance programs.
I. Title.

341.1
:338
C65a

Technical assistance programs.
U.S. Congress. House. Committee on Govern-
ment Operations.
Agency for International Development Contract
Operations, Office of Research, Evaluation and
Planning Assistance Staff ... report by the Com-
mittee on Government Operations. Washington,
Govt. Print. Off., 1962.
pts.

At head of title: 87th Cong., 2d sess.
House. Report no. 2436.

1. Technical assistance   programs.

341.1
:338
C653
1965
H-R

TECHNICAL ASSISTANCE PROGRAMS.
U.S. CONGRESS. HOUSE. COMMITTEE ON
FOREIGN AFFAIRS.
FOREIGN ASSISTANCE ACT OF 1965.
REPORT ON H.R. 7750. WASHINGTON, GOVT.
PRINT. OFF., 1965.
93P. (89TH CONGRESS, 1ST SESSION.
HOUSE. REPORT NO. 321)

1. TECHNICAL ASSISTANCE PROGRAMS.
I. TITLE.

VF
341.1
:338
C653

Technical assistance programs.

U. S. *Congress. House. Committee on Foreign Affairs.*
The Mutual security act and overseas private investment;
preliminary report of the Subcommittee on Foreign Economic Policy. Washington, U. S. Govt. Off., 1953.

ix, 87 p. illus. 23 cm.

At head of title: 83d Cong., 1st sess. Subcommittee print.

1. U. S.—Commercial policy. 2. Investments, American. 3. Technical assistance. 4. Economic assistance. I. Title.

HF1455.A55   338.91   53-61407

Library of Congress   (3)

341.1
:338
C65e

Technical assistance programs.
U.S. Congress. Joint Economic Committee.
Economic policies toward less developed
countries, by Raymond F. Mikesell and Robert
Loring Allen. Subcommittee on Foreign Economic
Policy of the Joint Economic Committee, Congress
of the United States. Washington, Govt. Print.
Off., 1961.
95p.

At head of title: 87th Cong., 1st sess.

1. Technical assistance programs. 2. Underdeveloped
countries. I. Mikesell, Raymond F. II. Allen,
Robert Loring.

321
C65

Technical assistance programs.
U.S. Congress. Senate.
A review of United States foreign policy and operations, by Allen J. Ellender. Washington, Govt. Print. Off., 1958.
361p. tables.

At head of title: 85th Cong., 2d sess. Senate document no. 78.

1. International relations. 2. Technical assistance programs. I. Ellender, Allen J

341.1
:338
C653
1964
S-R

TECHNICAL ASSISTANCE PROGRAMS.
U.S. CONGRESS. SENATE. COMMITTEE ON FOREIGN RELATIONS.
FOREIGN ASSISTANCE ACT OF 1964, REPORT ON H.R. 11380...TO AMEND FURTHER THE FOREIGN ASSISTANCE ACT OF 1961. WASHINGTON, GOVT. PRINT. OFF., 1964.
2PTS. (88TH CONGRESS, 2D SESSION. SENATE. REPORT NO. 1188)

1. TECHNICAL ASSISTANCE PROGRAMS.
I. TITLE.

341.1
:338
C653
1965
S-H

TECHNICAL ASSISTANCE PROGRAMS.
U.S. CONGRESS. SENATE. COMMITTEE ON FOREIGN RELATIONS.
FOREIGN ASSISTANCE, 1965. HEARINGS, EIGHTY-NINTH CONGRESS, FIRST SESSION. WASHINGTON, GOVT. PRINT. OFF., 1965.
772P.
HEARINGS HELD MAR. 9-APR. 7, 1965.

1. TECHNICAL ASSISTANCE PROGRAMS.
I. TITLE.

341.1
:338
C65F
1964
S-R

TECHNICAL ASSISTANCE PROGRAMS.
U.S. CONGRESS. SENATE. COMMITTEE ON APPROPRIATIONS.
FOREIGN AID AND RELATED AGENCIES APPROPRIATION BILL, 1964. REPORT TO ACCOMPANY H.R. 9499. WASHINGTON, GOVT. PRINT. OFF., 1963.
25P. (88TH CONGRESS, 1ST SESSION. SENATE. REPORT NO. 785)

1. TECHNICAL ASSISTANCE PROGRAMS.
I. TITLE.

341.1
:338
C653
1961
S-R

TECHNICAL ASSISTANCE PROGRAMS,
U.S. CONGRESS. SENATE. COMMITTEE ON FOREIGN RELATIONS.
FOREIGN ASSISTANCE ACT OF 1961.
REPORT... ON S. 1983. WASHINGTON, GOVT. PRINT. OFF., 1961.
125P. (87TH CONGRESS, 1ST SESSION. REPORT NO. 612)

1. TECHNICAL ASSISTANCE PROGRAMS.
I. TITLE.

341.1
:338
C653
1965
S-R

TECHNICAL ASSISTANCE PROGRAMS.
U.S. CONGRESS. SENATE. COMMITTEE ON FOREIGN RELATIONS.
FOREIGN ASSISTANCE ACT OF 1965.
REPORT... ON S. 1837...TOGETHER WITH MINORITY VIEWS. WASHINGTON, GOVT. PRINT. OFF., 1965.
72P. (89TH CONGRESS, 1ST SESSION. SENATE. REPORT NO. 170)

1. TECHNICAL ASSISTANCE PROGRAMS.
I. TITLE.

341.1
:338
C65F
1965
S-R

TECHNICAL ASSISTANCE PROGRAMS.
U.S. CONGRESS. SENATE. COMMITTEE ON APPROPRIATIONS.
FOREIGN ASSISTANCE AND RELATED AGENCIES APPROPRIATION BILL, 1965. REPORT TO ACCOMPANY H.R. 11812. WASHINGTON, GOVT. PRINT. OFF., 1964.
20P. (88TH CONGRESS, 2D SESSION. SENATE. REPORT NO. 1605)

1. TECHNICAL ASSISTANCE PROGRAMS.
I. TITLE.

341.1
:338
C65
1962
S-H

Technical assistance programs.
U.S. Congress. Senate. Committee on Foreign Relations.
Foreign assistance act of 1962. Hearings before the Committee on Foreign Relations, United States Senate, Eighty-seventh Congress, second session, on S. 2996, to amend further the Foreign assistance act of 1961, as amended, and for other purposes. Washington, Govt. Print. Off., 1962.
643p.
Hearings held Apr. 5-18, 1962.
1. Technical assistance programs. I. Title.

341.1
:338
C653
1967
S-H

TECHNICAL ASSISTANCE PROGRAMS.
U.S. CONGRESS. SENATE. COMMITTEE ON FOREIGN RELATIONS.
FOREIGN ASSISTANCE ACT OF 1967.
HEARINGS... NINTIETH CONGRESS, FIRST SESSION, ON S. 1872... WASHINGTON, GOVT. PRINT. OFF., 1967.
393P.
HEARINGS HELD JUNE 12-JULY 26, 1967.

1. TECHNICAL ASSISTANCE PROGRAMS.
I. TITLE.

341.1
:338
C65F
1966
S-R

TECHNICAL ASSISTANCE PROGRAMS.
U.S. CONGRESS. SENATE. COMMITTEE ON APPROPRIATIONS.
FOREIGN ASSISTANCE AND RELATED AGENCIES APPROPRIATION BILL, 1966. REPORT TO ACCOMPANY H.R. 10871. WASHINGTON, GOVT. PRINT. OFF., 1965.
20P. (89TH CONGRESS, 1ST SESSION. SENATE. REPORT NO. 708)

1. TECHNICAL ASSISTANCE PROGRAMS.
I. TITLE.

341.1
:338
C653
1962
S-R

TECHNICAL ASSISTANCE PROGRAMS.
U.S. CONGRESS. SENATE. COMMITTEE ON FOREIGN RELATIONS.
FOREIGN ASSISTANCE ACT OF 1962.
REPORT... ON S. 2996 TO AMEND FURTHER THE FOREIGN ASSISTANCE ACT OF 1961, AS AMENDED, AND FOR OTHER PURPOSES. WASHINGTON, GOVT. PRINT. OFF., 1962.
95P. (87TH CONGRESS, 2D SESSION. SENATE. REPORT NO. 1535)

1. TECHNICAL ASSISTANCE PROGRAMS.
I. TITLE.

341.1
:338
C653
1966
S-H

TECHNICAL ASSISTANCE PROGRAMS.
U.S. CONGRESS. SENATE. COMMITTEE ON FOREIGN RELATIONS.
FOREIGN ASSISTANCE, 1966. HEARINGS, EIGHTY-NINTH CONGRESS, SECOND SESSION, ON S. 2859 AND S. 2861. WASHINGTON, GOVT. PRINT. OFF., 1966.
752P.
HEARINGS HELD APRIL 6-MAY 11, 1966.

1. TECHNICAL ASSISTANCE PROGRAMS.
I. TITLE.

341.1
:338
C65f
S-H

TECHNICAL ASSISTANCE PROGRAMS.
U.S. Congress. Senate. Committee on Appropriations.
Foreign assistance and related programs appropriations. Hearings: 19
Washington, Govt. Print. Off., 19
v.

For Library holdings see main entry.

1. Technical assistance programs.
2. Underdeveloped countries. I. Title.

341.1
:338
C653
1963
S-H

TECHNICAL ASSISTANCE PROGRAMS.
U.S. CONGRESS. SENATE. COMMITTEE ON FOREIGN RELATIONS.
FOREIGN ASSISTANCE ACT OF 1963.
HEARINGS... EIGHTY-EIGHTH CONGRESS, 1ST SESSION, ON S. 1276, A BILL TO AMEND FURTHER THE FOREIGN ASSISTANCE ACT OF 1961. WASHINGTON, GOVT. PRINT. OFF., 1963.
764P.
HEARINGS HELD JUNE 11-JULY 11, 1963.

1. TECHNICAL ASSISTANCE PROGRAMS.
I. TITLE.

341.1
:338
C653
1966
S-R

TECHNICAL ASSISTANCE PROGRAMS.
U.S. CONGRESS. SENATE. COMMITTEE ON FOREIGN RELATIONS.
FOREIGN ECONOMIC ASSISTANCE.
REPORT... ON S. 3584 TO AMEND FURTHER THE FOREIGN ASSISTANCE ACT OF 1961 AS AMENDED, AND FOR OTHER PURPOSES TOGETHER WITH INDIVIDUAL VIEWS AND MINORITY VIEWS. WASHINGTON, GOVT. PRINT. OFF., 1966.
55P. (89TH CONGRESS, 2D SESSION. SENATE. REPORT NO. 1359)

1. TECHNICAL ASSISTANCE PROGRAMS.
I. TITLE.

341.1
:338
C65
1963
S-H

Technical assistance programs.
U.S. Congress. Senate. Committee on Banking and Currency.
Area redevelopment act amendments, 1963. Hearings before a subcommittee of the Committee on Banking and Currency, United States Senate, Eighty-eighth Congress, first session, on S. 1163. A bill to amend certain provisions of the Area redevelopment act. Washington, U.S. Govt. Print. Off., 1963.
377p.

1. Technical assistance programs.
I. Title.

341.1
:338
C65
1963
S-R

Technical assistance programs.
U.S. Congress. Senate. Committee on Foreign Relations.
Foreign assistance act of 1963. Report of the Committee on Foreign Relations, United States Senate on H.R. 7885 to amend further the Foreign assistance act of 1961, as amended and for other purposes. Washington, Govt. Print. Off., 1963.
83p. (88th Cong., 1st sess. Senate. Report no. 588)

1. Technical assistance programs.
I. Title.

341.1
:338
C65
S-H

Technical assistance programs.
U.S. Congress. Senate. Committee on Foreign Relations.
Hearing before a subcommittee of the Committee on Foreign Relations ..., 84th Congress, 1st & 2d session on technical assistance programs. 2pts. Washington, Govt. Print. Off., 1955-56.

Hearings held Feb. 17-24, March 2-4, 1955 and Jan. 23, 1956.

1. Technical assistance programs.

341.1
:338
C653
1967
S-R

TECHNICAL ASSISTANCE PROGRAMS.
U.S. CONGRESS. SENATE. COMMITTEE ON FOREIGN RELATIONS.
FOREIGN ASSISTANCE ACT OF 1967.
REPORT... ON S. 1872 TOGETHER WITH INDIVIDUAL VIEWS. WASHINGTON, GOVT. PRINT. OFF., 1967.
116P. (90TH CONGRESS, 1ST SESSION. SENATE. REPORT NO. 499)

1. TECHNICAL ASSISTANCE PROGRAMS.
I. TITLE.

341.1
:338
C653
1964
S-H

TECHNICAL ASSISTANCE PROGRAMS.
U.S. CONGRESS. SENATE. COMMITTEE ON FOREIGN RELATIONS.
FOREIGN ASSISTANCE, 1964. HEARINGS... EIGHTY-EIGHTH CONGRESS, SECOND SESSION, ON S. 2659 (AND OTHER BILLS) TO FURTHER THE FOREIGN ASSISTANCE ACT OF 1961, AS AMENDED, AND FOR OTHER PURPOSES. WASHINGTON, GOVT. PRINT. OFF., 1964.
628P.
HEARINGS HELD MAR. 31-JUNE 23, 1964.

1. TECHNICAL ASSISTANCE PROGRAMS.
I. TITLE.

341.1
:338
C653M

TECHNICAL ASSISTANCE PROGRAMS.
U.S. CONGRESS. SENATE. COMMITTEE ON FOREIGN RELATIONS.
MILITARY ASSISTANCE AND SALES ACT. REPORT ON S. 3583 TO PROMOTE THE FOREIGN POLICY, SECURITY, AND GENERAL WELFARE OF THE UNITED STATES BY ASSISTING PEOPLES OF THE WORLD IN THEIR EFFORTS TOWARD INTERNAL AND EXTERNAL SECURITY TOGETHER WITH MINORITY VIEWS. WASHINGTON, GOVT. PRINT. OFF., 1966.
35P. (89TH CONGRESS, 2D SESSION. SENATE. REPORT NO. 1358)

1. TECHNICAL ASSISTANCE PROGRAMS.
(CONTINUED ON NEXT CARD)

341.1
:338
C653M
U.S. CONGRESS. SENATE. COMMITTEE ON FOREIGN RELATIONS. MILITARY ASSISTANCE...1966. (CARD 2)

2. INTERNATIONAL RELATIONS. I. TITLE.

341.1
1338
C65
1956
S-H
U.S. CONGRESS. SENATE. COMMITTEE ON LABOR AND PUBLIC WELFARE. AREA REDEVELOPMENT....1956. (CARD 2)

HEARINGS HELD JAN. 4 - APR. 26, 1956.

1. TECHNICAL ASSISTANCE PROGRAMS.
2. EMPLOYMENT. I. TITLE.

VF
690
H68
IME
no. 18
1956
Technical assistance programs.

U.S. Housing and Home Finance Agency. Office of the Administrator. International Housing Service.
Aided self-help in housing improvement. Rev. Washington, Nov. 1956.
35 p. illus. (Its Ideas and methods exchange no. 18)

Bibliography: p. 33-35.

1. Aided self-help housing. 2. Technical assistance programs.

341.1
:338
C65m
S-H
Technical assistance programs.

U.S. Congress. Senate. Committee on Foreign Relations.
Mutual security act of 1959. Hearings before the Committee on Foreign Relations, United States Senate, Eighty-sixth Congress, first session on S. 1451, to amend further the Mutual security act of 1954, as amended, and for other purposes. Washington, Govt. Print. Off., 1959.
2 pts.
Hearings held: Apr. 23, May 14, 1959.
1. Technical assistance programs. I. Title.

341.1
1338
C657
TECHNICAL ASSISTANCE PROGRAMS.
U.S. CONGRESS. SENATE. COMMITTEE ON RULES AND ADMINISTRATION.
STUDY OF FOREIGN AID EXPENDITURES.
REPORT TO ACCOMPANY S. RES. 57. GOVT. PRINT. OFF., 1967.
14P. (90TH CONGRESS, 1ST SESSION. SENATE. REPORT NO. 44)

1. TECHNICAL ASSISTANCE PROGRAMS.
2. TECHNICAL ASSISTANCE PROGRAMS - CHILE.
I. TITLE: FOREIGN AID EXPENDITURES.

690
H68
IME
no.18
1961
Technical assistance programs.

U.S. Housing and Home Finance Agency. Office of the Administrator. Office of International Housing.
Aided self-help in housing improvement. Rev. Washington, 1961.
35p. (Its Ideas and methods exchange no. 18)

Bibliography: p. 33-35.

1. Aided self-help housing. 2. Technical assistance programs.

341.1
:338
C65m
S-R
1960
Technical assistance programs.
U.S. Congress. Senate. Committee on Foreign Relations.
The mutual security act of 1960. Report on S. 3058. Washington, Govt. Print. Off., 1960.
65p. (86th Cong., 2d sess. Senate. Report no. 1286)

1. Technical assistance programs.

341.1
1338
E26
TECHNICAL ASSISTANCE PROGRAMS.
U.S. ECONOMIC DEVELOPMENT ADMINISTRATION.
REPORT. 1ST - 1965/66-
WASHINGTON, GOVT. PRINT. OFF., 1966-
1 V. ANNUAL.

REPORT YEAR ENDS JUNE 30.
AT HEAD OF TITLE: ECONOMIC DEVELOPMENT ADMINISTRATION AND OFFICE OF REGIONAL ECONOMIC DEVELOPMENT.

1. TECHNICAL ASSISTANCE PROGRAMS.
2. REGIONAL PLANNING. I. U.S.
(CONTINUED ON NEXT CARD)

341.1
:338
H68
1958
Technical assistance programs.
U.S. Housing and Home Finance Agency. Office of the Administrator. International Housing Service.
Catalog of programs of international cooperation in housing and town and country planning. Washington, 1958.
67p.

1. Technical assistance programs. 2. City planning. 3. Regional planning. 4. Housing projects. I. Title.

341.1
:338
C65
1957
S-R
Technical assistance programs.

U.S. Congress. Senate. Committee on Foreign Relations.
Technical assistance. Final report... pursuant to the provisions of S.Res. 214, 83d Congress, 2d session; S.Res. 36 and S.Res. 133, 84th Congress, 1st session; and S.Res. 162, 84th Congress, 2d session [Extended by S.Res. 60 and 99 of the 85th Congress.] Washington, Govt. Print. Off., 1957.

(See Card No. 2)

341.1
1338
E26
U.S. ECONOMIC DEVELOPMENT ADMINISTRATION. REPORT....1966- (CARD 2)

OFFICE OF REGIONAL ECONOMIC DEVELOPMENT.

341.1
:338
H68
1952
Technical assistance programs.
U.S. Housing and Home Finance Agency. Office of the Administrator. Office of International Housing.
Catalog of projects of international cooperation in housing and community development and related fields. Washington, 1952.
20p. map.

"Unofficial."
1. Technical assistance programs. 2. City planning. 3. Regional planning. 4. Housing projects. I. Title.

341.1
:338
C65
1957
S-R
U.S. Congress. Senate. Committee on Foreign Relations... Technical assistance. Final report...1957. (Card No. 2)

668 p.

85th Congress, 1st session. Report no. 139.

1. Technical assistance programs.

301.158
F22
Technical assistance programs.

U.S. Federal Extension Service.
Rural youth clubs around the world. A handbook for developing programs. [Prepared in cooperation with the] Agency for International Development. Washington, For sale by Supt. of Docs., Govt. Print. Off., 1967.
36p.

1. Youth. 2. Technical assistance programs. 3. Social service, Rural. I. U.S. Agency for International Development. II. Title.

341.1
:338
H68
1956
Technical assistance programs.
U.S. Housing and Home Finance Agency. Office of the Administrator. International Housing Service.
Catalog of projects of international cooperation in housing and town and country planning. Washington, 1956.
54p.

"Unofficial."

1. Technical assistance programs. 2. City planning. 3. Regional planning. 4. Housing projects. I. Title.

341.1
:338
C65
1956
S-R
Technical assistance programs.

U.S. Congress. Senate. Committee on Foreign Relations.
Technical assistance and related programs. Washington, Govt. Print. Off., 1956.
30p. (84th Cong. 2d sess. Senate. Report no. 1956)

1. Technical assistance programs.

341.1
:338
F67
Technical assistance programs.

U.S. Foreign Operations Administration. Office of Industrial Resources.
Question and answer service. In cooperation with Office of Technical Services, United States Department of Commerce. Washington, 1955.
14p. illus.

1. Technical assistance programs. I. U.S. Office of Technical Services.

341.1
:338
H68
1957
Technical assistance programs.
U.S. Housing and Home Finance Agency. Office of the Administrator. Office of International Housing.
Catalog of projects of international cooperation in housing and town and country planning. Washington, 1957.
54p.

"Unofficial."

1. Technical assistance programs. 2. City planning. 3. Regional planning. 4. Housing projects.

341.1
:338
C65
1956
S-H
TECHNICAL ASSISTANCE PROGRAMS.
U.S. CONGRESS. SENATE. COMMITTEE ON LABOR AND PUBLIC WELFARE.
AREA REDEVELOPMENT. HEARINGS BEFORE THE SUBCOMMITTEE ON LABOR OF THE COMMITTEE ON LABOR AND PUBLIC WELFARE, UNITED STATES SENATE, EIGHTY-FOURTH CONGRESS, SECOND SESSION, ON S. 2663, A BILL TO ESTABLISH AN EFFECTIVE PROGRAM TO ALLEVIATE CONDITIONS OF EXCESSIVE UNEMPLOYMENT IN CERTAIN ECONOMICALLY DEPRESSED AREAS. WASHINGTON, GOVT. PRINT. OFF., 1956.
2 PTS. (1170 P.)

(CONTINUED ON NEXT CARD)

VF
728.1
H68ai
Technical assistance programs.
U.S. Housing and Home Finance Agency.
Aids to private entrepreneurs seeking overseas building opportunities. Washington, 1963.
4p.

1. Housing. 2. Technical assistance programs. I. Title: Overseas building opportunities. II. Title.

341.1
:338
H68h
Technical assistance programs.
U.S. Housing and Home Finance Agency. Office of the Administrator. Office of International Housing.
Helpful hints for ICA-financed team members. [Washington, 1959]
1v.

1. Technical assistance programs. 2. Housing. I. U.S. International Cooperation Administration.

Technical assistance programs.

332.72
H68hou
1964
U.S. Housing and Home Finance Agency.
Office of International Housing.
Housing loans, grants, and investment
guaranties. Rev. Washington, 1964.
21p.

1. Mortgage finance. 2. Investments.
3. Technical assistance programs.

Technical assistance program.

690
:1336.18
I57
U.S. International Cooperation Administration.
Adiestramiento del dirigente en la construccion de viviendas por esfuerzo propio
con ayuda, por Keith H. Hinchcliff. Mexico
City, Regional Technical Aids Center for
Latin America, 1958.
42p. diagrs.

(Continued on next card)

VF   Technical assistance programs.
341.1 U.S. International Cooperation Administra-
:338   tion.
I57f   Fact Sheet, mutual security in action.
1957/60 Washington, Govt. Print. Off., 1957- 1960.
12 nos.

Contents.-Brazil (Inter-American series 57;
Dept. of State pub. 6951) -Cambodia (Far East-
ern series 85; Dept. of State pub. 6931) -Ceylon
(Near and Middle Eastern series 47; Dept. of
State pub. 6936) -India (Near and Middle Eastern
series 46; Dept. of   State pub. 6910)

(Continued on next card)

Technical assistance programs.

690
H68
IME
no.18
Span.
1961
U.S. Housing and Home Finance Agency.
International Housing Service.
Mejoramiento de la vivenda por autosyuda
subsidiada. Rev. [n.p.] Centro Regional
de Ayuda Tecnica, 1965.
34p. (Its Ideas and methods exchange
no. 18, rev. Spanish)
Translation of Aided self-help in housing improvement.

1. Aided self-help housing. 2. Technical assistance programs.

690
:1336.18
I57
U.S. International Cooperation Administration. Adiestramiento del...(Card 2)

Translation of author's Leader training for
aided self-help housing.

1. Aided self-help housing.   2. Technical
assistance program. I. Hinchcliff, Keith
Harry.

VF
341.1 U.S. International Cooperation Administra-
:338   tion. Fact Sheet, ... 1957-) (Card 2)
I57f
1957/60
-Jordan (Near and Middle Eastern series 44; Dept. of
State pub. 6897) -The Philippines (Far Eastern series
84; Dept. of State pub. 6908) -Spain (European and
British Commonwealth series 58; Dept. of State pub.
6913) -Turkey (Near and Middle Eastern series 45;
Dept. of State pub. 6898) -Vietnam (Far Eastern
series 83; Dept. of State pub. 6896)

(Continued on next
card)

Technical assistance programs.

690
H68
IME
no.18
Span.
U.S. Housing and Home Finance Agency. Office
of the Administrator. International Housing
Service.
Mejoramiento de la vivienda por esfuerzo
propio con ayuda. Rev. Mexico, Centro Regional de Ayuda Tecnica, 1958.
38p. illus. (Its Ideas and methods exchange no. 18, Spanish)
Translation of Aided self-help in housing improvement.
1. Aided self-help housing. 2. Technical assistance programs.

341.1
:338
I57a
Technical assistance programs.

U.S. International Cooperation Administration.
Americans on a new frontier, U.S. technicians
lend a hand abroad. Washington, Govt. Print.
Off., 1960.
29p. illus. (Dept. of State Publication
6921; Economic cooperation series 55)

1. Technical assistance programs.

VF
341.1 U.S. International Cooperation Administra-
:338   tion. Fact Sheet ...1957. (Card 3)
I57f
1957/60
-Korea (Far Eastern series 91; Dept. of State pub.
6975) -Republic of China (Far Eastern series 93;
Dept. of State pub. 6998) -Chile (Inter-American
series 58; Dept. of State pub. 6969)

1. Technical assistance programs.

Technical assistance programs.

341.1
:338
H68p
U.S. Housing and Home Finance Agency.
Office of the Administrator. Office
of International Housing.
Prospects for United States builders
in overseas operations. Washington, 1961.
28p.

1. Technical assistance programs.
2. Building industry.

341.1
:338
I573co
Technical assistance programs.

U.S. International Cooperation Administration.
Community development and national change.
Summary of Conference, Endicott House, Decem-
ber 13-15, by Irwin T. Sanders, sponsored by
Center for International Studies, Massachusetts
Institute of Technology, assisted by Interna-
tional Cooperation Administration and Asso-
ciates for International Research, Inc.
Washington, 1958.
70p.   (Continued on Card 2)

Technical assistance programs.

VF
341.1 U.S. International Cooperation
:338   Administration.
I57f   Fact sheet, mutual security in action:
Jordan Jordan. Rev. Washington, Govt. Print.
1961 Off., 1961.
9p. (U.S. Dept. of State. Near and
Middle Eastern series 61)

1. Technical assistance programs.
(Series)

VF
728.1 TECHNICAL ASSISTANCE PROGRAMS.
H68hudi U.S. Dept. of Housing and Urban Development.
Office of International Affairs.
HUD international programs and activities.
Wash., 1971.
folder. (HUD-269-SF)

1. Federal housing programs. 2. Technical
assistance programs. I. Title.

341.1
:338
I573co
U.S. International Cooperation Administration.
Community development and... (Card 2)

1. Technical assistance programs. 2. Economic
development. I. Sanders, Irwin T
II. Massachusetts Institute of Technology. Center for International Study. III. Associates
for International Research.

Technical assistance programs.

VF
341.1 U.S. International Cooperation Administration.
:338   Fact sheet; mutual security in action,
I57f   Turkey. Rev. Washington, Govt. Print. Off.,
Turkey 1961.
1961 10p. (U.S. Dept. of State. Near
and Middle Eastern series 63)

1. Technical assistance programs.
(Series)

Technical assistance programs.

VF
341.1 U.S. Dept. of Housing and Urban
:338   Development.
H681   International programs of the
Department of Housing and Urban
Development. Wash., 1965.
Folder.

1. Technical assistance programs.
I. Title.

301.15
I57c
Technical assistance programs.

U.S. International Cooperation Administra-
tion.
The community development guidelines of the
International Cooperation Administration.
[Washington, 1956]
4p.

1. Community development. 2. Technical
assistance programs.

Technical assistance programs.

341.1
:338
(73:347)
I57
U.S. International Cooperation Administration.
Mutual security legislation and related
documents; with explanatory notes and cross-
references; printed for the use of the
International Cooperation Administration.
[Washington] Dec. 1955.
175 p.

1. Technical assistance programs.
2. National defense.   I. Title.

VF
341.1 Technical assistance programs.
:338
I57s U.S. Interdepartmental Committee on Scientific
and Cultural Cooperation.
Scientific & technical cooperation in the
American republics under the Interdepartmental
Committee on Scientific and Cultural Cooperation,
1939-1949. [Washington, Dept. of State, 1950?]
145 p.

Processed.

1. Technical assistance programs. I. Title.

341.1
:338
I573c
Technical assistance programs.

U.S. International Cooperation Administration.
Counterpart funds and ICA foreign currency
accounts. Washington, 1957.
22p. tables.

1. Technical assistance programs. 2. Foreign
exchange. I. Title. II. Title: ICA Foreign currency
accounts.

355.58
I57
Technical assistance programs.

U.S. International Cooperation Administration.
The mutual security program, fiscal year,

a summary presentation. In cooperation with
Dept. of State and Dept. of Defense. Washington,
v. diagrs.

For complete information see shelf list.

1. National defense. 2. Technical assistance
programs.

Technical assistance programs. VF 341.1 :338 I573p U.S. International Cooperation Administration. Principles of technical cooperation, by D. A. Fitzgerald. Washington, Govt. Print. Off., 1959. 8p. (Economic cooperation series 48) 1. Technical Assistance programs. 2. International relations— I. Fitzgerald, D. A.	Technical assistance programs. VF 341.1 :338 I573w U.S. International Cooperation Administration. Working with people, examples of U.S.technical assistance. Washington, Govt. Print. Off., 1959. 17p. (Its Economic cooperation series 49) 1. Technical assistance programs.	Technical assistance programs. VF 351(016) L41 no.1 U.S. Library of Congress. Legislative Reference Service. Point four. Washington, D.C., Jan. 1950. [32]p. (Its Public affairs abstracts. New series, no.1) 1.Technical assistance programs. I.Series: Public affairs abstracts. New series.
Technical assistance programs. 341.1 :338 I573 U.S.International Cooperation Administration. Technical cooperation, a report on how the United States and more than 50 nations of the Free World today are combining their skills and knowledge to benefit many millions of people. Washington, Jan. 1957. 37 p. illus. 1. Technical assistance programs. 2. Economic development.	Technical assistance programs. VF 341.1 :338 I57w U. S. International Cooperation Administration. Working with people, examples of U. S. technical cooperation. Washington, Govt. Print. Off., 1960. 31p. (Dept. of State Publication 6942; Economic cooperation series 56) 1. Technical assistance programs	Technical assistance programs. VF 341.1 L41 U.S. Library of Congress. Legislative Reference Service. Point four; background and program. (International Technical Cooperation Act of 1949.) Prepared for the use of the Committee on Foreign Affairs of the House of Representatives...largely from materials supplied by the Department of State. July 1949. Washington, Govt. Print. Off., 1949. v, 25 p. tables. (Continued on next card)
Technical assistance programs. VF 630 I57 U.S. International Cooperation Administration. Technical cooperation in agriculture. Rev. Washington, 1959. 22p. illus. (Dept. of State publication 6846. Economic cooperation series 53) 1. Agriculture. 2. Technical assistance programs. (Series)	Technical assistance programs. VF 341.1 :338 I57t U.S. International Cooperation Administration. Office of Public Reports. Technical cooperation through American universities. Washington [Govt. print. off., 1957] 40 p. illus. 1. Technical assistance programs. 2. Universities and colleges.	U.S. Library of Congress. Legislative Reference Service. Point four...1949. (Card 2) Committee print. John Kee, Chairman. 1.Technical assistance programs. I.U.S.Congress. House. Committee on Foreign Affairs.
Technical assistance programs. VF 370 I57t U.S. International Cooperation Administration. Technical cooperation in education. Washington, 1960. 31p. illus. (U.S. Dept. of State. Economic cooperation series 58) U.S. Dept. of State. Publication 7024. 1. Education. 2. Technical assistance programs. (Series)	Technical assistance programs. 341.1 :338 I573f U.S. International Cooperation Administration. United States of America Operations Mission to Iran. Followup evaluation study of Iranian participants who received training in the United States under ICA sponsorship. Teheran, 1956. 43p. 1. Technical assistance programs.	Technical assistance programs. 341.1 :338 M87 U.S. Mutual Security Agency. Report to Congress on the Mutual Security Program. Washington, Govt. Print. Off., v. maps. semiannual. For complete information see shelf list. 1. Technical assistance programs. 2. National defense.
Technical assistance programs. VF 341.1 :338 I573h U. S. International Cooperation Administration. Technical cooperation in health. Washington, 1959. 28p. illus. (Dept. of State Publication 6855. Economic cooperation series 54) 1. Technical assistance programs. 2. Public health.	Technical assistance programs. VF 341.1 :338 I572 U.S. International Development Advisory Board. Conclusions and recommendations of the International Development Advisory Board; report to Harold E. Stassen, Director of Foreign Operations, regarding the United States participation in technical cooperation programs for underdeveloped countries. [Washington] Dec. 1953. 27 p. Processed. 1.Technical assistance programs. 2.Under-developed countries. I.U.S. Foreign Operations Administration.	Technical assistance programs. 058.7 :327 P21 U.S. Peace Corps. Peace Corps factbook & directory, 1966. Washington, D.C., 1967. 1v. For complete information see main card. 1. U.S. Peace Corps - Direct. 2. International organizations. 3. Technical assistance programs. I. Title.
Technical assistance programs. VF 341.1 :338 I57tec U.S. International Cooperation Administration. Technical cooperation in industry. Washington, Govt. Print. Off., 1960. 23p. illus. (U.S. Dept. of State. Economic cooperation series 57) 1. Technical assistance programs. (Series)	Technical assistance programs. VF 330 I573 U.S. International Development Advisory Board. A new emphasis on economic development abroad; a report to the President of the United States on ways, means and reasons for U.S. assistance to international economic development. Washington [1957] 18 p. 1. Economic development. 2. Technical assistance programs.	Technical assistance programs. 341.1 P21 U.S. Peace Corps. Report, Wash., 19 v. annual. For Library holdings see main entry. 1. International organizations. 2. Technical assistance programs.
Technical assistance programs. VF 341.1 :338 I57te U.S. International Cooperation Administration. Technical cooperation, the dramatic story of helping others to help themselves. Washington, Govt. Print. Off., 1959. 58p. illus. (Dept. of State Publication 6815, Economic cooperation series 52) 1. Technical assistance programs. 2. Economic development.	Technical assistance programs. 341.1:338 I57 U.S. International Development Advisory Board. Partners in progress; a report to the President. [Washington, D.C., Govt. Print. Off.] 1951. v, 120 p. charts, tables. Nelson A. Rockefeller, Chairman. Explanatory press release, dated Mar. 10, 1951, attached inside front cover. Text of Point Four, p.91-92; Act for International Development, p.93-101. 1.Technical assistance programs. I.Title.	Technical assistance programs. 341.1 :338 P72 U.S. President. Report to Congress on lend-lease operations, Message from the President of the United States transmitting the report to Congress on lend-lease operations, Washington, Govt. Print. Off., v. tables. annual. For complete information see shelflist. At head of title: -- Cong., -- sess. House. Document no. --. (Continued on next card)

341.1
:338
P72   U.S. President.   Report to Congress on
       lend lease ....   (Card 2)

    1. Technical assistance programs. 2. U.S. Presi-
dent - Messages.   I. Title: Lend lease operations.

341.1
I338   TECHNICAL ASSISTANCE PROGRAMS.
P72S   U.S. PRESIDENT, 1963-1969 (JOHNSON)
        SUPPLEMENT TO MESSAGE RELATIVE TO
        FOREIGN AID. COMMUNICATION FROM THE
        PRESIDENT OF THE UNITED STATES...
        WASHINGTON, GOVT. PRINT. OFF., 1965.
        3P. (89TH CONGRESS, 1ST SESSION.
        HOUSE OF REPRESENTATIVES. DOCUMENT NO.
        161)

    1. TECHNICAL ASSISTANCE PROGRAMS.
    2. U.S. PRESIDENT - MESSAGES.
    I. TITLE.

Technical assistance programs.

VF
341.1   U.S. Dept. of State. Bureau of Public
I338   Affairs.
871ai   Aid in action, how U.S. aid lends a
        hand around the world. Washington, Govt.
        Print. Off., 1961.
           63p. (U.S. Dept. of State: General
        foreign policy series 172; Publication 7221)

    1. Technical assistance programs.

Technical assistance programs.

355.58
P72f U.S. President, 1961—   (Kennedy)
       Final annual report on the operations of the
    mutual security program. Message from the
    President of the United States transmitting the
    final annual report on the operations of the
    Mutual Security Program for the period ending
    June 30, 1961. The report was prepared under the
    direction of the Administrator of the Agency for
    International Development as coordinator of the
    Foreign Assistance Program, with participation by
    the Department of State and the Department of
    Defense. Washington,   Govt. Print. Off., 1962.
       48p.   (87th Cong.,
    2d sess. House.   Document 432)
    1. National defense. 2.   Technical assistance programs.

341.1
I338   TECHNICAL ASSISTANCE PROGRAMS.
A32v   U.S. Regional Technical Aid Center.
French   Manuel pratique de l-equipement rural (IV)
        amenagement de la ferme. 2d ed. Paris,
        1963.
           113p. (Its Collection: techniques
        Americaines no. 105)
           Translation of: Village technology handbook
        no. 2, published by U.S. Agency for
        International Development.
           1. Technical assistance programs.
        2. Farm buildings - France. I. U.S.
        Agency for International Development.

Technical assistance programs.

330
(5)   U.S. Dept. of State. Bureau of Public Affairs.
871b   Background: the subcontinent of South Asia;
1962   Afghanistan, Ceylon, India, Nepal, Pakistan.
        Rev. Washington, 1962.
           76p. (U.S. Dept. of State. Near and
        Middle Eastern Series 69, Rev.)

        Department of State Publication 7410.

           1. Economic conditions - Asia. 2. Technical
        assistance programs.   (Series)

Technical assistance programs.

341.1
:338 U.S. President, 1961-   (Kennedy)
P72o   Our Foreign assistance act; message from the
    President of the United States relative to
    our Foreign assistance act. Washington, Govt.
    Print. Off., 1963.
       15p.
    At head of title: 88th Cong. 1st sess.
    House. Document no. 94.

       1. Technical assistance programs.
       2. U.S. President - Messages.

341.1   Technical assistance programs.
:338   U.S. Dept. of State.
871e   Economic development of underdeveloped
        countries. Washington, Govt. Print. Off.,
        1958.
           15p.

           1. Technical assistance programs. 2. Under-
        developed countries.

Technical assistance programs.

351
871co   U.S. Dept. of State. Bureau of Public
           Affairs.
           The Country Team; an illustrated profile
        of our American missions abroad. Washington,
        For sale by the Supt. of Documents, Govt.
        Print. Off., 1967.
           69p.   (U.S. Dept. of State, Foreign
        Service series 136)
           U.S. Dept of State Publication 8193.

           1. Federal government. 2. International
        relations. 3. American Embassy. 4. Technical
        assistance   programs.
        I. Title.

Technical assistance program.

341.1
:338   U.S. President, 1963-   (Johnson)
P72r   Foreign assistance, from the President
        of the United States, transmitting rec-
        ommendations relative to foreign assistance.
        Washington, Govt. Print. Off., 1964.
           44p.
        At head of title: 88th Cong., 2d sess.
        House Document no. 250.

           1. Technical assistance program. I. Title.

341.1   Technical assistance programs.
:338   U.S. Dept. of State.
871ex   Expanding private investment for free world
        economic growth. A report and recommendations
        prepared pursuant to Section 413 (c) of the
        Mutual Security Act of 1954, as amended, by
        Ralph I. Straus. Washington, 1959.
           [72]p. diagrs., tables.
           Bibliography: p. 67-[72]

           1. Technical assistance programs. 2. In-
        vestments.   I. Straus, Ralph I.

Technical assistance programs.

VF
341.1   U.S. Dept. of State. Bureau of Public
:338   Affairs.
157f   Fact sheet. Wash., Govt. Print. Off.,
1963   1963-
           v.
           Contents:-Burma (Far Eastern series 119;
        Dept. of State pub. 7474)-Cambodia, (Far
        Eastern series 117; Dept. of State pub. 7471)-
        Indonesia (Far Eastern series 121; Dept. of
        State pub. 7267)-Laos (Far Eastern series
        123; Dept. of State pub. 7484)-Malaya (Far
        Eastern series 120; Dept. of State pub. 7475)-
        The   (Cont'd. on next card)

341.1   TECHNICAL ASSISTANCE PROGRAMS.
I338   U.S. PRESIDENT, 1963-1969 (JOHNSON)
P72FO   FOREIGN AID. MESSAGE FROM THE
1967   PRESIDENT OF THE UNITED STATES....
H-D   WASHINGTON, GOVT. PRINT. OFF., 1967.
           10P. (90TH CONGRESS, 1ST SESSION.
        HOUSE OF REPRESENTATIVES. DOCUMENT 55)

           1. TECHNICAL ASSISTANCE PROGRAMS.
           2. U.S. PRESIDENT - MESSAGES.
           I. TITLE.

341.1   Technical assistance programs.
:338
871   U.S. Dept. of State.
           Point four; cooperative program for aid in
        the development of economically under-developed
        areas [prepared by the Dept. of State with
        assistance of an Interdepartmental Advisory
        Committee on Technical Assistance and of the
        staff of the National Advisory Council]
        [Washington, 1949]
           157 p.
           Cover title.
           1.Technical assistance programs. 2.Under-
        developed countrie.

VF
341.1   U.S. Dept. of State. Bureau of Public
:338   Affairs. Fact sheet...(Card 2)
157f
1963

        Phillippines (Far Eastern series 122; Dept.
        of State pub. 7480)-Southeast Asia (Far
        Eastern series 118; Dept. of State
        pub. 7473)-Viet-Nam (Far Eastern series
        116; Dept. of State pub. 7469)

    1. Technical   assistance programs.
(Series)

341.1   TECHNICAL ASSISTANCE PROGRAMS.
:338   U.S. PRESIDENT, 1963-1969 (LYNDON B.
P72FO   JOHNSON)
1965   FOREIGN AID. MESSAGE FROM THE
H-D   PRESIDENT OF THE UNITED STATES...,
        WASHINGTON, GOVT. PRINT. OFF., 1965.
           8P. (89TH CONGRESS, 1ST SESSION.
        HOUSE OF REPRESENTATIVES. DOCUMENT NO.
        53)

           1. TECHNICAL ASSISTANCE PROGRAMS.
           2. U.S. PRESIDENT - MESSAGES.
           I. TITLE.

341.1   Technical assistance programs.
:338
871a   U.S. Dept. of State. Bureau of Public
1962   Affairs.
           An act for international development; a
        program for the decade of development.
        Summary of presentation. Washington, 1961.
           189p. (U.S. Dept. of State. General
        foreign policy series 174)

           U.S. Dept. of State. Publication 174.

           1. Technical assistance programs.

VF
341.1   U.S. Dept. of State. Bureau of Public
:338   Affairs. Fact sheet ...(Card 3)
157f
1963

        Ghana (African series 35; Dept. of State pub.
        7556)-Korea (Far Eastern series 114; Dept. of
        State pub. 7559)-Israel (Near and Middle Eastern
        series 71; Dept. of State pub. 7574)-Jordan
        (Near and Middle Eastern series 73; Dept. of
        State pub. 7591)-Tunisia (African series 39; Dept.
        of State pub. 7589)-Morocco (African series no. 38;
        Dept. of State pub. 7583)-Nigeria (African series
        37; Dept. of State   pub. 7572)-Congo (African
        series 36; Dept.   of State pub. 7571)

341.1   TECHNICAL ASSISTANCE PROGRAMS.
:338   U.S. PRESIDENT, 1963-1969 (LYNDON B
P72FO   JOHNSON)
1966   FOREIGN AID. MESSAGE FROM THE
H-D   PRESIDENT OF THE UNITED STATES...,
        WASHINGTON, GOVT. PRINT. OFF., 1966.
           10P. (89TH CONGRESS, 2D SESSION.
        HOUSE OF REPRESENTATIVES. DOCUMENT NO.
        374)

           1. TECHNICAL ASSISTANCE PROGRAMS.
           2. U.S. PRESIDENT - MESSAGES.
           I. TITLE.

341.1   Technical assistance programs.
:338
871a   U.S. Dept. of State. Bureau of Public
           Affairs.
           An act for international development;
        a program for the decade of development.
        Summary presentation. Washington, 1961.
           189p. (U.S. Dept. of State. General
        foreign policy series 169)

           U.S. Dept. of State. Publication 7205)

           1. Technical assistance programs.
        2. Underdeveloped   countries.

VF
341.1   Technical assistance programs.
:338   U.S. Dept. of State. Bureau of Public
157f   Affairs.
1962   Fact sheet; aid in action. Wash., Govt. Print.
        Off., 1962.
           2 v.   (Analyzed)

           Contents:-Mexico (Inter-American series 76;
        Dept.of State pub. 7310)-Columbia (Inter-Amer-
        ican series 77; Dept. of State pub. 7397)

           1. Technical assistance programs. (Series)

VF
341.1
:338
I57f
1961

U.S. Dept. of State. Bureau of Public
Affairs.
Fact sheet: mutual security in action.
Wash., Govt. Print. Off., 1961.
6 v.

Contents:-Burma (Far Eastern series 109;
Dept. of State pub. 7263)-Jordan (Near and
Middle Eastern series 61; Dept. of State
pub. 7184)-Morocco (African series 17; Dept.
of State pub. 7227)-Nepal (Near and Middle
Eastern series 66; Dept. of State pub. 7273)
(Cont'd. on next card)

VF
341.1
:338
T22

Technical assistance programs.
U.S. Technical Cooperation Administration.
Community Services Staff.
Methods of obtaining community participation
in self-help activities. [Washington] May
1953.
9, 4 p.

Appendix: Introducing and inducing change in
folk practices.
Processed.

1. Technical assistance programs. 2. Community
development.

341.1
:338
(60)
E55

Technical assistance programs - Africa.
Ellender, Allen J
United States foreign operations in Africa.
Washington, Govt. Print. Off., 1962.
803p.

At head of title: 88th Cong., 1st sess.
Senate. Doc. no. 8.

1. Technical assistance programs - Africa.

VF
341.1
:338
I57f
1961

U.S. Dept. of State. Bureau of Public
Affairs. Fact sheet: mutual security
in action...(Card 2)

-Sudan (African series 18; Dept. of State
pub. 7251)-Turkey (Near and Middle Eastern
series 63; Dept. of State pub. 7208)

1. Technical assistance programs.

658.564
(016)
066

U.S. OFFICE OF TECHNICAL SERVICES.
CATALOG OF TECHNICAL REPORTS:
COMPUTERS, 1937-58. WASHINGTON, 1959.
19P.

1. AUTOMATION - BIBLIOGRAPHY.
I. TITLE.

341.1
:338
(60)
N17

Technical assistance programs - Africa.
National Research Council.
Recommendations for strengthening science
and technology in selected areas of Africa,
south of the Sahara. Prepared for the International Cooperation Administration. Wash.,
National Academy of Sciences, National
Research Council, 1959.
[159]p.

1. Technical assistance programs - Africa.
2. Underdeveloped countries. 3. Natural
resources - Africa. I. Title. II. U.S.
International Cooperation Administration.

VF
341.1
:338
S71n

Technical assistance programs.
U.S. Dept. of State. Bureau of Public
Affairs.
A new program for a decade of development
for underdeveloped areas of the world.
Washington, 1961.
40p. (U.S. Dept. of State. General
foreign policy series 165)

U.S. Dept. of State. Publication 7190.

1. Technical assistance programs.
2. Underdeveloped countries.

FILM

Technical assistance programs.
United World Film Corporation.
We build a town. 1956?
16 mm., black and white, sound, 20 min.

Cost: $37.44.

1. Aided self-help housing - India. 2.
Technical assistance programs. I. Title.
3. Films.

330
(60)
UN1

Technical assistance programs - Africa.
United Nations. (Economic Commission for
Africa)
Industrial growth in Africa. New York, 1963.
100p. (United Nations. [Document]
E/CN.14/CNR/1/Rev.1)

1. Economic development - Africa.
2. Technical assistance programs - Africa.
I. Title.

VF
341.1
:338
S71o

Technical assistance programs.
U.S. Dept. of State. Bureau of Public
Affairs.
The organization for economic cooperation
and development, by Dean Rusk. [Washington]
1961.
6p. (Its Series S - no. 1)
Address before the Government-Industry Conference, Washington, D.C., 1961.

1. Technical assistance programs. I. Rusk, Dean.
II. Government Industry Conference, Washington, D. C.,
1961.

VF
341.1
:338
W45

Technical assistance programs.
Wilson, G M
The Colombo plan. London, Central Office of
Information, 1957.
9p.

Lecture delivered in Rome at the invitation of
the Societa Italiana per L'Organizzazione
Internazionale, June 1957.

1. Technical assistance programs. I. Title.
II. U.K. Central Office of Information. (Reference
Division)

341.1
:338
(60)
C65

Technical assistance programs - Africa.
U.S. Congress. House. Committee on Foreign
Affairs.
Report of the Special Study Mission to
Africa, south and east of the Sahara, by Frances
P. Bolton. Washington, Govt. Print. Off., 1956.

At head of title: Committee Print. 84th
Congress, 2d session.

1. Technical assistance programs - Africa.
I. Bolton, Frances P II. Title: Special Study
Mission to Africa, south and east of the
Sahara.

341.1
:338
S71f

Technical assistance programs.
U.S. Dept. of State. Bureau of
Public Affairs.
Foreign aid; facts and fallacies.
Washington, 1961.
52p. ([U.S.] Dept. of State
Publication 7239; General foreign
policy series 176)

1. Technical assistance programs.

VF
341.1
:338
(58)
D62

Technical assistance programs - Afghanistan.
Dodge, J Robert
Reports on specific projects requiring
architectural and engineering services in
Afghanistan. Washington, Housing and Home
Finance Agency, International Housing Service,
May 1957.
1 v.

Submitted to Osborne T. Boyd, Housing
Division, ICA.

(see card 2)

VF
341.1
:338
(60)
S71a

Technical assistance programs - Africa.
U.S. Dept. of State. Bureau of Public
Affairs.
Africa. Rev. Washington, Govt. Print. Off.,
1963.
9p. (U.S. Dept. of State. African series
34; Publication 7540)

Reprinted from a section of The Department of
State 1963.

1. Technical assistance programs - Africa.

341.1
:338
S71h

Technical assistance programs.
U.S. Dept. of State. Bureau of Public
Affairs.
Highlights of President Kennedy's new
act for international development. Washington, 1961.
44p. (U.S. Dept. of State. Publication
no. 7211; General foreign policy series 170)

1. Technical assistance programs. 2. Economic
development. 3. U.S. Agency for
International Development.

VF
341.1
:338
(58)
D62

Technical assistance programs - Afghanistan.
Dodge, J Robert
Reports on... May 1957. (card 3)

International Housing Service. II. U.S.
International Cooperation Administration.
United States of America Operations Mission
to Afghanistan.

341.1
:338
(60)
S71

Technical assistance programs - Africa.
U.S. Dept. of State. Bureau of Public Affairs.
The role of the United States in Africa,
our interests and operations, by James K.
Penfield. Washington, Govt. Print. Off.,
1959.
9p. (Its Publication 6858. Near and
Middle Eastern series 43)

Reprinted from the Department of State
Bulletin of June 8, 1959.

1. Technical assistance programs -
Africa. I. Penfield, James K.

VF
341.1
:338
S71t

Technical assistance programs.
U.S. Dept. of State. Bureau of Public
Affairs.
Technical assistance under the international agencies. Washington, 1951.
13p. (Its Publication 4256) (International
organization and conference series I, 16)

1. Technical assistance programs.

330
(58)
S71
1967

Technical assistance programs - Afghanistan.
U.S. Dept. of State. Bureau of Public
Affairs.
Background notes: Afghanistan. Rev.
Washington, 1967.
7p. (U.S. Dept. of State. Publication
7795)

1. Economic conditions - Afghanistan.
2. Technical assistance programs - Afghanistan.
I. Title.

VF
341.1
:338
(016)
S71
Suppl.
2

Technical assistance programs - Africa.
U.S. Department of State. Division of Library
and Reference Services.
Point four, Near East and Africa; a selected
bibliography of studies on economically underdeveloped countries. Washington, D.C. [Govt.
Print. Off.] Jan. 2, 1951.
136 p. (Its Bibliography no. 56)

Cover title.
Processed.

1. Technical assistance programs-Africa. 2. Technical
assistance programs-Asia I. Series.

Technical assistance programs - Africa.

728.1
(6)
I57
U.S. International Cooperation Admin'stration.
Africa housing team report: summary.
Washington, 1961.
9p.

1. Housing - Africa. 2. Technical assistance programs - Africa.

TECHNICAL ASSISTANCE PROGRAMS -
BIBLIOGRAPHY.

330
(016)
B17
1967
Bronson, Jack
Technology for underdeveloped areas; an annotated bibliography, 1st. ed. Oxford, New York, Pergamon Press, 1967.
81p. (International series of monographs in library and information science, v.6)

1. Underdeveloped countries - Bibl.
2. Technical assistance programs - Bibl.
I. Title.

Technical assistance programs - Ceylon.

330
(548.7)
S71
U.S. Dept. of State. (Public Services Div.)
Background; Ceylon, 1957. Washington, Govt. Print. Off., 1957.
[16]p. illus., maps. (Its Near and Middle Eastern series 21)

1. Economic conditions - Ceylon. 2. Technical assistance programs - Ceylon.

Technical assistance programs - Asia.

341.1
:338
(5)
C65
Conference on Commercial Development Training, Bandarawela, Ceylon, 1959.
Community development training, conference summary, by Jean Ogden. [n.p., 1960]
69p.

1. Technical assistance programs - Asia.
2. Community development - Congresses - Asia.
I. Ogden, Jean.

Technical assistance programs - Bibliography.

341.1
:338
(016)
K17
Katz, Saul M
A selected list of U.S. readings on development. Prepared for the United Nations Conference on the Application of Science and Technology for the Benefit of the Less Developed Areas, by Saul M. Katz and Frank McGowan. Washington, Agency for International Development, 1963.
363p.

1. Technical assistance programs - Bibl. I. McGowan, Frank, Jt. au. II. U.S. Agency for International Development. III. United Nations Conference on the Application of Science and Technology for the Benefit of the Less Developed Areas, Geneva, 1962.

711.4
(83)
F63
Fogle, David P
City planning in Valdivia, the Valdivia city plan. A final report to the United States A.I.D. Mission to Chile and the illustrious city of Valdivia and the Ministry of Public Works' Section of Urban Planning. Valdivia, Chile, 1962.
44p.

1. City planning - Chile. 2. Technical assistance programs - Chile. I. U.S. Agency for International Development.

Technical assistance programs - Asia.

728.1
(5)
UNa
United Nations. (Technical Assistance Program)
Asia and the Far East Seminar on Housing through Non-profit Organizations, Copenhagen, 31 July - 27 August, 1956. New York, 1958.
86p. tables. (ST/TAA/Ser.C/29,ILO/TAP/INT/R.1)

1. Housing - Asia. 2. Technical assistance programs - Asia. I. International Labour Organization.

Technical assistance programs - Bibliography.

711.583
(016)
S62
Sociological Abstracts.
Community development abstracts. Prepared for Agency for International Development. New York, [1964?]
281p.
On cover: Rural and Community Development Service, Office of Technical Cooperation and Research, Dept. of State, Agency for International Development.

1. Community development - Bibl. 2. Technical assistance programs - Bibl. 3. International relations - Bibl. I. U.S. Agency for International Development. II. Title.

TECHNICAL ASSISTANCE PROGRAMS - CHILE.

711.4
(83)
F74
Friedmann, John.
Urban and regional development in Chile; a case study of innovative planning. Santiago, Chile, Ford Foundation Urban and Regional Development Advisory Program in Chile, 1969.
251p.
1. City planning - Chile. 2. Chile - City planning. 3. Technical assistance programs - Chile. 4. Chile - Technical assistance programs. I. Ford Foundation. (Urban and Regional Development Advisory Program in Chile) II. Title.

Technical assistance programs - Asia.

VF
341.1
:338
(5)
S71
U. S. Dept. of State.
The Colombo plan, what it is, how it works. Washington, Govt. Print. Off., 1958.
11p. (Its Publication 6700)

Economic cooperation series 46.

1. Technical assistance programs - Asia. I. Title.

Technical assistance programs - Bibliography.

VF
341.1
:338
(016)
S71
U.S. Department of State. Division of Library and Reference Services.
Point four; a selected bibliography of materials on technical cooperation with foreign governments. Washington, D.C. [Govt. Print. Off.] Nov. 15, 1950.
10 p. (Its Bibliography no. 54)

Cover title.
Processed.

1.Technical assistance programs-Bibl. I.Series.

Technical assistance programs - Chile.

711.4
(83)
N18
Navarrette, Francis G
City planning in Puerto Montt. A final report to the United States A.I.D. Mission to Chile and the Ministry of Public Works' Section of Urban Planning. Puerto Montt, Chile, Publications Service, 1962.
20p.

1. City planning - Chile. 2. U.S. Agency for International Development. 3. Technical assistance programs - Chile.

Technical assistance programs - Asia.

VF
341.1
:338
(016)
S71
Suppl.
3
U.S. Department of State. Division of Library and Reference Services.
Point four, Far East; a selected bibliography of studies on economically underdeveloped countries. Washington, D.C. [Govt. Print. Off.] Jan. 15, 1951.
46 p. (Its Bibliography no. 57)

Cover title.
Processed.

1.Technical assistance programs-Asia. I.Series.

Technical assistance programs - Brazil.

728.1
(81)
I57
U.S. Agency for International Development.
Guanabara housing and urban development program. Report and recommendations by A.I.D. Housing and Urban Development Team, July 1, 1966. Bernard Wagner (team leader) and others. [Washington] 1966.
28p.

1. Housing - Brazil. 2. City planning - Brazil. 3. Technical assistance programs - Brazil. I. Wagner, Bernard. II. U.S. Dept. of Housing and Urban Development. III. Title.

Technical assistance programs - Chile.

352
(83)
N18
Navarrette, Francis G
A study of the Puerto Montt municipal administration. Puerto Montt, Chile, Housing and Planning Div., USAID, 1962.
17p.

1. Municipal government - Chile. 2. Technical assistance programs - Chile. I. U.S. Agency for International Development.

Technical assistance programs - Asia.

VF
341.1
:338
(016)
S71
Suppl.
2.
U.S. Department of State. Division of Library and Reference Services.
Point four, Near East and Africa; a selected bibliography of studies on economically underdeveloped countries. Washington, D.C. [Govt. Print. Off.] Jan. 2, 1951.
136 p. (Its Bibliography no. 56)

Cover title.
Processed.

1.Technical assistance programs-Africa. 2.Technical assistance programs-Asia. I.Series.

Technical assistance programs - Brazil.

VF
341.1
:338
C65
Condliffe, J B
Point four and the world economy. New York, N.Y., Foreign Policy Association, c1950.
62 p. charts. (Headline series, no.79)

Bibliography: p. 62.
Contents.-Point Four: Economic development, by J.B.Condliffe.-Brazil: A case study, by Harold H. Hutcheson.
1.Technical assistance programs. 2.Technical assistance programs - Brazil.
I.Hutcheson, Harold F. II.Ser.

TECHNICAL ASSISTANCE PROGRAMS - CHILE.

728.1
(83)
R61
ROBINSON, HAROLD.
HOUSING; A PROGRAM OF TECHNICAL ASSISTANCE, FINAL REPORT JUNE 1957 - JULY 1959, BY HAROLD ROBINSON, USOM /CHILE. SANTIAGO, 1959.
84P.

APPENDICES: NO.1-60.

1. HOUSING - CHILE. 2. TECHNICAL ASSISTANCE PROGRAMS - CHILE. I. U.S. OPERATIONS MISSION TO CHILE.

Technical assistance programs- Bibliography.

744
(016)
A24
Ackerman, Jean Marie.
Guide to films on international development. Beverly Hills, Calif., Film Sense; Wash., Society for International Development, 1967.
53p.
"Commentaries appeared first in the International development review."
1. Films - Bibl. 2. Economic development - Bibl. 3. Technical assistance programs - Bibl. I. Film Sense. II. Society for International Development. III. Title.

Technical assistance programs - Brazil.

VF
341.1
:338
(81)
C62
U.S. Operations Mission in Brazil.
Point 4 in Brazil, by Howard R. Cottam. Washington, 1959.
18p. (Dept. of State Publication 6741) (Inter-American series 54)
Address delivered by Mr. Cottam before the School of Economic and Administrative Science of the University of Sao Paulo at Sao Paulo, Brazil, August 1958.

1. Technical assistance programs - Brazil.
I. Cottam, Howard

TECHNICAL ASSISTANCE PROGRAMS - CHILE.

341.1
:338
(8)
C653A
1960
H-H
U.S. CONGRESS. HOUSE. COMMITTEE ON FOREIGN AFFAIRS.
AMERICAN REPUBLICS COOPERATION ACT AND OTHER SUBJECTS, HEARINGS, EIGHTY-SIXTH CONGRESS, SECOND SESSION, ON H.R. 13021, A BILL TO PROVIDE FOR ASSISTANCE IN THE DEVELOPMENT OF LATIN AMERICA AND IN THE RECONSTRUCTION OF CHILE. WASHINGTON, GOVT. PRINT. OFF., 1960.
50P.
1. TECHNICAL ASSISTANCE PROGRAMS - LATIN AMERICA. 2. TECHNICAL ASSISTANCE PROGRAMS - CHILE. I. TITLE.

341.1
:338
(8)
C65IN
1961
H-H

TECHNICAL ASSISTANCE PROGRAMS - CHILE.
U.S. CONGRESS. HOUSE. COMMITTEE ON
APPROPRIATIONS.
INTER-AMERICAN PROGRAMS FOR 1961,
DENIAL OF 1962 BUDGET INFORMATION;
INTER-AMERICAN PROGRAM FOR SOCIAL
PROGRESS, CHILEAN RECONSTRUCTION AND
REHABILITATION PROGRAM. HEARINGS BEFORE
THE SUBCOMMITTEE ON THE COMMITTEE ON
APPROPRIATIONS, HOUSE OF
REPRESENTATIVES, EIGHTY-SEVENTH
CONGRESS, FIRST SESSION. WASHINGTON,
GOVT. PRINT. OFF., 1961.
354P.

(CONTINUED ON NEXT CARD)

332.72
(83)
I57r

Technical assistance programs - Chile.
U. S. International Cooperation
Administration. Operations Mission to
Chile.
Report of housing finance team of David L.
Krooth and Arthur H. Courshon. Santiago,
Chile, 1958.
46p.

1. Mortgage finance - Chile. 2. Technical assistance programs - Chile.
I. Krooth, David. L. II. Courshon,
Arthur H.

VF
341.1
:338
(861)
062

Technical assistance programs - Colombia.
U.S. Operations Mission to Colombia.
Point four in Colombia, by Charles P.
Fossum. Washington, 1960.
10p. (U.S. Dept. of State. Inter-American
series 61)

U.S. Dept of State Publication 7071.
Address before the American Society of
Bogota, at Bogota, Colombia, on July 26,
1960.

1. Technical assistance programs - Colombia.
I. Fossum, Charles P.   II. Title. (Series)

341.1
:338
(8)
C65IN
1961
H-H

U.S. CONGRESS. HOUSE. COMMITTEE ON
APPROPRIATIONS. INTER-AMERICAN
PROGRAMS FOR ...1961.   (CARD 2)
1. TECHNICAL ASSISTANCE PROGRAMS -
LATIN AMERICA. 2. TECHNICAL ASSISTANCE
PROGRAMS - CHILE. I. TITLE.

728.1
(83)
062

Technical assistance programs - Chile.
U.S. Operations Mission to Chile.
Housing, a program of technical assistance. Final report, June 1957-July 1959.
Santiago, Chile, 1959.
1v. illus., tables.

Cover title: Chile's solution to a global problem.

1. Housing - Chile. 2. Technical assistance programs - Chile.

VF
341.1
:338
I57f
Colom-
bia
1962

Technical assistance programs - Colombia.
U.S. Dept. of State. Bureau of Public
Affairs.
Fact sheet; aid in action, Colombia. Washington, Govt. Print. Off., 1962.
13p. (U.S. Dept. of State. Publication
no. 7297. Inter-American series 77)

1. Technical assistance programs - Colombia.
I. Title.   (Series)

341.1
:338
(8)
C65I
1961
S-H

TECHNICAL ASSISTANCE PROGRAMS - CHILE.
U.S. CONGRESS. SENATE. COMMITTEE ON
APPROPRIATIONS.
INTER-AMERICAN SOCIAL AND ECONOMIC
COOPERATION PROGRAM AND THE CHILEAN
RECONSTRUCTION AND REHABILITATION
PROGRAM. HEARINGS... EIGHTY-SEVENTH
CONGRESS, FIRST SESSION ON H.R. 6518...
WASHINGTON, GOVT. PRINT. OFF., 1961.
100P.

1. TECHNICAL ASSISTANCE PROGRAMS -
LATIN AMERICA. 2. TECHNICAL ASSISTANCE
PROGRAMS - CHILE. I. TITLE.

341.1
:338
(8)
P72A

TECHNICAL ASSISTANCE PROGRAMS - CHILE.
U.S. PRESIDENT, 1961-1963 (KENNEDY)
APPROPRIATION FOR INTER-AMERICAN FUND
FOR SOCIAL PROGRESS AND REHABILITATION
OF CERTAIN AREAS OF SOUTHERN CHILE;
MESSAGE... WASHINGTON, GOVT. PRINT.
OFF., 1961.
7P. (87TH CONGRESS, 1ST SESSION.
HOUSE OF REPRESENTATIVES. DOCUMENT NO.
105)

1. TECHNICAL ASSISTANCE PROGRAMS -
LATIN AMERICA. 2. TECHNICAL ASSISTANCE
PROGRAMS - CHILE. 3. U.S.
PRESIDENT - MESSAGES.

341.1
:338
N17
1963

Technical assistance programs - Congresses.
National Conference on International
Economic and Social Development,
Washington, D.C. 1963.
Yardsticks for international development.
Highlights of the tenth annual meeting.
Washington, 1963.
35p.

1. Technical assistance programs -
Congresses.   2. Underdeveloped   countries.

341.1
:338
(8)
C65I
1961
S-R

TECHNICAL ASSISTANCE PROGRAMS - CHILE.
U.S. CONGRESS. SENATE. COMMITTEE ON
APPROPRIATIONS.
INTER-AMERICAN SOCIAL AND ECONOMIC
COOPERATION PROGRAM AND THE CHILEAN
RECONSTRUCTION AND REHABILITATION
PROGRAM. WASHINGTON, GOVT. PRINT. OFF.,
1961.
8P. (87TH CONGRESS, 1ST SESSION.
SENATE. REPORT. NO. 201)

1. TECHNICAL ASSISTANCE PROGRAMS -
LATIN AMERICA. 2. TECHNICAL ASSISTANCE
PROGRAMS - CHILE. I. TITLE.

711.14
(83)
V27

Technical assistance programs - Chile.
Vera, Luis.
Agricultural land inventory techniques;
experience of the OAS/Chile aerophoto-
grammetric project. Washington, Pan American
Union, General Secretariat of the Organization
of American States, 1964.
123p.   (Pan American Union. General
Secretariat of the Organization of American
States. Technical manuals, II)

(Continued on next card)

341.1
:338
UNs

Technical assistance programs - Congresses.
United Nations Conference on the Application
of Science and Technology for the Benefit
of the Less Developed Areas, Geneva, 1962.
Science, technology, and development.
United States papers prepared for the United
Nations... Geneva, 1962.
12 v.
Contents:-v. 1. Natural resources; energy, water and
river basin development.-v. 2. Natural resources;
minerals and mining, mapping and geodetic control.-
v. 3. Agriculture.-v. 4. Industrial development.-
v. 5. Transportation.-   v. 6. Health and
nutrition.-v. 7.   Social problems of

(Continued on next card)

341.1
:338
(8)
C653A

TECHNICAL ASSISTANCE PROGRAMS - CHILE.
U.S. CONGRESS. SENATE. COMMITTEE ON
FOREIGN RELATIONS.
AMERICAN REPUBLICS COOPERATION ACT...
REPORT TO ACCOMPANY S. 3861.
WASHINGTON, GOVT. PRINT. OFF., 1960.
5P. (86TH CONGRESS, 2D SESSION.
SENATE. REPORT NO. 1838)

1. TECHNICAL ASSISTANCE PROGRAMS -
LATIN AMERICA. 2. HOUSING - LATIN
AMERICA. 3. TECHNICAL ASSISTANCE
PROGRAMS - CHILE. I. TITLE.

711.14
(83)
V27

Vera, Luis. Agricultural land inventory
techniques... (Card 2)

1. Land use - Chile. 2. Agriculture -
Chile. 3. Economic development - Chile.
4. Technical assistance programs - Chile.
5. Photogrammetry. I. Pan American Union.
II. Title.

341.1
:338
UNs

United Nations Conference on the Application
of Science and Technology for the Benefit
of the Less Developed Areas, Geneva, 1962.
Science, technology, and development...1962.
(Card 2)
development and urbanization.-v. 8. Organizations,
planning, and programming for economic development.-
v. 9. Scientific and technological policy, planning
and organization.-v. 10. International cooperation
and problems of transfer and adaptation.-v. 11.
Human resources. Training of scientific and
technical personnel.-v. 2. Communications.

(Continued on next card)

341.1
:338
C657

TECHNICAL ASSISTANCE PROGRAMS - CHILE.
U.S. CONGRESS. SENATE. COMMITTEE ON
RULES AND ADMINISTRATION.
STUDY OF FOREIGN AID EXPENDITURES.
REPORT TO ACCOMPANY S. RES. 57. GOVT.
PRINT. OFF., 1967.
14P. (90TH CONGRESS, 1ST SESSION.
SENATE. REPORT NO. 44)

1. TECHNICAL ASSISTANCE PROGRAMS.
2. TECHNICAL ASSISTANCE PROGRAMS - CHILE.
I. TITLE: FOREIGN AID EXPENDITURES.

330
(51)
B71b

Technical assistance programs - China.
U.S. Dept. of State. Bureau of Public
Affairs.
Background notes; Republic of China. Rev.
Washington, 1967.
8p. (U.S. Dept. of State. Publication
no. 7791)

1. Economic conditions - China.
2. Technical assistance programs - China.
I. Title.

341.1
:338
UNs

United Nations Conference on the Application
of Science and Technology for the Benefit
of the Less Developed Areas, Geneva, 1962.
Science, technology, and development...1962
(Card 3)

1. Technical assistance programs - Congresses.
2. Sociology, Urban. 3. Community development.
4. Transportation. I. Title: Social problems
of development and   urbanization.

341.1
:338
(83)
G25

TECHNICAL ASSISTANCE PROGRAMS - CHILE.
U.S. GENERAL ACCOUNTING OFFICE.
DEFICIENCIES IN ADMINISTRATION OF THE
EARTHQUAKE RECONSTRUCTION AND
REHABILITATION PROGRAM FOR CHILE; AGENCY
FOR INTERNATIONAL DEVELOPMENT,
DEPARTMENT OF STATE; REPORT TO THE
CONGRESS OF THE UNITED STATES BY THE
COMPTROLLER GENERAL OF THE UNITED
STATES. WASHINGTON, 1964.
2, 72L.

1. TECHNICAL ASSISTANCE PROGRAMS -
CHILE. 2. EARTHQUAKES - CHILE.

728.1
(661)
S15

Technical assistance programs -
Colombia.
Salaun, Yves.
El problema de la vivienda en Colombia.
New York, United Nations, 1956.
81p. ([United Nations. Document]
TAA 173/13/06, TAA/col/1.)

At head of title: Programa de Asistencia
Tecnica.

1. Housing - Colombia. 2. Technical
assistance programs - Colombia. I. United
Nations.

VF
341.1
:338
(7286)
I57

Technical assistance programs - Costa Rica.
U.S. International Cooperation Administration. United States of America Operations Mission to Costa Rica.
El Punto cuatro en accion en Costa Rica.
[San Jose] 195-.
40p. illus.

1. Technical assistance programs - Costa
Rica.

058.7
:341.1
:338
S71

Technical assistance programs - Directory.
U.S. Dept. of State. Office of Public Affairs.
   Guide to technical assistance services of
United States voluntary agencies abroad, 1949-
1951. [Washington, Govt. Print. Off., Apr.
1952]
   114 p. (Its Publication 4422; International
information and cultural series 21)
   Includes Latin America, Africa, Near East,
Far East.
   Processed.

ICA
Library

Technical assistance programs - Greece.
   Munkman, C A
   American aid to Greece. A report on
the first ten years. New York,
Frederick A. Praeger, 1958.
   306p.

   1. Technical assistance programs -
Greece.

670
(595)
I57

Technical assistance programs - Indonesia.
U. S. International Cooperation
   Administration.
   Cottage and small industries in
Indonesia. Washington, 1958.
   23p. illus. (Small industry series.
Cottage industries bulletin no. 4)

   1. Industry - Indonesia. 2. Technical
assistance programs - Indonesia.

728.1
(7293)
C15

Technical assistance programs - Dominican
   Republic.
Callaway, Thomas R
   A housing and urban development program for
the Dominican Republic. Prepared for the
Agency for International Development, by
T.R. Callaway, Div. of International Affairs,
Dept. of Housing and Urban Development, and
Byron R. Hanke, Federal Housing Administra-
tion. Santo Domingo, D.R., 1966.
   18p.

1. Housing - Dominican Republic. 2. Technical
assistance programs - Dominican Republic. 3. Federal housing programs.   I. Hanke, Byron R.
II. U.S. Agency   for International
Development.   III. Title.

728.1
(499)
I57

Technical assistance programs - Greece.

U.S. International Cooperation Administration.
   United States of America Operations Mission
   to Greece.
   The Greek housing situation, by Barton P.
Jenks, Labor Housing Advisor. Athens, 1957.
   66 p.

   "Source materials": p. 65-66.

   1. Housing - Greece. 2. Technical Assistance
programs - Greece. I. Jenks, Barton P

711.4
(55)
G41

Technical assistance programs - Iran.
Gibbs, Leon L
   Plan, City of Shiraz, Fars Ostan, Iran.
Shiraz, Iran, United States Operation Mission,
1960.
   26p.

   1. City planning - Iran. 2. Technical
assistance programs - Iran. I. U.S.
Operations Mission to Iran. II. Title.

341.1
:338
(62)
062

Technical assistance programs - Egypt.
U.S. Operations Mission to Egypt.
   Followup and evaluation study of returned
International Cooperation Administration
participants in Egypt who have received
training in the United States, by John B.
Stabler and E. Theodore Mogannam. Washington, 1957.
   32p.

   Conducted by the United States Operation
Mission to Egypt Training Staff and cooperating USOM/Egypt Technicians during the period
from December 1954 - to October 1956.
   1. Technical assistance   programs - Egypt.
I. Stabler, John B. II. Mogannam, E. Theodore.

972.94
U54

Technical assistance programs - Haiti.
United Nations. Mission of Technical Assistance
   to the Republic of Haiti.
   Mission to Haiti; report.   Lake Success, N.Y.,
July 1949.
   xvii, 327 p.   illus.   maps (2 col. fold. in
pocket), graphs, tables. (U.N. Publications. 1949
IIB. 2.)

   1. Haiti-Econ. condit. 2. Technical assistance pro-
grams-Haiti. I. Title.

VF
341.1
:338
I57f
Iran

Technical assistance programs - Iran.

U.S. International Cooperation Administration.
   Fact sheet, mutual security in action,
Iran. Washington, Govt. Print. Off., 1959.
   folder. (Its Near and Middle Eastern
series 38)

   1. Technical assistance programs - Iran.
(Series)

VF
341.1
:338
I57f
Ethiopia

Technical assistance programs - Ethiopia.
U.S. International Cooperation Administration.
   Fact sheet, mutual security in action,
Ethiopia. Washington, Govt. Print. Off.,
1959.
   folder. (Its Near and Middle Eastern
series 37)

   1. Technical assistance programs - Ethiopia.
(Series)

711.4
(54)
F67

Technical assistance programs - India.

Ford Foundation.
   Drafting a new blueprint for India's
largest urban center; Calcutta metropolitan
plan project. New Delhi, India, 1964.
   24p.   (Program letter 133)

   1. City planning - India. 2. Technical
assistance programs - India. 3. Industrial
location - India. 4. Economic base studies -
India. I. Calcutta, India. Metropolitan
Plan Project.

327
L18

Technical assistance programs (Israel)

Laufer, Leopold.
   Israel and the developing countries: new
approaches to cooperation. New York, Twentieth Century Fund, 1967.
   298p.

   1. International relations. 2. Technical
assistance programs (Israel) 3. Underdeveloped countries. I. Twentieth Century Fund.
II. Title.

330
(4)
C65s

Technical assistance programs - Europe.

U.S. Congress. House. Committee on
   Foreign Affairs.
   Special study mission to Europe. Part II.
A study of European economic regionalism, a
new era in free world economic politics.
Report...of the Committee on Foreign Affairs
pursuant to H. Res. 113, a resolution authorizing the Committee on Foreign Affairs to
conduct thorough studies and investigations
of all matters coming within the jurisdiction
of the Committee. Washington, Govt. Print.
Off., 1960.
    (continued on next card)

341.1
:338
(54 and 59)
c65

Technical assistance programs - India.
U.S. Congress. House. Committee on
   Foreign Affairs.
   Report of the special study mission to
Pakistan, India, Thailand, and Indochina,
pursuant to H.Res. 113. Washington, Govt.
Print. Off., May 12, 1953.
   104 p. graphs, maps, tables. (83d
Congress. House Report no. 412)

   Hon. Chester E. Merrow, Chairman.

728.1
(5694)
R61

Technical assistance programs - Israel.

Robinson, Harold
   Housing: an increasing rather than
decreasing problem; report to the government
of Israel. Tel-Aviv, The United States of
America Operations Mission to Israel, June 1956.
   152p.   plans, tables.

   At head of title: Technical Assistance
Program, USOM Housing Report.

   1. Housing-Israel. I. International Cooperation
Administration. United   States of America
Operations Mission to   Israel. 2. Technical
assistance programs - Israel.

330
(4)
C65s

U.S. Congress. House. Committee on
   Foreign Affairs. Special ... 1960. (card 2)

   176p. (86th Cong., 2d sess. House.
Report no. 1226)

   1. Economic development - Europe.
2. Technical assistance programs - Europe.

728.1
(54)
W13
pt.2

Technical assistance programs - India.
Wegner, Bernard.
   Housing in India. Part II. Observation,
ideas, [and] recommendations. New Delhi,
1964.
   10p.

   1. Housing - India. 2. Technical assistance programs - India. 3. Housing in
the tropics. I. Title.

VF
341.1
:338
I57f
Israel

Technical assistance programs - Israel.
U.S. International Cooperation Administration.
   Fact sheet, mutual security in action:
Israel. Washington, Govt. Print. Off.,
1960.
   folder. (U.S. Dept. of State. Bureau
of Public Affairs. Near and Middle Eastern
Series 51)

   1. Technical assistance programs - Israel. (Series)

690
H68
IME
no.60

Technical assistance programs - Ghana.

U.S. Housing and Home Finance Agency.
   Office of International Housing.
   Village markets in Ghana; a study on the
planning of village markets and stalls. For
use of United States A.I.D. Missions. Washington, 1963.
   42p. (Ideas and methods exchange no. 60)
   At head of title: 302 urbanization and
local community planning and development
community facilities.

   1. Shopping centers. 2. Technical
assistance   programs - Ghana.
I. Title.   II. U.S. Agency for
International   Development. III. Title:
Local community planning and development
community facilities.

341.1
:338
(54 and 59)
c65

Technical assistance programs - Indochina.
U.S. Congress. House. Committee on
   Foreign Affairs.
   Report of the special study mission to
Pakistan, India, Thailand, and Indochina,
pursuant to H.Res. 113. Washington, Govt.
Print. Off., May 12, 1953.
   104 p. graphs, maps, tables. (83d
Congress. House Report no. 412)

   Hon. Chester E. Merrow, Chairman.

341.1
:338
(6668)
C65

TECHNICAL ASSISTANCE PROGRAMS - IVORY COAST.
Colwell, Robert C
   Ivory Coast Republic, Africa: pre-investment
survey, February 10 - March 8, 1971, Abidjan,
Ivory Coast, by Robert C. Colwell and others.
Wash., Agency for International Development,
1971.
   51p.
   At head of title: Report to the Office of
Housing, Agency for International Development.
   Author is Director, Planning-Programming-
Budgeting Staff, Dept. of Housing and Urban
Development.

    (Cont'd on next card)

341.1
:338
(6668)
C65

Colwell, Robert C   Ivory Coast...1971.
(Card 2)

1. Technical assistance programs - Ivory
Coast. 2. Underdeveloped countries.
I. U.S. Agency for International Development.
II. Title.

Technical assistance programs - Latin America.

332.72
(8)
E55

Elliot, Sean M
Financing Latin American housing;
domestic savings mobilization and U.S. assistance
policy. New York, Praeger, 1968.
216p.
Bibliography: p. 207-216.
At head of title: Praeger special studies in
international economics and development.
1. Mortgage finance - Latin America. 2. Mortgage finance - Savings banks. 3. Housing - Latin
America. 4. Technical assistance programs -
Latin America. I.   Title.

341.1
:338
I57o
pt. E

Technical assistance programs - Latin America.
Inter-American Housing and Planning Center.
Cursillo de introduccion institucional.
E. Las investigaciones de CINVA, por Rene
Eyheralde Frias. Edicion preliminar. Bogota,
Colombia, 1958.
12p. (Its Ensenanza 5 E)

1. Technical assistance programs - Latin
America. I. Frias, Rene Eyheralde.

728.1
(6668)
H68

Technical assistance programs - Ivory Coast.
U.S. Housing and Home Finance Agency.
Housing in the Ivory Coast, by Thomas R.
Callaway. For Agency for International
Development. [Washington] 1964.
80p.

1. Housing - Ivory Coast. 2. Technical
assistance programs - Ivory Coast.
I. Callaway, Thomas R. II. U.S. Agency for
International Development.

334
(8)
F68

Technical assistance programs - Latin America.
Foundation for Cooperative Housing, Washington,
D.C.
Ingredients for a successful self sustaining
cooperative housing program; a program. A
study prepared for the Agency for International
Development. Washington, D.C., 1965.
32p.

1. Cooperative housing - Latin America.
2. Mortgage finance - Latin America. 3. Technical
assistance programs - Latin America. I. U.S.
Agency for International Development. II. Title.

341.1
:338
I57o
pt. F

Technical assistance programs - Latin America.
Inter-American Housing and Planning Center.
Cursillo de introduccion institucional.
F. El adiestramiento en el CINVA, por Jorge
A. Videla. Edicion preliminar. Bogota,
Colombia, 1958.
9p. (Its Ensenanza 5-F)

1. Technical assistance programs - Latin
America. I. Videla, Jorge A

728.1
(6668)
H68
1966

Technical assistance programs - Ivory Coast
U.S. Dept. of Housing and Urban Develop-
ment.
Housing in the Ivory Coast, by Thomas R.
Callaway. Washington, U.S. Dept. of
Housing and Urban Development, Div. of
International Affairs, 1966.
53p. (Country report series)
Issued as a service to the Agency for
International Development.

1. Housing - Ivory Coast. 2. Housing in the tropics.
3. Technical assistance programs. I. Callaway,
Thomas R. II. U.S.   Agency for
International Develop-   ment. III. Title.

341.1
:338
(8)
G71

Technical assistance programs - Latin America.
Grace, J Peter.
It is not too late in Latin America: pro-
posals for action now. [n.p. 1962?]
74p.
Bibliography: p. 69-74.

1. Technical assistance programs - Latin
America. 2. Economic conditions - Latin
America. 3. Underdeveloped countries.
I. Title.

341.1
:338
I571

Technical assistance programs - Latin America.
Inter-American Economic and Social Council.
Coordinating Committee on Technical Assistance.
Program of technical cooperation of the
Organization of American States. 1951 -
Washington, Pan American Union, 1951 -
v.

For full information see shelf list card.

1.Technical assistance programs-Latin America.
I.Organization of American States.

VF
341.1
:338
(53)
062

Technical assistance programs - Jordan.
U.S. Operations Mission to Jordan.
Point four in Jordan, by Norman Burns.
Washington, 1960.
12p. (U.S. Dept. of State.
Near and Middle East series 59)

U.S. Dept. of State. Publication 7078.
Text of an address given before the
Chamber of Commerce, Jerusalem on June
14, 1960.
1. Technical assistance programs - Jordan. I. Burns,
Norman. (Series)

332
(8)
I57a
1961/68

TECHNICAL ASSISTANCE PROGRAMS - LATIN AMERICA.
Inter-American Development Bank.
Activities, 1961-1968. Washington [1969?]
144p.

1. Banks and banking - Latin America.
2. Economic development - Latin America.
3. Technical assistance programs - Latin
America.

341.1
:338
K71

TECHNICAL ASSISTANCE PROGRAMS - LATIN
AMERICA.
KRAUSE, WALTER.
THE UNITED STATES AND LATIN AMERICA:
THE ALLIANCE FOR PROGRESS PROGRAM.
AUSTIN, TEX., 1963.
35P. (TEXAS. UNIVERSITY. BUREAU OF
BUSINESS RESEARCH. STUDIES IN
LATIN-AMERICAN BUSINESS)

1. TECHNICAL ASSISTANCE PROGRAMS -
LATIN AMERICA. 2. ECONOMIC DEVELOPMENT
- LATIN AMERICA. I. TITLE.
II. TITLE: ALLIANCE FOR PROGRESS
PROGRAM. III. TEXAS. UNIVERSITY.
BUREAU OF BUSINESS RESEARCH.

728
:333
(8)
C17

TECHNICAL ASSISTANCE PROGRAMS - LATIN
AMERICA.
CARNOY, ALAN.
DEMOCRACIA SI; A WAY TO WIN THE COLD
WAR. FOREWORD BY ANGUS WARD. NEW YORK,
VANTAGE PRESS, 1962.
269P.

1. HOME OWNERSHIP - LATIN AMERICA. 2.
HOUSING - LATIN AMERICA. 3. TECHNICAL
ASSISTANCE PROGRAMS - LATIN AMERICA. I.
TITLE.

341.1
:338
I57c
pt. A

Technical assistance programs - Latin America.
Inter-American Housing and Planning Center.
Cursillo de introduccion institucional.
A. La cooperacion Interamericana en vivienda,
por Cesar Graces Vernaza. Edicion preliminar.
Bogota, Colombia, 1958.
6p. (Its Ensenanza no. 5 A)

1. Technical assistance programs - Latin
America. 2. Housing - Latin America.
I. Graces Vernaza, Cesar.

341.1
:338
(8)
M12

Technical assistance programs - Latin America.
McClellan, John L
Special report on Latin America. United States
activities in Mexico, Panama, Peru, Chile,
Argentina, Brazil, and Venezuela, by Senator
John L. McClellan, Mike Mansfield, and others.
Washington, Govt. Print. Off., 1962.
62p.
At head of title: 87th Cong., 2d sess.
Senate. Document no. 80.

1. Technical assistance programs - Latin America.
I. Mansfield, Mike, jt. au.

330
C31ur

Technical assistance programs - Latin America.
[Chase Manhattan Bank, New York]
Urbanization in Latin America. New York,
Chase Manhattan Bank, Economic Research Div.,
1967.
17p.

1. Economic conditions - Latin America.
2. Technical assistance programs - Latin
America. I. Title.

341.1
:338
I57c
pt. B

Technical assistance programs - Latin America.
Inter-American Housing and Planning Center.
Cursillo de introduccion institucional. B.
La Organizacion de los Estados Americanos y
el Programa de Cooperacion Tecnica, la Union
Panamericana y el CINVA. Edicion preliminar.
Bogota, Colombia, 1958.
29p. (Its Ensenanza 5-B)

1. Technical assistance programs - Latin
America.

341.1
:338
(8)
M15

Technical assistance programs - Latin America.
Mansfield, Mike.
Latin America and United States
policies. Report of Senator Mike
Mansfield on a study mission to Latin
America. Washington, Govt. Print.
Off., 1962.
35p.
At head of title: 85th Cong., 2d sess.
Senate. Document no. 82.

1. Technical assistance programs - Latin
America. I. Title.

341.1
:338
(8)
C65c

Technical assistance programs - Latin America.
Committee for Economic Development.
(Research and Policy Committee)
Cooperation for progress in Latin
America. A statement on national policy.
New York, 1961.
56p.

1. Technical assistance programs - Latin
America. 2. Economic development - Latin
America.

341.1
:338
I57c
pt.D

Technical assistance programs - Latin America.
Inter-American Housing and Planning Center.
Cursillo de introduccion institucional.
D. El intercambio cientifico y documentacion
del CINVA, por Luis Floren. Edicion preliminar. Bogota, Colombia, 1958.
15p. (Its Ensenanza no. 5-D)

1. Technical assistance programs - Latin
America. I. Floren Luis.

341.1
:338
(8)
M67

Technical assistance programs - Latin America.
Mora, Jose A
Social and political progress of the
Alliance; education, health, land, housing,
community development. [Washington] Pan
American Union. Office of the Assistant
Secretary for Cultural, Scientific, and
International Affairs, 1963.
12p. (Pan American Union. Information
series no. 1, 1963)

1. Technical assistance programs - Latin America.
2. Economic development - Latin America. I. Pan
American Union.

Technical assistance programs - Latin America.
341.1 National Planning Association.
:338 Technical cooperation in Latin America.
(8) TC /- - / /Washington, May 1955-June 1956/
N17 _ v. illus., tables.
TC Contents - no. 1. Organization of U.S.
Government for technical cooperation. -no.2
Technical cooperation - sowing the seeds of
progress - no. 3. Role of universities in
technical cooperation. -no.4. Case study of the
agricultural program of Acar in Brazil, by
Arthur T. Moser. -no. 5. Administration of bilateral
technical cooperation. -no.7. Recommendations for
the future. (over)

728.1
S62 Special Conference on International Housing
1966 and Urban Growth, Washington, D.C., 1966.
(Card 2)

La vivienda cooperativa; Nuevas perspecti
vas para solucionar, el problema de la habitacion en America Latina.

1.Cooperative housing-Latin America.
2. Technical assistance programs-Latin America.
I. Foundation for Cooperative Housing, Wash.,
D.C.

TECHNICAL ASSISTANCE PROGRAMS - LATIN
341.1 AMERICA.
:338 U.S. CONGRESS. HOUSE. COMMITTEE ON
(8) FOREIGN AFFAIRS.
C653A AMERICAN REPUBLICS COOPERATION ACT AND
1960 OTHER SUBJECTS, HEARINGS, EIGHTY-SIXTH
H-H CONGRESS, SECOND SESSION, ON H.R.
13021, A BILL TO PROVIDE FOR ASSISTANCE
IN THE DEVELOPMENT OF LATIN AMERICA AND
IN THE RECONSTRUCTION OF CHILE.
WASHINGTON, GOVT. PRINT. OFF., 1960.
50P.

1. TECHNICAL ASSISTANCE PROGRAMS -
LATIN AMERICA. 2. TECHNICAL ASSISTANCE
PROGRAMS - CHIL E. I. TITLE.

Technical assistance programs - Latin America.
341.1
073 Organization of American States.
Informe anual de Secretario General al
Consejo de la Organizacion
Washington, Union Panamericana,
v. annual. (Documentos officiales
de la OEA)

For complete information see shelflist.

1. International organizations. 2. Technical
assistance programs - Latin America.

Technical assistance programs - Latin
341.1 America.
:338 Spector, Paul.
(8) Communication and motivation in community
S62 development: an experiment, by Paul Spector
and others. Report of Phase 1, submitted
to the Agency for International Development.
Washington, Dept. of State, Agency for
International Development, 1963.
114p.

1. Technical assistance programs - Latin
America. 2. Community development - Latin
America. I. U.S. Agency for
International Development.

TECHNICAL ASSISTANCE PROGRAMS - LATIN
341.1 AMERICA.
:338 U.S. CONGRESS. HOUSE. COMMITTEE ON
(8) FOREIGN AFFAIRS.
C653P PROVIDING FOR ASSISTANCE IN THE
DEVELOPMENT OF LATIN AMERICA AND IN THE
RECONSTRUCTION OF CHILE... REPORT TO
ACCOMPANY H.R. 13021. WASHINGTON,
GOVT. PRINT. OFF., 1960.
8P. (86TH CONGRESS, 2D SESSION.
HOUSE. REPORT NO. 2163)

1. TECHNICAL ASSISTANCE PROGRAMS -
LATIN AMERICA. 2. HOUSING - LATIN
AMERICA. 3. H OUSING - CHILE.

Technical assistance programs - Latin
341.1 America.
:338 Pan American Union. (Dept. of Public
(8) Information.)
P15 Provisional listing of Alliance for
Progress projects. Prepared by the Dept.
of Public Information, Pan American Union,
Organization of American States. Washington,
1963.
72p.

1. Technical assistance programs -
Latin America. I. Alliance for
Progress.

Technical assistance programs - Latin America.
330
(8) U.S. Agency for International Development.
A32 Latin American growth trends; seven years
of the Alliance for Progress. Washington,
1968.
64p.

1. Economic development - Latin America.
2. Technical assistance programs - Latin
America. I. Title: Alliance for Progress.
II. Title.

TECHNICAL ASSISTANCE PROGRAMS - LATIN
330 AMERICA.
(8) U.S. CONGRESS. HOUSE. COMMITTEE ON
C651S FOREIGN AFFAIRS.
SPECIAL STUDY MISSION TO LATIN AMERICA:
PERU, ECUADOR, COLOMBIA, PANAMA, COSTA
RICA. REPORT OF SPECIAL STUDY MISSION,
COMPRISING ARMISTEAD I. SELDEN, JR.,
CHAIRMAN AND OTHERS. PURSUANT TO H.
RES. 60, EIGHTY-SEVENTH CONGRESS.
WASHINGTON, GOVT. PRINT. OFF., 1963.
66P. (88TH CONGRESS, 1ST SESSION.
HOUSE. REPORT NO. 223)

1. ECONOMIC D EVELOPMENT - LATIN
AMERICA. 2. T ECHNICAL ASSISTANCE
(CONTINUED ON NEXT CARD)

Technical assistance programs - Latin America.
341.1
:338 Pan American Union.
(8) Provisional listing of Alliance for
P15 Progress projects, supplement no. 1-
Suppl. 1963-

Washington, Alliance for Progress Information
Team, 1963-
v.

At head of title: Alliance for Progress.
Special report.
(Cont'd. on next card)

Technical assistance programs - Latin America.
341.1
:338 U.S. Agency for International Development.
(8) Report prepared by the Government of the
157 United States of America for the Inter-American
Committee on the Alliance for Progress and the
4th annual meetings of the Inter-American
Economic and Social Council. Wash., 1966.
58p.

1. Technical assistance programs - Latin
America. 2. Economic development - Latin
America. 3. International relations.
I. Title: Alliance for Progress. II. Inter-
American Economic and Social Council.

U.S. CONGRESS. HOUSE. COMMITTEE ON
330 FOREIGN AFFAIRS. SPECIAL STUDY
(8) MISSION ...1963. (CARD 2)
C651S

PROGRAMS - LATIN AMERICA. I. SELDEN,
ARMISTEAD I., JR.

341.1
:338 Pan American Union. Provisional listing
(8) of Alliance of ... (Card 2)
P15
Suppl. Issue no. 1- 1963- prepared by
the Alliance for Progress Information
Special Program Team, Pan American Union,
Organization of American States.

For complete information see shelflist.

1. Technical assistance programs - Latin America.
I. Organization of American States.

TECHNICAL ASSISTANCE PROGRAMS - LATIN
341.1 AMERICAN.
:338 U.S. AGENCY FOR INTERNATIONAL
(8) DEVELOPMENT.
A32S SAMPLE AGREEMENTS FOR HOUSING GUARANTY
PROGRAM. WASHINGTON, 1963.
1 V.

1. TECHNICAL ASSISTANCE PROGRAMS -
LATIN AMERICAN. 2. MORTGAGE FINANCE -
FORMS. I. TITLE.

Technical assistance programs - Latin America.
341.1
:338 U.S. Congress. House. Committee on
(8) Government Operations.
C65u United States aid operations in Latin
America. Hearings before a subcommittee of
the Committee on Government Operations,
House of Representatives, Eighty-seventh
Congress, first session. Washington,
Govt. Print. Off., 1963.
305p.
Hearings held Nov. 27-Dec. 11, 1961.

1. Technical assistance programs - Latin
America. I. Title.

Technical assistance programs - Latin America.
330
(8) Revista Vision.
R28 Conferencia Economica de la OEA. Buenos
Aires, 1957.
16p.

Serie de articulos editados por la
Revista Vision.

1. Economic development-Latin America.
2. Technical assistance programs - Latin
America. I. Organization of American
States.

TECHNICAL ASSISTANCE PROGRAMS - LATIN
341.1 AMERICA.
:338 U.S. CONGRESS. HOUSE. COMMITTEE ON
(8) APPROPRIATIONS.
C65IN INTER-AMERICAN PROGRAMS FOR 1961,
1961 DENIAL OF 1962 BUDGET INFORMATION:
H-H INTER-AMERICAN PROGRAM FOR SOCIAL
PROGRESS, CHILEAN RECONSTRUCTION AND
REHABILITATION PROGRAM. HEARINGS BEFORE
THE SUBCOMMITTEE ON THE COMMITTEE ON
APPROPRIATIONS, HOUSE OF
REPRESENTATIVES, EIGHTY-SEVENTH
CONGRESS, FIRST SESSION. WASHINGTON,
GOVT. PRINT. OFF., 1961.
354P.

(CONTINUED ON NEXT CARD)

TECHNICAL ASSISTANCE PROGRAMS - LATIN
341.1 AMERICA.
:338 U.S. CONGRESS. SENATE. COMMITTEE ON
(8) APPROPRIATIONS.
C65I INTER-AMERICAN SOCIAL AND ECONOMIC
1961 COOPERATION PROGRAM AND THE CHILEAN
S-H RECONSTRUCTION AND REHABILITATION
PROGRAM. HEARINGS... EIGHTY-SEVENTH
CONGRESS, FIRST SESSION ON H.R. 6518...
WASHINGTON, GOVT. PRINT. OFF., 1961.
100P.

1. TECHNICAL ASSISTANCE PROGRAMS -
LATIN AMERICA. 2. TECHNICAL ASSISTANCE
PROGRAMS - CHIL E. I. TITLE.

Technical assistance programs-Latin America.
728.1
S62 Special Conference on International Housing
1966 and Urban Growth, Washington, D.C., 1966.
[The Conference] Washington, Foundation
for Cooperative Housing, 1966.
Kit. (12 pieces)
Partial Contents: Un programe: componentes
para el exito de un programe autosuficiente
de viviendas cooperativas.--Construion,
investment guaranties, training will high-
light FCH program: emphasis on building in
country institutions.--Cooperativas de
viviendas.-- An international program for
cooperative housing.
(Cont'd on next card)

341.1 U.S. CONGRESS. HOUSE. COMMITTEE ON
:338 APPROPRIATIONS. INTER-AMERICAN
(8) PROGRAMS FOR ...1961. (CARD 2)
C65IN 1. TECHNICAL ASSISTANCE PROGRAMS -
1961 LATIN AMERICA. 2. TECHNICAL ASSISTANCE
H-H PROGRAMS - CHILE. I. TITLE.

TECHNICAL ASSISTANCE PROGRAMS - LATIN
341.1 AMERICA.
:338 U.S. CONGRESS. SENATE. COMMITTEE ON
(8) APPROPRIATIONS.
C65I INTER-AMERICAN SOCIAL AND ECONOMIC
1961 COOPERATION PROGRAM AND THE CHILEAN
S-R RECONSTRUCTION AND REHABILITATION
PROGRAM. WASHINGTON, GOVT. PRINT. OFF.,
1961.
8P. (87TH CONGRESS, 1ST SESSION.
SENATE. REPORT. NO. 201)

1. TECHNICAL ASSISTANCE PROGRAMS -
LATIN AMERICA. 2. TECHNICAL ASSISTANCE
PROGRAMS - CHIL E. I. TITLE.

Technical assistance programs - Latin America.

341.1
:338
(8)
C 65
1960
S-H

U.S. Congress. Senate. Committee on
Foreign Relations.
American republics cooperation act and other
subjects. Hearings before the Committee on
Foreign Relations, United States Senate, Eighty-
sixth Congress, second session on S. 3839, a
bill to provide for assistance in the development of Latin America and in the reconstruction
of Chile, and for other purposes. Washington,
Govt. Print. Off., 1960.
91p.

1. Technical assistance programs - Latin America.
I. Title.

Technical assistance programs - Latin America.

VF
341.1
:338
(016)
S71
Suppl.1

U.S. Department of State, Division of Library
and Reference Services.
Point four, Latin America and European
dependencies in the Western Hemisphere; a
selected bibliography of studies on economically
underdeveloped countries. Washington [Govt.
Print. Off.] Dec. 1950.
110 p. (Its Bibliography no. 55)

Processed.

Technical assistance programs - Mexico.

VF
341.1
:338
157f
Mexico.
1962

U.S. Dept. of State. Bureau of Public Affairs.
Fact sheet aid in action, Mexico. Washington,
Govt. Print. Off., 1962.
13p. (Dept. of State. Inter-American
series 76)

Dept. of State. Publication no. 7310.

1. Technical assistance programs - Mexico.

TECHNICAL ASSISTANCE PROGRAMS - LATIN
AMERICA.

341.1
:338
(8)
C653A

U.S. CONGRESS. SENATE. COMMITTEE ON
FOREIGN RELATIONS.
AMERICAN REPUBLICS COOPERATION ACT...
REPORT TO ACCOMPANY S. 3861.
WASHINGTON, GOVT. PRINT. OFF., 1960.
5P. (86TH CONGRESS, 2D SESSION.
SENATE. REPORT NO. 1838)

1. TECHNICAL ASSISTANCE PROGRAMS -
LATIN AMERICA. 2. HOUSING - LATIN
AMERICA. 3. TECHNICAL ASSISTANCE
PROGRAMS - CHILE. I. TITLE.

Technical assistance programs - Latin
America.

341.1
:338
(8)
P72

U.S. President, 1963-   (Johnson)
Freedom, peace and progress for the
Americas. [Washington] Organization of
American States, Pan American Union, General
Secretariat, Office of the Assistant Secre-
tary for Cultural, Scientific and Infor-
mational Affairs, Ideological and Political
March of the Alliance for Progress, 1963.
10p. (Pan American Union. Information
series no. 3, 1963)

(Cont'd. on next card)

Technical assistance programs - Middle East.

341.1
:338
(56)
UN

United Nations. (Dept. of Economic and
Social Affairs. Div. for Public
Administration)
Administrative problems of rapid urban
growth in the Arab States. Report of a
United Nations workshop held at Beirut,
Lebanon 11 to 22 March 1963. New York,
United Nations, 1964.
153p. (United Nations [Document]
ST/TAO/M/21)

(Cont'd. on next card)

TECHNICAL ASSISTANCE PROGRAMS - LATIN
AMERICA.

341.1
:338
(8)
C65L

U.S. CONGRESS. SENATE. COMMITTEE ON
FOREIGN RELATIONS.
LATIN AMERICAN SUMMIT CONFERENCE.
HEARINGS... NINETIETH CONGRESS, FIRST
SESSION ON S.J. RES. 53... MARCH 17 AND
21, 1967. WASHINGTON, GOVT. PRINT.
OFF., 1967.
161P.

HEARINGS HELD MARCH 17 AND 21, 1967.
1. TECHNICAL ASSISTANCE PROGRAMS -
LATIN AMERICA. 2. INTERNATIONAL
RELATIONS. I. TITLE.

341.1
:338
(8)
P72

U.S. President, 1963-   (Johnson)
Freedom, peace and progress ... (Card 2)

1. Technical assistance programs - Latin
America. I. U.S. President - Messages.
I. Organization of American States.

341.1
:338
(56)
UN

United Nations. (Dept. of Economic and
Social Affairs. Div. for Public
Administration)   Administrative
problems ...   (Card 2)

At head of title: United Nations
Technical Assistance Programme.

1. Technical assistance programs -
Middle East. 2. City growth - Middle
East. I. Title.

Technical assistance programs - Latin America.

728.1
(8)
468p
1965

U.S. Housing and Home Finance Agency.
Office of International Housing.
Proposed minimum standards for permanent
low-cost housing and for the improvement of
existing substandard areas. Prepared for the
Agency for International Development (PASA no.
60-65) Rev. Washington, 1965.
90p.

1. Low-income housing - Latin America.
2. Technical assistance programs - Latin
America. 3.   Family income and
expenditure -   Housing - Latin
America. I.   U.S. Agency for
International   Development.

TECHNICAL ASSISTANCE PROGRAMS - LATIN
AMERICA.

330
(8)
P72

U.S. PRESIDENT, 1963-1969 (JOHNSON)
LATIN AMERICAN SUMMIT CONFERENCE.
MESSAGE FROM THE PRESIDENT OF THE UNITED
STATES... MARCH 13, 1967. WASHINGTON,
GOVT. PRINT. OFF., 1967.
7P. (90TH CONGRESS, 1ST SESSION.
HOUSE. DOCUMENT NO. 84)

1. ECONOMIC DEVELOPMENT - LATIN AMERICA.
2. TECHNICAL ASSISTANCE PROGRAMS - LATIN
AMERICA. 3. U.S. PRESIDENT - MESSAGES.
I. TITLE.

Technical assistance programs - Middle East.

330
(56)
S71

U.S. Dept. of State. (Public Services Div.)
Background; a look at the Middle East:
Washington, Govt. Print. Off., 1958.
16p. illus., maps. (Its Near and Middle
Eastern series 24)

This Backgrounder except for minor editorial
changes is the text of a speech delivered by
Deputy Under Secretary of State, Robert Murphy,
on March 14, 1957.

1. Economic conditions - Middle East. 2. Technical assistance   programs - Middle East.

TECHNICAL ASSISTANCE PROGRAMS - LATIN
AMERICA.

341.1
:338
(8)
P72A

U.S. PRESIDENT, 1961-1963 (KENNEDY)
APPROPRIATION FOR INTER-AMERICAN FUND
FOR SOCIAL PROGRESS AND REHABILITATION
OF CERTAIN AREAS OF SOUTHERN CHILE,
MESSAGE... WASHINGTON, GOVT. PRINT.
OFF., 1961.
7P. (87TH CONGRESS, 1ST SESSION.
HOUSE OF REPRESENTATIVES. DOCUMENT NO.
105)

1. TECHNICAL ASSISTANCE PROGRAMS -
LATIN AMERICA. 2. TECHNICAL ASSISTANCE
PROGRAMS - CHILE. 3. U.S.
PRESIDENT - MESSAGES.

Technical assistance programs - Latin
America - Bibliography.

341.1
:338
(8)
P15p

Pan American Union. (Columbus Memorial
Library)
Provisional guide to writings on the
Alliance for Progress. Revision 1.
Washington, Alliance for Progress In-
formation Team, Pan American Union, 1964.
11p. (Special report)

Originally prepared by the Columbus
Memorial Library and the Alliance for
Progress Information Team.

1. Technical assistance   programs - Latin
America - Bibl.   I. Alliance for
Progress.

Technical assistance programs - Pakistan.

330
(549)
F67

Ford Foundation.
Design for Pakistan. A report on
assistance to the Pakistan Planning
Commission by the Ford Foundation and
Harvard University. New York, 1965.
36p.

1. Economic planning - Pakistan. 2. Technical
assistance programs - Pakistan. I. Harvard
University.   II. Title.

Technical assistance programs - Latin
America.

VF
341.1
:338
(8)
S71

U.S. Dept. of State. Bureau of Public
Affairs.
The American Republics in partnership.
75 years of international cooperation...
[Commemorating the 75th anniversary of the
Inter-American system] Washington, Govt.
Print. Off., 1965.
15p. (U.S. Dept. of State. Publication
no. 7833. Inter-American series 91)
1. Technical assistance programs - Latin
America. 2. International relations.
I. Title.

Technical assistance programs - Lebanon.

341.1
:338
(5694)
1575l

U.S. International Cooperation Administration.
United States of America. Operations Mission
to Lebanon.
Lebanon. Progress report, 1956/57-
Beirut, Lebanon, Lebanon American Embassy.
v. illus.

Report year ends June 30.

For complete information see shelflist.

1. Technical assistance programs - Lebanon.
2. Economic development - Lebanon.

Technical assistance programs - Pakistan.

334
(549)
P14

Pakistan. Planning Commission.
(Physical Planning and Housing Section)
Housing through non-profit organizations.
Karachi, Trade and Industry House, 1965.
134p. (Study no. P.P. & H. 23)

1. Cooperatives - Pakistan. 2. Technical
assistance programs - Pakistan. I. Title.

Technical assistance programs - Latin America.

VF
327
S71o

U.S. Dept. of State.
Our southern partners, the story of our
Latin American relations. Washington, 1954.
48p. illus., maps. (Its Inter-American
series no. 49)

1. International relations. 2. Technical
assistance programs - Latin America.

Technical assistance programs - Liberia

690
(666)
A55

Annis, Fred V
Government building activities in Liberia,
1954-1956; completion report. [Monrovia?
Nov. 1956]
76 p. illus., maps.
Part of the United States Operations Mission
to Liberia.

1. Building construction - Liberia. 2. Technical assistance programs - Liberia. I. U.S. International Cooperation Administration. United States of America Operations Mission to Liberia.

Technical assistance programs - Pakistan.

341.1
:338
(54 and 59)
c65

U.S. Congress. House. Committee on
Foreign Affairs.
Report of the special study mission to
Pakistan, India, Thailand, and Indochina,
pursuant to H.Res. 113. Washington, Govt.
Print. Off., May 12, 1953.
104 p. graphs, maps, tables. (83d
Congress. House Report no. 412)

Hon. Chester E. Merrow, Chairman.

Technical assistance programs - Panama.

VF
728.1
(862)
A55
Alliance for Progress.
Program for change; Panama City, Colon,
Santiago, Panama. [Washington] [1967?]
Folder.

1. Housing - Panama. 2. Technical assistance
programs - Panama.

Technical assistance programs - South
and Southeast Asia.

341.1
:338
(548.7)
C65c
Colombo. Colombo Plan Bureau.
The Colombo Plan story; 10 years
of progress, 1951-1961. [n.p.]
1961.
44p.

1. Technical assistance programs -
South and Southeast Asia. I. Title.

Technical assistance programs - Sudan.

330
(662)
871
U.S. Dept. of State. (Public Services
Div.)
Background; the Sudan Middle East bridge
to Africa. Washington, Govt. Print. Off.,
1958.
20p. illus. (Its Near and Middle Eastern
series 28)

1. Economic conditions - Sudan. 2. Technical assistance programs - Sudan. I.Title.
The Sudan, Middle East bridge to Africa.

341.1
:338
C653H
TECHNICAL ASSISTANCE PROGRAMS - PANAMA.
U.S. CONGRESS. HOUSE. COMMITTEE ON
FOREIGN AFFAIRS.
THE HOUSING INVESTMENT GUARANTY
PROGRAM AND THE ECONOMIC AID PROGRAM IN
PANAMA. REPORT OF THE STAFF SURVEY TEAM
OF THE SUBCOMMITTEE FOR REVIEW OF THE
MUTUAL SECURITY PROGRAMS. WASHINGTON,
GOVT. PRINT. OFF., 1963.
24P. (88TH CONGRESS, 1ST SESSION.
COMMITTEE PRINT.)
1. TECHNICAL ASSISTANCE PROGRAMS -
PANAMA. 2. HOUSING - PANAMA. 3. U.S.
AGENCY FOR INTERNATIONAL DEVELOPMENT.

341.1
:338
(548.7)
065
Technical assistance programs - South
and Southeast Asia.
Colombo. Bureau for Technical Cooperation.
Colombo Plan Information Unit.
Change in Asia: the Colombo Plan, 1956.
Ceylon. [1957]
71 p. illus.

1. Technical assistance programs - South
and Southeast Asia. II.Title: Colombo
Plan 1956.

341.1
:338
(529)
M65
Technical assistance programs - Taiwan.
Montgomery, John D
Rural improvement and political develop-
ment: JCRR [Sino-American Joint Commission
on Rural Reconstruction] model, by John D
Montgomery and others. Wash., Comparative
Administration Group, American Society for
Public Administration, 1966.
39p. (American Society for Public
Administration. Papers in comparative
public administration. Special series:
no. 7)

(Cont'd on next card)

Technical assistance programs - Peru.

341.1
:338
(85)
F68
Foundation for Cooperative Housing.
Community action for better neighborhoods.
Prepared for the Agency for International
Development. Washington, 1967.
66p.

1. Technical assistance programs - Peru.
2. Community development - Citizen participation. 3. Community facilities - Peru.
I. U.S. Agency for International Development. II. Title.

341.1
:338
(5)
871b
Technical assistance programs - South Asia.
U.S. Dept. of State. Bureau of Public
Affairs.
Background: the subcontinent of South Asia.
Afghanistan, Ceylon, India, Nepal, Pakistan.
Washington, Govt. Print. Off., 1959.
72p. illus., maps. (Its Near and Middle
Eastern series 41)

1. Economic development - South Asia.
2. Technical assistance programs - South
Asia.

341.1
:338
(529)
M65
Montgomery, John D. Rural improvement
and political development...1966
(Card 2)

1. Technical assistance programs - Taiwan.
2. Rural planning - Taiwan.
3. Agriculture - Taiwan. I. Sino-American
Joint Commission on Rural Reconstruction.
II. American Society for Public Administration. III. Title.

Technical assistance programs - Peru.

341.1
:338
(85)
065u
H-R
U.S. Congress. House. Committee on
Government Operations.
United States aid operations in Peru.
Fourth report by the Committee on Govern-
ment Operations. Washington, Govt. Print.
Off., 1961.
39p. (87th Cong., 1st sess. House.
Report no. 795)

1. Technical assistance programs - Peru.

Technical assistance program - Southeast Asia.

330
(5)
S71
U.S. Dept. of State. Bureau of Public
Affairs.
Background, Southeast Asia, area of
challenge, change, and progress. Washington, Govt. Print. Off., 1959.
15p. illus. (Its Far Eastern series
82)

1. Economic conditions - Southeast Asia.
2. Technical assistance program - Southeast
Asia. (Series)

Technical assistance programs - Thailand.

VF
711.4
(593)
C85
Cullers, Samuel J
Final report. Contract between the
Government of Thailand and Samuel J. Cullers.
Bangkok, Thailand, Ministry of Interior,
1961.
20p.

1. City planning - Thailand. 2. Technical
assistance programs - Thailand. I. Thailand.
Ministry of Interior.

Technical assistance programs - Peru.

341.1
:338
(85)
C65u
U.S. Congress. House. Committee on
Government Operations.
United States aid operations in Peru.
Hearings before a subcommittee of the
Committee on Government Operations, House
of Representatives, Eighty-seventh Congress,
first session. Washington, 1961.
488p.
Hearings held Nov. 14, 1960, Mar.-May 1961.

1. Technical assistance
programs - Peru.

Technical assistance programs - Southeast Asia.

VF
341.1
:338
I57f
Southeast
Asia
1963
U.S. Dept. of State. Bureau of Public Affairs.
Fact sheet aid in action, Southeast Asia.
Washington, Govt. Print. Off., 1963.
[16]p. (Dept. of State. Far Eastern Series
118)

Dept. of State. Publication no. 7473.

1. Technical assistance programs -
Southeast Asia.

341.1
:338
(593)
I57
Technical assistance programs - Thailand.
International Bank for Reconstruction and
Development.
A public development program for Thailand.
Report of a Mission organized by the Inter-
national Bank for Reconstruction and De-
velopment at the request of the Government
of Thailand. Baltimore, Johns Hopkins
Press, 1959.
301. maps, tables.

1. Technical assistance programs - Thailand. 2. Economic development -
Thailand.

Technical assistance programs - Puerto Rico.

341.1
:338
(7295)
J63
Johnson, Byron L
Remarks by Special Assistant to the
Assistant Administrator for Latin America,
agency for International Development, Dept.
of State; before a meeting of directors of
ACTION, Inc., Feb. 1962, San Juan, Puerto
Rico. New York, ACTION, inc., The National
Council for Good Cities, 1962.
4p.

1. Technical assistance programs -
Puerto Rico.

341.1
:338
(46)
S61
Technical assistance programs - Spain.
Spanish Building Materials and Standardi-
zation Study Team.
First report on observations to the
Housing and Home Finance Agency and the
International Cooperation Administration.
[Washington] 1958.
1v.

Period covers: January 28, 1957 - March
13, 1958.

1. Technical assistance programs - Spain. 2. International relations.   I. U.S.
International   Cooperation
Administration.   II. U.S. Housing
and Home Finance   Agency.

711.4
(593)
L47
1960
Technical assistance programs - Thailand.
Litchfield Whiting Bowne and Associates.
Greater Bangkok plan, 2533. [In cooperation
with] the City Planning Consultants, Adams,
Howard and Greeley of Cambridge, Massachusetts
[and Thailand, Ministry of Interior] New York,
1960.
210p.
"Support and advice of the United States
Operations Mission to Thailand..."

1. Master plan - Thailand. 2. Technical assistance
programs - Thailand.   I. Adams, Howard and
Greeley, Cambridge,   Mass. II. Thailand.
Ministry of Interior.

Technical assistance programs - South America.

330
(8)
C651e
U.S. Congress. Joint Economic Committee.
Economic policies and programs in South
America [by] Subcommittee on Inter-American
Economic Relationships of the Joint Economic
Committee, Congress of the United States.
Washington, Govt. Print. Off., 1962.
123p.

At head of title: 87th Cong., 2d sess.

1. Economic policy - Latin America.
2. Technical assistance programs - South
America.

International
Cooperation
Administration
Technical assistance programs - Spanish
America.
Glick, Philip M
The administration of technical
assistance; growth in the Americas.
Chicago, University of Chicago Press,
1957.
390p. tables. (National Planning
Association. Studies of technical co-
operation in Latin America)

Bibliographical footnotes.

1. Technical assistance programs -
Spanish America. I.Title.

341.1
:338
(54 and 59)
c65
Technical assistance programs - Thailand.
U.S. Congress. House. Committee on
Foreign Affairs.
Report of the special study mission to
Pakistan, India, Thailand, and Indochina,
pursuant to H.Res. 113. Washington, Govt.
Print. Off., May 12, 1953.
104 p. graphs, maps, tables. (83d
Congress. House Report no. 412)

Hon. Chester E. Merrow, Chairman.

Technical assistance programs - Thailand.

VF
341.1 U.S. Dept. of State. Bureau of Public
:338   Affairs.
S71ec   Economic assistance and progress in Thailand, by U. Alexis Johnson. Washington, Govt. Print. Off., 1960.
          11p. (Dept. of State. Far Eastern series 95)

1. Technical assistance programs - Thailand.
I. Johnson, U. Alexis.   (Series)

Technical assistance programs (France)

341.1 France. Embassy. U.S. (Press and
:338   Information Div.)
F71   Cultural and technical cooperation.
Suppl. Supplement to France aid and cooperation.
        New York, 1965.
          47p.

1. Technical assistance programs (France)
I. Title. II. Title: France aid and cooperation.

Technical assistance programs (U.K.)

330   U.K. British Information Services.
U54br   (Reference Division)
          Britain and economic development overseas. New York, 1960.
          32p. (I.D. 1349)

1. Technical assistance programs (U.K.) 2. Underdeveloped countries.

Technical assistance programs - Tunisia.

VF
341.1 U.S. International Cooperation Administration.
:338   Fact sheet; mutual security in action,
I57t   Tunisia. Washington, Govt. Print. Off.,
Tunisia 1959.
          folder. (Its Near and Middle Eastern series no. 33)

1. Technical Assistance programs - Tunisia.   (Series)

Technical assistance programs (France)

341.1 France. Embassy. U.S. (Press and
:338   Information Div.)
F71   France aid and cooperation. New York, 1962.
          56p.

1. Technical assistance programs (France)
2. Underdeveloped countries.

Technical assistance programs (U.K.)

341.1 U.K. Central Office of Information.
:338   Reference Div.
U54c   Community development. London, H.M.S.O., 1966.
          40p. (U.K. Central Office of Information Reference pamphlet 76)
          At head of title: Britain and the developing countries.
          Bibliography: p. 40

1. Technical assistance programs (U.K.)
2. Underdeveloped countries. I. Title.
II. Title: Britain and the developing countries.

341.1 Technical assistance programs - Tunisia.
:338
(611)   U.S. Operations Mission to Tunisia.
062   United States aid program to Tunisia.
          [Washington] 1960.
          1v. tables.

1. Technical assistance programs - Tunisia.

---

330   TECHNICAL ASSISTANCE PROGRAMS (GERMANY)
(016)   Entwicklungsländer-Studien. Bd. 1-
E57   Bonn, Deutsche Stiftung für Entwicklungsländer, 1966-
          v.

INDEXES:
Vols. 1-3, 1966. ov.

1. Economic development - Bibl.
2. Underdeveloped countries - Bibl.
3. Technical assistance programs (Germany)
I. Deutsche Stiftung für Entwicklungsländer.

Technical assistance programs (U.K.)

330   U.K. British Information Services.
U54e   (Reference Division)
          Economic development in the United Kingdom dependencies. Rev. New York, 1959.
          48p. (I.D. 1243 rev.)

1. Economic development. 2. Technical assistance programs (U.K.)

Technical assistance programs - Turkey.

330   U.S. Dept. of State. Bureau of Public
(56)   Affairs.
S71b   Background notes: Turkey. Rev. Washington, 1967.
          4p. (U.S. Dept. of State. Publication no. 7850)

1. Economic conditions - Turkey. 2. Technical assistance programs - Turkey.
I. Title.

Technical assistance programs (Israel)

341.1 Israel Institute of Applied Social
:338   Research.
(5694)   Evaluation survey of Israel participants in the aid training program.
I 77   Sponsored by the Technical Assistance Dept. of the Prime Minister's Office, and the United States Agency for International Development. Jerusalem, 1962.
          65p.

1. Technical assistance programs (Israel)
I. U.S. Agency for International Development.

Technical assistance programs (U.K.)

VF
341.1 U.K. British Information Services.
:338   Fact sheets on the Colombo plan. New
U54fa   York, 1958-
          v.

For complete information see shelflist.

1. Technical assistance programs (U.K.)
I. Title: The Colombo plan.

341.1 Technical assistance programs - Vietnam.
:338   Scigliano, Robert.
(59)   Technical assistance in Vietnam; the Michigan State University experience, by Robert
824   Scigliano and Guy H. Fox. New York, Praeger, 1965.
          78p. (Praeger special studies in international economics and development)
          Bibliography: p. 73-78.
          1. Technical assistance programs - Vietnam.
2. Economic development - Vietnam. I. Fox, Guy H., jt. au. II. Michigan State University.
III. Title.

Technical assistance programs - Union of South Africa.

VF
352   American Embassy, Pretoria.
(68)   Views of editors of non-white publications on recent unrest in Natal, on the
A52   Government's "Bantustan" scheme, and on U.S. programs in Africa. Pretoria, 1959.
          [3]p. (American Embassy, Pretoria. Foreign service dispatch no. 91, 1959)

"Official use only."

1. Federal government - Union of South Africa.
2. Technical assistance programs - Union of South Africa. (Series: American Embassy, Pretoria. Foreign service dispatch no. 91, 1959)

Technical assistance programs (U.K.)

341.1 U.K. British Information Services.
:338   Investment in progress, Britain's
U54i   contribution to overseas development,
1958   by Duncan Crow. London, 1958.
          40p.

Partial contents: The Columbo plan.

1. Technical assistance programs (U.K.) 2. Underdeveloped countries. I. Crow, Duncan. II. Title: The Columbo plan.

Technical assistance programs (France)

341.1 Caisse Centrale de Cooperation Economique.
:338   Les operations du F.A.C., [Fonds d'Aide et
(44)   de Coopération] du F.I.D.E.S. [Fonds d'Investissement pour le Développement Economique
C14   et Social des Territoires d'Outre-Mer] du F.I.D.O.M. [Le Fonds d'Investissement des Départements d'Outre-Mer] et de la Caisse Centrale de Cooperation Economique en 1961.
        2d ed. Paris, 1962.
          1v.

1. Technical assistance programs (France)

Technical assistance programs (USSR)

341.1 Committee for Economic Development.
:338   The new role of the Soviets in the world
C65n   economy. A supplementary paper of the Committee for Economic Development, by Michael Sapir.
        Washington, 1958.
          64p. illus., tables. (Its Supplementary paper no. 5)

1. Technical assistance programs (USSR)
2. Underdeveloped countries. I. Sapir, Michael.
(Series)

Technical assistance programs (U.K.)

341.1 U.K. British Information Services.
:338   Investment in progress, Britain's contribution to overseas development, by Duncan
U54i   Crow. London, 1960.
1960   40p. illus.

Partial contents:- The Colombo plan.

1. Technical assistance programs (U.K.) 2. Underdeveloped countries. I. Crow, Duncan. II. Title: The Colombo plan.

Technical assistance programs (France)

690   Fédération Nationale du Batiment et des
(44)   Activitiés Annexes.
F22r   Rapport des missions de productivité du batiment de France aux Etats-Unis. Paris, [1951?]
          285p.

1. Building industry - France. 2. Housing - France. 3. Technical assistance programs - France.

Technical assistance programs (USSR)

341.1 U.S. Dept. of State.
:338   The Sino-Soviet economic offensive in the less
S71s   developed countries. Washington, Govt. Print. Off., 1958.
          111p. illus., tables. (Its Publication no.6632) (European and British Commonwealth series 51)

1. Technical assistance programs (USSR)
2. Underdeveloped countries. I. Title.

Technical assistance programs (U.K.)

341.1 U.K. British Information Services.
:338   (Reference Division)
(41)   Political development in the United
U54p   Kingdom dependencies. Rev. New York, 1959.
1959   28p. (I.D. 1286)

1. Technical assistance programs (U.K.) 2. Underdeveloped countries.

Technical assistance programs (UK)

341.1
:338
(41)
U54p
U.K. British Information Services. (Reference Division)
Political development in the United Kingdom dependencies. New York, 1958.
28p. map.

1. Technical assistance programs (UK)
2. Underdeveloped countries.

Technical assistance programs (U.K.) - Africa.

VF
341.1
:338
(60)
U54
U.K. British Information Services. (Reference Division)
British colonial policy and achievement in Africa. New York, 1959.
12p. (Its I.D. 1321)

1. Technical assistance programs (U.K.) - Africa. I. Title.

Technical assistance programs (UN)

341.1
:338
UNr
United Nations Conference on the Application of Science and Technology for the Benefit of the Less Developed Areas.
Report of the Secretary-General, 19

Geneva, 19
v. (United Nations. [Document]

At head of title: United Nations. Economic and Social Council. Session   Agenda item

For complete   information see shelflist.   (Cont'd on next card)

Technical assistance programs (U.K.)

341.1
:338
(41)
U54p
1961
U.K. British Information Services. (Reference Div.)
Political development in the United Kingdom dependencies. Rev. New York, 1961.
26p. (I.D. 1286 (rev.))

1. Technical assistance programs (U.K.)
2. Underdeveloped countries.

Technical assistance programs (U. K.) - Africa.

341.1
:338
(60)
U54r
U.K. British Information Services.
Regional co-operation in British East Africa. New York, 1959.
13p. map, tables. (Its I.D. 1337)

1. Technical assistance programs (U.K.) - Africa. I. Title.

341.1
:338
UNr
United Nations Conference on the Application of Science and Technology... (Card 2)

1. Technical assistance programs (UN) I. United Nations. (Economic and Social Council)

Technical assistance programs (U.K.)

341.1
:338
U54r
no.3
U.K. British Information Services. (Economics Div.)
Technical assistance. Facts on Britain's aid to less developed countries, no. 3. New York, 1963.
9p. (Reference papers no. 3; ID 1446-3)

1. Technical assistance programs (U.K.)
2. Underdeveloped countries.

Technical assistance programs (U. K.) - Africa.

VF
341.1
:338
(60)
U54u
U.K. British Information Services.
United Kingdom aid to Africa. New York, 1959.
7p. tables.

1. Technical assistance programs (U.K.) - Africa.

Technical assistance programs (U.N.)

VF
341.1
:338
S38
Shuster, George N
The task of peaceful cooperation. Remarks by chairman of the U.S. delegation before the 55th meeting of the Executive Board of the United Nations Educational, Scientific and Cultural Organization. [Washington] 1959.
3p.
Reprinted from the Dept. of State Bulletin, Jan. 1960.
1. Technical assistance programs (U.N.) I. United Nations   Educational, Scientific and Cultural   Organizations.

Technical assistance programs (U.K.)

341.1
:338
(41)
U54un
U.K. British Information Services.
The U.K. dependencies in brief. Rev. New York,
v. map, tables.

For complete information see shelflist.

1. Technical assistance programs (U.K.) 2. British Commonwealth of Nations.

Technical assistance programs (U.K.) - South and South East Asia.

341.1
:338
U54r
no.4
U.K. British Information Services. (Economics Div.)
The Colombo plan for South and South East Asia. Facts on Britain's aid to less developed countries, no. 4. New York, 1963.
5p. (Reference paper no. 4; ID1446-4)

1. Technical assistance programs (U.K) - South and South East Asia. 2. Underdeveloped countries. I. Title.

Technical assistance programs (UN)

341.1
:338
UNun
United Nations. (Economic and Social Council)
United Nations development decade: activities of the United Nations and related agencies in the immediate future. Note by the Secretary-General. [Geneva] 1963.
189p. (United Nations [Document] E/3776)
At head of title: Thirty-sixth session agenda item 6(a)

1. Technical assistance programs (UN) 2. United Nations.

Technical assistance programs (U.K.)

341.1
:338
(41)
U54uni
U.K. British Information Services.
The United Kingdom dependencies 1957-58—
Swindon, Eng., 1958—
nos. tables.

For complete information see shelflist.

1. Technical assistance programs (U.K.)
2. British Commonwealth of Nations.

Technical assistance programs (UN)

341.1
:338
UNc
No. 1
United Nations. (Bureau of Social Affairs)
Current activities of the United Nations, its regional economic commissions and the specialized agencies in the fields of housing, building and planning. First report. Geneva, 1957.
[44]p.

1. Technical assistance programs (UN) 2. Housing.

Technical assistance programs (UN) - Asia.

711.417
R23
1960
Regional Seminar on Public Administration Problems of New and Rapidly Growing Towns in Asia, New Delhi, India, 1960.
Public administration problems of new and rapidly growing towns in Asia. Co-sponsored by the United Nations [and others] with the co-operation of the Indian Institute of Public Administration. New York, United Nations, 1962.
90p. (United Nations. [Document] ST/TAO/M/181)

(Cont'd on next card)

Technical assistance programs (U.K.)

696.1
U54s
no.3
pt.6
U.K. Ministry of Housing and Local Government.
Service cores in high flats; cold water services. London, H.M. Stat. Off., 1965.
40p. (Its Design bulletin 3, pt. 6)

1. Plumbing. I. Title: Cold water services.

Technical assistance programs (U.N.)

341.1
:338
UNe
United Nations. (Economic and Social Council, Technical Assistance Committee)
Expanded programme of technical assistance. New York,
v. tables. (E/TAC/—)

For complete information see shelf list.

1. Technical assistance programs (U.N.)

Technical assistance programs (UN) - Asia.

711.417
R23
1960
Regional Seminar on Public Administration Problems of New and Rapidly Growing Towns in Asia, New Delhi, India, 1960.   Public administration...   (Card 2)

At head of title: United Nations technical assistance programme.

1. New towns - Congresses. 2. Technical assistance programs (UN) - Asia. 3. Community development - Asia. I. United Nations. II. Indian   Institute of Public Administration.

Technical assistance programs (U. K.) - South and Southeast Asia.

341.1
:338
(5487)
U54
pt. 1
U.K. British Information Services.
The Colombo plan. I. Britain's part. London [1962]
32p.

1. Technical assistance programs (U. K.) - South and Southeast Asia. 2. Underdeveloped countries. I. Title.

Technical assistance programs (UN)

341.1
:338
UNc
no. 2
United Nations. (Bureau of Social Affairs)
Housing, building and planning; current activities of the United Nations, its regional economic commissions and the specialized agencies. Bangkok, Thailand, 1958.
[41]p. (E/CN.11/I&NR/HBWP.5/L.6)
Economic Commission for Asia and the Far East. Working paper no. 2.
Second report on Current activities in housing, building and planning of the United Nations.
1. Technical assistance programs (UN) 2. Housing.

Technical assistance programs (U.N.) - Latin America.

341.1
:338
(8)
A57
Anstee, M J
Los programas de cooperacion y asistencia tecnica de las N.U. Bogota, Centro Interamericano de Vivienda y Planeamiento, Servicio de Intercambio Cientifico y Documentacion, 1958.
18p. (Publicaciones del CINVA. Serie: Resumenes de clase, no. 9)

1. Technical assistance programs (U.N.) - Latin America. I. Inter-American Housing and Planning   Center. II. Title.

727.1
(8)
S25
1964

Technical assistance programs (UN) - Latin America.
Seminario Sobre la Situación de las Construcciónes Escolares en America Latina, Mexico, D.F., 1964.
Informe final. Mexico, D.F., 1964.
36p.

At head of title: Centro Regional de Construcciónes Escolares para America Latina.

1. Schools - Latin America. 2. Technical assistance programs (UN) - Latin America. I. Centro Regional de Construcciónes Escolares para America Latina.

VF
341.1
:338
T22

U.S. Technical Cooperation Administration. (Community Services Staff.)
Methods of obtaining community participation in self-help activities. [Washington] May 1953.
9, 4 p.

Appendix: Introducing and inducing change in folk practices.
Processed.

1. Technical assistance programs. 2. Community development.

711.417
(54)
G15a

U. S. Technical Cooperation Administration.
Adams, Howard and Greeley.
Report on a revised plan for the town and region of Gandhidham, Kutch, India. Prepared for the Government of India Ministry of Transport and the United States Department of State, Technical Cooperation Administration ... in collaboration with the Office of the Administrator, United States Housing and Home Finance Agency. [Boston, Mass.] Aug. 1952.
51 l.   map (fold)

1. New towns-India-Gandhidham. I. India. Ministry of Transport. II.U. Technical Cooperation Administration. Il d. Housing and Home Finance Agency. Office of the Administrator.

534.83
S23te

Technical background for noise abatement in HUD's operating programs.
Schultz, Theodore J
Technical background for noise abatement in HUD's operating programs. Cambridge, Mass., Bolt, Beranek and Newman, 1971.
210p. (Rept. no. 2005R)
Bibliography: p. 179-210.
Prepared for U.S. Dept. of Housing and Urban Development, under Contract no. H-1228. Revised under Contract no. H-1498.
1. Noise. I. U.S. Dept. of Housing and Urban Development. II. Bolt, Beranek and Newman. III. Title.

VF
728
:551.5
L22
8pan.

U.S. Technical Cooperation Administration.
Lee, Douglas H   K
Objetivos fisiologicos en la construccion de viviendas en climas calidos. Mexico, Centro Regional de Ayuda Tecnica, 1959.
84p. illus., diagrs., tables.

Translation of Physiological objectives in hot weather housing.

1. Architecture and climate. I. U.S. Housing and Home Finance Agency. Office of the

(Continued on next card)

VF
35
(016)
T22

U.S. Technical Cooperation Administration.
Selected bibliography for public administration representatives. [Washington?] Rev. July 1953.
39 p.

Processed.

1. Public administration - Bibliography.

VF
728
:551.5
L22
8pan.

Lee, Douglas H   K   Objetivos fisiolo-gicos en la ... (Card 2)

Administrator. International Housing Advisory Service. II. U.S. Institute of Inter-American Affairs. III. U.S. Technical Cooperation Administration. IV. Title: Hot weather housing, physiological objectives of.

691
I55

U.S. Technical Cooperation Administration.
Illinois Institute of Technology. Armour Research Foundation.
Survey on construction materials demonstration and training center. Final report to Technical Cooperation Administration, Dept. of State. Chicago, 1951.
245p. illus., maps, tables.

1. Building materials. I. Title. II. U.S. Technical Cooperation Administration.

728.1
:333.63
N17R

TECHNICAL BULLETIN.
NATIONAL ASSOCIATION OF HOME BUILDERS.
RENTAL HOUSING SERVICE, 1957-1959.
WASHINGTON, 1957-1959.
1 V. (LOOSELEAF) IRREGULAR.

CONTENTS.- INFORMATION BULLETINS, NO. 1, JULY 1957- NO. 13, OCTOBER 29, 1959.- TECHNICAL BULLETIN, NO. 1, JULY 1957- NO. 10, AUGUST 1959.
LAST BULLETIN PUBLISHED: OCTOBER 1959.
1. RENTAL HOUSING. I. TITLE.
II. TITLE: I NFORMATION BULLETIN.
III. TITLE: TECHNICAL BULLETIN.

VF
728
:551.5
L22

U.S. Technical Cooperation Administration.
Lee, Douglas H   K
Physiological objectives in hot weather housing; an introduction to the principles of hot weather housing design. Prepared ... under a contract with the U.S. Department of State, Technical Cooperation Administration, Institute of Inter-American Affairs. Published by the United States of America, Housing and Home Finance Agency, Office of the Administrator, International Housing Activities Staff. Washington [Govt. Print. Off.] June 1953.
xi, 79 p.   illus., graphs, maps, tables.
(Continued on next card)

728.1
(7286)
E76

U. S. Technical Cooperation Administration.
Espino, Rafaela
La vivienda en Costa Rica. Housing in Costa Rica. Prepared by Rafaela Espino and Leonard Currie. Cambridge, Mass., The Architects Collaborative, Nov. 1951.
xiv, 104 p. illus.

Spanish and English.
Contract between T.C.A., H.H.F.A., and F.S.A., and The Architects Collaborative for the Government of Costa Rica.
(Continued on next card)

690.015
H68
TB

Technical bulletins.
U.S. Housing and Home Finance Agency. Office of the Administrator. Division of Housing Research.
Technical bulletins, no. 1-17.
Washington, Nov. 1947 - June 1951.
17 pts.

Preceded by U.S. National Housing Agency. O.A. Technical Division. Technical bulletins.
690.015 N17 TB

Lee, Douglas H   K   Physiological objectives in hot weather housing ... June 1953. (Card 2)

Bibliography: p. 78-79.

1. Architecture and climate. I.U.S. Housing and Home Finance Agency. Office of the Administrator. International Housing Activities Staff. II.U.S. Institute of Inter-American Affairs. III.U.S. Technical Cooperation Administration. IV.Title. V.Title: Hot weather housing, Physiological objectives in.

Espino, Rafaela   La vivienda en Costa Rica....
1951. (Card 2)

Bibliography: p. [105]
Processed.

1. Housing-Costa Rica. I. Currie, Leonard, jt. au. II. The Architects Collaborative. III. U.S. Technical Cooperation Administration. IV. U.S. Housing and Home Finance Agency. Office of the Administrator. International Housing Activities Office. V. U.S. Federal Security Agency.

330
(8)
C65

U.S. Technical Cooperation Administration.
Columbia Federal Savings and Loan Association.
Capital formation in Latin America; a statement of needs, proposed methods and uses for improving the economic development; submitted ... to the Technical Cooperation Administration of the Department of State, U.S.A. [Washington] Dec. 1951.
2 v.
"The report was planned and written by Ormond E. Loomis with the assistance of Bion H. Francis."
Bibliography: Part IX, 8 p.

(over)

63
:33
C65

U.S. Technical Cooperation Administration.
Conference on World Land Tenure Problems, 1951.
[Report of the Conference held] at the University of Wisconsin, Madison, Wisconsin, U.S.A., October 8 to November 20, 1951.
Madison, Wis., 1951.
v.

Sponsors: The University of Wisconsin, the Economic Cooperation Administration, the Technical Cooperation Administration, United States Department of State, the United States Department
(continued on next card)

VF
341.1
:338
(8)
N17
TC

Technical cooperation in Latin America.
National Planning Association.
Technical cooperation in Latin America.
TC 1-5,7 [Washington , May 1955-June 1956]
6 v. illus., tables.
Contents - no. 1. Organization of U.S. Government for technical cooperation.-no.2. Technical cooperation - sowing the seeds of progress - no.3. Role of universities in technical cooperation. -no.4. Case study of the agricultural program of Acar in Brazil, by Arthur T. Moser. -no. 5 Administration of bilateral technical cooperation.-no.7. Recommendations for the future.

728.1
(62)
L47

U.S. Technical Cooperation Administration.
Little (Arthur D.) inc.
Demonstration of stabilized mud brick in Egyptian village housing. Washington, Technical Aids Branch, Office of Industrial Resources, International Cooperation Administration, [195-?]
58p.
Cover title.
"Prepared for the Technical Cooperation Administration."
1. Housing - Egypt. 2. Earth wall construction.
I. U.S. Technical Cooperation Administration.

Conference on World Land Tenure Problems, 1951.
[Report ...] ... 1951. (Card 2)

of Agriculture.
Contents.-Pt.1.Papers.-Pt.2.Papers.-Pt.4.Handbook of references.
1. Land reform. 2. Population. 3. Economic conditions 4. Cooperatives. I. Wisconsin. University. II.U.S. Economic Cooperation Administration. III.U.S. Technical Cooperation Administration. IV.U.S. Dept of State. V.U.S. Dept. of Agriculture.

697.942
W15

TECHNICAL DATA ON HUMIDIFICATION.
WALTON LABORATORIES, INC.
TECHNICAL DATA ON HUMIDIFICATION.
IRVINGTON, N.J., N.D.
1 V. (VARIOUS PAGINGS)

1. HUMIDITY. I. TITLE.

697
(03)
L45
Technical dictionary of heating, ventilation,
    Sanitary engineering.
Lindeke, Wolfgang, ed.
    Technical dictionary of heating, ventilation,
sanitary engineering, edited by Wolfgang Lindeke
and others. Oxford, Pergamon Press, 1970.
    182p.

    1. Heating - Dictionaries. 2. Ventilation -
Dictionaries. 3. Sanitation - Dictionaries.
I. Title.

727.1
(68)
S68T
TECHNICAL HIGH SCHOOLS.
SOUTH AFRICAN COUNCIL FOR SCIENTIFIC AND
INDUSTRIAL RESEARCH.
    TECHNICAL HIGH SCHOOLS. PRETORIA,
1964.
    67P. (SCHOOL BUILDINGS SERIES REPORT
NO. 21)

    1. SCHOOLS - UNION OF SOUTH AFRICA.
2. ARCHITECTURE. I. TITLE.

328
L41t
Technical information for Congress.
U.S. Library of Congress. Legislative
    Reference Service.
    Technical information for Congress. Report to
the Subcommittee on Science, Research, and Devel-
opment of the Committee on Science and Astronau-
tics, U.S. House of Representatives, Ninety-first
Congress, first session. Prepared by the Science
Policy Research Division, Legislative Reference
Service, Library of Congress. Wash., Govt.
Print. Off., 1969.
    521p.
    At head of title: 91st Cong., 1st sess.
House. Document   no. 91-137.
        (Cont'd on next card)

620
A52t
Technical Division handbook.
American Society of Civil Engineers.
    Technical Division handbook, 19

    New York, 19
    v.

    For Library holdings see main entry.

    1. Engineering. 2. Building societies.
I. Title.

720
T36
Technical illustration.
Thomas, T   A
    Technical illustration. 2d ed. New York,
McGraw-Hill, 1968.
    203p.

    1. Architectural drawing. I. Title.

328
L41t
U.S. Library of Congress. Legislative
    Reference Service.   Technical...1969.
        (Card 2)

    1. U.S. Congress. 2. Documentation.
I. U.S. Congress. House. Committee on Science
and Astronautics. II. Title.

690
(415)
S95
Technical documentation for the building
    industry.
Symposium on Technical Documentation
    for the Building Industry, Dublin, 1967.
    Technical documentation for the
building industry, sponsored by An
Foras Forbartha Teoranta, the National
Institute for Physical Planning and
Construction Research. Edited by: Pierce
T. Pigott and Lindsay N. Johnston. Dublin,
National Institute for Physical Planning
and Construction Research, 1967.
    306p.
    A project for the Government of Ireland
assisted by   the United Nations
Special Fund   and the United Nations.
    (Cont'd on next card)

600.15
U54c
Technical information and service act.
    U. S. *Congress. Senate. Committee on Expenditures in the
Executive Departments.*
    Technical information and services act. Hearings before the
Committee on Expenditures in the Executive Departments,
United States Senate, Eightieth Congress, first session, on S.
498, a bill to provide for the coordination of agencies dissemi-
nating technological and scientific information, and for the
more efficient and orderly administration of a program to make
the discoveries of engineers, inventors, scientists, and technicians more readily available to American industry and business,

        (Continued on next card)
            47-31888*
    [8]

728.3
T22
TECHNICAL JOURNALS, LTD., WESTMINSTER,
ENG.
    HOUSES FOR WORKERS. WESTMINSTER, 1917.
135P.

    1. HOUSE PLANS. I. TITLE.

690
(415)
S95
Symposium on Technical Documentation for
    the Building Industry, Dublin, 1967.
    Technical...1967.   (Card 2)

    1. Building industry - Ireland.
2. Building documentation. I. Pigott,
Pierce T., ed. II. Ireland (Eire)
National Institute for Physical
Planning and Construction Research.
III. United Nations. IV. Title.

600.15
U54c
Technical information and service act.
    U. S. *Congress. Senate. Committee on Expenditures in the
Executive Departments.*   Technical information and
services act. Hearings ... (Card 2)
and for other purposes. May 19, 20, 21, 22, 23, and 28, 1947.
Washington, U. S. Govt. Print. Off., 1947.
    iv, 241 p. 24 cm.
    George D. Aiken, chairman.

    1. Research, Industrial. 2. Research—U. S. 3. Science and state—
U. S. I. Title.

    T176.A5 1947   507   47-31888*
    Library of Congress   [8]

026
M12t
Technical libraries in cooperative programs.
McGraw-Hill Technical Writing Service.
    Technical libraries in cooperative
programs. Washington, D.C. International
Cooperation Administration, Office of
Industrial Resources, Technical Aids Branch,
1960.
    97p.
    Under contract with the U.S. Dept. of Com-
merce, Office of Technical Services.
    1. Libraries. I. U.S. Dept. of Commerce. Office
of Technical Services. II. U.S. International
Cooperation Administra-   tion. III. Title.

378
H17
Technical education in the junior college;
    new programs for new jobs.
Harris, Norman C
    Technical education in the junior college;
new programs for new jobs. Wash., American
Association of Junior Colleges, 1964.
    102p.

    Bibliography: p. 93-102.

    1. Universities and colleges.
2. Vocational guidance. 3. Occupations.
I. American Association of Junior Colleges.
II. Title.

658.564
T42
TECHNICAL INFORMATION CENTER
    ADMINISTRATION.
TICA CONFERENCE, DREXEL INSTITUTE OF
    TECHNOLOGY, 1964.
    TECHNICAL INFORMATION CENTER
ADMINISTRATION. EDITED BY ARTHUR W.
ELIAS. WASHINGTON, SPARTAN BOOKS,
1964.
    171P. (DREXEL INSTITUTE SCIENCE
SERIES)

    SPONSORED BY THE DREXEL INSTITUTE OF
TECHNOLOGY, INFORMATION SCIENCE DEPT.

    1. AUTOMATI ON. 2. MANAGEMENT -
AUTOMATION.   I. ELIAS, ARTHUR W.,
        (CONTINUED ON NEXT CARD)

331
(747)
N28t
Technical manpower in New York State.
New York (State) Dept. of Labor.
    Technical manpower in New York State.
In cooperation with the State Education Dept.,
State University of New York. [Albany]
1964.
    2 v. (Its Div. of Research and Statistics
special bulletin 239)
Suppl. ------ Supplement v.1, A-B. 1967-

    1. Labor supply - New York (State)
2. Occupations - New York (State)
3. Employment - New York (State) I. New
York (State)   University. II.
Title.

658
F17m
Technical field operations.
Farkas, L   L
    Management of technical field operations.
New York, McGraw-Hill, 1970.
    265p.

    1. Management. I. Title. II. Title:
Technical field operations.

658.564
T42
TICA CONFERENCE, DREXEL INSTITUTE OF
    TECHNOLOGY, 1964. TECHNICAL
    INFORMATION ...1964.   (CARD 2)

    ED. II. DREXEL INSTITUTE OF
TECHNOLOGY. INFORMATION SCIENCE DEPT.
III. TITLE.

362.6
I308
I57
TECHNICAL MATERIALS FOR AN INTERVIEW
    SURVEY OF THE AGING.
ILLINOIS. UNIVERSITY. SMALL HOMES
    COUNCIL-BUILDING RESEARCH COUNCIL.
    TECHNICAL MATERIALS FOR AN INTERVIEW
SURVEY OF THE AGING, BY BERNARD
PHILLIPS. URBANA, 1962.
    94P. (ITS RESEARCH REPORT 62-3)

    1. OLD AGE - SURVEYS. I. PHILLIPS,
BERNARD. II. TITLE. III. TITLE: AN
INTERVIEW SURVEY OF THE AGING.

362.6
W34t
Technical guide for community and State.
White House Conference on Aging, Wash., 1971.
    Technical guide for community and State;
White House Conferences on Aging; a guide
designed for the use of State units on aging
and community committees charged with responsi-
bility for organizing and conducting White House
Conferences on Aging at these levels. Wash.,
1970.
    47p.

    1. Old age. I. Title.

711.33
A52
A technical information exchange on State
    and metropolitan planning.
American Institute of Planners.
    A technical information exchange on
State and metropolitan planning. Final
report. Wash., 1969.
    40p.
    Bibliography: Appx. H.
    U.S. Dept. of Housing and Urban
Development. Urban Planning Research and
Demonstration Project.
    1. State planning. 2. Metropolitan area
planning. I. U.S. HUD-UPRDP. II. Title.

699.83
T22
Technical Meeting Concerning Wind Loads on
    Buildings and Structures, National Bureau
of Standards, 1969.
    Proceedings. R.D. Marshall and H.C.S. Thom,
editors. Wash., National Bureau of Standards,
1970.
    164p. (Building science series 30)

    1. Buildings - Wind stresses. I. U.S.
National Bureau of Standards. II. Marshall,
R.D., ed. III. Thom, H.C.S., ed.
IV. Title: Wind   loads on buildings and
structures.

690.22
377t Technical notes on brick and tile construction.
Structural Clay Products Institute.
Technical notes on brick and tile construction.
v.1, no.1, 1950-
v. Monthly. Notebook.

An up-to-date notebook contains a broken sequence
of volumes and numbers. Old issues are discarded
as they are superseded by new and revised material
on the same subject published in later issues.

SEE SERIAL RECORD

---

285 TECHNICAL PLANNING ASSOCIATES,
WINCHESTER, CONN. TOWN PLANNING AND
ZONING COMMISSION.
WINCHESTER, CONNECTICUT NEIGHBORHOOD
ANALYSIS. B, TECHNICAL PLANNING
ASSOCIATES. WINCHESTER, 1969. 49P. (HUD
701 REPORT)

1. NEIGHBORHOOD PLANNING - WINCHESTER,
CONN. I. TECHNICAL PLANNING ASSOCIATES.
II. HUD. 701. WINCHESTER, CONN.

711.4
(7439) Technical Planning Associates. The compre-
B25 hensive plan... 1959. (Card 2)
appen-
dix
Vermont economics study by Wm. N. Kinnard, Jr.
U.S. Urban Renewal Administration,
Urban Planning Assistance Program.

1. Master plan - Bellows Falls, Vt. I.
Bellows Falls, Vt. Planning Commission.
II. U.S. URA-UPAP. Bellows Falls, Vt.

699.85
T22 TECHNICAL OPERATIONS RESEARCH.
THE EFFECT OF INTERIOR PARTITIONS ON
THE DOSE RATE IN A MULTISTORY
WINDOWLESS BUILDING, BY ALBERT W.
STARBIRD AND OTHERS. BURLINGTON,
MASS., 1963.
54P. (ITS REPORT NO. TO-B-63-6)

SUBMITTED TO OFFICE OF CIVIL DEFENSE,
DEPT. OF DEFENSE.

1. PROTECTIVE CONSTRUCTION.
2. ATOMIC BOMB . I. STARBIRD,
ALBERT W.

711.4
(74426) Technical Planning Associates, New Haven,
A31 Conn.
Agawam, Massachusetts, the master plan.
Prepared for the Agawam Planning Board.
New Haven, 1962.
61p.
Prepared for Massachusetts Department of
Commerce.
U.S. Urban Renewal Adm. UPAP.

1. Master plan - Agawam, Mass.
I. Agawam, Mass. Planning
Board. II. U.S. URA-UPAP.
Agawam, Mass.

711.4
(7436) Technical Planning Associates, New Haven, Conn.
R15 The comprehensive plan, Randolph, Vermont.
Prepared for the Randolph Planning Commission
and the Vermont Development Commission. New
Haven, Conn., 1960.
1v.

U.S. Urban Renewal Adm. UPAP.

1. Master plan - Randolph, Vt. I. Randolph, Vt.
Planning Commission. II. U.S. URA-UPAP.
Randolph, Vt.

311.2
I52 Technical paper on sample design.
India. Secretariat.
Technical paper on sample design, by A.S.
Roy and A. Bhattacharyya, 1968. Delhi, Manager
of Publications, 1968.
50p. (Its National Sample survey no.
125)
At head of title: The National sample
survey, a nineteenth round, July 1964-
June 1965.
1. Sampling (Statistics) 2. Statistics -
India. I. Title.

711.4
(7439) Technical Planning Associates, New Haven Conn.
T22 Bellows Falls, Vermont plan of development.
Prepared for the Bellows Falls Planning Commission and the Vermont Development Commission. New Haven, 1959.
11p. maps.
U.S. Urban Renewal Administration, Urban
Planning Assistance Program.
1. City planning - Bellows Falls, Vt.
I. Bellows Falls, Vt. Planning Commission. II. U.S. URA-UPAP. Bellows Falls,
Vt.

711.4
(7469) Technical Planning Associates, New Haven, Conn.
T22 Danbury Connecticut plan of development, pre-
pared for the Danbury City Planning Commission
and the Connecticut Development Commission.
[New Haven] 1958.
1v. diagrs., maps, tables.
U.S. Urban Renewal Administration, Urban
Planning Assistance Program.
1. City planning - Danbury, Conn. I. Danbury,
Conn. City Planning Commission. II. U.S.
URA-UPAP.

VF
690.015 Technical papers.
H68
T U.S. Housing and Home Finance Agency. Office of
the Administrator. Division of Housing
Research.
Housing research papers, no. 1-
Washington, D.C., Feb. 1948-
v. irregular.

Title varies: no. 1-14, Technical papers;
no. 15- Housing research papers.

For full information see main entry.

711.3
(7441) Technical Planning Associates, New Haven, Conn.
T22r Berkshire County, Massachusetts: a regional
planning study. Prepared for the Berkshire
County Commissioners and the Massachusetts
Dept. of Commerce. New Haven, 1959.
3v. diagrs., maps, tables.

Volume 1 has title: A pilot plan for Berkshire County,
Massachusetts.
U.S. Urban Renewal Administration, Urban Planning
Assistance Program.

1. Regional planning - Berkshire Co., Mass. I. U.
URA-UPAP. Berkshire Co., Mass.

711.5
(7441) Technical Planning Associates, New Haven, Conn.
:347) Draft of zoning by-law. Prepared for
T22 Adams [Mass.] Planning Board. [New Haven,
Conn., 1960?]
23p.
U.S. Urban Renewal Adm. UPAP.

1. Zoning legislation - Adams, Mass.
I. Adams, Mass. Planning Board.
II. U.S. URA-UPAP. Adams, Mass.

711.4
(7467) Technical Planning Associates.
H15 Hamden; pilot study for a town plan. New
Haven, Conn. [1949]
3c. 11p. maps.

1. City planning - Hamden, Conn.

711.3
(7441) Technical Planning Associates, New Haven, Conn.
T22 Berkshire County, Massachusetts: the
regional plan. Prepared for the Berkshire
County Commissioners and the Massachusetts
Dept. of Commerce. New Haven, 1959.
64p. maps, tables.

U.S. Urban Renewal Administration, Urban
Planning Assistance Program.

1. Regional planning - Berkshire Co., Mass. I. U.S.
URA-UPAP. Berkshire Co., Mass.

711.4
(7448) Technical Planning Associates, New Haven,
M17 Conn.
Marshfield, Massachusetts: the master
plan. New Haven, 1962.
[11]p.
"This pamphlet contains a summary of
the Master plan report prepared for the
Marshfield Planning Board and the
Massachusetts Department of Commerce."
U.S. Urban Renewal Adm. UPAP.

1. Master plan - Marshfield, Mass.
I. Marshfield, Mass. Planning
Board. II. U.S. URA-UPAP.
Marshfield, Mass.

5484 TECHNICAL PLANNING ASSOCIATES.
STOWE, VT. PLANNING COMMISSION.
PLAN OF DEVELOPMENT. TECHNICAL
PLANNING ASSOCIATES. STOWE, 1964.
12P. (HUD 701 REPORT)

-- -- SUPPLEMENTARY MATERIAL IN
ENVELOPE.

1. CITY PLANNING - STOWE, VT.
I. TECHNICAL PLANNING ASSOCIATES.
II. HUD. 701. STOWE, VT.

711.4
(7439) Technical Planning Associates, New Haven, Conn.
B25 The comprehensive plan, Bellows Falls, Vermont. Prepared for the Bellows Falls Plan
Commission and the Vermont Development Commission. New Haven, 1959.
75p. maps, tables.
U.S. Urban Renewal Administration, Urban
Planning Assistance Program.
1. Master plan - Bellows Falls, Vt. I. Bellows Falls, Vt. Planning Commission. II. U.S.
URA-UPAP.

711.4
(7448) Technical Planning Associates, New Haven,
M17m Conn.
Marshfield, Massachusetts: the master
plan. Prepared for the Marshfield
Planning Board and the Massachusetts
Department of Commerce. New Haven, 1962.
53p.
U.S. Urban Renewal Adm. UPAP.

1. Master plan - Marshfield, Mass.
I. Marshfield, Mass. Planning Board.
II. U.S. URA- UPAP. Marshfield,
Mass.

5466 TECHNICAL PLANNING ASSOCIATES.
STOWE, VT. PLANNING COMMISSION.
REPORT OF THE PLAN OF DEVELOPMENT. BY
TECHNICAL PLANNING ASSOCIATES, NEW HAVEN,
CONN. STOWE, 1964.
86L. (HUD 701 REPORT)

1. CITY PLANNING - STOWE, VT.
I. TECHNICAL PLANNING ASSOCIATES.
II. HUD. 701. STOWE, VT.

711.4
(7439) Technical Planning Associates, New Haven,
B25 Conn.
appen- The comprehensive plan, Bellows Falls,
dix Vermont. Appendix. Prepared for the Bellows Falls Planning Commission and the Vermont Development Commission. New Haven,
1959.
1v. tables.
Contents:-Proposed zoning ordinance.-Sug-
gested subdivision regulations.-Question-
naire survey tabulation.-Southeastern

711.4
(7441) Technical Planning Associates, New Haven, Conn.
A21a Master plan for Adams, Massachusetts.
Prepared for the Adams Planning Board and
Massachusetts Dept. of Commerce. [New
Haven, Conn.] 1959.
40p.

U.S. Urban Renewal Adm. UPAP.

1. Master plan - Adams, Mass I. Adams, Mass.
Planning Board. II. U.S. URA-UPAP. Adams, Mass.

711.4
(7444)
A73   Technical Planning Associates, New Haven,
       Conn.
        Master plan for Ashland, Massachusetts.
Prepared for the Ashland Planning Board and
Massachusetts Dept. of Commerce. New Haven,
Conn., [1959]
      18p.   maps, tables.

      U.S. Urban Renewal Administration, Urban
Planning Assistance Program.

1. Master plan - Ashland, Mass. I. Ashland, Mass.
Planning Board. II. U.S.   URA-UPAP. Ashland,
Mass.

388
:331
F73   Technical Planning Associates, New Haven, Conn.
     Fredericksen, Nils.
       The New Haven commuter service, it is
expendable. Prepared in collaboration with
Technical Planning Associates of New Haven.
Norwalk, Conn., South Western Regional
Planning Agency [1966?]
     29p.
     U.S. Housing and Urban Development. UPAP.

     1. Journey to work. 2. Transportation - New
Haven. I. Technical Planning Associates, New
Haven, Conn. II. South Western Regional
Planning Agency,   Norwalk, Conn.
III. Title.   IV. U.S. HUD-UPAP.
New Haven.

711.4
(7461)
T22p   Technical Planning Associates, New Haven, Conn.
      Plan of development, Winchester, Connecticut.
Prepared for Connecticut Development Commission
and Winchester Planning and Zoning Commission.
New Haven, 1957.
     20p.   diagrs., maps, tables

     U.S. Urban Renewal Administration, Urban
Planning Assistance Program.

     1. City planning - Winchester, Conn. I. Win-
chester, Conn. Planning and Zoning Commission. II. U. S.   URA-UPAP.

711.4
(7445)
T66   Technical Planning Associates, New Haven,
     Conn.
       Master plan for Topsfield, Massachusetts.
[Prepared for Topsfield Planning Board and
Massachusetts Department of Commerce] New
Haven, 1961.
     1v.

      U.S. Urban Renewal Adm. UPAP.

     1. Master plan - Topsfield, Mass.
I. Topsfield,   Mass. Planning
Board. II. U.S.   URA-UPAP.
Topsfield,   Mass.

711.4
(7462)
T22   Technical Planning Associates, New Haven,
     Conn.
       Newington, Connecticut plan of develop-
ment. Prepared for the Newington Town Plan
Commission and the Connecticut Development
Commission. New Haven, Conn., 1958.
     22p. diagrs., maps.
     On cover: Summary report.
     U.S. Urban Renewal Administration, Urban
Planning Assistance Program.
     1. City planning - Newington, Conn. I.
Newington, Conn.   Town Plan Commission.
II. U.S.   URA-UPAP.

711.5
(7447:347)
T22   Technical Planning Association, New Haven,
draft   Conn.
       Proposed draft - zoning ordinance, North
Adams, Mass. Rev. New Haven, Conn., Sept. 1956.
     28 p. maps.

     1.Zoning legislation - North Adams, Mass.
     2.City planning - North Adams, Mass.

711.4
(74426)
L82   Technical Planning Associates, New Haven,
     Conn.
       Master plan, Ludlow, Massachusetts.
[Prepared for Ludlow Planning Board]
New Haven, 1964.
     68p.
     U.S. Urban Renewal Adm. UPAP.

     1. Master plan - Ludlow, Mass.
I. Ludlow, Mass. Planning Board.
II. U.S. URA-UPAP. Ludlow, Mass.

711.4
(74423)
N67   Technical Planning Associates, New Haven,
     Conn.
       Northampton, Massachusetts, the master
plan. [Prepared for] Northampton Planning
Board. New Haven, 1963.
     1v.

     Prepared in cooperation with Massachusetts
Department of Commerce.
     U.S. Urban Renewal Adm. UPAP.

     1. Master   plan - Northampton,
Mass.   I. Northampton, Mass.
Planning   Board. II. U.S.
URA-UPAP   Northampton, Mass.

711.4
(7441)
L22   Technical Planning Associates, New Haven,
     Conn.
       Report on the Master plan, Lee Massa-
setts. Prepared for Lee Planning Board and
Massachusetts Department of Commerce. New
Haven, 1958.
     45p. diagrs., maps, tables.

     U.S. Urban Renewal Administration, Urban Planning
Assistance Program.
     1. Master plan - Lee, Mass. I.Lee, Mass. Planning
Board. II. Massachusetts Dept. of Commerce. III.
U.S. URA-UPAP.

711.4
(7444)
T28   Technical Planning Associates, New Haven,Conn.
appendix   Master plan report, including capital
budget, subdivision regulations, zoning
by-law. Prepared for Tewksbury Planning
Board and Massachusetts Department of
Commerce. New Haven, 1958.
     1v. diagrs., maps, tables.

     U.S. Urban Renewal Administration, Urban
Planning Assistance Program.

1. Master plan - Tewksbury, Mass. 2. Zoning legislation-
Tewksbury, Mass. 3.   Subdivision regulation -
Tewksbury, Mass. I.   Tewksbury, Mass. Planning
Board. II. U.S. URA-UPAP. Tewksbury, Mass.

711.4
(74365)
T22p   Technical Planning Associates, New Haven,
     Conn.
       Pilot plan 1959. Does Windsor want to
grow? Retail trade. Residential growth.
New Haven, 1959.
     5p. maps.
     U.S. Urban Renewal Administration, Urban
Planning Assistance Program.
     1. City planning - Windsor, Vt. I. U.S.
URA-UPAP. Windsor, Vt.

711.4
(7447)
N67   Technical Planning Associates.
       Report on the master plan, North Adams,
Massachusetts. Prepared for North Adams
Planning Board and Massachusetts Depart-
ment of Commerce. New Haven, Conn., 1957.
     62p. tables.

     U.S. Urban Renewal Administration, Urban
Planning Assistance Program.

     (Continued on next card)

711.4
(7444)
A73   Technical Planning Associates, New Haven,
Append.   Conn.
       Master plan report, including capital bud-
get, zoning by-law. Appendix. Prepared
for Ashland Planning Board and Massachusetts Dept. of Commerce. New Haven, Conn.,
1959.
     1v. maps, tables.

     U.S. Urban Renewal Administration, Urban
Planning Assistance Program.

1. Master plan - Ashland, Mass. I. Ashland, Mass.
Planning Board. II.   U.S. URA-UPAP.
Ashland, Mass.

711.4
(7466)
T22   Technical Planning Associates, New Haven,
     Conn.
       Pilot plan, Westbrook, Connecticut. Pre-
pared for Connecticut Development Commis-
sion and Westbrook Planning and Zoning
Commission. New Haven, 1959.
     [9]p. diagrs., map, table.
     U.S. Urban Renewal Administration, Urban
Planning Assistance Program.
     1. City planning - Westbrook, Conn.
I. Westbrook, Conn Planning and Zoning
Commission.   II. U.S. URA-UPAP.

711.4
(7447)
N67   Technical Planning Associates. Report on
      the master plan ... (Card 2)

     1. Master plan - North Adams, Mass.
I. North Adams, Mass. Planning Board.
II. U.S. Urban Renewal Administration.
Urban Planning Assistance Program.

711.4
(7445)
T66   Technical Planning Associates, New Haven,
summary   Conn.
       Master plan summary report, Topsfield,
Massachusetts. Prepared for Topsfield
Planning Board and Massachusetts Department
of Commerce New Haven, 1961.
     6p.

      U.S. Urban Renewal Adm. UPAP.

     1. Master plan - Topsfield, Mass.
I. Topsfield,   Mass. Planning
Board.   II. U.S. URA-UPAP.
Topsfield,   Mass.

711.4
(74365)
T22   Technical Planning Associates, New Haven,
     Conn.
       The pilot plan, Windsor, Vermont. Pre-
pared for the Windsor Planning Commission
and the Vermont Development Commission.
New Haven, 1959.
     1v. diagrs., tables.
     U.S. Urban Renewal Administration,
Urban Planning Assistance Program.
     1. City planning - Windsor, Vt. I. Wind-
sor, Vt. Planning Commission. II. U.S.
URA-UPAP.   Windsor, Vt.

711.4
(7444)
T28   Technical Planning Associates, New Haven, Conn.
       Report on the Master plan, Tewksbury, Massa-
chusetts. Prepared for Tewksbury Planning
Board and Massachusetts Department of Commerce.
New Haven, 1958.
     20p. maps.

     U.S. Urban Renewal Administration, Urban
Planning Assistance Program.
     1. Master plan - Tewksbury, Mass. I. Tewks-
bury, Mass. Planning Board. II. U.S.
URA-UPAP

711.4
(7466)
M42   Technical Planning Associates, New Haven.
       Middletown, Connecticut, the plan of
development. [Prepared for] Middletown City
Plan Commission. New Haven, 1965.
     65p.
     Prepared in cooperation with Connecticut
Development Commission.
     U.S. Urban Renewal Adm. UPAP.

     1. Master plan - Middletown, Conn.
I. Middletown, Conn. City Plan Commission.
II. U.S. URA-UPAP. Middletown, Conn.

711.4
(74365)
T22   Technical Planning Associates, New Haven, Conn.
       A plan of development for Randolph.
Prepared for the Randolph Planning Com-
mission and the Vermont Development
Association. [New Haven] 1960.
     [10]p.

     U.S. Urban Renewal Adm. UPAP.

1. City planning - Randolph, Vt. I. Randolph, Vt.
Planning Commission.   II. U.S. URA-UPAP.
Randolph, Vt.

711.4
(7467)
T22   Technical Planning Associates, New Haven,
     Conn.
       Report on the updating of the plan of de-
velopment, Cheshire, Connecticut. Prepared
for the Cheshire Town Planning Commission.
New Haven, 1958.
     33p. maps

     U.S. Urban Renewal Administration, Urban
Planning Assistance Program.
     1. City planning - Cheshire, Conn.
I. Cheshire, Conn. Town Planning Commis-
sion. II. U.S.   URA-UPAP.

711.5
(7441)
T22
Technical Planning Associates.
Report to the Adams Planning Board on preliminary planning studies. [New Haven] 1957.
[12]p. tables.
U.S. Urban Renewal Administration, Urban Planning Assistance Program.
1. City planning - Adams, Mass. I. Adams, Mass. Planning Board. II. U.S. Urban Renewal Administration. Urban Planning Assist-   ance Program.

070.44
B14
TECHNICAL PUBLICATIONS.
BAKER, C
TECHNICAL PUBLICATIONS, THEIR PURPOSE, PREPARATION AND PRODUCTION. NEW YORK, JOHN WILEY, 1955.
302P.
1. REPORT WRITING.   I. TITLE.

VF
697.9
(016)
U54
1949
U.S. Office of Technical Services.
Bibliography of reports on air conditioning, refrigeration, and ventilation.   Washington, D.C. 1949.
5 p.   (1B 87)
Processed.
1.Air conditioning-Bibliog. 2.Refrigeration-Bibliog 3.Ventilation-Bibliog.

711.4
(7444)
W14s
Technical Planning Associates, New Haven, Conn.
Summary of report on the master plan for Wakefield. [Prepared in cooperation with] Wakefield Town Planning Board. New Haven, 1962.
5p.
U.S. Urban Renewal Adm. UPAP.
1. Master plan - Wakefield, Mass. I. Wakefield, Mass. Town Planning Board. II. U.S. URA-UPAP. Wakefield, Mass.

070.44
W24
The technical report.
Weil, B H ed.
The technical report ; its preparation, processing, and use in industry and government. New York, Reinhold, 1954.
xii, 485 p.   illus., forms , graphs.
Includes bibliographies.
1. Report writing. 2. Indexing. 3. Graphic methods. I. Title.

VF
691.54
(016)
J17
1949
U.S. Office of Technical Services.
Joseph, Leslie B.
Bibliography of reports on cements and concrete Washington, D.C. 1949.
25 p.   (SB-1)
Processed..
1.Cement-Bibliog. 2.Concrete-Bibliog. I.U.S: Office of Technical Services.

711.4
(7461)
T22t
Technical Planning Associates, New Haven, Conn.
Thomaston, Connecticut. [Prepared for] Thomaston Planning Commission. New Haven, 1957.
9p. diagrs., maps, tables.
U.S. Urban Renewal Administration, Urban Planning Assistance Program.
1. City planning - Thomaston, Conn. I. Thomaston, Conn. Planning Commission. II. U.S. URA-   UPAP.

690.015
H68
R
Technical reprint series.
U.S. Housing and Home Finance Agency. Office of the Administrator. Division of Housing Research.
Housing research reprints, no. 1-
Feb. 1950-   Washington, Govt. Print. Off., 1950-
pts.
Title varies: no. 1-9, Technical reprint series; no. 10- Housing research reprint series.
For full information see shelf list card.
1.Building research. I.Title. II.Title: Technical reprint series.

VF
69
(016)
T22
U.S. Office of Technical Services.
Bibliography of reports on construction (including building materials other than cements and concrete) comp. by Eric A. Tietz. Washington, Mar. 1949.
13 p.   (Its SB-8)
Processed.
1.Building construction-Bibl. 2.Building materials-Bibl. I.Tietz, Eric A., comp.

711.4
(7469)
T22t
Technical Planning Associates, New Haven, Conn.
Town of Danbury, Connecticut: plan of development. Prepared for the Danbury Town Planning Commission and the Connecticut Development Commission. New Haven, 1960.
4 | p.
--- Appendix
U.S. Urban Renewal Adm. UPAP.
1. City planning - Danbury, Conn. I. Danbury, Conn. Town Planning Commission. II. U.S. URA-UPAP.   Danbury, Conn.

015
(016)
0330
U.S. OFFICE OF TECHNICAL SERVICES.
OSRD REPORTS; A BIBLIOGRAPHY AND INDEX OF A NUMBERED SERIES AVAILABLE FROM THE OFFICE OF TECHNICAL SERVICES. WASHINGTON, 1947.
105P.
1. RESEARCH - BIBLIOGRAPHY. I. U.S. OFFICE OF SCIENTIFIC RESEARCH AND DEVELOPMENT. II. TITLE.

VF Concrete aggregates 1953
DATE OF REQUEST 3/9/53 AUG 24 1953 L. C. CARD NO.
AUTHOR U. S. Dept. of Commerce, Technical Service Office.
TITLE Bibliography of reports on lightweight aggregates and foam concrete.
SERIES
EDITION | PUB. DATE 1950 | PAGING p 4.
PUBLISHER U. S. Dept. of Commerce, Technical Service Office, Washington 25, D. C.
RECOMMENDED BY | REVIEWED IN USGP 1/53, p. 76
ORDER RECORD

711.4
(7444)
W14
Technical Planning Associates, New Haven, Conn.
Wakefield, Massachusetts: the master plan. Prepared for Wakefield Town Planning Board and Massachusetts Department of Commerce. New Haven, 1961.
57p.
U.S. Urban Renewal Adm. UPAP.
1. Master plan - Wakefield, Mass. I. Wakefield, Mass. Town Planning Board.   II. U.S. URA-UPAP.   Wakefield, Mass.

U.S. Office of Technical Services.
1965-
see
U.S. Clearinghouse for Federal Scientific and Technical Information.

691.322
(016)
T22
U.S. Office of Technical Services.
Bibliography of reports on lightweight aggregates and foam concrete. Washington, 1950.
11p.
1.Concrete - Bibliographies.

711.4
(74426)
W45
Technical Planning Associates, New Haven, Conn.
Wilbraham, Massachusetts: the master plan. Prepared for Wilbraham Planning Board and Massachusetts Department of Commerce. New Haven, 1963.
1v.
U.S. Urban Renewal Adm. UPAP.
1. Master plan - Wilbraham, Mass. II. Wilbraham, Mass. Planning Board. II. U.S. URA-   UPAP. Wilbraham, Mass.

697.8
(016)
T22
U.S. Office of Technical Services.
Air pollution and purification. Washington, 1961.
10p.
1. Air pollution - Bibliography.

VF Wallboard
DATE OF REQUEST 3/9/53 MAR 24 1953 L. C. CARD NO.
AUTHOR U. S. Dept. of Commerce, Technical Services Office.
TITLE Bibliography of reports on manufacture of board from wood wastes.
SERIES
EDITION | PUB. DATE 1952 | PAGING p.2
PUBLISHER U. S. Dept. of Commerce, Technical Service Office, Washington 25, D. C.
RECOMMENDED BY | REVIEWED IN USGP 1/53, p. 78
ORDER RECORD

691.542
D15
Technical properties of cements containing free calcium oxide.
Danyushevskii, S I
Technical properties of cements containing free calcium oxide, by S.I. Danyushevskii et al. Garston, Eng., Building Research Station, 1971.
5p. (Library communication no. 1622)
Translated from the Russian and reprinted from Tsement, 1970, (7), 15-17.
1. Portland cement. I. U.K. Building Research Station. II. Title. (Series)

VF air conditioning
DATE OF REQUEST 10/16/53 OCT 27 L. C. CARD NO.
AUTHOR U.S. Office of Technical Services.
TITLE Bibliography of reports on air conditioning and ventilation.
SERIES
EDITION | PUB. DATE June 1953 | PAGING 4 p.
PUBLISHER
RECOMMENDED BY FML | REVIEWED IN USGP 7/53 p.96
ORDER RECORD

VF Paints
DATE OF REQUEST 3/6/53 MAR 24 1953 L. C. CARD NO.
AUTHOR U. S. Dept. of Commerce, Technical Service Office.
TITLE Bibliography of reports on paints, varnishes and lacquers.
SERIES
EDITION | PUB. DATE 1950 | PAGING 6 p.
PUBLISHER U. S. Dept. of Commerce, Technical Service Office., Washington 25, D. C.
RECOMMENDED BY | REVIEWED IN USGP 1/53, p. 75
ORDER RECORD

VF
691.6
(016)
U54
1950
U.S. Office of Technical Services.
Bibliography of reports on plexiglas and fiber-glas. Washington, D.C., 1950.
6 p. (1B-116)

Processed.

1.Plexiglas. 2.Fiberglas.

538.56
(016)
T22co
U.S. Office of Technical Services.
Computer research: medicine, human engineering, and learning machines. Washington, Dept. of Commerce, Office of Technical Services, 1961.
14p. (OTS selective bibliography, SB-473)

1. Automation - Bibl.

VF
693.068
:389.6
T22
U.S. Office of Technical Services.
Dimensional coordination of buildings, and materials and equipment on the modular system; report. [Washington] Mar. 1948.
74 p. illus., diagrs.
Industrial Research and Development Division contract no. Cac-47-3, final report, Mar. 1948, Modular Service Association.
ASA project A62 committees: p. 2.
Contains Apr. 1947 and Dec. 1947 issues of Modular Grid Lines.
"Directory of manufacturers of manufacturers of modular products:" 68-72. (Continued on next card)

VF
691.116
(016)
U54
1947
U.S. Office of Technical Services.
Bibliography of reports on plywood. Washington, D.C. 1947?
13 p.

Processed.

1.Plywood-Bibliog.

538.56
(016)
T22c
2c
U.S. Office of Technical Services.
Computers. (Supplement to CTR-371)
Washington, Dept. of Commerce, Office of Technical Services, 1961.
31p. (OTS selective bibliography, SB-472)

538.56
(016)
T22c
Suppl.
2c
-- --- Supplement.

1.Automation - Bibl. I. Title.

U.S. Office of Technical Services. Dimensional coordination of buildings, and material and equipment on the modular system...1948.
(Card 2)

1.Modular coordination. 2.Modular coordination-Direct. 3.ASA project A62. I.Modular Grid Lines. II.Modular Service Association. III.Title.

VF Statistical Methods 1953
DATE OF REQUEST 3/9/53   MAR 24 1953   L.C. CARD NO.
AUTHOR U. S. Dept. of Commerce, Technical Services Office.
TITLE Bibliography of reports on statistical analysis in engineering and research.
SERIES
EDITION | PUB. DATE 1952 | PAGING 8 p.
PUBLISHER U. S. Dept. of Commerce, Technical Service Office.
RECOMMENDED BY | REVIEWED IN TRSGP 1/53, p. 80
ORDER RECORD

691.7;
1620.19
(016)
633
U.S. OFFICE OF TECHNICAL SERVICES.
CORROSION. WASHINGTON, DEPARTMENT OF COMMERCE, 1963.
61P. (ITS. SELECTIVE BIBLIOGRAPHY SB-401, SUPPL.1)

1. CORROSION - BIBLIOGRAPHY.

R
058.7
F67
1960
U.S. Office of Technical Services.
Directory of national associations of businessmen, by Jay Judkins. Washington, 1960.
81p.

"Supplements the basic directory of 1949, National associations of the United States."

1. Associations - Directories. I. Judkins, Jay. II. Title: National Associations of the United States.

VF
691.4
(016)
U54
1949
U.S. Office of Technical Services.
Bibliography of reports on tiles. Washington D.C., 1949.
2 p. (1B 108)

Processed.

1.Tile-Bibliog.

352.6
H68
U. S. Office of Technical Services.
U. S. Housing and Home Finance Agency. Office of the Administrator. Division of Housing Research.
The cost of municipal services in residential areas, by William L. C. Wheaton and Morton J. Schussheim. Washington, Govt. Print. Off., 1955.
v, 105 p. tables. (PB111652)

Published by U. S. Dept. of Commerce, Office of Technical Services.

699.85
A76
U. S. Office of Technical Services.
U. S. Atomic Energy Commission.
The effects of atomic bomb blasts on elevated tanks and standpipes. [Washington, Office of Technical Services, Department of Commerce] May 1954.
103 p. diagrs., graphs, tables. (Its WASH-182)

"This report presents the results of a research investigation conducted by the Pittsburgh-Des Moines Steel Company for the Atomic Energy Commission."-cf. p. vi.

VF
691.116
(016)
U54
1950
U.S. Office of Technical Services.
Bibliography of reports on veneers. Washington, D.C., 1950.
3 p. (1B-109)

Processed.

1.Veneers.

U. S. Housing and Home Finance Agency. Office of the Administrator. Division of Housing Research. The cost of....
1955. (Card 2)

A study prepared by the Department of Regional Planning, Harvard University (HHFA Research Project O-U-68).

1. Municipal services. 2. Housing research contracts. I. Wheaton, William L. C. II. Schussheim, Morton J. III. U.S. Office of Technical Services. IV. Harvard Universit' Dept. of Regional Planning. V. Title. VI. Title: Residential areas, The cost of municipal services in.

699.85
A76
U. S. Atomic Energy Commission. The effects of atomic bomb blasts...May 1954.(Card 2)

"References": p. 103.

1.Atomic bomb. I.Pittsburgh-Des Moines Steel Company. II.U.S. Office of Technical Services. III.Title.

VF
628.1
(016)
U54
1947
U.S. Office of Technical Services.
Bibliography of reports on water supply and sewage disposal. Washington, D.C., 1947.
3 p.

Processed.

1.Water supply-Bibliog. 2.Sewage and sewage disposal-Bibliog.

538.56
(016)
T22d
2c
U.S. Office of Technical Services.
Data processing and programming. Washington, Dept. of Commerce, Office of Technical Services, 1961.
26p. (Its OTS selective bibliography, SB-474)

538.56
(016)
T22d
Suppl.
2c
-- --- Supplement.

1. Automation - Bibl. I. Title.

691.16
(016)
T22
2c
U.S. OFFICE OF TECHNICAL SERVICES.
EXPANDED PLASTICS. WASHINGTON, 1963.
12P. (ITS SELECTIVE BIBLIOGRAPHY SB524)

1. PLASTICS - BIBLIOGRAPHY.
I. TITLE.

VF Wood
DATE OF REQUEST 3/9/53   MAR 24 1953   L.C. CARD NO.
AUTHOR U. S. Dept. of Commerce, Technical Service Office.
TITLE Bibliography of reports on wood preservation.
SERIES
EDITION | PUB. DATE 1951 | PAGING 7 p.
PUBLISHER U. S. Dept. of Commerce, Technical Service Office.
RECOMMENDED BY | REVIEWED IN MCUSGP 1/53, p. 79
ORDER RECORD

691.018.44
T22
U.S. Office of Technical Services.
Development of fire retardant paints and paint systems, by Harvey Miller. Washington, 1952.
121p. illus., diagrs., tables. (PB 111939)

1. Building materials - Fire resistance.
2. Paints and painting. I. Miller, Harvey.

308
:728.1
H68
U.S. Office of Technical Services.
U. S. Housing and Home Finance Agency. Office of the Administrator. Division of Housing Research.
How to make and interpret locational studies of the housing market, by Maurice R. Brewster and William A. Flinn and Ernest H. Jurkat. Washington, Govt. Print. Off., 1955.
vii, 66 p. forms, graphs, maps, tables. (PB111653)

Published by U. S. Department of Commerce, Office of Technical Services.

U. S. Housing and Home Finance Agency.
Office of the Administrator. Division of Housing Research. How to make and... 1955. (Card 2)

A report based largely upon a study by the State Engineering Experiment Station, Georgia Institute of Technology (HHFA Research Project 0-E-69).

1. Housing market analysis. 2. Housing surveys. 3. Survey methods. 4. Housing research contracts. I. Brewster, Maurice P II. Flinn, Wm. A. III. Jurkat, Ernest H. .V. Georgia. State Engineering Experiment Station. V. U. S. Office of Technical Services. VI. Title. VII. Title:

500.15 (016) T22o
U.S. Office of Technical Services.
OTS selective bibliography

Washington, Dept. of Commerce, Office of Technical Services.
v. (P.L. Translation Program; SB)

For complete information see shelflist.

1. Scientific research - Bibl. I. Title: Translation Program.

691.7 :620.19 (016) T22
U.S. OFFICE OF TECHNICAL SERVICES.
RUST PREVENTION AND REMOVAL, 1934-59. WASHINGTON, 1959.
4P. (ITS CATALOG OF TECHNICAL REPORTS CTR-305)

1. CORROSION - BIBLIOGRAPHY. I. TITLE.

---

027 (016) J63
U.S. OFFICE OF TECHNICAL SERVICES. JOHN CRERAR LIBRARY, CHICAGO. INDUSTRIAL TECHNICAL LIBRARY - A BIBLIOGRAPHY. PREPARED BY THE JOHN CRERAR LIBRARY IN COOPERATION WITH THE OFFICE OF TECHNICAL SERVICES, U.S. DEPT. OF COMMERCE. WASHINGTON, INTERNATIONAL COOPERATION ADMINISTRATION, 1960.
264P.

1. LIBRARIES - BIBLIOGRAPHY. I. U.S. OFFICE OF TECHNICAL SERVICES. II. TITLE.

3041 Concrete aggregates
Accession No.
Ordered JUL 6 1950
Phone
Received JUL 18 1950
Author (surname first) U.S. Dept. of Commerce Office of Technical Services
Title Perlite; methods of producing expanded light-weight aggregate from this new material Wash., D.C.
Date 1950 List Price 25¢ Est. Cost gratis
Edition or Series Order PB 100 497
Reviewed in O.S. newsletter
H-305 (2-50) HOUSING AND HOME FINANCE AGENCY: Office of the Administrator

---

VF 690.24 (016) U54 1949
U.S. Office of Technical Services.
Special bibliography of reports on roof construction and roofing materials. Washington, D.C 1949.
2 p. (IB-100)

Processed.

1. Roofs and roofing.

538.56 (016) T221
U.S. Office of Technical Services.
Information storage and retrieval. Washington, Dept. of Commerce, Office of Technical Services, 1961.
13p. (OTS selective bibliography, SB-475)

538.56 (016) T221 Suppl.
-- --- Supplement.

1. Automation - Bibl. I. Title.

VF 621.643 T22
U.S. Office of Technical Services.
Plastic drain and sewer pipe and fittings (effective January 4, 1960) With the cooperation of the National Bureau of Standards. Washington, Govt. Print. Off., 1960.
12p. diagrs., tables. (Commercial standard CS228-60)

1. Pipes. 2. Plastics. I. U.S. National Bureau of Standards.

690.25 T22
U.S. Office of Technical Services.
Strip oak flooring; a recorded voluntary standard of the trade published by the U.S. Department of Commerce. Washington, 1960.
20p.
Commercial standard Cs56-60; supersedes CS56-49.

1. Floors and flooring. 2. Standardization.

699.81 (016) F22
U.S. Office of Technical Services.
Federal Fire Council. Library material, 19

Washington, Office of Technical Services, Dept. of Commerce, 19
v.

For complete information see shelflist.

1. Fire prevention - Bibl. I. U.S. Office of Technical Services.

341.1 :338 F67
U.S. Office of Technical Services.
U.S. Foreign Operations Administration. Office of Industrial Resources.
Question and answer service. In cooperation with Office of Technical Services, United States Department of Commerce. Washington, 1955.
14p. illus.

1. Technical assistance programs. I. U.S. Office of Technical Services.

---

69 B84 1952
U.S. Office of Technical Services.
Building Research Advisory Board.
Study of conservation in building construction final report; performed ... under contract DPA-3 between the Defense Production Administration and the National Academy of Sciences. Washington, Govt. Print. Off., June 1952.
23, 106, 103 p. tables. (U.S. Office of Technical Services. PB-111006)

1. Building construction. I.U.S. Defense Production Administration. II. National Academy of Sciences. III. U.S. Office of Technical Services. IV. Title: Conservation in building construction.

---

010 T22
U.S. Office of Technical Services.
List of selective bibliographies. Washington, Dept. of Commerce, Office of Technical Services, 1963.
folder.

1. Bibliography.

658.562 (016) T22
U.S. OFFICE OF TECHNICAL SERVICES. RELIABILITY AND QUALITY CONTROL. WASHINGTON, 1962.
36P. (ITS SELECTIVE BIBLIOGRAPHY 405, REV)

REPORTS AND TRANSLATIONS ADDED TO THE OTS COLLECTION DURING THE PERIOD 1950 TO SEPTEMBER 1962.

1. QUALITY CONTROL - BIBLIOGRAPHY. I. TITLE.

VF 690.015 G72 1948
U.S. Office of Technical Services.
Green, John C
Technology and housing; statement before the Joint Committee on Housing, 80th Congress, 2d session, Jan. 21, 1948. [Washington, Office of Technical Services? 1948]
11 p.
Processed.

1. Building research. 2. Housing research. I. U.S. Office of Technical Services. II. U.S. Congress. Joint Committee on Housing. III. Title.

500.15 (016) T22
U.S. Office of Technical Services.
List of translations in process for fiscal year
Washington, Dept. of Commerce, Office of Technical Services.
v. (P.L. Translation Program)

For complete information see shelflist.

1. Scientific research - Bibl. I. Title: Translation Program.

690.015 L25
U.S. Office of Technical Services.
Lendrum, James Thoburn.
Research report on a study of construction methods. A report of an investigation conducted by the Small Homes Council in cooperation with the Office of Technical Services, United States Dept. of Commerce, by James T. Lendrum and Gerhard C. Rettber [Urbana] 1948.
[107] l. plans. (Illinois. University. Small Homes Council. Technical series, index no. E2.1R)

1. Building research. 2. Building methods. I. Rettberg, Gerhard Christoph, joint author. II. U.S. Office of Technical Services. III. Series.

697.133 :690.25 B17
U.S. Office of Technical Services.
Bareither, Harlan D
Temperature and heat loss characteristics of concrete floors laid on the ground. A report of an investigation conducted by the Small Homes Council and the Department of Mechanical engineering of the University of Illinois in cooperation with the Office of Technical Services, United States Department of Commerce, by Harlan D. Bareither, Arthur N. Fleming and Bryce E. Alberty. [Urbana, Ill., Small Homes Council] Aug. 1948.
50 l. illus.
Processed.

500.15 T22
U.S. OFFICE OF TECHNICAL SERVICES. NEW PLASTIC MATERIALS THROUGH GOVERNMENT RESEARCH, BY JAMES KANEGIS, CHIEF, CHEMICAL SECTION. WASHINGTON, 1958.
93P.

1. GOVERNMENTAL RESEARCH. 2. PLASTICS. I. KANEGIS, JAMES. II. TITLE.

---

690 I55 E2.1R
U.S. Office of Technical Services.
Illinois. University. Small Homes Council.
Research report on construction methods, by J. T. Lendrum and G. C. Rettberg. Urbana, Ill., 1948.
1 v. illus., diagrs. (Its Index no. E2.1R)
"In cooperation with the office of Technical Services, United States Department of Commerce."

1. Building methods. 2. Modular coordination. I. U.S. Office of Technical Services.

699.82 P25w
U.S. Office of Technical Services.
Pennsylvania. State College. Engineering Experiment Station.
Water vapor transfer through building materials; a report of an investigation conducted ... in cooperation with the Office of Technical Services, United States Department of Commerce, by F. A. Joy, E. R. Queer, R. E. Schreiner. State College, Pa., Dec. 1948.
81 p. illus., graphs. (Its Bull. 61)
Bibliography: p. 69-79.
(over)

728
:392
H68
    U.S. Office of Technical Services.
    U. S. Housing and Home Finance Agency.
    Office of the Administrator. Division
of Housing Research.
    What people want when they buy a house,
by Edward T. Paxton.   Washington, Govt. Print.
Off., 1955.
    x, 126 p.   tables.   (PB111654)

    Published by U. S. Dept. of Commerce,
Office of Technical Services.

VF
308
:67
T22
    U.S. Office of Technical Services. Area Development
    Division.
    What will new industry mean to my town? a summary
of two case studies on the impact of new industry on
small towns, by Wesley C. Calef and Charles Daoust.
[Washington, Govt. Print. Off., April 1955]
    19 p.

    Bibliography: p. 18-19.

    1.Impact of industry. I.Calef, Wesley C

538.56
J65
    Technical writing.
    Jones S   O
    Technical writing: a key to computerized
information retrieval. Santa Monica, Calif.,
Douglas Aircraft Co., inc., 1967.
    18p. (U.S. Defense Documentation Center.
Defense Supply Agency. 1967. AD653-726)
    Distributed by: U.S. Clearinghouse for
Federal Scientific and Technical Information.

    1. Automation. 2. Documentation. 3. Report writing. I. U.S. Defense Supply Agency.
II. Douglas Aircraft Co., inc. III. Title.

    U. S. Housing and Home Finance Agency.
    Office of the Administrator. Division
of Housing Research. What people want...
1955. (Card 2)

    A guide for architects and builders based
principally on a survey by the Survey Research
Center, Institute for Social Research, University of Michigan (HHFA Research Project O-T-84)
and a study by the Small Homes Council, University of Illinois (HHFA Research Project O-T-37).

VF
728.1
A52t
    Technical services for non-profit organizations to sponsor housing.
    Action Council for Better Cities.
    Technical services for non-profit
organizations to sponsor housing. New
York, Local Development Services Div.,
Urban America, inc., the Action Council
for Better Cities, 1965.
    [5]p.

    1. Housing. I. Title.

070.44
S54
    TECHNICAL WRITING.
    SMITH, RICHARD W
    TECHNICAL WRITING; A GUIDE TO
MANUALS, REPORTS, PROPOSALS, ARTICLES,
ETC., IN INDUSTRY AND THE GOVERNMENT.
NEW YORK, BARNES AND NOBLE, 1963.
    181P. (COLLEGE OUTLINE SERIES. NO.
43)

    1. REPORT WRITING.   I. TITLE.

    U.S. Office of Technical Services. Area Development Division.

    see also

    U.S. Office of Area Development.
    U.S. Bureau of Foreign and Domestic Commerce.
    Office of Industry and Commerce. Area
Development Division.

025.2
C67t
    A technical services manual for small libraries.
    Corbin, John Boyd.
    A technical services manual for small libraries.
Metuchen, N.J., Scarecrow Press, 1971.
    206p.

    Bibliography: p. 188-197.

    1. Book selection. 2. Cataloging. I. Title.

070.44
W24b
    Technical writing.
    Waisman, Herman M
    Basic technical writing. 2d ed. Columbus,
Ohio, Charles E. Merrill, 1968.
    498p.

    1. Report writing. I. Title: Technical
writing. II. Title.

330
(7673)
T22
pt. 11
sec. 2C
    U.S. Office of Technical Services. Area
    Development Division.
    Manufacturing; an economic base study supplement prepared for the Arkansas-White-Red Basins
Inter-Agency Committee, by David Brown. Tulsa,
Okla., July 1954.
    188 p. (Arkansas-White-Red Basins report part
II, section 2C)
    ———— Bibliography supplement. June 1954.
   46 p.   (section 2C-1)
    1. Economic base studies-Arkansas Valley. 2.
Industry-Arkansas   Valley. 3. Industry-
Bibliography.
                     (see card 2)

690
(7286)
C67
    TECHNICAL SPECIFICATIONS FOR THE
    CONSTRUCTION OF HOUSES.
    INSTITUTIO NACIONAL DE VIVIENDA Y
URBANISMO.
    TECHNICAL SPECIFICATIONS FOR THE
CONSTRUCTION OF HOUSES.   SAN JOSE,
COSTA RICA, 1965.
    23P.

    INVU-ROHRMOSER PROJECT.

    1. BUILDING CONSTRUCTION - COSTA RICA
- STANDARDS AND SPECIFICATIONS.
    2. HOUSING PROJECTS - COSTA RICA -
STANDARDS AND SPECIFICATIONS.
I. ROHRMOSER P ROJECT.   II. TITLE.

603
M85
    Technics and civilization.
    Mumford, Lewis, 1895–
    Technics and civilization, by Lewis Mumford. New York,
Harcourt, Brace and company [1934]
    xi, 495 p. front., plates. 24½ cm.
    "First edition."
    Bibliography: p. 447-474.

    1. Industrial arts—Hist. 2. Civilization—Hist. 3. Machinery—Hist. 4. Social conditions—Hist. 5. Inventions—Hist. 6. Power (Mechanics)—Hist. I. Title.

    Library of Congress   T15.M8   34—11680
                        [49z⁴5]   609

330
(7673)
T22
pt. II
sec. 2C
    U.S. Office of Technical Services. Area
    Development Division.
    Manufacturing. July 1954. (card 2)

    I. Arkansas-White-Red Basins. Inter-Agency
Committee. II. Brown, David   (series)

603
M45
    TECHNICAL SPELLER & DEFINITION FINDER.
    MILES, AETNA.
    TECHNICAL SPELLER & DEFINITION FINDER.
1ST ED. INDIANAPOLIS, H.W. SAMS, 1965.
    288P. (A HOWARD W. SAMS PHOTOFACT
PUBLICATION, SDM-1)

    1. TECHNOLOGY - DICTIONARIES.   I. TITLE.

728.1
(5694)
S59
    Technion magazine.
    Slyper, Joseph L
    Social aspects of housing in Israel.
New York, American Technion Society,
1968.
    [2]p.
    Detached from: Technion magazine,
March, 1968. p. 10-12.
    1. Housing - Israel. 2. Housing -
Social aspects. I. Technion magazine.
II. Title.

711.4
:67
T22
    U.S. Office of Technical Services. Area Development Division.
    Organized industrial districts; a tool for
community development, by Theodore K. Pasma.
Washington, Govt. Print. Off., June 1954.
    vii, 111 p.   illus., charts, maps, tables.

    "Selected sources": p. 108-109.

    1. Industrial districts.   I. Pasma,
Theodore K.   II. Title.

339.3
P72t
    Technical studies.
    U.S. President's Commission on Income Maintenance Programs.
    Technical studies. Wash., 1970.
    316p.

    1. Income. 2. Public assistance.
I. Title.

058.7
:330
(5694)
T22
    Technion yearbook, 1966;
    v.22
    New York, American Technion Society, 1966
/ v.

    For complete information see main card.

    1. Economic development - Israel -
Yearbooks. I. American Technion Society.

330
(7673)
T22
pt. 2
sec. 2A
    U.S. Office of Technical Services. Area
    Development Division.
    Population trends and prospects; an economic
base study report prepared for the Arkansas-
White-Red Basins Inter-Agency Committee, by
David Brown. Tulsa, Okla., June 1954.
    113 p. / maps (Arkansas-White-Red Basins
report, part II, section 2A)
    1. Economic base studies - Arkansas Valley.
2. Population - Arkansas Valley. I. Arkansas-
White-Red Basins Inter-Agency Committee.
II. Brown, David.   (Series)

    Technical writing

    see

    Report writing

332.72
F22TE
NOV.1937
    TECHNIQUE FOR A MORTGAGE EXPERIENCE
    STUDY.
    U.S. FEDERAL HOUSING ADMINISTRATION.
DIVISION OF ECONOMICS AND
STATISTICS.
    TECHNIQUE FOR A MORTGAGE EXPERIENCE
STUDY, NOVEMBER 1, 1937. [N.P.] 1937.
    25L.

    1. MORTGAGE FINANCE. 2. SURVEY
METHODS. I. TITLE.

TECHNIQUE FOR A MORTGAGE EXPERIENCE
STUDY.
332.72 U.S. FEDERAL HOUSING ADMINISTRATION.
F22TE   TECHNIQUE FOR A MORTGAGE EXPERIENCE
STUDY. WASHINGTON, DIVISION OF
ECONOMICS AND STATISTICS, FEDERAL
HOUSING ADMINISTRATION, 1937.
67 ℓ.

1. MORTGAGE FINANCE. 2. SURVEY
METHODS. I. TITLE.

TECHNIQUE FOR A SURVEY OF LOW-RENT
HOUSING NEEDS.
728.1   U.S. HOUSING AUTHORITY.
:338.63   TECHNIQUE FOR A SURVEY OF LOW-RENT
H68T   HOUSING NEEDS. WASHINGTON, 1940.
140L.

1. RENTAL HOUSING - SURVEYS.
2. SURVEY METHODS. I. TITLE.

VF   A technique for urban rehabilitation.
711.585 Weinberg, Robert C
(77132)   A technique for urban rehabilitation.
W24   Journal of the American Institute of Planners.
6p. Autumn, 1944.

TECHNIQUE FOR A REAL ESTATE ACTIVITY
SURVEY.
333.33 U.S. CENTRAL STATISTICAL BOARD.
C25   TECHNIQUE FOR A REAL ESTATE ACTIVITY
SURVEY. PREPARED JOINTLY BY
COORDINATING COMMITTEE OF THE CENTRAL
STATISTICAL BOARD AND THE WORKS
PROGRESS ADMINISTRATION, AND THE
DIVISION OF ECONOMICS AND STATISTICS,
FEDERAL HOUSING ADMINISTRATION.
WASHINGTON, 1937.
v.
1. REAL PROPERTY. 2. SURVEY METHODS.
I. TITLE. II. U.S. FEDERAL HOUSING ADM
INISTRATION. III.   U.S. WORKS PR
OGRESS ADMINISTRATIC

Technique for calculating optimum takeoff and
climbout trajectories for noise abatement.
534.83 Erzberger, Heinz.
:E79   Technique for calculating optimum takeoff
and climbout trajectories for noise abatement,
by Heinz Erzberger and Homer Q. Lee. Wash,
National Aeronautics and Space Administration,
1969.
24p. (NASA TN D-5182)
CFSTI.

1. Noise. 2. Air transportation. I. Lee,
Homer Q., jt. au. II. U.S. National Aeronautics and Space Administration. III. Title.

The technique of clear writing.
070.44 Gunning, Robert.
G85   The technique of clear writing. New York,
McGraw-Hill, 1952.
289p.

1. Report writing. 2. English language -
Grammar. I. Title.

728.1 TECHNIQUE FOR A REAL PROPERTY SURVEY.
:308   U.S. FEDERAL HOUSING ADMINISTRATION.
F22TE   TECHNIQUE FOR A REAL PROPERTY SURVEY.
SUPPLEMENT TO THE TECHNIQUE. PREPARED
JOINTLY BY: DIVISION OF SOCIAL
RESEARCH, THE WORKS PROGRESS
ADMINISTRATION, DIVISION OF RESEARCH AND
INFORMATION, UNITED STATES HOUSING
AUTHORITY, AND THE DIVISION OF ECONOMICS
AND STATISTICS, FEDERAL HOUSING
ADMINISTRATION. WASHINGTON, 1938.
49.

1. HOUSING SU   RVEYS. 2. REAL
PROPERTY - SURV   EYS. I. TITLE.
(CONTINUED ON NEXT CARD)

Technique for determining vacancy rates in
nonfarm rental housing units.
728.1   Carman, James M
:308   Technique for determining vacancy rates in
C17   nonfarm rental housing units. Berkeley, Center for Real Estate and Urban Economics, Institute of Urban and Regional Development,
University of California, 1968.
195p.
HUD contract no. H-819.
1. Vacancy surveys. 2. Rental housing -
Alameda County, Calif. I. California. University. Center   for Real Estate and Urban
Economics.   II. Title.

---

352   The technique of municipal administration.
I57te   Institute for Training in Municipal Administration, Chicago.
The technique of municipal administration.
3rd ed. Chicago, International City Managers'
Association, c1947, 1951.
603p. (Municipal management series [no. 1])

Bibliography: p. 579-587.

1. Municipal government. 2. Public
administration. I. Title. (Series)

728.1   U.S. FEDERAL HOUSING ADMINISTRATION.
:308   TECHNIQUE FOR A ...1938.   (CARD 2)
F22TE

II. U.S. WORKS PROGRESS
ADMINISTRATION. III. U.S. HOUSING
AUTHORITY.

A technique for investigation of clay micro-
structure.
690.015 Pusch, Roland.
(485)   A technique for investigation of clay micro-
S82   structure. Stockholm, Statens institut for
R28   byggnadsforskning, 1968.
1968   963-986p. (Stockholm. Statens institut for
byggnadsforskning. Rapport 28:1968)
Bibliography: p. 984-985.
Reprinted from J. Microscopie (1967), 963-
986.
1. Building research - Sweden. 2. Sweden -
Building research. 3. Clay. 4. Soils.
I. Stockholm. Statens institut for
byggnadsforskn   ing. II. Title.

---

352   The technique of municipal administration.
I57te   Institute for Training in Municipal Administra-
1958   tion, Chicago.
The technique of municipal administration.
4th ed. Chicago, International City Managers'
Association, 1958.
441p. (Municipal management series [no. 1])

Bibliography: p. 420-426.

1. Municipal government. 2. Public
administration. I. Title. (Series)

333.33 TECHNIQUE FOR A REAL PROPERTY SURVEY.
:308   U.S. WORKS PROGRESS ADMINISTRATION.
W67   DIV. OF SOCIAL RESEARCH.
TECHNIQUE FOR A REAL PROPERTY SURVEY,
TABULATION INSTRUCTIONS FOR DWELLING
SURVEY. WASHINGTON, 1938.
1 v. (W.P.A. TECHNICAL SERIES,
RESEARCH, STATISTICAL, AND SURVEY
PROJECT CIRCULAR NO. 6)

1. REAL PROPERTY - SURVEYS.
2. HOUSING SURVEYS. 3. SURVEY METHODS.
I. TITLE.

Technique for preparing plans by progressive
stages developed by Urban Section of the
VF   National Resources Planning Board.
711.4   American Municipal Association.
A52   Action for cities; a guide for community
planning. Published under the sponsorship of
American Municipal Association, American Society
of Planning Officials, International City
Managers' Association. Chicago, Public
Administration Service, 1943.
77 p.   diagrs.   (Public Administration
Service. [Publication] no. 86)
Bibliographical footnotes.

(Continued on next card)

---

720   Techniques et Architecture.
(44)   Amenagement de la region de la défense 2.
T22a   Paris, 1968.
151p. (No. special 1-29 series)

1. Architecture - France.
I. Title.

728.1 TECHNIQUE FOR A RESURVEY OF HOUSING.
:308   U.S. FEDERAL HOUSING ADMINISTRATION.
F22T   (DIVISION OF ECONOMICS AND STATISTICS)
TECHNIQUE FOR A RESURVEY OF HOUSING.
WASHINGTON, 1939.
142 ℓ.

1. HOUSING SURVEYS. 2. SURVEY METHODS.
I. TITLE.

American Municipal Association.   Action for
cities...1943.   (Card 2)

Technique for preparing plans by progressive
stages developed by Urban Section of the
National Resources Planning Board, used in Corpus Christi,
Texas, Salt Lake City, Utah, and Tacoma, Washington.-Foreword.

1. City planning-Handbooks, manuals, etc.
I. American Society of Planning Officials.
II. International City Managers' Assoc. III. Public
Administration Service IV. U.S. National Resources
Planning Board. Urban Section. V. Title.

---

720   Techniques & Architecture.
(44)   Un bureau d'études l'OTH [Omnium
T22   Technique de l'Habitation] Paris,
1961.
259p.

Numéro spécial.

1. Architecture - France.

TECHNIQUE FOR A SURVEY OF LOW-RENT
HOUSING NEEDS.
728.1   U.S. FEDERAL WORKS AGENCY.
:308   TECHNIQUE FOR A SURVEY OF LOW-RENT
F22TEC   HOUSING NEEDS. WASHINGTON, FEDERAL
WORKS AGENCY, UNITED STATES HOUSING
AUTHORITY, RESEARCH AND STATISTICS
DIVISION, 1940.
140P.

1. HOUSING SURVEYS. I. TITLE.

A technique for projection of occupational
educational requirements for state educational
370   planning areas.
M67   Morsch, William C
A technique for projection of occupational-
educational requirements for state educational
planning areas. [Washington] National Center
for Educational Statistics, Div. of Operations
Analysis, Office of Education, Dept. of Health,
Education, and Welfare, 1966.
[17]p. (U.S. Office of Education. Technical
note no. 7)

1. Education. 2. Employment. 3. Education - Automation. I. U.S. National Center
for Educational   Statistics. II. U.S.
Office of   Education. III. Title.

Techniques for estimating local and regional
multiplier effects of changes in the level of
major governmental programs.
331   Isard, Walter.
I71   Techniques for estimating local and regional
multiplier effects of changes in the level of
major governmental programs, by Walter Isard
and Stanislaw Czamanski. Ithaca, N.Y., Center
for Housing and Environmental Studies, Div.
of Urban Studies, 1965.
19-45p. (Cornell University. Center for
Housing and Environmental Studies. Article
reprints no. 23)
Reprinted from Peace Research Society: Papers,
III, Chicago Conference, 1965.

(Continued on next card)

331
I71   Isard, Walter   Techniques for estimating
local...1955.   (Card 2)
1. Employment - Research. 2. Economic
base studies. 3. Grants-in-aid. I. Czamanski,
Stanislaw, jt. au. II. Cornell University.
Center for Housing and Environmental Studies.
III. Title.

658
B82T   TECHNIQUES FOR THE DEVELOPMENT OF A
WORK MEASUREMENT SYSTEM.
U.S. BUREAU OF THE BUDGET.
TECHNIQUES FOR THE DEVELOPMENT OF A
WORK MEASUREMENT SYSTEM.   WASHINGTON,
1951.
65P. (ITS MANAGEMENT BULLETIN)

1. MANAGEMENT. I. TITLE. II. TITLE:
A WORK MEASUREMENT SYSTEM.

320
S17   Techniques of political analysis.
Sargent, Lyman Tower.
Techniques of political analysis: an introduc-
tion, by Lyman Tower Sargent and Thomas Zant.
Belmont, Calif., Wadsworth Pub. Co., 1970.
103p. (Wadsworth series in politics)

1. Political science. I. Zant, Thomas, jt. au.
II. Title.

311
N17   Techniques for examining statistical and power-
spectral properties of random time histories.
U.S. National Aeronautics and Space Administration.
Techniques for examining statistical and power-
spectral properties of random time histories, by
Herbert A. Leybold. Washington, Office of
Technical Services, 1965.
43 p. (NASA Technical note TN D-2714)

1. Stat. I. Leybold, Herbert A. II. Title.
III. Title: Random time histories.

725.23
B79   Techniques for the survey and evaluation of
live floor loads and fire loads in modern
Bryson, J   O
Techniques for the survey and evaluation
of live floor loads and fire loads in modern
office buildings, by J.O. Bryson and D.
Gross. Wash., Building Research Div.,
Institute for Applied Technology, National
Bureau of Standards, 1967.
30p. (Its Building science series 16)
Bibliography: p. 27-28.
1. Office buildings. 2. Floors and
flooring. 3. Loads. 4. Fire prevention.
I. Gross, D.,   jt. au. II. U.S.
Institute for   Applied Technology.
Building   Research Div.
III. Title.

311
L11
1954   Techniques of preparing major BLS statistical
series.
U. S. Bureau of Labor Statistics.
Techniques of preparing major BLS statistical
series.   [Washington, Govt. Print. Off.] Dec.
1954.
126 p.   forms, tables.   (Its Bulletin
no. 1168)

Edited by Benjamin Lipstein.
83d Congress, 2d Session. House document no.
448.
Includes bibliographies.
1. Statistics. I. Lipstein, Benjamin. II. Title.

020
L46   Techniques for machine-assisted cataloging
of books...
Lipetz, B   A
Techniques for machine-assisted cataloging
of books, by B.A. Lipetz and others. Prepared
for Electronic Research Directorate, Air
Force Cambridge Research Laboratories (AFCRL),
Air Force Office of Aerospace Research
(AFOAR), U.S. Air Force, Bedford, Mass.
Lexington, Mass., Itek Corp., 1962.
1vp. (Document AD 636 977 [and] Special
report no. 3 rev.)
Distributed by U.S. Clearinghouse for Federal
Scientific and Technical Information.
1. Library science   - Automation. 2. Cata-
loging. I. U.S. Air   Force, Bedford, Mass.
II. Itek Corp.   III. Title.

720
S15   Techniques of evaluation for designers.
Sanoff, Henry.
Techniques of evaluation for designers,
by Henry Sanoff, with the assistance of
Gary Coates and others. Raleigh, N.C.,
Design Research Laboratory, School of Design.
North Carolina State University, 1968.
66p.
At head of title: A research laboratory
monograph.
Bibliography: p. 54-66.
1. Architecture - Designs and plans.
I. North. Caro-   lina. University.
State College   of Agriculture and
Engineering,   Raleigh. II. Title.

311
L11   Techniques of preparing major BLS
statistical series.
U. S. Bureau of Labor Statistics.
Techniques of preparing major BLS
statistical series.   Washington,
Govt. Print. Off. [1950]
72 p.   forms, tables.   (Its
Bulletin no. 993)

693.5
829   Techniques for making large concrete units..
Seymour-Walker, K   J
Techniques for making large concrete units-
a survey, and some development work at the
Building Research Station. Garston, Eng.,
Building Research Station, Ministry of
Technology, 1965.
17p.   (U.K. Building Research
Station. Building research current papers.
Construction series 21)

1. Concrete construction. 2. Pipes. I. U.K.
Building Research Station. II. Title.

334.1
I57t   Techniques of financing cooperative and non-
profit housing developments in selected
countries.
International Cooperative Housing Development
Association.
Techniques of financing cooperative and
non-profit housing developments in selected
countries. Wash., 1967.
1v.
Prepared under contract with the United
Nations, Centre for Housing, Building, and
Planning.
1. Cooperative housing. 2. Mortgage fi-
nance. I. United Nations. (Center for
Housing,   Building, and Planning)
II. Title.

370
J82   Techniques of reading.
Judson, Horace.
Techniques of reading. An integrated program
for improved comprehension and speed, by Horace
Judson in consultation with Kenneth P. Baldridge,
the Reading Laboratory. New York, Harcourt,
Brace & World, 1954.
406p.

1. Education. I. Baldridge, Kenneth P.
II. Title.

711.585
(795L9)
P67t   Techniques for measuring blight;
Portland, Or. City Planning Commission.
Techniques for measuring blight; a
description of the appraisal methods used
to measure urban blight in Portland.
Portland, 1965.
26p.
U.S. Dept. of Housing and Urban Development. CRP.

1. Slums - Portland, Or. 2. Urban
renewal - Portland, Or. I. Title.
II. Title: Appraisal methods used to
measure   urban blight in
Portland.   III. U.S. HUD - CRP.
Portland, Or.

002
V42   Techniques of information retrieval.
Vickery, B   C
Techniques of information retrieval. Hamden,
Conn., Archon Books, 1970.
262p.

Bibliography: p. 245-257.

1. Documentation. 2. Indexing.
3. Abstracting. I. Title.

658.3
L17   The techniques of supervision.
Lateiner, Alfred R
The techniques of supervision.   New London,
Connecticut, National Foremen's Institute [1954].
207p.

744
M45   Techniques for producing visual instruct-
ional media.
Minor, Ed
Techniques for producing visual instruct-
ional media, by Ed Minor and Harvey R.
Frye. New York, McGraw-Hill, 1970.
305p.

Bibliography: p. 233-245.

1. Visual aids. I. Frye, Harvey R.,
jt. au. II. Title.

333.33
G66   TECHNIQUES OF INVESTMENT PROPERTY
EXCHANGING.
GOOD, SHELDON F   , ED.
TECHNIQUES OF INVESTMENT PROPERTY
EXCHANGING. CHICAGO, INTERNATIONAL
TRADERS CLUB, EXCHANGE DIVISION OF THE
NATIONAL INSTITUTE OF REAL ESTATE
BROKERS, 1965.
31P.

1. REAL ESTATE BUSINESS. I. NATIONAL
INSTITUTE OF REAL ESTATE BROKERS. II.
TITLE. III. TITLE: INVESTMENT
PROPERTY EXCHANGING.

388
M29t
v.1   Techniques of transport planning.
Meyer, John R   ed.
Techniques of transport planning. Vol. 1,
Pricing and project evaluation. Ed. by John
R. Meyer and Mahlon R. Straszheim. Wash.,
Brookings Institution, Transport Research Pro-
gram, 1971.
343p.
Bibliography: p. 317-336.

1. Transportation. I. Meyer, John R., ed.
II. Straszheim, Mahlon R., jt. ed.
III. Brookings Institution. Transport
Research Program.   IV. Title. V. Title:
Pricing and project evaluation.

331.86
M17   Techniques for on-the-job learning.
Matthies, Leslie H
Techniques for on-the-job learning.
Colorado Springs, Colo., Systemation, inc.,
[1969?]
9p.

1. Apprenticeship. 2. Occupations.
I. Title: On-the-job learning. II. Systemation, inc. III. Title.

712
W22   Techniques of landscape architecture.
Weddle, A   E   ed,
Techniques of landscape architecture. Edit-
ed for the Institute of Landscape Architects.
New York, American Elsevier Pub. Co., 1967.
Laf.   226p.

1. Landscape architecture. 2. Site planning.
I. Institute of Landscape Architects.
II. Title.

388
M29t
v.2   Techniques of transport planning.
Meyer, John R   ed.
Techniques of transport planning. Vol. 2:
Systems analysis and simulation models.
David T. Kresge and Paul O. Roberts. With
special contributions by Donald N. Dewees and
others. Wash., Brookings Institution, Trans-
port Research Program, 1971.
228p.
1. Transportation. I. Kresge, David T.
II. Brookings Institution. Transport Research
Program. III. Title.

658
M45t
Techniques of value analysis and engineering.
Miles, Lawrence D
Techniques of value analysis and engineering. New York, McGraw-Hill, 1961.
267p.
Bibliography: p. 250-253.

1. Industrial management. 2. Quality control. 3. Accounting. I. Title: Value analysis. II. Title.

658
M45t
1972
Techniques of value analysis and engineering.
Miles, Lawrence D
Techniques of value analysis and engineering. 2d ed. New York, McGraw-Hill, 1972.
366p.

1. Industrial management. 2. Quality control. 3. Building costs. I. Title. II. Title: Value analysis and engineering.

651.4
A75T
TECHNIQUES OF WORK SIMPLIFICATION.
U.S. DEPT. OF THE ARMY.
TECHNIQUES OF WORK SIMPLIFICATION; MORE EFFECTIVE USE OF MANPOWER, EQUIPMENT, MATERIALS, SPACE. WASHINGTON, GOVT. PRINT. OFF., 1956. 22P. CHARTS. (ITS PAMPHLET NO. 20-300)

1. OFFICE MANAGEMENT. I. TITLE.

628.515
(79455)
R22
Techniques to reduce nitrogen in drainage...
U.S. Bureau of Reclamation. Region 2.
Techniques to reduce nitrogen in drainage effluent during transport. Bio-engineering aspects of agricultural drainage, San Joaquin Valley, California. Prepared for Water Quality Office, Environmental Protection Agency. Wash., Govt. Print. Off., 1971.
48p. (Water pollution control research series)
1. Water pollution - San Joaquin Valley, Calif. I. U.S. Environmental Protection Agency. II. Title.

320
(44)
M29
Technocracy.
Meynaud, Jean.
Technocracy. Translated by Paul Barnes. New York, Free Press, 1969.
315p.

Bibliography: p. 304-306.

1. Political science - France. I. Barnes, Paul, tr. II. Title.

658.562
T46
Technological applications of statistics.
Tippett, L H C
Technological applications of statistics. New York, John Wiley & Sons, Inc., [c1950].
ix, 189 p. charts, graphs, tables. (Wiley publications in statistics)

Bibliography: p.185-186.
"This book is a "write-up" of a course of lectures given at the Massachusetts Institute of Technology". Pref.

1.Statistics. 2.Qual control. I.Title.

600
M27
Technological change.
Mesthene, Emmanuel G
Technological change; its impact on man and society. Cambridge, Mass., Harvard University Press, 1970.
127p. (Harvard studies in technology and society)

Bibliography: p. 96-124.

1. Technology. 2. Man - Influence of environment. I. Title.

608
N67
Technological change.
Nordhaus, William D
Invention, growth, and welfare; a theoretical treatment of technological change. Cambridge, Mass., M.I.T. Press, 1969.
168p. (M.I.T. monographs in economics, 10)
Bibliography: p. 155-164.

1. Inventions. 2. Economic development.
I. Title. II. Title: Technological change.

538.56
C65AU
TECHNOLOGICAL CHANGE.
U.S. CONGRESS. JOINT ECONOMIC COMMITTEE.
AUTOMATION AND TECHNOLOGICAL CHANGE. HEARINGS BEFORE THE SUBCOMMITTEE ON THE ECONOMIC STABILIZATION OF THE JOINT COMMITTEE ON THE ECONOMIC REPORT PURSUANT TO SEC. 5(A) OF PUBLIC LAW 304 (79TH CONGRESS) WASHINGTON, GOVT. PRINT. OFF., 1955.
644P.
HEARINGS HELD OCT. 14-15, 17-18, 14-28, 1955.
1. AUTOMATION. I. TITLE: TECHNOLOGICAL CHANGE. TECHN

385
065
1961
Technological change and the future of the railways.
Conference on Technological Change and the Future of the Railways, Northwestern University, 1961.
Technological change and the future of the railways. Selected papers from a three-day conference conducted by the Transportation Center at Northwestern University, Evanston, Illinois. Editors: Robert S. Nelson and Edward M. Johnson. [Evanston, Ill., 1961]
239p.

1. Railroads - Congresses. I. Nelson, Robert S., ed. II. Title. III. Northwestern University. Transportation Center.

691.116
W17
Technological changes in plywood occupations.
Washington (State) Employment Security Dept.
Technological changes in plywood occupations. [Olympia] 1968.
70p.

1. Plywood. 2. Lumber industry. I. Title.

600
E87
Technological forecasting.
European Conference on Technological Forecasting, University of Strathclyde, 1968.
Technological forecasting. Edited by R.V. Arnfield. Edinburg, Edinburgh U.P., 1969.
417p.

1. Technology. 2. Economic forecasting. I. Arnfield, R.V., ed. II. Glasgow. University of Strathclyde. III. Title.

711.4
A52ne
no. 7
Technological forecasting.
Jantsch, Erich.
Technological forecasting in perspective (A framework for technological forecasting, its techniques and organisation; a description of activities and annotated bibliography) Paris, Organisation for Economic Co-operation and Development, 1966.
493p. (Working document DAS/SPR/66.12)
Bibliography: p. 347-437.
AIP/Ewald notebooks, Basic book no. 7

1. City planning. 2. Scientific research. 3. Economic forecasting. 4. Sociology. I. Organisation for Economic Co-operation and Development. II. Title.

658
711.4
L42
Technological forecasting.
Lien, Arthur P
Technological forecasting: tools, techniques, applications, by Arthur P. Lien and others. New York, American Management Association, 1968.
27p. (American Management Association. Management bulletin no. 115)

1. Industrial management. I. American Management Association. III. Title. (Series)

600.15
F72
Laf.
Technological forecasting.
Prehoda, Robert W.
Designing the future; the role of technological forecasting, by Robert W. Prehoda. Foreword by Sir George Thomson. 1st ed. Philadelphia, Chilton Book Co., 1967.
310p.
Bibliography: p. 287-291.
1. Industrial research. 2. Automation. 3. Architecture. 4. Housing research. 5. Research. I. Title. II. Title: Technological forecasting.

330
A97
Technological forecasting and long-range planning.
Ayres, Robert U
Technological forecasting and long-range planning. New York, McGraw-Hill, 1969.
237p.

1. Economic planning. 2. Economic forecasting. 3. Scientific research. I. Title.

690.015
(41
:016)
U541
no.
218
Technological forecasting and project evaluation.
U.K. Building Research Station.
Technological forecasting and project evaluation. Garston, Eng., 1969.
7p. (Its Library bibliography 218)

1. Building industry - Bibl. 2. Building costs - Bibl. I. Title.

600
B74
Technological forecasting for industry and government.
Bright, James Rieser, ed.
Technological forecasting for industry and government; methods and applications. Englewood Cliffs, N.J., Prentice-Hall, 1968.
484p.

Bibliography: p. 451-474.

1. Technology. 2. Economic forecasting. 3. Industrial management. I. Title.

301.15
R67t
Technological injury.
Rose, John, 1917- ed.
Technological injury; the effect of technological advances on environment, life, and society. London, Gordon and Breach Science Publishers, 1969.
224p.

1. Man - Influence of environment.
2. Natural resources. 3. Technology. I. Title.

330
B51
Technological innovation in civilian public areas.
Black, Ronald P
Technological innovation in civilian public areas. Prepared by Ronald P. Black and Charles W. Foreman. Prepared for: U.S. Arms Control and Disarmament Agency. Falls Church, Va., Analytic Services, inc., 1967.
95p. (ACDA/E-118)
Bibliography: Appendix E.
1. Economic conditions. 2. National defense. 3. Impact of industry. 4. Impact of military installations. I. Foreman, Charles W., jt. au. II. U.S. Arms Control and Disarmament Agency. III. Analytic Services. IV. Title.

336.2
C65te
Technological innovation: its environment and management.
U.S. Dept. of Commerce.
Technological innovation: its environment and management [by the] Panel on Invention and Innovation. Washington, For sale by the Supt. of Documents, Govt. Print. Off., 1967.
83p.

1. Taxation. 2. Economic development. 3. Finance. I. Title.

330
(746)
C65v

Technological Innovation on the Future of
Connecticut, University of Connecticut, 1968.
Conference on the Influence of
Technological Innovation on the Future
of Connecticut, University of Connecticut,
1968.
Vantage point: 2000 A.D. Report on a
Conference... Hartford, Connecticut
Research Commission, 1968.
32p.

1. Economic development - Conn. 2. Man -
Influence of environment. I. Connecticut.
Research   Commission. II. Title.

500.15
A52.2
1965

AMERICAN UNIVERSITY. INSTITUTE ON
RESEARCH ADMINISTRATION, 10TH, 1965.
THE FUNDAMENTAL ...1965.   (CARD 2)

I. VOLLMER, HOWARD M., ED.
II. U.S. AIR FORCE. OFFICE OF
SCIENTIFIC RESEARCH. III. TITLE.

351
C61

TECHNOLOGY.
Coates, Vary Taylor.
Examples of technology assessments for
the Federal Government. Wash., Program
of Policy Studies in Science and Technology,
George Washington University, 1969.
44p. (George Washington University.
Program of Policy Studies in Science and
Technology. Staff discussion paper 208)
Prepared for hearings before the
Subcommittee on Science, Research, and
Development, Committee on Science and
Astronautics, U.S. House of Representa-
tives, Nov   18-Dec. 12, 1969.
1. Federal   (Cont'd on next card)

600
F27

Technological man.
Ferkiss, Victor C
Technological man: the myth and the reality.
New York, George Braziller, 1969.
336p.

Bibliography: p. 295-327.

1. Technology. 2. Man - Influence of
environment. I. Title.

360
B71

TECHNOLOGY.
Braden, William.
The age of aquarius; technology and the
cultural revolution. Chicago, Quadrangle Books,
1970.
306p.

1. Social conditions. 2. Technology.
3. Social change. I. Title.

351
C61

Coates, Vary Taylor. Examples...1969.
(Card 2)

government. 2. Technology. 3. Scientific research. I. George Washington
University. Program of Policy Studies
in Science and Technology. II. Title.

VF
690.015
C31

Technological research and construction
markets.
Chamber of Commerce of the United States.
(Construction and Civic Development Dept.)
Technological research and construction
markets.   Washington, May 1954.
24 p.

"Building Research Institute ... for the
advancement of building science in the United
States."-p. 20.
1.Building research. 2.Building industry.
3.Building Research Institute. I.Title.

600
B74

TECHNOLOGY.
Bright, James Rieser, ed.
Technological forecasting for industry and
government; methods and applications.
Englewood Cliffs, N.J., Prentice-Hall, 1968.
484p.

Bibliography: p. 451-474.

1. Technology. 2. Economic forecasting.
3. Industrial management. I. Title.

500.15
C65pr

TECHNOLOGY.
Conference on Space, Science, and Urban Life,
Oakland, Calif., 1963.
Proceedings, supported by the Ford Foundation and the National Aeronautics and Space
Administration in cooperation with the University of California and the city of Oakland.
Wash., National Aeronautics and Space Administration, 1963.
254p. (NASA SP-37)
1. Scientific research. 2. Technology.
3. Metropolitan areas. I. Ford Foundation.
II. U.S. Natio   nal Aeronautics and Space
Administra   tion. III. Title: Space,
science, and   urban life.

608
N17
1937

Technological trends and national policy.
U.S. National Resources Committee.
Technological trends and national policy,
including the social implications of new
inventions. June 1937. Report of the Subcommittee
on Technology.   Washington, Govt. Print. Off.,
1937.
388 p.   graphs, tables.

Bibliographical footnotes.
"Construction industrien:" p. 367-388.
1.Inventions. 2.Building methods. I.Title.

330
B74

TECHNOLOGY.
British Association for the Advancement of
Science.
Economics and technical change; papers pre-
sented to Section F (Economics) and jointly
to Sections F and G (Engineering) at the 1968
Annual Meeting of the British Association for
the Advancement of Science. Edited by E.M.
Hugh-Jones. New York, A.M. Kelley, 1969.
179p.

1. Economic conditions. 2. Technology.
I. High-Jones, Edward Maurice, ed. II. Title.

330
D21

TECHNOLOGY.
De Brigard, Raul.
Some potential societal developments, 1970-
2000, by Raul de Brigard and Olaf Helmer.
Middletown, Conn., Institute for the Future,
1970.
134p. (IFF report R-7)

1. Economic forecasting. 2. Technology.
3. Social conditions. I. Helmer, Olaf, jt. au.
II. Institute for the Future. III. Title.

711.417
(753)
C71

Technologies study...

Crane, David A
Technologies study: the application
of technological innovation in the
development of a new community, FLNT
(Fort Lincoln New Town) Prepared by
David A. Crane, architect, and Keyes,
Lethbridge and Condon for Edward J.
Logue, principal development consul-
tant, District of Columbia Redevelopment
Land Agency; National Capital Planning
Commission, and District of Columbia
Government. [Wash.?] 1968.
246p.   (Cont'd on next card)

693
B84

TECHNOLOGY.
Building Research Advisory Board.
New technologies in the development
of housing for lower-income families. A
special advisory report to the Office of
Urban Technology and Research, Dept. of
Housing and Urban Development. Wash.,
National Research Council, National Academy
of Sciences; National Academy of Engineering,
1969.
26p.
1. Building methods. 2. Technology.
I. U.S. Dept. of Housing and Urban Development. Office   of Urban Technology
and Research.   II. Title.

658.564
D42

TECHNOLOGY.
Diebold, John.
Man and the computer; technology as an
agent of social change. New York, Praeger,
1969.
157p.

Bibliography: p. 155-157.

1. Automation. 2. Technology.
I. Title.

711.417
(753)
C71

Crane, David A   Technologies...1968.
(Card 2)

Bibliography: p. 239-246.
1. Planned communities - District of
Columbia. 2. Community development -
District of Columbia. 3. Prefabricated
construction - District of Columbia.
I. Title. II. Title: Fort Lincoln new
town. III. Keys, Lethbridge and Condon.

301.15
C31s

TECHNOLOGY.
Chartrand, Robert L
Systems technology applied to social and
community problems. New York, Spartan Books,
1971.
478p.
Originally prepared for the Subcommittee on
Employment, Manpower, and Poverty of the
Committee on Labor and Public Welfare of the
United States Senate.
Bibliography: p. 443-468.
1. Man - Influence of environment.
2. Technology. I. U.S. Congress. Senate.
Committee on Labo   r and Public Welfare.
II. Title.

360
D25e

TECHNOLOGY.
Denver. University. Research Institute.
The environment and the action in technology
transfer, 1970-1980. Report of a conference
sponsored by Denver Research Institute, University of Denver, Snowness-at-Aspen, Colorado,
Sept. 26-28, 1969. Denver, Denver Research
Institute, University of Denver, 1969.
45p.

1. Science and civilization. 2. Technology.
I. Title.

500.15
A52.2
1965

TECHNOLOGY.
AMERICAN UNIVERSITY. INSTITUTE ON
RESEARCH ADMINISTRATION, 10TH, 1965.
THE FUNDAMENTAL RESEARCH ACTIVITY IN
A TECHNOLOGY-DEPENDENT ORGANIZATION; A
SELECTION OF PAPERS PRESENTED AT THE
TENTH INSTITUTE ON RESEARCH
ADMINISTRATION HELD 26-29 APRIL, 1965,
WASHINGTON, D.C. EDITED BY HOWARD M.
VOLLMER. WASHINGTON, AIR FORCE OFFICE
OF SCIENTIFIC RESEARCH, 1965.
103P.

1. SCIENTIFI   C RESEARCH.
2. TECHNOLOGY.
(CONTINUED ON NEXT CARD)

301
C31

TECHNOLOGY.
Chaszar, Edward.
Science and technology in the theories of
social and political alienation. Wash., 1969.
65p. (George Washington University. Program
of Policy Studies in Science and Technology.
Staff discussion paper 401)

1. Sociology. 2. Technology. 3. Social
conditions. I. George Washington University.
Program of Policy Studies in Science and Technology. II. Title.

Ref.
030.1
E52b

Technology.

Encyclopedia Britanica.
Britannica perspectives. Chicago, 1968.
3v.

1. Encyclopedias and dictionaries.
2. Man - Influence of environment.
3. Social sciences. 4. Technology.
5. Science. I. Title.

600
E53
TECHNOLOGY.
ENGINEERS JOINT COUNCIL.
NATIONAL ENGINEERING AFFAIRS:
ENVIRONMENTAL POLLUTION, NATURAL
RESOURCES, TECHNICAL INFORMATION. SUMMARY
REPORT ON A SEMINAR SPONSORED BY ENGINEERS
JOINT COUNCIL, JANUARY 16-18, 1966,
WASHINGTON, D.C. NEW YORK, 1966.
44P.

1. TECHNOLOGY. 2. AIR POLLUTION.
3. NATURAL RESOURCES. I. TITLE.

301.15
I57p
TECHNOLOGY.
International Symposium on Remote Sensing
of Environment.
Proceedings,

Ann Arbor, Mich., Center for Remote Sensing
Information and Analysis, Willow Run
Laboratories, Institute of Science and
Technology, University of Michigan, 19
v.
Sponsored by Center for Remote Sensing
Information and Analysis, Willow Run
Laboratories, Institute of Science and
(Cont'd on next card)

301.15
M19
TECHNOLOGY.
Mayo, Louis H
The relationship of technology assessment to
environmental management. Wash., 1969.
34p. (George Washington University. Program
of Policy Studies in Science and Technology.
Staff discussion paper 206)

1. Man - Influence of environment. 2. Technology. I. George Washington University. Program
of Policy Studies in Science and Technology.
II. Title.

600
E87
TECHNOLOGY.
European Conference on Technological Forecasting,
University of Strathclyde, 1968.
Technological forecasting. Edited by R.V.
Arnfield. Edinburg, Edinburgh U.P., 1969.
417p.

1. Technology. 2. Economic forecasting.
I. Arnfield, R.V., ed. II. Glasgow. University
of Strathclyde. III. Title.

301.15
I57p
TECHNOLOGY.
International Symposium on Remote Sensing
of Environment. Proceedings,

Technology, University of Michigan and
others.

1. Man - Influence of environment.
2. Technology. 3, International relations.
I. Michigan. University. Institute of
Science and Technology.

500
M19
TECHNOLOGY.
Mayo, Louis H
Scientific method, adversarial system and
technology assessment. Wash., Program of
Policy Studies in Science and Technology,
George Washington University, 1970.
110p. (George Washington University. Program
of Policy Studies in Science and Technology.
Monograph no. 5)
Revision of paper presented at the Engineering
Foundation Research Conference, Andover,
New Hampshire, August 1969.
1. Science. 2. Technology. I. George
Washington University. Program of Policy
Studies in Science and Technology. II. Title.
III. Title; Adversarial system.

600
F27
TECHNOLOGY.
Ferkiss, Victor C
Technological man: the myth and the reality.
New York, George Braziller, 1969.
336p.

Bibliography: p. 295-327.

1. Technology. 2. Man - Influence of
environment. I. Title.

500
J65
TECHNOLOGY.
Jones, Ernest M
Advocacy in technology assessment. Wash.,
Program of Policy Studies in Science and
Technology, George Washington University, 1970.
77p. (George Washington University. Program
of Policy Studies in Science and Technology.
Staff discussion paper 209)

1. Science. 2. Technology. I. George
Washington University. Program of Policy
Studies in Science and Technology. II. Title.

360
M19
TECHNOLOGY.
Mayo, Louis H
Social impact analysis: 1970. Wash., George
Washington University, Program of Policy Studies
in Science and Technology, 1971.
50p. (Staff discussion paper 210)

1. Social conditions. 2. Technology.
2. Man - Influence of environment. I. George
Washington University. Program of Policy
Studies in Science and Technology. II. Title.

368
F42
TECHNOLOGY.
Fields, Gordon B
The influence of insurance on technolog-
ical development. Wash., Program of Policy
Studies in Science and Technology, George
Washington University, 1969.
28p. (George Washington University.
Program of Policy Studies in Science and
Technology. Staff discussion paper 405)

1. Insurance. 2. Technology. I. George
Washington University. Program of Policy
Studies in   Science and Technology.
II. Title.

301.15
K17
TECHNOLOGY.
Kasper, Raphael G
Some comments on technology assessment and
the environment. Wash., Program of Policy
Studies in Science and Technology, George
Washington University, 1970.
13p. (George Washington University. Program
of Policy Studies in Science and Technology.
Occasional paper no. 18)
Presented at a panel discussion entitled
What to do about the environment, Nov. 19,
1970, George Washington University.
1. Man - Influence of environment.
2. Technology.   I. George Washington
University. Program of Policy Studies in
Science and Technology. II. Title.

600
M19
TECHNOLOGY.
Mayo, Louis H
Some legal, jurisdictional, and
operational implications of a congressional
technology assessment component. A
statement by Louis H. Mayo before the
Subcommittee on Science, Research, and
Development, Committee on Science and
Astronautics, U.S. House of Represent-
atives, Dec. 2, 1969. Wash., Program of
Policy Studies in Science and Technology,
George Washington University, 1969.
56p.   (George Washington
(Cont'd on next card)

600
G42
TECHNOLOGY.
GIEDION, SIEGFRIED.
MECHANIZATION TAKES COMMAND, A
CONTRIBUTION TO ANONYMOUS HISTORY. NEW
YORK, OXFORD UNIVERSITY PRESS, 1948.
743P.

1. TECHNOLOGY. 2. SCIENCE AND
CIVILIZATION. I. TITLE.

600
K17
TECHNOLOGY.
Kasper, Raphael G   ed.
Technology assessment; understanding the
social consequences of technological appli-
cations. New York, Praeger, 1972.
291p. (Praeger special studies in U.S.
economic and social development)
Published in cooperation with the Program of
Policy Studies in Science and Technology,
George Washington University.
1. Technology. 2. Man - Influence of environ-
ment. I. George Washington University. Program
of Policy Studies in Science and Technology.
II. Title.

600
M19
Mayo, Louis H   Some...1969. (Card 2)

University. Program of Policy Studies in
Science and Technology. Staff discussion
paper 207)

1. Technology. 2. U.S. Congress.
3. Governmental research. I. U.S.
Congress. House. Committee on Science
and Astronautics. II. George Washington
University. Program on Policy Studies.
III. Title.

330
G67
TECHNOLOGY.
Gordon, Theodore J
Forecasts of some technological and scientific
developments and their societal consequences,
by Theodore J. Gordon and Robert H. Ament.
Middletown, Conn., Institute for the Future,
1969.
98p. (IFF report R-6)

1. Economic forecasting. 2. Technology.
3. Social conditions. I. Ament, Robert H., jt.
au. II. Institute for the Future. III. Title.

500
K51
Technology.
Klaw, Spencer.
The new brahmins; scientific life in America.
New York, William Morrow, 1968.
315p.
Bibliography: p. 279-302.

1. Scientists. 2. Science. 3. Technology.
I. Title.

600
M27
TECHNOLOGY.
Mesthene, Emmanuel G
Technological change; its impact on man
and society. Cambridge, Mass., Harvard
University Press, 1970.
127p. (Harvard studies in technology
and society)

Bibliography: p. 96-124.

1. Technology. 2. Man - Influence of
environment. I. Title.

301.15
H15t
TECHNOLOGY.
Hall, Cameron P
Technology and people. Valley Forge, Pa.,
Judson Press, 1969.
159p.

Bibliography: p. 157-159.

1. Man - Influence of environment.
2. Technology. I. Title.

301.15
M12f
TECHNOLOGY.
McHale, John.
The future of the future. New York,
Braziller, 1969.
322p.

Bibliography: p. 301-317.

1. Man - Influence of environment.
2. Technology. 3. Sociology. I. Title.

600
M67t
TECHNOLOGY.
Mottur, Ellis R
Technology assessment and citizen action.
Presented in the Professional Seminar Series on
Technology Assessment, May 26, 1970. Wash.,
Program of Policy Studies in Science and
Technology, George Washington University, 1971.
27p. (George Washington University. Program
of Policy Studies in Science and Technology.
Occasional paper no. 10)
1. Technology. 2. Community development -
Citizen participation. I. George Washington
University. Program of Policy Studies in
Science and Technology. II. Title.

600
M67
TECHNOLOGY.
Mottur, Ellis R
Technology assessment and environmental engineering. Presented to the eighth annual meeting of the Society of Engineering Science, inc., Wash., Nov. 11, 1970. Wash., Program of Policy Studies in Science and Technology, George Washington University, 1971.
21p. (George Washington University. Program of Policy Studies in Science and Technology. Occasional paper no. 9)
1. Technology. 2. Man - Influence of environment. I. George Washington University. Program of Policy Studies in Science and Technology. II. Title.

658.564
P17
TECHNOLOGY.
Parkman, Ralph.
Cybernation and man: a course development project; final report to the Division of Higher Education Research, U.S. Office of Education. San Jose, Calif., School of Engineering, San Jose State College, 1967.
142p.
Bibliography: p. 99-142.
1. Automation. 2. Technology. I. California. State College, San Jose. School of Engineering. II. U.S. Office of Education. III. Title.

500
S24
TECHNOLOGY.
Scientific American resource library: readings in the physical sciences and technology. San Francisco, W.H. Freeman, 1969-
v.
Vols. 1-3; are Scientific American offprint no. 201/246; 247-290; 291/326.
1. Science. 2. Technology. I. Scientific American. II. Scientific American offprint. III. Title: Physical sciences and technology.

360
M85
v.2
TECHNOLOGY.
Mumford, Lewis.
The myth of the machine, vol. 2. The pentagon of power. New York, Harcourt, Brace Jovanovich, 1970.
496p.
Bibliography: p. 439-469.
1. Social conditions. 2. Technology. 3. Science and civilization. I. Title. II. Title: The pentagon of power.

VF
352.6
P25
TECHNOLOGY.
Pendleton, William C
Technology and cities; a foundation viewpoint. New York, Ford Foundation, 1968.
13p.
1. Municipal services. 2. Technology. I. Ford Foundation. II. Title.

330
C65d
no.6
TECHNOLOGY.
U.S. Dept. of Commerce.
Do you know your economic ABC's? Science and technology for mankind's progress. A simplified explanation of science and technology and how they are applied to further economic growth. [Wash.] 1967.
46p. (Booklet, no. 6)
Bibliography: p. 40-43.
1. Economics. 2. Technology. 3. Scientific research. I. Title: Science and technology for mankind's progress. II. Title.

600
N17p
TECHNOLOGY.
National Academy of Engineering.
The process of technological innovation; symposium sponsored by the National Academy of Engineering, April 24, 1968. Wash., National Academy of Sciences, 1969.
103p. (National Academy of Sciences. Publication 1726)
1. Technology. I. Title.

VF
600
P72
TECHNOLOGY.
Prehoda, Robert W
The growing role of technological forecasting. Wash., World Future Society, 1967.
[3]p.
In: The Futurist, June, 1967, p. 33-35.
1. Technology. 2. Economic forecasting. I. Futurist. II. Title.

500.15
C65CRE
1962
H-R
TECHNOLOGY.
U.S. CONGRESS. HOUSE. COMMITTEE ON SCIENCE AND ASTRONAUTICS.
CREATION OF THE OFFICE OF SCIENCE AND TECHNOLOGY (REORGANIZATION PLAN NO. 2, 1962) STAFF STUDY... EIGHTY-SEVENTH CONGRESS, SECOND SESSION. WASHINGTON, GOVT. PRINT. OFF., 1962.
85P.
1. SCIENTIFIC RESEARCH. 2. TECHNOLOGY. 3. U.S. OFFICE OF SCIENCE & TECHNOLOGY (PROPOSED)

600
N17s
TECHNOLOGY.
National Academy of Engineering. Committee on Public Engineering Policy.
A study of technology assessment. Wash., Committee on Science and Astronautics, U.S. House of Representatives, 1969.
208p.
Committee print.
1. Technology. I. U.S. Congress. House. Committee on Science and Astronautics. II. Title.

330
R61
TECHNOLOGY.
Roberts, Edward Baer.
Exploratory and normative technological forecasting: a critical appraisal. [n.p.] 1969.
27p. (Massachusetts Institute of Technology. Sloan (Alfred P.) School of Management. Research program on the management science and technology no. 378-69)
1. Economic forecasting. 2. Technology. I. Title.

301.15
C657
Technology.
U.S. Congress. House. Committee on Science and Astronautics.
Managing the environment; report of the Subcommittee on Science, Research and Development to the Committee on Science and Astronautics, U.S. House of Representatives. Washington, Govt. Print. Off., 1968.
59p.
1. Man - Influence of environment. 2. Scientific research. 3. Technology. I. Title.

600
N17
TECHNOLOGY.
National Academy of Sciences.
Technology: processes of assessment and choice. Wash., Govt. Print. Off., 1969.
163p.
Report of the National Academy of Sciences to the Committee on Science and Astronautics, U.S. House of Representatives.
1. Technology. 2. Scientific research. I. U.S. Congress. House. Committee on Science and Astronautics. II. Title.

658
R65
Technology.
Roman, Daniel D
Research and development management: the economics and administration of technology. New York, Appleton-Century-Crofts, 1968.
450p. (Administration series)
Bibliography: p. 434-442.
1. Management. 2. Technology. I. Title.

500.15
C65tec
1970
H-H
TECHNOLOGY.
U.S. Congress. House. Committee on Science and Astronautics.
Technology assessment. Hearings before the Subcommittee on Science, Research, and Development of the Committee on Science and Astronautics, U.S. House of Representatives, Ninety-first Congress, first session. Wash., Govt. Print. Off., 1970.
562p. (no. 13)
Hearings held Nov. 18 - Dec. 12, 1969.
1. Scientific research. 2. Technology. I. Title.

331
(747)
N28m
TECHNOLOGY.
New York (State) Dept. of Labor.
Manpower impacts of electronic data processing. New York, Dept. of Labor, Div. of Research and Statistics, 1968.
117p. (Its Publication B-171)
1. Employment - New York (State) 2. Labor supply - Automation. 3. Technology. 4. Automation. I. Title.

301.15
R67t
TECHNOLOGY.
Rose, John, 1917- ed.
Technological injury; the effect of technological advances on environment, life, and society. London, Gordon and Breach Science Publishers, 1969.
224p.
1. Man - Influence of environment. 2. Natural resources. 3. Technology. I. Title.

500.15
C65CR
1962
S-H
TECHNOLOGY.
U.S. CONGRESS. SENATE. COMMITTEE ON GOVERNMENT OPERATIONS.
CREATE A COMMISSION ON SCIENCE AND TECHNOLOGY. HEARING, EIGHTY-SEVENTH CONGRESS, SECOND SESSION, ON S. 2771. WASHINGTON, GOVT. PRINT. OFF., 1962.
2PTS.
PAGED CONTINUOUSLY.
1. SCIENTIFIC RESEARCH. 2. TECHNOLOGY. 3. U.S. COMMISSION ON SCIENCE AND TECHNOLOGY (PROPOSED)

002
P15
TECHNOLOGY.
Panel on Science and Technology.
The management of information and knowledge; a compilation of papers prepared for the eleventh meeting of the Panel on Science and Technology. [Wash.] Committee on Science and Astronautics, U.S. House of Representatives; for sale by the Superintendent of Docs., U.S. Govt. Print. Off., 1970.
130p.
1. Documentation. 2. Scientific research. 3. Technology. I. U.S. Congress. House. Committee on Science and Astronautics. II. Title.

658.564
R81a
TECHNOLOGY.
Rubin, Martin L ed.
Advanced technology: input and output. Princeton, N.J., Auerbach Pub., 1970.
361p. (Handbook of data processing management, vol. 4)
Thomas Harrell, technical editor.
1. Automation. 2. Management - Automation. 3. Technology. I. Title. (Series: Handbook of data processing management, vol. 4)

500.15
C65CR
1959
S-H
TECHNOLOGY.
U.S. CONGRESS. SENATE. COMMITTEE ON GOVERNMENT OPERATIONS.
CREATE A DEPARTMENT OF SCIENCE AND TECHNOLOGY. HEARINGS BEFORE THE SUBCOMMITTEE ON REORGANIZATION AND INTERNATIONAL ORGANIZATIONS... EIGHTY-SIXTH CONGRESS, FIRST SESSION, ON S. 676... AND S. 586... WASHINGTON, GOVT. PRINT. OFF., 1959.
2PTS.
1. SCIENTIFIC RESEARCH. 2. TECHNOLOGY. 3. U.S. DEPT. OF SCIENCE AND TECHNOLOGY (PROPOSED)

500.15
C65ES
1963
S-R

TECHNOLOGY.
U.S. CONGRESS. SENATE. COMMITTEE ON GOVERNMENT OPERATIONS.
ESTABLISHMENT OF A COMMISSION ON SCIENCE AND TECHNOLOGY. REPORT... ON S. 816. WASHINGTON, GOVT. PRINT. OFF., 1963.
62P. (88TH CONGRESS, 1ST SESSION. SENATE. REPORT NO. 16)

1. SCIENTIFIC RESEARCH.
2. TECHNOLOGY. 3. U.S. COMMISSION ON SCIENCE AND TECHNOLOGY (PROPOSED)

500.15
N17NA

TECHNOLOGY.
U.S. NATIONAL BUREAU OF STANDARDS.
NATIONAL STANDARD REFERENCE DATA SYSTEM; PLAN OF OPERATION, BY EDWARD L. BRADY AND MERRILL B. WALLENSTEIN. WASHINGTON, GOVT. PRINT. OFF., 1964.
12P. (ITS PUBLICATION NSRDS-NBS 1)

1. SCIENTIFIC RESEARCH.
2. TECHNOLOGY. I. BRADY, EDWARD L.
II. WALLENSTEIN, MERRILL B.
III. TITLE.

Ref.
500
(016)
A66

Technology - Bibliography.
Applied Science & Technology Index, 1958-
New York, Wilson, 1959-
v. quarterly. cumulated annually

Formerly: Industrial arts index, 1913-1957.
SEE SHELF LIST FOR LIBRARY HOLDINGS.

1. Science - Bibliography. 2. Technology - Bibliography. 3. Science - Periodicals. 4. Technology - Periodicals.

rds

500.15
C65ES
1962
S-H

TECHNOLOGY.
U.S. CONGRESS. SENATE. COMMITTEE ON GOVERNMENT OPERATIONS.
ESTABLISHMENT OF A COMMISSION ON SCIENCE AND TECHNOLOGY. REPORT... ON S. 2771. WASHINGTON, GOVT. PRINT. OFF., 1962.
52P. (87TH CONGRESS, 2D SESSION. REPORT NO. 1828)

1. SCIENTIFIC RESEARCH.
2. TECHNOLOGY. 3. U.S. COMMISSION ON SCIENCE AND TECHNOLOGY (PROPOSED)

500.15
N17st

Technology.
U.S. National Bureau of Standards.
Status report: National Standard Reference Data System. Edward L. Brady, ed. Wash., For sale by the Supt. of Docs., Govt. Print. Off., 1968.
129p. (Its Technical note 448)
Bibliography: p. 116-120.

1. Scientific research. 2. Technology.
I. Brady, Edward L., ed. II. Title: National Standard Reference Data System.

658
(016)
H65

TECHNOLOGY - BIBLIOGRAPHY.
Holman (John F.) & Co., Washington, D.C.
A small selected management and technical library; bibliography. Washington, Dept. of State, Agency for International Development, Communications Resources Division [1962]
61p.
Code B-16.
"Prepared ... for the technical aids program."

1. Industrial management - Bibl.
2. Technology - Bibl. I. Title.

351
C653AC
1958
S-H

TECHNOLOGY.
U.S. CONGRESS. SENATE. COMMITTEE ON GOVERNMENT OPERATIONS.
SCIENCE AND TECHNOLOGY ACT OF 1958. HEARINGS BEFORE A SUBCOMMITTEE... EIGHTY-FIFTH CONGRESS, SECOND SESSION, ON S. 3126... WASHINGTON, GOVT. PRINT. OFF., 1958. 2PTS.

HEARINGS HELD MAY 2-JUNE 26, 1958.

1. U.S. EXECUTIVE DEPARTMENTS - REORGANIZATION. 2. SCIENTIFIC RESEARCH. 3. TECHNOLOGY.
I. TITLE.

711
N17t

TECHNOLOGY.
U.S. National Resources Committee.
Technology and planning. Washington, Govt. Print. Off., 1937.
31 p.

1. Planning. 2. Technology. I. Title.

301.15
(016)
M42

TECHNOLOGY - BIBLIOGRAPHY.
Michigan. University. Architectural Research Laboratory.
Environmental impacts of new technology: an annotated bibliography, by Charles N. Ehler. Ann Arbor, 1969.
167p. (Environmental design and research
1. Supplemental research publications)
1. Man - Influence of environment - Bibl.
2. Scientific research - Bibl. 3. Technology - Bibl. I. Ehler, Charles N.
II. Title.

600
C657
1972
S-H

TECHNOLOGY.
U.S. Congress. Senate. Committee on Rules and Administration.
Office of Technology Assessment for the Congress. Hearing before the Subcommittee on Computer Services, Ninety-second Congress, second session on S. 2302 and H.R. 10243, to establish an Office of Technology Assessment for the Congress as an aid in the identification and consideration of existing and probable impacts of technological application; to amend the National Science Foundation Act of 1950; and for other purposes. Wash.,
(Cont'd on next card)

500.15
P72sc

TECHNOLOGY.
U.S. President's Task Force on Science Policy.
Science and technology; tools for progress [Wash.] 1970.
48p.

1. Scientific research. 2. Technology.
I. Title.

018
N28

Index
Suppl.

TECHNOLOGY - BIBLIOGRAPHY.
New York. Engineering Societies Library.
Classed subject catalog. Boston, G.K. Hall, 1963.
v.

------ Index. Boston, G.K. Hall, 1963.
356p.
------ Supplement. Boston, G.K. Hall. 19
6v.
1. Library catalogs. 2. Engineering - Bibl.
3. Technology - Bibl. 4. Science - Bibl.
I. Universal Decimal Classification. II. Title.

600
C657
1972

U.S. Congress. Senate. Committee on Rules and Administration. Office of...
1972. (Card 2)

Govt. Print. Off., 1972.
120p.
Hearing held March 2, 1972.

1. Technology. 2. Scientific research.
I. Title. 3. U.S. Congress.

300
071

TECHNOLOGY.
Urban Institute.
The struggle to bring technology to cities. Wash., 1971.
79p.

1. Science and civilization. 2. Metropolitan areas. 3. Technology. I. Title.

500
(016)
W15

TECHNOLOGY - BIBLIOGRAPHY.
Walford, A.J.
Guide to reference material; Volume I, Science and technology. 2d ed. London, Library Association, 1966.
v.

1. Science - Bibliography.
2. Technology - Bibliography.
I. Title.

eb

500.15
C65te
1970
S-H

TECHNOLOGY.
U.S. Congress. Senate. Select Committee on Small Business.
Technology transfer. Hearings before the Subcommittee on Science and Technology of the Select Committee on Small Business, United States Senate, Ninety-first Congress, second session on review of technology transfer programs administered by various executive departments and agencies. Wash., Govt. Print. Off., 1970.
pts. pt. 1
1. Governmental research. 2. Technology.
3. Business. I. Title.

360
V15v

TECHNOLOGY
Values and the future; the impact of technological change on American values. Ed. by Kurt Baier and Nicholas Rescher. New York, Free Press, 1969.
527p.

Bibliography: p. 472-512.

1. Social conditions. 2. Technology.
I. Baier, Kurt, ed. II. Rescher, Nicholas, jt. ed.

Ref.
607
(03)
C31

TECHNOLOGY - DICTIONARIES.
Chambers's technical dictionary. Edited by C.F. Tweney and L.E.C. Hughes. 3rd ed. revised with supplement. New York, Macmillan, 1958.
1028 p.

1. Technology - Dictionaries. 2. Engineering - Dictionaries. 3. Building construction - Dictionaries. 4. Manufacturing - Dictionaries.

ep

607
N17

Technology.
U.S. National Aeronautics and Space Administration. (Technology Utilization Div.)
Seals and sealing techniques; a compilation. Wash., 1967.
14p. (Its SP-5905(01))

At head of title: Technology utilization.
1. Technology. I. Title.

608
W15

Technology.
Wall Street journal.
The innovators; how today's inventors shape your life tomorrow. Princeton, N.J., Dow Jones Books, 1968.
110p.

1. Inventions. 2. Scientific research.
3. Technology. 4. Patents. I. Title.

500
(03)
M12

Technology - Encyclopedias and dictionaries.
McGraw-Hill encyclopedia of science and technology. New York, McGraw-Hill Book Co., 19
v.
-- --- Readers' guide. New York, 19
v.
-- --- Study guide. New York, 19
v.
-- --- Yearbook, 19
v. New York, 19
For Library holdings see main entry.
1. Science - Encyclopedias and dictionaries.
2. Technology - Encyclopedias and dictionaries. 3. Encyclopedias and dictionaries.

603
M45
TECHNOLOGY - DICTIONARIES.
MILES, AETNA.
THE TECHNICAL SPELLER & DEFINITION FINDER.
1ST ED. INDIANAPOLIS, H.W. SAMS, 1965.
288P. (A HOWARD W. SAMS PHOTOFACT
PUBLICATION, SDH-1)

1. TECHNOLOGY - DICTIONARIES. I. TITLE.

500
(03)
C65
1965
TECHNOLOGY - DICTIONARIES.
U.S. COMMITTEE ON SCIENTIFIC AND
TECHNICAL INFORMATION.
COSATI SUBJECT CATEGORY LIST
(DOD-MODIFIED). WASHINGTON, DEFENSE
DOCUMENTATION CENTER, DEFENSE SUPPLY
AGENCY, 1965.
69P.

1. SCIENCE - DICTIONARIES.
2. TECHNOLOGY - DICTIONARIES. I. TITLE.
II. TITLE: SUBJECT CATEGORY LIST.

Ref.
500
(016)
A66
Technology - Periodicals.
Applied Science & Technology Index, 1958-
New York, Wilson, 1959-
v.   quarterly. cumulated annually

Formerly: Industrial arts index, 1913-1957.
SEE SHELF LIST FOR LIBRARY HOLDINGS.

1. Science - Bibliography. 2. Technology - Biblio
graphy. 3. Science - Periodicals. 4.
Technology - Periodicals.

rdz

603
(03)
N28
TECHNOLOGY - DICTIONARIES
Newmark, Maxim.
Illustrated technical dictionary, containing standard technical definitions of current terms in the applied sciences,
graphic and industrial arts, and mechanical trades; including
air navigation, meteorology, shipbuilding, synthetics and plastics; with illustrations, technical data, and interconversion
tables. Edited by Maxim Newmark ... New York, The
Philosophical library [1944]
3 p. l., vi, 352 p. illus., diagrs. 23½ᶜᵐ.

1. Technology—Dictionaries.

44-8419

Library of Congress   T9.N4
[18]   608

058.7
:600
(016)
I57
TECHNOLOGY - DIRECTORIES - BIBLIOGRAPHY.
Internationale Bibliographie der Fach-
adressbücher Wirtschaft, Wissenschaft,
Technik.
München-Pullach, Verlag Dokumentationen
der Technik.
v. (Handbuch der technischen
Dokumentation und Bibliographie, 5. Bd.)
Began with 1962 edition.
Compilers: I.O. Saur and others.
Kept up to date by supplements.

1. Tech-   nology - Direct -
Bibl.   (Cont'd on next card)

058.7
:500.15
L41d
TECHNOLOGY - RESEARCH - DIRECTORIES.
U.S. Library of Congress. Reference Department.
Directories in science and technology; a
provisional checklist. Washington, G.P.O., 1963.
65 p.

1. Scientific research - Directories. 2. Technology - Research - Directories. 3. Automation -
Directories.

c.2

I. Title.

cj

030.8
(46)
S25
TECHNOLOGY - DICTIONARIES.
Sell, Lewis L
English-Spanish comprehensive technical
dictionary of aircraft-automobile-electricity-
radio-television-petroleum-steel products.
New York, 1944.
1477p.
Section I.
1. English language - Dict. - Spanish.
2. Spanish language - Dict. - English.
3. Science - Dict. 4. Technology - Dict.

058.7
:600
(016)
I57
Internationale Bibliographie der Fach-
adressbücher Wirtschaft, Wissenschaft,
Technik. München...   (Card 2)

2. Industry - Direct - Bibl. 3. Science -
Direct - Bibl. I. Title: International
bibliography of economics-, science- and
technique- directories. (Series:
Handbuch der technischen Dokumentation
und Bibliographie, 5. Bd.)

500.15
823
Technology and change; the new Heraclitus.
Schon, Donald A
Technology and change; the new Heraclitus.
[The impact of invention and innovation on
American social and economic development]
New York, Delacorte Press, 1967.
248p. (A Seymour Lawrence book)
Bibliography: p. 247-248.

1. Scientific research. 2. Industrial
research. 3. Economic development.
I. Title.

058.7
:500
S62
TECHNOLOGY - DIRECTORIES.
Special Libraries Association.
Translators and translations: services and
sources in science and technology, edited by
Frances E. Kaiser. 2d ed. New York, 1965.
214 p.

1. Science - Directories.
2. Technology - Directories.
I. Title.
II. Kaiser, Frances E., ed.

ct

600
:330
C65
1963
S-H
TECHNOLOGY - ECONOMIC EFFECT.
U.S. CONGRESS. SENATE. SELECT
COMMITTEE ON SMALL BUSINESS.
THE ROLE AND EFFECT OF TECHNOLOGY IN
THE NATION'S ECONOMY. HEARINGS...
EIGHTY-EIGHTH CONGRESS, FIRST SESSION. A
REVIEW OF THE EFFECT OF GOVERNMENT
RESEARCH AND DEVELOPMENT ON ECONOMIC
GROWTH. WASHINGTON, GOVT. PRINT. OFF.,
1963-64.
6 V.

1. TECHNOLOGY - ECONOMIC EFFECT.
I. TITLE: TECHNOLOGY IN THE NATIONAL
ECONOMY.

VF
352.6
P25
Technology and cities.
Pendleton, William C
Technology and cities; a foundation
viewpoint. New York, Ford Foundation, 1968.
13p.

1. Municipal services. 2. Technology.
I. Ford Foundation. II. Title.

058.7
:500
UN
1969
TECHNOLOGY - DIRECTORIES.
United Nations Educational Scientific and
Cultural Organization.
World guide to technical information and
documentation services. New York, 1969.
287p.

1. Science - Direct. 2. Documentation -
Direct. 3. Technology - Direct. I. Title.

600
(09)
M85
TECHNOLOGY - HISTORY.
MUMFORD, LEWIS.
THE MYTH OF THE MACHINE; TECHNICS AND
HUMAN DEVELOPMENT. NEW YORK, HARCOURT,
BRACE, 1966.
342P. ILLUS.

BIBLIOGRAPHY: P.297-323.

1. TECHNOLOGY - HISTORY. I. TITLE.

300
M47
Technology and growth.
Mishan, Ezra J
Technology and growth: the price we pay.
New York, Praeger, 1970.
193p. (Books that matter)

1. Science and civilization. 2. Economic
policy. I. Title.

058.7
:500
L41d
TECHNOLOGY - DIRECTORY.
U.S. Library of Congress. Science and
Technology Division.
A directory of information resources in the
United States physical sciences engineering, by
the U.S. Library of Congress, Science and
Technology Division, National Referral Center.
Washington, Govt. Print. Off., 1971.
803p.
Cover title: Physical sciences engineering.
1. Science - Direct. 2. Technology - Direct.
3. Engineering - Direct. I. Title. II. Title:
Physical sciences engineering.

500.15
:347
C653
1965
H-H
TECHNOLOGY - LAW AND LEGISLATION.
U.S. CONGRESS. HOUSE. COMMITTEE ON
INTERSTATE AND FOREIGN COMMERCE.
STATE TECHNICAL SERVICES ACT OF 1965.
HEARINGS BEFORE THE SUBCOMMITTEE ON
COMMERCE AND FINANCE...EIGHTY-NINTH
CONGRESS, FIRST SESSION, ON H.R.
3420.... WASHINGTON, GOVT. PRINT. OFF.,
1965.
130P. (SERIAL NO. 89-15)

HEARINGS HELD: JUNE 1-3, 1965.
1. SCIENTIFIC RESEARCH - LAW AND
LEGISLATION. 2. TECHNOLOGY - LAW
AND LEGISLATION. I. TITLE.

VF
690.015
G72
1948
Technology and housing.
Green, John C
Technology and housing; statement before the
Joint Committee on Housing, 80th Congress, 2d
session, Jan. 21, 1948. [Washington, Office of
Technical Services? 1948]
11 p.
Processed.

1.Building research. 2.Housing research. I.U.S.
Office of Technical Services. II.U.S. Congress.
Joint Committee on Housing. III.Title.

500
(03)
C65
1964
TECHNOLOGY - DICTIONARIES.
U.S. COMMITTEE ON SCIENTIFIC AND
TECHNICAL INFORMATION.
COSATI SUBJECT CATEGORY LIST. 1ST ED.
WASHINGTON, FEDERAL COUNCIL FOR SCIENCE
AND TECHNOLOGY, 1964.
55P.

1. SCIENCE - DICTIONARIES.
2. TECHNOLOGY - DICTIONARIES. I. TITLE.
II. TITLE: SUBJECT CATEGORY LIST.

500.15
:347
C655
1965
H-R
TECHNOLOGY - LAW AND LEGISLATION.
U.S. CONGRESS. HOUSE. COMMITTEE ON
INTERSTATE AND FOREIGN COMMERCE.
STATE TECHNICAL SERVICES ACT OF 1965.
REPORT TO ACCOMPANY H.R. 3420.
WASHINGTON, GOVT. PRINT. OFF., 1965.
26P. (89TH CONGRESS, 1ST SESSION.
HOUSE OF REPRESENTATIVES. REPORT NO.
187)

1. SCIENTIFIC RESEARCH - LAW AND
LEGISLATION. 2. TECHNOLOGY - LAW AND
LEGISLATION. I. TITLE.

301
W45t
Technology and human values; our identity, our
unconscious, our religion, our games, our...
Wilkinson, John.
Technology and human values; our identity,
our unconscious, our religion, our games,
our names, by John Wilkinson and others.
New York, Center for the Study of Democratic
Institutions, 1966.
43p.
An occasional paper on the role of tech-
nology in the free-society.

1. Sociology. 2. Political science.
3. Economic conditions. 4. Automation -
Social effect. I. Center for the
Study of Demo-   cratic Institutions.
II. Title.

331
.J13
Technology and jobs.
Jaffe, A   J
Technology and jobs; automation in perspective, by A.J. Jaffe and Joseph Froomkin. New York, Frederick A. Praeger, 1968. 284p.

1. Employment. 2. Automation - Economic effect. 3. Labor productivity. I. Froomkin, Joseph, jt. au. II. Title.

301.15
H15t
Technology and people.
Hall, Cameron P
Technology and people. Valley Forge, Pa., Judson Press, 1969. 159p.

Bibliography: p. 157-159.

1. Man - Influence of environment. 2. Technology. I. Title.

711
N17t
Technology and planning.
U.S. National Resources Committee. Technology and planning. [Washington, Govt. Print. Off., 1937] 31 p.

1. Planning. 2. Technology. I. Title.

728.1
(436)
A87
Tendencies and policies in the field of housing, building and planning.
Austria. Federal Ministry of Construction and Technology. (Housing Section) Tendencies and policies in the field of housing, building and planning; Austrian contribution for the report. [Vienna, 1969] [26]p.
1. Housing - Austria. 2. Building industry - Austria. 3. Regional planning - Austria. I. Title.

538.56
N17t
v.1
Technology and the American economy.
U.S. National Commission on Technology, Automation, and Economic Progress. Technology and the American economy. Vol. 1. Wash., For sale by the Supt. of Doc., Govt. Print. Off., 1966. 115p.
Report to the President.
1. Automation. 2. Governmental research. 3. Social science research. 4. Economic development. I. Title.

711.4
E53
1966
Technology and the city matrix.
Engineering Foundation Research Conference, University of California, Santa Barbara, 1966. Technology and the city matrix. New York, Engineering Foundation, 1966. 18p.

1. City planning. 2. Model cities. I. Engineering Foundation, New York. II. Title.

728.1
A17
v. 3
Technology and the impact on public policy.
ABT Associates.
Technology and the impact on public policy. [In-Cities Experimental Housing Research and Development Project, Phase I] Vol. 3. Prepared by ABT Associates, inc. and Daniel, Mann, Johnson and Mendenhall. Cambridge, Mass., 1968. 1v.
Prepared for U.S. Dept. of Housing and Urban Development under contract no. H-969.
1. Low-income housing. 2. Experimental houses. I. Daniel, Mann, Johnson and Mendenhall. II. Title. III. Title: In-Cities Experimental Housing Research and Development Project. IV. U.S. Dept. of Housing and Urban Development. In-Cities Experimental Housing Research...

697.8
B82t
Technology and the pollution problem.
Bueche, Arthur M
Technology and the pollution problem. Testimony before the Subcommittee on Science Research and Development on "The adequacy of technology for pollution abatement." U.S. House of Representatives. Wash. D.C., Aug. 9. 1966. Schenectady. N.Y., General Electric, 1966. [8]p.

1. Air pollution. 2. Water pollution. 3. General Electric Co. I. Title.

711.4
H25
Technology and the study of the city.
Helmer, O
Technology and the study of the city, by O. Helmer and others. Washington, Task Force on Economic Growth and Opportunity, Chamber of Commerce, 1968. 59p.

1. City planning. 2. City growth. I. U.S. Chamber of Commerce. II. Title.

538.56
N17t
v.1
Appx.
pt.5
excerpt
Technology and urban needs: a statement from the Engineering Foundation Research Conference on the Social Consequences of Technology.
Alcott, James
Technology and urban needs: a statement from the Engineering Foundation Research Conference on the Social Consequences of Technology. Kansas City, Mo., Midwest Research Institute, 1966. 24p.
Prepared for the National Commission on Technology, Automation, and Economic Progress as a part of the...Commission report to the President," appx. pt. 5, Applying technology to unmet needs, p. 31-41.

(Cont'd on next card)

538.56
N17t
v.1
Appx.
pt.5
excerpt
Alcott, James. Technology and urban needs: a statement from the Engineering Foundation Research Conference...1966. (Card 2)

1. Automation. 2. City planning. 3. Governmental research. 4. Economic development. I. U.S. National Commission on Technology, Automation, and Economic Progress. II. Engineering Foundation Research Conference on the Social Consequences of Technology. III. Title.

388
M29
Technology and urban transportation.
Meyer, John R
Technology and urban transportation, by John R. Meyer and others. [Washington] 1962. 131p.

1. Transportation. 2. Journey to work. I. Title.

396
B14
Technology and women's work.
Baker, Elizabeth Faulkner.
Technology and woman's work. New York, Columbia University Press, 1964. 460p.

Bibliography: p. 443-450.

1. Women. 2. Employment - Woman. I. Title.

600
K17
Technology assessment.
Kasper, Raphael G   ed.
Technology assessment; understanding the social consequences of technological applications. New York, Praeger, 1972. 291p. (Praeger special studies in U.S. economic and social development)
Published in cooperation with the Program of Policy Studies in Science and Technology, George Washington University.
1. Technology. 2. Man - Influence of environment. I. George Washington University. Program of Policy Studies in Science and Technology. II. Title.

500.15
C65tec
1970
H-H
Technology assessment.
U.S. Congress. House. Committee on Science and Astronautics. Technology assessment. Hearings before the Subcommittee on Science, Research, and Development of the Committee on Science and Astronautics, U.S. House of Representatives, Ninety-first Congress, first session. Wash., Govt. Print. Off., 1970. 562p. (no. 13)
Hearings held Nov. 18 - Dec. 12, 1969.
1. Scientific research. 2. Technology. I. Title.

500.15
C65t
Technology assessment.
U.S. Congress. House. Committee on Science and Astronautics. Technology assessment. Statement of Emilio Q. Daddario Chairman, Subcommittee on Science, Research, and Development of the Committee on Science and Astronautics, U.S. House of Representatives, Ninetieth Congress, first session. Serial I. Wash., Govt. Print. Off., 1967. 19p.

1. Scientific research. I. Daddario, Emilio Q.   II. Title.

600
M67t
Technology assessment and citizen action.
Mottur, Ellis R
Technology assessment and citizen action. Presented in the Professional Seminar Series on Technology Assessment, May 26, 1970. Wash., Program of Policy Studies in Science and Technology, George Washington University, 1971. 27p. (George Washington University. Program of Policy Studies in Science and Technology. Occasional paper no. 10)
1. Technology. 2. Community development - Citizen participation. I. George Washington University. Program of Policy Studies in Science and Technology. II. Title.

600
M67
Technology assessment and environmental engineering.
Mottur, Ellis R
Technology assessment and environmental engineering. Presented to the eighth annual meeting of the Society of Engineering Science, inc., Wash., Nov. 11, 1970. Wash., Program of Policy Studies in Science and Technology, George Washington University, 1971. 21p. (George Washington University. Program of Policy Studies in Science and Technology. Occasional paper no. 9)
1. Technology. 2. Man - Influence of environment. I. George Washington University. Program of Policy Studies in Science and Technology. II. Title.

500.15
C65t
1967
Technology assessment seminar.
U.S. Congress. House. Committee on Science and Astronautics. Technology assessment seminar. Proceedings before the Subcommittee on Science, Research, and Development of the Committee on Science and Astronautics, U.S. House of Representatives, Ninetieth Congress, first session. Wash., Govt. Print. Off., 1967. 184p. (no. 7)
Proceedings held Sept. 21-22, 1967.
1. Scientific research. I. Title.

330
N25
Technology, economic growth, and public policy.
Nelson, Richard R
Technology, economic growth, and public policy, by R.R. Nelson and others. A Rand Corporation and Brookings Institution study. Wash., Brookings Institution, 1967. 238p.
Bibliography: p. 212-228.

1. Economic development. 2. Scientific research. 3. Employment - Research. 4. Housing research. 5. Automation. I. Rand Corp. II. Brookings Institution, Wash. D.C. III. Title.

382
T22
The Technology factor in international trade.
Edited by Raymond Vernon. New York, National Bureau of Economic Research; distributed by Columbia University Press, 1970. 493p. (Universities-National Bureau conference series, 22)

1. Commercial policy. I. National Bureau of Economic Research. II. Vernon, Raymond, ed. III. Universities-National Bureau Committee for Economic Research.

711.4
F12

Technology for the city: the modern city is a
child of technology, undisciplined, unhealthy.
Eberhard, John P
Technology for the city: the modern city is
a child of technology, undisciplined, unhealthy,
unscrubbed, without charm. But the fault is
not technology's. In International science
and technology, Sept. 1966. p. 18-29, 84-85.

1. City planning. I. International science
and technology.   II. Title.

698
M17t

Technology of paints, varnishes and lacquers.
Martens, Charles R   ed.
Technology of paints, varnishes and
lacquers. New York, Reinhold., 1968.
744p.

1. Paints and painting. 2. Varnish and
varnishing. I. Title.

600
N17

Technology: processes of assessment and
choice.
National Academy of Sciences.
Technology: processes of assessment and
choice. Wash., Govt. Print. Off., 1969.
163p.
Report of the National Academy of Sciences
to the Committee on Science and Astronautics,
U.S. House of Representatives.

1. Technology. 2. Scientific research.
I. U.S. Congress. House. Committee on
Science and Astronautics. II. Title.

330
(016)
B17
1967

Technology for underdeveloped areas.
Baranson, Jack.
Technology for underdeveloped areas; an
annotated bibliography, 1st. ed. Oxford,
New York, Pergamon Press, 1967.
81p. (International series of monographs
in library and information science, v.6)

1. Underdeveloped countries - Bibl.
2. Technical assistance programs - Bibl.
I. Title.

388
B27

The technology of urban transportation.
Berry, Donald S
The technology of urban transportation, by
Donald S. Berry and others. [Evanston, Ill.]
Published for the Transportation Center
at Northwestern University, by Northwestern
University Press, 1963.
145p. (Metropolitan transportation series)
Bibliography: p. 128-139.

1. Transportation. 2. Parking. 3. Streets.
I. Northwestern   University.
Transportation   Center. II. Title.

339.5
T22

2C.

Technology review.
Energy technology to the year 2000: a
special symposium published by Technology
review. Cambridge, Mass., M.I.T., 1971-72.
1v.
Reprinted from Technology review, Oct./Nov.
1971, pp. 17-48; Dec. 1971, pp. 33-60; Jan.
1972, pp. 9-48.
1. Power resources. 2. Atomic energy.
3. Air pollution. I. Massachusetts Institute
of Technology. II. Title.

341.1
1338
A32v

Technology handbook.
U.S. Agency for International Development.
(Communications Resources Div.)
Village technology handbook. Washington,
1964.
2v. (Its C-11-12)

1. Technical assistance programs.
2. Water-supply. 3. Tools. I. Title.
II. Title: Technology handbook.

538.56
T22

Technology Planning Center, inc.
A compendium of information planning concepts and applications. Ann Arbor, Mich.,
[1966?]
1v.

1. Automation. 2. City planning - Automation. 3. Public administration - Automation.
I. Title.

620.015
M17m

Technology Status and Trends Symposium. 2d, Marshall
Space Flight Center, 1966.
U.S. National Aeronautics and Space Administration. (Office of Technology Utilization)
Nondestructive testing: trends and techniques; proceedings of the second Technology
Status and Trends Symposium, Marshall Space
Flight Center, Oct. 26-27, 1966. Washington,
1967.
123p. (Its SP-5082)
1. Engineering research. 2. Building
materials. I. Technology Status and Trends
Symposium. 2d, Marshall Space Flight Center,
1966. II. Title.

628.1
A24

Technology in American water development.
Ackerman, Edward A
Technology in American water development, by
Edward A. Ackerman and George O.G. Löf. Pub-
lished for Resources for the Future, Inc.
Baltimore, The Johns Hopkins Press, 1959.
710p. illus.

Bibliography: p. 667-672.

1. Water resources. 2. Water supply.
I. Löf, George O. G., jt. au. II. Resources for the Future. III. Title.

628.1
(754)
W27d

Technology Planning Center.
West Virginia. Dept. of Natural Resources
(Div. of Water Resources)
A design for a West Virginia water resources
plan. Charleston, 1967.
62p.
Technology Planning Center, consultant.
Bibliography: p. 58-62.

1. Water resources - W. Va. I. Technology
Planning Center. II. Title.

500.15
C65te
1970
S-H

Technology transfer.
U.S. Congress. Senate. Select Committee
on Small Business.
Technology transfer. Hearings before the
Subcommittee on Science and Technology of
the Select Committee on Small Business,
United States Senate, Ninety-first
Congress, second session on review of
technology transfer programs administered by
various executive departments and agencies.
Wash., Govt. Print. Off., 1970.
pts. pt. 1
1. Governmental research. 2. Technology.
3. Business.   I. Title.

370
265t

Technology in education.
U.S. Congress. Joint Economic Committee.
Technology in education. Hearings before
the Subcommittee on Economic Progress of the
Joint Economic Committee, Congress of the
United States, Eighty-ninth Congress, second
session. Wash., For sale by the Supt. of Doc.,
Govt. Print. Off., 1966.
273p.

Hearings held June 6-13, 1966.

1. Education. 2. Education - Automation.
I. Title.

711.33
(774)
T22

Technology Planning Center, Ann Arbor, Mich.
Interagency information reconnaissance study.
Prepared for Office of Economic Expansion,
State Resource Planning Division, Michigan
Dept. of Commerce. Ann Arbor, Mich., 1966.
41p. (Michigan. Dept. of Commerce.
State Resource Planning Program. Technical
rept. no. 4)
U.S. Housing and Urban Development. UPAP.

1. State planning - Michigan. 2. State
planning - Automation. I. Michigan. State
Resource   Planning Division.
II. U.S. HUD   UPAP. Mich.

600.15
R672

Technology transfer, process and policy...
Rosenbloom, Richard S
Technology transfer, process and policy;
an analysis of the utilization of techno-
logical by-products of military and space
R & D, and a statement by the NPA CAR-RAND
Committee. Wash., National Planning Associa-
tion, 1965.
39p. (National Planning Association.
Special report no. 62)

1. Industrial research. 2. Governmental
research.   3. Automation.
I. National   Planning Association.
II. Title.

728.1
N176b
no.20

Technology in the city.
Fleisher, Aaron.
Technology in the city. [n.p.] 1968.
24p. (Background paper [no. 20] for U.S.
National Commission on Urban Problems)

1. Housing. 2. Transportation.
I. U.S. National Commission on Urban
Problems. II. Title.

628.1
(774)
T22

Technology Planning Center, Ann Arbor, Mich.
Strategy for Michigan water resources
management; a systems approach. Prepared for
State of Michigan Joint Legislative Committee
on Water Resources Planning, East Lansing,
Michigan. Project director, J.S. Kellogg.
Staff, Robert R. Kley and others. Ann Arbor,
Mich., 1966.
87p.

1. Water resources - Michigan. 2. Water-
supply engineering. I. Kellott, James C.
II. Michigan.   Joint Legislative
Committee on   Water Resources
Planning.   III. Title.

691.16
T22

2C

Technomic Publishing Co.
U.S. plastics in building and construction;
marketing guide and company directory.
Stamford, Conn., 1971.
65p.

1. Plastics. I. Title.

600
1330
C65
1963
S-H

TECHNOLOGY IN THE NATIONAL ECONOMY.
U.S. CONGRESS. SENATE. SELECT
COMMITTEE ON SMALL BUSINESS.
THE ROLE AND EFFECT OF TECHNOLOGY IN
THE NATION'S ECONOMY. HEARINGS...
EIGHTY-EIGHTH CONGRESS, FIRST SESSION. A
REVIEW OF THE EFFECT OF GOVERNMENT
RESEARCH AND DEVELOPMENT ON ECONOMIC
GROWTH. WASHINGTON, GOVT. PRINT. OFF.,
1963-64.
6 V.

1. TECHNOLOGY - ECONOMIC EFFECT.
I. TITLE: TECHNOLOGY IN THE NATIONAL
ECONOMY.

4352

TECHNOLOGY PLANNING CENTER, ANN ARBOR,
MICH.
MICHIGAN. WATER RESOURCES COMMISSION.
WATER RESOURCE PLANNING METHODOLOGIES
AND TECHNIQUES INVESTIGATION. PREPARED
BY TECHNOLOGY PLANNING CENTER, INC. ANN
ARBOR, CA 1968.
51P. (ITS WRC-PI,6) HUD 701 REPORT)

1. WATER RESOURCES - MICHIGAN.
I. TECHNOLOGY PLANNING CENTER, ANN ARBOR,
MICH. II. HUD. 701. MICHIGAN.

614
(7471)
P17

Technomics, incorporation.
Parks, Robert B
Community health services for New York
City; a case study in urban medical
delivery; prepared by Technomics, inc., including the final report of the Commission
on the Delivery of Personal Health Services
to the Mayor of New York City. Foreword by
Gerard Piel, Chairman of the Commission.
New York, Frederick A. Praeger, 1968.
675p. (Praeger special studies economic
and social development)
Bibliography: p. 595-631.

1. Public health - New York (City)
I. Technomics, inc.
(Cont'd on next card)

614
(7471)   Parks, Robert B   Community health...1968.
P17   (Card 2)

   II. New York (City) Mayor's Commission on
the Delivery of Personal Health Services.
III. Title.

1808   TEC-SEARCH, INC.
          LOCKPORT, ILL. PLANNING COMMISSION.
          COMPREHENSIVE PLAN, BY TEC-SEARCH, INC.
          LOCKPORT, ILL., 1969.
          112P. (HUD 701 REPORT)

          1. MASTER PLAN - LOCKPORT, ILL.
          I. TEC-SEARCH, INC.   II. HUD. 701.
          LOCKPORT, ILL.

1853   TEC-SEARCH, INC.
          WALNUT, ILL. PLANNING COMMISSION.
          OBJECTIVE AND POLICIES, BY TEC-SEARCH,
          INC. WALNUT, ILL., 1968.
          8P. (HUD 701 REPORT)

          1. CITY PLANNING - WALNUT, ILL.
          I. TEC-SEARCH, INC.   II. HUD. 701.
          WALNUT, ILL.

332.2
T22   Teck, Alan.
           Mutual savings banks and savings and loan
         associations: aspects of growth. New York,
         Columbia University Press, 1968.
           192p.

           Bibliography: p. 179-188.

           1. Savings-banks. 2. Savings and loan
         associations. I. Title.

---

532   TEC-SEARCH, INC.
FOLIO   BUREAU CO., ILL. PLANNING BOARD.
          COMPREHENSIVE PLAN, BY TEC-SEARCH,
          INC. PRINCETON, ILL., 1969.
          115P. (HUD 701 REPORT)

          1. MASTER PLAN - BUREAU CO., ILL.
          I. TEC-SEARCH, INC.   II. HUD. 701.
          BUREAU CO., ILL.

---

593   TEC-SEARCH, INC.
          HOOPESTON, ILL. CITY PLAN COMMISSION.
          PRELIMINARY GOALS, OBJECTIVES AND
          POLICIES FOR HOOPESTON, ILL., BY
          TEC-SEARCH, INC. HOOPESTON, ILL., 1968.
          15P. (HUD 701 REPORT)

          1. CITY PLANNING - HOOPESTON, ILL.
          I. TEC-SEARCH, INC.   II. HUD. 701.
          HOOPESTON, ILL.

711
(81)   SOMBRA, SEVERINO.
S6b   TECNICA DE PLANEJAMENTO.
           TECNICA DE PLANEJAMENTO. 3 EDIÇÃO.
         COM INTRODUÇÃO E BIBLIOGRAFIA. RIO DE
         JANEIRO, ASSOCIAÇÃO BRASILEIRIA DE
         PLANEJAMENTO, 1952.
           53P.

           1. PLANNING - BRAZIL.   I. TITLE.

1845   TEC-SEARCH, INC.
          SOUTH ELGIN, ILL. PLAN COMMISSION.
          COMPREHENSIVE PLAN. BY TEC-SEARCH,
          INC. SOUTH ELGIN, ILL., 1968.
          79P. (HUD 701 REPORT)

          1. MASTER PLAN - SOUTH ELGIN, ILL.
          I. TEC-SEARCH, INC.   II. HUD. 701.
          SOUTH ELGIN, ILL.

1847   TEC-SEARCH, INC.
          SOUTH ELGIN, ILL. PLAN COMMISSION.
          A REPORT ON A SUBDIVISION REGULATIONS
          ORDINANCE. BY TEC-SEARCH, INC. SOUTH
          ELGIN, ILL., 1968.
          47P. (HUD 701 REPORT)

          1. SUBDIVISION REGULATION - SOUTH
          ELGIN, ILL. I. TEC-SEARCH, INC.
          II. HUD. 701. SOUTH ELGIN, ILL.

711.552   Técnicas de ordenacion del mercado y precios
(46)   del suelo urbano.
S61   Spain. Ministerio de la Vivienda.
           Técnicas de ordenación del mercado y precios
         del suelo urbano. Madrid, 1966.
           84p.   (Resumenes monograficos de docu-
         mentos, no. 7)

           1. Business districts - Spain. 2. Shopping
         centers. 3. Land use - Spain. I. Title.

1852   TEC-SEARCH, INC.
          WALNUT, ILL. PLANNING COMMISSION.
          COMPREHENSIVE PLAN, BY TEC-SEARCH, INC.
          WALNUT, ILL., 1969.
          104P. (HUD 701 REPORT)

          1. MASTER PLAN - WALNUT, ILL.
          I. TEC-SEARCH, INC.   II. HUD.
          701. WALNUT, ILL.

Folio   Tec-Search, inc.
711.4   Village of Hoffman Estates, Illinois com-
(7731)   prehensive plan report - 1968. Wilmette,
H63   Ill., 1968.
1968   168p.
          U.S. Dept. of Housing and Urban Development.
          UPAP. Ill. P-136.

            1. Master plan - Hoffman Estates, Ill.
          I. Hoffman Estates Ill. Plan Commission.
          II. Title. III. U S. HUD-UPAP. Hoffman
          Estates, Ill.

---

591   TEC-SEARCH, INC.
          HOOPESTON, ILL. CITY PLAN COMMISSION.
          ANALYSIS OF THE SUBDIVISION ORDINANCE,
          BY TEC-SEARCH, INC. HOOPESTON, ILL., 1970.
          5P. (HUD 701 REPORT)

          1. SUBDIVISION REGULATION - HOOPESTON,
          ILL. I. TEC-SEARCH, INC.   II. HUD.
          701. HOOPESTON, ILL.

5665   TEC-SEARCH.
          MOUNT VERNON, IND. PLAN COMMISSION.
          MASTER PLAN. BY TEC-SEARCH. MOUNT
          VERNON, IND., 1963.
          139P. (HUD 701 REPORT)

          1. MASTER PLAN - MOUNT VERNON, IND.
          I. TEC-SEARCH.   II. HUD. 701. MOUNT
          VERNON, IND.

5703   TEC-SEARCH, INC.
          ZIONSVILLE, IND. PLAN COMMISSION.
          VILLAGE PLAN. BY TEC-SEARCH, INC.,
          1967.
          167P. (HUD 701 REPORT)

          1. CITY PLANNING - ZIONSVILLE, IND.
          I. TEC-SEARCH, INC.   II. HUD. 701.
          ZIONSVILLE, IND.

---

592   TEC-SEARCH, INC.
          HOOPESTON, ILL. CITY PLAN COMMISSION.
          ANALYSIS OF THE ZONING ORDINANCE, BY
          TEC-SEARCH, INC. HOOPESTON, ILL., 1970.
          12P. (HUD 701 REPORT)

          1. ZONING - HOOPESTON, ILL.
          I. TEC-SEARCH, INC.   II. HUD. 701.
          HOOPESTON, ILL.

711.5   Tec-Search. (Planning Div.)
(7731   Matteson planning program. Evanston,
:347)   Ill., 1960-61.
T22   8 nos. in 1 v. (Technical report 60-
          13-T5-T10)

            Contents:-Technical report T5: Zoning
          workshop guide. Review of existing ordinance.
          -no.T6: Proposed comprehensive amendment to
          the Matteson Zoning Ordinances (3 pts.:
          preliminary 2 pts.-no.T7: Proposed
          comprehensive amendment to the Matteson

                              (Continued on next card)

1846   TEC-SEARCH, INC.
          SOUTH ELGIN, ILL. PLAN COMMISSION.
          ZONING ORDINANCE. BY TEC-SEARCH, INC.
          SOUTH ELGIN, ILL., 1968.
          59P. (HUD 701 REPORT)

          1. ZONING - SOUTH ELGIN, ILL.
          I. TEC-SEARCH, INC.   II. HUD. 701.
          SOUTH ELGIN, ILL.

---

590   TEC-SEARCH, INC.
          HOOPESTON, ILL. CITY PLAN COMMISSION.
          COMPREHENSIVE PLAN, BY TEC-SEARCH, INC.
          HOOPESTON, ILL., 1970.
          1 V. (HUD 701 REPORT)

          1. MASTER PLAN - HOOPESTON, ILL.
          I. TEC-SEARCH, INC.   II. HUD. 701.
          HOOPESTON, ILL.

711.5   Tec-Search. (Planning Div.) Matteson
(7731   planning program. (Card 2)
:347)
T22   subdivision regulations (2 pts.: preliminary,
          final)-no.T8: Population and economic bases.-
          no.T9: Community facilities.-no.T10: Public
          improvements program.
            U.S. Urban Renewal Adm. UPAP.
          1. Zoning legislation - Matteson, Ill. 2. Subdivision
          regulation - Matteson, Ill. 3. Community facilities -
          Matteson, Ill. I. Matteson, Ill. Plan Commission.
          II. U.S. Urban Renewal   Adm. UPAP.

1854   TEC-SEARCH, INC.
          WALNUT, ILL. PLANNING COMMISSION.
          ZONING ORDINANCE, BY TEC-SEARCH, INC.
          WALNUT, ILL., 1968.
          61P. (HUD 701 REPORT)

          1. ZONING - WALNUT, ILL.
          I. TEC-SEARCH, INC.   II. HUD. 701.
          WALNUT, ILL.

5181
5182   TEC-SEARCH.
ALBION, IND. PLANNING COMMISSION.
ZONING ORDINANCE; SUBDIVISION
REGULATIONS. BY TEC-SEARCH. ALBION,
IND., 1968.
2 V. (HUD 701 REPORT)

1. ZONING - ALBION, IND.
I. TEC-SEARCH. II. HUD. 701. ALBION,
IND.

5160
5161   TEC-SEARCH.
AVILLA, IND. PLAN COMMISSION.
ZONING ORDINANCE; SUBDIVISION
REGULATIONS. BY TEC-SEARCH. AVILLA,
IND., 1968.
2 V. (HUD 701 REPORT)

1. ZONING - AVILLA, IND.
I. TEC-SEARCH. II. HUD. 701. AVILLA,
IND.

6064   TEC-SEARCH. URBAN RESOURCES PLANNING
DIVISION.
WALNUT, ILL. PLANNING COMMISSION.
RECOMMENDED OFFICIAL MAP AND STANDARDS
ORDINANCE. TECHNICAL ASSISTANCE PROVIDED
BY URBAN RESOURCES PLANNING DIVISION,
TEC-SEARCH, WILMETTE, ILL. WALNUT, 1969.
5L. (HUD 701 REPORT)

1. ORDINANCES - WALNUT, ILL.
I. TEC-SEARCH. URBAN RESOURCES PLANNING
DIVISION. II. HUD. 701. WALNUT, ILL.

2705-
2710   TECUMSEH, MICH. PLANNING COMMISSION.
COMPREHENSIVE PLAN STUDY: 1,
RECREATION, COMMUNITY FACILITIES AND
THOROFARE PLAN; 2, FUTURE LAND USE PLAN;
3, COSTS AND REVENUE RETURN AND PUBLIC
IMPROVEMENT PROGRAM; 4, SUGGESTED DRAFT
OF REVISED SUBDIVISION STANDARDS; 5,
SUGGESTED DRAFT OF REVISED ZONING
STANDARDS; 6, PROJECT COMPLETION REPORT,
BY STATE OF MICHIGAN, DEPARTMENT OF
COMMERCE, COMMUNITY PLANNING DIVISION.
PREAPRED BY VILICAN-LEMAN AND
ASSOCIATES, INC. TECUMSEH, MICH.,
1968-69.
(CONTINUED ON NEXT CARD)

2705-
2710   TECUMSEH, MICH. PLANNING COMMISSION.
COMPREHENSIVE PLAN ... 8-69. (CARD 2)

6 V. (HUD 701 REPORT)

1. CITY PLANNING - TECUMSEH, MICH.
I. VILICAN-LEMAN AND ASSOCIATES.
II. MICHIGAN. DEPT. OF COMMERCE.
COMMUNITY PLANNING DIV. III. HUD.
701. TECUMSEH, MICH.

534.83
C653   TEDDINGTON, ENGLAND. NATIONAL
PHYSICAL LABORATORY.
CONFERENCE ON NOISE. NATIONAL PHYSICAL
LABORATORY, 1961.
THE CONTROL OF NOISE. PROCEEDINGS OF
A CONFERENCE HELD AT THE NATIONAL
PHYSICAL LABORATORY ON 26TH, 27TH AND
28TH JUNE, 1961. LONDON, H.M.
STATIONERY OFF., 1962.
434P. (TEDDINGTON, ENGLAND. NATIONAL
PHYSICAL LABORATORY SYMPOSIUM. NO. 12)

1. NOISE. I. TEDDINGTON, ENGLAND.
NATIONAL PHYSICAL LABORATORY.
II. TITLE.

VF
699.844.1
:690.225   Teddington, England. National Physical Labora-
A77   Aston, G   H   tory.
The sound insulation of partitions. London, H. M. Stationery Off., 1948.
24 p. 25 cm.
At head of title: National Physical Laboratory.
"References": p. 11.

1. Soundproofing.   I. Teddington, Eng. National Physical Labo-
ratory. II. Title.
TH1725.A8   693   50-16089
Library of Congress   [1]

LAW
T   Tedrow, Joseph Herbert.
Tedrow's regulation of transportation;
pratice and procedure before the Interstate
Commerce Commission. 6th ed. [Rev. by]
Mervin L. Fair and John Guandolo. Dubuque,
Iowa, W. C. Brown Co., 1964.
445p. (Brown transportation series)
Bibliography: p. 3-6.

1. U.S. Interstate Commerce Commission -
Rules and practice. 2. Transportation -
Legislation. I.   Fair, Marvin Luke.
II. Guandolo, John.   III. Title. IV.
Title: Regulation   of transportation.

LAW
T   Tedrow's regulation of transportation; practice
and procedure before the Interstate Commerce
Commission.
Tedrow, Joseph Herbert.
Tedrow's regulation of transportation;
pratice and procedure before the Interstate
Commerce Commission. 6th ed. [Rev. by]
Mervin L. Fair and John Guandolo. Dubuque,
Iowa, W. C. Brown Co., 1964.
445p. (Brown transportation series)
Bibliography: p. 3-6.

1. U.S. Interstate Commerce Commission -
Rules and practice. 2. Transportation -
Legislation. I.   Fair, Marvin Luke.
II. Guandolo, John.   III. Title. IV.
Title: Regulation   of transportation.

691.328.2
B79   Tee-beams.
Bryson, J   O
Flexural behavior of prestressed concrete
composite tee-beams, by J.O. Bryson and E.F.
Carpenter. Wash., U.S. National Bureau of
Standards, 1970.
12p. (U.S. National Bureau of Standards.
Building science series, 31)

1. Concrete, Prestressed. 2. Concrete
construction. I. Carpenter, E.F., jt. au.
II. U.S. National Bureau of Standards.
III. Title. IV. Title: Tee-beams.

331
(764)
C31   Teenage employment.
Champagne, Joseph E
Teenage employment: a study of low income
youth in Houston, Texas, by Joseph E. Champagne
and Robert L. Prater. Houston, Center for
Human Resources, University of Houston, 1969.
22p.

1. Employment - Houston, Tex. 2. Youth.
I. Prater, Robert L., jt. au. II. Title.
III. Houston. University. Center for Human
Resources.

699.82
R27   Teesdale, L   V
Research Correlation Conference. 4th, Washington,
D.C., 1952.
Condensation control in building as related
to paints, papers, and insulating materials,
Feb. 26 and 27, 1952. Washington, Building
Research Advisory Board, Div. of Engineering and
Industrial Research, National Research Council,
Sept. 1952.
118 p.   illus.   (Building Research Advisory
Board. Research Conference report no. 4)
(Continued on next card)

Research Correlation Conference. 4th, Washington,
D.C., 1952.   Condensation control ... 1952.
(Card 2)

Conference participants included Tyler S.
Rogers, chairman, Leonard Haeger, J. S. Long,
E. R. McLaughlin, R. S. Dill, Joseph Orendorff,
Kenneth Sargent.
Bibliography: p. 111-113.
Partial contents. -Technological aspects of
condensation contro[l] in building structure, by
(Continued on next card)

Research Correlation Conference. 4th, Washington,
D.C., 1952.   Condensation control ... 1952.
(Card 3)
Partial contents, continued.
C. E. Lund. -The movement of moisture in building
materials, by J. D. Babbitt. -Water permeability
of paint materials for wall construction, by E. J.
Dunn. -Paper and foil films, by Floyd Newkirk. -
Influence of construction methods and materials
on condensation prob[le]ms, by L. C. Teesdale.

699.82
T22C   TEESDALE, L   V
CONDENSATION IN WALLS AND ATTICS.
MADISON, WIS., U.S. FOREST PRODUCTS
LABORATORY, 1937.
9L.

REPRINTED FROM AMERICAN BUILDER AND
BUILDING AGE, DEC. 1937.

1. MOISTURE CONDENSATION. I. U.S.
FOREST PRODUCTS LABORATORY, MADISON,
WIS.

VF
699.82
F67   Teesdale, L   V
R1196   U.S. Forest Service. Forest Products Laboratory,
Madison, Wis.
Condensation problems in modern buildings, by
L. V. Teesdale. Rev.   Madison, Wis., May 1941.
9 p.   (Its no. R1196)
Presented before Conference on Air
Conditioning, University of Illinois, Urbana,
March 8-9, 1939.
Processed.

1. Moisture condensation. I. Teesdale, L. V.
II. Title.

VF
699.82
F67   Teesdale, L   V
R1196   U.S. Forest Service. Forest Products Laboratory,
1953   Madison, Wis.
Condensation problems in modern buildings, by
L. V. Teesdale. Rev. Sept. 1953.   Madison,
Wis., 1953.
12 p. diagrs., graphs, tables.   (Its
no. R1196)

Processed.

1. Moisture condensation. I. Teesdale, L. V.
II. Title.

VF
690
F67   Teasdale, L. V.
U.S. Forest Service. Forest Products Laboratory,
Madison, Wis.
[Frame dwelling construction practices]
Madison, Wis. [1952?]
8 v.   illus. tables.

Contents: -pt.1. Current housing construction
practices in the Central, Lake and Northeastern
States, by L. O. Anderson, O.C. Heyer, L.V.
Teesdale. -pt. 2. Current housing construction
practices in West Coast states, by L.V. Teesdale,
W.G. Youngquist. -pt.3. Current housing practices

VF
690
F67   U.S. Forest Service. Forest Products Laboratory,
Madison, Wis. [Frame dwelling construction
practices] [1952?]   (Card 2)

in the Southeastern and Southern states, by O.C.
Heyer, T.B. Heebink. -pt.4. A survey of exterior
painting on low cost houses, by F.L. Browne. -
pt.5. A survey of exterior painting on recently
built houses in southern Arizona, by F.L. Browne. -
pt.6. Cause of paint peeling on wood siding of
houses in Seattle, by Laurence V. Teesdale. -
pt.7. Suggestions for improved service of exterior

VF
690
F67   U.S. Forest Service. Forest Products Laboratory,
Madison, Wis. [Frame dwelling construction
practices] [1952?]   (Card 3)

paint on FHA-insured houses, by F. L. Browne. -
pt.8. Heavy snows and cold weather may cause
roof leaks, by L. V. Teesdale.

Final report, Research project O-T-24.
Housing and Home Finance Agency. Project
director: R. F. Luxford, Staff technician:
William A. Russell.
Typewritten.

VF
690
F67   U.S. Forest Service. Forest Products Laboratory,
Madison, Wis. [Frame dwelling construction
practices] [1952?]   (Card 4)

1. Building methods. 2. Paints and painting.
3. Winter construction. 4. Housing research
contracts. I. Luxford, R.F. II. Russell, Wm. A. III. U.S.
Housing and Home Finance Agency, Office of the Admini-
strator, Division of Housing Research. IV. Title.
V. Anderson, L.O. VI. Heyer, O.C. VII. Teesdale, L.V.
VIII. Youngquist, W. G. IX. Heebink, T.B. X. Browne, F.L.
XI. Title: Current housing construction practices.
(Over)

690.24
F67 Teesdale, L V
U.S. Forest Service. Forest Products
Laboratory, Madison, Wis.
Heavy snows and cold weather may cause
roof leaks, by L. V. Teesdale. Madison,
Wis., [1951]
1v.

"Work was done in cooperation with the
Housing and Home Finance Agency."

1. Roofs and roofing. I. Teesdale, L. V.
II. U.S. Housing and Home Finance Agency.

U. S. Forest Service. Forest Products.
Laboratory. Wood-frame house...1955 (card 2)

W. A. Russell. Project directors: L.V. Teesdale
and R. F. Luxford.
Bibliography: p.214-217.
"Glossary of housing terms": p.217-227.
1. Wood construction. 2. Wood framing 3. Housing
research contracts. I. Anderson, L. O. II. Heyer,
O. C. III. U.S. Housing and Home Finance Agency.
Office of the Administrator. Div. of Housing
Research. IV. Russell, William A. V. Teesdale, L.
V. VI Luxford, R. F. VII. Title.

690.091.82
:613.5 Teitz, Michael B
(7471) Housing code enforcement in New York City,
T24 by Michael B. Teitz and Stephen R. Rosenthal.
New York, New York City Rand Institute, 1971.
58p. (R-648-NYC)

1. Housing law enforcement - New York (City)
I. Rosenthal, Stephen R., jt. au.
II. New York City Rand Institute. III. Title.

VF
691.11 Teesdale, L V
:620.193.82 U.S. Dept. of Agriculture.
A37p Preventing cracks in new wood
floors, by L. V. Teesdale and J. S.
Mathewson. Rev. Washington, 1952.
6p. illus. (Its Leaflet no. 56)

1. Floors and flooring. I. Teesdale,
L. V. II. Mathewson, J. S.

VF
728.1 Teeter, Herman B
:362.6 New ideas in old folks' homes. Reprint
T22 from Together, Nov. 1960. p. 45-48.

1. Housing for the aged.

388
I57pu Institute of Public Administration.
Public Urban Locator Service (PULSE) back-
ground and conference proceedings, Oct. 24,
1968. [New York] 1968.
466p.
CFSTI. PB 180 116.
Work performed by Institute of Public
Administration and Teknekron, Inc.
U.S. Mass Transportation Demonstration
Grant Program. HUD contract no. H-1030.
1. Transportation. 2. Communication
systems. I. Teknekron, inc. II. U.S.
Mass Transportation Demonstration
Grant Program. III. Title.

VF
691.55 Teesdale, L V
F67 U.S. Forest Service. Forest Products Laboratory,
Madison, Wis.
How plastering affects the moisture content of
structural and finish woodwork, by L. V. Teesdale.
Rev. Madison, Wis., Apr. 1950.
4 p. (Its R1274)

Processed.

1.Plaster and plastering. I.Teesdale, L. V.
II.Title.

332.72 TEEVAN, JOHN M
R87 RUSSELL, HORACE.
THE PACKAGE MORTGAGE, BY HORACE
RUSSELL AND JOHN M. TEEVAN.

(IN LEGAL BULLETIN OF THE UNITED
STATES SAVINGS AND LOAN LEAGUE, V. 12,
NO. 2, MARCH 1946. P.17-34)

1. MORTGAGE FINANCE. I. TEEVAN,
JOHN M. II. U.S. SAVINGS AND LOAN
LEAGUE.

Teknillisen Korkeakoulun Ylioppilaskunta.
see Helsingfors. Suomen Teknillinen Korkeakoulu.

VF
699.82 Teesdale, L V
F67 U.S. Forest Service. Forest Products Laboratory,
R1710 Madison, Wis.
Remedial measures for building condensation
difficulties, by L. V. Teesdale. Madison, Wis.,
Sept. 1947.
14 p. illus., graphs, map, tables. (Its
no. R1710)
Presented at Humidity and Comfort Symposium,
Pennsylvania State College, State College, Pa.,
Sept. 30, 1947.
Processed.
1.Moisture condensa I.Teesdale, L. V.
II.Title.

658
T24 TEICHROEW, DANIEL.
AN INTRODUCTION TO MANAGEMENT SCIENCE,
DETERMINISTIC MODELS. NEW YORK, WILEY,
1964.
713P.

1. INDUSTRIAL MANAGEMENT. I. TITLE:
MANAGEMENT SCIENCE. II. TITLE:
DETERMINISTIC MODELS.

621.39 Telecommunications.
N17 National Academy of Engineering.
Reports on selected topics in telecommunica-
tions. Final report to the Dept. of Housing
and Urban Development by the Committee on
Telecommunications National Academy of
Engineering. Rev. Wash., National Academy
of Sciences, 1969.
141p.
Contract no. H-932.

1. Communication systems. I. U.S. Dept. of
Housing and Urban Development. II. Title:
Telecommunications.

699.82 TEESDALE, L V
T22 SUGGESTED METHODS OF TESTING
MATERIALS USED AS VAPOR BARRIERS UNDER
CONCRETE SLABS AND AS GROUND COVER IN
CRAWL SPACES, BY L.V. TEESDALE, T.C.
SCHEFFER AND R.F. LUXFORD. REV.
MADISON, WIS., U.S. FOREST PRODUCTS
LABORATORY, 1959.
11P.

1. MOISTURE CONDENSATION.

510
H68 Teichroew, Daniel, joint author
Howell, James E
Mathematical analysis for business
decisions, by James E. Howell and
Daniel Teichroew. Homewood, Ill.,
Richard D. Irwin, 1963.
320 p.

1. Mathematics. 2. Business. I. Title.
II. Teichroew, Daniel, jt. au.

621.39 Telecommunications and the computer.
M17 Martin, James.
Telecommunications and the computer.
Englewood Cliffs, N.J., Prentice-
Hall, 1969.
470p. (Prentice-Hall series in automatic
computation)

1. Communication systems - Automation.
I. Title.

VF
699.86 Teesdale, L V
F67 U.S. Forest Service. Forest Products Laboratory,
R1740 Madison, Wis.
Thermal insulation made of wood-base materials
its application and use in houses, by L. V.
Teesdale. Madison, Wis., Oct. 1949.
40 p. plates, tables. (Its R1740)

Bibliography: p. 38-40.
Processed.

1.Insulating materials. I.Teesdale, L. V. II.Title.

339.5
T24 Teitelbaum, Perry D
Energy cost comparisons: theoretical and
practical problems in comparing nuclear and
conventional energy costs, with particular
reference to less developed areas. Washington,
Resources for the Future, inc., 1963.
222p. (Resources for the Future, inc.
Reprint number 38)
Reprinted from Science, technology, and
development - United States papers prepared for
the United Nations Conference on the Application
of Science and Technology for the Benefit of the
Less Developed Areas, Vol. I, Natural resources - Energy, water, and river basin
(Continued on next card)

621.39 Telecommunications for enhanced
N17t metropolitan function and form.
National Academy of Engineering.
Committee on Telecommunications.
Telecommunications for enhanced
metropolitan function and form; report to
the Director of Telecommunications
Management. Wash., 1969.
85p.

1. Communication systems. I. Title.

694.1
F67 Teesdale, L V
U. S. Forest Service. Forest Products
Laboratory.
Wood-frame house construction, by L. O.
Anderson and O. C. Heyer. Washington, Govt.
Print. Off., 1955.
235 p. illus, diagrs., maps, tables.
(U. S. Dept. of Agriculture. Agriculture hand-
book no. 73)

Prepared under the housing research program
of the Office of the Administrator, Housing and
Home Finance Agency Staff technician:
(continued on next card)

339.5
T24 Teitelbaum, Perry D
Energy...1963. (Card 2)

development (Washington: U.S. Government
Printing Office, 1963)

1. Power resources. 2. Atomic energy.
3. Underdeveloped countries. 4. Technical
assistance programs. I. Resources for the
Future, inc. II. Title.

621.39 Telecommunications in urban development.
D67 Dordick, H S
Telecommunications in urban development,
by H.S. Dordick and others. Santa Monica,
Calif., Rand Corp., 1969.
170p. (RM-6069-RC)

Bibliography: p. 169-170.

1. Communication systems. I. Rand Corp.
II. Title.

621.39
C65r
1970
H-H

U.S. OFFICE OF TELECOMMUNICATIONS POLICY
(PROPOSED).
U.S. Congress. House. Committee on
Government Operations.
Reorganization plan no. 1 of 1970 (Office
of Telecommunications Policy) Hearings
before a Subcommittee of the Committee on
Government Operations, House of
Representatives, Ninety-first Congress,
second session. Wash., Govt. Print. Off.,
1970.
133p.

Hearings held March 9-10, 1970.
(Cont'd on next card)

621.39
M17t

Teleprocessing network organization.
Martin, James.
Teleprocessing network organization.
Englewood Cliffs, N.J., Prentice-Hall, 1970.
290p. (Prentice-Hall series in automatic
computation)

1. Communication systems. I. Title.
II. Title: Network organization.

323.25
M17 *ma*

U.S. National Commission on the Causes and
Prevention of Violence. Mass media...1969.
(Card 2)

Prepared by Paul L. Briand, Jr.

1. Civil disorders. 2. Communication
systems. 3. Television. I. Briand, Paul
L., Jr. II. Title. III. Title: Violence
and the media.

621.39
C65r
1970
H-H

U.S. Congress. House. Committee on
Government Operations.
Reorganization plan...1970. (Card 2)

1. Communication systems. 2. U.S. Office
of Telecommunications Policy (Proposed)
3. U.S. Executive departments -
Reorganization. I. Title.

388
T25m

10c

Teletrans Corp.
Mass-transit for cities of the 20th century.
Detroit, 1965.
1v.

1. Transportation. 2. Journey to work.
I. Title.

621.397
Z27

TELEVISION.
Zerilli-Marimo, Guido.
Uomo televisione e libertà. Roma, 1970.
309p.

1. Television. 2. Communication
systems.

614.8
:643
T25

2c.

Teledyne Brown Engineering.
A design guide for home safety. Prepared
for the Research and Technology Div., U.S.
Dept. of Housing and Urban Development.
Huntsville, Ala., 1972.
1v.

1. Home accidents. I..U.S. Dept. of
Housing and Urban Development. Office of
Research and Technology. II. Title.

621.39
S45

TELEVISION.
Singer, Arthur L   Jr.
Issues for study in cable communications; an
occasional paper from the Alfred P. Sloan
Foundation. New York, 1970.
19p.

1. Communication systems. 2. Television.
I. Alfred P. Sloan Foundation. II. Title.

621.397
(016)
A74

TELEVISION - BIBLIOGRAPHY.
Atkin, Charles K   ed.
Television and social behavior; an annotated
bibliography of research focusing on tele-
vision's impact on children, ed. by Charles K.
Atkin and others. Rockville, Md., National
Institute of Mental Health, 1971.
150p. (U.S. Public Health Service publica-
tion no. 2099)
Bibliography: p. 127-141.
At head of title: National Clearinghouse
for Mental Health Information.
1. Television — Bibl. 2. Education - Bibl.
I. U.S. National Clearinghouse for Mental
Health Information. II. Title.

551
(016)
T25

TELEDYNE INDUSTRIES, INC.
BIBLIOGRAPHY OF ARRAY LITERATURE.
GARLAND, TEX., GEOTECHNICAL CORP., 1965.
114, 16P.

1. EARTHQUAKES - BIBLIOGRAPHY.
2. COMMUNICATION SYSTEMS - BIBLIOGRAPHY.
3. NOISE - BIBLIOGRAPHY. I. TITLE.
II. TITLE: ARRAY LITERATURE.

621.397
T17

TELEVISION.
Tate, Charles.
Cable television in the cities: community
control, public access, and minority ownership. Wash., Urban Institute, 1971.
184p.

Bibliography: p. 180-184.

1. Television. I. Urban Institute.
II. Title.

621.397
T25

Television - Directories.
Television factbook, 19-
Washington, D. C., Television Digest, Inc.,
19
1v. annual

Vol. I Stations
Vol.II Services
See main card for Library holdings.
1. Television. 2. Television - Directories.
3. Advertising.

020
S23

Telefacsimile in libraries.
Schieber, William D
Telefacsimile in libraries: a report of an
experiment in facsimile transmission and an
analysis of implications for interlibrary loan
systems, by William D. Schieber and Ralph M.
Shoffner. Los Angeles, Institute of Library
Research, University of California, 1968.
137p.
CFSTI. PB 182 813.
1. Library science. I. Shoffner, Ralph M.,
jt. au. II. California. University. University at Los An   geles. Institute of Library Rese   arch. III. Title.
IV. Title: In   terlibrary loan systems.

621.397
T25

Television.
Television factbook, 19-
Washington, D. C., Television Digest, Inc.,
19
v. annual

Vol. 1 Stations
Vol. II Services
See main card for library holdings.
1. Television. 2. Television - Directories.
3. Advertising.

389.6
C17

Television: a program for action.
Carnegie Commission on Educational Television.
Public television: a program for action.
Report and recommendations. New York.
Carnegie Corporation 1967.
254p. (A Bantam book)

1. Communication systems. 2. Education -
Films. 3. Visual aids. I. Title. II. Title:
Television: a program for action.

621.39
F22T

TELEGRAMS.
U.S. FEDERAL PUBLIC HOUSING AUTHORITY.
PERSONNEL DIVISION.
TELEGRAMS. WASHINGTON, 1944.
22P.

1. COMMUNICATIONS SYSTEMS. I. TITLE.

621.39
F22

Television.
U.S. Federal Communications Commission.
Report,
19
Wash., Govt. Print. Off., 19
v. annual

For Library holdings see main entry.

1. Communication systems. 2. Television.

621.397
(016)
A74

Television and social behavior.
Atkin, Charles K   ed.
Television and social behavior; an annotated
bibliography of research focusing on tele-
vision's impact on children, ed. by Charles K.
Atkin and others. Rockville, Md., National
Institute of Mental Health, 1971.
150p. (U.S. Public Health Service publica-
tion no. 2099)
Bibliography: p. 127-141.
At head of title: National Clearinghouse
for Mental Health Information.
1. Television - Bibl. 2. Education - Bibl.
I. U.S. National Clearinghouse for Mental
Health Information. II. Title.

658.800.15
M47

TELEPHONE INTERVIEWING.
MITCHELL, GLEN H
TELEPHONE INTERVIEWING.
WOOSTER, O., OHIO AGRICULTURAL
EXPERIMENT STATION, 1957.
15P. (OHIO AGRI. EXPERIMENT
STATION, DEPT. OF AGRI. ECONOMICS
AND RURAL SOCIOLOGY MONOGRAPH
SERIES NO. A.E. 279)

1. MARKETING RESEARCH. I. TITLE.

323.25
M17 *ma*

TELEVISION.
U.S. National Commission on the Causes and
Prevention of Violence.
Mass media hearings: a report to the
National Commission on the Causes and Pre-
vention of Violence. Wash., Govt. Print.
Off., 1969.
463p. (Its Task force reports)
Number 9A on spine.
Cover title: Violence and the media.
Hearings on the mass media before the
National Commission on the Causes and Pre-
vention of Violence, October 16 - Dec. 20,
1968.
(Cont'd on next card)

621.397
T25

Television factbook, 19-
Washington, D. C., Television Digest, Inc.,
19
v. annual

Vol. I Stations
Vol. II Services
See main card for Library holdings.

1. Television. 2. Television - Directories.
3. Advertising.

312
C25
HI21

Television sets in households in the
United States.

U.S. Bureau of the Census.
Current housing reports.
housing characteristics: Television sets
in households in the United States. No. 1-
June 1955 - Washington, Sept. 1955-
pts. graphs, tables.

1. Title. II. Title: Television sets
in households in the United States.

058.7
:621.39
B76r

Television yearbook.

Radio annual and television yearbook.

New York, Radio Daily Corp.,
v.

Editor in chief: Charles A.
Alicoate.
For complete information see shelflist.

I. Alicoate, Charles A., ed. II. Title:
Television yearbook.

674
F67s

Telford, C   J

U.S. Forest Service. Forest Products Laboratory,
Madison, Wis.
Small sawmill operator's manual, by C. J. Tel-
ford. Washington, Govt. Print. Off., 1952.
121p. illus., tables.
Agriculture handbook no. 27.

1. Lumber industry. I. Telford, C   J
II. Title: Sawmill operator's manual.

711.552
(79494)
D68

Telford, Edward T   District VII freeways.

Downtown Business Men's Association, Los
Angeles.
Downtown Los Angeles gives you more ad-
vantages as a business location. Los
Angeles, 1963.
kit. (8 pieces)

Partial contents: L.A. renaissance;
freeway service, key factor in downtown
growth, renewal, by M. Stark. (Reprint
from California highways and public
works, Sept.-Oct. 1961) Los
Angeles centropolis, 1980.
no. 1-3. (Cont'd. on next card)

711.552
(79494)
D68

Downtown Business Men's Association, Los
Angeles. Downtown Los Angeles...
(Card 2)

District VII freeways, by Edward T.
Telford (Reprint from California highways
and public works, Mar.-Apr. 1963)

1. Business districts - Los Angeles.
2. Urban renewal - Economic effect.
3. Streets - Los Angeles. 4. Highways -
California. I. Stark, Milton. L.A.
renaissance. II. Los Angeles
centropolis, 1980. III. Telford,
Edward T.   District VII freeways.

388
(79494)
T25

Telford, Edward T
People on the move. Supplemental
remarks on mass transportation aspects
of the Greater Los Angeles Freeway
System. Remarks made before the
Collier Committee, Los Angeles, October
2, 1962. Los Angeles, Administrative
Offices, 1962.
26p.
1. Transportation - Los Angeles. 2. Highways -
Los Angeles.

697
:551:5
861
1950

Telkes, Maria
Space Heating with Solar Energy, Massachusetts
Institute of Technology, Aug. 21-26, 1950.
Course-symposium, sponsored by Space Heating
Committee, Cabot Solar Energy Research Project
at M. I. T.   Cambridge, Mass. [1951?]
1 v. (loose-leaf)   diagrs.
Abstracts of papers by Hoyt C. Hottel,
Lawrence B. Anderson, Eugene Ayres, Paul A.
Siple, Albert G. H. Dietz, George O. G. Lof,
George F. Keck, Maria Telkes, August L.
Hesselschwerdt, George V. Parmelee, E. R. Ambrose.

697.8
F56se

Teller, A   J

Florida. University. Engineering and Indus-
trial Experiment Station.
Selection of air pollution control equip-
ment, by A. J. Teller. Gainesville, Fla.,
1961.
7p.   (Its Technical paper no. 205)
Engineering progress at the University of
Florida, vol. XV, no. 9, Sept. 1961.
Reprinted from Industrial water & wastes,
Jan.-Feb. 1961.

1. Air pollution.   I. Teller, A. J.

64

TELLER, ALASKA. CITY COUNCIL.
CAPITAL IMPROVEMENTS PROGRAM: FY
1967-68, 1973-74. BY ALASKA CONSULTANTS.
TELLER, ALASKA, 1968.
32P. (HUD 701 REPORT)

1. CAPITAL IMPROVEMENT PROGRAMS - TELLER,
ALASKA. I. ALASKA CONSULTANTS. II. HUD.
701. TELLER, ALASKA.

61

TELLER, ALASKA. CITY COUNCIL.
COMPREHENSIVE DEVELOPMENT PLAN. BY
ALASKA CONSULTANTS. TELLER, 1968.
105P. (HUD 701 REPORT)

1. MASTER PLAN - TELLER, ALASKA.
I. ALASKA CONSULTANTS. II. HUD. 701.
TELLER, ALASKA.

62

TELLER, ALASKA. CITY COUNCIL.
SUBDIVISION CONTROL REGULATIONS. BY
ALASKA CONSULTANTS. DRAFT. TELLER, 1968.
9P. (HUD 701 REPORT)

1. SUBDIVISION REGULATION - TELLER,
ALASKA. I. ALASKA CONSULTANTS. II. HUD.
701. TELLER, ALASKA.

63

TELLER, ALASKA. CITY COUNCIL.
ZONING ORDINANCE. BY ALASKA CONSULTANTS.
DRAFT. TELLER, ALASKA, 1968.
26P. (HUD 701 REPORT)

1. ZONING - TELLER, ALASKA. I. ALASKA
CONSULTANTS. II. HUD. 701. TELLER,
ALASKA.

VF
360
J12

Telling it like it is.

Jackson, Luther P
Telling it like it is. A dramatic reading
based on the words of the poor. Sponsored by
the Health and Welfare Council of the National
Capital Area as presented on September 29,
1966, at Howard University. Washington, 1966.
16p.

1. Social welfare. 2. Social conditions.
I. Howard University, Washington, D.C.
II. Title.

370
(74461)
N67

Telling the story of the cooperative plan
at Northeastern University.

Northeastern University, Boston.
Telling the story of the co-operative
plan at Northeastern University. "I'm
a co-op." Boston [1966]
23p.

1. Education - Boston. 2. Universities
and colleges. I. Title.

728.1
(46)
861te
94p.

Temas de vivienda social, economica y rural.

Spain. Ministerio de la Vivienda.
Temas de vivienda social, economica y
rural. Madrid, 1966.
(Abreviaturas de articulos de
revistas no. 6)

1. Housing - Spain. 2. Housing - Social
aspects. 3. Farm housing. I. Title.

920
:720
T25

TEMKO, ALLAN.
EERO SAARINEN. NEW YORK, G. BRAZILLER,
1962.
127P. (MAKERS OF CONTEMPORARY
ARCHITECTURE)

1. ARCHITECTS. 2. SAARINEN, EERO,
1910-1961.

34

TEMPE, ARIZ. PLANNING AND ZONING
COMMISSION.
GENERAL PLAN, 1967. SUMMARY ED. TEMPE,
VAN CLEVE ASSOCIATES, 1967.
FOLDER (HUD 701 REPORT)

1. CITY PLANNING - TEMPE, ARIZ. I. VAN
CLEVE ASSOCIATES. II. HUD. 701. TEMPE,
ARIZ.

32

TEMPE, ARIZ. PLANNING AND ZONING
COMMISSION.
PROPOSED ZONING ORDINANCE. PREPARED BY
VAN CLEVE ASSOCIATES. DRAFT. TEMPE, 1968.
1 V. (HUD 701 REPORT)

1. ZONING LEGISLATION - TEMPE, ARIZ.
I. VAN CLEVE ASSOCIATES. II. HUD. 701.
TEMPE, ARIZ.

31

TEMPE, ARIZ. PLANNING AND ZONING
COMMISSION.
SUBDIVISION ORDINANCE. PREPARED BY VAN
CLEVE ASSOCIATES. DRAFT. TEMPE, 1968.
1 V. (HUD 701 REPORT)

1. SUBDIVISION REGULATION - TEMPE, ARIZ.
I. VAN CLEVE ASSOCIATES. II. HUD. 701.
TEMPE, ARIZ.

33

TEMPE, ARIZ. PLANNING AND ZONING
COMMISSION.
TEMPE GENERAL PLAN, 1967. TEMPE, VAN
CLEVE ASSOCIATES, 1967.
80P. (HUD 701 REPORT)

1. CITY PLANNING - TEMPE, ARIZ. I. VAN
CLEVE ASSOCIATES. II. HUD. 701. TEMPE,
ARIZ.

21-
30

TEMPE, ARIZ. PLANNING DEPT.
THE COMPREHENSIVE PLANNING PROGRAM: 1.
POPULATION; 2. HOUSING AND RESIDENTIAL
ENVIRONMENT; 3. ECONOMICS; 4. LAND USE; 5.
COMMUNITY FACILITIES; 6. UTILITIES; 7.
INDUSTRIAL DEVELOPMENT; 8. STREETS AND
THOROUGHFARES; 9. COMMERCIAL DEVELOPMENT;
10. TOWARD SOUND LAND PLANNING AND
DEVELOPMENT. PREPARED BY TEMPE PLANNING
DEPARTMENT AND OTHERS. TEMPE, ARIZ.,
1965-68.
10 V. (HUD 701 REPORT)
1. MASTER PLAN - TEMPE, ARIZ.
I. HUD. 701. TEMPE, ARIZ.

720
(52)
T25

Tempel, Egon.
New Japanese architecture. New York,
Praeger Publishers, 1969.
220p.

1. Architecture - Japan. I. Title.

VF
697.353
:691.8
F67

**Temperature variation on the surface of a
sandwich panel in which copper heating
tubes are embedded (exploratory test).**
U.S. Forest Service. Forest Products Laboratory,
Madison, Wis.
Temperature variation on the surface of a
sandwich panel in which copper heating tubes are
embedded (exploratory test), by J. S. Mathewson.
(In cooperation with the National Housing Agency).
Madison, Wis. [1947]
7 l./plates.
Not for publication.
Processed.
1.Heating-Radiant. 2. Panels. 3.Housing research
constructs. I.Mathewson J. S. II.U.S. National
Housing Agency.   III.Title.

728.3
T25

Temple Industries, inc.
A folio of homes designed in the "Viewpoint
1965" program of Temple Industries. Diboll,
Texas, 1965.
1v.

Cover title.

1. Architecture, Domestic - Design.
2. Architecture, Modern. I. Title: Viewpoint
1965.

551.5
:614
W45

Temperature and human life.
Winslow, Charles Edward Amory, 1877-
Temperature and human life, by C.-E. A. Winslow and
L. P. Herrington. Princeton, Princeton Univ. Press, 1949.
xiv, 272 p. illus. 23 cm.
"References": p. 260-266.

1. Temperature—Physiological effect. 2. Air conditioning. 3. Animal heat.   i. Herrington, Lovic Pierce, 1907-   joint author.

QP82.W5   612.5   49—8993*
Library of Congress   [52]5]

VF
697.001.5
D62

**Temperatures and related conditions in
Wisconsin farmhouses.**
Dodge, J   Robert
Temperatures and related conditions in
Wisconsin farmhouses, by J. Robert Dodge and
M. J. LaRock.   Washington [Govt. Print. Off.]
Mar. 1952.
81 p.   illus.   (U.S. Dept. of Agriculture.
Technical bulletin no. 1002).

1.Heating research. I.LaRock, M. J., jt. au.
II.Title. III.Series.

312
(748)
P25p

Temple University.
Pennsylvania. State Planning Board.
The population of Pennsylvania;
projections to 1980. Estimates by county
for 1965, 1970, 1975, 1980, by age, sex,
and race. Projections developed by Temple
University, Office of Research and
Specialized Services. [Harrisburg] 1963.
190p.

U.S. Urban Renewal Adm. UPAP.

1. Population - Pennsylvania. I. Temple
University.   II. U.S. URA-
UPAP.   Pennsylvania.

697.0015
H15

**TEMPERATURE CONDITIONS IN THREE
HOUSES FOLLOWING SIMULATED POWER**
HANDEGORD, G   O
TEMPERATURE CONDITIONS IN THREE
HOUSES FOLLOWING SIMULATED POWER
SHUT-OFF, BY G.O. HANDEGORD, H.W.
ORR AND R.G. NICHOLSON. OTTAWA,
1964.
18L. (NATIONAL RESEARCH COUNCIL,
CANADA. DIVISION OF BUILDING
RESEARCH. INTERNAL REPORT NO. 291)
1. HEATING RESEARCH. I. ORR,
H.W., JT. AU. II. NICHOLSON, R.G.,
JT. AU. III. NATIONAL RESEARCH
COUNCIL, CAN ADA. DIVISION OF
BUILDING RES   EARCH. IV. TITLE.

VF
691.8
F67L
P7

**Temperatures attained in "Lincoln" house-wall
panels when exposed to sunshine.**
U.S. Forest Service. Forest Products Laboratory,
Madison, Wis.
Temperatures attained in "Lincoln" house-wall
panels when exposed to sunshine, by Leslie E.
Downs. Madison, Wis. [1946]
14 l./plates, table.

Not for publication.
In cooperation with the National Housing Agency.
At head of title: Progress report no. 7.
Processed.

333.65
T25
3c.

Temple University. Center for Social Policy
and Community Development.
Model curricula and training techniques
for use in training para-professional
employees of public housing authorities.
Prepared under contract with the U.S.
Dept. of Housing and Urban Development.
Wash., U.S. Dept. of Housing and Urban
Development, 1972.
227p.
Bibliography: p. 56-58.

(Cont'd on next card)

696.1
N17t

Temperature distribution in an electric
water heater.
National Association of Plumbing Contractors.
Temperature distribution in an electric
water heater, by F. M. Dawson and E. C.
Lundquist. Washington, 1954.
19p. illus., diagrs.

1. Plumbing.   I. Dawson, F.M. II. Lundquist,
E. C.   III. Title.

VF
697
S45

Temperatures in southern farmhouses.
Simons, Joseph Winslow, 1908-
Factors affecting temperatures in southern farmhouses, by
Joseph W. Simons and Frank B. Lanham. Rev. Washing-
ton [U.S. Govt. Print. Off.] 1951.
91 p. illus. 23 cm. (U. S. Dept. of Agriculture. Technical
bulletin no. 822)
Cover title.
"Literature cited": p. 90-91.
1. [Farm houses—Heating] 2. [Farm houses—Ventilation] 3. [Farm
houses—Southern States] 4. Farm buildings. 5. Heating. 6. Ventila-
tion.   I. Lanham, Frank Bristol, 1915-   joint author. II. Title.
III. Title: Temperatures in southern farmhouses. (Series)
S21.A72 rev. no. 822, 1951   697   Agr 51-271

U. S. Dept. of Agr. Libr.   1Ag84Te no. 822 1951
for Library of Congress   [75]†

333.65
T25

Temple University. Center for Social Policy
and Community Development. Model curricula
...1972.   (Card 2)

1. Housing management. 2. Local housing
authorities. I. U.S. Dept. of Housing and
Urban Development. II. Title.

697
M85t

Temperature distribution in domestic
heating systems.
Muncey, R   W
Temperature distribution in domestic
heating systems, by R.W. Muncey and B.C.
Bautovich. Melbourne, Commonwealth
Scientific and Industrial Research
Organization, 1969.
[3]p. (Australia. Commonwealth
Scientific and Industrial Research
Organization. Division of Building
Research. D.B.R. reprint no. 453)
Reprinted from: Australian refrigeration,
air condition-   ing, and Heating, 1969,
p. 47-49.
(Cont'd on next card)

693.5
H27t

**Temperatures within battery moulds during
curing.**
Herbert, M   R   M
Temperatures within battery moulds during
curing. Garston, Eng., Building Research
Station, Ministry of Technology, 1967.
[3]p. (U.K. Building Research Station
Building research current papers. Construction series 33)
Reprinted from: Industrialised building
systems and components, 1966, vol. 3, no. 11,
p. 44, 45, 47.

1. Concrete construc-   tion. 2. Coordinated
components.   II. Title.
I. U.K. Building   Research Station.

332.72
(748)
P25f

Temple University. Bureau of Economic
Business Research.
Pennsylvania. Dept. of Commerce.
(Bureau of Community Development)
Financing lower-middle income housing.
Harrisburg, Pa., 1964.
107p.

Consultant for this Project: Temple
University, Bureau of Economic and
Business Research.
U.S. Urban Renewal Adm. Demonstration
Grant Program.

(Cont'd. on next
card)

697
M85t

Muncey, R   W   Temperature
...1969.   (Card 2)

1. Heating. I. Bautovich, B.C.,
jt. au. II. Australia. Commonwealth
Scientific and Industrial Research
Organization. (Division of Building
Research) III. Title.

711
(016)
C65
no.219

Temkin, Sanford.
An evaluation of comprehensive planning
literature with an annotated bibliography.
Philadelphia, Research for Better Schools, 1971.
86p. (Council of Planning Librarians.
Exchange bibliography no. 219)

1. Planning - Bibl. I. Research for Better
Schools. II. Title. (Series: Council of
Planning Librarians. Exchange bibliography
no. 219)

332.72
(748)
P25f

Pennsylvania. Dept. of Commerce.
(Bureau of Community Development)
Financing lower-middle income housing ...
(Card 2)

1. Mortgage finance - P... 2. Low-income
housing. 3. Family income and expenditure -
Housing. I. Temple University. Bureau of
Economic Business Research. II. U.S.
URA. Demonstration Grant Program.

628.1
M17t

Temperature prediction in stratified water.
Massachusetts Institute of Technology.
Ralph M. Parsons Laboratory for Water
Resources and Hydrodynamics.
Temperature prediction in stratified water;
mathematical model-user's manual (supplement
to report 16130DJH01/71) [Prepared for]
Environmental Protection Agency. Cambridge,
Mass., 1971.
125p. (Water pollution control research
series)
Bibliography: p. 120-121.
1. Water-supply. I. U.S. Environmental
Protection   Agency. II. Title.

352.1
(755)
L21

Temple, David G
League of Virginia Counties.
Virginia county finance, 1947-1956, by
David G. Temple. Charlottesville, League of
Virginia Counties and Bureau of Public Admin-
istration, U. of Va., 1958.
45p. graphs. (Joint report no. 1)

1. County finance - Virginia. I. Temple,
David G II. Virginia. University.
Bureau of Public Administration.

VF
33
(748)
T25

Temple University. Bureau of Economic and
Business Research.
The northeast industrial area of Pennsylvania;
an economic base study. [Philadelphia, Sept.
1952]
44 p.   tables. (Temple University.
School of Business and Public Administration.
Economics and business bulletin, v. 5, no. 1)

1.Economic base studies-Pennsylvania.
2.Industrial location.

362.6
T25P
TEMPLE UNIVERSITY. SCHOOL OF BUSINESS
AND PUBLIC ADMINISTRATION.
THE PHILADELPHIA AREA OLDER WORKER
STUDY, A SUMMARY. PHILADELPHIA, BUREAU
OF ECONOMIC AND BUSINESS RESEARCH,
TEMPLE UNIVERSITY, 1956.
56P. (ITS ECONOMICS AND BUSINESS
BULLETIN, V.9, NO.2)

1. OLD AGE - EMPLOYMENT. 2. LABOR
SUPPLY - PHILADELPHIA.

728.1
1940.42
F22SP
TEMPORARY DWELLING UNITS.
U.S. FEDERAL PUBLIC HOUSING AUTHORITY.
SPECIFICATION FOR THE LABOR AND
MATERIALS NECESSARY FOR THE
CONSTRUCTION OF WAR DORMITORIES AND
APARTMENTS, TEMPORARY DWELLING UNITS,
COMMUNITY FACILITIES, ELIZABETH CITY,
NORTH CAROLINA. N.C. 31081-T, N.C.
31082, N.C. 31083. WASHINGTON, 1942.
1 V. (VARIOUS PAGINGS)

1. DEFENSE HOUSING - STANDARDS AND
SPECIFICATIONS. 2. BUILDING
CONSTRUCTION - LABOR REQUIREMENTS.
I. ELIZABETH CITY, N.C.
(CONTINUED ON NEXT CARD)

728.1
1362.6
C65T
1964
S-R
TEMPORARY EXTENSION OF INSURED
HOUSING LOAN PROGRAM.
U.S. CONGRESS. SENATE. COMMITTEE ON
BANKING AND CURRENCY.
TEMPORARY EXTENSION OF INSURED
HOUSING LOAN PROGRAM FOR ELDERLY IN
RURAL AREAS. REPORT TO ACCOMPANY H.J.
RES. 1041. WASHINGTON, GOVT. PRINT.
OFF., 1964.
4P. (88TH CONGRESS, 2D SESSION.
SENATE. REPORT NO. 1108)

1. HOUSING FOR THE AGED. 2. DIRECT
LOANS FOR HOUSING. I. TITLE.

360
1308
T25
TEMPLE UNIVERSITY. SCHOOL OF MEDICINE.
DEPT. OF PSYCHIATRY.
THE MEN ON SKID ROW; A STUDY OF
PHILADELPHIA'S HOMELESS MAN POPULATION.
PHILADELPHIA, GREATER PHILADELPHIA
MOVEMENT, 1960.
218L.

1. SOCIAL SURVEY - PHILADELPHIA.
2. SOCIAL WELFARE - PHILADELPHIA.
I. TITLE.

728.1
1940.42
F22SP
U.S. FEDERAL PUBLIC HOUSING AUTHORITY.
SPECIFICATION FOR THE ...1942. (CARD 2)

II. TITLE: WAR DORMITORIES AND
APARTMENTS. III. TITLE: TEMPORARY
DWELLING UNITS.

333.63
C653
1950
H-H
DEC.4
TEMPORARY EXTENSION OF RENT CONTROL.
U.S. CONGRESS. HOUSE. COMMITTEE ON
BANKING AND CURRENCY.
TEMPORARY EXTENSION OF RENT CONTROL.
HEARINGS, EIGHTY-FIRST CONGRESS, SECOND
SESSION, ON H.R. 9763... WASHINGTON,
GOVT. PRINT. OFF., 1950.
51P.
HEARINGS HELD DECEMBER 4, 1950.

1. RENT CONTROL. I. TITLE.

331
C6533
1961
H-R
TEMPORARY EXTENDED UNEMPLOYMENT
COMPENSATION ACT OF 1961...
U.S. CONGRESS. CONFERENCE COMMITTEES.
1961.
TEMPORARY EXTENDED UNEMPLOYMENT
COMPENSATION ACT OF 1961... CONFERENCE
REPORT TO ACCOMPANY H.R. 4806.
WASHINGTON, GOVT. PRINT. OFF., 1961.
6P. (87TH CONGRESS, 1ST SESSION.
HOUSE. REPORT NO. 183)

1. EMPLOYMENT. I. TITLE.
II. TITLE: UNEMPLOYMENT COMPENSATION
ACT OF 1961.

FOLIO
728.1
1355.1
F22TE
TEMPORARY HOUSING FOR VETERANS.
U.S. FEDERAL PUBLIC HOUSING AUTHORITY.
TEMPORARY HOUSING FOR VETERANS; A
REPORT ON THE FEDERAL PUBLIC HOUSING
AUTHORITY RE-USE PROGRAM UNDER TITLE V
OF THE LANHAM ACT AS AMENDED.
WASHINGTON, 1947.
40L.

1. VETERANS' HOUSING. I. TITLE.

5423
TEMPLETON, MASS. PLANNING BOARD.
MASTER PLAN. BY METCALF AND EDDY.
TEMPLETON, 1967.
317P. (HUD 701 REPORT)

1. CITY PLANNING - TEMPLETON, MASS.
I. METCALF AND EDDY. II. HUD. 701.
TEMPLETON, MASS.

331
C65T
1961
H-R
NO.27
TEMPORARY EXTENDED UNEMPLOYMENT
COMPENSATION ACT OF 1961.
U.S. CONGRESS. HOUSE. COMMITTEE ON
WAYS AND MEANS.
TEMPORARY EXTENDED UNEMPLOYMENT
COMPENSATION ACT OF 1961. REPORT TO
ACCOMPANY H.R. 4806. WASHINGTON, GOVT.
PRINT. OFF., 1961.
42P. (87TH CONGRESS, 1ST SESSION.
HOUSE. REPORT NO. 27)

1. EMPLOYMENT. I. TITLE.

728.1
1355
(083.74)
W17
Temporary housing, general construction.
U.S. War Department (Office of the Quartermaster
General, Construction Division).
Standard specifications for temporary
housing; general construction. Revised
March 1, 1941. [Washington, Govt. Print. Off.]
June 1941.
159 p.

1.Military housing - Standards and specifications. I.Title: Temporary housing, general
construction.

728.1
(41)
U541T
TEMPORARY ACCOMMODATION.
U.K. MINISTRY OF HEALTH.
TEMPORARY ACCOMMODATION. MEMORANDUM
FOR THE GUIDANCE OF LOCAL AUTHORITIES.
LONDON, H.M. STAT. OFF., 1944.
32P.

AT HEAD OF TITLE: MINISTRY OF HEALTH,
MINISTRY OF WORKS.

1. HOUSING - U.K. I. U.K. MINISTRY
OF WORKS. II. TITLE.

331
C65T
1961
S-R
NO.27
TEMPORARY EXTENDED UNEMPLOYMENT
COMPENSATION ACT OF 1961...
U.S. CONGRESS. SENATE. COMMITTEE ON
FINANCE.
TEMPORARY EXTENDED UNEMPLOYMENT
COMPENSATION ACT OF 1961... REPORT...
TO ACCOMPANY H.R. 4806. WASHINGTON,
GOVT. PRINT. OFF., 1961.
27P. (87TH CONGRESS, 1ST SESSION.
SENATE. REPORT NO. 69)

1. EMPLOYMENT. I. TITLE.
II. TITLE: UNEMPLOYMENT COMPENSATION
ACT OF 1961.

690.091.82
N17T
TEMPORARY HOUSING SPECIFICATIONS
AUGUST, NOVEMBER, 1942.
U.S. NATIONAL HOUSING AGENCY.
TEMPORARY HOUSING SPECIFICATIONS
AUGUST, NOVEMBER, 1942. WASH.,
1942.
1 V.

1. BUILDING STANDARDS. I. TITLE.

728.1
1355
884
TEMPORARY AND SEMI-PERMANENT BUILDINGS.
BUILDING RESEARCH ADVISORY BOARD.
STUDY OF TEMPORARY AND SEMI-PERMANENT
BUILDINGS ON NAVAL ESTABLISHMENTS.
CONDUCTED BY THE BUILDING RESEARCH
ADVISORY BOARD FOR THE BUREAU OF YARDS
AND DOCKS, U.S. NAVY, UNDER CONTRACT
NO. NOY-76733, NOVEMBER 30, 1953.
WASHINGTON, 1953.
1 V.

COVER TITLE: A STUDY OF TEMPORARY AND
SEMI-PERMANENT BUILDINGS IN THE 5TH
NAVAL DISTRICT AND THE POTOMAC RIVER
NAVAL COMMAND.
(CONTINUED ON NEXT CARD)

388
C65U
1967
H-R
TEMPORARY EXTENSION OF EMERGENCY
PROVISIONS.
U.S. CONGRESS. HOUSE. COMMITTEE ON
BANKING AND CURRENCY.
TEMPORARY EXTENSION OF EMERGENCY
PROVISIONS OF URBAN MASS TRANSPORTATION
PROGRAM... REPORT TO ACCOMPANY H.J. RES.
601. WASHINGTON, GOVT. PRINT. OFF., 1967.
2P. (90TH CONGRESS, 1ST SESSION.
HOUSE. REPORT NO. 352)

1. TRANSPORTATION. I. TITLE.

330
S268
U.S. TEMPORARY NATIONAL ECONOMIC
COMMITTEE.
SCOVILLE, JOHN WATSON, COMP.
FACT AND FANCY IN THE T.N.E.C.
MONOGRAPHS; REVIEWS OF THE 43 MONOGRAPHS
ISSUED BY THE TEMPORARY NATIONAL ECONOMIC
COMMITTEE, COMPILED BY JOHN
SCOVILLE...AND NOEL SARGENT...SPONSORED
BY THE NATIONAL ASSOCIATION OF
MANUFACTURERS. NEW YORK, 1942.
812P.

1. ECONOMIC CONDITIONS. 2. U.S.
TEMPORARY NATIONAL ECONOMIC COMMITTEE.
INVESTIGATION OF CONCENTRATION OF
ECONOMIC POWER. MONOGRAPHS.
(CONTINUED ON NEXT CARD)

728.1
1355
884
BUILDING RESEARCH ADVISORY BOARD. STUDY
OF ...1953. (CARD 2)

1. MILITARY HOUSING. 2. EMERGENCY
HOUSING. I. U.S. BUREAU OF YARDS AND
DOCKS. II. TITLE: TEMPORARY AND
SEMI-PERMANENT BUILDINGS.

728.1
(73
1347)
C65
1950
H-R
NO.3143
TEMPORARY EXTENSION OF HOUSING AND
RENT ACT OF 1947.
U.S. CONGRESS. HOUSE. COMMITTEE ON
BANKING AND CURRENCY.
TEMPORARY EXTENSION OF HOUSING AND
RENT ACT OF 1947, AS AMENDED. REPORT
TO ACCOMPANY H.R. 9763. WASHINGTON,
GOVT. PRINT. OFF., 1950.
2P. (81ST CONGRESS, 2D SESSION.
HOUSE OF REPRESENTATIVES REPORT NO.
3143)

1. HOUSING LEGISLATION. 2. RENT
CONTROL. I. TITLE. II. TITLE:
HOUSING AND RENT ACT OF 1947.

330
S268
SCOVILLE, JOHN WATSON, COMP. FACT AND
FANCY ...1942. (CARD 2)

I. SARGENT, NOEL, JT. COMP.
II. NATIONAL ASSOCIATION OF MANUFACTURERS
OF THE UNITED STATES OF AMERICA.
III. TITLE.

Temporary National Economic Committee.

see

U.S. Congress. Temporary National Economic
Committee.

TEMPORARY UNEMPLOYMENT COMPENSATION
331   ACT AMOUNTS.
C65RES   U.S. CONGRESS. HOUSE. COMMITTEE ON
1963   WAYS AND MEANS.
H-R   RESTORATION OF TEMPORARY UNEMPLOYMENT
COMPENSATION ACT AMOUNTS. REPORT TO
ACCOMPANY H.R. 8821. WASHINGTON,
GOVT. PRINT. OFF., 1963.
12P. (88TH CONGRESS, 1ST SESSION.
HOUSE. REPORT NO. 860)

1. EMPLOYMENT. I. TITLE: TEMPORARY
UNEMPLOYMENT COMPENSATION ACT AMOUNTS.

---

658   TEN COMMANDMENTS OF GOOD ORGANIZATION.
A52TE   AMERICAN MANAGEMENT ASSOCIATION.
TEN COMMANDMENTS OF GOOD ORGANIZATION.
NEW YORK, 1941.
BROADSIDE (IN FOLDER)

1. MANAGEMENT. I. TITLE.

VF   Temporary shelter acts.
728.1
:940.42   U.S. National Housing Agency. (Office of the
(73:347)   Administrator. Office of the General
N17   Counsel)
Temporary shelter acts; extracts from
Public Laws 9, 73 and 353, 77th Congress.
[Washington] Feb. 1943.
5 p.

1. Housing legislation - Wartime.
I. Title.

TEMPORARY UNEMPLOYMENT COMPENSATION
331   ACT OF 1958.
C65TEMA   U.S. CONGRESS. HOUSE. COMMITTEE ON
1958   WAYS AND MEANS.
H-R   TEMPORARY UNEMPLOYMENT COMPENSATION
ACT OF 1958. REPORT TO ACCOMPANY
H.R. 12065. WASHINGTON, GOVT. PRINT.
OFF., 1958.
38P. (85TH CONGRESS, 2D SESSION.
HOUSE. REPORT NO. 1656)

1. EMPLOYMENT. I. TITLE.
II. TITLE: UNEMPLOYMENT COMPENSATION
ACT.

Ref.   10,000 jokes, toasts, & stories...
808.8
C66   Copeland, Lewis
10,000 jokes, toasts, & stories, edited by
Lewis and Faye Copeland. Garden City, N. Y.,
Garden City Books, 1940.
1020 p.

I. Title. II. Copeland, Faye.
1. Quotations.

ct

---

360   The temporary society.
B25   Bennis, Warren G
The temporary society, by Warren G. Bennis and
Philip E. Slater. New York, Harper & Row, 1968.
147p.

Bibliography: p. 129-139.

1. Social conditions. I. Slater, Philip E.
jt. au. II. Title.

TEMPORARY UNEMPLOYMENT COMPENSATION
331   AND AID.
C657TEM   U.S. CONGRESS. HOUSE. COMMITTEE ON
1961   WAYS AND MEANS.
H-H   TEMPORARY UNEMPLOYMENT COMPENSATION
AND AID, TO DEPENDENT CHILDREN OF
UNEMPLOYED PARENTS. HEARINGS,
EIGHTY-SEVENTH CONGRESS, FIRST
SESSION, ON H.R. 3864... AND H.R.
3865. WASHINGTON, GOVT. PRINT. OFF.,
1961.
423P.
HEARINGS HELD FEB. 15-17, 1961.

1. EMPLOYMENT. I. TITLE.
II. TITLE: U. NEMPLOYMENT
(CONTINUED ON NEXT CARD)

Ten year forecast of housing starts, 1957-
690   1966.
(083.41)   Housing Securities, inc.
H68   Ten year forecast of housing starts
1957-1966. New York, 1957.
1v.

1. Building construction - Statistics.
I. Title.

---

331   Temporary summer employment.
C65te   U.S. Congress. Senate. Committee on
1965   Post Office and Civil Service.
S-H   Temporary summer employment. Hearing
before the Subcommittee on Civil Service of
the Committee on Post Office and Civil
Service, United States Senate, Eighty-
ninth Congress, first session on H. R.
242. An act to extend the apportionment
requirement in the Civil Service act of
January 18, 1883, to temporary summer
employment, and for other purposes.
Washington, Govt. Print. Off., 1965.
49p.

1. Employment. 2. Federal civil service.
3. Title.

---

331   U.S. CONGRESS. HOUSE. COMMITTEE ON
C657TEM   WAYS AND MEANS. TEMPORARY
1961   UNEMPLOYMENT COMPENSATION ...1961.
H-H   (CARD 2)

COMPENSATION AND AID TO DEPENDENT
CHILDREN.

Ten-year master plan for water, electric &
628.16   sewerage systems.
B51   Black, Crow and Eidsness, inc.
Engineering report for City of Gainesville,
Florida. Ten-year master plan for water,
electric & sewerage systems. Gainesville, Fla.,
1965.
1v.

1. Water-supply engineering. 2. Electricity.
3. Sewers. 4. Master plan - Gainesville, Fla.
I. Gainesville, Fla. II. Title. III. Title:
Ten-year master plan for water, electric &
sewerage systems.

---

331   TEMPORARY UNEMPLOYMENT COMPENSATION.
C65TEMP   U.S. CONGRESS. CONFERENCE
1959   COMMITTEES, 1959.
H-R   TEMPORARY UNEMPLOYMENT COMPENSATION.
MAR.25   CONFERENCE REPORT TO ACCOMPANY H.R.
5640. WASHINGTON, GOVT. PRINT. OFF.,
1959.
3P. (86TH CONGRESS, 1ST SESSION.
HOUSE. REPORT NO. 257)

1. EMPLOYMENT. I. TITLE.
II. TITLE: UNEMPLOYMENT COMPENSATION.

TEMPORARY UNEMPLOYMENT COMPENSATION
331   ACT OF 1958...
C65TEMP   U.S. CONGRESS. SENATE. COMMITTEE ON
1958   FINANCE.
S-R   TEMPORARY UNEMPLOYMENT COMPENSATION
ACT OF 1958... REPORT TO ACCOMPANY HR
12065. WASHINGTON, GOVT. PRINT. OFF.,
1958.
2PTS. IN 1 V. (85TH CONGRESS, 2D
SESSION. SENATE. REPORT NO. 1625)
CONTENTS.-[PT.1]

1. EMPLOYMENT. I. TITLE.
II. TITLE: UNEMPLOYMENT COMPENSATION,
1958.

A ten year plan for housing older people in
728.1   Michigan.
:362.6   Michigan. Commission on Aging.
(774)   A ten year plan for housing older
M41   people in Michigan. A report prepared
by the Task Force on Senior Citizen
Housing. [Detroit] 1964.
1v.

Bibliography: p. 39-59.

1. Housing for the aged - Mich.
2. Housing and health. I. Title.

---

331   TEMPORARY UNEMPLOYMENT COMPENSATION.
C65TEMP   U.S. CONGRESS. SENATE. COMMITTEE ON
1959   FINANCE.
S-H   TEMPORARY UNEMPLOYMENT COMPENSATION,
HEARING ... EIGHTY-SIXTH CONGRESS,
FIRST SESSION, ON H.R. 5640, AN ACT
TO EXTEND THE TIME DURING WHICH
CERTAIN INDIVIDUALS MAY CONTINUE TO
RECEIVE TEMPORARY UNEMPLOYMENT
COMPENSATION. WASHINGTON, GOVT.
PRINT. OFF., 1959.
81P.
1. EMPLOYMENT. I. TITLE.
II. TITLE: U NEMPLOYMENT
COMPENSATION.

Ten blocks from the White House....
323.25   Gilbert, Ben W   ed.
G45   Ten blocks from the White House; anatomy of
the Washington riots of 1968, by Ben W. Gilbert
and the Staff of the Washington Post. New
York, Frederick A. Praeger, 1968.
245p.

1. Civil disorders. 2. Law enforcement.
3. Race relations. 4. Minority groups.
I. Washington Post. II. Title. III. Title:
Washington riots of 1968.

VF   A ten year plan for the economic and social
33   development of the Belgian Congo.
(675)   Wigny, Pierre
W43   A ten year plan for the economic and social
development of the Belgian Congo. 2d ed. New
York, Belgian Government Information Center, 1951.
72 p. illus., map. (Art, life and
science in Belgium, no. 16)

1.Economic planning-Belgian Congo. 2.Social
conditions-Belgian Congo. I.Title.

---

331   TEMPORARY UNEMPLOYMENT COMPENSATION.
C65TEMP   U.S. CONGRESS. SENATE. COMMITTEE ON
1959   FINANCE.
S-R   TEMPORARY UNEMPLOYMENT COMPENSATION.
REPORT TOGETHER WITH SUPPLEMENTAL
VIEWS TO ACCOMPANY H.R. 5640.
WASHINGTON, GOVT. PRINT. OFF., 1959.
13P. (86TH CONGRESS, 1ST SESSION.
SENATE. REPORT NO. 135)

1. EMPLOYMENT. I. TITLE.
II. TITLE: UNEMPLOYMENT COMPENSATION.

A ten city study of public welfare
practices relating to housing assistance
360   and shelter allowances.
D47   District of Columbia. Dept. of Public Welfare.
A ten city study of public welfare practices
relating to housing assistance and shelter
allowances. Washington, 1965.
34p.

Donald D. Brewer, director.

1. Social welfare. 2. Public assistance.
I. Title.

VF   A ten year plan for the economic and social
33   development of the Belgian Trust Territory
(6751)   of Ruanda-Urundi.
B25   Belgium. *Ministère des colonies.*
A ten year plan for the economic and social development
of the Belgian Trust Territory of Ruanda-Urundi. New
York, Belgian Govt. Information Center, 1952.
83 p. illus. 23 cm. (Art, life and science of Belgium, no. 24)

1. Ruanda-Urundi—Economic policy.— 2. Ruanda-Urundi—Soc.
condit. I. Title.
HC557.R8A54 1952   *309.23   338.9675   52-3152 ‡

Library of Congress   [2]

727
C31
A 10-year plan to save the schools.
Changing education.
A 10-year plan to save the schools.
Wash., American Federation of Teachers,
AFL-CIO, 1968.
48p.

Changing education, Summer/Fall, 1968.

1. Schools. 2. Education. I. Title.

330
(8)
I57t
Ten years of work in Latin America.
Inter-American Development Bank.
Ten years of work in Latin America.
Washington, D.C., 1969.
60p.

1. Economic development - Latin America.
I. Title.

VF
728.1
:336.18
(74811)
H68
Tenant assignment in public housing.
Housing Association of Delaware Valley.
Tenant assignment in public housing.
Philadelphia, 1968.
4p. (Its Special memo. no. 34)

1. Public housing - Philadelphia.
2. Minority groups - Housing -
Philadelphia. 3. Tenant selection.
I. Title.

VF
711.4
N175
A ten-year program for metropolitan areas.
National Planning Association.
A ten-year program for metropolitan areas;
joint statement of the NPA Board of Trustees
and Standing Committees. Washington [1957]
16 L.

1. Metropolitan area planning.
I. Title.

711.585
(7471)
R44T
A TEN YEARS' WAR.
RIIS, JACOB AUGUST, 1849-1914.
A TEN YEARS' WAR; AN ACCOUNT OF THE
BATTLE WITH THE SLUM IN NEW YORK.
BOSTON, HOUGHTON, MIFFLIN, 1900.
267P.

1. SLUMS - NEW YORK (CITY)
I. TITLE.

333.65
UN
TENANT EDUCATION
UNITED NATIONS. BUREAU OF TECHNICAL
ASSISTANCE OPERATIONS.
MEETING OF GROUP OF EXPERTS ON
HOUSING MANAGEMENT AND TENANT EDUCATION,
WELLINGTON, NEW ZEALAND, 9 TO 23 MARCH
1963. NEW YORK, UNITED NATIONS, 1964.
155P. (ST/TAO/SER/C 61)

BIBLIOGRAPHY: P.148-155.

1. HOUSING MANAGEMENT. 2. PUBLIC
HOUSING. I. TITLE: TENANT EDUCATION.

628.1
F22t
A ten-year program of Federal water resources
research.
U.S. Federal Council for Science and
Technology. (Committee on Water Resources
Research)
A ten-year program of Federal water
resources research. Wash., Office of Science
and Technology, Executive Office of the
President, for sale by the Supt. of Doc.,
Govt. Print. Off., 1966.
88p.

1. Water resources. 2. Water-supply
engineering. 3. Governmental research.
4. Power resources.
I. Title.

325.2
S25
The tenacity of prejudice.
Selznick, Gertrude J
The tenacity of prejudice; anti-Semitism in
contemporary America, by Gertrude J. Selznick
and Stephen Steinberg. New York, Harper and
Row, 1969.
248p. (Patterns of American prejudice.
v. 4)
Series based on the University of California
five-year study of anti-Semitism in the United
States conducted by Survey Research Center,
under grant from the Anti-Defamation league of
B'nai B'rith.
1. Race relations. 2. Minority groups.
I. Steinberg, Stephen, jt. au. II. Title:
Anti-Semitism in contemporary America.
III. Title.

711.585
:308
(7471)
G72
Tenant households in the West side urban
renewal area of New York City,
Greenleigh Associates.
Report of the diagnostic survey of
tenant households in the West side urban
renewal area of New York City. New York,
1965.
150p.

1. Urban renewal - Surveys - New York
(City) 2. Relocation - New York (City)
3. Neighborhood rehabilitation - New York
(City) 4. Public assistance - New York
(City) I. Title: Tenant households
in the West side urban renewal
area of New York City.

956.43
C96
A ten-year programme of development for Cyprus.
Cyprus. Government.
A ten-year programme of development for Cyprus.
Nicosia, Cyprus Govt. Print. Off., 1946.
viii, 143 p. tables.

1. Cyprus. 2. Housing-Cyprus. I. Title.

3799
TENAFLY, N.J. PLANNING BOARD.
COMPREHENSIVE PLAN FOR THE BOROUGH OF
TENAFLY, BERGEN COUNTY, NEW JERSEY;
TECHNICAL REPORT, V. 2, SPECIAL STUDIES.
PREPARED BY KENDREE AND SHEPHERD PLANNING
CONSULTANTS. TENAFLY, 1969.
89P. (HUD 701 REPORT)

1. CITY PLANNING - TENAFLY, N.J.
I. KENDREE AND SHEPHERD PLANNING
CONSULTANTS. II. HUD 701 TENAFLY,
N.J.

333.323
S15
Tenant-landlord problems.
Santa Clara County, Calif. Planning Dept.
Tenant-landlord problems; the joint
cities-county housing element program.
San Jose, 1970.
18p.

Bibliography: p. 15-18.

1. Landlord and tenant. I. Title.

353
C657t
1971
J-H
10-year record of the Advisory Commission on
Intergovernmental Relations.
U.S. Advisory Commission on Intergovernmental
Relations.
10-year record of the Advisory Commission
on Intergovernmental Relations. Joint hearing
before the Intergovernmental Relations Subcommittees of the House and Senate Committees
on Government Operations, Congress of the
United States, Ninety-second Congress, first
session. Wash., Govt. Print. Off., 1972.
118p.
Hearing held November 16, 1971.
(Cont'd on next card)

2644
TENAFLY, N.J. PLANNING BOARD.
COMPREHENSIVE PLAN FOR THE BOROUGH OF
TENAFLY, NEW JERSEY; TECHNICAL REPORT,
3, PLAN PROPOSALS, SEPT. 1969. PREPARED
BY KENDREE AND SHEPHERD PLANNING
CONSULTANTS. TENAFLY, 1969.
53P. (HUD 701 REPORT)

1. CITY PLANNING - TENAFLY, N.J.
I. KENDREE AND SHEPHERD PLANNING
CONSULTANTS. II. HUD 701 TENAFLY,
N.J.

333.323
N17
Tenant/landlord relations.
National Association of Housing and Redevelop-
ment Officials. Potomac Chapter.
Tenant/landlord relations; the proceedings
of a workshop sponsored by the Potomac
Chapter, National Association of Housing
and Redevelopment Officials, April 9, 1970.
Wash., 1970.
32p. (NAHRO publication no. N545)

1. Landlord and tenant. I. Title.

353
C657t
1971
J-H
10-year record of the Advisory Commission on
Intergovernmental Relations.
U.S. Advisory Commission on Intergovernmental
Relations. 10-year record...1972. (Card 2)

1. Intergovernmental relations. I. Title.
II. U.S. Congress. House. Committee
on Government Operations. III. U.S. Congress.
Senate. Committee on Government Operations.

2643
TENAFLY, N.J. PLANNING BOARD.
COMPREHENSIVE PLAN, INTERIM REPORT:
THE SHOPPING CENTER. BY KENDREE AND
SHEPHERD PLANNING CONSULTANTS. TENAFLY,
1969.
18L. (HUD 701 REPORT)

1. CITY PLANNING - TENAFLY, N.J.
I. KENDREE AND SHEPHERD PLANNING
CONSULTANTS. II. HUD 701 TENAFLY,
N.J.

333.65
H68T
TENANT MAINTENANCE.
U.S. HOUSING AUTHORITY.
TENANT MAINTENANCE, PRELIMINARY DRAFT
FOR DISCUSSION PURPOSES. WASHINGTON,
1940.
17L.

1. HOUSING MANAGEMENT. 2. LANDLORD
AND TENANT. I. TITLE.

711.585
(74552)
E17t
Ten year relocation plan.
East Providence, R I. Dept. of Planning and
Urban Development.
Ten year relocation plan, 1966-1975. East
Providence, [1965?]
40p. (Technical report, 9)
U.S. Dept. of Housing and Urban Develop-
ment. CRP.
Project no. R.I. R-14 (CR)
1. Relocation - East Providence, R.I.
I. U.S. HUD-CRP. East Providence, R.I.
II. Title.

352.6
E22
TENANT ACTIVITIES IN FOUR PUBLIC
HOUSING PROJECTS.
EDELMAN, KATE.
SUMMARY OF FINDINGS WITH RESPECT TO
COMMUNITY FACILITIES AND THEIR RELATION
TO TENANT ACTIVITIES IN FOUR PUBLIC
HOUSING PROJECTS. WASHINGTON, U.S.
HOUSING AUTHORITY, 1938.
1 V. (VAROUS PAGINGS)

1. COMMUNITY FACILITIES.
2. COMMUNITY STRUCTURE. I. TITLE:
TENANT ACTIVITIES IN FOUR PUBLIC HOUSING
PROJECTS.

728.1
1940.42
F22TEN
TENANT MAINTENANCE IN WAR HOUSING.
U.S. FEDERAL PUBLIC HOUSING
AUTHORITY. REGION V.
TENANT MAINTENANCE IN WAR HOUSING.
CLEVELAND, OHIO, 1943.
22L. (ITS PROJECT SERVICES
BULLETIN NO. 3)

1. DEFENSE HOUSING - MAINTENANCE AND
MODERNIZATION. I. TITLE.

728.1
:336.18
(7295)
P82t

The tenant; our most valuable resource.
Puerto Rico. Urban Renewal and Housing Corp.
The tenant; our most valuable resource. San Juan, [1967?]
[26] p.
1. Public housing - Puerto Rico.
2. Social welfare - Puerto Rico.
I. Title.

711.585
(77866)
S142

TENANT RELOCATION.
ST. LOUIS. HOUSING AUTHORITY.
TENANT RELOCATION; LOW RENT HOUSING PROJECT CLINTON-PEABODY TERRACE, SOUTH HOUSING AREA. ST. LOUIS, 1941.
66P. (ST. LOUIS. HOUSING AUTHORITY PROJECT NO. 1-2)

1. RELOCATION - ST. LOUIS.
2. HOUSING - ST. LOUIS. I. TITLE.

728.1
:336.18
J65

TENANT SELECTION.
JONES, HARRY WILMER.
STATEMENT OF CONCLUSIONS WITH RESPECT TO THE YIELD INSURANCE AND TENANT ELIGIBILITY FOR PUBLIC HOUSING PROVISIONS OF THE TAFT-ELLENDER-WAGNER HOUSING BILL. NEW YORK, COLUMBIA UNIVERSITY, 1948.
17L.

1. PUBLIC HOUSING. 2. TENANT SELECTION. 3. TAFT-ELLENDER-WAGNER HOUSING BILL. I. TITLE.

333.323
M17

Tenant participation, for what.
Marcuse, Peter.
Tenant participation, for what. Wash., 1970.
82p. (Urban Institute. Working paper 112-20)

Bibliography: p. 80-82.

1. Landlord and tenant. I. Urban Institute.
II. Title.

711.585
N17t

Tenant relocation and the highway program.
National Highway Users Conference.
Tenant relocation and the highway program. A report by NHUC's Research Dept. Washington, 1963.
18p.
"The 1962 Federal-aid highway act has provided, for the first time that Federal funds may be used for tenant relocation."

1. Relocation. 2. Highways - Finance.
3. Highways - Social effect. I. Title.

LAW
T

Tenant selection.
Kuchler, Frances W   H
Landlord, tenant and co-op housing. Rev. 3d ed. New York, Oceania Publications, 1960.
93p. (Legal almanac series, no. 11)
First ed. published in 1954 under title: Landlord and tenant.

1. Tenant selection. 2. Cooperative housing. I. Title.

VF
333.63
N24

Tenant power.
Neighborhood Legal Services.
Tenant power. [Wash., 1970?]
[12]p.

1. Tenant selection. I. Title.

VF
711.585
(7471)
N28te

Tenant relocation and the housing program.
New York, N.Y. City Administrator.
Tenant relocation and the housing program. New York, 1954.
15 l.

Report is dated May 20, 1954; on cover: reprinted 6/10/54.
Processed.

1.Relocation-New York, N.Y. I.Title.

LAW
T
L215ha

Tenant selection.
LeBlanc, Nancy E
A handbook of landlord-tenant procedures and law, with forms. New York, Mobilization for Youth, 1966.
51p.

1. Low-income housing - New York (City)
2. Forms (Law) 3. Public assistance - New York (City) 4. Tenant selection. I. Mobilization for Youth. II. Title. III. Title: Landlord-tenant procedures and law, with forms.

333.323
(016)
H68S

TENANT RELATIONS.
U.S. HOUSING AUTHORITY.
SELECTED BIBLIOGRAPHY ON TENANT RELATIONS. WASHINGTON, 1941.
8L.

1. LANDLORD AND TENANT - BIBLIOGRAPHY. I. TITLE: TENANT RELATIONS.

711.585
(7471)
N28t

Tenant relocation report.
New York, N.Y. City Planning Commission.
Tenant relocation report ... adopted January 20, 1954. New York, 1954.
79 p. 8 maps   graphs, tables.

1.Relocation-New York, N.Y. I.Title.

333.323
L28

TENANT SELECTION.
Levi, Julian H
Model residential landlord-tenant code, by Julian H. Levi and others. [Chicago] American Bar Foundation, 1968.
1v.
Prepared for the Legal Services Program of the Office of Economic Opportunity.
1. Landlord and tenant.
2. Tenant selection. I. American Bar Foundation. II. U.S. Office of Economic Opportunity. III. Title.

Tenant relocation

see

Relocation.

VF
711.585
(794)
M12

Tenant relocation without bonus payments.
McCoy, G   T
Tenant relocation without bonus payments. Reproduced from American Highways, April 1958, p. 45-46, 23.

1. Relocation - California. I. Title.

333.323
L28
1969

TENANT SELECTION.
Levi, Julian H
Model residential landlord-tenant code; tentative draft prepared as a research project of the American Bar Foundation, by Julian H. Levi and others. [Chicago] American Bar Foundation, 1969.
97p.

1. Landlord and tenant. 2. Tenant selection. I. American Bar Foundation. II. Title.

728.1
:336.18
(77866)
S14CA

TENANT RELOCATION.
ST. LOUIS, MO. HOUSING AUTHORITY.
CARR SQUARE VILLAGE, LOW RENT HOUSING PROJECT, NORTH HOUSING AREA, TENANT RELOCATION. ST. LOUIS, 1941.
57P.

1. PUBLIC HOUSING - ST. LOUIS.
I. TITLE. II. TITLE: TENANT RELOCATION.

647.1
C34
1947

Tenant selection.
Chicago, Ill. Housing Authority.
What is a low income family? An analysis of incomes of urban families of various types. Chicago, 1947.
24 p. graphs.

Prepared by John M. Ducey, Director of Planning, with the assistance of Harry Schaffner and Shirley Hillmer.

1.Family income and expenditure. 2.Survey methods. 3.Tenant selection. I.Ducey, John M. II.Title.

333.65
M22m
1963

Tenant selection.
Meeting of Group of Experts on Housing Management and Tenant Education, Wellington, New Zealand, 1963.
Meeting...under the sponsorship of the Bureau of Technical Assistance Operations and the Bureau of Social Affairs in cooperation with the Government of New Zealand. New York, United Nations, 1964.
155p. (United Nations. [Document] ST/TAO/SER.C/61)
Bibliography: p. 148-155.

1. Housing management - Congresses.
2. Tenant selection. I. United Nations. (Bureau of Social Affairs)

728.1
:336.18
(77866)
S14C

TENANT RELOCATION.
ST. LOUIS, MO. HOUSING AUTHORITY.
CLINTON-PEABODY TERRACE, LOW RENT HOUSING PROJECT, SOUTH HOUSING AREA, TENANT RELOCATION. ST. LOUIS, 1941.
66P.

1. PUBLIC HOUSING - ST. LOUIS, MO.
I. TITLE. II. TITLE: TENANT RELOCATION.

VF
728.1
:336.18
(74811)
H68

Tenant selection.
Housing Association of Delaware Valley.
Tenant assignment in public housing. Philadelphia, 1968.
4p. (Its Special memo. no. 34)

1. Public housing - Philadelphia.
2. Minority groups - Housing - Philadelphia. 3. Tenant selection.
I. Title.

333.65
M22m
1964
Spanish

TENANT SELECTION.
Meeting of Group of Experts on Housing Management and Tenant Education, Wellington, N.Z., 1964.
Junta de un grupo de expertos en administracion de viviendas y en educacion de inquilinos. Bajo los auspicios de la Direccion de Ayuda Tecnica y la Direccion de Asuntos Sociales y la cooperacion del Gobierno de Nueva Zelandia. New York, Naciones Unidas, 1964, 1968.
79p.
1. Housing management. 2. Tenant selection.
I. United Nations. (Bureau of Social Affairs)

Tenant selection.

Mackay, Richard Vance, 1909–
  The law of landlord and tenant. New York, Oceana Publications ₁1949₎
  71 p. 20 cm. (Legal almanac series, no. 11)

  Tenant selection
  1. Landlord and tenant—U. S.

                                                49–9044*
  Library of Congress   ₁15₎

728.1   Tenant selection.
:336.18 National Association of Housing Officials.
·061.3   Middle Atlantic Regional Council, Annual
N175   meeting, New York, May 10-11, 1951.
·1951   [Papers.   New York?] 1951.
              1 v. (various pagings)

     Contents.-Individual gas furnaces, H. J.
   Mackay.-Income limits and rent schedules, R.
   George Dodds.-Reaching lowest income families,
   Ellis Ash.-Streamlining tenant selection
   procedures, John P. Prescott.-Maximum income
   limits and rents, Lawrence N. Bloomberg.-
                               ₍continued on next card)

     National Association of Housing Officials.
   Middle Atlantic Regional Council, Annual
   meeting, New York, May 10-11, 1951.
   [Papers.]   (Card 2)
        Contents continued.
   Human rights in slum clearance, Charles Abrams.-
   Newly activated local housing authorities, Leo A.
   Geary.-The new Federal-local assistance contract,
   Murray M. Bisgaier.-Eligibility and maintenance
   policies governing Lanham projects, Florence T.
   Conlon.-Priorities for construction and main-
   tenance, Gerald J. Carey.

LAW   Tenant selection.
  T   National Conference on Legal Rights of Tenants,
N17   Washington, D.C., 1966.
C657te Tenants' rights: legal tools for better hous-
       ing. Sponsored by: Dept. of Housing and Urban
       Development, Dept. of Justice [and] Office of
       Economic Opportunity. Washington, Govt. Print.
       Off., 1967.
          44p.

     1. Tenant selection. 2. Low income housing.
   3. Housing law enforcement. 4. Grants-in-aid.
   I. U.S. Dept. of Housing and Urban Development.
   II. U.S. Dept.   of Justice.
   III. U.S. Office   of Economic Oppor-
   tunity.   IV. Title.

VF   TENANT SELECTION.
333.63   Neighborhood Legal Services.
N24   Tenant power. [Wash., 1970?]
             [12]p.

     1. Tenant selection. I. Title.

Tenant selection.
728.1
:336.18 New York (City) Housing and Redevelopment
(7471)   Board. (Bureau of Planning and Program
N28oc   Research)
no.11   Analysis of applications for new limited
         profit housing company developments. Pre-
         pared by Rhoda Radisch. New York, 1966.
            4p. (Its Occasional memo no. 11)

     1. Public housing - New York (City)
   2. Tenant selection. I. Radisch, Rhoda.
   II. Title: Limited-profit housing company
   developments.

Tenant selection.
728.1
:336.18 New York (City) Housing and Redevelopment
(7471)   Board. (Planning and Program Research
N28cit   Division)
         The City Mitchell-Lama Program: tenant
       selection policies. Prepared by Louis Winnick
       and Frank S. Kristof. New York, 1961.
          6p. (Its Report no. 2)

     1. State aided housing programs - New York
   (City) 2. Public housing projects. 3. Tenant
   selection. I. Winnick, Louis. II. Kristof,
   Frank S., jt. au. III. Title. (Series)

728.1   Tenant selection.
:336.18 Schermer (George) Associates.
S23p   Public housing is the tenants. Rethink-
         ing management's responsibility and role in
         tenant and community relations. Prepared
         by George Schermer Associates and K.C.
         Jones, for the National Association of Hous-
         ing and Redevelopment Officials.
         Washington, 1967.
           [107]p.   (Issue 3)
           On cover: Changing concepts of the
         tenant-management relationship.

                                (Cont'd on next card)

728.1
:336.18 Schermer (George) Associates. Public hous-
S23p   ing is the tenants. Rethinking manage-
         ment's responsibility and role in tenant
         and community relations...1967. (Card 2)

     1. Public housing. 2. Housing manage-
   ment. 3. Tenant selection. I. National
   Association of Housing and Redevelopment
   Officials. II. Title. III. Jones,
   Kenneth C., jt.au. IV. Title: Changing
   concepts of the tenant-managemnt
   relationship.

           TENANT SELECTION.
333.323 U.K. Central Housing Advisory Committee.
U54   Selection of tenants and transfers and
         exchanges. Third report of the Housing
         Management Sub-Committee of the Central
         Housing Advisory Committee. Issued by the
         Ministry of Housing and Local Government.
         London, H.M.S.O., 1949.
           28p.
           1. Tenant selection. I. U.K. Ministry
         of Housing and Local Government. II. Title.

           Tenant selection.
333.323
U54   U.K. Central Housing Advisory Committee.
1955   (Housing Management Sub-Committee)
        Unsatisfactory tenants. London, H. M.
        Stat. Off., 1955.
          32p.

          1. Landlord and tenant.

          2. Tenant selection.

           TENANT SELECTION.
333.323 U.S. FEDERAL EMERGENCY ADMINISTRATION
F22   OF PUBLIC WORKS (MANAGEMENT
           DIVISION)
         MANUAL OF TENANT SELECTION PROCEDURE.
         MANUAL OF INITIAL RENTING AND
         OCCUPANCY PROCEDURES. WASHINGTON, N.D.
         1 V. (VARIOUS PAGINGS)

         COVER TITLE: HANDBOOK FOR TENANT
         SELECTION AND INITIAL RENTING. PART
         I. INSTRUCTIONS.

           1. TENANT S ELECTION. 2. HOUSING
         MANAGEMENT.   I. TITLE.
                              (CONTINUED ON NEXT CARD)

333.323 U.S. FEDERAL EMERGENCY ADMINISTRATION
F22   OF PUBLIC WORKS (MANAGEMENT
           DIVISION) MANUAL OF TENANT ... N.D.
                                      (CARD 2)

         II. TITLE: MANUAL OF INITIAL RENTING
         AND OCCUPANCY PROCEDURE. III. TITLE:
         HANDBOOK FOR TENANT SELECTION AND
         INITIAL RENTING.

728.1   TENANT SELECTION.
1940:42 U.S. FEDERAL WORKS AGENCY (DIVISION
F22MA   OF DEFENSE HOUSING)
         MANUAL FOR TENANT SELECTION AND
         RENTING IN DEFENSE HOUSING
         DEVELOPMENTS FOR INDUSTRIAL WORKERS.
         WASHINGTON, 1941.
           13L.

           1. DEFENSE HOUSING. 2. HOUSING
         MANAGEMENT. 3. TENANT SELECTION.

333.323 TENANT SELECTION.
H68   U.S. HOUSING AUTHORITY.
         MANUAL OF TENANT SELECTION.
         PRELIMINARY. WASHINGTON, 1938.
           48L.

           1. TENANT SELECTION.

333.323 TENANT SELECTION.
H68P   U.S. HOUSING AUTHORITY.
         POLICIES AND PROCEDURES FOR TENANT
         SELECTION FOR USHA-AIDED RURAL
         HOUSING PROJECTS. WASHINGTON, 1941.
         1 V. [VARIOUS PAGINGS]

           1. TENANT SELECTION.   I. TITLE.
         II. TITLE: RURAL HOUSING PROJECTS.

           Tenant services personnel; 48 job descriptions
           from large housing authorities.
728.1   National Association of Housing and Redevelop-
:336.18   ment Officials.
N17te   Tenant services personnel; 48 job descrip-
         tions from large housing authorities. Wash.,
         1970.
           51p. (NAHRO publication no. N543)

           1. Local housing authorities. I. Title.
         II. Title: Job descriptions from large
         housing authorities

728.1   Tenants Association of University John Hope
:325   Homes.
(758231)   University homes, Atlanta, Georgia. 25th
T25   Anniversary edition, 1962.
             1v.

           1. Minority groups - Housing - Atlanta.
         2. Public housing - Atlanta.

           Tenant's handbook.
VF
333.65   Thailand. Housing Bureau.
T31   Tenant's handbook. [Bangkok?] 1965.
             1v.

           Text in Thai.

           1. Housing management. 2. Housing -
         Thailand. I. Title.

           TENANT'S HANDBOOK FOR FAMILIES LIVING
           IN PROJECTS.
333.65   PITTSBURGH. HOUSING AUTHORITY.
P47   TENANT'S HANDBOOK FOR FAMILIES LIVING
         IN PROJECTS OF THE HOUSING AUTHORITY
         OF THE CITY OF PITTSBURGH. PITTSBURGH,
         N.D.
           12P.

           1. HOUSING MANAGEMENT.   I. TITLE.

333.323 THE TENANT'S HOME COMPANION.
966   OPPENHEIM, BEATRICE.
           LOOK BEFORE YOU LEASE: THE TENANT'S
         HOME COMPANION. NEW YORK, VANGUARD
         PRESS, 1940.
           86P.

           1. LANDLORD AND TENANT.   I. TITLE.
         II. TITLE: THE TENANT'S HOME
         COMPANION.

VF 728.1 (74811) C34 Tenants League of Philadelphia.

Childs, Bernard.
The amazing case of Mr. Binns; a documentary history. Philadelphia, Tenants League of Philadelphia, 1940.
33p.

1. Housing - Philadelphia. 2. Rents. I. Tenants League of Philadelphia.

690.015 (41 :016) U541 no.234 Tendering documents with a production bias.
U.K. Building Research Station.
Tendering documents with a production bias. Garston, Eng., 1970.
3p. (Its Library bibliography no. 234)

1. Building costs - Bibl. I. Title. (Series)

VF 690.091.82 :613.5 (749) N28 The tenement house act.
New Jersey. Laws, statutes, etc.
The tenement house act: revised statutes of New Jersey, approved 1937 [as amended]. Newark, N.J., State Board of Tenement House Supervision, 1942.
70 p.

Title 55, subtitle 1, chapters 1-13.
"Digest of 1943 amendments to the tenement house act" attached inside front cover.

1. Housing codes-N.J. I. Title.

690.091.82 :613.5 H68t Tenants' remedies.
U.S. Dept. of Housing and Urban Development. Office of General Counsel.
Tenants' remedies; provisions of State laws relating to rent withholding, rent receivership and certain other rights of occupants of unfit housing. [Wash.] 1969.
7p.

1. Housing law enforcement. 2. Landlord and tenant. I. Title.

725.83 (79461) T25 TENEMENT COMMITTEE, INC.
FUNDING PROPOSAL FOR A COMMUNITY CENTER & CLINIC FACILITY. SAN FRANCISCO, 1966.
11P.

1. COMMUNITY CENTERS - SAN FRANCISCO. I. TITLE.

690.091.82 :613.5 (7471) B85 TENEMENT HOUSE ADMINISTRATION. BUREAU OF MUNICIPAL RESEARCH, NEW YORK.
TENEMENT HOUSE ADMINISTRATION, STEPS TAKEN TO LOCATE AND TO SOLVE PROBLEMS OF, ENFORCING THE TENEMENT HOUSE LAW. NEW YORK, BUREAU OF MUNICIPAL RESEARCH, 1909.
175P.

1. HOUSING LAW ENFORCEMENT - NEW YORK (CITY) I. TITLE.

---

630 (75861) R16 TENANTS OF THE ALMIGHTY.
RAPER, ARTHUR FRANKLIN.
TENANTS OF THE ALMIGHTY. FSA PHOTOGRAPHS BY JACK DELANO. NEW YORK, MACMILLAN, 1943.
403P.
THE STORY OF GREENE COUNTY, GEORGIA, AND ITS UNIFIED FARM PROGRAM.—CF. FOREWORD.

1. AGRICULTURE - GREENE CO., GA. 2. SOCIOLOGY, RURAL - GREENE CO., GA. I. TITLE.

711.585 (79461) T25F TENDERLOIN COMMITTEE, INC.
A FUNDING PROPOSAL FOR THE TENDERLOIN PROJECT. SAN FRANCISCO, 1966.
VI P.

1. NEIGHBORHOOD REHABILITATION - SAN FRANCISCO. I. TITLE.

728.1 (7471) D23 The tenement house problem.
DeForest, Robert W , ed.
The tenement house problem, including the report of the New York State Tenement House Commission of 1900; ed. by Robert W. DeForest and Lawrence Veiller. New York, The MacMillan Company, 1903.
2 v. illus., plans, tables.

1. Slums - New York, N. Y. 2. Housing codes - New York. 3. Slums - Social effect. 4. Housing and health. 5. Housing law enforcement. I. Veiller, Lawrence, jt. ed. II. Title.

333.323 F51 The tenant's rights movement.
Flaum, Thea K
The tenant's rights movement, by Thea K. Flaum and Elizabeth C. Salzman. Chicago, Urban Research Corp., 1969.
57p.

Bibliography: p. 56-57.

1. Landlord and tenant. I. Salzman, Elizabeth C., jt. au. II. Urban Research Corp. III. Title.

711.585 (79461) T25 TENDERLOIN COMMITTEE.
PROPOSAL FOR CONFRONTING THE TENDERLOIN PROBLEM: AN ANSWER TO EMOTIONAL NEEDS. SUBMITTED TO THE ECONOMIC OPPORTUNITIES COUNCIL. SAN FRANCISCO, 1966.
8P.

1. SLUMS - SAN FRANCISCO. 2. SOCIAL CONDITIONS - SAN FRANCISCO. I. TITLE: THE TENDERLOIN PROBLEM.

690.091.82 :613.5 S72 The tenement landlord.
Sternlieb, George.
The tenement landlord. New Brunswick, N.J. Urban Studies Center, Rutgers, The State University, 1966.
269p.
Bibliography; p. 267-270.

U.S. Housing and Urban Development. Demonstration Grant Program.

1. Housing law enforcement. 2. Slums. 3. Rental housing. 4. Minority groups - Housing. I. Rutgers University, New Brunswick, N.J. Urban Studies Center. (Cont'd on next card)

VF 728.1 (016) H17 The tenants' views on housing, a list of references.
Harvard University. Departments of Landscape Architecture and Regional Planning. Library.
The tenants' views on housing: a list of references, compiled ... by Katherine McNamara. [Cambridge, Mass.] June 1945.
3 l.

Processed.

1. Housing-Bibl. 2. Family living requirements-Bibl. I. McNamara, Katherine. II. Title.

711.585 (79461) H15 THE TENDERLOIN GHETTO.
HANSEN, EDWARD.
THE TENDERLOIN GHETTO: THE YOUNG REJECT IN OUR SOCIETY, BY EDWARD HANSEN, MARK FORRESTER, AND FRED BIRD. SAN FRANCISCO, GLIDE URBAN CENTER, 1966.
33P.

1. SLUMS - SAN FRANCISCO. 2. SOCIAL CONDITIONS - SAN FRANCISCO. I. FORRESTER, MARK, JT. AU. II. BIRD, FRED, JT. AU. III. TITLE. IV. TITLE: THE YOUNG REJECT IN OUR SOCIETY.

690.091.82 :613.5 S72 Sternlieb, George. The tenement landlord. (Card 2)

II. Title. III. U.S. HUD-Demonstration Grant Program.

690.031 (41) M47 A tender-based building price index.
Mitchell, Robert.
A tender-based building price index. London, Dept. of the Environment, 1971.
[3]p.

Reprints of articles by staff of the Department selected by the Library Service.

Reprinted for the Dept. of the Environment from the Chartered surveyor, vol. 104, no. 1, July 1971, pp. 34-6.

(Cont'd on next card)

711.585 (79461) T25 THE TENDERLOIN PROBLEM.
TENDERLOIN COMMITTEE.
PROPOSAL FOR CONFRONTING THE TENDERLOIN PROBLEM: AN ANSWER TO EMOTIONAL NEEDS. SUBMITTED TO THE ECONOMIC OPPORTUNITIES COUNCIL. SAN FRANCISCO, 1966.
8P.

1. SLUMS - SAN FRANCISCO. 2. SOCIAL CONDITIONS - SAN FRANCISCO. I. TITLE: THE TENDERLOIN PROBLEM.

628.44 (7471) C65 Tenement refuse disposal systems and artificial illumination of communal areas.
Conrad Engineers, inc.
Tenement refuse disposal systems and artificial illumination of communal areas. Los Angeles, 1967.
1v.
PB 180 879.
Federal Housing Administration contract no. FH-940.

1. Refuse and refuse disposal - New York (City) 2. Lighting. I. U.S. Federal Housing Administration. II. Title.

690.031 (41) M47 Mitchell, Robert. A tender-based building price...1971. (Card 2)

1. Building costs - U.K. I. U.K. Dept. of the Environment. II. Title.

728.1 (77311) C47 Tenement conditions in Chicago.
City Homes Association, Chicago, Ill.
Tenement conditions in Chicago; report by the investigating committee of the City Homes Association. Text by Robert Hunter. Chicago, 1901.
208 p. illus, graphs, tables.

Bibliography: p. 203-204.

1. Slums-Chicago, Ill. I. Hunter, Robert. II. Title.

728.1 (77311) A11 The tenements of Chicago, 1908-1935.
Abbott, Edith.
The tenements of Chicago, 1908-1935. New York, Arno Press & The New York Times, 1970, c1936.
505 p. (The rise of urban America)

1. Housing - Chicago. I. Title. (Series: The rise of Urban America)

699.85: TENER, R K
168
IOWA. ENGINEERING EXPERIMENT STATION.
A STUDY OF LOADS ON UNDERGROUND
STRUCTURES; FINAL REPORT, BY D.A. VAN
HORN AND R.K. TENER. AMES, IOWA.
I v. (VARIOUS PAGINGS)

1. PROTECTIVE CONSTRUCTION.
2. CIVILIAN DEFENSE. I. VAN HORN, D.A.
II. TENER, R.K.

Tennant, Robert J   jt. au.
711.585
(77311)   Berry, Brian J   L
B27   Chicago commercial reference handbook;
Hand-   statistical supplement to Commercial
book   structure and commercial blight, by
         Brian J.L. Berry and Robert J. Tennant.
         Chicago, 1963.
         278p. (Chicago. University. Dept.
         of Geography. Research paper no. 86)

         "A study made under contract with the
         Community Renewal Program of the City of
         Chicago."   (Cont'd. on next card)

353
(768)   Tennessee. Commission for Human Development.
T25r   Reports. 2nd - 3rd.   1968/70.

        Nashville, 1970 -
        1 v.

        For Library holdings see main entry.

        1. State government - Tenn. 2. Social
        conditions - Tenn.

690.015
(485)   Tengvall, Ivar.
S82   Jordtryck mot moyfylld murad
R6   källarvägg (Earth pressure on counter-
1968   fort masonry wall), av Ivar Tengvall and
         others. Stockholm, Statens institut
         för byggnadsforskning, 1968.
         16p. (Rapport fran Byggforskningen
         1968:6)
         Reviderat särtryck av tre artiklar ur
         Väg- och vattenbyggaren 2:1968.

         1. Building research - Sweden.
         2. Soils.   3. Walls. I. Stock-
         holm   Statens institut
                        (Cont'd on next card)

711.585
(77311)   Berry, Brian J   L   Chicago commer-
B27   cial reference handbook ... (Card 2)
Hand-
book   U.S. Urban Renewal Adm. CRP.

         1. Urban renewal - Chicago. 2. Business
         districts - Chicago. I. Tennant, Robert
         J., jt. au. II. Chicago. Community
         Renewal Program. III. Chicago. Universi-
         ty. IV. Title. V. U.S. URA-CRP.
         Chicago.

Tennessee. Commission on Intergovernmental Cooperation
353   Tennessee. State Planning Commission.
(768)   Interstate compacts; a summary of compacts
T25I   to which Tennessee is signatory and resume of
         selected compacts to which Tennessee is elegible.
         Nashville, 1967.
         1v.

         1. Intergovernmental relations.-Tenn.
         2. State planning - Tenn. I. Tennessee Commission
         on Intergovernmental Cooperation. II. Title.

690.015
(485)   Tengvall, Ivar.
S82   Jordtryck...1968.   (Card 2)
R6
1968   för byggnadsforskning. II. Title:
         Earth pressure on counterfort masonry
         wall.

362.6
T25
        Tenner, Irving.
        Financial administration of municipal utili-
        ties. Chicago, Public Administration Service,
        1947.
        152p.

        1.Municipal finance. 2.Public utilities.
        I.Public Administration Service.

Class No.
planning file   Tennessee.
                Community Services Commission

Accession No.   Title
Ordered   A future for Nashville; summary of
Source   findings and recommendations of the
Received   Community Services Commission for Davidson
                County and the City of Nashville.
Cost   Nashville,
Purchase Order No.   Date   June 1952   20
Date   Edition or Series
L. C. No.   Recommended by
                Reviewed by

H-305 (2-50)   HOUSING AND HOME FINANCE AGENCY, Office of the Administrator   16-61187-1

690.015
(485)   Tengvik, Nils
S82   Byggnadsforskningen i Sverige; en
M1   sammanställning.   Stockholm, Statens Kommitté
         för Byggnadsforskning, 1945.
         234 p.   (Sverige. Statens Kommitté för
         Byggnadsforskning. Meddelanden, nr. 1)

         1.Building research-Sweden. I.Sverige. Statens
         Kommitté för Byggnadsforskning.

---

657   Tenner, Irving, 1908-   jt. auth.
C31   Chatters, Carl Hallack, 1898-
1940   Municipal and governmental accounting, by Carl H. Chatters
         ... and Irving Tenner ... New York, Prentice-Hall, inc., 1940.
         xviii, 794 p. incl. tables, forms. 24cm. (The co-ordinated accounting
series)
         Bibliography : p. 549-577.

         1. Accounting.
         I. Tenner, Irving, 1908-   joint author. II. Title.

         Library of Congress   HJ9801.C45   40-5481
         (45b^2)   351.72

Tennessee. Court of appeals.

        South western reporter. Second series. Cases argued and
        determined in the courts of Arkansas, Kentucky, Missouri,
        Tennessee, Texas, with key number annotations. v. 1, (2d-
                    Feb./Mar 1928-   St. Paul,
        Minn., West publishing co., 1928-
        v.   26 cm.   For Additions or Holdings
        Vols. 1-52: Permanent edition.   See Continuation File
        Subtitle varies: v. 1-63. Cases argued and determined in the Supreme
        courts of Arkansas, Missouri, Tennessee, and Texas; Courts of
        appeal of Kentucky and Missouri; courts of civil and criminal
        appeals and Commission of appeals of Texas.

                    (Continued on next card)
                                    28-17744
                    (40r3281)

690.015
(485)   Tengvik, Nils
S82   Byggnadsmaterial från jord-och stenin-
M20   dustrien: produktion, kvalitet, distribution och
         prissättning. Building materials from the clay
         and stone industry: production, quality,
         distribution and pricing. Summary in English.
         Stockholm, Statens Kommitté för Byggnads-
         forskning, 1952.
         61 p.   graphs.   (Sweden. Statens Kommitté
         för Byggnadsforskning. Meddelanden, nr. 20)

         Bibliography: p. 42-45.
         1.Building materials-Sweden. I.Sweden. Statens
         Kommitté för   Byggnadsforskning.

---

657   Tenner, Irving
C31   Municipal and governmental accounting.
1955   3d ed.   Englewood Cliffs, N. J., Prentice-
         Hall (1955).
         569 p.   (Prentice-Hall accounting
         series).

         1.Accounting. I.Title.

Tennessee. Court of appeals.

        South western reporter. Second series ... 1928-
                                    (Card 2)
        v. 64-66. Cases argued and determined in the Supreme courts of
           Arkansas, Missouri, Tennessee, and Tennessee; Courts of civil and criminal
           appeals and Commission of appeals of Texas.
        v. 67-   Cases argued and determined in the courts of Arkansas,
           Kentucky, Missouri, Tennessee, Texas.

        1. Law reports, digests, etc.—Southwest, Old. I. Arkansas. Su-
        preme court. II. Missouri. Supreme court. III. Tennessee. Supreme
        court. IV. Texas. Supreme court. V. Kentucky. Court of appeals.
        VI. Missouri. Court of appeals. VII. Texas. Court of civil appeals.
        VIII. Texas. Court of criminal appeals. IX. Texas. Commissioners of
        appeals. X. Tennessee. Court of appeals. XI. West publishing co.,
        St. Paul.

        Library of Congress   28-17744
                    (49r3281)

---

325   TenHouten, Diana L   jt. au.
(79494) Tomlinson, T M
T65   Los Angeles Riot Study. Method: Negro
         reaction survey, by T. M. Tomlinson and
         Diana L. TenHouten. Los Angeles, Institute
         of Government and Public Affairs, University
         of California, 1967.
         13p. (MR-95)
         Contract with the Office of Economic
         Opportunity.
         1. Minority groups - Los Angeles.
         2. Social surveys - Los Angeles. 3. Race
         relations. 4. Social welfare - Los Angeles.
         4. Employment   - Negroes. I. TenHouten,
         Diana L., jt.   u. II. California.
         University.   (Cont'd on next card)

---

657   Tenner, Irving.
C31   Municipal and governmental accounting.
1960   4th ed. Englewood Cliffs, N. J., Prentice-
         Hall, 1960.
         592 p.   (Prentice-Hall accounting series).

         1. Accounting. I. Title.

339.5   Tennessee. Dept. of Finance and
(768)   Administration.
T25   Tennessee, its resources and economy.
v.1   Vol. 1. The Tennessee economy. Nashville,
         1965.
         41p.   (Its Publication no. 331a)

         1. Natural resources - Tenn. 2. Economic
         conditions - Tenn.

---

325   Tomlinson, T M   Los Angeles Riot
(79494) Study...1967.   (Card 2)
T65

         University at Los Angeles, Institute of
         Government and Public Affairs,   III.Title.

Tennessee.

VF
Heating.   Annexation
Housing-U.S.-Tenn.
Population.
School plant planning.
Sewage disposal.
State planning.
Taxation.
Tennessee Valley Authority.
Real property-Taxation.
State Finance

339.5   Tennessee. Dept. of Finance and
(768)   Administration.
T25   Tennessee, its resources and economy.
v.2   Vol. 2. Tennessee's natural resources.
         Nashville, 1966.
         (70)p. (Its Publication no. 331b)

         1. Natural resources - Tenn. 2. Economic
         conditions - Tenn. I. Title.

LAW
S   Tennessee. General Assembly.
        Legislative apportionment in Tennessee;
     1901-1961. Nashville, 1961.
        73p.

        1. Apportionment. I. Title.

Tennessee. Laws, statutes, etc. ... Acts ... (Card 2)
     Library has:
     1935 reg. pub. Jan.-Apr. 1935
     1935 ex. pub. & priv. July-Aug. 1935 (1st spec.)
     1937 reg. pub. and 1936 extra Jan.-May 1937, Dec. 1936
     1937 reg. priv. v.1 Jan.-May 1937
     1937 pub. & priv. 2d extra Oct. 1937
     1939 reg. pub. Jan.-Mar. 1939
     1941 reg. pub. Jan.-Mar. 1941

                    (Continued on next card)

Tennessee. Laws, statutes, etc.
     Tennessee code, annotated; the official
     Tennessee code as enacted by the seventy-
     ninth general assembly, chapter 6, public acts
     1955, effective Jan 1, 1956 ...Indianapolis,
     Bobbs-Merrill co. 1955-

        Kept up to date with cumulative pocket
     supplements.
        Contents on front lining-papers.

6221
     TENNESSEE. GOVERNOR'S SEWART AIR FORCE
        BASE REDEVELOPMENT COMMITTEE.
        SEWART AIR FORCE BASE -- CONVERSION TO
     CIVILIAN PURPOSES. NASHVILLE, 1969.
     119P. (HUD 701 REPORT)

        1. AIRPORTS - TENNESSEE. I. HUD.
     701. TENNESSEE.

Tennessee. Laws, statutes, etc. ... Acts ... (Card 3)

     1943 reg. pub. Jan.-Feb. 1943
     1944 pub. extra Apr. 1944
     1945 pub. Jan.-Mar. 1945
     1945 reg. priv. Jan.-Mar. 1945
     1947 reg. pub. Jan.-Mar. 1947

VF
711.3   Tennessee. Laws, statutes, etc.
(768:347)   Tennessee planning legislation,
T25   1935-1963. Prepared by Anne Sternheimer.
1963   [Nashville] Tennessee State Planning
             Commission, 1963.
                44p. (Publication no. 327)
             Reprinted from Tennessee Code
             annotated (as amended through 1962)

                1. State planning legislation -
             Tennessee. 2. Zoning legislation -
             Tenn. I. Tennessee. State Planning
             Commis-   sion. II. Title.

330
(768)   Tennessee. Governor's Study Committee for
T25to   Economic Development.
             To build a climate of confidence.
2c   Nashville, 1972.
             63p.

                1. Economic development - Tenn. 2. Commun-
             ity development - Tenn. I. Title.

Tennessee. *Laws, statutes, etc.*
     Annotated Code of Tennessee, 1934; containing all acts of
     a general and public nature in force January 1, 1934, includ-
     ing also the state and federal constitutions and rules of Ap-
     pellate courts, compiled and annotated by Samuel C. Wil-
     liams ... Indianapolis, The Bobbs-Merrill company [*1934-35]
        8 v. 26 cm.
        Kept up to date with cumulative pocket supplements to be inserted
     in perpetual-revision-binder at end of each volume.
        Contents on front lining-papers.

        I. Williams, Samuel Cole, 1864-   ed.
                              (Continued on next card)
                                           34—1354
                  [50r39f1]

R
711.3   Tennessee. Law, statutes, etc.
(768   Tennessee planning legislation, 1935-
:347)   1967. Prepared by Nicholas Beehan, Jr.
T25   Nashville, Tennessee State Planning
             Commission, 1967.
                49p. (Bulletin no. 353)
             Reprinted from Tennessee code annotated
             and attached amendments of the 85th General
             Assembly (Recessed May 26, 1967)

        1. State planning legislation - Tennessee.
     2. Zoning legislation - Tennessee.
     I. Tennessee. State   Planning Commission.
     II. Title.

Tennessee. Dept. of Highways.
388
(768551)   Metropolitan Government of Nashville and
M27n   Davidson County. Metropolitan Plan-
             ning Commission.
             Nashville metropolitan area transpor-
          tation study; a reevaluation of the 1980
          major route plan. Prepared by State of
          Tennessee, Dept. of Highways, Research
          and Planning Division and the Metro-
          politan Government of Nashville and David-
          son County, Metropolitan Planning Commis-
          sion, Dept. of Public Works, Traffic and
          Parking Board in cooperation with U.S.
          Dept. of Commerce, Bureau of Public
                    (Continued on next card)

352
(768)   Tennessee. Laws, statutes, etc.
T25   A bill to be entitled: An act to authorize
        and to provide for the consolidation of all, or
        substantially all, governmental and corporate
        functions of municipal corporations and of
        counties having a population of 200,000 or
        more according to the Federal census of 1950
        or any subsequent Federal census; and for said
        purpose to authorize and provide for the
        creation and establishment of charter commis-
        sions authorized to propose charters for metro-
        politan govern-   ments; and for said
        purpose to   authorize and
                              (Continued on next
                                     card) ..

362.6   TENNESSEE. LEGISLATURE. LEGISLATIVE
T255   COUNCIL COMMITTEE.
             FINAL REPORT: PROBLEMS OF THE AGED
        AND CHRONICALLY ILL STUDY. NASHVILLE,
        1960.
             46 (A20) P.

        1. OLD AGE. I. TITLE.

388
(768551)   Metropolitan Government of Nashville and
M27n   Davidson County. Metropolitan Plan-
             ning Commission. Nashville Metropo-
             litan...1965. (Card 2)

          Roads. Nashville, 1965.
             64p.

                1. Transportation - Nashville. 2. Metro-
             politan areas - Nashville. I. Tennessee.
          Dept. of Highways. II. U.S. Bureau of
          Public Roads. III. Title.

352
(768)   Tennessee. Laws, statutes, etc.
T25   a bill to be ... 1957.   (Card 2)

          provide for the creation and functioning of
        metropolitan governments. Nashville, [1957]
        12p.
             Chapter 120, Public acts of 1957.
             U.S. Urban Renewal Adm. UPAP.

        1. Metropolitan government - Tennessee. I. U.S.
     URA-UPAP. Tennessee.

711.73   TENNESSEE. LEGISLATURE. LEGISLATIVE
T25   COUNCIL COMMITTEE.
             STUDY ON AUTOMOBILE JUNK YARDS AND
        HIGHWAY BEAUTIFICATION 1964. FINAL
        REPORT OF THE LEGISLATIVE COUNCIL
        COMMITTEE. NASHVILLE, TENNESSEE, 1964.
             22L.

             1. HIGHWAYS. I. TITLE: AUTOMOBILE
        JUNK YARDS AND HIGHWAY BEAUTIFICATION.

Tennessee. Dept. of Highways.
711.73
(768)   Smith (Wilbur) and Associates.
S54   Statistical evaluation of mathematical
        projection model, Chattanoga, Tennessee.
        Prepared for the Tennessee Dept. of Highways,
        in cooperation with U.S. Dept. of Commerce,
        Bureau of Public Roads. New Haven, 1961.
             26p.

        1. Highways - Tennessee.
     2. Traffic surveys. 3. Journey to work.
     I. Tennessee. Dept. of Highways.

526.8
(76855)   Tennessee. Laws, statutes, etc.
T25   Chapter no. 330, private acts of 1959.
        Official map, Davidson County, Tennessee.
        [Nashville] 1959.
             10p.

             U.S. Urban Renewal Adm. UPAP.

             1. Maps and mapping - Davidson Co., Tenn.
        I. U.S. URA-UPAP. Davidson Co., Tenn.

712.21
(768)   Tennessee. Legislature. Legislative Council.
T25s   Study on bond financing of parks and
        recreational facilities. Final report of the
        Legislative Council Committee. Nashville,
        1968.
             77p. (FR - 1968 - B13)

        1. Parks - Tenn. 2. State bonds.
     3. Recreation - Tenn. I. Title: Bond financ-
     ing of parks and recreational facilities.

Tennessee. Laws, statutes, etc.
     ... Acts ...
Nashville, 19
     v. 23cm.

                    (Continued on next card)

526.8
(768551)   Tennessee. Laws, statutes, etc.
T25c   Chapter 356, private acts of 1959.
        Official map, City of Nashville, Tennessee.
        [Nashville] 1959.
             10p.

             U.S. Urban Renewal Adm. UPAP.

             1. Maps and mapping - Nashville, Tenn.
        I. U.S. URA-UPAP. Nashville, Tenn.

058.7
:353   Tennessee. Office of Local Government.
(768)   Services to local governments. 2d. ed.
T25   Nashville, 1969.
             91p.
2c
             1. State government - Tenn. - Direct.
     2. Local government - Tenn. I. Title.

697.8
R61a

Tennessee. Dept. of Public Health.
U.S. Robert A. Taft Sanitary Engineering
Center.
Appraisal of air pollution in Tennessee.
Report of a cooperative survey by the U.S.
Public Health Service and the State of
Tennessee Dept. of Public Health, Dec. 1956-
July 1957. Cincinnati, 1957.
85p. maps, tables.

1. Air pollution. I. Tennessee. Dept. of Public
Health.

711.5
(76856)
F71

Tennessee. State Planning Commission.
Franklin, Tenn. Municipal Planning Commission.
An analysis of zoning, Franklin, Tennessee.
Assisted by Tennessee State Planning Commis-
sion, Middle Tennessee Office. Franklin, 1958.
35p. maps. (MTO Publication 58-10)
U.S. Urban Renewal Administration, Urban
Planning Assistance Program.
1. Zoning - Franklin, Tenn. I. Tennessee.
State Planning Commission. II. U.S. Urban
Renewal Administration. Urban Planning
Assistance Program.

711.4
:370
(768865)
A73

Tennessee. State Planning Commission.
Athens, Tenn. Regional Planning Commission.
Athens school report. Assisted by the
Tennessee State Planning Commission, East
Tennessee Office. Athens, 1956.
17p. diagrs.

U.S. Urban Renewal Administration, Urban
Planning Assistance Program.

1. City planning - Athens, Tenn. 2. Education. I. Tennessee. State Planning Commission.
II. U.S. Urban Renewal Administration.

362.6
(768)
T25M

TENNESSEE. DEPT. OF PUBLIC HEALTH.
MINIMUM STANDARDS AND REGULATION FOR
NURSING HOMES AND HOMES FOR AGED, 1964.
NASHVILLE, TENN., 1965.
40P.

1. NURSING HOMES - TENNESSEE -
STANDARDS AND SPECIFICATIONS. I. TITLE

352.5
M17

Tennessee. State Planning Commission.
Maryville, Tenn. Regional Planning Com-
mission.
Annexation and Maryville. Prepared by
East Tennessee Office, Tennessee State
Planning Commission. Maryville, 1957.
38p. map, tables.

U.S. Urban Renewal Administration,
Urban Planning Assistance Program.
1. Annexation - Maryville, Tenn. I. Ten-
nessee. State Planning Commission. II. U.S.
Urban Renewal   Administration. Urban
Planning Assist-   ance Program.

526.8
(768865)
A73

Tennessee. State Planning Commission.
Athens, Tenn. Regional Planning Commission.
Athens, Tennessee base maps. Prepared by
Southeast Tennessee Office, Tennessee State
Planning Commission. Athens, 1957.
1v. maps.

U.S. Urban Renewal Administration,
Urban Planning Assistance Program.

1. Athens, Tenn. - Maps. 1. Tennessee.
State Planning Commission. II. U.S. Urban
Renewal Administration. Urban Planning
Assistance Program.

362
(768)
T25

Tennessee. Dept. of Public Health.
Tennessee State plan for construction of
hospitals and medical facilities, 1969.
Nashville, 1969.
1v.

Cover title.

1. Hospitals - Tenn. I. Title.

352.5
D92

Tennessee. State Planning Commission.
Dyersburg, Tenn. Regional Planning Commission.
Annexation study, Dyersburg, Tennessee. With
the assistance of the West Tennessee Office of
the Tennessee State Planning Commission. Dyersburg, 1956.
38p. maps, tables.

U.S. Urban Renewal Administration, Urban
Planning Assistance Program.

1. Annexation - Dyersburg, Tenn. I. Tennessee.
State Planning Commission. II. U.S. Urban Re-
newal Administration. Urban Planning Assistance
Program.

526.8
(76879)
T25

Tennessee. State Planning Commission.
Base map, South Pittsburg, Tenn.
South Pittsburg, 1958.
map.
U.S. Urban Renewal Administration, Urban
Planning Assistance Program.

1. Maps and mapping - South Pittsburg,
Tenn. I. U.S. URA-UPAP. South Pittsburg, Tenn.

690
(768)
T25

Tennessee. State Building Commission.
Building program 1953-1958. Nashville,
[1958?]
1v. illus.

Frank G. Clement, Governor.

1. Building construction - Tennessee.
2. Public buildings - Tennessee.

352.5
M67

Tennessee. State Planning Commission.
Morristown, Tenn. Regional Planning Commission.
Annexation study for Morristown, Tennessee.
Morristown, 1957.
23p. maps, tables.

In cooperation with Tennessee State Planning
Commission.

U.S. Urban Renewal Administration, Urban

(Continued on next card)

712.25
(763)
B22

Tennessee. State Planning Commission.
Beech River (Tenn.) Watershed Development
Authority.
Beech River watershed development plan
and program proposals with technical
assistance of Tennessee State Planning
Commission and Tennessee Valley Authority.
Nashville, 1965.
143p.

1. Recreation - Tenn. 2. Water-supply -
Tenn. I. Tennessee. State Planning
Commission.   II. Tennessee Valley
Authority.

711.14
(76896)
B74

Tennessee. State Planning Commission.
Bristol, Tenn. Planning Commission.
Analysis of Bristol land use. Prepared
by Upper East Tennessee Office, Tennessee
State Planning Commission. Bristol, 1957.
31p. diagrs., maps, tables.

U.S. Urban Renewal Administration, Urban
Planning Assistance Program.

(Continued on next card)

352.5
M67

Morristown, Tenn. Regional Planning Commission. Annexation study ... (Card 2)

Planning Assistance Program.

1. Annexation - Morristown, Tenn. I. Ten-
nessee. State Planning Commission. II. U.S.
Urban Renewal Administration. Urban Planning
Assistance Program.

VF
711.552
(016)
Q81

Tennessee. State Planning Commission.
Qualls, William H   comp.
A bibliography for the central business
district. [n.p] Upper East Tennessee Office
of the Tennessee State Planning Commission
[1955]
11 L.

1. Business districts - Bibl. 2. Traffic -
Bibl. I. Tennessee. State Planning Commission.

711.14
(76896)
B74

Bristol, Tenn. Planning Commission. Analysis of Bristol land ... (Card 2)

1. Land use - Bristol, Tenn. I. Tennessee.
State Planning Commission. II. U.S. Urban
Renewal Administration. Urban Planning Assist-
ance Program.

711.4
(768551)
N17A

TENNESSEE. STATE PLANNING COMMISSION.
ANY AGE, ANY TALENT. CHILDREN CAN
THINK CONSTRUCTIVELY ABOUT THEIR
COMMUNITIES. NASHVILLE, 1948.
5P.

1. CITY PLANNING - NASHVILLE.

352.5
B74

Tennessee. State Planning Commission.
Bristol, Tenn. Planning Commission.
Bristol, Tennessee annexation study.
Prepared by the Upper East Tennessee Of-
fice, Tennessee State Planning Commission.
Bristol, 1958.
42p. map, tables.
U.S. Urban Renewal Administration, Urban
Planning Assistance Program.
1. Annexation - Bristol, Tenn. I. Tennessee.
State Planning Commission. II. U.S. Urban Re-
newal Administration. Urban Planning Assist-
ance Program.

VF
690.091.82
:613.5
T25

Tennessee. (State) Planning Commission.
An analysis of selected housing ordinances
[compiled by Louise Nunnelly and Charlotte Orr
Moores] [Nashville? Nov. 1956]
40 p. (Its Publication no. 265)

3c

1. Housing codes. I. Nunnelly, Louise, Comp.
II. Moores, Charlotte Orr.

711.4
:330
(768865)
A73

Tennessee. State Planning Commission.
Athens, Tenn. Regional Planning Commission.
Athens, its people and economy. Assisted
by the Tennessee State Planning Commission,
East Tennessee Office. Athens, 1956.
21p. maps, tables.

U.S. Urban Renewal Administration, Urban
Planning Assistance Program.

1. City planning - Athens, Tenn. 2. Eco-
nomic conditions - Athens, Tenn. I. Tennessee.
State Planning Commission. II. U.S. Urban
Renewal Administration.

526.8
(76896)
B74

Tennessee. State Planning Commission.
Bristol, Tenn. Planning Commission.
Bristol, Tennessee base maps. Prepared
by Upper East Tennessee Office, Tennessee
State Planning Commission. Bristol, 1957.
1v. maps.

U.S. Urban Renewal Administration, Urban
Planning Assistance Program.

1. Bristol, Tenn. - Maps. I. Tennessee.
State Planning Commission. II. U.S. Urban
Renewal Administration. Urban Planning
Assistance Program.

352
(76837)
W18

Tennessee. State Planning Commission.
Waverly, Tenn. Regional Planning Commission.
A capital improvements program for Waverly, Tennessee. Assisted by the Tennessee State Planning Commission, Middle Tennessee Office. Waverly, 1957.
22p. diagrs., tables. (MTO publication no. 57-27)

U.S. Urban Renewal Administration,

(Continued on next card)

711.552
(76813)
U54

Union City, Tenn. Regional Planning Commission. Central business ... (Card 2)

Urban Planning Assistance Program.

1. Business districts - Union City, Tenn. I. Tennessee. State Planning Commission. II. U.S. Urban Renewal Administration. Urban Planning Assistance Program.

711
(016)
C65
no. 76

Tennessee. State Planning Commission.
Ledyard, Julia.
Citizen participation in planning, with a preface by Harold Miller. [Nashville] Tennessee State Planning Commission, 1969.
14p. (Council of Planning Librarians. Exchange bibliography no. 76)

1. Planning – Bibl. 2. Planning Citizen participation – Bibl. I. Tennessee. State Planning Commission. II. Title. (Series: Council of Planning Librarians. Exchange bibliography no. 76.)

352
(76837)
W18

Waverly, Tenn. Regional Planning Commission. A capital ... (Card 2)

Urban Planning Assistance Program.

1. Capital improvement programs - Waverly, Tenn. I. Tennessee. State Planning Commission. II. U.S. Urban Renewal Administration. Urban Planning Assistance Program.

711.552
(768585)
L28

Tennessee. State Planning Commission.
Lewisburg, Tenn. Planning Commission.
Central business zone study for Lewisburg, Tennessee. Prepared by Tennessee State Planning Commission, Middle Tennessee Office. Lewisburg, 1958.
11p. maps, tables. (MTO Publication no. 58-6)
U.S. Urban Renewal Administration, Urban Planning Assistance Program.
1. Business districts - Lewisburg, Tenn. I. Tennessee. State Planning Commission. II. U.S. Urban Renewal Administration. Urban Planning Assistance Program.

711.4
(768)
T25C

TENNESSEE. STATE PLANNING COMMISSION.
CITIZEN PARTICIPATION IN URBAN COMMUNITY PLANNING. NASHVILLE, 1948. 73P. (ITS PUBLICATION NO. 188)

PREPARED WITH THE ASSISTANCE OF THE TENNESSEE VALLEY AUTHORITY.

1. CITY PLANNING - TENNESSEE. I. TENNESSEE VALLEY AUTHORITY. II. TITLE.

352.1
(76856)
F71

Tennessee. State Planning Commission.
Franklin, Tenn. Municipal Planning Commission.
Capital improvements program, Franklin, Tennessee. Prepared by the Tennessee State Planning Commission, Middle Tennessee Office. Franklin, 1958.
26p. diagrs., tables. (MTO Publication 58-21)

U.S. Urban Renewal Administration, Urban Planning Assistance Program.

1. Capital improvement programs - Franklin, Tenn. I. Tennessee. State Planning Commission. II. U.S. URA-UPAP. Franklin, Tenn.

VF
711.552
Q81

Tennessee. State Planning Commission.
Qualls, William H
A checklist of the problems of the central business district. [n.p.] Upper East Tennessee. Office of the Tennessee State Planning Commission [n.d.]
20 L.

1. Business districts. 2. Traffic. I. Tennessee. State Planning Commission.

711.585
(76815)
T25
3c

Tennessee. State Planning Commission.
Citizen participation in urban renewal, by William Bishop Nixon and Joseph M. Boyd, jr. Nashville, Tenn., 1957.
245p. illus.

"A report of a Demonstration project conducted in Dyersburg, Tenn., to explore methods of creating understanding and enlisting support and participation on the part of citizens for launching an urban renewal program in a small community."

(Continued on Card 2)

352.1
(76858)
S32

Tennessee. State Planning Commission.
Shelbyville, Tenn. Regional Planning Commission.
Capital improvements program, Shelbyville, Tennessee. [Assisted by Tennessee State Planning Commission] Shelbyville, 1958.
29p. diagrs., tables. (MTO Publication 58-22)
U.S. Urban Renewal Administration, Urban Planning Assistance Program.
1. Capital improvement programs - Shelbyville, Tenn. I. Tennessee. State Planning Commission. II. U.S. Urban Renewal Administration. Urban Planning Assistance Program.

DATE OF REQUEST 3/6/53 MAR 1	L. C. CARD NO. 53-26269
AUTHOR Tennessee State Planning Commission	
TITLE For tomorrow; 1951-52 annual report.	
SERIES	
EDITION	PUB. DATE 1952	PAGING 61 p.
PUBLISHER State Planning Commission Nashville, Tennessee	
RECOMMENDED BY	REVIEWED IN
	ORDER RECORD

711.585
(76815)
T25

Tennessee. State Planning Commission.
Citizen participation in urban renewal. 1957. (Card 2)

1. Urban renewal – Dyersburg, Tenn. 2. Urban renewal – Citizen participation. I. Nixon, William Bishop. II. Boyd, Joseph M., jr. III. U.S. Urban Renewal Administration. Demonstration Grant Program.

352.1
(768464)
S67

Tennessee. State Planning Commission.
Springfield, Tenn. Municipal-Regional Planning Commission.
A capital improvements study for Springfield, Tennessee. Assisted by Tennessee State Planning Commission, Middle Tennessee Office. Springfield, 1959.
1v. diagrs., maps, tables. (MTO Publication no. 59-8)

U.S. Urban Renewal Administration, Urban Planning Assistance Program.

(Continued on next card)

Class No. Municipal Finance	Author (surname first) Tennessee State Planning Commission
Accession No.	Title Capital budget, a case history
Ordered SEP 21 1950	Place Publisher
Source	Address
Received DEC 26 1950	Date 10/50 Pages 75p. List Price Est. Cost Processed
Cost	
Purchase Order No.	Edition or Series Pub. No. 210
Date	Recommended by
L.C. No.	Reviewed in Tenn Planner 4/50 p.163

H-305 (2-50)   HOUSING AND HOME FINANCE AGENCY: Office of the Administrator   16-61107-1   GPO

352.1
(76845)
C51

Tennessee. State Planning Commission.
Clarksville, Tenn. Regional Planning Commission.
Clarksville capital improvements program. Assisted by Tennessee State Planning Commission, Middle Tennessee Office. Clarksville, 1959.
49p. diagrs., tables. (MTO Publication 59-19)
U.S. Urban Renewal Administration, Urban Planning Assistance Program.
1. Capital improvement programs - Clarksville, Tenn. I. U.S. URA-UPAP. Clarksville, Tenn. II. Tennessee. State Planning Commission.

352.1
(768464)
S67

Springfield, Tenn. Municipal-Regional Planning Commission. A capital improvements ... 1959. (Card 2)

1. Capital improvement programs - Springfield, Tenn. I. Tennessee. State Planning Commission. II. U.S. Urban Renewal Administration. Urban Planning Assistance Program.

352.1
(768467)
T25

Tennessee. State Planning Commission.
Capital improvements program, Cookeville, Tennessee. Nashville, 1969.
51p.

U.S. Dept. of Housing and Urban Development. UPAP. HUD project no. Tenn. P-97.

1. Capital improvement programs - Cookeville, Tenn. I. U.S. HUD-UPAP. Cookeville, Tenn. II. Title.

727.1
(768845)
C51

Tennessee. State Planning Commission.
Clarksville, Tenn. Regional Planning Commission.
Clarksville community facilities plan, a survey and plan for Clarksville's public schools and recreation areas. Prepared by Middle Tennessee Office, Tennessee State Planning Commission. Clarksville, 1958.
53p. diagrs., maps, tables. (MTO Publication 58-12)
U.S. Urban Renewal Administration, Urban Planning Assistance Program.
(Continued on next card)

711.552
(76813)
U54

Tennessee. State Planning Commission.
Union City, Tenn. Regional Planning Commission.
Central business district, Union City, Tennessee. With the assistance of the Tennessee State Planning Commission, West Tennessee Office. Union City, 1957.
35p. illus., maps, tables.

U.S. Urban Renewal Administration,

(Continued on next card)

DATE OF REQUEST 3/3/55 Cat	L. C. CARD NO.
AUTHOR Tenn. State Planning Comm.	
TITLE A checklist of the problems of the central business district.	
SERIES	
EDITION	PUB. DATE undated	PAGING 20p.
PUBLISHER	
RECOMMENDED BY NBL	REVIEWED IN Mur. City, 4/55, p.197.
	ORDER RECORD

727.1
(768845)
C51

Clarksville, Tenn. Regional Planning Commission. Clarksville community facilities ... 1958. (Card 2)

1. Schools - Clarksville, Tenn. I. Tennessee. State Planning Commission. II. U.S. Urban Renewal Administration. Urban Planning Assistance Program.

711.14
(76845)
C51

Tennessee. State Planning Commission.
Clarksville, Tenn. Regional Planning Commission.
Clarksville, land use. Prepared by Tennessee State Planning Commission. Clarksville, 1958.
1v. maps.

U.S. Urban Renewal Administration, Urban Planning Assistance Program.

1. Land use - Clarksville, Tenn. I. Tennessee. State Planning Commission. II. U.S. Urban Renewal Administration. Urban Planning As— —stance Program.

711.14
(76873)
C54

Clinton, Tenn. Regional Planning Commission. Clinton land ... (Card 2)

Planning Assistance Program.

1. Land use - Clinton, Tenn. I. Tennessee. State Planning Commission. II. U.S. Urban Renewal Administration. Urban Planning Assistance Program.

352.6
(76895)
R63

Tennessee. State Planning Commission.
Rogersville, Tenn. Regional Planning Commission.
Community facilities plan, Rogersville, Tennessee. A staff report to the Rogersville Regional Planning Commission, by Upper East Tennessee Office, Tennessee State Planning Commission, Rogersville, 1960.
29p.

U.S. Urban Renewal Adm. UPAP.
1. Community facilities - Rogersville, Tenn. I. Tennessee. State Planning Commission. II. U.S. URA-UPAP. Rogersville, Tenn.

711.14
(76859)
C65c

Tennessee. State Planning Commission.
Columbia, Tenn. Regional Planning Commission.
Columbia land use plan, by the Tennessee State Planning Commission, Middle Tennessee Office. Columbia, 1959.
43p. maps, tables. (MTO Publication 59-1)

U.S. Urban Renewal Administration, Urban Planning Assistance Program.
(Continued on next card)

VF
711.14
(76873)
C54

Tennessee. State Planning Commission.
Clinton, Tenn. Municipal Planning Commission.
The Clinton master plan. Clinton, Tenn., Oct. 1950.
29 p. illus., maps(part fold.)
Technical assistance from the Tennessee State Planning Commission, East Tennessee Office, and Tennessee Valley Authority, Division of Regional Studies.
1.Master plan-Clinton, Tenn. 2.City planning-Clinton, Mass. I.Tennessee. State Planning Commission. II.Tennessee Valley Authority. Division of Regional Studies.

711.4
(76864)
T85

Tennessee. State Planning Commission.
Tullahoma, Tenn. Planning Commission.
Comprehensive plan, Tullahoma, Tenn., 1957.
36p. maps, diagrs. (MTO Publication no. 57-5)

"Assisted by Tennessee State Planning Commission, Middle Tennessee Office."

1.Master plan - Tullahoma, Tenn.
I.Tennessee. State Planning Commission.

711.14
(76859)
C65c

Columbia, Tenn. Regional Planning Commission. Columbia land use ... 1959, (Card 2)

1. Land use - Columbia, Tenn. I. Tennessee. State Planning Commission. II. U.S. Urban Renewal Administration. Urban Planning Assistance Program.

526.8
1711.14
(76859)
T25

Tennessee. State Planning Commission.
Columbia existing land use. Nashville, 1957.
1v. maps.

U.S. Urban Renewal Administration, Urban Planning Assistance Program.

1. Columbia, Tenn. - Maps. 2. Land use - Maps and mapping - Columbia, Tenn. I. U.S. Urban Renewal Administration. Urban Planning Assistance Program.

628.1
(768)
S78

Tennessee. State Planning Commission.
Stuart, Leslie B
Comprehensive water and sewer plan, 1970-1990, Upper Cumberland Development District. [Nashville] Tennessee State Planning Commission, 1971.
197p.
U.S. Dept. of Housing and Urban Development. UPAP. HUD project no. Tenn. P-129.
1. Water supply - Tenn. 2. Sewerage and sewage disposal - Tenn. I. Tennessee. State Planning Commission. II. U.S. Dept. of Housing and Urban Development - UPAP. Upper Tenn. III. Title.

711.5
(76845)
C51

Tennessee. State Planning Commission.
Clarksville, Tenn. Regional Planning Commission.
Clarksville zoning study, an analysis of sixteen years of zoning in Clarksville and a proposed revised zoning ordinance and map. Prepared by Middle Tennessee Office, Tennessee State Planning Commission. Clarksville, 1957.
53p. maps, tables. (MTO publication no. 57-10)

(Continued on next card)

711.14
(76859)
C65

Tennessee. State Planning Commission.
Columbia, Tenn. Regional Planning Commission.
Columbia land use analysis. Prepared by Middle Tennessee Office, Tennessee State Planning Commission. Columbia, 1957.
19p. maps, tables. (MTO publication no. 57-32)

U.S. Urban Renewal Administration, Urban Planning Assistance Program.

(Continued on next card)

711
(016)
C65
no.42

Tennessee. State Planning Commission.
Tucker, Dorothy.
Computers and information systems in planning and related governmental functions. [Nashville] Tennessee State Planning Commission, 1968.
21p. (Council of Planning Librarians. Exchange bibliography no. 42)

1. Planning - Bibl. 2. Planning - Automation - Bibl. 3. Automation - Bibl. I. Tennessee. State Planning Commission. II. Title. Series: Council of Planning Librarians. Exchange bibliogrpahy no. 42)

711.5
(76845)
C51

Clarksville, Tenn. Regional Planning Commission. Clarksville ... (Card 2)

U.S. Urban Renewal Administration, Urban Planning Assistance Program.

1. Zoning - Clarksville, Tenn. I. Tennessee. State Planning Commission. II. U.S. Urban Renewal Administration. Urban Planning Assistance Program.

711.14
(76859)
C65

Columbia, Tenn. Regional Planning Commission. Columbia land ... (Card 2)

1. Land use - Columbia, Tenn. I. Tennessee. State Planning Commission. II. U.S. Urban Renewal Administration. Urban Planning Assistance Program.

352
(76867)
C66

Tennessee. State Planning Commission.
Cookeville, Tenn. Regional Planning Commission.
Cookeville revised capital improvement program 1958-1964. With Middle Tennessee Office, Tennessee State Planning Commission. Cookeville, 1957.
38p. tables. (MTO publication no. 57-44)

U.S. Urban Renewal Administration, Urban
(Continued on next card)

DATE OF REQUEST 12/11/51   L. C. CARD NO.

AUTHOR Tennessee. State Planning Commission.

TITLE Clinton capital budget—a public works timetable.

SERIES

EDITION   PUB. DATE 2/51   PAGING 40 p.

PUBLISHER   same

RECOMMENDED BY   REVIEWED IN
—Curr Lit 10/8/51 p. 3

ORDER RECORD

388
(76859)
T25

Tennessee. State Planning Commission.
Columbia traffic and parking survey. A report to the Columbia Municipal Regional Planning Commission. Columbia, 1958.
32p. diagrs., maps, tables. (MTO Publication 58-25)

U.S. Urban Renewal Adm. UPAP.

1. Traffic - Columbia, Tenn. I. Columbia, Tenn. Regional Planning Commission. II. U.S. Urban Renewal Administration. Urban Planning Assistance Program. Columbia, Tenn.

352
(76867)
C66

Cookeville, Tenn. Regional Planning Commission. Cookeville revised ... (Card 2)

Planning Assistance Program.

1. Capital improvement programs - Cookeville, Tenn. I. Tennessee. State Planning Commission. II. U.S. Urban Renewal Administration. Urban Planning Assistance Program.

711.14
(76873)
C54

Tennessee. State Planning Commission.
Clinton, Tenn. Regional Planning Commission.
Clinton land use survey and analysis. Prepared by Tennessee State Planning Commission, East Tennessee Office. Clinton, 1957.
29p. maps, tables.

U.S. Urban Renewal Administration, Urban
(Continued on next card)

3984

TENNESSEE. STATE PLANNING COMMISSION.
ELIZABETHTON, TENN. REGIONAL PLANNING COMMISSION.
COMMUNITY FACILITIES PLAN. BY TENNESSEE STATE PLANNING COMMISSION. ELIZABETHTON, TENN., 1970.
87P. (HUD 701 REPORT)

1. COMMUNITY FACILITIES - ELIZABETHTON, TENN. I. TENNESSEE. STATE PLANNING COMMISSION. II. HUD. 701. ELIZABETHTON, TENN.

526.8
(76875)
C76

Tennessee. State Planning Commission.
Crossville, Tenn. Municipal Planning Commission.
Crossville, Tennessee base maps. Prepared by East Tennessee Office, Tennessee State Planning Commission. Crossville, 1956.
1v. maps.

(Continued in next card)

526.8
(76875)
C76

Crossville, Tenn. Municipal Planning Commission. Crossville, ... (Card 2)

U.S. Urban Renewal Administration, Urban Planning Assistance Program.

1. Crossville, Tenn. - Maps.   I. Tennessee. State Planning Commission. II. U.S. Urban Renewal Administration. Urban Planning Assistance Program.

388
(768984)
E54d

Elizabethton, Tenn. Regional Planning Commission. Downtown ... (Card 2)

Urban Planning Assistance Program.

1. Traffic - Elizabethton, Tenn.
2. Business districts - Elizabethton, Tenn.   I. Tennessee. State Planning Commission. II. U.S. Urban Renewal Administration. Urban Planning Assistance Program.

352.6
(76815)
D92

Dyersburg, Tenn. Regional Planning Commission. Dyersburg ... (Card 2)

1. Public utilities - Dyersburg, Tenn. I. Tennessee. State Planning Commission. II. U.S. Urban Renewal Administration. Urban Planning Assistance Program.

4414

TENNESSEE. STATE PLANNING COMMISSION. COOKEVILLE, TENN. MUNICIPAL-REGIONAL PLANNING COMMISSION. COOKEVILLE'S HOUSING PROBLEMS AND PROSPECTS. BY TENNESSEE STATE PLANNING COMMISSION. COOKEVILLE, TENN., 1969. 105P. (HUD 701 REPORT)

1. HOUSING - COOKEVILLE, TENN. I. TENNESSEE. STATE PLANNING COMMISSION. II. HUD. 701. COOKEVILLE, TENN.

352.5
(755725)
T25

Tennessee. State Planning Commission. Draft of fringe area study for Bristol, Virginia. A staff report to the Bristol, Virginia Planning Commission. Bristol, 1958. 18p. map, tables.

U.S. Urban Renewal Adm. UPAP.

1. Fringe areas - Bristol, Va. I. Bristol, Va. Planning Commission. II. U.S. Urban Renewal Administration. Urban Planning Assistance Program. Bristol, Va.

330
(76824)
M12

Tennessee. State Planning Commission. McKenzie, Tenn. Municipal-Regional Planning Commission. Economic analysis for McKenzie, Tennessee. Assisted by the Tennessee State Planning Commission, West Tennessee Office. McKenzie, 1957. 46p. tables.

U.S. Urban Renewal Administration, Urban Planning Assistance Program.

(Continued on next card)

711.73
(76883)
D19

Tennessee. State Planning Commission. Dayton, Tenn. Municipal Planning Commission. Dayton major road plan. Assisted by the Tennessee State Planning Commission, East Tennessee Office. Dayton, 1957. 4p. map.

U.S. Urban Renewal Administration, Urban Planning Assistance Program.

1. Highways - Dayton, Tenn.   I. Tennessee. State Planning Commission. II. U.S. Urban Renewal Administration. Urban Planning Assistance Program.

647.1
T25

TENNESSEE. STATE PLANNING COMMISSION. DYERSBURG CAPITAL BUDGET, A CASE HISTORY. NASHVILLE, TENN., 1950. 75P. (ITS PUBLICATION NO. 210)

1. BUDGETS AND EXPENDITURES. I. TITLE.

330
(76824)
M12

McKenzie, Tenn. Municipal-Regional Planning Commission. Economic ... (Card 2)

1. Economic conditions - McKenzie, Tenn. I. Tennessee. State Planning Commission. II. U.S. Urban Renewal Administration. Urban Planning Assistance Program.

526.8
(76883)
D19

Tennessee. State Planning Commission. Dayton, Tenn. Municipal Planning Commission. Dayton, Tennessee base maps. Prepared by East Tennessee Office, Tennessee State Planning Commission. Dayton, 1956. 1v. maps.

U.S. Urban Renewal Administration, Urban Planning Assistance Program.

1. Dayton, Tenn.-Maps.   I. Tennessee. State Planning Commission. II. U.S. Urban Renewal Administration. Urban Planning Assistance Program.

352.1
(76815)
D92

Tennessee. State Planning Commission. Dyersburg, Tenn. Regional Planning Commission. Dyersburg capital budget program 1956-1961. [With the assistance of the Tennessee State Planning Commission, Division of State Planning] Dyersburg, 1956. 22p. tables.

U.S. Urban Renewal Administration, Urban

(Continued on next card)

330
(76813)
U54

Tennessee. State Planning Commission. Union City, Tenn. Regional Planning Commission. Economic base study for Union City. Assisted by the Tennessee State Planning Commission, West Tennessee Office. Union City, 1956. 28p. tables.

U.S. Urban Renewal Administration, Urban Planning Assistance Program.

1. Economic base studies - Union City, Tenn. I. Tennessee. State Planning Commission. II. U.S. Urban Planning Assistance Program. Urban Planning Assistance Program.

711
(016)
C65
no.191

Tennessee. State Planning Commission. Burt, Eleanor, comp. Directory of planning libraries. 3d ed. [Nashville] Tennessee State Planning Commission, 1971. 87p. (Council of Planning Librarians. Exchange bibliography no. 191)

1. Planning - Bibl. 2. Planning libraries - Direct. I. Tennessee. State Planning Commission II. Title. (Series: Council of Planning Librarians. Exchange bibliography no. 191)

352.1
(76815)
D92

Dyersburg, Tenn. Regional Planning Commission. Dyersburg capital budget...(Card 2)

Planning Assistance Program.

1. Municipal finance - Dyersburg, Tenn. 2. Capital improvement programs - Dyersburg. Tenn. I. Tennessee. State Planning Commission. II. U.S. Urban Renewal Administration. Urban Planning Assistance Program.

Class No. *[handwritten]*
Recorded
U.S.-Ten

Accession No.

JUN 3 0 1950
Source
tto
Received
JUL 1 2 1950
Cost

Purchase Order No.

Date

L. C. No.

Author (surname first) *Tennessee State Planning Commission*
Title *Economic data sheets on Tenn. communities. Data on 80 cities ....*
Place *Nashville 3* Publisher *Industrial Development*
Address *17 7th Ave, N.*   Div.
Date *1947 -* Paging
Cost List Price Est. Cost *gratis*
Edition or Series
Recommended by
Reviewed in *Ind. A   Dev. 1948-49*

H-305 (2-50) HOUSING AND HOME FINANCE AGENCY: Office of the Administrator   16—61187-1 GPO

Class No. *City*

Accession No.

Ordered
JUN 3 0 1950
Source
tto
Received
Cost

Purchase Order No.

Date

L. C. No.

Author (surname first) *Tennessee State Planning Commission*
Title *Directory of Tennessee industries*
Place *Nashville 3* Publisher *Industrial Development*
Address *17 7th Ave, N.*   Division
Date *1949* Paging *286* List Price *5.00* Est. Cost *gratis*
Edition or Series *TSPC Pub. 200*
Recommended by
Reviewed in *Ind. A   Dev. 48-49 Vol. I*

H-305 (2-50) HOUSING AND HOME FINANCE AGENCY: Office of the Administrator   16—61187-1 GPO

627.4
(76815)
D92

Tennessee. State Planning Commission. Dyersburg, Tenn. Regional Planning Commission. Dyersburg flood study. With the assistance of Tennessee State Planning Commission, West Tennessee Office. Dyersburg, 1957. 16p. illus., maps.

U.S. Urban Renewal Administration, Urban Planning Assistance Program.

1. Flood control - Dyersburg, Tenn.   I. Tennessee. State Planning Commission. II. U.S. Urban Renewal Administration. Urban Planning Assistance Program.

330
(76815)
D92

Tennessee. State Planning Commission. Dyersburg, Tenn. Regional Planning Commission. Economic survey for Dyersburg Tennessee. [With the assistance of the Tennessee State Planning Commission, West Tennessee Office] Dyersburg, 1956. 34p. tables.

U.S. Urban Renewal Administration, Urban Planning Assistance Program.

1. Economic condition - Dyersburg, Tenn. I. Tennessee. State Planning Commission. II. U.S. Urban Renewal Administration. Urban Planning Assistance Program.

388
(768984)
E54d

Tennessee. State Planning Commission. Elizabethton, Tenn. Regional Planning Commission. Downtown congestion traffic and parking problems and proposals. Assisted by the Upper East Tennessee Office, Tennessee State Planning Commission. Elizabethton, 1957. 69p. maps, tables.

U.S. Urban Renewal Administration,

(Continued on next card)

352.6
(76815)
D92

Tennessee. State Planning Commission. Dyersburg, Tenn. Regional Planning Commission. Dyersburg utilities study. With the assistance of the Tennessee State Planning Commission, West Tennessee Office. Dyersburg, 1957. 13p. maps, diagrs., tables.

U.S. Urban Renewal Administration, Urban Planning Assistance Program.

(Continued on next card)

VF
330
(768585)
T25

Tennessee. State Planning Commission. (Middle Tennessee Office.) An economic survey, Lewisburg, Tennessee. [Nashville, Tenn.] Sept. 1955. 19 p. charts.

Urban Planning Assistance Program

1. Economic base studies - Lewisburg, Tenn.

330
(768464)
S67

Tennessee. State Planning Commission.
Springfield, Tenn. Municipal—Regional
Planning Commission.
Economic survey of Springfield, Tenn-
essee. Assisted by Tennessee State
Planning Commission, Middle Tennessee
Office. Springfield, 1957.
91p. illus., diagrs., maps, tables.
(MTO publication no. 57-13)

U.S. Urban Renewal Administration,
(Continued on next card)

330
(768464)
S67

Springfield, Tenn. Municipal—Regional
Planning Commission. Econonomic survey
of Springfield, ... (Card 2)

Urban Planning Assistance Program.

1. Economic base studies - Springfield,
Tenn. I. Tennessee. State Planning Commission. II. U.S. Urban Renewal Administration. Urban Planning Assistance
Program.

330
(768)
T25e

Tennessee. State Planning Commission.
An economic survey of the tri-counties of
Upper East Tennessee. Prepared by Bristol
Tennessee Regional Planning Commission and
others; assisted by ... Upper East Tennessee Office. Nashville, 1956.
77p. illus., tables.

U.S. Urban Renewal Administration, Urban

(Continued on next card)

330
(768)
T25e

Tennessee. State Planning Commission. An
economic survey of the ... (Card 2)

Planning Assistance Program.

1. Economic conditions - Tenn. I. U.S.
Urban Renewal Administration. Urban Planning Assistance Program.

330
(768164)
T85

Tennessee. State Planning Commission.
Tullahoma, Tenn. Planning Commission.
Econonic survey of Tullahoma, Tennessee.
Prepared by the Tennessee State Planning
Commission, Middle Tennessee Office. Tulla-
homa, 1957.
19p. diagrs., tables. (MTO publication
no. 57-47)

U.S. Urban Renewal Administration, Urban
Planning Assistance Program.
(Continued on next card)

330
(768164)
T85

Tullahoma, Tenn. Planning Commission. Economic survey of Tullahoma, ... (Card 2)

1. Economic base studies - Tullahoma,
Tenn. I. Tennessee. State Planning Commission. II. U.S. Urban Renewal Administration. Urban Planning Assistance
Program.

352.5
E54

Tennessee. State Planning Commission.
Elizabethton, Tenn. Regional Planning
Commission.
Elizabethton annexation study. Assisted
by the Tennessee State Planning Commission,
Upper East Tennessee Office. Elizabethton,
1956.
43p. maps, tables.

U.S. Urban Renewal Administration,
Urban Planning Assistance Program.

(Continued on next card)

352.5
(768984)
E54

Elizabethton, Tenn. Regional Planning
Commission. Elizabethton ... (Card 2)

1. Annexation - Elizabethton, Tenn.
I. Tennessee. State Planning Commission.
II. U.S. Urban Renewal Administration.
Urban Planning Assistance Program.

627.4
(768984)
E54

Tennessee. State Planning Commission.
Elizabethton, Tenn. Regional Planning
Commission.
Elizabethton flood study; proposals
for meeting the flood problems at
Elizabethton, Tennessee. Prepared by
the Upper East Tennessee Office, Ten-
nessee State Planning Commission.
Elizabethton, 1957.
32p. maps, diagrs.

U.S. Urban Renewal Administration,
(Continued on next
card)

627.4
(768984)
E54

Elizabethton, Tenn. Regional Planning
Commission. Elizabethton ...(Card 2)

Urban Planning Assistance Program.

1. Flood control - Elizabethton, Tenn.
I. Tennessee. State Planning Commission.
II. U.S. Urban Renewal Administration.
Urban Planning Assistance Program.

728.1
(768984)
E54

Tennessee. State Planning Commission.
Elizabethton, Tenn. Regional Planning Com-
mission.
Elizabethton housing study. Assisted by
Upper East Tennessee Office, Tennessee State
Planning Commission. Elizabethton, 1956.
26p. maps, tables.

U.S. Urban Renewal Administration, Urban
Planning Assistance Program.

(Continued on next card)

728.1
(768984)
E54

Elizabethton, Tenn. Regional Planning Commission. Elizabethton housing...(Card 2)

1. Housing - Elizabethton, Tenn. I. Tenne-
ssee. State Planning Commission. II. U.S.
Urban Renewal Administration. Urban Planning
Assistance Program.

711.14
(768984)
E54

Tennessee. State Planning Commission.
Elizabethton, Tenn. Regional Planning
Commission.
Elizabethton land use. Prepared by the
Upper East Tennessee Office, Tennessee
State Planning Commission. Elizabethton,
1957.
44p. maps, diagrs., tables.

U.S. Urban Renewal Administration,
(Continued on next
card)

711.14
(768984)
E54

Elizabethton, Tenn. Regional Planning
Commission. Elizabethton ... (Card 2)

Urban Planning Assistance Program.

1. Land use - Elizabethton, Tenn.
I. Tennessee. State Planning Commission.
II. U.S. Urban Renewal Administration.
Urban Planning Assistance Program.

711.73
(768984)
E54

Tennessee. State Planning Commission.
Elizabethton, Tenn. Regional Planning Commission.
Elizabethton major road plan. Assisted by
the Tennessee State Planning Commission, Upper
East Tennessee Office. Elizabethton, 1956.
6p. maps.

U.S. Urban Renewal Administration, Urban
Planning Assistance Program.

1. Highways - Elizabethton, Tenn. I. Tenne-
ssee. State Planning Commission. II. U.S.
Urban Renewal Administration. Urban Planning
Assistance Program.

727.1
(768984)
E54

Tennessee. State Planning Commission.
Elizabethton, Tenn. Regional Planning Com-
mission.
The Elizabethton school system, a planning
analysis. [Prepared for ... by the Tennessee
State Planning Commission, Upper East Tennessee
Office] Elizabethton, 1956.
53p. maps, tables.

U.S. Urban Renewal Administration, Urban
Planning Assistance Program.

(Continued on next card)

727.1
(768984)
E54

Elizabethton, Tenn. Regional Planning Commission. The Elizabethton school ... (Card 2)

1. Schools - Elizabethton, Tenn. I. Tennessee. State Planning Commission. II. U.S.
Urban Renewal Administration. Urban Planning Assistance Program.

711.14
(76823)
T72

Tennessee. State Planning Commission.
Trenton, Tenn. Municipal Planning Commis-
sion.
Existing land use survey and analysis,
Trenton, Tennessee. With the assistance
of the Tennessee State Planning Commission,
West Tennessee Office. Trenton, 1957.
13p. map, tables.

U.S. Urban Renewal Administration, Urban
Continued on next card)

711.14
(76823)
T72

Trenton, Tenn. Municipal Planning Commission. Existing land ... (Card 2)

Planning Assistance Program.

1. Land use - Trenton, Tenn. I. Tennessee. State Planning Commission. II. U.S.
Urban Renewal Administration. Urban Planning Assistance Program.

352.1
(76875)
C76

Tennessee. State Planning Commission.
Crossville, Tenn. Municipal Planning Commission.
A fiscal analysis of Crossville, Tennessee.
Assisted by Tennessee State Planning Commission, East Tennessee Office. Crossville,
1957.
54p. diagrs., tables.

U.S. Urban Renewal Administration, Urban

(Continued on next card)

352.1
(76875)
C76

Crossville, Tenn Municipal Planning Commission. A fiscal analysis ... (Card 2)

Planning Assistance Program.

1. Municipal finance - Crossville, Tenn.
I. Tennessee. State Planning Commission.
II. U.S. Urban Renewal Administration.
Urban Planning Assistance Program.

352.1
(76887)
C52
Tennessee. State Planning Commission.
Cleveland, Tenn. Planning Commission.
A fiscal analysis of the City of Cleveland, Tennessee. A staff report ... prepared by Tennessee State Planning Commission, East Tennessee Office. Cleveland, 1957.
51p. tables.

U.S. Urban Renewal Administration, Urban

(Continued on next card)

Tennessee. State Planning Commission.

711.585
(76813)
U54
Union City, Tenn. Regional Planning Commission.
General community renewal plan, Union City, Tennessee. Prepared by Tennessee State Planning Commission, West Tennessee Office. Union City, 1958.
44p. illus., maps, tables.

U.S. Urban Renewal Administration, Urban Planning Assistance Program.
1. Urban renewal - Union City, Tenn. I. Tennessee. State Planning Commission. II. U.S. URA-UPAP. Union City, Tenn.

Tennessee. State Planning Commission.

690.091.82
:613.5
(76856)
F71
Franklin, Tenn. Municipal Planning Commission.
Housing code, Franklin, Tennessee. Assisted by Tennessee State Planning Commission, Middle Tennessee Office. Franklin 1957.
16p. (MTO Publication no. 57-20)

U.S. Urban Renewal Administration,
(Continued on next card)

352.1
(76887)
C52
Cleveland, Tenn. Planning Commission. A fiscal analysis of ... (Card 2)

Planning Assistance Program.

1. Municipal finance - Cleveland, Tenn. I. Tennessee. State Planning Commission. II. U.S. Urban Renewal Administration. Urban Planning Assistance Program.

Tennessee. State Planning Commission.

312
(76896)
K45
Kingsport, Tenn. Regional Planning Commission.
Growing Kingsport, potential residential development and population growth. By the Tennessee State Planning Commission, Upper East Tennessee Office. Kingsport, 1958.
58p. diagr., map, tables.
"A preliminary staff report."

U.S. Urban Renewal Administration,
(Continued on next card).

690.091.82
:613.5
(76856)
F71
Franklin, Tenn. Municipal Planning Commission. Housing code, ...(Card 2)

Urban Planning Assistance Program.

1. Housing codes - Franklin, Tenn. I. Tennessee. State Planning Commission. II. U.S. Urban Renewal Administration. Urban Planning Assistance Program.

627.4
(768)
T25
Tennessee. State Planning Commission.
Flood damage prevention for Tennessee, by Harold V. Miller. A survey of Tennessee's flood situation, trends in vulnerability, and a proposed program for action. Nashville, 1960.
94p. (Its Publication no. 309)

1. Flood control - Tennessee. I. Miller, Harold V.

312
(76896)
K45
Kingsport, Tenn. Regional Planning Commission. Growing ... (Card 2)

Urban Planning Assistance Program.

1. Population - Kingsport, Tenn.
2. City growth - Kingsport, Tenn. I. Tennessee. State Planning Commission. II. U.S. Urban Renewal Administration. Urban Planning Assistance Program.

Tennessee. State Planning Commission.

728.1
(76896)
K45
Kingsport, Tenn. Regional Planning Commission.
Housing in the Kingsport Area. A preliminary report by the Tennessee State Planning Commission to the Kingsport Regional Planning Commission. [Kingsport] 1956.
48p. maps, tables.

U.S. Urban Renewal Administration, Urban
(Continued on next page)

VF
627.4
S45
Tennessee. State Planning Commission.
Siler, Robert Wilson, Jr.
Flood problems and their solution through urban planning programs. [Nashville, Tenn.] Tennessee State Planning Commission, Sept. 1955.
vii, 48 p. illus.
A Special Publication of the American Society of Planning Officials.
1. Flood control. I. Tennessee. State Planning Commission. II. Title.

330
(75)
T25
Tennessee. State Planning Commission.
A guide for organizing development districts under Tennessee enabling legislation for participation in Appalachian regional development act, Economic development act, Regional planning, housing act of 1968. Nashville, 1969.
40p.
1. Economic development - Appalachian region. I. Title.

728.1
(76896)
K45
Kingsport, Tenn. Regional Planning Commission. Housing in the ... (Card 2)

Planning Assistance Program.

1. Housing - Kingsport, Tenn. I. Tennessee. State Planning Commission. II. U.S. Urban Renewal Administration. Urban Planning Assistance Program.

711.4
(76892)
M67
Tennessee. State Planning Commission.
Morristown, Tenn. Regional Planning Commission.
Future land use plan, capital improvement plan and comprehensive plan for Morristown, Tennessee. Assisted by Tennessee State Planning Commission. Morristown, 1956.
27p. maps, tables.

U.S. Urban Renewal Administration, Urban Planning Assistance Program.

(Continued on next card)

526.8
(76884)
R61
Roane Co., Tenn. Regional Planning Commission.
Harriman, Tennessee base maps. Prepared by the East Tennessee Office, Tennessee State Planning Commission. Harriman, Tenn., 1958.
1v. maps.

U.S. Urban Renewal Adm. UPAP.
1. Maps and mapping - Harriman, Tenn.
I. Tennessee. State Planning Commission.
II. U.S. Urban Renewal Administration. Urban Planning Assistance Program. Roane Co., Tenn.

Tennessee. State Planning Commission.

728.1
(76892)
M67
Morristown, Tenn. Regional Planning Commission.
Housing report for Morristown. Assisted by the Tennessee State Planning Commission. Morristown, 1956.
11p.
U.S. Urban Renewal Adm. UPAP.
1. Housing - Morristown, Tenn.
I. Tennessee. State Planning Commission.
II. U.S. URA-UPAP. Morristown, Tenn.

711.4
(76892)
M67
Morristown, Tenn. Regional Planning Commission. Future land ... (Card 2)

1. Master plan - Morristown, Tenn.
2. Land use - Morristown, Tenn. 3. Capital improvement programs — Morristown, Tenn. I. Tennessee. State Planning Commission. II. U.S. Urban Renewal Administration. Urban Planning Assistance Program.

690.091.82
:613.5
(76813)
U54
Tennessee. State Planning Commission.
Union City, Tenn. Regional Planning Commission.
Housing code for Union City, Tennessee. With the assistance of the Tennessee State Planning Commission, West Tennessee Office. Union City, 1957.
30p.

U.S. Urban Renewal Administration,
(Continued on next card)

308
:728.1
(76815)
D92
Tennessee. State Planning Commission.
Dyersburg, Tenn. Regional Planning Commission.
Housing survey and analysis for Dyersburg, Tennessee. Prepared by Tennessee State Planning Commission, West Tennessee Office. Dyersburg, 1957.
33p. maps, tables.

U.S. Urban Renewal Administration, Urban Planning Assistance Program.
(Continued on next card)

526.8
(76847)
T25
Tennessee. State Planning Commission.
Gallatin, Tennessee sectional base maps.
Scale 1" = 400'. Nashville, 1957.
1v. maps.

U.S. Urban Renewal Administration, Urban Planning Assistance Program.

1. Maps and mapping - Gallatin, Tenn.
I. U.S. Urban Renewal Administration. Urban Planning Assistance Program.

690.091.82
:613.5
(76813)
U54
Union City, Tenn. Regional Planning Commission. Housing code ... (Card 2)

Urban Planning Assistance Program.

1. Housing codes - Union City, Tenn.
I. Tennessee. State Planning Commission.
II. U.S. Urban Renewal Administration. Urban Planning Assistance Program.

308
:728.1
(76815)
D92
Dyersburg, Tenn. Regional Planning Commission. Housing survey ... (Card 2)

1. Housing surveys - Dyersburg, Tenn.
I. Tennessee. State Planning Commission. II. U.S. Urban Renewal Administration. Urban Planning Assistance Program.

728.1
(76813)
U54
Tennessee. State Planning Commission.
Union City, Tenn. Regional Planning Commission.
Housing survey and analysis, Union City, Tennessee. With the assistance of the Tennessee State Planning Commission, West Tennessee Office. Union City, 1957
51p. maps, tables.

U.S. Urban Renewal Administration, Urban
(Continued on next card)

727.1
(76837)
W18
Tennessee. State Planning Commission.
Waverly, Tenn. Regional Planning Commission.
Humphreys County school survey. With technical assistance provided by the Tennessee State Planning Commission, Middle Tennessee Office. Waverly, 1958.
40p. diagrs., maps, tables. (MTO Publication no. 58-13)
U.S. Urban Renewal Administration, Urban Planning Assistance Program.

1. Schools - Humphreys Co., Tenn. I. Tennessee. State Planning Commission. II. U.S. URA-UPAP.

712.25
(76896)
K45
Kingsport, Tenn. Regional Planning Commission. Kingsport public ... (Card 2)

1. Recreation - Kingsport, Tenn. I. Tennessee. State Planning Commission. II. U.S. Urban Renewal Administration. Urban Planning Assistance Program.

728.1
(76813)
U54
Union City, Tenn. Regional Planning Commission. Housing survey ... (Card 2)

Planning Assistance Program.

1. Housing surveys - Union City, Tenn. I. Tennessee. State Planning Commission. II. U.S. Urban Renewal Administration. Urban Planning Assistance Program.

360
(768)
T25
Tennessee. State Planning Commission.
The incidence of poverty; social and economic conditions in Tennessee, by Jerry J. Williams and Leo T. Surls. Nashville, State Planning Office, Tennessee State Planning Commission, 1965.
36p.
U.S. Urban Renewal Adm. UPAP.

1. Social conditions - Tennessee. 2. Economic conditions - Tennessee. I. Williams, Jerry J. II. Surls, Leo T. III. Title. IV. U.S. URA-UPAP. Tenn.

711.14
(76896)
K45k
Tennessee. State Planning Commission.
Kingsport, Tenn. Regional Planning Commission. Kingsport, Tennessee; future land use plan. [A staff report to the Kingsport Regional Planning Commission, by Upper East Tennessee Office, Tennessee State Planning Commission] Kingsport, 1959.
29p. maps, tables.
U. S. Urban Renewal Administration, Urban Planning Assistance Program.

1. Land use - Kingsport, Tenn. I. Tennessee. State Planning Commission. II. U. S. URA-UPAP. Kingsport, Tenn.

711.4
:728.1
(768865)
A73
Tennessee. State Planning Commission.
Athens, Tenn. Regional Planning Commission. Housing survey for Athens. Assisted by the Tennessee State Planning Commission. Athens, 1956.
9p. map.

U.S. Urban Renewal Administration, Urban Planning Assistance Program.

1. City planning - Athens, Tenn. 2. Housing surveys - Athens, Tenn. I. Tennessee. State Planning Commission. II. U.S. Urban Renewal Administration.

711.33
(016)
T25
Tennessee. State Planning Commission.
Index to information available from state agencies, compiled by Mary Coleman Harbison and Betty Currie Tilley. [Nashville?] 1955.
1 v. (Its Publication no. 261)

1. State planning - Bibliographies. I. Harbison, Mary Coleman. II. Tilley, Betty Currie

---

526.8
(76896)
T25
Tennessee. State Planning Commission.
Kingsport, Tennessee base maps. Kingsport, 1957.
1v. maps.

U.S. Urban Renewal Administration, Urban Planning Assistance Program.

1. Maps and mapping - Kingsport, Tenn. I. U.S. Urban Renewal Administration. Urban Planning Assistance Program.

728.1
T25
2c.
Tennessee. State Planning Commission.
Housing survey procedures: a guide for small Tennessee communities, comp. by Louise Nunnelly. [Nashville] 1956.
52 p. (Its Publication no. 266)

1. Housing surveys. I. Nunnelly, Louise, comp.

Class No.
Indus.
location -
Accession No.

Received

Purchase Order No.
Date

L. C. No.

Author (surname first) *Tennessee State Planning Commission*
Title *Industrial buildings available in Tennessee*
Place *Nashville 3* Publisher *Industrial Development*
Address *41 7th Ave N.* *O.W.*
Date *9/49* Paging *9* List Price Est. Cost *gratis*
Edition or Series
Recommended by
Reviewed in *Ind. V. D. Tenn. 1948-49*

H-305 (2-50)   HOUSING AND HOME FINANCE AGENCY: Office of the Administrator 10-61167-1 gpo

---

352.5
(768836)
K45
Tennessee. State Planning Commission.
Kingston, Tenn. Municipal Planning Commission. Kingston fringe-area study. Assisted by the Tennessee State Planning Commission, East Tennessee Office. Kingston, 1957.
21p. maps, tables.

U.S. Urban Renewal Administration, Urban
(Continued on next card)

352
(768)
T25h
Tennessee. State Planning Commission.
How to become a city, procedures under each of Tennessee's uniform charters by Ellen Muhr. Nashville, 1960.
11p. (TSPC Publication no. 306)

1. Municipal government - Tennessee. I. Muhr, Ellen.

711.4
:670
(768)
T25
Tennessee. State Planning Commission.
Industrial site survey of Carter Co., Sullivan Co., Washington Co. A report of the Upper East Tennessee Regional Planning Commission. Nashville, 1959.
106p. maps, tables.

1. Industrial location - Tennessee. I. U.S. URA-UPAP.

352.5
(768836)
K45
Kingston, Tenn. Municipal Planning Commission. Kingston fringe-...(Card 2)

Planning Assistance Program.

1. Fringe areas - Kingston, Tenn. I. Tennessee. State Planning Commission. II. U.S. Urban Renewal Administration. Urban Planning Assistance Program.

727.1
(76823)
H85
Tennessee. State Planning Commission.
Humboldt, Tenn. Municipal-Regional Planning Commission.
Humboldt school study. With the assistance of the Tennessee State Planning Commission, West Tennessee Office. Humboldt, 1957.
45p. maps, tables.

U.S. Urban Renewal Administration,
(Continued on next card)

353
(768)
T25i
Tennessee. State Planning Commission.
Interstate compacts; a summary of compacts to which Tennessee is signatory and resume of selected compacts to which Tennessee is elegible. Nashville, 1967.
1v.

1. Intergovernmental relations.-Tenn. 2. State planning - Tenn. I. Tennessee Commission on Intergovernmental Cooperation. II. Title.

727.1
(76896)
K45k
Tennessee. State Planning Commission.
Kingsport, Tenn. Regional Planning Commission.
Kingsport; toward a school and recreation plan. Prepared by Upper East Tennessee Office, Tennessee State Planning Commission. Kingsport, 1957.
17p. maps, tables.
U.S. Urban Renewal Administration, Urban Planning Assistance Program.
1. Schools - Kingsport, Tenn. 2. Recreation - Kingsport, Tenn. I. Tennessee. State Planning Commission. II. U.S. Urban Renewal Administration. Urban Planning Assistance Program.

727.1
(76823)
H85
Humboldt, Tenn. Municipal-Regional Planning Commission. Humboldt ...(Card 2)

Urban Planning Assistance Program.

1. Schools - Humboldt, Tenn. I. Tennessee. State Planning Commission. II. U.S. Urban Renewal Administration. Urban Planning Assistance Program.

712.25
(76896)
K45
Tennessee. State Planning Commission.
Kingsport, Tenn. Regional Planning Commission.
Kingsport public recreation areas. Report by the Tennessee State Planning Commission to the Kingsport Regional Planning Commission. Kingsport 1956.
58p. maps, tables.

U.S. Urban Renewal Administration, Urban Planning Assistance Program.
(Continued on next card)

711.14
(76875)
C76
Tennessee. State Planning Commission.
Crossville, Tenn. Municipal Planning Commission.
Land use analysis, Crossville, Tennessee. Prepared by East Tennessee Office, Tennessee State Planning Commission. Crossville, 1957.
29p. maps.

U.S. Urban Renewal Administration, Urban Planning Assistance Program.

(Continued on next card)

711.14
(76875)
C76
Crossville, Tenn. Municipal Planning Commission. Land use analysis ... (Card 2)

1. Land use - Crossville, Tenn. I. Tennessee. State Planning Commission. II. U.S. Urban Renewal Administration. Urban Planning Assistance Program.

711.14
(76885)
M17
Maryville, Tenn. Regional Planning Commission. Land use ...(Card 2)

Urban Planning Assistance Program.

1. Land use - Maryville, Tenn. I. Tennessee. State Planning Commission. II. U.S. Urban Renewal Administration. Urban Planning Assistance Program.

711.14
(768924)
W34
Tennessee. State Planning Commission. White Pine, Tenn. Regional Planning Commission. Land use analysis, White Pine planning region. Assisted by Tennessee State Planning Commission, East Tennessee Office. White Pine, 1957. 12p. maps.

U.S. Urban Renewal Administration, Urban Planning Assistance Program.

(Continued on next card)

Tennessee. State Planning Commission.
711.14
(76861)
P85
Pulaski, Tenn. Planning Commission. A land use analysis for Pulaski, Tennessee. Prepared by Middle Tennessee Office, Tennessee State Planning Commission. Pulaski, 1957. 11p. maps (MTO Publication no. 57-33)

U.S. Urban Renewal Administration, Urban Planning Assistance Program.
1. Land use - Pulaski, Tenn. I. Tennessee. State Planning Commission. II. U.S. Urban Renewal Administration. Urban Planning Assistance Program.

711.14
(76854)
L21
Lebanon, Tenn. Municipal-Regional Planning Commission. Land use analysis of Lebanon, Tennessee. Assisted by Tennessee State Planning Commission, Middle Tennessee Office. Lebanon, 1957. 11p. maps, tables. (MTO publication no. 57-39)

U.S. Urban Renewal Administration,

(Continued on next card)

711.14
(768924)
W34
White Pine, Tenn. Regional Planning Commission. Land use analysis, ...(Card 2)

1. Land use - White Pine, Tenn. I. Tennessee. State Planning Commission. II. U.S. Urban Renewal Administration. Urban Planning Assistance Program.

Tennessee. State Planning Commission.
711.14
(76892)
M67
Morristown, Tenn. Regional Planning Commission. Land use analysis for the City of Morristown, Tennessee. Assisted by Tennessee State Planning Commission, East Tennessee Office. Morristown, 1957. 20p. diagrs., maps.

U.S. Urban Renewal Administration, Urban Planning Assistance Program.

(Continued on next card)

711.14
(76854)
L21
Lebanon, Tenn. Municipal-Regional Planning Commission. Land use ...(Card 2)

Urban Planning Assistance Program.

1. Land use - Lebanon, Tenn. I. Tennessee. State Planning Commission. II. U.S. Urban Renewal Administration. Urban Planning Assistance Program.

Tennessee. State Planning Commission.
711.14
(76815)
D92
Dyersburg, Tenn. Regional Planning Commission. Land use plan, Dyersburg. [With the assistance of the Tennessee State Planning Commission, West Tennessee Office] Dyersburg, 1956. [15]p. illus., tables. diagrs.

U.S. Urban Renewal Administration, Urban Planning Assistance Program.

1. Land use - Dyersburg, Tenn. I. Tennessee. State Planning Commission. II. U.S. Urban Renewal Administration. Urban Planning Assistance Program.

711.14
(76892)
M67
Morristown, Tenn. Regional Planning Commission. Land use analysis ... (Card 2)

1. Land use - Morristown, Tenn. I. Tennessee. State Planning Commission. II. U.S. Urban Renewal Administration. Urban Planning Assistance Program.

711.14
(76864)
T85
Tennessee. State Planning Commission. Tullahoma, Tenn. Planning Commission. Land use analysis of Tullahoma, Tennessee. Prepared by Tennessee State Planning Commission, Middle Tennessee Office. Tullahoma, 1957. 12p. maps, tables. (MTO publication no. 57-42)

U.S. Urban Renewal Administration,

(Continued on next card)

Tennessee. State Planning Commission.
711.14
(76813)
U54
Union City, Tenn. Regional Planning Commission. Land use plan for Union City, Tennessee. With the assistance of the Tennessee State Planning Commission. Union City, 1956. 31p. maps, tables.

U.S. Urban Renewal Administration, Urban Planning Assistance Program.

1. Land use - Union City, Tenn. I. Tennessee. State Planning Commission. II. U.S. Urban Renewal Administration. Urban Planning Assistance Program.

Tennessee. State Planning Commission.
711.14
(76856)
F71
Franklin, Tenn. Municipal Planning Commission. Land use analysis, Franklin, Tennessee. Prepared by the Tennessee State Planning Commission, Middle Tennessee Office. Franklin, 1957. 12p. maps, tables. (MTO Publication no. 57-34)

U.S. Urban Renewal Administration, Urban
(Continued on next card)

711.14
(76864)
T85
Tullahoma, Tenn. Planning Commission. Land use analysis of ... (Card 2)

Urban Planning Assistance Program.

1. Land use - Tullahoma, Tenn. I. Tennessee. State Planning Commission. II. U.S. Urban Renewal Administration. Urban Planning Assistance Program.

711.14
(768865)
A73
Tennessee. State Planning Commission. Athens, Tenn. Regional Planning Commission. Land use survey and analysis for Athens, Tennessee. [Assisted by] Tennessee State Planning Commission, Southeast Tennessee Office. Athens, 1958. 13p. diagrs., maps, tables.

U.S. Urban Renewal Administration, Urban Planning Assistance Program.

1. Land use - Athens, Tenn. I. Tennessee. State Planning Commission. II. U.S. Urban Renewal Administration. Urban Planning Assistance Program.

711.14
(76856)
F71
Franklin, Tenn. Municipal Planning Commission. Land use ... (Card 2)

Urban Planning Assistance Program.

1. Land use - Franklin, Tenn. I. Tennessee. State Planning Commission. II. U.S. Urban Renewal Administration. Urban Planning Assistance Program.

Tennessee. State Planning Commission.
711.14
(76888)
S82
Sweetwater, Tenn. Regional Planning Commission. Land use analysis, Sweetwater, Tennessee. [Prepared for the Sweetwater Regional Planning Commission, by the East Tennessee State Planning Commission, East Tennessee Office] Sweetwater, 1959. 24p. maps.

U.S. Urban Renewal Administration, Urban Planning Assistance Program.

(Continued on next card)

711.14
(76883)
D19
Tennessee. State Planning Commission. Dayton, Tenn. Municipal Planning Commission. Land use survey and analysis for Dayton, Tennessee. Assisted by the Tennessee State Planning Commission, East Tennessee Office. Dayton, 1957. 25p. maps.

U.S. Urban Renewal Administration, Urban Planning Assistance Program.

(Continued on next card)

Tennessee. State Planning Commission.
711.14
(76885)
M17
Maryville, Tenn. Regional Planning Commission. Land use analysis, Maryville, Tennessee. Prepared by East Tennessee Office, Tennessee State Planning Commission. Maryville, 1957. 33p. maps.

U.S. Urban Renewal Administration,

(Continued on next card)

711.14
(76888)
S82
Sweetwater, Tenn. Regional Planning Commission. Land use... 1959. (Card 2)

1. Land use - Sweetwater, Tenn. I. Tennessee. State Planning Commission. II. U.S. Urban Renewal Administration. Urban Planning Assistance Program. Sweetwater, Tenn.

711.14
(76883)
D19
Dayton, Tenn. Municipal Planning Commission. Land use survey ... (Card 2)

1. Land use - Dayton, Tenn. I. Tennessee. State Planning Commission. II. U.S. Urban Renewal Administration. Urban Planning Assistance Program.

711.14
(76847)
G15
Tennessee. State Planning Commission.
Gallatin, Tenn. Municipal-Regional Planning Commission.
Land use survey and analysis for Gallatin, Tennessee. Assisted by the Tennessee State Planning Commission, Middle Tennessee Office. Gallatin, 1958.
25p. maps. (MTO Publication no. 58-17)

U.S. Urban Renewal Administration, Urban Planning Assistance Program.
1. Land use - Gallatin, Tenn. I. Tennessee. State Planning Commission. II. U.S. Urban Renewal Administration. Urban Planning Assistance Program.

711.14
(76812)
R42
Tennessee. State Planning Commission.
Ridgely, Tenn. Municipal-Regional Planning Commission.
Land use survey and analysis, Ridgely, Tennessee. With the assistance of the Tennessee State Planning Commission, West Tennessee Office. Ridgely, 1957.
13p. map, tables.

U.S. Urban Renewal Administration, Urban Planning Assistance Program.
(Continued on next card)

711.73
(76828)
B65
Bolivar, Tenn. Municipal Regional Planning Commission. Major road ... (Card 2)

Planning Assistance Program.

1. Highways - Bolivar, Tenn. 2. Street planning - Bolivar, Tenn. I. Tennessee. State Planning Commission. II. U.S. Urban Renewal Administration. Urban Planning Assistance Program.

711.14
(76824)
M12
Tennessee. State Planning Commission.
McKenzie, Tenn. Municipal-Regional Planning Commission.
Land use survey and analysis for McKenzie, Tennessee. Assisted by the Tennessee State Planning Commission, West Tennessee Office. McKenzie, 1957.
16p. map, tables.

U.S. Urban Renewal Administration,
(Continued on next card)

711.14
(76812)
R42
Ridgely, Tenn. Municipal-Regional Planning Commission. Land use ... (Card 2)

1. Land use - Ridgely, Tenn. I. Tennessee. State Planning Commission. II. U.S. Urban Renewal Administration. Urban Planning Assistance Program.

711.73
(76815)
D92
Tennessee. State Planning Commission.
Dyersburg, Tenn. Regional Planning Commission.
Major road plan for Dyersburg planning region. [With the assistance of the Tennessee State Planning Commission, West Tennessee Office] Dyersburg, 1956.
8p. maps.

U.S. Urban Renewal Administration, Urban Planning Assistance Program.
(Continued on next card)

711.14
(76824)
M12
McKenzie, Tenn. Municipal-Regional Planning Commission. Land use ...(Card 2)

Urban Planning Assistance Program.
1. Land use - McKenzie, Tenn. I. Tennessee. State Planning Commission. II. U.S. Urban Renewal Administration. Urban Planning Assistance Program.

711.14
(76842)
T25£
Tennessee. State Planning Commission.
Lawrenceburg land use survey. Lawrenceburg, Tenn., 1958.
1v. maps.

U.S. Urban Renewal Administration, Urban Planning Assistance Program.
1. Land use - Maps - Lawrenceburg, Tenn. I. U.S. URA-UPAP. Lawrenceburg, Tenn.

711.73
(76815)
D92
Dyersburg, Tenn. Regional Planning Commission. Major road plan for Dyersburg...(Card 2)

1. Highways - Dyersburg, Tenn. 2. Street planning - Dyersburg, Tenn. I. Tennessee. State Planning Commission. II. U.S. Urban Renewal Administration. Urban Planning Assistance Program.

711.14
(76823)
M45
Tennessee. State Planning Commission.
Milan, Tenn. Municipal-Regional Planning Commission.
Land use survey and analysis for Milan, Tennessee. With the assistance of the Tennessee State Planning Commission, West Tennessee Office. Milan, 1957.
15p. map, tables.

U.S. Urban Renewal Administration, Urban Planning Assistance Program.
(Continued on next card)

312
(76854)
L21
Tennessee. State Planning Commission.
Lebanon, Tenn. Municipal-Regional Planning Commission.
Lebanon's population and economy. Assisted by the Tennessee State Planning Commission, Middle Tennessee Office. Lebanon, 1957.
28p. diagrs., tables. (MTO publication no. 57-35)

U.S. Urban Renewal Administration,
(Continued on next card)

711.73
(76815)
N28
Tennessee. State Planning Commission.
Newbern, Tenn. Municipal-Regional Planning Commission.
Major road plan for Newbern planning region. With the assistance of the Tennessee State Planning Commission, West Tennessee Office. Newbern, 1957.
10p. map.

U.S. Urban Renewal Administration, Urban
Continued on next card)

711.14
(76823)
M45
Milan, Tenn. Municipal-Regional Planning Commission. Land use ... (Card 2)

1. Land use - Milan, Tenn. I. Tennessee. State Planning Commission. II. U.S. Urban Renewal Administration. Urban Planning Assistance Program.

312
(76854)
L21
Lebanon, Tenn. Municipal-Regional Planning Commission. Lebanon's ...(Card 2)

Urban Planning Assistance Program.
1. Population - Lebanon, Tenn. 2. Economic conditions - Lebanon, Tenn. I. Tennessee. State Planning Commission. II. U.S. Urban Renewal Administration. Urban Planning Assistance Program.

711.73
(76815)
N28
Newbern, Tenn. Municipal-Regional Planning Commission. Major road ... (Card 2)

Planning Assistance Program.
1. Street planning - Newbern, Tenn. 2. Highways - Newbern, Tenn. I. Tennessee. State Planning Commission. II. U.S. Urban Renewal Administration. Urban Planning Assistance Program.

711.14
(76824)
M17
Tennessee. State Planning Commission.
Martin, Tenn. Regional Planning Commission.
Land use survey and analysis, Martin, Tennessee. With the assistance of the Tennessee State Planning Commission, West Tennessee Office. Martin, 1957.
9p. map, tables.

U.S. Urban Renewal Administration,
(Continued on next card)

711.33
(768)
T25
Tennessee. State Planning Commission.
Local planning in Tennessee.
Nashville. 1940-49, 1951/52, 1956/57
v. illus.

1940/41-2c
1941/42-3c
1942/45-3c
1945/46-3c
1946/46-3c
1948/49-3c
1956/57-3c

1. State planning - Tenn. 2. City planning - Tenn. 3. County planning - Tenn. I. Title.

711.73
(76861)
P85
Tennessee. State Planning Commission.
Pulaski, Tenn. Municipal-Regional Planning Commission.
Major road plan for Pulaski, Tennessee, by Tennessee State Planning Commission, Middle Tennessee Office. Pulaski, 1958.
18p. diagrs., maps. (MTO Publication no. 58-5)

U.S. Urban Renewal Administration, Urban Planning Assistance Program.
1. Highways - Pulaski, Tenn. I. Tennessee. State Planning Commission. II. U.S. Urban Renewal Administration. Urban Planning Assistance Program. Pulaski, Tenn.

711.14
(76824)
M17
Martin, Tenn. Regional Planning Commission. Land use ...(Card 2)

Urban Planning Assistance Program.
1. Land use - Martin, Tenn. I. Tennessee. State Planning Commission. II. U.S. Urban Renewal Administration. Urban Planning Assistance Program.

711.73
(76828)
B65
Tennessee. State Planning Commission.
Bolivar, Tenn. Municipal-Regional Planning Commission.
Major road plan for Bolivar planning region. With the assistance of the Tennessee State Planning Commission, West Tennessee Office. Bolivar, 1957.
16p. maps.

U.S. Urban Renewal Administration, Urban
(Continued on next card)

711.73
(76824)
821
Tennessee. State Planning Commission.
Sharon, Tenn. Municipal-Regional Planning Commission.
Major road plan for Sharon, Tennessee. With the assistance of the Tennessee State Planning Commission, West Tennessee Office. Sharon, 1957.
12p. maps.

U.S. Urban Renewal Administration, Urban Planning Assistance Program.
(Continued on next card)

711.73
(76284)   Sharon, Tenn. Municipal-Regional Planning
S21   Commission. Major road ... (Card 2)

         1. Highways - Sharon, Tenn. 2. Street
planning - Sharon, Tenn. I. Tennessee. State
Planning Commission. II. U.S. Urban Renewal
Administration. Urban Planning Assistance
Program.

               Tennessee. State Planning Commission.
711.74
(76888)   Sweetwater, Tenn. Regional Planning Commis-
S82   sion.
             Major road plan for the Sweetwater, Tennes-
see planning region. Prepared by Tennessee
State Planning Commission, East Tennessee
Office. Sweetwater, 1958.
   5p. maps.

   U.S. Urban Renewal Administration, Urban
Planning Assistance Program.

               (Continued on next card)

711.74
(76888)   Sweetwater, Tenn. Regional Planning Commis-
S82   sion. Major road... 1958. (Card 2)

         1. Highways - Sweetwater, Tenn. I. Tennes-
see. State Planning Commission. II. U.S.
Urban Renewal Administration. Urban Planning Assistance Program. Sweetwater,
Tenn.

711.74   Tennessee. State Planning Commission.
(76895)   Rogersville, Tenn. Regional Planning Com-
R63   mission.
             Major road plan, Rogersville, Tennessee.
[Prepared by Upper East Tennessee Office,
Tennessee State Planning Commission]
Rogersville, 1958.
   1v. maps.
   U.S. Urban Renewal Administration, Urban
Planning Assistance Program.
   1. Highways - Rogersville, Tenn. I. Ten-
nessee. State Planning Commission. II. U.S.
Urban Renewal Administration. Urban Planning
Assistance   Program. Rogersville,
Tenn.

             Tennessee. State Planning Commission.
711.73
(76823)   Humboldt, Tenn. Municipal-Regional Plan-
H85   ning Commission.
             Major road plan for the Humboldt, Ten-
nessee planning region. With the assistance of the Tennessee State Planning Commission, West Tennessee Office. Humboldt,
1957.
   8p. maps.

   U.S. Urban Renewal Administration,
               (Continued on next
                         card)

711.73
(76823)   Humboldt, Tenn. Municipal-Regional Plan-
H85   ning Commission. Major ... (Card 2)

Urban Planning Assistance Program.

         1. Highways - Humboldt, Tenn.
I. Tennessee. State Planning Commission. II. U.S. Urban Renewal Administration. Urban Planning Assistance
Program.

711.73   Tennessee. State Planning Commission.
(768924) White Pine, Tenn. Regional Planning Com-
W34   mission.
             Major road plan for the White Pine plan-
ning region. Assisted by Tennessee State
Planning Commission, East Tennessee Office. White Pine, 1957.
   5p. diagrs.

   U.S. Urban Renewal Administration,
Urban Planning Assistance Program.

               (Continued on next card)

711.73
(76892u) White Pine, Tenn. Regional Planning Com-
W34   mission. Major road ... (Card 2)

         1. Street planning - White Pine, Tenn.
I. Tennessee. State Planning Commission.
II. U.S. Urban Renewal Administration.
Urban Planning Assistance Program.

             Tennessee. State Planning Commission.
711.73
(76856)   Franklin, Tenn. Municipal Planning Com-
F71   mission.
             Major road plan, Franklin, Tennessee.
Assisted by Tennessee State Planning Commission, Middle Tennessee Office. Franklin, 1957.
   13p. maps. (MTO PPublication no. 57-28)

   U.S. Urban Renewal Administration, Urban
               (Continued on next
                         card)

711.73
(76856)   Franklin, Tenn. Municipal Planning Com-
F71   mission. Major road ... (Card 2)

Planning Assistance Program.

         1. Highways - Franklin, Tenn. I. Ten-
nessee. State Planning Commission.
II. U.S. Urban Renewal Administration.
Urban Planning Assistance Program.

             Tennessee, State Planning Commission.
711.73
(768585) Lewisburg, Tenn. Planning Commission.
L28   Major road plan, Lewisburg, Tennessee.
Assisted by Tennessee State Planning
Commission, Lewisburg, 1956.
   7p. map. (MTO Publication no. 56-6)
   U.S. Urban Renewal Administration, Urban
Planning Assistance Program.

   1. Highways - Lewisburg, Tenn. I.
Tennessee, State Planning Commission.
II. U.S. Urban Renewal Administration.

             Tennessee. State Planning Commission.
711.73
(76873)   Clinton, Tenn. Regional Planning Commis-
C54   sion.
             Major road plan of the Clinton, Tennessee,
planning region. Assisted by the Tennessee
State Planning Commission, East Tennessee
Office. Clinton, 1957.
   15p. maps.
   U.S. Urban Renewal Administration,
Urban Planning Assistance Program.
               (Continued on next card)

711.73
(76873)   Clinton, Tenn. Regional Planning Com-
C54   mission. Major road ... (Card 2)

         1. Highways - Clinton, Tenn. 2. Street
planning - Clinton, Tenn. I. Tennessee. State Planning Commission. II.
U.S. Urban Renewal Administration. Urban
Planning Assistance Program.

             Tennessee. State Planning Commission.
711.74
(768865) Athens, Tenn. Regional Planning Commission.
A73   Major street plan, Athens, Tennessee.
[Assisted by] Tennessee State Planning Com-
mission, Southeast Tennessee Office.
Athens, 1957.
   13p. maps.
   U.S. Urban Renewal Administration,
Urban Planning Assistance Program.
   1. Street planning - Athens, Tenn. 2.
Business districts - Athens, Tenn. I.
Tennessee. State Planning Commission. II. U.S.
Urban Renewal Administration. Urban Plan-
ning Assistance   Program.

             Tennessee. State Planning Commission.
711.74
(76885)   Maryville, Tenn. Regional Planning
M17   Commission.
             Major streets in Maryville. Assisted
by Tennessee State Planning Commission,
East Tennessee Office. Maryville, 1957.
   12p. maps.

   U.S. Urban Renewal Administration,
Urban Planning Assistance Program.
               (Continued on next card)

711.74
(76885)   Maryville, Tenn. Regional Planning Com-
M17   mission. Major streets ... (Card 2)

         1. Street planning - Maryville, Tenn.
I. Tennessee. State Planning Commission. II. U.S. Urban Renewal Administration. Urban Planning Assistance Program.

             Tennessee. State Planning Commission.
330
(76864)   Manchester, Tenn. Regional Planning
M15   Commission.
             Manchester's economic base. Prepared
by Tennessee State Planning Commission,
Middle Tennessee Office. Manchester,
1957.
   38p. diagrs., tables. (MTO Publication
no. 57-38)

   U.S. Urban Renewal Administration, Urban
               (Continued on next
                         card)

330
(76864)   Manchester, Tenn. Regional Planning Com-
M15   mission. Manchester's ... (Card 2)

Planning Assistance Program.

         1. Economic base studies - Manchester,
Tenn. I. Tennessee. State Planning Commission. II. U.S. Urban Renewal Administration. Urban Planning Assistance Program.

353
(768)   Tennessee. State Planning Commission.
T25m   Manual on capital budgeting. Nashville,
1960.
   63p. (Its Publication no. 308)

   1. State finance - Tennessee.

526.8   Tennessee. State Planning Commission.
(76824)   Martin, Tenn. Regional Planning Commis-
M17   sion.
             Martin base map, Martin, Tennessee. With
the assistance of the Tennessee State Planning Commission, West Tennessee Office.
Martin, 1957.
   3p. map.

   U.S. Urban Renewal Administration,
               (Continued on next
                         card)

526.8
(76824)   Martin, Tenn. Regional Planning Commis-
M17   sion. Martin base map,... (Card 2)

Urban Planning Assistance Program.

         1. Maps and mapping - Martin, Tenn.
I. Tennessee. State Planning Commission.
II. U.S. Urban Renewal Administration.
Urban Planning Assistance Program.

Tennessee. State Planning Commission.

330 Maryville, Tenn. Municipal Planning Commis-
(76885) sion.
M17   Maryville: its people and economy. Assisted
by Tennessee State Planning Commission, East
Tennessee Office. Maryville, 1957.
45p. diagrs., maps, tables.
U.S. Urban Renewal Administration, Urban
Planning Assistance Program.
1. Economic conditions - Maryville, Tenn.
2. Population - Maryville, Tenn. I. Tennessee. State Planning Commission. II. U.S.
Urban Renewal Administration. Urban Planning
Assistance   Program.

526.8
(76892) Tennessee. State Planning Commission.
T25   Morristown, Tennessee base maps. Morris-
town, 1956.
1v. maps.
U.S. Urban Renewal Administration, Urban
Planning Assistance Program.
1. Morristown, Tenn. - Maps.
I. U.S. Urban Renewal Administration,
Urban Planning Assistance Program.

711.14
(76857) Murfreesboro, Tenn. Regional Planning Com-
M87   mission. Murfreesboro land ... (Card 2)

Planning Assistance Program.

1. Land use - Murfreesboro, Tenn. I. Ten-
nessee. State Planning Commission. II. U.S.
Urban Renewal Administration. Urban Planning
Assistance Program.

526.8
(76885) Tennessee. State Planning Commission.
T25   Maryville, Tennessee base maps. Maryville,
1956.
1v. maps.
U.S. Urban Renewal Administration, Urban
Planning Assistance Program.
1. Maps and mapping - Maryville, Tenn.
I. U.S. Urban Renewal Administration.
Urban Planning Assistance Program.

VF - Municipal services
DATE OF REQUEST 9/25/53   OCT 12 1953 CARD NO.
AUTHOR
Tennessee. State Planning Commission.
TITLE
Municipal services to fringe area residents, a survey
of Tennessee practices.
SERIES

EDITION   PUB. DATE 1953   PAGING 37 p.
PUBLISHER

RECOMMENDED BY   REVIEWED IN
MML   AC 9/53 p.165
                        ORDER RECORD

DATE OF REQUEST 10/20/52 NOV 7 1952 CARD NO.
AUTHOR
Tennessee. State Planning Commission.
TITLE
Murfreesboro, Tenn. - Capital budget. A six-year
program of public improvements.
SERIES   No. 237.

EDITION   PUB. DATE May 1952   PAGING 61 p.
PUBLISHER   same

RECOMMENDED BY   REVIEWED IN
                        Pity p. 377 10/52
                        ORDER RECORD

Tennessee. State Planning Commission.

727.1 Maryville, Tenn. Municipal Planning Commis-
(76885) sion.
M17   Maryville's school program. Prepared by
the East Tennessee Office, Tennessee State
Planning Commission. Maryville, 1957.
39p. maps.

U.S. Urban Renewal Administration, Urban
Planning Assistance Program.
1. Schools - Maryville, Tenn. I. Tennessee.
State Planning Commission. II. U.S. Urban
Renewal Administration. Urban Planning Assist-
ance Program.

711.5
(76867) Tennessee. State Planning Commission.
:347)   Municipal zoning ordinance, Cookeville,
T25   Tennessee, 1969. Nashville, 1969.
41p.
Cover title.
U.S. Dept. of Housing and Urban Development. UPAP. HUD project no. Tenn. P-97.
1. Zoning legislation - Cookeville, Tenn.
I. U.S. HUD-UPAP. Cookeville, Tenn.
II. Title.

Tennessee. State Planning Commission.

727.1 Murfreesboro, Tenn. Regional Planning Com-
(76857) mission.
M87   Murfreesboro's public schools, a survey
and plan. With technical assistance provided
by the Middle Tennessee Office, Tennessee
State Planning Commission. Murfreesboro,
1957.
40p. illus., diagrs., maps, tables.

U.S. Urban Renewal Administration, Urban

(Continued on next card)

711.14
(768) Tennessee. State Planning Commission.
T27   Melton Hill reservoir, comprehensive
plan for land use development. Nashville, Tenn., 1960.
82p. maps. (Its Publication no. 310)

1. Land use - Tennessee.

Tennessee. State Planning Commission.

711.14 Murfreesboro, Tenn. Regional Planning
(76857) Commission.
M87m   Murfreesboro future land use plan. With
assistance of the Tennessee State Planning
Commission, Middle Tennessee Office. Murfreesboro, 1958.
18p. maps. (MTO Publication no. 58-20)
U.S. Urban Renewal Administration, Urban
Planning Assistance Program.
1. Land use - Murfreesboro, Tenn. I. Tennessee. State Planning Commission. II. U.S.
Urban Renewal Administration. Urban
Planning   Assistance Program.

727.1 Murfreesboro, Tenn. Regional Planning
(76857) Commission. Murfreesboro's public
M87   schools, a survey ... (Card 2)

Planning Assistance Program.

1. Schools - Murfreesboro, Tenn. I. Ten-
nessee. State Planning Commission. II. U.S.
Urban Renewal Administration. Urban Planning
Assistance Program.

690.091.82
:613.5
(768) Tennessee. State Planning Commission.
T25   A minimum housing ordinance: suggested
standards for small Tennessee communities.
1956.
22 p.

1. Housing codes - Tenn.
3c

Tennessee. State Planning Commission

728.1 Murfreesboro, Tenn. Regional Planning Com-
(76857) mission.
M87   Murfreesboro housing survey and neighborhood analyses; a study which examines the extent and causes of substandard housing and
proposes action on a broad front to eliminate
slums and protect sound neighborhoods from the
spread of blight. [In cooperation with] the
Murfreesboro Housing Authority. Murfreesboro, 1958.
1v. maps. (MTO Publication no. 58-3)

(Continued on next
card)

711.581
(76895) Tennessee. State Planning Commission.
R63   Rogersville, Tenn. Regional Planning
Commission.
Neighborhood analysis, Rogersville,
Tennessee. A staff report to the Rogers-
ville Regional Planning Commission, by Upper
East Tennessee Office, Tennessee State
Planning Commission. Rogersville, 1959.
21p. illus., maps, table.

U.S. Urban Renewal Administration, Urban
Planning Assistance Program.

1. Neighborhood plan-   ning - Rogersville, Tenn.
I. Tennessee. State   Planning Commission.
II. U.S. URA-UPAP.   Rogersville, Tenn.

---

330 Tennessee. State Planning Commission.
(76892) Morristown, Tenn. Regional Planning Commission.
M67   Morristown, its people and economy. Assisted
by the Tennessee State Planning Commission.
Morristown, 1956.
22p. tables.

U.S. Urban Renewal Administration, Urban
Planning Assistance Program.

1. Economic base studies - Morristown, Tenn.
2. City growth - Morristown, Tenn. I. Tennessee. State Planning Commission. II. U.S.
Urban Renewal Administration. Urban Planning
Assistance Pro-   gram.

728.1 Murfreesboro, Tenn. Regional Planning Com-
(76857) mission. Murfreesboro housing ...1958(Card 2)
M87
U.S. Urban Renewal Administration, Urban
Planning Assistance Program.
"With the assistance of the Tennessee State
Planning Commission, Middle Tennessee Office."
1. Housing surveys - Murfreesboro, Tenn.
2. Neighborhood rehabilitation - Murfrees-
boro, Tenn. I. Tennessee. State Planning
Commission. II. Murfreesboro, Tenn. Housing
Authority. III.   U.S. Urban Renewal Ad-
ministration.   Urban Planning Assist-
ance Program.

711.581
(76845) Tennessee. State Planning Commission.
C51   Clarksville, Tenn. Regional Planning
Commission.
Neighborhood analyses and plan for
residential neighborhood units, Clarks-
ville, Tennessee. A staff report by the
Tennessee State Planning Commission to the
Clarksville Regional Planning Commission."
Clarksville, 1957.
100p. maps, tables. (MTO publication
no. 57-43)

U.S. Urban Renewal Administration,
(Continued on next card)

727.1 Tennessee. State Planning Commission.
(76892) Morristown, Tenn. Regional Planning Commis-
M67   sion.
Morristown school report. Assisted by the
Tennessee State Planning Commission. Morristown, 1956.
13p. diagrs., maps.

U.S. Urban Renewal Administration, Urban
Planning Assistance Program.
1. Schools - Morristown, Tenn. I. Tennessee.
State Planning Commission. II. U.S. Urban Renewal Administration. Urban Planning Assistance Program.

Tennessee. State Planning Commission.

711.14
(76857) Murfreesboro, Tennessee. Regional Planning
M87   Commission.
Murfreesboro land use survey and analysis.
Prepared by the Tennessee State Planning
Commission, Middle Tennessee Office.
Murfreesboro, 1957.
9p. maps. (MTO publication no. 57-29)

U.S. Urban Renewal Administration, Urban

(Continued on next card)

711.581
(76845) Clarksville, Tenn. Regional Planning Com-
C51   mission. Neighborhood ... (Card 2)

Urban Planning Assistance Program.

1. Neighborhood planning - Clarksville,
Tenn. I. Title. II. Tennessee. State Plan-
ning Commission. III. U.S. Urban Renewal
Administration. Urban Planning Assistance
Program.

711.585
(76847)
G15

Tennessee. State Planning Commission.
Gallatin, Tenn. Municipal-Regional
Planning Commission.
A neighborhood analysis for Gallatin,
Tennessee. Prepared by Tennessee State
Planning Commission, Middle Tennessee
Office. Gallatin, 1957.
19p. map. (MTO Publication no.
57-48)

U.S. Urban Renewal Administration,

(Continued on next
card)

526.8
(768695)
T25

Tennessee. State Planning Commission.
Newport, Tennessee: base map. Newport,
1958.
1v. maps.

U.S. Urban Renewal Administration, Urban
Planning Assistance Program.

1. Maps and mapping - Newport, Tenn.
I. U.S. URA-UPAP.

712.25
(76879)
T25

Tennessee. State Planning Commission.
A plan for development, Nickajack
reservoir area. [Prepared in cooperation
with] Marion County Planning Commission
and Tennessee Valley Authority.
Nashville, 1965.
88p.

1. Recreation - Marion Co., Tenn.
2. Open space land. 3. County planning -
Marion Co., Tenn. I. Marion County,
Tenn. Planning Commission.
II. Tennessee Valley Authority.

711.585
(76847)
G15

Gallatin, Tenn. Municipal-Regional Planning Commission. A neighbor- ...(Card 2)

Urban Planning Assistance Program.

1. Neighborhood rehabilitation -
Gallatin, Tenn. I. Tennessee. State
Planning Commission. II. U.S. Urban
Renewal Administration. Urban Plan-
ning Assistance Program.

711.4
(768)
T25n

Tennessee. State Planning Commission.
Newsletters, brochures, summary of
activities. Tenn. P-118 project. Nashville,
1969-70.
1v.
Partial contents.-Community problems in
town and country.-Your town considers: Planning,
zoning, subdivision control, capital improvements.-Tennessee. State Planning Commission.
Local planning news: vol. 1, nos. 3-6, May-Dec.,
1969; vol. 2, nos. 1-4, Jan.-April, 1970.
1. City planning - Tenn. 2. State planning -
Tenn.

711.74
(76883)
D19

Tennessee. State Planning Commission.
Dayton, Tenn. Municipal Planning Commission.
A plan for street naming and property numbering in Dayton, Tennessee. Assisted by the
Tennessee State Planning Commission, East Tennessee Office. Dayton, 1957.
4p. map.

U.S. Urban Renewal Administration, Urban
Planning Assistance Program.

(Continued on next card)

711.581
(76854)
L21

Tennessee. State Planning Commission.
Lebanon, Tenn. Municipal-Regional Planning Commission.
A neighborhood analysis for Lebanon,
Tennessee. Assisted by the Tennessee
State Planning Commission, Middle Tennessee Office. Lebanon, 1958.
28p. maps. (MTO Publication no. 58-
26)

U.S. Urban Renewal Administration, Urban Planning Assistance Program.

1. Neighborhood planning - Lebanon, Tenn. I. Tennessee. State Plan- ning Commission.
II. U.S. URA-UPAP. Lebanon, Tenn.

526.8
(76884)
R61

Tennessee. State Planning Commission
Roane County, Tenn. Regional Planning Commission.
Oliver Springs, Tennessee base maps. Prepared by East Tennessee Office, Tennessee
State Planning Commission. Oliver Springs,
1958.
1v. maps.

U.S. Urban Renewal Administration, Urban
Planning Assistance Program.

1. Maps and mapping - Oliver Springs, Tenn.
I. Tennessee. State Planning Commission.
II. U.S. Urban Renewal Administration.
Urban Planning Assistance Program.
Oliver Springs, Te...

711.74
(76883)
D19

Dayton, Tenn. Municipal Planning Commission. A plan for ... (Card 2)

1. Streets - Dayton, Tenn. 2. House numbering. I. Tennessee. State Planning
Commission. II. U.S. Urban Renewal Administration. Urban Planning Assistance
Program.

711.585
(76856)
F71

Tennessee. State Planning Commission.
Franklin, Tenn. Municipal Planning Commission.
A neighborhood analysis of Franklin,
Tennessee. Prepared by the Tennessee
State Planning Commission, Middle Tennessee Office. Franklin, 1957.
23p. maps, tables. (MTO Publication no. 57-49)

U.S. Urban Renewal Administration,
(Continued on next
card)

711.74
(76834)
P17p

Tennessee. State Planning Commission.
Paris, Tenn. Municipal Planning Commission.
Paris, Tennessee street classification and
improvement program. Prepared by the West
Tennessee Office, Tennessee State Planning
Commission. Paris, 1957.
28p. maps, tables.

U.S. Urban Renewal Administration,
Urban Planning Assistance Program.

(Continued on next card)

4406
4407
4408

TENNESSEE. STATE PLANNING COMMISSION.
JONESBORO, TENN. REGIONAL PLANNING
COMMISSION.
PLANNING: 1, LAND USE; 2, SUMMARY OF
LAND USE PLAN; 3, ANNUAL REPORT. BY
TENNESSEE STATE PLANNING COMMISSION.
JONESBORO, TENN., 1969.
3 V. (HUD 701 REPORT)

1. LAND USE - JONESBORO, TENN.
2. CITY PLANNING - JONESBORO, TENN.
I. TENNESSEE. STATE PLANNING COMMISSION.
II. HUD. 701. JONESBORO, TENN.

711.585
(76856)
F71

Franklin, Tenn. Municipal Planning Commission. A neighborhood ... (Card 2)

Urban Planning Assistance Program.

1. Neighborhood rehabilitation - Franklin, Tenn. I. Tennessee. State Planning
Commission. II. U.S. Urban Renewal Administration, Urban Planning Assistance
Program.

711.74
(76834)
P17p

Paris, Tenn. Municipal Planning Commission.
Paris, Tennessee street ... (Card 2)

1. Streets - Paris, Tenn. I. Tennessee.
State Planning Commission. II. U.S. Urban
Renewal Administration. Urban Planning
Assistance Program.

627.4
(768585)
T25

Tennessee. State Planning Commission.
(Middle Tennessee Office)
Planning for flood damage prevention, Lewisburg,
Tennessee. [Lewisburg] June 1956.
37 p. maps, tables. (Its MTO publication
no. 56-12)
c. 2. Reprint of June 1956 as TSPC publication no. 277.
1. Flood control - Lewisburg, Tenn. 2. City
planning - Lewisburg, Tenn.

711.14
(76815)
N28

Tennessee. State Planning Commission.
Newbern, Tenn. Municipal-Regional Planning
Commission.
Newbern land use survey and analysis, New-
bern, Tennessee. With the assistance of the
Tennessee State Planning Commission, West
Tennessee Office. Newbern, 1957.
13p. map.

U.S. Urban Renewal Administration, Urban
(Continued on next card)

711.729
P17

Tennessee. State Planning Commission.
Paris, Tenn. Municipal Planning Commission.
Parking and traffic study for central business district, Paris, Tennessee. (Proposed)
Prepared by the West Tennessee Office, Tennessee State Planning Commission. Paris, 1957.
11p. maps, tables.

U.S. Urban Renewal Administration, Urban
Planning Assistance Program.

(Continued on next card)

712.25
(768)
T25P

TENNESSEE. STATE PLANNING COMMISSION.
PLANNING FOR RECREATION. NASHVILLE,
1953.
37P. (ITS PUBLICATION NO. 252)

1. RECREATION - TENNESSEE. I. TITLE.

711.14
(76815)
N28

Newbern, Tenn. Municipal-Regional Planning
Commission. Newbern land ... (Card 2)

Planning Assistance Program.

1. Land use - Newbern, Tenn. I. Tennessee. State Planning Commission. II. U.S.
Urban Renewal Administration. Urban Planning Assistance Program.

711.729
P17

Paris, Tenn. Municipal Planning Commission.
Parking and traffic study ... (Card 2)

1. Parking - Paris, Tenn. 2. Business districts - Paris, Tenn. I. Tennessee. State
Planning Commission. II. U.S. Urban Renewal Administration. Urban Planning
Assistance Program.

VF - Recreation planning

DATE OF REQUEST 8/18/53   L.C. CARD NO.

AUTHOR
Tennessee. State Planning Commission.

TITLE
Planning for recreation - a guide for Tennessee
communities.

SERIES

EDITION   PUB. DATE June 1953   PAGING 37 p.
PUBLISHER

RECOMMENDED BY   REVIEWED IN
    MWL   City 8/53 p.159
ORDER RECORD

Row 1

371.7
(76887)
C52

Tennessee. State Planning Commission.
Cleveland, Tenn. Planning Commission.
Planning for recreation, a study of the recreational facilities and programs of Cleveland, Tennessee. With Tennessee State Planning Commission, East Tennessee Office. Cleveland, 1957.
43p. maps, tables.

U.S. Urban Renewal Administration, Urban

(Continued on next card)

3970

TENNESSEE. STATE PLANNING COMMISSION.
POPULATION IN TENNESSEE. NASHVILLE,
1970.
1 V. (HUD 701 REPORT)

1. POPULATION - TENN. I. HUD. 701.
TENNESSEE.

Class No.	Author (surname first) Tennessee State Planning
Industrial location	Commission
Accession No.	Title Potential plant sites in East
Ordered JUN 3 0 1950	Tennessee
Source ttv	Place Nashville 3 Publisher Industrial Development
Received JUL 1 2 1950	Div.
	Address 717 7th Ave. N.
Purchase Order No.	Date 1946 Paging 6 List Price Est. Cost gratis
Date	Edition or Series
L. C. No.	Recommended by
	Reviewed in Ind. Rev. Dema. 1948-49

H-305 (2-50) HOUSING AND HOME FINANCE AGENCY Office of the Administrator 10-61167-1 GPO

Row 2

371.7
(76887)
C52

Cleveland, Tenn. Planning Commission.
Planning for recreation, ... (Card 2)

Planning Assistance Program.

1. Recreation - Cleveland, Tenn. I. Tennessee. State Planning Commission. II. U.S. Urban Renewal Administration. Urban Planning Assistance Program.

711.4
:312
(76815)
D92

Tennessee. State Planning Commission.
Dyersburg, Tenn. Regional Planning Commission.
Population study for Dyersburg. [Assisted by the Tennessee State Planning Commission, West Tennessee Office] Dyersburg, 1956.
[19]p. maps, diagrs.

U.S. Urban Renewal Administration, Urban Planning Assistance Program.

1. City planning - Dyersburg, Tenn. 2. Population - Dyersburg, Tenn. I. Tennessee. State Planning Commission. II. U.S. Urban Renewal Administration. Urban Planning Assistance Program.

711.14
(76867)
C66

Tennessee. State Planning Commission.
Cookeville, Tenn. Regional Planning Commission.
A preliminary land use plan for the Cookeville region. Prepared by the Tennessee State Planning Commission, Middle Tennessee Office. Cookeville, 1957.
11p. maps. (MT publication no. 57-31)

U.S. Urban Renewal Administration, Urban

(Continued on next card)

Row 3

712.25
(768984)
E54

Tennessee. State Planning Commission.
Elizabethton, Tenn. Regional Planning Commission.
Planning for recreation. A survey prepared for ... by the Upper East Tennessee Office, Tennessee State Planning Commission. Elizabethton, 1956.
55p. maps, tables.

U.S. Urban Renewal Administration, Urban Planning Assistance Program.

(Continued on next card)

312
(76824)
M12

Tennessee. State Planning Commission.
McKenzie, Tenn. Municipal-Regional Planning Commission.
Population study for McKenzie, Tennessee. Assisted by the Tennessee State Planning Commission, West Tennessee Office. McKenzie, 1957.
22p. diagrs., maps, tables.

U.S. Urban Renewal Administration, Urban

(Continued on next card)

711.14
(76867)
C66

Cookeville, Tenn. Regional Planning Commission. A preliminary ... (Card 2)

Planning Assistance Program.

1. Land use - Cookeville, Tenn. I. Tennessee. State Planning Commission. II. U.S. Urban Renewal Administration. Urban Planning Assistance Program.

Row 4

712.25
(768984)
E54

Elizabethton, Tenn. Regional Planning Commission. Planning for ... (Card 2)

1. Recreation - Elizabethton, Tenn. I. Tennessee. State Planning Commission. II. U.S. Urban Renewal Administration. Urban Planning Assistance Program.

312
(76824)
M12

McKenzie, Tenn. Municipal-Regional Planning Commission. Population ... (Card 2)

1. Population - McKenzie, Tenn. I. Tennessee. State Planning Commission. II. U.S. Urban Renewal Administration. Urban Planning Assistance Program.

352.1
(768)
T25p

Tennessee. State Planning Commission.
Preparing a municipal capital budget; a TSPC staff guide. Prepared by Jerry P. Lee and others. Nashville, 1966.
54p. (Its Publication no. 340)

1. Municipal finance - Tennessee.
2. State finance - Tennessee. I. Lee, Jerry P. II. Title.

Row 5

628.44
(768)
T25

TENNESSEE. STATE PLANNING COMMISSION.
PLANNING GARBAGE AND REFUSE FACILITIES FOR THE SMALL COMMUNITY.
NASHVILLE, TENN., 1948.
34P.

1. REFUSE AND REFUSE DISPOSAL - TENNESSEE.

312
(76813)
U54

Tennessee. State Planning Commission.
Union City, Tenn. Regional Planning Commission.
Population study for Union City. Assisted by the Tennessee State Planning Commission, West Tennessee Office. Union City, 1956.
16p. tables.

U.S. Urban Renewal Administration, Urban Planning Assistance Program.

1. Population - Union City, Tenn. I. Tennessee. State Planning Commission. II. U.S. Urban Renewal Administration. Urban Planning Assistance Program.

3971

TENNESSEE. STATE PLANNING COMMISSION.
A PROGRAM FOR STATE PLANNING IN TENNESSEE. NASHVILLE, 1968.
96L. (HUD 701 REPORT)

1. STATE PLANNING - TENNESSEE.
I. HUD. 701. TENNESSEE.

Row 6

312
:330
(768)
T25

Tennessee. State Planning Commission.
Population and economy, an analysis, Humboldt, Milan, Trenton. Jackson, 1958.
92p. diagrs., maps, tables.

U.S. Urban Renewal Administration, Urban Planning Assistance Program.

Prepared for Humboldt Municipal-Regional Planning Commission, Milan Municipal-

(Continued on next card)

312
(76824)
M17

Tennessee. State Planning Commission.
Martin, Tenn. Regional Planning Commission.
Population study, Martin, Tennessee. With the assistance of the Tennessee State Planning Commission, West Tennessee Office. Martin, 1957.
19p. diagrs., tables.

U.S. Urban Renewal Administration, Urban

(Continued on next card)

711.4
:352.6
(768865)
A73

Tennessee. State Planning Commission.
Athens, Tenn. Regional Planning Commission.
Programming public improvements. [Assisted by Tennessee State Planning Commission, Division of State Planning] Athens, 1956.
37p. tables.

U.S. Urban Renewal Administration, Urban Planning Assistance Program.

1. City planning - Athens, Tenn. 2. Municipal services - Athens, Tenn. I. Tennessee. State Planning Commission. II. U.S. Urban Renewal Administration.

Row 7

312
:330
(768)
T25

Tennessee. State Planning Commission.
Population and economy ... (Card 2)

Regional Planning Commission, Trenton Municipal-Regional Planning Commission.

1. Population - Tenn. 2. Economic base studies - Tenn. I. U.S. Urban Renewal Administration. Urban Planning Assistance Program.

312
(76824)
M17

Martin, Tenn. Regional Planning Commission. Population ... (Card 2)

Planning Assistance Program.

1. Population - Martin, Tenn. I. Tennessee. State Planning Commission. II. U.S. Urban Renewal Administration. Urban Planning Assistance Program.

711.74
N28

Tennessee. State Planning Commission.
Newbern, Tenn. Municipal Regional Planning Commission.
A property identification system for Newbern, Tennessee. With the assistance of the Tennessee State Planning Commission, West Tennessee Office. Newbern, 1957.
12p. maps.

U.S. Urban Renewal Administration, Urban

(Continued on next card)

711.74
N28
Newbern, Tenn. Municipal Regional Planning
Commission. A property ... (Card 2)

Planning Assistance Program.

1. House numbering.   I. Tennessee.
State Planning Commission. II. U.S. Urban
Renewal Administration. Urban Planning
Assistance Program.

711.74
(76896)
B74
Tennessee. State Planning Commission.
Bristol, Tenn. Planning Commission.
Proposed revision of city major
street plan, planning region major road
plan for Bristol, Tennessee. Prepared by
the Upper East Tennessee Office, Tennessee State Planning Commission.
Bristol, 1957.
25p. diagrs., maps.

U.S. Urban Renewal Administration,
(Continued on next card)

333.38
(76837)
N28
Tennessee. State Planning Commission.
New Johnsonville, Tenn. Regional Plan-
ning Commission.
Proposed subdivision regulations, New
Johnsonville, Tennessee. Assisted by the
Tennessee State Planning Commission, Middle
Tennessee Office. New Johnsonville, 1957.
18p. forms, map. (MTO publication
no. 57-24)

U.S. Urban Renewal Administration, Urban
(Continued on next card)

627.4
(76873)
C54
Tennessee. State Planning Commission.
Clinton, Tenn. City Planning Commission.
Proposals for adjusting to flood
conditions at Clinton, Tennessee, ...
assisted by Tennessee State Planning
Commission. Clinton, Tenn., July 1956.
12 p. maps.

1. Flood control - Clinton, Tenn.
2. City planning - Clinton, Tenn.
I. Tennessee. State Planning Commission.

711.74
(76896)
B74
Bristol, Tenn. Planning Commission. Proposed revision of ... (Card 2)

Urban Planning Assistance Program.

1. Street planning - Bristol, Tenn.
2. Highways - Bristol, Tenn.   I. Tennessee. State Planning Commission.
II. U.S. Urban Renewal Administration.
Urban Planning Assistance Program.

333.38
(76837)
N28
New Johnsonville, Tenn. Regional Planning
Commission. Proposed ... (Card 2)

Planning Assistance Program.

1. Subdivision regulation - New Johnsonville, Tenn.   I. Tennessee. State Planning Commission. II. U.S. Urban Renewal
Administration. Urban Planning Assistance
Program.

690.091.82
:613.5
(76815)
D92
Tennessee. State Planning Commission.
Dyersburg, Tenn. Regional Planning Commission.
Proposed housing code for Dyersburg, Tennes-
see. Prepared by the Tennessee State Planning
Commission, West Tennessee Office. Dyersburg,
1957.
20p.
U.S. Urban Renewal Administration, Urban
Planning Assistance Program.
1. Housing codes - Dyersburg, Tenn.   I. Ten-
nessee. State Planning Commission. II. U.S.
Urban Renewal Administration. Urban Planning
Assistance Program.

627.4
(76896)
K45
Tennessee. State Planning Commission.
Kingsport, Tenn. Planning Commission.
Proposed revisions to zoning ordinance
and subdivision regulations for adjusting
to flood conditions at Kingsport, Tennessee...
assisted by Tennessee State Planning Commission. [Kingsport, Tenn.] June 1956.
[9] p. charts, maps.

(See Card No. 2)

333.38
(76873)
N67
Tennessee. State Planning Commission.
Norris, Tenn. Municipal Planning Commis-
sion.
Proposed subdivision standards, Norris,
Tennessee. Prepared by East Tennessee
Office, Tennessee State Planning Commis-
sion. Norris, 1957.
19p.

U.S. Urban Renewal Administration, Urban
Planning Assistance Program.
(Continued on next card)

711.74
(76834)
P17
Tennessee. State Planning Commission.
Paris, Tenn. Municipal Planning Commission.
Proposed major street plan, Paris, Tenn-
essee. [Prepared] by the West Tennessee
Office, Tennessee State Planning Commission.
Paris, 1958.
11p.

U.S. Urban Renewal Administration, Urban
Planning Assistance Program.

1. Street planning - Paris, Tenn.   I. Tenn-
essee. State Planning Commission. II. U.S.
Urban Renewal Administration.   Urban Planning
Assistance pro-   gram.

627.4
(76896)
K45
Kingsport, Tenn. Planning Commission.
Proposed revisions to zoning...1956.
(Card No. 2)

Partial contents:-Proposals for flood
damage prevention requirements to be
included in the subdivision regulations
for Kingsport, Tenn.

1. Flood control - Kingsport, Tenn.
2. City planning - Kingsport, Tenn. I.
Tennessee. State Planning Commission.

333.38
(76873)
N67
Norris, Tenn. Municipal Planning Commission. Proposed subdivision ... (Card 2)

1. Subdivision regulation - Norris, Tenn.
I. Tennessee. State Planning Commission.
II. U.S. Urban Renewal Administration.
Urban Planning Assistance Program.

711.5
(76815)
:347)
D92
Tennessee. State Planning Commission.
Dyersburg, Tenn. Planning Commission.
Proposed revised zoning ordinance, Dyersburg,
Tennessee. With the assistance of the Tennessee
State Planning Commission. Dyersburg, 1956.
60p. maps, tables.

U.S. Urban Renewal Administration, Urban Planning Assistance Program.

1. Zoning legislation - Dyersburg, Tenn. I.
Tennessee. State Planning Commission. II. U.S.
Urban Renewal Administration. Urban Planning
Assistance Program.

711.74
(768585)
L28
Tennessee. State Planning Commission.
Lewisburg, Tenn. Regional Planning Com-
mission.
Proposed street improvement program for
Lewisburg, Tennessee. Prepared by Middle
Tennessee Office, Tennessee State Plan-
ning Commission. Lewisburg, 1956.
1v. maps, tables. (MTO publication
no. 56-14)

U.S. Urban Renewal Administration, Urban
Planning Assistance Program.
(Continued on next card)

711.4
:711.5
(768865)
A73
1956
Tennessee. State Planning Commission.
Athens, Tenn. Regional Planning Commission.
Proposed zoning ordinance for Athens,
Tennessee. Assisted by the Tennessee State
Planning Commission, East Tennessee Office.
Athens, 1956.
17p. maps.

U.S. Urban Renewal Administration, Urban
Planning Assistance Program.
1. City planning - Athens, Tenn. 2. Zoning
legislation - Athens, Tenn. I. Tennessee.
State Planning Commission. II. U.S. Urban Renewal Administra-   tion.

711.5
(76857
:347)
M87
Tennessee. State Planning Commission.
Murfreesboro, Tenn. Regional Planning
Commission.
Proposed revised zoning ordinance, Mur-
freesboro, Tennessee. Assisted by Middle
Tennessee Office, Tennessee State Plan-
ning Commission. Murfreesboro, 1957.
20p. map. (MTO publication no. 57-26)

U.S. Urban Renewal Administration, Urban
(Continued on next card)

711.74
(768585)
L28
Lewisburg, Tenn. Regional Planning Commission. Proposed street ... (Card 2)

1. Street planning - Lewisburg, Tenn.
I. Tennessee. State Planning Commission.
II. U.S. Urban Renewal Administration.
Urban Planning Assistance Program.

711.5
(76892)
:347)
M67
Tennessee. State Planning Commission.
Morristown, Tenn. Regional Planning Commission.
Proposed zoning ordinance for Morristown,
Tennessee. Assisted by Tennessee State Planning
Commission. Morristown, 1956.
9p. tables.

U.S. Urban Renewal Administration, Urban
Planning Assistance Program.

1. Zoning legislation - Morristown, Tenn.
I. Tennessee. State Planning Commission.
II. U.S. Urban Renewal Administration. Urban
Planning Assistance Program.

711.5
(76857
:347)
M87
Murfreesboro, Tenn. Regional Planning
Commission. Proposed ... (Card 2)

Planning Assistance Program.

1. Zoning legislation - Murfreesboro,
Tenn.   I. Tennessee. State Planning
Commission. II. U.S. Urban Renewal Ad-
ministration. Urban Planning Assistance
Program.

333.38
(76867)
T25
Tennessee. State Planning Commission.
Proposed subdivision regulations for
Cookeville, Tenn. Nashville, Tennessee
State Planning Commission, Middle
Tennessee Office, 1969.
23p.

U.S. Dept. of Housing and Urban Devel-
opment. UPAP. HUD project no. Tenn.
P-97.
1. Subdivision regulation - Cookeville,
Tenn. I.   U.S. HUD-UPAP.
Cookeville,   Tenn. II. Title.

711.5
(76861
:347)
P85
Tennessee. State Planning Commission.
Pulaski, Tenn. Municipal-Regional Planning
Commission.
Proposed zoning ordinance revisions for
Pulaski, Tennessee. [Prepared by Tennessee
State Planning Commission, Middle Tennessee
Office] Pulaski, 1958.
22p. diagrs., maps, tables. (MTO Publi-
cation no. 58-19)
U.S. Urban Renewal Administration, Urban
Planning Assistance Program.
1. Zoning legislation - Pulaski, Tenn.
I. Tennessee. State Planning Commission.
II. U.S. Urban   Renewal Administra-
tion. Urban   Planning Assistance
Program.   Pulaski, Tenn.

4430
4431   TENNESSEE. STATE PLANNING COMMISSION.
MILLINGTON, TENN. MUNICIPAL PLANNING
COMMISSION.
PUBLIC IMPROVEMENT PROGRAM; ANNEXATION
STUDY. BY TENNESSEE STATE PLANNING
COMMISSION. MILLINGTON, TENN., 1964.
2 V. (HUD 701 REPORT)

    1. CITY PLANNING - MILLINGTON, TENN.
I. TENNESSEE. STATE PLANNING COMMISSION.
II. HUD. 701. MILLINGTON, TENN.

712.25
(768)
T25   Tennessee. State Planning Commission. A
public recreation plan...[1962] (Card 2)

    Tennessee; inventory and plan for develop-
ment, 1962-? v. 1. Maps. v. 2. Text.

    U.S. Urban Renewal Adm. UPAP.

    1. Recreation - Tennessee. I. Title.
II. U.S. URA-   UPAP.
Tennessee.

711.3
(76812)
T25   Tennessee. State Planning Commission.
Reelfoot, plan for comprehensive development, by Otis M. Trimble and Walter L.
Criley. Nashville, 1958.
85p. illus., maps. (Its Publication
no. 291)

    1. Regional planning - Reelfoot Lake Area.
I. Trimble, Otis M. II. Criley, Walter L.
III. Title.

352.1
(76854)
L21   Tennessee. State Planning Commission.
Lebanon, Tenn. Municipal-Regional Planning Commission.
Public improvements for Lebanon, Tennessee, by Tennessee State Planning Commission [Middle Tennessee Office] Lebanon,
1957.
45p. tables. (MTO publication no.
57-23)

    U.S. Urban Renewal Administration, Urban

    (Continued on next card)

727.1
(76896)
K45   Tennessee. State Planning Commission.
Kingsport, Tenn. Regional Planning Commis-
sion.
Public schools in the Kingsport area.
Report to the Kingsport Regional Planning
Commission, by the Upper East Office, Ten-
nessee State Planning Commission. [Kings-
port] 1956.
87p. maps, tables.
U.S. Urban Renewal Administration, Urban
Planning Assistance Program.

    (Continued on next card)

711.3
(768)
T25   Tennessee. State Planning Commission.
Regional planning approach for Camden, New
Johnsonville and Waverly. Nashville, 1957.
27p. illus., diagrs., maps.

    U.S. Urban Renewal Administration, Urban
Planning Assistance Program.

    1. Regional planning - Tenn. I. U.S.
Urban Renewal Administration. Urban Planning Assistance Program.

352.1
(76854)
L21   Lebanon, Tenn. Municipal-Regional Planning
Commission. Public ... (Card 2)

    Planning Assistance Program.

    1. Capital improvement programs - Lebanon,
Tenn. I. Tennessee. State Planning Commission. II. U.S. Urban Renewal Administration. Urban Planning Assistance Program.

727.1
(76896)
K45   Kingsport, Tenn. Regional Planning Commission. Public ... (Card 2)

    1. Schools - Kingsport, Tenn. I. Ten-
nessee. State Planning Commission.
II. U.S. Urban Renewal Administration.
Urban Planning Assistance Program.

628.1
(768)
T25r   Tennessee. State Planning Commission.
Reservoir shore line development in
Tennessee; a study of problems and
opportunities. Nashville, 1958.
77p.

    1. Water resources - Tenn. 2. Recreation -
Tenn. 3. Land use - Tenn. I. Title.

352.1
(76864)
T85   Tennessee. State Planning Commission.
Tullahoma, Tenn. Planning Commission.
Public improvements for Tullahoma, Ten-
nessee. Prepared by the Tennessee State
Planning Commission, Middle Tennessee Of-
fice. Tullahoma, 1957.
14p. tables. (MTO publication no. 57-46)
U.S. Urban Renewal Administration, Urban
Planning Assistance Program.
    1. Capital improvement programs - Tullahoma,
    (Continued on next card)

R
711
(016)
T25   Tennessee. State Planning Commission.
Publications of the Tennessee State Planning
Commission, 1950-1959, comp. by Ellen Muhr.
Nashville, 1959.
36p. (Its Publication no. 304)

    1. Planning - Bibliography. I. Muhr,
Ellen, comp.

352.1
(76812)
R42   Tennessee. State Planning Commission.
Ridgely, Tenn. Municipal-Regional Planning
Commission.
Ridgely Tennessee fiscal analysis. Assisted
by Tennessee State Planning Commission.
Ridgely, 1957.
29p. diagrs., tables.
U.S. Urban Renewal Administration, Urban
Planning Assistance Program.
    1. Municipal finance - Ridgely, Tenn. I. Ten-
nessee. State Planning Commission. II. U.S.
Urban Renewal Administration. Urban Planning
Assistance   Program.

352.1
(76864)
T85   Tullahoma, Tenn. Planning Commission.
Public improvements ... (Card 2)

    Tenn. 2. Municipal finance - Tullahoma,
Tenn. I. Tennessee. State Planning Commission. II. U.S. Urban Renewal Administration. Urban Planning Assistance
Program.

711
(016)
T25
1966   Tennessee. State Planning Commission
Publications of the Tennessee State
Planning Commission, 1959-1966, by Nicholas
Beehan and Mamie Ruth Willis. Nashville,
1966.
20p. (Its Publication no. 330)

    1. Planning - Bibl. 2. Tennessee. State
Planning Commission - Publications.
I. Beehan, Nicholas. II. Willis, Mamie Ruth.

526.8
(76884)
R61r   Tennessee. State Planning Commission.
Roane County, Tenn. Regional Planning Commission.
Rockwood, Tennessee base maps. Prepared
by East Tennessee Office, Tennessee State
Planning Commission. Rockwood, 1958.
1v. map.

    U.S. Urban Renewal Administration, Urban
Planning Assistance Program.

    1. Maps and mapping - Rockwood, Tenn. I.
Tennessee. State Planning Commission. II.
U.S. Urban Renewal Administration. Urban
Planning Assist-   ance Program. Rockwood,
Tenn.

371.7
(768885)
M17   Tennessee. State Planning Commission.
Maryville, Tenn. Recreation Study Committee.
Public recreation, a study of public recreation and plan for community action in Maryville, Alcoa and Blount County. In cooperation with Division of State Planning, Tennessee State Planning Commission and Division of State Parks, Tennessee Department of
Conservation. Maryville, 1957.
45p. maps, tables.

    1. Recreation - Blount Co., Tenn. I. Ten-
nessee. State Planning Commission.

371.7
(76843)
T25   Tennessee. State Planning Commission.
A recreation plan for Lewis County, Tennessee, by Otis M. Trimble. Nashville,
1958.
67p. illus., maps.

    1. Recreation - Lewis Co., Tenn.
I. Trimble, Otis M.

711.14
(76895)
R61   Tennessee. State Planning Commission.
Rogersville, Tenn. Regional Planning
Commission.
Rogersville, Tennessee; land use. A report
to the Rogersville Planning Commission, by
the Upper East Tennessee Office, Tennessee
State Planning Commission. Rogersville,
1958.
1v. diagrs., maps, tables.

    U.S. Urban Renewal Administration, Urban
Planning Assistance Program.

    1. Land use - Rogersville, Tenn. I. Tennessee. State
Planning Commission.   II. U.S. URA-UPAP.
Rogersville, Tenn.

712.25
(768)
T25   Tennessee. State Planning Commission.
A public recreation plan and program for
Tennessee. [Nashville, 1962]
2v in 3. (Its Publication no. 230, 322-
323)
Bibliography: pt. 1, p.96; pt. 2, v. 2,
p.241-251.
Contents.-pt. 1. Municipal and county
recreation in Tennessee; a survey and some
recommended standards, 1961-1962.-pt 2.
Public Outdoor recreation resources in
    (Cont'd. on next card)

371.7
(76813)
U54   Tennessee. State Planning Commission.
Union City, Tenn. Regional Planning Commission.
Recreation study for Union City. Assisted
by the Tennessee State Planning Commission.
Union City, 1956.
52p. illus., maps.

    U.S. Urban Renewal Administration, Urban
Planning Assistance Program.

    1. Recreation - Union City, Tenn. I.
Tennessee. State Planning Commission.

628
T25   Tennessee. State Planning Commission.
Sanitary service charges in
Tennessee. Nashville, 1955.
106 p. (Its Publication no. 260)

    1. Sanitation. 2. Sewerage and sewage
disposal - Tennessee. 3. Water supply.

628
T25
1947

TENNESSEE. STATE PLANNING COMMISSION.
SANITARY SERVICE CHARGES IN TENNESSEE.
NASHVILLE, 1947.
75P. (ITS PUBLICATION NO. 183)

1. SANITATION.   2. SEWERAGE AND SEWAGE
DISPOSAL - TENNESSEE.   3. WATER SUPPLY.

526.8
:711.14
(76864)
T25a

Tennessee. State Planning Commission.
Section index and existing land use,
Tullahoma, Tennessee. [n.p.] 1957.
1v. maps.
U.S. Urban Renewal Administration, Urban
Planning Assistance Program.

1. Tullahoma, Tenn. - Maps. 2. Land use -
Maps and mapping - Tullahoma, Tenn. I. U.S.
Urban Renewal Administration. Urban Plan-
ning Assistance Program.

711.581
(76858)
S32

Shelbyville, Tenn. Regional Planning Commission. Shelbyville neighborhood
analysis ... 1959.   (Card 2)

Planning Assistance Program.

1. Neighborhood planning - Shelbyville,
Tenn. I. Tennessee. State Planning Commission. II. U.S. Urban Renewal Administration. Urban Planning Assistance
Program.   Shelbyville, Tenn.

628
T25
1957

2c.

Tennessee. State Planning Commission.
Sanitary service charges in Tennessee.
Nashville, 1957.
162p. (Its Publication no. 281)

1. Sanitation. 2. Sewers. 3. Refuse
and refuse disposal - Tenn. I. Title.

711.4
(76858)
S32

Tennessee. State Planning Commission.
Shelbyville, Tenn. Regional Planning Com-
mission.
Shelbyville community facilities plan.
Assisted by Tennessee State Planning Commis-
sion, Middle Tennessee Office. Shelbyville,
1958.
57p. maps, tables. (MTO Publication no.58-1)
U.S. Urban Renewal Administration, Urban
Planning Assistance Program.
1. Community facilities - Shelbyville, Tenn.
2. Schools - Shelbyville, Tenn. I. Tennessee.
State Planning   Commission. II. U.S. URA-
UPAP. Shelby-   ville, Tenn.

711.14
(76842)
L18

Tennessee. State Planning Commission.
Lawrenceburg, Tenn. Regional Planning
Commission.
A sketch land use plan for Lawrence-
burg, Tennessee, by Tennessee State Plan-
ning Commission, Middle Tennessee Office.
Lawrenceburg, 1957.
24p. diagrs., maps. (MTO publication
no. 57-40)
U.S. Urban Renewal Administration,
(Continued on next
card)

628
T25
1961

2c.

Tennessee. State Planning Commission.
Sanitary service charges in Tennessee
1961. Nashville, 1961.
61p.. (Its Publication no. 316)

1. Sanitation. 2. Sewerage and sewage
disposal - Tennessee. 3. Water-supply.

711.14
(76858)
S32s

Tennessee State Planning Commission.
Shelbyville, Tenn. Regional Planning Com-
mission.
Shelbyville land use plan. Assisted by
Tennessee State Planning Commission, Middle
Tennessee Office. Shelbyville, 1958.
10p. maps, tables. (MTO Publication
no. 58-23)
U.S. Urban Renewal Administration, Urban
Planning Assistance Program.

(Continued on next card)

711.14
(76842)
L18

Lawrenceburg, Tenn. Regional Planning
Commission. A sketch ... (Card 2)

Urban Planning Assistance Program.

1. Land use - Lawrenceburg, Tenn.
I. Tennessee. State Planning Commission. II. U.S. Urban Renewal Administration. Urban Planning Assistance
Program.

628.4
T25

Tennessee. State Planning Commission.
Sanitary services in Tennessee, by
Dorothy Tucker. Nashville, 1963.
66p. (Its Publication no. 326)

1. Sanitation.   2. Sewerage
and sewage disposal - Tennessee. 3. Water-
supply - Tennessee. I. Tucker, Dorothy.

711.14
(76858)
S32s

Shelbyville, Tenn. Regional Planning Commission. Shelbyville land...1958 (Card

1. Land use - Shelbyville, Tenn.   I.
Tennessee State Planning Commission.
II. U.S. Urban Renewal Administration.
Urban Planning Assistance Program.
Shelbyville, Tenn.

711.5
(76837)
W18

Tennessee. State Planning Commission.
Waverly, Tenn. Regional Planning Commission.
A sketch regional zoning plan for the Waverly and New Johnsonville Planning Regions,
by ... and New Johnsonville Regional Planning Commission. Assisted by Tennessee
State Planning Commission, Middle Tennessee
Office. Waverly, 1957.
33p. maps, tables. (MTO Publication no.
57-30)
U.S. Urban Renewal Administration, Urban

(Continued on next card)

628.4
T25
1965

Tennessee. State Planning Commission.
Sanitary services in Tennessee, by Dorothy
Tucker. Nashville, 1965.
70p. (Its Publication no. 339)

1. Sanitation.   2. Sewerage
and sewage disposal - Tennessee. 3. Water-
supply - Tennessee. I. Tucker, Dorothy.

711.14
(76858)
S32

Tennessee. State Planning Commission.
Shelbyville, Tenn. Regional Planning Commis-
sion.
Shelbyville land use survey and analysis,
by the Tennessee State Planning Commission,
Middle Tennessee Office. Shelbyville, 1957.
1v. maps, tables. (MTO Publication no.
57-25)
U.S. Urban Renewal Administration, Urban
Planning Assistance Program.
(Continued on next card)

711.5
(76837)
W18

Waverly, Tenn. Regional Planning Commission. A sketch regional ... (Card 2)

Planning Assistance Program.

1. Zoning - Waverly and New Johnsonville
Planning regions.   I. Tennessee.   State
Planning Commission. II. U.S. Urban Re-
newal Administration. Urban Planning As-
sistance Program. III. New Johnsonville,
Tenn. Regional Planning Commission.

727.1
(76813)
U54

Tennessee. State Planning Commission.
Union City, Tenn. Regional Planning Com-
mission.
School study for Union City, Tennessee.
With the assistance of Tennessee State
Planning Commission, West Tennessee Of-
fice. Union City, 1957.
29p. diagrs., maps, tables.

U.S. Urban Renewal Administration,

(Continued on next card)

711.14
(76858)
S32

Shelbyville, Tenn. Regional Planning Commission. Shelbyville land ... (Card 2)

1. Land use - Shelbyville, Tenn. I. Tennessee. State Planning Commission. II. U.S.
Urban Renewal Administration. Urban Planning Assistance Program.

711.14
(76853)
S54

Tennessee. State Planning Commission.
Smithville, Tenn. Planning Commission.
Smithville land use survey and plan. [Pre-
pared by the Tennessee State Planning Com-
mission, Middle Tennessee Office] Smithville,
1958.
12p. maps. (MTO Publication no. 58-9)
U.S. Urban Renewal Administration, Urban
Planning Assistance Program.
1. Land use - Smithville, Tenn. I. Tennes-
see. State Planning Commission. II. U.S.
Urban Renewal   Administration. Urban
Planning As-   sistance Program.
Smithville,   Tenn.

727.1
(76813)
U54

Union City, Tenn. Regional Planning Commission. School study ... (Card 2)

Urban Planning Assistance Program.

1. Schools - Union City, Tenn. I. Tennessee. State Planning Commission. II. U.S.
Urban Renewal Administration. Urban Planning Assistance Program.

711.581
(76858)
S32

Tennessee. State Planning Commission.
Shelbyville, Tenn. Regional Planning Commission.
Shelbyville neighborhood analysis and
plan. [Prepared for the Shelbyville Regional
Planning Commission by the Tennessee State
Planning Commission, Middle Tennessee Of-
fice] Shelbyville, 1959.
34p. illus., maps. (MTO Publication 59-2
59-21)
U.S. Urban Renewal Administration, Urban

(Continued on next card)

526.8
(76853)
T25

Tennessee. State Planning Commission.
Smithville, Tennessee. Tennessee base
maps. Smithville, 1958.
1v.

U.S. Urban Renewal Administration, Urban
Planning Assistance Program

1. Maps and mapping - Smithville, Tenn.
I. U.S. URA-UPAP. Smithville, Tenn.

352.1
(768)
T25
Tennessee. State Planning Commission.
Sources of municipal revenue, by Anna Sternheimer. Nashville, 1959.
69p. tables. (Its Publication no. 297)

A revision of two earlier reports of the same title, publication numbers 169 by Eleanor Keeble, December 1946 and 229 by Margaret Pouder, November 1951.

1. Municipal finance - Tennessee. I. Sternheimer, Anna.

388
(768464)
S67
Springfield, Tenn. Municipal-Regional Planning Commission. Springfield traffic and parking... 1959 (Card 2)

1. Traffic surveys - Springfield, Tenn. I. Tennessee. State Planning Commission. II. U.S. Urban Renewal Administration. Urban Planning Assistance Program.

711.74
(76824)
S31
Sharon, Tenn. Municipal-Regional Planning Commission. Street ... (Card 2)

1. Streets - Sharon, Tenn. 2. Street planning - Sharon, Tenn. I. Tennessee. State Planning Commission. II. U.S. Urban Renewal Administration. Urban Planning Assistance Program.

711.14
(768464)
S67
Tennessee. State Planning Commission.
Springfield, Tenn. Municipal Regional Planning Commission.
Springfield land use analysis. Prepared by Tennessee State Planning Commission, Middle Tennessee Office. Springfield, 1957.
12p. maps, tables. (MTO publication no. 57-36)

U.S. Urban Renewal Administration, Urban Planning Assistance Program.

(Continued on next card)

711.5
(768464
:347)
S67
Tennessee. State Planning Commission.
Springfield, Tenn. Municipal-Regional Planning Commission.
Springfield zoning ordinance revision. Prepared by Tennessee State Planning Commission, Middle Tennessee Office. Springfield, 1958.
20p. maps, table. (MTO Publication no. 58-14)

U.S. Urban Renewal Administration, Urban Planning Assistance Program.

(Continued on next card)

711.74
(76813)
U54
Tennessee. State Planning Commission.
Union City, Tenn. Regional Planning Commission.
Street classification and improvement program, Union City, Tennessee. With the assistance of the Tennessee State Planning Commission. Union City, 1956.
30p. maps.

U.S. Urban Renewal Administration, Urban Planning Assistance Program.

1. Street planning - Union City, Tenn. I. Tennessee. State Planning Commission. II. U.S. Urban Renewal Administration. Urban Planning Assistance Program.

711.14
(768464)
S67
Springfield, Tenn. Municipal Regional Planning Commission. Springfield ... (Card 2)

1. Land use - Springfield, Tenn. I. Tennessee. State Planning Commission. II. U.S. Urban Renewal Administration. Urban Planning Assistance Program.

711.5
(768464
:347)
S67
Springfield, Tenn. Municipal-Regional Planning Commission. Springfield zoning ordinance ... 1958. (Card 2)

1. Zoning legislation - Springfield, Tenn. I. Tennessee. State Planning Commission. II. U.S. Urban Renewal Administration. Urban Planning Assistance Program.

711.74
(76815)
D92
Tennessee. State Planning Commission.
Dyersburg, Tenn. Regional Planning Commission.
Street classification and improvement program. [With the assistance of the Tennessee State Planning Commission, West Tennessee Office] Dyersburg, 1956.
16p. map.

U.S. Urban Renewal Administration, Urban Planning Assistance Program.
1. Streets - Dyersburg, Tenn. I. Tennessee. State Planning Commission. II. U.S. Urban Renewal Administration. Urban Planning Assistance Program.

526.8
:711.14
(768464)
T25
Tennessee. State Planning Commission.
Springfield land use survey. Nashville, 1957.
1v. maps.

U.S. Urban Renewal Administration, Urban Planning Assistance Program.

1. Springfield, Tenn. Maps. 2. Land use - Maps and mapping - Springfield, Tenn. I. U.S. Urban Renewal Administration. Urban Planning Assistance Program.

711
(016)
C65
no. 71
Tennessee. State Planning Commission.
Violi, Louis C
State planning in the United States. [Nashville] State Planning Div., Tennessee State Planning Commission, 1969.
27p. (Council of Planning Librarians. Exchange bibliography no. 71)

1. Planning - Bibl. 2. State Planning - Bibl. I. Tennessee. State Planning Commission. II. Title. (Series: Council of Planning Librarians. Exchange bibliography no. 71)

711.74
(76875)
C76
Tennessee. State Planning Commission.
Crossville, Tenn. Municipal Planning Commission.
Street naming and property numbering in Crossville. Assisted by Tennessee State Planning Commission East Tennessee Office. Crossville, 1957.
15p. maps.

U.S. Urban Renewal Administration, Urban

(Continued on next card)

711.4
(768464)
S67
Tennessee. State Planning Commission.
Springfield, Tenn. Municipal-Regional Planning Commission.
Springfield neighborhood analysis. Prepared by Middle Tennessee Office, Tennessee State Planning Commission. Springfield, 1957.
12p. maps, tables. (MTO publication no. 57-45)

U.S. Urban Renewal Administration, Urban Planning Assistance Program.

(Continued on next card)

711.74
(76828)
B65
Tennessee. State Planning Commission.
Bolivar, Tenn. Municipal-Regional Planning Commission.
Street classification and improvement program, Bolivar, Tennessee. With the assistance of the Tennessee State Planning Commission, West Tennessee Office. Bolivar, 1957.
30p. maps.

U.S. Urban Renewal Administration, Urban Planning Assistance Program.

(Continued on next card)

711.74
(76875)
C76
Crossville, Tenn. Municipal Planning Commission. Street naming ... (Card 2)

Planning Assistance Program.

1. Streets - Crossville, Tenn. 2. House numbering. I. Tennessee. State Planning Commission. II. U.S. Urban Renewal Administration. Urban Planning Assistance Program.

711.4
(768464)
S67
Springfield, Tenn. Municipal Regional Planning Commission. Springfield neighborhood analysis. ... Card 2)

1. City planning - Springfield, Tenn. 2. Neighborhood rehabilitation - Springfield, Tenn. I. Tennessee. State Planning Commission. II. U.S. Urban Renewal Administration. Urban Planning Assistance Program.

711.74
(76828)
B65
Bolivar, Tenn. Municipal-Regional Planning Commission. Street ... (Card 2)

1. Street planning - Bolivar, Tenn. I. Tennessee. State Planning Commission. II. U.S. Urban Renewal Administration. Urban Planning Assistance Program.

330
(76873)
C54
Tennessee. State Planning Commission.
Clinton, Tenn. Regional Planning Commission.
A study, economic base and population, Clinton, Tennessee. Prepared by the Tennessee State Planning Commission. Clinton, 1957.
36p. tables.

U.S. Urban Renewal Administration,

(Continued on next card)

388
(768464)
S67
Tennessee. State Planning Commission.
Springfield, Tenn. Municipal-Regional Planning Commission.
Springfield traffic and parking survey, by the Tennessee State Planning Commission, Middle Tennessee Office. Springfield, 1959.
36p. diagrs., maps. (MTO Publication 59-2)

U.S. Urban Renewal Administration, Urban Planning Assistance Program.

(Continued on next card)

711.74
(76824)
S31
Tennessee. State Planning Commission.
Sharon, Tenn. Municipal-Regional Planning Commission.
Street classification and improvement program for Sharon, Tenn. With the assistance of the Tennessee State Planning Commission, West Tennessee Office. Sharon, 1957.
31p. maps.

U.S. Urban Renewal Administration, Urban Planning Assistance Program.

(Continued on next card)

330
(76873)
C54
Clinton, Tenn. Regional Planning Commission. A study, ... (Card 2)

Urban Planning Assistance Program.

1. Economic base studies - Clinton, Tenn. 2. Population - Clinton, Tenn. I. Tennessee. State Planning Commission. II. U.S. Urban Renewal Administration. Urban Planning Assistance Program.

711.74
(76887)
C52

Tennessee. State Planning Commission.
Cleveland, Tenn. Planning Commission.
A study of street naming and property numbering in Cleveland, Tennessee. With Tennessee State Planning Commission, East Tennessee Office. Cleveland, 1957.
26p. maps.

U.S. Urban Renewal Administration, Urban Planning Assistance Program.

(Continued on next card)

711.583
T25
2 c.

Tennessee. State Planning Commission.
Subdivision improvement costs: who pays for what; a summary of existing practices, comp. by Anna Sternheimer. Nashville, 1958.
95p. tables.

1. Community development. 2. Community facilities. 3. Subdivision. I. Sternheimer, Anna, comp.

333.38
(76856)
F71

Franklin, Tenn. Municipal Planning Commission. Subdivision ... (Card 2)

Urban Planning Assistance Program.

1. Subdivision regulation - Franklin, Tenn. I. Tennessee. State Planning Commission. II. U.S. Urban Renewal Administration. Urban Planning Assistance Program.

711.74
(76887)
C52

Cleveland, Tenn. Planning Commission. A study of street ... (Card 2)

1. Streets - Cleveland, Tenn. 2. House numbering. I. Tennessee. State Planning Commission. II. U.S. Urban Renewal Administration. Urban Planning Assistance Program.

333.38
(768)
T25s

Tennessee. State Planning Commission.
Subdivision regulations, a model set of standards for Tennessee communities. Nashville, 1953.
18p. diagrs. (Its Publication no. 248)

1. Subdivision regulation - Tennessee.

333.38
(76824)
S31

Tennessee. State Planning Commission.
Sharon, Tenn. Municipal-Regional Planning Commission.
Subdivision regulations for Sharon, Tennessee planning region. With the assistance of the Tennessee State Planning Commission, West Tennessee Office. Sharon, 1957.
30p. maps.

U.S. Urban Renewal Administration, Urban Planning Assistance Program.

(Continued on next card)

330
(76887)
C52

Tennessee. State Planning Commission.
Cleveland, Tenn. Planning Commission.
A study of the economic base and population of Cleveland, Tennessee. With Tennessee State Planning Commission, East Tennessee Office. Cleveland, 1957.
29p. diagrs.

U.S. Urban Renewal Administration, Urban Planning Assistance Program.

(Continued on next card)

333.38
(76815)
D92

Tennessee. State Planning Commission.
Dyersburg, Tenn. Regional Planning Commission.
Subdivision regulations, Dyersburg, Tennessee. [With the assistance of the Tennessee State Planning Commission, West Tennessee Office] Dyersburg, 1956.
41p. maps, tables.

U.S. Urban Renewal Administration, Urban Planning Assistance Program.

1. Subdivision regulation - Dyersburg, Tenn. I. Tennessee. State Planning Commission. II. U.S. Urban Renewal Administration. Urban Planning Assistance Program.

333.38
(76824)
S31

Sharon, Tenn. Municipal-Regional Planning Commission. Subdivision ... (Card 2)

1. Subdivision regulation - Sharon, Tenn. I. Tennessee. State Planning Commission. II. U.S. Urban Renewal Administration. Urban Planning Assistance Program.

330
(76887)
C52

Cleveland, Tenn. Planning Commission. A study of the economic ... (Card 2)

1. Economic base studies - Cleveland, Tenn. 2. Population - Cleveland, Tenn. I. Tennessee. State Planning Commission. II. U.S. Urban Renewal Administration. Urban Planning Assistance Program.

333.38
(76837)
W18

Tennessee. State Planning Commission.
Waverly, Tenn. Regional Planning Commission.
Subdivision regulations, effective Jan. 3, 1957. Waverly, Tenn., 1957.
8p. diagrs., maps. (MTO Publication no. 57-2)

"Assisted by the Tennessee State Planning Commission."

1. Subdivision regulation - Waverly, Tenn. I. Tennessee. State Planning Commission.

333.38
(76858)
S32

Tennessee. State Planning Commission.
Shelbyville, Tenn. Regional Planning Commission.
Subdivision regulations for the Shelbyville planning region. Assisted by the Tennessee State Planning Commission, Middle Tennessee Office, Shelbyville, 1957.
18p. diagrs., maps. (MTO Publication 57-11)
1. Subdivision regulation - Shelbyville, Tenn. I. Tennessee. State Planning Commission. II. U.S. Urban Renewal Administration. Urban Planning Assistance Program.

330
(76883)
D19

Tennessee. State Planning Commission.
Dayton, Tenn. Municipal Planning Commission.
A study of the economic base of Dayton and Rhea county, including an informal survey of Rhea County manufacturers. Assisted by the Tennessee State Planning Commission, East Tennessee Office. Dayton, 1957.
16p. diagrs., tables.

U.S. Urban Renewal Administration, Urban
(Continued on next card)

333.38
(76828)
B65

Tennessee. State Planning Commission.
Bolivar, Tenn. Municipal Regional Planning Commission.
Subdivision regulations for Bolivar, Tennessee planning region. With the assistance of the Tennessee State Planning Commission, West Tennessee Office. Bolivar, 1957.
38p. diagrs., maps.

U.S. Urban Renewal Administration, Urban
(Continued on next card)

333.38
(76812)
R42

Tennessee. State Planning Commission.
Ridgely, Tenn. Municipal-Regional Planning Commission.
Subdivision regulations, Ridgely, Tennessee. With the assistance of the Tennessee State Planning Commission, West Tennessee Office. Ridgely, 1957.
30p. diagrs., maps.

U.S. Urban Renewal Administration, Urban Planning Assistance Program.

(Continued on next card)

330
(76883)
D19

Dayton, Tenn. Municipal Planning Commission. A study of the ... (Card 2)

Planning Assistance Program.

1. Economic base studies - Dayton, Tenn. I. Tennessee. State Planning Commission. II. U.S. Urban Renewal Administration. Urban Planning Assistance Program.

333.38
(76828)
B65

Bolivar, Tenn. Municipal Regional Planning Commission. Subdivision ... (Card 2)

Planning Assistance Program.

1. Subdivision regulation - Bolivar, Tenn. I. Tennessee. State Planning Commission. II. U.S. Urban Renewal Administration. Urban Planning Assistance Program.

333.38
(76812)
R42

Ridgely, Tenn. Municipal-Regional Planning Commission. Subdivision ... (Card 2)

1. Subdivision regulation - Ridgely, Tenn. I. Tennessee. State Planning Commission. II. U.S. Urban Renewal Administration. Urban Planning Assistance Program.

352.5
(76892)
M67

Tennessee. State Planning Commission
Morristown, Tenn. Regional Planning Commission.
A study of the Morristown fringe area. Assisted by the Tennessee State Planning Commission. Morristown, 1956.
10p. maps.

U.S. Urban Renewal Administration, Urban Planning Assistance Program.
1. Fringe areas - Morristown, Tenn. I. Tennessee. State Planning Commission. II. U.S. Urban Renewal Administration. Urban Planning Assistance Program

---

333.38
(76856)
F71

Tennessee. State Planning Commission
Franklin, Tenn. Municipal Planning Commission.
Subdivision regulations for Franklin, Tennessee. Assisted by Tennessee State Planning Commission, Middle Tennessee Office. Franklin, 1957.
30p. diagrs., maps. (MTO Publication no. 57-21)

U.S. Urban Renewal Administration,
(Continued on next card)

333.38
(76853)
S54

Tennessee. State Planning Commission.
Smithville, Tenn. Planning Commission.
Subdivision standards. Prepared by the Tennessee State Planning Commission, Middle Tennessee Office. Smithville, 1958.
1v. (MTO Publication no. 58-24)

U.S. Urban Renewal Administration, Urban Planning Assistance Program.
1. Subdivision regulation - Smithville, Tenn. I. Tennessee. State Planning Commission. II. U.S. Urban Renewal Administration. Urban Planning Assistance Program.

333.38
(76892)
M67
Tennessee. State Planning Commission.
Morristown, Tenn. Regional Planning Commission.
Subdivision standards for Morristown, Tennessee, and surrounding area. Assisted by Tennessee State Planning Commission. Morristown, 1956.
18p. diagrs., maps.

U.S. Urban Renewal Administration, Urban Planning Assistance Program.

1. Subdivision regulation - Morristown, Tenn.
I. Tennessee. State Planning Commission. II.
U.S. Urban Renewal Administration. Urban Planning Assistance   Program.

Class No. [handwritten]
U.S. Tenn [handwritten]
Accession No. [handwritten]
Ordered
JUN 20 1950
Received
JUL 12 1960
Purchase Order No.
Date
L. C. No.

Author (surname first) *Tennessee State Planning Commission* [handwritten]
Title *Summary of economic data on Tennessee communities* [handwritten]
Place *Nashville 3* [handwritten] Publisher *Industrial Development Div* [handwritten]
Address *417 7th Ave, N,* [handwritten]
Date *5/48* [handwritten] Paging *8* [handwritten] List Price   Est. Cost *gratis* [handwritten]
Edition or Series
Recommended by
Reviewed in *Ind. D. of Tenn. 1948-49* [handwritten]

H-305 (2-50)   HOUSING AND HOME FINANCE AGENCY; Office of the Administrator   16—61187-1   GPO

330
(768)
T25t
Tennessee. State Planning Commission.
Tennessee and national economic growth.
Nashville, Tenn. 1967.
89p. (Its Publication no. 357)

1. Economic base studies - Tennessee. 2.
Social conditions - Tennessee. 3. Labor-supply - Tennessee. 4. Employment - Tennessee. 5. Population - Tennessee. I. Title.

711.4
:333.38
(768865)
A73
Tennessee. State Planning Commission.
Athens, Tenn. Regional Planning Commission.
Subdivision standards for the Athens, Tennessee, planning region [proposed] Assisted by the Tennessee State Planning Commission, East Tennessee Office. Athens, 1956.
24p. maps.

Urban Renewal Administration, Urban Planning Assistance Program.

1. City planning - Athens, Tenn. 2. Subdivision. I. Tennessee. State Planning Commission. II. U.S. Urban Renewal Administration.

4439
4440
TENNESSEE, STATE PLANNING COMMISSION.
MOUNT CARMEL, TENN. REGIONAL PLANNING COMMISSION.
SUMMARY OF PUBLIC IMPROVEMENTS AND CAPITAL BUDGET; ANNUAL REPORT. BY TENNESSEE STATE PLANNING COMMISSION.
MOUNT CARMEL, TENN., 1969.
2 V. (HUD 701 REPORT)

1. CITY PLANNING - MOUNT CARMEL, TENN.
I. TENNESSEE, STATE PLANNING COMMISSION.
II. HUD. 701. MOUNT CARMEL, TENN.

728.1
(768.347)
T25
2c.
Tennessee. State Planning Commission.
Tennessee housing legislation, 1935-1955.
Nashville [1956]
61 p.

1. Housing legislation - Tennessee.
2. Urban renewal - Tennessee.

333.38
(768)
T25
2c.
Tennessee. State Planning Commission.
Subdivision standards for use by Tennessee local planning commissions as a guide to adoption of a set of standards for their community. Nashville, 1959.
20p. diagrs. (Its Publication no. 298)
U.S. Urban Renewal Adm. UPAP.

1. Subdivision regulation - Tennessee.
I. Urban Renewal Administration. Urban Planning Assistance Program. Tennessee.

Tennessee. State Planning Commission.
727.1
(76815)
D92
Dyersburg, Tenn. Regional Planning Commission.
Survey of Dyersburg schools, Dyersburg, Tenn. 1957; a preliminary report. Prepared by the Tennessee State Planning Commission, West Tennessee Office. Dyersburg, 1958.
23p. maps, tables.

U.S. Urban Renewal Administration,
(Continued on next card)

LAW
S
Tennessee. State Planning Commission.
Tennessee housing legislation, 1935-1965.
Prepared by Nicholas Beeman. Nashville, 1966.
50p. (Its Publication no. 338)
Reported from Tennessee code annotated (as amended through 1965)

1. Housing legislation - Tennessee.
2. Local housing authorities - Tennessee.
I. Beehan, Nicholas. II. Title.

333.38
(768924)
W34
Tennessee. State Planning Commission.
White Pine, Tenn. Regional Planning Commission.
Subdivision standards for White Pine, Tennessee and surrounding area. Assisted by Tennessee State Planning Commission, East Tennessee Office. White Pine, 1957.
22p.
U.S. Urban Renewal Administration, Urban Planning Assistance Program.

(continued on next card)

727.1
(76815)
D92
Dyersburg, Tenn. Regional Planning Commission. Survey of ... (Card 2)

Urban Planning Assistance Program.

1. Schools - Dyersburg, Tenn. I. Tennessee. State Planning Commission. II.
U.S. Urban Renewal Administration. Urban Planning Assistance Program.

VF
711.4
(7685)
T25e
Tennessee. State Planning Commission.
Tennessee P - 1 Project completion report.
[Nashville, Tenn.] May 1957.
16 p. (Its publication no. 276)

Report to HHFA and project financed by Urban Planning Assistance Grant.

1. City planning - Tennessee.

333.38
(768924)
W34
White Pine, Tenn. Regional Planning Commission. Subdivision ... (Card 2)

1. Subdivision regulation - White Pine, Tenn. I. Tennessee. State Planning Commission. II. U.S. Urban Renewal Administration, Urban Planning Assistance Program.

371.7
(76892)
M67
Tennessee. State Planning Commission.
Morristown, Tenn. Regional Planning Commission.
A survey of public recreation in Morristown. Assisted by the Tennessee State Planning Commission. Morristown, 1956.
13p. map.

U.S. Urban Renewal Administration, Urban Planning Assistance Program.
1. Recreation - Morristown, Tenn. I. U.S. Urban Renewal Administration. Urban Planning Assistance Program. II. Tennessee. State Planning Commis-   sion.

VF
711.4
(7685)
T25
Tennessee. State Planning Commission.
Tennessee P-2 project completion report.
[Nashville, Tenn.] April 1957.
5 p.

Report to HHFA on project financed by Urban Planning Assistance Grant.

1. City planning - Franklin, Tenn. 2. City planning - Lebanon, Tenn.

333.38
(76873)
C54
Tennessee. State Planning Commission.
Clinton, Tenn. Regional Planning Commission.
Subdivision standards of the Clinton, Tennessee planning region. Assisted by the Tennessee State Planning Commission, East Tennessee Office. Clinton, 1957.
46p. diagrs., maps.

U.S. Urban Renewal Administration, Urban Planning Assistance Program.

(Continued on next card)

711.4
:371.7
(768865)
A73
Tennessee. State Planning Commission.
Athens, Tenn. Regional Planning Commission.
A survey of recreation in Athens. Assisted by the Tennessee State Planning Commission, East Tennessee Office. Athens, 1956.
16p. map, diagr.

U.S. Urban Renewal Administration, Urban Planning Assistance Program.

1. City planning - Athens, Tenn. 2. Recreation - Athens, Tenn. I. Tennessee. State Planning Commission. II. U.S. Urban Renewal Administration.

VF
711.4
(768)
T25
1958
Tennessee. State Planning Commission.
Tennessee P-4 project completion report, May 1958. Nashville 1958.
40p. (Its Publication no. 285)

U.S. Urban Renewal Adm. UPAP.

1. City planning - Tennessee.
I. U.S. URA-UPAP. Tennessee.

333.38
(76873)
C54
Clinton, Tenn. Regional Planning Commission. Subdivision ... (Card 2)

1. Subdivision regulation - Clinton, Tenn. I. Tennessee. State Planning Commission. II. U.S. Urban Renewal Administration. Urban Planning Assistance Program.

526.8
(76888)
T25
Tennessee. State Planning Commission.
Sweetwater, Tennessee base map. Sweetwater, Tenn., 1959.
1v. maps.

U.S. Urban Renewal Administration, Urban Planning Assistance Program.

1. Maps and mapping - Sweetwater, Tenn.
I. U.S. URA-UPAP. Sweetwater, Tenn.

711.33
(768)
T25t
Tennessee. State Planning Commission.
Tennessee P-10 project completion report.
Nashville, 1960.
8p. (Its Publication no. 300)

U.S. Urban Renewal Administration, Urban Planning Assistance Program.

1. State planning - Tennessee. I. U.S. URA-UPAP.

711.33
(768) Tennessee. State Planning Commission.
T25t   Tennessee P-12 project completion
1961   report. [Nashville] 1961.
     14p. (Its Publication no. 314)

     U.S. Urban Renewal Adm. UPAP.

     1. State planning - Tennessee. I. U.S.
URA-UPAP. Tennessee.

VF
353.
(768) Tennessee. State Planning Commission.
T25t   Tennessee's finances. A quick summary of
    taxes, total income, expenditures,1956/57,
1957/58-
   Nashville. 1958-
     folder. diagrs.

     For complete information see shelf list.

     1. State finance - Tennessee.

711.4
:388   Athens, Tenn. Regional Planning Commission.
(768865) Traffic, parking and ... (Card 2)
A73
1957

     1. City planning - Athens, Tenn. 2. Traf-
fic - Athens, Tenn. 3. Business districts -
Athens, Tenn. I. Tennessee. State Planning
Commission. II. U.S. Urban Renewal Administration. Urban Planning Assistance Program.

S
       Tennessee. State Planning Commission.
      The Tennessee planner. v. 1-
    Jan./Feb. 1940-
   [Nashville] Tennessee State Planning Commission.
       v. in   illus., ports., maps (part col.) 28 cm. bimonthly
    (irregular)
    Supersedes Tennessee plan topics.
    INDEXES:
     Vols. 2-6, Jan. 1941-June 1946, with v. 3-6.
   For full information see Periodicals Kardex file.

    1. Tennessee—Economic policy—Period. 2. Regional planning—
Tennessee.   I. Tennessee. State Planning Commission.

    HC107.T3T43   338.91   51-28506
    Library of Congress   [1]

711.3
(768) Tennessee. State Planning Commission.
T25t   Tennessee's larger urban areas. Nashville,
1967.
     115p. (Its Publication no. 354)
     U.S. Urban Renewal Adm. UPAP.

     1. Metropolitan areas - Tennessee.
2. Population - Tennessee. 3. Employment -
Tennessee. 4. Economic base studies -
Tennessee. I. U.S. HUD-UPAP. II. Title.

388
(76857) Murfreesboro, Tenn. Regional Planning
M87   Commission.
     Traffic and parking in Murfreesboro,
Tennessee. [A report to the Murfreesboro
Regional Planning Commission, by Tennessee
State Planning Commission, Middle Tennessee
Office.] Murfreesboro, 1960.
     27p. diagrs., maps, tables. (MTO
Publication 59-20)

     U.S. Urban Renewal Administration, Urban
Planning Assistance Program.

     (Continued on next card)

VF   Tennessee. State Planning Commission.
711.3   Tennessee. Laws, statutes, etc.
(768:347)   Tennessee planning legislation,
T25   1935-1963. Prepared by Anne Sternheimer.
1963   [Nashville] Tennessee State Planning
     Commission, 1963.
     44p. (Publication no. 327)
     Reprinted from Tennessee Code
annotated (as amended through 1962)

     1. State planning legislation -
Tennessee. 2. Zoning legislation -
Tenn. I. Tennessee. State Planning
Commis-   sion. II. Title.

      Tennessee. State Planning Commission.
711.4   Elizabethton, Tenn. Regional Planning
(768984) Commission.
E54   Toward a comprehensive plan for Elizabethton. Prepared by Upper East Tennessee Office,
Tennessee State Planning Commission. Elizabethton, 1958.
     87p. diagrs., maps. tables.

     U.S. Urban Renewal Administration, Urban
Planning Assistance Program.

     1. City planning - Elizabethton, Tenn. I.
Tennessee. State Planning Commission. II.
U.S. Urban   Renewal Administration.
Urban Planning   Assistance Program.

388
(76857) Murfreesboro, Tenn. Regional Planning
M87   Commission. Traffic and ... 1960. (Card 2)

     1. Traffic - Murfreesboro, Tenn. 2. Parking -
Murfreesboro, Tenn. I. Tennessee. State Planning
Commission. II. U.S. URA-UPAP. Murfreesboro, Tenn.

R   Tennessee. State Planning Commission.
711.3   Tennessee. Law, statutes, etc.
(768   Tennessee planning legislation, 1935-
:347)   1967. Prepared by Nicholas Beehan, Jr.
T25   Nashville, Tennessee State Planning
     Commission, 1967.
     49p. (Bulletin no. 353)
     Reprinted from Tennessee code annotated
and attached amendments of the 85th General
Assembly (Recessed May 26, 1967)

1. State planning legislation - Tennessee.
2. Zoning legislation - Tennessee.
I. Tennessee. State   Planning Commission.
II. Title.

      Tennessee. State Planning Commission.
712.21
(76896) Bristol, Tenn. Planning Commission.
B74   Toward a park and recreation plan, Bristol,
Tennessee. Prepared by the Upper East Tennessee Office, Tennessee State Planning Commission. Bristol, 1958.
     47p. diagrs., maps, tables.

     U.S. Urban Renewal Administration, Urban
Planning Assistance Program.
     1. Parks - Bristol, Tenn. I. Tennessee.
State Planning Commission. II. U.S. Urban
Renewal Adminis-   tration. Urban Planning
Assistance Pro-   gram.

      Tennessee. State Planning Commission.
711.4   Athens, Tenn. Regional Planning Commission.
:388   Traffic, parking and circulation, Athens,
(768865) Tennessee. Assisted by the Tennessee State
A73   Planning Commission, East Tennessee Office.
     Athens, 1956.
     7p. map.

     U.S. Urban Renewal Administration, Urban
Planning Assistance Program.

     1. City planning - Athens, Tenn. 2. Traffic -
Athens, Tenn. I. Tennessee. State Planning
Commission. II. U.S. Urban Renewal Adminis-
tration.

VF   Tennessee. State Planning Commission.
711.3   Tennessee. Law, Statutes, etc.
(768:347)   Tennessee planning legislation, 1956;
T25   reprinted from Tennessee Code Annotated.
     Nashville, Tenn., Tennessee State Planning
     Commission, 1956.
     52 p.

1.State planning legislation - Tennessee. 2.Zoning
legislation - Tenn. I.Tennessee. State Planning
Commission.

3994   TENNESSEE STATE PLANNING COMMISSION.
3995   ERWIN, TENN. REGIONAL PLANNING
3996   COMMISSION.
3997   TOWN OF ERWIN, UNICOI COUNTY, TENNESSEE:
    1, TRANSPORTATION PLAN; 2, COMMUNITY
FACILITIES; 3, BIENNIAL REPORT; 4,
SUMMARY REPORT OF SUBDIVISION
REGULATIONS, COMMUNITY FACILITIES,
TRANSPORTATION. BY TENNESSEE STATE
PLANNING COMMISSION, UPPER EAST TENNESSEE
OFFICE. ERWIN, TENN., 1969.
    4 v. (HUD 701 REPORT)
    1. CITY PLANNING - ERWIN, TENN.
I. TENNESSEE STATE PLANNING COMMISSION.
II. HUD. 701   ERWIN, TENN.

388
(76892) Morristown, Tenn. Regional Planning Commission.
M67   Traffic, parking and circulation report.
     Assisted by the Tennessee State Planning Com-
mission. Morristown, 1956.
     15p. diagrs., maps.

     U.S. Urban Renewal Administration, Urban
Planning Assistance Program.

     1. Traffic - Morristown, Tenn. 2. Street
planning - Morristown, Tenn. I. U.S. Urban
Renewal Administration. Urban Planning Assistance Program. II. Tennessee. State Planning
Commission.

Class No.	Author (surname first) *Tennessee State Planning*
Popula-	*Commission*
U.S. Tenn.	Title *Tennessee Population and employment*
Accession No.	*data*
Ordered	
JUN 3 0 1958	Place *Nashville 3* Publisher *Industrial Development*
JUL 1 2 1950	Address *1017 7th Ave N.* *Division*
Cost	Pages *8* List Price Est. Cost *gratis*
Purchase Order No.	
Date	Edition or Series
L. C. No.	Recommended by
	Reviewed in *Ind. G. D. of Tenn. 1948-49*

H-305 (2-50)   HOUSING AND HOME FINANCE AGENCY; Office of the Administrator   10—61167-1   GPO

      Tennessee. State Planning Commission.
388
(768984) Elizabethton, Tenn. Regional Planning Com-
E54   mission.
     Traffic and parking, Elizabethton, Tennes-
see. [A report to ... by Upper East Tennessee
Office, Tennessee State Planning Commission]
Elizabethton, 1956.
     33p. maps, tables.
     U.S. Urban Renewal Administration,
Urban Planning Assistance Program.

     1. Traffic - Elizabethton, Tenn. 2. Park-
ing - Elizabethton, Tenn. I. Tennessee. State
Planning Commission. II. U.S. Urban Renewal
Administration   Urban Planning Assistance
Program.

      Tennessee. State Planning Commission.
388
(76896) Kingsport, Tenn. Regional Planning Commis-
K45   sion.
     Traffic, parking and major streets in Kings-
port, Tennessee, by Upper East Tennessee Office, Tennessee State Planning Commission.
Kingsport, 1956.
     62p. maps, tables.

     U.S. Urban Renewal Administration, Urban
Planning Assistance Program.

     (Continued on next card)

712.21
(768) Tennessee. State Planning Commission.
T25   The Tennessee River gorge, its scenic
    preservation. A report to the 1961
    General Assembly. Nashville, 1961.
     104p. illus., maps. (Its Publica-
tion no. 311)

     1. Parks - Tennessee.

      Tennessee. State Planning Commission.
711.4
:388   Athens, Tenn. Regional Planning Commission.
(768865) Traffic, parking and circulation and cen-
A73   tral business district renewal for Athens.
1957   [Assisted by] Tennessee State Planning
Commission, Southeast Tennessee Office.
Athens, 1957.
     32p. diagrs., maps.

     U.S. Urban Renewal Administration. Urban
Planning Assistance Program.

     (Continued on next card)

      Tennessee. State Planning Commission.
388
(76896) Kingsport, Tenn. Regional Planning Com-
K45   mission. Traffic, parking ... (Card 2)

     1. Traffic - Kingsport, Tenn. 2. Street
planning - Kingsport, Tenn. I. Tennessee.
State Planning Commission. II. U.S. Urban
Renewal Administration. Urban Planning
Assistance Program.

711.74
(76887)
C52t

Tennessee. State Planning Commission.
Cleveland, Tenn. Planning Commission.
Traffic, parking, Cleveland, Tennessee and the official major street plan. With Tennessee State Planning Commission, East Tennessee Office. Cleveland 1957.
37p. maps, tables.
U.S. Urban Renewal Administration, Urban Planning Assistance Program.

(Continued on next card)

711
(016)
T25u

Tennessee. State Planning Commission.
Unnumbered publications and studies, Local Planning Office, Tennessee State Planning Commission. Supplement no. 1, July 1, 1958-Dec. 31, 1959. Nashville, 1960.
12p.

Not to be listed in any book review or bibliographic publication.

1. Planning - Bibliography.

352.6
(768984)
E54

Elizabethton, Tenn. Regional Planning Commission. Utilities survey ... (Card 2)

Planning Assistance Program.

1. Public utilities - Elizabethton, Tenn. I. Tennessee. State Planning Commission. II. U.S. Urban Renewal Administration. Urban Planning Assistance Program.

711.74
(76887)
C52t

Cleveland, Tenn. Planning Commission.
Traffic, parking, ... (Card 2)

1. Street planning - Cleveland, Tenn. 2. Traffic - Cleveland, Tenn. 1. Tennessee. State Planning Commission. II. U.S. Urban Renewal Administration. Urban Planning Assistance Program.

Tennessee. State Planning Commission.

711.14
(76896)
K45

Kingsport, Tenn. Regional Planning Commission.
The use of land in Kingsport, by the Upper East Tennessee Office, Tennessee State Planning Commission. Kingsport, 1957.
57p. diagrs., maps, tables.
U.S. Urban Renewal Administration,

(Continued on next card)

711.4
:352.6
(768865)
A73u

Athens, Tenn. Regional Planning Commission. Utilities survey for Athens, Tennessee. Assisted by the Tennessee State Planning Commission, East Tennessee Office. Athens, 1956.
6p. maps.

Urban Renewal Administration, Urban Planning Assistance Program.

1. City planning - Athens, Tenn. 2. Public utilities - Athens, Tenn. I. Tennessee. State Planning Commission. II. U.S. Urban Renewal Administration.

711.4
(76823)
T72

Tennessee. State Planning Commission.
Trenton, Tenn. Municipal Planning Commission.
Trenton base map, Trenton, Tennessee. With the assistance of the Tennessee State Planning Commission, West Tennessee Office. Trenton, 1957.
7p. map.
U.S. Urban Renewal Administration, Urban

(Continued on next card)

711.14
(76896)
K45

Kingsport, Tenn. Regional Planning Commission. The use of land ...(Card 2)

Urban Planning Assistance program.

1. Land use - Kingsport, Tenn. I. Tennessee. State Planning Commission. II. U.S. Urban Renewal Administration. Urban Planning Assistance Program.

352.6
(76892)
M67

Tennessee. State Planning Commission.
Morristown, Tenn. Regional Planning Commission.
Utilities survey for Morristown. Assisted by the Tennessee State Planning Commission. Morristown, 1956.
14p. maps, tables.
U.S. Urban Renewal Administration, Urban Planning Assistance Program.
1. Public utilities - Morristown, Tenn. 2. Community facilities - Morristown, Tenn. I. Tennessee. State Planning Commission. II. U.S. Urban Renewal Administration. Urban Planning Assistance Program.

711.4
(76823)
T72

Trenton, Tenn. Municipal Planning Commission. Trenton base ... (Card 2)

Planning Assistance Program.

1. City planning - Trenton, Tenn. 2. Trenton, Tenn. - Maps. I. Tennessee. State Planning Commission. II. U.S. Urban Renewal Administration. Urban Planning Assistance Program.

Tennessee. State Planning Commission.

352.6
(76861)
P85

Pulaski, Tenn. Municipal-Regional Planning Commission.
Utilities, Pulaski, Tennessee. [Prepared by the Tennessee State Planning Commission, Middle Tennessee Office] Pulaski, 1958.
29p. maps, tables. (MTO Publication no. 58-11)
U.S. Urban Renewal Administration, Urban Planning Assistance Program.
1. Public utilities - Pulaski, Tenn. I. Tennessee. State Planning Commission. II. U.S. Urban Renewal Administration. Urban Planning Assistance Program.

352.6
(76823)
H85

Tennessee. State Planning Commission.
Humboldt, Tenn. Municipal-Regional Planning Commission.
Utilities survey, Humboldt, Tennessee. With the assistance of Tennessee State Planning Commission, West Tennessee Office. Humboldt, 1957.
26p. maps, diagrs., tables.
U.S. Urban Renewal Administration, Urban Planning Assistance Program.

(Continued on next card)

Folio
711.73
(768)
T25

Tennessee. State Planning Commission.
U.S. 41 scenic route. A plan for development. Prepared for the Southeast Tennessee Development District. Chattanooga, 1971.
57p.

1. Highways - Tenn. I. Southeast Tennessee Development District. II. Title.

352.6
(76854)
L21

Tennessee. State Planning Commission.
Lebanon, Tenn. Municipal-Regional Planning Commission.
Utilities study for Lebanon, Tennessee, by Tennessee State Planning Commission, Middle Tennessee Office. Lebanon, 1957.
15p. maps. (MTO publication no. 57-41)
U.S. Urban Renewal Administration,

(Continued on next card)

352.6
(76823)
H85

Humboldt, Tenn. Municipal-Regional Planning Commission. Utilities ... (Card 2)

1. Public utilities - Humboldt, Tenn. I. Tennessee. State Planning Commission. II. U.S. Urban Renewal Administration. Urban Planning Assistance Program.

DATE OF RECORD ___ L. C. CARD NO.
8-27-? AUG 20 1951
AUTHOR
Tennessee State Planning Commission.
TITLE
Uniform subdivision regulations, Sullivan County, Tenn.
SERIES
EDITION | PUB. DATE 6-51 | PAGING 16p. Maps.
PUBLISHER
Effective June 1, 1951
RECOMMENDED BY
REVIEWED IN Amer. City, p. 173, 8-51
ORDER RECORD

352.6
(76854)
L21

Lebanon, Tenn. Municipal-Regional Planning Commission. Utilities ...(Card 2)

Urban Planning Assistance Program.

1. Public utilities - Lebanon, Tenn. I. Tennessee. State Planning Commission. II. U.S. Urban Renewal Administration. Urban Planning Assistance Program.

352.6
(76813)
U54

Tennessee. State Planning Commission.
Union City, Tenn. Regional Planning Commission.
Utilities survey, Union City, Tennessee. With the assistance of the Tennessee State Planning Commission. Union City, 1957.
7p. maps.
U.S. Urban Renewal Administration, Urban Planning Assistance Program.
1. Public utilities - Union City, Tenn. I. Tennessee. State Planning Commission. II.U.S. Urban Renewal Administration. Urban Planning Assistance Program.

711.4
(76813)
U54

Tennessee. State Planning Commission.
Union City, Tenn. Regional Planning Commission.
Union City capital budget improvement program, a study. With the assistance of the Tennessee State Planning Commission. Union City, 1956.
23p. tables.
U.S. Urban Renewal Administration, Urban Planning Assistance Program.
1. Capitol improvement programs - Union City, Tenn. I. Tennessee. State Planning Commission. II. U.S. Urban Renewal Administration. Urban Planning Assistance Program.

352.6
(768984)
E54

Tennessee. State Planning Commission.
Elizabethton, Tenn. Regional Planning Commission.
Utilities survey, Elizabethton, Tennessee. Assisted by the Upper East Tennessee Office, Tennessee State Planning Commission. Elizabethton, 1956.
20p. maps, tables.
U.S. Urban Renewal Administration, Urban

(Continued on next card)

526.8
:711.14
(76837)
T25

Tennessee. State Planning Commission.
Waverly land use map. [Nashville] 1959.
1v. maps.

U.S. Urban Renewal Administration, Urban Planning Assistance Program.

1. Land use - Maps - Waverly, Tenn. I. U.S URA-UPAP. Waverly, Tenn.

330
(768)
T25

Tennessee. State Planning Commission.
Weaving the fabric. It's easy to show children the threads of life, but to weave the whole fabric of life is another question. Here is a new way to deal with the interrelationships of subject matter fields. Nashville, 1951.
    1v. (Its publication 216-B)

    1. Economic conditions - Tennessee.

[Card with handwritten notes]

Class No. *City Te. Plann*
Accession No.
Ordered SEP 21 1950
Received SEP 29 1950

Author (surname first) *Tenn. State Planning Commission*
Planning Legislation 1936-1950 3) What Makes
Place Nashville 3 New Tennessee Nick
Address 417 7th Ave. North *Index to Vol. X*
Edition or Series *3rd*
Reviewed by *Tenn. Pl. 6/50 p.182*

H-305 (2-50)   HOUSING AND HOME FINANCE AGENCY: Office of the Administrator   16-61187-1   GPO

526.8
(768924)
W34

Tennessee. State Planning Commission.
White Pine, Tennessee base maps. White Pine, 1956.
    1v. maps.

    U.S. Urban Renewal Administration, Urban Planning Assistance Program.

    1. White Pine, Tenn. - Maps. I. U.S. Urban Renewal Administration. Urban Planning Assistance Program.

[Card with printed form]

Class No. VF: State finance
Accession No.
Ordered
Source
Received 1/13/53
Cost
Purchase Order No.

Author (surname first) Tennessee. State Planning Commission.
Title Your money and mine.; state finances, 1951-1952.
Place Nashville
Date 12/53 Paging 61 proc.
Edition or Series Its Publication no. 245

H-305 (2-50)   HOUSING AND HOME FINANCE AGENCY: Office of the Administrator   16-61187-1   GPO

711.5
(76853
:347)
S54

Tennessee. State Planning Commission.
Smithville, Tenn. Planning Commission. Zoning for Smithville; a proposed zoning ordinance. Assisted by the Tennessee State Planning Commission, Middle Tennessee Office. Smithville, 1957.
    26p. maps, table. (MTO Publication, no. 57-16)

    U.S. Urban Renewal Administration, Urban Planning Assistance Program.

    (Continued on next card)

711.5
(76853
:347)
S54

Smithville, Tenn. Planning Commission. Zoning for ... 1957. (Card 2)

    1. Zoning legislation - Smithville, Tenn. I. Tennessee. State Planning Commission. II. U.S. Urban Renewal Administration. Urban Planning Assistance Program.

711.4
:711.5
(768865)
A73
1957

Tennessee. State Planning Commission.
Athens, Tenn. Regional Planning Commission. Zoning ordinance of Athens. In cooperation with Tennessee State Planning Commission, East Tennessee Office. Athens, 1957.
    36p. map

    U.S. Urban Renewal Administration, Urban Planning Assistance Program.

    1. City planning - Athens, Tenn. 2. Zoning legislation - Athens, Tenn. I. Tennessee. State Planning Commission. II. U.S. Urban Renewal Administration.

711.5
(768865
:347)
E76

Tennessee. State Planning Commission.
Etowah, Tenn. Municipal-Regional Planning Commission.
Zoning ordinance of the city of Etowah, Tennessee. Assisted by the Tennessee State Planning Commission, East Tennessee Office. Etowah, 1956.
    11p. map.

    U.S. Urban Renewal Administration, Urban Planning Assistance Program.
      (Continued on next card)

711.5
(768865
:347)
E76

Etowah, Tenn. Municipal-Regional Planning Commission.
Zoning ordinance ... (Card 2)

    1. Zoning legislation - Etowah, Tenn. I. Tennessee. State Planning Commission. II. U.S. Urban Renewal Administration. Urban Planning Assistance Program.

711.4
M45

Tennessee. State Planning Commission.
Miller, Harold V
Meeting problems of urban growth, an address before the Governor's Conference on Metropolitan and Urban Problems, Denver, Colorado, January 17, 1958. [Denver] 1958.
    8p.

    1.City growth. 2.Tennessee. State Planning Commission.

R
711
(016)
T25
1966

Tennessee. State Planning Commission - Publications.
Tennessee. State Planning Commission
Publications of the Tennessee State Planning Commission, 1959-1966, by Nicholas Beehan and Mamie Ruth Willis. Nashville, 1966.
    20p. (Its Publication no. 330)

    1. Planning - Bibl. 2. Tennessee. State Planning Commission - Publications. I. Beehan, Nicholas. II. Willis, Mamie Ruth.

534.83
T25

Tennessee. State University, Memphis.
Effects of noise on wildlife and other animals. [Prepared] for the U.S. Environmental Protection Agency, Office of Noise Abatement and Control. Wash., Govt. Print. Off., 1971.
    74p. (NTID 300.5)
    Bibliography: p. 58-74.

    1. Noise. I. U.S. Environmental Protection Agency. II. Title.

728.1
(768191)
C17

Tennessee. State University, Memphis. Bureau of Business and Economic Research.
Cartee, P Charles.
The underhoused of Memphis, by P. C. Cartee and others. Prepared for Housing, Real Estate, and Urban Land Studies Program, Graduate School of Business Administration, University of California, Los Angeles. Sponsored by Life Insurance Association of America. Memphis, Bureau of Business and Economic Research, Div. of Urban and Regional Studies, Memphis State University, 1970.
    86p.
    1. Housing - Memphis. 2. Housing market -

    (Cont'd on next card)

728.1
(768191)
C17

Cartee, P Charles. The underhoused... 1970. (Card 2)

Memphis. I. California. University. University at Los Angeles. Housing, Real Estate, and Urban Land Studies Program. II. Tennessee. State University, Memphis. Bureau of Business and Economic Research. III. Title.

711
(016)
C65
no. 162

Tennessee. State University, Memphis. Div. of Urban and Regional Studies.
Dean, Robert D
Development planning for water resources by Robert D. Dean and Carolyn Wilson. Memphis, Tenn., Div. of Urban and Regional Studies, Memphis State University, 1970.
    22p. (Council of Planning Librarians. Exchange bibliography no. 162)
    1. Planning - Bibl. 2. Water resources - Bibl. I. Tennessee. State University, Memphis. Div. of Urban and Regional Studies. II. Wilson, Carolyn, jt. au. III. Title. (Series: Council of Planning Librarians. Exchange biblio graphy no. 162)

712.21
E17

Tennessee. State University, Memphis. Div. for Regional and Urban Studies.
Easterwood, C B
The socio-economic impacts of the proposed Potomac National River on the contiguous counties, by C.B. Easterwood and others. Prepared for the National Park Service. Memphis Bureau of Business and Economic Research, Div. for Regional and Urban Studies, Memphis State University, 1969.
    114p.
    Bibliography: p. 111-114.
    1. Parks. 2. Rivers. I. U.S. National Park Service. II. Tennessee. State University Memphis. Div. for Regional and Urban Studies. III. Title.

711
(016)
C65
no.178

Tennessee. State University, Memphis. Div. of Urban and Regional Studies.
Dean, Robert D
Urbanization, industrialization and the development process. Memphis, Tenn., Div. of Urban and Regional Studies, Memphis State University, 1971.
    29p. (Council of Planning Librarians. Exchange bibliography no. 178)

    1. Planning - Bibl. 2. City planning - Bibl. 3. Industrial development - Bibl. I. Tennessee. State University, Memphis. Div. of Urban and Regional Studies. II. Title. (Series: Council Planning Librarians. Exchange biblio graphy no. 178)

Tennessee. Supreme court.

... The South western reporter ... Comprising all the current decisions of the Supreme courts of Arkansas, Missouri, Tennessee and Texas, Courts of appeals of Kentucky and Missouri, courts of civil and criminal appeals and Commission of appeals of Texas, with key-number annotations ... Aug./Dec. 1886-Jan./Feb. 1928. St. Paul, West publishing co., 1887-1928.
    300 v. 23-26½cm.
    Vols. 11-300: Permanent edition.
    Title varies: v. 1-112, The Southwestern reporter ... v. 113-114, The Southwestern reporter (annotated) ... v. 125-178, The Southwestern reporter, with key-number annotations ...
      (Continued on next card)
         2—732
      [44r37n2]

Tennessee. Supreme court.

... The South western reporter ... 1887-1928. (Card 2)
    v. 179-276, The South western reporter ...
    v. 277-300, The South western reporter ...
    Subtitle varies: v. 1-14, Containing all the current decisions of the Supreme courts of Missouri, Arkansas, and Tennessee, Court of appeals in Kentucky, and Supreme court and Court of appeals (criminal cases) of Texas.
    v. 15-19, Containing all the current decisions of the Supreme courts of Missouri, Arkansas, and Tennessee, Court of appeals of Kentucky, and Supreme court and Court of appeals of Texas.
    v. 20-34, Containing all the current decisions of the Supreme courts of Missouri, Arkansas, and Tennessee, Court of appeals of Kentucky, and Supreme court, Court of criminal appeals, and Courts of civil appeals of Texas.
      (Continued on next card)
         2—732
      [48r37p2]

Tennessee. Supreme court.

... The South western reporter ... 1887-1928. (Card 3)
    v. 35-36, Containing all the current decisions of the Supreme courts of Missouri, Arkansas, and Tennessee, Court of appeals of Kentucky, Supreme court, Court of criminal appeals, and Courts of civil appeals of Texas, and Court of appeals of Indian territory.
    v. 67-104, Containing all the current decisions of the Supreme and appellate courts of Arkansas, Kentucky, Missouri, Tennessee, and Indian territory.
    v. 105-292, Comprising all current decisions of the Supreme and appellate courts of Arkansas, Kentucky, Missouri, Tennessee, and Texas.
    v. 293-300, Comprising all the current decisions of the Supreme courts of Arkansas, Missouri, Tennessee and Texas, Courts of appeals of Kentucky and Missouri, courts of civil and criminal appeals and Commission of appeals of Texas.
      (Continued on next card)
         2—732
      [48r37p2]

Tennessee. Supreme court.

... The South western reporter ... 1887-1928. (Card 4)
    At head of title: v. 5-300, National reporter system. State series.

    1. Law reports, digests, etc.—Southwest. Old. I. Arkansas. Supreme court. II. Missouri. Supreme court. III. Tennessee. Supreme court. IV. Texas. Supreme court. V. Kentucky. Court of appeals. VI. Missouri. Court of appeals. VII. Texas. Court of civil appeals. VIII. Texas. Court of criminal appeals. IX. Texas. Commissioners of appeals. X. Texas. Court of appeals. XI. Indian territory. Court of appeals. XII. West publishing co., St. Paul. XIII. National reporter system.

    Library of Congress   [48r37p2]
         2—732

Tennessee. Supreme court.

South western reporter. Second series. Cases argued and determined in the courts of Arkansas, Kentucky, Missouri, Tennessee, Texas, with key number annotations. v. 1, [2d-Feb./Mar. 1928- St. Paul, Minn., West publishing co., 1928-

v. 26 cm. **For Additions or Holdings**

Vols. 1-52: Permanent edition see Continuation File
Subtitle varies: v. 1-63, Cases argued and determined in the Supreme courts of Arkansas, Missouri, Tennessee, and Texas; Courts of appeal of Kentucky and Missouri; courts of civil and criminal appeals and Commission of appeals of Texas.

(Continued on next card)
28—17744
[49r38i1]

Tennessee. Supreme court.

South western reporter. Second series ... 1928-
(Card 2)

v. 64-66, Cases argued and determined in the Supreme courts of Arkansas, Missouri, Tennessee, and Texas: Courts of appeals of Kentucky, Missouri and Tennessee; courts of civil and criminal appeals and Commission of appeals of Texas.
v. 67- Cases argued and determined in the courts of Arkansas, Kentucky, Missouri, Tennessee, Texas.

1. Law reports, digests, etc.—Southwest, Old. I. Arkansas. Supreme court. II. Missouri. Supreme court. III. Tennessee. Supreme court. IV. Texas. Supreme court. V. Kentucky. Court of appeals. VI. Missouri. Court of appeals. VII. Texas. Court of civil appeals. VIII. Texas. Court of criminal appeals. IX. Texas. Commissioners of appeals. X. Tennessee. Court of appeals. XI. West publishing co., St. Paul.

Library of Congress [49r38i1]
28—17744

VF
624.131
T25
Tennessee. University. (Dept. of Botany)
Rate and depth of thaw in arctic soils, by J. V. Drew and others. [Knoxville, 1958]
[5]p. (Its Reprint no. 183)
Transactions, American Geophysical Union, vol. 39, no. 4, Aug. 1958. p. 697-701.

1. Soils. 2. Frozen ground. I. Drew, J. V.

VF–Bldg. materials
DATE OF REQUEST 10/21/54 L. C. CARD NO.

AUTHOR Tennessee. University.

TITLE Tennessee building material dealers cost of doing business. Survey.

SERIES

EDITION PUB. DATE 1954 PAGING 12 p.
PUBLISHER

RECOMMENDED BY MML REVIEWED IN
DataGuide, 10/54, p.9
ORDER RECORD

628.515
(016)
H45
Tennessee. University. Center for Business and Economic Research.
Hinote, Hubert.
Benefit-cost analysis for water resources projects; a selected annotated bibliography. Rev. Knoxville, Tenn., Center for Business and Economic Research, College of Business Administration, University of Tennessee, 1969. 148p.

1. Water pollution - Bibl. 2. Water resources - Bibl. I. Tennessee. University. Center for Business and Economic Research. II. Title.

628.515.
T29b
Texas. University. Center for Research in Water Resources.
Bactericidal effects of algae on enteric organisms, by Ernst M. Davis and Earnest F. Gloyna. Austin, 1970.
132p. (U.S. Federal Water Quality Administration. Water pollution control research series)
Bibliography: p. 54-58.
1. Water pollution. 2. Water-supply. I. Davis, Ernst M. II. Gloyna, Earnest F., jt. au. III. U.S. Federal Water Quality Administration. IV. Title.

Tennessee. University. Division of Extension. Municipal Technical Advisory Service.
see
Tennessee. University. Municipal Technical Advisory Service.

351.712
(768)
T25
Tennessee. University. Municipal Technical Advisory Service.
Bid data on current municipal public works, by M. U. Snoderly. In cooperation with the Tennessee Municipal League. Technical bulletin no. 27-29; 31-32; 35-36; 41; Knoxville. 43-52; '54/'55; 57; 59
20 v. 69

For complete information see shelflist.

1. Public works - Tennessee. I. Snoderly, M. U. II. Tennessee Municipal League.

VF
070.44
T25
2C
Tennessee. University. Municipal Technical Advisory Service.
How to make reports, by Pan Dodd Wheeler. In cooperation with the Tennessee Municipal League. [Knoxville] 1957.
42 p. (Its Technical bulletin no. 20)

1. Report writing. 2. Municipal services. I. Wheeler, Pan Dodd. II. Tennessee Municipal League. III. Title.

352
(768)
T25i
Tennessee. University. Municipal Technical Advisory Service.
Ideas for a better city, comp. by Mary Bush. In cooperation with the Tennessee Municipal League. Knoxville, Tenn., 1957-1969 13 v. annual.
Items which have appeared in Tennessee Town and City and have been extracted from publications in the field of municipal government.
For complete information see shelflist.
1. Municipal government - Tennessee. I. Tennessee Municipal League. II. Bush, Mary, comp.

2c-67
sc-69

352.5
T25
Tennessee. University. Municipal Technical Advisory Service.
Tennessee. University. Bureau of Public Administration.
Kingsport and annexation, by Roy S. Nicks and others. Knoxville, Tenn., 1956. 153p. map, tables.

1. Annexation - Kingsport, Tenn. I. Nicks, Roy S. II. Tennessee. University. Municipal Technical Advisory Service. III. Tennessee Municipal League.

628.1
(768)
T25
Tennessee. University. Municipal Technical Advisory Service.
Municipal water works operating data for Tennessee, by W. T. Chaffin and M. U. Snoderly. In cooperation with the Tennessee Municipal League. Knoxville, 1960. 24p. tables. (Its Technical bulletin no. 39)

1. Water—supply - Tennessee. I. Chaffin, W. T. II. Snoderly, M. U. III. Tennessee Municipal League.

353
(768)
T25
Tennessee. University. Municipal Technical Advisory Service.
Revenues and expenditures of 79 Tennessee towns and cities, 1956, by William T. Chaffin and Kenneth E. Spence. In cooperation with Tennessee Municipal League. Knoxville, 1958. 33p. tables. (Its Technical bulletin no. 33)

1. State finance - Tennessee. I. Chaffin, William T. II. Spence, Kenneth E. III. Tennessee Municipal League.

353
(768)
T25
1957
Tennessee. University. Municipal Technical Advisory Service.
Revenues and expenditures of 107 Tennessee towns and cities 1957, by William T. Chaffin and John B. Berg. In cooperation with the Tennessee Municipal League. Knoxville, 1959. 45p. tables. (Its Technical bulletin no. 34)

1. State finance - Tennessee. I. Chaffin, William T. II. Berg, John B. III. Tennessee Municipal League.

353
(768)
T25
1958
Tennessee. University. Municipal Technical Advisory Service.
Revenues and expenditures of 139 Tennessee towns and cities, 1958 comp. by William T. Chaffin and George T. Morton. In cooperation with the Tennessee Municipal League. Knoxville, Tenn., 1960. 64p. tables. (Its Technical bulletin no. 38)

1. State finance - Tennessee. I. Chaffin, William T. II. Morton, George T. III. Tennessee Municipal League.

353
(768)
T25
1959
Tennessee. University. Municipal Technical Advisory Service.
Revenues and expenditures of 81 Tennessee towns and cities, 1959, comp. by Inslee Burnett. In cooperation with Tennessee Municipal League. Knoxville, Tenn., 1961. 39p. (Its Technical bulletin no. 42)

1. State finance - Tennessee. I. Burnett, Inslee, comp. II. Tennessee Municipal League.

353
(768)
T25
1960
Tennessee. University. Municipal Technical Advisory Service.
Revenues and expenditures of 78 Tennessee towns and cities, 1960, comp. by Inslee Burnett. In cooperation with Tennessee Municipal League. Knoxville, Tenn., 1962. 43p. (Its Technical bulletin no. 46)

1. State finance - Tennessee. I. Burnett, Inslee, comp. II. Tennessee Municipal League.

347
(768)
T25
Tennessee. University. Municipal Technical Advisory Service.
Sample code of ordinances for small cities and towns in Tennessee, by Don W. Ownby. In cooperation with the Tennessee Municipal League. Nashville, 1961. 137p.

1. Ordinances - Tennessee. I. Ownby, Don W. II. Tennessee Municipal League.

VF
352
T25
Tennessee. University. Municipal Technical Advisory Service.
Thoughts on metropolitan areas, by Lee S. Greene. Knoxville, Tenn., 1957. pamphlet.

1. Metropolitan areas. I. Greene, Lee S

353
(768:347)
H62
Tennessee. University. Bureau of Public Administration.
Hobday, Victor C
An analysis of 1953 Tennessee home rule amendments, number 6 and number 7. Knoxville, Tenn., Bureau of Public Administration, University of Tennessee, Sept. 1956. p.

1. State government - Tennessee. 2. Municipal government - Tennessee. 3. Intergovernmental relations - Tennessee. I. Tennessee Municipal League. II. Tennessee University. Bureau of Public Administration.

711.4
:670
S721
Tennessee. University. Bureau of Public Administration.
Stephenson, Charles M
Industrial sites; a community problem. Knoxville, Tenn., Bureau of Public Administration, Univ. of Tenn., 1961. 19p.

1. Industrial location. 2. Community development. I. Tennessee. University. Bureau of Public Administration.

352.5
T25
Tennessee. University. Bureau of Public
Administration.
Kingsport and annexation, by Roy S.
Nicks and others. Knoxville, Tenn., 1956.
153p. map, tables.

1.Annexation - Kingsport, Tenn. I.Nicks,
Roy S II.Tennessee. University. Municipal
Technical Advisory Service. III.Tennessee
Municipal League.

728.1
:336:18
L17
TENNESSEE. UNIVERSITY. BUREAU OF
PUBLIC ADMINISTRATION.
LARSEN, WILLIAM F
NEW HOMES FOR OLD, PUBLICLY OWNED
HOUSING IN TENNESSEE. KNOXVILLE,
TENN., PUBLISHED BY THE DIVISION OF
UNIVERSITY EXTENSION FOR THE BUREAU OF
PUBLIC ADMINISTRATION, UNIVERSITY OF
TENNESSEE, 1948.
83P. (UNIVERSITY OF TENNESSEE
RECORD. EXTENSION SERIES, V. 24, NO.
7)
1. PUBLIC HOUSING - TENNESSEE.
I. TITLE. II. TENNESSEE.
UNIVERSITY. BUREAU OF PUBLIC
ADMINISTRATIO.

Class No.
School

Author (Surname first)
NOT RUSH

Annexation No.
plant please

Title

Ordered

Or

Received 1950

Edition, Series   Place   Publisher

Cost

Date   11/49   Vols.   49p

Charged to   Recommended by

Date of bill   Address

L. C. No.   Reviewed in

330
(75)
G17
Tennessee. Office of Urban and Federal
Affairs.
Garriott, William C
A study of the ability of Tennessee
Appalachian Counties to pay for projects
partially funded by Federal grants, for
the Tennessee Appalachian Staff of the Office
of Urban and Federal Affairs, State of
Tennessee. [Nashville] 1967.
49p.
On cover: Resource Development Internship
project.
Bibliography: p. 45-47.

1. Economic   development - Appalachian region.   (Cont'd on next card)

330
(75)
G17
Garriott, William C   A study...1967.
(card 2)
2. Local government - Appalachian
region. 3. Grants-in-aid. I. Tennessee.
Office of Urban and Federal Affairs.
II. Title.

Tennessee and national economic growth.

330
(768)
T25t
Tennessee. State Planning Commission.
Tennessee and national economic growth.
Nashville, Tenn., 1967.
89p. (Its Publication no. 357)

1. Economic base studies - Tennessee. 2.
Social conditions - Tennessee. 3. Labor-
supply - Tennessee. 4. Employment - Tennessee. 5. Population - Tennessee. I. Title.

Ref
DATE OF REQUEST 1/22/53 Rec'd 2/4/53   L.C. CARD NO.

AUTHOR University of Tennessee. Municipal Technical
Advisory Service.

TITLE Directory, Tennessee Municipal Officials

SERIES

EDITION   PUB. DATE 1952   PAGING 63 pp

PUBLISHER Tennessee Municipal League

RECOMMENDED BY   REVIEWED IN Planning Current
Literature, 12/29/52-pg.4.
ORDER RECORD

351.712
(768)
T25
Tennessee Municipal League.
Tennessee. University. Municipal Technical
Advisory Service.
Bid data on current municipal public
works, by M. U. Snoderly. In cooperation
with the Tennessee Municipal League.
Technical bulletin no. 53.   July 1967.
Knoxville. no.58 July 1968.
3 v.

For complete information see shelflist.

1. Public works - Tennessee. I. Snoderly, M. U.
II. Tennessee Municipal League.

352
(768)
T25i
Tennessee Municipal League.
Tennessee. University. Municipal Technical
Advisory Service.
Ideas for a better city, comp. by Mary
Bush. In cooperation with the Tennessee
Municipal League. Knoxville, Tenn.
v. annual.
Items which have appeared in Tennessee
Town and City and have been extracted from
publications in the field of municipal govern-
ment.
For complete information see shelflist.
1. Municipal   government - Tennessee.
I. Tennessee   Municipal League.
II. Bush, Mary,   comp.

352.5
T25
Tennessee Municipal League.
Tennessee. University. Bureau of Public
Administration.
Kingsport and annexation, by Roy S.
Nicks and others. Knoxville, Tenn., 1956.
153p. map, tables.

1.Annexation - Kingsport, Tenn. I.Nicks,
Roy S II.Tennessee. University. Municipal
Technical Advisory Service. III.Tennessee
Municipal League.

VF
070.44
T25
Tennessee Municipal League.
Tennessee. University. Municipal Technical
Advisory Service.
How to make reports, by Pan Dodd Wheeler.
In cooperation with the Tennessee Municipal
League. [Knoxville] 1957.
42 p. (Its Technical bulletin no. 20)

1.Report writing. 2.Municipal services.
I.Wheeler, Pan Dodd. II.Tennessee Municipal
League. III.Title.

352
E55
Tennessee. University. Municipal Technical
Advisory Service.
Ellison, Gerry, ed.
Ideas for a better city/1970. Selected by
the staff of the Municipal Technical Advisory
Service. Edited by Gerry Ellison and Jackie
Kersh. [n.p.] Municipal Technical Advisory
Service, Div. of Continuing Education,
University of Tennessee, in cooperation with
the Tennessee Municipal League, 1971.
16p.
1. Municipal government. 2. Municipal govern-
ment - Bibl. I. Kersh, Jackie, jt. ed.
II. Tennessee. University. Municipal Technical
Advisory Service.   III. Tennessee Municipal
League.   IV. Title.

Tennessee housing legislation, 1935-1965.

LAW
S
Tennessee. State Planning Commission.
Tennessee housing legislation, 1935-1965.
Prepared by Nicholas Beehan. Nashville, 1966.
50p.   (Its Publication no. 338)
Reported from Tennessee code annotated
(as amended through 1965)

1. Housing legislation - Tennessee.
2. Local housing authorities - Tennessee.
I. Beehan, Nicholas. II. Title.

352
E55
Tennessee Municipal League.
Ellison, Gerry, ed.
Ideas for a better city/1970. Selected by
the staff of the Municipal Technical Advisory
Service. Edited by Gerry Ellison and Jackie
Kersh. [n.p.] Municipal Technical Advisory
Service, Div. of Continuing Education,
University of Tennessee, in cooperation with
the Tennessee Municipal League, 1971.
16p.
1. Municipal government. 2. Municipal govern-
ment - Bibl. I. Kersh, Jackie, jt. ed.
II. Tennessee. University. Municipal Technical
Advisory Service.   III. Tennessee Municipal
League.   IV. Title.

DATE OF REQUEST Munographt
DEC 2 6 1950   L.C. CARD NO.

AUTHOR
Bureau of Public Adm., Univ. of Tenn.

TITLE Greenville's government: A study of the organizatio
and administration of the government of Greenville,
Tennessee.
SERIES

EDITION   PUB. DATE 10/50   PAGING 159p.

PUBLISHER

same   Processed

RECOMMENDED BY   REVIEWED IN
Tenn.Govt. 9-10/50 Pg. 2
ORDER RECORD

339.5
(768)
T25
Tennessee, its resources and economy.
Tennessee. Dept. of Finance and
Administration.
Tennessee, its resources and economy.
Vol. 2. Tennessee's natural resources.
Nashville, 1966.
[70]p. (Its Publication no. 331b)

1. Natural resources - Tenn. 2. Economic
conditions - Tenn. I. Title.

628.1
(768)
T25
Tennessee Municipal League.
Tennessee. University. Municipal Technical
Advisory Service.
Municipal water works operating data for
Tennessee, by W. T. Chaffin and M. U.
Snoderly. In cooperation with the Tennessee
Municipal League. Knoxville, 1960.
24p. tables. (Its Technical bulletin
no. 39)

1. Water-supply - Tennessee. I. Chaffin, W. T.
II. Snoderly, M. U.   III. Tennessee Municipal
League.

312
(768)
K56
Tennessee. University. Bureau of Sociological
Research.
Knox, John Ballenger.
The people of Tennessee; a study of population trends.
Prepared for the Bureau for Sociological Research, with
the assistance of Jerry W. Combs, Jr., and others, With
an introd. by William E. Cole. Knoxville, University of
Tennessee Press, 1949.
xvi, 191 p. Illus., maps. 24 cm.
Bibliography: p. 178,-187.

1. Tennessee—Population. I. Tennessee. University. Bureau of
Sociological Research. II. Title.

HB3525.T2K5   312   49—48571*
Library of Congress   [50r5]

353
(768:347)
H62
Tennessee Municipal League.
Hobday, Victor C
An analysis of 1953 Tennessee home rule
amendments, number 6 and number 7. Knoxville,
Tenn., Bureau of Public Administration,
University of Tennessee, Sept. 1956.
p.

1. State government - Tennessee. 2. Municipal government - Tennessee. 3. Intergovernmental relations - Tennessee. I. Tennessee
Municipal League. II. Tennessee University.
Bureau of   Public Administration.

353
(768)
T25
Tennessee Municipal League
Tennessee. University. Municipal Technical
Advisory Service.
Revenues and expenditures of 79 Tennessee
towns and cities, 1956, by William T. Chaffin
and Kenneth E. Spence. In cooperation with
Tennessee Municipal League. Knoxville, 1958.
33p. tables. (Its Technical bulletin no. 33)

1. State finance - Tennessee. I. Chaffin, William
T   II. Spence, Kenneth F. III.Tennessee Municipal League.

353
(768)
T25
1959

Tennessee Municipal League.

Tennessee. University. Municipal Technical Advisory Service.
Revenues and expenditures of 107 Tennessee towns and cities 1957, by William T. Chaffin and John B. Berg. In cooperation with the Tennessee Municipal League. Knoxville, 1959.
45p. tables. (Its Technical bulletin no. 34)

1. State finance - Tennessee. I. Chaffin, William T. II. Berg, John B. III. Tennessee Municipal League.

353
(768)
T25
1958

Tennessee Municipal League.

Tennessee. University. Municipal Technical Advisory Service.
Revenues and expenditures of 139 Tennessee towns and cities, 1958, comp. by William T. Chaffin and George T. Morton. In cooperation with the Tennessee Municipal League. Knoxville, Tenn., 1960.
64p. tables. (Its Technical bulletin no.38)

1. State finance - Tennessee. I. Chaffin, William T. II. Morton, George T. III. Tennessee Municipal League.

353
(768)
T25
1959

Tennessee Municipal League.

Tennessee. University. Municipal Technical Advisory Service.
Revenues and expenditures of 81 Tennessee towns and cities, 1959, comp. by Inslee Burnett. In cooperation with Tennessee Municipal League. Knoxville, Tenn., 1961.
39p. (Its Technical bulletin no. 42)

1. State finance - Tennessee. I. Burnett, Inslee, comp. II. Tennessee Municipal League.

353
(768)
T25
1960

Tennessee Municipal League.

Tennessee. University. Municipal Technical Advisory Service.
Revenues and expenditures of 78 Tennessee towns and cities, 1960, comp. by Inslee Burnett. In cooperation with Tennessee Municipal League. Knoxville, Tenn., 1962.
43p. (Its Technical bulletin no. 46)

1. State finance - Tennessee. I. Burnett, Inslee, comp. II. Tennessee Municipal League.

347
(768)
T25

Tennessee Municipal League.

Tennessee. University. Municipal Technical Advisory Service.
Sample code of ordinances for small cities and towns in Tennessee, by Don W. Ownby. In cooperation with the Tennessee Municipal League. Nashville, 1961.
137p.

1. Ordinances - Tennessee. I. Ownby, Don W. II. Tennessee Municipal League.

711.4
(768)
T25

Tennessee Municipal League.
Tennessee municipal policy; preventing substandard urban growth, adopted at the 25th annual conference of the Tennessee Municipal League in Knoxville, June 7-9, 1964. Knoxville, 1964.
[3]p.
Pre-printed from Tennessee town and city August 1964.

1. City planning - Tennessee. I. Tennessee town and city.

---

s

The Tennessee planner. v. 1-
Jan./Feb. 1940-
[Nashville] Tennessee State Planning Commission.

v. in illus., ports., maps (part col.) 23 cm. bimonthly (irregular)

Supersedes Tennessee plan topics.
INDEXES:
Vols. 2-6, Jan. 1941-June 1946, with v. 3-6.
For full information see Periodicals Kardex file.
1. Tennessee—Economic policy—Period. 2. Regional planning—Tennessee. I. Tennessee. State Planning Commission.

HC107.T3T43   338.91   51-28506
Library of Congress   [1]

VF
711.4
C16

Tennessee planning legislation. In Caplow, Theodore, City planning. Minneapolis, Minn., c1950. p. 189-201.

Contents.-Municipal planning act.-Municipal zoning act.-Municipal subdivision control act.-Urban redevelopment act.
Reprinted from Tennessee State Planning Commission pamphlet issued in 1945.
1.City planning legislation-Tenn. 2.Zoning legis.-Tenn. 3.Urban redevelopment legislation-Tenn.

VF
711.3
(768:347)
T25
1963

Tennessee planning legislation, 1935-1963.
Tennessee. Laws, statutes, etc.
Tennessee planning legislation, 1935-1963. Prepared by Anne Sternheimer. [Nashville] Tennessee State Planning Commission, 1963.
44p. (Publication no. 327)
Reprinted from Tennessee Code annotated (as amended through 1962)

1. State planning legislation - Tennessee. 2. Zoning legislation - Tenn. I. Tennessee. State Planning Commission. II. Title.

R
711.3
(768:347)
T25

Tennessee planning legislation, 1935-1967.
Tennessee. Law, statutes, etc.
Tennessee planning legislation, 1935-1967. Prepared by Nicholas Beehan, Jr. Nashville, Tennessee State Planning Commission, 1967.
49p. (Bulletin no. 353)
Reprinted from Tennessee Code annotated and attached amendments of the 85th General Assembly (Recessed May 26, 1967)

1. State planning legislation - Tennessee. 2. Zoning legislation - Tennessee. I. Tennessee. State Planning Commission. II. Title.

333.33
(768)
R21

TENESSEE REAL ESTATE.
REAL ESTATE BOARD OF MEMPHIS.
TENESSEE REAL ESTATE, EDITED BY MAHLON LYNN TOWNSEND. KNOXVILLE, TENN., UNIVERSITY OF TENNESSEE PRESS, 1958.
304P.
APPENDIX OF REAL ESTATE FORMS, P.223-285. GLOSSARY, P.287-295.

1. REAL ESTATE BUSINESS - TENNESSEE. I. TOWNSEND, MAHLON LYNN, ED. II. TITLE.

627.4
T25t

Tennessee Valley Authority. (Government Research Branch)
The Tennessee River Valley, a case study by A. J. Gray, chief community planner, Government Research Branch and Victor Roterus, director, Office of Area Development, U.S. Dept. of Commerce. Prepared by Office of International Housing, Office of the Administrator, Housing and Home Finance Agency for the use of United States Operations Missions. Washington [Housing Division, International Cooperation Administration, 1960]
15p. maps. (Continued on next card)

627.4
T25t

Tennessee Valley Authority. (Government Research Branch) The Tennessee...1960.
(Card 2)

1. Flood control - Tennessee Valley. 2. Regional planning - Tennessee Valley. I. Gray, A.J. II. Roterus, Victor. III. U.S. Housing and Home Finance Agency. Office of the Administrator. Office of International Housing. IV. Title.

362
(768)
T25

Tennessee State plan for construction of hospitals and medical facilities.
Tennessee. Dept. of Public Health.
Tennessee State plan for construction of hospitals and medical facilities, 1969. Nashville, 1969.
1v.

Cover title.

1. Hospitals - Tenn. I. Title.

711.585.1
(76867)
C66m

7c

Tennessee Technological University, Cookeville.
Cookeville, Tenn. City Demonstration Agency.
Mid planning statement, Cookeville, Tennessee. Prepared in cooperation with the Tennessee Technological University, technical consultants. Cookeville, 1970.
70p.
U.S. Dept. of Housing and Urban Development. Model Cities Program.
1. Model cities - Cookeville, Tenn. I. Tennessee Technological University, Cookeville. II. U.S. HUD-Model Cities Program.

711
(016)
C65
no.190

Tennessee Technological University.
Lancaster, Joel R
A selected bibliography of geographical references and related research in outdoor recreation and tourism: 1930-1971, by Joel R. Lancaster and Leland L. Nicholls. Cookeville, Tenn., Tennessee Technological University, 1971.
41p. (Council of Planning Librarians. Exchange bibliography no. 190)
1. Planning - Bibl. 2. Recreation - Bibl. I. Nicholls, Leland L., jt. au. II. Tennessee Technological University. III. Title. (Series: Council of Planning Librarians. Exchange bibliography no. 190)

711.4
(768)
T25

Tennessee town and city.
Tennessee Municipal League.
Tennessee municipal policy; preventing substandard urban growth, adopted at the 25th annual conference of the Tennessee Municipal League in Knoxville, June 7-9, 1964. Knoxville, 1964.
[3]p.
Pre-printed from Tennessee town and city August 1964.

1. City planning - Tennessee. I. Tennessee town and city.

Tennessee Valley Authority.

do not subdivide for divisions, sections, etc. except for the Technical Library.

Tennessee Valley Authority

see also

Valley authorities.

VF
627.4
T25
1955

Tennessee Valley Authority.
TVA, a national asset. Knoxville, Tennessee, 1955.
8p.

1. Flood control - Tennessee Valley.

VF
339.5
E53
1958

Tennessee Valley Authority.
Engstrom, Le Roy.
TVA and the river. An address by Chief, TVA River Control Branch, at a joint meeting of the Engineers Club of Western North Carolina and Greenville Section of A.S.M.E., in Asheville, N.C. on Nov. 19, 1951. Rev. 1958. [Asheville, N.C.] 1958.
12p.

1. Power resources
2. Floods. I. Tennessee Valley Authority.

728.69
T25T
TENNESSEE VALLEY AUTHORITY.
  TVA DEMOUNTABLE COTTAGES.
KNOXVILLE, TENN., 1941.
  6L.

  1. DEMOUNTABLE HOUSES. I. TITLE.

711.4
(768)
T25C
TENNESSEE VALLEY AUTHORITY.
TENNESSEE. STATE PLANNING COMMISSION.
CITIZEN PARTICIPATION IN URBAN
COMMUNITY PLANNING. NASHVILLE, 1948.
73P. (ITS PUBLICATION NO. 188)

  PREPARED WITH THE ASSISTANCE OF THE
TENNESSEE VALLEY AUTHORITY.

  1. CITY PLANNING - TENNESSEE.
I. TENNESSEE VALLEY AUTHORITY.
II. TITLE.

728.1
(76873)
G71
TENNESSEE VALLEY AUTHORITY.
GRANDGENT, LOUIS.
  HOUSES AT NORRIS, TENNESSEE;
  A REVIEW OF COSTS. KNOXVILLE,
TENNESSEE VALLEY AUTHORITY, DIVISION
OF LAND PLANNING AND HOUSING, 1936.
  31L.

  1. HOUSING - NORRIS, TENN.
I. TENNESSEE VALLEY AUTHORITY.

VF
728.69
T25
Tennessee Valley Authority. (Department of
  Regional Studies)
  TVA Demountable houses for defense workers;
a report. Knoxville, Tenn., July 1941.
  10 L., illus., diagrs., plans.

  1. Demountable houses. 2. Housing - Wartime.

VF
711.4
(76873)
C54
Tennessee Valley Authority.
Clinton, Tenn. Municipal Planning Commission.
  The Clinton master plan. Clinton, Tenn.,
Oct. 1950.
  29 p. illus., maps(part fold.)
  Technical assistance from the Tennessee State
Planning Commission, East Tennessee Office, and
Tennessee Valley Authority, Division of Regional
Studies.
  1. Master plan-Clinton, Tenn. 2. City planning-
Clinton, Mass. I. Tennessee. State Planning
Commission. II. Tennessee Valley Authority.
Division of Regional Studies.

LAW
T
B282Le
Tennessee Valley Authority.
Beuchert, Edward W
  A legal view of the flood plain. [Cambridge]
Harvard Law School, 1961.
  81p.

  "Reproduced by the Tennessee Valley Authority."

  1. Flood control. I. Tennessee Valley
Authority. II. Harvard University. Law
School. III. Title.

VF
627.4
T25
Tennessee Valley Authority.
  TVA, flood control. Rev. [Knoxville]
1958.
  11p. illus., map.

  1. Flood control - Tennessee Valley.

VF
711.4
C31
Tennessee Valley Authority.
Chapin, F Stuart, Jr.
  Communities for living. By F. Stuart Chapin,
Jr., in collaboration with Sam Schiller. Athens,
Ga., University of Georgia Press, 1941.
  ix, 56 p. illus., diagrs.
  Prepared for the Advisory Panel on Regional
Materials of Instruction for the Tennessee Valley.
  1. City planning. I. Schiller, Sam, jt. au. II. Ad-
visory Panel on Regional Materials of Instruction
for the Tennessee Valley. III. Tennessee Valley
Authority. Dept. of Regional Studies. IV. Georgia.
University. V. Title.

651.4
T25
TENNESSEE VALLEY AUTHORITY.
  MANUAL OF FILE OPERATION STANDARDS.
4TH ED. CHATTANOOGA, 1956.
  1 V. (VARIOUS PAGINGS)

  1. OFFICE PROCEDURES. I. TITLE:
FILE OPERATION STANDARDS.

VF
711.3
(73)
T25
Tennessee Valley Authority.
  TVA, 1950. Washington, U. S. Govt. Print. Off., 1950.
  iv, 64 p. illus., map. 23 cm.

  TK1425.M8T4 1950   333.91   50-60463

  Library of Congress   [5]

627.4
(016)
T25
1963
TENNESSEE VALLEY AUTHORITY.
  FLOOD DAMAGE PREVENTION; AN INDEXED
BIBLIOGRAPHY. KNOXVILLE, TENN.,
TENNESSEE VALLEY AUTHORITY, TECHNICAL
LIBRARY, 1963.
  28P.

  1. FLOODS - BIBLIOGRAPHY. I. TITLE.

628.1
(768)
T25n
Tennessee Valley Authority.
  Nature's consent gift; a report on the
water resource of the Tennessee Valley.
Knoxville, Tenn., 1963.
  76p.

  1. Water resources - Tennessee Valley.
I. Title.

VF
339.5
T25
Tennessee Valley Authority.
  TVA today, 1965-1966. Knoxville, Tenn.
Direct requests to TVA Information Office,
1965.
  28p.

  1. Tennessee Valley Authority. 2. Power
resources. 3. Electricity.

627.4
(75574)
T25
Tennessee Valley Authority. (Division of Water
  Control Planning)
  Floods on Powell River and South Fork
Powell River in vicinity of Big Stone Gap,
Virginia Knoxville, Tenn., April 1956.
  24 L. Charts, maps, tables.

  Contents.-I. Flood histories to April 1, 1955.
II. Maximum floods of reasonable regional
expectancy.

  1. Floods - Big Stone Gap, Va.

628.1
(768)
T25n
1966
Tennessee Valley Authority.
  Nature's consent gift; a report on the
water resource of the Tennessee Valley.
Knoxville, Tenn., 1966.
  72p.

  1. Water resources - Tennessee Valley.
2. Water-supply - Tennessee Valley.
3. Water pollution - Tennessee Valley.
I. Title.

712.25
(763)
R22
Tennessee Valley Authority.
Beech River (Tenn.) Watershed Development
  Authority.
  Beech River watershed development plan
and program proposals with technical
assistance of Tennessee State Planning
Commission and Tennessee Valley Authority.
Nashville, 1965.
  143p.

  1. Recreation - Tenn. 2. Water-supply -
Tenn. I. Tennessee. State Planning
Commission.   II. Tennessee Valley
Authority.

627.4
(76199)
T25
Tennessee Valley Authority. (Division of
  Water Control Planning)
  Floods on Tennessee River and Cypress
and Cox Creeks in vicinity of Florence, Alabama.
Knoxville, Tenn., May 1956.
  39 L. Illus., graphs, maps, tables.

  Contents.-I. Flood histories to May 1, 1956.
- II. Maximum floods of reasonable regional
expectancy.

  1. Floods - Florence, Ala.

712.25
(768)
T25o
Tennessee Valley Authority.
  Outdoor recreation for a growing nation;
TVA's experience with man-made reservoirs.
Knoxville, Tenn., 1961.
  116p.

  1. Recreation - Tennessee Valley.
2. Tennessee Valley Authority.

628.16
T25C
TENNESSEE VALLEY AUTHORITY.
  THE CHICKAMAUGA PROJECT, A
COMPREHENSIVE REPORT ON THE PLANNING,
DESIGN, CONSTRUCTION, AND INITIAL
OPERATIONS OF THE CHICKAMAUGA PROJECT.
KNOXVILLE, 1942.
  451P. (ITS TECHNICAL REPORT NO. 6)

  PREPARED BY GEORGE E. TOMLINSON.
P. 301.
  1. WATER-SUPPLY ENGINEERING.
2. WATER-SUPPLY - TENNESSEE.
I. TOMLINSON, GEORGE EDMUND, 1906-
II. TITLE.

697
(76873)
G71
TENNESSEE VALLEY AUTHORITY.
GRANDGENT, LOUIS.
  HEATING AT NORRIS, TENNESSEE; A
STUDY OF THERMAL EFFICIENCY IN
HOUSING. KNOXVILLE, TENNESSEE VALLEY
AUTHORITY, 1938.
  42P.

  1. HEATING - NORRIS, TENN.
I. TENNESSEE VALLEY AUTHORITY.

712.25
(76879)
T25
Tennessee Valley Authority.
Tennessee. State Planning Commission.
  A plan for development, Nickajack
reservoir area. [Prepared in cooperation
with] Marion County Planning Commission
and Tennessee Valley Authority.
Nashville, 1965.
  88p.

  1. Recreation - Marion Co., Tenn.
2. Open space land. 3. County planning -
Marion Co., Tenn. I. Marion County,
Tenn.   Planning Commission.
II. Tennessee   Valley Authority.

VF
029
T25

[Tennessee Valley Authority. *Office of Chief Conservation Engineer. Division of Chemical Engineering.*]
Preparation of research and engineering reports, by M. A. Tschantre [chief, Administrative Section] Wilson Dam, Ala., 1950.
33 l. illus. 28 cm.
Bibliography: leaf 22-23.

Report

1. Technical writing. I. Tschantre, Maurice Albert. II. Title.
2. Engineering research.
T11.T37   651.78   51-60422
Library of Congress   [2]

VF
388
T25r
1959

Tennessee Valley Authority.
River traffic and industrial growth.
Rev. Knoxville, Tenn., 1959.
16p.

1. Transportation - Tennessee Valley.
2. Industrial location - Tennessee Valley. I. Title.

627
T25T

TENNESSEE VALLEY AUTHORITY.
TVA 25TH ANNIVERSARY PROGRESS THRU RESOURCE DEVELOPMENT. A REPORT TO THE NATION FROM THE TENNESSEE VALLEY AUTHORITY ON ITS FIRST TWENTY-FIVE YEARS, 1933-1958. [N.P., 195]
20P.

1. TITLE.

· VF
711.3
T25p

Tennessee Valley Authority.
Profile of a region; some characteristics and general trends, Tennessee Valley States. [Knoxville, Tenn.] Tennessee Valley Authority, Government Relations and Economics Staff, 1958.
19p.

1. Regional planning - Tenessee Valley.

627
T25s

TENNESSEE VALLEY AUTHORITY.
THE SCENIC RESOURCES OF THE TENNESSEE VALLEY. A DESCRIPTIVE AND PICTORIAL INVENTORY. PREPARED BY THE TENNESSEE VALLEY, DEPARTMENT OF REGIONAL PLANNING STUDIES. KNOXVILLE, 1938.
222P.

1. TENNESSEE VALLEY AUTHORITY.
I. TITLE.

627.4
T25t
Span.

Tennessee Valley Authority. (Government Research Branch)
El Valle del Rio Tennessee, estudio de un caso, por A. J. Gray, jefe de planificacion de la comunidad, Government Research Branch, Tennessee Valley Authority y Victor Roterus, director, Office of Area Development, U.S. Department of Commerce. [Preparado por Housing and Home Finance Agency, Office of International Housing, Office of the Administrator, para la International Cooperation Administration] Mexico, Centro Regional de Ayuda Tecnica, 1960.
(Continued on next card)

627.4
C65p

Tennessee Valley Authority.
U.S. Congress. Senate. Committee on Public Works.
A program for reducing the national flood damage potential. Washington, Govt. Print. Off., 1959.
70p.
At head of title: 86th Cong. 1st sess.
Memorandum of the Chairman to members of the Committee on a report from T.V.A.

1. Flood control. I. Tennessee Valley Authority.

627
T25

[Tennessee Valley Authority]
A short history of the Tennessee Valley Authority, 1933-1956. [Knoxville, Tenn.] 1956.
[6]p.

1. Tennessee Valley Authority.
2. Power resources.

627.4
T25t
Span.

Tennessee Valley Authority. (Government Research Branch) El Valle...1960. (Card 2)
18p. illus., maps.

Translation of The Tennessee River Valley.

1. Flood control - Tennessee Valley. 2. Regional planning - Tennessee Valley. I. Gray, A.J. II. Roterus, Victor. III. U.S. Housing and Home Finance Agency. Office of the Administrator. Office of International Housing. IV. Title.

VF
333.63
T25

Tennessee Valley Authority. (Social and Economic Division. Research Section.)
Rental rated for dwellings in Norris, Tennessee. Submitted by T. Levron Howard.
Knoxville, Tenn., June 1937.
17 l. tables.

Confidential, not for publication.
Mimeographed.

1. Rents, Norris, Tenn. I. Howard, T. Levron.

697
P87

TENNESSEE VALLEY AUTHORITY.
PURNELL, W H
STUDIES IN THE HEATING OF SMALL HOUSES.
KNOXVILLE, 1939.
55P.

AT HEAD OF TITLE: TENNESSEE VALLEY AUTHORITY, DEPARTMENT OF REGIONAL PLANNING STUDIES, COMMUNITY PLANNING DIVISION.

1. HEATING. I. TENNESSEE VALLEY AUTHORITY.

627
T25v

Tennessee Valley Authority.
Valley with a future Knoxville, 1960.
18p.

1. Tennessee Valley Authority.
2. Power resources.

712.25
(768)
T25R

TENNESSEE VALLEY AUTHORITY.
RECREATION DEVELOPMENT OF THE TENNESSEE RIVER SYSTEM; MESSAGE FROM THE PRESIDENT OF THE UNITED STATES TRANSMITTING A REPORT ON THE RECREATION DEVELOPMENT OF THE TENNESSEE RIVER SYSTEM. WASHINGTON, U.S. GOVT. PRINT. OFF., 1940.
99P. (76TH CONGRESS, 3D SESSION. HOUSE OF REPRESENTATIVES. DOCUMENT NO. 565)

1. RECREATION - TENNESSEE VALLEY.

V
6-14-56

DATE OF REQUEST electrical appliances C. CARD NO.

AUTHOR
Tennessee Valley Authority

TITLE
Survey of electrical appliances in homes and farms of TVA area, 1955.

SERIES

EDITION | PUB. DATE 12-55 | PAGING 20 p. ill.

PUBLISHER

RECOMMENDED BY M. L. | REVIEWED IN Mthly Cat, p 100
4-56

ORDER RECORD

VF
627
B52

Tennessee Valley Authority.
Blee, C E
TVA Tennessee River history. Based on the paper: Development of the Tennessee River waterway, by Chief engineer, Tennessee Valley Authority, before the American Society of Civil Engineers, Centennial meeting in Chicago, Illinois, Sept. 12, 1952. [Chicago?] 1959.
[8]p.

1. Tennessee Valley Authority.
I. Title.

353.1
T 25

Tennessee Valley Authority.
Report, 1970-71/

Muscle Shoals, Tenn., 19
annual.

1970(Sept.) 2v.
For Library holdings see main entry.
1971 v.1+2
1. Authorities. 2. Tennessee Valley Authority.

627.4
T25t

Tennessee Valley Authority. (Government Research Branch)
The Tennessee River Valley, a case study by A. J. Gray, chief community planner, Government Research Branch and Victor Roterus, director, Office of Area Development, U.S. Dept. of Commerce. Prepared by Office of International Housing, Office of the Administrator, Housing and Home Finance Agency for the use of United States Operations Missions. Washington [Housing Division, International Cooperation Administration, 1960]
15p. maps.
(Continued on next card)

728.1
:336.18
G26
1935

Tennessee Valley Authority.
Conference on Low Cost Housing, Atlanta, Ga., May 3, 4, 1935.
Proceedings. Under the auspices of the Dept. of Architecture, Georgia School of Technology, the University of Georgia. [Atlanta, Ga.] 1935.
126 p. plan (fold.) (Georgia School of Technology. Bulletin)

1. Public housing-U.S. 2. Tennessee Valley Authority. I. Georgia. University. Georgia School of Technology. Dept. of Architecture.

336.185
T25

Tennessee Valley Authority.
Report on Section 13 of the TVA Act.
[Knoxville] Dec. 1944.
136 p.

1940 amendment provided for payments in lieu of taxes.
Processed.

1. Payments in lieu of taxes.

627.4
T25t

Tennessee Valley Authority. (Government Research Branch) The Tennessee...1960. (Card 2)

1. Flood control - Tennessee Valley. 2. Regional planning - Tennessee Valley. I. Gray, A.J. II. Roterus, Victor. III. U.S. Housing and Home Finance Agency. Office of the Administrator. Office of International Housing. IV. Title.

627
H62

TENNESSEE VALLEY AUTHORITY.
Hodge, Clarence Lewis.
The Tennessee Valley Authority, national experiment in regionalism, Washington, American University Press, 1938.
272 p.
Bibliography p. 249-26

1. Tennessee Valley Authority. 2. Regional planning.

330
N67w
Tennessee Valley Authority.
North Carolina. State University.
Agricultural Policy Institute.
Workshop on problems of chronically depressed rural areas, Asheville, N.C., April 1965. Raleigh, 1965.
235p. (Its series 19)
Sponsored by the Agricultural Policy Institute, North Carolina State University in cooperation with the Tennessee Valley Authority.
1. Economic development. 2. Poverty. 3. Agriculture. I. Tennessee Valley Authority. II. Title: Problems of chronically depressed rural areas. III. Title.

353.1
T25
TENNESSEE VALLEY AUTHORITY.
Tennessee Valley Authority.
Report, 19

Muscle Shoals, Tenn., 19

v. annual.

For Library holdings see main entry.

1. Authorities. 2. Tennessee Valley Authority.

711.3
N17r
Tennessee Valley Authority.
U.S. National Resources Committee.
Regional factors in national planning and development. Washington, Govt. Print. Off., Dec. 1935.
223 p. maps.

1.Regional planning. 2.Metropolitan area planning. 3.Tennessee Valley Authority. 4.Decentralization.

711.3
I57
Tennessee Valley Authority.
International Conference on Regional Planning Development, 1st, London, 1955.
Report of the proceedings of the conference held at Bedford College, London, 28th September to 2nd October, 1955. Brussels, published by the Provisional Committee for the International Centre for Regional Planning and Development, [1955]
[246p.]

(Continued on next page)

627
T25s
TENNESSEE VALLEY AUTHORITY.
TENNESSEE VALLEY AUTHORITY.
THE SCENIC RESOURCES OF THE TENNESSEE VALLEY. A DESCRIPTIVE AND PICTORIAL INVENTORY. PREPARED BY THE TENNESSEE VALLEY DEPARTMENT OF REGIONAL PLANNING STUDIES. KNOXVILLE, 1938.
222P.

1. TENNESSEE VALLEY AUTHORITY.
I. TITLE.

VF
711.3
(73:016)
T25
1952
Tennessee Valley Authority - Bibliography.
Tennessee Valley Authority. Technical Library.
A bibliography for the TVA program.[compiled by Bernard L. Foy] Knoxville, Tenn., Oct. 1952.
34 p.

Processed.

1.Tennessee Valley Authority-Bibl. I.Foy, Bernard L.

711.3
I57
International Conference on Regional Planning Development, 1st, London, 1955. Report of the proceedings . . . (Card 2)

1. Regional planning. 2. Regional planning - Italy. 3. Volta River Project, Gold Coast. 4. Tennessee Valley Authority. I. International Centre for Regional Planning and Development.

627
T25
Tennessee Valley Authority.
[Tennessee Valley Authority]
A short history of the Tennessee Valley Authority, 1933-1956. [Knoxville, Tenn.] 1956.
[6]p.

1. Tennessee Valley Authority.
2. Power resources.

VF
711.3
(73:016)
T25
1953
Tennessee Valley Authority - Bibliography.
Tennessee Valley Authority. Technical Library.
A bibliography for the TVA program [compiled by Bernard L. Foy] Knoxville, Tenn., July 1953.
37 p.

Processed.

1.Tennessee Valley Authority-Bibl. I.Foy, Bernard L.

711.3
L45
TENNESSEE VALLEY AUTHORITY.
LILIENTHAL, DAVID ELI, 1899-
TVA; DEMOCRACY ON THE MARCH. NEW YORK, HARPER, 1944.
248P.

"SOME REFERENCES FOR TECHNICIANS": P. 227-241.

1. REGIONAL PLANNING. 2. TENNESSEE VALLEY AUTHORITY.

VF
339.5
T25
Tennessee Valley Authority.
Tennessee Valley Authority.
TVA today, 1965-1966. Knoxville, Tenn. Direct requests to TVA Information Office, 1965.
28p.

1. Tennessee Valley Authority. 2. Power resources. 3. Electricity.

VF
711.3
(73:016)
T251
Tennessee Valley Authority-Bibl.
Tennessee Valley Authority. Technical Library.
An index bibliography of the Tennessee Valley Authority; cumulative supplements, Knoxville, Tenn.,

v.

For full information see shelf list card. Compiled by Bernard L. Foy.
Magazine articles.
Processed.
1.Tennessee Valley Authority-Bibl. I.Foy, Bernard L.

711.3
M17
Tennessee Valley Authority.
Martin, Roscoe C   ed.
TVA, the first twenty years; a staff report. Kingsport, Tenn., Univ. of Alabama press and Univ. of Tennessee press., 1956.
282p.

1. Tennessee Valley Authority.

627
T25v
Tennessee Valley Authority.
Tennessee Valley Authority.
Valley with a future. Knoxville, 1960.
18p.

1. Tennessee Valley Authority.
2. Power resources.

VF
711.3
(73:016)
T25
1951
Tennessee Valley Authority - Bibliography.
Tennessee Valley Authority. Technical Library.
The TVA program; a bibliography of selected readings, compiled by Bernard L. Foy. Rev. Knoxville, Tenn., Sept. 1951.
24 p.

Includes list of films available from TVA.
Processed.

1.Tennessee Valley Authority-Bibl. I.Foy, Bernard L.

330
(76193)
S32
Tennessee Valley Authority.
Shelton, Barrett.
The Decatur story; an address, United Nations Scientific Conference on the Conservation and Utilization of Resources, Lake Success, New York, September 5, 1949. [n.p.] Tennessee Valley Authority, 1949.
11 p.
1.Economic base studies - Decatur, Ala. 2.Tennessee Valley Authority. I.United Nations Scientific Conference on the Conservation and Utilization of Resources, Lake Success, New York, 1949. II.Title.

627.4
G25
Tennessee Valley Authority.
U.S. General Accounting Office.
Audit report of Tennessee Valley Authority
letter from the Comptroller General of the United States transmitting a report on the audit of the Tennessee Valley Authority. Washington, Govt. Print. Off.,
v. tables.

For complete information see shelflist. Issued in the Congressional series as House Documents.

1. Tennessee Valley Authority.

VF
711.3
(73:016)
T25
1952
Tennessee Valley Authority. Technical Library.
A bibliography for the TVA program.[compiled by Bernard L. Foy] Knoxville, Tenn., Oct. 1952.
34 p.

Processed.

1.Tennessee Valley Authority-Bibl. I.Foy, Bernard L.

712.25
(768)
T25o
Tennessee Valley Authority.
Tennessee Valley Authority.
Outdoor recreation for a growing nation; TVA's experience with man-made reservoirs. Knoxville, Tenn., 1961.
116p.

1. Recreation - Tennessee Valley.
2. Tennessee Valley Authority.

711.4
N17f
1939
Tennessee Valley Authority.
U.S. National Resources Planning Board.
Federal relations to local planning. Washington, Dec. 1939.
364 p. chart (fold.) (Its Circular 14)
Mimeographed.

VF
711.3
(73:016)
T25
1953
Tennessee Valley Authority. Technical Library.
A bibliography for the TVA program [compiled by Bernard L. Foy] Knoxville, Tenn., July 1953.
37 p.

Processed.

1.Tennessee Valley Authority-Bibl. I.Foy, Bernard L.

627.4 (016) T25
Tennessee Valley Authority. Technical Library.
Flood damage prevention; an indexed bibliography. Knoxville, 1963.
28p.

1. Flood control - Bibl.

362.6 H21pa no. 9
The TVA preretirement program.
Schultz, E B
The TVA preretirement program. Washington, Dept. of Health, Education, and Welfare, Special Staff on Aging, 1961.
18p. (U.S. Dept. of Health, Education, and Welfare. Special Staff on Aging. Patterns for progress in aging. Case study no. 9)

1. Old age. I. U.S. Dept. of Health, Education, and Welfare. (Special Staff on Aging) II. Title. (Series)

325.2 B19
Tension in the cities/three programs for survival.
Bayton, James A
Tension in the cities/three programs for survival. Philadelphia, Chilton Book Co., 1969.
270p.
Bibliography: p. 249-255.
1. Race relations. 2. Municipal government - Atlanta. 3. Municipal government - New York (City) 4. Municipal government - District of Columbia. 5. Civil disorders. 6. Law enforcement. I. Title.

VF 627.4 (016) T25 1966
Tennessee Valley Authority. Technical Library.
Flood damage prevention; an indexed bibliography. Knoxville, Tenn., 1966.
37p.

1. Flood control - Bibl. I. Title.

---

627 T25T
TVA 25TH ANNIVERSARY.
TENNESSEE VALLEY AUTHORITY.
TVA 25TH ANNIVERSARY; PROGRESS THRU RESOURCE DEVELOPMENT. A REPORT TO THE NATION FROM THE TENNESSEE VALLEY AUTHORITY ON ITS FIRST TWENTY-FIVE YEARS, 1933-1958. [N.P., 1958]
20P.

1. TITLE.

691.110.15 F67t
Tension parallel-to-grain properties.
U.S. Forest Products Laboratory, Madison, Wis.
Tension parallel-to-grain properties of southern pine dimension lumber, by D.V. Doyle and L.J. Markwardt. Madison, 1967.
36p. (U.S. Forest Service research paper, FPL 84)

1. Wood - Research. 2. Strength of materials. I. Doyle, D.V. II. Markwardt, L.J. III. Title.

627.4 (016) T25 1967
Tennessee Valley Authority. Technical Library.
Flood damage prevention; an indexed bibliography. 5th ed. Knoxville, Tenn., 1967.
39p.

1. Flood control - Bibl. I. Title.

711.3 (768) T25t
Tennessee's larger urban areas.
Tennessee. State Planning Commission.
Tennessee's larger urban areas. Nashville, 1967.
115p. (Its Publication no. 354)
U.S. Urban Renewal Adm. UPAP.

1. Metropolitan areas - Tennessee. 2. Population - Tennessee. 3. Employment - Tennessee. 4. Economic base studies - Tennessee. I. U.S. HUD-UPAP. II. Title.

690.22 W66
A tentative design method for the composite action of heavily loaded brick panel walls.
Wood, R H
A tentative design method for the composite action of heavily loaded brick panel walls supported on reinforced concrete beams, by R.H. Wood and L.G. Simms. Garston, Eng., Building Research Station, 1969.
6p. (U.K. Building Research Station. Current paper CP 36/69)
1. Walls. 2. Brick construction. 3. Concrete, Reinforced. I. Simms, L.G., jt. au. II. U.K. Building Research Station. III. Title.

VF 711.3 (73:016) T25i
Tennessee Valley Authority. Technical Library.
An index bibliography of the Tennessee Valley Authority; cumulative supplements, Knoxville, Tenn.,
v.
For full information see shelf list card.
Compiled by Bernard L. Foy.
Magazine articles.
Processed.
1. Tennessee Valley Authority-Bibl. I. Foy, Bernard L.

VF 388 T25
Tennyson, E L
When is rapid transit economically justified? 1961.
[5]p.
Reprinted from the May 11th issue of Public utilities fortnightly, Washington, D.C. p. 657-661.

1. Transportation.

333.332 (7471) N28 1935
TENTATIVE LAND VALUE MAPS OF THE CITY OF NEW YORK FOR 1935.
NEW YORK (CITY) DEPT. OF TAXES AND ASSESSMENTS.
TENTATIVE LAND VALUE MAPS OF THE CITY OF NEW YORK FOR 1935. NEW YORK, 1934.
172P.

1. REAL PROPERTY - VALUATION - NEW YORK CITY. 2. TAXATION - NEW YORK CITY. I. TITLE.

627.4 T25pr
Tennessee Valley Authority. Technical Library.
A program for reducing the national flood damage potential; excerpts from newspaper stories, editorials, magazines and other publications. Knoxville, Tenn., 1960.
18p.

1. Flood control.

---

330 (76379) T25
Tensas Parish, La. Planning Board.
Tensas Parish resources and facilities; survey. Published in cooperation with State of Louisiana Dept. of Public Works, Planning Division. Baton Rouge, 1949.
81p. illus., maps, tables.

1. Economic conditions - Tensas Parish, La. 2. Community facilities - Tensas Parish, La. I. Louisiana. Dept. of Public Works.

333.332 (7471) N28 1942/43
TENTATIVE LAND VALUE MAPS OF THE CITY OF NEW YORK FOR THE FISCAL
NEW YORK (CITY) TAX DEPT.
TENTATIVE LAND VALUE MAPS OF THE CITY OF NEW YORK FOR THE FISCAL YEAR JULY 1, 1942-JUNE 30, 1943. NEW YORK, 1942.
182P.

1. REAL PROPERTY - VALUATION - NEW YORK CITY. 2. TAXATION - NEW YORK CITY. I. TITLE.

VF 711.3 T25
Tennessee Valley Authority. Technical Library.
TVA as a symbol of resource development in many countries; a digest and selected bibliography of information. Knoxville, Tenn., Jan. 1952.
55 p. illus.
"To provide some concept of the scope and magnitude of foreign projects or plans which have been influenced by the TVA example" - Foreword.
Includes bibliographies.
Processed.
1. Regional planning. 2. Water resources. I. Title.

691.322 L28t
Tensile splitting tests.
Lewis, R K
Tensile splitting tests on structural lightweight concrete with "Shalite" aggregate. Melbourne, Australia, Commonwealth Scientific and Industrial Research Organization, Div. of Building Research, 1967.
15p. (Australia. Commonwealth Scientific and Industrial Research Organization, Div. of Building Research. Report C3.3.2)

1. Concrete aggregates. 2. Strength of materials. I. Australia. Commonwealth Scientific and Industrial Research Organization. (Div. of Building Research) II. Title.

VF 690.25 A52
Tentative method of test for flammability of finished textile floor covering materials.
American Society for Testing and Materials.
Tentative method of test for flammability of finished textile floor covering materials. Philadelphia, 1970.
3p. (ASTM designation D2859-70T)
Reprinted from the Annual book of ASTM standards.

1. Floors and flooring. 2. Fire prevention. I. Title.

VF 711.3 (73:016) T25 1951
Tennessee Valley Authority. Technical Library.
The TVA program; a bibliography of selected readings, compiled by Bernard L. Foy. Rev. Knoxville, Tenn., Sept. 1951.
24 p.
Includes list of films available from TVA.
Processed.

1. Tennessee Valley Authority-Bibl. I. Foy, Bernard L.

---

720 O77 V.2
Tensile structure.
Otto, Frei, ed.
Tensile structure; vol. 2: design, structure, and calculation of buildings of cables, nets, and membranes. Cambridge, Mass., M.I.T. Press, 1969.
171p.

1. Architecture - Designs and plans. 2. Structural engineering. I. Title.

---

657 S67
A TENTATIVE SET OF BROAD ACCOUNTING PRINCIPLES.
SPROUSE, ROBERT T
A TENTATIVE SET OF BROAD ACCOUNTING PRINCIPLES FOR BUSINESS ENTERPRISES, BY ROBERT T. SPROUSE AND MAURICE MOONITZ. NEW YORK, AMERICAN INSTITUTE OF CERTIFIED PUBLIC ACCOUNTANTS, 1962.
87P. (AMERICAN INSTITUTE OF CPAS. ACCOUNTING RESEARCH STUDY NO. 3)
BIBLIOGRAPHY: P. 84-87.

1. ACCOUNTING. I. MOONITZ, MAURICE, JT. AU. II. TITLE.

690.091.82
(94)
A87
1970
Tentative uniform home building code.
Australia. Dept. of Housing.
Tentative uniform home building code.
Canberra, 1970.
61p.

1. Building codes - Australia.
I. Title. II. Title: Uniform building code.

690
T27
TERBORGH, GEORGE.
FLUCTUATIONS IN HOUSING CONSTRUCTION.
WASHINGTON, CYCLICAL VARIATIONS SECTION,
SUB-COMMITTEE ON RESEARCH AND STATISTICS,
CENTRAL HOUSING COMMITTEE, 1937.
14L.

1. BUILDING CYCLES. 2. HOUSING MARKET.
I. TITLE.

352.1
T27
no.1
Terhune, George A
Local governmental budgeting practices in
the United States and Canada. Chicago,
Municipal Finance Officers Association of the
United States and Canada, 1966.
26p. (MFOA Committee on Budgeting. Report
no. 1. Accounting publication no. 13-1)

1. Municipal finance. 2. Budget. 3. Local
government - Finance. I. Municipal Finance
Officers Association of the United States
and Canada. II. Title.

711.3
(74645)
H85
Tenzer, Morton J   jt. au.
Hultgren, Roger.
Organizational development for the Windham
Regional Planning Agency, by Roger Hultgren and
Morton J. Tenzer. Storrs, Conn. Institute of
Urban Research, University of Connecticut, 1971.
80p. (Urban research report no. 20)
U.S. Dept. of Housing and Urban Development.
UPAP.
HUD project Conn. P-127.
1. Metropolitan area planning - Windsor, Conn.
I. Tenzer, Morton J., jt. au. II. Connecticut.
University. Institute of Urban Research.
III. Windham, Conn. Regional Planning
Agency. IV. Title. V. U.S. HUD-UPAP.
Windsor, Conn.

332.571.2
M12
TERBORGH, GEORGE WILLARD.
MACHINERY AND ALLIED PRODUCTS
INSTITUTE.
INFLATION AND POSTWAR PROFITS.
CHICAGO, 1949.
37P. (ITS PAMPHLETS AND ECONOMIC
BRIEFS)
THE AUTHOR IS ... GEORGE
TERBORGH. PRELIM. PAGE [5]

1. INFLATION. 2. PRICES.
I. TERBORGH, GEORGE WILLARD.
II. TITLE. III. TITLE: POSTWAR
PROFITS.

Terhune, George A   jt. au.

352
(79494)
L21
Leask, Samuel, Jr.
Metropolitan government for Los Angeles;
a workable solution, by Samuel Leask, Jr.
and George A. Terhune. [Los Angeles] 1961.
15p.

1. Metropolitan government - Los Angeles.
I. Terhune, George A., jt. au.

728.1
(62)
T26
Teodorovitch, B
Housing problems in the Egyptian countryside;
translated and published by the International
Centre for Basic Training in the Arab World.
[n,p.] International Centre for Basic Training
in the Arab World. [1955?]
1 v. illus., diagrs.

In Arabic.
Bibliography contains works in English.

1. Housing - Egypt. I. International Centre
for Basic Training in the Arab World.

657
T27
TERBORGH, GEORGE.
REALISTIC DEPRECIATION POLICY.
CHICAGO, MACHINERY AND ALLIED PRODUCTS
INSTITUTE, 1954.
197P.

1. ACCOUNTING. 2. DEPRECIATION AND
OBSOLESCENCE. I. TITLE.

352.1
T27
no.2
Terhune, George A
Performance and program budgeting practices
in the United States and Canada. Chicago,
Municipal Finance Officers Association of
the United States and Canada, 1966.
12p. (MFOA Committee on Budgeting.
Report no. 2. Accounting publication no.
13-2)
1. Municipal finance. 2. Budget. 3. Local
government - Finance. I. Municipal Finance
Officers Association of the United States and
Canada. II. Title.

691.542
T26
Teoreanu, I
Correlations between the mineralizing
effect of substances on Portland cement
clinker formation and the periodic system
of the elements, by I. Teoreanu and Tran
van Huynh. Garston, Eng., Building
Research Station, 1971.
[11]p. (Library communication no. 1650)
Translated from the German.
1. Portland cement. I. Tran van Huynh,
jt. au. II. U.K. Building Research Station.
III. Title. (Series)

334.1
(016)
T27
1942
Tereshtenko, V   J
Bibliographical review of literature on
cooperative housing, by V. J. Tereshtenko and
research staff of the cooperative project.
New York, Work Projects Administration, 1942.
267 p. (U.S. Works Projects Administration
for the City of New York. Studies of the
cooperative project. Series E. Cooperative
housing, v. 1)
"Published with the assistance of the Edward
A. Filene Good Will Fund, Inc."
Official project   165-2-97-49.
Annotated.   (Continued on next card)

301.36
T27
Terkel, Studs.
Division street: America. New York, Pantheon
Books, 1967.
381p.

1. Sociology, Urban. 2. Democracy.
3. City growth. 4. Race relations. I. Title.

711.4
(46)
E77
TEORIA DE LA CIUDAD.
ESTEVE, GABRIEL ALOMAR.
TEORIA DE LA CIUDAD. IDEAS
FUNDAMENTALES PARA UN URBANISMO
HUMANISTA. MADRID, TALLERES GRAFICOS
MARISAL, 1947.
240P.

1. CITY PLANNING - SPAIN. 2. CITY
GROWTH. I. TITLE.

Tereshtenko, V.J.   Bibliographical review of
literature on cooperative housing...1942.
(Card 2)

1. Cooperative housing-Bibl. I. U.S. Work Projects
Administration for the City of New York.
II. Edward A. Filene Good Will Fund, inc.

332
(7471)
R61
Robbins, Sidney Martin.
Money metropolis; a locational study of
financial activities in the New York region,
by Sidney M. Robbins and Nestor E. Terleckyj, with the collaboration of Ira O.
Scott, Jr. Cambridge, Mass., Harvard Univ.
Press, 1960.
294p. charts, tables. (New York metropolitan region study)

1. Finance - New York metropolitan area. I. Terleckyj, Nestor E. II. Title. (Series: New York
metropolitan region study)

331.2
N17NA
ANAL.
TERBORGH, GEORGE.
AN ANALYSIS OF THE NATHAN REPORT
ENTITLED "A NATIONAL WAGE POLICY FOR
1947." WASHINGTON, 1946.
13, 14P. (MACHINERY & PRODUCTS
INSTITUTE. BULLETIN NO. 1965)

1. WAGES AND SALARIES. I. NATHAN,
ROBERT ROY. A NATIONAL WAGE POLICY FOR
1947. (SERIES: MACHINERY & PRODUCTS
INSTITUTE. BULLETIN NO. 1965)

334
1347
T27
TERESHTENKO, VALERY, J
LITERARY DEVELOPMENT OF COOPERATIVE
PRINCIPLES AND DATA. 2D ED. NEW YORK,
DIVISION OF STUDY OF COOPERATION, U.S.
WORKS PROGRESS ADMINISTRATION, 1939.
42L. (SERIES A, PT.1)

1. COOPERATIVES - LAW AND LEGISLATION.
I. U.S. WORKS PROGRESS ADMINISTRATION.
NEW YORK (CITY) II. TITLE.

600.15
N17R
TERLECKYJ, NESTOR E.
NATIONAL INDUSTRIAL CONFERENCE BOARD.
RESEARCH AND DEVELOPMENT: ITS GROWTH
AND COMPOSITION, BY NESTOR E.
TERLECKYJ. NEW YORK, 1963.
115P. (ITS STUDIES IN BUSINESS
ECONOMICS, NO. 82.)

1. INDUSTRIAL RESEARCH. I. TITLE.
II. TERLECKYJ, NESTOR E.

332.72
369
TERBORGH, GEORGE W
GRAY, JOHN H
FIRST MORTGAGES IN URBAN REAL ESTATE
FINANCE, BY JOHN M. GRAY AND GEORGE W.
TERBORGH. WASHINGTON, BROOKINGS
INSTITUTION, MAY 1929.
76P. (ITS PAMPHLET SERIES NO. 2)

1. MORTGAGE FINANCE. I. TERBORGH,
GEORGE W. II. BROOKINGS INSTITUTION.

352.1
T27
no.3
Terhune, George A
Capital budgeting practices in the United
States and Canada. Chicago, Municipal
Finance Officers Association of the United
States and Canada, 1966.
14p. (MFOA Committee on Budgeting.
Report no. 3. Accounting publication no.
13-3)

1. Municipal finance. 2. Budget.
3. Local government - Finance. I. Municipal
Finance Officers Association of the United
States and   Canada. II. Title.

351
T27
Terleckyj, Nestor E
Significance of productivity measurement in
the Federal Government. A lecture given at
the United States Civil Service Commission,
Executive Seminar Center, Kings Point, New
York, Dec. 5, 1963. Washington, Executive
Office of the President, Bureau of the Budget,
1963.
15p.

1. Federal government. 2. Management.
I. Title: Productivity
measurement in   the Federal Government.

332   TERM LENDING TO BUSINESS.
J12T   JACOBY, NEIL HERMAN, 1909-
     TERM LENDING TO BUSINESS, BY NEIL H.
JACOBY AND RAYMOND J. SAULNIER. NEW
YORK, NATIONAL BUREAU OF ECONOMIC
RESEARCH, 1942.
     163P. (FINANCIAL RESEARCH PROGRAM OF
THE NATIONAL BUREAU OF ECONOMIC RESEARCH.
STUDIES IN BUSINESS FINANCING)

     1. INSTALLMENT FINANCE. I. SAULNIER,
RAYMOND JOSEPH, 1908- , JT. AU.
II. TITLE.

     The term structure of interest rates:
     expectations and behavior patterns.
332.6   Malkiel, Burton Gordon.
M15   The term structure of interest rates:
     expectations and behavior patterns.
Princeton, N.J., Princeton University
Press, 1966.

   271 p.

   Bibliography: p. 253-260.

Laf.   1. Bond yields. 2. Interest rates.
     I. Title

     Terminal planning and design.
388   California. University. Institute of
(016)   Transportation and Traffic Engineering.
C15   Terminal planning and design. Berkeley,
no. 10   Calif., 1957.
     8p. (Its Library references no. 10)

     1. Transportation - Bibliography.
     2. Architecture - Design. I. Title.

---

630   TERMINATION OF THE BRACERO PROGRAM.
:331   MCELROY, ROBERT CECIL.
M22   TERMINATION OF THE BRACERO PROGRAM:
SOME EFFECTS ON FARM LABOR AND MIGRANT
HOUSING NEEDS BY ROBERT C. MCELROY AND
EARLE E. GAVETT. WASHINGTON, U.S.
DEPT. OF AGRICULTURE, ECONOMIC RESEARCH
SERVICE, 1965.
     29P. (AGRICULTURAL ECONOMIC REPORT NO.
77)
     1. AGRICULTURAL LABORERS. 2. HOUSING
FOR MIGRANT WORKERS. I. GAVETT, EARLE
EDWARD, JT. AU. II. U.S. AGRICULTURE
DEPARTMENT. ECONOMIC RESEARCH SERVICE.
III. TITLE.

     Termites

     see also

     Insects
     Rodents

691.11   TERMITES.
:620.197   AMERICAN WOOD PRESERVERS' INSTITUTE.
A52S   SPECIFICATIONS FOR THE PROTECTION
AGAINST DECAY AND TERMITES IN
RESIDENTIAL CONSTRUCTION WITH THE USE
OF PRESSURE TREATED WOODS. CHICAGO,
1959.
     1 V.

     1. WOOD PRESERVATION. 2. TERMITES.
I. TITLE.

VF
691.11
:620.193.82   Termites.
B19b   Baxter (J.H.) and Co.
     Baxco chemonited pressure treated lumber.
Case study number one: How to protect a
school building against termites in a
highly infested area, Daves Avenue School,
Los Gatos, Calif., by John M. Evans.
San Francisco. [1954]
     [2] p. illus.

     "Reprinted from Architectural Forum,
May 1954."
       (See Card No. 2)

VF
691.11
:620.193.82
B19b   Baxter (J.H.) and Co. (Card No. 2)
     Baxco chemonited pressure ...

     A.I.A. file no. 19a3.

     1. Termites. I. Title: Chemonited
pressure treated lumber. II. Evans, John M.

VF   Termites
691.11
:620.193.82   Baxter (J. H.) and Co.
B19   Before you buy or build a home look
under the floor! San Francisco [1957]
   [14] p.

     1. Termites. 2. Dry rot.

691.11   Termites.
:620.197   Building Research Advisory Board.
B84   Addendum to protection against decay
Addend.   and termites in residential construction.
1958   Conducted... for the Federal Housing Administration under Contract no. HA-fh ( ) 743,
Feb. 11, 1958. Report edited by Robert M.
Dillon. Washington, 1958.
     33p. (National Academy of Sciences
publication 448, addend.)
       (Continued on next card)

691.11   Building Research Advisory Board.   Addendum
:620.197   to protection against ... (Card 2)
B84
Addend.
1958   1. Termites. 2. Wood preservation.
I. Dillon, Robert M ed. II. U.S.
Federal Housing Administration. III. Title:
Decay and termites in residential construc-
tion.

691.11   Termites.
:620.197   Building Research Advisory Board.
B84   A study of protection against decay and
termites in residential construction; conducted
by the Building Research Advisory Board for the
Federal Housing Administration under Contract
No. HA-fh-646 (Amendment No. 1), May 10, 1956;
Report edited by Robert M. Dillon, Staff
Architect. Washington, National Academy of
Sciences, 1956.
     60 p. maps. (NAS publication 448)

VF   Termites.
691.11
:620.193.82   California. Agricultural Experiment
C15   Station. Extension Service.
     Termite control; prevention and
control of the western subterranean
termite, by Walter Ebeling and Roy J.
Pence. Berkeley, 1958.
     16p. illus. (Its Circular 469)

     1. Termites. I. Ebeling, Walter.
II. Pence, Roy J

624.131   TERMITES.
C34   CHISHOLM, R D
     THE ESTIMATION OF ALDRIN AND
CHLORDANE RESIDUES IN SOILS TREATED
FOR TERMITE CONTROL, BY R. D. CHISHOLM
AND OTHERS. WASHINGTON, U.S.
AGRICULTURAL RESEARCH SERVICE, 1962.
     8P. (ARS-33-73)

     1. SOILS. 2. TERMITES. I. U.S.
AGRICULTURAL RESEARCH SERVICE.
II. TITLE: ALDRIN AND CHLORDANE
RESIDUES IN SOILS. III. CHLORDANE
RESIDUES IN SOILS.

595.7   Termites.
F71   Franco, E J Sampaio
     Les petites colonies de reticulitermes
lucifugus (Rossi) en rapport avec les
essais laboratoriaux. Lisboa, Portugal,
Ministerio das Obras Publicas, Laboratorio
Nacional de Engenharia Civil, 1965.
     32-41p. (Portugal. Laboratorio
Nacional de Engenharia Civil. Memoria no.
242)
     English summary.

     1. Insects.   2. Termites.
I. Portugal.   Laboratorio de
Engenharia   Civil.

VF
690.37   Termites.
F71   Guidot, Daniel
EMay1950   Les termites, ennemis no. 1 de l'habitat
intertropical. [Paris, France] Centre Scientifique et Technique du Batiment, Service de
l'Habitat Intertropical [May 1950]
     28 l. diagrs. (France. Centre
Scientifique et Technique du Batiment. Service
de l'Habitat Intertropical. Etudes.)
     Bibliography: p. 28.
     Mimeographed.

     1. Termites. I. Ser.

691.11   TERMITES.
:620.193.82   HARRIS, WILLIAM VICTOR.
H17   TERMITES; THEIR RECOGNITION AND
CONTROL. LONDON, LONGMANS, 1961.
     187P. (TROPICAL AGRICULTURE
SERIES)

     INCLUDES BIBLIOGRAPHY.

     1. TERMITES. 2. WOOD
PRESERVATION.

595.7   TERMITES.
H17   HARTNACK, HUGO.
     202 COMMON HOUSEHOLD PESTS OF NORTH
AMERICA. CHICAGO, HARTNACK PUB. CO.,
1939.
     319P.

     1. INSECTS. 2. RODENTS.
3. TERMITES.

691.11   Termites.
:620.193.82   Holmgren, Lars.
H65   Resistance of Ethiopian timber to
termite attack. Addis Ababa, Ethiopia,
Building Centre, 1963.
     4p. (Haile Sellassie I University
Building Centre. Addis Ababa, Report no.
1, 1963)

     1. Termites. 2. Forests and forestry. I. Haile
Sellassie I Uni-   versity. Addis
Ababa.

691.11   TERMITES.
:620.193.82   Howse, P E
H68   Termites: a study in social behavior.
London, Hutchinson University Library, 1970.
     150p.

     Bibliography: p. 136-144.

     1. Termites.

---

690   Termites.
I55   Illinois. University. Small Homes Council.
P2.5   Termite control. Urbana, Ill., 1963.
     8p. (Its Circular series, index no. P2.5)

     Material in circular by Donald H. Percival.

     1. Termites. I. Percival, Donald H.
(Series)

VF
691.11
:620.193.82
I52

Termites.
India. National Buildings Organisation.
Termites and termite proofing. New
Delhi, 1959.
16p. (Its Technical information
series no. 14)

1. Termites.

691.11
:620.193.82
868

Termites.
South African Council for Scientific and
Industrial Research.
Report of the Committee on the
Production of Building Timbers in South
Africa against termites, wood-boring
beetles and fungi. Pretoria, 1950.
218p. (Series DR3 Reeks)

1. Termites. 2. Insects.

VF
691.11
:620.193.82
A37

Termites.
U.S. Dept. of Agriculture.
Soil treatment an aid in termite
control. Rev. Washington, Govt.
Print. Off., 1960.
folder. (Its Leaflet 324)

1. Termites.

691.11
:620.193.82
K53

TERMITES.
KOFOID, CHARLES A.
TERMITES AND TERMITE CONTROL.
2D REV. ED. BERKELEY, UNIVERSITY
OF CALIFORNIA PRESS, 1934.
795P.

1. TERMITES. I. TITLE.

691.11
:620.193.82
S68

Termites.
South African Council for Scientific
and Industrial Research. National
Building Research Institute.
Report of the Committee on the
Protection of Building Timbers in South
Africa against termites, wood-boring
beetles and fungi. Pretoria, 1950.
218p. (Series DR3 Reeks)

1. Termites.

VF
691.11
:620.193.82
A37s

Termites.
U.S. Dept. of Agriculture.
Subterranean termites, their prevention and control in buildings. Washington, Govt. Print. Off., 1960.
30p. illus., diagrs. (Its Home and
garden bulletin no. 64)

Supersedes Farmers' bulletin no. 1911, 1993.

1. Termites.

690.015
L68

Termites.
Louisiana. Engineering Experiment Station.
Low-cost housing research. Baton Rouge,
La., 1947-1949.
4 pts. illus. (LCHR)

Contents.-2. How to build a house of concrete
... or concrete masonry.-3. Termites.-4. Let's build
a house!-5. The "great-little" house: great
livability, little in cost.

691.11
:620.193.82
S59

TERMITES.
SNYDER, THOMAS ELLIOTT.
OUR ENEMY THE TERMITE. ITHACA,
COMSTOCK PUB. CO., 1935.
196P.

1. TERMITES. I. TITLE.

VF
691.11
:620.193.82
E57

Termites.
U.S. Bureau of Entomology and Plant Quarantine
An investigation of the effectiveness of
structural methods for preventing damage by
subterranean termites to buildings in the Gulf
States. Gulfport, Miss., Forest Insect
Laboratory, Jan. 1951.
1 v.(various pagings) illus., diagrs.,
tables.
Final report, Research Project no. 1950-STR-18
Housing and Home Finance Agency.
Project director, T. E. Snyder; staff
technician, Robert Michel.
Typewritten.

691.11
:620.193.82
L68

TERMITES.
LOUISIANA. STATE UNIVERSITY AND
AGRICULTURAL AND MECHANICAL
COLLEGE. LOW-COST HOUSING
RESEARCH.
TERMITES - WHAT ARE THEY, HOW
TO FIND THEM. BATON ROUGE, LA.,
1947.
8P. (ITS BULLETIN NO. 3)

1. TERMITES.

VF
690.37
F71
T1949

Termites.
Gt. Brit. Ministry of Supply.
Conservation des matériaux en zones tropicales.
[Paris, France] Centre Scientifique et Technique du
Bâtiment, Service de l'Habitat Intertropical, 1949.
58 l. (France. Centre Scientifique et Tech-
rique du Bâtiment. Service de l'Habitat Intertropi-
cal. Traductions.)
English title: Tropic proofing.
Mimeographed.
1. Building materials-Tropics. 2. Termites. I. Gt. Brit.
Dept. of Scientific and Industrial Research. II. Ser

VF
691.8
E57

Termites.
U.S. Bureau of Entomology and Plant Quarantine.
Report of accelerated laboratory termite test
of Lincoln Industries insulating panels [by]
R. Joseph Kowal. Gulfport, Miss. [1947]
3 l./illus. table.
In cooperation with National Housing Agency.
Copy 2 has identical text but lacks
illustrations.
Typewritten.
1. Panels. 2. Termites. 3. Housing research contracts
I. Kowal, R Joseph. II. U.S. National Housing
Agency. III. Title: Lincoln Industries insulating
panels.

VF
691.11
:620.193.82
M12

Termites.
MacGregor, W D
The protection of buildings and timber against
termites. London, H.M. Stationery Off., 1950.
v, 4 p. diagrs., plates. (Gt. Brit.
Forest Products Research bulletin no. 24)

Bibliography.

1. Termites I. Series.

VF
691.11
:620.193.82
A37d
1951

Termites.
U.S. Agricultural Research Administration.
Decay and termite damage in houses.
Rev. Washington, 1951.
26p. illus. (Farmers bulletin no.
1993, rev.)

1. Termites.

648.7
A75

Termites.
U.S. Dept. of the Army.
Insect and rodent control, repairs and utilities
Washington, Govt. Print. Off., Oct. 1947.
156 p. illus., diagrs. (Its Technical
manual, TM 5-632)

Bibliography: p. 144-146.

1. Insects. 2. Rodents. 3. Termites. I. Series.

VF
691
P76

Termites.
Progressive Architecture.
Structural engineering techniques for
architects and engineers. 3rd ed. [New York,
Reinhold, 1953]
112 p. illus., diagrs., graphs, plans,
tables.

"...Structural engineering reports ... selected
from past issues of Progressive Architecture".

VF
691.11
:620.193.82
A37c

Termites.
U.S. Dept. of Agriculture.
Control of nonsubterranean termites,
by Thomas E. Snyder. Washington, 1950.
16p. illus. (Farmers bulletin no.
2018)

1. Termites. I. Snyder, Thomas E.

VF
69
P22
TC2

Termites.
U.S. Federal Housing Administration.
Protection against termites: good construction,
termite barriers, wood preservation. [Washington
1939]
24 p. illus., diagrs. (Its Technical
circular no. 2)

Cover title.

1. Termites. I. Title. II. Series.

VF
691.11
:620.193.82
P87

Termites.
Purdue University. Agricultural Extension Service.
The prevention and control of termites, by J. J. Davis. 4th ed. Lafayette, Ind., 1950.
16p. illus., diagrs. (Its Extension
bulletin no. 225)

1. Termites. I. Davis, J. J. II.
Illinois. Agricultural Experiment Station.

VF
691.11
:620.193.82
A37c
1966

TERMITES.
U.S. DEPT. OF AGRICULTURE.
CONTROL OF NONSUBTERRANEAN
TERMITES, BY THOMAS E. SNYDER.
WASHINGTON, GOVT. PRINT. OFF.,
1966.
16P. (ITS FARMERS' BULLETIN
NO. 2018)

1. TERMITES. I. SNYDER, THOMAS
E.

691.11
:620.193.82
F22

TERMITES.
U.S. Federal Housing Administration.
Termites and decay guide. Wash., 1970.
25p. (Its Technical standards training
guide no. 3)

Bibliography: p. 21-25.

1. Termites. 2. Wood preservation.
I. Title.

691.11
:620.193.82
F67R
TERMITES.
U.S. FOREST INSECT LABORATORY, BELTSVILLE, MD.
RECOMMENDATIONS FOR PROTECTING WOOD IN NEW CONSTRUCTION FROM ATTACK BY SUBTERRANEAN TERMITES. REV. BELTSVILLE, MD., DIVISION OF FOREST INSECT RESEARCH, FOREST INSECT LABORATORY, 1959.
5P.

1. TERMITES. 2. WOOD PRESERVATION.

691.11
:620.197
F67
TERMITES.
U.S. FOREST PRODUCTS LABORATORY, MADISON, WIS.
COMPARISON OF WOOD PRESERVATIVES IN STAKE TESTS, PROGRESS REPORT.
MADISON, WIS.
V. ANNUAL.
For Library holdings see main entry
1. WOOD PRESERVATION. 2. TERMITES. I. TITLE.

VF
691.11
:620.193.82 Termites.
F67
1931
U.S. Forest Service. Forest Products Laboratory, Madison, Wis.
Fungus and termite damage in buildings, by Carl Hartley and Willis W. Wagener. Madison, Wis., June 1931.
8 p. (Its no. R1090)
Reprint from The Octagon, a Journal of the A.I.A., June 1931.
Processed.
1.Termites. 2.Dry rot. I.Hartley, Carl. II.Wagener, Willis W. III.Title.

691.11
:620.193.82
(016)
S59
TERMITES - BIBLIOGRAPHY.
SNYDER, THOMAS ELLIOTT.
ANNOTATED SUBJECT HEADING BIBLIOGRAPHY OF TERMITES, 1350 B.C. TO A.D. 1954. WASHINGTON, SMITHSONIAN INSTITUTION, 1954.
305P.

------. SUPPL., 1955-60. 1961.
137P.

1. TERMITES - BIBLIOGRAPHY. I. SMITHSONIAN INSTITUTION.

691.11
:620.193.82
F22
. Termites and decay guide.
U.S. Federal Housing Administration.
Termites and decay guide. Wash., 1970.
25p. (Its Technical standards training guide no. 3)

Bibliography: p. 21-25.

1. Termites. 2. Wood preservation. I. Title.

691.11
:620.193.82
K53
TERMITES AND TERMITE CONTROL.
KOFOID, CHARLES A.
TERMITES AND TERMITE CONTROL. 2D REV. ED. BERKELEY, UNIVERSITY OF CALIFORNIA PRESS, 1934.
795P.

1. TERMITES. I. TITLE.

LAW
T
P217fa
Terner, Benjamin B
Pearl, Laurence D
Fair housing laws: halfway mark, by Laurence D. Pearl and Benjamin B. Terner. Wash., 1965.
[18]p.

Reprinted from Georgetown law journal, Fall 1965, p. 156-172.

1. Housing legislation. 2. Minority groups - Housing. I. Terner, Benjamin B., jt. au. II. Georgetown law journal. III. Title.

LAW
T
P217g
Terner, Benjamin B.
Pearl, Lawrence D
Survey: fair housing laws; design for equal opportunity, by Lawrence D. Pearl and Benjamin B. Terner. Reproduced from Stanford law review, July, 1964. [p.1-51]

Reprinted by U.S. Housing and Home Finance Agency, Washington, D.C.

1. Housing legislation. 2. Housing surveys. 3. Minority groups - Housing. I. Terner, Benjamin B., jt. au. II. Stanford law review. III. U.S. Housing and Home Finance Agency. IV. Title.

LAW
T
P217su
Terner, Benjamin B   jt. au.
Pearl, Laurence D
Survey: fair housing laws, design for equal opportunity, by Laurence D. Pearl and Benjamin B. Terner. [Stanford, Calif.] Leland Stanford Junior Univ., 1964.
849-899p.
Reprinted from the Stanford law review, vol. 16, no. 4, July 1964.
c. 2 Reprinted by HHFA. 51p.
1. Housing. 2. Minority groups - Housing. I. Terner, Benjamin B., jt. au. II. Title: Fair housing laws.   III. Title. IV. Stanford law review. V. U.S. Housing and Home Finance Agency.

330
(744)
T27
TERNER, IAN DONALD.
THE ECONOMIC IMPACT OF A MILITARY INSTALLATION ON THE SURROUNDING AREA: A CASE STUDY OF FORT DEVENS AND AYER, MASSACHUSETTS. BOSTON, 1965.
140P. (FEDERAL RESERVE BANK OF BOSTON. RESEARCH REPORT, NO. 30)

1. ECONOMIC CONDITIONS - MASSACHUSETTS. 2. HOUSING - WAR TIME.

690
H68
IME
no.66
Terner, Ian Donald.
U.S. Dept. of Housing and Urban Development. Industrialized housing, by Ian Donald Terner and John F.C. Turner. In conjunction with OSTI, the Organization for Social and Technical Innovation, Cambridge, Massachusetts. Prepared for the U.S. Agency for International Development. Wash., U.S. Dept. of Housing and Urban Development, Office of International Affairs, 1972.
1v. (Ideas and methods exchange no. 66)

Bibliography: p. A-7 - A-12.

(Cont'd on next card)

690
H68
IME
no.66
U.S. Dept. of Housing and Urban Development. Industrialized...1972.   (Card 2)

1. Prefabricated construction. I. Turner, John F.C., jt. au. II. Organization for Social and Technical Innovation. III. U.S. Agency for International Development. IV. Terner, Ian Donald. V. Title.

728.1
(8)
M47
Terner, Ian Donald, jt. au.
Mitchell, Neal B   Jr.
Squatter housing: criteria for development, directions for policy, by Neal B. Mitchell, Jr. and Ian Donald Terner. [New York] United Nations, 1967.
26p. (United Nations. Information Document no. 19)
At head of title: United Nations Seminar on Prefabrication of Houses for Latin America.
1. Housing - Latin America. 2. Prefabricated construction. 3. Housing in the tropics. I. Terner, Ian Donald, jt. au. II. United Nations. III. Title.

5088-
5094
TERRA ALTA, W. VA. PLANNING COMMISSION.
COMPREHENSIVE DEVELOPMENT PLAN: 1, PHASE I, BASIC RESEARCH; 2, PHASE I, WORK PROGRAM; 3, PHASE II, THE PLAN; 4, SUMMARY; 5, PROPOSED ZONING STANDARDS; 6, PROPOSED SUBDIVISION REGULATIONS; 7, CAPITAL BUDGET AND PUBLIC IMPROVEMENTS PROGRAM. BY CANDEUB, FLESSIG AND ASSOCIATES. TERRA ALTA, W. VA., 1968-69.
7 V. (HUD 701 REPORT)

1. MASTER PLAN - TERRA ALTA, W. VA. II. CANDEUB, FLESSIG AND ASSOCIATES. III. HUD. 701. I. TERRA ALTA, W. VA.

712
A41
TERRACES.
Ajay, Betty.
Betty Ajay's guide to home landscaping. Illustrations by Abe Ajay. New York, McGraw-Hill, 1970.
208p.

1. Landscape architecture. 2. Terraces. 3. Trees. I. Title.

Terraces
American Home (RG 5/49 - 2/52)
5/49, p.35
3/50, p.32-35
5/50, p.34-35
6/50, p.30-31
8/50, p.90
7/51, p.78-80
8/51, p.34-35

Terraces
Better Homes and Gardens (RG 5/49 - 2/52)
1/49, p.32-33   6/51, p.218-221
5/49, p.185   8/51, p.50-51
6/49, p.8   9/51, p.231
7/49, p.42-43   10/51, p.318-320
4/50, p.18   6/50, p.66-67
7/50, p.17
9/50, p.46-47
p.202
5/51, p.72-73
p.265

712
B72
Terraces.
Brett, William S
Small city gardens, by William S. Brett and Kay Grant. London, New York, Abelard-Schuman, 1967.
159p.

1. Landscape architecture. 2. Trees. 3. Terraces. I. Grant, Kay, jt. au. II. Title.

712
E24
Terraces.
Eckbo, Garrett.
Urban landscape design. New York, McGraw-Hill, 1964.
248p.

1. Landscape architecture. 2. Terraces. 3. Architecture - Design. 4. Open space land. 5. Recreation.   I. Title.

Terraces
Good Housekeeping (RG 5/49 - 2/52)
7/49, p.76-77
11/49, p.68-69
5/50, p.83-86
4/51, p.106-109

Terraces
House and Garden (RG 5/49-2/52)
6/49, p.90-95
6/50, p.74-83
p.88-97
7/50, p.52-57
p.72-77
7/51, p.34-37
8/51, p.30-31
1/52, p.90

Terraces
House Beautiful (RG 5/49 - 2/52)
1/49, p.42-45   9/51, p.134-135
11/49, p.210-211√   p.138-140
3/50, p.94-96√   2/52, p.82-83√
9/50, p.186√
10/50, p.244-245
2/51, p.53-59√
    p.62-67
6/51, p.84-85√
7/51, p.44-45
    p.54-55

VF
33
(77245) Indiana. Economic Council.
I52   Economic survey of the Terre Haute area.
    Indianapolis, Ind., July 1951- May 1952.
    2 pts.   graphs, tables.   (Its Bulletin
    no. 14, ...)
    Contents.-pt.1.General direction of the
    survey, by A. Philip Sundal.-pt.2.[Analysis
    of industrial activity]

    1.Terre Haute, Ind.-Econ. condit. I.Sundal,
    A. Philip. II.Series.

Terre Haute, Ind. - Economic conditions.

Terraces
Ladies Home Journal (RG 5/49-2/52)
3/50, p.260√

362.6
T27   Terreberry, Shirley M
    Survey of the health, welfare and recrea-
    tion needs of the aging in Herman Gardens
    Housing Project. Detroit, 1958.
    47p. tables.

    "Sponsored by Neighborhood Service
    Organization and United Community Service
    of Metropolitan Detroit."

    1.Old age. 2.Housing for the aged -
    Detroit. I.Title: Herman Gardens
    Housing Project.

711.3
(967) Guam. Dept. of Land Management. (Div.
G81   of Planning)
    The Agana urban region planning project;
    general plans for Tamuning, Barrigada,
    Agana, Sinajana, Agana Heights, Asan, Piti.
    Prepared for the Territorial Planning Com-
    mission. Agana, 1960.
    22p. maps, tables.

    U.S. Urban Renewal Administration.
    Urban Planning Assistance Program.

    1. Regional planning - Guam. 2. Territories and
    possessions. I. Guam. Territorial Plan-
    ning Commission. II. U.S. URA-UPAP.
    Guam.

Territories and possessions.

Terraces
Popular Science (RG 5/49 - 2/52)
10/50, p.183-184

325.3
T27   Terrell, John Upton.
    American Indian almanac. New York, World
    Pub. Co., 1971.
    494p.

    Bibliography: p. 455-466.

C,I,E.O

    1. Indians. I. Title.

351
(7297) Virgin Islands. Governor.
V47   Report
    Washington, Govt. Print. Off.,
    v. tables. annual.

    Report year ends June 30.
    For complete information see shelflist.

    1. Territories and possessions.

Territories and possessions.

712
S85s   TERRACES.
    Sunset Books.
    Sunset garden and patio building book, by
    the editors of Sunset Books and Sunset Magazine.
    New ed. Menlo Park, Calif., Lane Books, 1970.
    96p.

    1. Landscape architecture. 2. Terraces.
    3. Fences. I. Title: Garden and patio building
    book.

711.73
(967) Territorial highway study.
T71   U.S. Dept. of Transportation.
    Territorial highway study: Guam, American
    Samoa, Virgin Islands. Report of the
    Secretary of Transportation to the United
    States Congress pursuant to Section 29(b),
    Public law 90-495, the Federal aid highway
    act of 1968. Wash., Govt. Print. Off.,
    1970.
    116p.
    At head of title: 91st Cong., 2d sess.
    Senate. Document no. 91-62.
    1. Highways - Guam. 2. Highways -
    American Samoa. 3. Highways -
    Virgin Islands. I. Title.

351
H66
Rept.18   Territories and possessions - U.S.
    U. S. Commission on Organization of the Executive Branch
    of the Government.
    Administration of overseas affairs; a report to the Con-
    gress, March 1949. [Washington, U. S. Govt. Print. Off.,
    1949]
    50 p. 28 cm.
    "Federal-State relations; a report to the Congress, March 1949":
    p. [19]-39.
    "Federal research; a report to the Congress, March 1949": p. [41]-
    50.
    Herbert Hoover, chairman.

    (Continued on next card)
    [20]   49-46294*

301.15
L45   Terracide; America's destruction of her
    living environment.
    Linton, Ron M
    Terracide; America's destruction of her
    living environment. Boston, Little, Brown,
    1970.
    376p.

    Bibliography: p. 355-362.

    1. Man - Influence of environment. 2. Natu-
    ral resources. 3. Air pollution. 4. Water
    pollution. I. Title.

U. S. Commission on Organization of the Executive Branch
of the Government. Administration of overseas affairs
... [1949]   (Card 2)
    Issued also as House Document no. 140, 81st Cong., 1st sess., under
    title: Overseas administration, Federal-State relations, Federal re-
    search. Letter from the chairman.

    1. U. S.—Territories and possessions. 2. World War, 1939-1945—
    Occupied territories. 3. Federal government. 4. Governmental research—Federal.
    I. U. S.
    Commission on Organization of the Executive Branch of the Govern-
    ment. Federal-State relations. II. U. S. Commission on Organiza-
    tion of the Executive Branch of the Government. Federal research.
    III. Hoover Commission reports.
    JV502.A52 1949   353.8   49-46294*
    ——— Copy 2.   JK643.O47A55 no. 18
    Library of Congress   [20]

690.241.53
A87   Terracotta roofing tile deterioration
    in Australia.
    Australia. Commonwealth Scientific and
    Industrial Research Organization. (Div.
    of Building Research)
    Terracotta roofing tile deterioration
    in Australia, cause of and remedy for a
    sea-side problem, by W. F. Cole. Mel-
    bourne, 1959.
    7p. illus., table. (Its Reprint
    no. 136)

    Reprinted from The British Clayworker,
    Sept. 1959. p. 180-185.

    1. Title. 2. Roofs and roofing.
    I. Cole, W. F.

651.4
T27m   Terry, George R
    Managing office services. Homewood, Ill.,
    Dow Jones-Irwin, 1966.
    174p.

    1. Office management. I. Title.

691.41
M12   TERRACRETE.
    MACDONALD, FRANCIS.
    TERRACRETE; BUILDING WITH
    RAMMED-EARTH-CEMENT. CHESTERTOWN, MD.,
    1939.
    46P.

    1. EARTH WALL CONSTRUCTION.
    I. TITLE.

002
:711 Territorial Planning, Housing, Information,
T27   International Group for Co-operation and
    Research on Documentation.
    Report, 1st- session of the group,
    1966-
    Paris, 1967-
    /v. (Its Doc. ref.AG-1-CR)

    For complete information see main card.

    1. Planning documentation. 2. Housing documenta-
    tion. 3. Documenta- tion.

651.4
T27   Terry, George Robert.
    Office management and control. Chicago, R. D. Irwin,
    1949.
    xvi, 808 p. illus. 24 cm.
    "Selected references": p. 770-791.

    1. Office management.

    HF5547.T4   651   49-9026 rev*
    Library of Congress   [r50n5]

651.4
T27
1958
TERRY, GEORGE ROBERT.
OFFICE MANAGEMENT AND CONTROL.
CHICAGO, R.D. IRWIN, 1949.
769P. ILLUS.

1. OFFICE MANAGEMENT.

624.131
T27V
TERZAGHI, KARL.
VARIETIES OF SUBMARINE SLOPE
FAILURES. CAMBRIDGE, HARVARD
UNIVERSITY, DIVISION OF ENGINEERING
AND APPLIED PHYSICS, 1956.
16P. (HARVARD SOIL MECHANICS SERIES
NO. 52)

REPRINTED FROM PUBLICATION NO. 25 OF
THE NORWEGIAN GEOTECHNICAL INSTITUTE
AND ORIGINALLY PUBLISHED IN THE
PROCEEDINGS OF THE EIGHTH TEXAS
CONFERENCE ON SOIL MECHANICS AND
FOUNDATION ENGINEERING, SEPTEMBER
(CONTINUED ON NEXT CARD)

VF
699.86
S17
A test hut study of two types of insulation.
Saskatchewan. University. Dept. of Mechanical
Engineering.
A test hut study of two types of insulation,
by N. B. Hutcheon, W. H. Ball, and E. E. Brooks.
Saskatoon, April 1953.
37 l., plates. tables. (Report PRH-4)

Processed.

1.Insulation. I.Hutcheon N. B. II.Ball, W. H.
III.Brooks, E. E. IV.Title.

VF
728.1
:613.5
T27
Terry, Luther L
Health and psychological aspects of the city.
Excerpts from a speech delivered, 96th Annual
Convention of the American Institute of Archi-
tects, St. Louis, Mo., June 17, 1964. Wash-
ington, Govt. Print. Off., 1965.
[11] p. (U.S. Public Health Service.
Publication no. 1249)

1. Housing and health. I. American Insti-
tute of Architects. Annual Convention, 96th,
St. Louis, 1964. II. U.S. Public Health
Service. III. Title.

624.131
T27V
TERZAGHI, KARL. VARIETIES OF
SUBMARINE ...1956. (CARD 2)

1956.

1. SOILS. I. TITLE: SUBMARINE
SLOPE FAILURES.

668.3
G42t
Test methods for sealed glazing units.
Gjelsvik, Tore.
Test methods for sealed glazing units;
Norwegian experience with accelerated tests
and their correlation with field experience.
Oslo, Norwegian Building Research Institute,
1969.
[5] p. (Oslo. Norges Byggforsknings-
institutt. Reprint 168.
Reprint from Glass digest, May 1969.

1. Adhesives. I. Oslo. Norges Byggforskningsinstitutt. II. Title.

336.2
(480)
K14
Tervola, V.
Kaksonen, V
Tilastomatemaattisten menetelmien käytöstä
erässä arvioimis - ja suunnittelutehtävissä
(The use of statistics in some taxation and
planning problems) by V. Kaksonen et V. Tervola.
Helsinki, State Institute for Technical
Research, 1967.
98p. (Finland. State Institute for Tech-
nical Research. Tiedotus. Sarja 3 - Rakennus
(Building) 114)
1. Taxation - Finland. 2. Economic condi-
tions - Finland - Statistics. I. Finland. State
Institute for Technical Research. II. Tervola, V

333.71
(7469)
G72
TERZO, FREDERICK C
GREATER BRIDGEPORT REGIONAL PLANNING
AGENCY.
OPEN SPACE NEEDS AND RESOURCES,
1960-2000, BY H.C. CHUNG AND FREDERICK
C. TERZO. TRUMBULL, CONN., 1965.
74P.

U.S. URBAN RENEWAL ADM. UPAP.
BIBLIOGRAPHY: P.73-74.

1. OPEN SPACE LAND - CONNECTICUT.
2. RECREATION - CONNECTICUT.
3. REGIONAL PL ANNING - CONNECTICUT.
I. TITLE. II. CHUNG, H.C.
(CONTINUED ON NEXT CARD)

691.71
W66
Test of a multi-storey rigid steel frame.
Wood, R H
Test of a multi-storey rigid steel frame,
by R.H. Wood and others. Garston, Eng.,
Building Research Station, Ministry of Public
Building and Works, 1968.
107-119p. (U.K. Building Research Station.
Building research current paper 53/68)
Reprinted from: The structural engineer,
April, 1968.

1. Steel. 2. Structural engineering.
I. U.K. Building Research Station. II. Title.

624
(07)
T27
TERZAGHI, KARL.
ENGINEERING GEOLOGY ON THE JOB AND IN
THE CLASSROOM. PAST AND FUTURE OF
APPLIED SOIL MECHANICS. CAMBRIDGE,
HARVARD UNIVERSITY, 1961.
97-137P. (HARVARD SOIL MECHANICS
SERIES NO. 62)

REPRINTED FROM JOURNAL OF THE BOSTON
SOCIETY OF CIVIL ENGINEERS, V. 48, APRIL
1961.

1. CIVIL ENGINEERING - STUDY AND
TEACHING. 2. SOILS. I. TITLE.
(CONTINUED ON NEXT CARD)

333.71
(7469)
G72
GREATER BRIDGEPORT REGIONAL PLANNING
AGENCY. OPEN SPACE NEEDS ...1965.
(CARD 2)

III. TERZO, FREDERICK C. IV. U.S.
URBAN RENEWAL ADMINISTRATION. V. U.S.
URA-UPAP. BRIDGEPORT, CONN.

691.8
M45t
A test of bond quality in glued lumber
panels.
Miller, D G
A test of bond quality in glued lumber
panels, by D.G. Miller and P. George.
Ottawa, Dept. of Forestry and Rural
Development, Forestry Branch, 1968.
10p. (Canada. Dept. of Forestry and
Rural Development. Departmental
publication no. 1246)
1. Panels. 2. Adhesives. 3. Veneers.
4. Furniture. I. George, P., jt. au.
I. Canada. Dept. of Forestry and rural
Development. II. Title.

624
(07)
T27
TERZAGHI, KARL. ENGINEERING GEOLOGY ON
...1961. (CARD 2)

II. TITLE: PAST AND FUTURE OF APPLIED
SOIL MECHANICS.

312
(743)
T27
Tesauro (S.J.) and Co.
People and homes in the American market.
Cross-tabulations of population and housing
characteristics from the 1960 Decennial
census, Vermont. Detroit, Data Processing
Center, S.J. Tesauro and Co., 1961.
10p.

1. Population - Vermont. 2. Housing
market - Vermont.

388
T74te
Test of gas turbine rail car.
Tri-State Transportation Commission
(Connecticut-New Jersey-New York)
Test of gas turbine rail car; a summary
report on part one of the mass transportation
demonstration grant project. Long Island
Railroad; July 1967-May 1968. New York, 1969.
14p.
INT-MTD 12.
U.S. Dept. of Housing and Urban Develop-
ment. Mass Transportation Demonstration Grant
Program.
1. Transportation - Conn.-N.J.-N.Y. area.
2. Journey to work. 3. Railroads -
Conn.-N.J.-N.Y. I. Title. II. Title:
Gas turbine rail car.
(Cont'd on next card)

624.131
T27
Terzaghi, Karl.
Soil mechanics in engineering practice, by
Karl Terzaghi and Ralph B. Peck. 2d ed. New
York, J. Wiley, 1967.
729p.
Bibliography: p.682-702.

1. Soils. 2. Engineering. 3. Foundations
(Building) I. Peck, Ralph B., jt. au. II. Title.

728.1
H687HOUS
1966
TESONE, S L
U.S. DEPT. OF HOUSING AND URBAN
DEVELOPMENT.
HOUSING FOR THE PHYSICALLY
HANDICAPPED; A GUIDE FOR PLANNING AND
DESIGN. DRAFT BY S.L. TESONE.
WAHSINGTON, 1966.
98L.

1. HOUSING FOR THE HANDICAPPED.
I. TESONE, S.L. II. TITLE.

388
T74te
Tri-State Transportation Commission
(Connecticut-New Jersey-New York) Test
of gas turbine...1969. (Card 2)

III. U.S. HUD Mass Transportation
Demonstration Grant Program.

624.131
T278
TERZAGHI, KARL.
STABILITY OF STEEP SLOPES ON HARD
UNWEATHERED ROCK. LONDON, INSTITUTION
OF CIVIL ENGINEERS, 1962.
20P. (HARVARD SOIL MECHANICS SERIES
NO. 69)

EXCERPT FROM GEOTECHNIQUE, DECEMBER
1962.

1. SOILS. I. TITLE.

691.54
B65
Test apparatus for automatically measuring
the setting time of cement.
Bombled, J P
Test apparatus for automatically measuring
the setting time of cement. Garston, Eng.,
Building Research Station, 1969.
[6]p. (U.K. Building Research Station.
Library communication no. 1507)

Translated from the German.

1. Cement. I. U.K. Building Research
Station. II. Title. (Series)

VF
697.3
:621.415
S54t
Test results for year's operation of
heat pump in Seattle.
Smith, George S
Test results for year's operation of heat
pump in Seattle American Artisan, p. 89-
92, May 1949. illus., tables.
University of Washington Engineering
Experiment Station Reprint no. 23.
1. Heat pumps. 2. Heating research.
I. Title. II. Series: Washington. Univ.
Engineering Experiment Station. Reprints.

699.8
W34
A test rig for establishing the dimensional needs of weatherproof joints.
Whiting, R W
A test rig for establishing the dimensional needs of weatherproof joints. Garston, Eng., Building Research Station, 1970.
4p. (U.K. Building Research Station. Current paper 26/70)

1. Insulation. I. U.K. Building Research Station. II. Title.

388
(74885)
M62
MPC Corp. Testing and evaluation transit expressway: Mass Transportation Demonstration Project...1967. (Card 2)

1. Transportation - Allegheny Co., Pa. 2. Engineering. I. U.S. Dept. of Housing and Urban Development. Mass Transportation Demonstration Grant Program. II. Title.

058.7
:620.1
U54
1944
Testing laboratories - Directory.
U.S. Treasury Department. Procurement Division.
Directory of inspection services and testing laboratories of the Federal government, compiled ...for the use of government purchasing agencies. [Washington, D.C.] 1944.
261 p.

Mimeographed.
Revision of Directory compiled by the Procurement Division and National Bureau of Standards, 1935

1.Testing laboratories-Direct.

370
L95
Test scores and what they mean.
Lyman, Howard B
Test scores and what they mean. Englewood Cliffs, N.J., Prentice-Hall, 1963.
223p.

Bibliography: p. 187-189.

1. Education. I. Title.

VF
690.015
F22
R11
Testing and inspection of building materials.
Federal Construction Council.
Testing and inspection of building materials. Washington, National Academy of Sciences-National Research Council. Sept. 1954.
27 p. (Its Technical report no. 11)

"...Prepared in cooperation with the Building Research Advisory Board."

1. Building materials - Testing. I. Title. (Series)

620.1
(68)
U541
Testing laboratories - Union of South Africa.
Union of South Africa. Bureau of Standards.
Inspection and testing services for industry. Pretoria [1965]
[32]p.

1. Testing laboratories - Union of South Africa. 2. Industrial research - Union of South Africa. I. Title.

690.022
S23
Testa, Carlo, jt. au.
Schmid, Thomas.
Systems building; an international survey of methods, by Thomas Schmid and Carlo Testa. New York, Praeger, 1969.
239p.

1. Prefabricated construction. 2. Building methods. I. Testa, Carlo, jt. au. II. Title.

658.27
D18
THE TESTING AND INSPECTION OF ENGINEERING MATERIALS.
DAVIS, HARMER ELMER, 1905-
THE TESTING AND INSPECTION OF ENGINEERING MATERIALS BY HARMER E. DAVIS, AND OTHERS. 3D ED. NEW YORK, MCGRAW-HILL, 1964.
475P. (MCGRAW-HILL CIVIL ENGINEERING SERIES)

1. MATERIALS - TESTING. I. TITLE.

620.1
(68)
U54
Rept.
Testing laboratories - Union of South Africa.
Union of South Africa. Council of South African Bureau of Standards.
Report (Jaarverslag),
[Pretoria]

v. annual

Eleventh report covers the period from January 1, 1956 - August 16, 1956.
Includes reports of the activities of the Bureau of Standards.

(see card 2)

711.4
(748111)
T65
Testimony presented to the second annual public hearing of the Philadelphia City
Toll, Seymour I   Planning Commission.
Testimony presented to the second annual public hearing of the Philadelphia City Planning Commission, Jan. 30, 1968. Philadelphia, Citizens' Council on City Planning, 1968.
20p.

1. City planning - Philadelphia. I. Philadelphia. City Planning Commission. II. Citizens' Council on City Planning, Philadelphia. III. Title.

VF
699.81
A52t
Testing and maintenance of dry pipe valves.
American Insurance Association.
Testing and maintenance of dry pipe valves. New York, 1968.
7p. (No. 13B)

1. Fire prevention. 2. Pipes. I. Title.

620.1
(68)
U54
Rept.
Union of South Africa. Council of South African Bureau of Standards. Report (Jaarverslag) 1956. (card 2)

1. Testing laboratories - Union of South Africa. I. Union of South Africa. Bureau of Standards.

VF
728.1
T27
Testimonial to Robert C. Weaver, December 16, 1968, Washington, D.C. Washington, D.C., 1968.
4p.
John W. Gardner, chairman.
2C
1. U.S. Dept. of Housing and Urban Development. 2. Weaver, Robert Clifton. I. Gardner, John W.

658
C65t
1971
S-H
Testing characteristics of consumer products.
U.S. Congress. Senate. Committee on Commerce.
Testing characteristics of consumer products. Hearing before the Consumer Subcommittee of the Committee on Commerce, United States Senate, Ninety-first Congress, second session on S. 3286... Wash., Govt. Print. Off., 1971.
31p.
Hearing held March 5, 1970.
1. Buying. I. Title.

311.2
E67
TESTS FOR THE VALIDITY OF THE ASSUMPTION THAT THE UNDERLYING
EPSTEIN, BENJAMIN.
TESTS FOR THE VALIDITY OF THE ASSUMPTION THAT THE UNDERLYING DISTRIBUTION OF LIFE IS EXPONENTIAL. ISSUED AS TECHNICAL REPORT BY OFFICE OF ASSISTANT SECRETARY OF DEFENSE (SUPPLY AND LOGISTICS) WASHINGTON, GOVT. PRINT. OFF., 1960.
1 V. (QUALITY CONTROL AND RELIABILITY HANDBOOK (INTERIM H 108)
BIBLIOGRAPHY: P. 100-101.
1. SAMPLING (STATISTICS) I. TITLE. II. QUALITY CON   TROL AND RELIABILITY HANDBOOK (INTER   IM) H 108.

027
A52t
The testing and evaluation of record players for libraries.
American Library Association. Library Technology Project
The testing and evaluation of record players for libraries; a report based on a study conducted for the Library Technology Project by Consumers' Research, inc. [Chicago] 1962.
72p. (Its LTP publications, no. 5)

1. Libraries. I. Consumers' Research. I. Title. II. Title: Record players for   libraries.

VF
691.32
U54t
Testing concrete.
U.K. Ministry of Public Building and Works.
Testing concrete. 2d ed. London, H.M.S.O., 1970.
folder. (Its Advisory leaflet no. 43)

1. Concrete. I. Title.

693.97
R61
Tests of a full-scale rigid-jointed...
Roberts, E H
Tests of a full-scale rigid-jointed multi-storey steel frame in high-yield steel (BS 4360, Grade 50), by E.H. Roberts and R.F. Smith, Garston, Eng., Building Research Station, 1971.
56p. (U.K. Building Research Station. Current paper CP 36/71)

1. Steel construction. 2. Strains and stresses. I. Smith, R.F., jt. au. II. U.K. Building Research Station. III. Title.

388
(74885)
M62
Testing and evaluation of the transit expressway.
MPC Corp.
Testing and evaluation of the transit expressway: Mass Transportation Demonstration Project conducted between Port Authority of Allegheny County, Pittsburgh, and U.S. Dept. of Housing and Urban Development. Pittsburgh, 1967.
272p.
U.S. Dept. of Housing and Urban Development. Mass Transportation Demonstration Grant Program.

(Cont'd on next card)

VF
620.1
U54
NBSC483
Testing laboratories
U.S. National Bureau of Standards.
Testing by the National Bureau of Standards; Policy, Information, fee schedule. Washington, D.C., U.S. G.P.O., 1949.
v1, 93 p. (Its circular 483)

1.Testing laboratories.

VF
699.86
F67
Tests of fiberized low-density hardwood for use in building boards and papers.
U.S. Forest Service. Forest Products Laboratory, Madison, Wis.
Tests of fiberized low-density hardwood for use in building boards and papers, by C. E. Hrubesky, F. J. Spinar, and E. A. Anderson. (In cooperation with National Housing Agency). Madison, Wis. [1947]
9 l./tables.
Not for publication.
At head of title: Project 9000-6B. Processed.

311.2
M12
Tests of homogeneity for correlated samples.
Madansky, Albert.
Tests of homogeneity for correlated samples.
Santa Monica, Calif., Rand Corporation, 1962.
43 p. (AD no. 6061 96)

1. Statistics. 2. Sampling (Statistics). I. Rand Corporation. II. Title.

593.5
G74
Tests on lightweight concrete columns.
Grimer, P J
Tests on lightweight concrete columns.
Gerston, Eng., Building Research Station, Ministry of Technology [1966?]
[18p.] (U.K. Building Research Station. Building research current papers. Engineering Series 27)
Reprinted from: Structural concrete, Nov/Dec. 1965. p. 503-20.

1. Concrete construction. 2. Concrete aggregates. I. U.K. Building Research Station. II. Title.

711.4
(7444)
T28
appendix
Tewksbury, Mass. Planning Board.
Technical Planning Associates, New Haven, Conn.
Master plan report, including capital budget, subdivision regulations, zoning by-law. Prepared for Tewksbury Planning Board and Massachusetts Department of Commerce. New Haven, 1958.
1v. diagrs., maps, tables.

U.S. Urban Renewal Administration, Urban Planning Assistance Program.

1. Master plan - Tewksbury, Mass. 2. Zoning legislation-Tewksbury, Mass. 3. Subdivision regulation - Tewksbury, Mass. I. Tewksbury, Mass. Planning Board. II. U.S. URA-UPAP. Tewksbury, Mass.

VF
697
N17t
Tests of modified warm air heating system in Martin Fultz Development, Lincoln, Ill.
U.S. National Bureau of Standards.
Tests of modified warm air heating system in Martin Fultz Development, Lincoln, Illinois, by P. R. Achenbach and S. D. Cole. [Washington] Dec. 1951.
14 l./illus., graphs, tables.
Prepared under Research Project no. 1950-ME-7, Housing and Home Finance Agency.
Project director, R. S. Dill staff technician, Robert Thulman.
Typewritten.

691.328.2
S72t
Tests on prestressed reinforced concrete beams.
Stevens, R F
Tests on prestressed reinforced concrete beams. Garston, Eng., Building Research Station, 1970.
[6]p. (U.K. Building Research Station. Current paper CP 8/70)
Reprinted from: Concrete, Nov., 1969. p. 457-462.
1. Concrete, Prestressed. 2. Concrete, Reinforced. I. U.K. Building Research Station. II. Title.

711.4
(7444)
T28
Tewksbury, Mass. Planning Board.
Technical Planning Associates, New Haven, Conn.
Report on the Master plan, Tewksbury, Massachusetts. Prepared for Tewksbury Planning Board and Massachusetts Department of Commerce. New Haven, 1958.
20p. maps.

U.S. Urban Renewal Administration, Urban Planning Assistance Program.

1. Master plan - Tewksbury, Mass. I. Tewksbury, Mass. Planning Board. II. U.S. URA-UPAP

691.116
J63t
Tests of power-driven fasteners for plywood...
Johnson, James W
Tests of power-driven fasteners for plywood, by James W. Johnson and Thomas J. Albert. Madison, Wis., Forest Products Research Society, 1962.
589-595p.
Presented at the 16th annual meeting of the Forest Products Research Society, session 19, Wood Engineering, Spokane, Wash., June 20, 1962.
Reprinted from: Forest products journal, Dec., 1962.
1. Plywood. I. Albert, Thomas J., jt. au. II. Forest Products Research Society. Annual Meeting, 16th, Spokane, Wash., 1962. III. Title.

691.41
A37U
TETER, W C
U.S. AGRICULTURAL RESEARCH SERVICE.
USE OF STABILIZED EARTH BLOCK IN FARM CONSTRUCTION, BY N.C. TETER AND OTHERS. WASHINGTON, GOVT. PRINT. OFF., 1964.
12P. (ITS TECHNICAL BULLETIN NO. 1305)

1. EARTH WALL CONSTRUCTION. I. TETER, W.C.

355.58
(764)
T29
TEXANS ON THE ALERT.
TEXAS. EXECUTIVE DEPT. DIV. OF DEFENSE AND DISASTER RELIEF.
TEXANS ON THE ALERT FOR CIVIL DEFENSE AND DISASTER RELIEF; ACTION PLAN FOR LOCAL GROUPS; A FAMILY PROTECTION PLAN, A PLAN FOR EMERGENCY MASS CARE. N.P., 1957.
53P.

BIBLIOGRAPHY: P.50-53.

1. CIVILIAN DEFENSE. 2. DISASTER SERVICES. I. TITLE: TEXANS ON THE ALERT.

VF
699.86
F67t
Tests of pulp-mill waste for use in building boards and papers.
U.S. Forest Service. Forest Products Laboratory, Madison, Wis.
Tests of pulp-mill waste for use in building boards and papers, by C. E. Hrubesky, F. J. Spinar and E. A. Anderson. (In cooperation with the National Housing Agency). Madison, Wis. [1947]
8 l./table.
Not for publication.
Typewritten.
1. Insulating materials. 2. Wood-Research.
3. Housing research contracts. I.Hrubesky, C. E. II.Spinar, F. J. III.Anderson, E. A. IV.U.S. National Housing Agency. V.Title.

711.4
(41)
T27
Tetlow, John.
Homes, towns, and traffic, by John Tetlow and Anthony Goss. New York, Praeger, 1968.
272p.

Bibliography: p. 263-266.

1. City planning - U.K. 2. Traffic - U.K. I. Title.

711.585.1
(76756)
T29
Texarkana, Ark. Office of City Manager.
Application to the Department of Housing and Urban Development for a grant to plan a comprehensive city demonstration program. Texarkana, Ark., 1967.
1v.
Selected to receive the first HUD Model Cities Program planning grants.

1. Model cities - Texarkana, Ark. I. U.S. HUD - Model Cities Program first planning grants.

690.015
(485)
S82
1971
R2
Tests on concrete slabs.
Kinnunen, Sven.
Försök med betongplattor understödda av pelare vid fri kant (Tests on concrete slabs supported on columns at free edges) Stockholm, Statens Institut för Byggnadsforskning, 1971.
103p. (Rapport R2:1971)
English summary.

1. Building research - Sweden. 2. Concrete construction. I. Stockholm. Statens Institut för Byggnadsforskning. II. Title: Tests on concrete slabs.

628.515
K63
Tetra Tech, inc.
Koh, Robert C Y
Mathematical models for the prediction of temperature distributions resulting from the discharge of heated water into large bodies of water, by Robert C.Y. Koh and Loh Nien Fan. [Prepared] for the Water Quality Office, Environmental Protection Agency. Pasadena, Calif., Tetra Tech, inc., 1970.
219p. (Water pollution control research series)
1. Water pollution. I. Fan, Loh-Nien, jt. au. II. Tetra Tech, inc. III. U.S. Environmental Protection Agency. IV. Title.

711.585.1
(764)
T29
1967
Texarkana, Tex. Office of City Manager.
Application to the Department of Housing and Urban Development for a grant to plan a comprehensive city demonstration program. Texarkana, Tex., 1967.
1v.
Selected to receive HUD Model Cities Program planning grant.

1. Model cities - Texarkana, Tex. I. U.S. HUD - Model Cities Program.

693.5
S65
Tests on joints between precast concrete members.
Somerville, G
Tests on joints between precast concrete members, by G. Somerville and P. Burhouse. Garston, Eng., Building Research Station, Ministry of Public Building and Works, 1966.
18p. (U.K. Building Research Station. Building research current papers. Engineering papers 45)
Reprinted from Proceedings of the Institution of Structural Engineers' Conference, 1966.
1. Concrete construction. 2. Prefabricated construction. I. Burhouse, P., jt. au. II. U.K. Building Research Station. III. Title.

728(52)
T27
Tetsuro, Yoshida.
Das japanische Wohnhaus. Berlin, Wasmuth [1935]
viii, 193 p. illus., diagrs., plans, tables.

1. Architecture, Domestic-Japan.

6247
6248
6249
TEXARKANA, ARK. CITY PLANNING COMMISSION.
PLANNING: 1, PLANS FOR THE CENTRAL AREA; 2, PLANS FOR GROWTH; 3, MAPS. TEXARKANA, ARK., 1964.
3 V. (HUD 701 REPORT)

1. CITY PLANNING - TEXARKANA, ARK. I. HUD 701. TEXARKANA, ARK.

621.6
H43
Tests on large culvert pipe.
Highway Research Board.
Tests on large culvert pipe. Presented at the thirty-third annual meeting, January 12-15, 1954. Wash., 1955.
18p. (Its Bulletin 102)

1. Pipes. 2. Concrete, Reinforced. I. Title.

332
P74i
Tew, Brian.
Princeton University. (International Finance Section)
The International Monetary Fund: its present role and future prospects, by Brian Tew. Princeton, N.J., 1961.
41p. (Its Essays in international finance no. 36)

1. International Monetary Fund. I. Tew, Brian.

330
(76756)
A74
Texarkana, Ark. City Planning Commission.
Arkansas. University. City Planning Div.
Planning unit study; basic planning data for Texarkana, Arkansas. Prepared for [Texarkana] City Planning Commission. Fayetteville, Ark., 1964.
1 v.
U.S. Urban Renewal Adm. UPAP.

1. Economic base studies - Texarkana, Ark. I. Texarkana, Ark. City Planning Commission. II. U.S. URA-UPAP. Texarkana, Ark.

711.4
(76756)
A74p

Texarkana, Ark. City Planning Commission.
Arkansas. University. City Planning Div.
Plans for action. Suggested regulations
and procedures for executing the long
range plans for Texarkana, Arkansas. Prepared for [Texarkana] City Planning Commission. Fayetteville, Ark., 1964.
105p.
U.S. Urban Renewal Adm. UPAP.

1. City planning - Texarkana, Ark.
I. Texarkana, Ark. City Planning Com-
mission. II. U.S. URA-UPAP. Texarkana,
Ark.

526.8
(76756)
A74

Texarkana, Ark. City Planning Commission.
Arkansas. University. City Planning Div-
ision.
Texarkana, Arkansas. Prepared for City
Planning Commission. Fayetteville, Ark.,
1956.
7 maps.
U.S. Urban Renewal Administration, Urban
Planning Assistance Program.
(Continued on next card)

526.8
(76756)
A74

Arkansas. University. City Planning Division. Texarkana, ... (Card 2)

1. Maps and mapping - Texarkana, Ark.
I. Texarkana, Ark. City Planning Commission. II. U.S. Urban Renewal Administration. Urban Planning Assistance
Program.

728.1
:336.18
(764)
T29R

TEXARKANA, TEX. HOUSING AUTHORITY.
REPORT, 1941-42 — 55-57

TEXARKANA.
6 v. BIENNIAL (1955-59, TRIENNIAL)

1941-42
1943-44
1945-47
1948-50
1951-54
1955-57 - 2v.

1. PUBLIC HOUSING - TEXARKANA, TEX.

Texas.

VF
Air conditioning.
Housing-U.S.-Texas.
School plant planning.
Sewage disposal.

693.5
T29

Texas. Agricultural Experiment Station.
Concrete tilt-up construction on the
farm, by Otto R. Kunze and Price Hobgood.
College Station, Texas, 1957.
12p. illus., diagrs. (Its Bulletin 874)

1. Concrete construction. I. Kunze,
Otto R II. Hobgood, Price. III. Title:
Tilt-up construction on the farm.

643.52
S72

TEXAS. AGRICULTURAL EXPERIMENT STATION.
STEWART, B R
DURABILITY OF MATERIALS AND METHODS
FOR CONSTRUCTING TUB AND SHOWER
ENCLOSURES, BY B. W. STEWART AND
OTHERS. COLLEGE STATION, TEXAS,
AGRICULTURAL EXPERIMENT STATION, 1962.
7P.

1. BATHROOMS. I. TEXAS. AGRICULTURAL
EXPERIMENT STATION.

690.25
T29

Texas. Agricultural Experiment Station.
Indentation and recovery tests of
common resilient floor coverings, by
B. R. Stewart and others. College
Station, Tex., 1960.
7p. illus. (Its Bulletin 961)

1. Floors and flooring. I. Stewart, B. R.

362.5
L28po

Texas. Agricultural Experiment Station.
Lever, Michael F
Poverty among nonwhite families in Texas and
the nation: a comparative analysis, by Michael
F. Lever and W. Kennedy Upham. College Station,
Dept. of Agricultural Economics and Sociology,
Texas A. & M. University, Texas Agricultural
Experiment Station, 1968.
110p. (Texas. Agricultural Experiment
Station. Departmental information report 68-4)
Bibliography: p. A-1 - A-11.
1. Poverty. 2. Minority groups. I. Texas.
Agricultural Experiment Station. II. Upham, W.
Kennedy, jt. au.

690.22
T29

Texas. Agricultural Experiment Station.
Scrub-resistance characteristics of
kitchen and bathroom wall-surfacing
materials, by O. R. Kunze and others.
College Station, Tex., 1960.
14p. diagrs. (Its Bulletin 962)

1. Walls. I. Kunze, O. R.

728.1
:362.6
S78

Texas. Agricultural Experiment Station.
Stubbs, Alice C
A small house for the aged or handicapped,
by Alice C. Stubbs and Billy R. Stewart.
[College Station, Texas] Agricultural and
Mechanical College of Texas, Texas
Agricultural Extension Service, 1962.
6p. (Study plan 4)

1. Housing for the aged. 2. Housing
for the handicapped. I. Stewart, Billy T.,
jt. au. II. Texas. Agricultural Experiment
Station.

Texas. Commissioners of appeals.
... The South western reporter ... 1887-1928. (Card 3)
v. 35-36, Containing all the current decisions of the Supreme courts
of Missouri, Arkansas, and Tennessee, Court of appeals of Kentucky, Supreme court, Court of criminal appeals, and Courts of
civil appeals of Texas, and Court of appeals of Indian territory.
v. 67-104, Containing all the current decisions of the Supreme and
appellate courts of Arkansas, Kentucky, Missouri, Tennessee,
Texas, and Indian territory.
v. 105-292, Comprising all current decisions of the Supreme and
appellate courts of Arkansas, Missouri, Tennessee and Texas,
Texas.
v. 293-300, Comprising all the current decisions of the Supreme
courts of Arkansas, Missouri, Tennessee and Texas, Courts of appeals of Kentucky and Missouri, courts of civil and criminal appeals and Commission of appeals of Texas.

(Continued on next card)
2—732
[48r37p2]

Texas. Commissioners of appeals.
... The South western reporter ... 1887-1928. (Card 4)
At head of title: v. 5-300, National reporter system. State series.

1. Law reports, digests, etc.—Southwest, Old. I. Arkansas. Supreme court. II. Missouri. Supreme court. III. Tennessee. Supreme
court. IV. Texas. Supreme court. V. Texas. Court of civil appeals.
VI. Missouri. Courts of appeals. VII. Texas. Court of civil appeals.
VIII. Texas. Court of criminal appeals. IX. Texas. Commissioners
of appeals. X. Texas. Court of appeals. XI. Indian territory. Court
of appeals. XII. West publishing co., St. Paul. XIII. National reporter
system.

Library of Congress   [48r37p2]
2—732

Texas. Commissioners of appeals.
South western reporter. Second series. Cases argued and
determined in the courts of Arkansas, Kentucky, Missouri,
Tennessee, Texas, with key number annotations. v. 1, [2d-
Feb./Mar. 1928- St. Paul,
Minn., West publishing co., 1928-
v. 26 cm.   For Additions or Holdings
Vols. 1-52: Permanent edition Continuation File
Subtitle varies: v. 1-63, Cases argued and determined in the Supreme
courts of Arkansas, Missouri, Tennessee, and Texas; Courts of
appeal of Kentucky and Missouri; courts of civil and criminal
appeals and Commission of appeals of Texas.

(Continued on next card)
28—17744
[49r38I]

Texas. Commissioners of appeals.
South western reporter. Second series ... 1928-
(Card 2)
v. 64-66, Cases argued and determined in the Supreme courts of
Arkansas, Missouri, Tennessee and Texas; Courts of appeals of
Kentucky, Missouri and Tennessee; courts of civil and criminal
appeals and Commission of appeals of Texas.
v. 67- Cases argued and determined in the courts of Arkansas,
Kentucky, Missouri, Tennessee, Texas.

1. Law reports, digests, etc.—Southwest, Old. I. Arkansas. Supreme court. II. Missouri. Supreme court. III. Tennessee. Supreme
court. IV. Texas. Supreme court. V. Kentucky. Court of appeals.
VI. Missouri. Court of appeals. VII. Texas. Court of civil appeals.
VIII. Texas. Court of criminal appeals. IX. Texas. Commissioners of
appeals. X. Tennessee. Court of appeals. XI. West publishing co.,
St. Paul.

Library of Congress   [49r38I]
28—17744

Texas. Constitution.
Texas. Laws, statutes, etc.
Vernon's annotated Revised civil statutes of the
state of Texas, revision of 1925...comprising all
laws of a general and permanent nature with annotations from state and federal courts... Kansas City,
Mo., Vernon law book company, 1926-
v. 26cm.
"Kept to date by cumulative annual pocket parts."

I, Texas. Constitution. II. Vernon law book
company, Kansas City, Mo.

Texas. Commissioners of appeals.
... The South western reporter ... Comprising all the current decisions of the Supreme courts of Arkansas, Missouri,
Tennessee and Texas, Courts of appeals of Kentucky and
Missouri, courts of civil and criminal appeals and Commission of appeals of Texas, with key-number annotations ...
Aug./Dec. 1886–Jan./Feb. 1928. St. Paul, West publishing
co., 1887-1928.
300 v. 23-26½ᶜᵐ.
Vols. 11-300: Permanent edition.
Title varies: v. 1-112, The Southwestern reporter ...
v. 113-114, The Southwestern reporter (annotated) ...
v. 125-178, The Southwestern reporter, with key-number annotations ...

(Continued on next card)
[44r37n2]
2—732

Texas. Commissioners of appeals.
... The South western reporter ... 1887-1928. (Card 2)
v. 179-276, The Southwestern reporter ...
v. 277-300, The Southwestern reporter ...
Subtitle varies: v. 1-14, Containing all the current decisions of the
Supreme courts of Missouri, Arkansas, and Tennessee, Court of
appeals in Kentucky, and Supreme court and Court of appeals
(criminal cases) of Texas.
v. 15-19, Containing all the current decisions of the Supreme courts
of Missouri, Arkansas, and Tennessee, Court of appeals of Kentucky, and Supreme court and Court of appeals of Texas.
v. 20-34, Containing all the current decisions of the Supreme courts
of Missouri, Arkansas, and Tennessee, Court of appeals of Kentucky, and Supreme court, Court of criminal appeals, and Courts
of civil appeals of Texas.

(Continued on next card)
2—732
[48r37p2]

Texas. Court of appeals.
... The South western reporter ... Comprising all the current decisions of the Supreme courts of Arkansas, Missouri,
Tennessee and Texas, Courts of appeals of Kentucky and
Missouri, courts of civil and criminal appeals and Commission of appeals of Texas, with key-number annotations ...
Aug./Dec. 1886–Jan./Feb. 1928. St. Paul, West publishing
co., 1887-1928.
300 v. 23-26½ᶜᵐ.
Vols. 11-300: Permanent edition.
Title varies: v. 1-112, The Southwestern reporter ...
v. 113-114, The Southwestern reporter (annotated) ...
v. 125-178, The Southwestern reporter, with key-number annotations ...

(Continued on next card)
[44r37n2]
2—732

Texas. Court of appeals.
... The South western reporter ... 1887-1928. (Card 2)
v. 179-276, The Southwestern reporter ...
v. 277-300, The Southwestern reporter ...
Subtitle varies: v. 1-14, Containing all the current decisions of the
Supreme courts of Missouri, Arkansas, and Tennessee, Court of
appeals in Kentucky, and Supreme court and Court of appeals
(criminal cases) of Texas.
v. 15-19, Containing all the current decisions of the Supreme courts
of Missouri, Arkansas, and Tennessee, Court of appeals of Kentucky, and Supreme court and Court of appeals of Texas.
v. 20-34, Containing all the current decisions of the Supreme courts
of Missouri, Arkansas, and Tennessee, Court of appeals of Kentucky, and Supreme court, Court of criminal appeals, and Courts
of civil appeals of Texas.

(Continued on next card)
2—732
[48r37p2]

Texas. Court of appeals.

... The South western reporter ... 1887–1928. (Card 3)

v. 85–86, Containing all the current decisions of the Supreme courts of Missouri, Arkansas, and Tennessee, Court of appeals of Kentucky, Supreme court, Court of criminal appeals, and Courts of civil appeals of Texas, and Court of appeals of Indian territory.
v. 67–104, Containing all the current decisions of the Supreme and appellate courts of Arkansas, Kentucky, Missouri, Tennessee, Texas, and Indian territory.
v. 105–292, Comprising all current decisions of the Supreme and appellate courts of Arkansas, Kentucky, Missouri, Tennessee, and Texas.
v. 293–300, Comprising all the current decisions of the Supreme courts of Arkansas, Missouri, Tennessee and Texas, Courts of civil and criminal appeals of Kentucky and Missouri, courts of civil and criminal appeals and Commission of appeals of Texas.

(Continued on next card)

[48r37p2]   2—732

Texas. Court of appeals.

... The South western reporter ... 1887–1928. (Card 4)

At head of title: v. 5–300, National reporter system. State series.

1. Law reports, digests, etc.—Southwest, Old. I. Arkansas. Supreme court. II. Missouri. Supreme court. III. Tennessee. Supreme court. IV. Texas. Supreme court. V. Texas. Court of civil appeals. VI. Missouri. Courts of appeals. VII. Texas. Court of criminal appeals. IX. Texas. Commissioners of appeals. X. Texas. Court of appeals. XI. Indian territory. Court of appeals. XII. West publishing co., St. Paul. XIII. National reporter system.

2—732

Library of Congress   [48r37p2]

Texas. Court of civil appeals.

... The South western reporter ... Comprising all the current decisions of the Supreme courts of Arkansas, Missouri, Tennessee and Texas, Courts of appeals of Kentucky and Missouri, courts of civil and criminal appeals and Commission of appeals of Texas, with key-number annotations ... Aug./Dec. 1886–Jan./Feb. 1928. St. Paul, West publishing co., 1887–1928.
800 v. 23–26½ᵐ.

Vols. 11–300: Permanent edition.
Title varies: v. 1–112, The Southwestern reporter ...
v. 113–114, The Southwestern reporter (annotated) ...
v. 125–178, The Southwestern reporter, with key-number annotations ...

(Continued on next card)

[44r37n2]   2—732

Texas. Court of civil appeals.

... The South western reporter ... 1887–1928. (Card 2)

v. 179–276, The Southwestern reporter ...
v. 277–800, The South western reporter ...
Subtitle varies: v. 1–14, Containing all the current decisions of the Supreme courts of Missouri, Arkansas, and Tennessee, Court of appeals in Kentucky, and Supreme court and Court of appeals (criminal cases) of Texas.
v. 15–19, Containing all the current decisions of the Supreme courts of Missouri, Arkansas, and Tennessee, Court of appeals of Kentucky, and Supreme court and Court of appeals of Texas.
v. 20–34, Containing all the current decisions of the Supreme courts of Missouri, Arkansas, and Tennessee, Court of appeals of Kentucky, and Supreme court, Court of criminal appeals, and Courts of civil appeals of Texas.

(Continued on next card)

[48r37p2]   2—732

Texas. Court of civil appeals.

... The South western reporter ... 1887–1928. (Card 3)

v. 85–86, Containing all the current decisions of the Supreme courts of Missouri, Arkansas, and Tennessee, Court of appeals of Kentucky, Supreme court, Court of criminal appeals, and Courts of civil appeals of Texas, and Court of appeals of Indian territory.
v. 67–104, Containing all the current decisions of the Supreme and appellate courts of Arkansas, Kentucky, Missouri, Tennessee, Texas, and Indian territory.
v. 105–292, Comprising all current decisions of the Supreme and appellate courts of Arkansas, Kentucky, Missouri, Tennessee, and Texas.
v. 293–300, Comprising all the current decisions of the Supreme courts of Arkansas, Missouri, Tennessee and Texas, Courts of appeals of Kentucky and Missouri, courts of civil and criminal appeals and Commission of appeals of Texas.

(Continued on next card)

[48r37p2]   2—732

Texas. Court of civil appeals.

... The South western reporter ... 1887–1928. (Card 4)

At head of title: v. 5–300, National reporter system. State series.

1. Law reports, digests, etc.—Southwest, Old. I. Arkansas. Supreme court. II. Missouri. Supreme court. III. Tennessee. Supreme court. IV. Texas. Supreme court. V. Kentucky. Court of appeals. VI. Missouri. Courts of appeals. VII. Texas. Court of civil appeals. VIII. Texas. Court of criminal appeals. IX. Texas. Commissioners of appeals. X. Texas. Court of appeals. XI. Indian territory. Court of appeals. XII. West publishing co., St. Paul. XIII. National reporter system.

2—732

Library of Congress   [48r37p2]

Texas. Court of civil appeals.

South western reporter. Second series. Cases argued and determined in the courts of Arkansas, Kentucky, Missouri, Tennessee, Texas, with key number annotations. v. 1, [2d–Feb./Mar. 1928– St. Paul, Minn., West publishing co., 1928–
v. 26 cm.   For Additions or Holdings
Vols. 1–52: Permanent edition. See Continuation File
Subtitle varies: v. 1–63, Cases argued and determined in the Supreme courts of Arkansas, Missouri, Tennessee, and Texas; Courts of appeal of Kentucky and Missouri; courts of civil and criminal appeals and Commission of appeals of Texas.

(Continued on next card)

[49r38l1]   28—17744

Texas. Court of civil appeals.

South western reporter. Second series ... 1928–
(Card 2)

v. 64–66, Cases argued and determined in the Supreme courts of Arkansas, Missouri, Tennessee, and Texas: Courts of appeals of Kentucky, Missouri and Tennessee; courts of civil and criminal appeals and Commission of appeals of Texas.
v. 67–   Cases argued and determined in the courts of Arkansas, Kentucky, Missouri, Tennessee, Texas.

1. Law reports, digests, etc.—Southwest, Old. I. Arkansas. Supreme court. II. Missouri. Supreme court. III. Tennessee. Supreme court. IV. Texas. Supreme court. V. Kentucky. Court of appeals. VI. Missouri. Courts of appeals. VII. Texas. Court of civil appeals. VIII. Texas. Court of criminal appeals. IX. Texas. Commissioners of appeals. X. Tennessee. Court of appeals. XI. West publishing co., St. Paul.

28—17744

Library of Congress   [49r38l1]

Texas. Court of criminal appeals.

... The South western reporter ... Comprising all the current decisions of the Supreme courts of Arkansas, Missouri, Tennessee and Texas, Courts of appeals of Kentucky and Missouri, courts of civil and criminal appeals and Commission of appeals of Texas, with key-number annotations ... Aug./Dec. 1886–Jan./Feb. 1928. St. Paul, West publishing co., 1887–1928.
800 v. 23–26½ᵐ.

Vols. 11–300: Permanent edition.
Title varies: v. 1–112, The Southwestern reporter ...
v. 113–114, The Southwestern reporter (annotated) ...
v. 125–178, The Southwestern reporter, with key-number annotations ...

(Continued on next card)

[44r37n2]   2—732

Texas. Court of criminal appeals.

... The South western reporter ... 1887–1928. (Card 2)

v. 179–276, The Southwestern reporter ...
v. 277–300, The South western reporter ...
Subtitle varies: v. 1–14, Containing all the current decisions of the Supreme courts of Missouri, Arkansas, and Tennessee, Court of appeals in Kentucky, and Supreme court and Court of appeals (criminal cases) of Texas.
v. 15–19, Containing all the current decisions of the Supreme courts of Missouri, Arkansas, and Tennessee, Court of appeals of Kentucky, and Supreme court and Court of appeals of Texas.
v. 20–34, Containing all the current decisions of the Supreme courts of Missouri, Arkansas, and Tennessee, Court of appeals of Kentucky, and Supreme court, Court of criminal appeals, and Courts of civil appeals of Texas.

(Continued on next card)

[48r37p2]   2—732

Texas. Court of criminal appeals.

... The South western reporter ... 1887–1928. (Card 3)

v. 85–86, Containing all the current decisions of the Supreme courts of Missouri, Arkansas, and Tennessee, Court of appeals of Kentucky, Supreme court, Court of criminal appeals, and Courts of civil appeals of Texas, and Court of appeals of Indian territory.
v. 67–104, Containing all the current decisions of the Supreme and appellate courts of Arkansas, Kentucky, Missouri, Tennessee, Texas, and Indian territory.
v. 105–292, Comprising all current decisions of the Supreme and appellate courts of Arkansas, Kentucky, Missouri, Tennessee, and Texas.
v. 293–300, Comprising all the current decisions of the Supreme courts of Arkansas, Missouri, Tennessee and Texas, Courts of appeals of Kentucky and Missouri, courts of civil and criminal appeals and Commission of appeals of Texas.

(Continued on next card)

[48r37p2]   2—732

Texas. Court of criminal appeals.

... The South western reporter ... 1887–1928. (Card 4)

At head of title: v. 5–300, National reporter system. State series.

1. Law reports, digests, etc.—Southwest, Old. I. Arkansas. Supreme court. II. Missouri. Supreme court. III. Tennessee. Supreme court. IV. Texas. Supreme court. V. Kentucky. Court of appeals. VI. Missouri. Courts of appeals. VII. Texas. Court of civil appeals. VIII. Texas. Court of criminal appeals. IX. Texas. Commissioners of appeals. X. Texas. Court of appeals. XI. Indian territory. Court of appeals. XII. West publishing co., St. Paul. XIII. National reporter system.

2—732

Library of Congress   [48r37p2]

Texas. Court of criminal appeals.

South western reporter. Second series. Cases argued and determined in the courts of Arkansas, Kentucky, Missouri, Tennessee, Texas, with key number annotations. v. 1, [2d–Feb./Mar. 1928– St. Paul, Minn., West publishing co., 1928–
v. 26 cm.   For Additions or Holdings
Vols. 1–52: Permanent edition. See Continuation File
Subtitle varies: v. 1–63, Cases argued and determined in the Supreme courts of Arkansas, Missouri, Tennessee, and Texas; Courts of appeal of Kentucky and Missouri; courts of civil and criminal appeals and Commission of appeals of Texas.

(Continued on next card)

[49r38l1]   28—17744

Texas. Court of criminal appeals.

South western reporter. Second series ... 1928–
(Card 2)

v. 64–66, Cases argued and determined in the Supreme courts of Arkansas, Missouri, Tennessee, and Texas: Courts of appeals of Kentucky, Missouri and Tennessee; courts of civil and criminal appeals and Commission of appeals of Texas.
v. 67–   Cases argued and determined in the courts of Arkansas, Kentucky, Missouri, Tennessee, Texas.

1. Law reports, digests, etc.—Southwest, Old. I. Arkansas. Supreme court. II. Missouri. Supreme court. III. Tennessee. Supreme court. IV. Texas. Supreme court. V. Kentucky. Court of appeals. VI. Missouri. Courts of appeals. VII. Texas. Court of civil appeals. VIII. Texas. Court of criminal appeals. IX. Texas. Commissioners of appeals. X. Tennessee. Court of appeals. XI. West publishing co., St. Paul.

28—17744

Library of Congress   [49r38l1]

LAW
T
T292p

Texas. Criminal Justice Council.
Policies and procedures governing grants for comprehensive law enforcement planning to councils of government and regional planning commissions in Texas under the Omnibus crime control and safe streets act of 1968.
[Austin] 1968.
30p.

1. Law enforcement – Tex. I. Title.

727.1   TEXAS. ENGINEERING EXPERIMENT STATION.
[764] EDUCATIONAL FACILITIES LABORATORIES.
E28B   BELAIRE ELEMENTARY SCHOOL, SAN ANGELO,
       TEXAS. PREPARED BY EVANS CLINCHY.
       RESEARCH BY THE ARCHITECTURAL RESEARCH
       GROUP, TEXAS ENGINEERING EXPERIMENT
       STATION, COLLEGE STATION, TEXAS. NEW
       YORK, 1960.
       19P. (ITS PROFILES OF SIGNIFICANT
       SCHOOLS)

       1. SCHOOLS – SAN ANGELO, TEX. I. CLINCHY,
       EVANS. II. TEXAS. ENGINEERING
       EXPERIMENT STATION. III. TITLE.

333.38   Texas. Engineering Experiment Station.
T29   A case for south living, by Robert
          F. White. College Station, Tex., 1960.
          11p. diagrs. (Its Reprint 102)

          Reprinted from the Autumn 1959 issue
          of Landscape architecture.

          1. Subdivision. I. White, Robert F.

697.9   Texas. Engineering Experiment Station.
T29d   Design for natural ventilation in hot
         humid weather, by Robert H. Reed. College
         Station, Tex., 1953.
         [11]p. illus., diagrs. (Its Reprint
         80)

         Reprinted from Building Research
         Institute. Housing and building in hot-
         humid and hot-dry climates, 1953.

         1. Ventilation.   I. Reed, Robert H.
         II. Building   Research
         Institute.   Housing and build-
         ing in hot-humid   and hot-dry climate

697.9   Texas. Engineering Experiment Station.
T29e   Effects of landscape development on the
         natural ventilation of buildings and their
         adjacent areas, by Robert F. White. College
         Station, Tex., 1954.
         16p. illus., diagrs. (Its Research
         report 45)

         1. Ventilation. 2. Landscape architecture.
         I. White, Robert F.

696.92   Texas. Engineering Experiment Station.
T29e   Effects of nearby walks and concrete
          areas on indoor natural lighting, by
          Bob H. Reed. College Station, Tex.,
          1956.
          [5]p. tables. (Its Reprint 64)

          Reprinted from Illuminating engineering,
          vol. LI, no. 7, July 1956. p. 532–536.

          1. Daylight. I. Reed, Robert H.

DATE OF REQUEST   4/26/55 | L.C. CARD NO.

AUTHOR   Texas. Engr. Experiment Station.

TITLE   An evaluation of plant location factors in Texas,
         by L. S. Paine.

SERIES   Research report #49.

EDITION | PUB. DATE   210/54 | PAGING   25p.

PUBLISHER

RECOMMENDED BY   Ed. | REVIEWED IN   Pbn.DataGuide, 3/55, p.9.
                                            ORDER RECORD

VF
697.9
T29

Texas. Engineering Experiment Station.
Natural air flow around buildings, by
Benjamin H. Evans. College Station, Texas,
1957.
15 p. illus., diagrs. (Its Research
report 59)
Bibliography: p. 13.

1.Ventilation. 2.Architecture and climate.
I.Evans, Benjamin H II.Title.

Texas. Engineering Experiment Station.
Research reports.

VF
727
C18
1952

no.
36 Caudill, W. W. Geometry of classrooms as
related to natural lighting and
natural ventilation. July 1952.

711.33
(764)
T29e

Texas. Office of the Governor.
Establishment and use of state planning
regions; official memorandum. Austin, 1968.
3p.

1. State planning - Tex. I. Title.

697.9
T29n

Texas. Engineering Experiment Station.
Natural ventilation by Bob F. Reed.
College Station, Tex., [1953?]
[5]p. illus. (Its Reprint 81)

Reprinted from Building Research Institute. Windows and glass in the exterior
of buildings, [n.d.]

1. Ventilation. 2. Windows. I. Reed,
Robert H. II. Building Research Institute.
Windows and glass in the exterior
of buildings.

Texas. Engineering Experiment Station.
Research Reports.

VF
697.9
T29

no.
59 Evans, Benjamin H. Natural air flow
around buildings, March 1957.

Texas. Office of the Governor. Planning
Agency Council for Texas.
see Texas. Planning Agency Council for
Texas.

VF
727
C18

Texas. Engineering Experiment Station.
Caudill, William W
Your schools; an approach to long-range
planning of school buildings. [College
Station, Tex.] Texas Engineering Experiment
Station [1950?]
43 p. illus., diagrs., graphs.

Cover title: Take a good look at your
schools.
Bibliography: p. 43.

1.Schools. I.Texas Engineering Experiment
Station.II.Title.

353
(764)
T29e

Texas. Executive Dept.
Executive budget, 1972/73

Austin, 19

|v. biennial.

For Library holdings see main entry.

1. State finance - Texas. I. Title.

362.6
T46R

TEXAS. GOVERNOR'S COMMITTEE, WHITE
HOUSE CONFERENCE ON AGING.
TIPS, CHARLES R
A REPORT FROM ITALY ON THE AGING.
AUSTIN, GOVERNOR'S COMMITTEE, WHITE
HOUSE CONFERENCE ON AGING, 1960.
7P.

REPORT MADE ROME, ITALY, SEPTEMBER,
1960.

1. OLD AGE. I. TEXAS. GOVERNOR'S
COMMITTEE, WHITE HOUSE CONFERENCE ON
AGING.

VF
697.353
E22

Texas. Engineering Experiment Station. Bulletins.
no.
29 Eddy, J.R.D. A study of thermal radiation.
1937.

VF
697.9
:06
A47

110 Proceedings of the fourth annual air
conditioning conference. Jan. 1949.

355.58
(07)
T29

TEXAS. EXECUTIVE DEPT. DIVISION OF
DEFENSE AND DISASTER RELIEF.
CURRICULUM GUIDE FOR CIVIL DEFENSE
AND DISASTER RELIEF EDUCATION.
AUSTIN, TEX., 1956.
11P.

1. CIVILIAN DEFENSE - STUDY AND
TEACHING. 2. DISASTER SERVICES -
STUDY AND TEACHING. I. TITLE.

362.6
T29

2c

TEXAS. GOVERNOR'S COMMITTEE, WHITE
HOUSE CONFERENCE ON AGING.
RETIREMENT HOUSING AND NURSING HOMES,
A GUIDE TO FEDERAL FINANCING AIDS. 1961.
39P.

1. NURSING HOMES. 2. NURSING HOMES -
TEXAS. I. TITLE.

VF
727
(016)
C18
VF
691.41
B87
VF
697.9
621.63
S26

Texas. Engineering Experiment Station. Research
reports.
no. 1. Caudill, W.W. Bibliography on school
architecture. 1948.

6. Burkhart, E. J. Investigation of soils
and building techniques for rammed-earth
construction.

13. Scoates, W. D. Some practical considerations
in attic fan design: part 1. Housings.
May 1950.

699.81
T29

Texas. Executive Dept. Division of
Defense and Disaster Relief.
Firefighting for the householder, by
A. J. Fogaley. Austin, 1957.
58p. illus.

1.Fire prevention. I.Fogaley, A J
II.Title.

628.1
(764)
T29

Texas. Dept. of Health.
Safe water for farm and suburban homes.
Austin, Tex., [1956?]
36 p. illus., tables, diagrs.

1.Water supply - Texas. I.Title.

VF
696.92
V29
VF
697.9
165
VF
697.9
C18

Texas. Engineering Experiment Station. Research
reports.
no. 21. Vezey, E.E. The feasibility of using models
for predetermining natural lighting.
Jan. 1951.

33 Holleman, T. R. Air flow through
conventional window openings. Nov.1951.

22 Caudill, W.W. Some general considerations
in the natural ventilation of buildings.
Feb. 1951.

355.58
(764)
T29

TEXAS. EXECUTIVE DEPT. DIV. OF
DEFENSE AND DISASTER RELIEF.
TEXANS ON THE ALERT FOR CIVIL DEFENSE
AND DISASTER RELIEF; ACTION PLAN FOR
LOCAL GROUPS, A FAMILY PROTECTION PLAN,
A PLAN FOR EMERGENCY MASS CARE. N.P.,
1957.
53P.

BIBLIOGRAPHY: P.50-53.

1. CIVILIAN DEFENSE. 2. DISASTER
SERVICES. I. TITLE: TEXANS ON THE
ALERT.

691.32
I82

Texas. Highway Dept.
Ivey, Don L
Air void systems in ready mixed concrete, by
Don L. Ivey and Patrick H. Torrans. Sponsored
by the Texas Highway Dept. in cooperation with
the Dept. of Transportation, Federal Highway
Administration, Bureau of Public Roads.
College Station, Texas Transportation Institute,
Texas A. & M. University, 1969.
50p. (Research report no. 103-4F; study
2-5-66-103)

1. Concrete. I. Torrans, Patrick H., jt. au.
II. Texas. Highway Dept. III. Texas
Transportation Institute.

VF
697.9
S54
VF
72
(07)
M22

Texas. Engineering Experiment Station. Research
reports.
no.
26 Smith, E. G. The feasibility of using models
for predetermining natural ventilation.
June 1951.

32 McCutchan, G. An experiment in architectural
education through research. Nov. 1951.

630
:331
T29

Texas. Good Neighbor Commission.
Texas migrant labor; annual report, 1969-71

[Austin] 19

3 v.
For Library holdings see main entry.

1. Agricultural laborers. 2. Labor supply -
Tex. I. Title.

DATE OF REQUEST 7/31/52   L.C. CARD NO.
TTH-Texas   AUG 7 1952
AUTHOR
Texas. Highway Department.
TITLE
Dallas metropolitan area traffic survey unit cost
data.
SERIES
EDITION   PUB. DATE 1952   PAGING 9 p.
PUBLISHER
same, Austin, Texas.
RECOMMENDED BY   REVIEWED IN
    L-Curr Lit 7/14/52 p.6
ORDER RECORD

388
(764)
T29e
Texas. Highway Dept.
Amarillo urban transportation plan: origin-destination survey. Vol. 1-2. Prepared in cooperation with U.S. Dept. of Commerce Bureau of Public Roads. Amarillo, Tex., 1964.
2 v.
1. Transportation - Amarillo, Tex. 2. Journey to work. I. U.S. Bureau of Public Roads. II. Title.

711.73
(764)
B83
Texas. Highway Department.
Buffington, Jesse L
An economic impact study of interstate highway 35E on Waxahachie, Texas. Sponsored by the Texas Highway Dept. in cooperation with the U.S. Dept. of Commerce, Bureau of Public Roads. College Station, Tex., 1966.
50p. (Texas Transportation Institute. Bulletin no. 35)
Research report number 4-6. Economic impact of the interstate system on selected areas in Texas. Research study number 2-10-57-4.
1. Highways - Economic effect. I. Buffington, Jesse L.
(Cont'd on next card)

711.73
(764)
B83
Buffington, Jesse L   An economic impact study...1966.   (Card 2)
II. U.S. Bureau of Public Roads. III. Texas. Highway Dept. IV. Title.

388
(764)
T29e
Texas. Highway Dept. (Planning Survey Div.)
El Paso metropolitan area traffic survey. In cooperation with the City of El Paso, Texas and the U.S. Department of Commerce, Bureau of Public Roads. San Antonio, 1958.
48p. illus., diagrs., maps.
1. Traffic surveys - El Paso metropolitan area.

691.421
(015)
T29
Texas. Highway dept.
Texas Transportation Institute.
Clay, aggregate, and concrete, by Eugene Buth and others. Sponsored by the Texas Highway Dept. in cooperation with the U.S. Dept. of Commerce, Bureau of Public Roads. College Station, Tex., 1967.
34p. (Its Research report no. 71-3 (final); Deleterious materials in concrete research study 2-5-63-71)
1. Clay - Research. 2. Concrete--Research. I. Buth, Eugene. II. U.S. Bureau of Public Roads. III. Texas. Highway Dept.   IV. Title.

711.73
(764)
P17
Texas. Highway Dept.
Park, Ross A
A computer technique for perspective plotting of roadways, by Ross A. Park and Neilon J. Rowan. Sponsored by the Texas Highway Dept. in cooperation with the U.S. Dept. of Transportation, Federal Highway Administration, Bureau of Public Roads. College Station, Tex., Texas Transportation Institute, Texas A & M University, 1967.
27p. (Texas Transportation Institute. Research report number 19-3; Channelization research   study number 2-8-60-19)
(Cont'd on next card)

711.73
(764)
P17
Park, Ross A   A computer technique...1967.   (Card 2)
Distributed by U.S. Clearinghouse for Federal Scientific and Technical Information as PB 177535.
1. Highways - Texas. 2. Transportation-Automation. I. Rowan, Neilon J., jt. au. II. Texas Transportation Institute. III. Texas. Highway Dept. IV. Title.

388
(764)
T29h
Texas. Highway Dept.
Houston-Harris County, designing a transportation system with you in mind. A preview of the Cooperative Houston Metropolitan Area Transportation Study. [Houston, Tex.] 1962.
24p.
Prepared in cooperation with U.S. Bureau of Public Roads, Automotive Safety Foundation, Texas Transportation Institute, Texas A and M College.
(Cont'd on next card)

388
(764)
T29h
Texas. Highway Dept. Houston-Harris County, designing a transportation system with you in mind...1962.
(Card 2)
1. Transportation - Houston-Harris Co., Tex. 2. City growth - Houston-Harris Co., Tex. 3. Houston Metropolitan Area Transportation Study. I. Title.

388
(764)
T29l
v.1
Texas. Highway Dept.
Lubbock urban transportation plan, Lubbock, Texas, Hub of the Plains, origin destination survey. Sponsoring agencies: City of Lubbock, County of Lubbock, in cooperation with the U.S. Dept. of Commerce, Bureau of Public Roads. [Austin, Tex.] 1964.
56p.   (Vol. 1)
1. Transportation - Lubbock, Tex. 2. Traffic surveys. 3. Journey to work. I. U.S. Bureau of Public Roads. II. Title.

711.14
(764)
T29p
Texas. Highway Dept.
Projection of land use and population, City of Houston, County of Harris. A basic study upon which traffic patterns and volumes to the year 1980 were based. Houston, Tex., 1961.
1 v.   (Houston Metropolitan Area Transportation Study report no. 2)
1. Land use - Houston, Tex. 2. Population - Houston, Tex. 3. Transportation - Houston, Tex. I. Title. II. Houston Metropolitan Area Transportation Study.

330
(764)
J65
Texas. Highway Dept.
Jones, Joe H
San Angelo: urban growth influencing transportation planning. Sponsoring agencies: the City of San Angelo and Tom Green County, Texas Highway Dept., in cooperation with U.S. Dept. of Commerce, Bureau of Public Roads. Austin, Bureau of Business Research, University of Texas, 1965.
86p.   (Texas. University. Bureau of Business Research. Area economic survey no. 26)
(Cont'd on next card)

330
(764)
J65
Jones, Joe H. San Angelo: urban growth influencing transportation planning...1965.   (Card 2)
1. Economic base studies - San Angelo, Tex. 2. Transportation - San Angelo, Tex. I. Texas. University. Bureau of Business Research. II. Texas. Highway Dept. III. Title.

388
(764)
T29
Texas. Highway Dept. (Highway Planning Survey)
San Antonio metropolitan area traffic survey, 1956. San Antonio, 1956.
170p. illus., maps, tables.
1. Traffic surveys - San Antonio. I. U.S. Bureau of Public Roads.

624.131
(016)
C31
TEXAS. HIGHWAY DEPARTMENT.
CHAN, PAUL C
SOIL DYNAMICS AND SOIL RHEOLOGY: AN ANNOTATED BIBLIOGRAPHY, BY PAUL C. CHAN AND T.J. HIRSCH. COLLEGE STATION, TEXAS TRANSPORTATION INSTITUTE, 1966.
23P. (TEXAS TRANSPORTATION INSTITUTE. RESEARCH REPORT 33-5)
RESEARCH PROJECT NO. 2-5-62-33; PILING BEHAVIOR SPONSORED BY THE TEXAS HIGHWAY DEPARTMENT IN COOPERATION WITH THE U.S. BUREAU OF PUBLIC ROADS.
(CONTINUED ON NEXT CARD)

624.131
(016)
C31
CHAN, PAUL C SOIL DYNAMICS AND ...
1966.   (CARD 2)
1. SOILS - BIBLIOGRAPHY. I. HIRSCH, T.J., JT. AU. II. U.S. BUREAU OF PUBLIC ROADS. III. TEXAS. HIGHWAY DEPARTMENT. IV. TITLE.

625.7
T29
1962
TEXAS. HIGHWAY DEPARTMENT.
STANDARD SPECIFICATIONS FOR ROAD AND BRIDGE CONSTRUCTION; ADOPTED BY THE STATE HIGHWAY DEPARTMENT OF TEXAS, JANUARY 2, 1962. AUSTIN, 1962.
813P.
1. ROAD CONSTRUCTION - STANDARDS AND SPECIFICATIONS. 2. BRIDGES - STANDARDS AND SPECIFICATIONS.

711.14
(764)
T29
Texas. Highway Dept. (Study Office Staff)
Technical report on land use, population distribution, trip forecasting, Dallas-Fort Worth Regional Transportation Study. [Fort Worth] Tex., 1966.
158p.
Prepared in cooperation with U.S. Dept. of Commerce, Bureau of Public Roads.
1. Land use - Dallas-Fort Worth. 2. Automation. 3. Transportation - Dallas-Fort Worth. 4. Population - Dallas-Fort Worth. I. Dallas-Fort Worth Regional Transportation Study.

312.8
T29
[Texas. Highway Dept.] Study Office Staff.
Technical report on population forecasts, Dallas-Fort Worth Regional Transportation Study. Prepared in cooperation with U.S. Dept. of Commerce, Bureau of Public Roads. [Fort Worth, Tex.] 1965.
33p.
1. Population forecasting. I. Dallas-Fort Worth Regional Transportation Study.

VF
711.73
(764)
T29t
Texas. Highway Dept.
Texas and the interstate highway system. Austin, Tex., 1957.
39p. illus.
1. Highways - Texas.

VF
711.73
(764)
T29
Texas. Highway Dept.
Texas official highway travel map. Austin, Tex., 1958
folder
1. Highways - Texas - Maps.

Texas. Highway Dept.

711.73
(764)
H21   Heathington, Kenneth W
    Traffic volume analysis of urban free-
ways, by Kenneth W. Heathington and Paul R.
Tutt. [Prepared] in cooperation with the
U.S. Dept. of Commerce, Bureau of Public
Roads. [Austin,Texas] Texas Highway Dept.
1966.
    56p. (Texas. Highway Dept. Departmental
Research. Report no. SS 5.0)
    1. Highways - Texas. 2. Traffic surveys -
Texas. 3. Transportation - Statistics. I. Tutt,
Paul R., jt. au. II. Texas. Highway Dept.
IV. Title.

388
T29   Texas. Legislative Council.
    Balanced transportation for Texas cities; a
report to the 60th Legislature. Austin, Tex.,
1966.
    87p.

    1. Transportation - Texas. I. Title.

728.1
:325   TEXAS. PLANNING BOARD.
(764)   LOW INCOME HOUSING FOR SOUTHERN TEXAS
T29   CONDITIONS. AUSTIN, 1938.
    44P.

    PREPARED BY A SPECIAL SUBCOMMITTEE OF
THE BOARDS' COMMITTEE ON GOVERNMENT AND
SOCIAL ASPECTS.

    1. MINORITY GROUPS - HOUSING - TEXAS.
2. PUBLIC HOUSING - TEXAS. I. TITLE.

388
(764)   Texas. Highway Dept.
T29t   Tyler urban transportation study. Vol. 1.
v.1   Origin-destination survey. Sponsoring
agencies: City of Tyler, County of Smith
[and] Texas Highway Dept. in cooperation
with U.S. Dept. of Commerce, Bureau of
Public Roads. [Austin?] 1964.
    1 v.

    1. Transportation - Tyler, Tex.
2. Journey to work. 3. Transportation -
Statistics.   I. U.S. Bureau of
Public Roads.   II. Title.

352.5
(764)   TEXAS. LEGISLATIVE COUNCIL.
T29   MUNICIPAL ANNEXATION; A REPORT TO THE
57TH LEGISLATURE. AUSTIN, 1962.
    77P. (ITS STAFF RESEARCH REPORT. NO.
56-6)

    1. ANNEXATION - TEXAS. I. TITLE.

2C

058.7
:352   Texas. Div. of Planning Coordination.
(764)   Directory of councils of governments and
T29   regional planning commissions in Texas.
[Austin] 1968.
    92p.

    1. Local government - Tex. - Direct.
2. Intergovernmental relations - Tex. -
Direct. 3. Metropolitan area planning - Tex.
- Direct. I. Title: Councils of governments
and regional planning commissions in Texas.

625.7
(016)   TEXAS. HIGHWAY DEPT.
T29   TEXAS TRANSPORTATION INSTITUTE.
    VIBRATORY PILE DRIVING. TEXAS
TRANSPORTATION INSTITUTE, TEXAS HIGHWAY
DEPARTMENT: COOPERATIVE RESEARCH, IN
COOPERATION WITH THE DEPARTMENT OF
COMMERCE, BUREAU OF PUBLIC ROADS, N.P.,
1963.
    6P. PHOTOCOPIED IN 4 L. (SURVEY OF
LIBRARY FACILITIES PROJECT.
BIBLIOGRAPHY, 63-16)

    1. ROAD CONSTRUCTION - BIBLIOGRAPHY.
I. TEXAS. HIGHWAY DEPT. II. TITLE:
PILE DRIVING.

352.5
T29   Texas. [Legislature.] Legislative Council.
    Municipal annexation; prepared by the
staff of the Texas Legislative Council.
Austin, Tex., Sept, 1954.
    82, XXV p.

    1.Annexation - Texas. 2.Municipal Services -
Texas.

058.7
:352   Texas. Div. of Planning Coordination.
(764)   Directory of regional councils in Texas,
T29d   19 70;
2c, 1970   Austin, 1970-
    1 v.

    For Library holdings see main entry.

    1. Local government - Texas - Direct.
2. Intergovernmental relations - Texas -
Direct.

Criminal Pro.

Texas. *Laws, statutes, etc.*
    Vernon's annotated Code of criminal procedure of the state
of Texas, revision of 1925, including all laws of general application passed by the regular session of the 39th Legislature,
with historical notes, notes of decisions and references to forms
... Kansas City, Mo., Vernon law book company, 1926-50.
    3 v. 26 cm.
    On cover: Vernon's annotated criminal statutes of the state of Texas.
    "Annotations are complete to August 1, 1925 and include volumes 272
South western reporter, 5 Federal reporter (second series) 45 Supreme
court reporter."
    Kept up to date by Cumulative quarterlies. cf. Pref.
    1. Criminal procedure—Texas. I. Vernon law book company, Kan-
sas City, Mo. II. Title.
    26—23212
Library of Congress   [40r28f1]

711.74
(764)   Texas. Legislative Council.
T29   State assistance to Texas municipalities
for arterial streets; a report to the 60th
Legislature. Austin, Tex., 1966.
    73p. (Its Report no. 59-1)

    1. Streets - Texas. 2. Municipal
finance - Texas. I. Title.

711.33
(764)   Texas. Div. of Planning Coordination.
T29d   Division of Planning Coordination. Austin,
1968.
    [8]p.

    1. State planning - Tex. 2. Texas. Div.
of Planning Coordination.

Penal

Texas. *Laws, statutes, etc.*
    Vernon's annotated Penal code of the state of Texas, re-
vision of 1925, including subsequent laws of general application through the   session of the
Legislature, with historical notes and notes of decisions ...
Kansas City, Mo., Vernon law book company, 1926-
    3 v. 26¼ cm.
    On cover: Vernon's annotated criminal statutes of the state of
Texas.
    "Kept to date by cumulative annual pocket parts."
    1. Criminal law—Texas. 2. Criminal procedure—Texas. I. Ver-
non law book company, Kansas City, Mo. II. Title. III. Title: Ver-
non's annotated criminal statutes of the state of Texas.
For Additions or Holdings
See Continuation File   38—14104
    Library of Congress   [48f1]

711.3
(764)   Texas. Legislature.
T29   Texas Research League.
    Metropolitan Texas: a workable approach
to its problems. Austin, Texas, 1967.
    79p.
    A report to Governor John Connally and
the 60th Texas Legislature.

    1. Metropolitan area planning - Texas.
2. Intergovernmental relations - Texas.
3. Local government - Texas. I. Connally,
John. II. Texas. Legislature. III. Title.

711.33
(764)   Texas. Div. of Planning Coordination.
T29p   Planning regions for the State of Texas.
Austin, 1968.
    21p.

3c

    1. State planning - Tex. 2. Metropolitan
area planning - Tex. I. Title.

Civil

Texas. Laws, statutes, etc.
    Vernon's annotated Revised civil statutes of the
state of Texas, revision of 1925 ... comprising all
laws of a general and permanent nature with annotations from state and federal courts ... Kansas City,
Mo., Vernon law book company, 1926-
    22 v. 26cm.
    "Kept to date by cumulative annual pocket parts."

    II. Vernon law book company, Kansas City, Mo.
I. Texas. Constitution.

Texas. Legislature. Legislative Council.
see Texas. Legislative Council.

353
(764)   Texas. Div. of Planning Coordination.
T29p   Procedures and policies governing State
of Texas grants...metropolitan and rural
regional planning commissions in Texas, 1969
2c, '69   Austin 1968
    1 v.
    For Library holdings see main entry.

    1. State finance - Tex. 2. Intergovern-
mental relations - Tex. 3. Local government -
Finance - Tex. I. Title.

General

Texas. Laws, statutes, etc.
    Vernon's annotated statutes of the state of
Texas, comprising all laws of a general and permanent nature with annotations from state and
federal courts. Index ... Kansas City, Mo.,
Vernon law book company, 1941.
    2 v. 26cm.
    "Kept to date by cumulative annual pocket parts."

    I. Vernon law book company, Kansas City, Mo.

353
(764)   Texas. Planning Agency Council for Texas.
T29   Catalog of state services to local governments. Austin, 1966.
2c   196p.
    At head of title: The State of Texas.

    1. Local government - Texas. 2. State
government - Texas. 3. Intergovernmental
relations - Texas. I. Title.

058.7
:711.33   Texas. Div. of Planning Coordination.
(764)   Regional councils and economic development
T29   districts in Texas. Directors and maps.
[Austin] 1969.
    [6]p.

    1. State planning - Texas - Direct.
I. Title.

711.33
(764)
T29u

Texas. Div. of Planning Coordination.
Urban and regional development planning in Texas. Condensed proceedings of the Comprehensive Planning Workshop for Regional Councils, Houston, May 15 and 16, 1969. [Austin] 1969.
94p.
Sponsored by the Office of the Governor, Div. of Planning Coordination, U.S. Dept. of Housing and Urban Development and others.
Condensed and edited by: Elbert V. Borden.
1. State planning - Tex. 2. City Planning - Tex. I. U.S. Dept. of Housing and Urban Development. II. Borden, Elbert V. III. Title.

Texas. Supreme court.
... The South western reporter ... 1887-1928. (Card 3)
v. 85-86, Containing all the current decisions of the Supreme courts of Missouri, Arkansas, and Tennessee, Court of appeals of Kentucky, Supreme court, Court of criminal appeals, and Courts of civil appeals of Texas, and Court of appeals of Indian territory.
v. 87-104, Containing all the current decisions of the Supreme and appellate courts of Arkansas, Kentucky, Missouri, Tennessee, Texas, and Indian territory.
v. 105-292, Comprising all current decisions of the Supreme and appellate courts of Arkansas, Kentucky, Missouri, Tennessee, and Texas.
v. 293-300, Comprising all the current decisions of the Supreme courts of Arkansas, Missouri, Tennessee and Texas, Courts of appeals of Kentucky and Missouri, courts of civil and criminal appeals and Commission of appeals of Texas.

(Continued on next card)
[48r37p2]
2—732

711.33
(764)
T29d

TEXAS. DIV. OF PLANNING COORDINATION.
Texas. Div. of Planning Coordination.
Division of Planning Coordination. Austin, 1968.
[8]p.

1. State planning - Tex. 2. Texas. Div. of Planning Coordination.

Texas. Supreme court.
... The South western reporter ... 1887-1928. (Card 4)
At head of title: v. 5-300, National reporter system. State series.

1. Law reports, digests, etc.—Southwest, Old. I. Arkansas. Supreme court. II. Missouri. Supreme court. III. Tennessee. Supreme court. IV. Texas. Supreme court. V. Kentucky. Court of appeals. VI. Missouri. Courts of appeals. VII. Texas. Court of civil appeals. VIII. Texas. Court of criminal appeals. IX. Texas. Commissioners of appeals. X. Texas. Court of appeals. XI. Indian territory. Court of appeals. XII. West publishing co., St. Paul. XIII. National reporter system.

Library of Congress   [48r87p2]   2—732

628.515
T29

Texas. University.
Use of new analytical methods in water resource development. For the Water Quality Administration, Dept. of the Interior. Austin, Tex., Dept. of Mechanical Engineering, University of Texas, 1970.
13p. (U.S. Federal Water Quality Administration. Water pollution control research series 16110 FZE 09/70)
Bibliography: p. 11-12.
1. Water pollution. 2. Water resources. I. U.S. Federal Water Quality Administration. II. Title.

362.6
(016)
T29

Texas. State Library.
Through the looking glass at 4 groups of books for senior citizens. 1. Housing, 2. Health, 3. Care of the aged, and 4. Employment. Austin, [1968?]
[5]p.

1. Old age - Bibliography. I. Title.

Texas. Supreme court.
South western reporter. Second series. Cases argued and determined in the courts of Arkansas, Kentucky, Missouri, Tennessee, Texas, with key number annotations. v. 1, [2d- Feb./Mar. 1928– St. Paul, Minn., West publishing co., 1928.
v. 26 cm.
For Additions or Holdings See Continuation File
Vols. 1-52: Permanent edition.
Subtitle varies: v. 1-68, Cases argued and determined in the Supreme courts of Arkansas, Missouri, Tennessee, and Texas; Courts of appeal of Kentucky and Missouri; courts of civil and criminal appeals and Commission of appeals of Texas.

(Continued on next card)
[49r3811]   28—17744

378
:500.15
T29

Texas. University. Balcones Research Center.
Report,
Austin, Tex.
v. semiannual.

Editor: 1955 - Fred D. Thompson.

Period covered by report, June 20-Dec. 20; Dec. 20-June 20.
1. Universities and colleges - Research facilities. 2. Scientific research.

VF
712.21
(764)
T29

Texas. State Parks Board.
Guide to Texas state parks. Austin, Tex., [1958]
folder. illus.

1. Parks - Texas.

Texas. Supreme court.
South western reporter. Second series ... 1928- (Card 2)
v. 64-86, Cases argued and determined in the Supreme courts of Arkansas, Missouri, Tennessee, and Texas: Courts of appeals of Kentucky, Missouri and Tennessee; courts of civil and criminal appeals and Commission of appeals of Texas.
v. 67- Cases argued and determined in the courts of Arkansas, Kentucky, Missouri, Tennessee, Texas.
1. Law reports, digests, etc.—Southwest, Old. I. Arkansas. Supreme court. II. Missouri. Supreme court. III. Tennessee. Supreme court. IV. Texas. Supreme court. V. Kentucky. Court of appeals. VI. Missouri. Court of appeals. VII. Texas. Court of civil appeals. VIII. Texas. Court of criminal appeals. IX. Texas. Commissioners of appeals. X. Tennessee. Court of appeals. XI. West publishing co., St. Paul.

Library of Congress   [49r3811]   28—17744

914.015
W18

Texas. University. Bureau of Business Research.
Waugh, Robert E
The American traveler more darkness than light? Austin, Tex., Bureau of Business Research, University of Texas, 1962.
54p.

1. Travel - Research. I. Texas. University. Bureau of Business Research.

336.211
(764)
T29t

Texas. State Tax Study Commission.
Taxation in Texas; our property taxes: a research staff study. Austin, 1958.
26p. illus., tables. (Its Report no. 6)

1. Real property - Taxation - Texas. 2. Taxation - Texas.

691.400.15
A25

Texas. University.
Acme All-Ceramic Home Research Program.
Bulletin no. 1-   1950-
Austin, Tex., Acme Brick Co., Univ. of Texas, 1950-
1 v. (loose-leaf) illus.

Some issues mimeographed.
For full information see shelf list card.

1. Building research. 2. Building materials—Ceramic. I. Texas. University.

Texas. University. Bureau of Business Research. Bibliographies.

VF
658.800.15
(016)
T36
no.
8 Thompson, R. B. A selected and annotated bibliography of marketing research. Nov. 1951.

711.552.1
(016)
T29
13 Holmes, Jack D. L. A selected and annotated bibliography of shopping centers. 1957. Rev. 1960.

Texas. Supreme court.
... The South western reporter ... Comprising all the current decisions of the Supreme courts of Arkansas, Missouri, Tennessee and Texas, Courts of appeals of Kentucky and Missouri, courts of civil and criminal appeals and Commission of appeals of Texas, with key-number annotations ... Aug./Dec. 1886-Jan./Feb. 1928. St. Paul, West publishing co., 1887-1928.
300 v. 23-26]cm.
Vols. 11-300: Permanent edition.
Title varies: v. 1-112, The Southwestern reporter ...
v. 113-114, The Southwestern reporter (annotated) ...
v. 125-178, The Southwestern reporter, with key-number annotations ...

(Continued on next card)
[44r87u2]   2—732

Texas. University. Bureau of Business Research. Bibliographies.

301.15
(764)
T29
no.
15 Texas. University. Bureau of Business Research. The Texas IDX; sources of information and services on community development. 1967.

Texas. Supreme court.
... The South western reporter ... 1887-1928. (Card 2)
v. 179-276, The Southwestern reporter ...
v. 277-300, The Southwestern reporter ...
Subtitle varies: v. 1-14, Containing all the current decisions of the Supreme courts of Missouri, Arkansas, and Tennessee, Court of appeals in Kentucky, and Supreme court and Court of appeals (criminal cases) of Texas.
v. 15-19, Containing all the current decisions of the Supreme courts of Missouri, Arkansas, and Tennessee, Court of appeals of Kentucky, and Supreme court and Court of appeals of Texas.
v. 20-34, Containing all the current decisions of the Supreme courts of Missouri, Arkansas, and Tennessee, Court of appeals of Kentucky, and Supreme court, Court of criminal appeals, and Courts of civil appeals of Texas.

(Continued on next card)
[48r37p2]   2—732

020
:538.56
D15

Texas. University.
Dale, A   G
A programming system for automatic classification with applications in linguistic and information retrieval research, by A.G. Dale and others. Prepared for National Science Foundation. Austin, Tex., Linguistics Research Center. The University of Texas, 1964.
18p. (Texas University. Linguistics Research Center. LRC 64 WTM-4)
1. Library science - Automation. 2. Documentation. I. Texas. University. II. Title.

659.11
T19

Texas. University. (Bureau of) Business Research
Community relations in Texas industry, by Stanley A. Arbingast, Al. E. Cudlipp, Jr., Anne K. Schuler. Austin, Texas, 1955.
100 p. forms, tables.

Bibliography: p. 99-100.

1. Industry. - Texas. 2. Community relations. I. Arbingast, Stanley A.

658
H87

TEXAS. UNIVERSITY. BUREAU OF BUSINESS
RESEARCH.
HUTTON, CLIFFORD E
CONTROLLERSHIP FUNCTION AND TRAINING.
AUSTIN, BUREAU OF BUSINESS RESEARCH,
UNIVERSITY OF TEXAS, 1962.
144P. (BUREAU OF BUSINESS RESEARCH,
UNIVERSITY OF TEXAS. RESEARCH MONOGRAPH
NO. 24)

1. MANAGEMENT - STUDY AND TEACHING.
2. ACCOUNTING - STUDY AND TEACHING.
I. TITLE. II. TEXAS. UNIVERSITY.
BUREAU OF BUSINESS RESEARCH.

330
(764)
J55

Texas. University. Bureau of Business
Research.
Jones, Joe H
San Angelo: urban growth influencing
transportation planning. Sponsoring agen-
cies: the City of San Angelo and Tom Green
County, Texas Highway Dept., in cooperation
with U.S. Dept. of Commerce, Bureau of
Public Roads. Austin, Bureau of Business
Research, University of Texas, 1965.
86p. (Texas. University. Bureau of
Business Research. Area economic survey
no. 26)

(Cont'd on next card)

325
(764)
B76

Texas. University. Bureau of Business Research.
Browning, Harley L
A statistical profile of the Spanish-surname population of Texas, by Harley L.
Browning and S. Dale McLemore. Austin, University of Texas, Bureau of Business Research,
1964.
83p.
1. Minority groups - Texas. I. McLemore, S.
Dale, jt. au. II. Texas. University. Bureau
of Business Research. III. Title. IV. Title:
Spanish-surname population of Texas.

VF
308
T29

Texas. University. Bureau of
Business Research.
An economic survey method for small
areas [by] Alfred G. Dale. Austin, Texas,
1955.
47 p.

Bibliography: p. 42-47.

1. Survey methods. I. Dale, Alfred G.
II. Title.

330
(764)
J65

Jones, Joe H. San Angelo: urban growth
influencing transportation planning...
1965. (Card 2)

1. Economic base studies - San Angelo,
Tex. 2. Transportation - San Angelo, Tex.
I. Texas. University. Bureau of Business
Research. II. Texas. Highway Dept.
III. Title.

VF
600.15
T29

Texas. University. Bureau of Business Researc

Texas. University. Texas Industrial and
Commercial Research Council.
Technical research in business, chemistry,
engineering, geology; to industrialize Texas
and Texans. ⌐Austin? c1939⌐
28 p. illus., maps, diagrs.

Cover title: Research for resources,
industry, commerce.

(Continued on next card)

33
(764)
T29d

Texas. University. Bureau of Business Research.
An economic survey of Denton County, Texas;
a study of resources, industrial potential, and
population growth, by John R. Stockton and others.
Austin, Texas, 1953.
1 v.(various pagings) graphs, maps, tables.

Processed.

1.Economic base studies-Denton Co., Texas.
I.Stockton, John R.

658.3
(016)
C51

TEXAS. UNIVERSITY. BUREAU OF
BUSINESS RESEARCH.
CLARK, CHARLES T
SELECTED AND ANNOTATED BIBLIOGRAPHY OF
PERSONNEL ADMINISTRATION. REV.
AUSTIN, 1958.
27P. (BUREAU OF BUSINESS RESEARCH,
UNIVERSITY OF TEXAS BIBLIOGRAPHY SERIES
1)

1. PERSONNEL MANAGEMENT - BIBLIOGRAPHY.
I. TEXAS. UNIVERSITY. BUREAU OF
BUSINESS RESEARCH.

Texas. University. Texas Industrial and
Commercial Research Council. Technical
research in business, chemistry, engineering,
geology.. ⌐c1939⌐ (Card 2)

1.Industrial research. 2.Economic research.
3.Engineering research. I.Title: Research for
resources, industry, commerce. II.Texas. University.
Bureau of Business Research. III.Texas.
University. Bureau of Engineering Research.

330
(7641)
T29

Texas. University. Bureau of Business
Research.
An economic survey of Dallas County, Texas;
a study of resource utilization, industrial
development potentials, population growth and
water use by Richard C. Henshaw, Jr. and
Alfred G. Dale. Austin, Tex., 1955.
207 L. graphs.

1.Economic base studies - Dallas Co., Tex.
I.Henshaw, Richard C

711.552.1
(016)
T29

Texas. University. Bureau of Business
Research.
A selected and annotated bibliography
of the planned suburban shopping center,
by Jack D. L. Holmes. Austin, 1957.
55p. (Its Bibliography series no. 13)

1.Shopping centers - Bibliographies.
I.Holmes, Jack D L (Series)

330
(764)
T29t

Texas. University. Bureau of Business
Research.
The Texas economy to 1957; resources
for tomorrow, by Richard C. Henshaw, jr.
and Alfred G. Dale. [Austin, Tex] 1956.
30p. graphs, tables.

1.Economic conditions - Texas. 2.Economic
forecasting. I.Henshaw, Richard C
II.Dale, Alfred G

33
(764)
T29

Texas. University. Bureau of Business Research.
On the economy of Texas, by Elmer H. Johnson.
[Austin, Texas] 1953.
1v.

Articles Published in the Texas Business
Review, Dec. 1938-Dec. 1945.

1.Economic base studies-Texas. I.Johnson, Elmer H.

711.552.1
(016)
T29
1960

Texas. University. Bureau of Business
Research.
Selected and annotated bibliography of
the planned suburban shopping center, by
Jack D. L. Holmes. Rev. Austin, 1960.
59p. (Its Bibliography series no. 13)

1. Shopping centers - Bibliography. I. Holmes,
Jack D. L. (Series)

341.1
:338
K71

TEXAS. UNIVERSITY. BUREAU OF
BUSINESS RESEARCH.
KRAUSE, WALTER.
THE UNITED STATES AND LATIN AMERICA:
THE ALLIANCE FOR PROGRESS PROGRAM.
AUSTIN, TEX., 1962.
35P. (TEXAS. UNIVERSITY. BUREAU OF
BUSINESS RESEARCH. STUDIES IN
LATIN-AMERICAN BUSINESS)

1. TECHNICAL ASSISTANCE PROGRAMS -
LATIN AMERICA. 2. ECONOMIC DEVELOPMENT
- LATIN AMERICA. I. TITLE.
II. TITLE: ALLIANCE FOR PROGRESS
PROGRAM. III. TEXAS. UNIVERSITY.
BUREAU OF BUSINESS RESEARCH.

330
(764)
R91

TEXAS. UNIVERSITY. BUREAU OF
BUSINESS RESEARCH.
RYAN, ROBERT H
GEORGETOWN; URBAN NUCLEATION ON THE
TEXAS BLACKLANDS BY ROBERT H. RYAN AND
OTHERS. PREPARED THROUGH THE
COOPERATION OF THE TEXAS STATE
DEPARTMENT OF HEALTH. AUSTIN, BUREAU OF
BUSINESS RESEARCH, UNIVERSITY OF TEXAS,
1964.
134L. (BUREAU OF BUSINESS RESEARCH,
UNIVERSITY OF TEXAS. AREA ECONOMIC
SURVEY, NO. 23)

1. ECONOMIC CONDITIONS -
GEORGETOWN, TEX. 2. POPULATION -
(CONTINUED ON NEXT CARD)

VF - Industrial location - Texas
DATE OF REQUEST 9/20/54   L C CARD NO.
SEP 27 1954

AUTHOR
Texas. University. Bureau of Business Research.

TITLE A selected and annotated bibliography of Texas
industrialization, by Stanley A. Arbingast [and]
Frank T. Cadena.

SERIES Bibliography series 7.

| EDITION Rev. | PUB. DATE [1954] | PAGING 54 p. |
| PUBLISHER | | |

RECOMMENDED BY M&L   REVIEWED IN CSP 8/54 p. 277

ORDER RECORD

330
(764)
(016)
T29

Texas. University. Bureau of Business
Research.
The Texas IDX; sources of information and
services on community development. Austin,
Tex., 1967.
92p. (Its Bibliography series no. 15)
1. Economic development - Texas - Bibl.
2. Community development - Texas. 3. Industrial location - Texas. I. Title.

330
(764)
R91

RYAN, ROBERT H GEORGETOWN....1964.
(CARD 2)

GEORGETOWN, TEX. I. TEXAS.
UNIVERSITY. BUREAU OF BUSINESS RESEARCH.
II. TITLE. III. TITLE: URBAN
NUCLEATION ON THE TEXAS BLACKLANDS.

658
S67

TEXAS. UNIVERSITY. BUREAU OF BUSINESS
RESEARCH.
SORD, BURNARD H
MANAGERIAL PLANNING AND CONTROL, AS
VIEWED BY LOWER LEVELS OF SUPERVISION, BY
BURNARD H. SORD AND GLENN A. WELSCH.
AUSTIN, BUREAU OF BUSINESS RESEARCH,
UNIVERSITY OF TEXAS, 1964.
XV, 237P. (UNIVERSITY OF TEXAS. BUREAU
OF BUSINESS RESEARCH. RESEARCH MONOGRAPH
NO. 27)

1. MANAGEMENT. 2. PERSONNEL MANAGEMENT.
I. WELSCH, GLENN A., JT. AU. II. TEXAS.
UNIVERSITY. BUREAU OF BUSINESS
RESEARCH. III. TITLE.

VF - Industrial location
DATE OF REQUEST 3/29/55   L C CARD NO.

AUTHOR
Texas. Univ. Bureau of Business Research.

TITLE Why 122 manufacturers located plants in Texas.

SERIES Texas Industry Series #3.

| EDITION | PUB. DATE Dec. 1954 | PAGING 29p. |
| PUBLISHER | | |

RECOMMENDED BY M&L   REVIEWED IN 's.Data Guide, 2/55, p.11.

ORDER RECORD

625.7
T29A TEXAS. UNIVERSITY. CENTER FOR HIGHWAY
RESEARCH.
ANALYSIS OF DISCONTINUOUS ORTHOTROPIC
PAVEMENT SLABS SUBJECTED TO COMBINED
LOADS, BY W. RONALD HUDSON AND HUDSON
MATLOCK. AUSTIN, TEX., 1965.
93L.

BIBLIOGRAPHY: P. 75-77.
PREPARED FOR PRESENTATION AT THE 45TH
ANNUAL MEETING OF THE HIGHWAY RESEARCH
BOARD, JAN. 21, 1966.
SPONSORED BY   TEXAS HIGHWAY
DEPARTMENT AND   THE U.S. BUREAU OF
(CONTINUED ON NEXT CARD)

625.7 TEXAS. UNIVERSITY. CENTER FOR HIGHWAY
T29A   RESEARCH. ANALYSIS OF DISCONTINUOUS
...1965.   (CARD 2)

PUBLIC ROADS.

1. ROAD CONSTRUCTION. 2. LOADS.
I. HUDSON, W. RONALD. II. MATLOCK,
HUDSON. III. HIGHWAY RESEARCH BOARD.

691.32
T29C   TEXAS. UNIVERSITY. CENTER FOR
FEB.1964 HIGHWAY RESEARCH.
RELATIONSHIP BETWEEN CRITICAL
MECHANICAL PROPERTIES AND AGE FOR
STRUCTURAL LIGHT WEIGHT CONCRETE, BY
W.B. LEDBETTER AND J. NEILS
THOMPSON. AUSTIN, TEX., 1964.
124L. (REPORT NO. 1, PROJECT
3-8-63-65)

1. CONCRETE. I. LEDBETTER,
WILLIAM B. II. THOMPSON, J. NEILS.

628.515
T29b   Texas. University. Center for Research in
Water Resources.
Bactericidal effects of algae on enteric
organisms, by Ernst M. David and Earnest F.
Gloyna. Austin, 1970.
132p. (U.S. Federal Water Quality Adminis-
tration. Water pollution control research
series)
Bibliography: p. 54-58.

1. Water pollution. 2. Water-supply.
I. Davis, Ernst M. II. Gloyna, Earnest F.,
jt. au. III. U.S. Federal Water Quality
Administration. IV. Title.

628.515
(746)   Texas. University. Center for Research
T29   in Water Resources.
Design guides for biological wastewater
treatment processes, by the City of Austin,
Texas and Center for Research in Water
Resources, Environmental Health Engineering
Dept., the University of Texas. Prepared
for the Environmental Protection Agency.
Wash., Govt. Print. Off., 1971.
221p. (Water pollution control research
series)
Bibliography: p. 211-218.
(Cont'd on next card)

628.515
(746)   Texas. University. Center for Research
T29   in Water Resources. Design guides...
1971.   (Card 2)

1. Water pollution - Austin, Tex.
I. U.S. Environmental Protection Agency.
II. Title.

551.49
T29   TEXAS. UNIVERSITY. CENTER FOR
RESEARCH IN WATER RESOURCES.
A STUDY OF SOME EFFECTS OF
URBANIZATION ON STORM RUNOFF FROM A
SMALL WATERSHED, TECHNICAL REPORT TO
THE TEXAS WATER COMMISSION. BY WILLIAM
H. ESPEY, JR. AND OTHERS. AUSTIN,
CENTER FOR RESEARCH IN WATER RESOURCES,
HYDRAULIC ENGINEERING LABORATORY, DEPT.
OF CIVIL ENGINEERING, UNIVERSITY OF
TEXAS, 1965.
109L.

BIBLIOGRAPHY: P. 92-96.
(CONTINUED ON NEXT CARD)

551.49
T29   TEXAS. UNIVERSITY. CENTER FOR
RESEARCH IN WATER RESOURCES. A STUDY
OF ...1965.   (CARD 2)

1. HYDROLOGY. 2. STORMS. I. ESPEY,
WILLIAM H. II. TITLE: STORM RUN-OFF.

339.5
(764)
T29r Texas. University. Bureau of Economic
Geology.
Report, 1968, 69

Austin, 19

2 v. annual.
For Library holdings see main entry.

1. Natural resources - Texas.
2. Geology - Texas.

TEXAS. UNIVERSITY. BUREAU OF
VF   ENGINEERING RESEARCH.
711.4 LEIPZIGER, HUGO.
L24A THE ARCHITECTONIC CITY IN THE AMERICAS.
SIGNIFICANT FORMS, ORIGINS, AND
PROSPECTS. AUSTIN, TEX., 1944.
98P. (TEXAS. UNIVERSITY. BUREAU OF
MUNICIPAL RESEARCH. MUNICIPAL STUDIES,
NO. 21; BUREAU OF ENGINEERING RESEARCH.
ENGINEERING RESEARCH SERIES NO. 39)

UNIVERSITY OF TEXAS PUBLICATION NO.
4407.

1. ARCHITECTURE - HISTORY.
2. ARCHITECTURE - TEXAS.
(CONTINUED ON NEXT CARD)

VF
711.4 LEIPZIGER, HUGO. THE ARCHITECTONIC CITY
L24A   ...1944.   (CARD 2)

3. ARCHITECTURE - MEXICO.
4. ARCHITECTURE - SOUTH AMERICA.
I. TEXAS. UNIVERSITY. BUREAU OF
MUNICIPAL RESEARCH. II. TEXAS.
UNIVERSITY. BUREAU OF ENGINEERING
RESEARCH.

VF - Heating - Solar
DATE OF REQUEST 9/20/54   L.C. CARD NO.
AUTHOR Texas. University. Bureau of Engineering
Research.
TITLE Controlling roof solar heat effects in buildings of
the South-est; some observations and calculations,
by Wayne B. Long, W. R. Woolrich [and] R. K. Bacon.
SERIES   Reprint 7.
EDITION | PUB. DATE 1950 | PAGING 35-38 p.
PUBLISHER
RECOMMENDED BY HWL | REVIEWED IN MCSP 7/54 p. 241
ORDER RECORD

VF - Foundations
DATE OF REQUEST 9/20/54   L.C. CARD NO.
AUTHOR Texas. University. Bureau of Engineering
Research.
TITLE The design of building footings on expansive clay
soils, by Raymond F. Dawson.
SERIES   Reprint 17.
EDITION | PUB. DATE [1952] | PAGING 6 p.
PUBLISHER
RECOMMENDED BY HWL | REVIEWED IN MCSP 7/54 p. 241
ORDER RECORD

VF - Foundations
DATE OF REQUEST 9/20/54   L.C. CARD NO.
AUTHOR Texas. University. Bureau of Engineering
Research.
TITLE The movement of small houses erected on an
expansive clay soil, by Raymond F. Dawson.
SERIES   Reprint 20.
EDITION | PUB. DATE [1953] | PAGING 346-350 p.
PUBLISHER
RECOMMENDED BY HWL | REVIEWED IN MCSP 7/54 p. 241
ORDER RECORD

VF
728   TEXAS. UNIVERSITY. BUREAU OF
:551.5 ENGINEERING RESEARCH.
(016) PRELIMINARY BIBLIOGRAPHY OF HOUSING
B84P   AND BUILDING IN HOT-HUMID AND HOT-DRY
SUPPL. CLIMATES; 1953 SUPPLEMENT (OCTOBER 1952
1953   THROUGH DECEMBER 1953) PUBLISHED UNDER
THE JOINT SPONSORSHIP OF THE BUREAU OF
ENGINEERING RESEARCH... AND THE
COMMITTEE ON TROPICAL HOUSING AND
BUILDING, BUILDING RESEARCH ADVISORY
BOARD. AUSTIN, TEXAS, 1954.
115P.

1. ARCHITECTURE AND CLIMATE -
(CONTINUED ON NEXT CARD)

VF
728   TEXAS. UNIVERSITY. BUREAU OF
:551.5 ENGINEERING RESEARCH. PRELIMINARY
(016) BIBLIOGRAPHY ...1954.   (CARD 2)
B84P
SUPPL. BIBLIOGRAPHY. 2. HOUSING -
1953   BIBLIOGRAPHY. 3. BUILDING
CONSTRUCTION - BIBLIOGRAPHY.
4. HOUSING IN THE TROPICS -
BIBLIOGRAPHY. I. BUILDING RESEARCH
ADVISORY BOARD.

VF
728   Texas. University. Bureau of Engineering
:551.5 Research.
(016) Preliminary bibliography of housing and
B84p   building in hot-humid and hot-dry climates.
Suppl. 1954 supplément (January through December 1954).
1954   Published under the joint sponsorship of the
Bureau of Engineering Research ... and the
3c   Committee on Tropical Housing and Building,
Building Research Advisory Board. Austin,
Texas [1955]
xi, 160 p.

1.Architecture and climate - Bibl. 2.Housing - Bibl.
3.Building construction - Bibl. 4.Housing in the tropics-
Bibl. I.Building Research Advisory Board.

690.37   Texas. University. Bureau of Engineering
R272   Research.
R   Research on livability in warm climates. Research
reports, no. 1-   [Austin, Tex., Clay
Products Association of the Southwest,
1951-
rts.
For full information see Periodical Kardex file.
Irregular.

1.Architecture, Domestic-Tropics. 2.Building
research. I.Acme all ceramic home research program. II.Clay Products Association of the Southwest. III.Texas. University. Bureau of Engineering
Research.

VF - Floors & flooring
DATE OF REQUEST 9/20/54   L.C. CARD NO.
AUTHOR Texas. University. Bureau of Engineering
Research.
TITLE Shear resistance of tile-concrete floor joists, by
J. Neils Thompson and Phil M. Ferguson.
SERIES   Circular 16A.
EDITION | PUB. DATE 1951 | PAGING 229-236 p.
PUBLISHER
RECOMMENDED BY HWL | REVIEWED IN MCSP 7/54 p. 241
ORDER RECORD

690.37   Texas. University. Bureau of Engineering
M42   Research.
Mid-Southwest Conference on Tropical Housing and
Building.
[Proceedings] University of Texas, Austin,
Texas, April 8 and 9, 1952. Austin, Bureau of
Engineering Research [Univ. of Texas, 1953]
115 p. illus., diagrs., graphs.

Includes bibliographies.
Partial contents.-The vertical movement of
House No. 1 on a "honeycomb" foundation of the
ceramic housing project, Austin, Texas, by Raymond
F. Dawson.-A study of the effect of foundation
(Continued on next card)

Mid-Southwest Conference on Tropical Housing and
Building. [Proceedings ... 1953] (Card 2)

movements on ceramic walls in semi-arid climates,
by J. Neils Thompson.-Study of design criteria for
floating or structural concrete slab floors laid
on grade, K. O. Small.-Human bioclimatology and
energy in arid and humid tropical zones, by Konrad
Buettner.-The making of bioclimatical charts and
their use in designing structures for livability
(Summary only), by Victor Olgyay.-Attachments,
appendages, and devices for external control of
(Continued on next card)

Mid-Southwest Conference on Tropical Housing and Building. [Proceedings ... 1953] (Card 3)

solar heat (Summary only), by W. W. Dornberger.-
Means of breeze control, by Charles Granger.-
Means of sun control, by Harwell H. Harris.-
Recommended lighting procedures in tropical houses
and buildings for maximum effectiveness and
livability, by H. D. Weisser.-Effect of evapo-
rative roof cooling on room temperature of a
house, by R. A. Bacon.-Some observations on
thermal research data obtained from the Acme
ceramic housing project at Austin, Texas, by
                    (continued on next card)

728.1
T29

TEXAS CONFERENCE ON HOUSING. 1ST,
AUSTIN, 1940. TRANSCRIPT OF
PROCEEDINGS....1940.   (CARD 2)

UNIVERSITY. COLLEGE OF ENGINEERING,
DEPT. OF AGRICULTURE.

362.5
Z87

Texas. University. Hogg Foundation for
    Mental Health.
Zurcher, Louis A   Jr.
    Poverty warriors: the human experience of
planned social intervention. With a foreword
by Gardner Murphy. Austin, University of
Texas Press, 1970.
    442p. (The Hogg Foundation research series)
    Bibliography: p. 410-427.

    1. Poverty. 2. Social service. I. Texas.
University. Hogg Foundation for Mental
Health. II. Title.

Mid-Southwest Conference on Tropical Housing and Building. [Proceedings ... 1953] (Card 4)

Wayne E. Long and F. E. Giesecke.-Recent studies
of livability factors in heating and cooling the
individual in tropical climates, by W. R. Woolrich.
Processed.

1.Architecture and climate. 2.Foundations.
3.Concrete floors. 4.Solar radiation. 5.Venti-
lation. 6.Lighting. 7.Air conditioning. 8.Heating.
9.Housing research. I.Texas. University. Bureau of
Engineering Research.

691.32
T29C
JAN.1965

TEXAS. UNIVERSITY. CENTER FOR
    HIGHWAY RESEARCH.
    CRITICAL MECHANICAL PROPERTIES OF
STRUCTURAL LIGHTWEIGHT CONCRETE AND
THE EFFECTS OF THESE PROPERTIES ON
THE DESIGN OF THE PAVEMENT STRUCTURE,
FINAL REPORT, COOPERATIVE HIGHWAY
RESEARCH PROGRAM, BY WILLIAM
LEDBETTER AND OTHERS. AUSTIN, TEX.,
1965.
    82L. (RESEARCH REPORT NO. 55-3F,
PROJECT 3-8-63-55)

    1. CONCRET   E. 2. ROAD
                (CONTINUED ON NEXT CARD)

711.4
:67
(72:764)
T29

Texas. University. *Institute of Latin-American Studies.*
    Basic industries in Texas and northern Mexico; conference
sponsored by the Institute of Latin American Studies of the
University of Texas, June 9-11, 1949. Austin, University
of Texas Press, 1950.
    183 p. illus., maps (1 fold.) tables. 25 cm. (*Its* Latin-American
studies, 9)
    CONTENTS.—The role of Nacional Financiera in the development of
industry in northern Mexico, by P. Reina Hermosillo.—A survey of
the Texas chemical industry, by W. A. Cunningham.—Some problems
of relocation facing the steel industry, by M. J. Barloon.—Five years
of achievement at Altos Hornos Steel Company, by H. R. Pape.—
Problems of utilizing coal resources in the industrialization of north-
                    (Continued on next card)
                                        A 50-9464
                    [10]†

VF
500.15
T29

Texas. University. Bureau of Engineering
    Research.
Texas. University. Texas Industrial and
    Commercial Research Council.
    Technical research in business, chemistry,
engineering, geology; to industrialize Texas
and Texans. [Austin? c1939]
    28 p.   illus., maps, diagrs.

    Cover title: Research for resources,
industry, commerce.

                    (Continued on next card)

691.32
T29C
JAN.1965

TEXAS. UNIVERSITY. CENTER FOR
    HIGHWAY RESEARCH. CRITICAL
    MECHANICAL ...1965.   (CARD 2)

    CONSTRUCTION.   I. LEDBETTER, WILLIAM.

Texas. University. *Institute of Latin-American Studies.*
Basic industries in Texas and northern Mexico ... 1950.
(Card 2)   CONTENTS—Continued.
ern Mexico, by J. A. de Silva.—Problems of Texas-Mexico trade, by
E. Nunnally.—Brief sketch of the industrial development of Monter-
rey, by V. Garza, Jr.—The oil industry in the northeast of Mexico,
by A. J. Bermúdez.—The oil industry and resources of Texas, by R. J.
González.—Mexico's irrigation possibilities along the northeastern
zone bordering the State of Texas, by A. Rodriguez L.—Some problems
of the Texas industrial water supply, by R. K. Cassell.—Planning the
hydroelectric development of northern Mexico, by A. Paez Urquidi.—
The El Mante Refinery in the national sugar industry, by J. C.
Ramírez.
    I. Industrial location-Texas.
    1. Texas—Indus. 2. Mexico—Indus.   I. Title.   (Series)
    2. Industrial location-Mexico.
    F1401.T45 no. 9   338   A 50-9464
Texas. Univ. Library
for Library of Congress   [10]†

Texas. University. Texas Industrial and
    Commercial Research Council.   Technical
    research in business, chemistry, engineering,
    geology.. [c1939] (Card 2)

1.Industrial research. 2.Economic research.
3.Engineering research. I.Title: Research for
resources,industry,commerce. II.Texas. University.
Bureau of Business Research. III.Texas.
University. Bureau of Engineering Research.

691.32
T29V

TEXAS. UNIVERSITY. CENTER FOR HIGHWAY
    RESEARCH.
    VOLUME CHANGES IN UNRESTRAINED
STRUCTURAL LIGHTWEIGHT CONCRETE, BY
JAMES T. HOUSTON, J. NEILS THOMPSON.
AUSTIN, TEX., 1964.
    55L. (RESEARCH REPORT NO. 55-2,
PROJECT 3-8-63-55)

    1. CONCRETE.   I. HOUSTON, JAMES T.
II. THOMPSON, J. NEILS.   III. TITLE:
LIGHTWEIGHT CONCRETE.

352
T29

TEXAS. UNIVERSITY. INSTITUTE OF PUBLIC
    AFFAIRS.
    FORMS OF CITY GOVERNMENT. 5TH ED.
AUSTIN, 1959.
    36P. (PUBLIC AFFAIRS SERIES, NO. 38)

    1. MUNICIPAL GOVERNMENT. I. TITLE.

VF
500.15
(41)
W66

Texas. University. Bureau of Engineering Research.
    Circulars.

no.8 Woolrich, W.R. The organization and adminis-
    tration of civil scientific research in
    Great Britain. 1950.

728.1
:362.6
(764)
W66

Texas. University. Hogg Foundation for
    Mental Health.
Woods, Frances Jerome, Sister.
    A community experiment in establishing a senior
center. Prepared in collaboration with Alice
Calverley. Austin, Tex., Hogg Foundation for
Mental Health, University of Texas, 1964.
    24p.

    1. Housing for the aged - Texas. 2. Old age.
I. Calverley, Alice, jt. au. II. Texas.
University. Hogg Foundation for Mental Health.

Census
B 835
T31
1956

Texas. University. Institute of Public
    Affairs.
Gillespie, John.
    Government in metropolitan Austin. Austin,
Texas, Institute of Public Affairs, University
of Texas, 1956.
    82 p. (Texas. University. Institute of
Public Affairs. Public Affairs series no. 26)

    1. Metropolitan areas - Austin, Texas.
I. Texas. University. Institute of Public
Affairs.

VF
711.4
L24
1942

VF
711.4
L24
1944

**Texas. University. Bureau of Engineering
    Research. Engineering research series.**

no. Leipziger, H. The city, the housing and the
34   community plan. Oct. 1942.

no. Leipziger, H. The architectonic city in
39   America. 1944.

728.1
:362.6
(764)
C17

Texas. University. Hogg Foundation for Mental
    Health.
Carp, Frances Merchant.
    A future for the aged; Victoria Plaza and its
residents. Foreword by Marie C. McGuire,
Commissioner, Public Housing Administration.
Austin, Tex., Published for the Hogg Foundation
for Mental Health, by the University of Texas
Press, 1966.
    287p.   (Texas. University. Hogg Foundation
Research series)

    Bibliography: p. [277]-279.

                    (Cont'd on next card)

352
(764)
B17

Texas. University. Institute of Public
    Affairs.
Barnes, Philip W
    Metropolitan coalitions: a study of Councils
of Governments in Texas. Austin, Institute of
Public Affairs, 1969.
    113p. (Public affairs series no. 76)
    Bibliography: p. 106-113.

    1. Metropolitan government - Tex. 2. City
planning - Tex. I. Texas. University.
Institute of Public Affairs. II. Title.

728.1
T29

TEXAS. UNIVERSITY. COLLEGE OF
    ENGINEERING. DEPT. OF AGRICULTURE.
TEXAS CONFERENCE ON HOUSING. 1ST,
AUSTIN, 1940.
    TRANSCRIPT OF PROCEEDINGS. AUSTIN,
DEPARTMENT OF ARCHITECTURE, COLLEGE OF
ENGINEERING, THE UNIVERSITY OF TEXAS,
1940.
    70L.

    ON COVER: HOUSING. FIRST TEXAS
CONFERENCE ON THE PROBLEMS OF HUMAN
HABITATION, APRIL 12 AND 13, 1940.

    1. HOUSING - CONGRESSES.
    2. HOUSING - TE   XAS. I. TEXAS.
                (CONTINUED ON NEXT CARD)

728.1
:362.6
(764)
C17

Carp, Frances Merchant. A future for the
    aged; Victoria Plaza and its residents...
                    (Card 2)

    1. Housing for the aged - San Antonio, Tex.
2. Old age. I. McGuire, Marie C.
II. Texas. University. Hogg Foundation for
Mental Health.

711.729
(764)
T29

Texas. University. Institute of Public
    Affairs.
    Parking, traffic and transportation in
Texas cities, by C. E. Schermbeck. Austin,
Tex., 1956.
    46p. (Its Public affairs series no. 25)

    1.Parking - Texas. 2.Traffic - Texas.
I.Schermbeck, C. E.

333.332
I57p

Texas. University. Institute of Public Affairs.
Institute for Tax Assessors, University of Texas.
Proceedings.
19

Austin, Institute of Public Affairs, University of Texas, 19
v.
For Library holdings see main entry.
1. Appraisal. 2. Real property. I. Texas. University. Institute of Public Affairs.

301.15
T29c

TEXAS. UNIVERSITY. BUREAU OF MUNICIPAL RESEARCH.
CITY IN SOCIETY. AUSTIN, TEX., 1945. 30P.

1. CITY GROWTH. 2. MUNICIPAL GOVERNMENT.

VF
308
:312
T28

Texas. University. Bureau of Research in the Social Sciences.
The use of city directories in the study of urban populations: a methodological note. Austin, Texas, Jan. 8, 1942.
29 p. forms. (Texas. University. Publication no. 4202)

Method used in study made by the University. Population mobility in Austin, Tex.

1. Survey methods. I. City directories.

336.2
A52s

Texas. University. Institute of Public Affairs.
Anderson, Lynn F
State-local fiscal effort, a measurement. Austin, Tex., Institute of Public Affairs, University of Texas, 1960.
6p.

Public affairs comment, vol. VI, no. 6, Nov., 1960.

1. Taxation. I. Texas. University. Institute of Public Affairs.

VF
711.4
L24
1942

Texas. University. Bureau of Municipal Research.
Municipal studies.
no. Leipziger, H. The city, the housing and
19　the community plan. Oct. 1942.

339.5
(764)
T29

Texas. University, Austin. School of Architecture.
The Texas aggregates research project. Austin, [1969?]
59p.

1. Natural resources - Texas. I. Title: Aggregates research project. II. Title.

711.585
(764)
T29

2c

Texas. University. Institute of Public Affairs.
Urban renewal for Texas, by C. E. Schermbeck. Austin, Tex., 1957.
41p. (Its Public affairs series no. 34)

1. Urban renewal - Texas. I. Schermbeck, C E

Texas. University. Bureau of Municipal Research.
352(764)
M12
[no.]
12. MacCorkle, S.A. Police and allied powers of municipalities in Texas. 1938.

301.15
T29

Texas. University. School of Architecture.
Texas Conference on Our Environmental Crisis, University of Texas, 1965.
Texas Conference on Our Environmental Crisis [papers] Austin, School of Architecture, University of Texas, 1966.
N.c.1
Laf.c.2
255p.

1. Community structure. 2. Sociology. 3. Man - Influence of environment. I. Texas. University. School of Architecture. II. Title. III. Title: Our environmental crisis.

336.211
(764)
T29

Texas. University. Institute of Urban Studies
The Texas property tax; an information report on the tax and its impact on urban development. Arlington, Tex., 1970.
45p.

1. Real property - Taxation - Tex. I. Title.

VF
312
(764)
R67d

Texas. University. Bureau of Research in the Social Sciences.
Rosenquist, Carl M
Family mobility in Dallas, Texas, 1923-1938 [by] Carl M. Rosenquist and Walter Gordon Browder. Austin, Tex., Univ. of Texas, Mar. 1942.
96 p. tables. (Texas. University. Publication no. 4209)
Conducted by the Bureau of Research in the Social Sciences with the assistance of the Work Projects Administration (Official project no. 665-66-3-183).

711
(016)
C65
no.129

Texas. University. School of Law Library.
Boner, Marian O
The merchant and the poor: a selected bibliography. [Austin] University of Texas, School of Law Library, 1970.
5p. (Council of Planning Librarians. Exchange bibliography no. 129)
1. Planning - Bibl. 2. Buying - Bibl. 3. Installment finance - Bibl. I. Texas. University. School of Law Library. II. Title. (Series: Council of Planning Librarians. Exchange bibliography no. 129)

628.515
T29p

Texas. University. Medical Branch.
Phosphorus removal and disposal from municipal wastewater. [Prepared] for the Environmental Protection Agency. Galveston, Tex., 1971.
121p. (Water pollution control research series)

1. Water pollution. I. U.S. Environmental Protection Agency. II. Title.

VF
312
(764)
R67h

Texas. University. Bureau of Research in the Social Sciences.
Rosenquist, Carl M
Family mobility in Houston, Texas, 1922-1938 [by] Carl M. Rosenquist and Walter Gordon Browder. Austin, Tex., Univ. of Texas, June 1942.
96 p. maps, tables. (Texas. University. Publication no. 4224)
Part of Project no. 54 of the Bureau of Research in the Social Sciences, sponsored by the Univ. of Texas, the city of Houston, and the Work Projects Administration (Official project no. 665-66-3-183).

711
(016)
C65
no.128

Texas. University. School of Law Library.
Boner, Marian O
Poverty and housing: a selected bibliography [Austin] University of Texas, School of Law Library, 1970.
5p. (Council of Planning Librarians. Exchange bibliography no. 128)
1. Planning - Bibl. 2. Housing market - Bibl. 3. Minority groups - Housing - Bibl. I. Texas. University. School of Law Library. II. Title. (Series: Council of Planning Librarians. Exchange bibliography no. 128)

VF
711.4
L24A

TEXAS. UNIVERSITY. BUREAU OF MUNICIPAL RESEARCH.
LEIPZIGER, HUGO.
THE ARCHITECTONIC CITY IN THE AMERICAS. SIGNIFICANT FORMS, ORIGINS, AND PROSPECTS. AUSTIN, TEX., 1944.
98P. (TEXAS. UNIVERSITY. BUREAU OF MUNICIPAL RESEARCH. MUNICIPAL STUDIES, NO. 21; BUREAU OF ENGINEERING RESEARCH. ENGINEERING RESEARCH SERIES NO. 39)
UNIVERSITY OF TEXAS PUBLICATION NO. 4407.
1. ARCHITECTURE - HISTORY.
2. ARCHITECTURE - TEXAS.
(CONTINUED ON NEXT CARD)

VF
312
(764)
B76

Texas. University. Bureau of Research in the Social Sciences.
Browder, Walter Gordon
The pattern of internal mobility in Texas; a subregional analysis. Austin, Tex., Univ. of Texas, Sept. 1944.
164 p. tables. (Texas. University. Publications no. 4434)

Bibliography: p. 83-85.
Study conducted under the auspices of the Bureau of Research in the Social Science of the University and the Works Projects Administration (Official Project no. 665-66-3-183).
(Continued on next card)

711
(016)
C65
no.130

Texas. University. School of Law Library.
Boner, Marian O
Social legislation: a selected bibliography. [Austin] University of Texas, School of Law Library, 1970.
3p. (Council of Planning Librarians. Exchange bibliography no. 130)
1. Planning - Bibl. 2. Social welfare - Bibl. I. Texas. University. School of Law Library. II. Title. (Series: Council of Planning Librarians. Exchange bibliography no. 130)

VF
711.4
L24A

LEIPZIGER, HUGO. THE ARCHITECTONIC CITY ...1944. (CARD 2)
3. ARCHITECTURE - MEXICO.
4. ARCHITECTURE - SOUTH AMERICA. I. TEXAS. UNIVERSITY. BUREAU OF MUNICIPAL RESEARCH. II. TEXAS. UNIVERSITY. BUREAU OF ENGINEERING RESEARCH.

VF
312
(764)
T29

Texas. University. Bureau of Research in the Social Sciences.
Population mobility in Austin, Texas, 1929-1931. Austin, Texas, University of Texas, July 15, 1941.
78 p. maps, tables. (Texas. University. Publication no. 4127)

1. Population shifts - Austin, Tex.

VF
600.15
T29

Texas. University. Texas Industrial and Commercial Research Council.
Technical research in business, chemistry, engineering, geology; to industrialize Texas and Texans. [Austin? c1939]
28 p. illus., maps, diagrs.

Cover title: Research for resources, industry, commerce.

(Continued on next card)

Texas. University. Texas Industrial and Commercial Research Council. Technical research in business, chemistry, engineering, geology.. c1939 (Card 2)

1.Industrial research. 2.Economic research. 3.Engineering research. I.Title: Research for resources,industry,commerce. II.Texas. University. Bureau of Business Research. III.Texas. University. Bureau of Engineering Research.

628.1
(764)
T29p

Texas. Water Development Board. Laws and programs pertaining to water and related land resources, comp. by Donald B. Yarbrough. Austin, 1969. 34p. (Its Report 89)

1. Water resources - Tex. 2. Land use - Tex. I. Yarbrough, Donald B., comp. II. Title.

378
D72
n.6.

Texas Agricultural and Mechanical University. Research Institute. Drew, Donald R The definition of the role of the universities in the solution of urban problems, by Donald R. Drew and others. College Station, Texas A & M Research Foundation, Texas A & M University, 1969. 1v.

CFSTI. PB 183 959.

1. Universities and colleges - Research services to neighboring communities. I. Texas Agricultural and Mechanical University. Research Institute. II. Title.

352
(75)
W45
2c.

Texas. University. University at El Paso. Wingfield, Clyde J ed. Urbanization in the Southwest; a symposium. El Paso, Texas Western Press, the University of Texas, 1968. 87p. (Texas. University. University at El Paso. Public affairs series no. 1)

1. City growth - Southern states. 2. Municipal government - Southern states. I. Texas. University. University at El Paso. II. Title.

628.1
(764)
T29t

Texas. Water Development Board. The Texas water plan; summary. Austin, Texas, 1968. 2c. 50p.

1. Water resources - Texas. I. Title.

059
(764)
T29

Texas almanac and State industrial guide, 1972/73;

[Galveston] A.H. Belo Corp., 1971— 1 v.

For Library holdings see main entry.

1. Almanacs - Texas. I. Title: [Texas] state industrial guide.

728.1
(764)
M49

Texas. Urban Development Commission. Mixon, John. Housing issues in Texas; papers prepared for the Texas Urban Development Commission, by John Mixon and others. Arlington, Tex., Texas Urban Development Commission, 1971. 73p.

1. Housing - Tex. I. Texas. Urban Development Commission. II. Title.

624.131.3
R62

TEXAS. BOARD OF WATER ENGINEERS. ROCKWELL, WILLIAM L A STUDY OF THE MOVEMENT OF MOISTURE IN SOILS, BASED ON DATA COLLECTED BY THE BUREAU OF IRRIGATION INVESTIGATIONS OF THE UNITED STATES DEPARTMENT OF AGRICULTURE CO-OPERATING WITH THE TEXAS BOARD OF WATER ENGINEERS, BY WILLIAM L. ROCKWELL. WASHINGTON, 1915. 46L.

1. SOILS - TESTING. I. TEXAS. BOARD OF WATER ENGINEERS. (CONTINUED ON NEXT CARD)

T20
(07)
G74

Texas Architectural Foundation. Grillo, Paul Jacques. Architecture at Rice; general plan, by Paul Jacques Grillo and others. Sponsored by the Texas Architectural Foundation. Houston, Texas, 1963. [63]p. (Rice University, Houston. Dept. of Architecture. Architecture at Rice, series no. 10. Three cities)

1. Architecture - Study and teaching. 2. City planning - Study and teaching. I. Texas Architectural Foundation. II. Rice University, Houston. III. Title.

628.1
(764)
W66

TEXAS. WATER COMMISSION. WOOD, LEONARD A ANALOG MODEL STUDY OF GROUND WATER IN THE HOUSTON DISTRICT, TEXAS, BY LEONARD A. WOOD AND R.K. GABRYSCH. WITH A SECTION ON DESIGN, CONSTRUCTION, AND USE OF ELECTRIC ANALOG MODELS, BY EUGENE P. PATTEN. AUSTIN, TEXAS, 1965. 103P. (ITS BULLETIN 6508)

BIBLIOGRAPHY: P.99-103.

1. WATER SUPPLY - TEXAS. 2. HYDROLOGY - TEXAS. I. TITLE. II. TEXAS. WATER COMMISSION.

624.131.3
R62

ROCKWELL, WILLIAM L A STUDY OF... 1915. (CARD 2)

II. U.S. BUREAU OF IRRIGATION INVESTIGATIONS. III. TITLE: MOISTURE IN SOILS.

728.1
(85)
T76

Texas Architectural Foundation. Troy, Robert D Lima, Peru; a study of housing in an arid coastal region, 1967-1968. Sponsored by the American Institute of Architects and the Texas Architectural Foundation. [Lubock, Tex.] 1969. 55p. (International Center for Arid and Semi-arid Land Studies. Special report no. 13) 1. Housing - Peru. 2. Housing in the tropics. I. American Institute of Architects. II. Texas Architectural Foundation. III. International Center for Arid and Semi-arid Land Studies. IV. Title.

628.1
(764)
M24

TEXAS. WATER COMMISSION. MEIER, WILBUR L ANALYSIS OF UNITE HYDROGRAPHS FOR SMALL WATERSHEDS IN TEXAS. AUSTIN, TEXAS WATER COMMISSION, 1964. 58L. (TEXAS WATER COMMISSION BULLETIN 6414)

1. WATER SUPPLY - TEXAS. I. TITLE: HYDROGRAPHS. II. TEXAS. WATER COMMISSION.

628.1
(764)
F22

Texas. Water Quality Board. U.S. Federal Water Pollution Control Administration. Water quality standards summary. Wash., 1969. 43p.

On cover: Texas Water Quality Board.

1. Water resources - Tex. 2. Water pollution - Tex. I. Texas. Water Quality Board. II. Title.

711
(016)
C65
no.220

Texas Christian University, Fort Worth. Dept. of Geography. Ray, William W A bibliography of dissertations, theses, and thesis alternatives in planning: 1965-1970. Fort Worth, Tex., Texas Christian University, Dept. of Geography, 1971. 72p. (Council of Planning Librarians. Exchange bibliography no. 220)

1. Planning - Bibl. I. Texas Christian University, Fort Worth. Dept. of Geography. II. Title. (Series: Council of Planning Librarians. Exchange bibliography no. 220)

628.1
T29

TEXAS. WATER COMMISSION. RULES, REGULATIONS AND MODES OF PROCEDURE. 1964 REVISION. AUSTIN, 1964. 147P.

1. WATER-SUPPLY - LAWS AND LEGISLATION. 2. WATER-SUPPLY - TEXAS.

026
R61

Texas. Woman's University, Denton. Robisheaux, Judy. The Federal Library Committee: a paper. Denton, Texas Woman's University, Graduate School of Library Science, 1971. 59p. Thesis (M.L.S.) - Texas Woman's University. Bibliography: p. 56-59.

1. Libraries. 2. Federal government. I. Texas. Woman's University, Denton. II. Title.

728.1
:613.5
W67p

Texas Christian University, Fort Worth. Institute of Behavioral Research. Wortham, John L A pilot methodological study of the cost of debilitating conditions in urban areas, by J.L. Wortham and F. Durham. Final report, Dept. of Health, Education, and Welfare, Public Health Service, Bureau of State Service. Fort Worth, Tex., Institute of Behavioral Research, Texas Christian University, 1966. 114p. Bibliography: p. [104]-108.

(Cond't on next card)

628.1
(746)
G26

Texas. Water Development Board. U.S. Geological Survey. (Water Resources Div.) Basic data for urban hydrology study, Austin, Texas. Austin, 1967. 59p. Prepared in cooperation with the Texas Water Development Board.

1. Water-supply - Austin, Tex. 2. Hydrology. I. Texas. Water Development Board. II. Title.

339.5
(764)
T29

The Texas aggregates research project. Texas. University, Austin. School of Architecture. The Texas aggregates research project. Austin, [1969?] 59p.

1. Natural resources - Texas. I. Title: Aggregates research project. II. Title.

728.1
:613.5
W67p

Wortham, John L. A pilot methodological study of the cost of debilitating conditions in urban areas...1966 (Card 2)

1. Housing and health. 2. Public health. I. Durham, Floyd, jt. au. II. U.S. Public Health Service. III. Texas Christian University, Fort Worth. Institute of Behavioral Research. IV. Title.

690.091.82 Texas City Managers Association.
:613.5 Liverman, Ralph L
(764) Concentrated code enforcement, Federal-
L48 city participation. Galveston, Texas
City Managers Association, 1967.
1v.
E. H. Denton, Assistant to the city
manager.
1. Housing law enforcement - Fort Worth,
Tex. 2. Neighborhood rehabilitation -
Fort Worth, Tex. I. Texas City Managers
Association. II. Denton, E. H.
III. Title.

711.4
(764) Texas City, Tex. City Planning Commission.
T29ma Master plan for Texas City: schools, parks,
public buildings, utilities. [Prepared through
the cooperation of the Texas State Dept. of
Health] Houston, Tex., 1959.
94p. (Interim report phase 4)
Planning consultants: Chas. R. Haile Associates
and Caldwell and Caldwell.
U.S. Urban Renewal Adm. UPAP.
1. Master plan - Texas City, Tex. 2. Schools -
Texas City, Tex. 3. Parks - Texas City, Tex.
4. Public buildings -   Texas City, Tex.
5. Public utilities -   Texas City, Tex.
I. Caldwell and   Caldwell. II. U.S.
URA-UPAP. Texas City,   Tex.

728.1 TEXAS CONFERENCE ON HOUSING. 1ST,
T29 AUSTIN, 1940.
TRANSCRIPT OF PROCEEDINGS. AUSTIN,
DEPARTMENT OF ARCHITECTURE, COLLEGE OF
ENGINEERING, THE UNIVERSITY OF TEXAS,
1940.
70L.

ON COVER: HOUSING. FIRST TEXAS
CONFERENCE ON THE PROBLEMS OF HUMAN
HABITATION, APRIL 12 AND 13, 1940.

1. HOUSING - CONGRESSES.
2. HOUSING - TEXAS. I. TEXAS.
(CONTINUED ON NEXT CARD)

Texas City, Tex. City Planning and Zoning
Commission

see

Texas City, Tex. City Planning Commission

711.4
(764) Texas City, Tex. City Planning Commission.
T29z Master plan report for Texas City: zoning,
land subdivision control. [Prepared through
the cooperation of the Texas State Dept. of
Health] Houston, Tex., 1959.
36p. (Interim report, stage 2)
Planning consultants: Caldwell and Caldwell
and Chas. R. Haile Associates.
U.S. Urban Renewal Adm. UPAP.
1. Master plan - Texas City, Tex. 2. Zoning - Texas
City, Tex. 3. Subdivision regulation - Texas City,
Tex. I. U.S. URA-   UPAP. Texas City,
Tex. II. Caldwell and   Caldwell.

728.1 TEXAS CONFERENCE ON HOUSING. 1ST,
T29 AUSTIN, 1940. TRANSCRIPT OF
PROCEEDINGS....1940.   (CARD 2)

UNIVERSITY. COLLEGE OF ENGINEERING.
DEPT. OF AGRICULTURE.

711.4
(764) Texas City, Tex. City Planning Commission.
T29h Master plan for Texas City: historical
background and characteristics, economic
base, population, land use. [Prepared through
the cooperation of the Texas State Dept. of
Health] Houston, 1959.
80p. (Interim report phase 1)
Planning consultants: Caldwell and Caldwell
and Chas. R. Haile Associates.
U.S. Urban Renewal Adm. UPAP.
(Continued on next card)

711.4
(764) Texas City, Tex. City Planning Commission.
T29 The master plan, Texas City, 1958-1983.
Prepared through the cooperation of the
Texas State Dept. of Health. Houston, Tex.,
[1958]
241p.
Planning consultants: Caldwell and Caldwell
and Chas. R. Haile Associates.

1. Master plan - Texas City, Tex.
I. U.S. URA-UPAP. Texas City, Tex.
II. Caldwell and Caldwell.

711.585 TEXAS CONFERENCE ON METROPOLITAN
(764) PROBLEMS. UNIVERSITY OF TEXAS, 1958.
T291 PROCEEDINGS. AUSTIN, TEXAS,
INSTITUTE OF PUBLIC AFFAIRS,
UNIVERSITY OF TEXAS, 1958.
102P.

1. URBAN RENEWAL - TEXAS.

711.4
(764) Texas City, Tex. City Planning Commission.
T29h Master plan for Texas City...1959 (Card 2)

1. Master plan - Texas City, Tex. 2. Economic base
studies - Texas City, Tex. 3. Population - Texas
City, Tex. 4. Land use - Texas City, Tex. I. U.S.
URA-UPAP. Texas City, Tex. II. Caldwell and Caldwell.

711.4
(764) Texas City, Tex. City Planning Commission.
T29r Recommended zoning ordinance text for Texas
City, Texas. Developed as a part of the
comprehensive master plan. [Prepared through
the cooperation of the Texas State Dept. of
Health] Houston, Tex., 1959.
41p.
Prepared and recommended by Caldwell and
Caldwell and Chas. R. Haile Associates,
planning consultants.
1. Master plan - Texas City, Tex. 2. Zoning
legislation - Texas   City, Tex.
I. Caldwell and   Caldwell. II. U.S.
URA-UPAP. Texas City,   Tex.

301.15
T29 Texas Conference on Our Environmental Crisis,
University of Texas, 1965.
Texas Conference on Our Environmental Crisis
[papers] Austin, School of Architecture, Uni-
versity of Texas, 1966.
N.cl 255p.
Laf.c.2
1. Community structure. 2. Sociology. 3. Man -
Influence of environment. I. Texas. University.
School of Architecture. II. Title. III. Title:
Our environmental crisis.

711.4
(764) Texas City, Tex. City Planning Commission.
T29c Master plan for Texas City, Texas: capital
improvement program. Prepared through the
cooperation of the Texas State Dept. of Health.
Houston, Tex., 1959.
38p. (Interim report no. 5)
Planning consultants: Caldwell and Caldwell
and Chas. R. Haile Associates.
U.S. Urban Renewal Adm. UPAP.

1. Master plan - Texas City, Tex. 2. Capital
improvement programs - Texas City, Tex. I. U.S.
URA-UPAP. Texas City,   Tex.
II. Caldwell and   Caldwell.

Class No. *Modular wood* Author (Surname first) *Texas Housing Co.*
NOT RUSH 1/30/52
Accession No.
Title *Engineered houses.*
2/7/50 ltr.
Of
                9001 Denton Drive
Received FEB 20 1950 Edition or Series Place *Dallas Texas* Publisher
Cost   Date *n.d. (1949?)* Vols. *4p. illus* List Price Est. Cost
Charged to   Recommended by
Date of bill   Address
L. C. No.   Reviewed in
                        A.R., p. 174,
                        Jan. 1950.

Texas Conference on Our Environmental Crisis.
301.15 Papers.
T29 Texas Conference on Our Environmental Crisis,
University of Texas, 1965.
Texas Conference on Our Environmental Crisis
[papers] Austin, School of Architecture, Uni-
versity of Texas, 1966.
N.cl 255p.
Laf.c.2
1. Community structure. 2. Sociology. 3. Man -
Influence of environment. I. Texas. University.
School of Architecture. II. Title. III. Title:
Our environmental crisis.

711.4
(764) Texas City, Tex. City Planning Commission.
T29m Master plan for Texas City: major thorough-
fares and highways, automobile parking and
central business district plan. [Prepared
through the cooperation of the Texas State
Dept. of Health] Houston, Tex., 1959.
40p. (Interim report, phase 3)
Planning consultants: Chas. R. Haile
Associates and Caldwell and Caldwell.
U.S. Urban Renewal Adm. UPAP.
(Continued on next card)

333.38
(764) Texas City, Tex. City Planning Commission.
T29 Subdivision rules and regulations, City of
Texas City, Texas. With the cooperation of
the Texas State Dept. of Health. Houston,
Tex., 1959.
16p.

Planning consultants: Chas. R. Haile
Associates, Inc. and Caldwell and Caldwell.
U.S. Urban Renewal Adm. UPAP.
1. Subdivision regulation - Texas City,
Tex. I. U.S. URA-UPAP. Texas City, Tex.
II. Caldwell and   Caldwell.

711.4 TEXAS ELECTRIC SERVICE CO. AREA
:670 DEVELOPMENT DIVISION.
(016) BIBLIOGRAPHY OF INDUSTRIAL DEVELOPMENT
T29 MATERIAL INCLUDING SOURCES OF
INFORMATION FOR ASSEMBLING INDUSTRIAL
DEVELOPMENT MATERIAL. NEWARK, DEL.,
AMERICAN INDUSTRIAL DEVELOPMENT COUNCIL,
1957.
1 V.

SUPPL. ------ SUPPLEMENT. FORT WORTH,
TEX., 1958.
67P.

(CONTINUED ON NEXT CARD)

711.4
(764) Texas City, Tex. City Planning Commission.
T29m Master plan for Texas City...1959. (Card 2)

1. Master plan - Texas City, Tex. 2. Streets -
Texas City, Tex. 3. Parking - Texas City, Tex.
4. Business districts - Texas City, Tex. I. U.S.
URA-UPAP. Texas City, Tex. II. Caldwell and
Caldwell.

LAW
T TEXAS CIVIL JUDICIAL COUNCIL.
T291a ADMINISTRATIVE PROCEDURE LAWS IN THE
UNITED STATES: A COMPARATIVE STUDY.
AUSTIN, TEX., 1957.
29P.

1. ADMINISTRATIVE PROCEDURE.

711.4 TEXAS ELECTRIC SERVICE CO. AREA
:670 DEVELOPMENT DIVISION. BIBLIOGRAPHY OF
(016) INDUSTRIAL ....1957. (CARD 2)
T29 1. INDUSTRIAL DEVELOPMENT -
BIBLIOGRAPHY. I. TITLE.

362.6
T46
TEXAS GOVERNOR'S COMMITTEE, WHITE HOUSE CONFERENCE ON AGING.
TIPS, CHARLES R
THE CARE OF THE AGED IN EUROPE.
REPORT TO TEXAS GOVERNOR'S ADVISORY COMMITTEE ON AGING. AUSTIN, GOVERNOR'S COMMITTEE, WHITE HOUSE CONFERENCE ON AGING, 1961.
21P.

1. OLD AGE. I. TEXAS GOVERNOR'S COMMITTEE, WHITE HOUSE CONFERENCE ON AGING.

630
:331
T29
Texas migrant labor.
Texas. Good Neighbor Commission.
Texas migrant labor; annual report, 19

[Austin] 19

v.
For Library holdings see main entry.

1. Agricultural laborers. 2. Labor supply – Tex. I. Title.

347
(764)
T29
Texas Research League.
A program design for law enforcement and criminal justice planning in North Central Texas. A report to the North Central Texas Council of Governments. Austin, 1969.
63p.

1. Law enforcement – Tex. I. North Central Texas Council of Governments. II. Title.

Class No. *Modular Coordination*
Accession No.
Ordered SEP 2 2 1950
Received OCT 6 1950
Purchase Order No.
Date
L. C. No. Reviewed in *Arch* Record 10/50 p. 158

Author (surname first) *Texas House Co.*
Title *Town and Country Engineered Houses*
Place *Dallas 9, Tex.* Publisher
Address *9001 Denton Dr.*
Date Paging *4* List Price Est. Cost
Edition or Series
Recommended by

H-305 (2-50)   HOUSING AND HOME FINANCE AGENCY: Office of the Administrator   10—61187-1   GPO

Class No. *Sewage Disposal*
Accession No.
JUL 28 1950
Source
Received AUG 4 1950
Date
Purchase Order No.
Date
L. C. No. Reviewed in *Kans* Govt. Jl. 7/50 p. 18

Author (surname first) *Texas Municipalities, League*
Title *Sewage service charges + related information of Texas cities + towns*
Place *Austin, Tex.* Publisher
Address *2200 Guadalupe St.*
Date Paging *38* List Price Est. Cost
Edition or Series
Recommended by

H-305 (2-50)   HOUSING AND HOME FINANCE AGENCY: Office of the Administrator   10—61187-1   GPO

711.33
(764)
T29
Texas Research League.
Regional planning, cooperation and development in the lower Rio Grande Valley. A report to the Lower Rio Grande Valley Development Council. Austin, 1967.
62p.

1. State planning – Texas. I. Lower Rio Grande Valley Development Council. II. Title.

330
(764)
r016)
T29
The Texas IDX; sources of information.
Texas. University. Bureau of Business Research.
The Texas IDX; sources of information and services on community development. Austin, Tex., 1967.
92p. (Its Bibliography series no. 15)
1. Economic development – Texas – Bibl. 2. Community development – Texas. 3. Industrial location – Texas. I. Title.

728.1
(764)
T29
TEXAS PLANNING BOARD.
LOW INCOME HOUSING FOR SOUTHERN TEXAS CONDITIONS. AUSTIN, TEX., 1938.
44P.

1. LOW INCOME HOUSING – TEXAS.

325.3
T29
TEXAS. STATE AUDITOR.
AUDIT REPORT, ALABAMA-COUSHATTA INDIAN RESERVATION, LIVINGSTON, TEXAS. August 1st
AUSTIN, TEX., 19..
v.

1. INDIANS. I. TITLE: ALABAMA-COUSHATTA INDIAN RESERVATION.

Texas Industrial and Commercial Research Council

see

Texas. University. Texas Industrial and Commercial Research Council.

336.211
(764)
T 29
The Texas property tax.
Texas. University. Institute of Urban Studies
The Texas property tax; an information report on the tax and its impact on urban development. Arlington, Tex., 1970.
45p.

1. Real property – Taxation – Tex. I. Title.

332.72
W45p
Texas Savings and Loan League.
Williams, Edward E Jr.
Prospects for the savings and loan industry to 1975. Austin, Tex., Texas Savings and Loan League, 1968.
117p.
Bibliography: p. 111-7.

1. Savings and loan associations. 2. Mortgage finance. I. Texas Savings and Loan League. II. Title.

378
G65
TEXAS INSTITUTIONAL INBREEDING RE-EXAMINED.
GOLD, DAVID.
TEXAS INSTITUTIONAL INBREEDING RE-EXAMINED. BY DAVID GOLD AND STANLEY LIEBERSON. IOWA CITY, IOWA, UNIVERSITY OF IOWA, 1961.
506-509P. (IOWA. UNIVERSITY. REPRINT NO. 3)
AT HEAD OF TITLE: IOWA URBAN COMMUNITY RESEARCH CENTER.
REPRINTED FROM THE AMERICAN JOURNAL OF SOCIOLOGY, V. 66, NO. 5, MARCH 1961.

1. UNIVERSITIES AND COLLEGES. I. LIEBERSON, STANLEY, JT. AU.
(CONTINUED ON NEXT CARD)

728.1
:613.5
L28R
TEXAS PUBLIC HEALTH ASSOCIATION.
LEUKHARDT, JOHN C
REQUIREMENTS FOR HEALTHFUL HOUSING. TRANSCRIPT OF A PAPER PRESENTED AT THE ANNUAL MEETING OF THE TEXAS PUBLIC HEALTH ASSOCIATION, FORT WORTH, TEXAS, OCTOBER 1, 1940. DALLAS, HOUSING AUTHORITY OF THE CITY OF DALLAS, 1940.
14L.

1. HOUSING AND HEALTH. I. TEXAS PUBLIC HEALTH ASSOCIATION.

362.6
C656
TEXAS SOCIETY ON AGING.
COMMUNITY MENTAL HEALTH SERVICES FOR OLDER PEOPLE, REPORT OF A CONFERENCE, DALLAS, TEXAS, MARCH 18-20, 1964. SPONSORED BY TEXAS SOCIETY ON AGING AND OTHERS. DALLAS, TEXAS, 1964.
62P.

1. OLD AGE. 2. HEALTH. I. TEXAS SOCIETY ON AGING. I. TITLE.

378
G65
GOLD, DAVID. TEXAS INSTITUTIONAL INBREEDING ...1961. (CARD 2)

II. IOWA. UNIVERSITY. IOWA URBAN COMMUNITY RESEARCH CENTER. III. TITLE.

353
(764)
T29c
Texas Research League.
Citizen participation in the North Central Texas Council of Governments; a report to the North Central Texas Council of Governments. Austin, Tex., 1967.
32p.
1. Intergovernmental relations – Texas. 2. Community development – Citizen participation. 3. Local government – Texas. I. North Central Texas Council of Governments. II. Title.

728.1
:325
(764)
G56
Texas Southern University.
Gloster, Jessee E
The changing residential housing values resulting from racial transition of a selected community in Houston, Texas; a research project. [Houston] Texas Southern University. 1961.
33p.

1. Minority groups – Housing – Houston, Tex. I. Texas Southern University.

551.5
(016)
T29
TEXAS INSTRUMENTS, INC.
AN INVENTORY OF GEOGRAPHIC RESEARCH OF THE HUMID TROPIC ENVIRONMENT. DALLAS, 1965.
1 v.

CONTENTS.– VOL. 1: KWIC INDEX: HUMID TROPIC ENVIRONMENTAL LITERATURE.

1. CLIMATOLOGY – BIBLIOGRAPHY. 2. HUMIDITY. I. TITLE. II. TITLE: KWIC INDEX. III. TITLE: HUMID TROPIC ENVIRONMENTAL LITERATURE.

711.3
(764)
T29
Texas Research League.
Metropolitan Texas: a workable approach to its problems. Austin, Texas, 1967.
79p.
A report to Governor John Connally and the 60th Texas Legislature.

1. Metropolitan area planning – Texas. 2. Intergovernmental relations – Texas. 3. Local government – Texas. I. Connally, John. II. Texas. Legislature. III. Title.

331
G56
Texas Southern University.
Gloster, Jesse E
Unemployment and the central city; a research project, by Jesse E. Gloster, [n.p.] 1968.
43p.
1. Employment. 2. Employment – Negroes. 3. Employment – Houston. I. Texas Southern University. II. Title.

059
(764)
T29
[Texas] state industrial guide.
Texas almanac and State industrial guide,
19

[Galveston] A.H. Belo Corp., 19
v.

For Library holdings see main entry.

1. Almanacs - Texas. I. Title: [Texas] state industrial guide.

325
K56
Texas Technological College.
Knowlton, Clark S ed.
Indian and Spanish American adjustments to arid and semiarid environments; a symposium held during the fortieth annual meeting of the Southwestern and Rocky Mountain Division of the American Association for the Advancement of Science, April 2, 1964. Lubbock, Tex. Lubbock, Tex., 1964.
89p. (Texas Technological College. Committee on Desert and Arid Zone Research. Contribution no. 7)

(Cont'd on next card)

325
K56
Knowlton, Clark S ed. Indian and Spanish...1964. (Card 2)

1. Minority groups. 2. Man - Influence of environment. I. Texas Technological College. II. American Association for the Advancement of Science. Southwestern and Rocky Mountain Div. Meeting, 40th, Lubbock, 1964. III. Title.

628.1
W32
TEXAS TECHNOLOGICAL COLLEGE, LUBBOCK, TEX.
WHETSTONE, GEORGE A
RE-USE OF EFFLUENT IN THE FUTURE, WITH AN ANNOTATED BIBLIOGRAPHY. AUSTIN, TEXAS WATER DEVELOPMENT BOARD, 1965.
187P. (TEXAS WATER DEVELOPMENT BOARD. REPORT 8)

PREPARED BY THE TEXAS TECHNOLOGICAL COLLEGE FOR THE TEXAS WATER DEVELOPMENT BOARD.

1. WATER SUPPLY - BIBLIOGRAPHY. I. TEXAS TECHNO LOGICAL COLLEGE, LUBBOCK, TEX. II. TITLE.

628.44
T29
Texas Tech. University, Lubbock.
Water Resources Center.
Characteristics of wastes from Southwestern cattle feedlots. [Prepared] for the Environmental Protection Agency. Lubbock, 1971.
87p. (Water pollution control research series)

Bibliography: p. 77-83.
1. Refuse and refuse disposal. I. U.S. Environmental Protection Agency. II. Title.

628.515
T29po
Texas Tech University, Lubbock. Water Resources Center.
Potential pollution of the Ogallala by recharging Playa Lake water; pesticides, by Dan M. Wells and others. [Wash.] Environmental Protection Agency, 1970.
36p. (Water pollution control research series)

1. Water pollution. I. Wells, Dan M. II. U.S. Environmental Protection Agency. III. Title.

691.32
I82
Texas Transportation Institute.
Ivey, Don L
Air void systems in ready mixed concrete, by Don L. Ivey and Patrick H. Torrans. Sponsored by the Texas Highway Dept. in cooperation with the Dept. of Transportation, Federal Highway Administration, Bureau of Public Roads. College Station, Texas Transportation Institute, Texas A. & M. University, 1969.
50p. (Research report no. 103-4F; study 2-5-66-103)

1. Concrete. I. Torrans, Patrick H., jt. au. II. Texas. Highway Dept. III. Texas Transportation Institute.

711.73
:330
(764)
T29c
Texas Transportation Institute.
Changes in land value, land use, and business activity along a section of the Interstate Highway system in Austin, Texas. An interim report on one of a series of studies of the economic impact of the Interstate Highway system on local areas, by C. V. Wootan and C. R. Haning. College Station, Tex., 1960.
46p. (Its Bulletin no. 13)

1. Highways - Austin, Tex. - Economic effect. I. Wootan, C. V. II. Haning, C. R.

711.73
:330
(764)
T29ch
Texas Transportation Institute.
Changes in land value, land use, and business activity along a section of the Interstate Highway system in Temple, Texas. An interim report on one of a series of studies of the economic impact of the Interstate Highway System on local areas, by C. V. Wootan and H. G. Meuth. College Station, Tex., 1960.
33p. (Its Bulletin no. 14)

1. Highways - Temple, Tex. - Economic effect. I. Wootan, C. V. II. Meuth, H. G.

691.421
(015)
T29
Texas Transportation Institute.
Clay, aggregate, and concrete, by Eugene Buth and others. Sponsored by the Texas Highway Dept. in cooperation with the U.S. Dept. of Commerce, Bureau of Public Roads. College Station, Tex., 1967.
34p. (Its Research report no. 71-3 (final); Deleterious materials in concrete research study 2-5-63-71)
1. Clay - Research. 2. Concrete-- Research. I. Buth, Eugene. II. U.S. Bureau of Public Roads. III. Texas. Highway Dept. IV. Title.

Texas Transportation Institute.
711.73
(764)
P17
Park, Ross A
A computer technique for perspective plotting of roadways, by Ross A. Park and Neilon J. Rowan. Sponsored by the Texas Highway Dept. in cooperation with the U.S. Dept. of Transportation, Federal Highway Administration, Bureau of Public Roads. College Station, Tex., Texas Transportation Institute, Texas A & M University, 1967.
27p. (Texas Transportation Institute. Research report number 19-3; Channelization research study number 2-8-60-19)
(Cont'd on next card)

711.73
(764)
P17
Park, Ross A A computer technique... 1967. (Card 2)

Distributed by U.S. Clearinghouse for Federal Scientific and Technical Information as PB 177535.
1. Highways - Texas. 2. Transportation-Automation. I. Rowan, Neilon J., jt. au. II. Texas Transportation Institute. III. Texas. Highway Dept. IV. Title.

691.32
B87
TEXAS TRANSPORTATION INSTITUTE.
BUTH, EUGENE.
CORRELATION OF CONCRETE PROPERTIES WITH TESTS FOR CLAY CONTENT OF AGGREGATE, BY EUGENE BUTH AND OTHERS. COLLEGE STATION, TEXAS TRANSPORTATION INSTITUTE, 1964.
20P. (RESEARCH REPORT NO. 71-1. BULLETIN NO. 32)

1. CONCRETE. 2. CLAY. I. TEXAS TRANSPORTATION INSTITUTE.

691.41
W65
Texas Transportation Institute.
Wolfskill, Lyle A
Earthen home construction; a field and library compilation with an annotated bibliography, by Lyle A. Wolfskill and others. Prepared for the Agency for International Development under the technical supervision of the Office of International Housing, Housing and Home Finance Agency. College Station, Tex., Texas Transportation Institute, 1962.
36p. (Texas Transportation Institute. Bulletin no. 18)

(Continued on next card)

691.41
W65
Wolfskill, Lyle A
Earthen home construction ... 1962. (Card 2)

Bibliography: p. 31-36.

1. Earth wall construction. I. U.S. Housing and Home Finance Agency. Office of the Administrator. Office of International Housing. II. Texas Transportation Institute.

711.73
:330
(764)
T29
Texas Transportation Institute.
Economic impacts of expressways in San Antonio, a study of the effects of a 3.7-mile expressway near downtown San Antonio, Texas, on land values and land use, by William G. Adkins and Alton W. Tieken. College Station, Tex., 1958.
47p. illus., diagrs., tables. (Its Bulletin no. 11)

(Continued on next card)

711.73
:330
(764)
T29
Texas Transportation Institute. Economic impacts of ... (Card 2)

1. Highways - San Antonio - Economic effect. 2. Real property - Valuation. I. Adkins, William G. II. Tieken, Alton W. III. U.S. Bureau of Public Roads.

711.73
:330
(764)
T29e
Texas Transportation Institute.
Effects of the Dallas central expressway on land values and land use; a study of the influence of an urban expressway on land prices, tax valuations of real property, land use, and attitudes of businessmen and residents along its route, by William G. Adkins. College Station, Tex. 1957
87p. illus., diagrs., tables. (Its Bulletin 6)
1. Highways - Dallas - Economic effect. 2. Real property - Valuation. I. Adkins, William G.

333.332
(764)
T29
Texas Transportation Institute.
Farm land value and rural roads service in Ellis County, Texas 1955-58, by William G. Adkins and others. A special report to the Bureau of Public Roads, United States Dept. of Commerce. College Station, Tex., 1960.
27p. (Its Bulletin no. 12)

1. Real property - Valuation - Ellis Co., Tex. 2. Highways - Ellis County, Tex. - Economic effect. I. U.S. Bureau of Public Roads. II. Adkins, William G.

Texas Transportation Institute.
VF
691.41
W65h
Wolfskill, Lyle A
Handbook for building homes of earth, by Lyle A. Wolfskill and others. Prepared for the Agency for International Development under the technical supervision of the Office of International Housing, Housing and Home Finance Agency. College Station, Tex., Texas Transportation Institute. [1963]
159p. (Texas Transportation Institute. Bulletin no. 21)
(Cont'd. on next card)

VF
691.41
W65h
Wolfskill, Lyle A Handbook for building homes ... (Card 2)

1. Earth wall construction. I. U.S. Housing and Home Finance Agency. Office of International Housing. II. Texas Transportation Institute.

699.86
H47
Texas Transportation Institute.
   Hirsch, T J
   Impact load-deformation properties of pile cushioning materials, by T. J. Hirsch and Thomas C. Edwards. College Station, Texas Transportation Institute, Texas A&M University, 1966.
Laf.
   12p.
   Sponsored by the Texas Highway Dept. in co-operation with the U.S. Dept. of Commerce, Bureau of Public Roads.
   Distributed by U.S. Clearinghouse for Technical Information as document PB 173 352.
   1. Insulating materials. 2. Loads. I. Texas Transportation Institute. II. U.S. Clearinghouse for Federal Scientific and Technical Information. III. Title.

691.32
H117
Texas Transportation Institute.
   Harper, William J
   Interim report on the influence of design, construction and traffic on compaction of hot-mix asphaltic concrete, by William J. Harper and Bob M. Gallaway. College Station, Texas Transportation Institute, 1967.
   40p. (Texas A & M University. Texas Transportation Institute. Research report 90-1; Research study no. 2-6-65-90)
   1. Concrete. I. Gallaway, Bob M., jt. au. II. Texas Transportation Institute. III. Title: Influence of design, construction and traffic on compaction of hot-mix asphaltic concrete.

711.73
:330
(764)
T29p
Texas Transportation Institute.
   Preliminary study of the Economic impact of a section of San Antonio's Loop 13 Expressway, by Russell H. Thompson and others. A special report to the Bureau of Public Roads, United States Dept. of Commerce. College Station, Tex., 1960.
   39p.
   1. Highways - San Antonio - Economic effect. I. Thompson, Russell H. II. U.S. Bureau of Public Roads.

711.73
:330
(764)
T29pr
Texas Transportation Institute.
   A preliminary study of the economic impact of Stemmons Freeway, a section of interstate 35 E, Dallas, Texas, by Russell G. Thompson and others. A special report to the Bureau of Public Roads, United States Dept. of Commerce. College Station, Tex., 1960.
   40p.
   1. Highways - Dallas - Economic effect. I. Thompson, Russell G. II. U.S. Bureau of Public Roads.

693.55
N24
Texas Transportation Institute.
   Neidermeyer, J
   Properties of lightweight concrete. Prepared in cooperation with Bureau of Public Roads. College Station, Texas Transportation Institute, 1966.
Laf.
   21p.
   Distributed by U.S. Clearinghouse for Federal Scientific and Technical Information as document PB 174 318.
   1. Concrete, Reinforced. 2. Concrete aggregates. I. Texas Transportation Institute. II. U.S. Clearinghouse for Federal Scientific and Technical Information. III. Title.

624.131
(016)
T29
Texas Transportation Institute.
   Stabilization of soils. College Station, Tex., 1968.
   52p. (Its Survey of library facilities project bibliography no. 194)
   CFSTI. PB 178 856.
   Prepared in cooperation with the U.S. Dept. of Transportation, Federal Highway Administration, Bureau of Public Roads and the Texas Highway Dept.
   1. Soils - Bibl. I. Title.

628.1
(764)
T29t
The Texas water plan.
   Texas. Water Development Board.
   The Texas water plan; summary. Austin, Texas, 1968.
   20p.
   1. Water resources - Texas. I. Title.

4643
TEXOMA REGIONAL PLANNING COMMISSION.
SOLID WASTE MANAGEMENT PLAN, FOR THE GRAYSON COUNTY AREA. SHERMAN, TEX., 1969. 77P. (HUD 701 REPORT)
   1. REFUSE AND REFUSE DISPOSAL - GRAYSON CO., TEX. I. HUD. 701. GRAYSON CO., TEX.

711.5
:347
B14
1966
The text of a model zoning ordinance with commentary.
   Beir, Fred H
   The text of a model zoning ordinance with commentary, by Fred H. Beir and Ernest R. Bartley. 3d ed. Chicago, American Society of Planning Officials, 1966.
   99p.
   "First appeared in 1958 as a publication of the University of Florida Public Administration Clearing Service."
   1. Zoning legislation. I. Bartley, Ernest R., jt. au. II. American Society of Planning Officials. III. Title. IV. Title: Model zoning ordinance.

360
N17t
Textbook for welfare.
   National Foundation of Health, Welfare and Pension Plans.
   Textbook for welfare, pension trustees, and administrators; eleventh annual conference, San Francisco, 1965. Elm Grove, Wis., 1965.
   593p. (vol. 7)
   1. Social welfare. 2. Insurance. 3. Public health. 4. Pensions. 5. Trusts and trustees. I. Title.

691.11
(07)
P15
Textbook of wood technology.
   Panshin, A J
   Textbook of wood technology, by A.J. Panshin and Carl de Zeeuw. Vol. 1, structure, identification, uses, and properties of the commercial woods of the United States and Canada. 3d ed. New York, McGraw-Hill, 1970.
   705p. (American forestry series)
   1. Wood - Study and teaching. I. de Zeeuw, Carl, jt. au. II. Title.

370
R212
Textes choisis sur l'économie de l'éducation.
   Readings in the economics of education; a selection of articles, essays and texts from the works of economists, past and present, on the relationships between economics and education. Textes choisis sur l'économie de l'éducation: articles, essais et autres textes tirés des oeuvres anciennes ou récentes, d'économistes qui traité des rapports entre économie et éducation. Editorial advisory committee: Mary Jean Bowman and others. Paris, Unesco, 1968.
   945p.
   (Cont'd on next card)

370
R212
Readings in the...1968.   (Card 2)
   English and/ or French.
   1. Education - Economic effect. I. Bowman, Mary Jean. ed. II. United Nations Educational Scientific and Cultural Organisation. III. Title: Textes choisis sur l'économie de l'éducation.

728.1
(75636)
T29
Textile Workers Union of America.
   Carolina textile workers seek modern housing; a report on new housing needs in Erwin, North Carolina. New York, 1957.
   17p.
   1. Housing - Erwin, N. C.

728.1
:670
T29
TEXTILE WORKERS UNION OF AMERICA. RESEARCH DEPARTMENT.
COTTON MILL WORKERS' HOUSING. HIGH POINT, N.C. NEW YORK, 1944. 17L. (HOUSING STUDY NO. 1)
   1. COMPANY HOUSING - HIGH POINT, N.C. I. TITLE.

691.322
T29l
Teychenne, D C
   Lightweight aggregates; their properties and use in concrete in the U.K. Garston, Eng., Building Research Station, Ministry of Public Building and Works, 1968.
   15p. (U.K. Building Research Station. Current paper 73/68)
   Bibliography: p. 14-15.
   Reprint from: Volume I of the Proceedings of the International Congress of Lightweight Concrete, London, May 27-29, 1968, pp. 23-27.
   1. Concrete aggregates. I. U.K. Building Research Station. II. Title.

691.32
T29sp
Teychenne, D C
   Specification of concrete with special reference to the proposed unified code. Garston, Eng., Building Research Station, 1968.
   [9]p. (Current paper no. 58/68)
   Reprinted from: The Structural engineer, 1968, vol. 46 (5), May, p. 131-139.
   1. Concrete - Standards and specifications. I. U.K. Building Research Station. II. Title.

691.322
T29
Teychenne, D C
   Structural concrete made with lightweight aggregates. Garston, Eng., Building Research Station, Ministry of Public Building and Works, 1967.
   111-122p. (U.K. Building Research Station. Building research current papers. Engineering papers 48)
   Reprinted from: Concrete, April 1967.
   1. Concrete aggregates. 2. Concrete construction. I. U.K. Building Research Station. II. Title.

691.32
T29s
Teychenne, D C
   A survey of crushed stone sands for concrete. Garston, Eng., Ministry of Public Building and Works, Building Research Station, 1968.
   5p. (Building Research Station. Current paper 11)
   Reprinted from: British Granite and Whinstone Federation Journal, 1967, p. 53-60.
   1. Concrete. I. U.K. Building Research Station. II. Title.

691
(41)
N28
Teychenne, D C jt. au.
   Newman, A J
   A technical and historical review of the sand grading requirements in British Standard 882 by A. J. Newman and D. C. Teychenne. Garston, Eng., Building Research Station, Dept. of Scientific and Industrial Research, 1964.
   [3]p. (U.K. Building Research Station. Building research current papers. Engineering series 18)
   Reprinted from: Cement, lime and gravel, vol. 39 (10), p. 336-8.
   (Continued on next card)

691
(41)
N28
Newman, A J   A technical and historical review of the sand grading requirements in British Standard 882...1964.   (Card 2)
   1. Building materials - U.K. 2. Building standards - U.K. I. Teychenne, D. C., jt. au. II. U.K. Building Research Station.

691.32
T29
Teychenné, D C
The verisbility of the strength of concrete and its treatment in codes of practice. Gerston, [Eng.] Building Research Station, Ministry of Technology, 1966.
13p. (U.K. Building Research Station. Building research current papers. Engineering series 32)
Reprinted from: Structural Concrete, 1966, vol. 3 (January/February), pp.3047.

1. Concrete. 2. Concrete, Reinforced.
I. U.K.   Building Research
Station.   II. Title.

Thailand. Ministry of Interior.
711.4
(593)
L47t
Litchfield Whiting Bowne and Associates.
Bangkok-Thonburi city planning project; land use. A study of existing land use within and immediately outside the municipalities of Bangkok and Thonburi. [In cooperation with] consultants to the Ministry of Interior, Government of Thailand. New York, 1960.
20p. (Technical monograph)

1. City planning - Thailand. 2. Land use - Thailand. I. Thailand. Ministry of   Interior.

711.4
(593)
L47t
Litchfield Whiting Bowne and Associates.
Bangkok-Thonburi city planning project; travel time...1959.   (Card 2)

1. City planning - Thailand.
2. Transportation - Thailand. 3. Journey to work. I. Thailand. Ministry of Interior. II. Adams, Howard and Greeley.

312
(016)
T31
THADEN, J F
ANNOTATED BIBLIOGRAPHY OF COMMUNITY STUDIES WITH DEMOGRAPHIC ANALYSIS. EAST LANSING, 1963.
12L. (INSTITUTE FOR COMMUNITY DEVELOPMENT AND SERVICES, MICHIGAN STATE UNIVERSITY, BIBLIOGRAPHIC SERIES NO. 4)

1. POPULATION - BIBLIOGRAPHY.
2. COMMUNITY PLANNING - BIBLIOGRAPHY.

Thailand. Ministry of Interior.
711.4
(593)
L47m
Litchfield Whiting Bowne and Associates.
Bangkok-Thonburi city planning project; maps and boundaires, including administrative divisions and land areas. [In cooperation with] Adams, Howard and Greeley, city planning consultants to the Ministry of Interior, Government of Thailand. New York, 1960.
1 v.   (Technical monograph)

1. City planning - Thailand. 2. Maps and mapping -   Thailand. 3. Land use -   Thailand. I. Thailand.
Ministry of   Interior.

Thailand. Ministry of Interior.
711.4
(593)
L47v
Litchfield Whiting Bowne and Associates.
Bangkok-Thonburi city planning project; vehicle registrations. [In cooperation with] Adams, Howard and Greeley, city planning consultants of Thailand. New York, 1958.
12p. (Technical monograph; Traffic motor vehicle registration 7a)

1. City planning - Thailand. 2. Traffic - Thailand. I.Thailand. Ministry of Interior.

362.6
T31
Thaden, J   F
Michigan's 600,000 senior citizens. East Lansing, Mich., Michigan State University, Institute for Community Development and Services, Continuing Education Service, 1960.
9p. (Michigan State University. Institute for Community Development and Services. Technical bulletin B-10)

1. Old age. I. Michigan State University. Institute for Community Development and Services.

Thailand. Ministry of Interior.
711.4
(593)
L47p
Litchfield Whiting Bowne and Associates.
Bangkok-Thonburi city planning project; population. An analysis of past, present and future population of the Bangkok-Thonburi Metropolitan area in the context of National and Greater Metropolitan area data and trends. [In cooperation with] Adams, Howard and Greeley, city planning consultants to the Ministry of Interior, Government of Thailand. New York, 1959.
62p. (Technical monograph)

Cont'd. on next card)

Thailand. Ministry of Interior.
VF
711.4
(593)
C85
Cullers, Samuel J
Final report. Contract between the Government of Thailand and Samuel J. Cullers. Bangkok, Thailand, Ministry of Interior, 1961.
20p.

1. City planning - Thailand. 2. Technical assistance programs - Thailand. I. Thailand. Ministry of Interior.

330
(593)
H25
Thailand.
Henderson, John W
Area handbook for Thailand, by John W Henderson and others. Wash., Govt. Print. Off., 1971.
413p.
Bibliography: p. 329-391.
One of a series of handbooks prepared by Foreign Area Studies (FAS) of The American University.
1. Economic conditions - Thailand. I. American University, Washington, D.C. Foreign Area Studies. II. Title: Thailand. III. Title.

711.4
(593)
L47p
Litchfield Whiting Bowne and Associates.
Bangkok-Thonburi city planning project; population. An analysis...1959. (Card 2)

1. City planning - Thailand. 2. Population - Thailand. I. Thailand. Ministry of Interior.

Thailand. Ministry of Interior.
711.4
(593)
L47
1960
Litchfield Whiting Bowne and Associates.
Greater Bangkok plan, 2533. [In cooperation with] the City Planning Consultants, Adams, Howard and Greeley of Cambridge, Massachusetts [and Thailand, Ministry of Interior] New York, 1960.
210p.
"Support and advice of the United States Operations Mission to Thailand..."

1. Master plan - Thailand. 2. Technical assistance programs - Thailand.   I. Adams, Howard and Greeley, Cambridge,   Mass. II. Thailand, Ministry of Interior.

VF
333.65
T31
Thailand. Housing Bureau.
Tenant's handbook. [Bangkok?] 1965.
1v.

Text in Thai.

1. Housing management. 2. Housing - Thailand. I. Title.

Thailand. Ministry of Interior.
711.4
(593)
L47tr
Litchfield Whiting Bowne and Associates.
Bangkok-Thonburi city planning project; traffic volumes and characteristics. A report on the existing traffic volumes and character of traffic in the Bangkok-Thonburi Metropolitan area in January and March, 1959. [In cooperation with] Adams, Howard and Greeley, city planning consultants to the Ministry of Interior, Government of Thailand. New York, 1960.
(Cont'd. on next card)

690.25
R87
Thames, Gena.
Rutgers University. College of Agriculture.
Flooring materials, by Gena Thames. New Brunswick, N.J., 1960.
12p. (New Jersey Extension bulletin 338)

1. Floors and flooring.   I. Thames, Gena.

Thailand. Ministry of Interior.
711.4
(593)
L47e
Litchfield Whiting Bowne and Associates.
Bangkok-Thonburi city planning project; education, an inventory and analysis of existing educational facilities, and recommended standards for school sites. [In cooperation with] Adams, Howard and Greely, city planning consultants to the Ministry of Interior, Government of Thailand. New York, 1960.
16p. (Technical monograph)

1. City planning - Thailand.
2. Education -   Thailand.
I. Thailand.   Ministry of Interior.

711.4
(593)
L47tr
Litchfield Whiting Bowne and Associates.
Bangkok-Thonburi city planning project; traffic volumes...1960. (Card 2)

32p. (Technical monograph)

1. City planning - Thailand. 2. Traffic - Thailand. I. Thailand. Ministry of Interior. II. Adams, Howard and Greeley.

711.585
(7457)
C15
Thames Street renewal area.
Candeub, Fleissig and Associates.
Thames Street renewal area; general neighborhood renewal plan. Newport, R.I., Redevelopment Agency, [1964?]
19 p.

1. Neighborhood rehabilitation - Newport, R.I. I. Newport, R.I. Redevelopment Agency. II. Title.

Thailand. Ministry of Interior.
711.4
(593)
L47h
Litchfield Whiting Bowne and Associates.
Bangkok-Thonburi city planning project; historical growth. [In cooperation with] Adams, Howard and Greeley, city planning consultants to the Ministry of Interior, Government of Thailand. New York, 1959.
17p. (Technical monograph)

1. City planning - Thailand. 2. City planning - History. I. Thailand. Ministry of Interior. II. Adams, Howard and Greeley.

Thailand. Ministry of Interior.
711.4
(593)
L47t
Litchfield Whiting Bowne and Associates.
Bangkok-Thonburi city planning project; travel time. A study of the time factor in alternate forms of transportation serving the Bangkok Metropolitan area and an evaluation of the city's road system in terms of traffic travel time. [In cooperation with] Adams, Howard and Greeley, city planning consultants to the Ministry of Interior, Government of Thailand. New York, 1959.
5p. (Technical monograph)
(Cont'd. on next card)

711.583
(41)
P44
Thamesmead report.
Pike, Alexander.
Thamesmead report.
[London, n.p.] 1966.
12p.

1. Community development - U.K.
I. Title.

711.73
K43
Tharp, K   J   jt. au.
Kihlberg, Jaakko K
    Accident rates as related to design elements of rural highways, by Jaakko K. Kihlberg and K.J. Tharp. Washington, Highway Research Board, Division of Engineering, National Research Council, National Academy of Sciences, National Academy of Engineering, 1968.
    173p. (National Cooperative Highway Research program report 47; National Research Council publication 1581)
    Research sponsored by the American Association of State Highway Officials in cooperation with the Bureau   of Public Roads.

VF
691.12
(016)
H68
(Building materials - Thatch.
U.S. Housing and Home Finance Agency. Office of the Administrator. International Housing Activities Staff.
    Bibliography on thatch. [Prepared ... in cooperation with the Library]   Washington [Jan. 1954]
    4 p.

    Processed.

    1.Building materials-Thatch. I.U.S. Housing and Home Finance Agency. Office of the Adminis-trator. Library.

301
T32
Thelen, Herbert A
    Dynamics of groups at work. Chicago, University of Chicago Press, 1958.
    379p.

    "Selected readings": p. 369-370.

    1. Sociology. 2. Management. 3. Urban re-newal - Citizen participation. I. Title.

711.73
K43
Kihlberg, Jaakko K
    Accident...1968.   (Card 2)

    Bibliography: p. 174-175.

    1. Highways. 2. Accidents.
I. Tharp, K. J., jt. au. II. U.S. Bureau of Public Roads. III. Title. IV. Highway Research Board.

424
T31
THAYER, LEE O
    ADMINISTRATIVE COMMUNICATION. HOMEWOOD, ILL., R.D. IRWIN, 1961.
    344P. (THE IRWIN SERIES IN MANAGEMENT)

    1. ENGLISH LANGUAGE. I. TITLE.

711.581
(77311)
C34n
Thelen, Herbert A
Chicago. University.
    Neighbors in action; a manual for com-munity leaders, by Herbert A. Thelen and Bettie Belk Sarchet. Chicago, 1954.
    70p. illus.

    1. Neighborhood planning - Hyde Park-Kenwood area.
2. Community development - Citizen participation.
I. Thelen, Herbert A. II. Sarchet, Bettie Belk.

744
A77
Tharpe, Josephine M.
Association of Research Libraries.
    Interim report. Part one: Determination of the environmental conditions required in a library for the effective utilization of micro-forms, by Donald C. Holmes. Part two (interim report): Determination of an effective system of bibliographic control of microform publications, by Felix Reichmann and Josephine M. Tharpe. Wash., 1970.
    90p.
    Bibliography: p. 25-26.
             (Cont'd on next card)

728.1
(85)
W42
Thayer, Lee O
Wichita, Kan. University. College of Business Administration and Industry.
    Hogares Peruanos S.A.: a study of private U.S. enterprise in foreign housing, by Lee O. Thayer. Wichita, 1960.
    41p.

    1. Housing - Peru. I. Thayer, Lee O.

674
T32
THELEN, ROLF.
    KILN DRYING HANDBOOK. WASHINGTON, 1929.
    96P. (U.S. DEPT. OF AGRICULTURE. BULLETIN NO. 1136)

    1. LUMBER INDUSTRY. 2. WOOD.
I. TITLE.

744
A77
Association of Research Libraries. Interim report...1970.   (Card 2)

    1. Films. 2. Library sciences. I. Holmes, Donald C. Determination of the environmental conditions required in a library for the effective utilization of microforms.
II. Reichmann, Felix. Determination of an effective system of bibliographic control of microform publications. III. Tharpe, Josephine M.

538.56
(016)
A75c
Thayne, Rulon L   comp.
U.S. Armed Services Technical Information Agency.
    Computers and data processing systems, comp. by Rulon L. Thayne and others. Arlington, Va., 1962.
    463p. (Publication no. AD 291 850)

    1. Automation - Bibliography. 2. Documenta-tion. I. Thayne,   Rulon L., comp.   II. Title.

912
025
Thematic atlas of the world.
General Drafting Co.
    Man's domain; a thematic atlas of the world. Norman J.W. Thrower, ed. 2d ed. New York, McGraw-Hill, 1970.
    80p.

    1. Atlases. I. Thrower, Norman J.W., ed.
II. McGraw-Hill. III. Title: Thematic atlas of the world. IV. Title.

VF
691.12
F67
(Building materials - Thatch.
Forbes, Ruth Dorothea.
    Thatched roofs; selected references. Washington, 1958.
    sheet. 27 cm. (U. S. Dept. of Agriculture. Library. Library list no. 58)
    Revision of Bibliography on thatched roofs compiled by Claire Hirschfeld and issued by the Bureau of Agricultural Engineering in 1938.

    1. Roofs, Thatched. Bibl. 2. Hirschfeld, Etta Claire. Bibliography on thatched roofs. (Series)
                    Agr 53-131
U. S. Dept. of Agr. Libr.   1.916L612 no. 58
for Library of Congress   [3*]

649
C65t
Their daily bread ...
Committee on School Lunch Participation.
    Their daily bread; a study of the National School Lunch Program. New York, 1968
    135p.
    Florence Robin, Director.
    Sponsoring organizations: Church Women United and others.

    1. Children. 2. Schools. 3. Agriculture.
I. Church Women United. II. Robin, Florence. III. Title.

728.1
N17TH
THEMES FOR HOUSING PROGRAMS.
U.S. NATIONAL HOUSING AGENCY.
    THEMES FOR HOUSING PROGRAMS. WASHINGTON, 1946.
    21P.

    1. FEDERAL HOUSING PROGRAMS.
I. TITLE.

VF
691.12
(016)
R69
(Building materials - Thatch.
Royal Institute of British Architects. Library.
    Bibliography on thatch. [London? Jan. 1952]
    3 p.

    Processed.

R
920
:320
W36
Theis, Paul A.
Who's who in American politics; a biographical directory of United States political leaders, 1st ed.-
    1967-68-
    New York, R.R. Bowker, 1967-
    v.
    Edited 1967-68-   by Paul A. Theis and Edmund L. Henshaw.
    For complete information see main card.

    1. Political science - Biog. I. Theis, Paul A. ed. II. Henshaw, Edmund L., jt. ed.

323.25
T32
Themis House Workshop on Research Problems in Community Violence, Waltham, Mass., 1968.
    Problems in research on community violence. Edited by Ralph W. Conant and Molly Apple Levin. New York, Praeger, 1969.
    97p. (Praeger special studies in U.S. economic and social development)
    Sponsored jointly by the Lemberg Center for the Study of Violence and the Applied Research Branch, Division of Extramural Research Programs, of the National Institute of Mental Health.
             (Cont'd on next card)

VF
691
H68l
no.1
(Building materials - Thatch.
U.S. Housing and Home Finance Agency. Office of International Housing.
    Grasses, their use in building. Washington, Publications and Technical Services Branch, Agency for International Development, 1964.
    5p. (Its Leaflet no. 1)

    1. Building materials - Thatch.
I. U.S. Agency for International Develop-   ment. II. Title.

328
L13
Laf.
Theiss, J   William.
Lahr, Raymond M
    Congress; power and purpose on Capitol Hill, by Raymond M. Lahr and J. William Theis. Boston, Allyn and Bacon, 1967.
    288p.
    Bibliography: p. 270-273.

    1. U.S. Congress. 2. Federal government. 3. Political science. I. Theis, J. William. II. Title.

323.25
T32
Themis House Workshop on Research Problems in Community Violence, Waltham, Mass., 1968.
    Problems...1969.   (Card 2)

    Bibliography by Charles Tilly: p. 89-97.

    1. Civil disorders. I. Conant, Ralph Wendell, 1926- ed. II. Levin, Molly Apple, ed. III. Brandeis University. Lemberg Center for the Study of Violence. IV. U.S. National Institute of Mental Health. V. Title.

333.38
T32 Theobald, A   D
Financial aspects of subdivision develop-
ment. Chicago, Institute for Economic
Research, 1930.
88p. (Institute for Economic Research.
Studies in land economics. Research mono-
graph no. 3)

1. Subdivision. I. Institute for Economic
Research. II. Title.

Theodore, Rose.
331
L1lu U. S. Bureau of Labor Statistics.
Union security and checkoff provisions
in major union contracts 1958-59, by Rose Theodore
Washington, Govt. Print. Off., 1960.
16p. tables. (Its Bulletin no. 1272)

At head of title: 86th Cong., 2d sess.
House. Document no. 340.

1. Labor relations. I. Theodore, Rose.

699.81
F84 The theoretical calculation of temperature-
rise of thermally protected steel column
exposed to the fire.
Fujii, Seiichi
The theoretical calculation of temperature-
rise of thermally protected steel column
exposed to the fire. Tokyo, Building Research
Institute, Ministry of Construction, Japanese
Government, 1963.
16p. (Japan. Building Research Institute.
BRI occasional report no. 10)

1. Fire prevention. 2. Steel construction.
I. Japan. Building Research Institute.
II. Title.

360
T32a Theobald, Robert.
An alternative future for America; essays
and speeches of Robert Theobald. Edited by
Kendall College. Chicago, Swallow Press,
1968.
186p.

1. Social conditions. 2. Civil rights.
3. Economic conditions. I. Title.

301
(03)
T32 Theodorson, Achilles G   jt. au.
Theodorson, George A
A modern dictionary of sociology, by
George A. Theodorson and Achilles G.
Theodorson.   New York, Thomas Y.
Crowell, 1969.
469p.

1. Sociology - Dictionaries.
I. Theodorson, Achilles G., jt. au.
II. Title.

691.32
H47 Theoretical treaty of the relation between a
mixing ratio and breaking strength of
concrete.
Hiraga, Ken-ichi
Theoretical treaty of the relation between
a mixing ratio and breaking strength of concrete. Tokyo, Building Research Station,
Ministry of Construction, Japanese Government,
1966.
83p. (Japan. Building Research Institute.
BRI occasional report no. 26)

1. Concrete. I. Japan. Building Research
Institute. II. Title.

658
A52r
no.62 Theobald, Robert.
Business potential in the European
Common Market. New York, American
Management Association, 1963.
72p. (American Management Association.
AMA research study 62)

1. Management. 2. Business.
3. European Common Market (1955-
3. Economic development - Europe.
I. American   Management
Association.

301
(03)
T32 Theodorson, George A
A modern dictionary of sociology, by
George A. Theodorson and Achilles G.
Theodorson.   New York, Thomas Y.
Crowell, 1969.
469p.

1. Sociology - Dictionaries.
I. Theodorson, Achilles G., jt. au.
II. Title.

711.583
S15 Theories of community development.
Sanders, Irwin T
Theories of community development. Wash.,
Agency for International Development, 1958.
96p. (Readings in community development)
Reprint from Community development review,
vol. no. 9, June, 195 .
Training program developed in part under
grant from U.S. Dept. of Housing and Urban
Development.
1. Community development. I. U.S. Agency
for International Development. II. U.S.
Dept. of Housing and Urban Development.
III. Title.

331.26
T32 Theobald, Robert. ed.
Committed spending; a route to economic
security. New York, Doubleday, 1968.
199p.

1. Guaranteed annual income. 2. Economic
forecasting. 3. Social conditions. I. Title.

332
F74t A theoretical framework for monetary analysis.
Friedman, Milton.
A theoretical framework for monetary analysis.
New York, National Bureau of Economic Research,
1971.
69p. (NBER occasional paper 112)

Bibliography: p. 62-65.

1. Money. I. National Bureau of Economic
Research. II. Title. III. Title: Monetary
Analysis.

728.1
:325
K14 Theories of residential location and
realities of race.
Kain, John F
Theories of residential location and
realities of race. Cambridge, Mass.,
Harvard University, 1969.
35p. (Harvard University. Program on
Regional and Urban Economics. Discussion
paper no. 47)

1. Minority groups - Housing. 2. Housing
market. I. Harvard University. Program
on Regional and Urban Economics. II. Title.

339.3
T32 Theobald, Robert, ed.
The guaranteed income; next step in economic
evolution? [1st ed.] Garden City, N.Y.,
Doubleday, 1966.
233p.

1. Income. 2. Family income and expenditure.
I. Title.

697
H85 Theoretical and practical aspects of thermal
comfort.
Humphreys, M   A
Theoretical and practical aspects of thermal
comfort, by M.A. Humphreys and J.F. Nicol.
Garston, Eng., Building Research Station, 1971.
[13]p. (Current paper no. 14/71)

1. Heating. I. U.K. Building Research
Station. II. Nicol, J.F., jt. au. III. Title.

720.36
B15 Theory and design in the first machine age.
Banham, Reyner.
Theory and design in the first machine age. New York,
Praeger [1960]
338 p. illus. 23 cm. (Books that matter)
Includes bibliographies.

1. Architecture, Modern—20th cent.   I. Title.

NA680.B25 1960   722.9   60-8831 ‡
Library of Congress

658
A52r
no. 53 Theobald, Robert.
Profit potential in the developing
countries. New York, American Management
Association, 1962.
299p. (American Management Association.
AMA research study no. 53)

1. Management. 2. Economic development.
3. International relations. I. American
Management Association.

624.131
J85t Theoretical soil mechanics with practical
applications to soil mechanics and foundation engineering.
Jumikis, Alfreds R
Theoretical soil mechanics with practical
applications to soil mechanics and foundation
engineering. New York, Van Nostrand, 1969.
432p.

1. Soils. I. Title.

330
(73)
065
v.31 The theory and empirical analysis of production.
Brown, Murray, ed.
The theory and empirical analysis of production. [Papers presented at the Conference
on Production Relations, New York, October 1965].
New York, National Bureau of Economic Research,
distributed by Columbia Univ. Press, 1967.
515p. (Conference on Research in Income and
Wealth. Studies in income and wealth, v.31)

1. Income. 2. Economic conditions.
I. Conference on Research in Income and Wealth.
II. National Bureau of Economic Research.
III. Title.

360
T32 Theobald, Robert, ed.
Social policies for America in the seventies;
nine divergent views. Garden City, N.Y.,
Doubleday, 1968.
216p.
Anchor -- ----Another issue. Garden City, N.Y., Anchor
Books, Doubleday, 1969.
210p.

1. Social conditions. 2. Social welfare.
3. Minority groups. I. Title.

352
(54)
R13 Theories of administrative and political devel-
opment and rural institutions in India and...
Rahman, A   T   R
Theories of administrative and political
development and rural institutions in India and
Pakistan. New York, Southeast Asia Development
Advisory Group, Asia Society, 1967.
26p. (SEADAG papers on problems of develop-
ment in Southeast Asia. No. 21)
Paper presented at a meeting of the SEADAG
Development Administration Seminar in Carmel,
California, Nov. 23-25, 1967.
1. Local government - India. 2. Local govern-
ment - Pakistan. I. Southeast Asia Development
Advisory Group.   II. Title.

658
J63t The theory and management of systems.
Johnson, Richard A
The theory and management of systems, by
Richard A. Johnson and others. 2d ed.
New York, McGraw-Hill, 1967.
513p. (McGraw-Hill series in management)

Bibliography: p. 489-502.

1. Management. I. Title.

333.63   Theory and measurement of rent.
N28   New York University. Graduate School of Business
    Administration.
    Theory and measurement of rent by Joseph S.
    Keiper _and others_ With a foreword by Raymond
    Moley. 1st ed.   Philadelphia, Chilton Co.,
    Book Division, 1961.
    194 p.

    1. Rents. 2. Real property - Taxation.
    I. Title. II. Keiper, Joseph S.

    Theory and practice of presswork.
655
G68p   U.S. Government Printing Office.
1962   Theory and practice of presswork. Rev.
    Washington, For sale by the Supt. of
    Documents, Govt. Print. Off., 1963.
    220p.   (Its Training series)

    1. Printing and publishing. I. Title.
    II. Title: Presswork.

    Theory of business finance.
658.1
W27   Weston, John Frederick, comp.
    Theory of business finance; advanced readings,
    by J. Fred Weston and Donald H. Woods.
    Belmont, Calif., Wadsworth Pub. Co., 1967.
    482p.

    1. Corporations - Finance. 2. Finance.
    I. Woods, Donald H., jt. au. II. Title.

300.15   Theory and methods of social research.
G15   Galtung, Johan.
    Theory and methods of social research. Oslo,
    Universitetsforlaget, New York, Columbia
    University Press, etc., 1967.
    534p. (Basic social science monographs no. 1)
    Scandinavian university books.

    1. Social science research. 2. Social
    sciences - Statistics. I. Title.

---

350   Theory and practice of public administra-
C31   Charlesworth, James C   ed.   ion...
    Theory and practice of public administration;
    scope, objectives, and methods. Philadelphia,
    American Academy of Political and Social Science,
    1968.
    336p. (Monograph [no.] 8)
    Cosponsor: American Society for Public
    Administration.
    1. Public administration. I. Title.
    II. American Academy of Political and Social
    Science. III. American Society of Public
    Administration.

    Theory of documentation.
002
P27   Perry, James W
    Theory of documentation and strategy of
    searching; mathematical formulation of basic
    procedures in documentation, by James W.
    Perry and William Goffman, Western Reserve
    University. \Washington]Air Force Office of
    Scientific Research, 1960.
    49p. (Air Force Office of Scientific
    Research TN-60-366)
    1. Documentation. 2. Library science -
    Automation. I. U.S. Air Force. Office of
    Scientific Research. II. Western Reserve
    University.   III. Goffman, William,
    jt. au.   IV. Title.

    Theory and practice of bookbinding.
655
G68b   U.S. Government Printing Office.
1962   Theory and practice of bookbinding. Rev.
    Washington, For sale by the Supt. of
    Documents, Govt. Print. Off., 1963.
    244p. (Its Training series)

    1. Printing and publishing. I. Title.
    II. Title: Bookbinding.

    The theory and practice of reinforced concrete.
693.55
D85   Dunham, Clarence W
    The theory and practice of reinforced
    concrete. 2d ed.   New York, McGraw-Hill, 1944.
    558 p.   illus., diagrs., graphs, tables.

    Bibliographical footnotes.

    1.Reinforced concrete Construction-Tables,
    calculations, etc. I.Title.

    The theory of economic growth.
330
L28t   Lewis, W   Arthur.
    The theory of economic growth. New
    York, Harper Torchbooks, 1970.
    453p.

    1. Economic development. I. Title.

    The theory and practice of commercial policy.
381
B31   Bhagwati, Jagdish.
    The theory and practice of commercial policy;
    departures from unified exchange rates. Prince-
    ton, N.J., Dept. of Economics, Princeton
    University, 1968.
    74p. (Princeton University. International
    Finance Section. Special papers in inter-
    national economics no. 8)
    1. Commercial policy. 2. Economics. I. Prince-
    ton University. (International Finance Section)
    II. Title.

---

690   Theory and practice of shell structures.
F47t   Fischer, Ladislav.
    Theory and practice of shell structures.
    Berlin, Munich, Ernst & Sohn, 1968.
    541p.

    Translation of Theorie and Praxis der
    Schalenkonstruktionen.

    1. Owner-built houses. 2. Roofs and
    roofing. 3. Structural engineering. I. Title.
    II. Title: Shell structures.

---

510   Theory of equations.
U76   Uspensky, J   V
    Theory of equations. New York, McGraw-Hill
    Book Company, 1948.
    353 p.

    1. Mathematics. I. Title.

    Theory and practice of composition.
655
G68c   U.S. Government Printing Office.
1962   Theory and practice of composition. Rev.
    Washington, For sale by the Supt. of
    Documents, Govt. Print. Off., 1963.
    242p.   (Its Training series)

    1. Printing and publishing. I. Title.

---

360   Theory and practice of social planning.
K13t   Kahn, Alfred J
    Theory and practice of social planning.
    New York, Russell Sage Foundation, 1969.
    348p.

    Companion volume to Studies in social
    Policy and planning.

    1. Social conditions. 2. Social welfare.
    I. Title.

---

332   The theory of forward exchange.
863   Sohmen, Egon.
    The theory of forward exchange. Princeton,
    N.J., International Finance Section, Dept. of
    Economics, Princeton University, 1966.
    55p.   (Princeton University. Inter-
    national Finance Section. Princeton studies
    in international finance no 17)

    1. Finance. 2. Foreign exchange.
    I. Princeton University. (International
    Finance Section) II. Title.

---

624   Theory and practice of foundation engineering.
G66   Goodman, Louis J
    Theory and practice of foundation engineering,
    by Louis J. Goodman and R.H. Karol. New York,
    Macmillan, 1968.
    433p. (Macmillan series in civil engineering)

    1. Structural engineering. 2. Architecture -
    Designs and plans. 3. Foundations (Building)
    4. Civil engineering. I. Karol, R.H., jt. au.
    II. Title.

300.15   Theory building.
D81   Dubin, Robert.
    Theory building. New York, Free Press,
    1969.
    298p.
    Bibliography: p. 280-282.

    1. Social science research. I. Title.

---

510   THE THEORY OF GAMES.
R15   RAND CORPORATION.
    THE THEORY OF GAMES, BY RICHARD BELLMAN.
    SANTA MONICA, CALIFORNIA, 1957.
    19P.

    1. MATHEMATICS.   I. BELLMAN, RICHARD.
    II. TITLE.

---

655   Theory and practice of lithography.
G68l   U.S. Government Printing Office.
    Theory and practice of lithography.
    Washington, For sale by the Supt. of
    Documents, Govt. Print. Off., 1964.
    109p.   (Its Training series)

    Glossary: p. 77-109.

    1. Printing and publishing. I. Title.
    II. Title: Lithography.

690.248 Theory of beams.
I84   Iwinski, T
    Theory of beams; the application of the
    Laplace transformation method to engineering
    problems. Translated from the Polish by
    E.P. Bernat. New York, Pergamon Press,
    1958.
    85p. (International series of monographs
    on electronics and instrumentation)

    1. Trusses. 2. Structural engineering.
    3. Strains and stresses. I. Title.
    II. Title: Laplace transformation.

---

624   Theory of inelastic structures.
L45   Lin, T   H
    Theory of inelastic structures. New York,
    Wiley, 1968.
    454p.

    1. Structural engineering. I. Title.
    II. Title: Inelastic structures.

325.2
B51
THEORY OF MINORITY-GROUP RELATIONS.
BLALOCK, HUBERT M
TOWARD A THEORY OF MINORITY-GROUP
RELATIONS. NEW YORK, WILEY, 1967.
227P.

BIBLIOGRAPHICAL FOOTNOTES.

1. RACE RELATIONS. 2. MINORITY
GROUPS. I. TITLE. II. TITLE: THEORY
OF MINORITY-GROUP RELATIONS.

336
M87t
The theory of public finance; a study in public
economy.
Musgrave, Richard A
The theory of public finance; a study in
public economy. New York, McGraw-Hill, 1959.
628p.

1. Finance. 2. Taxation. 3. Money.
4. Investments. 5. Monopolies. I. Title.

333.332
J27
THE THEORY OF REAL PROPERTY
VALUATION.
JERRETT, HERMAN DANIEL.
THE THEORY OF REAL PROPERTY
VALUATION. 1ST ED. SACRAMENTO,
CALIF., 1938.
309P.

1. REAL PROPERTY - VALUATION.
I. TITLE.

301.15
M12t
The theory of social change.
McLeish, John.
The theory of social change; four views
considered. New York, Schocken Books, 1969.
95p.

Bibliography: p. 88-90.

1. Social change. I. Title.

690.4
T45
Theory of structures.
Timoshenko, S
Theory of structures, by S. Timoshenko and D.H.
Young. 1st ed. New York, McGraw-Hill, c1945.
xiv, 488 p. diagrs., tables.

1. Structural engineering. I. Young, D   H
jt. au. II. Title.

691.328
W66t
The theory of the strip method for design of
slabs.
Wood, R   H
The theory of the strip method for design of
slabs, by R.H. Wood and G.S.T. Armer. Garston,
Eng., Building Research Station, 1968.
311p. (U.K. Building Research Station.
Current paper CP84/68)
Reprinted from: Proceedings of the Institution
of Civil Engineers, 1968, Vol. 41 (October),
pp. 285-311.
1. Concrete, Reinforced. 2. Loads. I. Armer,
G.S.T., jt. au.   II. U.K. Building Re-
search Station.   III. Title.

388
H27s
Theory of traffic flow.
Herman, Robert.
Single-lane traffic theory and experiment,
by Robert Herman and R.B. Potts. Amsterdam,
Elsevier, 1961.
120-146p.
Reprinted from Theory of traffic flow
(1961) 120.

1. Traffic. 2. Highways - Research.
I. Potts, R.B., jt. au. II. Theory of traffic
flow. III. Title.

712.25
(79461)
S15T
THERE ARE NO STRANGERS HERE.
SAN FRANCISCO. RECREATION COMMISSION.
THERE ARE NO STRANGERS HERE:
HOUSING AND RECREATION JOIN HANDS. A
REPORT TO JOSEPHINE D. RANDALL,
SUPERINTENDENT, SAN FRANCISCO
RECREATION DEPARTMENT, COMPILED BY
ALTA SIMS BUNKER... SAN FRANCISCO,
1947.
23P.
1. RECREATION - SAN FRANCISCO.
2. COMMUNITY DEVELOPMENT - SAN
FRANCISCO. I. BUNKER, ALTA SIMS,
COMP. II. T   ITLE. III. TITLE:
HOUSING AND R   ECREATION JOIN HANDS.

360
H47
There shall be no poor.
Hirsch, Richard G
There shall be no poor. Foreword by Hubert
H. Humphrey, Vice President of the United
States. New York, Commission on Social Action
of Reform Judaism, 1965.
109p. (Issues of conscience no. 6)

1. Social welfare. 2. Social conditions.
3. Church and social problems. I. Humphrey,
Hubert Horatio. II. Commission on Social
Action of Reform Judaism. III. Title.

691.32
L68
The thermal and acoustic properties of light-
weight concretes.
Loudon, A   G
The thermal and acoustic properties of light-
weight concretes, by A.G. Ludon and E.F. Stacy.
Garston, Eng., Building Research Station,
Ministry of Technology, 1966.
10p. (U.K. Building Research Station.
Building research current papers. Design
series 45)
Reprinted from: Structural concrete, March/
April 1966. pp. 58-76.

1. Concrete. I. U.K. Building Research
Station. II. Title.

620.1
F56
Thermal buckling of conical shells.
Florida. University. Engineering and Indus-
trial Experiment Station.
Thermal buckling of conical shells, by S.Y.
Lu and L.K. Chang [and] Dynamic stability of
heated conical and cylindrical shells, by C.L.
Sun and S.Y. Lu. Gainesville, 1969.
31p. (Its Technical papers no. 424 and
425)
At head of title: Engineering progress at
the University of Florida, Vol. XXIII, no.
1, Jan. 1969.
No. 424 reprinted from AIAA journal,
p. 1877-1822.
(Cont'd on next card)

620.1
F56
Florida. University. Engineering and Industrial Experiment Station.   Thermal buckling...1969.   (Card 2)

No. 425 reprinted from Developments in
mechanics, Vol. 4. Proceedings of the tenth
Midwestern Mechanics Conference, Aug. 1967,
p. 305-327.

1. Strength of materials. I. Title.
II. Title: Conical shells.

VF
699.86
P25
1952
Thermal characteristics and effects of
condensation within frame walls.
Pennsylvania. State College. Engineering
Experiment Station.
Thermal characteristics and effects of
condensation within frame walls ... by A. W.
Sherdon.   State College, Pa., June 1952.
33 l.   plate, tables.

Progress report no. 1, Research Project no.
1-T-89, Housing and Home Finance Agency.
Project director, E. R. Queer; staff
technician, William A. Russell.
Processed.

VF
699.86
P25
1953
Thermal characteristics and effects of
condensation within frame walls.
Pennsylvania. State College. Engineering
Experiment Station.
Thermal characteristics and effects of
condensation within frame walls ... by F. A.
Joy.   State College, Pa., July 1953.
43 l.   plates, tables.

Final report, Research Project no. 1-T-89,
Housing and Home Finance Agency.
Project director, E. R. Queer; staff
technician, William A. Russell.
Processed.

697
A52mi
Thermal comfort conditions.
American Society of Heating, Refrigerating
and Air-Conditioning Engineers.
Thermal comfort conditions. New York, 1966.
2p. (ASHRAE standard 55-66)

1. Heating. 2. Air conditioning. I. Title.

699.8
S68
THERMAL CONDITIONS IN DWELLINGS.
SOUTH AFRICAN COUNCIL FOR SCIENTIFIC AND
INDUSTRIAL RESEARCH. NATIONAL
BUILDING RESEARCH INSTITUTE.
THE INFLUENCE OF CEILING INSULATION ON
INDOOR THERMAL CONDITIONS IN DWELLINGS
OF HEAVYWEIGHT CONSTRUCTION UNDER SOUTH
AFRICAN CONDITIONS, BY F.J. LOTZ AND
S.J. RICHARDS. PRETORIA, 1964.
16P. (ITS BULLETIN 35)

C.S.I.R. RESEARCH REPORT NO. 214.
1. INSULATION.   I. LOTZ, F.J.
II. RICHARDS, S   J.   III. TITLE:
THERMAL CONDITIONS IN DWELLINGS.

691.42
A75
Thermal conductivity of masonry materials.
Arnold, Pamela J
Thermal conductivity of masonry materials.
Garston, Eng., Building Research Station, 1970.
[8]p. (U.K. Building Research Station.
Current paper 1/70)
Reprinted from: The Journal of the Institution
of Heating and Ventilating Engineers, 1969,
vol. 37 (August), pp. 101-108 and 117.

1. Bricks. 2. Concrete. 3. Heat transmission. I. U.K. Building Research Station.
II. Title.

VF
699.86
F67
R1952
1953
Thermal conductivity of paper honeycomb cores.
U.S. Forest Service. Forest Products Laboratory,
Madison, Wis.
Thermal conductivity of paper honeycomb cores
and sound absorption of sandwich panels, by D. J.
Fahey, M. E. Dunlap and R. J. Seidl. Madison,
Wis., Sept. 1953.
10 p. illus., tables. (Its no. R1952)

Processed.

1. Insulating materials. 2. Soundproofing. 3. Panels.
I. Fahey, D. J. II. Dunlap, M. E. III. Seidl, R. J.
IV. Title.

VF
691.8
F67u
P8
Thermal conductivity, vapor transmissions and
condensation tests of the Lincoln honey-
comb plastic wall panel.
U.S. Forest Service. Forest Products Laboratory,
Madison, Wis.
Thermal conductivity, vapor transmissions and
condensation tests of the Lincoln honey-comb
plastic wall panel, by M. E. Dunlap. Madison,
Wis. [1946]
11 l. plates, tables.
Not for publication.
In cooperation with the National Housing
Agency.
At head of title: Progress report no. 8.
Processed.

697.3
R63
THERMAL DESIGN OF BUILDINGS.
ROGERS, TYLER STEWART.
THERMAL DESIGN OF BUILDINGS; A GUIDE
TO ECONOMICALLY SOUND THERMAL DESIGN OF
HEATED, AIR CONDITIONED, OR REFRIGERATED
BUILDINGS FOR USE BY ARCHITECTS, HOME
BUILDERS, AND BUILDING OWNERS DURING
PRELIMINARY DESIGN STAGES. NEW YORK,
WILEY, 1964.
196P.

1. THERMAL RADIATION. 2. HEATING.
3. AIR CONDITIONING. I. TITLE.

697.9
T37
1970
Thermal environmental engineering.
Threlkeld, James L
Thermal environmental engineering. 2d ed.
Englewood Cliffs, N.J., Prentice-Hall, 1970.
495p.

1. Air conditioning. 2. Heating.
3. Ventilation. I. Title.

691.32
H65
THE THERMAL EXPANSION OF CONCRETE.
BONNELL, DAVID GLYNWYN ROBERT.
THE THERMAL EXPANSION OF CONCRETE, BY
D.G.R. BONNELL AND F.C. HARPER.
LONDON, H.M. STAT. OFF., 1951.
24P. (U.K. BUILDING RESEARCH
STATION. NATIONAL BUILDING STUDIES.
TECHNICAL PAPER NO. 7)

1. CONCRETE. I. HARPER, F.C., JT.
AU. II. U.K. BUILDING RESEARCH
STATION. III. TITLE.

699.844
C56
THERMAL INSULATION OF BUILDINGS.
CLOSE, PAUL DUNHAM.
SOUND CONTROL AND THERMAL INSULATION
OF BUILDINGS. NEW YORK, REINHOLD PUB.
CORP., 1966.
502P.

1. SOUNDPROOFING. 2. HEATING.
3. INSULATION. I. TITLE.
II. TITLE: THERMAL INSULATION OF
BUILDINGS.

697.3
.V15
Laf.
Thermal performance of buildings.
Van Straaten, J F
Thermal performance of buildings. New York,
Elsevier Pub. Co., 1967.
311p.
Bibliogrpahy: p. 248-297.

1. Thermal radiation. 2. Heat transmission.
3. Ventilation. I. Title.

699.8
P76
Thermal insulation.
Probert, S D ed.
Thermal insulation, edited by S.D.
Probert and D.R. Hub. Amsterdam,
Elsevier, 1968.
121p.
Revised selection of papers presented
to a Symposium on thermal insulation held
at the Welsh College of Advanced Technology,
Cardiff, 4-6 Oct., 1965.
1. Insulation. 2. Thermal radiation.
3. Heating. I. Title. II. Hub, D.R., jt.
ed.

690.015
P87
v.1
no.4
Thermal insulation of houses.
Purdue University. Better Homes in America.
Thermal insulation of houses, by B.F. Betts.
Lafayette, Ind., 1936.
25p. (Home information Bulletin no. 4)

In looseleaf binder with other numbers in
series.

1. Insulation. I. Betts, B.F. II. Title.

628.515
N17b
Thermal pollution.
National Symposium on Thermal Pollution,
Portland, Or., 1968.
Biological aspects of thermal pollution;
proceedings. Edited by Peter A. Krenkel
and Frank L. Parker. Sponsored by the
Federal Water Pollution Control Administration
and Vanderbilt University. [Nashville, Tenn.]
Vanderbilt University Press, 1969.
407p.
1. Water pollution. I. Title. II. Title:
Thermal pollution. II. Krenkel, Peter A.,
ed. III. Parker, Frank L., jt. ed.
IV. U.S. Federal Water Pollution
Control Administration. V. Vanderbilt
University.

699.8
M15
Thermal insulation.
Malloy, John F
Thermal insulation. New York, Van Nostrand
Reinhold, 1969.
546p. (Van Nostrand Reinhold environmental
engineering series)

1. Insulation. I. Title.

699.8
E53
Thermal insulation of industrial buildings.
Engineering Equipment Users Association.
(Panel C/6, Thermal Insulation of Industrial
Buildings)
Thermal insulation of industrial buildings.
London, Constable [1966]
xi, 80p. 15 plates, tables, diagrs. 25 1/2
cm. (E.E.A.U. handbook no. 14) 30/-
Bibliography: p. 80. (B66-4700)
1. Insulation. 2. Insulating materials.
3. Industrial buildings. I. Title.

628.515
C657t
Thermal pollution...
U.S. Congress. Senate. Committee on
Public Works.
Thermal pollution, 1968. Hearings before
the Subcommittee on Air and Water Pollution
of the Committee on Public Works, United
States Senate, Ninetieth Congress, second
session, on the extent to which environmental factors are considered in selecting
powerplant sites, with particular emphasis
on the ecological effects of the discharge
of waste heat into rivers, lakes, estuaries,
and coastal waters. Wash., Govt. Print. Off.,
1968.
4pts.
(Cont'd on next card)

699.86
U54
Thermal insulation.
U.K. Ministry of Public Building and Works.
Thermal insulation. London, H.M.S.O., 1968.
folder. (Its Advisory leaflet 34)

1. Insulating materials. I. Title.

690.015
H68
T32
The thermal insulating value of airspaces.
U.S. Housing and Home Finance Agency. Office of
the Administrator. Division of Housing
Research.
The thermal insulating value of airspaces.
[Washington, Govt. Print. Off., Apr. 1954]
32 p. illus., diagrs., graphs, tables.
(Housing research paper 32)
Based on data compiled under Research Project
no. 1950-ME-12 at National Bureau of Standards.
1. Insulation. 2. Housing research contracts.
I. Title. II. Title: Airspaces, The thermal
insulating value of I. Series.

628.515
C657t
U.S. Congress. Senate. Committee on
Public Works. Thermal pollution...
1968. (Card 2)

Hearings held: Washington, D.C., Portland,
Me., Montpelier, Vt., Miami, Fla.; Feb. 6-
Apr. 19, 1968.
Includes bibliographies.
1. Water pollution. 2. Water pollution -
Bibl. 3. Power resources. 4. Public
utilities. I. Title.

697
O57
THERMAL INSULATION FOR BUILDINGS.
OLSEN, FREDERIK.
THERMAL INSULATION FOR BUILDINGS.
PARIS, ORGANISATION FOR ECONOMIC
CO-OPERATION AND DEVELOPMENT, 1962.
146P.

1. HEATING. 2. INSULATION.
I. ORGANISATION FOR ECONOMIC CO-OPERATION
AND DEVELOPMENT. II. TITLE.

VF
699.86
N17
The thermal insulating value of air spaces.
U.S. National Bureau of Standards.
The thermal insulating value of air spaces,
by H. E. Robinson [and] F. J. Powlitch.
Washington, Jan. 1954.
19 p. figures, graphs, tables. (NBS
Report 3030)
Prepared under Research project no. 1950-ME-
12, HHFA.
Project director: R. S. Dill; Staff
technician: Robert Thulman.
(over)

VF
690.015
P42
R9
Thermal properties of a floor in contact with
the ground.
Mackey, C O
Thermal properties of a floor in contact with
the ground. New York, John B. Pierce
Foundation, Jan. 1944.
23 p. tables. (John B. Pierce
Foundation. Research study 9)

"Thermal studies."

1. Concrete floors. I. Title.
II. John B. Pierce Foundation.

699.86
L28
Thermal insulation from wood for
buildings...
Lewis, Wayne C
Thermal insulation from wood for buildings:
effects of moisture and its control. Madison,
Wis., U.S. Dept. of Agriculture, Forest Service,
Forest Products Laboratory, 1968.
42p. (U.S. Forest Service. Research note
FPL 86)

1. Insulating materials. 2. Insulation.
3. Wood. I. U.S. Forest Products Laboratory,
Madison, Wis. II. Title.

VF
690.015
(41)
U54t
no.3
Thermal insulation in building.
U.K. Ministry of Works.
The importance of thermal insulation
in building, by A. G. Sutton. London,
H.M. Stationery Off., 1957.
11 p. (Its Technical notes no. 3)

1. Insulation. I. Sutton, A. G.
II. Title: Thermal insulation in
building. (Series)

624.131.3
N18
THERMAL PROPERTIES OF SOIL.
U.S. NAVAL CIVIL ENGINEERING
LABORATORY, PORT HUENEME, CALIF.
THE DEVELOPMENT, FABRICATION, AND
EVALUATION OF A DEVICE FOR THE
MEASUREMENT OF THERMAL PROPERTIES OF
SOIL. PORT HUENEME, CALIF., 1966.
242L.

AN INVESTIGATION CONDUCTED AT
VIRGINIA POLYTECHNIC INSTITUTE.
1. SOILS - TESTING. I. VIRGINIA
POLYTECHNIC INSTITUTE. II. TITLE:
THERMAL PROPERTIES OF SOIL.

VF
699.86
F67
R1740
1958
THERMAL INSULATION MADE OF WOOD-BASE
MATERIALS.
U.S. FOREST PRODUCTS LABORATORY,
MADISON, WIS.
THERMAL INSULATION MADE OF WOOD-BASE
MATERIALS; ITS APPLICATION AND USE IN
HOUSES BY L.V. TEESDALE. REV., 1958.
MADISON, 1958.
41P. (ITS REPORT NO. 1740)

1. INSULATING MATERIALS. I. TITLE.
II. TITLE: WOOD-BASE MATERIALS.

VF
699.86
F67
R1740
Thermal insulation made of wood-base materials
its application and use in houses.
U.S. Forest Service. Forest Products Laboratory,
Madison, Wis.
Thermal insulation made of wood-base materials
its application and use in houses, by L. V.
Teesdale. Madison, Wis., Oct. 1949.
40 p./plates, tables. (Its R1740)

Bibliography: p. 38-40.
Processed.

1. Insulating materials. I. Teesdale, L. V. II. Title

355.58
B27
THERMAL RADIATION.
BERMAN, WILLIAM H.
FEDERAL AND STATE RESPONSIBILITIES
FOR RADIATION PROTECTION: THE NEED FOR
FEDERAL LEGISLATION, BY WILLIAM H.
BERMAN AND LEE M. HYDEMAN. ANN ARBOR,
MICH., UNIVERSITY OF MICHIGAN LAW
SCHOOL, 1959.
120P.

1. CIVILIAN DEFENSE. 2. THERMAL
RADIATION. I. HYDEMAN, LEE M., JT. AU.
II. MICHIGAN UNIVERSITY. LAW SCHOOL.
III. TITLE: RADIATION PROTECTION.

355.58
(794)
C15R

THERMAL RADIATION.
CALIFORNIA. ASSEMBLY. INTERIM COMMITTEE ON PUBLIC HEALTH. SUBCOMMITTEE ON RADIATION PROTECTION. RADIATION PROTECTION IN CALIFORNIA. SACRAMENTO, 1961.
72P. (ASSEMBLY INTERIM COMMITTEE REPORTS, 1959-61, V. 9, NO. 23)

1. CIVILIAN DEFENSE - CALIFORNIA. 2. THERMAL RADIATION. I. TITLE.

697.3
M85t

Muncey, R W   The thermal response of temperature or...(Card 2)

1. Thermal radiation. 2. Heat transmission. I. Australia. Commonwealth Scientific and Industrial Research Organization. (Div. of Building Research)

697.3
A76E

THERMAL RADIATION.
U.S. ATOMIC ENERGY COMMISSION. AN EXPERIMENTAL EVALUATION OF THE RADIATION PROTECTION AFFORDED BY A LARGE MODERN CONCRETE OFFICE BUILDING, BY J.A. BATTER, JR. AND OTHERS. OAK RIDGE, TENN., 1960.
61P.

AT HEAD OF TITLE: CEX-59-1, CIVIL EFFECTS EXERCISE.

1. THERMAL RADIATION. 2. CIVILIAN DEFENSE. I. BATTER, J.F. II. TITLE.

697.
1662.6
O66

Thermal radiation.
Goodale, Thomas. Improvement of the performance of carbon smoke generators by the choice of fuels and fuel additives. Final report. For Office of Civil Defense through U.S. Naval Radiological Defense Laboratory. Burlingame, Calif., URS Systems Corp., 1968.
1v. (URS Systems Corp. URS 678-4)

1. Fuel. 2. Thermal radiation. I. URS Systems Corp. II. U.S. Office of Civil Defense. III. U.S. Naval Radiological Defense Laboratory. IV. Title.

699.8
P76

Thermal radiation.
Probert, S D ed. Thermal insulation, edited by S.D. Probert and D.R. Hub. Amsterdam, Elsevier, 1968.
121p.
Revised selection of papers presented to a symposium on thermal insulation held at the Welsh College of Advanced Technology, Cardiff, 4-6 Oct., 1965.
1. Insulation. 2. Thermal radiation. 3. Heating. I. Title. II. Hub, D.R., jt. ed.

697.3
A76EXP

THERMAL RADIATION.
U.S. ATOMIC ENERGY COMMISSION. EXPERIMENTAL EVALUATION OF THE RADIATION PROTECTION AFFORDED BY RESIDENTIAL STRUCTURES AGAINST DISTRIBUTED SOURCES, BY J.A. AUXIER AND OTHERS. OAK RIDGE, TENNESSEE, 1959.
133P.

AT HEAD OF TITLE: CEX-58-1, CIVIL EFFECTS EXERCISE.

1. THERMAL RADIATION. 2. CIVILIAN DEFENSE. I. AUXIER, J.A. II. TITLE.

690.015
(485)
S82
R16
1967

Thermal radiation.
Göstring, Bo. Plattapparat för bestämning av värmelednings-förmåga hos byggnadsmaterial [Hot plate apparatus for determination of thermal conductivity of building materials] Stockholm, 1967.
8p. (Sweden. Statens Kommitté för Byggnadsforskning. Rapport 16:67)
English summary.
Särtryck ur tidskriften VVS 3:1967
1. Building research - Sweden. 2. Heat transmission. 3. Building materials. 4. Thermal radiation.

699.85
R12

THERMAL RADIATION.
RADIATION EFFECTS INFORMATION CENTER, COLUMBUS, OHIO.
THE EFFECT OF NUCLEAR RADIATION ON ELASTOMERIC AND PLASTIC COMPONENTS AND MATERIALS, BY R.W. KING AND OTHERS. COLUMBUS, 1961.
1 V. (VARIOUS PAGINGS)

1. PROTECTIVE CONSTRUCTION. 2. THERMAL RADIATION. I. KING, R.W.

697.3
A76EX

THERMAL RADIATION.
U.S. ATOMIC ENERGY COMMISSION. EXPERIMENTAL EVALUATION OF THE RADIATION PROTECTION AFFORDED BY TYPICAL OAK RIDGE HOMES AGAINST DISTRIBUTED SOURCES, BY T.D. STICKLER AND J.A. AUZIER. OAK RIDGE, TENN., 1960.
51P.

AT HEAD OF TITLE: CEX-59-13, CIVIL EFFECTS EXERCISE.
1. THERMAL RADIATION. 2. CIVILIAN DEFENSE. I. STICKLER, J.D. II. AUZIER, J.A. III. TITLE.

697.3
L68

Thermal radiation.
Loudon, A G U-values in the 1970 guide. Garston, Eng., Building Research Station, Ministry of Public Building and Works, 1968.
167-174p. (U.K. Building Research Station. Current paper CP 79/68)
Reprinted from: Journal of the Institution of Heating and Ventilating Engineers, Sept., 1968 pp. 167-174.
1. Thermal radiation. 2. Walls. 3. Roofs and roofing. I. Title. II. U.K. Building Research Station.

697.3
R63

THERMAL RADIATION.
ROGERS, TYLER STEWART.
THERMAL DESIGN OF BUILDINGS, A GUIDE TO ECONOMICALLY SOUND THERMAL DESIGN OF HEATED, AIR CONDITIONED, OR REFRIGERATED BUILDINGS FOR USE BY ARCHITECTS, HOME BUILDERS, AND BUILDING OWNERS DURING PRELIMINARY DESIGN STAGES. NEW YORK, WILEY, 1964.
196P.

1. THERMAL RADIATION. 2. HEATING. 3. AIR CONDITIONING. I. TITLE.

697.3
A76

THERMAL RADIATION.
U.S. ATOMIC ENERGY COMMISSION. HEALTH ASPECTS OF NUCLEAR WEAPONS TESTING. WASHINGTON, GOVT. PRINT. OFF., 1964.
56P.

BIBLIOGRAPHY: P. 55-56.

1. THERMAL RADIATION. 2. ATOMIC BOMB. 3. HEALTH. I. TITLE.

697.3
M85

Thermal radiation.
Muncey, R W Properties of the lunar surface as revealed by thermal radiation. Melbourne, Australia, Commonwealth Scientific and Industrial Research Organization, Div. of Building Research, 1963.
24-31p. (Australia. Commonwealth Scientific and Industrial Research Organization. Div. of Building Research. D.C.R. reprint no. 245)
Reprinted from the Australian journal of physics, vol. 16, no. 1, Mar. 1963, p. 24-31. (Cont'd. on next card).

355.58
UN

Thermal radiation.
United Nations. (General Assembly) Report of the United Nations Scientific Committee on the effects of atomic radiation. New York, 1962.
442p.
Official records: Seventeenth Session, Supplement no. 16 (A/5216)

1. Thermal radiation. 2. Civilian defense.

355.58
C48fi

Thermal radiation.
U.S. Office of Civil Defense. Fire aspects of civil defense. Evaluation report, by Welmer E. Strope and John F. Christian. Wash., Govt. Print. Off., 1964.
109. (TR-25)

1. Civilian defense. 2. Fire prevention. 3. Thermal radiation. I. Strope, Welmer E. II. Christian, John F. III. Title.

697.3
M85

Muncey, R W Properties of the lunar surface as revealed...(Card 2)

1. Thermal radiation. I. Australia. Commonwealth Scientific and Industrial Research Organization. (Div. of Building Research)

697.3
A75

THERMAL RADIATION.
U.S. ARMY. COLD REGIONS RESEARCH AND ENGINEERING LABORATORY.
DAILY SUMS OF GLOBAL RADIATION FOR CLOUDLESS SKIES, BY S.J. BOLSENGO. HANOVER, N.H., 1964.
124P. (ITS RESEARCH REPORT NO. 160)

1. THERMAL RADIATION. I. BOLSENGO, S.J. II. TITLE. III. TITLE: GLOBAL RADIATION.

355.58
D23E

THERMAL RADIATION.
U.S. DEPT. OF DEFENSE.
THE EFFECTS OF ATOMIC WEAPONS. PREPARED FOR AND IN COOPERATION WITH THE U.S. DEPT. OF DEFENSE AND THE U.S. ATOMIC ENERGY COMMISSION, UNDER THE DIRECTION OF THE LOS ALAMOS SCIENTIFIC LABORATORY, JUNE 1950. WASHINGTON, GOVT. PRINT. OFF., 1950.
456P.
1. ATOMIC BOMB. 2. THERMAL RADIATION. 3. CIVILIAN DEFENSE. 4. U.S. ATOMIC ENERGY COMMISSION. 5. U.S. SCIENTIFIC LABORATORY, LOS ALAMOS, N.M.

697.3
M85t

Thermal radiation.
Muncey, R W The thermal response of a building to sudden changes of temperature or heat flow. Melbourne, Australia, Commonwealth Scientific and Industrial Research Organization, 1963.
123-128p. (Australia. Commonwealth Scientific and Industrial Research Organization. Div. of Building Research. D.B.R. reprint no. 250)
Reprinted from the Australian journal of applied science vol. 14, no. 2, June 1963. p. 123-128. (Cont'd. on next card).

697.3
A76C

THERMAL RADIATION.
U.S. ATOMIC ENERGY COMMISSION. COMPARATIVE NUCLEAR EFFECTS OF BIOMEDICAL INTEREST, BY CLAYTON S. WHITE AND OTHERS. OAK RIDGE, TENN., 1961.
83P.

BIBLIOGRAPHY: P. 81-83.
AT HEAD OF TITLE: CEX-58-8, CIVIL EFFECTS STUDY.

1. THERMAL RADIATION. 2. CIVILIAN DEFENSE. 3. HEALTH. I. WHITE, CLAYTON S. II. TITLE.

355.58
D23

Thermal radiation.
U.S. Dept. of Defense. The effects of nuclear weapons. Washington, Govt. Print. Off., 1957.
579 p. illus., tables.

Editor: Samuel Glasstone.

1. Civilian defense. 2. Thermal radiation. 3. Atomic bomb. I. Title.

Thermal radiation.

355.58
D23
1962   U.S. Dept. of Defense.
The effects of nuclear weapons. Rev.
Washington, U.S. Atomic Energy Commission,
1962.
730p. (Dept. of the Army pamphlet no. 39-3)
Editor: Samuel Glasstone.

1. Civilian defense. 2. Thermal radiation.
I. Glasstone, Samuel, ed. I. Title. II. U.S.
Atomic Energy Commission.

699.81
N18I   THERMAL RADIATION.
U.S. NAVAL CIVIL ENGINEERING
LABORATORY.
IGNITION OF FIRES AND FIRE SPREAD BY
THERMAL RADIATION, BY F.W. BROWN.
PORT HUENEME, CALIF., U.S. NAVAL CIVIL
ENGINEERING LABORATORY, 1962.
22P. (TECHNICAL NOTE N-442)

1. FIRE PROTECTION. 2. THERMAL
RADIATION. I. BROWN, F.W.

628.1
D27   The thermal stability of modified water.
Deryagin, B   V
The thermal stability of modified water, by
B.V. Deryagin and others. Garston, Eng.,
Building Research Station, 1970.
4p. (U.K. Building Research Station.
Library communication no. 1572)
Translated from the Russian [and reprinted
from] Doklady Akademii Nauk SSSR, 1970, 191 (4),
859-61.
1. Water-supply. I. U.K. Building Research
Station. II. Title. (Series)

697.3
F22   THERMAL RADIATION.
U.S. FEDERAL RADIATION COUNCIL.
REVISED FALLOUT ESTIMATES FOR
1964-1965 AND VERIFICATION OF THE 1963
PREDICTIONS. WASHINGTON, GOVT. PRINT.
OFF., 1964.
29P. (ITS REPORT NO. 6)

1. THERMAL RADIATION. I. TITLE:
FALLOUT ESTIMATES FOR 1964-65.

697.3
.V15   Thermal radiation.
Van Straaten, J F
Laf.   Thermal performance of buildings. New York,
Elsevier Pub. Co., 1967.
311p.
Bibliogrpahy: p. 248-297.

1. Thermal radiation. 2. Heat transmission.
3. Ventilation. I. Title.

690.22
B21   Thermal transmittance of wall constructions.
Beard, R
Thermal transmittance of wall constructions;
a review of relevant information, by R. Beard
and A. Dinnie. London, Clay Products Technical
Bureau, 1968.
15p. (Clay Products Technical Bureau.
Technical note, vol. 2, no. 5)

1. Walls. 2. Heat transmission. I. Dinnie,
A., jt. au. II. Clay Products Technical Bureau.
III. Title.

355.58
F67   THERMAL RADIATION.
U.S. FOREST SERVICE.
EFFECTS OF MASS FIRES ON PERSONNEL IN
SHELTERS. BY A. BROIDO AND A.W.
MCMASTERS. BERKELEY, CALIF., 1960.
84P. (PACIFIC SOUTHWEST FOREST AND
RANGE EXPERIMENT STATION, TECHNICAL
PAPER 50)

1. CIVILIAN DEFENSE. 2. THERMAL
RADIATION. I. BROIDO, A.
II. MCMASTERS, A.W.

697.3
A77   THERMAL RADIATION - CONGRESSES.
ASSOCIATION FOR APPLIED SOLAR ENERGY.
PROCEEDINGS OF THE WORLD SYMPOSIUM ON
APPLIED SOLAR ENERGY, 1955. MENLO PARK,
CALIF., STANFORD RESEARCH INSTITUTE,
1956-
V.
For Library holdings see main entry
CONFERENCE SPONSORED IN COOPERATION
WITH STANFORD RESEARCH INSTITUTE AND THE
UNIVERSITY OF ARIZONA.

1. THERMAL RADIATION - CONGRESSES.
2. HEATING, SOLAR - CONGRESSES.
I. STANFORD RESEARCH INSTITUTE.
(CONTINUED ON NEXT CARD)

VF
697.3
:621.415
S15   Thermodynamic criteria for heat pump
performance.
Sandfort, John F
Thermodynamic criteria for heat pump
performance. Heating, Piping & Air Conditioning, p.105-110, Sept. 1949. charts.
diagrs.
Reprint, Iowa Engineering Experiment
Station. Engineering report no. 1.

1. Heat pumps. I. Title. II. Series.

697.3
N17   THERMAL RADIATION.
U.S. NATIONAL ADVISORY COMMITTEE ON
RADIATION.
RADIOACTIVE CONTAMINATION OF THE
ENVIRONMENT: PUBLIC HEALTH ACTION.
REPORT TO THE SURGEON GENERAL, U.S.
PUBLIC HEALTH SERVICE. WASHINGTON, 1962.
11P.

NEWS RELEASE STATEMENT BY SURGEON
GENERAL ATTACHED, DATED JUNE 5, 1962.

1. THERMAL RADIATION. 2. AIR
POLLUTION. I. TITLE.

697.3
A77   ASSOCIATION FOR APPLIED SOLAR ENERGY.
PROCEEDINGS OF ...1956- (CARD 2)

STANFORD UNIVERSITY. II. ARIZONA.
UNIVERSITY. III. TITLE: WORLD
SYMPOSIUM ON APPLIED SOLAR ENERGY.

697.133
S85   Thermodynamic foundation of finite
elastic locking medium.
Sun, C   T
Thermodynamic foundation of finite
elastic locking medium. Ames, Engineering
Research Institute, Iowa State University,
1968.
58p. (Iowa. State University of Science
and Technology, Ames. Engineering Research
Institute. Engineering research report
70)
Bibliography: p. 57-58.
1. Heat transmission. I. Iowa. State
University of Science and Technology. Ames.
Engineering Research Institute. II.
Title.

699.85
N17E   THERMAL RADIATION.
U.S. NATIONAL BUREAU OF STANDARDS.
AN ENGINEERING METHOD FOR CALCULATING
PROTECTION AFFORDED BY STRUCTURES
AGAINST FALLOUT RADIATION, BY CHARLES
EISENHAUER. WASHINGTON, GOVT. PRINT.
OFF., 1964.
20P. (ITS MONOGRAPH 76)

1. PROTECTIVE CONSTRUCTION.
2. THERMAL RADIATION. I. TITLE.
II. EISENHAUER, CHARLES.

691.771
A58t   Thermal resistance of aluminum siding.
Aluminum Siding Association.
Thermal resistance of aluminum siding.
Chicago, 1963.
16p.

1. Aluminum. I. Title.

690.015
N17t   Thermo-osmosis.
National Research Council, Canada.
Division of Building Research.
Thermo-osmosis, by P. Habib, tr. by
D. A. Sinclair. Ottawa, 1957.
21p. diagrs., graphs. (Its Technical
translation TT-708)

"From Ann. Inst. Tech. Batiment et
Trav. Publ. (110): 130-136, 1957."

1. Building research. I. Habib, P
II. Title. (Series)

699.85
N17ST   THERMAL RADIATION.
U.S. NATIONAL BUREAU OF STANDARDS.
STRUCTURE SHIELDING AGAINST FALLOUT
RADIATION. WASHINGTON, 1962.
7L.

1. PROTECTIVE CONSTRUCTION.
2. THERMAL RADIATION. I. TITLE.

690.24
C85   Thermal shock resistance for built up membranes.
Cullen, William C
Thermal-shock resistance for built-up mem-
branes, by William C. Cullen and Thomas H. Boone.
Washington, U.S. Dept. of Commerce, National
Bureau of Standards, 1967.
13p. (National Bureau of Standards. Building
science series, 9)
1. Roofs and roofing. 2. Insulation. 3. Build-
ing materials. I. Boone, Thomas H., jt. au.
II. U.S. National Bureau of Standards.
III. Title.

355.58
K13o   Thermonuclear war.
Kahn, Herman.
On thermonuclear war. Princeton, N.J.,
Princeton Univ. Press, 1960.
651p.
Published for the Center of International
Studies, Woodrow Wilson School of Public and
International Affairs - Princeton University.

1. National defense. 2. Atomic bomb.
I. Title: Thermonuclear war. II. Princeton
University. (Center of Internation-
al Studies)

699.85
N17STR   THERMAL RADIATION.
U.S. NATIONAL BUREAU OF STANDARDS.
STRUCTURE SHIELDING AGAINST FALLOUT
RADIATION FROM NUCLEAR WEAPONS, BY L.V.
SPENCER. WASHINGTON, GOVT. PRINT.
OFF., 1962.
13P. (NBS MONOGRAPH 42)

1. PROTECTIVE CONSTRUCTION.
2. THERMAL RADIATION. I. SPENCER, L.V.
II. TITLE.

624.131
J86   THERMAL SOIL MECHANICS.
JUMIKIS, ALFREDS R
THERMAL SOIL MECHANICS. NEW
BRUNSWICK, N.J., RUTGERS UNIVERSITY
PRESS, 1966.
267P.

1. FROZEN GROUND. I. TITLE.

621.6
B84   Thermoplastic piping for portable water
distribution systems.
Building Research Advisory Board.
Thermoplastic piping for potable water dis-
tribution systems. Prepared by Task Group
T-52 of the Federal Construction Council,
Building Research Advisory Board, Div. of
Engineering, National Research Council. Wash.,
National Academy of Science, 1971.
52p. (BRAB-Federal Construction Council.
Technical report no. 61)

1. Pipes. 2. Water - Supply. I. Federal
Construction Council. II. Title.

697
M45   THERMOSTATIC CONTROL.
      MILES, V   C
      THERMOSTATIC CONTROL, PRINCIPLES AND
      PRACTICE. LONDON, NEWNES, 1965.
      215P.

      1. HEATING.   2. AIR CONDITIONING.
      I. TITLE.

      Thesaurus of English words and phrases.
R
030.8 Roget, Peter Mark, 1779-1869.
.R63t   The original Roget's thesaurus of English
1965   words and phrases. New ed., completely rev.
       and modernized by Robert A. Dutch. New York,
       St. Martin's Press, 1965.
          1405p.
          For the first time American spelling and
       usage are incorporated in the original Roget.

          1. English language. I. Dutch, Robert A.,
       ed. II. Title: Thesaurus of English words
       and phrases. 2. English language - Dictionaries.

658
(016) THESES.
F52   FLECHSIG, THEODORE S
       THE PREDICTIVE VALUE OF CONSUMER
       BUYING INTENTIONS; A STUDY OF AGGREGATE
       TIME SERIES. NEW BRUNSWICK, N.J., 1963.
       94 ℓ .
       BIBLIOGRAPHY: P. 92-94.
       SUBMITTED IN PARTIAL FULFILLMENT OF
       THE REQUIREMENTS OF THE STONIER GRADUATE
       SCHOOL OF BANKING CONDUCTED BY THE
       AMERICAN BANKERS ASSOCIATION AT RUTGERS,
       THE STATE UNIVERSITY.

       1. BUYING.   2. THESES.   I. TITLE.
       II. AMERICAN BANKERS ASSOCIATION.
                    (CONTINUED ON NEXT CARD)

711.583
(74461) Thernstrom, Stephan.
T32   Poverty, planning, and politics in the
         New Boston: the origins of ABCD. New York,
         Basic Books, 1969.
           190p.

         1. Community development - Boston.
         2. Urban renewal - Boston. I. Title.

Ref.
808.8   ...Thesaurus of quotations.
F96   Fuller, Edmund
          2500 anecdotes for all occasions: a new
       classified collection of the best anecdotes
       from ancient times to the present day.
       Garden City, N. Y., Doubleday, 1943.
          495 p.

          Originally published as Thesaurus of anec-
       dotes.

          1. Quotations. I. Title. II. Title:...Thesaurus
       of quotations.
                                          ct

658
(016) FLECHSIG, THEODORE S THE PREDICTIVE
F52   VALUE ...1963.   (CARD 2)

       III. TITLE: CONSUMER BUYING
       INTENTIONS.

711.4
(09)   Thernstrom, Stephen, ed.
Y15   Yale Conference on the Nineteenth-Century
        Industrial City, New Haven, 1968.
          Nineteenth-century cities; essays in the new
       urban history. Edited by Stephan Thernstrom and
       Richard Sennett. New Haven, Yale University
       Press, 1969.
          430p. (Yale studies of the city, 1)

          1. City planning - History. 2. City growth.
       3. Community structure. I. Thernstrom, Stephen,
       ed. II. Sennett, Richard, jt. ed. III. Title.

711.437
032   These things we tried.
       Ogden, Jean (Carter)
          These things we tried; a five-year experiment
       in community development initiated and carried out
       by the Extension Division of the University of
       Virginia, by Jean Carter Ogden and Jesse Switzer
       Ogden.   University, Va., Univ. of Virginia,
       Extension Division, Oct. 15, 1947.
          x, 432 p.   illus., tables.   (Virginia.
       University. Extension series. v. 25, no. 6)
          "Publications of the special projects":
       p. [414]-424.

029
T87   Theses.
       Turabian, Kate L
          A manual for writers of term papers, theses
       and dissertations. Rev. Chicago, U. of
       Chicago Press, 1958.
          82p. tables.

          1. Style manuals. 2. Theses.   I. Title.

029
A75T   THESAURUS OF ASTIA DESCRIPTORS.
       U.S. ARMED SERVICES TECHNICAL
       INFORMATION AGENCY.
       THESAURUS OF ASTIA DESCRIPTORS.   2D
       ED. ARLINGTON, VA., 1962.
       673P.

       1. INDEXING.   2. TECHNOLOGY -
       CATALOGING.   I. TITLE.

362.4
P72t   These, too, must be equal.
       U.S. President's Committee on Mental
       Retardation.
          These, too, must be equal; America's
       needs in habilitation and employment of the
       mentally retarded. Wash., 1969.
          22p.
          President's Committee on Mental
       Retardation/President's Committee on
       Employment of the Handicapped.
          1. Handicapped. 2. Housing for the
       handicapped. I. U.S. President's Committee
       on Employment of the Handicapped. II. Title.

Ref.
029   Theses.
T87   Turabian, Kate L
1967   A manual for writers of term papers, theses,
       and dissertations. 3d ed rev. Chicago,
       University of Chicago Press, 1967.
          164p. (Phoenix books)

          1. Style manuals, 2. Theses. I. Title.

025.3   Thesaurus of descriptive terms and code book.
834   U.S. Bureau of Ships.
          Bureau of Ships technical library, thesaurus
       of descriptive terms and code book. 1st ed.
       Washington, U.S. Bureau of Ships, Navy Dept.,
       1963.
          1v. (NAVSHIPS-250-210-1)

          1. Cataloging. 2. Automation. 3. Documentation.
       I. Title: Thesaurus of descriptive terms and
       code book.

016
B51   THESES.
       Black, Dorothy M   comp.
          Guide to lists of master's theses, compiled by Dorothy M.
       Black. Chicago, American Library Association, 1965.
          144 p. 24 cm.

          1. Theses.
                              I. Title.

       Z5055.U49B55   016.011   65-24955
       Library of Congress   [14-1]

332
A52   Theses - Bibliography
1956   American Bankers Association. Graduate School of
       Banking.
          Cumulative catalogue of theses, 1937-1956.
       New York [1956]
          199p.

          Annotated.

332
(016) Supplement,
A52
Suppl

020
538.56   Thesaurus of engineering and scientific terms
E53   Engineers Joint Council.
          Thesaurus of engineering and scientific
       terms. A list of engineering and related
       scientific terms and their relationships
       for use as a vocabulary reference in index-
       ing and retrieving technical information.
       1st ed. New York, 1967.
          690p.
          Major revision of Thesaurus of engineer-
       ing terms, Engineers Joint Council, May
       1964.
          Prepared in joint operation with the
       U.S. Dept.   of Defense.

                 (Cont'd on next card)

R
029   Theses.
C15   Campbell, William Giles.
          A form book for thesis writing. Boston,
       Houghton Mifflin, 1939.
          1v. diagrs., tables.

          1. Style manuals.   2. Theses.

332
(016) Theses - Bibliography.
A52   American Bankers Association. Graduate School of
1951   Banking.
          Cumulative catalogue of theses, 1937-1951.
       New York [1951?]
          169 p.

          Annotated.

          1. Banks and banking-Bibl. 2. Theses-Bibl.

020
538.56   Engineers Joint Council.   Thesaurus of
E53   engineering...1967.   (Card 2)

          1. Library science - Automation.
       2. Cataloging. 3. Engineering - Dict.
       I. U.S. Dept. of Defense. II. Title.
       III. Title: Engineering and scientific
       terms.

388
F22   Theses.
       Fedel, Robert F
          Techniques and factors relating to future
       rapid transit demand. Boston, 1962.
          139p.
          Thesis-Massachusetts Institute of
       Technology.

          1. Transportation. 2. Journey to work.
       3. Theses. I. Massachusetts Institute of
       Technology.

332
(016) Theses - Bibliography.
A52   American Bankers Association. Stonier
1961   Graduate School of Banking.
          Cumulative catalog of theses, 1937-1961.
       New York [1962?]
          185p.
          Annotated.
       -- ---Supplement. New York, 1965.
          45p.

          1. Banks and banking - Bibl.
       2. Theses - Bibl.

016
A52

THESES - BIBLIOGRAPHY.
American doctoral dissertations, 1955/56-
Compiled for the Association of Research
Libraries. Ann Arbor, Mich., University
Microfilms, 1957-
   v. annual. (Dissertation abstracts,

SEE SHELF LIST FOR LIBRARY HOLDINGS
Title varies. Index to American doctoral
dissertations, v. 16, 1955/56-v. 23, 1962/63;
American doctoral dissertations, v. 24, 1963/64-

1. Theses - Bibliography. I. Association of
Research Libraries. II. Title: Index to American doctoral dissertations.

016
G26
1967

THESES - BIBLIOGRAPHY.
Georgia Tech Library Staff Association.
Theses and dissertations accepted in partial
fulfillment of the requirements for graduate
degrees by the Georgia Institute of Technology.
Atlanta, 1967.
   16p.
   Fourth supplement to the anniversary edition.

1. Theses - Bibl. 2. City planning - Bibl.
I. Georgia Institute of Technology. II. Title.

658.3
(016)
C48D
1957

THESES - BIBLIOGRAPHY.
U.S. CIVIL SERVICE COMMISSION. LIBRARY
DISSERTATION AND THESES RELATING TO
PERSONNEL ADMINISTRATION ACCEPTED BY
AMERICAN COLLEGES AND UNIVERSITIES,
1955. WASHINGTON, 1957.
   20P.

1. PERSONNEL MANAGEMENT -
BIBILIOGRAPHY. 2. THESES -
BIBLIOGRAPHY.

VF
500
(016)
G26

Theses - Bibliography.
Georgia. State Engineering Experiment Station.
Theses and dissertations accepted in partial
fulfillment of the requirements for graduate
degrees by the Georgia Institute of Technology,
1962, compiled and edited by the Georgia Tech
Library Staff Association, Prince Gilbert
Memorial Library. Atlanta, Engineering Experiment Station, Georgia Institute of Technology,
1962.
   8p. (Its Bulletin 22. Suppl. no. 5)

1. Thesis - Bibl. 2. Science - Bibl.

500.15
(016)
I55

Theses - Bibliography.
Illinois Institute of Technology.
Publications from the Illinois Institute of
Technology, v. 5-
Chicago, Dec. 1956-
   v. annual
References to theses by graduate students
and to scientific and scholarly works
published by the staff: College and Graduate
School, Armour Research Foundation, Institute
of Gas Technology.

(see card 2)

020
(016)
U54

Theses - Bibliography.
University Microfilms, inc.
Dissertations in library science,
1951-1966. [Ann Arbor, Mich., 1967?]
   16p.

1. Library science - Bibl.
2. Theses - Bibl. I. Title.

016
G26a

Theses - Bibliography.
Georgia Institute of Technology.
(Graduate Div.)
Abstracts of theses,

Atlanta,
   v. biennial (Its vol.

For complete information see shelf
list.

1. Theses - Bibl. 2. Engineering
research - Bibl. 3. City
planning - Bibl.

500.15
(016)
I55

Illinois Institute of Technology.
Publications... Dec. 1956 - (card 2)

1. Theses - Bibliography. 2. Scientific
research - Bibliography. I. Illinois
Institute of Technology. Armour Research
Foundation. II. Illinois Institute of
Technology. Institute of Gas Technology.

711.4
(016)
V15

Theses - Bibliography.
Vance, Mary.
Abstracts of student theses in city and
regional planning. Compiled and edited by
American Institute of Planners. Washington, American Institute of Planners, 1965.
   83p. (American Institute of Planners.
Issue I)

1. City planning - Bibl. 2. Regional
planning - Bibl. 3. Theses - Bibl.
I. American Institute of Planners, Washington. II. Title.

016
G26
1963

Theses - Bibliography.
Georgia Institute of Technology. Library.
The anniversary edition of theses and
dissertations accepted in partial fulfillment
of the requirements for graduate degrees by
the Georgia Institute of Technology, 1925-
1963. Atlanta, 1963.
   120p.
"Supersedes previous lists of theses published by the
Engineering Experiment Station as Bulletin 22 and its
Supplements 1 through 5."
   1. Theses - Bibliography. 2. City planning -
Bibliography. I. Title.

016
K42

Theses - Bibliography.
Kidder, Frederick Elvyn, comp.
Theses on Pan American topics; prepared by
candidates for doctoral degrees in universities
and colleges in the United States and Canada.
Compiled by Frederick Elvyn Kidder and Allen
David Bushong. Pan American Union, General
Secretariat of the Organization of American
States, 1962.
   124p. (Pan American Union. Columbus Memorial
Library. Bibliographic series, no. 5, 4th ed.)
1. Theses - Bibl. I. Bushong, Allen David, jt. comp.
II. Pan American Union. Columbus Memorial
Library.

016
G26
1965

Theses and dissertations accepted in partial
fulfillment of the requirements for graduate...
Georgia Tech Library Staff Association.
Theses and dissertations accepted in partial
fulfillment of the requirements for graduate
degrees by the Georgia Institute of Technology.
Atlanta, 1965.
   10p.
   Second supplement to the anniversary
edition.

1. Theses - Bibl. 2. City planning -
Bibl. I. Georgia Institute of Technology.
II. Title.

016
G26
1964

Theses - Bibliography.
Georgia Tech Library Staff Association.
Theses and dissertations accepted in
partial fulfillment of the requirements for
graduate degrees by the Georgia Institute
of Technology, 1964. Atlanta, Price Gilbert
Memorial Library, Georgia Institute of
Technology, 1964.
   10p.
   First supplement to the anniversary edition.

1. Theses - Bibl. 2. Engineering research - Bibl.
3. City planning - Bibl.

711.4
(016)
L14

Theses- Bibliography.
Lakshmanan, Teresa Romanowska.
Survey of urban geographical research in
progress in the United States and Canada in
1963/64. Washington, 1965.
   148p.
   Thesis - Catholic University.
   1. City planning - Bibl. 2. City growth -
Bibl. 3. Theses - Bibl. I. Title: Urban geographical research in progress in the United
States and Canada.

016
G26
1966

Theses and dissertations accepted in partial fulfillment of the requirements for graduate degrees.
Georgia Tech Library Staff Association.
Theses and dissertations accepted in partial fulfillment of the requirements for
graduate degrees by the Georgia Institute of
Technology. Atlanta, 1966.
   14p.
   Third supplement to the anniversary
edition.

1. Theses - Bibl. 2. City planning -
Bibl. I. Georgia Institute of Technology.
II. Title.

016
G26
1965

Theses - Bibliography.
Georgia Tech Library Staff Association.
Theses and dissertations accepted in partial
fulfillment of the requirements for graduate
degrees by the Georgia Institute of Technology.
Atlanta, 1965.
   10p.
   Second supplement to the anniversary
edition.

1. Theses - Bibl. 2. City planning -
Bibl. I. Georgia Institute of Technology.
II. Title.

VF
728
.392
(016)
A37

Theses - Bibliography.
U.S. Dept. of Agriculture. (Agricultural
Research Service.)
Titles of completed theses in home economics
and related fields in colleges and universities
of the United States, 1952-1953. Washington,
Dec. 1953.
   iv, 48 p. tables.
   In cooperation with Office of Education.
Processed.
1.Family living requirements. 2.Theses-Bibl.
I.U.S. Office of Education. II.Title.

016
G26
1967

Theses and dissertations accepted in partial
fulfillment of the requirements for...
Georgia Tech Library Staff Association.
Theses and dissertations accepted in partial
fulfillment of the requirements for graduate
degrees by the Georgia Institute of Technology.
Atlanta, 1967.
   16p.
   Fourth supplement to the anniversary edition.

1. Theses - Bibl. 2. City planning - Bibl.
I. Georgia Institute of Technology. II. Title.

016
G26
1966

Theses - Bibliography.
Georgia Tech Library Staff Association.
Theses and dissertations accepted in partial fulfillment of the requirements for
graduate degrees by the Georgia Institute of
Technology. Atlanta, 1966.
   14p.
   Third supplement to the anniversary
edition.

1. Theses - Bibl. 2. City planning -
Bibl. I. Georgia Institute of Technology.
II. Title.

658.3
(016)
C48d

Theses - Bibliography.
U.S. Civil Service Commission. Library.
Dissertations and theses relating to
personnel administration. Wash., 1965.
   28p.

1. Personnel management - Bibl.
2. Theses - Bibl. I. Title.

VF
711(016)
A52
1949

Thesis titles on planning.
American Society of Planning Officials.
Thesis titles on planning. Chicago, Ill.
[Nov. 1949]
   25 l.

Mimeographed.

1.Planning-Bibl. 2.City planning-Research. I.Title.

5476
5477
5478   THETFORD, VT. PLANNING COMMISSION.
COMPREHENSIVE PLAN: BASIC STUDIES
REPORT; PROPOSED ZONING REGULATIONS;
PROPOSED SUBDIVISION REGULATIONS. BY
E.H. LORD-WOOD ASSOCIATES. THETFORD,
1965.
  3 V. (HUD 701 REPORT)

------ SUPPLEMENTARY MATERIAL IN
ENVELOPE.

1. CITY PLANNING - THETFORD, VT.
I. LORD-WOOD (E.H.) ASSOCIATES.
II. HUD. 701. THETFORD, VT.

728.1
T32   THEY LIKE [FHA] TITLE I LOANS.
[MADISON, WIS.] 1957.
  11-14P.
ARTICLE FROM JULY 1957 OF CREDIT UNION
BRIDGE.

1. DIRECT LOANS FOR HOUSING. 2. U.S.
FEDERAL HOUSING ADMINISTRATION.
I. CREDIT UNION BRIDGE. II. TITLE:
TITLE I LOANS.

690.015
(485)   Thiberg, Sven. Beskrivnings-...1969.
S82   (Card 2)
R18
1969   2. Building documentation.
3. Architecture, Domestic - Designs and
plans. I. Stockholm. Statens Institut
för Byggnadsforskning. II. Title:
System for description and evaluation
of features of housing and urban areas.

5464   THETFORD, VT. PLANNING COMMISSION.
COMPREHENSIVE PLAN DIGEST, 1965. BY
E.H. LORD-WOOD ASSOCIATES. THETFORD,
1965.
  6P. (HUD 701 REPORT)

------ SUPPLEMENTARY MATERIAL IN
ENVELOPE.

1. CITY PLANNING - THETFORD, VT.
I. LORD-WOOD (E.H.) ASSOCIATES.
II. HUD. 701. THETFORD, VT.

           They preach what they practice.
VF
301   Willis, Jeannie.
W45   They preach what they practice. When
customers moved to the suburbs, department
stores followed them with branch stores.
So have many churches. But what happens
to a church which does not move? Reproduced
from the Episcopalian, Oct. 1962, p. 46-52.

1. Church and social problems. I. Title.

690.015
(485)   Thiberg, Sven.
S82   The determination of dimensions by full-
R46   scale laboratory tests. Stockholm, National
1968   Swedish Institute for Building Research, 1968.
  86p. (Stockholm. Statens institut för
byggnadsforskning. Rapport 46:1968)
  Bibliography: p. 81-86.
  1. Building research - Sweden. 2. Sweden -
Building research. I. Stockholm, Statens
institut för byggnadsforskning. II. Title.

331
L11T   THEY ARE AMERICAN.
  U.S. DEPT. OF LABOR.
    THEY ARE AMERICA ! A REPORT TO THE
AMERICAN PEOPLE. WASHINGTON, GOVT.
PRINT. OFF., 1957.
  83P.

1. LABOR SUPPLY. I. TITLE.

325
B65   THEY SEEK A CITY.
  BONTEMPS, ARNAL WENDELL, 1902-
    THEY SEEK A CITY, 1ST ED. GARDEN CITY,
N.Y., DOUBLEDAY, DORAN, 1945.
  266P.

AT HEAD OF TITLE: ARNA BONTEMPS AND
JACK CONROY.
  A SELECTED LIST OF REFERENCES AND
SOURCES : P.253-258.

1. NEGROES. 2. MINORITY GROUPS -
HOUSING. I. CONROY, JACK, JT. AU.
II. TITLE.

690.015
(485)   Thiberg, Sven.
S82   Non-institutional housing for the elderly.
R5   Stockholm, 1967.
1967   36p. (Sweden. Statens Kommitté för
Byggnadsforskning. Rapport 5:1967)

1. Building research - Sweden. 2. Housing for the aged - Sweden. I. Sweden.
Statens Kommitté för Byggnadsforskning.

325
(09)
R22   They came in chains; Americans from Africa.
  Redding, Jay Saunders.
    They came in chains; Americans from Africa.
Ed. by Louis Adamic. Philadelphia, Lippincott,
1969.
  320p.

Bibliography: p. 304-308.

1. Negroes - History. I. Adamic, Louis, ed.
II. Title.

325.2
H15   They've been neglected too long.
  Hall, Nathaniel B
    They've been neglected too long. New York,
Vantage Press, 1969.
  79p.

Bibliography: p. 78-79.

1. Race relations. 2. Social conditions.
I. Title.

690.015
(485)   Thiberg, Sven.
S82   Orientation and floor-level; a study in
R35   preferences of dwellers in point-blocks, by
1966   Sven Thiberg and Surya Kant Misra. Stockholm,
National Swedish Institute for Building
Research, 1966.
  19p. (Sweden. National Swedish
Institute for Building Research. Report
35:1966)
  1. Building research - Sweden. 2. Architecture, Domestic - Design. 3. Family
living require-   ments. I. Misra, Surya
Kant, jt.au.   II. Sweden. Statens
Kommitté för   Byggnadsforskning.

VF
320
C31t   They grade the Congress.
  Chamber of Commerce of the United States.
    They grade the Congress: a summary of rat-
ings of the U.S. House of Representatives
and the U.S. Senate,

Washington, 19

v.

For complete information see main card.

1. Political science. 2. U.S. Congress.
I. Title.

420.1
(016)
L41   Thibault, Charles D ed.
  U.S. Library of Congress. Science and
Technology Division.
    Materials research abstracts, a review of
the Air Force materials research and develop-
ment. Edited by Charles D. Thibault.
[Washington] Published for Directorate of
Materials Processes, Aeronautical Systems
Division, Wright-Patterson Air Force Base,
Ohio, 1962.
  534p.

1. Strength of materials - Bibl.
I. Thibault,   Charles D., ed.
II. U.S. Air   Force. III. Title

693.002.22
(485)   Thiberg, Sven.
T34   Rommål, plantyper, hustyper för indus-
triell bygging - orientering om svenske
forskningsprosjekte. (Room dimensions,
types of design, and types of building construction - a description of some Swedish
research projects) Oslo, Norges Byggforskningsinstitutt, 1967.
  9 p. (Oslo. Norges Byggforskningsinstitutt. Saertrykk 141)
  Saertrykk fra Byggmesteren nr. 5/1967.
  1. Prefabricated construction. 2. Room
sizes. I. Oslo. Norges Byggforskningsinstitutt.
II. Title.

331
F68t   They have the power: we have the people.
  U.S. Equal Employment Opportunity Commission.
    They have the power: we have the people; the
status of equal employment opportunity in
Houston, Tex., 1970. [Wash., 1970]
  103p. (An equal employment opportunity
report)

1. Employment - Minority groups.
I. Title.

690.015
(485)
S 82
R41
1970   Thiberg, Alice.
    Planutformning av bostadsrum; förslag till
måttunderlag och dimensioneringsprinciper
samt planexempel (Room layouts; draft of
dimensional guide and dimensioning principles
illustrated by examples of plans) Stockholm,
1970.
  88p. (Stockholm. Statens Institut för
Byggnadsforskning. Rapport R41:1970)
  1. Building research - Sweden. 2. Space
considerations. I. Stockholm. Statens
Institut för Byggnadsforskning. II. Title:
Room layouts.

690.015
(485)   Thiberg, Sven.
S82   Samhällsplanering för rörelsehindrade
R50   - boende i invalidbostäder (Town planning
1968   for the disabled - special housing)
Stockholm, Statens Institut för Byggnads-
forskning, 1968.
  35p. (Stockholm. Statens Institut for
Byggnadsforskning. Rapport 50:1968)
  English summary.
  1. Building research - Sweden. 2. Sweden -
Building research. 3. Housing for the
handicapped. I. Stockholm. Statens
Institut för   Byggnadsforskning.
II. Title: Town planning for the
disabled -   special housing.

728.3
(41)
H68   THEY KNOW WHAT THEY WANT.
  HOUSE-BUILDING INDUSTRIES' STANDING
COMMITTEE.
    THEY KNOW WHAT THEY WANT:
DEMONSTRATION - PERMANENT HOUSES 1946.
LONDON, 1946.
  56P.

1. MODEL HOUSES - U.K.
2. ARCHITECTURE, DOMESTIC - DESIGNS AND
PLANS. I. TITLE.

690.015
(485)
S82
R18
1969   Thiberg, Sven.
    Beskrivnings- och värderingssystem för
bostads- och stadsdelsegenskaper
(System for description and evaluation of
features of housing and urban areas)
Stockholm, Statens Institut for
Byggnadsforskning, 1969.
  54p. (Stockholm. Statens Institut för
Byggnadsforskning. Rapport 18:1969)
  English summary.

  1. Build-   ing research - Sweden.
              (Cont'd on next card)

  Thibodaux, La. Regional Planning Commission.
711.4   Martin (Dan S.) and Associates.
(76339)   Economic base analysis and population fore-
M17m   cast, Thibodaux planning region, Thibodaux,
pt. 1   Louisiana. [Prepared for] Thibodaux Regional
Planning Commission. New Orleans, 1957.
  2 p. diagrs., maps tables.
  Chapter 1 of the Master plan.
  U.S. Urban Renewal Administration, Urban
Planning Assistance Program.
  1. Master plan - Thibodaux, La. 2. Economic
base studies - Thibodaux, La. 3. Population -
Thibodaux, La. I. Thibodaux, La. Regional Plan-
ning Commission. II. U.S. Urban Renewal
Administration.   Urban Planning Assistance
Program.

Thibodaux, La. Regional Planning Commission.

711.4 Martin (Dan S.) and Associates.
(76339) (76339) Land use analysis and land use plan, Thibo-
M17m daux planning region, Thibodaux, Louisiana.
pt. 2 [Prepared for] Thibodaux Regional Planning
Commission. New Orleans, 1957.
22p. maps, tables.
Chapter 2 of the Master plan.
U.S. Urban Renewal Administration, Urban
Planning Assistance Program.
1. Master plan - Thibodaux, La. 2. Land use -
Thibodaux, La. I. Thibodaux, La. Regional Plan-
ning Commission. II. U.S. Urban Renewal Ad-
ministration. Urban Planning Assistance
Program.

Thibodaux, La. Regional Planning Commission.

711.4 Martin (Dan S.) and Associates.
(76339) Major street plan, Thibodaux planning
M17m region, Thibodaux, Louisiana. [Prepared for]
pt. 3 Thibodaux Regional Planning Commission. New
Orleans, 1957.
16p. diagrs., maps.
Chapter [3] of the Master plan.
U.S. Urban Renewal Administration, Urban
Planning Assistance Program.
1. Master plan - Thibodaux, La. 2. Street
planning - Thibodaux, La. I. Thibodaux, La.
Regional Planning Commission. II. U.S. Urban
Renewal Administration. Urban Planning Assist-
ance Program. Thibodaux, La.

Thibodaux, La. Regional Planning Commission.

333.38 Martin (Dan S.) and Associates.
(76339) Subdivision regulations, Thibodaux plan-
M17 ning region, Louisiana. Prepared for the
Thibodaux Regional Planning Commission.
[New Orleans] 1959.
20p.
U.S. Urban Renewal Administration, Urban Planning
Assistance Program.
1. Subdivision regulation - Thibodaux, La. I.
Thibodaux, La. Regional Planning Commission.
II. U.S. URA-UPAP. Thibodaux, La.

711.5 Thibodaux, La. Regional Planning Commission
(76339 Martin (Dan S.) and Associates.
:347) Zoning ordinance, Thibodaux, Louisiana.
M17 [Prepared for Thibodaux Regional Planning
Commission] New Orleans, 1958.
1v. maps.

U.S. Urban Renewal Administration, Urban
Planning Assistance Program.

1. Zoning legislation - Thibodaux, La. I. Thibodaux,
La. Regional Planning Commission. II. U.S. URA-UPAP.
Thibodaux, La.

Thick particleboards with pulp chip cores...

690.24 U.S. Forest Products Laboratory, Madison,
F67t Wis.
Thick particleboards with pulp chip cores;
possibilities as roof decking, by Bruce G.
Heebink and Wayne C. Lewis. Madison, 1967.
13p. (U.S. Forest Service. Research note
FPL-0174)
1. Roofs and roofing. I. Heebink,
Bruce G. II. Lewis, Wayne C. III. Title.

711.4 THIEL, PHILIP.
T34 THE PROBLEM OF SEQUENTIAL
CONNECTEDNESS IN THE URBAN ENVIRONMENT.
SEATTLE. UNIVERSITY OF WASHINGTON,
DEPT. OF URBAN PLANNING, 1963.
29L. (URBAN PLANNING DEVELOPMENT
SERIES, NO. 1)

1. CITY PLANNING. I. TITLE.

628.1 Thiele, Heinrich J
(791) Present and future water use and its
T34 effect on planning in Maricopa County,
Arizona. A study for the Maricopa County
Board of Supervisors and the Maricopa County
Planning and Zoning Dept. Scottsdale, Ariz.,
1965.
60p.

Bibliography: p. 57-60.

1. Water-supply - Maricopa Co., Ariz. 2. County
planning - Maricopa Co., Ariz. 3. Land use -
Maricopa Co., Ariz. I. Maricopa County,
Ariz. Planning and Zon- ing Dept. II. Title.

---

308 Thigpenn, James A
A52 Improvement of land title records.
1969 (In American Congress on Surveying and
Mapping. Papers from the 29th annual meeting.
1969. p. 29-37)

1. Land titles. I. Title.

728.1 THIMMES, JAMES G
T34 HOUSING FOR AMERICA, STATEMENT BY
JAMES G. THIMMES, PRESIDENT'S ADVISORY
COMMITTEE ON HOUSING. WASH., CIO
HOUSING COMMITTEE, 1954.
8P.

1. HOUSING. I. U.S. PRESIDENTS'
ADVISORY COMMITTEE ON HOUSING.

VF Thin-walled cylindrical and barrel-shaped
691.116 plywood shells.
F67 U.S. Forest Service. Forest Products Laboratory,
no.1323 Madison, Wis.
A comparison of the buckling strength of thin-
walled cylindrical and barrel-shaped plywood
shells, by Edward W. Kuenzi. Madison, Wis.,
June 1943.
3 p. illus., graph, table. (Its no. 1323)

Processed.

1.Plywood. I.Kuenzi, Edward W. II.Title;Thin-walled
cylindrical and barrel-shaped plywood shells.

VF Thin-walled plywood cylinders in bending.
691.116 U.S. Forest Service. Forest Products Laboratory,
F67 Madison, Wis.
no.1502 Thin-walled plywood cylinders in bending, by
Edward W. Kuenzi. Madison, Wis., Feb. 1944.
4 p. diagr., graphs, table. (Its no. 1502)

Processed.

1.Plywood. I.Kuenzi, Edward W. II.Title.

Thin-walled structures.

623 Chilver, A H ed.
C34 Thin-walled structures; a collection of
papers on the stability and strength of thin-
walled structural members and frames. New York,
Ref. J. Wiley, 1967.
303p.

1. Structural engineering. 2. Strength of
materials. 3. Walls. I. Title.

Think big about small parks.

VF Hoving, Thomas P F
712.21 Think big about small parks. Reproduced
(7471) from the New York Times magazine, April 10,
H68 1966.
[5]p.

1. Parks - New York (City) 2. Recreation -
New York (City) I. New York Times magazine.
II. Title.

389.1 Think metric.
U54 U.K. Ministry of Public Building and Works.
Think metric. London, H.M.S.O., 1969.
[6] p.
CI/SfB (F7)
Leaflet suggests guide lines for learning
and appreciating metric units of measurements.

1. Metric system. 2. Building industry -
U.K. I. Title.

Thinking ahead; fiasco of urban renewal.

711.585 Anderson, Martin.
A522t Thinking ahead; fiasco of urban
renewal. Reproduced from Harvard
business review, Jan./Feb. 1965.
[11]p.

1. Urban renewal. 2. Urban renewal -
Social effect. I. Harvard business
review. II. Title.

Thinking about cities.

352 Pascal, Anthony H ed.
P17t Thinking about cities: new perspectives on
urban problems. Anthony H. Pascal, editor.
Belmont, Calif., Dickenson Pub. Co., 1970.
188p.
Papers originally presented at the Workshop
on Urban Programs held at the Rand Corporation
in 1967-68. Jointl6 sponsored by Rand and the
Ford Foundation.
1. Municipal government. 2. Race relations.
3. Civil disorders. I. Rand Corp. II. Title.

728.1 Thinking about housing.
I75 Isler, Morton L
Thinking about housing; a policy research
agenda. Wash., Urban Institute, 1970.
47p.

1. Housing. I. Urban Institute. II. Title.

362.6 THINKING OF BUILDING A NURSING HOME.
B14 BAINUM, ROBERT.
THINKING OF BUILDING A NURSING HOME
FAIRFAX, VA., 1963.
132P.

COLLECTION OF BUSINESS FORMS USED AT
WHEATON NURSING HOME, WHEATON, MD.
P.80-132.

1. NURSING HOMES. I. WHEATON NURSING
HOME, WHEATON, MD. II. TITLE.

728.1 Thiokol Chemical Corp.
(76212) Forest Heights low income home ownership
T34 program. Research and final report. Submitted
to Office of Research and Technology, U.S.
Dept. of Housing and Urban Development.
Ogden, Utah, 1970.
1v.
U.S. Dept. of Housing and Urban Development.
Low-Income Housing Demonstration Project.
Contract no. H-1019. Project LIHD-Miss.-1.
1. Low-income housing - Gulfport, Miss.
2. Home ownership. I. Title. II. U.S. HUD-
Low-Income Housing Demonstration Project.
Gulfport, Miss.

Third Australian Building Research Congress,
691 1967.
(95) Brealey, T B
B72 The use of local resources for building in
New Guinea. Melbourne, Div. of Building Re-
search, Commonwealth Scientific and Industrial
Research Organization, 1967.
4p. (Australia. Commonwealth Scientific
and Industrial Research Organization, Div. of
Building Research. Reprint no. 401)
Reprinted from Proceedings of the third
Australian Building Research Congress, 1967.
1. Building materials - New Guinea.
2. Housing in the tropics. I. Australia.
Commonwealth Scientific and Industrial
Research Organi zation. (Div. of Building
(Cont'd on next card)

---

691 Brealey, T B The use of local re-
(95) sources...1967. (Card 2)
B72
Research) II. Third Australian Building Research Congress, 1967. III. Title.

920
T17

The third door.
Tarry, Ellen.
The third door; the autobiography of an American Negro woman. New York, Guild Press, 1966.
374p.

1. Tarry, Ellen. 2. Negroes. I. Title.

Thirty fourth street-midtown assn.   NOT RUSH

What are the nation's cities doing about traffic and parking?
Summary of developments to aid parking; short description of situation in 44 cities.

Ordered 4-1-49

Received 8-9

NYC, NY   *above author*
Dec. 1948   16p.

116 W. 34 St., N. Y. C., NY.

362.6
C15t

This is CAHA.
California Association of Homes for the Aging.
This is CAHA; an introduction to the Association and the homes and persons it serves. Sacramento, 1970.
24p.

1. Old age. 2. Nursing homes - Calif. I. Title.

658
:538.56
A52

The third generation computer; software issues, information input, access...
American Management Association.
The third generation computer; software issues, information input, access, and retrieval, management information systems. New York, American Management Association, Administrative Services Div., 1966.
64p.   (Its AMA management bulletin 79)

1. Management - Automation. I. Title. (Series)

711.4
N17th

31 minds explore our government.
National Association of Home Builders.
31 minds explore our environment. A report of the Committee on Environmental Design. Washington, 1965.
23p.

1. City planning. I. Title.

331
(77717)
I68

This is Cherokee County.
Iowa. Employment Security Commission.
This is Cherokee County; an Iowa manpower report. Des Moines, 1970.
19p.

1. Labor supply - Cherokee Co., Iowa.
2. Employment - Cherokee Co., Iowa. I. Title

629.136
N64

The third London airport with particular reference to Foulness.
Noise Abatement Society.
The third London airport with particular reference to Foulness.
[n.p., 1969?]
78p.

Suppl.   — —— Supplement.
[7]p.

1. Airports. 2. Site selection - U.K. 3. Noise. I. Title.

728.3
P65TH

34 OUTSTANDING DESIGNS PLUS 16 VACATION HOMES.
POLLMAN, RICHARD B
34 OUTSTANDING DESIGNS PLUS 16 VACATION HOMES. DETROIT, HOME PLANNERS, INC., 1962.
48P. (DESIGNS FOR CONVENIENT LIVING, BOOK NO. 4)

1. ARCHITECTURE, DOMESTIC - DESIGNS AND PLANS. I. TITLE.

331
(77856)
I68

This is Clarke County.
Iowa. Employment Security Commission.
This is Clarke County; an Iowa manpower report. Des Moines, 1969.
21p.

1. Labor supply - Clarke Co., Iowa.
2. Employment - Clarke Co., Iowa. I. Title.

711.3
(7526)
B15th

The third million.
Baltimore Regional Planning Council.
The third million; Baltimore regional progress report, 1969-1970. [Baltimore, 1969]
28p.
Bibliography: p. 26-28.

U.S. Dept. of Housing and Urban Development. UPAP.

1. Metro-   politan area planning -
Baltimore.   I. U.S. HUD-UPAP.
Baltimore.   II. Title.

647.1
:728.1
W67

THE 39 STEPS.
WORKSHOP 221, INC., WASHINGTON, D.C.
THE 39 STEPS: A BRAND-NEW, UNIQUE AND COMPLETE OPERATIONAL GUIDE FOR HOUSING, REHABILITATION, RELOCATION, AND MODERATE INCOME HOUSING UNDER SECTION 221. WASHINGTON, 1961.
1 V.

1. FAMILY INCOME AND EXPENDITURE - HOUSING. 2. URBAN RENEWAL. I. HAAS, JOHN H. II. TITLE. III. TITLE: MODERATE INCOME HOUSING UNDER SECTION 221.

VF
332.72
F17t

This is FHA.
U.S. Farmers Home Administration.
This is FHA. [Wash.] 1971.
folder. (PA-973)

1. Mortgage finance. I. Title.

628.44
S51

Third pollution; the national problem of solid waste disposal.
Small, William E
Third pollution; the national problem of solid waste disposal. New York, Praeger, 1971.
173p.
Bibliography: p. 159-164.

1. Refuse and refuse disposal. I. Title.

658.3
:770
T34

This, Leslie E   ed.
Training film index; films on audio-visual aids, communications, community action and citizen responsibility, human behavior and human relations, leadership, supervision, training methodology, miscellaneous. Washington, Leadership Resources, 1961.
26p. (Learning about leadership series)

1. Films - Bibliography. 2. Personnel management films. I. Title.

330
(74811)
D42

This is greater Philadelphia.
Dickinson, William B
This is greater Philadelphia. Philadelphia, 1954.
46 p. illus.

"Reprinted from the Evening and Sunday Bulletin, Philadelphia."

1. Economic conditions - Philadelphia. 2. Metropolitan areas - Philadelphia. I. Title.

339.5
I57c
1966

The third wave: America's new conservation.
U.S. Dept. of the Interior.
The third wave: America's new conservation. Washington, For sale by the Supt. of Documents, Govt. Print. Off., 1966.
128p. (Conservation yearbook no. 3)

1. Natural resources. 2. Open space land. 3. Landscape architecture. I. Title. II. Title: America's new conservation. (Series: Conservation yearbook no.3)

301.15
F15

This endangered planet.
Falk, Richard A
This endangered planet; prospects and proposals for human survival. New York, Random House, 1971.
495p.

Bibliography: p. 474-483.

1. Man - Influence of environment.
2. Natural resources. I. Title.

728.1
:336.18
(755521)
N67

THIS IS IT.
NORFOLK, VA. REDEVELOPMENT AND HOUSING AUTHORITY.
THIS IS IT. NORFOLK, VA., 1946.
48P.
FIRST PRINTED REPORT OF THE AUTHORITY

1. PUBLIC HOUSING - NORFOLK, VA. I. TITLE.

325
G41

The $30 billion Negro. London, Macmillan, 1969
Gibson, D   Parke.
The $30 billion Negro. London, Macmillan, 1969.
311p.
Bibliography: p. 271-279.

1. Negroes. 2. Marketing. 3. Advertising. 4. Buying. I. Title.

674
H67

This fascinating lumber business.
Horn, Stanley Fitzgerald, 1889-
This fascinating lumber business. Indianapolis, Bobbs-Merrill [1951]
313 p. illus., map. 28 cm.

1. Lumber trade—U. S. 2. Lumbering—U. S.   I. Title.

HD9755.H6 1951   674   51-14101

Library of Congress   [20]

728.1
H68t

This is Operation Breakthrough.
U.S. Dept. of Housing and Urban Development.
This is Operation Breakthrough. A new program designed to utilize modern techniques of production, marketing and management to provide housing for all income levels through a partnership of labor, consumers, private enterprise, and local, State and Federal governments. Washington, 1968.
22p.
HUD news, Jul. 10, 1969.
1. Federal housing programs. I. Title. II. Title: Operation Breakthrough.

VF
728.1
H68th
This is Operation Breakthrough.
U.S. Dept. of Housing and Urban Development.
This is Operation Breakthrough. Wash.,
1969.
folder. (HUD-13-RT)

1. Housing. 2. Building methods.
3. Operation Breakthrough. I. Title.

312
W17t
This U.S.A.; an unexpected family portrait...
Wattenberg, Ben J
This U.S.A.; an unexpected family
portrait of 194,067,296 Americans drawn
from the census, by Ben J. Wattenberg in
collaboration with Richard M. Scammon.
Garden City, N.Y., Doubleday, 1965.
520p.

1. Population. 2. Social conditions.
3. Economic conditions. 4. Housing
statistics. 5. Minority groups.
I. Scammon,   Richard M., jt. au.
II. Title.

American Public Works Association.   An evaluation
of household food waste disposers...1951.
(Card 2)

Garbage grinders: selected references, compiled
by the Municipal Reference Library, Detroit Public
Library, reprinted p. 29-32.
Mimeographed.

1.Refuse and refuse disposal. I.Clarke, Samuel M.
II.Anderson, Robert L. III.Zimmer, Edward J.
IV.Tholin, A.L. V.Anderson, Norval E. VI.Series.

VF
351.7
:728.1
F22t
This is the FHA.
U.S. Federal Housing Administration.
This is the FHA; insurance programs for
home financing, property improvement, rental
housing, urban renewal, cooperative housing.
Washington [Govt. Print. Off. 1956]
16 p.

1.U.S. Federal Housing Administration. I.Title.

697.8
A95
This vital air; this vital water.
Aylesworth, Thomas G
This vital air; this vital water. Man's
environmental crisis. Chicago, Rand McNally,
1968.
192p.

1. Air pollution. 2. Water pollution.
3. Noise. I. Title.

699.83
T22
Thom, H C S ed.
Technical Meeting Concerning Wind Loads on
Buildings and Structures, National Bureau
of Standards, 1969.
Proceedings. R.D. Marshall and H.C.S. Thom,
editors. Wash., National Bureau of Standards,
1970.
164p. (Building science series 30)

1. Buildings - Wind stresses. I. U.S.
National Bureau of Standards. II. Marshall,
R.D., ed. III. Thom, H.C.S., ed.
IV. Title: Wind   loads on buildings and
structures.

697.8
U54
This is UOP.
Universal Oil Products Co. [Air Correction
Div.]
This is UOP. Greenwich, Conn., 1967.
1v.   (looseleaf)

1. Air pollution. 2. Petroleum industry.
3. Air pollution. I. Title.

728.69
K17
This wonderful world of mobile home living.
Karr, Harrison M
This wonderful world of mobile home living.
Beverly Hills, Calif., Trail-R-Club of
America, 1968.
175p. (Book no. 1)

Bibliography: p. 149-150.

1. Mobile homes. I. Trail-R-Club of
America. II. Title.

628.3
P81s
Thoman, John R
U.S. Public Health Service.
Statistical summary of sewage works in the
United States, by John R. Thoman and Kenneth
H. Jenkins. Washington, Govt. Print. Off.,
1958.
40p. tables. (Its Publication no. 609)

1. Sewerage and sewage disposal.
I. Thoman John R   II. Jenkins,
Kenneth h

728.1
:336.18
(792)
W17
This is Washington Terrace [Utah]
[Ogden, Utah] 1947.
Washington Terrace Non-Profit Housing
Corp., Ogden, Utah.
This is Washington Terrace [Utah]
[Ogden, Utah] 1947.
76p.

1. Public housing - Utah. I. Title.

VF
728.1
:362.6
D18t
Thistles in Paradise...
Davidson, Bill.
Thistles in Paradise; the truth about re-
tirement housing. In Saturday evening post,
January 16, 1965. p. 19-25.

1. Housing for the aged. 2. Building costs.
I. U.S. Housing and Home Finance Agency.
II. Saturday   evening post. III. Title.

628.44
P81
Thoman, J. R.
U.S. Public Health Service. Environmental Health
Center.
Studies on household sewage disposal systems;
2   in a series of research reports on
individual sewage disposal systems.   Cincinnati,
1949 - 1950
2 v.   illus.

Includes bibliographies.
Program begun by Public Health Service and
Housing and Home Finance Agency in 1947.
(Continued on next card)

325
(09)
C72
This is what we found.
Creger, Ralph.
This is what we found; how a white father
and son in Little Rock came to champion equal
rights and opportunities for Negroes, by
Ralph and Carl Creger. New York, Lyle Stuart,
1960.
64p.

Bibliography: p. 60-64.

1. Negroes - History. 2. Race relations.
I. Creger,   Carl, jt. au. II. Title.

331.2
T36
THOLE, HENRY C
ARE WAGES HIGH IN DETROIT   BY HENRY
C. THOLE AND HAROLD C. TAYLOR.
KALAMAZOO, W.E. UPJOHN INSTITUTE FOR
EMPLOYMENT RESEARCH, 1963.
86P. (STUDIES OF THE MICHIGAN ECONOMY)

1. WAGES AND SALARIES. I. TAYLOR,
HAROLD C., JT. AU. II. UPJOHN
INSTITUTE FOR EMPLOYMENT RESEARCH.
III. TITLE.

U.S. Public Health Service. Environmental Health
Center. Studies on household sewage disposal
systems ... 1949 -   (Card 2)

Contributors: pt.1.S. R. Weibel, C. P. Straub,
J. R. Thoman.-pt.2.T. W. Bendixen, M. Berk, J. P.
Sheehy, S. R. Weibel.

1.Sewerage and sewage disposal. I.U.S. Housing and
Home Finance Agency. II.Bendixen, T. W. III.Berk,
M. IV.Sheehy, J. P. V.Straub, C. P. VI.Thoman,
J. R. VII.Weibel, S. R.

301.15
H81
This land of ours; ...
Hubbard, Alice Harvey.
This land of ours; community and conserva-
tion projects for citizens. New York, Mac-
millan, 1960.
272p.

1. Community development - Citizen participation.
2. Natural resources. I. Title.

VF
658
(016)
W28
Thole, Henry C
W. E. Upjohn Institute for Community Research.
Management controls; an annotated bibliography,
by Henry C. Thole.   Kalamazoo, Mich., Dec. 1953.
40 p.

1.Management-Bibl. I.Thole, Henry C. II.Title.

728.1
:670
B19
Thomas, Andrew J
Bayonne Housing Corp.
Industrial housing, by Andrew J. Thomas.
Bayonne, N. J., 1925.
61p. illus.

1.Company housing. I.Thomas, Andrew J

301.15
H15th
This little planet.
Hamilton, Michael, ed.
This little planet. With an introduction
by Edmund S. Muskie. New York, Charles
Scribner's, 1970.
241p.

1. Man - Influence of environment.
2. Natural resources. 3. Air pollution.
4. Water pollution. 5. Land use.
I. Title.

VF
628.44
A52
Tholin, A. L.
American Public Works Association.
An evaluation of household food waste
disposers, presented at the spring meeting
of the Chicago Metropolitan Chapter on
March 7, 1951, Southwest Side Sewage
Treatment Plant. Chicago, Ill. [May 1951]
32 l.   (Public Works Engineers' Special
report no. 13)
Panel: Samuel M. Clarke, chairman, Robert L.
Anderson, Edward J. Zimmer, A.L. Tholin, Norval
E. Anderson.
(continued on next card)

658
(016)
A52t
Thomas, Bernadine H   comp.
American Management Association.
Ten-year index of AMA publications
(1954-1963) compiled by Bernadine H.
Thomas and Vera Kohn. New York, 1964-
v.
For complete information see main card.
1. American Management Association -
Publications. 2. Management - Bibl.
I. Thomas, Bernadine H., comp. II. Kohn,
Vera, comp.

657.47
:690
M42

Thomas, D. A.
Michigan. University. School of Business
Administration.
[Cost accounting systems for home builders]
prepared by R. L. Brummet and D. A. Thomas.
Washington, Dec. 1951 - Feb. 1952.
2 pts.   forms, tables.

Contents.-part 1. Record keeping for the
small home builder.-part 2. Accounting
procedures for home builders.

657.47
:690
M42

Michigan. University. School of Business
Administration. [Cost accounting
systems for home builders] (Card 2)

Final report, Research project no. 0-E-52,
Housing and Home Finance Agency.
Project director: Herbert F. Taggert;
Staff technician: George Kinzie.

Processed.

657.47
:69
B78

Thomas, D. A., jt. au.
Brummet, R   L
Record keeping for the small home builder,
prepared by R.L. Brummet and D.A. Thomas, under the
supervision of H.F. Taggert.   Washington, Housing
and Home Finance Agency, Office of the Administrator, Division of Housing Research, January 1952.
85 p. + full size forms in separate envelope.
forms(part fold.), tables.

(Continued on next card)

Brummet, R   L   Record keeping for
the small home builder...1952.   (Card 2)

HHFA research project no. 0-E-52 at University
of Michigan School of Business Administration; Max
Lipowitz, staff technician.

1.Contractors-Accounting. I.Thomas, D.A., jt. au.
II.Taggert, H.F. III.Michigan. University. School
of Business Administration. IV.U.S. Housing and
Home Finance Agency. Office of the Administrator.
Division of Housing Research. V.Title.

333.32
(41)
T36

THOMAS, D   LLEUFER.
THE WELSH LAND COMMISSION: A DIGEST
OF ITS REPORT, BY D. LLEUFER THOMAS...
LONDON, WHITTAKER, 1896.
465P.

1. LAND TENURE - U.K.   2. U.K.
WELSH LAND COMMISSION.

778
A52

Thomas, David.
American Management Association.
Interviewing the potential employee;
an audio training aid for more effective
employment interviewing, by P. W. Maloney
and David Thomas. New York, 1961.
Record.   (AMA recording no. 9018001)
—— Interviewing the potential employee;
designed to accompany AMA recording
no. 9018001. 31p.
1. Visual aids. 2. Personnel management. I. Maloney,
P. W. II. Thomas,   David. III. Title.

33(04)
M47

Thomas, Dorothy Swayne
Economic essays in honor of Wesley Clair
Mitchell, presented to him by his former
students on the occasion of his sixtieth
birthday.   New York, N.Y., Columbia Univ.
Press, 1935.
ix, 519 p.

Contents.-Recent efforts of the Federal
government in the field of low-rental housing,
by Asher Achinstein.-Genesis and import of the
collective-bargaining provisions of the Recovery
act, by Paul F. Brissenden.-Long cycles in

(Continued on next card)

Economic essays in honor of Wesley Clair
Mitchell...1935.   (Card 2)
(Contents cont'd)
residential construction, by Arthur F. Burns.-
Purchasing power of the masses and business
depressions, by Paul H. Douglas.-Obstacles to
the statistical approach in economics and the
social sciences with special reference to England,
by P. Sargant Florence.-The Marxian right to the
whole product, by Abram L. Harris.-Some reflections on retail prices, by Oswald W. Knauth.-.
Relation between capital goods and finished

(Continued on next card)

Economic essays in honor of Wesley Clair
Mitchell...1935.   (Card 3)
(Contents cont'd)
products in the business cycle, by Simon Kuznets.-
Some basic problems in index-number theory, by
Edward E. Lewis.-Urban decentralization, by
Robert J. McFall.-Some aspects of economic
planning, by P.W. Martin.-On the changing
structure of economic life, by Frederick C.
Mills.-The role of the middle class in social
development; facism, populism, communism, social-
ism, by David J. Saposs.-On the current skepticism

(Continued on next card)

Economic essays in honor of Wesley Clair
Mitchell...1935.   (Card 4)
(Contents cont'd)
toward systematic economics, by Horace Taylor.-
Economic and social aspects of internal migrations:
an exploratory study of selected Swedish communities, by Dorothy Swaine Thomas.-The problem
of overcapacity, by Willard L. Thorp.-Plateaus of
prosperity and plains of depression, by Clark
Warburton.

388
:538.56
T36

Thomas, Edwin N
Further comments on the analysis of non-
residential trip generation, by E.N.
Thomas and others. Research supported by
the U.S. Bureau of Public Roads, Urban
Planning Div., Urban Development Branch.
Evenston, Ill., Transportation Center, at
Northwestern University, 1966.
131p.

1. Transportation-Automation. 2. Journey to work.
I. Northwestern University. II. Title: Analysis of
non-residential trip   generation.

388.015
T36

Thomas, Edwin N
Introduction to a systems approach to trans-
portation problems; by Edwin N. Thomas and
Joseph L. Schofer. Evanston, Ill., Trans-
portation Center, Northwestern University,
1966.
65p. (Research report)
Prepared for a seminar hosted by the Chicago
Area Transportation Study sponsored by the
Committee on Urban Transportation Systems
Evaluation (UTP-4) of the Highway Research
Board as part   of Project 8-4, Criteria
for evalua   ting alternative
(Cont'd on next card)

388.015
T36

Thomas, Edwin N   Introduction...1966.
(Card 2)

transportation plans: National Cooperative
Highway Research Program; Highway Research
Board, NAS-NRC.
1. Transportation - Research. 2. Journey
to work. I. Schofer, Joseph L., jt. au.
II. Northwestern University. Transportation
Center. III. Title.

378
T36

Thomas, Edwin N
University responses to urban conditions:
supportive relationships between HUD and the
university. Chicago, Center for Urban
Studies, University of Illinois, 1968.
66p. (Illinois. University. Center for
Urban Studies. Occasional paper series no. 2)
Prepared under contract with the Dept. of
Housing and Urban Development.
1. Universities and colleges - Research
services to neighboring communities.
I. Illinois. University. Center for Urban
Studies.   II. U.S. Dept. of Housing
and Urban Deve   lopment. III. Title.

614.8
:690
T36

Thomas, F   G
Basic parameters and terminology in the
consideration of structural safety.
Garston, Eng., Building Research Station,
Dept. of Scientific and Industrial Research,
1964.
7p. (U.K. Building Research Station.
Building research current papers.
Engineering series 20)
Reprinted from: C.I.B Bulletin, 1964
(3), pp. 4-12.

(Continued on next card)

614.8
:690
T36

Thomas, F   G
and terminology...1964.   Basic parameters
(Card 2)

1. Building construction - Accidents.
I. U.K. Building Research Station.

691.328.2
I57
1949

Thomas, Frederick G
Conference on Pre-stressed Concrete, London,
Feb., 1949.
Pre-stressed concrete: proceedings of the
conference arranged by the joint committee on
materials and their testing of technical
institutions and societies in Great Britain and
held under the auspices of the Institution of
Civil Engineers.   London, Institution of Civil
Engineers, 1949.
132 p.   illus.
Contents.-Pre-stressed concrete, by Frederick
G. Thomas.-Bibliogra   p. 72-82.-Discussion.

690
(41)
U54STU

THOMAS, F   G
UNITED KINGDOM. DEPT. OF SCIENTIFIC
AND INDUSTRIAL RESEARCH.
STRUCTURAL REQUIREMENTS FOR HOUSES,
BY F.G. THOMAS. LONDON, H.M.
STATIONERY OFF., 1948.
8P. (ITS NATIONAL BUILDING STUDIES
SPECIAL REPORT NO. 1)

1. BUILDING CONSTRUCTION - UNITED
KINGDOM. 2. STRUCTURAL ENGINEERING.
I. THOMAS, F.G.   II. TITLE.

625.7
U54s
pt.3

Thomas, F   G   jt. au.
Short, A
Studies on bridge-deck systems.   III.
Tests on model slab-and-girder bridge-
deck systems, by A. Short and F.G. Thomas.
London, H.M. Stationery Office, 1963.
70p. (U.K. Building Research Station.
National Building Studies. Research paper
37)

1. Bridges. 2. Building methods.
I. Thomas, F.G., jt. au. I. U.K. Building
Research Station

624.131
T36

Thomas, H   S   H
The design, construction and performance of
a vibrating-wire earth pressure cell, by
H.S.H. Thomas and W.H. Ward. Garston, Eng.,
Building Research Station, 1969.
[16] p. (U.K. Building Research Station.
Current paper 13/69)
Reprinted from: Geotechnique, Mar. 1969,
p. 39-51.

1. Soils. 2. Strains and stresses.
I. Ward, W.H., jt. au. II. U.K. Building
Research Stati on. III. Title.

623
T36

Thomas, H   S   H
The measurement of strain in tunnel linings
using the vibrating-wire technique. Garston,
Eng., Building Research Station, Ministry of
Technology, 1966.
8p. (U.K. Building Research Station.
Building research current papers. Engineering
series 34)
Reprinted from: Strain, 1966, vol. 2(July),
p. 16-21.

1. Structural engineering. I. U.K. Building Research   Station. II. Title.
III. Title: Tunnel linings.

VF
690.015
F22
R8

Thomas, Harold A.

National Academy of Sciences. Committee on Sanitary Engineering and Environment.
Effects of detergents on sewage and sewage treatment at military installations. [Washington] National Research Council, May 1954.
10 p. (Federal Construction Council. Technical report no. 8)
Bibliography: p. 10.

1.Sewerage and sewage disposal. I.Thomas, Harold A. II.Title. Series.

690.22
T36h Thomas, K
Hamilton College: construction of residences in loadbearing brickwork, by K. Thomas and D. Marshall. London, Clay Products Technical Bureau, 1966.
7p. (CPTB Technical note. Vol. 1, no. 11)

1. Walls. 2. Brick construction. 3. Foundations (Building) 4. Universities and colleges - Buildings. I. Clay Products Technical Bureau, London. II. Marshall, D. jt.au.

301.36 THOMAS, LEWIS FRANCIS, JT. AU.
Q82 QUEEN, STUART ALFRED, 1890-
THE CITY; A STUDY OF URBANISM IN THE UNITED STATES, BY STUART ALFRED QUEEN ... AND LEWIS FRANCIS THOMAS ... 1ST ED. NEW YORK, MCGRAW-HILL, 1939.
500P. (MCGRAW-HILL PUBLICATIONS IN SOCIOLOGY)

1. SOCIOLOGY, URBAN. 2. HOUSING. I. THOMAS, LEWIS FRANCIS, JT. AU. II. TITLE.

628.1
T365 THOMAS, HAROLD E
THE CONSERVATION OF GROUND WATER. NEW YORK, MCGRAW-HILL, 1951.
327P.

1. WATER RESOURCES. I. TITLE.

693.2
H17 Thomas, K jt. au.
Haseltine, B A
Loadbearing brickwork; design for accidental forces, by B.A. Haseltine and K. Thomas. London, Clay Products Technical Bureau, 1969.
11p. (Clay Products Technical Bureau. Technical note, v.2, no.6)

1. Brick construction. I. Thomas, K., jt. au. II. Clay Products Technical Bureau. III. Title.

VF
693.068
:389.6
T36 Thomas, M Hartland
Cheaper building: the contribution of modular coordination. Journal of the Royal Society of Arts (London), p. 98-120, Jan. 9, 1953.

1. Modular coordination. I. Title.

712.25
(77132)
T36 THOMAS, HELEN O.
PLANNING FOR LEISURE TIME ACTIVITIES AND FACILITIES IN THE PORTLAND-OUTHWAITE HOUSING PROJECT, CLEVELAND, OHIO. CLEVELAND, 1937.
117L.

THESIS (M.S.) - WESTERN RESERVE UNIVERSITY.

1. RECREATION - CLEVELAND, OHIO. I. TITLE: LEISURE TIME ACTIVITIES AND FACILITIES.

Thomas, K ., jt. au.

690.22
B71 Bradshaw, R E
Modern developments in structural brickwork, by R.E. Bradshaw and K. Thomas. Paper presented at the sixth annual Conference of Municipal Surveyors. London, Clay Products Technical Bureau, 1968.
15p. (CPTB Technical note. Vol. 2, no. 3)

1. Walls. 2. Brick construction. I. Clay Products Technical Bureau, London. II. Thomas, K., jt. au. III. Title.

551.5
(71)
C15 Thomas, Morley K
Canada. National Research Council.
Climatological atlas of Canada, prepared by Morley K. Thomas. Ottawa, Dec. 1953.
256 p. graphs, maps, tables. (N.R.C. no. 3151)

A joint publication of the Division of Building Research, National Research Council, and the Meteorological Division, Department of Transport, Canada.
1.Climate-Canada. I.Thomas, Morley K. II.Canada. Dept. of Transport. Meteorological Division. III.Title.

VF
728.1
:631
N28 Thomas, Howard E
New York. State University. College of Agriculture.
Housing for migrant farm workers [by Ruby M. Loper and Howard E. Thomas. Ithaca, N.Y., Cornell University, June 1953]
31 p. illus., plans. (Cornell miscellaneous bulletin 15)

1.Housing for migrant workers. I.Loper, Ruby M. II.Thomas, Howard E. III.New York. State University. College of Home Economics.

690.22
T36 Thomas, K
Movement joints in brickwork. London, Clay Products Technical Bureau, 1966.
7p. (Clay Products Technical Bureau. CPTB technical note, vol. 1, no. 10.)

1. Walls. 2. Bricks. I. Clay Products Technical Bureau, London. I. Title.

350
T36 Thomas, Norman C
Rule 9: politics, administration, and civil rights. New York, Random House, 1966.
121p. (Studies in political science)

1. Public administration. 2. Real estate business - Michigan. 3. Civil rights. 4. Political science. 5. Minority groups - Michigan. I. Title. II. Title: Politics, administration, and civil rights.

63
:331
T36 Thomas, Howard E
Migrant farm labor in Colorado; a study of migratory families. Report prepared by Howard E. Thomas and Florence Taylor. New York, National Child Labor Committee, Nov. 1951.
116 1. tables.

Prepared for the Colorado Survey Committee on Migrant Labor.
"How the migrants live:" p. 35-47.
Mimeographed.

(Continued on next card)

325
(764)
K88so Thomas, Katheryn A jt. au.
Kuvlesky, William P
Social ambitions of Negro boys and girls from a metropolitan ghetto, by William P. Kuvlesky and Katheryn A. Thomas. New York Academic Press, 1971.
[11]p.
Reprinted from: Journal of vocational behavior, 1, 177-187 (1971)
Bibliography: p. 186-187.

1. Negroes - Houston. I. Thomas, Katheryn A., jt. au. II. Title.

534.83
H62 Thomas, P jt. au.
Hoch, R
Effect of reflection on sound-pressure spectra of jets, by R. Hoch and P. Thomas. Garston, Eng., Building Research Station, 1969.
[11]p. (U.K. Building Research Station. Library communication no. 1523)
Translated from the French and reprinted from: Revue d'acoustique, 1969, (5), 47-54.

1. Noise. I. Thomas, P., jt. au. II. U.K. Building Research Station. III. Title. (Series)

Thomas, Howard E. Migrant farm labor in Colorado...Nov. 1951. (Card 2)

1.Agricultural laborers.2.Housing for migrant workers.I.Taylor,Florence.II.National Child Labor Committee.III.Colorado. Survey Committee on Migrant Labor.

312
(762)
M47e Thomas, Leila H
Mississippi. Agricultural Experiment Station.
Estimated population trends in Mississippi, 1950-56, by Harold A. Pedersen and Leila H. Thomas. State College, Miss., 1957.
17p. illus., tables. (Its Bulletin 550)

1.Population - Miss. I.Pedersen, Harold A II.Thomas, Leila H

699.81
T36 Thomas, P H
Movement of smoke in horizontal corridors against an air flow, by P.H. Thomas, Ministry of Technology and Fire Offices' Committee, Joint Fire Research Organisation. [n.p. 1970?]
[9]p.
Reprinted from: Institute of Fire Engineers quarterly.

1. Fire prevention. 2. Air pollution. I. Title.

628.3
P81mu Thomas, John R
U.S. Public Health Service.
Municipal sewage treatment needs, by John R. Thomas and Kenneth H. Jenkins. Washington, 1958.
16p. tables. (Its Publication no. 619)

1. Sewerage and sewage disposal. I. Thomas, John R. II. Jenkins, Kenneth H.

058.7
:658
851 Thomas, Leonard N
U.S. Small Business Administration.
U.S. Government purchasing and sales directory; a guide for selling or buying in the Government market, by Karl G. Fox and Leonard N. Thomas. Washington, For sale by the Supt. of Documents, Govt. Print. Off., 1965.
138p.

1. Buying - Direct. I. Fox, Karl G. II. Thomas, Leonard N. III. Title: Government purchasing and sales directory. IV. Title.

690.031
T36 Thomas, Paul I
1971 How to estimate building losses and construction costs. 2d ed. Englewood Cliffs, N.J., Prentice-Hall, 1971.
452p.

Bibliography: p. xi-xiv.

1. Building costs - Estimates. I. Title.

325
(7471)
T36
Thomas, Piri.
Down these mean streets. New York,
New American Library, 1967.
317p.

c.1 E.O. 1. Minority groups - New York (City)
I. Title.

388
:331
T36j
Thomas, Ray.
Journey to work. [London, PEP
[Political and Economic Planning] 1968
419p.

Planning, vol. XXXIV, no. 504, Nov.
1968.

1. Journey to work. 2. Transportation -
U.K. I. Political and Economic Planning.

720
T36
Thomas, T A
Technical illustration. 2d ed. New York,
McGraw-Hill, 1968.
203p.

1. Architectural drawing. I. Title.

728.1
1940.42
T36
THOMAS, R J
HOUSING FOR DEFENSE. DETROIT,
MICH., INTERNATIONAL UAW-CIO, 1941.
63P.

1. DEFENSE HOUSING. 2. COOPERATIVE
HOUSING.

711.417
(41)
T36
Thomas, Ray.
London's new towns; a study of self-
contained and balanced communities.
London, PEP [Political and Economic
Planning] 1969.
131p. (PEP [Political and Economic
Planning] vol. XXXV; broadsheet 510;
Planning, April 1969 10/)

4c

1. New towns - U.K. - London.
I. Political and Economic Planning.
II. Title.

388
:331
T36
Thomas, Thomas C
The value of time for passenger cars; an
experimental study of commuters' values. Pre-
pared for Bureau of Public Roads, U.S. Dept. of
Transportation, Menlo Park, Calif., Stanford
Research Institute, 1967.
150p. (SRI Project 5074)
Distributed by U.S. Clearinghouse for Feder-
al Scientific and Technical Information as
document PB 175 731.
1. Journey to work. 2. Traffic surveys.
3. Highways - Research. I. Stanford Research
Institute. II. U.S. Clearinghouse for Federal
Scientific and Technical Information.
III. Title.

728.1
1940.42
T36
1942
THOMAS, R J
HOUSING FOR DEFENSE. DETROIT,
MICH., INTERNATIONAL UAW-CIO, 1942.
47P.

2C.

1. DEFENSE HOUSING. 2. COOPERATIVE
HOUSING.

628.1
T36
Thomas, Richard E
Domestic water use in suburban homes, by
Richard E. Thomas and Thomas W. Bendixen.
Final report to the Federal Housing Admin-
istration. Cincinnati, Public Health
Service, Robert A. Taft Sanitary Engineering
Center, 1962.
51p.

3c

1. Water-supply. I. Bendixen, Thomas W., jt. au.
II. U.S. Federal Housing Administration. III. U.S.
Robert A. Taft Sanitary Engineering Center.
Technical Studies Pro- gram.

728.1
1308
(79461)
T36
THOMAS, TREVOR.
SAN FRANCISCO'S HOUSING MARKET, OPEN
OR CLOSED; CIVIL RIGHTS INVENTORY OF
SAN FRANCISCO. PART II, HOUSING. A
REPORT BY TREVOR THOMAS, BASED UPON A
SURVEY... FOR THE COUNCIL FOR CIVIC
UNITY OF SAN FRANCISCO... SAN
FRANCISCO, COUNCIL FOR CIVIC UNITY OF
SAN FRANCISCO, 1960.
47P.

1. HOUSING MARKET - SAN FRANCISCO.
I. COUNCIL FOR CIVIC UNITY OF SAN
FRANCISCO. II. TITLE.
(CONTINUED ON NEXT CARD)

728.1
:940.42
I57w
Thomas, R J
International Union, United Automobile,
Aircraft and Agricultural Implement
Workers of America (UAW-CIO)
Housing for defense, by R. J. Thomas.
Detroit, 1941.
63p.

1. Defense housing. I. Thomas, R. J.

705
:670
T36
Thomas, Richard K
Three-dimensional design: a cellular
approach. New York, Van Nostrand Reinhold,
1969.
96p.

1. Design, Industrial. 2. Architecture -
Designs and plans. 3. Visual aids. I. Title.

728.1
1308
(79461)
T36
THOMAS, TREVOR. SAN FRANCISCO'S
HOUSING ...1960. (CARD 2)

III. TITLE: CIVIL RIGHTS INVENTORY OF
SAN FRANCISCO.

647.1
M87
Thomas, R J , jt. au.
Murray, Philip
Living costs in World War II, 1941-1944, by
Philip Murray [and] R. J. Thomas. Washington,
Congress of Industrial Organizations, June 1944.
161 p., 76 p.

1.Cost and standard of living. I.Congress of
Industrial Organizations. II.Thomas, R. J., jt. au.

Ref.
030.8
015c
Thomas, Robert C.
Gale Research Company.
Code names dictionary; a guide to code names,
slang, nicknames, journalese, and similar terms....
Edited by Frederick G. Ruffner and Robert C.
Thomas. Introd. by Eric Partridge. Detroit,
Mich., 1963.
555 p.

1. English language - Dictionaries.
I. Title. II. Ruffner,
Frederick G. III. Thomas, Robert C.
IV. Partridge, Eric.

350
T36c
Thomas, Uwe.
Computerized data banks in public administra-
tion: trends and policy issues. Paris,
Organisation for Economic Co-operation and
Development, 1970.
71p.

Bibliography: p. 67-71.

1. Public administration - Automation.
I. Organisation for Economic Cooperation and
Development. II. Title. III. Title: Data
banks in public administration.

728.1
T36
THOMAS, R J
POLITICS IN HOUSING. DETROIT,
INTERNATIONAL UNION, UNITED AUTOMOBILE,
AIRCRAFT AND AGRICULTURAL IMPLEMENT
WORKERS OF AMERICA (UAW-CIO), 1944.
18P. (PUBLICATION NO. 42)

2c

"AN ADDRESS BEFORE THE FIRST NATIONAL
CONVENTION OF THE PUBLIC HOUSING
CONFERENCE... ST. LOUIS, MO., MARCH 25,
1944."
1. HOUSING. 2. FEDERAL HOUSING
PROGRAMS. I. NATIONAL PUBLIC
HOUSING CONFERENCE. II. TITLE.

325
(74811)
P34
Thomas, Robert M ed.
Philadelphia. Commission on Human Relations.
Non-white residential patterns; analysis
of changes in the non-white residential
patterns in Philadelphia from 1950 to 1958,
by Lary Groth, ed. by Robert M. Thomas.
Philadelphia, 1959.
13p. maps.

1. Minority groups - Philadelphia.
I. Groth, Lary. II. Thomas, Robert M., ed.

378
E28ho
Thomas, Virginia F
U.S. Office of Education.
Home economics in degree-granting
institutions, 1957-1958, by Virginia F.
Thomas. Washington, 1958.
38p. tables. (Its Misc. 2557 - rev.
1958)

1. Universities and colleges.
2. Old age - Study and teaching.
I. Thomas, Virginia F.

711.417
(41)
T36
Thomas, Ray.
Aycliffe to Cumbernauld; a study of
seven new towns in their regions. London,
PEP (Political and Economic Planning) ,1969.
[161]p. (Political and Economic Planning.
vol. XXXV; Broadsheet 516, Dec., 1969,
20/- p. 801-962)

1. New towns - U.K. I. Political and
Economic Planning. II. Title.

334.1
T36
THOMAS, ROLLAND JAY.
CO-OP HOUSING DO'S AND DON'TS; A
PRACTICAL GUIDE IN THE ORGANIZATION AND
DEVELOPMENT OF UNION SPONSORED
NON-PROFIT HOUSING, BY R. J. THOMAS.
N.P., INTERNATIONAL UNION UAW-CIO,
HOUSING DEPT., 1947.
1 V.

1. COOPERATIVE HOUSING. 2. NONPROFIT
HOUSING ORGANIZATIONS. I. TITLE.

362.6
(747)
T36
Thomas, William C Jr.
Nursing homes and public policy; drift
and decision in New York State. Ithaca,
Cornell University Press, 1969.
287p.

1. Nursing homes - New York (State)
I. Title.

33
(73)
F22
P8

Thomas, Woodlief
U.S. Federal Reserve System. Board of Governors.
Federal reserve policy. Washington, Nov.
1947.
119 p. graphs, tables. (Its Postwar
economic studies, no. 8)
Contents.-Three decades of Federal reserve
policy, Karl R. Bopp.-Impact of the war on the
member banks, 1939-1946, Robert V. Rosa.-Selective
instruments of national credit policy, Carl E.
Parry.-Problems of postwar monetary policy,
Woodlief Thomas and Ralph A. Young.

Thomas M. Cooley lectures.
see Michigan. University. Law School. The
Thomas M. Cooley lectures.

690.015
(485)
S82
1971
R10

Thomasson, Per-Olof, jt. au.
Baehre, Rolf.
Plåtpaneler i byggnadsteknisk användning
förstyvade plattfälts funktion och bärförmåga
(Sheet metal panels in building construction
function and load-bearing capacity of stiffened
plates), av. Rolf Baehre och Per-Olof Thomasson.
Stockholm. Statens Institut för Byggnadsfor-
skning, 1971.
50p. (Rapport R10:1971)
English summary.
Bibliography: p. 40-48.

(Cont'd on next card)

2297
2298

THOMAS, MICH. PLANNING COMMISSION.
STUDY REPORT: 1. POPULATION, HOUSING
AND URBANIZATION STUDIES, LAND USE SURVEY
AND ANALYSIS; 2. COMMUNITY FACILITIES
STUDY. PREPARED BY RAYMOND W. MILLS AND
ASSOCIATES. MIDLAND, MICH. 1968-69.
2 V. (HUD 701 REPORT)

2299

-- --- SUPPLEMENTARY MATERIAL.
1 ENV.

1. CITY PLANNING - THOMAS, MICH.
I. MILLS (RAYMOND W.) AND ASSOCIATES.
II. HUD. 701. THOMAS, MICH.

R
058.7
:67
T36

Thomas' register of American manufacturers,
ed. for 1971
New York, Thomas pub. co., 1971-
18 v.
Contents. vols. 1-6, A-Z-Products and Services.
v.-7 Companies, local offices, telephones.
v.-8 Index, trade names... vols. 9-and 10-Files
catalogs of companies A-Z.

Library keeps latest ed. only.
mc Nally-Loug; x5580
1. Manufact-ers - Direct. 2. Buyers'
guides.

690.015
(485)
S82
1971
R10

Baehre, Rolf. Platpaneler...1971. (Card 2)

1. Building research - Sweden. 2. Panels.
3. Steel construction. I. Thomasson, Per-Olof,
jt. au. II. Stockholm. Statens Institut för
Byggnadsforskning. III. Title: Sheet metal
panels...

5442

THOMAS ASSOCIATES.
STOW, MASS. PLANNING BOARD.
MASTER PLAN. PREPARED BY THOMAS
ASSOCIATES. STOW, 1966.
23P. (HUD 701 REPORT)

1. MASTER PLAN - STOW, MASS.
I. THOMAS ASSOCIATES. II. HUD. 701.
STOW, MASS.

VF
526.8
(74811)
C47c

Thomas Skelton Harrison Foundation.
Citizens' Council on City Planning,
Philadelphia.
Comprehensive plan for North Philadelphia.
Report. Philadelphia, 1962.
map.
Prepared in cooperation with the Thomas
Skelton Harrison Foundation.

1. Maps and mapping - Philadelphia.
I. Thomas Skelton Harrison Foundation.

272

THOMASTON, CONN. PLANNING COMMISSION.
A PLANNING STUDY FOR THE TOWN OF
THOMASTON, CONNECTICUT. THOMASTON, 1970.
113P. (HUD 701 REPORT)

1. CITY PLANNING - THOMASTON, CONN.
I. HUD. 701. THOMASTON, CONN.

711.4
(7441)
W45

Thomas Associates.
Master plan for the town of Williamstown,
Massachusetts. [Prepared for Williamstown
Planning Board] [n.p.] 1963.
244p.

U.S. Urban Renewal Adm. UPAP.

1. Master plan - Williamstown, Mass.
I. Williamstown, Mass. Planning Board.
II. U.S. URA-UPAP. Williamstown, Mass.

VF
526.8
(74811)
C47

Thomas Skelton Harrison Foundation.
Citizens' Council on City Planning,
Philadelphia.
Comprehensive plan for Olney-Oak Land.
Report. Philadelphia, 1962.
map.

Prepared in cooperation with the
Thomas Skelton Harrison Foundation.

1. Maps and mapping - Philadelphia.
I. Thomas Skelton Harrison Foundation.
2. Master plan - Philadelphia.

274

THOMASTON, CONN. PLANNING COMMISSION.
SUBDIVISION REGULATIONS OF THE TOWN OF
THOMASTON, CONNECTICUT. THOMASTON, 1970.
32P. (HUD 701 REPORT)

1. CITY PLANNING - THOMASTON, CONN.
I. HUD. 701. THOMASTON, CONN.

624.131
M17so

Thomas Associates.
Massachusetts. Dept. of Commerce. (Div. of
Planning)
Soils interpretation for community planning,
by Stephen J. Zayack and Charles W. Upham.
Prepared in cooperation with Thomas Associates,
community planners. [Boston?] 1963.
2v.
Contents:-v. 1. Case study for town of
Hanover, Plymouth County, Mass.-v. 2. Effectu-
ation of soils interpretation for town of
Hanover, by Thomas Associates.
1. Soils. 2. Community development -
Hanover, Mass. I. Zayack, Stephen J.
II. Upham, Charles W. III. Thomas Associates.

VF
711.4
(74811)
P34com

Thomas Skelton Harrison Foundation.
Citizens' Council on City Planning,
Philadelphia.
Comprehensive plan for near Northeast
Philadelphia. Prepared in cooperation with
the Thomas Skelton Harrison Foundation.
Philadelphia, 1962.
Map.

1. Master plan - Philadelphia. 2. Maps
and mapping - Philadelphia. I. Thomas
Skelton Harrison Foundation.

711.4
(7461)
T22t

Thomaston, Conn. Planning Commission.
Technical Planning Associates, New Haven,
Conn.
Thomaston, Connecticut. [Prepared for]
Thomaston Planning Commission. New Haven,
1957.
9p. diagrs., maps, tables.
U.S. Urban Renewal Administration, Urban
Planning Assistance Program.
1. City planning - Thomaston, Conn.
I. Thomaston, Conn. Planning Commission.
II. U.S. URA-UPAP.

628.44
T36

Thomas, Dean & Hoskins, inc.
Comprehensive study of solid waste
disposal in Cascade County, Montana. Final
report on a solid waste demonstration.
Wash., U.S. Public Health Service,
Environmental Health Service, Bureau of
Solid Waste Management, 1970.
187p. (U.S. Public Health Service.
Publication no. 2002)

Bibliography: p. 155-157.

(Cont'd on next card)

697.7
T36

THOMASON, HARRY E 1923-
SOLAR HOUSE MODELS, BY HARRY E.
THOMASON. BARRINGTON, N.J., EDMUND
SCIENTIFIC CO., 1965.
35P. (POPULAR OPTICS LIBRARY)

BIBLIOGRAPHY: P.35.

1. HEATING, SOLAR. 2. MODEL HOUSES.
I. TITLE.

1034

THOMASTON - UPSON COUNTY PLANNING
COMMISSION.
INITIAL HOUSING ELEMENT STUDY FOR UPSON
COUNTY. BY ADLEY ASSOCIATES, INC., FOR
THE CHATTAHOOCHEE - FLINT AREA PLANNING
AND DEVELOPMENT COMMISSION. LAGRANGE,
GA., 1970.
37L. (HUD 701 REPORT)

1. HOUSING - UPSON CO., GA. I. ADLEY
ASSOCIATES, INC. II. HUD. 701. UPSON
CO., GA.

628.44
T36

Thomas, Dean & Hoskins, inc.
Comprehensive...1970. (Card 2)

1. Refuse and refuse disposal.
I. U.S. Public Health Service. II. Title.

697
:551.5
T36

Thomason, Harry E
Solar space heating and air conditioning
in the Thomason home. [Washington, 1961?]
[15]p.

Reprinted from Solar energy, vol. IV,
no. 4, Oct. 1960.

1. Heating, Solar. 2. Air conditioning.

1036

THOMASTON - UPSON COUNTY PLANNING
COMMISSION.
MAJOR THOROUGHFARE PLAN FOR UPSON
COUNTY, GEORGIA. BY ADLEY ASSOCIATES,
INC., FOR THE CHATTAHOOCHEE - FLINT AREA
PLANNING AND DEVELOPMENT COMMISSION, 1970.
50L. (HUD 701 REPORT)

1. HIGHWAYS - UPSON CO., GA. I. ADLEY
ASSOCIATES, INC. II. HUD. 701. UPSON
CO., GA.

1035

THOMASTON = UPSON COUNTY PLANNING
COMMISSION.
PROPOSED SUBDIVISION REGULATIONS FOR
UPSON COUNTY. BY ADLEY ASSOCIATES, INC.,
FOR THE CHATTAHOOCHEE = FLINT AREA
PLANNING AND DEVELOPMENT COMMISSION.
LAGRANGE, GA., 1970.
45L. (HUD 701 REPORT)

1. SUBDIVISION REGULATION = UPSON CO.,
GA. I. ADLEY ASSOCIATES, INC.
II. HUD. 701. UPSON CO., GA.

711.4
(761245)
T36

Thomasville, Ala. City Planning Commission. Thomasville, Alabama: ... (Card 2)

1. City planning - Thomasville, Ala.
2. Zoning legislation - Thomasville, Ala.
I. Alabama. State Planning and Industrial
Development Board. II. U.S. Urban Re-
newal Administration. Urban Planning
Assistance Program.

711.585
H68e

Thompson, Albert.
U.S. Housing and Home Finance Agency. Office of the Administrator.
An evaluation of the Section 221 relocation
housing program. A report to the Housing Administrator. Prepared under the supervision
of Albert Thompson. Washington, 1959.
48p.

Cover-title.

1. Relocation. I. Thompson, Albert.
2. Mortgage finance. II. Title: 221 relocation
housing programs.

711.4
(761245)
T36t

Thomasville, Ala. City Planning Commission.
Thomasville, Alabama: community facilities plan. Parks and playgrounds, schools,
public building and Industrial Development -
Board. Thomasville, 1958.
27p. maps, tables.

U.S. Urban Renewal Administration, Urban
Planning Assistance Program.

1. Community facilities - Thomasville,
Ala. I. U.S. URA-UPAP. Thomasville, Ala.

711.5
(758981
:347)
S68

Thomasville, Ga. Planning Commission.
Southwest Georgia Planning and Development
Commission.
Zoning ordinance for Thomasville,
Georgia. Thomasville, Ga., Thomasville-
Thomas County Planning Commission, 1970.
86p.
U.S. Dept. of Housing and Urban Devel-
opment. Comprehensive Planning Grant
Program. HUD project no. Ga. P-149.
1. Zoning legislation - Thomasville, Ga.
I. Thomasville, Ga. Planning Commission.
II. U.S. HUD-Comprehensive Planning
Grant Program. Thomasville,
Ga.

711
(016)
C65
no.202

2c

Thompson, Bryan.
Ethnic groups in urban areas; community
formation and growth: a selected bibliography.
[Detroit] Wayne State University, Dept. of
Geography, 1971.
18p. (Council of Planning Librarians.
Exchange bibliography no. 202)

1. Planning - Bibl. 2. Minority groups -
Housing - Bibl. I. Wayne State University,
Detroit. Dept. of Geography. II. Title.
(Series: Council of Planning Librarians.
Exchange bibliography no. 202)

711.4
(761245)
T36la

Thomasville, Alabama. City Planning Commission.
Thomasville, Alabama: land subdivision
regulations and manual. [In cooperation
with Alabama State Planning and Industrial
Development Board] Thomasville, 1956.
29p. diagrs.

U.S. Urban Renewal Administration, Urban

(Continued on next card)

3626

THOMASVILLE, N.C. PLANNING BOARD AND
ZONING COMMISSION.
ZONING ORDINANCE. THOMASVILLE, N.C.,
1967.
67P. (HUD 701 REPORT)

1. ZONING = THOMASVILLE, N.C. I. HUD.
701. THOMASVILLE, N.C.

325
T36

Thompson, Daniel C
The Negro leadership class. Foreword by
Martin Luther King, Jr. Englewood Cliffs,
N.J., Prentice Hall, 1963.
174p. (A Spectrum book)

1. Negroes. 2. Civil rights. 3. Minority groups - New Orleans. I. Title.

711.4
(761245)
T36la

Thomasville, Alabama. City Planning Commission. Thomasville, ... (Card 2)

Planning assistance Program.

1. City planning - Thomasville, Ala. 2.
Subdivision regulation - Thomasville, Ala.
I. Alabama. State Planning and Industrial
Development Board. II. U.S. Urban Renewal
Administration. Urban Planning Assistance
Program.

3625

THOMASVILLE, N.C. PLANNING COMMISSION.
POPULATION AND ECONOMY. THOMASVILLE,
N.C., 1964.
87P. (HUD 701 REPORT)

1. CITY PLANNING = THOMASVILLE, N.C.
I. HUD. 701. THOMASVILLE, N.C.

Thompson, Donald S.

Vice President
Federal Reserve Bank of Cleveland
Cleveland, Ohio

Member Housing Research Advisory Committee, Apr.1950

711.4
(761245)
T36l

Thomasville, Ala. City Planning Commission.
Thomasville, Alabama: long range land use
plan. [In cooperation with Alabama State
Planning and Industrial Development Board]
Thomasville, 1956.
1v. charts, diagrs., maps.

U.S. Urban Renewal Administration, Urban
Planning Assistance Program.
1. City planning - Thomasville, Ala. 2.
Land use- Thomasville, Ala. I. Alabama State
Planning and Industrial Development Board.
II. U.S. Urban Renewal Administration.
Urban Planning Assistance Program.

301.15
T36

2C

Thomlinson, Ralph.
Urban structure; the social and spatial
character of cities. New York, Random House,
1969.
335p.

Bibliography: p. 306-317.

1. Community structure. 2. Sociology, Urban.
3. City planning. I. Title.

690.091.82
(41)
B45

Thompson, E., jt. au.
Binns, G D
Knight's building regulations, by G.D.
Binns and E. Thompson London, Charles
Knight and Company, 1967.
1v. (loose-leaf)

1 Building codes - U.K. I. Thompson, E.,
jt. au. II. Title.

711.74
(761245)
T36

Thomasville, Ala. City Planning Commis-
sion.
Thomasville, Alabama: major street plan.
[In cooperation with] Alabama State Plan-
ning and Industrial Development Board.
Thomasville, 1958.
1v. diagrs., maps, tables.
U.S. Urban Renewal Administration, Urban
Planning Assistance Program.
1. Street planning - Thomasville, Ala.
I. U.S. URA-UPAP. Thomasville,
Ala.

334.1
(71)
A75

THOMPKINSVILLE, NOVA SCOTIA.
ARNOLD, MARY ELLICOTT.
THE STORY OF TOMPKINSVILLE. NEW YORK,
COOPERATIVE LEAGUE, 1940.
102P.

1. COOPERATIVE HOUSING = NOVA SCOTIA.
2. THOMPKINSVILLE, NOVA SCOTIA.
I. TITLE: THOMPKINSVILLE.

Thompson (Edward) company.

U.S. Laws, statutes, etc.
United States code annotated. St. Paul, West Pub. Co.,
1927-   For additions or Holdings
v. 25 cm.   See Continuation File
Comprises all laws of a general and permanent nature under arrangement of the official Code of laws of the United States, with annotations from Federal and State courts.
The laws are arranged under fifty numbered titles. Many of the
titles are subdivided and issued in several volumes.
"Prepared by the editorial staffs of Edward Thompson Company
and West Publishing Co."
Kept up to date by supplementary pamphlets and cumulative
annual pocket parts.

Continued on next card)
41—5629*

711.4
(761245)
T36

Thomasville, Ala. City Planning Commission.
Thomasville, Alabama: zoning ordinance.
[In cooperation with Alabama State and In-
dustrial Development Board] Thomasville,
Ala., 1957.
209p. tables, maps.

U.S. Urban Renewal Administration, Urban
Planning Assistance Program.

(Continued on next card)

Class No. 19 Foreign file Bibliographies
Author (surname first) *Thompson, A.*
Accession No.
Ordered
Source
Place *London*   Publisher *Society for Cultural Relations*
Address
Received 11/16/50
Cost
Date *1949*   Paging *8*
Purchase Order No.   Edition or Series
Date   Recommended by
L. C. No.   Reviewed in

Title *a short bibliography of books and articles on architecture & town planning in the USSR*
List Price   Est. Cost
Processed.

11-305 (2-50)   HOUSING AND HOME FINANCE AGENCY: Office of the Administrator   16—61187-1   gpo

---

Thompson (Edward) company.

U.S. Laws, statutes, etc.   United States code annotated
... 1927-   (Card 2)
———— Constitution of the United States annotated;
annotations from Federal and State courts. St. Paul, West
Pub. Co. [19
v. 25 cm.
Kept up to date by cumulative annual pocket parts and replacement vols.

———— General index. St. Paul, West Pub. Co. [1935]
xlvii, 1787 p. 26 cm.
Kept up to date by cumulative annual pocket parts.
Superseded by Index [1949]

Continued on next card)
41—5629*

Thompson (Edward) company.

U. S. *Laws, statutes, etc.* United States code annotated ... 1927-　(Card 3)　United States code annotated

———— Index. St. Paul, West Pub. Co. [1949]

4 v.　25 cm.

Kept up to date by cumulative annual pocket parts.

———— Tables. St. Paul, West Pub. Co., 1929.

vii, 376 p.　25 cm.

Kept up to date by cumulative annual pocket parts.

I. Thompson (Edward) Company. II. West Publishing Co., St. Paul. III. Title.

Sct. Library
Stg. Board
Library of Congress　[40r40j1]　　41—5629*

FOLIO
711.3
(41)
T36

THOMPSON, FRANCIS LONGSTRETH, 1890-
MERSEYSIDE PLAN 1944.　A REPORT PREPARED IN CONSULTATION WITH A TECHNICAL COMMITTEE OF THE MERSEYSIDE ADVISORY JOINT PLANNING COMMITTEE AT THE REQUEST OF THE MINISTER OF TOWN AND COUNTRY PLANNING. LONDON, H.M. STAT. OFF., 1945.
72P.

1. REGIONAL PLANNING - U.K.
2. RECONSTRUCTION - U.K.　3. CITY PLANNING - U.K. - LIVERPOOL.
I. TITLE.

728.1
N177
1940

Thompson, George N

Land, materials, and labor costs.　*In* National Resources Planning Board, Housing, the continuing problem.　Washington, 1940.　p. 117-217.

Contents.-Location factors in housing programs, by Jacob Crane.-Site planning, by Frederick Bigger.-The significance of small-house design, by Pierre Blouke.-Building materials and the cost of housing, by Theodore J. Kreps.-Labor and the cost of housing, by Mercer G. Evans.-Building regulations and the housing problem, by George N. Thompson.

362.5
D28

Thompson, Elizabeth J ., jt. au.
Deutscher, Irwin.
Among the people; encounters with the poor. Edited by Irwin Deutscher and Elizabeth J. Thompson.　New York, Basic Books, 1968.
408p.

1. Poverty.　2. Minority groups.
I. Title.　II. Thompson, Elizabeth J., jt. au.

711.6
T36

THOMPSON, FRANCIS LONGSTRETH.
SITE PLANNING IN PRACTICE; AN INVESTIGATION OF THE PRINCIPLES OF HOUSING ESTATE DEVELOPMENT. WITH A FOREWORD BY RAYMOND UNWIN. LONDON, H. FROWDE, 1923.
257P. (OXFORD TECHNICAL PUBLICATIONS).

1. SITE PLANNING.

LAW
T
T365C

THOMPSON, GEORGE WASHINGTON, 1864-.
COMMENTARIES ON THE MODERN LAW OF REAL PROPERTY... ADAPTING SPECIAL TOPICS FROM THE WORKS OF LEONARD A. JONES. INDIANAPOLIS, BOBBS-MERRILL, 1957-65
14V. in 13

1. REAL PROPERTY.　2. FORMS (LAW)
I. JONES, LEONARD A.　II. TITLE.

630
(016)
P15

Thompson, Edgar T

Pan American Union. Dept. of Cultural Affairs. (Social Science Section)
The plantation: a bibliography, by Edgar T. Thompson. Washington, 1957.
93p. (Its Social science monographs no. 4)

"A joint publication of the Research and Training Program for the study of man in the tropics (Columbia University) and the Pan American Union."

1. Agriculture - Bibliographies.
I. Thompson, Edgar T II. Title.

658.3
T36

2c.

Thompson, Frank J
Two approaches to the politics of personnel policy.　Wash., Urban Institute, 1970.
81p. (Workings paper no. 107-14)

Research conducted through contract with University of California, Oakland Project. Draft.

1. Personnel management.　I. Urban Institute.
II. California. University. Oakland Project.
III. Title.

VF
697.3
:621.415
P25p
1950

Thompson, H.H. jt. au.
Penrod, Estel B
Performance of an earth heat pump on intermittent operation by E.B. Penrod, E.L. Dunning, and H.H. Thompson. Transaction of the Kentucky Academy of Science, p. 82-99, Oct. 1950. diagrs., tables.

Reprint.

351.712
F67n
pt.4

Thompson, Edward T
The worst public-works problem. Detached from Fortune, December 1958.　p. 102/
(Fortune. A new decade of public works, pt. IV)

1. Public works. (Series)

LAW
T
W455TR

THOMPSON, GEORGE J
WILLISTON, SAMUEL, 1861-
A TREATISE ON THE LAW OF CONTRACTS. REV. ED. BY SAMUEL WILLISTON AND GEORGE J. THOMPSON.　NEW YORK, BAKER, VOORHIS, 1938.
5-9V.

VOLUMES DISCARDED AS CORRESPONDING (BY SECTIONS) VOLUMES OF REV. 3D ED. ARE RECEIVED.

1. CONTRACTS.　2. FORMS.
I. THOMPSON, G GEORGE J.

728
:551.5
A37

Thompson, Harold J
U.S. Agricultural Research Service.
Some effects of construction and climatic factors on heating five expansible farmhouses, by Harold J. Thompson and Joseph W. Simons. Washington, 1961.
22p. (ARS 42-46)

1. Architecture and climate.　2. Farm housing. I. Thompson, Harold J.　II. Simons, Joseph W.

020
(03)
A52

Thompson, Elizabeth H.
American Library Association. (Editorial Committee. Subcommittee on Library Terminology)
A. L. A. glossary of library terms, with a selection of terms in related fields. Prepared under the direction of the Committee on Library Terminology, by Elizabeth H. Thompson. Chicago, 1943.
159p.

1. Library science - Glossary.　I. Thompson, Elizabeth H　II. Title.

VF
699.81
R27

Thompson, George N.
Research Correlation Conference. 2d, Washington, D.C., 1950.
Fire resistance of non-load-bearing exterior walls, National Academy of Sciences, Nov. 21, 1950. Washington, Building Research Advisory Board, Div. of Engineering and Industrial Research, National Research Council, Feb. 1951.
60 p.　illus., diagrs.　(Research Advisory Board. Research Conference report no. 2)

(Continued on next card)

5873

THOMPSON (HERMAN) ASSOCIATES. LINN CO., IOWA. REGIONAL PLANNING COMMISSION.
A REGIONAL OPEN SPACE CONCEPT. BY HERMAN THOMPSON ASSOCIATES. CEDAR RAPIDS, IOWA, 1969.
67L. (HUD 701 REPORT)

1. OPEN SPACE LAND - LINN CO., IOWA.
I. THOMPSON (HERMAN) ASSOCIATES.
II. HUD. 701. LINN CO., IOWA.

327
N17

Thompson, Elizabeth M
National Education Association. Committee on International Relations.
Other lands, other peoples, a country-by-country fact book for Americans entertaining visitors from abroad, by Elizabeth M. Thompson. Washington, 1960.
1v.

1. International relations.　I. Thompson, Elizabeth M.　II. Title.

Research Correlation Conference. 2d, Washington, D.C., 1950.　Fire resistance...1951.
(Card 2)

Bibliography: p. 58-60, prepared by Clement R. Brown and Fred L. Mayer of the Science Division, Library of Congress.
Partial contents.-The background of requirements for fire resistance of exterior non-load-bearing walls, George N. Thompson.-The wall - what do we want?, J. Walter Severinghaus.-The viewpoint of the research director, Robert L.

(Continued on next card)

691.32
T29C
FEB.1964.

THOMPSON, J NEILS.
TEXAS. UNIVERSITY. CENTER FOR HIGHWAY RESEARCH.
RELATIONSHIP BETWEEN CRITICAL MECHANICAL PROPERTIES AND AGE FOR STRUCTURAL LIGHT WEIGHT CONCRETE, BY W.B. LEDBETTER AND J. NEILS THOMPSON. AUSTIN, TEX., 1964.
124L. (REPORT NO. 1, PROJECT 3-8-63-65)

1. CONCRETE.　I. LEDBETTER, WILLIAM B.　II. THOMPSON, J. NEILS.

674
V47

Thompson, Emmett F.
Virginia Polytechnic Institute.
Linear programming over time to establish least-cost wood procurement procedures, by E.F. Thompson and others. Blacksburg, 1968.
70p. (Virginia Polytechnic Institute. Research Division bulletin 29)
Cover title.

1. Wood-using industries.　2. Building materials - Prices.　I. Thompson, Emmett F.　II. Title.

Research Correlation Conference. 2d, Washington, D.C., 1950.　Fire resistance...1951.
(Card 3)

Davison.-Costs of exterior non-load-bearing walls, J.P.H. Perry.-The viewpoint of the code official, Emil J. Szendy.-Fire hazards and fire protection, James K. McElroy.-Proposed restrictions for exterior non-load-bearing walls with respect to fire safety, John W. Dunham.-The sandwich-type spandrel wall, Nolan D. Mitchell.

691.32
T29V

THOMPSON, J NEILS.
TEXAS. UNIVERSITY. CENTER FOR HIGHWAY RESEARCH.
VOLUME CHANGES IN UNRESTRAINED STRUCTURAL LIGHTWEIGHT CONCRETE, BY JAMES T. HOUSTON, J. NEILS THOMPSON. AUSTIN, TEX., 1964.
55L. (RESEARCH REPORT NO. 55-2, PROJECT 3-8-63-55)

1. CONCRETE.　I. HOUSTON, JAMES T.　II. THOMPSON, J. NEILS.　III. TITLE: LIGHTWEIGHT CONCRETE.

658
P47
THOMPSON, JAMES D , ED.
PITTSBURGH. UNIVERSITY. ADMINISTRATIVE
SCIENCE CENTER.
COMPARATIVE STUDIES IN ADMINISTRATION,
EDITED BY JAMES D. THOMPSON AND OTHERS.
PITTSBURGH, UNIV. OF PITTSBURGH PRESS,
1959.
224P. (ITS SERIES IN COMPARATIVE
ADMINISTRATION NO. 1)

BIBLIOGRAPHICAL FOOTNOTES.

1. MANAGEMENT. I. THOMPSON, JAMES D.,
ED. II. TITLE.

368
T36
Thompson, Kenneth R
Reinsurance; a digest on some aspects of the
practice of reinsurance and excess insurance
and a legal treatise on the subject. 4th ed.
Philadelphia, Spectator, 1966.
560p.

2c

1. Insurance. I. Title.

691.51
I55
THOMPSON, MARSHALL R
ILLINOIS. UNIVERSITY. ENGINEERING
EXPERIMENT STATION.
FACTORS INFLUENCING THE PLASTICITY
AND STRENGTH OF LIME-SOIL MIXTURES, BY
MARSHALL R. THOMPSON. URBANA, 1967.
20P. (ITS BULLETIN 492. ILLINOIS
COOPERATIVE HIGHWAY RESEARCH PROGRAM,
SERIES NO. 73)

1. LIME. I. THOMPSON, MARSHALL R.

658
T36
Thompson, James D
Organizations in action: social science
bases of administrative theory. New York,
McGraw-Hill, 1967.
192p.

Bibliography: p. 165-177.

1. Industrial management. I. Title.
II. Title: Social science bases of administrative theory.

728.1
(945)
T36
2c.
THOMPSON, LINDSAY.
VICTORIAN HOUSING - TODAY AND
TO-MORROW. MELBOURNE, 1965.
36P.

1. HOUSING - VICTORIA, AUSTL.
2. PLANNING - VICTORIA, AUSTL.
I. TITLE.

625.7
I55L
THOMPSON, MARSHALL R
ILLINOIS. UNIVERSITY. ENGINEERING
EXPERIMENT STATION.
A LIME STABLIZED TEST ROAD IN RANDOLPH
COUNTY, ILLINOIS, BY MARSHALL R.
THOMPSON AND GEORGE W. HOLLON. URBANA,
1962.
43L. (CIVIL ENGINEERING STUDIES:
HIGHWAY ENGINEERING SERIES NO. 10;
ILLINOIS COOPERATIVE HIGHWAY RESEARCH
PROGRAM SERIES NO. 10)

1. ROAD CONSTRUCTION. 2. LIME.
I. THOMPSON, MARSHALL R.

711.4
T36
2C
Thompson (J. Walter) Co.
Interurbia; the changing face of
America. [New Haven, Conn., 1957]
33p. illus.

1. Metropolitan areas. 2. City growth.

308
:67
V47
Thompson, Lorin A.
Virginia. University. *Bureau of Population and Economic
Research.*
The impact of a new manufacturing plant upon the socio-
economic characteristics and travel habits of the people in
Charlotte County, Virginia; an analysis of the characteristics of a rural county and the preliminary changes associated with the establishment of a new manufacturing plant.
Prepared by the Bureau of Population and Economic Research, University of Virginia, in cooperation with the Division of Traffic and Planning, Virginia Dept. of Highways,
and the U. S. Bureau of Public Roads. [Charlottesville]
1951.

(Continued on next card)
A 52-9502

352.1
(771391)
Y68
Thompson, Norman H
Youngstown, Ohio. City Planning Commission.
Youngstown's 1962-1967 capital improve-
ments program, by Norman H. Thompson and
Irwin E. Jones. Youngstown, Ohio, 1962.
36p. (CPC report, no. 62-2)

1. Capital improvement programs -
Youngstown, Ohio. I. Thompson, Norman H.
II. Jones, Irwin E.

312
T36bp
1941
THOMPSON (J. WALTER) COMPANY.
POPULATION AND ITS DISTRIBUTION, THE
UNITED STATES MARKETS. 6TH ED. NEW
YORK, MCGRAW-HILL, 1941.
429 P. (WORLD MARKETS SERIES)

1. POPULATION. 2. MARKETING.
3. ADVERTISING. 4. STATISTICS.

Virginia. University. *Bureau of Population and Economic
Research.* The impact of a new manufacturing plant
... 1951. (Card 2)

1 v. (various pagings) maps, diagrs, tables. 28 cm.
On cover: Preliminary copy, not for distribution.
"Initial report of Part I of the Charlotte County Research Project."

1. Traffic surveys - Charlotte Co., Va. 2. Charlotte Co., Va. - Soc.
condit. 3. Roads - Charlotte Co., Va. I. Title.

HE371.V8C45   *301.35 323.354   A 52-9502
Virginia. State Library
for Library of Congress   [11]†

312
T36bp
1961
THOMPSON (J. WALTER) COMPANY.
POPULATION AND ITS DISTRIBUTION, THE
UNITED STATES MARKETS. 8TH ED. NEW
YORK, MCGRAW-HILL, 1961.
471 P. (WORLD MARKETS SERIES)

1. POPULATION. 2. MARKETING.
3. ADVERTISING. 4. STATISTICS.

312.8
(755)
T36
THOMPSON, LORIN ANDREW.
FISCAL SURVEY OF THE NORTHERN VIRGINIA
REGION, SEPTEMBER 1955. REPORT ON
OUTLOOK FOR POPULATION INCREASES IN
NORTHERN VIRGINIA, 1960 AND 1965, FOR
THE NORTHERN VIRGINIA REGIONAL PLANNING
AND ECONOMIC DEVELOPMENT COMMISSION.
CHARLOTTESVILLE, VA., 1955.
26L.
PRESS RELEASE.
1. POPULATION FORECASTING - NORTHERN
VIRGINIA. I. NORTHERN VIRGINIA
REGIONAL PLANNING AND ECONOMIC
DEVELOPMENT COMMISSION. II. TITLE.

699.81
T36F
THOMPSON, NORMAN J.
FIRE BEHAVIOR AND SPRINKLERS, BY
NORMAN J. THOMPSON. BOSTON, NATIONAL
FIRE PROTECTION ASSOCIATION, 1964.
157P.

1. FIRE PREVENTION. I. TITLE.
II. TITLE: SPRINKLERS.

362
P25
THOMPSON, JOHN D   JT. AU.
PELLETIER, ROBERT J
YALE INDEX MEASURES DESIGN EFFICIENCY,
BY ROBERT J. PELLETIER AND JOHN D.
THOMPSON.

(IN THE MODERN HOSPITAL, VOL. 95, NO. 5
NOV. 1960, P.73-77.)

1. HOSPITALS. I. THOMPSON, JOHN D.,
JT. AU. II. YALE UNIVERSITY. III. THE
MODERN HOSPITAL. IV. TITLE.

VF
312(755)
T36
Thompson, Lorin Andrew, 1902-
Virginia. University. *Bureau of Population and Economic
Research.*
Population changes in Virginia [by] Lorin A. Thompson,
director, Bureau of Population and Economic Research,
Univ. of Virginia. [Charlottesville, 1949]

9 p. maps, tables. 33 cm.
Caption title.
"Analyzes the changes which have occurred in the cities and coun-
ties of Virginia since 1940."

1. Virginia - Population. I. Thompson, Lorin Andrew, 1902-
II. Title. 2. Population shifts - Va.

A 49-4282*
Virginia. State Library
for Library of Congress   [2]

658.800.15
(016)
T36
1957
THOMPSON, RALPH BURNHAM.
MARKETING RESEARCH; A SELECTED
AND ANNOTATED BIBLIOGRAPHY.
AUSTIN, TEXAS. BUREAU OF BUSINESS
RESEARCH, UNIVERSITY OF TEXAS, 1957.
41P.

1. MARKETING RESEARCH.
I. UNIVERSITY OF TEXAS. BUREAU OF
BUSINESS RESEARCH. II. TITLE.

FF-UK-Housing for the aged
DATE OF REQUEST 3/31/53   L. C. CARD NO.
MAY
AUTHOR
Thompson, Kenneth, John Vaughan-Morgan and Angus Maude
TITLE
The care of old people.
SERIES

EDITION   PUB. DATE 1952   PAGING 90p.
PUBLISHER
London, Conservative Political Centre

RECOMMENDED BY   REVIEWED IN
                  Lib Ctr Rev 11-12/52 p.21
ORDER RECORD

301.36
(016)
B25
Thompson, Marcia, jt. au.
Bell, Gwen.
Social activities in urban space: an annotated bibliography of behavioral implications
for environmental design, by Gwen Bell and
Marcia Thompson. Pittsburgh, Publications
Office, Graduate School of Public and International Affairs, University of Pittsburgh,
1971.
139p.
1. Sociology, Urban - Bibl. 2. Community
structure - Bibl. I. Thompson, Marcia, jt.
au. II. Pittsburgh. University. Graduate
School of Public and International
Affairs. III. Title.

VF
658.800.15
(016)
T36
1951
Thompson, Ralph Burnham
A selected and annotated bibliography of
marketing research. Rev. [Austin, Tex.]
Univ. of Texas, Nov. 1951.
32 p. (Texas. University. Bureau of
Business Research. Bibliography no. 8)

1. Marketing research - Bibl. I. Series.

699.83
T36

THOMPSON, ROBERT A
    PROTECTION OF SMALL BUILDINGS AGAINST HIGH VELOCITY WINDS. GAINESVILLE, 1949. 52P. (FLORIDA. UNIVERSITY, GAINESVILLE. ENGINEERING AND INDUSTRIAL EXPERIMENT STATION. BULLETIN SERIES NO. 28)

    COVER TITLE: ENGINEERING PROGRESS AT THE UNIVERSITY OF FLORIDA, V. 3, NO. 7, SEPTEMBER, 1949.

    1. BUILDINGS   - WIND STRESSES.

Thompson, Stewart.

658
A52r
no. 32

American Management Association.
    Management creeds and philosophies, by Stewart Thompson. New York, 1958.
    127p. (AMA research study no. 32)

    1. Management. I. Thompson, Stewart.

312
T36EF

THOMPSON, WARREN S
    THE EFFECT OF HOUSING UPON POPULATION GROWTH. NEW YORK, 1938.
    [359] -368P.
    REPRINTED FROM THE MILBANK MEMORIAL FUND QUARTERLY, V. 16, NO. 4, OCT. 1938.

    1. POPULATION. 2. HOUSING - SOCIAL ASPECTS. I. MILBANK MEMORIAL FUND QUARTERLY. II. TITLE.

Class No.
Slum construction

Author (surname first)
Thompson, Robert A

Accession No.

Ordered
Protection of small buildings against high velocity winds

Source
Place   Publisher *Fla. U.*

Received *11/14/50*
Cost

Purchase Order No.
Date *9/49*   Pages *52*   List Price   Est. Cost

Date
Edition or Series *Fla. Eng. & Ind. Exp. Sta. Bull. 28*

L. C. No.
Recommended by
Reviewed in

11-305 (2-50)   HOUSING AND HOME FINANCE AGENCY: Office of the Administrator   16—61187-1   GPO

511.8
T62

Thompson, T   P
Todhunter, Ralph
    ... Text-book on compound interest and annuities-certain. 4th ed. rev. by R. C. Simmonds and T. P. Thompson. Cambridge, University Press [1937]
    xiv, 270 p. tables.

    Reprinted 1950.
    Published for the Institute of Actuaries.

1.Compound interest. I.Simmonds, R. C. II. Thompson, T. P. III.Institute of Actuaries.

312
T36e

Thompson, Warren Simpson.
    Estimates of future population of the United States, 1940-2000. Prepared by Warren S. Thompson and P.K. Whelpton of the Scripps Foundation for Research in Population Problems, for the Committee on Population Problems of the National Resources Planning Board. Washington, Govt. Print. Off., 1943.
    137 p.

3c

    1. Population. 2. Population forecasting. I. Whelpton, Pascal Kidder, jt. au. II. U.S. National Resources Planning Board. Committee on Population Problems. III.   Title.

711.3
(79647)
T36

Thompson (Ronald) and Associates.
    The metropolitan plan for the cities of Pocatello and Alameda, the Village of Chubbuck, and Bannock County, Idaho. Prepared under contract for the Bannock County Regional Planning Commission. Butte, Mont., 1961.
    115p.

    U.S. Urban Renewal Adm. UPAP.

      (Cont'd. on next card)

658.564
M21c

Thompson, Van B   jt. au.
Meacham, Alan D   ed.
    Computer applications service. Edited by Alan D. Meacham and Van B. Thompson. Detroit, American Data Processing, 1962-
    2v. (loose-leaf) semi annual.

    Library has: v.1-7   in 2

    1. Automation. I. Thompson, Van B., jt. au. II. Title.

VF
312
T36

Thompson, Warren S
    The growth of metropolitan districts in the United States: 1900-1940. Washington, Govt. Print. Off., 1948.
    vi, 61 p. map, tables.
    Dr. Warren S. Thompson is Director of the Scripps Foundation for Research in Population Problems.
    1.City growth. I.U.S. Bureau of the Census. II.Scripps Foundation for Research in Population Problems. III.Title.

711.3
(79647)
T36

Thompson (Ronald) and Associates.   The metropolitan plan ...   (Card 2)

    1. Metropolitan area planning - Pocatello, Idaho. 2. Metropolitan area planning - Alameda, Idaho. I. Bannock Co., Idaho. Regional Planning Commission. II. U.S. URA-UPAP. Bannock Co., Idaho.

538.56
M21

Thompson, Van B   jt. ed.
Meacham, Alan D   ed.
    Total systems. Edited by Alan D. Meacham and Van B. Thompson. Enoch J. Hage and Maurice F. Ronayne, coordinating editors. 1st ed. Detroit, American Data Processing, 1962.
    200p.   (Data processing library series)

    1. Automation. I. Thompson, Van B., jt. ed. II. Title.

312
(771)
T36

Thompson, Warren S
    Migration within Ohio, 1935-40; a study in the re-distribution of population. Oxford, Ohio, Scripps Foundation for Research in Population Problems, Miami Univ., c1951.
    227 p. graphs, tables. (Scripps Foundation studies in population distribution)

2c

    Processed.

    1.Population shifts-Ohio. I.Series.

711.73
:330
(764)
T29pr

Thompson, Russell G
Texas Transportation Institute.
    A preliminary study of the economic impact of Stemmons Freeway, a section of interstate 35 E, Dallas, Texas, by Russell G. Thompson and others. A special report to the Bureau of Public Roads, United States Dept. of Commerce. College Station, Tex., 1960.
    40p.

    1. Highways - Dallas - Economic effect. I. Thompson, Russell G. II. U.S. Bureau of Public Roads.

330
:(69)
T36

Thompson, Virginia.
    The Malagasy Republic; Madagascar today, by Virginia Thompson and Richard Adloff. Stanford, Calif., Stanford University Press, 1965.
    504p.

    Bibliography: p. 485-494.

    1. Economic conditions - Malagasy Republic. 2. History - Malagasy Republic. 3. Political science - Malagasy Republic. I. Adloff, Richard, jt. au. II. Title.

711(73)
:06
A52
A1951

Thompson, Warren S
    Planning for an aging population.   In ASPO Planning. Chicago, 1952. p. 89-105.

    Contents.—Our old people, Warren S. Thompson.—State Planning for the aged, Walter E. Keyes.—Reporter's summary, Andre Faure.

711.73
:330
(764)
T29p

Thompson, Russell H
Texas Transportation Institute.
    Preliminary study of the Economic impact of a section of San Antonio's Loop 13 Expressway, by Russell H. Thompson and others. A special report to the Bureau of Public Roads, United States Dept. of Commerce. College Station, Tex., 1960.
    39p.

    1. Highways - San Antonio - Economic effect. I. Thompson, Russell H. II. U.S. Bureau of Public Roads.

728.1
(41)
T36

Thompson, W
    The housing handbook. London, National Housing Reform Council, 1903.
    101p.
    A practical manual for the use of officers, members, and committees of local authorities, ministers of religion, members of Parliament, and all social or municipal reformers interested in the housing of the working classes.

    1. Housing - U.K. 2. U.K. - Housing. 3. Company housing. I. National Housing Reform Council, London. II. Title.

312
T36p

Thompson, Warren S
    Plenty of people [basic facts of population]. Lancaster, Pa., Jacques Cattell Press, 1944.
    246p. (War and peace series)

    1. Population. I. Title.

658
A52r
no. 54

Thompson, Stewart.
    How companies plan, by Stewart Thompson, with the assistance of George H. Haas. New York, American Management Association, 1962.
    215p. (AMA research study 54)

    Bibliography: p. 205-210.

    1. Management. I. Haas, George H., jt. au. II. American Management Association.

711.4
P27

Thompson, Warren S.
    The atomic threat.   In Peterson, E.T., Cities are abnormal. Norman, Okla., 1946. p. 226-238.

    1.Decentralization. I.Title.

312
827
Prelim.

Thompson, Warren S
Scripps Foundation for Research in Population Problems.
    Population growth in standard metropolitan areas, 1900-1950, with an analysis of urbanized areas, by Donald J. Bogue. Oxford, Ohio, June 1952.
    105 p. charts, tables.
    Final report, Research project no. 0-U-66, Housing and Home Finance Agency.
    Project director: Warren S. Thompson; Staff technician: Edmond Hoben.

      (See Card No. 2)

312
827
Prelim.   Scripps Foundation for Research in Population
             Problems.
               Population growth in standard metropolitan
             areas, 1900-1950, with an analysis of urbanized
             areas, by Donald J. Bogue. 1952. (Card No. 2)

               1.Population. 2.Metropolitan areas. 3.
             Housing research contracts. I.Bogue, Donald J.
             II.Thompson, Warren. III. Hoben, Edmond. IV.
             HHFA. OA. Div. of Housing Research. V.Title.

312
T36po   Thompson, Warren Simpson, 1887-
               Population trends in the United States, by
             Warren S. Thompson and P.K. Whelpton. New
             York, McGraw-Hill, 1933.
               415 p. (Recent social trends monographs).

               1. Population.   I. Whelpton, P.K., jt.
             au. II. Title.

Folio
711.4 Thompson (Ronald) and associates.
(786)   Master plan, Missoula urban area. Prepared
M47   for Missoula City-County Planning Board.
             Butte, Mont., 1961.
               85p.
               Prepared in cooperation with Montana State
             Planning Board.
               U.S. Urban Renewal Adm. UPAP.

               1. Master plan - Missoula, Mont. I. Missoula,
             Mont. City-County Planning Board. II. U.S.
             URA-UPAP. Missoula, Mont.

711.4   Thompson, Warren S.
(77178) Cincinnati, Ohio. City Planning Commission.
C45   The population of the Cincinnati metropolitan
no. 1   area. Cincinnati, Dec. 1945.
               157 p. graphs, maps, tables. (Cincinnati
             metropolitan master plan study, no. 1)

               "Results of the studies made by [Scripps]
             Foundation are presented by Dr. Warren S.
             Thompson...in this report." p. 1
               Cover title: Population.
               Processed.

312.1
T36   Thompson, Warren S
               Research memorandum on internal migration
             in the depression. Prepared under the
             direction of the Committee on Studies in
             Social Aspects of the Depression. New York,
             1937.
               86 p. (Social Science Research Council.
             Bulletin, 30)

               1. Population shifts. I. Title: Migration
             in the depression.   (Series) Social Science
             Research Council. Bulletin, 30.

Thompson Ramo Woolridge.
 see   TRW Systems Group.

312
T36   Thompson, Warren S
1942   Population problems. 3d ed.   New York,
             McGraw-Hill, c1942.
               xi, 471 p. graphs, tables. (McGraw-Hill
             publications in sociology)

               "References" at the end of each chapter.

               1.Population.

301.15   Thompson, Wayne E
157   Institute for Local Self Government,
             Berkeley, Calif.
               Organizing cities to solve "people prob-
             lems." An interview with Wayne E. Thompson,
             former City Manager of Oakland. Berkeley,
             Calif., Institute for Local Self Govern-
             ment, 1966.
               87p.

               1. Community development - Citizen partici-
             pation. 2. Municipal government. 3. Local
             government.   I. Thompson, Wayne E.
             II. Title.

711.73   Thomson, J Michael.
(41)   Motorways in London. Report of a working
T36   party. Published for the London Amenity and
             Transport Association. Beverly Hills,
             Calif., Sage Publications, 1969.
               194p.

               1. Highways - U.K. - London. I. London
             Amenity and Transport Association.
             II. Title.

312.015 THOMPSON, WARREN SIMPSON.
T36   POPULATION PROBLEMS. 4TH ED. NEW
             YORK, McGRAW-HILL, 1953.
               488P.

               1. POPULATION.   2. TITLE.

301.36
T36   Thompson, Wilbur R
1965   A preface to urban economics. Published
             for Resources for the Future, Inc. Balti-
             more, Johns Hopkins Press, 1965.
               413p.

               1. Sociology, Urban. 2. Economic develop-
             ment. 3. City growth. 4. Housing. 5. Urban
             renewal. 6. City planning. 7. Social
             conditions. I. Resources for the Future.
             II. Title: Urban economics. III. Title.

Folio   Thomson, John W   Cast iron buildings.
720   The Origins of cast iron architecture in
074   America. New introd. by W. Knight Sturges.
             New York, Da Capo Press, 1970.
               1v. (Da Capo Press series in architecture
             and decorative art, vol. 13)
               Bibliography: p. [xi]-xii.
               Comprised of reprints of the 1865 ed. of
             illustrations of iron architecture made by
             the Architectural Iron Works of the city of
             New York, by D.D. Badger, and of the 1856
             ed. of Cast iron buildings: their con-
             struction and advantages, by James
                           (Cont'd on next card)

312   Thompson, Warren S.
827p
Prelim.   Scripps Foundation for Research in Population
             Problems.
               Population redistribution within metropolitan
             areas of the United States: 1900-1950 [by]
             Amos H. Hawley. Oxford, Ohio, 1952.
               229 p., 1 L., graphs, tables.

               Report prepared under research contract
             No. O-U-66, Housing and Home Finance Agency.
             Project Director: Warren S. Thompson;
             Staff technician: Edmond Hoben.

                    (See Card No. 2)

301.36
T36   Thompson, Wilbur R
2c   A preface to urban economics; toward a
             conceptual framework for study and research.
             Preliminary. Washington, Resources for the
             Future, 1963.
               320p.

               1. Sociology, Urban. 2. Economic research.
             I. Resources for the Future. II. Title:
             Urban economics. III. Title.

Folio   The Origins...1970.   (Card 2)
720
074   Bogardus, who attributes authorship to J.W.
             Thomson.

               1. Architecture. 2. Iron. 3. Metal-work.
             I. Bogardus, James, 1800-1874. II. Badger,
             Daniel D. Illustrations of iron architec-
             ture. III. Thomson, John W. Cast iron
             buildings. IV. Title: Cast iron architec-
             ture in America.

312
827p
Prelim. Scripps Foundation for Research in Population
             Problems. Population redistribution ...
               1952.   (Card No. 2)

               Published as: Hawley, A. H. Changing shape
             of metropolitan America. 1956. 312 827p

               1.Metropolitan areas. 2.City growth. 3.
             Population. 4.Housing research contracts.
             I.Hawley, Amos H. II.HHFA. OA. Div. of
             Housing Research. III.Title. IV.Thompson,
             Warren S. V. Hoben, Edmond.

333.33
T36   Thompson, Willard M
               The effectiveness of salesmanship in selling
             real estate. Sacramento, Calif., Sacramento
             State College, [1967?]
N.a.1   101p.
Laf.a.2   1. Real estate business. 2. Real property.
             I. California. State College, Sacramento.
             Bureau of Business Research. II. Title.
             III. Title: Salesmanship in selling real estate.

711.5   Thomson, Ga. Planning Commission.
(75863)   Draft of proposed comprehensive zoning
:347)   ordinance for Thomson, Georgia, by Sydney
T36   Carter. Prepared under contract with Georgia
             Dept. of Commerce. Augusta, Ga., 1960.
               36p. map.
               U.S. Urban Renewal Adm. UPAP.

               1. Zoning legislation - Thomson, Ga.
             I. U.S. URA-UPAP. Thomson, Ga.

VF   Thompson, Warren S
312   U.S. National Resources Committee.
N17   Population statistics. 3.Urban data.
1937   Material prepared for a study of population
             problems. Washington, Govt. Print. Off.,
             Oct. 1937.
               52 p. tables.

               Contents.-Urban population changes, by Warren
             S. Thompson.-Metropolitan regions, by Louis Wirth
             and Lewis Copeland.
               1.Population. I.Copeland, Lewis. II.Thompson,
             Warren S. III.Wirth, Louis.

Folio   Thompson, N.Y. City Planning Board.
711.4 Sargent-Webster-Crenshaw & Folley.
(74735)   A comprehensive plan for the town of
T36   Thompson. Prepared for the New York State
             Dept. of Commerce [in cooperation with
             Thompson Planning Board] Syracuse, N.Y.,
             1964.
               137p.
               U.S. Urban Renewal Adm. UPAP.

               1. Master plan - Thompson, N.Y.
             I. Thompson, N.Y. City Planning Board.
             II. U.S. URA- UPAP. Thompson, N.Y.

333.38   Thomson, Ga. Planning Commission.
(75863)   Draft of proposed subdivision regu-
T36   lations for Thomson, Georgia, by Sydney
             Carter. Prepared under contract with
             Georgia Dept. of Commerce. Rev. Augusta,
             Ga., 1960.
               19p.
               U.S. Urban Renewal Adm. UPAP.

               1. Subdivision regulation - Thomson, Ga.
             I. U.S. URA-UPAP. Thomson, Ga.

352.1
(75863)
T36
Addendum
    Thomson, Ga. Planning Commission.
       Thomson, Georgia: addendum to capital improvements program, by Sydney Carter. Prepared under contract with Georgia Dept. of Commerce. Augusta, Ga. [1960]
       5p.

       U.S. Urban Renewal Adm. UPAP.

       1. Capital improvement programs - Thomson, Ga. I. U.S. URA-UPAP. Thomson, Ga.

711.14
(75863)
T36f
    Thomson, Ga. Planning Commission.
       Thomson, Georgia: future land use plan, by Sydney Carter. Prepared under contract with the Georgia Dept. of Commerce. Thomson, 1960.
       17p.

       U.S. Urban Renewal Adm. UPAP.

       1. Land use - Thomson, Ga. I. Carter, Sydney. II. U.S. URA-UPAP. Thomson, Ga.

1026
    THOMSON - MCDUFFIE COUNTY PLANNING COMMISSION.
       MUNICIPAL SERVICES, FACILITIES, AND FINANCES. BY CENTRAL SAVANNAH RIVER AREA PLANNING AND DEVELOPMENT COMMISSION. AUGUSTA, GA., 1969.
       68P. (HUD 701 REPORT)

       1. MUNICIPAL SERVICES - THOMSON, GA. I. CENTRAL SAVANNAH RIVER AREA PLANNING & DEVELOPMENT COMMISSION. II. HUD. 71. THOMSON, GA.

352.6
(75863)
T36
Addendum
    Thomson, Ga. Planning Commission.
       Thomson, Georgia: addendum to community facilities plan, by Sydney Carter. Prepared under contract with the Georgia Dept. of Commerce. Augusta, Ga. [1960?]
       8p.

       U.S. Urban Renewal Adm. UPAP.

       1. Community facilities - Thomson, Ga. I. U.S. URA-UPAP. Thomson, Ga.

388
(75863)
T36
    Thomson, Ga. Planning Commission.
       Thomson, Georgia: transportation study, transportation survey, central business district, major street plan, by Sydney Carter. Prepared under contract with the Georgia Dept. of Commerce. Thomson, 1960.
       32p.

       U.S. Urban Renewal Adm. UPAP.

       1. Transportation - Thomson, Ga. 2. Business districts - Thomson, Ga.   I. U.S. URA-UPAP.   Thomson, Ga.

334.1
(485)
H93
    Thoors, Sten.
    Hyresgästernas Sparkasse- och Byggnadsföreningars Riksförbund.
       Innerstad; en granskning av aktuella problem vid innerstadens förnyelse utförd, av Curt Strehlenert och Sten Thoors. [Stockholm] 1960.
       71p.

       1. Cooperative housing - Sweden. I. Strehlenert, Curt. II. Thoors, Sten.

711.4
(75863)
T36
    Thomson, Ga. Planning Commission.
       Thomson, Ga.: addendum to continuing planning programs, by Sydney Carter. Prepared under contract with Georgia Dept. of Commerce. Augusta, Ga. [1960]
       4p.

       U.S. Urban Renewal Adm. UPAP.

       1. City planning - Thomson, Ga. I. U.S. URA-UPAP. Thomson, Ga.

336.2
T36
    Thomson, John Cameron.
       Taxation for growth, based on a statement on national policy issued by the Research and Policy Committee of the Committee for Economic Development. New York, Committee for Economic Development, 1957.
       20 p. illus.

       1. Taxation. I. Committee for Economic Development. II. Title.

630
R65
    Thorbecke, Erik, ed.
    The Role of agriculture in economic development; a conference of the Universities-National Bureau Committee for Economic Research. Erik Thorbecke, editor. New York, National Bureau of Economic Research; distributed by Columbia University Press, 1969.
       480p. (Universities-National Bureau Conference series, no. 21)

       1. Agriculture. 2. Economic development. I. Thorbecke, Erik, ed. II. Universities-National Bureau of Economic Research.

711.581
(75863)
T36
    Thomson, Ga. Planning Commission.
       Thomson, Georgia: addendum to neighborhood analyses, by Sydney Carter. Prepared under contract with the Georgia Dept. of Commerce. Augusta, Ga., [1960?]
       16p.

       U.S. Urban Renewal Adm. UPAP.

       1. Neighborhood planning - Thomson, Ga. I. U.S. URA-UPAP. Thomson, Ga.

VP
330
(07)
C655
    Thomson, J Cameron.
    Committee for Economic Development.
       The work of the Business-Education Committee, Committee for Economic Development, by J. Cameron Thomson. New York, 1960.
       [9]p.

       1. Economic planning - Study and teaching. I. Thomson, J. Cameron.

628.2
T36
    THORN, ROLAND BERKELEY, ED.
       THE DESIGN OF LAND DRAINAGE WORKS; A COLLECTION OF PAPERS, SELECTED, ANNOTATED, AND ARR. IN THE FORM OF A DESIGN HANDBOOK. LONDON, BUTTERWORTHS, 1959.
       235P.

       1. DRAINAGE. I. TITLE: LAND DRAINAGE WORKS.

711.14
(75863)
T36
    Thomson, Ga. Planning Commission.
       Thomson, Georgia: an analysis of existing land use, community facilities, neighborhood analysis, by Sydney Carter. Prepared under contract with the Georgia Dept. of Commerce. Thomson, 1960.
       47p.

       U.S. Urban Renewal Adm. UPAP.

    1. Land use - Thomson, Ga. 2. Community facilities - Thomson, Ga. 3. Neighborhood planning - Thomson, Ga. I. U.S. URA-UPAP.   Thomson, Ga.

711.73
(41)
T36
    Thomson, J Michael.
       Motorways in London. Report of a working party. Published for the London Amenity and Transport Association. Beverly Hills, Calif., Sage Publications, 1969.
       194p.

       1. Highways - U.K. - London. I. London Amenity and Transport Association. II. Title.

551.49
T36
    THORN, ROLAND BERKELEY.
       RIVER ENGINEERING AND WATER CONSERVATION WORKS. LONDON, BUTTERWORTHS, 1966.
       520P.

       1. HYDROLOGY. 2. RIVERS. 3. WATER RESOURCES. I. TITLE.

352.1
(75863)
T36
    Thomson, Georgia. Planning Commission.
       Thomson, Georgia: capital improvements, planning administration, by Sydney Carter. Prepared under contract with the Georgia Dept. of Commerce. Thomson, 1960.
       18p.

       U.S. Urban Renewal Adm. UPAP.

    1. Capital improvement programs - Thomson, Ga. 2. City planning administration - Thomson, Ga. I. Carter, Sydney.   II. U.S. URA-UPAP. Thomson, Ga.

020
T 36
    Thomson, Sarah Katharine.
       Interlibrary loan procedure manual. Chicago, Interlibrary Loan Committee, Reference Services Div., American Library Association, 1970.
       116p.

       Bibliography: p. 111-113.

       1. Library science. I. American Library Association. II. Title.

624.131
T36s
    Thornburn, Thomas H
       Stabilization of soils with inorganic salts and bases: a review of the literature. A report of the investigation of use of admixtures for chemical (and physico-chemical) stabilization of natural soils for road building, by Thomas H. Thornburn and Romeo Mura. Conducted by the Soil Mechanics Laboratory, University of Illinois and others. Urbana, University of Illinois, 1969.
       36p. (Illinois. University. Dept. of
(Cont'd on next card)

330
(75863)
T36
    Thomson, Ga. Planning Commission.
       Thomson, Georgia: economic base survey and population study by Sydney Carter. Prepared under contract with the Georgia Dept. of Commerce. Thomson, 1960.
       30p.

       U.S. Urban Renewal Adm. UPAP.
    1. Economic base studies - Thomson, Ga. 2. Population - Thomson, Ga. I. Carter, Sydney. II. U.S. URA-UPAP. Thomson, Ga.

1025
    THOMSON - MCDUFFIE COUNTY PLANNING COMMISSION.
       COMPLETION REPORT, URBAN PLANNING ASSISTANCE PROGRAM, PROJECT GEORGIA NO. P-89. PREPARED BY STATE PLANNING AND PROGRAMMING BUREAU, STATE OF GEORGIA. ATLANTA, 1970.
       3L. (HUD 701 REPORT)

       1. CITY PLANNING - THOMSON, GA. I. GEORGIA. STATE PLANNING AND PROGRAMMING BUREAU. II. HUD. 701. THOMSON, GA.

624.131
T36s
    Thornburn, Thomas H   Stabilization of...1969.   (Card 2)

       Civil Engineering. Civil engineering studies; soil mechanics series no. 14; Illinois Cooperative Highway Research Program series no. 81)

       1. Soils. 2. Road construction. 3. Road construction - Bibl. 4. Soils - Bibl. I. Mura, Romeo, jt. au. II. Illinois. University. III. Title.

301.36
T360
THORNDIKE, EDWARD L
144 SMALLER CITIES. NEW YORK,
HARCOURT, BRACE AND CO., 1940.
135P.

1. SOCIOLOGY, URBAN. I. TITLE.

711
(016)
C65
no.181
Thornton, Barbara.
Gaming techniques for city planning: a
bibliography. [New Haven] Yale University
Art Library, 1971.
14p. (Council of Planning Librarians.
Exchange bibliography no. 181)

1. Planning – Bibl. 2. City planning –
Bibl. I. Yale University. Art Library.
II. Title. (Series: Council of Planning
Librarians. Exchange bibliography no. 181)

711.74
(7426)
P51
A thoroughfare plan for the City of Ports-
mouth, New Hampshire.
Planning and Renewal Associates.
A thoroughfare plan for the City of Ports-
mouth, New Hampshire. Prepared ... for New
Hampshire State Planning and Development
Commission, Concord, N.H. under section 701
of the Housing act of 1954. Newton Centre,
Mass., 1956.
22p.n maps, tables.

(Continued on next card)

301.36
T36Y
THORNDIKE, EDWARD L
YOUR CITY. NEW YORK, HARCOURT,
BRACE & CO., 1939.
204P.

1. SOCIOLOGY, URBAN. I. TITLE.

693.5
T36
no.3

Laf.
Thornton, H T
Field soniscope tests of concrete; report 3,
ten-year summary of results. Vicksburg, Miss.
U.S. Army Engineer Waterways Experiment Station
Corps of Engineers, 1967.
1v. (U.S. Waterways Experiment Station,
Vicksburg, Miss. Technical memorandum no. 6-
383)

1. Concrete construction. 2. Strains and
stresses. I. U.S. Waterways Experiment Station,
Vicksburg, Miss. II. Title.

711.74
(7426)
P51
Planning and Renewal Associates. A thoroughfare plan for the ... (Card 2)

1. Street planning – Portsmouth, N. H.
I. New Hampshire. State Planning and De-
velopment Commission. II. U.S. Urban
Renewal Administration. Urban Planning
Assistance Program. III. Title.

551
(72)
T36
THORNLEY, J H
MEXICO CITY'S EARTHQUAKE DAMAGE, BY
J.H. THORNLEY AND PEDRO ALBIN, JR. NEW
YORK, AMERICAN SOCIETY OF CIVIL
ENGINEERS, 1957.
76-80P.

REPRINTED FROM CIVIL ENGINEERING, V.
27, NO. 10, OCTOBER 1957.

1. EARTHQUAKES – MEXICO. I. TITLE.
II. ALBIN, PEDRO, JT. AU.

VF
691.42
T36
Thornton, John C
Relation between bond and the surface
physics of masonry units. Journal of the
American Ceramic Society. p. 105-120.
April 1953. illus.
Reprint.
Presented at the Fifth-fourth annual
meeting, the American Ceramic Society,
Pittsburgh, Pa., April 29, 1952.

1. Bricks.

388
(764)
D15
1965
Thoroughfares: a guide plan for streets: City
of Dallas.
Dallas. Dept. of City Planning.
Thoroughfares: a guide plan for streets: City
of Dallas. Prepared for the city Plan Commission. Dallas, 1965.
1 v.

1. Transportation – Dallas. 2. Streets –
Dallas. I. Title.

312.1
(73)
T36

2C.
THORNTHWAITE, CHARLES WARREN.
INTERNAL MIGRATION IN THE UNITED
STATES, BY C. WARREN THORNTHWAITE
ASSISTED BY HELEN I. SLENTZ.
PHILADELPHIA, UNIVERSITY OF PENNSYLVANIA
PRESS, 1934.
52P. (STUDY OF POPULATION
REDISTRIBUTION, INDUSTRIAL RESEARCH
DEPT., WHARTON SCHOOL OF FINANCE AND
COMMERCE, UNIVERSITY OF PENNSYLVANIA)

1. POPULATION. 2. POPULATION SHIFTS.
3. SOCIAL CONDITIONS – U.S.
I. SLENTZ, HELEN IRENE, JT. AU.
(CONTINUED ON NEXT CARD)

VF
697.3
:621.415
P25p
1951
Thornton, R.C., jt. au.
Penrod, Estel B
Performance of an earth heat pump
operating intermittently on the cooling
cycle by E.B. Penrod and R.C. Thornton.
Transactions of the Kentucky Academy of
Science, p. 156-172, Aug. 1951.
Reprint.

338
T36
THORP, WILLARD LONG.
BUSINESS ANNALS, UNITED STATES, ENGLAND,
FRANCE, GERMANY, AUSTRIA, RUSSIA, SWEDEN,
NETHERLANDS, ITALY, ARGENTINA, BRAZIL,
CANADA, SOUTH AFRICA, AUSTRALIA, INDIA,
JAPAN, CHINA. NEW YORK, 1926.
380 P. (NATIONAL BUREAU OF ECONOMIC
RESEARCH. PUBLICATIONS, NO. 8)

1. BUSINESS CYCLES. I. TITLE. II.
NATIONAL BUREAU OF ECONOMIC RESEARCH.

312.1
(73)
T36
THORNTHWAITE, CHARLES WARREN. INTERNAL
MIGRATION IN ...1934. (CARD 2)

II. TITLE. III. TITLE: MIGRATION IN
THE UNITED STATES.

320
H86
Thornton, Robert L jt. comp.
Hupman, Richard D comp.
Nomination and election of the President and
Vice President of the United States, including
the manner of selecting delegates to national
political conventions. Compiled by Richard D.
Hupman and Robert L. Thornton, under the direc-
tion of Francis R. Valeo. Wash., Govt. Print.
Off., 1972.
273p.

Suppl. -- --- Supplement. 1972. 107p.

1. U.S. Presidents. 2. Elections.
I. Thornton, Robert L., jt. comp. II. Title.

VF
728.6
T36
Thorpe, Alice C
Family use of farm homes; a study of activities
carried on by and preferences of family members,
by Alice C. Thorpe and Irma H. Gross. East
Lansing, Mich., Agricultural Experiment Station,
Dept. of Home Management, Apr. 1952.
63 p. graphs, tables. (Michigan.
Agricultural Experiment Station. Technical
bulletin 227)

1.Family living requirements. 2.Farm housing.
I.Gross, Irma H., jt. au. II.Title. III.Series.

627.4
B87
Thornthwaite (C. W.) Associates. Laboratory
of Climatology.
Burton, Ian.
The shores of megalopolis: costal occupence
and human adjustment to flood hazard, by Ian
Burton and others. Elmer, N.J., 1965.
603p. (C. W. Thornthwaite Associates.
Laboratory of Climatology. Publications in
Climatology, v. 13, no. 3)
Final report, Office of Naval Research.
Contract nonr 40-43(00) NR 388-073.

1. Floods. 2. Storms. I. Thornthwaite
(C. W.) Associates. Laboratory of
Climatology.

5570
THORNTON, COLO. CITY COUNCIL.
1987 DEVELOPMENT POLICY AND PLAN.
THORNTON, COLO., 1966.
64P. (HUD 701 REPORT)

1. CITY PLANNING – THORNTON, COLO.
I. HUD. 701. THORNTON, COLO.

VF
728.6
T36h
Thorpe, Alice C.
How homes are used on farms and in small
cities; a comparative study of the activities
carried on in the homes, by Alice C. Thorpe
and Irma H. Gross. East Lansing, Michigan,
Agricultural Experiment Station, Michigan State
University, Dec. 1955.
52 p. graphs, tables. (Michigan
Agricultural Experiment Station. Technical
Bulletin 254)

1. Family living requirements. 2. Farm housing.
I. Gross, Irma H. II. Title. III. Series.

332.72
T36
THORNTON, ALLAN FITZHUGH.
THE ECONOMIC IMPACT OF FEDERAL
HOUSING ADMINISTRATION INSURANCE
PROGRAMS. WASHINGTON, 1965.
189L.
PHOTOCOPY OF TYPESCRIPT.
THESIS (PH.D.) – AMERICAN UNIVERSITY.

1. U.S. FEDERAL HOUSING
ADMINISTRATION. 2. MORTGAGE FINANCE.
3. HOUSING – ECONOMIC EFFECT.
I. TITLE.

711.73
(756622)
G72t
Thoroughfare plan.
Greensboro, N.C. Dept. of Planning
Thoroughfare plan, Greensboro, North
Carolina. Greensboro, N.C., 1965.
48p.

1. Highways – Greensboro, N.C.
2. Traffic – Greensboro, N.C. I. Title.

VF
392
T36
Thorpe, Alice C
Patterns of family interaction in farm and
town homes. East Lansing, Mich., Michigan
State University, Agricultural Experiment
Station, April 1957.
37 p. (Michigan. Agricultural Experiment
Station. Technical bulletin 260)

1.Family. (Series.)

VF
728.1
:325
(016)
T36

Tlorpe, Margaret Peterson
The racial restrictive covenant, an annotated bibliography. Seattle, Wash., Municipal Reference Library, Oct. 1948.
12 l.

Processed.

1. Deed restrictions. 2. Minority groups-Housing-Bibl. I. Seattle. Public Library. Municipal Reference Library.

370
:325
C51

Clark, Donald Henry, 1930–
Those children; case studies from the inner-city school, by Donald H. Clark and others. Belmont, Calif., Wadsworth Pub. Co., 1970.
334p.

Bibliography: p. 331–334.

1. Education – Minority groups. I. Title. II. Title: Case studies from the inner-city school.

647.1
L11
no.1570-6

Three budgets for a retired couple in urban areas of the United States, 1967-68.
U.S. Bureau of Labor Statistics.
Three budgets for a retired couple in urban areas of the United States, 1967-68. Washington, U.S. Dept. of Labor, Bureau of Labor Statistics, 1970.
74p. (Its Bulletin no. 1570-6)

1. Family income and expenditure. 2. Old age. I. Title.

624
D15
no.11

Thorsen, Jens.
Dansk Ingeniørforening. Byggerationaliseringsudvalget Montagebyggeri. El-installationer i montagebyggeri. Electrical installations in prefab buildings, av Mogens Voltelen og Jens Thorsen. København, Kommission hos Teknisk Forlag, 1958.
11p. diagrs. (Its Publikation nr. 11; Arbejdsudvalg 4: Fuger, tolerencer og installationer)

English summary.

1. Electric apparatus and appliances. I. Voltelen, Mogens. II. Thorsen, Jens.

VF
711.13
W12

Those empty spaces.
Wadham, Samuel MacMahon, 1891–
Those empty spaces; the problems of decentralisation. Sydney, Commonwealth Office of Education [1950]
32 p. illus. maps. 24 cm. (Platypus pamphlet no. 6)
Bibliography: p. 31.

1. Australia—Population. 2. Industries, Location of—Australia. I. Title. (Series)

HB2135.W3   51-36694
Library of Congress   [3]

647.1
L11
no.1570-6
1969-70

Three budgets for a retired couple...
U.S. Bureau of Labor Statistics.
Three budgets for a retired couple in urban areas of the United States, 1969-70. Wash., U.S. Dept. of Labor, Bureau of Labor Statistics, 1971.
29p. (Its Bulletin no. 1570-6, Supplement)

1. Family income and expenditure. 2. Old age. I. Title.

VF
352(792)
T36

Thorsen, Thomas W
The Utah Municipal League, by Thomas W. Thorsen and Evan A. Iverson. [Salt Lake City] Institute of Government, Univ. of Utah, 1949.
12 p. 23 cm. (Utah. University. Institute of Government. Institute publications, 7)
"Institute publications" inside back cover.
Municipal leagues-Utah.
1. Utah Municipal League. I. Iverson, Evan Amos, joint author. II. Title. III. (Series)
JS303.U8U828 1949   352.0792   49-45443*
Library of Congress   [2]

388
W63t

Thoughts about congestion toll pricing for public transport facilities.
Wohl, Martin.
Thoughts about congestion toll pricing for public transport facilities, preliminary draft, by Martin Wohl, Urban Institute, Wash., D.C. [n.p.] [1969?]
34p.
Draft of paper to appear in Highway Research Board publication.

1. Transportation. 2. Journey to work. 3. Highways. I. Highway Research Board. II. Title.

647.1
L11t
Suppl.

Three budgets for an urban family of ...
U.S. Bureau of Labor Statistics.
Three budgets for an urban family of four persons, 1969-70. Wash., 1972.
30p. (Its Bulletin no. 1570-5, suppl.)

1. Family income and expenditure. I. Title.

Class No.	Author (surname first)
Real property –Valuation	Thorson, Ivan A
Accession No.	Title
Ordered	Our confused handling of lease interests in present day appraisal practice?
Source	Place Publisher
Received	Address
Cost	Date 1950 Paging 15 List Price Est. Cost
Purchase Order No.	Edition or Series
Date	Recommended by
L. C. No.	Reviewed in

11-305 (1-56) HOUSING AND HOME FINANCE AGENCY: Office of the Administrator 16—61167-1 GPO

808.8
F67

Thoughts on the business of life.
Forbes magazine.
The Forbes scrapbook of thoughts on the business of life. New York, Forbes, 1968.
574p.

Selections from the "Thoughts on the business of life" page in Forbes magazine.

1. Quotations. I. Title: Thoughts on the business of life.

388
(7471)
T74t

Three decades of service; a pictorial review of accomplishments.
Triborough Bridge and Tunnel Authority.
Three decades of service; a pictorial review of accomplishments. New York, 1966.
77p.

1. Transportation – New York (City)
2. Triborough Bridge and Tunnel Authority.
I. Title.

333.332
T36

Thorson, Ivan August, 1884–
Simplified appraisal system; land economics. Los Angeles, Realty Research Bureau [1949]
288 p. 20 cm.
Replaces the author's Land economics and simplified appraisal system.
Bibliography: p. [277]-284.

1. Real property—Valuation. 2. Real property—California. I. Title.
HD1387.T52   333.3   49-5094*
Library of Congress   [2]

352
E92

The threads of public policy.
Eyestone, Robert.
The threads of public policy: a study in policy leadership. Indianapolis, Bobbs-Merrill, 1971.
197p. (Urban governors series)

Bibliography: p. 178-182.

1. Municipal government. I. Title.

301.15
P27

The three-dimensional city.   Anal.
Hoch, Irving.
The three-dimensional city; contained urban space.
(In Perloff, Harvey S., ed. The quality of the urban environment. 1969. p. 75-135)

1. Land use. I. Title.

711.585
(7471)
C47REL

THORSON, PHIL.
CITIZEN'S HOUSING COUNCIL OF NEW YORK. THE RELATION OF TAX DELINQUENCY IN SLUM AREA TO THE HOUSING PROBLEM; REPORT AND RECOMMENDATIONS OF THE COMMITTEE ON TAXATION...BY PHIL THORSON. NEW YORK, 1942.
35P.

1. SLUMS. 2. REAL PROPERTY – TAXATION. 3. HOUSING – NEW YORK (CITY) I. THORSON, PHIL. II. TITLE.

711.4
(7471)
N28t

The threatened city.
New York (City) Mayor's Task Force on Urban Design.
The threatened city. A report on the design of the City of New York, by James M. Clark and others. William S. Paley, Chairman. New York, 1967.
51p.

1. City planning - New York. 2. Architecture, Modern. 3. Architecture - New York. I. Clark, James M. II. Paley, William S. III. Title.

705
:670
T36

Three-dimensional design.
Thomas, Richard K
Three-dimensional design: a cellular approach. New York, Van Nostrand Reinhold, 1969.
96p.

1. Design, Industrial. 2. Architecture - Designs and plans. 3. Visual aids. I. Title.

332.72
(489)
T36

Thorsteinsson, Th
Mortgaging of real estate in Denmark. Copenhagen, 1949.
39p. tables.

1. Mortgage finance - Denmark. I. Credit Association of Estate Owners in the Danish Islands.

339.5
H17

Three approaches to environmental resource analysis.
Harvard University. Landscape Architecture Research Office.
Three approaches to environmental resource analysis. Wash., Conservation Foundation, 1967.
102p.

Bibliography: p. 93-102.

1. Natural resources. I. Conservation Foundation. II. Title.

323.4
M2

Three-fifths of a man.
McKissick, Floyd.
Three-fifths of a man. London, MacMillan, 1969.
223p.

Foreword by Justice William O. Douglas.
Bibliography: p. 209-214.

1. Civil rights. 2. Minority groups. 3. Race relations. I. Title.

711.437
L15

Three iron mining towns.
Landis, Paul Henry.
Three iron mining towns; a study in cultural change. New York, Arno Press and the New York Times, 1970, 1938.
148p. (The rise of urban America)

1. Villages. 2. Social conditions. 3. Community structure. I. Title. (Series: The rise of urban America)

728.1
H11

3'Rs of housing.
Haas, John H
3'Rs of housing. A guide to housing rehabilitation, relocation housing, and refinancing. Washington, D.C., General Improvement Contractors Association, 1962.
104p.

1. Housing. 2. Mortgage finance. I. General Improvement Contractors Association, Washington, D.C. II. Title.

330
(499)
G72

Three years of national resurgence.
Greece. Ministry to the Prime Minister.
Foreign Press Div.
Three years of national resurgence; 21 April 1967 - 21 April 1970. Athens, 1970.
45p.

1. Economic development - Greece. I. Title.

336
C65th
1970
S-H

#395 billion debt limit.
U.S. Congress. Senate. Committee on Finance.
#395 billion debt limit. Hearing before the Committee on Finance, United States Senate, Ninety-first Congress, second session on H.R. 17802, an act to increase the public debt limit set forth in section 21 of the Second liberty bond act. Wash., Govt. Print. Off., 1970.
67p.
Hearing held June 18, 1970.

1. Budget. 2. Finance. I. Title.

711.4
(77419)
T37

Three Rivers, Mich. Planning Commission.
Bagby, Scott.
A long range plan for the Three Rivers area; St. Joseph County, Michigan. [Prepared with the assistance of] Robert Boetman and Marsha Rickner and the Three Rivers, Mich. Planning Commission. Grand Rapids, Mich., 1957.
61p.

1. City planning - Three Rivers, Mich. I. Boetman, Robert. II. Three Rivers, Mich. Planning Commission.

697.9
T37
1970

Threlkeld, James L
Thermal environmental engineering. 2d ed. Englewood Cliffs, N.J., Prentice-Hall, 1970.
495p.

1. Air conditioning. 2. Heating. 3. Ventilation. I. Title.

VF
694.183
V47
E81

Three-member joints for nailed trussed rafters.
Stern, E George
Design of nailed structures, by E. George Stern and Paul W. Stoneburner. Blacksburg, Virginia Polytechnic Institute, Sept. 1952.
67 p. illus. (Virginia Polytechnic Institute. Engineering Experiment Station series no. 81)

Bulletin of the Virginia Polytechnic Institute, v. 45, no. 6.
Includes references.
(Continued on next card)

647.1
L11t

Three standards of living for an urban family of four persons.
U.S. Bureau of Labor Statistics.
Three standards of living for an urban family of four persons. Wash., U.S. Dept. of Labor, Bureau of Labor Statistics, 1967.
92p. (U.S. Bureau of Labor Statistics. Bulletin no. 1570-5)
Bibliography: p. 91-92.

1. Family income and expenditure. I. Title.

362.6
(74461)
W45

THRESHER, IRENE K   , JT. AU.
WILLIAMS, CONSTANCE
IF YOU NEED A NURSING HOME; POINTS TO CONSIDER IN CHOOSING A NURSING HOME IN THE BOSTON AREA, BY CONSTANCE WILLIAMS AND IRENE K. THRESHER. BOSTON, SPECIAL SERVICE DEPT., WOMEN'S EDUCATION AND INDUSTRIAL UNION, 1962.
67P.

1. NURSING HOMES - BOSTON. I. THRESHER, IRENE K., JT. AU. II. TITLE.

Stern, E George. Design of nailed structures ... Sept. 1952. (Card 2)

Contents.-Fundamental considerations in the design of nailed structures.-Three-member joints for nailed trussed rafters.-Nailed vs. bolted vs. connectored trussed rafters.
1.Nails and nailing. I.Stoneburner, Paul W. II.Title. III.Title: Three-member joints for nailed trussed rafters. IV.Title: Nailed vs. bolted vs. connectored trussed rafters. V.Series.

658.564
S728

THREE SYSTEMS OF INFORMATION RETRIEVAL.
STEVENS, NORMAN D
A COMPARATIVE STUDY OF THREE SYSTEMS OF INFORMATION RETRIEVAL. NEW BRUNSWICK, N.J., GRADUATE SCHOOL OF LIBRARY SERVICE, RUTGERS-THE STATE UNIVERSITY, 1961.
149P

1. AUTOMATION. I. TITLE. II. RUTGERS UNIVERSITY. GRADUATE SCHOOL OF LIBRARY SERVICE. III. TITLE: THREE SYSTEMS OF INFORMATION R ETRIEVAL.

100
D27

THRESHOLD LOGIC.
DERTOUZOS, MICHAEL L.
THRESHOLD LOGIC; A SYNTHESIS APPROACH BY MICHAEL L. DERTOUZOS. CAMBRIDGE, M.I.T. PRESS, 1965.
256P. (M.I.T. RESEARCH MONOGRAPH NO. 32)

1. LOGIC. I. TITLE. II. TITLE: A SYNTHESIS APPROACH.

728.1
(41)
M67
1937

Three million houses.
Morgan-Webb, Charles
Three million houses. New York, Committee for the Nation [c1937]
197 p. illus.

1.Housing-U.K. I.Committee for the Nation. II.Title.

362.5
A32

Three tenant families.
Agee, James.
Let us now praise famous men; three tenant families, by James Agee and Walker Evans. New York, Ballantine Books, 1960.
428p.

1. Poverty. 2. Agricultural laborers. 3. Social conditions - Ala. I. Evans, Walker, jt. au. II. Title. III. Title: Three tenant families.

658.564
H15

Threshold logic implementation of a modular computer system design.
Hampel, D
Threshold logic implementation of a modular computer system design by D. Hampel and others. Prepared by RCA Corporation for Electronics Research Center. Wash., National Aeronautics and Space Administration, 1970.
70p. (NASA CR-1663)

1. Automation. I. U.S. National Aeronautics and Space Administration. II. Radio Corporation of America. III. Title.

312.1
A85

Three papers on quality of urban environment.
Ault, Gary L
Three papers on quality of urban environment, by Gary L. Ault and others. St. Louis, Institute for Urban and Regional Studies, Washington University, 1967.
52p. (U.S. Economic Development Administration. Working paper EDA [Water Resources Investment Project] Working paper DRA 7)
1. Population shifts. 2. Economic development. I. U.S. Economic Development Administration. II. Washington University, St. Louis. Institute for Urban and Regional Studies. III. Title.

711.585
R611

3000 FAMILIES MOVE TO MAKE WAY FOR STUYVESANT TOWN.
ROBERTS, ROSEMOND G
3000 FAMILIES MOVE TO MAKE WAY FOR STUYVESANT TOWN; A STORY OF TENANT RELOCATION BUREAU, INC. NEW YORK, JAMES FELT & CO., 1946.
23P.

1. SLUM CLEARANCE. 2. URBAN RENEWAL. I. TITLE: STUYVESANT TOWN. II. TITLE.

711.4
:538.56
T37

Threshold of planning information systems; selected papers presented at the ADP workshops conducted at the ASPO national planning conference, Houston, April 1967. Chicago, American Society of Planning Officials [1967]
108p.

1. City planning - Automation. I. American Society of Planning Officials.

728.1
:336.18
H11t

3 R's for public housing: (Re-think, Re-vise, Re-organize)
Haas, John
3 R's for public housing: (Re-think, Re-vise, Re-organize) Washington, Workshop 221, inc. [1963?]
9p.

1. Public housing. I. Workshop 221, inc., Washington, D.C. II. Title.

VF
332.725
F22t

Three ways to finance home improvements through FHA.
U.S. Federal Housing Administration.
Three ways to finance home improvements through FHA. Wash., 1967.
10p. (HUD consumer bulletin IP-37)

1. Property improvement loans. 2. Houses - Maintenance and modernization. I. Title. (Series)

DATE OF REQUEST 2/20/53   MAY 7 1953 C. CARD NO.

AUTHOR
Thrift, Eric W.
TITLE Report on planning and development for the city of Yorkton, Saskatchewan, Canada.
SERIES

EDITION PUB. DATE 1952 PAGING
PUBLISHER illus., maps
Yorkton, City Planning Committee
RECOMMENDED BY
REVIEWED IN ... 10-11/52 p.5
ORDER RECORD

VF
332.72
O29
    Thrift and home ownership.
Geyer, Don
    Thrift and home ownership; a venture in
free enterprise. Seattle, Wash., Seattle
City League of Savings and Loan Associations,
1954.
    50 p.

    Bibliography: p. 47-50.

    1. Savings and loan associations. I. Title.

330
(47)
E81
    Through Soviet windows.
Evans, Joseph E
    Through Soviet windows. New York, Dow
Jones, 1957.
    124p.

    1. Economic conditions - U.S.S.R.
I. Title.

697.5
D25a
    Thulman, Robert.
    Denver. University. Institute of Industrial
Research.
    Development of static pressure design data
for low-pressure forced warm-air heating systems,
covering the period: March 5, 1952 to April 30,
1952. Washington, May 28, 1952.
    114 L. figures, graphs, tables.

    Bibliography: p. 100-102.

    Final report, Research project 1-T-95,
Housing and Home Finance Agency.

332.72
(8)
C65
    Thrift institution development in Latin
America.
    U.S. Congress. Joint Economic Committee.
    Thrift institution development in Latin
America. A staff study prepared for the use
of the Subcommittee on Inter-American Economic
Relationships of the Joint Economic Committee,
Congress of the United States. Wash., Govt.
Print. Off., 1970.
    92p.
    At head of title: 91st Cong., 2d sess.
Joint committee print.
    1. Savings and loan associations - Latin
America. 2. Credit. I. Title.

362.6
(016)
T29
    Through the looking-glass at 4 groups of
books for senior citizens.
    Texas. State Library.
    Through the looking glass at 4 groups of
books for senior citizens. 1. Housing, 2.
Health, 3. Care of the aged, and 4. Employment.
Austin, [1968?]
    [5]p.

    1. Old age - Bibliography. I. Title.

697.5
D25a
    Denver. University. Institute of Industrial
Research. Development of static pressure
design data for low-pressure ... May 28, 1952.
    (Card 2)

    Project director: George Lof; Staff
technician: Robert Thulman.

    Processed.

332.72
(41)
B25
1935
    The thrifty three millions.
    Bellman, *Sir* Harold, 1886-
    The thrifty three millions; a study of the building society
movement and the story of the Abbey road society, by Sir
Harold Bellman ... London [The Abbey road building so-
ciety] 1935.
    xii, 357, [1] p. plates, ports., facsims., tables. 22½ᶜᵐ.

    1. Building societies.
2. Building and loan associations-Gt. Brit. 2. Building and loan
associations. 3. Abbey Road Building Society. I. Title.

    [Full name: Sir Charles Harold Bellman]

    35-11723

    Library of Congress   HG2156.G75B43
    [3]   332.320942

912
G25
    Thrower, Norman J W ed.
    General Drafting Co.
    Man's domain; a thematic atlas of the world.
Norman J.W. Thrower, ed. 2d ed. New York,
McGraw-Hill, 1970.
    80p.

    1. Atlases. I. Thrower, Norman J.W., ed.
II. McGraw-Hill. III. Title: Thematic atlas
of the world. IV. Title.

728.2
I55
Prelim
    Thulman, Robert
    Illinois Institute of Technology.
    Research and design development for a
multi-story, multi-family dwelling; progress
report no. 1. Chicago, Sept. 1951.
    53 p. illus., tables.

    Bibliography: p. 52-53.

    Project no. 1-T-99, Housing and Home
Finance Agency. Project director: E. I.
Fiesenheiser; staff technician: Robert
Thulman.
    (over)

LAW
T
T3761
    Throckmorton, Archibald Hall, 1876-1938.
    ... Illustrative cases on equity jurisprudence, by Archibald
H. Throckmorton ... 2d ed. ... A companion book to Eaton
on equity, 2d ed. St. Paul, Minn., West publishing co., 1923.
    x, 611 p. 23½ᶜᵐ. (Hornbook case series)

    1. Equity-U. S.-Cases. I. Eaton, James Webster, 1856-1901.
Handbook of equity jurisprudence.
    23-11192

    Library of Congress
    —— Copy 2.
    Copyright A 752246   [a41d1]

620
T38
    THUESEN, HOLGER GEORGE.
    ENGINEERING ECONOMY. 2ND ED., ENGLEWOOD
CLIFFS, N.J., PRENTICE-HALL, 1957.
    581P.

    BIBLIOGRAPHY, P. 553-556.

    1. ENGINEERING. 2. INDUSTRIAL
MANAGEMENT. I. TITLE.

697
N17p
    Thulman, Robert.
    U.S. National Bureau of Standards.
    Performance of a gas-fired warm air furnace
installed in the attic of a one-story house,
by O. N. McDorman and P. R. Achenbach. Washington, March 1952.
    20 p. illus., graphs, tables. (NBS
Report 1499)
    Prepared under Research Project No. 1950-
ME-7, Housing and Home Finance Agency.
    Project director: R. S. Dill.
    Staff technician: Robert Thulman.
    (over)

[1753 o]
2 V.
    Throckmorton, Archibald Hall, 1876-1938, ed.
    Ohio. *Laws, statutes, etc.*
    Throckmorton's Ohio code, annotated. Baldwin's 1948
revision, complete to January 1, 1948, William Edward
Baldwin, editor-in-chief... Cleveland, Banks-Baldwin Co.
[1948]
    5 v. (various pagings) facsim. 28 cm.

    "Index to the Ohio General code" has special t.-p.
    On cover: Baldwin's blue book.
    "Will be kept to date with Baldwin's Ohio code service."

    I. Baldwin, William Edward, 1883- ed. II. Throckmorton,
Archibald Hall, 1876-1938, ed.
    49-3957*

    Library of Congress   [3]

690.015
H68
R9
    Thulman, Robert K
    Application of the floor furnace in the heating
of small houses. Washington, Govt. Print. Off.,
July 1950.
    9 p. diagrs. (U.S. Housing and Home
Finance Agency. Office of the Administrator.
Division of Housing Research. Technical reprint
series no. 9)

    Reprinted from HHFA Technical bulletin no. 10,
May-July 1949.
    1. Heating. 2. Furnaces. I. Title.

697.353
N17d
    Thulman, Robert
    U.S. National Bureau of Standards.
    [Development of testing and rating
procedures for baseboard radiators and
convectors] by George O. Raiche [and]
Paul R. Achenbach. Washington, January
1952 - May 1952.
    2 pts. illus., diagrs., tables.
(NBS reports 1392 & 1653)
    Contents.-pt. 1. Tests of Vulcan steel
baseboard Radi-vectors, manufactured by
Vulcan Radiator Co., Hartford, Conn.-

VF
624.2
T74
    Throgs neck bridge.
    Triborough Bridge and Tunnel Authority.
    Throgs neck bridge. [New York, 1957]
    12 p. illus.

    1. Bridges. I. Title.

VF
697.5
D25
    Thulman, Robert
    Denver. University. Institute of Industrial
Research.
    Development of static pressure design data for
low-pressure forced warm air heating systems.
Denver, Colo., Aug. 1951.
    32 l. tables.

    Bibliography: p. 27-31.
    Progress report no. 1, Research Project no.
1-T-95, Housing and Home Finance Agency.

    (Continued on next card)

697.353
N17d
    U.S. National Bureau of Standards.
    [Development of testing and rating
procedures ...] Jan.1952-May 1952.
    (Card 2)

    pt. 2. Performance of a steel baseboard
convector manufactured by Kritzer Radiant
Coils, Inc., Chicago, Ill.
    Final report, Research project no. 1-T-125,
Housing and Home Finance Agency.

711.583
(79549)
T37
    Throop, Vincent M
    The suburban zone of metropolitan
Portland, Oregon. Chicago, Univ. of
Chicago, 1948.
    244p.
    Thesis: University of Chicago.

    1. Suburbs - Portland, Or.
I. Chicago. University. II. Title.

    Denver. University. Institute of Industrial
Research. Development of static pressure
design data ... Aug. 1951. (Card 2)

    Project director, George Lof; staff
technician, Robert Thulman.
    Processed.
    1. Heating-Warm air. 2. Heating research.
3. Housing research contracts. I. Lof, George.
II. Thulman, Robert. III. U.S. Housing and Home
Finance Agency. O.A. Division of Housing
Research. IV. Title.

697.353
N17d
    U.S. National Bureau of Standards.
    [Development of testing and rating
procedures ...] Jan.1952-May 1952.
    (Card 3)

    Project director: R.S. Dill; Staff
technician: Robert Thulman.

    Processed.

697.922
N17
Thulman, Robert
U.S. National Bureau of Standards.
[Duct materials - criteria for substitutes for metal. Washington] 1952-1953.
3 pts. illus., diagrs., graphs, tables.

Final report, Research Project no. 1-T-102, Housing and Home Finance Agency.
Contents.-pt.1.Fire hazard tests of substitute duct materials, by A. C. Hutton and D. Gross.-pt.2.Criteria for substitute duct materials, by O. N. McDorman, A. C. Hutton [and] . .

(Continued on next card)

U.S. National Bureau of Standards. [Duct materials ...] 1952-1953. (Card 2)

P. R. Achenbach.-pt.3.Simulated use tests of substitute duct materials, by O. N. McDorman [and] P. R. Achenbach.
Project director, R. S. Dill; staff technician, Robert Thulman.
Processed.

VF
697
N17ha
Thulman, Robert
U.S. National Bureau of Standards.
The Harvey-Whipple oil-burning furnace, model VCF-75 ... by B. A. Peavy [and] P. R. Achenbach. [Washington] Oct. 1951.
13 l. illus., graphs, tables.

Prepared under Research Project no. 1950-ME-7, Housing and Home Finance Agency.
Project director, R. S. Dill; staff technician, Robert Thulman.
Processed.

VF
697
N17a
Thulman, Robert.
U.S. National Bureau of Standards.
The heating and ventilating system at reflection point, by P. R. Achenbach [and] S. D. Cole. [Washington, Nov. 1953]
15 l. graphs, tables.

Research Project 1950-ME-7, Housing and Home Finance Agency.
Project director, R. S. Dill; staff technician Robert Thulman.
Processed.

VF
690.015
H68
T13
Thulman, Robert K
Performance of masonry chimneys for houses.
Washington, D.C., U.S. Housing and Home Finance Agency, Office of the Administrator, Division of Standardized Building Codes and Materials, Aug. 1949.
46 p. illus., charts, diagrs., tables.
(U.S. Housing and Home Finance Agency. Office of the Administrator. Technical Office. Technical paper no. 13)
Processed.

(Continued on next card)

Thulman, Robert K   Performance of masonry chimneys for houses...1949. (Card 2)

1.Chimneys. I.U.S. Housing and Home Finance Agency. Office of the Administrator. Division of Standardized Building Codes and Materials. II.Title.

VF
697
N17r
Thulman, Robert.
U.S. National Bureau of Standards.
Report on the tests of radiant glass heating panels manufactured by continental Radiant Glass Heating Corporation. Washington, May 24, 1950.
37, 14 p. figures, graphs, tables.

Prepared under Research Project no. 1950 - ME-7, Housing and Home Finance Agency.
Project director: R. S. Dill; HHFA Technician: Robert Thulman.

Processed.

728.2
I55
Thulman, Robert
Illinois Institute of Technology.
Research and design development for a multi-story, multi-family dwelling. Chicago, June 1952.
147 l. drawing file. illus., diagrs., graphs, plans, tables.

Final report, Research Project no. 1-T-99, Housing and Home Finance Agency.
Project director, E. I. Fiesenheiser; staff technician, Robert Thulman.
Processed.

VF
697.353
N17
Thulman, Robert.
U.S. National Bureau of Standards.
A study of a ceiling panel heating system, by O. N. McDorman, Minoru Fujii [and] P. R. Achenbach. [Washington] Apr. 1954.
11 l. plates, tables.

Final report, Research Project no. 1-T-124, Housing and Home Finance Agency.
Project director, R. S. Dill; staff technician, Robert Thulman.
Processed.

VF
697
N17t
Thulman, Robert
U.S. National Bureau of Standards.
Tests of modified warm air heating system in Martin Fultz Development, Lincoln, Illinois, by P. R. Achenbach and S. D. Cole. [Washington] Dec. 1951.
14 l. illus., graphs, tables.

Prepared under Research Project no. 1950-ME-7, Housing and Home Finance Agency.
Project director, R. S. Dill staff technician, Robert Thulman.
Typewritten.

VF
699.86
N17
Thulman, Robert.
U.S. National Bureau of Standards.
The thermal insulating value of air spaces, by H. E. Robinson [and] F. J. Powlitch.
Washington, Jan. 1954.
19 p. figures, graphs, tables. (NBS Report 3030)
Prepared under Research project no. 1950-ME-12, HHFA.
Project director: R. S. Dill; Staff technician: Robert Thulman.

(over)

697.9
N17
Thulman, Robert
U.S. National Bureau of Standards.
Ventilation measurements ... by C. W. Coblentz M. A. Barron [and] P. R. Achenbach. [Washington Apr. 1953.
44 p. plates, tables.

References: p. 44.
Research Project no. 1950-ME-14, Housing and Home Finance Agency.
Project director: R. S. Dill; staff technician, Robert Thulman.
Processed.

699.8
T38
THULMAN, ROBERT K
A PROPOSED BASIS FOR DETERMINING MINIMUM REQUIREMENTS FOR INSULATION.
WASHINGTON, U.S. FEDERAL HOUSING ADMINISTRATION, 1940.
15L.

1. INSULATION. I. U.S. FEDERAL HOUSING ADMINISTRATION.

Thunblad, Gunnar.
690.015
(485)
S82
R50
Sweden. Statens Kommitte för Byggnadsforskning.
Arbetskraftatgang vid traditionella byggen och monteringsbyggen [Labor requirements for traditional building versus unit construction] av Hans G. Rahm och Gunnar Thunblad. Stockholm, 1959.
94p. diagrs., tables. (Its Rapport 50)
English summary.
1. Building construction - Labor requirements. I. Rahm, Hans G. II. Thunblad, Gunnar.

Thunblad, Gunnar, jt. au.
690.015
(485)
S82
R87
Jernström, Sven.
Arbetskraftatgang vid traditionella byggen och monteringsbyggen (Utredning 2) (Labour consumption for traditional building versus assembly building) av Sven Jernström och Gunnar Thunblad. Stockholm, Statens råd för Byggnadsforskning, 1962.
16p. (Sweden. Statens Kommitte för Byggnadsforskning. Rapport 87)
English summary.

(Continued on next card)

690.015
(485)
S82
R87
Jernström, Sven.   Arbetskraftatgang vid traditionella byggen...1962. (Card 2)

1. Building research - Sweden.
2. Building construction - Labor requirements. I. Thunblad, Gunnar, jt. au. II. Sweden. Statens Kommitte for Byggnadsforskning.

331
(743)
V27
THURBER, HARRIS.
VERMONT. DEPT. OF EMPLOYMENT SECURITY.
SPECIAL STUDY OF THE LONG-TERM UNEMPLOYED MARRIED SECONDARY WAGE EARNERS. ANALYSIS BY HARRIS THURBER, IN COOPERATION WITH RESEARCH AND STATISTICS. MONTPELIER, 1962.
1 V.

1. EMPLOYMENT - VERMONT. I. THURBER, HARRIS. II. TITLE: LONG-TERM UNEMPLOYED MARRIED SECONDARY WAGE EARNERS.

339.3
C657
Thurow, Lester C
U.S. Congress. Joint Economic Committee.
The American distribution of income: a structural problem. A study prepared for the use of the Joint Economic Committee, Congress of the United States, by Lester C. Thurow and Robert E.B. Lucas. Wash., Govt. Print. Off., 1972.
50p.
At head of title: 92d Cong., 2d sess. Joint Committee print.
1. Income. 2. Family income and expenditure. I. Thurow, Lester C. II. Lucas, Robert E.B. III. Title.

339.3
T38
Thurow, Lester C
The American distribution of income: a structural problem. A study prepared for the use of the Joint Economic Committee, Congress of the United States, by Lester C. Thurow and Robert E. B. Lucas. Wash., Govt. Print. Off., 1972.
50p.
At head of title: 92d Cong., 2d sess. Joint committee print.
1. Income. I. Lucas, Robert E.B. II. U.S. Congress. Joint Economic Committee. III.Title.

362.5
T38

C.1,E.O.
Thurow, Lester C
Poverty and discrimination. Wash., Brookings Institution, 1969.
214p. (Brookings Institution. Studies in social economics)

Bibliography: p 201-208.

1. Poverty. 2. Race relations. I. Brookings Institution. II. Title.

336.18
T38
Thursby, Vincent V
Federal grant-in-aid programs in Florida, by V. V. Thursby and A. M. Hartsfield.
Tallahassee, Institute of Governmental Research, Florida State University, 1964.
175p. (Florida State University. Florida government series no. 3)

1. Grants-in-aid. 2. Governmental research. I. Hartsfield, Annie Mary, jt. au. II. Florida State University. Institute of Governmental Research. III. Title.

620
045   THURSTON, GEORGE B
OKLAHOMA. STATE UNIVERSITY. RESEARCH
FOUNDATION.
MEASUREMENT OF THE DYNAMIC AND FLEXURAL
RESPONSE OF BEAMS AND PLATES, BY JOE F.
GUESS AND GEORGE B. THURSTON. STILLWATER,
OKLA., 1963.
47L. (AD 422665)

   1. ENGINEERING.   2. BUILDING MATERIALS.
3. VIBRATION.   I. TITLE.   II. GUESS,
JOE F.   III. THURSTON, GEORGE B.

362.6
I57   Tibbitts, Clark.
International Association of Gerontology.
Aging and social health in the United States
and Europe. Report of an international seminar
held at Merano, Italy, July 9-13, 1957. Compiled and edited by Clark Tibbitts. Ann Arbor,
Mich., Div. of Gerontology, Univ. of Michigan,
1959.
186p. tables.

   Partial contents: Housing and the social
health of older people in the United States, by

(Continued on next
card)

362.6
T41C   TIBBITTS, CLARK.
THE COMPOSITION AND CHARACTERISTICS OF
THE OLDER POPULATION. N.P., 1962.
15P.

   1. OLD AGE.   2. HOUSING FOR THE AGED.

651.4
T38   THURSTON, PHILIP H
SYSTEMS AND PROCEDURES RESPONSIBILITY;
AN ADMINISTRATIVE VIEW OF THE DIVISION
OF RESPONSIBILITY BETWEEN OPERATING
PEOPLE AND SPECIALISTS FOR SYSTEMS AND
PROCEDURE WORK. BOSTON, DIVISION OF
RESEARCH, GRADUATE SCHOOL OF BUSINESS
ADMINISTRATION, HARVARD UNIVERSITY, 1959.
110P.

   1. OFFICE MANAGEMENT.   2. OFFICE
PROCEDURES.   I. TITLE.

362.6
I57   International Association of Gerontology.
Aging and social ... (Card 2)

   Wilma Donahue and E. Everett Ashley, III, p. 141-
155.

   1. Old age. 2. Housing for the aged.   I. Tib-
bitts, Clark. II. Donahue, Wilma. III. Ashley,
E. Everett III. IV. Title: Housing and the
social health of older people in the United
States. V. Seminar on Aging and Social Health,
Merano, Italy, 1957.

362.6
T41h   Tibbitts, Clark, ed.
Handbook of social gerontology; societal
aspects of aging. Chicago, Univ. of Chicago
Press, 1960.
770p.

Partial contents:-Housing and community settings for
older people, by Walter K. Vivrett.

   1. Old age. I. Vivrett, Walter K. II. Title.
III. Title: Housing and community settings for older
people.

711.585
(753)
T38   Thursz, Daniel.
Where are they now? A study of the
impact of relocation on former residents of
Southwest Washington who were served in an
HWC (Health and Welfare Council) demonstration project. Washington, Health and Welfare Council of the National Capital Area,
1966.   PB 176 260
148p.
Bibliography: p. 110-113.

   1. Relocation - District of Columbia. 2. Housing -
District of Columbia.   I. Health and Wel-
fare Council of   the National Capital
Area. II. Title.

362.6
C653a   Tibbitts, Clark, ed.
1962   Conference on Aging, University of Michigan,
1962.
Aging and the economy. Edited by Harold
L. Orbach and Clark Tibbitts. Pref. by
Wilma Donahue. Ann Arbor, University of
Michigan Press, 1963.
237p.

   1. Old age. I. Orbach, Harold L., ed.
II. Tibbitts, Clark, ed. III. Title.

VF
362.6
T41m   Tibbitts, Clark.
Middle aged and older people in American
society. Address before the Training
Institute for Public Welfare Specialists in
Aging, Cleveland, Ohio, June 13, 1965.
Wash., Dept of Health, Education, and
Welfare, Administration on Aging, 1965.
30p.
OA-227.

   1. Old age. 2. Old age - Social service.
I. Training Institute   for Public Welfare
Specialists in Aging,   Cleveland, 1965.
II. Title.

388
(4971)
T39   Thyagarajan, S
Belgrade transportation and land use study;
an overview. Detroit, Div. of International
Urban Studies, Center for Urban Studies,
Wayne State University, 1971.
45p. (Belgrade transportation and land use
study no. 1)

   1. Transportation - Yugoslavia. 2. Land
use - Yugoslavia. II. Wayne State University,
Detroit. Div. of International Urban
Studies. III. Title.

362.6
M42A   TIBBITTS, CLARK.
MICHIGAN. UNIVERSITY. DIVISION OF
GERONTOLOGY.
AGING IN THE MODERN WORLD, A GUIDEBOOK
FOR LEADERS; A SERIES OF ADULT STUDY
DISCUSSION PROGRAMS, PREPARED BY CLARK
TIBBITTS AND WILMA DONAHUE. ANN ARBOR,
MICH., UNIV. OF MICHIGAN, 1957.
68P.

   1. OLD AGE.   I. TIBBITTS, CLARK.
II. DONAHUE, WILMA.   III. TITLE.

362.6
W17n   Ware, George W
The new guide to happy retirement. Introd.
by Clark Tibbitts. Illus. by Ben Murow.
New York, Crown Publishers, 1968.
352p.

   1. Old age. 2. Social security.
3. Recreation. 4. Housing for the aged.
I. Tibbitts, Clark. II. Title.

DATE OF REQUEST 4/10/52 1952   L. C. CARD NO.
AUTHOR
Thye, L. S. and K. N. Capen.
TITLE
Farm houses as farm families want them.
SERIES
EDITION   PUB. DATE 951   PAGING 8 p.
PUBLISHER
U.S. Dept. of Agri., Office of Info.
RECOMMENDED BY   REVIEWED IN
Bibliography of Agri. 1/52
ORDER RECORD p. 152

362.6
M42AG   TIBBITTS, CLARK.
MICHIGAN. UNIVERSITY. DIVISION OF
GERONTOLOGY.
AGING IN THE MODERN WORLD, A STUDY
DISCUSSION SERIES FOR ADULTS; A HANDBOOK
FOR GROUP MEMBERS, PREPARED UNDER THE
DIRECTION OF CLARK TIBBITTS AND WILMA
DONAHUE. ANN ARBOR, MICH., UNIV. OF
MICHIGAN, 1957.
175P.

   READING LIST AT END OF EACH SECTION.

   1. OLD AGE.   I. TIBBITTS, CLARK.
II. DONAHUE, WILMA.   III. TITLE.

362.6
C65po   Tibbitts, Clark, jt. ed.
Conference on Aging, University of Michigan,
14th, 1961.
Politics of age. Proceedings. Edited by
Wilma Donahue and Clark Tibbitts. Ann Arbor,
University of Michigan, Division of Geron-
tology, 1962.
226p.

   1. Old age. I. Donahue, Wilma, ed. II. Tibbitts,
Clark, jt. ed. III. Title.

690.5
:551.5
(016)
T41   Tibbetts, D C comp.
A bibliography on cold weather construction, compiled by D.C. Tibbetts, revised by
G.G. Boileau. Ottawa, Division of Building Research, National Research Council,
1965.
[29]p. (National Research Council,
Canada. Division of Building Research.
Bibliography no. 10)

   1. Winter construction - Bibl. 2. Archi-
tecture and climate - Bibl. I. Boileau,
G. G.   II. National Research
Council,   Canada. Division of
Building   Research.

362.6
M42AGI   TIBBITTS, CLARK.
MICHIGAN. UNIVERSITY. DIVISION OF
GERONTOLOGY.
AGING IN THE MODERN WORLD, SELECTIONS
FROM THE LITERATURE OF AGING FOR
PLEASURE AND INSTRUCTION; A BOOK OF
READINGS, COMPILED BY CLARK TIBBITTS.
ANN ARBOR, MICH., UNIVERSITY OF
MICHIGAN, 1957.
246P.

   BIBLIOGRAPHY: P.235-245.

   1. OLD AGE.
   I. TIBBITTS, CLARK.   II. TITLE.

362.6
T41s   Tibbitts, Clark, ed.
Social and psychological aspects of aging,
edited by Clark Tibbitts and Wilma Donahue.
New York, Columbia University Press, 1962.
952p.
Partial contents.-The need for research
toward meeting the housing needs of the el-
derly, by E. Everett Ashley, III, Director,
Statistical Reports and Development Branch,
Housing and Home Finance Agency, and M.
Carter McFarland, Director, Div. of Economic
and Program Studies, Housing and Home
Finance Ag-   ency.
(Cont'd on next card)

690.5
:551.5
(71)
N171   Tibbetts, D.C., jt. author.
National Research Council, Canada.
Division of Building Research.
Winter construction, by C. R. Crocker and
D. C. Tibbetts. Ottawa [n.d.]
26 p. tables. (Its Better building
bulletin no. 6)

   1. Winter construction. I. Crocker, C. R.
II. Tibbetts, D. C., jt. author.

362.6
T41   Tibbitts, Clark, ed.
Aging in today's society, ed. by Clark
Tibbitts and Wilma Donahue. Englewood Cliff,
N.J., Prentice-Hall, 1960.
418p. (Prentice-Hall sociology series)

   1. Old age. I. Donahue, Wilma, jt. ed.

362.6
T41s   Tibbitts, Clark, ed.
Social and psychological...1962 (Card 2)

   1. Old age. 2. Housing for the aged.
I. Donahue, Wilma, jt. ed. II. Title.

362.6
A52
Jan.1952
Tibbitts, Clark, 1903 –   ed.
American Academy of Political and Social Science, *Phila-delphia.*
 Social contribution by the aging, edited by Clark Tibbitts, chairman, Committee on Aging and Geriatrics, Federal Security Agency, Washington, D. C., with the assistance of the Committee. Philadelphia, 1952.
  vi, 258 p. diagrs. 24 cm. (*Its* Annals, v. 279)
  Bibliographical footnotes.
   Housing our older citizens, by Hertha Kraus, p. 126–138.
   1. Old age.   I. Tibbitts, Clark, 1903–   ed. II. Title. (Series)
  H1.A4 vol. 279   *301.43   52–7045
  ——— Copy 2.   HQ1060.A53
  Library of Congress   [25]

658.564
T42
TICA CONFERENCE, DREXEL INSTITUTE OF TECHNOLOGY, 1964.
TECHNICAL INFORMATION CENTER ADMINISTRATION. EDITED BY ARTHUR W. ELIAS. WASHINGTON, SPARTAN BOOKS, 1964.
  171P. (DREXEL INSTITUTE SCIENCE SERIES)

  SPONSORED BY THE DREXEL INSTITUTE OF TECHNOLOGY, INFORMATION SCIENCE DEPT.

  1. AUTOMATION.   2. MANAGEMENT - AUTOMATION.   I. ELIAS, ARTHUR W.
         (CONTINUED ON NEXT CARD)

614.7
P25
Tideman, T. Nicolaus jt. au.
Peltzman, Sam.
 Local versus national pollution control, by Sam Peltzman and T. Nicolaus Tideman. Cambridge, Mass., Program on Regional and Urban Economics, 1971.
  10p.

  1. Pollution. 2. Man - Influence of environment. I. Tideman, T. Nicolaus, jt. au. II. Harvard University. Program on Regional and Urban Economics. III. Title.

362.6
T4180
TIBBITTS, CLARK.
 SOCIAL GERONTOLOGY. PREPARED FOR PRESENTATION AT THE ELEVENTH ANNUAL CONFERENCE ON AGING, UNIVERSITY OF MICHIGAN, JUNE 23, 1958. REVISED. WASHINGTON, U.S. DEPT. OF HEALTH, EDUCATION, AND WELFARE, 1958.
  38P.

  1. OLD AGE.   I. TITLE.

658.564
T42
TICA CONFERENCE, DREXEL INSTITUTE OF TECHNOLOGY, 1964. TECHNICAL INFORMATION ...1964.   (CARD 2)

  ED.   II. DREXEL INSTITUTE OF TECHNOLOGY. INFORMATION SCIENCE DEPT. III. TITLE.

388
T42
Tideman, T   Nicolaus.
 Rational bases for potential and transport cost models of location. Cambridge, Mass., Program on Regional and Urban Economics, Harvard University, 1968.
  9p. (Harvard University. Program on Regional and Urban Economics. Discussion paper no. 38)
  1. Transportation - Finance. 2. Industrial location. I. Harvard University. Program on   Regional and Urban Economics.   II. Title.

650
:325
T42
Tideman, T   Nicolaus.
 Efficiency in minority enterprise programs. Cambridge, Mass., Harvard University, Program on Regional and Urban Economics, 1972.
  13p. (Discussion paper no. 72)

C.1, E.O.

  1. Business - Minority groups. I. Harvard University. Program on Regional and Urban Economics. II. Title.

711.73
(016)
P81
TICKNOR, MARGARET, COMP.
U.S. BUREAU OF PUBLIC ROADS. LIBRARY.
A BIBLIOGRAPHY OF HIGHWAY PLANNING REPORTS. COMPILED BY MARGARET TICKNOR. WASHINGTON, GOVT. PRINT. OFF., 1950.
  48P.

  1. HIGHWAYS - BIBLIOGRAPHY.
  I. TICKNOR, MARGARET, COMP.

330
T42
Tiebout, Charles M
 The community economic base study. New York, Committee for Economic Development, 1962.
  86p. (Committee for Economic Development. Supplementary paper no. 16)
330   -- --- Summary. New York, 1962.
T42   4p.
Summary
  1. Economic base studies. 2. Community development.   I. Committee for Economic   Development.
(Series)

362.6
T46
TIPS, CHARLES R
 THE CARE OF THE AGED IN EUROPE. REPORT TO TEXAS GOVERNOR'S ADVISORY COMMITTEE ON AGING. AUSTIN, GOVERNOR'S COMMITTEE, WHITE HOUSE CONFERENCE ON AGING, 1961.
  21P.

  1. OLD AGE.   I. TEXAS GOVERNOR'S COMMITTEE, WHITE HOUSE CONFERENCE ON AGING.

VF
711.552
(016)
T42
Ticknor, Margaret
 Business districts, central and decentralized: some representative publications.   Washington, Bureau of Public Roads, June 1951.
  26 p.

  Annotated.
  Processed.

  1.Business districts-Bibl. 2.Shopping centers-Bibl. I.U.S. Bureau of Public Roads.

VF
621.643
T42
Tiedeman, Walter D
 A study of plastic pipe for potable water supplies, directed by Walter D. Tiedeman ... and assisted by Nicholas A. Milone. Ann Arbor, Mich., National Sanitation Foundation, June 1955.
  90 p. illus., tables.

  "Review of literature": p. 75-79.

  Research partly financed by ... the Society of the Plastics Industry.

  1.Plastics. 2.   pipes. I.Milone, Nicholas A , jt. au.

VF
728.1
:613.5
A52
Tiboni, Emil A.
American Public Health Association. Committee on the Hygiene of Housing.
 An appraisal method for measuring the quality of housing: A yardstick for health officers, housing officials and planners. New York, N.Y., 1945-1950.
  3 v. in 5 pts.   diagrs.,forms, maps, tables.

  Parts 1 and 2 prepared by Allan Twichell; Part 3 prepared by Anatole A. Solow, Allan Twichell and Emil A. Tiboni.
  Contents.-Pt.1. Nature and uses of the method. 1945.-Pt.2.Appraisal   dwelling conditions:
                              (Continued on next card).

VF
330
N17
P89
Tickton, Sidney G
 The budget in transition. A staff study prepared for the NPA Business Committee. Wash., National Planning Association, 1955.
  50p. (National Planning Association. Planning pamphlets no. 89)

  1. Budget. 2. Federal government. I. National Planning Association. II. Title. (Series)

711.73
:330
(764)
T29
Tieken, Alton W
Texas Transportation Institute.
 Economic impacts of expressways in San Antonio, a study of the effects of a 3.7-mile expressway near downtown San Antonio, Texas, on land values and land use, by William G. Adkins and Alton W. Tieken. College Station, Tex. 1958.
  47p. illus., diagrs., tables. (Its Bulletin no. 11)

             (Continued on next card)

American Public Health Association. Commission on the Hygiene of Housing. An appraisal method for measuring the quality of housing 1945-1950.   (Card 2)

Contents cont'd.-v.A.Survey director's manual.1946. v.B.Field procedures.1946.v.C.Office procedures. 1946.-Pt.3.Appraisal of neighborhood environment: Manual of survey procedures. 1950.

1.Building inspection-Handbooks,manuals, etc. 2.Neighborhood surveys-Handbooks, manuals, etc. I.Twichell, Allan. II.Solow, Anatole A. III.Tiboni, Emil A. IV.Title.

711.14
(79463)
R42
pt. 1
Tideland reclamation report. Part 1.
Richmond, Calif. City Planning Commission.
 Tideland reclamation report. Part 1. Richmond, Calif., 1962.
  65p.

  1. Land use - Richmond, Calif. 2. Water-supply - Richmond, Calif. I. Title.

711.73
:330
(764)
T29
Texas Transportation Institute.   Economic impacts of   ...   (Card 2)

  1. Highways - San Antonio - Economic effect. 2. Real property- Valuation.   I. Adkins, William G. II. Tieken, Alton W. III. U.S. Bureau of Public Roads.

711.585
(74811)
T41
Tiboni, Emil A
 Philadelphia's plan of action for housing and neighborhood improvement. [Prepared in cooperation with Philadelphia Dept. of Public Health, National Association of Redevelopment and Housing Officials.] Philadelphia, 1955.
3c.
  19p.

  1. Urban renewal - Philadelphia. 2. Neighborhood rehabilitation - Philadelphia.   3. Housing - Philadelphia   I. Title.

711.14
T42
Tideman, T   Nicolaus.
 Land use control through administered compensation. Cambridge, Mass., Harvard University, 1970.
  10p. (Harvard University. Program on Regional and Urban Economics. Discussion paper no. 59)

  1. Land use. 2. Eminent domain. I. Harvard University. Program on Regional and Urban Economics.

697.133
A75
TIEN, CHI.
U.S. ARMY. COLD REGIONS RESEARCH AND ENGINEERING LABORATORY.
 LAMINAR HEAT TRANSFER OVER A MELTING PLATE - THE MODIFIED LEVEQUE PROBLEM, BY YIN-CHAO YEN AND CHI TIEN. HANOVER, N.H., 1964.
  19P. (ITS RESEARCH REPORT 125)

  1. HEAT TRANSMISSION.   I. YEN, YIN-CHAO. II. TIEN, CHI. III. TITLE.

728.1
(94)
T42
TIERNEY, JOHN L
AMERICAN AND AUSTRALIAN HOUSING; MR.
JOHN TIERNEY'S VISIT. MELBOURNE,
COMMONWEALTH DEPT. OF WORKS AND HOUSING,
1946.
1 V. (VARIOUS PAGINGS)

TEXT OF RADIO BROADCAST AND TWO
NEWSPAPER ARTICLES BY JOHN TIERNEY.

1. HOUSING - AUSTRALIA. I. TITLE.

LAW
T
T456L
TIFFANY, HERBERT THORNDIKE.
THE LAW OF REAL PROPERTY. 3D ED., BY
BASIL JONES. CHICAGO, CALLAGHAN, 1939.
6 V.

1. REAL PROPERTY. I. JONES, BASIL.

711.4
(77392)
T45
Tilden, Ill. Planning Commission.
General Planning and Resource Consultants.
A comprehensive community plan, Tilden,
Illinois. Prepared for the Tilden Planning
Commission. St. Louis, 1965.
20p.
Prepared for Illinois Department of Busi-
ness and Economic Development.
U.S. Urban Renewal Adm. UPAP.

1. Master plan - Tilden, Ill.
I. Tilden, Ill. Planning Commission.
II. U.S. URA-UPAP. Tilden, Ill.

332.72
T42F
TIERNEY, JOHN L
"FAIR VALUE" AND THE DEFICIENCY
JUDGMENT. [CHICAGO, 1940?]
181-195P.
REPRINTED FROM THE JOURNAL OF LAND &
PUBLIC UTILITY ECONOMICS.

1. MORTGAGE FORECLOSURE - PROCEDURES.
2. REAL PROPERTY - VALUATION.
I. TITLE.

LAW
T
T456TR
TIFFANY, HERBERT THORNDIKE.
A TREATISE ON THE LAW OF LANDLORD AND
TENANT. CHICAGO, CALLAGHAN, 1912.
2 V.

1. LANDLORD AND TENANT.

729.69
C68
Tile.
Council of America, inc.
American standard specifications for glazed
ceramic wall tile, ceramic mosaic tile, quarry
tile and pavers installed in portland cement
mortars including requirements for related
division. New York, 1958.
28p. (AIA file nos. 23A and 23P; ASA A108.
1-1958, A108. 2-1958, A108. 3-1958)

1. Tile. 2. Cement. I. American Standards
Association. II. Title.

332.72
T42
TIERNEY, JOHN L
REAL ESTATE APPRAISAL IN FORECLOSURE
CASES. CHICAGO, 1940.
[4]P.
REPRINTED FROM THE JULY 1940 ISSUE OF
THE APPRAISAL JOURNAL.

1. MORTGAGE FORECLOSURE - PROCEDURES.
2. APPRAISAL. I. TITLE.

S. L

711.4
(77124)
T43
Tiffin, Ohio. City Planning Commission.
Bartholomew (Harland) and Associates.
The final report upon the comprehensive
plan, Tiffin, Ohio. Prepared for the Tiffin
City Planning Commission. St. Louis, 1965.
135p.

U.S. Urban Renewal Adm. UPAP.

1. Master plan - Tiffin, Ohio. I. Tiffin,
Ohio. City Planning Commission. II. U.S.
URA-UPAP. Tiffin, Ohio.

VF
690.015
(489)
D15
A35
Tile.
Denmark. Statens Byggeforskningsinstitut.
Teglprodukter. [Tile and brick
products] København, 1956.
36 p. / tables (Its Anvisning no. 35)

1. Tile. 2. Bricks.

658
A52r.
no.59
Tietjen, Karl H
Organizing the product-planning function.
New York, American Management Association.
1963.
77p. (American Management Association.
AMA research study 59)

1. Industrial management.

1033
TIFTON, GA. PLANNING COMMISSION.
SUBDIVISION REGULATIONS FOR TIFTON,
GEORGIA. BY COASTAL PLAIN AREA PLANNING
AND DEVELOPMENT COMMISSION. TIFTON, GA.,
1970.
33L. (HUD 701 REPORT)

1. SUBDIVISION REGULATION - TIFTON, GA.
I. COASTAL PLAIN AREA PLANNING AND
DEVELOPMENT COMMISSION. II. HUD 701.
TIFTON, GA.

701.8
F12
Tile.
Facing Tile Institute.
Color-engineered facing tile; the scien-
tific approach to color specification.
Washington, [1960?]
29p. illus., diagrs.

1. Color. 2. Tile.

VF
69
(016)
T22
Tietz, Eric A   comp.
U.S. Office of Technical Services.
Bibliography of reports on construction
(including building materials other than cements
and concrete) comp. by Eric A. Tietz.
Washington, Mar. 1949.
13 p. (Its SB-8)

Processed.
1.Building construction-Bibl. 2.Building
materials-Bibl. I.Tietz, Eric A., comp.

711.4
1670
(75888)
T43
Tifton County, Ga. Chamber of Commerce. (Industry Development Committee)
A survey for industry of Tifton, Georgia.
Tifton, 1958.
39p. illus., maps, tables.

1. Industrial location - Tifton, Ga.

690.241.53
M17
Tile.
Martin, K G
Paving tiles reduce flat roof temperatures.
[Melbourne] 1963.
[6]p. (Australia. Commonwealth Scientific
and Industrial Research Organization. D.B.R.
Reprint no. 240)

Reprinted from Building materials, March,
1963, vol. 4, no. 3. p. 34-37, 70-72.

1. Tile. I. Australia. Commonwealth Scientific and
Industrial Research   Organization
(Div. of Building   Research)

301.15
T42
Tietze, Frederick J   ed.
The changing metropolis, edited by
Frederick J. Tietze and James E. McKeown.
Boston, Houghton Mifflin, 1964.
210p. (Houghton Mifflin research
series no. 10)

1. City growth. 2. Sociology, Urban.
3. Population. I. McKeown, James E, jt. ed.
II. Title.

332
C65t
Tight money and rising interest rates.
Conference on Economic Progress.
Tight money and rising interest rates, and
the damage they are doing. Washington,
1960.
77p. diagrs.

1. Finance. 2. Interest rates. I. Title.

620
P58
Tile.
Plummer, Harry C
Brick and tile engineering. McLean Va.,
Structural Clay Products Institute, 1962.
466p.
Bibliography: p. 454-459.

1. Engineering. 2. Bricks. 3. Tile.
I. Structural Clay Products Institute, McLean,
Va. II. Title.

LAW
T
T455h
Tiffany, Francis B
Handbook of the law of principal and agent.
St. Paul, West Pub. Co., 1903.
609p. [The Hornbook series 26]

1. Agency (Law) I. Title.

332.72
C25t
Tighter control needed on occupancy of
Federally subsidized housing.
U.S. General Accounting Office.
Tighter control needed on occupancy of
Federally subsidized housing: Dept. of Housing
and Urban Development. Report to the Congress
by the Comptroller General of the United
States. Wash., 1970.
43p. (B-114860)

1. Mortgage finance. 2. Family income and
expenditure. 3. U.S. Dept. of Housing and
Urban Development. I. Title.

691
P67
E94
1962
Tile.
Portugal. Laboratório Nacional de
Engenharia Civil.
Telhas cerâmicas; ensaio de absorção de
agua. [Burnt clay roofing tiles water
absorption test] Lisboa, 1962.
[3]p. (Its Especificacoes E94-1962)

English summary.

1. Building materials - Standards and
specifications. 2. Tile. 3. Roofs and
roofing.

Tile.

691
P67
E89-
1962
Portugal. Laboratório Nacional de
Engenharia Civil.
Telhas cerâmicas caracteristicas e recepcao.
[Burnt clay roofing tiles characteristics and
acceptance] Lisboa, 1962.
3p. (Especificacoes E89-1962; serie
B, Seccao 3)
English summary.

1. Building materials - Standards and
specifications.   2. Clay.   3. Tile.

691.421
T18
Tauber, E   Some new ceramic finishes...
1967.   (Card 2)

II. Australian Building Research Congress,
3d, 1967. III. Title.

Tile construction.

VF
729.69
A87
Australia. Commonwealth Scientific and Industrial Research Organization. (Division of
Building Research)
Failures of wall and floor tiling, their
causes and prevention, by E. H. Waters. Melbourne, 1958.
22p. illus. (Its Report no. R5)

1. Tile construction. 2. Floors and flooring.
3. Walls. I. Waters, E   H

Tile.

691
P67
E93-
1962
Portugal. Laboratório Nacional de Engenharia
Civil.
Telhas cerâmicas ensaio da orelha de aramar.
[Burnt clay roofing tiles test of the wiring
lug] Lisboa, 1962.
[2]p. (Its Especificacoes E93-1962; Serie
B, Seccao 5)
English summary.

1. Building materials - Standards and
specifications. 2. Tile.

330
UNes
TILE.
United Nations. (Industrial Development Organi-
zation)
The establishment of the brick and tile
industry in developing countries, by H.W.H. West.
New York, United Nations, 1969.
122p. (United Nations. [Document] ID/15)

1. Underdeveloped countries. 2. Brick
industry. 3. Tile. I. West, H.W.H. II. Title.

Tile construction.

VF
693.068.32
A37
pt.2
Australia. Commonwealth Scientific and
Industrial Research Organization. (Div.
of Building Research)
Studies in tile bonding. II. The effect
of a layer of neat cement on the strength
of the tile/mortar bond, by E. H. Waters.
Melbourne, 1960.
7p. (Its Technical paper no. 10)

1. Tile construction. I. Waters, E. H.

Tile.

691
P67
E92-
1962
Portugal. Laboratório Nacional de
Engenharia Civil.
Telhas cerâmicas ensaio de flexao.
[Burnt clay roofing tiles bending test]
Lisboa, 1962.
2p. (Especificacoes E92-1962; Serie
B, Seccao 5)
English summary.

1. Building materials - Standards and
specficiations. 2. Tile.

VF
666.7
L11
Tile industry
U.S. Bureau of Labor Statistics.
Case study data on productivity and factory
performance: brick and tile (by the stiff mud
process). Prepared for the Foreign Operations
Administration, Industrial and Technical
Assistance Division. [Washington, Govt. Print.
Off.] Oct. 1953.
85 p. illus., graph, tables. (Its
Report no. 43)

Processed.

1.Brick industry.   e 2. Tile. 3.Clay.
I.U.S. Foreign Operations Administration.

Tile construction.

690.015
(485)
S82
R105
Ericsson, Alvar.
Läggning och sättning av keramiska
plattor; en sammanställning av nyare
undersökningar (Tile fixing; a summary
of recent investigations) Stockholm,
Statens råd för Byggnadsforskning,
1964.
39p. (Sweden. Statens Kommitté
för Byggnadsforskning. Rapport no. 105)
English summary.

1. Building research - Sweden. 2. Tile construction.   I. Sweden.
Statens Kommitté   för Byggnadsforskning.

Tile.

691
P67
E91-
1962
Portugal. Laboratório Nacional de
Engenharia Civil.
Telhas cerâmicas ensaio de resis-
tencia ao frio. [Burnt clay roofing
tiles freezing test] Lisboa, 1962.
[3]p. (Especificacoes E91-1962;
Serie B, Seccao 5)
English summary.

1. Building materials - Standards and
specifications. 2. Tile.

VF
691.4
(016)
U54
1949
Tile - Bibliographies
U.S. Office of Technical Services.
Bibliography of reports on tile.   Washington,
D.C., 1949.
2 p.   (1B 108)

Processed.

1.Tile-Bibliog.

693
F71
Tile construction.
Frankl, Lee.
The masonry house; step-by-step construction in tile and
brick [by] Training-Thru-Sight Associates: Lee Frankl, in
cooperation with Structural Clay Products Institute. New
York, Duell, Sloan & Pearce [1950]
124 p. illus. 28 cm. (Basic industrial series)

1.Brick construction. 2 Masonry-Building-Brick. 3. Tile construction. I. Train-
ing-Thru-Sight Associates, New York. II. Title. (Series)
III.Structural Clay Products Institute.
TH1199.F7   690
Library of Congress   [20]   50-8592

729.69
S61
TILE.
Spangler, B D
The failure of floor tile systems; an inves-
tigation. Prepared for the Technical Studies
Program of the Dept. of Housing and Urban
Development, Federal Housing Administration.
[Gainesville, Fla.] Dept. of Civil Eginneer-
ing, Engineering and Industrial Experiment
Station, University of Florida, 1968.
27p.
1. Tile. 2. Tile construction. 3. Floors and
flooring. I. Florida. University. Engineering
and Industrial   Experiment Station.
II. Title.   III. U.S. Federal Housing
Administratio   n Technical Studies Program.

Tile - Standards and specifications.

693.068.32
IA52
American Standards Association.
American standard specifications for installation of ceramic tile with dry-set portland
cement mortar including American Standard
specification for dry-set portland cement
mortar A118.1-1959. Sponsor: Tile Council of
America, inc. New York, 1960.

20p. (AIA file numbers 23A and 23P; ASA A-
108.5-1960)
1. Tile - Standards and specifications.
2. Clay - Standards and specifications
3. Cement - Standards and specifications.
I. Tile Council   of America, inc.
II. Title.

VF
693.068.32
G71
Suppl.
Tile construction.
Graf, Donald Thornton, comp.
... Thin setting bed methods and materials.
Complementary to the Tile hand book.   [New
York] Tile Council of America [c1952]
21 p.   (K400)

At head of title: Genuine clay tile unequalled
for performance and beauty throughout seventy
centuries.
AIA 23A.
1.Tile construction. I.Tile Council of America.

VF
691.4
S77
R5
Tile
Structural Clay Products Research Foundation.
Space division in schools, by S. E. Hubbard.
Geneva, Ill., June 1956.
18 p.   graphs, tables.   (Its Research
report no. 5)

1.Schools. 2.Tile. 3.Walls. I.Title. II.Hubbard,
S   E

690.241.53
W67
TILE, ROOFING.
WORCESTER, WOLSEY GARNET, 1876-
THE MANUFACTURE OF ROOFING TILES.
EDWARD ORTON, JR., COLLABORATOR AND
EDITOR. COLUMBUS, OHIO, 1910.
476P. (OHIO. GEOLOGICAL SURVEY.
4TH SERIES. BULLETIN 11)

1. TILE, ROOFING. I. ORTON,
EDWARD, 1863-1932. II. TITLE.

VF
693.068.32
G71
Tile construction.
Graf, Donald Thornton, comp.
Tile handbook ... [combines the data formerly contained
in the Tile handbook T-1 with the Basic specification for
tilework K-300. Ossining? N. Y., 1951]
48 p. diagrs. 28 cm.
Cover title.
At head of title: AIA-23A.

1.Tile construction. I. American Institute of Architects.

TH8531.G7   693.3
Library of Congress   [1]   51-19674

Tile.

691.421
T18
Tauber, E
Some new ceramic finishes and cladding
materials. Melbourne, Div. of Building
Research, Commonwealth Scientific and Indus-
trial Research Organization, 1967.
2p. (Australia. Commonwealth Scientific
and Industrial Research Organization, Div.
of Building Research. Reprint no. 394)
Reprinted from Proceedings of the third
Australian Building Research Congress, 1967.
1. Clay. 2. Tile. 3. Building materials.
I. Australia. Commonwealth Scientific and
Industrial Re   search Organization.
(Div. of Buildi   ng Research)
(Cont'd on next card)

VF
668.3
A87e
Tile construction.
Australia. Commonwealth Scientific and
Industrial Research Organization.
Epoxy resin will mend faulty tiling;
a method of repair which saves the cost of
demolishing affected areas, by E.N. Mattison
and L.V. Sokolich. [Melbourne] 1963.
68-69p.   (Its Div. of Building Research.
D.B.R. reprint no. 254)
Reprinted from Building materials
magazine, vol. 4, no. 51, June-July, 1963.
p. 68-69.
1. Adhesives.   2. Tile construction.
I. Mattison, E.N.   II. Sokolich, L.V.

693.2
G71
Tile construction
Graham, Frank D
Audels masons and builders guide; a practical
illustrated trade assistant on modern construction
for bricklayers, stone masons, cement workers,
plasterers and tile setters ... by Frank D. Graham
[and] Thomas J. Emery.   New York, Audel [1950-
1951]
3 v.   illus., diagrs.

1.Bricklaying. 2.Tile construction. 3.Concrete
construction. I.Title.

Tile construction.

VF
693.2
G85
Gunsallus, Brooke L
Manufacturing brick and tile to serve your community, by Brooke L. Gunsallus and others. U.S. Dept. of Commerce cooperating with U.S. Dept. of Agriculture. Washington, Govt. Print. Off., 1946.
59p. (U.S. Dept. of Commerce. Industrial (Small business) series no. 49)
1. Brick construction. 2. Tile construction. I. U.S. Dept. of Agriculture. II. U.S. Dept. of Commerce.

693.2
S77p
TILE CONSTRUCTION.
STRUCTURAL CLAY PRODUCTS INSTITUTE.
POCKET GUIDE: BRICK AND TILE CONSTRUCTION. 4TH ED. WASHINGTON, 1959.
129P.
1. BRICK CONSTRUCTION. 2. TILE CONSTRUCTION. I. TITLE.

Tile construction.

VF
691.421
W15
Walton, J D
Felted ceramics, by J.D. Walton and R.R. Sulliven. Presented at the 67th Annual Meeting of the American Ceramic Society in Philadelphia, May 3, 1965 (Society Symposium 2, no. 5-82-65) [Philadelphia?] American Ceramic Society, 1966.
586-589p.
Reprinted from the American Ceramic Society bulletin, June 7, 1966.
1. Clay. 2. Tile construction. I. Sulliven, R.R., jt. au. II. American Ceramic Society. 67th Meeting, Philadelphia, 1966. III. Title.

Tile construction.

VF
729.69
O72
Oregon. Forest Products Research Center.
Floor tile from planer shavings, by C. H. Burrows. Corvallis, 1958.
22p. illus. (Its Information circular no. 12)
1. Tile construction. 2. Floors and flooring. I. Burrows, C. H. (Series)

Tile construction.

693.5
S77s
Structural Clay Products Institute.
Structural design of combination tile and concrete slabs, by Guillermo Enciso and Richard La Vigne. Washington, 1960.
24p. diagrs., tables.
1. Concrete construction. 2. Tile construction. I. Enciso, Guillermo. II. La Vigne, Richard.

Tile construction.

693.2
W27
West, Miriam E
Productivity and employment in selected industries; brick and tile. Philadelphia, Works Progress Administration, National Research Project, in cooperation with National Bureau of Economic Research, 1939.
212p. (U.S. Works Progress Administration, National Research Project. Report no. N-2)
1. Brick construction. 2. Tile construction. 3. Employment. I. U.S. Works Progress Administration. National Research Project.

693.2
P58
1950
Tile construction.
Plummer, Harry Custer, 1897-
Brick and tile engineering; handbook of design. [1st ed.] Washington, Structural Clay Products Institute, ⁺1950.
vii, 302 p. illus. 24 cm.
"A revised edition of those sections of [Principles of] brick engineering [by the author with L. J. Reardon] and [Principles of] tile engineering [by the author with E. F. Wanner] ... which deal with unreinforced masonry."
Bibliography: p. 383-387.
construction.
1. Bricks. 2. Building, Brick. 3. Tile construction. 4. Title.
I. Structural Clay Products Institute.
TA432.P48   693.2   51-905
Library of Congress   [10]

690.22
S77t
TILE CONSTRUCTION
Structural Clay Products Institute.
Technical notes on brick and tile construction.
v.1, no.1, 1950-
v. monthly. Notebook.
An up-to-date notebook contains a broken sequence of volumes and numbers. Old issues are discarded as they are superseded by new and revised material on the same subject published in later issues.
SEE SERIAL RECORD.

691.4
B74
Tile construction - Handbooks, manuals, etc.
Brick and Tile Association of Oklahoma.
The 7 easy steps to build a fireproof all-ceramic home. Oklahoma City, Okla. [1948]
82 p. illus., diagrs.
1. Brick construction - Handbooks, manuals, etc.
2. Tile construction - Handbooks, manuals, etc.
3. Fireproof construction.

693.068.32
P58
Tile construction.
Plummer, Harry Custer, 1897-
Principles of tile engineering; handbook of design, by Harry C. Plummer and Edwin F. Wanner. Washington, Structural Clay Products Institute, ⁺1947.
453 p. illus. 24 cm.
1. Tile construction. I. Wanner, Edwin F., 1900- joint author. II. Title: Tile engineering.
TH1083.P59   693.8   49-6460*
Library of Congress   [15]

VF
691.4
877
R
Tile construction.
Structural Clay Products Research Foundation.
Research report No. 1-   Chicago, Ill.
1953 -
v.
1. Brick construction. 2. Tile construction.
Anals. for 1-3, 5

693.068.32
T45a
TILE CONSTRUCTION - STANDARDS AND SPECIFICATIONS.
Tile Council of America.
American National Standard Specifications for: ceramic tile installed with chemical resistant, water cleanable tile-setting and -grouting epoxy; A108.6-1969. Chemical resistant, water cleanable tile-setting and -grouting epoxy; A118.3-1969. Princeton, N.J., 1969. [14]p. (Its Tile work 9, ceramic tile)
Approved Dec. 17, 1959, American National Standards Institute.
1. Tile Construction - Standards and specifications. — I. American National Standards Institute. II. Title.

691.421
S45
Tile constriction.
Simms, L   G
The strength of walls built in the laboratory with some types of clay bricks and blocks. Gerston, Eng., Building Research Station, Ministry of Technology, 1965.
11p. (U.K. Building Research Station. Building research current papers. Engineering series no. 24)
Reprinted from Transactions of the British Ceramic Society, July 1965, p. 81-92.
(Continued on next card)

693.068.32
T45
Tile construction.
Tile Council of America.
American standard specifications for glazed ceramic wall tile, ceramic mosaic tile, quarry tile and pavers installed in Portland cement mortars, including requirements for related divisions. New York, 1958.
28p. tables.
Approved as American standard by the American Standards Association, October 16, 1958.
1. Tile construction. 2. Building standards.

693.068.32
T45h
Tile construction - Standards and specifications.
Tile Council of America.
Handbook for ceramic tile installation,
19   New York, 19
v.
For Library holdings see main entry.
1. Tile construction - Standards and specifications. 2. Portland cement. I. Title.

691.421
S45
Simms, L   G   The strength of walls built in the laboratory...1965. (Card 2)
1. Clay. 2. Tile construction. 3. Walls. I. U.K. Building Research Station. II. Title.

VF
690.013
(68)
U54
Tile construction.
Union of South Africa. Council of South African Bureau of Standards.
Standard specification for concrete roofing tiles. Johannesburg, 1956.
[24] p. (Its S.A.B.S. 542-1956)
English and Dutch.
1. Building standards - Union of South Africa
2. Tile construction. 3. Roofs and roofing. I. Title.

693.068.32
T45uni
Tile construction - Standards and specifications.
Tile Council of America, inc.
USA standard specifications for: ceramic tile installed with dry-set portland cement mortar A108.5-1967; dry-set portland cement mortar A118.1-1967. Approved [by] United States of America Standards Institute, with suggested guide outline form for specifiers. New York, 1968.
16p.
On cover: 9 tile work.
1. Tile construction - Standards and specifications. 2. Portland cement. I. Title. II. Title: Ceramic tile installed with dry-set portland cement mortar.

729.69
S61
TILE CONSTRUCTION.
Spangler, B   D
The failure of floor tile systems; an investigation. Prepared for the Technical Studies Program of the Dept. of Housing and Urban Development, Federal Housing Administration. [Gainesville, Fla.] Dept. of Civil Engineering, Engineering and Industrial Experiment Station, University of Florida, 1968.
27p.
1. Tile. 2. Tile construction. 3. Floors and flooring. I. Florida. University. Engineering and Industrial Experiment Station. II. Title. III. U.S. Federal Housing Administration Technical Studies Program.

690.013
(68)
U54st
Tile construction.
Union of South Africa. Council of South African Bureau of Standards.
Standard specification for glazed ceramic wall tiles and fittings. Johannesburg, 1956.
[20] p. illus., tables. (Its S.A.B.S. 22-1956)
English and Dutch.
1. Building standards - Union of South Africa. 2. Tile construction. 3. Walls.

693.068.32
T45un
Tile construction - Standards and specifications.
Tile Council of America, inc.
USA standard specifications for ceramic tile installed with water resistant organic adhesives A108.4-1968. Approved Feb. 14, 1968, United States of America Standards Institute. Including related standard: USA standard for organic adhesives for installation of ceramic tiles USAS A136.1-1967 with suggested guide outline form for specifiers. New York, 1968.
24p.
On cover: 9 tile work. USAS A108.4-1968.
1. Tile construction - Standards and specifications. 2. Adhesives. 3. Waterproofing. I. Title.

693.068.32
T45u Tile Council of America, inc. ations.
USA standard specifications for: glazed
ceramic wall tile installed with portland
cement mortar A108.1-1967; ceramic mosaic tile
installed with portland cement mortar A108.2-
1967; quarry tile and paver tile installed with
portland cement mortar A108.2-1967;quarry tile
and paver tile installed with portland cement
mortar A108.3-1967. Approved [by] United States
of America Standards Institute, with suggested
guide outline form for specifiers. New York,
1967.
20p.
1. Tile construc tion - Standards and
specifications. (Cont'd on next card)

693.068.32
T45 Tile Council of America.
American standard specifications for glazed
ceramic wall tile, ceramic mosaic tile,
quarry tile and pavers installed in Portland
cement mortars, including requirements for
related divisions. New York, 1958.
28p. tables.

Approved as American standard by the
American Standards Association, October 16,
1958.
1. Tile construction. 2. Building standards.

693.068.32
T45u Tile Council of America, inc.
USA standard specifications for: glazed
ceramic wall tile installed with portland
cement mortar A108.1-1967; ceramic mosiac tile
installed with portland cement mortar A108.2-
1967; quarry tile and paver tile installed with
portland cement mortar A108.2-1967;quarry tile
and paver tile installed with portland cement
mortar A108.3-1967. Approved [by] United States
of America Standards Institute, with suggested
guide outline form for specifiers. New York,
1967.
20p.
1. Tile construc tion - Standards and
specifications. (Cont'd on next card)

693.068.32
T45u Tile Council of America, inc. USA
Standard...1967. (Card 2)

2. Walls. 3. Portland cement. I. Title.

Tile Council of America, inc.
693.068.32
IA52 American Standards Association.
American standard specifications for installation of ceramic tile with dry-set portland
cement mortar including American Standard
specification for dry-set portland cement
mortar A118.1-1959. Sponsor: Tile Council of
America, inc. New York, 1960.

20p. (AIA file numbers 23A and 23P; ASA A-
108.5-1960)
1. Tile - Standards and specifications.
2. Clay - Standards and specifications.
3. Cement - Stan dards and specifications.
I. Tile Council of America, inc.
II. Title.

693.068.32
T45u Tile Council of America, inc. USA
Standard...1967. (Card 2)

2. Walls. 3. Portland cement. I. Title.

668.3
U54u TILE CONSTRUCTION - STANDARDS AND
SPECIFICATIONS.
United States of America Standards Institute.
USA standard for organic adhesives for
installation of ceramic tile. Type I. Organic
adhesives for installation of ceramic tile
in interior areas requiring prolonged water
resistance. Type II. Organic adhesives for
installation of ceramic tile in interior areas
requiring intermittent water resistance.
Sponsor: Adhesive and Sealant Council.
New York, 1967.
10p.
At head of title: USAS A136.1-1967.

(Cont'd on next card)

VF
693.068.32
G71 Tile Council of America.
Suppl. Graf, Donald Thornton, comp.
... Thin setting bed methods and materials.
Complementary to the Tile hand book. [New
York] Tile Council of America [c1952]
21 p. (K400)

At head of title: Genuine clay tile unequalled
for performance and beauty throughout seventy
centuries.
AIA 23A.
1.Tile construction. I.Tile Council of America.

693.068.32
P58 Tile engineering.
Plummer, Harry Custer, 1897-
Principles of tile engineering; handbook of design, by
Harry C. Plummer and Edwin F. Wanner. Washington,
Structural Clay Products Institute, °1947.
453 p. illus. 24 cm.

1. Tile construction. I. Wanner, Edwin F., 1900- joint author. II. Title: Tile engineering.

TH1083.P59 698.3 49-6460*
Library of Congress [15]

668.3
U54u United States of America Standards Institute.
USA standard...1967. (Card 2)

1. Adhesives - Standards and specifications.
2. Tile construction - Standards and
specifications. I. Adhesive and Sealant
Council. II. Title: Organic adhesives for
installation of ceramic tile.

693.068.32
T45h Tile Council of America.
Handbook for ceramic tile installation,
1969. New York, 1969-
1y.
For Library holdings see main entry.

1. Tile construction - Standards and
specifications. 2. Portland cement. I. Title.

VF
690.013
(41) Tile flooring and slab flooring.
G72 United Kingdom. Ministry of Works. Council for
CP202 Codes of Practice for Buildings.
General series: Tile flooring and slab
flooring. London, British Standards Institution,
1951.
28 p. tables. (British standard code of
practice. CP 202)

1.Floors and flooring. 2.Building standards-U.K.
I.Title. II.Series.

693.068.32
U54 TILE CONSTRUCTION - STANDARDS AND
SPECIFICATIONS.
United States of America Standards Institute.
USA standard specification for ceramic
tile approved June 7, 1967, United States
of America Standards Institute. Sponsor:
Tile Council of America. New York, 1967.
10p.

1. Tile construction - Standards and
specifications. I. Tile Council of America.
II. Title. III. Title: Ceramic tile.

693.068.32
U54 Tile Council of America.
United States of America Standards Institute.
USA standard specification for ceramic
tile approved June 7, 1967, United States
of America Standards Institute. Sponsor:
Tile Council of America. New York, 1967.
10p.

1. Tile construction - Standards and
specifications. I. Tile Council of America.
II. Title. III. Title: Ceramic tile.

VF Tile flooring and slab flooring.
690.013
(41) U.K. Ministry of Works. Council for Codes
G72 of Practice for Buildings.
CP Tile flooring and slab flooring. London,
draft British Standards Institution, 1958.
8/14/58 12p.

CY (BLCP) 6621. (Revision of C.P. 202 :1951)
VF690.013(41)G72 CP202.
Issued for comment only.

1. Floors and flooring. 2. Building standards - U.K. I.British Standards Institution.
II.Title.

693.068.32
U54u TILE CONSTRUCTION - STANDARDS AND
SPECIFICATIONS.
United States of American Standards Institute.
USA standard specifications for: electrically conductive ceramic tile installed with
conductive dry-set portland cement mortar.
With suggested guide outline form for specifiers. Sponsor: Tile Council of America.
New York, 1967.
8p.
1. Tile construction - Standards and
specifications. 2. Portland cement.
I. Title: Ceramic tile installed with
conductive dry-set portland cement mortar.

693.068.32
T45un Tile Council of America, inc.
USA standard specifications for ceramic
tile installed with water resistant organic
adhesives A108.4-1968. Approved Feb. 14,
1968, United States of America Standards
Institute. Including related standard: USA
standard for organic adhesives for installation of ceramic tiles USAS A136.1-1967 with
suggested guide outline form for specifiers.
New York, 1968.
24p.
On cover: 9 tile work. USAS A108.4-1968.

1. Tile con struction - Standards
and specifica tions. 2. Adhesives.
3. Waterproof ing. I. Title.

Tile construction.
VF
690.013 U.K. Ministry of Works. Council for
(41) Codes of Practice for Buildings.
G72 British standard code of practice on
CP wall tiling. Part 1: Internal wall
draft tiling under normal conditions. London,
10/23/61 British Standards Institution, 1961.
16p. (British draft code of practice)
AB (BLCP) 5005.
Issued for comment only.

1. Tile construction. 2. Walls. I. British
Standards Institution.

693.068.32
T45a Tile Council of America.
American National Standard
Specifications for: ceramic tile installed
with chemical resistant, water cleanable
tile-setting and -grouting epoxy:
A108.6-1969. Chemical resistant, water
cleanable tile-setting and -grouting
epoxy; A118.3-1969. Princeton, N.J., 1969.
[14]p. (Its Tile work 9, ceramic tile)
Approved Dec. 17, 1959, American National
Standards Institute.
1. Tile Construction - Standards and
specifications. I. American National
Standards Institute. II. Title.

693.068.32
T45uni Tile Council of America, inc.
USA standard specifications for: ceramic
tile installed with dry-set portland cement
mortar A118.1-1967; dry-set portland cement
mortar A118.1-1967. Approved [by] United
States of America Standards Institute, with
suggested guide outline form for specifiers.
New York, 1968.
16p.
On cover: 9 tile work.
1. Tile construction - Standards and
specifications. 2. Portland cement.
I. Title. II. Title: Ceramic tile
installed with dry-set portland cement
mortar.

Tile construction.
VF
690.013 U.K. Ministry of Works. Council for
(41) Codes of Practice for Buildings.
G72 Wall tiling. Part I: Internal wall
CP tiling under normal conditions. London,
draft British Standards Institution, 1961.
10/23/61 16p. (British draft code of practice)
AB (BLCP) 5005.
Issued for comment only.
1. Tile construction. 2. Walls.
I. British Standards Institution.

Ref.
808.8
M14

Tilghman, Tench Francis.

Magill, Frank N.
Magill's quotations in context, edited by Frank N. Magill and Tench Francis Tilghman. New York, Harper, 1965.
1256 p.

1. Quotations. I. Title. II. Tilghman, Tench Francis.

ct

711.33
(016)
T25

Tilley, Betty Currie
Tennessee. State Planning Commission.
Index to information available from state agencies, compiled by Mary Coleman Harbison and Betty Currie Tilley. [Nashville?] 1955.
1 v. (Its Publication no. 261)

1. State planning - Bibliographies.

693.5
C65M

TILT-UP CONSTRUCTION.
COLLINS, FRANK THOMAS.
MANUAL OF TILT-UP CONSTRUCTION. 5TH (I.E. 6TH) ED. BERKELEY, AVAILABLE FROM KNOW-HOW PUBLICATIONS, 1965.
148P.

1. CONCRETE CONSTRUCTION. I. TITLE: TILT-UP CONSTRUCTION.

697.942
N17A

TILL, C E
NATIONAL RESEARCH COUNCIL, CANADA.
AN APPLICATION OF THE DUNMORE ELECTRIC HYGROMETER TO HUMIDITY MEASUREMENT AT LOW TEMPERATURE, BY G.O. HANDEGORD AND C.E. TILL. OTTAWA, 1965.
P.280-284. (ITS DBR RESEARCH PAPER NO. 259)

REPRINTED FROM INTERNATIONAL SYMPOSIUM ON HUMIDITY AND MOISTURE, PROCEEDINGS, V. I, CHAPTER 28, WASHINGTON, D C., 1963.

(CONTINUED ON NEXT CARD)

930.9
P56

Tillinghast, William H.
Ploetz' epitome of history, translated and enlarged by William H. Tillinghast. Revised under the editorship of Harry Elmer Barnes. New York, Blue Ribbon Books, 1925.
855 p.

1. History. I. Tillinghast, William H. II. Barnes, Harry Elmer.

ct

693.5
P67

TILT-UP CONSTRUCTION.
PORTLAND CEMENT ASSOCIATION.
TILT-UP CONSTRUCTION; A MODERN METHOD OF BUILDING WITH REINFORCED CONCRETE. CHICAGO, 1952.
31P.

1. CONCRETE CONSTRUCTION.
2. CONCRETE, REINFORCED. I. TITLE.

697.942
N17A

NATIONAL RESEARCH COUNCIL, CANADA. AN APPLICATION ...1965.   (CARD 2)
1. HUMIDITY. I. HANDEGORD, G.O.
II. TILL, C.E.

312.1
(7512)
T45

Tilly, Charles.
Migration to an American city. [Wilmington, Del.] Agricultural Experiment Station and Div. of Urban Affairs, University of Delaware, in cooperation with Farm Population Branch, Economic Research Service, U.S. Dept. of Agriculture, 1965.
52p.

1. Population shifts - Wilmington, Del. I. Delaware. University. Division of Urban Affairs.   II. U.S. Economic Research   Service. III. Title.

VF
693.5
S77

Tilt-up construction.
Structural Engineers Association of Southern California.
Tilt-up construction. [Los Angeles, Calif.] Sept. 1950.
[3] p. (Its Technical bulletin no. 2)

At head of title: Report of Special Committee.

1. Concrete construction. I. Title.

3686

TILLAMOOK CO., OR. PLANNING COMMISSION.
A PROPOSED PRELIMINARY COMPREHENSIVE PLAN. TILLAMOOK CO., OR., 1969.
32P. (HUD 701 REPORT)

1. MASTER PLAN - TILLAMOOK CO., OR.
I. HUD. 701. TILLAMOOK CO., OR.

728.1
:325
(7512)
T45

3 cl

Tilly, Charles.
Race and residence in Wilmington, Delaware, by Charles Tilly and others. [New York] Bureau of Publications, Teachers College, Columbia University, 1965.
145p.

Bibliography: p. 135-140.

1. Minority groups - Housing - Wilmington, Del.
2. Housing - Wilmington, Del. - Social aspects. I. Title.

C. 2 in E.D. coll.

693.5
T29

Tilt-up construction on the farm.
Texas. Agricultural Experiment Station.
Concrete tilt-up construction on the farm, by Otto R. Kunze and Price Hobgood. College Station, Texas, 1957.
12p. illus., diagrs. (Its Bulletin 874)

1. Concrete construction. I. Kunze, Otto R   II. Hobgood, Price. III. Title: Tilt-up construction on the farm.

378
M22b

Tillery, Dale, jt. au.
Medsker, Leland L
Breaking the access barriers; a profile of two-year colleges, by Leland L. Medsker and Dale Tillery. With a commentary by Joseph P. Cosand. New York, McGraw-Hill, 1971.
183p.
Bibliography: p. 163-168.
Fourth of a series of profiles sponsored by the Carnegie Commission on Higher Education.

1. Universities and colleges. I. Tillery, Dale, jt. au. II. Title.

VF
331.252
F85

Tilove, Robert.
Fund for the Republic.
Pension funds and economic freedom, by Robert Tilove. New York, 1959.
91p. diagrs., tables.

1. Pension funds. I. Tilove, Robert.

Timber

see

Forests and forestry
Lumber industry

690.59
(016)
N17

Tilleux, Eugene A.
National Association of Home Builders.
Improving America's housing; a bibliography of American, British and foreign language publications on the maintenance, repair and improvement of housing [compiled by Eugene A. Tilleux.   Washington, 1955]
75 p.

1. Houses - Maintenance and modernization - Bibliography. 2. Neighborhood rehabilitation - Bibliography. I. Tilleux, Eugene A. II. Title.

711.73
(797)
T45

Tilse, Frances E
The highway system and the impact of population and industrial growth in a changing economy: State of Washington. [Olympia] Industrial Development Subcommittee of the Joint Committee on Highways, 1968.
348p.
Bibliography: p. 343-348.
1. Highways - Wash. (State) I. Washington (State) Joint Committee on Highways. II. Title.

691.110.15
B67

Timber.
Bosman, D   L
The management of research and development for results in the TRU. Pretoria, Timber Research Unit, South African Council for Scientific and Industrial Research, 1969.
84-87p. (South African Council for Scientific and Industrial Research. Houtim 21)
Timber, vol. 6, no. 6, March 1969, p. 9-12.

1. Wood - Research. I. South African Council for Scientific and Industrial Research. II. Timber. III. Title.

058.7
:728.100.15
B84
1952
Prelim.

Tilleux, Eugene A.
Building Research Advisory Board.
A survey of housing research.
[Washington, National Academy of Sciences - National Research Council] April 1952.
1 v. (unpaged) forms, tables.

Final report. Research Project No. O-T-59.
Housing and Home Finance Agency.
Project director: William H. Scheick;
Staff technician: Eugene A. Tilleux.
Processed.

697.8
T45

TILSON, SEYMOUR.
AIR POLLUTION. NEW YORK, CONOVER-MAST PUBLICATIONS, 1965.
UNPAGED.

REPRINTED FROM INTERNATIONAL SCIENCE AND TECHNOLOGY, JUNE 1965.

1. AIR POLLUTION.

691.11
U54

Timber.
U.K. Ministry of Public Building and Works.
Care in the use of timber. 3d ed. London, H.M.S.O., 1970.
folder. (Advisory leaflet no. 29)

1. Wood. I. Title: Timber. II. Title.

VF
694.1
(083.74) American Institute of Timber Construction.
A52
Timber construction standards.
Timber construction standards; standard specifications and codes for architects, engineers, fabricators, contractors and others concerned with engineered timber construction. 1st ed. Washington, 1954.
1 v. (various pagings)

1. Wood construction. I. Title.

Vf Wood construction
DATE OF REQUEST 2/4/53   L. C. CARD NO.

AUTHOR
Timber Engineering Company
TITLE
Architects aids for better homes and other wood construction.

EDITION	PUB. DATE	PAGING
PUBLISHER		AIA 19-B-5
same, Washington, D.C.		

RECOMMENDED BY
TECO Trip-L-Grip framing anchors
REVIEWED IN
Timber Merchant 1/53 p.41
ORDER RECORD

694
T45
Timber Engineering Company.
Timber design and construction handbook. New York, F. W. Dodge Corporation [1956]
622 p.   illus., diagrs., tables.

1. Wood construction. 2. Wood framing. 3. Wood construction - Standards and specifications. 4. Plywood. I. Title.

691.11 Timber content of two-storey houses.
A74 Atkinson, J   E
Timber content of two-storey houses, by J.E. Atkinson and C.R. Honey. Garston, Eng., Building Research Station, Ministry of Public Building and Works, 1968.
26-27,29-30, 33p. (U.K. Building Research Station, Building research current papers. Current paper 6/68)
Reprinted from: Industrialized building. July 1967.
1. Wood. 2. Housing. 3. Architecture, Domestic - Designs and plans.
I. Honey, C   R.   jt. au. II. U.K. Building Research   Station. III. Title.

VF - Wood construction
DATE OF REQUEST 3/19/54   L. C. CARD NO.
MAR 29
AUTHOR
Timber Engineering Company.
TITLE
Building better homes with wood.

SERIES

EDITION	PUB. DATE	PAGING
PUBLISHER		

RECOMMENDED BY
NDL
REVIEWED IN
3/54 p.145
ORDER RECORD

FOLIO
728.3
T45 TIMBER ENGINEERING COMPANY, WASHINGTON, D.C.
TWENTY-THREE GARDEN APARTMENT DESIGNS, NEW IDEAS IN ARCHITECTURAL TREATMENT, PLANNING AND STRUCTURAL FRAMING FOR MILITARY HOUSING, SUBURBAN APARTMENTS, LOW-COST PUBLIC HOUSING. WASHINGTON, 1950.
25P.

1. ARCHITECTURE, DOMESTIC - DESIGNS AND PLANS. 2. HOUSE PLANS. I. TITLE: GARDEN APARTMENT DESIGNS.

634.9 U.K. Forest Products Research Laboratory.
U54 Timber decay and its control. London, H.M.S.O., 1962.
12p. (Its Leaflet no. 39)

1. Forests and forestry. 2. Lumber industry.
I. Title.

Timber decay and its control.

DE 1850 Trusses
Class No. Cop.1   Author (surname first) Timber Engineering Co.
Wood construction
Accession No.   Title Clear span Teco trussed rafters in modern home planning
Ordered   Place Wash, D.C.   Publisher
SEP 18 1950
Source   Address
None
Received
SEP 25 1950   Date   Paging 8   List Price   Est. Cost
Purchase Order No.   Edition or Series
Date   Recommended by
L. C. No.   Reviewed in Jour. of Bldg. & Contractor 9/5/50
H-305 (2-50)   HOUSING AND HOME FINANCE AGENCY: Office of the Administrator

---

VF
694.1
T45
Timber Engineering Company.
Typical designs of timber structures; a reference for use of architects and engineers. 1949 ed. Washington [1948]
114 p. illus. 28 x 35 cm.

Wood construction
1. Building, Wooden.   I. Title.

TH1101.T58   694.1   19-2734*
Library of Congress

694
T45 Timber Engineering Company.
Timber design and construction handbook. New York, F. W. Dodge Corporation [1956]
622 p.   illus., diagrs., tables.

1. Wood construction. 2. Wood framing. 3. Wood construction - Standards and specifications. 4. Plywood. I. Title.

VF - Trusses
DATE OF REQUEST 8/29/52   L. C. CARD NO.

AUTHOR
Timber Engineering Co., Washington, D.C.
TITLE
Lank-Teco truss bulletin and Modern timber roof trusses

SERIES

EDITION	PUB. DATE	PAGING
PUBLISHER		
same		

RECOMMENDED BY
REVIEWED IN
H-R 8/21/52 p.52
ORDER RECORD

VF
674
T45 Timber Engineering Co.
Typical lumber designs, with quantities and material lists for light and heavy frame structures. 1958 ed. Washington, Govt. Print. Off., 1958.
15p. illus., diagrs., tables.

1. Lumber industry.

Timber Development Association, *London.*
Constructional research bulletin. no. 1- London, 1948?-
no. illus. 28 cm.

For full information see Periodical Kardex file.

research.
1. Building - Collected works. 2. Wood construction.
I. Title.
TH7.T5   690.72   49-54859*
Library of Congress

DATE OF REQUEST 9/24/54   L. C. CARD NO.
SEP 17 1954
AUTHOR
Timber Engineering Co.
TITLE
One hundred years of engineering progress with wood.

SERIES

EDITION	PUB. DATE 1954	PAGING
PUBLISHER		

RECOMMENDED BY
NDL
REVIEWED IN
H-R 9/9/54 p.57
ORDER RECORD

Wood construction
DATE OF REQUEST 7/25/52   L. C. CARD NO.
JUL
AUTHOR
Timber Engineering Co., Washington, D.C.
TITLE
Wood frame trussed rafters.

SERIES

EDITION	PUB. DATE	PAGING 12 p.
PUBLISHER		
same		

RECOMMENDED BY
REVIEWED IN
Prac Bldr 5/52 p.446
ORDER RECORD

UK Wood construction
DATE OF REQUEST 4/1/54   L. C. CARD NO.
JUN 28 1954
AUTHOR
Timber Development Association.
TITLE
Timbers for house building, compiled by Gerald Hart.

SERIES

EDITION	PUB. DATE 1954	PAGING 51 p.
PUBLISHER		
73 Cannon St., London, England.		

RECOMMENDED BY
NDL
REVIEWED IN
Bldg Mat Digest 3/54 p. 106
ORDER RECORD

Timber Engineering Co
Prize winning designs, eight family garden-type apartments of wood frame construction Washington, D.C. 1950 22p. Illus., plans.

Jury report, Mar. 15, 1952

Arch - Domes - Des + plans - Multi - fam.

694.1 Timber frame houses.
(481) Birkeland, Øivind.
B47 Småhus av tre - fundamenter, bjelkelag, tak og bindingsverk m.m. [Timber frame houses and their foundations] av Øivind Birkeland et al. Oslo, Norges Byggforskningsinstitutt, 1970.
19p. (Saertrykk 198)
Saertrykk fra Teknisk ukeblad nr. 15/70; Byggmesteren nr. 12/70; Bygge nr. 9/70.
1. Wood construction - Norway. 2. Foundations (Building) I. Oslo. Norges Byggnadsforskning. II. Title: Timber frame houses.

Class No.   Author (surname first)
cat-Ros.   Timber Engineering Company.

Accession No.   Title
Ordered   Advancements in wood research and timber engineering.
Source   Place Publisher
Received 12/4/52   DC
Cost   Date 11/52 Paging 31   List Price   Est. Cost
Purchase Order No.   Edition or Series
Date   Recommended by
L. C. No.   Reviewed in
H-305 (2-50)   HOUSING AND HOME FINANCE AGENCY: Office of the Administrator

---

Class No.   Author (surname first) Timber Engineering Co.
School plant planning
Accession No.   Title School buildings your tax dollars can afford.
Ordered
Source   Place Wash., D.C.   Publisher
Received 9/25/50   Address
Cost   Date 1950 Paging 20   Illus., diagrs. List Price   Est. Cost
Purchase Order No.   Edition or Series
Date   Recommended by
L. C. No.   Reviewed in
H-305 (2-50)   HOUSING AND HOME FINANCE AGENCY: Office of the Administrator

---

634.9 Timber income potential from small forests...
F17t Farrell, John H
Timber income potential from small forests in the Missouri Ozarks. Columbus, Ohio, U.S. Forest Service. Central States Forest Experiment Station, 1964.
74p. (U.S. Forest Service. Research paper CS-11)
Bibliography: p. 35-39.
1. Forests and forestry. I. U.S. Forest Experiment Station. Central States Forest Experiment Station, Columbus, Ohio.   II. Title.

691.11
845

Silvester, Frederick D

Timber; its mechanical properties and factors affecting its structural use.
Timber; its mechanical properties and factors affecting its structural use. 1st ed. New York, Pergamon Press, 1967.

Ref.   151p. (Pergamon series of monographs on furniture and timber, vol. 8)
Bibliography: p. 139-141.

1. Wood. 2. Wood - Testing. 3. Lumber industry. I. Title.

634.9
(748)
F27

Ferguson, Roland H

The timber resources of Pennsylvania.
The timber resources of Pennsylvania. Upper Darby, Pa., Northeastern Forest Experiment Station, Forest Service, U.S. Dept. of Agriculture, 1968.
147p. (U.S. Forest Service resources bulletin NE-8)

1. Forests and forestry - Pa.
I. U.S. Northeastern Forest Experiment Station, Upper Darby, Pa. II. Title.

694.1
B46

Björk, S O

Timber structures.
Timber structures (Träkonstruktioner) Garston, Eng., Building Research Station, Ministry of Public Building and Works, 1969.
5p. (U.K. Building Research Station. Library communication 1479)
Translated from the Swedish Byggmastaren, 1968, (3), 23-26.

1. Wood construction. I. U.K. Building Research Station. II. Title.

690.015
(485)
882
R23-
1965

Jensson, Ingvar.

Timber joints.
Timber joints. Stockholm, National Swedish Institute for Building Research, 1965.
1v. (Sweden. Statens Kommitté för Byggnadsforskning. Rapport 23-65)

1. Building research-Sweden. 2. Nails and nailing - Bibl. I. Title. II. Sweden. Statens Kommitté för Byggnadsforskning.

634.9
(771)
D21

DeBald, Paul S

The timber resources of the Ohio Hill Country.
The timber resources of the Ohio Hill Country, by Paul S. DeBald and Roger E. McCay. Upper Darby, Pa., Northeastern Forest Experiment Station, 1969.
75p. (U.S. Forest Service. Resource bulletin NE-14)

1. Forests and forestry - Ohio. I. McCay, Roger E., jt. au. II. U.S. Northeastern Forest Experiment Station, Upper Darby, Pa. III. Title.

725.13
(76624)
T45

Timberlake and Kanady.
A study and recommendations for the municipal building of Ponca City, Oklahoma. [Prepared for] Board of Commissioners of Ponca City and the Oklahoma Dept. of Commerce and Industry. Ponca City, Okla., [1960?]
16p.

U.S. Urban Renewal Adm. UPAP.

1. Public buildings - Ponca City, Okla. I. U.S. URA-UPAP. Ponca City, Okla.

333
B15

Banzhaf (George) and Co.

Timber policy.
Study of public land timber policy. Prepared for Public Land Law Review Commission. Milwaukee, 1969.
2v.

1. Public lands. 2. Forests and forestry. 3. Land use. I. U.S. Public Land Law Review Commission. II. Title: Timber policy.

690.24
B79

Bryant, P A V

Timber roof trusses;
Timber roof trusses; a development study. Pretoria, South African Council for Scientific and Industrial Research, 1967.
11p. (C.S.I.R. Reference no. RU I.48)
Bibliography: p. 10-11.

1. Roofs and roofing. I. South African Council for Scientific and Industrial Research. II. Title.

728
:333
T45
1970

3C

Timberlane Homeownership Conference, Seattle, 1970.
[The Conference] Washington, U.S. Dept. of Housing and Urban Development, Federal Housing Administration, 1970.
37p.

1. Home ownership. I. U.S. Dept. of Housing and Urban Development.

691.11
:620.197
C62

Cockcroft, R

Timber preservatives and methods of treatment.
Timber preservatives and methods of treatment. Princes Risborough, Eng., Forest Products Research Laboratory, 1971.
6p. (Timberlab papers no. 46, 1971)

1. Wood preservation. I. U.K. Forest Products Research Laboratory. II. Title.

VF
690.015
(94)
A87
D29

Dalgleish, D

Timber roof trusses for domestic buildings.
Timber roof trusses for domestic buildings. Sydney, Australia, Commonwealth Experimental Building Station, Sept. 1949.
6 [8] 7 p. (Australia. Commonwealth Experimental Building Station, Duplicated document no. 29)
Processed.

VF
690
T45

Time.
Building; finish your-own house. Detached from Time, Nov. 7, 1960, p. 94-95.

1. Owner-built houses.

634.9
F67t

U.S. Forest Service.

Timber resources for America's future.
Timber resources for America's future. Washington, Govt. Print. Off., 1958.
713p. tables, charts, diagrs. (Its Forest resource report no. 14)

1. Forests and forestry. I. Title.

VF
694.1
U54t

U.K. Ministry of Public Building and Works.

Timber sizes for small buildings; part two.
Timber sizes for small buildings; part two. 2d ed. London, H.M.S.O., 1970.
folder. (Its Advisory leaflet no. 56)

1. Wood construction. I. Title.

711.585
T45

3c.

Time.
The city; under the knife or all for their own good. In Time, vol. 84, no. 19, November, 1964. p. [60]-75.

On cover: Urban renewal: remaking the American city.

1. Urban renewal. 2. Architecture - Design. 3. Apartment houses. I. Title: Urban renewal: remaking the American City. II. Title.

634.9
G15t

Gansner, David A

The timber resources of Kentucky.
The timber resources of Kentucky. Upper Darby, Pa., Northeastern Forest Experiment Station, 1968.
97p. (U.S. Forest Service. Resource bulletin NE-9)

1. Forests and forestry. I. U.S. Northeastern Forest Experiment Station. II. Title.

694.1
C152

CALIFORNIA. UNIVERSITY. INSTITUTE OF ENGINEERING RESEARCH.
ACTION OF TIMBER STRUCTURES SUBJECTED TO LATERAL LOADS. REPORT TO DIVISION OF ARCHITECTURE, STATE DEPARTMENT OF PUBLIC WORKS, SACRAMENTO, CALIFORNIA, BY G.E. TROXELL AND V. BERTERO. BERKELEY, CALIF., 1959.
19P.

1. WOOD CONSTRUCTION. 2. STRUCTURAL ENGINEERING. I. TROXELL, GEORGE EARL. II. BERTERO, V. III. CALIFORNIA. DEPT. OF PUBLIC
(CONTINUED ON NEXT CARD)

159
M12

McCay, James T

Time.
The management of time. Englewood Cliffs, N.J., Prentice-Hall, 1969.
176p.

Bibliography: p. 168-170.

1. Psychology. I. Title. II. Title: Time.

634.9
(747)
F27

Ferguson, Roland H

The timber resources of New York.
The timber resources of New York, by Roland H. Ferguson and Carl E. Mayer. Upper Darby, Pa., U.S. Northeastern Forest Experiment Station, 1970.
193p. (U.S. Forest Service resource bulletin NE-20)
1. Forests and forestry, New York (State). I. Mayer, Carl, jt. au. II. U.S. Northeastern Forest Experiment Station, Upper Darby, Pa. III. Title.

694.1
C152

CALIFORNIA. UNIVERSITY. INSTITUTE OF ENGINEERING RESEARCH. ACTION OF TIMBER ...1959.   (CARD 2)

WORKS. (DIVISION OF ARCHITECTURE)
IV. TITLE. IV. TITLE: TIMBER STRUCTURES.

711.4
W21ci

Weaver, Robert Clifton.

Time.
Cities; hope for the heart. In Time; the weekly news magazine, Mar. 4, 1966. p. 29-33.

Cover title: First Negro in the Cabinet trying to save the cities, Secretary Weaver.

1. City planning. 2. City growth. 3. Metropolitan areas. 4. Race relations. I. Time. II. Title.

690.25
U54T
TIME AND COST STUDIES ON FIVE FLOOR
SYSTEMS.
ILLINOIS. UNIVERSITY. SMALL HOMES
COUNCIL.
TIME AND COST STUDIES ON FIVE FLOOR
SYSTEMS, BY RUDARD A. JONES AND DONALD
H. PERCIVAL. URBANA, 1963.
62P. (ITS RESEARCH REPORT 63-2)

1. FLOORS AND FLOORINGS. I. JONES,
RUDARD A. II. PERCIVAL, DONALD H.
III. TITLE.

351.88
W25
The time for decision.
Welles, Sumner.
The time for decision. New York, Harper
[1944]
431 p. map.

——— A time of progress for older Americans.

362.6
P72t
U.S. President's Council on Aging.
A time of progress for older Americans.
1965-1966-1967 report of the President's
Council on Aging. Wash., For sale by the
Supt. of Docs., Govt. Print. Off., 1968.
57p. (U.S. Dept. of Health, Education,
and Welfare. Administration on Aging.
Publication no. 137)

1. Old age. 2. Public health. 3. Family
income and expenditure. I. Title.

VF
651.4
(016)
L15
Time and motion study - Bibliography.
Lansing Library Service, Oakland, Calif.
Work simplification; a bibliography.
[Oakland, Calif., Dec. 1950]
5 p.

Library Workshop, Work Simplification Clinic,
Univ. of California School of Librarianship
Alumni Association.
June 1951 supplement attached.
Processed.
1.Office management-Bibl. 2.Time and motion study-
Bibl. I.California. University. School of
Librarianship. II.Tit.

VF
693.068
:389.6
A52t
Time for decision in the building industry.
American Standards Association.
Time for decision in the building industry.
[New York, 1950?]
[12] p. illus.

LAW
U.S.
TIME OFF FOR VOTING UNDER STATE LAWS.
U.S. BUREAU OF LABOR STANDARDS.
TIME OFF FOR VOTING UNDER STATE LAWS.
REV. 1962. WASHINGTON, GOVT. PRINT.
OFF., 1962.
22P. (ITS BULLETIN NO. 138)

1. LABOR LAWS AND LEGISLATION.
I. TITLE. II. TITLE: VOTING UNDER
STATE LAWS.

690
(016)
N17t
Time and motion study in the construction
industry.
National Research Council, Canada.
Time and motion study in the construction industry, a selected annotated bibliography, by D. A. Williams and M. E. Sterling.
Ottawa, 1958.
8p. (Its Technical Information Service
report no. 57)

1. Building industry - Bibliography.
I. Williams, D. A. II. Sterling, M. E.
III. Title.

711.14
R63
THE TIME LAG OF FACTORS INFLUENCING
LAND DEVELOPMENT.
ROGERS, ANDREI.
THE TIME LAG OF FACTORS INFLUENCING
LAND DEVELOPMENT. CHAPEL HILL, CENTER
FOR URBAN AND REGIONAL STUDIES,
UNIVERSITY OF NORTH CAROLINA, 1963.
31L.

1. LAND USE. I. TITLE.

658.3
N17TI
TIME OFF WITH PAY.
NATIONAL INDUSTRIAL CONFERENCE BOARD,
INC.
TIME OFF WITH PAY, BY MITCHELL MEYER
AND MICHAEL E. EDMONDS. NEW YORK, 1965.
84P. (ITS STUDIES IN PERSONNEL
POLICY, NO. 196)

1. PERSONNEL MANAGEMENT. 2. WAGES
AND SALARIES. I. MEYER, MITCHELL.
II. EDMONDS, MICHAEL E., JT. AU.
III. TITLE.

301.15
P27
Time and space use. Anal.
Chapin, F Stuart.
Patterns of time and space use, by F. Stuart
Chapin, Jr. and Thomas H. Logan.
(In Perloff, Harvey S., ed. The quality
of the urban environment. 1969. p. 305-332)

1. Sociology. I. Logan, Thomas H., jt. au.
II. Title. III. Title: Time and space use.

728.1
:333.63
D25t
Time lags in the rental housing market.
De Leeuw, Frank.
Time lags in the rental housing market, by
Frank de Leeuw and Nkanta F. Ekanem. Wash.,
Urban Institute, 1970.
57p. (Urban Institute. Working paper
112-19)
Bibliography: p. 56-57.
Draft.
1. Rental housing. 2. Housing market.
I. Ekanem, Nkanta F., jt. au. II. Urban
Institute. III. Title.

301.158
L48
TIME ON THEIR HANDS.
LIVERPOOL NEW ESTATES: ALLIED COUNCIL
OF SOCIAL WELFARE.
A REPORT ON THE NEED FOR THE
PROVISION OF JUVENILE SOCIAL CENTRES:
A SOCIAL SURVEY OF LIVERPOOL'S NEW
HOUSING ESTATES... AT THE REQUEST OF
THE LIVERPOOL JUVENILE ORGANIZATIONS'
COMMITTEE. LIVERPOOL, 1937.
96P.

ON COVER: TIME ON THEIR HANDS.

1. YOUTH. 2. COMMUNITY
FACILITIES. 3. JUVENILE
(CONTINUED ON NEXT CARD)

728.1
:325
(7731)
A17
THE TIME BOMB THAT EXPLODED IN CICERO.
ABRAMS, CHARLES.
THE TIME BOMB THAT EXPLODED IN CICERO,
SEGREGATED HOUSING'S INEVITABLE
DIVIDEND. NEW YORK, 1951.
8P.

REPRINT FROM COMMENTARY, NOV. 1951.

1. MINORITY GROUPS - HOUSING -
CICERO, ILL. I. TITLE.

728.1
:347
T45
TIME MAGAZINE.
THE NATIONAL HOUSING ACT: ITS
BACKGROUND, ITS PROVISIONS, ITS
POSSIBILITIES. NEW YORK, PUB. JOINTLY
BY TIME AND THE ARCHITECTURAL FORUM,
1934.
15P.

1. HOUSING LEGISLATION.
I. ARCHITECTURAL FORUM. II. TITLE.

301.158
L48
LIVERPOOL NEW ESTATES: ALLIED COUNCIL
OF SOCIAL WELFARE. A REPORT ON ...
1937. (CARD 2)

DELINQUENCY. I. TITLE: TIME ON
THEIR HANDS. II. TITLE: JUVENILE
SOCIAL CENTRES.

691.328
C22
Time-dependent behaviour of reinforced
concrete structures.
Cederwall, Krister.
Time-dependent behaviour of reinforced con-
crete structures. Stockholm, Statens Institut
for Byggnadsforskning, 1971.
173p. (Document D3:1971)
Bibliography: p. 169-173.

1. Concrete, Reinforced. 2. Concrete
construction. I. Stockholm. Statens Institut
för Byggnadsforskning. II. Title.

VF
711.583
T45
Time Magazine.
Suburbia U.S.A. Detached from Time
Magazine, June 20, 1960. p. 14-18.

Cover title: One-third of a nation:
U.S. Surbia, 1960.

1. Suburbs.

711.400.15
C72
Time-Oriented Metropolitan Model.
Crecine, John P
A dynamic model of urban structure. Santa
Monica, Calif., Rand Corp., 1968.
61p. (P-3803)
Partial contents.-History of T.O.M.M.
(Time-Oriented Metropolitan Model)

1. City planning - Research. 2. Industrial
location. I. Rand Corp. II. Title.
III. Title: Time-Oriented Metropolitan
Model.

332
G71
Time deposits in monetary analysis.
Gramley, Lyle E
Time deposits in monetary analysis, by Lyle
E. Gramley and Samuel B. Chase. Wash.,
Brookings Institution, 1965.
1380-1404p. (Brookings Institution.
Reprint 108)
Reprinted from the Federal Reserve bulletin,
Oct. 1965.

1. Banks and banking. 2. Finance. I. Chase,
Samuel B., jt. au. II. Brookings Institution.
III. Title.

699.81
G15
Time of evacuation by stairs in high
buildings.
Galbreath, M
Time of evacuation by stairs in high
buildings. Ottawa, National Research Council
of Canada, Div. of Building Research, 1969.
6p. (National Research Council, Canada.
Div. of Building Research. Fire research
note no. 8)
Reprinted from: Fire fighting in Canada,
Feb. 1969.
1. Fireproof construction. I. National
Research Council, Canada. Div. of Building
Research. II. Title.

69
A72
1950
Time-saver standards.
Architectural record.
Time-saver standards, a manual of essential architectural
data for architects, engineers, draftsmen, builders, and other
technicians. Ed. no. 2, new enl. ed. New York, F. W. Dodge
Corp. [1950]
884 p. illus. 29 cm.

"An Architectural record book."

construction
1. Building—Tables, calculations, etc. 2. Building—Handbooks,
manuals, etc. I. Title.
TH151.A72 1950   690.2   51-1937
Library of Congress [10]

69
A72
1946

Time-saver standards

Architectural record.
Time-saver standards, a manual of essential architectural data, for architects, engineers, draftsmen, builders and other technicians. Ed. no. 1 ... An Architectural record book. New York, N. Y., F. W. Dodge corp. [1946]
4 p. l., 648 p. illus., tables, diagrs. 28½ x 22½ cm.
"First complete edition in book form [of the series of Time-saver standards published monthly in the Architectural record]"
1. Building—Tables, calculations, etc. 2. Building—Handbooks, manuals, etc. I. Title.
TH151.A72   690.2   47—2660
© 27Dec46; 2c 24Mar47; publisher; A11443.

Library of Congress   [48g5]

690
A72
1954

TIME-SAVER STANDARDS.
ARCHITECTURAL RECORD.
TIME-SAVER STANDARDS, A MANUAL OF ESSENTIAL ARCHITECTURAL DATA, FOR ARCHITECTS, ENGINEERS, DRAFTSMEN, BUILDERS AND OTHER TECHNICIANS. 3D ED. AN ARCHITECTURAL RECORD BOOK. NEW YORK, F.W. DODGE, CORP., 1954.
888P.

1. BUILDING CONSTRUCTION.   I. TITLE.

720
C15
1966

Time-saver standards; a handbook of architectural design.
Callender, John Hancock, ed.
Time-saver standards; a handbook of architectural design. 4th ed. New York, McGraw-Hill, 1966.
1299p.

1. Architecture – Design. 2. Architecture, Modern. I. Title: A handbook of architectural design. II. Title.

625.7
H43t

Time-saving methods in highway engineering.
Highway Research Board.
Time-saving methods in highway engineering (fourteenth and final installment) Chapter 14: Summary, selected references, and subject index. Washington, July 1956.
p. 362-383

Selected References: p. 365-369.

1. Road construction. 2. Highways. I. Title.

658.564
S12

Time-sharing and batch processing.
Sackman, Harold.
Man-computer problem solving; experimental evaluation of time-sharing and batch processing. Princeton, N.J., Auerbach Publishers, 1970.
272p.
Bibliography: p. 262-268.

1. Automation. I. Title. II. Title: Time-sharing and batch processing.

311
W15

Time series.
Wallis, W   Allen.
A significance test for time series; and other ordered observations, by W. Allen Wallis and Geoffrey H. Moore. New York, National Bureau of Economic Research, 1941.
59 p. (National Bureau of Economic Research. Technical paper 1)
Bibliography: p. 57-59.

1. Stat. I. Title. II. Title: Time series. III. Moore, Geoffrey H., jt. au. IV. Series: National Bureau of Economic Research. Technical paper 1.

728.1
:336.18
(747)
N28oc
no.7

Time series analysis of project development costs of the Mitchell-Lama Program.
New York (City) Housing and Redevelopment Board. (Bureau of Planning and Program Research)
Time series analysis of project development costs of the Mitchell-Lama Program. Prepared by David Talmas. New York, 1963.
5p. (Its Occasional memo no. 7)
1. Public housing – New York (City) 2. Public housing projects. 3. State aided housing programs – New York (City) I. Talmas, David. II. Title.

658.83
A71

The time-service approach to physical distribution.
Arbury (James N.) and Associates.
The time-service approach to physical distribution. New York, American Management Association, Purchasing Div., 1967.
15p.   (American Management Association. Management bulletin no. 99)

1. Marketing. 2. Buying. I. American Management Association. II. Title. (Series)

658.564
W45

Time-sharing computer systems.
Wilkes, M   V
Time-sharing computer systems. New York, American Elsevier Publishing Co., 1968.
102p. (Computer monograph series 5)

Bibliography: p. 97-99.

1. Automation. I. Title.

658.564
A82a

Time sharing reports.
Auerbach Info, inc.
Auerbach time sharing reports. Philadelphia, 1969-
v. (loose-leaf)
Updated by quarterly supplements.

1. Automation. I. Title: Time sharing reports.

658.564
B82

Time-sharing services and utilities.
Bueschel, Richard T
Commercial time-sharing services and utilities, by Richard T. Bueschel and others. New York, American Management Association, 1969.
95p.

1. Automation. 2. Management. I. American Management Association. II. Title. III. Title: Time-sharing services and utilities.

658
H17m

Time study; design and measurement of work.
Barnes, Ralph Mosser.
Motion and time study; design and measurement of work. 6th ed. New York, John Wiley & Sons, 1968.
799p.
Bibliography: p. 769-788.

1. Management. 2. Job analysis. 3. Labor productivity. I. Title: Time study; design and measurement of work. II. Title.

658.511
I57

TIME STUDY PRACTICE AND PROCEDURE.
U.S. INTERNATIONAL COOPERATION ADMINISTRATION.
TIME STUDY PRACTICE AND PROCEDURE. WASHINGTON, TECHNICAL AIDS BRANCH, OFFICE OF INDUSTRIAL RESOURCES, INTERNATIONAL COOPERATION ADMINISTRATION, 1960.
52P. (ITS TRAINING MANUAL NO. 111)

1. JOB ANALYSIS.   2. PERSONNEL MANAGEMENT.   I. TITLE.

323.4
C65ti

N.c.1
Laf.
c.2

A time to listen, a time to act.
U.S. Commission on Civil Rights.
A time to listen, a time to act. Voices from the ghettos of the Nation's cities. Washington, Govt. Print. Off., 1967.
133p.

1. Civil rights. 2. Slums – Social effect. 3. Minority groups. 4. Race relations. I. U.S. President's Commission on Civil Disorders. II. Title.

300.15
K25

A time to speak.
Kelman, Herbert C
A time to speak: on human values and social research. San Francisco, Jossey-Bass, 1968.
349p.

Bibliography: p. 333-339.

1. Social science research. I. Title. II. Title: Human values and social research.

808
B87

Time to speak up
Butler, Jessie Haver.
Time to speak up; a speaker's handbook for women. Foreword by Nancy Astor. 2d rev. ed. New York, Harper & Brothers, 1957.
249p.
Bibliography: p. 247-249.

1. English language. I. Title. II. Title: A speaker's handbook for women.

640
M15

Time use in household tasks by Indiana families.
Manning, Sarah L
Time use in household tasks by Indiana families. Lafayette, Ind., Purdue University, Agricultural Experiment Station, 1968.
48p.   (Research bulletin no. 837)

1. Home economics. 2. Household equipment. I. Indiana. Agricultural Experiment Station. II. Title.

332
M85
1970

The timeless rights and the contemporary problems.
Municipal Finance Officers Association of the United States and Canada.
The timeless rights and the contemporary problems. Special conference issue no. 1 [of the Bond buyer concerning the] 64th annual conference of the Municipal Finance Officers Association of the U.S. and Canada, May 24-28, 1970, Miami Beach, Fla. New York, Bond buyer, 1970.
no.
Partial contents.–Housing crisis: what it means to our cities, by Preston Martin.–Housing needs: unmatched challenge, unique opportunity, by George Romney, Secretary, U.S. Dept. of
(Cont'd on next card)

332
M85
1970

Municipal Finance Officers Association of the United States and Canada. The timeless...1970. (Card 2)

Housing and Urban Development.

1. Banks and banking. 2. Operation Breakthrough. 3. Housing. I. Bond buyer. II. Martin, Preston. Housing crisis: what it means to our cities. III. Romney, George. Housing needs: unmatched challenge, unique opportunity. IV. Title.

Ref.
910
T45

The Times, *London.*
Index-gazetteer of the world. [1st American ed.] Boston, Houghton Mifflin, 1966 [*1965]
xxxi, 964 p. 31 cm.
Includes map references to The Times atlas of the world. Mid-century ed.

1. Geography—Dictionaries. 2. Atlases   —Indexes. I. Title
G103.T5 1966   910.003   66-4080

Library of Congress   [5]

Folio
912
B17t

The Times, London.
Bartholomew (John) and Son, ltd.
The Times atlas of the world. Comprehensive ed., produced and published by the Times in collaboration with John Bartholomew & Son, ltd. Edinburgh. 2d ed., rev. Boston, Houghton Mifflin, 1971.
272p. illus.

1. Atlases. I. The Times, London. II. Title.

Folio
912
B17t
The Times atlas of the world.
Bartholomew (John) and Son, ltd.
The Times atlas of the world. Comprehensive
ed., produced and published by the Times in
collaboration with John Bartholomew & Son, ltd.
Edinburgh. 2d ed., rev. Boston, Houghton
Mifflin, 1971.
272p. illus.

1. Atlases. I. The Times, London. II. Title.

330
(85)
S23
Schreiner, Dean F   An integrated growth
model...1968.   (Card 2)

Bibliography: p. 42-43.

1. Economic development - Peru. I. Timmons,
John F., jt. au. II. Iowa. State University
of Science and Technology, Ames. III. Title.

6391
TINICUM TOWNSHIP, PA. PLANNING
COMMISSION.
COMPREHENSIVE PLAN. MEDIA, PA.,
DELAWARE COUNTY PLANNING COMMISSION, 1968.
33P. (HUD 701 REPORT)

1. CITY PLANNING - TINICUM TOWNSHIP, PA.
I. HUD. 701. TINICUM TOWNSHIP, PA.

VF
728.3
(5487)
T45
Times of Ceylon.
The ideal home exhibition. A Times of
Ceylon Supplement. Colombo, Ceylon, July 25,
1959.
20p. illus. (American Embassy, Colombo,
Ceylon. Foreign service dispatch no. 136,
1959, encl. no. 2)

1. Model houses - Ceylon. (Series: American
Embassy, Colombo, Ceylon. Foreign service dispatch no. 136, 1959, encl. no. 2)

301.36
T45

2 C.
Timms, Ducan.
The urban mosaic; towards a theory of
residential differentiation. Cambridge [Eng.]
University Press, 1971.
277p. (Cambridge geographical studies, 2)

Bibliography: p. 254-269.

1. Sociology, Urban. 2. Social change.
I. Title.

352.1
M85s
1963C
Tinsley, W   E
Getting the best price for your bonds.
Chicago, Municipal Finance Officers
Association of the United States and
Canada, 1963.
8p. (Municipal Finance Officers
Association of the United States and
Canada. Special bulletin 1963C)

In ring binder 352.1 M85s

1. Municipal bonds.   I. Municipal
Officers Associa-   ation of
the United   States and
Canada.

658.564
W17
Timesharing system design concepts.
Watson, Richard W
Timesharing system design concepts. New
York, McGraw-Hill, 1970.
270p. (McGraw-Hill computer science series)

Bibliography: p. 254-259.

1. Automation. I. Title. II. Title: System
design concepts.

620
T45
TIMOSHENKO, STEPHEN.
ENGINEERING MECHANICS, BY S. TIMOSHENKO
AND D.H. YOUNG. 4TH ED. NEW YORK,
McGRAW-HILL. 1956.
478P.

1. ENGINEERING.   I. YOUNG, D.H.
II. TITLE.

510
T45
Tintner, Gerhard.
Mathematics and statistics for economists,
by Gerhard Tintner and Charles B. Millham.
2d ed. New York, Holt, Rinehart and Winston,
1970.
485p.

1. Mathematics. 2. Economics.
3. Statistics. I. Millham, Charles B.,
jt. au.

VF
352
(759121)
T45
Times-Union and Journal, Jacksonville,
Fla.
Building the future with consolidation.
Detached from Times-Union and Journal,
Sunday, July 2, 1967.
[20]p.

1. Local government - Jacksonville, Fla.
2. Intergovernmental relations - Jacksonville, Fla.
I. Jacksonville, Fla. Ordinance, etc. II. Title.

620.1
T45
Timoshenko, Stephen, 1878–
Strength of materials, by S. Timoshenko ... 2d ed. New York,
D. Van Nostrand company, inc. 1940-41.
2 v. Illus, diagrs. 24 cm.

CONTENTS.—pt. I. Elementary theory and problems.—pt. II. Advanced theory and problems.

1. Strength of materials.

Library of Congress   TA405.T5   30—16661
                           [49r37q1]   620.11

5238
TIOGA CO., PA. PLANNING COMMISSION.
SPECIAL STUDY: PLANNING GOALS AND
OBJECTIVES FOR THE TIOGA-HAMMOND AND
COWANESQUE RESERVOIR COMPLEXES.
WELLSBORO, PA., 1969.
100P. (HUD 701 REPORT)

1. WATER-SUPPLY - TIOGA CO., PA.
I. HUD. 701. TIOGA CO., PA.

LAW
T
Timing and procedures in registering securities.
Practising Law Institute.
Timing and procedures in registering
securities, by Ralph H. Demmler. New York,
1957.
153-168p.

Bound with: Israels, Carlos L. and Raymond
J. Gorman. Corporate Practice. New York,
1957.

1. Securities. I. Demmler, Ralph H.
II. Title.

690.4
T45

2 c.
Timoshenko, S
Theory of structures, by S. Timoshenko and D.H.
Young. 1st ed.   New York, McGraw-Hill, c1945.
xiv, 488 p.   diagrs., tables.

1.Structural engineering. I.Young, D
jt. au. II.Title.

5220-
5232
TIOGA CO., PA. PLANNING COMMISSION.
TIOGA COUNTY COMPREHENSIVE PLAN: 1,
POPULATION REPORT; 2, HISTORICAL
DEVELOPMENT; 3, COMMUNITY FACILITIES
STUDY; 4, GOVERNMENT AND FISCAL
ANALYSIS; 5, ECONOMIC BASE STUDY; 6,
PHYSICAL FEATURES AND NATURAL RESOURCES;
7, HOUSING; 8, AN INVENTORY OF EXISTING
LAND USE; 9, AN INVENTORY OF EXISTING
TRANSPORTATION FACILITIES; 10, EXTERNAL
INFLUENCE FACTORS; 11, RELATED STUDIES
OF AN AREA-WIDE SCOPE; 12, DEVELOPMENT
AIDS PROGRAM; 1   3, DEVELOPMENT OF
ALTERNATIVES AN   D ESTABLISHMENT OF
                    (CONTINUED ON NEXT CARD)

728.1
1362.6
T454
TIMKO, GEORGE A
HOUSING AND MORTGAGE LENDING PROGRAM
FOR SENIOR CITIZENS. LOS ANGELES,
CALIFORNIA SAVINGS AND LOAN
ASSOCIATION, 1962.
53P.

1. HOUSING FOR THE AGED.
2. MORTGAGE FINANCE.

620.1
:534.15
T45
Timoshenko, Stephen, 1878–
Vibration problems in engineering, by S. Timoshenko ...
2d ed. New York, D. Van Nostrand company, inc. [1937]
ix, [1], 470 p. illus., diagrs. 23½ cm.

1. Vibration. 2. Mechanics, Applied.

                                     37—22225
Library of Congress   TA355.T55 1937
                           [50h½]   620.1123

5220-
5232
TIOGA CO., PA. PLANNING COMMISSION.
TIOGA COUNTY ...1969.   (CARD 2)

POLICIES, STANDARDS AND OBJECTIVES.
WELLSBORO, PA., 1969.
13 V. (HUD 701 REPORT)

1. MASTER PLAN - TIOGA CO., PA.
I. HUD. 701. TIOGA CO., PA.

330
(85)
S23
Timmons, John F   jt. au.
Schreiner, Dean F
An integrated growth model for the basic sec-
tors and dependant residentiary sectors of
Southern Peru, by Dean F. Schreiner and John F.
Timmons. Ames, Dept. of Economics, Iowa State
University, 1968.
51p. (Iowa. State University of Science and
Technology, Ames. International studies in
economics. Monograph no. 7)
Iowa-Peru Program.
In cooperation with the College of Law, Univer-
sity of Iowa, and the Agency for International
Development.
                        (Cont'd on next card)

338
T45
Tinbergen, Jan
Statistical testing of business cycle theories.
I. A method and its application to investment
activity. Geneva, League of Nations, 1939.
164 p.

1. Business cycles. 2. Investments. I. Title.

658.562
T46
Tippett, L   H   C
Technological applications of statistics.
New York, John Wiley & Sons, Inc., [c1950].
ix, 189 p. charts, graphs, tables. (Wiley
publications in statistics)

Bibliography: p.185-186.
"This book is a "write-up" of a course of lec-
tures given at the Massachusetts Institute of
Technology". Pref.

1.Statistics. 2.Quality control. I.Title.

629.136
T15
Tippetts-Abbett-McCarthy-Stratton.
Airport layout plan; Dallas Fort Worth
Regional Airport. New York, 1965.
87p.

1. Airports. 2. Space considerations.
I. Title: Dallas-Fort Worth Regional Airport.
II. Title.

362.6
T46
Tips, Charles R
The care of the aged in Europe. Report
to Texas Governor's Advisory Committee on
on Aging. Austin, Governor's Committee,
White House Conference on Aging, 1961.
21p.

1. Old age. I. Texas Governor's Committee, White House Conference on Aging.

711.585
:308
S62
Tishler, Izhak, jt. au.
Soen, Dan.
Urban renewal; social surveys, by Dan Soen
and Izhak Tishler. Tel Aviv, Institute for
Planning and Development, 1968.
143p.

1. Urban renewal - Surveys. I. Tishler,
Izhak, jt. au. II. Israel. Institute for
Planning and Development. III. Title.

FOLIO
711.333
(74775)
B76
Tippetts-Abbett-McCarthy-Stratton.
Comprehensive plan, Broome County, 1980.
[Prepared in cooperation with] Broome
County Planning Board. New York, 1963.
85p.

U.S. Urban Renewal Adm. UPAP.

1. Master plan - Broome Co., N.Y. 2. County
planning - Broome Co., N.Y. I. Broome Co., N.Y.
Planning Board. II. U.S. URA-UPAP. Broome Co.,
N.Y.

362.6
T46R
A REPORT FROM ITALY ON THE AGING.
AUSTIN, GOVERNOR'S COMMITTEE, WHITE
HOUSE CONFERENCE ON AGING, 1960.
7P.

REPORT MADE ROME, ITALY, SEPTEMBER,
1960.

1. OLD AGE. I. TEXAS. GOVERNOR'S
COMMITTEE, WHITE HOUSE CONFERENCE ON
AGING.

VF
Savings
banks-
Housing
investments
Tishman, Paul.
Address...before the Savings Banks Mortgage and Real Estate Forum of Groups IV
and V, Yale Club, New York City, Jan.27,
1953. New York, Paul Tishman Co., Inc.,
1953. 8p. Mimeo.

Proposes formation of Savings Bank
Housing Foundation to initiate all
projects (for middle income groups),
purchase land, approve plans, award
contracts, supervise construction and
manage com_____pleted project.
Individual _____ savings banks will hold
stocks in the ____ Foundation.

388
T46
1962
Tippetts-Abbett-McCarthy-Stratton.
Estimating traffic patterns in urban
areas, by Thomas J. Frater and others.
Presented at International Road Federation,
4th World Meeting, Madrid, Spain, October
14-20, 1962. New York, 1962.
21p.

1. Traffic - Congresses. 2. Transportation -
Congresses. I. Frater, Thomas J. II. International
Road Federation,   4th World Meeting,
Madrid, 1962.

658.3
A75T
TIPS TO SUPERVISORS.
U.S. DEPT. OF THE ARMY.
TIPS TO SUPERVISORS. INDIANAPOLIS,
INC., 1957?
29P.

1. PERSONNEL MANAGEMENT. I. TITLE.

3963
3964
3965
3966
3967
TISHOMINGO, OKLA. PLANNING COMMISSION.
COMPREHENSIVE DEVELOPMENT PLAN: 1, THE
PLANNING DOCUMENT; 2, CAPITAL
IMPROVEMENTS PROGRAM; 3, ZONING
ORDINANCE; 4, SUBDIVISION ORDINANCE; 5,
SUPPLEMENTARY REPORT. BY ASSOCIATED
PLANNERS, LITTLE ROCK, ARK. TISHOMINGO,
OKLA., 1968-1969.
5 V. (HUD 701 REPORT)

1. MASTER PLAN - TISHOMINGO, OKLA.
I. ASSOCIATED PLANNERS, LITTLE ROCK, ARK.
II. HUD. 701. TISHOMINGO, OKLA.

FOLIO
711.4
:670
(7471)
T46
Tippetts-Abbett-McCarthy-Stratton.
Flatlands urban industrial park, preliminary plan. Prepared for the City of
New York Urban Renewal Board. New York,
1959.
32p. diagrs., maps, tables.

1. Industrial districts - New York (City)
I. New York (City) Urban Renewal Boardd.
II. Title.

711.4
(77766)
T46
Tipton, Iowa. City Planning and Zoning
Commission.
Bartholomew (Harland) and Associates.
Comprehensive plan, Tipton, Iowa.
Prepared for Tipton, Iowa, City Planning
and Zoning Commission and Iowa Development
Commission. St. Louis, 1964.
1v.

U.S. Urban Renewal Adm. UPAP.

1. Master plan - Tipton, Iowa.
I. Tipton, Iowa. City Planning and Zoning
Commission. II. U.S. URA-UPAP. Tipton,
Iowa.

LAW
S
CALIF.
TITLE GUARANTEE AND TRUST CO., LOS
ANGELES.
CALIFORNIA LAND TITLES; A MANUAL OF
CALIFORNIA LAND LAW FOR BROKERS, ESCROW
AGENTS, BANKS, TITLE AND TRUST
COMPANIES, AND ALL PERSONS INTERESTED
IN REAL ESTATE. REV. ED. LOS ANGELES,
1936.
227P.

1. LAND TITLES. I. TITLE.

711.73
(753)
T46
Tippetts-Abbett-McCarthy-Stratton.
The joint development of housing and freeways. A study of the feasibility of developing housing to accommodate site residents
over the center leg of the inner loop freeway.
[Prepared in cooperation with] Dept. of Highways and Traffic, District of Columbia [and]
U.S. Dept. of Commerce, Bureau of Public
Roads. Wash., 1967.
1v.

1. Highways - District of Columbia. 2. Housing -
District of Columbia. 3. Site planning.
I. Title.

711.73
M17
TIRES.
MARYLAND. STATE ROADS COMMISSION.
EFFECTS OF CARBIDE STUDDED TIRES ON
ROADWAY SURFACES, BY ALLAN LEE AND
OTHERS. BALTIMORE, 1965.
118P.

1. HIGHWAYS. I. LEE, ALLAN.
II. TITLE: TIRES.

Title insurance

see

Land titles.

728.1
:336.18
(7526)
T46
TIPPETTS-ABBETT-MCCARTHY-STRATTON.
RESEARCH STUDY: DEVELOPMENT OF THE
GEORGE STREET SITE, MC 2-18, FOR THE
HOUSING AUTHORITY OF BALTIMORE CITY.
NEW YORK, 1956.
1 V.

1. PUBLIC HOUSING - BALTIMORE.
2. BALTIMORE. HOUSING AUTHORITY.
I. TITLE: GEORGE STREET SITE.

728.1
(471)
T47
Tirinen, Arvo.
Pääomamenojen vaikutus asumiskustannuksiin.
Vuokralaisten keskusliitto r.y.n. toimeksian-
nosta kirjoittanut [The influence of capital
expenditures on the cost of housing] Helsinki,
1958.
83p. diagrs., tables.

1. Housing - Finland. 2. Housing costs -
Finland.

Title insurance.

LAW
T
Roberts, Ernest F   Jr., ed.
Public regulation of title insurance
companies and abstracters, by E.F. Roberts
and others. Villanova, Pa., Villanova
University Press, 1961.
346p.

1. Insurance. 2. Land titles. I. Title.
II. Title: Title insurance.

5126
TIPPETTS - ABBETT - MCCARTHY - STRATTON.
SNOHOMISH CO., WASH. PLANNING COMMISSION.
SNOHOMISH RIVER BASIN PLANNING STUDY.
BY TIPPETTS - ABBETT - MCCARTHY -
STRATTON. EVERETT, WASH., 1968.
93P. (HUD 701 REPORT)

1. COUNTY PLANNING - SNOHOMISH CO.,
WASH. I. TIPPETTS - ABBETT - MCCARTHY -
STRATTON. II. HUD. 701. SNOHOMISH
CO., WASH.

694.183
T47
TISCH, ARTHUR S
STEEL, ALUMINUM, STAINLESS STEEL AND
NON-FERROUS THREADED NAILS IN
RESIDENTIAL CONSTRUCTION. PRESENTED
AT THE BUILDING RESEARCH INSTITUTE
CONFERENCE ON SIGNIFICANCE OF
MECHANICAL FASTENERS IN RESIDENTIAL
CONSTRUCTION, NOVEMBER 19-21, 1963.
WASHINGTON, D.C., 1963.
7L.

1. NAILS AND NAILING. I. TITLE.
II. BUILDING RESEARCH INSTITUTE.

728.1
T32
TITLE I LOANS.
THEY LIKE [FHA] TITLE I LOANS.
[MADISON, WIS.] 1957.
11-14P.
ARTICLE FROM JULY 1957 OF CREDIT UNION
BRIDGE.

1. DIRECT LOANS FOR HOUSING. 2. U.S.
FEDERAL HOUSING ADMINISTRATION.
I. CREDIT UNION BRIDGE. II. TITLE:
TITLE I LOANS.

728.1
:361
C65
1956
S-R
NO.1406

TITLE I LOANS FOR DISASTER AREAS.
U.S. CONGRESS. SENATE. COMMITTEE ON
BANKING AND CURRENCY.
TITLE I LOANS FOR DISASTER AREAS;
REPORT TO ACCOMPANY S.J. RES. 113.
WASHINGTON, GOVT. PRINT. OFF., 1956.
3P. (84TH CONGRESS, 2D SESSION.
SENATE. REPORT NO. 1406)

1. EMERGENCY HOUSING. 2. U.S.
FEDERAL HOUSING ADMINISTRATION.
3. NATIONAL HOUSING ACT. I. TITLE.

VF
728.1
:355.1
F22

Title V housing.
U.S. Federal Public Housing Authority.
Handbook of information: Title V
Housing. Washington, Feb. 1956.
1 v.

1. Veterans' housing. 2. Housing
management. I. Title: Title V housing.

333.34
C65
1946
S-H

U.S. CONGRESS. SENATE. COMMITTEE ON
THE JUDICIARY. TITLE TO LANDS ...
1946. (CARD 2)

1946. WASHINGTON, GOVT. PRINT. OFF.,
1946.
315P.

SUPPLEMENTAL TO THE JOINT HOUSE AND
SENATE HEARINGS HELD ON JUNE 18, 19,
AND 20, 1945 ISSUED AS SERIAL NO. 5 OF
THE HEARINGS BEFORE THE COMMITTEE ON
THE JUDICIARY, HOUSE OF
REPRESENTATIVES, SEVENTY-NINTH
(CONTINUED ON NEXT CARD)

332.72
F22TIT

TITLE I OPERATION GUIDE FOR QUALIFIED
LENDING INSTITUTIONS.
U.S. FEDERAL HOUSING ADMINISTRATION.
TITLE I OPERATION GUIDE FOR QUALIFIED
LENDING INSTITUTIONS. WASHINGTON,
GOVT. PRINT. OFF., 1957.
1 V.

CONTENTS.-- 1. TITLE I REGULATIONS.--
2. DEALER'S GUIDE.-- 3. OPERATING
FORMS.-- 4. SUPPLEMENTARY INSTRUCTIONS.

1. MORTGAGE FINANCE. I. TITLE.
II. DEALER'S GUIDE.

728.1
1940.42
F22TI

TITLE VI OF THE NATIONAL HOUSING
ACT.
U.S. FEDERAL HOUSING ADMINISTRATION.
TITLE VI OF THE NATIONAL HOUSING
ACT. PUBLIC LAW 24 - 77TH CONGRESS,
CHAPTER 31 - 1ST SESSION, H.R. 3575,
MARCH 28, 1941. INCLUDING ALL
AMENDMENTS TO JUNE 15, 1946.
WASHINGTON, 1946.
12P.

1. DEFENSE HOUSING. 2. INSURANCE.
I. TITLE.

333.34
C65
1946
S-H

U.S. CONGRESS. SENATE. COMMITTEE ON
THE JUDICIARY. TITLE TO LANDS ...
1946. (CARD 3)

CONGRESS.

1. LAND TITLES. 2. PETROLEUM
INDUSTRY. I. TITLE.

332.72
F22TI

TITLE I PUBLICATIONS LOOSELEAF
NOTEBOOK.
U.S. FEDERAL HOUSING ADMINISTRATION.
TITLE I PUBLICATIONS LOOSELEAF
NOTEBOOK NOTEBOOK CONTAINING VARIOUS
PAMPHLETS DEALING WITH TITLE I.
WASHINGTON, U.S.F.H.A., 1936-1953.
24 ITEMS

1. U.S. FEDERAL HOUSING
ADMINISTRATION. 2. MORTGAGE FINANCE.
I. TITLE.

323.4
065t

Title VI, one year after; a survey of desegregation of health and welfare services in the
U.S. Commission on Civil Rights.   South.
Title VI, one year after; a survey of
desegregation of health and welfare services
in the South. Wash., Govt. Print. Off., 1966.
51p.

1. Civil rights. 2. Public health.
3. Social welfare. I. Title.

691.11
(03)
T47

TITMUSS, F H
COMMERCIAL TIMBERS OF THE WORLD; A
CONCISE ENCYCLOPEDIA OF WORLD TIMBERS.
3D ED. LONDON, TECHNICAL PRESS, 1965.
277P.

1. WOOD -- DICTIONARIES. I. TITLE.

711.585
N17TI

TITLE I REDEVELOPMENT.
NATIONAL ASSOCIATION OF HOUSING AND
REDEVELOPMENT OFFICIALS.
TITLE I REDEVELOPMENT; THE FIRST
FOUR YEARS AND DEFENSE CONSIDERATIONS,
BY FRANCIS L. HOUSER. WASHINGTON,
1954.
37P.

1. URBAN RENEWAL. 2. DEFENSE
HOUSING. I. HOUSER, FRANCIS.
II. TITLE.

332.72
G71

TITLE VII OFFERS SECURITY AND RETURNS.
GRAY, THOMAS S
TITLE VII OFFERS SECURITY AND RETURNS.
WASHINGTON, 1949.
[4]P.
REPRINTED FROM THE SECOND QUARTER
1949 FHA INSURED MORTGAGE PORTFOLIO.

1. MORTGAGE FINANCE. I. U.S.
FEDERAL HOUSING ADMINISTRATION.
II. TITLE.

360
T47

Titmuss, Richard M
Commitment to welfare. New York, Pantheon
Books, 1968.
272p.

1. Social welfare I. Title.

VF
711.585
N171
S8

Title I redevelopment: the first four years
and defense considerations.
Hauser, Francis L
Title I redevelopment: the first four years
and defense considerations. Washington, Na-
tional Association of Housing and Redevelopment
Officials, June 1954.
37 P. (National Association of Housing
Officials, Special publication no. 8)
NAHRO Publication N356.

1. Urban redevelopment. 2. Federal housing
programs. I. Title. II. Title: Defense
considerations, Title I. redevelopment.
III. Ser.

VF
728
392
(016)
A37

Titles of completed theses in home economics
and related fields in colleges and univer-
sities of the United States, 1952-1953.
U.S. Dept. of Agriculture. (Agricultural
Research Service.)
Titles of completed theses in home economics
and related fields in colleges and universities
of the United States, 1952-1953. Washington,
Dec. 1953.
iv, 48 p. tables.
In cooperation with Office of Education.
Processed.
1. Family living requirements. 2. Theses-Bibl.
I. U.S. Office of Education. II. Title.

6029
6030
6031
6032
6033

TITONKA, IOWA. PLANNING AND ZONING
COMMISSION.
COMPREHENSIVE PLANNING PROGRAM: 1,
PRELIMINARY PLANNING REPORT; 2, TECHNICAL
REPORT; 3, ZONING ORDINANCE; 4,
SUBDIVISION REGULATIONS; 5, SUMMARY
REPORT. BY WALLACE, HOLLAND, KASTLER,
AND SCHMITZ. TITONKA, IOWA, 1968-69.
5 V. (HUD 701 REPORT)

1. MASTER PLAN - TITONKA, IOWA.
I. WALLACE, HOLLAND, KASTLER, AND SCHMITZ.
II. HUD 701 - TITONKA, IOWA.

728.1
711.585
(7471)
N28

Title I Slum clearance projects.
New York, N. Y. Comptroller.
Report to the Board of Estimate on
Title I Slum clearance projects and tax
exempt housing projects [by] Lawrence E.
Gerosa, Comptroller. New York, May 9, 1956.
6, 45, 3 p. tables.

Processed.

1. Urban redevelopment - New York, N. Y. 2. Housing
projects - New York, N. Y. 3. Tax incentives. I. Gerosa,
Lawrence E. New York, N.Y. Board of Estimate.
III. Title: Tax exempt housing projects. IV. Title:
Title I Slum Clearance projects.

Title records.
Patton, Rufford Guy, 1876-
Land titles; a treatise on title records, records as muni-
ments of title, priorities, incumbrance shown by county, state
and federal records or existing in pais, proof of title,
examination of title, and the nature of titles required to
fulfill contracts for sale or security, by Rufford G. Patton ...
and Carroll G. Patton ... Kansas City, Mo., Vernon law
book company [*1938].
viii, 1472 p. diagr. 26 cm.
"Table of cases cited": p. 1097-1335.
1. Land titles-U. S. I. Patton, Carroll Gray, 1908-   joint
author. II. Title: Title records.

38—23524
Library of Congress   [51e]

2711-
2716

TITTABAWASSEE, MICH. TOWNSHIP PLANNING
COMMISSION.
COMPREHENSIVE COMMUNITY PLAN: 1,
ZONING ORDINANCE; 2, SUBDIVISION
ORDINANCE; 3, BASIC STUDIES REPORT; 4,
PRELIMINARY PLAN AND REPORT; 5, CAPITAL
IMPROVEMENTS PROGRAM; 6, FINAL REPORT.
BY RAYMOND W. MILLS AND ASSOCIATES,
INC. MIDLAND, MICH., 1965-67.
6 V. (HUD 701 REPORT)
1. MASTER PLAN - TITTABAWASSEE, MICH.
I. MILLS (RAYMOND W.) AND ASSOCIATES.
II. HUD 701 - TITTABAWASSEE, MICH.

DATE OF REQUEST 5/7/53   MAY 22 1953   L C. CARD NO.
5/7/53
AUTHOR Los Angeles, California. Title Insurance and Trust
Company.
TITLE When you subdivide, what to do, how to do it.

SERIES

EDITION   PUB. DATE 1953   PAGING 25 pp.
PUBLISHER
Los Angeles, Calif.
RECOMMENDED BY   REVIEWED IN
Gov't Res. Notes 4/53, p.10
ORDER RECORD

333.34
C65
1946
S-H

TITLE TO LANDS BENEATH TIDAL AND
NAVIGABLE WATERS.
U.S. CONGRESS. SENATE. COMMITTEE ON
THE JUDICIARY.
TITLE TO LANDS BENEATH TIDAL AND
NAVIGABLE WATERS. HEARINGS BEFORE THE
COMMITTEE ON THE JUDICIARY, UNITED
STATES SENATE, SEVENTY-NINTH CONGRESS,
SECOND SESSION, ON S.J. RES. 48 AND
H.J. RES. 225, JOINT RESOLUTIONS TO
QUIET THE TITLES OF RESPECTIVE STATES,
AND OTHERS, TO LANDS BENEATH TIDEWATERS
AND LANDS BENEATH NAVIGABLE WATERS
WITHIN THE BOUNDARIES OF SUCH STATES
AND TO PREVENT FURTHER CLOUDING OF
SUCH TITLES. FEBRUARY 5, 6, AND 7,
(CONTINUED ON NEXT CARD)

625.7
H43s

Tittle, Robert H
Highway Research Board.
Salvaging old pavements by resurfacing;
presented at the Thirtieth annual meeting,
January 9, 1951, by Robert H. Tittle.
Washington, 1952. National Research Council.
35 p. illus. (Its Bulletin 47)

1. Road construction. I. Title.
II. Tittle, Robert H. (Series)

330
(79455)
C17
Titus, Charles B
Carr, Robert A
Profile analysis of the San Joaquin Valley, by Robert A. Carr, Sarah G. Bedrosian and Charles B. Titus. Fresno, Calif., Fresno State College, Bureau of Business Research and Service, 1967.
121p. (Fresno State College. Bureau of Business Research and Service. Study no. 16)
1. Economic conditions - San Joaquin Co., Calif. 2. Economic development - San Joaquin Co., Calif.
(Cont'd on next card)

330
(79455)
C17
Carr, Robert A   Profile analysis of the San Joaquin Valley...1967. (Card 2)
I. Bedrosian, Sarah G. II. Titus, Charles B. III. California. State College, Fresno. Bureau of Business Research and Service. IV. Title.

058.7
:05
U54
1965
Titus, Edna Brown
Union List of Serials in Libraries of the United States and Canada, edited by Edna Brown Titus. 3rd ed. New York, H.W. Wilson, 1965.
5 v.
Contents:-v.1. A-B. -v.2. C-G. -v.3. H-M. -v.4. N-R. -v.5. S-Z.
1. Periodicals - Directories. I. Titus, Edna Brown.

658.564
D25
TITUS, HAROLD A   , JT. AU.
DEMETRY, JAMES S
LINEAR CONTROL SYSTEM OPTIMIZATION USING A MODEL-BASED INDEX OF PERFORMANCE, RESEARCH REPORT. SUBMITTED BY JAMES S. DEMETRY AND HAROLD A. TITUS. MONTEREY, CALIF., 1964.
49L. (U.S. NAVAL POST GRADUATE SCHOOL, MONTEREY, CALIF. RESEARCH PAPER 48)
1. AUTOMATION. I. TITUS, HAROLD A., JT. AU. II. U.S. NAVAL POST GRADUATE SCHOOL, MONTEREY, CALIF. III. TITLE.

LAW
T
K157Le
Titus, James E
Kansas. University. Governmental Research Center.
Legislative apportionment in Kansas: 1960, by James W. Drury and James E. Titus. Lawrence, Kan., 1960.
47p. maps, tables. (Its Citizen's pamphlet no. 26)
1. Apportionment. I. Drury, James W. II. Titus, James E. III. Title.   (Series)

711.585.1
(75927)
T47
1968
Titusville, Fla. Office of the City Manager
Application to the Department of Housing and Urban Development for a grant to plan a comprehensive model cities program. Titusville, Fla., 1968.
1v.
1. Model cities - Titusville, Fla. I. U.S. Model Cities Program.

333.38
(74897)
T47
Titusville, Pa. Ordinances, etc.
Land subdivision regulations.
[Titusville, 1958]
[15]p.
U.S. Urban Renewal Adm. UPAP.
1. Subdivision regulation - Titusville, Pa. I. U.S. URA-UPAP. Titusville, Pa.

711.5
(74897
:347)
T47
Titusville, Pa. Ordinances, etc.
Proposed amendment to zoning ordinance no. 1288 of the City of Titusville.
[Titusville, 1959]
1v.
U.S. Urban Renewal Adm. UPAP.
1. Zoning legislation - Titusville, Pa. I. U.S. URA-UPAP. Titusville, Pa.

690.091.82
:613.5
(74897)
R62
Titusville, Pa. Planning and Zoning Commission.
Rodgers (Clifton E.) and Associates.
Proto-type housing code, Planning Commission of the City of Titusville. Beaver Falls, Pa., [n.d.]
13p.
U.S. Urban Renewal Adm. UPAP.
1. Housing codes - Titusville, Pa. I. Titusville, Pa. Planning and Zoning Commission. II. U.S. URA-UPAP. Titusville, Pa.

711.4
(74897)
T47
Titusville, Pa. Planning and Zoning Commission.
Rodgers (Clifton E.) and Associates.
Titusville, Pennsylvania comprehensive city plan. Prepared for the Planning and Zoning Commission, City of Titusville. Beaver Falls, Pa., 1959.
68p.
U.S. Urban Renewal Adm. UPAP.
1. Master plan - Titusville, Pa. I. Titusville, Pa. Planning and Zoning Commission. II. U.S. URA-UPAP. Titusville, Pa.

691.32
T48
Tiusanen, K
The strength of extremely dry and set mature concrete; an experimental study on the effect of vacuum-wetting high-pressure-wetting and oven-drying on the strength of concrete, by K. Tiusanen and S.E. Pihlajavaara. Helsinki, State Institute for Technical Research, 1969.
24p. (Finland. State Institute for Technical Research. Tiedotus, sarja III - Rakennus 139)
1. Concrete. 2. Strength of materials. I. Pihlajavaara, S.E., jt. au. II. Finland. State Institute for Technical Research. III. Title.

362.6
T48
Tiven, Marjorie Bloomberg.
Older Americans: special handling required. Wash., National Council on the Aging, 1971.
118p.
Bibliography: p. 115-118.
Prepared for U.S. Dept. of Housing and Urban Development and U.S. Dept. of Health, Education and Welfare under HUD Contract, H-1294.
1. Old age. I. National Council on the Aging. II. U.S. Dept. of Housing and Urban Development. III. Title.

526.8
(7456)
T48
Tiverton, R.I.
[Maps] [Tiverton, 1958]
5 maps.
U.S. Urban Renewal Adm. UPAP.
1. Maps and mapping - Tiverton, R.I. I. U.S. URA-UPAP. Tiverton, R.I.

711.14
(7456)
R36£
Tiverton, R.I. Planning Board.
Rhode Island. Development Council.
Land use study. [Prepared for Tiverton, R.I. Planning Board] Providence, 1957.
1v. maps. (Tiverton worksheet no. 6)
U.S. Urban Renewal Administration, Urban Planning Assistance Program.
1. Land use - Tiverton, R.I. I. Tiverton, R.I. Planning Board. II. U.S. Urban Renewal Administration. Urban Planning Assistance Program. Tiverton, R.I.

333.38
(7456)
R36
Tiverton, R.I. Planning Board.
Rhode Island. Development Council.
Subdivision regulations, Tiverton, Rhode Island. [In cooperation with] Tiverton Planning Board. Final draft. Providence, 1958.
8p. (Its Community Assistance Program. Tiverton worksheet no. 15)
U.S. Urban Renewal Adm. UPAP.
1. Subdivision regulation - Tiverton, R.I. I. Tiverton, R.I. Planning Board. II. U.S. URA-UPAP. Tiverton, R.I.

711.5
(7456
:347)
T48
Tiverton, R.I. Planning Board.
Tiverton proposed zoning ordinance. Tiverton, 1958.
19p. map.
U.S. Urban Renewal Administration, Urban Planning Assistance Program.
1. Zoning legislation - Tiverton, R.I. I. U.S. URA-UPAP. Tiverton, R.I.

3163
3164
TIVOLI, N.Y. PLANNING BOARD.
ZONING ORDINANCE; SUBDIVISION REGULATIONS. BY SARGENT-WEBSTER-CRENSHAW AND FOLLEY. TIVOLI, N.Y., CA. 1971.
2 V. (HUD 701 REPORT)
1. ZONING - TIVOLI, N.Y. I. SARGENT-WEBSTER-CRENSHAW AND FOLLEY. II. HUD. 701. TIVOLI, N.Y.

728.1
(519)
T44
Tjioe, B Khing.
Housing and productivity: casualty and measurement, by B. Khing Tjioe and Leland S. Burns. Los Angeles, International Housing Productivity Study, Housing, Real Estate and Urban Land Studies Program, Graduate School of Business Administration, Division of Research, University of California, 1966.
155-174p. (Reprint no. IHPS-8)
Reprinted from the Social Statistics Section, Proceedings of the American Statistical Association, 1966.
(Cont'd on next card)

728.1
(519)
T44
Tjioe, B Khing.   Housing productivity
...1966.   (Card 2)
1. Housing. 2. Labor productivity. I. Burns, Leland S., jt. au. II. American Statistical Association. III. California. University. University at Los Angeles. International Housing Productivity Study. IV. Title.

728.1
(519)
T44r
Tjioe, B Khing.
Report on productivity in relation to housing conditions and community facilities in Hambaek, Korea, by B. Khing Tjioe and Leland S. Burns. Rev. Los Angeles, International Housing Productivity Study, Real Estate Research Program, Graduate School of Business Administration, University of California, 1966.
77p.
"Not for publication."
(Cont'd on next card)

728.1
(519)
T44r
Tjioe, B Khing. Report on productivity...1966. (Card 2)
1. Housing - Korea. 2. Labor productivity - Korea. 3. Housing and health. I. Burns, Leland S., jt. au. II. California. University. University at Los Angeles. Real Estate Research Program. III. Title.

728.1
(73:347)
C65t
1967
H-H

To amend and extend laws relating to housing and urban development.
U.S. Congress. House. Committee on Banking and Currency.
To amend and extend laws relating to housing and urban development. Hearings before the Subcommittee on Housing of the Committee on Banking and Currency, House of Representatives, Ninetieth Congress, first session on H.R. 8068, a bill to amend and extend laws relating to housing and urban development, and for other purposes. Wash., Govt. Print. Off., 1967.
803p.
Hearings held April 18-21, 24-27, 1967.
(Cont'd on next card)

728.1
(744)
B74

TO COMPLETE THE HOUSING PICTURE.
BRIGHAM, HARRY R
TO COMPLETE THE HOUSING PICTURE.
BOSTON, 1948.
103-107P.
IN THE BAR BULLETIN, V. 19, NO. 4, APRIL 1948.
REPLY TO ARTICLE BY HAROLD AND JOHN I. ROBINSON ENTITLED :THE MASSACHUSETTS HOUSING PICTURE - 1911-1947.

1. HOUSING - MASSACHUSETTS.   I. TITLE.

388
(748)
P25to

To go or not to go?
Pennsylvania. Governor's Committee for Transportation
To go or not to go? Pennsylvania on the move. [Harrisburg, 1970]
[12]p.

1. Transportation - Pa. I. Title.

728.1
(73:347)
C65t
1967
H-H

U.S. Congress. House. Committee on Banking and Currency.   To amend and extend laws relating to housing and urban development...1967.   (Card 2)

1. Housing legislation. 2. Public housing. 3. Urban renewal. I. Title.

323.4
P14

To do justice...
Pain, William,   ed.
To do justice; the heroic struggle for human rights. Detroit, Pyramid Publications, 1965.
104p.

1. Civil rights. 2. Race relations. I. Title. II. Title: The heroic struggle for human rights.

712.25
(797)
W17t

To have and to hold.
Washington (State) Interagency Committee for Outdoor Recreation.
To have and to hold; Washington's outdoor recreation heritage. Summary of first official revision, Washington Statewide Outdoor Recreation and Open Space Plan. Olympia, 1970.
37p.

1. Recreation - Washington (State)
2. Open space - Washington (State) I. Title.

332.3
C65t
1970
H-H

To amend the Small business act.
U.S. Congress. House. Committee on Banking and Currency.
To amend the Small business act. Hearing before the Committee on Banking and Currency, House of Representatives, Ninety-first Congress second session on H.R. 19828, a bill to help small business and combat inflation. Wash., Govt. Print. Off., 1970.
12p.
Hearing held Nov. 25, 1970.
1. Small business. I. Title.

658.802
C657e
1971
S-H

To establish a consumer protection agency.
U.S. Congress. Senate. Committee on Government Operations.
To establish a consumer protection agency. Hearings before the Subcommittee on Executive Reorganization and Government Research of the Committee on Government Operations, United States Senate, Ninety-second Congress, first session on S. 1177 and H.R. 10835. Wash., Govt. Print. Off., 1972.
Hearings held Nov. 4-5, 1971.
1. Consumer protection. I. Title.

614
H21t
1966

To improve medical care.
U.S. Dept. of Health Education, and Welfare.
To improve medical care; a guide to Federal financial aid for the development of medical care services facilities personnel. Rev. ed. Washington, For sale by the Supt. of Docs., Govt. Print. Off., 1966.
96p.

1. Public health. 2. Medical research. I. Title.

728.1
(73:347)
C657t
1970
H-H

To amend title VII of the Housing and urban development act of 1965.
U.S. Congress. House. Committee on Banking and Currency.
To amend title VII of the Housing and urban development act of 1965. Hearings before the Committee on Banking and Currency, House of Representatives, Ninety-first congress, second session on H.R. 17795... Wash., Govt. Print. Off., 1970.
1v.
Hearings held June 12, 15, 1970.
1. Housing legislation. I. Title.

323.25
N17e

To establish justice, to insure domestic tranquility.
U.S. National Commission on the Causes and Prevention of Violence.
To establish justice, to insure domestic tranquility. Wash., 1969.

338p.

1. Civil disorders. 2. Law enforcement. I. Title.

VP
353
A28ad
1964

To improve the effectiveness of the American Federal system through increased cooperation...
U.S. Advisory Commission on Intergovernmental Relations.
To improve the effectiveness of the American Federal system through increased cooperation among National, State, and local levels of government. Washington, 1964.
61p.

1. Intergovernmental relations. 2. Federal government. I. Title.

325.2
Y68

To be equal.
Young, Whitney M
To be equal. New York, McGraw-Hill, 1964.
256p.

1. Race relations. 2. Negroes. 3. Social conditions. I. Title.

338.53
C657
1971
H-H

To extend standby powers of the President to stabilize wages and prices...
U.S. Congress. House. Committee on Banking and Currency.
To extend standby powers of the President to stabilize wages and prices and the authority of the Federal Reserve Board and the Federal Home Loan Bank Board to establish flexible interest rates on time deposits. Hearings before the Committee on Banking and Currency, House of Representatives, Ninety-second Congress, first session on H.R. 4246, a bill to extend until March 31, 1973, certain provisions of law relating to
(Cont'd on next card)

368
C65t
1966
H-H

TO INCORPORATE THE AMERICAN ACADEMY OF ACTUARIES.
U.S. CONGRESS. HOUSE. COMMITTEE ON THE JUDICIARY.
TO INCORPORATE THE AMERICAN ACADEMY OF ACTUARIES. HEARINGS BEFORE SUBCOMMITTEE NO. 4... EIGHTY-NINTH CONGRESS, SECOND SESSION ON H.R. 4-70, H.R. 5987, AND S. 1154... FEBRUARY 1-, 1966. WASHINGTON, 1966.
99P. (SERIAL NO 19)

1. INSURANCE.   . TITLE. II. TITLE: AMERICAN ACADEMY OF ACTUARIES.

330
(768)
T25to

To build a climate of confidence.
Tennessee. Governor's Study Committee for Economic Development.
To build a climate of confidence. Nashville, 1972.
63p.

1. Economic development - Tenn. 2. Community development - Tenn. I. Title.

351
C657to
1971
S-H

To extend the reorganization act.
U.S. Congress. Senate. Committee on Government Operations.
To extend the reorganization act. Hearing before the Subcommittee on Executive Reorganization and Government Research of the Committee on Government Operations, United States Senate, Ninety-second Congress, first session on S. 878. Wash., Govt. Print. Off., 1971.
17p.
Hearing held March 24, 1971.
1. U.S. Executive departments - Reorganization. I. Title.

351
C65t

To increase the maximum rates on per diem allowance.
U.S. Congress. Senate. Committee on Post Office and Civil Service.
To increase the maximum rates on per diem allowance. Hearing before the Subcommittee on Civil Service of the Committee on Post Office and Civil Service, United States Senate, Eighty-seventh Congress, first session on S. 470, a bill to increase the maximum rates of per diem allowance for employees of the government traveling on official business, and for other purposes. Washington, Govt. Print. Off., 1961.
37p.
Hearing held   May 1, 1961.
1. Federal government.   I. Title.

727.3
E282t

TO BUILD OR NOT TO BUILD.
EDUCATIONAL FACILITIES LABORATORIES.
TO BUILD OR NOT TO BUILD; A REPORT ON THE UTILIZATION AND PLANNING OF INSTRUCTIONAL FACILITIES IN SMALL COLLEGES. BASED ON RESEARCH BY JOHN X. JAMRICH. NEW YORK, 1962.
38P.

BOUND WITH: SPACE UTILIZATION WORKBOOK.

1. UNIVERSITIES AND COLLEGES - BUILDINGS. 2. SPACE CONSIDERATIONS. I. JAMRICH, JOHN X. II. TITLE.

338.53
C657
1971
H-H

U.S. Congress. House. Committee on Banking and Currency. To extend...1971. (Card 2)

interest rates, mortgage credit controls, and cost-of-living stabilization. Wash., Govt. Print. Off., 1971.
226p.

Hearings held Feb. 23-26, 1971.

1. Price regulation. 2. Wages and salaries. I. Title.

339.5
(794)
C15

To know our land.
California. University.
To know our land. Berkeley, 1967.
16p.

1. Natural resources - Calif. 2. Open space land. I. Title.

320
C25to
   To live as men; an anatomy of peace.
   Center for the Study of Democratic
     Institutions.
     To live as men; an anatomy of peace.
   Papers by Paul Tillich and others. Santa
   Barbara, Calif., 1965.
     67p.

     1. Democracy. 2. Social conditions.
   I. Title.

698
C65
1970
H-H
   U.S. Congress. House. Committee on Banking
     and Currency. To...1970.   (Card 4)

out an effective plan for eliminating the cause
of lead-based paint poisoning. Wash., Govt.
Print. Off., 1970.
   294p.
   Hearings held July 22-23, 1970.

     1. Paints and painting. 2. Health. I. Title.
II. Title: Lead-based paint poisoning.

628.515
(768191)
M25
   To shape up three rivers.
   Memphis and Shelby County Planning Commission.
     To shape up three rivers; an environmental
   campaign. Memphis, [1971]
   folder.

     1. Water pollution - Memphis.
   I. Title.

339.5
B78
   To live on earth.
   Brubaker, Sterling.
     To live on earth: man and his environment in
   perspective. Baltimore, Published for Resources
   for the Future, inc., by the Johns Hopkins Press,
   1972.
     202p.   (A Resources for the Future study)

     Bibliography: p. 191-193.

     1. Natural resources. 2. Population.
   I. Resources for the Future. II. Title.

332
C657t
1972
H-H
   To provide for a modification in the par...
   U. S. Congress. House. Committee on
   Banking and Currency.
     To provide for a modification in the par
   value of the dollar. Hearings, Ninety-second
   Congress, second session on H.R. 13120, a
   bill to provide for a modification in the
   par value of the dollar, and for other
   purposes. Wash., Govt. Print. Off., 1972.
     230p.
     Hearings held March 1-6, 1972.

     1. Money. I. Title.

711.3
(764)
W32
   To wear a city's crown.
   Wheeler, Kenneth W
     To wear a city's crown; the beginnings of
   urban growth in Texas, 1836-1865.
   Cambridge, Mass., Harvard University Press,
   1968.
     222p.

     Bibliography: p. 169-189.

     1. City growth - Tex. I. Title.

VF
061.6
I55
   To our sponsors.
   Illinois Institute of Technology. Armour
     Research Foundation.
     To our sponsors ... by Francis Godwin.
   Chicago [c1945]
     32 p.

728.1
(60)
A37
   To provide housing for the lowest income
     groups.
   Afro-Asian Housing Congress. 3d, Dar Es-
     Salam, 1969.
     To provide housing for the lowest income
   groups; [programme of the] Third Congress to
   be held in Dar Es-Salam, Tanzania, Sept.,
   1969. Cairo, Afro-Asian Housing Organi-
   zation, 1969.
     12p. (Afro-Asian Housing Organization.
   Bulletin 11)
     1. Housing - Africa. 2. Housing - Asia.
   I. Afro-Asian Housing Organization.
   II. Title.

362.5
B79
   To whom it may concern; poverty, humanity,
     community.
   Bryant, M   Darrol.
     To whom it may concern; poverty, humanity,
   community. Philadelphia, Fortress Press, 1969.
     54p.

     Bibliography: p. 51-54.

     1. Poverty. 2. Church and social problems.
   I. Title.

370
C81
   To make a difference; teaching in the inner
     city.
   Cuban, Larry.
     To make a difference; teaching in the inner
   city. New York, Free Press, 1970.
     261p.

     1. Education. 2. Education - Negroes.
   I. Title.

725.1
C657t
1971
S-H
   To review the proposed demolition of the old
     Post Office Building...
   U.S. Congress. Senate. Committee on Public
     Works.
     To review the proposed demolition of the old
   Post Office Building and other landmark buildings
   Hearing before the Subcommittee on Public
   Buildings and Grounds, Ninety-second Congress,
   first session. Wash., Govt. Print. Off., 1971.
     98p.
     Hearing held April 21, 1971.

     1. Public buildings. 2. Demolition. I. Title.

360
H47s
   Toastmistress.
   Hitt, Patricia Reilly.
     Small, splendid efforts, by
   Patricia Reilly Hitt, Dept. of Health,
   Education, and Welfare. [n.p.] 1969.
     [4]p.

     From: Toastmistress, Sept., 1969,
   p. 6-9.

     1. Social service. 2. Community de-
   velopment - Citizen participation. I.
   Toastmistress. II. Title.

698
C65
1970
H-H
   To provide Federal assistance for eliminating
     the causes of lead-based paint poisoning.
   U.S. Congress. House. Committee on Banking
     and Currency.
     To provide Federal assistance for eliminating
   the causes of lead-based paint poisoning. Hearings before the Subcommittee on Housing of the
   Committee on Banking and Currency, House of
   Representatives, Ninety-first Congress, second
   session, on H.R. 17260, a bill to provide Federal
   financial assistance to help cities and communities of the United States to develop and carry
   out intensive local programs to eliminate the
   causes of lead-based paint poisoning and to
     (Cont'd on next card)

628.515
C65sa
   To save America's small lakes.
   U.S. Congress. House. Committee on
     Government Operations.
     To save America's small lakes (water
   pollution control and abatement) Third report
   by the Committee on Government Operations.
   Wash., Govt. Print. Off., 1967.
     20p. (90th Cong., 1st sess. House. Rept.
   no. 594)

     1. Water pollution. I. Title.

614
T61
1947
   Tobey, James Alner, 1894-
     Public health law ... 3d ed. New York, The Common-
   wealth Fund, 1947.
     xxi, 419 p. 24 cm.

     "Selected bibliography": p. [381]-388.

     1. Hygiene, Public—U. S. [1. Public health—U. S. I. U. S.
   Laws, statutes, etc. II. Title.
     RA445.T63 1947   614.0973   Med 47—2423
   U. S. Army Medical Libr.   [WA548T628p 1947]
   for Library of Congress   [48q7]†

698
C65
1970
H-H
   U. S. Congress. House. Committee on Banking
     and Currency. To...1970. (Card 2)

require an effective plan for the elimination of
lead-based paint poisoning as a condition of
Federal assistance under certain other programs;
H.R. 13254, a bill to provide Federal financial
assistance to help cities and communities of the
United States develop and carry out intensive
local programs to eliminate the causes of lead-
based paint poisoning; H.R. 14734, a bill to provide that Federal assistance to a state or local
     (Cont'd on next card)

325
P72
1947
   To secure these rights.
   U. S. *President's Committee on Civil Rights.*
     To secure these rights, the report of the President's Com-
   mittee on Civil Rights. Washington, U. S. Govt. Print.
   Off., 1947.
     xii, 178 p. illus., maps. 25 cm.
     Charles E. Wilson, chairman.

     1. Civil rights—U. S.   I. Wilson, Charles Erwin, 1886-
   II. Title.
     JC599.U5A32 1947   323.4   47—46486*
   Library of Congress   [52b²]

VF Port of New York Authority
DATE OF REQUEST APR 27 195? | L C CARD NO.
   4/20/53
AUTHOR
   Tobin, Austin J.
TITLE The Administration of a Port Authority; Address
   before Greater Philadelphia-South Jersey council,
   Philadelphia, Oct. 3, 1952/
SERIES
EDITION | PUB. DATE | PAGING 19p.
PUBLISHER Reprinted from Bond Buyer, 10-7-
   52
RECOMMENDED BY | REVIEWED IN
ORDER RECORD

698
C65
1970
H-H
   U. S. Congress. House. Committee on Banking
     and Currency. To...1970. (Card 3)

government or agency for rehabilitation or
renovation of housing and for enforcement of
local or state housing codes under the urban
renewal program, the public housing program,
or the model cities programs, or under any
other program involving the provision by state
or local governments of housing or related
facilities, shall be made available only on
condition that the recipient submit and carry
     (Cont'd on next card)

360
K25
   To seek a newer world.
   Kennedy, Robert F
     To seek a newer world. [1st ed.] Garden City,
   N.Y., Doubleday, 1967.
     233p.

     1. Social conditions. 2. Urban renewal.
   I. Title.

VF
353.1
T61
   Tobin, Austin J
     Authorities as a governmental technique,
   by Executive Director, the Port of New York
   Authority, before the 3d annual Institute,
   the place of authorities in the life of
   New Jersey citizens. Sponsored by the New
   Jersey Council for Social Studies, and the
   Bureau of Governmental Research at Rutgers
   University, March 26, 1963. [n.p.] 1953.
     32p.   (Cont'd. on next card)

VF
353.1   Tobin, Austin J   Authorities as a
T61   governmental technique...(Card 2)

      1. Authorities. 2. Political science.
I. New Jersey Council for Social Studies.
II. Rutgers University. Bureau of Govern-
mental Research. III. Port of New York
Authority.

384
T61   Tobin, Austin J
      The airport's influence on air transport
development, by Executive Director, the Port
of New York Authority, An address before th
Association of German Airports, May 9, 1962.
Hamburg. [n.p.] 1962.
      17p.

      1. Air transportation. I. Association of
German Airports. II. Port of New York
Authority.

388
:331   Tobin, Austin J
T61   The commuter problem and business. An
address at a seminar held at Fordham University School of Business on April 15,
1959. [New York] Port of New York
Authority, 1959.
      10p.

      1. Journey to work. I. Port of New York
Authority.

383
(747)   Tobin, Austin J
T61   Financial condition and future plans of the
Port of New York Authority, by Executive
Director, the Port of New York Authority. An
address before the Municipal Forum of New York,
the Municipal Bond Club of New York, and the
Bond Club of New Jersey. New York, 1962.
      13p.

      1. Port of New York Authority.

VF
332.6   Tobin, Austin J
T61   Immunity of municipal bonds, current
problems.   Address before the Municipal
Forum of New York, October 29, 1959.
New York, 1959.

      1. Municipal bonds.   I. Municipal
Forum of New York.

Class No.	Author (surname first)
VF Mort fin	Tobin, Howard J
Accession No.	Title The life insurance company viewpoint
Ordered	
Source	Place Publisher
Received	Address
Cost	Date 1951 Paging 5p List Price Mimeo Est. Cost
Purchase Order No.	Edition or Series
Date	Recommended by
L. C. No.	Reviewed in Add'l Med. Winter

H-305 (2-50)   HOUSING AND HOME FINANCE AGENCY: Office of the Administrator   10—61187-1   GPO

711.552
(77595)   Tobin, Howard J., jt. author.
T92

  Hyder, K. Lee
      Proposals for downtown Milwaukee, by K.
Lee Hyder and Howard J. Tobin. Chicago, Urban
Land Institute, Aug. 1941.
      89 p. illus., charts, maps, tables.

      1. Business districts - Milwaukee.
I. Tobin, Howard J., jt. author. II. Urban
Land Institute, Chicago.

691.32
T62   Tobio, J   M
      Medidas y ensayos no destructivos.
Madrid, Consejo Superior de Investigaciones
Cientificas, Patronato Juan de la
Cierva de Investigacion Tecnica, 1964.
      51p. (Spain. Instituto Eduardo Torroja
de la Construcción y del Cemento.
Monografias no. 237)
      English summary.

      1. Concrete. I. Spain. Consejo Superior de
Investigaciones Cientificas. Instituto Eduardo
Torroja de la   Construcción y del
Cemento.

628.1
(46)   Tobio, Jose M
861   Spain. Consejo Superior de Investigaciones
Cientificas. Instituto Tecnico de la Construccion y del Cemento.
      Potabilizacion del agua de mar, por Jose
Laorden y Jose M. Tobio. Madrid, 1960.
      70p. illus., diagrs., tables. (Its
Numero 204)
      English summary.

      1. Water-supply - Spain.   I. Laorden, Jose.
II. Tobio, Jose M.

      Tobyhanna.
  Rodgers, Clifton E
      Tobyhanna - new town development.
Beaver Falls, Pa.? 1952?
      65 p.

      $5.00-letter 3/52.

711.417
(74825)   Tobyhanna, Pa. Planning and Zoning
R63   Commission.
  Rodgers, Clifton E
      Tobyhanna [Pa.] new town development.
[Prepared in cooperation with] Tobyhanna
Planning and Zoning Commission.
Harrisburg, Pa., 1951.
      65p.

      1. Planned communities - Tobyhanna,
Pa. I. Tobyhanna, Pa. Planning and
Zoning Commission.

711.4
(75813)   Toccoa-Stephens County Joint
T62   Planning Commission.
  Bartholomew (Harland) and Associates.
      Comprehensive plan, Toccoa-Stephens
County, Georgia. Prepared for Toccoa
-Stephens County Joint Planning Commis-
sion. Atlanta, 1959.
      85p. maps, tables.

      U.S. Urban Renewal Administration.
Urban Planning Assistance Program.

      1. Master plan - Toccoa, Ga. I. Toccoa-Stephens
County Joint Planning Commission. II. U.S.
URA-UPAP. Toccoa, Ga.

711.14
(75813)   Toccoa-Stephens County Joint Planning
B17   Commission.
  Bartholomew (Harland) and Associates
      Land use and zoning, City of Toccoa,
Georgia. Prepared for Toccoa-Stephens
County Joint Planning Commission.
Atlanta, 1959
      lv. maps, tables.

      U.S. Urban Renewal Administration,
Urban Planning Assistance Program

      1. Land use - Toccoa, Ga. 2. Zoning - Toccoa, Ga.
I. Toccoa-Stephens County Joint Planning Commission.
II. U.S. URA-UPAP.   Toccoa, Ga.

352.1
(75813)   Toccoa-Stephens County Joint Planning
B17   Commission.
  Bartholomew (Harland) and Associates.
      Public improvements and administration
of the comprehensive plan. [Prepared for]
Toccoa-Stephens County Joint Planning
Commission [Under contract with Georgia
Dept. of Commerce] Atlanta, 1959.
      lv. tables.

      U.S. Urban Renewal Administration,
Urban Planning Assistance Program.

      1. Capital improvement programs - Toccoa, Ga.
2. Subdivision regulation - Toccoa, Ga. I. Toccoa-
Stephens County Joint   Planning Commission.
II. U.S. URA-UPAP.   Toccoa, Ga.

1027-
1032   TOCCOA - STEPHENS COUNTY PLANNING
      COMMISSION.
      TOCCOA, GEORGIA, COMPREHENSIVE PLAN,
REPORT: 1, POPULATION AND ECONOMIC BASE
STUDY: 2, NEIGHBORHOOD ANALYSES: 3,
EXISTING LAND USE ANALYSIS, FUTURE LAND
USE PLAN, MAJOR THOROUGHFARE PLAN,
COMMUNITY FACILITIES PLAN, PUBLIC
IMPROVEMENT PROGRAM 4, ZONING ORDINANCE
AND SUBDIVISION REGULATIONS 5, CENTRAL
BUSINESS DISTRICT STUDY 5, CONTINUING
PLANNING PROGRAM. BY GEORGIA MOUNTAINS
PLANNING AND DE   VELOPMENT COMMISSION.
TOCCOA, GA., 19   6.
         (CONTINUED ON NEXT CARD)

1027-
1032   TOCCOA - STEPHENS COUNTY PLANNING
      COMMISSION. TOCCOA, GEORGIA,
      COMPREHENSIVE ... 969.   (CARD 2)

      6 V. (HUD 701 REPORT)

      1. MASTER PLAN - TOCCOA, GA.
I. GEORGIA MOUNTAINS PLANNING &
DEVELOPMENT COMMISSION. II. HUD. 701.
TOCCOA, GA.

551
T62   TOCHER, DON.
      EARTHQUAKE ENERGY AND GROUND BREAKAGE.
SANTA CLARA, CALIF., SEISMOLOGICAL SOCIETY
OF AMERICA, 1958.
      P.147-153.

      REPRINTED FROM BULLETIN OF THE
SEISMOLOGICAL SOCIETY OF AMERICA, V. 48,
APRIL 1958.
      1. EARTHQUAKES. 2. EARTHQUAKES -
CALIF.   3. EARTHQUAKES - NEVADA.
I. TITLE. II. CALIFORNIA. UNIVERSITY.
SEISMOGRAPHIC STATION.
III. SEISMOLOGICAL SOCIETY OF AMERICA.

551
(794)   TOCHER, DON.
C15E   CALIFORNIA. UNIVERSITY. SEISMOGRAPHIC
      STATIONS.
      EARTHQUAKES IN NORTHERN CALIFORNIA,
NEVADA AND OREGON AND REGISTRATION OF
EARTHQUAKES AT BERKELEY, MOUNT HAMILTON,
PALO ALTO, SAN FRANCISCO, FERNDALE,
FRESNO, MINERAL, ARCATA, REON,
CORVALLIS, SHASTA, MANZANITA LAKE,
FALLON AND YERINGTON FROM APRIL 1, 1957
TO JUNE 30, 1957, BY DON TOCHER.
BERKELEY, UNIVERSITY OF CALIFORNIA
PRESS, 1959.
      85-137P. (ITS BULLETIN, V. 27,
NO. 2)
         (CONTINUED ON NEXT CARD)

551
(794)   CALIFORNIA. UNIVERSITY. SEISMOGRAPHIC
C15E   STATIONS. EARTHQUAKES IN NORTHERN ...
      1959.   (CARD 2)
      1. EARTHQUAKES - CALIFORNIA.
I. TOCHER, DON.

658
T62   Tocher, K D
      The art of simulation London, English
Universities Press, 1963.
      184p. (Electrical engineering series)

      1. Industrial management - Automation.
2. Automation. I. Title.

712.23
NTt   Tocks Island national recreation area.
  U.S. National Park Service.
      Tocks Island national recreation area.
A proposal. [Prepared in cooperation
with] Delaware River Basin Commission.
[Washington] Dept. of the Interior,
National Park Service. 1965.
      25p.

      1. National parks and reserves.
2. Recreation. 3. Delaware River Basin
Commission.   I. Title.

628.44
T62

Tocks Island Regional Advisory Council.
Tocks Island regional-interstate solid waste management study; application for an inter-state study and investigation grant under the Federal solid waste disposal act of 1965.
n.p. 1967.
28p.
Submitted to the U.S. Public Health Service.
1. Refuse and refuse disposal. I. U.S. Public Health   Service. II. Title.

628.44
T62

Tocks Island regional-interstate solid waste management study.
Tocks Island Regional Advisory Council.
Tocks Island regional-interstate solid waste management study; application for an inter-state study and investigation grant under the Federal solid waste disposal act of 1965.
n.p. 1967.
28p.
Submitted to the U.S. Public Health Service.
1. Refuse and refuse disposal. I. U.S. Public Health   Service. II. Title.

628.44
(748)
C15

Tocks Island regional-interstate solid waste management study.
Candeub, Fleissig and Associates.
Tocks Island regional-interstate solid waste management study. Study design. Newark, 1968.
25p.

1. Refuse and refuse disposal - Tocks Island Region, Pa. I. Title.

360
T62

Tocqueville, Alexis de
Democracy in America. Edited by J.P. Mayer. A new translation by George Lawrence. Garden City, N.Y., Doubleday, 1969.
778p.

1. Social conditions. 2. Political science. I. Mayer, J.P., ed. II. Title.

711.4
N17t

The "Today" show, Robert Weaver [Administrator U.S. Housing and Home Finance Agency]
National Broadcasting Company Network.
The "Today" show, Robert Weaver [interviewed. Administrator, U.S. Housing and Home Finance Agency] interviewed. [New York] 1964.
8p.

1. City planning. I. Weaver, Robert Clifton. II. U.S. Housing and Home Finance Agency.   III. Title.

301
W15

TODAY'S CHANGING SOCIETY.
WALTON, CLARENCE C   ED.
TODAY'S CHANGING SOCIETY: A CHALLENGE TO INDIVIDUAL IDENTITY. NEW YORK, INSTITUTE OF LIFE INSURANCE, 1967.
136P.

REPORT OF AN ARDEN HOUSE CONFERENCE SPONSORED BY COLUMBIA UNIVERSITY AND THE INSTITUTE OF LIFE INSURANCE.

1. SOCIOLOGY. I. INSTITUTE OF LIFE INSURANCE. II. COLUMBIA UNIVERSITY. III. TITLE. IV. TITLE: A CHALLENGE TO INDIVIDUAL IDE_NTITY.

371.4
S82

TODAY'S HANDBOOK FOR LIBRARIANS.
SWEENEY, MARY AGNES, 1901-
TODAY'S HANDBOOK FOR LIBRARIANS.
READY REFERENCE DATA WITH LISTS OF SOURCES OF INFORMATION ABOUT INDUSTRIAL EMPLOYMENT AND TRAINING OPPORTUNITIES, OPPORTUNITIES IN THE ARMED SERVICES AND THE QUALIFICATIONS THEY DEMAND, REHABILITATION, AND OTHER SOCIAL AND EMOTIONAL PROBLEMS INVOLVING INDIVIDUAL READJUSTMENT AND GUIDANCE. BY MARY A. SWEENEY ... CHICAGO, AMERICAN LIBRARY ASSOCIATION, 1944.
99P.

(CONTINUED ON NEXT CARD)

371.4
S82

SWEENEY, MARY AGNES, 1901- TODAY'S HANDBOOK ...1944.   (CARD 2)

REPRODUCED FROM TYPE-WRITTEN COPY.

1. VOCATIONAL GUIDANCE.
2. OCCUPATIONS. 3. VOCATIONAL GUIDANCE - BIBLIOGRAPHY. I. AMERICAN LIBRARY ASSOCIATION. II. TITLE.

800
M87

Today's Negro voices.
Murphy, Beatrice M   ed.
Today's Negro voices: an anthology by young Negro poets. New York, Julian Messner, 1970.
141p.

1. Literature. 2. Negroes. I. Title.

371.7
(77311)
T62

TODD, ARTHUR J
THE CHICAGO RECREATION SURVEY 1937; A PROJECT SPONSORED JOINTLY BY THE CHICAGO RECREATION COMMISSION AND NORTHWESTERN UNIVERSITY. CHICAGO, 1937-40.
5 V.

v.1-1c
v.2-2c
v.3-2c
v.4
v.5

CONDUCTED UNDER THE AUSPICES OF THE WORKS PROGRESS ADMINISTRATION, NATIONAL YOUTH ADMINISTRATION, ILLINOIS EMERGENCY RELIEF COMMISSION.

1. RECREATI ON - CHICAGO, ILL.
(CONTINUED ON NEXT CARD)

371.7
(77311)
T62

TODD, ARTHUR J THE CHICAGO RECREATION, 1937-40.   (CARD 2)

I. CHICAGO, ILL. RECREATION COMMISSION. II. NORTHWESTERN UNIVERSITY.

551.49
T62

TODD, DAVID KEITH, 1923-
GROUND WATER HYDROLOGY. NEW YORK, WILEY, 1959.
336P.

1. HYDROLOGY. I. TITLE.

628.1
(03)
T62

Todd, David Keith.
The water encyclopedia; a compendium of useful information on water resources. Port Washington, N.Y., Water Information Center, 1970.
559p.

c.1 Ref.

1. Water resources - Encyclopedias.
2. Hydrology. I. Title.

614
(79461)
T62

Todd, Frank Morton. (Historian for the Committee)
Eradicating plague from San Francisco. Report of the Citizens' Health Committee and an account of its work, with brief descriptions of the measures taken, copies of ordinances in aid of sanitation, articles by sanitarians on the nature of plague and the best means of getting rid of it facsimiles of circulars issued by the committee and a list of subscribers to the health fund. San Francisco, C.A. Murdock, 1909.
313p.   (Cont'd on next card)

614
(79461)
T62

Todd, Frank Morton. (Historian for the Committee) Eradicating plague from San Francisco. Report of the Citizens' Health Committee and an account of its work...1909.   (Card 2)

1. Public health - San Francisco.
2. Sanitation. 3. Rodents. 4. San Francisco. Citizens' Health Committee. I. Title.

728.1
†308
(7445)
R26

TODD, ROBERT E
THE REPORT OF THE LAWRENCE SURVEY, STUDIES IN RELATION TO LAWRENCE, MASSACHUSETTS, MADE IN 1911 ... BY ROBERT E. TODD AND FRANK B. SANBORN AT THE PROCUREMENT OF THE WHITE FUND. LAWRENCE, 1912.
263P.

CONTENTS.- PT.I. HOUSING CONDITIONS, BY R.E. TODD.- PT.II. PUBLIC HEALTH, BY F.B. SANBORN.

1. HOUSING S URVEYS - LAWRENCE, MASS. 2. HOU SING AND HEALTH.
(CONTINUED ON NEXT CARD)

728.1
†308
(7445)
R26

THE REPORT OF THE LAWRENCE SURVEY, STUDIES IN RELATION TO LAWRENCE, MASSACHUSETTS, MADE IN 1911 ... BY ROBERT E. TODD AND FRANK B. SANBORN AT THE PROCUREMENT OF THE WHITE FUND. LAWRENCE, 1912. 263P....   (CARD 2)

I. TODD, ROBERT E. II. SANBORN, FRANK BERRY, 1865-

312
K15

Todd, Thomas R   jt.au.
Kenwit, Edmond L
Recent population trends and their highway implications, by E.L. Kenwit and Thomas R. Todd. [n.p.] 1961.
33p.
Reprinted from Highway Research Board. Proceedings, vol. 40, 1961. (711.73N177, 1961)

1. Population. 2. Population shifts.
3. Transportation - Statistics. I. Todd, Thomas R., jt.au. II. Highway Research Board. III. Title.

362.6
W34
1971
no.3

Todhunter, E   Neige.
White House Conference on Aging, Washington, 1971. Nutrition; background, by E. Neige Todhunter Issues, by the Technical Committee on Nutrition, with the collaboration of the author. Wash., 1971.
35p. [no. 3]
Cover title: Background and issues; nutrition.
Bibliography: p. 31-35.

1. Old age. 2. Health. I. Todhunter, E. Neige. II. Title.

332
T62

Todhunter, Ralph
... Text-book on compound interest and annuities -certain. 4th ed. rev. by R. C. Simmonds and T. P. Thompson. Cambridge, University Press [1937]
xiv, 270 p.   tables.

Reprinted 1950.
Published for the Institute of Actuaries.

1. Compound Interest. I. Simmonds, R. C. II. Thompson, T. P. III. Institute of Actuaries.

301.15
T63

Toffler, Alvin.
Future shock. New York, Random House, 1970.
505p.

Bibliography: p. 461-483.

1. Man - Influence of environment.
2. Social conditions. 3. Social change. I. Title.

332.72
T63
TOFFLER, ALVIN.
NEW PITFALLS FOR HOME BUYERS. NEW YORK, MCCALL CORP., 1962.
6P.

ARTICLE IN REDBOOK, OCTOBER 1962, P.64, 151-155.

2c
1. MORTGAGE FORECLOSURES.
~~I. REDBOOK. II. TITLE.~~

697.8
J63
TOGETHER WE CAN CHECK THE BLIGHT OF AIR POLLUTION.
JOHN WOOD COMPANY. (AIR POLLUTION CONTROL DIVISION)
TOGETHER WE CAN CHECK THE BLIGHT OF AIR POLLUTION. A PARTNERSHIP FOR LOCAL CONTROL. FLORHAM PARK, N.J., 1961.
20P.

1. AIR POLLUTION. I. TITLE.

352
(52)
T64
1970
Tokyo. Metropolitan Government.
An administrative perspective of Tokyo. Tokyo, 1970.
64p.

1. Metropolitan government - Japan.
2. Metropolitan area planning - Japan. I. Title.

727
T63
Toffler, Alvin, ed.
The schoolhouse in the city. New York, Frederick A. Praeger, 1968.
255p.

Published in cooperation with Educational Facilities Laboratories.

1. Schools. I. Educational Facilities Laboratories. II. Title.

966
U54
1950
Togoland.
United Nations. Trusteeship Council.
Report of the United Nations Visiting Mission to Trust Territories in West Africa and related documents. New York, 1951.
138 p. map.

Official records of the Seventh session (1 June - 21 July 1950) Suppl. no. 2(T/798)

1. Cameroons. 2. Togoland.

336
(52)
T64
Tokyo. Metropolitan Government.
Budget of Tokyo for fiscal 1969.

Tokyo, 19

1v.

For Library holdings see main entry.

1. Budget - Japan - Tokyo.

628.44
T63
Toftner, Richard O
Developing a state solid waste management plan. Wash., U.S. Bureau of Solid Waste Management, 1970.
50p. (U.S. Public Health Service publication no. 2031)

1. Refuse and refuse disposal.
I. U.S. Bureau of Solid Waste Management. II. Title.

711
(016)
C65
no.
138

2c
Toizer, Alfred.
Survey of recent housing studies: an annotated guide. Philadelphia, City Planning Commission, 1970.
39p. (Council of Planning Librarians. Exchange bibliography no. 138)

1. Planning - Bibl. 2. Federal housing programs - Bibl. 3. Housing - Philadelphia Bibl. I. Philadelphia. City Planning Commission. II. Title. (Series: Council of Planning Librarians. Exchange Bibliography no. 138)

728.1
(52)
T64
Tokyo. Metropolitan Government.
Housing report,
Tokyo,
V. illus., tables. annual.

In Japanese, with English summary.

For complete information see shelflist.

1. Housing - Japan

628.44
T63i
Toftner, Richard O
Intergovernmental approaches to solid waste management, by Richard O. Toftner and Robert M. Clark. Wash., U.S. Environmental Protection Agency, Solid Waste Management Office, 1971.
17p. (SW-47ts)

1. Refuse and refuse disposal.
2. Intergovernmental relations. I. Clark, Robert M., jt. au. II. U.S. Environmental Protection Agency. III. Title.

312
(74811)
P34
Toizer, Alfred.
Philadelphia. Community Renewal Program.
Trends in population, housing and socio-economic characteristics. Prepared under the direction of Alfred Toizer, of the Philadelphia City Planning Commission. Philadelphia, 1963.
25p.

U.S. Urban Renewal Adm. CRP.

1. Population - Philadelphia. 2. Housing - Philadelphia. 3. Economic conditions - Philadelphia. I. Toizer, Alfred. II. U.S. URA-CRP. Philadelphia.

352
(52)
R61
Tokyo. (Metropolitan Government.)
Robson, William A
Report on Tokyo Metropolitan Government. Tokyo, Tokyo Metropolitan Government [and] Tokyo Institute for Municipal Research, 1967.
113p.

1. Metropolitan government - Japan. 2. Metropolitan areas - Japan. I. Tokyo. Metropolitan Government. II. Tokyo Institute for Municipal Research. III. Title.

691.32
H15b
Togba, David, jt. au.
Hansen, Henry.
Betongfasthet bestemt ved hjelp av Schmidthammer (Strength of concrete in compression determined by the Schmidthammer) av Henry Hansen og David Togba. Oslo, Norges Byggforskningsinstitutt, 1968.
[3]p. (Oslo. Norges Byggforskningsinstitutt. Saertrykk 154)
Saertrykk fra Betongen idag, nr. 1, 1968.
1. Concrete. 2. Strength of materials. I. Togba, David, jt. au. II. Oslo. Norges Byggforsknings institutt. III. Title: Strength of con crete in compression determined by the Schmidthammer.

621.32
M17
Tokhadze, I L jt. au.
Matveev, A B
Determining luminosity in terms of threshold increments, by A.B. Matveev and I.L. Tokhadze. Garston, Eng., Building Research Station, 1968.
[7]p. (Library communication no. 1428)
Translated from the Russian and reprinted from Svetotekhnika, 1965, 11 (12), 10-14.

1. Lighting. I. Tokhadze, I.L., jt. au. II. U.K. Building Research Station. III. Title. (Series)

352
(52)
R61
Tokyo Institute for Municipal Research.
Robson, William A
Report on Tokyo Metropolitan Government. Tokyo, Tokyo Metropolitan Government [and] Tokyo Institute for Municipal Research, 1967.
113p.

1. Metropolitan government - Japan. 2. Metropolitan areas - Japan. I. Tokyo. Metropolitan Government. II. Tokyo Institute for Municipal Research. III. Title.

VF
728.1
:336.18
G47
Together.
Girl Scouts of the United States of America.
Together: girl scouts and public housing. New York, 1969.
folder.

1. Public housing. 2. Community development - Citizen participation. I. Title.

711.4
(74827)
E55
Tokmakian, Harold.
Emmaus, Pa. Planning Commission.
Planning and zoning for the borough of Emmaus, Lehigh County, Pennsylvania, by Russell VanNest Black with Harold Tokmakian. Emmaus, 1957.
38p. maps, tables.

U.S. Urban Renewal Administration, Urban Planning Assistance Program.
1. City planning - Emmaus, Pa. 2. Zoning - Emmaus, Pa. I. Black, Russell VanNest. II. Tokmakian, Harold. III. U.S. URA-UPAP. Emmaus, Pa.

711.585
(79463)
B17
Tolan, John H Jr.
Barrett Homes.
The Plaza Richmond; a study of 1957-58 sales in the pilot project redevelopment area, comp. and edited by John H. Tolan, Jr. Richmond, Calif., 1958
35p. illus.

1. Urban renewal - Richmond, Calif. 2. Family income and expenditure - Richmond, Calif. 3. House plans. I. Tolan, John H jr.

301
L15
Together.
Lane, Martha A
Wisconsin's Indians: too long forgotten. [n.p.] 1970.
[6]p.

Detached from: Together, Jan. 1970, p. 28-33.

1. Indians. I. Together. II. Title.

352
(52)
T64
Tokyo. Metropolitan Government.
An administrative perspective of Tokyo. Tokyo, 1969.
72p.

1. Metropolitan government - Japan - Tokyo. 2. Metropolitan areas - Japan - Tokyo. 3. Metropolitan area planning - Japan - Tokyo. I. Title.

652
T65
TOLBERT, MARGUERITE.
LETTER WRITING FOR YOU, BY M. TOLBERT AND SARAH WITHERS. COLUMBIA, S.C., STATE DEPT. OF EDUCATION, 1947.
111P.

1. LETTER WRITING. I. WITHERS, SARAH, JT. AU.

628.44
K14
Tolciss, J   jt. au.
Kaiser, E   R
    Incineration of automobile bodies and
bulky waste materials, by E.R. Kaiser and
J. Tolciss. Presented at annual meeting of
American Public Works Association, New York,
N.Y., August 17, 1960. New York, New York
University, College of Engineering, Research
Div., 1960.
    20p. (New York University. College of
Engineering. Research Div. Technical
report 764.1)
    Prepared for National Institutes of Health,
U.S. Public   Health Service.
                    (Continued on next card)

711.585
(77113)
T65
TOLEDO. CHAMBER OF COMMERCE.
    THIS ALSO IS TOLEDO. TOLEDO, 1945.
    15P.

    1. SLUMS - TOLEDO.

728.1
:336.18
(77113)
T65
Toledo. Metropolitan Housing Authority.
    Report, 1943-44, 48-49; 1955/56; 1960/63; 1963/64;
    69/70, 70/71
    Toledo, 19

    9 v. annual.

    For Library holdings see main entry.

    1. Public housing - Toledo.

628.44
K14
Kaiser, E   R   Incineration of auto-
    mobile...1960.   (Card 2)

    1. Refuse and refuse disposal. I. New
York University. College of Engineering.
II. Tolciss, J., jt. au. III. American
Public Works Association, New York,
IV. Title.

711.4
(77112)
T65

2c
TOLEDO, OHIO. CHAMBER OF COMMERCE.
METROPOLITAN PLANNING COMMITTEE.
PRELIMINARY SKETCH FOR A MASTER PLAN
OF THE CITY OF TOLEDO AND THE
METROPOLITAN AREA. TOLEDO, 1947.
116P.

    1. MASTER PLAN - TOLEDO.

728.1
P17
Toledo. Metropolitan Housing Authority.
Pastalan, Leon A
    Vistula Manor demonstration housing for the
physically disabled. Final report. Prepared
for Toledo Metropolitan Housing Authority.
Toledo, Research Foundation, University of
Toledo, 1969.
    84p.
    U.S. Dept. of Housing and Urban Development.
Low-Income Housing Demonstration Project.
    1. Housing for the handicapped. I. Toledo.
University. Research Foundation. II. Toledo.
Metropolitan Housing Authority. III. Title.
IV. U.S. HUD-Low-   Income Housing
Demonstration Gran   t Project. Toledo.

628.44
K14s
Tolciss, J   jt. au.
Kaiser, E   R
    Smokeless burning of automobile bodies, by
E.R. Kaiser and J. Tolciss. Presented at
annual meeting of Air Pollution Control
Association, New York, N.Y., June 12, 1961.
New York, New York University, College of
Engineering, Research Division, 1961.
    31p. (New York University. College of
Engineering, Research Division. Technical
report 764.2)
    1. Refuse and refuse disposal. I. New York
University. College of Engineering.

                    (Cont'd on next card)

711.585.1
(77113)
T65
Toledo. Office of City Manager.
    Application to the Department of Housing
and Urban Development for a grant to plan a
comprehensive city demonstration program
for Toledo, Ohio. Toledo, 1967.
    1v.
    Selected to receive the first HUD Model
Cities Program planning grants.

    1. Model cities - Toledo, Ohio. I. U.S.
HUD - Model Cities Program first planning
grants.

690.091.82
(77113)
T65
TOLEDO, OHIO. ORDINANCES, ETC.
    BUILDING CODE. CHAPTER X OF THE
TOLEDO MUNICIPAL CODE. AMENDED
THROUGH APRIL 16, 1966. TOLEDO,
1966.
    1 V.

    1. BUILDING CODES - TOLEDO.

628.44
K14s
Kaiser, E   R   Smokeless burning...1961.
                    (Card 2)

    II. Tolciss, J., jt. au. III. American
Public Works Association, New York, Aug.,
1960. IV. U.S. National Institute of
Health. V. Title.

711.585.1
(77113)
T65m
Toledo. Office of the City Manager.
    Model cities program; activity report,
1st-   1969
    Toledo, 1969 -
    1 v.
    U.S Dept. of Housing and Urban Development
Model Cities Program.
    For Library holdings see main entry.
    1. Model cities - Toledo. I. U.S.
HUD - Model Cities Program.

690.091.82
:613.5
(77113)
T65
1953
Toledo, Ohio. Ordinances, etc.
    Housing regulation controlling supplied
facilities, maintenance, and occupancy of dwelling
units.   The Toledo City Journal, p. 1555-1561,
Dec. 5, 1953.
    Adopted by the Toledo District Board of
Health, Nov. 24, 1953; supercedes Regulation 6-45,
dated Nov. 20, 1945.
    Clipping.
    1. Housing codes-Toledo, Ohio.

    Toledo, Ohio.

VF
Neighborhoods.
Traffic, transit & highways.

711.74
(77113)
T65
TOLEDO. CITY PLAN COMMISSION.
    MAJOR STREET REPORT. TOLEDO, 1924.
    72P.

    1. STREETS - TOLEDO.   2. CITY
PLANNING - TOLEDO.

Ph-Ohio-Toledo
DATE OF REQUEST 6/22/54   JUN 28 1964   L. C. CARD NO.

AUTHOR   Toledo, Ohio. Ordinances, etc.

TITLE   Ordinance creating a "Housing Improvement and Urban
Renewal Commission".

SERIES

| EDITION | PUB. DATE | PAGING |
| PUBLISHER | | |

RECOMMENDED BY   MWL   REVIEWED IN   Munic News 6/15/54 p. 49
                            ORDER RECORD

    Toledo.
    see also
Greater Toledo Municipal League.

711.585
:659.11
T65
Toledo. Board of Community Relations.
    Report, 1963
    Toledo, 1963
    1 v.   annual.

    For complete information see shelf list.

    1. Community relations.

Toledo (Ohio) Plan Commission

    see also

Toledo-Lucas County (Ohio) Plan Commission

352.1
(77113)
T65
Toledo. Capital Improvements Committee.
    Capital improvement program,
Toledo,
    v.   maps, tables. annual.

    For complete information see shelflist.

1. Capital improvement programs - Toledo.

DATE OF REQUEST   3/23/51   MAY 31 1951   L. C. CARD NO.
AUTHOR
    Toledo (Ohio) Housing and Urban Redevelopment Comm.
TITLE   City of Toledo, Ohio: Application preliminary
advance for a slum clearance and urban redevelopment
SERIES   program.
EDITION   PUB. DATE 4/51   PAGING 43pp.
PUBLISHER   same

RECOMMENDED BY   REVIEWED IN
                JRL 5/15/51, p/ 2
            ORDER RECORD

711.4
(77113)
T65
Toledo. Plan Commission.
    Report, 1957
    Toledo, 1957
    1 v.   annual.

    For complete information see main card.

    1. City planning - Toledo.

711
(016)
C65
no.185

Toledo. University.
Winters, William R   Jr.
Minority enterprise and marketing: an annotated bibliography, by William R. Winters, Jr., and others. [Toledo] University of Toledo, 1971.
39p. (Council of Planning Librarians. Exchange bibliography no. 185)

1. Planning - Bibl. 2. Business - Minority groups - Bibl. I. Toledo. University. II. Title. (Series: Council of Planning Librarians. Exchange bibliography no. 185)

693.5
:691.8
:690.22
T65
Prelim.

Toledo. University. Research Foundation.
An investigation... Sept. 1950. (card 2)

1. Concrete blocks. 2. Walls. 3. Building materials - Testing. I. Selden, John K II. U.S. Army. (Corps of Engineers)

690.591
N17r

Toledo. Urban Renewal Agency.
National Association of Housing and Redevelopment Officials.
Rehabilitation operational guide and training manual. Prepared for the Urban Renewal Agency, City of Toledo, Ohio by Harold Taylor and Marian Wojciechowski. Wash., 1971.
140p. (NAHRO publication no. N547)

1. Houses - Maintenance and modernization. 2. Housing law enforcement. I. Toledo. Urban Renewal Agency. II. Taylor, Harold. III. Wojciechowski, Marian, jt. au. IV. Title.

693.5
:691.8
:690.22
T65

Toledo. University. Research Foundation.
Concrete masonry investigation: volume change characteristics of blocks and wallettes, 1950-52; combined report on wallettes #1-130, by J.K. Selden [and others] Toledo, Ohio, July 1953.
109 L. photos, tables.
Contents.-v.1. Final report to Office of the Chief of Engineers, Wallettes #1-78: Volume change characteristics of blocks and wallettes.-v. 2. Final report to Housing and Home Finance Agency, Wallettes #79-130: Investigation of the relationship betwee   shape, strength and

(see card 2)

693.5
:691.8
T65r

Toledo. University. Research Foundation.
Relation of shrinkage to moisture content in concrete blocks, by George L. Kalousek [and others] Toledo, Ohio, April 30, 1952.
26 L.   plates, graphs, tables.

Final report, Research project no. 1950-Str-22, Housing and Home Finance Agency.
Project director: John K. Selden; Staff director: William A. Russell.

Processed.

Toledo, Oreg.

VF
Housing-U.S.-Oreg.

693.5
:691.8
:690.22
T65

Toledo. University. Research Foundation.
Concrete masonry investigation. July 1953. (card 2)
Contents continued: treatment of concrete masonry units and the shrinkage and cracking of wall specimens.-v. 3. Combined photographs, tables and curves.
Final report, Research contract no. I-T-110, Housing and Home Finance Agency.
Project director: John K. Selden; staff technician, William A. Russell.

(see card 3)

690.015
YS8
T20

Toledo. University. Research Foundation.
Relation of shrinkage to moisture content in concrete masonry units. [Washington, Govt. Print. Off., Mar. 1953]
28 p. (Housing and Home Finance Agency. O.A Division of Housing Research. Housing research paper 25)

HHFA project no. 1950-STR-22. Dr. George L. Kalousek supervised laboratory work and preparation of the final report. William A. Russell, Staff technician.
(Continued on next card)

711.14
(79533)
072 l

Toledo, Or. City Planning Commission.
Oregon. University. Bureau of Municipal Research and Service.
Land use in Toledo. Prepared for the Toledo City Planning Commission. Eugene, Or., 1959.
10p.

U.S. Urban Renewal Adm. UPAP.

1. Land use - Toledo, Or. I. Toledo, Or. City Planning Commission. II. U.S. URA-UPAP. Toledo, Or.

VF
693.5
:691.8
T65

Toledo. University. Research Foundation.
[Development of test methods for prediction of shrinkage in concrete masonry units, including identification of curing process, by gas absorption or other methods.] Toledo, Ohio, Apr. 1953.
2 pts.   illus., graphs, tables.

Contains bibliography.
Pt.1.Simplified method for the determination of surface area of concrete products, by L. F. Gleysteen [and] G. L. Kalousek.-pt.2.Physical
(continued on next card)

Toledo. University. Research Foundation.
Relation of shrinkage ... 1953.   (Card 2)

"This report covers only the first of a series of investigations aimed at the reduction of shrinkage cracking of concrete masonry unit construction."

1.Housing research contracts. 2.Concrete blocks. I.Kalousek, George L. II.Title. III.Title: Shrinkage, relation of, to moisture content in masonry units. IV.Russell, William A. V.Series. VI.U.S. Housing and   Home Finance Agency. Office of the Administrato   Division of Housing Research.

312
(79533)
T65

Toledo, Or. City Planning Commission.
Population trends in Toledo. [In cooperation with the Bureau of Municipal Research and Service, University of Oregon] Toledo, 1959.
13p. maps, tables.

U.S. Urban Renewal Administration, Urban Planning Assistance Program.

1. Population - Toledo, Or. I. Oregon. University. Bureau of Municipal Research and Service.   II. U.S. URA-UPAP.

Toledo. University. Research Foundation.
[Development of test methods ...] 1953.
(Card 2)

properties of high-pressure steam-cured concrete block. (Reprint, Journal of the American Concrete Institute, p. 745-756, April 1953; attached to front cover of pt. 1)
Final report, Research Project no. 1-T-122, Housing and Home Finance Agency.
(Continued on next card)

693.5
:691.8
T65s

Toledo. University. Research Foundation.
Simplified method for the determination of surface area of concrete products, by L. F. Gleysteen and G. L. Kalousek. Toledo, 1953.
12p.
Final report (Part 1 of 2 parts) Research project no. 251. Housing and Home Finance Agency.

1. Concrete blocks. 2. Housing research projects. I. Gleysteen, L. F. II. Kalousek, G. L. III. U.S. Housing and Home Finance Agency. Office of the Administrator. Div. of   Housing Research.

711.74
(79533)
072

Toledo, Or. City Planning Commission.
Oregon. University. Bureau of Municipal Research and Service.
A preliminary major street plan for Toledo. In cooperation with the Toledo City Planning Commission. Eugene, Or., 1959.
3p. map.

U.S. Urban Renewal Administration, Urban Planning Assistance Program.

1. Street planning - Toledo, Or. I. Toledo, Or. City Planning Commission. II.U.S. URA-UPAP. Toledo, Or.

Toledo. University. Research Foundation.
[Development of test methods ...] 1953.
(Card 3)

Project director, John K. Selden; staff technician, William A. Russell.
Processed (pt.1)
1.Concrete blocks. 2.Concrete. 3.Housing research contracts. I.Gleysteen, L. F. II.Kalousek, G. L. III.Selden, John K. IV.Russell, William A. V.U.S. Housing and Home Finance Agency. O.A. Division of Housing Research. VI.Title. VII.Title: Simplified method for the determination of surface area of concrete products. V Title: Physical properties of high-pressure ste cured concrete block.

728.1
P17

Toledo. University Research Foundation.
Pastalan, Leon A
Vistula Manor demonstration housing for the physically disabled. Final report. Prepared for Toledo Metropolitan Housing Authority. Toledo, Research Foundation, University of Toledo, 1970.
84p.
U.S. Dept. of Housing and Urban Development. Low-Income Housing Demonstration Project.
1. Housing for the handicapped. I. Toledo. University. Research Foundation. II. Toledo. Metropolitan Housing Authority. III. Title. IV. U.S. HUD-Low-   Income Housing Demonstration Gran   t Project. Toledo.

333.38
(79533)
T65

Toledo, Or. City Planning Commission.
Oregon. University. Bureau of Municipal Research and Service.
Proposed subdivision ordinance for Toledo, Oregon. Prepared for the Toledo City Planning Commission. Preliminary draft. [Eugene, Or.] 1960.
13p.

U.S. Urban Renewal Adm. UPAP.

1. Subdivision regulation - Toledo, Or. I. Toledo, Or. City Planning Commission. II. U.S. URA-UPAP. Toledo, Or.

693.5
:691.8
:690.22
T65
Prelim.

Toledo. University. Research Foundation.
An investigation into the volume change characteristics of concrete block masonry wallettes and individual unites; progress report #1: Preliminaries, Department of the Army Contract DA 49-129 ENG 50... by John K. Selden. Toledo, Ohio, Sept. 1950.
21 L. charts
Part 1 of an investigation, part 2 of which was done under HHFA contract 1-T-110.

(see card 2)

693.55
T65

Toledo. University. Research Foundation.
Welded wire mesh for horizontal mortar joint reinforcing; a study of its effectiveness in reducing widths of shrinkage cracks in concrete masonry walls, by John K. Selden and William G. Rohr; sponsored by Adrian Peerless, Inc., Adrian, Mich. Toledo, Ohio, Dec. 1952.
1 v. graphs, tables.

1.Reinforced concrete construction. I.Selden, John K

711.74
(79533)
T65

Toledo, Or. City Planning Commission.
A street plan for Toledo. In cooperation with the Bureau of Municipal Research and Service, University of Oregon. [Toledo] 1960.
23p.

U.S. Urban Renewal Adm. UPAP.

1. Street planning - Toledo, Or. I. Oregon. University. Bureau of Municipal Research and Service. II. U.S.   URA-UPAP. Toledo, Or.

352.5
072

Toledo, Or. City Planning Commission.
Oregon. University. Bureau of Municipal
Research and Service.
A study of selected factors related to
future annexation of Toledo. Prepared for
the Toledo City Planning Commission. Eugene,
Or., 1959.
11p. maps.

U.S. Urban Renewal Administration, Urban
Planning Assistance Program.

1. Annexation - Toledo, Or. I. Toledo, Or. City
Planning Commission. II. U.S. URA-UPAP. Toledo, Or.

352.6
(77113)
T65

Toledo-Lucas County (Ohio) Plan
Commission.
Planning research studies. Prepared for
the Capital Improvements Committee.
[Toledo] 1960.
[31]p. (Its report no. 33)

Contents:-no. 1. The zoo.-no. 2. Forest
Cemetery.-no. 3. House of correction.-
no. 4. Fire stations.-
no. 6. Urban renewal.-

1. Capital improvement programs - Toledo-Lucas Co.,
Ohio. 2. Community facilities - Toledo-
Lucas Co., Ohio. I. Title.

550
(77113)
F67

Toledo regional area.
Forsythe, Jane.
A study of physical features for the Toledo
regional area. Preliminary. Bowling Green,
Ohio, Bowling Green State University, Geology
Dept., 1967.
111p. (Regional report 8.2, July 1967)
Prepared for the Toledo Regional Area Plan
for Action.
1. Geology - Toledo. 2. City planning -
Toledo. I. Toledo Regional Area Plan for Ac-
tion. II. Ohio. State University, Bowling
Green. III. Title: Physical features for
the Toledo re gional area. IV. Title:
Toledo regi onal area.

711.552
(79533)
072

Toledo, Or. City Planning Commission.
Oregon. University. Bureau of Municipal
Research and Service.
A study of the Toledo central business
district. Prepared for the Toledo City
Planning Commission. Eugene, Or., 1959.
5p. diagrs., maps.

U.S. Urban Renewal Administration, Urban Planning
Assistance Program.

1. Business districts - Toledo, Or. I. Toledo, Or.
City Planning Commission. II. U.S. URA-
UPAP. Toledo, Or.

312
(77112)
T65

Toledo-Lucas County, Ohio. Plan Commissions.
Population report. Toledo, O., 1957.
22p. illus., diagrs., maps.

1.Population - Toledo-Lucas Co., Ohio.
2.City growth - Toledo, Ohio.

693.5
(485)
S88

Tolerance measurements in precast concrete...
Suu, V
Tolerance measurements in precast concrete
construction at Norrköping. Garston, Eng.,
Building Research Station, 1971.
[9]p. (Library communication no. 1621)
Translated from the Swedish.

1. Concrete construction - Sweden.
I. U.K. Building Research Station.
II. Title. (Series)

711.5
(79533
:347)
T65

Toledo, Or. Ordinances, etc.
Toledo zoning ordinance. Revised
preliminary draft. [Toledo] 1960.
21p.

U.S. Urban Renewal Adm. UPAP.

1. Zoning legislation - Toledo, Or.
I. U.S. URA-UPAP. Toledo, Or.

728.69
T65

Toledo-Lucas County (Ohio) Plan
Commssions.
A study of motel-apartments. Toledo, 1964.
58p. (Planning research study 2-64)

1. Tourist courts. 2. Apartment houses -
Ohio.

711.4
(74811)
T65

Toll, Seymour I
Testimony presented to the second annual
public hearing of the Philadelphia City
Planning Commission, Jan. 30, 1968.
Philadelphia, Citizens' Council on City
Planning, 1968.
20p.

1. City planning - Philadelphia. I.
Philadelphia. City Planning Commission.
II. Citizens' Council on City Planning.
Philadelphia. III. Title.

VF
325
B76

Toledo Blade.
Brower, William
"15,000,000 Americans;" a personal inquiry
into the status of the one-tenth of our
population that constitutes what is called "the
Negro problem." [Toledo, Ohio, Toledo Blade,
c1951]
43 p.

Reprinted from the Toledo Blade.

1.Minority groups. 2.Race relations. I.Toledo
Blade.

711.3
(77112)
T65

Toledo-Lucas County, Ohio. Plan Commissions.
Report,
Toledo,
v. illus., maps. annual

For complete information see shelflist.

1. County planning - Lucas Co., Ohio. 2. City
planning - Toledo.

711.5
T65

4G.

Toll, Seymour I
Zoned American. New York, Grossman
Publishers, 1969.
370p.

Bibliography: p. 311-332.

1. Zoning. I. Title.

312
(77113)
T65

Toledo-Lucas County (Ohio) Plan
Commissions.
Data and trends of Toledo and County.
1960 population and housing census and
other sources. [Toledo, 1964?]
12p. (Population studies; Report no.
41)

1. Population - Toledo-Lucas Co., Ohio.
2. Housing - Toledo-Lucas Co.,
Ohio.

711.4
(77112)
T65T

TOLEDO-LUCAS COUNTY, OHIO. PLAN
COMMISSIONS.
TOLEDO'S FUTURE IN THE MAKING, A
PROGRESS REPORT. TOLEDO, 1949.
18P.

1. CITY PLANNING - TOLEDO, OHIO.

058.7
:388
A52

Toll bridges, ferries, domestic steamship
lines, and toll roads.
American Automobile Association.
Directory of toll bridges, ferries, domestic
steamship lines, and toll roads. Wash.,
1968.
56p.

1. Transportation - Direct. 2. Highways.
3. Bridges. I. Title. II. Title: Toll bridges,
ferries, domestic steamship lines, and toll
roads.

711.552
(77112)
T65
pt. 4

Toledo-Lucas County, Ohio. Plan Commissions.
Downtown study. Part 4. Plan for
tomorrow. Toledo, 1959.
37p. illus., maps. (Its Report no. 25)

1. Business districts - Toledo.

711.333
(77112)
T65

TOLEDO-LUCAS COUNTY (OHIO) PLAN
COMMISSIONS.
WHAT ABOUT OUR FUTURE. A PREVIEW OF
PLANNING FOR TOLEDO AND LUCAS COUNTY
ADOPTED BY THE TOLEDO AND LUCAS COUNTY
PLAN COMMISSION, DECEMBER 8, 1944.
TOLEDO, 1944.
45P.

1. COUNTY PLANNING - LUCAS CO., OHIO.
2. CITY PLANNING - TOLEDO. I. TITLE.

336
:651t

The toll of rising interest rates...
Conference on Economic Progress.
The toll of rising interest rates;
the one great waste in the Federal
budget. Washington, 1964.
89p.

1. Interest rates. 2. Budget.
I. Title.

711.581
(77112)
T65

TOLEDO-LUCAS, OHIO. COUNTY PLAN
COMMISSIONS.
NEIGHBORHOODS PLANNED FOR GOOD
LIVING... SUBDIVISION STANDARDS AND
REGULATIONS. TOLEDO, 1946.
37P.

1. NEIGHBORHOOD PLANNING -
TOLEDO-LUCAS CO., OHIO. I. TITLE.

550
(77113)
F67

Toledo Regional Area Plan for Action.
Forsythe, Jane.
A study of physical features for the Toledo
regional area. Preliminary. Bowling Green,
Ohio, Bowling Green State University, Geology
Dept., 1967.
111p. (Regional report 8.2, July 1967)
Prepared for the Toledo Regional Area Plan
for Action.
1. Geology - Toledo. 2. City planning -
Toledo. I. Toledo Regional Area Plan for Ac-
tion. II. Ohio. State University, Bowling
Green. III. Title: Physical features for
the Toledo re gional area. IV. Title:
Toledo regi onal area.

336.18
(016)
T65

Tolmachev, Mirjana, comp.
Federal revenue sharing; a bibliography of
recent material in the State Library of
Pennsylvania. 2d. ed. Harrisburg General
Library Bureau, State Library, Pennsylvania
Dept. of Education, 1971.
[4]p.

1. Grants-in-aid - Bibl. 2. State finance -
Bibl. I. Pennsylvania. State Library,
Harrisburg. II. Title. III. Title: Revenue
sharing.

388
(748)
P25p
no. 8

Tomazinis, Anthony Rudolf.
An introduction to mathematical models. Philadelphia, Penn Jersey Transportation Study, 1960.
18p. (Penn Jersey Transportation Study, Philadelphia. PJ paper no. 8)

1. Transportation - Pennsylvania.
2. Transportation - New Jersey. (Series: Penn Jersey Transportation Study, Philadelphia. PJ paper no. 8)

658.564
T65c

Tomeski, Edward Alexander.
The computer revolution; the executive and the new information technology. London, Macmillan, 1970.
276p.

Bibliography: p. 257-263.

1. Automation. 2. Management - Automation.
I. Title.

Tomorrow a new world.

711.417
C65t

Conkim, Paul K
Tomorrow a new world: the New Deal community program. Ithaca, N.Y., Cornell University Press, 1959.
350p.

Published for the American Historical Association.

1. Planned communities. 2. Community development. I. Title: The New Deal community program. II. Title.

388
(748)
P25p
no.15

Tomazinis, Anthony R
A new method of trip distribution in an urban area. Presented at the 41st annual meeting of the Highway Research Board (Origin and Destination Committee) Washington, D.C. - January 10, 1962. Philadelphia, Penn Jersey Transportation Study, 1962.
51p. (Pen Jersey Transportation Study. PJ paper no. 15)
1. Transportation - Pa.-N.J.-Del.
2. Journey to work. I. Penn Jersey Transportation Study. II. Highway Research Board. Meeting Washington, Jan. 1962.
(Cont'd on next card)

658.564
T65

Tomlin, Roger.
Managing the introduction of computer systems. London, New York, McGraw-Hill, 1970.
186p. (McGraw-Hill European series in management and marketing)

1. Automation. 2. Management.
I. Title.

Tomorrow belongs to Oklahoma.

330
(766)
A24

Ackerman, Ray.
Tomorrow belongs to Oklahoma. Oklahoma City, Semco Color Press, 1964.
26p.

1. Economic development - Oklahoma.
2. City growth - Oklahoma City. I. Title.

388
(748)
P25p
no.15

Tomazinis, Anthony R   A new method...1962.
(Card 2)

III. Title. (Series: Penn Jersey Transportation Study, Philadelphia. PJ paper no. 15)

628.16
T25c

TOMLINSON, GEORGE EDMUND, 1906 -
TENNESSEE VALLEY AUTHORITY.
THE CHICKAMAUGA PROJECT, A COMPREHENSIVE REPORT ON THE PLANNING, DESIGN, CONSTRUCTION, AND INITIAL OPERATIONS OF THE CHICKAMAUGA PROJECT. KNOXVILLE, 1942.
451P. (ITS TECHNICAL REPORT NO. 6)

PREPARED BY GEORGE E. TOMLINSON.
P. 301.
1. WATER - SUPPLY ENGINEERING.
2. WATER - SUPPLY - TENNESSEE.
I. TOMLINSON, GEORGE EDMUND, 1906 -
II. TITLE.

711.4
(7468)
N28

TOMORROW IS HERE.
NEW HAVEN. CITY PLAN COMMISSION.
TOMORROW IS HERE. NEW HAVEN, 1944.
16L.

1. CITY PLANNING - NEW HAVEN.
I. TITLE.

388
(748)
P25p
no. 6

Tomazinis, Anthony Rudolf.
Spatial parameters affecting urban traffic. Presented at the Origin and Destination Survey Committee Meeting, Highway Research Board, Washington, D.C., 1961. Philadelphia, Penn Jersey Transportation Study, 1961.
31p. (Penn Jersey Transportation Study, Philadelphia. PJ paper no. 6)
1. Transportation - Pennsylvania. 2. Transportation - New Jersey. (Series: Penn Jersey Transportation Study, Philadelphia. PJ paper no. 6)

690.21
T65

Tomlinson, M   J
Foundation design and construction. 2d ed. London, Pitman, 1970.
785p.

1. Foundations (Building) I. Title.

362.6
A742

TOMORROW IS TODAY.
ARIZONA CONFERENCE ON REHABILITATION OF THE AGING, PHOENIX, 1960.
TOMORROW IS TODAY; REHABILITATION PROBLEMS OF OUR SENIOR CITIZENS. EDITED BY DAVID WAYNE SMITH. TUCSON, UNIVERSITY OF ARIZONA PRESS, 1960.
60P.

1. OLD AGE - ARIZONA. I. SMITH, DAVID WAYNE, ED. II. TITLE: REHABILITATION PROBLEMS OF OUR SENIOR CITIZENS. III. TITLE.

534.83
T65

Tomboulian, Roger.
Research and development of a sonic boom simulation device. Wash., National Aeronautics and Space Administration, 1969.
43p. (NASA CR-1378)
Prepared by General Applied Science Laboratories, inc; for Langley Research Center, National Aeronautics and Space Administration. CFSTI.
1. Noise. 2. Air transportation. I. General Applied Science Laboratories. II. U.S. National Aeronautics and Space Administration. III. Title.

690.21
T65
1964

TOMLINSON, MICHAEL JOHN.
FOUNDATION DESIGN AND CONSTRUCTION. NEW YORK, WILEY, 1964.
749P.

1. FOUNDATIONS (BUILDING) I. TITLE.

711.4
(77311)
H45

Tomorrow's Chicago.
Hillman, Arthur, 1909-
Tomorrow's Chicago, by Arthur Hillman & Robert J. Casey. [Chicago, University of Chicago Press [1953]
x, 182 p. illus., maps. 24 cm.
Bibliography: p. [173]-177.

1. Cities and towns - Planning - Chicago.   I. Casey, Robert Joseph, 1890-   joint author.   II. Title.
Full name: William Arthur Hillman.

NA9127.C4H53   711.09773   53-6507

Library of Congress   [10]

R
058.7
(05)
U54

Tome, Martha, ed.
A Union list of serials in the libraries of the consortium of universities of the Metropolitan Washington area. Martha Tome, editor and Joseph T. Popecki, general editor. Washington, D.C., Distributed by Catholic University of America Press, 1967.
370p.

1. Periodicals - Direct. 2. Libraries - District of Columbia. I. Catholic University of America. II. Tome, Martha, ed. III. Popecki, Joseph T. ed. IV. Title.

325
(79494)
T65

Tomlinson, T M
Los Angeles Riot Study. Method: Negro reaction survey, by T. M. Tomlinson and Diana L. TenHouten. Los Angeles, Institute of Government and Public Affairs, University of California, 1967.
13p. (MR-95)
Contract with the Office of Economic Opportunity.
1. Minority groups - Los Angeles.
2. Social surveys - Los Angeles. 3. Race relations. 4. Social welfare - Los Angeles.
4. Employment - Negroes. I. TenHouten, Diana L., jt. au. II. California. University. (Cont'd on next card)

330
(762)
M47t

Mississippi. Economic Council.
Tomorrow's county. Jackson, 1967.
20p.

1. Economic development - Mississippi
2. County government - Mississippi.
I. Title.

691.542
B51e

Tomes, L   A   jt. au.
Blaine, Raymond Leonard, 1905-
Exploratory studies of early strength development in portland cement pastes and mortars, by R.L. Blaine and L.A. Tomes. Wash., U.S. National Bureau of Standards, 1970.
11p. (Building science series no. 28)

1. Portland cement. I. Tomes, L.A., jt. au. II. U.S. National Bureau of Standards. III. Title.

325
(79494)
T65

Tomlinson, T M   Los Angeles Riot
Study...1967.   (Card 2)

University at Los Angeles, Institute of Government and Public Affairs.   III. Title.

728.3
H21

TOMORROW'S HOME.
HEATH, ANNABELLE.
WHAT MRS. AMERICA WANTS IN TOMORROW'S HOME. WASHINGTON, HOUSING AND HOME FINANCE AGENCY, 1956.
9P.
ADDRESS BY MISS ANNABELLE HEATH, ASSISTANT ADMINISTRATOR, HHFA, AT THE FIFTH ANNUAL MEETING, BUILDING RESEARCH INSTITUTE, SHERATON-BROOK HOTEL, NIAGARA FALLS, ONTARIO.

1. HOUSE PLANS. I. TITLE.
II. TITLE: TOMORROW'S HOME.

728.3
N25

Tomorrow's house.
Nelson, George
   Tomorrow's house; a complete guide for the home-builder [by] George Nelson [and] Henry Wright. New York, Simon and Schuster, 1946 [c1945]
   214 p.   illus., diagrs.

1.Architecture, Domestic-Design. I.Wright, Henry, jt. au. II.Title.

330
C31

Tomorrow's trade.
Chase, Stuart
   When the war ends; guide lines to America's future as reported to the Twentieth Century Fund. New York, Twentieth Century Fund, 1942-1946.
   6 v.

   Contents.-v.1. The road we are travelling, 1914-1942.-v.2.Goals for America: A budget of our needs and resources.-v.3.Where's the money coming from? Problems of postwar finance.-v.4. Democracy under pressure: Special interests vs. the public welfare.-v.5.Tomorrow's trade: problems of our foreign commerce.-v.6. For this we fought.

VF
351.7
(016)
T65
1950

Tompkins, Dorothy C
   National defense in 1950—the Federal program; a selected bibliography. Berkeley, Calif., University of California, Bureau of Public Administration, Nov. 1950.
   37 l. (California. University. Bureau of Public Administration. Defense bibliographies no.1)

   Mimeographed.

I.Title. II.California. University. Bureau of Public Adminis-   tration.

658
Y68
1967

Tomorrow's management.
Young, John D
   Tomorrow's management. [An address at the] Civil Service Commission Executive Seminar on Management of Organizations, Kings Point, New York, Sept. 1, 1967. [n.p.] 1967.
   29p.

   1. Management. 2. Federal government. 3. Intergovernmental relations. 4. Automation. I. Civil Service Commission Executive Seminar on Management of Organizations, King Point, N.Y., 1967. II. Title.

388
S68

Tomorrow's transportation.
Southern Research Institute.
   Proceedings: Tomorrow's transportation, a conference on future technological trends, Sept. 29-30, 1960. Sponsored by Southern Research Institute. Birmingham, Ala., 1960.
   96p.

   1. Transportation. I. Title: Tomorrow's transportation.

362.6
T65S

TOMPKINS, DOROTHY C
   THE SENILE AGED PROBLEM IN THE UNITED STATES. BERKELEY, 1955.
   82P. (CALIFORNIA. UNIVERSITY. BUREAU OF PUBLIC ADMINISTRATION. LEGISLATIVE PROBLEMS NO. 1)

   BIBLIOGRAPHY: P.55-59.

   1. OLD AGE. I. TITLE.

331
(083.41)
L11t

Tomorrow's manpower needs.
U.S. Bureau of Labor Statistics.
   Tomorrow's manpower needs; national manpower projections and a guide to their use as a tool in developing state and area manpower projections. Wash., U.S. Dept. of Labor, Bureau of Labor Statistics, 1969.
   4v. (Its Bulletin no. 1606)
   Contents.-vol. I, Developing area manpower projections.-vol. II, National trends and outlook: industry employment and occupational structure.-vol. III, National trends and outlook: occupational employment. vol. IV, The national industry occupational matrix and other manpower data.
   (Cont'd on next card)

388
H68t

Tomorrow's transportation; new systems for the urban future.
U.S. Dept. of Housing and Urban Development.
   Tomorrow's transportation; new systems for the urban future. Wash., 1968.
   100p.

   1. Transportation. 2. Journey to work. I. Title.

353
(016)
T65S

TOMPKINS, DOROTHY C
   STATE AND LOCAL FINANCE AND TAXATION: A BIBLIOGRAPHY OF MATERIALS PUBLISHED 1941-1946. BERKELEY, BUREAU OF PUBLIC ADMINISTRATION, UNIVERSITY OF CALIFORNIA, 1946.
   97P. (CALIFORNIA. UNIVERSITY. BUREAU OF PUBLIC ADMINISTRATION. POSTWAR BIBLIOGRAPHIES NO. 2)

   SELECTION FROM THE FINANCE SECTION OF THE BUREAU OF PUBLIC ADMINISTRATION'S CATALOG.

   (CONTINUED ON NEXT CARD)

331
(083.41)
L11t

U.S. Bureau of Labor Statistics.
   Tomorrow's manpower needs...1969.
   (Card 2)

   1. Labor supply - Statistics. 2. Occupations - Statistics. 3. Employment - Statistics. I. Title.

388
H17

Tomorrow's transportation systems.
Harmon, George M   ed.
   Tomorrow's transportation systems. Proceedings of the 17th annual Transportation Conference and Salzberg Memorial Lecture of Syracuse University's College of Business Administration and College of Engineering. Syracuse, N.Y., Syracuse University, Business Research Center, 1965.
   71p. (Salzberg lecture series no. 17)

   1. Transportation. I. Syracuse University, Business Research Center. II. Title.
   (Series; Salzberg lecture series no. 17)

353
(016)
T65S

TOMPKINS, DOROTHY C. STATE AND LOCAL ...
1946.   (CARD 2)

   1. STATE FINANCE - BIBLIOGRAPHY. 2. LOCAL GOVERNMENT - FINANCE - BIBLIOGRAPHY. 3. TAXATION - BIBLIOGRAPHY. I. CALIFORNIA. UNIVERSITY. BUREAU OF PUBLIC ADMINISTRATION.

728.3
N25

TOMORROW'S SMALL HOUSE.
NEW YORK. MUSEUM OF MODERN ART.
   TOMORROW'S SMALL HOUSE. NEW YORK, N.D.
   20P.

   REPRINTED FROM THE BULLETIN OF THE MUSEUM OF MODERN ART, V. 12, NO. 5.

   1. ARCHITECTURE, DOMESTIC - DESIGNS AND PLANS. 2. HOUSE PLANS. I. TITLE.

551.4
(016)
G26

Tompkin, Jessie M
U.S. Geological Survey.
   Landslides; a selected annotated bibliography. Compiled by Jessie M. Tompkin and Severine H. Britt. Wash., 1965.
   53p. (Highway Research Board. Bibliography no. 10)
   Sponsored for publication by the Committee on Landslide Investigations of the Highway Research Board.

   1. Landslides - Bibl. I. Tompkin, Jessie M. II. Britt, Severine H. III. Highway Research Board.

353
(016)
T65

Tompkins, Dorothy C
   State government and administration; a bibliography, by Dorothy C. Tomkins, Bureau of Public Administration, University of California. Chicago Public Administration Service, 1954.
   269p.

   1. State government - Bibl. I. California. University. Bureau of Public Administration. II. Public Administration Service. III. Title.

325
L12t

Tomorrow's tomorrow: the black woman.
Ladner, Joyce A
   Tomorrow's tomorrow: the black woman. Garden City, N.Y., Doubleday, 1971.
   304p.

   Bibliography: p. 289-297.

   1. Negroes. 2. Woman. I. Title.

355.58
(016)
C15

Tompkins, Dorothy C.
California. University. Bureau of Public Administration.
   Civil defense in the states; a bibliography, compiled by Dorothy C. Tompkins. [Berkeley, Calif.] April 1953.
   56 p. (Its Defense bibliographies, no. 3)

   Processed.

   1.Civilian defense-Bibl. I.Tompkins, Dorothy C. II.Title.

331.892
(016)
T65

Tompkins, Dorothy C   comp.
   Strikes by public employees and professional personnel: a bibliography. Berkeley, Institute of Governmental Studies, University of California, 1967.
   92p.

   1. Strikes - Bibl. 2. Labor relations - Bibl. I. Californai. University. Institute of Governmental Studies. II. Title.

728.1
(05)
T65

Tomorrow's Town, v.1, no.1 - v.6, no.2. New York, National Committee on the Housing Emergency, Inc., Apr. 1943 - Mar. 1948.
   51 pts. in 1.   illus.

   1.Housing-Period. 2.Public housing. I.National Committee on the Housing Emergency, Inc.

VF
351.1
.C15

Tompkins, Dorothy C   comp.
California. University. Bureau of Public Administration.
   Loyalty-security programs for federal employees, a selected bibliography, compiled by Dorothy C. Tompkins. Berkeley, Calif., Dec. 1955.
   69p.

360
(016)
C15

TOMPKINS, DOROTHY CAMPBELL.
CALIFORNIA. UNIVERSITY. INSTITUTE OF GOVERNMENTAL STUDIES.
   WHITE COLLAR CRIME - A BIBLIOGRAPHY, COMPILED BY DOROTHY CAMPBELL TOMPKINS. BERKELEY, 1967.
   85P.

   1. SOCIAL CONDITIONS - BIBLIOGRAPHY. I. TOMPKINS, DOROTHY CAMPBELL. II. TITLE.

347
S15
Tompkins, John S   jt. au.
Salerno, Ralph.
    The crime confederation; Cosa Nostra and
allied operations in organized crime, by
Ralph Salerno and John S. Tompkins. Garden
City, N.Y., Doubleday, 1969.
    424p.

    1. Law enforcement. I. Tompkins, John S.,
jt. au. II. Title. III. Title: Cosa Nostra
and allied operations.

711.4
(769685)
T65
                Tompkinsville, Ky. Planning Commission.
Kentucky. Dept. of Commerce. Div. of
    Planning and Zoning.
    General plan, Tompkinsville, Kentucky.
[Prepared for Tompkinsville Planning Com-
mission] Corbin, Ky., 1963.
    84p.

    1. Master plan - Tompkinsville, Ky.
I. Tompkinsville, Ky. Planning Commission.
II. U.S. URA-UPAP. Tompkinsville, Ky.

LAW
T
T657ar
        Tomson, Bernard, 1909-
    Architectural & engineering law ₁by₁ Bernard Tomson &
Norman Coplan. 2d ed. New York, Reinhold Pub. Corp.
₁1967₁
    x, 382 p. 24 cm.

                Law and legislation
    1. Architects — Legal status, laws, etc. — U. S. 2. Engineers
Legal status, laws, etc.—U. S.   I. Coplan, Norman, joint author.
II. Title. *Law and legislation*

    KF2925.T6 1967   340   67-27161
    Library of Congress   ₅₁

711.4
(79728)
T65
            Tonasket, Wash. Planning Commission.
Joint Planning Office, Wenatchee, Wash.
    Comprehensive plan, town of Tonasket,
[Washington] [Prepared for Town of Tonasket
Planning Commission] Wenatchee, Wash., 1964.
    30p.
    Prepared in cooperation with Washington
State Department of Commerce and Economic
Development.
    U.S. Urban Renewal Adm. UPAP.

    1. Master plan - Tonasket, Wash.
I. Tonasket, Wash. Planning Commission.
II. U.S.   URA-UPAP.
Tonasket,   Wash.

339.5
(7449)
M17s
        Toner, R   C
    Marine Research Foundation.
    A summary of the study of the marine
resources of Barnstable County,
Massachusetts, by G. C. Matthiessen [and]
R. C. Toner. [Prepared for Division of
Planning, Massachusetts Department of
Commerce] Edgartown, Mass. [1963?]
    31p.
    Cape Cod planning program: a sector of
the Massachusetts State plan.
    U.S. Urban Renewal Adm. UPAP.

                (Continued on
                next card)

339.5
(7449)
M17s
        Marine Research Foundation. A summary of
    the study of the marine resources of
    Barnstable County...[1963?] (Card 2)

    1. Natural resources - Barnstable Co.,
Mass. 2. State planning - Mass.
I. Matthiessen, G. C. II. Toner, R. C.
III. U.S. URA-UPAP. Barnstable Co.,
Mass.

510
T65
    TONER, JAMES V
        MATHEMATICS OF FINANCE.   NEW YORK,
    N.Y., RONALD PRESS, C1926.
    142P.

    1. MATHEMATICS.   I. TITLE.

658.564
R156A
        TONGE, F   M
    RAND CORP.
        SOME REFLECTIONS ON A SURVEY OF
    RESEARCH PROBLEMS IN COMPUTER SOFTWARE,
    BY F.M. TONGE. SANTA MONICA, CALIF.,
    1965.
        22P. (ITS MEMORANDUM RM-4467-PR.
    AD 614 417)

        1. AUTOMATION.   I. TITLE.
    I. TONGE, F.M.

020
E92
    Tonks, Peter, jt. au.
Eyre, John.
    Computers and systems; an introduction for
librarians, by John Eyre and Peter Tonks.
Hamden, Conn., Linnet Books, 1971.
    127p.

    Bibliography: p. 123-124.

    1. Library science - Automation. I. Tonks,
Peter, jt. au. II. Title.

728.1
(47)
T65
    Tonsky, D   G
    Développement et efficacité économique
de la construction des maisons en grands
panneaux en URSS. Moscou, Centre d'Information
Technique et Scientifique pour la Construction
civile et l'Architecture, 1967.
    29p.

    1. Housing - USSR. 2. Panels.

711.4
W42
    Tony Garnier: the Cite industrielle.
Wiebenson, Dora.
    Tony Garnier: the Cite industrielle.
New York, Braziller, 1969.
    127p. (Planning and cities)

    Bibliography: p. 117-121.

    1. City planning. 2. Industrial districts.
3. Garnier, Tony. Une cite industrielle.
I. Title.

301.15
B67t
    Too many; a study of earth's biological
        limitations.
Borgstrom, Georg.
    Too many; a study of earth's biological
limitations. London, MacMillan, 1969.
    368p.

    Bibliography: p. 351-357.

    1. Man - Influence of environment.
2. Natural resources. I. Title.

LAW
T
T664c
    Tooke, Charles Wesley, 1870-
    Cases on the law of municipal corporations, by Charles W.
Tooke ... 1931 ed. (2d printing, 1933) Chicago, The Foun-
dation press, inc. ₁1933₁ °1931.
    xiii, 896 p. 25½ᵐ. ₁OCH university casebook series₁
    Published 1926 under title: A selection of cases on the law of munici-
pal corporations.

    1. Municipal corporations—Cases. 2. Municipal corporations—U. S.
I. Title.
                                37-8051
    Library of Congress   ₂₁

698
026
    Tooke, W   Raymond.
Georgia. State Engineering Experiment Station.
    Coatings adherence measurement by an angular
scribe-stripping technique, by W. R. Tooke,
and Jose R. Montalvo. Atlanta, 1966.
    12p. (Its Reprint no. 178)

    Reprinted from Journal of paint technology,
Jan. 1966. p. 18-28.

    1. Paints and painting. 2. Varnish and
varnishing. 3. Veneers. I. Montalvo, Jose R.
II. Tooke, W.   Raymond.
III. Journal of   paint technology.
IV. Title.

362.6
H21t
            A tool for community action.
    U.S. Dept. of Health, Education and Welfare.
        Administration on Aging.
        A tool for community action. Title III
    of the Older Americans act. Wash., 1968.
        14p. (Its AoA publication no. 258)
        Cover title: Communities in action for
    older Americans; a report of progress under
    Title III of the Older Americans act.
        1. Old age. 2. Social welfare. I. Title:
    Communities in action for older Americans.
    II. Title.

690.591
S231
    TOOLS.
    SCHAEFER, CLEMENS THOMAS, 1886-
        THE HANDY MAN'S HANDBOOK; A HANDBOOK
    ON GENERAL MECHANICAL OPERATIONS,
    INCLUDING WOOD, METAL, ELECTRICAL, AND
    PLUMBING WORK. TOOLS, THEIR USE AND
    ABUSE; FOR THE HANDY MAN IN THE HOME,
    APARTMENT, OR PUBLIC BUILDINGS, ON THE
    FARM, AND IN THE FACTORY. 9TH ED.
    NEW YORK, HARPER, 1931.
        273P.

        1. HOUSES - MAINTENANCE AND
    MODERNIZATION. 2. TOOLS.
    I. TITLE.

621.9
U54c
    TOOLS.
    U.K. Dept. of the Environment.
        Care of small plant and hand tools. 3d ed.
    London, H.M.S.O., 1971.
        folder. (Advisory leaflet no. 22)

        1. Tools. I. Title.

621.9
U54po
    TOOLS.
    U.K. Dept. of the Environment.
        Powered hand tools 1: electric tools. 2d ed.
    rev. London, H.M.S.O., 1971.
        folder. (Advisory leaflet no. 18)

        1. Tools. 2. Electric apparatus and appli-
    ances. I. Title.

621.9
U54p
1971
    TOOLS.
    U.K. Dept. of the Environment.
        Powered hand tools 3; safety and maintenance.
    2d ed. rev. London, H.M.S.O., 1971.
        folder. (Advisory leaflet no. 20)

        1. Tools. 2. Building construction -
    Accidents. I. Title.

VF
1690
U54ca
    Tools.
    U.K. Ministry of Public Building and Works.
        Care of builders' tools. London, 1969.
        folder. (Its Advisory leaflet 33)

        1. Building construction. 2. Tools.
    I. Title.

621.9
U54
    Tools.
    U.K. Ministry of Public Buildings and Works.
        Pneumatic tools; powered hand tools 2. 2d ed.
    London, H.M.S.O., 1969.
        folder. (Its Advisory leaflet no. 19)

        1. Tools. I. Title: Powered hand tools
    II. Title.

341.1
:338
A32v
Tools.
U.S. Agency for International Development.
(Communications Resources Div.)
Village technology handbook. Washington,
1964.
2v.   (Its C-11-12)

1. Technical assistance programs.
2. Water-supply. 3. Tools. I. Title.
II. Title: Technology handbook.

301.15
H85
TOP LEADERSHIP.
HUNTER, FLOYD.
TOP LEADERSHIP, U.S.A. CHAPEL HILL,
UNIVERSITY OF NORTH CAROLINA PRESS,
1959.
268P.

1. COMMUNITY STRUCTURE.
2. PERSONNEL MANAGEMENT.   I. TITLE.

711.4
(781631)
T66p
Topeka-Shawnee County (Kan.) Regional
Planning Commission.
Parks, recreation areas and open spaces.
Topeka, Kan., 1962.
174p.   (Master plan report no. 2)

1. Master plan - Topeka-Shawnee Co., Kan.
2. Parks - Topeka-Shawnee Co., Kan.
3. Open space land. I. Title.

621.9
U54p
TOOLS.
U.K. Ministry of Public Building and Works.
Powered hand tools 3; safety and maintenance.
2d ed. London, H.M.S.O., 1970.
folder. (Advisory leaflet no. 20)

1. Tools. 2. Building construction -
Accidents. I. Title.

351.1
C657to
1971
H-H
Top-level positions for economic stabilization
program.
U.S. Congress. House. Committee on Post
Office and Civil Service.
Top-level positions for economic stabiliza-
tion program. Hearing before the Subcommittee
on Manpower and Civil Service... Ninety-second
Congress, first session on H.R. 11902, a bill
to provide for additional positions in grades
GS-16, 17, and 18, to carry out the functions
of the Economic stabilization act of 1970.
Wash., Govt. Print. Off., 1971.
39p.

1. Federal civil service. I. Title.

956
TOPEKA-SHAWNEE COUNTY (KAN.) REGIONAL
PLANNING COMMISSION.
TOPEKA AREA PLANNING STUDY, ECONOMIC
BASE REPORT.
PREPARED BY LARRY SMITH AND COMPANY.
TOPEKA, 1969.
1 V. (HUD 701 REPORT)

1. REGIONAL PLANNING—TOPEKA, KAN.
2. ECONOMIC BASE STUDIES - TOPEKA, KAN.
I. SMITH (LARRY) AND CO.   II. HUD
701, TOPEKA, KAN.

VF
621.9
L11
Tools.
U.S. Bureau of Labor Standards.
Use hammers the safe way. Washington, 1951.
12p. illus. (U.S. Dept. of Labor Bulletin
no. 127)

1. Tools.

658.1
H6b
TOP-MANAGEMENT ORGANIZATION AND
CONTROL.
HOLDEN, PAUL EUGENE, 1893-
TOP-MANAGEMENT ORGANIZATION AND
CONTROL; A RESEARCH STUDY OF THE
MANAGEMENT POLICIES AND PRACTICES OF
THIRTY-ONE LEADING INDUSTRIAL
CORPORATIONS, CONDUCTED UNDER THE
AUSPICES OF THE GRADUATE SCHOOL OF
BUSINESS, STANFORD UNIVERSITY, BY PAUL
E. HOLDEN ... LOUNSBURY S. FISH ...
AND HUBERT L. SMITH ... STANFORD
UNIVERSITY, CALIF., STANFORD UNIVERSITY
PRESS; LONDON, H. MILFORD, OXFORD
UNIVERSITY PRES S, C1941.
239P.
(CONTINUED ON NEXT CARD)

312
C6bT
TOPICAL INDEX OF POPULATION CENSUS
REPORTS.
U.S. BUREAU OF THE CENSUS.
TOPICAL INDEX OF POPULATION CENSUS
REPORTS, 1900-1930. WASH., 1934.
76P.

1. CENSUS - POPULATION.   I. TITLE.
II. TITLE: INDEX OF POPULATION CENSUS
REPORTS, 1900-1930.

621.9
W17
Tools.
U.S. War Department.
Maintenance and care of hand tools.
Washington, Govt. Print. Off., April 19, 1945.
116 p. illus. (Its Technical manual
TM 9-867)

1.Tools. I.Title.

658.1
H65
HOLDEN, PAUL EUGENE, 1893-
TOP-MANAGEMENT ORGANIZATION ...1941.
(CARD 2)

1. CORPORATIONS.   2. INDUSTRY.
I. FISH, LOUNSBURY SPAIGHT, JT. AU.
II. SMITH, HUBERT L., JT. AU.
III. TITLE.

711.14
U54t
Topographical planning design processes.
U.K. National Coal Board.
Topographical planning design processes:
first special process. [n.p.] [1970?]
v.
Cover title: Planning the design of
settled topographies: means of thinking
creatively about realities as features of
localities.

1. Land use. 2. Landscape architecture.
I. Title.

621.9
W15
Tools.
Wander, R
Cartridge-operated fixing tools; some safe-
ty considerations. Garston, Eng., Building
Research Station, Ministry of Technology,
1967.
7p. (U.K. Building Research Station.
Building research current papers. Construc-
tion series 36)
Reprinted from: The Illustrated carpenter
and builder, 1967, vol. 156 (Jan. 27) p. 194-6.
1. Tools. 2. Building construction - Accidents.
I. U.K. Building   Research Station.
II. Title.

Topeka, Kansas

VF:
Parking

624.131
S64t
A toposequence of soils in tonalite..
U.S. Soil Conservation Service.
A toposequence of soils in tonalite grus
in the Southern California peninsular range,
by Wiley D. Nettleton and others. Wash.,
1968.
41p. (U.S. Dept. of Agriculture. Soil
survey investigations report no. 21)

1. Soils. I. Nettleton, Wiley D.
II. Title.

331.2
F69
TOP EXECUTIVE COMPENSATION.
FOX, HARLAND.
TOP EXECUTIVE COMPENSATION, BY HARLAND
FOX. NEW YORK, 1964.
77P. (NATIONAL INDUSTRIAL CONFERENCE
BOARD PERSONNEL POLICY STUDY NO. 193)

1. WAGES AND SALARIES.   2. MANAGEMENT.
I. NATIONAL INDUSTRIAL CONFERENCE BOARD.
II. TITLE.

728.1
:336.18
(78161)
T66
TOPEKA, KAN. HOUSING AUTHORITY.
REPORT, 1 - 3d
TOPEKA, 1962-64
2 V. ANNUAL.
1961162-2c,
1961164
1. PUBLIC HOUSING - TOPEKA, KAN.

711.4
(7445)
T66
Topsfield, Mass. Planning Board.
Technical Planning Associates, New Haven,
Conn.
Master plan for Topsfield, Massachusetts.
[Prepared for Topsfield Planning Board and
Massachusetts Department of Commerce] New
Haven, 1961.
1v.

U.S. Urban Renewal Adm. UPAP.

1. Master plan - Topsfield, Mass.
I. Topsfield,   Mass. Planning
Board. II. U.S.   URA-UPAP.
Topsfield,   Mass.

658
S74
TOP MANAGEMENT ORGANIZATION IN
DIVISIONALIZED COMPANIES.
STIEGLITZ, HAROLD.
TOP MANAGEMENT ORGANIZATION IN
DIVISIONALIZED COMPANIES, BY HAROLD
STIEGLITZ AND ALLEN R. JANGER. NEW YORK,
1965.
188P. (NATIONAL INDUSTRIAL CONFERENCE
BOARD. STUDIES IN PERSONNEL POLICY NO.
195)

1. MANAGEMENT.   I. JANGER, ALLEN R.,
JT. AU.   II. NATIONAL INDUSTRIAL
CONFERENCE BOARD.   III. TITLE.

FOLIO
711.4
(781631)
T66
Topeka-Shawnee County (Kan.) Regional
Planning Commission.
Neighborhood analysis for the Topeka-
Shawnee County Regional Planning Area.
[Prepared in cooperation with] Topeka-
Shawnee County, Kan. Board of Commis-
sioners. Topeka, Kan., 1965.
1v.   (Master plan report 5)
U.S. Urban Renewal Adm. UPAP.

1. Master plan - Topeka-Shawnee Co.,Kan.
2. Neighborhood rehabilitation - Topeka-
Shawnee Co.   Kan. I. U.S. URA-
UPAP.   Topeka-Shawnee Co.,
Kan.

711.4
(7445)
T66
summary
Topsfield, Mass. Planning Board.
Technical Planning Associates, New Haven,
Conn.
Master plan summary report, Topsfield,
Massachusetts. Prepared for Topsfield
Planning Board and Massachusetts Department
of Commerce New Haven, 1961.
6p.

U.S. Urban Renewal Adm. UPAP.

1. Master plan - Topsfield, Mass.
I. Topsfield,   Mass. Planning
Board.   II. U.S. URA-UPAP.
Topsfield,   Mass.

658
T67

Torgersen, Paul E
    A concept of organization. New York, American Book-Van Nostrand-Reinhold, 1969.
    173p.

    1. Management. I. Title. II. Title: Organization.

030.8
(46)
L17

Toro y Gisbert, Miguel de.
    Larousse, Pierre, 1817-1875.
    Pequeño Larousse ilustrado, por Miguel de Toro y Gisbert... refundido y aumentado por Ramón García-Pelayo y Gross. 60.000 artículos, 5.000 ilustraciones en negro, 100 mapas, 75 grabados en color. 3ª tirada. Paris, Editorial Larousse, 1967.
    1664p.

    1. Spanish language - Dictionaries - English.
    2. English language - Dictionaries - Spanish.
    I. Toro y Gisbert, Miguel de. II. García-Pelayo y Gross, Ramon, ed. III. Title.

728.1
:336.18
(713541)
T67H
1947/64

TORONTO. HOUSING AUTHORITY.
    THE HOUSING AUTHORITY OF TORONTO OPENS THE DOOR TO BETTER LIVING: A REVIEW OF PROGRESS 1947-1964.
    TORONTO, 1964.
    32P.

    1. PUBLIC HOUSING - TORONTO.
    2. TORONTO. HOUSING AUTHORITY.

657
M67

TORGERSON, HAROLD W
    MORTGAGE BANKERS ASSOCIATION OF AMERICA.
    HOME-STUDY SYLLABUS FOR ANALYSIS OF FINANCIAL STATEMENTS. A CORRESPONDENCE COURSE BY HAROLD W. TORGERSON, 1955. REV. 1963. CHICAGO, 1963.
    1 V.

    1. ACCOUNTING. I. TORGERSON, HAROLD W.
    II. TITLE.

Toronto.
    see also
Municipality of Metropolitan Toronto.

728.1
:336.18
(713541)
T67H
1947/65

TORONTO. HOUSING AUTHORITY.
    THE HOUSING AUTHORITY OF TORONTO PROVIDES BETTER LIVING FOR OUR COMMUNITY: A REVIEW OF PROGRESS 1947-1965. TORONTO, 1965.
    32P.

    1. PUBLIC HOUSING - TORONTO.
    2. TORONTO. HOUSING AUTHORITY.

658.564
045

TORGERSON, PAUL E
    OKLAHOMA. STATE UNIVERSITY. OFFICE OF ENGINEERING RESEARCH, STILLWATER.
    A DIGITAL COMPUTER SOLUTION TO THE TRANSIT OPERATOR ASSIGNMENT PROBLEM, BY PAUL E. TORGERSON AND SAMY E.G. ELIAS. STILLWATER, OKLA., 1961.
    45L. (ITS ENGINEERING REPORT NO. 120)

    1. AUTOMATION. 2. TRANSPORTATION.
    I. TORGERSON, PAUL E. II. ELIAS, SAMY E.G. III. TITLE.

711.585
(71)
T67

Toronto, Ont. Advisory Committee on the Urban Renewal Study.
    Urban renewal; a study of the city of Toronto, 1956. Toronto, 1956.
    1 v. (various pagings) illus., plans.

    For summary statement see: Community Planning Association of Canada. Urban renewal; a study of the city of Toronto, 1956.
    VF 711.585 (71) C65

    1. Urban renewal - Toronto, Ont.

728.1
:336.18
(713541)
T67H
1947/64

TORONTO. HOUSING AUTHORITY.
    TORONTO. HOUSING AUTHORITY.
    THE HOUSING AUTHORITY OF TORONTO OPENS THE DOOR TO BETTER LIVING: A REVIEW OF PROGRESS 1947-1964. TORONTO, 1964.
    32P.

    1. PUBLIC HOUSING - TORONTO.
    2. TORONTO. HOUSING AUTHORITY.

551.5
S45

Torn land.
Simpson, Paige Shoaf.
    Torn land, by Paige Shoaf Simpson and Jerry H. Simpson, Jr. Lynchburg, Va., Bell Co., 1970.
    429p.

    1. Storms. 2. Disaster services.
    I. Simpson, Jerry H., Jr., jt. au. I. Title.

711.4
(713541)
T67RE

TORONTO. CITY PLANNING BOARD.
    REPORT, 1943-47

    TORONTO, 1944-48

    4 V.

    1. CITY PLANNING - TORONTO.

728.1
:336.18
(713541)
T67H
1947/65

TORONTO. HOUSING AUTHORITY.
    TORONTO. HOUSING AUTHORITY.
    THE HOUSING AUTHORITY OF TORONTO PROVIDES BETTER LIVING FOR OUR COMMUNITY: A REVIEW OF PROGRESS 1947-1965. TORONTO, 1965.
    32P.

    1. PUBLIC HOUSING - TORONTO.
    2. TORONTO. HOUSING AUTHORITY.

361
(7443)
N17

TORNADO IN WORCESTER.
    NATIONAL RESEARCH COUNCIL. COMMITTEE ON DISASTER STUDIES.
    TORNADO IN WORCESTER; AN EXPLORATORY STUDY OF INDIVIDUAL AND COMMUNITY BEHAVIOR IN AN EXTREME SITUATION, BY ANTHONY F.C. WALLACE. WASHINGTON, NATIONAL RESEARCH COUNCIL, 1956.
    166P. (ITS DISASTER STUDIES NO. 3)

    1. DISASTER SERVICES - WORCESTER, MASS. I. WALLACE, ANTHONY F.R.
    II. TITLE.

690.091.82
(713)
T67

Toronto, Can. Council.
    A by-law to regulate the erection and provide for the safety of buildings, no. 9868. (Approved by the Ontario Municipal Board by Order no. P.F.B. 765, dated Feb. 25, 1942, pursuant to Section 3 of the City of Toronto Act, 1939) Toronto, 1950.
    300 p.

    Enacted Dec. 1923, rev. to Feb. 1947.

    1. Building codes-Canada.

728.1
(485)
T67

Toronto. Metropolitan Housing Authority.
    Housing in Sweden. [Prepared in cooperation with] Ontario Association of Housing Authorities, and the National Board of Housing, Sweden. Toronto, 1962.
    39p.

    1. Housing - Sweden. 2. Housing - Netherlands. 3. Housing - Denmark.
    I. Sweden. National Board of Housing.
    II. Ontario Association of Housing Authorities.

Tornadoes

    see

Storms
Wind resistance

386
(713541)
T67p

Toronto. Harbour Commissioners.
    The port of Toronto story. Toronto, Trade Development Dept., [1962?]
    8p.

    1. Harbors - Canada - Toronto.
    I. Title.

728.1
(41)
T67

Toronto. Metropolitan Housing Authority.
    Housing in the United Kingdom. [Prepared in cooperation with] Ontario Association of Housing Authorities, and the British Ministry of Housing and Local Government. Toronto, 1962.
    81p.

    1. Housing - U.K. I. Ontario Association of Housing Authorities. II. U.K. Ministry of Housing and Local Government.

551.5
W45

TORNADOES.
    U.S. WEATHER BUREAU.
    TORNADOES. WASHINGTON, GOVT. PRINT. OFF., 1965.
    13P. ILLUS.

    1. STORMS. I. TITLE.

386
(713541)
T67

Toronto. Harbour Commissioners.
    Report, 1965

    Toronto, 1966

    1 v. annual.

    For Library holdings see main entry.

    1. Harbors - Canada - Toronto.

728.1
:336.18
(71)
T67

Toronto. Metropolitan Housing Authority.
    Relating public housing abroad to Canadian public housing. [Prepared in cooperation with] Ontario Association of Housing Authorities and the British Ministry of Housing and Local Government.
    Toronto, 1962.
    46p.

    1. Public housing - Canada. 2. Housing - U.K.
    3. Housing - Sweden. 4. Mortgage finance - Canada. I. Ontario Association of Housing Authorities. II. U.K. Ministry of Housing and Local Government.

728.1
:336.18　Toronto.　Metropolitan Housing Authority.
(713541)　　Report,
T67　　　　Toronto,
　　　　　　　v.　illus.　annual.

For complete information see shelflist.

1. Public housing - Toronto.

728.1
:336.18　　Toronto.　Metropolitan Housing Authority.
(713541)　　The social implications of public
T67s　　housing in metropolitan Toronto, 1963.
　　　　　　93p.

　　　　　1. Public housing - Social effect -
　　　　Toronto metropolitan area.　I. Title.

388　　　Toronto.
(713541)　Metropolitan Toronto and Region Transportation
T67g　　Study.
　　　　Growth and travel, past and present; a study
　　of the basic components of growth in the
　　Toronto-centered region, and their relation-
　　ship to travel characteristics and demand.
　　Toronto, 1966.
　　　　94p.
　　　On cover: First report of a series.
　　　1. Transportation - Canada - Toronto.
　　2. Canada -　　　　　Transportation. 3. Jour-
　　ney to work.　　　　I. Title.

VF　　Toronto.　Metropolitan Toronto Council.
.301.15
(713541)　Allen, William R
A55　　　　An address by William R. Allen, Q.C.,
　　　　Chairman of Metropolitan Toronto Council,
　　　　to the Advertising and Sales Club of
　　　　Toronto.　Toronto, 1968.
　　　　10p.

　　　　　1. City growth - Canada - Toronto.
　　I. Metropolitan Toronto Council.
　　II. Advertising and Sales Club, Toronto.

　　　　Toronto.　Municipal Council.
711.585
(718)　　Project Planning Associates, Toronto.
P76　　City of St. John's (Newfoundland) urban
　　　　renewal study.　Prepared for the Municipal
　　　　Council.　Toronto, Maclean-Hunter, 1961.
　　　　84p.

　　　　　1. Urban renewal - Newfoundland.
　　I. Toronto.　　　　　Municipal Council.

711.3　　Toronto.　Bureau of Municipal Research.
(71)　　　The centennial study and training programme
T67cen　　on metropolitan problems.　Report of the
　　　　Seminar-Conference stage held in Toronto, Aug.
　　6-16, 1967.　Toronto, 1967.
　　　　57p.

　　　　1. City growth - Canada. 2. Canada - City
　　growth. 3. Metropolitan areas.　I. Title.

711.3　　Toronto.　Bureau of Municipal Research.
T67c　　　The centennial study and training programme
　　　　on metropolitan problems.　Toronto, 1968.
　　　　[8]p.
　　　　Prepared with the co-operation of the
　　　United Nations Public Administration Branch.

　　　　1. City growth. 2. Metropolitan areas.
　　I. United Nations. II. Title.

352　　Toronto.　Bureau of Municipal Research.
G67　　Gorynski, Juliusz.
　　　　The functional metropolis and systems of
　　government, by Juliusz Gorynski and Zygmunt
　　Rybiki. Toronto, Bureau of Municipal Research,
　　1967.
　　　　59p. (Toronto. Bureau of Municipal
　　Research. Paper no. 2)
　　　　1. Metropolitan government. 2. Intergovern-
　　mental relations. 3. Public administration. I. Rybiki
　　Zygmut, jt. au. II. Toronto. Bureau of Municipal
　　Research. III. Title.

　　　　Toronto. Bureau of Municipal Research.
728.1
S19　　Sazanami, Hidehiko.
　　　　Housing in metropolitan areas. Toronto,
　　Bureau of Municipal Research, 1967.
　　　　91p. (Toronto.　Bureau of Municipal Research.
　　Paper no. 10)
　　　　At head of title: Centennial study and
　　training programme on metropolitan problems.
　　　　1. Housing. 2. Metropolitan areas.
　　I. Toronto. Bureau of Municipal Research.
　　II. Title.

　　　　Toronto. Bureau of Municipal Research.
352
D86　　Dupré, J　　　Stefan.
　　　　Intergovernmental relations and the metro-
　　politan area. Toronto, Bureau of Municipal
　　Research, 1967.
　　　　39p. (Toronto.　Bureau of Municipal
　　Research. Paper no. 5)

　　　　At head of title: Centennial study and
　　training programme on metropolitan problems.

　　　　1. Intergovernmental relations.
　　2. Metropolitan areas.　3. Metropolitan govern-
　　ments. I. Toronto.　Bureau of Municipal
　　Research.　　　II. Title.

　　　　Toronto. Bureau of Municipal Research.
388
K14m　　Kain, John F
　　　　Metropolitan area transportation. Toronto,
　　Bureau of Municipal Research, 1967.
　　　　62p. (Toronto. Bureau of Municipal
　　Research. Paper no. 6)

　　　　Centennial Study and Training Programme
　　on Metropolitan Problems.

　　　　1. Transportation. 2. Journey to work.
　　I. Toronto.　Bureau of Municipal Research.
　　II. Title.

　　　　Toronto. Bureau of Municipal Re-
　　　　　　　search.
711.14
(713541)　Civic affairs.
C48　　　Municipalities as landlords and land
　　development partners.　Toronto, Bureau
　　of Municipal Research, 1967.
　　　　14p.
　　　　Entire issue: Nov., 1967.

　　　　1. Land use - Toronto. 2. Real
　　property - Toronto. I. Toronto. Bureau
　　of Municipal Research. II. Title.

VF　　Toronto. Bureau of Municipal Research.
352
(713541)　Neighbourhood participation in local
T67n　　government; a study of the City of Toronto.
　　　　Toronto, 1970.
　　　　15p.
　　　　Civic affairs, Jan., 1970.

　　　　1. Local government - Can. - Toronto.
　　2. Community development - Citizen
　　participation. I. Civic affairs.
　　II. Title.

388　　Toronto.　Bureau of Municipal Research.
(713541)　Transportation. Who plans? Who pays?
T67t　　Toronto, 1970.
　　　　24p.

　　　　Civic affairs, Autumn, 1970.

　　　　1. Transportation - Toronto. I. Title.
　　II. Civic affairs.

　　　　Toronto.　Planning Board.
　　　　see also　Municipality of Metropolitan Toronto.
(Planning Board)

728.2
(713541)　Toronto.　Planning Board.
J67　　　Apartment survey, 1961.　Toronto, 1962.
　　　　14p.

　　　　　1. Apartment houses - Toronto.
　　I. Title.

711.4
(713541)　Toronto.　Planning Board.
T67c　　　The changing city; a forecast of plan-
　　ning issues for the City of Toronto, 1956-
　　1980.　Toronto, 1959.
　　　　48p.　Illus., diagrs., maps.

　　　　1. City planning - Toronto.

711.5
(713541)　TORONTO. PLANNING BOARD.
1347)　A GUIDE TO THE REVISED RESIDENTIAL
T67G　　ZONING STANDARDS.　TORONTO, 1956.
　　　　26P.

　　　　1. ZONING LEGISLATION - TORONTO.

308
:728.1　Toronto.　Planning Board.
(713541)　The market for new housing in the
T67　　Metropolitan Toronto area.　Prepared by
　　Housing Research Section, Research Division,
　　Metropolitan Toronto Planning Board.
　　Toronto, 1962.
　　　　35p.

　　　　1. Housing market - Toronto.
　　2. Metropolitan areas - Toronto.

711.4
(713541)　TORONTO.　CITY PLANNING BOARD.
T67M　　THE MASTER PLAN FOR THE CITY OF
　　TORONTO AND ENVIRONS... TORONTO, 1943.
　　8L.

　　　　1. MASTER PLAN - TORONTO.

352
(713541)　Toronto.　Planning Board.
T67　　　Metropolitan Toronto 1967; prepared for
1967　　the Metropolitan Toronto Council by the
　　staff of the Metropolitan Toronto Planning
　　Board. 1967. [n.p.] 1967.
　　　　36p.

　　　　1. Metropolitan government - Toronto.
　　2. Community facilities - Toronto.
　　3. Statistics - Toronto. I. Title.

352
(713541)
T67
1970

Toronto. Planning Board.
Metropolitan Toronto 1970. Prepared
for the Metropolitan Toronto Council by
the staff of the Metropolitan Toronto
Planning Board. Toronto, 1970.
36p.

1. Metropolitan government - Toronto.
2. Community facilities - Toronto.
I. Title.

711.581
(713541)
T67e

Toronto. Planning Board.
Plan for Eglinton. Toronto, 1964.
23p.
On cover: Draft.
1. Neighborhood planning - Canada - Toronto.
2. Canada - Neighborhood planning. I. Title:
Eglinton. II. Title.

711.729
:308
T67

Toronto. Planning Board.
Report on the residential parking survey.
Toronto, 1966.
3p.
Report to Committee on Buildings and
Development.
File no. 02.20.05.
Includes Apartment parking survey questionnaire.

1. Parking - Surveys. I. Title: Residential
parking survey.

388
(713541)
T67

Toronto. Planning Board.
Metropolitan Toronto transportation
research program. Prepared by the
Metropolitan Toronto Planning Board.
Consultants: Traffic Research Corporation
(K.C.S. Ltd) Toronto, 1962.
79p. (Report no. 1)
Bibliography: p. i-iii.

1. Transportation - Toronto.
2. Journey to work.

711.581
(713541)
T67r

Toronto. Planning Board.
Plan for Rosedale. Toronto, 1960.
12p.

1. Neighborhood planning - Canada - Toronto.
2. Canada - Neighborhood planning. I. Title:
Rosedale. II. Title.

711.5
(713541)
T67

Toronto. Planning Board.
Residential zoning. Proposed revision
of standards. Toronto, 1956.
22p.

1. Zoning - Toronto. I. Title.

711.4
(713541)
T67o

Toronto. Planning Board.
The official plan of the Metropolitan
Toronto planning area. Toronto, 1959.
272p. maps, tables.

"Draft."

1. Master plan - Toronto.

711.581
(713541)
T67d

Toronto. Planning Board.
Plan for the Don. Toronto, 1963.
24p.

1. Neighborhood planning - Canada - Toronto.
2. Canada - Neighborhood planning. I. Title:
The Don. II. Title.

711.5
(713541
:347)
T67

TORONTO. PLANNING BOARD.
RESIDENTIAL ZONING STANDARDS:
ILLUSTRATED GUIDE. TORONTO, 1956.
18P.

1. ZONING LEGISLATION - TORONTO.
I. TITLE.

711.3
(713541)
T67
Suppl.

Toronto. Planning Board.
Official plan of the Metropolitan Toronto
Planning Area. Toronto, 1965.
19p.
...... Supplement. Toronto, 1965
22p.

1. Master plan - Canada - Toronto.
2. Canada - Master plan. I. Title.

711.4
(713541)
T67p

Toronto. Planning Board.
Proposed plan for Toronto. Toronto, 1967.
4pts.
Contents.-pt. 1. Proposals for a new plan
for Toronto.-pt. 2. Review of submissions.-pt.
3. Proposed plan for Toronto.-pt.4. Submissions received.

1. City planning - Canada - Toronto.
2. Canada - City planning. I. Title.

711.585
(713541)
T67R

TORONTO. PLANNING BOARD.
THE ROLE OF PRIVATE ENTERPRISE IN
URBAN RENEWAL; A STUDY CARRIED OUT BY
MURRAY V. JONES UNDER CONTRACT WITH
THE METROPOLITAN TORONTO PLANNING
BOARD. TORONTO, 1966.
303P.

1. URBAN RENEWAL - TORONTO.
I. JONES, MURRAY V. II. TITLE.

711.4
(713541)
T67o
1965

Toronto. Planning Board.
Official plan of the Metropolitan
Toronto planning area. Toronto, 1965.
21p.
-- ----Supplement. 1966.
22p.

1. Master plan - Toronto.

711.585
(713541)
R67

Toronto. Planning Board.
Rose, Albert.
Prospects for rehabilitation of housing
in central Toronto. Report of research
[prepared for] City of Toronto Planning
Board and Central Mortgage and Housing
Corporation. Toronto, 1966.
122p.

1. Neighborhood rehabilitation - Toronto. 2. Slum
clearance - Toronto. 3. Community development -
Citizen participation. I. Toronto. Planning
Board. II. Central Mortgage and Housing Corp.
III. Title.

711.14
(713541)
T67

Toronto. Planning Board.
South side of the Civic Square.
Toronto, 1958.
[12]p.

1. Land use - Toronto. I. Title.

711.581
(713541)
T67

Toronto. Planning Board.
Plan for Deer Park. Toronto, 1961.
25p.

1. Neighborhood planning - Canada - Toronto.
2. Canada - Neighborhood planning. I. Title:
Deer Park. II. Title.

711.5
(713541
:347)
T67R

TORONTO. PLANNING BOARD.
REPORT ON RESIDENTIAL STANDARDS,
APRIL 1956. TORONTO, 1956.
24P.

1. ZONING - TORONTO. I. TITLE:
RESIDENTIAL STANDARDS.

711.4
(71)
T67

Toronto, Canada. City Planning Board.
A submission to the Royal Commission on
Canada's economic prospects, presented by
His Worship Mayor Nathan Phillips. Toronto,
Canada, Jan. 1956.
78 p. tables.

1.City planning - Toronto, Canada. I.Canada.
Royal Commission on Canada's Economic Prospects.

711.552
(713541)
T67

Toronto. Planning Board.
Plan for downtown Toronto. [Prepared]
in cooperation with the City of Toronto
Redevelopment Advisory Council. Toronto,
1963.
60p.

1. Business districts - Toronto.
I. Title.

388
(713541)
T67r

Toronto. Planning Board.
Report on the metropolitan Toronto
transportation plan. Toronto, 1964.
82p.
1. Transportation - Canada - Toronto.
2. Canada - Transportation. 3. Journey to
work. 4. Highways - Canada - Toronto.
5. Canada - Highways. I. Title: Metropolitan
Toronto transportation plan.

711.4
(713541)
T67

Toronto. Planning Board.
Township of Toronto. Toronto, 1957-
v. illus., maps.

1. City planning - Toronto.

727
I(713541)
T67

2c-v.1-2

Toronto. School Board.
Study of educational facilities. SEF
T1-Introduction to the first SEF building
system. SEF T2. Specifications for the
first SEF building system. Toronto, 1968.
2v. (loose-leaf)

1. Schools - Toronto. 2. Building construction - Toronto. 3. Building methods.
4. Building costs - Toronto. I. Title.

534.83
A27

Toronto. University. Institute for
Aerospace Studies.
Aerodynamic noise. Proceedings of AFOSR-
UTIAS Symposium held at Toronto 20-21 May
1968. Sponsored by Air Force Office of
Scientific Research, Office of Aerospace
Research, United States Air Force and
Institute for Aerospace Studies, University
of Toronto. Toronto, University of Toronto
Press, 1969.
442p.
1. Noise. 2. Air transportation.
I. U.S. Air Force. Office of Scientific
Research. II. Toronto. University.
Institute for Aerospace Studies.

331
T67

2c

Torpey, William G
Optimum utilization of scientific and
engineering manpower. Alexandria, 1970.
324p.

1. Labor supply. 2. Science. 3. Engineering.
I. Title.

711.585
(713541)
T67

2c.

Toronto. Social Planning Council. (Committee on Housing)
Urban renewal and housing for unattached
persons. Toronto, 1964.
17p.

1. Urban renewal - Toronto. 2. Housing
for single persons. 3. Public housing -
Toronto. I. Title.

025.3
C65

Toronto. University. School of Library Sci-
ence.
Colloquium on the Anglo-American Cataloging
Rules, University of Toronto, 1967.
The code and the cataloguer; proceedings of
the Colloquium on the Anglo-American Cataloging
Rules held at the School of Library Science,
University of Toronto on March 31 and April
1, 1967. Edited by Katherine H. Packer and
Delores Phillips; supervising editor: Katherine
L. Ball. Toronto, University of Toronto Press,
1969.
122p.

(Cont'd on next card)

691.32
I82

Ivey, Don L
Air void systems in ready mixed concrete, by
Don L. Ivey and Patrick H. Torrans. Sponsored
by the Texas Highway Dept. in cooperation with
the Dept. of Transportation, Federal Highway
Administration, Bureau of Public Roads.
College Station, Texas Transportation Institute,
Texas A. & M. University, 1969.
50p. (Research report no. 103-4F; study
2-5-66-103)

1. Concrete. I. Torrans, Patrick H., jt. au.
II. Texas. Highway Dept. III. Texas
Transportation Institute.

Torrans, Patrick H   jt. au.

711.4
(713541)
T67R

1947

TORONTO. TORONTO AND SUBURBAN
PLANNING BOARD.
REPORT OF THE TORONTO AND SUBURBAN
PLANNING BOARD, 1947- . TORONTO,
1947-
1V.

1. CITY PLANNING - TORONTO.

025.3
C65

Colloquium on the Anglo-American Cataloging
Rules, University of Toronto, 1967. The code
...1969.   (Card 2)

1. Cataloging. I. Packer, Katherine H., ed.
II. Phillips, Delores, ed. III. Spalding,
Charles Sumner, 1912-. IV. Toronto. Univer-
sity. School of Library Science. V. Title.

370
:308
A52

Torrence, Lois E
American University, Washington, D.C.
A survey and analysis of earned doctorates,
1916-1966, by Lois E. Torrence. Washington,
1969.
114p.

1. Education - Surveys. 2. Universities and
colleges. 3. Employment - Surveys.
I. Torrence, Lois E. II. Title.

711
(016)
C65
no.209

Toronto. University.
Andrews, Howard F
Working notes and bibliography on central
place studies, 1965-1969. Toronto, University
of Toronto, 1971.
41p. (Council of Planning Librarians. Exchange bibliography no. 209)
1. Planning - Bibl. 2. City growth - Bibl.
I. Toronto. University. II. Title. III. Title:
Central place studies. (Series: Council of
Planning Librarians. Exchange bibliography
no. 209)

308
:728.1
(71)
T67

3c.

Toronto. University. School of Social Work.
An experimental study of local housing
conditions and needs; a report, by Albert Rose.
[Ottawa, Central Mortgage and Housing Corporation, 1955.]
150 p. forms, map, tables.

Cover title: Local housing conditions and
needs.

Bibliography: p. 144-150.

333.34
F47

Torrens system.
Fisher, Anne Reeploeg.
The Torrens system - how to escape the
title insurance gouge. Seattle, 1968.
31p.

1. Torrens system. 2. Insurance.

711
(016)
C65
no.230

Toronto. University.
Andrews, Howard F
Working note on non-spatial consumer behavior.
Toronto, University of Toronto, 1971.
43p. (Council of Planning Librarians. Ex-
change bibliography no. 230)
1. Planning - Bibl. 2. Buying - Bibl.
I. Toronto. University. II. Title. III. Title:
Consumer behavior. (Series: Council of Planning
Librarians. Exchange bibliography no. 230)

308
:728.1
(71)
T67

Toronto. University. School of Social Work.
An experimental study of local housing
conditions and needs. Ottawa. 1955. (Card 2)

1.Housing surveys - Canada. 2.Family living
requirements. 3.Survey methods. I.Rose, Albert.
II.Central Mortgage and Housing Corporation.
III.Title: Local housing conditions and needs.

691
A75

Torsional waves in composite rods.
Armenàkas, Anthony E
Torsional waves in composite rods. Gaines-
ville, Fla., Florida University, Engineering and
Industrial Experiment Station, 1965.
8p. (Florida. University. Engineering
and Industrial Experiment Station. Technical
paper no. 335)
Engineering progress at the University of
Florida, Oct. 1965.
Reprinted from the Journal of the Acoustical
Society of America. Sept. 1965. p. 439-446.

1. Building mate-   rials. I. Florida.
University. Engi-   neering and Industrial Experiment   Station. II. Title.

711.585
I(71)
T67u

4c

Toronto. University. Centre for Urban and
Community Studies.
Urban renewal; papers presented at the
Inaugural Seminar of the Centre for Urban and
Community Studies. Toronto, 1968.
225-329p.
Reprinted from: University of Toronto law
journal, Vol. XVIII, no. 3, 1968.

1. Urban renewal - Canada. 2. Canada -
Urban renewal. I. Title.

711
(016)
C65
no.232

Toronto. University. Dept. of Urban and
Regional Planning.
Waterhouse, Alan.
Urban development in mediaeval Europe: a
bibliography. Toronto, University of Toronto,
Dept. of Urban and Regional Planning, 1971.
20p. (Council of Planning Librarians.
Exchange bibliography no. 232)

1. City planning - Europe - Bibl. I. Toronto.
University. Dept. of Urban and Regional
Planning. II. Title. (Series: Council of
Planning Librarians. Exchange bibliography
no. 232)

Torrens system

see also

Land titles.

628.1
(54)
L22

Toronto. University. Dept. of Geography.
Lee, Terence R
Residential water demand and economic develop-
ment. Toronto, Published for the University of
Toronto, Dept. of Geography by the University
of Toronto Press, 1969.
151p. (University of Toronto. Dept. of
Geography. Research publications, 2)

1. Water-supply - India. 2. Economic conditions - India. I. Toronto. University. Dept.
of Geography. II. Title.

711
(016)
C65
no. 96

Toronto. University. Dept of Urban and
Regional Planning.
Hodge, Gerald.
Urbanization in regional development: a
selected bibliography. Toronto, Dept. of
Urban and Regional Planning, University of
Toronto, 1969.
13p. (Council of Planning Librarians.
Exchange bibliography no. 96)
1. Planning - Bibl. 2. City growth -
Bibl. 3. Economic development - Bibl.
I. Toronto. University. Dept. of Urban
and Regional Planning. II. Title.
(Series: Council of Planning Librarians.
Exchange bibliography no. 96)

VF
333.34
A74

Torrens system.
Arkansas. Legislative Council. (Research
Department.)
An analysis of the torrens system of land title
registration. Little Rock, Ark., 1952.
14 p.

Staff report on Council proposal no. 11.
Processed.

1.Torrens system.

333.34
B97
TORRENS SYSTEM.
BYRNE, M MARTHA.
ANALYSIS OF JOHN L. FINCK'S PAMPHLET TITLED "THE TORRENS FALLACY", PREPARED BY MARTHA BYRNE, REGISTER, NEW YOUR COUNTY, WITH THE ASSISTANCE OF THE U.S. WORKS PROGRESS ADMINISTRATION FOR THE CITY OF NEW YORK. OFFICIAL PROJECT 465-97-3-46 "ANALYSIS OF ALL LAWS AFFECTING REAL ESTATE." N.P., 1938
34L.
1. TORRENS SYSTEM. 2. FINCK, JOHN L. THE TORRENS FALLACY. I. U.S. WORKS PROGRESS — ADMINISTRATION FOR THE CITY OF NE W YORK.

1133
TORRINGTON, CONN. COMMUNITY DEVELOPMENT ACTION PLAN AGENCY.
STUDY ON HANDLING OF INDUSTRIAL REFUSE, SLUDGE, AND OIL. TORRINGTON, CONN., 1968.
1 V. (HUD 701 REPORT)
1. REFUSE AND REFUSE DISPOSAL - TORRINGTON, CONN. I. HUD. 701. TORRINGTON, CONN.

693.5
:691.215
T67
1963
Torroja Miret, Eduardo. Sobre el comportamiento...   (Card 2)
1. Concrete, Reinforced. I. Spain. Consejo Superior de Investigaciones Cientificas. Instituto Eduardo Torroja de la Construcción y del Cemento.

333.34
C15
Torrens system.
California. State Lands Commission.
Report on land title law of state of California, pursuant to the Budget act of 1949 and section 6211 of the Public resources code. [Sacramento, Calif.] Jan. 1953.
313 p.   tables.

Includes bibliographies.
Processed.

1.Land titles. 2.Torrens system. I.Title: Land title law of state California.

1130
1131
TORRINGTON, CONN. COMMUNITY DEVELOPMENT ACTION PLAN AGENCY.
WORKING PAPERS, TORRINGTON COMMUNITY DEVELOPMENT ACTION PLAN. TORRINGTON, 1970.
2 V. (HUD 701 REPORT)
1. COMMUNITY DEVELOPMENT - TORRINGTON, CONN. I. HUD. 701. TORRINGTON, CONN.

620.1
C65
NO.16
TORSION FATIGUE.
COLUMBIA UNIVERSITY. INSTITUTE FOR THE STUDY OF FATIGUE AND RELIABILITY.
ON SECOND ORDER STRAIN ACCUMULATION IN TORSION FATIGUE, BY MARIA RONAY. NEW YORK, 1965.
51P. (ITS TECHNICAL REPORT NO. 16)
1. STRENGTH OF MATERIALS. I. RONAY, MARIA. II. TITLE: TORSION FATIGUE.

VF
333.34
C25
Torrens system.
Central Housing Committee. Sub-Committee on Law and Legislation.
Land title procedure, with particular referenc to the legal costs of home mortgage loans. Washington, D.C., Aug. 1936.
68 p. (Its Special report no. 3)

Mimeographed.

1.Land titles-U.S. 2.Torrens system. I.Title.

VF
33(746)
C65
Torrington, Conn. - Economic conditions
Columbia. University. Summer Engineering School.
The town of Torrington, a student survey of the community. New York, N.Y. 1948.
ii, 36 p.   diagrs., maps, tables.

Bibliographical footnotes.

1.Public utilities-Survey-Torrington, Conn.
2.Economic base studies-Torrington, Conn.
3.Torrington, Conn.-Econ. condit.

691.328
H78t
Torsion of structural concrete - interaction surface for combined torsion...
Hsu, Thomas T
Torsion of structural concrete - interaction surface for combined torsion, shear, and bending in beams without stirrups. Skokie, Ill., Portland Cement Association, Research and Development Laboratories, 1968.
27p. (Portland Cement Association. Research and Development Laboratories. Development Dept. Bulletin D138)
Bibliography: p. [28-30]
Reprinted from Journal of the American Concrete Institute. Jan., 1968, proceedings vol. 65, pp. 51-   60.
(Cont'd on next card)

362
(7471)
T67
Torres, Aida.
Service utilization and patient characteristics: the Gouverneur Health Services Program of Beth Israel Medical Center, New York City, Sponsored by Beth Israel Medical Center, New York City and others. New York, Gouverneur Economic Research Project. 1967.
120p.
Bibliography: p. 119-122.
1. Hospitals - New York (City) 2. Sick.
3. Public health - New York (City) I. Beth Israel Medical   Center, N.Y. (City)
II. Gouverneur   Economic Research Project, New   York, N.Y. III. Title.

DATE OF REQUEST 6/16/52   L. C. CARD NO.
VF: Fans   JUL 22 1952
AUTHOR
Torrington Manufacturing Company.
TITLE
How to have comfort from moving air.   (XPAC 102)
SERIES
EDITION 3d   PUB. DATE 1952   PAGING 200 p.
PUBLISHER
RECOMMENDED BY   REVIEWED IN
                           AC 6/52 p. 250
ORDER RECORD

691.328
H78t
Hsu, Thomas T   C   Torsion of structural concrete...1968.   (Card 2)
1. Concrete, Reinforced. I. Portland Cement Association. II. American Concrete Institute. Journal. III. Title.

711.4
H68s
Torrey, Volta.
U.S. Dept. of Housing and Urban Development. Science and the city. Prepared by Volta Torrey. Washington, Govt. Print. Off., 1967.
43p. (HUD MP-39)

1. City planning. 2. City growth.
I. Torrey, Volta. II. Title.

691.322
861
Torroja, Eduardo.
Spain. Consejo Superior de Investigaciones Cientificas. Instituto Tecnico de la Construccion y del Cemento.
Estudio de ensayos de flexion simple y compuesta (con una armadura siempre en traccion) por Eduardo Torroja y Jose M. Urcelay. Madrid, 1959.
25p.   tables. (Its Numero 201)

English summary.

1. Concrete. I. Torroja, Eduardo. II. Urcelay, Jose, M.

691.32
H78
Torsion of structural concrete; plain concrete rectangular sections.
Hsu, Thomas T   C
Torsion of structural concrete; plain concrete rectangular sections. Skokie, Ill., Portland Cement Association, Research and Development Laboratories, 1968.
203-238p. (Portland Cement Association. Research and Development Laboratories Development Dept. Bulletin D134)
Bibliography: p. 239-241
Reprinted from: Torsion of structural concrete, American Concrete Institute, Publication SP-18, 203-238 (1968)
(Cont'd on next card)

712
Y17
Torrington, Conn. Beautification Committee.
Yarwood and Block, inc.
A more beautiful Torrington. Simsbury, Conn., 1969.
28p.
Prepared for: The Beautification Committee, City of Torrington, Connecticut.
Bibliography: app. J, p. 1-3.
1. Landscape architecture. 2. City planning - Torrington, Conn. I. Torrington, Conn. Beautification Committee.
II. Title.

693.55
861m
Torroja, E
Spain. Consejo Superior de Investigaciones Cientificas. Instituto Tecnico de la Construccion y del Cemento.
El metodo del momento tope, para la flexión y la compresión simples o compuestas en hormigón armado, por E. Torroja et al. I parte. Secciones rectangulares con simple o doble armadura. Madrid, 1961.
32p. (Its Numero 213)
English summary.

1. Reinforced   concrete construction.
I. Torroja, E.

691.32
H78
Hsu, Thomas T   C   Torsion...1968.   (Card 2)
1. Concrete. 2. Concrete, Reinforced. 3. Strains and stresses.
I. Portland Cement Association. II. American Concrete Institute. III. Title.

1132
TORRINGTON, CONN. COMMUNITY DEVELOPMENT ACTION PLAN AGENCY.
FISCAL ANALYSES OF TAXES, MUNICIPAL SERVICES, AND CAPITAL IMPROVEMENTS. TORRINGTON, CONN., 1969.
1 V. (HUD 701 REPORT)
1. MUNICIPAL FINANCE - TORRINGTON, CONN. I. HUD. 701. TORRINGTON, CONN.

693.5
:691.215
T67
1963
Torroja Miret, Eduardo.
Sobre el comportamiento anelástico del hormigón armado en piezas prismáticas.
2d ed. Madrid, Consejo Superior de Investigaciones Cientificas, Patronato Juan de la Cierva de Investigacion Tecnica, 1963.
99p. (Spain. Instituto Eduardo Torroja de la Construcción y del Cemento. Monografías no. 54)
Bibliography: p. 89-93.
English   summary.
(Cont'd. on next card)

691.328.2
H78
Torsion of structural concrete uniformly...
Hsu, Thomas T
Torsion of structural concrete uniformly prestressed rectangular members without web reinforcement. Skokie, Ill., Portland Cement Association, Research and Development Laboratories, 1968.
44p. (Portland Cement Association. Research and Development Laboratories. Development Dept. bulletin D140)
Reprinted from Journal of the Prestressed Concrete Institute, April, 1968.
1. Concrete, Prestressed. 2. Strength of materials. I.   Portland Cement Association. II. Title.

620.1
P24
Torsional flexural buckling of thin-
walled sections under eccentric load.
Peköz, Teoman B
Torsional flexural buckling of thin-
walled sections under eccentric load.
With a contribution by N. Celebi. A
research project sponsored by the
American Iron and Steel Institute.
Ithaca, N.Y., Dept. of Structural
Engineering, School of Civil Engineering,
Cornell University, 1969.
75p. (Cornell engineering research
bulletin 69-1)
(Cont'd on next card)

620.1
P24
Peköz, Teoman B   Torsional
flexural...1969.   (Card 2)

Bibliography: p. 68-69.

1. Strength of materials. 2. Loads.
3. Steel construction. I. Cornell
University. School of Civil Engineering.
II. Title.

LAW   Torts.
T
A52
L184to
American law institute.
Restatement of the law of torts, as adopted and
promulgated by the American law institute at Wash-
ington, D.C., May 11, 1934... St. Paul, American
law institute, 1935- 1939.
4v. 23cm.

LAW
T
A52
L184TD
2D
TORTS.
AMERICAN LAW INSTITUTE.
RESTATEMENT OF THE LAW, SECOND:
TORTS 2D, AS ADOPTED AND PROMULGATED BY
THE AMERICAN LAW INSTITUTE AT
WASHINGTON, D.C., MAY 25, 1963 AND MAY
22, 1964. REV. AND ENL. ST. PAUL,
1965-66.
5 V.

INCLUDES 3 VOLS. OF APPENDIX.

1. TORTS.

LAW
T
C177DE
TORTS.
CARTER, J   HOWARD.
DEFAMATION ACTIONS, BY J. HOWARD
CARTER, AND ANDREW L. HUGHES.
LITIGATION INVOLVING DECEDENTS'
ESTATES, BY JAMES N. VAUGHAN. NEW
YORK, PRACTISING LAW INSTITUTE, 1964.
70, 52P.

1. TORTS. 2. PROBATE LAW AND
PRACTICE. I. HUGHES, ANDREW L.
II. VAUGHAN, JAMES N. III. TITLE.
IV. TITLE: DECEDENTS' ESTATES.

LAW
T
C665
TORTS.
COOLEY, THOMAS M
A TREATISE ON THE LAW OF TORTS OR THE
WRONGS WHICH ARISE INDEPENDENTLY OF
CONTRACT. 4TH ED. BY D. AVERY HAGGARD.
CHICAGO, CALLAGHAN, 1932.
3 V.

1. TORTS. I. HAGGARD, D. AVERY.

LAW
T
G157NE
TORTS.
GANS, ALFRED W
A LAWYER'S QUICK APPROACH TO
NEGLIGENCE CASES AND TORT PROCEDURES.
SAN FRANCISCO, AMERICAN LAW REPORTS,
1963.
1 V.

1. NEGLIGENCE (LAW). 2. TORTS.
I. AMERICAN LAW REPORTS.

LAW   Torts.
T
G677ne
Gottlieb, Irvin M
A new approach to the handling of tort claims
against the sovereign. Vienna, Va., Coiner
Publications, 1967.
79p.
On cover: A special report.

1. Torts. I. Title.

LAW   Torts.
T
G677un
Gottlieb, Irvin M
"Uncle Sam" as a landlord under the Federal
tort claims act, by Irvin M. Gottlieb and
Paul H. Gantt. Vienna, Va., Coiner Publications,
ltd., 1967.
145p.
At head of title: A special report.

1. Public lands. 2. Public buildings.
3. Real property. 4. Torts. I. Gantt, Paul
H., jt. au. II. Title.

LAW
T
J197HA
TORTS.
JAYSON, LESTER S
HANDLING FEDERAL TORT CLAIMS:
ADMINISTRATIVE AND JUDICIAL REMEDIES.
NEW YORK, MATTHEW BENDER, 1968.
2 V.

COVER TITLE: PERSONAL INJURY:
HANDLING FEDERAL TORT CLAIMS.

1. TORTS. I. TITLE: PERSONAL
INJURY.

LAW
T
P767
1955
TORTS.
PROSSER, WILLIAM L
HANDBOOK OF THE LAW OF TORTS. 2D ED.
ST. PAUL, WEST PUB. CO., 1955.
989P.

1. TORTS.

LAW
T
P767
TORTS.
PROSSER, WILLIAM L
HANDBOOK OF THE LAW OF TORTS. 4TH ED.
ST. PAUL, WEST PUB. CO., 1971.
1208P. (HORNBOOK SERIES)

1. TORTS.

LAW
T
S724DI
TORTS.
STEIN, JACOB A
DISTRICT OF COLUMBIA CASEFINDER:
TORTS. VIENNA, VA., COINER, 1966.
314P.

1. TORTS. I. TITLE.

368
C65imp
1966
H-H
Torts.
U.S. Congress. House. Committee on the
Judiciary.
Improvement of procedures in claims settlement and Government litigation. Hearing
before Subcommittee No. 2 of the Committee on
the Judiciary, House of Representatives,
Eighty-ninth Congress, second session on H.R.
13650 to amend the Federal tort claims act to
authorize increased agency consideration of
tort claims against the Government, and for
other purposes. H.R. 13651 to avoid unnec-
essary litigation   by providing for the
collection of   claims of the United

(Continued on   next card)

368
C65imp
1966
H-H
U.S. Congress. House. Committee on the
Judiciary. Improvement of procedures in
claims settlement and Government litiga-
tion...1966.   (Card 2)

States, and for other purposes. H.R.13652 to
establish a statute of limitations for certain
actions brought by the Government. H.R.14182
to provide for judgments for costs against the
United States. Wash., Govt. Print. Off.,
1966.
35p.

1. Insurance. 2. Torts.   I. Title: Claims
settlement and Govern-   ment litigation.

325.3
B87
The tortured Americans.
Burnette, Robert.
The tortured Americans. Englewood Cliffs,
N.J. Prentice-Hall, 1971.
176p.

1. Indians. 2. Federal government.
I. Title.

711.3
T67
Toscano, James V
The chief elected official in the
Penjerdel region; a self portrait.
Philadelphia, Pennsylvania-New Jersey-
Delaware Metropolitan Project, 1964.
47p.

1. Regional planning - Penjerdel region.
I. Pennsylvania-New Jersey-Delaware
Metropolitan Project.

330.15
N176
NO.44
TOSTLEBE, ALVIN S
THE GROWTH OF PHYSICAL CAPITAL IN
AGRICULTURE, 1870-1950. NEW YORK, 1954.
92P. (NATIONAL BUREAU OF ECONOMIC
RESEARCH. OCCASIONAL PAPER 44)

1. AGRICULTURE - STATISTICS.
2. FINANCE. I. TITLE.

312
(78883)
D25t
Total population and minority group
population.
Denver Regional Council of Governments.
Total population and minority group popula-
tion: estimates and projections. Denver SMSA.
Denver, 1969.
[4] p.
U.S. Dept. of Housing and Urban Develop-
ment. UPAP.

1. Population - Denver. 2. Minority groups -
Denver. I. Title. II. U.S. HUD-UPAP.
Denver.

538.56
M21
Total systems.
Meacham, Alan D   ed.
Total systems. Edited by Alan D. Meacham
and Van B. Thompson. Enoch J. Hage and
Maurice F. Ronayne, coordinating editors.
1st ed. Detroit, American Data Processing,
1962.
200p. (Data processing library series)

1. Automation. I. Thompson, Van B., jt.
ed. II. Title.

658
S76
A total systems approach to management
control.
Stokes, Paul M
A total systems approach to management
control. New York, American Management
Association, 1968.
160p.

1. Management. 2. Management - Automation.
I. American Management Association. II. Title.

711.5
(74923)
M67

Totowa, N.J. Planning Board.
Morrow Planning Associates.
Development study and proposed zoning of lands adjoining State highway #46 in Totowa Borough, New Jersey. Prepared for the Totowa Borough Planning Board. [Ridgewood, N.J., 1959?]
10p.

U.S. Urban Renewal Adm. UPAP.

1. Zoning - Totowa, N.J. I. Totowa, N.J. Planning Board. II. U.S. URA-UPAP. Totowa, N.J.

711.4
(74923)
T67
no. 3

Totowa, N. J. Planning Board.
Morrow Planning Associates.
Master plan, Borough of Totowa, New Jersey. [Prepared for] the Planning Board. Ridgewood, N.J., 1959.
35p. maps, tables. (Title VII master plan studies report no. 3)

U.S. Urban Renewal Administration, Urban Planning Assistance Program.

1. Master plan - Totowa, N.J. I. Totowa, N.J. Planning Board. II. U.S. URA-UPAP. Totowa, N. J.

336.211
(74923)
M67

Totowa, N.J. Planning Board.
Morrow Planning Associates.
Studies of tax exempt property in the Borough. [Memorandum] to the Planning Board, Borough of Totowa. [Ridgewood, N.J.] 1959.
2p.

U.S. Urban Renewal Adm. UPAP.

1. Real property - Taxation - Totowa, N.J. I. Totowa, N.J. Planning Board. II. U.S. URA-UPAP.   Totowa, N.J.

711.585
(74923)
M57

Totowa, N.J. Planning Board.
Morrow Planning Associates.
Urban renewal recommendations. Memorandum to Planning Board, Borough of Totowa. [Ridgewood, N.J.] 1959.
[2]p.

U.S. Urban Renewal Adm. UPAP.

1. Urban renewal - Totowa, N.J. I. Totowa, N.J. Planning Board. II. U.S. URA-UPAP. Totowa, N.J.

711.33
(788)
T67

Totschek, Robert A
Outline of proposed planning guide for the Inter-County Regional Planning Commission. Santa Monica, Calif., System Development Corp., 1967.
47p. (System Development Corp. Technical memo TM-3483/000/00)

1. State planning - Colorado. 2. County planning - Colorado. I. Inter-County Regional Planning Commission, Denver. II. System Development Corp. III. Title.

711.4
(016)
A55

Totschek, Robert A., jt. au.
Almendinger, Vladimir V
Urban and regional information systems: a selected bibliography, by Vladimir V. Almendinger and Robert A. Totschek. Santa Monica, Calif., System Development Corp., 1968.
128p. (System Development Corporation. Technical memorandum (TM series) TM-L-3595/001/00)
1. City planning - Bibl. I. Totschek, Robert A., jt. au. II. System Development Corporation. III. Title.

727
T67

Totten, W Fred.
The community school; basic concepts, function, and organization, by W. Fred Totten and Frank J. Manley. Galien, Mich., Allied Education Council, 1969.
278p.
Bibliography: p. 268-274.

1. Schools. 2. Education. I. Manley, Frank J., jt. au. II. Title.

697.942
T67

Tottle, H F
Strong-room climate. [n.p.] 1956.
[11] p.

Reprinted from Archivist, 1956. 387-97.

1. Humidity. 2. Archives. I. Title.

325.3
M12

Touch the earth.
McLuhan, T C
Touch the earth; a self-portrait of Indian existence. New York, Outerbridge & Dienstfrey, 1971.
185p.

Bibliography: p. 179-185.

1. Indians. I. Title.

325.3
T68

Touche Ross & Co.
Proposal to the Dept. of Housing and Urban Development to provide planning and development assistance to the Blackfoot Tribal Construction Company. Denver, 1971.
18p.

1. Indians. I. Title. II. Title: Blackfoot Tribal Construction Co.

711.4
T68w

TOUGH, ROSALIND.
WHAT'S BEHIND HOUSING. NEW YORK, 1949.
25-38P.

REPRINTED FROM SOCIAL SERVICE REVIEW, V. 23, NO. 1, MARCH 1949.

1. CITY PLANNING. 2. HOUSING LEGISLATION. I. SOCIAL SERVICE REVIEW.

712.21
(7471)
T74

A tour of Staten Island improvements and the next steps
Triborough Bridge and Tunnel Authority.
A tour of Staten Island improvements and the next steps. New York, Published by the Triborough Bridge and Tunnel Authority with the cooperation of other agencies, 1965.
20p.

1. Parks - New York (City) 2. Metropolitan areas - New York (City) I. Title.

914
L49

Tourism and recreation.
Little (Arthur D.) inc.
Tourism and recreation; a state-of-the art study. Prepared for the Office of Regional Development Planning. Washington, U.S. Dept. of Commerce, Economic Development Administration, [1967]
301p.

1. Travel. 2. Recreation. 3. Economic development. 4. Regional planning. I. U.S. Economic Development Administration. II. Title.

910
A72

THE TOURIST BUSINESS.
U.S. OFFICE OF AREA DEVELOPMENT.
YOUR COMMUNITY CAN PROFIT FROM THE TOURIST BUSINESS. WASHINGTON, GOVT. PRINT. OFF., 1957.
25P.

1. TRAVEL. 2. REAL PROPERTY - VALUATION. I. TITLE. II. TITLE: THE TOURIST BUSINESS.

Tourist courts.
VF
711.585
(75552)
A21

Adams, Frank.
Golden boy's touch, Futterman aids city. Norfolk, Va., 1959.
1p. illus.

Reprinted from Virginian-Pilot and the Portsmouth Star, July 26, 1959, by Norfolk Redevelopment and Housing Authority.

1. Urban renewal - Norfolk, Va. 2. Tourist courts. I. Futterman, Robert Allen. II. Norfolk, Va. Redevelopment and Housing Authority.

Tourist courts.
647.7
A52

Alexandria, Va. Dept. of City Planning and Urban Renewal.
Parking requirements for hotels and motels. Alexandria, 1966.
3p. (Its Special study. Rept. no. 2)

1. Hotels. 2. Tourist courts. 3. Parking.

Tourist courts.
728.69
A72

Architectural Record.
Motels, hotels, restaurants and bars. 2d ed. New York, F. W. Dodge, 1960.
327p. illus., diagrs.

1. Tourist courts. 2. Hotels. 3. Architecture - Design.

Tourist courts.
728.69
B72

Brener, Stephen W
Hotel sales and operations. Englewood Cliffs, N.J., Prentice-Hall, 1960.
211-235p.

Reprinted from the Real estate encyclopedia.

1. Tourist courts.

VF
728.69
(794)
C15t

Tourist courts,
California. Laws, statutes, etc.
State auto and trailer park act (Health and safety code, Division 13, Part 2) and California administrative code (Title 8, Chapter 9, Article 3). Sacramento, Calif., Dept. of Industrial Relations, Division of Housing, 1952.
48 p. diagrs., plans, tables.

1. Trailers. 2. Tourist courts. I. California. Dept. of Industrial Relations. Division of Housing.

5/53

VF
728.69
(794)
C15a

Tourist courts.
California. Laws, statutes, etc.
State auto court, resort and motel act. (Health and safety code, Division 13, Part 2). Sacramento, Calif., Dept. of Industrial Relations, Division of Housing, 1952.
34 p. diagrs., tables.

1. Tourist courts. I. California. Dept. of Industrial Relations. Division of Housing.

5/53

VF
728.69
(794)
C15a
1954

Tourist courts.
California. Laws, statutes, etc.
State auto court, resort and motel act. Health and safety code division 13, part 2. Sacramento, Dept. of Industrial Relations, Division of Housing, 1954.
34p. diagrs. tables.

1. Tourist courts. I. California. Dept. of Industrial Relations. Division of Housing.

VF
728.69
C31

Tourist courts.

Charleston County, S. C. Ordinances, etc.
Regulations controlling the operation and
use of trailer camps or parks and tourist
courts... 1943?
10 p.

1.Trailers. 2.Tourist courts.

728.69
M67

TOURIST COURTS.

Morgan, Howard Edwin.
The motel industry in the United States:
small business in transition. Prepared
under the Small Business Administration
Management Research Grant Program. Project
director: Harold J. Hoflich. Tucson,
Bureau of Business and Public Research,
University of Arizona, 1964.
218p. (Small business management
research reports)

Bibliography: p. 214-218.
(Cont'd on next card)

Tourist courts - Bibliography.

VF
728.69
(016)
M67

Morgan, Howard Edwin.
Motels: bibliography. Washington,
Small Business Administration, 1962.
8p. (U.S. Small Business Administration.
Small business bulletin no. 66)

1. Tourist courts - Bibl. I. U.S.
Small Business Administration. II. Title.

VF
728.69
(757711)
C65

Tourist courts.

Columbia, S.C. Ordinances, etc.
An ordinance to regulate trailer coaches and
trailer coach parks within the city of Columbia,
South Carolina. Columbia, S.C., City Council
[Aug. 1953]
7 l.

Processed.

1.Trailers. 2.Tourist courts.

728.69
M67

Morgan, Howard Edwin. The motel...1964.
(Card 2)

1. Tourist courts. I. Arizona.
University. Bureau of Business and Public
Research. II. Title.

Tourist courts - Directories.

R
910
A52w

American Automobile Association.
Western tour book, including western Canada.
Washington,
v. illus., maps. annual.

For complete information see shelflist.

1. Travel. 2. Hotels - Directories. 3. Tourist
courts - Directories.

712.25
(746)
C65

Tourist courts.

Connecticut. Agricultural Experiment Station,
Storrs.
Recreation, by Walter C. McKain, Jr. and
James R. Weir. In cooperation with the
Connecticut State Highway Department and
Bureau of Public Roads, U.S. Dept. of Com-
merce. Storrs, Conn., 1960.
[5]p. (Its Progress report 35)

"The social and economic effects of the Connecticut Turnpike on Eastern Connecticut."
1. Recreation - Connecticut. 2. Tourist courts.
I. McKain, Walter C., Jr. II. Weir,
James R.

VF
690.091.82
:613.5
(742)
N28

Tourist courts.

New Hampshire. State Dept. of Health.
Sanitary laws and regulations governing
tourist and trailer camps, trailer coaches, hotels,
inns, lodging houses, apartment and tenement
houses, tourist homes, stores, offices, theaters
and public halls, roadside places and public fairs.
Concord, N.H., 1953.
20 p.

1.Housing codes-N.H. 2.Trailers. 3.Tourist
courts.

R
058.7
:647.7
H67

Tourist courts - Directories.

Hotel and motel red book, 19
New York, American Hotel Association
Directory Corporation, 19
v.
Library keeps latest ed. only.

1. Hotels - Direct. 2. Tourist courts -
Direct. I. American Hotel Association
Directory Corporation.

647.7
E24

Tourist courts.

Eckert, Fred W
Economic factors and case studies in
hotel and motel valuation. Chicago,
American Institute of Real Estate
Appraisers, 1962.
86p.

1. Hotels. 2. Tourist courts.
I. American Institute of Real Estate
Appraisers. II. Title.

VF
728.69
868m

Tourist courts.

South Dakota. University. Business
Research Bureau.
The motel industry of South Dakota, by
C. S. Van Doren. Vermillion, S.D.,
1959.
46p. diagrs., tables. (Its Bulletin
no. 64)

1. Tourist courts. I. Van Doren, C.S.
(Series)

711.3
(7946)
N17

Toward a Bay area regional organization.
Nathan, Harriet, ed.
Toward a Bay area regional organization.
Report of the September 14, 1968 Conference
presented by University Extension and the
Institute of Governmental Studies of the
University of California, Berkeley, on
behalf of the Joint Committee on Bay Area
Regional Organization. Edited by Harriet
Nathan and Stanley Scott. San Francisco,
Institute of Governmental Studies,
University of California, 1969.
272p. (Cont'd on next card)

VF
728.69
F72

Tourist courts.

Frey, Jerry B , Jr.
The Motel Story. [Chicago, Mortgage
Bankers Association of America, 1955]
[22] p. graphs, maps, tables.

Bibliography: p. 22

1955 Certificate of Merit Award,
Mortgage Bankers Association of America and
School of Commerce, Northwestern University.
1. Tourist courts. I. Title.

728.69
T65

Tourist courts.

Toledo-Lucas County (Ohio) Plan
Commissions.
A study of motel-apartments. Toledo, 1964.
58p. (Planning research study 2-64)

1. Tourist courts. 2. Apartment houses -
Ohio.

711.3
(7946)
N17

Nathan, Harriet, ed. Toward a Bay...1969.
(Card 2)

1. Metropolitan area planning -
San Francisco Bay area. I. Scott,
Stanley, jt. ed. II. California.
University. Institute of Governmental
Studies. III. Title.

647.7
L18

TOURIST COURTS.

Laventhol Krekstein Horwath & Horwath.
Lodging industry; report on hotel and motor
hotel operations,
19
Philadelphia, 19
v. annual.
For Library holdings see main entry.

1. Hotels. 2. Tourist courts. I. Title.

711.5
(41)
U54
no.9

TOURIST COURTS.

U.K. Ministry of Housing and Local
Government. (Welsh Office)
Petrol filling stations and motels.
London, H.M.S.O., 1969.
[2]p. (Development control policy note 9)

1. Zoning - U.K. 2. Tourist courts.
I. Title.

711.4
(74812)
H17

Toward a better Hatboro.

Community Planning Associates, Princeton, N.J.
Toward a better Hatboro, by Carl G.
Lindbloom and others. Princeton, N. J.,
1957.
41p. maps, tables.

Sponsored by the Hatboro Committee for
Community Advancement.
1. City planning - Hatboro, Pa.
2. Community development - Hatboro, Pa.
I.Lindbloom, Carl G II.Title.
III.Hatboro, Pa. Committee for Community
Advancement.

728.69
M12t

Tourist courts.

McKain, Walter C Jr.
Tourist facilities along the Connecticut
turnpike. Storrs, Conn., Agricultural
Experiment Station, in cooperation with the
Connecticut State Highway Dept. and Bureau
of Public Roads, U.S. Dept. of Commerce,
1962.
10p. (Storrs Agricultural Experiment
Station. Progress report 48)

1. Tourist courts. I. Connecticut.
Agricultural Experiment
Station, Storrs.

647.7
G68

Tourist courts.

U.S. Board of Governors of the Federal
Reserve System.
The postwar boom in hotels and motels, by
Royel Shipp and Robert Moore Fisher. [Wash.]
1965.
41p. (Staff economic studies)

1. Hotels. 2. Tourist courts. I. Shipp,
Royel. II. Fisher, Robert Moore.
III. Title.

362.6
P72to

Toward a brighter future for the elderly.
U.S. President's Task Force on the Aging.
Toward a brighter future for the elderly;
the report of the President's Task Force
on the Aging. [Wash] 1970.
60p.

1. Old age. I. Title.

712
W15   Wallace, McHarg, Roberts and Todd.
       Toward a comprehensive landscape plan for
       Washington, D.C. A report prepared for the
       National Capital Planning Commission. New
       York, 1967.
       40p.

       1. Landscape architecture. I. U.S. National
       Capital Planning Commission. II. Title.

691.32
M12   McHenry, Douglas. Toward a generalized...1966.
       (Card 2)

       1. Concrete. 2. Structural engineering.
       I. Portland Cement Association. II. Title.

712
W42   Toward a more livable city.
       Wichita-Sedgwick County (Kan.)
       Metropolitan Area Planning Commission.
       Toward a more livable city; an urban
       beautification plan for Wichita Kansas.
       Wichita, [1969?]
       91p.

       1. Landscape architecture. I. Title.

360
H17t   Harrington, Michael.
       Toward a democratic left; a radical program
       for a new majority. New York, MacMillan, 1968.
       314p.

       1. Social conditions. 2. Economic conditions.
       3. Minority groups. I. Title.

Toward a high-energy civilization.
500.15
G25   General Electric Forum for National Security
       and Free World Progress.
       Toward a high-energy civilization.
       Schenectady, N.Y., General Electric, 1967.
       24p.
       Entire issue: January-March 1967.
       Partial contents: A systems approach to the
       cities, by C.A. Doxiadis.--New approach to city
       building, by James W. Rouse.--New approach to
       metropolitan transportation, by W.J. Ronan.

       1. Scientific research. 2. City planning. 3. City
       growth. I. Doxiadis,   Constantinos A. A
       systems approach to   the cities. II.Title.

711.3
T68   Toward a national urban policy. Edited by
       Daniel P. Moynihan. New York, Basic Books,
       1970.
       348p.

       1. Metropolitan areas. 2. Economic
       policy. 3. City planning. I. Moynihan,
       Daniel Patrick, ed.

728.6
B87T   TOWARD A FARM HOUSING POLICY.
       BURROUGHS, ROY J
       TOWARD A FARM HOUSING POLICY.
       [MADISON] 1948.
       22P.
       REPRINTED FROM LAND ECONOMICS, V. 24,
       NO. 1, FEB. 1948.

       1. FARM HOUSING.   I. TITLE.

379
H21t   U.S. Dept. of Health, Education, and
       Welfare.
       Toward a long-range plan for federal
       financial support for higher education.
       Toward a long-range plan for federal
       financial support for higher education; a
       report to the President. Wash., U.S.
       Dept. of Health, Education, and Welfare,
       Office of the Assistant Secretary for
       Planning and Evaluation, 1969.
       73p.
       1. Education - Finance. 2. Universities
       and colleges. I. Title.

711.3
T68   Toward a national urban policy, by Daniel
1969   P. Moynihan. [n.p.] 1969.
       38p.

       1. Metropolitan areas. 2. Economic
       policy. 3. City planning. I. Moynihan,
       Daniel Patrick.

728.1
:325   Baum, Daniel Jay.
(77252) Toward a free housing market. In collabora-
B18   tion with Karen Orloff Kaplan. Coral Gables,
       Fla., University of Miami Press, 1971.
       241p.

       1. Minority groups - Housing - Indianapolis.
       I. Kaplan, Karen Orloff, jt. au. II. Title.

Folio
973   Philadelphia 1976 Bicentennial Corp.
(74811) Toward a meaningful bicentennial.
P34   Philadelphia, 1969.
       60p.

       1. Philadelphia. Bicentennial
       Exhibition, 1976. 2. Public buildings -
       Philadelphia. 3. Architecture - Phila-
       delphia. I. Title.

711.4
(776579) Minneapolis. City Planning Commission.
M45to Toward a new city: a preliminary report on
       Minneapolis' Urban Design Pilot Study.
       Toward a new city: a preliminary report
       on Minneapolis' Urban Design Pilot Study.
       A joint study by the Planning Commission,
       Minneapolis Chapter, American Institute of
       Architects and others. Minneapolis, Urban
       Design Study, Community Renewal Program,
       1965.
       28p.
       U.S. Urban Renewal Adm. CRP.

       1. City planning - Minneapolis. 2. Landscape
       architecture. I. Title.   II. American Institute
       of Architects,   Minneapolis Chapter.

711.015
A22   ADELSON, MARVIN.
       TOWARD A FUTURE FOR PLANNING.
       TOWARD A FUTURE FOR PLANNING. SANTA
       MONICA, CALIF., SYSTEM DEVELOPMENT
       CORPORATION, 1966.
       17P. ON 5L.

       1. PLANNING - RESEARCH.
       2. AUTOMATION.   I. SYSTEM DEVELOPMENT
       CORPORATION.   II. TITLE.

728.1
:308   Kaiser, Edward John.
K14   Toward a model of residential developer
       locational behavior. Chapel Hill, Center for
       Urban and Regional Studies, University of
       North Carolina, 1966.
       291p. (Environmental policies and urban
       development thesis series no. 4)
       Thesis (Doctor of Philosophy) - University
       of North Carolina.
       Bibliography: p. 284-291.
       1. Housing market. 2. Subdivision. I. North
       Carolina. University. II. Title. (Series:
       Environmental policies and urban development
       thesis series no. 4)

728.1
S23t   Schussheim, Morton J
       Toward a new housing policy.
       Toward a new housing policy; the legacy of
       the sixties. New York, Committee for Economic
       Development, 1969.
       64p. (CED supplementary paper no. 29)

       1. Housing. 2. Federal housing programs.
       I. Committee for Economic Development.
       II. Title.

658
M17t   Markel, Gene A
       Toward a general methodology for systems evaluation.
       Toward a general methodology for systems
       evaluation. Sponsored by Information Systems
       Branch, Office of Naval Research. State
       College, Pa., HRB-Singer, inc., 1965.
       73p. (U.S. Defense Documentation Center.
       Defense Supply Agency. AD 619 373)
       Bibliography: p. 27-63.
       1. Management. 2. Automation. I. U.S.
       Office of Naval Research. II. HRB-Singer,
       inc. III. Title.

728.1
:308   Armiger, Louis Earl, Jr.
A75   Toward a model of the residential location
       decision process: a study of recent and
       prospective buyers of new and used homes.
       Chapel Hill, Center for Urban and Regional
       Studies, University of North Carolina, 1966.
       134p. (Environmental policies and urban
       development thesis series no. 5)
       Thesis (Master of Regional Planning) -
       University of North Carolina.
       Bibliography: p. 130-134.
       1. Housing market. I. North Carolina.
                          (Cont'd on next card)

350
M17t   Marini, Frank, ed.
       Toward a new public administration.
       Toward a new public administration; the
       Minnowbrook perspective. Scranton, Pa., Chandler
       Pub. Co., 1971.
       372p. (Chandler publications in political
       science)

       1. Public administration. I. Title:
       Minnowbrook perspective. II. Title.

691.32
M12   McHenry, Douglas
       Toward a generalized treatment of delayed
       elasticity in concrete.
       Toward a generalized treatment of delayed
       elasticity in concrete. Skokie, Ill., Portland
       Cement Association, Research and Development
       Laboratories, 1966.
       269-283p. (Portland Cement Association.
       Research and Development Laboratories.
       Development Dept. Bulletin D 132)
       Bibliography: p. 284-286.
       Reprint from Publications International
       Association for Bridge and Structural Engineer-
       ing, Zurich Vol. 26, pp. 269-283. (1966)
                          (Continued on next card)

728.1
:308   Armiger, Louis Earl, Jr. Toward...1966.
A75   (Card 2)

       University. Center for Urban and Regional
       Studies. II. Title. (Series: Environmental
       policies and urban development series no. 5)

649
M17   Martin, John M
       Toward a political definition of juvenile
       delinquency.
       Toward a political definition of juvenile
       delinquency. Wash., U.S. Social and Rehabili-
       tation Service, Youth Development and Delin-
       quency Prevention Administration, 1970.
       17p.

       1. Juvenile delinquency. I. U.S. Youth
       Development and Delinquency Prevention
       Administration. II. Title.

728.1
P76
TOWARD A POSTWAR HOUSING PROGRAM.
PRODUCERS' COUNCIL, INC.
TOWARD A POSTWAR HOUSING PROGRAM,
PREPARED AND ISSUED FOR CONSIDERATION IN
DETERMINING SUITABLE POSTWAR HOUSING
LEGISLATION. WASHINGTON, 1944.
2c.
98P.
REISSUED AUGUST 1, 1944, PREPARED BY
FREDERIC M. BABCOCK.

1. HOUSING. 2. FEDERAL HOUSING
PROGRAMS. I. BABCOCK, FREDERIC M.
II. TITLE.

325.2
B51
TOWARD A THEORY OF MINORITY-GROUP
RELATIONS.
BLALOCK, HUBERT M
TOWARD A THEORY OF MINORITY-GROUP
RELATIONS. NEW YORK, WILEY, 1967.
227P.

BIBLIOGRAPHICAL FOOTNOTES.

1. RACE RELATIONS. 2. MINORITY
GROUPS. I. TITLE. II. TITLE: THEORY
OF MINORITY-GROUP RELATIONS.

728.1
P72t
Toward better housing for low income families.
U.S. President's Task Force on Low Income
Housing.
Toward better housing for low income families:
the report of... Wash., Govt. Print. Off., 1970.
20p.

1. Low-income housing. 2. Federal housing
programs. I. Title.

159
M17
1968
Toward a psychology of being.
Maslow, Abraham Harold.
Toward a psychology of being. 2d ed.
Princeton, N.J., Van Nostrand, 1968.
240p. (Van Nostrand insight books 5)

Bibliography: p. 223-237.

1. Psychology. I. Title.

333.65
C25
TOWARD A UNIFORM ACCOUNTING SYSTEM IN
HOUSING MANAGEMENT.
U.S. CENTRAL HOUSING COMMITTEE.
TOWARD A UNIFORM ACCOUNTING SYSTEM IN
HOUSING MANAGEMENT. REPORT NO. 1 OF
THE SUB-COMMITTEE ON OPERATION AND
MANAGEMENT, BASED ON REPORT NO. 1 OF
THE ACCOUNTING SECTION. WASHINGTON,
1936.
1 V.

1. HOUSING MANAGEMENT.
2. ACCOUNTING. I. TITLE.

658.3
C65t
Toward better utilization of scientific and
engineering talent; a program for action.
Committee on Utilization of Scientific
and Engineering Manpower.
Toward better utilization of scientific
and engineering talent; a program for
action. Washington, National Academy
of Sciences, Printing and Publishing
Off., 1964.
153p. (Publication no. 1191)

1. Personnel management. 2. Scientific
research. 3. Engineering research.
I. National Academy of Sciences.
II. Title.

728.1
B11T
TOWARD A RATIONAL POSTWAR HOUSING
PROGRAM FOR THE CONSTRUCTION
BABCOCK, FREDERICK M
TOWARD A RATIONAL POSTWAR HOUSING
PROGRAM FOR THE CONSTRUCTION INDUSTRY.
[N.P.] 1943.
13L.
ADDRESS DELIVERED AT 20TH ANNUAL
MEETING OF THE PRODUCERS' COUNCIL,
CINCINNATI, MAY 26, 1943.

1. HOUSING. 2. BUILDING INDUSTRY.
I. PRODUCERS' COUNCIL. II. TITLE.

FILM
Toward a uniform plumbing code.
United World Films, Inc. Castle Films
Division.
Toward a uniform plumbing code.
16 mm. black and white, sound.

Cost: $30.48.

1. Films. 2. Plumbing codes. I. Title.

360
L42
Toward community: a criticism of contemporary
capitalism.
Lichtman, Richard.
Toward community: a criticism of contemporary capitalism. New York, Center
for the Study of Democratic Institutions,
1966.
58p.
An occasional paper on the role of the
economic order in the free society.

1. Social conditions. 2. Democracy.
I. Center for the Study of Democratic
Institutions. II. Title.

339.5
F11
Toward a rational power policy.
Fabricant, Neil.
Toward a rational power policy; energy,
politics, and pollution. A report by the
Environmental Protection Administration of
the City of New York. Prepared and written
by Neil Fabricant and Robert Marshall Hall-
man. New York, George Braziller, 1971.
292p.
1. Power-resources. 2. Air pollution.
3. Water pollution. 4. Atomic energy.
I. Hallman, Robert Marshall, jt. au.
II. New York (City) Environmental Protection
Administration. III. Title.

VF
336.18
R42
Toward a workable Federalism.
Richardson, Elliot L
Toward a workable Federalism. An address
by the Honorable Elliot L. Richardson, Secretary of Health, Education, and Welfare, before
the National Association of Counties annual
meeting, Atlanta, Georgia, July 27, 1970.
Wash., U.S. Dept. of Health, Education, and
Welfare, 1970.
12p.

1. Grants-in-aid. 2. Intergovernmental
relations. I. U.S. Dept. of Health, Education,
and Welfare. II. Title.

711.4
L28t
Toward decision-making rules for urban
planners.
Lewin, P H
Toward decision-making rules for urban
planners. Garston, Eng., Building Research
Station, Ministry of Public Building and
Works, 1968.
437-442p. (U.K. Building Research Station.
Building research current papers. Current
paper 41/68)
Reprinted from the Journal of the Town
Planning Institute, December, 1967.
1. City planning. I. U.K. Building
Research Station. II. Title.

711.73
E43
Toward a simulation of land use for highway inter-
change communities.
Eighmy, Thomas H
Toward a simulation of land use for highway
interchange communities, by T.H. Eighmy and
John J. Coyle. University Park, Institute for
Research on Land and Water Resources, Penn-
sylvania State University, 1967.
44p. (Pennsylvania. State University.
Institute for Research on Land and Water Re-
sources. Research publication no. 51, pre-
viously referred to as Research report no. 11)
1. Highways. 2. Land use - Automation.
I. Coyle, John J., jt. au. II. Pennsylvania.
State University. Institute for Research
on Land and Water Resources. III. Title.

330
T68
2c.
Toward an age of greatness. Wash., State
Committees on Voter Education, 1965.
[141]p.
Partial contents:-Toward a strong urban
America, by Robert C. Weaver.
Designed and produced by Maurer,
Fleisher, Zon and Associates, Wash., D.C.

1. Economic development. 2. Housing.
3. Town planning. 4. Civil rights.
5. Social welfare. I. Weaver, Robert
Clifton. Toward a strong urban
America. II. State Committees on
Voter Education, Wash., D.C. III.
Maurer, Fleisher, Zon and Associates.

301
C657
Toward economic development for native
American communities.
U.S. Congress. Joint Economic
Committee.
Toward economic development for
native American communities: a compendium
of papers submitted to the Subcommittee on
Economy in Government of the Joint
Economic Committee, Congress of the United
States. Wash., Govt. Print. Off., 1969.
v.
At head of title: 91st Cong., 1st sess.
Joint committee print.
1. Indians. 2. Economic development.
I. Title.

360
H21t
Toward a social report.
U.S. Dept. of Health, Education, and
Welfare.
Toward a social report. Wash., 1969.
101p.

1. Social conditions. 2. Sociology,
Urban. I. Title.

332.748
F52
Toward assessing the need for international
reserves.
Fleming, J Marcus.
Toward assessing the need for international
reserves. Princeton, N.J., International
Finance Section, Dept. of Economics, 1967.
26p. (Princeton University. International Finance Section. Essays in international finance no. 58)

1. Foreign exchange. 2. Money.
I. Princeton University. (International
Finance Section) II. Title.

362.5
S32
Toward economic security for the poor.
Sheppard, Harold L
A search for new directions in the war
against poverty. Staff paper. A reprint of the
Appendix paper in Toward economic security for
the poor, prepared by the Subcommittee on
Employment, Manpower, and Poverty of the Com-
mittee on Labor and Public Welfare, United
States Senate (90th Congress, 2d sess)
Kalamazoo, Mich., W.E. Upjohn Institute for
Employment Research, 1968.
79-[99]p.

1. Poverty. (Cont'd on next card)

711.14
(756622)
S54
Toward a theory of landowner behavior on
the urban periphery.
Smith, John Edward.
Toward a theory of landowner behavior on
the urban periphery. Chapel Hill, N.C.,
Center for Urban and Regional Studies,
University of North Carolina, 1967.
159p. (Environmental policies and urban
development thesis series no. 6)
Thesis (Master of Regional Planning) -
University of North Carolina.
Bibliography: p. 155-159.
1. Land use - Greensboro, N.C. 2. City
growth - Greensboro, N.C. I. North Carolina.
University. Center for Urban and
Regional Studies. II. Title.

360
M17to
Toward balanced growth.
U.S. National Goals Research Staff.
Toward balanced growth: quantity with
quality. Wash., 1970.
228p.

1. Social conditions. 2. Economic conditions. 3. Economic development.
4. Economic policy. I. Title.
5. Population growth.

362.5
S32
Sheppard, Harold L A search for new
directions...1968. (Card 2)

2. Economic conditions. I. Upjohn Institute
for Employment Research. II. Title. III. Title:
New directions in the war against poverty.
IV. Title: Toward economic security for the
poor. V. U.S. Congress. Senate. Committee
on Labor and Public Welfare.

711.14
C34   Toward efficient programs of land use controls.
Childs, Gerald L
Toward efficient programs of land use controls. Boston Urban Land Research Analysts Corp., 1967.
1v. (ULRAC monograph no. 1)
Bibliography: section VI [9-11]

1. Land use. I. Title. II. Urban Land Research Analysts Corp.

711.14
U71t   Toward efficient programs of land use controls.
Urban Land Research Analysts Corp.
Toward efficient programs of land use controls, by William L. Letwin and others. Lexington, Mass., 1969.
168p.

Bibliography: p. 166-168.
U.S. Dept. of Housing and Urban Development. Urban Planning Research and Demonstration Project.
1. Land use. I. Title. II. Letwin, William L. III. U.S. HUD-UPRDP.

331
C48t   Toward equal opportunity in Federal employment.
U.S. Civil Service Commission.
Toward equal opportunity in Federal employment. A report to the President from the United States Civil Service Commission. Wash., 1969.
[8]p.

1. Employment. 2. Federal civil service. 3. Minority groups. I. Title.

728.1
:325
(758231)
G26   Toward equal opportunity in housing in Atlanta, Georgia.
Georgia. State Advisory Committee to the United States Commission on Civil Rights.
Toward equal opportunity in housing in Atlanta, Georgia. Atlanta, 1968.
77p.

1. Minority groups - Housing - Atlanta. I. Title.

F
:25
(775)
:47t   Toward equal opportunity with equal results.
Wisconsin. Dept. of Industry, Labor and Human Relations.
Toward equal opportunity with equal results. Madison, [1969?]
folder.

1. Minority groups - Wis. I. Title.

325
S42   Toward equality, Baltimore's progress report.
Sidney Hollander Foundation, Baltimore.
Toward equality, Baltimore's progress report; a chronicle of progress since World War II toward the achievement of equal rights and opportunities for Negroes in Maryland. Baltimore, 1960.
92p.

1. Negroes. 2. Minority groups - Baltimore. I. Title.

728.6
F17   Toward farm security;
U.S. Farm Security Administration
Toward farm security; the problem of rural poverty and the work of the Farm Security Administration; prepared under the direction of the FSA Personnel Training Committee for FSA employees, by Joseph Gaer. [Washington] Govt. Print. Off., 1956.
246 p. illus., charts.
Bibliography: p.220-237

336
H47   Toward Federal program budgeting.
Hirsch, Werner Z
Toward Federal program budgeting. Los Angeles, University of California, Institute of Government and Public Affairs, 1967.
259-269p. (California. University. University at Los Angeles. Institute of Government and Public Affairs. Reprint no. 31)
Reprinted from Public administration review Dec. 1966.

1. Budget. 2. Federal government. 3. Management. I. Title. II. California. University. University at Los Angeles. Institute of Government and Public Affairs. III. Public administration review.

352.1
(7471)
N28t
1965   Toward fiscal strength; overcoming New York City's financial dilemma.
New York (City) Temporary Commission on City Finances.
Toward fiscal strength; overcoming New York City's financial dilemma. Second interim report. New York, 1965.
83p.

1. Municipal finance - New York (City) I. Title.

LC   Toward freedom from want, from India to Mexico.
Hatch, Duane Spencer
Toward freedom from want; from India to Mexico. [Bombay, India] Geoffrey Cumberlege, Oxford Univ. Press. [1949]
x, 303p. illus.

Bibliography: p. 297-299.

728.1
(756)
M12t   Toward good housing for all North Carolinians.
Mace, Ruth L
Toward good housing for all North Carolinians. Final report ... review of the State's current housing situation; summary of related statewide public and private low-income housing activities; recommendations. Raleigh, N.C., Dept. of Administration, State Planning Task Force, 1968.
95p.

U.S. Dept. of Housing and Urban
(Cont'd on next card)

728.1
(756)
M12t   Mace, Ruth L   Toward...1968. (Card 2)

Development. Low-income Housing Demonstration Program.

1. Low-income housing - N.C. I. North Carolina. State Planning Task Force. II. U.S. HUD-Low-income Housing Demonstration Program. N.C. III. Title.

VF
728.1
:362.6
N17   Toward good housing for the aging.
National Association of Housing and Redevelopment Officials.
Toward good housing for the aging; selected articles from the Journal of Housing. Chicago, 1956
40 p.
Bibliography: p. 38-40.

1. Housing for the aged. I. Title.

331
B87   Toward greater industry and government involvement in manpower development.
Burt, Samuel M
Toward greater industry and government involvement in manpower development, by Samuel M. Burt and Herbert E. Striner. Kalamazoo, Mich., W.E. Upjohn Institute for Employment Research, 1968.
21p. (Upjohn Institute for Employment Research. Staff paper)

1. Employment. 2. Education. 3. Labor supply. I. Striner, Herbert E., jt. au. II. Upjohn Institute for Employment Research. III. Title.

370
L87   Toward improved urban education.
Lutz, Frank W ed.
Toward improved urban education. Worthington, Ohio, Charles A. Jones Pub. Co., 1970.
343p.

Bibliography: p. 334-336.

1. Education. I. Title. II. Title: Urban education.

378
E74   Toward increasing the social relevance of the contemporary university.
Ericson, Richard F
Toward increasing the social relevance of the contemporary university. Wash., George Washington University, Program of Policy Studies in Science and Technology, Cybernetic Studies Group, 1969.
31p.
A resume of the philosophic bases and the activities of the interdisciplinary systems and cybernetics project since 1967, and plans for the future.
1. Universities and colleges. I. George Washington University. Program of Policy Studies in Science and Technology. II. Title.

331
E68   Toward job equality for women.
U.S. Equal Employment Opportunity Commission
Toward job equality for women. Wash., 1969.
11p.

1. Employment. I. Title.

332.748
H15   Toward limited exchange-rate flexibility.
Halm, George N
Toward limited exchange-rate flexibility. Princeton, N.J., International Finance Section, Dept. of Economics, Princeton University, 1969.
33p. (Princeton University. International Finance Section. Princeton studies in international finance no. 73)

1. Foreign exchange. I. Title. II. Princeton University. (International Finance Section)

338.8
065
M8   Toward more housing.
U.S. Congress. Temporary National Economic Committee.
Toward more housing. Washington, Govt. Print. Off., 1941.
223 p. charts(fold.), graphs, tables.
(Its Investigation of concentration of economic power monograph no. 8)

Senate committee print, 76th Cong., 3d sess., 1941.
Includes bibliographies.
(Continued on next card)

U.S. Congress. Temporary National Economic Committee. Toward more housing ... 1941. (Card 2)

Contents.-pt.1.Some economic aspects of housing, by Peter A. Stone.-pt.2.The relation of productivity to low-cost housing, by R. Harold Denton.

1.Building industry. 2.Building costs. 3.Mortgage finance. 4.Housing research I.Stone, Peter A. II.Denton, R. Harold. III.Title.

370
F67t   Toward mutual understanding...
U.S. Board of Foreign Scholarships.
Toward mutual understanding... a report on academic exchanges, a report to the U.S. Congress on academic exchanges.
19   Wash.
v. annual.
For Library holdings see main entry.

1. Educational exchanges. I. Title.

711.417
(73)
S72
Toward new towns for America.
Stein, Clarence S
    Toward new towns for America. With an introd.
by Lewis Mumford.   Liverpool, Univ. of Liverpool
agents for the Western Hemisphere: Public Administration Service, Chicago, 1951.
    245 p.   illus.

    Bibliography: p. 229-235.

    1.New towns. 2.Greenbelt, Md. I.Mumford, Lewis.
II.Title.

628.1
R46
Toward the optimization of investment-pricing
    decisions.
Riordan, Courtney.
    Toward the optimization of investment-pricing
decisions: a model for urban water supply
treatment facilities. [Ithaca, N.Y.] Dept. of
City and Regional Planning, Cornell University,
1969.
    304p. (Cornell dissertations in planning)
    Bibliography: p. 296-304.
    Thesis (Ph.D.) - Cornell University.

    1. Water-supply. 2. Municipal finance.
I. Cornell. University. Dept. of City and
Regional Planning.   II. Title.

330
G15t
Towards a strategy for conservation in a
    world of technological change.
Gannon, Colin A
    Towards a strategy for conservation in a
world of technological change. Philadelphia,
Regional Science Research Institute, 1968.
    43p. (Regional Science Research Institute.
Discussion paper series no. 24)
    Bibliography: p. 42-43.

    1. Economic development. I. Title.
II. Regional Science Research Institute,
Philadelphia.

711.417
(73)
S72
1957
Toward new towns for America.
Stein, Clarence S
    Toward new towns for America. With
an introd. by Lewis Mumford. New York,
Reinhold Pub. Corp., 1957.
    263p.

    Bibliography: p. 249-253.

    1. New towns. 2. Greenbelt, Md.
I. Mumford, Lewis. II. Ti .

711.585
(74927)
J27
Toward the seventies; a progress report of
    the Jersey City Redevelopment Agency.
Jersey City. Redevelopment Agency.
    Toward the seventies; a progress report
of the Jersey City Redevelopment Agency.
Jersey City, [1970?]
    25p.

    1. Urban renewal - Jersey City, N.J.
I. Title.

388
(794)
L47
Towards a systems transportation network.
Litton Industries. Economic Development Div.
    Proposal to the Div. of Highways, Dept. of
Public Works, State of California for a
Work Program to design and develop specifi-
cations for an integrated study of transpor-
tation in California. Beverly Hills, Calif.,
1964.
    1v.
    Cover title: Toward a systems approach for
a California integrated transportation network.
    1. Transportation - Calif. 2. Journey to
work. 3. Transportation - Finance. I. California.
Dept. of Public Works.   II. Title. III. Title:
Toward a systems transportation network.

711.417
(73)
S72
1966
Toward new towns for America.
Stein, Clarence S
    Toward new towns for America. With an
introduction by Lewis Mumford. Cambridge,
Mass., M.I.T. Press, 1966.
    263p.
    Paperback ed.
    Bibliography: p. 249-255.

    1. New towns. 2. Planned communities.
I. Mumford, Lewis.   II. Title.

339.5
A52
Toward the sociological analysis of natural
    resources and society.
Andrews, Wade H
    Toward the sociological analysis of natural
resources and society. Logan, Utah State University, Institute for Social Science Research
on Natural Resources, 1968.
    [15] p. (Utah. State University, Logan.
Institute for Social Science Research on
Natural Resources. Special paper no. 1)
    1. Natural resources. 2. Man - Influence of
environment. I. Utah. State University of Agriculture and Applied Science, Logan. Institute for Social   Science Research on Natural Resour   ces. II. Title.

330
(54)
S45
Towards and integrated society.
Singh, Tarlok
    Toward an integrated society; reflections on
planning, social policy and rural institutions.
Westport, Conn., Greenwood, 1969.
    554p. (Contributions in economics and
economic history, no. 6)

    1. Economic policy - India. 2. Social
conditions - India. 3. Rural planning -
India. I. Title.

711.13
N25
Toward policies for balanced growth.
Nelson, Donald L   ed.
    Toward policies for balanced growth; a
lecture series sponsored by the Graduate
School, U.S. Department of Agriculture.
Wash., Graduate School Press, U.S. Dept.
of Agriculture, 1971.
    88p.

    1. Decentralization. 2. Population
density. 3. City growth. 4. Rural planning.
I. U.S. Dept. of Agriculture. Graduate
School. II. Title.

711.4
A52ne
no.1
Toward the year 2000: work in progress.
Daedalus.
    Toward the year 2000: work in progress.
Richmond, American Academy of Arts and
Sciences, 1967.
    1002p.
    Partial contents: Planning and predicting;
or what to do when you don't know the names
of the variables, by Leonard J. Duhl.
    Also participating in Working session:
Charles M. Haar and Robert C. Wood.
    Issued as Vol. 96, no. 3 of the Proceedings
of the American Academy of Arts and Sciences.

    (continued on next card)

308
(78883:016) Towards an urban sociology of Denver.
S72
    Sternberg, Barbara, 1923-
        Towards an urban sociology of Denver, a select and anno-
    tated bibliography with interpretative comments. [Denver]
    University of Denver Press, 1949 [i. e. 1950]
        vi, 109 p. 21 cm. (Denver. University. Publications. Studies in
    social sciences, no. 1)

        1.Social surveys-Denver-Bibl.
        1. Denver—Soc. condit.—Bibl.   I. Title.   II.Series: Denver.
    University. Studies in social sciences, no. 1.

    Z7165.U6D35   016.309178   50-2855
    Library of Congress   [3]

551
(798)
N17t
Toward reduction of losses from earthquakes.
National Research Council. (Committee on
    the Alaska Earthquake)
    Toward reduction of losses from earth-
quakes; conclusions from the great Alaska
earthquake of 1964. Washington, National
Academy of Sciences, 1969.
    34p.
                - Alaska.
    1. Earthquakes. 2. Earthquake resistant
construction. I. Title. II. Title: The
great Alaska earthquake of 1964.

711.4
A52ne
no.1
Daedalus. Toward the year 2000...1967.

    AIP/Ewald notebooks, Basic book no. 1.

    1. City planning. 2. Scientific research.
3. Sociology. 4. Economic development.
5. Political science. 6. Universities and
colleges. 7. Church and social problems.
I. American Academy of Arts and Sciences.
II. Duhl, Leonard J. Planning and predicting;
or what to do when you don't know the names
of the variables. III. Title.

362
(41)
W47
Towards economic design of water and sanitary
    services for hospitals.
Wise, A   F   E
    Towards economic design of water and sani-
tary services for hospitals. Garston, Eng.,
Building Research Station Ministry of Tech-
nology, 1966.
    12p.   (U.K. Building Research Station.
Building research current papers. Engineer-
ing series 25)
    Paper presented to the Hospital Engineering
Service Symposium of the I.H.V.E., January,
1966.

    1. Hospitals - U.K.   2. Water-supply.
3. Sanitation.   I. U.K. Building
Research Station.   II. Title.

330
W45
Toward social welfare.
Wilcox, Clair
    Toward social welfare; an analysis of
programs and proposals attacking poverty,
insecurity, and inequality of opportunity.
Homewood, Ill., Irwin, 1969.
    402p.

    Bibliography: p. 381-391.

    1. Economic policy. 2. Social welfare.
I. Title.

728.100.15
E77
Towards a habitable world; task, problems, and
    methods, acceleration.
Ettinger, Jan van.
    Towards a habitable world; task, problems
and methods, acceleration. Published for
Bouwcentrum Rotterdam. Amsterdam, Elsevier,
1960.
    318p. illus., diagrs., tables.

    1. Housing research. 2. Building construction.
I. Bouwcentrum. II. Title.

628.2
L45
Towards general method for the design of
    drainage systems in large buildings.
Lillywhite, M   S   T
    Towards general method for the design of
drainage systems in large buildings, by
M.S.T. Lillywhite and A.F.E. Wise.
Garston, Eng., Building Research Station,
1969.
    22p. (U.K. Building Research Station.
Current paper 27/69)
    Paper presented at a meeting of the
Institution of Public Health Engineers,
Caxton Hall, Westminster, London, 6th
Feb. 1969.
    1. Drainage.   I. Wise, A.F.E., jt. au.
                    (Cont'd on next card)

332.72
(71)
O57
TOWARD THE IMPROVEMENT OF MORTGAGE
    MARKETING.
ONTARIO TITLE INSURANCE AGENCY LIMITED.
    TOWARD THE IMPROVEMENT OF MORTGAGE
MARKETING. TORONTO, 1958.
    20L.

    SUPPLEMENT: CANADIAN MORTGAGES AND
THE UNITED STATES INVESTOR. 4L.

    1. MORTGAGE FINANCE - CANADA.
I. TITLE.

339.5
N17t
Towards a national materials policy.
U.S. National Commission on Materials Policy.
    Towards a national materials policy; basic
data and issues, an interim report. Wash.,
1972.
    63p.

    1. Natural resources. 2. Building materials.
I. Title.

628.2
L45
Lillywhite, M   S   T   Towards
    general...1969.   (Card 2)

    II. U.K. Building Research Station.
III. Title.

690
I57t Towards industrialised building.
1965 International Council for Building Research
Studies and Documentation.
Towards industrialised building; proceedings
of the third CIB Congress, Copenhagen, 1965.
Amsterdam, New York, Elsevier Pub. Co., 1966.
493p.

1. Building industry. 2. Prefabricated construction. I. Title. II. Title: Industrialised
building.

VF - Office management
DATE OF REQUEST 12/29/54   L.C. CARD NO.
AUTHOR Tower, Ralph B.
TITLE Handbook of small business finance [with list of
publications for further study].
SERIES Small business management series #15.
EDITION   PUB. DATE Sept. 1954   PAGING 71p.
PUBLISHER

RECOMMENDED BY   REVIEWED IN
    SBA   Monthly Catalog, 11/54, p.66
ORDER RECORD

TOWN   (definition)

Used in New York State to indicate a unit of rural
administration similar to the township of many other
parts of the country.

(N.Y.S. Commerce Review, p. 11   footnote)

Towards information retrieval.

538.56
F14 Fairthorne, Robert Arthur.
Towards information retrieval.
London, Butterworths, 1961.
211p.

1. Automation. 2. Documentation.
I. Title.

621.9 Tower cranes for building.
:690 U.K. Building Research Station.
(47) Tower cranes for building. Garstone, Eng.,
U54 1971.
[57]p. (Library communication no. 1601)

Translated from the Russian.

1. Building equipment - U.S.S.R. I. Title.
(Series)

352
I57t International Union of Local Authorities.
Town affiliation. Papers presented at
the World Conference of Local Governments,
Washington, D.C., June 15-20, 1961. The
Hague, M. Nijhoff, for the International
Union of Local Authorities, 1962.
45p. (Its [Publication] 70)

1. Local government. I. Title.
II. World Conference of Local Governments
Washington, D.C., 1961.

711.4 Towards new planning and building legislation
(485) in Sweden.
S82t Sweden. National Board of Urban Planning.
Towards new planning and building legislation
in Sweden. Stockholm, 1968.
12p. (Its Statens planverk information in
English no. 1)

1. City planning - Sweden. 2. Building
industry - Sweden. I. Title.

621.9 Tower cranes in Finland.
:690 Saarinen, Erkki.
S11 Suomen torninosturit (Tower cranes in
Finland) por Erkki Saarinen e Raimo Salokangas.
Helsinki, State Institute for Technical
Research, 1970.
46p. (Finland. State Institute for
Technical Research. Tiedotus. Sarja 3 -
Rakennus 147)
English summary.
1. Building equipment. I. Salokangas,
Raimo, jt. au. II. Finland. State Institute
for Technical Research. III. Title: Tower
cranes in Finland.

711.4 Towns and cities.
(09) Jones, Emrys.
J65 Towns and cities. London, New York,
Oxford University Press, 1966.
152p.
Bibliography: p[143] - 145.

1. City planning - Hist. 2. Metropolitan
areas. I. Title.

Towards postal excellence.

351.7
:383 U.S. President's Commission on Postal
P72 Organization.
Towards postal excellence. The report.
Wash., For sale by the Supt. of Docs., Govt.
Print Off., 1968.
212p.

1. Postal service. 2. Management.
3. U.S. Post Office Dept. 4. Labor
relations. I. Title.

352.6 Tower lines and residential property.
(746) Kinnard, William N.
K45 Tower lines and residential property
values. Storrs, Conn., Center for Real
Estate and Urban Economic Studies, Univer-
sity of Connecticut, 1967.
[16]p. (Connecticut. University.
Center for Real Estate and Urban Economic
Studies. Reprint series no. 3)
Reprinted from: The Appraisal Journal,
Apr. 1967, p. 269-283.

(Cont'd on next card)

711.4 Town and city monographs.
:67 Massachusetts. Dept. of Commerce. Division of
(744) Research.
M171 Town and city monographs, no. 1-
Boston, 1955-
    nos. in   v.
Index   Index
    Library lacks nos.

For complete contents see Shelf list card.

1. Industrial location - Mass. I. Title.
2. Economic conditions - Mass.

647.1 TOWARDS SOLVING THE LOW-INCOME PROBLEM
(754) OF SMALL FARMERS.
W27 WEST VIRGINIA. AGRICULTURAL EXPERIMENT
STATION, MORGANTOWN.
TOWARDS SOLVING THE LOW-INCOME PROBLEM
OF SMALL FARMERS IN THE APPALACHIAN
AREA, BY ANTHONY L. PAVLICK.
MORGANTOWN, W. VA., 1964.
71P. (ITS BULLETIN 499T)

1. FAMILY INCOME AND EXPENDITURE -
WEST VIRGINIA. 2. ECONOMIC CONDITIONS
- WEST VIRGINIA. I. PAVLICK, ANTHONY L.
II. TITLE.

352.6
(746) Kinnard, William N.
K45 Tower lines and residential property
values. 1967.
    (Card 2)

1. Public utilities - Conn. 2. Real
property - Valuation. 3. Public utilities -
Surveys. I. Connecticut. University.
Center for Real Estate and Urban Economic
Studies. II. Title.

711.4 Town and country planning.
(41) Keeble, Lewis.
K22 Principles and practice of town and country
1969 planning. 4th ed. London, Estates Gazette,
1969.
415p.

Bibliography: p. 399-403.

1. City planning - U.K. 2. Regional
planning - U.K. I. Title. II. Title:
Town and country planning.

711.3 Tower, F Carlisle.
(7471) Regional Plan Association, New York.
R23 The Lower Hudson, by F. Carlisle Towery
in collaboration with Philip Israel, under
the supervision of Stanley B. Tankel and
Boris Pushkarev. Edited by William B.
Shore. A report of the second Regional
plan. New York, 1966.
78p.
"Sequel to the Regional plan of New York
and its environs."

1. Metropolitan area planning - New York (City)
2. Regional planning - New York metropolitan
area. I. Towery, F. Carlisle. II. Shore,
William B., ed. III. Title.

VF
621.315 Towers
P67
Portugal. Laboratório Nacional de
Engenharia Civil.
Experimental study of towers for
high tension lines [by] J. Ferry Borges
and J. Arga e Lima. Lisbon, 1956.
14 p. illus. (Its Report no. 86)

Reprinted from the Preliminary Publication of the V Congress of the International
Association of Bridge and Structural Engineering.
1. Structural engineering. I. Ferry, Borges, J
I. Title: Towers

711.4 (41)
F63 Town and country planning.

Fogarty, Michael Patrick.
Town and country planning. London, New York, Hutchinson's University Library, 1948.
221 p. diagr. (on lining-paper) 19 cm. (Hutchinson's university
library: Politics)
"Note on further reading": p. 215-216.

1. City planning-Gt. Brit.
2. Cities and towns - Planning - Gt. Brit.   I. Title.

NA9185.F6   711   49—14322*
Library of Congress   [50d2]

728.1 TOWER, JOHN G
:347 U.S. FEDERAL HOUSING ADMINISTRATION.
F22 REPLY TO SENATOR JOHN G. TOWER,
CONCERNING THE VARIOUS MULTIFAMILY
HOUSING PROGRAMS OF THE FEDERAL HOUSING
ADMINSTRATION. WASHINGTON, 1963.
1 V. (VARIOUS PAGINGS)

CONTAINS INFORMATION CONCERNING
CHANGES IN THE LAW AND REGULATIONS WITH
RESPECT TO MULTIFAMILY SECTIONS OF THE
NATIONAL HOUSING ACT.
1. HOUSING LEGISLATION. I. NATIONAL
HOUSING ACT. II. TOWER, JOHN G.

VF
728.1 Town, George.
:362.6 Loans for group housing. (Reproduced
T68 from Harvest years. July 1964. p.36-
38)

"Story on the Direct loan program,
the newest addition to the HHFA's
portfolio of aids to retirement housing."

1. Housing for the aged.
2. U.S.   Housing and Home
Finance   Agency.
I. Title.

711.4 TOWN AND COUNTRY PLANNING.
(41) MCALLISTER, GILBERT.
M21 TOWN AND COUNTRY PLANNING; A STUDY OF
PHYSICAL ENVIRONMENT; THE PRELUDE TO
POST-WAR RECONSTRUCTION, BY GILBERT
MCALLISTER AND ELIZABETH GLEN
MCALLISTER. WITH A FOREWORD BY THE RT.
HON. ARTHUR GREENWOOD. LONDON, FABER
AND FABER, 1941.
176P.

1. CITY PLANNING - U.K. 2. HOUSING -
U.K. I. MCALLISTER, ELIZABETH GLEN.
II. TITLE.

711.4
(41)
T68T
TOWN AND COUNTRY PLANNING.
TOWN PLANNING INSTITUTE, LONDON.
TOWN AND COUNTRY PLANNING,
COMPENSATION AND BETTERMENT, REPORT OF
COMMITTEE OF THE INSTITUTE, APPROVED BY
THE COUNCIL OF THE INSTITUTE, 31ST MAY,
1940. LONDON, EDE & TOWNSEND, 1940.
60P.

1. CITY PLANNING - U.K. 2. EMINENT
DOMAIN. I. TITLE.

711
(41:347)
E52
Town and Country Planning Act, 1947 (U.K.)
Encyclopaedia of the law of planning, compulsory
purchase and compensation; general editor,
E. J. Rimmer.   London, Sweet & Maxwell
[1949]
2 v. in 3 (loose-leaf)

Current.
Contents.-v.1.Planning, by D. Heap and H. J.
Brown.-v.2.Compulsory purchase and compensation,
by R. D. Stewart-Brown.

711.4
(41)
R45
TOWN AND COUNTRY PLANNING ASSOCIATION.
RILEY, DENIS W
THE CITIZEN'S GUIDE TO TOWN AND
COUNTRY PLANNING. REV. ED. LONDON,
TOWN & COUNTRY PLANNING ASSOCIATION,
1966.
68P.

BIBLIOGRAPHY: P.56-57.

1. CITY PLANNING - UNITED KINGDOM.
I. TOWN AND COUNTRY PLANNING ASSOCIATION.
II. TITLE.

711.4
(41)
U54
1951
Town and country planning.
U.K. British Information Services.
(Reference Div.)
Town and country planning. New York, 1951.
31p.   (I.D. 920, rev.)

1. City planning - U.K. I. Title.

711.4
(41:347)
H11
Town and Country Planning Act, 1947
(United Kingdom)
Haar, Charles Monroe, 1921–
Land planning law in a free society; a study of the British
town and country planning act. Cambridge, Harvard Uni-
versity Press, 1951.
xiii, 213 p. illus., maps. 25 cm. (Harvard legal studies)
Bibliographical references included in "Notes" (p. [173]-210)

1. Cities and towns—Planning—Gt. Brit. 2. Regional planning—
Gt. Brit. 3. Land—Gt. Brit.   I. Title.   (Series)

711.172   51-6659
Library of Congress   [7]

711.4
(41)
T685
TOWN AND COUNTRY PLANNING ASSOCIATION.
CONFERENCE, LONDON, 1943.
COUNTRY TOWNS IN THE FUTURE ENGLAND; A
REPORT OF THE CONFERENCE REPRESENTING
LOCAL AUTHORITIES, ARTS AND AMENITIES
ORGANIZATIONS AND MEMBERS OF THE TOWN
AND COUNTRY PLANNING ASSOCIATION ON THE
23RD OF OCTOBER, 1943, EDITED BY STANLEY
BARON. LONDON, FABER AND FABER LIMITED,
1944.
140P.

1. CITY PLANNING - U.K. I. BARON,
STANLEY, ED.   II. TITLE.

VF
711.4
(41)
U54to
Town and country planning.
U.K. Labour Publications Dept.
Town and country planning. London,
Labour Party, Transport House, 1947.
16p.

1. City planning - U.K. I. Title.

711.333
(41)
U54
1956
Town and Country Planning Act, 1947 (U.K.)
U.K. County Borough of East Ham. (County
Council)
Development plan: (prepared in accordance
with Section 5 of the Town and Country
Planning Act, 1947) written statement.
Essex, Eng., 1956.
[15]p. tables.

Plan submitted to the Minister of Housing
and Local Government.

(See Card No. 2)

VF
711.3
(41)
T68
Town and Country Planning Association.
Green belts: their establishment and
safeguarding; a memorandum by the executive
of the Town and Country Planning Association
prepared at the request of the Minister of
Housing and Local government. London [Jan.1956]
8 p.

1.Title.

711
(41:347)
H21
Town and Country Planning Act, 1932 (U.K.)
Heap, Desmond
Planning law for town and country, being a
critical dissertation on the Town and Country
Planning Act, 1932, and on the regulations and
orders made thereunder and a number of enactments
having relation thereto. With an introd. by Sir
Raymond Unwin.   London, Sweet & Maxwell, 1938.
208 p.
1.City planning legislation-U.K. 2.Town and
Country Planning Act, 1932 (U.K.) I.Title.

711.333
(41)
U54
1956
U.K. County Borough of East Ham. (County
Council) Development plan. 1956. (Card No.2

711.333
(41)
U54
1956
map
With this is issued: 3 maps: - 1. Designation area no. 1. - 2. Town map. - 3. Programme
map.

1.County planning - U.K. 2.Town and Country
Planning Act, 1947 (U.K.)

728.1
(41)
R67
Town and Country Planning Association.
Roskill, O W
Housing in Britain. A survey commissioned
by the Town and Country Planning Association.
London, Town and Country Planning Association,
1964.
150p.

1. Housing - U.K. 2. Housing - Social
aspects. 3. City planning - U.K. I. Town
and Country Planning Association.

Town and Country Planning Act, 1947 (U.K.)

see also

City planning - U.K.
Regional planning - U.K.

711.333
(41)
U54
1952
Town and Country Planning Act, 1947.
(U.K.)
U.K. County Borough of East Ham. (Engineer
and Surveyor's Department)
Town and Country Planning Act of 1947.
Development plan, 1952: written analysis, an
analysis of the planning problems in the
county borough. [Essex, Eng.] 1952.
1 v. maps, tables.

1.County planning - U.K. 2.Town and Country
Planning Act, 1947. (U.K.)

711.417
(41)
B27
TOWN AND COUNTRY PLANNING
ASSOCIATION.
BEST, ROBIN H
LAND FOR NEW TOWNS; A STUDY OF LAND
USE, DENSITIES, AND AGRICULTURAL
DISPLACEMENT. LONDON, TOWN AND
COUNTRY PLANNING ASSOCIATION, 1964,
REPRINTED 1966.
59P.

1. PLANNED COMMUNITIES - U.K.
2. REGIONAL PLANNING. I. TOWN AND
COUNTRY PLANNING ASSOCIATION.
II. TITLE.

Law
T
C518La
Town and Country Planning Act, 1947
(U. K.)
Clarke, John J
Law of housing and planning, by
John J. Clarke and Leslie Scott. 5th ed.
London, Isaac Pitman, 1949.
547 p.

Bibliography: p. 497-512.

1.Housing legislation - U.K.
2. Town and Country Planning Act, 1947
(U.K.) I.Scott, Leslie, jt. au.

VF
728.1
:061.3
I57
1950
no. 4
Town and country planning and industry.
International Federation for Housing and Town
Planning. 20th Congress, Amsterdam, 1950.
Town and country planning and industry.
L'aménagement des villes et de la campagne, et
l'industrie.   Amsterdam [1950?]
78 p.   ([Congress report no. 4])

English with summaries in French.
Sections by L.H.J. Angenot, Waclaw Ostrowski,
Boleslaw Malisz, the Earl of Verulam, Max Werner.
1.Industrial location. I.Title.

VF
728.69
M68
Town and Country Planning Association.
Movable Dwelling Conference, 1947-9.
Movable dwellings; report. London, Town
and Country Planning Association, 1950.
96 p.

"Convened in Oct. 1947 by the Caravan Club of
Great Britain and Ireland and the Town and Country
Planning Association:" p.7.

I.Caravan Club of Great Britain and Ireland.
II.Town and Country Planning Association.

711
(41:347)
C51
Town and Country Planning Act, 1947 (U.K.)
Clarke, John J
A synopsis of the Town and Country
Planning Act, 1947. London, Pitman,
1949.
28 p.

Bibliography: p. 28.

1.Town and Country Planning Act, 1947 (U.K.)
2.City planning - U.K. 3.Regional planning -
U.K.

Cat.
DATE OF REQUEST   12/9/54   L. C. CARD NO.

AUTHOR
Town and country planning association;

TITLE Bibliography of publications referring to the
development of country towns in Great Britain.

SERIES

| EDITION | PUB. DATE 1952? | PAGING 7p. |

PUBLISHER

RECOMMENDED BY   REVIEWED IN
              MML   Lon.Cur.Lit.,11/1/54,p.5.

ORDER RECORD

711.417
(41)
T68
Town and Country Planning Association.
New towns, an exhibition arranged by
the Town and Country Planning Association
and the fifteen New Town Development C
Corporations. London, 1959.
59p. illus., diagrs., tables.

1. New towns - U.K.

711.14
(41)
T68
Town and Country Planning Association.
Planning Britain's land; a summary of Town and country planning act, 1947. London, 1947.
15p.

1. Land use - U.K. I. Title.

711.3
(945)
T68
2c.
Town and Country Planning Association of Victoria.
Let's plan. [Melbourne, 1944?]
92 p. illus.

1.Regional planning-Australia. 2.City planning-Australia. 3.Housing-Australia. I.Title.

711.4
(41)
T68
Town and country planning summer school, Bangor, 1952.
Town Planning Institute
Town and country planning summer school, Bangor. 1952: report of proceedings. London [1953?]
viii, 115 p.

Partial contents.-The place of housing in town and country planning, by George Pepler.-Design in its relation to economic factors, by Gordon Stephenson.-The development of new towns, by W. O. Hart.

711.3
825
1964
Town and Country Planning Association.
Seminar on Metropolitan Planning, Ditchley Park, Eng., 1964.
The regional city; an Anglo-American discussion of metropolitan planning, edited by Derek Senior. Chicago, Aldine Pub. Co., 1966.
192p.
Sponsored by the Ditchley Foundation in collaboration with the Town and Country Planning Association.

(Cont'd on next card)

711
(41)
U54t
1958
Town and country planning bill.
U.K. Ministry of Housing and Local Government.
Town and country planning bill. Explanatory memorandum. London, H.M. Stat. Off., 1958.
24p. (American Embassy, London. Foreign service dispatch no. 1058, 1958, enclosure no. 2)

1. City planning - U.K. 2. Regional planning - U.K. 3. Land use - U.K. I. Title. II. Series: American Embassy, London. Foreign service dispatch no. 1058, 1958, enclosure no. 2.

711.3
(05)
T68
Town and Country Planning Technical Broadsheet, no.1-24. [Edinburgh, Dept. of Health for Scotland, June 1948-Sept. 1949]
24 pts. in 1.

1.Regional planning-Period. 2.Survey methods. 3.Maps and mapping.

711.3
825
1964
Seminar on Metropolitan Planning, Ditchley Park, Eng., 1964. The regional city; an Anglo-American discussion of metropolitan planning...1966.
(Card 2)

1. Metropolitan area planning. 2. City planning. 3. City planning - U.K. 4. Urban renewal - Social effect. I. Senior, Derek, ed. II. Ditchley Foundation, Ditchley Park, Eng. III. Town and Country Planning Association. IV. Title.

711.4
(41)
U54t
1947
Town and country planning bill, explanatory memorandum, 1947.
U.K. Ministry of Town and Country Planning.
Town and country planning bill, explanatory memorandum, 1947. London, H.M. Stat. Off., 1947.
22p. (Cmd. 7006)

1. City planning - U.K. 2. Regional planning - U.K. I. Title.

711
(41)
A77t
Town and country planning textbook.
Association for Planning and Regional Reconstruction...Town and country planning textbook, ed. by APRR. With an introd. by W.G.Holford. London, Architectural Press [1950]
xx, 613 p. diagrs., maps, tables.

Bibliography: p.577-591.

1.City planning. 2.City planning-Gt. Brit. 3.Regional planning-Gt. Brit. I.Holford,W.G. Analytics: Taylor, E. G. R.; Forrester, J.; Whittle, Jack.

VF
728
B18
Town and Country Planning Association.
Bauer, Catherine, 1905-
Social questions in housing & town planning. London, University of London Press [1952]
35 p. 22 cm.

For full information see main entry card.

1. Housing - U.S. 2. Title.

Full name: Catherine Krouse Bauer.

HD7293.B35   331.833   53-23112 †

Library of Congress   [3]

711
(41)
U54
1967
Town and country planning in Britain.
U.K. Central Office of Information. (Reference Div.)
Town and country planning in Britain., 1967. London, H.M.S.O., 1968.
31p. (Its Reference pamphlet 9)
Bibliography: p. 31-32.
Prepared for U.K. British Information Services.

1. Planning - U.K. 2. U.K. - Planning. I. U.K. British Information Services. II. Title.

711.4
B68
Town and country tomorrow.
Boumphrey, Geoffrey Maxwell, 1894-
Town and country tomorrow, by Geoffrey Boumphrey. With an introduction by Herbert J. Manzoni ... London, New York [etc.] T. Nelson and sons ltd. [1940]
xvi, 17-200 p. front., plates, diagrs. 18½ cm. (Half-title: Discussion books. General editors: Richard Wilson ... and A. J. J. Ratcliff ... no. 74)
"First published, 1940."

1.City planning. I.Title.
2.Cities and towns—Planning. III. Title

A 41—1629

Harvard univ. Library for Library of Congress   [2]

711
(41)
U54
1968
Town and country planning in Britain.
U.K. Central Office of Information. (Reference Div.)
Town and country planning in Britain. Rev. New York, 1968.
32p.

Bibliography: p. 31-32.
Prepared for U.K. British Information Services.
1. Planning - U.K. I. U.K. British Information Services. (Reference Div.) II. Title.

VF
711.3
A37
Town and country, U.S.A...
U.S. Dept. of Agriculture.
Town and country, U.S.A.; a year-end report by the Secretary, 1967;
Washington, D.C., 1967-
v.
1967-   by Secretary Freeman.
For complete information see main card.

1. Rural planning. 2. Population shifts. I. Freeman, Orville. II. Title.

711.4
(41)
U54
1949
Towns and country planning in Britain...
U.K. British Information Services. (Reference Div.)
Town and country planning in Britain; the main problems, Barlow, Scott, and Uthwatt reports, the Planning acts, 1947, replanning in action, new towns. New York, 1949.
43p. (I.D. 920)

1. City planning - U.K. I. Title.

711.4
(09)
Z82
Town and square from the agora to the village green.
Zucker, Paul
Town and square from the agora to the village green. New York, Columbia University Press, 1959.
287p.
Bibliography: p. [256]-275.

1. City planning - Hist. 2. Shopping centers. I. Title.

711.3(41)
T58
Town and country planning association. *Conference, Oxford,* 1941.
Replanning Britain; being a summarized report of the Oxford conference of the Town and country planning association, spring, 1941, edited by F. E. Towndrow ... London, Faber and Faber limited [1941]
173 p. 22 cm.
"First published in September Mcmxli."
1. Regional planning—Gt. Brit. 2. Regional planning—Congresses. 3. Cities and towns—Planning. 4. Industries, Location of. 5. Agriculture—Gt. Brit. I. Towndrow, Frederic Edward, 1897- ed. II. Title. 4. Industrial location.

Harvard univ. Library for Library of Congress   HT407.T68 1941   A 42-1790

[a45] 3, †   300.142

711.4
(41)
C865
TOWN AND COUNTRY PLANNING IN ENGLAND AND WALES.
CULLINGWORTH, J B
TOWN AND COUNTRY PLANNING IN ENGLAND AND WALES; AN INTRODUCTION. TORONTO, UNIVERSITY OF TORONTO PRESS, 1964.
301P.

1. CITY PLANNING - U.K. I. TITLE.

720
(47)
K66
Town and revolution.
Kopp, Anatole.
Town and revolution; Soviet architecture and city planning, 1917-1935. Translated by Thomas E. Burton. London, Thames and Hudson, 1970.
274p.

Bibliography: p. 261-267.

1. Architecture - U.S.S.R. 2. City planning - U.S.S.R. I. Title.

711
:308
S54

Town building.

Smith, Bernard.
   Town building. Dallas, Tex.,
Holland's Southern Institute for Town Service,
1939.
   150 p. illus.

   1. Community development manuals. I. Title.

711.4
G41
1959

Town design.

Gibberd, Frederick.
   Town design. 3d ed. New York, Praeger,
1959.
   316p. illus., diagrs., maps.

   1. City planning.   2. Housing.   3. Shopping
centers.   4. Industrial location. I. Title.

711.4
S54ci

The town in American history.

Smith, Page.
   As a city upon a hill: the town in
American history. New York. Alfred, A.
Knopf, 1966.
   332p.

   1. City planning - History. 2. City
growth. 3. Church and social problems.
4. Sociology, Urban. I. Title. II. Title:
The town in American history.

711.417
(41)
A15

A TOWN CALLED ALCAN.

ALCAN INDUSTRIES LIMITED.
   A TOWN CALLED ALCAN. BANBURY, 1964.
24P.

   1. NEW TOWNS - U.K.   2. ALUMINUM.
3. CITY PLANNING - U.K.   I. TITLE.

711.4
G41
1967

Town design.

Gibberd, Frederick.
   Town design. 5th ed. New York,
Frederick A. Praeger, 1967.
   372p.   (Books that matter)

   1. City planning. 2. Architecture -
Design. 3. Landscape architecture.
4. Industrial location. 5. Housing.
I. Title.

FOLIO
711.4
F52

TOWN IN TRANSITION.

FLEWELLING, RALPH CARLIN, 1894-
   TOWN IN TRANSITION. LOS ANGELES, 1945.
20P.

   1. CITY PLANNING.   I. TITLE.

711.585
(41)
U54

Town centres approach to renewal.

U.K. Ministry of Housing and Local
Government.
   Town centres approach to renewal.
[In cooperation with] Ministry of
Transport. London, H.M. Stat.
Office, 1962.
   21p.   (Its Planning bulletin 1)

   1. Urban renewal - U.K. I. Title.
II. U.K. Ministry of Transport.

711.585
(794)
T68

TOWN HALL, LOS ANGELES.
   THE NEED FOR URBAN REDEVELOPMENT
LEGISLATION IN CALIFORNIA. A REPORT
BY THE REGIONAL PLANNING AND
DEVELOPMENT SECTION, REGINALD D.
JOHNSON, CHAIRMAN. LOS ANGELES, 1944.
34P.

   1. URBAN RENEWAL - CALIFORNIA.
I. JOHNSON, REGINALD D.

711.4:67
W45

The town in which we want to build a plant.

Williams, S   B
   The town in which we want to build a plant,
an address before the 5th Annual Conference.
Association of State Planning & Development
Agencies. Hotel New Yorker, New York City, May
9, 1950.
   10 l.
   Author is Director of Public Relations, Sylvania
Electric Products, Inc.
   Processed.
   1. Industrial location. I. Title.

711.552
(41)
U54

Town centres; cost and control of redevelopment.

U.K. Ministry of Housing and Local
Government.
   Town centres; cost and control of re-
development. [Prepared in cooperation with]
Ministry of Transporrt. London, H.M.
Stationery Off., 1963.
   12p.   (Its Planning bulletin 3)

   1. Business districts - U.K.
I. Title.

058.7
1(794)
T68

Town Hall of California.
   Report to members; with a list of members
June 1968   Los Angeles, 1968
   1v.

   For Library holdings see main entry.

   1. Town Hall of California - Direct.

352
(744)
M17

Town meeting.

Massachusetts. University. Bureau of
Government Research.
   Guide for establishing a representative
town meeting. Amherst, Mass., 1957.
   32p.

   1. Municipal government - Mass. I. Title:
Town meeting.

711.552
(41)
U54t

Town centres; current practice.

U.K. Ministry of Housing and Local
Government.
   Town centres; current practice.
[Prepared in cooperation with] the
Ministry of Transport. London, H.M.
Stationery Off., 1963.
   1v.   (Its Planning bulletin 4)

   1. Business districts - U.K.   2. City planning - U.K.
3. Urban renewal - U.K.   I. U.K. Ministry
of Transport.   II. Title.

058.7
1(794)
T68

Town Hall of California - Directories.

Town Hall of California.
   Report to members; with a list of members
       Los Angeles,
   v.

   For Library holdings see main entry.

   1. Town Hall of California - Direct.

Folio
711.4
(43)
T68

Town plan for the development of Selb.
   Town planning, by Walter Gropius and the
Architects Collaborative, inc. Traffic
planning, by Kurt Leibbrand and Verkehrs-und
Industrieplanung GmbH. Cambridge, Mass.,
MIT Press, 1969.
   72p.
   Translation of Entwicklungsplan der Stadt Selb.
   1. City planning - Germany. I. Gropius,
Walter. II. Leibbrand, Kurt. III. Verkehrs-
und Industrieplanung GMBH. IV. Architects
Collaborative, inc.

352
H21

Town clerks and city managers: blood brothers
or distant cousins?

Headrick, T   E
   Town clerks and city managers: blood
brothers or distant cousins? Washington,
American Society for Public Administration,
1964.
   10p. (American Society for Public Adm.
Occasional papers)
   Reproduced from the Journal of Local
Administration Overseas, Vol. III; no. 3,
July, 1964.

   1. City manager government. I. American
Society for   Public
Administration.   II. Title.

720
H66

TOWN HOUSES.

HOPE, ALICE.
   TOWN HOUSES.   NEW YORK, HAYDEN BOOK
COMPANY, 1965.
159P.

   1. ARCHITECTURE - DESIGNS AND PLANS -
U.K.   I. TITLE.

711.4
(492)
N27t

Town planning and ground exploitation in
Amsterdam.

Netherlands. Dept. of Public Works.
   Town planning and ground exploitation in
Amsterdam. Amsterdam, 1967.
   39p.

   1. City planning - Netherlands. 2. Land
use - Netherlands. 3. City growth - Netherlands.
I. Title.

330
S51

A town comes to life.

U.S. Small Business Administration.
   A town comes to life. Washington, Govt.
Print. Off., 1963.
   20 p.

   1. Econ. development. 2. Industrial districts -
Redevelopment. I. Title. 3. Small business.

728.1
(016)
N17t

Town houses.

National Housing Center. Library
   Town houses; a selected list of references
including periodical articles through July
1969. Wash., 1969.
   13p. (Reference list # L-83)

   1. Housing - Bibl. I. Title.

728.1
(6668)
I86

Town planning and rural housing...

Ivory Coast. Ministry of Information.
   Town planning and rural housing modernization in the Ivory Coast. Abidjan, Press
and General Documentation, 1968.
   1v.

   1. Housing - Ivory Coast. 2. Rural
planning - Ivory Coast. 3. Social
welfare - Ivory Coast. I. Title.

243   TOWN PLANNING ASSOCIATES.
WINFIELD, ALA. CITY PLANNING COMMISSION.
SUBDIVISION REGULATIONS, BY TOWN
PLANNING ASSOCIATES. WINFIELD, ALA., 1970.
1 V. (HUD 701 REPORT)

1. SUBDIVISION REGULATION - WINFIELD,
ALA. I. TOWN PLANNING ASSOCIATES.
II. HUD. 701. WINFIELD, ALA.

711.4   Town planning in industrial districts...
1670
(47)   Davidovich, V G
D18   Town planning in industrial districts
(engineering and economics). Edited by I.V.
Bordukov. Translated from Russian by A.
Skotnicki. Published pursuant to an agreement
with the National Science Foundation.
Jerusalem, Israel Program for Scientific
Translation, 1968.
314p. (National Science Foundation. TT
67-51378)
On title page: Gosudarstvennoe Izdatel'stvo
Literatury po Stroitel'stvu, Arkhitekture i
Stroitel'nym Mat   erialam, Moskva 1960.

(Cont'd on next card)

TOWN PLANNING IN THE VICINITY OF
534.83   AIRPORTS WITH SPECIAL REFERENCE TO
V15T   VAN NIEKERK, C G
TOWN PLANNING IN THE VICINITY OF
AIRPORTS WITH SPECIAL REFERENCE TO THE
PROBLEM OF NOISE; A PAPERETTE PRESENTED
TO THE FORTIETH ANNUAL CONFERENCE,
INSTITUTE OF MUNICIPAL ENGINEERS (SOUTH
AFRICAN DISTRICT) PRETORIA, SOUTH
AFRICAN COUNCIL FOR SCIENTIFIC AND
INDUSTRIAL RESEARCH, N.D.
7L.
1. NOISE. 2. AIRPORTS.
I. INSTITUTION OF MUNICIPAL ENGINEERS,
SOUTH AFRICAN   DISTRICT. II. TITLE.

---

242   TOWN PLANNING ASSOCIATES.
WINFIELD, ALA. CITY PLANNING COMMISSION.
ZONING ORDINANCE, BY TOWN PLANNING
ASSOCIATES. WINFIELD, ALA., 1970.
40P. (HUD 701 REPORT)

1. ZONING - WINFIELD, ALA. I. TOWN
PLANNING ASSOCIATES. II. HUD. 701.
WINFIELD, ALA.

711.4
1670   Davidovich, V G   Town planning...1968.
(47)   (Card 2)
D18
Distributed by U.S. Clearinghouse for
Federal Scientific and Technical Information.
Bibliography: p. 298-314.

1. Industrial districts - U.S.S.R. 2. New
towns - U.S.S.R. 3. City planning - U.S.S.R.
4. U.S.S.R. - Industrial districts.
5. U.S.S.R. - New towns. 6. U.S.S.R. - City
planning. I. Gosudarstvennoe Izadel'stvo
Literatury po Str   oitel'stvu, Arkhitekture i Stroitel'   nym Materialam,
Moscow.   (Cont'd on next card)

711.4   Town planning in Uganda.
(676.1)
K25   Kendall, Henry
Town planning in Uganda; a brief description
of the efforts made by government to control
development of urban areas from 1915 to 1955.
London, Eng., Published by the Crown Agents,
for Overseas Governments and Administrations ...
on behalf of the Government of Uganda, 1955.
91 p. illus., maps.

1. City planning - Uganda. I. Title.

Town-planning; avenida del generalismo zone.
VF
711.4   Spain. Ministerio de la Vivienda.
(46)   Town-planning; avenida del generalismo
S61t   zone. Enlargement of the axle, joining
the north with the southern part of the city.
Madrid, 1963.
[12]p.

1. City planning - Spain. I. Title.

711.4
1670   Davidovich, V G   Town planning...1968.
(47)   (Card 3)
D18
II. U.S. National Science Foundation.
IV. Title.

711.4   Town-planning in South America.
(8)
W42   Wiener, Paul Lester
Urbanisme en Amerique du Sud. Town-planning
in South America [by] Paul Lester Wiener, Jose Luis
Sert.   L'Architecture d'Aujourd'hui, no. 33, 1951.
55 p.   illus., maps.

Reprint.
1. City planning-South America.
I. Sert, Jose Luis. II. Title: Town-planning in
South America. III. Title: South America, Town-
planning in.

720
(49)   Town Planning Conference, [Moscow], 1960.
T68   Architecture and planning. Reproduced
1960   from Soviet architecture information
bulletin, Winter, 1960-1961. General
editor: H.C. Creighton. London, Society
for Cultural Relations with the USSR, 1961.
25p. (S C R Soviet Information Library)

1. Architecture - USSR. 2. City planning -
USSR.   I. Creighton, H.C., ed.
II. Society for   Cultural Relations with
the USSR.

711.4   Town planning in London.
(41)
O57   Olsen, Donald J
Town planning in London; the eighteenth
and nineteenth centuries. New Haven,
Yale University Press, 1964.
245p.   (Yale historical publications.
Miscellany, 80)

1. City planning - U.K. (London)
2. Architecture - Conservation and
restoration. 3. Architecture - History.
4. New towns - U.K. I. Title.

VF
711.585
:33   Town Planning Institute. (Research Committee.)
(41)   The economics of central area redevelopment.
T68   London, July 1952.
18 p.

1. Industrial districts-Redevelopment. 2. Urban
redevelopment-U.K. I. Title.

690.015   Town planning for the disabled; outdoor mo-
(485)   bility.
S82   Olsson, Tommy.
R7   Samhällsplanering för rörelsehindrade;
1969   förflyttning utomhus (Town planning for the
disabled; outdoor mobility) Stockholm,
Statens Institut för Byggnadsforskning, 1969.
73p. (Stockholm. Statens Institut för
Byggnadsforskning. Rapport 7:1969)
English summary.
1. Building research - Sweden. 2. Sweden -
Building research. 3. Handicapped. I. Stockholm.
Statens Institut för Byggnadsforskning.
II. Title: Town planning for the disabled;
outdoor mobili   ty.

711.4   TOWN PLANNING IN PRACTICE.
U58T   UNWIN, SIR RAYMOND, 1863-
TOWN PLANNING IN PRACTICE; AN
INTRODUCTION TO THE ART OF DESIGNING
CITIES AND SUBURBS. NEW YORK, CENTURY
CO., 1932.
416P.

1. CITY PLANNING.   I. TITLE.

711.4   TOWN PLANNING INSTITUTE, LONDON.
T68   EXAMINATION BROCHURE CONTAINING PAPERS
ON MANY SUBJECTS READ BEFORE THE
INSTITUTE AND ELSEWHERE, AND PREPARED
FOR THE USE OF CANDIDATES FOR TOWN
PLANNING EXAMINATIONS. LONDON, 1931.
107P.

1. CITY PLANNING.   2. CITY PLANNING -
U.K.

690.015   Town planning for the disabled - special
(485)   housing.
S82   Thiberg, Sven.
R50   Samhällsplanering för rörelsehindrade
1968   - boende i invalidbostäder (Town planning
for the disabled - special housing)
Stockholm, Statens Institut för Byggnadsforskning, 1968.
35p. (Stockholm. Statens Institut för
Byggnadsforskning. Rapport 50:1968)
English summary.
1. Building research - Sweden. 2. Sweden -
Building research. 3. Housing for the
handicapped. I. Stockholm. Statens
Institut för   Byggnadsforskning.
II. Title: To   wn planning for the
disabled -   special housing.

711.4   Town planning in practice.
U58t   Unwin, Raymond.
1971   Town planning in practice; an introduction
to the art of designing cities and suburbs.
New York, Benjamin Blom, 1971.
416p.

Bibliography: p. 405-411.

1. City planning. I. Title.

744
(016)   The Town Planning Institute.
T68   Film catalogue. London, 1963.
20p.

1. Films - Bibl. 2. City planning - Films.

711.4   Town planning in Hungary
(4391)   Hungarian Institute for Town and Regional
H85   Planning and Research, Budapest.
Town planning in Hungary, by Pal Virach.
Prepared on behalf of the Ministry of
Building and Urban Development. Budapest,
1968.
28p.

1. City planning - Hungary. I. Virach,
Pal. II. Hungary. Ministry of Building
and Urban Development. III. Title.

711.4   Town-planning in the Netherlands since 1900.
(492)   Blijstra, R.
B54   Town-planning in the Netherlands since
1900. Amsterdam, P.N. Van Kempen & Zoon
[1963?]
74p.

1. City planning - Netherlands.
2. Architecture - Netherlands. I. Title.

711.4   TOWN PLANNING INSTITUTE, LONDON.
M45l   Milan. Centro di Documentazione.
L'organizzazione professionale dei planners
in Gran Bretagna, a cura di Piergiorgio
Marabelli. Milano, Italy, 1967.
85p. (Its Documento n. 1, nuova serie)
Bibliography: p. 74-88.
English summary.
1. City planning as a profession. 2. Town
Planning Institute, London. I. Marabelli,
Piergiorgio, ed.

711.015
(41)
T68

TOWN PLANNING INSTITUTE.
PLANNING RESEARCH. A REGISTER OF
RESEARCH OF INTEREST TO THOSE
CONCERNED WITH TOWN AND COUNTRY
PLANNING. LONDON, 1961.
158P.

1. PLANNING - UNITED KINGDOM -
RESEARCH. 2. CITY PLANNING - UNITED
KINGDOM.

711
(41:06)
T68

Town Planning Institute.
Yearbook, 1957/58-
London, 1957-
v. annual

For complete information see shelf list.

1. City planning - U.K. - Yearbooks.

711.417
(41)
P87T

TOWN THEORY AND PRACTICE.
PURDOM, CHARLES BENJAMIN, 1883- ED.
TOWN THEORY AND PRACTICE, BY W.R.
LETHABY, GEORGE L. PEPLER AND OTHERS
... EDITED WITH AN INTRODUCTION, BY
C.B. PURDOM. LONDON, BENN BROTHERS,
1921.
139P.

A SHORT BIBLIOGRAPHY : P. 137-139.

1. GARDEN CITIES - U.K. 2. CITY
PLANNING - U.K. I. LETHABY, WILLIAM
RICHARD, 1857- II. TITLE.

VF
614
C72

Town Planning Institute, London.
Crew, F   A   E
Public health in relation to town and
country planning. [London, Eng., Town
Planning Institute, 1950]
18 l.

Paper read at the Town and Country Planning
Summer School, 1950.

1.Public health-U.K. 2.Housing and health.
I.Town Planning Institute, London.

711.4
G87s

Town planning Institute of Canada.
Guttenberg, Albert Z
The social uses of city planning; a prelimi-
nary inquiry. Toronto, Town Planning Insti-
tute of Canada, 1968.
14p.
Reprinted from: Plan (Journal of the Town
Planning Institute of Canada) March, 1968.

1. City planning - Social aspects.
I. Town planning Institute of Canada.
II. Plan. III. Title.

711.3(41)
T58

Towndrow, Frederic Edward, 1897-   ed.
Town and country planning association. *Conference, Oxford, 1941.*
Replanning Britain; being a summarized report of the Oxford conference of the Town and country planning association,
spring, 1941, edited by F. E. Towndrow ... London, Faber and
Faber limited [1941]
173 p. 22ᶜᵐ.
"First published in September Mcmxli."
1. Regional planning—Gt. Brit. 2. Regional planning—Congresses.
3. Cities and towns—Planning. 4. Industries, Location of. 5. Agriculture—Gt. Brit.   I. Towndrow, Frederic Edward, 1897-   ed. II. Title.
4. Industrial location.
Harvard univ. Library   A 42-1790
for Library of Congress   [845][3]†
HT407.T68 1941
300.142

711.4
(41)
083
1951

Town Planning Institute.
Oxford. University. Town and Country Planning
Summer School, Sept. 17-22, 1951.
Report of proceedings. London, Town
Planning Institute [1951]
102 p. illus.

Partial contents.-A critical analysis of the
working of the Town and Country Planning Act of
1947, by Henry W. Wells.-Some design problems and
trends in the planning of towns, by Anthony
Minoprio.-Public influences on planning, by
F. J. Osborn.

624.8
(711.73)
G65

TOWN PLANNING INSTITUTE OF NEW
ZEALAND.
GOLDIE, G N T
THE INFLUENCE OF TRAFFIC SAFETY AND
CONTROL PROBLEMS ON PLANNING.
WELLINGTON, N.Z., TOWN PLANNING
INSTITUTE OF NEW ZEALAND, 1939.
14P.

IN PLANNING, SER. NO. 2, BULLETIN
NO. 15, JULY 1939.

1. TRAFFIC SAFETY. 2. PLANNING.
I. TOWN PLANNING INSTITUTE OF NEW
ZEALAND.

388
:308
T68
Appx.

Towne (Robin M.) and Associates.
An investigation of the effect of freeway
traffic noise on apartment rents. Appendix.
Prepared for the Oregon State Highway
Commission, State Highway Dept. and the U.S.
Dept. of Commerce, Bureau of Public Roads.
Seattle, 1966.
1v.
Distributed by: Clearinghouse for Federal
Scientific and Technical Information as
Document PB 176 345.
1. Traffic surveys. 2. Noise. 3. High-
ways - Economic effect. I. Oregon. State
Highway Commission. II. Title.

711.4
(41)
T68R

TOWN PLANNING INSTITUTE, LONDON.
REPORT OF THE NATIONAL SURVEY AND
NATIONAL PLANNING COMMITTEE, APPROVED BY
THE COUNCIL OF THE INSTITUTE 20TH MAY,
1938. LONDON, 1938.
36P.

1. CITY PLANNING - U.K. 2. ECONOMIC
POLICY - U.K.

711
(931)
L22

TOWN-PLANNING INSTITUTE OF N.Z.
LEE, JOHN
PLAN   D HOUSING. WELLINGTON,
TOWN-PLAN   INSTITUTE OF N.Z., 1937.
8P. (PL.   ING, SERIES NO. 2.
BULLETIN NO. 5)

1. PLANNING - NEW ZEALAND. 2. PUBLIC
HOUSING - NEW ZEALAND.
I. TOWN-PLANNING INSTITUTE OF N.Z.

388
:308
T68

Towne (Robin M.) and Associates.
An investigation of the effect of freeway
traffic noise on apartment rents. Prepared for
the Oregon State Highway Commission, State
Highway Dept. and the U.S. Dept. of Commerce,
Bureau of Public Roads. Seattle, 1966.
121p.
Distributed by Clearinghouse for Federal
Scientific and Technical Information as PB
176 344.
1. Traffic surveys. 2. Noise. 3. Highways - Economic effect. I. Oregon. State
Highway Commis   sion. II. Title.

711.4
(41)
T68T

TOWN PLANNING INSTITUTE, LONDON.
TOWN AND COUNTRY PLANNING,
COMPENSATION AND BETTERMENT, REPORT OF
COMMITTEE OF THE INSTITUTE, APPROVED BY
THE COUNCIL OF THE INSTITUTE, 31ST MAY,
1940. LONDON, EDE & TOWNSEND, 1940.
60P.

1. CITY PLANNING - U.K. 2. EMINENT
DOMAIN. I. TITLE.

711
(931)
P87

TOWN-PLANNING INSTITUTE OF N.Z.
PUTT, CHARLES E   H
HOUSING IN RELATION TO CIVIC
DEVELOPMENT. WELLINGTON, TOWN-PLANNING
INSTITUTE OF N.Z., 1937.
PTS. (PLANNING, SERIES NO. 2,
BULLETIN NO. 9.)
For Library holdings see main entry.
1. PLANNING - NEW ZEALAND.
I. TOWN-PLANNING INSTITUTE OF N.Z.
II. TITLE.

711.583
(74811)
N28

The Towne Gardens; a community of convenience.
New Eastwick Corp., Philadelphia.
The Towne Gardens; a community of convenience. Philadelphia, 1967.
kit. (4 pieces)
Contents: [no.1] The Towne Gardens; a
community of convenience.-[no.2] Questions
and answers about the Towne Gardens. [no.3]
House plans.] [no.4 Architectural drawings]

1. Community development. 2. Aluminum.
3. Building materials - Philadelphia.
4. House plans. I. Title.

711.4
(41)
T68

Town Planning Institute.
Town and country planning summer school,
Bangor, 1952; report of proceedings. London
[1953?]
viii, 115 p.

Partial contents.-The place of housing in town
and country planning, by George Pepler.-Design in
its relation to economic factors, by Gordon
Stephenson.-The development of new towns, by W. O.
Hart.

(Continued on next card)

711.4
C41

Town planning problems in the reconstruction of badly damaged towns.
Ciborowski, A
Town planning problems in the reconstruction of badly damaged towns. Translated
from the German by D.R. Gray. Garston, Eng.,
Ministry of Public Building and Works,
Building Research Station, 1968.
5p. (Library communication no. 1422)

1. City planning. 2. Reconstruction.
I. U.K. Building Research Station.
II. Title.

711.585
(41)
T68B

TOWNROE, BERNARD STEPHEN, 1885-
BRITAIN REBUILDING; THE SLUM AND
OVERCROWDING CAMPAIGNS. LONDON, F.
MULLER LTD., 1936.
180P.

1. URBAN RENEWAL - U.K. 2. SLUM
CLEARANCE - U.K. I. TITLE.

Town Planning Institute. Town and country planning
summer school, Bangor, 1952 ... (Card 2)

1.City planning. 2.Housing. 3.New towns-U.K.
I.Pepler, George. II.Stephenson, Gordon. III.Hart,
W. O. IV.Titl.

728.1
V24H

THE TOWN PLANNING REVIEW.
VEILLER, LAWRENCE.
THE HOUSING PROBLEM IN THE UNITED
STATES. LIVERPOOL, UNIVERSITY PRESS OF
LIVERPOOL, 1929.
228-256P.
REPRINTED FROM THE TOWN PLANNING
REVIEW, 13, NO. 4. DEC., 1929.

1. HOUSING. I. THE TOWN PLANNING
REVIEW. II. TITLE.

300:2
(41)
T68

TOWNROE, BERNARD STEPHEN.
THE BUILDING OF A NEW BRITAIN; THE
BUILDING INDUSTRIES' RESPONSIBILITY FOR
RECONSTRUCTION. REV. ED., JULY 1943.
LONDON BUILDING INDUSTRIES NATIONAL
COUNCIL, 1943.
18P.

1. RECONSTRUCTION - U.K. 2. BUILDING
INDUSTRY - U.K. I. BUILDING INDUSTRIES
NATIONAL COUNCIL. II. TITLE.

728.1
(41)
T68
TOWNROE, BERNARD STEPHEN, 1885-
A HANDBOOK OF HOUSING; HOW TO MEET THE PROBLEM. WITH CONTRIBUTIONS BY FOUR EX-MINISTERS OF HEALTH, THE DIRECTOR-GENERAL OF HOUSING, THE FORMER DIRECTOR OF THE BUILDING RESEARCH BOARD. LONDON, METHUEN, 1924.
178P.

1. HOUSING - U.K.   I. TITLE.

711.4
(41)
C85
Townscape.

Cullen, Gordon.
Townscape. New York, Reinhold Pub. Corp., 1961.
315p.

1. City planning - U.K. I. Title.

693.5:691.8
D15
Townsend, Gilbert, 1880-   joint author.

Dalzell, James Ralph, 1900-
Concrete block construction for home and farm, by J. Ralph Dalzell and Gilbert Townsend. Illus by Arthur E. Burke. Chicago, American Technical Society, 1951.
216 p. illus. 22 cm.
"Adapted and enlarged from sections of the authors' ... Masonry simplified."

1. Concrete blocks. 2. Concrete construction.   I. Townsend, Gilbert, 1880-   joint author. II. Title.

TH1491.D3   693.5   51-2175

Library of Congress   [20]

711.585
(41)
T68
Townroe, Bernard Stephen.
The slum problem. New York, Longmans, Green and Co., 1928.
220p.

2c

1. Housing - U. K. 2. Company housing - U. K. 3. Slums - U. K. I. Title.

701
L45
Townscape painting and drawing.

Links, J G
Townscape painting and drawing. New York, Harper & Row, 1972.
261p.

1. Art. I. Title.

693.5
:691.8
D15
1957
Townsend, Gilbert, jt. au.

Dalzell, J Ralph.
Concrete block construction for home and farm, by J. Ralph Dalzell and Gilbert Townsend. Contributor to 2d ed., Edward Matzke. Chicago, American Technical Society, 1957.
Laf.   216p.

1. Concrete blocks. I. Townsend, Gilbert, jt. au. II. American Technical Society. III. Title.

711.4
.670
(016)
T68
Townroe, P M
Industrial location and regional economic policy; a selected bibliography. Birmingham, Eng., Centre for Urban and Regional Studies, University of Birmingham, 1968.
43p. (Birmingham, Eng. University. Centre for Urban and Regional Studies. Occasional paper no. 2)
1. Industrial location - Bibl. 2. Industrial location - U.K. - Bibl. 3. U.K. - Industrial location - Bibl. I. Birmingham, Eng. University. Centre for Urban and Regional Studies.   II. Title.

624
T68
TOWNSEND, CHARLES L
STUDIES AND PROCEDURES FOR THE CONTROL OF CRACKING IN MASS CONCRETE STRUCTURES. DENVER, COLORADO, 1964.
101P. (U.S. BUREAU OF RECLAMATION. TECHNICAL MEMORANDUM NO. 664)

1. STRUCTURAL ENGINEERING. 2. CONCRETE CONSTRUCTION. I. U.S. BUREAU OF RECLAMATION.

728
T68
TOWNSEND, GILBERT.
HOW TO PLAN A HOUSE, BY GILBERT TOWNSEND AND J. RALPH DALZELL. 3D ED. REV. CONTRIBUTOR TO 3D ED. REXFORD BATTENBERG. CHICAGO, AMERICAN TECHNICAL SOCIETY, 1958.
591P.
2C.
1. ARCHITECTURE, DOMESTIC. I. DALZELL, J. RALPH, JT. AU. II. TITLE.

711.4
(09)
R17
1951
TOWNS AND BUILDINGS DESCRIBED IN DRAWINGS AND WORDS.
RASMUSSEN, STEEN EILER, 1898-
TOWNS AND BUILDINGS DESCRIBED IN DRAWINGS AND WORDS. CAMBRIDGE, MASS., HARVARD UNIVERSITY PRESS, 1951.
203P.

1. CITY PLANNING - HISTORY. 2. ARCHITECTURE. I. TITLE.

362.6
T68
Townsend, Claire.
Old age; the last segregation. New York, Grossman, 1971.
229p. (Ralph Nader's study group report on nursing homes)

2C

1. Old age. 2. Nursing homes. I. Nader, Ralph. II. Title.

690.26
T68
Townsend, Gilbert
Stair building; design and construction, bevels and face molds, self-help questions.   Chicago, Ill., American Technical Society, 1947 [c1940]
200 p.   illus., diagrs., plans.

1. Stairs.

711.4
(09)
R17
Towns and buildings described in drawings and words.
Rasmussen, Steen Eiler, 1898-
Towns and buildings described in drawings and words. Cambridge, Mass., M.I.T. Press, 1969.
203p.
First Danish edition: 1949.

1. City planning - History. 2. Architecture. I. Title.

691.421
(016)
M27
TOWNSEND, D C
METCALF, J B
VARVED CLAYS; A SELECTIVE BIBLIOGRAPHY TO 1960, BY J.B. METCALF AND D.L. TOWNSEND. KINGSTON, ONTARIO, QUEEN'S UNIVERSITY, CIVIL ENGINEERING DEPARTMENT, 1961.
44P. (QUEEN'S UNIVERSITY. C.E. RESEARCH REPORT NO. 18)

1. CLAY - BIBLIOGRAPHY. I. TOWNSEND, D.C. II. TITLE.

697.8
F56r
v. 2
Townsend, H D
Florida. University. Engineering and Industrial Experiment Station.
Register of air pollution analyses; a record of community air sampling and analyses performed in the United States and Territories during the period Jan. 1, 1956 to June 30, 1959. Volume 2. Comp. for the U.S. Public Health Service by H. D. Townsend and E. R. Hendrickson. Washington, Govt. Print. Off., 1961.
247p.
U.S. Public Health Service publication no. 610, vol. 2.
1. Air pollution.   I. U.S. Public Health Service.   II. Townsend, H. D. III. Hendrickson,   E. R.

711.4
B87t
Towns in the making.
Burke, Gerald.
Towns in the making. New York, St. Martin's Press, 1971.
193p.

Bibliography: p. 181-184.

1. City planning. I. Title.

691.421
Q82
TOWNSEND, D L
QUEEN'S UNIVERSITY. DEPARTMENT OF CIVIL ENGINEERING. KINGSTON, ONTARIO.
TRIAXIAL SHEAR TESTS ON ARTIFICIAL VARVED CLAYS, BY D.L. TOWNSEND AND G.C.W. GAY. KINGSTON, ONTARIO, 1964.
56L.

ONTARIO JOINT HIGHWAY RESEARCH PROGRAMME SPONSORED BY ONTARIO DEPARTMENT OF HIGHWAYS.
1. CLAY. I. TOWNSEND, D.L. II. GAY, G.C. W. III. ONTARIO. DEPARTMENT OF HIGHWAYS.

VF
330
(5694)
A52
Townsend, Lewis R
American Embassy, Tel Aviv.
Weekly economic review - 37, by Lewis R. Townsend. Tel Aviv, Israel, 1959.
9p. (American Embassy, Tel Aviv. Foreign service dispatch no. 168, 1959)

"Official use only."

1. Economic conditions - Israel. I. Townsend, Lewis R. (Series: American Embassy, Tel Aviv. Foreign service dispatch no. 168, 1959)

711.4
W65t
TOWNS, TIME, AND REGIONALISM.
WOLFE, M R
TOWNS, TIME, AND REGIONALISM. SEATTLE, UNIVERSITY OF WASHINGTON, DEPT. OF URBAN PLANNING, 1963.
113L. (URBAN PLANNING DEVELOPMENT SERIES NO. 2)

1. CITY PLANNING. I. TITLE.

334.1
(4)
F22
Townsend, Dwight D.
U.S. Federal Housing Administration.
Report on cooperative housing in Europe, by Dwight D. Townsend. Washington, 1957.
15p.

1. Cooperative housing - Europe. I. Townsend, Dwight D.

333.33
(768)
R21
TOWNSEND, MAHLON LYNN, ED.
REAL ESTATE BOARD OF MEMPHIS.
TENESSEE REAL ESTATE, EDITED BY MAHLON LYNN TOWNSEND. KNOXVILLE, TENN., UNIVERSITY OF TENNESSEE PRESS, 1958.
304P.
APPENDIX OF REAL ESTATE FORMS, P.223-285. GLOSSARY, P.287-295.

1. REAL ESTATE BUSINESS - TENNESSEE. I. TOWNSEND, MAHLON LYNN, ED. II. TITLE.

621.6
W65
Townsend, Merrill, jt. au.
Wolf, Erik W
    Corrugated metal pipe; structural design criteria and recommended installation practice, by Erik W. Wolf and Merrill Townsend. Rev. [Wash.] Bureau of Public Roads, 1970.
    26p.

    1. Pipes. 2. Culverts. I. Townsend, Merrill, jt. au. I. U.S. Bureau of Public Roads. II. Title.

711.333
(75271)
B15t
Towson [Md.] a new urban center.
Baltimore County, Md. Redevelopment and Rehabilitation Commission.
    Towson [Md.] a new urban center.
    Towson, Md., 1964.
    44p.

    1. City planning - Towson, Md.
    2. Business districts - Towson, Md.
    I. Title.

300
T69
Toynbee, Arnold.
    Surviving the future. New York, Oxford University Press, 1971.
    164p.

4 c

    1. Science and civilization. 2. Social conditions. I. Title.

362.6
(41)
T68
Townsend, Peter.
    The last refuge; a survey of residential institutions and homes for the aged in England and Wales. London, Routledge and Paul, 1962.
    552p.
    Bibliography: p. 530-539.

2c

    1. Housing for the aged - U.K.
    2. Nursing homes - U.K. I. Title.

614
C68
Toxic substances.
U.S. Council on Environmental Quality.
    Toxic substances. Wash., 1971.
    25p.

    Bibliography: p. 23-25.

    1. Health. 2. Man - Influence of environment. I. Title.

332.6
T69
Tozzi, Jim J
    Establishing priorities for public investments. Wash., Systems Analysis Group (Civil Functions), Office of the Secretary of the Army, 1969.
    21p.

    1. Investments. 2. Federal government. I. U.S. Army. II. Title.

362.6
(41)
W66
TOWNSEND, PETER, JT. AU.
WOODROFFE, CAROLINE.
    NURSING HOMES IN ENGLAND AND WALES; A STUDY OF PUBLIC RESPONSIBILITY, BY CAROLINE WOODROFFE AND PETER TOWNSEND. LONDON, NATIONAL CORPORATION FOR THE CARE OF OLD PEOPLE, 1961.
    71P.

    1. NURSING HOMES - U.K. I. TOWNSEND, PETER, JT. AU. II. TITLE.

658.802
C657t
1972
S-H
The toxic substances control act of 1971 and amendment.
U.S. Congress. Senate. Committee on Commerce.
    The toxic substances control act of 1971 and amendment. Hearings before the Subcommittee on the Environment, Ninety-second Congress, first session on S. 1478, to amend the Federal hazardous substances act as amended, and for other purposes. Wash., Govt. Print. Off., 1972.
    pts.

    1. Consumer protection. I. Title.

711.14
M17
Trace, Michael, jt. au
March, Lionel.
    The land use performance of selected arrays of built forms, by Lionel March and Michael Trace. Cambridge, Eng., University of Cambridge, School of Architecture, Centre for Land Use and Built Form Studies, [1968?]
    83p. (Cambridge, Eng. University. Centre for Land Use and Built Form Studies. Working paper no. 2)
    Prepared under the sponsorship of the Ministry of Public Building and Works.
    Bibliography: p. 81-83.
                (Cont'd on next card)

VF
323.4
C655
Townsend, Richard, comp.
U.S. Commission on Civil Rights.
    Civil rights and land development; background on housing for Negroes in Cleveland, Ohio. Origin and relative contemporary significance of main activities affecting equal opportunity, 1800-1965. Wash., 1966.
    chart.
    Richard Townsend, comp.
    Incomplete, uncolored version.

    1. Civil rights. 2. Land use - Cleveland.
    2. Statistical presentation. 3. Minority groups - Housing - Cleveland.
    I. Townsend, Richard, comp. II. Title.

628.515
L42
Toxicity and fate of insecticide residues in water...
Lichtenstein, E
    Toxicity and fate of insecticide residues in water; insecticide residues in water after direct applications or by leaching of agricultural soil, by E.P. Lichtenstein and others. [Chicago, American Medical Association] 1966.
    199-212p.
    Reprinted from Archives of environmental health, Feb., 1966.

    1. Water pollution. I. Archives of environmental health. II. American Medical Association. III. Title.

711.14
M17
March, Lionel. The land use...[1968?]
                (Card 2)

    1. Land use. 2. Architecture - Designs and plans. I. Trace, Michael, jt. au.
    II. Cambridge, Eng. University. Centre for Land Use and Built Form Studies. III. Title.

658
T68
Townsend, Robert
    Up the organization. New York, Alfred A. Knopf, 1970.
    202p.

3c

    1. Management. I. Title.

711.14
(79473)
S15s
TRW Systems Group (Thompson Ramo Wooldridge)
    Santa Clara County property subsystem requirements analysis and design study reports. Redondo Beach, Calif., 1967.
    1v.

    1. Land use - Santa Clara County, Calif.
    2. Land use - Automation. I. Title.

658.3
T71
Tracey, William R
    Evaluating training and development systems. New York, American Management Association, 1968.
    304p. (AMA management bookshelf)

    1. Personnel management. I. Title: Training and development systems. II. Title.

711.4
(7444)
C65
Townsend, Mass. Planning Board.
Community Planning Service.
    Townsend, Mass. town plan summary. Boston, 1969.
    10p.

    U.S. Dept. of Housing and Urban Development. UPAP.

    1. City planning - Townsend, Mass.
    I. Townsend, Mass. Planning Board.
    II. U.S. HUD-UPAP. Townsend, Mass.

Folio
301.15
T69c
Toynbee, Arnold, ed.
    Cities of destiny. New York, McGraw-Hill, 1967.
    376p.

2 C

    Bibliography: p. 362-363.

    1. City growth. 2. City planning - History. I. Title.

712.25
L22
Trachsel, Alfred, jt. au.
Ledermann, Alfred.
    Creative playgrounds and recreation centers, by Alfred Ledermann and Alfred Trachsel. 2d ed. New York, Frederick A. Praeger, 1968.
    175p.
    English and German.

    1. Recreation. 2. Children. I. Trachsel, Alfred, jt. au. II. Title. III. Title: Playgrounds and recreation centers.

352
(781)
K15
Township government in Kansas.
Kansas. University. Governmental Research Center.
    Township government in Kansas, by James W. Drury. [Lawrence, Kans.] 1954.
    66 p. graphs, map, tables. (Its Governmental research series no. 10)

    1. Local government. I. Drury, James W. II. Title.

301.15
T69
Toynbee, Arnold.
    Cities on the move. New York, Oxford University Press, 1970.
    257p.

4c.

    1. City growth. 2. City planning - History. I. Title.

353
(787)
T71
Trachsel, Herman H
    The government and administration of Wyoming, by Herman H. Trachsel and Ralph M. Wade. New York, Thomas Y. Crowell, 1953.
    381p. (American Commonwealths series, v. 48)

    Bibliography: p. 368-371.

    1. State government - Wyo. I. Wade, Ralph M., jt. au. II. Title.

800
T71
Trachtenberg, Alan.
The city; American experience, by Alan Trachtenberg and others. New York, Oxford University Press, 1971.
620p.

Bibliography: p. iv-vi.

1. Literature. 2. Metropolitan areas. I. Title.

628.515
T71
TRACOR, inc.
Estuarine modeling: an assessment. Capabilities and limitations for resource management and pollution control. [Prepared] for the Water Quality Office, Environmental Protection Agency. Austin, Tex., 1971.
497p. (Water pollution control research series)

1. Water pollution. I. U.S. Environmental Protection Agency. II. Title.

VF
312.2
C25
Tract data compared for a 25-percent sample and a complete census.
U.S. Bureau of the Census.
Tract data compared for a 25-percent sample and a complete census, prepared by Max A. Bershad and Blanche S. Sirken. Washington, U.S. Dept. of Commerce, 1956.
30 p. tables. (Its Working paper no. 3)

1.Sampling. 2.Census. I.Bershad, Max A. II.Title.

689
690
691
692
TRACY, CALIF. CITY PLANNING COMMISSION. COMMUNITY GENERAL PLAN PROGRAM: 1, BASIC DETERMINANTS; 2, CENTRAL AREA PLAN; 3, FINANCIAL PLAN; 4, REVIEW OF DEVELOPMENT REGULATIONS. BY GRUNWALD, CRAWFORD AND ASSOCIATES. TRACY, CALIF., 1969-1970.
4 V. (HUD 701 REPORT)

1. MASTER PLAN - TRACY, CALIF. I. GRUNWALD, CRAWFORD AND ASSOCIATES. II. HUD. 701. TRACY, CALIF.

711.4
(79455)
T71
Tracy, Calif. City Planning Commission.
Tracy general plan, by Lawrence Livingston, Jr. and Elizabeth Gavain. Tracy, 1959.
20p.

U.S. Urban Renewal Adm. UPAP.

1. City planning - Tracy, Calif. I. Livingston, Lawrence, Jr. II. Gavain, Elizabeth. III. U.S. URA-UPAP. Tracy, Calif.

381
P72t
Trade agreements with the European Economic Community, the United Kingdom, Norway, and Sweden.
U.S. President, 1961-   (Kennedy)
Trade agreements with the European Economic Community, the United Kingdom, Norway, and Sweden. Message from The President of the United States transmitting copies of trade agreements with the European Economic Community, the United Kingdom, Norway, and Sweden, including schedules signed on behalf of the United States on March 5 and 7, 1962 and reporting actions taken with respect to peril points.
242p.
At head of title: 87th Cong., 2d sess. House Document no. 358.
1. Commercial policy. I. Title.

Trade and professional associations

see

Associations

332.2
N17MU
TRADE ASSOCIATION MONOGRAPHS.
NATIONAL ASSOCIATION OF MUTUAL SAVINGS BANKS.
MUTUAL SAVINGS BANKING; BASIC CHARACTERISTICS AND ROLE IN THE NATIONAL ECONOMY. A MONOGRAPH PREPARED FOR THE COMMISSION ON MONEY AND CREDIT. ENGLEWOOD CLIFFS, N.J., PRENTICE-HALL, 1962.
273P.

1. SAVINGS - BANKS. I. TITLE. II. COMMISSION ON MONEY AND CREDIT. III. SERIES.

VF
658.800.15
P17
Trade association opportunities in marketing research.
Pasma, Theodore K
Trade association opportunities in marketing research. Washington, Govt. Print. Off., 1948.
79 p. (U.S. Bureau of Foreign and Domestic Commerce. Industrial series no. 78)

Prepared in the Office of Domestic Commerce.

1.Marketing research. I.U.S. Bureau of Foreign and Domestic Commerce. Office of Domestic Commerce. II.Title. III.Series.

061.3
(41)
M45
Trade associations and professional bodies of the United Kingdom.
Millard, Patricia, ed.
Trade associations and professional bodies of the United Kingdom. 3d ed. Oxford, Eng., Pergamon, 1966.
372p.

1. Associations - U.K. 2. U.K. - Associations. I. Title.

330.15
N17o
no.67
Trade balances during business cycles.
Mintz, Ilse.
Trade balances during business cycles: U.S. and Britain since 1880. New York, 1959.
99 p. (National Bureau of Economic Research. Occasional paper 67).

1. Finance. 2. Finance - U.K. 3. Business cycles. I. Title. II. National Bureau of Economic Research. Occasional paper, no. 67.

711.552
(763991)
S37
1965
Trade center of the Ark-La-Tex- region.
Shreveport, La. Metropolitan Planning Commission of Caddo Parish.
Downtown Shreveport. A development plan for the trade center of the Ark-La-Tex region. [Prepared in cooperation with] Downtown Shreveport Unlimited and the City of Shreveport, Louisiana. Shreveport, 1965.
39p.

1. Business districts - Shreveport, La. 2. Master plan - Shreveport, La. I. Downtown Shreveport Unlimited. II. Title. III. Title: Trade center of the Ark- Le-Tex region.

333.33
S32
TRADE-IN FINANCING.
SHEPHERD, DAVID LEROY.
TRADE-IN FINANCING. PREPARED FOR THE GRADUATE SCHOOL OF SAVINGS AND LOAN, INDIANA UNIVERSITY. JOLIET, ILL., 1959.
26 l.

1. TRADE-IN HOUSES. 2. MORTGAGE FINANCE. I. TITLE.

333.33
C152
TRADE-IN HOUSES.
CALIFORNIA REAL ESTATE ASSOCIATION.
HOME TRADE-IN WORKBOOK. LOS ANGELES, CALIF., 1965.
33P.

1. TRADE-IN HOUSES. 2. REAL ESTATE BUSINESS. I. TITLE.

333.33
H68
TRADE-IN HOUSES.
HOUSE AND HOME.
TRADE-INS CAN BECOME BIG BUSINESS. [N.P.] 1953.
156-160P.
FROM HOUSE AND HOME, OCT. 1953.

1. TRADE-IN HOUSES. I. TITLE.

VF
333.33
M45
"Trade-in" houses.
Minneapolis Honeywell Regulator Company (Home Products Division)
[Booklets] Nos. 1-6. [Minneapolis, n.d.]
6 v.

Contents: - No.1. A future for you trading homes? -No.2. They're trading homes in Detroit. No.3. Oregon's real tall realtor has traded homes for years. -No.4. Thirty years of trading homes in Fort Wayne -No.5. A trail-blazing home trader from Dallas. -No.6. The Baltimore plan makes home trading big business.

333.33
N17RE
TRADE-IN HOUSES.
NATIONAL ASSOCIATION OF REAL ESTATE BOARDS.
REAL ESTATE TRADER'S HANDBOOK. 1ST REV. ED. CHICAGO, NATIONAL INSTITUTE OF REAL ESTATE BROKERS OF NAREB, 1956.
152P.

1. TRADE-IN HOUSES. I. TITLE. II. NATIONAL ASSOCIATION OF REAL ESTATE BOARDS.

333.33
N17p
Trade-in houses.
National Gypsum Co.
Plain facts about trade-in housing by John Peter. 2d ed. Buffalo, 1958.
35p.

1. Trade-in houses. I. Peter, John.

333.33
N17CO
TRADE-IN HOUSES.
NATIONAL INSTITUTE OF REAL ESTATE BROKERS.
HOME TRADE-IN HANDBOOK. 1ST ED. CHICAGO, NATIONAL TRADERS CLUB, EXCHANGE DIVISION OF THE NATIONAL INSTITUTE OF REAL ESTATE BROKERS, 1966.
86P.

1. TRADE-IN HOUSES. I. TITLE.

333.33
R24
TRADE-IN HOUSES.
REID, GARE B JR.
FINANCING OF TRADE-IN HOUSING. PREPARED FOR GRADUATE SCHOOL OF SAVINGS AND LOAN, INDIANA UNIVERSITY. DETROIT, SURETY FEDERAL SAVINGS AND LOAN ASSOCIATION, 1961.
36P.

1. TRADE-IN HOUSES. 2. MORTGAGE FINANCE - MICHIGAN. I. SURETY FEDERAL SAVINGS AND LOAN ASSOCIATION. II. TITLE.

333.33
R25
TRADE-IN-HOUSES.
Reno, Richard R
Profitable real estate exchanging and counseling. Englewood Cliffs, N.J., Prentice-Hall, 1965.
301 p.

1. Real estate business. 2. Trade-in-houses. I. Title: Real estate exchanging and counseling.

333.73
S32
TRADE-IN HOUSES.
SHEPHERD, DAVID LEROY.
TRADE-IN FINANCING. PREPARED FOR THE
GRADUATE SCHOOL OF SAVINGS AND LOAN,
INDIANA UNIVERSITY. JOLIET, ILL., 1959.
26 ℓ.

1. TRADE-IN HOUSES. 2. MORTGAGE
FINANCE. I. TITLE.

G91.771
F32
TRADE PRACTICE RULES FOR THE
RESIDENTIAL ALUMINUM SIDING
U.S. FEDERAL TRADE COMMISSION.
TRADE PRACTICE RULES FOR THE
RESIDENTIAL ALUMINUM SIDING INDUSTRY.
PROMULGATED APRIL 6, 1962.
[WASHINGTON, 1962]
13P. (FTC L-4616)

1. ALUMINUM. I. TITLE.

658
A52r
no.63
Trade unions.
Blum, Albert A
Management and the white-collar union.
New York, American Management Association,
1964.
111p. (American Management Association.
AMA research study 63)

1. Management. 2. Trade unions.
I. American Management
Association.

333.33
S76
TRADE-IN HOUSES.
STONE, DAVID V
HOW TO OPERATE A REAL ESTATE TRADE-IN
PROGRAM. ENGLEWOOD CLIFFS, N.J.,
PRENTICE-HALL [1962]
189P.
BIBLIOGRAPHY: P. 179-180.

1. TRADE-IN HOUSES. I. TITLE.

LAW
T
P173S8
TRADE SECRET.
PATENT RESOURCES GROUP.
SOFTWARE PROTECTION BY TRADE SECRET,
CONTRACT, PATENT, LAW, PRACTICE AND
FORMS. WASHINGTON, 1969.
358P.

PARTIAL CONTENTS.- WHY PROTECT
COMPUTER PROGRAMS.

1. AUTOMATION. 2. PATENTS.
3. COPYRIGHT (LAW) 4. CONTRACTS.
I. TITLE. II. TITLE: TRADE SECRET.
III. TITLE: COMPUTER PROGRAMS.

331.881
C65
Trade-unions.
Committee for Economic Development.
Union powers and union functions: toward
a better balance. A statement on national
policy. New York, 1964.
43p.

1. Trade-unions. 2. Labor relations.
I. Title.

VF
332.72
F22Las
Trade-in-houses.
U.S. Federal Housing Administration.
(Office of Public Information)
FHA assistance for home trade-ins.
Washington, 1964.
[2]p. (Its Consumer bulletin, FHA
no. 793)

1. Mortgage finance. 2. Trade-in-
houses. (Series)

658
A52tra
Trade secrets; a management overview.
American Management Association.
Trade secrets; a management overview.
New York, 1965.
24p. (AMA management bulletin no. 64)

1. Management. 2. Industrial management.
3. Patents. I. Title. (Series)

331:881
E26
TRADE-UNIONS.
Economisch Instituut voor de
Bouwnijverheid.
Toetredingen niet-fabriekmatig
bouwbedrijf, 1969/70. Amsterdam, 1970.
28p. (Publikatie nr. 25 in de serie
''de bouwproduktie'')

1. Trade-unions.

VF
332.72
F22Las
1966
Trade-in-houses.
U.S. Federal Housing Administration.
How FHA helps on home trade-ins.
Washington, 1966.
[2]p. (Its Consumer bulletin, FHA
no. 793. HUD IP-5)

1. Mortgage finance. 2. Trade-in-
houses. (Series)

331.881
I57
Trade union activities in the field of housing
and building.
International Confederation of Free Trade
Unions.
Trade union activities in the field of hous-
ing and building. Brussels, 1966.
46p. (Know your facts series)

1. Trade-unions. 2. Housing. 3. Building
industry. I. Title.

330
G15
Trade-unions.
Galbraith, John Kenneth.
The new industrial state. Boston, Houghton
Mifflin, 1967.
427p.

1. Economic development. 2. Economic planning. 3. Industrial research. 4. Industrial
management. 5. Marketing research. 6. Trade-
unions. I. Title.

333.33
(016)
N17t
Trade-in houses - Bibl.
National Housing Center. Library.
Trade-in housing, a selected list
of references, 1959-1961. Washington,
1961.
2p. (Its Reference list no. 42)

1. Trade-in houses - Bibl.

330.15
N17o
no.92
Trade union membership.
Troy, Leo.
Trade union membership, 1897-1962. New
York, 1965.
21,65 p. (National Bureau of Economic
Research. Occasional paper 92).

1. Trade-unions. I. Title. II. National
Bureau of Economic Research. Occasional
paper, no. 92.

331
G15
Trade unions.
Galenson, Walter.
Labor and trade unionism: an
interdisciplinary reader, by Walter
Galenson and Seymour Martin Lipset.
New York, Wiley, 1960.
379p.

1. Labor-supply. 2. Labor relations.
3. Trade unions. I. Lipset, Seymour Martin,
jt. au. II. Title.

333.33
H68
TRADE-INS CAN BECOME BIG BUSINESS.
HOUSE AND HOME.
TRADE-INS CAN BECOME BIG BUSINESS.
[N.P.] 1953.
156-160P.
FROM HOUSE AND HOME, OCT. 1953.

1. TRADE-IN HOUSES. I. TITLE.

331.881
B17
Trade-unions.
Barkin, Solomon.
The decline of labor movement and
what can be done about it. Santa Barbara,
Calif., Center for the Study of Democratic
Institutions, 1961.
75p.

1. Trade-unions. I. Center for the
Study of Democratic Institutions.

331
G84
TRADE-UNIONS.
Guidebook to labor relations, 19

Chicago, Commerce Clearing House, 19

v.
For Library holdings see main entry.

1. Labor relations. 2. Trade-unions.
3. Labor laws and legislation. I. Commerce
Clearing House.

381
C65t
Trade policy toward low-income countries.
Committee for Economic Development.
Trade policy toward low-income countries.
A statement on national policy by the Research
and Policy Committee of the Committee for
Economic Development. Prepared in association
with CEPES-the European Committee for Economic
and Social Progress and others. New York,
1967.
44p.

1. Commercial policy. I. Title.

330.15
N17o
no.105
TRADE-UNIONS.
Bartell, H Robert.
Pension funds of multiemployer industrial
groups, unions, and nonprofit organizations.
by H. Robert Bartell and Elizabeth T. Simpson.
New York, 1968.
52 p. (National Bureau of Economic Research.
Occasional paper 105).

1. Pensions. 2. Trade-unions. 3. Social
security. I. Simpson, Elizabeth T. II. Title.
III. National Bureau of Economic Research.
Occasional paper, no. 105.

331.881
I57
Trade-unions.
International Confederation of Free Trade
Unions.
Trade union activities in the field of hous-
ing and building. Brussels, 1966.
46p. (Know your facts series)

1. Trade-unions. 2. Housing. 3. Building
industry. I. Title.

325
J12

TRADE-UNIONS.
Jacobson, Julius, ed.
The Negro and the American labor movement. Garden City, N.Y., Doubleday, 1968.
430p.
Anchor Books edition.

1. Negroes. 2. Employment - Negroes.
3. Trade-unions. I. Title: American labor movement. II. Title.

690.072
073

Trade unions.
Organisation for Economic Co-operation and Development.
The role of trade unions in housing; regional trade union seminar, Hamburg, 17-19 January, 1967. Supplement to the final report. Paris, 1967.
94p.
At head of title: International seminars 1967-1.
1. Building industry - Labor relations.
2. Trade unions. I. Regional Trade Union Seminar, Hamburg, 1967. II. Title.

330.15
N17o
no.92

TRADE-UNIONS.
Troy, Leo.
Trade union membership, 1897-1962. New York, 1965.
21,65 p. (National Bureau of Economic Research. Occasional paper 92).

1. Trade-unions. I. Title. II. National Bureau of Economic Research. Occasional paper, no. 92.

331
(77434)
L23

Trade unions
Leggett, John C
Class, race, and labor; working class consciousness in Detroit. New York, Oxford University Press, 1968.
252p.
Bibliography: p. 228-238.

1. Labor supply - Detroit. 2. Trade unions. 3. Employment - Detroit. 4. Race relations. 5. Labor relations. I. Title.

VF
331.881
P25

Trade unions.
Pennsylvania Economy League.
Background for decision, a union shop for Philadelphia's city employees? In association with the Bureau of Municipal Research. Philadelphia, 1960.
10p.

Reprinted from Citizens business, May and June 1960.

1. Trade unions. 2. Municipal government - Philadelphia.

331.881
L118E

TRADE-UNIONS.
U.S. BUREAU OF LABOR STATISTICS.
BENEFICIAL ACTIVITIES OF AMERICAN TRADE-UNIONS. WASHINGTON, GOVT. PRINT. OFF., 1928.
229p. (ITS BULLETIN NO. 465. MISCELLANEOUS SERIES)

PREPARED BY FLORENCE E. PARKER.

1. TRADE-UNIONS. I. PARKER, FLORENCE E. II. TITLE.

325
M17

Trade-unions.
Marshall, F Ray
The Negro and apprenticeship, by F. Ray Marshall and Vernon M. Briggs, Jr. Baltimore, Johns Hopkins Press, 1967.
283p.

1. Negroes. 2. Apprenticeship. 3. Building trades. 4. Trade-unions. 5. Youth. I. Briggs, Vernon M., jt. au. II. Title.

331.881
R17

Trade unions.
Raskin, Bernard.
On a true course; the story of the National Maritime Union of America, AFL-CIO. Washington, Merkle Press, 1967.
162p.

1. Trade unions. 2. Labor relations.
3. Harbors. I. National Maritime Union of America. II. American Federation of Labor and Congress of Industrial Organizations. III. Title.

331
L11neg

TRADE UNIONS.
U.S. Bureau of Labor Statistics.
Negotiation impasse, grievance, and arbitration in Federal agreements. Wash., Govt. Print. Off., 1970.
78p. (Its Bulletin 1661)

1. Labor relations. 2. Trade unions.
3. Federal civil service. I. Title.

690
(774)
M42

Trade unions.
Michigan. Civil Rights Commission.
Employment distribution study of the construction industry in Michigan. Detroit, 1966.
95p.

1. Building industry - Michigan.
2. Employment - Michigan. 3. Employment - Negroes. 4. Trade unions. I. Title.

711.585
(77434)
R18

Trade-unions.
Ravitz, Mel.
Neighborhood conservation and the trade union member. In Metropolitan Research Bureau of Detroit Newsletter, vol. 2, no. 1, December 1961. p. 1-5.

1. Neighborhood rehabilitation - Detroit.
2. Trade-unions. I. Detroit. Metropolitan Research Bureau. Newsletter.

331.881
L11

Trade unions.
U.S. Bureau of Labor Statistics.
Union constitution provisions; election and tenure of national and international union officers, 1958. Qualifications for office, nominating and election procedures, term of office, presidential salaries, removal procedures, by Harry P. Cohany and Irving P. Phillips. Washington, Govt. Print. Off., 1958.

(Continued on next card)

331.881
N17

Trade-unions.
National Institute of Municipal Law Officers.
The latest developments on labor unions and municipalities. (Transcript of NIMLO Labor Relations Seminar, work paper, position papers, transcript of papers, by the Union, city and state experts, questions and answers at two-day seminar) Washington, 1968.
206p. (Its Report no. 153)

1. Trade-unions. 2. Labor relations.
3. Municipal government. I. Title.

331.881
R23
1967

Trade unions.
Regional Trade Union Seminar, Hamburg, 1967.
The role of trade unions in housing, Hamburg 17-19th, 1967. Final report. Paris, Organisation for Economic Co-operation and Development, 1968.
207p. (International seminars 1967-1)

1. Trade unions. 2. Housing. 3. Labor relations. I. Organisation for Economic Co-operation and Development. II. Title.

331.881
L11

Trade-unions.
U.S. Bureau of Labor Statistics. Union constitution provisions:...(Card 2)

37p. (Its Bulletin no. 1239)

85th Cong., 2d sess. House document no. 446.
1. Labor relations. 2. Trade unions.
I. Phillips, Irving Philip. II. Title.
III. Title: Election and tenure of national and international union officers, 1958.

352
N17P

TRADE-UNIONS.
NATIONAL INSTITUTE OF MUNICIPAL LAW OFFICERS, WASHINGTON, D.C.
POWER OF MUNICIPALITIES TO ENTER INTO LABOR UNION CONTRACTS, A SURVEY OF LAW AND EXPERIENCE, PREPARED BY CHARLES S. RHYNE... WASHINGTON, 1941.
78P. (ITS REPORT NO. 76)

1. MUNICIPAL GOVERNMENT.
2. TRADE-UNIONS. I. RHYNE, CHARLES S. II. TITLE.

VF
323.4
R87c

TRADE UNIONS.
Rustin, Bayard.
Conflict or coalition? The civil rights struggle and the trade union movement today. From an address before the Eighth Constitutional Convention of the American Federation of Labor and the Congress of Industrial Organizations, Oct. 3, 1969. New York, A. Philip Randolph Institute, 1969.
12p.

1. Civil rights. 2. Trade unions.
I. Randolph (A. Philip) Institute.
II. Title.

331.2
L11U

TRADE UNIONS.
U.S. BUREAU OF LABOR STATISTICS.
UNION SCALES OF WAGES AND HOURS IN THE BUILDING TRADES IN 70 CITIES, MAY 15, 1937. PREPARED BY INDUSTRIAL RELATIONS DIVISION. WASHINGTON, GOVT. PRINT. OFF., 1938.
67P. (ITS BULLETIN NO. 657)

1. WAGES AND SALARIES. 2. BUILDING TRADES. 3. TRADE UNIONS. I. TITLE.

331
(7471)
N28m

Trade-unions.
New York (City) Temporary Commission on City Finances.
Municipal collective bargaining; relations between the City of New York and public employee organizations, by George H. Deming and others. New York, 1966.
65p. (Its Staff paper 8)

1. Labor relations - New York (City)
2. Trade-unions. 3. Wages and salaries.
I. Deming, George H. II. Title.

330.15
N17o
no.56

TRADE-UNIONS.
Troy, Leo.
Distribution of union membership among the states, 1939 and 1953. New York, 1957.
32 p. illus. (National Bureau of Economic Research. Occasional paper 56).

1. Trade-unions. I. Title. II. National Bureau of Economic Research. Occasional paper, no.56.

331.881
W21

Trade-unions.
Weaver, Robert Clifton.
Recent events in Negro union relationships. Chicago, 1944.
234-249 p.

Reprinted from the Journal of political economy, vol. III, no. 3, Sept. 1944.

1. Trade-unions. 2. Labor relations.
3. Employment - Negroes.

331
W651 TRADE UNIONS.
WOLMAN, LEO.
INDUSTRY = WIDE BARGAINING.
IRVINGTON=ON=HUDSON, N.Y., FOUNDATION FOR
ECONOMIC EDUCATION, 1948.
63P.

1. LABOR RELATIONS.   2. TRADE UNIONS.
I. TITLE.

332
G68T TRADING IN FEDERAL FUNDS.
U.S. BOARD OF GOVERNORS OF THE FEDERAL
RESERVE SYSTEM.
TRADING IN FEDERAL FUNDS; FINDINGS OF A
THREE=YEAR SURVEY, BY DOROTHY M.
NICHOLS. WASHINGTON, 1965.
116P. ILLUS. (FEDERAL RESERVE
TECHNICAL PAPERS)

1. BANKS AND BANKING.   I. NICHOLS,
DOROTHY M.   II. TITLE.

Traffic.
388
A52m American Automobile Association.
Metro, toward a brighter traffic
future for cities and suburbs. Washington, [1961]
28p.

1. Traffic. 2. Highways.

058.7   TRADE=UNIONS = DIRECTORIES.
:331.881 U.S. DEPARTMENT OF LABOR.
L112   REGISTER OF REPORTING LABOR
ORGANIZATIONS, JUNE 30, 1960.
WASHINGTON, GOVT. PRINT. OFF., 1960.
5PTS.
CONTENTS.= PT. 1. WESTERN STATES.=
PT. 2. MIDDLE WEST=ROCKY MOUNTAIN
STATES.= PT. 3. GREAT LAKES STATES.=
PT. 4. SOUTHEASTERN STATES.= PT. 5.
NORTHEASTERN STATES.

1. TRADE=UNIONS = DIRECTORIES.
I. TITLE.

658.8
868t Trading stamps: theory and practice.
South Dakota. University. Business Research Bureau.
Trading stamps: theory and practice, by
H. L. Grathwohl. Vermillion, S. D., 1958.
64p. (Its Bulletin no. 60)

1. Marketing. I. Grathwohl, H. L.
II. Title.

711.73 TRAFFIC.
A52U AMERICAN INSTITUTE OF PLANNERS.
COMMITTEE ON URBAN TRANSPORTATION.
URBAN FREEWAYS. NEW YORK, AMERICAN
TRANSIT ASSOCIATION, 1947.
38P.

1. HIGHWAYS.   2. TRAFFIC.
I. TITLE: FREEWAYS.

R
058.7   Trade unions - Directories.
:331.881
L11   U.S. Bureau of Labor Statistics.
Directory of national and international
labor unions in the United States,

Washington, Govt. Print. Off.
v. (Its Bulletin)

Title varies.

For complete information see shelflist.

1.Trade unions - Directories. I.Title.
II.Title: National and international labor
unions in the United States.

360
(72) Tradition and growth.
A84 Avila, Manuel.
Tradition and growth; a study of four Mexican
villages. Chicago, University of Chicago Press,
1969.
219p.

1. Social conditions - Mexico. 2. Economic
development - Mexico. I. Title.

388
A52d American Municipal Association.
Developing the transportation plan.
Chicago, Public Administration Service, 1964.
90p.

"A handbook sponsored by the American
Municipal Association for use in conjunction
with the basic planning guide, Better
transportation for your city, and the
procedure manuals developed by the
National Committee on Urban Transportation."
(Continued on next
card)

331.881   Trade-unions - Hist.
A52 American Federation of Labor and Congress
of Industrial Organizations.
Our first 50 years, 1908-1958; an
informal narrative of the Building and
Construction Trades Department, AFL-CIO.
[Washington] Ransdell, 1958.
56p.

1. Trade-unions - Hist.
2. Labor relations. 3. Building trades.
I. Title.

323.25   The tradition of violence in our society.
:S64 Spiegel, John P
The tradition of violence in our society.
Waltham, Mass., Lemberg Center for the Study of
Violence, Brandeis University, 1968.
12p. (Reprint series)
Ed. Washington star, Oct. 13, 1968.

1. Civil disorders. 2. Minority groups.
I. Title. II. Brandeis University. Lemberg
Center for the Study of Violence. III. Washington
star.

388
A52d American Municipal Association. Developing
the transportation plan... 1964.
(Card 2)

Bibliography: p. 80-89.

1. Transportation. 2. Traffic.
I. Public Administration Service, Chicago.
II. Title.

331.881   Trade unions - History.
(07) U.S. Bureau of Labor Statistics.
L11b   Brief history of the American labor
movement. Washington, Govt. Print.
Off., 1964.
100p. (Its Bulletin no. 1000)

1. Trade unions - Hist. 2. Labor
relations. I. Title.

728.3 TRADITIONAL AND CONTEMPORARY PLANS.
P65EI POLLMAN, RICHARD B
88 TRADITIONAL AND CONTEMPORARY PLANS.
DETROIT, HOME PLANNERS, INC., 1965.
94P. (DESIGNS FOR CONVENIENT LIVING,
BOOK NO. 55)

1. ARCHITECTURE, DOMESTIC = DESIGNS
AND PLANS. I. TITLE: TRADITIONAL AND
CONTEMPORARY PLANS.

VF   Traffic.
388 American Society of Planning Officials.
A52mo Moving the masses in modern cities;
significant facts and fallacies on the
growing problem of traffic congestion.
New York City [1962?]
32p.

1. Transportation. 2. Traffic.

331.881   TRADE=UNIONS - HISTORY.
(09) Werstein, Irving.
W27 Pie in the sky, an American struggle; the
Wobblies and their times. New York,
Delacorte Press, 1969.
139p.

Bibliography: p. 135-136.

1. Trade-unions - History. I. Title.

690.031   Traditional building costs; the target for
B47   system building.
Bishop, D
Traditional building costs; the target for
system building. Garston, Eng., Building
Research Station, Ministry of Technology,
1966.
34-37p. (U.K. Building Research
Station. Building research current papers.
Design series no. 42)

Reprinted from the National builder,
Jan., 1966.

1. Building   costs. 2. Building
research.   I. U.K. Building
Research Sta-   tion. II. Title.

Traffic.
388
A52me American Transit Association.
Manual of transit and traffic studies.
New York, 1947.
73p.

1. Transportation. 2. Journey to work.
3. Parking. 4. Traffic. I. Title.

VF
341.1   Trading ideas with the world.
:338 U.S. Advisory Commission on Educational Exchange.
A28   Trading ideas with the world; international
educational and technical exchange. Washington,
Govt. Print. Off., 1949.
88 p./map. illus., charts, graphs, tables.

Dept. of State publication 3551, International
information and cultural series 7.

1.Technical assistance programs. I.Title.

Traffic
see also
Transportation.

388
A52on Anderson, Robert L.
On the statistical distribution
function theory of traffic flow, by
Robert L. Anderson and others. Balti-
more, Operations Research Society of
America, 1962.
180-196p.
Reprinted from Operations research,
March-April, 1962.

1. Traffic. 2. Highways - Research.
I. Operations Research Society of
America.   II. Operations
Research.   III. Title.

388
A57
TRAFFIC.
Antoniou, Jim.
Environmental management; planning for traffic.
London, McGraw-Hill, 1971.
171p.

1. Traffic. 2. Transportation. I. Title.

Traffic.
388
A87t
Automotive Safety Foundation.
Traffic control and roadway elements; their relationship to highway safety. Prepared in cooperation with the U.S. Bureau of Public Roads. Washington, D.C., 1963.
124p.
Bibliography: p. 86-111.

1. Traffic. 2. Traffic safety. 3. Traffic regulations. I. U.S. Bureau of Public Roads. II. Title.

Traffic.
388
B42v
Bidwell, J   B
Vehicles and drivers; 1980. For presentation at the SAE Annual Meeting, Detroit, Michigan, Jan. 12-16, 1959. New York, Society of Automotive Engineers, 1959.
11p.
1. Traffic. 2. Highways. I. Society of Automotive Engineers. Meeting, Detroit, 1959. II. Title.

Traffic.
388
B42
Bierley, Robert L
The traffic pacer system, by Robert L. Bierley and Jon Parkinson. Warren, Mich., Research Laboratories, General Motors Corp., 1963.
42p. (General Motors Corp., Research Laboratories. GMR-406)

1. Traffic. I. Parkinson, Jon, jt. au. II. General Motors Corp. III. Title.

534.83
B47
TRAFFIC.
Birgersson, Lisbeth.
Trafikbuller i stadsmiljö - några bullerreducerande åtgärder i Schweiz, by Lisbeth Birgersson & Trad Wrigglesworth. Stockholm, 1970.
[4]p. (Stockholm. Statens Institut för Byggnadsforskning. Byggforskningen informerar B4: 1970)

1. Noise. 2. Traffic. I. Wrigglesworth, Trad, jt. au. II. Stockholm. Statens Institut for Byggnadsforskning.

711.585
B87
Traffic.
Burton, Hal
The city fights back; a nation-wide survey of what cities are doing to keep pace with traffic, zoning, shifting population, smoke, smog and other problems. Narrated and edited by Hal Burton from material developed by the Central Business District Council of the Urban Land Institute. New York, Citadel Press [c1954]
318 p.   plates, graphs, tables.

Bibliography: p. 313-318.

351.81
C15
NO.35
TRAFFIC.
CALIFORNIA. UNIVERSITY. INSTITUTE OF TRANSPORTATION AND TRAFFIC ENGINEERING.
VEHICLE QUEUES IN MIXED TRAFFIC STREAMS; PROGRESS REPORT, BY ROBERT M. OLIVER AND OTHERS. BERKELEY, CALIF., 1962.
12P. (ITS RESEARCH REPORT NO. 35)

1. TRAFFIC. 2. TRAFFIC - SURVEYS. I. TITLE. II. OLIVER, ROBERT M.

351.81
C15
NO.34
TRAFFIC.
CALIFORNIA. UNIVERSITY. INSTITUTE OF TRANSPORTATION AND TRAFFIC ENGINEERING.
VEHICLE SPACE-OCCUPANCY IN MOVING STREAMS OF TRAFFIC; PROGRESS REPORT, BY ROBERT M. OLIVER AND OTHERS. BERKELEY, CALIF., 1962.
16P. (ITS RESEARCH REPORT NO. 34)

1. TRAFFIC. 2. TRAFFIC - SURVEYS. 3. HIGHWAYS. I. TITLE. II. OLIVER, ROBERT M.

351.81
C15
NO.37
TRAFFIC.
CALIFORNIA. UNIVERSITY. UNIVERSITY AT LOS ANGELES. INSTITUTE OF TRANSPORTATION AND TRAFFIC ENGINEERING.
WAVE THEORIES OF TRAFFIC FLOW, BY LOUIS A. PIPES. LOS ANGELES, 1964.
21P. (ITS RESEARCH REPORT NO. 37)

1. TRAFFIC. 2. TRAFFIC - SURVEYS. I. TITLE. II. PIPES, LOUIS A.

352.6
C31me
TRAFFIC.
Chaiken, Jan M
Methods for allocating urban emergency units, by Jan M. Chaiken and Richard C. Larson. New York, New York City Rand Institute, 1971.
55p. (R-680-HUD/NSF)
Bibliography: p. 51-55.
Study sponsored in part by the U.S. Dept. of Housing and Urban Development. Contract no. H-1056.
1. Municipal services. 2. Traffic. I. New York City Rand Institute. II. Larson, Richard C., jt. au. III. U.S. Dept. of Housing and Urban Development. IV. Title.

352.6
C31n
TRAFFIC.
Chaiken, Jan M
The number of emergency units busy at alarms which require multiple servers. New York, New York City Rand Institute, 1971.
15p. (R-531-NYC/HUD)
Study sponsored by City of New York and U.S. Dept. of Housing and Urban Development.

1. Municipal services 2. Traffic. I. New York City Rand Institute. II. Title. III. Title: Emergency units. IV. U.S. Dept. of Housing and Urban Development.

388
C31ho
Traffic.
Chamber of Commerce of the United States.
How bypasses affect business. Washington [1956?]
24p.

1. Traffic. 2. Highways. I. Title.

388
C31h
Traffic.
Chamber of Commerce of the United States. (Transportation and Communication Dept.)
How to get the most out of our streets. Washington, [1954]
51p. illus., diagrs., maps.

1. Traffic.

388
C31s
Traffic.
Chamber of Commerce of the United States. (Transportation and Communication Dept.)
Solutions to the problem of merchandise pickup and delivery in business districts. Washington, 1951.
24p.

1. Traffic. 2. Business districts.

388
C315
Traffic.
Chandler, Robert E
Traffic dynamics: studies in car following, by Robert E. Chandler and others. Baltimore, Operations Research Society of America, 1958.
165-184p.
Reprinted from Operations research, Mar.-Apr., 1958.

1. Traffic. 2. Highways - Research. I. Operations Research Society of America. II. Operations research. III. Title.

VF
711.585
:388
C51
Traffic.
Claire, William H
Redevelopment and traffic.   Traffic Engineering Magazine, Nov. 1953.   [3] p.

Reprint.

1. Urban redevelopment. 2. Traffic.

388
C52
Traffic.
Cleveland, Donald E
Traffic characteristics at regional shopping centers, by Donald E. Cleveland and Edward A. Mueller, Yale University, Bureau of Highway Traffic, 1961.
28p.

1. Traffic. 2. Shopping centers. I. Mueller, Edward A., jt. au. II. Yale University. Bureau of Highway Traffic.

711.73
C65e
TRAFFIC.
Colony, David C
Estimating traffic noise levels and acceptability for freeway design, by David C. Colony. [n.p.] [1969?]
26p.
Paper presented at the 49th annual meeting of the Highway Research Board, Wash., D.C., Jan. 12-16, 1970.

1. Highways. 2. Traffic. 3. Noise. I. Highway Research Board. II. Title.

388
C65
Traffic.
Columbia University. Institute for Urban Land Use and Housing Studies.
Urban traffic, a function of land use, by Robert B. Mitchell and Chester Rapkin. New York, Columbia Univ. Press, 1954.
xvii, 226 p.   illus., graphs, tables.
(Its Publications)

1. Traffic. 2. Land use. 3. City Planning. I. Mitchell, Robert B. II. Rapkin, Chester. III. Title.

534.83
C66
TRAFFIC.
Cook, David I
Trees may help solve the traffic noise problem, by David I. Cook and David F. Van Haverbeke. Wash. U.S. Forest Service, 1969.
[2]p.

Reprinted from: Univ. Nebr. Quart. 116(2): p. 11-12.

1. Noise. 2. Traffic. 3. Trees. I. Van Haverbeke, David R., jt. au. II. Title.

388
E81
Traffic.
Evans, David H
The highway merging and queuing problem, by David H. Evans and others. Baltimore, Operations Research Society of America, 1964.
832-857p.
Reprinted from Operations research, Nov.-Dec., 1964.
Bibliography: p. 856-857.
1. Traffic. 2. Highways - Research. I. Operations Research Society of America. II. Operations research. III. Title.

388
G17e   Gardels, Keith.
        Automatic car controls for electronic high-
        ways. Warren, Mich. Research Laboratories
        General Motors Corp., 1960.
        12p. (General Motors Corp. Research
        Laboratories. GMR-276)

        1. Highways - Research. 2. Traffic.
        I. General Motors Corp. II. Title.

388
G19   Gazis, Denos C
        Car-following theory of steady-state traffic
        flow, by Denos C. Gazis and others. Baltimore,
        Operations Research Society of America, 1959.
        499-505p.
        Reprinted from Operations research, July-
        Aug., 1959.

        1. Traffic. 2. Highways - Research.
        I. Operations Research Society of America.
        II. Operations research. III. Title.

388
G19d   Gazis, Denos C
        Density oscillations between lanes of a
        multilane highway, by Denos C. Gazis and
        others. Baltimore, Operations Research
        Society of America, 1962.
        658-667p.
        Reprinted from Operations research, Sept.-
        Oct., 1962.

        1. Traffic. 2. Highways - Research.
        I. Operations Research Society of America.
        II. Operations research. III. Title.

388
G19m   TRAFFIC.
        Gazis, Denos C
        Mathematical theory of automobile traffic.
        Wash., American Association for the
        Advancement of Science, 1967.
        273-281p.

        In: Science, July 21, 1967, p. 273-281.

        1. Traffic. I. Science. II. Title.

388
G25tr   General Electric Co.
        Traffic assignment by electronic computer.
        Phoenix, Ariz., [1965?]
        [10] p.

        1. Traffic. 2. Automation. I. Title.

388
G27   Gerlough, Daniel L.
        Use of Poisson distribution in highway
        traffic; the probability theory applied to
        distribution of vehicles on two-lane
        highways [by] André Schuhl. Saugatuck,
        Conn., 1955.
        75 p.   graphs.

        Bibliographies.

        1. Traffic. I. Schuhl, André. II. Title: Poisson
        and traffic.

711.4
G78   Gruen, Victor, 1903-
        The heart of our cities; the urban
        crisis: diagnosis and cure. New York,
        Simon and Schuster, 1964.
        368p.

        Bibliography: p. 348-351.

        1. City planning. 2. Suburbs.
        3. Transportation. 4. Journey to work.
        5. Traffic. 6. Shopping centers. I. Title.

711.14
G78   Gruen (Victor) Associates.
        A review of transportation aspects of land
        use control, [by] Harold Marks and Salem Spitz
Laf.   [of] Victor Gruen Associates. [Wash.]
        Highway Research Board, 1966.
        41p. (National Cooperative Highway Re-
        search Program report no. 31)
        Research sponsored by the American Associ-
        ation of State Highway Officials in co-
        operation with the Bureau of Public Roads.

        1. Land use. 2. Highways. 3. Traffic.
        4. Transportation.
                              (Cont'd on next card)

711.14
G78   Gruen (Victor) Associates.   A review of
        transportation aspects of land use control...
                              (Card 2)
        I. Marks, Harold. II. Spitz, Salem.
        III. Highway Research Board. IV. American
        Association of State Highway Officials. V. Title.

711.73
H13r   Hafstad, Lawrence R
        Research as applied to traffic engineering.
        Detroit, Institute of Traffic Engineers,
        1957.
        1v.

        1. Highways. 2. Traffic. I. Institute of
        Traffic Engineers. Meeting, 27th, Detroit,
        Sept., 1957. II. Title.

388
H24   Heikoff, Joseph Meyer, 1917-
        Urban highway planning liaison. Urbana,
        1963.
        42p. (University of Illinois.
        Engineering Experiment Station. Technical
        report no. 7)
        University of Illinois bulletin, v. 61,
        no. 8.

        Bibliography: p. 40-42.

        1. Traffic. 2. Highways - Economic effect.
        I. Title.

388
H27b   Herman, R
        Behavior of traffic leaving a signalized
        intersection, by R. Herman and others.
        [London, Pointeverall, ltd.] 1964.
        529-533p.

        Reprinted from Traffic engineering and
        control, 1964.

        1. Traffic. 2. Highways. I. Traffic
        engineering and control. II. Title.

388
H27c   Herman, Robert.
        Comments on the highway-crossing
        problem, by Robert Herman and George
        Weiss. Warren, Mich., Research Labora-
        tories, General Motors Corp., 1961.
        828-840p.
        Reprinted from Operations research,
        Nov.- Dec., 1961

        1. Traffic. 2. Highways - Research.
        I. Weiss, George, jt. au. II. General
        Motors Corp. III. Operations research.
        IV. Title.

VF
388
H27ma   Herman, Robert.
        Mathematical theory of traffic flow.
        Warren, Mich. Research Laboratories, General
        Motors Corp., 1960.
        67-79p.

        Reprinted from 1960 Proceedings, Institute of
        Traffic Engineers.

        1. Traffic. 2. Mathematics. I. General Motors
        Corp. Research Laboratories. II. Institute of
        Traffic Engineers. Proceedings, 1960.
        III. Title.

388
H27m   Herman, Robert.
        Microscopic and macroscopic aspects of
        single lane traffic flow, by Robert Herman and
        Richard Rothery. Warren, Mich., Research
        Laboratories, General Motors Corp., 1962.
        74-93p.
        Reprinted from Journal of Operations Research
        Society of Japan, Dec., 1962.

        1. Traffic. 2. Highways - Research.
        I. Rothery, Richard, jt. au. II. Operations
        Research Society of Japan. III. General
        Motors Corp. IV. Title.

388
H27p   Herman, R
        Problem of the amber signal light, by R.
        Herman and others.
        Reprinted from Traffic engineering and
        control, Sept. 1963. p. 298-304.

        1. Traffic. I. Traffic engineering and
        control. II. Title.

388
H27s   Herman, Robert.
        Single-lane traffic theory and experiment,
        by Robert Herman and R.B. Potts. Amsterdam,
        Elsevier, 1961.
        120-146p.
        Reprinted from Theory of traffic flow
        (1961) 120.

        1. Traffic. 2. Highways - Research.
        I. Potts, R.B., jt. au. II. Theory of traffic
        flow. III. Title.

388
H27t   Herman, Robert.
        Traffic dynamics: analysis of stability in
        car following, by Robert Herman and others.
        Baltimore, Operations Research Society of
        America, 1959.
        86-106p.
        Reprinted from Operations research,
        Jan.-Feb., 1959.

        1. Traffic. 2. Highways - Research.
        I. Operations Research Society of America.
        II. Operations research. III. Title.

388
H27v   Herman, Robert.
        Vehicular traffic flow, by Robert Herman
        and Keith Gardels. New York, Scientific
        American, 1963.

        Reprinted from Scientific American, Dec., 1963

        1. Traffic. 2. Highways. I. Scientific
        American. II. Gardels, Keith, jt. au.
        III. Title.

VF
711.73
H43   Highway Research Board.
        Directional channelization and determina-
        tion of pavement widths; presented at the
        Thirty-second annual meeting January 13-16,
        1953. Washington, National Research
        Council, 1953.
        49 p.   illus., charts, diagrs.   (Its
        Bulletin 72)
        Contents.-Directional channelization design,
        W. R. Bellis.-Determining widths of pavements
        in channelized intersections, L. F. Heuperman,
        with appendix: Path of vehicles on curves and

VF
711.73
H43   Highway Research Board.   Directional
        channelization and determination ...
        January 13-16, 1953. (Card 2)

        minimum width of turning lanes.

        1. Highways. 2. Traffic. I. Bellis, W. R.
        II. Heuperman, L. F. III. Title.

VF
388
H43e

Traffic.
Highway Research Board.
Effects of traffic control on street capacity; presented at the thirty-fourth annual meeting, January 11-14, 1955. Washington, 1956.
52 p. illus. (Its Bulletin 112)
Contents.-Capacities of narrow streets with manual control and signal control.-Capacities of one-way and two-way streets with signals and stop signs.-Starting delay and time spacing of vehicles entering signalized intersection.-Effect of parked vehicle on traffic capacity of signalized intersection.
1. Traffic.

388
H43w

Traffic.
Highway Research Board.
Weighing vehicles in motion, by O.K. Normann and R.C. Hopkins; presented at the 31st annual meeting, January 1952. Washington, 1952.
27 p. illus. (Its Bulletin 50)
1.Traffic. I.Normann, O.K. II.Title.

388
I57
1950

Traffic.
Institute of Traffic Engineers.
Traffic engineering handbook, ed. by Henry K. Evans. 2d ed. New Haven, Conn., 1950.
514 p. illus., graphs, tables.

1. Traffic. I. Evans, Henry K., ed. II. Title.

388
H43f

Traffic.
Highway Research Board.
Factors influencing travel patterns.
Washington, 1955.
94p. graphs maps, tables. (Its Bulletin 119)
Contents.-Trends in traffic diversion on Edens Expressway, William J. Mortimer.-Objective and subjective correlates of expressway use, E. Wilson Campbell and Robert McCargar
(Continued on Card 2)

388
H63d

TRAFFIC.
HOFFMAN, GEORGE A
ON MINIMIZING THE LAND USED BY AUTOMOBILES AND BUSES IN THE URBAN CENTRAL CORE: UNDERGROUND HIGHWAYS AND PARKING FACILITIES. SANTA MONICA, CALIF., RAND CORPORATION, 1964.
30P.

1. TRAFFIC. 2. HIGHWAYS. 3. LAND USE. I. TITLE. II. RAND CORP.

388
I57tr

Traffic.
Institute of Traffic Engineers.
Traffic planning and other considerations for pedestrian malls. An informational report. Washington, 1966.
66p.
Bibliography: p. 65-66.

1. Traffic. 2. Parking. 3. Retail trade. I. Title.

388
H43f

Highway Research Board. Factors influencing travel patterns.... (Card 2)

-Induced traffic on Chesapeake Bay Bridge, Ernest W. Bunting. -Intracity traffic movements, F. Houston Wynn. -Evaluation of intercity-travel desire, Willa Mylroie.

1. Traffic. 2. Traffic surveys - Cook County, Ill. 3. Traffic surveys - Washington. 4. Traffic surveys - Maryland. I. Title: Travel patterns.

690.015
(485)
S 82
R20
1970

TRAFFIC.
Ingemansson, Stig.
Bullerproblem vid trafikleder, en litteraturstudie och förslag till beräkningmetodik (Traffic noise, study of literature and draft of calculation methods) av Stig Ingemansson och Sten Ljunggren. Stockholm, 1970.
188p. (Stockholm. Statens Institut för Byggnadsforskning. Rapport 20:1970)
English summary.
1. Building research - Sweden. 2. Noise. 3. Traffic. I. Ljunggren, Sten, jt. au. II. Stockholm. Statens Institut för Byggnadsforskning. III. Title: Traffic noise.

711.4
I572

Traffic.
Inter-American Congress of Municipalities, 3d meeting, New Orleans, 1950.
North American reports. Chicago, Public Administration Clearing House, 1950.
1 v.

Bound with Spanish version: Ponencias norteamericanas, sometidas a la III Reunion del Congreso Interamericano de Municipios.

Contents.-Relations between municipalities and central governments, Rowland Egger.-Housing and   the municipalities.,
(see card 2)

388
H43hi

TRAFFIC.
Highway Research Board.
Highway capacity manual, 1965. Wash., 1965.
411p. (Its Special report 87)

National Academy of Sciences, National Research Council, publication 1328.

1. Traffic. 2. Highways. I. Title.

690.015
(485)
S82
R52
1969

TRAFFIC.
Ingemansson, Stig.
Störningsmått för trafikbuller. Minimiavstand trafikled - bebyggelse i plan, oskärmad terräng (Physical scales of traffic noise. Minimum distance between road and dwellings in level unshielded terrain) av Stig Ingemansson och Sven-Olof Benjegard. Stockholm, 1969.
23p. (Stockholm. Statens Institut för Byggnadsforskning. Rapport 52:1969)
English summary.
1. Building research - Sweden. 2. Noise.
(Cont'd on next card)

711.4
I572

Inter-American Congress of Municipalities, 3d meeting.. North American reports.
1950. (card 2)

Contents continued: Herbert Emmerich.-City planning - its present status in the United States of America, Walter H. Blucher. - Traffic problems in cities - suggestions for their solution, J. Stannard Baker.
1. Intergovernmental relations. 2. City planning. 3. Housing. 4. Traffic.

388
H433t

Traffic.
Highway Research Board.
Travel forecasting; 8 reports presented at the 42nd annual meeting, January 7-11, 1963. Washington, Highway Research Board of the Division of Engineering and Industrial Research, National Academy of Sciences, National Research Council, 1963.
166p. (Highway research record no. 38)
National Research Council Publication 1158.

1. Highways. 2. Traffic. 3. Journey to work. 4. Transportation. I. Title.

690.015
(485)
S82
R52
1969

Ingemansson, Stig. Störningsmått för...1969. (Card 2)

3. Traffic. I. Benjegard, Sven-Olof, jt. au. II. Stockholm. Statens Institut för Byggnadsforskning. III. Title: Physical scales of traffic noise.

388
I573

TRAFFIC.
INTERNATIONAL HOUSING AND TOWN PLANNING. 17TH CONGRESS, STOCKHOLM, 1939. URBANISME ET TRAFIC LOCAL. TOWN PLANNING AND LOCAL TRAFFIC. FRANKFURT AM MAIN, 1939.
1 v. (VARIOUS PAGINGS)

TEXT IN FRENCH, ENGLISH AND GERMAN.

1. TRAFFIC. 2. CITY PLANNING.

VF
388
H43

Traffic.
Highway Research Board.
Urban traffic congestion, presented at the thirty-third annual meeting January 12-15, 1954. Washington, National Research Council, 1954.
39 p. illus., graphs, tables. (Its Bulletin 86)
Contents.-Economic costs of traffic congestion, John W. Gibbons and Albert Proctor.-Urban congestion index principles, C. A. Rothrock.-Discussion.
Bibliography: p. 23-25.

388
I57F

TRAFFIC.
INSTITUTE OF TRAFFIC ENGINEERS.
FREEWAY OPERATIONS, NEW INFORMATION ON EMERGING RESPONSIBILITIES. WASHINGTON, 1961
88P.

AN OUTGROWTH OF THE 12 REGIONAL SEMINARS ON FREEWAY OPERATIONS.

1. TRAFFIC.

711.74
I57

TRAFFIC.
INTERNATIONAL RESEARCH CENTER FOR URBAN ANTHROPOLOGY.
THE URBAN-PROMENADE-NETWORK: A CONTRIBUTION TOWARDS THE HUMANIZATION OF MODERN URBAN LANDSCAPES. BERLIN, WEST GERMANY, 1966.
55P.

1. STREETS. 2. TRAFFIC. I. TITLE.

VF
388
H43v

Traffic.
Highway Research Board.
Vehicle operation as affected by traffic control and highway type; presented at the thirty-fourth annual meeting, January 11-14, 1955. Washington, 1955.
62 p. illus. (Its Bulletin 107)
References.
Contents.-Operating characteristics of a passenger car on selected routes.-Analysis of flow on an urban thorofare.-Economics of operation on limited-access highways.
1. Traffic. I. Title.

388
I57
1965

TRAFFIC.
INSTITUTE OF TRAFFIC ENGINEERS.
TRAFFIC ENGINEERING HANDBOOK. 3D ED. WASHINGTON, 1965.
770P.

1. TRAFFIC. I. TITLE. II. INSTITUTE OF TRAFFIC ENGINEERS.

388
J67

Traffic.
Jorgensen, Niels O
Some aspects of the urban traffic assignment problem. Berkeley, University of California, Institute of Transportation and Traffic Engineering, 1963.
37p. (Graduate report)

Thesis (M.E.) - University of California.

1. Traffic. 2. Journey to work. I. California. University. Institute of Transportation and Traffic Engineering.

Traffic.

388
K22   Keefer, Louis E
    Urban travel patterns for airports, shopping centers, and industrial plants. Research is sponsored by the American Association of State Highway Officials in cooperation with the Bureau of Public Roads. [Washington] Highway Research Board, Div. of Engineering, National Academy of Sciences-National Academy of Engineering 1966.
    116p.   (National cooperative highway research program report 24)
    Bibliography: p. 92-101.

(Cont'd on next card)

Traffic.

388
M29u   Meyer, John Robert.
    The urban transportation problem, by J. R. Meyer and others. Cambridge, Harvard University Press, 1965.
    427p.   (A Rand Corporation research study)

    1. Traffic. 2. Journey to work. 3. Transportation. I. Title. II. Rand Corp.

621.39   TRAFFIC.
P81   Public Urban Locator Service (PULSE): background and conference proceedings, Oct., 1968, Wash., D.C. Sponsored by U.S. Dept. of Housing and Urban Development, Office of Urban Transportation. New York, Institute of Public Administration and Teknekron, Inc., [1969]
    466p.
    U.S. Mass Transportation Demonstration Grant Program.
    HUD contract no. H-1030.
    CFSTI. PB180116.
    1. Communication systems. 2. Traffic. 3. Transportation. I. Institute of Public Administration.

(Cont'd on next card)

388
K22   Keefer, Louis E. Urban travel patterns for airports, shopping centers, and industrial plants...1966.   (Card 2)

    1. Traffic. 2. Journey to work. 3. Transportation - Automation. 4. Land use. I. Highway Research Board. II. American Association of State Highway Officials. IV. Title.

Traffic.

388
O57   Olson, Paul L
    Driver response to the amber phase of traffic signals, by Paul L. Olson and Richard W. Rothery Warren, Mich., Research Laboratories, General Motors Corp., 1961.
    650-663p.
    Reprinted from Operations research, Sept.-Oct., 1961.

    1. Traffic. 2. Highways - Research. I. Rothery, Richard W., jt. au. II. General Motors Corp. III. Operations research. IV. Title.

621.39
P81   Public Urban Locator...[1969]   (Card 2)

    II. U.S. Dept. of Housing and Urban Development. III. U.S. Mass Transportation Demonstration Grant Program.

Traffic - Addresses, lectures, etc.

388
K25   Kennedy, Norman.
    Access control for city and county arterials, by Norman Kennedy and Wolfgang S. Homburger, Engineer, Institute of Transportation and Traffic Engineering, University of California, Berkeley.   [Berkeley Calif.?] 1962.
    6p.
    "A paper prepared for presentation at the 1962 Northwest Roads and Street Conference, at Oregon State University, Corvallis, Oregon, February 8, 1962.
    1. Traffic - Addresses, lectures, etc. I. Homburger, Wolfgang S., jt. au. III. Northwest Roads and Street Conference, Corvallis, Or., 1962.

534.83   TRAFFIC.
O73   Organisation for Economic Cooperation and Development.
    Urban traffic noise; strategy for an improved environment. Report of the Consultative Group on Transportation Research to the governments of member countries. Paris, 1969.
    56p.
    Bibliography: p. 52-55.

    1. Noise. 2. Traffic. I. Title.

VF
711.552   Traffic.
Q81   Qualls, William H
    A checklist of the problems of the central business district. [n.p.] Upper East Tennessee. Office of the Tennessee State Planning Commission [n.d.]
    20 L.

    1. Business districts. 2. Traffic. I. Tennessee. State Planning Commission.

711.73   TRAFFIC.
K25P   KENTUCKY HIGHWAY CONFERENCE, UNIVERSITY OF KENTUCKY, 1962.
    PROCEEDINGS. LEXINGTON, UNIVERSITY OF KENTUCKY, 1962.
    112P. (KENTUCKY ENGINEERING EXPERIMENT STATION. BULLETIN NO. 64, V. 16, NO. 4)

    1. HIGHWAYS. 2. TRAFFIC. 3. BRIDGES. I. KENTUCKY. ENGINEERING EXPERIMENT STATION.

388
O82
1966   Owen, Wilfred.
    The metropolitan transportation problem. Rev. A Brookings Institution study. Garden City, N.Y., Anchor Books, 1966.
    266p.

    1. Transportation. 2. Traffic. 3. Journey to work. 4. Railroads. I. Brookings Institution. II. Title.

388
R15   Rand Corp.
    Transportation for future urban communities: a study prospectus. Santa Monica, Calif., 1961.
    48p.   (Research memo RM-2824-FF)

    1. Transportation. 2. Journey to work. 3. Traffic. 4. Automation. I. Title.

690.015
1(485)
S82
R38
1968   Kihlman, Tor.
    Trafikbullerstudier (Traffic noise studies) Stockholm, Statens Institut för Byggnadsforskning, 1968.
    51p. (Stockholm. Statens Institut för Byggnadsforskning. Rapport 38:1968)
    English summary.
    Bibliography: p. 15, 28, 46-47.
    1. Building research - Sweden. 2. Sweden - Building research. 3. Noise. 4. Traffic. I. Stockholm. Statens Institut for Byggnadsforskning. II. Title: Traffic noise studies.

Traffic.

388
P17   Passenger Belt Conveyors, inc.
    Is downtown traffic strangling your city? Carveyor passenger conveyor system to ease today's traffic problems today! [n.p., 1961?]
    15p.

    1. Transportation. 2. Traffic.

388
R47   Ritter, Paul.
    Planning for man and motor. New York, Macmillan, 1964.
    384p.

    A Pergamon press book.

    Parts in French and German.

    1. Transportation. 2. Traffic. 3. Journey to work. I. Title.

Traffic.

534.83
L15   Langdon, F J
    The traffic noise index: a method of controlling noise nuisance, by F.J. Langdon and W.E. Scholes. Garston, Eng., Building Research Station, Ministry of Public Building and Works, 1968.
    8p. (U.K. Building Research Station. Building research current papers, Current paper 38/68)
    Version of this paper in the Architects' journal, April 1968.
    1. Noise. 2. Traffic. 3. Highways - Social effect. I. Scholes, W.E. jt. au. II. U.K. Building Research Station. III. Title.

Traffic.

388
P74   Prigogine, I
    On a generalized Boltzmann-like approach for traffic flow, by I. Prigogine and others. Brussels, Belgium, Academie royale des sciences des lettres et des beaux-arts de Belgique, 1962.
    805-814p.
    Extrait du Bulletin de l'Academie royale de Belgique (Classe des Sciences) Seance du 6 Octobre 1962.
    1. Traffic. I. Academie royale des sciences des lettres et des beaux arts de Belgique. Brussels. II. Title.

388
R67a   Rothery, R
    Analysis of experiments on single-lane bus flow, by R. Rothery and others. Baltimore, Operations Research Society of America, 1964.
    913-933p.
    Reprinted from Operations research, Nov.-Dec., 1964.

    1. Traffic. 2. Highways. I. Operations Research Society of America. II. Operations research. III. Title.

388
L24tr   TRAFFIC.
  Leibbrand, Kurt.
    Transportation and town planning. Translated by Nigel Seymer. Cambridge, Mass., M.I.T., 1970.
    381p.

    Bibliography: p. 367-370.

    1. Transportation. 2. City planning. 3. Traffic. I. Title.

388
(7471)   TRAFFIC.
P67S   PORT OF NEW YORK AUTHORITY.
    SOLUTION METHODS FOR WAITING LINE PROBLEMS. NEW YORK, 1958.
    38P. CHARTS.

    BIBLIOGRAPHY: P.37-38.

    1. TRAFFIC. I. TITLE.

711.730.15   Traffic.
R82   Rude, R G
    Formulation of a technique for evaluating urban highway needs, by R.G. Rude and J.C. Oppenlander. [Lafayette, Ind.] Joint Highway Research Project, Engineering Experiment Station, Purdue University [1968]
    112-137p.

    1. Highways. 2. Traffic. I. Purdue University. Engineering Experiment Station. II. Title.

388
S23
Traffic.
Schmidt, Robert E
  Highway traffic estimation.   Saugatuck,
Conn., Eno Foundation for Highway Traffic
Control, 1956.
    247 p.   graphs, tables.

  Bibliographies.

  1.Traffic. I.Campbell, M   Earl, jt.
author. II.Eno Foundation for Highway Traffic
Control. III.Title.

211.73
S71
Traffic.
Stauffer, Robert N
  GMR auto-control system. Warren, Mich.
Research Laboratories, General Motors Corp.,
1959.
    11p. (General Motors Corp. Research
Laboratories. GMR-205)

  1. Highways. 2. Traffic. I. General
Motors Corp. II. Title.

VF
388
T71
Traffic.
Traffic engineering.
  Traffic planning in urban renewal projects.
Technical notes. (Reproduced from Traffic
engineering, Jan. 1961)
    [15]p.

  1. Traffic. 2. Urban renewal.

534.83
S23d
TRAFFIC.
Scholes, W   E
  Designing against noise from road traffic,
by W.E. Scholes and J.W. Sargent. Garston,
Eng., Building Research Station, 1971.
    22p. (Current paper 20/71)

  1. Noise. 2. Traffic. I. Sargent, J.W.,
jt. au. II. U.K. Building Research Station.
III. Title.

690.015
(485)
S82
R36E
1968
TRAFFIC.
Stockholm. Statens Institut for Byggnads-
forskning.
  Traffic noise in residential areas — study
by the National Swedish Institute for Building
Research and the National Swedish Institute
of Public Health. Stockholm, 1968.
    179p. (Its Report 36E)

  1. Building research – Sweden. 2. Noise.
3. Traffic.

388
T74pr
TRAFFIC.
Tri-State Transportation Commission
  Projecting vehicle miles of travel in a
metropolitan region. New York, 1967.
    25p. (Interim technical report 4070-8078)

  1. Transportation. 2 Traffic. I. Title.

534.83
S23t
TRAFFIC.
Scholes, W   E
  Traffic noise criteria. [Garston,
Eng.] Building Research Station, 1969.
    9p. (U.K. Building Research Station.
Current paper 38/69)

  1. Noise. 2. Traffic. I. U.K.
Building Research Station. II. Title.

388
S76c
Traffic.
Stonex, K   A
  Colloquy on law, traffic & engineering
technology. Prepared for Colloquy on Re-
search Frontiers in Motor Vehicle & Traffic
Laws. Sponsored by the Highway Research Board
of the National Research Council, Feb. 2-3,
1965. Warren, Mich., GM Engineering Staff,
General Motors Corp., 1965.
    7p.

  1. Traffic. 2. Law enforcement. I. General
Motors Corp. II. Title

388
T76
TRAFFIC.
TROEDSSON, CARL B
  THE CITY, THE AUTOMOBILE AND MAN.
STOCKHOLM, FLANDERS, 1957.
    50P. ILLUS.

  NA 9108 .T7

  1. TRAFFIC.   I. TITLE.

388
S76
Traffic.
Stonex, K   A
  Research as applied to traffic and trans-
portation. For presentation at the tenth
Missouri Traffic Conference, University
of Missouri, Columbia, Missouri, May 21, 1958.
Milford, Mich., General Motors Corp., 1958.
    12p.

  Bibliography: p. 13-14.

  1. Transportation. 2. Traffic. I. Missouri
Traffic Conference, 10th, Columbia, 1958.
II. General   Motors Corp. III. Title.

388
S27
Traffic.
Sessions, Gordon.
  Getting the most from city streets. Wash.,
Highway Research Board, Div. of Engineering,
National Research Council, National Academy
of Sciences, National Academy of Engineering,
1967.
    46p.

  1. Traffic. 2. Streets. I. Title.
II. Highway Research Board. III. Title:
Improved street utilization through traffic
engineering.

LC
Traffic.
Troedsson, Carl B
  The city, the automobile and man.
[Stockholm] Flanders 1957.
    50p. illus.

  NA 9108 .T7

  1.Traffic. I.Title.

711.73
S54h
Traffic.
Smith (Wilbur) and Associates.
  Highway travel in Washington-New York-Boston
Megalopolis. Distributed by: Clearinghouse for
Federal Scientific and Technical Information.
Prepared for U.S. Dept. of Commerce.
Washington, 1963.
    172p.   (PB 166 881)

  1. Highways. 2. Traffic. 3. Journey to
work. I. U.S. Clearinghouse for Federal
Scientific and Technical Information.
II. Title. III. Title: Washington-New York-
Boston Megalopolis.

388
S86
TRAFFIC.
Suomen Arkkitehtiliiton Asemakaava- ja
Standardisoimislaitos.
  Liikenne, moottoriajoneuvojen melun
torjuminen (Traffic, prevention of motor
traffic noise) Helsinki, 1968.
    11p.

  1. Traffic. 2. Noise.

388
(41)
U54c
Traffic.
U.K. Ministry of Transport.
  Cars for cities. A study of trends in the
design of vehicles with particular reference
to their use in towns. Reports of the
Steering Group and Working Group appointed by
the Minister of Transport. London, H.M.S.O.,
1967.
    107p.

  1. Transportation – U.K. 2. Traffic.
3. Air pollution. I. Title.

388
S54m
TRAFFIC.
Smith (Wilbur) and Associates.
  Motor trucks in the metropolis. Prepared under
commission from the Automobile Manufacturers
Association. New Haven, 1969.
    208p.
    Bibliography: p. 195-199.

  1. Traffic. 2. Transportation. I. Title.
II. Title: Trucks.

VF
388
895
Traffic
Symposium: Urban Traffic Congestion. Virginia
  Law Review, p. 831-872, Nov. 1950; p. 989-1055,
Dec. 1950.

  Reprint.

  1.Traffic. 2.Parking. I.Title: Urban Traffic
Congestion.

388
UN
1970
TRAFFIC.
United Nations. (Economic Commission for Asia
  and the Far East)
  Urban transportation in the renewal of
American cities; an information paper. Workshop
on Urban Traffic and Transportation, Bangkok,
Thailand, December 8-17, 1970. Presented by
the Dept. of Housing and Urban Development.
Washington, D.C., 1970.
    14p.
  1. Transportation. 2. Traffic. I. Workshop
on Urban Traffic and Transportation, Bangkok,
1970. II. U.S. Dept. of Housing and Urban
Development. III.   Title.

388
S71
Traffic.
Sterk, M   C
  Computer simulation of street traffic.
Washington, Distributed by U.S. Dept. of
Commerce, Office of Technical Services, 1961.
    88p. (U.S. National Bureau of Standards.
Technical note 119)

  1. Traffic. 2. Automation. I. U.S.
National Bureau of Standards. II. Title.

711.74
T71
Traffic.
Traffic engineering.
  Tentative standards for subdivision
streets. Wash., Institute of Traffic
Engineers, 1964.
    16p.

  A reprint from Traffic engineering,
September, 1964, by Berton-Aschmen
Associates.

  1. Streets. 2. Traffic. 3. Subdivision
design.   I. Berton-Aschmen
Associates.

388
C65RE
1958
H-H
TRAFFIC.
U.S. CONGRESS. HOUSE. COMMITTEE ON
INTERSTATE AND FOREIGN COMMERCE.
RESEARCH NEEDS IN TRAFFIC SAFETY,
HEARINGS BEFORE A SUBCOMMITTEE,
EIGHTY-FIFTH CONGRESS, SECOND SESSION.
WASHINGTON, GOVT. PRINT. OFF., 1958.
    299P.

  HEARINGS HELD APRIL 23, 1958.

  1. TRAFFIC.   I. TITLE.

658.564
P82
TRAFFIC.
U.S. BUREAU OF PUBLIC ROADS.
CALIBRATING AND TESTING A GRAVITY
MODEL FOR ANY SIZE URBAN AREA.
WASHINGTON, 1963.
1 V. (VARIOUS PAGINGS)

1. AUTOMATION. 2. TRAFFIC.
I. TITLE.

Traffic.
388
V67
Votaw, David F
Elementary sampling for traffic engineers,
by David F. Votaw, and Herbert S. Levinson.
Saugatuck, Conn., the Eno Foundation for
Highway Traffic Control, 1962.
128p.

1. Traffic. I. Levinson, Herbert S., jt. au.
II. Eno Foundation for Highway Traffic Control.

711.333
(74885) Pittsburgh Regional Planning Association.
P47p   Preliminary report...1959. (Card 2)

1. Master plan - Allegheny Co., Pa. 2. Land use -
Allegheny Co., Pa. 3. Population - Allegheny Co.,
Pa. 4. Economic conditions - Allegheny Co., Pa.
5. Traffic - Allegheny Co., Pa. 6. Business
districts - Allegheny Co., Pa. 7. Publi utilities
- Allegheny Co., Pa. 8. Schools - Allegheny Co.,
Pa. 9. Recreation - Allegheny Co., Pa. 10. Housing
- Allegheny Co., Pa. 11. Urban renewal - Allegheny
- Allegheny Co., Pa.
(Continued on next
card)

Traffic.
388
P81
U.S. Bureau of Public Roads.
Traffic assignment manual: for application
with a large, high speed computer.
Washington, U.S. Dept. of Commerce, Bureau
of Public Roads, Office of Planning, Urban
Planning Div., 1964.
1v.

1. Traffic. 2. Automation. I. Title.

Traffic.
388
W17s
Werner, Stanley Leon.
Stochastic choice of mode in urban travel:
a study in binary choice. [Evanston, Ill.]
Published for the Transportation Center,
at Northwestern University by Northwestern
University Press, 1962.
90p. (Metropolitan transportation
series)
Bibliography: p. [87]-88.

1. Traffic. I. Northwestern University.
Transportation   Center. II. Title.

711.333
(74885) Pittsburgh Regional Planning Association.
P47p   Preliminary report...1959. (Card 3)

Co., Pa. 12. Public utilities - Allegheny Co.,
Pa. I. Steel Valley Regional Planning Commission. II. U.S. URA-UPAP. Allegheny Co.,
Pa.

388
T71rep
TRAFFIC.
U.S. Dept. of Transportation.
Report on urban area traffic operations
improvement programs (TOPICS) Report of the
Secretary of Transportation to the United
States Congress..., 19
Wash., Govt. Print. Off., 19
v.
Published in the Congressional series as
Senate documents.
For Library holdings see main entry.
1. Traffic. I. Title: Urban area traffic
operations improv   ement programs.

388
W24
Weiss, George.
Statistical properties of low-density
traffic, by George Weiss and Robert
Herman. Providence, R.I., Brown
University, 1962.
121-130p.
Reprinted from Quarterly of applied
mathematics, July, 1962.

1. Traffic. 2. Highways - Research.
I. Herman, Robert, jt. au. II. Brown
University, Providence, R.I.
III. Quarterly   of applied mathematics. IV. Title.

Traffic - Allendale, N.J.
711.4
(74921) Community Planning Associates.
A55m   Borough of Allendale: master plan
no. 1   studies: physical features, land use
and traffic. West Trenton, N.J., 1959.
10p. (Borough of Allendale master
plan studies memo. no. 1)

U.S. Urban Renewal Adm. UPAP.

1. Master plan - Allendale, N.J. 2. Land use -
Allendale, N.J. 3. Traffic - Allendale, N.J.
I. U.S. URA-UPAP.   Allendale, N.J.

388
U78
TRAFFIC.
Utudjian, E
Il mondo sotterraneo; incontri di studio con
la partecipazione di E. Utudjian e W.J.
Armento. Anno accademico 1966-67. Napoli,
Istituto di Architettura e Urbanistica,
Universita di Napoli, Facolta di Ingegneria,
1967.
92p. (Naples. Universita. Istituto di
Architettura e Urbanistica. [Pubblicazioni]
12)
1. Transportation. 2. Journey to work.
3. Traffic. 4.   Soils. I. Armento, W.J.,
jt. au.
(Cont'd on next card)

Traffic.
711.73
W63
Wohl, Martin.
Traffic system analysis [by] Martin Wohl [and]
Brian V. Martin. New York, McGraw-Hill, [1967]
558p. (McGraw-Hill series in transportation)

Includes bibliographies.

1. Highways - Economic effect. 2. Journey to
work. 3. Traffic. I. Martin, Brian V., jt. au.
II. Title.

388
(74827) TRAFFIC - ALLENTOWN, PA.
A55   Allentown, Pa. City Planning Commission.
1969   Plan for traffic circulation. Allentown,
1969.
72p.

1. Traffic - Allentown, Pa. I. Title.

388
U78
Utudjian, E   Il mondo sotterraneo...1967.
(Card 2)

II. Naples. Universita istituto di
Architettura e Urbanistica. III. Title.

388
Y15
Traffic.
Yale University. Bureau of Highway Traffic.
Bibliography of traffic engineering literature (selected, annotated and indexed).
New Haven, Conn., 1954.
237 p.

Compilers: Kathryn Childs Cassidy and
Cele Kagan.

1. Traffic. I. Caddidy, Kathryn Childs.
II. Kagan, Cele. III. Title: Traffic Engineerin
literature, Bibliography of.

388
(74827) Traffic - Allentown, Pa.
A55   Allentown, Pa. City Planning Commission.
Plan for traffic circulation; tri-point
concept as a traffic solution for the
city of Allentown, Pennsylvania. Allentown,
1964.
21p.

1. Traffic - Allentown, Pa.
2. Transportation - Allentown, Pa.

388
V66g
Traffic.
Voorhees, Alan M
A general theory of traffic movement. The
1955 past Presidents award paper. New Haven,
Institute of Traffic Engineers, 1956.
16p.

1. Traffic. 2. Journey to work.
I. Institute of Traffic Engineers, New Haven.
II. Title.

711.73
(75294) Traffic - Allegany County, Md.
S23   Segoe (Ladislas) and Associates.
A report upon the major highway plan,
Allegany County, Maryland. Prepared for
the Allegany County Planning and Zoning
Commission. [n.p.] 1961.
19p. (Comprehensive master plan
series)

1. Highways - Allegany County, Md.
2. Traffic - Allegany County, Md.
3. Journey to work. 4. Master plan -
Allegany County,   Md. I. Allegany
Co., Md.   Planning and
Zoning   Commission.

711.333
(755295) Traffic - Arlington Co., Va.
A75r   Arlington Co., Va. Office of Planning.
Rosslyn, Arlington Co., Va.
Arlington, 1965.
16p.

1. County planning - Arlington Co.,
Va. 2. Traffic - Arlington Co., Va.
I. Title.

388
V66
Traffic.
Voorhees, Alan M
Traffic patterns and land use alternatives,
by Alan M. Voorhees and others. Prepared for
presentation at Highway Research Board 41st
annual meeting, Wash., D.C., Jan. 1962. [Washington] 1962.
17p.

1. Traffic. 2. Land use. I. Highway Research
Board.

711.333
(74885) Traffic - Allegheny Co., Pa.
P47p   Pittsburgh Regional Planning Association.
Preliminary report; part of a master plan
report for the Steel Valley Regional Planning
Commission representing the Boroughs of
Homestead, Munhall, West Homestead, West
Mifflin and Whitaker in Allegheny County,
Pennsylvania. Stage II. Pittsburgh, 1959.
13 pts.
Prepared under Program of the Bureau of
Community Development.
U.S. Urban Renewal Adm. UPAP.
(Continued on next
card)

388
(795461) Traffic - Astoria, Or.
072   Oregon. University. Bureau of Municipal
Research and Service.
Traffic circulation. Memorandum to
Astoria City Planning Commission. Eugene,
Or., 1959.
3p.
U.S. Urban Renewal Administration, Urban Planning
Assistance Program.

1. Traffic - Astoria, Or. I. Astoria, Or. City
Planning Commission. II. U.S. URA-UPAP. Astoria,
Or.

711.4 :388 (768865) A73 1957	**Traffic - Athens, Tenn.** Athens, Tenn. Regional Planning Commission. Traffic, parking and circulation and central business district renewal for Athens. [Assisted by] Tennessee State Planning Commission, Southeast Tennessee Office. Athens, 1957. 32p. diagrs., maps. U.S. Urban Renewal Administration. Urban Planning Assistance Program. (Continued on next card)
711.4 :388 (768865) A73 1957	Athens, Tenn. Regional Planning Commission. Traffic, parking and ... (Card 2) 1. City planning - Athens, Tenn. 2. Traffic - Athens, Tenn. 3. Business districts - Athens, Tenn. I. Tennessee. State Planning Commission. II. U.S. Urban Renewal Administration. Urban Planning Assistance Program.
711.4 :388 (768865) A73	**Traffic - Athens, Tenn.** Athens, Tenn. Regional Planning Commission. Traffic, parking and circulation, Athens, Tennessee. Assisted by the Tennessee State Planning Commission, East Tennessee Office. Athens, 1956. 7p. map. U.S. Urban Renewal Administration, Urban Planning Assistance Program. 1. City planning - Athens, Tenn. 2. Traffic - Athens, Tenn. I. Tennessee. State Planning Commission. II. U.S. Urban Renewal Administration.
711.4 (758231) A75c draft	**Traffic - Atlanta.** Atlanta. Metropolitan Planning Commission. Transportation Policy Project. Central Atlanta, 1957 street use and traffic plan. Outlines and interim drafts relating to a plan; report to be completed in August 1957. Atlanta, 1957. 1v. U.S. Urban Renewal Administration, Urban Planning Assistance Program. (U.R.A. Prof. Ga. P-3, I.A.3c) 1. City planning - Atlanta. 2. Traffic - Atlanta. I. U.S. Urban Renewal Administration.
711.4 (758231) A75c	**Traffic - Atlanta.** Atlanta. Metropolitan Planning Commission. Transportation Policy Project. Central Atlanta, 1957 street use and traffic plan. Progress report, May-August, 1957. Atlanta, 1957. 1v. Partial contents:-Downtown expressway ramp connections as proposed by State Highway Department of Georgia at the public hearings of May 23, 1957, by Karl A. Bevins.-Central (Continued on next card)
711.4 (758231) A75c	Atlanta. Metropolitan Planning Commission. Transportation Policy... (Card 2) Atlanta street capacity study procedure, by James M. Schafer and Richard H. Sears, Jr. (Issued also as a separate - 711.4 (758231) A75tra) U.S. Urban Renewal Administration, Urban Planning Assistance Program. (U.R.A. Proj. Ga. P-3, I.A.3.c.) 1. City planning - Atlanta. 2. Traffic - Atlanta. I. Bevins, Karl A II. U.S. Urban Renewal Administration.
711.4 (758231) A75ce	**Traffic - Atlanta.** Atlanta. Metropolitan Planning Commission. Transportation Policy Project. Central Atlanta 1957 street use plan. Guide to computations forecasting downtown street traffic volumes resulting from expressway completion, by Richard H. Sears, Jr. Atlanta, 1957. 12p. U.S. Urban Renewal Administration, Urban (Continued on next card)

711.4 (758231) A75ce	Atlanta. Metropolitan Planning Commission. Transportation Policy Project...(Card 2) Planning Assistance Program. (URA Proj. P-3, I. A. 2) 1. City planning - Atlanta. 2. Traffic - Atlanta. 3. Transportation - Atlanta. I. Sears, Richard H. Jr. II. U.S. Urban Renewal Administration. Urban Planning Assistance Program.
711.4 (758231) A75r	**Traffic - Atlanta.** Atlanta. Metropolitan Planning Commission. Transportation Policy Project. Revised through traffic procedures, by Robert C. Stuart and Richard H. Sears, Jr. Atlanta, 1957. 5p. U.S. Urban Renewal Administration, Urban Planning Assistance Program. (URA (Continued on next card)
711.4 (758231) A75r	Atlanta. Metropolitan Planning Commission. Transportation Policy...(Card 2) Proj. Ga. P-3, I. A. 2) 1. City planning - Atlanta. 2. Transportation - Atlanta. 3. Traffic - Atlanta. I. Stuart, Robert C. II. Sears Richard H., Jr. III. U. S. Urban Renewal Administration. Urban Planning Assistance Program.
711.4 (758231) A75s	**Traffic - Atlanta.** Atlanta. Metropolitan Planning Commission. Transportation Policy Project. Street use traffic assignment procedures, by E. Wilson Campbell. Atlanta, 1957. 10p. U.S. Urban Renewal Administration, Urban Planning Assistance Program. (URA Proj. P-3, I. A. 2) 1. City planning - Atlanta. 2. Traffic - Atlanta. I. Campbell, E. Wilson. II. U.S. Urban Renewal Administration. Urban Planning Assistance Program.
711.4 (758231) A75w	**Traffic - Atlanta** Atlanta. Traffic and Safety Council. What's to be done to cure downtown traffic jams? Discussion at Traffic Forum presented by the Atlanta Traffic and Safety Council at Atlanta, Ga. Dec. 1955. Atlanta, 1955. 15p. illus. U.S. Urban Renewal Administration, Urban Planning Assistance Program. 1. City planning - Atlanta. 2. Traffic - Atlanta. I. U.S. Urban Renewal Administration.
711.4 (78882) A87 Sect. 3	**Traffic - Aurora, Colo.** Aurora, Colo. Planning Dept. Traffic and transportation: comprehensive plan, section 3, by Richard H. Sundell. Denver, 1959. 11p. U.S. Urban Renewal Adm. UPAP. 1. Master plan - Aurora, Colo. 2. Traffic - Aurora, Colo. 3. Transportation - Aurora, Colo. I. Sundell, Richard H. II. U.S. URA-UPAP. Aurora, Colo.
388 (747245) L62	**Traffic - Automation.** Lockwood, Kessler and Bartlett. Traffic study, the heartland of Nassau County, N.Y. Prepared by Lockwood, Kessler and Berlett, inc., and Alan M. Voorhees & Associates, inc. Vincent A. van Pragg, computer consultant. Syosset, N.Y., 1966. 78p. Prepared in cooperation with the Nassau County, Dept. of Public Works. (Cont'd on next card)

388 (747245) L62	Lockwood, Kessler and Bartlett. Traffic study, the heartland of Nassau County, N.Y...1966. (Card 2) 1. Traffic - Nassau Co., N.Y. 2. Traffic - Automation. I. Nassau Co., N.Y. Dept. of Public Works. II. Voorhees (Alan M.) and Associates, jt.au. III. Title.
VP 711.73 (7526) B15j	**Traffic - Baltimore.** Baltimore. Planning Commission. The Jones Falls expressway. Baltimore, 1951. folder. maps. 1. Highways - Baltimore. 2. Traffic - Baltimore.
388 (7526) M67	TRAFFIC - BALTIMORE. MOSES, ROBERT. BALTIMORE ARTERIAL REPORT. REPORT TO THE MAYOR AND CITY COUNCIL, BALTIMORE, MD., OCT. 9, 1944. CONSULTING ENGINEERS: W. ERLE ANDREWS, MADIGAN-HYLAND, PARSONS, BRINCKERHOFF, HOGAN, AND MACDONALD. NEW YORK 1944. 39P. 1. TRAFFIC - BALTIMORE. 2. HIGHWAYS - BALTIMORE. I. TITLE.
711.417 (7526) V66m	**Traffic - Baltimore metropolitan area.** Voorhees (Alan M.) and Associates. Multi-purpose centers for the Baltimore region: traffic analysis. Prepared for the Regional Planning Council, Baltimore, Maryland. Baltimore, 1964. 6p. U.S. Urban Renewal Adm. UPAP. 1. Planned communities - Baltimore metropolitan area. 2. Traffic - Baltimore. I. Baltimore Regional Planning Council. II. U.S. URA-UPAP. Baltimore.
388 (016) C15 no.12	**Traffic - Bibliography.** California. University. Institute of Transportation and Traffic Engineering. Relationship of city planning and traffic engineering. Berkeley, Calif., 1958. 4p. (Its Library references no. 12) 1. Traffic engineering - Bibliography. 2. City planning - Bibliography. 3. Transportation - Bibliography.
388 (016) C15 no. 4	**Traffic - Bibl.** California. University. Institute of Transportation and Traffic Engineering. Some basic references on traffic engineering. Berkeley, Calif., 1956. 11p. (Its Library references no. 4) 1. Transportation - Bibl. 2. Traffic - Bibl.
388 (016) C15 no. 16	**Traffic - Bibl.** California. University. Institute of Transportation and Traffic Engineering. Some references on traffic engineering. Rev. ed. Berkeley, Calif., 1959. 26p. (Its Library references no. 16) 1. Transportation - Bibl. 2. Traffic - Bibl.

Traffic - Bibliography.

388
(016)
C31
Chamber of Commerce of the United States.
(Transportation and Communication Dept.)
A bibliography of publications in the
field of street and highway traffic.
Washington, 1950.
19p.

1. Traffic - Bibliography.

Traffic - Bibliographies.

VF
711.552
(016)
B87
U.S. Business and Defense Services Administration.
Basic information sources on downtown
shopping districts; compiled in the Office of
Distribution. Washington, Dec. 1955.
11 p.   (Its Business Service Bulletin No.
BSB-135)

1.Business districts - Bibliographies. 2.Parking -
Bibliographies. 3.Traffic - Bibliographies. I.Title:
Downtown shopping districts. (Series.)

Traffic - Bordentown, N.J.

388
(74961)
P25t
Pennsylvania. University. Fels Institute
of Local and State Government. (Govern-
ment Consulting Service)
Traffic, streets and parking, City of
Bordentown, Burlington County, New Jersey.
[Philadelphia] 1958.
9p.

U.S. Urban Renewal Adm. UPAP.

1. Traffic - Bordentown, N.J. 2. Parking -
Bordentown, N.J.   I. U.S. URA-UPAP.
Bordentown,   N.J.

TRAFFIC - BIBLIOGRAPHY.

711
(016)
C65
no. 81
Dickey, John W
Traffic control systems for urban areas.
[Blacksburg, Va.] Center for Urban and
Regional Studies, Virginia Polytechnic
Institute, 1969.
21p. (Council of Planning Librarians.
Exchange bibliography no. 81)

1. Planning - Bibl. 2. Traffic - Bibl.
I. Virginia Polytechnic Institute. II. Title.
(Series: Council of Planning Librarians.
Exchange bibliography no. 81)

Traffic - Bibliography.

388
(016)
H21
U.S. Dept. of Health, Education, and Welfare.
Library.
Traffic and the senior citizen, selected
references. Compiled by Dorothy M. Jones.
Washington, 1964.
16p. (Its Bibliographic series: 64-2)

1. Traffic - Bibl. 2. Old age - Bibl.
I. Jones,   Dorothy M., comp.

Traffic - Boston.

388
(74461)
A87
Automotive Safety Foundation.
A comparative legal study of Boston's
regulations and the nationally recommended
model traffic ordinance. Washington, 1961.
60p.

A companion report to "better street
traffic management for Boston."

1. Traffic - Boston. 2. Transportation -
Legislation.

Traffic - Bibliography.

VF
352
(016)
M17
Massachusetts Federation of Taxpayers Associations
Inc.
A taxpayer's library; books and pamphlets
helpful in studying city and town government in
Massachusetts.   Boston, May 1948.
iii, 28 p.

Processed.

1.Municipal government-Bibl. 2.Municipal
government-Mass.-Bibl. 3.Citizen participation
in government-Bibl. 4.City manager government-

(Continued on next card)

Traffic - Bibliography.

388
(016)
H21
1965
U.S. Health, Education, and Welfare.
Library.
Traffic and the senior citizen, selected
references. Compiled by Dorothy M. Jones.
Rev. Wash., U.S. Dept. of Health, Education,
and Welfare, Office of Aging, 1965.
15p.   (OA no. 308, no. 8)

1. Traffic - Bibl. 2. Accidents - Bibl.
3. Old age - Bibl. I. Jones, Dorothy M.,
comp. II. Title.

Traffic - Boston.

388
(74461)
G72
Greater Boston Chamber of Commerce. (Urban
Transportation Committee)
A report on Boston traffic. Boston, 1957.
23p. tables

1. Traffic - Boston.

Massachusetts Federation of Taxpayers Associations
Inc. A taxpayer's library ... 1948 (Card 2)

Bibl. 5.Municipal finance-Bibl. 6.Parking-Bibl.
7.Traffic-Bibl. 8.Building codes-Bibl. 9.Building
inspection-Bibl. 10City planning-Bibl. 11.Sewerage
and sewage disposal-Bibl. 12.Schools-Bibl.
I.Title.

TRAFFIC - BIBLIOGRAPHY.

388
(016)
L41
U.S. LIBRARY OF CONGRESS. LEGISLATIVE
REFERENCE SERVICE.
CURRENT DEVELOPMENT IN URBAN MASS
TRANSPORTATION TECHNOLOGY, SELECTED
REFERENCES, 1950-1960, BY CATHERINE S.
CORRY. WASHINGTON, 1960.
35L.

1. TRANSPORTATION - BIBLIOGRAPHY.
2. TRAFFIC - BIBLIOGRAPHY. I. CORRY,
CATHERINE S   II. TITLE.

Traffic - Boston metropolitan area.

FOLIO
388
(74461)
H19
Hayden, Harding and Buchanan, inc.,
Boston.
Inner belt and expressway system,
Boston Metropolitan Area, 1962. Prepared
for the Massachusetts Dept. of Public
Works in cooperation with U.S. Dept.
of Commerce, Bureau of Public Roads.
A joint venture report by Hayden,
Harding and Buchanan and Charles A.
Maguire and Associates. Boston,
1962.
1v.

1. Traffic -
area. I. Maguire   Boston metropolitan
Associates.   (Charles A.) and

Traffic - Bibliography.

711
(016)
C65
no. 58
Pollock, Leslie S
Driver distraction as related to physical development abutting urban streets:
an empirical inquiry into the design
of the motorist's visual environment
(thesis abstract and bibliography)
Urbana, University of Illinois, Dept. of
Urban Planning, 1968.
4p. (Council of Planning Librarians.
Exchange bibliography no. 58)

1. Planning - Bibl.
(Continued on next card)

TRAFFIC - BIBLIOGRAPHY.

388
(016)
W45
WILLIAMS, LESLIE, COMP.
LIBRARY CLASSIFICATION AND SAMPLE
BIBLIOGRAPHY OF TRAFFIC ENGINEERING
MATERIALS. NEW HAVEN, CONN., BUREAU OF
STREET TRAFFIC RESEARCH, YALE
UNIVERSITY, 1940.
58P. (YALE TRAFFIC BUREAU SERIES NO.
1)

1. TRAFFIC - BIBLIOGRAPHY. I. YALE
UNIVERSITY. BUREAU FOR STREET TRAFFIC
RESEARCH.

Traffic - Boulder, Colo.

388
(788631)
B21
Bean (Trafton) and Associates.
Traffic, transportation and parking,
City of Boulder, Colorado. Prepared under
contract for the Colorado State Planning
Div. [Denver] 1960.
71p.

U.S. Urban Renewal Adm. UPAP.

1. Traffic - Boulder, Colo. 2. Parking - Boulder,
Colo. 3. Transportation - Boulder, Colo. I. U.S.
URA-UPAP. Boulder,   Colo.

711
(016)
C65
no. 58
Pollock, Leslie S   Driver...1968.
(Card 2)

2. Streets - Bibl. 3. Traffic - Bibl.
I. Illinois. University. Dept. of Urban
Planning. II. Title. (Series: Council
of Planning Librarians. Exchange bibliography no. 58)

Traffic - Bloomingdale, N.J. Planning Board.

711.4
(74923)
B56m
no. 8
Candeub (Isadore) and Associates.
Traffic circulation in Bloomingdale, New
Jersey. Report to the Bloomingdale Planning
Board. Newark, N.J., 1959.
8p. (Bloomingdale master plan memo-
randum no. 8)
U.S. Urban Renewal Adm. UPAP.

1. Master plan - Bloomingdale, N.J. 2. Traffic -
Bloomingdale, N.J. Planning Board. I. U.S. URA-
UPAP. Bloomingdale, N.J.

Traffic - Brookline, Mass.

711.729
(7447)
B76
Brookline, Mass. Planning Board.
Parking and traffic study. Brookline,
Mass., Brookline Planning Board for Board
of Selectmen, 1963.
24p. (Brookline Planning Board for
Board of Selectmen initial report no. 1)

Adams, Howard and Greeley, Planning
Consultants.

1. Parking - Brookline, Mass. 2. Traffic - Brookline, Mass. I. Adams, Howard and Greeley.

Traffic - Bibl.

VF
711.552
(016)
Q81
Qualls, William H   comp.
A bibliography for the central business
district. [n.p] Upper East Tennessee Office
of the Tennessee State Planning Commission
[1953]
11 L.

1. Business districts - Bibl. 2. Traffic -
Bibl. I. Tennessee State Planning Commission.

TRAFFIC - BLUEFIELD, W. VA.

5000
BLUEFIELD, W. VA. PLANNING COMMISSION.
TRAFFIC AND PARKING IN DOWNTOWN. BY
ALAN M. VOORHEES AND ASSOCIATES.
BLUEFIELD, W. VA., 1966.
50P. (HUD 701 REPORT)

1. TRAFFIC - BLUEFIELD, W. VA.
I. VOORHEES (ALAN M.) AND ASSOCIATES.
II. HUD. 701. BLUEFIELD, W. VA.

Traffic - Brownwood, Tex.

388
(764)
C18
Caudill, Rowlett and Scott.
Elements of the Brownwood plan 1958-1980:
circulation. [Prepared for] City Planning
Commission, Brownwood, Texas [under contract
with Texas State Dept. of Health] [Houston,
Tex.] 1959.
62p.

U.S. Urban Renewal Adm. UPAP.

1. Traffic - Brownwood, Tex. I. Brownwood,
Tex. City Planning Commission. II. U.S.
URA-UPAP. Brownwood,   Tex.

Traffic - Buffalo, N. Y.

VF
388
(74797) Buffalo, N. Y. Division of Safety.
B83　　Curb regulations for primary and secondary
streets. Buffalo, 1957.
[9] p. maps.

1. Traffic - Buffalo, N. Y. I. Title.

Traffic - Chicago.

FOLIO
388
(77311) Chicago Transit Authority.
C34t　　Traffic trends in downtown Chicago with
Suppl. suggestions for improvements. 1962
1962 supplement to March 1960 publication.
Chicago, 1963.
1v.

1. Traffic - Chicago. 2. Business
districts - Chicago.

Traffic - Clinton, Tenn.

711.729 Clinton, Tenn. Regional Planning Commission
C54　　A study, parking and traffic, Clinton, Ten-
nessee. Assisted by the Tennessee State
Planning Commission, East Tennessee Office.
Clinton, 1958.
35p. diagrs., maps, tables.
U.S. Urban Renewal Administration, Urban
Planning Assistance Program.
1. Parking - Clinton, Tenn. 2. Traffic -
Clinton, Tenn. I. U. S. Urban Renewal Ad-
ministration. Urban Planning Assistance
Program.

Traffic - Buffalo, N. Y.

Folio
388
(74797) Buffalo, N. Y. Division of Safety.
B83m　　Moving people in downtown Buffalo:
Pt. 1 traffic, transit improvements, part 1.
Buffalo, 1949.
[27] p. maps.

1. Traffic - Buffalo, N. Y. I. Title.

Traffic - Chicago.

388
(77311) McLean, Elizabeth J
M12　　Traffic planning for urban renewal
projects in Chicago, Illinois. Prepared
for Institute of Traffic Engineers,
Committee 6-C. [Chicago] 1962.
10p.

1. Traffic - Chicago. 2. Transportation -
Chicago. I. Institute of Traffic Engineers.

Traffic - Columbia, Tenn.

388
(76859) Tennessee. State Planning Commission.
T25　　Columbia traffic and parking survey. A
report to the Columbia Municipal Regional
Planning Commission. Columbia, 1958.
32p. diagrs., maps, tables. (MTO
Publication 58-25)
U.S. Urban Renewal Adm. UPAP.

1. Traffic - Columbia, Tenn. I. Columbia, Tenn.
Regional Planning Commission. II. U.S. Urban
Renewal Administration. Urban Planning Assistance
Program. Columbia, Tenn.

Traffic - Butler, N.J.

388
(74974) Bagby, Scott.
B13　　Highway, street and traffic study for
the Borough of Butler, Morris County, New
Jersey, by Scott Bagby and Robert Catlin.
Denville, N.J., (1958
6p.

U.S. Urban Renewal Administration,
Urban Planning Assistance Program.

1. Traffic - Butler, N.J. I. Catlin, Robert, jt. au.
II. U.S. URA-UPAP. Butler, N.J.

Traffic - Cincinnati.

711.552
(77178) Cincinnati. City Planning Commission.
C45　　Cincinnati central business district
pt. 1 plan. Part 1. Circulation. Cincinnati,
1958.
140p.

1. Business districts - Cincinnati.
2. Traffic - Cincinnati.

Traffic - Congresses.

388
I57p
Institute of Traffic Engineers.
Proceedings of the　　annual meeting

New Haven, Conn.,
v.

1. Traffic - Congresses.

Traffic - California.

388
(794) Metzger, William L
M27　　An analysis of intercity passenger traffic
movement within the California corridor
through 1980. Final report. Prepared by
William L. Metzger and Howard R. Ross.
South Pasadena, Calif., Southern California
Laboratories of Stanford Research Institute,
1966.
1 v.

1. Transportation - California. 2. Traffic - California. I. Ross, Howard R., jt.
au. II. Stanford Research Institute. III. Title.

Traffic - Clanton, Ala.

711.4
(76181) Clanton, Ala. City Planning Commission.
C51　　Clanton, Alabama: major thoroughfare
plan. [Prepared in cooperation with]
Alabama State Planning and Industrial
Development Board. Clanton, 1961.
26p.
U.S. Urban Renewal Adm. UPAP.

1. Master plan - Clanton, Ala. 2. Streets
- Clanton, Ala. 3. Traffic -
Clanton, Ala. I. U.S. URA-
UPAP. Clanton, Ala.

Traffic - Congresses.

388
I572 Inter-American Traffic Seminar, Pan-American
1961 Union, Washington, D.C., 1961.
Use of traffic signs (Topic 3 of the Agenda)
Report of the Permanent Secretariat. Wash-
ington, D.C., 1961.
4p. (Doc. 18, English)
At head of title: Pan American Highway
Congresses, 1st Inter-American Traffic Seminar,
Pan American Union, Washington, D.C., 1961.
1. Traffic - Congresses. 2. Traffic
safety. I. Pan American Union.

Traffic - Canandaigua, N.Y.

711.4
(74786) Candeub (Isadore) and Associates.
C15　　Master plan study for the City of Canan-
no.5 daigua, New York. Report 5. Traffic and
parking survey and plan. Prepared for the
Canandaigua City Planning Commission and
the New York State Dept. of Commerce.
Newark, N. J., 1958.
42p. maps, tables.

U.S. Urban Renewal Administration, Urban Planning
Assistance Program.

(Continued on next card)

Traffic - Claremont, Calif.

388
(79493) Faustman, D　　Jackson.
F18　　Master traffic plan, City of Claremont,
California. [Prepared for the City Council
of the City of Claremont, California]
Claremont, 1957.
51p. diagrs., tables.

U. S. Urban Renewal Administration, Urban
Planning Assistance Program.

1. Traffic - Claremont, Calif. I. Claremont, Calif.
City Council. II. U. S. URA-UPAP. Claremont, Calif.

Traffic - Congresses.

388
T46 Tippetts-Abbett-McCarthy-Stratton.
1962　　Estimating traffic patterns in urban
areas, by Thomas J. Fratar and others.
Presented at International Road Federation,
4th World Meeting, Madrid, Spain, October
14-20, 1962. New York 1962.
21p.

1. Traffic - Congresses. 2. Transportation -
Congresses. I. Fratar, Thomas J. II. International
Road Federation,　　4th World Meeting,
Madrid, 1962.

711.4
(74786) Candeub (Isadore) and Associates.　　Master
C15　　plan study for ... 1958. (Card 2)
no.5

1. Master plan - Canandaigua, N.Y. 2. Traffic -
Canandaigua, N.Y. 3. Parking - Canandaigua, N. Y.
I. Canandaigua, N. Y. City Planning Commission.
II. U.S. URA-UPAP. Canandaigua, N. Y.

Traffic - Cleveland, Tenn.

711.74
(76887) Cleveland, Tenn. Planning Commission.
C52t　　Traffic, parking, Cleveland, Tennessee
and the official major street plan. With
Tennessee State Planning Commission, East
Tennessee Office. Cleveland 1957.
37p. maps, tables.
U.S. Urban Renewal Administration, Urban
Planning Assistance Program.

(Continued on next card)

Traffic - Costa Rica.

388
(7286) Instituto Nacional de Vivienda Y Urbanismo.
I57　　Estudios de transito en el area metropoli-
tana de San Jose. San Jose, Costa Rica,
[1960]
93p.

1. Traffic - Costa Rica.

Traffic - Center Line, Mich.

711.4
(77429) Vilican-Leman & Associates.
C25m　　Thorofares and parking study; a master
no.5 plan report for the city of Center Line,
Michigan. Prepared for Center Line
Planning Commission. Southfield, Mich.,
1963.
43p. (Its Master plan rept. no. 5)
U.S. Urban Renewal Adm. UPAP.

1. Master plan - Center Line, Mich.
2. Traffic - Center Line, Mich. 3. Park-
ing - Center Line, Mich. I.
Center Line, Mich. Planning
Commission. II. U.S. URA-UPAP.
Center Line, Mich.

711.74
(76887) Cleveland, Tenn. Planning Commission.
C52t　　Traffic, parking, ... (Card 2)

1. Street planning - Cleveland, Tenn.
2. Traffic - Cleveland, Tenn. I. Tennessee. State Planning Commission. II.
U.S. Urban Renewal Administration. Urban
Planning Assistance Program.

Traffic - Dade Co., Fla.

388
(75938) Dade County, Fla. Traffic and Transpor-
D12 tation Dept.
A study of traffic and transportation
in Metropolitan Dade County 1958.
Miami, 1959.
54p. illus., diagrs., maps, tables.

1. Traffic - Dade Co., Fla. 2. Transportation - Dade Co., Fla.

VF
388
(74797) Buffalo, N. Y. Division of Safety.
B83   Curb regulations for primary and secondary
         streets. Buffalo, 1957.
         [9] p. maps.

         1. Traffic - Buffalo, N. Y. I. Title.

Folio
388
(74797) Buffalo, N. Y. Division of Safety.
B83m   Moving people in downtown Buffalo:
Pt. 1   traffic, transit improvements, part 1.
        Buffalo, 1949.
        [27] p. maps.

        1. Traffic - Buffalo, N. Y. I. Title.

388
(74974) Bagby, Scott.
B13   Highway, street and traffic study for
         the Borough of Butler, Morris County, New
         Jersey, by Scott Bagby and Robert Catlin.
         Denville, N.J., (1958
         6p.

         U.S. Urban Renewal Administration,
         Urban Planning Assistance Program.

         1. Traffic - Butler, N.J. I. Catlin, Robert, jt. au.
         II. U.S. URA-UPAP. Butler, N.J.

Traffic - Butler, N.J.

Traffic - California.

388
(794)   Metzger, William L
M27   An analysis of intercity passenger traffic
         movement within the California corridor
         through 1980. Final report. Prepared by
         William L. Metzger and Howard R. Ross.
         South Pasadena, Calif., Southern California
         Laboratories of Stanford Research Institute,
         1966.
         1 v.

         1. Transportation - California. 2. Traf-
         fic - California. I. Ross, Howard R., jt.
         au. II. Stanford Research Insti-
         tute. III. Title.

Traffic - Canandaigua, N.Y.

711.4
(74786) Candeub (Isadore) and Associates.
C15   Master plan study for the City of Canan-
no.5   daigua, New York. Report 5. Traffic and
         parking survey and plan. Prepared for the
         Canandaigua City Planning Commission and
         the New York State Dept. of Commerce.
         Newark, N. J., 1958.
         42p. maps, tables.

U.S. Urban Renewal Administration, Urban Planning
Assistance Program.

         (Continued on next card)

711.4
(74786) Candeub (Isadore) and Associates. Master
C15   plan study for ... 1958. (Card 2)
no.5

         1. Master plan - Canandaigua, N.Y. 2. Traffic -
         Canandaigua, N. Y. 3. Parking - Canandaigua, N. Y.
         I. Canandaigua, N. Y. City Planning Commission.
         II. U.S. URA-UPAP. Canandaigua, N. Y.

Traffic - Center Line, Mich.

711.4
(77439) Vilican-Leman & Associates.
C25m   Thorofares and parking study; a master
no.5   plan report for the city of Center Line,
         Michigan. Prepared for Center Line
         Planning Commission. Southfield, Mich.,
         1963.
         42p.   (Its Master plan rept. no. 5)
         U.S. Urban Renewal Adm. UPAP.

         1. Master plan - Center Line, Mich.
         2. Traffic - Center Line, Mich. 3. Park-
         ing - Center Line, Mich. I.
         Center Line, Mich. Planning
         Commission.   II. U.S. URA-UPAP.
         Center Line, Mich.

Traffic - Chicago.

FOLIO
388
(77311) Chicago Transit Authority.
C34t   Traffic trends in downtown Chicago with
Suppl.   suggestions for improvements. 1962
1962   supplement to March 1960 publication.
         Chicago, 1963.
         1v.

         1. Traffic - Chicago. 2. Business
         districts - Chicago.

Traffic - Chicago.

388
(77311) McLean, Elizabeth J
M12   Traffic planning for urban renewal
         projects in Chicago, Illinois. Prepared
         for Institute of Traffic Engineers,
         Committee 6-C. [Chicago] 1962.
         10p.

         1. Traffic - Chicago. 2. Transportation -
         Chicago. I. Institute of Traffic Engineers.

Traffic - Cincinnati.

711.552
(77178) Cincinnati. City Planning Commission.
C15   Cincinnati central business district
pt. 1   plan. Part I. Circulation. Cincinnati,
         1958.
         140p.

         1. Business districts - Cincinnati.
         2. Traffic - Cincinnati.

Traffic - Clanton, Ala.

711.4
(76181) Clanton, Ala. City Planning Commission.
C51   Clanton, Alabama: major thoroughfare
         plan. [Prepared in cooperation with]
         Alabama State Planning and Industrial
         Development Board. Clanton, 1961.
         26p.
         U.S. Urban Renewal Adm. UPAP.

         1. Master plan - Clanton, Ala. 2. Streets
         - Clanton, Ala.   3. Traffic -
         Clanton, Ala.   I. U.S. URA-
         UPAP.   Clanton, Ala.

Traffic - Claremont, Calif.

388
(79493) Faustman, D   Jackson.
F18   Master traffic plan, City of Claremont,
         California. [Prepared for the City Council
         of the City of Claremont, California]
         Claremont, 1957.
         51p. diagrs., tables.

         U. S. Urban Renewal Administration, Urban
         Planning Assistance Program.

         1. Traffic - Claremont, Calif. I. Claremont, Calif.
         City Council. II. U. S. URA-UPAP. Claremont, Calif.

Traffic - Cleveland, Tenn.

711.74
(76887) Cleveland, Tenn. Planning Commission.
C52t   Traffic, parking, Cleveland, Tennessee
         and the official major street plan. With
         Tennessee State Planning Commission, East
         Tennessee Office. Cleveland 1957.
         37p. maps, tables.

         U.S. Urban Renewal Administration, Urban
         Planning Assistance Program.

         (Continued on next card)

711.74
(76887) Cleveland, Tenn. Planning Commission.
C52t   Traffic, parking, ... (Card 2)

         1. Street planning - Cleveland, Tenn.
         2. Traffic - Cleveland, Tenn. I. Ten-
         nessee. State Planning Commission. II.
         U.S. Urban Renewal Administration. Urban
         Planning Assistance Program.

Traffic - Clinton, Tenn.

711.729
C54   Clinton, Tenn. Regional Planning Commission.
         A study, parking and traffic, Clinton, Ten-
         nessee. Assisted by the Tennessee State
         Planning Commission, East Tennessee Office.
         Clinton, 1958.
         35p. diagrs., maps, tables.

         U.S. Urban Renewal Administration, Urban
         Planning Assistance Program.
         1. Parking - Clinton, Tenn. 2. Traffic -
         Clinton, Tenn. I. U.S. Urban Renewal Ad-
         ministration.   Urban Planning Assistance
         Program.

Traffic - Columbia, Tenn.

388
(76859) Tennessee. State Planning Commission.
T25   Columbia traffic and parking survey. A
         report to the Columbia Municipal Regional
         Planning Commission. Columbia, 1958.
         32p. diagrs., maps, tables. (MTO
         Publication 58-25)

         U.S. Urban Renewal Adm. UPAP.

         1. Traffic - Columbia, Tenn. I. Columbia, Tenn.
         Regional Planning Commission. II. U.S. Urban
         Renewal Administration. Urban Planning Assistance
         Program. Columbia,   Tenn.

Traffic - Congresses.

388
I57p   Institute of Traffic Engineers.
         Proceedings of the   annual meeting

         New Haven, Conn.,
              v.

         1. Traffic - Congresses.

Traffic - Congresses.

388
I572   Inter-American Traffic Seminar, Pan-American
1961   Union, Washington, D.C., 1961.
         Use of traffic signs (Topic 3 of the Agenda)
         Report of the Permanent Secretariat. Wash-
         ington, D.C., 1961.
         4p. (Doc. 18, English)
         At head of title: Pan American Highway
         Congresses, 1st Inter-American Traffic Seminar,
         Pan American Union, Washington, D.C., 1961.

         1. Traffic - Congresses. 2. Traffic
         safety. I. Pan American Union.

Traffic - Congresses.

388
746   Tippetts-Abbett-McCarthy-Stratton.
1962   Estimating traffic patterns in urban
         areas, by Thomas J. Frater and others.
         Presented at International Road Federation,
         4th World Meeting, Madrid, Spain, October
         14-20, 1962. New York, 1962.
         21p.

         1. Traffic - Congresses. 2. Transportation -
         Congresses. I. Frater, Thomas J. II. International
         Road Federation,   4th World Meeting,
         Madrid, 1962.

Traffic - Costa Rica.

388
(7286) Instituto Nacional de Vivienda Y Urbanismo.
I57   Estudios de transito en el area metropoli-
         tana de San Jose. San Jose, Costa Rica,
         [1960]
         93p.

         1. Traffic - Costa Rica.

Traffic - Dade Co., Fla.

388
(75938) Dade County, Fla. Traffic and Transpor-
D12   tation Dept.
         A study of traffic and transportation
         in Metropolitan Dade County 1958.
         Miami, 1959.
         51p. illus., diagrs., maps, tables.

         1. Traffic - Dade Co., Fla. 2. Trans-
         portation - Dade Co., Fla.

Traffic - Dade Co., Fla.

388.
(75938) [Miami, Fla. Dept. of Engineering]
M41   Magic City Center comprehensive traffic
and circulation plan 1960 through 1985;
City of Miami and metropolitan Dade County,
1960. Miami, Fla., 1960.
29p.

1. Traffic - Miami, Fla. 2. Traffic -
Dade Co., Fla. I. Title.

Traffic - Davenport, Iowa.

Folio
388   Iowa. State Highway Commission. (Div.
(777691) of Planning)
I68   Davenport; origin and destination,
traffic report. Prepared in cooperation
with the U.S. Dept. of Commerce, Bureau
of Public Roads. Davenport, Iowa, 1963.
119p.

1. Traffic - Davenport, Iowa. 2. Journey to work. 3. Transportation - Davenport, Iowa. I. Title.

Traffic - Dayton, Tenn.

711.729
(76883) Dayton, Tenn. Regional Planning Commission.
D19   Dayton parking and traffic study. [Assisted
by Southeast Tennessee Office, Tennessee State
Planning Commission] Dayton, 1959.
36p. diagrs., maps, tables.
U.S. Urban Renewal Administration, Urban Planning
Assistance Program.

1. Parking - Dayton, Tenn. 2. Traffic - Dayton,
Tenn. I. U.S. URA-UPAP. Dayton, Tenn.

711.3   TRAFFIC - DETROIT, MICH.
(77434) CONFERENCE ON LOCAL PLANNING AND
C65   ZONING, DETROIT, 1952.
   CONFERENCE PROCEEDINGS; COOPERATIVE
PLANNING FOR REGIONAL DEVELOPMENT.
DETROIT, DETROIT METROPOLITAN AREA
REGIONAL PLANNING COMMISSION, 1952.
77P.

1. REGIONAL PLANNING - DETROIT, MICH.
2. CITY PLANNING - DETROIT, MICH.
3. ZONING - DETROIT, MICH.
4. TRAFFIC - DETROIT, MICH.
I. DETROIT METROPOLITAN AREA
REGIONAL PLANNING COMMISSION.

711.4
(77434) Detroit. City Plan Commission.
D27t   Central business district study; land
no.7   use, trafficways and transit. A basis for
the development of a long range guide for
growth in downtown Detroit. Detroit, 1956.
1v. (Its Master plan technical report,
second series no. 7)

1. Master plan - Detroit. 2. Business
districts - Detroit. 3. Land use - Detroit.
4. Traffic - Detroit. 5. Transportation -
Detroit. I. Title.

Traffic - Detroit metropolitan area.

388
(77434) Detroit Metropolitan Area Regional Plan-
D27d   ning Commission.
   Development of comprehensive studies of
mass transit and trucking in the Detroit
region, by Leland E. Jolgren. Detroit,
1959.
20p. map, tables.
U.S. Urban Renewal Administration, Urban Planning
Assistance Program.

1. Transportation - Detroit metropolitan area. 2.
Traffic - Detroit metro-   politan area.
I. Jolgren, Leland E.   II. U.S. URA-UPAP.
Detroit.

Traffic - Detroit metropolitan area.

388
(77434) Detroit Metropolitan Area Traffic Study.
D27   Report. J. D. Carroll, Jr., study
director. [Detroit, 1956]
2v.
   Contents:-pt.1. Data summary and interpretation, July 1955.-pt.2. Future traffic
and a long range expressway plan, March 1956.

1. Traffic - Detroit metropolitan area.
I. Carroll, J. D., Jr.

534.83   TRAFFIC - DISTRICT OF COLUMBIA.
S29   SEXTON-SEXTON ASSOCIATES.
   STREET AND HIGHWAY TRAFFIC NOISE.
WASHINGTON, D.C. PREPARED FOR DEPT. OF
HIGHWAYS AND TRAFFIC. WASHINGTON, 1961.
1 V. (UNPAGED)

1. NOISE. 2. TRAFFIC - DISTRICT OF
COLUMBIA. I. TITLE.

Traffic - District of Columbia.

388
(753) U.S. Bureau of Public Roads.
P81   Increasing the traffic-carrying capability
of urban arterial streets: the Wisconsin
Avenue study [in Washington, D.C.] by the
Division of Traffic Operations Research,
Office of Research, Bureau of Public Roads.
Reported by Arthur A. Carter, Jr., head,
Highway Capacity Project. Washington, 1962.
388   54p.
(753)   -- Appendix. Washington, 1962.
P81   143p.
Appendix
   1. Traffic - District of Columbia. 2. Streets -
District of Columbia.   I. Carter, Arthur A.
II. Wisconsin Avenue study,   Washington, D.C.

Traffic - D. C.

388
(753) U.S. President's Committee for Traffic
P72   Safety.
   Traffic needs of the District of Columbia,
by Alvin C. Welling. [Washington] 1958.
13p.

At head of title: Eastern Regional
Conference of Citizens Leaders. Atlantic
City, March 1958.

1. Traffic - D. C. I. Welling, Alvin C

Traffic - District of Columbia metropolitan
area.

388
(753) Little (Arthur D.)
L47   Transportation planning in the District of
Columbia, 1955 to 1965: a review and
critique. A report to the Policy Advisory
Committee to the District Commissioners.
[Wash.] 1966.
68p.
Bibliography: p. b1-b24.

1. Transportation - District of Columbia metropolitan area. 2. Transportation - Economic effect.
3. Traffic - District of   Columbia metropolitan
area. I. District of   Columbia. Board of
Commissioners.   II. Title.

Traffic - District of Columbia
metropolitan area.

VF
388   Metropolitan Area Traffic Council.
(7531) Action program. Washington, 1959.
M27   11p.

1. Traffic - District of Columbia metropolitan area.

Traffic - District of Columbia metropolitan area.

388
(7531) Washington Metropolitan Area Transit
W17re   Commission.
   Recommendations for immediate transit
improvement. The report of the WMATC
Advisory Committee. Washington, 1964.
45p.

1. Transportation - District of
Columbia metropolitan area. 2. Journey
to work.   3. Traffic -
District of   Columbia
metro-   politan area.

Traffic - Dover, N.H.

388
(7425) Dover, N. H. Planning Board.
D68   Traffic study report of the City of
Dover, New Hampshire, comp. by the
City Planning Board. Dover, 1950.
32p. maps, tables.

1. Traffic - Dover, N.H.

Traffic - East Hanover, N.J.

388
(74974) Community Planning Associates.
C65   Addendum to traffic study for East
Hanover Township East-West freeway (special
study comments). Prepared for the Township
Planning Board. West Trenton, N.J., 1960.
2p.

U.S. Urban Renewal Adm. UPAP.

1. Traffic - East Hanover, N.J. I. East Hanover, N.J.
Township Planning Board. II. U.S. URA-UPAP. East
Hanover, N.J.

Traffic - Economic effect.

388
A72 Architectural forum.
   Traffic in cities. New York, Urban America
inc., 1968. p. 47-108.

Special edition, Jan. - Feb. 1968.

1. Transportation. 2. Traffic - Economic
effect. I. Urban America, inc. II. Title.

Traffic - Economic effect.

Ref.
388 Franklin Institute, Philadelphia. Journal.
F71n   New concepts in urban transportation
systems. Lancaster, Pa., 1968.
1v.
   Partial contents: The Federal role by
guest editor, Ralph Warburton, Special
Assistant to the Secretary U.S. Dept. of
Housing and Urban Development.
Entire special issue: Nov. 1968.

1. Transportation. 2. Journey to work.
3. Traffic - Economic effect. I. Warburton,
Ralph, ed. The   Federal role.
II. U.S. Dept.   of Housing and Urban
Development.   III. Title.

Traffic - Economic effect.

VF
388
H43 Highway Research Board.
   Urban traffic congestion, presented at the
thirty-third annual meeting January 12-15,
1954. Washington, National Research Council,
1954.
39 p. illus., graphs, tables. (Its
Bulletin 86)
   Contents.-Economic costs of traffic
congestion, John W. Gibbons and Albert Proctor.-
Urban congestion index principles, C. A.
Rothrock.-Discussion.
Bibliography: p. 23-25.

Traffic - Economic effect.

388
M12 McGregor, Franklin T
   An economic analysis of diamond vs clover-
leaf interchange design. Graduate report.
Berkeley, University of California,
Institute of Transportation and Traffic
Engineering, 1961.
26p.

Thesis (M.S.) - University of California.

1. Traffic - Economic effect. 2. Road
construction. I. California. University.
Institute of   Transportation and
Traffic Engin-   ing.

Traffic - Elizabethton, Tenn.

388
(768984) Elizabethton, Tenn. Regional Planning
E54d   Commission.
   Downtown congestion traffic and parking
problems and proposals. Assisted by the
Upper East Tennessee Office, Tennessee
State Planning Commission. Elizabethton, 1957.
69p. maps, tables.

U.S. Urban Renewal Administration,
(Continued on next card)

Traffic - Elizabethton, Tenn.

388
(768984) Elizabethton, Tenn. Regional Planning
E54d   Commission. Downtown ... (Card 2)

Urban Planning Assistance Program.

1. Traffic - Elizabethton, Tenn.
2. Business districts - Elizabethton,
Tenn. I. Tennessee. State Planning
Commission. II. U.S. Urban Renewal Ad-
ministration. Urban Planning Assistance
Program.

Traffic - Elizabethton, Tenn.

388
(768984) Elizabethton, Tenn. Regional Planning Com-
E54   mission.
     Traffic and parking, Elizabethton, Tenne-
ssee. [A report to ... by Upper East Tennessee
Office, Tennessee State Planning Commission]
Elizabethton, 1956.
     33p. maps, tables.
     U.S. Urban Renewal Administration,
Urban Planning Assistance Program.
     1. Traffic - Elizabethton, Tenn. 2. Park-
ing - Elizabethton, Tenn. I. Tennessee. State
Planning Commission. II. U.S. Urban Renewal
Administration   Urban Planning Assistance
Program.

Traffic - Germany.

625.7
(43)   Forschungsgesellschaft für das
F67   Strassenwesen. (Germany)
     Strassenbau- und Strassenverkehrsforschung
1967/1968. [Research in road construction and
traffic engineering] Bericht über die
Tätigkeit der Arbeitsgruppen und
Arbeitsausschüsse der Forschungsgesellschaft
für das Strassenwesen E.V. für die Ziet vom
10.OKT. 1966 bis 17. OKT. 1968 Bearbeitet von
Ernst Goerner und Herbert Kuhn. Köln, 1968.
     289p.
     1. Road construction - Germany. 2. Traffic -
Germany. 3. Germany - Road construction.
4. Germany - Traffic. I. Goerner,
Ernst.

Traffic - Hattiesburg, Miss.

388
(76281) Mississippi. State Highway Dept. (Traffic
M47   and Planning Division)
     Motor vehicle volume study, Hattiesburg,
Mississippi, 1956. In cooperation with U.S.
Dept. of Commerce, Bureau of Public Roads and
the City of Hattiesburg. Jackson, 1958.
     134. illus., diagrs., maps, tables.
     1. Traffic - Hattiesburg, Miss. I. U.S.
Bureau of Public Roads.

Traffic - Erie, Pa.

388
(74899) Pennsylvania. Dept. of Highways. Planning
P25   and Traffic Division.
     Erie metropolitan area traffic survey.
/Harrisburg/ 1950.
     1v. maps, tables

     1. Traffic - Erie, Pa.

Traffic - Germany.

711.4
:388   Germany (Federal Republic, 1949-)
(43)   Bundesministerium für Wohnungsbau.
G27   Die autogerechte Stadt. Ein Weg aus dem
Verkehrs-Chaos [Cities planned for (automobile) traffic, by] Hans Bernhard Reichow.
Ravensburg, Otto Maier Verlag, 1959.
     91p. illus., maps.

     1. City planning - Germany. 2. Traffic - Germany.
I. Reichow, Hans Bernhard.

Traffic - Hightstown, N.J.

388
(74965) Community Housing and Planning Associates.
C65   Traffic and trafficways. (A preliminary
report on circulation in the Borough of
Hightstown) [New York] 1958.
     16p. (Master plan series)

     U.S. Urban Renewal Adm. UPAP.

     1. Traffic - Hightstown, N.J. I. U.S.
URA-UPAP. Hightstown, N.J.

Traffic - Farmingdale, N. Y.

711.4
(74725) Voorhis (Edwin S.) and Son.
F17   Master plan, Village of Farmingdale,
v. 2   New York. Volume II. Traffic, parking
and circulation. Rockville Centre, N.Y.,
1959.
     77p.

     U.S. Urban Renewal Adm. UPAP.

     1. Master plan - Farmingdale, N.Y.
2. Traffic - Farmingdale, N.Y. 3. Parking
- Farmingdale, N.Y. I. U.S. URA-UPAP.
Farmingdale,   N.Y.

Traffic - Germany.

388
(43)   Hamburg. Baubehörde.
H15f   Fussgänger in Hamburg. Hamburg, 1961.
     26p. (Its Schriften zum Bau-, Wohnungs- und
Siedlungswesen no. 35)

     1. Traffic - Germany.

Traffic - Hillsdale, N.J.

711.4
(74921) Community Planning Associates.
H45   Borough of Hillsdale master plan studies:
no. 3   traffic and circulation. Memorandum #3.
[Prepared for the Borough Planning Board]
West Trenton, N.J., 1959.
     8p.
     U.S. Urban Renewal Adm. UPAP.

     1. Master plan - Hillsdale, N.J. 2. Traffic -
Hillsdale, N.J. I. Hillsdale, N.J. Borough Planning Board. II. U.S. URA-UPAP. Hillsdale, N.J.

Traffic - Fort Collins, Colo.

711.4
(78868) Fort Collins, Colo. Planning and Zoning
F67p   Board.
pt.3   Traffic and transportation, City of Fort
Collins, Colorado, by Harold Beier. Preliminary comprehensive plan reports part
3. Fort Collins, 1958.
     41p.

     U.S. Urban Renewal Adm. UPAP.

     1. Master plan - Fort Collins, Colo. 2. Traffic -
Fort Collins, Colo. 3. Transportation - Fort Col-
lins, Colo. I. Beier, Harold. II. U.S.
URA-UPAP. Fort Collins, Colo.

Traffic - Germany.

388
(43)   Hannover. Universität. Institut für
H15fl   Verkehrswirtschaft, Strasenwesen und
Städtebau.
     Fliessender und ruhender Individualverkehr;
Beispiel für 8000 Einwohner: Lüneburg-Kalten-
moor. Hannover, 1969.
     1v. (Die Demonstrativbauvorhaben des
Bundesministeriums für Wohnungswesen und
Städtebau. Informationen Nr. 17)
     Bibliography: p. 70-72.
     1. Transportation - Germany. 2. Germany -
Transportation. 3. Traffic - Germany.
4. Germany - Traffic. 5. Parking -
Germany. 6. Germany - Parking.

Traffic - Hull, Mass.

388
(74481) Advance Planning Associates.
A28   Circulation and parking study for the Town
of Hull. Prepared for the Hull Planning
Board and the Massachusetts Dept. of Commerce.
Cambridge, Mass., 1960.
     24p.
     U.S. Urban Renewal Adm. UPAP.

     1. Traffic - Hull, Mass. 2. Parking -
Hull, Mass. I. Hull, Mass. Planning Board.
II. U.S. URA-UPAP. Hull, Mass.

Traffic - Franklin Lakes, N.J.

711.4
(74921) Community Planning Associates.
F71p   Borough of Franklin Lakes master plan
studies: population, housing, and traffic.
Memorandum #3 [to Franklin Lakes Planning
Board] West Trenton, N.J., 1959.
     10p.
     U.S. Urban Renewal Adm. UPAP.

     1. Master plan - Franklin Lakes, N.J. 2. Population -
Franklin Lakes, N.J. 3. Housing - Franklin Lakes, N.J.
4. Traffic - Franklin Lakes, N.J. I. Franklin Lakes,
N.J. Planning Board. II. U.S. URA-UPAP.
Franklin Lakes, N.J.

Traffic - Greensboro, N.C.

711.73
(756622) Greensboro, N.C. Dept. of Planning
G72t   Thoroughfare plan, Greensboro, North
Carolina. Greensboro, N.C., 1965.
     48p.

     1. Highways - Greensboro, N.C.
2. Traffic - Greensboro, N.C. I. Title.

TRAFFIC - ILLINOIS.

388
(773) GREENWOOD, GEORGE WATKINS.
G72   TRAFFIC LINKAGE PATTERNS BETWEEN A
METROPOLITAN AREA AND THE COMMUNITIES
WITHIN ITS REGION OF INFLUENCE. URBANA,
UNIVERSITY OF ILLINOIS, ENGINEERING
PUBLICATIONS OFFICE, 1966.
     101P. (UNIVERSITY OF ILLINOIS.
ENGINEERING EXPERIMENT STATION.
BULLETIN 488)

     1. TRAFFIC - ILLINOIS. I. TITLE.

Traffic - Gainesville, Fla.

388
(75979) Florida. University.
F56   Traffic, parking and registration of motor
vehicles, adopted by the Board of Control
March 15, 1956, amended June 27, 1957. Regulations to take effect July 1, 1957. Gainesville, 1957.
     17p.

     University record, vol. LII, no. 8.

     1. Traffic - Gainesville, Fla. 2. Parking -
Gainesville, Fla.

Traffic - Greensburg, Pa.

711.4
(74881) Central Westmoreland Regional Planning
G72   Commission.
no. 7   Circulation and transportation.
Greensburg, Pa., 1959.
     15p. (Greater Greensburg planning area
master plan report no. 7)
     U.S. Urban Renewal Adm. UPAP.

     1. Master plan - Greensburg, Pa. 2. Traffic -
Greensburg, Pa. 3. Transportation - Greensburg,
Pa. I. U.S. URA-UPAP. Greensburg, Pa.

Transportation - Illinois.

388
(773) Illinois. Div. of Highways.
I55   Instructions for the evaluation of the
transportation plan contained in the typical
community plan. [Evanston, Ill.] Dept. of
Public Works and Building, Div. of Highways,
Bureau of Research and Planning, 1962.
     [27]p.

     1. Transportation - Illinois. 2. Road
construction. I. Title.

TRAFFIC - GERMANY.

388
(43) Borner, Holger.
B67   Stadtebau und Raumordnung ohne verkehrs-
politische Konzeption? Vortrag und Diskussion
am 22. Mai 1968 in Karlsruhe. Anhang
Literaturnachweis über Stadtverkehr und
Stadtebau voon Lorenz Mainczyk. Köln-Mulheim,
Deutscher Verband für Wohnungswesen, Stadtebau
und Raumplanung, 1968.
     55p. (Deutscher Verband für Wohnungswesen,
Stadtebau und Raumplanung. Kleine schriften
no. 4)
     Bibliography: p. 47-55.
     1. Traffic - Germany. 2. Streets -
Germany. I. Deutscher Verband für
Wohnungswesen, Stadtebau und Raumplan-
ung.

Traffic - Haddonfield, N.J.

388
(74987) Pennsylvania. University. Fels Institute
P25   of Local and State Government. (Government Consulting Service)
     Preliminary traffic analysis and circula-
tion proposals, Haddonfield Borough, New
Jersey. Planning memorandum (work draft
for Planning Board use only) [Philadelphia]
1958.
     9p.
     U.S. Urban Renewal Adm. UPAP.
     1. Traffic - Haddonfield, N.J. I. Haddonfield, N.J.
Planning Board. II. U.S. URA-
UPAP. Haddonfield, N.J.

TRAFFIC - INDIA.

Folio
388
(54)   West Bengal. Calcutta Metropolitan Planning
W27   Organization.
     Traffic and transportation plan for the
Calcutta metropolitan district, 1966-1986.
[Prepared in cooperation with the] Ford
Foundation and others. Calcutta, West Bengal,
India, 1967.
     178p.

     1. Traffic - India. 2. Transportation - India.
I. Ford Foundation. II. Title.

Row 1, Column 1

711.4
(77418)
K15
CPR

Traffic - Kalamazoo, Mich.
Kalamazoo, Mich. City Planning Commission.
City plan report no. 1-
Kalamazoo, Mich., Dec. 1950-
pts. illus.

For full information see main entry.

Row 1, Column 2

LAW
T

Traffic - Law and legislation.
Association of Washington Cities.
Washington traffic statutes adopted by
reference in ordinance no. _____ in the City
(Town) of _____. In Coopera-
tion with the Bureau of Governmental Research
and Services, University of Washington.
Seattle, 1968.
18p.
Supplement to University of Washington Information bulletin no. 283, May 1968.

1. Traffic - Law and legislation.
I. Washington (State) University. Bureau of
Governmental Research and Services.
II. Title.

Row 1, Column 3

388
(79494)
T19n

Traffic - Los Angeles.
Taylor, S Sam.
New attacks on traffic tangles. An
address by Los Angeles City Traffic
Engineer. Los Angeles, Dept. of Traffic,
1962.
26p.

1. Traffic - Los Angeles. 2. Journey
to work. I. Los Angeles. Dept. of
Traffic.

Row 2, Column 1

388
(7429)
N28

Traffic - Keene, N.H.
New Hampshire. State Planning and Develop-
ment Commission.
Traffic circulation study and plan, Keene,
New Hampshire, by Elliot G. Hansen. A re-
port to Keene City Planning Board. Concord,
N. H., 1960.
47p. maps, tables.

U.S. Urban Renewal Administration, Urban Planning
Assistance Program.

1. Traffic - Keene, N.H. I. Hansen, Elliot G.
II. Keene, N.H. City Planning Board. III. U.S.
URA-UPAP. Keene, N.H.

Row 2, Column 2

388
(74893)
L18

Traffic - Lawrence Co., Pa.
Lawrence County, Pa. Regional Planning
Commission.
Traffic and circulation, Lawrence County,
Pennsylvania. [A study of transportation
facilities.] New Castle, Pa., 1963.
71p. (Its Data report 6)

U.S. Urban Renewal Adm. UPAP.

1. Transportation - Lawrence Co., Pa.
2. Traffic - Lawrence Co., Pa. I. U.S.
URA-UPAP. Lawrence Co., Pa.

Row 2, Column 3

388
(79494)
B25

Traffic - Lunenburg, Mass.
Benjamin, Allen.
Circulation plan for Lunenburg, Massachusetts; a portion of the general plan
study. Wayland, Mass., 1960.
16p.

U.S. Urban Renewal Adm. UPAP.

1. Traffic - Lunenburg, Mass.
I. U.S. URA-UPAP. Lunenburg,
Mass.

Row 3, Column 1

388
(76896)
K45

Traffic - Kingsport, Tenn.
Kingsport, Tenn. Regional Planning Commission.
Traffic, parking and major streets in Kingsport, Tennessee, by Upper East Tennessee Office, Tennessee State Planning Commission.
Kingsport, 1956.
62p. maps, tables.

U.S. Urban Renewal Administration, Urban
Planning Assistance Program.

(Continued on next card)

Row 3, Column 2

711.333
(74827)
L23t

Traffic - Lehigh Co., Pa.
Lehigh-Northampton Counties (Pa.)
Joint Planning Commission.
Traffic and transportation; a comprehen-
sive research report. [n.p.] 1963.
130p.
U.S. Urban Renewal Adm. UPAP.

1. Master plan - Lehigh-Northampton Counties, Pa.
2. Traffic - Lehigh Co., Pa. 3. Traffic - Northampton
Co., Pa. 4. Transportation - Lehigh Co., Pa.
5. Transportation - Northampton Co., Pa.
I. U.S. URA-UPAP, Lehigh-Northampton
Counties, Pa.

Row 3, Column 3

711.4
(764)
M12

Traffic - McAllen, Tex.
Caudill, Rowlett and Scott.
Circulation plan of McAllen, Texas; an element
of the comprehensive plan. Prepared for McAllen
City Planning Commission [under the supervision
of the Texas State Dept. of Health] [Houston,
Tex.] 1959.
62p.
At head of title: Economic, population, land
use.
U.S. Urban Renewal Adm. UPAP.

1. Master plan - McAllen, Tex. 2. Traffic - McAllen,
Tex. I. McAllen, Tex. City Planning Com-
mission. II. U.S. URA-UPAP. McAllen,
Tex.

Row 4, Column 1

388
(76896)
K45

Kingsport, Tenn. Regional Planning Commission. Traffic, parking ... (Card 2)

1. Traffic - Kingsport, Tenn. 2. Street
planning - Kingsport, Tenn. I. Tennessee.
State Planning Commission. II. U.S. Urban
Renewal Administration. Urban Planning
Assistance Program.

Row 4, Column 2

388
(76947)
K25

TRAFFIC - LEXINGTON, KY.
KENTUCKY. ENGINEERING EXPERIMENT
STATION. LEXINGTON.
A STUDY OF TRAVEL PATTERNS IN TWO
LEXINGTON, KY., RESIDENTIAL AREAS, BY
HAROLD G. MAYS AND JOHN O. GIBBS.
LEXINGTON, 1962.
130P. (ITS BULLETIN, V. 16, NO. 3,
MARCH 1962)

1. TRAFFIC - LEXINGTON, KY.
I. GIBBS, JOHN O., JT. AU.

Row 4, Column 3

711.74
(76197)
M12

Traffic - Madison, Ala.
Madison, Ala. Town Planning Commission.
Madison, Alabama thoroughfare plan.
[Prepared in cooperation with the]
Alabama State Planning and Industrial
Development Board. Madison, 1963.
17p.

U.S. Urban Renewal Adm. UPAP.

1. Streets - Madison, Ala. 2. Traffic
- Madison, Ala. I. U.S.
URA-UPAP. Madison, Ala.

Row 5, Column 1

388
(74974)
C15

Traffic - Kinnelon, N.J.
Candeub (Isadore) and Associates.
Traffic analysis and plan, Kinnelon,
New Jersey. [Kinnelon] 1959.
24-36p. (Kinnelon planning memorandum
no. 6)

U.S. Urban Renewal Adm. UPAP.

1. Traffic - Kinnelon, N.J. I. U.S. URA-
UPAP. Kinnelon, N.J.

Row 5, Column 2

711.4
(767731)
L47

Traffic - Little Rock, Ark.
Little Rock, Ark. Planning Commission.
Report,
Little Rock,
v. annual.
"The activities of the Traffic and
Planning Departments have been combined
within this report."

1. City planning - Little Rock, Ark. 2. Traffic -
Little Rock, Ark. I. Little Rock, Ark. Traffic
Engineering Dept. Annual report.

Row 5, Column 3

388
(77584)
W47s

Traffic - Madison, Wis.
Wisconsin. State Highway Commission.
Street and highway traffic: Madison
and environs, 1956. Madison, 1956.
119p. maps.

1. Traffic - Madison, Wis.
I. U.S. Bureau of Public Roads.

Row 6, Column 1

388
(76885)
K56

Traffic - Knoxville, Tenn.
Knoxville-Knox County, Tenn. Metropolitan
Planning Commission.
Metropolitan Knoxville traffic and circula-
tion. With the assistance of Wilbur Smith
and Associates. Knoxville, Tenn., 1959.
100p. diagrs., maps.
U.S. Urban Renewal Adm. UPAP.

1. Traffic - Knoxville, Tenn. I. Smith (Wilbur) and
Associates. II. U.S. URA-UPAP. Knoxville, Tenn.

Row 6, Column 2

388
(78882)
L47

Traffic - Littleton, Colo.
Littleton, Colo. City Planning Commission.
Recommendations for a traffic and trans-
portation system, Littleton, Colorado.
Littleton, 1957.
9p.

[Prepared by] Development Planning
Associates.
U.S. Urban Renewal Adm. UPAP.

1. Traffic - Littleton, Colo. 2. Transportation -
Littleton, Colo. I. Development Plan-
ning Associates. II. U.S. URA-UPAP.
Littleton, Colo.

Row 6, Column 3

388
(74961)
P25

Traffic - Maple Shade, N.J.
Pennsylvania. University. Fels Institute
of Local and State Government. (Government Consulting Service)
Analysis of traffic pattern and volumes,
Maple Shade Township. Planning memorandum
to Maple Shade Planning Board. Philadelphia, 1957.
6p.

U.S. Urban Renewal Adm. UPAP.

1. Traffic - Maple Shade, N.J.
I. Maple Shade, N.J. Planning Board.
II. U.S. URA-UPAP. Maple Shade, N.J.

Row 7, Column 1

711.4
(74796)
L15
no. 2

Traffic - Lancaster, N.Y.
Tryon and Schwartz and Associates.
A preliminary report on trafficways,
Town of Lancaster, N.Y. Prepared for the
Town Planning Board. Buffalo, 1959.
27p. (Lancaster master plan report
no. 2)

U.S. Urban Renewal Adm. UPAP.

1. Master plan - Lancaster, N.Y. 2. Traffic -
Lancaster, N.Y. I. Lancaster, N.Y. Town Planning
Board. II. U.S. URA-UPAP.
Lancaster, N.Y.

Row 7, Column 2

388
(79494)
C15s

Traffic - Los Angeles.
California. Dept. of Public Works. (Div.
of Highways)
A special report on transportation and
the accomplishments of the California Freeway-Expressway System in the Los Angeles
area. Prepared for the Assembly Interim
Committee on Transportation and Commerce.
[Los Angeles] 1963.
21p.

1. Transportation - Los Angeles.
2. Traffic - Los Angeles.

Row 7, Column 3

711.73
(76824)
M17

Traffic - Martin, Tenn.
Martin, Tenn. Regional Planning Commission.
Martin traffic circulation system, major
road plan, major street plan. Martin, 1958.
15p. diagrs., maps.
U.S. Urban Renewal Administration, Urban
Planning Assistance Program.

1. Highways - Martin, Tenn. 2. Traffic -
Martin, Tenn. I. U.S. Urban Renewal Ad-
ministration. Urban Planning Assistance
Program.

Traffic - Maryville, Tenn.

388   Maryville, Tenn. Planning Commission.
(76885)   Traffic and parking in Maryville, Tennessee.
M17   Assisted by the Tennessee State Planning Commission, East Tennessee Office. Maryville, 1958.
    39p. diagrs., maps, tables.
    U.S. Urban Renewal Administration, Urban Planning Assistance Program.
    1. Traffic - Maryville, Tenn. I. U.S. Urban Renewal Administration. Urban Planning Assistance Program.

711.74
(776)   Borchert, John R   Projection of population ...   (Card 2)
B67

    1. Highways - Minnesota. 2. Traffic - Minnesota. 3. Population - Minnesota. I. Minnesota. University. II. Minnesota. Highway Dept.

Traffic - Nashville.

388
(768551)   Nashville Metropolitan Area Transportation Study.
N17do   Downtown cordon count, Cumberland River screenline count. Nashville, 1959.
    37p.

    Traffic census, 1959.

    1. Transportation - Nashville. 2. Traffic - Nashville. 3. Business districts - Nashville.

Traffic - Meriden, Conn.

711.4
(74467)   Candeub and Fleissig.
M27   Circulation plan. Submitted to the
no. 2   Meriden City Planning Commission. Newark, N.J., 1959.
    22p. (Meriden, Conn. Master plan report no. 2)

    1. Master plan - Meriden, Conn. 2. Traffic - Meriden, Conn. I. Meriden, Conn. City Planning Commission.

Traffic - Mississippi.

388
(762)   Mississippi. State Highway Dept. (Traffic
M47   and Planning Division)
    Mississippi highway traffic study, 1957. Prepared by the Traffic and Planning Division, Mississippi State Highway Department in cooperation with U. S. Department of Commerce, Bureau of Public Roads. [Jackson] 1958.
    108p. illus.

    1. Traffic - Mississippi. 2. Highways - Mississippi. I. U. S. Bureau of Public Roads.

Traffic - Nashville.

388
(768551)   Nashville Metropolitan Area Transportation Study.
N17t   Travel time study #2. Level of street service: major arterial streets, 1959. Nashville, 1960.
    26p.

    1. Transportation - Nashville. 2. Journey to work. 3. Traffic - Nashville.

Traffic - Metuchen, N.J.

711.4
(74941)   Candeub (Isadore) and Associates.
M27   Traffic plan. Prepared for the Metuchen
no. 3   Planning Board and the Dept. of Conservation and Economic Development of the State of New Jersey. Newark, 1958.
    18p. maps. (Metuchen, N.J. master plan report no. 3)

U.S. Urban Renewal Administration, Urban Planning Assistance Program.

1. Master plan - Metuchen, N. J. 2. Traffic - Metuchen, N. J. I. Metuchen, N.J. Planning Board. II. U.S. URA-UPAP. Metuchen, N.J.

Traffic - Morristown, Tenn.

388
(76892)   Morristown, Tenn. Regional Planning Commission.
M67   Traffic, parking and circulation report. Assisted by the Tennessee State Planning Commission. Morristown, 1956.
    15p. diagrs., maps.
    U.S. Urban Renewal Administration, Urban Planning Assistance Program.
    1. Traffic - Morristown, Tenn. 2. Street planning - Morristown, Tenn. I. U.S. Urban Renewal Administration. Urban Planning Assistance Program. II. Tennessee. State Planning Commission.

Traffic - Nassau Co., N.Y.

388
(747245)   Lockwood, Kessler and Bartlett.
L62   Traffic study, the heartland of Nassau County, N.Y. Prepared by Lockwood, Kessler and Barlett, inc., and Alan M. Voorhees & Associates, inc. Vincent A. van Preeg, computer consultant. Syosset, N.Y., 1966.
    78p.
    Prepared in cooperation with the Nassau County, Dept. of Public Works.

    (Cont'd on next card)

Traffic - Miami, Fla.

388
(75938)   [Miami, Fla. Dept. of Engineering]
M41   Magic City Center comprehensive traffic and circulation plan 1960 through 1985; City of Miami and metropolitan Dade County, 1960. Miami, Fla., 1960.
    29p.

    1. Traffic - Miami, Fla. 2. Traffic - Dade Co., Fla. I. Title.

Traffic - Murfreesboro, Tenn.

388
(76857)   Murfreesboro, Tenn. Regional Planning
M87   Commission.
    Traffic and parking in Murfreesboro, Tennessee. [A report to the Murfreesboro Regional Planning Commission, by Tennessee State Planning Commission, Middle Tennessee Office.] Murfreesboro, 1960.
    27p. diagrs., maps, tables. (MTO Publication 59-20)

    U.S. Urban Renewal Administration, Urban Planning Assistance Program.

    (Continued on next card)

388
(747245)   Lockwood, Kessler and Bartlett. Traffic
L62   study, the heartland of Nassau County, N.Y...1966.   (Card 2)

    1. Traffic - Nassau Co., N.Y. 2. Traffic - Automation. I. Nassau Co., N.Y. Dept. of Public Works. II. Voorhees (Alan M.) and Associates, jt.au. III. Title.

Traffic - Middlesex, N.J.

388
(74941)   New Jersey. Dept. of Conservation and
N28   Economic Development. (Div. of Planning and Development)
    Middlesex Borough, Middlesex County, New Jersey: preliminary master plan studies. Thoroughfares and traffic, public transportation, railroads and freight service, airports and air service. Prepared for the Middlesex Planning Board. Trenton, 1958.
    14p.
    U.S. Urban Renewal Adm. UPAP.
1. Traffic - Middlesex, N.J. 2. Transportation - Middlesex, N.J. I. Middlesex, N.J. Planning Board. II. U.S. URA-UPAP. Middlesex, N.J.

388
(76857)   Murfreesboro, Tenn. Regional Planning
M87   Commission. Traffic and ... 1960. (Card 2)

    1. Traffic - Murfreesboro, Tenn. 2. Parking - Murfreesboro, Tenn. I. Tennessee. State Planning Commission. II. U.S. URA-UPAP. Murfreesboro, Tenn.

Traffic - Nassau Co., N.Y.

388
(747245)   Nassau County, N.Y. Planning Commission.
N17   Transportation centers for Nassau County. Mineola, N.Y., 1965.
    36p.

    1. Transportation - Nassau Co., N.Y. 2. Traffic - Nassau Co., N.Y. I. Title.

Traffic - Milwaukee.

711.73
(77595)   Milwaukee. Dept. of City Development.
M45   Planning guide for the urban highway and street system, city of Milwaukee. Prepared in cooperation with the Dept. of Public Works. Milwaukee [1965?]
    [80] p. (Master plan program. Traffic and transportation studies)

    1. Highways - Milwaukee. 2. Streets - Milwaukee. 3. Master plan - Milwaukee. 4. Traffic - Milwaukee. I. Milwaukee. Dept. of Public Works.

Traffic - Nashville metropolitan area.

388
(768551)   Metropolitan Government of Nashville and
M27e   Davidson County. Metropolitan Planning Commission.
    Experimental bus lines in metropolitan Nashville. [Prepared in cooperation with] Nashville Metropolitan Traffic and Parking Commission. Nashville, 1966.
    81p.
    U.S. Dept. of Housing and Urban Development. Mass Transportation Demonstration Grant Program.

    (Cont'd on next card)

Traffic - New Bedford, Mass.

388
(74485)   De Leuw, Cather & Co.
D25   General circulation plan and off-street parking standards for New Bedford, Massachusetts. [Prepared in cooperation with City Planning Department of New Bedford and Department of Public Works of the Commonwealth of Massachusetts] Boston, 1964.
    1 v.
    U.S. Urban Renewal Adm. UPAP.

1. Traffic - New Bedford, Mass. 2. Parking - New Bedford, Mass. I. New Bedford, Mass. City Planning Dept. II. U.S. URA-UPAP. New Bedford, Mass.

Traffic - Minnesota.

711.74
(776)   Borchert, John R
B67   Projection of population and highway traffic in Minnesota. [Minneapolis] Dept. of Agricultural Economics and Dept. of Geography, University of Minnesota, 1963.
    53p.

    Minnesota Highway Research Project, under contract with Minnesota Highway Dept. in cooperation with U.S. Bureau of Public Roads.

    (Cont'd. on next card)

388
(768551)   Metropolitan Government of Nashville and
M27e   Davidson County. Metropolitan Planning Commission. Experimental bus lines in metropolitan Nashville...1966. (Card 2)

    1. Transportation - Nashville metropolitan area. 2. Traffic - Nashville metropolitan area. 3. Journey to work. I. Nashville. Metropolitan Traffic and Parking Commission. II. U.S. Dept. of Housing and Urban Development. Mass Transportation Demonstration Grant Program. III. Title: Bus lines in Metropolitan Nashville.

388
(7471)   TRAFFIC - NEW YORK (CITY)
B17   BARTHOLOMEW (HARLAND) AND ASSOCIATES.
    PLANS FOR MAJOR TRAFFIC THOROUGHFARES AND TRANSIT, LOWER EAST SIDE, NEW YORK CITY, PREPARED FOR THE LOWER EAST SIDE PLANNING ASSOCIATION. NEW YORK, 1932.
    118P.

    BIBLIOGRAPHY: P. 118.

    1. TRAFFIC - NEW YORK (CITY) 2. CITY PLANNING - NEW YORK (CITY) I. LOWER EAST SIDE PLANNING ASSOCIATION, NEW YORK.

711.6
C51p
no. 2

Traffic - New York (City)

Clark and Rapuano, New York.
Preparation of the site for the World's Fair 1964-1965, by Clark and Rapuano and others. Second supplementary report: maintenance of traffic during arterial construction. New York, 1960.
9p.

Prepared for Triborough Bridge and Tunnel Authority.

1. Site planning. 2. Traffic - New York (City) I. Triborough Bridge and Tunnel Authority.

388
(747)
S34

Traffic - New York (State)

Shiatte, Kenneth W
Composite networks, a new planning and testing tool. Prepared in cooperation with the U.S. Dept. of Commerce, Bureau of Public Roads, the Housing and Home Finance Agency [and others] Albany, N.Y., Subdivision of Transportation Planning and Programming, State Department of Public Works, 1965.
25p.

1. Traffic - New York (State) 2. Automation. I. U.S. Housing and Home Finance Agency. II. New York (State) Dept. of Public Works.

711.333
(74827)
L23t

Traffic - Northampton Co., Pa.

Lehigh-Northampton Counties (Pa.)
Joint Planning Commission.
Traffic and transportation; a comprehensive research report. [n.p.] 1963.
130p.

U.S. Urban Renewal Adm. UPAP.

1. Master plan - Lehigh-Northampton Counties, Pa. 2. Traffic - Lehigh Co., Pa. 3. Traffic - Northampton Co., Pa. 4. Transportation - Lehigh Co., Pa. 5. Transportation - Northampton Co., Pa. I. U.S. URA-UPAP, Lehigh-Northampton Counties, Pa.

388
(7471)
C63

Traffic - New York (City)

Cohen, Lawrence B
Work staggering for traffic relief; an analysis of Manhattan's central business district. New York, Frederick A. Praeger, 1968.
646p. (Praeger special studies in U.S. economic and social development)

1. Traffic - New York (City) 2. Journey to work. 3. Business districts - New York (City) I. Title.

388
(7472)
P21

TRAFFIC - NEW YORK METROPOLITAN REGION.

Peat, Marwick, Livingston & Co.
The Queens-Long Island traffic demand model. New York, 1968.
1v.
Prepared for: Queens-Long Island Mass Transportation Demonstration Program.
U.S. Dept. of Housing and Urban Development. Mass Transportation Demonstration Grant Program.

1. Traffic - New York metropolitan region. 2. Journey to work. 3. Transportation - New York metropolitan region. I. Title. II. Queens-Long Island Mass Transportation Program. III. U.S. HUD - Mass Transportation Demonstration Grant Program.

711.73
(79466)
O14

Traffic - Oakland, Calif.

Oakland, Calif. City Planning Dept.
Trafficways in the Oakland central district; a study of vehicular circulation in downtown Oakland; a technical report. Oakland, 1964.
25p.

1. Traffic - Oakland, Calif. 2. Business districts - Oakland, Calif. I. Title.

711.585
(7471)
D68

Traffic - New York (City)

Downtown-Lower Manhattan Association.
Lower Manhattan, recommended land use, redevelopment areas, traffic improvements. 1st report. New York, 1958.
48p. illus., maps.

1. Urban renewal - New York (City) 2. Land use - New York (City) 3. Traffic - New York (City)

388
(7471)
T74

Traffic - New York metropolitan area.

Triborough Bridge and Tunnel Authority.
Traffic, earnings and feasibility of the Long Island Sound crossing, by Robert Moses. Joint report of the Madigen-Hyland, inc. and the Triborough Bridge and Tunnel Authority. New York, 1965.
25p.

1. Traffic - New York metropolitan area. I. Moses, Robert. II. Madigen-Hyland, inc.

388
(74946)
C65

Traffic - Ocean, N.J.

Community Housing and Planning Associates.
The circulation system; a preliminary report on the circulation system in Ocean Township, New Jersey. [New York] 1958.
31p. (Master plan series)

U.S. Urban Renewal Administration, Urban Planning Assistance Program.

1. Traffic - Ocean, N.J. I. U.S. URA-UPAP. Ocean, N.J.

711.585
(7471)
D68
1963

Traffic - New York (City)

Downtown-Lower Manhattan Association.
Major improvements; land use, transportation, traffic, Lower Manhattan. New York, 1963.
44p.

1. Urban renewal - New York (City) 2. Land use - New York (City) 3. Traffic - New York (City) 4. Business districts - New York (City)

388
(74275)
N28

Traffic - Newport, N.H.

New Hampshire. State Planning and Development Commission.
Traffic and circulation study, Newport, New Hampshire. [Concord] 1957.
15p. maps, charts.

U.S. Urban Renewal Administration, Urban Planning Assistance Program.

1. Traffic - Newport, N. H. I. U.S. Urban Renewal Administration. Urban Planning Assistance Program.

711.73
(74991)
N28

Traffic - Oldmans, N.J.

New Jersey. Dept. of Conservation and Economic Development. (Div. of Planning and Development)
Oldmans Township, Salem County, New Jersey; preliminary master plan studies. Supplement to the Study on thoroughfares and traffic. Prepared for the Oldmans Planning Board. Trenton, 1950.
4p. map.

U.S. Urban Renewal Administration, Urban Planning Assistance Program.
(Continued on next card)

711.4
(7471)
R23
v.3

Traffic - New York, N.Y.

Lewis, Harold MacLean, 1888-
Highway traffic, including a program, by Nelson P. Lewis, for a study of all communication facilities within the region of New York and its environs ... By Harold M. Lewis ... in consultation with Ernest P. Goodrich ... New York, Regional plan of New York and its environs, 1927.
172 p. front., illus., maps (1 fold.) diagrs. 28½ᵐ. (Half-title: Regional survey of New York and its environs, vol. III)
A revised edition of "Highway traffic in New York and its environs", published, 1925, as monograph no. 1 of the Engineering series of the Regional plan of New York and its environs.
Bibliography: p. 167-168.

1. Traffic-New York, N.Y. 2. Traffic regulations-New York, N.Y. I. Goodrich, Ernest Payson, 1874- joint author. II. Lewis, Nelson Peter, 1856-1924. III. Title.

Library of Congress   HE5634.N5L4 1927
Copy 2.
Copyright A 1018042   [32k1]   28—1274

388
(756)
H67

Traffic - N.C.

Horn, J W
Effects of commercial roadside development on traffic flow in North Carolina, by J.W. Horn and others. [Raleigh] State College, Dept. of Engineering Research, 1961.
76-93p. (North Carolina. State College. Reprint bulletin no. 93)
Reprinted from Highway Research Board. Bulletin 303 (1961)

1. Traffic - N.C. 2. Highways - N.C. - Economic effect. 3. Small business. I. North Carolina. State College. Dept. of Engineering Research.

711.73
(74991)
N28

New Jersey. Dept. of Conservation and Economic Development. (Div. of Planning and Development) Oldmans Township, Salem County ... 1958. (Card 2)

1. Highways - Oldmans, N. J. 2. Traffic - Oldmans, N. J. I. Oldmans, N.J. Planning Board. II. U.S. Urban Renewal Administration. Urban Planning Assistance Program. Oldmans, N. J.

VF
388
(7471)
M67

Traffic - New York (City)

Moses, Robert.
Building for traffic in the New York area. Reprinted from Traffic Engineering, August, 1959.
folder. illus.

1. Traffic - New York (City)

711.729
(756)
N67

Traffic - North Carolina.

North Carolina. Dept. of Conservation and Development. (Div. of Community Planning)
Off-street parking for North Carolina cities. [Raleigh] 1964.
42p.
U.S. Urban Renewal Adm. UPAP.

1. Parking - North Carolina. 2. Traffic - North Carolina. I. Title. II. U.S. URA-UPAP. North Carolina.

711.4
(74921)
P15
no. 8

Traffic - Palisades Park, N.J.

Candeub (Isadore) and Associates.
Traffic plan for Palisades Park, New Jersey. Report to the Palisades Park Planning Board. Newark, N.J., 1959.
9p. (Palisades Park master plan memorandum no. 8)
Prepared with the assistance of the New Jersey Expanded State and Regional Planning Program.
U.S. Urban Renewal Adm. UPAP.

1. Master plan - Palisades Park, N.J. 2. Traffic - Palisades Park, N.J. I. Palisades Park, N.J. Planning Board. II. U.S. URA-UPAP. Palisades Park, N.J.

728.1
:388
(7471)
M67

Traffic - New York (City)

Moses, Robert.
Housing and traffic relief. Detached from the Westsider, Winter 1957, p. 42.

1. Housing - New York (City) 2. Traffic - New York (City)

388
(7459)
N67

Traffic - North Kingstown, R.I.

North Kingstown, R.I. Planning Commission.
Circulation study, North Kingstown, Rhode Island. North Kingstown, 1958.
28p.

U.S. Urban Renewal Adm. UPAP.

1. Traffic - North Kingstown, R.I. I. U.S. URA-UPAP. North Kingstown, R.I.

711.74
(74921)
R19

Traffic - Park Ridge, N.J.

Raymond and May Associates.
Street and traffic plan [Park Ridge, N.J.] Pleasantville, N.Y., 1959.
13p. (Park Ridge memorandum no. 4)

U.S. Urban Renewal Adm. UPAP.

1. Street planning - Park Ridge, N.J. 2. Traffic - Park Ridge, N.J. I. U.S. URA-UPAP. Park Ridge, N.J.

388
(74981)
C65
Traffic - Paulsboro, N.J.
Community Housing and Planning Associates.
The circulation system. (A preliminary report on circulation in Paulsboro, New Jersey) [New York] 1959.
31p. (Master plan series)

U.S. Urban Renewal Adm. UPAP.

1. Traffic - Paulsboro, N.J. I. U.S. URA-UPAP. Paulsboro, N.J.

711.4
(74733)
P68
no. 4
Traffic - Poughkeepsie, N.Y.
Candeub (Isadore) and Fleissig.
Traffic plan. Submitted to City of Poughkeepsie, New York. Newark, N.J., 1960.
26p. (Poughkeepsie master plan report no. 4)

U.S. Urban Renewal Adm. UPAP.

1. Master plan - Poughkeepsie, N.Y.
2. Traffic - Poughkeepsie, N.Y. I. U.S. URA-UPAP. Poughkeepsie, N.Y.

711.73
(74762)
R65
Traffic - Rome, N.Y.
Rome, N.Y. City Planning Board.
Major thoroughfare plan. Rome, 1957.
37p. maps, charts.

1. Street planning - Rome, N.Y.
2. Traffic - Rome, N.Y.

711.73
(74811)
F34p
Traffic - Philadelphia.
Philadelphia. City Planning Commission.
Philadelphia's first expressway, the Schuylkill expressway system. Philadelphia, 1949.
1v. illus., maps.

1. Highways - Philadelphia.
2. Traffic - Philadelphia.

388
(7295)
P52
Traffic - Puerto Rico.
Pleasants, W W
Design proposal for a grade separation structure to increase the capacity of a major urban arterial. San Juan, P.R., 1966.
13p.

1. Traffic - Puerto Rico. 2. Streets - Puerto Rico. 3. Highways - Puerto Rico. I. Title.

711.74
(74974)
B13
Traffic - Roxbury, N.J.
Bagby, Scott.
A street and traffic study for the Township of Roxbury, by Scott Bagby and Robert Catlin. [Roxbury, 1959?]
7p.

U.S. Urban Renewal Adm. UPAP.

1. Streets - Roxbury, N.J. 2. Traffic - Roxbury, N.J. I. Catlin, Robert. II. U.S. URA-UPAP. Roxbury, N.J.

388
(74811)
P34
Traffic - Philadelphia.
Philadelphia. Urban Traffic and Transportation Board.
Plan and program 1955. Conclusions and recommendations of the Board, report of staff to the Board. Philadelphia, 1956.
124p. illus., map.

1. Transportation - Philadelphia.
2. Traffic - Philadelphia.

711.74
(74921)
M45
TRAFFIC - RADBURN, N.J.
Miller, A
Radburn and its validity today. Garston, Eng., Building Research Station, 1969.
14p. (U.K. Building Research Station. Current paper 36/69)
Reprinted from: The Architect and building news, 1969, Mar. 13, pp. 40-47; 1969, Mar. 27, pp. 30-35.
1. Streets - Radburn, N.J. 2. Traffic - Radburn, N.J. I. U.K. Building Research Station. II. Title.

388
(789)
B17
Traffic - Ruidoso, N.M.
Bartholomew (Harland) and Associates.
Traffic and parking surveys, Village of Ruidoso, New Mexico. For Village Planning and Zoning Commission. St. Louis Mo., 1959.
18p.

U.S. Urban Renewal Adm. UPAP.

1. Traffic - Ruidoso, N.M. 2. Parking - Ruidoso, N.M. I. U.S. URA-UPAP. Ruidoso, N.M.

388
(74811)
P34u
Traffic - Philadelphia.
Philadelphia. Urban Traffic and Transportation Board.
UTTB April 1956-May 1960. Philadelphia [1960]
1v.

1. Transportation - Philadelphia.
2. Traffic - Philadelphia.

388
(756551)
C74
TRAFFIC - RALEIGH, N.C.
Cribbins, Paul D
Exploration of volume - capacity - speed relationships on urban arterial streets; final report, by Paul D. Cribbins and others. Raleigh, Highway Research Program, North Carolina State University at Raleigh, 1968.
51p.
Prepared in cooperation with North Carolina State Highway Commission and U.S. Bureau of Public Roads.
(Cont'd on next card)

388
(79656)
I21
Traffic - St. Anthony, Idaho.
Idaho. Dept. of Highways.
1959 origin-destination traffic study, St. Anthony, Idaho. Prepared by Idaho Highway Planning Survey, in cooperation with U.S. Dept. of Commerce, Bureau of Public Roads. [n.p.] 1959.
[16]p.

1. Traffic - St. Anthony, Idaho.

388
(791)
P36
Traffic - Phoenix, Ariz.
Arizona. Highway Department.
Better roads for tomorrow, Phoenix-Maricopa County, traffic study. Phoenix, Ariz., 1956-1957.
125p.

1. Traffic - Phoenix, Ariz.
2. Transportation - Phoenix, Ariz.

388
(756551)
C74
Cribbins, Paul D   Exploration of...1968.   (Card 2)

1. Traffic - Raleigh, N.C. 2. Streets - Raleigh, N.C. I. North Carolina. State University, Raleigh. Highway Research Program. II. Title.

312
815es
Traffic - San Diego metropolitan area.
San Diego Metropolitan Area Transportation Study.
Estimating future auto and truck trips for populations,-2.5 million, -2.0 million. Participants: California Div. of Highways, District XI, County of San Diego Planning Department, City of San Diego Planning Department, Traffic Engineering, Transportation Research. San Diego, Calif., 1959.
1v. tables.

U.S. Urban Renewal Administration,

(Continued on next card)

711.4
(74832)
P47
no. 5-7
Traffic - Pittston, Pa.
Candeub & Associates.
Master plan, Pittston, Pennsylvania. Reports: no. 5, Community facilities plan; no. 6, Traffic survey and plan; no. 7, Parking survey and plan. Submitted to the Pittston City Planning and Zoning Commission. Scranton, Pa., 1960.
60p.
U.S. Urban Renewal Adm. UPAP.

1. Master plan - Pittston, Pa. 2. Traffic - Pittston, Pa. 3. Parking - Pittston, Pa. I. Pittston, Pa. City Planning and Zoning Commission. II. U.S. URA-UPAP. Pittston, Pa.

711.4
(74946)
R17
no. 1
1957
Traffic - Raritan (Monmouth Co.) N.J.
Community Planning Associates.
Township of Raritan [Monmouth Co., N.J.] land use, population, traffic. In cooperation with Township Planning Board. Princeton, N.J., [1957]
31p. (Township of Raritan master plan studies, phase 1)
U.S. Urban Renewal Adm. UPAP.
1. Master plan - Raritan (Monmouth Co.) N.J.
2. Land use - Raritan (Monmouth Co.) N.J.
3. Population - Raritan (Monmouth Co.) N.J.
4. Traffic - Raritan (Monmouth Co.) N.J.
I. Raritan (Monmouth Co.) N.J. Planning Board. II. U.S. URA-UPAP. Raritan (Monmouth Co.) N.J.

312
815es
San Diego Metropolitan Area Transportation Study. Estimating future ... 1959. (Card 2)

Urban Planning Assistance Program.

1. Population density. 2. Traffic - San Diego metropolitan area. I. U.S. Urban Renewal Administration. Urban Planning Assistance Program. San Diego, Calif.

720
(469)
L47
Travel - Portugal.
Lisbon. Camara Municipal.
[Edicões da Camara Municipal de Lisboa] Lisbon, 1951.
Kit (10 pieces)
Partial contents:- Casas da Câmara de Lisboa por L.P. De Macedo e N. De Araujo.- Chafarizes de Lisboa.- Esculturas de Lisboa.- Igrejas e mosteiros de Lisboa.- Janelas de Lisboa.- Museus de Lisboa.-

1. Architecture - Portugal. 2. Travel - Portugal. I. De Macedo, Luis Pastor. II. De Araujo, Norberto.

388
(7425)
G66
Traffic - Rochester, N.H.
Goodkind and O'Dea.
Circulation plan for Rochester, New Hampshire. [Prepared for the Rochester Planning Board] Hamden, Conn., 1960.
9p.

U.S. Urban Renewal Administration, Urban Planning Assistance Program.

1. Traffic - Rochester, N.H. I. Rochester, N.H. Planning Board. II. U.S. URA-UPAP. Rochester, N.H.

388
(79461)
C15
Traffic - San Francisco.
California. Legislature. Assembly. Interim Committee on Reclamation of Tide Lands and Related Traffic Problems.
Report on San Francisco Bay vehicular crossing. San Francisco, 1949.
40p.

1. Traffic - San Francisco. 2. Traffic regulations - San Francisco.

Traffic - San Francisco.

VF
388
:331
S15c

San Francisco. Dept. of City Planning.
The cost of driving to work in San Francisco. San Francisco, 1951.
11p.   (Its Planning monograph no. 9)

c.2
Re-
print

c. 2. Reprinted by American Society of
Planning Officials, Planning Advisory Service as a Special report.

1. Journey to work. 2. Traffic - San
Francisco. I. American Society of
Planning Offic-   ials.

Traffic - San Francisco.

388
:331
S15d

San Francisco. Dept. of City Planning.
Daily trips in San Francisco.... An
analysis of survey data-1913, 1926, 1937,
1947, and 1954. Prepared by William A.
Proctor and others. San Francisco, 1955.
106p.
Cover title: Daily trips in San Francisco;
to work...to shop...to play...from Bay area
counties.

1. Journey to work. 2. Traffic - San
Francisco. I. Proctor, William A.

Traffic - San Francisco.

VF
388
(79461)
S15s

San Francisco. [Dept. of City Planning]
San Francisco reappraises its freeways.
San Francisco, 1959.
13p.

1. Transportation - San Francisco.
2. Traffic - San Francisco. 3. Streets -
San Francisco.

Traffic - San Francisco.

Folio
388
(79461)
S15t

San Francisco. Dept. of City Planning.
Trafficways in San Francisco; a
reappraisal. [In cooperation with] Dept.
of Public Works. San Francisco, 1960.
50p.

1. Traffic - San Francisco.
I. San Francisco. Dept. of Public
Works.

Traffic - Sangamon Co., Ill.

VF
711.14
(77356)
G72

Greater Springfield, Ill. Plan Commission.
Guide plan for future land use and circulation. Springfield, Ill., 1957.
7 p. maps.

1.Land use - Sangamon Co., Ill. 2.Traffic -
Sangamon Co., Ill. I.Sangamon County, Ill.
Plan Commission.

Traffic - Seaside, Or.

388
(79546)
072t

Oregon. University. Bureau of Municipal
Research and Service.
Traffic and parking problems in the area
west of North Downing Street and North
Franklin Street between Second Avenue and
Twelfth Avenue. Memorandum to Seaside City
Planning Commission. Eugene, Or., 1959.
19p.
U.S. Urban Renewal Adm. UPAP.
1. Traffic - Seaside, Or. 2. Parking - Seaside, Or.
I. Seaside, Or.   City Planning
Commission. II. U.S.   URA-UPAP.
Seaside, Or.

Traffic - Seaside, Or.

388
(79546)
072

Oregon. University. Bureau of Municipal
Research and Service.
Traffic volume pattern on the bridges
over the Necanicum River. Memorandum
to Seaside City Planning Commission.
Eugene, Or., 1959.
4p.

U.S. Urban Renewal Adm. UPAP.

1. Traffic - Seaside, Or. I. Seaside, Or. City
Planning Commission.   II. U.S. URA-
UPAP. Seaside, Or.

Traffic - Seaside, Or.

388
(79546)
072v

Oregon. University. Bureau of Municipal
Research and Service.
Vehicle accumulation in the area west
of the Necanicum River. Memorandum to
Seaside City Planning Commission. Eugene,
Or., 1959.
[2]p.

U.S. Urban Renewal Adm. UPAP.

1. Traffic - Seaside,   Or. I. Seaside,
Or. City Planning   Commission.
II. U.S. URA-UPAP.   Seaside, Or.

Traffic - Seaside, Or.

388
(79546)
S21

[Seaside, Or. City Planning Commission]
Manual traffic volume count and analysis.
Seaside, 1957.
[5]p.

U.S. Urban Renewal Adm. UPAP.

1. Traffic - Seaside, Or. I. U.S.
URA-UPAP. Seaside, Or.

Traffic - Sharpsville, Pa.

388
(74895)
S32t

Shenango Valley Regional Planning Commission.
Traffic control signs, Borough of
Sharpsville, Mercer County, Pennsylvania.
[Prepared for] Sharpsville Borough Planning
Commission. Sharon, Pa., 1959.
13p.

U.S. Urban Renewal Adm. UPAP.

1. Traffic - Sharpsville, Pa. I. Sharpsville, Pa.
Planning Commission. II. U.S. URA-UPAP.
Sharpsville, Pa.

Traffic - Social effect.

388
C65con
1967

Conference on Transportation Engineering.
[The Conference] Reproduced from the
Sciences (New York Academy of Sciences)
Oct. 1967. p. 2-5.

1. Transportation. 2. Journey to work.
3. Traffic - Social effect.

Traffic - Social effect.

388
:538.56
M17

Martin, Brian V
Principles and techniques of predicting
future demand for urban area transporta-
tion, by Brian V. Martin, Frederick W.
Memmott and Alexander J. Bone. Cambridge,
Massachusetts Institute of Technology
Press, 1965.
214p. (Massachusetts Institute of
Technology. Report no.3)
Bibliography: p. B.1-B.8.

1. Transportation - Automation. 2. Journey to work.
3. Traffic - Social   effect. I. Title.
II. Memmott, Frederick   W. III. Bone,
Alexander J.

Traffic - South Pittsburg, Tenn.

711.729
S68

South Pittsburg, Tenn. Planning Commission.
South Pittsburg parking and traffic study
with major road plan. [Assisted by the
Southeast Tennessee Office, Tennessee State
Planning Commission] South Pittsburg, 1959.
25p. diagrs., tables.
U.S. Urban Renewal Administration, Urban
Planning Assistance Program.
1. Parking - South Pittsburg, Tenn. 2.
Traffic - South Pittsburg, Tenn. I. U.S.
Urban Renewal Adm' 'stration. Urban Plan-
ning Assist-   ance Program. South
Pittsburg,   Tenn.

Traffic - Spain.

388
(46)
S61

Spain. Ministerio de la Vivienda.
Trafico y urbanismo: fasciculo: " El
problema del tráfico en relación con el
urbanismo" Madrid, 1966.
50p. (Resumenes monograficos de
documentos, numero 9)

1. Traffic - Spain. 2. City planning-
Spain.

TRAFFIC - SPAIN.

388
(46)
S61
pt.2

Spain. Ministerio de la Vivienda.
Trafico y urbanismo: fasciculo II: soluciones,
principios teóricos, realizaciones y experiencias.
Madrid, 1966.
80p. (Its Resumenes monograficos de documentos
numero 10)

1. Traffic - Spain. 2. City planning -
Spain.

Traffic - Stanislaus Co., Calif.

711.74
(79457)
S71

Stanislaus Cities-County Advance Planning
Staff.
Stanislaus Cities-County major street
and traffic study for the communities of
the Stanislaus urban region. Modesto,
Calif., 1959.
15p. diagrs., maps, tables.
For study purposes only.
U.S. Urban Renewal Administration, Urban
Planning Assistance Program.

(Continued on next card)

711.74
(79457)
S71

Stanislaus Cities-County Advance Planning
Staff. Stanislaus Cities-County major
street and ... 1959. (Card 2)

1. Street planning - Stanislaus Co., Calif.
2. Traffic - Stanislaus Co., Calif. I. U.S.
Urban Renewal Administration. Urban Planning Assistance Program.

Traffic - Stanislaus Co., Calif.

711.74
(79457)
S71s

Stanislaus Cities-County Advance Planning
Staff.
Stanislaus Cities-County major street and
traffic study for the communities of the
Stanislaus urban region. Modesto, Calif.,
1960.
1v. diagrs., maps, tables. (Its Survey
series report no. 8)

U.S. Urban Renewal Administration, Urban
Planning Assistance Program.

1. Street planning -   Stanislaus Co., Calif.
2. Traffic -   Stanislaus Co., Calif.
I. U.S. URA-UPAP. Stanislaus Co., Calif.

Traffic - Study and teaching.

388
(07)
G25

General Electric Co.
Manual for traffic study. Phoenix, Ariz.,
[1965?]
76p.

1. Traffic - Study and teaching.
2. Automation. I. Title.

Traffic - Sunapee Harbor, N.H.

711.4
(74275)
S85

New Hampshire. State Planning and Development Commission.
A plan for the improvement of Sunapee Harbor.
Preliminary study on: conservation and rehabilitation, traffic circulation and parking. A
report to Sunapee Planning Board by Elliot G.
Hansen. [Concord, N. H.] 1958.
7p.
U.S. Urban Renewal Administration.

(Continued on next card)

711.4
(74275)
S85

New Hampshire. State Planning and Development Commission.   A plan...(Card 2)

1. City planning - Sunapee Harbor, N.H.
2. Traffic - Sunapee Harbor, N. H.
I. Hansen, Elliot G. II. Sunapee, N.H.
Planning Board. III. U.S. Urban
Renewal Administration.

351.81 TRAFFIC - SURVEYS.
C15   CALIFORNIA. UNIVERSITY. UNIVERSITY AT
NO.37   LOS ANGELES. INSTITUTE OF
        TRANSPORTATION AND TRAFFIC
        ENGINEERING.
        WAVE THEORIES OF TRAFFIC FLOW, BY
        LOUIS A. PIPES. LOS ANGELES, 1964.
        21P. (ITS RESEARCH REPORT NO. 37)

        1. TRAFFIC. 2. TRAFFIC - SURVEYS.
        I. TITLE. II. PIPES, LOUIS A.

                Traffic - Thailand.
711.4
(593)   Litchfield Whiting Bowne and Associates.
L47tr   Bangkok-Thonburi city planning project;
        traffic volumes and characteristics. A
        report on the existing traffic volumes
        and character of traffic in the Bangkok-
        Thonburi Metropolitan area in January and
        March, 1959. [In cooperation with] Adams,
        Howard and Greeley, city planning con-
        sultants to the Ministry of Interior,
        Government of Thailand. New York, 1960.
                        (Cont'd. on next card)

---

388   TRAFFIC - U.K.
(41)   TRIPP, HERBERT ALKER, 1883-
T74   TOWN PLANNING AND ROAD TRAFFIC, BY H.
        ALKER TRIPP. FOREWORD BY PATRICK
        ABERCROMBIE... LONDON, ARNOLD, 1943.
        118P.

        1. TRAFFIC - U.K. 2. CITY PLANNING -
        U.K.

690.015 TRAFFIC - SWEDEN.
(485)   Stockholm. Statens Institut för Byggnads-
S 82   forskning.
R46   SVRs Plananvisningskommitté rekommendationer
1969   för tekniska och ekonomiska utredningar vid
        upprättande av planförslag. Del 3,
        trafikförhållanden (Planning Committee of
        the Swedish Society of Civil Engineers
        recommendations for technical and economic
        surveys in the compiling planning proposals.
        Part 3. Traffic conditions) Stockholm, 1969.
        77p. (Its Rapport 46:1969)
        English summary.

                        (Cont'd on next card)

711.4
(593)   Litchfield Whiting Bowne and Associates.
L47tr   Bangkok-Thonburi city planning pro-
        ject; traffic volumes...1960. (Card 2)

        32p. (Technical monograph)

        1. City planning - Thailand. 2. Traffic -
        Thailand. I. Thailand. Ministry of Interior.
        II. Adams, Howard and Greeley.

                Traffic - U.K.
711.6
U54c   U.K. Ministry of Housing and Local Govern-
        ment.
        Cars in housing 1; some medium density
        layouts. London, H.M.S.O., 1966.
        52p. (Its Design bulletin 10)

        1. Site planning. 2. Traffic - U.K.
        3. U.K. - Traffic. I. Title.

690.015 Stockholm. Statens Institut för Byggnads-
(485)   forskning. Rekommendationer...1969.
S 82   (Card 2)
R46
1969   Bibliography: p. 75-77.

        1. Building research - Sweden.
        2. Traffic - Sweden.

711.4
(593)   Litchfield Whiting Bowne and Associates.
L47v   Bangkok-Thonburi city planning project;
        vehicle registrations. [In cooperation with]
        Adams, Howard and Greely, city planning
        consultants of Thailand. New York, 1958.
        12p. (Technical monograph; Traffic motor
        vehicle registration 7a)

        1. City planning - Thailand. 2. Traffic -
        Thailand. I.Thailand. Ministry of Interior.

                Traffic - U.K.
388
(41)   U.K. Ministry of Transport. (Scottish
U54a   Development Dept.)
        Advisory memorandum on urban traffic
        engineering techniques. London, H.M.S.O., 1965.
        92p.
        Reprinted 1966.

        1. Traffic - U.K. 2. Traffic safety. I. Title.
        II. Title: Traffic engineering techniques.

                Traffic - Sweden.
690.015
(485)   Westelius, Orvar.
S82   Trafikrörelsers sammansättning - en
R29   undersökning i Uppsala 1965 (Travel - pattern
1968   within an urban area). Stockholm, Statens
        institut för byggnadsforskning, 1968.
        74p. (Stockholm. Statens institut för
        byggnadsforskning. Rapport 29:1968)
        English summary.
        1. Building research - Sweden. 2. Sweden -
        Building research. 3. Traffic - Sweden.
        4. Sweden - Traffic. I. Stockholm. Statens
        institut för byggnadsforskning. II. Title:
        Travel-pattern   within an urban area.

                Traffic - Trenton, N. J.
711.552
(74966) Candeub (Isadore) and Fleissig.
C15t   Trenton central district area circula-
        tion plan. Trenton, 1958.
        32p. illus., maps.

        Sponsored jointly with the Greater Trenton
        Council.

        1. Business districts - Trenton, N. J. 2.
        Streets - Trenton, N. J. 3. Traffic - Tren-
        ton, N. J. I. Trenton, N. J. Greater
        Trenton Council.

                Traffic - U.K.
388
(41)   U.K. Ministry of Transport.
U54b   Better use of town roads; the report of a
        study of the means of restraint of traffic on
        urban roads. London, H.M.S.O., 1967.
        50p.

        1. Traffic - U.K. 2. Highways - U.K.
        I. Title.

---

388   Traffic - Tacoma.
(797781) Smith (Wilbur) and Associates.
S54   New Tacoma project; traffic planning
        study. Prepared for City of Tacoma,
        Office of Urban Renewal. San Francisco,
        1963.
        51p.

        1. Traffic - Tacoma. 2. Parking - Tacoma.
        I. Tacoma. Office of Urban Renewal.

330.15 TRAFFIC - U.K.
N178   HULTGREN, THOR.
NO.40   TRANSPORT AND THE STATE OF TRADE IN
        BRITAIN. [NEW YORK] 1953.
        114P. (NATIONAL BUREAU OF ECONOMIC
        RESEARCH. OCCASIONAL PAPER 40)

        1. TRANSPORTATION - U.K. 2. TRAFFIC
        - U.K. I. TITLE. II. SERIES:
        NATIONAL BUREAU OF ECONOMIC RESEARCH.
        OCCASIONAL PAPER, NO. 40.

                Traffic - U.K.
388
(41)   U.K. Ministry of Transport.
U54   Traffic in towns; a study of the long term
        problems of traffic in urban areas. Report
        of the Steering Group and Working Group
        appointed by the Minister of Transport. London,
        H.M. Stat. Off., 1963.
        223p.

        Report of Working Group in the Ministry is
        led by Colin D. Buchanan.

        1. Traffic - U.K. 2. Parking - U.K. 3. Transpor-
        tation - U.K.   4. Journey to work.
        I. Buchanan (Colin D.)   Report.

711.4   Traffic - Tacoma, Wash.
(797781)
T12   Tacoma, Wash. City Planning Commission.
          Preliminary report: major thoroughfares.
        Tacoma, 1955.
        16 p. maps, diagrs.

        1. Traffic - Tacoma, Wash. 2. Community
        development - Tacoma, Wash.

---

388   TRAFFIC - U.K.
(41)   INTERNATIONAL SYMPOSIUM ON THE THEORY OF
I57   ROAD TRAFFIC FLOW. ED, LONDON, 1963.
        PROCEEDINGS. EDITED BY JOYCE ALMOND.
        PARIS, ORGANISATION FOR ECONOMIC
        CO-OPERATION AND DEVELOPMENT, 1955.
        406P.

        1. TRAFFIC - U.K. I. ALMOND, JOYCE,
        ED. II. TITLE: ROAD TRAFFIC FLOW.

711.73 TRAFFIC - VIRGINIA.
(755)   SMITH (WILBUR) AND ASSOCIATES.
S54   HIGHWAY TRANSPORTATION IN THE
        WASHINGTON METROPOLITAN AREA OF
        VIRGINIA. NEW HAVEN, CONN., 1953.
        103P.

        1. HIGHWAYS - VIRGINIA. 2. TRAFFIC
        - VIRGINIA. 3. HIGHWAYS - DISTRICT OF
        COLUMBIA.

                Traffic - Texas.
711.729
(764)
T29   Texas. University. Institute of Public
          Affairs.
          Parking, traffic and transportation in
        Texas cities, by C. E. Schermbeck. Austin,
        Tex., 1956.
        46p. (Its Public affairs series no. 25)

        1.Parking - Texas. 2.Traffic - Texas.
        I.Schermbeck, C. E.

711.4   TRAFFIC - U.K.
(41)   Tetlow, John.
T27   Homes, towns, and traffic, by John Tetlow and
        Anthony Goss. New York, Praeger, 1968.
        272p.

        Bibliography: p. 263-266.

        1. City planning - U.K. 2. Traffic - U.K.
        I. Title.

---

388   TRAFFIC - WASHINGTON, D.C.
(753)   SEXTON, BURTON H
S29   ANALYSIS OF COMMUTER SERVICE ON
        RAILROADS AND INTER-CITY BUSSES SERVING
        THE WASHINGTON NATIONAL CAPITAL REGION,
        FOR MASS TRANSPORTATION SURVEY SPONSORED
        BY NATIONAL CAPITAL PLANNING COMMISSION,
        NATIONAL CAPITAL REGIONAL PLANNING
        COUNCIL. WASHINGTON, GOVT. PRINT. OFF.,
        1956.
        33P.

        1. TRANSPORTATION - WASHINGTON, D.C.
        2. TRAFFIC - WASHINGTON, D.C.
        I. U.S. NATIONAL CAPITAL PLANNING
                        (CONTINUED ON NEXT CARD)

388
(753)
SP9
SEXTON, BURTON H ANALYSIS OF COMMUTER
...1956.   (CARD 2)

COMMISSION.   II. U.S. NATIONAL CAPITAL
REGIONAL PLANNING COUNCIL.   III. TITLE:
MASS TRANSPORTATION SURVEY.

388
(74981)
W66
Woodbury, N.J. City Planning Board. Recommendations for ... 1958. (Card 2)

U.S. Urban Renewal Administration, Urban
Planning Assistance Program.

1. Traffic - Woodbury, N. J. 2. Business districts -
Woodbury, N.J. I. Mitchell, Robert A.   II. Penn-
sylvania. University. Fels Institute of Local and
State Government. (Government Consulting Service)
III. U.S. URA-UPAP.   Woodbury, N. J.

3600-
3605
TRAFFIC AND PLANNING ASSOCIATES.
MOORESVILLE, N.C. PLANNING AND ZONING
BOARD.
COMPREHENSIVE PLAN: 1. POPULATION AND
ECONOMY STUDY; 2. NEIGHBORHOOD ANALYSIS;
3. LAND USE SURVEY AND ANALYSIS; 4.
INITIAL HOUSING ELEMENT; 5. SUBDIVISION
REGULATIONS; 6. ZONING ORDINANCE. BY
TRAFFIC AND PLANNING ASSOCIATES.
MOORESVILLE, N.C. 1959-71.
6 V. (HUD 701 REPORT)

1. MASTER PLAN - MOORESVILLE, N.C.
I. TRAFFIC AND   PLANNING ASSOCIATES.
II. HUD. 701.   MOORESVILLE, N.C.

Traffic - Washington (State)

LAW
T
Association of Washington Cities.
Traffic ordinance for Washington cities.
Prepared in cooperation with the Bureau of
Governmental Research and Services [University
of Washington] Seattle, 1968.
22p.
Supplement to University of Washington
Information bulletin, no. 284, May 1968.

1. Traffic - Washington (State) I. Washington
(State) University. Bureau of Governmental
Research and Services. II. Title.

388
(75667)
854c
Traffic - Winston-Salem, N.C.
Smith (Wilbur) and Associates.
Central area traffic plan, Winston-
Salem, North Carolina. Prepared for
city of Winston-Salem, in cooperation
with City-County Planning Board, Winston-
Salem, N.C., City-County Planning Board,
1962.
54p.

1. Traffic - Winston-Salem, N.C.
2. Parking - Winston-Salem, N.C.
I. Winston-   County Planning Board.
City-

3622
TRAFFIC AND PLANNING ASSOCIATES.
STATESVILLE, N.C. PLANNING BOARD.
INITIAL HOUSING ELEMENT. BY TRAFFIC
AND PLANNING ASSOCIATES. STATESVILLE,
N.C. 1970.
13P. (HUD 701 REPORT)

1. HOUSING - STATESVILLE, N.C.
I. TRAFFIC AND PLANNING ASSOCIATES.
II. HUD. 701. STATESVILLE, N.C.

Traffic - Washington (State) - Legislation.

LAW
S
Association of Washington Cities.
Washington traffic statutes. In cooperation
with the Bureau of Governmental Research and
Services. Seattle, University of Washington,
1964.
89p. (Its Information bulletin no. 260)
Bulletin supersedes Information bulletin no.
244, published in September, 1962.

1. Traffic - Washington (State) - Legislation.
I. Washington (State) University. Bureau of
Governmental   Research
Studies.

388
I57y
Traffic - Yearbooks.
Institute of Traffic Engineers.
Yearbook.
Washington,
v. annual.

1. Traffic - Yearbooks.

3619
3620
TRAFFIC AND PLANNING ASSOCIATES.
STATESVILLE, N.C. REDEVELOPMENT
COMMISSION.
PLANNING PROGRAM: , NEIGHBORHOOD
ANALYSIS; 2. ZONING ORDINANCE. BY
TRAFFIC AND PLANNING ASSOCIATES.
STATESVILLE, N.C. 1970.
2 V. (HUD 701 REPORT)

1. CITY PLANNING - STATESVILLE, N.C.
I. TRAFFIC AND PLANNING ASSOCIATES.
II. HUD. 701. STATESVILLE, N.C.

388
(71)
854
Traffic - Winnipeg, Can.
Smith (Wilbur) and Associates.
Traffic, transit, parking, Metropolitan
Winnipeg. New Haven, 1957.
319p. (No. 817)

-- --- Addendum report. New Haven, 1959.
16p.

1. Traffic - Winnipeg, Can. 2. Parking -
Winnipeg, Can. I. Greater Winnipeg, Can.
Metropolitan Planning Commission.

Traffic accidents

see

Traffic safety

3069-
3070
TRAFFIC AND PLANNING ASSOCIATES.
GASTON CO., N.C. REGIONAL PLANNING
COMMISSION.
PLANNING PROGRAM: , POPULATION AND
ECONOMY; 2. LAND USE SURVEY AND
ANALYSIS. BY TRAFFIC AND PLANNING
ASSOCIATES. GASTONIA. N.C. 1968.
2 V. (HUD 701 REPORT)

1. COUNTY PLANNING - GASTON CO., N.C.
I. TRAFFIC AND PLANNING ASSOCIATES.
II. HUD. 701. GASTON CO., N.C.

388
(71)
854
Summary
Traffic - Winnipeg, Can.
Smith (Wilbur) and Associates.
Traffic, transit, parking, metropolitan
Winnipeg. Summary report. New Haven
[1957?]
13p.

1. Traffic - Winnipeg, Can.
2. Parking - Winnipeg, Can. I. Greater
Winnipeg, Can. Metropolitan Planning
Commission.

711.73
H15t
Traffic accidents and congestion.
Halsey, Maxwell.
Traffic accidents and congestion. New
York, Wiley, 1941.
408p.

Bibliography: p. 343-359.

1 Traffic safety. I. Title.

388
(016)
H21
1965
Traffic and the senior citizen, selected
references.
U.S. Health, Education, and Welfare.
Library.
Traffic and the senior citizen, selected
references. Compiled by Dorothy M. Jones.
Rev. Wash., U.S. Dept. of Health, Education,
and Welfare, Office of Aging, 1965.
15p. (OA no. 308, no. 8)

1. Traffic - Bibl. 2. Accidents - Bibl.
3. Old age - Bibl. I. Jones, Dorothy M.,
comp. II. Title.

388
(775)
D62
Traffic - Wisconsin.
Dodge, William H
Transportation in the Wisconsin economy.
Madison, Wis., University of Wisconsin,
School of Commerce, Bureau of Business
Research and Service, 1955.
103p.

At head of title: Wisconsin Commerce
reports, vol. 4, no. 4, August, 1955.

1. Transportation - Economic effect - Wisconsin.
2. Traffic - Wisconsin. I. Wisconsin. University.
Bureau of Business   Research and Service.

3621
TRAFFIC AND PLANNING ASSOCIATES.
STATESVILLE, N.C. PLANNING AND ZONING
BOARD.
CAPITAL IMPROVEMENTS PROGRAM. BY
TRAFFIC AND PLANNING ASSOCIATES.
STATESVILLE, N.C. 1970.
30P. (HUD 701 REPORT)

1. CAPITAL IMPROVEMENT PROGRAMS -
STATESVILLE, N.C. I. TRAFFIC AND
PLANNING ASSOCIATES. II. HUD. 701.
STATESVILLE, N.C.

388
(492)
N27t
Traffic and transport in particular in the
urban areas.
Netherlands. Ministry of Housing and Physical
Planning.
Traffic and transport in particular in the
urban areas. The Hague, Information Service,
1970.
23p.

1. Transportation - Netherlands. I. Title.

388
(74981)
W66
Traffic - Woodbury, N. J.
Woodbury, N.J. City Planning Board.
Recommendations for improvement of traffic movements in the central business district of Woodbury, New Jersey. With the
technical assistance of Government Consulting Service, Fels Institute of Local and
State Government, University of Pennsylvania, and Robert A. Mitchell. Woodbury,
1958.
13p. maps.

(Continued on next card)

3040-
3043
TRAFFIC AND PLANNING ASSOCIATES.
CLEVELAND CO., N.C. PLANNING BOARD.
COMPREHENSIVE PLAN: 1. COMMUNITY
POTENTIAL STUDY; 2. ZONING ORDINANCE; 3.
SUBDIVISION REGULATIONS; 4. INITIAL
HOUSING ELEMENT. BY TRAFFIC AND
PLANNING ASSOCIATES. SHELBY, N.C., 1970.
4 V. (HUD 701 REPORT)

1. COUNTY PLANNING - CLEVELAND CO.,
N.C. I. TRAFFIC AND PLANNING
ASSOCIATES. II. HUD. 701. CLEVELAND
CO., N.C.

Folio
388
(54)
W27
Traffic and transportation plan for the Calcutta
metropolitan district.
West Bengal. Calcutta Metropolitan Planning
Organization.
Traffic and transportation plan for the
Calcutta metropolitan district, 1966-1986.
[Prepared in cooperation with the] Ford
Foundation and others. Calcutta, West Bengal,
India, 1967.
187p.

1. Traffic - India. 2. Transportation - India.
I. Ford Foundation. II. Title.

388
325tr   General Electric Co.

Traffic assignment by electronic computer.

Traffic assignment by electronic computer.
Phoenix, Ariz., [1965?]
[10] p.

1. Traffic. 2. Automation. I. Title.

388
671   Osborne, Henry W

A traffic engineer looks at rapid transit.

A traffic engineer looks at rapid transit.
Presented to the Institute for Rapid Transit,
Annual Meeting, Washington, D.C., May 19, 1965.
[n.p.] 1965.
7p.
1. Transportation. 2. Journey to work.
3. Highways. I. Institute for Rapid Transit.
Meeting, Washington, 1965. II. Title.

388
157
1965   TRAFFIC ENGINEERING HANDBOOK.
INSTITUTE OF TRAFFIC ENGINEERS.
TRAFFIC ENGINEERING HANDBOOK. 3D ED.
WASHINGTON, 1965.
770P.

1. TRAFFIC. I. TITLE. II. INSTITUTE
OF TRAFFIC ENGINEERS.

388
P61   U.S. Bureau of Public Roads.

Traffic assignment manual:

Traffic assignment manual: for application
with a large, high speed computer.
Washington, U.S. Dept. of Commerce, Bureau
of Public Roads, Office of Planning, Urban
Planning Div., 1964.
1v.

1. Traffic. 2. Automation. I. Title.

388
:308
(7472)
E24   Edie, L C

Traffic engineering.

Analysis of single lane traffic flow, by
L.C. Edie and others. Warren, Mich., Research Laboratories, General Motors Corp.,
1963.
[7]p.
Reprinted from: Traffic engineering, Jan.,
1963.
1. Traffic surveys - New York metropolitan
region. I. Title. II. General Motors Corp.
III. Traffic engineering.

388
157
1950   Traffic engineering handbook.
Institute of Traffic Engineers.
Traffic engineering handbook, [ed. by]
Henry K. Evans. 2d ed. New Haven, Conn.,
1950.
514 p. illus., graphs, tables.

1. Traffic. I. Evans, Henry K., ed. II. Title.

DATE OF REQUEST   6/16/52   L. C. CARD NO.

TTH-Missouri   JUN 24 195_

AUTHOR
Traffic Associates.

TITLE
A traffic study of the "Old Town" central business
district, Independence, Missouri.

SERIES

EDITION	PUB. DATE	PAGING 108 p.

PUBLISHER

RECOMMENDED BY | REVIEWED IN
Urban Land News & Trends 5/52
ORDER RECORD   p.6

711.74
T71   Traffic engineering.
Tentative standards for subdivision
streets. Wash., Institute of Traffic
Engineers, 1964.
16p.

A reprint from Traffic engineering,
September, 1964, by Barton-Aschmen
Associates.

1. Streets. 2. Traffic. 3. Subdivision
design. I. Barton-Aschman
Associates.

388
Y15   Traffic engineering literature, Bibliography
of.
Yale University. Bureau of Highway Traffic.
Bibliography of traffic engineering lit-
erature (selected, annotated and indexed).
New Haven, Conn., 1954.
237 p.

Compilers: Kathryn Childs Cassidy and
Cele Kagan.

1. Traffic. I. Cassidy, Kathryn Childs.
II. Kagan, Cele. III. Title: Traffic Engineering
literature, Bibliography of.

388
A87t   Traffic control and roadway elements; their
relationship to highway safety.
Automotive Safety Foundation.
Traffic control and roadway elements; their
relationship to highway safety. Prepared in
cooperation with the U.S. Bureau of Public
Roads. Washington, D.C., 1963.
124p.
Bibliography: p. 86-111.

1. Traffic. 2. Traffic safety. 3. Traffic
regulations. I. U.S. Bureau of Public Roads.
II. Title.

S

Traffic engineering - Periodical.

Traffic quarterly; an independent journal for better traffic.
v. 1 - 3 - Jan. 1947- 1949 -
Saugatuck, Conn., Eno Foundation for Highway Traffic
Control.

v. plates, maps, diagrs. 26 cm.

For full information see Periodical Kardex file.

1. Traffic engineering—Period. I. Eno Foundation for Highway
Traffic Control.

HE331.T74   388.3   50-1781
Library of Congress   [2]

388
(41)
U54a   Traffic engineering techniques.
U.K. Ministry of Transport. (Scottish
Development Dept.)
Advisory memorandum on urban traffic
engineering techniques. London, H.M.S.O., 1965.
92p.
Reprinted 1966.

1. Traffic - U.K. 2. Traffic safety. I. Title.
II. Title: Traffic engineering techniques.

711
(016)
C65
no. 81   Dickey, John W

Traffic control systems for urban areas.

Traffic control systems for urban areas.
[Blacksburg, Va.] Center for Urban and
Regional Studies, Virginia Polytechnic
Institute, 1969.
21p. (Council of Planning Librarians.
Exchange bibliography no. 81)

1. Planning - Bibl. 2. Traffic - Bibl.
I. Virginia Polytechnic Institute. II. Title.
(Series: Council of Planning Librarians.
Exchange bibliography no. 81)

VF
388
T71   Traffic engineering.
Traffic planning in urban renewal projects.
Technical notes. (Reproduced from Traffic
engineering, Jan. 1964)
[15]p.

1. Traffic. 2. Urban renewal.

388
A72   Traffic in cities.
Architectural forum.
Traffic in cities. New York, Urban America
inc., 1968. p. 47-108.

Special edition, Jan. - Feb. 1968.

1. Transportation. 2. Traffic - Economic
effect. I. Urban America, inc. II. Title.

388
H27t   Herman, Robert.

Traffic dynamics: analysis of stability in
car following.

Traffic dynamics: analysis of stability in
car following, by Robert Herman and others.
Baltimore, Operations Research Society of
America, 1959.
86-106p.
Reprinted from Operations research,
Jan.-Feb., 1959.

1. Traffic. 2. Highways - Research.
I. Operations Research Society of America.
II. Operations research. III. Title.

388
H27b   Herman, R

Traffic engineering and control.

Behavior of traffic leaving a signalized
intersection, by R. Herman and others.
[London, Pointeverall, ltd.] 1964.
529-533p.

Reprinted from Traffic engineering and
control, 1964.

1. Traffic. 2. Highways. I. Traffic
engineering and control. II. Title.

388
(773)
G72   GREENWOOD, GEORGE WATKINS.
TRAFFIC LINKAGE PATTERNS BETWEEN A
METROPOLITAN AREA.

TRAFFIC LINKAGE PATTERNS BETWEEN A
METROPOLITAN AREA AND THE COMMUNITIES
WITHIN ITS REGION OF INFLUENCE. URBANA,
UNIVERSITY OF ILLINOIS, ENGINEERING
PUBLICATIONS OFFICE, 1966.
101P. (UNIVERSITY OF ILLINOIS.
ENGINEERING EXPERIMENT STATION.
BULLETIN 488)

1. TRAFFIC - ILLINOIS. I. TITLE.

388
C315   Chandler, Robert E

Traffic dynamics...

Traffic dynamics: studies in car following,
by Robert E. Chandler and others. Baltimore,
Operations Research Society of America, 1958.
165-184p.
Reprinted from Operations research, Mar.-
Apr., 1958.

1. Traffic. 2. Highways - Research.
I. Operations Research Society of America.
II. Operations research. III. Title.

388
H27p   Herman, R

Traffic engineering and control.

Problem of the amber signal light, by R.
Herman and others.
Reprinted from Traffic engineering and
control, Sept. 1963. p. 298-304.

1. Traffic. I. Traffic engineering and
control. II. Title.

690.015
(485)
S 82
R 20
1970   Ingemansson, Stig.

Traffic noise.

Bullerproblem vid trafikleder, en litteraturstudie och förslag till beräkningmetodik
(Traffic noise, study of literature and draft
of calculation methods) av Stig Ingemansson
och Sten Ljunggren. Stockholm, 1970.
188p. (Stockholm. Statens Institut för
Byggnadsforskning. Rapport 20:1970)
English summary.
1. Building research - Sweden. 2. Noise.
3. Traffic. I. Ljunggren, Sten, jt. au.
II. Stockholm. Statens Institut för
Byggnadsforskning. III. Title: Traffic
noise.

534.83　Traffic noise criteria.
S23t　Scholes, W　E
　　　　Traffic noise criteria. [Garston,
　　Eng.] Building Research Station, 1969.
　　9p. (U.K. Building Research Station.
　　Current paper 38/69)

　　1. Noise. 2. Traffic. I. U.K.
Building Research Station. II. Title.

690.015　Traffic noise studies.
1(485)
S82　Kihlman, Tor.
R38　　Trafikbullerstudier (Traffic noise studies)
1968　Stockholm, Statens Institut för Byggnads-
　　forskning, 1968.
　　51p. (Stockholm. Statens Institut för
　　Byggnadsforskning. Rapport 38:1968)
　　English summary.
　　Bibliography: p. 15, 28, 46-47.
　　1. Building research - Sweden. 2. Sweden -
Building research. 3. Noise. 4. Traffic.
I. Stockholm. Statens Institut for
Byggnadsforskning. II. Title: Traffic
noise studies.

LAW　Traffic ordinance for Washington cities.
S　Association of Washington Cities.
　　Traffic ordinance for Washington cities.
　　[Prepared] in cooperation with the Bureau of
　　Governmental Research and Services. Seattle,
　　University of Washington, 1964.
　　89p. (Its Information bulletin no. 259)

　　1. Traffic regulations - Washington (State)
I. Washington (State) University. Bureau of
Governmental Research and Services. II. Title.

LAW　Traffic ordinace for Washington cities.
T　Association of Washington Cities.
　　Traffic ordinance for Washington cities.
　　Prepared in cooperation with the Bureau of
　　Governmental Research and Services [University
　　of Washington] Seattle, 1968.
　　22p.
　　Supplement to University of Washington
　　Information bulletin, no. 284, May 1968.

　　1. Traffic - Washington (State) I. Washington
(State) University. Bureau of Governmental
Research and Services. II. Title.

388　The traffic pacer system,
B42　Bierley, Robert L
　　　　The traffic pacer system, by Robert L.
　　Bierley and Jon Parkinson. Warren, Mich.,
　　Research Laboratories, General Motors
　　Corp., 1963.
　　42p. (General Motors Corp., Research
　　Laboratories. GMR-406)

　　1. Traffic. I. Parkinson, Jon, jt. au.
II. General Motors Corp. III. Title.

388　Traffic planning and other considerations for
I57tr　　pedestrian malls.
　　Institute of Traffic Engineers.
　　　　Traffic planning and other considerations
　　for pedestrian malls. An informational report.
　　Washington, 1966.
　　66p.
　　Bibliography: p. 65-66.

　　1. Traffic. 2. Parking. 3. Retail trade.
I. Title.

1022　TRAFFIC PLANNING ASSOCIATES, INC.
　　SLASH PINE AREA PLANNING AND DEVLEOPMENT
　　COMMISSION.
　　REGIONAL HIGHWAY PLAN; SLASH PINE AREA
　　REGIONAL TRANSPORTATION STUDY. PREPARED
　　BY TRAFFIC PLANNING ASSOCIATES, INC.
　　ATLANTA, STATE PLANNING BUREAU, 1969.
　　87L. (HUD 701 REPORT)

　　1. HIGHWAYS - GEORGIA. I. TRAFFIC
PLANNING ASSOCIATES, INC. II. HUD.
701. GEORGIA.

470-　TRAFFIC PLANNING ASSOCIATES, ATLANTA,
483　　GA.
　　SLASH PINE AREA PLANNING AND DEVELOPMENT
　　COMMISSION.
　　　SLASH PINE AREA REGIONAL TRANSPORTATION
　　STUDY. A, PRELIMINARY TRANSPORTATION
　　PLAN: B, TECHNICAL MEMORANDUM: 1,
　　TRAFFIC SIMULATION MODEL EXISTING TRAVEL
　　PATTERNS; 2, TRAFFIC SIMULATION MODEL
　　TRIP GENERATION MODEL; 3, TRAFFIC
　　SIMULATION MODEL CALIBRATION; 4, TRAFFIC
　　ASSIGNMENTS; C, RECOMMENDED HIGHWAY PLAN:
　　1, ATKINSON COUNTY; 2, BACON COUNTY; 3,
　　BEN HILL COUNTY; 4, BRANTLEY COUNTY; 5,
　　CHARLTON COUNTY; 6, CLINCH COUNTY; 7,
　　COFFEE COUNTY; 8 , PIERCE COUNTY; 9,
　　　　　　　　　(CONTINUED ON NEXT CARD)

470-　SLASH PINE AREA PLANNING AND DEVELOPMENT
483　COMMISSION. SLASH PINE AREA ...1969.
　　　　　　　　　　　　　　　　　(CARD 2)

　　WARE COUNTY. ATLANTA, TRAFFIC PLANNING
　　ASSOCIATES, INC., 1969.
　　14 V. (HUD 701 REPORT)

　　1. TRANSPORTATION - GEORGIA.
I. TRAFFIC PLANNING ASSOCIATES, ATLANTA,
GA. II. HUD. 701. GEORGIA.

S
Traffic quarterly; an independent journal for better traffic.
　v.1- 3-　Jan. 1947-1949-
Saugatuck, Conn., Eno Foundation for Highway Traffic
Control.

　　v. plates, maps, diagrs. 26 cm.

For full information see Periodical Kardex file.

　　1. Traffic engineering—Period.　I. Eno Foundation for Highway
Traffic Control.

HE331.T74　　　　388.3　　　　50-1781
Library of Congress

351.81　TRAFFIC REGULATION.
C15　CALIFORNIA. UNIVERSITY. UNIVERSITY AT
NO.40　LOS ANGELES. INSTITUTE OF
　　TRANSPORTATION AND TRAFFIC
　　ENGINEERING.
　　EFFECTIVENESS OF TRAFFIC SAFETY FILMS
　　IN RELATION TO EMOTIONAL INVOLVEMENT,
　　BY EDWARD LEVONIAN. LOS ANGELES,
　　CALIF., INSTITUTE OF TRANSPORTATION AND
　　TRAFFIC ENGINEERING, 1965.
　　187P. (ITS RESEARCH REPORT 40)

　　BIBLIOGRAPHY: P.177-187.
　　1. TRAFFIC R EGULATION. 2. FILMS.
I. TITLE. II. LEVONIAN, EDWARD.

351.81　TRAFFIC REGULATION.
C15　CALIFORNIA. UNIVERSITY. UNIVERSITY AT
NO.45　LOS ANGELES. INSTITUTE OF
　　TRANSPORTATION AND TRAFFIC
　　ENGINEERING.
　　STATISTICAL ANALYSIS OF ACCIDENT DATA
　　AS A BASIS FOR PLANNING SELECTIVE
　　ENFORCEMENT; PHASE I REPORT, BY ROBERT
　　BRENNER, GARY R. FISHER, AND WALTER W.
　　MOSHER. LOS ANGELES, CALIF., INSTITUTE
　　OF TRANSPORTATION AND TRAFFIC
　　ENGINEERING, 1966.
　　68P. (ITS RESEARCH REPORT NO. 45)

　　1. TRAFFIC R EGULATIONS.
　　　　　　　(CONTINUED ON NEXT CARD)

351.81　CALIFORNIA. UNIVERSITY. UNIVERSITY AT
C15　LOS ANGELES. INSTITUTE OF
NO.45　TRANSPORTATION AND TRAFFIC
　　ENGINEERING. STATISTICAL ANALYSIS OF
　　...1966.
　　　　　　　　　　　　　　　(CARD 2)

　　2. TRAFFIC SAFETY. I. TITLE.
II. BRENNER, ROBERT. III. FISHER,
GARY R. IV. MOSHER, WALTER W.

LAW　TRAFFIC REGULATIONS.
T
A527di　American Automobile Association.
　　Digest of motor laws. Summary of regula-
　　tions governing registration and operation
　　of passenger cars in the United States,
　　Canal Zone, Guam, Puerto Rico, and Provinces
　　of Canada. Wash., 1972.
　　198p.

　　1. Traffic regulations. I. Title.
II. Title: Motor laws.

388　Automotive Safety Foundation.
A87t　　Traffic control and roadway elements; their
　　relationship to highway safety. Prepared in
　　cooperation with the U.S. Bureau of Public
　　Roads. Washington, D.C., 1963.
　　124p.
　　Bibliography: p. 84-111.

　　1. Traffic. 2. Traffic safety. 3. Traffic
regulations. I. U.S. Bureau of Public Roads.
II. Title.

388　Traffic regulations.
B18　Bauer, John.
　　Transit modernization and street traffic
　　control, a program of municipal responsibility
　　and administration, by John Bauer and Peter
　　Costello. Chicago, Public Administration
　　Service, 1950.
　　271p.

　　1. Traffic regulations. I. Costello, Peter,
jt. au. II. Title.

351.81　TRAFFIC REGULATIONS.
C15　CALIFORNIA. UNIVERSITY. UNIVERSITY AT
NO.48　LOS ANGELES. INSTITUTE OF
　　TRANSPORTATION AND TRAFFIC
　　ENGINEERING.
　　CAR FOLLOWING MODELS AND THE
　　FUNDAMENTAL DIAGRAM OF ROAD TRAFFIC, BY
　　LOUIS A. PIPES. LOS ANGELES, CALIF.,
　　INSTITUTE OF TRANSPORTATION AND TRAFFIC
　　ENGINEERING, 1966.
　　16L. (ITS RESEARCH REPORT 48)

　　BIBLIOGRAPHY: P.15-16.
　　1. TRAFFIC R EGULATIONS. I. TITLE.
II. PIPES, LOUIS A.

351.81　TRAFFIC REGULATIONS.
C15　CALIFORNIA. UNIVERSITY. UNIVERSITY AT
NO.41　LOS ANGELES. INSTITUTE OF
　　TRANSPORTATION AND TRAFFIC
　　ENGINEERING.
　　DEVELOPMENT OF AN EXPEDITIOUS METHOD
　　FOR OFF-SITE TESTING OF FREEWAY SIGN
　　FORMATS (SIGN TESTER) FINAL REPORT, BY
　　SLADE HULBERT AND CHARLES K. WOJCIK.
　　LOS ANGELES, CALIF., INSTITUTE OF
　　TRANSPORTATION AND TRAFFIC ENGINEERING,
　　1965.
　　14L. (ITS RESEARCH REPORT 41)

　　1. TRAFFIC R EGULATIONS.
　　　　　　　(CONTINUED ON NEXT CARD)

351.81　CALIFORNIA. UNIVERSITY. UNIVERSITY AT
C15　LOS ANGELES. INSTITUTE OF
NO.41　TRANSPORTATION AND TRAFFIC
　　ENGINEERING. DEVELOPMENT OF AN ...
　　1965.
　　　　　　　　　　　　　　　(CARD 2)

　　2. TRAFFIC SAFETY. I. TITLE.
II. HULBERT, SLADE. III. WOJCIK,
CHARLES K.

351.81　TRAFFIC REGULATIONS.
C15　CALIFORNIA. UNIVERSITY. UNIVERSITY AT
NO.47　LOS ANGELES. INSTITUTE OF
　　TRANSPORTATION AND TRAFFIC
　　ENGINEERING.
　　EXPLORATORY WORK ON THE PROBLEM OF
　　REDUCED VISIBILITY; FINAL REPORT, BY
　　SLADE HULBERT. LOS ANGELES, CALIF.,
　　INSTITUTE OF TRANSPORTATION AND TRAFFIC
　　ENGINEERING, 1966.
　　10L. (ITS RESEARCH REPORT NO. 47)

　　1. TRAFFIC REGULATIONS. 2. TRAFFIC
SAFETY. I. TITLE. II. HULBERT,
SLADE.

351.81　TRAFFIC REGULATIONS.
C15　CALIFORNIA. UNIVERSITY. UNIVERSITY AT
NO.42　LOS ANGELES. INSTITUTE OF
　　TRANSPORTATION AND TRAFFIC
　　ENGINEERING.
　　SIGNING A FREEWAY TO FREEWAY
　　INTERCHANGE (GUIDE SIGNS); FINAL
　　REPORT, BY SLADE HULBERT. LOS ANGELES,
　　CALIF., INSTITUTE OF TRANSPORTATION AND
　　TRAFFIC ENGINEERING, 1965.
　　20L. (ITS RESEARCH REPORT NO. 42)

　　1. TRAFFIC REGULATIONS. 2. TRAFFIC
SAFETY. I. TITLE. II. HULBERT,
SLADE.

351.81
C15
NO.43
TRAFFIC REGULATIONS.
CALIFORNIA. UNIVERSITY. UNIVERSITY AT
LOS ANGELES. INSTITUTE OF
TRANSPORTATION AND TRAFFIC
ENGINEERING.
TANGENTIAL OFF-RAMPS ON FREEWAYS:
FINAL REPORT, BY SLADE HULBERT. LOS
ANGELES, CALIF., INSTITUTE OF
TRANSPORTATION AND TRAFFIC ENGINEERING,
DEPARTMENT OF ENGINEERING, DECEMBER,
1965.
8P. ILLUS. (ITS RESEARCH REPORT 43)
1. TRAFFIC REGULATIONS. 2. TRAFFIC
SAFETY. I. TITLE. II. HULBERT,
SLADE.

VF
388,009,182 Traffic regulations - Kansas.
(781)
K15
Kansas. State Highway Commission.
Manual for uniform traffic control devices for
streets and highways in Kansas. Topeka, Printed
by F. Voiland, Jr., state printer, 1950-
2 pts. illus. (part col.)

Contents.-pt.1. Signs and markings.-pt.2.
Traffic signals and islands.

1. Traffic regulations-Kansas.

LAW
8
Traffic regulations - Washington (State)
Association of Washington Cities.
Traffic ordinance for Washington cities.
[Prepared] in cooperation with the Bureau of
Governmental Research and Services. Seattle,
University of Washington, 1954.
89p. (Its Information bulletin no. 259)

1. Traffic regulations - Washington (State)
I. Washington (State) University. Bureau of
Governmental Research and Services. II. Title.

614.8
:711.73
341
TRAFFIC REGULATIONS.
GIBBONS, JOHN W   ED.
HIGHWAY SAFETY AND TRAFFIC CONTROL.
PHILADELPHIA, 1958.
209P. (THE ANNALS OF THE AMERICAN
ACADEMY OF POLITICAL AND SOCIAL
SCIENCE. V. 320)

1. TRAFFIC SAFETY. 2. TRAFFIC
REGULATIONS. I. AMERICAN ACADEMY OF
POLITICAL AND SOCIAL SCIENCE.
II. TITLE.

351.81
(776579)
M45
TRAFFIC REGULATIONS - MINNEAPOLIS.
Minneapolis Planning and Development.
Design concepts; signs on the streets.
Metro Center '85, environmental design for
central Minneapolis. Minneapolis, 1969.
10p.
U.S. Dept. of Housing and Urban Development.
CRP.

1. Traffic regulations - Minneapolis.
I. Title. II. Title: Signs. III. U.S.
HUD-CRP. Minneapolis.

LAW
8
Traffic regulations - Washington (State) -
Legislation.
Association of Washington Cities.
Washington traffic statutes. In cooperation
with the Bureau of Governmental Research and
Services. Seattle, University of Washington,
1964.
89p. (Its Information bulletin no. 260)
Bulletin supersedes Information bulletin no.
244, published in September, 1962.

1. Traffic regulations - Washington (State) -
Legislation. I. Washington (State) University.
Bureau of Governmental   Research Studies.

351.81
H43d
TRAFFIC REGULATIONS.
Highway Research Board.
Design of sign supports and structures. 6
reports. Wash., 1971.
66p. (Highway research record no. 346)

1. Traffic regulations. I. Title.

351.81
(776579)
M45d
TRAFFIC REGULATIONS - MINNEAPOLIS.
Minneapolis Planning and Development.
Design recommendations; street name signs
Metro center '85, environmental design for
central Minneapolis. Minneapolis, 1969.
93p.

1. Traffic regulations - Minneapolis.
I. Title. II. Title: street name signs.

Traffic Research Corporation.

see also

Peat, Marwick, Livingston and Co.

351.81
H43
TRAFFIC REGULATIONS.
Highway Research Board.
Design of traffic safety barriers. 10
reports. Wash., 1971.
141p. (Highway research record no. 343)

1. Traffic regulations. I. Title.

351.81
(776579)
M45i
TRAFFIC REGULATIONS - MINNEAPOLIS.
Minneapolis Planning and Development.
Inventory and analysis; signs in the
streets. [Metro center '85, environmental
design for central Minneapolis] Minneapolis,
1968.
25p.
U.S. Dept. of Housing and Urban Development.
CRP.
1. Traffic regulations - Minneapolis.
I. Title. II. Title: Signs. III. U.S.
HUD-CRP. Minneapolis.

538.56
T71
Traffic Research Corp.
Reliability test report: "Polimetric" land use
forecasting model. Presented to the Boston
Regional Planning Project, Mass Transportation
Commission, Massachusetts Dept. of Public Works,
in cooperation with the Urban Renewal Adm. of
the Housing and Home Finance Agency and the
Dept. of Commerce, Bureau of Public Roads.
New York, 1963.
44p.
U.S. Urban Renewal Adm. UPAP.
1. Automation. 2. Land use. I. Massachusetts.
Mass Transportation   Commission. II. U.S.
URA-UPAP.

711.4
H17
v.9
Traffic regulations.
Malcher, Fritz, 1888-1938.
The steadyflow traffic system, by Fritz Malcher. Cambridge,
Harvard university press, 1935.
ix, 91 p. front. (port.) illus., maps, diagrs. 25ᵐ. (Half-title: Harvard city planning studies. IX)
Preface signed: Theodora Kimball Hubbard ... Henry Vincent Hubbard.
4. City planning.
1. Streets. 2. Roads. 3. Traffic regulations. 4. Cities and towns
Planning. i. Hubbard, Mrs. Theodora (Kimball) 1887-   ii. Hubbard, Henry Vincent, 1875-   iii. Title. iv. Title: Traffic system. Ser.
36—1420
Library of Congress   HE371.A3M35
——— Copy 2.
Copyright A 90142   [36p5]   388.3

351.81
(776579)
M45v
TRAFFIC REGULATIONS - MINNEAPOLIS.
Minneapolis Planning and Development.
Visual communication study. [Metro center
'85, environmental design for central
Minneapolis] Work program. Rev. Minneapolis,
1969.
6p.
U.S. Dept. of Housing and Urban Development.
CRP.

1. Traffic regulations - Minneapolis.
I. Title. II. U.S. HUD-CRP. Minneapolis.

711.14
T71
Traffic Research Corp.
Review of existing land use forecasting
techniques. Presented to the Boston Regional
Planning Project, Mass Transportation Commis-
sion, Mass. Dept. of Public Works, in coopera-
tion with the Urban Renewal Administration of
the Housing and Home Finance Agency and the
Dept. of Commerce, Bureau of Public Roads.
New York, 1963.
107p.
Bibliography: p. 83-93.

(Continued on next card)

614.8
:711.73
P72
TRAFFIC REGULATIONS.
PRESIDENT'S HIGHWAY SAFETY CONFERENCE,
WASHINGTON, D.C., 1949.
COMMITTEE REPORTS: ACCIDENT
RECORDS, EDUCATION, ENFORCEMENT,
ENGINEERING, LAWS AND ORDINANCES,
MOTOR VEHICLE ADMINISTRATION,
ORGANIZED PUBLIC SUPPORT, PUBLIC
INFORMATION, AND THE ACTION PROGRAM.
WASHINGTON, GOVT. PRINT. OFF., 1949.
9 V.

1. TRAFFIC SAFETY. 2. TRAFFIC
REGULATIONS.

388
(79461)
C15
Traffic regulations - San Francisco.
California. Legislature. Assembly.
Interim Committee on Reclamation of
Tide Lands and Related Traffic
Problems.
Report on San Francisco Bay vehicular
crossing. San Francisco, 1949.
40p.

1. Traffic - San Francisco. 2. Traffic
regulations -   - San Francisco.

711.14
T71
Traffic Research Corp. Review of existing land
use forecasting techniques... 1963.
(Card 2)

U.S. Urban Renewal Adm. UPAP.

1. Land use. 2. Automation. I. Boston
Regional Planning Project. II. Massachusetts.
Mass Transportation Commission. III. U.S.
URA-UPAP.

351.81
S76
TRAFFIC REGULATIONS.
Stover, Vergil G
Final/summary report on the traffic
assignment study. Sponsored by the Texas
Highway Dept. in cooperation with the U.S.
Bureau of Public Roads. College Station,
Transportation Institute, Texas A & M
University, 1969.
20p.

1. Traffic regulations. I. U.S. Bureau
of Public Roads. II. Transportation
Institute.

711.729
(41)
U54p
Traffic regulations - U.K.
U.K. Ministry of Transport.
Parking, the next stage. A new look by the
Ministry of Transport at London's parking
problem: July 1963. London, H.M.S.O., 1963.
47p.

1. Parking - U.K. 2. Traffic regulations -
U.K. I. Title.

Folio
388
(7531)
G45
Traffic, revenue and operating cost.
Gilman (W.C.) and Co.
Traffic, revenue and operating costs; by
W.C. Gilman & Co. and Alan M. Voorhees and
Associates. Rev. McLean, Va., 1969.
106p.
Prepared for the Washington Metropolitan
Area Transit Authority.
1. Transportation - District of Columbia
metropolitan area. 2. Journey to work.
3. Traffic surveys - District of Columbia
metropolitan area. I. Title. II. Voorhees
(Alan M.) and Associates. III. Washington
Metropolitan   Area Transit Authority.

614.8
:711.73 Automotive Safety Foundation.
A87   Better street traffic management for
         Boston; study and recommendations of the
         Automotive Safety Foundation. Washington,
         1961.
         39p.

         1. Traffic safety.

614.8
:711.73 Automotive Safety Foundation.
A87h   Highway safety program management.
         Transcripts of Regional Safety Program
         Management Seminars conducted for the
         National Highway Safety Bureau, Federal
         Highway Administration. Wash., 1968.
         125p.
         Bibliography: p. 114-116.

         1. Traffic safety. 2. Highways.
         I. U.S. National Highway Safety Bureau.
         II. Title.

388
A87t   Automotive Safety Foundation.
       Traffic control and roadway elements; their
       relationship to highway safety. Prepared in
       cooperation with the U.S. Bureau of Public
       Roads. Washington, D.C., 1963.
       124p.
       Bibliography: p. 86-111.

       1. Traffic. 2. Traffic safety. 3. Traffic
       regulations. I. U.S. Bureau of Public Roads.
       II. Title.

614.8
:711.73 Blackman, Allan.
B51   The role of city planning in child pe-
         destrian safety. Berkeley, Calif. Institute
         of Urban and Regional Development, Center
         for Planning and Development Research, Uni-
         versity of California. [1966?]
         48p.
         Bibliography: p. 43-48.

         1. Traffic safety. 2. City planning -
         Calif. 3. Children. I. California. Uni-
         versity. Center for Planning and Development
         Research.   II. Title.

351.81 TRAFFIC SAFETY.
C15   CALIFORNIA. UNIVERSITY. UNIVERSITY AT
NO.41 LOS ANGELES. INSTITUTE OF
       TRANSPORTATION AND TRAFFIC
       ENGINEERING.
       DEVELOPMENT OF AN EXPEDITIOUS METHOD
       FOR OFF-SITE TESTING OF FREEWAY SIGN
       FORMATS (SIGN TESTER) FINAL REPORT, BY
       SLADE HULBERT AND CHARLES K. WOJCIK.
       LOS ANGELES, CALIF., INSTITUTE OF
       TRANSPORTATION AND TRAFFIC ENGINEERING,
       1965.
       14L. (ITS RESEARCH REPORT 41)

       1. TRAFFIC REGULATIONS.
                       (CONTINUED ON NEXT CARD)

351.81 CALIFORNIA. UNIVERSITY. UNIVERSITY AT
C15   LOS ANGELES. INSTITUTE OF
NO.41 TRANSPORTATION AND TRAFFIC
       ENGINEERING. DEVELOPMENT OF AN ...
       1965.   (CARD 2)

       2. TRAFFIC SAFETY.   I. TITLE.
       II. HULBERT, SLADE.   III. WOJCIK,
       CHARLES K.

351.81 TRAFFIC SAFETY.
C15   CALIFORNIA. UNIVERSITY. UNIVERSITY AT
NO.47 LOS ANGELES. INSTITUTE OF
       TRANSPORTATION AND TRAFFIC
       ENGINEERING.
       EXPLORATORY WORK ON THE PROBLEM OF
       REDUCED VISIBILITY; FINAL REPORT, BY
       SLADE HULBERT. LOS ANGELES, CALIF.,
       INSTITUTE OF TRANSPORTATION AND TRAFFIC
       ENGINEERING, 1966.
       10L. (ITS RESEARCH REPORT NO. 47)

       1. TRAFFIC REGULATIONS. 2. TRAFFIC
       SAFETY. I. TITLE. II. HULBERT,
       SLADE.

351.81 TRAFFIC SAFETY.
C15   CALIFORNIA. UNIVERSITY. UNIVERSITY AT
NO.42 LOS ANGELES. INSTITUTE OF
       TRANSPORTATION AND TRAFFIC
       ENGINEERING.
       SIGNING A FREEWAY TO FREEWAY
       INTERCHANGE (GUIDE SIGNS); FINAL
       REPORT, BY SLADE HULBERT. LOS ANGELES,
       CALIF., INSTITUTE OF TRANSPORTATION AND
       TRAFFIC ENGINEERING, 1965.
       20L. (ITS RESEARCH REPORT NO. 42)

       1. TRAFFIC REGULATIONS. 2. TRAFFIC
       SAFETY. I. TITLE. II. HULBERT,
       SLADE.

351.81 TRAFFIC SAFETY.
C15   CALIFORNIA. UNIVERSITY. UNIVERSITY AT
NO.45 LOS ANGELES. INSTITUTE OF
       TRANSPORTATION AND TRAFFIC
       ENGINEERING.
       STATISTICAL ANALYSIS OF ACCIDENT DATA
       AS A BASIS FOR PLANNING SELECTIVE
       ENFORCEMENT; PHASE I REPORT, BY ROBERT
       BRENNER, GARY R. FISHER, AND WALTER W.
       MOSHER. LOS ANGELES, CALIF., INSTITUTE
       OF TRANSPORTATION AND TRAFFIC
       ENGINEERING, 1966.
       68P. (ITS RESEARCH REPORT NO. 45)

       1. TRAFFIC REGULATIONS.
                       (CONTINUED ON NEXT CARD)

351.81 CALIFORNIA. UNIVERSITY. UNIVERSITY AT
C15   LOS ANGELES. INSTITUTE OF
NO.45 TRANSPORTATION AND TRAFFIC
       ENGINEERING. STATISTICAL ANALYSIS OF
       ...1966.   (CARD 2)

       2. TRAFFIC SAFETY. I. TITLE.
       II. BRENNER, ROBERT.   III. FISHER,
       GARY R.   IV. MOSHER, WALTER W.

351.81 TRAFFIC SAFETY.
C15   CALIFORNIA. UNIVERSITY. UNIVERSITY AT
NO.43 LOS ANGELES. INSTITUTE OF
       TRANSPORTATION AND TRAFFIC
       ENGINEERING.
       TANGENTIAL OFF-RAMPS ON FREEWAYS;
       FINAL REPORT, BY SLADE HULBERT. LOS
       ANGELES, CALIF., INSTITUTE OF
       TRANSPORTATION AND TRAFFIC ENGINEERING,
       DEPARTMENT OF ENGINEERING, DECEMBER,
       1965.
       8P. ILLUS. (ITS RESEARCH REPORT 43)
       1. TRAFFIC REGULATIONS. 2. TRAFFIC
       SAFETY. I. TITLE. II. HULBERT,
       SLADE.

614.8
:711.73 CALIFORNIA. UNIVERSITY. UNIVERSITY
C15   AT LOS ANGELES. INSTITUTE OF
       TRANSPORTATION AND TRAFFIC
       ENGINEERING.
       WRONG-WAY DRIVING OFF-RAMP STUDIES,
       BY SLADE HULBERT AND JINX BEERS. LOS
       ANGELES, CALIF., INSTITUTE OF
       TRANSPORTATION AND TRAFFIC
       ENGINEERING, DEPARTMENT OF
       ENGINEERING, UNIVERSITY OF CALIFORNIA,
       1965.
       25P. (ITS RESEARCH REPORT 39)

       1. TRAFFIC SAFETY. 2. HIGHWAYS
                       (CONTINUED ON NEXT CARD)

614.8
:711.73 CALIFORNIA. UNIVERSITY. UNIVERSITY
C15   AT LOS ANGELES. INSTITUTE OF
       TRANSPORTATION AND TRAFFIC
       ENGINEERING. WRONG-WAY DRIVING
       OFF-RAMP ...1965.   (CARD 2)

       3. RESEARCH. I. TITLE. II. HULBERT,
       SLADE.   III. BEERS, JINX.

711.73
C67   Cornell Aeronautical Laboratory.
       A projection of technology applicable to
       the future highway system of the Boston-
       Washington corridor. Prepared for U.S.
       Dept. of Commerce, Office of Undersecretary
       for Transportation Policy, Buffalo, N.Y.,
       Cornell Aeronautical Laboratory of Cornell
       University, 1964.
       256p.   (PB 166 878)
       Distributed by Clearinghouse for Federal
       Scientific and Technical Information.

       (Continued on   next card)

711.73
C67   Cornell Aeronautical Laboratory. A projec-
       tion of technology applicable to the future
       highway system...1964.   (Card 2)

       1. Highways - Boston-New York-Washington
       Corridor. 2. Transportation - Economic
       effect. 3. Traffic safety. I. Title: Future
       highway system of the Boston-Washington
       Corridor. II. Title.

711.73
E56   Eno Foundation for Highway Traffic Control.
       Roadside hazards. Saugatuck, Conn., 1968.
       28p.
       Contents.-The need for highway safety
       consciousness, by John A. Blatnik,--An
       evaluation of roadside hazards on the inter-
       state system, by Charles W. Prisk.

       1. Highways. 2. Traffic safety.
       I. Blatnik, John A. The need for highway
       safety consciousness. II. Prisk, Charles
       W. An evaluation of roadside hazards on
       the interstate system. III. Title.

614.8
:711.73 Eno Foundation for Highway Traffic Control.
E56   Traffic safety; a national problem. A
       symposium sponsored by the National Academy
       of Engineering held in Washington, D.C.,
N.a.1 April 28, 1966. Saugatuck, Conn., 1967.
Laf.c.2 164p.

       1. Traffic safety. I. National Academy
       of Engineering, Wash. D.C. II. Title.

388
F67   Ford Motor Company
       Freedom of the American road. [Dearborn,
       Mich., 1956]
       120 p.   illus., maps.

       1.Traffic safety. 2.Highways. I.Title.

384
F76   TRAFFIC SAFETY.
       Fromm, Gary.
       Aviation safety. Wash., Brookings
       Institution, 1969.
       [29]p. (Brookings Institution. Reprint
       152)
       Reprinted from: Law and contemporary
       problems, vol. 33, no. 3 (Summer 1968)
       p. [590]-618.
       1. Air transportation. 2. Traffic
       safety. I. Brookings Institution.
       II. Title.

614.8
:711.73 TRAFFIC SAFETY.
G41   GIBBONS, JOHN W ED.
       HIGHWAY SAFETY AND TRAFFIC CONTROL.
       PHILADELPHIA, 1958.
       209P. (THE ANNALS OF THE AMERICAN
       ACADEMY OF POLITICAL AND SOCIAL
       SCIENCE, V. 320)

       1. TRAFFIC SAFETY. 2. TRAFFIC
       REGULATIONS. I. AMERICAN ACADEMY OF
       POLITICAL AND SOCIAL SCIENCE.
       II. TITLE.

614.8
:711.73 TRAFFIC SAFETY.
G65   GOLDIE, G N
       THE INFLUENCE OF TRAFFIC SAFETY AND
       CONTROL PROBLEMS ON PLANNING.
       WELLINGTON, N.Z., TOWN PLANNING
       INSTITUTE OF NEW ZEALAND, 1939.
       14P.

       IN PLANNING, SER. NO. 2, BULLETIN
       NO. 15, JULY 1939.

       1. TRAFFIC SAFETY. 2. PLANNING.
       I. TOWN PLANNING INSTITUTE OF NEW
       ZEALAND.

711.73
H15
Traffic safety.
    Halsey, Maxwell
      State traffic safety; its organization, administration and programming. Saugatuck, Conn., The Eno Foundation for Highway Traffic Control, 1953.
      280 p. illus., charts, forms, tables.

    1.Traffic safety. I. Eno Foundation for Highway Traffic Control. II.Title.

VF
612.84
H43
Traffic safety.
    Highway Research Board.
      Night visibility; presented at the thirty-first annual meeting, January 1952. Washington, 1952.
      77 p. illus. (Its Bulletin 56)
      Bibliographies.
      Contents.-Determination of windshield levels requisite for driving visibility.-Effect of exposure to sunlight on night-driving visibility.-Effect of pattern distribution on perception of relative motion in low levels of illumination.- Vision at levels of night road illumination.- Spherical lens optics applied to retrodirective reflection.   (over)

614.8
:711.73
H82
TRAFFIC SAFETY.
    Huelke, Donald F
      A study of pedestrian fatalities in Wayne County, Michigan, by Donald F. Huelke and Rollin A. Davis. Ann Arbor, Mich., Highway Safety Research Institute, University of Michigan, 1969.
      52p. (HSRI report no. Bio-9)

      Bibliography: p. 21-22.
    1. Traffic safety. I. Davis, Rollin A., jt. au. II. Michigan. University. Highway Safety Research Institute. III. Title: Pedestrian fatalities. IV. Title.

711.73
H15t
Traffic safety.
    Halsey, Maxwell.
      Traffic accidents and congestion. New York, Wiley, 1941.
      408p.

      Bibliography: p. 343-359.

    1 Traffic safety. I. Title.

VF
612.84
H43n
Traffic safety.
    Highway Research Board.
      Night visibility; presented at the annual meeting, January 12-15, 1954. Washington, 1954.
      75 p. illus. (Its Bulletin 89)

      Bibliography.

    1. Traffic safety. 2. Visibility.

614.8
:711.73
I57
Traffic safety.
    Institute of Traffic Engineers.
      A program for school crossing protection adopted by the Board of Direction as a recommended practice, Aug. 12, 1962. Wash., 1962.
      22p. (Its RP-3)

    1. Traffic safety. 2. Schools. I. Title.

VF
614.8
:711.73
H43d
Traffic safety.
    Highway Research Board.
      Driver characteristics and accidents; presented at the thirty-second annual meeting, January 13-16, 1953. Washington, 1953.
      54 p. illus., graphs (Its Bulletin 73)
      Contents.-The A.T.A. case-interview plan as a method for driver improvement.-Assapling study of driver on the highways for the 24-hr. period. -Relationship of preventable to nonpreventable accidents in the trucking industry.-Rapid-deceleration test of chest-level safety belt.

    1. Traffic safety. I. Title.

VF
614.8
:711.73
H43rr
Traffic safety.
    Highway Research Board.
      Road roughness and slipperiness; some factors and test methods; presented at the thirty-fifth annual meeting, January 17-20, 1956. Washington, 1956.
      84 p. illus. (Its Bulletin 139)

    1. Traffic safety. I. Title.

388
I572
1961
Traffic safety.
    Inter-American Traffic Seminar, Pan-American Union, Washington, D.C., 1961.
      Use of traffic signs (Topic 3 of the Agenda) Report of the Permanent Secretariat. Washington, D.C., 1961.
      4p. (Doc. 18, English)
      At head of title: Pan American Highway Congresses, 1st Inter-American Traffic Seminar, Pan American Union, Washington, D.C., 1961.

    1. Traffic - Congresses. 2. Traffic safety. I. Pan American Union.

VF
612.84
H43e
Traffic safety.
    Highway Research Board.
      Effect of tinted windshields and vehicle headlighting on night visibility; presented at the thirty-second annual meeting, January 13-16, 1953. Washington, 1953.
      61 p. illus. (Its Bulletin 68)

    1. Traffic safety. 2. Visibility.

VF
614.8
:711.73
H43r
Traffic safety.
    Highway Research Board.
      Road-user characteristics; presented at the annual meeting, January 1952. Washington, 1952.
      66 p. (Its Bulletin 60)
      Bibliographies.
      Contents.-Development of criteria of safe motor vehicle operations.-Relation between psychological tests and driver performance.-Age and sex relation to accidents.-Human factors in highway-transport safety.-Analysis of certain variables related to sign legibility.-35-Millimeter airphotos for the study of driver behavior.   (over)

614.8
:711.73
L47c
Traffic safety.
    Little (Arthur D.) inc.
      Cost-effectiveness in traffic safety. New York, Praeger, 1968.
      167p. (Praeger special studies in U.S. economic and social development)
      Bibliography: p. 161-167.

    1. Traffic safety. I. Title.

VF
614.8
:711.73
H43h
Traffic safety.
    Highway Research Board.
      Highway accidents and related factors; presented at the thirty-third annual meeting, January 12-15, 1954. Washington, 1954.
      54 p. graphs, tables (Its Bulletin 91)

      Contains references.
      Contents.-Psychology of trip geography, Heinz Haber, Robert Brenner and Slade Hulbert.- Rural intersection accidents, William J. Miller, Jr.-Effect of shoulder width on accidents on two-lane tangents D.M.Belmont.-Effect of

---

VF
6148
:711.73
H43
Traffic safety.
    Highway Research Board.
      Statistical analysis of highway accidents, presented at the thirty-fourth annual meeting, January 11-14, 1955. Washington, 1956.
      31 p. charts (Its Bulletin 117)

      Contents: Accidents versus width of paved shoulders on California two-lane tangents-1951 and 1952, by D. M. Belmont. --Application of statistical quality-control techniques to analysis of highway-accident data, by Monroe Norden.
    1. Traffic safety. I. Title.

614.8
:711.73
L47
TRAFFIC SAFETY.
    LITTLE (ARTHUR D.) INC.
      THE STATE OF THE ART OF TRAFFIC SAFETY. A CRITICAL REVIEW AND ANALYSIS OF THE TECHNICAL INFORMATION ON FACTORS AFFECTING TRAFFIC SAFETY. CAMBRIDGE, MASS., 1966.
      624P.

      PREPARED FOR THE AUTOMOBILE MANUFACTURERS ASSOCIATION, INC. DISTRIBUTED BY U.S. CLEARINGHOUSE FOR FEDERAL SCIENTIFIC AND TECHNICAL INFORMATION A S DOCUMENT PB 175 613.

      (CONTINUED ON NEXT CARD)

VF
614.8
:711.73
H43h
Traffic safety.
    Highway Research Board. Highway accidents and related factors. 1954. (card 2)
      Contents continued.- enforcement on vehicle speeds, James Stannard Baker.-Automobile-barrier impacts, D.M. Severy and J.H. Mathewson.

    1. Traffic safety. I. Title.

VF
614.8
:711.73
H43ta
Traffic safety.
    Highway Research Board.
      Traffic-accident studies, presented at the thirty-second annual meeting, January 13-16, 1953. Washington, 1953.
      53 p. illus., graphs. (Its Bulletin 74)

      Contents: Traffic-Accident trends.- Relation between number of accidents and traffic volume at divided-highway intersections.-Interstate highway-accident study. -Relation of traffic signals to intersection accidents.
    1. Traffic safety.

614.8
:711.73
L47
LITTLE (ARTHUR D.) INC. THE STATE OF ...1966. (CARD 2)
    1. TRAFFIC SAFETY. 2. ACCIDENTS. I. AUTOMOBILE MANUFACTURERS ASSOCIATION. II. U.S. CLEARINGHOUSE FOR FEDERAL SCIENTIFIC AND TECHNICAL INFORMATION. III. TITLE.

VF
614.8
:711.73
H43m
Traffic safety.
    Highway Research Board
      Median design: effect on traffic behavior; presented at the thirty-fifth annual meeting, January 17-20, 1956. Washington, 1956.
      26 p. illus. (Its Bulletin 137)

    1. Traffic safety. I. Title.

VF
614.8
:711.73
H43t
Traffic safety.
    Highway Research Board.
      Traffic accidents and violations; presented at the thirty-fourth annual meeting, January 11-14, 1955. Washington, 1954.
      54 p. illus., graphs (Its Bulletin 120)
      Contents.-Role of roadway elements in Pennsylvania Turnpike accidents.-Relation of accidents to speed habits and other driver characteristics.-The habitual traffic violator. -Comparison of types of traffic violations for different years.-Automobile-crash injuries.
    1. Traffic safety.

711.73
M14
Traffic safety.
    Maiolo, John R
      Guidelines for estimating the adoption of highway protection measures, by J. R. Maiolo and H. Kirk Dansereau. University Park, Pa. Institute for Research on Land and Water Resources, Pennsylvania State University, 1967.
      20p. (Pennsylvania. State University. Research publication no. 52)

    1. Highways. 2. Traffic safety. I. Dansereau, H. Kirk., jt. au. II. Pennsylvania. State University. Institute for Research on Land and Water Resources. III. Title.

388
N17re   National Citizens' Commission on Inter-
national Cooperation.
Report of the Committee on Transportation.
[Wash.] Govt. Print. Off., 1965.
29p.   (Document 4. Final draft)
For presentation at the White House
Conference on International Cooperation,
Wash., Nov. 28-Dec. 1, 1965.

1. Transportation. 2. Traffic safety.
3. International relations. I. White House
Conference on International
Cooperation,   Wash., D.C., 1965.

614.8   TRAFFIC SAFETY.
:711.73 PRESIDENT'S HIGHWAY SAFETY CONFERENCE,
P72   WASHINGTON, D.C., 1949.
COMMITTEE REPORTS: ACCIDENT
RECORDS, EDUCATION, ENFORCEMENT,
ENGINEERING, LAWS AND ORDINANCES,
MOTOR VEHICLE ADMINISTRATION,
ORGANIZED PUBLIC SUPPORT, PUBLIC
INFORMATION, AND THE ACTION PROGRAM.
WASHINGTON, GOVT. PRINT. OFF., 1949.
9 V.

1. TRAFFIC SAFETY.   2. TRAFFIC
REGULATIONS.

Traffic safety.
690.015
(485)   Tynelius, Sven.
882   Fri sikt i gathörn (Clear view at street
R30   corners), av Sven Tynelius and Carl-Olof
1966   Berglund. Stockholm, Statens Institut för
Byggnadsforskning, 1966.
99p.   (Sweden. Statens Kommitté för
Byggnadsforskning. Rapport 30: 1966)
English summary.

1. Building research - Sweden.
2. Traffic safety. I. Berglund, Carl-
Olof, jt.au. II. Sweden. Statens Kommitté
för Byggnadsfor-   skning.

VF
711.73 Traffic safety.
N17   National Committee for Traffic Safety.
Building traffic safety into residential
developments.   [Chicago, Ill., 1950?]
40 p.   illus., diagrs.

1.Traffic safety. 2.Street planning. I.Title.

614.8   TRAFFIC SAFETY.
:711.73 PRESIDENT'S HIGHWAY SAFETY CONFERENCE,
P72N   WASHINGTON, D.C., 1949.
1949-50 INVENTORY AND GUIDE FOR
ACTION. WASHINGTON, GOVT. PRINT.
OFF., 1949.
76P.

1. TRAFFIC SAFETY.

Traffic safety.
388
(41)   U.K. Ministry of Transport. (Scottish
W54a   Development Dept.)
Advisory memorandum on urban traffic
engineering techniques. London, H.M.S.O., 1965.
92p.
Reprinted 1966.

1. Traffic - U.K. 2. Traffic safety. I. Title.
II. Title: Traffic engineering techniques.

Traffic safety.
388
N17b   National Committee on Urban Transportation,
no. 3E   District of Columbia.
Maintaining accident records. Chicago,
Public Administration Service, 1958.
18p.   (Procedure manual no. 3E)
"For use in conjunction with [its] Better
transportation for your city ... "

1. Transportation. 2. Traffic safety.
I. Public Administration Service.

614.8   Traffic safety.
:711.73 Stonex, K A
S76   Scientific highway design for
safer motoring. For presentation at
the Greenbrier Meeting, Detroit
Section, Society of Automotive
Engineers, Sept. 9-10-11, 1960.
New York, Society of Automotive
Engineers, 1960.
18p.

1. Traffic safety. 2. Highways -
Research. I. Society of Automotive
Engineers. II. Title. III. Title:
Highway   design for safer
motoring.

711.73   Traffic safety.
UNe   United Nations. (Economic Commission for
Europe. Inland Transport Committee)
European agreement on road markings done
at Geneva on 13 December 1957. [Geneva]
7p.   (E/ECE/303; E/ECE/TRANS/501)

English and French.

1.Traffic safety. I.Title: Road markings.

VF
614.8   National Safety Council.
:711.73 Doubtful about driving? Here's how
N17d   to avoid accidents. Chicago, [n.d.]
folder.

1. Traffic safety.

614.8   TRAFFIC SAFETY.
:711.73 Sweden. National Board of Urban Planning.
S82   Principles for urban planning with respect
to road safety; the SCAFT guidelines 1968.
In collaboration with the National Road
Administration. Stockholm, 1968.
34p. (Sweden. Statens Planverk. Publication no. 5 (English))

1. Traffic safety. I. Title.

614.8   United Nations. (Economic Commission
(083.41) for Europe)
:4)   Statistics of road traffic accidents in
UN   Europe, 1956,
Statistiques des accidents de la circulation routiere en Europe, 1956-
Geneva, 1958
v.   (E/ECE/32", (393); ECE/TRANS-
506,(516)
For complete information see shelflist.

1. Accidents - Statistics. 2 Traffic safety.

VF
614.8   National Safety Council.
:711.73 Worried about walking? Here's how to
N17   avoid accidents. Chicago, [n.d.]
folder.

1. Traffic safety.

VF
711.6   Sweden. Statens Kommitté för Byggnadsfor-
882   skning.
Bilar pa tomtmark. Stockholm, 1963.
[6]p.   (Its Blad 1963:1)

1. Site planning. 2. Traffic safety.

614.8   Traffic safety.
:711.73 U.S. Dept. of Commerce.
C65   The Federal role in highway safety: letter
from the Secretary of Commerce transmitting
the report on the investigation and study
made to determine what action can be taken
by the Federal Government to promote the
public welfare by increasing highway safety in the United States, pursuant to section 117 of the Federal-aid highway act of
1956, and under the general authority of
section 307 of title 23 of the United
States Code, entitled Highways. Washington, Govt.   Print. Off., 1959.
232p.
1. Traffic   safety.   2. Highways.

Traffic safety.
711.73
(749)   New Jersey. State Highway Dept.
N28h1   Highway spot improvements. Trenton, 1965.
93p.

1. Highways - New Jersey. 2. Traffic
safety. I. Title.

VF
711.4   Sweden. Statens Kommitté för Byggnadsfor-
882   skning.
Trafikolyckor i bostadsomraden.
Stockholm, 1963.
[4]p.   (Its Blad 1963:12)

1. Residential areas. 2. Traffic safety.

614.8   TRAFFIC SAFETY.
C65   U.S. CONGRESS. HOUSE. COMMITTEE ON
INTERSTATE AND FOREIGN COMMERCE.
TO ESTABLISH A NATIONAL ACCIDENT
PREVENTION CENTER.   HEARINGS,
EIGHTY-SEVENTH CONGRESS, SECOND SESSION
ON H.R. 133. WASHINGTON, GOVT. PRINT.
OFF., 1962.
328P.

HEARINGS HELD FEBRUARY 6-21, 1962.
1. ACCIDENTS. 2. ACCIDENTS -
STATISTICS. 3. TRAFFIC SAFETY.
I. U.S. NATIONAL ACCIDENT PREVENTION
CENTER (PROPOSED)

614.8   Traffic safety.
:711.73 New York (State) Legislature. Joint
N28   Legislative Committee on Motor Vehicles
and Traffic Safety.
Death or life? Albany, 1963.
72p.   (Its Legislative document (1963)
no. 76)

1. Traffic safety. 2. Accidents.
I. Title.

711.73   Traffic safety.
(7471) Triborough Bridge and Tunnel Authority.
T74s   Safety and our highways, by Robert
Moses. New York, 1966.
10p.

Reprinted from Newsday, June and
September 1966 in the interest of safer
and saner road travel.

1. Highways - New York (City) 2. Traffic safety. I. Moses, Robert. II. Newsday. III. Title.

614.8   Traffic safety.
:711.73 U.S. Congress. Senate. Committee on
C65f   Government Operations.
Federal role in traffic safety. Hearings
before the Subcommittee on Executive
Reorganization of the Committee on Government Operations, United States Senate,
Eighty-ninth Congress, first session.
Traffic safety: examination and review of
efficiency, economy, and coordination of
public and private agencies' activities
and the role of the Federal government.
Wash., Govt. Print. Off., 1966.
2 pts.   (Continued on
next card)

614.8
:711.73
C65f
U.S. Congress. Senate. Committee on
Government Operations. Federal role in
traffic safety. Hearings...1966.
(Card 2)
Hearings held March 22, 25, 26, 1966.

1. Traffic safety. I. Title.

388
(016)
C15
no. 11
Traffic safety- Bibl.
California. University. Institute of
Transportation and Traffic Engineering.
Traffic safety. Berkeley, Calif., 1957.
14p. (Its Library references no. 11)

1. Transportation - Bibl.
2. Traffic safety - Bibl.

614.8
:711.73
E56

N.a.1
Laf.c.2
Traffic safety; a national problem.
Eno Foundation for Highway Traffic Control.
Traffic safety; a national problem. A
symposium sponsored by the National Academy
of Engineering held in Washington, D.C.,
April 28, 1966. Saugatuck, Conn., 1967.
164p.

1. Traffic safety. I. National Academy
of Engineering, Wash., D.C. II. Title.

614.8
:711.73
C65f
1968
S-R
Traffic safety.
U.S. Congress. Senate. Committee on
Government Operations.
Federal role in traffic safety. Report
of the Committee on Government Operations,
United States Senate made by its Sub-
committee on Executive Reorganization.
Washington, Govt. Print. Off., 1968.
34p. (90th Cong. 2d sess. Senate.
Report no. 951)

1. Traffic safety. 2. Federal government. I. Title.

388
(016)
M17
Traffic safety - Bibliography.
Massachusetts Institute of Technology.
Bibliography of high speed ground transport. Part 1 A of [Survey of technology
for high speed ground transport] Prepared
for the U.S. Dept. of Commerce. Cambridge,
Mass., 1965.
82p.

1. Transportation - Bibl. 2. Traffic
safety - Bibl. I. Title.

388
(747245)
L62
Traffic study, the heartland of Nassau
County, N.Y.
Lockwood, Kessler and Bartlett.
Traffic study, the heartland of Nassau
County, N.Y. Prepared by Lockwood,
Kessler and Berlett, inc., and Alan M.
Voorhees & Associates, inc. Vincent A.
van Pragg, computer consultant. Syosset,
N.Y., 1966.
78p.
Prepared in cooperation with the Nassau
County, Dept. of Public Works.

(Cont'd on next card)

614.8
:711.73
C65H
1966
S-H
TRAFFIC SAFETY.
U.S. CONGRESS. SENATE. COMMITTEE ON
PUBLIC WORKS.
HIGHWAY SAFETY ACT OF 1966.
HEARINGS BEFORE THE SUBCOMMITTEE ON
PUBLIC ROADS... ON S. 3052.
WASHINGTON, GOVT. PRINT. OFF., 1966.
282P.

1. TRAFFIC SAFETY. I. TITLE.

711.73
(016)
T87
Traffic safety - Bibliography.
Turner, Laura R
Highway safety, 1960-1965: an annotated
bibliography, by Laura R. Turner and Louise
Philpot. Charlottesville, Virginia Highway
Research Council, 1966.
82p.
Sponsored jointly by the Virginia Dept.
of Highways and the University of Virginia.

1. Highways - Bibl. 2. Traffic safety -
Bibl. I. Philpot, Louise, jt. au.
II. Virginia Dept. of Highways.
III. Title. IV. Virginia Highway
Research Council.

388
(747245)
L62
Lockwood, Kessler and Bartlett. Traffic
study, the heartland of Nassau County,
N.Y...1966. (Card 2)

1. Traffic - Nassau Co., N.Y.
2. Traffic - Automation. I. Nassau Co.,
N.Y. Dept. of Public Works. II. Voorhees
(Alan M.) and Associates, jt.su.
III. Title.

614.8
:711.73
C657
1971
H-H
TRAFFIC SAFETY.
U.S. Congress. House. Committee on
Public Works.
Interstate 75 safety projects in Northern
Kentucky. Hearing before the Subcommittee
on Investigations and Oversight...Ninety-
second Congress, first session. Wash.,
Govt. Print. Off., 1972.
107p.
Hearing held Sept. 24, 1971.

1. Traffic safety. I. Title.

614.8
:711.73
(016)
N17b
TRAFFIC SAFETY - BIBLIOGRAPHY.
U.S. National Bureau of Standards.
Bibliography on motor vehicle and traffic
safety. Wash., 1971.
220p.

1. Traffic safety - Bibl.

351.81
C15
NO.35
TRAFFIC SURVEYS.
CALIFORNIA. UNIVERSITY. INSTITUTE OF
TRANSPORTATION AND TRAFFIC
ENGINEERING.
VEHICLE QUEUES IN MIXED TRAFFIC
STREAMS; PROGRESS REPORT, BY ROBERT M.
OLIVER AND OTHERS. BERKELEY, CALIF.,
1962.
12P. (ITS RESEARCH REPORT NO. 35)

1. TRAFFIC. 2. TRAFFIC - SURVEYS.
I. TITLE. II. OLIVER, ROBERT M.

614.8
:711.73
C65H
1966
S-R
TRAFFIC SAFETY.
U.S. CONGRESS. SENATE. COMMITTEE ON
PUBLIC WORKS.
HIGHWAY SAFETY ACT OF 1966. REPORT
TO ACCOMPANY S. 3052. WASHINGTON,
GOVT. PRINT. OFF., 1966.
27P. (89TH CONGRESS, 2D SESSION.
SENATE. REPORT NO. 1302)

1. TRAFFIC SAFETY. I. TITLE.

614.8
:711.73
(016)
N17h
TRAFFIC SAFETY - BIBLIOGRAPHY.
U.S. National Highway Safety Bureau.
Highway safety literature; annual cumulation
19

highway safety bibliography. Wash., 19
v.
For Library holdings see main entry.

1. Traffic safety - Bibl. I. Title.
II. Title: Highway safety bibliography.

351.81
C15
NO.34
TRAFFIC SURVEYS.
CALIFORNIA. UNIVERSITY. INSTITUTE OF
TRANSPORTATION AND TRAFFIC
ENGINEERING.
VEHICLE SPACE-OCCUPANCY IN MOVING
STREAMS OF TRAFFIC; PROGRESS REPORT, BY
ROBERT M. OLIVER AND OTHERS.
BERKELEY, CALIF., 1962.
16P. (ITS RESEARCH REPORT NO. 34)

1. TRAFFIC. 2. TRAFFIC - SURVEYS.
3. HIGHWAYS. I. TITLE. II. OLIVER,
ROBERT M.

388
N17r
Traffic safety.
U.S. National Transportation Safety Board.
Report to Congress, 1st-
1967-
Washington, National Transportation Safety
Board, Dept. of Transportation, 1958-
v. annual.

For complete information see main card.

1. Transportation. 2. Traffic safety.
I. U.S. Dept. of Transportation.

614.8
:711.73
(016)
N17hi
TRAFFIC SAFETY - BIBLIOGRAPHY.
U.S. National Highway Safety Bureau.
Highway safety literature; annual cumulation,
19

human factors bibliography. [Wash.] 19
v.
For Library holdings see main entry.

1. Traffic safety - Bibl. I. Title.
II. Title: Human factors bibliography.

388
:308
C65
Traffic surveys.
Coleman, Francis E
Evaluation of some of the elements of auto-
driver trip productions. A paper prepared by
Francis E. Coleman, Connecticut Highway Dept.
for presentation at 42nd annual meeting, Highway Research Board. [n.p.] 1963.
1v.

1. Traffic surveys. I. U.S. Highway
Research Board.

711.73
(489)
V17
TRAFFIC SAFETY.
Varming, Michael.
Motorveje i landskabet. København,
Statens Byggeforskningsinstitut, 1970.
118p. (SBI-byplanlaegning 12)
English summary.

Bibliography: p. 93-105.

1. Highways - Denmark. 2. Traffic safety.
I. Denmark. Statens Byggeforskningsinstitut.

614.8
:711.73
(016)
N17
TRAFFIC SAFETY - BIBLIOGRAPHY.
U.S. National Highway Safety Bureau.
Highway safety literature; annual cumulation
19

related areas bibliography. Wash., 19
v.
For Library holdings see main entry.

1. Traffic safety - Bibl. I. Title.
II. Title: Related areas bibliography.

388
F27
TRAFFIC SURVEYS.
Fertal, Martin J
Modal split; documentation of nine methods
for estimating transit usage, by Martin
J. Fertal and others. Chicago, U.S.
Bureau of Public Roads, Office of
Planning, 1966.
136p.
Bibliography: p. 134-136.
1. Transportation - Automation.
2. Journey to work. 3. Traffic surveys.
I. U.S. Bureau of Public Roads.
II. Title.

728.1
:303
F45

TRAFFIC SURVEYS.
Fink, Ira Stephen.
An approach to surveying housing and transportation patterns of college and university students, by Ira Stephen Fink and David Bradwell. Berkeley, Calif., University of California, 1971.
1v.

1. Housing surveys. 2. Traffic surveys. I. Bradwell, David, jt. au. II. Title.

388
H43t

Traffic surveys.
Highway Research Board.
Traffic assignment; presented at the 31st annual meeting, January 1952. Washington, 1952.
70 p. illus. (Its Bulletin 61)
References.

1. Traffic surveys.

388
:331
L16

Lapin, Howard S
Structuring the journey to work. Philadelphia, University of Pennsylvania Press, 1964.
227p. (Publications in the city planning series)
Bibliography: p. 215-221.

1. Journey to work. 2. Traffic surveys. I. Title.

388
G17

Traffic surveys.
Garrison, W L
A prolegomenon to the forecasting of transportation development, by W.L. Garrison and D.F. Marble. Final report of study conducted at Northwestern University for U.S. Army Aviation Materiel Laboratories, Fort Eustis, Virginia. Processed for U.S. Defense Documentation Center, Defense Supply Agency. [Wash.?] U.S. Dept. of Commerce, National Bureau of Standards, Institute for Applied Technology, 1965.
[64]p. (AD-621 514)
Distributed by U.S. Clearinghouse for Federal Scientific and Technical Information. (Cont'd on next card)

388
H43t
1959

Traffic surveys.
Highway Research Board.
Trip characteristics and traffic assignment. Presented at the 38th annual meeting January 5-9, 1959. Washington, 1959.
135p. (Its Bulletin no. 224)
National Research Council. Publication 684.

1. Traffic surveys. 2. Journey to work.

388
:308
M22

McConochie, W R
Study of terminal transfer facilities in conjunction with urban freeways, for Minnesota Dept. of Highways and Bureau of Public Roads. Chicago, DeLeuw, Cather and Co., 1967.
54p.
U.S. Clearinghouse for Federal Scientific and Technical Information document PB 175 759.

1. Traffic surveys. 2. Transportation. 3. Highways. (Cont'd on next card).

388
G17

Garrison, W.L. A prolegomenon to the forecasting of transportation development... (Card 2)

1. Transportation. 2. Traffic surveys. I. Marble, D.F., jt. au. II. Northwestern University. III. U.S. Defense Documentation Center for Scientific and Technical Information IV. U.S. Clearinghouse for Federal Scientific and Technical Information. V. Title.

388
H433

Traffic surveys.
Highway Research Board.
Trip generation and urban freeway planning. Presented at the 38th annual meeting January 5-9, 1959. Washington, 1959.
125p. (Its Bulletin no. 230)
National Research Council. Publication 690.

1. Traffic surveys. 2. Journey to work.

388
:308
M22

McConochie, W R Study of terminal transfer facilities in conjunction with urban freeways...1967. (Card 2)

4. Urban renewal. I. DeLeuw, Cather & Co., Chicago. II. Minnesota. Dept. of Highways. III. U.S. Bureau of Public Roads. IV. U.S. Clearinghouse for Federal Scientific and Technical Information. V. Title.

388
:308
H25

Traffic surveys.
Hemmens, George C
The structure of urban activity linkages. Chapel Hill, Center for Urban and Regional Studies, Institute for Research in Social Science, University of North Carolina, 1966.
54p. (An Urban studies research monograph)

1. Traffic surveys. 2. Journey to work. I. North Carolina. University. Institute for Research in Social Science. II. Title.

FOLIO
388
H68w

Traffic surveys.
Houston, Tex. Public Service Dept.
World-wide transit study, by Clinton Owsley, Director. Houston, Tex., 1963.
1v.

1. Transportation. 2. Traffic surveys. 3. Journey to work. I. Owsley, Clinton. II. Title.

388
:308
M17

Traffic surveys.
Massachusetts Institute of Technology.
Survey of technology for high speed ground transport. Part 1 [of the Northeast Corridor Transportation Project] Prepared for the United States Dept. of Commerce. Cambridge, Mass., 1965.
271p. (PB 168 648)
Distributed by Clearinghouse for Federal Scientific and Technical Information.

1. Traffic surveys. 2. Transportation. 3. Journey to work. I. Northeast Corridor Transportation Project. II. Title.

388
H43o

Traffic surveys.
Highway Research Board.
Origin and destination; 4 reports. Wash., Highway Research Board, Div. of Engineering, National Academy of Sciences-National Academy of Engineering, National Research Council, 1966.
88p. (Its Highway research record no. 141)
National Research Council. Publication 1385.

1. Transportation. 2. Journey to work. 3. Traffic surveys.

711.73
(772)
I52

Traffic surveys.
Indiana. State Highway Commission. (Urban Planning Section)
Urban planning facts in Indiana. Indianapolis, 1964.
v.
Contents:-Series 1. The Federal aid highway act of 1962.-Series 3. Coordination.-Series 4. Status of planning, September 1, 1964.-Series 5. Data collection and analysis forms.

1. Highways - Indiana. 2. Transportation - Indiana. 3. Traffic surveys. I. Title: Federal aid highway act of 1962. II. Title.

388
(786)
M65

Traffic surveys.
Montana. State Highway Commission.
Urban transportation survey of Great Falls, Montana. Conducted by Planning Survey, Div. of Montana State Highway Commission in cooperation with U.S. Dept. of Commerce, Bureau of Public Roads and the city of Great Falls. [Helena, Mont.] 1961-1965.
4v.

1. Transportation - Great Falls, Mont. 2. Highways - Great Falls, Mont. 3. Parking - Great Falls, Mont. 4. Traffic surveys. I. U.S. Bureau of Public Roads.

388
:308
H43

TRAFFIC SURVEYS.
Highway Research Board.
Origin and destination technology; 9 reports. Wash., 1968.
96p. (Highway research record no. 250; National Research Council publication 1397)

1. Traffic surveys. 2. Journey to work. I. Title.

388
:308
I57

International Research and Technology Corp.
Study of major urban activity circulation systems and their impact on congested areas. Final report. Wash., 1971.
1v. (IRT-205-R)
Prepared for U.S. Dept. of Housing and Urban Development under Contract H-1067.

1. Traffic surveys. I. U.S. Dept. of Housing and Urban Development. II. Title.

388
N17b
no.3A

Traffic surveys.
National Committee on Urban Transportation, District of Columbia.
Measuring traffic volumes. Chicago, Public Administration Service, 1958.
39p. graphs. (Procedure manual 3A)
"For use in conjunction with [its] Better transportation for your city ... "

1. Transportation. 2. Traffic surveys. I. Public Administration Service.

VF
308
:388
H43

Traffic surveys.
Highway Research Board.
Traffic assignment by mechanical methods; presented at the thirty-fifth annual meeting, January 17-20, 1956. Washington, 1956.
77 p. (Its Bulletin 130)

1. Traffic surveys.

388
:308
K22

TRAFFIC SURVEYS.
Keefer, Louis E
Urban travel patterns for hospitals, universities, office buildings, and capitols, by Louis E. Keefer and others. [Wash.] Highway Research Board, Div. of Engineering, 1969.
144p. (National Cooperative Highway Research Program report 62)
Bibliography: p. 137-144.

1. Traffic surveys. I. Title.

388
:308
(766)
045

TRAFFIC SURVEYS.
OKLAHOMA. DEPT. OF HIGHWAYS.
MANUAL OF PROCEDURE FOR CONDUCTING AN ECONOMIC SURVEY, PREPARED BY OKLAHOMA STATE HIGHWAY DEPARTMENT OF STATISTICS. OKLAHOMA CITY, 1956.
1 v.

1. TRAFFIC SURVEYS. I. TITLE.

388 (79537) 072 Introduction
Traffic surveys.
Oregon. State Highway Dept.
An introduction to Salem Area Transportation Study. [Prepared] in cooperation with the U.S. Dept. of Commerce, Bureau of Public Roads. Salem, Oregon State Highway Commission, 1964.
12p.

1. Transportation - Salem, Or. 2. Master plan - Salem, Or. 3. Traffic surveys. 4. Journey to work. I. Salem (Or.) Area Transportation Study. II. U.S. Bureau of Public Roads. III. Title.

---

388 :331 T11
Traffic surveys.
Taafe, Edward J
The peripheral journey to work; a geographic consideration, by Edward J. Taaffe and others. [Evanston, Ill.] Published for the Transportation Center at Northwestern University, by Northwestern University Press, 1963.
125p.

1. Journey to work. 2. Traffic surveys. I. Northwestern University. Transportation Center. II. Title.

---

388 C52r
Traffic surveys.
U.S. Clearinghouse for Federal Scientific and Technical Information.
Report of the Panel on Transportation Research and Development of the Commerce Technical Advisory Board, to the Secretary of Commerce. Springfield, Va., 1965.
90p. (PB 167 186)

1. Transportation. 2. Traffic surveys. 3. Governmental research. I. U.S. Panel on Transportation Research and Development. II. Title.

---

388 (79537) 072
Traffic surveys.
Oregon. State Highway Dept.
Salem Area Transportation Study. Survey conducted in cooperation with U.S. Dept. of Commerce, Bureau of Public Roads. Salem, Oregon, State Highway Commission, 1961-
v.
Cover title: A study in Salem's transportation.
Contents:-Vol. 1. Factual data report.-Vol. 2. Data projection - 1982.
U.S. Dept. of Housing and Urban Development. UPAP.

(Continued on next card)

---

388 (764) T29ℓ v.1
Traffic surveys.
Texas. Highway Dept.
Lubbock urban transportation plan, Lubbock, Texas, Hub of the Plains, origin destination survey. Sponsoring agencies: City of Lubbock, County of Lubbock, in cooperation with the U.S. Dept. of Commerce, Bureau of Public Roads. [Austin, Tex.] 1964.
56p. (Vol. 1)

1. Transportation - Lubbock, Tex. 2. Traffic surveys. 3. Journey to work. I. U.S. Bureau of Public Roads. II. Title.

614.8 I711.73 C65S 1957 H-H
TRAFFIC SAFETY.
U.S. CONGRESS. HOUSE. COMMITTEE ON INTERSTATE AND FOREIGN COMMERCE. SURFACE TRANSPORTATION; SAFETY LEGISLATION HEARINGS, EIGHTY-FIFTH CONGRESS, FIRST SESSION ON BILLS TO PROVIDE FOR GREATER SAFETY IN SURFACE TRANSPORTATION. WASHINGTON, GOVT. PRINT. OFF., 1957.
241P.

HEARINGS HELD MARCH 28, 29 AND APRIL 1, AND 12, 1957.

1. TRAFFIC SAFETY. I. TITLE.

---

388 (79537) 072
Oregon. State Highway Dept. Salem Area Transportation Study...1961. (Card 2)

1. Transportation - Salem, Or. 2. Master plan - Salem, Or. 3. Traffic surveys. 4. Journey to work. I. Title. II. U.S. HUD-UPAP. Salem, Or.

---

388 :331 T36
Traffic surveys.
Thomas, Thomas C
The value of time for passenger cars; an experimental study of commuters' values. Prepared for Bureau of Public Roads, U.S. Dept. of Transportation, Menlo Park, Calif., Stanford Research Institute, 1967.
150p. (SRI Project 5074)
Distributed by U.S. Clearinghouse for Federal Scientific and Technical Information as document PB 175 731.
1. Journey to work. 2. Traffic surveys. 3. Highways - Research. I. Stanford Research Institute. II. U.S. Clearinghouse for Federal Scientific and Technical Information. III. Title.

---

388 :308 V63
TRAFFIC SURVEYS.
Vogt, Ivers and Associates.
Social and economic factors affecting intercity travel. Cincinnati, 1969.
68p. (National Cooperative Highway Research Program report 70)
Research sponsored by the American Association of State Highway Officials in cooperation with the Bureau of Public Roads.

1. Traffic surveys. I. U.S. Bureau of Public Roads. II. Title.

---

388 S38
TRAFFIC SURVEYS.
Shunk, C A
The journey to work: a singular basis for travel pattern surveys, by G.A. Shunk and others. [Lafayette, Ind.] Purdue University, 1968.
[20]p. (Purdue University. Engineering reprints. Civil engineering CE 263)
Reprinted from: Highway research record 240 (1968) p. 32-51.
1. Transportation. 2. Journey to work. 3. Traffic surveys. I. Purdue University. II. Title.

---

388 :308 T68 Appx.
Traffic surveys.
Towne (Robin M.) and Associates.
An investigation of the effect of freeway traffic noise on apartment rents. Appendix. Prepared for the Oregon State Highway Commission, State Highway Dept. and the U.S. Dept. of Commerce, Bureau of Public Roads. Seattle, 1966.
1v.
Distributed by: Clearinghouse for Federal Scientific and Technical Information as Document PB 176 345.
1. Traffic surveys. 2. Noise. 3. Highways - Economic effect. I. Oregon. State Highway Commission. II. Title.

---

388 W45a
Traffic surveys.
Wilson, Nigel H M
CARS; computer aided routing system. Cambridge, School of Engineering, Massachusetts Institute of Technology, 1967.
80p. (Massachusetts Institute of Technology. Dept. of Civil Engineering. Research report #R67-12)

1. Transportation. 2. Traffic surveys. 3. Journey to work. I. Massachusetts Institute of Technology (School of Engineering) II. Title.

711.73 (768) 854
Traffic surveys.
Smith (Wilbur) and Associates.
Statistical evaluation of mathematical projection model, Chattanoga, Tennessee. Prepared for the Tennessee Dept. of Highways, in cooperation with U.S. Dept. of Commerce, Bureau of Public Roads. New Haven, 1961.
26p.

1. Highways - Tennessee. 2. Traffic surveys. 3. Journey to work. I. Tennessee. Dept. of Highways.

---

388 :308 T68
Traffic surveys.
Towne (Robin M.) and Associates.
An investigation of the effect of freeway traffic noise on apartment rents. Prepared for the Oregon State Highway Commission, State Highway Dept. and the U.S. Dept. of Commerce, Bureau of Public Roads. Seattle, 1966.
121p.
Distributed by Clearinghouse for Federal Scientific and Technical Information as PB 176 344.
1. Traffic surveys. 2. Noise. 3. Highways - Economic effect. I. Oregon. State Highway Commission. II. Title.

---

388 :308 W63
TRAFFIC SURVEYS.
Wohl, Martin.
A methodology for forecasting peak and off-peak travel volumes, by Martin Wohl. The Urban Institute, Wash., D.C. [n.p.] [1969?]
98p.
Draft of paper to appear in Highway Research Board publication.

1. Traffic surveys. 2. Transportation. 3. Journey to work. I. Highway Research Board. II. Title.

---

388 :308 S78
Traffic surveys.
Studies of weaving and merging traffic: a symposium. Weaving practices on one-way highways, by F. Houston Wynn. Merging traffic characteristics applied to acceleration lane design, by Stewart M. Gourlay. A study of merging vehicular traffic movements, by Richard I. Strickland. [n.p.] Bureau of Highway Traffic, Yale University, published with funds from Eno Foundation for Highway Traffic Control, 1948.
130p. (Yale highway traffic series. Technical report no. 4)

Continued on next card)

---

388 :308 T74
TRAFFIC SURVEYS.
Tri-State Transportation Commission. (Connecticut-New Jersey-New York)
Direct traffic estimation method; systematic inputs and method of computation. New York, 1967.
20p. (Its Interim technical report 4075-7111)

1. Traffic surveys. 2. Transportation. 3. Journey to work. I. Title.

---

308 :388 Y17
Traffic surveys.
Yale University. Bureau of Highway Traffic.
Quality and theory of traffic flow; a symposium by Bruce D. Greenshields and others. New Haven, 1961.
188p.

1. Traffic surveys. 2. Journey to work. I. Greenshields, Bruce D.

---

388 :308 S78
Studies of weaving and merging traffic: a symposium...1948. (Card 2)

1. Traffic surveys. 2. Journey to work. I. Wynn, F. Houston. II. Gourlay, Stewart M. III. Strickland, Richard I. IV. Yale University. Bureau of Highway Traffic.

711.729 (41) U54
Traffic surveys.
U.K. Ministry of Housing and Local Government.
Parking in town centers. London, H.M. Stat. Off., 1965.
46p. (Its Design bulletin no. 7)
At head of title: Ministry of Housing and Local Government. Ministry of Transport, Scottish Development Dept. The Welsh Off.

1. Parking - U.K. 2. Traffic surveys.

---

388 (758231) A75 no.1
Traffic surveys - Atlanta.
Atlanta. Metropolitan Planning Commission.
Physical inventory: automotive and transit facilities. Atlanta, 1956.
63p. maps, tables. (Transportation policy project report no. 1)
U.S. Urban Renewal Administration, Urban Planning Assistance Program.

1. Transportation - Atlanta. 2. Traffic surveys - Atlanta. I. U.S. Urban Renewal Administration. Urban Planning Assistance Program.

384
M27a
· Traffic surveys - Baltimore.
Metropolitan Washington Council of Governments.
Air travel demand in the Washington-Baltimore region, 1970-1990; a summary report. Wash., 1968.
21p.
U.S. Dept. of Housing and Urban Development. UPAP.
HUD project no. D.C. P-3.
1. Air transportation. 2. Airports. 3. Traffic surveys - District of Columbia metropolitan area. 4. Traffic surveys - Baltimore. I. Title. II. Baltimore. Regional Planning Council.
(Cont'd on next card)

308
:67
V47
1956
Virginia. University. Bureau of Population and Economic Research. The impact of...
1956. (card 2)
244 p. graphs, tables.
Have also abridged ed., 1956 [n.p]
308.67 V47 1956 abridged.
1. Impact of industry. 2. Journey to work. 3. Traffic surveys - Charlotte Co., Va. I. U.S. Bureau of Public Roads.

FOLIO
388
(7531)
D25
Traffic surveys - District of Columbia.
De Leuw, Cather and Co.
Mass transportation survey, National Capital region: civil engineering report for the National Capital Planning Commission and the National Capital Regional Planning Council. Chicago, 1 59.
98p. illus., maps, tables.
1. Transportation - District of Columbia, metropolitan area. 2. Traffic surveys - District of Columbia metropolitan area. I. U.S. National Capital Planning Commission. II. U.S. National Capital Regional Planning Council.

384
M27a
Metropolitan Washington Council of Governments. Air travel...1968. (Card 2)
IV. U.S. HUD-UPAP. District of Columbia metropolitan area. V. U.S. HUD-UPAP. Baltimore.

VF
388
(77311)
C34
Traffic surveys - Chicago, Ill.
Chicago. Bureau of Streets.
Cordon count data on the central business district, May 1948. Cooperating agency, Chicago Association of Commerce. Chicago, Traffic Engineering Division, Bureau of Streets, Dept. of Streets & Electricity [1948]
14 l. 28 cm.
Cover title.
"The eighteenth of a series of cordon counts taken since 1926."
Ill.
1. Traffic surveys—Chicago. I. Title.
HE372.C4 1948   388.3   50-16692
Library of Congress [1]

711.73
:330
(7531)
G26
Traffic surveys - District of Columbia metropolitan area.
George Washington University, Washington, D.C.
Parkway impact study; an investigation of the effects of parkways in the National Capital Region. Prepared ... under terms of National Parks Service, in cooperation with the Bureau of Public Roads [and others.] [Washington] 1962.
152p.
(Cont'd. on next card)

388
(763181)
S54
TRAFFIC SURVEYS - BATON ROUGE, LOUISIANA.
Smith (Wilbur) and Associates.
Metropolitan area transportation study, Baton Rouge. Columbia, S.C., 1967-68.
3v.
1. Transportation - Baton Rouge, La. 2. Journey to work. 3. Traffic surveys - Baton Rouge, La. I. Title.

388
:308
(77311)
S17
TRAFFIC SURVEYS - CHICAGO.
Sato, Kathalie G
Methods for estimating trip destination by trip purpose. Chicago, Chicago Area Transportation Study, 1966.
60p.
1. Traffic surveys - Chicago. 2. Journey to work. I. Chicago Area Transportation Study. II. Title.

711.73
:330
(7531)
G26
George Washington University, Washington, D.C. Parkway impact study ...
(Card 2)
1. Highways - Economic effect - District of Columbia. 2. Transportation - District of Columbia metropolitan area. 3. Traffic surveys - District of Columbia metropolitan area. 4. Journey to work. I. U.S. Bureau of Public Roads. II. Title. III. U.S. National Parks Service.

711
(016)
C65
no.173
TRAFFIC SURVEYS - BIBLIOGRAPHY.
Stutz, Frederick P
Research on intra-urban social travel: introduction and bibliography. San Diego, San Diego State College, Dept. of Geography, 1971.
12p. (Council of Planning Librarians. Exchange bibliography no. 173)
1. Planning - Bibl. 2. Traffic surveys - Bibl. I. California. State College, San Diego. II. Title: Intra-urban social travel. (Series: Council of Planning Librarians. Exchange bibliography no. 173)

388
(77311)
T15
TRAFFIC SURVEYS - CHICAGO.
Talvitie, Antti Petri.
An econometric model for downtown work trips. Chicago, Chicago Area Transportation Study, 1971.
123p.
1. Transportation - Chicago. 2. Traffic surveys - Chicago. I. Chicago Area Transportation Study. II. Title.

Folio
388
(7531)
G45
Traffic surveys - District of Columbia metropolitan area.
Gilman (W.C.) and Co.
Traffic, revenue and operating costs; by W.C. Gilman & Co. and Alan M. Voorhees and Associates. Rev. McLean, Va., 1969.
106p.
Prepared for the Washington Metropolitan Area Transit Authority.
1. Transportation - District of Columbia metropolitan area. 2. Journey to work. 3. Traffic surveys - District of Columbia metropolitan area. I. Title. II. Voorhees (Alan M.) and Associates. III. Washington Metropolitan Area Transit Authority.

Folio
388
(777621)
I68
Traffic surveys - Cedar Rapids, Iowa.
Iowa. State Highway Commission. (Div. of Planning)
Cedar Rapids metropolitan area; origin and destination, traffic report. Prepared in cooperation with the U.S. Dept. of Commerce, Bureau of Public Roads. Cedar Rapids, Iowa, 1965.
145p.
1. Transportation - Cedar Rapids metropolitan area. 2. Journey to work. 3. Traffic surveys - Cedar Rapids, Iowa. I. U.S. Bureau of Public Roads. II. Title.

388
(77178)
O34
Traffic surveys - Cincinnati, Ohio.
Ohio. Dept. of Highways.
Report on the Cincinnati metropolitan traffic survey; a study of traffic movements, 1946, conducted by U.S. Public Roads Administration, Ohio Department of Highways, Kentucky Department of Highways [and] city of Cincinnati, Ohio. [Columbus, 1946]
156 p. maps (part fold.)
1.Traffic surveys-Cincinnati, O. I.Title: Cincinnati metropolitan traffic survey. II.U.S. Public Roads Administration.

384
M27a
Traffic surveys - District of Columbia metropolitan area.
Metropolitan Washington Council of Governments.
Air travel demand in the Washington-Baltimore region, 1970-1990; a summary report. Wash., 1968.
21p.
U.S. Dept. of Housing and Urban Development. UPAP.
HUD project no. D.C P-3.
1. Air transportation. 2. Airports. 3. Traffic surveys - District of Columbia metropolitan area. 4. Traffic surveys - Baltimore. I. Title. II. Baltimore. Regional Planning Council.
(Cont'd on next card)

:330
H43
Traffic surveys - Charlotte Co., Va.
Highway Research Board.
Some economic effects of highway improvement, presented at the 32d annual meeting, January 13-16, 1953. Washington, 1953.
21 p. (Its Bulletin 67)
Contents.-Economic evaluation of two Indiana bypasses.-Socio-economic relationships of highway travel of residences of a rural area.
1.Highways - Economic effect. 2.Highways-Indiana. 3.Traffic surveys - Charlotte Co., Va. (Series)

388
H43f
Traffic surveys - Cook County, Ill.
Highway Research Board.
Factors influencing travel patterns. Washington, 1955.
94p. graphs, maps, tables. (Its Bulletin 119)
Contents.-Trends in traffic diversion on Edens Expressway, William J. Mortimer.-Objective and subjective correlates of expressway use, E. Wilson Campbell and Robert McCargar
(Continued on Card 2)

384
M27a
Metropolitan Washington Council of Governments. Air travel...1968. (Card 2)
IV. U.S. HUD-UPAP. District of Columbia metropolitan area. V. U.S. HUD-UPAP. Baltimore.

308
:67
V47
1956
Traffic surveys - Charlotte Co., Va.
Virginia. University. Bureau of Population and Economic Research.
The impact of industry in a southern rural county; changes in road use, travel habits and socio-economic characteristics in Charlotte County, Virginia, five years after the establishment of a new manufacturing plant, prepared... in cooperation with the Division of Traffic and Planning, Virginia Department of Highways, and the U.S. Bureau of Public Roads. [Charlottesville, Va.] 1956
(see card 2)

388
H43f
Highway Research Board.   Factors influencing travel patterns.... (Card 2)
Induced traffic on Chesapeake Bay Bridge, Ernest W. Bunting. -Intracity traffic movements, F. Houston Wynn. -Evaluation of intercity-travel desire, Willa Mylroie.
1. Traffic. 2. Traffic surveys - Cook County, Ill. 3. Traffic surveys - Washington. 4. Traffic surveys - Maryland. I. Title: Travel patterns.

FOLIO
388
(7531)
S54
Traffic surveys - District of Columbia metropolitan area.
Smith (Wilbur) and Associates.
Mass transportation survey, National Capital region: traffic engineering study, 1958. New Haven? 1959.
125p. diagrs., maps, tables.
Report submitted to the National Capital Planning Commission and the National Capital Regional Planning Council.
1. Transportation - District of Columbia metropolitan area. 2. Traffic surveys - District of Columbia metropolitan area. I. U.S. National Capital Planning Commission. II. U.S. National Capital Regional Planning Council.

Traffic surveys - El Paso metropolitan area.

388
(764)
T29e
Texas. Highway Dept. (Planning Survey Div.)
El Paso metropolitan area traffic survey.
In cooperation with the City of El Paso,
Texas and the U.S. Department of Commerce,
Bureau of Public Roads. San Antonio, 1958.
48p. illus., diagrs., maps.

1. Traffic surveys - El Paso metropolitan
area.

Traffic surveys - Iowa.

388
(777)
W41
Wiant, Rex H
A simplified method for forecasting urban
traffic, by Rex H. Wiant, Traffic and Highway
Planning Department, Division of Planning, Iowa
State Highway Commission, Ames, Iowa. [n.p.]
1961.
33p.
For presentation at Highway Research Board,
Origin and Destination Surveys Committee
Meeting, Jan. 1961.

1. Traffic surveys - Iowa. 2. Journey to work.
I. Iowa. State Highway   Commission.

TRAFFIC SURVEYS - MARYLAND.

388
:308
(752)
M17
Maryland. Bureau of Highway Statistics.
Traffic trends, 19

[Annapolis] 19

v. annual.

For Library holdings see main entry.
1. Traffic surveys - Md. I. Title.

TRAFFIC SURVEYS = FERNDALE, MICH.

3588
FERNDALE, MICH. CITY PLAN COMMISSION.
TRAFFIC STUDY. BY PARKINS, ROGERS AND
ASSOCIATES, INC. DETROIT, 1969.
43L. (HUD 701 REPORT)

1. TRAFFIC SURVEYS = FERNDALE, MICH.
I. PARKINS, ROGERS AND ASSOCIATES.
II. HUD. 701. FERNDALE, MICH.

Traffic surveys - Lafayette, Ia.

388
(763471)
S54
Smith (Wilbur) and Associates.
Lafayette metropolitan area transportation study. Prepared for Louisiana Dept.
of Highways in cooperation with U.S. Dept.
of Transportation, Federal Highway Administration, Bureau of Public Roads, and
Lafayette Parish and City of Lafayette.
Columbia, S.C., 1967.
2v.
Contents.-v.1 Inventory of current
travel demands and facilities.-v.2:
Future travel demands and recommended
transportation   plan.

(Cont'd on next card)

Traffic surveys - Morristown, Tenn.

711.73
(76892)
M67
Morristown, Tenn. Regional Planning Commis-
sion.
Detailing of major road plan, Morristown.
Traffic survey of July 15, 1958. Morristown,
1958.
68p. diagrs., maps, tables.
U.S. Urban Renewal Administration, Urban
Planning Assistance Program.

1. Highways - Morristown, Tenn. 2. Traffic
surveys - Morristown, Tenn. I. U.S. Urban
Renewal Administration. Urban Planning
Assistance Program.

TRAFFIC SURVEYS = FLINT, MICH.

711.4
(77437)
F54c
FLINT, MICH. CITY PLANNING BOARD.
A COMPREHENSIVE CITY PLAN FOR FLINT,
MICHIGAN. FLINT, FLINT INSTITUTE OF
RESEARCH AND PLANNING, 1937
PTS.

CONTENTS.=PT.1. TRAFFIC SURVEY AND
THOROUGHFARE PLAN.

1. CITY PLANNING = FLINT, MICH.
2. TRAFFIC SURVEYS - FLINT, MICH.
3. STREETS = FLINT, MICH.

388
(763471)
S54
Smith (Wilbur) and Associates.
Lafayette metropolitan area...1967.
(Card 2)

1. Transportation - Lafayette, La.
2. Journey to work. 3. Highways -
Lafayette, La. 4. Traffic surveys -
Lafayette, La. I. Louisiana. Dept. of
Highways. II. Title.

TRAFFIC SURVEYS - NETHERLANDS.

388
:308
(492)
D25
Delft. Technische Hogeschool.
De verkeersproduktie van de Bomenwijk.
Delft, Netherlands, 1965.
57p.

1. Traffic surveys - Netherlands.

Traffic surveys - Hartford, Conn.

388
:308
(7463)
C65
Connecticut. State Highway Dept.
Hartford area traffic study report.
Prepared by Planning Research Unit,
Division of Planning, Connecticut Highway
Dept. in cooperation with the Bureau of
Public Roads, United States Dept. of
Commerce. Hartford, 1961.
v.1

1. Traffic surveys - Hartford, Conn.
2. Journey to work. I. Title.

Traffic surveys - Lake Charles, La.

388
(763541)
L68
Louisiana. *Dept. of Highways (1942-)*
Traffic survey of Lake Charles metropolitan area, by
Louisiana Dept. of Highways and local governmental units,
in cooperation with U. S. Public Roads Administration,
1947. [Baton Rouge? 1947?]
vii, 63 p. col. illus., col. maps. 22 x 28 cm.

1. Traffic surveys—Lake Charles, La. I. U.S. Public Roads
Administration.
HE372.L25 1947   388.3   49-47362*
Library of Congress   [1]

Traffic surveys - New York metropolitan region

388
:308
(7472)
E24
Edie, L C
Analysis of single lane traffic flow, by
L.C. Edie and others. Warren, Mich., Research Laboratories, General Motors Corp.,
1963.
[7]p.
Reprinted from: Traffic engineering, Jan.,
1963.
1. Traffic surveys - New York metropolitan
region. I. Title. II. General Motors Corp.
III. Traffic engineering.

Traffic surveys - Hastings, Neb.

388
(782397)
H67
Hoskins (Harold) and Associates.
Traffic survey and urban development
plan for Hastings, Nebraska. In cooperation with U.S. Dept. of Commerce, Bureau
of Public Roads and State of Nebraska, Dept.
of Roads and Irrigation. Lincoln, 1954.
1v. maps, tables.

1. Traffic surveys - Hastings, Neb.
I. Nebraska. Dept. of Roads and Irrigation.

Traffic surveys - Manhattan, Kan.

388
(78128)
K15
Kansas. State Highway Commission.
Origin-destination survey, Manhattan,
Kansas. [Topeka] 1955.
59p. illus., plates, tables.

"In cooperation with U.S. Dept. of Commerce,
Bureau of Public Roads."

1. Traffic surveys - Manhattan, Kan.

Traffic surveys - New Orleans metropolitan
area.

FOLIO
388
(76335)
L68
Louisiana. Dept. of Highways.
New Orleans; metropolitan area trans-
portation study, 1959-1960, 1960-1980.
Vol. 1. Characteristics of existing traffic.
Vol. 2. Outlook for the future. By
Louisiana Dept. of Highways, Traffic and
Planning Section, in cooperation with
Bureau of Public Roads, Dept. of Commerce,
[Baton Rouge?] 1960.
2v.

1. Transportation - New Orleans metropolitan area.
2. Traffic surveys -   New Orleans metropolitan area.

Traffic surveys - Hattiesburg, Miss.

388
(76281)
M47t
Mississippi. State Highway Dept. (Traffic
and Planning Division)
Traffic survey, Hattiesburg, Mississippi
[1956] In cooperation with U.S. Dept. of
Commerce Bureau of Public Roads and the
city of Hattiesburg. Jackson, 1958.
119p. Illus., maps, tables.

1. Traffic surveys - Hattiesburg, Miss.
I. U.S. Bureau of Public Roads.

Traffic surveys - Maryland.

388
H43f
Highway Research Board.
Factors influencing travel patterns.
Washington, 1955.
94p. graphs, maps, tables. (Its Bulletin
119)

Contents.-Trends in traffic diversion on
Edens Expressway, William J. Mortimer.-
Objective and subjective correlates of express-
way use, E. Wilson Campbell and Robert McCargar

(Continued on Card 2)

Traffic surveys - New York (City)

388
:308
(7471)
N28
New York (City) Transit Authority.
The effect of the 1966 transit strike on the
travel behavior of regular transit users. Prepared from a survey made by Berrington and
Company, division of Day and Zimmerman, Inc.
[n.p., 1967?]
116p.
U.S. Dept. of Housing and Urban Development.
Mass Transportation Demonstration Grant Program.

(Cont'd on next card)

Traffic survey - Hawaii.

388
(969)
H18
Hawaii. Territorial Highway Department.
Traffic census, 1953 - Prepared by
the Hawaii Highway Planning Survey, Territorial
Highway Department... in cooperation with the
U.S. Department of Commerce, Bureau of Public
Roads. [Honolulu] 1954 -
v. in   diagrs., maps, tables.
Contents.-[pt. 1] Island of Hawaii.-[pt. 2]
Island of Kauai -[pt. 3] Islands of Maui and
Molokai. - [pt. 4] Island of Oahu.
1. Traffic survey - Hawaii. I. U.S.
(Bureau of) Public   Roads.

388
H43f
Highway Research Board.   Factors influencing
travel patterns.... (Card 2)

-Induced traffic on Chesapeake Bay Bridge,
Ernest W. Bunting. -Intracity traffic movements,
F. Houston Wynn. -Evaluation of intercity-
travel desire, Willa Mylroie.

1. Traffic. 2. Traffic surveys - Cook County,
Ill. 3. Traffic surveys - Washington. 4.
Traffic surveys - Maryland. I. Title: Travel
patterns.

388
:308
(7471)
N28
New York (City) Transit Authority. The effect
of the 1966 transit strike on the travel
behavior of regular transit users...[1967?]
(Card 2)

1. Traffic surveys - New York (City)
2. Transportation - New York (City) 3. Journey
to work. I. Berrington and Co. II. Title.
III. U.S. HUD-Demonstration Grant Program.

388
:331
N28m

Traffic surveys - N.Y.

New York (State) Dept. of Public Works.
(Subdivision of Transportation Planning
and Programming)
A model-choice model--description of basic
concepts. Prepared by Hohn R. Hamburg and
Charles Guinn. Albany, N.Y., 1966.
19p. (Its Publication TP00-130-01)

1. Journey to work. 2. Traffic surveys
- N.Y. I. Hamburg, Charles R. II. Guinn,
Charles. III. Title.

711
(7946)
P17

Traffic surveys - San Francisco Bay area.

Parsons, Brinckerhoff, Hall and MacDonald.
Technical reference on procedures used in
physical planning studies for the San
Francisco Bay area rapid transit survey,
1953-1955. New York, 1955.
61p.

1. Planning - San Francisco Bay area.
2. Traffic surveys - San Francisco Bay area.
I. Title: San Francisco Bay area rapid transit survey, 1953-1955.

388
(79562)
072

Traffic surveys - The Dalles, Or.

Oregon. Highway Dept.
Traffic survey, City of the Dalles,
1956. Salem, Or., 1957.
221p. illus. maps. (Its Technical
report no. 57-3)

Prepared in cooperation with City of the
Dalles, Wasco Co. and Bureau of Public Roads.

1.Traffic surveys - The Dalles, Or. I.U.S.
Bureau of Public Roads.

388
(7472)
T74

TRAFFIC SURVEYS - NEW YORK METROPOLITAN
AREA.

Tri-State Transportation Commission.
(Connecticut-New Jersey-New York)
Findings of the taxi survey. New York,
1968.
12p. (Its Technical bulletin, vol. IV,
no. 3, April, 1968)

1. Transportation - New York
metropolitan area. 2. Traffic surveys -
New York metropolitan area. I. Title:
Taxi survey.

388
(768464)
S67

Traffic surveys - Springfield, Tenn.

Springfield, Tenn. Municipal-Regional
Planning Commission.
Springfield traffic and parking survey,
by the Tennessee State Planning Commission, Middle Tennessee Office. Springfield, 1959.
36p. diagrs., maps. (MTO Publication 59-2)

U.S. Urban Renewal Administration,
Urban Planning Assistance Program.

(Continued on next card)

388
H43f

Traffic surveys - Washington.

Highway Research Board.
Factors influencing travel patterns.
Washington, 1955.
94p. graphs, maps, tables. (Its Bulletin
119)

Contents.-Trends in traffic diversion on
Edens Expressway, William J. Mortimer.-
Objective and subjective correlates of express-
way use, E. Wilson Campbell and Robert McCargar

(Continued on Card 2)

Folio
388
:308
(76985)
E28

Traffic surveys - Owensboro, Ky.

Edwards and Kelcey, inc.
Urban transportation needs, study for
Owensboro, Kentucky. [Prepared in coopera-
tion with the] Kentucky Dept. of highways.
Newark, N.J., 1966.
68p.

1. Traffic surveys - Owensboro, Ky.
2. Streets - Owensboro, Ky. I. Kentucky.
Dept. of Highways. II. Title.

388
(768464)
S67

Springfield, Tenn. Municipal-Regional
Planning Commission. Springfield traffic and parking... 1959 (Card 2)

1. Traffic surveys - Springfield, Tenn.
I. Tennessee. State Planning Commission.
II. U.S. Urban Renewal Administration.
Urban Planning Assistance Program.

388
H43f

Highway Research Board. Factors influencing
travel patterns.... (Card 2)

-Induced traffic on Chesapeake Bay Bridge,
Ernest W. Bunting. -Intracity traffic movements,
F. Houston Wynn. -Evaluation of intercity-
travel desire, Willa McIroie.

1. Traffic. 2. Traffic surveys - Cook County,
Ill. 3. Traffic surveys - Washington. 4.
Traffic surveys - Maryland. I. Title: Travel
patterns.

388
(77866)
045

Traffic surveys - St. Louis metropolitan
area

Gilman, (W.C.) & Co.
The radial express and suburban cross-
town bus rider, being a detailed evalua-
tion of the sources of patronage of seven
new radial express bus routes and an out-
lying suburban crosstown local bus service,
St. Louis (Mo.-Ill.) metropolitan area.
Final report. New York, 1966.
1 v.
Prepared in cooperation with the Bi-State
Development Agency of the Missouri-Ill.
Metropolitan District.
U.S. Dept. of Housing and Urban
Develop- ment. Mass Trans-
portation Demonstration Grant
Program. (Cont'd on next card)

388
:308
(485)
W27

TRAFFIC SURVEYS - SWEDEN.

Westelius, Orvar.
The individual's pattern of travel in an
urban area; a study of the relationship between the individual's choice of destination
and the choice of location for different
types of business establishments. Stockholm,
Statens Institut for Byggnadsforskning, 1972.
202p. (Document D2:1972)

1. Traffic surveys - Sweden. 2. Industrial
location - Sweden. I. Stockholm. Statens
Institut for Byggnadsforskning. II. Title.

388
(77593)
W47
1956

Traffic surveys - Waukesha, Wis.

Wisconsin. State Highway Commission.
Report of the Waukesha traffic survey,
1956. Waukesha, Wis., 1956.
118p. illus., graphs, maps.

1.Traffic surveys - Waukesha, Wis.
I.U.S. Bureau of Public Roads.

388
(77866)
345

Gilman, W.C. & Co. The radial express and
suburban crosstown bus rider...1966.
(Card 2)

1. Transportation - St. Louis
metropoli- tan area. 2. Journey to work. 3. Traffic
surveys - St. Louis metropolitan area.
I. Bi-State Development Agency of the
Missouri-Illinois Metropolitan District.
II. Title. III. U.S. HUD, Mass Transportation Demonstration Grant Program.

388
(74765)
N28

Traffic surveys - Syracuse, N.Y. metropolitan.

New York (State) Dept. of Public Works.
(Subdivision of Transportation Planning
and Programming)
A prospectus for a comprehensive transportation study in the Syracuse metropolitan area. Albany, 1966.
31p. (Its Publication RP50-000-01)

1. Transportation - Syracuse, N.Y. metropolitan area. 2. Journey to work.
3. Traffic surveys - Syracuse, N.Y. metropolitan area. I. Title.

388
(77593)
W47
1955
Suppl.

Traffic surveys - Waukesha, Wis.

Wisconsin. State Highway Commission.
Traffic information. Supplement to the
Waukesha traffic survey. Waukesha, Wis.,
1955.
106p. map, tables.

1.Traffic surveys - Waukesha, Wis.

388
(764)
T29

Traffic surveys - San Antonio.

Texas. Highway Dept. (Highway Planning
Survey)
San Antonio metropolitan area traffic
survey, 1956. San Antonio, 1956.
170p. illus., maps, tables.

1.Traffic surveys - San Antonio.
I.U.S. Bureau of Public Roads.

388
:308
(797781)
W17

TRAFFIC SURVEYS - TACOMA, WASH.

Washington (State) Dept. of Highways.
Origin and destination traffic survey,
Tacoma, Wash., 1948-1949. Olympia, Wash.,
[1950?]
54p.
Conducted by the State of Washington Dept.
of Highways in cooperation with Dept. of
Commerce, Bureau of Public Roads and the City
of Tacoma Dept. of Public Works.
1. Traffic surveys - Tacoma, Wash. 2. Journey to work. I. Tacoma. Dept. of Public
Works. II. Title.

308
:388
(7447)
C15

Traffic surveys - Wellesley, Mass.

Campbell (Bruce) and Associates.
Town of Wellesley, Massachusetts;
traffic and parking survey. Prepared
for the Town of Wellesley Planning Board
and the Massachusetts Dept. of Commerce.
Boston, 1960.
1v. maps, tables.
U.S. Urban Renewal Adm. UPAP.

1. Traffic surveys - Wellesley, Mass.
2. Parking surveys - Wellesley, Mass.
I. Wellesley, Mass. Planning Board. II. U.S.
URA-UPAP. Welles- ley, Mass.

711.73
(7946)
C15

TRAFFIC SURVEYS - SAN FRANCISCO BAY AREA.

California. University. Institute of
Transportation and Traffic Engineering.
Bay area freeway operations study. Special
report. Interim report no. 1-3. Conducted
in cooperation with U.S. Dept. of Transportation, Federal Highway Administration,
Bureau of Public Roads. Berkeley, 1968.
3 nos.
1. Highways - San Francisco Bay area.
2. Traffic surveys - San Francisco Bay area.
I. Title.

711.73
(764)
H21

Traffic surveys - Texas.

Heathington, Kenneth W
Traffic volume analysis of urban free-
ways, by Kenneth W. Heathington and Paul R.
Tutt. [Prepared] in cooperation with the
U.S. Dept. of Commerce, Bureau of Public
Roads. [Austin, Texas] Texas Highway Dept.
1966.
56p. (Texas. Highway Dept. Departmental
Research Report no. SS 5.0)
1. Highways - Texas. 2. Traffic surveys -
Texas. 3. Transportation - Statistics. I. Tutt,
Paul R., jt. au. II. Texas. Highway Dept.
IV. Title.

308
:388
(7447)
C15w

Traffic surveys - Wellesley, Mass.

Campbell (Bruce) and Associates.
Wellesley traffic and parking survey.
Data submission no. Prepared for
Massachusetts Dept. of Commerce and the
Wellesley Planning Board. Boston, 1960.
1v. diagrs.

U.S. Urban Renewal Adm. UPAP.

1. Traffic surveys - Wellesley, Mass.
2. Parking surveys - Wellesley, Mass.
I. Massachusetts. Dept. of Commerce.
II. Wellesley, Mass. Planning Board.
III. U.S. URA- UPAP. Wellesley, Mass.

388
(775)
S68t
Traffic surveys - Wis.
Southeastern Wisconsin Regional Planning Commission.
Truck and taxi survey. Land use-transportation study. Rev. Waukesha, Wis., 1964.
49p. (Its Procedural manual no. 3)
Prepared in cooperation with State Highway Commission of Wisconsin, the U.S. Dept. of Commerce, Bureau of Public Roads.
U.S. Urban Renewal Adm. UPAP.

1. Transportation - Wis. 2. Traffic surveys - Wis. I. Title. II. U.S. URA-UPAP. Wis.

711.73
W63
Traffic system analysis.
Wohl, Martin.
Traffic system analysis [by] Martin Wohl [and] Brian V. Martin. New York, McGraw-Hill, [1967]
558p. (McGraw-Hill series in transportation)

Includes bibliographies.

1. Highways - Economic effect. 2. Journey to work. 3. Traffic. I. Martin, Brian V., jt. au. II. Title.

534.83
L15
The traffic noise index: a method of controlling noise nuisance.
Langdon, F J
The traffic noise index: a method of controlling noise nuisance, by F.J. Langdon and W.E. Scholes. Garston, Eng., Building Research Station, Ministray of Public Building and Works, 1968.
8p. (U.K. Building Research Station. Building research current papers, Current paper 38/68)
Version of this paper in the Architects' Journal, April 1968.
1. Noise. 2. Traffic. 3. Highways - Social effect. I. Scholes, W.E. jt. au. II. U.K. Building Research Station. III. Title.

388
:308
(752)
M17
Traffic trends.
Maryland. Bureau of Highway Statistics.
Traffic trends, 19
[Annapolis] 19
v. annual.

For Library holdings see main entry.
1. Traffic surveys - Md. I. Title.

711.73
(764)
H21
Traffic volume analysis of urban freeways.
Heathington, Kenneth W
Traffic volume analysis of urban freeways, by Kenneth W. Heathington and Paul R. Tutt. [Prepared] in cooperation with the U.S. Dept. of Commerce, Bureau of Public Roads. [Austin, Texas] Texas Highway Dept. 1966.
56p. (Texas. Highway Dept. Departmental Research. Report no. SS 5.0)
1. Highways - Texas. 2. Traffic surveys - Texas. 3. Transportation - Statistics. I. Tutt, Paul R., jt. au. II. Texas. Highway Dept. IV. Title.

711.73
(79466)
O14
Trafficways in the Oakland central district; a study of vehicular circulation in downtown Oakland; a technical report.
Oakland, Calif. City Planning Dept.
Trafficways in the Oakland central district; a study of vehicular circulation in downtown Oakland; a technical report. Oakland, 1964.
25p.

1. Traffic - Oakland, Calif.
2. Business districts - Oakland, Calif.
I. Title.

366
TRAFTON BEAN AND ASSOCIATES.
GRAND CO., COLO. REGIONAL PLANNING COMMISSION.
DEVELOPMENT STANDARDS FOR USE IN GRAND COUNTY, COLORADO. PREPARED BY TRAFTON BEAN AND ASSOCIATES. DENVER, 1970.
69L. (HUD 701 REPORT)

1. LAND USE - GRAND CO., COLO.
I. TRAFTON BEAN AND ASSOCIATES. II. HUD. 701. GRAND CO., COLO.

367
FOLIO
TRAFTON BEAN AND ASSOCIATES.
GRAND CO., COLO. REGIONAL PLANNING COMMISSION.
GRAND COUNTY COMPREHENSIVE PLAN; SUMMARY REPORT. PREPARED BY TRAFTON BEAN AND ASSOCIATES. DENVER, 1970.
44P. (HUD 701 REPORT)

1. MASTER PLAN - GRAND CO., COLO.
I. TRAFTON BEAN AND ASSOCIATES.
II. HUD. 701. GRAND CO., COLO.

711.585
(74461)
T85
TRAGEDY OF A VERTICAL SLUM.
TUNLEY, ROUL.
TRAGEDY OF A VERTICAL SLUM. PHILADELPHIA, CURTIS PUB. CO., 1963.
5P.

REPRODUCED FROM THE SATURDAY EVENING POST, JUNE 29-JULY 6, 1963, P.89-93.

1. SLUMS - BOSTON. 2. PUBLIC HOUSING - BOSTON. I. TITLE.

711.585
1659.11
T71
TRAGER, BERNARD H
JEWISH COMMUNITY RELATIONS AND THE NCRAC, 1944-1957; AN ADDRESS ... TO THE NCRAC PLENARY SESSION, JUNE 22, 1957. NEW YORK, NATIONAL COMMUNITY RELATIONS ADVISORY COUNCIL, 1957.
23P.

1. COMMUNITY RELATIONS. I. NATIONAL COMMUNITY RELATIONS ADVISORY COUNCIL. II. TITLE.

711.585
(861)
O12
Trail, B C City Council.
Oberlander, H Peter.
A study for urban renewal in Trail, B.C., by H. Peter Oberlander and R.J. Cave. Prepared for the City Council. Trail, B.C., Corporation of the City of Trail, 1959.
85p.

1. Urban renewal - British Columbia. I. Cave, R.J., jt. au. II. Trail, B.C. City Council.

728.69
N85m
Trail-R-Club of America.
Nulsen, Robert H
The mobile home manual; a complete mobile home and travel trailer how-to-do-it book. Beverly Hills, Calif., Trail-R-Club of America, 1967-70.
2v.

1. Mobile homes. I. Trail-R-Club of America. II. Title.

728.69
K17
Trail-R-Club of America.
Karr, Harrison M
This wonderful world of mobile home living. Beverly Hills, Calif., Trail-R-Club of America, 1968.
175p. (Book no. 1)

Bibliography: p. 149-150.

1. Mobile homes. I. Trail-R-Club of America. II. Title.

728.69
T71
Trailer Coach Association.
Annual report, 1968-69 [and other publications] [Anaheim, Calif.] [1970?]
kit (16 pieces)

Partial contents.-The investment potential of mobile home parks.-Mobile homes may be the answer to low-cost housing problem.

1. Mobile homes.

728.69
G45
Trailer Coach Association.
Gillies, James
Another look at mobile home parks and municipal fiscal problems. [Anaheim, Calif.] Trailer Coach Association, 1968.
24p.

1. Mobile homes. I. Trailer Coach Association. II. Title.

728.69
C65a
Trailer Coach Association.
Construction Industries Research, inc.
An appraisal of mobile home living; the parks and the residents. 1. Factors influencing social patterns in mobile home parks. 2. Mobile home parks and municipal costs and revenues. Prepared under direction of James Gillies. Anaheim, Calif., Trailer Coach Association, 1967.
15p.

1. Mobile homes. I. Gillies, James. II. Trailer Coach Association. III. Title.

728.69
W27
Trailer Coach Association.
Western Economic Research Co.
The Hemet report. [Anaheim, Calif.] Trailer Coach Association, 1970.
18p.

1. Mobile homes. I. Trailer Coach Association. II. Title.

621.6
W27
TRAILER COACH DRAINAGE AND VENT SYSTEMS.
WESTERN PLUMBING OFFICIALS ASSOCIATION. (TRAILER STANDARDS COMMITTEE)
MATERIALS AND PROPERTY STANDARDS; PLASTIC DRAIN AND VENT PIPE-DRAINAGE FITTINGS FOR TRAILER COACH DRAINAGE AND VENT SYSTEMS; ABS-TYPE 1 AND 1A. REV. SOUTH PASADENA, CALIF., 1961.
5L.
1. PIPES - STANDARDS AND SPECIFICATIONS. 2. MOBILE HOMES. I. TITLE: DRAIN AND VENT PIPE - DRAINAGE FITTINGS. II. TITLE: TRAILER COACH DRAINAGE AND VENT SYSTEMS.

Class No.	Author (surname first)
VF TRAILERS	TRAILER COACH INDUSTRY. WAR ACTIVITIES COMMITTEE
Accession No.	Title
Ordered	Use of the trailer coach in a period of national mobilization
Source	Place ... Publisher
Received 3. 4.53	Address
Cost	Date 11-15-60 Paging 18 p. List Price Est. Cost
Purchase Order No.	Edition or Series
Date	Recommended by
L. C. No.	Reviewed in

H-305 (2-50) HOUSING AND HOME FINANCE AGENCY: Office of the Administrator 16—61157-1 GPO

728.69
T71H
TRAILER COACH MANUFACTURERS ASSOCIATION.
HOMES FOR THE MOBILE POPULATION.
CHICAGO, 1951.
25P.

1. TRAILERS AND TRAILER COURTS.

728.69
T71M
TRAILER COACH MANUFACTURERS ASSOCIATION.
MOBILE WAR HOUSING; SAVING MANPOWER, MATERIALS, MONEY; A FACTUAL PRESENTATION. WASH., 1942.
1 V.

1. TRAILERS AND TRAILER COURTS. 2. DEFENSE HOUSING. I. TITLE.

728.69
T71MO
TRAILER COACH MANUFACTURERS ASSOCIATION.
MOBILE WAR HOUSING, SAVING MANPOWER,
MATERIALS, MONEY, A FACTUAL
PRESENTATION. N.P., 1943.
14P.

1. TRAILERS AND TRAILER COURTS.
2. MOBILE HOMES.   I. TITLE.

728.69
B21
BEAUCHAMP, GEORGE E   TRAILER COURTS AND
...1960.   (CARD 2)

II. SEMINAR ON HOUSING AND LIVING
ARRANGEMENTS FOR THE LATER YEARS.
III. TITLE.   IV. TITLE: RETIREMENT
TOWNS.

728.69
B21
TRAILERS AND TRAILER COURTS.
BEAUCHAMP, GEORGE E
TRAILER COURTS AND RETIREMENT TOWNS.
NEW YORK, NATIONAL COUNCIL ON THE
AGING, THE LIBRARY, 1960.
5P.

PHOTOCOPY OF TYPESCRIPT.
PAPER GIVEN AT SEMINAR ON HOUSING AND
LIVING ARRANGEMENTS FOR THE LATER
YEARS, HELD AT LAKE MOHONK MOUNTAIN
HOUSE, N.Y., JUNE 13-18, 1960.

1. TRAILERS AND TRAILER COURTS.
I. NATIONAL CO UNCIL ON THE AGING.
                (CONTINUED ON NEXT CARD)

728.69
T71TR
TRAILER COACH MANUFACTURERS ASSOCIATION.
TRAILER COACHES, THEIR PLACE IN WAR
HOUSING. N.P., 1942.
12P.

1. TRAILERS AND TRAILER COURTS.
2. DEFENSE HOUSING.

728.69
(79482)
F72
TRAILER PARKS AND FRESNO COUNTY.
FRESNO COUNTY, CALIF. PLANNING
COMMISSION.
TRAILER PARKS AND FRESNO COUNTY.
FRESNO, CALIFORNIA, 1960.
22L.

1. MOBILE HOMES - FRESNO CO., CALIF.
I. TITLE.

728.69
B21
BEAUCHAMP, GEORGE E   TRAILER COURTS AND
...1960.   (CARD 2)

II. SEMINAR ON HOUSING AND LIVING
ARRANGEMENTS FOR THE LATER YEARS.
III. TITLE.   IV. TITLE: RETIREMENT
TOWNS.

728.69
T71T
TRAILER COACH MANUFACTURERS.
ASSOCIATION. LEGISLATIVE AND PARK
PLANNING COMMITTEE.
TRAILER COACH PARKS AND THEIR PLACE
IN THE FUTURE OF AMERICA. WASH., 1945.
1 V.

1. TRAILERS AND TRAILER COURTS.
I. TITLE.

728.69
A52
Trailer storage.
Alexandria, Va. Dept. of City Planning and
Urban Renewal.
Trailer storage. Alexandria, 1966.
6p.   (Its Special study. Rept. no. 4)

1. Trailers and trailer courts - Model
laws and ordinances. I. Title.

VF
728.69
(794)
C15t
Trailers. & Trailer courts
California. Laws, statutes, etc.
State auto and trailer park act (Health and
safety code, Division 13, Part 2) and California
administrative code (Title 8, Chapter 9, Article
3).   Sacramento, Calif., Dept. of Industrial
Relations, Division of Housing, 1952.
48 p.   diagrs., plans, tables.
1.Trailers. 2.Tourist courts. I.California. Dept.
of Industrial Relations. Division of Housing.

5/53

728.69
T71T
TRAILER COACH PARKS AND THEIR PLACE
IN THE FUTURE OF AMERICA.
TRAILER COACH MANUFACTURERS
ASSOCIATION. LEGISLATIVE AND PARK
PLANNING COMMITTEE.
TRAILER COACH PARKS AND THEIR PLACE
IN THE FUTURE OF AMERICA. WASH., 1945.
1 V.

1. TRAILERS AND TRAILER COURTS.
I. TITLE.

728.69
S87
TRAILER TOPICS MAGAZINE.
A SURVEY OF THE MOBILE HOME CONSUMER.
CHICAGO, TRAILER TOPICS MAGAZINE,
1959.
34P.

SUMMARY OF QUESTIONNAIRE PREPARED AND
CODED BY C.M. EDWARDS, DIRECTOR,
MICHIGAN STATE UNIVERSITY MOBILE HOMES
EDUCATION PROGRAM.

1. MOBILE HOMES.   I. EDWARDS, C.M.
II. MICHIGAN   STATE UNIVERSITY.
MOBILE HOMES E DUCATION PROGRAM.
                (CONTINUED ON NEXT CARD)

VF
728.69
C31
Trailers. & Trailer courts

Charleston County, S. C. Ordinances, etc.
Regulations controlling the operation and
use of trailer camps or parks and tourist
courts... 1943?
10 p.

1.Trailers. 2.Tourist courts.

728.69
A87
TRAILER COACH REGULATIONS.
AUTOMOBILE CLUB OF SOUTHERN CALIFORNIA.
(LICENSE DEPT.)
SUMMARY OF TRAILER COACH REGULATIONS
1955-1956, UNITED STATES AND CANADA.
LOS ANGELES, 1955.
86P.

1. MOBILE HOMES.   I. TITLE: TRAILER
COACH REGULATIONS.

728.69
S87
A SURVEY OF THE MOBILE HOME CONSUMER.
CHICAGO, TRAILER TOPICS MAGAZINE,
1959.   ....   (CARD 2)

III. TRAILER TOPICS MAGAZINE.
IV. TITLE: THE MOBILE HOME CONSUMER.

VF
728.69
(757711)
C65
Trailers. & Trailer courts
Columbia, S.C. Ordinances, etc.
An ordinance to regulate trailer coaches and
trailer coach parks within the city of Columbia,
South Carolina.   Columbia, S.C., City Council
[Aug. 1953]
7 l.

Processed.

1.Trailers. 2.Tourist courts.

728.69
P81
Trailer court sanitation
U.S. Public Health Service (Division of Sanita-
tion)
Trailer court sanitation, with suggested
ordinances and regulations.   [Chicago]
Mobile Homes Manufacturer's Association, 1953.
29 p.   illus., plans.

"References": p.19

728.69
T71S
TRAILER TRANSPORT CO.
SOLVING THE NATION'S NUMBER ONE
PROBLEM. FLINT, MICH., 1943.
1 V.

1. TRAILERS AND TRAILER COURTS.
2. HOUSING.

728.1
:362.6
(746)
065f
Trailers and trailer courts.
Connecticut. Commission on Services for
Elderly Persons.
Feasibility and costs of developing a plan
for a model mobilehome park to be occupied
by retired persons and their spouses.
Special act no. 259, 1965 session. Hartford,
1966.
30p.
A Joint Study Commission: Commission on
Services for Elderly Persons and Public
Works Dept.
1. Housing for the   aged - Conn.
2. Trailers and trailer   courts.
I. Connecticut. Public   Works Dept. II. Title.

728.69
B21
TRAILER COURTS AND RETIREMENT TOWNS.
BEAUCHAMP, GEORGE E
TRAILER COURTS AND RETIREMENT TOWNS.
NEW YORK, NATIONAL COUNCIL ON THE
AGING, THE LIBRARY, 1960.
5P.

PHOTOCOPY OF TYPESCRIPT.
PAPER GIVEN AT SEMINAR ON HOUSING AND
LIVING ARRANGEMENTS FOR THE LATER
YEARS, HELD AT LAKE MOHONK MOUNTAIN
HOUSE, N.Y., JUNE 13-18, 1960.

1. TRAILERS   AND TRAILER COURTS.
I. NATIONAL CO UNCIL ON THE AGING.
                (CONTINUED ON NEXT CARD)

058.7
:728.69
W66
Trailering parks and campgrounds.
Woodall's trailering parks and campgrounds,
19

New York, Simon and Schuster, 19

v.
For Library holdings see main entry.

1. Trailers and trailer courts - Direct.
2. Parks - Direct. I. Title: Trailering
parks and campgrounds.

690
(746
:083.41)
C65
Trailers and trailer courts.
Connecticut. Public Works Dept.
Housing Div.
Housing units by units in structure
and trailers by town and county, April 1,
1960. Hartford, 1960.
12p.   (Housing report no. 2)

1. Building construction - Statistics -
Conn. 2. Trailers and trailer courts.

728.69   Trailers and trailer courts.
C65   Consumer Council.
    Living in a caravan; a Consumer Council
study. London, H.M.S.O., 1967.
Lef.   50p.   (S.O. code no. 88-5705)

    1. Trailers and trailer courts. 2. Site
selection - U.K. 3. Public utilities -
U.K. I. Title.

690.015   Trailers. & Trailer courts
H68   Housing Research. No. 1 - 7.   Washington, Govt.
H   Print. Off., Fall 1951 - Apr. 1954.
    7 nos.   illus., diagrs., graphs, maps, plans,
tables.

    Publication of U.S. Housing and Home Finance
Agency, Office of the Administrator, Division of
Housing Research.

    Trailers and trailer courts.
VF   Mobile Homes Manufacturers Association.
728.69   Homes for the mobile population.
M61   [Chicago, n.d.]
    [14] p.   illus.

    1.Trailers and trailer courts. I.Title.

VF   Trailers and trailer courts.
728.69
C87   Curtis Publishing Co. (Research Department)
    Market for passenger trailer coaches.
Philadelphia, 1957.
    3 p.

    1.Trailers and trailer courts. I.Title.

        Trailers and trailer courts.
728.69
J85   July Town Planners.
    Trailer park regulations, Buckley, Washington.
[n.p.] 1960.
    [1]p.
    Prepared under general supervision of
Washington State Dept. of Commerce and Economic
Development.
    U.S. Urban Renewal Adm. UPAP.

    1. Trailers and trailer courts. I. U.S.
URA-UPAP. Buckley, Wash.

728.69   Trailers.& Trailer courts
:332.72   Natale, Ralph M.
N17   Mobile home financing. [Washington, School of
    Consumer Banking, c1956]
    xi, 84 p.   illus.

    Submitted in partial fulfillment of the
requirements of the School of Consumer Banking
sponsored by the Consumer Bankers Association
at the University of Virginia, Charlottesville,
Virginia, August, 1955.
    Bibliography: 81-84

VF   Trailers and trailer courts.
728.69
D68o   Douglas, Alaska. Ordinances, etc.
    Outline of standards and requirements for
an ordinance regulating use and occupancy of
trailers and mobile homes and the development
of mobile home parks. [Douglas, 1958?]
    2p.
U.S. Urban Renewal Administration, Urban Planning
Assistance Program.

1. Trailers and trailer courts. I. U.S. URA-UPAP.
Douglas, Alaska.

        Trailers and trailer courts.
728.69
M12   McPherson, L   D   comp.
    Regulation of: I. - House trailers and
their locations. II. - Plumbing in house
trailers, trailer parks or buildings any-
where for any use. Washington, 1949.
    104p.

    1. Trailers and trailer courts.

        Trailers and trailer courts.
728.69
N17m   National Association of Real Estate Boards.
    Mobile homes and residential land use, by
Dean W. Dittmer and Catherine E. Martini.
Washington, 1960.
    17p.   tables.

    1. Trailers and trailer courts. I. Dittmer, Dean W.
II. Martini, Catherine   E.

711.333   Trailers and trailer courts.
(74796)
E74c   Erie County, N. Y. Planning Board.
    [Comprehensive plan for community
development] Buffalo, N. Y., 1957.
    Pieces in folder.

    Partial contents: -Minimum residential
lot size requirements in Erie County towns.
-Color code for land use maps. -Suggested
text for town or village zoning ordinance.
-Present municipal services in Erie County
-Suggested text for house trailer and trailer
camp ordinance. -Suggested text for town or
            (See Card No. 2)

        Trailers and trailer courts.
728.69
M25.   Meloan, Taylor W
    Mobile homes: the growth and business
practices of the industry. Homewood, Ill.,
Richard D. Irwin, 1954.
    143 p. illus., map. (Indiana University.
School of Business Study no. 37)
    Bibliography: p. 131 - 138.
    Appendix (p. 121-130) - Recommended
Standards for trailer courts by the Housing
and Home Finance Agency.

    1.Trailers and trailer courts. I.Title.
II.U.S. Housing   and Home Finance Agency.

VF   Trailers. & Trailer courts
690.091.82
:613.5   New Hampshire. State Dept. of Health.
(742)   Sanitary laws and regulations governing
N28   tourist and trailer camps, trailer coaches, hotels,
    inns, lodging houses, apartment and tenement
    houses, tourist homes, stores, offices, theaters
    and public halls, roadside places and public fairs.
    Concord, N.H., 1953.
    20 p.

    1.Housing codes-N.H. 2.Trailers. 3.Tourist
courts.

711.333   Erie County, N. Y. Planning Board. [Comprehen-
(74796   sive plan for community development] 1957.
E74c

            (Card No. 2)

    village subdivision regulations. -A planned
street tree program for an attractive commonwealth.

    1.Community development - Erie County, N. Y.
2.County planning - Erie County, N. Y. 3.Master
plan - Erie County, N. Y. 4.Trailers and trailer
courts.

728.69
M42   Trailers. &Trailer courts
    Michelon, L   C
    How to build and operate a mobile-home park.
[Chicago, Mobile Homes Manufacturers Ass'n, 1955.]
    122 p.   illus., plates.

    1. Trailers. I. Mobile Homes Manufacturers Associa-
tion. II. Title. III. Title: Mobile-home park,
How to build and operate.

711.4   Trailers and trailer courts.
N67   Norton, Perry L   ed.
no.1   A forum on technical problems in an expand-
    ing urban society. Lexington, Mass., Chandler-
    Davis, 1959.
    249p. (Urban problems and techniques no. 1)

    Contents:-The planning aspects of annexation
and of service areas, by Maxine Kurtz.-Seeking
action consesus through research; the Cleveland Metropolitan Services Commission, by
J.A. [Dolph] Norton.-How important is recreation planning, by Kenneth R. Anderson.-
                (Continued on
                    next card)

        Trailers and trailer courts.
728.69
F56   Florida. University. Public Administration
    Clearing Service.
    Mobile home parks and comprehensive com-
munity planning, by Ernest R. Bartley and
Frederick H. Bair, Jr. Gainesville, Fla.,
1960.
    147p. illus., diagrs. (Its Studies in
public administration no. 19)

1. Trailers and trailer courts. I. Bartley,
Ernest R. II. Bair, Frederick H., Jr.

VF
728.69   Trailers.& Trailer courts
:336.2   Michigan. State College. Bureau of Business
M42   Research.
    The taxation of mobile homes, by Richard D.
Duke [and] Avery A. Haak.   [East Lansing, Mich.,
1955?]
    38 p.   tables.

    Sponsored by Michigan Trailer Parks Association.

    1. Trailers. I. Duke, Richard D. II. Haak,
Avery A. III. Michigan Trailer Parks Association.
IV. Title.

711.4
N67   Norton, Perry L   ed.   A forum on ...
no.1   (Card 2)

    .Toward permanent agrarian greenbelts for the
Garden State, by John Brewer Moore.-The role
of the planner in a Recreation Department, by
Gregory Bassett.-Techniques in central busi-
ness district research, by Raymond E. Murphy.-
Utilities in and out of planning, by Charles
D. Laidlaw.-The planning consultant looks at
"701", by Herbert H. Smith.-Industrial per-
formance standards: a proposal, by O. Wayne
Noble.-
                (Continued on
                    next card)

        Trailers and trailer courts.
728.69
H19   Hayes, Richard L
    How to live like a retired millionaire on
less than $200 a month. A fascinating
true story of country club living for
retired people of modest means. Beverly
Hills, Calif., Trail-R-Club of America,
1962.
    64p.

    1. Trailers and trailer courts.
    2. Housing for the aged. I. Title.

        Trailers and trailer courts.
728.69
M61b   Mobilehome Dealers National Association.
    Brookhill; a residential mobilehome
development. [n.p.] 1960.
    34p.

    1. Trailers and trailer courts.

711.4
N67   Norton, Perry L   ed.   A forum on ...(Card 3)
no.1

    Columbus, Ohio adopts performance standards as
the basis for modern control of industrial
nuisances, by Edmond M. Loewe.-Attacking smog
through zoning, by Gordon Whitnall.-Trailers,
trailer parks and zoning cases, by Stephen
Sussna.

    1. City growth. 2. City planning. 3. An-
nexation. 4. Metropolitan areas.

                (Continued on
                    next card)

711.4
N67
no.1
Norton, Perry L ed. A forum ... (Card 4)

5. Business districts. 6. Zoning. 7. Recreation. 8. Air pollution. 9. Trailers and trailer courts. 10. Public utilities. 11. Industrial location - Columbus, Ohio. (Series)

Trailers and trailer courts.

728.69
P89
Puyallup, Wash. Ordinances, etc.
Proposed trailer park ordinance for the Town of Puyallup. [Puyallup, 1958?]
[1]p.

U.S. Urban Renewal Adm. UPAP.

1. Trailers and trailer courts. I. U.S. URA-UPAP. Puyallup, Wash.

728.69
T71TR
TRAILERS AND TRAILER COURTS.
TRAILER COACH MANUFACTURERS ASSOCIATION.
TRAILER COACHES, THEIR PLACE IN WAR HOUSING. N.P., 1942.
12P.

1. TRAILERS AND TRAILER COURTS.
2. DEFENSE HOUSING.

728.69
N85A
TRAILERS AND TRAILER COURTS.
NULSEN, ROBERT HOVEY.
ALL ABOUT PARKS FOR MOBILE HOMES AND TRAILERS, A GUIDE FOR SELECTING THE PARK THAT IS BEST FOR YOU. 1ST ED. BEVERLY HILLS, CALIF., TRAIL-R-CLUB OF AMERICA, 1960.
199P.

1. MOBILE HOMES. 2. TRAILERS AND TRAILER COURTS. I. TITLE.

728.69
(79498)
S15
pt. 1
Trailers and trailer courts.
San Diego, Calif. City Planning Department.
Houses on wheels. Part I. An initial study of mobile home activity in the City of San Diego, 1959.
71p. illus., diagrs., maps, tables.

1. Trailers and trailer courts.

728.69
T71S
TRAILERS AND TRAILER COURTS.
TRAILER TRANSPORT CO.
SOLVING THE NATION'S NUMBER ONE PROBLEM. FLINT, MICH., 1943.
1 V.

1. TRAILERS AND TRAILER COURTS.
2. HOUSING.

728.69
022
Trailers and trailer courts.
Ocean County, N. J. Planning Board.
Mobile homes and parks in the community planning process. [Toms River, N.J., 1959]
23p. tables. (Its Bulletin 6)

1. Trailers and trailer courts.

728.69
S68t
Trailers and trailer courts.
South Saskatchewan River Development Commission.
Trailer parks for construction workers, South Saskatchewan River Development Region, by Jean Downing. Regina, Can, 1960.
53p. maps, tables.

1. Trailers and trailer courts. I. Downing, Jean.

728.69
T74
Trailers and trailer courts.
Tri-County Regional Planning Commission. (Peoria, Tazewell, Woodford Counties, Ill.)
The mobile home and its place. Peoria, Ill., 1967.
24p.

1. Trailers and trailer courts. 2. Trailers and trailer courts - Taxation. I. Title.

728.69
078
Trailers and trailer courts.
[Orting, Wash. Planning Commission]
Trailer park regulations, Orting, Washington. [Orting] 1960.
[1]p.

Prepared under general supervision of Washington State Dept. of Commerce and Economic Development.
U.S. Urban Renewal Adm. UPAP.

1. Trailers and trailer courts.
I. U.S. URA-UPAP. Orting, Wash.

728.69
T71H
TRAILERS AND TRAILER COURTS.
TRAILER COACH MANUFACTURERS ASSOCIATION.
HOMES FOR THE MOBILE POPULATION.
CHICAGO, 1951.
25P.

1. TRAILERS AND TRAILER COURTS.

711.5
(41)
U54
no. 8
TRAILERS AND TRAILER COURTS.
U.K. Ministry of Housing and Local Government. (Welsh Office)
Caravan sites. London, H.M.S.O., 1969.
[3]p. (Its Development control policy note, 8)

1. Zoning - U.K. 2. Trailers and trailer courts. I. Title.

VF
728.69
(74821)
P25
Trailers and trailer courts.
Pennsylvania. University. Institute for Urban Studies.
Trailer parks and trailer residents in Bucks County (Bristol-Morrisville, Pennsylvania) critical defense housing area, prepared by Don J. Hager. Philadelphia, Pa. Sept. 1952.
33 L.

Bibliography: p. 1-2

Prepared under research contract no. 1-E-121,

(see card 2)

728.69
T71M
TRAILERS AND TRAILER COURTS.
TRAILER COACH MANUFACTURERS ASSOCIATION.
MOBILE WAR HOUSING; SAVING MANPOWER, MATERIALS, MONEY, A FACTUAL PRESENTATION. WASH., 1942.
1 V.

1. TRAILERS AND TRAILER COURTS.
2. DEFENSE HOUSING. I. TITLE.

728.69
F22m
Trailers and trailer courts.
U.S. Federal Housing Administration.
Mobile home courts. Washington, Nov. 1955.
9 p. plans. (Land planning bulletin No. 5.)

VF
728.69
(74821)
P25
Pennsylvania. University. Institute for Urban Studies.
Trailer parks and trailer... Sept. 1952. (card 2)

Housing and Home Finance Agency.
"Draft - not for publicity nor publication."

1. Trailers and trailer courts. 2. Housing research contracts. I. Hager, Don J II U.S. Housing and Home Finance Agency. Office of the Administrator. Div. of Housing Research.

728.69
T71MO
TRAILERS AND TRAILER COURTS.
TRAILER COACH MANUFACTURERS ASSOCIATION.
MOBILE WAR HOUSING; SAVING MANPOWER, MATERIALS, MONEY; A FACTUAL PRESENTATION. N.P., 1943.
14P.

1. TRAILERS AND TRAILER COURTS.
2. MOBILE HOMES. I. TITLE.

VF
728.69
H68
Nov.
1952
Trailers & trailer courts
U.S. Housing and Home Finance Agency. Office of the Administrator. Division of Plans and Programs.
Recommended standards for trailer courts. Washington, Govt. Print. Off., Nov. 1952.
24 p.

"Housing research."
Issued by Division of Plans and Programs and Division of Housing Research.
Ralph R. Kaul, special adviser.

Film
TRAILERS AND TRAILER COURTS.
Promise of tomorrow. Mobile home community planning film. (Filmstrip) [Arlington, Va.] Mobile Homes Association, inc., 1970.

13 1/2 min. 16mm.
Cost: $100 a print.
Rent: $100 a week.

1. Mobile homes. 2. Trailers and trailer courts. I. Mobile Homes Association, inc. Arlington, Va.

728.69
T71T
TRAILERS AND TRAILER COURTS.
TRAILER COACH MANUFACTURERS ASSOCIATION. LEGISLATIVE AND PARK PLANNING COMMITTEE.
TRAILER COACH PARKS AND THEIR PLACE IN THE FUTURE OF AMERICA. WASH., 1945.
1 V.

1. TRAILERS AND TRAILER COURTS.
I. TITLE.

355.58
H68gu
1965
Trailers and trailer courts.
U.S. Housing and Home Finance Agency. Office of Program Policy.
Guides for the inventory and use of existing stocks of tents and trailers (mobile homes) for emergency housing, by Defense Planning Staff. Rev. [Washington] Govt. Print. Off., 1965.
6p.

"HHFA staff document."

1. Civilian defense. 2. Trailers and trailer courts. I. Title.

355.58
H68gu
1967
Trailers and trailer courts.
U.S. Dept. of Housing and Urban Development.
Assistant Secretary for Demonstrations and Intergovernmental Relations.
Guides for the inventory and use of existing stocks of tents and trailers (mobile homes) for emergency housing, by Defense Planning Staff. [Washington] Govt. Print. Off., 1967.
7p. (Its Operating instruction no. 1)
"HUD staff document."
Reprinted 1967.

1. Civilian defense. 2. Trailers and trailer courts. I. Title.

728.69
B14
Trailers and trailer courts - Model laws and ordinances.
Beir, Fredrick H
Local regulation of mobile home parks, travel trailer parks and related facilities. Chicago, Mobile Homes Research Foundation, 1965.
94p.

1. Trailers and trailer courts - Model laws and ordinances. I. Mobile Homes Research Foundation. II. Title.

LAW
8
Trailers and trailer courts - Model laws and ordinances.
California. Laws, statutes, etc.
Trailer park act. California health and safety code, division 13, part 2. Rules and regulations to implement, interpret, and make specific, California Administrative Code, title 8, chapter 9, article 2 (including standards for gas piping installations) San Francisco, State of California, Dept. of Industrial Relations, Division of Housing, 1960.
47p. diagrs.

1. Trailers and trailer courts - Model laws and ordinances. I. California. Dept. of Industrial Relations. (Division of Housing)

712.25
W47d
TRAILERS AND TRAILER COURTS.
Wisconsin. Bureau of Commercial Recreation.
Developing campgrounds for recreational vehicles. Appleton, Wis., Dept. of Local Affairs and Development, Div. of Economic Development, Bureau of Commercial Recreation, 1969.
23p. (Its Recreational development series no. 2)

1. Recreation. 2. Trailers and trailer courts. I. Title: Campgrounds for recreational vehicles.

VF
728.69
C15ru
Trailers and trailer courts - Model laws and ordinances.
California. Laws, statutes, etc.
Rules and regulations for electrical standards in trailer parks. (California Administrative Code, title 8, chapter 9, article 5, effective July 14, 1956) 2d ed. Sacramento, Department of Industrial Relations, Division of Housing, 1957.
[12]p. tables.

1. Trailers and trailer courts - Model laws and ordinances. I. California. Dept. of Industrial Relations. (Div. of Housing)

728.69
D68
Trailers and trailer courts - Model laws and ordinances.
Dover, N. H. Ordinances, etc.
Mobilehome park regulations. Dover, 1956.
27p.

1. Trailers and trailer courts - Model laws and ordinances.

VF
728.69
(016)
S51
Trailers and trailer courts - Bibliography.
U.S. Small Business Administration.
Mobile homes, bibliography, by Edward L. Wilson. Washington, 1960.
4p. (Small business bulletin no. 41)

1. Trailers and trailer courts - Bibliography. I. Wilson, Edward L.

VF
728.69
C15ru
1959
Trailers and trailer courts - Model laws and ordinances.
California. Laws, statutes, etc.
Rules and regulations for electrical standards in trailer parks. California administrative code, title 8, chapter 9, article 5, effective July 14, 1956. Rev. Sacramento, Cali Dept. of Industrial Relations, Div. of Housing, 1959.
14p. diagrs., tables.

1. Trailers and trailer courts - Model laws and ordinances. I. California. Dept. of Industrial Relations. (Div. of Housing)

728.69
H25
Trailers and trailer courts - Model laws and ordinances.
Hendrickson, Einar H
Municipal regulation of mobile homes (trailers) and mobile home parks in the State of Washington. Seattle, Bureau of Governmental Research and Services, University of Washington, in cooperation with Association of Washington Cities, 1964.
192p. (Washington (State) University. Bureau of Governmental Research and Services. Report no. 152)

(Cont'd. on next card)

VF
728.69
(016)
S51
1962
Trailers and trailer courts - Bibliography.
U.S. Small Business Administration.
Mobile homes, bibliography, by Edward L. Wilson. Rev. Washington, 1962.
4p. (Small Business bulletin no. 41. [rev.])

1. Trailers and trailer courts - Bibliography. I. Wilson, Edward L.

VF
728.69
C15rul
Trailers and trailer courts - Model laws and ordinances.
California. Laws, statutes, etc.
Rules and regulations for independent trailer coaches. (California Administrative Code, Title 8, Chapter 9, Article 3) 6th ed. Sacramento, Department of Industrial Relations, Division of Housing, 1958.
[18]p. illus.

1. Trailer and trailer courts - Model laws and ordinances. I. California. Dept. of Industrial Relations. (Div. of Housing)

728.69
H25
Hendrickson, Einar H Municipal regulation of mobile home parks ... (Card 2)

Bibliography: p. 190-192.

1. Trailers and trailer courts - Model laws and ordinances. I. Association of Washington Cities. II Washington (State) University. Bureau of Government Research and Services. (Series)

VF
728.69
(016)
S51
1963
Trailers and trailer courts - Bibliography.
Wilson, Edward L
Mobile homes. Rev. Washington, Small Business Administration, 1963.
8p. (U.S. Small Business Administration. Small business bulletin no. 41, rev.)

1. Trailers and trailer courts - Bibl. I. U.S. Small Business Administration. II. Title.

VF
728.69
C15p
Trailers and trailer courts - Model laws and ordinances.
California. Laws, statutes, etc.
Rules and regulations for plumbing installations in trailer parks accommodating independent trailer coaches. (California administrative code, title 8, chapter 9, article 3, amended July 1958) Sacramento, Dept. of Industrial Relations, Division of Housing, 1959.
15p. diagrs.

1. Trailers and trailer courts - Model laws and ordinances. 2. Plumbing. I. California. Dept. of Industrial Relations. (Div. of Housing)

LAW
T
H622La
Trailers and trailer courts - Model laws and ordinances.
Hodes, Barnet.
The law of mobile homes, by Barnet Hodes and G. Gale Robertson. New York, Commerce Clearing House, 1957.
464p.

1. Trailers and trailer courts - Model laws and ordinances. I. Robertson, G. Gale, jt.au. II. Commerce Clearing House. III. Title.

058.7
:728.69
W66
TRAILERS AND TRAILER COURTS - DIRECTORIES.
Woodall's trailering parks and campgrounds, 19
New York, Simon and Schuster, 19
v.
For Library holdings see main entry.

1. Trailers and trailer courts - Direct. 2. Parks - Direct. I. Title: Trailering parks and campgrounds.

VF
728.69
C15r
Trailers and trailer courts - Model laws and ordinances.
California. Laws, statutes, etc.
Rules and regulations for structures in trailer parks. (California Administrative Code, Title 8, Chapter 9, Article 4, amended July 1956) Sacramento, Department of Industrial Relations, Division of Housing, 1957.
[15]p.

1. Trailers and trailer courts - Model laws and ordinances. I. California. Dept. of Industrial Relations. (Div. of Housing)

LAW
T
H622La
1965
Trailers and trailer courts - Model laws and ordinances.
Hodes, Barnet.
The law of mobile homes, by Barnet Hodes and G. Gale Robertson. 2d ed. New York Commerce Clearing House, 1965.
623p.

1. Trailers and trailer courts - Model laws and ordinances. I. Robertson, G. Gale, jt.au. II. Commerce Clearing House. III. Title.

728.69
A52
Trailers and trailer courts - Model laws and ordinances.
Alexandria, Va. Dept. of City Planning and Urban Renewal.
Trailer storage. Alexandria, 1966.
6p. (Its Special study. Rept. no. 4)

1. Trailers and trailer courts - Model laws and ordinances. I. Title.

VF
728.69
C15
Trailers and trailer courts - Model laws and ordinances.
California. Laws, statutes, etc.
Trailer Park Act. (California health and safety code, Division 13, part 2) Minimum requirements for construction and operation of trailer parks, applicable in all parts of the State. Sacramento, Department of Industrial Relations. Division of Housing, 1958.
41p. diagrs.

1. Trailers and trailer courts - Model laws and ordinances. I. California. Dept. of Industrial Relations. (Div. of Housing)

VF
728.69
H62
Trailers and trailer courts - Model laws and ordinances.
Hodes, Barnet
Suggested model ordinance regulating mobile home parks; prepared for Mobile Homes Manufacturers Association. Rev. Chicago, Ill., Mobile Home Manufacturers Association, Jan. 1956.
[8]p.

1. Trailers and trailer courts - Model laws and ordinances. I. Mobile Home Manufacturers Association.

728.69 K51 — Trailers and trailer courts - Model laws and ordinances.
Klamath Falls, Or. Ordinances, etc.
An ordinance regulating trailers and trailer parks. Klamath Falls, 1959.
11p.

U.S. Urban Renewal Administration, Urban Planning Assistance Program.

1. Trailers and trailer courts - Model laws and ordinances. I. U.S. URA-UPAP. Klamath Falls, Or.

728.69 065 — Trailers and trailer courts - Standards and specifications.
[Goldendale, Wash.] Ordinances, etc.
Trailer code ordinance. [Goldendale, 1959?]
[6]p.

U.S. Urban Renewal Adm. UPAP.

1. Trailers and trailer courts - Standards and specifications. I. U.S. URA-UPAP. Goldendale, Wash.

728.69 H17 — Trailers and trailer courts - Surveys.
Harrel, William B
Mobile homes survey: a survey of mobile homes and the taxation problems they cause. by William B. Harrel and Robert L. Nutt. Harrisburg, Pa., Pennsylvania State Association of Boroughs and Municipal Assessors' Association of Pennsylvania, Local Government Center [1966?]
17p.

(Cond't on next card)

728.69 M22 — Trailers and trailer courts - Model laws and ordinances.
Medford, Or. Ordinances, etc.
City of Medford trailer park regulations. [Medford] 1960.
[19]p.

U.S. Urban Renewal Adm. UPAP.

1. Trailers and trailer courts - Model laws and ordinances. I. U.S. URA-UPAP. Medford, Or.

728.69 F22 — Trailers and trailer courts - Standards and specifications.
U.S. Federal Housing Administration.
Minimum property requirements for mobile home courts. [Washington] October 1955.
1 v.

728.69 H17 — Harrel, William B. Mobile homes survey: a survey of mobile homes and the taxation problems they cause...[1966?] (Card 2)

1. Trailers and trailer courts - Taxation.
2. Trailers and trailer courts - Surveys.
I. Nutt, Robert L., jt. au. II. Pennsylvania State Association of Boroughs. III. Municipal Assessors' Association of Pennsylvania. IV. Title.

728.69 S68 — Trailers and trailer courts - Model laws and ordinances.
South Kingstown, R.I. Ordinances, etc.
An act to authorize the town of South Kingstown to enact ordinances regulating and licensing trailer parks and other tourist accommodations. South Kingstown, [1956]
1v.
U.S. Urban Renewal Administration, Urban Planning Assistance Program.
1. Trailers and trailer courts - Model laws and ordinances. I. U.S. Urban Renewal Administration. Urban Planning Assistance Program.

728.69 F22 1961 — Trailers and trailer courts - Standards and specifications.
U.S. Federal Housing Administration.
Minimum property requirements for mobile home courts. Washington, 1961.
1v. (FHA 2424)

1. Trailers and trailer courts - Standards and specifications. 2. Site planning. I. Title.

728.69 H17 — Trailers and trailer courts - Taxation.
Harrel, William B
Mobile homes survey: a survey of mobile homes and the taxation problems they cause. by William B. Harrel and Robert L. Nutt. Harrisburg, Pa., Pennsylvania State Association of Boroughs and Municipal Assessors' Association of Pennsylvania, Local Government Center [1966?]
17p.

(Cond't on next card)

728.69 A52H — TRAILERS AND TRAILER COURTS - SOCIAL EFFECT.
AMERICAN MUNICIPAL ASSOCIATION.
THE HOUSE TRAILER: ITS EFFECT ON STATE AND LOCAL GOVERNMENT. A REPORT PREPARED IN COOPERATION WITH THE AMERICAN PUBLIC WELFARE ASSOCIATION, AMERICAN SOCIETY OF PLANNING OFFICIALS, AND NATIONAL ASSOCIATION OF HOUSING OFFICIALS. CHICAGO, 1937.
57P. (ITS REPORT NO. 115. REPORT NO. 114, REV.)

1. TRAILERS AND TRAILER COURTS - SOCIAL EFFECT. I. TITLE.

728.69 F22ST — TRAILERS AND TRAILER COURTS - STANDARDS AND SPECIFICATIONS.
U.S. FEDERAL PUBLIC HOUSING AUTHORITY.
STANDARDS FOR WAR TRAILER PROJECTS, BY FEDERAL PUBLIC HOUSING AUTHORITY. WASHINGTON, 1942.
21L.

1. TRAILERS AND TRAILER COURTS - STANDARDS AND SPECIFICATIONS. I. TITLE.

728.69 H17 — Harrel, William B. Mobile homes survey: a survey of mobile homes and the taxation problems they cause...[1966?] (Card 2)

1. Trailers and trailer courts - Taxation.
2. Trailers and trailer courts - Surveys.
I. Nutt, Robert L., jt. au. II. Pennsylvania State Association of Boroughs. III. Municipal Assessors' Association of Pennsylvania. IV. Title.

VF 728.69 (794) C15 p — Trailers and trailer courts - Standards and specifications
California. Laws, Statutes, etc.
Plumbing regulations for independent trailer coaches; California administrative code, Title 8, Chapter 9, Article 3. 3d ed. San Francisco, 1956.
1 v. diagrs.

— Same. 2d ed. 1954.

1. Plumbing codes - California. 2. Trailers and trailer courts - Standards and specifications. I. California. (Dept. of) Industrial Relations. (Division of) Housing.

728.69 H68R — TRAILERS AND TRAILER COURTS - STANDARDS AND SPECIFICATIONS.
U.S. HOUSING AND HOME FINANCE AGENCY.
RECOMMENDED STANDARDS FOR TRAILER COURTS. WASH., GOVT. PRINT. OFF., 1954.
24P.

1. TRAILERS AND TRAILER COURTS - STANDARDS AND SPECIFICATIONS.

728.69 034 — Trailers and trailer courts - Taxation.
Ohio. Dept. of Taxation.
Taxation of house trailers in Ohio and other states. Columbus, Ohio, 1958.
18p.

1. Trailers and trailer courts - Taxation. I. Title.

VF 728.69 (794) C15r — Trailers and trailer courts - Standards and specifications.
California. Laws, statutes, etc.
Rules and regulations for structures in trailer parks (California Administrative Code, title 8, chapter 9, article 4) Sacramento, Calif., State of California, Department of Industrial Relations, Division of Housing, 1954.
19p.

728.69 P81M — TRAILERS AND TRAILER COURTS - STANDARDS AND SPECIFICATIONS.
U.S. PUBLIC HEALTH SERVICE.
MOBILE HOME PARK SANITATION, WITH A SUGGESTED ORDINANCE. CHICAGO, PRINTED BY MOBILE HOME MANUFACTURERS ASSOCIATION, 1960.
28P.

1. TRAILERS AND TRAILER COURTS - STANDARDS AND SPECIFICATIONS. I. MOBILE HOME MANUFACTURERS ASSOCIATION. II. TITLE.

728.69 P27 — Trailers and trailer courts - Taxation.
Peterson, J R
Mobile homes in Georgia. A study of the personal property taxes levied on mobile homes in the metropolitan areas of Georgia and the significance of the mobile home industry to the state. Prepared for the Georgia Mobile Home Association in cooperation with the Georgia Department of Industry and Trade and the Mobile Home Manufacturers Association, by J. R. Peterson and Harvey Diamond. Atlanta,

(Continued on next card)

VF 728.69 (794) C15s — Trailers and trailer courts - Standards and specifications.
California. Laws, Statutes, etc.
State trailer park act (Health and safety code, division 13, part 2) Sacramento, Calif., State of California, Department of Industrial Relations, Division of Housing, 1954.
36p. diagrs.

1. Trailers and trailer courts - Standards and specifications. I. California. Dept. of Industrial Relations. Div. of Housing.

728.69 P81 — Trailers and trailer courts - Standards and Specifications.
U. S. Public Health Service (Division of Sanitation)
Trailer court sanitation, with suggested ordinances and regulations. /Chicago/ Mobile Homes Manufacturer's Association, 1953.
29 p. illus., plans.

"References": p. 19.

728.69 P27 — Peterson, J R Mobile homes in Georgia. A study of the personal property taxes levied on mobile homes...1965. (Card 2)

Engineering Experiment Station, Georgia Institute of Technology, 1965.
29p.

1. Trailers and trailer courts - Taxation. I. Georgia Mobile Home Association. II. Georgia. State Engineering Experiment Station.

728.69
T74 Trailers and trailer courts - Taxation.
Tri-County Regional Planning Commission.
(Peoria, Tazewell, Woodford Counties, Ill.)
The mobile home and its place. Peoria, Ill.,
1967.
24p.

1. Trailers and trailer courts. 2. Trailers
and trailer courts - Taxation. I. Title.

U. S. *Congress. Senate. Committee on Post Office and
Civil Service.* Training and education in the Federal
Government ... (Card 2)
the period of the national emergency. Washington, U. S.
Govt. Print. Off., 1953.
iii, 24 p. 24 cm. (83d Cong., 1st sess. Senate. Document no. 31)

1. Employees, Training of. 2. Civil service - U. S. I. Title.
(Series: U. S. 83d Cong., 1st sess., 1953. Senate. Document no. 31)

JK718.A54 1953c *351.3 351.1 53-60654
Library of Congress [2]

711.585.1
T71 Training Corporation of America.
Final report and proposal for resident
observer study and report on model cities
program. Submitted to Department of
Housing and Urban Development, Contracts
and Agreements Division. Wash., 1970.
pts.
HUD contract H-1006, RFP HUD-27-68.
1. Model cities. I. U.S. HUD. Model
Cities Program. II. Title: Resident
observer study.

711
(016)
C65 Trails.
no.175 Marsh, John S
Recreation trails in Canada: a comment and
bibliography on trail development and use with
special reference to the Rocky Mountain
National Parks and proposed Great Divide Trail.
Calgary, Alta., Geography Dept., University of
Calgary, 1971.
17p. (Council of Planning Librarians.
Exchange bibliography no. 175)
1. Planning - Bibl. 2. Recreation - Bibl.
I. Calgary, Alta. University. II. Title.
III. Title: Trails. (Series: Council of
Planning Librarians. Exchange bibliography
no. 175)

LAW
T The training and employment of offenders.
F723tra Freedman, Marcia.
The training and employment of offenders, by
Marcia Freedman and Nick Pappas. [Report] sub-
mitted to the President's Commission on Law
Enforcement and Administration of Justice.
[n.p.] 1967.
63p.
Bibliography: [p. 64-70]
1. Vocational guidance. 2. Juvenile delin-
quency. 3. Law enforcement. I. Pappas, Nick,
jt. au. II. U.S. President's Commission on
Law Enforcement and Administration of Justice.
III. Title.

614
(79492)
P81 Training course environmental health survey
report and recommendations greater...
U.S. Public Health Service. (Bureau
of State Services)
Training course environmental health
survey report and recommendations greater
San Buenaventura, California; a report
of an environmental health survey of the
City of San Buenaventura, California and
adjacent areas of Ventura County conducted
as a training exercise during presentation
of the course Urban Planning for Environmental Health, February 24-29, 1964.
Wash., 1964.
78p. (Continued on next card)

VF
339.5
T71 Train, Russell E
America the beautiful. An address by the
President, the Conservation Foundation,
before the 90th annual meeting of the American Forestry Association held jointly with
the National Council of State Garden Clubs,
Grand Teton National Park, Wyoming, Sept. 6,
1965. Wash., Conservation Foundation, 1965.
[20]p.

1. Natural resources. I. Conservation
Foundation. II. American Forestry
Association. III. Title.

331
C65tr Training and jobs for the urban poor.
Committee for Economic Development.
Training and jobs for the urban poor. A
statement on national policy by the Research
and Policy Committee of the Committee for
Economic Development. New York, 1970.
78p.

1. Employment. 2. Education - Minority
groups. 3. Employment - Minority groups.
I. Title.

614
(79492)
P81 U.S. Public Health Service. (Bureau of
State Services) Training...1964. (Card 2)

Conducted by the California State Dept.
of Public Health and the Robert A. Taft
Sanitary Engineering Center.
1. Public health - San Buenaventura,
Calif. I. California. Dept. of Public
Health. II. U.S. Robert A. Taft Sanitary
Engineering Center. III. Title.

658
C71 Training and development handbook.
Craig, Robert L ed.
Training and development handbook, edited by
Robert L. Craig and Lester R. Bittel. Sponsored
by the American Society for Training and
Development. New York, McGraw-Hill, 1967.
650p.
1. Management. 2. Personnel management.
3. Vocational guidance. 4. Education. I. Bittel,
Lester R., jt. ed. II. American Society for
Training and Development. III. Title.

058.7
:711.583 Training and technical assistance directory.
N17 National Association for Community Development.
NACD training and technical assistance
directory. [n.p.] 1970.
112p.

1. Community development - Direct.
I. Title: Training and technical assistance
directory.

614
(66155)
P81 Training course environmental health
survey report and recommendation...
U.S. Public Health Service.
Training course environmental
health survey report and recommendation: Rochester-Olmsted County,
Minnesota. A report of an environmental health survey conducted as a training exercise during presentation of
the course Urban planning for environmental health, September 21 - 26, 1964,
in Rochester-Olmsted County, Minnesota. Co-sponsored by Minnesota Dept.
of Health and others. [n.p.] 1964.
114p.
(Cont'd on next card)

658.3
T71 Training and development systems.
Tracey, William R
Evaluating training and development
systems. New York, American Management
Association, 1968.
304p. (AMA management bookshelf)

1. Personnel management. I. Title:
Training and development systems.
II. Title.

711.585.1
073 Training and technical assistance in planning and evaluation to model cities.
Organization for Social and Technical
Innovation.
Training and technical assistance in
planning and evaluation to model cities.
City summaries final report. [Prepared in
cooperation with] Marshall Kaplan, Gans and
Kahn and CONSULTEC, inc. Cambridge, Mass.,
[1972]
178p.
U.S. Dept. of Housing and Urban Development.
Model Cities Administration contract no.H-1097.
1. Model Cities. I. Kaplan (Marshall), Gans
and Kahn. II. CONSULTEC, inc. III. U.S. Dept.
of Housing and Urban Development. Model
Cities Administration. IV. Title

614
(66155)
P81 U.S. Public Health Service. Training
course...1964. (Card 2)

Cover title: An application of the
environmental health planning guide,
by the students attending the course,
Urban planning for environmental
health. Survey of Rochester, Minnesota.

1. Public health - Rochester, Minn.
2. Housing and health. I. Title:
Environ- mental health planning guide. II. Title: Urban
(Cont'd on next card)

658.3
(016)
M27 TRAINING AND EDUCATION FOR MANPOWER
DEVELOPMENT.
MESICS, EMIL A
TRAINING AND EDUCATION FOR MANPOWER
DEVELOPMENT; BUSINESS, INDUSTRY,
GOVERNMENT, SERVICE ORGANIZATIONS,
EDUCATIONAL INSTITUTIONS; AN ANNOTATED
BIBLIOGRAPHY. ITHACA, N.Y., 1964.
99P. (NEW YORK STATE SCHOOL OF
INDUSTRIAL AND LABOR RELATIONS, CORNELL
UNIVERSITY. BIBLIOGRAPHY SERIES NO. 7)

1. PERSONNEL MANAGEMENT - BIBLIOGRAPHY.
I. TITLE. II. NEW YORK STATE SCHOOL
OF INDUSTRIAL AND LABOR RELATIONS,
CORNELL UNIVERSITY.

362.6
W34 Training; background.
1971 White House Conference on Aging, Washington, 1971.
no.11 Training; background, by James E. Birren.
Issues, by the Technical Committee on Training,
with the collaboration of the author. Wash.,
1971.
81p. [no. 11]
Cover title: Background and issues; training.
Bibliography: p. 79-81.

1. Old age. 2. Old age - Education.
I. Birren, James E. II. Title.

614
(66155)
P81 U.S. Public Health Service. Training
course...1964. (Card 3).

planning for environmental health.
III. Minnesota. Dept. of Health.
IV. Title.

351.1
C65 Training and education in the Federal Govern-
no.31 ment.
U. S. *Congress. Senate. Committee on Post Office and
Civil Service.*
Training and education in the Federal Government. A
report with conclusions and recommendations made as a
result of the investigation into the personnel needs and practices of the various governmental agencies being conducted
by the Subcommittee on Federal Manpower Policies pursuant to Senate resolution 53, as amended by Senate resolutions 206 and 288, with the purpose of formulating policies
for the most effective utilization of civilian personnel during

(Continued on next card) 53-60654
[2]

728.1
H68 Training conferences, HHFA.
U.S. Housing and Home Finance Agency.
Housing and Home Finance Agency training
conferences, April 16-20 and June 4-6, 1956.
[Washington, 1957]
278 p.

1.U.S. Housing and Home Finance Agency.
2.Federal housing programs. 3.Urban renewal.
4.Mortgage insurance. 5.Housing - Study and
teaching. I.Title: Training conferences, HHFA.

658.78
I57 Training course in material handling
for use in supervisory training
programs.
U.S. International Cooperation
Administration. Office of Industrial
Resources.
Training course in material handling
for use in supervisory training programs;
outline with reference material to assist
in the development of supervisors. Washington, 1956.
82 p. illus. (Its Technical bulletin
no. 11)

1. Materials handling. 2. Personnel
management. I. T

058.7 TRAINING COURSES IN AUTOMATIC DATA
:538.56 PROCESSING.
882 U.S. BUREAU OF THE BUDGET.
1961 DIRECTORY OF ORIENTATION AND
TRAINING COURSES IN AUTOMATIC DATA
PROCESSING. WASHINGTON, 1961.
12P. (ISSUE NO. 3)

PREVIOUSLY TITLED :DIRECTORY OF:
EXECUTIVE ORIENTATION COURSES.

1. AUTOMATION - DIRECTORIES.
2. AUTOMATION - STUDY AND TEACHING.
I. TITLE. II. TITLE: TRAINING
COURSES IN AU TOMATIC DATA
PROCESSING.

658.3 Training group leaders.
A28 Adult Education Association of the U.S.A.
Training group leaders. A practical aid
to leaders in education, government, welfare,
health, farm, labor, religion, industry, and
the community. Chicago, 1956.
48p. (Leadership pamphlet no. 8)

1. Personnel management. I. Title.

711.585 Training Institute in Residential Rehabilita-
M12res tion. University of Minn., 1965.
McFarland, M Carter, ed.
Residential rehabilitation, edited by
M. Carter McFarland and Walter K. Vivrett.
A compilation of papers presented at the
Training Institute in Residential Rehabilita-
tion, University of Minnesota, Minneapolis,
July 19-30, 1965. Minneapolis, School of
Architecture, University of Minnesota, 1966.
331p.
U.S. Dept. of Housing and Urban Develop-
ment. Demonstration Grant Program.
Partial contents:- Residential rehabilita-
tion: an over-   view, by M. C.
McFarland.

(Cont'd on next card)

728.1 TRAINING CURRICULUM.
B11 BABCOCK, FREDRICK M
TRAINING CURRICULUM, FHA MULTIPLE
HOUSING PROGRAMS REPORT. WASHINGTON,
1961.
1 V.

REPORT PREPARED UNDER CONTRACT NO. HA
(—) FH-841, DATED SEPT. 1, 1961
BETWEEN F.M. BABCOCK AND FHA.

1. HOUSING. 2. FEDERAL HOUSING
PROGRAM. I. TITLE.

---

360 Training home economics program assistants to
(07) work with low income families.
F22 U.S. Federal Extension Service.
Training home economics program assistants
to work with low income families. Prepared
under direction of Janalyce Rouls, consultant
and others. Washington, For sale by Supt. of
Long. Doc.,Govt. Print. Off., 1965.
110p. (PA-681)

1. Social welfare - Study and teaching.
2. Family income and expenditure. 3. Home economics.
I. Rouls, Janalyce. II. Title. III. Title:
Home economics program assistants.

711.585 McFarland, M Carter, ed. Residential
M12res rehabilitation...1966. (Card 2)

Residential rehabilitation potential through
the urban renewal program by R.E. McCabe,
Assistant Commissioner for Field Operations,
Urban Renewal Administration.--Rehabilitation
standards, by M.C. Farland.
Editor is Ass't Commissioner for Office of
the Assistant Commissioner for Programs.

(Cont'd on next card)

658.3 Training director's handbook.
(07) Bureau of Business Practice.
B87 The BBP training director's handbook.
Waterford, Conn., 1970-

v. (loose-leaf)

1. Personnel management - Study and teaching.
I. Title. II. Title: Training director's
handbook.

---

029 Training in indexing; a course of the Society
T71 of Indexers. Edited by G. Norman Knight.
Cambridge, Mass., M.I.T. Press, 1969.
219p.

Bibliography: p. 202-203.

1. Indexing. I. Knight, Gilfred Norman,
1891- ed. II. Society of Indexers.

711.585 McFarland, M Carter, ed. Residential
M12res rehabilitation...1966. (Card 3)

1. Neighborhood rehabilitation. 2. Urban renewal.
I. Vivrett, Walter K., jt.ed. II. McCabe, Robert E.
Residential rehabilitation potential through the
urban renewal program. III. McFarland, M. Carter.
Rehabilitation standards. IV. Training Institute in
Residential Rehabilitation. University of Minn.,
1965. V. Title. VI. U.S. Housing and Urban
Development, Demonstration Grant Program.

658.3 Training film index.
:770. This, Leslie E ed.
T34 Training film index; films on audio-visual
aids, communications, community action and
citizen responsibility, human behavior and
human relations, leadership, training
methodology, miscellaneous. Washington, Leadership Resources, 1961.
26p. (Learning about leadership series)

1. Films - Bibliography. 2. Personnel
management films. I. Title.

362.6 Training in social gerontology and its
(07) application.
H21t U.S. Dept. of Health, Education, and
Welfare. (Office of Aging)
Training in social gerontology and its
application; a suggested university curricu-
lum. Prepared by the Division of Research and
Training of the Office of Aging. Washington
Govt. Print. Off., 1965.
21p. (OA-222)

1. Old age - Study and teaching. 2. Housing for the aged - Study and teaching.
3. Social welfare - Study and teaching.
I. Title.

362.6 Training manual for human service technicians
L68t Lowy, Louis. working with...
Training manual for human service tech-
nicians working with older people. Developed
under the auspices of United Community
Services of Metropolitan Boston and Boston
University, School of Social Work. Boston,
Boston University Bookstores, 1968.
2 pts.
1. Old age. 2. Social service. I. United
Community Services of Metropolitan Boston.
II. Boston University. School of Social
Work. III. Title.

658.3 Training first-line supervisors.
B87p Bureau of National Affairs, Washington, D.C.
no.78 Training first-line supervisors. Wash.,
1966.
13p. (Its Personnel policies forum
survey no. 78)

1. Personnel management. I. Title.

VF Training Institute for Public Welfare
362.6 Specialists in Aging, Cleveland, 1965.
T41m Tibbitts, Clark.
Middle aged and older people in American
society. Address before the Training
Institute for Public Welfare Specialists in
Aging, Cleveland, Ohio, June 13, 1965.
Wash., Dept of Health, Education, and
Welfare, Administration on Aging, 1965.
30p.
OA-227.

1. Old age. 2. Old age - Social service.
I. Training Institute for Public Welfare
Specialists in Aging, Cleveland, 1965.
II. Title.

690.091.83 A training manual in field inspection of build-
C65t ings and structures.
Colling, R C , ed.
A training manual in field inspection
of buildings and structures; by R. C. Colling
and Hal Colling under the direction of Rolland
P. Cravens and Arthur G. Clark; from material
developed by the First Institute for Training
Technical Personnel. Los Angeles, International
Conference of Building Officials [1956]
174 p. illus., diagrs., forms.

301.15 Training for community development.
(07) Anderson, C David, ed.
A52 Training for community development. Vol.
v.1 1. An introduction to the theory of
community development. A curriculum for
village level workers in the traditional
society. New York, S.A.R., Associated
Educational Services Corporation, 1968.
173p.
1. Community development - Study and
teaching. 2. Community development -
Bolivia. I. Associated Educational
Services Corp. II. Title.

362.6 Training Institute for Public Welfare
H21pl Specialists on Aging, Cleveland, 1965.
1965 U.S. Dept. of Health, Education, and
Welfare.
Planning welfare services for older people.
Papers presented at the Training Institute
for Public Welfare Specialists on Aging,
Cleveland, Ohio, June 13-24, 1965.
Washington, U.S. Dept. of Health, Education,
and Welfare, Welfare Administration, Bureau
of Family Services, for sale by the Supt. of
Documents, Govt. Print. Off., 1966.
198p.

(Cont'd on next card)

690.091.83 A training manual in field inspection of
I57 buildings and structures.
International Conference of Building
Officials.
A training manual in field inspection
of buildings and structures. Pasadena,
Calif., 1968.
174p.

1. Building inspection.
I. Title: Field inspection of buildings
and structures. II. Title.

711.585.1 Training for model neighborhood residents.
H68mod U.S. Dept. of Housing and Urban Development.
no.10 Training for model neighborhood residents.
Wash., 1971.
66p. (Model cities management series
bulletin no. 10)
Cover title: Citizens training.

1. Model cities. I. Title: Citizens
training. II. Title. (Series: Model cities
management series bulletin no. 10)

362.6 U.S. Dept. of Health, Education, and
H21pl Welfare. Planning welfare services for
1965 older people...1966. (Card 2)

1. Old age - Social service. 2. Social
welfare - Study and teaching. I. Training
Institute for Public Welfare Specialists
on Aging, Cleveland, 1965. II. Title.

---

370 Training methodology.
(016) U.S. Public Health Service.
P81 (Health Services and Mental Health
Administration)
Training methodology; an annotated
bibliography. [Wash.] 1969.
4 pts. (U.S. Public Health Service.
Publication no. 1862, pts. I-IV)
Contents.-Part I: Background theory
and research.-Part II: Planning and
administration.-Part III: Instructional
methods and techniques.-Part IV:
Audiovisual theory, aids, and
equipment. (Cont'd on next card)

333.65
W66
A training model for low rent housing
management.
Wood, W Kent.
A training model for low rent housing
management. A training kit for instructors.
[n.p., 1971?]
191p.
Developed pursuant to a Stokes, Wood and
Associates contract with the Dept. of Housing
and Urban Development in cooperation with the
Dept. of Health, Education, and Welfare.
1. Housing management. 2. Low income
housing. I. Stokes, Wood and Associates.
II. U.S. Dept. of Housing and Urban
Development. III. Title.

331.86
B74
Training of operatives.
British Specialist Team on the Training of
Industrial Operatives.
Training of operatives; report of one of four
specialist teams which visited the United States
of America in 1951 to study problems of training
for industry. London, Anglo-American Council on
Productivity, Oct. 1951.
52 p.
1. Apprenticeship. I. Anglo-American Council on
Productivity. II. Title.

VF
333.65
N17t
A training program for housing management.
National Association of Housing Officials.
(Management Division.)
A training program for housing management;
learning from practical experience. Chicago, Ill
March 1941.
22 p. (Its publication no. NM 131)
Bibliography: p. 19-20.
1. Housing management - Study and teaching.
I. Title.

728.1
:362.6
V63
Training needs in managing housing for
the elderly.
Vogelsang, Frederick.
Training needs in managing housing for
the elderly. Final report to the
Administration on Aging by the National
Association of Housing and Redevelopment
Officials. [Chicago] National Association
of Housing and Redevelopment Officials,
1968.
157p.
1. Housing for the aged. 2. Housing
management. I. National Association
(Cont'd on next card)

651.5
(07)
A76
TRAINING OF RECORDS PERSONNEL.
U.S. ATOMIC ENERGY COMMISSION.
MANUAL OF SUGGESTED PROCEDURES FOR THE
TRAINING OF RECORDS PERSONNEL.
WASHINGTON, RECORDS MANAGEMENT BRANCH,
ATOMIC ENERGY COMMISSION, 1948
VARIOUS PAGING.
1. RECORDS MANAGEMENT - STUDY AND
TEACHING. 2. PERSONNEL MANAGEMENT -
STUDY AND TEACHING. I. TITLE:
TRAINING OF RECORDS PERSONNEL.

711.4
(07)
H68T
TRAINING PROGRAM FOR STUDENT PLANNERS.
U.S. HOUSING AND HOME FINANCE AGENCY.
TRAINING PROGRAM FOR STUDENT PLANNERS.
(STUDENT TRAINEE - STUDENT ASSISTANT)
WASHINGTON, 1959.
5P.
1. CITY PLANNING - STUDY AND TEACHING.
2. FEDERAL CIVIL SERVICE. I. TITLE.

728.1
:362.6
V63
Vogelsang, Frederick. Training...1968.
(Card 2)
of Housing and Redevelopment Officials.
II. U.S. Administration on Aging.
III. Title.

658.3
(016)
T71
TRAINING OFFICERS CONFERENCE.
TRAINING MATERIALS BIBLIOGRAPHY.
WASHINGTON, 1957.
72P.
1. PERSONNEL MANAGEMENT - BIBLIOGRAPHY.

711.5
:347
T71
Training, Research and Development, inc.
Career ladder and curriculum guide. Wash.,
[1971?]
45p.
U.S. Dept. of Housing and Urban Development,
Office of Small Town Services and Intergovern-
mental Relations, Community Development Training
Program. Contract no. H-1285.
1. Zoning legislation. I. U.S. Dept. of
Housing and Urban Development. II. Title.

711
(016)
C65
no.206
The training of citizen-agents of planned
community change.
Bolton, Charles K
A selected bibliography for the training of
citizen-agents of planned community change, by
Charles K. Bolton and Kenneth E. Corey.
Cincinnati, Institute for Research and Training
in Higher Education, University of Cincinnati,
1971.
31p. (Council of Planning Librarians.
Exchange bibliography no. 206)
A revised edition of CPL Exchange bibliography
no. 125 of April 1970.
1. Planning - Bibl. 2. Community development - Citizen participation - Bibl.
(Cont'd on next card)

720.07
B74
THE TRAINING OF THE ARCHITECT.
BRIGGS, MARTIN SHAW, 1882-.
THE TRAINING OF THE ARCHITECT.
LONDON, H.M. STATIONERY OFF., 1943.
50P. (BOARD OF EDUCATION.
EDUCATIONAL PAMPHLETS, NO. 118)
1. ARCHITECTS. 2. ARCHITECTURE -
STUDY AND TEACHING. I. TITLE.

690.091.82
:613.5
T71
Training, Research and Development, inc.
Handbook for training; code enforcement
and zoning inspection personnel. Wash.,
[1971?]
163p.
U.S. Dept. of Housing and Urban Develop-
ment, Office of Small Town Services and
Intergovernmental Relations, Community
Development Training Program. Contract no.
H-1285.
Bibliography: p. 149-163.
(Cont'd on next card)

711
(016)
C65
no.206
Bolton, Charles K A selected...1971.
(Card 2)
I. Corey, Kenneth E., jt. comp. II. Cincinnati.
University. Institute for Research and
Training in Higher Education. III. Title: The
training of citizen-agents of planned community
change. (Series: Council of Planning Librari-
ans. Exchange bibliography no. 206)

351.74
B17
Training police as specialists in family
crisis intervention.
Bard, Morton.
Training police as specialists in family
crisis intervention. Wash., National Institute of Law Enforcement and Criminal Justice,
1970.
65p. (PR 70-1, May, 1970)
1. Police. 2. Family. I. U.S. National
Institute of Law Enforcement and Criminal
Justice. II. Title.

690.091.82
:613.5
T71
Training, Research and Development, inc.
Handbook for ... [1971?] (Card 2)
1. Housing law enforcement. I. U.S.
Dept. of Housing and Urban Development.
II. Title.

658.3
H68t
Training of finance analysts.
U.S. Housing and Home Finance Agency.
Office of the Administrator. Div. of
Personnel.
Training of finance analysts. Washington,
1959.
12p.
Training guide.
"The material in this training guide was
developed by the Finance Branch, Community
Facilities Administration."
(Continued on next card)

658.3
H68t
1962
Training program, finance analysts guide.
U.S. Housing and Home Finance Agency. Office
of the Administrator. Div. of Personnel.
Training program, finance analysts guide.
Washington [1962?]
12p.
"The material in this training guide was
developed by the Finance Branch, Community
Facilities Administration."
1. Personnel management. 2. Accounting -
Study and teaching. I. U.S. Community
Facilities Administration.
II. Title.

658.3
S67
TRAINING SUPERVISORS IN HUMAN
RELATIONS.
SPRIEGEL, WILLIAM ROBERT, 1893-.
TRAINING SUPERVISORS IN HUMAN
RELATIONS, BY W.R. SPRIEGEL AND EDWIN
W. MUMMA. AUSTIN, BUREAU OF BUSINESS
RESEARCH, UNIVERSITY OF TEXAS, 1961.
43P. (UNIVERSITY OF TEXAS. BUREAU OF
BUSINESS RESEARCH. PERSONNEL STUDY NO.
13)
1. PERSONNEL MANAGEMENT. I. MUMMA,
EDWIN W., JT. AU. II. TITLE.

658.3
H68t
U.S. Housing and Home Finance Agency.
Office of the Administrator. Div. of
Personnel. Training of ... (Card 2)
1. Personnel management. 2. Accounting -
Study and teaching. I. U.S. Community
Facilities Administration. II. Title.

690.591
N17tr
Training program for housing maintenance
employees.
National Association of Housing and Redevel-
opment Officials.
Training program for housing maintenance
employees; developed and prepared by the
Housing Authority of New Orleans. Wash.,
1970.
35p. (NAHRO publication no. N544)
1. Houses - Maintenance and modernization.
I. New Orleans. Housing Authority.
II. Title.

362.5
S28
Training the poor.
Sewell, D O
Training the poor; a benefit-cost analysis of
manpower programs in the U.S. antipoverty
program. Kingston, Ont., Industrial Relations
Centre, Queen's University, 1971.
153p. (Kingston, Ont. Queen's University.
Industrial Relations Centre. Research series:
no. 12)
Bibliography: p. 147-153.
1. Poverty. 2. Labor supply. 3. Education -
Minority groups. I. Kingston, Ont. Queen's
University. Industrial Relations Centre.
II. Title.

371.4
831

Training the poor for new careers.

Shaffer, Anatole.
Training the poor for new careers, by Anatole Shaffer and Harry Specht. Walnut Creek, Contra Costa Council of Community Services, 1966.
57p. (Contra Costa Council of Community Services. Monograph no. 105)

1. Vocational guidance. 2. Occupations. 3. Social service. I. Specht, Harry, jt. au. II. Contra Costa Co., Calif. Council of Community Services. III. Title.

690.592
F71

Training-Thru-Sight Associates, New York.
Frankl, Lee.
Home repairs made easy; the complete illustrated guide with 2056 easy-to-follow pictures, by Training-Thru-Sight Associates: Lee Frankl. [1st ed.] Garden City, N. Y., N. Doubleday [1949].

ix, 488 p. illus. 29 cm.

"List of selected publications": p. 423–424.

1. Houses—Maintenance and modernization. 1. Building—Repair and reconstruction. I. Training-Thru-Sight Associates, New York. II. Title.

TH3401.F7   643.7   49–0036*

Library of Congress   [10]

693
F71

Training-Thru-Sight Associated, New York.
Frankl, Lee.
The masonry house; step-by-step construction in tile and brick [by] Training-Thru-Sight Associates: Lee Frankl, in cooperation with Structural Clay Products Institute. New York, Duell, Sloan & Pearce [1950].

124 p. illus. 28 cm. (Basic industrial series)

1. Brick construction. 2. Masonry. 3. Building, Brick. 3. Tile construction. I. Training-Thru-Sight Associates, New York. II. Title. (Series) III. Structural Clay Products Institute.

TH1199.F7   690   50–8592

Library of Congress   [20]

694
F71s

Training-Thru-Sight Associates, New York.
Frankl, Lee
Small house carpentry: framing, sheathing, insulation. Training-Thru-Sight Associates. New York, N.Y., Prentice-Hall [c1948].
99 p. illus., diagrs. (part fold.), plans. (Basic industrial series)

1. Carpentry. 2. Wood framing. I. Training-Thru-Sight Associates, New York. II. Title.

694
F71

Training-Thru-Sight Associates, New York.
Frankl, Lee.
Exterior-interior finish for the small house. Training-Thru-Sight Associates: Lee Frankl. New York, Prentice-Hall [1950].

105 p. illus., plans. 28 cm. (Basic industrial series)

Methods developed by Small Homes Council used for this Industry Engineered House.

1. Building, Wooden. 2. Carpentry. 3. Architecture—Details. I. Training-Thru-Sight Associates, New York. II. Title. (Series)
For full tracings see main entry.

TH5607.F7   694   50–7855

Library of Congress   [50o7]

690.592
F71h

Training-Thru-Sight Associates, New York.
Frankl, Lee.
How to expand and improve your home; the complete, step-by-step illustrated guide for expanding, altering, and modernizing your home, by Training-Thru-Sight Associates: Lee Frankl. New York, Simmons-Boardman [1951].

ix, 245 p. illus. 28 cm.

1. Houses—Maintenance and modernization. 1. Building—Repair and reconstruction. I. Training-Thru-Sight Associates, New York. II. Title.

TX301.F7   643.7   51–9598

Library of Congress   [10]

658
(061.3)
I57
1962

Training today for the world of tomorrow.

Institute of the Training Officers Conference, Washington, D.C., 1962.
Training today for the world of tomorrow. Proceedings of the annual Institute of the Training Officers Conference. A summary of the Institute held April 24, 1962, at the International Conference Room, U.S. Dept. of State, Washington, D.C. Washington, 1962.
44p.

1. Management - Congresses. 2. Personnel management - Congresses. I. Title.

658.3
(07)
A52T

TRAINING UNDERSTUDIES.

AMERICAN MANAGEMENT ASSOCIATION.
TRAINING UNDERSTUDIES. NEW YORK, 1952.
11P.

1. PERSONNEL MANAGEMENT - STUDY AND TEACHING. I. TITLE.

388
V15

Trains, tracks, and travel.

Van Metre, Thurman W
Trains, tracks and travel, by Thurman W. Van Metre and Russel Gordon Van Metre. Rev. 9th ed. New York, Simmons-Boardman, 1960.
501 p.

1. Transportation. 2. Railroads. I. Van Metre, Russel Gordon, jt. au. II. Title.

699.85
I55T

TRAJECTORY ANALYSIS FOR STRUCTURAL FRAGMENTS.

IIT RESEARCH INSTITUTE, CHICAGO.
TRAJECTORY ANALYSIS FOR STRUCTURAL FRAGMENTS, BY EDWARD B. AHLERS. CHICAGO, 1965.
94L. (ITS STRUCTURES RESEARCH MEMORANDUM NO. SRM-65-1)

DISTRIBUTED AS AN ADDENDUM TO THE FINAL REPORT ON DEBRIS CLEARANCE STUDY, PUBLISHED SEPT. 1963.

1. PROTECTIVE CONSTRUCTION. I. AHLERS, EDWARD B. II. TITLE.

627.41
(78883)
H67

Trajectory of a tragedy, Denver area, June 16-17, 1965.

Hotchkiss, inc.
Trajectory of a tragedy, Denver area, June 16-17, 1965. Denver, 1965.
30p.

1. Floods - Denver. I. Title.

691.542
T26

Tran van Huynh, jt. au.

Teoreanu, I
Correlations between the mineralizing effect of substances on Portland cement clinker formation and the periodic system of the elements, by I. Teoreanu and Tran van Huynh. Garston, Eng., Building Research Station, 1971.
[11]p. (Library communication no. 1650)
Translated from the German.
1. Portland cement. I. Tran van Huynh, jt. au. II. U.K. Building Research Station. III. Title. (Series)

325
L12

Trans-action.

Ladner, Joyce.
The new Negro ideology...What "black power" means to Negroes in Mississippi. St. Louis, Washington University, 1967.
[12]p.
Reprinted from: Trans-action, Nov., 1967.
1. Minority groups. 2. Civil rights. 3. Political science. I. Trans-action. II. Washington University, St. Louis. III. Title.

362.5
P45

Transaction.

Pilisuk, Marc, ed.
Poor Americans: how the white poor live, edited by Marc Pilisuk and Phyllis Pilisuk. [n.p.] Aldine Publishing Co., 1971.
192p.

Essays appearing originally in Transaction magazine.

1. Poverty. I. Pilisuk, Phyllis, jt. ed. II. Transaction. III. Title.

699.81
S159

TRANS-ATTACK FIRE SUPPRESSION.

SALZBERG, F
AN APPROACH TO TRANS-ATTACK FIRE SUPPRESSION IN URBAN AREAS, FINAL REPORT BY F. SALZBERG, G.L. MAATMAN AND F.J. VODVARKA FOR OFFICE OF CIVIL DEFENSE. CHICAGO, IIT RESEARCH INSTITUTE, TECHNOLOGY CENTER, 1964.
114p.

BIBLIOGRAPHY: P.98-101.

1. FIRE PROTECTION (MUNICIPAL) 2. ATOMIC BOMB. I. MAATMAN, G.L., JT. AU. II. VODVARKA, FRANK J.
(CONTINUED ON NEXT CARD)

699.81
S159

SALZBERG, F. AN APPROACH TO ...1964.   (CARD 2)

JT. AU. III. ILLINOIS INSTITUTE OF TECHNOLOGY, RESEARCH INSTITUTE. IV. TITLE: TRANS-ATTACK FIRE SUPPRESSION.

551.4
N17AV

TRANS-CANADA HIGHWAY.

NATIONAL RESEARCH COUNCIL, CANADA. DIVISION OF BUILDING RESEARCH.
AVALANCHE DEFENCES FOR THE TRANS-CANADA HIGHWAY AT ROGERS PASS, BY P. SCHAERER. OTTAWA, 1962.
32P. (ITS TECHNICAL PAPER NO. 141)

JOINT PAPER OF THE DEPARTMENT OF PUBLIC WORKS AND THE NATIONAL RESEARCH COUNCIL.

1. LANDSLIDES. I. SCHAERER, P. II. TITLE. III. TITLE: TRANS-CANADA HIGHWAY.

711.581
(76756)
T71

TransCentury Corp.
Texarkana community survey. Wash., [1968]
38p.

1. Neighborhood surveys - Texarkana, Ark. 2. Neighborhood surveys - Texarkana, Tex.

336
A522

TRANSCRIPT OF SPEECHES.

AMERICAN FINANCE CONFERENCE, INC.
TRANSCRIPT OF SPEECHES. ANNUAL CONVENTION. CHICAGO, 1958
V. ANNUAL.
For Library holdings see main entry.
TITLES VARIES SLIGHTLY.

1. FINANCE. 2. CREDIT. I. TITLE.

332.748
M12t

The transfer gap of the United States.

Machlup, Fritz.
The transfer gap of the United States. Princeton, N.J., International Finance Section, Dept. of Economics, Princeton University, 1968.
195-238p. (Reprints in international finance no. 11)

1. Foreign exchange. I. Title. II. Princeton University. (International Finance Section)

388
(016)
S97

Trans-ocean transportation of high value packaged cargo.

Systems Analysis and Research Corp.
Trans-ocean transportation of high value packaged cargo. Bibliography. Prepared for the Under Secretary for Transportation, U.S. Dept. of Commerce, Wash., D.C. Cambridge, Mass., 1966.
64p.
Distributed by U.S. Clearinghouse for Federal Scientific and Technical Information. as Document PB 173 007
1. Transportation - Bibl. I. U.S. Commerce. II. Title.

728.1
:336.18
(77434)
C65
1963
S-R
NO.508

TRANSFER OF CERTAIN PROPERTY
PURCHASED.
U.S. CONGRESS. SENATE. COMMITTEE ON
BANKING AND CURRENCY.
TRANSFER OF CERTAIN PROPERTY
PURCHASED FOR LOW-RENT HOUSING
PROJECT IN DETROIT, MICH. REPORT TO
ACCOMPANY H.R. 772. WASHINGTON,
GOVT. PRINT. OFF., 1963.
2P. (88TH CONGRESS, 1ST SESSION.
SENATE. REPORT NO. 508)

1. PUBLIC HOUSING - DETROIT, MICH.
2. URBAN RENEWAL - DETROIT, MICH.
I. TITLE.

361
W67
1936

Transient.
U.S. Works Progress Administration. Div. of
Social Research.
A survey of the transient and homeless
population in 12 cities, September 1935 and
September 1936; prepared by M. Starr
Northrop, Malcolm J. Brown, Katherine Gordon
... Washington, 1937.
52 p. tables (Its Research bulletin)

1. Public assistance. I. Northrop, M
Starr II. Title: Transient.

388
(7531)
O65tr
1963
H-R

Transit development program for the
National Capital region; report to
accompany H.R. 8929.
U.S. Congress. House. Committee on the
District of Columbia.
Transit development program for the
National Capital region; report to
accompany H.R. 8929. [Washington]
Govt. Print. Off., 1963.
59p. (88th Cong., 1st sess.
House. Report no. 1005)

"Publications of the Joint Committee on
Washington Metropolitan Problems relating
to transportation in the National Capital
(Cont'd. on next
card)

728.1
:336.18
(77434)
C65
1963
H-R
NO.649

TRANSFER OF CERTAIN PROPERTY
PURCHASED FOR LOW-RENT HOUSING
U.S. CONGRESS. HOUSE. COMMITTEE ON
BANKING AND CURRENCY.
TRANSFER OF CERTAIN PROPERTY
PURCHASED FOR LOW-RENT HOUSING PROJECT
IN DETROIT, MICH. REPORT TO ACCOMPANY
H.R. 772. WASHINGTON, GOVT. PRINT.
OFF., 1963.
3P. (88TH CONGRESS, 1ST SESSION.
HOUSE OF REPRESENTATIVES. REPORT NO.
649)

1. PUBLIC HOUSING - DETROIT, MICH.
2. URBAN RENEWAL - DETROIT, MICH.
I. TITLE.

361
W67

The transient unemployed.
U.S. Works Progress Administration. (Division of
Social Research.)
The transient unemployed; a description and
analysis of the transient relief population, by
John N. Webb. Washington, 1935.
132 p. (Its Research monograph III)

1.U.S. Federal Emergency Relief Administration.
(Transient Division) 2.Public assistance. I.Webb,
John N II.Title.

388
(7531)
O65tr
1963
H-R

U.S. Congress. House. Committee on the
District of Columbia. Transit development program ... (Card 2)

region": p. 50.

1. Transportation - District of Columbia
metropolitan area. I. Title.

333.33
(75238)
M87

The transfer of farm and open country real
estate in Cecil County, Md.
Murray, Ray A
The transfer of farm and open country
real estate in Cecil County, Md., 1964,
by Ray A. Murray and Edwin I. Cissel.
College Park, Univ. of Maryland, Agricultural Experiment Station, 1967.
27p. (Maryland. Agricultural Experiment
Station. Miscellaneous publication 625)
1. Real property - Cecil Co., Md. 2. Open
space land. 3. Land use - Cecil Co., Md.
4. Farm mortgages. I. Cissel, Edwin I., jt.
au. II. Maryland. Agricultural Experiment
Station. III. Title.

LAW
T
L427
L230

TRANSILL, CHARLES C
U.S. LIBRARY OF CONGRESS. LEGISLATIVE
REFERENCE SERVICE.
DOCUMENTS ILLUSTRATIVE OF THE
FORMATION OF UNION OF THE AMERICAN
STATES, SELECTED, ARRANGED, AND INDEXED
BY CHARLES C. TANSILL. WASHINGTON,
GOVT. PRINT. OFF., 1927.
1115P. (69TH CONGRESS, 1ST SESSION.
HOUSE. DOCUMENT NO. 398)

1. CONSTITUTION. 2. FEDERAL
GOVERNMENT - HISTORY. I. TRANSILL,
CHARLES C. II. TITLE.

388
(77157)
B17t

Transit in Columbus.
Battelle Memorial Institute.
Transit in Columbus; a summary report to
Advisory Committee on Transit, April 16,
1968. Columbus, Ohio, 1968.
20p.

1. Transportation - Columbus, Ohio.
I. Title.

333.33
(75231)
M17

The transfer of farm and open country real estate
in Caroline County, Maryland.
Maryland. Agricultural Experiment Station.
The transfer of farm and open country
real estate in Caroline County, Maryland,
1964, by Ray A. Murray and Edwin I. Cissel.
College Park, Md., 1967.
25p. (Its Miscellaneous publication no.
622)

1. Real property - Caroline Co., Md.
2. Land use - Caroline Co., Md. 3. Vacant
land. 4. Agriculture - Caroline Co., Md.
I. Murray, A. II. Cissel, Edwin I.
III. Title.

388
:538.56
C15

Transim general purpose transportation...
California. University. Dept. of Engineering.
Transim general purpose transportation
system stimulator; user's manual. Prepared
for the Undersecretary for Transportation,
U.S. Department of Commerce, Washington,
D.C. Los Angeles, 1966.
1v. (Its Report no. 66-6)

1. Transportation - Automation.
I. Title.

388
B18

Transit modernization and street traffic control,
a program of municipal responsibility and
administration.
Bauer, John.
Transit modernization and street traffic
control, a program of municipal responsibility
and administration, by John Bauer and Peter
Costello. Chicago, Public Administration
Service, 1950.
271p.

1. Traffic regulations. I. Costello, Peter,
jt. au. II. Title.

351.1
O65tt
1967
H-R

Transfer of retirement credits.
U.S. Congress. House. Committee on Post
Office and Civil Service.
Transfer of retirement credits to social
security system. Part I. Hearings before
the Subcommittee on Retirement, Insurance,
and Health Benefits of the Committee on Post
Office and Civil Service, House of Representa-
tives, Ninetieth Congress, first session on
H.R. 6784, a bill to amend subchapter 83 of
Title 5, United States Code. Wash., Govt.
Print. Off., 1967.
99p. (Serial no. 90-10)
Hearings held: March 21-22, 1967.
1. Federal civil service. 2. Social
security. 3. Old age. I. Title.

659
C51

Transit advertising.
Clarke, George T
Transit advertising. New York, Transit
Advertising Association, 1970.
91p.

1. Advertising. 2. Transportation.
3. Journey to work. I. Transit Advertising
Association. II. Title.

388
(745)
R36

Transit plan.
Rhode Island. Statewide Comprehensive
Transportation and Land Use Planning
Program.
Transit plan: future mass transit services
and facilities for the State of Rhode
Island. Providence, 1969.
105p. (Its Report no. 9)
U.S. Mass Transportation Demonstration
Grant Program. R.I. P-22; R.I. P-30.
1. Transportation. 2. Journey to
work. I. U.S. Mass Transportation Demon-
stration Grant Program. R.I. II. Title.

333.33
A37

TRANSFERS OF FARM REAL ESTATE.
U.S. BUREAU OF AGRICULTURAL ECONOMICS.
TRANSFERS OF FARM REAL ESTATE; NUMBER
OF PROPERTIES AND ACREAGE TRANSFERRED,
BY TYPE OF TRANSFER, AND AVERAGE
CONSIDERATION IN BONA FIDE SALES. DATA
FOR 414 SELECTED COUNTIES FOR 1933 OR
EARLIER YEARS. WASHINGTON, 1936.
115P.

1. REAL ESTATE BUSINESS. I. TITLE.
II. TITLE: FARM REAL ESTATE.

388
:331
T71

Transit-Advertising Association.
Fact book; information about employed
persons who use transit as their primary
means of going to and from work. New York,
1963.
[30]p.

1. Journey to work.

388
(77311)
C34tr

Transit planning study; Chicago central area.
Chicago Transit Authority.
Transit planning study; Chicago central
area. Chicago, 1968.
v.
Bibliography: p. 191-192.
U.S. Dept. of Housing and Urban Development.
Mass Transportation Demonstration Grant Program. HUD project no. P-Ill-3254
(City of Chicago)
1. Transportation - Chicago. 2. Journey
to work. I. Title. II. U.S. Mass Transportation Demonstration Grant Program.

370
E28t
1969

Transformation of the schoolhouse.
Educational Facilities Laboratories.
Transformation of the schoolhouse. New York,
1969.
48p.

Annual report for 1969.
Bibliography: p. 39-48.

1. Education. I. Title.

659
C51

Transit Advertising Association.
Clarke, George T
Transit advertising. New York, Transit
Advertising Association, 1970.
91p.

1. Advertising. 2. Transportation.
3. Journey to work. I. Transit Advertising
Association. II. Title.

388
(7531)
O65tr

Transit program for the National Capital
Region.
U.S. Congress. House. Committee on the
District of Columbia.
Transit program for the National Capital
Region. Hearings before the Subcommittee
No. 6 of the Committee on the District of
Columbia, House of Representatives, Eighty-
eighth Congress, first session on H.R. 6633
and H.R. 7240, to authorize the prosecution
of a transit development program for the
National Capital Region. Washington,
Govt. Print. Off., 1963.
462p. (Cont'd. on next card)

383
(7531)
C65tr

U.S. Congress. House. Committee on the District of Columbia. Transit program for the National Capital Region...
(Card 2)

Hearings held July 9-31, 1963.

1. Transportation - District of Columbia Metropolitan Area. 2. Journey to work. I. Title.

058.7
:500
S62

Translators and translations: services and sources in science and technology.

Special Libraries Association.
Translators and translations: services and sources in science and technology, edited by Frances E. Kaiser. 2d ed. New York, 1965.
214 p.

1. Science - Directories.
2. Technology - Directories.
I. Title.
II. Kaiser, Frances E., ed.

at

388
H12

Transport and national goals.
Haefele, Edwin T ed.
Transport and national goals. Wash., Brookings Institution, Transport Research Program, 1969.
201p.

1. Transportation. 2. Economic planning. I. Brookings Institution. Transport Research Program. II. Title.

388
C65tra

Transit usage forecasting techniques...

Consad Research Corp.
Transit usage forecasting techniques: a review and new directions. Final report to New Systems Study Project, Urban Transportation Administration, U.S. Dept. of Housing and Urban Development. Pittsburgh, 1968.
170p.
Contract no. H-811.
Bibliography: p. 161-170.

1. Transportation
2. Journey to work. I. U.S. Dept. of Housing and Ur   ban Development. Urban Transpor   tation Administration. II. Title.

628.1
(747)
N28
no. 5

Transmission and distribution of water.
New York (State) Office for Local Government.
Transmission and distribution of water. Albany, 1970.
12p. (Its Water utility management information series for local officials. Water utility management bulletin no. 5)

1. Water-supply - New York (State)
I. Title.

624.131
F45t

Transport and retention of virus-sized particles in porous media.
Filmer, Robert William.
Transport and retention of virus-sized particles in porous media, by R.W. Filmer and A.T. Corey. Fort Collins, Colo., Colorado State University, 1966.
37p. (Colorado. State University, Fort Collins. Sanitary engineering papers no. 1)
Bibliography: p. 3.-32.
1. Soils. I. Colorado. State University, Fort Collins. II. Corey, A.T., jt. au. III. Title.

---

i0.7
v.5

Transition zoning.

Comey, Arthur Coleman, 1886-
Transition zoning, by Arthur C. Comey. Cambridge, Harvard university press, 1933.
xiv, 150 p. front., plates, diagrs. 25ᵐ. (Half-title: Harvard city planning studies. v)

"Compilation of transition clauses": p. 91-143.

1.Zoning. 1. Cities and towns—Planning—Zone system. 2. Cities and towns—U. S. 1. Title. II.Ser.

Library of Congress   NA9050.C6
——— Copy 2.   33—12551

Copyright A 62584   [34g3]   T11

333.332
K45

Transmission line rights of way and residential values: an analysis...
Kinnard, William N
Transmission line rights of way and residential values: an analysis of the impact of overhead electric transmission rights of way, both on the value of adjacent residential properties and on the development of affected land for residential purposes, by William N. Kinnard and G. Ross Stephens. Storrs, Conn., University of Connecticut, Institute of Urban Research, 1965.
2v.   (Connecticut urban research reports no. 7)

(Continued on   next card)

330.15
N178/
NO.40

TRANSPORT AND THE STATE OF TRADE IN BRITAIN.
HULTGREN, THOR.
TRANSPORT AND THE STATE OF TRADE IN BRITAIN. [NEW YORK] 1953.
114P. (NATIONAL BUREAU OF ECONOMIC RESEARCH. OCCASIONAL PAPER 40)

1. TRANSPORTATION - U.K. 2. TRAFFIC - U.K. I. TITLE. II. SERIES: NATIONAL BUREAU OF ECONOMIC RESEARCH. OCCASIONAL PAPER, NO. 40.

728.1
(783)
R67

Transitional housing experiment; Rosebud Indian Reservation.
Rosebud Sioux Tribal Council.
Report on the transitional housing experiment; Rosebud Indian Reservation. Report based on excerpts from findings and conclusions of Richard G. Pates, Project Administrator and reports of Kirschner Associates, inc. Wash., U.S. Dept. of Housing and Urban Development, 1968.
43p.
U.S. Dept. of Housing and Urban Development. Low Income Housing Demonstration Program.
CFSTI.   (Cont'd on next card)

333.332
K45

Kinnard, William N   Transmission line rights of way and residential values... 1965.   (Card 2)

Bibliography: p. [151]-154.

1. Real property - Valuation. 2. Public utilities. 3. Eminent domain. I. Connecticut. University. Institute of Urban Research. II. Title.

388
F76

Transport investment and economic development.
Fromm, Gary, ed.
Transport investment and economic development. Washington, Brookings Institution, Transport Research Program, 1965.
314p.
Papers prepared for a series of Harvard University seminars, which are part of the Brookings Transport Research Program.
Bibliography: p.277-305.

1. Transportation - Economic effect. 2. Economic development. I. Brook-   ings Institution, Washington, D.C.   II. Title.

728.1
(783)
R67

Rosebud Sioux Tribal Council.   Report on the transitional...1968.   (Card 2)

1. Low income housing - S.D. 2. Housing - Indians. I. Pates, Richard G. II. Kirschner Associates, inc. III. U.S. HUD-Low Income Housing Demonstration Program. S.D. IV. Title: Transitional housing experiment; Rosebud Indian Reservation.

699.844
S31

The transmission loss of multi-layer structures.
Sharp, B H S
The transmission loss of multi-layer structures, by B.H.S. Sharp and J.W. Beauchamp. Garston, Eng., Building Research Station, 1969.
383-392p. (U.K. Building Research Station. Current paper 31/69)
Reprinted from: Journal of sound and vibration, May, 1969, pp. 383-392.
1. Architectural acoustics. 2. Panels. I. Beauchamp, J.W., jt. au. II. U.K. Building Research   Station. III. Title.

301.15
P27

Transport: key to the future of cities.   Anal.
Owen, Wilfred.
Transport: key to the future of cities.
(In Perloff, Harvey S., ed. The quality of the urban environment. 1969. p. 205-337)

1. Transportation. 2. Journey to work. I. Title.

500.15
(016)
T22

Translation Program.

U.S. Office of Technical Services.
List of translations in process for fiscal year
Washington, Dept. of Commerce, Office of Technical Services.
v. (P.L. Translation Program)

For complete information see shelflist.

1. Scientific research - Bibl.
I. Title: Translation Program.

699.844/
C37

TRANSMISSION OF SOUND THROUGH WALL FLOOR STRUCTURES.
CHRISLER, V L
TRANSMISSION OF SOUND THROUGH WALL FLOOR STRUCTURES, BY V. L. CHRISLER AND W. F. SNYDER. WASHINGTON, 1929.
541-559P. (U.S. BUREAU OF STANDARDS RESEARCH PAPER NO. 48)

1. ARCHITECTURAL ACOUSTICS.
I. SNYDER, W. F., JT. AU.   II. TITLE.

534.83
P87

Transport noise and town planning.
Purkis, H J
Transport noise and town planning. Garston, Eng., Building Research Station, Dept. of Scientific and Industrial Research, 1964.
13p. (U.K. Building Research Station. Building research current papers. Design series 25)
Reprinted from: Journal of sound and vibration, vol. (3) 1964, pp. 323-34.

1. Noise.   2. City planning.
I. U.K.   Building Research
Station.   II. Title.

500.15
(016)
T22o

Translation Program.

U.S. Office of Technical Services.
OTS selective bibliography
Washington, Dept. of Commerce, Office of Technical Services.
v. (P.L. Translation Program; SB)

For complete information see shelflist.

1. Scientific research - Bibl. I. Title: Translation Program.

699.81
F67f
v.2

Transport and combustion of firebrands.
U.S. Forest Service.
Transport and combustion of firebrands, by Carlos Sanchez Tarifa, et al. Madrid, Instituto Nacional de Tecnica Aeroespacial "Esteban Terradas", 1967.
90p. (v. 2 of 2)
Final report of work sponsored by U.S. Forest Service and conducted by Instituto Nacional de Tecnica Aeroespacial. V.1 entitled: Open fires.
1. Fire prevention. I. Madrid. Instituto Nacional de Tecnica Aeroespacial "Esteban Terradas." II. Sanchez Tarifa, Carlos. III. Title.

690.015
(485)
S82
1971
R36

Transport of industrialised building units.
Ugander, Mikael.
Transporter av byggelement; hanterings- och förflyttningskostnader för systemtransporter med lastbil [Transport of industrialized building units; handling and haulage costs relating to transport system by road of units in industrialized building systems] Stockholm, Statens Institut för Byggnadsforskning, 1971.
174p. (Rapport R36:1971)
Bibliography: p. 142-147.

(Cont'd on next card)

690.015
(485)
S82
1971
    Ugander, Mikael. Transporter av...1971.
                        (Card 2)
      1. Prefabricated construction.
2. Transportation. I. Stockholm. Statens
Institut för Byggnadsforskning. II. Title:
Transport of industrialised building units.

691.771   Transportation.
A58alu   Aluminum Association.
      Aluminum; the performance metal for
rapid transit. New York, 1967.
    [10]p.

      1. Aluminum. 2. Transportation.
I. Title: The performance metal for rapid
transit.

           Transportation.
388
A52c   American Municipal Association.
      The collapse of commuter service, a threat
to the survival of America's metropolitan
areas. A survey of mass transportation in
five selected cities: New York, Chicago, Philadelphia, Boston, and Cleveland. Washington,
1960.
    29p.   tables.

    1. Transportation.

---

388   Transport policy.
(41)   U.K. Ministry of Transport.
U54t   Transport policy. Presented to Parliament
by the Minister of Transport, by Command of
Her Majesty. London, H.M. Stat. Off., 1966.
    36p.   ([U.K. Parliament. Papers by
command] cmnd. 3057)

      1. Transportation - U.K. 2. Railroads -
U.K. I. Title.

---

388   Transportation.
A521   American Academy of Political and Social
Jan.   Science.
1963   Transportation renaissance. Special
editor, George Fox Mott. Philadelphia, 1963.
    214p.   (Its Annals, v. 345)

    1. Transportation. I. Mott, George Fox, ed.

---

388   Transportation.
A52   American Municipal Congress. 36th, Denver,
    1959.
      Better urban transportation. Proceedings
of the Thirty-sixth annual meeting at
Denver, Colorado, Nov. 28-Dec. 2, 1959.
Washington, American Municipal Association,
1959.
    102p.

      1. Transportation. I. American
Municipal   Association.

     TRANSPORT TECHNOLOGY FOR DEVELOPING
            REGIONS.
388   SOBERMAN, RICHARD M
(87)   TRANSPORT TECHNOLOGY FOR DEVELOPING
S61   REGIONS; A STUDY OF ROAD TRANSPORTATION
IN VENEZUELA. CAMBRIDGE, MASS., M.I.T.
PRESS, 1966.
    177P. (A PUBLICATION OF THE JOINT
CENTER FOR URBAN STUDIES OF THE
MASSACHUSETTS INSTITUTE OF TECHNOLOGY AND
HARVARD UNIVERSITY)

    1. TRANSPORTATION - VENEZUELA.
I. JOINT CENTER FOR URBAN STUDIES.
II. TITLE.

---

388   Transportation.
A52ur   American Association of State Highway
    Officials.
      Urban transportation planning. Papers
presented at the annual AASHO meeting in
Detroit, December 1, 1960. Wash., 1960.
    9p.
      Contents.-The urban transportation challenge,
by Don Hummel.-Detroit's workable program, by
Glenn C. Richards.-North Carolina organizes,
by W.F. Babcock.-Interrelation with city
planning, by John T. Howard.-The national
highway program, by E. H. Holmes.

    (Continued on next card)

---

388   Transportation.
A52d   American Municipal Association.
      Developing the transportation plan.
Chicago, Public Administration Service, 1964.
    90p.

      "A handbook sponsored by the American
Municipal Association for use in conjunction
with the basic planning guide, Better
transportation for your city, and the
procedure manuals developed by the
National Committee on Urban Transportation."
                 (Continued on next
                      card)

               Transportation

                 see also

            Air transportation
            Traffic
            Parking
            Journey to work
            Railroads

---

388   American Association of State Highway
A52ur   Officials. Urban transportation...1960.
                    (Card 2)

      1. Transportation. 2. Highways.
3. Journey to work. I. American Association
of State Highway Officials. Meeting, Detroit,
1960. II. Hummel, Don. The urban transportation challenge. III. Title.

---

388   American Municipal Association. Developing
A52d   the transportation plan... 1964.
                    (Card 2)

      Bibliography: p. 80-89.

      1. Transportation. 2. Traffic.
I. Public Administration Service, Chicago.
II. Title.

---

388   TRANSPORTATION.
A17   ABT Associates..
      Qualitative aspects of urban personal
travel demand. Prepared for U.S. Dept.
of Housing and Urban Development Urban
Transportation Administration, 1968.
    139p.
    Contract no. H-810.

      1. Transportation. 2. Journey to work.
I. U.S. Dept. of Housing and Urban
Development. II. Title.

---

388   Transportation.
A52o   American Association of State Highway
    Officials. Committee on Urban
    Transportation Planning.
      Organizational procedures of 17
urban transportation studies. [New York,
n.p.] 1963.
    60p.
      Report summarizes data on selected urban
transportation studies...In cooperation with
the U.S. Bureau of Public Roads.
1. Transportation. 2. Journey to work. I. U.S.
Bureau of Public   Roads.

VF
388   Transportation.
A52mb   American Society of Planning Officials.
      Moving the masses in modern cities;
significant facts and fallacies on the
growing problem of traffic congestion.
New York City [1962?]
    32p.

      1. Transportation. 2. Traffic.

362.4   TRANSPORTATION.
A17   ABT Associates, inc.
      Transportation needs of the handicapped.
Prepared for Dept. of Transportation, Office
of Economics and Systems Analysis. Cambridge,
Mass., 1969.

    1v.
    Cover title: Travel barriers.

      1. Handicapped. 2. Transportation. I. Title.

---

388   Transportation.
A52tr   American Automobile Association.
      Transportation and tomorrow's cities.
Wash., 1969.
    20p.

      1. Transportation. 2. Journey to work.
3. Highways.

---

388   Transportation.
A527   American Transit Association.
      Expressway bus operations, 1963. A
compilation based on the submissions of
two dozen interested properties regarding
their experiences with transit bus operations on expressways in urban metropolitan
areas. Edited by W.S. Rainville. Rev.
New York, 1963.
    96p.

      1. Transportation. I. Rainville,
W.S., ed.   2. Journey to
work.   II. Title.

---

388   Transportation.
A55   Allott, Gordon.
      Urban transit: paper or progress; delivered
at the third International Conference on Urban
Transportation. [Pittsburgh] WABCO Mass Transit
Center, Westinghouse Air Brake Co. [1968]
    6p.

      1. Transportation. 2. Journey to work.
I. Westinghouse Air Brake Co. II. International
Conference on Urban Transportation, 3d, 1968.
III. Title.

VF
388   Transportation.
A52u   American Automobile Association.
      Urban transportation, guidelines to
improvement. Washington, [1961?]
    [8]p.

      1. Transportation.

---

388   Transportation.
A52ms   American Transit Association.
      Manual of transit and traffic studies.
New York, 1947.
    73p.

      1. Transportation. 2. Journey to work.
3. Parking. 4. Traffic. I. Title.

388
A52P   TRANSPORTATION.
AMERICAN TRANSIT ASSOCIATION.
POSTWAR PATTERNS OF CITY GROWTH. NEW
YORK, 1944.
32P.

1. TRANSPORTATION.   2. CITY GROWTH.

388
A78   Atwell, Albert A
The autoline; a missing link in city to city
transportation, by Albert A. Atwell and Robert
F. McLean. For presentation at the 1961 SAE
International Congress and Exposition of Automotive Engineering, Detroit, Michigan, January
9-13, 1961. New York, Society of Automotive
Engineers, 1961.
12p. (Society of Automotive Engineers, inc.
266D)
1. Transportation. I. Society of Automotive
Engineers International Congress and Exposition
of Automotive   Engineering, Detroit,
1961. III. McLean,   Robert F., jt. au.
IV. Title.

Transportation.

388
B17j   Barton-Aschman Associates.
Joint project concepts: integrated trans-
portation corridors. Chicago, 1968.
129p.
Bibliography: p. 123-129.
U.S. HUD-UPRDP.

1. Transportation. I. Title: Integrated
transportation corridors. II. U.S. HUD-
UPRDP.

388
A52TO   TRANSPORTATION.
AMERICAN TRANSIT ASSOCIATION.
TO-MORROW'S CITIES. NEW YORK, N.D.
32P.

REPRINTED FROM PASSENGER TRANSPORT.

1. TRANSPORTATION.   2. CITY PLANNING.

Transportation.

388
A87a   Automobile Manufacturers Association.
Automobile facts and figures

Detroit,
v.   annual.

For complete information see shelflist.

1. Transportation. 2. Transportation —
Statistics.

Transportation.

388
B17m   Battelle Memorial Institute. Columbus Laboratories.
Monographs on potential RD & D projects
summary report. Prepared for New Systems
Study Project, Urban Transportation Administration, Dept. of Housing and Urban Development, Columbus, Ohio, 1968.
1v.
On cover: Study in new systems of urban
transportation.
Project staff - Kaj L. Nielsen, manager.

(Cont'd on next card)

Transportation.

388
A52t   American Transit Association.
Transit fact book; annual summary of
basic data and trends in the transit
industry of the United States.

New York,
v.   annual.

For complete information see shelflist.

1. Transportation.

Transportation.

388
A87u   Automobile Manufacturers Association.
Urban transportation issues and trends.
Detroit, 1963.
35p.

1. Transportation. 2. Metropolitan areas.
3. Journey to work.

388
B17m   Battelle Memorial Institute. Columbus
Laboratories.   Monographs...1968.
(Card 2)

1. Transportation. 2. Transportation
- Automation. I. U.S. Dept. of Housing and
Urban Development. II. Nielsen, Kaj L.
III. Title. IV. Title: Study in new systems
of urban transportation.

Transportation.

R
388   American Transit Association.
A52t   Urban transit industry; historical record.
1962   New York, 1963.
suppl. [16]p.

"Supplements the 1962 edition of the Transit
fact book."

1. Transportation. I. Title.

Transportation.

388
A87d   Automobile Manufacturers Association.
The dynamics of urban transportation; a
national symposium sponsored by Automobile
Manufacturers Association, inc., Oct. 23-24,
1962. Detroit, 1962.
1v.
Contents:-Panel 1. Interaction of urban transportation and land use.-Panel 2. Transportation service
to downtown areas.-Panel 3. Planning urban regional
transportation facilities.-Panel 4. Financing and
implementing urban transportation systems.

1. Transportation.

Transportation.

388
B17u   Battelle Memorial Institute. Columbus
Laboratories.
Urban goods: movement demand, by David
N. Goss and others; final report. Prepared
for New Systems Study Project, Urban Transportation Administration, Dept. of Housing
and Urban Development, Wash., D.C., Columbus, Ohio, Battelle Memorial Institute,
Columbus Laboratories, 1967.
232p.
On cover: Study in new systems of urban
transportation.

Transportation.

388
A52l   Ames, Ardee.
A look at urban transportation. Wash.,
National League of Cities, 1966.
28p.
Reprinted from Nation's cities.

1. Transportation. I. National League
of Cities. I. Title.

Transportation.

388
A87   Automotive Safety Foundation.
Transportation in tomorrow's
cities. Washington, 1960.
15p. (ASF rept. no. 9)

1. Transportation.

388
B17u   Battelle Memorial Institute. Columbus
Laboratories. Urban goods... 1967.
(Card 2)
1. Transportation. 2. Transportation
- Automation. I. U.S. Dept. of Housing
and Urban Development. II. Goss, David N.
III. Title. IV. Title: Study in new systems
of urban transportation.

388
A57   TRANSPORTATION.
Antoniou, Jim.
Environmental management; planning for traffic.
London, McGraw-Hill, 1971.
171p.

1. Traffic. 2. Transportation. I. Title.

Transportation.

388
A87ur   Automotive Safety Foundation.
Urban freeway development in twenty
major cities. Washington, D.C., 1964.
45p.

1. Transportation. 2. Transportation -
Statistics. 3. City growth. 4. Population. I. Title. 5. Highways.

Transportation.

388
B22   Bechtel Corp.
Dynamics of vehicle-structure interaction,
rapid transit structures. Prepared for
Parsons, Brinckerhoff, Tudor, Bechtel...in
cooperation with C. F. Scheffey. Berkeley,
Calif., 1964.
1v.

Bibliography: p. 1A-4A.
U.S. Housing and Home Finance Agency. Mass
Transportation Demonstration Grant Program.

(Continued on
next card)

388
A72   Transportation.
Architectural forum.
Traffic in cities. New York, Urban America
inc., 1968. p. 47-108.

Special edition, Jan. - Feb. 1968.

1. Transportation. 2. Traffic - Economic
effect. I. Urban America, inc. II. Title.

388
B17   TRANSPORTATION.
Barton-Aschman Associates.
Guidelines for new systems of urban
transportation. Prepared for the U.S.
Dept. of Housing and Urban Development.
v.1-3
[Washington] 1968-
v.
Contents:v.1. Urban needs and potentials.
v.2. A collection of papers. v.3.
Annotated bibliography.
1. Transportation. 2. Journey to work.
I. U.S. Dept.   of Housing and Urban
Development.   II. Title.

388
B22   Bechtel Corp. Dynamics of... (Card 2)

1. Transportation. 2. Journey to work.
I. Parsons, Brinckerhoff, Tudor, Bechtel.
II. Scheffey, C.F. III. Title. IV. U.S.
Housing and Home   Finance Agency.
Mass Transporta-   tion Demonstration
Grant Program.

VF
711.4
F67a
no.2

Bello, Francis
The city and the car. Detached from Fortune, Oct., 1957, p. 157-163/
(Fortune. Exploding Metropolis series no. 2)

1. City planning. 2. Transportation.
I. Title. (Series)

388
B69

Transportation.
Boys, J A
Supplemental studies of urban transportation systems analysis, by J.A. Boys and others. Conducted under contract with the Office of the Secretary, Dept. of Housing and Urban Development. Santa Barbara, Calif., General Research Corp., 1968.
162p. (CR-777-2)
Bibliography: p. 161-162.
HUD contract no. H-777.
1. Transportation. 2. Journey to work. I. Title. II. Title: Urban transportation systems analysis. III. General Research Corp. IV. U.S. Dept. of Housing and Urban Develop ment.

388
B83

Transportation.
Bugge, William A
"A highway engineer looks at rapid transit". Address delivered before the 1964 Institute for Rapid Transit Annual Meeting, Washington, D.C., [n.p.] 1964.
15p.

1. Transportation. 2. Journey to work. 3. Highways. I. Institute for Rapid Transit. Meeting, Washington, 1964. II. Title.

534.83
B25

TRANSPORTATION.
Bender, Erich K
Noise generated by subways aboveground and in stations, by Erich K. Bender and Manfred Heckl. Cambridge, Mass., Bolt, Beranek and Newman, 1970.
57p. (Report no. OST-ONA-70-1)

1. Noise. 2. Transportation. 3. Journey to work. I. Heckl, Manfred. II. Bolt, Beranek, and Newman. III. Title.

388
B71p

TRANSPORTATION.
Braman, J D
Planning for mobility; regional councils and transportation planning. Wash., National Service to Regional Councils, 1969.
7p.

Highlights of remarks at the Ohio Valley Workshop, Cincinnati, Ohio, Nov. 14, 1969.

1. Transportation. I. Title.

388
C15

Transportation.
California. University. Institute of Business and Economic Research. (Real Estate Research Program)
Influence of transportation changes on urban land uses and values, by Paul F. Wendt. Berkeley, 1960.
13p. (Its Reprint no. 21)
Reprinted from Some evaluations of highway improvement impacts, Highway Research Board Bulletin 268, 1960.
1. Transportation   2. Land use. 3. Real property-   Valuation. I. Wendt, Paul F.   (Series)

388
B27u

Transportation.
Berggren Transportation System Co.
Uniflow; a mass transit system concept, by Lloyd E. Berggren. Minneapolis, 1966.
28p.

1. Transportation. 2. Journey to work. 3. Railroads. 4. Automation. I. Title.

388
B71

Transportation.
Branch, Melville C
Transportation developments, cities, and planning. Based on paper presented at the Joint Planning Conference of the American Society of Planning Officials and the Community Planning Association of Canada, Toronto, Canada, April 25-29, 1965. Chicago, American Society of Planning Officials, 1965.
29p.
Bibliography: p. 27-29.
1. Transportation. 2. City planning. I. American   Society of Planning Officials.

388
(016)
C15
no. 15

Transportation.
California. University. Institute of Transportation and Traffic Engineering. Airport terminal design. Berkeley, Calif., 1959.
5p. (Its Library references no. 15)

1. Transportation. 2. Airports - Bibl.

388
B27

Transportation.
Berry, Donald S
The technology of urban transportation, by Donald S. Berry and others. [Evanston, Ill.] Published for the Transportation Center at Northwestern University, by Northwestern University Press, 1963.
145p. (Metropolitan transportation series)
Bibliography: p. 128-139.

1. Transportation. 2. Parking. 3. Streets. I. Northwestern University. Transportation Center. II. Title.

711.4
B72

Transportation.
Breese, Gerald William, ed.
An approach to urban planning, edited by Gerald Breese and Dorothy E. Whiteman. Princeton, Princeton University Press, 1953.
147 p. 20 cm.

Bibliography: p. 111-147.
For full information see main entry card.

1. Cities and towns - Planning. I. Whiteman, Dorothy E., joint ed. II. Title.

NA9040.B73   711   52-13142 ‡
Library of Congress   [10]

388
C15p

TRANSPORTATION.
California. University. Institute of Transportation and Traffic Engineering.
Planning methodology for new systems of transportation, with a summary of alternatives, by Lawrence Vance and others. Berkeley, 1969.
117p. (Special report)
Prepared for Bay Area Transportation Study Commission.
U.S. Dept. of Housing and Urban Development. UPAP.
1. Transportation. I. Bay Area Transportation Study Commission. II. Vance, Lawrence. III. Title. IV. U.S. Dept. of Housing and Urban Development. UPAP.

388
B58

Transportation.
Blumenfeld, Hans.
The modern metropolis: its origins, growth, characteristics, and planning. Selected essays. Edited by Paul D. Spreiregen. Cambridge, Mass., M.I.T. Press, 1967.
377p.

1. City planning. 2. Metropolitan area planning. 3. City growth. 4. Urban renewal. 5. Architecture. 5. Transportation. I. Spreiregen, Paul D., ed. II. Title.

VF
388
B76

Transportation.
Browne, Alan K
The place of transit in the business life of the community. Pittsburgh, WABCO Mass Transit Center, 1963.
10p.

An address by a vice president of Bank of America, in San Francisco, before American Transit Association, Western Regional Conference, San Francisco, Calif., Apr., 1963.
1. Transportation. 2. Journey to work. I. American Transit Association, Western Regional Conference, San Francisco, 1963. II. Westinghouse Air Brake Co.

388
C15t

TRANSPORTATION.
Cantilli, Edmund J ed.
Transportation and aging; selected issues, ed. by Edmund J. Cantilli and June L. Shmelzer. Wash., Div. of Information, Administration on Aging, 1970.
208p.
Based on proceedings of the Interdisciplinary Workshop on Transportation and Aging, Wash., D.C. May 24-26, 1970.
1. Transportation. 2. Old age. I. Shmelzer, June L., jt. ed. II. U.S. Dept. of Health, Education, and Welfare (Administration on aging) III. Title. IV. Interdisciplinary Workshop on Transportation and Aging, Wash., 1970.

711..4
B69

TRANSPORTATION.
Boyce, David E
Metropolitan plan evaluation methodology, by David E. Boyce and others. Prepared for U.S. Bureau of Public Roads. Philadelphia, Institute for Environmental Studies, University of Pennsylvania, 1969.
112p.
Bibliography: p. 102-112.
1. Land use. 2. Transportation. I. Pennsylvania. University. Institute for Environmental Studies. II. Title.

385
B82

Transportation.
Budd Co.
First tour of the new Budd 160 mph. train. Philadelphia, 1965.
1v.

1. Railroads. 2. Transportation. 3. Journey to work. I. Title.

388
C17t

TRANSPORTATION.
Carnegie-Mellon University, Pittsburgh. Transportation Research Institute.
Latent demand for urban transportation. Final report. Prepared for U.S. Dept. of Housing and Urban Development. Pittsburgh, 1968.
259p. (Study D-3)
Contract H-813.
Bibliography: p. 255-259.
1. Transportation. 2. Journey to work. I. U.S. Dept. of Housing and Urban Development. II. Title.

711.3
B69

TRANSPORTATION.
Boyce, David E
Metropolitan plan making; an analysis of experience with the preparation and evaluation of alternative land use and transportation plans, by David E. Boyce and others. Philadelphia, 1970.
475p. (Regional Science Research Institute. Monograph series no. 4)
Bibliography: p. 427-432.

1. Metropolitan area planning. 2. Land use. 3. Transportation. I. Regional Science Research Institute. II. Title.

388
B82

TRANSPORTATION.
Buel, Ronald A
Dead end: the automobile in mass transportation. Englewood Cliffs, N.J., Prentice-Hall, 1972.
305p.

1. Transportation. I. Title. II. Title: Automobile in mass transportation.

388
C17

Transportation.
Carnegie-Mellon University, Pittsburgh. Transportation Research Institute.
Urban rapid transit; concepts and evaluation, by Lester A. Hoel and others. Pittsburgh, 1968.
241p. (Its Research report no. 1)

Bibliography: p. 237-241.

1. Transportation. 2. Journey to work. I. Hoel, Lester A. II. Title.

388
C17a
TRANSPORTATION.
Carnegie-Mellon University. Transportation
Research Institute.
Advanced urban transportation systems. Pro-
ceedings of the Carnegie-Mellon Conference on
Advanced Urban Transportation Systems, May 25-
27, 1970. Ed. by Mary Anne Williamson.
Pittsburgh, 1970.
148p. (T.R.I. research report 5)

1. Transportation. 2. Journey to work.
I. Williamson, Mary Anne, ed. II. Title.

712.25
C31
TRANSPORTATION.
Charles River Associates.
Urban transportation and recreation.
New York, Institute of Public Administration,
1970.
1v.
Submitted to the U.S. Dept. of Housing and
Urban Development. Project no. DC-D6-12-69.

1. Recreation. 2. Transportation. 3. Parks.
I. Institute of Public Administration.
II. U.S. Dept. of Housing and Urban Develop-
ment. III. Title.

388
C655
Transportation.
Committee for Economic Development.
Developing metropolitan transportation
policies: a guide for local leadership. A
statement on National policy by the Research
and Policy Committee. New York, 1965.
99p.

1. Transportation. 2. Transportation -
Economic effect. 3. Community development.
I. Title.

388
C31x
Transportation.
Chalk, O Roy.
Transportation and metropolitan develop-
ment. [Washington] 1960.
5p.

1. Transportation. 2. Metropolitan areas.

388
C32
Transportation.
Cheaney, E S
A national urban transportation test and
evaluation center, by E.S. Cheaney and J.T.
Herridge. Summary report. Prepared for New
Systems and Study Project, Urban Transportation
Administration, Dept. of Housing and Urban
Development. Columbus, Ohio, Battelle Memorial
Institute, 1968.
32p.
Bibliography: F-1 - F-6.
HUD contract no. H-778 (task 7)
1. Transportation. 2. Journey to work.
I. Title. II. Herridge, J.T., jt.
au. III. Battelle Memorial Institute.
IV. U.S. Dept. of Housing and Urban
Development.

388
C65p
Transportation.
Conference on New Approaches to Urban
Transportation, 2d, Washington, D.C., 1967.
[Proceedings] Washington, U.S. Dept. of
Housing and Urban Development. [1968?]
104p.

Partial contents.-Welcome, by Charles M.
Haar.-Keynote address, by Peter A. Lewis.-
The urban transportation demonstration program, by Thomas H. Floyd, Jr.-Rapid transit
and urban survival, by J.D. Braman.-Reviving
commuter rail service, by James M. Loconto.

(Continued on next card)

VF
312
:383
C31
Transportation.
Chalmers University of Technology, Gothenburg,
Sweden.
Transportation and city-building, by
Carl Birger Troedsson. Gothenburg, Sweden,
Elanders Boktryckeri Aktiebolag, 1954.
30 p. illus., charts. (Its transac-
tion no. 146 [Avd. Arkitektur 2])

1.City growth. 2.Transportation. I.Troedsson, Carl
Birger.

388
C32p
TRANSPORTATION.
Cheaney, E S
A program to evaluate advanced tech-
nology for buses, by E.S. Cheaney and C.W.
Vigrass. Columbus, Ohio, Battelle Memorial
Institute, Columbus Laboratories, 1967.
18p. (Battelle Memorial Institute.
Columbus Laboratories. Monograph no. 11)
Prepared for New Systems Study Project,
Urban Transportation Administration, Dept.
of Housing and Urban Development.
Contract no. H-778.
(Cont'd on next card)

388
C65p
Conference on New Approaches, 1967...
(Card 2)

-Putting new spokes on urban transit networks,
by George Krambles.-Adapting bus systems to
present urban needs, by John C. Kohl.-New
kinds of services, by Michael Blurton.- New
movements by new methods, by Leland Hazard.
-Transportation and employment opportunity,
by William F. Hibbard.-Transit shapes the city,
and urban transportation, by Robert C. Weaver.

(Continued on next card)

388
C31b
Transportation.
Chamber of Commerce of the United States.
(Transportation and Communication Dept.)
Business views on local transit; an
analysis of how 1,129 Chambers of Commerce
view the need for a federal subsidy program.
Washington, 1963.
13p.

1. Transportation. 2. Taxation.
3. Grants-in-aid.

388
C32p
Cheaney, E S A program
to evaluate...1967. (Card 2)

1. Transportation. 2. Journey to work.
I. Vigrass, C.W., jt. au. II. Battelle
Memorial Institute. (Columbus Laboratories)
III. U.S. Dept. of Housing and Urban
Development. Urban Transportation
Administration. IV. U.S. Mass Trans-
portation Demonstration Grant Program.
V. Title: Buses. VI. Title.

388
C65p
Conference on New Approaches, 1967...
(Card 3)

1. Transportation. 2. Journey to work.
I. Haar, Charles M. II. Lewis, Peter A.
III. Floyd, Thomas H., Jr. The urban
transportation demonstration program.
IV. Weaver, Robert Clifton. Transit shapes
the city. V. Weaver, Robert Clifton.
Urban transportation award. VI. Title:
New approaches to urban transportation.

388
C31r
Transportation.
Chamber of Commerce of the United States.
Relation of highways and motor transport
to other transportation agencies, report
of Special Committee IV. Washington, 1923.
44p.

1. Transportation. 2. Highways.

388
C34
Transportation.
Chilton, E G
Buffeting of trains entering a tunnel. Pre-
pared for Parsons, Brinckerhoff-Tudor-Bechtel.
Final report. Menlo Park, Calif., Stanford
Research Institute, 1963.
42p.
U.S. Housing and Home Finance Agency. Mass
Transportation Demonstration Grant Program.
1. Transportation. 2. Railroads. I. Stanford
Research Institute. II. U.S. Housing and Home
Finance Agency. Mass Transportation
Demonstration Grant Program.
III. Title.

388
C65ed
Transportation.
Conference on Poverty and Transportation,
Brookline, Mass 1968.
Edited transcript of the Conference on
Poverty and Transportation, June 7, 1968,
sponsored by the Department of Housing and
Urban Development and the Department of
Transportation. Brookline, Mass., American
Academy of Arts and Sciences, 1968.
1v.

1. Transportation. 2. Social conditions.
3. Minority groups. 4. Employment.
I. Title: Poverty and transporta-
(Cont'd on next card)

388
C31
Transportation.
Chamber of Commerce of the United States.
(Transportation and Communication Dept.)
Urban transportation. Report of Committee on
Urban Transportation. Washington, 1948.
33p.

1. Transportation.

659
C51
TRANSPORTATION.
Clarke, George T
Transit advertising. New York, Transit
Advertising Association, 1970.
91p.

1. Advertising. 2. Transportation.
3. Journey to work. I. Transit Advertising
Association. II. Title.

388
C65ed
Conference on Poverty and Transportation,
(Brookline, Mass 1968. (Card 2)

tion. II. U.S. Dept. of Housing and Urban
Development. III. U.S. Dept. of Transporta-
tion. IV. American Academy of Arts and
Sciences.

VF
388
C31c
Transportation.
The Changing times.
The cost of getting to work; whether you
go by car, bus, cab, train or shanks' mare,
the true cost will surprise you. This
suggests ways to save. Reproduced from The
Changing times, the Kiplinger magazine,
May 1961, p. 7-11.

1. Transportation. 2. Journey to work.
I. Title.

VF
388
C651
Transportation.
Colwell, Robert C
Interactions between transportation and
urban economic growth, a paper by Robert C.
Colwell, Economic Advisor, Urban Renewal
Administration, Housing and Home Finance
Agency for the Highway Research Board 42nd
annual meeting, January 9, 1963, Washington,
D.C. Wash., 1962.
17p.
1. Transportation. 2. City growth. I.
Highway Research Board. II. U.S. Urban
Renewal Administration.

388
C65s
TRANSPORTATION.
Conference on Poverty and Transportation,
Brookline, Mass., 1968.
Summary and conclusions and papers pres-
ented. Brookline, Mass., American Academy of
Arts and Sciences, 1968.
1v.
Sponsored by the Dept. of Housing and Urban
Development and the Dept. of Transportation
under contract no. EH-11-6845.

1. Transportation. 2. Poverty. 3. Journey
to work. I. American Academy of Arts and
Sciences. II. U.S. Dept. of Housing
and Urban Development.

301.15
C65co

TRANSPORTATION.
College-Industry Conference, New Orleans, 1968.
Urban America challenges engineering; report. Wash., American Society for Engineering Education, 1969.
74p. (American Society for Engineering Education. Industry-engineering education series, monograph I-1)
Sponsored by the Relations with Industry Division of the American Society for Engineering Education.

⌒ (Cont'd on next card)

388
C66

TRANSPORTATION.
Cooper, Norman L
Urban transportation: an answer. Bloomington, Ind., Bureau of Business Research, Graduate School of Business, Indiana University, 1971.
66p. (Institute for Urban Transportation series 1)

Bibliography: p. 61-66.

1. Transportation. I. Indiana. University. Bureau of Business Research. II. Title.

Transportation.

388
D15

Danielson, Michael N
Federal metropolitan politics and the commuter crisis. New York, Columbia University Press, 1965.
244p. (Metropolitan political series no. 2)

1. Transportation. 2. Metropolitan area planning. 3. Intergovernmental relations. 4. Suburbs. 5. Journey to work. 6. U.S. Housing and Home Finance Agency. I. Title.

301.15
C65co

College-Industry Conference, New Orleans, 1968. Urban America...1969. (Card 2)

1. Man - Influence of environment. 2. City planning. 3. Transportation. I. American Society for Engineering Education. II. Title.

388
C67

Transportation.
Cornell Aeronautical Laboratory.
Bi-modal urban transtportation system study. Prepared for the U.S. Dept. of Housing and Urban Development. Buffalo, 1968.
2v. (Its CAL v.1 report no. VJ-2431-v-2)
On cover: Study in new systems of urban transportation.
1. Transportation. I. U.S. Dept. of Housing and Urban Development. II. Title. III. Title: Study in new systems of urban transportation.

388
D18c

Transportation.
Davis, Harmer E
Community values as affected by transportation, summary remarks, Session I, by Director, Institute of Transportation and Traffic Engineering, University of California. [n.p] 1963.

"Presented at the 42nd Annual Meeting of the Highway Research Board, Washington, D.C., Jan. 9, 1963."

1. Transportation. I. Highway Annual Meeting, 1963. 2. Community development Research Board. Washington, D.C.,

---

388
C65con
1967

Transportation.
Conference on Transportation Engineering. [The Conference] Reproduced from the Sciences (New York Academy of Sciences) Oct. 1967. p. 2-5.

1. Transportation. 2. Journey to work. 3. Traffic - Social effect.

388
:331
C67

Transportation.
Cornell University. Housing Research Center.
The journey to work; a guide for delineating labor and housing supply areas for defense plants. [Ithaca, N.Y.] Dec. 1952.
157 l. forms, graphs, tables.
...Part 1. World War II Experience. Nov. 1952.
Bibliography: p. 151-157.
Final report, Research Project no. 1-E-116, Housing and Home Finance Agency.
Project directors, L. P. Adams and T. W. Mackesey; staff technician, Edmond H. Hoben. Processed.

VF
388
D18na

Transportation.
Davis, Harmer E
National and metropolitan systems, by Director, Institute of Transportation and Traffic Engineering, University of California. [n.p.] 1963.
6p.

"Presented at the session on Graduate Studies at the Annual Meeting of the American Society for Engineering Education, Philadelphia, Pennsylvania, June 19, 1963."

1. Transportation. I. California. University. Transportation and Institute of Traffic Engineering.

711.33
(746)
C65t

Transportation.
Connecticut Interregional Planning Program.
Transportation. Prepared in cooperation with the Bureau of Public Roads. Hartford, 1966.
101p.
At the head of title: Connecticut: choices for action.

U.S. Dept. of Housing and Urban Development. UPAP.
1. State planning - Conn. 2. Transportation - Conn. I. Title. II. Title: Connecticut: choices for action. III. U.S. HUD-UPAP. Conn.

388
C68

Transportation.
Cowley, R D
A public official's attitude to rapid transit; an address to the Institute of Rapid Transit. [n.p.], 1964.
13p.

1. Transportation. 2. Journey to work. I. Institute of Rapid Transit, Meeting, Washington, 1964. II. Title.

388
D18n

Transportation - (Addresses, lectures, etc.)
Davis, Harmer E
Notes and comments on a proposed national transportation study, by Harmer Davis, Director, Institute of Transportation and Traffic Engineering, University of California. Berkeley, Calif., 1962.
10p.
Prepared for discussion at a meeting of the Committee on Origin and Destination Surveys, Highway Research Board, Washington, D.C., Jan. 8, 1962.
1. Transportation - Addresses, lectures, etc. I. Highway Research Board.

388
C65d

Transportation.
Consad Research Corp.
Design for impact studies: Northeast Corridor Transportation Project. Prepared in cooperation with Center for Regional Economic Studies, University of Pittsburgh, Pittsburgh, Pa. Prepared for the U.S. Dept. of Commerce, Office of the Under Secretary for Transportation. Pittsburgh, 1965.
1v.
On cover: Preliminary report.
Bibliography.

1. Transportation. 2. Land use. 3. Automation. I. Pittsburgh. University. Center for Regional Economic Studies. II. Title.

388
C72

TRANSPORTATION.
Creighton, Roger L
Urban transportation planning. Urbana, University of Illinois, 1970.
375p.

1. Transportation. I. Title.

VF
388
D18r

Transportation.
Davis, Harmer E
Role of research in transportation, by Director, Institute of Transportation and Traffic Engineering, University of California. [n.p.] 1963.
4p.

Remarks presented at the Western Regions Research and Development Conference, sponsored by the U.S. Bureau of Public Roads, San Francisco, Feb. 19, 1963.

1. Transportation. I. California. University. Institute of Transportation and Traffic Engineering.

388
C65m

Transportation.
Consad Research Corp.
Impact studies: Northeast Corridor Transportation Project. Vol. I. Background overview, and summary. Vol. II. Models, results, and technical discussion. Final report. Prepared for Northeast Corridor Transportation Project, U.S. Dept. of Transportation. Pittsburgh, 1968.
2v.
Bibliography: p. 367-375.
CFSTI PB 176 478; PB-177761/1
1. Transportation. 2. Railroads. I. Northeast Corridor Transportation Project. II. Title.

388
C76

TRANSPORTATION.
CROWDED STREETS, A SYMPOSIUM ON PUBLIC TRANSPORTATION. WASHINGTON, URBAN LAND INSTITUTE, 1955.
77P. (TECHNICAL BULLETIN NO. 26)

1. TRANSPORTATION. 2. STREETS. (SERIES) URBAN LAND INSTITUTE. TECHNICAL BULLETIN NO. 26)

388
D18

Transportation.
Davis, Harmer E
Some aspects of urban transportation planning, by Harmer E. Davis and W. Norman Kennedy. [Berkeley, Calif.] Institute of Transportation and Traffic Engineering, University of California, 1961.
10p.
A paper prepared for presentation at the Symposium on Urban Survival and Traffic, King's College, University of Durham, England, April 10-14, 1961.
1. Transportation. I. Kennedy, W. Norman, jt. au. II. Symposium on Urban Survival and Traffic, University of Durham, England, 1961.

388
C65tra

Transportation
Consad Research Corp.
Transit usage forecasting techniques: a review and new directions. Final report to New Systems Study Project, Urban Transportation Administration, U.S. Dept. of Housing and Urban Development. Pittsburgh, 1968.
170p.
Contract no. H-811.
Bibliography: p. 161-170.

1. Transportation - 2. Journey to work. I. U.S. Dept. of Housing and Urban Development. Urban Transportation Administration. II. Title.

388
C87

Transportation.
Currey, Neil J
A trucker looks at rapid transit. Presented before the 4th Annual Meeting, Institute for Rapid Transit, May 19, 1965, Washington, D.C. [n.p.] 1965.
9p.

1. Transportation. 2. Journey to work. 3. Highways. I. Institute for Rapid Transit. Meeting, 4th, Washington, 1965. II. Title.

711.4
:670
D18t

Transportation.
Davis, Harmer E
Transportation and land use planning as related to industrial development. Paper prepared for presentation at annual meeting of the California State Chamber of Commerce, Industrial Development Section, Nov. 29, 1962. San Francisco, Calif., 1962.
11p.

1. Industrial districts - Redevelopment. 2. Transportation. 3. Land use. I. California. State Chamber of Commerce.

388
D18ur
TRANSPORTATION.
Davis, Harmer E
Urban transportation planning: development and prospects, by Harmer E. Davis, Director, Institute of Transportation and Traffic Engineering, University of California. [n.p.] 1968.
7p.
Prepared for the Syracuse Transportation Conference, Syracuse University, Nov. 18, 1968.

1. Transportation. I. Title.

711.4
D61
TRANSPORTATION.
Dober, Richard P
Environmental design. New York, Van Nostrand Reinhold, 1969.
278p.

1. City planning. 2. Open space land. 3. Transportation. I. Title.

388
E58
TRANSPORTATION.
Enviromerrics, inc.
The river basin model the transportation sector. [Prepared] for the Office of Research and Monitoring, Environmental Protection Agency. Wash., Govt. Print. Off., 1971.
94p. (Water pollution control research series)

1. Transportation. I. U.S. Environmental Protection Agency. II. Title.

388
D18u
Transportation.
Davis, Harmer E
The urban transportation planning process capabilities and potentials, by director [of the] Institute of Transportation and Traffic Engineering, University of California. A paper ... at the session on Urban Transportation at the Jubilee Conference of the New Zealand Institution of Engineers, Wellington, New Zealand, 11 Feb., 1964. [n.p.] 1964.
19p.   (Cont'd on next card)

388
D65
TRANSPORTATION.
Domencich, Thomas A
Free transit; a Charles River Associates research study, by Thomas A. Domencich and Gerald Kraft. Lexington, Mass., Heath Lexington Books, 1970.
104p.

1. Transportation. 2. Transportation - Boston. I. Charles River Associates. II. Kraft, Gerald, jt. au. III. Title.

388
F22
Transportation.
Fedel, Robert F
Techniques and factors relating to future rapid transit demand. Boston, 1962.
139p.
Thesis—Massachusetts Institute of Technology.

1. Transportation. 2. Journey to work. 3. Theses. I. Massachusetts Institute of Technology.

388
D18u
Davis, Harmer E   The urban transportation planning process capabilities and potentials ...   (Card 2)

1. Transportation. I. New Zealand Institution of Engineers Jubilee Conference, Wellington, N.Z., 1964. II. California. University. Institute of Transportation and Traffic Engineering.

388
D67
TRANSPORTATION.
Dot Zero.
Transportation graphics: where am I going? How do I get there? Symposium, Oct. 23, 1967, New York City. New York, Dot Zero, 1968.
46p.

Entire issue: no. 5, Fall 1968.

1. Transportation. 2. Visual aids. I. Title.

VF
711.73
:330
F25
TRANSPORTATION.
Fellman, Gordon.
Field work as an appropriate method for evaluating community values in regard to transportation planning. [n.p.] [1969?]
22p.
Paper to be submitted to the 49th annual meeting of the Highway Research Board (Community Values Committee) by Gordon Fellman, Dept. of Sociology, Brandeis University, Waltham, Mass.
1. Highways -   Economic effect. 2. Transportation. I.   Highway Research Board. II. Title.

388
D19
Transportation.
Day and Zimmerman, inc., Philadelphia.
Potential near term improvements in urban transportation. Prepared for U.S. Department of Housing and Urban Development. [Philadelphia] 1968.
304p.
On cover: Study in new systems of urban transportation.
1. Transportation. 2. Eminent domain. 3. Transportation - Automation. I. U.S. Dept. of Housing and Urban Development. II. Title.   III. Title: Study on new systems of   urban transportation.

388
E28b
Transportation.
Edwards, L   K
Baseline system definition: urban gravity-vacuum-transit, by L. K. Edwards and R. E. Skov, Tube Transit Corporation. Silver Spring Md., Applied Physics Laboratory, Johns Hopkins University, 1968.
1v. (Johns Hopkins University. Applied Physics Laboratory. Contractor report. BFM-097)
1. Transportation. 2. Transportation - Research. I. Johns Hopkins University. Applied Physics Laboratory. II. Tube Transit Corp. III. Skov,   R.E., jt. au. IV. Title.

388
F42
Transportation.
Fichter, Donn.
Small car automatic transit. Prepared for presentation at the forty-seventh annual meeting of the Highway Research Board, Washington, D.C, January 15-19, 1968. Albany, Subdivision of Transportation Planning and Programming, New York State Dept. of Transportation, 1968.
28p.
Publication TP60022-1.
1. Transportation. 2. Journey to work. I. Highway Research Board. Meeting, 47th, Washington, 1968. II. New York (State) Dept. of Transportation. III. Title.

388
D25
Transportation.
Delisi, Samuel P
Legal and regulatory aspects of coordinated transportation service. Prepared for Office of the Under Secretary for Transportation, U.S. Dept. of Commerce, Washington, D.C. Pittsburgh, Graduate School of Business, University of Pittsburgh, 1966.
154p.
1. Transportation. I. U.S. Dept. of Commerce. II. Pittsburgh. University. Graduate School of Business. III. Title.

910
E35
TRAVEL.
Ehlers, Joseph H
Far horizons - the travel diary of an engineer. New York, Carlton Press, 1966.
189p. (A reflection book)

1. Travel. I. Title. II. Title: Travel diary of an engineer.

388
F47
Transportation.
Fitch (Lyle C.) and Associates.
Urban transportation and public policy. Based on memoranda prepared by Alan Cripe and others. San Francisco, Chandler Pub. Co., 1964. (Chandler publications in political science)
279p. (Chandler publications in political science)
"Based upon a 1961 study prepared by the Institute of Public Administration for the U.S. Department of Commerce and the Housing and Home Finance Agency."
1. Transportation.   I. Cripe, Alan. II. Title. III. Institute of Public   tute of Public Administration, New   York.

388
D27
1967
Transportation.
Design in Urban Transportation Conference, Washington, D.C., 1967.
The Conference. Sponsored by the Dept. of Housing and Urban Development. Washington, 1967.
kit.   (8 pieces)

Contents:- [no.1] Visual and graphic presentations of transportation design in relation to function and to the city. Recent developments in Boston.-[no.2] Designing the subway Kiosk to compliment the architec-   ture of the city, by C. Hilgenhurst   [no.3] Transit design (Cont'd on next card)

'388
E57
TRANSPORTATION.
Enright, J   J
An investigation of steel wheelrail noise and techniques for its suppression. Columbus, Ohio, Battelle Memorial Institute, Columbus Laboratories, 1967.
15p. (Battelle Memorial Institute. Columbus Laboratories. Monograph no. 15)
Prepared for New Systems Study Project, Urban Transportation Administration, Dept. of Housing and Urban Development.
U.S. Mass Transportation Demonstration Grant Program.   Contract no. H-778.
(Cont'd on next card)

728.1
N176b
no.20
TRANSPORTATION.
Fleisher, Aaron.
Technology in the city. [n.p.] 1968.
24p. (Background paper [no. 20] for U.S. National Commission on Urban Problems)

1. Housing. 2. Transportation. I. U.S. National Commission on Urban Problems. II. Title.

388
D27
1967
Design in Urban Transportation Conference. Washington, D.C., 1967. The Conference.
(Card 2)

[no.4] Bay Area Rapid Transit District, by B.R. Stokes.-[no.5] Remarks of D.G. Hammond.-[no.6] Massachusetts Bay Transportation Authority. We're quite proud of your new South Shore car.-[no.7] The next fifty years 1967-2017.-[no.8] Keynote address. Asst. Secretary of U.S. HUD Charles M. Haar.-
1. Transportation.   2. Journey to work. 3. Art. I. Haar,   Charles M. II. U.S. Dept. of Housing and   Urban Development.

388
E57
Enright, J   J   an investigation ...1967.   (Card 2)

1. Transportation. 2. Journey to work. 3. Railroads. 4. Noise. I. Battelle Memorial Institute. (Columbus Laboratories) II. U.S. Dept. of Housing and Urban Development. Urban Transportation Administration. III. U.S. Mass Transportation Demonstration Grant Program. IV. Title.

388
F67t
Transportation.
Forbes.
Transportation: what President Johnson wants to do. Editor, James W. Michaels. New York, N.Y., 1965.
72p.

Entire issue June 15, 1965.

1. Transportation. I. U.S. President, 1963-   (Johnson) Transportation.

16

Transportation.

388
F67u
Forbes.
The U.S.' lopsided transportation budget.
New York, Forbes, inc., 1968.
[6] p.

Reprinted from Forbes magazine, Oct. 1,
1968.

Cover title: Transportation troubles,
getting worse?

1. Transporta   tion. I. Title.
II. Title: Transportation troubles,
getting worse?

Transportation.

388
G25a General Electric Co.
America is going places. Erie,
Pa., [1962?]
51p.

1. Transportation. 2. Journey
to work.

VF
388
G25me   General Motors Corp.
Metro mobility. Detroit, [1968?]
[22] p.

1. Transportation. 2. Highways.
3. Journey to work. I. Title.

Transportation.

711.4
F67e Fortune.
The exploding metropolis, by the editors of
Fortune. New York, Doubleday,
193p. illus.
Originally appeared as a series of articles
in Fortune magazine during the winter and
spring of 1957-58. VF-711.4F67a.

1. City planning. 2. Municipal government.
3. Transportation. 4. Urban renewal.

Transportation.

388
G25an General Electric Co. (Transportation Systems
Div.)
Analysis and requirements of electronic
command and control systems. Prepared for
Urban Transportation Administration, Dept.
of Housing and Urban Development, Erie, Pa.,
Marketing Operation, General Electric Co.,
Transportation Systems Div., 1967.
114p.
1. Transportation. 2. Journey to work.
3. Transportation - Automation. I. U.S.
Dept. of Housing and Urban Development.
II. Title.

Transportation.

388
G25m General Motors Corp.
Metro-mode: a new approach to rapid transit.
Prepared in [cooperation] with the Southeastern Wisconsin Regional Planning Commission. Detroit, Mich., 1967.
16p.

1. Transportation. 2. Journey to work.
I. Southeastern Wisconsin Regional Planning
Commission. II. Title.

Transportation.

711.4
F67a Fortune.
The exploding metropolis: a series of
articles from Fortune during the winter and
spring of 1957-58. New York.
6 nos. (clippings) in 1 v. (analyzed)
See main entry for list of anals.
See also its Exploding metropolis. New York,
Doubleday,   (711.4 F67e)

1. City planning. 2. Municipal government.
3. Transportation. 4. Urban renewal.

Transportation.

388
G25st General Electric Co. Transportation Systems
Div.
A study of command control systems for
urban transportation. Prepared for Urban
Transportation Administration, Dept. of
Housing and Urban Development, Wash. D.C.,
Erie, Pa., Transportation Equipment Projects
and Marketing Operation, General Electric Co.,
Transportation Systems Div., 1968.
360p.
H.W. Merritt, Director.
On cover: Study in new systems of urban
transportation.
(Cont'd on next card)

Transportation.

388
G25n General Motors Corp.
New systems implementation study, final
study. Prepared for the U.S. Dept. of Housing
and Urban Development, Urban Transportation
Administration, by E.T. Canty and others.
[Detroit] 1968.
3v. (Its Research publication GMR-710B)
Contents: v.1. Summary and conclusions.--
v.2. Planning and evaluation methods.--v.3.
Case studies.
On cover: Study in new systems of Urban
Transportation.
1. Transporta   tion. 2. Transporta-
tion - Research.   3. Transportation -
Automation.   (Cont'd on next card)

Transportation.

Ref.
388 Franklin Institute, Philadelphia. Journal.
F71n New concepts in urban transportation
systems. Lancaster, Pa., 1968.
1v.
Partial contents: The Federal role by
guest editor, Ralph Warburton, Special
Assistant to the Secretary U.S. Dept. of
Housing and Urban Development.
Entire special issue: Nov. 1968.

1. Transportation. 2. Journey to work.
3. Traffic - Economic effect. I. Warburton,
Ralph, ed. The   Federal role.
II. U.S. Dept.   of Housing and Urban
Development.   III. Title.

388
G25st General Electric Co. Transportation Systems
Div.   A study of command and control
systems...1968.   (Card 2)

1. Transportation. 2. Transportation -
Automation. I. Merritt, H.W. II. U.S. Dept.
of Housing and Urban Development. III. Title.
IV. Title: Study in new systems of urban
transportation.

388
G25n General Motors Corp.   New systems...1968.
(Card 2)

I. Canty, E.T. II. U.S. Dept. of Housing
and Urban Development.
III. Title. IV. Title: Study in new
systems of urban transportation.

Transportation.

388
G17 Gerrison, W   L
A prolegomenon to the forecasting of trans-
portation development, by W.L. Gerrison and
D.F. Marble. Final report of study conducted
at Northwestern University for U.S. Army Avia-
tion Materiel Laboratories, Fort Eustis,
Virginia. Processed for U.S. Defense Docu-
mentation Center, Defense Supply Agency.
[Wash.?] U.S. Dept. of Commerce, National
Bureau of Standards, Institute for Applied
Technology, 1965.
[64]p.   (AD-621 514)
Distributed   by U.S. Clearing-
house for Federal   Scientific and Technical Information.   (Cont'd on next card)

Transportation.

388
G25su General Electric Co. (Transportation
Systems Div.)
Survey of electronic command and control
systems. Prepared for Urban Transportation
Administration, U.S. Dept. of Housing and
Urban Development, Washington, D.C. Erie,
Pa., Transportation Equipment Projects and
Marketing Operation, General Electric Co.,
Transportation Systems Div., 1967.
1v.
1. Transportation. 2. Journey to work.
3. Transportation - Automation. I. U.S.
Dept. of Hous   ing and Urban Develop-
ment.   II. Title.

Transportation.

388
G25s General Research Corp.
Systems analysis of urban transportation.
Prepared for the U.S. Dept. of Housing and
Urban Development. Santa Barbara, Calif., 1968.
4v.   (E-777)
On cover: Study in new systems of urban
transportation.
Contents: v.1. Summary. v.2. Cases for study.--
v.3. Network flow analyses.-- v.4. Supporting
analyses.
1. Transportation. 2. Transportation - Re-
search. 3. Journey to work. 4. Transportation -
Automation. I. U.   S. Dept. of Housing
and Urban Develop   ment.
(Cont'd on next card)

388
G17 Gerrison, W.L. A prolegomenon to the fore-
casting of transportation development...
(Card 2)

1. Transportation. 2. Traffic surveys.
I. Marble, D.F., jt.au. II. Northwestern
University. III. U.S. Defense Documentation
Center for Scientific and Technical Information
IV. U.S. Clearinghouse for Federal Scientific
and Technical Information. V. Title.

Transportation.

388
G25tra General Electric Corp.
Transportation Systems Div. General electric
aerial transport system; transportation for a
supersonic age. Technical report. Erie, Penn.,
General Electric, Transportation Systems
Division, 1967.
27p. (Its GEA-8603)

1. Transportation. 2. Journey to work.
I. Title.

388
G25s General Research Corp.   Systems analysis...
1968.   (Card 2)

II. Title. III. Title: Study in new systems
of urban transportation.

388
G15 TRANSPORTATION.
Ganz, Alexander.
Emerging patterns of urban growth and travel.
Cambridge, Mass., Massachusetts Institute of
Technology, Project Transport, Highway Trans-
portation Program, 1968.
198p. (Transport report 68-1)

1. Transportation. 2. City growth.
I. Massachusetts Institute of Technology.
Project Transport. II. Title.

Transportation.

VF
388 The General Electric Forum for National
G25t Security and Free World Progress.
Transportation and National strength.
Schenectady, N.Y., General Electric, 1962.
34p. (Vol. 5, no. 4, Oct.-Nov., 1962)

1. Transportation.

Transportation.

388
G26 George, Patricia Conway.
Mass transit; problem and promise.
Minneapolis, Walker Art Center, 1968.
40p.

Entire issue: Design quarterly 71.

1. Transportation. 2. Journey to work.
I. Title. II. Design quarterly.

388. TRANSPORTATION.
G267 GEORGIA. STATE COLLEGE OF BUSINESS
ADMINISTRATION. BUREAU OF BUSINESS AND
ECONOMIC RESEARCH.
URBAN TRANSPORTATION DILEMMA. BY
STEPHEN PARANKA. ATLANTA, 1961.
42L. (ITS RESEARCH PAPER SERIES, NO.
21)

1. TRANSPORTATION. I. PARANKA,
STEPHEN. II. TITLE.

Transportation.
711.73
G76 Grossman, David A
Area development and highway transportation,
by David A. Grossman, Director, Community
Development Branch of Urban Renewal Administra-
tion, Washington, D.C. and Melvin R. Levin,
Advance Planning Associates, Cambridge, Mass.
A paper prepared for the Highway Research Board,
42nd annual meeting, Jan. 1963, Washington, D.C.
19p.
Bibliography: p. 17-19.
1. Highways. 2. Transportation. I. Levin, Melvin R.
II. U.S. Urban Renewal Administration.
III. Highway Research Board.

Transportation.
388
H11a Haase, R H
Analysis of some land transportation
vehicles: today and tomorrow. Santa Monica,
Calif., Rand Corp., 1962.
27p.
"This paper was prepared for presentation
at the 32nd annual meeting of the Institute
of Traffic Engineers, held at the Denver
Hilton Hotel, Denver, Colorado, August 13-
17, 1962."

1. Transportation. I. Title: Land
transportation vehicles.
II. Rand Corp.

388
G48 Givens, W R
A study of the applicability of air-pad
support for urban transportation vehicles.
Columbus, Ohio, Battelle Memorial Institute,
Columbus Laboratories, 1967.
9p. (Battelle Memorial Institute.
Columbus Laboratories. Monograph no. 19)
Prepared for New Systems Study Project,
Urban Transportation Administration, Dept. of
Housing and Urban Development.
U.S. Mass Transportation Demonstration
Grant Program. Contract no. H-778.
(Cont'd on next card)

Transportation.
711.4
G78 Gruen, Victor, 1903-
The heart of our cities; the urban
crisis: diagnosis and cure. New York,
Simon and Schuster, 1964.
368p.

Bibliography: p. 348-351.

1. City planning. 2. Suburbs.
3. Transportation. 4. Journey to work.
5. Traffic. 6. Shopping centers. I. Title.

Transportation.
388
H11 Haase, R H
Performance of land transportation vehicles,
by R. H. Haase and W.H.T. Holden. Santa
Monica, Calif., Rand Corp., 1964.
138p. (Rand Corp Memo. RM-3966-RC)

Bibliography: p. 137-138.

1. Transportation. 2. Journey to work.
I. Holden, W.H.T., jt. au. II. Rand Corp.
III. Title. IV. Title: Land transportation
vehicles.

388
G48 Givens, W R A study of
the...1967. (Card 2)

1. Transportation. 2. Journey to work.
3. Air transportation. I. Battelle
Memorial Institute. Columbus
Laboratories. II. U.S. Dept. of Housing
and Urban Development. Urban
Transportation Administration. III. U.S.
Mass Transportation Demonstration Grant
Program. IV. Title.

711.14 Transportation.
G78 Gruen (Victor) Associates.
A review of transportation aspects of land
use control, [by] Harold Marks and Salem Spitz
[of] Victor Gruen Associates. [Wash.]
Laf. Highway Research Board, 1966.
41p. (National Cooperative Highway Research Program report no. 31)
Research sponsored by the American Association of State Highway Officials in cooperation with the Bureau of Public Roads.

1. Land use. 2. Highways. 3. Traffic.
4. Transportation. (Cont'd on next card)

388
H12 Haefele, Edwin T ed.
Transport and national goals. Wash.,
Brookings Institution, Transport Research
Program, 1969.
201p.

1. Transportation. 2. Economic planning.
I. Brookings Institution. Transport Research
Program. II. Title.

388
G65ef TRANSPORTATION.
Golenberg. Marvin.
The effect of land use planning and transport
pricing policies in express transit planning.
by Marvin Golenberg and Robert Keith. [n.p.]
[1969?]
31p
1. Transportation. 2. Journey to work.
3. Land use. I. Keith, Robert, jt. au.
II. Highway Research Board. III. Title.

711.14
G78 Gruen (Victor) Associates. A review of
transportation aspects of land use control...
(Card 2)
I. Marks, Harold. II. Spitz, Salem.
III. Highway Research Board. IV. American
Association of State Highway Officials. V. Title.

Transportation.
388
:331 Haney, Dan G
H15 The value of time for passenger cars: a
theoretical analysis and description of preliminary experiments. Final report. Prepared
for: Bureau of Public Roads, U.S. Dept. of
Transportation. Menlo Park, Calif., Stanford
Research Institute, 1967.
v.
Distributed by U.S. Clearinghouse for
Federal Scientific and Technical Information
as PB 175 653.
1. Journey to work. 2. Transportation.
I. Stanford Research Institute. II. U.S.
Bureau of Public Roads. III. Title.

711.4 TRANSPORTATION.
G67C GORDON, CHARLES.
COORDINATION OF CITY PLANNING, HIGHWAY
DEVELOPMENT AND URBAN TRANSIT.
WASHINGTON, U.S. CHAMBER OF COMMERCE,
1945.
16P.

1. CITY PLANNING. 2. TRANSPORTATION.
I. U.S. CHAMBER OF COMMERCE.

Transportation.
388
G78 Grumman Aircraft Engineering Corp.
Study of hydrofoil seacraft. Phase I
Technical report for U.S. Dept. of Commerce,
Maritime Administration. Prepared in fulfill-
ment of the requirements of Contract no. MA-
1730 by Grumman Aircraft Engineering Corp.,
Bethpage, New York, and its affiliate Dynamic
Development Inc., Babylon, New York. Bethpage,
New York, 1958.
2v. (PB 161759)
Distributed by U.S. Dept. of Commerce,
(Office of Technical Services)
(Cont'd on next card)

Transportation.
388
H17 Harmon, George M ed.
Tomorrow's transportation systems. Proceed-
ings of the 17th annual Transportation Con-
ference and Salzberg Memorial Lecture of
Syracuse University's College of Business
Administration and College of Engineering.
Syracuse, N.Y., Syracuse University, Business
Research Center, 1965.
71p. (Salzberg lecture series no. 17)

1. Transportation. I. Syracuse University.
Business Research Center. II. Title.
(Series; Salzberg lecture series no. 17)

388
G72 TRANSPORTATION.
Greco, William L
Major aspects of the urban transportation
planning process. Lafayette, Ind., Purdue
Univ., 1969.
51p. (Joint Highway Research Project,
Purdue University. Interim-summary report
no. 14)
Prepared in cooperation with Indiana State
Highway Commission and U.S. Bureau of
Public Roads.

1. Transportation. I. Joint Highway
Research Project, Purdue
University. II. Title

388
G78 Grumman Aircraft Engineering Corp.
Study of hydrofoil seacraft...
(Card 2)

1. Transportation. I. U.S. Dept. of
Commerce, (Office of Technical Services)
II. U.S. Maritime Administration.
III. Title. IV. Title: Hydrofoil seacraft.

388
H19a TRANSPORTATION.
Hazard, H R
A study of the applicability of the
linear electric motors to urban
transportation. Columbus, Ohio, Battelle
Memorial Institute, Columbus Laboratories,
1967.
12p. (Battelle Memorial Institute.
Columbus Laboratories. Monograph no. 17)
Prepared for New Systems Study Project,
Urban Transportation Administration, Dept.
of Housing and Urban Development.
(Cont'd on next card)

VF
388
G74 Transportation.
Griffin, C W Jr.
Car snobs, commuters, and chaos. Reproduced
from the Harper's Magazine, July, 1962. p. [53]
-58.

1. Transportation. 2. Journey to work.
I. Title.

388
G87 TRANSPORTATION.
Gutheim, Frederick.
The future city and its transportation.
Wash., 1969.
21p.

1. Transportation. 2. Journey to work.
I. Title.

388
H19a Hazard, H R A study of
the...1967. (Card 2)

U.S. Mass Transportation Demonstration
Grant Program. Contract no. H-778.
1. Transportation. 2. Journey to work.
3. Electricity. 4. Engineering. I. Battelle
Memorial Institute. (Columbus Laboratories)
II. U.S. Dept. of Housing and Urban
Development. Urban Transportation
Administration. III. U.S. Mass
Transportation Demonstration Grant Program.
IV. Title.

388
H19
Transportation.
Hazard, Leland.
The central city, island of excellence, the role of rapid transit. Address before the 1965 Carnegie Conference, Pittsburgh, Pa. Pittsburgh, WABCO Mass Transit Center, Westinghouse Air Brake Co., 1965.
17p.
Reprint.

1. Transportation. 2. Journey to work.
I. Carnegie Conference, Pittsburgh, 1965.
II. Westinghouse   Air Brake Co.

388
H43co
Transportation.
Highway Research Board.
Component elements of the planning process; 6 reports. Papers presented at the 45th annual meeting, 1966. Washington, Highway Research Board, Div. of Engineering and Industrial Research, National Academy of Sciences, National Research Council, 1966.
24p.   (Its Highway research record no. 137)
National Research Council. Publication 1381.

(Cont'd on next card)

388
H43h
Transportation.
Highway Research Board.
Highway corridor planning and land acquisition, 9 reports. Wash., Highway Research Board, Div. of Engineering, National Research Council, National Academy of Sciences, National Academy of Engineering, 1967.
76p. (National Research Council. Publication 1444. Highway research record no. 166)

1. Transportation. 2. Highways. 3. Land acquisition. I. Title.

388
H21
Transportation.
Hearle, Edward F   R
Have we learned anything from transportation studies? Santa Monica, Calif., Rand Corp., 1963.
10p.   (P-2740.)

1. Transportation. I. Rand Corp.

388
H43co
Highway Research Board. Component elements of the planning process; 6 reports...1966.
(Card 2)

Partial contents:-Urban renewal and urban transportation: contrasting concepts and methods, by S. Leigh Curry, Chief Counsel Urban Renewal Administration.

1. Transportation. 2. Land use. 3. Urban renewal. I. Curry, S. Leigh. Urban renewal and urban transportation;contrasting concepts and methods.

711.730.15
H43hi
Transportation.
Highway Research Board.
Highway research and urban transportation planning in other countries; 4 reports. Subject area, 90 highway research (general) Wash., Highway Research Board, Div. of Engineering, National Research Council, National Academy of Sciences, National Academy of Engineering, 1967.
Laf.   36p. (Highway research record no. 169; National Research Council Publication 1449;
Contents: A preliminary analysis of current research projects in nineteen countries, by Robert O. Swain

(Cont'd on next card)

388
H25t
TRANSPORTATION.
Hellman, Hal.
Transportation in the world of the future. New York, M. Evans and Co., distributed in association with J.B. Lippincott Co., 1968.
187p.

Bibliography: p. 177-181.

1. Transportation. I. Title.

388
H43d
Transportation.
Highway Research Board.
Design and performance criteria for improved nonrail urban mass transit vehicles and related urban transportation. A report to the United States Dept. of Housing and Urban Development. Wash., 1968.
109p.

1. Transportation. 2. Journey to work.
I. U.S. Dept. of Housing and Urban Development. II. Title. III. Title: Nonrail urban mass transit vehicles.

711.730.15
H43hi
Highway Research Board.   Highway research and urban transportation planning...1967.
(Card 2)

Road research in Canada, by Gordon D. Campbell.-The road capacity of city centers, by R.J. Smeed.-Urban development and expressways in Tokyo, by Masao Yamada.

1. Highways - Research. 2. Transportation.
3. City planning. I. Title.

388
H25
Transportation.
Henderson, Clark.
New concepts for mass transit. Menlo Park, Calif., Stanford Research Institute, 1961.
18p.

1. Transportation. I. Stanford Research Institute.

388
H43ec
Transportation.
Highway Research Board.
Economic forecasting; 6 reports. Presented at the 44th annual meeting, January 11-15, 1965. Wash., Highway Research Board, Div. of Engineering and Industrial Research, National of Sciences-National Research Council, 1966.
96p.   (Its Highway research record no. 106)
National Research Council. Publication 1323.

1. Transportation.   2. City planning.
3. Highways -   Finance.

711.73
H43hig
Transportation.
Highway Research Board.
Highways and environmental quality. 6 reports. Washington, D.C., Highway Research Board, Div. of Engineering. National Research Council, National Academy of Sciences, National Academy of Engineering. 1967.
38p. (Highway research record no. 182)
National Research Council. Publication 1513.

1. Highways. 2. Transportation. 3. Land use. I. National Research Council.
II. Title.

388
H25f
Transportation.
Hennes, Robert Graham.
Fundamentals of transportation engineering, by Robert G. Hennes and Martin Ekse. 2d ed. New York, McGraw-Hill, 1969.
613p. (McGraw-Hill civil engineering series)

1. Transportation. 2. Civil engineering.
I. Title. II. Ekse, Martin, jt. au.

388
H43fr
Transportation.
Highway Research Board.
Freight transportation; 9 reports. Presented at the 43rd annual meeting, January 13-17, 1964 and 44th annual meeting January 11-15, 1965. Washington, 1965.
120p. (Highway Research Record no. 82; Publication 1267)

1. Transportation. I. Title.

711.73
H43j
TRANSPORTATION.
Highway Research Board.
Joint development and multiple use of transportation rights-of-way; proceedings of a conference held Nov. 14-15, 1968, Wash., D.C. Wash., Highway Research Board, Div. of Engineering and Industrial Research, National Academy of Sciences-National Research Council, 1968.
198p. (Its Special report 104)
National Research Council. Publication 1459.
1. Highways.   2. Land acquisition.
3. Transport-   ation. I. National
Research   Council. II. Title.

388
H27
Transportation.
Herbert, Evan.
Transporting people. The hardest difficulties to deal with come at the interface where transportation systems (almost) meet. Can new technology improve the flow? Reproduced from International science and technology, October 1965. p. 30-42.

1. Transportation. I. International science and technology. II. Title.

388
H43g
Transportation.
Highway Research Board.
Geometric highway design, 4 reports. Wash., Highway Research Board, Div. of Engineering, National Research Council, National Academy of Engineering, 1967.
93p. (National Research Council. Publication 1503. Highway research record no. 172)

1. Transportation. 2. Highways. I. Title.

388
H43o
1967
Transportation.
Highway Research Board.
Origin and destination; advances in transportation planning, 8 reports. Wash., Highway Research Board, Div. of Engineering, National Research Council, National Academy of Sciences, National Academy of Engineering, 1967.
128p. (National Research Council. Publication 1443. Highway research record no. 165)

1. Transportation. 2. Highways. 3. Journey to work. I. Title.

388
H43c
Transportation.
Highway Research Board.
Community values as affected by transportation, 7 reports. Presented at the 42nd annual meeting, January 7-11, 1963. Washington, Highway Research Board of the Div. of Engineering and Industrial Research, National Academy of Sciences, National Research Council, 1963.
100p.   (Its Highway research record no. 2)
National Research Council. Publication 1065

1. Transportation.   2. Journey to work.   I. National Research Council.

388
H43ge
Transportation.
Highway Research Board.
Geometric aspects of highways, 5 reports. Wash., Highway Research Board, Div. of Engineering, National Academy of Sciences, National Academy of Engineering, 1967.
145p. (National Research Council. Publication 1440. Highway research record no. 165)

1. Transportation. 2. Highways. I. Title.

388
H43o
Transportation.
Highway Research Board.
Origin and destination; 4 reports. Wash., Highway Research Board, Div. of Engineering, National Academy of Sciences-National Academy of Engineering, National Research Council, 1966.
88p.   (Its Highway research record no. 141)
National Research Council. Publication 1385.

1. Transportation. 2. Journey to work.
3. Traffic surveys.

711.417
H43
Transportation.
Highway Research Board.
Planned communities; 5 reports. Presented at the 44th annual meeting, January 11-15, 1965. Wash., Highway Research Board of the Div. of Engineering and Industrial Research, National Academy of Sciences, National Research Council, 1965.
51p. (Highway research record no. 97)
National Research Council. Publication no. 1313.
Contents:-Planned communities, by R. C. Weaver.-The Bluffs: a planned community on
(Continued on next card)

711.417
H43
Highway Research Board. Planned communities; 5 reports...1965. (Card 2)
the Irvine Ranch, Newport Beach, Calif., by K. C. Albright.-Columbia, Md., a new town for America, by W. E. Finley.-Lessons to be learned from Europe, by W. Von Eckardt.-Transportation planning criteria for new towns, by H. K. Evans.
1. Planned communities. 2. Land use. 3. Transportation. 4. Community planning. I. Weaver, Robert Clifton. Planned communities.

388
H43p
Transportation.
Highway Research Board.
Planning and development in urban transportation, 1959. Papers presented at the 38th annual meeting, January 5-9, 1959. Washington, 1959.
66p. illus., diagrs., tables. (Its Bulletin 221)
Partial contents.-General planning, urban renewal, and highways, by Richard L. Steiner, Commissioner, Urban Renewal Administration, p. 37-39.
(Continued on next card)

388
H43p
Highway Research Board. Planning and Development in urban transportation ...1959(Card 2)

1. Transportation. 2. Urban renewal. 3. Highways. I. Steiner, Richard L.

388
H43pl
TRANSPORTATION.
Highway Research Board.
Planning and evaluation of transportation systems. 17 reports. [Wash.] 1971.
210p. (Highway research record no. 348)

1. Transportation. I. Title.

388
H43pu
TRANSPORTATION.
Highway Research Board.
Public transportation to airports. 7 reports. Wash., 1970.
36p. (Its Highway research record no. 330)

1. Transportation. 2. Highways. I. Title.

388
H437
TRANSPORTATION.
Highway Research Board.
Transportation and community values; report of a conference held at Warrenton, Va., March 2-5, 1969. Wash., 1969.
178p. (Its Special report 105)
Bibliography: p. 171-173.

1. Transportation. I. Title.

388
H43tra
Transportation.
Highway Research Board. (Special Committee on Urban Transportation Research.)
Transportation and other urban development and renewal programs. Panel no. 4.
[n.p., 1961]
[9]p.

1. Transportation. 2. Urban renewal.

388
H43tran
Transportation.
Highway Research Board.
Transportation system analysis and evaluation of alternate plans; 9 reports. Washington, Highway Research Board, Div. of Engineering. National Research Council, National Academy of Sciences-National Academy of Engineering, 1967.
132p. (Highway research record no. 180)
National Research Council. Publication 151.
H.e.1
Laf.e.2
1. Transportation. 2. Journey to work. I. Title.

388
H43tr
Transportation.
Highway Research Board.
Travel characteristics in urban areas; presented at the thirty-seventh annual meeting, January 6-10, 1958. Washington, National Research Council, 1958.
130p. diagrs., tables. (Its Bulletin 203)

Contents:-Travel characteristics of two San Diego subdivision developments, by Edward M. Hall.-Factors affecting trip generation of residential land-use areas, by Gordon B. Sharpe, Walter G.
(Continued on next card)

388
H43tr
Highway Research Board. Travel characteristics ... 1958. (Card 2)
Hansen, and Lamelle B. Hamner.-Forecasting peak hours of travel, by Alan M. Voorhees.-Transportation usage study, by William J. Mortimer.-Evaluating trip forecasting methods with an electronic computer, by G.L. Brokke and W. L. Mertz.-Center city goods movement: an aspect of congestion, by Edgar M. Horwood.-Travel patterns in 50 cities, by Frank B. Curran and Joseph T. Stagmaier.

1. Transportation.

388
H433t
Transportation.
Highway Research Board.
Travel forecasting; 8 reports presented at the 42nd annual meeting, January 7-11, 1963. Washington, Highway Research Board of the Division of Engineering and Industrial Research, National Academy of Sciences, National Research Council, 1963.
166p. (Highway research record no. 38)
National Research Council Publication 1158.

1. Highways. 2. Traffic. 3. Journey to work. 4. Transportation. I. Title.

388
H43trav
Transportation.
Highway Research Board.
Travel to commercial centers. Presented at the thirty-second annual meeting. January 13-16, 1953. Washington, D.C., 1953.
38p. (Its Bulletin no. 79)
National Research Council. Publication 281.

1. Transportation. 2. Shopping centers.

711.14
H43u
Transportation.
Highway Research Board.
Urban land use: concepts and models; 6 reports. Wash., Highway Research Board, National Academy of Engineering, National Academy of Sciences-National Research Council, 1967.
84p. (Its Highway research record no. 207)
National Research Council. Publication 1539

1. Land use. 2. City growth. 3. Transportation. 4. Highways. 5. Journey to work. I. Title.

388
H43urb
TRANSPORTATION.
Highway Research Board.
Urban mass transportation planning; 7 reports. Wash., 1968.
77p. (Highway research record no. 251)
National Research Council. Publication, 1398.

1. Transportation. 2. Journey to work. I. Title.

388
H43ur
Transportation.
Highway Research Board.
Urban transportation planning techniques and concepts, 1965; 4 reports presented at the 44th annual meeting, January 11-15, 1965. Washington, Highway Research Board, Division of Engineering and Industrial Research, National Academy of Sciences, National Research Council, 1965.
114p. (Highway research record no. 102)
National Research Council. Publication 1319.

(Continued on next card)

388
H43ur
Highway Research Board. Urban transportation planning techniques and concepts. 1965...1965. (Card 2)

1. Transportation. 2. Air transportation. 3. Journey to work. I. National Research Council. II. Title.

388
H43tru
Transportation.
The Highway User.
The truth about city freeways! Washington, D.C., National Highway Users Conference, 1962.
40p.

Special issue, December, 1962.

1. Highways. 2. Transportation. I. National Highway Users Conference, Wash., D.C.

385
H45
Transportation.
Hilton, George W
The electric interurban railways in America, by George W. Hilton and John F. Due. Stanford, Calif., Stanford University Press, 1960.
463p.

1. Railroads. 2. Transportation. I. Due, John F., jt. au. II. Title.

388
H47
TRANSPORTATION.
Hitt, William D
The development of a course of instruction in urban transportation management. Columbus, Ohio, Battelle Memorial Institute, Columbus Laboratories, 1967.
11p. (Battelle Memorial Institute. Columbus Laboratories. Monograph no. 3)
Prepared for New Systems Study Project, Urban Transportation Administration, Dept. of Housing and Urban Development.
U.S. Mass Transportation Demonstration Grant Program. Contract no. H-778.
(Cont'd on next card)

388
H47
Hitt, William D The development ...1967. (Card 2)

1. Transportation. 2. Journey to work. 3. Management. I. Battelle Memorial Institute. (Columbus Laboratories) II. U.S. Dept. of Housing and Urban Development. Urban Transportation Administration. III. U.S. Mass Transportation Demonstration Grant Program. IV. Title.

520.333
H62   Hoch, Irving.
    The economics of vertical transportation,
air rights and land use. [n.p., 1968?]
    1v.

    1. Air rights. 2. Land use. 3. Transportation.
4. Elevators. I. Title. II. Title: Vertical
transportation.

---

388   TRANSPORTATION.
H62   Hoess, J   A
    Unconventional heat engines for urban
vehicles. Columbus, Ohio, Battelle
Memorial Institute, Columbus Laboratories,
1967.
    8p.   (Battelle Memorial Institute.
Columbus Laboratories, Monograph no. 16)
    Prepared for New Systems Study Project,
Urban Transportation Administration, Dept.
of Housing and Urban Development.
    U.S. Mass Transportation Demonstration
Grant Program.   Contract no. H-778.
      (Cont'd on next card)

388
H62   Hoess, J   A   Unconventional
    heat...1967.   (Card 2)

    1. Transportation.   2. Journey to work.
3. Highways. 4. Air pollution.
5. Engineering. I. Battelle Memorial
Institute. (Columbus Laboratories).
II. U.S. Dept. of Housing and Urban
Development. Urban Transportation
Administration. III. U.S. Mass
Transportation Demonstration Grant
Program. IV.   Title.

388
H63   Hoffman, George A
    Automobiles: today and tomorrow. Santa
Monice, Calif., Rand Corp., 1962.
    84p.   (Memorandum RM-2922-FF)

    1. Transportation. I. Rand Corp.
II. Title.

388
H63e   Hoffman, George A
    The electric automobile. Los Angeles,
University of California, Institute of
Government and Public Affairs, 1966.
    34-40p.   (California. University.
University at Los Angeles. Institute of
Government and Public Affairs. Reprint no. 30)
    Reprinted from Scientific American,
Oct., 1966.

    1. Transportation.   2. Air pollution.
I. California.   University. University
at Los Angeles. Insti-   tute of Government and
Public Affairs.   II. Title.

     Transportation -(Addresses)
VF
388   Holmes, E   H
H65u   Urban transportation planning and the National
Highway Program, by Assistant Commissioner for
Research, Bureau of Public Roads. [Address] at
Special Committee on Urban Planning Seminars,
AASHO 1960 annual meeting, Detroit, Mich.,
Dec. 1, 1960. [n.p.] 1960.
    9p.

    1. Transportation - Addresses. I. U.S.
Bureau of Public Roads.

     Transportation.
388
H65n   Homburger, Wolfgang S
    New developments in urban transportation
technology. A paper prepared for presentation at the ninth annual California Conference
on City and Regional Planning, Vallejo, Calif.,
May 5, 1961.
    9p.

    1. Transportation. I. California Conference on
City and Regional Planning, 9th, Vallejo,
Calif., 1961.

     Transportation.
383
E65   Homburger, Wolfgang S
    Recent trends in rapid transit. Remarks
prepared for presentation at the annual
meeting of the Special Libraries' Association,
San Francisco, California, May 31, 1961.
    7p.

    Bibliography: p. 6-7.

    1. Transportation. I. Special Libraries
Association.

     Transportation.
388
H65   Homburger, Wolfgang S   ed.
1967   Urban mass transit planning. Berkeley,
Institute of Transportation and Traffic Engineering, University of California, 1967.
    212p. (California. University. Institute
of Transportation and Traffic Engineering.
Course notes)
    Bibliography: p. 204-212.
    1. Transportation. 2. Transportation - Study
and teaching. 3. Journey to work. I. California.
University. Institute of Transportation and
Traffic Engineering. II. Title.

     Transportation.
388
H668   Hoover, Edgar M
    Motor metropolis: some observations on
urban transportation in America. Pittsburgh,
University of Pittsburgh, 1965.
    13p.   (University of Pittsburgh. Center
for Regional Economic Studies. Reprint no 2)

    1. Transportation. 2. Journey to work.
I. Pittsburgh. University. Center for
Regional Economic Studies. II. Title.

     Transportation.
388
H66   Hopkins, Richard C
    Long-range research and development
program for individual transportation
systems, by Richard C. Hopkins and others.
Presented before the Special Committee on
Electronic Research, at the 42nd annual
Meeting of the Highway Research Board, Wash.,
January 1963. Washington, Office of
Research and Development, Bureau of Public
Roads, 1963.
    153-180p.
          ((Cont'd. on next card)

388
H66   Hopkins, Richard C   Long-range research
    and development ...   (Card 2)

    In Public roads; a journal of highway
research, vol. 32, no. 7, April 1963.

    1. Transportation. I. Highway
Research Board. I. U.S. Bureau of
Public Roads.

     TRANSPORTATION.
Folio
711.73
H68 m   Household Goods Carriers' Bureau.
    Mileage guide, containing maps and charts
for determining distances in highway miles
between points within the United States....
No. ..
Washington, Rand McNally,
    v. irregular.
    SEE SHELF LIST FOR LIBRARY HOLDINGS
    Each edition cancels the previous one.

    1. Highways.   2. Travel.
3. Transportation. Title: Mileage guide.
                          ml/jb

     Transportation.
711.4
H68b   U.S. Dept. of Housing and Urban Development.
    Building a better America. Washington, For
sale by the Supt. of Doc., Govt. Print. Off.,
1967.
    43p.

    1. City planning. 2. Housing. 3. Community
facilities. 4. Urban renewal. 5. Transportation.
I. Title.

     Transportation.
388
H68ca   U.S. Dept. of Housing and Urban Development. Urban Transportation Administration.
    Capital grants and loans for urban mass
transportation; information for applicants.
Washingtn, D.C., 1966.
    15 p.

    1. Transportation.   2. Grants-in-aid.
I. Title.

     Transportation.
FOLIO
388
H68w   Houston, Tex. Public Service Dept.
    World-wide transit study, by Clinton
Owsley, Director. Houston, Tex., 1963.
    1v.

    1. Transportation. 2. Traffic surveys.
3. Journey to work. I. Owsley, Clinton.
II. Title.

     Transportation.
385
H83   Huff, David L
    A topological model of consumer space
preferences. Based on a paper presented
before the Regional Science Association.
Washington, 1959.
    25p.   diagrs.

    1. Transportation. 2. Family income and
expenditure.

     Transportation.
388
H83   Rugsted, Reidar.
    Bruk av køanalyse pa laste- og transporter
beider (Queue theory applied to the solution
of loading and transportation problems in civil
engineering) Oslo, Norges Byggforskningsinstitutt, 1967.
    44p.   (Oslo. Norges Byggforsknings-
institutt. Rapport 49)

    1. Transportation. 2. Loads. 3. Building
methods. I. Oslo. Norges Byggforskningsinstitutt. (Series)

     Transportation.
388
H87   Hurter, Arthur P
    Transportation and the spatial distribution
of economic activity, by A.P. Hurter and L.N.
Moses. Research report. Evanston, Ill.,
Transportation Center at Northwestern
University, [1962?]
    27p.
    Paper to be published by the University
of Illinois Press in Essays in regional
economic science.

    1. Transportation.   2. Automation.
I. Moses, Leon N.

     Transportation.
388
I52   Industrial design.
    Mass transportation on the move. New York,
1966.
    [14]p.
    Reprinted from Industrial design, Nov. 1966.

    1. Transportation. I. Title.

     Transportation.
388
I57r   Institute for Rapid Transit, Chicago.
    Rapid transit reference manual. Prepared in
cooperation with the IRT Public Information
Committee. 1st ed. Chicago, 1967.
    1v.
    Summary of the U.S. Dept. of Housing and
Urban Development financial aid to Urban mass
transportation; pt. III.

    1. Transportation.   2. Grants-
in-aid. I. U.S. Dept. of Housing and Urban
Development. II. Title.

388
I57pu
TRANSPORTATION.
Institute of Public Administration.
Public Urban Locator Service (PULSE) background and conference proceedings, Oct. 24, 1968. [New York] 1968.
466p.
CFSTI. PB 180 116.
Work performed by Institute of Public Administration and Teknekron, Inc.
U.S. Mass Transportation Demonstration Grant Program. HUD contract no. H-1030.
1. Transportation. 2. Communication systems. I. Teknekron, inc. II. U.S. Mass Transportation Demonstration Grant Program. III. Title.

388
I57t
Transportation.
Institute of Public Administration, New York.
The transportation picture in selected urban areas. A supplement to Urban transportation and public policy. Prepared for U.S. Dept. of Commerce and Housing and Home Finance Agency. New York, 1961.
175p.
On cover: Appendix volume.
See also 388H68ur
1. Transportation. 2. Metropolitan areas. I. U.S. Dept. of Commerce. II. U.S. Housing and Home Finance Agency. III. Title. IV. Title: Urban transportation and public policy.

388
I57o
Transportation.
Institute of Traffic Engineers.
Capacities and limitations of urban transportation modes; an information report. Washington, 1965.
36p.
1. Transportation. 2. Journey to work. I. Title.

711.73
I57
TRANSPORTATION.
Institute of Traffic Engineers.
System considerations for urban freeways; an informational report. Wash., 1967.
48p.
1. Highways. 2. Transportation. I. Title.

388
I57o
Transportation.
International Conference on Urban Transportation.
Official proceedings, 1st- 1966-
Pittsburgh, 1966-
v.
For complete information see main card.
Sponsored 19 by the Urban Transportation Council of the Chamber of Commerce of Greater Pittsburgh.
1. Transportation. I. Pittsburgh. Chamber of Commerce of Greater Pittsburgh. Urban Transportation Council.

388
I57u
TRANSPORTATION.
International Federation for Housing and Planning. 28th Congress, Tokyo, 1966.
Urban transportation and urban pattern. Housing standards for low and lowest income groups in relation to the national level of economic and social development. The Hague, 1966.
265p.
English, French, and German.
1. Transportation. 2. Housing. 3. Family income and expenditure - Housing. I. Title.

388
I57i
TRANSPORTATION.
International Union of Public Transport. International Congress.
Brussels, 19
nos.
1. Transportation. 2. Journey to work. 3. Railroads.

690.015
(485)
S82
R30
1969
TRANSPORTATION.
Jonson, Jan-Ake.
Externa transporter av betongelement till bostadshus (External transport of concrete units for residential buildings) Stockholm, Statens Institut för Byggnadsforskning, 1969.
193p. (Stockholm. Statens Institut för Byggnadsforskning. Rapport 30:1969)
English summary.
Bibliography: p. 192-93.
1. Building research - Sweden. 2. Concrete construction. 3. Transportation. I. Title: External transport of concrete units for residential buildings. II. Stockholm. Statens Institut för Byggnadsforskning.

388
K14c
Transportation.
Kain, John F
A contribution to the urban transportation debate: an econometric model of urban residential and travel behavior.
[n.p.] 1962.
37p.
1. Transportation. 2. Land use. 3. Journey to work.

388
K52
TRANSPORTATION.
Klein, G E
Methods of evaluation of the effects of transportation systems on community values; final report, by G.E. Klein and others. Menlo Park, Calif., Stanford Research Institute, 1971.
290p.
Bibliography: p. R-3 - R-19.
Prepared for Dept. of Housing and Urban Development. HUD contract H-1122.
1. Transportation. I. Stanford Research Institute. II. U.S. Dept. of Housing and Urban Development. III. Title.

388
K14f
Transportation.
Kain, John F
A first approximation to a Rand model for study of urban transportation, by John F. Kain and J.R. Meyer. Santa Monica, Calif., Rand Corp., 1961.
52p. (Rand Corp. Memorandum RM-2878-FF)
1. Transportation. I. Meyer, J.R., jt. au. II. Rand Corp.

388
K14h
TRANSPORTATION.
Kain, John F
How to improve urban transportation at practically no cost. [Cambridge, Mass.] Harvard University, Program on Regional and Urban Economics, 1970.
34p. (Harvard University. Program on Regional and Urban Economics. Discussion paper no. 60)
1. Transportation. 2. Journey to work. I. Harvard University. Program on Regional and Urban Economics. II. Title. (Series: Harvard University. Program on Regional and Urban Economics. Discussion paper no. 60)

388
K14m
Transportation.
Kain, John F
Metropolitan area transportation. Toronto, Bureau of Municipal Research, 1967.
62p. (Toronto. Bureau of Municipal Research. Paper no. 6)
Centennial Study and Training Programme on Metropolitan Problems.
1. Transportation. 2. Journey to work. I. Toronto. Bureau of Municipal Research. II. Title.

388
K14re
TRANSPORTATION.
Kain, John F
A re-appraisal of metropolitan transport planning. Seattle, Wash., University of Washington, Center for Urban and Regional Research, 1969.
23p. (Washington (State) University. Center for Urban and Regional Research. Reprint no. 16. [Program on Regional and Urban Economics. Discussion paper no. 20]
1. Transportation. 2. Journey to work. I. Washington (State) Center for Urban and Regional Research. II. Title.

388
K14r
Transportation.
Kain, John F
A report on an urban transportation model, some progress and some problems. Santa Monica, Calif., Rand Corp., 1962.
26p.
"Prepared for presentation at the first Annual Meeting of the Western Section of the Regional Science Association, Berkeley, Calif., June 29, 1962."
1. Transportation. I. Regional Science Association. Meeting, Berkeley, Calif., 1962. Papers. II. Rand, Corp.

388
K14
v.21
no.1
Transportation.
Kaiser aluminum news.
The rise of the city. Oakland, Calif., Kaiser Aluminum and Chemical Corp 1963.
35p.
Entire issue, vol. 21, no. 1.
1. Transportation. 2. Transportation - San Francisco. I. Kaiser Aluminum and Chemical Corporation.

388
K17
TRANSPORTATION.
KARREMAN, HERMAN F
METHODS FOR IMPROVING WORLD TRANSPORTATION ACCOUNTS, APPLIED TO 1950-1953. NEW YORK, NATIONAL BUREAU OF ECONOMIC RESEARCH, 1961.
121P. (NATIONAL BUREAU OF ECONOMIC RESEARCH. TECHNICAL PAPER 15)
1. TRANSPORTATION. I. TITLE. II. NATIONAL BUREAU OF ECONOMIC RESEARCH.

388
K25o
Transportation.
Kennedy, Norman.
The organization of metropolitan transit agencies by Norman Kennedy and Wolfgang S. Homburger. Berkeley, University of California, Institute of Transportation and Traffic Engineering, 1961.
41p. (California. University. Institute of Transportation and Traffic Engineering. Research report no. 32)
1. Transportation. I. Homburger, Wolfgang S., jt. au. II. California. University. Institute of Transportation and Traffic Engineering.

388
K65
TRANSPORTATION.
Koltnow, Peter G
Successful cities; six case studies in transportation progress. Wash., Transportation Development Div., Highway Users Federation for Safety and Mobility, 1971.
39p.
1. Transportation. 2. Journey to work. 3. Highways. I. Highway Users Federation for Safety and Mobility. (Transportation Development Div.)

388
K71
TRANSPORTATION.
Kraft, Gerald.
The role of transportation in regional economic development. A Charles River Associates Research Study, by Gerald Kraft and others. Lexington, Mass., D.C. Heath and Co., 1971.
129p.
Bibliography: p. 95-129.
1. Transportation. 2. Economic development. I. Charles River Associates Research Study. II. Title.

388
L15d
TRANSPORTATION.
Lampert, Seymour.
Developing area transportation study. Program formulation. Long Beach, Calif., Systems Associates, 1968.
139p.
CFSTI. AD 673 432.
1. Transportation. 2. Journey to work. I. Systems Associates. II. Title.

388
L15

Lang, A Scheffer.
    Urban rail transit: its economics and technology, by A. Scheffer Lang and Richard M. Soberman, Cambridge, Mass., Massachusetts Institute of Technology, 1964.
    139p.

    Published for the Joint Center for Urban Studies of the Massachusetts Institute of Technology and Harvard University.

1. Transpor-   tation. I. Title.
II. Soberman,   Richard M., jt. au.
III. Joint Center   for Urban Studies.

388
L17

TRANSPORTATION.
Larson, Roy E
    Transportation, 1983; the Minnesota Experimental city, by Roy E. Larson and Robert J. Reid, North Star Research and Development Institute. [n.p.] [1969?]
    30p.

    1. Transportation. 2. Transportation - Minn.
3. Journey to work. I. Reid, Robert J., jt. au.
II. Highway Research Board. III. Title.

388
L28

TRANSPORTATION.
Levin, Melvin R
    Bureaucrats in collision: case studies in area transportation planning, by Melvin R. Levin and Norman A. Abend. Cambridge, MIT Press, 1971.
    295p.
    Bibliography: p. 277-281.

    1. Transportation. I. Abend, Norman A., jt. au. II. Title.

388
:331
L15

Transportation.
Lansing, John B
    Automobile ownership and residential density, by John B. Lansing and Gary Hendricks. Prepared for Bureau of Public Roads, Federal Highway Adm., U.S. Dept. of Transportation. Ann Arbor, University of Michigan, Survey Research Center, Institute for Social Research, 1967.
    230p.

    1. Journey to work. 2. Population density.
3. Transportation. I. Hendricks, Gary, jt. au.
II. U.S. Federal   Highway Adm.
        (Cont'd on next card)

388
L21

TRANSPORTATION.
Leathers, Nancy J
    Residential location and mode of transportation to work: a model of choice. Oxford, Pergamon, 1967.
    [27]p.

    Reprinted from: Transportation research, vol. 1, pp. 129-155.

    Bibliography: p. 153-155.

    1. Transportation. 2. Journey to work.
I. Title.

388
L47

Transportation.
Li, Shu-t'ien.
    Regional aspects of transportation centers, by Shu-t'ien Li. New York, American Society of Civil Engineers, 1965.
    25p.
    Prepared for ASCE Transportation Engineering Conference, Minneapolis, Minnesota, May 17-21, 1965 as Conference preprint 219.
    1. Transportation. 2. Journey to work.
3. Highways. I. American Society of Civil Engineers. II. ASCE Transportation Engineering Conference, Minneapolis, 1965. III. Title.

388
:331
L15

Lansing, John B   Automobile ownership and residential density...1967.   (Card 2)

III. Michigan. University. Institute for Social Research. IV. Title.

330
L22s

Transportation.
Lecht, Leonard A
    Goals, priorities, and dollars; the next decade. New York, Free Press, London, Collier-Macmillan, 1966.
    365p.
Add. copy, AIP/Ewald notebooks (711.4 A52ne no. 10)
    1. Economic conditions. 2. Economic forecasting. 3. National income. 4. Social welfare. 5. Housing. 6. City planning.
7. Transportation. 8. International relations. I. Title.

388:331
L42

Transportation.
Liepmann, Kate K
    The journey to work; its significance for industrial and community life, by Kate K. Liepmann, PH. D., with a foreword by A. M. Carr-Saunders ... London, K. Paul, Trench, Trubner & co., ltd. [1944]
    xii, 190 p. incl. tables. fold. maps, fold. diagr. 22½ cm. (International library of sociology and social reconstruction. Editor: Dr. Karl Mannheim)
    "First published 1944."
    "The study has been approved by the University of London for the award of the degree of Ph. D."—Pref.
    Bibliographical foot-notes.
    1. Traffic and engineering. 2. Industries, Location of. 3. Cities and towns—Planning. I. Title.
    For tracing see main entry.   44—3511
    Library of Congress   HD7895.T72L5
    [a51j₁]   331.83

711.417
L15

TRANSPORTATION.
Lansing, John B
    Planned residential environments, by John B. Lansing and others. A report prepared for the U.S. Dept. of Transportation, Bureau of Public Roads. Ann Arbor, University of Michigan, Institute for Social Research, Survey Research Center, 1970.
    269p.
    Bibliography: p. 265-269.
    1. Planned communities. 2. Transportation.
I. U.S. Bureau of Public Roads. II. Michigan. University. Survey Research Center.
III. Title.

388
L24tr

TRANSPORTATION.
Leibbrand, Kurt.
    Transportation and town planning. Translated by Nigel Seymer. Cambridge, Mass., M.I.T., 1970.
    381p.

    Bibliography: p. 367-370.

    1. Transportation. 2. City planning.
3. Traffic. I. Title.

388
L44

Transportation.
Líkař, Otakar.
    The allocation of production units and their optimum size. [n.p., 1965?]
    25p.

    1. Transportation. 2. Automation.
I. Title.

388
L157r

Transportation.
Lansing, John B
    Residential location and urban mobility: a multivariate analysis, by John B. Lansing and Nancy Barth. Prepared for the U.S. Dept. of Commerce, Bureau of Public Roads. [Ann Arbor] University of Michigan, Survey Research Center, Institute for Social Research, 1964.
    98p.

    (Cont'd on next card)

388
L24

TRANSPORTATION.
Leis, R D
    The development and demonstration of a family of practical moving-way transport systems for pedestrians. Columbus, Ohio, Battelle Memorial Institute, Columbus Laboratories, 1967.
    17p. (Battelle Memorial Institute. Columbus Laboratories. Monograph no. 13)
    Prepared for New Systems Study Project, Urban Transportation Administration, Dept. of Housing and Urban Development.
    U.S. Mass Transportation Demonstration Grant Program.   Contract no. H-778.
    (Cont'd on next card)

388
L440

Transportation.
Líkař, Otakar.
    The optimum allocation of capacities from the viewpoint of the minimization of transport costs. [n.p., 1965?]
    24p.

    1. Transportation. 2. Automation.
3. Journey to work. I. Title.

388
L157r

Lansing, John B. Residential location and urban mobility: a multivariate analysis...
    (Card 2)

    1. Transportation. 2. City growth.
3. Journey to work. 4. Population shifts.
5. Family income and expenditure. I. Barth, Nancy, jt.au. II. Title. III. Michigan. University. Institute for Social Research.
IV. U.S. Bureau of Public Roads.

388
L24

Leis, R D   The development and demonstration...1967.   (Card 2)

    1. Transportation. 2. Journey to work.
I. Battelle Memorial Institute. (Columbus Laboratories) II. U.S. Dept. of Housing and Urban Development. Urban Transportation Administration. III. U.S. Mass Transportation Demonstration Grant Program. IV. Title:
Pedestrians. V. Title.

388
L44s

Transportation.
Líkař, Otakar.
    Solution of allocation problems by the column minima method. [n.p., 1965?]
    7p.

    1. Transportation. 2. Automation.
3. Journey to work. I. Title.

388
L15r

Transportation.
Lansing, John B
    Residential location and urban mobility: the second wave of interviews. Prepared for the U.S. Dept. of Commerce, Bureau of Public Roads. Ann Arbor, Michigan University, Survey Research Center, Institute for Social Research, 1966.
    [152]p.

    1. Transportation. 2. City growth.
3. Journey to work. 4. Residential areas.
I. U.S. Bureau of   Public Roads.
II. Michigan   University. Institute for Social   Research. III. Title.

388
L24t

TRANSPORTATION.
Leisch, Jack E
    Transportation systems in the future development of metropolitan areas: the permanent corridor concept. [Toronto, De Leuw, Cather and Co. of Canada, ltd., 1968]
    27p.

    For presentation at the 48th annual meeting of the Highway Research Board, Jan. 1969.

    1. Trans-   portation. 2. Journey to work.   I. Title.

388
L61

TRANSPORTATION.
Lobdell, Norman E
    Application of improved management methods to the urban transportation industry. Columbus, Ohio, Battelle Memorial Institute, Columbus Laboratories, 1967.
    4p. (Battelle Memorial Institute. Columbus Laboratories. Monograph no. 4)
    Prepared for New System Study Project, Urban Transportation Administration, Dept. of Housing and Urban Development.
    U.S. Mass Transportation Demonstration Grant Program.   Contract no. H-778.
    (Cont'd on next card)

388
L61

TRANSPORTATION.
Lobdell, Norman E   Application of
improved...1967.   (Card 2)

1. Transportation. 2. Journey to work.
I. Battelle Memorial Institute. (Columbus
Laboratories) II. U.S. Dept. of Housing
and Urban Development. Urban Transportation
Administration. III. U.S. Mass
Transportation Demonstration Grant Program.
IV. Title.

388
L61g

TRANSPORTATION.
Lobdell, Norman E
Grouped road vehicles. Columbus, Ohio,
Battelle Memorial Institute, Columbus
Laboratories, 1967.
5p. (Battelle Memorial Institute.
Columbus Laboratories. Monograph no. 8)
Prepared for New Systems Study Project,
Urban Transportation Administration, Dept. of
Housing and Urban Development.
U.S. Mass Transportation Demonstration
Grant Program. Contract no. H-778.
(Cont'd on next card)

388
L61g

Lobdell, Norman E   Grouped
road...1967.   (Card 2)

1. Transportation. 2. Journey to work.
3. Highways. I. Battelle Memorial Institute.
(Columbus Laboratories) II. U.S. Dept. of
Housing and Urban Development. Urban
Transportation Administration. III. U.S.
Mass Transportation Demonstration Grant
Program. IV. Title.

711.15
L61

TRANSPORTATION.
Lobdell, Norman E
Land use involving transportation
rights-of-way. Columbus, Ohio, Battelle
Memorial Institute, Columbus Laboratories,
1967.
6p. (Battelle Memorial Institute.
Columbus Laboratories. Monograph no. 5)
Prepared for New Systems Study Project,
Urban Transportation Administration, Dept.
of Housing and Urban Development.
U.S. Mass Transportation Demonstration
Grant Program. Contract no. H-778.
(Cont'd on next card)

711.15
L61

Lobdell, Norman E   Land use
involving...1967.   (Card 2)

1. Air rights. 2. Land use. 3. Highways.
4. Transportation. 5. Journey to work.
I. Battelle Memorial Institute. (Columbus
Laboratories) II. U.S. Dept. of Housing
and Urban Development. Urban Transportation
Administration. III. U.S. Mass
Transportation Demonstration Grant Program.
IV. Title.

388
L61m

TRANSPORTATION.
Lobdell, N   E
Models of urban transportation.
Columbus, Ohio, Battelle Memorial Institute,
Columbus Laboratories, 1967.
5p. (Battelle Memorial Institute.
Columbus Laboratories. Monograph no. 9)
Prepared for New Systems Study Project,
Urban Transportation Administration, Dept.
of Housing and Urban Development.
U.S. Mass Transportation Demonstration
Grant Program. Contract no. H-778.
(Cont'd on next card)

388
L61m

Lobdell, N   E   Models of
urban...1967.   (Card 2)

1. Transportation. 2. Journey to
work. I. Battelle Memorial Institute.
(Columbus Laboratories). II. U.S. Dept.
of Housing and Urban Development.
Urban Transportation Administration. III. U.S.
Mass Transportation Demonstration Grant
Program. IV. Title.

388
L61o

TRANSPORTATION.
Lobdell, Norman E
Operations analysis of augmented-
guideway systems. Columbus, Ohio,
Battelle Memorial Institute, Columbus
Laboratories, 1967.
7p. (Battelle Memorial Institute.
Columbus Laboratories. Monograph no. 6)
Prepared for New Systems Study Project,
Urban Transportation Administration, Dept.
of Housing and Urban Development.
U.S. Mass Transportation Demonstration
Grant Program. Contract no. H-778.
(Cont'd on next card)

388
L61o

Lobdell, Norman E   Operations
analysis...1967.   (Card 2)

1. Transportation. 2. Journey to work.
3. Highways. I. Battelle Memorial
Institute. (Columbus Laboratories)
II. U.S. Dept. of Housing and Urban
Development. Urban Transportation
Administration. III. U.S. Mass
Transportation Demonstration Grant Program.
IV. Title.

388
L62e

Transportation.
Locklin, David Philip, 1897-
Economics of transportation. 6th ed.
Homewood, Ill., R.D. Irwin, 1966.
882p. (The Irwin series in economics)

1. Transportation. 2. Transportation -
Economic effect. 3. Railroads. I. Title.

388
L62

Transportation.
Loewenstein, Louis K
The location of residences and work places in
urban areas. New York, Scarecrow, 1965.
331p.

Bibliography: p. 312-324.

1. Transportation. 2. Journey to work.
3. Business districts. 4. Residential areas.
I. Title.

388
L66

TRANSPORTATION.
Loomis, J   P
Potential application of the helicopter
in urban mass transportation. Columbus,
Ohio, Battelle Memorial Institute, Columbus
Laboratories, 1967.
11p. (Battelle Memorial Institute.
Columbus Laboratories. Monograph no. 18)
Prepared for New Systems Study Project,
Urban Transportation Administration, Dept.
of Housing and Urban Development.
U.S. Mass Transportation Demonstration
Grant Program. Contract no. H-778.
(Cont'd on next card)

388
L66

Loomis, J   P   Potential
application...1967.   (Card 2)

1. Transportation. 2. Journey to work.
3. Air Transportation. I. Battelle
Memorial Institute. (Columbus Laboratories)
II. U.S. Dept. of Housing and Urban
Development. Urban Transportation
Administration. III. U.S. Mass
Transportation Demonstration Grant Program.
IV. Title.

388
L85

TRANSPORTATION.
Luna, Charles.
The UTU [United Transportation Union]
handbook of transportation in America.
New York, Popular Library, 1971.
282p.

Bibliography: p. 236-276.

1. Transportation. 2. Federal government.
I. United Transportation Union. II. Title.

388
L91

Transportation.
Lybrand, Ross Bros. & Montgomery United
Research, inc.
Cost accounting system for ground modes
of common transportation carriers. Prepared
for the Under Secretary of Transportation.
Washington, 1966.
v.
Contents: v.1. Railroad manual. v.2. Motors
manual. v.3. Barge manual.
Distributed by U.S. Clearinghouse for Federal
Scientific and Technical Information.
1. Transportation. 2. Accounting. 3. Rail-
roads. 4. Harbors.   I. U.S. Dept. of
Commerce. II. Title.

388
308
M22

Transportation.
McConcochie, W   R
Study of terminal transfer facilities in
conjunction with urban freeways, for
Minnesota Dept. of Highways and Bureau of
Public Roads. Chicago, DeLeuw, Cather and
Co., 1967.
54p.
U.S. Clearinghouse for Federal Scientific
and Technical Information   document PB
175 759.

1. Traffic surveys. 2. Transportation.
3. Highways.   (Cont'd on next card)

388
308
M22

McConcochie, W   R   Study of
terminal transfer facilities in conjunction
with urban freeways.. 1967.   (Card 2)

4. Urban renewal. I. DeLeuw, Cather & Co.,
Chicago. II. Minnesota Dept. of Highways.
III. U.S. Bureau of Public Roads. IV. U.S.
Clearinghouse for Federal Scientific and
Technical Information. V. Title.

621.39
M12

Transportation.
McLuhan, Herbert Marshall.
Understanding media; the extensions of man.
1st ed. New York, McGraw-Hill, 1964.
359p.
Bibliography: p. [391]-365.

1. Communication systems. 2. Education.
3. Transportation. 4. Automation.
I. Title. II. Title: The extensions of
man.

388
M25

Transportation.
McMonagle, J   Carl
The impact of highway transportation on
regional and community development, by J.
Carl McMonagle and Robert B. Hotaling.
[East Lansing, Mich.] Institute for Communi-
ty Development and Services, Michigan State
University, 1964.
12p. (Michigan. State University.
Institute for Community Development and
Services. Technical bulletin B-42)

(Continued on
next card)

388
M25

McMonagle, J   Carl. The impact of highway transportation on regional and
community development...1964. (Card 2)

1. Transportation. 2. Highways - Economic
effect. I. Hotaling, Robert B., jt. au.
II. Michigan. State University. Institute
for Community Development and Services.

388
M14

Transportation .
Makofski, R   A
Performance criteria and technical feasibility of the urban gravity-vacuum-transit
system, by R.A. Makofski and others. Silver
Spring Md., Applied Physics Laboratory,
1968.
226p. (Johns Hopkins University. Applied
Physics Laboratory. Technical memo. TG-984)

1. Transportation. 2. Transportation -
Research. I. Johns Hopkins University.
Applied Physics Laboratory. II. Title.

388
(744)
M17ur

Transportation.
Massachusetts. Bureau of Transportation
Planning and Development.
The urban transportation planning process
in Massachusetts. Prepared in cooperation
with U.S. Dept. of Commerce, Bureau of
Public Roads. Boston, 1964.
[20]p. (Its Informational bulletin no.
2)
Massachusetts. Dept. of Public Works.
Publication no. 419.

1. Transportation. 2.   Boston Regional
Planning Project. I.   U.S. Bureau of
Public Roads.   II. Title.

388
M17h

Transportation.
Massachusetts Institute of Technology.
High speed ground transport. Part 2.
High priority research tasks for high speed
ground transport. Prepared for the U.S.
Dept. of Commerce. Distributed by: U.S.
Clearinghouse for Federal Scientific and
Technical Information. Cambridge, Mass.,
1965.
[62]p. (PB 169 121)

1. Transportation. 2. Journey to work.
I. U.S. Clearinghouse for Federal Scien-
tific and Tech- nical Information.
II. Title.

388
:308
M17

Transportation.
Massachusetts Institute of Technology.
Survey of technology for high speed
ground transport. Part 1 [of the Northeast
Corridor Transportation Project] Prepared
for the United States Dept. of Commerce.
Cambridge, Mass., 1965.
271p. (PB 168 648)
Distributed by Clearinghouse for Federal
Scientific and Technical Information.

1. Traffic surveys. 2. Transportation. 3. Journey
to work. I. Northeast   Corridor
Transportation Project.   II. Title.

388
M19

Transportation.
Mayo (Robert B.) and Associates.
Tunneling; the state of the art; a review
and evaluation of current tunneling techniques
and costs, with emphasis on their application
to urban rapid-transit systems in the U.S.A.;
prepared for the U.S. Dept. of Housing and
Urban Development. Lancaster, Pa., 1968.
263p.
Distributed by U.S. Clearinghouse for Federal
Scientific and Technical Information as document PB 178 036.
1. Transportation. 2. Building methods.
3. Soils. I. U.S.   Dept. of Housing and
Urban Development.   II. Title.

388
M29t
v.1

TRANSPORTATION.
Meyer, John R   ed.
Techniques of transport planning. Vol. 1,
Pricing and project evaluation. Ed. by John
R. Meyer and Mahlon R. Straszheim. Wash.,
Brookings Institution, Transport Research Pro-
gram, 1971.
343p.
Bibliography: p. 317-336.

1. Transportation. I. Meyer, John R., ed.
II. Straszheim, Mahlon R., jt. ed.
III. Brookings Institution. Transport
Research Program.   IV. Title. V. Title:
Pricing and project evaluation.

388
M29t
v.2

TRANSPORTATION.
Meyer, John R   ed.
Techniques of transport planning. Vol. 2:
Systems analysis and simulation models.
David T. Kresge and Paul O. Roberts. With
special contributions by Donald N. Dewees and
others. Wash., Brookings Institution, Trans-
port Research Program, 1971.
228p.
1. Transportation. I. Kresge, David T.
II. Brookings Institution. Transport Research
Program. III. Title.

388
M29

Transportation.
Meyer, John R
Technology and urban transportation, by
John R. Meyer and others. [Washington] 1962.
131p.

1. Transportation. 2. Journey to work.
I. Title.

388
M29u

Transportation.
Meyer, John Robert.
The urban transportation problem, by J. R.
Meyer and others. Cambridge, Harvard
University Press, 1965.
427p. (A Rand Corporation research
study)

1. Traffic. 2. Journey to work.
3. Transportation. I. Title. II. Rand
Corp.

388
M42

Transportation.
Michigan State University, East Lansing.
Highway Traffic Safety Center.
Papers presented at the Urban Transportation
Conference, February 18-20, 1959. East Lansing,
1959.
1v.

Partial contents:-Organizing a transportation
planning program, by Wilbur E. Smith.-The Federal government's interest in urban transportation studies, by Gordon B. Sharpe.-Carrying
out the plan, by Edward M. Hall.-Inventory of
the physical street system, by

(Continued on next
card)

388
M42

Michigan State University, East Lansing. Highway Traffic Safety Center. Papers... (Card 2)

Alfred Berarducci.-The work of the National
Committee on Urban Transportation, by Glenn C.
Richards.-Carrying out the plan, by W. A.
Rusch.-Transit service and your community, by
Walter S. Rainville, Jr.-Transit service in
the plan, by Walter S. Rainville, Jr.

1. Transportation.

388
M42s

Transportation.
Midler, J L
A stochastic dynamic multimode transpor-
tation model. Prepared for United States
Air Force Project Rand. Santa, Monica,
Calif., Rand Corp., 1967.
31p. (Rand Corp. Memo. RM-5250-PR AD 655
344)

1. Transportation. 2. Transportation -
Automation. I. Rand Corp. II. Title.

388
M42sp

Transportation.
Midwest Research Institute.
Special transportation requirements in
small cities and towns, final report, by
Bruce W. Macy and others. Prepared for the
U.S. Dept. of Housing and Urban Development.
[Kansas City, Mo.] 1968.
87p.
On cover: Study in new systems of urban
transportation.
1. Transportation. 2. Transportation -
Statistics. I. U.S. Dept. of Housing and
Urban Development. II. Macy, Bruce W.
III. Title.
(Cont'd on next card)

388
M42sp

Midwest Research Institute. Special
transportation requirements...1968.
(Card 2)

IV. Title: Study in new systems of urban
transportation. V. Title: Transportation
requirements in small cities and towns.

711.3
M47

Transportation.
Mitchell, Robert B
Metropolitan planning for land use and
transportation; a study, by Robert B.
Mitchell, professor of City Planning, University of Pennsylvania. Washington, Govt.
Print. Off., 1961.
47p.
Date on title page: 1959.
"Under contract with the Special Assistant
to the President for Public Works Planning."
1. Metropolitan area planning. 2. Land use.
3. Transportation. I. U.S. Special Assistant to
the President for Public Works Planning.

388
M66

Transportation
Moody's transportation manual; railroads,
airlines, shipping, traction, bus and truck
lines. American and Foreign, 1966-68.
New York, Moody's Investors Service, 19
3v, weekly; annual

For library holdings see main entry

Weekly looseleaf issuances are recorded in
Kardex

(Cont'd on next card)

388
M66

Moody's transportation manual...19-   (card 2)

1. Transportation   2. Investments
I. St. Clair, Frank J. ed.

388
M67u

TRANSPORTATION.
Morin, Donald A
Urban transportation planning course; the
role of transit in transportation systems.
Lecture 8.9, Oct. 16, 1968. [Wash.] U.S. Bureau
of Public Roads, 1968.
1v. (loose-leaf)

1. Transportation. 2. Journey to work.
I. U.S. Bureau of Public Roads. II. Title.

388
:331
M67s

TRANSPORTATION.
Morrall, J   F
A study of the journey to work by
central business district workers,
by J.F. Morrall, and B.G. Hutchinson.
[n.p.] [1969?]
99-114p.

1. Journey to work. 2. Transportation.
3. Business districts. I. Hutchinson,
B.G., jt. au. II. Title.

388
M672

Transportation.
Moses, Leon N
Urban transportation subsidies and the
problems of mature central cities, by
Director of Research, Transportation Center,
and Professor of Economics, Northwestern
University. [n.p.] 1963.
10p.
1. Transportation. 2. City growth.
I. Northwestern University. Transportation
Center.

388
M67

Transportation.
Mossman, Frank H   ed.
Principles of urban transportation. In
cooperation with the American Transit Association. East Lansing, Mich., Press of Western
Reserve University, 1951.
236p.

1. Transportation. 2. Journey to work.
I. American Transit Association.

388
M67t

Transportation.
Mott, George Fox, ed.
Transportation century. [A compilation of
essays from various authors] Baton Rouge,
Louisiana State University Press, 1966.
279p.
Partial contents: President Johnson's
Transportation message of Mar. 2, 1966.

1. Transportation. 2. U.S. Dept. of Transportation. 3. U.S. President - Messages.
I. Title.

Transportation.

352
N17ame National Association of County Officials.
American county platform; transportation.
Washington [1966?]
6p.

1. County government. 2. Transportation. 3. Highways. I. Title.

388
N17b National Committee on Urban Transportation,
District of Columbia.
Better transportation for your city; a
guide to the factual development of urban
transportation plans. Chicago, Public
Administration Service, 1958.
96p. illus., charts, maps.

see also its Procedure manual.
1. Transportation. I. Public Administration
Service. II. Title.

388
N17b National Committee on Urban Transportation. District of Columbia.
no. 5A Inventory of the physical street system.
Chicago, Public Administration Service, 1958.
21p. (Procedure manual 5A)
"For use in conjunction with [its] Better
transportation for your city ... "

1. Streets. 2. Transportation. I. Public
Administration Service.

Transportation.

388
N17bu National Association of Motor Bus Owners.
Bus facts; a summary of facts and figures
on the intercity-bus industry.
Washington, D.C.,
v.

For complete information see shelf list.

1. Transportation. I. Title.

Transportation.

388
N17b National Committee on Urban Transportation,
no. 2B District of Columbia.
Conducting a home interview origin-
destination survey. Chicago, Public
Administration Service, 1954.
109p. (Procedure manual no. 2B)
Cover-title.
"For use in conjunction with [its] Better
transportation for your city ... "

1. Transportation. 2. Journey to work.
I. Public Administration Service.

Transportation.

388
N17b National Committee on Urban Transportation,
no. 3E District of Columbia.
Maintaining accident records. Chicago,
Public Administration Service, 1958.
18p. (Procedure manual no. 3E)
"For use in conjunction with [its] Better
transportation for your city ... "

1. Transportation. 2. Traffic safety.
I. Public Administration Service.

Transportation.

388
N17pu National Association of Real Estate Boards.
National Institute of Real Estate Brokers.
Public transportation and your community.
Sponsor: John J. Herd [and] Albert M.
Greenfield & Co., Philadelphia. Chicago,
1958.
63p.

1. Transportation. 2. Journey to work.
I. Title.

Transportation.

388
N17b National Committee on Urban Transportation, District of Columbia.
no. 3c Conducting a limited parking study. Chicago,
Public Administration Service, 1958.
35p. maps. (Procedure manual no. 3c)

"For use in conjunction with [its] Better
transportation for your city ... "

1. Transportation. 2. Parking. I. Public
Administration Service.

Transportation.

388
N17b National Committee on Urban Transportation,
no. 3A District of Columbia.
Measuring traffic volumes. Chicago, Public
Administration Service, 1958.
39p. graphs. (Procedure manual 3A)

"For use in conjunction with [its] Better
transportation for your city ... "

1. Transportation. 2. Traffic surveys.
I. Public Administration Service.

388
N17nb TRANSPORTATION.
National Bureau of Economic Research.
The NBER urban simulation model. [New York,
1964?]
2v.
Vol.I: The Model description, by Gregory K.
Ingram and others.
Vol.II: Supporting empirical studies, ed. by
John F. Kain.
Report supported by HUD grant number NY-MTD-15,
Administered by the Office of Urban Transportation
Development and Liaison, Div. of Systems Research
and Development.

(Cont'd on next card)

Transportation.

388
N17b National Committee on Urban Transportation,
no.1A District of Columbia.
Determining street use. Chicago, Public
Administration Service, 1958.
7p. (Procedure manual no. 1A)

"For use in conjunction with [its] Better
transportation for your city ... "

1. Transportation. 2. Street planning.
I. Public Administration Service.

Transportation.

388
N17b National Committee on Urban Transportation,
no. 4A District of Columbia.
Measuring transit service. Chicago,
Public Administration Service, 1958.
27p. (Procedure manual no. 4A)
"For use in conjunction with [its]
transportation for your city ... "

1. Transportation. I. Public
Administration Service.

388
N17nb National Bureau of Economic Research. The NBER
urban...[1964?] (Card 2)

1. Transportation. 2. Land use. 3. City
planning. I. U.S. Dept. of Housing and Urban
Development. II. Ingram, Gregory K.
III. Kain, John F., ed. IV. Title: Urban
simulation model. V. Title.

Transportation.

388
N17b National Committee on Urban Transportation,
no. 3B District of Columbia.
Determining travel time. Chicago, Public
Administration Service, 1958.
24p. illus., maps, tables. (Procedure manual 3B)
"For use in conjunction with [its] Better
transportation for your city ... "
1. Transportation. I. Public Administration
Service.

Transportation.

388
N17b National Committee on Urban Transportation, District of Columbia.
no. 2A Origin-destination and land use. Chicago,
Public Administration Service, 1958.
46p. diagrs., maps. (Procedure
manual 2A)

"For use in conjunction with [its] Better
transportation for your city ... "

1. Transportation. 2. Land use.
I. Public Administration Service.

388
N17o TRANSPORTATION.
National Bureau of Economic Research.
Overview of land use-transportation models in
planning and survey of land use models in five
metropolitan areas, by James Brown and others.
[New York, 1966?]
1v.
U.S. Dept. of Housing and Urban Development.
Mass Transportation Demonstration Grant Program.
1. Transportation. 2. Journey to work.
3. Land use. I. Title. II. Brown, James.
III. U.S. Mass Transportation Demonstration
Grant Program.

Transportation.

388
N17b National Committee on Urban Transportation,
no. 10A District of Columbia.
Developing project priorities for
transportation improvements. Chicago,
Public Administration Service, 1959.
9p. (Procedure manual no. 10A)
"For use in conjunction with [its] Better
transportation for your city ... "

1. Transportation. I. Public
Administration Service.

Transportation.

388
N17b National Committee on Urban Transportation,
District of Columbia.
Procedure manual (analyzed)

For complete information see shelflist.
For use in conjunction with its Better
transportation for your city.

1. Transportation.

388
N17re Transportation.
National Citizens' Commission on Inter-
national Cooperation.
Report of the Committee on Transportation.
[Wash.] Govt. Print. Off., 1965.
29p. (Document 4. Final draft)
For presentation at the White House
Conference on International Cooperation,
Wash., Nov. 28-Dec. 1, 1965.

1. Transportation. 2. Traffic safety.
3. International relations. I. White House
Conference on International
Cooperation, Wash., D.C., 1965.

Transportation.

388
N17b National Committee on Urban Transportation,
no. 11A District of Columbia.
Improving transportation administration.
Chicago, Public Administration Service, 1958.
20p. (Procedure manual no. 11A)
"For use in conjunction with [its] Better
transportation for your city ... "

1. Transportation. I. Public Administration Service.

Transportation.

388
N17b National Committee on Urban Transportation,
no. 8A District of Columbia.
Recommended standards, warrants, and objectives
for transit services and facilities. Chicago,
Public Administration Service, 1958.
20p. (Procedure manual 8A)

"For use in conjunction with [its] Better
transportation for your city ... "

1. Transportation. I. Public Administration
Service.

Transportation.

388
N17b
no.7A
National Committee on Urban Transportation,
District of Columbia.
Standards for street facilities and
services. Chicago, Public Administration
Service, 1958.
27p. maps, tables. (Procedure
manual 7A)
"For use in conjunction with [its] Better
transportation for your city ... "

1. Transportation. 2. Streets. I. Public
Administration Service.

Transportation.

388
N17u
National Research Council.
U.S. transportation, resources, performance
and problems; a collection of papers prepared
for the Transportation Research Conference,
convened by the National Academy of Sciences
at Woods Hole, Mass., August, 1960. Washington,
National Academy of Sciences, National Research
Council, 1961.
319p. (Its Publication 841-S (Supplement
to publication 841))

1. Transportation. I. Transportation
Research Conference,
Woods Hole, Mass.

Transportation.

711.4
A52ne
no.12
The New scientist.
The world in 1984. The complete New
scientist series, edited by Nigel Calder.
Baltimore, Penguin, 1965.
2v. (Penguin A720-A721)
AIP/Ewald notebooks, Basic book no. 12.

1. City planning. 2. Scientific research.
3. Economic forecasting. 4. Transportation.
I. Calder, Nigel, ed. II. Title.

Transportation.

388
N17c
National Conference Co-ordinating Metropolitan
Area Transportation.
A lesson for tomorrow. Mansfield, Ohio,
Ohio Brass Co., 1958.
19p. illus.

1. Transportation. 2. Metropolitan areas.

Transportation.

388
N17e
1963
National Research Council. Meeting.
Washington, D.C., 1963.
Engineering and the behavioral sciences.
A presentation of papers and panel discussion
from the joint Annual Meeting of the Div. of
Behavioral Sciences and the Div. of Engineer-
ing and Industrial Research, held in Washing-
ton, D.C., 9 April 1963. Washington,
National Academy of Sciences, National
Research Council, 1963.
39p.

1. Transportation -
Congresses. 2. Engineering -
I. Title.

Transportation.

388
N28
Newcomb (Robinson) Associates, Washington,
D.C.
Report on urban transportation.
Washington, Under Commission from the
American Automobile Association, Special
Committee on Urban Transportation, 1960.
91p.

1. Transportation. 2. Highways.
I. American Automobile Association.

Transportation.

388
N17g
National geographer.
Geography and planning. Allahabad, India,
Dept. of Geography, University of Allahabad,
1963.
[15]p.
Reprints.
Special issue; National geographer, vol. 5,
1962.
Contents:-Geographic aspects of transpor-
tation planning for the rural-urban fringe,
by R.I. Wolfe.
(Cont'd. on next card)

Transportation.

711.729
N17
National Research Council. Highway Research
Board.
Parking as a factor in business. Washington
1953 [c1954]
xxv, 321 p. in 6 pts. illus., graphs, maps,
tables. (Its Special report 11)
Bibliographical footnotes.
Contents.-Preface [and] foreword, a review of
major findings.-pt.1.Attitudes toward parking and
related conditions in Columbus, by C. T. Jonassen.-
pt.2.Economic relationships of parking to business
in Seattle metropolitan area, by Louis C. Wagner.-
(Continued on next card)

Transportation.

388
N67fu
Norling, A H
Future transportation needs. Cambridge,
Mass., United Research, inc., 1963.
1v.

Distributed by U.S. Clearinghouse for
Federal Scientific and Technical Information as N 64 25006.

1. Transportation. 2. Journey to work.
I. United Research, inc. II. Title.

388
N17g
National geographer. Geography and planning
... (Card 2)

1. Transportation. I. Title.
II. Wolfe, Roy I. Geographic aspects of
transportation planning for the rural-urban
fringe.

National Research Council. Highway Research
Board. Parking as a factor in business ...
1953 [c1954] (Card 2)

pt.3.Relationship between downtown automobile-
parking conditions and retail-business decentralization, by William J. Watkins.-pt.4.Central city
property values in San Francisco and Oakland, by
Paul F. Wendt.-pt.5.Trends in economic activity
and transportation in San Francisco bay area, by
David A. Revzan.

TRANSPORTATION.

388
N671
North American Rockwell Corp.
Implementation requirements for four ad-
vanced urban transportation systems. Final
report by Transportation System Technology,
M.A. Sulkin, Program Manager. Los Angeles,
1968.
211p. (NA-63-807)
Prepared for the U.S. Dept. of Housing
and Urban Development. Contract H-779,
Phase II.
U.S. Mass Transportation Demonstration
Grant Program.
CFSTI. PB 183 939.
(Cont'd on next card)

TRANSPORTATION.

388
N17na
National Motor Freight Traffic Association.
National motor freight classification;
classes and rules applying on freight
traffic covered by tariffs governed by
this classification as such tariffs may
provide,
Wash., American Trucking Asso., 19-

v.

For Library holdings see main entry.
Supple- ments,
(Cont'd on next card)

Transportation.

VF
383
N17
National Resources Planning Board.
The future of transportation. [Washington,
Govt. print. off.] Sept. 1942.
43 p.

1. Transportation.

388
N671
North American Rockwell Corp. Implemen-
tation...1968. (Card 2)

1. Transportation. 2. Journey to work.
I. Sulkin, M.A. II. U.S. Dept. of
Housing and Urban Development. III. U.S.
Mass Transportation Demonstration Grant
Program. IV. Title.

388
N17na
National Motor Freight Traffic Association.
National...19- (Card 2)

Wash. 19
v.

1. Transportation. 2. Tariff.
I. American Trucking Association.
II. Title.

TRANSPORTATION.

388
N17n
1966
National Transportation Symposium, San
Francisco, 1966.
1966 National Transportation Symposium,
San Francisco, Calif., May 1-6, 1966.
Sponsored by Aviation and Space Division of
the American Society of Mechanical Engineers
and others. New York, American Society of
Mechanical Engineers, United Engineering
Center, 1966.
457p.
1. Transportation. I. American Society
of Mechanical Engineers. Aviation
and Space Div.

TRANSPORTATION.

388
N67p
North American Rockwell Corp.
Preliminary implementation requirements for
dual-mode bus system. Los Angeles, Los Angeles
Division of North American Rockwell Corp., 1968.
57p. (NA 68-350)
U.S. Dept. of Housing and Urban Development.
Mass Transportation Demonstration Grant Program.
Contract H-779, Amendment no. 4.
1. Transportation. 2. Journey to work.
I. Title: Dual mode bus system. II. U.S. Mass
Transportation Demonstration Grant Program.

Transportation.

388
N17t
National Research Council.
Transportation design considerations.
Selections from the proceedings of the
Transportation Research Conference, convened
by the National Academy of Sciences at Woods
Hole, Massachusetts, August, 1960.
Washington, National Academy of Sciences,
National Research Council, 1961.
243p. (Its Publication 841)

1. Transportation I. Transportation
Research Conference, Woods Hole,
Mass., 1960.

TRANSPORTATION.

388
N17nat
National Urban Coalition.
A national perspective on center city
transportation; 21 cities. Wash., 1970.
149p. (Report no. UMTA-DC-MTD-6-71)

Financed in part through Mass Transportation
Demonstration Grant DC-MTD-6.

1. Transportation. 2. Business districts.
I. Title. II. U.S. Mass Transportation
Demonstration Grant Program.

Transportation - Addresses.

388
N67m
North, Clyde B
Metropolitan transportation. Prepared for
delivery June 21, 1960, Metropolitan Transportation Panel, conducted by Northwestern University
Transportation Center, Evanston, Ill., June 21,
1960.
6p.

1. Transportation - Addresses. I. Northwestern University. Transportation Center.

Transportation.
388
N67 Northwest Road Building and Traffic
Engineering Conference, Seattle, 1961.
Some observations on urban transport
planning and research, by Harmer E.
Davis. Seattle, 1961.
9p.

1. Transportation. I. Davis, Harmer E.

Transportation.
388
O71 Osborne, Henry W
A traffic engineer looks at rapid transit.
Presented to the Institute for Rapid Transit,
Annual Meeting, Washington, D.C., May 19, 1965.
[n.p.] 1965.
7p.
1. Transportation. 2. Journey to work.
3. Highways. I. Institute for Rapid Transit.
Meeting, Washington, 1965. II. Title.

Transportation.
388
082t Owen, Wilfred.
Transportation and the city. Pittsburgh,
Institute of Local Government, Graduate School
of Public and International Affairs, University of Pittsburgh, 1966.
24p. (Twelfth annual Wherrett lecture
on local government)

1. Transportation. 2. Journey to work.
3. Federal government. I. Wherrett lecture
on local government. II. Pittsburgh. University. Graduate School of Public and International Affairs. III. Title.

Transportation.
388
N677 Northwestern University. Transportation
Center.
Growth and change in metropolitan areas
and their relations to metropolitan transportation: a research summary, by Mark
Reinsberg. Evanston, Ill., 1961.
23p.

1. Transportation. I. Reinsberg, Mark.

TRANSPORTATION.
388
082a Owen, Wilfred.
The accessible city, by Wilfred Owen with
the assistance of Inai Bradfield. Wash.,
Brookings Institution, 1972.
150p.
Bibliography: p. 141-143.

1. Transportation. 2. City planning.
3. Journey to work. I. Bradfield, Inai.
II. Brookings Institution. III. Title.

Transportation.
388
P15 Pan American Union.
A survey of factors which effect transportation cost. Prepared in the Dept. of
Economic Affairs of the Pan American Union,
General Secretariat, Organization of
American States. Wash., 1964.
76p.

1. Transportation. 2. Title.

TRANSPORTATION.
388
N67n Norton, Hugh S
National transportation policy: formation
and implementation. Berkeley, Calif.,
McCutchan Pub. Corp., 1966.
249p.

1. Transportation. I. Title.

Transportation.
388
082f Owen, Wilfred.
A fable; how the cities solved their transportation problems. Washington, Urban America,
Ref. inc., 1967.
23p.

1. Transportation. 2. Urban renewal.
I. Urban America, inc. II. Title.

Folio Transportation.
388
(758231) Parsons, Brinckerhoff, Quade and Douglas.
P17p A plan and program of rapid transit for
the Atlanta Metropolitan Region. A report of Metropolitan Atlanta Transit
Study Commission, to the city of Atlanta
and the counties of Clayton, Cobb, Dekalb,
Fulton and Gwinnett. New York, 1962.
117p.
U.S. Urban Renewal Adm. UPAP.
1. Transportation. 2. Journey to work. I. Atlanta.
Metropolitan Transit Study Commission. II. U.S.
URA-UPAP. Atlanta.

TRANSPORTATION.
658.564
O45 OKLAHOMA. STATE UNIVERSITY. OFFICE
OF ENGINEERING RESEARCH, STILLWATER.
A DIGITAL COMPUTER SOLUTION TO THE
TRANSIT OPERATOR ASSIGNMENT PROBLEM,
BY PAUL E. TORGERSON AND SAMY E.G.
ELIAS. STILLWATER, OKLA., 1961.
45L. (ITS ENGINEERING REPORT NO.
120)

1. AUTOMATION. 2. TRANSPORTATION.
I. TORGERSON, PAUL E. II. ELIAS,
SAMY E.G. III. TITLE.

Transportation.
388
082 Owen, Wilfred
The metropolitan transportation problem.
Washington, Brookings Institution, 1956.
301 p. illus., graphs, tables, maps.

Bibliographical footnotes.

1. Transportation. 2. City planning.
I. Brookings Institution. II. Title.

Transportation.
388
P17 Passenger Belt Conveyors, inc.
Is downtown traffic strangling your city?
Carveyor passenger conveyor system to ease
today's traffic problems today! [n.p.,
1961?]
15p.

1. Transportation. 2. Traffic.

Transportation.
388
O44 Oi, Walter Y
An analysis of urban travel demands, by
Walter Y. Oi and Paul W. Shuldiner.
[Evanston] Published for the Transportation Center, at Northwestern University, by
Northwestern University Press, 1962.
281p.

Bibliography: p. 275-278.

1. Transportation. I. Shuldiner, Paul W., jt. au.
II. Northwestern University. Transportation Center.
III. Title.

Transportation.
388
082 Owen, Wilfred.
1966 The metropolitan transportation problem.
Rev. A Brookings Institution study. Garden
City N.Y., Anchor Books, 1966.
266p.

1. Transportation. 2. Traffic.
3. Journey to work. 4. Railroads.
I. Brookings Institution. II. Title.

Transportation
WF
534.83 Paterson, W H
:388 Noise control in Toronto's new subway, by
P17 W. H. Paterson and T. D. Northwood. Noise
control, v. 2, no. 5, Sept. 1956, p. 28-32, 62.
illus.
Reprinted by National Research Council of
Canada as Research paper no. 28 of the Division
of Building Research.

1. Noise. 2. Transportation. I. Northwood, T.D., jt.
Au.

TRANSPORTATION.
388
073 Organisation for Economic Cooperation and
Development.
The urban transportation planning process.
Paris, 1971.
351p.

Bibliography: p. 343-351.

1. Transportation. I. Title.

Transportation.
388
082s Owen, Wilfred.
Strategy for mobility. Washington,
Brookings Institution, Transport Research
Program, 1964.
249p.
Bibliography: p. 229-236.

1. Transportation. 2. Technical
assistance programs. 3. Economic development. I. Brookings
Institution. II. Title.

TRANSPORTATION.
388
P21e Peat, Marwick, Livingston & Co.
Evaluation of a bus transit system in a selected
urban area. [n.p.] 1963.
142p.

Prepared for Bureau of Public Roads.

1. Transportation. 2. Transportation –
Baltimore. 3. Journey to work. I. Title.

Transportation.
388
075 Orlando, Martin.
Technical and managerial capabilities.
A summary. New York, Martin-Marietta, Corp.
[196??]
11p. (Martin-Marietta Corp. OR 3630)

1. Transportation. 2. Transportation – Automation. 3. Journey to work. I. Martin-
Marietta Corp. II. Title.

TRANSPORTATION. Anal.
301.15
P27 Owen, Wilfred.
Transport: key to the future of cities.
(In Perloff, Harvey S., ed. The quality
of the urban environment. 1969. p. 205-337)

1. Transportation. 2. Journey to work.
I. Title.

Transportation.
388
P21 Peat, Marwick, Livingston & Co., New York.
Projection of urban personal transportation
demand. Prepared for the U.S. Dept. of Housing
and Urban Development. New York, 1968.
72p.
At head of title: Study in new systems of
urban transportation.
1. Transportation. 2. Journey to work.
3. Transportation – Automation. I. U.S. Dept.
of Housing and Urban Development. II. Title.
III. Title: Study in new systems of urban
transportation.

388
P21s
TRANSPORTATION.
Peat, Marwick, and Livingston.
Sensitivity analysis of the evaluation of a bus transit system in a selected urban area. Prepared for Bureau of Public Roads. [n.p.] 1970.
62p.

1. Transportation. 2. Transportation - Baltimore. 3. Journey to work. I. Title.

711.4
P272
TRANSPORTATION.
PERRING, KATHERINE.
URBAN LAND USE AND THE NEW MOBILITY, BY KATHERINE PERRING AND MELVILLE C. BRANCH, JR. [NEW YORK 1942]
P.44-46.
REPRINTED FROM THE AMERICAN CITY, MAY 1942.

1. CITY PLANNING. 2. TRANSPORTATION. I. BRANCH, MELVILLE C. JR., JT. AU. II. TITLE.

388
P79
TRANSPORTATION.
Prytula, George.
Community mobility systems. Wash., Urban Land Institute, 1970.
32p. (ULI special report)

1. Transportation. 2. Journey to work. I. Urban Land Institute. II. Title.

388
P21c
TRANSPORTATION.
Peat, Marwick, Mitchell & Co.
A case for bus transit in urban areas. [n.p.] 1970.
20p.

Based on a study for Bureau of Public Roads, Federal Highway Administration.

1. Transportation. 2. Journey to work. I. U.S. Bureau of Public Roads. II. Title.

711.585
P27t
Transportation.
Pestalozzi, Gerold.
Transportation and land use. Berkeley, Calif., Institute of Transportation and Traffic Engineering, University of California, 1962.
13p.

Cover title: Graduate report.
Thesis (M.S.)-University of California, Berkeley.

1. Transportation. 2. Land use. I. California. University. Institute of Transportation and Traffic Engineering.

621.39
P81
TRANSPORTATION.
Public Urban Locator Service (PULSE): background and conference proceedings, Oct., 1968, Wash., D.C. Sponsored by U.S. Dept. of Housing and Urban Development, Office of Urban Transportation. New York, Institute of Public Administration and Teknekron, Inc., [1969]
466p.
U.S. Mass Transportation Demonstration Grant Program.
HUD contract no. H-1030.
CFSTI. PB 180116.
1. Communication systems. 2. Traffic. 3. Transportation. I. Institute of Public Administration.
(Cont'd on next card)

388
P25m
Transportation.
Pell, Claiborne de Borda.
Megalopolis unbound; the supercity and the transportation of tomorrow. New York, Frederick A. Praeger, 1966.
233p.

Bibliography: p. 222-226.

1. Transportation. 2. Highways. 3. Railroads. 4. Airports. I. Title.

388
P34
Transportation.
Philadelphia. Office of the Mayor.
Public transit authority: a study of five cities, compiled and written by the Mayor's Transit Study Task Force. Philadelphia, Office of the Mayor, [1963?]
49p.

1. Transportation. 2. Journey to work. I. Title.

621.39
P81
Public Urban Locator...[1969]   (Card 2)

II. U.S. Dept. of Housing and Urban Development. III. U.S. Mass Transportation Demonstration Grant Program.

388
P25
Transportation.
Pell, Claiborne.
Remarks of Senator Claiborne Pell (D.R.I.) before the National Housing Conference Convention, Washington, D. C. Washington, 1965.
8p.

1. Transportation. 2. Housing. I. National Housing Conference, Wash., D. C., 1965.

388
P43
Transportation.
Pignataro, Louis J
An analysis of results from HHFA/HUD Mass transportation demonstration projects, by Louis J. Pignataro and Raymond S. Niedowski. New York, American Society of Mechanical Engineers, 1967.
12p. (67-Tran-20)
An ASME publication.
1. Transportation. I. Niedowski, Raymond S., jt. au. II. American Society of Mechanical Engineers. III. U.S. Dept. of Housing and Urban Development. Mass Transportation Demonstration Grant Program. IV. Title.

711.73
R12
TRANSPORTATION.
Rae, John B
The road and the car in American life. Cambridge, Mass., MIT Press, 1971.
390p.

Bibliography: p. 375-382.

1. Highways. 2. Transportation. I. Title.

388
(748)
P25p
no.18
Transportation.
Penn Jersey Transportation Study.
Regional data. Philadelphia, Penn Jersey Transportation Study, 1962.
8p. (Penn Jersey Transportation Study. PJ paper no. 18)

1. Transportation - Pa.-N.J.-Del. 2. Journey to work. 3. Transportation. I. Title. (Series: Penn Jersey Transportation Study. Philadelphia. P.J. paper no. 18)

VF
624.2
P67
Transportation.
Port of New York Authority.
George Washington Bridge lower level scheduled for completion 1962 to improve service by increasing traffic capacity 75 percent. New York [1960?]
[8]p. illus., map.

1. Bridges. 2. Transportation.

388
R14
Transportation.
Rainville, Walter S   Jr.
Capacity of urban transportation modes, by Walter S. Rainville, Jr. and Wolfgang S. Homburger.
37-55 p.

Part of the Journal of the Highway Division, Proceedings of the American Society of Civil Engineers, Vol. 89, no. HW1, Proc. Paper 3489, April, 1963, p. 37-55.

1. Transportation. 2. Highways. I. American Society of Civil Engineers. II. Homburger, Wolfgang S., jt. au

---

711.4
P275
Transportation.
Perloff, Harvey S
Common goals and the linking of physical and social planning. For the ASPO (American Society of Planning Officials)-CPAC (Community Planning Association of Canada) Joint Planning Conference, Pomeroy Memorial Lecture, April 28, 1965. [Washington?] 1965.
26p.

1. City planning - Social aspects.

(Continued   on next card)

388
P68
Transportation.
Power systems for electric vehicles; a symposium sponsored by the U.S. Dept. of Health, Education, and Welfare, Columbia University and Polytechnic Institute of Brooklyn, April 6-8, 1967. Cincinnati, U.S. Dept. of Health, Education and Welfare, Public Health Service, Bureau of Disease Prevention and Environmental Control, National Center for Air Pollution Control, 1967.
323p. (Public Health Service. Publication 999-AP-37)

(Cont'd on next card)

388
R15m
Transportation.
Rams, Edwin M
Means of access and the socio-economic structure of urban areas in the United States. Written for Highway Research Board, National Academy of Sciences. [Washington] 1965.
28p.

1. Transportation. 2. Highways - Economic effect. 3. Highways - Social effect. I. Highway Research Board. II. Title.

711.4
P275
Perloff, Harvey S   Common goals and the linking...1965.   (Card 2)

2. Land use. 3. Transportation. I. American Society of Planning Officials. II. Community Planning Association of Canada. III. Pomeroy Memorial Lecture. IV. Title.

711.4
:670
P74
Transportation.
Princeton University Conference.
Urban development and urban transportation; papers presented at a meeting of the Princeton University Conference, April 30 and May 1, 1957. Princeton, N. J., 1957.
62p.

1. Industrial location. 2. Transportation. I. Title.

388
R15
Transportation.
Rand Corp.
Transportation for future urban communities: a study prospectus. Santa Monica, Calif., 1961.
48p. (Research memo RM-2824-FF)

1. Transportation. 2. Journey to work. 3. Traffic. 4. Automation. I. Title.

Transportation.

388
R22   Reck, Franklin M
        A car traveling people; how the auto-
      mobile has changed the life of Americans,
      a study of social effects. [Detroit,
      Automobile Manufacturers Association,
      1945?]
        48p.

        1. Transportation. I. Automobile
      Manufacturers Association.

Transportation.

388
R61   Roberts, John M
        Expressive self-testing in driving, by
      John M. Roberts and others. Ithaca, N.Y.,
      Center for Housing and Environmental Studies,
      Division of Urban Studies, Cornell University,
      1966.
        [10]p.   (Cornell University. Center for
      Housing and Environmental Studies. Division
      of Urban Studies. Article 17, reprints)
        Reprinted from Human organizations, Spring
      1966, p. 54-63.

                    (Cont'd on next card)

Transportation.

388
R67a Ross, Howard R
        U.S. passenger transportation; an inventory
      of resources and an analysis of capabilities
      of surface modes. Prepared for: Office of
      Civil Defense, Dept. of the Army. Menlo
      Park, Calif., Stanford Research Institute, 1967.
        76p. (U.S. Defense Documentation Center.
      Defense Supply Agency. Document] AD655 567)
        Distributed by U.S. Clearinghouse for Federal
      Scientific and Technical Information.
        1. Transportation. 2. Civilian defense.
      I. U.S. Defense Supply Agency. II. U.S.
      Clearinghouse for Federal Scientific and
      Technical Infor   mation. III. Stanford
      Research Institu   te. IV. Title.

Transportation.

VF
388
R21   Reinsberg, Mark.
        Facts, theories, opinions on private
      carriage; a research summary. Evanston, Ill.,
      Transportation Center, Northwestern University,
      1963.
        6p.

        Reprinted from National Defense transportation
      journal, January-February, 1963.

        1. Transportation. 2. Railroads.
      I. Northwestern   University.
      Transportation   Center.

388
R61   Roberts, John M.   Expressive self-testing in
        driving...1966.
                            (Card 2)

        1. Transportation. 2. Sociology, Urban.
      I. Cornell University. Center for Housing and
      Environmental Studies. Division of Urban
      Studies. II. Title.

Transportation.

388
S15   Salmon, V
        Noise control in the Bay Area Rapid Transit
      System, by V. Salmon and S. K. Oleson. Pre-
      pared for Parsons, Brinckerhoff-Tudor-Bechtel,
      San Francisco, Calif. Interim report. Menlo
      Park, Calif., Stanford Research Institute,
      1965.
        109p.

        U.S. Housing and Home Finance Agency. Mass
      Transportation Demonstration Grant Program.

                    (Continued on
                      next card)

388
R23   TRANSPORTATION.
        Regional Economic Development Institute,
      Pittsburgh.
        Transportation requirements and effects
      of new communities. Prepared for the
      U.S. Dept. of Housing and Urban
      Development. Pittsburgh, 1968.
        102p.
        1. Transportation. 2. Planned
      communities. I. U.S. Dept. of Housing
      and Urban   Development. II. Title.

388
R611 TRANSPORTATION.
        Roberts, Paul O
        Interregional transport models. Cambridge,
      Mass., 1969.
        14p. (Harvard University. Program on
      Regional and Urban Economics. Discussion
      paper no. 48)
        1. Transportation. I. Harvard University.
      Program on Regional and Urban Economics.
      II. Title.

388
S15   Salmon, V   Noise control... (Card 2)

        1. Transportation. 2. Noise. 3. Railroads.
      4. San Francisco Bay Area Rapid Transit Dis-
      trict. I. Stanford Research Institute.
      II. U.S. Housing and Home Finance Agency.
      Mass Transportation Demonstration Grant Pro-
      gram. III. Oleson, S.K., jt. au. IV. Title.

388
R27   TRANSPORTATION.
        Resource Management Corp.
        External costs and benefits analyses, NECTP,
      by Paul F. Dienemann and Armando M. Lago. [Pre-
      pared for Northeast Corridor Transportation Pro-
      ject] Office of High Speed Ground Transportation,
      Federal Railway Administration, U.S. Department of
      Transportation. Wash., Govt. Print. Off., 1969.
        101p. ([DOT] Report no. NECTP-224)
        This volume is one of a set of 17 reports
      supporting the Northeast Corridor Transportation
      Project Report of December 1969 (NECTP-209)
        1. Transportation. 2. Railroads. 3. Air
      transportation.   I. U.S. Northeast Corridor
      Transportation Pro   ject. II. Dienemann, Paul
      F. III. Lago, Armando M., jt. au. IV. Title.

388
R62   TRANSPORTATION.
        Roeseler, W   G
        Transportation planning and urban renewal.
      New York, Howard, Needles, Tammen & Bergendoff,
      1966.
        15p.
        Presented at the Road Gang, American Concrete
      Pipe Association luncheon meeting,
      1966, Wash., D.C.

        1. Transportation. 2. Urban renewal.
      3. City planning. I. Title.

388
S15W TRANSPORTATION.
        SANTA CLARA CO., CALIF. CITY PLANNING
      COMMISSION.
        WAR TRANSIT SURVEY SAN JOSE, 1943.
        20P.

        1. TRANSPORTATION.

388
R42   Transportation.
        Richards, Brian.
        New movement in cities. London, Studio
      Vista, New York, Reinhold, 1966.
        96p.

        1. Transportation. 2. Journey to work.
      3. City planning - Social aspects. I. Title.

388
R67d TRANSPORTATION.
        Rosinger, George.
        Design of urban transportation for the
      user, by George Rosinger and others.
      Columbus, Ohio, Battelle Memorial Institute,
      Columbus Laboratories, 1967.
        22p. (Battelle Memorial Institute.
      Columbus Laboratories. Monograph no. 1)
        Bibliography: p. 19-22.
        Prepared for New Systems Study Project,
      Urban Transportation Administration, Dept. of
      Housing and Urban Development.
                            (Cont'd on next card)

388
S23b TRANSPORTATION.
        Scheel, Jerold W
        Bus operation in single lane platoons and
      their ventilation needs for operation in
      tunnels, by Jerold W. Scheel and James E.
      Foote. Warren, Mich., Research Labor-
      atories, General Motors Corp., 1968.
        30p. (General Motors Corp. Research
      Laboratories. Research publication GMR
      808)
        1. Transportation. 2. Journey to work.
      3. Ventilation. I. Foote, James E., jt. au.
      II. General   Motors Corp.
      III. Title.

388
R47   Transportation.
        Ritter, Paul.
        Planning for man and motor. New York,
      Macmillan, 1964.
        384p.

        A Pergamon press book.

        Parts in French and German.

        1. Transportation. 2. Traffic. 3. Journey
      to work. I. Title.

388
R67d Rosinger, George. Design of urban
        transportation...1967. (Card 2)

        U.S. Mass Transportation Demonstration
      Grant Program. Contract no. H-778.

        1. Transportation. 2. Journey to work.
      I. Battelle Memorial Institute. (Columbus
      Laboratories). II. U.S. Dept. of Housing
      and Urban Development. Urban Transportation
      Administration. III. U.S. Mass Transpor-
      tation Demonstration Grant Program.
      IV. Title.

388
S23r TRANSPORTATION.
        Schmidt, Randall W   S
        Regional urban mass transportation; prob-
      lems, proposals, solutions. [Philadelphia]
      Graduate Division of the Wharton School, Uni-
      versity of Pennsylvania, 1968.
        210p.
        Thesis (Master of Governmental Administra-
      tion) - Wharton School, University of Penn-
      sylvania.
        Bibliography: p. 198-210.
        1. Transportation. 2. Journey to work.
      I. Pennsylvan   ia. University. Wharton
      School of Fi   nance and Commerce.
      II. Title.

Transportation.

VF
388
R48   Rivers, Robert L
        An appraisal of the urban transit
      situation. Reproduced from the Quarterly
      review, Economics and business, vol. 2,
      no. 4, November 1962. p. 41-51.

        1. Transportation. 2. Journey to work.

Transportation.

VF
388
R67   Ross, Howard R
        New transportation technology. Reproduced
      from International science and technology,
      Nov. 1966.
        [10]p.

        1. Transportation. 2. Journey to work.
      3. Grants-in-aid. I. International science
      and technology. II. Title.

388
S23f TRANSPORTATION.
        Schneider, Jerry B
        Locating ambulance dispatch centers in an
      urban region: a man-computer interactive prob-
      lem - solving approach, by Jerry B. Schneider
      and John G. Symons, Jr. Philadelphia, Regional
      Science Research Institute, 1971.
        40p. (RSRI discussion paper series: no. 49)

        1. Transportation. 2. Health. I. Regional
      Science Research Institute, Philadelphia.
      II. Symons, John G., Jr., jt. au. III. Title.

388
S23a   TRANSPORTATION.
Schneider, Kenneth R
    Autokind vs. mankind; an analysis of tyranny;
A proposal for rebellion; a plan for reconstruc-
tion. Illustrated by Richard D. Hedman.
New York, W.W. Norton, 1971.
267p.

    1. Transportation. 2. Highways.
I. Title.

388
S23m   Transportation.
Schneider, Lewis M
    Marketing urban mass transit; a comparative
study of management strategies. Boston, Div.
of Research, Graduate School of Business
Administration, Harvard University, 1965.
217p.
    Bibliography: p. [201]-210.
    Based on the thesis...in partial fulfill-
ment of the requirements of the degree of
Doctor of Business Administration...

1. Transportation. 2.   Management. 3.
Journey to work.   I. Harvard
University.   II. Title.

711.400.15   Transportation.
823   Schnore, Leo F   ed.
    Urban research and policy planning. Edited
by Leo F. Schnore and Henry Fagin. Vol. 1
Urban affairs annual reviews. Beverly Hills,
California., Sage Publications, 1967.
638p.
    Bibliography: p. [603]—630.
    Partial contents: The evolving goals of the
Department of Housing and Urban Development,
by R.C. Weaver, Secretary, Department of Housing and Urban Development.

        (Cont'd on next card)

711.400.15
823   Schnore, Leo F   Urban research and policy
planning...1967.   (Card 2)

    1. City planning - Research. 2. City growth.
3. Sociology, Urban. 4. Housing - Social
aspects. 5. Transportation. I. Fagin, Henry,
jt.au. II. Weaver, Robert Clifton. The
evolving goals of the Dept. of Housing and
Urban Development. III. Title.
IV. Series: Urban affairs annual review. Vol.1.

301.15   Transportation.
824   Scientific American.
Per.ed.   Cities. Edited by Dennis Flanagan. New
York, 1965.
280p.
301.15   Another issue.
824   Entire issue, September 1965. 211p.
    Contents: The urbanization of the human
population, by K. Davis.--The origin and
evolution of cities, by G. Sjoberg.--The
modern metropolis, by Hans Blumenfeld.--
Calcutta: a premature metropolis, by N. K.
Bose.--Stockholm: a planned city, by G.

        (Continued on
         next card)

301.15
824   Scientific American. Cities...1965.
Per.ed.   (Card 2)

    Sidenbladh.--Ciudad Guayana: a new city, by
L. Rodwin.--New York: a metropolitan region,
by B. Chinitz.--The uses of land in cities,
by C. Abrams.--Transportation in cities, by
J. W. Dyckman.--The metabolism of cities, by
A. Wolman.--The renewal of cities, by N.
Glazer.--The city as environment, by K. Lynch.
Add. copy, AIP/Ewald notebooks (711.4 A52ne no.15)
1. City growth.   2.   Metropolitan areas.
3. Land use. 4. Urban   renewal. 5. Transportation. 6. City   planning.

300.15   Transportation.
S27   Scripps Foundation for Research in Population
Problems.
    Needed urban and metropolitan research.
Donald J. Bogue, editor. [Oxford, Ohio] Scripps
Foundation for Research in Population Problems,
Miami University and Population Research and
Training Center, University of Chicago [c1953]
    x, 88 p.   (Scripps Foundation studies in
population distribution, no. 7)

388
824   Transportation.
Seip, Norman W
    The key to better living; balanced trans-
portation. A speech [given] at the annual
meeting of the Aerospace Research Applications
Center and Indiana Executive Program at Indiana
University, November 1966. Erie, Pa., General
Electric, Transportation Systems Div., 1967.
19p.   (GEA-8473)

    1. Transportation. I. General Electric Co.
II. Title.

388
S31a   TRANSPORTATION.
Shaffer, Margaret T
    Attitude techniques in action, by Margaret
T. Shaffer, Urban Sciences Corp., Bethesda, Md.
[n.p.] [1969?]
    Prepared for presentation at the 49th annual
meeting of the Highway Research Board, Wash.,
D.C., Jan., 1970.

    1. Transportation. 2. Journey to work.
I. Highway Research Board. II. Title.

388
S38   TRANSPORTATION.
Shunk, G   A
    The journey to work: a singular basis
for travel pattern surveys, by G.A.
Shunk and others. [Lafayette, Ind.]
Purdue University, 1968.
    [20]p.   (Purdue University. Engineering
reprints. Civil engineering CE 263)
    Reprinted from: Highway research record
240 (1968) p. 32-51.
    1. Transportation. 2. Journey to
work. 3. Traffic surveys. I. Purdue
University.   II. Title.

VF
388   Transportation - (Addresses)
S45   Singer, Russell E
    Transportation: key to downtown's future;
[text of address, at the Downtown Development
Committee Session of the National Retail
Merchants Association's 51st annual convention,
New York City, 1962] Washington, American
Automobile Association, 1962.
12p.   (Stock no. 2568)

    1. Transportation - Addresses. I. American
Automobile   Association.

VF
388   Transportation - (Addresses)
S45f   Singer, Russell E
    Fallacies & facts about urban
transportation. Washington,
American Automobile Association,
1962.
11p.

    1. Transportation - Addresses.
I. American Automobile Association.

388
S52r   Transportation.
Smerk, George M   ed.
    Readings in urban transportation. Blooming-
ton, Indiana University Press, 1968.
336p.

    1. Transportation. 2. Journey to work.
I. Title: Urban transportation. II. Title.

388
852   Transportation.
Smerk, George M
    Urban transportation; the Federal role.
Bloomington, Indiana University Press,
1965.
336p.

    Bibliography: p. 309-325.

    1. Transportation. 2. Federal government.
3. U.S. Dept. of Urban Affairs. (Proposed)
4. Grants-in-aid. I. Title.

388
S54e   Transportation.
Smith (Wilbur) and Associates.
    Evaluation of bus transit demand in middle
sized urban areas. Final report: first phase.
Prepared for U.S. Dept. of Commerce, Bureau of
Public Roads. Wash., U.S. Dept. of Commerce,
National Bureau of Standards, Institute for
Applied Technology. 1966.
    258p. (PB 173 665)
    Distributed by Clearinghouse for Federal
Scientific and Technical Information.
    Bibliography: p. 249-258.

         (Cont'd on next card)

388
854e   Smith (Wilbur) and Associates.   Evaluation
of bus transit demand in middle sized urban
areas...1966.   (Card 2)

    1. Transportation. 2. Transportation - Re-
search. 3. Journey to work. I. U.S. Bureau of
Public Roads. II. U.S. Clearinghouse for
Federal Scientific and Technical Information.
III. Title.

388
S54m   TRANSPORTATION.
Smith (Wilbur) and Associates.
    Motor trucks in the metropolis. Prepared under
commission from the Automobile Manufacturers
Association. New Haven, 1969.
208p.
    Bibliography: p. 195-199.

    1. Traffic. 2. Transportation. I. Title.
II. Title: Trucks.

388
854   Transportation.
Smith (Wilbur) and Associates.
    Transportation and parking for tomorrow's
cities. New Haven, 1966.
393p.
    "Prepared...under commission from the Auto-
mobile Manufacturers Association."

    1. Transportation. 2. Parking. e. Journey
to work. 4. Highways. 5. City planning.
I. Automobile Manufacturers Association.
II. Title.

388
862   TRANSPORTATION.
Société pour l'Avancement et l'Utilisation de
la Recherche Opérationnelle Civile.
    Etude d'une methode de prevision technologique
normative; exemple d'application à la recherche
de nouveaux moyens de transport en commun en
zone urbaine. Annexe technique. [Paris] 1969.
1v.

    1. Transportation. I. Title.

388
867   Transportation.
Sorsby, William Quinn.
    The American city 1967 nationwide inventory
of governmental mass transit facilities.
New York, Buttenheim Pub., Corp., 1967.
20p.   (Report no. SD-1084)
    At head of title: Municipal government,
Marketing report; the American city magazine.
    Inventory based on 200 telephone interviews
made by the American city magazine, Research
Dept. and the Municipal index, with transit
management officials on information from the
U.S. Dept. of Housing and Urban Development,
p.8.

         (Cont'd on next card)

388
867   Sorsby, William Quinn.   The American city
1967 nationwide inventory of governmental
mass transit facilities.1967.   (Card 2)

    1. Transportation. 2. Municipal government.
I. American city magazine. II. U.S. Dept. of
Housing and Urban Development. III. Title.

Transportation.

388
S68
Southern Research Institute.
Proceedings: Tomorrow's transportation, a conference on future technological trends, Sept. 29-30, 1960. Sponsored by Southern Research Institute. Birmingham, Ala., 1960.
96p.

1. Transportation. I. Title: Tomorrow's transportation.

Transportation.

388
S71t
Stanford University. Graduate School of Business.
Transportation and tomorrow. From the 1964 and 1965 sessions of the Transportation Management Program and the 19th and 20th annual forums of the National Defense Transportation Association. Edited by Karl M. Ruppenthal and Henry A. McKinnell. Stanford, Calif., 1966.
180p. (Stanford transportation series)

1. Transportation. 2. Railroads. 3. Harbors. 4. Air transportation. I. Ruppenthal, Karl M., ed. II. McKinnell, Henry A., ed. III. National Defense Transportation Association. IV. Title.

TRANSPORTATION.

388
S77
Straszheim, Mahlon R
Transportation policy as an i... ...ment for altering regional development patterns - misdirected emphasis? Cambridge, Mass., Program on Regional and Urban Economics, 1969.
34p. (Harvard University. Program on Regional and Urban Economics. Discussion paper no. 52)

1. Transportation. 2. Economic development. I. Harvard University. Program on Regional and Urban Economics. II. Title.

Transportation.

388
S68p
Southwest Transportation Seminar, San Diego, Calif.
Proceedings, 19

San Diego, State College, Bureau of Business and Economic Research, School of Business Administration, 19
v. annual.
For complete information see main card.
1. Transportation. 2. Commercial policy.
I. California. State College, San Diego. Bureau of Business and Economic Research.

711.14
S72u
TRANSPORTATION.
Stewart, W Don
An urban area use model to maximize return. Final report. Lafayette, Ind., Joint Highway Research Project; Purdue University and Indiana State Highway Commission, 1969.
223p.

1. Land use. 2. City planning.
3. Transportation. I. Joint Highway Research Project, Purdue University and Indiana State Highway Commission. II. Title.

Transportation.

388
S87
Surveys & Research Corp., Washington, D.C.
The role of transportation in area development and redevelopment. Draft report. Wash., 1962.
51p.
Bibliography: p. i-viii.

1. Transportation. 2. Journey to work.
3. Highways. I. Title.

388
S71fut
TRANSPORTATION.
Stanford Research Institute.
Future urban transportation systems: descriptions, evaluations, and programs, by Clark Henderson and others. Prepared for Urban Transportation Administration, Dept. of Housing and Urban Development. Final report 1. Menlo Park, Calif., 1968.
426p.
At head of title: Study in new systems of urban transportation.
U.S. Mass Transportation Demonstration Grant Program. Contract no. H-776.
1. Transportation 2. Journey to work.
I. Henderson, Clark. II. Title. III. U.S. Mass Transportation Demonstration Grant Program.

388
S76b
TRANSPORTATION.
Stone, Tabor R
Beyond the automobile: reshaping the transportation environment. Englewood Cliffs, N.J., Prentice-Hall, 1971.
148p. (A Spectrum book)

1. Transportation. 2. Journey to work.
3. Subways. I. Title.

Transportation.

339.5
895
1967
Symposium on Power Systems for Electric Vehicles, New York, 1967.
Extended abstracts. [Prepared] under the joint sponsorship of the U.S. Dept. of Health, Education and Welfare, Columbia University, [and] Polytechnic Institute of Brooklyn, New York, Law School, Columbia University, 1967.
1 v.
Partial contents: The electric car, by K.W.C. Jeremy.
Henry, B. Linford, Chairman.

(Cont'd on next card)

388
S71f
Transportation.
Stanford Research Institute.
Future urban transportation systems: desired characteristics. Edited by Dan G. Haney. Prepared for Urban Transportation Administration, Dept. of Housing and Urban Development, Washington, D.C. Menlo Park, Calif., 1967.
128p. (Memorandum report MR-1)
Stewart P. Blake, Executive director.
1. Transportation. I. Haney, Dan G., ed. II. U.S. Dept. of Housing and Urban Development. III. Title.

711.73
S76m
Transportation.
Stonex, K A
Motor vehicle inspection problems from the engineer's viewpoint. National Automobile Meeting, March 19-21, 1963, Detroit, Michigan. New York, Society of Automotive Engineers, inc., 1963.
8p.

1. Highways. 2. Accidents. 3. Transportation. I. Society of Automotive Engineers. II. Title.

339.5
895
1967
Symposium on Power Systems for Electric Vehicles...1967.

1. Power resources 2. Fuel. 3. Transportation. I. U.S. Dept. of Health, Education and Welfare. II. Columbia University. Law School. III. Polytechnic Institute, Brooklyn.

388
S71fu
Transportation.
Stanford Research Institute.
Future Urban Transportation systems: impacts on urban life and form. Final report I, by Clark Henderson and others. Final report II, by Robert A. Burco and David A. Curry. Prepared for Urban Transportation Administration, Dept. of Housing and Urban Development, Wash., D.C., Menlo Park, Claif., 1968.
2v.
On cover: Study in new systems of urban transportation.
1. Transporta—tion. 2. Journey to work. (Cont'd on next card)

711.73
S76p
Transportation.
Stonex, K A
Priority needs in highway and vehicle research. National Engineers' Week, Boston, Massachusetts, Feb. 19, 1964. Warren, Mich., GM Engineering Staff, General Motors Corp., 1964.
8p.

1. Highways. 2. Transportation. I. General Motors Corp. II. Title.

388
S97
Transportation.
Systems Analysis and Research Corp.
Cost-based freight rates: desirability and feasibility. Prepared for the Under Secretary for Transportation, U.S. Department of Commerce, Wash, D.C. Cambridge, Mass., 1966.
1v.
Distributed by U.S. Clearinghouse for Federal Scientific and Technical Information as Document PB 173 209.
1. Transportation. 2. Railroads. I. U.S. Dept. of Commerce. II. Title.

388
S71fu
Stanford Research Institute. Future Urban Transportation systems...1968.
(Card 2)

3. Transportation - Automation. I. Henderson, Calrk. II. Burco, Robert A. III. Curry, David A. IV. U.S. Dept. of Housing and Urban Development. V. Title. VI. Title: Study in new systems of urban transportation.

388
S76
Transportation.
Stonex, K A
Research as applied to traffic and transportation. For presentation at the tenth Missouri Traffic Conference, University of Missouri, Columbia, Missouri, May 21, 1958. Milford, Mich., General Motors Corp., 1958.
12p.

Bibliography: p. 13-14.

1. Transportation. 2. Traffic. I. Missouri Traffic Conference, 10th, Columbia, 1958. II. General Motors Corp. III. Title.

388
T19
Transportation.
Tax Foundation.
Urban mass transportation in perspective. New York, 1968.
48p. (Its Research publication no. 14 (new series))

1. Transportation. 2. Journey to work.
I. Title.

388
S71u
TRANSPORTATION.
Stanford Research Institute journal.
Uptown to downtown in 1980. In Stanford Research Institute journal, August 1968, p. 4-13.
Research was supported by the U.S. Dept. of Housing and Urban Development under contract no. 4-776.
1. Transportation. 2. Journey to work.
I. U.S. Dept. of Housing and Urban Development. II. Title.

388
S77f
TRANSPORTATION.
Straszheim, Mahlon R
The Federal mass-transit capital grant program. Cambridge, Mass., 1969.
29p. (Harvard University. Program on Regional and Urban Economics. Discussion paper no. 53)

1. Transportation. 2. Journey to work.
3. Grants-in-aid. I. Harvard University. Program on Regional and Urban Economics. II. Title.

388
T25m
Transportation.
Teletrans Corp.
Mass-transit for cities of the 20th century. Detroit, 1965.
1v.

1. Transportation. 2. Journey to work.
I. Title.

Transportation.

VF
388
T25
Tennyson, E   L
     When is rapid transit economically
justified? 1961.
     [5]p.

     Reprinted from the May 11th issue of Public
utilities fortnightly, Washington, D.C. p. 657-
661.

     1. Transportation.

Transportation.

388
T81
Tube Transit, inc.
     Gravity-vacuum transit system as presented
at EXPO '67. Palo Alto, Calif., 1967.
     1v.

     1. Transportation. 2. Journey to work.
I. Title.

341.1
:338
UNs
United Nations Conference on the Application
     of Science and Technology for the Benefit
     of the Less Developed Areas, Geneva, 1962.
     Science, technology, and development...1962.
                                   (Card 2)
development and urbanization.-v. 8. Organizations,
planning, and programming for economic development.-
v. 9. Scientific and technological policy, planning
and organization.-v. 10. International cooperation
and problems of transfer and adaptation.-v. 11.
Human resources. Training of scientific and
technical personnel.-v. 12. Communications.

                         (Continued on next card)

388
(713541)
T67t
        Transportation.
     Toronto. Bureau of Municipal Research.
     Transportation. Who plans? Who pays?
Toronto, 1970.
     24p.

     Civic affairs, Autumn, 1970.

     1. Transportation - Toronto. I. Title.
II. Civic affairs.

388
T81t
     Transportation.
     Tube Transit, inc.
     Tube Transit, inc. presents gravity-vacuum
transportation (GVT) [n.p.] 1965.
     51p.

     1. Transportation. 2. Journey to work.
I. Title: Gravity-vacuum transportation
(GVT)

341.1
:338
UNs
United Nations Conference on the Application
     of Science and Technology for the Benefit
     of the Less Developed Areas, Geneva, 1962.
     Science, technology, and development...1962
                                   (Card 3)

     1. Technical assistance programs - Congresses.
2. Sociology, Urban. 3. Community development.
4. Transportation. I. Title: Social problems
of development and   urbanization.

388
T71t
     Transportation.
     Transportation Association of America.
     Transportation, facts and trends;
statistical analysis showing the importance
of, and trends in transportation in the
United States, including both for-hire and
private carriage. 1st ed. Washington,
1964.
     21p.

     1. Transportation.   I. Title.

388
T87
     Transportation.
     Turner, Daniel L
     The fundamentals of transit planning for
cities. [New York] National Conference on
City Planning, 1922.
     20p.

     1. Transportation. I. Title.

697.8
A23
     TRANSPORTATION.
     U.S. Ad Hoc Committee on the Cumulative
     Regulatory Effects on the Cost of Automotive
     Transportation.
     Cumulative regulatory effects on the cost of
automotive transportation (RECAT) Final report
of the Ad Hoc Committee. Prepared for Office
of Science and Technology. [Wash.] 1972.
     1v.

     1. Air pollution. 2. Transportation.
I. U.S. Office of Science and Technology.
II. Title.

534.33
T71t
     TRANSPORTATION.
     Transportation noises; a symposium on
acceptability criteria. Ed. by James D.
Chalupnik. Seattle, University of Washington Press, 1970.
     358p.

     1. Noise. 2. Transportation.
I. Chalupnik, James D., ed.

690.015
(485)
S82
1971
R36
     TRANSPORTATION.
     Ugander, Mikael.
     Transporter av buggelement; hanterings-
och förflyttningskostnader för systemtransporter med lastbil (Transport of industrialized building units; handling and
haulage costs relating to transport system
by road of units in.industrialized building
systems) Stockholm, Statens Institut för
Byggnadsforskning, 1971.
     174p. (Rapport R36:1971)
     Bibliography: p. 142-147.

                         (Cont'd on next card)

388
A28
     Transportation.
     U.S. Advisory Commission on Intergovern-
     mental Relations.
     Intergovernmental responsibilities for
mass transportation facilities and services
in metropolitan areas; a commission report.
Washington, 1961.
     54p.

     1. Transportation. 2. Intergovernmental
relations.

388
:308
T74
     TRANSPORTATION.
     Tri-State Transportation Commission.
     (Connecticut-New Jersey-New York)
     Direct traffic estimation method; systematic
inputs and method of computation. New York,
1967.
     20p. (Its Interim technical report
4075-7111)

     1. Traffic surveys. 2. Transportation.
3. Journey to work. I. Title.

690.015
(485)
S82
1971
     Ugander, Mikael. Transporter av...1971.
                                   (Card 2)
     1. Prefabricated construction.
2. Transportation. I. Stockholm. Statens
Institut för Byggnadsforskning. II. Title:
Transport of industrialised building units.

647.1
A37t
     Transportation.
     U.S.(Department of) Agriculture. (Bureau of
     Home Economics)
     Family expenditures for automobile and
other transportation, five regions. Washington,
Govt. Print. Off., 1941.
     272 p. tables. (Its Miscellaneous pub.
no. 415)
     At head of title: Consumer purchases study.
     "In cooperation with the Work Projects
Administration".

1.Family income and expenditure. 2.Transportation.
I.U.S. Work Projects Administration. II.Consumer
purchases study.

388
T74t
     TRANSPORTATION.
     Tri-State Transportation Commission.
     (Connecticut-New Jersey-New York)
     The intermodal transportation of van-size
containers. New York, 1967.
     32p. (Its Interim technical report 4055-8081)

     1. Transportation. 2. Highways.
3. Railroads. 4. Air transportation.
I. Title.

388
UN
1970
     TRANSPORTATION.
     United Nations. (Economic Commission for Asia
     and the Far East)
     Urban transportation in the renewal of
American cities; an information paper. Workshop
on Urban Traffic and Transportation, Bangkok,
Thailand, December 8-17, 1970. Presented by
the Dept. of Housing and Urban Development.
Washington, D.C., 1970.
     14p.
     1. Transportation. 2. Traffic. I. Workshop
on Urban Traffic and Transportation, Bangkok,
1970. II. U.S. Dept. of Housing and Urban
Development. III.   Title.

VF
623
U54
AE10.2A
     Transportation.
     U.S. Army. Corps of Engineers.
     Transportation facilities: Railroad lay-out
data. Washington, D.C., Govt. Print. Off.,
Sept. 1947.
     19 p. diagrs., tables. (Its Engineering
manual for War Department construction. Pt. X,
chap. 2, appendix A)

     1.Transportation. 2.Railroads. I.Series:
Engineering manual for War Department construction

388
T74pr
     TRANSPORTATION.
     Tri-State Transportation Commission
     Projecting vehicle miles of travel in a
metropolitan region. New York, 1967.
     25p. (Interim technical report 4070-8078)

     1. Transportation. 2. Traffic. I. Title.

341.1
:338
UNs
     Transportation.
     United Nations Conference on the Application
     of Science and Technology for the Benefit
     of the Less Developed Areas, Geneva, 1962.
     Science, technology, and development,
United States papers prepared for the United
Nations... Geneva, 1962.
     12 v.
Contents:-v. 1. Natural resources; energy, water and
river basin development.-v. 2. Natural resources;
minerals and mining, mapping and geodetic control.-
v. 3. Agriculture.-v. 4. Industrial development.-
v. 5. Transportation.-   v. 6. Health and
nutrition.-v. 7.   Social problems of

                         (Continued on next card)

VF
623
U54
AE10.1
     Transportation.
     U. S. Army. Corps of Engineers.
     Transportation facilities: Roads, walks and
open storage areas. Washington, D.C., Govt. Print.
Off., May 1947.
     36 p. diagrs., graphs, tables. (Its
Engineering manual for War Department construction.
Pt. X, chap. 1)

     1.Transportation. I.Series: Engineering manual for
War Department construction.

388
C25c
Transportation.
U.S. Bureau of the Census.
Census of transportation, current status and future plans. Presented as supplement to statement of Richard M. Scammon, Director, Bureau of the Census before the Subcommittee on Census and Government Statistics of the Committee on Post Office and Civil Service. Washington, 1964.
26p.

1. Transportation. 2. Census - Transportation.   I. Scammon, Richard M. II. Title.

388
C65CO
1965
H-R
TRANSPORTATION.
U.S. CONGRESS. CONFERENCE COMMITTEES, 1965.
COMMERCE DEPARTMENT TRANSPORTATION RESEARCH. CONFERENCE REPORT TO ACCOMPANY S. 1588. WASHINGTON, GOVT. PRINT. OFF., 1965.
7P. (89TH CONGRESS, 1ST SESSION. HOUSE OF REPRESENTATIVES. REPORT NO. 1017)

1. TRANSPORTATION. 2. RAILROADS. I. TITLE.

388
C65m
Transportation.
U.S. Congress. House. Committee on Banking and Currency.
Metropolitan mass transportation. Hearings before Subcommittee no. 1 of the Committee on Banking and Currency, House of Representatives, Eighty-sixth Congress, second session on metropolitan mass transportation legislation. Washington, Govt. Print. Off., 1960.
92p.

Hearings held June 29-30, 1960.

1. Transportation.   I. Title

388
C25p
Transportation.
U.S. Bureau of the Census.
PICADAD; a system for machine processing of geographic and distance factors in transportation and marketing data, by D. E. Church. Washington, U.S. Dept. of Commerce, Bureau of the Census, 1965.
16p.
PICADAD; PI stands for place identification. CA stands for the characteristics and area of the place. DAD stands for the computed distance and direction.
1. Transportation.   2. Marketing.
3. Automation.   I. Church, Donald E.
II. Title.

388
C65T
1966
H-R
TRANSPORTATION.
U.S. CONGRESS. CONFERENCE COMMITTEES, 1966.
DEPARTMENT OF TRANSPORTATION ACT... CONFERENCE REPORT TO ACCOMPANY H.R. 15963. WASHINGTON, GOVT. PRINT. OFF., 1966.
29P. (89TH CONGRESS, 2D SESSION. HOUSE. REPORT NO. 2236)

1. TRANSPORTATION.   I. U.S. DEPT. OF TRANSPORTATION (PROPOSED)

388
C65SEC
1962
C-P
TRANSPORTATION.
U.S. CONGRESS. HOUSE. COMMITTEE ON BANKING AND CURRENCY.
SECTION-BY-SECTION SUMMARY OF THE URBAN MASS TRANSPORTATION ACT OF 1962 (AS AGREED TO BY COMMITTEE) H.R. 11158, EIGHTY-SEVENTH CONGRESS, SECOND SESSION. WASHINGTON, GOVT. PRINT. OFF., 1962.
4P.

AT HEAD OF TITLE: COMMITTEE PRINT.
1. TRANSPORTATION. I. TITLE: URBAN MASS TRANSPORTATION ACT OF 1962.

VF
388
C25pl
Transportation.
U.S. Bureau of the Census.
Plans for 1963 census of transportation. Washington, U.S. Dept. of Commerce, Bureau of the Census, 1962.
12p.

1. Transportation.

728.1
(73:347)
065
1966
H-H
Transportation.
U.S. Congress. House. Committee on Banking and Currency.
Demonstration cities, housing and urban development, and urban mass transit. Hearings before the Subcommittee on Housing of the Committee on Banking and Currency, House of Representatives, Eighty-ninth Congress, second session on H.R. 12341, a bill to assist city demonstration programs for rebuilding slum and blighted areas and for providing the public facilities and services necessary to improve the general welfare of the   people who live in these areas,   H.R. 12946, a bill
(Cont'd on next card)

388
C65SECT
1963
TRANSPORTATION.
U.S. CONGRESS. HOUSE. COMMITTEE ON BANKING AND CURRENCY.
SECTION-BY-SECTION SUMMARY OF THE URBAN MASS TRANSPORTATION ACT OF 1963, H.R. 3881, EIGHTY-EIGHTH CONGRESS, FIRST SESSION. WASHINGTON, GOVT. PRINT. OFF., 1963.
4P.

AT HEAD OF TITLE: COMMITTEE PRINT.

1. TRANSPORTATION. 2. URBAN MASS TRANSPORTATION ACT OF 1963.

388
C52r
Transportation.
U.S. Clearinghouse for Federal Scientific and Technical Information.
Report of the Panel on Transportation Research and Development of the Commerce Technical Advisory Board, to the Secretary of Commerce. Springfield, Va., 1965.
90p. (PB 167 186)

1. Transportation. 2. Traffic surveys. 3. Governmental research. I. U.S. Panel on Transportation   Research and Development.   II. Title.

728.1
(73:347)
065
1966
H-H
U.S. Congress. House. Committee on Banking and Currency. Demonstration cities, housing and urban development.
(Card 2)

to provide incentives to planned metropolitan development and to otherwise assist urban development, H.R. 13064, a bill to amend and extend laws relating to housing and urban development, H.R. 9256, a bill to amend the National housing act... Wash., Govt. Print. Off., 1966.
2 pts.
Hearings   held Feb. 28-May 9, 1966.   (Cont'd on next card)

388
C65U
1967
H-R
TRANSPORTATION.
U.S. CONGRESS. HOUSE. COMMITTEE ON BANKING AND CURRENCY.
TEMPORARY EXTENSION OF EMERGENCY PROVISIONS OF URBAN MASS TRANSPORTATION PROGRAM... REPORT TO ACCOMPANY H.J. RES. 601. WASHINGTON, GOVT. PRINT. OFF., 1967.
2P. (90TH CONGRESS, 1ST SESSION. HOUSE. REPORT NO. 352)

1. TRANSPORTATION.   I. TITLE.

388
C65f
Transportation.
U.S. Dept. of Commerce.
Federal transportation policy and program. Washington, Govt. Print. Off., 1960.
32p.

1. Transportation.   I. Title.

728.1
(73:347)
065
1966
H-H
U.S. Congress. House. Committee on Banking and Currency. Demonstration Cities, housing and urban development.
(Card 3)

1. Housing legislation. 2. Model cities. 3. Transportation. 4. Urban renewal. I. Title. II. U.S. Department of Housing and Urban Development.

388
C657ur
1972
H-H
TRANSPORTATION.
U.S. Congress. House. Committee on Banking and Currency.
Urban mass transportation. Hearing before the Subcommittee on Housing, Ninety-second Congress, second session on providing financial assistance for the operating expenses of urban mass transportation. Wash., Govt. Print. Off., 1972.
116p.
Hearing held February 23, 1972.
1. Transportation. 2. Journey to work. I. Title.

351
H66
1955
Rept.16A
Transportation.
U. S. Commission on Organization of the Executive Branch of the Government, 1953-1955.
Report on transportation, prepared ... by the Subcommittee on Transportation of the Committee on Business Organization for the Department of Defense, March 1955. [Washington, Govt. Print. Off., 1955.]
362 p.   charts (1 fold.), maps (fold.), tables.

1.Transportation. I.Hoover Commission reports.

728.1
(73:347)
065
1965
H-H
Transportation.
U.S. Congress. House. Committee on Banking and Currency.
Housing and urban development act of 1965. Hearings before the Subcommittee on Housing, of the Committee on Banking and Currency, House of Representatives, Eighty-ninth Congress, first session on H.R. 5840 and related bills. A bill to assist in the provision of housing for low and moderate-income families, to promote orderly urban development, to improve living environ-   ment in urban areas, and to   extend and amend laws relat-   ing to housing, (Continued   on next card)

388
C65u
1970
H-H
TRANSPORTATION.
U.S. Congress. House. Committee on Banking and Currency.
Urban mass transportation. Hearings before the Subcommittee on Housing of the Committee on Banking and Currency, House of Representatives, Ninety-first Congress, second session on H.R. 6663... S. 3154...H.R. 7006...H.R. 13463...H.R. 16261... Wash., Govt. Print. Off., 1970.
732p.
Hearings held March 3-12, 1970.
1. Transportation. I. Title.

351
H66
1955
Rept.16
Transportation.
U. S. Commission on Organization of the Executive Branch of the Government, 1953-1955.
Transportation; a report to the Congress, March 1955. [Washington, Govt. Print. Off., 1955].
126 p.   tables.

1.Transportation. I.Hoover Commission reports.

728.1
(73:347)
065
1965
H-H
U.S. Congress. House. Committee on Banking and Currency. Housing and urban development act of 1965...1965. (Card 2)

urban renewal, urban mass transportation, and community facilities. Washington, Govt. Print. Off., 1965.
2 pts.
Hearings; March 25-31; April 1-7, 1965.

1. Housing legislation. 2. Public housing. 3. Urban renewal.   4. Transportation. 5. Community facili-   ties. II. Title.

388
C65
1962
C-P
TRANSPORTATION.
U.S. CONGRESS. HOUSE. COMMITTEE ON BANKING AND CURRENCY.
THE URBAN MASS TRANSPORTATION ACT OF 1962. H.R. 11158, EIGHTY-SEVENTH CONGRESS, SECOND SESSION. WASHINGTON, GOVT. PRINT. OFF., 1962.
40P.

AT HEAD OF TITLE: SUBCOMMITTEE PRINT.

1. TRANSPORTATION. I. TITLE.

388
C65U
1964
H-R

TRANSPORTATION.
U.S. CONGRESS. HOUSE. COMMITTEE ON
BANKING AND CURRENCY.
URBAN MASS TRANSPORTATION ACT OF 1964
AMENDMENTS. CONFERENCE REPORT TO
ACCOMPANY S. 3700. WASHINGTON, GOVT.
PRINT. OFF., 1966.
6P. (89TH CONGRESS, 2D SESSION.
HOUSE. REPORT NO. 1869)

1. TRANSPORTATION. I. TITLE.

388
C65
1962
H-R

TRANSPORTATION.
U.S. CONGRESS. HOUSE. COMMITTEE ON
BANKING AND CURRENCY.
URBAN MASS TRANSPORTATION ACT OF 1962.
REPORT ... ON H.R. 11158. WASHINGTON,
GOVT. PRINT. OFF., 1962.
24P. (87TH CONGRESS, 2D SESSION.
HOUSE OF REPRESENTATIVES. REPORT NO.
1961)

1. TRANSPORTATION. I. TITLE.

388
C65COM
1965
H-R
ADD.

TRANSPORTATION.
U.S. CONGRESS. HOUSE. COMMITTEE ON
INTERSTATE AND FOREIGN COMMERCE.
COMMERCE DEPARTMENT TRANSPORTATION
RESEARCH. ADDENDUM TO HEARINGS...ON
H.R. 5863, EIGHTY-NINTH CONGRESS,
FIRST SESSION. WASHINGTON, GOVT.
PRINT. OFF., 1965.
11P.

HEARINGS HELD MAY 19 - JUNE 30, 1965.

1. TRANSPORTATION. 2. RAILROADS.
I. TITLE.

388
C65U
1966
H-R

TRANSPORTATION.
U.S. CONGRESS. HOUSE. COMMITTEE ON
BANKING AND CURRENCY.
URBAN MASS TRANSPORTATION ACT OF 1966.
REPORT TO ACCOMPANY H.R. 14810.
WASHINGTON, GOVT. PRINT. OFF., 1966.
16P. (89TH CONGRESS, 2D SESSION.
HOUSE. REPORT NO. 1487)

1. TRANSPORTATION. I. TITLE.

388
C65
1963
H-R

Transportation.
U.S. Congress. House. Committee on
Banking and Currency.
Urban mass transportation act of 1963.
Washington, Govt. Print. Off., 1963.
30p. (88th Cong. 1st session. House.
Report no. 204)

1. Transportation. 2. Federal government.

388
C65COM
1965
H-R

TRANSPORTATION.
U.S. CONGRESS. HOUSE. COMMITTEE ON
INTERSTATE AND FOREIGN COMMERCE.
COMMERCE DEPARTMENT TRANSPORTATION
RESEARCH. REPORT TO ACCOMPANY H.R.
5863. WASHINGTON, GOVT. PRINT. OFF.,
1965.
29P. (89TH CONGRESS, 1ST SESSION.
HOUSE. REPORT NO. 845)

1. TRANSPORTATION. 2. RAILROADS.
I. TITLE.

388
C65
1961
H-H

Transportation.
U.S. Congress. House. Committee on
Banking and Currency.
Urban mass transportation--1961. Hearings
before Subcommittee No. 3 of the Committee on
Banking and Currency, House of Representatives,
Eighty-seventh Congress, 1st session. Wash-
ington, Govt. Print. Off., 1961.
194p.

Hearings held June 27-28, 1961.

1. Transportation.

388
C65
1963

Transportation.
U.S Congress. House. Committee on
Banking and Currency.
Urban mass transportation act of 1963.
Hearings before the Committee on Banking
and Currency, House of Representatives,
Eighty-eight Congress, first session on
H.R. 3881, a bill to authorize the Housing
and Home Finance Administrator to provide
additional assistance for the development
of comprehensive and coordinated mass
transportation systems in metropolitan
and other urban areas, and for other
purposes.

(Cont'd. on next card)

388
C65g

Transportation.
U.S. Congress. House. Committee on Interstate
and Foreign Commerce.
Guaranteed loans for common carriers. Hearings
before a subcommittee of the Committee on Interstate and Foreign Commerce, House of Representatives, Eighty-fifth Congress, second session on
H.R. 11527, a bill to amend the Interstate
commerce act by adding thereto a new part V, to
provide for a temporary program of assistance
to enable common carriers subject to such act to
finance improvementents and developments, and
for other purposes. Washington, Govt. Print.
Off., 1958.
167p.
Hearings held   Apr. 28-May 7, 1958.
1. Transportation. 2. Railroads. I. Title.

LAW
U.S.

Transportation.
U.S. Congress. House. Committee on Banking
and Currency.
The urban mass transportation act of 1962.
H.R. 11158, a bill to authorize the Housing and
Home Finance Administrator to provide additional
assistance for the development of comprehensive
and coordinated mass transportation systems in
metropolitan and other urban areas, and for
other purposes. Subcommittee no. 3, Committee
on Banking and Currency, House of Representatives, Eighty-seventh Congress, second session,
April 23, 1962. Washington, Govt. Print. Off.,
1962.
40p.   (Continued on next card)

388
C65
1963
H-H

U.S. Congress. House. Committee on Banking
and Currency. Urban mass transportation
act of 1963...(Card 2)

Washington, Govt. Print. Off., 1963.
708p.
Hearings held Feb. 27-March 18, 1963.

1. Transportation.

388
C657
1968
H-R

Transportation.
U.S. Congress. House. Committee on
Interstate and Foreign Commerce.
High-speed ground transportation extension;
report together with separate views to
accompany H.R. 16024. Washington, Govt.
Print. Off., 1968.
13p. (90th Cong., 2d sess. House. Report
no. 1606)

1. Transportation. I. Title.

LAW
U.S.

U.S. Congress. House. Committee on Banking
and Currency. The urban mass transportation
act of 1962 ... 1962.   (Card 2)

1. Transportation. I. Title.

388
C65au
1961
H-R

Transportation.
U.S. Congress. House. Committee on the
District of Columbia.
Authorizing the National Capital Transportation Agency to carry out part 1 of its transit
development program and to further the objectives of the act approved July 14, 1960 (74
Stat. 537) Mr. McMillan, from the Committee
on District of Columbia, submitted the
following Report [to accompany S. 2397]
[Washington] Govt. Print. Off., 1961.
7p. (87th Cong., 1st sess. House.
Rept. no. 1207)
1. Transportation.   I. U.S. National
Capital Transporta-   tion Agency.

388
C65t
1962
H-H

Transportation.
U.S. Congress. House. Committee on Interstate
and Foreign Commerce.
Transportation acts amendments--1962. Hearings
before the Committee on Interstate and Foreign
Commerce, House of Representatives, Eighty-
seventh Congress, second session on H.R. 11583
a bill to exempt certain carriers from minimum
rate regulation in the transportation of bulk
commodities, agricultural and fishery products,
and passengers, and for other purposes, H.R.
11584 a bill to provide for strengthening and
improving the national transportation system,
and for other pur-   poses. Wash., Govt.
Print. Off.,   1962.
736p.
     (Continued on next card)

388
C65
1962
H-H

Transportation.
U.S. Congress. House. Committee on
Banking and Currency.
Urban mass transportation act of 1962.
Hearings before Subcommittee no. 3 of the
Committee on Banking and Currency, House of
Representatives, Eighty-seventh Congress,
second session on H.R. 11158, a bill to authorize
the Housing and Home Finance Administrator to
provide additional assistance for the development of comprehensive and coordinated mass
transportation systems in metropolitan and
other urban areas,   and for other
purposes. Wash-   ington, Govt. Print.
Off., 1962.
896p.   (Continued on next card)

388
C65
1966

U.S. CONGRESS. HOUSE. COMMITTEE ON
GOVERNMENT OPERATIONS.
DEPARTMENT OF TRANSPORTATION ACT.
REPORT TO ACCOMPANY H.R. 15963.
WASHINGTON, GOVT. PRINT. OFF., 1966.
106P. (89TH CONGRESS, 2D SESSION.
HOUSE. REPORT NO. 1701)

1. TRANSPORTATION. 2. U.S. DEPT. OF
TRANSPORTATION (PROPOSED)

388
C65t
1962
H-H

U.S. Congress. House. Committee on Interstate and Foreign Commerce. Transportation
acts amendments--1962...1962.   (Card 2)

Hearings held June 26 - Aug. 10, 1962.

1. Transportation.

388
C65
1962
H-H

U.S. Congress. House. Committee on Banking
and Currency. Urban mass transportation act
of 1962 ... 1962.   (Card 2)

Hearings held May 1-4, 7-11, 1962.

1. Transportation.

388
C65t
1966
H-H

Transportation.
U.S. Congress. House. Committee on
Government Operations.
Creating a Department of Transportation.
(Part 1-2)Hearings before a subcommittee of
the Committee on Government Operations, House
of Representatives, Eighty-ninth Congress,
second session on H.R. 13200. A bill to
establish a Department of Transportation, and
for other purposes. Wash., Govt. Print.
Off., 1966.
2 pts.
Hearings held Apr. 6-June 21, 1966.

1. U.S. Dept. of   Transportation
(Proposed) 2. Trans-   portation.

88
C65COM
1964
H-R

TRANSPORTATION.
U.S. CONGRESS. HOUSE. COMMITTEE ON
INTERSTATE AND FOREIGN COMMERCE.
TRANSPORTATION AMENDMENTS OF 1964.
REPORT ON H.R. 9903 TOGETHER WITH
SUPPLEMENTAL VIEWS. WASHINGTON, GOVT.
PRINT. OFF., 1964.
107P. (88TH CONGRESS, 2D SESSION.
HOUSE OF REPRESENTATIVES. REPORT NO.
1144)

1. TRANSPORTATION. I. TITLE.

388
C65t
1963
H-H

Transportation.

U.S. Congress. House. Committee on Interstate and Foreign Commerce.
Transportation act, 1963. Hearings before the Committee on Interstate and Foreign Commerce, House of Representatives, Eighty-eighth Congress, first session on H.R. 4700, a bill to exempt certain carriers from minimum rate regulation in the transportation of bulk commodities, agricultural and fishery products and passengers, and for other purposes; H.R. 4701, a bill to provide for
(Cont'd on next card)

388
C65
1970
J-R

TRANSPORTATION.

U.S. Congress. Joint Economic Committee.
Federal transportation expenditure. Report of the Subcommittee on Economy in Government of the Joint Economic Committee, Congress of the United States together with separate views. Wash., Govt. Print. Off., 1970.
28p.

At head of title: 91st Cong., 2d sess.
Joint Committee print.

1. Transportation. 2. Finance.

388
C65
1961
S-H

Transportation.

U.S. Congress. Senate. Committee on Banking and Currency.
Urban mass transportation, 1961. Hearings before a subcommittee of the Committee on Banking and Currency, United States Senate, Eighty-seventh Congress, first session on S. 345, a bill to authorize the Administrator of HHFA to assist state and local governments and their public instrumentalities in planning and providing for necessary community facilities to preserve and improve essential mass transporta-   tion services in
(Continued on next card)

388
C65t
1963
H-H

U.S. Congress. House. Committee on Interstate and Foreign Commerce. Transportation act, 1963. Hearings...(Card 2)

strengthening and improving the national transportation system and for other purposes. Washington, Govt. Print. Off., 1963.
pts.

Hearings held April 30, May 1-9, 1963.

1. Transpor-   tation.

388
C657
1968
S-H

TRANSPORTATION.

U.S. Congress. Senate. Committee on Banking and Currency.
Effect of railroad mergers on commuter transportation. Hearings before the Subcommittee on Housing and Urban Affairs ... Ninetieth Congress, second session, on solutions to problems of improved commuter service in mass transportation. Wash., Govt. Print. Off., 1968.
249p.
Hearings held March 26-28, 1968.
1. Transportation. 2. Journey to work.
3. Railroads.   I. Title.

388
C65
1961
S-H

U.S. Congress. Senate. Committee on Banking and Currency.
Urban mass...1961.   (Card 2)

urban and metropolitan areas. Washington, Govt. Print. Off., 1961.
449p.

Hearings held March 20-22, 1961.

1. Transportation.

388
C65C
1961
H-H

TRANSPORTATION.

U.S. CONGRESS. HOUSE. COMMITTEE ON POST OFFICE AND CIVIL SERVICE.
CENSUS OF TRANSPORTATION. HEARINGS BEFORE THE SUBCOMMITTEE ON CENSUS AND GOVERNMENT STATISTICS OF THE COMMITTEE ON POST OFFICE AND CIVIL SERVICE, HOUSE OF REPRESENTATIVES, EIGHTY-SEVENTH CONGRESS, FIRST SESSION. JULY 18 AND 19, 1961. WASHINGTON, GOVT. PRINT. OFF., 1961.
176P.

1. TRANSPORTATION.   I. TITLE.

388
C657cm
1971
S-H

TRANSPORTATION.

U.S. Congress. Senate. Committee on Banking, Housing and Urban Affairs.
Emergency urban mass transit legislation. Hearings before the Subcommittee on Housing and Urban Affairs of the Committee on Banking, Housing and Urban Affairs, United States Senate. Ninety-second Congress on emergency urban mass transit legislation. Wash., Govt. Print. Off., 1972.
184p.
Hearings held April 6, 1971, Jan. 31, and Feb. 1-2, 1972.
1. Transporta-   tion. 2. Journey to work. I. Title.

388
C65
1962
S-H

Transportation.

U.S. Congress. Senate. Committee on Banking and Currency.
Urban mass transportation, 1962. Hearings before a subcommittee of the Committee on Banking and Currency, United States Senate, Eighty-seventh Congress, second session on bills to authorize the Housing and Home Finance Agency to provide additional assistance for the development of mass transportation systems, and for other purposes. Washington, Govt. Print. Off., 1962.
533p.
Hearings held   Apr. 24-27, 1962.
1. Transporta-   tion.

388
C65tr
1963
H-H

Transportation.

U.S. Congress. House. Committee on Public Works.
Transportation planning in certain urban areas. Hearings before the Subcommittee on Roads of the Committee on Public Works, House of Representatives, Eighty-eighth Congress, first session. Washington, Govt. Print. Off., 1963.
305p.

Hearings held June 25-27, July 9-10, 1963.

1. Transportation.

388
C657
1969
S-H

TRANSPORTATION.

U.S. Congress. Senate. Committee on Banking and Currency.
Mass transportation - 1969. Hearings before the Subcommittee on Housing and Urban Affairs of the Committee on Banking and Currency, United States Senate, Ninety-first Congress, first session on S. 676, S. 1032, S. 2656, S. 2821, and S. 3154, bills to amend the Urban mass transportation act of 1964, and for other purposes. Wash., Govt. Print. Off., 1969.
631p.
(Cont'd on next card)

388
C65
1962
S-R

Transportation.

U.S. Congress. Senate. Committee on Banking and Currency.
Urban mass transportation act of 1962. Report of the Committee on Banking and Currency, United States Senate to accompany S. 3615 together with individual views. Washington, Govt. Print. Off., 1962.
35p.   (87th Cong. 2d sess. Senate. Report no. 1852)

1. Transportation.   I. Title.

336.2
C657t
1968
H-R

Transportation.

U.S. Congress. House. Committee on Ways and Means.
Tax adjustment act of 1968. Report to accompany H.R. 15414. Washington, 1968.
14p. (90th Cong., 2d sess. House. Report no. 1104)

1. Taxation. 2. Communication systems.
3. Transportation. I. Title.

388
C657
1969
S-H

U.S. Congress. Senate. Committee on Banking and Currency. Mass transportation...1969.   (Card 2)

Hearings held July-Nov., 1969.

1. Transportation. 2. Journey to work.
I. Title.

388
C65
1963
S-H

Transportation.

U.S. Congress. Senate. Committee on Banking and Currency.
Urban mass transportation, 1963. Hearings before a subcommittee of the Committee on Banking and Currency, United States Senate, Eighty-eighth Congress, first session on S. 6 and S. 917, a bill to authorize the Housing and Home Finance Agency to provide additional assistance for the development of mass transportation systems, and for other purposes. Washington, Govt. Print. Off., 1963.
484p.
(Cont'd. on next card)

388
C65COM
1965
H-H

TRANSPORTATION.

U.S. CONGRESS. INTERSTATE AND FOREIGN COMMERCE COMMITTEE.
COMMERCE DEPARTMENT TRANSPORTATION RESEARCH. HEARINGS BEFORE THE SUBCOMMITTEE ON TRANSPORTATION AND AERONAUTICS, EIGHTY-NINTH CONGRESS, FIRST SESSION, ON H.R. 5863.... WASHINGTON, GOVT. PRINT. OFF., 1965.
193P.

HEARINGS HELD MAY 19-JUNE 30, 1965.

1. TRANSPORTATION. 2. RAILROADS.
I. TITLE.

388
C657
1970
S-H

TRANSPORTATION.

U.S. Congress. Senate. Committee on Banking and Currency.
Mass transportation - 1970. Hearings before the Subcommittee on Housing and Urban Affairs of the Committee on Banking and Currency, United States Senate, Ninety-first Congress, second session, on S. 676 and S. 3499, bills to provide financial assistance to mass transit systems. Wash., Govt. Print. Off., 1970.
60p.
Hearings held   Apr. 8-9, 1970.
1. Trans-   portation. 2. Journey to work.   I. Title.

388
C65
1963
S-H

U.S. Congress. Senate. Committee on Banking and Currency. Urban mass transportation, 1963...(Card 2)

Hearings held: Feb. 28, March 1-11, 1963.

1. Transportation.

388
C65r

Transportation.

U.S. Congress. Joint Committee on Washington Metropolitan Problems.
Rapid transit systems in six metropolitan areas, by Gunther M. Gottfeld. Staff report prepared for the Joint Committee on Washington Metropolitan Problems, Congress of the United States. Washington, Govt. Print. Off., 1959.
39p.

At head of title: 86th Cong., 1st sess.

1. Transportation. I. Gottfeld, Gunther M.

388
C65U
1967
S-R

TRANSPORTATION.

U.S. CONGRESS. SENATE. COMMITTEE ON BANKING AND CURRENCY.
TEMPORARY EXTENSION OF EMERGENCY PROVISIONS OF URBAN MASS TRANSPORTATION PROGRAM... REPORT TO ACCOMPANY S.J. RES. 90. WASHINGTON, GOVT. PRINT. OFF., 1967.
2P. (90TH CONGRESS, 1ST SESSION. SENATE. REPORT NO. 347)

1. TRANSPORTATION.   I. TITLE: URBAN MASS TRANSPORTATION.

388
C65
1963
S-R
NO.82

TRANSPORTATION.

U.S. CONGRESS. SENATE. COMMITTEE ON BANKING AND CURRENCY.
URBAN MASS TRANSPORTATION ACT OF 1963. REPORT TO ACCOMPANY S. 6 TOGETHER WITH INDIVIDUAL VIEWS. WASHINGTON, GOVT. PRINT. OFF., 1963.
58P. (88TH CONGRESS, 1ST SESSION. SENATE. REPORT NO. 82)

1. TRANSPORTATION.   I. TITLE.

388
C65
1960
S-R

TRANSPORTATION.
U.S. CONGRESS. SENATE. COMMITTEE ON BANKING AND CURRENCY.
MASS TRANSPORTATION ACT OF 1960, REPORT TO ACCOMPANY S. 3278. WASHINGTON, GOVT. PRINT. OFF., 1960.
23P. (86TH CONGRESS, 2D SESSION. SENATE. REPORT NO. 1591)

1. TRANSPORTATION. I. TITLE.

388
C65H
1970
S-H

TRANSPORTATION.
U.S. Congress. Senate. Committee on Commerce.
High-speed ground transportation. Hearing before the Subcommittee on Surface Transportation of the Committee on Commerce, United States Senate, Ninety-first Congress, second session on S. 3730, to extend for one year the act of September 30, 1965, as amended by the act of July 24, 1968... Wash., Govt. Print. Off., 1970.
39p.
Hearing held June 4, 1970.
1. Transportation. 2. Railroads. I. Title.

388
C65u
1962
S-H

Transportation.
U.S. Congress. Senate. Committee on Commerce.
Urban mass transportation--1962. Hearings before the Committee on Commerce, United States Senate, Eighty-seventh Congress, second session on S. 3615, a bill to authorize the Housing and Home Finance Administrator to provide additional assistance for the development of comprehensive and coordinated mass transportation systems, both public and private, in metropolitan and other urban areas, and for other purposes. Washington, Govt. Print. Off., 1962.
163p.
Hearings held   Sept. 17-20, 1962.
1. Transporta-   tion.

388
C65U
1966
S-R

TRANSPORTATION.
U.S. CONGRESS. SENATE. COMMITTEE ON BANKING AND CURRENCY.
URBAN MASS TRANSPORTATION AMENDMENTS OF 1966. REPORT TOGETHER WITH MINORITY VIEWS TO ACCOMPANY S. 3700. WASHINGTON, GOVT. PRINT. OFF., 1966.
10P. (89TH CONGRESS, 2D SESSION. SENATE. REPORT NO. 1436)

1. TRANSPORTATION. I. TITLE.

388
C65H
1965
S-R

TRANSPORTATION.
U.S. CONGRESS. SENATE. COMMITTEE ON COMMERCE.
HIGH-SPEED GROUND TRANSPORTATION. REPORT TO ACCOMPANY S. 1588. WASHINGTON, GOVT. PRINT. OFF., 1965.
16P. (89TH CONGRESS, 1ST SESSION. SENATE. REPORT NO. 497)

1. TRANSPORTATION. 2. RAILROADS. I. TITLE.

388
C65
1963
S-H
MAR.

TRANSPORTATION.
U.S. CONGRESS. SENATE. COMMITTEE ON COMMERCE.
URBAN MASS TRANSPORTATION, 1963. HEARINGS BEFORE THE SUBCOMMITTEE ON SURFACE TRANSPORTATION, EIGHTY-EIGHTH CONGRESS, FIRST SESSION, ON S. 807, S. 6, AND S. 917... WASHINGTON, GOVT. PRINT. OFF., 1963.
308P.

HEARING HELD MARCH 19-22, 1963.

1. TRANSPORTATION. I. TITLE.

388
C65c
1962
S-H

Transportation.
U.S. Congress. Senate. Committee on Commerce.
Control of illegal interstate motor carrier transportation (Amendments to Interstate commerce act) Hearings before the Surface Transportation Subcommittee of the Committee on Commerce, United States Senate, Eighty-seventh Congress, second session on S. 2560 and S. 2764 strengthening the role of authorized transportation services and therby improving the relative status of interstate common carriers by all modes of transportation in order to make more adequate our national   transportation system. Washington, Govt.   Print. Off., 1962.
303p.   (Continued on next card)

388
C65na
1970
S-H

TRANSPORTATION.
U.S. Congress. Senate. Committee on Commerce.
National transportation act. Hearings before the Committee on Commerce, United States Senate, Ninety-first Congress, second session on S. 924 and S. 2425, to develop a comprehensive national transportation system. Wash., Govt. Print. Off., 1970.
401p.

Hearings held Feb. 26-May 13, 1970.

1. Transportation. I. Title.

388
C65
1963
S-R

TRANSPORTATION.
U.S. CONGRESS. SENATE. COMMITTEE ON COMMERCE.
URBAN MASS TRANSPORTATION ACT OF 1963. REPORT TOGETHER WITH MINORITY AND INDIVIDUAL VIEWS TO ACCOMPANY AN AMENDMENT IN THE NATURE OF A SUBSTITUTE INTENDED TO BE PROPOSED TO THE BILL S. 6. WASHINGTON, GOVT. PRINT. OFF., 1963.
23P. (88TH CONGRESS, 1ST SESSION. SENATE. REPORT NO. 83)

1. TRANSPORTATION. I. TITLE.

388
C65c
1962
S-H

U.S. Congress. Senate. Committee on Commerce.
Control of illegal interstate motor carrier transportation ... 1962.   (Card 2)

Hearings held Feb. 7-25, 1962.

1. Transportation.

388
C65n

Transportation.
U.S. Congress. Senate. Committee on Commerce.
National transportation policy. Report of the Committee on Commerce, United States Senate by its Special Study Group on Transportation Policies in the United States (pursuant to S. Res. 29, 151, and 244 of the 86th Congress). Washington, Govt. Print. Off., 1961.
732p. (87th Cong. 1st sess. Senate. Report no. 445)
John P. Doyle, staff director, Transportation Study   Group.
1. Transportation.   I. Doyle, John P.

388
C65au
1961
S-R

Transportation.
U.S. Congress. Senate. Committee on the District of Columbia.
Authorizing the National Capital Transportation Agency to carry out part 1 of its transit development program and to further the objectives of the act approved July 14, 1960 (74 Stat. 537) Mr. Bible, from the Committee on the District of Columbia, submitted the following report [to accompany S. 2397] Washington, Govt. Print. Off., 1961.
8p. (87th Cong., 1st sess. Senate. Report no. 855)
1. Transportation.   I. U.S. National
Capital Transportation   Agency.

388
C65fe
1963
S-H

Transportation.
U.S. Congress. Senate. Committee on Commerce.
Federal-aid-to-airports program. Hearings before the Aviation Subcommittee of the Committee on Commerce, U.S. Senate, Eighty-eighth Congress, first session on S. 1153, a bill to extend the time for making grants thereunder, and for other purposes. Washington, Govt. Print. Off., 1963.
198p. (88th Cong. 1st sess. Senate. Report no. 1153)   (Cont'd. on next card)

388
C65PR
1962
S-H

TRANSPORTATION.
U.S. CONGRESS. SENATE. COMMITTEE ON COMMERCE.
PROPOSED AMENDMENTS OF FEDERAL TRANSPORTATION LAWS. HEARINGS ON S. 3242 AND S. 3243, EIGHTY-SEVENTH CONGRESS, SECOND SESSION. WASHINGTON, GOVT. PRINT. OFF., 1962.

1. TRANSPORTATION.

388
C65e

Transportation.
U.S. Congress. Senate. Committee on Government Operations.
Establish a Department of Transportation. Hearings before the Committee on Government Operations, United States Senate, Eighty-ninth Congress, second session, on S. 3010, a bill to establish a Dept. of Transportation and for other purposes. Wash., Govt. Print. Off., 1966.
4 pts.
Hearings held Mar.-June, 1966.

1. Transporta-   tion. 2. U.S. Dept.
of Transportation   (Proposed)

389
C65fe
1963
S-H

U.S. Congress. Senate. Committee on Commerce. Federal-aid-to-airports...(Card 2)

Hearing held April 9, 10, and 23, 1963.

1. Transportation. 2. Airports.
I. Title.

388
C65T
1964
S-H

TRANSPORTATION.
U.S. CONGRESS. SENATE. COMMITTEE ON COMMERCE.
TRANSPORTATION ACT AMENDMENTS -- 1963. HEARINGS, EIGHTY-EIGWTH CONGRESS, FIRST SESSION, BEFORE THE SURFACE TRANSPORTATION SUBCOMMITTEE ON S. 1061 AND 1062. WASHINGTON, GOVT. PRINT. OFF., 1964.
2 V. (1079P.)

1. TRANSPORTATION. I. TITLE.

388
C65E
1966
S-R
REPT.1659

TRANSPORTATION.
U.S. CONGRESS. SENATE. COMMITTEE ON GOVERNMENT OPERATIONS.
ESTABLISHING A DEPARTMENT OF TRANSPORTATION AND FOR OTHER PURPOSES. REPORT TOGETHER WITH ADDITIONAL VIEWS TO ACCOMPANY S. 3010. WASHINGTON, GOVT. PRINT. OFF., 1966.
43P. (89TH CONGRESS, 2D SESSION. SENATE. REPORT NO. 1659)

1. TRANSPORTATION. I. U.S.
DEPT. OF TRANSPORTATION (PROPOSED)

388
C65H
1965
S-H

TRANSPORTATION.
U.S. CONGRESS. SENATE. COMMITTEE ON COMMERCE.
HIGH-SPEED GROUND TRANSPORTATION. HEARINGS BEFORE THE SUBCOMMITTEE ON SURFACE TRANSPORTATION, EIGHTY-NINTH CONGRESS, FIRST SESSION, ON S. 1588... WASHINGTON, GOVT. PRINT. OFF., 1965.
183P.

HEARINGS HELD JUNE 14, 15 AND 16, 1965.

1. TRANSPORTATION. 2. RAILROADS.
I. TITLE.

388
C65
1962
S-R
NO.2119

TRANSPORTATION.
U.S. CONGRESS. SENATE. COMMITTEE ON COMMERCE.
URBAN MASS TRANSPORTATION. REPORT TO ACCOMPANY S. 3615. WASHINGTON, GOVT. PRINT. OFF., 1962.
1P. (87TH CONGRESS, 2D SESSION. SENATE. REPORT NO. 2119)

1. TRANSPORTATION. I. TITLE.

388
C65E
1966
S-R
REPT.1660

TRANSPORTATION.
U.S. CONGRESS. SENATE. COMMITTEE ON GOVERNMENT OPERATIONS.
ESTABLISHING A DEPARTMENT OF TRANSPORTATION, AND FOR OTHER PURPOSES. REPORT TO ACCOMPANY H.R. 15963. WASHINGTON, GOVT. PRINT. OFF., 1966.
1L. (89TH CONGRESS, 2D SESSION. SENATE. REPORT NO. 1660)

1. TRANSPORTATION. I. U.S.
DEPT. OF TRANSPORTATION (PROPOSED)

697.8
C657a
1972
S-H

TRANSPORTATION.
U.S. Congress. Senate. Committee on
Public Works.
Alternatives to the gasoline-powered in-
ternal combustion engine. Hearing before
the Panel on Environmental Science and
Technology of the Subcommittee on Air and
Water Pollution. Ninety-second Congress,
second session. Wash., Govt. Print. Off.,
1972.
132p.
Hearing held March 14, 1972.
1. Air pollution. 2. Transportation.
I. Title.

388
C657w
1972
S-H

TRANSPORTATION.
U.S. Congress. Senate. Committee on Public
Works.
Wider buses and the interstate highway
system. Hearings before the Subcommittee on
Roads, Ninety-second Congress, first and second
sessions on H.R. 4354, an act to amend Section
127 of Title 23 of the United States Code relating to vehicle width limitations on the interstate system in order to increase such
limitations for motorbuses. Wash., Govt. Print.
Off., 1972.
354p.
Hearings held December 13-February 14,
1972.
1. Transportation. I. Title.

LAW
U.S.

Transportation.
U.S. Housing and Home Finance Agency.
Federal laws: assistance to mass transportation; excerpts from the Housing act
of 1949, the Housing act of 1954, the
housing amendments of 1955 as amended
through June 30, 1961. Washington, 1961.
7p.

1. Transportation. I. Title.

388
C65e

Transportation.
U.S. Congress. Senate. Committee on
Public Works.
Electric vehicles and other alternatives
to the internal combustion engine. Joint
Hearings before the Committee on Commerce
and the Subcommittee on Air and Water Pollution of the Committee on Public Works,
United States Senate, Ninetieth Congress,
first session on S. 451, a bill to amend the
clean air act in order to authorize an
investigation and study to determine means
of propelling vehicles so as not to contrib-
ute to air   pollution and
(Cont'd on next card)

629.136
F22p

Transportation.
U.S. Federal Aviation Agency.
Planning the metropolitan airport system.
[Washington] 1965.
13p.   (Its Advisory circular AC no:
AC 150/50-70-2 airports)

1. Airports. 2. Transportation.
I. Title.

711.3
H68h

Transportation.
U.S. Housing and Home Finance Agency.
Office of Metropolitan Development.
HHFA program activity in metropolitan
areas, 1963-1965. [Washington] 1965.
25p.

"For internal use only."

1. Metropolitan area planning.
2. Transportation. I. Title.

388
C65e

Transportation.
U.S. Congress. Senate. Committee on
Public Works. Electric vehicles and other
alternatives to the internal combustion
engine...1967.   (Card 2)

S. 453, a bill to authorize a program of
research, development, and Demonstration
projects for electrically powered vehicles.
Wash., For sale by the Supt. of Doc.,
Govt. Print. Off., 1967.
550p.
Hearings held March 14-17, and April 10,
April 10, 1967.
(Cont'd on next card)

383
:336.18
F22

Transportation.
U.S. Federal Coordinator of Transportation.
Section of Research.
Public aids to transportation. Washington,
Govt. Print. Off., 1938-1940.
4 v. tables.
Contents: -v. 1. General comparative
analysis and public aids to scheduled air transportation.-v. 2. Aids to railroads and related
subjects.-v.3. Public aids to transportation by
water. -v. 4. Public aids to motor vehicle
transportation.
Contains bibliographies.
1. Trans-   portation. I. Title.

388
H68ur

Transportation.
U.S. Housing and Home Finance Agency.
Urban transportation; joint report to the
President by the Housing and Home Finance
Administrator and the Secretary of Commerce.
Washington, 1962.
18p.

Robert C. Weaver, Administrator.

Letter of transmittal to the President
from the Secretary of Commerce and the
Housing and Home Finance Administrator.

1. Transportation.   I. Weaver, Robert C.
II. U.S. Dept. of   Commerce. III. Title.

388
C65e

U.S. Congress. Senate. Committee on
Public Works. Electric vehicles and other
alternatives to the internal combustion
engine...1967.   (Card 3)

1. Transportation. 2. Air pollution.
I. U.S. Congress. Senate. Committee on
Commerce. II. Title.

388
F22tr

TRANSPORTATION.
U.S. Federal Highway Administration.
Transportation planning data for urbanized
areas; based on 1960 census; a summary.
Wash., 1971.
13p.

1. Transportation. I. Title.

388
H68ci

Transportation.
U.S. Dept. of Housing and Urban Development.
Cities on the move. HUD's urban transportation programs help urbanites move into the
21st century. Washington, Govt. Print. Off.,
1967.
27p.   (Its HUD IP-64)

1. Transportation. 2. Journey to work.
3. City planning. 4. Public utilities. I. Title.

711.73
C65F
1966
H-R

TRANSPORTATION.
U.S. CONGRESS. HOUSE. COMMITTEE ON
PUBLIC WORKS.
FEDERAL-AID HIGHWAY ACT OF 1966.
REPORT ... ON H.R. 14359. WASHINGTON,
GOVT. PRINT. OFF., 1966.
58P. (89TH CONGRESS, 2D SESSION.
HOUSE. REPORT NO. 1704)

1. HIGHWAYS. 2. TRANSPORTATION.
I. TITLE.

Folio
388
F22t

TRANSPORTATION.
U.S. Federal Highway Administration.
Transportation planning data for urbanized
areas, based on 1960 census. Wash., U.S. Dept.
of Transportation, Federal Highway Administration, Office of Highway Planning, Urban Planning
Div., 1970.
664p.

1. Transportation. I. Title.

VF
720
H68
1968

Transportation.
U.S. Dept. of Housing and Urban Development.
Design awards. 1968 HUD design awards for
urban transportation. Washington, 1968.
folder. MT/MP-65)

1. Architecture - Designs and plans.
2. Transportation. I. Title. II. Title:
Awards for urban transportation.

388
C657
1970
S-H

TRANSPORTATION.
U.S. Congress. Senate. Committee on
Banking and Currency.
Mass transportation - 1970. Hearings
before the Subcommittee on Housing and
Urban Affairs of the Committee on Banking
and Currency, United States Senate, Ninety-
first Congress, second session, on S. 676
and S. 3499, bills to provide financial
assistance to mass transit systems. Wash.,
Govt. Print. Off., 1970.
60p.
Hearings   held Apr. 8-9, 1970.
1. Trans-   portation. 2. Journey to work.   I. Title.

388
F22u

TRANSPORTATION.
U.S. Federal Highway Administration.
Urban transportation planning; general information and introduction to system 360. Wash.,
1972.
1v.

1. Transportation. I. Title.

388
H68g

U.S. Dept. of Housing and Urban Development.
Grants for research and training in urban
transportation; information for applicants
(interim guide) Wash., Dept. of Housing and
Urban Transportation, 1968.
13p.

1. Transportation. I. U.S. Dept. of
Transportation. II. Title. III. Title:
Urban transportation.

711.73
C65u
1970
S-H

TRANSPORTATION.
U.S. Congress. Senate. Committee on Public
Works.
Use of highway funds for public transportation. Hearings before the Subcommittee on
Roads of the Committee on Public Works, United
States Senate, Ninety-first Congress, second
session on S. 3293, a bill to amend title 23
of the United States Code, to provide for the
use of highway funds for public transportation
Wash., Govt. Print. Off., 1970.
65p.
Hearings held May 14-18, 1970.
1. Highways.   2. Transportation.
3. Journey to   work. I. Title.

711.4
G25p

TRANSPORTATION.
U.S. General Accounting Office.
Progress and problems of urban and transpor-
tation planning. Report to the Congress by the
Comptroller General of the United States.
Department of Housing and Urban Development;
Department of Transportation. Wash., 1971.
36p. (B-174182)

1. City planning. 2. Transportation.
I. U.S. Dept. of Housing and Urban Development.
II. U.S. Dept. of Transportation. III. Title.

VF
388
H68h

Transportation.
U.S. Dept. of Housing and Urban Development.
HUD's role in urban transportation. Wash.
[1968]
Folder. (Its M/IP-78, Dec. 1968)

1. Transportation. 2. Journey to work.
I. Title.

388
H68s

TRANSPORTATION.
U.S. Dept. of Housing and Urban Development.
A summary of Urban transportation demonstration projects. Washington, 1967.
63p.

1. Transportation. 2. Management.
3. Grants-in-aid. I. Title. II. Title:
Urban transportation demonstration projects.

388
H68ms

Transportation.
U.S. Dept. of Housing and Urban Development.
Urban Transportation Administration.
Mass transportation demonstration program:
information for applicants. Wash., 1966.
5p.

1. Transportation. I. Title.

388
N17tr

TRANSPORTATION.
U.S. National Resources Planning Board.
Transportation and national policy. Washington, Govt. Print. Off., 1942.
513 p.
"Includes..., a summary report of findings and
recommendations prepared by Dr. Ralph J. Watkins,
director of the study ... and a series of staff
and agency contributions prepared by a group
of specialists." - Letter of transmittal.

1. Transportation. I. Watkins, Ralph James.

500
H68
1966
Summary

Transportation.
U.S. Dept. of Housing and Urban Develop-
ment.
Summer Study on Science and Urban Develop-
ment, held at the National Academy of Sci-
ence Summer Study Center, Woods Hole, Mass.,
June, 1966. Summary reports and recommen-
dations. Sponsored by the Department of
Housing and Urban Development and the
Office of Science and Technology, Executive
Office of the President. Washington, 1966.
Kit. (7 pieces)
Contents: [no.1] Transportation Panel.-
(Cont'd on next card)

---

355 .58
I52e

Transportation.
U.S. Industrial College of the Armed Forces.
The economics of national security. Washington, 1960.
22v.

Contents:-v.1. The nature of economic mobilization.
-v.2. Basic economics; refresher notes -v.3. Public
support, morale and security.-v.4. Principles of administration.-v.5. Human resources.-v.6. Natural resources.-v.7. Energy resources.-v.8. Research and
development.-v.9. Transportation.-v.10. Electric
power, gas, and telecommunications.-v.11. Requirements.-v.12. Procure-   ment.-v.13.
(Continued on next
card)

388
N17r

Transportation.
U.S. National Transportation Safety Board.
Report to Congress, 1st-
1967-
Washington, National Transportation Safety.
Board, Dept. of Transportation, 1958-
v.
annual.

For complete information see main card.

1. Transportation. 2. Traffic safety.
I. U.S. Dept. of Transportation.

500
H68
1966
Summary

U.S. Dept. of Housing and Urban Development. Summer Study on Science and Urban
Development...1966   (Card 2)

[no.2]Health Services Panel.-[no.3]Environ-
mental Engineering Panel.-[no.4] Rehabilitation Panel report.-[no.5] New Housing
Panel.-[no.6] Transcript of summary report
of Summer Study on Science and Urban
Development.-[no.7] Working papers of the
Summer Study on Science and Urban Development.
(Cont'd on next card)

355.58
I52e

U.S. Industrial College of the Armed Forces.
The economics of national security. Washington... 1960.   (Card 2)

Production.-v.14. Military supply management.-v.15.
Economic warfare and economic intelligence.-v.16.
United States economic foreign policy.-v.17. Mutual
security.-v.18. Psychological aspects of global
conflict.-v.19. Administration of mobilization
WWII -v.20. Economic stabilization.-v.21. Recon-
version and partial mobilization.-v.22. Retrospect
and prospect.
1. National defense.   2. Public administration. 3. Transporta-   tion. 4. Economic
policy.

712.25
O87or

TRANSPORTATION.
U.S. Bureau of Outdoor Recreation.
ORRV (Off road recreation vehicles)
Wash., 1971.
123p.

Bibliography: p. 82-99.

1. Recreation. 2. Transportation. I. Title.

500
H68
1966
Summary

U.S. Dept. of Housing and Urban Development. Summer Study on Science and Urban
Development...1966.   (Card 3)

1. Science. 2. City planning. 3. Housing. 4. Mortgage finance. 5. Urban
renewal. 6. Transportation. I. Summer
Study on Science and Urban Development.
Woods Hole, Mass., 1966. II. U.S. Office
of Science and Technology.

388
I58

TRANSPORTATION.
U.S. BOARD OF INVESTIGATION AND RESEARCH.
PUBLIC AIDS TO DOMESTIC TRANSPORTATION;
LETTER ... TRANSMITTING THE REPORT, SEPT.
18, 1944. WASHINGTON, GOVT. PRINT. OFF.,
1945.
1026P. (79TH CONGRESS, 1ST SESSION.
HOUSE. DOCUMENT NO. 159)

1. TRANSPORTATION.   I. TITLE.

712.25
O87s
no. 23

Transportation.
U.S. Outdoor Recreation Resources Review
Commission.
Projections to the years 1976 and 2000:
economic growth, population, labor force
and leisure, and transportation, by Com-
mission staff. Washington, Govt. Print.
Off., 1962.
434p. (ORRRC study report 23)
Add. copy, AIP/Ewald notebooks (711.4 A52ne no.13)
"The population studies are by the
Commission staff, economic projections,
by the National Planning Association,
(Cont'd. on next card)

388
H68t

Transportation.
U.S. Dept. of Housing and Urban Development.
Tomorrow's transportation; new systems for
the urban future. Wash., 1968.
100p.

1. Transportation. 2. Journey to work.
I. Title.

388
N17f

Transportation.
U.S. National Capital Transportation Agency.
Foreign rail rapid transit systems.
Washington, 1963.
36p.

1. Transportation. 2. Journey to work.
I. Title.

712.25
O87s
no. 23

U.S. Outdoor Recreation Resources Review
Commission. Projections to the years
1976 and 2000 ... 1962. (Card 2)

labor force and leisure projections by
the Bureau of Labor Statistics, U.S.
Dept. of Labor and the transportation
study by A.J. Goldenthal."

1. Recreation. 2. Economic development.
3. Transportation. 4. Population.
I. Goldenthal, A.J. II. Title. (Series
U.S. Outdoor   Recreation Resources
Review   Commission. ORRRC
study   report 23,)

388
H68urb

Transportation.
U.S. Dept. of Housing and Urban
Development.
Urban mass transportation planning require-
ments guide. Washington, 1966.
9p.

1. Transportation. I. Title.

388
N174

Transportation.
U.S. National Capital Transportation
Agency.
United States rapid transit systems, by
Robert L. Abrams. Washington, 1965.
21p.

1. Transportation. 2. Journey to work.
I. Abrams, Robert L.

351
P72reo
1968
no.2

Transportation.
U.S. President, 1963-   (Johnson)
Reorganization plan no. 2, 1968 for
transportation. Message from the President of the United States to the Congress
of the United States, transmitting reorganization plan no. 2 of 1968 transferring certain functions of the Dept.
of Transportation, Washington, Govt.
Print. Off., 1968.
5p.
Issued as House. Document no. 262.
90th Cong. 2d sess.
(Continued on next card)

R
388
H68e

Transportation.
U.S. Dept. of Housing and Urban Development.
Urban Transportation Administration.
Capital improvement grants and loans under
the Urban mass transportation act of 1964;
directory of projects Jan. 1, 1967. Wash.,
1967.
11p.
1. Transportation. 2. Grants-in-aid. I. Title.

697.8
N17mai

TRANSPORTATION.
U.S. National Industrial Pollution Control
Council.
Maintaining vehicular emission control
system integrity. Sub-Council report.
Wash., 1971.
13p.

1. Air pollution. 2. Transportation.
I. Title.

351
P72reo
1968
no.2

Transportation.
U.S. President, 1963-   (Johnson)
Reorganization plan no. 2, 1968.
(Card 2)

1. U.S. Executive departments - Reorganization. 2. Transportation. 3. U.S. Dept.
of Housing and Urban Development -
Reorganization. 4. U.S. Dept. of Transportation - Reorganization. I. Title.

388 P72

Transportation.

U.S. President, 1961- (Kennedy)
The transportation system of our nation.
Message from the President of the United States,
relative to the transportation system of our
nation. [Washington, Govt. Print. Off.] 1962.
17p. (87th Cong., 2d sess. House.
Document no. 384)

1. Transportation. 2. U.S. President -
Messages.

VF 388 P72p

Transportation - Legislation.

U.S. President, 1963 (Johnson)
Proposed Dept. of Transportation. Message
from the President of the United States,
transmitting a proposal for a Cabinet-Level
Dept. of Transportation consolidating various
existing transportation agencies. Wash.,
Govt. Print. Off., 1966.
14p.
At head of title: 89th Cong.
Document no. 399.

1. U.S. Dept. of Transportation (Proposed)
2. Transportation - Legislation.
3. U.S. President - Messages. I. Title.

---

388 P72PR

TRANSPORTATION.

U.S. PRESIDENT, 1963-1969 (JOHNSON)
PROPOSED LEGISLATION FOR HIGH-SPEED
GROUND TRANSPORTATION RESEARCH AND
DEVELOPMENT. COMMUNICATION FROM THE
PRESIDENT OF THE UNITED STATES...
WASHINGTON, GOVT. PRINT. OFF., 1965.
4P. (89TH CONGRESS, 1ST SESSION.
HOUSE OF REPRESENTATIVES. DOCUMENT NO.
101)

1. TRANSPORTATION. I. TITLE.
II. TITLE: GROUND TRANSPORTATION.

---

388 P72u

Transportation.

U.S. President, 1963- (Johnson)
Urban mass transportation; message from the
President of the United States transmitting
report to the President on urban transportation
organization by the Dept. of Housing and Urban
Development and the Dept. of Transportation.
Washington, Govt. Print. Off., 1968.
10p.

At head of title: 90th Cong., 2d sess. House.
Document no. 281.
1. Transportation. 2. U.S. Executive departments - Reorganization. 3. U.S. President -
Messages. I. Title.

---

388 P72r

TRANSPORTATION.

U.S. President, 1969- (Nixon)
Revenue sharing for transportation. Message
from the President of the United States proposing a system of special revenue sharing for
transportation. Wash., Govt. Print. Off., 1971.
9p.
At head of title: 92d Cong., 1st sess.
House. Document no. 92-71.

1. Transportation. 2. Grants-in-aid.
I. Title.

---

388 N17

Transportation.

U.S. Bureau of Public Roads.
Parking study manual: instructions for a
comprehensive study. Washington, 1949.
1v. diagrs., tables.

Rev. ed. 1958 issued as National Committee
on Urban Transportation, District of Columbia.
Procedure manual 3D. 388 N17b no.3D.

1. Transportation. 2. Parking.

---

388 N17b no.3D

Transportation.

U.S. Bureau of Public Roads.
Parking study manual: instructions for a
comprehensive study. Rev. ed. Ann Arbor,
1958.
161p. tables. (National Committee on
Urban Transportation, District of Columbia.
Procedure manual 3D)
For use in conjunction with [its] Better
transportation for your city ...
1st ed. 388 N17.
1. Transportation. 2. Parking. I. National Committee on Urban Transportation, District of Columbia. II. Public
Administration Service.

---

388 P81p

Transportation.

U.S. Bureau of Public Roads.
Population, economic, and land use studies
in urban transportation planning; a discussion
of current practice. Prepared by Jacob Silver
and Joseph R. Stowers. Washington, U.S. Dept.
of Commerce, Bureau of Public Roads, 1964.
27p.

1. Transportation. 2. Economic conditions.
I. Silver, Jacob. II. Stowers, Joseph R.
III. Title.

624.2 P81 v.5

Transportation.

U.S. Bureau of Public Roads.
Standard plans for highway bridges. Vol. 5.
Typical pedestrian bridges. Wash., For sale
by the Supt. of Doc., Govt. Print. Off., 1965.
1v.

1. Bridges. 2. Transportation. I. Title.
II. Title: Pedestrian bridges.

VF 388 P81u

Transportation.

U.S. Bureau of Public Roads.
Urban transportation planning. Wash.,
U.S. Dept. of Commerce, Bureau of Public
Roads, 1963.
8p. (Its Instructional memorandum
50-2-63)
Suppl. -- --Guidlines... Wash., U.S. Dept. of
Commerce, Bureau of Public Roads, 1963.
10p.

1. Transportation. I. Title.

---

388 T71c

TRANSPORTATION.

U.S. Dept. of Transportation.
Capital grants for urban mass transportation; information for applicants. Wash., U.S.
Dept. of Transportation, Urban Mass Transportation Administration, 1968.
10p.

1. Transportation. 2. Journey to work.
I. Title.

534.83 T71f

Transportation.

U.S. Dept. of Transportation.
Federal aircraft noise abatement plan,
FY 19[69-70]
Wash., Govt. Print. Off., 19[69-
1v. annual.

For Library holdings see main entry.

1. Noise. 2. Airports. I. Title.

VF 711.73 T71

Transportation.

U.S. Dept. of Transportation.
The Federal Highway Administration.
Created April 1, 1967, as part of the Dept.
of Transportation. Washington, U.S. Dept.
of Transportation, Federal Highway Administration, 1967.
folder.

1. U.S. Federal Highway Administration.
2. Highways. 3. Transportation.

---

388 T71m

TRANSPORTATION.

U.S. Dept. of Transportation.
Metropolitan transportation planning seminars.
Wash., 1971.
48p.

Sponsored by the American Institute of Planners
for the Dept. of Transportation, Office of the
Assistant Secretary for Environment and Urban
Systems.

1. Transportation. I. American Institute of
Planners. II. Title.

---

388 T71r

TRANSPORTATION.

U.S. Dept. of Transportation.
Report, 19
Washington, Govt. Print. Off., 19
v. annual.

For Library holdings see main entry.

1. U.S. Dept. of Transportation.
2. Transportation. 3. Journey to work.

---

388 T71u

TRANSPORTATION.

U.S. Dept. of Transportation. (Office
of Planning and Program Review)
Urban commutation alternatives. Wash.,
1968.
70p.

1. Transportation. 2. Journey to work.
I. Title.

---

388 U54

Transportation.

Universities-National Bureau Committee for
Economic Research.
Transportation economics: a conference of the
Committee. New York, National Bureau of
Economic Research. Distributed by Columbia
University Press, 1965.
451p. (National Bureau of Economic
Research. Special conference series no. 17)

1. Transportation. 2. Transportation -
Economic effect. 3. Railroads. I. National
Bureau of Economic Research. II. Title.

---

388 U78

TRANSPORTATION.

Utudjian, E
Il mondo sotterraneo; incontri di studio con
la partecipazione di E. Utudjian e W.J.
Armento. Anno accademico 1966-67. Napoli,
Istituto di Architettura e Urbanistica,
Universita di Napoli, Facolta di Ingegneria,
1967.
92p. (Naples. Universita. Istituto di
Architettura e Urbanistica. [Pubblicazioni]
12)
1. Transportation. 2. Journey to work.
3. Traffic. 4. Soils. I. Armento, W.J.,
jt. au. (Cont'd on next card)

---

388 U78

Utudjian, E Il mondo sotterraneo...1967.
(Card 2)

II. Naples. Universita. Istituto di
Architettura e Urbanistica. III. Title.

---

388 V15

Transportation.

Van Metre, Thurman W
Trains, tracks and travel, by Thurman W.
Van Metre and Russel Gordon Van Metre.
Rev. 9th ed. New York, Simmons-Boardman,
1960.
501p.

1. Transportation. 2. Railroads.
I. Van Metre, Russel Gordon, jt. au.
II. Title.

711.4 V27 1966

Transportation.

Vernon, Raymond.
The myth and reality of our urban problems.
(A publication of the Joint Center for Urban
Studies of the Massachusetts Institute of
Technology and Harvard University) Cambridge,
Mass., Harvard University Press, 1966.
90p.
Issued in 1962 as the Stafford Little Lec-
ture.

1. City planning. 2. Regional planning.
3. Housing. 4. Transportation. 5. Low-
income housing. 6. Social science research.
I. Stafford Little Lectures.
II. Joint Center for Urban
Studies. III. Title.

388
V43
TRANSPORTATION.
Vigrass, J   William.
A program to establish an urban transportation information and analysis center. Columbus, Ohio, Battelle Memorial Institute, Columbus Laboratories, 1967.
18p. (Battelle Memorial Institute. Columbus Laboratories. Monograph no. 10)
Prepared for New Systems Study Project, Urban Transportation Administration, Dept. of Housing and Urban Development.
(Cont'd on next card)

388
W25
Wendt, Paul F   The use...1969.   (Card 2)
au. II. California. University. Center for Real Estate and Urban Economics. III. Title. (Series)

388
W45f
TRANSPORTATION.
Wilcox, J   P
Flywheel energy-storage systems for transit buses. Columbus, Ohio, Battelle Memorial Institute, Columbus Laboratories, 1967.
14p. (Battelle Memorial Institute. Columbus Laboratories. Monograph no. 12)
Prepared for New Systems Study Project, Urban Transportation Administration, Dept. of Housing and Urban Development.
U.S. Mass Transportation Demonstration Grant Program.   Contract no. H-778.
(Cont'd on next card)

388
V43
Vigrass, J   William. A program to...1967.   (Card 2)

1. Transportation. 2. Journey to work. I. Battelle Memorial Institute. (Columbus Laboratories). II. U.S. Dept. of Housing and Urban Development. Urban Transportation Administration. III. U.S. Mass Transportation Demonstration Grant Program. IV. Title.

Transportation.

388
W27
Westinghouse Air Brake Co.
Rapid transit concepts. Pittsburgh, WABCO Mass Transit Center [1963?]
[21]p.

1. Transportation.

388
W45f
Wilcox, J   P   Flywheel energy...1967.   (Card 2)

1. Transportation. 2. Journey to work. I. Battelle Memorial Institute. (Columbus Laboratories). II. U.S. Dept. of Housing and Urban Development. Urban Transportation Administration. III. U.S. Mass Transportation Demonstration Grant Program. IV. Title: Buses. V. Title.

388
W15
TRANSPORTATION.
Wang, Chuan F
Alternative for maximum utilization of urban transportation system. [n.p.] 1970.
40p.

Research supported by a grant to the University of Pittsburgh from the Dept. of Housing and Urban Development, Project no. PENN-R-11-8-69.

1. Transportation. I. Pittsburgh. University. II. U.S. Dept. of Housing and Urban Development. III. Title.

388
W27s
Transportation.
Westinghouse Air Brake Co.
Study of evolutionary urban transportation. Organizations participating: Westinghouse Air Brake and others. Prepared for the U.S. Dept. of Housing and Urban Development. [Pittsburgh] 1968.
v.   (v.1. v.2. Appendices 1, 2, and 3. [and] v.3. Appendix 4)
At head of title: Study in new systems of urban transportation.

1. Transportation. 2. Transportation - Automation. 3. Journey to work. 4. Transportation - Statistics.
(cont'd on next card)

330.15
N17o
no.65
TRANSPORTATION.
Williams, Ernest W
Freight transportation in the Soviet Union: a comparison with the United States, by Ernest W. Williams, Jr., assisted by George Novak. New York, 1959.
38 p. (National Bureau of Economic Research. Occasional paper 65).

1. Transportation - U.S.S.R. 2. Transportation. I. Title. II. National Bureau of Economic Research. Occasional paper 65.

388
W17
Transportation.
Washington Center for Metropolitan Studies.
The impact of design: transportation and the metropolis. Sponsored by the Housing and Home Finance Agency and the Bureau of Public Roads. Washington, 1962.
295p.
Papers of Symposium containing statements and discussions on problems of coordination of transportation planning with urban planning. Held in Washington, D.C., Oct. 29-Nov., 1962.
Cover title.   (Cont'd. on next card)

388
W27s
Westinghouse Air Brake Co.   Study of evolutionary urban transportation...1968.   (Card 2)

I. U.S. Dept. of Housing and Urban Development. II. Title. III. Title: Study in new systems of urban transportation.

VF
388
W45s
Transportation - (Addresses)
Williams, Harrison A
Some fallacies about mass transportation. Address by United States Senator from New Jersey, before the thirty-first annual meeting of the National Housing Conference, Washington, D.C., 1962. Washington, 1962.
9p.

1. Transportation - Addresses. I. National Housing Conference, 31st, Washington, D.C., 1962.

388
W17
Washington Center for Metropolitan Studies.
The impact of design: transportation and the metropolis...(Card 2)

1. Transportation. 2. City planning. I. Title. II. U.S. Housing and Home Finance Agency.

388
W27w
Transportation.
Westinghouse Electric Corp.
The Westinghouse Transit Expressway; a concept in rapid transit for metropolitan areas. Pittsburgh, Westinghouse Industrial Systems, 1962.
14p.

1. Transportation. I. Title: Rapid transit for metropolitan areas.

388
W45n
TRANSPORTATION.
Wilson, A   G
New directions in strategic transportation planning, by A.G. Wilson and others. [n.p.] Organization for Economic Cooperation and Development, Directorate for Scientific Affairs, 1969.
260p.

At head of title: Centre for Environmental Studies.

1. Transportation. I. Centre for Environmental Studies. II. Organi-
(Cont'd on next card)

388
L65
Transportation.
Weltner, Charles Longstreet.
Address to The Institute for Rapid Transit Washington, D.C., May 14, 1964. [n.p.] 1964.
1v.

1. Transportation. 2. Journey to work. I. Institute for Rapid Transit. Meeting, Washington, 1964.

362.6
W34
1971
no.2
TRANSPORTATION.
White House Conference on Aging, Washington, 1971.
Transportation; background, by Joseph S. Revis. Issues, by the Technical Committee on Transportation, with the collaboration of the author. Wash., 1971.
51p. [no. 2]
Cover title: Background and issues; transportation.
Bibliography: p. 49-51.
1. Old age. 2. Transportation. I. Revis, Joseph S. II. Title.

388
W45n
Wilson, A   G   New...1969.   (Card 2)

zation for Economic Cooperation and Development. Directorate for Scientific Affairs. III. Title.

388
W25
TRANSPORTATION.
Wendt, Paul F
The use of land development simulation models in transportation planning, by Paul F. Wendt and Michael A. Goldberg. Berkeley, Calif., Center for Real Estate and Urban Economics, Institute of Urban and Regional Development, University of California, 1969.
[10]p. (California. University. Center for Real Estate and Urban Economics. Reprint no. 59)
Reprinted from: Highway research record 284 (1969)
1. Transportation. 2. Journey to work. 3. Land use. I.   Goldberg, Michael A., jt.
(Cont'd on next card)

388
W34
Transportation.
Whitener, Basil L
Address by member of Congress before the Institute for Rapid Transit, 3rd Annual Meeting, Washington, D.C., May 14, 1964. [Chicago] Institute for Rapid Transit, 1964.
8p.

1. Transportation. 2. Journey to work. I. Institute for Rapid Transit. Meeting, 3d, Washington, 1964.

388
W45
Transportation.
Wilson, G   Lloyd.
The elements of transportation economics. New York, Simmons-Boardman Publishing Corporation, 1950.
178p.

1. Transportation.   I. Title.

388
W45a
Transportation.
Wilson, Nigel H M
CARS; computer aided routing system.
Cambridge, School of Engineering, Massachusetts Institute of Technology, 1967.
80p. (Massachusetts Institute of Technology. Dept. of Civil Engineering. Research report #R67-12)

1. Transportation. 2. Traffic surveys. 3. Journey to work. I. Massachusetts Institute of Technology (School of Engineering) II. Title.

534.83
W95t
TRANSPORTATION.
Wyle Laboratories.
Transportation noise and noise from equipment powered by internal combustion engines. Wash., U.S. Environmental Protection Agency, Office of Noise Abatement and Control, 1971.
1v. (NTID300.13)

1. Noise. 2. Transportation. I. U.S. Environmental Protection Agency. II. Title.

388
(79461
1657)
L18
TRANSPORTATION - ACCOUNTING.
LAVE, CHARLES A
A BENEFIT COST ANALYSIS OF THE BAY AREA RAPID TRANSIT SYSTEM. PREPARED FOR DELIVERY AT THE 1966 ANNUAL MEETING OF THE AMERICAN POLITICAL SCIENCE ASSOCIATION. WASHINGTON, AMERICAN POLITICAL SCIENCE ASSOCIATION, 1966.
9P.

1. TRANSPORTATION - ACCOUNTING. 2. TRANSPORTATION - SAN FRANCISCO. I. TITLE. II. AMERICAN POLITICAL SCIENCE ASSOCIATION.

388
W45t
Transportation.
Wingo, Lowdon, Jr.
Transportation and urban land. Washington, Resources for the Future, 1961.
132p. (RFF regional studies)

1. Transportation. 2. Journey to work. I. Resources for the Future.

388
Y15u
Transportation.
Yale University. Bureau of Highway Traffic.
Urban transportation administration, by Thomas H. Seburn and Bernard L. Marsh. New Haven, Conn., 1959.
134p. diagrs., tables.

Partial contents:-Urban highway planning and urban renewal programs.

1. Transportation. 2. Highways. I. Seburn, Thomas J. II. Marsh, Bernard L.

388
:657
U54
Transportation - Accounting.
United Research, inc.
Responsibility accounting system and work measurement for the motor carrier industry. Prepared for Office of Transportation Research, Office of the Under Secretary for Transportation, U.S. Dept. of Commerce, Wash., D.C. Cambridge, Mass., 1966.
1v.
CFSTI PB 173202-2

1. Transportation - Accounting. I. U.S. Dept. of Transportation. II. Title.

388
W63
Leaf.
Transportation.
Wohl, Martin.
Evaluation of mutually exclusive design projects, by Martin Wohl and Brian V. Martin. Subject area: urban transportation administration, urban transportation systems, transportation economics. Wash., Highway Research Board, Div. of Engineering, National Research Council, National Academy of Sciences, National Academy of Engineering, 1967.
106p. (Highway Research Board. Special report 92)
National Research Council. Publication 1446.
1. Transportation. I. Martin, Brian V., jt. au. II. Highway Research Board. III. Title.

388
:331
Y68
TRANSPORTATION.
Young, Gifford A
Commuters, stay home. New York, American Institute of Aeronautics and Astronautics, 1971.
9p. (AIAA paper no. 71-490)

[Presented to] Urban Technology Conference, New York Coliseum, May 24-26, 1971.

1. Journey to work. 2. Transportation. I. American Institute of Aeronautics and Astronautics. II. Title.

388
(60)
D69
Transportation - Africa.
Doxiadis Associates.
Toward an African transport plan. Athens, 1964.
[6]p. (Its Bulletin no. 63)

1. Transportation - Africa. 2. Economic conditions - Africa. I. Title: African transport plan.

388
:308
W63
TRANSPORTATION.
Wohl, Martin.
A methodology for forecasting peak and off-peak travel volumes, by Martin Wohl. The Urban Institute, Wash., D.C. [n.p.] [1969?]
98p.
Draft of paper to appear in Highway Research Board publication.

1. Traffic surveys. 2. Transportation. 3. Journey to work. I. Highway Research Board. II. Title.

388
Z27n
Transportation.
Zettel, Richard M
Notes on transportation planning metropolitan areas, by Richard M. Zettel, research economist, Institute of Transportation and Traffic Engineering, University of California, Berkeley. Prepared for annual meeting of Western Section Regional Science Association. University of California, Berkeley. June 30, 1962.
6p.
1. Transportation. I. Regional Science Association, Western Section. Berkeley, Calif.

388
(798)
A51a
Transportation - Alaska.
Alaska. Dept. of Commerce. Div. of Tourism and Economic Development.
Alaska passenger traffic survey.
Juneau, Alaska,
v. charts.

Issued 1957 by Alaska. Resource Development Board; in 1958, Alaska. Dept. of Natural Resources.
For complete information see shelflist.

1. Transportation - Alaska. I. Title

388
W63t
TRANSPORTATION.
Wohl, Martin.
Thoughts about congestion toll pricing for public transport facilities, preliminary draft, by Martin Wohl, Urban Institute, Wash., D.C. [n.p.] [1969?]
34p.
Draft of paper to appear in Highway Research Board publication.

1. Transportation. 2. Journey to work. 3. Highways. I. Highway Research Board. II. Title.

388
Z27p
Transportation.
Zettel, Richard M
Planning for better urban transportation, by research economist, Institute of Transportation and Traffic Engineering, University of California, Berkeley. A paper prepared for presentation at the 40th annual conference of the American Municipal Association, Houston, Texas, July 12, 1963. [Berkeley, Calif.?] 1963.
9p.
1. Transportation. I. California. University. Institute of Transportation and Traffic Engineering. II. American Municipal Association.

388
(798)
A51a1
Transportation - Alaska.
Alaska. Dept. of Economic Development and Planning.
Alaska transportation facilities. Juneau, 1965.
17p.

1. Transportation - Alaska. I. Title.

388
W63u
TRANSPORTATION.
Wohl, Martin
The urban transportation problem: a brief analysis of our objectives and the prospects for current proposals. Wash., Urban Institute, 1970.
18p. (Urban Institute. Working paper 450-6)

1. Transportation. 2. Journey to work. I. Urban Institute, Wash., D.C. II. Title.

388
Z27
Transportation.
Zettel, Richard M
Summary review of major metropolitan area transportation studies in the United States, by Richard M. Zettel and others. Berkeley, University of California, 1962.
66p. (California. University. Institute of Transportation and Traffic. Special report)

1. Transportation. I. California. University. Institute of Transportation and Traffic Engineering.

388
(798)
A51
Transportation - Alaska.
Alaska. International Rail and Highway Commission.
Transportation requirements for the growth of northwest North America. Letter from the Chairman, Alaska International Rail and Highway Commission, transmitting the final report of the Alaska International Rail and Highway Commission, pursuant to public law 884, 84th Congress. Washington, Govt. Print. Off., 1961.
3v.
At head of 1st sess. title: 87th Cong., no. 176. House. Document (Continued on next card)

388
w63w
TRANSPORTATION.
Wohl, Martin.
What kind of transport will the urban public use: today and tomorrow? Wash., Urban Institute, 1971.
13p. (Urban Institute paper, 450-8)

1. Transportation. I. Urban Institute. II. Title.

388
Z84
Transportation.
Zwick, Charles J
Models of urban change: their role in urban transportation research. Santa Monica, Calif., 1962.
17p.
"This paper was prepared for presentation at the annual meeting & Transportation Engineering Conference of the American Society of Civil Engineers in Detroit, Michigan, October 8-12, 1962."

1. Transportation. I. Rand Corp. II. Title: Urban transportation.

388
(798)
A51
Transportation - Alaska.
Alaska. International Rail and Highway Commission. Transportation...1961. (Card 2)

Volume 2. Research report by Battelle Memorial Institute on an integrated transport system to encourage economic development of northwestern North America.

1. Transportation - Alaska. I. Battelle Memorial Institute.

388 (9) N17
TRANSPORTATION - ALASKA.
NATIONAL RESEARCH COUNCIL, CANADA. DIVISION OF BUILDING RESEARCH.
TRANSPORTATION AND ECONOMIC POTENTIAL IN THE ARCTIC, BY K.B. WOODS AND R.F. LEGGET. OTTAWA, 1960.
435-458P. (ITS DBR TECHNICAL PAPER NO. 113)

REPRINTED FROM TRAFFIC QUARTERLY, OCTOBER 1960.
1. TRANSPORTATION - ARCTIC AND ANTARCTIC. 2. TRANSPORTATION - ALASKA.
3. TRANSPORTATION - CANADA. I. WOODS, K.B. II. LEGGET, R.F.

---

388 (764) T29a
Transportation - Amarillo, Tex.
Texas. Highway Dept.
Amarillo urban transportation plan; origin-destination survey. Vol. 1-2 Prepared in cooperation with U.S. Dept. of Commerce Bureau of Public Roads. Amarillo, Tex., 1964.
2 v.

1. Transportation - Amarillo, Tex.
2. Journey to work. I. U.S. Bureau of Public Roads. II. Title.

---

388 (762) M47ur
Mississippi-Arkansas-Tennessee Council of Governments. Urban mass...1968.(Card 2)

I. Title. II. U.S. Dept. of Housing and Urban Development. Mass Transportation Demonstration Grant Program. Miss.-Ark.-Tenn.

---

388 C65a
Transportation - Alaska.
U.S. Congress.
Alaskan and Hawaiian transportation. Joint hearings before the Senate and House Committees on Interstate and Foreign Commerce, Congress of the United States, Eighty-sixth Congress, first session on S. 1507 [etc.] Washington, Govt. Print. Off., 1961.
508p.
Hearings held Oct. 20-Nov. 18, 1959.

1. Transportation - Alaska. 2. Transportation - Hawaii.   I. U.S. Congress. Senate. Committee on Inter-   state and Foreign Commerce.   II. U.S. Congress. House.   Committee on Inter-state and Foreign Commerce.

---

388 (798) A52
TRANSPORTATION - ANCHORAGE, ALASKA.
Anchorage Transit System, inc.
Final report on the Mass Transportation Demonstration Grant contract no. H-543, Project no. Alaska MTD-1, between the City of Anchorage, Alaska, and the United States of America. Anchorage, [1968?]
118p.
U.S. Mass Transportation Demonstration Grant Program.
1. Transportation - Anchorage, Alaska.
2. Journey to work. 3. Streets - Anchorage, Alaska. I.   U.S. Mass Transportation Demons   tration Grant Program Anchorage,   Alaska.

---

388 (762) M47urb
Transportation - Arkansas.
Mississippi-Arkansas-Tennessee Council of Governments.
UMT (urban mass transportation) program planning requirements; supplemental documentation MATCOG. Regular program planning requirements. Memphis, 1968.
13p.
U.S. Dept. of Housing and Urban Development. Mass Transportation Demonstration Grant Program.
1. Transportation - Mississippi.
2. Transportation - Arkansas. 3. Transportation - Tennessee. 4. Journey to work.
(Continued on next card).

---

388 (75526) A52r
TRANSPORTATION - ALEXANDRIA, VA.
Alexandria, Va. Dept. of Planning and Regional Affairs.
Expected impact of rapid transit. Part I. General patterns. Part II. Impact in Alexandria. Special report. Alexandria, 1969.
9p. (Its Report no. 19)

1. Transportation - Alexandria, Va.
2. Journey to work. I. Title.

---

388 (77435) M42
Transportation - Ann Arbor, Mich.
Michigan. State Highway Dept.
Ann Arbor-Ypsilanti urban area transportation study. Preliminary report. Lansing, Mich., 1966.
1 v.

1. Transportation - Ann Arbor, Mich.
2. Transportation - Ypsilanti, Mich. I. Title.

---

388 (762) M47urb
Mississippi-Arkansas-Tennessee Council of Governments. UMT...1968.   (Card 2)

I. U.S. Dept. of Housing and Urban Development. Mass Transportation Demonstration Grant Program Miss.-Ark.-Tenn. II. Title.

---

388 (75526) A52
Transportation - Alexandria, Va.
Alexandria. Dept. of City Planning and Urban Renewal.
Rail transit; relationship to other planning considerations. Alexandria, Va., 1966.
9p. (Its Special Study. Report no. 10)

1. Transportation - Alexandria, Va.
2. Journey to work. 3. Railroads - Alexandria, Va. I. Title.

---

388 (9) N17
TRANSPORTATION - ARCTIC AND ANTARCTIC.
NATIONAL RESEARCH COUNCIL, CANADA. DIVISION OF BUILDING RESEARCH.
TRANSPORTATION AND ECONOMIC POTENTIAL IN THE ARCTIC, BY K.B. WOODS AND R.F. LEGGET. OTTAWA, 1960.
435-458P. (ITS DBR TECHNICAL PAPER NO. 113)

REPRINTED FROM TRAFFIC QUARTERLY, OCTOBER 1960.
1. TRANSPORTATION - ARCTIC AND ANTARCTIC. 2. TRANSPORTATION - ALASKA.
3. TRANSPORTATION - CANADA. I. WOODS, K.B. II. LEGGET, R.F.

3025- 3026
TRANSPORTATION - ASHEVILLE, N.C.
ASHEVILLE, N.C. METROPOLITAN PLANNING BOARD.
ASHEVILLE TRANSPORTATION STUDY AREA: 1. POPULATION AND ECONOMIC DATA; 2. LAND USE PROJECTIONS. BY RUST ENGINEERING COMPANY. ASHEVILLE, N.C., 1969.
2 V. (HUD 701 REPORT)

1. TRANSPORTATION - ASHEVILLE, N.C. I. RUST ENGINEERING COMPANY. II. HUD. 701. ASHEVILLE, N.C.

---

388 (74885) M62
Transportation - Allegheny Co., Pa.
MPC Corp.
Testing and evaluation of the transit expressway; Mass Transportation Demonstration Project conducted between Port Authority of Allegheny County, Pittsburgh, and U.S. Dept. of Housing and Urban Development. Pittsburgh, 1967.
272p.
U.S. Dept. of Housing and Urban Development. Mass Transportation Demonstration Grant Program.

(Cont'd on next card)

---

388 (762) M47u
Transportation - Arkansas.
Mississippi-Arkansas-Tennessee Council of Governments.
Urban mass transportation grant program; regular program planning requirements. Memphis, 1968.
48p.
U.S. Dept. of Housing and Urban Development. Mass Transportation Demonstration Grant Program.
1. Transportation - Mississippi. 2. Transportation - Arkansas. 3. Transportation - Tennessee. 4. Journey to work. I. U.S. Dept.
of Housing and   Urban Development. Mass Transportation   Demonstration Grant Pro-gram.   (Cont'd on next card)

Folio 388 (756881) S54
Transportation - Asheville metropolitan area.
Smith (Wilbur) and Associates.
A master highway transportation plan, Asheville metropolitan area. Prepared for North Carolina State Highway Commission and the City of Asheville. New Haven, 1961.
109p.

1. Transportation - Asheville metropolitan area. I. North Carolina. State Highway Commission.

---

388 (74885) M62
MPC Corp. Testing and evaluation transit expressway; Mass Transportation Demonstration Project...1967. (Card 2)

1. Transportation - Allegheny Co., Pa.
2. Engineering. I. U.S. Dept. of Housing and Urban Development. Mass Transportation Demonstration Grant Program. II. Title.

---

388 (762) M47u
Mississippi-Arkansas-Tennessee Council of Governments. Urban mass transportation...1968.   (Card 2)

Mississippi. II. U.S. Dept. of Housing and Urban Development. Mass Transportation Demonstration Grant Program. Arkansas. III. U.S. Dept. of Housing and Urban Development. Mass Transportation Demonstration Grant Program. Tennessee. IV. Title.

711.4 (758231) A75cen
Transportation - Atlanta.
Atlanta. City Planning Dept.
Central Atlanta. Atlanta, 1962.
28p.   Map inserted in pocket of back cover

1. City planning - Atlanta.
2. Transportation - Atlanta.

---

388 (74827) A55
Transportation - Allentown, Pa.
Allentown, Pa. City Planning Commission.
Plan for traffic circulation; tri-point concept as a traffic solution for the city of Allentown, Pennsylvania. Allentown, 1964.
21p.

1. Traffic - Allentown, Pa.
2. Transportation - Allentown, Pa.

---

388 (762) M47ur
Transportation - Arkansas.
Mississippi-Arkansas-Tennessee Council of Governments.
Urban mass transportation program planning requirements; supplementary material, MATCOG. Memphis, 1968.
18p.
U.S. Dept. of Housing and Urban Development. Mass Transportation Demonstration Grant Program.
1. Transportation - Mississippi. 2. Transportation - Arkansas. 3. Transportation - Tennessee. 4. Journey to work. (Cont'd on next card)

---

388 (758231) A75 no. 2
Transportation - Atlanta.
Atlanta. Metropolitan Planning Commission.
Assignment of costs: automotive and transit facilities. Atlanta, 1956.
40p. map, tables. (Transportation policy project report no. 2)
U.S. Urban Renewal Administration, Urban Planning Assistance Program.
1. Transportation - Atlanta. I. U.S. Urban Renewal Administration. Urban Planning Assistance Program.

711.4
(758231)
A75au
Transportation - Atlanta.
Atlanta. Metropolitan Planning Commission.
Evaluation of services: automotive and
transit facilities, by John Geiger.
Atlanta. [1957]
41p. table. (Its Transportation Policy
Project report no. 3)

U.S. Urban Renewal Administration, Urban
Planning Assistance Program.

(Continued on next card)

711.4
(758231)
A75te
Transportation - Atlanta.
Atlanta. Metropolitan Planning Commission.
A tentative model of the present and
future transportation network, metropolitan
Atlanta, 1955-1980. Atlanta, 1956.
7p. (Its Transportation policy summary
report no. 1)

U.S. Urban Renewal Administration, Urban
Planning Assistance Program.

1. City planning - Atlanta. 2. Transportation - Atlanta. I. U.S. Urban Renewal
Administration.

711.4
(758231)
A75ce
Atlanta. Metropolitan Planning Commission.
Transportation Policy Project...(Card 2)

Planning Assistance Program. (URA Proj.
P-3, I. A. 2)

1. City planning - Atlanta. 2. Traffic -
Atlanta. 3. Transportation - Atlanta. I.
Sears, Richard H. Jr. II. U.S. Urban Renewal
Administration. Urban Planning Assistance
Program.

711.4
(758231)
A75au
Atlanta. Metropolitan Planning Commission.
Evaluation of services:... (Card 2)

Preliminary draft for Commission review.

Not for public release.

1. City planning - Atlanta. 2. Transportation - Atlanta. I. U.S. Urban Renewal
Administration. II. Geiger, John.

711.4
(758231)
A75cent
Transportation - Atlanta.
Atlanta. Metropolitan Planning
Commission.
Transportation policy project.
Central Atlanta street capacity study
procedure, by James M. Schafer and
Richard H. Sears, Jr. Atlanta, 1957.
3p.
"This project financed by
appropriations of DeKalb and Fulton
Counties and the city of Atlanta, with
assistance from U.S. Urban Renewal
Administration."
(Continued on
next card)

711.4
(758231)
A75i
Transportation - Atlanta.
Atlanta. Metropolitan Planning Commission.
Transportation Policy Project. Impact of
trends on the greater Atlanta region.
Atlanta, 1957.
1v.

U.S. Urban Renewal Administration. Urban
Planning Assistance Program. (U.R.A. Proj.
Ga. P-3, I.A.1)

1. City planning - Atlanta. 2. Transportation - Atlanta. I. U.S. Urban Renewal Administration.

711.4
(758231)
A75
aut
Transportation - Atlanta.
Atlanta. Metropolitan Planning Commission.
Future requirements: automotive and transit
facilities, by John Geiger. Atlanta, 1957.
26p. maps, tables. (Its Transportation
Policy Project report no. 4)

U.S. Urban Renewal Administration, Urban
Planning Assistance Program.

Preliminary draft for Commission review.
(Continued on next card)

711.4
(758231)
A75cent
Atlanta. Metropolitan Planning
Commission. Transportation policy
project...1957. (Card 2)

1. City planning - Atlanta.
2. Transportation - Atlanta.
I. Schafer, James M. II. Sears,
Richard H. III. U.S. URA-UPAP.
Atlanta.

711.4
(758231)
A75r
Transportation - Atlanta.
Atlanta. Metropolitan Planning Commission.
Transportation Policy Project. Revised
through traffic procedures, by Robert C.
Stuart and Richard H. Sears, Jr.
Atlanta, 1957.
5p.

U.S. Urban Renewal Administration,
Urban Planning Assistance Program. (URA
(Continued on next card)

711.4
(758231)
A75
aut
Atlanta. Metropolitan Planning Commission.
Future requirements:... (Card 2)

Not for public release.

1. City planning - Atlanta. 2. Transportation - Atlanta. I. U.S. Urban Renewal
Administration. II. Geiger, John.

711.4
(758231)
A75d
July
1957
Transportation - Atlanta
Atlanta. Metropolitan Planning Commission.
Transportation Policy Project. Discus-
sion and decision. Atlanta, 1957.
1v.

U.S. Urban Renewal Administration, Urban
Planning Assistance Program. (U.R.A. Proj.
Ga. P-3, I.A.1)

1. City planning - Atlanta. 2. Transportation - Atlanta. I. U.S. Urban Renewal
Administration.

711.4
(758231)
A75r
Atlanta. Metropolitan Planning Commission.
Transportation Policy...(Card 2)

Proj. Ga. P - 3, I. A. 2)

1. City planning - Atlanta. 2. Transporta-
tion - Atlanta. 3. Traffic - Atlanta. I.
Stuart, Robert C. II. Sears Richard H., Jr.
III. U. S. Urban Renewal Administration.
Urban Planning Assistance Program.

711.4
(758231)
A75ma
Transportation - Atlanta.
Atlanta. Metropolitan Planning Commission.
Major transportation policy alternatives
available to greater Atlanta. Atlanta,
1956.
10p.

U.S. Urban Renewal Administration, Urban
Planning Assistance Program.

1. City planning - Atlanta. 2. Transportation - Atlanta. I. U.S. Urban Renewal
Administration.

711.4
(758231)
A75d
Oct.
1957
Transportation - Atlanta.
Atlanta. Metropolitan Planning Commission.
Transportation Policy Project. Discus-
sion and decision. Atlanta, 1957.
1v.

U.S. Urban Renewal Administration, Urban
Planning Assistance Program. (U.R.A. Proj.
Ga. P-3, I.A.1)

1. City planning - Atlanta. 2. Transportation - Atlanta. I. U.S. Urban Renewal
Administration.

388
(758231)
A75e
no.1
Transportation - Atlanta.
Atlanta Region Metropolitan Planning
Commission.
Access to central Atlanta. Atlanta,
1959.
39p. (Its Expressway policy study.
Report no. 1)

1. Transportation - Atlanta. 2. Highways - Atlanta metropolitan area.

388
(758231)
A75
no.1
Transportation - Atlanta.
Atlanta. Metropolitan Planning Commission.
Physical inventory: automotive and transit
facilities. Atlanta, 1956.
63p. maps, tables. (Transportation
policy project report no. 1)

U.S. Urban Renewal Administration, Urban
Planning Assistance Program.

1. Transportation - Atlanta. 2. Traffic
surveys - Atlanta. I. U.S. Urban Renewal
Administration. Urban Planning Assistance
Program.

711.4
(758231)
A75a
Transportation - Atlanta.
Atlanta. Metropolitan Planning Commission.
Transportation Policy Project. Atlanta
area, 1957, transportation objectives.
Atlanta, 1957.
1v.

U.S. Urban Renewal Administration, Urban
Planning Assistance Program. (U.R.A. Proj.
Ga. P-3, I.A.3.c.)

1. City planning - Atlanta. 2. Transportation - Atlanta. I. U.S. Urban Renewal
Administration.

388
(758231)
A75e
no.2
Transportation - Atlanta.
Atlanta Region Metropolitan Planning
Commission.
Crosstown and by-pass expressways.
Atlanta, 1959.
40p. (Expressway policy study.
Report no. 2)

1. Transportation - Atlanta.
2. Journey to work. 3. Highways -
Atlanta.

VF
711.3
(758231)
A75
Transportation - Atlanta.
Atlanta. Metropolitan Planning
Commission.
Regional development plan: land use and
transportation; city of Atlanta, [Counties
of] Clayton, Cobb, Dekalb, Fulton,
Gwinnett, Atlanta, 1962.
folder.

1. Metropolitan area planning - Atlanta.
2. Land use - Atlanta. 3. Transportation -
Atlanta. I. Title.

711.4
(758231)
A75ce
Transportation - Atlanta.
Atlanta. Metropolitan Planning Commission.
Transportation Policy Project. Central
Atlanta 1957 street use plan. Guide to computations forecasting downtown street traffic
volumes resulting from expressway completion,
by Richard H. Sears, Jr. Atlanta, 1957.
12p.

U.S. Urban Renewal Administration, Urban
(Continued on next card)

388
(758231)
A75r
Transportation - Atlanta.
Atlanta Transit System.
Rapid... Atlanta. Atlanta, 1960.
27p. illus.

1. Transportation - Atlanta.

388
(758231)
G26

Transportation - Atlanta.

Georgia Institute of Technology.
Downtown Atlanta radial transit; a
graduate project in complex systems
design. Submitted by students at the
Georgia Institute of Technology.
Completed Spring quarter. Atlanta, 1967.
225p.
Bibliography: p. 224-225.
1. Transportation - Atlanta. 2. Journey
to work. 3. Business districts - Atlanta.
I. Title.

391

TRANSPORTATION - ATLANTA METROPOLITAN
AREA.
METROPOLITAN ATLANTA COUNCIL OF LOCAL
GOVERNMENTS, INC.
REGIONAL VEHICLE OPERATIONS EDUCATION
FOR METROPOLITAN ATLANTA: A PRELIMINARY
STUDY. ATLANTA, 1969.
15L. (HUD 701 REPORT)

1. TRANSPORTATION - ATLANTA METROPOLITAN
AREA. I. HUD. 701. ATLANTA
METROPOLITAN AREA.

711.4
(78882)
A87
Sect. 3

Transportation - Aurora, Colo.

Aurora, Colo. Planning Dept.
Traffic and transportation: comprehensive plan, section 3, by Richard H.
Sundell. Denver, 1959.
11p.

U.S. Urban Renewal Adm. UPAP.

1. Master plan - Aurora, Colo. 2. Traffic - Aurora,
Colo. 3. Transportation - Aurora, Colo. I. Sundell,
Richard H. II. U.S. URA-UPAP. Aurora, Colo.

Folio
388
(758231)
A75re
no.4

Transportation - Atlanta metropolitan
area.

Atlanta Region Metropolitan Planning
Commission.
Atlanta region comprehensive plan:
rapid transit. Atlanta, 1961.
31p. (Its Report no. 4)

1. Transportation - Atlanta metropolitan
area. 2. Journey to work. 3. Master
plan - Atlanta.

399

TRANSPORTATION - ATLANTA METROPOLITAN
AREA.
METROPOLITAN ATLANTA TRANSIT STUDY
COMMISSION.
IMPLEMENTING RAPID TRANSIT FOR THE
ATLANTA METROPOLITAN REGION, BY PARSONS,
BRINCKERHOFF, QUADE & DOUGLAS. NEW YORK,
1962.
30L. (HUD 701 REPORT)

1. TRANSPORTATION - ATLANTA METROPOLITAN
AREA. I. PARSONS, BRINCKERHOFF, QUADE &
DOUGLAS. II. ATLANTA REGION METROPOLITAN
PLANNING COMMISSION. III. HUD. 701.
ATLANTA METROPOLITAN AREA.

1598
1599

TRANSPORTATION - AUSTIN, MINN.
AUSTIN, MINN. PLANNING COMMISSION.
AUSTIN AREA COMPREHENSIVE DEVELOPMENT
AND TRANSPORTATION PLAN: 1, BASIC
STUDIES REPORT; 2, TRAVEL
CHARACTERISTICS. VOGT, SAGE, AND PFLUM,
CONSULTANTS. AUSTIN, MINN, 1969-70.
2 V. (HUD 701 REPORT)

1. TRANSPORTATION - AUSTIN, MINN.
I. VOGT, SAGE, AND PFLUM, CONSULTANTS.
II. HUD. 701. AUSTIN, MINN.

463
464

TRANSPORTATION - ATLANTA METROPOLITAN
AREA.
ATLANTA REGION METROPOLITAN PLANNING
COMMISSION.
PASSENGER CAR REGISTRATIONS: 1, 1961;
2, 1983. ATLANTA, HAMMER, GREENE, SILER
ASSOCIATES, 1962.
2 V. (HUD 701 REPORT)

1. TRANSPORTATION - ATLANTA METROPOLITAN
AREA. I. HAMMER, GREENE, SILER
ASSOCIATES. II. HUD. 701. ATLANTA
METROPOLITAN AREA.

453
FOLIO

TRANSPORTATION - ATLANTA METROPOLITAN
AREA.
METROPOLITAN ATLANTA TRANSIT STUDY
COMMISSION.
A PLAN AND PROGRAM OF RAPID TRANSIT
FOR THE ATLANTA METROPOLITAN REGION.
NEW YORK, PARSONS, BRINCKERHOFF, QUADE &
DOUGLAS, 1962.
117P. (HUD 701 REPORT)

1. TRANSPORTATION - ATLANTA
METROPOLITAN AREA. I. PARSONS,
BRINCKERHOFF, QUADE & DOUGLAS.
II. HUD. 701. ATLANTA METROPOLITAN
AREA.

388
c538.56
B17

Annex

Transportation - Automation.

Battelle Memorial Institute.
Feasibility of computer storage and
retrieval of freight tariff information -
Phase I. Columbus, Ohio, 1966.
54p.
... ...Technical annex. 1966. 282p.

1. Transportation - Automation. 2. Tariff.
I. U.S. Dept. of Commerce. II. Title.

454
FOLIO

TRANSPORTATION - ATLANTA METROPOLITAN
AREA.
ATLANTA REGION METROPOLITAN PLANNING
COMMISSION.
A PLAN AND PROGRAM OF RAPID TRANSIT
FOR METROPOLITAN ATLANTA, BY PARSONS,
BRINCKERHOFF, TUDOR, BECHTEL.
WASHINGTON, D.C., 1967.
77P. (HUD 701 REPORT)

1. TRANSPORTATION - ATLANTA
METROPOLITAN AREA. I. PARSONS,
BRINCKERHOFF, TUDOR, BECHTEL. II. HUD.
701. ATLANTA METROPOLITAN AREA.

710

TRANSPORTATION - ATLANTA METROPOLITAN
AREA.
METROPOLITAN ATLANTA TRANSIT STUDY
COMMISSION.
A PLAN AND PROGRAM OF RAPID TRANSIT FOR
THE ATLANTA METROPOLITAN REGION. PREPARED
BY PARSONS, BRINCKERHOFF, QUADE AND
DOUGLAS. ATLANTA, 1962.
1 V. (HUD 701 REPORT)

1. TRANSPORTATION - ATLANTA METROPOLITAN
AREA. I. PARSONS, BRINCKERHOFF, QUADE
AND DOUGLAS. II. HUD. 701. ATLANTA
METROPOLITAN AREA.

388
B17m

Transportation - Automation.

Battelle Memorial Institute. Columbus Laboratories.
Monographs on potential RD & D projects
summary report. Prepared for New Systems
Study Project, Urban Transportation Administration, Dept. of Housing and Urban Development, Columbus, Ohio, 1968.
1v.
On cover: Study in new systems of urban
transportation.
Project staff - Kaj L. Nielsen, manager.

(Cont'd on next card)

393

TRANSPORTATION - ATLANTA METROPOLITAN
AREA.
ATLANTA REGION METROPOLITAN PLANNING
COMMISSION.
RAPID TRANSIT FOR METROPOLITAN ATLANTA,
A SPECIAL SUMMARY REPORT. ATLANTA, 1967.
16P. (HUD 701 REPORT)

1. TRANSPORTATION - ATLANTA METROPOLITAN
AREA. I. HUD. 701. ATLANTA
METROPOLITAN AREA.

388
(758231)
P17i

Transportation - Atlanta metropolitan area.

Parsons, Brinckerhoff, Quade and Douglas.
Implementing rapid transit for the
Atlanta Metropolitan Region. A report
of the Metropolitan Atlanta Transit Study
Commission to the city of Atlanta and
counties of Clayton, Cobb, Dekalb, Fulton
and Gwinnett. New York, 1962.
30p.
Final draft.
U.S. Urban Renewal Adm. UPAP.

(Cont'd. on next card)

388
B17m

Transportation - Automation.

Battelle Memorial Inttitute. Columbus
Laboratories. Monographs...1968.
(Card 2)

1. Transportation. 2. Transportation -
Automation. I. U.S. Dept. of Housing and
Urban Development. II. Nielsen, Kaj L.
III. Title. IV. Title: Study in new systems
of urban transportation.

388
(758231)
A75reg

Transportation - Atlanta metropolitan area.

Atlanta Region Metropolitan Planning
Commission.
Regional development plan: land use
and transportation, City of Atlanta,
Clayton, Cobb, Dekalb, Fulton, and
Gwinnett County. Atlanta, 1962.
5p. on folded map.

1. Transportation - Atlanta metropolitan
area. 2. Master plan - Atlanta metropolitan area. 3. Land use -
Atlanta metropolitan area.

388
(758231)
P17i

Parsons, Brinckerhoff, Quade and Douglas.
Implementing rapid transit...(Card 2)

1. Transportation - Atlanta metropolitan
area 2. Journey to work. I. Metropoli-
tan Atlanta Transit Study Commission.
II. Atlanta Region Metropolitan Planning
Commission. III. U.S. URA-UPAP.
Atlanta.

388
B17u

Transportation - Automation.

Battelle Memorial Institute. Columbus
Laboratories.
Urban goods: movement demand, by David
N. Goss and others; final report. Prepared
for New Systems Study Project, Urban Transportation Administration, Dept. of Housing
and Urban Development, Wash., D.C., Columbus, Ohio, Battelle Memorial Institute,
Columbus Laboratories, 1967.
232p.
On cover: Study in new systems of urban
transportation.

711.3
(758231)
B76

Transportation - Atlanta metropolitan area.

Brown, Albert Yeates.
The influence of the Atlanta Region
Metropolitan Planning Commission on regional
decision-making. [Atlanta] 1960.
133p.
Bibliography: p. 125-133.
Thesis: George Washington University.

1. Metropolitan area planning - Atlanta.
2. City planning - Atlanta. 3. Transportation - Atlanta metropolitan area.
4. Metropolitan government - Atlanta.
5. Atlanta Region Metropolitan
Planning Commission.

388
(758231)
P17

Transportation - Atlanta metropolitan area.

Parsons, Brinckerhoff, Quade and Douglas.
A plan and program of rapid transit for
the Atlanta Metropolitan Region. Atlanta,
1962.
[10]p.
At head of title: Metropolitan Atlanta
Transit Study Commission.
U.S. Urban Renewal Adm. UPAP.

1. Transportation - Atlanta metropolitan
area. I. Metropolitan Atlanta Transit
Study Commission. II. U.S.
URA-UPAP. Atlanta.

388
B17u

Transportation - Automation.

Battelle Memorial Institute. Columbus
Laboratories. Urban goods... 1967.
(Card 2)

1. Transportation. 2. Transportation
- Automation. I. U.S. Dept. o f Housing
and Urban Development. II. Goss, David N.
III. Title. IV. Title: Study in new systems
of urban transportation.

Transportation - Automation.

388
:538.56
C15

California. University. Dept. of Engineering.
Transim general purpose transportation system stimulator; user's manual. Prepared for the Undersecretary for Transportation, U.S. Department of Commerce, Washington, D.C. Los Angeles, 1966.
1v.   (Its Report no. 66-6)

1. Transportation - Automation.
I. Title.

Transportation - Automation.

388
G25st

General Electric Co. Transportation Systems Div.   A study of command and control systems...1968.   (Card 2)

1. Transportation. 2. Transportation - Automation. I. Merritt, H.W. II. U.S. Dept. of Housing and Urban Development. III. Title. IV. Title: Study in new systems of urban transportation.

Transportation - Automation.

538.56
H43

Highway Research Board.
Information systems for land use and transportation planning; 8 reports. Washington, Highway Research Board, Div. of Engineering, National Research Council, National Academy of Sciences-National Academy of Engineering, 1967.
102p. (Its Highway research record no. 194)
National Research Council. Publication 1525.
1. Automation. 2. Land use - Automation. 3. Transportation - Automation. I. Title.

Transportation - Automation.

388
D19

Day and Zimmerman, inc., Philadelphia.
Potential near term improvements in urban transportation. Prepared for U.S. Department of Housing and Urban Development. [Philadelphia] 1968.
304p.
On cover: Study in new systems of urban transportation.
1. Transportation. 2. Eminent domain. 3. Transportation - Automation. I. U.S. Dept. of Housing and Urban Development. II. Title.   III. Title: Study on new systems of   urban transportation.

Transportation - Automation.

388
G25su

General Electric Co. (Transportation Systems Div.)
Survey of electronic command and control systems. Prepared for Urban Transportation Administration, U.S. Dept. of Housing and Urban Development, Washington, D.C. Erie, Pa., Transportation Equipment Projects and Marketing Operation, General Electric Co., Transportation Systems Div., 1967.
1v.
1. Transportation. 2. Journey to work. 3. Transportation - Automation. I. U.S. Dept. of Housing and Urban Development. II. Title.

Transportation - Automation.

388
K22

Keefer, Louis E
Urban travel patterns for airports, shopping centers, and industrial plants. Research is sponsored by the American Association of State Highway Officials in cooperation with the Bureau of Public Roads. [Washington] Highway Research Board, Div. of Engineering, National Academy of Sciences-National Academy of Engineering 1966.
116p.   (National cooperative highway research program report 24)
Bibliography: p. 92-101.

(Cont'd on next card)

TRANSPORTATION - AUTOMATION.

388
F27

Fertal, Martin J
Modal split; documentation of nine methods for estimating transit usage, by Martin J. Fertal and others. Chicago, U.S. Bureau of Public Roads, Office of Planning, 1966.
136p.
Bibliography: p. 134-136.
1. Transportation - Automation. 2. Journey to work. 3. Traffic surveys. I. U.S. Bureau of Public Roads. II. Title.

Transportation - Automation.

388
G25n

General Motors Corp.
New systems implementation study, final study. Prepared for the U.S. Dept. of Housing and Urban Development, Urban Transportation Administration, by E.T. Canty and others. [Detroit] 1968.
3v. (Its Research publication GMR-710B)
Contents: v.1. Summary and conclusions.-- v.2. Planning and evaluation methods.--v.3. Case studies.
On cover: Study in new systems of Urban Transportation.
1. Transportation. 2. Transportation - Research. 3. Transportation - Automation.
(Cont'd on next card)

Transportation - Automation.

388
K22

Keefer, Louis E. Urban travel patterns for airports, shopping centers, and industrial plants...1966.   (Card 2)

1. Traffic. 2. Journey to work. 3. Transportation - Automation. 4. Land use. I. Highway Research Board. II. American Association of State Highway Officials. IV. Title.

Transportation - Automation.

388
:538.56
F42

Fichter, Donn.
Individualized automatic transit and the city. Providence, 1964.
162p.

1. Transportation - Automation. 2. Streets. 3. Journey to work. 4. City planning. I. Title.

Transportation - Automation.

388
G25m

General Motors Corp.   New systems...1968.   (Card 2)

I. Canty, E.T. II. U.S. Dept. of Housing and Urban Development.
III. Title. IV. Title: Study in new systems of urban transportation.

TRANSPORTATION - AUTOMATION.

388
M15

Manheim, Marvin L
DODOTRANS I: A decision-oriented computer language for analysis of multimode transportation systems, by Marvin L. Manheim and Earl R. Ruiter, Transportation Systems Div., Dept. of Civil Engineering, Massachusetts Institute of Technology, Cambridge, Mass. [n.p.] [1969?]
58p.
For presentation to the 49th annual meeting, Highway Research Board, Wash., D.C., Jan., 1970.
1. Transportation - Automation. I. Ruiter, Earl R., jt. au. II. Highway Research Board.   III. Title.

Transportation - Automation.

388
G25an

General Electric Co. (Transportation Systems Div.)
Analysis and requirements of electronic command and control systems. Prepared for Urban Transportation Administration, Dept. of Housing and Urban Development, Erie, Pa., Marketing Operation, General Electric Co., Transportation Systems Div., 1967.
114p.
1. Transportation. 2. Journey to work. 3. Transportation - Automation. I. U.S. Dept. of Housing and Urban Development. II. Title.

Transportation - Automation.

388
G25s

General Research Corp.
Systems analysis of urban transportation. Prepared for the U.S. Dept. of Housing and Urban Development. Santa Barbara, Calif., 1968.
4v.   (R-777)
On cover: Study in new systems of urban transportation.
Contents: v.1. Summary. v.2. Cases for study.-- v.3. Network flow analyses. -- v.4. Supporting analyses.
1. Transportation. 2. Transportation - Research. 3. Journey to work. 4. Transportation - Automation. I. U.S. Dept. of Housing and Urban Development.
(Cont'd on next card)

Transportation - Automation.

388
:538.56
M17

Martin, Brian V
Principles and techniques of predicting future demand for urban area transportation, by Brian V. Martin, Frederick W. Memmott and Alexander J. Bone. Cambridge, Massachusetts Institute of Technology Press, 1965.
214p.   (Massachusetts Institute of Technology. Report no.3)
Bibliography: p. B.1-B.8.

1. Transportation - Automation. 2. Journey to work. 3. Traffic - Social effect. I. Title. II. Memmott, Frederick W. III. Bone, Alexander J.

TRANSPORTATION - AUTOMATION.

388
G25g

General Electric Co.
GE-400 series transportation program. Phoenix, Ariz., General Electric, Computer Dept., 1966.
62p.

1. Transportation - Automation.
2. Materials handling.

Transportation - Automation.

388
G25s

General Research Corp.   Systems analysis... 1968.   (Card 2)

II. Title. III. Title: Study in new systems of urban transportation.

Transportation - Automation.

388
(74)
M17

Massachusetts Institute of Technology.
The glideway system; a high-speed ground transportation system in the northeastern corridor of the United States. Cambridge, M.I.T. Press, 1966.
414p. (M.I.T. report no. 6)
"Designed as an interdepartmental student project in systems engineering at the Massachusetts Institute of Technology in the spring term, 1965."
Bibliography: p. 333-410.

1. Transportation - Northeastern States. 2. Electricity. 3. Transportation - Automation. I. Title.

Transportation - Automation.

388
G25st

General Electric Co. (Transportation Systems Div.)
A study of command control systems for urban transportation. Prepared for Urban Transportation Administration, Dept. of Housing and Urban Development, Wash. D.C., Erie, Pa., Transportation Equipment Projects and Marketing Operation, General Electric Co., Transportation Systems Div., 1968.
360p.
H.W. Merritt, Director.
On cover: Study in new systems of urban transportation.

(Cont'd on next card)

TRANSPORTATION - AUTOMATION.

388
(71)
G74

Grimble (L.G.) & Associates.
Description of a guided automated individual transportation system. Prepared for the Canadian Council on Urban and Regional Research. Sponsored by the City of Regina. Edmonton, Alberta, 1968.
53p.
1. Transportation - Canada. 2. Transportation - Automation. I. Canadian Council on Urban and Regional Research. II. Title.

Transportation - Automation.

388
(74461)
M17

Massachusetts Institute of Technology.
Project Metran; an integrated, evolutionary transportation system for urban areas. Interdepartmental Student Project in Systems Engineering at the Massachusetts Institute of Technology, Spring 1966. Mark E. Henson, editor. Cambridge, Mass., M.I.T. Press, 1966.
262p.   (M.I.T. report no. 8)

1. Transportation - Boston. 2. Transportation - Automation. 3. Engineering. 4. Journey to work. I. Henson, Mark E., ed.   II. Title.

388
M17c

TRANSPORTATION - AUTOMATION.
Massachusetts Institute of Technology, Urban Systems Laboratory.
CARS (Computer aided routing system); a prototype dial-a-bus system. Cambridge, Mass., 1969.
278p. (Its R69-53)
U.S. Mass Transportation Demonstration Grant Program.
HUD Mass.-MTD-5.

1. Transportation - Automation. 2. Journey to work. I. Title. II. U.S. Mass Transportation Demonstration Grant Program.

388
:538.56
S61

Transportation - Automation.
Space/Aeronautics.
Megalopolis transportation: Attacking the systems problem, by William S. Beller [and] High-speed ground transportation, by Frank Leary. New York, 1967.
31p.

Reprinted from Space/Aeronautics, Sept. 1967.

1. Transportation - Automation. I. Beller, William S. Attacking the systems problem. II. Leary, Frank. High-speed ground transportation. III. Title.

388
:538.56
V66ur

TRANSPORTATION - AUTOMATION.
Voorhees (Alan M.) and Associates.
Urban mass transit planning project. IBM System/360 computer programs general information manual. Prepared for Dept. of Housing and Urban Development. McLean, Va., 1968.
v.a. (Technical report no. 6)
1. Transportation - Automation. 2. Journey to work. I. U.S. Dept. of Housing and Urban Development. II. Title.

388
(774)
M62

Transportation - Automation.
Michigan. State Resource Planning Program.
Transportation: predictive procedures. Summary report. [Prepared in] cooperation with the Michigan Dept. of Commerce and others. Lansing, Mich., 1966.
38p. (Michigan. Dept. of Commerce. State Resource Planning Program. Technical report no. 9)
U.S. Dept. of Housing and Urban Development. UPAP.
1. Transportation - Michigan. 2. Transportation - Automation. I. Title. II. U.S. HUD-UPAP. Michigan.

388
(778781)
867

Transportation - Automation.
Springfield, Mo. Metropolitan Area Planning Dept.
Methods and procedures for tabulation of basic data for street, system analysis in the Springfield metropolitan area by key-sort data processing system, 1964. Springfield, Mo., 1964.
14p.
U.S. Urban Renewal Adm. UPAP.
Cover title: Springfield transportation study street and structure evaluation.

(Cont'd on next card)

388
:538.56
V66
v.1

Transportation - Automation.
Voorhees (Alan M.) and Associates.
Urban mass transit planning project.
Vol. 1. IBM 7090/94 computer programs general information manual. Prepared for Dept. of Housing and Urban Development. McLean, Va., 1967.
71p. (Technical report no. 3, vol. 1)
1. Transportation - Automation. 2. Journey to work. I. U.S. Dept. of Housing and Urban Development. II. Title.

388
M42s

Transportation - Automation.
Midler, J L
A stochastic dynamic multimode transportation model. Prepared for United States Air Force Project Rand. Santa, Monica, Calif., Rand Corp., 1967.
31p. (Rand Corp. Memo. RM-5250-PR AD 655 344)
1. Transportation. 2. Transportation - Automation. I. Rand Corp. II. Title.

388
(778781)
S67

Springfield, Mo. Metropolitan Area Planning Dept. Methods and procedures for tabulation of basic data for street...1964. (Card 2)

1. Transportation - Springfield, Mo.
2. Streets - Springfield, Mo. 3. Transportation - Automation. I. U.S. URA-UPAP. Springfield, Mo.

388
:538.56
V66
v.2

Transportation - Automation.
Voorhees (Alan M.) & Associates.
Urban mass transit planning project. Vol. 2. IBM 7090/94 computer programs users' reference manual. Prepared for Dept. of Housing and Urban Development. McLean, Va., 1967.
121p. (Technical report no. 3, v.2)
1. Transportation - Automation.
2. Journey to work. 3. Library science - Automation. I. U.S. Dept. of Housing and Urban Development. II. Title.

388
075

Transportation - Automation.
Orlando, Martin.
Technical and managerial capabilities. A summary. New York, Martin-Marietta, Corp. [1967?]
11p. (Martin-Marietta Corp. OR 3630)
1. Transportation. 2. Transportation - Automation. 3. Journey to work. I. Martin-Marietta Corp. II. Title.

388
S71fu

Transportation - Automation.
Stanford Research Institute.
Future Urban Transportation systems: impacts on urban life and form. Final report I, by Clark Henderson and others. Final report II, by Robert A. Burco and David A. Curry. Prepared for Urban Transportation Administration, Dept. of Housing and Urban Development, Wash., D.C., Menlo Park, Claif., 1968.
2v.
On cover: Study in new systems of urban transportation.
1. Transportation. 2. Journey to work. (Cont'd on next card)

388
:538.56
V66u

TRANSPORTATION - AUTOMATION.
Voorhees (Alan M.) and Associates.
Urban mass transit planning project. Computer program specifications. [Prepared] for Dept. of Housing and Urban Development. McLean, Va., 1966.
1v. (Technical report no.2)

1. Transportation - Automation. 2. Journey to work. I. U.S. Dept. of Housing and Urban Development. II. Title.

711.73
(764)
P17

Transportation - Automation.
Park, Ross A
A computer technique for perspective plotting of roadways, by Ross A. Park and Neilon J. Rowan. Sponsored by the Texas Highway Dept. in cooperation with the U.S. Dept. of Transportation, Federal Highway Administration, Bureau of Public Roads. College Station, Tex., Texas Transportation Institute, Texas A & M University, 1967.
27p. (Texas Transportation Institute. Research report number 19-3; Channelization research study number 2-8-60-19) (Cont'd on next card)

388
S71fu

Stanford Research Institute. Future Urban Transportation systems...1968. (Card 2)

3. Transportation - Automation. I. Henderson, Calrk. II. Burco, Robert A. III. Curry, David A. IV. U.S. Dept. of Housing and Urban Development. V. Title. VI. Title: Study in new systems of urban transportation.

388
:538.56
W27

Transportation - Automation.
West Virginia. University. College of Engineering.
The development of a mathematical model for optimizing the assignment of men and machine "run-cutting" in public transit, under the direction of Samy E.G. Elias. Morgentown, W.Va., 1966.
62p. (Its Series 67, no. 3-5. Research bulletin no. 81)
U.S. Dept. of Housing and Urban Development. Mass Transportation Demonstration Grant Program. Final report.
(Cont'd on next card)

711.73
(764)
P17

Park, Ross A   A computer technique... 1967. (Card 2)

Distributed by U.S. Clearinghouse for Federal Scientific and Technical Information as PB 177535.
1. Highways - Texas. 2. Transportation-Automation. I. Rowan, Neilon J., jt. au. II. Texas Transportation Institute. III. Texas. Highway Dept. IV. Title.

388
:538.56
T36

Transportation-Automation.
Thomas, Edwin N
Further comments on the analysis of non-residential trip generation, by E.N. Thomas and others. Research supported by the U.S. Bureau of Public Roads, Urban Planning Div., Urban Development Branch. Evanston, Ill., Transportation Center, at Northwestern University, 1966.
131p.

1. Transportation-Automation. 2. Journey to work. I. Northwestern University. II. Title: Analysis of non-residential trip generation.

388
:538.56
W27

Transportation - Automation.
West Virginia. University. College of Engineering. The development of a mathematical model for optimizing the the assignment of men and machine "run-cutting" in public transit...1966. (Card 2)

1. Transportation - Automation. I. Elias, Samy E.G. II. Title. III. U.S. Dept. of Housing and Urban Development. Mass Transportation Demonstration Grant Program.

388
P21

Transportation - Automation.
Peat, Marwick, Livingston & Co., New York.
Projection of urban personal transportation demand. Prepared for the U.S. Dept. of Housing and Urban Development. New York, 1968.
72p.
At head of title: Study in new systems of urban transportation.
1. Transportation. 2. Journey to work. 3. Transportation - Automation. I. U.S. Dept. of Housing and Urban Development. II. Title. III. Title: Study in new systems of urban transportation.

388
P81pr

TRANSPORTATION - AUTOMATION.
U.S. Bureau of Public Roads.
Program documentation, urban transportation planning, system 360. Wash., 1970.
614p.

1. Transportation - Automation. I. Title. II. Title: Urban transportation planning.

388
W27s

Transportation - Automation.
Westinghouse Air Brake Co.
Study of evolutionary urban transportation. Organizations participating: Westinghouse Air Brake and others. Prepared for the U.S. Dept. of Housing and Urban Development. [Pittsburgh] 1968.
v. (v.1 - v.2. Appendices 1, 2, and 3. [and] v.3. Appendix 4)
At head of title: Study in new systems of urban transportation.
1. Transportation. 2. Transportation - Automation. 3. Journey to work. 4. Transportation - Statistics. (Cont'd on next card)

388
W27s
Westinghouse Air Brake Co.   Study of evolutionary urban transportation...1968.
(Card 2)

I. U.S. Dept. of Housing and Urban Development. II. Title. III. Title: Study in new systems of urban transportation.

711.3
(7526)
B15
NO.9
TRANSPORTATION - BALTIMORE.
BALTIMORE REGIONAL PLANNING COUNCIL.
A PROJECTION OF PLANNING FACTORS FOR LAND USE AND TRANSPORTATION.
BALTIMORE, MARYLAND STATE PLANNING DEPT., 1963.
1 V. (VARIOUS PAGINGS) (ITS TECHNICAL REPORT NO. 9)

REPORT FINANCED THROUGH A GRANT FROM THE URBAN RENEWAL ADMINISTRATION AUTHORIZED UNDER SECTION 701 OF THE HOUSING ACT OF 1954.

1. REGIONAL PLANNING - BALTIMORE.
(CONTINUED ON NEXT CARD)

Transportation - Baltimore.

388
(7526)
P17
Persons, Brinkerhoff, Quade and Douglas.
Baltimore area mass transportation study.
Phase 1, report: Long range study program.
Phase 2, report: Long-range program. [Prepared in cooperation with] Metropolitan Transit Authority of Maryland. Baltimore, 1964-65.
2 v.
U.S. Urban Renewal Adm. UPAP.

1. Transportation - Baltimore. I. U.S. URA-UPAP. Baltimore.

1642
TRANSPORTATION - AUTOMATION - ST. LOUIS, MO.
EAST-WEST GATEWAY COORDINATING COUNCIL.
COORDINATED LAND USE AND TRANSPORTATION PLANNING PROGRAMS, GENERALIZED DATA FLOW ANALYSIS, ST. LOUIS METROPOLITAN AREA.
ST. LOUIS, 1968.
UNPAGED. (HUD 701 REPORT)

1. LAND USE - AUTOMATION - ST. LOUIS, MO. 2. TRANSPORTATION - AUTOMATION - ST. LOUIS, MO. I. HUD. 701. ST. LOUIS, MO.

711.3
(7526)
B15
NO.9
BALTIMORE REGIONAL PLANNING COUNCIL. A PROJECTION ...1963.   (CARD 2)

2. LAND USE - BALTIMORE.
3. TRANSPORTATION - BALTIMORE.
I. U.S. URA-UPAP. BALTIMORE.

388
P21e
TRANSPORTATION - BALTIMORE.
Peat, Marwick, Livingston & Co.
Evaluation of a bus transit system in a selected urban area. [n.p.] 1969
142p.

Prepared for Bureau of Public Roads.

1. Transportation. 2. Transportation - Baltimore. 3. Journey to work. I. Title.

388
(7526)
B15b
TRANSPORTATION - BALTIMORE.
Baltimore. Dept. of Planning.
Baltimore; transportation: facilities and services. Baltimore, 1970.
52p.

1. Transportation - Baltimore. 2. Journey to work.

388
(7526)
B51
Transportation - Baltimore.
Blair and Stein Associates.
Socio-economic impacts of the proposed East-West and Southwest expressways interstate routes 70 N and 95 on the City of Baltimore, For the State of Maryland Roads Commission. [Baltimore] 1962.
16p.
Cover title: Impacts of the East-West and Southwest expressways on the City of Baltimore.

1. Transportation - Baltimore.
2. Highways - Baltimore - Economic effect.

388
P21s
TRANSPORTATION - BALTIMORE.
Peat, Marwick, and Livingston.
Sensitivity analysis of the evaluation of a bus transit system in a selected urban area. Prepared for Bureau of Public Roads. [n.p.] 1970.
62p.

1. Transportation. 2. Transportation - Baltimore. 3. Journey to work. I. Title.

388
(7526)
B15
Transportation - Baltimore.
Baltimore. Dept. of Transit and Traffic.
Progress report, 19

Baltimore, 19

folder   annual.

For complete information see main card.

1. Transportation - Baltimore.

Folio
388
(7526)
D15
Transportation - Baltimore.
Daniel, Mann, Johnson, and Mendenhall.
Baltimore region rapid transit system; feasibility and preliminary engineering. Prepared for the Mass Transit Steering Committee, Regional Planning Council. Baltimore, 1968.
116p.
U.S. Dept. of Housing and Urban Development. Mass Transportation Demonstration Grant Program.
1. Transportation - Baltimore. 2. Journey to work. I. Baltimore Regional Planning Council. II. U.S. Dept. of Housing and Urban Development.
(Cont'd on next card)

388
(7526)
M27
Transportation - Baltimore metropolitan area.
Metropolitan Transit Authority of Maryland.
Forecast; a special report on Baltimore's Bus Transit Improvement Program. Baltimore, [1962?]
11p.
U.S. Urban Renewal Adm. UPAP.

1. Transportation - Baltimore metropolitan area. 2. Baltimore's Bus Transit Improvement Program. 3. Journey to work. I. U.S. URA-UPAP. Baltimore.

711.3
(7526)
B15
no. 7
Transportation - Baltimore.
Baltimore Regional Planning Council.
Baltimore-Washington interregional study, land use and transportation. [In cooperation with] National Capital Regional Planning Council. [Baltimore] 1960.
130p. (Its Technical report no. 7)
U.S. Urban Renewal Adm. UPAP.
1. Metropolitan area planning - Baltimore. 2. Metropolitan area planning - District of Columbia. 3. Transportation - Baltimore. 4. Transportation - District of Columbia. I. U.S. National Capital Regional Planning Council. II. U.S. URA-UPAP. Baltimore-Washington area.

Folio
388
(7526)
D15
Daniel, Mann, Johnson, and Mendenhall.
Baltimore region rapid transit system...
1968.   (Card 2)

Mass Transportation Demonstration Grant Program. III. Title.

388
(7526)
P17o
Transportation - Baltimore metropolitan area.
Persons, Brinkerhoff, Quade and Douglas.
Operation giant step; high speed rail-and-bus transit system proposed for Baltimore metropolitan area. A report submitted to the Metropolitan Transit Authority of Maryland. Baltimore, 1965.
20p.
U.S. Urban Renewal Adm. UPAP.

1. Transportation - Baltimore metropolitan area. 2. Metropolitan area planning - Baltimore. I. Metropolitan Transit Authority of Maryland. II. Title: Rail-and-bus transit system proposed for Baltimore metropolitan area. III. U.S. URA-UPAP. Baltimore metropolitan area.

711.3
(7526)
B15
no.7-8
Transportation - Baltimore.
Baltimore Regional Planning Council.
Baltimore-Washington interregional study, land use and transportation. Summary. [In cooperation with] National Capital Regional Planning Council. Baltimore, 1960.
[12]p. (Its Technical report no. 7-8)
U.S. Urban Renewal Adm. UPAP.

1. Metropolitan area planning - Baltimore. 2. Metropolitan area planning - District of Columbia. 3. Transportation - District of Columbia. 4. Transportation - Baltimore. 5. Land use - Baltimore. 6. Land use - District of Columbia.
(Cont'd on next card)

388
(75271)
M27
TRANSPORTATION - BALTIMORE CO., MD.
The Metro Flyer; a suburban express bus service to downtown, Towson area, Baltimore County-Baltimore City, Maryland. Final report. Participating agencies: Metropolitan Transit Authority of Maryland, U.S. Dept. of Housing & Urban Development, the McMahon Transportation Co., inc. Baltimore, Metropolitan Transit Authority of Maryland, 1967.
29p.
U.S. Dept. of Housing and Urban Development. Mass Transportation Demonstration Grant Program.
1. Transportation - Baltimore Co., Md.
(Cont'd on next card)

388
(763181)
S54
TRANSPORTATION - BATON ROUGE, LOUISIANA.
Smith (Wilbur) and Associates.
Metropolitan area transportation study, Baton Rouge. Columbia, S.C., 1967-68.

3v.

1. Transportation - Baton Rouge, La. 2. Journey to work. 3. Traffic surveys - Baton Rouge, La. I. Title.

711.3
(7526)
B15
no.7-8
Baltimore Regional Planning Council.
Baltimore-Washington interregional study, land use and transportation...1960.   (Card 2)

I. U.S. National Capital Regional Planning Council. II. U.S. URA-UPAP. Baltimore - Washington area.

388
(75271)
M27
The Metro Flyer; a suburban express bus service...1967.   (Card 2)

2. Journey to work. I. Metropolitan Transit Authority of Maryland. II. U.S. HUD Mass Transportation Demonstration Grant Program.

385
(016)
A77c
Transportation - Bibliography.
Association of American Railroads.
Commuters and rapid transit; reference list, 1959-1960. Washington, Association of American Railroads, Bureau of Railway Economics Library, 1961.
11p.

1. Railroads - Bibl. 2. Journey to work - Bibl. 3. Transportation - Bibl.

Transportation - Bibliography.

388
(016)
A77
Association of American Railroads.
Rapid transit: a brief reference list by
place, August 23, 1960. Washington,
Association of American Railroads, Bureau
of Railway Economics Library, 1960.

1. Transportation - Bibl. 2. Railroads
- Bibl.

Transportation - Bibliography.

388
(016)
C15
no. 14
California. University. Institute of
Transportation and Traffic Engineering.
Planning and design of heliports.
Berkeley, Calif., 1959.
5p. (Its Library references no. 14)

1. Transportation - Bibliography.

Transportation - Bibliography.

388
(016)
C15
no.7
California. University. Institute of
Transportation and Traffic Engineering.
Selected references on mass transit.
Berkeley, Calif., 1957.
7p. (Its Library references no. 7)

1. Transportation - Bibliography.

Transportation - Bibliography.

388
(016)
B51
Blaisdell, Ruth F   comp.
Sources of information in transportation.
Compiled by Ruth F. Blaisdell, Ronald J.
Booser and others. Evanston, Northwestern
University Press, published for the
Transportation Center at Northwestern
University, 1964.
262p.

1. Transportation - Bibl. 2. Highways -
Bibl. I. Booser, Ronald J., jt. comp.
II. Northwestern   University.
Transportation   Center.

Transportation - Bibl.

388
(016)
C15
no. 6
California. University. Institute of
Transportation and Traffic Engineering.
Protection and control of airport approaches.
Berkeley, Calif., 1956.
4p. (Its Library references no. 6)

1. Transportation - Bibl.
2. Air transportation - Bibl.
3. Airports - Bibl.

Transportation - Bibl.

388
(016)
C15
no. 17
California. University. Institute of
Transportation and Traffic Engineering.
Selected references on mass transit. Rev.
ed. Berkeley, Calif., 1959.
11p. (Its Library references no. 17)

1. Transportation - Bibl.

Transportation - Bibl.

388
(016)
C15
no. 13
California. University. Institute of
Transportation and Traffic Engineering.
Air traffic trends; passenger and
cargo. Berkeley, Calif., 1958.
19p. (Its Library references no. 13)

1. Transportation - Bibl. 2. Air
transportation - Bibl.

Transportation - Bibl.

388
(016)
C15
no. 8
California. University. Institute of
Transportation and Traffic Engineering.
References concerning highway engineering
manpower needs. Berkeley, Calif., 1957.
10p. (Its Library references no. 8)

1. Transportation - Bibl. 2. Road
construction - Bibl.

Transportation - Bibliography.

388
(016)
C15
no.32
California. University. Institute of
Transportation and Traffic Engineering.
Selected references on mass transit.
[Berkeley, Calif.] 1966.
28p. (Its Library references no. 32)

1. Transportation - Bibl. I. Title.

Transportation - Bibliography.

388
(016)
C15
no. 3
California. University. Institute of
Transportation and Traffic Engineering.
Controlled-access highway facilities.
Berkeley, Calif., 1956.
19p. (Its Library references no. 3)

1. Transportation - Bibliography.
2. Highways - Bibliography.

Transportation - Bibliography.

388
(016)
C15
no. 12
California. University. Institute of
Transportation and Traffic Engineering.
Relationship of city planning and traffic engineering. Berkeley, Calif., 1958.
4p. (Its Library references no. 12)

1. Traffic - Bibliography. 2. City
planning - Bibliography. 3. Transportation -
Bibliography.

Transportation - Bibl.

388
(016)
C15s
California. University. Institute of
Transportation and Traffic Engineering.
Serials received by the Institute of
Transportation and Traffic Engineering
Library. [Berkeley, Calif.] 1961.
19p.

1.

1. Transportation - Bibl.

Transportation - Bibliography.

388
(016)
C15
no. 21
California. University. Institute of
Transportation and Traffic Engineering.
Highway transportation subject headings
used by the Institute of Transportation and
Traffic Engineering Library, Berkeley,
Calif., 1960.
127p. (Its Library references no. 21)

1. Transportation - Bibliography.
2. Cataloging.

Transportation - Bibliography.

388
(016)
C15
no. 1
California. University. Institute of
Transportation and Traffic Engineering.
Road system designation. Berkeley, Calif.,
1955.
4p. (Its Library references no. 1)

1. Transportation - Bibliography.
2. Highways - Bibliography.

Transportation - Bibl.

388
(016)
C15
no. 4
California. University. Institute of
Transportation and Traffic Engineering.
Some basic references on traffic
engineering. Berkeley, Calif., 1956.
11p. (Its Library references no. 4)

1. Transportation - Bibl.
2. Traffic - Bibl.

Transportation - Bibliography.

388
(016)
C15
no. 20
California. University. Institute of
Transportation and Traffic Engineering.
Information sources for a highway
transportation library, comp. by Beverly
Sickok. Berkeley, Calif., 1960.
5p. (Its Library references no. 20)

1. Transportation - Bibl. 2. Highways -
Bibl. I. Hickok, Beverly, comp.

Transportation - Bibliography.

388
(016)
C15
no. 71
California. University. Institute of
Transportation and Traffic Engineering.
Selected list of recent acquisitions of the
Transportation Library. Berkeley, Calif.,
1961.
25p. (Its Library references no. 71)

1. Transportation - Bibl.

Transportation - Bibl.

388
(016)
C15
no. 9
California. University. Institute of
Transportation and Traffic Engineering.
Some references on congestion and delay
on arterial highways. Berkeley, Calif.,
1957.
2p. (Its Library references no. 9)

1. Transportation - Bibl.
2. Highways - Bibl.

Transportation - Bibliography.

388
(016)
C15
no. 19
California. University. Institute of Transportation and Traffic Engineering.
Metropolitan area problems. Berkeley,
1959.
17p. (Its Library references no. 19)

1. Metropolitan areas - Bibliography. 2. Transportation - Bibliography.

Transportation - Bibl.

388
(016)
C15
no. 5
California. University. Institute of
Transportation and Traffic Engineering.
Selected list of references on air
transportation in the Institute of Transportation and Traffic Engineering Library. Berkeley,
Calif., 1956.
17p. (Its Library references no. 5)

1. Transportation - Bibl.
2. Air transportation - Bibl.

Transportation - Bibl.

388
(016)
C15
no. 16
California. University. Institute of
Transportation and Traffic Engineering.
Some references on traffic engineering.
Rev. ed. Berkeley, Calif., 1959.
26p. (Its Library references no. 16)

1. Transportation - Bibl.
2. Traffic - Bibl.

388
(016)
C15
no. 10

Transportation - Bibliography.
California. University. Institute of
Transportation and Traffic Engineering.
Terminal planning and design. Berkeley,
Calif., 1957.
8p. (Its Library references no. 10)

1. Transportation - Bibliography.
2. Architecture - Design. I. Title.

388
(016)
C15
no.28

Transportation - Bibliography.
Chase, Karen, comp.
A selected bibliography on air cushion
vehicles and ground effect machines. [Los
Angeles] Institute of Transportation and
Traffic Engineering, University of
California, 1965.
6p. (California. University. Insti-
tute of Transportation and Traffic Engineer-
ing. Library reference no. 28)

1. Transportation - Bibl. 2. Air transportation -
Bibl. I. California. University. Institute of
Transportation and Traffic Engineer-
ing. II. Title.

388
(016)
K52

TRANSPORTATION - BIBLIOGRAPHY.
Kleiber, Michael C
New and novel passenger transportation
systems: a list of selected references, by
Michael C. Kleiber and Lawrence L. Vance, Jr.
Berkeley, University of California, Institute of
Transportation and Traffic Engineering, 1971.
23p. (California. University. Institute of
Transportation and Traffic Engineering. Library
references no. 38)
1. Transportation - Bibl. 2. Journey to work -
Bibl. I. Vance, Lawrence L., Jr., jt. au.
II. California. University. Institute of
Transportation and Traffic Engineering.
III. Title.

388
(016)
C15
no. 2

Transportation - Bibliography.
California. University. Institute of
Transportation and Traffic Engineering.
Toll roads. Berkeley, Calif., 1955.
15p. (Its Library references no. 2)

1. Transportation - Bibliography.
I. Title.

711
(016)
C65
no. 98
& 99

TRANSPORTATION - BIBLIOGRAPHY.
Dickey, John W
Mass transit. [Blacksburg, Va.] Center for
Urban and Regional Studies, Virginia Polytechnic
Institute, 1969.
96p. (Council of Planning Librarians. Ex-
change bibliography no. 98 and 99)

1. Planning - Bibl. 2. Transportation - Bibl.
I. Virginia Polytechnic Institute. II. Title.
(Series: Council of Planning Librarians. Ex-
change bibliography no. 98 and 99)

388
(016)
M17

Transportation - Bibliography.
Massachusetts Institute of Technology.
Bibliography of high speed ground transport. Part 1 A of [Survey of technology
for high speed ground transport] Prepared
for the U.S. Dept. of Commerce. Cambridge,
Mass., 1965.
82p.

1. Transportation - Bibl. 2. Traffic
safety - Bibl. I. Title.

388
(016)
C15
no. 11

Transportation - Bibl.
California. University. Institute of
Transportation and Traffic Engineering.
Traffic safety. Berkeley, Calif., 1957.
14p. (Its Library references no. 11)

1. Transportation - Bibl.
2. Traffic safety - Bibl.

711
(016)
C65
no. 78

TRANSPORTATION - BIBLIOGRAPHY.
Dickey, John W
Passenger transportation planning and design.
[Blacksburg, Va.] Center for Urban and Regional
Studies, Virginia Polytechnic Institute, 1969.
16p. (Council of Planning Librarians. Ex-
change bibliography no. 78)
1. Planning - Bibl. 2. Transportation - Bibl.
I. Virginia Polytechnic Institute. II. Title.
(Series: Council of Planning Librarians. Ex-
change bibliography no. 78)

388
(016)
M27

Transportation - Bibliography.
Metcalf, Kenneth N
Transportation information sources. An
annotated guide to publications, agencies
and other data sources concerning air, rail,
water, road, and pipeline transportation.
Detroit, Gale Research Co., 1965.
307p. (Management information guide
8)
Series editor: Paul Wasserman.

1. Transportation - Bibl. 2. Associations -
Bibl. I. Wasserman, Paul, ed. (Series:
Management information guide 8)

388
(016)
C15
no.34

Transportation - Bibl.
California. University. Institute of
Transportation and Traffic Engineering.
Transportation statistical sources; select-
ed references. Berkeley, Calif., 1967.
17p. (Its Library references no. 34)

1. Transportation - Bibl. 2. Transportation
- Statistics. 3. Railroads - Bibl. I. Title.

711
(016)
C65
no. 80

TRANSPORTATION - BIBLIOGRAPHY.
Dickey, John W
Transportation system synthesis.
[Blacksburg, Va.] Center for Urban and
Regional Studies, Virginia Polytechnic
Institute, 1969.
17p. (Council of Planning Librarians.
Exchange bibliography no. 80)

1. Planning - Bibl. 2. Transportation -
Bibl. I. Virginia Polytechnic Institute.
II. Title. (Series: Council of Planning
Librarians. Exchange bibliography no. 80)

711
(016)
C65
no.40

Transportation - Bibliography.
Northwestern University. Transportation
Center. (Library)
Journey to work; selected references 1960-
67. [Evanston, Ill.] 1968.
8p. (Council of Planning Librarians.
Exchange bibliography no. 40)

1. Planning - Bibl. 2. Journey to work -
Bibl. 3. Transportation - Bibl. I. Title.
(Series: Council of Planning Librarians.
Exchange bibliography no. 40)

R
388
(016)
C15
no.33

Transportation - Bibliography.
California. University. Institute of
Transportation and Traffic Engineering.
Transportation trends and forecasts;
selected references. [Berkeley, Calif.] 1967.
21p. (Its Library reference no. 33)

1. Transportation - Bibl. 2. Air transportation - Bibl. 3. Railroads - Bibl. I. Title.

388
(016)
F71

Transportation - Bibliography.
Franklin Institute Research Laboratories.
Science Information Services.
A selected and annotated survey of the
literature on transportation. Status,
structure, characteristics, problems, and
proposed solutions. Compiled by Jacob
Grauman and others. Philadelphia, Franklin
Institute, 1968.
202p. (Its Bibliographic series no. 1)
1. Transportation - Bibl. I. Title.

388
(016)
N67ur

TRANSPORTATION - BIBLIOGRAPHY.
Northwestern University. Transportation Center
Library.
Urban transportation planning references; a
checklist for library collections. Evanston,
Ill., 1970.
25p.

1. Transportation - Bibl. 2. Journey to work -
Bibl. I. Title.

388
(016)
C15
no. 22

Transportation - Bibliography.
California. University. Institute of Transportation and Traffic Engineering.
Urban growth and development and city planning. Berkeley, 1960.
7p. (Its Library references no. 22)

1. Transportation - Bibliography. 2. City planning - Bibliography.

388
(016)
H 42

TRANSPORTATION - BIBLIOGRAPHY.
Hickok, Beverly, comp.
Selected reports concerning transportation
policy, financing and development in the United
States. Berkeley, Calif., Institute of Transportation and Traffic Engineering, University
of California, 1969.
14p. (California. University. Institute
of Transportation and Traffic Engineering.
Library references no. 36)
1. Transportation - Bibl. I. California.
University. Institute of Transportation
and Traffic Engineering. II. Title.

VF
388
(016)
N67

Transportation - Bibliography.
Northwestern University. Transportation
Center.
Publications 1960. Evanston, Ill., 1960.
[4]p.

1. Transportation - Bibliography.

388
(016)
C15
no. 18

Transportation - Bibl.
California. University. Institute of
Transportation and Traffic Engineering.
Urban transportation. Berkeley, Calif.,
1959.
7p. (Its Library references no. 18)

no. 18-1   -- --- Supplement. Berkeley, Calif., 1968.
5p.

1. Transportation - Bibl.

350
(016)
I57
no.1

Transportation - Bibliography.
Institute of Public Administration,
New York.
Urban standards bibliography, by
Rodman T. Davis. No. 1. Water supply,
transportation, housing and elementary
education. New York, 1964.
9p.

1. Public administration - Bibl.
2. Water-supply - Bibl. 3. Transportation
- Bibl. 4. Housing - Bibl. 5. Education
- Bibl. I. Davis, Rodman
T. II. Title.

VF
388
(016)
N67
1964

Transportation - Bibliography.
Northwestern University. Transportation
Center.
Publications of the Transportation
Center at Northwestern University. Evanston,
Ill., 1964.
[4]p.

1. Transportation - Bibl. 2. Northwestern
University. Transportation
Center - Publications.

388
(016)
N67r
Transportation - Bibliography.
Northwestern University. Transportation Center.
A reference guide to metropolitan transportation; an annotated bibliography. Evanston, Ill., 1964.
42p.

1. Transportation - Bibl.　I. Title.

388.015
T71
Transportation - Bibliography.
Transportation Association of America.
Transportation research; a survey of current and potential transportation research projects. 3d ed. Washington, Research Staff of the Transportation Association of America, 1962.
50p.

1. Transportation - Research.
2. Transportation - Bibl.

388
(016)
W65
Transportation - Bibl.
Wolfe, Roy I
An annotated bibliography of the geography of transportation, by Roy I. Wolfe and Beverly Hickok. Berkeley, University of California, Institute of Transportation and Traffic Engineering, 1961.
61p.　(Information circular no. 29)

1. Transportation - Bibl.　2. Economic geography - Bibl.　I. Hickok, Beverly, jt. au.　II. California.　University.　Institute of Transportation and Traffic Engineering.

388
(016)
N 67u
TRANSPORTATION - BIBL.
Northwestern University. Transportation Center.
Urban transportation developments outside the United States; a bibliography prepared by the Transportation Center Library, Northwestern University, Evanston, 1970.
37p.

1. Transportation - Bibl.　2. Journey to work - Bibl.　I. Title.

R
388
(016)
C25
Transportation - Bibliography.
U.S. Bureau of the Census.
1963 census of transportation. Publication program. Washington, 19

v.　(Its Publication program no.

For complete information see main card.

1. Transportation - Bibl.　2. Census - Transportation.　3. U.S. Bureau of the Census - Publications.

388
(74776)
N28
Transportation - Binghamton, N.Y., metropolitan area.
New York. Dept. of Public Works.
A prospectus for the Binghamton Metropolitan Transportation Study. New York, 1963.
26p.

U.S.　Urban Renewal Adm.　UPAP.

1. Transportation - Binghamton, N.Y., metropolitan area.　I. Title: Binghamton, N.Y., Metropolitan Transportation Study.　II. U.S. URA-UPAP. Binghamton, N.Y.

VF
711.4
(016)
P34
Transportation - Bibliography.
Philadelphia.　Free Library.
A route through megalopolis.　A bibliography　Philadelphia, 1965.
12 p.

1. City planning - Bibl.　2. Urban renewal - Bibl.　3. Transportation - Bibl.　4. Films - Bibl.　I. Title.

388
(016)
L41
TRANSPORTATION - BIBLIOGRAPHY.
U.S. LIBRARY OF CONGRESS. LEGISLATIVE REFERENCE SERVICE.
CURRENT DEVELOPMENT IN URBAN MASS TRANSPORTATION TECHNOLOGY, SELECTED REFERENCES, 1950-1960, BY CATHERINE S. CORRY.　WASHINGTON, 1960.
35L.

1. TRANSPORTATION - BIBLIOGRAPHY.
2. TRAFFIC - BIBLIOGRAPHY.　I. CORRY, CATHERINE S　II. TITLE.

6046
TRANSPORTATION - BLACK HAWK CO., IOWA.
BLACK HAWK CO., IOWA.　METROPOLITAN PLANNING COMMISSION.
WATERLOO METROPOLITAN AREA TRANSPORTATION STUDY. BY ALAN M. VOORHEES AND ASSOCIATES. WATERLOO, IOWA, 1968.
45P.　(HUD 701 REPORT)

1. TRANSPORTATION - BLACK HAWK CO., IOWA.　2. TRANSPORTATION - WATERLOO, IOWA.　I. VOORHEES (ALAN M.) AND ASSOCIATES.　II. HUD. 701. BLACK HAWK CO., IOWA.　III. HUD. 701. WATERLOO, IOWA.

711
(016)
C65
no. 61
TRANSPORTATION - BIBLIOGRAPHY.
Robbins, Jane B
Access to airports: selected references. [Evanston, Ill.] Transportation Center Library at Northwestern University, 1968.
21p. (Council of Planning Librarians. Exchange bibliography no. 61)

1. Planning - Bibl. 2. Airports - Bibl.
3. Transportation - Bibl.　I. Northwestern University. Transportation Center. (Library)　II. Title. (Series: Council of Planning Librarians. Exchange bibliography no. 61)

388
(016)
758
Transportation - Bibliography.
U.S. Dept. of Housing and Urban Development. Library.
Urban public transportation: selected references. Washington, For sale by the Supt. of Documents, Govt. Print. Off., 1966.
20p.　(HUD MP-3)

1. Transportation - Bibl.　2. Journey to work.　I. Title.

6118
TRANSPORTATION - BLYTHEVILLE, ARK.
BLYTHEVILLE, ARK. CITY PLANNING COMMISSION.
MASS TRANSPORTATION STUDY FOR BLYTHEVILLE, ARK. PREPARED BY CITY PLANNING DIVISION, UNIVERSITY OF ARKANSAS. FAYETTEVILLE, ARK., 1966.
20L.　(HUD 701 REPORT)

1. TRANSPORTATION - BLYTHEVILLE, ARK.
I. ARKANSAS. UNIVERSITY. CITY PLANNING DIV.　II. HUD. 701. BLYTHEVILLE, ARK.

711
(016)
C65
no.218
TRANSPORTATION - BIBLIOGRAPHY.
Sloss, George J
Environmental aspects of transportation planning. Pittsburgh, Environmental Planning and Design, 1971.
18p. (Council of Planning Librarians. Exchange bibliography no. 218)
1. Planning - Bibl. 2. Transportation - Bibl.
3. Man - Influence of environment - Bibl.
I. Environmental Planning and Design.　II. Title. (Series: Council of Planning Librarians. Exchange bibliography no. 218)

R
388
(016)
P81
Transportation - Bibliography.
U.S. Bureau of Public Roads.
List of publishers and prices of periodicals most frequently referred to by the U.S. Bureau of Public Roads Library in Highways: current literature; Urban transportation research and planning: current literature. Rev. to　　　[Washington, 19　]
p.

1. Transportation - Bibl.　2. Highways - Bibl. I. Title.

388
(74461)
B67
Transportation - Boston.
Boston College. College of Business Administration.
Transportation facts and public policy for downtown Boston. Boston, 1959.
42p. diagrs., maps. (Studies of urban transportation)

1. Transportation - Boston.

388
(016)
S54
Transportation - Bibliography.
Smith, Charles L
Bibliography on electric automobiles and related subjects. Berkeley, Calif., 1968.
[4]p.

1. Transportation - Bibl.
2. Electricity - Bibl.
3. Air pollution - Bibl.

711
(016)
C65
no. 65
TRANSPORTATION - BIBLIOGRAPHY.
Wheeler, James O
Research on the journey to work: introduction and bibliography. [East Lansing, Mich.] Dept. of Geography, Michigan State University, 1969.
21p. (Council of Planning Librarians. Exchange bibliography no. 65)
1. Planning - Bibl. 2. Journey to work - Bibl. 3. Transportation - Bibl.　I. Michigan. State University. Dept. of Geography.
II. Title. (Series: Council of Planning Librarians.　　　　Exchange bibliography no. 65)

388
(74461)
B67t
Transportation - Boston.
Boston College. College of Business Administration. (Seminar Research Bureau)
Travel in the Boston region 1959-1980. Boston, 1960.
3v. diagrs., maps, tables. (Studies in urban transportation)

1. Transportation - Boston.　2. Travel.

388
(016)
S97
Transportation - Bibliography.
Systems Analysis and Research Corp.
Trans-ocean transportation of high value packaged cargo. Bibliography. Prepared for the Under Secretary for Transportation, U.S. Dept. of Commerce, Wash., D.C. Cambridge, Mass., 1966.
64p.
Distributed by U.S. Clearinghouse for Federal Scientific and Technical Information. as Document PB 173 007
1. Transportation - Bibl.　I. U.S. Commerce.　　II. Title.

388
(016)
W45u
TRANSPORTATION - BIBLIOGRAPHY.
Willis, Dawn E
Urban mass transportation; a bibliography. Wash., Dept. of Transportation, Office of Administrative Operations, Library Services Div., 1971.
140p. (Bibliographic list no. 6)

1. Transportation - Bibl.　I. U.S. Dept. of Transportation. Library Services Div.
II. Title.

388
(74461)
C31
Transportation - Boston.
Charles River Associates.
An evaluation of free transit service. Prepared for Office of Economics, Assistant Secretary for Policy Development, Dept. of Transportation, Wash., D.C. Cambridge, Mass., 1968.
172p.
CFSTI PB 179 845.

1. Transportation - Boston. 2. Journey to work.　I. Title. II. U.S. Dept. of Transportation.

388
D65
TRANSPORTATION - BOSTON.
Domencich, Thomas A
Free transit; a Charles River Associates research study, by Thomas A. Domencich and Gerald Kraft. Lexington, Mass., Heath Lexington Books, 1970.
104p.

1. Transportation. 2. Transportation - Boston. I. Charles River Associates. II. Kraft, Gerald, jt. au. III. Title.

388
(74461)
P51
pt.1
Transportation - Boston.
Planning Services Group, Cambridge, Mass.
Boston regional survey. [Part 1.] A bibliography of planning studies of the Boston metropolitan region. Prepared for the Mass Transportation Commission, Commonwealth of Massachusetts. Cambridge, 1962.
75p.
U.S. Urban Renewal Adm. UPAP.
1. Transportation - Boston. 2. Metropolitan area planning - Boston - Bibl. I. Massachusetts. Mass Transportation Commission. II. Title. III. U.S. URA-UPAP.   Boston.

VF
388
(74461)
Q84
Transportation - Boston.
Quincy Taxpayers Association.
South Shore transit plan first step toward Greater Boston transit system, by George A. Yarrington, Quincy, Mass., 1959.
4p.   illus. (Tips on taxes, vol. 27, no. 1)

1. Transportation - Boston. I. Yarrington, George A.

388
(74461)
L28
Transportation - Boston.
Levin, Melvin R
Boston Regional Survey, by Melvin R. Levin and others for the Mass Transportation Commission, 1963.
214p.
U.S. Housing and Home Finance Agency. Mass Transportation Demonstration Grant Program.
Planning Services Group, Cambridge, Mass., Consultants. (Cont'd on next card)

388
(74461)
P51
Pt.2
Ch.1
Transportation - Boston.
Planning Services Group, Cambridge, Mass.
Boston regional survey. Part 2. Regional overview: Ch. 1. Regional population trends. Prepared for the Mass Transportation Commission, Commonwealth of Massachusetts. Cambridge, 1962.
62p.
U.S. Urban Renewal Adm. UPAP.
1. Transportation - Boston. 2. Population - Boston. I. Massachusetts. Mass Transportation Commission. II. Title. III. U.S.   URA-UPAP. Boston.

388
(788631)
B21
Transportation - Boulder, Colo.
Bean (Trafton) and Associates.
Traffic, transportation and parking, City of Boulder, Colorado. Prepared under contract for the Colorado State Planning Div. [Denver] 1964.
71p.
U.S. Urban Renewal Adm. UPAP.
1. Traffic - Boulder, Colo 2. Parking - Boulder, Colo. 3. Transportation - Boulder, Colo. I. U.S. URA-UPAP. Boulder,   Colo.

388
(74461)
L28
Transportation - Boston.
Levin, Melvin R   Boston Regional Survey
...   (Card 2)

1. Transportation - Boston. 2. Economic base studies - Boston. 3. Land use - Boston. I. Massachusetts. Mass Transportation Comm. II. U.S. Housing and Home Finance Agency. Mass Transportation Demonstration Grant Program.

388
(74461)
P51
Pt.2
Ch.2
Transportation - Boston.
Planning Services Group, Cambridge, Mass.
The Boston regional survey. [Part 2. Regional] overview: ch. 2. Regional land land use patterns. Prepared for the Mass Transportation Commission, Commonwealth of Massachusetts. Cambridge, 1962.
55p.
U.S. Urban Renewal Adm. UPAP.
1. Transportation - Boston. 2. Land use - Boston. I. Massachusetts. Mass Transportation Commission. II. Title. III. U.S. URA-UPAP.   Boston.

388
(744)
B17
Transportation - Boston metropolitan area.
Barton-Aschman Associates.
North terminal area study, Boston, Cambridge, and Somerville, Massachusetts. A comprehensive plan of transportation facilities and related land development, by Barton-Aschman Associates and others. Evanston, Ill., 1962.
188p. [In cooperation with the] North Terminal Area Policy Committee.

1. Transportation - Boston metropolitan area. 2. Land use - Boston   metropolitan area

---

LAW
T
M175re
Transportation - Boston.
Massachusetts. Legislative Research Council.
Report relative to harbor regulation. Boston, 1965.
119p.   (Mass. Legislature. Senate. [Document] no. 1234)

1. Harbors - Boston. 2. Transportation - Boston. I. Title.

388
(74461)
P51
Pt.2
Ch.3
Transportation - Boston.
Planning Services Group, Cambridge, Mass.
Boston regional survey. [Part 2. Regional] overview: ch. 3. Economic base. Prepared for Mass Transportation Commission, Commonwealth of Massachusetts. Cambridge, 1962.
96p.
U.S. Urban Renewal Adm. UPAP.
1. Transportation - Boston. 2. Economic base studies - Boston. I. Massachusetts. Mass Transportation Commission. II. Title. III. U.S. URA-   UPAP. Boston.

388
(81)
L18
Transportation - Brazil.
Lave, Roy E   Jr.
A systems study of transportation in Northeast Brazil, by Roy E. Lave, Jr. and Donald W. Kyle. Stanford, Calif., Institute in Engineering-Economic Systems, Stanford University, 1966.
82p. (Stanford University. Institute in Engineering-Economic Systems. DPS-1)
Bibliography: p. 76-82.
1. Transportation - Brazil. 2. Railroads - Brazil. 3. Highways - Brazil. I. Kyle, Donald W., jt. au. II. Stanford University. III. Title.

388
(74461)
M17r
Transportation - Boston.
Massachusetts. Mass Transportation Commission.
Report on transit facilities utilizing Old Colony Line, Ashmont to South Braintree. Boston, Wright & Potter Print. Co., 1960.
25p. (Massachusetts. [General Court, 1959] House [of Representatives. Documents] no. 2600)

1. Transportation - Boston.

388
(74461)
P51
Pt.3
Ch.4
Transportation - Boston.
Planning Services Group, Cambridge, Mass.
Boston regional survey. Part 3. Transportation inventory: ch. 4. Highways. Prepared for the Mass Transportation Commission, Commonwealth of Massachusetts. Cambridge, 1962.
110p.
U.S. Urban Renewal Adm. UPAP.
1. Transportation - Boston. 2. Highways - Boston. I. Massachusetts. Mass Transportation Commission. II. Title. III. U.S. URA-UPAP.   Boston.

388
(711)
B74
Transportation - British Columbia.
British Columbia Research Council.
Rail-rapid transit for metropolitan Vancouver. Prepared for the Dept. of Highways, Province of British Columbia. Vancouver, B.C., 1962.
41p.

1. Transportation - British Columbia. 2. Journey to   work. I. British Columbia   Dept. of Highways. II. Title.

388
(74461)
M17
Transportation - Boston.
Massachusetts Institute of Technology.
Project Metran; an integrated, evolutionary transportation system for urban areas. Interdepartmental Student Project in Systems Engineering at the Massachusetts Institute of Technology, Spring term, 1966. Mark E. Hanson, editor. Cambridge, Mass., M.I.T. Press, 1966.
262p.   (M.I.T. report no. 8)

1. Transportation - Boston. 2. Transportation - Automation. 3. Engineering. 4. Journey   to work. I. Hanson, Mark E., ed.   II. Title.

388
(74461)
P51
Pt.3
Ch.5
Transportation - Boston.
Planning Services Group, Cambridge, Mass.
Boston regional survey. [Part 3.] Transportation inventory: ch. 5. Public transportation. Prepared for Mass Transportation Commission, Commonwealth of Massachusetts. Cambridge, 1962.
135p.
"First draft."
U.S. Urban Renewal Adm. UPAP.
1. Transportation - Boston. I. Massachusetts. Mass Transportation Commission. II. Title.   III. U.S. URA-UPAP. Boston.

388
(77132)
C52s
Transportation - Brooklyn.
Cleveland Transit System.
Southwest rapid transit extension to Brooklyn-Parma area; engineering and feasibility study. [Cleveland] 1963.
11p.
"A bus rapid transit supplementary report."

1. Transportation - Cleveland. 2. Journey to work.

711.4
(74461)
M29
Transportation - Boston.
Meyerson, Martin.
Boston: the job ahead, by Martin Meyerson and Edward C. Banfield. Cambridge, Mass., Harvard University Press, 1966.
121p.   (Publications of the Joint Center for Urban Studies)

1. City planning - Boston. 2. Metropolitan area planning - Boston. 3. Housing - Boston. 4. Harbors - Boston. 5. Landscape architecture - Boston. 6. Transportation - Boston. I. Banfield, Edward C., jt. au. II. Joint   Center for Urban Studies.   III. Title.

VF
388
(74461)
P56
Transportation - Boston.
Plotkin, A   B
The crisis in greater Boston's public transportation. Boston, 1964.
30p.
"A Boston Globe reprint."

1. Transportation - Boston.

711.73
(74884)
F19
Transportation - Brownsville, Pa.
Fayette County, Pa. Planning and Zoning Commission.
Brownsville, a report on major streets, parking, and transportation. Uniontown, Pa., 1959.
35, 9p.
U.S. Urban Renewal Adm. UPAP.
1. Street planning - Brownsville, Pa. 2. Transportation - Brownsville, Pa. I. U.S. URA-   UPAP. Brownsville, Pa.

388
(74797)
N67
TRANSPORTATION - BUFFALO.
Notess, Charles B
Suburbanization of industry, residential segregation, and access to employment opportunities; preliminary report, by Charles B. Notess and Robert E. Paaswell. Buffalo, Dept. of Civil Engineering, State University of New York at Buffalo, 1969.
1v.
Cover title: The mobility of inner city residents; a preliminary report.
Sponsor: New York State Science and Technology Foundation.
(Cont'd on next card)

388
(794)
M27
Transportation - California.
Metzger, William L
An analysis of intercity passenger traffic movement within the California corridor through 1980. Final report. Prepared by William L. Metzger and Howard R. Ross. South Pasadena, Calif., Southern California Laboratories of Stanford Research Institute, 1966.
1 v.
1. Transportation - California. 2. Traffic - California. I. Ross, Howard R., jt. au. II. Stanford Research Institute. III. Title.

388
(016)
C15
no.35
TRANSPORTATION - CALIF. - BIBLIOGRAPHY.
California. University. Institute of Transportation and Traffic Engineering.
Selected reports concerning transportation policy, financing and development in the state of California, compiled by Beverly Hickok. Berkeley, Calif., 1969.
20p. (Its Library references no. 35)

1. Transportation - Calif. - Bibl. I. Hickok, Beverly, comp. II. Title.

388
(74797)
N67
Notess, Charles B   Suburbanization of industry...1969.   (Card 2)

1. Transportation - Buffalo. 2. Journey to work. 3. Employment - Minority groups. I. Paaswell, Robert E., jt. au. II. New York (State) University, Buffalo. Dept. of Civil Engineering. III. New York (State) Science and Technology Foundation. IV. Title.

388
(794)
N67
Transportation - Calif.
North American Aviation. (Los Angeles Div.)
California integrated transportation study. Los Angeles, 1965.
5v. (NA-65-650)

1. Transportation - Calif.

388
(74988)
C68
Transportation - Camden, N.J.
Coverdale and Colpitts.
Camden rapid transit; route alternative study for the Greater Camden Movement. New York, 1962.
14p. Map in pocket on back cover.

1. Transportation - Camden, N.J. I. Greater Camden (N.J.) Movement.

629.136
C15r
Transportation - Calif.
California. Legislature. Assembly. Interim Committee on Transportation and Commerce.
Regional operation of airports and development of heliports, Nov. 22-23, 1965, San Francisco. Sacramento, Calif., 1965.
145p.

1. Airports. 2. Heliports. 3. Transportation - Calif. I. Title.

388
(794)
S68n
Transportation - California.
Southern California Rapid Transit District.
1967 SCRTD survey; a special bulletin on the operations of the Southern California Rapid Transit District. Venice, Calif., United Transit Boosters; Upper Montclair, N.J., Motor Bus Society, inc., 1967.
44p.

1. Transportation - Calif. I. Title.

388
(74988)
C68g
Transportation - Camden, N.J.
Coverdale and Colpitts.
Greater Camden Movement, transportation proposals. New York, 1962.
15p.

1. Transportation - Camden, N.J. 2. Transportation - Philadelphia. I. Greater Camden (N.J.) Movement.

388
(794)
C15
Transportation - California.
California. Legislature. Assembly. Interim Committee on Transportation and Commerce.
Southern California rapid transit financing. Los Angeles, 1965.
99p.

1. Transportation - California. 2. Journey to work. 3. Transportation - Finance. I. Title.

388
(794)
S68
Transportation - Calif.
Southern California Research Council.
An approach to an orderly and efficient transportation system for the Southern California metropolis. A study. Los Angeles, 1960.
48p. (SCRC Publications. Report no. 8)

1. Transportation - Calif. 2. Journey to work. 3. Automation. I. Title: Transportation system for the Southern California metropolis.

R
711.4
(71
:016)
C15
Transportation - Canada.
Canadian Council on Urban and Regional Research.
Urban and regional references; 1945-1962. Ottawa [1962?]
.... Supplement 1965-66.
103p.

1. City growth - Canada. 2. Population - Canada. 3. Economics - Canada. 4. Transportation - Canada. 5. Political science - Canada. 6. Public administration - Canada. I. Title.

388
(794)
E53
Transportation - California.
Engelbert, Ernest A   ed.
Transportation and metropolitan planning. Berkeley, California Chapter of the American Institute of Planners, University Extension, University of California, 1956.
81p. (Publication of the Southern California Planning Institute Publication. vol. 3)

1. Transportation - California. 2. Metropolitan area planning - California. I. American Institute of Planners. California Chapter. II. Southern California Planning Institute Publication. vol. 3

711.33
(794
:347)
S61
TRANSPORTATION - CALIF.
Spangle (William E.) and Associates.
An analysis of selected California laws affecting urban development, by William E. Spangle and Harold F. Wise, with Paul Sedway. Preliminary technical report. Menlo Park, Calif., 1965.
1v.
Bibliography: p. B-1 - B-4.
U.S. Housing and Home Finance Agency. UPAP.
1. State planning legislation - Calif. 2. Land use - Calif. 3. Transportation - Calif. I. U.S. HHFA-UP   AP. Calif. II. Title.

388
(71)
C15
Transportation - Canada.
Canadian Federation of Mayors and Municipalities.
Urban transportation; papers, summaries and reviews for the regional study groups and the first Canadian Urban Transportation Conference, 9-12 Feb., 1969, Toronto. Compiled and edited by John Steel. [Montreal] 1969.
397p.
1. Transportation - Canada. 2. Canada - Transportation. 3. Journey to work. I. Steel, John, ed. II. Canadian Urban Transportation Conference, 1st, Toronto, 1969. III. Title.

388
(794)
F17
Transportation - California.
Farmer, Richard N
Technical studies in transportation: transportation cost finding. Los Angeles, Dept. of Engineering, University of California, 1963.
47p. (California. University. University at Los Angeles, Dept. of Engineering. Report no. 63-65)

1. Transportation - Calif. I. California. University. University at Los Angeles.

388
(794)
T71
Transportation - Calif.
Transportation Association of Southern California.
LARTS [Los Angeles Regional Transportation Study] 1980 progress report. Los Angeles [1967?]
46p.
"Published in cooperation with the Dept. of Transportation, Federal Highway Administration, Bureau of Public Roads."
1. Transportation - Calif. 2. Land use - Calif. 3. Population - Calif. 4. Employment - Calif. I. U.S. Bureau of Public Roads. II. Los Angeles Regional Transportation Study. III. Title.

388
(71)
E22
Transportation - Canada.
Edens, H   J
Modal split and peak period model as applied in Ottawa Hull area transportation study (OHATS) Prepared for January 17th, 1966 meeting of Highway Research Board, Origin and Destination Committee Session, Chicago. DeLeuw, Cather & Company, 1966?
19p.

1. Transportation - Canada. 2. Journey to work. I. Highway Research Board. II. DeLeuw, Cather & Company. III. Title.

388
(794)
L47
Transportation - Calif.
Litton Industries. Economic Development Div.
Proposal to the Div. of Highways, Dept. of Public Works, State of California for a Work Program to design and develop specifications for an integrated study of transportation in California. Beverly Hills, Calif., 1964.
1v.
Cover title: Toward a systems approach for a California integrated transportation network.
1. Transportation - Calif. 2. Journey to work. 3. Transportation - Finance. I. California. Dept. of Public Works. II. Title. III. Title: Toward a systems transportation network.

388
(794)
T71r
TRANSPORTATION - CALIF.
Transportation Association of Southern California.
Report, 19

Los Angeles, 19
v. annual.
For Library holdings see main entry.

1. Transportation - Calif.

VF
388
(71)
G17
Transportation - Canada.
Gardiner, Frederick G
Q.C. "Sic Transit Gloria Mundi." Rapid transit, is it a thing of the past or is it our only hope for the future? An address... to the annual meeting Canadian Transit Association, on Tuesday, June 10th, 1958. [Toronto, Metropolitan Toronto Council] 1958. pamphlet.

1. Transportation - Canada.

388
(71)
G74

TRANSPORTATION - CANADA.
Grimble (L.G.) & Associates.
Description of a guided automated individual transportation system. Prepared for the Canadian Council on Urban and Regional Research. Sponsored by the City of Regina. Edmonton, Alberta, 1968.
53p.
1. Transportation - Canada. 2. Transportation - Automation. I. Canadian Council on Urban and Regional Research. II. Title.

388
(713541)
T67g

TRANSPORTATION - CANADA - TORONTO.
Metropolitan Toronto and Region Transportation Study.
Growth and travel, past and present; a study of the basic components of growth in the Toronto-centered region, and their relationship to travel characteristics and demand. Toronto, 1966.
94p.
On cover: First report of a series.
1. Transportation - Canada - Toronto. 2. Canada - Transportation. 3. Journey to work. I. Title.

711.729
(758725)
G26

Transportation - Chatham Co., Ga.
Georgia. State Highway Dept.
Chatham Urban Transportation Study. Savannah parking report. [Prepared] in cooperation with the U.S. Dept. of Commerce, Bureau of Public Roads and approved by the Technical Coordinating Committee. Savannah, 1965.
71p.
1. Parking - Savannah. 2. Transportation - Savannah. 3. Transportation - Chatham Co., Ga. 4. Chatham Urban Transportation Study. I. U.S. Bureau of Public Roads. III. Title.

388
(71)
L21

Transportation - Canada.
Lea (N.D.) & Associates.
Urban transportation developments in eleven Canadian metropolitan areas. Prepared for the Transportation Planning Committee of the Canadian Good Roads Association, Ottawa, 1966.
90p.
1. Transportation - Canada. 2. Metropolitan areas - Canada. I. Title.

388
(713541)
T67r

TRANSPORTATION - CANADA - TORONTO.
Toronto. Planning Board.
Report on the metropolitan Toronto transportation plan. Toronto, 1964.
82p.
1. Transportation - Canada - Toronto. 2. Canada - Transportation. 3. Journey to work. 4. Highways - Canada - Toronto. 5. Canada - Highways. I. Title: Metropolitan Toronto transportation plan.

388
(755521)
S54

TRANSPORTATION - CHESAPEAKE, VA.
Smith (Wilbur) and Associates.
Chesapeake Mass Transportation Demonstration Project. Final report. Prepared for City of Chesapeake, Va. Chesapeake, 1969.
73p.
U.S. Dept. of Housing and Urban Development Mass Transportation Demonstration Grant Program. VA-MTD-1.
1. Transportation - Chesapeake, Va. 2. Journey to work. I. U.S. Mass Transportation Demonstration Grant Program. Chesapeake, Va. II. Title.

388
(9)
N17

TRANSPORTATION - CANADA.
NATIONAL RESEARCH COUNCIL, CANADA. DIVISION OF BUILDING RESEARCH.
TRANSPORTATION AND ECONOMIC POTENTIAL IN THE ARCTIC, BY K.B. WOODS AND R.F. LEGGET. OTTAWA, 1960.
435-458P. (ITS DBR TECHNICAL PAPER NO. 113)
REPRINTED FROM TRAFFIC QUARTERLY, OCTOBER 1960.
1. TRANSPORTATION - ARCTIC AND ANTARCTIC. 2. TRANSPORTATION - ALASKA. 3. TRANSPORTATION - CANADA. I. WOODS, K.B. II. LEGGET, R.F.

711.73
(74008)
C16

Transportation - Cape May Co., N.J.
Cape May Co., N.J. Planning Board.
Highways and transportation. Cape May Court House, N.J., 1959.
134p. maps, tables.
U.S. Urban Renewal Administration, Urban Planning Assistance Program.
1. Highways - Cape May Co., N.J. 2. Transportation - Cape May Co., N.J. I. U.S. URA-UPAP. Cape May Co., N.J.

388
(77311)
A75r

Transportation - Chicago.
Arnold, Bion Joseph.
Recommendations and general plans for a comprehensive passenger subway system for the city of Chicago. Made and submitted to ... Member of the Committee on Local Transportation, of the City Council of the City of Chicago. [New York, McGraw, 1911.
75p.
1. Transportation - Chicago. I. Chicago. Committee on Local Transportation.

711.4
(71)
U71u

TRANSPORTATION - CANADA.
Urban Canada: problems and prospects. Research monograph[s prepared] for the Honourable R.K. Andras, Minister Responsible for Housing, Government of Canada. Ottawa, Central Mortgage and Housing Corp., 1971.
6v. (Research monographs no. 1-6)
Background research for Lithwick report.
Contents.-no. 1. Urban poverty, by N.H. Lithwick.-no. 2. Housing in Canada: market structure and policy performance, by L.B. Smith.-no. 3. The urban transport problem (Cont'd on next card)

388
(74742)
N28

New York (State) Dept. of Public Works.
A prospectus for a comprehensive transportation and regional development study in the Capital District. [Prepared] in cooperation with U.S. Dept. of Commerce, Bureau of Public Roads and Housing and Home Finance Agency. Albany, Upstate New York Transportation Studies, 1963.
36p.
1. Transportation - Capital District, N.Y. 2. Journey to work. 3. Metropolitan areas - Capital District, N.Y. I. U.S. Housing and Home Finance Agency. II. Title.

Transportation - Capital District, N.Y.

388
(77311)
A75

Transportation - Chicago.
Arnold, Bion Joseph.
Report on the engineering and operating features of the Chicago transportation problem submitted to the Committee on Local Transportation of the Chicago City Council. New York, McGraw, 1905.
316p.
1. Transportation - Chicago. I. Chicago. Committee on Local Transportation.

711.4
(71)
U71u

Urban Canada: problems and prospects...1971. (Card 2)
in Canada, 1970-2000, by D.J. Reynolds.-no. 4. The urban public economy, by W.I. Gillespie.-no. 5. The urban future, by A. Goracz and others.-no. 6. A survey of alternative urban policies, by L.D. Feldman and Associates.
1. City planning - Canada. 2. Sociology, Urban - Canada. 3. Housing - Canada. (Cont'd on next card)

Folio
388
(777621)
I68

Transportation - Cedar Rapids metropolitan area.
Iowa. State Highway Commission. (Div. of Planning)
Cedar Rapids metropolitan area; origin and destination, traffic report. Prepared in cooperation with U.S. Dept. of Commerce, Bureau of Public Roads. Cedar Rapids, Iowa, 1965.
145p.
1. Transportation - Cedar Rapids metropolitan area. 2. Journey to work. 3. Traffic surveys - Cedar Rapids, Iowa. I. U.S. Bureau of Public Roads. II. Title.

388
(77311)
B14p

TRANSPORTATION - CHICAGO.
Bailey, John A
A proposal for a regional transportation agency for the Chicago metropolitan area. Chicago, Center for Research in Urban Government, Loyola University, 1970.
20p. (Loyola University, Chicago. Study no. 14)
1. Transportation - Chicago. 2. Journey to work. I. Loyola University, Chicago. Center for Research in Urban Government. II. Title.

711.4
(71)
U71u

Urban Canada: problems and prospects...1971. (Card 3)
4. Poverty. 5. Transportation - Canada.
I. Lithwick, N. Harvey. Urban poverty. II. Smith, Lawrence B. Housing in Canada: market structure and policy performance. III. Reynolds, D.J. The urban transport problem in Canada, 1970-2000. IV. Gillespie, W. Irwin. The urban public economy. V. Goracz, A. The urban future. VI. Feldman (L.D.) and Associates. A survey of alternative urban policies.

388
(757911)
S54

Transportation - Charleston, South Carolina.
Smith (Wilbur) and Associates.
Charleston area transportation study. Travel demands and recommended transportation plan. Summary report. Prepared for South Carolina State Highway Dept. in cooperation with Charleston County Planning Board and U.S. Dept. of Transportation, Federal Highway Administration, Bureau of Public Roads. [New Haven] 1968.
20p.
1. Transportation - Charleston, S.C. 2. Journey to work. 3. Highways - Charleston, S.C. I. Charleston County, S.C. Planning Board. II. Title.

388
(77311)
B17

TRANSPORTATION - CHICAGO.
Barton-Aschman Associates.
High-accessibility corridors in the comprehensive plan of Chicago. Prepared for the Dept. of Development and Planning, Chicago. [Chicago] 1968.
78p.
Financed in part by U.S. Dept. of Housing and Urban Development, Renewal Assistance Administration.
1. Transportation - Chicago. 2. Journey to work. 3. Highways - Chicago. I. Chicago. Dept. of Development and Planning. II. U.S. Dept. of Housing and Urban Development. Renewal Assistance Administration. III. Title.

388
(71:083.41)
C15

Transportation - Canada - Statistics.
Canada. Dominion Bureau of Statistics.
Urban transit, 1960. Ottawa, Queen Printer and Controller of Stationery, 1961.
20p.
1. Transportation - Canada - Statistics.

388
(757911)
S54o

TRANSPORTATION - CHARLESTON, S.C.
Smith (Wilbur) and Associates.
Operation bus stop; feasibility study for Charleston-Columbia, S.C. Final report. Prepared for The Economic Development Administration. [n.p.] 1969.
144p.
CFSTI. PB 183 912.
1. Transportation - Charleston, S.C. 2. Transportation - Columbia, S.C. 3. Journey to work. I. Title.

711.585
(77311)
B17

Transportation - Chicago.
Barton-Aschman Associates.
Needs and opportunities for coordinating renewal and transportation improvement. A study prepared for the City of Chicago Community Renewal Program. Chicago, 1963.
124p.
U.S. Urban Renewal Adm. CRP.
1. Urban renewal - Chicago. 2. Transportation - Chicago. I. Chicago. Community Renewal Program. II. U.S. URA-CRP. Chicago.

388
(77311)
B27

Transportation - Chicago.

Berge, Stanley.
    Chicagoland's mass transportation dilemma.
Address delivered at meeting of the Rotary
Club of Chicago, December 2, 1958.
Chicago, Northwestern Univ., 1958.

1. Transportation - Chicago. I. Northwestern University.

388
(77311)
C342m

Transportation - Chicago.

Chicago Transit Authority.
    Metropolitan transit research, by
Werner W. Schroeder. Chicago, 1957.
403p.

1. Transportation - Chicago.
I. Schroeder, Werner W.

362
(77311)
M67r

Transportation - Chicago.

Morrill, Richard L
    Relationship between transportation
and hospital location and utilization.
Chicago, Regional Hospital Study, 1967.
    10p. (Chicago Regional Hospital Study.
Working paper # I.14)

1. Hospitals - Chicago. 2. Transportation - Chicago. I. Chicago Regional
Hospital Study. II. Title.

312(77311)
B72

Transportation - Chicago, Ill.

Breese, Gerald William.
    The daytime population of the central business district
of Chicago, with particular reference to the factor of transportation. [Chicago, Univ. of Chicago Press [1949]
    xxiii, 267 p. illus., maps (part fold.) 25 cm.
    "A publication of the Chicago Community Inventory."
    Bibliography: p. [247]-267.

2 [Ill.]
    1. Chicago—Population. 1. Chicago. University. Chicago Community Inventory. II. Title. 2. Transportation-Chicago, Ill.

HB3527.C4B7   312.9   49-10725*
Library of Congress   [5]

388
(77311)
C34r

Transportation - Chicago.

Chicago Transit Authority.
    Rapid transit cars. Series 2001-2180,
the air-conditioned fleet. Chicago, 1964.
12p.

1. Transportation - Chicago. 2. Journey
to work. I. Title.

388
(77311)
P17

Transportation - Chicago.

Parsons, Brinckerhoff, Quade and Douglas.
    Northwest Chicago corridor transportation
study. Engineering report. Chicago, 1962.
75p.

    Prepared in cooperation with the Chicago
and Northwestern Railway Co. and Chicago
Transit Authority.

1. Transportation - Chicago. I. Chicago
and Northwestern Railway Co. II. Chicago.
Transit Authority.

388
(77311)
B82

Transportation - Chicago.

Buck, Thomas.
    Skokie swift, the commuter's friend.
Chicago, Chicago Transit Authority, 1968.
65p. (Chicago Transit Authority.
Publication RP-x68222)
U.S. Dept. of Housing and Urban Development. Mass Transportation Demonstration
Grant Program.
    1. Transportation - Chicago. 2. Transportation - Skokie, Ill. 3. Journey to
work. I. Chicago Transit Authority.
II. Title. III. U.S. Dept. of Housing
and Urban Development. Mass Transportation Demonstration Grant Program.

388
(77311)
C34tr

TRANSPORTATION - CHICAGO.

Chicago Transit Authority.
    Transit planning study; Chicago central
area. Chicago, 1968.
    v.
    Bibliography: p. 191-192.
U.S. Dept. of Housing and Urban Development.
Mass Transportation Demonstration Grant Program. HUD project no. P-Ill-3254
(City of Chicago)
    1. Transportation - Chicago. 2. Journey
to work. I. Title. II. U.S. Mass Transportation Demonstration Grant Program.

388
(77311)
S68

Transportation - Chicago.

South Side Planning Board, Chicago.
    Employee transportation survey; a study
of the journey to work. Chicago, 1954.
30p.

1. Transportation - Chicago. 2. Journey
to work. I. Title.

388
(77311)
C34c

Transportation - Chicago.

Chicago. Dept. of City Planning.
    Coordinated transportation system for
Chicago area, mass transit. Preliminary.
[Prepared] in cooperation with Chicago
Transit Authority. Chicago, 1965.
19p.

1. Transportation - Chicago. I. Chicago
Transit Authority. II. Title.

388
(77311)
C65

Transportation - Chicago, Ill.

Commercial Club of Chicago. (Committee on
Chicago Harbor and Port Survey)
    The Harbor Plan of Chicago.
[Chicago] 1927.
    97 p. illus., maps, tables.

1. Transportation - Chicago, Ill.
2. Harbors.

388
(77311)
T15

TRANSPORTATION - CHICAGO.

Talvitie, Antti Petri.
    An econometric model for downtown work
trips. Chicago, Chicago Area Transportation
Study, 1971.
123p.

1. Transportation - Chicago. 2. Traffic
surveys - Chicago. I. Chicago Area Transportation Study. II. Title.

330
C34

Transportation - Chicago.

Chicago Area Transportation Study.
    Forecasting economic activity in the
Chicago region; a progress report (abstract),
by Irving J. Hoch. Chicago [1958]
12p. tables.

1. Economic forecasting. 2. Transportation
- Chicago. I. Hoch, Irving J

388
(77311)
K25

Transportation - Chicago, Ill.

Kelker, R F
    Report and recommendations on a physical
plan for a unified transportation system for
the City of Chicago; to the Committee on
Local Transportation of the City Council of the
City of Chicago. Chicago, Ill., 1923.
    175 p. / 17 plates. illus., charts, tables.

1. Transportation - Chicago, Ill. I.Chicago, Ill.-
City Council (Committee on Local Transportation).

388
(77311)
V47c

Transportation - Chicago.

Vise, Pierre de.
    Chicago at mid-century. The transportation
base; from portage to world port. Chicago,
Regional Hospital Study, 1967.
    12-74p. (Chicago Regional Hospital Study.
Working paper # II.3)

1. Transportation - Chicago. 2. City
growth - Chicago. I. Chicago Regional
Hospital Study. II. Title.

388
(77311)
C34u

TRANSPORTATION - CHICAGO.

Chicago Area Transportation Study.
    Updating the opportunity model for
continuing transportation planning.
Prepared by James P. Curry. Chicago,
1970.
    63p.
    Bibliography: p. 61-63.

1. Transportation - Chicago.
2. Journey to work. I. Curry, James
P. II. Title.

388
(77311)
L47

Transportation - Chicago.

Little, Arthur D
    Comparative economics of propane and
diesel buses; report to Chicago Transit
Authority. Chicago, 1960.
111p. (C-62924)

1. Transportation - Chicago.
I. Chicago Transit Authority.

388
(77311)
C34f

Transportation - Chicago metropolitan area.

Chicago Area Transportation Study.
    Final report. Vol. 1. Survey findings.
Vol. 2. Data projections. Vol. 3. Transportation plan. In cooperation with Bureau of
Public Roads. Chicago, 1962.
3 v.

1. Transportation - Chicago metropolitan
area.

388
(77311)
C34w

Transportation - Chicago.

Chicago Area Transportation Study.
    Work progress report, 19

Chicago,
    v. annual.

For complete information see main card.

1. Transportation - Chicago.

388
(77311)
M12

Transportation - Chicago.

McLean, Elizabeth J
    Traffic planning for urban renewal
projects in Chicago, Illinois. Prepared
for Institute of Traffic Engineers,
Committee 6-C. [Chicago] 1962.
10p.

1. Traffic - Chicago. 2. Transportation -
Chicago. I. Institute of Traffic Engineers.

388
(77311)
C34p

Transportation - Chicago Metropolitan Area.

Chicago Area Transportation Study.
    Planning and building expressways in
the Chicago Area; a brief description of
the governmental apparatus, by Eugene
Kramer. Chicago, 1958.
13p.

    In cooperation with U.S. Bureau of
Public Roads.

1. Transportation - Chicago Metropolitan Area. 2. Highways - Chicago
Metropolitan Area. I. Kramer, Eugene.

388
(77311)
I55

Transportation - Chicago metropolitan area.

Illinois. University.
A sector of a metropolis; a study of radial corridor development for the Chicago metropolitan region. A project by graduate students in architecture and city planning at the University of Illinois. Urbana, Ill., 1964.
1 v.

1. Transportation - Chicago metropolitan area. 2. Journey to work. 3. Metropolitan area planning - Chicago. I. Title.

388
(77132)
C52r

Transportation - Cleveland.

Cleveland. Transit Board.
Report, 19

Cleveland, 19
v.   annual.

For complete information see shelflist.

1. Transportation - Cleveland.
2. Highways - Cleveland.

388
(77157)
B17t

Transportation - Columbus, Ohio.

Battelle Memorial Institute.
Transit in Columbus; a summary report to Advisory Committee on Transit, April 16, 1968. Columbus, Ohio, 1968.
20p.

1. Transportation - Columbus, Ohio.
I. Title.

728.1
(83)
C34d

TRANSPORTATION - CHILE.

Chile. Ministerio de Vivienda y Urbanismo.
Direccion de planificacion del desarrollo urbano. Concepcion estudio pre-inversional de vivienda y desarrollo urbano. Primera etapa. [Santiago] 1968.
204p.

Appx. -- --- Anexos. [Santiago] 1968.
65p.

1. Housing - Chile. 2. Transportation - Chile. I. Title.

388
(77132)
C52

Transportation - Cleveland.

Cleveland. Transit System.
A modernization plan for the Cleveland Transit System. Cleveland,, 1944.
28p.

1. Transportation - Cleveland.

388
(77157)
B17

Transportation - Columbus, Ohio.

Bartholomew (Harland) and Associates.
Transportation, Columbus urban area. Prepared for the City Planning Commission and Franklin County Regional Planning Commission. St. Louis, 1956.
61p.
U.S. Urban Renewal Adm. UPAP.

1. Transportation - Columbus, Ohio. I. Columbus, Ohio. City Planning Commission. II. Franklin County, Ohio. Regional Planning Commission. III. U.S. URA-UPAP.   Columbus, Ohio.

388
(77178)
A75

Transportation - Cincinnati.

Arnold, Bion J
Report on an interurban electric railway terminal system for the city of Cincinnati. Submitted to the Cincinnati Interurban Rapid Transit Commission. Cincinnati, 1912.
163p.

1. Transportation - Cincinnati. 2. Cincinnati.   Interurban Rapid Transit   Commission.

388
(77132)
C52ra

Transportation - Cleveland.

Cleveland. Transit System.
Rapid transit progress in Cleveland. Cleveland [1964?]
[10]p.
Cover title.

1. Transportation - Cleveland.
2. Journey to work.

388
(77157)
C65

Transportation - Columbus, Ohio.

Columbus, Ohio. Development Committee.
Transportation Committee, annual report, 19
[Columbus, Ohio] 19
v.

For complete information see shelflist.

1. Transportation - Columbus, Ohio.
2. Parking - Columbus, Ohio

711.729
(77178)
K45

Transportation - Cincinnati.

Kinney (A.M.) Associates.
Presentation brochure for underground bus terminal and parking facility, Fountain and Government Square, Cincinnati, Ohio. Cincinnati, 1961.
1 v.

1. Parking - Cincinnati. 2. Transportation - Cincinnati.

388
(77132)
C52rep

Transportation - Cleveland.

Cleveland. Transit System.
Rapid transit to airport, proposed by City of Cleveland. Cleveland, 1961.
12p.
U.S. Housing and Home Finance Agency. Mass Transportation Demonstration Grant Program.

1. Transportation - Cleveland. 2. Airports. I. U.S. Housing and Home Finance Agency. Mass Transportation Demonstration Grant Program.   II. Title.

711.4
(7427)
C65m

Transportation - Concord, N.H.

Concord, N.H. City Planning Board.
Major thoroughfare plan, City of Concord, New Hampshire; a master plan report. Concord, N.H., 1963.
74p.

1. Master plan - Concord, N.H.
2. Transportation - Concord, N.H.
3. Streets - Concord, N.H.

388
(74275)
S54

Transportation - Claremont, N.H.

Smith (Wilbur) and Associates.
Master transportation plan, Claremont, New Hampshire. Prepared for New Hampshire Dept. of Public Works and Highways in cooperation with the U.S. Dept. of Commerce, Bureau of Public Roads. New Haven, 1961.
100p.

Summary -- ---Summary report. New Haven, 1961.
22p.

1. Transportation - Claremont, N.H. I. New Hampshire. Dept. of   Public Works and Highways.

388
(77132)
C89

TRANSPORTATION - CLEVELAND.

CUYAHOGA COUNTY, OHIO. BOARD OF COUNTY COMMISSIONERS.
CLEVELAND SUBWAY OPERATING AND ENGINEERING FEASIBILITY. CLEVELAND, 1955.
136P.

1. TRANSPORTATION - CLEVELAND.
I. TITLE.

711.73
A15u

Transportation - Congresses.

American Association of State Highway Officials.
Urban transportation planning papers presented at the 48th annual AASHO Meeting in Miami Beach, December 7, 1962. Washington, 1962.
17p.

1. Highways - Congresses. 2. Transportation - Congresses. I. American Association of State Highway Officials. Meeting, Miami Beach, 1962.   II. Title.

711.74
(77149)
C51t

Transportation - Clark County-Springfield, Ohio.

Clark County-Springfield, Ohio. Regional Planning Commission.
Transit study for Clark County and Springfield, Ohio. In cooperation with the Springfield Transit Authority. Springfield, Ohio, 1962.
30p.
U.S. Urban Renewal Adm. UPAP.

1. Transportation - Clark County-Springfield, Ohio. I. Springfield, Ohio. Transit Authority. II. U.S. URA-UPAP. Clark County-Springfield, Ohio.

3870

TRANSPORTATION - CLEVELAND-SEVEN COUNTY. MODEL CHOICE AND TRANSIT PLANNING CONFERENCE. CLEVELAND, 1966.
PROCEEDINGS, EDITED BY THE PUBLICATIONS SECTION OF THE CLEVELAND-SEVEN COUNTY TRANSPORTATION-LAND USE STUDY. CLEVELAND, 1966.
423P. (HUD 701 REPORT)

1. TRANSPORTATION - CLEVELAND-SEVEN COUNTY. I. CLEVELAND-SEVEN COUNTY TRANSPORTATION - LAND USE STUDY. II. HUD. 701. CLEVELAND-SEVEN COUNTY.

388
H43top

Transportation - Congresses.

Highway Research Board.
Top issues in urban research 1963. Presented at the 43rd annual meeting, January 13-17, 1964. Washington, Division of of Engineering and Industrial Research, National Academy of Sciences, National Research Council, 1965.
105p. (Highway research record no. 64)
National Research Council. Publication no. 1248.

(Continued on next card)

388
(77132)
B24

Transportation - Cleveland.

Beiswenger, Hoch, Arnold, and Associates.
Cleveland, Transit System; design report, rapid transit to airport. Cleveland, Cleveland Transit System, 1962.
56p.

1. Transportation - Cleveland.
2. Highways - Cleveland. I. Title.

388
(757911)
S54o

TRANSPORTATION - COLUMBIA, S.C.

Smith (Wilbur) and Associates.
Operation bus stop; feasibility study for Charleston-Columbia, S.C. Final report. Prepared for The Economic Development Administration. [n.p.] 1969.
144p.
CFSTI. PB 183 912.

1. Transportation - Charleston, S.C.
2. Transportation - Columbia, S.C.
3. Journey to work. I. Title.

388
H43top

Highway Research Board. Top issues in urban research 1963. (Card 2)

Contents:-Costs of urban transport systems of varying capacity and service, by M. Wohl.-System configurations in urban transportation planning, by H. S. Levinson and K. R. Roberts.-The development of a land-use data bank for transportation planning, by C. S. Hamilton.-Volume and characteristics of inter-city travel during Winter 1963, by D. E. Church.

1. Transportation -   Congresses. 2. Journey to work. 3. Transportation - Research.

Transportation - Congresses.

388
H43u Highway Research Board.
Urban transportation; demand and coordi-
nation. Presented at the 41st Annual Meeting
January 8-12, 1962. Washington, National
Academy of Sciences, National Research Council,
1962.
97p. (Its Bulletin 326)
Bibliography: p. 78-97.
National Research Council. Publication 1006.

1. Transportation - Congresses.

388
N21p National Conference on Private and Unregulated
Transportation, Northwestern University, 1962.
Private and unregulated carriage; selected
papers presented at a two-day conference
conducted by the Transportation Center at
Northwestern University, Evanston, Ill.
Evanston, Ill., Transportation Center,
Northwestern University, 1963.
155p.

1. Transportation - Congresses. I. Northwestern
University. Transportation Center.
II. Title.

388
S71p Stanford Research Institute Urban Transporta-
1964 tion Alternatives Symposium, Menlo Park,
Calif., 1964.
Proceedings, 1964.
Menlo Park, Calif., 1964.
/ v.

1. Transportation - Congresses. 2. Highways
- California. 3. Metropolitan area planning -
Calif. 4. Journey to work.

Transportation - Congresses.

388
746 Tippetts-Abbett-McCarthy-Stratton.
1962 Estimating traffic patterns in urban
areas, by Thomas J. Frater and others.
Presented at International Road Federation,
4th World Meeting, Madrid, Spain, October
14-20, 1962. New York, 1962.
21p.

1. Traffic - Congresses. 2. Transportation -
Congresses. I. Frater, Thomas J. II. International
Road Federation, 4th World Meeting,
Madrid, 1962.

Transportation - Congresses.

388
U71 Urban Transportation Planning Conference
Columbus, Ohio, 1962.
1962 Proceedings. AMA-AASHO-NACO action program: urban transportation planning program.
Cooperating agencies, American Association
of State Highway Officials, National Association of County Officials, American Municipal Association. Conference coordinator,
Ohio, Dept. of Highways. Columbus, Ohio,
Dept. of Highways, 1963.
93p.
1. Transportation - Congresses.
 I. Ohio. Dept. of
Highways.

Transportation - Conn.

388
(746) Connecticut. Employment Security Div.
C65c Commuting patterns in Connecticut.
[Hartford] Connecticut Labor Dept., Employment
Security Division, Dept. of Research and
Information, 1966.
88p.

1. Transportation - Conn. 2. Journey to
work. 3. Labor supply - Conn. I. Title.

Transportation - Conn.

711.33
(746) Connecticut Interregional Planning Program.
C65t Transportation. Prepared in cooperation
with the Bureau of Public Roads. Hartford,
1966.
101p.
At the head of title: Connecticut: choices
for action.

U.S. Dept. of Housing and Urban Development. UPAP.
1. State planning - Conn. 2. Transportation -
Conn. I. Title. II. Title: Connecticut:
choices for action. III. U.S. HUD-UPAP.
Conn.

1127 TRANSPORTATION - CONNECTICUT.
CONNECTICUT. STATE HIGHWAY DEPT.
HARTFORD-BLOOMFIELD RAIL BUS
FEASIBILITY STUDY. HARTFORD, 1968.
47L. (HUD 701 REPORT)

1. TRANSPORTATION - CONNECTICUT.
I. HUD. 701. CONNECTICUT.

---

281 TRANSPORTATION - CONNECTICUT.
CONNECTICUT. STATE HIGHWAY DEPT.
WATER TRANSPORTATION. HARTFORD, 1964.
45L. (P42 STAFF PAPER, NO. 251B; HUD
701 REPORT)

1. TRANSPORTATION - CONNECTICUT.
I. HUD. 701. CONNECTICUT.

Transportation - Connecticut.

388
T74 Tri-State Transportation Committee.
Interim report
[New York,
 Transport...
 ...]
For complete information see shelflist.

1. Transportation - Connecticut.
2. Transportation - New Jersey. 3. Transportation - New York.

Transportation - Conn.

388
T74ps Tri-State Transportation Commission.
(Connecticut-New Jersey-New York)
Park'n ride rail service: New Brunswick,
Newark, New York City: a final report on
the Mass Transportation Demonstration
Project October 27, 1963-April 24, 1965.
New York, 1967.
39p.
U.S. Dept. of Housing and Urban
Development. Mass Transportation Demon-
stration Grant Program.

(Cont'd on next card)

388
T74ps Tri-State Transportation Commission.
(Connecticut-New Jersey-New York) Park'n
ride rail service: New Brunswick, Newark,
New York...1967. (Card 2)

1. Transportation - Conn. 2. Parking -
Conn.-N.J.-N.Y. 3. Railroads - Conn.-N.J.-
N.Y. I. U.S. Dept. of Housing and Urban
Development. Mass Transportation Demon-
stration Grant Program.
II. Title.

Transportation - Connecticut.

388
T74p Tri-State Transportation Committee.
Prospectus. New York, 1962.
51p.
"The Tri-State Metropolitan Region, consists
of portions of the states of Connecticut, New
Jersey and New York."

1. Transportation - Connecticut.
2. Transportation - New Jersey. 3. Transportation - New York.

Transportation - Connecticut.

388
(746) Connecticut. Development Commission.
C65 Transportation; an analysis of the transportation of goods and people by rail,
highway, water, air and pipeline in
Connecticut. [Prepared in cooperation
with Connecticut Public Utilities
Commission and others.] Hartford, 1964.
114p. (Connecticut Interregional
Planning Program Technical report 153)

(Cont'd. on next card)

388
(746) Connecticut. Development Commission.
C65 Transportation; an analysis ... (Card 2)

Partial contents:-Appendix B. Description
of the Connecticut Interregional Planning
Program.
U.S. Urban Renewal Adm. UPAP.

1. Transportation - Connecticut.
I. Connecticut Interregional Planning
Program. II. U.S. URA-UPAP.
Connecticut.

711.333
(74896) Venango County, Pa. Planning Commission.
V25 Report
Franklin, Pa.
v.

For complete information see shelflist.

1. County planning - Venango Co., Pa.

Transportation - Conn.-N.J.-N.Y.

Folio
388 Edwards and Kelcey.
E28 Region-wide passenger potential study, 1963.
[Prepared] for the Tri-State Transportation
Committee (Connecticut-New Jersey-New York)
New York, 1963.
1v.
Prepared in cooperation with U.S. Dept. of
Commerce, Bureau of Public Roads and the Hous-
ing and Home Finance Agency.

1. Transportation - Conn.-N.J.-N.Y. I. Tri-
State Transporta- tion Committee

(Continued on next card)

Folio
388 Edwards and Kelcey. Region-wide passenger
E28 potential study, 1963...1963. (Card 2)

(Connecticut-New Jersey-New York) II. Title:
Passenger potential study. III. U.S. Housing and Home Finance Agency.

Transportation - Connecticut-New Jersey-New
York.

388
(746) Ronan, William J
R65 Tri-State transportation planning, by
Chairman, Tri-State Transportation Committee,
New York. In Newark commerce (Newark
Association of Commerce and Industry) vol. 7,
no. 4, September 1962. p. 18-20, 42-43.

1. Transportation - Connecticut-New Jersey-
New York. I. Newark commerce. II. Tri-State
Transportation Committee.
(Connecticut- New Jersey-New
York)

1759 TRANSPORTATION - CONN. - N.J. - N.Y.
TRI-STATE TRANSPORTATION COMMISSION.
(CONNECTICUT - NEW JERSEY - NEW YORK)
COMPLETION REPORT, PROJECT 3810,
COORDINATION WITH STATE AND LOCAL PLANS.
NEW YORK, 1970.
1 v. (HUD 701 REPORT)

1. TRANSPORTATION - CONN. - N.J. - N.Y.
I. HUD. 701. CONN. - N.J. - N.Y.

Transportation - Connecticut-New Jersey-
New York.

388
T74c Tri-State Transportation Committee
(Connecticut, New Jersey, and New York)
A consultant's report to the Tri-State
Transportation Committee on a reconnaissance
of the Tri-State Region and some ideas for a
development plan. New Haven, 1963.
48p.
U.S. Urban Renewal Adm. UPAP.

1. Transportation - Connecticut-New Jersey-
New York. I. Title. II. U.S. URA-UPAP.
Connecticut-New Jersey-New York.

388
T74co
Transportation - Connecticut-New Jersey-New York.
Tri-State Transportation Commission.
(Connecticut-New Jersey-New York)
Coordinated bus-rail service; Rockland County-Westchester County, New York City. A final report on the Mass Transportation Demonstration Project, Sept. 17, 1963-June 25, 1965. [Prepared in cooperation with the] U.S. Dept. of Housing and Urban Development and others. New York, 1967.
47p.
U.S. Dept. of Housing and Urban Development. Mass Transportation Demonstration Grant Program.

(Cont'd on next card)

388
T74co
Tri-State Transportation Commission.
(Connecticut-New Jersey-New York) Coordinated bus-rail service; Rockland County-Westchester County New York City...1967. (Card 2)

1. Transportation - Connecticut-New Jersey-New York. 2. Journey to work. I. Title. II. Title: Bus rail service. III. U.S. Dept. of Housing and Urban Development. Mass Transportation Demonstration Grant Program.

1760-
1764
TRANSPORTATION - CONN. - N.J. - N.Y.
TRI-STATE TRANSPORTATION COMMISSION.
(CONNECTICUT - NEW JERSEY - NEW YORK) INTERIM TECHNICAL REPORT: 1, LOCAL TRANSIT TRIP; 2, VEHICLE REGISTRATION FORECASTS; 3, VEHICLE TRIP PROJECTIONS, 1985, 2000; 4, VEHICLE TRIP PROJECTIONS 1990; 5, PARKING ANALYSIS. NEW YORK, 1969-70.
5 V. (HUD 701 REPORT)

1. TRANSPORTATION - CONN. - N.J. - N.Y. I. HUD. 701. CONN. - N.J. - N.Y.

1753
TRANSPORTATION - CONN.-N.J.-N.Y.
TRI-STATE TRANSPORTATION COMMISSION.
(CONNECTICUT-NEW JERSEY-NEW YORK)
LAND USE UPDATE - OUTSIDE MAJOR CITIES. NEW YORK, 1970.
1 V. (HUD 701 REPORT)

1. TRANSPORTATION - CONN.-N.J.-N.Y. I. HUD. 701. CONN., N.J., N.Y.

388
(746)
T74
Transportation - Connecticut-New Jersey-New York.
Tri-State Transportation Commission.
(Connecticut-New Jersey-New York)
Measure of a region. New York, 1967.
32p.

1. Transportation - Connecticut-New Jersey-New York. 2. Journey to work. 3. Land use - Connecticut-New Jersey-New York. I. Title.

1754
TRANSPORTATION - CONN. - N.J. - N.Y.
TRI-STATE TRANSPORTATION COMMISSION.
(CONNECTICUT - NEW JERSEY - NEW YORK) MONITORING OPEN SPACE ACTION. NEW YORK, 1970.
1 V. (HUD 701 REPORT)

1. TRANSPORTATION - CONN. - N.J. - N.Y. I. HUD. 701. CONN. - N.J. - N.Y.

388
T74pe
1971
TRANSPORTATION - CONNECTICUT - NEW JERSEY - NEW YORK.
Tri-State Regional Planning Commission.
(Connecticut-New Jersey-New York)
People-transportation-jobs. Public transport services to non-CBD employment concentrations. New York, 1971.
22p. (Progress report no. 5; INT-MTD-13) Mass Transportation Demonstration Grant Program.
1. Transportation - Connecticut-New Jersey-New York. I. U.S. Mass Transportation Demonstration Grant Program. N.Y. II. Title.

1752
TRANSPORTATION - CONN. - N.J. - N.Y.
TRI-STATE TRANSPORTATION COMMISSION.
(CONNECTICUT - NEW JERSEY - NEW YORK) RECREATION ASPECTS OF THE PASSAIC RIVER WATER DEVELOPMENT AND FLOOD CONTROL PROPOSAL OF THE CORPS OF ENGINEERS. NEW YORK, 1970.
5L. (HUD 701 REPORT)

1. TRANSPORTATION - CONN. - N.J. - N.Y. I. HUD. 701. CONN. - N.J. - N.Y.

1791
1792
TRANSPORTATION - CONN. - N.J. - N.Y.
TRI-STATE TRANSPORTATION COMMISSION.
(CONNECTICUT - NEW JERSEY - NEW YORK)
REGIONAL PROFILE: 12, HIGHWAY PROGRESS AND HIGHWAY STATUS MAP; 13, COUNTY TRAVEL PATTERNS. NEW YORK, 1969.
2 V. (HUD 701 REPORT)

1. TRANSPORTATION - CONN. - N.J. - N.Y. I. HUD. 701. CONN. - N.J. - N.Y.

388
(746)
T74u
TRANSPORTATION - CONNECTICUT-NEW JERSEY-NEW YORK.
Tri-State Transportation Commission.
(Connecticut-New Jersey-New York)
Urban corridor demonstration program. Interim report, Oct. 1970 - March 1971. New York, 1971.
45p.

1. Transportation - Conn.-N.J.-N.Y. 2. Highways. I. Title.

388
T74d
Transportation - Connecticut-New Jersey-New York.
Tri-State Transportation Committee
(Connecticut, New Jersey, and New York)
Designs for growth; a report on the Tri-State Transportation Committee, 1961-1966. [New York] 1967.
[30]p.
U.S. Dept. of Housing and Urban Development. UPAP.

1. Transportation - Connecticut-New Jersey-New York. I. Title. II. U.S. Dept. of Housing and Urban Development. UPAP. Connecticut-New Jersey-New York.

388
T74o
Transportation--Connecticut-New Jersey-New York.
Tri-State Transportation Committee.
(Connecticut, New Jersey, and New York)
Origin-destination survey. Park 'n ride station and service at New Brunswick, New Jersey on Pennsylvania Railroad. New York, 1963.
50p.
Participating agencies: New Jersey State Highway Dept., Div. of Railroad Transportation, Middlesex County, City of New Brunswick, Pennsylvania Railroad.

(Continued on next card)

388
T74o
Tri-State Transportation Committee.
(Connecticut, New Jersey, and New York)
Origin-destination survey...1963. (Card 2)

Submitted by Research Data Processing Corp., Traffic Research Corp., R.L.M. Associates. U.S. Housing and Home Finance Agency Mass Transportation Demonstration Program.

1. Journey to work. 2. Transportation--New Jersey-New York. I. U.S. Housing and Home Finance Agency. Mass Transportation Demonstration Grant Program.

388
T74o
1968
Transportation - Connecticut-New Jersey-New York.
Tri-State Transportation Commission.
(Connecticut-New Jersey-New York)
People, transportation, jobs; public transport services to non-CBD employment concentration. Prepared in cooperation with U.S. Dept. of Housing and Urban Development. New York, 1968.
21p. (Progress report no. 2. 2046-5620-6C; INT-MTD 13)
1. Transportation - Connecticut-New Jersey-New York. 2. Journey to work. 3. Employment - Connecticut-New Jersey-New York. I. Title. II. U.S. Dept. of Housing and Urban Development.

388
T74pu
Transportation - Conn.-N.J.-N.Y.
Tri-State Transportation Commission.
(Connecticut-New Jersey-New York)
Public transport services to non-CBD employment concentrations. New York, 1967.
26p. (Progress report no. 1. 2044-5620-5C)
U.S. Dept. of Housing and Urban Development. Mass Transportation Demonstration Project.
1. Transportation - Conn.-N.J.-N.Y. 2. Journey to work. I. Title. II. U.S. Dept. of Housing and Urban Development. Mass Transportation Demonstration Project.

388
(746)
T74r
TRANSPORTATION - CONN.-N.J.-N.Y.
Tri-State Transportation Committee.
(Connecticut-New Jersey-New York)
A region on the move: travel choices depend on destinations. New York, 1966.
20p. (Its Technical bulletin, vol. 11, no. 1, Feb., 1965)
U.S. Mass Transportation Grant Program.
1. Transportation - Conn.-N.J.-N.Y. 2. Journey to work. 3. Highways - Conn.-N.J.-N.J. I. U.S. Mass Transportation Demonstration Grant Program. II. Title.

711.3
T74
Transportation - Connecticut-New Jersey-New York.
Tri-State Transportation Commission.
(Connecticut-New Jersey-New York)
Regional development alternates. [Prepared in cooperation with U.S. Bureau of Public Roads] New York, 1967.
31p.
U.S. Dept. of Housing and Urban Development. UPAP.

1. Regional planning - Connecticut-New Jersey-New York. 2. Transportation - Connecticut-New Jersey-New York. I. U.S. Bureau of Public Roads. II. Title. III. U.S. HUD-UPAP. Connecticut-New Jersey-New York.

388
T74re
Transportation - Connecticut-New Jersey-New York.
Tri-State Transportation Commission.
(Connecticut-New Jersey-New York)
Regional profile, transit strike highlights. New York, 1967.
8p. (v.1, no. 4)
U.S. Housing and Urban Development. UPAP.
1. Transportation - Connecticut-New Jersey-New York. 2. Journey to work. I. Title. II. U.S. HUD-UPAP. Connecticut-New Jersey-New York.

388
T74rep
Transportation - Connecticut-New Jersey-New York.
Tri-State Transportation Commission.
(Connecticut-New Jersey-New York)
Report, 1967
New York, 1967-
1 v. annual.

For complete information see main card.
U.S. Dept. of Housing and Urban Development. UPAP.

1. Transportation - Connecticut-New Jersey-New York. I. U.S. HUD-UPAP. Connecticut-New Jersey-New York.

388
T74s
Transportation - Connecticut-New Jersey-New York.
Tri-State Transportation Commission.
(Connecticut-New Jersey-New York)
Station fare collection; Kew Gardens-Forest Hills, Queens County, New York; a final report on the Mass Transportation Demonstration Project, July 1, 1964-June 30, 1965. New York, 1966.
32p.
U.S. Dept. of Housing and Urban Development. Mass Transportation Demonstration Grant Program.

(Cont'd on next card)

388
T74s
Tri-State Transportation Commission. (Connecticut-New Jersey-New York) Station fare collection...1966. (Card 2)

1. Transportation - Connecticut-New Jersey-New York. I. U.S. Dept. of Housing and Urban Development. Mass Transportation Demonstration Grant Program. II. Title.

388
T74su　Tri-State Transportation Commission.
(Connecticut-New Jersey-New York)
Suburban service adjustment experiment; a
summary, Harlem Division, New York Central
Railroad, Westchester and Putnam Counties;
a final report on the Mass Transportation
Demonstration Grant Project. New York,
1967.
8p.
U.S. Dept. of Housing and Urban Develop-
ment. Mass Transportation Demonstration
Grant Program.

(Continued on next card)

388
T74su　Tri-State Transportation Commission.
(Connecticut-New Jersey-New York)
Suburban service adjustment...1967.
(Card 2)

1. Transportation - Conn.-N.J.-N.Y.
2. Journey to work. I. Title. II. U.S.
Dept. of Housing and Urban Development.
Mass Transportation Demonstration Grant
Program.

388
(746)
T74te　TRANSPORTATION - CONN.-N.J.-N.Y.
Tri-State Regional Planning Commission
(Connecticut-New Jersey-New York)
Test of fare restructuring in a multicarrier,
multizone bus transportation system.
Final report. New York, 1972.
17p.

1. Transportation - Conn.-N.J.-N.Y.
I. Title.

388
T74te　Tri-State Transportation Commission
(Connecticut-New Jersey-New York)
Test of gas turbine rail car; a summary
report on part one of the mass transportation
demonstration grant project. Long Island
Railroad; July 1967-May 1968. New York, 1969.
14p.
INT-MTD 12.
U.S. Dept. of Housing and Urban Develop-
ment. Mass Transportation Demonstration Grant
Program.
1. Transportation - Conn.-N.J.-N.Y. area.
2. Journey to work. 3. Railroads -
Conn.-N.J.-N.Y. I. Title. II. Title:
Gas turbine rail car.
(Cont'd on next card)

388
T74te　Tri-State Transportation Commission
(Connecticut-New Jersey-New York)　Test
of gas turbine...1969.　(Card 2)

III. U.S. HUD Mass Transportation
Demonstration Grant Program.

388
(746)
T74t　TRANSPORTATION - CONN.-N.J.-N.Y.
Tri-State Transportation Commission.
(Connecticut-New Jersey-New York)
Truck transportation. New York, 1968.
4p. (Its Regional profile, vol. 1, no. 8,
Jan., 1968)

U.S. Mass Transportation Demonstration Grant
Program.

1. Transportation - Conn.-N.J.-N.Y.
2. Highways - Conn.-N.J.-N.Y. I. U.S. Mass
Transportation Demonstration Grant Program.
II. Title.

711.74
(74834)
F19　Transportation - Connellsville, Pa.
Fayette County, Pa. Planning and Zoning
Commission.
Connellsville, a report on major streets
and transportation. In cooperation with
the Urban Planning Assistance Program,
Bureau of Community Development, Pennsylvania
Dept. of Commerce. [Uniontown, Pa.] 1959.
25p.
U.S. Urban Renewal Adm. UPAP.
1. Streets - Connellsville, Pa. 2. Transportation -
Connellsville, Pa. I. U.S. URA-
UPAP. Connellsville, Pa.

388
(75938)
D12　Transportation - Dade Co., Fla.
Dade County, Fla. Traffic and Transportation Dept.
A study of traffic and transportation
in Metropolitan Dade County 1958.
Miami, 1959.
54p. illus., diagrs., maps, tables.

1. Traffic - Dade Co., Fla. 2. Transportation - Dade Co., Fla.

VF
388
(75938)
D12t　Transportation - Dade Co., Fla.
Dade County, Fla. Transportation Advisory
Committee.
Transit authority urged by Committee.
Board sets July 19 hearing on plan for
unified system. Miami, Fla., 1960.
4p.

1. Transportation - Dade Co., Fla.

388
(764)
D15
1965　Transportation - Dallas.
Dallas. Dept. of City Planning.
Thoroughfares: a guide plan for streets: City
of Dallas. Prepared for the city Plan Commission. Dallas, 1965.
1 v.

1. Transportation - Dallas. 2. Streets -
Dallas. I. Title.

711.14
(764)
T29　Transportation - Dallas-Fort Worth.
Texas. Highway Dept. (Study Office Staff)
Technical report on land use, population
distribution, trip forecasting, Dallas-
Fort Worth Regional Transportation Study.
[Fort Worth] Tex., 1966.
158p.
Prepared in cooperation with U.S. Dept.
of Commerce, Bureau of Public Roads.

1. Land use - Dallas-Fort Worth. 2. Auto-
mation. 3. Transportation - Dallas-Fort
Worth. 4. Population - Dallas-Fort Worth.
I. Dallas-Fort Worth Regional
Transporta-tion Study.

388
(764)
D15　Transportation - Dallas metropolitan area.
Dallas. Dept. of City Planning.
Thoroughfares: Dallas metropolitan
area. Prepared for the Dallas Area
Master Plan Committee. Dallas, 1961.
154p.

1. Transportation - Dallas metropolitan
area.

711.4
(77691)
D18
Pt. 3　Transportation - Davenport, Iowa.
Bartholomew (Harland) and Associates.
Transportation and transit facilities,
Davenport, Iowa. St. Louis, June 1946.
16 p. charts, maps, tables.
Part 3 of the comprehensive plan of the
City of Davenport.

1.Master plan - Davenport, Iowa. 2. Transportation - Davenport, Iowa. I.Davenport, Iowa.
City Plan Commission.

555　TRANSPORTATION - DAVENPORT, IOWA.
BI-STATE METROPOLITAN PLANNING COMMISSION.
IOWA PORTION OF THE DAVENPORT-ROCK
ISLAND-MOLINE URBANIZED AREA
TRANSPORTATION STUDY: 3, FINANCIAL
RESOURCES. BY DE LEUW, CATHER AND
COMPANY. INTERIM REPORT. ROCK ISLAND,
ILL., 1969.
1 V. (HUD 701 REPORT)

1. TRANSPORTATION - DAVENPORT, IOWA.
I. DE LEUW, CATHER AND CO. II. HUD.
701. DAVENPORT, IOWA.

553
554　TRANSPORTATION - DAVENPORT, IOWA.
BI-STATE METROPOLITAN PLANNING COMMISSION.
IOWA PORTION OF THE DAVENPORT-ROCK
ISLAND-MOLINE URBANIZED AREA
TRANSPORTATION STUDY: 2, TERMINAL AND
TRANSFER FACILITIES AND PUBLIC
TRANSPORTATION; 4, TERMINAL AND TRANSFER
FACILITIES FORECASTS. BY DE LEUW, CATHER
AND COMPANY. INTERIM REPORT. ROCK
ISLAND, ILL., 1968-69.
2 V. (HUD 701 REPORT)

1. TRANSPORTATION - DAVENPORT, IOWA.
I. DE LEUW, CATHER AND CO. II. HUD.
701. DAVENPORT, IOWA.

598　TRANSPORTATION - DAVENPORT, IOWA.
BI-STATE METROPOLITAN PLANNING COMMISSION.
URBANIZED AREA TRANSPORTATION STUDY:
DAVENPORT, ROCK ISLAND, MOLINE. BY DE
LEUW, CATHER AND CO. ROCK ISLAND, ILL.,
1970.
14P. (HUD 701 REPORT)

1. TRANSPORTATION - DAVENPORT, IOWA.
2. TRANSPORTATION - ROCK ISLAND, ILL.
3. TRANSPORTATION - MOLINE, ILL. I. DE
LEUW, CATHER AND CO. II. HUD. 701.
DAVENPORT, IOWA. III. HUD. 701. ROCK
ISLAND, ILL. IV. HUD. 701. MOLINE,
ILL.

Folio
388
(777691)
I68　Transportation - Davenport, Iowa.
Iowa. State Highway Commission. (Div.
of Planning)
Davenport; origin and destination,
traffic report. Prepared in cooperation
with the U.S. Dept. of Commerce, Bureau
of Public Roads. Davenport, Iowa, 1963.
119p.

1. Traffic - Davenport, Iowa. 2. Journey to work. 3. Transportation - Davenport, Iowa. I. Title.

388
(768551)
M27　Transportation - Davidson Co., Tenn.
Metropolitan Government of Nashville and
Davidson County. Metropolitan Planning
Commission.
Study of interstate highway interchange
area development for Metropolitan
Nashville and Davidson County, Tennessee.
Nashville, 1965.
43p.

1. Transportation - Nashville. 2. Transportation - Davidson Co., Tenn. 3. Zoning - Nashville metropolitan area.
4. Highways - Economic effect.
I. Title.

388
(77358)
I55　Transportation - Decatur, Ill.
Illinois. University. Bureau of
Economic and Business Research.
University of Illinois-U.S. Dept. of
H.U.D. mass transportation demonstration
projects Ill-MTD-3,4. Kent, Ohio, Kent
State University, 1968.
160p.
U.S. Dept. of Housing and Urban Develop-
ment. Mass Transportation Demonstration
Grant Program.
1. Transportation - Decatur, Ill.
2. Transportation - Peoria, Ill. 3. Journey
to work. I. Ohio. State Univer-
sity, Kent. Center for Urban
Regionalsim. (Cont'd on next card)

388
(77358)
I55　Illinois. University. Bureau of
Economic and Business Research.
University...1968. (Card 2)

II. Illinois. University. Bureau of
Business and Economic Research. III. U.S.
HUD-Mass Transportation Demonstration Grant
Program. Ill.

388
(751)
D25n　TRANSPORTATION - DELAWARE RIVER BASIN.
Delaware Valley Regional Planning
Commission.
1985 regional transportation plan.
[Philadelphia] 1969.
66p. (Its Plan report no. 5)

Suppl.　——— Technical supplement. 1969.
135p.

U.S. Mass Transportation Demonstration
Grant Program.
1. Transportation - Delaware River Basin.
I. Title: Regional transportation
plan. II. U.S. Mass Transportation
Demonstration Grant Program.

388
(751)
D25o
TRANSPORTATION - DELAWARE RIVER BASIN.
Delaware Valley Regional Planning Commission.
Operations plan design for regional transportation planning; the continuing phase. [Philadelphia] 1969.
47p.
Prepared for: New Jersey Dept. of Transportation; Pennsylvania Dept. of Highways, in cooperation with U.S. Bureau of Public Roads.
1. Transportation - Delaware River Basin. 2. Journey to work. I. New Jersey. Dept. of Transportation. II. Pennsylvania. Dept. of Highways.   III. Title.

388
(751)
D25
Transportation - Delaware River Basin.
Delaware Valley Regional Planning Commission.
Transportation systems and policies for the 1985 region. Philadelphia, 1966.
1v. (DVRPC v.4)
1. Transportation - Delaware River Basin. 2. Journey to work. I. Title.

711.4
(78883)
D25L
Transportation - Denver.
Denver Planning Office.
Lower downtown Denver: expressway and adjacent redevelopment areas. Denver, 1958.
22p. maps. (Its Central area plan bulletin no. 6)
1. City Planning - Denver. 2. Business districts - Denver. 3. Transportation - Denver.

388
(78883)
D25
Transportation - Denver.
Denver. Transportation Committee.
Central area transportation study, Denver, Colorado; accessibility, circulation [and] terminals. Prepared for the Downtown Denver Master Plan Committee. Denver, 1963.
80p.
1. Transportation - Denver. 2. Business districts - Denver.

711.4
(78883)
D25
no. 3
Transportation - Denver.
Inter-County Regional Planning Commission, Denver.
Transportation in the Denver region / Denver, 1958.
60p. illus., maps. (Its Master plan report number 3)
U.S. Urban Renewal Adm. UPAP.
1. Master plan - Denver. 2. Transportation - Denver. I. U.S. URA-UPAP. Denver.

388
(78883)
C65
Transportation - Denver metropolitan area.
Colorado. Dept. of Highways. (Planning and Research Div.)
Denver metropolitan area transportation study. Land use report; summary edition. In cooperation with U.S. Dept. of Commerce, Bureau of Public Roads. Denver, 1961.
[16]p. (Maps included)
1. Transportation - Denver metropolitan area. 2. Land use - Denver metropolitan area. I. Title.

856-
862
TRANSPORTATION - DES MOINES.
CENTRAL IOWA REGIONAL PLANNING COMMISSION.
DES MOINES TRANSIT COMPANY: 1. MAXIMUM LOAD POINTS; 2. MAPS; 3. FARE STRUCTURE; 4. EXPRESS ROUTES AND EXTENSION; 5. OPERATING AND FINANCIAL DATA; 6. OPERATING DATA FOR SYSTEM; 7. OPERATING REVENUE. DES MOINES, 1968.
7 V. (HUD 701 REPORT)
1. TRANSPORTATION - DES MOINES.
I. HUD. 701. DES MOINES.

869
TRANSPORTATION - DES MOINES.
CENTRAL IOWA REGIONAL PLANNING COMMISSION.
DES MOINES URBAN AREA TRUCK TERMINAL INVENTORY. BY HOWARD, NEEDLES, TAMMEN AND BERGENDOFF. DES MOINES, 1969.
24L. (HUD 701 REPORT)
1. TRANSPORTATION - DES MOINES.
I. HOWARD, NEEDLES, TAMMEN AND BERGENDOFF.
II. HUD. 701. DES MOINES.

868
TRANSPORTATION - DES MOINES.
DES MOINES. TRAFFIC AND TRANSPORTATION DEPARTMENT.
AERAWIDE TOPICS PLAN. CENTRAL IOWA REGIONAL PLANNING COMMISSION. DES MOINES, 1969.
1 V. (HUD 701 REPORT)
1. TRANSPORTATION - DES MOINES.
I. CENTRAL IOWA REGIONAL PLANNING COMMISSION. II. HUD. 701. DES MOINES.

711.4
(77434)
D27t
no.7
Transportation - Detroit.
Detroit. City Plan Commission.
Central business district study; land use, trafficways and transit. A basis for the development of a long range guide for growth in downtown Detroit. Detroit, 1956.
1v. (Its Master plan technical report, second series no. 7)
1. Master plan - Detroit. 2. Business districts - Detroit. 3. Land use- Detroit. 4. Traffic - Detroit. 5. Transportation - Detroit. I. Title.

711.4
(77434)
D27M
N8-6
TRANSPORTATION - DETROIT.
DETROIT. CITY PLAN COMMISSION.
PROPOSED TRANSPORTATION PLAN. PART 1: MOTOR FREIGHT TERMINALS, PORT FACILITIES. DETROIT, 1948.
16P. (ITS MASTER PLAN REPORT NO. 6)
1. MASTER PLAN - DETROIT.
2. TRANSPORTATION - DETROIT.

388
(77434)
D27e
TRANSPORTATION - DETROIT.
Detroit Edison Co.
Elaboration of the land transportation system of UDA [Urban Detroit Area] Detroit, 1969.
66p. (UDA Research Project. Document DOX-USA-A 70)
A project of the Detroit Edison Co., Wayne State University and Doxiadis Associates.
1. Transportation - Detroit. 2. Land use - Detroit. I. UDA Research Project. II. Title.

388
(77434)
D27s
Transportation.- Detroit.
Detroit Metropolitan Area Regional Planning Commission.
Study design for comprehensive transportation and land use programs for the Detroit region. Developed in cooperation with Michigan State Highway Department [and others] Detroit, 1964.
97p.
U.S. Urban Renewal Adm. UPAP.
1. Transportation - Detroit. 2. Land use - Detroit. I. Title.   II. U.S. URA-UPAP. Detroit.

388
(77434)
D27g
Transportation - Detroit.
Detroit. Dept. of Street Railways.
Grand River Avenue transit survey, Detroit, Michigan. Final report. Detroit, 1963.
65p.
U.S. Housing and Home Finance Agency. Mass Transportation Demonstration Grant Program.
1. Transportation - Detroit. 2. Journey to work. I. U.S. Housing and Home Finance Agency. Mass Transportation Demonstration Grant Program.

Transportation - Detroit metropolitan area.
388
(77434)
D27d
Detroit Metropolitan Area Regional Planning Commission.
Development of comprehensive studies of mass transit and trucking in the Detroit region, by Leland E. Jolgren. Detroit, 1959.
20p. map, tables.
U.S. Urban Renewal Administration, Urban Planning Assistance Program.
1. Transportation - Detroit metropolitan area. 2. Traffic - Detroit metropolitan area.
I. Jolgren, Leland E.   II. U.S. URA-UPAP. Detroit.

1457
TRANSPORTATION - DETROIT METROPOLITAN AREA.
DETROIT METROPOLITAN AREA REGIONAL PLANNING COMMISSION.
LIVING PATTERNS AND ATTITUDES IN THE DETROIT REGION; A REPORT OF TALUS, THE DETROIT REGIONAL TRANSPORTATION AND LAND USE STUDY, BY JOHN B. LANSING AND GARY HENDRICKS, SURVEY RESEARCH CENTER, INSTITUTE FOR SOCIAL RESEARCH, THE UNIVERSITY OF MICHIGAN. DETROIT, 1967.
241P. (HUD 701 REPORT)
1. SOCIAL CONDITIONS - DETROIT METROPOLITAN AREA. 2. TRANSPORTATION - DETROIT METROPOLITAN AREA. 3. LAND
(CONTINUED ON NEXT CARD)

1457
DETROIT METROPOLITAN AREA REGIONAL PLANNING COMMISSION. LIVING PATTERNS AND ...1967.   (CARD 2)
USE - DETROIT METROPOLITAN AREA.
I. MICHIGAN. UNIVERSITY. INSTITUTE FOR SOCIAL RESEARCH. II. HUD. 701. DETROIT METROPOLITAN AREA.

1455
TRANSPORTATION - DETROIT METROPOLITAN AREA.
DETROIT METROPOLITAN AREA REGIONAL PLANNING COMMISSION.
PUBLIC TRANSPORTATION IN DETROIT - SOUTHEAST MICHIGAN REGION. PRELIMINARY AREA STUDY FOR METROPOLITAN FUND, INC. ON BEHALF OF DETROIT REGIONAL TRANSPORTATION AND LAND USE STUDY. DETROIT, 1967.
47L. (HUD 701 REPORT)
1. TRANSPORTATION - DETROIT METROPOLITAN AREA. I. METROPOLITAN FUND, INC. II. HUD. 701. DETROIT METROPOLITAN AREA.

1452
TRANSPORTATION - DETROIT METROPOLITAN AREA.
DETROIT METROPOLITAN AREA REGIONAL PLANNING COMMISSION.
STUDY DESIGN FOR A COMPREHENSIVE TRANSPORTATION AND LAND USE PROGRAM FOR THE DETROIT REGION. DEVELOPED IN COOPERATION WITH MICHIGAN STATE HIGHWAY DEPARTMENT. SUMMARY REPORT: A REGIONAL DEVELOPMENT PLAN FOR 1990. DETROIT, 1964.
25P. (HUD 701 REPORT)
1. TRANSPORTATION - DETROIT METROPOLITAN AREA. 2. LAND USE - DETROIT METROPOLITAN AREA. I. MICHIGAN. STATE HIGHWAY DEPT. II. HUD. 701. DETROIT METROPOLITAN AREA.

1456
TRANSPORTATION - DETROIT METROPOLITAN AREA.
DETROIT METROPOLITAN AREA REGIONAL PLANNING COMMISSION.
STUDY DESIGN FOR A COMPREHENSIVE TRANSPORTATION AND LAND USE PROGRAM FOR THE DETROIT REGION. DEVELOPED IN COOPERATION WITH MICHIGAN STATE HIGHWAY DEPARTMENT AND OTHERS. DETROIT, 1964.
97P. (HUD 701 REPORT)
1. TRANSPORTATION - DETROIT METROPOLITAN AREA. 2. LAND USE - DETROIT METROPOLITAN AREA. I. MICHIGAN. STATE HIGHWAY DEPT. II. HUD. 701. DETROIT METROPOLITAN AREA.

058.7
i.388
A52
Transportation - Directories.
American Automobile Association.
Directory of toll bridges, ferries, domestic steamship lines, and toll roads. Wash., 1968.
56p.
1. Transportation - Direct. 2. Highways. 3. Bridges. I. Title. II. Title: Toll bridges, ferries, domestic steamship lines, and toll roads.

Transportation - Directories.

058.7
:670
F67
pt.1

Fortune.
   The Fortune directory; the 500 largest
U.S. industrial corporations, and the 50
largest banks, merchandising, transportation,
life-insurance, and utility companies. New
York, 1967.
   40p.

   1. Industry - Direct. 2. Business - Direct.
3. Banks and banking - Direct. 4. Transportation - Direct. 5. Life insurance companies -
Direct. 6. Public utilities - Direct. I. Title:
500 largest U.S. industrial corporations.
II. Title.

Transportation - Directories.

R
058.7
:658
M27

Metropolitan management, transportation
and planning directory, 19

   Wheaton, Ill., Hitchcock Pub. Co., 19
   v.

For complete information see main card.

   1. Management - Direct. 2. Transportation -
Direct. 3. Planning - Direct. I. Hitchcock
Publishing Co.

Transportation - Direct.

058.7
:388
N67

Northwestern University. Transportation
Center.
   A directory of transportation education
in American colleges and universities.
Compiled by Gilbert James. Evanston, Ill.,
1961.
   49p.

   1. Transportation - Direct. 2. Transportation
- Study and teaching. I. James, Gilbert, comp.

Transportation - Directories.

058.7
:388
H68

U.S. Dept. of Housing and Urban Development.
Urban Transportation Administration.
   Directory of urban mass transportation
demonstration projects. Wash.,
   v.
   For complete information see main card.
   Kept up-to-date by press releases; these may
be consulted in the Urban Transportation Admin.

   1. Transportation - Direct. I. Title.
II. Title: Urban mass transportation demonstration projects.

TRANSPORTATION - DIRECTORIES.

058.7
:388
H68d

U.S. Dept. of Housing and Urban
Development.
   A directory of urban transportation
research and planning projects.
Washington, U.S. Dept. of Housing and
Urban Development, Office of Urban
Transportation Planning and Liason,
Div. of Systems Research and
Development, 1969.
   45p. (M/MP-92)
   1. Transportation - Direct. I. Title.

Transportation - Directories.

058.7
:388
P81

U.S. Bureau of Public Roads.
   Directory, urbanized area transportation
planning programs. Wash., 1967.
   47p.

   1. Transportation - Direct. 2. City
planning - Direct. I. Title.

Transportation - District of Columbia.

711.3
(7526)
B15
no. 7

Baltimore Regional Planning Council.
   Baltimore-Washington interregional study,
land use and transportation. [In cooperation
with] National Capital Regional Planning
Council. [Baltimore] 1960.
   130p. (Its Technical report no. 7)
   U.S. Urban Renewal Adm. UPAP.
   1. Metropolitan area planning - Baltimore.
2. Metropolitan area planning - District of
Columbia. 3. Transportation - Baltimore.
4. Transportation - District of Columbia.
I. U.S. National   Capital Regional Planning Council.   II. U.S. URA-UPAP.
Baltimore-   Washington area.

Transportation - District of Columbia.

711.3
(7526)
B15
no.7-8

Baltimore Regional Planning Council.
   Baltimore-Washington interregional study,
land use and transportation. Summary.
[In cooperation with] National Capital
Regional Planning Counci. Baltimore, 1960.
[12]p. (Its Technical report no. 7-8)
U.S. Urban Renewal Adm. UPAP.

   1. Metropolitan area planning - Baltimore. 2. Metropolitan area planning - District of Columbia.
3. Transportation - District of Columbia. 4. Transportation - Baltimore. 5. Land use - Baltimore.
6. Land use -   District of Columbia.
              (Cont'd on next card)

Transportation - District of Columbia.

711.3
(7526)
B15
no.7-8

Baltimore Regional Planning Council.
   Baltimore-Washington interregional study,
land use and transportation...1960.
                 (Card 2)

   I. U.S. National Capital Regional Planning
Council. II. U.S. URA-UPAP. Baltimore -
Washington area.

Transportation - District of Columbia.

388
(753)
D18

Davidson, H   O
   Feasibility analysis of rapid transit
vehicle systems, by H. O. Davidson and
others. Preliminary draft. Wash., U.S.
National Capital Transportation Agency,
1962.
   1v. (Operations Research, inc.
Technical report 173)

   1. Transportation - District of Columbia.
2. Journey to work. I. U.S. National
Capital Transportation Agency.
II. Operations   Research, inc.

Transportation - District of Columbia.

FOLIO
388
(7531)
D25

De Leuw, Cather and Co.
   Mass transportation survey, National Capital
region: civil engineering report for the National Capital Planning Commission and the
National Capital Regional Planning Council.
Chicago, 1 59.
   98p. illus., maps, tables.
   1. Transportation - District of Columbia,
metropolitan area. 2. Traffic surveys - District of Columbia metropolitan area. I. U.S.
National Capital Planning Commission. II.
U.S. National Cap-   ital Regional Planning
Council.

TRANSPORTATION - DISTRICT OF COLUMBIA.

388
(753)
D47r

District of Columbia. City Council.
   Report on the City Council approval of
the mass transportation and major
thoroughfare plans for the District of
Columbia. [Wash.] 1969.
   101p.
   1. Transportation - District of Columbia.
2. Journey to work. 3. Highways - District
of Columbia. I. Title: Mass transportation
and major thoroughfare plans for the
District of Columbia.

Transportation - District of Columbia.

VF
711.73
(753)
D47

District of Columbia Metropolitan Area
Highways Users Conference, 1962.
   Freeways move more people better;
pertinent facts about Washington's
transportation crisis. Washington,
D.C., 1962.
   15p.

   1. Highways - District of Columbia.
2. Transportation - District of Columbia.
I. Title.

Transportation - District of Columbia.

388
(753)
D47

District of Columbia Transit System.
   An area-wide system of monorail rapid
transit for Washington, D. C. and its environs. Washington, [1959]
   12p. illus., diagrs., maps.

   1. Transportation - District of Columbia.

Transportation - District of Columbia.

VF
388
(753)
F22b

Federal City Council.
   Balanced transportation policy statement. [Washington] 1964.
   folder.

   1. Transportation - District of
Columbia.

Transportation - District of Columbia.

VF
388
(753)
F22

Federal City Council.
   Transportation plan, National Capital
region, recommendations by the Federal
City Council. Washington, 1960.
   [14]p.

   1. Transportation - District of Columbia.

Transportation - District of Columbia.

388
(753)
G78

Gruen (Victor) Associates.
   Anacostia urban core; a study prepared for
the National Capital Planning Commission.
Washington, 1967.
   25p.

   1. Transportation - District of Columbia.
2. Journey to work. I. U.S. National Capital
Planning Commission. II. Title.

TRANSPORTATION - DISTRICT OF COLUMBIA
   METROPOLITAN AREA.

388
(7531)
M171

Maryland. Maryland-National Capital Park and
Planning Commission.
   Impact; a working document for metrospace
3. [Silver Spring, Md.] 1971.
   63p.
   Cover title.
   A symposium on metro area impact: Land use
policies and regulations, support systems...

   1. Transportation - District of Columbia
metropolitan area. 2. Journey to work.
I. Title.

TRANSPORTATION - DISTRICT OF COLUMBIA
   METROPOLITAN AREA.

388
(7531)
M17

Maryland. Maryland-National Capital Park and
Planning Commission.
   Metro impact. [Silver Spring, Md.] 1970.
   [28]p. (Metro impact series)

   1. Transportation - District of Columbia
metropolitan area. 2. Journey to work.
I. Title.

Transportation - District of Columbia.

388
(753)
O87

Our Nation's Capital; the city and the
freeway, a symposium, Washington, D.C.,
May 23, 1965. Wash., 1965.
   30p.

   1. Transportation - District of Columbia.
2. Highways - District of Columbia.
3. Journey to work.

Transportation - District of Columbia.

VF
711.3
(7531)
S85

Sunday Star.
   The new Washington; an era of
renaissance. Washington, the
Sunday Star, September 17, 1961, Section W.
   [20]p.

   1. Metropolitan area planning - District
of Columbia. 2. Transportation - District
of Columbia.

388
(753)
285

Transportation - District of Columbia.

Sunday Star.
Preview of 1970; the subway station to be built under 8th and G Streets N.W. by 1970. Washington, 1966.
27-33p.   (Section W)

Issue of October 30, 1966.

1. Transportation - District of Columbia.
2. Journey to work. I. Title.

388
(7531)
C65WME

TRANSPORTATION - DISTRICT OF COLUMBIA.
U.S. CONGRESS. SENATE. COMMITTEE ON THE JUDICIARY.
WASHINGTON METROPOLITAN TRANSIT COMPACT AMENDMENTS. REPORT TO ACCOMPANY H.J. RES. 693. WASHINGTON, GOVT. PRINT. OFF., 1962.
19P. (87TH CONGRESS, 2D SESSION. SENATE. REPORT 2156)

1. TRANSPORTATION - DISTRICT OF COLUMBIA.

VF
388
(753)
W17pr

Transportation - District of Columbia.
Washington Metropolitan Area Transit Authority.
Progress report, regional rapid rail. Washington, Office of Community Services, 1967.
folder.

1. Transportation - District of Columbia.
2. Journey to work. 3. Railroads.

388
(7531)
C65w
1966
H-R

TRANSPORTATION - DISTRICT OF COLUMBIA.
U.S. CONGRESS. HOUSE. COMMITTEE ON THE JUDICIARY.
WASHINGTON METROPOLITAN AREA TRANSIT AUTHORITY. REPORT TOGETHER WITH ADDITIONAL VIEWS TO ACCOMPANY H.J. RES 1163. WASHINGTON, GOVT. PRINT. OFF., 1966.
59P. (89TH CONGRESS, 2D SESSION. HOUSE. REPORT 1914)

1. TRANSPORTATION - DISTRICT OF COLUMBIA.

388
(7531)
C65w

Transportation - District of Columbia.
U.S. Congress. Senate. Committee on the Judiciary.
Washington metropolitan area transit regulation compact. Report to accompany H. J. Res. 402. Washington, Govt. Print. Off., 1960.
56p.   (86th Cong., 2d sess. Senate. Report no. 1906)

1. Transportation - District of Columbia.

VF
388
(753)
W17p

Transportation - District of Columbia.
Washington Metropolitan Area Transit Authority.
Proposed regional rapid rail transit system. Washington, Office of Community Services, 1967.
map.

1. Transportation - District of Columbia.
2. Railroads. 3. Journey to work.

388
(7531)
C65m

Transportation - District of Columbia.
U.S. Congress. Joint Committee on Washington Metropolitan Problems.
Metropolitan transportation. Staff report on investigation of status and prospects for the mass transportation survey. Washington, Govt. Print. Off., 1958.
34p. tables.

85th Cong. 2d sess.

1. Transportation - District of Columbia.

Folio
388
(7531)
W17t

Transportation - District of Columbia.
U.S. National Capital Planning Commission.
Transportation plan, National Capital Region. The mass transportation survey report, 1959. Washington, 1959.
[87]p. illus., maps. tables.

In cooperation with the National Capital Regional Planning Council.

1. Transportation - District of Columbia.
2. Journey to work.

388
(753)
W17pro

Transportation - District of Columbia.
Washington Metropolitan Area Transit Authority.
Proposed regional rapid rail transit plan & program. Washington, 1967.
39p.

1. Transportation - District of Columbia.
2. Highways - District of Columbia.
3. Journey to work. I. Title.

388
(753)
C65n

Transportation - District of Columbia.
U.S. Congress. Joint Committee on Washington Metropolitan Problems.
National Capital transportation act of 1960. Hearings before the Joint Committee on Washington Metropolitan Problems, Congress of the United States, Eighty-sixth Congress, second session pursuant to S. Con. Res. 101 on S. 3193 and H.R. 11135. Washington, Govt. Print. Off., 1960.
299p.   illus., maps.
Hearings held May 5 and 6, 1960.

1. Transportation -   District of Columbia.

385
(753)
W17
1965

Transportation - District of Columbia.
U.S. National Capital Transportation Agency.
Rail rapid transit for the Nation's Capital Transit development program 1965. Rev. Washington, 1965.
39p.

1. Railroads - District of Columbia.
2. Transportation - District of Columbia.
3. Journey to   work. I. Title.

VF
388
(7531)
W17ra

Transportation - District of Columbia.
Washington Metropolitan Area Transit Authority.
Rapid rail transit facts. Washington [1967?]
Folder.

1. Transportation - District of Columbia.
2. Journey to work. I. Title.

388
(753)
C65

Transportation - District of Columbia.
U.S. Congress. Senate. Committee on the District of Columbia.
Aiding in the development of a unified and integrated system of transportation for the National Capital region; to create a temporary National Capital Transportation Agency; to authorize negotiation to create an interstate agency; and for other purposes. Report to accompany S. 3193. Washington, Govt. Print. Off., 1960.
18p. (86th Cong., 2d sess. Senate. Report no. 1631)

1. Transportation -   District of Columbia.

388
(753)
W17

Transportation - District of Columbia.
U.S. National Capital Transportation Agency.
Report, 1st-   1965-
Wash., 1966-
v.   annual.

For complete information see main card.

1. Transportation - District of Columbia.
2. Journey to work.

388
(7531)
A21

Transportation - District of Columbia metropolitan area.
Adams, Howard and Greeley.
General development plan for the National Capital region. Prepared for the mass transportation survey as directed by the National Capital Planning Commission and the National Capital Regional Planning Council. Washington, 1959.
34p. maps. (in pocket)

(Continued on next card)

388
(753)
C654
1952
S-H

TRANSPORTATION - DISTRICT OF COLUMBIA.
U.S. CONGRESS. SENATE. COMMITTEE ON INTERSTATE AND FOREIGN COMMERCE.
WASHINGTON METROPOLITAN AREA TRANSIT PROBLEM. HEARINGS, EIGHTY-SECOND CONGRESS, SECOND SESSION, ON S. 1868 AND S.J. RES. 135, SUBMITTED MAY 21-22, 1952. WASHINGTON, GOVT. PRINT. OFF., 1952.
71P.

1. TRANSPORTATION - DISTRICT OF COLUMBIA. I. TITLE.

VF
388
(7531)
W17tra

Transportation - District of Columbia.
U.S. National Capital Transportation Agency.
Transportation Agency asks authority to buy land for stations, parking lots, and express transit. Washington, 1961.
[2]p.

1. Transportation - District of Columbia.

388
(7531)
A21

Adams, Howard and Greeley. General development plan for ... (Card 2)

1. Transportation - District of Columbia metropolitan area. 2. Land use - District of Columbia metropolitan area. I. U.S. National Capital Planning Commission. II. U.S. National Capital Regional Planning Council.

388
(7531)
C65WASH

TRANSPORTATION - DISTRICT OF COLUMBIA.
U.S. CONGRESS. SENATE. COMMITTEE ON THE JUDICIARY.
WASHINGTON METROPOLITAN AREA TRANSIT AUTHORITY COMPACT. REPORT TO ACCOMPANY S. 3488. WASHINGTON, GOVT. PRINT. OFF., 1966.
29P. (89TH CONGRESS, 2D SESSION. SENATE. REPORT 1491)

1. TRANSPORTATION - DISTRICT OF COLUMBIA.

VF
388
(753)
W17a

Transportation - District of Columbia.
Washington Metropolitan Area Transit Authority.
Authorized basic rapid rail transit system. Washington, D.C., Office of Community Services, 1967.
map.

1. Transportation - District of Columbia.
2. Journey to work. 3. Railroads.

388
(7531)
A56

Transportation - District of Columbia metropolitan area.
Alper, Jerome M
Transit regulation for the metropolitan area of Washington, D.C. Prepared for National Capital Planning Commission and National Capital Regional Planning Council. Washington, 1955.
56p.

1. Transportation - District of Columbia metropolitan area. I. U.S. National Capital Planning Commission. II. U.S. National Capital Regional Planning Council.

388
(7531)
B14
Bain, Henry.
Reverse-flow express bus service; a proposal for improved transit service between inner-city residential areas of Washington, D.C. and suburban employment centers in Montgomery County, Maryland. Wash., Washington Center for Metropolitan Studies, 1968.
60p. (Washington Center for Metropolitan Studies. Improving transportation in the Washington metropolitan area no. 1)

1. Transporta   tion - D.C. metropolitan area.
(Cont'd on next card)

Transportation - D.C. metropolitan area.

388
(7531)
B14
Bain, Henry.   Reverse-flow...1968.
(Card 2)

2. Journey to work. I. Washington Center for Metropolitan Studies. II. Title.

388
(7531
:016)
C51
1960
Transportation - District of Colombia metropolitan area.
Clark, David Sanders.
A guide to sources of information pertinent to planning a transportation system for the Washington metropolitan area. Prepared for the Northwest Committee for Transportation Planning. Washington, 1960.
44p.

1. Transportation - District of Columbia metropolitan area. I. District of Columbia. Northwest Committee for Transportation   Planning.

388
(7531
:016)
C51
1961
Transportation - District of Columbia metropolitan area.
Clark, David Sanders.
A guide to sources of information pertinent to planning a transportation system for the Washington metropolitan area. Prepared for the Northwest Committee for Transportation Planning. 2d ed. Washington, 1961.
38p.

1. Transportation - District of Columbia metropolitan area. I. District of Columbia. Northwest Committee for Transportation   Planning.

711.3
(7531)
E26r
1966
Transportation - District of Columbia metropolitan area.
Economic Associates.
The regional development guide, 1966-2000. Prepared for National Capital Regional Planning Council. Wash., 1966.
2pts. in 1v.
"Pt. 2, a very detailed technical appendix."
Contents:Appx.: no.1. Regional growth 1950-2000. no.2. Regional statistics, 1960-2000. no.3. NCRPC policies 1952-1966. no.4. NCRPC staff studies. no.5. Local zoning and planning standards.

(Cont'd on next card)

711.3
(7531)
E26r
1966
Economic Associates. The regional development guide, 1966-2000...1966. (Card 2)

1. Metropolitan area planning - District of Columbia. 2. Transportation - District of Columbia metropolitan area. 3. Population - District of Columbia metropolitan area. I. U.S. National Capital Regional Planning Council. II. Title.

388
(753)
D47i
Transportation - District of Columbia metropolitan area.
District of Columbia. Committee on Urban Conservation.
Issues confronting the Nation's Capital; freeways and our city; costs, displacement, suburban sprawl, alternatives. A handbook on transportation facts, National Capital region. Wash., 1965.
16p.

1. Transportation - District of Columbia metropolitan area. 2. Highways - District of Columbia metropolitan area. I. Title: Freeways and our   city. II. Title.

388
(7531)
C31
Transportation - District of Columbia
D.C. Transit System, Inc. Metropoleton Area
A modern all-bus rapid transit system for the Washington Metropolitan Area. A proposal for the Washington Metropolitan Air Transit Commission. Washington, D.C., 1964.
35 p.

1. Transportation - District of Columbia Metropolitan area. 2 Journey to work I. Title. II. Washington Metropolitan Area Transit Commission. III Title: Rapid transit system for the Washington Metropoleton Area.

388
(7531)
D47
Transportation - District of Columbia metropolitan area.
D.C. Transit System, inc., Washington, D.C.
Proposal for a demonstration model of a controlled high-speed Superail transit system for mass transportation, Washington, D.C., to Dulles International Airport. In collaboration with S. H. Bingham. [Washington] 1962.
83p.

1. Transportation - District of Columbia metropolitan area. 2. Railroads. I. Bingham, Sidney H. II. Title: Superail transit system for mass transportation, Washington, D.C. to Dulles International Airport.

388
(7531)
D47r
Transportation - District of Columbia metropolitan area.
District of Columbia Transit System.
A report to the President of the United States on transportation in the Washington metropolitan area and its environs. Washington, 1963.
16p.

1. Transportation - District of Columbia metropolitan area.

711.3
(7531)
E26
Transportation - District of Columbia metropolitan area.
Economic Associates.
Prospective growth of the Washington metropolitan area and its central core. Washington, 1963.
2v.   (NCTA technical report)

Reprinted August 1963, by National Capital Transportation Agency.

1. Metropolitan areas - District of Columbia. 2. Transportation - District of Columbia Metropolitan area. I. U.S. National Capital Transportation Agency.

711.3
(7531)
E26r
Transportation - District of Columbia metropolitan area.
Economic Associates.
Regional growth, 1950-2000: the regional development guide. Prepared for National Capital Regional Planning Council. Wash., 1966.
2 pts. in 1v.
"Pt. 2, a very detailed technical appendix."

1. Metropolitan areas - District of Columbia. 2. Transportation - District of Columbia metropolitan area. 3. Population - District of Columbia metropolitan area. 4. Metropolitan area planning - District of Columbia. I. U.S. National Capital Regional Planning Council.

711.73
:330
(7531)
G26
Transportation - District of Columbia metropolitan area.
George Washington University, Washington, D.C.
Parkway impact study; an investigation of the effects of parkways in the National Capital Region. Prepared ... under terms of National Parks Service, in cooperation with the Bureau of Public Roads [and others.] [Washington] 1962.
152p.
(Cont'd on next card)

711.73
:330
(7531)
G26
George Washington University, Washington, D.C.   Parkway impact study ...
(Card 2)

1. Highways - Economic effect - District of Columbia. 2. Transportation - District of Columbia metropolitan area. 3. Traffic surveys - District of Columbia metropolitan area. 4. Journey to work. I. U.S. Bureau of Public Roads. II. Title. III. U.S. National   Parks Service.

Folio
388
(7531)
G45
Transportation - District of Columbia metropolitan area.
Gilman (W.C.) and Co.
Traffic, revenue and operating costs; by W.C. Gilman & Co. and Alan M. Voorhees and Associates. Rev. McLean, Va., 1969.
106p.
Prepared for the Washington Metropolitan Area Transit Authority.

1. Transportation - District of Columbia metropolitan area. 2. Journey to work. 3. Traffic surveys - District of Columbia metropolitan area. I. Title. II. Voorhees (Alan M.) and Associates. III. Washington Metropolitan   Area Transit Authority.

388
(753)
L47
Transportation - District of Columbia metropolitan area.
Little (Arthur D.)
Transportation planning in the District of Columbia, 1955 to 1965: a review and critique. A report to the Policy Advisory Committee to the District Commissioners. [Wash.] 1966.
68p.
Bibliography: p. b1-b24.

1. Transportation - District of Columbia metropolitan area. 2. Transportation - Economic effect. 3. Traffic - District of   Columbia metropolitan area. I. District of   Columbia. Board of Commissioners.   II. Title.

388
(7531)
M27p
Transportation - District of Columbia metropolitan area.
Metropolitan Washington Council of Governments.
Preliminary regional forecasts for 1990, socio-economic characteristics by census tracts and traffic zones. Washington, 1967.
1v.
Distributed by U.S. Clearinghouse for Federal Scientific and Technical Information as PB 177 505.

1. Transportation - District of Columbia metropolitan area. 2. Journey to work. I. Metropolitan Washington Council of Governments.   II. Title.

388
(7531)
M277
Transportation - District of Columbia metropolitan area.
Metropolitan Washington Council of Governments.
Program design for comprehensive transportation planning. [Washington] Metropolitan Washington Council of Governments and National Capital Region Transportation Planning Board, 1967.
1v.
U.S. Dept. of Housing and Urban Development. UPAP.
Distributed by U.S. Clearinghouse for Federal Scientific and Technical Information. as [Document] PB 177 514.
(Continued on next card)

388
(7531)
M277
Metropolitan Washington Council of Governments. Program...1967. (Card 2)

1. Transportation - District of Columbia metropolitan area. I. U.S. National Capital Region Transportation Planning Board. II. U.S. Dept. of Housing and Urban Development. UPAP. III. Title.

388
(7531)
M87
TRANSPORTATION - DISTRICT OF COLUMBIA METROPOLITAN AREA.
Murin, William J
Mass transit policy planning: an incremental approach. Lexington, Mass., Heath Lexington Books, 1971.
123p. (Studies in social and economic process)

Bibliography: p. 105-112.

1. Transportation - District of Columbia metropolitan area. 2. Subways. 3. Journey to work. I. Title.

VF
388
(7531)
N17
Transportation - District of Columbia Metropolitan Area.
National Capitol Planning Commission.
Mass transportation survey. Part 1: Basic freeway plan, National Capitol Region. Washington, 1958.
folder. map.

Attached: Gigantic freeway plan urged for D.C. area, by George Beveridge; proposed freeway system includes both the loop and arterial types. Detached from the Sunday Star, Washington, D. C., Nov. 9, 1958.
1. Transportation - District of Columbia Metropolitan area. Highways - District of Columbia Metropolitan   politan area.

FOLIO 388 (7531) 854

Transportation - District of Columbia metropolitan area.

Smith (Wilbur) and Associates.
Mass transportation survey, National Capital region: traffic engineering study, 1958. New Haven? 1959.
125p. diagrs., maps, tables.

Report submitted to the National Capital Planning Commission and the National Capital Regional Planning Council.

1. Transportation - District of Columbia metropolitan area. 2. Traffic surveys - District of Columbia metropolitan area. I. U.S. National Capital Planning Commission. II. U.S. National Capital Regional Planning Council.

---

388 (7531) C65tr

Transportation - District of Columbia Metropolitan Area.

U.S. Congress. House. Committee on the District of Columbia.
Transit program for the National Capital Region. Hearings before the Subcommittee No. 6 of the Committee on the District of Columbia, House of Representatives, Eighty-eighth Congress, first session on H.R. 6633 and H.R. 7240, to authorize the prosecution of a transit development program for the National Capital Region. Washington, Govt. Print. Off., 1963.
462p. (Cont'd on next card)

---

388 (7531) C65

U.S. Congress. House. Committee on the Judiciary. District...1959-60. (Card 2)

in the Washington, District of Columbia, metropolitan area, and for other purposes. Washington, Govt. Print. Off., 1959-60.
2 pts. (Serial no. 11)

Hearings held Aug. 26, 1959 and Mar. 9, 1960.

1. Transportation - District of Columbia metropolitan area.

711.3 (7531) D47

Transportation - District of Columbia metropolitan area.

The Sunday Star.
METRO. City of tomorrow. (Detached from the Sunday Star, Washington, Oct. 6, 13, 20, 27, Nov. 3, 10, 17, 24, 1957)
8 pts. illus.

Contents: -[pt.I] New urban problem needs new answers, Oct. 6.-[pt.II] Washington area ponders its future, Oct. 13. -[pt. 3] Congestion forces new transit approach, Oct. 20. -[pt. 4] Potomac is key to future water supply, Oct. 27.-[pt.5] Human problems call for regional attack, Nov. 3.
(See Card No. 2)

---

388 (7531) C65tr

U.S. Congress. House. Committee on the District of Columbia. Transit program for the National Capital Region... (Card 2)

Hearings held July 9-31, 1963.

1. Transportation - District of Columbia Metropolitan Area. 2. Journey to work. I. Title.

---

388 (7531) C65WAS H-H

TRANSPORTATION - DISTRICT OF COLUMBIA METROPOLITAN AREA.

U.S. CONGRESS. HOUSE. COMMITTEE ON THE JUDICIARY.
WASHINGTON AREA TRANSIT COMPACT AMENDMENTS. HEARING BEFORE THE SUBCOMMITTEE NO. 3, 87TH CONGRESS, 2D SESSION, ON H.J. RES. 693 AND H.J. RES. 694. WASHINGTON, GOVT. PRINT. OFF., 1962.

1. TRANSPORTATION - DISTRICT OF COLUMBIA METROPOLITAN AREA.

711.3 (7531) D47

The Sunday Star. METRO. 1957. (Card No. 2)

-[pt.6] Area lacks unity in control of pollution, Nov. 10. -[pt. 7] Area seeks ways to keep open spaces, Nov. 17. -[pt. 8] Regional action wins wide acceptance, Nov. 24.

1.Metropolitan area planning - District of Columbia metropolitan area. 2.City planning - District of Columbia. 3.Urban renewal - District of Columbia. 4.Transportation - District of Columbia metropolitan area. 5.Regional planning
(See Card No. 3)

---

388 (7531) C65tr Suppl.

Transportation - District of Columbia metropolitan area.

U.S. Congress. House. Committee on the District of Columbia.
Transit program for the National Capital Region. Supplement to Hearings before Subcommittee no. 6 of the Committee on the District of Columbia, House of Representatives, Eighty-eighth Congress, first session on H.R. 6633, H.R. 7249, and H.R. 8929. To authorize the prosecution of a transit development program
(Cont'd on next card)

---

388 (7351) C65WS

TRANSPORTATION - DISTRICT OF COLUMBIA METROPOLITAN AREA.

U.S. CONGRESS. HOUSE. COMMITTEE ON THE JUDICIARY.
WASHINGTON METROPOLITAN AREA TRANSIT REGULATION COMPACT. REPORT TO ACCOMPANY H.J. RES. 402. WASHINGTON, GOVT. PRINT. OFF., 1960.
52P. (86TH CONGRESS, 2D SESSION. HOUSE REPORT 162.)

1. TRANSPORTATION - DISTRICT OF COLUMBIA METROPOLITAN AREA.

711.3 (7531) D47

The Sunday Star. METRO. 1957. (Card No. 3)

- District of Columbia metropolitan area. 6.Water pollution - District of Columbia metropolitan area. 7.Water supply - District of Columbia metropolitan area. I.Title.

---

388 (7531) C65tr Suppl.

U.S. Congress. House. Committee on the District of Columbia. Transit program for ... (Card 2)

for the National Capital Region. Washington, Govt. Print. Off., 1963.
89p.

Hearings held: July 9-31, 1963, Nov. 12-13, 1963.

1. Transportation - District of Columbia metropolitan area. 2. Journey to work.

---

388 (7531) C65WM

TRANSPORTATION - DISTRICT OF COLUMBIA METROPOLITAN AREA.

U.S. CONGRESS. HOUSE. COMMITTEE ON THE JUDICIARY.
WASHINGTON METROPOLITAN TRANSIT COMPACT AMENDMENTS. REPORT TO ACCOMPANY H.J. RES 693. WASHINGTON, GOVT. PRINT. OFF., 1962.
19P. (87TH CONGRESS, 2D SESSION. HOUSE. REPORT 1579)

1. TRANSPORTATION - DISTRICT OF COLUMBIA METROPOLITAN AREA.

VF 388 (7531) 885

Transportation - District of Columbia Metropolitan Area.

The Sunday Star.
Subway and road needs for 1980 outlined in survey, by George Beveridge. [With] Summary of mass transit program for Capital area. Washington, July 12, 1959.
clippings. illus.

1. Transportation - District of Columbia Metropolitan Area. I. Beveridge, George.

---

388 (7531) C65dis

Transportation - District of Columbia metropolitan area.

U.S. Congress. House. Committee on the Judiciary.
D.C. area transit compact. Hearings before Subcommittee no. 3 of the Committee on the Judiciary, House of Representatives, Eighty-ninth Congress, second session on H.J. Res. 1163, ... to grant the consent of Congress for the States of Virginia and Maryland and the District of Columbia to amend the Washington metropolitan area transit regulation compact to establish an organization empowered to provide transit facilities in the National Capital.
(Cont'd on next card)

---

388 (7531) C65f

Transportation - District of Columbia metropolitan area.

U.S. Congress. Joint Committee on Washington Metropolitan Problems.
Further progress on transportation and other metropolitan problems. Report of the Joint Committee on Washington Metropolitan Problems. Washington, Govt. Print. Off., 1960.
5p. (86th Cong., 2d sess. Senate. Report no. 1074)

1. Transportation - District of Columbia metropolitan area. 2. Metropolitan areas - District of Columbia.

---

388 (7531) C65tr 1963 H-R

Transportation - District of Columbia metropolitan area.

U.S. Congress. House. Committee on the District of Columbia.
Transit development program for the National Capital region; report to accompany H.R. 8929. [Washington] Govt. Print. Off., 1963.
59p. (88th Cong., 1st sess. House. Report no. 1005)

"Publications of the Joint Committee on Washington Metropolitan Problems relating to transportation in the National Capital
(Cont'd on next card)

---

388 (7531) C65dis

U.S. Congress. House. Committee on the Judiciary. D.C. area transit compact... 1966. (Card 2)

region and for other purposes and to enact said amendment for the District of Columbia. Wash., For Sale by the Dept. of Doc., Govt. Print. Off., 1966.
292p. (Serial no. 18)
Hearings held July 20-27, August 3, 1966.

1. Transportation - District of Columbia metropolitan area.

---

388 (7531) C65NAT

TRANSPORTATION - DISTRICT OF COLUMBIA METROPOLITAN AREA.

U.S. CONGRESS. JOINT COMMITTEE ON WASHINGTON AND METROPOLITAN PROBLEMS.
NATIONAL CAPITAL TRANSPORTATION ACT OF 1960. CONFERENCE REPORT TO ACCOMPANY H.R. 11135. WASHINGTON, GOVT. PRINT. OFF., 1960.
12P. (86TH CONGRESS, 2D SESSION. HOUSE. REPORT 2061)

1. TRANSPORTATION - DISTRICT OF COLUMBIA METROPOLITAN AREA.

---

388 (7531) C65tr 1963 H-R

U.S. Congress. House. Committee on the District of Columbia. Transit development program ... (Card 2)

region": p. 50.

1. Transportation - District of Columbia metropolitan area. I. Title.

---

388 (7531) C65di

Transportation - District of Columbia metropolitan area.

U.S. Congress. House. Committee on the Judiciary.
District of Columbia, Maryland, and Virginia mass transit compact. Hearings before Subcommittee no. 3 of the Committee on the Judiciary, House of Representatives, Eighty-sixth Congress, first session on H. J. Res. 402 granting the consent and approval of Congress for the states of Virginia and Maryland and the District of Columbia to enter into a compact related to the regulation of mass transit
(Continued on next card)

---

388 (7531) C65NAC

TRANSPORTATION - DISTRICT OF COLUMBIA METROPOLITAN AREA.

U.S. CONGRESS. JOINT COMMITTEE ON WASHINGTON AND METROPOLITAN PROBLEMS.
NATIONAL CAPITAL TRANSPORTATION ACT OF 1960. REPORT TO ACCOMPANY H.R. 11135. WASHINGTON, GOVT. PRINT. OFF., 1960.
26P. (86TH CONGRESS, 2D SESSION. HOUSE. REPORT 1962)

1. TRANSPORTATION - DISTRICT OF COLUMBIA METROPOLITAN AREA.

388
(7531)
C65n

Transportation - District of Columbia metropolitan area.
U.S. Congress. Joint Committee on Washington Metropolitan Problems.
National Capital Transportation Authority, preliminary draft for discussion purposes. Staff report prepared for the Joint Committee on Washington Metropolitan Problems, Congress of the United States. Washington, 1959.
31p.

At head of title: 86th Cong., 1st sess.

1. Transportation - District of Columbia metropolitan area.

388
(7531)
C65NA

U.S. CONGRESS. SENATE. COMMITTEE ON THE DISTRICT OF COLUMBIA. NATIONAL CAPITAL ...1961.   (CARD 2)

DEVELOPMENT PROGRAM AND TO FURTHER THE OBJECTIVES OF THE ACT APPROVED JULY 14, 1960. WASHINGTON, GOVT. PRINT. OFF., 1961.
34P.

1. TRANSPORTATION - DISTRICT OF COLUMBIA METROPOLITAN AREA. I. U.S. NATIONAL CAPITAL TRANSPORTATION AGENCY.

388
G25

Transportation - District of Columbia metropolitan area.
U.S. General Services Administration.
Federal employee parking and transportation survey, Washington metropolitan area. Washington, 1962.
3v.
Contents.-v.1. Improvements in public transportation.

1. Transportation - District of Columbia metropolitan area. 2. Parking - District of Columbia metropolitan area.

388
(7531)
C65o

Transportation - District of Columbia metropolitan area.
U.S. Congress. Joint Committee on Washington Metropolitan Problems.
Organization for transportation in the National Capital region. Selected documents prepared for the Joint Committee on Washington Metropolitan Problems, Congress of the United States. Washington, Govt. Print. Off., 1960.
111p.

At head of title: 86th Cong., 2d sess.

1. Transportation - District of Columbia metropolitan area.

388
(7531)
C65d

Transportation - District of Columbia metropolitan area.
U.S. Congress. Senate. Committee on the Judiciary.
District of Columbia, Maryland, and Virginia mass transit compact. Hearings before the special subcommittee of the Committee on the Judiciary, United States Senate, Eighty-sixth Congress, second session on H.J. Res. 402 granting the consent and approval of Congress for the states of Virginia and Maryland and the District of Columbia to enter into a compact related to   the regulation of mass
(Continued on next card)

VF
388
(7531)
M17m

Transportation - District of Columbia metropolitan area.
U.S. National Capital Transportation Agency.
Mass transit for Shirley highway seen in Roads Bureau, NCTA accord. Washington, 1961.
5p.

1. Transportation - District of Columbia metropolitan area.

388
(7531)
C65p

Transportation - District of Columbia metropolitan area.
U.S. Congress. Joint Committee on Washington Metropolitan Problems.
Preliminary financial and organizational report regarding metropolitan transportation. Washington, Govt. Print. Off., 1959.
25p.   tables.
Prepared by the Institute of Public Administration as part of the Washington mass transportation survey and cited in Chapter VII of the report.
At head of title: 86th Cong., 1st sess.
1. Transportation - District of Columbia metropolitan area. I. Institute of Public Administration.

388
(7531)
C65d

Transportation - District of Columbia metropolitan area.
U.S. Congress. Senate. Committee on the Judiciary. District...1960. (Card 2)

transit in the Washington, D.C. metropolitan area, and for other purposes. Washington, Govt. Print. Off., 1960.
131p.

Hearings held June 24-25, 1960.

1. Transportation - District of Columbia metropolitan area.

VF
388
(7531)
M17a

Transportation - District of Columbia metropolitan area.
U.S. National Capital Transportation Agency.
The NCTA plan for transportation in the National Capital Region; a program that meets the needs of the region at the least cost by giving people a choice of how to travel, by rapid transit or by automobile. Washington, 1962.
folder.

1. Transportation - District of Columbia metropolitan area.

388
(7531)
C65t

Transportation - District of Columbia metropolitan area.
U.S. Congress. Joint Committee on Washington Metropolitan Problems.
Transportation plan for the National Capital region. Hearings before the Joint Committee on Washington Metropolitan Problems, Congress of the United States, Eighty-sixth Congress, first session on report of the Washington mass transportation survey. Washington, Govt. Print. Off., 1960.
1070p. diagrs., maps.
Hearing held: Nov. 9-14, 1959.
1. Transportation - District of Columbia metropolitan area.

388
(7531)
C65wa

Transportation - District of Columbia metropolitan area.
U.S. Congress. Senate. Committee on the Judiciary.
Washington metropolitan area transit authority compact. Hearing before a special subcommittee of the Committee on the Judiciary, United States Senate, Eighty-ninth Congress, second session on S. 3488 to enact for the District of Columbia and grant the consent of Congress to the Interstate transit compact among Maryland, Virginia and the District of Columbia. Washington, Govt. Print. Off., 1966.
118p.
Hearing   held August 22, 1966.
(Cont'd on next card)

VF
388
(7531)
M17p

Transportation - District of Columbia metropolitan area.
U.S. National Capital Transportation Agency.
Proposed legislation authorizing the Agency to carry out Part one of the Transit Development Program for the National Capital region. [Washington, 1961]
[5]p.

1. Transportation - District of Columbia metropolitan area.

388
(7531)
C657

Transportation - District of Columbia metropolitan area.
U.S. Congress. Senate. Committee on Public Works.
Metropolitan area pilot transportation study. Study implementing Senate resolution 250 concerning: The relationship between highway facilities and other modes of commuter service in the movement of people to and from the Washington, D.C. area from areas beyond the proposed range of projected mass transit and urban freeway facilities and The feasibility of solid waste disposal using rail haul techniques. Presented by Mr. Jennings Randolph. Wash., Govt. Print. Off., 1968.
139p. (90th Cong. 2d sess. Senate
(Cont'd on next card)

388
(7531)
C65

Transportation - District of Columbia metropolitan area.
U.S. Congress. Senate. Committee on the Judiciary. Washington metropolitan area transit authority compact...1966. (Card 2)

1. Transportation - District of Columbia metropolitan area. I. Title.

388
(7531)
M17r

Transportation - District of Columbia metropolitan area.
U.S. National Capital Transportation Agency.
Recommendations for transportation in the National Capital region; finance and organization. A report to the President for transmittal to Congress. Washington, For sale by the Supt. of Documents, Govt. Print. Off., 1962.
92p.

1. Transportation - District of Columbia metropolitan area.

388
(7531)
C657

U.S. Congress. Senate. Committee on Public Works. Metropolitan...1968. (Card 2)

document no. 117)
Bibliography: p. 115-116.

1. Transportation - District of Columbia metropolitan area. 2. Journey to work. I. Title. II. Randolph, Jennings.

388
(7531)
C65

Transportation - District of Columbia Metropolitan Area.
U.S. Congress. Joint Committee on Washington Metropolitan Problems.
Washington Metropolitan Area transportation problems. Hearings before the Joint Committee on Washington Metropolitan Problems, Eighty-fifth Congress, second session, on transportation problems in Maryland, Virginia, and the Washington metropolitan area, May 22, 23 and June 10, 1958. Washington, Govt. Print. Off., 1958.
382p. illus., maps.
1. Transportation - District of Columbia Metropolitan Area. I. Title.

388
(7531)
M17st

Transportation - District of Columbia metropolitan area.
U.S. National Capital Transportation Agency.
A study of bus rapid transit operations of the National Capital Region. Prepared by NCTA staff with supplementary studies by Operations Research Incorporated, Kaiser Engineers, [and] Wilbur Smith & Associates. [Wash.] 1963.
102p. (NCTA technical report)

1. Transportation - District of Columbia metropolitan area. 2. Journey to work. I. Title: Bus rapid transit operations.

388
(7531)
C65NA

TRANSPORTATION - DISTRICT OF COLUMBIA METROPOLITAN AREA.
U.S. CONGRESS. SENATE. COMMITTEE ON THE DISTRICT OF COLUMBIA.
NATIONAL CAPITAL TRANSIT DEVELOPMENT PROGRAM. AUTHORIZE ACQUISITION AND PURCHASE OF MEDIAN STRIPS FOR MEMORIAL PARKWAY, ROUTE 66 AND ROUTE 95, FREEWAY TRANSIT STATIONS, PARKING LOTS IN METROPOLITAN WASHINGTON REGION. HEARING BEFORE THE SUBCOMMITTEE ON METROPOLITAN AREA PROBLEMS... EIGHTY-SEVENTH CONGRESS, FIRST SESSION, ON S. 2397, AUTHORIZING THE NATIONAL CAPITAL TRANSPORTATION AGENCY TO CARRY OUT PART 1 OF ITS TRANSIT
(CONTINUED ON NEXT CARD)

388
(7531)
E92

Transportation - District of Columbia metropolitan area.
U.S. Executive Office of the President.
Transportation in the Northeastern Megalopolitan Corridor. Task force report to an Executive Office Steering Committee. [Washington] 1962.
36p.

1. Transportation - District of Columbia metropolitan area. 2. Northeastern Megalopolitan Corridor.

388
(7531)
M17p

Transportation - D.C. metropolitan area.
Washington Metropolitan Area Transit Authority.
Proposed regional rapid rail transit plan and program. Washington, 1968.
39p.

1. Transportation - D.C. metropolitan area. 2. Traffic surveys. 3. Railroads - D.C. metropolitan area. I. Title. II. Title: Rapid rail transit plan and program.

388 (7531) W17re
Washington Metropolitan Area Transit Commission.
Recommendations for immediate transit improvement. The report of the WMATC Advisory Committee. Washington, 1964.
45p.

1. Transportation - District of Columbia metropolitan area. 2. Journey to work. 3. Traffic - District of Columbia metropolitan area.

---

388 (7531) V66
Voorhees (Alan M.) and Associates, inc. A systems...1969. (Card 2)

II. U.S. Mass Transportation Demonstration Grant Program. District of Columbia metropolitan area. III. Title.

VF 388 (7531) W17regi 1967
Transportation - District of Columbia metropolitan area.
Washington Metropolitan Area Transit Authority.
Regional rapid rail. Progress report. Washington, 1967.
folder.

1. Transportation - District of Columbia metropolitan area. 2. Railroads. I. Title: Regional rapid rail.

---

388 (7531) N17s
Transportation - District of Columbia metropolitan area.
U.S. National Capital Transportation Agency.
Summary report on the transit development program. [Washington] Govt. Print. Off., 1963.
42p.

1. Transportation - District of Columbia metropolitan area.

---

388 (7531) W17me
TRANSPORTATION - D.C. METROPOLITAN AREA.
Washington Metropolitan Area Transit Authority.
Metro; a rapid rail transit system for the National Capital Region. Wash., 1969.
44p.

1. Transportation - D.C. metropolitan area. 2. Journey to work. I. Title.

---

388 (7531) W17r
Transportation - District of Columbia metropolitan area.
Washington Metropolitan Area Transit Commission.
Report, 19
Washington, 19
v. annual.

For complete information see shelf list.

1. Transportation - District of Columbia metropolitan area.

---

388 (7531) N17tr
Transportation - District of Columbia metropolitan area.
U.S. National Capital Transportation Agency. Transit development program. Report on part 1. Washington, 1961.
1v.

1. Transportation - District of Columbia metropolitan area.

---

388 (7531) W17m
Transportation - District of Columbia metropolitan area.
Washington Metropolitan Area Transit Authority.
Metro; adopted regional rapid rail transit plan and program, Washington, 1968.
30p.

1. Transportation - District of Columbia metropolitan area. 2. Railroads - District of Columbia metropolitan area. 3. Journey to work. I. Title.

---

388 (7531) W17s
TRANSPORTATION - DISTRICT OF COLUMBIA METROPOLITAN AREA
Washington Metropolitan Area Transit Commission.
The scrip system of the D.C. Transit System, Washington, D.C. Final report. Wash., 1970.
63p.

Mass transportation Demonstration Project INT-MTD-15.

1. Transportation - District of Columbia metropolitan area. 2. Journey to work. I. Title. II. U.S. Mass Transportation Demonstration Grant Program.

---

388 (7531) N17tran
Transportation - District of Columbia metropolitan area.
U.S. National Capital Transportation Agency. Transportation in the National Capital Region, finance and organization. A report to the President for transmittal to Congress. Washington, Govt. Print. Off., 1962.
92p.
Appendices - Dr. Kohl has cop. in office
1. Transportation - District of Columbia metropolitan area.

---

388 (7531) W17met
TRANSPORTATION - DISTRICT OF COLUMBIA METROPOLITAN AREA.
Washington Metropolitan Area Transit Authority.
Metro. Info kit, Wash., 1969.
kit (28 pieces)

1. Transportation - District of Columbia metropolitan area. 2. Journey to work. 3. Railroads - District of Columbia metropolitan area. I. Title.

---

388 (7531) W17t
Transportation - District of Columbia metropolitan area.
Washington Metropolitan Area Transportation Study.
Technical procedures employed in the forecasting of 1980 internal person trips. Staff report. [Washington] 1963.
64p.

Bibliography: p. 62-64.

1. Transportation - District of Columbia metropolitan area. 2. Journey to work.

---

388 (7531) P72
Transportation - D.C. metropolitan area.
U.S. President, 1963- (Johnson)
Washington metropolitan area transit regulation compact. A communication from the President of the United States transmitting a draft of proposed legislation to grant the consent of Congress for the States of Virginia and Maryland and the District of Columbia to amend the Washington metropolitan area transit regulation compact to establish an organization empowered to provide transit facilities in the National Capital region and for other purposes and to enact said amendment for the District of

(Continued on next card)

---

388 (7531) W17
Transportation - District of Columbia metropolitan area.
Washington Metropolitan Area Transit Commission.
The minibus in Washington, D.C. Final report on a Mass Transportation Demonstration Project. Prepared under the direction of Government of the District of Columbia in conjunction with Washington Metropolitan Area Transit Commission. Based on materials developed by D.C. Highway Department and others. Washington, 1965.
71p.
U.S. Housing and Home Finance Agency.

(Continued on next card)

---

388 (7531) W17te
Transportation - District of Columbia metropolitan area.
Washington Metropolitan Area Transportation Study.
Technical procedures employed in the travel forecast for the 1965 interstate cost estimate. [Prepared in cooperation with] Maryland State Roads Commission ... the U.S. Dept. of Commerce, Bureau of Public Roads. Washington, 1964.
127p.
1. Transportation - District of Columbia metropolitan area. 2. Journey to work. 3. Automation. I. Maryland. State Roads Commission.

---

388 (7531) P72
U.S. President, 1963- (Johnson)
Washington metropolitan area transit regulation compact...1966. (Card 2)

Columbia. Washington, Govt. Print. Off., 1966.
30p. (89th Cong., 2d sess. House. Document no. 452)

1. Transportation - D.C. metropolitan area.

---

338 (753) W17
Washington Metropolitan Area Transit Commission. The minibus in Washington, D.C....1965. (Card 2)
Mass Transportation Demonstration Grant Program.
1. Transportation - District of Columbia metropolitan area. I. Title. II. U.S. Housing and Home Finance Agency. Mass Transportation Demonstration Grant Program.

VF 388 (7531) W17
Transportation - District of Columbia Metropolitan Area.
Washington Post and Times Herald.
Bus-rail system urged to avert traffic chaos. [and] Pooks Hill to downtown in 20 min. envisioned for 1970 in subway plan, by Jack Eisen. [With] Survey foresees outlays for transit, shift in offices. Detached from the Washington Post and Times Herald, Sunday July 12, 1959.
clippings. illus. maps.

1. Transportation - District of Columbia Metropolitan Area. I. Eisen, Jack.

---

388 (7531) V66
TRANSPORTATION - DISTRICT OF COLUMBIA METROPOLITAN AREA.
Voorhees (Alan M.) and Associates.
A systems analysis of transit routes and schedules. Prepared for Washington Metropolitan Area Transit Commission. McLean, Va., 1969.
101p.
U.S. Mass Transportation Demonstration Grant Program.
1. Transportation - District of Columbia metropolitan area. 2. Journey to work. I. Washington Metropolitan Area Transit Commission. (Cont'd on next card)

VF 388 (7531) W17reg
Transportation - District of Columbia metropolitan area.
Washington Metropolitan Area Transit Authority.
Regional metro system; adopted March 1, 1968 by the Washington Metropolitan Area Transit Authority. Wash., 1968.
map.

1. Transportation - District of Columbia metropolitan area. 2. Railroads - District of Columbia metropolitan area. 3. Journey to work. I. Title.

5821 5822 5823 5824
TRANSPORTATION - DUBUQUE, IOWA. DUBUQUE CO., IOWA. AREA PLANNING COMMISSION.
PLANNING AND ZONING PROGRAM: 1, PRELIMINARY TRANSPORTATION PLAN; 2, COUNTY TRANSPORTATION PLAN; 3, FINANCIAL RESOURCES INVENTORY; 4, FORECASTS. BY GREEN ENGINEERING CO. DUBUQUE, IOWA, 1968.
4 v. (HUD 701 REPORT)

1. TRANSPORTATION - DUBUQUE, IOWA. I. GREEN ENGINEERING CO. II. HUD. 701. DUBUQUE CO., IOWA.

57J5   TRANSPORTATION - DUVAL CO., FLA.
JACKSONVILLE-DUVAL AREA PLANNING BOARD.
PRELIMINARY LAND USE AND TRANSPORTATION
PLAN. BY BARBOUR-COOPERA AND ASSOCIATES,
INC. JACKSONVILLE, FLA., 1968.
71P. (HUD 701 REPORT)

1. LAND USE - DUVAL CO., FLA.
2. TRANSPORTATION - DUVAL CO., FLA.
I. BARBOUR-COOPER AND ASSOCIATES, INC.
II. HUD. 701. DUVAL CO., FLA.
III. HUD. 701. JACKSONVILLE, FLA.

---

388   Transportation - Economic effect.
F76   Fromm, Gary, ed.
Transport investment and economic develop-
ment. Washington, Brookings Institution,
Transport Research Program, 1965.
314p.
Papers prepared for a series of Harvard
University seminars, which are part of the
Brookings Transport Research Program.
Bibliography: p.277-305.

1. Transportation - Economic effect.   2. Economic
development.   I. Brook-   ings Institution,
Washington, D.C.   II. Title.

---

388   Kalachek, Edward D   ed.   Transportation
K15   ...1970.   (Card 2)

1. Transportation - Economic effect.
2. Employment - Minority groups.
I. Goering, John M., jt. au.
II. Washington University, St. Louis.
Institute for Urban and Regional Studies.
III. U.S. Mass Transportation Demonstration
Grant Program. IV. Title.

---

388   Transportation - Economic effect.
C655 Committee for Economic Development.
Developing metropolitan transportation
policies: a guide for local leadership. A
statement on National policy by the Research
and Policy Committee. New York, 1965.
99p.

1. Transportation. 2. Transportation -
Economic effect. 3. Community development.
. I. Title.

711.14   TRANSPORTATION - ECONOMIC EFFECT.
H25   Hemmens, George C
Urban development modeling. Wash., 1970.
34p. (George Washington University. Program
of Policy Studies in Science and Technology.
Monograph no. 6)
Prepared for Seminar no. 1 of a series on the
Application of computer simulation techniques
to social and political decision-making, March,
1970.
1. Land use. 2. Transportation - Economic
effect. I. George Washington University.
Program of Policy Studies in Science and Technology. II. Title.

---

388   Transportation - Economic effect.
L157t Lensing, John B
Transportation and economic policy. New
York, Free Press, 1966.
409p.

1. Transportation - Economic effect.
2. Highways - Finance 3. Air transportation.
4. Railroads. I. Title.

711.73   Transportation - Economic effect.
C67   Cornell Aeronautical Laboratory.
A projection of technology applicable to the
future highway system of the Boston-
Washington corridor. Prepared for U.S.
Dept. of Commerce, Office of Undersecretary
for Transportation Policy, Buffalo, N.Y.,
Cornell Aeronautical Laboratory of Cornell
University, 1964.
256p.   (PB 166 878)
Distributed by Clearinghouse for Federal
Scientific and Technical Information.

(Continued on   next card)

---

388   Transportation - Economic effect.
H67   Horwood, Edgar M
Community consequences of highway improve-
ment, by Edgar M. Horwood, Carl A. Zellner,
and Richard L. Ludwig. Research sponsored
by the American Association of State Highway
Officials in cooperation with the Bureau of
Public Roads. Washington, Highway Research
Board, Div. of Engineering and Industrial
Research, National Academy of Sciences,
National Research Council, 1965.
37p.   (National Cooperative Highway
Research Program. Report 18)

(Cont'd on next card)

---

388   Transportation - Economic effect.
(753) Little (Arthur D.)
L47   Transportation planning in the District of
Columbia, 1955 to 1965: a review and
critique. A report to the Policy Advisory
Committee to the District Commissioners.
[Wash.] 1966.
68p.
Bibliography: p. b1-b24.

1. Transportation - District of Columbia metropolitan area. 2. Transportation - Economic effect.
3. Traffic - District of   Columbia metropolitan
area. I. District of   Columbia. Board of
Commissioners.   II. Title.

711.73   Cornell Aeronautical Laboratory. A projec-
C67   tion of technology applicable to the future
highway system...1964.   (Card 2)

1. Highways - Boston-New York-Washington
Corridor. 2. Transportation - Economic
effect. 3. Traffic safety. I. Title: Future
highway system of the Boston-Washington
Corridor. II. Title.

---

388   Horwood, Edgar M. Community consequences of
H67   highway improvement...1965.   (Card 2)

1. Transportation - Economic effect.
2. Highways - Social effect. I. Zellner,
Carl A.   II. Ludwig, Richard L.
III. Highway Research Board. IV. Title.

---

388   Transportation - Economic effect.
L62e Locklin, David Philip, 1897-
Economics of transportation. 6th ed.
Homewood, Ill., R.D. Irwin, 1966.
882p.   (The Irwin series in economics)

1. Transportation. 2. Transportation -
Economic effect. 3. Railroads. I. Title.

·388   TRANSPORTATION - ECONOMIC EFFECT.
C71t   Crain, John L
Transportation effects on the National
Alliance of Businessmen Program. Menlo
Park, Stanford Research Institute, 1969.
26p.
Prepared for U.S. Housing and Urban
Development Dept. under Contract no. H-10-29
with the National Alliance of Businessmen.
U.S. Mass Transportation Demonstration
Grant Program.
CFSTI. PB 183 054.
1. Transportation - Economic effect.
(Cont'd on next card)

---

388   TRANSPORTATION - ECONOMIC EFFECT.
K141 Kain, John F
Interrelationships of transportation and
poverty: summary of Conference on
Transportation and Poverty, by John F.
Kain and John R. Meyer. Cambridge, Mass.,
Program on Regional and Urban Economics,
Harvard University, 1968.
24p. (Harvard University. Program on
Regional and Urban Economics. Discussion
paper no. 39)
Prepared for the American Academy of
Arts and   Sciences Conference on
(Cont'd on next card)

---

388   Transportation - Economic effect.
M22   Meck, J P
The role of economic studies in urban
transportation planning. Wash., U.S. Dept.
of Commerce, Bureau of Public Roads, 1965.
67p.
Bibliography: p. 65-67.

1. Transportation - Economic effect.
2. Economic conditions. I. U.S. Bureau of
Public Roads. II. Title.

---

388   Crain, John L   Transportation effects
C71t on...1969.   (Card 2)

2. Journey to work. I. Stanford Research
Institute. II. National Alliance of
Businessmen. III. U.S. Dept. of Housing
and Urban Development. IV. U.S. Mass
Transportation Demonstration Grant
Program. V. Title.

---

388   Kain, John F   Interrelationships...
K141 1968.   (Card 2)

Poverty and Transportation, June 7-8, 1968.

1. Transportation - Economic effect.
2. Poverty. I. Meyer, John R., jt. au.
II. Harvard University. Program on
Regional and Urban Economics. III. Title.

---

388   Transportation - Economic effect.
P22   Peck, Merton J
Competitive policy for transportation?
Washington, Brookings Institution, 1965.
244-272p.   (Brookings Institution.
Reprint no. 91)
Reprinted from Perspectives on anti-trust
policy, April 1965.

1. Transportation - Economic effect.
I. Brookings Institution. II. Title.

---

301   Transportation - Economic effect.
D67   Dorfman, Robert, ed.
Measuring benefits of government investments;
papers presented at a conference of experts held
November 7-9, 1963. Washington, Brookings
Institution, 1965.
429p. (Studies of government finance)

1. Sociology. 2. Social surveys. 3. Urban
renewal - Social effect. 4. Recreation.
5. Governmental research. 6. Transportation -
Economic effect.   I. Brookings Institution, Wash-   ington, D.C.

---

388   TRANSPORTATION - ECONOMIC EFFECT.
K15   Kalachek, Edward D   ed.
Transportation and central city unemploy-
ment. Edited by Edward D. Kalachek and
John M. Goering. St. Louis, Mo., Institute
for Urban and Regional Studies, Washington
University, 1970.
18p. (Washington University, St. Louis.
Institute for Urban and Regional Studies.
Working paper INS 5)
U.S. Dept. of Housing and Urban Develop-
ment. Mass Transportation Demonstration
Grant Program.   Contract no. H-1034)
(Cont'd on next card)

---

388   Transportation - Economic effect.
P23   Pegrum, Dudley F
Transportation; economics and public
policy. Homewood, Ill., Richard D. Irvin,
1963.
625p. (Irwin series of economics)
Bibliography: p. 601-610.

1. Transportation - Economic effect.

388
P65
Transportation - Economic effect.
Palenske, Karen R
The study of transportation requirement using national and multiregional input-output techniques. Cambridge, Harvard Economic Research Project, 1967.
71p.
Prepared for the Secretary of Transportation under contract.
Distributed by U.S. Clearinghouse for Federal Scientific and Technical Information as document PB 174 742
1. Transportation - Economic effect. 2. Industry - Statistics. I. Harvard Economic Research Project.   (Cont'd on next card)

388
(79549)
P67po
Portland-Vancouver Metropolitan Transportation Study. Social-economic study...1954. (Card 2)
1. Transportation - Portland, Or. metropolitan area. 2. Transportation - Vancouver, Wash. metropolitan area. 3. Transportation - Economic effect. 4. Journey to work. I. Oregon. University. Bureau of Municipal Research and Service. II. Oregon. State Highway Commission.

388
W17st
TRANSPORTATION - ECONOMIC EFFECT.
Washington (State) State University, Pullman.
A study of the social, economic and environmental impact of highway transportation facilities on urban communities. Prepared for Washington State Dept. of Highways in cooperation with the U.S. Bureau of Public Roads...Pullman, Highway Research Section, Engineering Research Div., Washington State University, 1968.
208p.
(Cont'd on next card)

388
P65
Palenske, Karen R   The study of transportation requirement...1967.   (Card 2)
II. U.S. Dept. of Transportation. III. U.S. Clearinghouse for Federal Scientific and Technical Information. IV. Title.

388
(77162)
S71
no.2
Transportation - Economic effect.
Preston (E.S.) and Associates.
SCATS procedure manual no. 2, population and economics. [Prepared for] Stark County Area Transportation Study. [n.p. 1966?]
42p.
1. Transportation - Stark Co., Ohio. 2. Population - Stark Co., Ohio. 3. Transportation - Economic effect. I. Stark County (Ohio) Transportation Study.

388
W17st
Washington (State) State University, Pullman. A study...1968. (Card 2)
1. Transportation - Economic effect. 2. Highways. I. Washington (State) Dept. of Highways. II. Title.

388
(79549)
P67
Transportation - Economic effect.
Portland-Vancouver Metropolitan Transportation Study.
Interim report 1-205, location. Prepared by the Technical Advisory Committee in cooperation with the U.S. Dept. of Commerce, Bureau of Public Roads, and U.S. Housing and Home Finance Agency. [Salem, Or.] State Highway Commission, 1964.
54p.
1. Transportation - Portland, Or. metropolitan area. 2. Transportation - Vancouver, Wash.
(Continued on next card)

382
S71
Transportation - Economic effect.
Stanford Research Institute. Management Services Div.
The economic feasibility of passenger hydrofoil craft in U.S. domestic and foreign commerce, by Den G. Haney and Stanton R. Smith. Prepared for Maritime Administration, U.S. Dept. of Commerce, Washington, D.C. Menlo Park, Calif., 1961.
220p.   (Cont'd. on next card)

388
W45e
Transportation - Economic effect.
Wildermuth, Bruno.
The effect of transportation on residential location. A report submitted for the course, CE 250, "Analysis of transportation systems." Berkeley, University of California, 1964.
21p.
At head of title: Institute of Transportation and traffic engineering. Graduate report.
1. Transportation - Economic effect. I. California. University. Institute of Transportation and Traffic Engineering. II. Title.

388
(79549)
P67
Portland-Vancouver Metropolitan Transportation Study. Interim report 1-205, location...1964. (Card 2)
metropolitan area. 3. Transportation - Economic effect. 4. Journey to work. I. Oregon. State Highway Commission. II. U.S. Housing and Home Finance Agency.

382
S71
Stanford Research Institute. Management Services Div.   The economic feasibility of passenger hydrofoil ... (Card 2)
SRI Project no. IMU-3532.
1. Commercial policy. 2. Transportation - Economic effect. I. Title. II. Title: Hydrofoil craft in U.S. domestic and foreign commerce. III. Haney, Den G.   IV. Smith, Stanton, R.V. V. U.S. Maritime Administration.

388
Z84d
Zwick, Charles J
The demand for transportation services in a growing economy. Santa Monica, Calif., Rand Corp., 1962.
10p.
"This paper was prepared for presentation at the 42nd Annual Meeting of the Highway Research Board, Washington, D.C., January 9, 1965."
1. Transportation - Economic effect. I. Rand Corp.

388
(79549)
P67p
v.1
Transportation - Economic effect.
Portland-Vancouver Metropolitan Transportation Study.
Portland-Vancouver Metropolitan Transportation Study. Vol. 1. Factual data report. Prepared in cooperation with the U.S. Dept. of Commerce, Bureau of Public Roads. Salem, Or., State Highway Commission, [1964?]
135p.
1. Transportation - Portland, Or. metropolitan area. 2. Transportation - Vancouver, Wash. metropolitan area. 3. Transportation -
(Continued on next card)

388
U54
Transportation - Economic effect.
Universities-National Bureau Committee for Economic Research.
Transportation economics: a conference of the Committee. New York, National Bureau of Economic Research. Distributed by Columbia University Press, 1965.
451p.   (National Bureau of Economic Research. Special conference series no. 17)
1. Transportation. 2. Transportation - Economic effect. 3. Railroads. I. National Bureau of Economic Research. II. Title.

388
(775)
D62
Transportation - Economic effect - Wisconsin.
Dodge, William H
Transportation in the Wisconsin economy. Madison, Wis., University of Wisconsin, School of Commerce, Bureau of Business Research and Service, 1955.
103p.
At head of title: Wisconsin Commerce reports, vol. 4, no. 1, August, 1955.
1. Transportation - Economic effect - Wisconsin. 2. Traffic - Wisconsin. I. Wisconsin. University. Bureau of Business Research and Service.

388
(79549)
P67p
v.1
Portland-Vancouver Metropolitan Transportation Study. Portland-Vancouver Metropolitan Transportation Study. Vol. 1...1964. (Card 2)
Economic effect. 4. Journey to work. I. Oregon. State Highway Commission.

385
(7437)
C65
Transportation - Economic effect.
U.S. Dept. of Commerce. (Transportation Research)
Studies on the economic impact of railway abandonment and service discontinuance. [Sect. 1] Implications of railway abandonments (a general survey), by W.B. Saunders Co. [Sect. 2] The economic impact of the discontinuance of the Rutland Railway (condensed version) by Boston University, Bureau of Business Research. Wash., For sale by the Supt. of Doc., Govt. Print. Off., 1965.
1 v.   (PB 167 640)
(Cont'd on next card)

388
(74892)
H43
Transportation - Ellwood City, Pa.
Hill (Carroll V.) & Associates.
Streets, parking, and transportation, Ellwood City, Pennsylvania. Prepared for the Ellwood City Borough Planning Commission. Dayton, Ohio, 1958.
56p.   ([Ellwood City, Pa.] rept. no. 3)
In cooperation with Bureau of Community Development, Pennsylvania Dept. of Commerce. U.S. Urban Renewal Adm. UPAP.
1. Transportation - Ellwood City, Pa. I. Ellwood City, Pa. Planning Commission. II. U.S. URA-UPAP. Ellwood City, Pa.

388
(79549)
P67po
Transportation - Economic effect.
Portland-Vancouver Metropolitan Transportation Study.
Social-economic study. Interim report 1-205, location. Prepared by Bureau of Municipal Research and Service, University of Oregon for Oregon State Highway Commission in cooperation with U.S. Dept. of Commerce, Bureau of Public Roads. [Salem, Or.?] 1954.
67p.
(Continued on next card)

385.
(7437)
C65
U.S. Dept. of Commerce. (Transportation Research) Studies on the economic impact of railway abandonment and service discontinuance...1965.   (Card 2)
Distributed by U.S. Clearinghouse for Federal Scientific and Technical Information.
1. Railroads - Rutland, Vt. 2. Transportation - Economic effect. I. Saunders (W.B.) & Co. Implications of railway abandonments. II. Boston University. Bureau of Business Research. The economic impact of the discontinuance of the Rutland Railway. III. U.S. Clearinghouse for Federal Scientific and Technical Information. IV. Title.

3362
TRANSPORTATION - ESSEX CO., N.J.
ESSEX CO., N.J. PLANNING BOARD.
TRAFFIC STUDY NO. 7: TRAFFIC, STREET AND HIGHWAY CLASSIFICATION REPORT. N.P., 1969.
1 V. (HUD 701 REPORT)
1. TRANSPORTATION - ESSEX CO., N.J. I. HUD. 701. ESSEX CO., N.J.

Transportation - Eugene-Springfield area.

331 (79531) 072   Oregon. University. Bureau of Municipal Research and Service.
    Industry-transportation study Eugene-Springfield area. Prepared through the cooperative efforts of the Bureau of Municipal Research and Service, University of Oregon, and the Central Lane County Planning Commission, Eugene, Oregon. Eugene, Or., 1961.
    pts.
    Contents:-pt. 1. Employment forecast.
    U.S. Urban Renewal Adm. UPAP.
1. Employment - Eugene-Springfield area, Or.
2. Transportation - Eugene-Springfield area. I. Central Lane County, Or. Planning Commission. II. Title. III. U.S. URA-UPAP. Eugene-Springfield, Or.

---

338 (784) F17   Fargo, N.D. City Planning Commission.
    Application of the Metropolitan Council of Governments and Planning Commissions, Cities of Fargo & West Fargo, North Dakota, Moorhead & Dilworth, Minnesota for a Mass Transportation Technical Study Grant... Fargo, 1970.
    1v.
    U.S. Dept. of Housing and Urban Development. Mass Transportation Demonstration Grant Program.
1. Transportation - Fargo, N.D. 2. Journey to work. I. U.S. Mass Transportation Demonstration Grant Program. Fargo, N.D.

TRANSPORTATION - FARGO, N.D.

Transportation - Finance.

388 N17b no. 6B   National Committee on Urban Transportation, District of Columbia.
    Cost accounting for streets and highways. Chicago, Public Administration Service, 1959.
    35p. (Procedure manual no. 6B)
    "For use in conjunction with [its] Better transportation for your city ... "
1. Transportation - Finance. I. Public Administration Service.

---

388 (79531) E83eu   Eugene-Springfield Area Transportation Study. (Technical Advisory Committee)
    Eugene-Springfield area transportation study. Minority report on the 1985 transportation plan interim report. Prepared by Jerry G. Olmstead. Eugene, 1967.
    8p.
    Oregon P-61.
1. Transportation - Eugene-Springfield metropolitan area. I. Olmstead, Jerry G. II. Title.

TRANSPORTATION - EUGENE-SPRINGFIELD METROPOLITAN AREA.

---

384 A47s   AirportTransit.
    Skylounge ground operations study. [Final report for Skylounge project, November 10, 1966-July 27, 1967. Prepared for System Development Corporation] Los Angeles, 1967.
    157p.
    Cover title.
    U.S. Mass Transportation Demonstration Grant Program. Subcontract no.: 67-59.
    (Cont'd on next card)

TRANSPORTATION - FINANCE.

---

388 N17b no. 6A   National Committee on Urban Transportation, District of Columbia.
    Financial records and reports. Chicago, Public Administration Service. 1958.
    102p. (Procedure manual no. 6A)
    "For use in conjunction with [its] Better transportation for your city ... "
1. Transportation - Finance. I. Public Administration Service.

Transportation - Finance.

---

388 (79531) E83   Eugene-Springfield Area Transportation Study. (Technical Advisory Committee)
    Eugene-Springfield Area Transportation Study, 1985 transportation plan. Interim report. Prepared in cooperation with U.S. Dept. of Transportation, Bureau of Public Roads and Dept. of Housing and Urban Development. Eugene, Or., 1967.
    38p.
1. Transportation - Eugene-Springfield Or. metropolitan area. I. U.S. Bureau of Public Roads. II. U.S. Dept. of Housing and Urban Development.

Transportation - Eugene-Springfield Or. metropolitan area.

---

384 A47s   AirportTransit. Skylounge...1967.
    (Card 2)
1. Air transportation. 2. Transportation - Finance. I. System Development Corp. II. U.S. Mass Transportation Demonstration Grant Program. III. Title: Skylounge project. IV. Title.

---

388 N17b no. 12A   National Committee on Urban Transportation, District of Columbia.
    Modernizing laws and ordinances. Chicago, Public Administration Service, 1958.
    78p. (Procedure manual no. 12A)
    "For use in conjunction with [its] Better transportation for your city ... "
1. Transportation - Finance. I. Public Administration Service.

Transportation - Finance.

---

388 (79531) E83e v. 1   Eugene-Springfield Area Transportation Study. (Technical Advisory Committee)
    Eugene-Springfield area transportation study. Vol. 1, factual data report. [Portland] Oregon State Highway Commission, [1968?]
    106p.
    Survey conducted in cooperation with U.S. Dept. of Transportation, Bureau of Public Roads, and Dept. of Housing and Urban Development.
    Oregon P-61.
1. Transportation - Eugene-Springfield metropolitan area. I. Oregon. State Highway Commission.
    (Cont'd on next card)

TRANSPORTATION - EUGENE-SPRINGFIELD METROPOLITAN AREA.

---

388 (794) C15   California. Legislature. Assembly. Interim Committee on Transportation and Commerce.
    Southern California rapid transit financing. Los Angeles, 1965.
    99p.
1. Transportation - California. 2. Journey to work. 3. Transportation - Finance. I. Title.

Transportation - Finance.

---

388 (77162) S71 no.8   Prestud (E.S.) and Associates.
    SCATS procedure manual no. 8, financial resources. [Prepared for] the Stark County Area Transportation Study. [n.p., 1966?]
    55p.
1. Transportation - Stark Co., Ohio. 2. Transportation - Finance. I. Stark County (Ohio) Area Transportation Study.

Transportation - Finance.

---

388 (79531) E83e v. 1   Eugene-Springfield Area Transportation Study. (Technical Advisory Committee) Eugene... [1968?]
    (Card 2)
II. U.S. Dept. of Housing and Urban Development. III. Title.

---

388 C78   Crumlish, Joseph D
    Notes on the state-of-the art of benefit-cost analysis as related to transportation systems. Washington, Technical Analysis Div., Institute for Applied Technology, National Bureau of Standards, for sale by the Supt. of Documents, Govt. Print. Off., 1966.
    41p. (U.S. National Bureau of Standards. NBS technical note no. 294)
1. Transportation - Finance. 2. Labor relations. I. U.S. National Bureau of Standards.

Transportation - Finance.

---

388 (744) M17m Suppl. no.3   Systems Analysis and Research Corp.
    Supplementary statistics and analysis relating to the Demonstration Project. Prepared under the direction of Joseph F. Maloney for the Mass Transportation Commission, Commonwealth of Massachusetts. Boston, 1964.
    234p.
    Supplement no. 3 to Mass transportation in Mass.
    (Cont'd. on next card)

---

388 (4) B76   Brookings Institution.
    The transport revolution in Europe, by Wilfred Owen. Washington, 1961.
    [32]p. (Its Reprint no. 53)
    Reprinted from Europe's needs and resources: trends and prospects in eighteen countries. Dec. 1961. Chap. 9. p. 279-311.
    Cover title.
1. Transportation - Europe. I. Owen, Wilfred.

Transportation - Europe.

---

388 (797) D25r   De Leuw, Cather and Company.
    Report to the Puget Sound Governmental Conference on a regional transit plan. San Francisco, 1966.
    49p.
    U.S. Urban Renewal Adm. UPAP.
1. Transportation - Washington (State) 2. Transportation - Finance. 3. Journey to work. I. Puget Sound Governmental Conference. II. U.S. URA- UPAP. Washington (State)

Transportation - Finance.

---

388 (744) M17m Suppl. no.3   Systems Analysis and Research Corp.
    Supplementary statistics and analysis relating to the Demonstration Project ...
    (Card 2)
    U.S. Housing and Home Finance Agency. Mass Transportation Demonstration Grant Program.
1. Transportation - Mass. 2. Transportation - Finance. I. Maloney, Joseph F. II. Massachusetts. Mass Transportation Commission. Mass transportation ... III. U.S. Housing and Home Finance Agency. Mass Transportation Demonstration Grant Program.

711.552 (77233) E81   Evansville-Vanderburgh (Ind.) Metropolitan Plan Commission.
    Design for downtown Evansville, 1942-1982. Evansville, Ind., 1963.
    66p.
    U.S. Urban Renewal Adm. UPAP.
1. Business districts - Evansville, Ind. 2. Transportation - Evansville, Ind. I. U.S. URA-UPAP. Evansville, Ind.

Transportation - Evansville, Ind.

---

388 (794) L47   Litton Industries. Economic Development Div.
    Proposal to the Div. of Highways, Dept. of Public Works, State of California for a Work Program to design and develop specifications for an integrated study of transportation in California. Beverly Hills, Calif., 1964.
    1v.
    Cover title: Toward a systems approach for a California integrated transportation network.
1. Transportation - Calif. 2. Journey to work. 3. Transportation - Finance. I. California. Dept. of Public Works. II. Title. III. Title: Toward a systems transportation network.

Transportation - Finance.

---

388 T42   Tideman, T Nicolaus.
    Rational bases for potential and transport cost models of location. Cambridge, Mass., Program on Regional and Urban Economics, Harvard University, 1968.
    9p. (Harvard University. Program on Regional and Urban Economics. Discussion paper no. 38)
1. Transportation - Finance. 2. Industrial location. I. Harvard University. Program on Regional and Urban Economics. II. Title.

TRANSPORTATION - FINANCE.

388.
C65AM
1962
S-R.
TRANSPORTATION - FINANCE.
U.S. CONGRESS. SENATE. COMMITTEE ON GOVERNMENT OPERATIONS.
AMENDMENT OF SECTION 109 OF THE FEDERAL PROPERTY AND ADMINISTRATIVE SERVICES ACT OF 1949; GENERAL SUPPLY FUND. REPORT TO ACCOMPANY H.R. 8100. WASHINGTON, GOVT. PRINT. OFF., 1962. 16P. (87TH CONGRESS, 2D SESSION. SENATE. REPORT NO. 1827)

1. TRANSPORTATION - FINANCE. I. FEDERAL PROPERTY AND ADMINISTRATIVE SERVICES ACT OF 1949.

388
H58
Jan.
1962
Transportation - Finance.
U.S. Housing and Home Finance Agency. Office of the Administrator. Office of Transportation.
Information on the Mass Transportation Demonstration Grant Program. [Washington] 1962.
5p.

1. Transportation - Finance. 2. Grants-in-aid. I. U.S. Housing and Home Finance Agency. Mass Transportation Demonstration Grant Program.

388
H58
Feb.
1962
Transportation - Finance.
U.S. Housing and Home Finance Agency. Office of the Administrator. Office of Transportation.
Information on the mass transportation loan program. Washington, 1962.
12p.

1. Transportation - Finance. 2. Grants-in-aid.

388
H58pt
Dec.
1962
Transportation - Finance.
U.S. Housing and Home Finance Agency. Office of the Administrator. Office of Transportation.
Program guide on the Mass Transportation Demonstration Grant Program. Rev. Washington, D.C., Govt. Print. Off., 1962.
5p.

1. Transportation - Finance. 2. Grants-in-aid. I. U.S. Housing and Home Finance Agency. Mass Transportation Demonstration Grant Program.

388
H58p
Transportation - Finance.
U.S. Housing and Home Finance Agency. Office of the Administrator. Office of Transportation.
Program guide on the mass transportation loan program. Washington, 1962.
4p.

1. Transportation - Finance. 2. Grants-in-aid.

388
H58p
Dec.
1962
Transportation - Finance.
U.S. Housing and Home Finance Agency. Office of the Administrator. Office of Transportation.
Program guide on the mass transportation loan program. Rev. Washington, Govt. Print. Off., 1962.
4p.

1. Transportation - Finance. 2. Grants-in-aid.

388
H58u
Transportation - Finance.
U.S. Housing and Home Finance Agency. Office of the Administrator. Office of Transportation.
Urban transportation; fact sheet on the Federal aids available to localities on problems of urban mass transportation. Washington, 1962.
4p.

1. Transportation - Finance. 2. Grants-in-aid.

388
H58u
Dec.
1962
Transportation - Finance.
U.S. Housing and Home Finance Agency. Office of the Administrator. Office of Transportation.
Urban transportation; fact sheet on the Federal aids available to localities on problems of urban mass transportation. Rev. Washington, Govt. Print. Off., 1962.
[3]p.

1. Transportation - Finance. 2. Grants-in-aid.

388
(7443)
P21
Transportation - Fitchburg, Mass.
Peat, Marwick, Livingston & Co.
Fitchburg-Leominster urban area transportation study. New York, 1967.
161p.

Bibliography: p. 159 - 160.
Prepared for: Massachusetts Dept. of Public Works in cooperation with the U.S. Dept. of Transportation, Federal Highway Administration, Bureau of Public Roads.
1. Transportation - Fitchburg, Mass.
2. Transportation - Leominster, Mass. I. Massachusetts. Dept. of Public Works. II. Title.

711.73
(759)
H68
Transportation - Florida.
Howard, Needles, Tammen, and Bergendoff.
Highway engineers' report to the East Central Florida Regional Planning Council. Kansas City, Kan., 1965.
198p.

U.S. Urban Renewal Adm. UPAP.

1. Highways - Florida. 2. Transportation - Florida. I. East Central Florida Regional Planning Council. II. Title. III. U.S. URA- UPAP. Florida.

388
(759)
P17
Transportation - Florida.
Parsons, Brinckerhoff, Quade and Douglas.
Transportation: mass transit. Report to the East Central Florida Regional Planning Council. New York, 1965.
14p.

U.S. Urban Renewal Adm. UPAP.

1. Transportation - Florida. 2. Journey to work. I. East Central Florida Regional Planning Council. III. U.S. URA-UPAP. Florida. II. Title.

711.4
(78868)
F67p
pt.3
Transportation - Fort Collins, Colo.
Fort Collins, Colo. Planning and Zoning Board.
Traffic and transportation, City of Fort Collins, Colorado, by Harold Beier. Preliminary comprehensive plan reports part 3. Fort Collins, 1958.
41p.

U.S. Urban Renewal Adm. UPAP.

1. Master plan - Fort Collins, Colo. 2. Traffic - Fort Collins, Colo. 3. Transportation - Fort Collins, Colo. I. Beier, Harold. II. U.S. URA-UPAP. Fort Collins, Colo.

388
(44)
C25
Transportation - France.
Centre d'Etudes et de Recherches sur l'Amenagement Urbain.
Etude de la demande de transport; note de synthese. Puteaux, France, Centre d'Etudes et de Recherches sur l'Amenagement Urbain, 1968.
35p.

1. Transportation - France. 2. France - Transportation. I. Title.

388
(44)
C25t
TRANSPORTATION - FRANCE.
Centre d'Etudes et de Recherches sur l'Amenagement Urbain.
Trans 18; une innovation importante en matiere de metro continu. Paris, [1969?]
[12]p.
Text in English and French.

1. Transportation - France. 2. Journey to work.

301.15
F42
TRANSPORTATION - FRANCE.
Fichelet, Monique.
Pour une approche ecologique de l'utilisation des moyens de transport. Analyse critique des methodes d'etude des deplacements de personnes dans les grandes agglomerations urbaines, par Monique Fichelet et al. Paris, Societe d'Etudes et de Recherches en Sciences Sociales, 1968-1969.
1v.
At head of title: Delegation Generale a la Recherche Scientifique & Technique. Service d'aide a la recherche et au developpement.

(Cont'd on next card)

301.15
F42
Fichelet, Monique. Pour une approche...1968-1969. (Card 2)

Action concertee urbanisation.

1. Man - Influence of environment.
2. Transportation - France. I. Societe d'etudes et de Recherches en Sciences Sociales. II. Title: Urbanization.

388
(44)
F71
TRANSPORTATION - FRANCE.
France. Ministere de l'Equipement et du Logement. (Direction de L'Amenagement Foncier et de l'Urbanisme)
Les transports urbains dans les villes nouvelles, colloque des 7 et 8 Janvier 1971. Compte rendu des debats. Paris, 1971.
221p.

1. Transportation - France. 2. New towns - France.

711.4
(44)
P17
Transportation - France.
Paris. Institut d'Amenagement et d'Urbanisme de la Region Parisienne.
Schema directeur d'amenagement et d'urbanisme de la Region de Paris. Paris, 1965.
221p.

1. City planning - France. 2. Transportation - France. 3. Industry - France.

388
(44)
S62
TRANSPORTATION - FRANCE.
Societe pour l'Advancement et l'Utilisation de la Recherche Operationnelle Civile.
Rapport de synthese; recherches sur l'analyse morphologique. Exemple d'application au probleme de transport interurbain. Paris, Delegation Generale a la Recherche Scientifique et Technique (D.G.R.S.T.) 1969.
10p.
1. Transportation - France. 2. Journey to work. I. France. Delegation Generale a la Recherche Scientifique et Technique. II. Title.

388
(44)
W27
Transportation - France.
Wetmore, Warren C
French company speeding development of aerotrain. [New York] McGraw-Hill, 1966.
[8]p.

Reprinted from Aviation week and space technology.

1. Transportation - France. 2. Airports. I. Title. II. Title: Aerotrain.

711.4
(44)
P17c
TRANSPORTATION - FRANCE - PARIS.
Paris. Institut d'Amenagement et d'Urbanisme de la Region Parisienne.
Cahiers. v. 1-
[Paris] 1964-
v.
For Library holdings see main entry.

1. City planning - France - Paris.
2. New towns - U.K. - London. 3. Transportation - France - Paris. 4. City planning - U.K.

4209
4210

TRANSPORTATION - FRANKLIN, MICH.
FRANKLIN, MICH. VILLAGE PLANNING
COMMISSION.
PRELIMINARY BASIC PLANNING STUDIES: 1,
COMMUNITY FACILITIES PLAN; 2,
TRANSPORTATION PLAN. BY PARKINS, ROGERS
AND ASSOCIATES, INC. DETROIT, 1969.
2 V. (HUD 701 REPORT)

1. COMMUNITY FACILITIES - FRANKLIN,
MICH. 2. TRANSPORTATION - FRANKLIN,
MICH. I. PARKINS, ROGERS AND ASSOCIATES.
II. HUD. 701. FRANKLIN, MICH.

388
(43)
D28

TRANSPORTATION - GERMANY.
Deutsche Akademie für Städtebau und
Landesplanung.
Stadtstruktur und Verkehr.
Forschungsarbeit der Deutschen Akademie
für Städtebau und Landesplanung.
Bearbeit von Sill und Seitz. Bad
Godesberg, Bundesministerium für
Wohnungswesen und Stadtebau, 1966.
75p.
Bibliography: p. 67-68.
1. Transportation - Germany. 2. City
planning -   Germany. 3. Journey to
      (Cont'd on next card)

385
(43)
Z45

TRANSPORTATION - GERMANY.
Zimniok, Klaus.
U-Bahn und S-Bahn in Munchen; planung und
Gestaltung eines modernen Verkehramittels, von
Klaus Zimniok und dem U-Bahn-Referat.
Eppstein im Taunus, Verlag Wolfgang Zimmer,
1968.
54p.
Nachdruk aus der Zeitschrift Bayerland, Heft
11/1967.

1. Railroads - Germany. 2. Transportation -
Germany. 3. Journey to work.

Transportation - Franklin, Va.
Franklin, Va. Town Planning Commission.
Transportation. Franklin, Va., May 1953.
31p. (Its Master plan study no.2)

Price: $1.50.

388
(43)
D28

Deutsche Akademie für Städtebau und
Landesplanung. Stadtstruktur...1966.
(Card 2)

work. I. Germany. (Federal Republic
1949-) Bundesministerium für
Wohnungswesen und Stadtebau. II. Title.

Transportation - Great Falls, Mont.
388
(786)
M65

Montana. State Highway Commission.
Urban transportation survey of
Great Falls, Montana. Conducted by
Planning Survey, Div. of Montana State
Highway Commission in cooperation with
U.S. Dept. of Commerce, Bureau of Public
Roads and the city of Great Falls.
[Helena, Mont.] 1961-1965.
4v.

1. Transportation - Great Falls, Mont. 2. Highways
- Great Falls, Mont. 3. Parking - Great Falls,
Mont. 4. Traffic   surveys.
I. U.S. Bureau of   Public Roads.

Transportation - Fresno, Calif.
388
(79482)
F72

Fresno-Clovis Area Planning Commission.
Meeting with Norman A. McSweyn, Manager,
Fresno City Lines, concerning transit element
for the preliminary general plan, Aug. 23,
1957, by Kenneth R. Schneider. Fresno, 1957.
[1]p.
U.S. Urban Renewal Adm. UPAP.

1. Transportation - Fresno, Calif.
I. Schneider, Kenneth R. II. U.S.
URA-UPAP. Fresno, Calif.

388
(43)
H15s

TRANSPORTATION - GERMANY.
Hamburg. Baubehörde.
Schnellbahnbau in Hamburg. Hamburg,
Baubehörde, Amt fur Ingenieurwesen,
1969.
81p. (Hamburger Schriften zum Bau-,
Wohnungs- und Siedlungswesen. Heft
49/1969)

1. Transportation - Germany. 2.
Journey to work. 3. Railroads -
Germany. 4. Subways - Germany. I.
Title.

Transportation - Great Falls, Mont.
388
(786)
851

Small, Cooley and Associates.
Great Falls transportation plan, 1964-1981.
[Pt. 1: Economic and population studies to
1981. Pt. 2: Land use study. Prepared] for
Great Falls City-County Planning Board and
Montana State Highway Commission in coopera-
tion with U.S. Dept. of Commerce, Bureau of
Public Roads. Denver, 1965.
153p.

1. Transportation - Great Falls, Mont. 2. Economic
base studies - Great Falls, Mont. 3. Population -
Great Falls, Mont.   4. Land use - Great
Falls, Mont.   I. Title.

388
(758)
G26

TRANSPORTATION - GA.
Georgia. State Planning Bureau.
Status of transportation in Georgia.
Atlanta, [1969?]
49p.
U.S. Dept. of Housing and Urban Development.
UPAP.
Bibliography: p. 43-44.

1. Transportation - Ga. I. Title. II. U.S.
HUD-UPAP. Ga.

388
(43)
H15

Transportation - Germany.
Hamburg. Baubehörde. Tiefbauamt.
U - Bahn - Bau in Hamburg. Hamburg, 1961.
28p. (Hamburg. Baubehörde. Schriften zum
Bau-, Wohnungs - und Siedlungswesen. No. 36)

1. Transportation - Germany.

Transportation - Great Lakes region.
388
(71)
S71

Stanford Research Institute.
Economic analyses of St. Lawrence Seaway
cargo movements and forecasts of future
cargo tonnage. Prepared for the Under
Secretary for Transportation, U.S. Department of Commerce, Wash., D.C. Menlo Park,
Calif., 1965.
184p.

Distributed by U.S. Clearinghouse for
Federal Scientific and Technical Information. as Document PB 169 965.
1. Transportation. -   Great Lakes region.
I. U.S. Dept. of   Commerce. II. Title.

470-
483

TRANSPORTATION - GEORGIA.
SLASH PINE AREA PLANNING AND DEVELOPMENT
COMMISSION.
SLASH PINE AREA REGIONAL TRANSPORTATION
STUDY. A, PRELIMINARY TRANSPORTATION
PLAN; B, TECHNICAL MEMORANDUM: 1,
TRAFFIC SIMULATION MODEL EXISTING TRAVEL
PATTERNS; 2, TRAFFIC SIMULATION MODEL
TRIP GENERATION MODEL; 3, TRAFFIC
SIMULATION MODEL CALIBRATION; 4, TRAFFIC
ASSIGNMENTS; C, RECOMMENDED HIGHWAY PLAN:
1, ATKINSON COUNTY; 2, BACON COUNTY; 3,
BEN HILL COUNTY; 4, BRANTLEY COUNTY; 5,
CHARLTON COUNTY; 6, CLINCH COUNTY; 7,
COFFEE COUNTY; 8, PIERCE COUNTY; 9,
     (CONTINUED ON NEXT CARD)

388
(43)
H15g

TRANSPORTATION - GERMANY.
Hamburger Verkehrsverbund.
Geschäftsbericht, 19

Hamburg, 19

2 v.

For Library holdings see main entry.

1. Transportation - Germany.

711.4
(74881)
G72
no. 7

Transportation - Greensburg, Pa.
Central Westmoreland Regional Planning
Commission.
Circulation and transportation.
Greensburg, Pa., 1959.
15p. (Greater Greensburg planning area
master plan report no. 7)

1. Master plan - Greensburg, Pa. 2. Traffic -
Greensburg, Pa. 3. Transportation - Greensburg,
Pa. I. U.S. URA-UPAP. Greensburg, Pa.

470-
483

SLASH PINE AREA PLANNING AND DEVELOPMENT
COMMISSION. SLASH PINE AREA ...1969.
     (CARD 2)

WARE COUNTY. ATLANTA, TRAFFIC PLANNING
ASSOCIATES, INC., 1969.
14 V. (HUD 701 REPORT)

1. TRANSPORTATION - GEORGIA.
I. TRAFFIC PLANNING ASSOCIATES, ATLANTA,
GA. II. HUD. 701. GEORGIA.

388
(43)
H15n

Transportation - Germany.
Hannover. Universität. Institut für
Verkehrswirtschaft, Strasenwesen und
Städtebau.
Fliessender und ruhender Individualverkehr;
Beispiel für 8000 Einwohner: Luneburg-Kalten-
moor. Hannover, 1969.
1v. (Die Demonstrativbauvorhaben des
Bundesministeriums für Wohnungswesen und
Städtebau. Informationen Nr. 17)
Bibliography: p. 70-72.
1. Transportation - Germany. 2. Germany -
Transportation. 3. Traffic - Germany.
4. Germany -   Traffic. 5. Parking -
Germany. 6. Ge   rmany - Parking.

388
(7463)
C31

Transportation - Hartford metropolitan area
Chave, Robert W
Factors effecting bus usage in the
Hartford metropolitan area. A summary
report. Hartford Capitol Region
Planning Agency, 1964.
[21]p.
U.S. Urban Renewal Adm. UPAP.

1. Transportation - Hartford metropolitan area. 2. Journey to work.
I. Capitol Region Planning Agency, Hartford. II. U.S.   URA-UPAP.
Hartford.

711.4
(75284)
G27

Transportation - Germantown, Md.
Maryland. Maryland-National Capital Park
and Planning Commission.
Master plan for Germantown, Montgomery
County, Maryland. Silver Spring, Md.,
1967.
48p.
Cover title: Master plan for Germantown;
a corridor city.

1. Master plan - Germantown, Md.
2. Transportation - Germantown, Md.

388
(43)
P15

TRANSPORTATION - GERMANY.
Pampel, F
The Hamburg transport community, an example
of coordination and integration in public
transport. Brussels, UITP (International Union
of Public Transport) 1969.
30p.

Paper presented to the 38th International
UITP Congress, London, 1969.

1. Transportation - Germany. I. International
Union of Public Transport. II. Title.

388
(969)
H180

TRANSPORTATION - HAWAII.
Hawaii. Dept. of Planning and Economic
Development.
Oahu transportation study. Honolulu
1967.
3v.
Contents.-v.1, Economic, population, and
land use.-v.2, Mass transportation
facilities travel patterns, volumes &
forecasts.-v.3, Plan development & plans.
U.S. Dept. of Housing and Urban
Development. UPAP.
1. Trans-   portation - Hawaii.
2. Journey   to work. I. U.S.
HUD-UPAP.   Hawaii. II. Title.

Transportation - Hawaii.

711.33
(969)
H18p

Hawaii. State Planning Office.
Progress report on state transportation and general plan. Prepared by State Planning Office and State Department of Transportation. Honolulu, 1960.
25p.

1. Master plan - Hawaii. 2. Transportation - Hawaii. I. Hawaii. Dept. of Transportation. II. Title.

Transportation - Houston-Harris Co., Tex.

388
(764)
T29h

Texas. Highway Dept.
Houston-Harris County, designing a transportation system with you in mind. A preview of the Cooperative Houston Metropolitan Area Transportation Study. [Houston, Tex.] 1962.
24p.
Prepared in cooperation with U.S. Bureau of Public Roads, Automotive Safety Foundation, Texas Transportation Institute, Texas A and M College.

(Cont'd on next card)

Transportation - India.

647.1
(54)
I52hous
1966

India. Secretariat.
Tables with notes on household non-mechanised transport, and utilisation of working animals, by S.K. Goswami and others. Delhi, Manager of Publications, 1966.
72p. (Indian Statistical Institute. National sample survey no. 105)
At head of title: The National sample survey, fifteenth round: July 1959- June 1960.
1. Family income and expenditure - India. 2. Transportation - India. I. Goswami, S. K. II. Indian Statistical (Continued on next card)

Transportation - Hawaii.

388
(969)
L18

Law and Wilson-Tudor Engineering Co.
State of Hawaii transportation plan. Prepared for the Department of Planning and Research and the Department of Transportation. Honolulu, 1961.
153p.

U.S. Urban Renewal Adm. UPAP.

1. Transportation - Hawaii. I. Hawaii. Dept. of Planning and Research. II. Hawaii. Dept. of Transportation. III. U.S. URA-UPAP. Honolulu.

Transportation - Houston-Harris

388
(764)
T29h

Texas. Highway Dept. Houston-Harris County, designing a transportation system with you in mind...1962.
(Card 2)

1. Transportation - Houston-Harris Co., Tex. 2. City growth - Houston-Harris Co., Tex. 3. Houston Metropolitan Area Transportation Study. I. Title.

647.1
(54)
I52hous
1966

India. Secretariat Tables with notes...
1966.
(Card 2)

Institute. III. Title: Utilization of working animals in India

---

Transportation - Hawaii.

388
C65a

U.S. Congress.
Alaskan and Hawaiian transportation. Joint hearings before the Senate and House Committees on Interstate and Foreign Commerce, Congress of the United States, Eighty-sixth Congress, first session on S. 1507 [etc.] Washington, Govt. Print. Off., 1961.
508p.
Hearings held Oct. 20-Nov. 18, 1959.
1. Transportation - Alaska. 2. Transportation - Hawaii. I. U.S. Congress. Senate. Committee on Interstate and Foreign Commerce. II. U.S. Congress. House. Committee on Interstate and Foreign Commerce.

Transportation - Howard Co., Md.

711.417
(75281)
V66p

Voorhees (Alan M.) and Associates.
The proposed transit system for Columbia. Washington, 1964.
14p.

1. Planned communities - Howard Co., Md. 2. Transportation - Howard Co., Md. 3. Journey to work.

Transportation - India.

388
(54)
I52

India. Secretariat.
Tables with notes on household transport operations, by K. G. Chandrasekharan Nair and others. Delhi, Manager of Publications, 1960.
42p. tables. Indian Statistical Institute. National sample survey no. 31)

1. Transportation - India. I. Indian Statistical Institute. II. Nair, K. G. Chandrasekharan. III. Title: Household transport operations.

Transportation - Hawaii - Congresses.

388
(969:061.3)
O13
1963

Oahu Development Conference, Oahu, Hawaii, 1963.
A transportation policy for Oahu. Honolulu, Hawaii, 1963.
[8]p.

1. Transportation - Hawaii - Congresses.

Transportation - Idaho Falls, Idaho.

Folio
388
(796531)
I21

Idaho. Dept. of Highways.
Idaho Falls urban transportation study. Sponsored by City of Idaho Falls, Bonneville Co., and Idaho Dept. of Highways. [Prepared] in cooperation with U.S. Dept. of Commerce, Bureau of Public Roads. Boise, Idaho, 1965.
52p.
1. Transportation - Idaho Falls, Idaho. 2. Streets - Idaho Falls, Idaho. I. U.S. Bureau of Public Roads. II. Title.

TRANSPORTATION - INDIA.

Folio
388
(54)
W27

West Bengal. Calcutta Metropolitan Planning Organization.
Traffic and transportation plan for the Calcutta metropolitan district, 1966-1986. [Prepared in cooperation with the Ford Foundation and others. Calcutta, West Bengal, India, 1967.
178p.

1. Traffic - India. 2. Transportation - India. I. Ford Foundation. II. Title.

Transportation - Honolulu.

711.4
(969)
H65w

Honolulu. Citizens Advisory Committee to the Waikiki-Diamond Head Development Plan.
The Waikiki plan; recommendations on goals and objectives, land use, transportation and implementation. [Prepared in cooperation with the] Honolulu Planning Dept. and Planning Commission. Honolulu, 1966.
12p.

1. City planning - Honolulu. 2. Land use-Honolulu. 3. Transportation - Honolulu. I. Honolulu. Planning Dept. II. Title.

Transportation - Houston, Tex.

711.14
(764)
T29p

Texas. Highway Dept.
Projection of land use and population, City of Houston, County of Harris. A basic study upon which traffic patterns and volumes to the year 1980 were based. Houston, Tex., 1961.
1 v. (Houston Metropolitan Area Transportation Study report no. 2)

1. Land use - Houston, Tex. 2. Population - Houston, Tex. 3. Transportation - Houston, Tex. I. Title. II. Houston Metropolitan Area Transportation Study.

Transportation - Indiana.

711.73
(772)
I52

Indiana. State Highway Commission.
(Urban Planning Section)
Urban planning facts in Indiana. Indianapolis, 1964.
v.
Contents:-Series 1. The Federal aid highway act of 1962.- Series 3. Coordination.-Series 4. Status of planning, September 1, 1964.-Series 5. Data collection and analysis forms.

1. Highways - Indiana. 2. Transportation - Indiana. 3. Traffic surveys. I. Title: Federal aid highway act of 1962. II. Title.

Transportation - Houston, Tex.

388
(764)
H68

Houston, Tex. Metropolitan Transportation and Transit Study.
Freeway phase. Preliminary report. Houston, Tex., 1961.
1 v.

1. Transportation - Houston, Tex. 2. Journey to work. 3. Highways - Houston, Tex. I. Title.

TRANSPORTATION - ILL.

388
(773)
I55m

Illinois. University. Bureau of Economic and Business Research.
Mass Transportation Demonstration Projects Ill. MTD 3,4. Urbana 1968.
160p.
U.S. Dept. of Housing and Urban Development. Mass Transportation Demonstration Grant Program.

1. Transportation - Ill. 2. Journey to work. I. U.S. Mass Transportation Demonstration Grant Program. II. Title.

Transportation - Indiana.

388
(772)
P87

Purdue University. Engineering Experiment Station. (Joint Highway Research Proj.)
A study of highway transportation in Indiana by transportation research staff, Joint Highway Research Project. [In cooperation with the State Highway Dept. of Indiana] Lafayette, Ind. 1959.
146p. illus., diagrs. (Purdue University. Engineering Extension Div. Extension series no. 98)

Engineering bulletin, Purdue Univ., vol. 43, no. 4.

1. Highways - Indiana. 2. Transportation - Indiana. (Series)

Transportation - Houston, Texas.

711.74
(764)
H68s

Houston, Texas. City Planning Commission.
A study of thoroughfare development in the southeast area of Metropolitan Houston and Harris County. Houston, 1963.
13p.

1. Streets - Houston, Tex. 2. Highways - Houston, Tex. 3. Transportation - Houston, Tex. 4. Journey to work. I. Title.

Transportation - Illinois.

388
(77321)
L14

Lake County, Ill. Transportation Study.
Planning for your transportation needs. Highland Park, Ill., [1965?]
9p.

[Prepared in cooperation with] Lake County, [Ill.] Regional Planning Commission and others.

1. Transportation - Illinois. I. Lake County, Ill. Regional Planning Commission. II. Title.

TRANSPORTATION - INDIANA.

1415-
1419

SOUTHWESTERN INDIANA AND KENTUCKY REGIONAL COUNCIL OF GOVERNMENTS. TRANSPORTATION AND DEVELOPMENT PLAN: 1. LAND USE SURVEY PROCEDURE MANUAL; 2. ADMINISTRATION PROCEDURE MANUAL, SECTION 1; 3. POPULATION AND ECONOMIC INVENTORY AND ANALYSIS MANUAL; 4. SOCIAL AND COMMUNITY VALUES SURVEY MANUAL; 5. PHYSICAL FEATURES SURVEY MANUAL. EVANSVILLE, IND., 1969-70.
5 v. (HUD 701 REPORT)

1. TRANSPORTATION - INDIANA. 2. TRANSPORTATION - KENTUCKY. (CONTINUED ON NEXT CARD)

1415• SOUTHWESTERN INDIANA AND KENTUCKY
1419 REGIONAL COUNCIL OF GOVERNMENTS.
TRANSPORTATION AND ...9-70. (CARD 2)

I. HUD. 701. INDIANA. II. HUD. 701.
KENTUCKY.

388
(77252)
B17

TRANSPORTATION - INDIANAPOLIS.
Barton-Aschman Associates.
Indianapolis Regional Transportation and
Development Study; IRTADS; summary of recom-
mendations. Chicago, 1968.
9p.
U.S. Dept. of Housing and Urban Develop-
ment. UPAP.

1. Transportation - Indianapolis. 2. Journey
to work. I. Title. II. U.S. HUD-UPAP.
Indianapolis.

388
(77252)
B17

Transportation - Indianapolis.
Barton-Aschman Associates.
A transportation and land development
plan for the Indianapolis region; a
summary report. Chicago, 1968.
149p.
Bibliography: p. 147-148.
U.S. Dept. of Housing and Urban
Development. UPAP.

1. Transportation - Indianapolis.
2. Land use - Indianapolis. I. U.S. HUD-
UPAP. Indianapolis. II. Title.

5608• TRANSPORTATION - INDIANAPOLIS.
5626 INDIANAPOLIS REGIONAL TRANSPORTATION AND
DEVELOPMENT STUDY.
TECHNICAL WORK PAPER: 1, FORECAST AND
PLANNING GUIDELINES; 2, TRANSIT NETWORK
CALIBRATION; 3, TRIP GENERATION
ANALYSIS; 4, TRAVEL CHARACTERISTICS; 5,
1985 TRAVEL FORECASTS; 6, AIR TRAVEL
STUDY; 7-8, ECONOMIC BASE; 9, LAND USE
IN 1985; 10, LAND USE INVENTORY; 11,
FINANCIAL RESOURCES FOR TRANSPORTATION
IMPROVEMENTS; 12, EMPLOYMENT INVENTORY;
13, POPULATION AND HOUSEHOLD INVENTORY;
14, PARKING IN DOWNTOWN INDIANAPOLIS;
15, CALIBRATION OF THE TRIP
(CONTINUED ON NEXT CARD)

5608• INDIANAPOLIS REGIONAL TRANSPORTATION AND
5626 DEVELOPMENT STUDY. TECHNICAL WORK
PAPER....6-67. (CARD 2)

GENERATION MODELS; 16, RAIL AND TERMINAL
ANALYSIS; 17, MAJOR STREET NETWORK
CALIBRATION; 18, STREET FACILITIES
INVENTORY; 19, TRANSIT INVENTORY.
INDIANAPOLIS, 1966-67.
19 V. (HUD 701 REPORT)

1. TRANSPORTATION - INDIANAPOLIS.
I. HUD. 701. INDIANAPOLIS.

---

769 TRANSPORTATION - INDIANAPOLIS.
770 MARION COUNTY, IND. COOPERATIVE HIGHWAY
COMMITTEE.
INDIANAPOLIS REGIONAL TRANSPORTATIONAL
AND DEVELOPMENT STUDY. FINAL REPORT, MAY
1968. CHICAGO, BARTON-ASCHMAN ASSOCIATES,
1968.
2 V. (HUD 701 REPORT)

1. TRANSPORTATION - INDIANAPOLIS.
I. BARTON-ASCHMAN ASSOCIATES. II. HUD.
701. INDIANAPOLIS.

388
(45)
F46

TRANSPORTATION - ITALY.
Fiorentini, Fausto.
I trasporti nella pianificazione territoriale.
Roma, 1967.
[50]p. (Centro di studi e piani economici.
Contributi occasionali 7)
Bibliography: p. [43-50]

1. Transportation - Italy. 2. City growth -
Italy. (Series: Centro di studi e piani
economici. Contributi occasionali 7)

690
(52)
082

Transportation - Japan.
Overseas Construction Association of Japan,
Inc.
Japan's construction, 1967. Tokyo, 1967.
210p.

1. Building industry - Japan. 2. Architecture - Japan. 3. Transportation - Japan.
I. Title.

388
(52)
UN
1963

Transportation - Japan.
United Nations. (Economic Commission for
Asia and the Far East)
Report of the United States Delegation to
the United Nations Economic Commission for
Asia and the Far East. Study week of the
New Tokaido Line, Tokyo, Japan (April 11 to
April 18, 1963 inclusive) Submitted to the
Secretary of State. [n.p.] 1963.
108p.
Laurence K. Walrath, Chairman.

1. Transportation - Japan. I. Walrath,
Laurence K.

388
(52)
Y13

TRANSPORTATION - JAPAN.
Yamada, Hiroyuki.
Urban transportation problem in contemporary
Japan: an introductory analysis. Kyoto,
Faculty of Economics, Kyoto University, 1968.
[28]p.

In Kyoto University economic review, Apr.
1968, p. 57-84.

1. Transportation - Japan. 2. Journey to
work. I. Title.

1140 TRANSPORTATION - JEFFERSON PARISH, LA.
1141 JEFFERSON, ORLEANS, AND ST. BERNARD
PARISHES, LA. REGIONAL PLANNING
COMMISSION.
COMPREHENSIVE REGIONAL PLANNING
PROGRAM; STUDY DESIGN AND TRANSPORTATION
AS A MAJOR ELEMENT: 1, FINAL REPORT; 2,
SUPPLEMENT TO FINAL REPORT. BY RADER AND
ASSOCIATES. NEW ORLEANS, 1966.
2 V. (HUD 701 REPORT)

1. TRANSPORTATION - JEFFERSON PARISH,
LA. 2. TRANSPORTATION - ORLEANS PARISH,
LA. 3. TRANSPORTATION - ST. BERNARD
PARISH, LA. I. RADER AND ASSOCIATES.
(CONTINUED ON NEXT CARD)

1140 JEFFERSON, ORLEANS, AND ST. BERNARD
1141 PARISHES, LA. REGIONAL PLANNING
COMMISSION. COMPREHENSIVE REGIONAL
PLANNING ...1966. (CARD 2)

II. HUD. 701. JEFFERSON PARISH, LA.
III. HUD. 701. ORLEANS PARISH, LA.
IV. HUD. 701. ST. BERNARD PARISH, LA.

4128 TRANSPORTATION - JOHNSTOWN, PA.
CAMBRIA CO., PA. PLANNING COMMISSION.
JOHNSTOWN AREA TRANSPORTATION STUDY;
PHASE I, DATA COLLECTION AND INVENTORIES.
BY WILBUR SMITH AND ASSOCIATES.
JOHNSTOWN, PA., 1969.
87P. (HUD 701 REPORT)

1. TRANSPORTATION - JOHNSTOWN, PA.
I. SMITH (WILBUR) AND ASSOCIATES.
II. HUD. 701. CAMBRIA CO., PA.
III. HUD. 701. JOHNSTOWN, PA.

388
(76798)
A74
1962

Transportation - Jonesboro, Ark.
Arkansas. University. City Planning
Division.
Jonesboro, Arkansas; transportation,
land use, population. Data book.
Prepared by Traffic Study Advisory
Commission, Arkansas State Highway Dept.
[and others] Jonesboro, 1962.
1v. (Rept. no. 3R-5)
U.S. Urban Renewal Adm. UPAP.
1. Transportation - Jonesboro, Ark. 2. Land use -
Jonesboro, Ark. 3. Population - Jonesboro, Ark.
I. U.S. URA-UPAP. Jonesboro, Ark.

388
(76798)
A74
1963

Transportation - Jonesboro, Ark.
Arkansas. University. City Planning
Div.
Jonesboro, Arkansas; transportation,
land use, population. Data book.
Prepared by Traffic Study Advisory Com-
mission, Arkansas State Highway Dept.
[and others] Jonesboro, 1963.
252p.
U.S. Urban Renewal Adm. UPAP.

1. Transportation - Jonesboro, Ark. 2. Land use -
Jonesboro, Ark. 3. Population -
Jonesboro, Ark. I. U.S. URA-
UPAP. Jonesboro, Ark.

6186 TRANSPORTATION - JONESBORO, ARK.
JONESBORO, ARK. PLANNING COMMISSION.
TRANSPORTATION, LAND USE, POPULATION:
DATA BOOK. REVIEW DRAFT. JONESBORO,
ARK., 1961.
1 V. (HUD 701 REPORT)

1. TRANSPORTATION - JONESBORO, ARK.
I. HUD. 701. JONESBORO, ARK.

6187 TRANSPORTATION - JONESBORO, ARK.
FOLIO JONESBORO, ARK. TRAFFIC STUDY ADVISORY
6188 COMMISSION.
FOLIO TRANSPORTATION, LAND USE, POPULATION:
1, DATA BOOK; 2, PLAN BOOK. JONESBORO,
ARK., 1962.
2 V. (HUD 701 REPORT)

1. TRANSPORTATION - JONESBORO, ARK.
I. ARKANSAS. UNIVERSITY. CITY PLANNING
DIV. II. HUD. 701. JONESBORO, ARK.

388
(77418)
K15

Transportation - Kalamazoo, Mich.
Kalamazoo Area Transportation Study.
Prospectus. (Rev. and approved by Policy
Committee, September, 1965) [Kalamazoo,
Mich.] 1965.
26p.

1. Transportation - Kalamazoo, Mich.
2. Journey to work. I. Kalamazoo, Mich.
Policy Committee.

388
(781)
K15

Transportation - Kansas.
Kansas. Engineering Experiment Station.
The use of digital computers in the economic
scheduling for both men and machine in public
transportation. Final report under direction
of Samy E. G. Elias. Manhattan, Kan., 1964.
61p. (Its Special report no. 49; Kansas
State University bulletin)
U.S. Housing and Home Finance Agency.
Mass Transportation Demonstration Grant
Program.
1. Transportation - Kansas. 2. Automation.
I. Elias, Samy E. G. II. U.S. Housing
and Home Finance
Agency. Mass
Transportation
Program. Demonstration Grant

388
(77841)
G45
v.2

Transportation - Kansas City, Mo.
Gilman (W.C.) and Co.
Study of transit service; Greater
Kansas City Metropolitan area. Volume II:
Conclusions and recommendations. Prepared
for Metropolitan Planning Commission,
Kansas City Region. New York, 1966.
1v.
U.S. Dept. of Housing and Urban Develop-
ment. UPAP.
U.S. Urban Renewal Adm. UPAP.
1. Transportation - Kansas City, Mo.
I. Kansas City, Mo. Metropolitan Planning
Commission. II. Title. III. U.S. HUD-
UPAP. Kansas City, Mo.

711.4
77841
H68

Transportation - Kansas City, Mo.
Howard, Needles, Tammen & Bergendoff.
Comprehensive development plan and
transportation study for the Kansas City
Metropolitan area in Missouri; a study
design prepared for the Transportation Plan-
ning Commission of Greater Kansas City,
Missouri. Kansas City, 1965.
46p.
U.S. Urban Renewal Adm. UPAP.
1. Master plan - Kansas City, Mo.
2. Transportation - Kansas City, Mo.
I. Kansas City, Mo. Transportation Planning
Commission. II. U.S. URA-UPAP.
III. Title.

711.4
(77841)
K15t

Transportation - Kansas City, Mo.

Kansas City, Mo. City Plan Commission.
Preliminary report, local transportation.
Kansas City, Mo., 1945.
146 p. plans.

1. Transportation - Kansas City, Mo.
2. Master plan - Kansas City, Mo.

388
(763471)
S54

Transportation - Lafayette, La.

Smith (Wilbur) and Associates.
Lafayette metropolitan area transportation study. Prepared for Louisiana Dept.
of Highways in cooperation with U.S. Dept.
of Transportation, Federal Highway Administration, Bureau of Public Roads, and
Lafayette Parish and City of Lafayette.
Columbia, S.C., 1967.
2v.
Contents.-v.1 Inventory of current
travel demands and facilities.-v.2:
Future travel demands and recommended
transportation   plan.

(Cont'd on next card)

388
(74893)
L18

Transportation - Lawrence Co., Pa.

Lawrence County, Pa. Regional Planning
Commission.
Traffic and circulation, Lawrence County,
Pennsylvania. [A study of transportation
facilities] New Castle, Pa., 1963.
71p. (Its Data report 6)

U.S. Urban Renewal Adm. UPAP.

1. Transportation - Lawrence Co., Pa.
2. Traffic - Lawrence Co., Pa. I. U.S.
URA-UPAP. Lawrence Co., Pa.

388
(77841)
H68

Transportation - Kansas City, Mo.

Howard, Needles, Tammen and Bergendoff.
Planning data file design for comprehensive regional and transportation planning
in the Kansas City Metropolitan area.
Kansas City, Mo., 1965.
30p.
U.S. Urban Renewal Adm. UPAP.

1. Transportation - Kansas City, Mo.
I. Title. II. U.S. URA-UPAP. Kansas
City, Mo.

388
(763471)
S54

Smith (Wilbur) and Associates.
Lafayette metropolitan area...1967.
(Card 2)

1. Transportation - Lafayette, La.
2. Journey to work. 3. Highways -
Lafayette, La. 4. Traffic surveys -
Lafayette, La. I. Louisiana. Dept. of
Highways. II. Title.

388
(74461)
A87

Transportation - Legislation.

Automotive Safety Foundation.
A comparative legal study of Boston's
regulations and the nationally recommended
model traffic ordinance. Washington, 1961.
60p.

A companion report to "Better street
traffic management for Boston."

1. Traffic - Boston. 2. Transportation -
Legislation.

1629

TRANSPORTATION - KANSAS CITY, MO.
KANSAS CITY, MO. TRANSPORTATION PLANNING
COMMISSION OF GREATER KANSAS CITY,
MISSOURI.
COMPREHENSIVE DEVELOPMENT PLAN AND
TRANSPORTATION STUDY FOR THE KANSAS CITY
METROPOLITAN AREA IN MISSOURI, A STUDY
DESIGN. PREPARED BY HOWARD, NEEDLES,
TAMMEN AND BERGENDOFF. KANSAS CITY, MO.,
1965.
46P. (HUD 701 REPORT)
1. TRANSPORTATION - KANSAS CITY, MO.
I. HOWARD, NEEDLES, TAMMEN AND BERGENDOFF.
II. HUD. 701. KANSAS CITY, MO.

388
(77321)
I55

Transportation - Lake County, Ill.

Illinois. Div. of Highways.
Lake County transportation study
and comprehensive highway plan for
coordinated urban and regional comprehensive transportation planning. Revised
prospectus. Prepared in cooperation with
Lake County Municipal League and others.
[Waukegan, Ill.] 1963.
34p.

1. Highways - Lake County, Ill.
2. Transpor-   tation - Lake
County,   Ill.

LAW
T
Guandolo

Transportation - Legislation.

Guandolo, John.
Transportation law. Dubuque, Iowa, Wm. C.
Brown, 1965.
838p. (Transportation series. Edited by
W. H. Thompson)

1. Transportation - Legislation. I. Title.

1628

TRANSPORTATION - KANSAS CITY, MO.
KANSAS CITY REGION METROPOLITAN PLANNING
COMMISSION.
WORK PAPER NO. 2, RELATION OF TRANSIT
PLANNING TO TRANSPORTATION PLANNING.
PREPARED BY BARTON-ASCHMAN ASSOCIATES.
KANSAS CITY, MO., 1967.
32L. (HUD 701 REPORT)

1. TRANSPORTATION - KANSAS CITY, MO.
I. BARTON-ASCHMAN ASSOCIATES. II. HUD.
701. KANSAS CITY, MO.

388
(8:016)
O73

Transportation - Latin America - Bibliography.

Organization of American States.
A guide to institutions in the Washington,
D.C., New York area containing bibliograph-
ical references on transportation in
Latin America. Washington, Organization of
American States, 1961.
108p. (Bibliographical compilation on
transportation in Latin America)

1. Transportation - Latin America -
Bibl.   2. Libraries.
I. Pan   American Union.
II. Title.

711.73
(347)
N17

Transportation - Law and legislation.

National Highway Users Conference.
Highway transportation legislation in 1967
(A summary of Federal and State activity)
Prepared by NHUC Legislative Reporting Service.
Wash., [1967?]
42p.

1. Highways - Law and legislation.
2. Transportation - Law and legislation.
I. Title.

1627

TRANSPORTATION - KANSAS CITY, MO.
KANSAS CITY REGION METROPOLITAN PLANNING
COMMISSION.
WORK PAPER, PRELIMINARY TRANSIT GOALS
AND OBJECTIVES. PREPARED BY
BARTON-ASCHMAN ASSOCIATES. KANSAS CITY,
MO., 1967.
21L. (HUD 701 REPORT)

1. TRANSPORTATION - KANSAS CITY, MO.
I. BARTON-ASCHMAN ASSOCIATES. II. HUD.
701. KANSAS CITY, MO.

LAW
T
G815T

TRANSPORTATION - LAW AND LEGISLATION.
GUANDOLO, JOHN.
TRANSPORTATION LAW. DUBUQUE, IOWA,
WM. C. BROWN, 1965.
839P.

1. TRANSPORTATION - LAW AND
LEGISLATION.

LAW
T
N28
S717rs

Transportation - Law and legislation.

New York (State) Legislature. Joint Legislative Committee on Interstate Cooperation.
Report of the Joint Legislative Committee on
Interstate Cooperation to the 1966 Legislature.
Special supplement: Legislative White Paper on
mass transportation. Albany, 1966.
86p. (Its Legislative document (1966)
no. 37A)

1. Transportation - New York metropolitan
area. 2. Transportation - Law and legislation.
3. Journey to work. I. Title: White Paper on
mass transporta-   tion.

1415-
1419

TRANSPORTATION - KENTUCKY.
SOUTHWESTERN INDIANA AND KENTUCKY
REGIONAL COUNCIL OF GOVERNMENTS.
TRANSPORTATION AND DEVELOPMENT PLAN:
1, LAND USE SURVEY PROCEDURE MANUAL; 2,
ADMINISTRATION PROCEDURE MANUAL, SECTION
1; 3, POPULATION AND ECONOMIC INVENTORY
AND ANALYSIS MANUAL; 4, SOCIAL AND
COMMUNITY VALUES SURVEY MANUAL; 5,
PHYSICAL FEATURES SURVEY MANUAL.
EVANSVILLE, IND., 1969-70.
5 V. (HUD 701 REPORT)

1. TRANSPORTATION - INDIANA.
2. TRANSPORTATION - KENTUCKY.
(CONTINUED ON NEXT CARD)

388
(7445)
L18

TRANSPORTATION - LAWRENCE, MASS.

Lawrence, Mass. City Planning Dept.
Final report on a mass transportation
technical study. Lawrence, 1969.
[20]p.
Prepared in cooperation with U.S. Dept.
of Housing and Urban Development.
U.S. Mass Transportation Demonstration
Grant Program. Mass. T9-2.
1. Transportation - Lawrence, Mass.
2. Journey to work. I. U.S. Dept. of
Housing and   Urban Development.
(Cont'd on next card)

624.2
N28

TRANSPORTATION - NEW YORK (CITY)
NEW YORK (CITY). TRIBOROUGH BRIDGE AND
TUNNEL AUTHORITY.
THREE DECADES OF SERVICE. PUBLISHED
ON THE THIRTIETH ANNIVERSARY OF THE
OPENING OF THE TRIBOROUGH BRIDGE, JULY
11, 1966. NEW YORK, 1966.
76P.

1. BRIDGES. 2. TRANSPORTATION - NEW
YORK (CITY)

1415-
1419

SOUTHWESTERN INDIANA AND KENTUCKY
REGIONAL COUNCIL OF GOVERNMENTS.
TRANSPORTATION AND ...9-70. (CARD 2)

I. HUD. 701. INDIANA. II. HUD. 701.
KENTUCKY.

388
(7445)
L18

Lawrence, Mass. City Planning Dept.
Final...1969.   (Card 2)

II. U.S. Mass Transportation
Demonstration Grant Program. Lawrence,
Mass.

LAW
T
T

Transportation - Legislation.

Tedrow, Joseph Herbert.
Tedrow's regulation of transportation;
practice and procedure before the Interstate
Commerce Commission. 6th ed. [Rev. by]
Marvin L. Fair and John Guandolo. Dubuque,
Iowa, W. C. Brown Co., 1964.
445p. (Brown transportation series)
Bibliography: p. 3-5.

1. U.S. Interstate Commerce Commission -
Rules and practice. 2. Transportation -
Legislation. I. Fair, Marvin Luke.
II. Guandolo, John.   III. Title. IV.
Title: Regulation of transportation.

388
(73:347)
C65

Transaction - ~~Legislation.~~
Laws and regulation

U.S. Congress. House. Committee on Interstate and Foreign Commerce.
Transportation act of 1958. Report of the Committee on Interstate and Foreign Commerce on H.R. 12832 together with supplemental views. Washington, Govt. Print. Off., 1958.
54p. tables. (85th Cong., 2d sess. House report no. 1922)

1. Transportation - Legislation. I. Title.

AUTOMOBILES - LAWS AND REGULATIONS - U.S.
Commerce clearing house.
Insurance law reporter ... Chicago, Commerce clearing house, inc., c1949.
3v. 25½x23½cm.

388
(79494)
C15t

TRANSPORTATION - LOS ANGELES.
California. Business and Transportation Agency.
Transportation-Employment Project. A research project to determine and test the relationship between a public transportation system and job and other opportunities of low income groups. Progress report no.
Los Angeles, 19
v.
U.S. Mass Transportation Demonstration Grant Program.
Contract no. H-730.
For Library holdings see main entry.
(Cont'd on next card)

LAW
U.S.

Transportation - Legislation.

U.S. Housing and Home Finance Agency.
Federal laws; assistance to urban mass transportation, Urban mass transportation act of 1964 and excerpts from the Housing act of 1949, the Housing act of 1954, the Housing amendments of 1955, as amended through October 15, 1964. Washington, For sale by the Supt. of Documents, Govt. Print. Off., 1964.
12p.

1. Transportation - Legislation. 2. Journey to work. I. U.S. Laws, statutes, etc. II. Title.

LAW
U.S.

Transportation - Legislation.

U.S. Housing and Home Finance Agency.
Federal laws; assistance to urban mass transportation, Urban mass transportation act of 1964 and excerpts from the Housing act of 1949, the Housing act of 1954, the Housing amendments of 1955, as amended through October 15, 1964. Washington, For sale by the Supt. of Documents, Govt. Print. Off., 1964.
12p.

1. Transportation - Legislation. 2. Journey to work. I. U.S. Laws, statutes, etc. II. Title.

388
(79494)
C15t

California. Business and Transportation Agency.
Transportation-Employment...19   (Card 2)

1. Transportation - Los Angeles. 2. Journey to work. 3. Employment - Los Angeles. I. Title. II. U.S. Mass Transportation Demonstration Grant Program - Los Angeles.

LAW
T
H683st

TRANSPORTATION - LAW AND LEGISLATION.
U.S. Dept. of Housing and Urban Development. Office of General Counsel.
State laws enacted in 19

of interest to the Dept. of Housing and Urban Development as reported by the Commerce Clearing House and other unofficial sources.
Wash., 19
v.
For Library holdings see main entry.
(Cont'd on next card)

LAW
U.S.

Transportation - Legislation.

U.S. Laws, statutes, etc.
Section-by-section summary of the Urban mass transportation act of 1964. (Public law 88-365) [Washington] 1964.
[6]p.

1. Transportation - Legislation. I. Urban mass transportation act of 1964.

388
(79494)
C15p

TRANSPORTATION - LOS ANGELES.
California. Dept. of Public Works.
Public transportation map of metropolitan Los Angeles. Sacramento, California Transportation-Employment Project, 1967.
map
U.S. Dept. of Housing and Urban Development. Mass Transportation Demonstration Grant Program.
1. Transportation - Los Angeles.
2. Journey to work. 3. Maps and mapping - Los Angeles. I. U.S. Mass Transportation Demonstration Grant Program. II. California Transportation - Employment Project. III. Title.

LAW
T
H683st

U.S. Dept. of Housing and Urban Development. Office of General Counsel.   State laws...
19   (Card 2)

1. Housing legislation. 2. Urban renewal legislation. 3. Transportation - Law and legislation. 4. State government. I. Commerce Clearing House. II. Title.

711.333
(74827)
L23t

Transportation - Lehigh Co., Pa.

Lehigh-Northampton Counties (Pa.)
Joint Planning Commission.
Traffic and transportation; a comprehensive research report. [n.p.] 1963.
130p.
U.S. Urban Renewal Adm. UPAP.

1. Master plan - Lehigh-Northampton Counties, Pa.
2. Traffic - Lehigh Co., Pa. 3. Traffic - Northampton Co., Pa. 4. Transportation - Lehigh Co., Pa.
5. Transportation - Northampton Co., Pa.
I. U.S. URA-UPAP. Lehigh-Northampton Counties, Pa.

388
(79494)
C15s

Transportation - Los Angeles.

California. Dept. of Public Works. (Div. of Highways)
A special report on transportation and the accomplishments of the California Freeway-Expressway System in the Los Angeles area. Prepared for the Assembly Interim Committee on Transportation and Commerce, [Los Angeles] 1963.
21p.

1. Transportation - Los Angeles.
2. Traffic - Los Angeles.

LAW
U.S.

Transportation - ~~Legislation.~~ Laws and regulations

U.S. Laws, statutes, etc.
Section-by-section summary of the Urban mass transportation act of 1964. (Public law 88-365) [Washington] 1964.
[6]p.

1. Transportation - Legislation. I. Urban mass transportation act of 1964.

388
(7443)
P21

Transportation - Leominster, Mass.

Peat, Marwick, Livingston & Co.
Fitchburg-Leominster urban area transportation study. New York, 1967.
161p.

Bibliography: p. 159 - 160.
Prepared for: Massachusetts Dept. of Public Works in cooperation with the U.S. Dept. of Transportation, Federal Highway Administration, Bureau of Public Roads.
1. Transportation - Fitchburg, Mass.
2. Transportation - Leominster, Mass. I. Massachusetts Dept. of Public Works. II. Title.

388
(79494)
C25

TRANSPORTATION - LOS ANGELES.
CENTRAL BUSINESS DISTRICT ASSOCIATION, LOS ANGELES.
PARKWAY TRANSIT LINES IN THE CENTRAL BUSINESS DISTRICT. LOS ANGELES, 1945.
26P.

1. TRANSPORTATION - LOS ANGELES.

Transportation - Legislation - California

AUTOMOBILES - LAWS AND ~~REGULATIONS~~ - CALIFORNIA

California. Laws, statutes, etc.
Vehicle code, annotated, of the State of California. Adopted March 25, 1935. With amendments up to and including those of the first extraordinary session of the fifty-seventh Legislature. Annotated and indexed by the publisher's editorial staff. San Francisco, Bancroft-Whitney Co., 1948.
xxxviii, 707 p. 24 cm. (Deering's California codes)

1. Automobiles—Laws and regulations—California.
I. Bancroft-Whitney Company, San Francisco. (Series)

388.3   48-4072*

Library of Congress   [2]

388
(78882)
L47

Transportation - Littleton, Colo.

Littleton, Colo. City Planning Commission.
Recommendations for a traffic and transportation system, Littleton, Colorado.
Littleton, 1957.
9p.

[Prepared by] Development Planning Associates.
U.S. Urban Renewal Adm. UPAP.

1. Traffic - Littleton, Colo. 2. Transportation - Littleton, Colo. I. Development Planning Associates. II. U.S. URA-UPAP.

388
(79494)
C68

Transportation - Los Angeles, Calif.
Coverdale and Colpitts, Consulting Engineers.
Report to the Los Angeles Metropolitan Transit Authority on a monorail rapid transit line for Los Angeles. New York, Jan. 15, 1954.
1 v. illus., graphs, maps, tables. Processed.

1. Transportation-Los Angeles, Calif. I. Los Angeles, Calif. Metropolitan Transit Authority. II. Title: Monorail rapid transit line for Los Angeles.

AUTOMOBILES - LAWS AND REGULATIONS - U.S.
Commerce clearing house.
Automobile cases ... v. 1949- Chicago, Commerce clearing house, 1949-
v. 25½cm. (Insurance case series)

For Additions or Holdings See Continuation File

388
(79494)
A27

TRANSPORTATION - LOS ANGELES.
Aerospace Corp.
Preliminary proposal for a Southern California transportation study design. Prepared by Transportation Systems Directorate for Southern California Association of Governments. El Segundo, Calif., 1970.
59p. (Aerospace report no. ATR-70(9990)-11)

1. Transportation - Los Angeles. I. Southern California Association of Governments. II. Title.

388
(79494)
D15

TRANSPORTATION - LOS ANGELES.
Daniel, Mann, Johnson, and Mendenhall.
Planning and economic considerations affecting transportation in the Los Angeles region. Prepared for Southern California Rapid Transit District.
Los Angeles, 1965.
1v.
Bibliography: p. B-1 - B-7.
1. Transportation - Los Angeles.
2. Journey to work. I. Southern California Rapid Transit District. II. Title.

Transportation - Los Angeles.

388
(79494)
F14
Fairman, Gibson W
Los Angeles Regional Transportation Study, prospectus, September, 1960. Los Angeles, California Division of Highways, 1960.
- 33p.
-- --- Appendix. 1969.
81p.

1. Transportation - Los Angeles.
I. California. Division of Highways.

Transportation - Los Angeles.

388
(79494)
T25
Telford, Edward T
People on the move. Supplemental remarks on mass transportation aspects of the Greater Los Angeles Freeway System. Remarks made before the Collier Committee, Los Angeles, October 2, 1962. Los Angeles, Administrative Offices, 1962.
26p.

1. Transportation - Los Angeles. 2. Highways - Los Angeles.

Transportation - Lubbock, Tex.

388
(764)
T29ℓ
v.1
Texas. Highway Dept.
Lubbock urban transportation plan, Lubbock, Texas. Hub of the Plains, origin destination survey. Sponsoring agencies: City of Lubbock, County of Lubbock, in cooperation with the U.S. Dept. of Commerce, Bureau of Public Roads. [Austin, Tex.] 1964.
56p. (Vol. 1)

1. Transportation - Lubbock, Tex.
2. Traffic survey. 3. Journey to work. I. U.S. Bureau of Public Roads. II. Title.

Transportation - Los Angeles.

388
(79494)
L67
Los Angeles. Central City Committee.
Transportation study. A joint report by the Los Angeles Central City Committtee and the Los Angeles City Traffic Department. Los Angeles, 1963.
23p. (Centropolis no. 3)
On cover: Los Angeles Centropolis, 1980.

1. Transportation - Los Angeles.
I. Los Angeles. City Traffic Dept.

388
(79494)
T71
TRANSPORTATION - LOS ANGELES.
Transportation Association of Southern California.
TASC prospectus. Published in cooperation with the Dept. of Transportation, Federal Highway Administration, Bureau of Public Roads. Los Angeles, 1969.
53p.

1. Transportation - Los Angeles. 2. Journey to work.

Transportation - Madison, Wis.

388
(77584)
M12
Madison, Wis. Committee to Study the Advisability and Feasibility of Operating a Municipally Owned Bus System.
Mass transit report, Madison, Wisconsin. Madison, 1959.
95p. maps, tables.

1. Transportation - Madison, Wis.

388
(79494)
L671
TRANSPORTATION - LOS ANGELES.
Los Angeles Regional Transportation Study.
An introduction to the Los Angeles Regional Transportation Study. Los Angeles, [1961?]
19p.

1. Transportation - Los Angeles. I. Title.

312
(79494)
P23
Transportation - Los Angeles metropolitan area.
Pegrum, Dudley F
Residential population and urban transport facilities in the Los Angeles metropolitan area. Los Angeles, Bureau of Business and Economic Research, University of California, 1964.
42p. (California. University. University at Los Angeles. Bureau of Business and Economic Research. Occasional paper no. 3)

(Cont'd. on next card)

1545-
1549
TRANSPORTATION - MANKATO, MINN.
MANKATO, MINN. PLANNING COMMISSION.
MANKATO AREA TRANSPORTATION AND PLANNING STUDY: 1, MOBILE HOME ORDINANCE, PRELIMINARY; 2-3, IMPLEMENTING ORDINANCE RECOMMENDATIONS: SUBDIVISION REGULATIONS, ZONING ORDINANCE; 4, CAPITAL IMPROVEMENTS AND FINANCIAL PROGRAM; 5, CHALLENGE FOR THE FUTURE. NASON, WEHRMAN, KNIGHT, AND CHAPMAN, INC. MANKATO, 1970.
5 V. (HUD 701 REPORT)

1. TRANSPORTATION - MANKATO, MINN.
I. NASON, WEHRMAN, KNIGHT, AND
(CONTINUED ON NEXT CARD)

Transportation - Los Angeles.

388
(79494)
L67L
Los Angeles Regional Transportation Study.
Los Angeles Regional Transportation Study. V.1. 1. Base year report, 1960. [Los Angeles] 1963.
--51p.
-- --- Appendix. 1969.
81p.

1. Transportation - Los Angeles.
2. Highways - Los Angeles. 3. Los Angeles Regional Transportation Study.

Appx.

312
(79494)
P23
Pegrum, Dudley F Residential population and urban transport ...
(Card 2)

1. Population - Los Angeles metropolitan area. 2. Transportation - Los Angeles metropolitan area. I. California. University. University at Los Angeles. Bureau of Business and Economic Research.

1545-
1549
MANKATO, MINN. PLANNING COMMISSION.
MANKATO AREA ...1970. (CARD 2)

CHAPMAN, INC. II. HUD. 701. MANKATO, MINN.

388
(79494)
L67t
TRANSPORTATION - LOS ANGELES.
Los Angeles Regional Transportation Study.
Transportation, 1970. Los Angeles, 1971. [16]p. (A Los Angeles Regional Transportation Study profile)

1. Transportation - Los Angeles.
I. Title.

388
(79494)
P23
Transportation - Los Angeles metropolitan area.
Pegrum, Dudley F
Urban transport and the location of industry in metropolitan Los Angeles. Los Angeles, Bureau of Business and Economic Research, University of California, 1963.
46p. (California. University. University at Los Angeles. Bureau of Business and Economic Research. Occasional paper no. 2)

(Cont'd. on next card)

1585-
1592
TRANSPORTATION - MANKATO, MINN.
MANKATO, MINN. PLANNING COMMISSION.
MANKATO AREA TRANSPORTATION AND PLANNING STUDY: 1, PROSPECTUS; 2, COMMUNITY FACILITIES PLAN; 3, TRIP GENERATION ANALYSIS; 4, TRANSPORTATION PLAN; 5, LAND USE ANALYSIS AND PRELIMINARY GUIDE PLAN; 6, LAND USE PLAN; 7, ECONOMY, POPULATION PROJECTIONS; 8, TRAVEL CHARACTERISTICS. MANKATO, 1969-70.
8 V. (HUD 701 REPORT)

1. TRANSPORTATION - MANKATO, MINN.
I. HUD. 701. MANKATO, MINN.

Transportation - Los Angeles.

388
(79494)
T19c
Taylor, S Sam.
Centropolis transportation 1980, Los Angeles vista. An address by Los Angeles City Traffic Engineer. Presented at the 38th Annual Meeting of the Downtown Businessmen's Association, Los Angeles, Calif., June 27, 1962. Los Angeles, Dept. of Traffic, 1962.
27p.

1. Transportation - Los Angeles.
I. Downtown Businessmen's Association, Los Angeles. 38th Meeting. 1962. II. Los Angeles. Dept. of Traffic.

388
(79494)
P23
Pegrum, Dudley F Urban transport and the location of industry...(Card 2)

1. Transportation - Los Angeles metropolitan area. 2. Industrial location - Los Angeles metropolitan area. I. California. University. University at Los Angeles. Bureau of Business and Economic Research.

Transportation - Massachusetts.

388
(744)
A28
Advance Planning Associates.
Transportation systems of Southeastern Massachusetts, by David A. Grossman and Melvin R. Levin. [Prepared] for the Southeastern Massachusetts Regional Planning District and the Massachusetts Dept. of Commerce. Cambridge, Mass., 1960.
62p. maps, tables. (Southeastern Mass. [regional planning program rept.] no. 6)

U.S. Urban Renewal Administration, Urban Planning Assistance Program.

(Continued on next card)

Transportation - Los Angeles.

388
(79494)
T19
Taylor, S Sam.
Minutes, not miles. An address by Los Angeles City Traffic Engineer. Presented to Los Angeles Chamber of Commerce (Construction Industry's Div.) Sept. 12, 1962. Los Angeles, Dept. of Traffic, 1962.
11p.

1. Transportation - Los Angeles.
2. Journey to work. I. Los Angeles. Dept. of Traffic.

1090
FOLIO
TRANSPORTATION - LOUISVILLE METROPOLITAN AREA.
LOUISVILLE AND JEFFERSON COUNTY, KY. PLANNING AND ZONING COMMISSION.
RAPID MASS TRANSIT STUDY, LOUISVILLE METROPOLITAN AREA. BY DE LEUW, CATHER AND COMPANY. LOUISVILLE, KY., 1969.
57P. (HUD 701 REPORT)

1. TRANSPORTATION - LOUISVILLE METROPOLITAN AREA. I. DE LEUW, CATHER AND COMPANY. II. HUD. 701. LOUISVILLE METROPOLITAN AREA.

388
(744)
A28
Advance Planning Associates. Transportation systems of Southeastern ... 1960. (Card 2)

1. Transportation - Massachusetts. 2. Regional planning - Massachusetts. I. Grossman, David A. II. Levin, Melvin R. III. Southeastern Massachusetts Regional Planning District. IV. U.S. URA-UPAP. Massachusetts.

388
(744)
D25
Transportation - Massachusetts.

De Leuw, Cather and Co.
Report to the Old Colony Area Transportation Commission on plans for improved suburban transit. Brookline, Mass., 1959.
1v. maps, tables.

1. Transportation - Massachusetts.   I. Massachusetts. Old Colony Area Transportation Commission.

388
(744)
M17m
Transportation - Mass.

Massachusetts. Mass Transportation Commission.
Mass transportation in Massachusetts. Final report on Mass Transportation Demonstration Project. Prepared under the direction of Joseph F. Maloney for the Mass Transportation Commission, Commonwealth of Massachusetts. Based on materials developed by the Mass Transportation Commission staff and Mckinsey and Co. and others. Boston, 1964.
144p.   (Cont'd. on next card)

388
(744)
M17m
Suppl.
no.3
Systems Analysis and Research Corp.
Supplementary statistics and analysis relating to the Demonstration Project ...
(Card 2)

U.S. Housing and Home Finance Agency. Mass Transportation Demonstration Grant Program.

1. Transportation - Mass. 2. Transportation - Finance. I. Maloney, Joseph F. II. Massachusetts. Mass Transportation Commission. Mass transportation ... III. U.S. Housing and Home Finance Agency. Mass Transportation Demonstration Grant Program.

5427
TRANSPORTATION - MASSACHUSETTS.
LOWER PIONEER VALLEY REGIONAL PLANNING COMMISSION.
COMMUTING PATTERN DATA. BY THE PLANNING SERVICES GROUP, CAMBRIDGE, MASSACHUSETTS. BOSTON, 1964.
1 V. (HUD 701 REPORT)

1. TRANSPORTATION - MASSACHUSETTS.
I. PLANNING SERVICES GROUP. II. HUD. 701. MASSACHUSETTS.

388
(744)
M17m
Massachusetts. Mass Transportation Commission.   Mass transportation in Massachusetts ...   (Card 2)

U.S. Housing and Home Finance Agency. Mass Transportation Demonstration Grant Program. Distributed by U.S. Clearinghouse for Federal Scientific and Technical Information as PB 174 422.
1. Transportation - Mass. I. Maloney, Joseph F. II. Mckinsey & Co. III. U.S. Housing and Home Finance Agency. Mass Transportation Demonstration Grant Program. IV. U.S. Clearinghouse for Federal Scientific and Technical Information.

388
(768191)
M25
Transportation - Memphis.

Memphis Transit Authority.
Mass transportation studies in Memphis, transit system's history, 1956-1965. Suburban ridership demonstration project. Memphis, 1965.
116p.

U.S. Housing and Home Finance Agency. Mass Transportation Demonstration Grant Program.

1. Transportation - Memphis. 2. Journey to work. I. U.S. Housing and Home Finance Agency. Mass Transportation Demonstration Grant Program. II. Title.

5432
TRANSPORTATION - MASSACHUSETTS.
LOWER PIONEER VALLEY REGIONAL PLANNING COMMISSION.
RECOMMENDED TRANSPORTATION ZONES. BY THE PLANNING SERVICES GROUP, CAMBRIDGE, MASSACHUSETTS. BOSTON, 1964.
24L. (HUD 701 REPORT)

-- ----. SUPPLEMENTARY MATERIAL IN ENVELOPE.

1. TRANSPORTATION - MASSACHUSETTS.
I. PLANNING SERVICES GROUP. II. HUD. 701. MASSACHUSETTS.

388
(744)
M17s
Transportation - Massachusetts.

Massachusetts. Old Colony Area Transportation Commission.
Second report of the Old Colony Area Transportation Commission relative to the Old Colony commuter problem. [Boston] 1959.
69p. (Massachusetts. Legislature. Senate. Report no. 480)

1. Transportation - Massachusetts.

FOLIO
711.33
(77677)
A38
no.6
Transportation - Mesabi and Vermilion Ranges, Minn.

Aguar, Jyring and Whiteman.
Transportation survey and analysis, regional planning area, Mesabi and Vermilion Ranges, Minnesota. [Prepared in cooperation with] Range Regional Planning Commission. Duluth, 1964.
16p. (Regional Planning Program for Mesabi and Vermilion Iron Ranges, series no. 6)

U.S. Urban Renewal Adm. UPAP.

(Continued on next card)

388
(744)
M17m
Suppl.
no.2
Transportation - Mass.

McKinsey & Co.
Supplementary analyses relating to rail demonstration project. Prepared for: Mass Transportation Commission, Commonwealth of Massachusetts. Washington, 1964.
1v.
Supplement no. 2, to Mass transportation in Massachusetts. A final report on a Mass Transportation Demonstration Project.
(Cont'd. on next card)

VF
388
(744)
M17t
Transportation - Mass.

Massachusetts. Dept. of Public Works.
Transportation planning process; basic elements for which inventories and analyses are required. [Boston] 1964.
[6]p.   (Its Informational bulletin no. 1)

1. Transportation - Mass.

FOLIO
711.33
(77677)
A38
no.6
Aguar, Jyring and Whiteman. Transportation...
(Card 2)

1. State planning - Mesabi and Vermilion Ranges, Minn. 2. Transportation - Mesabi and Vermilion Ranges, Minn. I. Minnesota Range Regional Planning Commission. II. U.S. URA-UPAP. Mesabi and Vermilion Ranges, Minn.

388
(744)
M17
Transportation - Massachusetts.

Massachusetts. Bureau of Transportation Planning and Development.
External zoning system manual. Prepared in cooperation with United States Dept. of Commerce, Bureau of Public Roads. Boston, 1964.
[22]p.   (Its Informational bulletin no. 3)
Massachusetts. Dept. of Public Works. Publication no. 435.

1. Transportation - Massachusetts. I. U.S. Bureau of Public Roads. II. Title.

388
(744)
M17m
Suppl.
no.4
Transportation - Mass.

Napolitan (Joseph) Associates.
A survey to determine factors which influence the public's choice of mode of transportation. Prepared under the direction of Joseph F. Maloney for the Mass Transportation Commission, Commonwealth of Massachusetts. Washington, 1964.
160p.
Supplement no. 4, to Mass transportation in Massachusetts.
(Cont'd. on next card)

353
C34
Transportation - Metropolitan areas.

Chinitz, Benjamin, ed.
City and suburb; the economics of metropolitan growth. Englewood Cliffs, N.J., Prentice-Hall, 1964.
181p.   (Modern economic issues)

Bibliography: p. 179-181.

1. Metropolitan areas. 2. Transportation - Metropolitan areas. 3. Sociology, Urban. 4. Suburbs. I. Title.

388
(744)
M17u
Transportation - Mass.

Massachusetts. Bureau of Transportation Planning and Development.
Urban transportation studies aerial photography inventory and description. Prepared in cooperation with the U.S. Dept. of Commerce, Bureau of Public Roads. Boston [1964?]
19p.   (Its Informational bulletin no. 4)
Massachusetts. Dept. of Public Works. Publication no. 501.

1. Transportation - Mass. 2. Aerial photography. I. U.S. Bureau of Public Roads. II. Title.

388
(744)
M17m
Suppl.
no.4
Napolitan (Joseph) Associates.   A survey to determine factors which ...
(Card 2)
U.S. Housing and Home Finance Agency. Mass Transportation Demonstration Grant Program.

1. Transportation - Mass. 2. Journey to work. I. Maloney, Joseph F. II. Massachusetts. Mass Transportation Commission. Mass Transportation. III. U.S. Housing and Home Finance Agency. Mass Transportation Demonstration Grant Program.

388
(083.41)
P81
Transportation - Metropolitan areas.

U.S. Bureau of Public Roads.
Selected statistics by standard metropolitan statistical areas for use in transportation planning. Washington, U.S. Dept. of Commerce, Bureau of Public Roads, 1964.
98p.

Unpublished tables developed by E. L. Kanwit and others.

1. Transportation - Statistics. 2. Transportation - Metropolitan areas. 3. Journey to work. I. Title. metropolitan statisti-   II. Title: Standard cal areas.

388
(744)
M17
Transportation - Massachusetts.

Massachusetts. Mass Transportation Commission.
Demonstration project progress report. Boston, 1963-
v.

U.S. Housing and Home Finance Agency. Mass Transportation Demonstration Grant Program.
For complete information see shelflist.

1. Transportation - Massachusetts. I. U.S. Housing and Home Finance Agency. Mass Transportation Demonstration Grant Program.

388
(744)
M17m
Suppl.
no.3
Transportation - Mass.

Systems Analysis and Research Corp.
Supplementary statistics and analysis relating to the Demonstration Project. Prepared under the direction of Joseph F. Maloney for the Mass Transportation Commission, Commonwealth of Massachusetts. Boston, 1964.
234p.
Supplement no. 3 to Mass transportation in Mass.
(Cont'd. on next card)

388
(774)
M42
Transportation - Michigan.

Michigan. State Resource Planning Program.
Transportation; predictive procedures. Summary report. [Prepared in] cooperation with the Michigan Dept. of Commerce and others. Lansing, Mich., 1966.
38p. (Michigan. Dept. of Commerce. State Resource Planning Program. Technical report no. 9)
U.S. Dept. of Housing and Urban Development. UPAP.

1. Transportation - Michigan. 2. Transportation - Automation. I. Title. II. U.S. HUD-UPAP. Michigan.

388
(774)
S68

TRANSPORTATION - MICHIGAN.
Southeastern Michigan Transportation Authority.
Report, 19

Detroit, 19

v. annual.
For Library holdings see main entry.

1. Transportation - Mich.

388
(77657)
M45re

Transportation - Minneapolis-St. Paul.
Minneapolis-St. Paul Metropolitan Transit
Commission.
Report, 19

St. Paul, 19
v. annual.

For Library holdings see main entry.

1. Transportation - Minneapolis-St.
Paul. 2. Journey to work.

388
(762)
M47urb

Mississippi-Arkansas-Tennessee Council
of Governments.
UMT (urban mass transportation) program
planning requirements; supplemental documentation MATCOG. Regular program planning
requirements. Memphis, 1968.
13p.
U.S. Dept. of Housing and Urban Development. Mass Transportation Demonstration
Grant Program.
1. Transportation - Mississippi.
2. Transportation - Arkansas. 3. Transportation
- Tennessee. 4. Journey to work.

(Continued on next card)

388
(74941)
N28

Transportation - Middlesex, N.J.
New Jersey. Dept. of Conservation and
Economic Development. (Div. of Planning
and Development)
Middlesex Borough, Middlesex County, New
Jersey: preliminary master plan studies.
Thoroughfares and traffic, public transpor-
tation, railroads and freight service, air-
ports and air service. Prepared for the
Middlesex Planning Board. Trenton, 1958.
14p.
U.S. Urban Renewal Adm. UPAP.
1. Traffic - Middlesex,   N.J. 2. Trans-
portation - Middlesex,   N.J.
I. Middlesex, N.J.   Planning Board.
II. U.S. URA-UPAP.   Middlesex, N.J.

388
(77657)
M45s

TRANSPORTATION - MINNEAPOLIS-ST. PAUL.
Minneapolis-St. Paul Metropolitan Transit
Commission.
Status report: transit program for the
twin cities area. St. Paul, 1970.
25p.
U.S. Mass Transportation Demonstration
Grant Program.
1. Transportation - Minneapolis-St. Paul.
2. Journey to work. I. Title. II. U.S.
Mass Transportation Demonstration Grant
Program. Minneapolis-St. Paul.

388
(762)
M47urb

Mississippi-Arkansas-Tennessee Council of
Governments. UMT...1968.

(Card 2)

I. U.S. Dept. of Housing and Urban Develop-
ment. Mass Transportation Demonstration
Grant Program Miss.-Ark.-Tenn.
II. Title.

388
(77657)
K42

Transportation - Minneapolis.
Kieffer, Stephen A
Transit and the twins, a survey of the
history of the transportation company in
Minneapolis and St. Paul; an analysis of the
role of public transportation in the growth of
the Twin Cities. Minneapolis, Twin City Rapid
Transit Co., 1958.
60p. illus., maps.

1. Transportation - Minneapolis. 2. Transportation - St. Paul.

388
(77657)
M45r

Transportation - Minneapolis-St. Paul.
Minnesota. Dept. of Highways.
The role of mass transit; Twin Cities
metropolitan area. In cooperation with
U.S. Dept. of Commerce, Bureau of Public
Roads. [Minneapolis] 1963.
80p.

1. Transportation - Minneapolis-St.
Paul. 2. Journey to work.

388
(762)
M47u

Transportation - Mississippi.
Mississippi-Arkansas-Tennessee Council of
Governments.
Urban mass transportation grant program;
regular program planning requirements.
Memphis, 1968.
48p.
U.S. Dept. of Housing and Urban Develop-
ment. Mass Transportation Demonstration
Grant Program.
1. Transportation - Mississippi. 2. Trans-
portation - Arkansas. 3. Transportation -
Tennessee. 4. Journey to work. I. U.S. Dept.
of Housing and   Urban Development. Mass
Transportation   Demonstration Grant Pro-
gram.   (Cont'd on next card)

5385

TRANSPORTATION - MINNEAPOLIS, MINN.
TWIN CITIES METROPOLITAN PLANNING
COMMISSION.
TRANSIT REPORT. SAINT PAUL, CA. 1960.
37L. (HUD 701 REPORT)

1. TRANSPORTATION - MINNEAPOLIS, MINN.
2. TRANSPORTATION - ST. PAUL, MINN.
I. HUD. 701. MINNEAPOLIS, MINN.
II. HUD. 701. ST. PAUL, MINN.

388
(77657)
M45t
v.1

Transportation - Minneapolis-St. Paul.
Minnesota. Dept. of Highways.
Twin Cities area transportation study.
Volume 1, Study findings. In cooperation
with U.S. Dept. of Commerce, Bureau of
Public Roads. [St. Paul] 1962.
99p.

1. Transportation - Minneapolis-St.
Paul. 2. Metropolitan area planning -
Minneapolis-St. Paul. I. Title.

388
(762)
M47u

Mississippi-Arkansas-Tennessee Council of
Governments. Urban mass transportation...1968. (Card 2)

Mississippi. II. U.S. Dept. of Housing and
Urban Development. Mass Transportation
Demonstration Grant Program. Arkansas.
III. U.S. Dept. of Housing and Urban Develop-
ment. Mass Transportation Demonstration
Grant Program. Tennessee. IV. Title.

VF
388
(77657)
M45j

Transportation - Minneapolis-St. Paul.
Minneapolis-St. Paul Metropolitan Planning
Commission.
The joint program; an inter-agency land
use transportation planning program for the
Twin Cities Metropolitan Area. St. Paul,
Twin Cities Metropolitan Planning Commission,
1962.
12p.
At head of title: What's this big joint
program I've been hearing about? asked
T.C. Mits.
U.S. Urban   Renewal Adm. UPAP.
1. Transportation -   Minneapolis-St. Paul.
2. Metropolitan area   planning - Minneapolis-
St. Paul. I. U.S. URA-   UPAP. Minneapolis-St. Paul.

VF
388
(77657)
C68

Transportation - Minneapolis-St. Paul
metropolitan area.
Council of Metropolitan Area Leagues of
Women Voters.
Exploring transportation for the Twin
Cities metropolitan area. Minneapolis,
1966.
30p.

1. Transportation - Minneapolis-St. Paul
metropolitan area. 2. Municipal bonds.
I. Title.

388
(762)
M47ur

Transportation - Mississippi.
Mississippi-Arkansas-Tennessee Council of
Governments.
Urban mass transportation program plann-
ing requirements; supplementary material,
MATCOG. Memphis, 1968.
18p.
U.S. Dept. of Housing and Urban Develop-
ment. Mass Transportation Demonstration
Grant Program.
1. Transportation - Mississippi. 2. Trans-
portation - Arkansas. 3. Transportation -
Tennessee. 4. Journey to work.

(Cont'd on next card)

388
(77657)
M45m

Transportation - Minneapolis-St. Paul.
Minneapolis-St. Paul Metropolitan Planning
Commission.
Mass transit in the Twin Cities metro-
politan area. Minneapolis, 1964.
28p. (Its Background document no. 4)

U.S. Urban Renewal Adm. UPAP.

1. Transportation - Minneapolis-St.
Paul. 2. Journey to work. I. U.S.
URA-UPAP. Minneapolis-St. Paul.

388
L17

TRANSPORTATION - MINN.
Larson, Roy E
Transportation, 1983; the Minnesota Experimental city, by Roy E. Larson and Robert J.
Reid, North Star Research and Development Institute. [n.p.] [1969?]
30p.

1. Transportation. 2. Transportation - Minn.
3. Journey to work. I. Reid, Robert J., jt. au.
II. Highway Research Board. III. Title.

388
(762)
M47ur

Mississippi-Arkansas-Tennessee Council of
Governments. Urban mass...1968.(Card 2)

I. Title. II. U.S. Dept. of Housing
and Urban Development. Mass Transportation
Demonstration Grant Program. Miss.-Ark.-
Tenn.

388
(77657)
M45
pt. 1

Transportation - Minneapolis-St. Paul.
Minneapolis-St. Paul Metropolitan Planning
Commission.
Metropolitan transportation study, part 1.
St. Paul, 1960.
81p. illus., maps, tables. (Its Metro-
politan planning report no. 8)
U.S. Urban Renewal Administration, Urban Planning
Assistance Program.

1. Metropolitan area planning - Minneapolis-St. Paul.
2. Transportation - Minneapolis-St. Paul. I. U.S.
URA-UPAP. Minneapolis-St. Paul.

2306
2307
2308
2309

TRANSPORTATION - MINNESOTA.
MINNESOTA. STATE PLANNING AGENCY.
MINNESOTA WATERBORNE TRANSPORTATION;
1. ECONOMIC SIGNIFICANCE AND OUTLOOK; 2.
MARKETING FARM CROPS; 3. IRON ORE AND
CONCENTRATES; 4. COMPENDIUM OF MINNESOTA
TAXES AND FEES. ST. PAUL, 1969.
4 V. (HUD 701 REPORT)

1. TRANSPORTATION - MINNESOTA.
I. HUD. 701. MINNESOTA.

TRANSPORTATION - MODEL CITIES

SEE

U.S. HUD. Model Cities Program. Model Cities
Transportation Project.

59* TRANSPORTATION - MOLINE, ILL.
BI-STATE METROPOLITAN PLANNING COMMISSION.
URBANIZED AREA TRANSPORTATION STUDY,
DAVENPORT, ROCK ISLAND, MOLINE. BY DE
LEUW, CATHER AND CO. ROCK ISLAND, ILL.,
1970.
14P. (HUD 701 REPORT)

1. TRANSPORTATION - DAVENPORT, IOWA.
2. TRANSPORTATION - ROCK ISLAND, ILL.
3. TRANSPORTATION - MOLINE, ILL. I. DE
LEUW, CATHER AND CO. II. HUD. 701.
DAVENPORT, IOWA. III. HUD. 701. ROCK
ISLAND, ILL. IV. HUD. 701. MOLINE,
ILL.

Transportation - Montreal.

388
(714281) Montreal. Transportation Commission.
M65 Urban transit in Montreal, 1861-1961.
Montreal, 1961.
1v.

English and French.

1. Transportation - Montreal.
I. Title.

Transportation - Nashville.

388
(768551) Metropolitan Government of Nashville and
M27 Davidson County. Metropolitan Planning
Commission.
Study of interstate highway interchange
area development for Metropolitan
Nashville and Davidson County, Tennessee.
Nashville, 1965.
43p.

1. Transportation - Nashville. 2. Transportation - Davidson Co., Tenn. 3. Zoning - Nashville metropolitan area.
4. High-   ways - Economic effect.
I. Title.

Transportation - Monmouth Co., N.J.

388
(74946) Monmouth County, N.J. Planning Board.
M65 Transportation report for Monmouth coastal
region. [Freehold, N.J.] 1959.
78p. (Report no. 4)

U.S. Urban Renewal Adm. UPAP.

1. Transportation - Monmouth Co., N.J.
I. U.S. URA-UPAP. Monmouth Co., N.J.

3330 TRANSPORTATION - MORRIS CO., N.J.
MORRIS CO., N.J. PLANNING BOARD.
MORRIS COUNTY TRANSPORTATION STUDY;
INTERIM REPORT, 20 YEAR WORK PROGRAM. BY
JAMES P. PURCELL ASSOCIATES. N.P., 1970.
48L. (HUD 701 REPORT)

1. TRANSPORTATION - MORRIS CO., N.J.
I. PURCELL (JAMES P.) ASSOCIATES.
II. HUD. 701. MORRIS CO., N.J.

Transportation - Nashville.

388
(768551) Nashville Metropolitan Area Transportation
N17do Study.
Downtown cordon count, Cumberland River
screenline count. Nashville, 1959.
37p.

Traffic census, 1959.

1. Transportation - Nashville. 2. Traffic
- Nashville. 3. Business districts -
Nashville.

Transportation - Monroe, Ga.

388
(75821) Monroe, Ga. Planning Commission.
M65 Monroe, Georgia: transportation,
central business district parking plan,
by Sydney Carter. Prepared under
contract with the Georgia Dept. of
Commerce. Monroe, 1960.
23p.

1. Transportation - Monroe, Ga.
2. Parking - Monroe, Ga. I. Carter,
Sydney. II. U.S. URA-UPAP. Monroe,
Ga.

Transportation - Mt. Holly, N.J.

388
(74961) Smith (Herbert H.) Associates.
827 Mass transportation considerations.
[Prepared in cooperation with] Pinelands
Regional Planning Board. Mt. Holly, N.J.,
1962.
21p. (Memorandum 10)

1. Transportation - Mt. Holly, N.J.
I. Pinelands Regional Planning Board,
Mt. Holly, N.J. II. Title.

Transportation - Nashville.

388
(768551) Nashville Metropolitan Area Transportation
N17d Study.
Downtown parking study. Prepared by
Nashville Parking Board; participating
agencies: Nashville Traffic Commission,
Tennessee Dept. of Highways, Nashville-
Davidson County Planning Commission.
Nashville, 1960.
72p.

1. Transportation - Nashville. 2. Park-
ing - Nashville. 3. Business districts -
Nashville.   I. Nashville. Parking
Board.

TRANSPORTATION - MONROE, La.

388
(763871) Smith (Wilbur) and Associates.
S54 Metropolitan area transportation study,
Monroe, La. Columbia, S.C., 1967/68.
3v.
Prepared for U.S. Bureau of Public Roads
and Ouachita Parish, Cities of Monroe and
West Monroe.
U.S. Mass Transportation Demonstration
Grant Program.
1. Transportation - Monroe, La.
2. Journey to work.
(Cont'd on next card)

---

388 TRANSPORTATION - NASHVILLE.
(768551) Nashville Urban Observatory.
N171 An inventory of private and public
transportation services in the social-
services system of Metropolitan Nashville,
Tennessee, by Transportation RAP Group.
Final report. Nashville, Tenn., 1971.
5p.
Preparation of this report supported in
part by grant from Dept. of Housing and
Urban Development, administered through
the National League of Cities.
(Cont'd on next card)

Transportation - Nashville.

388
(768551) Nashville Metropolitan Area Transportation
N17 Study.
Transit facts, [level of service and
general operating facts] 1959. Participating agencies: Nashville Transit Company,
Nashville Traffic Commission, Nashville
Transit Authority. Nashville, 1959.
11p.

1. Transportation - Nashville.

388
(763871) Smith (Wilbur) and Associates.
S54 Metropolitan...1967/68 (Card 2)

I. Monroe, La. Metropolitan Area
Transportation Study.
II. U.S. Mass Transportation Demonstration
Grant Program. III. Title.

388
(768551) Nashville Urban Observatory. An
N171 inventory...1971. (Card 2)

1. Transportation - Nashville.
I. U.S. Dept. of Housing and Urban
Development. II. Title.

Transportation - Nashville.

388
(768551) Nashville Metropolitan Area Transportation
N17tr Study.
Transportation administration. Nashville, 1961.
19p.

1. Transportation - Nashville. I. Title.

Transportation - Montreal.

388
(714281) Binns, Richard M
B45 A study of the transportation situation
in Montreal's central business district.
[Montreal] Montreal Transportation
Commission, 1962.
6p.

Cover-title.

1. Transportation - Montreal.
I. Montreal. Transportation Commission.

Transportation - Nashville.

388
(768551) Metropolitan Government of Nashville and
M27n Davidson County. Metropolitan Planning Commission.
Nashville metropolitan area transportation study; a reevaluation of the 1980
major route plan. Prepared by State of
Tennessee, Dept. of Highways, Research
and Planning Division and the Metropolitan Government of Nashville and Davidson County, Metropolitan Planning Commission, Dept. of Public Works, Traffic and
Parking Board in cooperation with U.S.
Dept. of Comm-   erce, Bureau of Public
(Continued on next card)

Transportation - Nashville.

388
(768551) Nashville Metropolitan Area Transportation
N17t Study.
Travel time study #2. Level of street
service: major arterial streets, 1959.
Nashville, 1960.
26p.

1. Transportation - Nashville. 2. Journey
to work. 3. Traffic - Nashville.

Transportation - Montreal.

388
(714281) Montreal. Transportation Commission.
M65f The first ten years, 1950-1960.
Montreal, [1961?]
39p.

French and English.

1. Transportation - Montreal.

388
(768551) Metropolitan Government of Nashville and
M27n Davidson County. Metropolitan Planning Commission. Nashville Metropolitan...1965. (Card 2)

Roads. Nashville, 1965.
64p.

1. Transportation - Nashville. 2. Metro-
politan areas - Nashville. I. Tennessee.
Dept. of Highways. II. U.S. Bureau of
Public Roads. III. Title.

Transportation - Nashville.

388
(768551) Smith (Wilbur) and Associates.
S54 Nashville Metropolitan Area Transporta-
vol.1 tion Study. Vol. 1. Origin-destination
survey and major route plan. Prepared
for the Tennessee Department of Highways
in cooperation with U.S. Dept. of Commerce, Bureau of Public Roads and City
of Nashville and Davidson County. New
Haven, Conn., 1961.
119p.

1. Nashville Metropolitan Area Transportation Study. 2. Transportation - Nashville.   3. Journey to work.

388
(768551)
V66

TRANSPORTATION - NASHVILLE.
Voorhees (Alan M.) and Associates.
Transportation accessibility from the Model Cities area. Prepared for the Nashville Model Cities Agency. McLean, Va., 1969.
66p.

1. Transportation - Nashville. 2. Journey to work. 3. Model cities - Nashville.
I. Nashville. Model Cities Agency.
II. Title.

388
(74893)
B51

TRANSPORTATION - NEW CASTLE, PA.
Blackson (John) Associates.
Mass transportation in a small city; final report. Pennsylvania Mass Transportation Demonstration Project. Prepared for the New Castle Area Transit Authority. New Castle, Pa., 1968.
32p.
U.S. Mass Transportation Demonstration Grant Program.
HUD Project PA-MTD-6.

1. Transportation - New Castle, Pa. (Cont'd on next card)

388
(749)
D25

Transportation - New Jersey.
Delaware River Port Authority.
Southern New Jersey rapid transit system, Haddonfield-Kirkwood Line. Report to Governor David L. Lawrence and Governor Robert B. Meyner and the Legislatures of Pennsylvania and New Jersey. Camden, N.J., 1961.
67p.
-- --- Supplement. Camden, N.J., 1962.
[5]p.

1. Transportation - New Jersey.
2. Transportation - Pennsylvania.

388
(768551)
M27e

Transportation - Nashville metropolitan area
Metropolitan Government of Nashville and Davidson County. Metropolitan Planning Commission.
Experimental bus lines in metropolitan Nashville. [Prepared in cooperation with] Nashville Metropolitan Traffic and Parking Commission. Nashville, 1966.
81p.
U.S. Dept. of Housing and Urban Development. Mass Transportation Demonstration Grant Program.

(Cont'd on next card)

388
(74893)
B51

Blackson (John) Associates.   Mass
Transportation...1968.   (Card 2)

2. Journey to work. I. New Castle, Pa. Area Transit Authority. II. Title.
III. U.S. Mass Transportation Demonstration Grant Program.

388
(748)
P25p
no. 14

Transportation - New Jersey.
Harris, Britton.
PJ area systems. Philadelphia, Penn Jersey Transportation Study, 1962.
11p. (Penn Jersey Transportation Study, Philadelphia. PJ paper no. 14)

1. Transportation - Pennsylvania.
2. Transportation - New Jersey.
(Series: Penn Jersey Transportation Study, Philadelphia. PJ paper no. 14)

388
(768551)
M27e

Metropolitan Government of Nashville and Davidson County. Metropolitan Planning Commission. Experimental bus lines in metropolitan Nashville...1966. (Card 2)

1. Transportation - Nashville metropolitan area. 2. Traffic - Nashville metropolitan area. 3. Journey to work.
I. Nashville. Metropolitan Traffic and Parking Commission. II. U.S. Dept. of Housing and Urban Development. Mass Transportation Demonstration Grant Program.
III. Title: Bus lines in Metropolitan Nashville.

330
(74)
K45

Transportation - New England.
Kinnard, William N   ed.
The New England region; problems of a mature economy; papers and proceedings of a conference held at the University of Connecticut, Nov. 18, 1967. Storrs, University of Conn., Center for Real Estate and Urban Economic Studies, School of Business Administration, 1968.
95p. (Connecticut. University. Center for Real Estate and Urban Economic Studies. General series; no.2)
1. Economic conditions - New England. 2. Industrial location - New England. 3. Housing - New England. 4. Transportation - New England.
I. Connecticut. University. Center for Real Estate and Urban Economic Studies.

388
(748)
P25p
no. 1

Transportation - New Jersey.
Harris, Britton.
Planning metropolitan transportation studies. Prepared for presentation at the Operations Research Society of America, Chicago. Philadelphia, Penn Jersey Transportation Study, 1961.
11p. (Penn Jersey Transportation Study, Philadelphia. PJ paper no. 1)

1. Transportation - Pennsylvania.
2. Transportation - New Jersey.
(Series: Penn Jersey Transportation Study, Philadelphia. PJ paper no. 1)

388
(747245)
N17

Transportation - Nassau Co., N.Y.
Nassau County, N.Y. Planning Commission.
Transportation centers for Nassau County. Mineola, N.Y., 1965.
36p.

1. Transportation - Nassau Co., N.Y.
2. Traffic - Nassau Co., N.Y. I. Title.

2386-
2390

TRANSPORTATION - NEW HAMPSHIRE.
NEW HAMPSHIRE. STATE PLANNING AND DEVELOPMENT COMMISSION.
INTER-CITY TRANSPORTATION: 1. COMPREHENSIVE TRANSPORTATION PLAN; 2. ECONOMIC FACTORS AND COMMUNITY OF INTEREST; 3. AIR TRANSPORTATION; 4. AIRPORTS AND AIRWAYS; 5. SURFACE TRANSPORTATION. CONCORD, N.H., 1966.
5 V. (HUD 701 REPORT)

1. TRANSPORTATION - NEW HAMPSHIRE.
II. HUD. 701. NEW HAMPSHIRE.

388
(748)
P25p
no. 7

Transportation - New Jersey.
Harris, Britton.
Regional growth model--activity distribution sub-model. Philadelphia, Penn Jersey Transportation Study, 1961.
12p. (Penn Jersey Transportation Study, Philadelphia. PJ paper no. 7)

1. Transportation - Pennsylvania.
2. Transportation - New Jersey. (Series: Penn Jersey Transportation Study, Philadelphia. PJ paper no. 7)

388
(747245)
T74

TRANSPORTATION - NASSAU CO., N.Y.
Tri-State Transportation Commission.
(Connecticut-New Jersey-New York)
People, transportation, jobs; public transport services to non-CBD employment concentrations. Participating agencies: Tri-State Transportation Commission, U.S. Department of Transportation, State of New York, Dept. of Transportation. New York, 1969.
36p. (Nassau and Suffolk Counties Progress report no. 3)
INT-MTD 13.
U.S. Dept. of Housing and Urban Development. Mass Transportation Demonstration Grant (Cont'd on next card)

388
:331
F73

Transportation - New Haven.
Fredericksen, Nils.
The New Haven commuter service, it is expendable. Prepared in collaboration with Technical Planning Associates of New Haven. Norwalk, Conn., South Western Regional Planning Agency [1966?]
29p.
U.S. Housing and Urban Development. UPAP.

1. Journey to work. 2. Transportation - New Haven. I. Technical Planning Associates, New Haven, Conn. II. South Western Regional Planning Agency, Norwalk, Conn.
III. Title. IV. U.S. HUD-UPAP. New Haven.

388
(748)
P25p
no. 3

Transportation - New Jersey.
Harris, Britton.
Some problems in the theory of intra-urban location. Philadelphia, Penn Jersey Transportation Study, 1961.
29p. (Penn Jersey Transportation Study, Philadelphia. PJ paper no. 3)

1. Transportation - Pennsylvania.
2. Transportation - New Jersey. (Series: Penn Jersey Transportation Study, Philadelphia. PJ paper no. 3)

388
(747245)
T74

Tri-State Transportation Commission.
(Connecticut-New Jersey-New York)
People, transportation, jobs...1969.
(Card 2)

Program.

1. Transportation - Nassau Co., N.Y.
2. Transportation - Suffolk Co., N.Y.
3. Journey to work. I. Title. II. U.S. HUD. Mass Transportation Demonstration Grant Program.

388
(7468)
C25

TRANSPORTATION - NEW HAVEN.
U.S. Bureau of the Census.
Census use study: area travel survey. Wash., 1970.
43p. (Its Census use study report no. 11)

1. Transportation - New Haven. 2. Journey to work. I. Title. II. Title: Area travel survey.

388
(748)
P25p
no. 13

Transportation - New Jersey.
Mulroney, Thomas B
PJ costs: April 1959 to July 1961; a summary of accounting methods and costs incurred during the first phases of PJ work. Philadelphia, Penn Jersey Transportation Study, 1962.
13p. (Penn Jersey Transportation Study, Philadelphia. PJ paper no. 13)

1. Transportation - Pennsylvania.
2. Transportation - New Jersey. 3. Accounting. (Series: Penn Jersey Transportation Study, Philadelphia. PJ paper no. 13)

388
(492)
N27t

TRANSPORTATION - NETHERLANDS.
Netherlands. Ministry of Housing and Physical Planning.
Traffic and transport in particular in the urban areas. The Hague, Information Service, 1970.
23p.

1. Transportation - Netherlands. I. Title.

388
(748)
P25p
no. 4

Transportation - New Jersey.
Almendinger, V
Topics in the regional growth model: 1. Philadelphia, Penn Jersey Transportation Study, 1961.
22p. (Penn Jersey Transportation Study, Philadelphia. PJ paper no. 4)

1. Transportation - Pennsylvania.
2. Transportation - New Jersey. 3. City growth. (Series: Penn Jersey Transportation Study, Philadelphia. PJ paper no. 4)

VF
385
(7472)
N28

Transportation - New Jersey.
New Jersey. Regional Planning Commission.
Report on improved rapid transportation for the Metropolitan Region of New York and New Jersey. Trenton, N. J., January 14, 1952.
21 p. (Its report no. 1)

1. Transportation - New Jersey. 2. Transportation - New York, N. Y. 3. Railroads - New Jersey. 4. Railroads - New York, N. Y. I. Title: Improved rapid transportation for the Metropolitan Region of New York and New Jersey.

Transportation - New Jersey.

388
:331
N28   New York-New Jersey Transportation Agency.
      Journey to work. New York, 1962.
      36p.
      "This study was undertaken to improve the
future of transportation within the core of
America's most vital urban area in accordance
with the objectives of the United States
Bureau of Public Roads."

      1. Journey to work. 2. Transportation -
New York. 2. Transportation - New Jersey.

Transportation - N.J.

388
(748)
P25p   Penn Jersey Transportation Study.
v.2   Philadelphia.
      Penn Jersey Transportation Study, Vol.
2. 1975 projections: foreground of the
future. Philadelphia, 1964.
      [105]p.   (P.J. reports, vol. 2)

      1. Transportation - Pennsylvania.
      2. Transportation - N.J.

Transportation - New Jersey.

VP
388
(747)
P67   Port of New York Authority.
      Facilities of the Port of New York
Authority. [New York, 1960]
      1v. illus.

      1. Transportation - New York (State) 2. Trans-
portation - New Jersey.

Transportation - New Jersey.

388
(749)
N28   Newark commerce. (The Magazine of Metropolitan North Jersey)
      Organizing the transportation mess. Newark,
N.J., 1967.
      40p.

      Entire issue: Spring 1967.

      1. Transportation - New Jersey. I. Title.

Transportation - New Jersey.

388
(748)
P25pe   Penn Jersey Transportation Study,
v.3   Philadelphia.
      Penn Jersey Transportation Study, Vol.
3. 1975 transportation plans.
Philadelphia, 1965.
      [114]p.   (P.J. reports, vol. 3)

      1. Transportation - Pennsylvania.
      2. Transportation - New Jersey.

Transportation - New Jersey.

388
P67f   Port of New York Authority.
      Financial report,
New York, N.Y.,
      v. illus.
      For complete information see shelf list.

      1. Transportation - New York (State)
      2. Transportation - New Jersey. 3. Au-
thorities.

Transportation - New Jersey.

388
(749)
P15   Palmer, Dwight R   G
      The impending breakthrough in transportation.
An address by Commissioner, New Jersey State
Highway Department, before the North Jersey
Conference, Regional Plan Association, Newark,
New Jersey, November 29, 1961. Trenton, New
Jersey State Highway Dept., Bureau of Public
Information, 1961.
      15p.

      1. Transportation - New Jersey. I. North Jersey
Conference, Regional   Plan Association,
Newark, 1961.

Transportation - New Jersey.

388
(748)
P25p   Penn Jersey Transportation Study,
no. 12   Philadelphia.
      Preliminary projections of population;
county totals for the Camden-Philadelphia-
Trenton-Wilmington metropolitan region.
Philadelphia, 1962.
      37p.   (Its PJ paper no. 12)

      1. Transportation - Pennsylvania.
      2. Transportation - New Jersey. 3. Population
(Series: Penn Jersey
Transportation   Study, Philadelphia.
PJ paper no.   12)

Transportation - New Jersey.

388
(747)
P67m   Port of New York Authority.
      Metropolitan rapid transit financing, legal,
administrative and financial studies. A
report to the metropolitan rapid transit
survey of New York and New Jersey. Sponsored
by the Port of New York Authority and the
Metropolitan Rapid Transit Commission of
New York and New Jersey. New York, 1957.
      137p.
      William Miller, governmental consultant.
      1. Transportation - New York. 2. Transportation -
New Jersey. 3. Journey   to work.

Transportation - New Jersey.

388
(748)
P25p   Penn Jersey Transportation Study, Philadelphia.
no. 10   Alternative transportation systems and
associated sets of policies. Philadelphia,
1961.
      44p.   (Its PJ paper no. 10)

      1. Transportation - Pennsylvania.
      2. Transportation - New Jersey.
(Series: Penn Jersey Transportation
Study, Philadelphia. PJ paper no. 10)

Transportation - New Jersey.

388
(748)
P25   Penn-Jersey Transportation Study.
      Prospectus. Philadelphia, 1959.
      1v. tables.

Suppl. -- --- Supplement. Philadelphia, 1962.
      36p.
Suppl. -- --- 1963-64 supplement. Philadelphia, 1963.
      28p.

      1. Transportation - Pennsylvania. 2. Transporta-
tion - New Jersey.

Transportation - New Jersey.

388
P67   Port of New York Authority.
      Report, 1957-
New York, 1958-
      v. illus., maps, tables. annual

      For complete information see shelf list.

      1. Transportation - New York (State)
      2. Transportation - New Jersey.

Transportation - New Jersey.

388
(748)
P25p   Penn Jersey Transportation Study, Philadelphia.
no. 9   Computation of accessibility measures.
to be used in sub-model no. 3. (Calculated in
submodel no. 2) of regional growth model.
Philadelphia, 1961.
      2p.   (Its PJ paper no. 9)

      1. Transportation - Pennsylvania.
      2. Transportation - New Jersey.   (Series:
Penn Jersey Transportation Study, Philadelphia.
PJ paper no. 9)

Transportation - New Jersey.

388
(748)
P25r   Penn-Jersey Transportation Study.
      Report on study procedures; data col-
lection phase. Philadelphia, 1961.
      30p.   (PJ report no. 1)

      1. Transportation - Pennsylvania.
      2. Transportation - New Jersey.

Transportation - New Jersey.

388
(748)
P25p   Tomazinis, Anthony R
no. 8   An introduction to mathematical models.
Philadelphia, Penn Jersey Transportation
Study, 1960.
      18p.   (Penn Jersey Transportation Study,
Philadelphia. PJ paper no. 8)

      1. Transportation - Pennsylvania.
      2. Transportation - New Jersey.   (Series:
Penn Jersey Transportation Study, Philadelphia.
PJ paper no. 8)

Transportation - New Jersey.

388
(748)
P25t   Penn Jersey Transportation Study,
no.2   Factoring procedures and accuracy
checks. Philadelphia, 1963.
      30p.   (Its Technical report no. 2)

      1. Transportation - Pennsylvania.
      2. Transportation - New Jersey.

Transportation - New Jersey.

388
(748)
P25s   Penn-Jersey Transportation Study, Philadelphia.
      Summary; state of the region. Philadelphia
[1967]
      [7] p.

      1. Transportation - Pennsylvania. 2.
Transportation - New Jersey. I. Title.

Transportation - New Jersey.

388
(748)
P25p   Tomazinis, Anthony Rudolf.
no. 6   Spatial parameters affecting urban traffic.
Presented at the Origin and Destination
Survey Committee Meeting, Highway Research
Board, Washington, D.C., 1961. Philadelphia,
Penn Jersey Transportation Study, 1961.
      31p.   (Penn Jersey Transportation Study,
Philadelphia. PJ paper no. 6)
      1. Transportation - Pennsylvania. 2. Transportation
- New Jersey.   (Series: Penn Jersey Transportation
Study, Philadelphia. PJ paper no. 6)

Transportation - New Jersey.

388
(748)
P25pe   Penn Jersey Transportation Study,
vol.1   Philadelphia.
      Penn Jersey Transportation Study. Vol.
1. The state of the [PJ] region.
Philadelphia, 1964.
      [156]p.   (PJ reports, vol. 1)

      1. Transportation - Pennsylvania.
      2. Transportation - New Jersey.

Transportation - New Jersey.

388
(748)
P25p   Penn Jersey Transportation Study, Philadelphia.
no. 11   Survey of county leadership and policy
development; report on procedures.
Philadelphia, 1961.
      4p.   (Its PJ paper no. 11)

      1. Transportation - Pennsylvania.
      2. Transportation - New Jersey. I. Title.
(Series: Penn Jersey Transportation Study,
Philadelphia.   PJ paper no. 11)

Transportation - New Jersey.

388
T74   Tri-State Transportation Committee.
      Interim report
[New York,
      v.
      For complete information see shelflist.

      1. Transportation - Connecticut.
      2. Transportation - New Jersey. 3. Transporta-
tion - New York.

Row 1, Column 1

388
T74p   Transportation - New Jersey.
Tri-State Transportation Committee.
Prospectus. New York, 1962.
51p.

"The Tri-State Metropolitan Region, consists of portions of the states of Connecticut, New Jersey and New York."

1. Transportation - Connecticut.
2. Transportation - New Jersey. 3. Transportation - New York.

Row 1, Column 2

388
(7471)
L21   Transportation - New York (City)
Leavens, John M
Runaway transit? Statement of Executive Director of the Citizens Budget Commission to the City Planning Commission on the proposed 1962 capital budget. New York, Citizens Budget Commission, 1961.
11p.

1. Transportation - New York (City)
2. Budget - New York (City) I. Citizens Budget Commission, New York.

Row 1, Column 3

388
:308   Transportation - New York (City)
(7471)   New York (City) Transit Authority.
N28   The effect of the 1966 transit strike on the travel behavior of regular transit users. Prepared from a survey made by Berrington and Company, division of Day and Zimmermen, Inc. [n.p., 1967?]
116p.
U.S. Dept. of Housing and Urban Development. Mass Transportation Demonstration Grant Program.

(Cont'd on next card)

Row 2, Column 1

388
T97   Transportation - New Jersey.
Tyson, David O
A close look at the transit crisis. [Trenton, 1961?]
9p.

Reprinted by: Bureau of Public Information, New Jersey State Highway Department, Trenton, New Jersey.

1. Transportation - New York.
2. Transportation - New Jersey.

Row 2, Column 2

711.4
(7471)
R23
v.4   Transportation - New York; N.Y.
Lewis, Harold MacLean
Transit and transportation, and a study of port and industrial areas and their relation to transportation. By Harold M. Lewis... with supplementary reports by William J. Wilgus and Daniel L. Turner... New York, Regional plan of New York and its environs, 1928.
226p. (Regional plan of New York and its environs. Survey volumes. v.4)
1.Transportation-New York, N.Y. I.Wilgus, William J. II.Turner, Daniel L.

Row 2, Column 3

388
:308   New York (City) Transit Authority. The effect
(7471)   of the 1966 transit strike on the travel
N28   behavior of regular transit users...[1967?]
(Card 2)

1. Traffic surveys - New York (City)
2. Transportation - New York (City) 3. Journey to work. I. Berrington and Co. II. Title.
III. U.S. HUD-Demonstration Grant Program.

Row 3, Column 1

388
(789)
B61   TRANSPORTATION - N.M.
Boatright, C   C
Transportation and communications in New Mexico. Santa Fe, State Planning Office, 1966.
58p.

U.S. Urban Renewal Administration. UPAP.

1. Transportation - N.M. I. New Mexico. State Planning Office. II. U.S. URA-UPAP. N.M.

Row 3, Column 2

388
(7471)
L47   Transportation - New York (City)
Little (Arthur D.) inc.
Queens-Long Island Mass Transportation Demonstration Program; a preliminary proposal by Edwards and Kelcey, Wyer, Dick & Co. [and] Arthur D. Little. Cambridge, Mass., 1964.
24p.

1. Transportation - New York (City)
2. Journey to work. I. Title.
II. Edwards and   Kelcey, Wyer, Dick & Co.

Row 3, Column 3

388
(7471)
N28f   Transportation - New York (City)
New York (City) Transit Authority.
49th Street modernization; revised application of the City of New York acting by the New York City Transit Authority for a mass transportation facilities grant under the urban mass transportation act of 1964, May 15, 1968. New York, 1968.
54p.

1. Transportation - New York(City)
2. Journey to work. I. Title.

Row 4, Column 1

4005   TRANSPORTATION = NEW MEXICO.
NEW MEXICO. STATE PLANNING OFFICE.
TRANSPORTATION AND COMMUNICATIONS.
SANTA FE, 1966.
58P. (HUD 701 REPORT)

1. TRANSPORTATION = NEW MEXICO.
I. HUD. 701. NEW MEXICO.

Row 4, Column 2

VF
388
(7471)
M57r   Transportation - New York (City)
Moses, Robert.
Remarks of Robert Moses at the opening of Alexander Hamilton Bridge, George Washington Bridge Bus Station, and sections of the Cross-Bronx Expressway. [New York] 1963.
5p.

1. Transportation - New York (City)

Row 4, Column 3

388
(7471)
N28p   Transportation - New York (City)
New York (City) Transit Authority.
Preliminary proposal for rapid transit expansion, Borough of Queens. New York, 1963.
24p.

1. Transportation - New York (City)
2. Journey to work.

Row 5, Column 1

POLIO
388
(76335)
L68   Transportation - New Orleans metropolitan area.
Louisiana. Dept. of Highways.
New Orleans: metropolitan area transportation study, 1959-1960, 1960-1980. Vol. 1. Characteristics of existing traffic. Vol. 2. Outlook for the future. By Louisiana Dept. of Highways, Traffic and Planning Section, in cooperation with Bureau of Public Roads, Dept. of Commerce, [Baton Rouge?] 1960.
2v.
1. Transportation - New Orleans metropolitan area.
2. Traffic surveys -   New Orleans metropolitan area.

Row 5, Column 2

VF
385
(7472)
N28   Transportation - New York, N.Y.
New Jersey. Regional Planning Commission.
Report on improved rapid transportation for the Metropolitan Region of New York and New Jersey. Trenton, N. J., January 14, 1952.
21 p. (Its report no. 1)

1.Transportation - New Jersey. 2. Transportation - New York, N. Y. 3.Railroads - New Jersey.
4.Railroads - New York, N. Y. I.Title: Improved rapid transportation for the Metropolitan Region of New York and New Jersey.

Row 5, Column 3

388
(7471)
N28m   Transportation - New York (City)
New York (City) City Planning Commission.
Metropolitan mobility; proposals for improved transportation to serve New York City. Comprehensive planning report. New York, 1965.
34p.

1. Transportation - New York (City)
2. Population shifts - New York (City)
3. Master plan - New York (City)
I. Title.

Row 6, Column 1

388
(76335)
N28   Transportation - New Orleans metropolitan area.
New Orleans Public Service.
A basic concept for rapid transit planning in the New Orleans metropolitan area. Rev. New Orleans, Public Service, inc., Transit Dept., Research Div., 1962.
45p.

1. Transportation - New Orleans metropolitan area. 2. Journey to work.

Row 6, Column 2

385
(7471)
N28   Transportation - New York (City)
New York (City) Office of the City Construction Co-ordinator.
Railroad grade crossing elimination program, the City of New York, New York, 1958.
8p. illus., map.

1.Railroads - New York (City) 2.Transportation - New York (City)

Row 6, Column 3

388
(7471)
N28t   Transportation - New York (City)
New York (City) Transit Authority.
Two-way radio communication; Mass Transportation Demonstration Project. Final report New York, 1966.
92p. (Project NY-MTD-8)

U.S. Dept. of Housing and Urban Development Mass Transportation Demonstration Grant Program.
1. Transportation - New York (City)
2. Communication systems. I. U.S. HUD-Mass Transportation Demonstration Grant Program.
II. Title.

Row 7, Column 1

388
(7471)
D15   Transportation - New York (City)
Danielson, Michael N
Federal-metropolitan politics and the commuter crisis. New York, Columbia University Press, 1965.
244 p. (Columbia University. Metropolitan politics series no. 2)

Bibliographical notes: p. 201-232.

1. Transportation - New York (City) 2. Journey to work. I. Title.

11

Row 7, Column 2

353.1
N28   Transportation - New York (City)
New York (City) Temporary Commission on City Finances.
Transportation authorities: fiscal and organizational relations with the City of New York, by R.G. Smith and others. New York, 1966.
69p. (Its Staff paper 7)

1. Authorities. 2. Transportation - New York (City) 3. Municipal finance - New York (City) I. Smith, Robert G. II. Title.

Row 7, Column 3

388
(7471)
N28   Transportation - New York (City)
New York (State) Legislature. Senate.
Committee on the Affairs of the City of New York.
Interim report on the inquiry into the public transit system of New York City, including minority report

Albany, 19
v. (Legislative document

For complete information see main card.

1. Transportation - New York (City)

388
(7471)
N28r

Transportation - New York (City)

New York (City) Transit Authority.
  Report

New York,
    v.   annual.

For complete information see main card.

  1. Transportation - New York (City)
2. Journey to work.

711.73
(7471)
T74p

Transportation - New York (City).
Triborough Bridge and Tunnel Authority.
  Plan to increase the capacity of the Miller Highway and Henry Hudson Parkway. New York, 1965.
  19p.
    Introduction by Robert Moses.

  1. Highways - New York (City)
2. Transportation - New York (City)
3. Journey to work. I. Title.

388
(7472)
H27

TRANSPORTATION - NEW YORK METROPOLITAN AREA.
HERRING, FRANK W
  METROPOLITAN GROWTH AND METROPOLITAN TRAVEL PATTERNS. NEW YORK, PORT OF NEW YORK AUTHORITY, 1961.
  28L.

  PRESENTED AT THE ANNUAL MEETING OF THE HIGHWAY RESEARCH BOARD, NATIONAL ACADEMY OF SCIENCES - NATIONAL RESEARCH COUNCIL, COMMITTEE ON URBAN RESEARCH, JANUARY 12, 1961.
  1. TRANSPORTATION - NEW YORK METROPOLITAN AREA. 2. CITY GROWTH.
I. TITLE.

388
(7471)
O75

TRANSPORTATION - NEW YORK (CITY)
Ornati, Oscar A
  Transportation needs of the poor; a case study of New York City, by Oscar A. Ornati and others. New York, Praeger, 1969.
  127p. (Labor economics and urban studies. Praeger special studies in U.S. economic and social development)

  1. Transportation - New York (City)
2. Journey to work. 3. Poor. I. Title.

388
(7471)
T74r

Transportation - New York (City)
Triborough Bridge and Tunnel Authority.
  Report,

New York,
  v. annual.

For complete information see main card.

  1. Transportation. - New York (City) 2. Bridges.
3. Highways - New York (City)

388
(7472)
G25

Transportation - New York metropolitan region.
General Steel Industries, inc.
  The challenge of the path car; the story of a unique project to design and build pacesetting new rapid transit cars for the Port Authority Trans-Hudson system. St. Louis [1968?]
  8p.

  1. Transportation - New York metropolitan region. 2. Journey to work. I. Title.

388
(7471)
P67

Transportation - New York (City).
Port of New York Authority.
  Trans-Hudson passenger travel, 1948-1954; a pilot study, by Frank W. Herring. [New York, 1955]
  30p. maps, tables.

  1. Transportation - New York (City)
I. Herring, Frank W

624.2
T74th

Transportation - New York (City)
Triborough Bridge and Tunnel Authority.
  Third tube. [New York] 1965.
  16p.

  1. Bridges. 2. Highways - New York (City) 3. Transportation - New York (City)

388
(7471
:016)
P67

Transportation - New York (City) - Bibl.

Port of New York Authority.
  A selected bibliography of the Port of New York Authority, 1921/56
New York, 1956
  v.

For complete information see main card.

  1. Port of New York Authority - Bibl.
2. Transportation - New York (City) - Bibl.

711.3
(7471)
R23

Transportation - New York, N.Y.
Regional Plan Association.
  Metropolis in the making; the next twenty-five years in the New York metropolitan region: Proceedings of the twenty-fifth anniversary celebration...held at the Roosevelt Hotel, New York, N.Y., on October 6, 1954. New York, 1955.
  88 p. plates.

  1. Regional planning - New York, N.Y.
2. Transportation - New York, N.Y. I. Title.

388
(7471)
T74t

Transportation - New York (City)
Triborough Bridge and Tunnel Authority.
  Three decades of service; a pictorial review of accomplishments. New York, 1966.
  77p.

  1. Transportation - New York (City)
2. Triborough Bridge and Tunnel Authority.
I. Title.

388
(747)
C72

TRANSPORTATION - NEW YORK (STATE).
Creighton, Roger L
  Statewide transportation planning: a key element in environmental design, by Roger L. Creighton and others. Prepared for presentation at the annual meeting of the American Association of State Highway Officials, Wichita, Kansas, Nov. 30, 1966. Albany, Planning and Research Bureau, Planning Div., New York State Dept. of Transportation, 1966.
  21p.
  Publication IP 070405.
          (Cont'd on next card)

VF
388
(7471)
S15

Transportation - New York (City)
Salisbury, Harrison E
  The commuter crisis. A series of three articles. Reprinted from the New York Times, March 2, 3, and 4, 1959.
  4p. illus.
    Contents:-no.1. Commuter crisis traced to upheavals of auto age.-no.2. Study finds cars choking cities as 'urban sprawl' takes over. -no.3. Existing commuter cures found to need direction.

  1. Transportation - New York (City)
2. Journey to work.

388
(7471)
T74tr

Transportation - New York (City)
Triborough Bridge and Tunnel Authority.
  Triborough Bridge, 1936-1966. [New York] 1966.
  [7]p.

  1. Transportation - New York (City)
2. Bridges. 3. Triborough Bridge.

388
(747)
C72

Creighton, Roger L   Statewide transportation...1966. (Card 2)

  Prepared in cooperation with the U.S. Bureau of Public Roads, the U.S. Dept. of Housing and Urban Development, and others.
  1. Transportation - New York (State)
I. New York (State) Dept. of Transportation. Planning Div. II. U.S. Dept. of Housing and Urban Development. III. Title.

388
(7471)
T74r
suppl.

Transportation - New York (City)
Triborough Bridge and Tunnel Authority.
  Financial and construction program 1967-1971

Financial supplement to the annual report. New York, 1967
  v. annual.
For complete information see main card.

  1. Transportation - New York (City)
2. Bridges. 3. Highways - New York (City)

388
(7472)
D64

Transportation - New York metropolitan area.
Doig, Jameson W
  Metropolitan transportation politics and the New York region. New York, Columbia University Press, 1966.
  327p.   (Metropolitan politics series, no. 6)

  Bibliography: p. [251]-311.

  1. Transportation - New York metropolitan area. 2. Journey to work. 3. Railroads.
I. Title.   (Series: Metropolitan politics series no. 6)

711.14
(747)
F27

Transportation - New York (State)
Ferguson, George.
  Land use measurement manual. Albany, Niagara Frontier Transportation Study. 1962.
  83p.   (Manual no. 120)

  1. Land use - New York (State)
2. Transportation - New York (State)
I. Niagara Frontier Transportation Study.

711.73
(7471)
T74

Transportation - New York (City)
  Triborough Bridge and Tunnel Authority.
  Lower Manhattan Elevated Expressway. Introduction by Robert Moses. New York, 1965.
  11p.

  1. Highways - New York (City)
2. Transportation - New York (City)
I. Moses, Robert. II. Title.

388
(7472)
M12

Transportation - New York (City) metropolitan area.
Madigan-Hyland, inc.
  A study of metropolitan New York transportation. Prepared for Triborough Bridge and Tunnel Authority. New York, Triborough Bridge and Tunnel Authority, 1967.
  33p.

  1. Transportation - New York (City) metropolitan area. I. Triborough Bridge and Tunnel Authority. II. Title.

388
(747)
H15

Transportation - New York
Hamburg, John R
  Contingency check manual for the home interview, truck-taxi, and external surveys, by John R. Hamburg and Frederick W. Memmott, III. Albany, Niagara, Frontier Transportation Study, 1962.
  40p.   (Manual no. 110.M5)

  1. Transportation - New York. 2. Journey to work. I. Memmott, Frederick W. III. II. Niagara Frontier Transportation Study.

388
(747)
N28
TRANSPORTATION - NEW YORK (STATE).
New York (State) Legislature.
Joint Committee on Mass Transportation.
Report to the legislature, 19

Albany, 19

    v.   annual. (Legislative document, document (19) no.
For Library holdings see main entry.
1. Transportation - New York (State)
2. Intergovernmental relations - New York (State) 3. Journey to work.

388
(747)
N28re
TRANSPORTATION - NEW YORK (STATE)
New York (State) Legislature. Joint Committee on Mass Transportation.
Report to the Legislature, 19

Albany, 19

    v.   annual. (Legislative document)
For Library holdings see main entry.

1. Transportation - New York (State)
2. Journey to work.

388
(747)
N28m
Transportation - New York (State)
New York (State) Metropolitan Commuter Transportation Authority.
Metropolitan transportation; a program for action. Report to Nelson A. Rockefeller Governor of New York. New York, 1968.
56p.

1. Transportation - New York (State)
2. Railroads - New York (State) 3. Journey to work. I. Title.

388
(747)
N28r
Transportation - New York (State)
New York (State) Metropolitan Commuter Transportation Authority.
Report, 1st-   1966-

New York, 1966-
  v.

For complete information see main card.

1. Transportation - New York (State)
2. Railroads - New York (State) 3. Journey to work.

388
(747)
N28
Transportation - New York (State)
New York (State) Office of Transportation.
Journey to work transportation analysis-Westchester, Putnam and Rockland counties.
[Albany] 1964.
40p.

1. Transportation - New York (State)
2. Journey to work. I. Title.

388
N28l
Transportation - New York.
New York (State) Office of Transportation.
Long Island journey-to-work report.
[Albany] 1963.
36p.

1. Journey to work. 2. Transportation - New York. I. Title.

388
(747)
N41
Transportation - New York (State)
Niagara Frontier Transportation Study.
Basic corridor plan for expressways in the Niagara Frontier. Albany, New York State Dept. of Public Works, 1965.
[8]p.
Prepared in cooperation with U.S. Dept. of Commerce, Bureau of Public Roads and U.S. Housing and Home Finance Agency.

1. Transportation - New York (State)
2. Highways - New York (State)

388
(747)
N41
Transportation - New York.
Niagara Frontier Transportation Study.
The basis of travel. Final report, vol. 1.
v.1 Albany, 1964.
38p.

1. Transportation - New York. 2. Journey to work. I. Title.

VF
388
(747)
P67
Transportation - New York (State).
Port of New York Authority.
Facilities of the Port of New York Authority. [New York, 1960]
1v. illus.

1. Transportation - New York (State) 2. Transportation - New Jersey.

388
P67f
Transportation - New York (State)
Port of New York Authority.
Financial report,
New York, N.Y.,
  v. illus.
For complete information see shelf list.

1. Transportation - New York (State)
2. Transportation - New Jersey. 3. Authorities.

388
(747)
P67m
Transportation - New York.
Port of New York Authority.
Metropolitan rapid transit financing, legal, administrative and financial studies. A report to the metropolitan rapid transit survey of New York and New Jersey. Sponsored by the Port of New York Authority and the Metropolitan Rapid Transit Commission of New York and New Jersey. New York, 1957.
137p.
William Miller, governmental consultant.
1. Transportation - New York. 2. Transportation - New Jersey. 3. Journey to work.

388
P67
Transportation - New York (State)
Port of New York Authority.
Report, 1957 -
New York, 1958 -
  v. illus., maps, tables. annual

For complete information see shelf list.

1. Transportation - New York (State)
2. Transportation - New Jersey.

388
(7472)
T74
TRANSPORTATION - NEW YORK METROPOLITAN AREA.
Tri-State Transportation Commission. (Connecticut-New Jersey-New York)
Findings of the taxi survey. New York, 1968.
12p. (Its Technical bulletin, vol. IV, no. 3, April, 1968)

1. Transportation - New York metropolitan area. 2. Traffic surveys - New York metropolitan area. I. Title: Taxi survey.

388
T74
Transportation - New York.
Tri-State Transportation Committee.
Interim report
[New York,
  v.

For complete information see shelflist.

1. Transportation - Connecticut.
2. Transportation - New Jersey. 3. Transportation - New York.

388
T74p
Transportation - New York.
Tri-State Transportation Committee.
Prospectus. New York, 1962.
51p.

"The Tri-State Metropolitan Region, consists of portions of the states of Connecticut, New Jersey and New York."

1. Transportation - Connecticut.
2. Transportation - New Jersey. 3. Transportation - New York.

388
T97
Transportation - New York.
Tyson, David O
A close look at the transit crisis.
[Trenton, 1961?]
9p.

Reprinted by: Bureau of Public Information, New Jersey State Highway Department, Trenton, New Jersey.

1. Transportation - New York.
2. Transportation - New Jersey.

LAW
T
N28
S717re
Transportation - New York metropolitan area.
New York (State) Legislature. Joint Legislative Committee on Interstate Cooperation.
Report of the Joint Legislative Committee on Interstate Cooperation to the 1966 Legislature. Special supplement: Legislative White Paper on mass transportation. Albany, 1966.
86p. (Its Legislative document (1966) no. 37A)

1. Transportation - New York metropolitan area. 2. Transportation - Law and legislation. 3. Journey to work. I. Title: White Paper on mass transportation.

388
(7472)
S54
Transportation - New York metropolitan area.
Smith (Wilbur) and Associates.
Shuttle bus service; Hunters Point Avenue to Manhattan. Final report. New York, 1968.
77p.
At head of title: Queens-Long Island Mass Transportation Demonstration Program. U.S. Dept. of Housing and Urban Development. Mass Transportation Demonstration Grant Program.

1. Transportation - New York metropolitan area. 2. Journey to work. I. Title. II. Title: Queens-Long Island Mass Transportation Demonstration Program. III. U.S. HUD- Mass Transportation Demonstration Program.

388
(7471)
M27
Transportation - New York-New Jersey Metropolitan area.
Metropolitan Rapid Transit Commission.
Rapid transit needs of the New York-New Jersey Metropolitan Area. Staff report. New York, 1957.
42p. maps, tables.

1. Transportation - New York-New Jersey Metropolitan Area.

388
(7471)
M27r
Transportation - New York-New Jersey Metropolitan Area.
Metropolitan Rapid Transit Commission.
Rapid transit for the New York-New Jersey Metropolitan Area. New York, 1958.
75p. maps.

1. Transportation - New York-New Jersey Metropolitan Area.

388
:331
N28
Transportation - New York New Jersey metropolitan area
New York-New Jersey Transportation Agency.
Journey to work. New York, 1962.
36p.
"This study was undertaken to improve the future of transportation within the core of America's most vital urban area in accordance with the objectives of the United States Bureau of Public Roads."

1. Journey to work. 2. Transportation - New York. 2. Transportation - New Jersey.

388
(7472)
P21
TRANSPORTATION – NEW YORK METROPOLITAN REGION.
Peat, Marwick, Livingston & Co.
The Queens-Long Island traffic demand model.
New York, 1968.
1v.
Prepared for: Queens-Long Island Mass
Transportation Demonstration Program.
U.S. Dept. of Housing and Urban Development.
Mass Transportation Demonstration Grant Program.

1. Traffic – New York metropolitan region.
2. Journey to work. 3. Transportation – New York
metropolitan region. I. Title. II. Queens-Long
Island Mass Transportation Program.
III. U.S. HUD – Mass Transportation
Demonstration Grant Program.

388
(7471)
P67m
Transportation – New York/New Jersey Metro-
politan Area.
Port of New York Authority.
Metropolitan transportation, 1980. A
framework for the long-range planning of
transportation facilities to serve the
New York-New Jersey Metropolitan Region.
New York, Port of New York Authority,
Comprehensive Planning Office, 1963.
380p.

1. Transportation – New York-New Jersey
Metropolitan Area.

388
(74932)
E22
Transportation – Newark, N.J.
Edwards and Kelcey, inc.
Transportation for the new Newark, by
Edwards and Kelcey, De Leuw, Cather &
Company. Prepared for the New Jersey
State Highway Department and Bureau of
Public Roads. Newark, N.J., 1961.
12p.

1. Transportation – Newark, N.J.
I. De Leuw, Cather & Company.
II. New Jersey. State Highway
Dept.

388
(74932)
N28
Transportation – Newark, N.J.
New Jersey. Dept. of Conservation and
Economic Development.
Newark area transportation study. Trenton,
1959.
83p.

1. Transportation – Newark, N.J.
I. Title.

711.73
(74932)
S54
Transportation – Newark, N.J.
Smith (Wilbur) and Associates.
Urban Land Institute background data:
highways and mass transit, Newark, New
Jersey. New Haven, 1965.
24p.

1. Highways – Newark, N.J. 2. Transportation – Newark, N.J. I. Title.

388
(74976)
N28
Transportation – Newton, N.J.
New Jersey. Dept. of Conservation and
Economic Development. (Div. of Planning
and Development)
Preliminary master plan studies, circula-
tion and transportation, by Paul L. Rex and
Arthur Morey. [Prepared for Town of Newton
Planning Board] Trenton, 1960.
12p.
New Jersey. Expanded State and Regional
Planning Program.
U.S. Urban Renewal Adm. UPAP.
1. Transportation – Newton, N.J. I. Rex,
Paul L. II. Morey, Arthur. III. Newton,
N.J. Planning Board. IV. U.S. URA-UPAP.
Newton, N.J.

711.333
(74827)
L23t
Transportation – Northampton Co., Pa.
Lehigh-Northampton Counties (Pa.)
Joint Planning Commission.
Traffic and transportation; a comprehen-
sive research report. [n.p.] 1963.
130p.
U.S. Urban Renewal Adm. UPAP.

1. Master plan – Lehigh-Northampton Counties, Pa.
2. Traffic – Lehigh Co., Pa. 3. Traffic – Northampton
Co., Pa. 4. Transportation – Lehigh Co., Pa.
5. Transportation – Northampton Co., Pa.
I. U.S. URA-UPAP, Lehigh-Northampton
Counties, Pa.

388
(74)
M17
Transportation – Northeastern States.
Massachusetts Institute of Technology.
The glideway system; a high-speed ground
transportation system in the northeastern
corridor of the United States. Cambridge,
M.I.T. Press, 1966.
414p. (M.I.T. Report no. 6)
"Designed as an interdepartmental student
project in systems engineering at the
Massachusetts Institute of Technology in the
spring term, 1965."
Bibliography: p. 333-410.

1. Transportation – Northeastern
States. 2. Electricity. 3. Transportation – Automation. I. Title.

388
(755)
N67
Transportation – Northern Va.
Northern Virginia Transportation Commission.
Report, 19
Arlington, Va., 19
v. annual.

Form complete information see main card.

1. Transportation – Northern Va.
2. Journey to work.

388
(481)
O75
Transportation – Norway.
Oslo. Transportøkonomisk Institutt.
Årsberetning 1965.

Oslo, 19
v.

For complete information see main card.

1. Transportation – Norway.

711
(481
:016)
N67
TRANSPORTATION – NORWAY – BIBLIOGRAPHY.
Norsk Institutt for By- og Regionforskning.
Planning in Norway; literature in English.
2. edition. Oslo, 1971.
18p.

1. Planning – Norway – Bibl. 2. Economic
planning – Norway – Bibl. 3. Transportation –
Norway – Bibl. I. Title.

601
TRANSPORTATION – OAHU, HAWAII.
OAHU, HAWAII. TRANSPORTATION STUDY STAFF.
OAHU TRANSPORTATION STUDY; SUMMARY
REPORT, 1985; RAPID-TRANSIT, AND
FREEWAY-ARTERIAL PLAN. HONOLULU, 1967.
34P. (HUD 701 REPORT)

1. TRANSPORTATION – OAHU, HAWAII.
I. HUD. 701. OAHU, HAWAII.

388
(79466)
L15
Transportation – Oakland, Calif.
Lambert, John L
Air cushion vehicles: Mass Transporta-
tion Demonstration Project, Port of
Oakland. Final report. [n.p.] 1967.
72p.
U.S. Dept. of Housing and Urban Develop-
ment. Mass Transportation Demonstration
Grant Program.

1. Transportation – Oakland, Calif.
2. Municipal services – Oakland, Calif.
I. U.S. Dept. of Housing and Urban
Development. Mass Transportation
Demonstration Grant Program.
II. Title.

388
:331
Y77
Transportation – Oakland, Calif.
Ystehede, Frederik
Express bus operations in the Oakland
area. Institute of Transportation and
Traffic Engineering graduate report.
Berkeley, Calif., Univ. of Calif., 1962.
32p.

Thesis (Master of Engineering in Transportation) – University of California.

1. Journey to work. 2. Transportation –
Oakland, Calif. I. California.
University. Institute of Trans-
portation and Traffic Engineering.

1191
TRANSPORTATION – OCEAN CITY, MD.
OCEAN CITY, MD. PLANNING AND ZONING
COMMISSION.
TRAFFIC AND TRANSPORTATION; PRELIMINARY
REPORT, PART OF THE COMPREHENSIVE PLAN.
BY HARLAND BARTHOLOMEW AND ASSOCIATES.
OCEAN CITY, 1968.
23L. (HUD 701 REPORT)

1. TRANSPORTATION – OCEAN CITY, MD.
I. BARTHOLOMEW (HARLAND) AND ASSOCIATES.
II. HUD. 701. OCEAN CITY, MD.

388
(792)
O32
v.1
Transportation – Ogden, Utah.
Ogden (Utah) Area Transportation Study.
Ogden Area Transportation Study. Vol.1
Inventory of existing conditions. A coopera-
tive study by Davis County, Utah and others,
in cooperation with Utah State Dept. of
Highways, U.S. Dept. of Commerce, Bureau of
Public Roads. Salt Lake City, Utah State
Dept. of Highways, 1966.
42p.

1. Transportation – Ogden, Utah. I. Utah.
Highway Dept. II. U.S. Bureau of Public
Roads.

388
(771)
C52
Transportation – Ohio.
Cleveland-Seven County.
Transportation-Land Use Study
Operations plan, by Robert C. Stuart and
others. Cleveland, 1966.
1v.
Preparation of manual was financed by U.S.
Urban Renewal Adm. and others.

1. Transportation – Ohio. 2. Land use –
Ohio. 3. Journey to work. I. U.S. Urban
Renewal Administration. II. Title.

388
(771)
O34
Transportation – Ohio.
Ohio. Legislative Service Commission.
Public mass transportation. Columbus,
Ohio, 1963.
36p. (Its Staff research report no. 54)

1. Transportation – Ohio.

352
(771)
O34
Transportation – Ohio.
Ohio. Legislative Service Commission.
Selected metropolitan area problems. Sec-
tion 1, The municipal income tax. Section
2, Mass transportation in Ohio. Section 3,
Alternative form of county government.
Columbus, 1959.
70p. tables. (Its Staff research
report no. 34)

1. Metropolitan areas – Ohio. 2. County
government – Ohio. 3. Transportation –
Ohio.

388
(76638)
S54
Transportation – Oklahoma City, Oklahoma.
Smith (Wilbur) and Associates.
Current public transit service and riding
patterns, Oklahoma City, Oklahoma. Interim
report. Prepared for Oklahoma City, Oklahoma
in cooperation with Oklahoma State Highway
Dept. and U.S. Dept. of Commerce, Bureau
of Public Roads as an interim report for
the Oklahoma City Area Regional Transportation Study (OCARTS) [n.p.] 1965.
50p.
1. Transportation – Oklahoma City, Okla.
2. Journey to work. I. Title. II. Oklahoma. State Highway Dept.
III. Oklahoma City Area Regional
Transportation Study.

711.4
(74795)
O52
no. 2
Transportation – Olean, N.Y.
Tryon and Schwartz and Associates.
A preliminary report on traffic and park-
ing, City of Olean, N.Y. For the City
Planning Board. Buffalo, N.Y., 1959.
52p. diagrs., maps. (Olean, N.Y. City
Planning Board. Master plan rept. no. 2)
U.S. Urban Renewal Administration. Urban
Planning Assistance Program.
1. Master plan – Olean, N.Y. 2. Transportation
– Olean, N.Y. I. Olean, N.Y. City
Planning Board. II. U.S. URA-UPAP.

Transportation - Oneida, N.Y.

388
(74762) Oneida, N.Y. City Planning Commission.
052   Transportation facilities, a master plan
report, City of Oneida, New York, by
Russell D. Bailey. Utica, N.Y., 1957.
31p. maps, tables.

U.S. Urban Renewal Administration, Urban
Planning Assistance Program.

~~1. Master plan - Oneida, N.Y.~~ 2. Transportation -
Oneida, N.Y. I. U.S. URA-UPAP. Oneida, N.Y.
II. Bailey, Russell D.

Transportation - Onondaga-Syracuse
metropolitan area.

388
(74765) Blair and Stein Associates.
B51   Transportation in the Onondaga-Syracuse
metropolitan area, for the Onondaga County
Dept. of Planning, and the New York State
Dept. of Commerce. Syracuse, N.Y., 1962.
35p.

U.S. Urban Renewal Adm. UPAP.

1. Transportation - Onondaga-Syracuse
metropolitan area. I. U.S. URA-UPAP.
Onondaga-Syracuse metropolitan area.

Transportation - Ontario.

388
(713) Ontario. Dept. of Planning and
057   Development. (Community Planning
1959   Branch)
The St. Lawrence area study: transportation. Preliminary report. Rev. Toronto,
1959.
52p.

1. Transportation - Ontario. I. Title.

1140   TRANSPORTATION - ORLEANS PARISH, LA.
1141   JEFFERSON, ORLEANS, AND ST. BERNARD
PARISHES, LA. REGIONAL PLANNING
COMMISSION.
COMPREHENSIVE REGIONAL PLANNING
PROGRAM; STUDY DESIGN AND TRANSPORTATION
AS A MAJOR ELEMENT; 1, FINAL REPORT; 2,
SUPPLEMENT TO FINAL REPORT. BY RADER AND
ASSOCIATES. NEW ORLEANS, 1966.
2 V. (HUD 701 REPORT)

1. TRANSPORTATION - JEFFERSON PARISH,
LA. 2. TRANSPORTATION - ORLEANS PARISH,
LA. 3. TRANSPORTATION - ST. BERNARD
PARISH, LA. I. RADER AND ASSOCIATES.
(CONTINUED ON NEXT CARD)

1140   JEFFERSON, ORLEANS, AND ST. BERNARD
1141   PARISHES, LA. REGIONAL PLANNING
COMMISSION. COMPREHENSIVE REGIONAL
PLANNING ...1966.   (CARD 2)

II. HUD. 701. JEFFERSON PARISH, LA.
III. HUD. 701. ORLEANS PARISH, LA.
IV. HUD. 701. ST. BERNARD PARISH, LA.

Transportation - Oxford, N.J.

711.4
(74978) New Jersey. Dept. of Conservation and
093t   Economic Development. (Div. of Planning
and Development)
Oxford Township, Warren County, New
Jersey preliminary master plan studies.
Thorofares and traffic, public transportation, railroads and freight service. Prepared for the Oxford Planning Board.
[Trenton] 1958.
9p.

U.S. Urban Renewal Adm. UPAP.

1. Master plan - Oxford, N.J. 2. Transportation - Oxford, N.J. I. Oxford, N.J.
Planning Board. II. U.S. URA-UPAP. Oxford, N.J.

Transportation - Penjerdel region.

388
F71 Frazier, Charles H
   Transportation: lubricant or friction to our
region's progress. Philadelphia, Penjerdel,
1962.
26p.

1. Transportation - Penjerdel region.
I. Pennsylvania-New Jersey-Delaware
Metropolitan Project.

Transportation - Pennsylvania.

388
(748) Almendinger, V
P25p   Topics in the regional growth model: 1.
no. 4   Philadelphia, Penn Jersey Transportation
Study, 1961.
22p. (Penn Jersey Transportation Study,
Philadelphia. PJ paper no. 4)

1. Transportation - Pennsylvania.
2. Transportation - New Jersey. 3. City
growth. (Series: Penn Jersey Transportation
Study, Philadelphia, PJ paper no. 4)

Transportation - Pennsylvania.

711.73
(7481) Bureau of Municipal Research, Philadelphia.
B87   Digest of Improved transportation for
Southeastern Pennsylvania; an analysis with
recommendations for planning, financing, and
administering Southeastern Pennsylvania's
road system, including relationships with
mass transportation. [U.S. URA-UPAP. In
cooperation with] Pennsylvania Economy League
(Eastern Div.) Prepared for Pennsylvania Dept.
(Continued on next card)

711.73
(7481) Bureau of Municipal Research, Philadelphia.
B87   Digest of ... 1960. (Card 2)

of Commerce and Study Commission of the
Philadelphia Metropolitan Area. Philadelphia, 1960.
24p. illus., diagrs.

1. Highways - Pennsylvania. 2. Transportation -
Pennsylvania. I. Pennsylvania Economy League.
(Eastern Div.)   II. U.S. URA-
UPAP. Pennsylvania.

711.73
(7481) Bureau of Municipal Research, Philadelphia.
B871   Improved transportation for southeastern
Pennsylvania. An analysis with recommendations for planning, financing, and administering, southeastern Pennsylvania's road
system, including relationships with mass
transportation. Prepared for Pennsylvania
Dept. of Commerce and Study Commission of
the Philadelphia Metropolitan Area. Philadelphia, Bureau of Municipal Research and
Pennsylvania Economy League, Eastern Div.
1960.   (Cont'd. on next card)
378p.

711.73
(7481) Bureau of Municipal Research, Philadelphia.
B871   Improved transportation for southeastern
Pennsylvania...(Card 2)

U.S. Urban Renewal Adm. UPAP.

1. Highways - Pennsylvania. 2. Transpor-
tation - Pennsylvania. I. Pennsylvania
Economy League. II. U.S. URA-UPAP.
Pennsylvania.

Transportation - Pennsylvania.

388
(749) Delaware River Port Authority.
D25   Southern New Jersey rapid transit system,
Haddonfield-Kirkwood Line. Report to
Governor David L. Lawrence and Governor
Robert B. Meyner and the Legislatures of
Pennsylvania and New Jersey. Camden, N.J.,
1961.
67p.
-- --- Supplement. Camden, N.J., 1962.
[5]p.

1. Transportation - New   Jersey.
2. Transportation -   Pennsylvania.

Transportation - Pennsylvania.

388
(748) Harris, Britton.
P25p   PJ area systems. Philadelphia, Penn
no. 14   Jersey Transportation Study, 1962.
11p. (Penn Jersey Transportation Study,
Philadelphia. PJ paper no. 14)

1. Transportation - Pennsylvania.
2. Transportation - New Jersey.
(Series: Penn Jersey Transportation Study,
Philadelphia. PJ paper no. 14)

Transportation - Pennsylvania.

388
(748) Harris, Britton.
P25p   Planning metropolitan transportation studies.
no. 1   Prepared for presentation at the Operations
Research Society of America, Chicago.
Philadelphia, Penn Jersey Transportation Study,
1961.
11p. (Penn Jersey Transportation Study,
Philadelphia. PJ paper no. 1)

1. Transportation - Pennsylvania.
2. Transportation - New Jersey.
(Series: Penn   Jersey
Transportation   Study, Philadelphia.
PJ paper no. 1)

Transportation - Pennsylvania.

388
(748) Harris, Britton.
P25p   Regional growth model--activity distribution
no. 7   sub-model. Philadelphia, Penn Jersey
Transportation Study, 1961.
12p. (Penn Jersey Transportation Study,
Philadelphia. PJ paper no. 7)

1. Transportation - Pennsylvania.
2. Transportation - New Jersey. (Series:
Penn Jersey Transportation Study, Philadelphia.
PJ paper no. 7)

Transportation - Pennsylvania.

388
(748) Harris, Britton.
P25p   Some problems in the theory of intra-urban
no. 3   location. Philadelphia, Penn Jersey
Transportation Study, 1961.
29p. (Penn Jersey Transportation Study,
Philadelphia. PJ paper no. 3)

1. Transportation - Pennsylvania.
2. Transportation - New Jersey. (Series:
Penn Jersey Transportation Study, Philadelphia.
PJ paper no. 3)

Transportation - Pennsylvania.

388
(748) Herbert, John D
P25p   A model for the distribution of residential
no.2   activity in urban areas, by John D. Herbert
and Benjamin H. Stevens. Philadelphia, Penn
Jersey Transportation Study [1963]
57p. (Penn Jersey Transportation Study
Philadelphia. PJ paper no. 2)

1. Transportation - Pennsylvania. 2. Land
use - Pennsylvania. 3. Land use - New Jersey.
I. Stevens, Benjamin H., jt. au. (Series:
Penn Jersey Transportation Study, Philadelphia.
PJ paper no. 2)

Transportation - Pennsylvania.

388
(748) Mulroney, Thomas B
P25p   PJ costs: April 1959 to July 1961; a
no. 13   summary of accounting methods and costs
incurred during the first phases of PJ work.
Philadelphia, Penn Jersey Transportation Study,
1962.
13p. (Penn Jersey Transportation Study,
Philadelphia. PJ paper no. 13)

1. Transportation - Pennsylvania.
2. Transportation - New Jersey. 3. Accounting.
(Series: Penn   Jersey Transportation
Study,   Philadelphia. PJ
paper no. 13)

Transportation - Pennsylvania.

388
(748) Penn Jersey Transportation Study, Philadelphia.
P25p   Alternative transportation systems and
no. 10   associated sets of policies. Philadelphia,
1961.
44p. (Its PJ paper no. 10)

1. Transportation - Pennsylvania.
2. Transportation - New Jersey.
(Series: Penn Jersey Transportation
Study, Philadelphia. PJ paper no. 10)

Transportation - Pennsylvania.

388
(748) Penn Jersey Transportation Study, Philadelphia.
P25p   Computation of accessibility measures.
no. 9   to be used in sub-model no. 3. (Calculated in
submodel no. 2) of regional growth model.
Philadelphia, 1961.
2p. (Its PJ paper no. 9)

1. Transportation - Pennsylvania.
2. Transportation - New Jersey. (Series:
Penn Jersey Transportation Study, Philadelphia.
PJ paper no. 9)

Transportation - Pennsylvania.

388 (748) P25t no.2
Penn Jersey Transportation Study,
Factoring procedures and accuracy
checks. Phialdelphia, 1963.
30p. (Its Technical report no. 2)

1. Transportation - Pennsylvania.
2. Transportation - New Jersey.

Transportation - Pennsylvania.

388 (748) P25s
Penn-Jersey Transportation Study, Philadelphia.
Summary; state of the region. Philadelphia
[1967]
[7] p.

1. Transportation - Pennsylvania. 2.
Transportation - New Jersey. I. Title.

Transportation - Pennsylvania-New Jersey-Delaware.

388 (748) P25p no. 16
Berryman, Russell G
Mass transportation post card survey.
Philadelphia, Penn Jersey Transportation
Study, 1962.
14p. (Penn Jersey Transportation Study.
PJ paper no. 16)
1. Transportation - Pa.-N.J. - Del.
2. Railroads - Pa.-N.J.- Del. 3. Journey
to work. I. Title. (Series: Penn Jersey
Transportation Study, Philadelphia. P.J.
paper no. 16)

Transportation - Pennsylvania.

388 (748) P25pe vol.1
Penn Jersey Transportation Study,
Philadelphia.
Penn Jersey Transportation Study. Vol.
1. The state of the [PJ] region.
Philadelphia, 1964.
[156]p. (PJ reports, vol. 1)

1. Transportation - Pennsylvania.
2. Transportation - New Jersey.

Transportation - Pennsylvania.

388 (748) P25p no. 11
Penn Jersey Transportation Study, Philadelphia.
Survey of county leadership and policy
development; report on procedures.
Philadelphia, 1961.
4p. (Its PJ paper no. 11)

1. Transportation - Pennsylvania.
2. Transportation - New Jersey. I. Title.
(Series: Penn Jersey Transportation Study,
Philadelphia. PJ paper no. 11)

Transportation - Pa.-N.J.-Del.

388 (748) H47
Hitchcock, S T
Federal responsibility in comprehensive
urban planning. Address at first meeting of
the PJ Civic Advisory Committee, Philadelphia, 20 April 1961. Philadelphia Penn
Jersey Transportation Study, 1961.
11p.
1. Transportation - Pa.-N.J.-Del.
2. Journey to work. 3. Highways - Pa.-N.J.-
Del. I. Penn Jersey Transportation Study.
II. Title.

Transportation - Pennsylvania.

388 (748) P25pe v.2
Penn Jersey Transportation Study.
Philadelphia.
Penn Jersey Transportation Study. Vol.
2. 1975 projections: foreground of the
future. Philadelphia, 1964.
[105]p. (P.J. reports, vol. 2)

1. Transportation - Pennsylvania.
2. Transportation - N.J.

TRANSPORTATION - PA.

388 (748) P25tr
Pennsylvania. Governor's Committee for
Transportation.
Transportation and Pennsylvania's future.
Summary report of the Governor's Committee
for Transportation. [Harrisburg] 1969.
44p.

1. Transportation - Pa. I. Title.

Transportation - Pa.-N.J.-Del.

388 (748) L65
Longmaid, David D
The importance of mass transportation to
the region; statement before the House
Appropriations Committee, March 12, 1965.
Philadelphia Penn Jersey Transportation
Study, 1965.
5p.
1. Transportation - Pa.-N.J.-Del.
2. Journey to work. I. Pennsylvania.
General Assembly. House. Appropriations
Committee. II. Title. III. Penn Jersey
Transportation Study.

Transportation - Pennsylvania.

388 (748) P25pe v.3
Penn Jersey Transportation Study,
Philadelphia.
Penn Jersey Transportation Study. Vol.
3. 1975 transportation plans.
Philadelphia, 1965.
[114]p. (P.J. reports, vol. 3)

1. Transportation - Pennsylvania.
2. Transportation - New Jersey.

Transportation - Pennsylvania.

388 (748) P25p no. 5
Perazich, George.
Recent economic changes in the five-county
Philadelphia region. Philadelphia, Penn
Jersey Transportation Study, 1961.
10p. (Penn Jersey Transportation Study,
Philadelphia. PJ paper no. 5)
"Prepared for presentation at the Pennsylvania
Conference of Economists, Franklin and Marshall
College, June 1961."
1. Transportation - Pennsylvania. 2. Economic
conditions - Statistics - Philadelphia.
I. Title: Economic changes in the five-
county Philadel- phia region.
(Series: Penn Jersey Transportation
Study, Philadelphia. PJ paper no. 5)

Transportation - Pennsylvania-New Jersey-Delaware.

388 (748) P25p no. 21
Mulroney, Thomas B Jr.
Penn Jersey position classification and
pay plan. Philadelphia, Penn Jersey
Transportation Study, 1964.
1v. (Penn Jersey Transportation Study.
PJ paper no. 21)

1. Transportation - Pa.-N.J.-Del.
2. Personnel management. 3. Wages and
salaries. I. Title. (Series: Penn Jersey
Transportation Study, Philadelphia. P.J.
paper no. 21)

Transportation - Pennsylvania.

388 (748) P25p no. 12
Penn Jersey Transportation Study,
Philadelphia.
Preliminary projections of population;
county totals for the Camden-Philadelphia-
Trenton-Wilmington metropolitan region.
Philadelphia, 1962.
37p. (Its PJ paper no. 12)

1. Transportation - Pennsylvania.
2. Transportation - New Jersey. 3. Population
(Series: Penn Jersey
Transportation Study, Philadelphia.
PJ paper no. 12)

Transportation - Pennsylvania.

388 (748) P25p no. 8
Tomazinis, Anthony R
An introduction to mathematical models.
Philadelphia, Penn Jersey Transportation
Study, 1960.
18p. (Penn Jersey Transportation Study,
Philadelphia. PJ paper no. 8)

1. Transportation - Pennsylvania.
2. Transportation - New Jersey. (Series:
Penn Jersey Transportation Study, Philadelphia.
PJ paper no. 8)

Transportation - Pennsylvania-New Jersey-Delaware.

388 (748) P25p no.18
Penn Jersey Transportation Study.
Regional data. Philadelphia, Penn Jersey
Transportation Study, 1962.
8p. (Penn Jersey Transportation Study.
PJ paper no. 18)

1. Transportation - Pa.-N.J.-Del.
2. Journey to work. 3. Transportation.
I. Title. (Series: Penn Jersey Transportation Study. Philadelphia. P.J. paper no.
18)

Transportation - Pennsylvania.

388 (748) P25
Penn-Jersey Transportation Study.
Prospectus. Philadelphia, 1959.
1v. tables.

Suppl. -- --- Supplement. Philadelphia, 1962.
36p.

Suppl. -- --- 1963-64 supplement. Philadelphia, 1963.
28p.

1. Transportation - Pennsylvania. 2. Transportation - New Jersey.

Transportation - Pennsylvania.

388 (748) P25p no. 6
Tomazinis, Anthony Rudolf.
Spatial parameters affecting urban traffic.
Presented at the Origin and Destination
Survey Committee Meeting, Highway Research
Board, Washington, D.C., 1961. Philadelphia,
Penn Jersey Transportation Study, 1961.
31p. (Penn Jersey Transportation Study,
Philadelphia. PJ paper no. 6)
1. Transportation - Pennsylvania. 2. Transportation
- New Jersey. (Series: Penn Jersey Transportation
Study, Philadelphia. PJ paper no. 6)

Transportation - Pennsylvania-New Jersey-Delaware.

388 (748) P25pr
Pennsylvania Economy League. (Eastern Div.)
Preliminary report on organization for
the administration of transportation
functions in the Pennsylvania-New Jersey
(and Delaware) region. Philadelphia,
Pennsylvania Economy League (Eastern Division) in association with the Bureau of
Municipal Research, 1963.
36p.
1. Transportation - Pa.-N.J.-Del.
2. Journey to work. I. Philadelphia.
Bureau of Municipal Research. II. Title.

Transportation - Pennsylvania.

388 (748) P25r
Penn-Jersey Transportation Study.
Report on study procedures; data collection phase. Philadelphia, 1961.
30p. (PJ report no. 1)

1. Transportation - Pennsylvania.
2. Transportation - New Jersey.

TRANSPORTATION - PA.

388 (748) P 25to
Pennsylvania. Governor's Committee for
Transportation.
To go or not to go? Pennsylvania on the
move. [Harrisburg, 1970]
[12]p.

1. Transportation - Pa. I. Title.

Transportation - Pa.-N.J.-Del.

388 (748) P25p no.17
Read, Edward.
PJ site rating survey, by Edward Read and
Robert C. Bingham. Philadelphia, Penn Jersey
Transportation Study, 1962.
13p. (Penn Jersey Transportation Study.
PJ paper no. 17)
1. Transportation - Pa.-N.J.-Del.
2. Land use - Pa.-N.J.-Del. 3. Site selection
Pa.-N.J.-Del. 4. Regional planning - Pa.-N.J.-
Del. I. Bingham, Robert C., jt. au. II. Title.
(Series: Penn Jersey Transportation Study,
Philadelphia. P.J. paper no. 17)

388
(748)
S24

Transportation - Pa.-N.J.-Del.

Seidman, David R
Report on the activities allocation model.
[Philadelphia, Penn Jersey Transportation
Study, 1964.
25p.

1. Transportation - Pa.-N.J.-Del.
2. Journey to work. I. Penn Jersey Transportation Study.

388
(77358)
I55

Illinois. University. Bureau of
Economic and Business Research.
University...1968.   (Card 2)

II. Illinois. University. Bureau of
Business and Economic Research. III. U.S.
HUD-Mass Transportation Demonstration Grant
Program. Ill.

388
(74811)
P34ph

Transportation - Philadelphia.

Philadelphia. City Planning Commission.
Philadelphia's comprehensive plan for
rapid transit. Philadelphia, 1966.
[7]p.

1. Transportation - Philadelphia.
2. Journey to work. I. Title.

388
(748)
P25p
no.15

Transportation - Pa.-N.J.-Del.

Tomazinis, Anthony R
A new method of trip distribution in an
urban area. Presented at the 41st annual
meeting of the Highway Research Board
(Origin and Destination Committee) Washington, D.C. - January 10, 1962. Philadelphia,
Penn Jersey Transportation Study, 1962.
51p. (Pen Jersey Transportation Study.
PJ paper no. 15)
1. Transportation - Pa.-N.J.-Del.
2. Journey to work. I. Penn Jersey Transportation Study. II. Highway Research
Board. Meeting Washington, Jan. 1962.

(Cont'd on next card)

352.5
(74811)
B78

Transportation - Philadelphia.

Brush, John E
Service centers and consumer trips;
studies on the Philadelphia metropolitan
fringe, by John E. Brush and Howard L.
Gauthier, Jr. Chicago, Dept. of Geography,
University of Chicago, 1968.
182p. (Chicago. University. Dept. of
Geography. Research paper no. 113)
Bibliography: p. 183-185.
1. Fringe areas - Philadelphia.
2. Transportation - Philadelphia.
3. Shopping centers. I. Gauthier, Howard
L., Jr. II.   Chicago. University.
III. Title.

388
(74811)
P34p

Transportation - Philadelphia.

Philadelphia. Dept. of Public Property.
Plan for South Philadelphia subway
extension, Broad Street to Oregon Avenue,
and municipal stadium with 3000 parking
spaces. Philadelphia [1962?]
[14]p.

1. Transportation - Philadelphia.
2. Public buildings - Philadelphia.
3. Parking - Philadelphia.

388
(748)
P25p
no.15

Tomazinis, Anthony R   A new method...1962.
(Card 2)

III. Title. (Series: Penn Jersey
Transportation Study, Philadelphia. PJ
paper no. 15)

388
(74988)
C68g

Transportation - Philadelphia.

Coverdale and Colpitts.
Greater Camden Movement, transportation
proposals. New York, 1962.
15p.

1. Transportation - Camden, N.J.
2. Transportation - Philadelphia.
I. Greater Camden (N.J.) Movement.

VF
388
(74811)
P34ra

Transportation - Philadelphia.

Philadelphia. Dept. of Public Property.
Rapid transit for Eastwick, the city within
a city; fast direct public transit is
programmed to link Center City, Thirtieth
Street Station, the University, West Philadelphia, New Eastwick [and] International
Airport. Philadelphia [1962?]
folder.

1. Transportation - Philadelphia.

388
(748)
P25p
no.19

Transportation - Pa.-N.J.-Del.

Watt, James E
Preliminary cost estimate of construction
and right-of-way for rail and highway
facilities in alternative regional trans-
portation plans, by James E. Watt, Jr. and
Marshall F. Reed, Jr. Philadelphia, Penn
Jersey Transportation Study, 1962.
10p. (Penn Jersey Transportation Study.
PJ paper no. 19)
1. Transportation - Pa.-N.J.-Del.
2. Highways - Pa.-N.J.-Del. 3. Railroads -
Pa.-N.J.-Del. 4. Land acquisition. I. Reed,
Marshall F.,   jt. au. II. Title.
(Series: Penn Jersey Transportation
Study. Philadel   phia. P.J. paper no. 19)

388
(74811)
K51

Transportation - Philadelphia.

Klauder (Louis T.) and Associates.
Plan for a high speed mass transit system
between Philadelphia and Camden and South
Jersey suburbs. Philadelphia, Urban Traffic
and Transportation Board, 1959.
25p. maps, tables.

1. Transportation - Philadelphia.
I. Philadelphia. Urban Traffic and Transportation Board.

388
(74811)
P34v

Transportation - Philadelphia.

Philadelphia. Dept. of Public Property.
Report on the proposed Northeast extension
of the Broad Street subway in the city of
Philadelphia. Philadelphia, 1960.
9p.

Louis T. Klauder and Associates,
Consulting engineers.

1. Transportation - Philadelphia.
I. Klauder (Louis T.) and Associates.

388
(748)
W42

Transportation - Pa.-N.J.-Del.

Wickstrom, George V
Transportation flow; simulation and
projection; an address given on December 12,
1961 to the Philadelphia Chapter, American
Society of Civil Engineers. [Philadelphia]
Penn Jersey Transportation Study, 1961.
6p.

1. Transportation - Pa.-N.J.-Del.
2. Journey to work. I. American Society of
Civil Engineers. Philadelphia Chapter.
II. Penn Jersey Transportation Study.
III. Title.

388
(748)
M19

Transportation - Philadelphia.

Mayors' Metropolitan Conference, Wilkes-
Barre & Scranton, Pa.
Regional mass transportation recommenda-
tions submitted to Mayors' William T.
Schmidt of Scranton and Frank Slattery of
Wilkes-Barre to assure maximum transporta-
tion in all dimensions for Northeastern
Pennsylvania Wilkes-Barre & Scranton, Pa.,
1967.
1v.
1. Transportation - Pa. 2. Journey to work.
I. Title.

388
(74811)
P34

Transportation - Philadelphia.

Philadelphia. Urban Traffic and Transportation Board.
Plan and program 1955. Conclusions
and recommendations of the Board, report
of staff to the Board. Philadelphia,
1956.
124p. illus., map.

1. Transportation - Philadelphia.
2. Traffic - Philadelphia.

320
F6LIO

TRANSPORTATION - PENSACOLA, FLA.

ESCAMBIA-SANTA ROSA REGIONAL PLANNING
COUNCIL.
PENSACOLA URBAN AREA TRANSPORTATION
STUDY. PENSACOLA, FLA., 1970.
91P. (HUD 701 REPORT)

1. TRANSPORTATION - PENSACOLA, FLA.
I. HUD. 701. PENSACOLA, FLA.

388
(74811)
P25

Transportation - Philadelphia.

Penn Jersey Transportation Study.
Regional planning: Functions, program,
structure, by H.W. Bruck, Director, Division
of Regional Planning. Philadelphia, 1963.
9p. (Its PJD background paper no. 3)
1. Transportation - Philadelphia.
2. Transportation - Trenton. 3. Transportation
- Wilmington, Del. 4. Regional planning - Pa.-
N.J.-Del. 5. Journey to work. I. Bruck,
H.W. II. Title.

388
(74811)
P34u

Transportation - Philadelphia.

Philadelphia. Urban Traffic and
Transportation Board.
UTTB April 1956-May 1960. Philadelphia
[1960]
1v.

1. Transportation - Philadelphia.
2. Traffic - Philadelphia.

388
(77358)
I55

Transportation - Peoria, Ill.

Illinois. University. Bureau of
Economic and Business Research.
University of Illinois-U.S. Dept. of
H.U.D. mass transportation demonstration
projects Ill-MTD-3,4. Kent, Ohio, Kent
State University, 1968.
160p.
U.S. Dept. of Housing and Urban Development. Mass Transportation Demonstration
Grant Program.
1. Transportation - Decatur, Ill.
2. Transportation - Peoria, Ill. 3. Journey
to work. I.   Ohio. State University, Kent.   Center for Urban
Regionalsim.   (Cont'd on next card)

Folio
388
(74811)
P34pr

Transportation - Philadelphia.

Philadelphia. Architects Committee.
The proposal for a covered below-grade
expressway through Philadelphia's historic
riverfront. [Prepared in cooperation with]
Committee to Preserve Philadelphia's
Historic Gateway. Philadelphia, 1965.
28p.

1. Transportation - Philadelphia.
2. Architecture - Conservation and
restoration. I. Title.

388
(74811)
S56

TRANSPORTATION - PHILADELPHIA.

Sloan, Anthony R
Reestablishing the link; a study of the
commuter rail station, by Anthony R. Sloan
and John W. Blatteau. Philadelphia, Southeastern Pennsylvania Transportation Authority,
1970.
66p.
1. Transportation - Philadelphia.
2. Journey-to-work. I. Blatteau, John W., jt.
au. II. Southeastern Pennsylvania
Transportation Authority. III. Title.

388
:331
P343
Transportation - Philadelphia-Trenton-Wilmington
metropolitan area.
Philadelphia. City Planning Commission.
The journey to work, Philadelphia-Trenton-Wilmington metropolitan area, 1960.
Philadelphia, 1965.
107p.   (Its Public information bulletin
no. 10)

1. Journey to work. 2. Transportation -
Philadelphia-Trenton-Wilmington metropolitan
area.

388
(791)
P36
Transportation - Phoenix, Ariz.
Arizona. Highway Department.
Better roads for tomorrow, Phoenix-Maricopa County, traffic study.
Phoenix, Ariz., 1956-1957.
125p.

1. Traffic - Phoenix, Ariz.
2. Transportation - Phoenix, Ariz.

388
(781981)
B87
Transportation - Pittsburgh, Kan.
Burgvin and Martin.
Pittsburgh, Kansas, transportation
survey. Prepared for the city of
Pittsburgh, in cooperation with
the State Highway Commission of Kansas
and the U.S. Dept. of Commerce, Bureau
of Public Roads. Topeka, Kan., 1962.
198p.

1. Transportation - Pittsburgh, Kan.
I. Kansas.   State Highway
Commis-   sion. II. U.S.
Bureau of   Public Roads.

388
(74886)
A75
Transportation - Pittsburgh.
Arnold, Bion Joseph.
Report on the Pittsburgh transportation
problem. Submitted to Hon. William A.
Magee, Mayor of the city of Pittsburgh.
Pittsburgh, 1910.
202p.

1. Transportation - Pittsburgh.
2. City planning - Pittsburgh.

388
(74886)
P47
Transportation - Pittsburgh.
Pennsylvania. Dept. of Highways.
Pittsburgh Area Transportation Study; final
report in two parts. Study conducted under
the sponsorship of Commonwealth of Pennsylvania, in cooperation with U.S. Dept. of
Commerce, Bureau of Public Roads. Pittsburgh,
Pittsburgh Area Transportation Study, 1961.
2v. Vol. 2, 1963, on spine 1962.
1. Transportation - Pittsburgh. I. Pittsburgh Area
Transportation Study.

388
(74886)
R17
TRANSPORTATION - PITTSBURGH.
Rattien, Stephen.
The Pittsburgh taxicab study; 1970; final
report, by Stephen Rattien and E. Joseph
Duckett. Pittsburgh, Environmental Health
Program, Graduate School of Public Health,
University of Pittsburgh, 1971.
195p.
Bibliography: p. 151-195.
Research supported by a grant from the Dept.
of Housing and Urban Development, Project no.
PENN-R11-8-69.
1. Transportati   on - Pittsburgh.
          (Cont'd on next card)

388
(74886)
R17
Rattien, Stephen.   The Pittsburgh...1971.
          (Card 2)

I. Duckett, E. Joseph, jt. au. II. Pittsburgh.
University. Environmental Health Program.
III. U.S. Dept. of Housing and Urban Development. IV. Title. V. Title: Taxicab study 1970.

388
(74886)
S23
TRANSPORTATION - PITTSBURGH.
Schwartz, Arthur.
Forecasting transit usage. Pittsburgh,
Pittsburgh Area Transportation Study, 1961.
22p.
Prepared for the 40th annual meeting, Highway Research Board, Wash., D.C., Jan. 9-13,
1961.
1. Transportation - Pittsburgh.
I. Pittsburgh Area Transportation Study.
II. Title.

388
(74886)
W27
Transportation - Pittsburgh.
Westinghouse Electric Co.
Westinghouse transit expressway TrEx.
South Park Demonstration Project picture
portfolio. Pittsburgh [1967?]
1v.
Transit Expressway South Park Demonstration Project sponsored by Federal Housing
and Home Finance Agency and others.
1. Transportation - Pittsburgh. 2. Journey
to work. I. U.S. Housing and Home Finance
Agency. II. Title: South Park Demonstration
Project.

385
(74886)
W74
Transportation - Pittsburgh.
Wright, Frank Joseph, 1919-
Transfer values of private metropolitan
transit systems; a study of Pittsburgh
railways. Pittsburgh, Duquesne University Press, 1964.
36p. (Bureau of Research, School of
Business Administration, Duquesne
University. Occasional papers, 1)
Bibliography: p. 35-36.

1. Railroads - Pittsburgh. 2. Transportation -
Pittsburgh. I. Title. (Series: Duquesne
University, Pittsburgh.   School of Business
Administration.   Bureau of Research.
Occasional papers, 1)

388
(7441)
C15
Transportation - Pittsfield, Mass.
Campbell (Bruce) and Associates, Boston.
Pittsfield urbanized area comprehensive
transportation study. Summary report.
Boston, 1966.
32p.
"Prepared for the Massachusetts Dept.
of Public Works in cooperation with the
U.S. Dept. of Commerce, Bureau of Public
Roads."
1. Transportation - Pittsfield, Mass.
2. Parking - Pittsfield, Mass. 3. Land use - Pittsfield Mass. I. Massachusetts. Dept. of Public
Works. II. U.S. Bureau   of Public Roads. III.
Title.

388
(76624)
B17
Transportation - Ponca City, Okla.
Barton (George W.) and Associates.
Transportation planning study of Ponca
City. [Prepared] for Ponca City, Oklahoma,
under contract with the State of Oklahoma
Dept. of Commerce and Industry. Evanston,
Ill., 1959.
49p.
U.S. Urban Renewal Adm. UPAP.
1. Transportation - Ponca City, Okla. I. U.S.
URA-UPAP. Ponca City, Okla.

4815
TRANSPORTATION = PORT HURON, MICH.
PORT HURON, MICH. TOWNSHIP PLANNING
COMMISSION.
TRANSPORTATION STUDY AND PLAN. BY
PARKINS, ROGERS AND ASSOCIATES, INC.
DETROIT, 1969.
9, 11P. (HUD 701 REPORT)

1. TRANSPORTATION = PORT HURON, MICH.
I. PARKINS, ROGERS AND ASSOCIATES.
II. HUD. 701. PORT HURON, MICH.

388
(79549)
P67
Transportation - Portland, Or. metropolitan
area.
Portland-Vancouver Metropolitan
Transportation Study.
Interim report 1-205, location. Prepared by the Technical Advisory Committee
in cooperation with the U.S. Dept. of
Commerce, Bureau of Public Roads, and
U.S. Housing and Home Finance Agency.
[Salem, Or.] State Highway Commission,
1964.
54p.

1. Transpor-   tation - Portland,
Or. metropol-   itan area. 2. Trans-
portation -   Vancouver, Wash.
(Continued on   next card)

388
(79549)
P67
Portland-Vancouver Metropolitan
Transportation Study. Interim report
1-205, location...1964.   (Card 2)

metropolitan area. 3. Transportation -
Economic effect. 4. Journey to work.
I. Oregon. State Highway Commission.
II. U.S.. Housing and Home Finance
Agency.

383
(79549)
P67p
v.1
Transportation - Portland, Or. metropolitan
area.
Portland-Vancouver Metropolitan
Transportation Study.
Portland-Vancouver Metropolitan Transportation Study. Vol. 1. Factual data
report. Prepared in cooperation with the
U.S. Dept. of Commerce, Bureau of Public
Roads. Salem, Or., State Highway Commission, [1964?]
135p.

1. Transportation - Portland, Or. metropolitan
area. 2. Transportation   - Vancouver, Wash.
metropolitan area. 3.   Transportation
(Continued on next   card)

383
(79549)
P67p
v.1
Portland-Vancouver Metropolitan
Transportation Study. Portland-
Vancouver Metropolitan Transportation
Study. Vol. 1...1964.   (Card 2)

Economic effect. 4. Journey to work.
I. Oregon. State Highway Commission.

388
(79549)
P67po
Transportation - Portland, Or. metropolitan area.
Portland-Vancouver Metropolitan
Transportation Study.
Social-economic study. Interim report
1-205, location. Prepared by Bureau of
Municipal Research and Service, University
of Oregon for Oregon State Highway
Commission in cooperation with the U.S.
Dept. of Commerce, Bureau of Public Roads.
[Salem, Or.?] 1964.
67p.

(Continued on
next card)

388
(79549)
P67po
Portland-Vancouver Metropolitan
Transportation Study. Social-
economic study...1964. (Card 2)

1. Transportation - Portland, Or.
metropolitan area. 2. Transportation -
Vancouver, Wash. metropolitan area.
3. Transportation - Economic effect.
4. Journey to work. I. Oregon.
University. Bureau of Municipal
Research and Service. II. Oregon.
State Highway   Commission.

388
(74552)
.845
Transportation - Providence-Pawtucket metropolitan area.
Simpson and Curtin, Philadelphia.
Acquisition and public operation of
transit services in Providence-Pawtucket
metropolitan area. [Prepared in cooperation with] Rhode Island Public Transit
Authority. Providence, 1965.
60p.
U.S. Urban Renewal Adm. Demonstration
Grant Program.

1. Transportation - Providence-Pawtucket metropolitan area. I. Rhode   Island. Public
Transit Authority. II.   U.S. Urban Renewal
Adm. Demonstration   Grant Program.

380
(76773)
P85m
Transportation - Pulaski Co., Ark.
Pulaski County, Ark. Metropolitan Area
Planning Commission.
A Metropolitan Port Authority for Pulaski
County. Metroplan. March, 1962. [Little
Rock, Ark.] 1962.
27p.

U.S. Urban Renewal Adm. UPAP.

1. Transportation - Pulaski Co., Ark.
2. Pulaski Co., Ark. Metropolitan Port
Authority. I. U.S. URA-UPAP. Pulaski, Ark.

6218   TRANSPORTATION - PULASKI CO., ARK.
PULASKI CO., ARK. METROPOLITAN AREA
PLANNING COMMISSION.
TRANSIT PLANNING STUDY. BY
BARTON-ASCHMAN ASSOCIATES. LITTLE ROCK,
ARK., 1967.
69P. (HUD 701 REPORT)

1. TRANSPORTATION - PULASKI CO., ARK.
I. BARTON-ASCHMAN ASSOCIATES. II. HUD.
701. PULASKI CO., ARK.

VF
330
(79739)
N25

Transportation - Pullman, Wash.

[Nelson (Harlan) and Associates]
Economic data; traffic, transportation and
parking. Supplemental material furnished
planning consultant by the City of Pullman.
[Pullman, Washington, 1960?]
6p.

1. Economic conditions - Pullman, Wash.
2. Transportation - Pullman, Wash.

388
(74816)
S54

TRANSPORTATION - READING, PA.
Smith (Wilbur) and Associates.
Transportation study; Reading model cities
neighborhood, Reading, Pennsylvania. Prepared for Reading Model Cities Agency.
New Haven, 1969.
53p.
U.S. Dept. of Housing and Urban Development. UPAP.

1. Transportation - Reading, Pa. 2. Journey
to work. 3. Model Cities - Reading, Pa.
I. U.S. HUD-UPAP, Reading, Pa.

388
(74741)
R25

TRANSPORTATION - RENSSELAER CO., N.Y.
Rensselaer County, N.Y. Dept. of Planning
and Promotion.
Transportation. Troy, N.Y., 1969.
4p.

U.S. Dept. of Housing and Urban Development.
UPAP. Project. N.Y. P-168.

1. Transportation - Rensselaer Co., N.Y.
I. U.S. HUD-UPAP. Rensselaer Co., N.Y.

711.73
(797)
R67

Transportation - Renton, Wash.

Ross, Lewis J
Renton arterials; a study of the highway
planning process in the State of Washing-
ton, by Lewis J. Ross and G. A. Riedesel.
Pullman, Wash., Division of Industrial
Research, Washington State University,
1964.
53p. (Washington (State) University.
Division of Industrial Research. Highway
Research Section. Publication H-22)

(Continued on
next card)

711.73
(797)
R67

Ross, Lewis J   Renton arterials...1964.
(Card 2)

1. Highways - Renton, Wash. 2. Trans-
portation - Renton, Wash. I. Riedesel,
G. A., jt. au. II. Washington (State)
University. Division of Industrial
Research. III. Title.

500.15
A52
1966

Transportation - Research.

American Institute of Aeronautics and Astronautics.
Annual meeting. Papers. New York, 1966.
6 pp.. (AIAA paper no. 66-856, 859,
913,944,985,1023)
Contents: A municipality adopts the systems
approach to major community problems, by
E.H. Ereth and R.L. Goe.-Megalopolis airport
requirements, by L.H. Quick.-The future of
reliability and maintainability, by L.W.
Bell.-A history of selected reliability and
maintainability committees and interested
government   agencies, by J. de S.
Coutinho.-   (Cont'd on next card)

500.15
A52
1966

American Institute of Aeronautics and Annual
meeting. Papers. (Card 2)

Historic review of transportation in the Northeast Corridor, by A.J. Bone.-Organizational
factors that influence technological innovation,
by Kenneth E. Knight.

1. Scientific research. 2. Governmental
research. 3. Transportation. 4. Automation. 5. Community development.
6. Airports. I. Bone, Alexander J. Historic
review of trans-   portation in the
Northeast   Corridor.
(Cont'd on next card)

500.15
A52
1966

American Institute of Aeronautics and Annual
meeting. Papers. (Card 3)

II. Ereth, Edward H. A municipality adopts the
systems approach to major community problems.
III. Quick, Leonard H. Megalopolis airport
requirements. IV. Bell, Leslie W. The future
of reliability and maintainability. V.
Coutinho, John de S. A history of selected
reliability and maintainability committees and
interested government agencies. VI. Knight,
Kenneth E. Organizational factors that influence techno-   logical innovation.

388.015
B17e

Transportation - Research.

Battelle Memorial Institute, Geneva Switzerland.
Electric town car. Geneva, 1964.
4p.

1. Transportation - Research. I. Title.

388.015
B17s

TRANSPORTATION - RESEARCH.
Battelle Memorial Institute. (Columbus
Laboratories)
. Summary report on methodology for RD&D
program planning. Prepared for System
Research Development Div., Dept. of Housing
and Urban Development. Columbus, Ohio, 1969.
1v. (Research report)
Contract no. H-778 (Task 8)
Kaj L. Nielsen, Project manager.
1. Transportation - Research. I. Nielsen,
Kaj L. II. U.S. Dept. of Housing and Urban
Development. III. Title: Methodology for
RD&D program   planning.

388.015
B25

TRANSPORTATION - RESEARCH.
Bendix Corp.
National Urban Transportation Research
and Test Center; an engineering study of the
establishment and operation. BSD 1238,
May 1968. [New York] 1968.
1v.

1. Transportation - Research. I. Title.

388.015
B68

Transportation - Research.

Bouladon, Gabriel A
Unified theory of transport and transfer
systems. Translation of an exposé given on
April 4, 1966 at Round Table on Transport, under
the auspices of the Délégation Générale à la
Recherche Scientifique et Technique, Paris.
[Geneva, Switzerland. Battelle Memorial Institute, 1967?]
21p.
illus.   Illustrations. 10p.
[1967?]
1. Transportation - Research. 2. Journey to
work. I. Battelle   Memorial Institute.
Geneva, Switzer-   land. II. Title.

388.015
C17

TRANSPORTATION - RESEARCH.
Catanese, Anthony J   ed.
New perspectives in urban transportation
research. Lexington, Mass., Lexington
Books, 1972.
273p.

Bibliography: p. 200-208.

1. Transportation - Research. 2. Journey
to work. I. Title.

388.015
C65

Transportation - Research.

Conference on Transportation Research,
Woods Hole, Mass., 1960.
Report of a study group convened by the
National Academy of Sciences at Woods Hole,
Massachusetts, August 1960. With assistance
from: the Rockefeller Foundation, the Na-
tional Science Foundation, the Office of
Civil and Defense Mobilization. Washington,
1960.
88p.

National Research Council Publication 840.

1. Transporta-   tion - Research.
I. National   Research Council.

388
E28b

Transportation - Research.

Edwards, L   K
Baseline system definition: urban gravity-
vacuum-transit, by L.K. Edwards and R.E.
Skov, Tube Transit Corporation. Silver Spring
Md., Applied Physics Laboratory, Johns Hopkins
University, 1968.
1v. (Johns Hopkins University. Applied
Physics Laboratory. Contractor report.
BFM-097)
1. Transportation. 2. Transportation -
Research. I. Johns Hopkins University.
Applied Physics Laboratory. II. Tube Transit
Corp. III. Skov,   R.E., jt. au.
IV. Title.

388
1025n

Transportation - Research.

General Motors Corp.
New systems implementation study, final
study. Prepared for the U.S. Dept. of Housing
and Urban Development, Urban Transportation
Administration, by E.T. Canty and others.
[Detroit] 1968.
3v. (Its Research publication GMR-710B)
Contents: v.1. Summary and conclusions.--
v.2. Planning and evaluation methods.--v.3.
Case studies.
On cover: Study in new systems of Urban
Transportation.
1. Transporta-   tion. 2. Transporta-
tion - Research.   3. Transportation -
Automation.   (Cont'd on next card)

388
G25m

General Motors Corp.   New systems...1968.
(Card 2)

I. Canty, E.T. II. U.S. Dept. of Housing
and Urban Development.
III. Title. IV. Title: Study in new
systems of urban transportation.

388
G25s

Transportation - Research.

General Research Corp.
Systems analysis of urban transportation.
Prepared for the U.S. Dept. of Housing and
Urban Development. Santa Barbara, Calif., 1968.
4v. (H-777)
On cover: Study in new systems of urban
transportation.
Contents: v.1. Summary. v.2. Cases for study.-
v.3. Network flow analyses.-- v.4. Supporting
analyses.
1. Transportation. 2. Transportation - Research. 3. Journey to work. 4. Transportation -
Automation. I. U.   S. Dept. of Housing
and Urban Develop-   ment.
(Cont'd on next card)

388
G25s

General Research Corp.   Systems analysis...
1968.   (Card 2)

II. Title. III. Title: Study in new systems
of urban transportation.

388
H43top

Transportation - Research.

Highway Research Board.
Top issues in urban research 1963.
Presented at the 43rd annual meeting, January 13-17, 196-. Washington, Division of
of Engineering and Industrial Research,
National Academy of Sciences, National Research Council, 1965.
105p. (Highway research record no.
64)
National Research Council. Publication
no. 1248.

(Continued on
next card)

388
H43top   Highway Research Board. Top issues in urban research 1963. (Card 2)

     Contents:-Costs of urban transport systems of varying capacity and service, by M. Wohl.-System configurations in urban transportation planning, by H. S. Levinson and K. R. Roberts.-The development of a land-use data bank for transportation planning, by C. S. Hamilton.-Volume and characteristics of inter-city travel during Winter 1963, by D. E. Church.

   1. Transportation -   Congresses. 2. Journey to work. 3. Trans-   portation - Research.

388
M14   Transportation - Research.

Makofski, R   A
    Performance criteria and technical feasibility of the urban gravity-vacuum-transit system, by R.A. Makofski and others. Silver Spring Md., Applied Physics Laboratory, 1968.
    226p. (Johns Hopkins University. Applied Physics Laboratory. Technical memo. TG-984)

    1. Transportation. 2. Transportation - Research. I. Johns Hopkins University. Applied Physics Laboratory. II. Title

---

388.015
073   TRANSPORTATION - RESEARCH.
Organisation for Economic Cooperation and Development.
    Future directions for research in urban transportation. Paris, 1969.
    158p.

    1. Transportation - Research. 2. Journey to work. I. Title.

388
854e   Transportation - Research.

Smith (Wilbur) and Associates.
    Evaluation of bus transit demand in middle sized urban areas. Final report: first phase. Prepared for U.S. Dept. of Commerce, Bureau of Public Roads. Wash., U.S. Dept. of Commerce, National Bureau of Standards, Institute for Applied Technology. 1966.
    258p. (PB 173 665)
    Distributed by Clearinghouse for Federal Scientific and Technical Information.
    Bibliography: p. 249-258.

      (Cont'd on next card)

388
854e   Smith (Wilbur) and Associates.   Evaluation of bus transit demand in middle sized urban areas...1966. (Card 2)

    1. Transportation. 2. Transportation - Research. 3. Journey to work. I. U.S. Bureau of Public Roads. II. U.S. Clearinghouse for Federal Scientific and Technical Information. III. Title.

388.015
S52   TRANSPORTATION - RESEARCH.
Snell, J
    Analysis of urban transportation research, by J. Snell and P. Schuldiner. Evanston, Ill., Transportation Center, Northwestern University, 1966.
    105p. (Research report)
    Prepared for the Urban Transportation Research Council, American Society of Civil Engineers.
    Bibliography: p. 95-105.
    1. Transportation - Research. 2. Journey to work.   I. Schuldiner, P., jt. au. II. Northwest   ern University. Transportation Center.   III. Urban Transportation Research Council. IV. Title.

388.015
S72   TRANSPORTATION - RESEARCH.
Steiss, Alan Walter.
    University research and training program in urban transportation at Virginia Polytechnic Institute and State University.
    Project completion report for the University Research and Training Program grant, 1969-1970. Final report. Blacksburg, Va., Div. of Environmental and Urban Systems, College of Architecture, Virginia Polytechnic Institute and State University, 1970.
    28p.

      (Cont'd on next card)

388.015
S72   Steiss, Alan Walter. University research ...1970. (Card 2)

    Prepared for U.S. Dept. of Housing and Urban Development (to 1969). Contract no. H-1070.

    1. Transportation - Research. I. Virginia Polytechnic Institute, Blacksburg. Div. of Environmental and Urban Systems. II. U.S. Dept. of Housing and Urban Development. III. Title.

388.015
T36   TRANSPORTATION - RESEARCH.
Thomas, Edwin N
    Introduction to a systems approach to transportation problems; by Edwin N. Thomas and Joseph L. Schofer. Evanston, Ill., Transportation Center, Northwestern University, 1966.
    65p. (Research report)
    Prepared for a seminar hosted by the Chicago Area Transportation Study sponsored by the Committee on Urban Transportation Systems Evaluation (UTP-4) of the Highway Research Board as part   of Project 8-4, Criteria for evalua   ting alternative
      (Cont'd on next card)

388.015
T36   Thomas, Edwin N   Introduction...1966. (Card 2)

transportation plans: National Cooperative Highway Research Program; Highway Research Board, NAS-NRC.
    1. Transportation - Research. 2. Journey to work. I. Schofer, Joseph L., jt. au. II. Northwestern University. Transportation Center. III. Title.

388.015
T71   Transportation - Research.

Transportation Association of America.
    Transportation research; a survey of current and potential transportation research projects. 3d ed. Washington, Research Staff of the Transportation Association of America, 1962.
    50p.

    1. Transportation - Research. 2. Transportation - Bibl.

388
(791)
T82   Transportation - Research.

Tucson Area Transportation Planning Agency.
    Tucson Area Transportation Study: Vol. 1. Inventory and analysis of existing conditions, 1960. Vol.2. Forecasts and the plan 1965. Sponsoring agencies, City of Tucson, County of Pima, State of Arizona in cooperation with U.S. Dept. of Commerce, Bureau of Public Roads. Tucson, Ariz., 1965.
    2v.
    Cover title on v.2. Forecasts and plans, 1980.

      (Cont'd on next card)

388
(791)
T82   Tucson Area Transportation Planning Agency. Tucson Area Transportation Study...1965. (Card 2)

    1. Transportation - Tucson, Ariz. 2. Transportation - Research. 3. Highways - Tucson, Ariz. 4. Land use - Tucson, Ariz. I. U.S. Bureau of Public Roads. II. Title.

388
(015)
W65   Transportation - Research.

Wolf, Robert A
    Metrotran-2000; a study of future concepts in metropolitan transportation for the year 2000. Final report. Buffalo, Cornell Aeronautical Laboratory, inc., 1967.
    1v. (Cornell Aeronautical Laboratory, inc. Technical report CAL no. 150)
    1. Transportation - Research. 2. Journey to work. I. Cornell Aeronautical Laboratory. II. Title.

058.7
:388.015
U71   TRANSPORTATION - RESEARCH - DIRECTORIES.
U.S. Urban Mass Transportation Administration.
    Directory of research development and demonstration projects, 19

    Wash., 19

      v.
    For Library holdings see main entry.

    1. Transportation - Research - Directories. 2. Journey to work.

388
(75529)
B14   TRANSPORTATION - RESTON, VA.
Bain, Henry.
    The Reston express bus; a case history of citizen action to improve urban transportation. Wash., Washington Center for Metropolitan Studies, 1969.
    67p. (Improving transportation in the Washington metropolitan area - no. 2)
    1. Transportation - Reston, Va. 2. Journey to work.

      I. Washington Center for Metropolitan Studies. II.   Title.

388
(745)
R36   TRANSPORTATION - RHODE ISLAND.
Rhode Island. Statewide Comprehensive Transportation and Land Use Planning Program.
    Transit plan: future mass transit services and facilities for the State of Rhode Island. Providence, 1969.
    105p. (Its Report no. 9)
    U.S. Mass Transportation Demonstration Grant Program. R.I. P-22; R.I. P-30.
    1. Transportation - R.I. 2. Journey to work. I. U.S. Mass Transportation Demonstration Grant Program. R.I. II. Title.

388
(745)
R36r
1972   TRANSPORTATION - RHODE ISLAND.
Rhode Island. Statewide Planning Program.
    Rhode Island transportation needs study, 1970-1990. Narrative report. Providence, 1972.
    16p.

    1. Transportation - R.I. I. Title.

388
(745)
R36r   TRANSPORTATION - RHODE ISLAND.
Rhode Island. Statewide Planning Program.
    Rhode Island transportation needs study, 1970-1990. Providence, 1971.
    77p. (Technical paper no. 19)

    1. Transportation - R.I. I. Title.

711.4
(764)
R42
no.3   Transportation - Richmond, Tex.
Johnson (Bernard) Engineers.
    Circulation. Report 3 of the comprehensive city plan, Richmond, Texas. Presented to the Planning Commission. Houston, 1964.
    45p.
    Prepared in cooperation with Texas State Department of Health.
    U.S. Urban Renewal Adm. UPAP.

    1. Master plan - Richmond, Tex. 2. Streets - Richmond, Tex. 3. Highways - Richmond, Tex. 4. Transportation -   Richmond, Tex. I. Richmond, Tex.   Planning Commission. II. U.S. URA-UPAP.   Richmond, Tex.

4865
FOLIO
4866
FOLIO
4867
FOLIO
4868
FOLIO   TRANSPORTATION - RICHMOND, VA.
RICHMOND, VA. REGIONAL PLANNING COMMISSION.
    RICHMOND REGIONAL AREA TRANSPORTATION STUDY: 1, CURRENT AND PROJECTED TRAVEL PATTERNS; 2, HIGHWAY TRANSPORTATION PLAN AND IMPLEMENTATION PROGRAM; 3, PUBLIC TRANSPORTATION, AN EVALUATION OF SERVICE LEVELS AND PATRONS' DEMANDS; 5, RECOMMENDED THOROUGHFARE PLAN, STREET INVENTORY, FUNCTIONAL PLANS, AND COST ESTIMATES. BY WILBUR SMITH AND ASSOCIATES, 1967-68.
    4 V. (HUD 7 01 REPORT)

      (CONTINUED ON NEXT CARD)

4865 RICHMOND, VA. REGIONAL PLANNING
FOLIO COMMISSION. RICHMOND REGIONAL AREA ...
4866 7-68. (CARD 2)
FOLIO
4867 1. TRANSPORTATION - VIRGINIA.
FOLIO 2. TRANSPORTATION - RICHMOND, VA.
4868 I. SMITH (WILBUR) AND ASSOCIATES.
FOLIO II. HUD. 701. VIRGINIA. III. HUD.
701. RICHMOND, VA.

711.3 Transportation - Richmond.
(755451) Stein and Marcou Associates.
S72 Analysis of the physical potential for
development of land in the Richmond region.
A report to the Richmond Regional
Planning Commission, Richmond, Virginia.
Wash. 1963.
73p.
U.S. Urban Renewal Adm. UPAP.

1. Metropolitan area planning - Richmond.
2. Land use - Richmond. 3. Transportation
- Richmond. I. Richmond. Regional
Planning Commission. II. Title.
III. U.S. UPA-UPAP. Richmond.

---

598 TRANSPORTATION - ROCK ISLAND, ILL.
BI-STATE METROPOLITAN PLANNING COMMISSION.
URBANIZED AREA TRANSPORTATION STUDY,
DAVENPORT, ROCK ISLAND, MOLINE. BY DE
LEUW, CATHER AND CO. ROCK ISLAND, ILL.,
1970.
14P. (HUD 701 REPORT)

1. TRANSPORTATION - DAVENPORT, IOWA.
2. TRANSPORTATION - ROCK ISLAND, ILL.
3. TRANSPORTATION - MOLINE, ILL. I. DE
LEUW, CATHER AND CO. II. HUD. 701.
DAVENPORT, IOWA. III. HUD. 701. ROCK
ISLAND, ILL. IV. HUD. 701. MOLINE,
ILL.

Transportation - Rockland Co., N.Y.
388
(74728) Rockland County, N.Y. Planning Board.
R62 Transportation study and highway plan,
Rockland County. With the cooperation of
Rockland County Highway Department. New
York, 1960.
1v.
U.S. Urban Renewal Adm. UPAP.

1. Transportation - Rockland Co., N.Y.
2. Highways - Rockland Co., N.Y.
I. Rockland Co., N.Y. Highway Department.
II. U.S. URA- UPAP. Rockland Co.,
N.Y.

1140 TRANSPORTATION - ST. BERNARD PARISH, LA.
1141 JEFFERSON, ORLEANS, AND ST. BERNARD
PARISHES, LA. REGIONAL PLANNING
COMMISSION.
COMPREHENSIVE REGIONAL PLANNING
PROGRAM; STUDY DESIGN AND TRANSPORTATION
AS A MAJOR ELEMENT: 1, FINAL REPORT; 2,
SUPPLEMENT TO FINAL REPORT. BY RADER AND
ASSOCIATES. NEW ORLEANS, 1966.
2 V. (HUD 701 REPORT)

1. TRANSPORTATION - JEFFERSON PARISH,
LA. 2. TRANSPORTATION - ORLEANS PARISH,
LA. 3. TRANSPORTATION - ST. BERNARD
PARISH, LA. I. RADER AND ASSOCIATES.
(CONTINUED ON NEXT CARD)

1140 JEFFERSON, ORLEANS, AND ST. BERNARD
1141 PARISHES, LA. REGIONAL PLANNING
COMMISSION. COMPREHENSIVE REGIONAL
PLANNING ...1966. (CARD 2)

II. HUD. 701. JEFFERSON PARISH, LA.
III. HUD. 701. ORLEANS PARISH, LA.
IV. HUD. 701. ST. BERNARD PARISH, LA.

1563 TRANSPORTATION - ST. CLOUD, MINN.
ST. CLOUD, MINN. PLANNING COMMISSION.
THOROUGHFARES AND TRANSPORTATION PLAN.
ST. CLOUD, MINN., 1967.
21L. (HUD 701 REPORT)

1. TRANSPORTATION - ST. CLOUD, MINN.
I. HUD. 701. ST. CLOUD, MINN.

Transportation - St. Louis metropolitan
area.
388
(77866) Gilman, (W.C.) & Co.
G45 The radial express and suburban crosstown bus rider, being a detailed evaluation of the sources of patronage of seven
new radial express bus routes and an outlying suburban crosstown local bus service,
St. Louis (Mo.-Ill.) metropolitan area.
Final report. New York, 1966.
1 v.
Prepared in cooperation with the Bi-State
Development Agency of the Missouri-Ill,
Metropolitan District.
U.S. Dept. of Housing and Urban
Develop- ment. Mass Transportation Demonstration Grant
Program. (Cont'd on next card)

388
(77866) Gilman, W.C. & Co. The radial express and
345 suburban crosstown bus rider...1966.
(Card 2)

1. Transportation - St. Louis metropolitan area. 2. Journey to work. 3. Traffic
surveys - St. Louis, metropolitan area.
I. Bi-State Development Agency of the
Missouri-Illinois Metropolitan District.
II. Title. III. U.S. HUD, Mass Transportation Demonstration Grant Program.

Transportation - St. Paul
388
(77657) Kieffer, Stephen A
K42 Transit and the twins, a survey of the
history of the transportation company in
Minneapolis and St. Paul; an analysis of the
role of public transportation in the growth of
the Twin Cities. Minneapolis, Twin City Rapid
Transit Co., 1958.
60p. illus., maps.

1. Transportation - Minneapolis. 2. Transportation - St. Paul.

5385 TRANSPORTATION - ST. PAUL, MINN.
TWIN CITIES METROPOLITAN PLANNING
COMMISSION.
TRANSIT REPORT. SAINT PAUL, CA. 1960.
37L. (HUD 701 REPORT)

1. TRANSPORTATION - MINNEAPOLIS, MINN.
2. TRANSPORTATION - ST. PAUL, MINN.
I. HUD. 701. MINNEAPOLIS, MINN.
II. HUD. 701. ST. PAUL, MINN.

Transportation - Salem, Or.
388
(79537) Oregon. State Highway Dept.
072 An introduction to Salem Area Transporta-
Introd. tion Study. [Prepared] in cooperation with
the U.S. Dept. of Commerce, Bureau of Public
Roads. Salem, Oregon State Highway Commission, 1964.
12p.

1. Transportation - Salem, Or. 2. Master
plan - Salem, Or. 3. Traffic surveys.
4. Journey to work. I. Salem (Or.) Area
Transportation Study. II. U.S.
Bureau of Public Roads.
III. Title.

388
(79537) Oregon. State Highway Dept.
072 Salem Area Transportation Study. Survey
conducted in cooperation with U.S. Dept. of
Commerce, Bureau of Public Roads. Salem,
Oregon, State Highway Commission, 1961-
v.
Cover title: A study in Salem's transportation.
Contents:-Vol. 1. Factual data report.-
Vol. 2. Data projection - 1982.
U.S. Dept. of Housing and Urban Development. UPAP.

(Continued on next card)

388
(79537) Oregon. State Highway Dept. Salem Area
072 Transportation Study...1961. (Card 2)

1. Transportation - Salem, Or. 2. Master
plan - Salem, Or. 3. Traffic surveys.
4. Journey to work. I. Title. II. U.S.
HUD-UPAP. Salem, Or.

388
(792) Smith (Wilbur) and Associates.
S54 SLATS (Salt Lake Area Transportation Study)
Prepared for Utah State Dept. of Highways,
Salt Lake County and others. Prepared in
cooperation with U.S. Dept. of Commerce,
Bureau of Public Roads. New Haven, 1963-
1965.
4v.

1. Transportation - Salt Lake Co., Utah.
2. Highways - Salt Lake Co., Utah. 3. Salt
Lake Area Transportation Study. I. Utah.
State Dept. of Highways. II. U.S.
Bureau of Public Roads.

Transportation - San Angelo, Tex.
330
(764) Jones, Joe H
J65 San Angelo: urban growth influencing
transportation planning. Sponsoring agencies: the City of San Angelo and Tom Green
County, Texas Highway Dept., in cooperation
with U.S. Dept. of Commerce, Bureau of
Public Roads. Austin, Bureau of Business
Research, University of Texas, 1965.
86p. (Texas. University. Bureau of
Business Research. Area economic survey
no. 26)

(Cont'd on next card)

330
(764) Jones, Joe H. San Angelo: urban growth
J65 influencing transportation planning...
1965. (Card 2)

1. Economic base studies - San Angelo,
Tex. 2. Transportation - San Angelo, Tex.
I. Texas. University. Bureau of Business
Research. II. Texas. Highway Dept.
III. Title.

Transportation - San Antonio.
388
(764) San Antonio Bexar County Urban Transportation
815 Study.
no.1 Mass transportation. [Prepared] in
cooperation with U.S. Dept. of Commerce,
Bureau of Public Roads. [San Antonio] 1966.
37p. (Its Report no.1)

1. Transportation - San Antonio.
2. Journey to work. I. U.S. Bureau of
Public Roads. II. Title.

711.4 Transportation - San Benito, Tex.
(764) Fowler and Grafe, inc.
S15 [San Benito] business district, thorough-
no.3 fares, and transportation. [Consultants:
Fowler and Grafe, inc. and Hare and Hare.
Prepared for San Benito City Planning Com-
mission] [Dallas?] 1964.
39p. (Its Comprehensive plan report 3)
Prepared in cooperation with Texas State
Department of Health.
U.S. Urban Renewal Adm. UPAP.

(Continued on next card)

711.4 Fowler and Grafe, inc. San Benito business
(764) district, thoroughfares...1964 (Card 2)
S15
no.3
1. Master plan - San Benito, Tex.
2. Business districts - San Benito, Tex.
3. Streets - San Benito, Tex. 4. Highways -
San Benito, Tex. 5. Transportation - San
Benito, Tex. I. Hare and Hare. II. San
Benito, Tex. City Planning Commission.
III. U.S. URA-UPAP. San Benito, Tex.

---

388 TRANSPORTATION - SAN BERNARDINO, CALIF.
(79495) Plotkin (H.M.) and Associates.
P56 A study to determine improvements to the San
Bernardino municipal transit system for increas-
ing employment opportunities to residents of
depressed areas. Prepared for the City of San
Bernardino. San Bernardino, Calif., 1968.
88p.
U.S. Mass Transportation Demonstration Grant
Program.
Bibliography: p. 84-85.
1. Transportation - San Bernardino, Calif.
2. Journey to work. 3. Employment -
San Bernardino, Calif.
(Cont'd on next card)

388
(79495) Plotkin (H.M.) and Associates.   A study...
P56   1968.   (Card 2)

I. Title. II. U.S. Mass Transportation
Demonstration Grant Program. San Bernardino,
Calif.

---

388   San Diego Metropolitan Area Transportation
(79498) Study.   Transportation ... 1959. (Card 2)
815

U.S. Urban Renewal Administration, Urban
Planning Assistance Program.

1. Transportation - San Diego metropolitan
area. I. Hall, Edward M. II. U.S. Urban
Renewal Administration. Urban Planning
Assistance Program. San Diego, Calif.

Transportation - San Francisco.

388
(79461) San Francisco Planning and Urban Renewal
S15m   Association.
    Market Street subway stations, a SPUR
report,
San Francisco,
       v.   (Its report no.

For complete information see main card.
1. Transportation - San Francisco.
2. Journey to work. I. Title: Subway
stations.

---

388   TRANSPORTATION - SAN DIEGO CO., CALIF.
(79498) San Diego County, Calif. Comprehensive
S15c   Planning Organization.
    Candidate transportation systems
background. Detailed study design.
San Diego, [1969?]
    23p.

Cover title.

1. Transportation - San Diego Co.,
Calif. 2. Journey to work. I. Title.

388
(79461) Ernst and Ernst.
E75   A report prepared for the Golden Gate
Authority Commission. [San Francisco]
1960.
    186p.

1. Transportation - San Francisco.
2. Authorities.

Transportation - San Francisco.

388
(79461) Begoe (Ladislas) and Associates.
823   Transportation plan for San Francisco.
A report to the City Planning Commission.
[Prepared in cooperation with the Dept. of
Public Works] and others. Cincinnati, 1948.
    1v.

1. Transportation - San Francisco.
I. San Francisco. City Planning Commission.
II. San Francisco. Dept. of Public Works.

---

388   TRANSPORTATION - SAN DIEGO COUNTY, CALIF.
(79498) San Diego County, Calif. Comprehensive
S15ca   Planning Organization.
    Candidate transportation systems. San Diego,
1971.
    196p.
    Preparation of report financed in part
through a comprehensive planning grant from
the Dept. of Housing and Urban Development.
Bibliography: p. 189-196.

1. Transportation - San Diego County, Calif.
I. U.S. HUD—Comprehensive Planning Grant
Program. San Diego Co., Calif. II. Title.

Transportation - San Francisco.

388
K14   Kaiser aluminum news.
v.21   The rise of the city. Oakland, Calif.,
no.1   Kaiser Aluminum and Chemical Corp 1963.
    35p.

Entire issue, vol. 21, no. 1.

1. Transportation. 2. Transportation -
San Francisco. I. Kaiser Aluminum and
Chemical   Corporation.

Transportation - San Francisco Bay area.

388
(79461) California. Highway Transportation Agency.
C15p   Prospectus for a San Francisco Bay Area
Transportation Study. Submitted to each
member of the State Legislature. Sacramento,
1962.
    25p.

1. Transportation - San Francisco Bay
area. I. California. San Francisco Bay
Area   Transportation
Study.

---

408   TRANSPORTATION - SAN DIEGO CO., CALIF.
SAN DIEGO CO., CALIF. COMPREHENSIVE
PLANNING ORGANIZATION.
TRANSIT SURVEY. SAN DIEGO, CALIF., 1970.
68P. (HUD 701 REPORT)

1. TRANSPORTATION - SAN DIEGO CO., CALIF.
I. HUD. 701. SAN DIEGO CO., CALIF.

---

388   TRANSPORTATION - SAN FRANCISCO.
(79461) LAVE, CHARLES A
[657]   A BENEFIT COST ANALYSIS OF THE BAY
L18   AREA RAPID TRANSIT SYSTEM. PREPARED
FOR DELIVERY AT THE 1966 ANNUAL MEETING
OF THE AMERICAN POLITICAL SCIENCE
ASSOCIATION. WASHINGTON, AMERICAN
POLITICAL SCIENCE ASSOCIATION, 1966.
9P.

1. TRANSPORTATION - ACCOUNTING.
2. TRANSPORTATION - SAN FRANCISCO.
I. TITLE. II. AMERICAN POLITICAL
SCIENCE ASSOCIATION.

Transportation - San Francisco Bay Area.

388
(79461) California. Legislature. Senate. Interim
C15f   Committee on San Francisco Bay Area Metropolitan Rapid Transit Problems.
Final report. Sacramento, 1957.
    29p.

1. Transportation - San Francisco Bay
Area.

---

388   Transportation - San Diego metropolitan area.
(79498) San Diego Metropolitan Area Transporta-
815n   tion Study.
    1959 collision index; a summary of high
accident locations. Participants: City of
San Diego, Police Dept., Transportation and
Traffic Engineering Division. San Diego,
1960.
    46p. tables.

1. Transportation - San Diego metropolitan area.
2. Accidents - Statistics.

Transportation - San Francisco.

VF
388   San Francisco. [Dept. of City Planning]
(79461) San Francisco reappraises its freeways.
815s   San Francisco, 1959.
    13p.

1. Transportation - San Francisco.
2. Traffic - San Francisco. 3. Streets -
San Francisco.

Transportation - San Francisco Bay area.

388
(79461) California. San Francisco Bay Area.
C15   Rapid Transit Commission.
    Report to the Legislature of the State
of California, December, 1957. [Sacramento,
1958]
    184p. tables.

Includes legislation.

1. Transportation - San Francisco Bay area.
I. California. Laws, Statutes, etc.

---

388   Transportation - San Diego metropolitan area.
(79498) San Diego Metropolitan Area Transporta-
815r   tion Study.
    Results of San Diego River screen line
counts, 1959. Participants: California
Division of Highways, District XI, County
of San Diego, Road Dept., City of San Diego,
Transportation and Traffic Engineering
Division. San Diego, 1960.
    8p. map, diagrs., tables.

"Traffic census 1959."

1. Transportation - San Diego metropolitan area.

Transportation - San Francisco.

388
(79461) San Francisco. Dept. of City Planning.
S15   Transportation Section of the Master
pt. 1   plan. I. The trafficways plan. San
Francisco, 1955.
    [12]p. map.

1. Transportation - San Francisco.

Transportation - San Francisco Bay Area.

711.3
(79461) California. University. Conference on City
C15   and Regional Planning.
    Moving people in metropolitan areas. Pro-
ceedings of the second annual University of
California Conference on City and Regional
Planning, San Francisco, Calif., June 18, 1954
Berkeley, Calif., Univ. of Calif. Dept. of
City and Regional Planning, 1955.
    35p.

1. Metropolitan area planning - San Francisco
Bay Area. 2. Transportation - San Francisco
Bay Area.

Transportation - San Diego metropolitan area.

388   San Diego Metropolitan Area Transportation
(79498) Study.
815   Transportation planning studies in the San
Diego metropolitan area, by Edward M. Hall.
Presented on Panel of Highway Division spon-
sored by Committee on Urban Transportation,
American Society of Civil Engineers, Los
Angeles, California, February 10, 1959. San
Diego, 1959.
    33p. diagrs., maps.

"A paper for ASCE meeting, February, 1959."

(Continued on next
card)

Transportation - San Francisco.

388
(79461) San Francisco. Transportation Technical
815r   Committee.
    Report on a plan for rapid transit in
San Francisco consonant with the Bay Area
Rapid Transit System. San Francisco, 1960.
    46p.

1. Transportation - San Francisco.

Transportation - San Francisco Bay Area.

353.1
G65   Golden Gate Authority Commission.
    Final report on the feasibility of a
regional agency to coordinate transportation
facilities serving the people of a nine-
county metropolitan region with recommendations
for a Golden Gate Transportation Commission for
the San Francisco Bay Area. Submitted to the
California State Legislature on Feb. 1, 1961.
San Francisco, 1961.
    24p.

1. Authorities.   2. Transportation -
San Francisco   Bay Area.

Transportation - San Francisco Bay area.

388
(7946)
K28
Kevany, Michael J
An information system for urban transportation planning; the BATSC [Bay Area Transportation Study Commission] approach. Santa Monica, Calif., 1968.
56p. (System Development Corp. Technical memo TM-3920/000/01)
U.S. Dept. of Housing and Urban Development, Contract California PD-1.
Bibliography: p. 55-56

(Cont'd on next card)

Transportation - San Francisco Bay Area.

388
(7946)
P17c
Parsons-Brinckerhoff-Tudor-Bechtel.
The composite report Bay Area Rapid Transit. Reports submitted to the San Francisco Bay Area Rapid Transit District describing the engineering, financial and economic phases of a rapid transit plan for Alameda, Contra Costa and San Francisco Counties. [San Francisco] 1962.
88p.

1. Transportation - San Francisco Bay Area.
2. Journey to work. I. San Francisco Bay Area Rapid   Transit District.

534.83
S15
TRANSPORTATION - SAN FRANCISCO BAY AREA.
Salmon, V
Noise control in the Bay area rapid transit system, by V. Salmon and S.K. Oleson. Final report. Menlo Park, Calif., Stanford Research Institute, 1966.
1v.
Prepared for Parsons Brinckerhoff-Tudor-Bechtel.
U.S. Dept. of Housing and Urban Development. Mass Transportation Demonstration Grant Program.
Contract   Z=23, SRI Project PH-4579.
1. Noise.   (Cont'd on next card)

388
(7946)
K28
Kevany, Michael J   An information...1968
(Card 2)

1. Transportation - San Francisco Bay area. I. Bay Area Transportation Study Commission. II. U.S. Dept. of Housing and Urban Development. III. System Development Corp. IV. Title.

Transportation - San Francisco Bay Area.

388
(7946)
P17e
Parsons, Brinckerhoff, Tudor, Bechtel, Engineers.
Engineering report to the San Francisco Bay Area Rapid Transit District. San Francisco, 1961.
87p.

Suppl.   ---- Supplement. San Francisco, 1961. 12p.

1. Transportation - San Francisco Bay Area. I. California. San   Francisco Bay Area Rapid Transit   Commission.

534.83
S15
Salmon, V   Noise control...1966.
(Card 2)

2. Transportation - San Francisco Bay area. I. Oleson, S.K., jt. au. II. Parsons Brinckerhoff-Tudor-Bechtel. III. U.S. HUD. Mass Transportation Demonstration Program. IV. Stanford Research Institute. V. Title.

Transportation - San Francisco Bay area.

388
(7946)
M13
Mahoney, Patrick J
Minority employment in the construction of BART [Bay Area Rapid Transit] [San Francisco] 1966.
37p.

1. Transportation - San Francisco Bay area.
2. Employment - San Francisco Bay area.
3. Labor relations. 4. Employment - Negroes. I. Title.

Transportation - San Francisco.

388
(79461)
P17
Parsons Brinckerhoff-Tudor-Bechtell.
Laboratory cars and support facilities. Final report. San Francisco, 1967.
52p. (Its Report no. 3)
U.S. Dept. of Housing and Urban Development. Demonstration Grant Program.
Distributed by U.S. Clearinghouse for Federal Scientific and Technical Information as PB-177 100.
1. Transportation - San Francisco.
2. Journey to work. I. U.S. Dept. of Housing and Urban Development. Demonstration Grant   Program. II. Title.

Transportation - San Francisco Bay Area.

388
(7946)
S15
San Francisco Bay Area Rapid Transit District.
Report,
San Francisco,
v.   annual.
For complete information see shelf list.

1. Transportation - San Francisco Bay Area.

388
(7946)
M17
TRANSPORTATION - SAN FRANCISCO BAY AREA.
Martin, Darryl B
Feasibility of an exclusive lane for buses on the San Francisco-Oakland Bay Bridge. [Sacramento] State of California, Business and Transportation Agency, Dept. of Public Works, Div. of Highways and Div. of Bay Toll Crossings, 1969.
30p.
To be presented at 49th annual meeting, Highway Research Board, Jan. 1970.

1. Transpor   tation - San Francisco Bay area. 2. Jo   urney to work.
(Cont'd on next card)

Transportation - San Francisco Bay Area.

FOLIO
388
(7946)
P17
Parsons, Brinckerhoff, Hall and MacDonald.
Regional rapid transit; a report to the San Francisco Bay Area Rapid Transit Commission, 1953-1955. New York, 1956.
106p.

1. Transportation - San Francisco Bay Area. I. California. San Francisco Bay Area Rapid Transit Commission.

388
(7946)
S15tr
Transportation - San Francisco Bay area.
San Francisco. Dept. of City Planning.
Transportation policy for San Francisco: recent trends and current developments, by William A. Proctor. San Francisco, 1967.
26p.

1. Transportation - San Francisco Bay area. 2. Population - San Francisco. I. Proctor, William A. II. Title.

388
(7946)
M17
Martin, Darryl B   Feasibility of an exclusive lane for buses...1969.   (Card 2)

I. California. Div. of Highways. II. Title: Buses. III. Title. IV. Highway Research Board

---

388
(7946)
P17t
TRANSPORTATION - SAN FRANCISCO BAY AREA.
Parsons Brinckerhoff-Tudor-Bechtel.
San Francisco Bay Area Rapid Transit District Demonstration Project.
Technical report no.1-
San Francisco, 1966-
nos. in
U.S. Mass Transportation Demonstration Grant Program.
Financed in part by U.S. Dept. of Housing and Urban Development.
For Library holdings see main card.
1. Transportation - San Francisco Bay area.
(Cont'd on next card)

Transportation - San Francisco Bay Area.

388
(7946)
S26
Scott, Stanley.
Organizing for a regional transportation study in the San Francisco Bay Area; objectives and alternatives, by Assistant Director, Bureau of Public Administration, University of California, Berkeley, California. [n.p.] 1962.
7p.

1. Transportation - San Francisco Bay Area.

Transportation - San Francisco Bay Area.

388
054
Oliver Tire and Rubber Co.
Report to BARTD (Bay Area Rapid Transit District) Prepared for Parsons Brinckerhoff-Tudor-Bechtel. Oakland, Calif., [1964?]
23p.

U.S. Housing and Home Finance Agency. Mass Transportation Demonstration Grant Program.

(Continued on next card)

388
(7946)
P17t
Parsons Brinckerhoff-Tudor-Bechtel. San Francisco...1966-   (Card 2)

2. Journey to work. 3. Railroads. I. U.S. Mass Transportation Demonstration Grant Program. II. U.S. Dept. of Housing and Urban Development. III. Title.

Transportation - San Francisco Bay area.

388
(7946)
B45
Simpson & Curtin.
Coordinated transit for the San Francisco Bay area, now to 1975; final report of Northern California Transit Demonstration Project. Philadelphia, 1967.
222p. (Cal MTO-5 and Cal MTO-6)

Abstract   ----Abstract report of Northern California Transit Demonstration Project. Philadelphia, 1967.
18p.
U.S. Dept. of Housing and Urban Development Mass Transportation Demonstration Grant Program.
(Cont'd on next card)

388
054
Oliver Tire and Rubber Co. Report to BARTD... [1964?]   (Card 2)

1. Transportation - San Francisco Bay Area.
2. Railroads. 3. Journey to work. I. Parsons Brinckerhoff-Tudor-Bechtel. II. U.S. Housing and Home Finance Agency. Mass Transportation Demonstration Grant Program.

Transportation - San Francisco Bay Area.

388
(7946)
R22
Reed, George E
Transportation; surface transportation on and around San Francisco Bay. Prepared for San Francisco Bay Conservation and Development Commission. San Francisco, San Francisco Bay Conservation and Development Commission, 1968.
181p.

Summary   .. ... Summary. San Francisco, 1968.
29p.
1. Transportation - San Francisco Bay Area. 2. Jour   ney to work. I. San Francisco Bay   Area Conservation and Development Commission. II. Title.

388
(7946)
B45
Simpson & Curtin.   Coordinated transit for the San Francisco Bay area...1967. (Card 2)

1. Transportation - San Francisco Bay area.
2. Journey to work. I. Northern California Transit Demonstration Project. II. U.S. HUD. Mass Transportation Demonstration Grant Program. III. Title.

Transportation - San Francisco Bay Area.

388
(7946) Stone and Youngberg.
S76   Rapid transit for the Bay area, the
four-county system; a summary of engineering,
financial and economic reports submitted to
the San Francisco Bay Area Rapid Transit
District. San Francisco, 1961.
48p.

    1. Transportation - San Francisco Bay
Area. I. California. San Francisco Bay
Area Rapid Transit Commission.

Transportation - San Francisco Bay area.

388
(7946) Ystebede, Fredrik.
Y77   Express bus operations in the Oakland area.
Berkeley, University of California, 1962.
32p.
    "Institute of Transportation and Traffic
Engineering. Graduate report."
    "A condensation of a research report
submitted ... as partial fulfillment of the
requirements for the degree of Master of
Engineering in transportation."

1. Transportation - San   Francisco Bay area.
I. Title.

Transportation - San Francisco Bay area.

388
(7946) Zettel, Richard M
Z27   Urban transportation in the San Francisco
Bay area. Berkeley, Institute of Governmental Studies, University of California,
1963.
51p. (The 1963 Franklin K. Lane Project)

    1. Transportation - San Francisco Bay
area. 2. Journey to work.

Transportation - Sangamon Co., Ill.

388
(77356) Sangamon County, Ill. Regional Planning
S15   Commission.
    Circulation plan. Springfield, Ill.,
1959.
24p. illus., maps. (Its Regional plan
report no. 3)
    U.S. Urban Renewal Administration, Urban
Planning Assistance Program.
    1. Transportation - Sangamon Co., Ill. 2.
Regional planning - Sangamon Co., Ill. I.
U.S. Urban Re-   newal Administration.
Urban Planning   Assistance Program.
Sangamon County,   Ill.

Transportation - Santa Barbara Co., Calif.

388
(79491) California. Div. Of Highways. (Urban Plan-
C17   ning Dept.)
    SCOTS [South Coast Transportation Study]
base year report, 1964. Santa Barbara,
Calif., 1967.
2v.
    Prepared in cooperation with the Dept. of
Transportation, Federal Highway Administratio
Bureau of Public Roads.
    1. Transportation - Santa Barbara Co., Cali
2. Population - Santa Barbara Co., Calif.
3. Journey to work. I. U.S. Bureau of Public
Roads.   II. Title.

388
(79491) TRANSPORTATION - SANTA BARBARA CO., CALIF.
S15   Santa Barbara Co., Calif. South Coast Transportation Study.
    SCOTS progress report; analysis and fore-
cast; 1990. Santa Barbara, 1969.
68p.

    1. Transportation - Santa Barbara Co.,
Calif. 2. Journey to work. I. Title.

Transportation - Savannah.

711.729
(758725) Georgia. State Highway Dept.
G26   Chatham Urban Transportation Study.
Savannah parking report. [Prepared] in
cooperation with the U.S. Dept. of Commerce, Bureau of Public Roads and
approved by the Technical Coordinating
Committee. Savannah, 1965.
71p.

    1. Parking - Savannah. 2. Transporta-
tion - Savannah. 3. Transportation -
Chatham Co., Ga. 4. Chatham Urban
Transporta-   tion Study. I. U.S.
Bureau of   Public Roads.
III. Title.

538
FOLIO TRANSPORTATION - SCOTT CO., IOWA.
BI-STATE METROPOLITAN PLANNING
COMMISSION.
RESEARCH AND ANALYSIS REPORT,
BACKGROUND PLANNING STUDIES FOR SCOTT
COUNTY AREA TRANSPORTATION PROGRAM. BY
CANDEUB, FLEISSIG AND ASSOCIATES.
CHICAGO, 1967.
1 V. (HUD 701 REPORT)

    1. TRANSPORTATION - SCOTT CO., IOWA.
I. CANDEUB, FLEISSIG AND ASSOCIATES.
II. HUD. 701. SCOTT CO., IOWA.

Transportation - Scranton.

711.4
(74832) Candeub (Isadore) and Associates.
S71   Master plan, Scranton, Pennsylvania.
Transportation facilities survey and
plan. Submitted to the Scranton City
Planning Commission. Scranton, 1959.
32p. (Scranton master plan report
14)

    1. Master plan - Scranton. 2. Trans-
portation - Scranton. I. Scranton.
City Planning Commission. II. Title.

Transportation - Seattle.

388
(797771) De Leuw, Cather & Co.
D25   Interim report to the Puget Sound
Governmental Conference on feasibility
of rapid transit operation within the
Seattle area. Seattle, 1965.
48p.

    1. Transportation - Seattle. I. Puget
Sound Governmental Conference, Seattle,
1965.

Transportation - Seattle.

388
(797771) De Leuw, Cather and Company.
D25   Summary of interim report to the Puget
Summary Sound Governmental Conference on feasibility of rapid transit operation within
the Seattle area. San Francisco, 1965.
[4]p.

    U.S. Urban Renewal Adm. UPAP.

    1. Transportation - Seattle.
I. Puget Sound Governmental Conference.
II. Title. III. U.S. URA-UPAP. Seattle.

711.4
(797771) TRANSPORTATION - SEATTLE.
821D SEATTLE. URBAN DESIGN ADVISORY BOARD.
DESIGNING A GREAT CITY; REPORT TO
THE SEATTLE CITY PLANNING COMMISSION.
SEATTLE, 1965.
46L.

    1. CITY PLANNING - SEATTLE.
2. OPEN SPACE - SEATTLE.
3. TRANSPORTATION - SEATTLE.
I. TITLE.

Transportation - Seattle.

388
(797771) Washington (State) University. Dept.
W17   of Civil Engineering.
    Seattle monorail. Washington, Housing
and Home Finance Agency, Office of
Transportation, 1962.
108p.
    U.S. Housing and Home Finance Agency.
Mass Transportation Demonstration Grant
Program.

(Continued on
next card)

388
(797771) Washington (State) University. Dept. of
W17   Civil Engineering. Seattle monorail...
1962. (Card 2)

    1. Transportation - Seattle. 2. Rail-
roads - Seattle. I. U.S. Housing and
Home Finance Agency. Office of
Transportation. II. Title. III. U.S.
Housing and Home Finance Agency. Mass
Transportation Demonstration Grant
Program.

Transportation - Shamong, N.J.

711.4
(74961) New Jersey. Dept. of Conservation and
S31t   Economic Development. (Div. of Planning
and Development)
    Shamong Township, Burlington County, New
Jersey: preliminary master plan studies.
Thorofares and traffic, transportation
service. Prepared for the Shamong Planning
Board. [Trenton] 1958.
6p.
    U.S. Urban Renewal Adm. UPAP.

1. Master plan - Shamong, N.J. 2. Transportation -
Shamong, N.J. I.   Shamong, N.J.
Planning Board.   II. U.S. URA-
UPAP. Shamong, N.J.

Transportation - Shenango Valley, Pa.

388
(74895) Shenango Valley Regional Planning Commission.
S32   Transportation in the Shenango Valley,
Mercer County, Pennsylvania. Sharon, Pa.,
1958.
36p. diagrs., maps.

    U.S. Urban Renewal Administration, Urban
Planning Assistance Program.

    1. Transportation - Shenango Valley, Pa.
I. U.S. Urban Renewal Administration.
Urban Planning Assistance Program.

TRANSPORTATION - SHREVEPORT, LA.

388
(763991) Howard, Needles, Tasman and Bergendoff.
H68   Shreveport metropolitan plan and transportation study. Prepared for Louisiana
Dept. of Highways in cooperation with
U.S. Bureau of Public Roads. Kansas City,
1968.
2v.

    1. Transportation - Shreveport, La.
2. Journey to work. I. Title.

Transportation - Skokie, Illinois.

388
(77311) Buck, Thomas.
B82   Skokie swift, the commuter's friend.
Chicago, Chicago Transit Authority, 1968.
65p. (Chicago Transit Authority.
Publication RP-x68222)
    U.S. Dept. of Housing and Urban Develop-
ment. Mass Transportation Demonstration
Grant Program.
    1. Transportation - Chicago. 2. Trans-
portation - Skokie, Ill. 3. Journey to
work. I. Chicago Transit Authority.
II. Title. III. U.S. Dept. of Housing
and Urban Deve-   lopment. Mass Transportation De-   monstration Grant Program.

Transportation - Skokie, Ill.

388
(7731) Greisdorf, Myron.
G72   A suburban mayor looks at rapid transit;
address before Institute for Rapid Transit,
third Annual Meeting, Washington, D.C.,
May 14. [n.p.] 1964.
6p.

    1. Transportation - Skokie, Ill.
2. Journey to work. I. Institute for Rapid
Transit. Meeting, Washington, 1964.
II. Title.

Transportation - South Carolina.

388
(757) Bennett, James W
B25   An analysis of the transportation complex
of the State of South Carolina; a study
prepared for the State Organization for
Associated Research, by James W. Bennett, Jr.
and others. Columbia, Bureau of Business and
Economic Research, School of Business Administration, University of South Carolina, 1961.
v. (SOAR report)
1. Transportation - South Carolina. I. South
Carolina State Organization for Associated Research.
II. South Carolina.   University. Bureau
of Business and   Economic Research.

TRANSPORTATION - SPAIN.

388
(46) Sociedad Privada Municipal, Barcelona.
S62   Memoria, 19

Barcelona, 19
v.
    Reports: 19   has title: Tranvias
de Barcelona. 19   Transportes de
Barcelona.
    For Library holdings see main entry.

    1. Transportation - Spain. I. Title:
Tranvias de Barcelona. II. Title: Transportes
de Barcelona.

388
(797371)
S66
pt.1

Transportation - Spokane.

Spokane. City Plan Commission.
Transportation. Part 1. Arterial
street plan. Spokane, City Plan
Commission, Traffic Engineering Dept.,
Dept. of Public Works and Utilities,
1964.
73p. (Report no. 12, City plan
series 1)

1. Transportation - Spokane.
2. Streets - Spokane.

388
(778781)
S67

Transportation - Springfield, Mo.

Springfield, Mo. Metropolitan Area
Planning Dept.
Methods and procedures for tabulation of
basic data for street, system analysis in
the Springfield metropolitan area by key-
sort data processing system, 1964.
Springfield, Mo., 1964.
14p.
U.S. Urban Renewal Adm. UPAP.
Cover title: Springfield transportation
study street and structure evaluation.

(Cont'd on next card)

388
(778781)
S67

Springfield, Mo. Metropolitan Area
Planning Dept. Methods and procedures
for tabulation of basic data for
street...1964. (Card 2)

1. Transportation - Springfield, Mo.
2. Streets - Springfield, Mo. 3. Transportation - Automation. I. U.S. URA-
UPAP. Springfield, Mo.

388
(77162)
S71
no.2

Transportation - Stark Co., Ohio.

Preston (E.S.) and Associates.
SCATS procedure manual no. 2, population
and economics. [Prepared for] Stark County
Area Transportation Study. [n.p. 1966?]
42p.

1. Transportation - Stark Co., Ohio.
2. Population - Stark Co., Ohio.
3. Transportation - Economic effect.
I. Stark County (Ohio) Transportation
Study.

388
(77162)
S71
no.3

Transportation - Stark Co., Ohio.

Preston (E.S.) and Associates.
SCATS procedure manual no. 3, land use.
[Prepared for] the Stark County Area Transportation Study, by E.S. Preston and
Associates and Candeub, Fleissig and Associates. [n.p. 1966?]
57p.

1. Transportation - Stark Co., Ohio.
2. Land use - Stark Co., Ohio. I. Stark
County (Ohio) Area Transportation Study.
II. Candeub, Fleissig and Associates.

388
(77162)
S71
no.6

Transportation - Stark Co., Ohio.

Preston (E.S.) and Associates.
SCATS procedure manual no. 6, terminal
and transfer facilities. [Prepared for]
the Stark County Area Transportation Study.
[n.p. 1966?]
63p.

1. Transportation - Stark Co., Ohio.
I. Stark County (Ohio) Area Transportation
Study.

388
(77162)
S71
no.7

Transportation - Stark Co., Ohio.

Preston (E.S.) and Associates.
SCATS procedure manual no. 7, governmental control measures. [Prepared for] the
Stark County Area Transportation Study.
[n.p. 1966?]
22p.

1. Transportation - Stark Co., Ohio.
2. Intergovernmental relations - Stark Co.,
Ohio. I. Stark County (Ohio) Area Transportation Study.

388
(77162)
S71
no.8

Transportation - Stark Co., Ohio.

Preston (E.S.) and Associates.
SCATS procedure manual no. 8, financial
resources. [Prepared for] the Stark County
Area Transportation Study. [n.p. 1966?]
55p.

1. Transportation - Stark Co., Ohio.
2. Transportation - Finance. I. Stark
County (Ohio) Area Transportation Study.

388
(77162)
S71
no.9

Transportation - Stark Co., Ohio.

Preston (E.S.) and Associates.
SCATS procedure manual no. 9, transportation system evaluation. Prepared for the
Stark County Area Transportation Study.
[n.p. 1966?]
20p.

1. Transportation - Stark Co., Ohio.
I. Stark County (Ohio) Area Transportation
Study.

388
(77162)
S71

Transportation - Stark Co., Ohio.

Stark County (Ohio) Area Transportation
Study.
SCATS. Canton, Ohio, 1966.
128p.

1. Transportation - Stark Co., Ohio.

388
A87a

Transportation - Statistics.

Automobile Manufacturers Association.
Automobile facts and figures

Detroit,
v. annual.

For complete information see shelflist.

1. Transportation. 2. Transportation -
Statistics.

388
A87ur

Transportation - Statistics.

Automotive Safety Foundation.
Urban freeway development in twenty
major cities. Washington, D.C., 1964.
45p.

1. Transportation. 2. Transportation -
Statistics. 3. City growth. 4. Population. I. Title. 5. Highways.

388
(016)
C15
no.34

Transportation - Statistics.

California. University. Institute of
Transportation and Traffic Engineering.
Transportation statistical sources; selected references. Berkeley, Calif., 1967.
17p. (Its Library references no. 34)

1. Transportation - Bibl. 2. Transportation
- Statistics. 3. Railroads - Bibl. I. Title.

711.73
(764)
H21

Transportation - Statistics.

Heathington, Kenneth W
Traffic volume analysis of urban free-
ways, by Kenneth W. Heathington and Paul R.
Tutt. [Prepared] in cooperation with the
U.S. Dept. of Commerce, Bureau of Public
Roads. [Austin, Texas] Texas Highway Dept.
1966.
56p. (Texas. Highway Dept. Departmental
Research. Report no. SS 5.0)
1. Highways - Texas. 2. Traffic surveys -
Texas. 3. Transportation - Statistics. I. Tutt,
Paul R., jt. au. II. Texas. Highway Dept.
IV. Title.

312
K15

Transportation - Statistics.

Kanwit, Edmond L
Recent population trends and their highway
implications, by E.L. Kanwit and Thomas R.
Todd. [n.p.] 1961.
33p.
Reprinted from Highway Research Board.
Proceedings, vol. 40, 1961. (711.73N177, 1961)

1. Population. 2. Population shifts.
3. Transportation - Statistics. I. Todd,
Thomas R., jt.au. II. Highway Research Board.
III. Title.

388
M42sp

Transportation - Statistics.

Midwest Research Institute.
Special transportation requirements in
small cities and towns, final report, by
Bruce W. Macy and others. Prepared for the
U.S. Dept. of Housing and Urban Development.
[Kansas City, Mo.] 1968.
87p.
On cover: Study in new systems of urban
transportation.
1. Transportation. 2. Transportation -
Statistics. I. U.S. Dept. of Housing and
Urban Development. II. Macy, Bruce W.
III. Title.

(Cont'd on next card)

388
M42sp

Midwest Research Institute. Special
transportation requirements...1968.
(Card 2)

IV. Title: Study in new systems of urban
transportation. V. Title: Transportation
requirements in small cities and towns.

388
(083.41)
N17

Transportation - Statistics.

National Research Council.
Selected statistics on the transportation
system of the U.S.A. A staff paper for
sessions "A" Transportation Research Study,
Woods Hole, Massachusetts, Aug. 1960. Washington, National Academy of Sciences-National
Research Council, 1960.
25p.

1. Transportation - Statistics.
I. Transportation Research Study, Woods
Hole, Mass., 1960.

388
(764)
T29t
v.1

Transportation - Statistics.

Texas. Highway Dept.
Tyler urban transportation study. Vol. 1.
Origin-destination survey. Sponsoring
agencies: City of Tyler, County of Smith
[and] Texas Highway Dept. in cooperation
with U.S. Dept. of Commerce, Bureau of
Public Roads. [Austin?] 1964.
1 v.

1. Transportation - Tyler, Tex.
2. Journey to work. 3. Transportation -
Statistics. I. U.S. Bureau of
Public Roads. II. Title.

388
(083.41)
C65

TRANSPORTATION - STATISTICS.

U.S. CONGRESS. HOUSE. COMMITTEE ON
POST OFFICE AND CIVIL SERVICE.
IMPROVING FEDERAL TRANSPORTATION
STATISTICS. REPORT... WASHINGTON,
GOVT. PRINT. OFF., 1962.
89P. (87TH CONGRESS, 2D SESSION.
HOUSE. REPORT NO. 1700)

1. TRANSPORTATION - STATISTICS.

388
(083.41)
I57

Transportation - Statistics.

U.S. Interstate Commerce Commission.
Report
on transport statistics in the United
States for the year ended Dec. 31,
Washington,
9 pts. annual.
Contents:-pt.1. Railroads, their lessors and pro-
prietary companies.-pt.2. The Pullman Company (sleep-
ing car companies).-pt.3 Railway Express Agency,
(Express company).pt.4. Electric railways.-pt.5.
Carriers by water.-pt.6. Oil pipe lines.-pt.7. Motor
carriers.-pt.8. Freight forwarders.-pt.9. Private
car lines.
For complete informa- tion see shelflist.
1. Transportation - Statistics.

16

Transportation - Statistics.

388 (083.41) F81 — U.S. Bureau of Public Roads.
Selected statistics by standard metropolitan statistical areas for use in transportation planning. Washington, U.S. Dept. of Commerce, Bureau of Public Roads, 1964.
98p.

Unpublished tables developed by E. L. Kanwit and others.

1. Transportation - Statistics. 2. Transportation - Metropolitan areas. 3. Journey to work. I. Title. II. Title: Standard metropolitan statistical areas.

TRANSPORTATION - SUFFOLK CO., N.Y.

388 (747245) T74 — Tri-State Transportation Commission. (Connecticut-New Jersey-New York)
People, transportation, jobs; public transport services to non-CBD employment concentrations. Participating agencies: Tri-State Transportation Commission, U.S. Department of Transportation, State of New York, Dept. of Transportation. New York, 1969.
36p. (Nassau and Suffolk Counties Progress report no. 3)
INT-MTD 13.
U.S. Dept. of Housing and Urban Development. Mass Transportation Demonstration Grant (Cont'd on next card)

Transportation - Surveys.

388 :308 C25c v.3 pt.2 — U.S. Bureau of the Census.
1963 census of transportation. [Vol. 3] Commodity transportation survey. Commodity groups, part 2. Washington, U.S. Dept. of Commerce, Bureau of the Census. For sale by the Supt. of Documents, Govt. Print. Off., 1966.
341p. (TC63-C3-2)
Cover title.
c.2 2 pts in IV. 471p

1. Transportation - Surveys. 2. Census - Transportation. I. Title. II. Title: Commodity transportation survey.

Transportation - Statistics.

388. W27s — Westinghouse Air Brake Co.
Study of evolutionary urban transportation. Organizations participating: Westinghouse Air Brake and others. Prepared for the U.S. Dept. of Housing and Urban Development. [Pittsburgh] 1968.
v. (v.1 v.2. Appendices 1, 2, and 3. [and] v.3. Appendix 4)
At head of title: Study in new systems of urban transportation.

1. Transportation. 2. Transportation - Automation. 3. Journey to work. 4. Transportation - Statistics.
(Cont'd on next card)

Transportation - Surveys.

388 (747245) T74 — Tri-State Transportation Commission. (Connecticut-New Jersey-New York)
People, transportation, jobs...1969. (Card 2)

Program.

1. Transportation - Nassau Co., N.Y. 2. Transportation - Suffolk Co., N.Y. 3. Journey to work. I. Title. II. U.S. HUD. Mass Transportation Demonstration Grant Program.

Transportation - Surveys.

388 :308 C25c v.3 pts.3&4 — U.S. Bureau of the Census.
1963 census of transportation. Vol. 3. Commodity transportation survey. Pt. 3: Shipper groups. Pt. 4: Production areas. Wash., For sale by the Supt. of Doc., Govt. Print. Off., 1966.
561p.
Have also Vol. 3. Commodity transportation survey. Pt. 3: Shipper TC63-C1, 317p.

1. Transportation - Surveys. 2. Census - Transportation. 3. Journey to work. I. Title. II. Title: Shipper groups. III. Title: Production areas.

---

388 W27s — Westinghouse Air Brake Co. Study of evolutionary urban transportation...1968. (Card 2)

I. U.S. Dept. of Housing and Urban Development. II. Title. III. Title: Study in new systems of urban transportation.

Transportation - Surveys.

388 :308 G45 — Gilman (W. C.) and Co.
A survey to evaluate the criteria which influence the purchase and use of a monthly transit pass and to determine reasons why transit non pass riders do not purchase a pass. Final report. Prepared for the Bi-State Development Agency. New York, 1964.
30p.
U.S. Housing and Home Finance Agency. Mass Transportation Demonstration Grant Program.
(Continued on next card)

Transportation - Surveys.

388 :308 C25c v.4 — U.S. Bureau of the Census.
1963 census of transportation. Vol. 4. Motor carrier survey. Wash., For sale by the Supt. of Doc., Govt. Print. Off., 1966.
27p. (TC63-M1)

1. Transportation - Surveys. 2. Census - Transportation. I. Title. II. Title: Motor carrier survey.

Transportation - Study and teaching.

388 H65 1967 — Homburger, Wolfgang S ed.
Urban mass transit planning. Berkeley, Institute of Transportation and Traffic Engineering, University of California, 1967.
212p. (California. University. Institute of Transportation and Traffic Engineering. Course notes)
Bibliography: p. 204-212.

1. Transportation. 2. Transportation - Study and teaching. 3. Journey to work. I. California. University. Institute of Transportation and Traffic Engineering. II. Title.

---

388 :308 G45 — Gilman (W.C.) and Co. A survey to evaluate the criteria which influence the purchase and use of a monthly transit pass...1964. (Card 2)

1. Transportation - Surveys. 2. Journey to work. I. Bi-State Development Agency, New York. II. U.S. Housing and Home Finance Agency. Mass Transportation Demonstration Grant Program. III. Title: The purchase and use of a monthly transit pass.

TRANSPORTATION - SURVEYS.

388 :308 1967 C25c v.1 — U.S. Bureau of the Census.
1967 census of transportation. Vol. 1. National travel survey. Wash., 1967.
94p.

1. Transportation - Surveys. 2. Census - Transportation. I. Title. II. Title: National travel survey.

Transportation - Study and teaching.

058.7 :388 N67 — Northwestern University. Transportation Center.
A directory of transportation education in American colleges and universities. Compiled by Gilbert James. Evanston, Ill., 1961.
49p.

1. Transportation - Direct. 2. Transportation - Study and teaching. I. James, Gilbert, comp.

Transportation - Surveys.

388 :308 C25c v.1 — U.S. Bureau of the Census.
1963 census of transportation. Vol. 1. Passenger transportation survey: pt. 1: National travel survey, pt. 2: Home-to-work travel survey. Wash., For sale by the Supt. of Doc., Govt. Print. Off., 1966.
106p.

1. Transportation - Surveys. 2. Census - Transportation. 3. Journey to work. I. Title. II. Title: National travel survey. III. Title: Home-to-work travel survey.

TRANSPORTATION - SURVEYS.

388 :308 1967 C25c v.2 — U.S. Bureau of the Census.
1967 census of transportation. Vol. 2. Truck inventory and use survey. Wash., 1967.
693p.

1. Transportation - Surveys. 2. Census - Transportation. I. Title. II. Title: Truck inventory and use survey.

Transportation - Study and teaching.

388 (07) N677 — Northwestern University. Transportation Center.
A national center for education, research, and service to the transportation industry and the Nation. Evanston, Ill., [1960]
51p.

1. Transportation - Study and teaching. I. Title.

Transportation - Surveys.

388 :308 C25c v.2 — U.S. Bureau of the Census.
1963 census of transportation. Vol. 2. Truck inventory and use survey. Wash., U.S. Dept. of Commerce, Bureau of the Census, 1965.
698p.
"Publication graphics and design developed by Stuart Freeman."

1. Transportation - Surveys. 2. Census - Transportation. I. Freeman, Stuart. II. Title. III. Title: Truck inventory and use survey.

TRANSPORTATION - SURVEYS.

388 :308 1967 C25c v.3 pt.1 — U.S. Bureau of the Census.
1967 census of transportation. Vol. 3 Commodity transportation survey, pt.1: Shipper groups. Wash., 1970.
1184p.

388 :308 1967 C25c TC67 C1- — -- --- Reprints.
v.
1. Transportation - Surveys. 2. Census - Transportation. I. Title. II. Title: Commodity transportation survey; shipper groups.

Transportation - Study and teaching.

388 (07) N677r — Northwestern University. Transportation Center.
Report,
[Evanston, Ill.]
v. annual.

For complete information see main card.

1. Transportation - Study and teaching.

Transportation - Surveys.

388 :308 C25c v.3 pt.1 — U.S. Bureau of the Census.
1963 census of transportation. Vol. 3. Commodity transportation survey, commodity groups, pt. 1. Wash., U.S. Dept. of Commerce, Bureau of the Census, 1966.
137p. (TC63-C3-1)
c.2. 2pts in IV. 471p

1. Transportation - Surveys. 2. Census - Transportation. I. Title. II. Title: Commodity transportation survey.

TRANSPORTATION - SURVEYS.

388 :308 1967 C25c v.3 pt2 — U.S. Bureau of the Census.
1967 census of transportation. Vol. 3: Commodity transportation survey, pt. 2: production areas and selected states. Wash., 1970.
878p.

388 :308 1967 C25c TC67 C2- — -- --- Reprints.
v.
1. Transportation - Surveys. 2. Census - Transportation. I. Title. II. Title: Commodity transportation survey; production areas and selected states.

388 :308 1967 C25c vo.3 pt.3	TRANSPORTATION - SURVEYS. U.S. Bureau of the Census. 1967 census of transportation. Vol. 3: Commodity transportation survey, pt.3: commodity groups. Wash., 1970. 633p.
388 :308 1967 C25c TC67 C3-	— — Reprints. v. 1. Transportation - Surveys. 2. Census - Transportation. I. Title. II. Title: Commodity transportation survey; commodity groups.

388 :308 C25 TC63	Transportation - Surveys. U.S. Bureau of the Census. Passenger transportation survey, national travel first 6 months of 1963— Washington, Dept. of Commerce, Bureau of the Census, 1964— v. (Preliminary report, Apr. 29, 1964 — TC63 (P)-P1 — Advance report TC 63(A)-P2 — At head of title: Census of trans- portation. For complete information see shelf list. 1. Transportation - Surveys. I. Title.

690.015 (485) S82 1971 R7	TRANSPORTATION - SWEDEN. Henriksson, Jan. Byggmaterialtransporter: kortidernas varia- tioner under dygnet pa trafikleder av olika typ. (Transportation of building materials: varia- tions in transportation time during a 24 hour period for streets of varying types) av Jan Henriksson och Lars Bjerkner. Stockholm, Statens Institut for Byggnadsforskning, 1971. 51p. (Rapport R7:1971) English summary. 1. Building research - Sweden. 2. Transpor- tation - Sweden. 3. Building materials - Sweden. I. Stock holm. Statens Institut (Cont'd on next card)

690.015 (485) S82 1971 R7	Henriksson, Jan. Byggmaterialtransporter... 1971. (Card 2) for Byggnadsforskning. II. Title: Transporta- tion of building materials. III. Bjerkner, Lars, jt. au.

388 (74765) C72	TRANSPORTATION - SYRACUSE, N.Y. Creamer, Trowbridge, Case & Basford. The Buttonwoods-Providence express and local shoppers' shuttle. Final report on Mass Demonstration Project RI-MTD-2, November 6, 1967 - October 31, 1968. Syracuse, N.Y., 1969. 39p. Cover title: Arriving late in suburbia. Participant agencies: Rhode Island Public Transit Authority; U.S. Dept. of Housing and Urban Development; Rhode Island Statewide Comprehensive Transportation and Land Use Planning Program. (Cont'd on next card)

388 (74765) C72	Creamer, Trowbridge, Case & Basford. The Buttonwoods-Providence . . . 1969. (Card 2) 1. Transportation - Syracuse, N.Y. 2. Employment - Syracuse, N.Y. I. Title. II. U.S. Mass Transportation Demonstration Grant Program. III. U.S. Dept. of Housing and Urban Development. IV. Title: Arriving late in suburbia.

388 (74765) S97	TRANSPORTATION - SYRACUSE, N.Y. Syracuse-Onondaga County Planning Agency. Job accessibility: a study of factors inhibiting employment. Syracuse, N.Y., 1969. 30p. U.S. Mass Transportation Demonstration Grant Program. 1. Transportation - Syracuse, N.Y. 2. Employment - Syracuse, N.Y. I. Title. II. U.S. Mass Transportation Demonstration Grant Program.

388 (74765) N28	Transportation - Syracuse, N.Y. metropolitan area. New York (State) Dept. of Public Works. (Subdivision of Transportation Planning and Programming) A prospectus for a comprehensive trans- portation study in the Syracuse metropoli- tan area. Albany, 1966. 31p. (Its Publication RP50-000-01) 1. Transportation - Syracuse, N.Y. metro- politan area. 2. Journey to work. 3. Traffic surveys - Syracuse, N.Y. metro- politan area. I. Title.

388 (797781) D25	Transportation - Tacoma. De Leuw, Cather & Co. Report on operation of Tacoma Transit System. San Francisco, 1965. 1v. 1. Transportation - Tacoma. 2. Journey to work.

388 (797781) G45	TRANSPORTATION - TACOMA. Gilman (W.C.) and Co. Tacoma Transit Company; review of service earnings and property. Jan. 28, 1949. New York, 1949. 72p. 1. Transportation - Tacoma. I. Title.

388 (759651) T15	TRANSPORTATION - TAMPA, FLA. Tampa Bay Regional Planning Council. Mass transit in the Tampa Bay region; summary report. St. Petersburg, Fla., [1970] folder. U.S. Dept. of Housing and Urban Develop- ment. UPAP. 1. Transportation - Tampa, Fla. 2. Journey to work. I. Title. II. U.S. HUD-UPAP. Tampa, Fla.

513	TRANSPORTATION - TAMPA BAY, FLA. TAMPA BAY, FLA. REGIONAL PLANNING COUNCIL. MASS TRANSIT CONCEPTS OF THE TAMPA BAY REGION. ST. PETERSBURG, FLA., 1970. 76P. (HUD 701 REPORT) 1. TRANSPORTATION - TAMPA BAY, FLA. I. HUD. 701. TAMPA BAY, FLA.

514	TRANSPORTATION - TAMPA BAY, FLA. TAMPA BAY, FLA. REGIONAL PLANNING COUNCIL. MASS TRANSIT IN THE TAMPA BAY REGION; SUMMARY REPORT. ST. PETERSBURG, FLA., 1970. 9P. (HUD 701 REPORT) 1. TRANSPORTATION - TAMPA BAY, FLA. I. HUD. 701. TAMPA BAY, FLA.

511	TRANSPORTATION - TAMPA BAY, FLA. TAMPA BAY, FLA. REGIONAL PLANNING COUNCIL. TAMPA BAY MASS TRANSIT: PLANNING FOR TOMORROW. ST. PETERSBURG, FLA., 1970. 106P. (HUD 701 REPORT) 1. TRANSPORTATION - TAMPA BAY, FLA. I. HUD. 701. TAMPA BAY, FLA.

512	TRANSPORTATION - TAMPA BAY, FLA. TAMPA BAY, FLA. REGIONAL PLANNING COUNCIL. TAMPA BAY MASS TRANS T: PLANNING FOR TOMORROW: SUMMARY REPORT. ST. PETERSBURG, FLA., 1970. 25P. (HUD 701 REPORT) 1. TRANSPORTATION - TAMPA BAY, FLA. I. HUD. 701. TAMPA BAY, FLA.

5450	TRANSPORTATION - TAUNTON, MASS. TAUNTON, MASS. PLANNING BOARD. A GENERAL DESIGN FOR COMPREHENSIVE DEVELOPMENT OF THE MILL RIVER PARKWAY, 1966. BY COMMUNITY PLANNING SERVICES, A DIVISION OF WHITMAN AND HOWARD. TAUNTON, 1966. 1 V. (HUD 701 REPORT) 1. TRANSPORTATION - TAUNTON, MASS. I. WHITMAN AND HOWARD. COMMUNITY PLANNING SERVICES. II. HUD. 701. TAUNTON, MASS.

388 (762) M47urb	Transportation - Tennessee. Mississippi-Arkansas-Tennessee Council of Governments. UMT (urban mass transportation) program planning requirements: supplemental documen- tation MATCOG. Regular program planning requirements. Memphis, 1968. 13p. U.S. Dept. of Housing and Urban Develop- ment. Mass Transportation Demonstration Grant Program. 1. Transportation - Mississippi. 2. Transportation - Arkansas. 3. Transportation - Tennessee. 4. Journey to work. (Continued on next card)

388 (762) M47urb	Mississippi-Arkansas-Tennessee Council of Governments. UMT...1968. (Card 2) I. U.S. Dept. of Housing and Urban Develop- ment. Mass Transportation Demonstration Grant Program Miss.-Ark.-Tenn. II. Title.

388 (762) M47ur	Transportation - Tennessee. Mississippi-Arkansas-Tennessee Council of Governments. Urban mass transportation program plann- ing requirements; supplementary material, MATCOG. Memphis, 1968. 18p. U.S. Dept. of Housing and Urban Develop- ment. Mass Transportation Demonstration Grant Program. 1. Transportation - Mississippi. 2. Trans- portation - Arkansas. 3. Transportation - Tennessee. 4. Journey to work. (Cont'd on next card)

388 (762) M47ur	Mississippi-Arkansas-Tennessee Council of Governments. Urban mass...1968.(Card 2) I. Title. II. U.S. Dept. of Housing and Urban Development. Mass Transportation Demonstration Grant Program. Miss.-Ark.- Tenn.

388 (762) M47u	Transportation - Tennessee. Mississippi-Arkansas-Tennessee Council of Governments. Urban mass transportation grant program; regular program planning requirements. Memphis, 1968. 48p. U.S. Dept. of Housing and Urban Develop- ment. Mass Transportation Demonstration Grant Program. 1. Transportation - Mississippi. 2. Trans- portation - Arkansas. 3. Transportation - Tennessee. 4. Journey to work. I. U.S. Dept. of Housing and Urban Development. Mass Transportation Demonstration Grant Pro- gram. (Cont'd on next card)

388
(762)
M47u
Mississippi-Arkansas-Tennessee Council of
Governments.   Urban mass transporta-
tion...1968.   (Card 2)

Mississippi. II. U.S. Dept. of Housing and
Urban Development. Mass Transportation
Demonstration Grant Program. Arkansas.
III. U.S. Dept. of Housing and Urban Develop-
ment. Mass Transportation Demonstration
Grant Program. Tennessee. IV. Title.

388
(71354l)
T67t
TRANSPORTATION - TORONTO.
Toronto. Bureau of Municipal Research.
Transportation. Who plans? Who pays?
Toronto, 1970.
24p.

Civic affairs, Autumn, 1970.

1. Transportation - Toronto. I. Title.
II. Civic affairs.

Transportation - U.K.

388
(41)
F67
Foster, C   D
The transport problem. London,
Blackie, 1963.
354p.

1. Transportation - U.K. 2. Journey
to work.

Transportation - Tennessee.

388
(768)
036
O'Donnell, Claude W
Cooperative transportation planning
in Tennessee by Claude W. O'Donnell
and William H. Wilson. Saugatuck, Conn.,
Eno Foundation for Highway Traffic
Control, 1962.
499-509p.

Reprint, Traffic quarterly, Oct. 1962.

1. Transportation - Tennessee. I. Wilson,
William H., jt. au.   II. Title.

388
(71354l)
T67
Transportation - Toronto.

Toronto. Planning Board.
Metropolitan Toronto transportation
research program. Prepared by the
Metropolitan Toronto Planning Board.
Consultants: Traffic Research Corporation
(K.C.S. Ltd) Toronto, 1962.
79p. (Report no. 1)
Bibliography: p. i-iii.

1. Transportation - Toronto.
2. Journey to work.

330.15
N178
NO.40
TRANSPORTATION - U.K.
HULTGREN, THOR.
TRANSPORT AND THE STATE OF TRADE IN
BRITAIN. [NEW YORK] 1953.
114P. (NATIONAL BUREAU OF ECONOMIC
RESEARCH. OCCASIONAL PAPER 40)

1. TRANSPORTATION - U.K. 2. TRAFFIC
- U.K. I. TITLE. II. SERIES:
NATIONAL BUREAU OF ECONOMIC RESEARCH.
OCCASIONAL PAPER, NO. 40.

VF
388
T25r
1959
Transportation - Tennessee Valley.

Tennessee Valley Authority.
River traffic and industrial growth.
Rev. Knoxville, Tenn., 1959.
16p.

1. Transportation - Tennessee Valley.
2. Industrial location - Tennessee
Valley. I. Title.

388
(74811)
P25
Transportation - Trenton.

Penn Jersey Transportation Study.
Regional planning: Functions, program,
structure, by H.W. Bruck, Director, Division
of Regional Planning. Philadelphia, 1963.
9p. (Its PJD background paper no. 3)
1. Transportation - Philadelphia.
2. Transportation - Trenton. 3. Transportation
- Wilmington, Del. 4. Regional planning - Pa.-
N.J.-Del. 5. Journey to work. I. Bruck,
H.W. II. Title.

711.4
(41)
R29
Transportation - U.K.

Reynolds, D   J
Economics, town planning and traffic.
London, Institute of Economic Affairs, 1966.
166p.

1. City planning - U.K. 2. City planning
- Economic effect. 3. Industrial location
- U.K. 4. Urban renewal - U.K. 5. Econom-
ic development - U.K. 6. Population
shifts - U.K. 7. Transportation - U.K.
I. Institute of Economic Affairs, London.
II. Title.

388
T29
Transportation - Texas.

Texas. Legislative Council.
Balanced transportation for Texas cities; a
report to the 60th Legislature. Austin, Tex.,
1966.
87p.

1. Transportation - Texas. I. Title.

388
(791)
E15
Transportation - Tucson, Ariz.

Ealy, William G
The transportation planning process in
Tucson. Denver Urban Transportation Planning
Conference, Sept. 19-20, 1962. [Tucson,
Ariz.] 1962.
12p.

1. Transportation - Tucson, Ariz.
I. Denver Urban Transportation Planning
Conference, 1962.

388
S31
Transportation - U.K.

Sharp, Clifford.
Problems of urban passenger transport;
with special reference to Leicester.
Leicester, Eng., Leicester University Press,
1967.
118p.

1. Transportation - U.K. 2. U.K. - Transportation. 3. Journey to work. 4. Railroads -
U.K. 5. U.K. - Railroads. I. Title.

711.4
(593)
L47t
Transportation - Thailand.

Litchfield Whiting Bowne and Associates.
Bangkok-Thonburi city planning project;
travel time. A study of the time factor
in alternate forms of transportation
serving the Bangkok Metropolitan area and
an evaluation of the city's road system
in terms of traffic travel time. [In
cooperation with] Adams, Howard and
Greeley, city planning consultants to
the Ministry of Interior, Government of
Thailand. New York, 1959.
5p. (Technical monograph)
(Cont'd. on next card)

388
(791)
T82
Tucson Area Transportation Planning Agency.
Tucson Area Transportation Study: Vol. 1.
Inventory and analysis of existing conditions,
1960. Vol.2. Forecasts and the plan 1965.
Sponsoring agencies, City of Tucson, County
of Pima, State of Arizona in cooperation
with U.S. Dept. of Commerce, Bureau of Public
Roads. Tucson, Ariz., 1965.
2v.
Cover title on v.2. Forecasts and plans,
1980.

(Cont'd on next card)

388
:331
S78
Transportation - U.K.

Sturt, Alan R
The relationship between distance and
commuting to central London, 1951-1961.
London, London School of Economics and
Political Science, Graduate Geography Dept.,
1968.
12p. (London School of Economics and
Political Science. Graduate School of Economics and Political Science. Discussion
paper no. 25)
1. Journey to work. 2. Transportation - U.K.
3. U.K. - Transportation. I. London School of
Economics and Political Science. Graduate
School of   Geography. II. Title.

711.4
(593)
L47t
Litchfield Whiting Bowne and Associates.
Bangkok-Thonburi city planning project;
travel time...1959.   (Card 2)

1. City planning - Thailand.
2. Transportation - Thailand. 3. Journey to
work. I. Thailand. Ministry of Interior.
II. Adams, Howard and Greeley.

388
(791)
T82
Tucson Area Transportation Planning Agency.
Tucson Area Transportation Study...1965.
(Card 2)

1. Transportation - Tucson, Ariz. 2. Trans-
portation - Research. 3. Highways - Tucson,
Ariz. 4. Land use - Tucson, Ariz. I. U.S.
Bureau of Public Roads. II. Title.

388
:331
T36j
TRANSPORTATION - U.K.

Thomas, Ray.
Journey to work. [London, PEP
[Political and Economic Planning] 1968
419p.

Planning, vol. XXXIV, no. 504, Nov.
1968.

1. Journey to work. 2. Transportation -
U.K. I. Political and Economic Planning.

388
(75963)
T36
Transportation - Thomson, Ga.

Thomson, Ga. Planning Commission.
Thomson, Georgia: transportation
study, transportation survey, central
business district, major street plan,
by Sydney Carter. Prepared under contract with the Georgia Dept. of Commerce.
Thomson, 1960.
32p.

U.S. Urban Renewal Adm. UPAP.

1. Transportation - Thomson, Ga. 2. Business
districts - Thomson, Ga.   I. U.S.
URA-UPAP.   Thomson, Ga.

388
(764)
T29t
v.1
Transportation - Tyler, Tex.

Texas. Highway Dept.
Tyler urban transportation study. Vol. 1.
Origin-destination survey. Sponsoring
agencies; City of Tyler, County of Smith
[and] Texas Highway Dept. in cooperation
with U.S. Dept. of Commerce, Bureau of
Public Roads. [Austin?] 1964.
1 v.

1. Transportation - Tyler, Tex.
2. Journey to work. 3. Transportation -
Statistics.   I. U.S. Bureau of
Public Roads.   II. Title.

711.3
(41)
U54s
Transportation - U.K.

U.K. H.M. Stationery Office.
South East England. Presented to
Parliament by the Secretary of State for
Industry, Trade and Regional Development,
and the Minister of Housing and Local
Government and Minister for Welsh Affairs
by Command of Her Majesty. London, 1964.
7p. (Cmnd. 2308)

1. Regional planning - U.K.
2. Transportation - U.K.

Transportation - U.K. 388 (41) U54c U.K. Ministry of Transport. Cars for cities. A study of trends in the design of vehicles with particular reference to their use in towns. Reports of the Steering Group and Working Group appointed by the Minister of Transport. London, H.M.S.O., 1967. 107p. 1. Transportation - U.K. 2. Traffic. 3. Air pollution. I. Title.	**Transportation - Vancouver, Wash. metropolitan area.** 388 (79549) P67 Portland-Vancouver Metropolitan Transportation Study. Interim report 1-205, location. Prepared by the Technical Advisory Committee in cooperation with the U.S. Dept. of Commerce, Bureau of Public Roads, and U.S. Housing and Home Finance Agency. [Salem, Or.] State Highway Commission, 1964. 54p. 1. Transpor- tation - Portland, Or. metropol- itan area. 2. Trans- portation - Vancouver, Wash. (Continued on next card)	5492 **TRANSPORTATION - VERMONT.** VERMONT. CENTRAL PLANNING OFFICE. TRANSPORTATION. BY SARGENT, WEBSTER, CRENSHAW AND FOLLEY. MONTPELIER, 1966. 130L. (HUD 701 REPORT) 1. TRANSPORTATION - VERMONT. I. SARGENT, WEBSTER, CRENSHAW AND FOLLEY. II. HUD. 701. VERMONT.
Transportation - U.K. 388 (41) U54 U.K. Ministry of Transport. Traffic in towns; a study of the long term problems of traffic in urban areas. Report of the Steering Group and Working Group appointed by the Minister of Transport. London, H.M. Stat. Off., 1963. 223p. Report of Working Group in the Ministry is led by Colin D. Buchanan. 1. Traffic - U.K. 2. Parking - U.K. 3. Transpor- tation - U.K. 4. Journey to work. I. Buchanan (Colin D.) Report.	388 (79549) P67 Portland-Vancouver Metropolitan Transportation Study. Interim report 1-205, location...1964. (Card 2) metropolitan area. 3. Transportation - Economic effect. 4. Journey to work. I. Oregon. State Highway Commission. II. U.S.. Housing and Home Finance Agency.	4998 **TRANSPORTATION - VERMONT.** VERMONT. CENTRAL PLANNING OFFICE. TRANSPORTATION. STATE OF VERMONT. MONTEPELIER, 1966. 130L. (HUD 701 REPORT) 1. TRANSPORTATION - VERMONT. I. HUD. 701. VERMONT.
Transportation - U.K. 388 (41) U54t U.K. Ministry of Transport. Transport policy. Presented to Parliament by the Minister of Transport, by Command of Her Majesty. London, H.M. Stat. Off., 1966. 36p. ((U.K. Parliament. Papers by command) cmnd. 3057) 1. Transportation - U.K. 2. Railroads - U.K. I. Title.	**Transportation - Vancouver, Wash. metropolitan area.** 388 (79549) P67p v.1 Portland-Vancouver Metropolitan Transportation Study. Portland-Vancouver Metropolitan Transportation Study. Vol. 1. Factual data report. Prepared in cooperation with the U.S. Dept. of Commerce, Bureau of Public Roads. Salem, Or., State Highway Commission, [1964?] 135p. 1. Transportation - Portland, Or. metropolitan area. 2. Transportation - Vancouver, Wash. metropolitan area. 3. (Continued on next card)	**Transportation - Virginia.** 388 (755) B17 pt.2 Bartholomew (Harland) and Associates. Economics, population, land use. Virginia Peninsula area comprehensive transportation planning study, pt. 2. Wash., 1965. 2 pts. Prepared in cooperation with Virginia Dept. of Highways and U.S. Dept. of Commerce, Bureau of Public Roads. pt. 2 Statistical appendix. 1.Transportation - Virginia. 2. Population - Virginia. 3. Land use - Virginia. 4. Economic conditions - Virginia.
Transportation - U.S.S.R. 711.4 (47) A41p no.10 Akademiia stroitel'stva i arkhitektury SSSR. Institut gradostroitel'stva i raionnoi planirovki. Gorodskoe dvizhenie i transport. Moskva, Gosudarstvennoe izdatelstvo literaturi po stroitelstvu, arkhitekture i stroitelnim materialam, 1963. 144p. (Problemi sovetskogo gradostroitel- stva no. 10) 1. City planning - U.S.S.R. 2. Transporta- tion - U.S.S.R. 3. U.S.S.R. - Transportation. 4. U.S.S.R. - City planning.	388 (79549) P67p v.1 Portland-Vancouver Metropolitan Transportation Study. Portland-Vancouver Metropolitan Transportation Study. Vol. 1...1964. (Card 2) Economic effect. 4. Journey to work. I. Oregon. State Highway Commission.	4865 FOLIO 4866 FOLIO 4867 FOLIO 4868 FOLIO **TRANSPORTATION - VIRGINIA.** RICHMOND, VA. REGIONAL PLANNING COMMISSION. RICHMOND REGIONAL AREA TRANSPORTATION STUDY: 1. CURRENT AND PROJECTED TRAVEL PATTERNS; 2. HIGHWAY TRANSPORTATION PLAN AND IMPLEMENTATION PROGRAM; 3. PUBLIC TRANSPORTATION, AN EVALUATION OF SERVICE LEVELS AND PATRONS' DEMANDS; 5. RECOMMENDED THOROUGHFARE PLAN, STREET INVENTORY, FUNCTIONAL PLANS, AND COST ESTIMATES. BY WILBUR SMITH AND ASSOCIATES, 1967-68. 4 V. (HUD 701 REPORT) (CONTINUED ON NEXT CARD)
Transportation - Union of Soviet Socialist Republics. 388 (47) H85 Hunter, Holland. Soviet transport experience: its lessons for other countries. Wash., Brookings Institution, Transport Research Program, 1968. 194p. 1. Transportation - Union of Soviet Socialist Republics. I. Brookings Institution. Transport Research Program. II. Title.	**Transportation - Vancouver, Wash. metropolitan area.** 388 (79549) P67po Portland-Vancouver Metropolitan Transportation Study. Social-economic study. Interim report 1-205, location. Prepared by Bureau of Municipal Research and Service, University of Oregon for Oregon State Highway Commission in cooperation with the U.S. Dept. of Commerce, Bureau of Public Roads. [Salem, Or.?] 1964. 67p. (Continued on next card)	4865 FOLIO 4866 FOLIO 4867 FOLIO 4868 FOLIO RICHMOND, VA. REGIONAL PLANNING COMMISSION. RICHMOND REGIONAL AREA ... 7-68. (CARD 2) 1. TRANSPORTATION - VIRGINIA. 2. TRANSPORTATION - RICHMOND, VA. I. SMITH (WILBUR) AND ASSOCIATES. II. HUD. 701. VIRGINIA. III. HUD. 701. RICHMOND, VA.
TRANSPORTATION - U.S.S.R. 330.15 N17o no.65 Williams, Ernest W Freight transportation in the Soviet Union: a comparison with the United States, by Ernest W. Williams, Jr., assisted by George Novak. New York, 1959. 38 p. (National Bureau of Economic Research. Occasional paper 65). 1. Transportation - U.S.S.R. 2. Transpor- tation. I. Title. II. National Bureau of Economic Research. Occasional paper 65.	388 (79549) P67po Portland-Vancouver Metropolitan Transportation Study. Social- economic study...1964. (Card 2) 1. Transportation - Portland, Or. metropolitan area. 2. Transportation - Vancouver, Wash. metropolitan area. 3. Transportation - Economic effect. 4. Journey to work. I. Oregon. University. Bureau of Municipal Research and Service. II. Oregon. State Highway Commission.	**Transportation - Wall, N.J.** 711.4 (74946) W15t New Jersey. Dept. of Conservation and Economic Development. (Div. of Planning and Development) Wall Township, Monmouth County, New Jersey: preliminary master plan studies. Thorough- fares and traffic, public transportation, air service, freight service. Prepared for the Wall Township Planning Board, Trenton, 1958. 20p. U.S. Urban Renewal Adm. UPAP. 1. Master plan - Wall, N.J. 2. Transporta- tion - Wall, N.J. I. Wall, N.J. Township Planning Board. II. U.S. URA-UPAP. Wall, N.J.
TRANSPORTATION - VANCOUVER, B.C. 388 (711) H62 HODGE, GERALD. JOBS, PEOPLE AND TRANSPORTATION, THEIR ROLE IN METROPOLITAN PHYSICAL DEVELOPMENT; A REPORT TO THE METROPOLITAN JOINT COMMITTEE, BY GERALD HODGE AND IRA M. ROBINSON. VANCOUVER, B.C., 1960. 134L. 1. TRANSPORTATION - VANCOUVER, B.C. I. ROBINSON, IRA M., JT. AU. II. TITLE.	**TRANSPORTATION - VENEZUELA.** 388 (87) S61 SOBERMAN, RICHARD M TRANSPORT TECHNOLOGY FOR DEVELOPING REGIONS; A STUDY OF ROAD TRANSPORTATION IN VENEZUELA. CAMBRIDGE, MASS., M.I.T. PRESS, 1966. 177P. (A PUBLICATION OF THE JOINT CENTER FOR URBAN STUDIES OF THE MASSACHUSETTS INSTITUTE OF TECHNOLOGY AND HARVARD UNIVERSITY) 1. TRANSPORTATION - VENEZUELA. I. JOINT CENTER FOR URBAN STUDIES. II. TITLE.	**Transportation - Wartime.** 388 :840.42 D23 U.S. Office of Defense Transportation. Civilian war transport; a record of the control of domestic traffic operations by the Office of Defense Transportation, 1941-1946. Washington, D. C., Govt. Print. Off. [1948] ix, 361 p. charts, graphs, tables. J. Monroe Johnson, Director. 1.Transportation-Wartime. I.Title.

711.585
N17
UDB2

Transportation - Wartime.
U.S. National Housing Agency. Office of the
Administrator. Division of Urban Studies.
The Radford, Virginia, housing-and-transportation plan; an example of coordinated programming
for war housing and transportation. Washington,
D.C., Aug. 31, 1942.
4 l. (Its Bulletin no. 2)

Mimeographed.

711.585
N17
UDB9

Transportation - Wartime.
U.S. National Housing Agency. Office of the
Administrator. Division of Urban Studies.
Transportation problems and war housing.
Washington, D.C., Dec. 1942.
15 p. (Its Bulletin no. 9)

"Bulletin no. 9...supersedes the former
bulletins 1, 5, and 7."-p.1.

711.585
N17
UDB1

Transportation - Wartime.
U.S. National Housing Agency. Office of the
Administrator. Division of Urban Studies.
Transportation problems in war housing
programs. Washington, D.C., July 27, 1942.
5 l. (Its Bulletin no. 1)

Superseded by Bulletin no. 9, Dec. 1942.
Mimeographed.

1.Transportation-Wartime. I.Title.

383
:940.42
(016)
L67

Transportation - Wartime. - Bibl.

Los Angeles Railway Corporation. Library.
Mass transportation in relation to national
defense; a selected bibliography. Los
Angeles, Aug. 1941.
20 L. (Los Angeles. Public Library.
Municipal Reference Library. Defense series,
no. 7)

1. Transportation - Wartime. - Bibl.
I. Title.

388
(753)
R27

TRANSPORTATION - WASHINGTON, D.C.
RESOURCES FOR THE FUTURE, INC.
THE WASHINGTON TRANSPORTATION PLAN;
TECHNICS OR POLITICS, BY LOWDON WINGO,
JR. AND HARVEY S. PERLOFF. WASHINGTON,
D.C., 1962.
8P. (ITS REPRINT NO. 34)

1. TRANSPORTATION - WASHINGTON, D.C.
I. TITLE. II. WINGO, LOWDON.
III. PERLOFF, HARVEY S., JT. AU.

388
(753)
S29

TRANSPORTATION - WASHINGTON, D.C.
SEXTON, BURTON H
ANALYSIS OF COMMUTER SERVICE ON
RAILROADS AND INTER-CITY BUSSES SERVING
THE WASHINGTON NATIONAL CAPITAL REGION,
FOR MASS TRANSPORTATION SURVEY SPONSORED
BY NATIONAL CAPITAL PLANNING COMMISSION,
NATIONAL CAPITAL REGIONAL PLANNING
COUNCIL. WASHINGTON, GOVT. PRINT. OFF.,
1956.
33P.

1. TRANSPORTATION - WASHINGTON, D.C.
2. TRAFFIC - WASHINGTON, D.C.
I. U.S. NATIONAL CAPITAL PLANNING
(CONTINUED ON NEXT

388
(753)
S29

SEXTON, BURTON H ANALYSIS OF COMMUTER
....1956. (CARD 2)
COMMISSION. II. U.S. NATIONAL CAPITAL
REGIONAL PLANNING COUNCIL. III. TITLE:
MASS TRANSPORTATION SURVEY.

388
(797)
D25

Transportation - Washington (State)
De Leuw, Cather & Company.
Interim report to the Puget Sound Governmental Conference on transit facilities required on the Third Lake Washington Bridge.
San Francisco, 1964.
14p.

U.S. Urban Renewal Adm. UPAP.

1. Transportation - Washington (State)
2. Bridges. I. Puget Sound Governmental
Conference. II. U.S. URA-UPAP. Washington (State)

388
(797)
D25r

Transportation - Washington (State)
De Leuw, Cather and Company.
Report to the Puget Sound Governmental
Conference on a regional transit plan.
San Francisco, 1966.
49p.

U.S. Urban Renewal Adm. UPAP.

1. Transportation - Washington (State)
2. Transportation - Finance. 3. Journey to
work. I. Puget Sound Governmental Conference.
II. U.S. URA-   UPAP. Washington
(State)

388
(7977)
J67

Transportation - Washington (State)
Joshi, Rajanikant N
Alternative patterns of development,
Puget Sound Region - 20, by R. N. Joshi
and Fred Utevsky. Preliminary draft.
Seattle, Puget Sound Regional Transportation Study, 1964.
18p. (Summary report and supplement
to Staff report no. 5)
Prepared in cooperation with the U.S.
Housing and Home Finance Agency.
1. Transportation - Washington (State)
I. Puget Sound   Regional Transportation Study.   II. Utevsky, Fred,
jt. au.   III. U.S. Housing
and Home   Finance Agency.

711.333
(74882)
W17
no.4

Transportation - Washington Co., Pa.

Hill (Carroll V.) and Associates.
Transportation and public services,
Greater Washington Region, Pennsylvania.
[Prepared for] Regional Planning
Commission of Greater Washington,
Pennsylvania. Dayton, Ohio, 1959.
36p. (Comprehensive plan rept. no.
4)
U.S. Urban Renewal Adm. UPAP.

(Cont'd. on next card)

711.333
(74882)
W17
no.4

Hill (Carroll V.) and Associates.
Transportation and public services ...
(Card 2)

1. Master plan - Washington Co., Pa.
2. Transportation - Washington Co.,
Pa. 3. Municipal services - Washington
Co., Pa. I. Greater Washington (Pa.)
Regional Planning Commission. II. U.S.
URA-UPAP. Washington Co., Pa.

388
(7467)
V66

Transportation-Waterbury, Conn.
Voorhees (Alan M.) and Associates.
A component of the Waterbury Area
Transportation Study. Results of Community
Planning Survey of the Central Naugatuck
Valley Region. Washington, 1962.
25p.
U.S. Urban Renewal Adm. UPAP.

1. Transportation - Waterbury, Conn.
2. Community development - Naugatuck,
Conn. I. Waterbury, Conn. Area Transportation Study.   II. U.S. URA-UPAP.
Waterbury,   Conn.

6046

TRANSPORTATION - WATERLOO, IOWA.
BLACK HAWK CO., IOWA. METROPOLITAN
PLANNING COMMISSION.
WATERLOO METROPOLITAN AREA
TRANSPORTATION STUDY. BY ALAN M.
VOORHEES AND ASSOCIATES. WATERLOO, IOWA,
1968.
45P. (HUD 701 REPORT)

1. TRANSPORTATION - BLACK HAWK CO.,
IOWA. 2. TRANSPORTATION - WATERLOO,
IOWA. I. VOORHEES (ALAN M.) AND
ASSOCIATES. II. HUD. 701. BLACK HAWK
CO., IOWA. III. HUD. 701.
WATERLOO, IOWA.

4906

TRANSPORTATION - WEBER CO., UTAH.
WEBER CO., UTAH. PLANNING COMMISSION.
TRANSPORTATION. OGDEN, 1968.
25P. (HUD 701 REPORT)

1. TRANSPORTATION - WEBER CO., UTAH.
I. HUD. 701. WEBER CO., UTAH.

388
(74727)
W27w

Transportation - Westchester Co., N.Y.

Westchester Co., N.Y. Dept. of Planning.
Westchester commuting patterns.
White Plains, N.Y., 1963.
47p.

1. Transportation - Westchester Co.,
N.Y. 2. Journey to work.

388
(79)
B56

TRANSPORTATION - WESTERN STATES.
Blood, Dwight.
Transportation in the Rocky Mountain West,
by Dwight Blood, Ronald Babcock and James
Hardee. Denver, Federation of Rocky Mountain
States, inc., 1970.
1v. (Regional planning program. Background
paper 1)
Preliminary draft- for review.

1. Transportation - Western states.
I. Federation of Rocky Mountain States.
II. Title.

388
(79)
T71

TRANSPORTATION - WESTERN STATES.
Transportation problems and policies in the
trans-Missouri west. Edited by Jack R.
Davidson and Howard W. Ottoson. Lincoln,
University of Nebraska Press [1967]
377p.
"Papers presented at a workshop on
transportation sponsored jointly by the
Great Plains Resource Economics Committee
and the Western Marketing Research
Committee...held at Denver, November 30
to December 2, 1965."

(Cont'd on next card)

711.4
(74974)
W31c

Transportation - Wharton, N.J.

New Jersey. Dept. of Conservation and
Economic Development. (Div. of Planning
and Development)
Wharton Borough, Morris County, New
Jersey; preliminary master plan studies.
Circulation and transportation, thorofares
and traffic, public transportation. Prepared for the Wharton Planning Board.
[Trenton] 1958.
13p.
U.S. Urban Renewal Adm. UPAP.
1. Master plan -   Wharton, N.J.
2. Transportation -   Wharton, N.J.
I. Wharton, N.J. Plan-   ning Board.
II. U.S. URA-UPAP.   Wharton, N.J.

388
(78186)
Wi2

Transportation - Wichita metropolitan area.

Wichita-Sedgwick County, Kan.
Metropolitan Area Planning Dept.
Prospectus for the conduct of a
comprehensive transportation study for
the Wichita metropolitan area.
[Wichita,] 1961.
11p.

1. Transportation - Wichita
metropolitan area.

388
(74832)
L89

Transportation - Wilkes-Barre/Hazleton, Pa.

Luzerne County, Pa. Planning
Commission.
Transportation report; Wilkes-Barre/
Hazleton metropolitan area of Pennsylvania.
[Wilkes-Barre] 1960.
76p.

U.S. Urban Renewal Adm. UPAP.

1. Transportation - Wilkes-Barre/
Hazleton, Pa. I U.S. URA-UPAP.
Wilkes-Barre/   Hazleton, Pa.

388
(74832)
L89t

Transportation - Wilkes-Barre/Hazleton, Pa. metropolitan area
Luzerne County, Pa. Planning Commission.
Trucking report. Part of the comprehensive plan of the Wilkes-Barre/Hazleton metropolitan area, Pennsylvania. Wilkes-Barre, Pa., 1961.
48p.
U.S. Urban Renewal Adm. UPAP.
1. Transportation - Wilkes-Barre/Hazleton, Pa. metropolitan area. 2. Master plan - Wilkes-Barre/Hazleton, Pa. metropolitan area. I. U.S. URA-UPAP. Wilkes-Barre/Hazleton, Pa. metropolitan area.

388
(775)
S68
v.2

Southeastern Wisconsin Regional Planning Commission. Land use-transportation study...1966. (Card 2)
1. Transportation - Wis. 2. Land use - Wis. 3. State planning - Wis. I. U.S. HUD-UPAP. Wis.

388
(74841)
Y67

Transportation - York Co., Pa.
York County, Pa. Planning Commission.
Mass transit study; a portion of the transportation section of the York County comprehensive plan and the York Area transportation study. York, Pa., 1965.
37p.
Prepared in cooperation with the Pennsylvania Dept. of Highways.
U.S. Urban Renewal Adm. UPAP.
1. Transportation - York Co., Pa. 2. Master plan - York Co., Pa. 3. Journey to work. I. Pennsylvania. Dept. of Highways. II. U.S. URA-UPAP. York Co., Pa.

388
(7512)
D25

Transportation - Wilmington, Del.
Delaware. University. Bureau of Economic and Business Research.
An analysis of mass transportation in Wilmington, Delaware, by Robert W. Lang, edited by Blaine G. Schmidt. [Newark, Del.] 1965.
73p.
1. Transportation - Wilmington, Del. 2. Journey to work. I. Lang, Robert W. II. Schmidt, Blaine G., ed. III. Title.

5344

TRANSPORTATION - WISCONSIN.
SOUTHEASTERN WISCONSIN REGIONAL PLANNING COMMISSION.
PROSPECTUS FOR A CONTINUING LAND USE TRANSPORTATION STUDY. WAUKESHA, WIS., CA. 1968.
39L. (HUD 701 REPORT)
1. LAND USE - WISCONSIN.
2. TRANSPORTATION - WISCONSIN. I. HUD. 701. WISCONSIN.

711.4
(771391)
Y68
no. 8

Transportation - Youngstown, Ohio.
Pace Associates.
Streets and transportation in Youngstown. Chicago, 195-.
40p. maps, tables. (Youngstown comprehensive plan report no. 8)
1. Master plan - Youngstown, Ohio. 2. Street planning - Youngstown, Ohio. 3. Transportation - Youngstown, Ohio. (Series)

388
(74811)
P25

Transportation - Wilmington, Del.
Penn Jersey Transportation Study.
Regional planning: Functions, program, structure, by H.W. Bruck, Director, Division of Regional Planning. Philadelphia, 1963.
9p. (Its PJD background paper no. 3)
1. Transportation - Philadelphia. 2. Transportation - Trenton. 3. Transportation - Wilmington, Del. 4. Regional planning - Pa.-N.J.-Del. 5. Journey to work. I. Bruck, H.W. II. Title.

5345

TRANSPORTATION - WISCONSIN.
SOUTHEASTERN WISCONSIN REGIONAL PLANNING COMMISSION.
STUDY DESIGN FOR THE CONTINUING LAND USE - TRANSPORTATION STUDY. WAUKESHA, WIS., 1967.
38L. (HUD 701 REPORT)
1. LAND USE - WISCONSIN.
2. TRANSPORTATION - WISCONSIN. I. HUD. 701. WISCONSIN.

388
(77435)
M42

Transportation - Ypsilanti, Mich.
Michigan. State Highway Dept.
Ann Arbor-Ypsilanti urban area transportation study. Preliminary report. Lansing, Mich., 1966.
1v.
1. Transportation - Ann Arbor, Mich. 2. Transportation - Ypsilanti, Mich. I. Title.

388
(758195)
W45

Transportation - Winder, Ga.
Winder, Ga. Planning Commission.
Transportation study, Winder, Georgia: major street plan, central business district, by Sydney Carter. Prepared under contract with the Georgia Dept. of Commerce. Winder, 1960.
65p. Addendum.
U.S. Urban Renewal Adm. UPAP.
1. Transportation - Winder, Ga. 2. Street planning - Winder, Ga. 3. Business districts - Winder, Ga. I. U.S. URA-UPAP. Winder, Ga.

388
(775)
S68t

Transportation - Wis.
Southeastern Wisconsin Regional Planning Commission.
Truck and taxi survey. Land use-transportation study. Rev. Waukesha, Wis., 1964.
49p. (Its Procedural manual no. 3)
Prepared in cooperation with State Highway Commission of Wisconsin, the U.S. Dept. of Commerce, Bureau of Public Roads.
U.S. Urban Renewal Adm. UPAP.
1. Transportation - Wis. 2. Traffic surveys - Wis. I. Title. II. U.S. URA-UPAP. Wis.

711.3
(4971)
A52
no.8

TRANSPORTATION - YUGOSLAVIA.
American-Yugoslav Project in Regional and Urban Planning Studies.
Development of transportation networks, by Lojze Gosar. Ljubljana, 1970.
30p. (Urbanisticni Institut. Spatial policies for regional development; a demonstration study of the Ljubljana region. Technical report no 8)
1. Regional planning - Yugoslavia. 2. Transportation - Yugoslavia. I. Urbanisticni Institut, Ljubljana. II. Gosar, Lojze. III. Title.

5346

TRANSPORTATION - WISCONSIN.
SOUTHEASTERN WISCONSIN REGIONAL PLANNING COMMISSION.
FIRST CONTINUING REGIONAL LAND USE - TRANSPORTATION STUDY, JULY 1, 1966, THROUGH DECEMBER 31, 1969. PROJECT COMPLETION REPORT. WAUKESHA, WIS., 1970.
38L. (HUD 701 REPORT)
1. LAND USE - WISCONSIN.
2. TRANSPORTATION - WISCONSIN. I. HUD. 701. WISCONSIN.

FOLIO
388
(775)
W47

Transportation - Wisconsin.
Wisconsin. Dept. of Resource Development.
Intercity transportation in Wisconsin. [Prepared in cooperation with] the State Highway Commission. Madison, 1962.
59p.
Consultant: Wilbur Smith and Associates.
U.S. Urban Renewal Adm. UPAP.
1. Transportation - Wisconsin. 2. Highways - Wisconsin. I. Wisconsin. State Highway Commission. II. Smith (Wilbur) and Associates.

711.3
(4971)
A52
no.12

TRANSPORTATION - YUGOSLAVIA.
American-Yugoslav Project in Regional and Urban Planning Studies.
The evaluation of alternative patterns of spatial organization for the Ljubljana urban region. Ljubljana Urbanisticni Institut SRS, 1970.
2pts. (Urbanisticni Institut, Ljubljana. Spatial policies for regional development; a demonstration study of the Ljubljana region. Technical report no. 12)
1. Regional planning - Yugoslavia. 2. Housing - Yugoslavia. 3. Industrial
(Cont'd on next card)

388
(775)
S68
v.1

Transportation - Wis.
Southeastern Wisconsin Regional Planning Commission.
Land use: transportation study. Vol. 1. Inventory findings, 1963. Waukesha, Wis., 1965.
192p. (Its Planning rept. no. 7, vol. 1)
U.S. Urban Renewal Adm. UPAP.
1. Transportation - Wis. 2. Land use - Wis. I. Title. II. U.S. URA-UPAP. Wis.

386
(775)
W66

Transportation - Wisconsin.
Wood, Donald F
Urban waterfront problems and development planning; aesthetic approach to future improvement. Madison, Wis., 1965.
[12]p.
Reprinted from the Dock and harbour authority, Oct. and Nov., 1965.
Distributed by Wisconsin Dept. of Resource Development.
1. Harbors - Wisconsin. 2. Transportation - Wisconsin. 3. Recreation - Wisconsin. I. Wisconsin. Dept. of Resource Development.

711.3
(4971)
A52
no.12

American-Yugoslav Project in Regional and Urban Planning Studies. The evaluation... 1970. (Card 2)
location - Yugoslavia. 4. Transportation - Yugoslavia. 5. Agriculture - Yugoslavia. I. Urbanisticni Institut, Ljubljana. II. Title.

388
(775)
S68
v.2

Transportation - Wis.
Southeastern Wisconsin Regional Planning Commission.
Land use-transportation study. Vol 2: Forecasts and alternative plans, 1990. Waukesha, Wis., 1966.
256p. (Its Planning report no. 7, vol. 2)
Prepared in cooperation with State Highway Commission of Wisconsin, the U.S. Dept. of Commerce, Bureau of Public Roads.
U.S. Housing and Urban Development. UPAP.
(Cont'd on next card)

1531

TRANSPORTATION - YELLOW MEDICINE CO., MINN.
YELLOW MEDICINE CO., MINN. PLANNING ADVISORY COMMISSION.
LAND FACILITIES TRANSPORTATION. GRANITE FALLS, MINN., 1969.
47L. (HUD 701 REPORT)
1. TRANSPORTATION - YELLOW MEDICINE CO., MINN. I. HUD. 701. YELLOW MEDICINE CO., MINN.

388
(4971)
T39

TRANSPORTATION - YUGOSLAVIA.
Thyagarajan, S
Belgrade transportation and land use study; an overview. Detroit, Div. of International Urban Studies, Center for Urban Studies, Wayne State University, 1971.
45p. (Belgrade transportation and land use study no. 1)
1. Transportation - Yugoslavia. 2. Land use - Yugoslavia. II. Wayne State University, Detroit. Div. of International Urban Studies. III. Title.

388
C65T
1966
H-R

U.S. DEPT. OF TRANSPORTATION (PROPOSED)
U.S. CONGRESS. CONFERENCE COMMITTEES,
1966.
DEPARTMENT OF TRANSPORTATION ACT...
CONFERENCE REPORT TO ACCOMPANY H.R.
15963. WASHINGTON, GOVT. PRINT. OFF.,
1966.
29P. (89TH CONGRESS, 2D SESSION.
HOUSE. REPORT NO. 2236)

1. TRANSPORTATION. I. U.S. DEPT. OF
TRANSPORTATION (PROPOSED)

388
T71c

U.S. Dept. of Transportation.
Capital grants for urban mass transportation; information for applicants. Wash., U.S.
Dept. of Transportation, Urban Mass Transportation Administration, 1968.
10p.

2c

1. Transportation. 2. Journey to work.
I. Title.

388
H68g

U.S. Dept. of Transportation.
U.S. Dept. of Housing and Urban Development.
Grants for research and training in urban
transportation; information for applicants
(interim guide) Wash., Dept. of Housing and
Urban Transportation, 1968.
13p.

1. Transportation. I. U.S. Dept. of
Transportation. II. Title. III. Title:
Urban transportation.

388
C65t
1966
H-H

U.S. Dept. of Transportation (Proposed)
U.S. Congress. House. Committee on
Government Operations.
Creating a Department of Transportation.
(Part 1-2) Hearings before a subcommittee of
the Committee on Government Operations, House
of Representatives, Eighty-ninth Congress,
second session on H.R. 13200. A bill to
establish a Department of Transportation, and
for other purposes. Wash., Govt. Print.
Off., 1966.
2 pts.
Hearings held Apr. 6-June 21, 1966.

1. U.S. Dept. of   Transportation
(Proposed) 2. Trans-   portation.

388
C65ed

U.S. Dept. of Transportation.

Conference on Poverty and Transportation,
Brookline, Mass 1968.
Edited transcript of the Conference on
Poverty and Transportation, June 7, 1968,
sponsored by the Department of Housing and
Urban Development and the Department of
Transportation. Brookline, Mass., American
Academy of Arts and Sciences, 1968.
1v.

1. Transportation. 2. Social conditions.
3. Minority   groups. 4. Employment.
I. Title: Poverty and transporta-
(Cont'd on next card)

711.73
T71h1

U.S. Dept. of Transportation.
Highway relocation assistance study; a study
transmitted by the Secretary of the Dept. of
Transportation to the Congress, as required by
the Federal-aid highway act of 1966 (Public
law 89-574, 89th Cong., Sept. 13, 1966)
Wash., Govt. Print. Off., 1967.
235p.
At head of title: 90th Cong., 1st sess.
Committee print no. 9.
1. Highways. I. U.S. Congress. House.
Committee on Public   Works. II. Title.

2c

388
C65
1966

U.S. DEPT. OF TRANSPORTATION (PROPOSED)
U.S. CONGRESS. HOUSE. COMMITTEE ON
GOVERNMENT OPERATIONS.
DEPARTMENT OF TRANSPORTATION ACT.
REPORT TO ACCOMPANY H.R. 15963.
WASHINGTON, GOVT. PRINT. OFF., 1966.
106P. (89TH CONGRESS, 2D SESSION.
HOUSE. REPORT NO. 1701)

1. TRANSPORTATION. 2. U.S. DEPT. OF
TRANSPORTATION (PROPOSED)

388
C65ed

Conference on Poverty and Transportation,
(Brookline, Mass 1968. (Card 2)

tion. II. U.S. Dept. of Housing and Urban
Development. III. U.S. Dept. of Transportation. IV. American Academy of Arts and
Sciences.

711.73
T71h

U.S. Dept. of Transportation.
Highway safety programs standards; a report
from the Secretary of the Dept. of Transportation to the Congress, as required by the
Highway safety act of 1966 (Public Law 89-564, 89th Cong., S. 3052, Sept. 9, 1966)
Printed for the use of the Committee on
Public Works. Washington, Govt. Print. Off.,
1967.
40p.
At head of title: 90th Cong., 1st sess.
Committee print no. 7.

388
C65e

U.S. Dept. of Transportation (Proposed)
U.S. Congress. Senate. Committee on
Government Operations.
Establish a Department of Transportation.
Hearings before the Committee on Government
Operations, United States Senate, Eighty-ninth Congress, second session, on S. 3010,
a bill to establish a Dept. of Transportation
and for other purposes. Wash., Govt. Print.
Off., 1966.
4 pts.
Hearings held Mar.-June, 1966.

1. Transporta-   tion. 2. U.S. Dept.
of Transportation   (Proposed)

388
1(74461)
C31

U.S. Department of Transportation.
Charles River Associates.
An evaluation of free transit service.
Prepared for Office of Economics, Assistant
Secretary for Policy Development, Dept.
of Transportation, Wash., D.C. Cambridge,
Mass., 1968.
172p.
CFSTI PB 179 845.

1. Transportation - Boston. 2. Journey
to work. I. Title. II. U.S. Dept. of
Transportation.

711.73
T71h

U.S. Dept. of Transportation. Highway safety
programs standards...1967. (Card 2)

1. Highways. 2. Accidents. I. U.S. Congress. House. Committee on Public Works.
II. Boyd, Allen S. III. Title.

388
C65E
1966
S-R
REPT.1659

U.S. DEPT. OF TRANSPORTATION
(PROPOSED)
U.S. CONGRESS. SENATE. COMMITTEE
ON GOVERNMENT OPERATIONS.
ESTABLISHING A DEPARTMENT OF
TRANSPORTATION AND FOR OTHER
PURPOSES. REPORT TOGETHER WITH
ADDITIONAL VIEWS TO ACCOMPANY S.
3010. WASHINGTON, GOVT. PRINT.
OFF., 1966.
43P. (89TH CONGRESS, 2D SESSION.
SENATE. REPORT NO. 1659)

1. TRANSPORTATION. I. U.S.
DEPT. OF TRANSPORTATION (PROPOSED)

534.83
T71f

U.S. Dept. of Transportation.
Federal aircraft noise abatement plan,
FY 1969-70 - 70/71 71/72

Wash., Govt. Print. Off., 1969-
2v. annual.

2c, 1969-70-in.   For Library holdings see main entry.
new.

71/72   1. Noise. 2. Airports. I. Title.

384
T71

U.S. Dept. of Transportation.
Joint DOT-NASA civil aviation research and
development policy study. Report. Wash., Dept.
of Transportation and National Aeronautics and
Space Administration, 1971.
1v. (DOT TST-10-4; NASA SP-265)

1. Air transportation. I. U.S. National
Aeronautics and Space Administration. II. Title.

388
C65E
1966
S-R
REPT.1660

U.S. DEPT. OF TRANSPORTATION
(PROPOSED)
U.S. CONGRESS. SENATE. COMMITTEE
ON GOVERNMENT OPERATIONS.
ESTABLISHING A DEPARTMENT OF
TRANSPORTATION, AND FOR OTHER
PURPOSES. REPORT TO ACCOMPANY H.R.
15963. WASHINGTON, GOVT. PRINT.
OFF., 1966.
1L. (89TH CONGRESS, 2D SESSION.
SENATE. REPORT NO. 1660)

1. TRANSPORTATION. I. U.S.
DEPT. OF TRANSPORTATION (PROPOSED)

534.83
T71

U.S. Dept. of Transportation.
Federal aircraft noise abatement program.
Summary status report. Wash., Office of Noise
Abatement, Dept. of Transportation, 1968.
26p.
Bibliography: p. 22-26.

1. Noise. 2. Airports. I. Title. II. Title:
Aircraft noise abatement program.

384
T71j

U.S. Dept. of Transportation.
Joint DOT-NASA civil aviation research and
development policy study. Supporting papers.
Wash., Dept. of Transportation and National
Aeronautics and Space Administration, 1971.
1v. (DOT TST-10-5; NASA SP-266)

1. Air transportation. I. U.S. National
Aeronautics and Space Administration. II. Title.

VF
388
P72p

U.S. Dept. of Transportation (Proposed)
U.S. President, 1963   (Johnson)
Proposed Dept. of Transportation. Message
from the President of the United States,
transmitting a proposal for a Cabinet-Level
Dept. of Transportation consolidating various
existing transportation agencies. Wash.,
Govt. Print. Off., 1966.
14p.
At head of title: 89th Cong.
Document no. 399.

1. U.S. Dept. of Transportation (Proposed)
2. Transportation -   Legislation.
3. U.S. President -   Messages. I. Title.

VF
711.73
T71

U.S. Dept. of Transportation.
The Federal Highway Administration.
Created April 1, 1967, as part of the Dept.
of Transportation. Washington, U.S. Dept.
of Transportation, Federal Highway Administration, 1967.
folder.

1. U.S. Federal Highway Administration.
2. Highways. 3. Transportation.

388
T71m

U.S. Dept. of Transportation.
Metropolitan transportation planning seminars.
Wash., 1971.
48p.

Sponsored by the American Institute of Planners
for the Dept. of Transportation, Office of the
Assistant Secretary for Environment and Urban
Systems.

1. Transportation. I. American Institute of
Planners. II. Title.

2c

711.73
T71n   U.S. Dept. of Transportation.
     National highway needs report. Communica-
tion from the Secretary of Transportation.
Wash., Govt. Print. Off., 1972-
     v.
     Published in the Congressional series as
House document no.

     1. Highways. I. Title.

330
(083.41)
T71   U.S. Dept. of Transportation.
     Socioeconomic projections for subregions of
the Northeast Corridor through 1980. Wash.,
Northeast Corridor Transportation Project,
Office of High-Speed Ground Transportation,
U.S. Dept. of Transportation, 1969.
     45p.

     1. Economic conditions - Statistics.
     2. Economic forecasting. I. Title.
     II. Northeast Corridor Transportation Project.

     U.S. Dept. of Transportation.
388
M67t   Mott, George Fox, ed.
     Transportation century. [A compilation of
essays from various authors] Baton Rouge,
Louisiana State University Press, 1966.
     279p.
     Partial contents: President Johnson's
Transportation message of Mar. 2, 1966.

     1. Transportation. 2. U.S. Dept. of Trans-
portation. 3. U.S. President - Messages.
I. Title.

711.4
G25p   U.S. Dept. of Transportation.
     U.S. General Accounting Office.
     Progress and problems of urban and transpor-
tation planning. Report to the Congress by the
Comptroller General of the United States.
Department of Housing and Urban Development;
Department of Transportation. Wash., 1971.
     36p. (B-174182)

     1. City planning. 2. Transportation.
I. U.S. Dept. of Housing and Urban Development.
II. U.S. Dept. of Transportation. III. Title.

388
P65   U.S. Dept. of Transportation.
     Polenske, Karen R
     The study of transportation requirement using
national and multiregional input-output techniques. Cambridge, Harvard Economic Research
Project, 1967.
     71p.
     Prepared for the Secretary of Transportation
under contract.
     Distributed by U.S. Clearinghouse for
Federal Scientific and Technical Information as
document PB 174 742
     1. Transportation - Economic effect. 2. Indus-
try - Statistics. I. Harvard Economic Research Project.   (Cont'd on next card)

351
C65REO
1967
H-H
PLAN
NO.1   U.S. DEPT. OF TRANSPORTATION.
     U.S. CONGRESS. HOUSE. COMMITTEE ON
GOVERNMENT OPERATIONS.
     REORGANIZATION PLAN NO. 1 OF 1967
(CERTAIN FUNCTIONS RELATING TO SHIP
MORTGAGES) HEARING BEFORE A
SUBCOMMITTEE, NINETIETH CONGRESS, FIRST
SESSION. WASHINGTON, GOVT. PRINT.
OFF., 1967.
     16P.

     HEARING HELD, MARCH 21, 1967.
     1. U.S. EXECUTIVE DEPARTMENTS -
REORGANIZATION. 2. U.S. DEPT. OF
TRANSPORTATION. I. TITLE.

388
T71r   U.S. Dept. of Transportation.
     Report, 2d-4th-5th   1967/68-1970-71

     Washington, Govt. Print. Off., 1969-72
     v. annual.
     For Library holdings see main entry.

     1. U.S. Dept. of Transportation.
     2. Transportation. 3. Journey to work.

388
P65   Polenske, Karen R   The study of transportation requirement...1967.   Card 2)

     II. U.S. Dept. of Transportation. III. U.S.
Clearinghouse for Federal Scientific and
Technical Information. IV. Title.

351
P72REO
1967
H-D
PLAN
NO.1   U.S. DEPT. OF TRANSPORTATION.
     U.S. PRESIDENT, 1963-1969 (JOHNSON)
     REORGANIZATION PLAN NO. 1 OF 1967.
MESSAGE FROM THE PRESIDENT OF THE
UNITED STATES, TRANSFERRING FROM THE
SECRETARY OF COMMERCE TO THE SECRETARY
OF TRANSPORTATION AUTHORITY TO APPROVE
THE SURRENDER OF CERTAIN SHIPS
DOCUMENTS. WASHINGTON, GOVT. PRINT.
OFF., 1967.
     2P. (90TH CONGRESS, 1ST SESSION.
HOUSE OF REPRESENTATIVES. DOCUMENT NO.
60)

     1. U.S. EXECUTIVE DEPARTMENTS -
     (CONTINUED ON NEXT CARD)

388
T71rep   U.S. Dept. of Transportation.
     Report on urban area traffic operations
improvement programs (TOPICS) Report of the
Secretary of Transportation to the United
States Congress..., 1969
     Wash., Govt. Print. Off., 1970
     1 v.
     Published in the Congressional series as
Senate documents.
     For Library holdings see main entry.
     1. Traffic. I. Title: Urban area traffic
operations improvement programs.

711.73
(967)
T71   U.S. Dept. of Transportation.
     Territorial highway study: Guam, American
Samoa, Virgin Islands. Report of the
Secretary of Transportation to the United
States Congress pursuant to Section 29(b),
Public law 90-495, the Federal aid highway
act of 1968. Wash., Govt. Print. Off.,
1970.
     116p.
     At head of title: 91st Cong., 2d sess.
Senate. Document no. 91-62.
     1. Highways - Guam. 2. Highways -
American Samoa. 3. Highways -
Virgin Islands. I. Title.

351
P72REO
1967
H-D
PLAN
NO.1   U.S. PRESIDENT, 1963-1969 (JOHNSON)
     REORGANIZATION PLAN ...1967. (CARD 2)

     REORGANIZATION. 2. U.S. DEPT. OF
TRANSPORTATION. I. TITLE.

388
N17r   U.S. Dept. of Transportation.
     U.S. National Transportation Safety Board.
     Report to Congress, 1st-
1967-
     Washington, National Transportation Safety
Board, Dept. of Transportation, 1958-
     v. annual.

     For complete information see main card.

     1. Transportation. 2. Traffic safety.
I. U.S. Dept. of Transportation.

388
T71u   U.S. Dept. of Transportation. (Office
of Planning and Program Review)
     Urban commutation alternatives. Wash.,
1968.
     70p.

     1. Transportation. 2. Journey to work.
I. Title.

388
T71r   U.S. DEPT. OF TRANSPORTATION.
     U.S. Dept. of Transportation.
     Report. 1967/68.   19

     Washington, Govt. Print. Off., 19
     v. annual.

     For Library holdings see main entry.

     1. U.S. Dept. of Transportation.
     2. Transportation. 3. Journey to work.

     U.S. Dept. of Transportation.
388
:657
U54   United Research, inc.
     Responsibility accounting system and work
measurement for the motor carrier industry.
Prepared for Office of Transportation
Research, Office of the Under Secretary for
Transportation, U.S. Dept. of Commerce, Wash.,
D.C. Cambridge, Mass., 1966.
     1v.
     CFSTI PB 173202-2

     1. Transportation - Accounting. I. U.S.
Dept. of Transportation. II. Title.

VF
351
M22   U.S. DEPT. OF TRANSPORTATION.
     Meet the Press, Sunday, Feb. 2, 1969.
     Guests: Robert H. Finch, Secretary, Dept.
of Health, Education, and Welfare; George
Romney, Secretary, Dept. of Housing and Urban
Development; John A. Volpe, Secretary, Dept.
of Transportation. Moderator: Lawrence E.
Spivak. [New York] National Broadcasting
Co., 1969.
     39p.
     Transcript.
     1. U.S. Dept. of Health, Education, and
Welfare. 2. U.S. Dept. of Transportation.
     (Cont'd on next card)

351.7
:8
C65t
H-H   U.S. DEPT. OF TRANSPORTATION - APPROPRIATIONS
AND EXPENDITURES.
     U.S. Congress. House. Committee on Appropria-
tions.
     Department of Transportation and related
agencies appropriations for 19   Hearings
before a Subcommittee on the Committee on
Appropriations, House of Representatives,
Wash., Govt. Print. Off., 19
     v in pts.
     For Library holdings see main entry.
     1. U.S. Executive departments - Appropria-
tions and expenditures. 2. U.S. Dept. of
Transportation - Appropriations and
expenditures.

711.73
:336
T71   U.S. Dept. of Transportation.
     A revised estimate of the cost of
completing the national system of
interstate and defense highways.
Communication from the Secretary of
Transportation transmitting a revised
estimate... Wash., Govt. Print. Off., 1970.
     18p. At head of title: 91st Cong.,
2d sess. House. Document no. 91-317.

     1. Highways - Finance. I. Title.

VF
351
M22   Meet the Press...1969.   (Card 2)

     3. U.S. Dept. of Housing and Urban
Development. 4. Federal housing programs.
I. Spivak, Lawrence E. II. National
Broadcasting Co.

351.7
:8
C65t
S-H   U.S. DEPT. OF TRANSPORTATION - APPROPRIATIONS
AND EXPENDITURES.
     U.S. Congress. Senate. Committee on Appropri-
ations.
     Department of Transportation and related
agencies appropriations for 19
     Hearings before the Subcommittee of the Commit-
tee on Appropriations, United States Senate...
Wash., Govt. Print. Off., 19
     v. in pts.
     For Library holdings see main entry.
     1. U.S. Executive departments -
Appropriations and expenditures. 2. U.S.
Dept. of Transportation - Appropriations and
expenditures.

U.S. Dept. of Transportation - Reorganization.

351
P72reo
1968
no.2

U.S. President, 1963-   (Johnson)
Reorganization plan no. 2, 1968 for
transportation. Message from the President of the United States to the Congress
of the United States, transmitting reorganization plan no. 2 of 1968 transferring certain functions of the Dept.
of Transportation, Washington, Govt.
Print. Off., 1968.
5p.
Issued as House. Document no. 262.
90th Cong. 2d sess.
(Continued on next card)

Transportation accessibility from the Model
Cities area.

388
(768551)
V66

Voorhees (Alan M.) and Associates.
Transportation accessibility from the Model
Cities area. Prepared for the Nashville Model
Cities Agency. McLean, Va., 1969.
66p.

1. Transportation - Nashville. 2. Journey
to work. 3. Model cities - Nashville.
I. Nashville. Model Cities Agency.
II. Title.

Transportation and central city
unemployment.

388
K15

Kalachek, Edward D   ed.
Transportation and central city unemploy-
ment. Edited by Edward D. Kalachek and
John M. Goering. St. Louis, Mo., Institute
for Urban and Regional Studies, Washington
University, 1970.
18p. (Washington University, St. Louis.
Institute for Urban and Regional Studies.
Working paper INS 5)
U.S. Dept. of Housing and Urban Develop-
ment. Mass Transportation Demonstration
Grant Program.   Contract no. H-1034)
(Cont'd on next card)

351
P72reo
1968
no.2

U.S. President, 1963-   (Johnson)
Reorganization plan no. 2,....1968.
(Card 2)

1. U.S. Executive departments - Reorganization. 2. Transportation. 3. U.S. Dept.
of Housing and Urban Development -
Reorganization. 4. U.S. Dept. of Transportation - Reorganization. I. Title.

388
C65T
1964
S-H

TRANSPORTATION ACT AMENDMENTS .
U.S. CONGRESS. SENATE. COMMITTEE ON
COMMERCE.
TRANSPORTATION ACT AMENDMENTS - 1963.
HEARINGS, EIGHTY-EIGHTH CONGRESS, FIRST
SESSION, BEFORE THE SURFACE
TRANSPORTATION SUBCOMMITTEE ON S. 1061
AND 1062. WASHINGTON, GOVT. PRINT. OFF.,
1964.
2 V. (1079P.)

1. TRANSPORTATION.   I. TITLE.

388
K15

Kalachek, Edward D   ed. Transportation
...1970.   (Card 2)

1. Transportation - Economic effect.
2. Employment - Minority groups.
I. Goering, John M., jt. ed.
II. Washington University, St. Louis.
Institute for Urban and Regional Studies.
III. U.S. Mass Transportation Demonstration
Grant Program. IV. Title.

U.S. Dept. of Transportation. Federal
Highway Administration.

see

U.S. Federal Highway Administration.

Transportation act of 1958.

388
(73:347)
C65

U.S. Congress. House. Committee on Interstate and Foreign Commerce.
Transportation act of 1958. Report of the
Committee on Interstate and Foreign Commerce
on H.R. 12832 together with supplemental views.
Washington, Govt. Print. Off., 1958.
54p. tables. (85th Cong., 2d sess. House
report no. 1922)

1. Transportation - Legislation. I. Title.

388
H437

Transportation and community values.
Highway Research Board.
Transportation and community values; report
of a conference held at Warrenton, Va., March
2-5, 1969. Wash., 1969.
178p. (Its Special report 105)

Bibliography: p. 171-173.

1. Transportation. I. Title.

U.S. Dept. of Transportation. Office of High-
Speed Ground Transportation. Northeast
Corridor Transportation Project

see

U.S. Northeast Corridor Transportation Project.

388
(768551)
N17tr

Transportation administration.
Nashville Metropolitan Area Transportation
Study.
Transportation administration. Nash-
ville, 1961.
19p.

1. Transportation - Nashville. I. Title.

388
L157t

Transportation and economic policy.
Lansing, John B
Transportation and economic policy. New
York, Free Press, 1966.
409p.

1. Transportation - Economic effect.
2. Highways - Finance 3. Air transportation.
4. Railroads. I. Title.

388
(016)
W45u

U.S. Dept. of Transportation. Library
Services Div.
Willis, Dawn E
Urban mass transportation; a bibliography.
Wash., Dept. of Transportation, Office of
Administrative Operations, Library Services
Div., 1971.
140p. (Bibliographic list no. 6)

1. Transportation - Bibl. I. U.S. Dept.
of Transportation. Library Services Div.
II. Title.

384
L24

Transportation: air facilities.
Leigh Fisher Associates.
Transportation: air facilities.
Prepared for the East Central Florida
Regional Planning Council. San Francisco,
1965.
76p.

U.S. Urban Renewal Adm. UPAP

1. Air transportation. I. East Central
Florida Regional Planning Council. II. Title.
III. U.S. URA-UPAP. Florida.

388
(77252)
B27

A transportation and land development plan
for the Indianapolis region.
Barton-Aschman Associates.
A transportation and land development
plan for the Indianapolis region; a
summary report. Chicago, 1968.
149p.
Bibliography: p. 147-148.
U.S. Dept. of Housing and Urban
Development. UPAP.

1. Transportation - Indianapolis.
2. Land use - Indianapolis. I. U.S. HUD-
UPAP. Indianapolis. II. Title.

U.S. Dept. of Transportation. Mass Transportation
Demonstration Grant Program.

see

U.S. Mass Transportation Demonstration Grant
Program.

88
C65COM
1964
H-R

TRANSPORTATION AMENDMENTS OF 1964.
U.S. CONGRESS. HOUSE. COMMITTEE ON
INTERSTATE AND FOREIGN COMMERCE.
TRANSPORTATION AMENDMENTS OF 1964.
REPORT ON H.R. 9903 TOGETHER WITH
SUPPLEMENTAL VIEWS. WASHINGTON, GOVT.
PRINT. OFF., 1964.
107P. (88TH CONGRESS, 2D SESSION.
HOUSE OF REPRESENTATIVES. REPORT NO.
1144)

1. TRANSPORTATION.   I. TITLE.

388
S54

Transportation and parking.
Smith (Wilbur) and Associates.
Transportation and parking for tomorrow's
cities. New Haven, 1966.
393p.
"Prepared...under commission from the Automobile Manufacturers Association."

1. Transportation. 2. Parking. e. Journey
to work. 4. Highways. 5. City planning.
I. Automobile Manufacturers Association.
II. Title.

U.S. Dept. of Transportation. Urban Mass
Transportation Administration.

see

U.S. Urban Mass Transportation Administration

388
C15t

Transportation and aging.
Cantilli, Edmund J   ed.
Transportation and aging; selected issues, ed.
by Edmund J. Cantilli and June L. Shmelzer. Wash.,
Div. of Information, Administration on Aging, 1970.
208p.
Based on proceedings of the Interdisciplinary
Workshop on Transportation and Aging, Wash., D.C.
May 24-26, 1970.
1. Transportation. 2. Old age. I. Shmelzer,
June L., jt. ed. II. U.S. Dept. of Health,
Education, and Welfare (Administration on aging)
III. Title. IV. Interdisciplinary Workshop on
Transportation and   Aging, Wash., 1970.

388
(748)
P25tr

Transportation and Pennsylvania's future.
Pennsylvania. Governor's Committee for
Transportation.
Transportation and Pennsylvania's future.
Summary report of the Governor's Committee
for Transportation. [Harrisburg] 1969.
44p.

1. Transportation - Pa. I. Title.

388
871t Stanford University. Graduate School of
Business.
Transportation and tomorrow. From the 1964
and 1965 sessions of the Transportation Management Program and the 19th and 20th annual
forums of the National Defense Transportation
Association. Edited by Karl M. Ruppenthal and
Henry A. McKinnell. Stanford, Calif., 1966.
180p. (Stanford transportation series)

1. Transportation. 2. Railroads. 3. Har-
bors. 4. Air transportation. I. Ruppenthal,
Karl M., ed. II. McKinnell, Henry
A., ed. III. National Defense
Transportation Association. IV. Title.

388
082t Owen, Wilfred.
Transportation and the city. Pittsburgh,
Institute of Local Government, Graduate School
of Public and International Affairs, University of Pittsburgh, 1966.
24p. (Twelfth annual Wherrett lecture
on local government)

1. Transportation. 2. Journey to work.
3. Federal government. I. Wherrett lecture
on local government. II. Pittsburgh. University. Graduate School of Public and International Affairs. III. Title.

388
L24tr Leibbrand, Kurt.
Transportation and town planning. Translated
by Nigel Seymer. Cambridge, Mass., M.I.T., 1970.
381p.

Bibliography: p. 367-370.

1. Transportation. 2. City planning.
3. Traffic. I. Title.

388
(016) California. University. Institute of
C15 Transportation and Traffic Engineering.
no. 2 Toll roads. Berkeley, Calif., 1955.
15p. (Its Library references no. 2)

1. Transportation - Bibliography.
I. Title.

VF
711.585 Transportation as an element in urban
N174 rehabilitation.
1939 Gordon, Charles
Transportation as an element in urban
rehabilitation. In The National Conference on
Planning, Boston, Massachusetts, May 15-16-17,
1939. [Boston, Mass., 1939] pt. 6.

I. Title.

388
T71t Transportation Association of America.
Transportation, facts and trends;
statistical analysis showing the importance
of, and trends in transportation in the
United States, including both for-hire and
private carriage. 1st ed. Washington,
1964.
21p.

1. Transportation. I. Title.

388.015
T71 Transportation Association of America.
Transportation research; a survey of
current and potential transportation
research projects. 3d ed. Washington,
Research Staff of the Transportation
Association of America, 1962.
50p.

1. Transportation - Research.
2. Transportation - Bibl.

728.1
(79494) Dove, Donald A.
D68 Housing and population; presents a method
for estimating distribution of housing units
and population by traffic zones or census
tracts. Los Angeles, Transportation Association of Southern California, 1965.
11p. (Los Angeles Regional Transportation Study. LARTS technical bulletin
1-6)
Cover title.
Burton E. Jones, Chairman.

(Continued on next card)

728.1
(79494) Dove, Donald A Housing and popula-
D68 tion; presents a method...1965 (Card 2)

U.S. Urban Renewal Adm. UPAP.

1. Housing - Los Angeles. 2. Population -
Los Angeles. I. Transportation Association
of Southern California. II. Los Angeles
Regional Transportation Study. III. U.S.
URA-UPAP. Los Angeles.

388
(794) Transportation Association of Southern
T71 California.
LARTS [Los Angeles Regional Transportation
Study] 1980 progress report. Los Angeles
[196?]
46p.
"Published in cooperation with the Dept.
of Transportation, Federal Highway Admini-
stration, Bureau of Public Roads."
1. Transportation - Calif. 2. Land use
- Calif. 3. Population - Calif. 4. Employment -
Calif. I. U.S. Bureau of Public Roads. II. Los
Angeles Regional Trans portation Study.
III. Title.

388
(794) Transportation Association of Southern California.
T71r Report, 1969

Los Angeles, 19

/v. annual.
For Library holdings see main entry.

1. Transportation - Calif.

388
(79494) Transportation Association of Southern
T71 California.
TASC prospectus. Published in cooperation
with the Dept. of Transportation, Federal
Highway Administration, Bureau of Public
Roads. Los Angeles, 1969.
53p.

1. Transportation - Los Angeles. 2. Journey
to work.

Transportation authorities: fiscal and organizational
353.1 relations with the City of New York.
N28 New York (City) Temporary Commission on
City Finances.
Transportation authorities: fiscal and
organizational relations with the City of
New York, by R.G. Smith and others. New York,
1966.
69p. (Its Staff paper 7)

1. Authorities. 2. Transportation -
New York (City) 3. Municipal finance -
New York (City) I. Smith, Robert G.
II. Title.

362.6 Transportation; background.
W34 White House Conference on Aging, Washington, 1971.
1971 Transportation; background, by Joseph S. Revis.
no.2 Issues, by the Technical Committee on Transportation, with the collaboration of the author.
Wash., 1971.
51p. [no. 2]
Cover title: Background and issues; transportation.
Bibliography: p. 49-51.
1. Old age. 2. Transportation. I. Revis,
Joseph S. II. Title.

398
:331 Worcester, Mass. Planning Dept.
W67 Transportation between poverty pockets and
employment. Worcester urban mass transporta-
tion technical study. Final report. Worcester,
1969.
1v.
U.S. HUD. Mass Transportation Demonstration
Grant Program. Contract no. H-1021.
NTIS. PB 193 152.
1. Journey to work. I. U.S. Dept of
Housing and Urban Development. II. U.S. Mass
Transportation Demonstration Grant Program.
Worcester, Mass. III. Title.

388
(747245) Nassau County, N.Y. Planning Commission.
N17 Transportation centers for Nassau
County. Mineola, N.Y., 1965.
26p.

1. Transportation - Nassau Co., N.Y.
2. Traffic - Nassau Co., N.Y. I. Title.

388
M67t Mott, George Fox, ed.
Transportation century. [A compilation of
essays from various authors] Baton Rouge,
Louisiana State University Press, 1966.
279p.
Partial contents: President Johnson's
Transportation message of Mar. 2, 1966.

1. Transportation. 2. U.S. Dept. of Transportation. 3. U.S. President - Messages.
I. Title.

629.136
T71 Transportation Consultants, inc.
Aids available for complete land use planning
around airports. Prepared for Federal Aviation
Agency. Washington, 1966.
Laf. 91p. (U.S. Defense Documentation Center,
Defense Supply Agency. AD 650271)
Distributed by U.S. Clearinghouse for Federal
Scientific and Technical Information.
1. Airports. 2. Land use. I. U.S. Clearing-
house for Federal Scientific and Technical
Information. II. U.S. Defense Documentation
Center. Defense Supply Agency. III. U.S. Federal
Aviation Agency. IV. Title.

629.136
T71c Transportation Consultants, Inc.
Compatible land use planning on and around
airports. Prepared for Federal Aviation
Agency. Processed for Defense Documentation
Center, Defense Supply Agency. [Wash.] U.S.
Dept. of Commerce, National Bureau of Stand-
ards, Institute for Applied Technology, 1966.
Laf. 102p.
Distributed by U.S. Clearinghouse for
Federal Scientific and Technical Information.

(Cont'd on next card)

629.136
T71c Transportation Consultants, Inc. Compatible
land use planning on and around airports...
(Card 2)

1. Noise. 2. Airports. 3. Land use.
I. U.S. Clearinghouse for Federal Scientific
and Technical Information. II. U.S. Defense
Documentation Center for Scientific and Tech-
nical Information. III. U.S. National
Bureau of Standards. IV. Title.

388
U54 Transportation economics.
Universities-National Bureau Committee for
Economic Research.
Transportation economics: a conference of the
Committee. New York, National Bureau of
Economic Research. Distributed by Columbia
University Press, 1965.
451p. (National Bureau of Economic
Research. Special conference series no. 17)

1. Transportation. 2. Transportation -
Economic effect. 3. Railroads. I. National
Bureau of Economic Research. II. Title.

388
C71t

Transportation effects on the National
Alliance of Businessmen Program.
Crain, John L
Transportation effects on the National
Alliance of Businessmen Program. Menlo
Park, Stanford Research Institute, 1969.
26p.
Prepared for U.S. Housing and Urban
Development Dept. under Contract no. H-10-29
with the National Alliance of Businessmen.
U.S. Mass Transportation Demonstration
Grant Program.
CFSTI. PB 183 054.
1. Transportation - Economic effect.
(Cont'd on next card)

388
D67

Transportation graphics: where am I going?
Dot Zero.
Transportation graphics: where am I going?
How do I get there? Symposium, Oct. 23, 1967,
New York City. New York, Dot Zero, 1968.
46p.

Entire issue: no. 5, Fall 1968.

1. Transportation. 2. Visual aids I. Title.

621.39
T71p

Transportation Institute.
The privacy battleground; the people's
forum (A forum report) June 14-16, 1971,
Wash. Jointly sponsored by AFL-CIO
Maritime Trades Dept. [n.p.] 1971.
93p.

1. Communication systems. I. American
Federation of Labor and Congress of Industrial
Organizations. II. Title.

388
C71t

Crain, John L   Transportation effects
on...1969.   (Card 2)

2. Journey to work. I. Stanford Research
Institute. II. National Alliance of
Businessmen. III. U.S. Dept. of Housing
and Urban Development. IV. U.S. Mass
Transportation Demonstration Grant
Program. V. Title.

711.73
:330
H43t

Transportation impacts and attitude surveys; 6 reports.
Washington, Highway Research Board, Division of En-
gineering, National Research Council, National Academy of
Sciences-National Academy of Engineering, 1967.
61 p. illus. 26 cm. (Highway research record no. 187)
National Research Council. Publication 1518.
"Papers sponsored by Committee on Economic Forecasting and
others."
Includes bibliographies.

(Continued on next card)
67-62772

388
(771)
C52

Transportation-Land Use Study.
Cleveland-Seven County.
Transportation-Land Use Study
Operations plan, by Robert C. Stuart and
others. Cleveland, 1966.
1v.
Preparation of manual was financed by U.S.
Urban Renewal Adm. and others.

1. Transportation - Ohio. 2. Land use -
Ohio. 3. Journey to work. I. U.S. Urban
Renewal Administration. II. Title.

388
(79494)
C15t

Transportation-Employment Project.
California. Business and Transportation Agency.
Transportation-Employment Project. A re-
search project to determine and test the rela-
tionship between a public transportation system
and job and other opportunities of low income
groups. Progress report no.
Los Angeles, 19
v.
U.S. Mass Transportation Demonstration Grant
Program.
Contract no. H-730.
For Library holdings see main entry.
(Cont'd on next card)

711.73
:330
H43t

Transportation impacts and attitude surveys ... 1967.
(Card 2)
CONTENTS.—Transportation implications of employment trends in
central cities and suburbs, by E. L. Kanwit and A. F. Eckartt.—High-
way impacts on downtown and suburban shopping, by D. K. Withe-
ford. — Highway development: attitudes and economic climate, by
H. K. Dansereau.—Mobility as a measure of neighborhood, by S. L.
Hill and B. Frankland.—Living patterns and attitude survey, by
C. F. Barnes, Jr.—Attitudes, community values, and highway plan-
ning, by M. T. Shaffer.
1. Highways - Economic effect.
I. Highway Research Board.

TE7.H5 no. 187   388.1'0973   67-62772
Library of Congress

LAW
T

Transportation law.
Guandolo, John.
Transportation law. Dubuque, Iowa, Wm. C.
Brown, 1965.
838p. (Transportation series. Edited by
W. H. Thompson)

1. Transportation - Legislation. I. Title.

388
(79494)
C15t

California. Business and Transportation Agency.
Transportation-Employment...19   (Card 2)

1. Transportation - Los Angeles. 2. Journey
to work. 3. Employment - Los Angeles.
I. Title. II. U.S. Mass Transportation
Demonstration Grant Program - Los Angeles.

388
(79)
B56

Transportation in the Rocky Mountain West.
Blood, Dwight.
Transportation in the Rocky Mountain West,
by Dwight Blood, Ronald Babcock and James
Hardee. Denver, Federation of Rocky Mountain
States, inc., 1970.
1v. (Regional planning program. Background
paper 1)
Preliminary draft- for review.

1. Transportation - Western states.
I. Federation of Rocky Mountain States.
II. Title.

388
(759)
P17

Transportation: mass transit.
Parsons, Brinckerhoff, Quade and Douglas.
Transportation: mass transit. Report to
the East Central Florida Regional Planning
Council. New York, 1965.
14p.

U.S. Urban Renewal Adm. UPAP.

1. Transportation - Florida. 2. Journey
to work. I. East Central Florida Regional
Planning Council. III. U.S. URA-UPAP.
Florida. II. Title.

388
T71t

Transportation, facts and trends.
Transportation Association of America.
Transportation, facts and trends;
statistical analysis showing the importance
of, and trends in transportation in the
United States, including both for-hire and
private carriage. 1st ed. Washington,
1964.
21p.

1. Transportation. I. Title.

388
H25t

Transportation in the world of the future.
Hellman, Hal.
Transportation in the world of the future.
New York, M. Evans and Co., distributed in
association with J.B. Lippincott Co., 1968.
187p.

Bibliography: p. 177-181.

1. Transportation. I. Title.

362.4
A17

Transportation needs of the handicapped.
ABT Associates, inc.
Transportation needs of the handicapped.
Prepared for Dept. of Transportation, Office
of Economics and Systems Analysis. Cambridge,
Mass., 1969.
1v.
Cover title: Travel barriers.

1. Handicapped. 2. Transportation. I. Title.

388
(748)
W42

Transportation flow; simulation and projection.
Wickstrom, George V
Transportation flow; simulation and
projection; an address given on December 12,
1961 to the Philadelphia Chapter, American
Society of Civil Engineers. [Philadelphia]
Penn Jersey Transportation Study, 1961.
6p.

1. Transportation - Pa.-N.J.-Del.
2. Journey to work. I. American Society of
Civil Engineers. Philadelphia Chapter.
II. Penn Jersey Transportation Study.
III. Title.

351.81
S76

Transportation Institute.
Stover, Vergil G
Final/summary report on the traffic
assignment study. Sponsored by the Texas
Highway Dept. in cooperation with the U.S.
Bureau of Public Roads. College Station,
Transportation Institute, Texas A & M
University, 1969.
20p.

1. Traffic regulations. I. U.S. Bureau
of Public Roads. II. Transportation
Institute.

388
(7471)
O75

Transportation needs of the poor.
Ornati, Oscar A
Transportation needs of the poor; a case
study of New York City, by Oscar A. Ornati
and others. New York, Praeger, 1969.
127p. (Labor economics and urban studies.
Praeger special studies in U.S. economic and
social development)

1. Transportation - New York (City)
2. Journey to work. 3. Poor. I. Title.

388
R15

Transportation for future urban communities:
a study prospectus.
Rand Corp.
Transportation for future urban communities:
a study prospectus. Santa Monica, Calif.,
1961.
48p. (Research memo Rm-2824-FF)

1. Transportation. 2. Journey to work.
3. Traffic. 4. Automation. I. Title.

621.39
T71

Transportation Institute.
The people's forum; the privacy battleground; June 14-16, 1971, Washington-Hilton
Hotel, Washington, D.C. Jointly sponsored
by AFL-CIO Maritime Trades Department;
Transpostation Institute. [n.p.] 1971.
34p.

1. Communication systems. I. American
Federation of Labor and Congress of
Industrial Organizations. Maritime Trades
Dept. I. Title.

388
(79494)
L67t

Transportation, 1970.
Los Angeles Regional Transportation Study.
Transportation, 1970. Los Angeles, 1971.
[16]p. (A Los Angeles Regional Transportation Study profile)

1. Transportation - Los Angeles.
I. Title.

388
L17
Transportation, 1983; the Minnesota Experimental city.
Larson, Roy E
Transportation, 1983; the Minnesota Experimental city, by Roy E. Larson and Robert J. Reid, North Star Research and Development Institute. [n.p.] [1969?]
30p.

1. Transportation. 2. Transportation - Minn. 3. Journey to work. I. Reid, Robert J., jt. au. II. Highway Research Board. III. Title.

388
R62
Transportation planning and urban renewal.
Roeseler, W G
Transportation planning and urban renewal. New York, Howard, Needles, Tammen & Bergendoff, 1966.
15p.
Presented at the Road Gang, American Concrete Pipe Association luncheon meeting, 1966, Wash., D.C.

1. Transportation. 2. Urban renewal. 3. City planning. I. Title.

388
(79)
T71
Transportation problems and policies in the trans-Missouri west. Edited by Jack R. Davidson and Howard W Ottoson. Lincoln, University of Nebraska Press [1967]
377p.
"Papers presented at a workshop on transportation sponsored jointly by the Great Plains Resource Economics Committee and the Western Marketing Research Committee...held at Denver, November 30 to December 2, 1965."

(Cont'd on next card)

VF
711.5
:534.83
W27
Transportation noise.
West Coast Noise Symposium, 2d, Los Angeles, 1955
Proceedings: Community noise. Noise control, p. 10-76, July 1956. illus., charts, tables.

Partial contents.-Fundamentals of community noise.-Transportation noise.-Planning, zoning and legislation for noise control.-Industrial noise.

1.Noise. 2.Zoning. I.Title: Transportation noise. II.Title: Community noise. III.Title: Industrial noise.

388
F22tr
Transportation planning data for urbanized...
U.S. Federal Highway Administration.
Transportation planning data for urbanized areas; based on 1960 census; a summary. Wash., 1971.
13p.

1. Transportation. I. Title.

388
(79)
T71
Transportation problems...[1967] (Card 2)

1. Transportation - Western states. I. Davidson, Jack R., ed. II. Ottoson, Howard W., jt. ed. III Great Plains Agricultural Council. Great Plains Resource Economics Committee. IV. Western Agricultural Economics Research Council. Western Marketing Research Committee.

534.83
W95t
Transportation noise and noise from equipment powered by internal combustion engines.
Wyle Laboratories.
Transportation noise and noise from equipment powered by internal combustion engines. Wash., U.S. Environmental Protection Agency, Office of Noise Abatement and Control, 1971.
1v. (NTID300.13)

1. Noise. 2. Transportation. I. U.S. Environmental Protection Agency. II. Title.

Folio
388
F22t
Transportation planning data for urbanized areas, based on 1960 census.
U.S. Federal Highway Administration.
Transportation planning data for urbanized areas, based on 1960 census. Wash., U.S. Dept. of Transportation, Federal Highway Administration, Office of Highway Planning, Urban Planning Div., 1970.
664p.

1. Transportation. I. Title.

711.585
N17
UDB9
Transportation problems and war housing.
U.S. National Housing Agency. Office of the Administrator. Division of Urban Studies.
Transportation problems and war housing. Washington, D.C., Dec. 1942.
15 p. (Its Bulletin no. 9)

"Bulletin no. 9...supersedes the former bulletins 1, 5, and 7."-p.1.

534.83
T71t
Transportation noises; a symposium on acceptability criteria. Ed. by James D. Chalupnik. Seattle, University of Washington Press, 1970.
358p.

1. Noise. 2. Transportation. I. Chalupnik, James D., ed.

388
(753)
L47
Transportation planning in the District of Columbia, 1955 to 1965.
Little (Arthur D.)
Transportation planning in the District of Columbia, 1955 to 1965: a review and critique. A report to the Policy Advisory Committee to the District Commissioners. [Wash.] 1966.
68p.
Bibliography: p. b1-b24.

1. Transportation - District of Columbia metropolitan area. 2. Transportation - Economic effect. 3. Traffic - District of Columbia metropolitan area. I. District of Columbia. Board of Commissioners. II. Title.

711.585
N17
UDB1
Transportation problems in war housing programs.
U.S. National Housing Agency. Office of the Administrator. Division of Urban Studies.
Transportation problems in war housing programs. Washington, D.C., July 27, 1942.
5 l. (Its Bulletin no. 1)

Superseded by Bulletin no. 9, Dec. 1942. Mimeographed.

690.015
(485)
S82
1971
R7
Transportation of building materials.
Henriksson, Jan.
Byggmaterialtransporter: kortidernas variationer under dygnet pa trafikleder av olika typ. (Transportation of building materials: variations in transportation time during a 24 hour period for streets of varying types) av Jan Henriksson och Lars Bjerkner. Stockholm, Statens Institut för Byggnadsforskning, 1971.
51p. (Rapport R7:1971)
English summary.
1. Building research - Sweden. 2. Transportation - Sweden. 3. Building materials - Sweden. I. Stockholm. Statens Institut
(Cont'd on next card)

388
S77
Transportation policy as an instrument for altering regional development patterns - misdirected emphasis?
Straszheim, Mahlon R
Transportation policy as an instrument for altering regional development patterns - misdirected emphasis? Cambridge, Mass., Program on Regional and Urban Economics, 1969.
34p. (Harvard University. Program on Regional and Urban Economics. Discussion paper no. 52)
1. Transportation. 2. Economic development. I. Harvard University. Program on Regional and Urban Economics. II. Title.

388
R23
Transportation requirements and effects of new communities.
Regional Economic Development Institute, Pittsburgh.
Transportation requirements and effects of new communities. Prepared for the U.S. Dept. of Housing and Urban Development. Pittsburgh, 1968.
102p.
1. Transportation. 2. Planned communities. I. U.S. Dept. of Housing and Urban Development. II. Title.

690.015
(485)
S82
1971
R7
Henriksson, Jan. Byggmaterialtransporter...
1971.   (Card 2)

för Byggnadsforskning. II. Title: Transportation of building materials. III. Bjerkner, Lars, jt. au.

388
(7946)
S15tr
Transportation policy for San Francisco.
San Francisco. Dept. of City Planning.
Transportation policy for San Francisco: recent trends and current developments, by William A. Proctor. San Francisco, 1967.
26p.

1. Transportation - San Francisco Bay area. 2. Population - San Francisco. I. Proctor, William A. II. Title.

388
M42sp
Transportation requirements in small cities and towns.
Midwest Research Institute.
Special transportation requirements in small cities and towns, final report, by Bruce W. Macy and others. Prepared for the U.S. Dept. of Housing and Urban Development. [Kansas City, Mo.] 1968.
87p.
On cover: Study in new systems of urban transportation.
1. Transportation. 2. Transportation - Statistics. I. U.S. Dept. of Housing and Urban Development. II. Macy, Bruce W. III. Title.

(Cont'd on next card)

388
I57t
The transportation picture in selected urban areas.
Institute of Public Administration, New York.
The transportation picture in selected urban areas. A supplement to Urban transportation and public policy. Prepared for U.S. Dept. of Commerce and Housing and Home Finance Agency. New York, 1961.
175p.
On cover: Appendix volume.
See also 388fi68ur
1. Transportation. 2. Metropolitan areas. I. U.S. Dept. of Commerce. II. U.S. Housing and Home Finance Agency.   III. Title.
IV. Title: Urban transportation and public policy.

388
(774)
M42
Transportation: predictive procedures.
Michigan. State Resource Planning Program.
Transportation: predictive procedures. Summary report. [Prepared in] cooperation with the Michigan Dept. of Commerce and others. Lansing, Mich., 1966.
38p. (Michigan. Dept. of Commerce. State Resource Planning Program. Technical report no. 9)
U.S. Dept. of Commerce and Housing and Urban Development. HPAP.
1. Transportation - Michigan. 2. Transportation - Automation. I. Title. II. U.S. HUD. HPAP. Michigan.

388
M42sp
Midwest Research Institute. Special transportation requirements...1968.
(Card 2)

IV. Title: Study in new systems of urban transportation. V. Title: Transportation requirements in small cities and towns.

388
N17u

Transportation Research Conference, Woods Hole, Mass.
National Research Council.
U.S. transportation, resources, performance and problems; a collection of papers prepared for the Transportation Research Conference, convened by the National Academy of Sciences at Woods Hole, Mass., August, 1960. Washington, National Academy of Sciences, National Research Council, 1961.
319p. (Its Publication 841-8 (Supplement to publication 841))
1. Transportation. I. Transportation Research Conference, Woods Hole, Mass.

388
N17t

Transportation Research Conference, Woods Hole, Mass., 1960.
National Research Council.
Transportation design considerations. Selections from the proceedings of the Transportation Research Conference, convened by the National Academy of Sciences at Woods Hole, Massachusetts, August, 1960. Washington, National Academy of Sciences, National Research Council, 1961.
243p. (Its Publication 841)
1. Transportation. I. Transportation Research Conference, Woods Hole, Mass., 1960.

Transportation Research Institute.
see
Carnegie-Mellon University, Pittsburgh. Transportation Research Institute.

388
(083.41)
N17

Transportation Research Study, Woods Hole, Mass., 1960.
National Research Council.
Selected statistics on the transportation system of the U.S.A. A staff paper for sessions "A" Transportation Research Study, Woods Hole, Massachusetts, Aug. 1960. Washington, National Academy of Sciences-National Research Council, 1960.
25p.
1. Transportation - Statistics. I. Transportation Research Study, Woods Hole, Mass., 1960.

388
(016)
C15
no.34

Transportation statistical sources.
California. University. Institute of Transportation and Traffic Engineering.
Transportation statistical sources; selected references. Berkeley, Calif., 1967.
17p. (Its Library references no. 34)
1. Transportation - Bibl. 2. Transportation - Statistics. 3. Railroads - Bibl. I. Title.

388
(7946)
R22

Transportation; surface transportation.
Reed, George E
Transportation; surface transportation on and around San Francisco Bay. Prepared for San Francisco Bay Conservation and Development Commission. San Francisco, San Francisco Bay Conservation and Development Commission, 1968.
181p.

Summary ... ... Summary. San Francisco, 1968.
29p.
1. Transportation - San Francisco Bay Area. 2. Journey to work. I. San Francisco Bay Area Conservation and Development Commission. II. Title.

388
H43tran

Transportation system analysis and evaluation of alternate plans.
Highway Research Board.
Transportation system analysis and evaluation of alternate plans; 9 reports. Washington, Highway Research Board, Div. of Engineering. National Research Council, National Academy of Sciences-National Academy of Engineering, 1967.
132p. (Highway research record no. 180) National Research Council. Publication 151.
N.e.1
Laf.e.2
1. Transportation. 2. Journey to work. I. Title.

388
(751)
D25

Transportation system and policies for the...
Delaware Valley Regional Planning Commission.
Transportation systems and policies for the 1985 region. Philadelphia, 1966.
1v. (DVRPC v.4)
1. Transportation - Delaware River Basin. 2. Journey to work. I. Title.

388
(794)
S68

Transportation system for the Southern California metropolis.
Southern California Research Council.
An approach to an orderly and efficient transportation system for the Southern California metropolis. A study. Los Angeles, 1960.
46p. (SCRC Publications. Report no. 8)
1. Transportation - Calif. 2. Journey to work. 3. Automation. I. Title: Transportation system for the Southern California metropolis.

711
(016)
C65
no. 80

Transportation system synthesis.
Dickey, John W
Transportation system synthesis. [Blacksburg, Va.] Center for Urban and Regional Studies, Virginia Polytechnic Institute, 1969.
17p. (Council of Planning Librarians. Exchange bibliography no. 80)
1. Planning - Bibl. 2. Transportation - Bibl. I. Virginia Polytechnic Institute. II. Title. (Series: Council of Planning Librarians. Exchange bibliography no. 80)

388
G25tra

Transportation Systems Div. General electric aerial transport system...
General Electric Corp.
Transportation Systems Div. General electric aerial transport system; transportation for a supersonic age. Technical report. Erie, Penn., General Electric, Transportation Systems Division, 1967.
27p. (Its GEA-8603)
1. Transportation. 2. Journey to work. I. Title.

388
L24t

Transportation systems in the future development of metropolitan areas.
Leisch, Jack E
Transportation systems in the future development of metropolitan areas: the permanent corridor concept. [Toronto, De Leuw, Cather and Co. of Canada, ltd., 1968]
27p.

For presentation at the 48th annual meeting of the Highway Research Board, Jan. 1969.
1. Transportation. 2. Journey to work. I. Title.

R
388
(016)
C15
no.33

Transportation trends and forecasts.
California. University. Institute of Transportation and Traffic Engineering.
Transportation trends and forecasts; selected references. [Berkeley, Calif.] 1967.
21p. (Its Library reference no. 33)
1. Transportation - Bibl. 2. Air transportation - Bibl. 3. Railroads - Bibl. I. Title.

388
F67u

Transportation troubles, getting worse?
Forbes.
The U.S.' lopsided transportation budget. New York, Forbes, inc., 1968.
[6] p.

Reprinted from Forbes magazine, Oct. 1, 1968.

Cover title: Transportation troubles, getting worse?
1. Transportation. I. Title. II. Title: Transportation troubles, getting worse?

388
(46)
S62

Transportes de Barcelona.
Sociedad Privada Municipal, Barcelona.
Memoria, 19

Barcelona, 19
v.
Reports: 19   has title: Tranvias de Barcelona. 19   Transportes de Barcelona.
For Library holdings see main entry.
1. Transportation - Spain. I. Title: Tranvias de Barcelona. II. Title: Transportes de Barcelona.

388
H27

Transporting people.
Herbert, Even.
Transporting people. The hardest difficulties to deal with come at the interface where transportation systems (almost) meet. Can new technology improve the flow? Reproduced from International science and technology, October 1965. p. 30-42.
1. Transportation. I. International science and technology. II. Title.

Transportokonomisk Institutt.
see also
Oslo. Transportokonomisk Institutt

Transvaal (Province)
1856-77, South African Republic; 1877-81, Transvaal (Colony); 1881 - Oct. 25, 1900, South African Repblic; Oct. 25, 1900 - May 31, 1910, Transvaal (Colony); May 31, 1910 - Transvaal (Province)

727
T71b

Transvaal (Province) Education Department. (School Buildings Committee)
Beplanning van laerskole. Planning of primary schools. Pretoria, 1957.
85p. illus., tables.

Text also in English.
1. Schools - Transvaal (Province)

727
T71o

Transvaal (Province) Education Department. (School Buildings Committee)
Die ontwerp van klaskamers en spesiale kamers vir hoerskole. Planning of classrooms and special rooms for high schools. Pretoria, 1958.
68p. illus., diagrs.

Text also in English.
1. Schools - Transvaal (Province)

727
T71

Transvaal (Province) Education Department.
Die terrein: keuse van terrein vir skool-en koshuisgeboue en die uitle van die speelterrain. The site: site selection for school and hostel buildings and the layout of playing grounds. Pretoria, 1957.
29 p. illus., tables. (Its verslag (report) no. 2)

Text also in English.
1. Schools - Transvaal (Province) 2. Site selection

VF
727
C15

Transvaal (Province) Education Department.

Calderwood, D M
The planning of grades rooms, by D. M. Calderwood and S. Nicholson. Johannesburg, 1957.
[8] p. illus., plans.

Research sponsored by the Transvaal Provincial Administration.

"Reprint from the South African Architectural Record, vol. 42, no. 7,

(See Card No. 2)

VF
727
C15

Calderwood, D M The planning of grades rooms. 1957. (Card No. 2)

Council for Scientific and Industrial Research, National Building Research Institute. Pretoria, July 1957."

1.Schools - Transvaal (Province).
I.Nicholson, S II.Transvaal (Province) Education Department.

691.11
F67t

Transverse strains during drying of 2-inch ponderosa pine.
U.S. Forest Service. Forest Products Laboratory, Madison, Wis.
Transverse strains during drying of 2-inch ponderosa pine. Madison, Wis., 1968.
26p. (Research paper FPL 83)

1. Wood. I. McMillen, John M. II. Title.

388
(46)
S62

Tranvias de Barcelona.
Sociedad Privada Municipal, Barcelona.
Memoria, 19

Barcelona, 19
v.
Reports: 19   has title: Tranvias
de Barcelona. 19   Transportes de
Barcelona.
For Library holdings see main entry.

1. Transportation - Spain. I. Title: Tranvias de Barcelona. II. Title: Transportes de Barcelona.

697.
:662.6
T71

TRAPNELL, W
THE BITUMINOUS COAL INDUSTRY WITH A SURVEY OF COMPETING FUELS.
WASHINGTON, FEDERAL EMERGENCY RELIEF ADMINISTRATION, DIVISION OF RESEARCH, STATISTICS AND FINANCE SECTIONAL ECONOMIC RESEARCH, 1935.
154P.

1. FUEL. I. TITLE.

332
T71

TRAPP, JOSEPH T
CREDIT INSURANCE, A FACTOR IN BANK LENDING. BALTIMORE, AMERICAN CREDIT INDEMNITY COMPANY OF NEW YORK, 1954.
96P.

1. BANKS AND BANKING. 2. INSURANCE. I. TITLE.

711.3
(6761)
T71

Trappe, P
Social change and development institutions in a refugee population (Development from below as an alternative: the case of the Nakapiripirit Settlement Scheme in Urganda) Prepared for the Institute and the Office of the High Commissioner by P. Trappe. Geneva, United Nations Research Institute for Social Development, 1971.
102p. (Report no. 71.2)
Bibliography: p. 93-95.
1. Rural planning - Uganda. I. United Nations Research Institute for Social Development. II. Title.

690.013
T71

Tratman, E E Russell.
Modern construction specifications and standards; a practical guide for civil engineers, contractors and other construction men; prepared ... in cooperation with the editorial staff of Engineering News-Record. New York, Engineering News-Record. [1938]
254 p. diagrs., tables.

1.Building construction - Contracts and specifications. 2.Building construction - Tables, calculations, etc. I.Engineering News-Record.
II.Title.

693.55
T71

Travaux.
Cent ans de béton armé 1849-1949. Paris, Editions Science & Industrie [1949]
214 p. illus.

"Supplément a la revue Travaux - no. 194 bis."

1.Reinforced concrete construction. I.Title.

351.712
(44)
T71

Travaux.
Travaux publics de France. Paris, Editions Science et Industrie, 1957.
112p. illus. (American Embassy, Paris. Foreign service dispatch no. 19, 1958, encl. no. 1)

Supplement a la Revue Travaux no. 273 bis.

1. Public works - France. (Series: American Embassy, Paris. Foreign service dispatch no. 19, 1958, encl. no. 1)

910
A21

Travel.
Adams, Alexander B
New York. 2d ed. New York, Bankers Trust Co., 1963.
68p.

1. Travel. 2. Harbors - New York (City)
I. Bankers Trust Co., New York. II. Title.

910
A51

Travel.
Alaska. Dept. of Economic Development and Planning.
Traveler profiles; a study of summer travel to Alaska during 1963 and 1964, by Charles E. Hinkson. Juneau, 1964.
37p.
U.S. Urban Renewal Adm. UPAP.

1. Travel. I. Hinkson, Charles E.
II. Title. III. U.S. URA-UPAP. Alaska.

712.25
(798)
A51a

Alaska. Dept. of Natural Resources.
(Div. of Lands)
Alaska campers 1964; an official publication of the State of Alaska. Prepared in cooperation with: Div. of Planning and Research, Dept. of Economic Development and Planning. [Juneau] 1964.
26p.
U.S. Urban Renewal Adm. UPAP.

1. Recreation - Alaska. 2. Natural resources. 3. Travel. I. Alaska. Dept. of Economic Development and Planning. II. Title. III. U.S. URA-UPAP. Alaska.

Ref.
910
A52al

Travel.
American Automobile Association.
Alaska and the Alaska highway, 19 /

Washington, D.C., 1968-
v. annual.

For Library holdings see main entry.

1. Travel.

R
910
A52c

Travel.
American Automobile Association.
California-Nevada tour book, including Baja, California. What to see, where to stay, where to dine; a catalog of complete travel information.
Washington,
v.

Keep latest edition only.

For complete information see shelflist.

1. Travel.

Ref.
910
A52gl

Travel.
American Automobile Association.
Great Lakes tour book, Illinois, Indiana, Michigan, Wisconsin, 19
what to see, where to stay, where to dine.
Washington, D.C., 19
v. annual.

For library holdings see main entry.

1. Travel.

R
910
A52m

Travel.
American Automobile Association.
Mideastern tour book, including Chicago, Ill. and New York City, N.Y. Washington,
v. annual.

Keep latest edition only.
For complete information see shelflist.

1. Travel.

R
910
A52nc

Travel.
American Automobile Association.
North Central tour book, including Manitoba and Western Ontario. What to see, where to stay, where to dine. A catalog of complete travel information.
Washington,
v. annual.
For complete information see shelflist.
Keep latest edition only.

1. Travel.

R
910
A52ne

Travel.
American Automobile Association.
Northeastern tour book, including eastern Canada. A descriptive catalog of places of interest.
Washington,
v. illus., maps. annual.

For complete information see shelflist.

1. Travel.

R
910
A52nw

Travel.
American Automobile Association.
Northwestern tour book, including western Canada. What to see, where to stay, where to dine; a catalog of complete travel information.
Washington,
v. illus., maps. annual.

For complete information see shelf list.

1. Travel.

R
910
A52sc

Travel.
American Automobile Association.
South Central tour book. What to see, where to stay, where to dine. A catalog of complete travel information.
Washington,
v. annual.

For complete information see shelflist.
Keep latest edition only.

1. Travel.

R
910
A52se   Travel.
American Automobile Association.
    Southeastern tour book, including West
Indies and other islands; a descriptive
catalog of places of interest,
Washington,
    1v. illus., maps. annual.

    For complete information see shelf list.

    1. Travel

R
910
A52sw   Travel.
American Automobile Association.
    Southwestern tour book, including Hawai-
ian Islands, Lower California, U.S. 30
through Wyoming, El Paso, Texas. What to see,
where to stay, where to dine. A catalog of
complete travel information.
Washington,
    v. illus., maps. annual.

    For complete information see shelf list.

    1. Travel.

R
910
A52w   Travel.
American Automobile Association.
    Western tour book, including western Canada.
Washington,
    v. illus., maps. annual.

    For complete information see shelflist.

    1. Travel. 2. Hotels - Directories. 3. Tourist
courts - Directories.

910
A74   Travel.
Arkansas. Industrial Development Commission.
    A photographic essay of Arkansas. [Little
Rock, Ark., 1958]
    1v.

    1. Travel. 2. Architecture - Ark.
I. Title.

526.8
(7531)
A77n   Travel.
Association of American Geographers.
    Nine geographical field trips in the
Washington, D.C. area. Wash., 1968.
    93p.
    Partial contents.-Washington, D.C. and
environs, by Jerome P. Pickard, Director,
Program Analysis and Evaluation Staff, HUD.

    1. Maps and mapping - D.C. metropolitian
area. 2. Travel. 3. Geography. I. Pickard,
Jerome P. II. Title.

388
(74461)
B67t   Travel.
Boston College. College of Business Administration. (Seminar Research Bureau)
    Travel in the Boston region 1959-1980.
Boston, 1960.
    3v. diagrs., maps, tables. (Studies
in urban transportation)

    1. Transportation - Boston. 2. Travel.

339
   TRAVEL.
EAST CENTRAL FLORIDA REGIONAL PLANNING
COUNCIL.
    TOURISM IN EAST CENTRAL FLORIDA, BY
ECONOMICS RESEARCH ASSOCIATES.
TITUSVILLE, FLA., 1969.
    68P. (HUD 701 REPORT)

    1. TRAVEL. 2. REGIONAL PLANNING -
FLORIDA. I. ECONOMICS RESEARCH
ASSOCIATES. II. HUD. 701. FLORIDA.

910
F22w   TRAVEL.
FEDERAL WRITERS' PROJECT. DISTRICT OF
COLUMBIA.
    WASHINGTON, CITY AND CAPITAL.
WASHINGTON, GOVT. PRINT. OFF., 1937.
1140P. (WORKS PROGRESS ADMINISTRATION.
AMERICAN GUIDE SERIES)

    1. TRAVEL. I. TITLE.

910
F42   Travel.
Fielding, Temple.
    Fielding's travel guide to Europe,

New York, William Sloane Associates, 1959.
    v. annual.

    For complete information see shelflist.

    1. Travel.

910
F56   Travel.
Florida. Development Commission. (Industrial
Services Division)
    [List of over 800 travel agents in the Latin
American area] Miami, [1959]
    42p.

    1. Travel.

910
F56f   Travel.
Florida. Development Commission.
    Florida package vacations, 1964.
Tallahassee, 1964.
    48p.

    1. Travel. 2. Economic conditions
- Florida. I. Title.

VF
650
(759)
F56   Travel - (Florida)
Florida. Development Commission.
    Florida tourist study,
Tallahassee,
    v. annual.
    Title varies: 1958-1959, Tourist studies
in Fla.-1960- Florida tourism report.

    For complete information see shelflist.

    1. Business - Florida. 2. Travel -
Florida.

914
F62   Travel.
Fodor, Eugene, ed.
    Austria 1958; illustrated edition with
maps. New York, David McKay Co., 1958.
    304p. (Fodor's modern guides)

    1. Travel. I. Title.

330
(969)
H18b   Travel.
Hawaii. Dept. of Economic Development.
    Bring your business imagination to Hawaii.
Honolulu, Hawaii, 1961.
    36p.

    1. Economic conditions - Hawaii.
2. Travel. I. Title.

910
H18   Travel.
Hawaii. Dept. of Planning and Research.
    Out-of-state travel by Hawaii residents,
1960-1961. Honolulu, 1961.
    11p. (Its Research report no. 11)

    1. Travel.

Folio
711.73
H68m   Travel
Household Goods Carriers' Bureau.
    Mileage guide no. 8, containing maps and charts
for determining distances in highway miles between
points within the United States,..
No.
Washington, Rand McNally,
    v. irregular
    See Shelf List For Library Holdings.
    Each edition cancels the previous one.
    1. Highways. 2. Travel. 3. Transportation.
I. Title: Mileage guide.

330
(7455)
L47   Travel.
Little, Arthur D
    A research and action program to aid in
the development of New Bedford's tourist
industry: a supplementary memorandum report
to "A study of the economic base of the city
of New Bedford." Cambridge, Mass. [1962?]
    10p.

    U.S. Urban Renewal Adm. UPAP.

    1. Economic base studies - New Bedford,
Mass. 2. Travel. I. U.S. URA-UPAP.
New Bedford, Mass.

914
L49   Travel.
Little (Arthur D.) inc.
    Tourism and recreation; a state-of-the art
study. Prepared for the Office of Regional
Development Planning. Washington, U.S. Dept.
of Commerce, Economic Development Administration,
[1967]
    301p.

    1. Travel. 2. Recreation. 3. Economic develop-
ment. 4. Regional planning. I. U.S. Economic
Development Administration. II. Title.

910
L87   TRAVEL.
LURIE, RICHARD G
    PASSPORTS AND PROFITS; PAN AM'S GUIDE TO
DOING BUSINESS IN 105 COUNTRIES. PREPARED
FOR PAN AMERICAN AIRWAYS; DISTRIBUTION BY
DOUBLEDAY & COMPANY, INC., GARDEN CITY,
N.Y. NEW YORK, PAN AMERICAN PUBLICATIONS,
1964.
    672P.

    1. TRAVEL. I. PAN AMERICAN AIRWAYS.
II. TITLE.

330
(764)
M13   Travel.
Maffitt, Peter C ed.
    Houston guide and handbook; metropolitan
Houston NASA-Galveston areas. Houston,
TIFCO Publications, TIFCO Inter-America
Corp., 1968.
    239p.

    1. Economic conditions - Houston, Tex.
2. Travel. I. Title.

712.25
087s
no. 18   Travel.
Martin, Betty Sullivan.
    A look abroad: the effect of foreign travel
on domestic outdoor recreation and a brief
survey of outdoor recreation in six countries,
by Betty Sullivan Martin, Donald N. Martin
Company. Report to the Outdoor Recreation
Resources Review Commission. Wash., Govt.
Print. Off., 1962.
    82p. (U.S. Outdoor Recreation Resources
Review Commission. ORRRC study report 18)
    1. Recreation. 2. Travel. I. Martin (Donald N.)
Co. (Series: U.S. Outdoor Recreation
Resources Review Commission. ORRRC
study report 18)

374 TRAVEL.
MIDDLE GEORGIA AREA PLANNING COMMISSION.
A COMPREHENSIVE PLAN FOR TOURISM IN THE
MIDDLE GEORGIA AREA, BY ADLEY ASSOCIATES,
INC. MACON, 1969.
65P. (HUD 701 REPORT)

1. TRAVEL. I. ADLEY ASSOCIATES, INC.
II. HUD. 701. GEORGIA.

351.1 Travel.
C657tr U.S. Congress. House. Committee on
1967 Government Operations.
H-H Travel expenses of government employees.
Hearing before a subcommittee of the Committee
on Government Operations, House of Representatives, Ninetieth Congress, first session on
H.R. 7713 to increase the maximum rate of per
diem allowance for employees of the government traveling on official business. Wash.,
Govt. Print. Off., 1967.
29p.
Hearings held Sept. 13, 1967.
1. Federal civil service.
2. Travel. I. Title.

---

910 TRAVEL - CONNECTICUT
F22C FEDERAL WRITERS' PROJECT. CONNECTICUT.
CONNECTICUT; A GUIDE TO ITS ROADS,
LORE, AND PEOPLE, WRITTEN BY WORKERS OF
THE FEDERAL WRITERS' PROJECT OF THE WORKS
PROGRESS ADMINISTRATION FOR THE STATE OF
CONNECTICUT; SPONSORED BY WILBUR L.
CROSS. BOSTON, HOUGHTON MIFFLIN COMPANY,
1938.
593P. (AMERICAN GUIDE SERIES)

SELECTED READING LIST : P. 562-565.

1. TRAVEL - CONNECTICUT

R Travel.
711.73 Rand, McNally & Co.
R15 Standard highway mileage guide, 1961-

Chicago, 1961-
v.

For complete information see shelflist.

1. Highways. 2. Travel. I. Title.

R Travel - Alaska.
910 Jacobin, Lou.
(798) Guide to Alaska and the Yukon; the
J12 authentic handbook of the 49th state.
13th ed. Anchorage, Alaska, Guide to
Alaska, 1962.
320p.

1. Travel - Alaska. 2. Economic
conditions - Alaska.

---

914 TRAVEL - CZECHOSLOVAKIA.
(437) Fodor's Czechoslovakia, 19
F62
New York, McKay, 19
v.

19 edited by Eugene Fodor.

1. Travel - Czechoslovakia.
I. Fodor, Eugene, ed. II. Title:
Czechoslovakia.

711.4 Travel.
(46) Spain. Ministerio de la Vivienda.
S61u Urbanismo, arquitectura y turismo y
arquitectura y paisaje. Madrid, 1966.
56p. (Abreviaturas de articulos de
revistas no. 3)

1. City planning - Spain. 2. Landscape
architecture. 3. Travel. I. Title.

---

915 TRAVEL - ASIA.
(52) Fodor, Eugene, ed.
F62 Fodor's Japan and East Asia. A definitive
handbook of the Far East and Southeast Asia.
Ed. by Eugene Fodor and Robert C. Fisher.
New York, McKay, 1971.
757p.

1. Travel - Japan. 2. Travel - Asia.
I. Fisher, Robert C., jt. ed.

---

910 TRAVEL - DELAWARE
F22D FEDERAL WRITERS' PROJECT. DELAWARE.
DELAWARE; A GUIDE TO THE FIRST STATE,
COMPILED AND WRITTEN BY THE FEDERAL
WRITERS' PROJECT OF THE WORKS PROGRESS
ADMINISTRATION FOR THE STATE OF DELAWARE
... SPONSORED BY EDWARD W. COOCH,
LIEUTENANT GOVERNOR. NEW YORK, VIKING
PRESS, 1938.
549P. (AMERICAN GUIDE SERIES)

BIBLIOGRAPHY: P. 530-538.

1. TRAVEL - DELAWARE

---

910 TRAVEL.
S77 STRUNSKY, SIMEON.
NO MEAN CITY. NEW YORK, DUTTON, 1944.
285P.

1. TRAVEL. 2. SOCIAL CONDITIONS - NEW
YORK (CITY) I. TITLE.

---

910 TRAVEL - AUGUSTA, GA.
F22G FEDERAL WRITERS' PROJECT. GEORGIA.
AUGUSTA. SPONSORED BY CITY COUNCIL OF
AUGUSTA. AUGUSTA, GA., TIDWELL PRINT
SUPPLY CO., 1938.
218P. (AMERICAN GUIDE SERIES)

1. TRAVEL - AUGUSTA, GA. I. AUGUSTA,
GA. CITY COUNCIL.

---

910 TRAVEL - ERIE, PA.
F22PEN FEDERAL WRITERS' PROJECT. PENNSYLVANIA.
ERIE; A GUIDE TO THE CITY AND COUNTY,
WRITTEN AND COMPILED BY THE ERIE COUNTY
UNIT OF THE FEDERAL WRITERS' PROJECT OF
THE WORKS PROGRESS ADMINISTRATION FOR
THE COMMONWEALTH OF PENNSYLVANIA.
SPONSORED BY CHARLIE R. BARBER, MAYOR
OF ERIE. PHILADELPHIA, WILLIAM PENN
ASSOCIATION, 1938
133P. (AMERICAN GUIDE SERIES)

1. TRAVEL - ERIE, PA. 2. TRAVEL -
ERIE CO., PA.

---

910 TRAVEL.
A72 U.S. OFFICE OF AREA DEVELOPMENT.
YOUR COMMUNITY CAN PROFIT FROM THE
TOURIST BUSINESS. WASHINGTON, GOVT.
PRINT. OFF., 1957.
25P.

1. TRAVEL. 2. REAL PROPERTY -
VALUATION. I. TITLE. II. TITLE: THE
TOURIST BUSINESS.

---

910 TRAVEL - CANADA.
(71) Frommer, Arthur.
F76 Dollar-wise guide to Montreal, Quebec and
the Laurentians, by Arthur Frommer and John
Godwin in cooperation with the Bank of Nova
Scotia. New York, Frommer/Pasmantier Pub.
Corp., 1967.
223p.

1. Travel - Canada. 2. Canada - Travel.
I. Godwin, John, jt. au. II. Title.

---

914 TRAVEL - EUROPE.
A52p American Automobile Association. (World-
1969 Wide Travel)
Map Planning map of Europe. Washington, 1969.

map. (no. 1030)

1. Travel - Europe. 2. Maps and
mapping - Europe. I. Title.

VF Travel.
712.25 U.S. Area Redevelopment Administration.
A72 Recreation and tourism development through
Federal programs. Washington, U.S. Dept. of
Commerce, Area Redevelopment Administration,
1965.
25p.

1. Recreation. 2. Travel. 3. National
parks and reserves. 3. Grants-in-aid.
I. Title.

---

910 TRAVEL - CHICAGO.
(77311) HARPER, WILLIAM HUDSON, ED.
H17 CHICAGO, A HISTORY AND FORECAST.
EDITOR, WM. HUDSON HARPER;
CONTRIBUTORS, MILO MILTON QUAIFE,
MABEL MCILVAINE. CHICAGO, THE CHICAGO
ASSOCIATION OF COMMERCE, 1921.
256P.

COVER-TITLE: CHICAGO, YESTERDAY,
TODAY, TOMORROW, 1673, 1921, 1973.

1. TRAVEL - CHICAGO.

---

914 TRAVEL - EUROPE.
A52w American Automobile Association. (World-
Wide Travel)
Where to stay in Europe, 19
Washing, 19
v.
For Library holdings see main entry.
Keep latest edition only.

1. Travel - Europe. I. Title.

---

351 Travel.
C657 U.S. Congress. House. Committee on
1967 Government Operations.
H-R Payment of travel expenses of applicants
for government employment in manpower-short-
age positions; report to accompany H.R. 9382.
Washington, Govt. Print. Off., 1967.
16p. (90th Cong., 1st sess. House. Report
no. 881)

1. Federal government. 2. Federal civil
service. 3. Travel. 4. Employment.
I. Title.

---

910 TRAVEL - CHICAGO - BIBLIOGRAPHY.
(016) FEDERAL WRITERS' PROJECT. ILLINOIS.
F221 SELECTED BIBLIOGRAPHY; ILLINOIS,
CHICAGO AND ITS ENVIRONS; FEDERAL
WRITERS' PROJECT, ILLINOIS, WORKS
PROGRESS ADMINISTRATION. CHICAGO, 1937.
58L. (AMERICAN GUIDE SERIES)

1. TRAVEL - ILLINOIS - BIBLIOGRAPHY.
2. TRAVEL - CHICAGO - BIBLIOGRAPHY.

---

914 TRAVEL - EUROPE.
(4) Europe on 5 dollars a day. 19
C87 New York, Arthur Frommer, inc., 19
v.
Vols. for 19 prepared by
Arthur Frommer.
19 Sightseeing commentaries by
Hope Arthur.
For Library holdings see main entry.
1. Travel - Europe. I. Frommer,
Arthur. II. Arthur, Hope.

Travel - Florida.

VF
610
(759)
F56
Florida. Development Commission.
Florida plant tours. Tallahassee,
Fla., [1962?]
[9]p.

1. Industry - Florida. 2. Travel -
Florida. I. Title.

910
(764)
F67
TRAVEL - FORT WORTH, TEX.
FORT WORTH IN PICTURES. FORT WORTH,
J.J. WALDEN, 1942.
148P.

1. TRAVEL - FORT WORTH, TEX.

914
(43)
A75f
1964
Travel - Germany.
Arntz, Helmut, 1912-
Facts about Germany. 5th ed. [Bonn]
Press and Information Office of the Federal
Government of Germany, 1964.
380p.

1. Travel - Germany. 2. Germany (Federal
Republic, 1949-   ) 3. Economic conditions - Germany. I. Title.

914
(43)
A75
1964
Travel - Germany.
Arntz, Helmut, 1912-
Germany in brief: historical development,
government and politics, economy, the arts,
statistics. 3d ed. [Bonn] Press and Information Office of the Federal Government of
Germany, 1964.
120p.

1. Travel - Germany. 2. Germany (Federal
Republic, 1949-   ) 3. Economic conditions - Germany.   I. Title.

914
(43)
B 12
TRAVEL - GERMANY.
Bad Mergentheim, Ger. Stadtische Kultur- und
Verkehrsamt.
Bad Mergentheim. Jubilaum 750 Jahre Deutscher
Orden in Mergentheim. Bad Mergentheim, 1970.
[56]p.
Bad Mergentheimer Blätter, drittes Heft,
1969/70.

1. Travel - Germany.

914
(43)
F62
TRAVEL - GERMANY.
Fodor, Eugene, ed.
Fodor's Germany. Illustrated edition with
atlas and city plans. New York, McKay, 1971.
427p.

1. Travel - Germany.

914
(43)
M81
TRAVEL - GERMANY.
MVA Reise- und Baderdienst.
Bad Mergentheim. Bad Mergentheim, 1965.
24p.

1. Travel - Germany. 2. Health.
3. Hospitals - Germany. 4. Recreation -
Germany.

910
(969)
H18o
Travel - Hawaii.
Hawaii. Dept. of Planning and Research.
Oahu residents vacationing on neighbor
islands, 1961. Honolulu, 1962.
12p.   (Its Research report 31)

1. Travel - Hawaii.

910
(969)
H18v
Travel - Hawaii.
Hawaii. Dept. of Planning and Research.
Visitor and hotel room projections
for Hawaii, 1948-1980. Honolulu, 1962.
6p.   (Its Research report 29)

1. Travel - Hawaii. 2. Business - Hawaii.
3. Hotels - Hawaii.

910
F221D
TRAVEL - IDAHO.
FEDERAL WRITERS' PROJECT. IDAHO.
IDAHO, A GUIDE IN WORD AND PICTURE,
PREPARED BY THE FEDERAL WRITERS'
PROJECTS OF THE WORKS PROGRESS
ADMINISTRATION. THE LIBRARY ED.
CALDWELL, CAXTON PRINTERS, 1937.
431P. (THE AMERICAN GUIDE SERIES)

1. TRAVEL - IDAHO.

910
F221DA
TRAVEL - IDAHO.
FEDERAL WRITERS' PROJECT. IDAHO.
THE IDAHO ENCYCLOPEDIA, COMPILED BY
THE FEDERAL WRITERS' PROJECT OF THE
WORKS PROGRESS ADMINISTRATION.
CALDWELL, CAXTON PRINTERS, LTD., 1938.
452P.

1. TRAVEL - IDAHO.

910
(016)
F221
TRAVEL - ILLINOIS - BIBLIOGRAPHY.
FEDERAL WRITERS' PROJECT. ILLINOIS.
SELECTED BIBLIOGRAPHY, ILLINOIS,
CHICAGO AND ITS ENVIRONS, FEDERAL
WRITERS' PROJECT, ILLINOIS, WORKS
PROGRESS ADMINISTRATION. CHICAGO, 1937.
58L. (AMERICAN GUIDE SERIES)

1. TRAVEL - ILLINOIS - BIBLIOGRAPHY.
2. TRAVEL - CHICAGO - BIBLIOGRAPHY.

910
(54)
M66
TRAVEL - INDIA.
Moorhouse, Geoffrey, 1931-
Calcutta. [1st American ed.] New York,
Harcourt Brace Jovanovich, 1972.
376p.
Bibliography: p. 348-350.

1. Travel - India. 2. Economic conditions -
India. I. Title.

910
F221
TRAVEL - INDIANA.
FEDERAL WRITERS PROJECT. INDIANA.
INDIANA. A GUIDE TO THE HOOSIER
STATE. COMPILED BY WORKERS OF THE
WRITERS' PROGRAM OF THE WORK PROJECTS
ADMINISTRATION IN THE STATE OF INDIANA.
NEW YORK, OXFORD UNIVERSITY PRESS, 1941.
548P. (AMERICAN GUIDE SERIES)

BIBLIOGRAPHY P. 509-523.

1. TRAVEL - INDIANA

711.333
(415)
I72
Ireland (Eire) National Institute for
Physical Planning and Construction Research.
Planning for amenity and tourism; illustrated by excerpts from the model amenity -
tourism study of County Donegal. Dublin, 1966.
110p. (Its Specimen development plan
manual 2-3)
A project of the Government of Ireland
assisted by the United Nations Special Fund
and the United Nations.
1. County planning - Ireland. 2. Travel -
Ireland. 3. Ireland - County planning.
4. Ireland - Tr   avel. I. United Nations.
II. Title.

910
(415)
UN
1962
Travel - Ireland.
United Nations. (Economic Commission for
Europe. Housing Committee)
Visit to Northern Ireland. Belfast,
H.M. Stat. Off., 1962.
1v.

1. Travel - Ireland.

915
(5694)
A57
TRAVEL - ISRAEL.
Anti-Defamation League of B'Nai B'Rith.
Israel handbook. New York. 1970.
192p.

Bibliography: p. 189-192.

1. Travel - Israel. I. Title.

915
(52)
F62
TRAVEL - JAPAN.
Fodor, Eugene, ed.
Fodor's Japan and East Asia. A definitive
handbook of the Far East and Southeast Asia.
Ed. by Eugene Fodor and Robert C. Fisher.
New York, McKay, 1971.
757p.

1. Travel - Japan. 2. Travel - Asia.
I. Fisher, Robert C., jt. ed.

910
F22K
TRAVEL - KENTUCKY.
FEDERAL WRITERS' PROJECT. KENTUCKY.
KENTUCKY; A GUIDE TO THE BLUEGRASS
STATE, COMPILED AND WRITTEN BY THE
FEDERAL WRITERS' PROJECT OF THE WORK
PROJECTS ADMINISTRATION FOR THE STATE OF
KENTUCKY. SPONSORED BY THE UNIVERSITY OF
KENTUCKY. NEW YORK, HARCOURT, BRACE AND
CO., 1939.
489P. (AMERICAN GUIDE SERIES)

1. TRAVEL - KENTUCKY.

VF
910
(519)
K67
Travel - Korea.
Korea. Ministry of Public Information.
Guide to Korea. Washington, D.C. The
Korean Research and Information Office,
[1962?]
24p.

1. Travel - Korea. 2. Economic
conditions - Korea.

910
F22MA
TRAVEL - MAINE.
FEDERAL WRITERS' PROJECT. MAINE.
MAINE, A GUIDE 'DOWN EAST,' WRITTEN BY
WORKERS OF THE FEDERAL WRITERS' PROJECT
OF THE WORKS PROGRESS ADMINISTRATION FOR
THE STATE OF MAINE, SPONSORED BY THE
MAINE DEVELOPMENT COMMISSION. BOSTON,
HOUGHTON MIFFLIN, 1937.
476P. (AMERICAN GUIDE SERIES)

1. TRAVEL - MAINE.

910
F22MAR TRAVEL - MARYLAND.
FEDERAL WRITERS' PROJECT. MARYLAND.
MARYLAND, A GUIDE TO THE OLD LINE
STATE, COMPILED BY WORKERS OF THE
WRITERS' PROGRAM OF THE WORK PROJECTS
ADMINISTRATION IN THE STATE OF
MARYLAND. SPONSORED BY HERBERT R.
O'CONOR, GOVERNOR OF MARYLAND. NEW
YORK, OXFORD UNIVERSITY PRESS, 1940.
561P. (AMERICAN GUIDE SERIES)

1. TRAVEL - MARYLAND.

910
(752)
M17
1969 TRAVEL - MD.
Maryland. Dept. of State Planning.
Maryland manual of coordinates. 3d
ed. Baltimore, 1969.
107p. (Its Publication no. 155)

1. Travel - Md. I. Title: Coordinates.
II. Title: Manual of coordinates.

910
F22MAS TRAVEL - MASSACHUSETTS.
FEDERAL WRITERS' PROJECT.
MASSACHUSETTS.
MASSACHUSETTS, A GUIDE TO ITS PLACES
AND PEOPLE, WRITTEN AND COMPILED BY THE
FEDERAL WRITERS' PROJECT OF THE WORKS
PROGRESS ADMINISTRATION FOR THE STATE
OF MASSACHUSETTS. BOSTON, HOUGHTON
MIFFLIN, 1937.
675P. (AMERICAN GUIDE SERIES)

1. TRAVEL - MASSACHUSETTS.

910
F22M TRAVEL - MISSISSIPPI
FEDERAL WRITERS' PROJECT. MISSISSIPPI.
MISSISSIPPI, A GUIDE TO THE MAGNOLIA
STATE, COMPILED AND WRITTEN BY THE
FEDERAL WRITERS' PROJECT OF THE WORKS
PROGRESS ADMINISTRATION. NEW YORK,
VIKING PRESS, 1938.
545P. (AMERICAN GUIDE SERIES)

BIBLIOGRAPHY: P. 523-530.

1. TRAVEL - MISSISSIPPI

910
F22NEW TRAVEL - MONROE COUNTY, N.Y.
FEDERAL WRITERS' PROJECT. NEW YORK
(STATE)
ROCHESTER AND MONROE COUNTRY. BY
FEDERAL WRITERS' PROJECT. WORKS
PROGRESS ADMINISTRATION, STATE OF NEW
YORK, SPONSORED BY THE CITY OF
ROCHESTER AND THE GENESEE BOOK CLUB.
ROCHESTER, N.Y., SCRANTOM'S, 1937.
460P. (AMERICAN GUIDE SERIES)

1. TRAVEL - ROCHESTER, N.Y.
2. TRAVEL - MONROE COUNTY, N.Y.
I. TITLE.

360
(492)
B 14 TRAVEL - NETHERLANDS.
Bailey, Anthony.
The light in Holland. New York, Knopf, 1970.
263p.

Bibliography: p. 261-263.

1. Social conditions - Netherlands.
2. Travel - Netherlands. I. Title.

914
(492)
R22 Travel - Netherlands.
Redeker, Hans.
Life in Holland. English text, Dorothy de
Graaf-Sherston and P. Lopes Cardozo.
Amsterdam, De Bezige Bij [1966]
1 v.

1. Travel - Netherlands. 2. Economic
conditions - Netherlands. I. Title.
II. Graaf-Sherston, Dorothy de.

914
(492)
V15 TRAVEL - NETHERLANDS.
Van Wel, F J
Portrait of Holland. Porträt von Holland.
Retrato de Holanda. [Amsterdam, 1970?]
128p.

1. Travel - Netherlands. 2. Architecture -
Netherlands. 3. Public buildings - Netherlands.
I. Title.

910
F22DE TRAVEL - NEW CASTLE, DEL.
FEDERAL WRITERS' PROJECT. DELAWARE.
NEW CASTLE ON THE DELAWARE, COMPILED
BY THE DELAWARE FEDERAL WRITERS'
PROJECT, WORKS PROGRESS ADMINISTRATION.
SPONSORED AND PUBLISHED BY THE NEW
CASTLE HISTORICAL SOCIETY. NEW CASTLE,
1936.
142P.

1. TRAVEL - NEW CASTLE, DEL.
I. TITLE.

910
F22NE TRAVEL - NEW HAMPSHIRE
FEDERAL WRITERS' PROJECT. NEW HAMPSHIRE.
NEW HAMPSHIRE, A GUIDE TO THE GRANITE
STATE, WRITTEN BY WORKERS OF THE FEDERAL
WRITERS' PROJECT OF THE WORKS PROGRESS
ADMINISTRATION FOR THE STATE OF NEW
HAMPSHIRE. BOSTON, HOUGHTON MIFFLIN,
1938.
559P. (AMERICAN GUIDE SERIES)

BIBLIOGRAPHY: P. 539-530.

1. TRAVEL - NEW HAMPSHIRE

910
F22N TRAVEL - NEW JERSEY.
FEDERAL WRITERS' PROJECT. NEW JERSEY.
NEW JERSEY. A GUIDE TO ITS PRESENT
AND PAST. COMPILED AND WRITTEN BY THE
FEDERAL WRITERS' PROJECT OF THE WORKS
PROGRESS ADMINISTRATION FOR THE STATE OF
NEW JERSEY. NEW YORK, THE VIKING PRESS,
1939.
735P. (AMERICAN GUIDE SERIES)

1. TRAVEL - NEW JERSEY.

917
B27 TRAVEL - NEW YORK (CITY)
Berenyi, John.
Up against New York; a handbook for survival
in the city. New York, William Morrow and Co.,
1971.
290p.

1. Travel - New York (City) 2. Metropolitan
areas - New York (City) I. Title.

910
F22NO TRAVEL - NORTH CAROLINA.
FEDERAL WRITERS' PROJECT. NORTH
CAROLINA.
NORTH CAROLINA, A GUIDE TO THE OLD
NORTH STATE, COMPILED AND WRITTEN BY THE
FEDERAL WRITERS' PROJECT OF THE FEDERAL
WORKS AGENCY, WORK PROJECTS
ADMINISTRATION FOR THE STATE OF NORTH
CAROLINA. SPONSORED BY NORTH CAROLINA
DEPARTMENT OF CONSERVATION AND
DEVELOPMENT. CHAPEL HILL, UNIVERSITY OF
NORTH CAROLINA PRESS, 1939.
601P. (AMERICAN GUIDE SERIES)

1. TRAVEL - N ORTH CAROLINA.

910
F22NOR TRAVEL - NORTH DAKOTA.
FEDERAL WRITERS' PROJECT. NORTH DAKOTA.
NORTH DAKOTA, A GUIDE TO THE NORTHERN
PRAIRIE STATE, WRITTEN BY WORKERS OF
THE FEDERAL WRITERS' PROJECT OF THE
WORKS PROGRESS ADMINISTRATION FOR THE
STATE OF NORTH DAKOTA, SPONSORED BY THE
STATE HISTORICAL SOCIETY OF NORTH
DAKOTA. FARGO, 1938.
371P. (AMERICAN GUIDE SERIES)

1. TRAVEL - NORTH DAKOTA.

910
B14 Travel - Northeastern States.
Bailey, Anthony.
Through the great city. New York, Macmillan,
1967.
276p.
N.c.1,2
Laf.c.3
"Most of the material...appeared originally in
the New Yorker in slightly different form."
Bibliography: p. 267-26*.

1. Travel - Northeastern States.
2. Sociology, Urban.

330
(713)
O57o Travel - Ontario.
Ontario. Dept. of Economics and Development.
Ontario, 67. Ontario, 1967.
99p.

1. Economic conditions - Ontario.
2. Social conditions - Ontario. 3. Travel -
Ontario. I. Title.

910
(713)
O57 Travel - Ontario, Can.
Ontario, Can. Dept. of Tourism and Information.
Ontario; friendly, familiar, foreign and
near. [n.p., 1965?]
1v.

1. Travel - Ontario, Can. I. Title.

910
F22L TRAVEL - NEW ORLEANS.
FEDERAL WRITERS' PROJECT. LOUISIANA.
NEW ORLEANS CITY GUIDE, WRITTEN AND
COMPILED BY THE FEDERAL WRITERS' PROJECT
OF THE WORKS PROGRESS ADMINISTRATION FOR
THE CITY OF NEW ORLEANS. BOSTON,
HOUGHTON MIFFLIN, 1938. 430P.

1. TRAVEL - NEW ORLEANS.

910
F22PE TRAVEL - PENNSYLVANIA.
FEDERAL WRITERS' PROJECT. PENNSYLVANIA.
PENNSYLVANIA, A GUIDE TO THE KEYSTONE
STATE, COMPILED BY WORKERS OF THE
WRITERS' PROGRAM OF THE WORK PROJECTS
ADMINISTRATION IN THE STATE OF
PENNSYLVANIA. CO-SPONSORED BY THE
PENNSYLVANIA HISTORICAL COMMISSION AND
THE UNIVERSITY OF PENNSYLVANIA. NEW
YORK, OXFORD UNIVERSITY PRESS, 1940.
660P. (AMERICAN GUIDE SERIES)

1. TRAVEL - PENNSYLVANIA.

330
(85)
R15 Travel - Peru.
Belaunde-Terry, Fernando.
Peru's own conquest. Introduction by
David A. Robinson. 1st ed. Lima, American
Studies Press, 1965.
219p.

1. Economic development - Peru. 2. Social
conditions - Peru. 3. Travel - Peru.

910
F22P TRAVEL - PHILADELPHIA
FEDERAL WRITERS' PROJECT. PENNSYLVANIA.
PHILADELPHIA, A GUIDE TO THE NATION'S
BIRTHPLACE, COMPILED BY THE FEDERAL
WRITERS' PROJECT, WORKS PROGRESS
ADMINISTRATION, FOR THE COMMONWEALTH OF
PENNSYLVANIA, SPONSORED BY THE
PENNSYLVANIA HISTORICAL COMMISSION... 1ST
ED. PHILADELPHIA, WILLIAM PENN
ASSOCIATION OF PHILADELPHIA, INC., 1937.
704P. (AMERICAN GUIDE SERIES)

BIBLIOGRAPHY: P. 690-691.

1. TRAVEL - PHILADELPHIA

910
(7295)
P82

TRAVEL - PUERTO RICO.
PUERTO RICO. DIRECCION: JULIAN DEVIS
ECHEANDIA; DIRECTOR ARTISTICO: LOUIS
DUCHESNE CAICEDO. BARRANQUILLA,
COLOMBIA, 1949.
420P. (COLECCION AMERICA, TOMO 10)

1. TRAVEL - PUERTO RICO.

910
F22GE

TRAVEL - SAVANNAH.
FEDERAL WRITERS' PROJECT. GEORGIA.
SAVANNAH; COMPILED AND WRITTEN BY
SAVANNAH UNIT, FEDERAL WRITERS' PROJECT
IN GEORGIA. WORKS PROGRESS
ADMINISTRATION. SPONSORED BY CHAMBER OF
COMMERCE. SAVANNAH, REVIEW
PRINT CO., 1937.
208P. (AMERICAN GUIDE SERIES)

1. TRAVEL - SAVANNAH.

914
(47)
R21

Travel - U.S.S.R.
Redro, P
Eaporizhzhia. Kiev, Vidavnitstvo
Mistetstvo, 1965.
81p.

1. Travel - U.S.S.R. 2. U.S.S.R. - Travel.

914.015
V18

Travel - Research.
Waugh, Robert E
The American traveler: more darkness than
light? Austin, Tex., Bureau of Business
Research, University of Texas, 1962.
54p.

1. Travel - Research. I. Texas.
University. Bureau of Business Research.

918
(9)
F62

TRAVEL - SOUTH AMERICA.
Fodor, Eugene, ed.
Fodor's South America, 1971. A comprehensive
handbook of the whole continent. New York,
McKay, 1971.
613p.

1. Travel - South America.

914
(47)
I57

Travel - U.S.S.R.
Intourist, Moscow.
The cities of the U.S.S.R. Visit the
Soviet Union. Moscow [1965?]
1v.

1. Travel - U.S.S.R. 2. Communism.
I. Title.

910
F22R

TRAVEL - RHODE ISLAND.
FEDERAL WRITERS' PROJECT. RHODE ISLAND.
RHODE ISLAND, A GUIDE TO THE SMALLEST
STATE, WRITTEN BY WORKERS OF THE FEDERAL
WRITERS' PROJECT OF THE WORKS PROGRESS
ADMINISTRATION FOR THE STATE OF RHODE
ISLAND. BOSTON, HOUGHTON MIFFLIN, 1937.
500P. (AMERICAN GUIDE SERIES)

1. TRAVEL - RHODE ISLAND.

910
(8)
W15

Travel - South America.
Waldo, Myra
Myra Waldo's travel guide to South
America. New York, Macmillan, 1968.
456p.

1. Travel - South America. 2. Economic
conditions - South America. I. Title.

914
(47)
U47

Travel - U.S.S.R.
Ukraine. Komitet po pechati.
Sovetskaia Ukraina. Kiev, 1967.
38p.

1. Travel - U.S.S.R. 2. U.S.S.R. -
Travel.

910
F22NEW

TRAVEL - ROCHESTER, N.Y.
FEDERAL WRITERS' PROJECT. NEW YORK
(STATE)
ROCHESTER AND MONROE COUNTRY. BY
FEDERAL WRITERS' PROJECT, WORKS
PROGRESS ADMINISTRATION, STATE OF NEW
YORK; SPONSORED BY THE CITY OF
ROCHESTER AND THE GENESEE BOOK CLUB.
ROCHESTER, N.Y., SCRANTOM'S, 1937.
460P. (AMERICAN GUIDE SERIES)

1. TRAVEL - ROCHESTER, N.Y.
2. TRAVEL - MONROE COUNTY, N.Y.
I. TITLE.

910
F22S

TRAVEL - SOUTH DAKOTA.
FEDERAL WRITERS' PROJECT. SOUTH DAKOTA.
A SOUTH DAKOTA GUIDE, COMPILED BY THE
FEDERAL WRITERS' PROJECT OF THE WORKS
PROGRESS ADMINISTRATION, STATE OF SOUTH
DAKOTA. SPONSORED BY THE STATE OF SOUTH
DAKOTA. PIERRE, 1938.
441P. (AMERICAN GUIDE SERIES)

1. TRAVEL - SOUTH DAKOTA.

VF
914
U54

Travel - U.S.S.R.
U.S.S.R.
Guide to the map of Kiev. Kiev, State
Publishing House for Literature on Building
and Architecture Ukranian SSR, 1958.
86p.

1. Travel - U.S.S.R. 3. Maps and mapping
- U.S.S.R.

720
(498)
B82b

TRAVEL - RUMANIA.
Bucharest. Institutul Proiect.
Bucuresti. Bucuresti [1962?]
1v.

1. Architecture - Rumania. 2. Travel -
Rumania.

VF
912
(611)
F71

Travel - Tunisia.
France. Office du Tourisme et de
l'Expansion Commerciale.
Tunisie, par Magdelaine Farisot.
[Paris] 1955.
217p. maps. (Les Guides bleus)

Le present ouvrage est un extrait du
volume Algerie-Tunisie publie dans la
collection Les Guides bleus.

1. Travel - Tunisia 2. Tunisia. I. Farisot,
Magdelaine.

914
(47)
U54

Travel - U.S.S.R.
U.S.S.R.
Leningrad. Moscow, Intourist [1965?]
[28] p. (no. 1730)

1. Travel - U.S.S.R. I. Intourist,
Moscow, U.S.S.R. II. Title.

910
F22F

TRAVEL - ST. AUGUSTINE, FLA.
FEDERAL WRITERS' PROJECT. FLORIDA.
SEEING ST. AUGUSTINE. SPONSORED BY
CITY COMMISSION OF ST. AUGUSTINE. ST.
AUGUSTINE, RECORD CO., 1937.
73P. (AMERICAN GUIDE SERIES)

1. TRAVEL - ST. AUGUSTINE, FLA.
I. ST. AUGUSTINE, FLA. CITY COMMISSION.

711.3
(41)
H25

TRAVEL - U.K.
Hempel Hempstead.
Official guide to the Borough of Hempel
Hempstead. Hempel Hempstead, 1970.
87p.

1. Metropolitan areas - U.K.
2. Travel - U.K.

947
U41

Travel - U.S.S.R.
U.S.S.R.
[U.S.S.R.] [n.p.] 1962, 1964.
Kit. (23 pieces)

1. Travel - U.S.S.R.

910
F22T

TRAVEL - SAN ANTONIO.
FEDERAL WRITERS' PROJECT. TEXAS.
SAN ANTONIO; AN AUTHORITATIVE GUIDE TO
THE CITY AND ITS ENVIRONS, COMPILED AND
WRITTEN BY THE FEDERAL WRITERS' PROJECT
OF THE WORKS PROGRESS ADMINISTRATION IN
THE STATE OF TEXAS; SAN ANTONIO
CONSERVATION SOCIETY, COOPERATING
SPONSOR. SAN ANTONIO, CLEGG CO., 1938.
106P. (AMERICAN GUIDE SERIES)

1. TRAVEL - SAN ANTONIO.

914
(41)
N14

TRAVEL - U.K. - LONDON.
NAIRN, IAN.
NAIRN'S LONDON. BALTIMORE, PENGUIN
BOOKS, 1966.
272P.

1. TRAVEL - U.K. - LONDON.
2. ARCHITECTURE - U.K. - LONDON.
I. TITLE: LONDON. II. TITLE.

910
F22V

TRAVEL - VERMONT
FEDERAL WRITERS' PROJECT. VERMONT.
VERMONT; A GUIDE TO THE GREEN MOUNTAIN
STATE, WRITTEN BY WORKERS OF THE FEDERAL
WRITERS' PROJECT OF THE WORKS PROGRESS
ADMINISTRATION FOR THE STATE OF VERMONT;
SPONSORED BY THE VERMONT STATE PLANNING
BOARD ... BOSTON, HOUGHTON MIFFLIN
COMPANY, 1937.
392P. (AMERICAN GUIDE SERIES)

BIBLIOGRAPHY: P. 372-379.

1. TRAVEL - VERMONT

914
(497?)
F62

TRAVEL - YUGOSLAVIA.
Fodor, Eugene, ed.
Fodor's Yugoslavia. Illustrated edition
with atlas and city plans. New York, McKay,
1971.
318p.

1. Travel - Yugoslavia.

690.015
(485)
S82
R29
1968

Travel-pattern within an urban area.
Westelius, Orvar.
Trafikrörelsers sammansättning - en
undersökning i Uppsala 1965 (Travel - pattern
within an urban area). Stockholm, Statens
institut för byggnadsforskning, 1968.
74p. (Stockholm. Statens institut för
byggnadsforskning. Rapport 29:1968)
English summary.
1. Building research - Sweden. 2. Sweden -
Building research. 3. Traffic - Sweden.
4. Sweden - Traffic. I. Stockholm. Statens
institut för byggnadsforskning. II. Title:
Travel-pattern   within an urban area.

370
N17p
no.30

Travers, Kenneth J
Teaching resources for low-achieving
mathematics classes, by Kenneth J. Travers
and others. Wash., U.S. Dept. of Health,
Education and Welfare, Office of Education,
National Center for Educational Communication,
1972.
34p. (Putting research into educational
practice. Report no.30)
Bibliography: p. 19-34.
1. Education. 2. Mathematics - Study and
teaching. I. U. S National Center for
Educational   Communication. II. Title.

351
G25RE

TRAVEL ADVANCES ISSUED AND
OUTSTANDING.
U.S. GENERAL ACCOUNTING OFFICE.
REPORT ON TRAVEL ADVANCES ISSUED AND
OUTSTANDING IN AMOUNTS IN EXCESS OF
TRAVELERS NEEDS, FEDERAL HOUSING
ADMINISTRAITON, HOUSING AND HOME FINANCE
AGENCY. WASHINGTON, 1963.
9P.

1. FEDERAL GOVERNMENT. 2. U.S.
HOUSING AND HOME FINANCE AGENCY.
I. TITLE: TRAVEL ADVANCES ISSUED AND
OUTSTANDING.

388
H43f

Travel patterns.
Highway Research Board.
Factors influencing travel patterns.
Washington, 1955.
94p. graphs, maps, tables. (Its Bulletin
119)

Contents.-Trends in traffic diversion on
Edens Expressway, William J. Mortimer.-
Objective and subjective correlates of express-
way use, E. Wilson Campbell and Robert McCargar
(Continued on Card 2)

728.69
W15

Travis, R W   jt. au.
Wang, P S
The characteristics, economic resources
and housing preferences of mobile home
occupants in Santa Clara County, by P.S.
Wang and R.W. Travis. San Jose, Calif., Real
Estate Research Bureau, School of Business,
San Jose State College, 1967.
95p.

1. Mobile homes. 2. Housing surveys.
3. Home ownership. I. Travis, R.W., jt. au. II.
California. State College, San Jose. Real
Estate Research Bureau. III. Title.

351
C48R

TRAVEL AND MOVING EXPENSES.
U.S. CIVIL SERVICE COMMISSION.
A REPORT ON OPERATIONS UNDER PL 85-749
ON PAYMENT OF TRAVEL AND MOVING EXPENSES
TO FIRST POST OF DUTY. PREPARED PURSUANT
TO A COMMITTEE REQUEST OF THE COMMITTEE
ON GOVERNMENT OPERATIONS, U.S. SENATE,
EIGHTY FIFTH CONGRESS. WASHINGTON, 1960.
1 V.

1. FEDERAL GOVERNMENT. I. TITLE:
TRAVEL AND MOVING EXPENSES. II. TITLE:
MOVING EXPENSES.

388
H43f

Highway Research Board.   Factors influencing
travel patterns.... (Card 2)

-Induced traffic on Chesapeake Bay Bridge,
Ernest A. Bunting. -Intracity traffic movements,
F. Houston Wynn. -Evaluation of intercity-
travel desire, Willa Mylroie.

1. Traffic. 2. Traffic surveys - Cook County,
Ill. 3. Traffic surveys - Washington. 4.
Traffic surveys - Maryland. I. Title: Travel
patterns.

728.1
1308
(79474)
C15

TRAVIS, ROBERT W
CALIFORNIA. STATE COLLEGE. SAN JOSE.
REAL ESTATE RESEARCH BUREAU.
A DEVELOPMENT OF HOUSING RESEARCH
TECHNIQUES AND ANALYSIS OF HOUSING
INVENTORY AND EST MATES OF NEEDS AND
TRENDS IN SAN JOSE, CALIFORNIA, BY
ROBERT W. TRAVIS. SAN JOSE, CALIF.,
1960.
98L.

FINAL REPORT ... INTERAGENCY
AGREEMENT 140, JU , 1, 1959, SUBMITTED
TO ... REAL E STATE COMMISSIONER,
STATE OF CALI FORNIA.
(CONTINUED ON NEXT CARD)

910
E35

Travel diary of an engineer.
Ehlers, Joseph H
Far horizons - the travel diary of an
engineer. New York, Carlton Press, 1966.
189p. (A reflection book)

1. Travel. I. Title. II. Title: Travel
diary of an engineer.

910
A51

Traveler profiles; a study of summer travel
to Alaska during 1963 and 1964.
Alaska. Dept. of Economic Development and
Planning.
Traveler profiles; a study of summer travel
to Alaska during 1963 and 1964, by Charles
E. Hinkson. Juneau, 1964.
37p.
U.S. Urban Renewal Adm. UPAP.

1. Travel. I. Hinkson, Charles E.
II. Title. III. U.S. URA-UPAP. Alaska.

728.1
1308
(79474)
C15

CALIFORNIA. STATE COLLEGE. SAN JOSE.
REAL ESTATE RESEARCH BUREAU. A
DEVELOPMENT ...1960.   (CARD 2)

... 1960 SUPPL. SAN JOSE, CALIF.,
1960.

1. HOUSING MARKET ANALYSIS - SAN
JOSE, CALIF. I. TRAVIS, ROBERT W.

351.1
O657tr
1967
H-H

Travel expenses of government employees.
U.S. Congress. House. Committee on
Government Operations.
Travel expenses of government employees.
Hearing before a subcommittee of the Committee
on Government Operations, House of Representatives, Ninetieth Congress, first session on
H.R. 7113 to increase the maximum rate of per
diem allowance for employees of the government traveling on official business. Wash.,
Govt. Print. Off., 1967.
29p.
Hearings held Sept. 13, 1967.
1. Federal   civil service.
2. Travel. I.   Title.

690.5
I551.5
T71

TRAVELERS RESEARCH CENTER, INC.
THE OPERATIONAL AND ECONOMIC IMPACT
OF WEATHER ON THE CONSTRUCTION INDUSTRY
OF THE UNITED STATES,
BY J.A. RUSSO AND OTHERS. HARTFORD,
1965.
103P.

REFERENCES: P. 101-103.

1. WINTER CONSTRUCTION. 2. BUILDING
INDUSTRY. I. RUSSO, JAMES A.

711.4
1670
(79473)
T71

TRAVIS, ROBERT W
A STUDY OF INDUSTRIAL SITE
DEVELOPMENT AND SITE CHOICE IN SANTA
CLARA COUNTY - 1950 TO 1959. SAN
JOSE, CALIF., STATE COLLEGE, REAL
ESTATE RESEARCH BUREAU, DIVISION OF
BUSINESS, 1960.
90L.

FINAL REPORT IN FULFILLMENT OF
INTERAGENCY AGREEMENT 263, DATED
OCTOBER 1, 1959.

1. INDUSTRI ALLOCATION - SANTA
(CONTINUED ON NEXT CARD)

351
O657t
1968
H-R

Travel expenses of government employees.
U.S. Congress. House. Committee on Govern-
ment Operations.
Travel expenses of government employees.
Report to accompany H.R. 13738. Washington,
1968.
25p. (90th Cong., 2d sess. House.
Report no. 1144)

1. Federal government. 2. Grants-in-aid.
I. Title.

352
R87

Travelers Research Corp.
Russo, John A
Assessment of priorities for computer appli-
cations in Capitol region municipalities and
school systems, by John A. Russo, Jr. and
Isadore Enger. Report to the Capitol Region
Council of Elected Officials. Hartford,
Travelers Research Corp., 1969.
19p.
U.S. Dept. of Housing and Urban Develop-
ment. UPAP; Project no. Conn. P-85.
1. Municipal government - Conn. 2. Municipal
government -   Automation. 3. Schools -
Conn.
(Cont'd on next card)

711.4
1670
(79473)
T71

TRAVIS, ROBERT W A STUDY OF ...1960.
(CARD 2)
CLARA CO., CALIF. I. CALIFORNIA.
STATE COLLEGE, SAN JOSE. REAL ESTATE
RESEARCH BUREAU.

388
H433t

Travel forecasting; 8 reports presented at the
42nd annual meeting, January 7-11, 1963.
Highway Research Board.
Travel forecasting; 8 reports presented at
the 42nd annual meeting, January 7-11, 1963.
Washington, Highway Research Board of the
Division of Engineering and Industrial Re-
search, National Academy of Sciences, National
Research Council, 1963.
166p.   (Highway research record no. 38)
National Research Council Publication 1158.

1. Highways. 2. Traffic. 3. Journey to work.
4. Transportation.   I. Title.

352
R87

Russo, John A   Assessment of priorities...
1969.   (Card 2)

I. Travelers Research Corp. II. Connecticut.
Capitol Region Council of Elected Officials.
III. Enger, Isadore, jt. au. IV. U.S. HUD-
UPAP. Conn. V. Title.

333.71
T71

Travis, Robert W
The use of greenbelt theory in Santa Clara
County, Calif. San Jose, Calif., State
College, Real Estate Research Bureau,
Div. of Business, 1962.
46p.

2c.

1. Open space land. 2. Land use - Santa
Clara Co., Calif. 3. County planning -
Santa Clara Co., Calif. I. California.
State College,   San Jose, Calif.
II. Title: Greenbelt theory
in Santa Clara   County, Calif.

650.015
T71

Traweek, Stella.
    A survey of university business and economic research reports. Prepared by Stella Traweek, Bureau of Business Research, the University of Texas, Austin, Texas for the Small Business Administration. Washington, Govt. Print. Off., 1961.
    642p.

    "A compilation of faculty and doctoral research projects in business and economics completed or in progress in university schools

                 (Continued on next card)

691.71
T72

Treadaway, K   W   J
    Inhibition of the corrosion of steel in concrete, by K.W.J. Treadaway and A.D. Russell. Garston, Eng., Building Research Station, Ministry of Public Building and Works, 1968.
    5p. (U.K. Building Research Station. Current paper CP 82/68)
    Reprinted from: Highways and public works. Aug., 1968. pp. 19-21; Sept., 1968. pp. 41-41.
    1. Steel. 2. Concrete. 3. Corrosion. I. Title. II. Russell, A.D., jt. au. III. U.K. Building Research Station.

VF
658.3
T72

U.S. Dept. of the Treasury.
    Better management through incentive awards. Washington, 1956.
    12p. (Its Management improvement series no. 2)

    1. Personnel management.

650.015
T71

Traweek, Stella. A survey of university business and economic reports...1961. (Card 2)

of business and departments of economics during the academic years 1957 through 1961."

    1. Business research. 2. Economic research. I. U.S. Small Business Administration. II. Texas. University. Bureau of Business Research.

691.328
E82

Treadaway, K.W.J., jt. au.
Everett, L   H
    The use of galvanized steel reinforcement in building, by L.H. Everett and K.W.J. Treadaway. Garston, Eng., Building Research Station, 1970.
    5p.
    Paper first published in the Proceedings of the 8th International Conference on Hot Dip Galvanising held in London, June 1967, by the Zinc Development Association.
    1. Concrete, Reinforced. I. Treadaway, K.W.J., jt. au. II. U.K. Building Research Station. III. Title.

351.72
T72
R

U.S. Treasury Dept.
    Combined statement of receipts, expenditures and balances of the United States government for the fiscal year ended June 1953-70
Washington,
    18 v.   tables.

    Latest two years only in OA Library.
    For full information see shelf list card.

VF
691.116
F67
R1026

Trayer, George W
U.S. Forest Service. Forest Products Laboratory, Madison, Wis.
    Floor panels with stressed plywood coverings, by George W. Trayer. Madison, Wis., Aug. 1934.
    4 p./illus. (Its R1026)

    Mimeographed.

    1.Plywood. 2.Floors and flooring. I.Trayer, George W.

551.5
C48

Treadwell, Mattie E
U.S. Office of Civil Defense. Region V. Denton, Texas.
    Hurricane Carla, September 3-14, 1961. Prepared by Mattie E. Treadwell. Wash., Govt. Print. Off., 1962.
    97p.
    Mattie E. Treadwell, OCD Texas State Dir. for Field Operations.

    1. Storms. 2. Wind resistance. 3. Disaster services. I. Treadwell, Mattie E. II. Title.

330
157D

U.S. TREASURY DEPARTMENT.
U.S. INTERNAL REVENUE SERVICE. DEPRECIATION GUIDELINES AND RULES, REVENUE PROCEDURE 62-21. WASHINGTON, GOVT. PRINT. OFF., 1964.
    92P. (IRS PUBLICATION NO. 456)
    1. ECONOMIC CONDITIONS.
2. DEPRECIATION AND OBSOLESCENCE.
I. U.S. TREASURY DEPARTMENT. II. TITLE. III. TITLE: REVENUE PROCEDURE 62-21.

VF
691.116
F67
R1025

Trayer, George W
U.S. Forest Service. Forest Products Laboratory, Madison, Wis.
    Plywood as a structural covering for frame walls and wall units, by G. W. Trayer. Madison, Wis., Aug. 1934.
    7 p./illus. (Its R1025)

    Mimeographed.

    1.Plywood. 2.Walls. I.Trayer, George W.

LAW
T
T721r

Treanor, Gerard F
    Riots and municipalities. Washington, National Institute of Municipal Law Officers, 1968.
    37p. (National Institute of Municipal Law Officers, Rept. no. 152)

    1. Social conditions. 2. Minority groups. 3. Municipal government. I. National Institute of Municipal Law Officers. II. Title.

336
T72

U.S. Treasury Dept.
    Digest of appropriations for the support of the government of the United States for the service of the fiscal year ending June 30,
Washington, Govt. Print. Off.,
    v.   annual.

    For complete information see shelflist.

    1. U.S. - Appropriations and expenditures.

VF
690.22
F67
1929

Trayer, George W
U.S. Forest Service. Forest Products Laboratory, Madison, Wis.
    The rigidity and strength of frame walls, by George W. Trayer. Madison, Wis., Oct. 1929.
    11 l.   illus.

    Processed.

    1.Walls. I.Trayer, George W. II.Title.

728.1
1940.42
D23T

TREASURER'S REPORT FOR THE YEAR ENDED DECEMBER 31.
DEFENSE HOMES CORPORATION.
    TREASURER'S REPORT FOR THE YEAR ENDED DECEMBER 31, 1942.
WASHINGTON, 1949.
    v.
    For Library holdings see main entry
    1. DEFENSE HOUSING. I. TITLE.

332.3
T72f

U.S. Treasury Dept.
    Federal credit programs. A report by the Secretary of the Treasury to the Congress as required by the participation sale act of 1966 (public law 89-429, 89th Congress, May 24, 1966) Committee on Banking and Currency, United States Senate. Wash., For sale by the Supt. of Doc., Govt. Print. Off., 1967.
    108p.
    At head of title: 90th Cong., 1st sess.

    1. Federal lending. I. U.S. Congress. Senate. Committee on Banking and Currency. II. Title.

691.11
F67w
1935

Trayer, George
U.S. Forest Service. Forest Products Laboratory, Madison, Wis.
    Wood handbook; basic information on wood as a material of construction with data for its use in design and specifications. Washington, Govt. Print. Off., Sept. 1935.
    326 p.   illus.
    Prepared by R. F. Luxford and George W. Trayer, with the assistance of other members of the Laboratory.
    Includes bibliographies.

657
B17

U.S. TREASURY DEPT.
BARTELT, EDWARD F
    ACCOUNTING PROCEDURES OF THE UNITED STATES GOVERNMENT; A SERIES OF PAPERS. CHICAGO, PUBLIC ADMINISTRATION SERVICE, 1941.
    155P.

    1. ACCOUNTING. 2. U.S. TREASURY DEPT.

336.18
T72

U.S. Treasury Dept.
    Federal revenue sharing with state and local governments: allocations to major counties, cities, and towns. A special report. New York, Commerce Clearing House, 1970.
    84p. (Urban affairs reports)

    1. Grants-in-aid. 2. Municipal finance. 3. State finance. I. Commerce Clearing House. II. Title.

VF
693.002.22
T72

Treacy, Moira.
    Housing takes shelter in the factory; the industry is being made over in the image of the big company - as huge demand goes unmet. New York, New York Stock Exchange, 1969.
    8-13p.
    In: Exchange, vol. XXX, no. 5, May, 1969, p. 8-13.
    1. Prefabricated construction. 2. Building industry. I. Exchange. II. Title.

690.591
T72

U.S. Dept. of the Treasury.
    Asset depreciation range (ADR) system. [Wash.] 1971.
    98p.

    1. Depreciation and obsolescence (Buildings) 2. Taxation. 3. Industry. I. Title.

332.3
T72

U.S. Treasury Dept.
    Final report on the Reconstruction Finance Corporation, pursuant to Section 6(c), Reorganization plan no. 1 of 1957. Washington, Govt. Print. Off., 1958.
    321p. tables.

    1. Reconstruction Finance Corp.

711.73
:336　U.S. Treasury Dept.
T72　　Financial condition and fiscal operations of
the Highway Trust Fund. Letter from Secretary
of the Treasury transmitting the ... annual
report on the financial condition and fiscal
operations of the Highway Trust Fund. Washington, Govt. Print. Off., 1961-
　　　pts.
　　For complete information see shelflist.
　　Issued in the Congressional Series as House
Documents.

　　1. Highways -　　　　Finance.

336.2
T72　U.S. Treasury Dept.
　　　Tax reform studies and proposals. Joint
publication: Committee on Ways and Means of the
U.S. House of Representatives and Committee on
Finance of the U.S. Senate. Wash., Govt. Print.
Off., 1969.
　　4pts.
　　At head of title: 91st Cong., 1st sess.
Committee Print.
　　1. Taxation. I. U.S. Congress. House.
Committee on Ways and Means. II. U.S. Congress.
Senate. Committee on Finance. III. Title.

336
T72　U.S. Treasury Dept. Bureau of Accounts.
　　　Receipt, appropriation, and other fund
account symbols and titles covering accounts
established by the Treasury Department, 1966/67

Washington, 1967-
　　2 v.

　　For complete information see main card.

　　1. Finance. I. Title.

332.3
T72L　U.S. TREASURY DEPT.
　　　LIQUIDATION OF RECONSTRUCTION FINANCE
CORPORATION: REPORT TO THE CONGRESS,
JUNE 30, 1957. WASHINGTON, 1958.
　　19P.

　　1. RECONSTRUCTION FINANCE CORPORATION.
I. TITLE.

351.7
:8　U.S. DEPT. OF THE TREASURY - APPROPRIATIONS
C65tr　　AND EXPENDITURES.
H-H　U.S. Congress. House. Committee on Appropria-
tions.
　　Departments of Treasury and Post Office and
Executive Office appropriations for 19

Hearings before a Subcommittee of the Committee
on Appropriations, House of Representatives.
Wash., Govt. Print. Off., 19
　　v. in pts.
　　For Library holdings see main entry.

　　　　　　　　　　(Cont'd on next card)

336.2
T72I　U.S. TREASURY DEPT. COMMITTEE ON
　　　INTERGOVERNMENTAL FISCAL RELATIONS.
INTERGOVERNMENTAL FISCAL RELATIONS.
WASHINGTON, 1943.
　　6 V.

　　1. TAXATION. I. TITLE.

651.4
T72　U.S. Dept. of the Treasury.
　　　Machinery for management improvement.
Washington, 1954.
　　22p. (Management improvement series
no. 1)

　　1. Office management.

351.7
:8　U.S. Congress. House. Committee on Appropria-
C65tr　tions. Departments...19　　(Card 2)
H-H
　　1. U.S. Executive departments - Appropriations
and expenditures. 2. U.S. Dept. of the Treasury
- Appropriations and expenditures. 3. U.S. Post
Office Dept. - Appropriations and expenditures.

336
(016)　U.S. TREASURY DEPARTMENT. LIBRARY.
T72　　CONSOLIDATED REVIEW OF CURRENT
INFORMATION. WASHINGTON, 1956-
　　3 V. ANNUAL.

1956
1957　　1. ECONOMIC CONDITIONS - BIBLIOGRAPHY.
1958　　2. FINANCE - BIBLIOGRAPHY.
3. INTERNATIONAL RELATIONS -
BIBLIOGRAPHY. I. TITLE.

351.72
T72　U.S. Dept. of the Treasury.
　　　Annual report of the Secretary of the
Treasury on the state of the finances for
the fiscal year ended June 30 1961-1971,
Washington,
　　11 v. tables.

sunpl. -- --- Statistical supplement 1966-69

appx. --- ---Statistical　　appendix 1968-71
1962 2R
1962　　1964
1963　　1965 2c.

351.7
:8　U.S. TREASURY DEPT. - APPROPRIATIONS AND
C65tr　　EXPENDITURES.
S-H　U.S. Congress. Senate. Committee on Appropriations.
　　Treasury, Post Office, and Executive Office
appropriations for fiscal year 19

Hearings before a Subcommittee of the Committee
on Appropriations, United States Senate...
Wash., Govt. Print. Off., 19
　　v.
　　For Library holdings see main entry.
　　1. U.S. Executive departments -
Appropriations　　　　and expenditures.
　　　　　　　　(Cont'd on next card)

VF
339.3
(016)　U.S. Treasury Department. Library.
T72　　National income and wealth in the U.S. and in
many countries abroad; references assembled in the
U.S. Treasury Department Library. [Washington]
Dec. 1950.
　　78 p.
2c.　　352.　---Suppl. Compiled by Leah Lenn, Washington, 1956.
　　Processed.

　　1.National income-Bibl.

657
T72.　U.S. TREASURY DEPT.
　　　REPORT ON FINANCIAL MANAGEMENT
IMPROVEMENT ACTIVITIES FOR THE FISCAL YEAR
ENDED JUNE 30, 1960. PREPARED BY
ACCOUNTING SYSTEMS DIVISION, BUREAU OF
ACCOUNTS, FISCAL SERVICE. WASHINGTON,
1960. 25L.

　　1. ACCOUNTING. I. TITLE: FINANCIAL
MANAGEMENT.

351.7
:8　U.S. Congress. Senate. Committee on Appropri-
C65tr　　ations. Treasury...19　　(Card 2)
S-H
　　2. U.S. Treasury Dept. - Appropriations and
expenditures. 3. U.S. Post Office Dept. -
Appropriations and expenditures.

058.7
:620.1　U.S. Treasury Department. Procurement Division.
U54　　Directory of inspection services and testing
1944　laboratories of the Federal government, compiled
...for the use of government purchasing agencies.
[Washington, D.C.] 1944.
　　261 p.

　　Mimeographed.
　　Revision of Directory compiled by the Procurement Division and National Bureau of Standards, 1935

　　1.Testing laboratories-Direct.

336
T72A　U.S. DEPT. OF THE TREASURY.
　　　REPORT TO THE SECRETARY OF THE TREASURY
ON IMPROVEMENTS IN FINANCIAL MANAGEMENT.
WASHINGTON, 1961-67
　　V. ANNUAL.
1961
1962
1963　　TITLE VARIES SLIGHTLY.
1964
1965　　1. FINANCE.
1966
1967

351
M66　U.S. Treasury Department - Reorganization.
Rept.11　U.S. Commission on Organization of the Executive Branch
of the Government.
　　Treasury Department; a report to the Congress, March
1949. [Washington, U.S. Govt. Print. Off., 1949]
　　87 p. 23 cm.

　　Herbert Hoover, chairman.
　　Issued also as House Document no. 115, 81st Cong. 1st sess., under
title: Treasury Department. Letter from the chairman.

　　　　　　Reorganization.
　　1. U.S. Treasury Dept.　I.Hoover Commission reports.

　　HJ263.A42 1949　　353.2　　　　49-46081*
　　　　　Copy 2.　　JK643.C47A55 no. 11
　　Library of Congress　　[15]

380
B82　U.S.Treasury Dept. Procurement Division.
　　　U.S. Bureau of the Budget.
　　　Standard commodity classification. Washing-
ton, Govt. Print. Off., 1943-45.
　　2 v. and Suppl. (Its Technical paper no.
26-28)
　　At head of title: Executive Office of the
President. Bureau of the Budget ... War Produc-
tion Board ... Department of the Treasury.
Procurement Division ...
　　Contents.- v. 1-Standard classified list of
commodities. - v. 2-Alphabetic index. - Supplement
to volume 2.

332
G25r　U.S. Treasury Dept. Study of Treasury tax
　　　and loan accounts.
　　U.S. General Accounting Office.
　　　Report on review of the Treasury Department
study of treasury tax and loan accounts, etc.
Letter from Comptroller General of the United
States transmitting a report on the review of
the Treasury Department study of treasury tax
and loan accounts, services rendered by banks
for the Federal Government; and other related
matters. Washington, Govt. Print. Off., 1962.
　　72p.
　　At head of title: 87th Cong. 2d sess.
House. Document　no. 421.
1. Finance. 2. Banks　　and banking. I. U.S.
Treasury Dept. Study　　of Treasury tax and
loan accounts.

336
T72p　U.S. Treasury Dept. Bureau of Accounts.
　　　Preliminary statement of receipts and
expenditures of the U.S. Government,

Washington,
　　v.

　　For complete information see shelf list.

　　1. Finance. 2. Federal government.

332
F45t　Treasury bills showing coupon issue yield
　　　equivalents discount rates and prices.
Financial Publishing Co.
　　Treasury bills showing coupon issue yield
equivalents discount rates and prices.
Boston, 1966.
　　366p.

Suppl.　... ...Supplement. Boston, Financial Pub. Co.,
1969.
　　127p.

　　1. Bond yield tables. 2. Interest rates.
I. Title.

332.72
C65EXC
S-R
NO.534

TREASURY BONDS.
U.S. CONGRESS. SENATE. COMMITTEE ON
BANKING AND CURRENCY.
EXCHANGING FNMA MORTGAGES FOR
TREASURY BONDS. REPORT TOGETHER WITH
MINORITY AND INDIVIDUAL VIEWS TO
ACCOMPANY S. RES. 130... WASHINGTON,
GOVT. PRINT. OFF., 1959.
15P. (86TH CONGRESS, 1ST SESSION.
SENATE. REPORT NO. 534)

1. MORTGAGE FINANCE. 2. U.S.
FEDERAL NATIONAL MORTGAGE ASSOCIATION.
I. TITLE: TREASURY BONDS.

728.3
A72
1954

A TREASURY OF CONTEMPORARY HOUSES.
ARCHITECTURAL RECORD.
A TREASURY OF CONTEMPORARY HOUSES,
SELECTED BY THE EDITORS OF ARCHITECTURAL
RECORD. NEW YORK, F.W. DODGE CORP.,
1954.
215P.

1. ARCHITECTURE, DOMESTIC - DESIGNS
AND PLANS. I. TITLE.

728(73)
P71

A treasury of early American homes.
Pratt, Richard.
A treasury of early American homes. New York, Whittlesey House [1949]
vii, 136 p. illus. (part col.) ports. 35 cm.
Previously published in the Ladies' home journal.
Bibliography: p. 134.

1. U. S. Historic houses, etc. 2. Architecture, Domestic U. S.
I. Title.

NA7205.P7   728.084   49—50069*
Library of Congress   [50†20]

808.8
W66

A treasury of the familiar.
Woods, Ralph Lewis, 1904-   ed.
A treasury of the familiar. With a foreword by John Kieran. New York, Macmillan,
1942.
751p.

1. Literature. I. Title.

691.11
:620.197
N17

TREATED LUMBER.
U.S. NATIONAL COMMITTEE ON WOOD
UTILIZATION.
TREATED LUMBER, ITS USES AND
ECONOMICS. REPORT OF THE NATIONAL
COMMITTEE ON WOOD UTILIZATION.
WASHINGTON, GOVT. PRINT. OFF., 1930.
42P.

AT HEAD OF TITLE: U.S. DEPT. OF
COMMERCE. WOOD UTILIZATION.
BIBLIOGRAPHY: P.39-42.
THE REPORT HAS BEEN PREPARED FOR
THE SUBCOMMITTEE ON TREATED LUMBER
BY PHILLIPS A. HAYWOOD CF. P.V.
(CONTINUED ON NEXT CARD)

691.11
:620.197
N17

U.S. NATIONAL COMMITTEE ON WOOD
UTILIZATION. TREATED LUMBER....
1930.   (CARD 2)
1. WOOD PRESERVATION. I. HAYWOOD,
PHILLIPS A. II. TITLE.

691.11
:620.197
B52t

Treating wood by the cold-soaking method.
Blew, J Oscar.
Treating wood by the cold-soaking method.
Rev. Madison, Wis., Forest Products Laboratory, 1961.
10p. (no. 1445)

1. Wood preservation. I. U.S. Forest
Products Laboratory, Madison, Wis.
II. Title.

LAW
T
W435t

A treatise on the Anglo-American system of
evidence in trials at common law...
Wigmore, John Henry.
A treatise on the Anglo-American system of
evidence in trials at common law, including the
statutes and judicial decisions of all jurisdictions of the United States and Canada. 3d ed.
Boston, Little, Brown, 1940.
10v.
Kept up to date with suppl., 1959- by Richmond
Rucker.

1. Evidence (Law) 2. Evidence (Law) - Canada.
I. U.S. Laws, statutes,   etc. II. Canada.
Laws, statutes, etc.   III. Title. IV. Title:
Anglo-American system   of evidence in trials
at common law.   V. Rucker, Richmond.

LAW

A treatise on the Anglo-American system of
evidence in trials at common law...
Wigmore, John Henry.
A treatise on the Anglo-American system
of evidence in trials at common law, including
the statutes and judicial decisions of all
jurisdictions of the United States and Canada.
2d ed. Boston, Little Brown, 1923-
v.
First edition has title: "A treatise on the
system of evidence in trials at common law.
—— Supplement to the 2d ed. 1923-33.
1395p.

(Continued on   next card)

LAW

Wigmore, John Henry. A treatise on the Anglo-
American system of evidence in trials at common
law...1923.   (Card 2)

"List of latest source examined:" p. XI-XV.
"Index of authors quoted or cited...covers both,
the Treatise and this supplement." p. 1371-1388.

1. Evidence (LAW) 2. Evidence (LAW)—Canada.
I. U.S. Laws, statutes, etc. II. Canada. Laws,
statutes, etc. III. Title. IV. Title: Anglo-
American system of   evidence in trials
at common law.

729
C31

A treatise on the decorative part of civil
architecture.
Chambers, Sir William, 1726-1796.
A treatise on the decorative part of civil
architecture. New York, B. Blom, 1968.
1v.
First ed. 1759 has title: A treatise on civil
architecture.
Reprint of the "Third edition, considerably
augmented" published in London in 1791.

1. Architectural details. 2. Architecture -
Designs and plans. I. Title. II. Title: Civil
architecture.

LAW
T
M223tr

A treatise on the law of public offices and
officers.
Mechem, Floyd Russell.
A treatise on the law of public offices and
officers. Chicago, Callaghan, 1890.
751p.

1. Administrative law - U. S.   I. Title.

LAW
T
C5162t

A treatise on the law of surveying and
boundaries.
Clark, Frank Emerson.
A treatise on the law of surveying and
boundaries. 3d ed., by John S. Grimes.
Indianapolis, Bobbs-Merrill, 1959.
1031p.

1. Surveying. I. Grimes, John S. II. Title.
III. Title: The law of surveying and boundaries.

712
D68

A treatise on the theory and practice of landscape
gardening.
Downing, Andrew Jackson.
A treatise on the theory and practice of
landscape gardening. With the 1859 sixth ed.
supplemented by Henry Winthrop Sargent and a
special appreciation by John O. Simonds, Jr.
New York, Funk & Wagnalls, 1967.
576p.
At head of title: A facsimile edition.

1. Landscape architecture. 2. Trees.
3. Site planning. 4. Rural planning. I. Title.
II. Title: Landscape gardening.

628.515
H67

Treatment of acid mine drainage.
Horizons, inc.
Treatment of acid mine drainage. [Prepared] for Federal Water Quality Administration. Cleveland, Ohio, 1970.
88p. (Water pollution control research
series)

1. Water pollution. I. U.S. Federal
Water Quality Administration. II. Title.

628.515
R29

Treatment of acid mine drainage by...
Rex Chainbelt, inc.
Treatment of acid mine drainage by
reverse osmosis. [Prepared] for the
Commonwealth of Pennsylvania, Dept. of
Mines and Mineral Industries and the
Federal Water Quality Administration.
Milwaukee, Wis., 1970.
35p. (Water Pollution control research
series)
1. Water pollution. I. Pennsylvania.
Dept. of Mines and Mineral Industries.
II. U.S. Federal Water Quality
Administration. III. Title.

628.44
B27

The treatment of industrial wastes.
Besselievre, Edmund B
The treatment of industrial wastes. New
York, McGraw-Hill, 1969.
493p.
Bibliography: p. 341-364.

1. Refuse and refuse disposal.
2. Water pollution. 3. Sewerage and sewage
disposal. I. Title. II. Title: Industrial
wastes.

331
M87

The treatment of seasonal unemployment
under unemployment insurance.
Murray, Merrill G
The treatment of seasonal unemployment under
unemployment insurance. Kalamazoo, Mich.,
W.E. Upjohn Institute for Employment Research,
1972.
84p. (Studies in unemployment insurance and
related problems)

1. Employment. 2. Insurance. I. Upjohn
Institute for Employment Research. II. Title.

628.515
E92

Treatment of sole leather vegetable tannery wastes.
Eye, J David.
Treatment of sole leather vegetable
tannery wastes. Separation, pretreatment,
and blending of the waste fractions from
a sole leather tannery for final treatment
in a stratefied anaerobic-aerobic lagoon
system. Wash., Federal Water Pollution
Control Administration, 1970.
112p. (Water pollution control research
series)
1. Water pollution. I. U.S. Federal
Water Pollution Control Administration.
II. Title.

628.515
D68t

Treatment of wastewater from the production
of polyhydric organics.
Dow Chemical Co.
Treatment of wastewater from the production
of polyhydric organices, by the Texas Division.
[Prepared] for the Office of Research and
Monitoring, Environmental Protection Agency.
Wash., Govt. Print. Off., 1971.
198p. (Water pollution control research
series)
Bibliography: p. 135-136.
1. Water pollution. I. U.S. Environmental
Protection Agency. II. Title.

628.515
A75

Treatment of waste water-waste oil mixtures.
ARMCO Steel Corp.
Treatment of waste water-waste oil mixtures.
Wash., U.S. Federal Water Pollution Control
Administration, 1970.
137p. (Water pollution control research
series 12010 EZV 02/70)

1. Water pollution. I. U.S. Federal Water
Pollution Control Administration. II. Title.

628.515
C65t

Treatment techniques for removing phosphorus from municipal wastewaters.

Convery, John J
Treatment techniques for removing phosphorus from municipal wastewaters. Presented at New York. Water Pollution Control Association, New York, New York. Cincinnati, Environmental Protection Agency, Water Quality Office, Advanced Waste Treatment Research Laboratory, 1970. 35p. (Water pollution control research series)

Bibliography: p. [36-38]

1. Water pollution. I. U.S. Environmental Protection Agency. II. Title. III. Title: Phosphorus.

Trees
see also
Landscape architecture

712.41
C25o
1968

TREES.
Central States Forest Tree Improvement Conference, 6th, Carbondale, Ill. and St. Louis, Mo., 1968.
Ornamental tree and shrub improvement-the forester's role. Proceedings. Edited by David T. Funk. Published in cooperation with Dept. of Forestry, School of Agriculture, Southern Illinois University. St. Paul, North Central Forest Experiment Station, 1968. 62p.
1. Trees. 2. Landscape architecture. I. U.S. North Central Forest Experiment Station. II. Funk, David T., ed. III. Title.

352.6
(74813)
T72

Tredyffrin, Pa. Planning Commission.
Community facilities plan for Tredyffrin Township. [Prepared in cooperation with] Pennsylvania Bureau of Community Development. Rev. Tredyffrin, 1961. 13p.

U.S. Urban Renewal Adm. UPAP.

1. Community facilities - Tredyffrin, Pa. I. U.S. URA-UPAP.   Tredyffrin, Pa.

VF
712.41
A37p

TREES.
U.S. Dept. of Agriculture.
Protecting shade trees during home construction. Rev. Wash., 1971. 7p. (Its Home and garden bulletin no. 104)

1. Trees. 2. Landscape architecture. 3. Site planning. I. Title.

534.83
C66

TREES.
Cook, David I
Trees may help solve the traffic noise problem, by David I. Cook and David F. Van Haverbeke. Wash. U.S. Forest Service, 1969.
[2]p.

Reprinted from: Univ. Nebr. Quart. 116(2): p. 11-12.

1. Noise. 2. Traffic. 3. Trees. I. Van Haverbeke, David R., jt. au. II. Title.

711.14
(74813)
T72

Tredyffrin, Pa. Planning Commission.
Land use plan for Tredyffrin Township, Chester County, Pennsylvania. [Prepared in cooperation with] Pennsylvania Bureau of Community Development] Rev. Tredyffrin, 1961. 32p.

U.S. Urban Renewal Adm. UPAP.

1. Land use - Tredyffrin, Pa. I. U.S. URA   URA-UPAP. Tredyffrin, Pa.

712
A41

TREES.
Ajay, Betty.
Betty Ajay's guide to home landscaping. Illustrations by Abe Ajay. New York, McGraw-Hill, 1970. 208p.

1. Landscape architecture. 2. Terraces. 3. Trees. I. Title.

712
D68

Trees.
Downing, Andrew Jackson.
A treatise on the theory and practice of landscape gardening. With the 1859 sixth ed. supplemented by Henry Winthrop Sargent and a special appreciation by John O. Simonds, Jr. New York, Funk & Wagnalls, 1967. 576p.
At head of title: A facsimile edition.

1. Landscape architecture. 2. Trees. 3. Site planning. 4. Rural planning. I. Title. II. Title: Landscape gardening.

711.4
(74813)
P25

Tredyffrin, Pa. Planning Commission.
Pennsylvania. University. Fels Institute of Local and State Government. (Government Consulting Service)
The preservation of open space in suburban municipalities. A planning memorandum prepared for the Tredyffrin Township Planning Commission by the Government Consulting Service. Pennsylvania, [n.p.] 1959. 9p.
1. City planning - Tredyffrin, Pa. 2. Land use - Tredyffrin, Pa. I. Title: Open space in suburban municipalities. II. Tredyffrin, Pa. Planning Commission.

595.7
A52

TREES.
ANDERSON, ROGER F
FOREST AND SHADE TREE ENTOMOLOGY. NEW YORK, WILEY, 1960. 428P.

1. INSECTS. 2. TREES. I. TITLE.

634.9
E77

Trees.
Essex, Burton L
Illinois' timber resource, by Burton L. Essex and David A. Gansner. St. Paul, Lake States Forest Experiment Station, Forest Service, U.S. Dept. of Agriculture, 1965. 56p. (U.S. Forest Service. Resource bulletin LS-3)

1. Forests and forestry. 2. Trees. I. Gansner, David A., jt. au. II. U.S. Forest Service. Central States Forest Experiment Station. III. Title.

388
(74813)
T72

Tredyffrin, Pa. Planning Commission.
Transportation plan for Tredyffrin Township, Chester County, Pa. [Prepared in cooperation with] Pennsylvania Bureau of Community Development. Tredyffrin, 1962. [8] l.

U.S. Urban Renewal Adm. UPAP.

1. Community facilities - Tredyffrin, Pa. I. U.S. URA-UPAP. Tredyffrin, Pa.

691
B69

Trees.
Boyce, Stephen G
Provisional grade specifications for hardwood growing-stock trees, by Stephen G. Boyce and Roswell D. Carpenter. Upper Darby, Pa., Northeastern Forest Experiment Station, Forest Service, U.S. Dept. of Agriculture, 1968.
12p. (U.S. Forest Service. Research paper NE-97)
1. Building materials - Standards and specifications. 2. Trees. I. Carpenter, Roswell D., jt. au. II. U.S. Northeastern Forest Experiment Station, Upper Darby, Pa. III. Title.

712.41
F68

TREES.
FOWLER, MARVIN EDWARD, 1904-
REDUCING DAMAGE TO TREES FROM CONSTRUCTION WORK. WASHINGTON, U.S. GOVT. PRINT. OFF., 1945. 26P. (U.S. DEPT. OF AGRICULTURE. FARMERS' BULLETIN NO. 1967)

1. TREES. I. TITLE.

920
1720
P17

TREE, MICHAEL.
PATTRICK, MICHAEL.
A CAREER IN ARCHITECTURE, BY MICHAEL PATTRICK AND MICHAEL TREE. LONDON, MUSEUM PRESS, 1961. 127P.

1. ARCHITECTS. 2. ARCHITECTURE - STUDY AND TEACHING. I. TREE, MICHAEL. II. TITLE.

712
B72

Trees.
Brett, William S
Small city gardens, by William S. Brett and Kay Grant. London, New York, Abelard-Schuman, 1967. 159p.

1. Landscape architecture. 2. Trees. 3. Terraces. I. Grant, Kay, jt. au. II. Title.

711.74
(758)
G26

Trees.
Georgia. University. Institute of Community and Area Development.
Street and highway landscape development, by Robert J. Hill. Athens, Ga., 1962. 28p.

1. Streets - Georgia. 2. Highways - Ga. 3. Landscape architecture. 4. Trees. I. Hill, Robert J. II. Title.

634.9
P47

Tree maintenance.
Pirone, P P
Tree maintenance. 3d ed. New York, Oxford University Press, 1959. 483p.

Second ed., 1948, has title: Maintenance of shade and ornamental trees.

Bibliography: p. 447-465.

1. Trees. I. Title.

712.41
C25

TREES.
CENTRAL ILLINOIS LIGHT COMPANY.
TREES. N.P., N.D. 18P.

1. TREES.

712.41
I55

TREES.
ILLINOIS. UNIVERSITY. SMALL HOMES COUNCIL - BUILDING RESEARCH COUNCIL.
PREVENTION AND TREATMENT OF CONSTRUCTION DAMAGE TO SHADE TREES, BY DONALD F. SCHOENENWEISS. URBANA, ILL., 1965. 8P. (ITS TECHNICAL NOTE NO. 1)

1. TREES. I. SCHOENENWEISS, DONALD F.

712.41
K25
TREES.
KENNARD, WILLIAM C
SOME FRUITS AND NUTS FOR THE TROPICS,
BY WILLIAM C. KENNARD AND HAROLD F.
WINTERS. WASHINGTON, U.S. GOVT.
PRINT. OFF., 1960.
135P. (AGRICULTURAL RESEARCH
SERVICE. MISCELLANEOUS PUBLICATION NO.
801)

1. TREES. I. WINTERS, HAROLD F.,
JT. AU. II. TITLE.

Trees.
VF
712.41
O31
Ogburn, Charlton, Jr.
The battle to save the trees. Detached
from Saturday Evening Post, Jan. 28, 1961.
p. 28, 29, 68-70.

1. Trees. 2. Subdivision. I. Saturday
Evening Post.

712.41
S76
TREES.
STOKER, JOHN W
STREET TREE PLANTING. THE
SELECTION, PLANTING AND CARE OF TREES
ALONG MUNICIPAL THOROUGHFARES. WITH
APPENDIX OF POWERS AND PROCEDURES,
ORDINANCES AND RULES. COMMONWEALTH OF
PENNSYLVANIA, DEPARTMENT OF INTERNAL
AFFAIRS, 1945.
35P.

1. TREES. I. PENNSYLVANIA. DEPT.
OF INTERNAL AFFAIRS.

634.9
K87
Trees.
Kurtenacker, R S
Appalachian hardwoods for pallets; a labora-
tory evaluation, by R.S. Kurtenacker and others.
Madison, Forest Products Laboratory, 1967.
Laf. 20p. (U.S. Forest Service. Research paper,
FPL 76)
1. Forests and forestry. 2. Trees. I. U.S.
Forest Service. Forest Products Laboratory.
Madison, Wis. II. Title.

712.41
O72
TREES.
OREGON. UNIVERSITY. BUREAU OF
MUNICIPAL RESEARCH AND SERVICE.
STREET TREES FOR CITIES. BY BUREAU
OF MUNICIPAL RESEARCH AND SERVICE... IN
COOPERATION WITH THE LEAGUE OF OREGON
CITIES. EUGENE, 1947.
16P. (ITS PLANNING BULLETIN NO. 1)

1. TREES. I. TITLE.

712.41
S97
Trees.
Syracuse, N.Y. Dept. of City Planning.
Trees in the city. Syracuse, N.Y.,
1960.
7p. (Its Planning information bulle-
tin, vol. 2, no. 1. April-May 1960)

1. Trees.

634.9
L17
TREES.
Lassen, L E
Sapwood thickness of Douglas-fir and
five other western softwoods, by L.E.
Lassen and E.A. Okkonen. Madison, Wis.,
U.S. Forest Products Laboratory, 1969.
16p. (U.S. Forest Service. Research
paper FPL 124)

1. Trees. 2. Wood preservation.
I. Okkonen, E.A., jt. au. II. U.S.
Forest Products Laboratory. Madison, Wis.
III. Title.

Trees.
712.41
P42
Pierson, Robert W
Trees for Bucks County communities.
Philadelphia, Philadelphia Electric Co.,
1959.
7p. illus.

Reprinted from the Bucks County Realtor,
Autumn issue, 1959.

1. Trees.

712.41
A37
TREES.
U.S. DEPT. OF AGRICULTURE.
PROTECTING SHADE TREES DURING HOME
CONSTRUCTION. WASHINGTON, GOVT.
PRINT. OFF., 1965.
8p. (ITS HOME AND GARDEN BULLETIN
NO. 104)

1. TREES.

712
L67
Trees.
Los Angeles. Dept. of City Planning.
Shrubs and trees for landscaping and
screening. Technical report. Los
Angeles [1960?]
1v.
1. Landscape architecture. 2. Trees.
I. Title.

634.9
P47
TREES.
Pirone, P P
Tree maintenance. 3d ed. New York, Oxford
University Press, 1959.
483p.

Second ed., 1948, has title: Maintenance of
shade and ornamental trees.

Bibliography: p. 447-465.

1. Trees. I. Title.

721.41
A37
Trees.
U.S. Agricultural Research Service.
Protecting trees against damage from
construction work. Wash., Govt. Print. Off.,
1964.
26p. (Agriculture information bulletin
no. 285)

1. Trees. I. Title.

634.9
M14
TREES.
Maini, J S ed.
Growth and utilization of poplars in
Canada, edited by J.S. Maini and J.H. Cayford.
[Ottawa] Dept. of Forestry and Rural
Development, Forestry Branch, 1968.
257p. (Canada. Dept. of Forestry and
Rural Development. Departmental publication
no. 1205)
1. Trees. I. Cayford, J.H., jt. ed.
I. Canada. Dept. of Forestry and Rural
Development. II. Title: Poplars.
III. Title.

634.9
P47
1948
TREES.
PIRONE, PASCAL POMPEY.
MAINTENANCE OF SHADE AND ORNAMENTAL
TREES. 2D ED. CORR. AND ENL. NEW YORK,
OXFORD UNIVERSITY PRESS, 1948.
436P.

1. TREES. I. TITLE: SHADE AND
ORNAMENTAL TREES.

721.41
F67
TREES.
U.S. Forest Service.
People, cities and trees. Wash., 1970.
[12]p.

1. Trees. I. Title.

712.41
M84
Trees.
Muirhead, Desmond.
The trees on your street. Portland, Or.,
Portland General Electric Company, [1963?]
36p.

1. Trees. 2. Street planning.
I. Portland General Electric Co.

712.41
P67
Trees.
Portland General Electric Co.
The trees on your street. Portland, Or.
[1963?]
6p.

1. Trees.

634.9
F67TR
TREES.
U.S. FOREST SERVICE.
TREES OF THE FOREST; THEIR BEAUTY AND
USE. WASHINGTON, GOVT. PRINT. OFF.,
1964.
24P.

1. TREES.

712.41
N28
TREES.
NEW JERSEY FEDERATION OF SHADE TREE
COMMISSIONS.
TREES FOR NEW JERSEY STREETS. REV.
ED. NEW BRUNSWICK, N.J. RUTGERS
COLLEGE OF AGRICULTURE, 1965.
50P.

1. TREES.

712.41
R23
TREES.
REHDER, ALFRED.
MANUAL OF CULTIVATED TREES AND SHRUBS,
HARDY IN NORTH AMERICA, EXCLUSIVE OF
THE SUBTROPICAL AND WARMER TEMPERATE
REGIONS. 2D ED. NEW YORK, MACMILLAN,
1940.
996P.

1. TREES. I. TITLE. II. TITLE:
TREES AND SHRUBS.

634.9
F67TR
Trees.
U.S. Forest Service. North Central Forest
Experiment Station, St. Paul.
Proceedings of the Eighth Lake States
Forest Tree Improvement Conference, Sept.
12-13, 1967. St. Paul, 1967.
60p. (U.S. Forest Service. Research
paper NC-23)
Bibliography: p. 59-60.

1. Forests and forestry. 2. Trees.
I. Title.

634.9
F6Th
Trees.
U.S. Forest Service. Northeastern Forest
Experiment Station.
Harvesting costs & returns under 4 cutting
methods in mature beech-birch-maple stands
in New England, by Stanley M. Filip. Upper
Darby, Pa., 1967.
14p. (U.S. Forest Service Research paper
NE-87)

1. Trees. 2. Forests and forestry.
3. Lumber industry. I. Filip, Stanley M.
II. Title.

634.9
F72
Trees.
U.S. President's Appalachian Regional Com-
mission.
Appalachia's forest resources - timber. A
Task Force report on the timber resources of
Appalachia. Washington, Govt. Print. Off.,
1963.
149p.

1. Forests and forestry. 2. Trees.
I. Title.

VF
712.41
V47
Trees
Virginia Electric and Power Co.
Trees are lovely. [Richmond, n.d.]
16p. illus.

1. Trees.

712.41
W95
TREES.
WYMAN, DONALD.
TREES FOR AMERICAN GARDENS. NEW
YORK, MACMILLAN, 1959.
376P.

1. TREES. I. TITLE.

721.41
Z46
Trees.
Zion, Robert L
Trees for architecture and the landscape.
New York, Reinhold Book Corp., 1968.
284p.

1. Trees. 2. Landscape architecture.

691.11
(016)
C65
no.150
Trees - Bibliography.
La Perriere, Louis R
Applications of aerial infrared imagery to
research on the Dutch Elm disease; with speci-
fic reference to urban areas, by Louis R.
LaPerriere and William A. Howard. Denver, Dept.
of Geography, University of Denver, 1970.
25p. (Council of Planning Librarians.
Exchange bibliography no. 150)
1. Planning - Bibl. 2. Trees - Bibl.
I. Howard, William A., jt. au. II. Denver.
University. Dept. of Geography. III. Title.
(Series: Council of Planning Librarians.
Exchange bibliography no. 150)

691.11
(016)
P76
Trees - Bibliography.
Pronin, Dimitri.
A literature survey of Populus species with
emphasis on P. tremuloides, by Dimitri Pronin
and Coleman L. Vaughan. Rev. ed. Madison,
Wis., U.S. Forest Products Laboratory,
1968.
67p. (U.S. Forest Service. Research note
FPL-0180 (revised))
1. Wood - Bibl. 2. Trees - Bibl. I. U.S.
Forest Products Laboratory, Madison Wis.
II. Vaughan, Coleman L., jt. au. III. Title.

712.41
R23
TREES AND SHRUBS.
REHDER, ALFRED.
MANUAL OF CULTIVATED TREES AND SHRUBS,
HARDY IN NORTH AMERICA, EXCLUSIVE OF
THE SUBTROPICAL AND WARMER TEMPERATE
REGIONS. 2D ED. NEW YORK, MACMILLAN,
1940.
996P.

1. TREES. I. TITLE. II. TITLE:
TREES AND SHRUBS.

712.41
W95
TREES FOR AMERICAN GARDENS.
WYMAN, DONALD.
TREES FOR AMERICAN GARDENS. NEW
YORK, MACMILLAN, 1959.
376P.

1. TREES. I. TITLE.

634.83
C66
Trees may help solve the traffic noise
problem.
Cook, David I
Trees may help solve the traffic noise
problem, by David I. Cook and David F.
Van Haverbeke. Wash. U.S. Forest Service,
1969.
[2]p.

Reprinted from: Univ. Nebr. Quart.
116(2): p. 11-12.

1. Noise. 2. Traffic. 3. Trees.
I. Van Haverbeke, David R., jt. au.
II. Title.

VF
634.9
A52t
Trees of the District of Columbia, including
some foreign trees.
American Forestry Association.
Trees of the District of Columbia, including
some foreign trees; how to know them, where
to see them; a pocket manual, by Wilbur R. Mattoon
and Susan S. Alburtis. Washington, 1941.
72p. illus.

First edition, 1923 has title: Forest trees of
the District of Columbia.

I. Mattoon, Wilbur R   II. Alburtis,
Susan S   III. Title.

634.9
A37
Trees; the yearbook of agriculture.
U.S. Dept. of Agriculture.
Trees; the yearbook of agriculture, 1949.
Washington, Govt. Print. Off., 1949.
944 p. illus.

Includes bibliographies.

1.Forests and forestry. I.Title: Yearbook of
agriculture, 1949. II.Title: Trees: the yearbook of agriculture.

658
M12
Trefethen, Florence N, Jt. ed.
McCloskey, Joseph F , ed.
Operations research for management, ed. by
Joseph F. McCloskey and Florence N. Trefethen.
Baltimore, Johns-Hopkins Press, 1954.
2v. diagrs., tables.

"Selected bibliography": p.383-401.

1.Operations research. I.Trefethen,
Florence N , jt. ed.

658
K26
TREGOE, BENJAMIN B , JT. AU.
KEPNER, CHARLES HIGGINS, 1922-
THE RATIONAL MANAGER. A SYSTEMATIC
APPROACH TO PROBLEM SOLVING AND DECISION
MAKING BY CHARLES H. KEPNER AND BENJAMIN
B. TREGOE. EDITED WITH AN INTROD. BY
PERRIN STRYKER. NEW YORK, MCGRAW-HILL,
1965.
275P.

ANNOTATED BIBLIOGRAPHY : P.243-252.

1. MANAGEMENT. I. TREGOE, BENJAMIN B.,
JT. AU. II. TITLE

694.1
(481)
G71
1958
Trehus.
Granum, Hans.
Trehus [Modern frame houses] av Hans
Granum og Sven Erik Lundby. Oslo, 1958.
255p. illus., diagrs. (Oslo. Norges
Byggforskningsinstitutt. Anvisning 8)

1. Wood construction - Norway. 2. Wood framing.
I. Lundby, Sven Erik, jt. au. II. Title.
III. Title: Modern frame houses. (Series)

694.1
(481)
G71
1961
Trehus 1961.
Granum, Hans.
Trehus 1961 [modern frame houses, by]
Hans Granum og Sven Erik Lundby. Rev.
Oslo, 1961.
283p. (Oslo. Norges Byggforskningsinsti-
tutt. Handbok 12)
English summary.

1. Wood construction - Norway. 2. Wood
framing. I. Lundby, Sven Erik, jt. au.
II. Title. III. Title: Modern frame houses.
IV. Oslo. Norges   Byggforskningsinstitutt.

694.1
(481)
G71
1965
Trehus 1965.
Granum, Hans.
Trehus 1965 [Modern frame houses, by]
Hans Branum og Sven Erik Lundby. Oslo,
Norges Byggforsknings institutt, 1964.
288p. (Oslo. Norges Byggforsknings-
institutt. Handbok 12)
English summary.

1. Wood construction - Norway. 2. Wood framing.
I. Lundby, Sven Erik, jt. au. II. Title.
III. Title: Modern frame houses. IV. Oslo.
Norges Byggforskningsin-   stitutt.

694.1
(481)
G71
Trehus i dag.
Granum, Hans
Trehus i dag. Modern frame houses. Av
Hans Granum og Sven Erik Lundby. Oslo, Johan
Grundt Tanum Forlag, 1952.
152 p. illus. (Norway. Norges Teknisk-
Naturvitenskaplige Forskningsråd. Byggeteknisk
utvalg. Anvisning nr. 1

English summary: p. 146-147.
Bibliography: p. 148-150.

694.1
(481)
A 72
Trehus 70, av O. Aschehoug et al.
Aschehoug, O
Trehus 70, av O. Aschehoug et al. Oslo,
Norges Byggforskningsinstitutt, 1970.
240p. (Oslo. Norges Byggforskningsinstitutt.
Handbok 22)
English summary.
Bibliography: p. 228-230.

1. Wood construction - Norway. I. Oslo.
Norges Byggforskningsinstitutt. II. Title.

VF
690.37
F71
EAug.1950
Tremblot, D
Recherche d'un parti pour une habitation dans
la zone intertropicale. [Paris, France] Centre
Scientifique et Technique du Bâtiment, Service de
l'Habitat Intertropical [Aug. 1950]
9 l. diagrs., plans. (France. Centre
Scientifique et Technique du Bâtiment. Service
de l'Habitat Intertropical. Etudes.)

Mimeographed.

1.Architecture, Domestic-Tropics. I.Ser.

DATE OF REQUEST 2/2/54   MAR 1 9 1954   L. C. CARD NO.

AUTHOR Tremco Manufacturing Co.   Cleveland, Ohio.

TITLE Floors and floor problems.

SERIES

EDITION   PUB. DATE   PAGING 24 p.

PUBLISHER

RECOMMENDED BY NHL   REVIEWED IN AR 1/54 p. 220

ORDER RECORD

DATE OF REQUEST 7/20/53   L. C. CARD NO.

AUTHOR Tremco Manufacturing Co.

TITLE Solving roof problems.

SERIES

EDITION   PUB. DATE [c 1952]   PAGING 32 p.

PUBLISHER 8701 Kinsman Rd., Cleveland, Ohio.

RECOMMENDED BY NHL   REVIEWED IN MAR 7/53 p.240

ORDER RECORD

Class No. Roofs

Author (surname first) Tremco Manufacturing Co.

Accession No.

Title Solving Roof Problems

Ordered JUN 1 1950 Source

Received JUN 12 1950

Cost   Date Ag 9   Paging 32   List Price   Est. Cost

Purchase Order No.

Date

L. C. No.   Place Cleveland 4, O. Publisher   Address 8701 Kinsman Rd.   Edition or Series   Recommended by   Reviewed in Jt. og g. May 1950 g. 182

H-305 (2-50)   HOUSING AND HOME FINANCE AGENCY: Office of the Administrator   16—61157-1   GPO

---

330 (016) N18

Trend analysis.

U.S. Naval Research Laboratory.
Trend analysis; a reading list of books and periodical articles, comp. by Mildred Benton, Librarian. Washington, 1955.
11p. (Its Bibliography no. 7)

1. Economics - Bibliographies. I. Benton, Mildred, comp. II. Title.

728.3 P65TR

TREND HOMES FOR THE SIXTIES.
POLLMAN, RICHARD B
TREND HOMES FOR THE SIXTIES. DETROIT, HOME PLANNERS, INC., 1961.
48P. (DESIGNS FOR CONVENIENT LIVING, BOOK NO. 35)

1. ARCHITECTURE, DOMESTIC - DESIGNS AND PLANS. I. TITLE.

---

331 (747) N28TR

TREND OF EMPLOYMENT IN NEW YORK STATE FACTORIES FROM 1914 TO 1939.
NEW YORK (STATE). DEPT. OF LABOR.
TREND OF EMPLOYMENT IN NEW YORK STATE FACTORIES FROM 1914 TO 1939. ALBANY, N.Y., 1940.
198P. (ITS SPECIAL BULLETIN NO. 206)

1. EMPLOYMENT - NEW YORK (STATE). I. TITLE.

333.332 (755) L21

THE TREND OF REAL ESTATE VALUES IN VIRGINIA CITIES AND COUNTIES.
LEAGUE OF VIRGINIA MUNICIPALITIES.
THE TREND OF REAL ESTATE VALUES IN VIRGINIA CITIES AND COUNTIES, 1931-1939. RICHMOND, VA., 1943.
15P.

1. REAL PROPERTY - VALUATION. I. TITLE.

---

711 (016) C65 no. 144

The trend to the metropolis.
Blumenfeld, Hans.
The trend to the metropolis: a bibliography. Ottawa Canadian Council on Urban and Regional Research, 1970.
9p. (Council of Planning Librarians. Exchange bibliography no. 144)

1. Planning - Bibl. 2. City growth - Bibl. 3. Metropolitan areas - Bibl. I. Title. (Series: Council of Planning Librarians. Exchange bibliography no. 144)

711.14 (41) T72

Trends.
The British Land Commission bill. Chicago, American Society of Planning Officials, 1967.
21p.

Entire issue of Trends, no. 1, 1967.

1. Land use - U.K. 2. Management - U.K. I. American Society of Planning Officials. II. Title.

330.15 N17o no.43

Trends and cycles in capital formation by United States railroads.
Ulmer, Melville J
Trends and cycles in capital formation by United States railroads, 1870-1950. New York, 1954.
70 p. (National Bureau of Economic Research. Occasional paper 43). Studies in capital formation and financing.
1. Railroads. 2. Finance. I. Title. II. Capital formation. III. National Bureau of Economic Research. Occasional paper, no. 43. IV. Studies in capital formation and financing.

330.15 N17o no.37

Trends and cycles in corporate bond financing.
Hickman, Walter Braddock.
Trends and cycles in corporate bond financing. New York, 1952.
37 p. (National Bureau of Economic Research. Occasional paper 37).

1. Finance. I. Title. II. Corporate bond financing. III. Bond financing. IV. National Bureau of Economic Research. Occasional paper, no. 37.

330.15 N17o no.85

Trends and cycles in the commercial paper market.
Selden, Richard T
Trends and cycles in the commercial paper market. [New York] 1963.
119 p. (National Bureau of Economic Research. Occasional paper 85).

1. Negotiable instruments. I. Title. II. Commercial paper market. III. National Bureau of Economic Research. Occasional paper, no. 85.

312.8 P42t

Trends and projections of future population growth in the United States.
Pickard, Jerome P
Trends and projections of future population growth in the United States, with special data on large urban regions and major metropolitan areas, for the period 1970-2000. Wash., U.S. Dept. of Housing and Urban Development, 1969.
27p. (U.S. Dept. of Housing and Urban Development. Program Analysis and Evaluation Staff. Technical paper no. 4)
Presented to the Ad Hoc Subcommittee on Urban Growth, Committee on Banking and Currency, U.S. House of Representatives, Wash., D.C., July 22, 1969.

(Cont'd on next card)

312.8 P42t

Pickard, Jerome P   Trends and projections...1969.   (Card 2)

HUD news.
Author is Director, Program Analysis and Evaluation Staff.

1. Population forecasting. 2. City growth. 3. Metropolitan areas - Statistics. 4. New towns - Statistics. I. U.S. Dept. of Housing and Urban Development. II. HUD news. III. Title.

VF 352 L28

Trends and prospects in local government finances.
Levy, Michael E
Trends and prospects in local government finances. Reproduced from the Conference board record, [New York] October 1966, p. 20-26.

1. Local government - Finance. 2. Grants-in-aid. I. Conference board record. II. Title.

---

330 158T

TRENDS IN AMERICAN PROGRESS.
INVESTORS SYNDICATE, MINNEAPOLIS.
TRENDS IN AMERICAN PROGRESS; FACTS AND FIGURES ABOUT THE GROWTH OF ECONOMIC LIFE IN AMERICA. MINNEAPOLIS, INVESTORS SYNDICATE, 1946.
66P.

1. ECONOMIC CONDITIONS. 2. STATISTICS. I. TITLE.

VF 352 C25 G-88 no.54

Trends in assessed valuations and sales ratios.
U.S. Bureau of the Census.
Trends in assessed valuations and sales ratios, 1956-1966. [Wash.] 1970.
23p. (Its State and local government special studies no. 54)

1. Real property - Valuation. I. Title.

691.328 H63

Trends in consumer demands for new grades of reinforcing steel.
Hognestad, Eivind.
Trends in consumer demands for new grades of reinforcing steel. Skokie, Ill., Portland Cement Association, Research and Development Laboratories, 1967.
9p. (Portland Cement Association. Research and Development Laboratories. Development Dept. Bulletin D 130)
Reprint from Proceedings, Fall Business Meeting. Concrete Reinforcing Steel Institute. Oct. 1967, p. 22-32.
1. Concrete, Reinforced. 2. Steel. I. Portland Cement Association. II. Title.

---

336 A74

TRENDS IN CORPORATE BOND QUALITY.
ATKINSON, THOMAS R
TRENDS IN CORPORATE BOND QUALITY. NEW YORK, NATIONAL BUREAU OF ECONOMIC RESEARCH, DISTRIBUTED BY COLUMBIA UNIVERSITY PRESS, 1967.
106P. (STUDIES IN CORPORATE BOND FINANCING, NO. 4)

1. FINANCE. I. TITLE.

---

330 IA1

Trends in economic growth.
U.S. Library of Congress. Legislative Reference Service.
Trends in economic growth; a comparison of the Western powers and the Soviet bloc; a study prepared for the Joint Committee on the Economic Report. Wash., Govt. Print. Off., 1955.
339 p. tables.
At head of title: 83d Congress, 2d sess. Joint Committee Print.
Bibliographical footnotes.
1. Economic conditions. 2. Economic conditions - U.S.S.R. I. Title. II. U.S. Congress. Joint Committee on the Economic Report.

FOLIO 621.3 N17T

TRENDS IN ELECTRIC UTILITY INDUSTRY EXPERIENCE.
NATIONAL COAL ASSOCIATION.
TRENDS IN ELECTRIC UTILITY INDUSTRY EXPERIENCE, 1946-1958. COMPARATIVE COAL, OIL AND GAS CONSUMPTION STATISTICS, AND OTHER RELATED DATA PERTAINING TO THE GENERATION OF ELECTRIC POWER. A STUDY BY THE DEPARTMENT OF COAL ECONOMICS. WASHINGTON, 1960.
87P.

1. ELECTRICITY - STATISTICS. I. TITLE.

380
S74 TRENDS IN EMPLOYMENT IN THE SERVICE INDUSTRIES.
STIGLER, GEORGE JOSEPH.
TRENDS IN EMPLOYMENT IN THE SERVICE INDUSTRIES. PRINCETON, N.J., PRINCETON UNIVERSITY PRESS, 1956.
167P. (NATIONAL BUREAU OF ECONOMIC RESEARCH. GENERAL SERIES, NO. 59)

1. SERVICE INDUSTRIES. 2. EMPLOYMENT. 3. ECONOMIC CONDITIONS. I. NATIONAL BUREAU OF ECONOMIC RESEARCH. II. TITLE.

728.1
:308
J27 TRENDS IN HOUSING DURING THE WAR AND POSTWAR PERIODS.
JESSUP, MARY FROST.
TRENDS IN HOUSING DURING THE WAR AND POSTWAR PERIODS. WASHINGTON, GOVT. PRINT. OFF., 1947.
13P. (SERIAL NO. R. 1875)

FROM THE MONTHLY LABOR REVIEW, JAN. 1947, BUREAU OF LABOR STATISTICS.

1. HOUSING MARKET. 2. HOUSING. 3. VETERANS' HOUSING. I. U.S. BUREAU OF LABOR STATISTICS. II. TITLE.

VF
690.57
:331
L11 Trends in man-hours expended per unit.
U.S. Bureau of Labor Statistics.
Trends in man-hours expended per unit: selected types of construction machinery, 1948 to 1949. [Washington] Jan. 1952.
14 p. graphs, tables.

Processed.

1.Building equipment-Labor requirements. I.Title.

LAW
T Trends in European corrections.
Conrad, John P.
Trends in European corrections. [Report] submitted to the President's Commission on Law Enforcement and Administration of Justice. [Washington, D.C.] 1967.
50p.

1. Law enforcement - Europe. I. U.S. President's Commission on Law Enforcement and Administration of Justice. II. Title.

312
N17t Trends in illegitimacy.
U.S. National Center for Health Statistics.
Trends in illegitimacy, United States 1940-1965. Vital and health statistics, data from the National Vital Statistics System. Washington. 1968.
90p. (U.S. Public Health Service. Publication no. 1000-Series 21-no. 15)

1. Population
2. Public health - Statistics. I. Title.

728.1
(79454)
C15 TRENDS IN MULTI-FAMILY HOUSING.
CALIFORNIA. STATE COLLEGE. SACRAMENTO. REAL ESTATE RESEARCH BUREAU.
TRENDS IN MULTI-FAMILY HOUSING, SACRAMENTO METROPOLITAN AREA, 1950-1970. A CASE STUDY OF A DIRECTIONAL GROWTH PROBLEM IN THE METROPOLITAN SACRAMENTO AREA. SACRAMENTO, CALIF., 1961.
272P.
BIBLIOGRAPHY: P.268-272.

1. APARTMENT HOUSES - SACRAMENTO, CALIF. I. TITLE.

332.72
(083.41)
F22T TRENDS IN FHA HOME MORTGAGE OPERATIONS 1935-1950.
U.S. FEDERAL HOUSING ADMINISTRATION.
TRENDS IN FHA HOME MORTGAGE OPERATIONS 1935-1950. SELECTED STATISTICAL TRENDS IN VOLUME AND CHARACTERISTICS OF HOME MORTGAGES... WASHINGTON, 1951.
20P.

1. MORTGAGE FINANCE - STATISTICS. I. TITLE. II. TITLE: HOME MORTGAGE OPERATIONS, 1935-1950.

711.4
:670
S72t Trends in industrial location and their impact on regional economic development.
Stevens, Benjamin H
Trends in industrial location and their impact on regional economic development; a report on research in progress, by Benjamin H. Stevens and others. Philadelphia, Regional Science Research Institute, 1969.
38p. (RSRI discussion paper no. 31)
Research under grant from the Economic Development Administration.

1. Industrial location. 2. Economic development. I. Regional Science Research Institute. II. Title.

FOLIO
333.5
R27T TRENDS IN NATURAL RESOURCE COMMODITIES.
RESOURCES FOR THE FUTURE.
TRENDS IN NATURAL RESOURCE COMMODITIES, STATISTICS FOR PRICES, OUTPUT, CONSUMPTION, FOREIGN TRADE AND EMPLOYMENT IN THE UNITED STATES, 1870-1957 BY NEAL POTTER AND FRANCIS T. CHRISTY, JR. BALTIMORE, PUBLISHED FOR RESOURCES FOR THE FUTURE, BY JOHNS HOPKINS PRESS, 1962.
568P.

1. NATURAL RESOURCES. 2. ECONOMIC CONDITIONS. I. POTTER, NEAL. II. CHRISTY, FRANCIS T. III. TITLE.

690
(75526)
A52n
1967 Trends in house construction.
Alexandria, Va. Dept. of Planning and Regional Affairs.
1967 construction trends, Alexandria, Va. and region. Alexandria, 1968.
7p. (Information bulletin no. 13)

1. Building industry - Alexandria, Va. 2. Trends in house construction. I. Title: Construction trends.

711.17
N174 Trends in land acquisition.
National Research Council. Highway Research Board.
Trends in land acquisition. Washington, 1955.
82 p. tables. (Its Bulletin 101)

728.1
:325
F22 Trends in occupied dwelling units, all races and nonwhite.
U.S. Federal Housing Administration.
Trends in occupied dwelling units, all races and nonwhite 1940, 1950, and 1956 and components of nonwhite housing inventory change, April 1950 to December, 1956 in selected standard metropolitan areas (SMA's) and cities Washington, 1959.
[3]p. tables.

1. Minority groups - Housing. I. Title.

728.1
:308
H68 Trends in house construction.
House and home.
Housing facts and trends. New York, McGraw-Hill, 1965.
201p.
Prepared in cooperation with F. W. Dodge Corporation.

1. Housing market. 2. Trends in house construction. 3. Building industry. 4. Building costs. 5. Rental housing. I. Title. II. Dodge (F. W.) Corp., New York.

VF
333.33
(781)
K15 Trends in land values in Kansas.
Kansas. State College. Agricultural Experiment Station.
Trends in land values in Kansas. Manhattan, 1956.
18 p. charts, tables. (Its Circular 341)

1. Real property - Kansas. 2. Real property - Valuation. I. Title.

338
S74 TRENDS IN OUTPUT AND EMPLOYMENT.
STIGLER, GEORGE JOSEPH.
TRENDS IN OUTPUT AND EMPLOYMENT. NEW YORK, 1947.
67P. (NATIONAL BUREAU OF ECONOMIC RESEARCH. TWENTY-FIFTH ANNIVERSARY SERIES, 4)

1. LABOR PRODUCTIVITY. I. NATIONAL BUREAU OF ECONOMIC RESEARCH. II. TITLE.

351.7
:728.1
F22 Trends in house construction.
U.S. Federal Housing Administration. Division of Research and Statistics.
FHA homes in metropolitan districts; characteristics of mortgages, homes, borrowers under the FHA plan, 1934-1940. Washington, Govt. Print. Off., 1942.
238 p. graphs, maps, tables.

1.U.S. Federal Housing Administration. 2.Rental housing. 3.Trends in house construction. 4.Mortgage finance. I.Title.

362.6
C65t
1969
S-H Trends in long-term care.
U.S. Congress. Senate. Special Committee on Aging.
Trends in long-term care. Hearings before the Subcommittee on Long-Term Care of the Special Committee on Aging, United States Senate, Ninety-first Congress, first session, Wash., Govt. Print. Off., 1970.
/pts. pt. 1 Washington, D.C.

1. Old age. 2. Nursing homes. I. Title.

658.83
A52t Trends in packaging technology and marketing.
American Management Association.
Trends in packaging technology and marketing. New York, 1968.
24 p. (AMA management bulletin no. 121)

1. Marketing. I. Title: Packaging. II. Title. (Series

OA
Archives Trends in house construction.
U.S. Housing and Home Finance Agency. Office of the Administrator.
Survey shows construction characteristics of new houses. Trends in selected characteristics of single family detached houses. Washington, Aug. 9, 1951.
2/8 p. tables. (HHFA-RP-no. 129)
Some results of HHFA 1950 Housing materials use survey.
1.Trends in house construction. I.Title: Trends in selected characteristics of..houses. II.1950 housing materials use survey.

VF
696.6
:331
L11 Trends in man hours expended per unit.
U.S. Bureau of Labor Statistics.
Trends in man hours expended per unit: household electrical appliances, 1939-1947. [Washington, D.C.] Apr. 1950.
77 p. charts, tables.

Processed.

1.Electric apparatus and appliances-Labor requirements. I.Title.

312
(794)
N17 TRENDS IN PROBLEMS OF URBAN POPULATION GROWTH IN CALIFORNIA.
U.S. NATIONAL RESOURCES PLANNING BOARD.
TRENDS IN PROBLEMS OF URBAN POPULATION GROWTH IN CALIFORNIA. BERKELEY, 1941.
28L.

1. POPULATION - CALIF. I. TITLE.

350
W34 TRENDS IN PUBLIC ADMINISTRATION.
WHITE, LEONARD DUPEE.
TRENDS IN PUBLIC ADMINISTRATION. NEW
YORK, MCGRAW-HILL, 1933.
365P. (RECENT SOCIAL TRENDS MONOGRAPHS)

1. PUBLIC ADMINISTRATION. I. TITLE.

VF
332.72 Trends in the savings and loan field.
:1083.41U.8. Home Loan Bank Board.
H65t Trends in the savings and loan field.
Washington,

v.

For full information see shelf list card.

Trends of vehicle dimensions and performance
characteristics.
711.73
S76t Stonex, K A
Trends of vehicle dimensions and performance
characteristics. [Prepared for] Society of
Automotive Engineers, Summer meeting, Atlantic
City, New Jersey, June 11-15, 1962. New
York, Society of Automotive Engineers, inc.,
1962.
14p.

1. Highways. I. Society of Automotive
Engineers. Meeting, Atlantic City, 1962.
II. Title.

727.1
S71 Trends in school planning.
Stanford University. School of Education.
School Planning Laboratory.
Trends in school planning. [Stanford,
Calif., Stanford Univ. Press, 1955].
119 p. illus.

Joh S. Peters, Editor.

312
C25t Trends in the income of families and persons
no.17 in the United States.
U.S. Bureau of the Census.
Trends in the income of families and persons
in the United States, 1947-1964, by Mary F.
Henson. Washington, Govt. Print. Off., 1967.
294p. (Its Technical paper no. 17)

1. Census. 2. Income. 3. Family income and
expenditure. I. Henson, Mary F. II. Title.

VF
728.1 Trends toward open occupancy.
:325 U.S. Public Housing Administration.
P81t Open occupancy in housing programs of the
Public Housing Administration; a trends record.
[No. 1] - As of Sept. 1952 -
Washington, Nov. 1952 -
nos. tables.

Processed.
Title varies: 1956- Trends toward open
occupancy.

01
Archives Trends in selected characteristics of houses.
U.S. Housing and Home Finance Agency. Office of
the Administrator.
Survey shows construction characteristics of
new houses. Trends in selected characteristics of
single family detached houses. Washington,
Aug. 9, 1951.
2+8 p. tables. (HHFA-RP-no. 129)
Some results of HHFA 1950 Housing materials use
survey.
1.Trends in house construction. I.Title: Trends in
selected characteristics of..houses.II.1950 housing
materials use survey.

VF
308 Trends in town - country relations.
(775) Kolb, J H
K65 Trends in town-country relations, by J.H. Kolb
and R.A. Polson. [Madison, Wis.] University of
Wisconsin, Agricultural Experiment Station, Sept.
1933.
37 p. diagrs., tables. (Wisconsin.
University. Agricultural Experiment Station.
Research bulletin 117)

1.Social surveys-Wis. I.Polson, R.A., jt. au.
II.Title. III.Series.

Trenger vi daginstitusjoner for barn?
649.1
A72 As, Dagfinn.
Trenger vi daginstitusjoner for barn?
Barnefamiliene i Nøtterøy kommune svarer
på spørreskjema. Bilag til utbyggings-
planen for daginstitusjoner for barn,
Nøtterøy kommune, 1968 (Day-care for
children; a questionnaire survey of parent
attitudes). Oslo, Norges Byggforskningsinstitutt, 1968.
52p. (Oslo, Norges Byggforskningsinstitutt Rapport no. 55)
English summary.

(Cont'd on next card)

312
C25 Trends in social and economic conditions in
P23 metropolitan areas.
no.27 U.S. Bureau of the Census.
Trends in social and economic conditions in
metropolitan areas. Wash., Govt. Print. Off.,
1969.
67p. (Its Series P23, no. 27)
At head of title: Current population
reports: special studies.
1. Census - Population - 1960.
2. Social conditions. 3. Economic conditions.
I. Title. (Series)

388
:331 Trends in travel to central business districts
S45 by residents of the Washington, D.C. area.
Silver, Jacob.
Trends in travel to the central business
district by residents of the Washington, D. C.
Metropolitan Area, 1948 and 1955. Washington, Bureau of Public Roads, 1959.
153-176p.

Public Roads, a Journal of Highway Research,
vol. 30, no. 7, 1959.

1. Journey to work. I. Title.

649.1
A72 As, Dagfinn. Trenger...1968 (Card 2)

1. Day nurseries. 2. Children.
3. Social surveys. 4. Public opinion
polls. I. Oslo. Norges Byggforskningsinstitutt. II. Title. (Series)

VF
336.2 Trends in the assessed value of taxable
(795) property in Oregon.
072 Oregon. University. Bureau of Municipal
Research and Service.
Memorandum on trends in the assessed
value of taxable property in Oregon, 1950-
1956. Eugene, Or., 1957.
14 p., tables.

1.Taxation - Oregon. 2.Real property -
Taxation - Oregon. I.Title: Trends in
the assessed value of taxable property in
Oregon.

711.585 TRENDS IN URBAN RESIDENTIAL
(79498) DEVELOPMENT.
H46 HIPPAKA, WILLIAM H
TRENDS IN URBAN RESIDENTIAL
DEVELOPMENT, BY WILLIAM H. HIPPAKA
AND LAWRENCE J. RINK. SAN DIEGO,
CALIF., SAN DIEGO STATE COLLEGE,
DIVISION OF BUSINESS ADMINISTRATION,
1960.
126L.

1. URBAN RENEWAL - SAN DIEGO COUNTY,
CALIF. I. CALIFORNIA. STATE
COLLEGE. SAN DIEGO. DIV. OF BUSINESS
ADMINISTRATION. II. TITLE.

Trenor, William R jt. au.
711.73
(016) Tummins, Marvin.
T85 Forecasting and estimating; a selected
annotated bibliography with special emphasis
on methodology (supplemented by a section of
unannotated entries), by Marvin Tummins and
William R. Trenor. Charlottesville, Va.,
Virginia Council of Highway Investigation and
Research. In cooperation with the U.S.
Bureau of Public Roads, 1961.
96p.
1. Highways - Bibliography. I. Trenor, William R.,
jt. au. II. Virginia Council of Highway
Investigation and Research. III. U.S.
Bureau of Public Roads.

690.022 Trends in the industrialization of building.
UN United Nations. (Dept. of Economic and Social
Affairs)
Trends in the industrialization of building.
New York, 1970.
58p. (United Nations [Document] ST/SOA/102)

1. Prefabricated construction. I. Title.

351
F74 Trends of federalism in theory and practice.
Friedrich, Carl J
Trends of federalism in theory and practice.
New York, Frederick A. Praeger, 1968.
193p.

1. Federal government. 2. Intergovernmental
relations. 3. Political science. I. Title:
Federalism in theory and practice. II. Title.

336
T72b Trentin, H George.
Budgeting general and administrative
expenses: a planning and control system, by
H. George Trentin and Reginald L. Jones.
New York, American Management Association,
Administrative Services Div., 1966.
15p. (American Management Association.
Management bulletin 74)

1. Budget. 2. Management. I. Jones,
Reginald L., jt. au. II. American
Management Associ- ation. III. Title.
(Series)

312.1 TRENDS IN THE RACIAL DISTRIBUTION ON
(7471) THE POPULATION.
N28 NEW YORK (CITY) COMMISSION ON HUMAN
RIGHTS.
TRENDS IN THE RACIAL DISTRIBUTION ON
THE POPULATION, OF THE CITY OF NEW YORK
BETWEEN 1950 AND 1957; AN ECOLOGICAL
ANALYSIS. REV. NEW YORK, 1962.
15P. (ITS RESEARCH REPORT NO. 1)
MAP SUPPLEMENTS (5) INSERTED.
COVER TITLE: NEW YORK CITY'S RACIAL
DISTRIBUTION.

1. POPULATION SHIFTS - NEW YORK (CITY)
I. TITLE. I I. TITLE: NEW YORK
CITY'S RACIAL DISTRIBUTION.

312
(77311) Trends of population in the region of
J27 Chicago.
Jeter, Helen Rankin.
Trends of population in the region of
Chicago. Prepared by the Local Community
Research Committee of the University of
Chicago and the Commonwealth Club of Chicago
for the Chicago Regional Planning Association.
Chicago, University of Chicago Press [c1927]
64 p.

1. Population - Chicago. I. Chicago Regional
Planning Association. II. Title.

711.585
(766821) Trenton, R W
T72 Economic and marketability studies; a
part of a Community Renewal Program for
the city of Muskogee, Oklahoma.
[Stillwater Okla.] 1963.
25p.
Prepared for the Muskogee Metropolitan
Area Planning Commission, city-county of
Muskogee, Oklahoma and the Department of
Commerce and Industry, State Planning
Agency.
U.S. Urban Renewal Adm. CRP.

(Cont'd on next card)

711.585
(766821)
T72
Trenton, R.W. Economic and marketability studies; a part of a community Renewal Program for the city of Muskogee, Oklahoma....1963. (Card 2)

1. Urban renewal - Muskogee, Okla. 2. Economic base studies - Muskogee, Okla. I. Title. II. Muskogee, Okla. Metropolitan Area Planning Commission. III. U.S. URA-CRP. Muskogee, Okla.

711.4
(74966)
T72r
Trenton. Central Planning Board. Report, 1961

Trenton, 19
v. annual.
For complete information see shelflist.

1. City planning - Trenton. 2. Urban renewal - Trenton.

728.1
:336.18
(76966)
T72s
TRENTON. HOUSING AUTHORITY. SCARCER THAN HESSIANS. TRENTON, 1948.
28P.

CONTAINS MONTHLY INCOME AND EXPENSE FOR CALENDAR YEAR 1947.

1. PUBLIC HOUSING - TRENTON.

2717-
2723
TRENTON, MICH. PLANNING COMMISSION. MASTER PLAN STUDY: 1, EXISTING LAND USE; 2, NEIGHBORHOOD PLANNING UNITS; 3, WATERFRONT MARINA; 4, RECREATION AND COMMUNITY FACILITIES; 5, MUNICIPAL COSTS AND REVENUES; 6, MASTER PLAN FOR FUTURE LAND USE; 7, PROJECT COMPLETION REPORT, BY STATE OF MICHIGAN, DEPARTMENT OF COMMERCE, COMMUNITY PLANNING DIVISION. PREPARED BY VILICAN-LEMAN AND ASSOCIATES, INC. SOUTHFIELD, MICH., 1968-69.
7 V. (HUD 7 01 REPORT)
(CONTINUED ON NEXT CARD)

711.585
(74966)
T72
Trenton, N.J. Greater Trenton Council. Report,

Trenton,
v. illus., maps. annual.
For complete information see shelflist.

1. Urban renewal - Trenton, N.J. 2. City planning - Trenton, N.J.

711.585.1
(74966)
T72
Trenton. Office of the Mayor. Application to the Department of Housing and Urban Development for a grant to plan a comprehensive city demonstration program. Trenton. 1967.
1v.
Selected to receive the first HUD Model Cities Program planning grants.

1. Model cities- Trenton. I. U.S. HUD- Model Cities Program first planning grants.

2717-
2723
TRENTON, MICH. PLANNING COMMISSION. MASTER PLAN ...8-69. (CARD 2)

1. MASTER PLAN - TRENTON, MICH. I. VILICAN-LEMAN AND ASSOCIATES. II. MICHIGAN. DEPT. OF COMMERCE. COMMUNITY PLANNING DIV. III. HUD. 701. TRENTON, MICH.

711.552
(74966)
C15
Trenton, N. J. Greater Trenton Council. Candeub (Isadore) and Fleissig. Trenton central business district economic study. Trenton, 1958.
1 v. tables, maps.

1. Business districts-Trenton, N.J. I. Trenton, N. J. Greater Trenton Council.

711.585
(74966)
T72c
Trenton, N.J. Office of the Mayor. City of Trenton, New Jersey: slum clearance and rehabilitation, a report. Trenton, 1953.
1v.

1. Slum clearance - Trenton, N.J.

2161
TRENTON, MO. CITY PLANNING COMMISSION. COMPREHENSIVE PLAN, BY HARE AND HARE. TRENTON, MO., 1970.
101P. (HUD 701 REPORT)

1. MASTER PLAN - TRENTON, MO. I. HARE AND HARE. II. HUD. 701. TRENTON, MO.

711.552
(74966)
C15t
Trenton, N. J. Greater Trenton Council. Candeub (Isadore) and Fleissig. Trenton central district area circulation plan. Trenton, 1958.
32p. illus., maps.

Sponsored jointly with the Greater Trenton Council.

1. Business districts - Trenton, N. J. 2. Streets - Trenton, N. J. 3. Traffic - Trenton, N. J. I. Trenton, N. J. Greater Trenton Council.

VP
690.091.82
:613.5
(74966)
T72
Trenton, N.J. Ordinances, etc.
... An ordinance establishing minimum standards governing the condition and maintenance of dwellings; establishing minimum standards governing supplied utilities and facilities and other physical things, and conditions essential to making dwellings safe, sanitary and fit for human habitation ... Trenton, N.J., Board of Commissioners, Dec. 1952.
1 l.
[Ordinance 780, passed Dec. 23, 1952]
1.Housing codes-Trenton N.J. 2.Housing law enforcement.

2162
TRENTON, MO. CITY PLANNING COMMISSION. PROPOSED SUBDIVISION REGULATIONS, BY HARE AND HARE. TRENTON, MO., 1970.
12P. (HUD 701 REPORT)

1. SUBDIVISION REGULATION - TRENTON, MO. I. HARE AND HARE. II. HUD. 701. TRENTON, MO.

711.4
(74966)
T72t
Trenton, N. J. Greater Trenton Council. Candeub (Isadore) and Fleissig. Trenton central district area plan. Trenton, 1959.
40p. illus., maps.

1. Master plan - Trenton, N. J. 2. Business districts - Trenton, N. J. I. Trenton, N. J. Greater Trenton Council.

711.585
(74966)
G27
Trenton. Dept. of Planning and Development. Gershen (Alvin E.) Associates. John Fitch Way III a middle income community in an urban setting. Trenton, 1968.
kit. (28 pieces)
U.S. Dept. of Housing and Urban Development. General Neighborhood Renewal Plan. Prepared for Trenton Dept. of Planning and Development.
1. Urban renewal - Trenton. 2. Family income and expenditure - Housing - Trenton. I. Trenton. Dept. of Planning and Development. II. Title: Middle income community. III. Title. IV. U.S. HUD-GNRP. Trenton.

2163
TRENTON, MO. CITY PLANNING COMMISSION. ZONING ORDINANCE STUDY AND SUGGESTED AMENDMENTS. TRENTON, MO., 1970.
1 V. (HUD 701 REPORT)

1. ZONING - TRENTON, MO. I. HUD. 701. TRENTON, MO.

711.4
(74966)
T72
Trenton, N.J. Greater Trenton Council. Candeub (Isadore) and Fleissig. Trenton Central district plan; Trenton and Mercer County economic study. Trenton, N.J., 1957.
31p. charts, tables.

1.Business districts - Trenton, N. J. 2.Economic base studies - Mercer Co., N. J. 3.City planning - Trenton, N. J. I.Trenton, N. J. Greater Trenton Council.

VP
711.4
(74966)
T77
Trenton, N.J. Planning Board. Official report on planning and zoning for metropolitan Trenton, by the Joint Planning Boards of Ewing Township, Lawrence Township and the city of Trenton, New Jersey. Trenton, N.J., 1952.
67 p. maps (fold.), tables.
Russell Vannest Black, Consultant.
1.City planning-Trenton, N.J. 2.Zoning-Trenton, N.J. 3.Housing-Trenton, N.J. I.Black, Russell Vannest.

Trenton, N. J.

VP
Housing-U.S.-N.J.

728.1
:336.18
(76966)
T72
TRENTON. HOUSING AUTHORITY. REPORT, 1938-39, 1940/41- 46/47
TRENTON.
8 V. ANNUAL.

1. PUBLIC HOUSING - TRENTON.

330
(016)
T72
Trenton, N.J. State College. Roscoe L West Library. Africa today, comp. by Parker Worley. Rev. ed. Trenton, 1959.
23p.

Earlier list prepared in 1956, by Doria M. Perry and Evald Rink.

1. Economic conditions - Africa - Bibliography. I. Worley, Parker. II. Title.

940
(016)
T72

Trenton, N. J. State College. (Roscoe L. West Library)
Europe today, a bibliography comp. by Felix E. Hirsch. rev. 3d ed. Trenton, 1960.
27p.

1. Bibliography - Europe. I. Hirsch, Felix E., comp.

711.4
(76823)
T72

Trenton, Tenn. Municipal Planning Commission. Trenton base ... (Card 2)

Planning Assistance Program.

1. City planning - Trenton, Tenn. 2. Trenton, Tenn. - Maps. I. Tennessee. State Planning Commission. II. U.S. Urban Renewal Administration. Urban Planning Assistance Program.

312
T72

Trewartha, Glenn Thomas.
A geography of population: world patterns. New York, Wiley, 1969.
186p.

Bibliography: p. 175-177.

1. Population. I. Title.

711.14
(76823)
T72

Trenton, Tenn. Municipal Regional Planning Commission.
Existing land use survey and analysis, Trenton, Tennessee. With the assistance of the Tennessee State Planning Commission, West Tennessee Office. Trenton, 1957.
13p. map, tables.

U.S. Urban Renewal Administration, Urban

(Continued on next card)

711.5
(76823
:347)
T72

Trenton, Tenn. Municipal-Regional Planning Commission.
Zoning ordinance, Trenton, Tennessee. Trenton, 1958.
47p. map.

U.S. Urban Renewal Administration, Urban Planning Assistance Program.

1. Zoning legislation - Trenton, Tenn. I. U.S. Urban Renewal Administration. Urban Planning Assistance Program. Trenton, Tenn.

551.5
T72

Trewartha, Glenn T
An introduction to weather and climate. 2d ed. New York, McGraw-Hill, c1943.
xi, 545 p. illus., charts (part fold., 1 col., 4 in pocket), diagrs., graphs, tables. (McGraw-Hill series in geography)

Includes references.

1. Weather. 2. Climate.

711.14
(76823)
T72

Trenton, Tenn. Municipal Planning Commission. Existing land ... (Card 2)

Planning Assistance Program.

1. Land use - Trenton, Tenn. I. Tennessee State Planning Commission. II. U.S. Urban Renewal Administration. Urban Planning Assistance Program.

VF
332.725
H68

Tres maneras de financiar las mejoras en su casa por medio de la FHA.
U.S. Dept. of Housing and Urban Development.
Tres maneras de financiar las mejoras en sucasa por medio de la FHA. Wash., Govt. Print. Off., 1968.
9p. (HUD consumer bulletin. IP-37-S)

1. Property improvement loans. 2. Mortgage finance. 3. Federal housing programs. I. Title.

027
L41pr

Trezza, Alphonse F., ed.
Library Equipment Institute, 3d. New York, 1966.
The procurement of library furnishings: specifications, bid documents, and evaluation; proceedings. Edited by Frazer G. Poole and Alphonse F. Trezza. Chicago, American Library Association, 1969.
150p.
Sponsored by the Library Administration Div., American Library Association.
1. Libraries. 2. Furniture. I. Poole, Frazer G., ed. II. Trezza, Alphonse F., ed. III. American Library Association. Library Administration Div. IV. Title.

711.14
(76823)
T72

Trenton, Tenn. Municipal-Regional Planning Commission.
Land use plan, Trenton, Tennessee. Trenton, 1959.
12p. map.

U.S. Urban Renewal Administration, Urban Planning Assistance Program.

1. Land use - Trenton, Tenn. I. U.S. URA-UP/AP. Trenton, Tenn.

VF
690.091.82
(74811)
P17

Tresolini, R John, jt. au.
Parratt, Spencer D
The administration of housing and building regulations in Philadelphia, by Spencer D. Parratt and R. John Tresolini. Philadelphia, Housing Association, 1952.
66 l.
Processed.
1. Building code administration. 2. Building codes- Philadelphia, Pa. I. Tresolini, R. John, jt. au. II. Philadelphia Housing Association.

002
B67

TRIAL: an information retrieval system.
Borman, Lorraine.
TRIAL: an information retrieval system for creating, maintaining, indexing, and retrieving from files of textual information; user's manual, by Lorraine Borman and others. Evanston, Ill., Vogelback Computing Center, Northwestern University, 1968.
[54]p. (U.S. Air Force Office of Scientific Research. AFOSR 69-0743 TR)
CFSTI. AD 684 626.
1. Documentation. 2. Library science. I. Northwestern University. Vogelback Computing (Cont'd on next card)

711.73
(76823)
T72

Trenton, Tenn. Municipal-Regional Planning Commission.
Major road and street plan, Trenton, Tennessee. Trenton, 1958.
16p. maps.

U.S. Urban Renewal Administration, Urban Planning Assistance Program.

1. Highways - Trenton, Tenn. 2. Street planning - Trenton, Tenn. I. U.S. URA-UPAP.

VF
728.1
:336.18
T72

Tretter, Maxwell H
Public housing finance. Harvard Law Review, p. 1325-1358, June 1941.

Reprint.

1. Public housing - financing.

002
B67

Borman, Lorraine. TRIAL...1968. (Card 2)

Center. II. U.S. Air Force. Office of Scientific Research. III. Title.

333.38
(76823)
T72

Trenton, Tenn. Municipal-Regional Planning Commission.
Subdivision regulations, Trenton, Tennessee. [Assisted by the Tennessee State Planning Commission, West Tennessee Office] Trenton, 1959.
40p. diagrs.

U.S. Urban Renewal Administration, Urban Planning Assistance Program.

1. Subdivision regulation - Trenton, Tenn. I. U.S. URA-UP Trenton, Tenn.

711.4
(669)
T72

Trevallion, B A W
Metropolitan Kano; report on the twenty year development plan 1963-1983. Oxford, Pergamon Press, 1966.
2v.
Vol. 2 consists of 2 col. maps in pocket.
"Prepared in 1963 for the Greater Kano Planning Authority."

1. City planning - Nigeria. 2. Economic conditions - Nigeria. I. Greater Kano Planning Authority. II. Title.

LAW
T
P728tr

Trial by agency.
Prettyman, E Barrett.
Trial by agency. Forward by Felix Frankfurter. Charlottesville, Va., The Virginia Law Review Association, 1959.
60p.

The Henry L. Doherty lectures.

1. Administrative law. 2. Administrative procedure. I. Title.

711.4
(76823)
T72

Trenton, Tenn. Municipal Planning Commission.
Trenton base map, Trenton, Tennessee. With the assistance of the Tennessee State Planning Commission, West Tennessee Office. Trenton, 1957.
7p. map.

U.S. Urban Renewal Administration, Urban

(Continued on next card)

711.585
(41)
M17

Marshall, Howard
Slum, by Howard Marshall, in collaboration with Avice Trevelyan. London, William Heinemann, 1933.
166p.

Trevelyan, Avice.

1. Slum clearance - U.K. 2. Housing - U.K. I. Trevelyan, Avice.

621.643
C76

Trial of plastics pipes for hot water services.
Crowder, J R
Trial of plastics pipes for hot water services, by J.R. Crowder and A. Rixon. Garston, Eng., Building Research Station, Ministry of Public Building and Works, 1968.
[4]p. (U.S. Building Research Station. Building research current papers. Current paper 7/68)
Reprinted from: British plastics, July, 1967.
1. Pipes. 2. Plastics. I. Rixon, A., jt. au. II. U.K. Building Research Station. III. Title.

224

TRIANA, ALA. TOWN PLANNING COMMISSION.
PUBLIC IMPROVEMENTS PROGRAM AND CAPITAL
IMPROVEMENTS BUDGET, BY ALABAMA
DEVELOPMENT OFFICE. TRIANA, ALA., 1970.
5p. (HUD 701 REPORT)

1. CAPITAL IMPROVEMENT PROGRAMS -
TRIANA, ALA. I. ALABAMA DEVELOPMENT
OFFICE. II. HUD. 701. TRIANA, ALA.

333.332
815 Sánchez-Arjona, José María Martínez.
Trías Bertran, Carlos, jt. au.
Valoración de terrenos sujetos a expropiación
en ejecución de los planes de vivienda y
urbanismo; discursos, enmiendas, proyecto y
texto definitivo de la ley, por José María
Martínez Sánchez-Arjona y Carlos Trías Bertran.
Madrid, Ministerio de la Vivienda, Secretaría
General Tecnica, 1962.
148p. (Spain. Ministerio de la Vivienda.
Conferencias y discursos 4)
1. Real property - Valuation. 2. Appraisal.
I. Trías Bertran, Carlos, jt. au.
II. Spain. Ministerio de la Vivienda.

332.72
(60)
T74
Tribe, M
The finance of housing in the public and
private sectors. [New York] United Nations,
Economic and Social Council, 1968.
21p. (United Nations. [Document] E/CN.14
HOU/31)
At head of title: United Nations Economic
and Social Council, Economic Commission for
Africa and German Foundation for Developing
Countries Meeting on Technical and Social
Problems of Urbanization (With Emphasis on
Financing of Housing) Addis Ababa,
(Cont'd on next card)

332.72
(60)
T74
Tribe, M   The finance...1968. (Card 2)

8-23 Jan. 1969.

1. Mortgage finance - Africa. I. United
Nations. (Economic Commission for
Africa) II. Title.

Triborough Bridge.
388
(7471) Triborough Bridge and Tunnel Authority.
T74tr   Triborough Bridge, 1936-1966. [New York]
1966.
[7]p.

1. Transportation - New York (City)
2. Bridges. 3. Triborough Bridge.

712.21
(7471) Triborough Bridge and Tunnel Authority.
T74a   Arterial recreation areas for New York.
New York, 1966.
[11]p.

1. Parks - New York (City)
2. Recreation - New York (City) I. Title.

711.73
(747) Triborough Bridge and Tunnel Authority.
T74   Cross Bronx Expressway, Alexander Hamilton
Bridge, George Washington Bridge bus
station. In cooperation with the Port of
New York Authority, Federal and State highway
agencies, and the City of New York. New York,
1963.
[8]p.

1. Highways - New York (State)
2. Bridges. I. Port of New York Authority.

711.74
(7471)
T74 [Triborough Bridge and Tunnel Authority]
Cross Manhattan arterials and related
improvements. [New York] 1959.
[15]p.   map.

1. Street planning - New York (City)

Triborough Bridge and Tunnel Authority.
712.21
(7471)
M67   Moses, Robert.
The expanding New York waterfront.
[New York] Triborough Bridge and Tunnel
Authority, 1964.
28p.

1. Parks - New York (City) I. Triborough
Bridge and Tunnel Authority.

388
(7471) Triborough Bridge and Tunnel Authority.
T74r   Financial and construction program 1967-1971
suppl.

Financial supplement to the annual report.
New York, 1967
/v. annual.
For complete information see main card.

1. Transportation - New York (City)
2. Bridges. 3. Highways - New York (City)

VF
352.6
(7471) Triborough Bridge and Tunnel Authority.
T74   The influence of public improvements
on property values [in] the city of New York
[by Robert Moses] New York, 1953.
2a   [17]p.

1. Community facilities - New York (City)
2. Public housing - New York (City)
3. Real property - New York (City) I. Moses,
Robert. II. Title.

Triborough Bridge and Tunnel Authority.
711.73
(747) Port of New York Authority.
P67   Joint study of arterial facilities, New
York-New Jersey metropolitan area. [In
cooperation with] Triborough Bridge and
Tunnel Authority. [New York, 1954?]
62p.
Cover title.
1. Highways - New York (State) 2. Highways -
New Jersey. I. Triborough Bridge and Tunnel
Authority.

711.73
(7471) Triborough Bridge and Tunnel Authority.
T74   Lower Manhattan Elevated Expressway.
Introduction by Robert Moses. New York,
1965.
11p.

1. Highways - New York (City)
2. Transportation - New York (City)
I. Moses, Robert. II. Title.

712.21
(7471) Triborough Bridge and Tunnel Authority.
T74m   Mill Rock, Wards Island, Randall's
Island, Flushing Meadow Park. New York,
1965.
24p.

1. Parks - New York (City)
2. Metropolitan areas - New York (City)

725.822.91
T74   Triborough Bridge and Tunnel Authority.
The New York Coliseum. New York,
1954.
[16]p.

1. Auditoriums. 2. Public buildings
- New York (City) I. Title.

725.822.91
T74
1966   Triborough Bridge and Tunnel Authority.
New York Coliseum. Tenth anniversary.
New York, 1966.
23p.

Robert Moses, Chairman.
Includes Triborough Bridge and Tunnel
Authority facilities booklet.

1. Auditoriums. 2. Public buildings -
New York (City) I. Moses, Robert.
II. Title.

VF
712.21
(7471) Triborough Bridge and Tunnel Authority.
T74o   Opening of Brooklyn-Queens Expressway
playgrounds. New York, 1967.
folder.

1. Parks - New York (City) 2. Recreation - New York (City) I. Title.

711.73
(7471) Triborough Bridge and Tunnel Authority.
T74p   Plan to increase the capacity of the
Miller Highway and Henry Hudson Parkway.
New York, 1965.
19p.
Introduction by Robert Moses.

1. Highways - New York (City)
2. Transportation - New York (City)
3. Journey to work. I. Title.

711.6   Triborough Bridge and Tunnel Authority.
C51p Clarke and Rapuano, New York.
no. 2   Preparation of the site for the World's
Fair 1964-1965, by Clarke and Rapuano and
others. Second supplementary report:
maintenance of traffic during arterial
construction. New York, 1960.
9p.

Prepared for Triborough Bridge and
Tunnel Authority.

1. Site planning. 2. Traffic - New York (City)
I. Triborough Bridge and Tunnel
Authority.

Triborough Bridge and Tunnel Authority.
352.6
(7471)
M67   Moses, Robert.
Public works and beauty; the philosophy
of Triborough. New York, Triborough
Bridge and Tunnel Authority, 1966.
16p.

1. Community facilities - New York
(City) I. Triborough Bridge and Tunnel
Authority. II. Title.

712.25
(7471) Triborough Bridge and Tunnel Authority.
T74   Reopening of New York City building; an
initial step in the restoration and
redevelopment of Flushing Meadow Park.
New York, 1966.
[6]p.

1. Recreation - New York (City)
2. Public buildings - New York (City)
I. Title.

388
(7471)
T74r

Triborough Bridge and Tunnel Authority.
Report, 1964-18

New York, 1965-
5 v.   annual.

For complete information see main card.

1. Transportation - New York (City)
2. Bridges. 3. Highways - New York
(City)

712.21
(7471)
T74

Triborough Bridge and Tunnel Authority.
A tour of Staten Island improvements
and the next steps. New York, Published
by the Triborough Bridge and Tunnel
Authority with the cooperation of other
agencies, 1965.
20p.

1. Parks - New York (City) 2. Metropolitan areas - New York (City) I. Title.

320
C657

Tributes to the President and Mrs. Lyndon
Baines Johnson in the Congress of the...
U.S. Congress. Senate.
Tributes to the President and Mrs. Lyndon
Baines Johnson in the Congress of the United
States. Wash., Govt. Print. Off., 1969.
185p. (91st Cong., 1st sess. Senate.
Document no. 91-7)
1. U.S. President, 1936-1969 (Johnson)
2. Johnson, Claudia Alta (Taylor)
I. U.S. Congress. II. Title.

711.73
(7471)
T74s

Triborough Bridge and Tunnel Authority.
Safety and our highways, by Robert
Moses. New York, 1966.
10p.

Reprinted from Newsday, June and
September 1966 in the interest of safer
and saner road travel.

1. Highways - New York (City) 2. Traffic safety. I. Moses, Robert. II. Newsday. III. Title.

388
(7471)
T74

Triborough Bridge and Tunnel Authority.
Traffic, earnings and feasibility of the
Long Island Sound crossing, by Robert
Moses. Joint report of the Madigan-Hyland,
inc. and the Triborough Bridge and
Tunnel Authority. New York, 1965.
25p.

1. Traffic - New York metropolitan area.
I. Moses, Robert. II. Madigan-Hyland, inc.

630
1331
812

Trice, Andrew H.
Sacramento, Calif. Redevelopment Agency.
Present and future requirements for agricultural labor from the Sacramento labor
market area, by Andrew H. Trice. Sacramento, 1958.
50p. diagrs., tables.

U.S. Urban Renewal Administration, Demonstration Grant Program.

1. Agricultural laborers. I. Trice, Andrew H.
II. U.S. Urban Renewal Administration. Demonstration Grant Program.

711.4
(7471)
M672

Triborough Bridge and Tunnel Authority.
Moses, Robert.
The saga of Flushing Meadow; the valley
of ashes. New York, Triborough Bridge
and Tunnel Authority, 1966.
20p.

1. City planning - New York (City)
2. Recreation - New York (City)
3. Parks - New York (City) I. Triborough Bridge and Tunnel Authority.
II. Title.

388
(7471)
T74tr

Triborough Bridge and Tunnel Authority.
Triborough Bridge, 1936-1966. [New York]
1966.
[7]p.

1. Transportation - New York (City)
2. Bridges. 3. Triborough Bridge.

728.1
1613.5
J15

TRICHTER, JEROME, JT. AU.
JAMES, GEORGE.
HEALTH AND HOUSING, BY GEORGE JAMES
AND JEROME TRICHTER. NEW YORK, 1966.
3L. (CO-OP CONTACT, UNITED HOUSING
FOUNDATION, NO. 11)

1. HOUSING AND HEALTH. I. TRICHTER,
JEROME, JT. AU.

388
(7472)
M12

Triborough Bridge and Tunnel Authority.
Madigan-Hyland, inc.
A study of metropolitan New York transportation. Prepared for Triborough Bridge
and Tunnel Authority. New York, Triborough
Bridge and Tunnel Authority, 1967.
33p.

1. Transportation - New York (City)
metropolitan area. I. Triborough Bridge
and Tunnel Authority. II. Title.

624.2
T74t

Triborough Bridge and Tunnel Authority.
Triborough Bridge and Tunnel Authority
facilities. New York, 1965.
30p.
Robert Moses, Chairman.

1. Bridges. 2. Engineering. I. Title.

628.515
N17t

Trickling filter treatment of fruit
processing waste waters.
National Canners Association. Research
Foundation.
Trickling filter treatment of fruit
processing waste waters. [Prepared] for
the Office of Research and Monitoring,
Environmental Protection Agency. Wash.,
Govt. Print. Off., 1971.
37p. (Water pollution control research
series)

1. Water pollution. I. U.S. Environmental Protection Agency. II. Title.

624.2
T74th

Triborough Bridge and Tunnel Authority.
Third tube. [New York] 1965.
16p.

1. Bridges. 2. Highways - New York
(City) 3. Transportation - New York
(City)

388
(7471)
T74t

Triborough Bridge and Tunnel Authority.
Triborough Bridge and Tunnel Authority.
Three decades of service; a pictorial
review of accomplishments. New York, 1966.
77p.

1. Transportation - New York (City)
2. Triborough Bridge and Tunnel Authority.
I. Title.

312
(76192)
T74

Tri-County (Ala.) Regional Planning
Commission.
Population and economic analyses.
[Prepared in cooperation with] Alabama
State Planning and Industrial Development
Board. [n.p.] 1962.
103p.
U.S. Urban Renewal Adm. UPAP.
(Cont'd. on next card)

388
(7471)
T74t

Triborough Bridge and Tunnel Authority.
Three decades of service; a pictorial
review of accomplishments. New York, 1966.
77p.

1. Transportation - New York (City)
2. Triborough Bridge and Tunnel Authority.
I. Title.

624.2
T74t

Triborough Bridge and Tunnel Authority
facilities.
Triborough Bridge and Tunnel Authority.
Triborough Bridge and Tunnel Authority
facilities. New York, 1965.
30p.
Robert Moses, Chairman.

1. Bridges. 2. Engineering. I. Title.

312
(76192)
T74

Tri-County (Ala.) Regional Planning
Commission.   Population and economic
analyses ...   (Card 2)

1. Population - Lawrence Co., Ala.
2. Population - Limestone Co., Ala.
3. Population - Morgan Co., Ala.
4. Economic base studies - Lawrence Co.,
Ala. 5. Economic base studies - Limestone
Co., Ala. 6. Economic base studies -
Morgan Co.,   Ala. I. U.S.
URA-UPAP.   Tri-County Region
(Ala.)

VF
624.2
T74

Triborough Bridge and Tunnel Authority.
Throgs neck bridge. [New York, 1957]
12 p. illus.

1. Bridges. I. Title.

920
C65t

Tributes to the Honorable Earl Warren.
U.S. Congress.
Tributes to the Honorable Earl Warren, Chief
Justice of the United States to commemorate the
occasion of his retirement from the Supreme
Court, June 23, 1969. Delivered in the House
of Representatives of the United States Senate.
Wash., Govt. Print. Off., 1970.
136p.
At head of title: 91st Cong., 2d sess. House.
Document no. 348.

1. Warren, Earl, 1891- 2. U.S. Supreme
Court. I. Title.

711.14
(76192)
T74

Tri-County (Ala.) Regional Planning
Commission.
Tri-County Region, Alabama: land use
maps. [Prepared in cooperation with the]
State Planning and Industrial Development
Board. [n.p.] 1962.
43p.

U.S. Urban Renewal Adm. UPAP.
1. Land use - Lawrence Co., Ala. 2. Land use -
Limestone Co., Ala. 3. Land use - Morgan Co., Ala.
I. U.S. URA-   UPAP. Tri-County
Region (Ala.)

333.38
(76192)
T74
Tri-County (Ala.) Regional Planning
Commission.
Tri-County Region, Alabama: subdivision
regulations and manual. [Prepared in
cooperation with] Alabama State Planning
and Industrial Development Board. [n.p.]
1961.
40p.
U.S. Urban Renewal Adm. UPAP.

1. Subdivision regulation - Lawrence Co., Ala.
2. Subdivision regulation - Limestone Co., Ala.
3. Subdivision regula-   tion -
Morgan Co., Ala.   I. U.S. URA-UPAP.
Alabama.

1838
TRI-COUNTY REGIONAL PLANNING COMMISSION.
(PEORIA, TAZEWELL, AND WOODFORD
COUNTIES, ILL.)
ECONOMIC BASE STUDY. PEORIA, ILL.,
1960.
161P. (HUD 701 REPORT)

1. ECONOMIC CONDITIONS - PEORIA CO.,
ILL. 2. ECONOMIC CONDITIONS - TAZEWELL
CO., ILL. 3. ECONOMIC CONDITIONS -
WOODFORD CO., ILL. I. HUD. 701.
PEORIA CO., ILL. II. HUD. 701.
TAZEWELL CO., ILL. III. HUD. 701.
WOODFORD CO., ILL.

628.1
(774)
S81
Swager, W L   Alternative... (Card 2)

1. Water resources - Mich. 2. Water-supply
engineering. I. Tri-County Regional Planning
Commission, Clinton, Eaton, Ingham County,
Mich. II. Battelle Memorial Institute.
III. U.S. URA-UPAP. Michigan.

711.3
(788)
T74
TRI-COUNTY (COL.) REGIONAL PLANNING
COMMISSION.
REPORT,   TO THE BOARDS
OF COUNTY COMMISSIONERS, ADAMS, ARAPAHOE,
AND JEFFERSON COUNTIES. DENVER,
GOVERNMENT CENTER, 1945-.
V. ANNUAL.

1. REGIONAL PLANNING - COLORADO.

728.69
T74
Tri-County Regional Planning Commission.
(Peoria, Tazewell, Woodford Counties, Ill.)
The mobile home and its place. Peoria, Ill.,
1967.
24p.

1. Trailers and trailer courts. 2. Trailers
and trailer courts - Taxation. I. Title.

4823
4824
TRI-COUNTY REGIONAL PLANNING COMMISSION,
LANSING, MICH.
ALTERNATIVE LONG RANGE WATER USE PLANS
FOR THE TRI-COUNTY REGION, MICHIGAN: 1,
A TECHNICAL-ECONOMIC REPORT; 2, A SUMMARY
REPORT. PREPARED BY BATTELLE MEMORIAL
INSTITUTE. LANSING, MICH., 1963-64.
2 V. (HUD 701 REPORT)

1. WATER-SUPPLY - MICHIGAN.
I. BATTELLE MEMORIAL INSTITUTE.
II. HUD. 701. MICHIGAN.

1837
TRI-COUNTY REGIONAL PLANNING
COMMISSION, PEORIA, ILL.
PRINCEVILLE, ILL. PLANNING COMMISSION.
COMPREHENSIVE PLAN. BY TRI-COUNTY
REGIONAL PLANNING COMMISSION. PEORIA,
ILL., 1969.
24P. (HUD 701 REPORT)

1. MASTER PLAN - PRINCEVILLE, ILL.
I. TRI-COUNTY REGIONAL PLANNING
COMMISSION, PEORIA, ILL. II. HUD. 701.
PRINCEVILLE, ILL.

1835-
1836
TRI-COUNTY REGIONAL PLANNING COMMISSION.
(PEORIA, TAZEWELL, AND WOODFORD
COUNTIES, ILL.)
PLANNING PROGRAM: 1, LOCAL GOVERNMENT
STUDY; 2, THE MOBILE HOME AND ITS PLACE.
PEORIA, ILL., 1970.
2 V. (HUD 701 REPORT)

1. LOCAL GOVERNMENT - ILLINOIS.
2. MOBILE HOMES - ILLINOIS. I. HUD.
701. ILLINOIS.

2956
TRI-COUNTY REGIONAL PLANNING
COMMISSION, LANSING, MICH.
BATH CHARTER TOWNSHIP, MICH. PLANNING
COMMISSION.
BACKGROUND FOR PLANNING. LANSING,
MICH., TRI-COUNTY REGIONAL PLANNING
COMMISSION, 1969.
100L. (HUD 701 REPORT)

1. MASTER PLAN - BATH CHARTER TOWNSHIP,
MICH. I. TRI-COUNTY REGIONAL PLANNING
COMMISSION, LANSING, MICH. II. HUD.
701. BATH CHARTER TOWNSHIP, MICH.

1831-
1833
TRI-COUNTY REGIONAL PLANNING COMMISSION.
(PEORIA, TAZEWELL, AND WOODFORD
COUNTIES, ILL.)
COMPREHENSIVE REGIONAL PLAN: 1,
POPULATION AND ECONOMIC BASE; 2,
HOUSING-COMMUNITY FACILITIES-LAND USE;
3, HIGHWAYS AND TRANSPORTATION. PEORIA,
ILL., 1962.
3 V. (HUD 701 REPORT)

1. MASTER PLAN - PEORIA CO., ILL.
2. MASTER PLAN - TAZEWELL CO., ILL.
3. MASTER PLAN - WOODFORD CO., ILL.
I. HUD. 701. PEORIA CO., ILL.
(CONTINUED ON NEXT CARD)

312
(773)
T74
Tri-County Regional Planning Commission.
(Peoria, Woodford, Tazewell Counties, Ill.)
Population projections. [Peoria, Ill.]
1967.
15p.
Projections to 1985.

1. Population - Illinois.
I. Title.

4822
TRI-COUNTY REGIONAL PLANNING COMMISSION,
LANSING, MICH.
BACKGROUND FOR PLANNING. PREPARED BY
ALAIEDON, VEVAY TOWNSHIPS AND CITY OF
MASON PLANNING COMMISSIONS. LANSING,
MICH., 1969.
171P. (HUD 701 REPORT)

1. CITY PLANNING - INGHAM CO., MICH.
I. HUD. 701. INGHAM CO., MICH.

1831-
1833
TRI-COUNTY REGIONAL PLANNING COMMISSION.
(PEORIA, TAZEWELL, AND WOODFORD
COUNTIES, ILL.) COMPREHENSIVE
REGIONAL ...1962.   (CARD 2)

II. HUD. 701. TAZEWELL CO., ILL.
III. HUD. 701. WOODFORD CO., ILL.

728.1
(771
(1308)
T74
TRI-COUNTY REGIONAL PLANNING COMMISSION
(MEDINA, SUMMIT, PORTAGE, COUNTIES,
OHIO)
A SURVEY OF ANALYSIS OF THE
PHYSICAL-ECONOMIC CHARACTERISTICS OF
SELECTED RECENT SUBURBAN RESIDENTIAL
DEVELOPMENTS AND THE SOCIO-ECONOMIC
CHARACTERISTICS OF THEIR INHABITANTS.
AKRON, OHIO, 1965. 103P. (ITS REGIONAL
PLANNING STUDY NO. 34)

1. HOUSING MARKET - OHIO. I. U.S.
URA-UPAP. OHIO. II. TITLE:
SUBURBAN RESIDENTIAL DEVELOPMENTS.

5965
TRI-COUNTY REGIONAL PLANNING
COMMISSION, LANSING, MICH.
LANSING CHARTER TOWNSHIP, MICH. PLANNING
COMMISSION.
BACKGROUND FOR PLANNING. PREPARED IN
COOPERATION WITH TRI-COUNTY REGIONAL
PLANNING COMMISSION. LANSING, MICH., CA.
1970.
1 V. (HUD 701 REPORT)

1. CITY PLANNING - LANSING CHARTER
TOWNSHIP, MICH. I TRI-COUNTY REGIONAL
PLANNING COMMISSION, LANSING, MICH.
II. HUD. 701. LANSING CHARTER TOWNSHIP,
MICH.

711.333
(773)
T74
Tri-County Regional Planning Commission.
(Peoria, Tazewell, Woodford Counties,
Ill.)
Comprehensive regional plan; a summary.
Peoria, Ill., 1962.
71p.
U.S. Urban Renewal Adm. UPAP.

1. County planning - Ill. 2. Master
plan - Ill. I. U.S. URA-UPAP. Ill.

711.5
(773)
C65
Tri-County Regional Planning Commission,
Peoria, Ill.
Community Studies.
Zoning and subdivision study. Prepared for
the Tri-County Regional Planning Commission.
Peoria, Ill., 1959.
242p. diagrs., maps, tables. (Regional
planning report no. 1)
U.S. Urban Renewal Administration, Urban Planning
Assistance Program.

1. Zoning - Illinois. I. Tri-County Regional Planning Commission, Peoria, Ill. II. U.S. URA-UPAP.
Peoria, Ill.

2772-
2777
TRI-COUNTY REGIONAL PLANNING
COMMISSION, LANSING, MICH.
WINDSOR, MICH. TOWNSHIP PLANNING
COMMISSION.
COMPREHENSIVE PLANNING PROGRAM: 1,
SUGGESTED SUBDIVISION REGULATION
ORDINANCE; 2, EXISTING LAND USE; 3,
BACKGROUND FOR PLANNING; 4,
COMPREHENSIVE DEVELOPMENT PLAN; 5,
PRELIMINARY PUBLIC IMPROVEMENTS PROGRAM;
6, PROPOSED WINDSOR TOWNSHIP ZONING
ORDINANCE. PREPARED BY TRI-COUNTY
REGIONAL PLANNING COMMISSION. LANSING,
MICH., 1966-68.
6 V. (HUD 701 REPORT)

(CONTINUED ON NEXT CARD)

711.5
(77352)
T74
Tri-County Regional Planning Commission,
Peoria, Ill.
A digest of the zoning and subdivision
study for Peoria, Woodford and Tazewell
counties. An interim report. Peoria,
1956.
15p.

1. Zoning - Illinois. 2. Subdivision
regulation - Illinois.

628.1
(774)
S81
Tri-County Regional Planning Commission,
(Clinton, Eaton, Ingham County, Mich.)
Swager, W L
Alternative long-range water use plans for
the Tri-County Region, Michigan. A technical
-economic report to Tri-County Regional Plan-
ning Commission, by W. L. Swager and others
Columbus, Ohio, Battelle Memorial Institute,
1963.
184p.
Bibliography: p. 167-169.
U.S. Urban Renewal Adm. UPAP.

(Continued on
next card)

2772-
2777
WINDSOR, MICH. TOWNSHIP PLANNING
COMMISSION. COMPREHENSIVE PLANNING
PROGRAM... 1966-68.   (CARD 2)

1. CITY PLANNING - WINDSOR, MICH.
I. TRI-COUNTY REGIONAL PLANNING
COMMISSION, LANSING, MICH. II. HUD.
701. WINDSOR, MICH.

4830

TRI-COUNTY REGIONAL PLANNING COMMISSION,
LANSING, MICH.
COOPERATION THROUGH PLANNING, A REVIEW
AND PROSPECTUS OF THE TRI-COUNTY REGIONAL
PLANNING COMMISSION, FISCAL YEARS,
1967-68, 1968-69, 1969-70. LANSING,
MICH., 1970.
19P. (HUD 701 REPORT)

1. REGIONAL PLANNING - MICHIGAN.
I. HUD. 701. MICHIGAN.

352.6
(774)
T74
pt.2

Tri-County Regional Planning Commission,
Lansing, Mich.
Cultural facilities, an inventory. Pt.
II. Community facilities study [Clinton,
Eaton, and Ingham Counties] Lansing, Mich.,
1964.
20p.

U.S. Urban Renewal Adm. UPAP.

1. Community facilities - Mich. 2. County planning -
Mich. 3. Libraries - Mich. 4. Community centers -
Mich. I. U.S. URA-   UPAP. Mich.

711.333
(774)
T74e

Tri-County Regional Planning Commission.
(Clinton, Eaton, Ingham Counties, Mich.)
Eaton County building needs study.
Phase 1. Existing and projected personnel
and space needs. Prepared for the Office
Space Committee, Eaton County Board of
Supervisors. [Lansing, Mich.] 1966.
38p.

1. County planning - Michigan. 2. Space
considerations. I. Title.

4831

TRI-COUNTY REGIONAL PLANNING COMMISSION,
LANSING, MICH.
ECONOMIC AND POPULATION BASE STUDY OF
THE LANSING TRI-COUNTY AREA, AN
INTERINDUSTRY RELATIONS ANALYSIS.
PREPARED BY BUREAU OF BUSINESS AND
ECONOMIC RESEARCH, COLLEGE OF BUSINESS
AND PUBLIC SERVICE, MICHIGAN STATE
UNIVERSITY, EAST LANSING, MICHIGAN. EAST
LANSING, 1960.
319P. (HUD 701 REPORT)

1. ECONOMIC BASE STUDIES - MICHIGAN.
I. MICHIGAN. STATE UNIVERSITY.
(CONTINUED ON NEXT CARD)

4831

TRI-COUNTY REGIONAL PLANNING COMMISSION,
LANSING, MICH. ECONOMIC AND POPULATION
...1960. (CARD 2)

BUREAU OF BUSINESS & ECONOMIC RESEARCH.
II. HUD. 701. MICHIGAN.

711.333
(774)
T74g

Tri-County Regional Planning Commission.
(Clinton, Eaton, and Ingram Counties, Mich.)
Growth and change. Preliminary develop-
ment proposals for the Tri-County region.
Lansing, Mich., 1965.
16p.

1. County planning - Michigan.
I. U.S. URA-UPAP. Michigan.

333.38
T74
pt.3

Tri-County Regional Planning Commission,
Lansing, Mich.
Guiding land subdividing. Part 3. Residential standards. Lansing, 1964.
42p.

1. Subdivision. 2. Residential areas.

4819
4820
4821

TRI-COUNTY REGIONAL PLANNING COMMISSION,
LANSING, MICH.
AN INVENTORY, JANUARY 1962: 1, OUTDOOR
RECREATION: 2, PUBLIC UTILITIES: 3,
TRANSPORTATION. LANSING, MICH., 1962.
3 V. (HUD 701 REPORT)

1. REGIONAL PLANNING - MICHIGAN.
I. HUD. 701. MICHIGAN.

4832

TRI-COUNTY REGIONAL PLANNING COMMISSION,
LANSING, MICH.
LAW, CRIME, AND JUSTICE: A PLANNING
PROPOSAL FOR CLINTON, EATON, AND INGHAM
COUNTIES, MICHIGAN PLANNING REGION 6.
LANSING, MICH., 1969.
73P. (HUD 701 REPORT)

1. LAW ENFORCEMENT - MICHIGAN.
I. HUD. 701. MICHIGAN.

4818

TRI-COUNTY REGIONAL PLANNING
COMMISSION. LANSING, MICH.
WINDSOR, MICH. TOWNSHIP PLANNING
COMMISSION.
PHYSICAL FEATURES, A BASIC STUDY OF THE
COMPREHENSIVE DEVELOPMENT PLAN. PREPARED
BY THE STAFF OF THE TRI-COUNTY REGIONAL
PLANNING COMMISSION. LANSING, MICH.,
1966.
7L. (HUD 701 REPORT)

1. CITY PLANNING - WINDSOR, MICH.
I. TRI-COUNTY REGIONAL PLANNING
COMMISSION. LANSING, MICH. II. HUD.
701. WINDSOR, MICH.

2999

TRI-COUNTY REGIONAL PLANNING
COMMISSION. LANSING, MICH.
DELHI CHARTER TOWNSHIP, MICH. PLANNING
COMMISSION.
PHYSICAL FEATURES, A BASIC STUDY OF THE
COMPREHENSIVE DEVELOPMENT PLAN. PREPARED
BY THE TRI-COUNTY REGIONAL PLANNING
COMMISSION. LANSING, MICH., 1966.
1 V. (HUD 701 REPORT)

1. NATURAL RESOURCES - DELHI CHARTER
TOWNSHIP, MICH. I. TRI-COUNTY REGIONAL
PLANNING COMMISSION, LANSING, MICH.
II. HUD. 701. DELHI CHARTER TOWNSHIP,
MICH.

3564

TRI-COUNTY REGIONAL PLANNING
COMMISSION, LANSING, MICH.
DELTA, MICH. TOWNSHIP PLANNING
COMMISSION.
PRELIMINARY COMPREHENSIVE DEVELOPMENT
PLAN. PREPARED BY TRI-COUNTY REGIONAL
PLANNING COMMISSION. LANSING, MICH.,
1965.
127P. (HUD 701 REPORT)

1. CITY PLANNING - DELTA, MICH.
I. TRI-COUNTY REGIONAL PLANNING
COMMISSION, LANSING, MICH. II. HUD.
701. DELTA, MICH.

711.333
(774)
T74

Tri-County Regional Planning Commission,
Lansing, Mich.
Report 1962/63-1966/67

Lansing,
4 v. annual.

For complete information see main card.

1. County planning - Michigan.

628.1
(774)
B17

Tri-County Regional Planning Commission,
Lansing, Mich.
Battelle Memorial Institute.
A summary of alternative long range water
use plans for the Tri-County Region, Michigan
[Clinton, Eaton, and Ingham Counties] A
summary report to Tri-County Regional Planning
Commission. Columbus, Ohio, 1964.
21p.

U.S. Urban Renewal Adm. UPAP.

1. Water resources - Michigan. I. Tri-County
Regional Planning   Commission,
Lansing, Mich.   II. U.S. URA-UPAP.
Mich.

3557-
3562

TRI-COUNTY REGIONAL PLANNING
COMMISSION, LANSING, MICH.
DELHI, MICH. TOWNSHIP PLANNING
COMMISSION.
URBAN PLANNING: 1, SUGGESTED
SUBDIVISION REGULATION ORDINANCE: 2,
EXISTING LAND USE: 3, BACKGROUND FOR
PLANNING: 4, COMPREHENSIVE DEVELOPMENT
PLAN: 5, PRELIMINARY PUBLIC IMPROVEMENTS
PROGRAM: 6, PROPOSED ZONING ORDINANCE.
PREPARED BY TRI-COUNTY REGIONAL PLANNING
COMMISSION. LANSING, MICH., 1966-68.
6 V. (HUD 701 REPORT)

1. CITY PLANNING - DELHI, MICH.
I. TRI-COUNTY REGIONAL PLANNING
(CONTINUED ON NEXT CARD)

3557-
3562

DELHI, MICH. TOWNSHIP PLANNING
COMMISSION. URBAN PLANNING....6-68.
(CARD 2)

COMMISSION, LANSING, MICH. II. HUD.
701. DELHI, MICH.

711.14
(771)
T74

Tri-County Regional Planning Commission,
Akron, Ohio.
Existing land use, 1959. Akron, 1961.
65p. (Its Regional planning study no. 12;
Physical inventories rept. no. 3)

U.S. Urban Renewal Adm. UPAP.

1. Land use - Ohio. 2. Regional planning -
Ohio. I. U.S. URA-UPAP. Ohio. (Series)

728.1
:308
(771)
T74

Tri-County Regional Planning Commission
(Medina, Summit, Portage, Ohio)
Housing survey and future needs.
Akron, 1964.
51p. (Its Regional study no. 33)

U.S. Urban Renewal Adm. UPAP.

1. Housing surveys - Ohio. I. U.S. URA-UPAP.
Ohio.

711.14
(77135)
T74

Tri-County Regional Planning Commission.
(Medina, Summit, Portage, Ohio)
Land use and thoroughfare plan, Twinsburg,
Ohio. Akron, Ohio, Tri-County Regional
Planning Commission, Community Assistance
Division, 1963.
67p. (Its Planning report no. 3)
Prepared in cooperation with Twinsburg
Planning Commission.
U.S. Urban Renewal Adm. UPAP.

1. Land use - Twinsburg, Ohio. 2. Highways - Twins-
burg, Ohio. I. Twins-   burg, Ohio. Planning
Commission. II. U.S.   URA-UPAP. Twinsburg,
Ohio.

711.4
:670
(771)
T74

Tri-County Regional Planning Commission,
Akron, Ohio.
Land with industrial potential. Akron, 1961.
[20]p. (Its Regional planning study no. 9;
Physical inventories rept. no. 4)
U.S. Urban Renewal Adm. UPAP.

1. Industrial location - Ohio. 2. Regional
planning - Ohio. I. U.S. URA-UPAP. Ohio.
(Series)

3437
3438
3439

TRI-COUNTY REGIONAL PLANNING
COMMISSION, AKRON, OHIO.
GARRETTSVILLE, OHIO. PLANNING COMMISSION.
MODEL ZONING REGULATIONS; MODEL
SUBDIVISION REGULATIONS; PROJECT
COMPLETION REPORT. BY TRI-COUNTY
REGIONAL PLANNING COMMISSION, AKRON,
OHIO. GARRETTSVILLE, OHIO, 1969-70.
3 V. (HUD 701 REPORT)

1. ZONING - GARRETTSVILLE, OHIO.
I. TRI-COUNTY REGIONAL PLANNING
COMMISSION, AKRON, OHIO. II. HUD. 701.
GARRETTSVILLE, OHIO.

Tri-County Regional Planning Commission, Akron, Ohio.
Physical inventories report. (Analyzed)

727.1
(771) no.
T74   1   Schools today and tomorrow. 1960.

333.71
(771) no.
T74   2   Recreation and open space. 1960.

711.14
(771) no.
T74   3   Existing land use, 1959. 1961.
                        (Continued on next card)

Tri-County Regional Planning Commission Akron,
Ohio. Physical ...   (Card 2)

711.4
:670
(771) no.
T74   4   Land with industrial potential. 1961.

352.6
(771) no.
T74   5   Public utility transmission lines. 1961.

388
T74pe   Tri-State Regional Planning Commission.
1971   (Connecticut-New Jersey-New York)
        People-transportation-jobs. Public
2C.   transport services to non-CBD employment
        concentrations. New York, 1971.
        22p. (Progress report no. 5; INT-MTD-13)
        Mass Transportation Demonstration Grant
        Program.
          1. Transportation - Connecticut-New Jersey-
        New York. I. U.S. Mass Transportation
        Demonstration Grant Program. N.Y.
        II. Title.

312
(771)   Tri-County Regional Planning Commission.
T74   (Medina, Summit, Portage Counties, Ohio)
        Population and labor force. Akron, 1964.
        103p.   (Its Regional planning study
        no. 28)
          U.S. Urban Renewal Adm. UPAP.
          1. Population - Ohio. 2. Labor supply -
        Ohio. 3. County planning - Ohio.
        I. Title. II. U.S. URA-UPAP.
        Ohio.

330
(771)   Tri-County Regional Planning Commission.
T74   (Medina, Summit, Portage Counties, Ohio)
no.4   Population and labor force of the Tri-
        County area. Akron, 1961.
        [82]p. (Its Regional planning study
        no. 11; Economic base rept. no. 4)
          U.S. Urban Renewal Adm. UPAP.
          1. Economic base studies - Ohio.
        2. Population - Ohio. 3. Labor supply -
        Ohio. 4. County planning - Ohio.
        I. Title.   II. U.S. URA-UPAP.
        Ohio.

352.6
(771)   Tri-County Regional Planning Commission, Akron,
T74   Ohio.
        Public utility transmission lines. Akron,
        1961.
        5p.   (Its Regional planning study no. 21;
        Physical inventories rept. no. 5)
          U.S. Urban Renewal Adm. UPAP.
          1. Public utilities - Ohio. 2. Regional
        planning - Ohio. I. U.S. URA-UPAP. Ohio.
        (Series)

712.25
(771)   Tri-County Regional Planning Commission.
T74   (Medina, Summit, Portage Counties, Ohio)
        Recreation and governmental agencies.
        Akron, 1962.
        130p.   (Its Regional planning study no.
        22)
          U.S. Urban Renewal Adm. UPAP.
          1. Recreation - Ohio. 2. County planning
        - Ohio. I. Title. II. U.S. URA-UPAP.
        Ohio.

333.71
(771)   Tri-County Regional Planning Commission,
T74   Akron, Ohio.
        Recreation and open space. Akron, 1960.
        34p.   (Its Regional planning study no. 9;
        Physical inventories rept. no. 2)
          U.S. Urban Renewal Adm. UPAP.
          1. Recreation - Ohio. 2. Open space
        land - Ohio. 3. Regional planning - Ohio.
        I. U.S. URA-UPAP. Ohio.   (Series)

711.333
(771)   Tri-County Regional Planning Commission.
T74   (Medina, Summit, Portage Counties, Ohio)
        Regional development guide. Akron, 1962.
        68p.   (Its Regional planning study no.
        23)
          U.S. Urban Renewal Adm. UPAP.
          1. County planning - Ohio. I. Title.
        II. U.S. URA-UPAP. Ohio.

711.14
(771)   Tri-County Regional Planning Commission.
T74r   (Medina, Summit, Portage Counties, Ohio)
        Regional land use plan. Akron, 1963.
        115p.   (Its Regional planning study
        no. 25)
          U.S. Urban Renewal Adm. UPAP.
          1. Land use - Ohio. 2. County planning
        - Ohio. I. Title. II. U.S. URA-UPAP.
        Ohio.

628.3
(771)   Tri-County Regional Planning Commission.
T74   (Medina, Summit, Portage Counties, Ohio)
        Sanitary sewage disposal plan. Akron,
        1963.
        [112]p.   (Its Regional planning study
        no. 26)
          U.S. Urban Renewal Adm. UPAP.
          1. Sewerage and sewage disposal - Ohio.
        2. County planning - Ohio. I. Title.
        II. U.S. URA-UPAP. Ohio.

727.1
(771)   Tri-County Regional Planning Commission,
T74   Akron, Ohio.
        Schools today and tomorrow. Akron, 1960.
        82p.   (Its Regional planning study no. 8;
        Physical inventories rept. no. 1)
          U.S. Urban Renewal Adm. UPAP.
          1. Schools - Ohio. 2. Regional planning -
        Ohio. I. U.S. URA-UPAP. Ohio.   (Series)

330
(771)   Tri-County Regional Planning Commission.
T74   (Medina, Summit, Portage Counties, Ohio)
no.3   Shopping habits in the Tri-County area.
        Akron, 1960.
        62p.   (Its Regional planning study no.
        10; Economic base rept. no. 3)
          U.S. Urban Renewal Adm. UPAP.
          1. Economic base studies - Ohio.
        2. Shopping centers. 3. County planning -
        Ohio. I. Title. II. U.S. URA-UPAP.
        Ohio.

711.3
(43)   Triebel, Wolfgang.
157   Institut für Bauforschung.
no.11   Wirtschaftliche Erschliessung neuer
        Wohngebiete -Massnahmen und Erfolge-
        Querschnittsbericht über Untersuchungen und
        Erfahrungen bei Demonstrativbauvorhaben des
        Bundesministeriums für Wohnungswesen und
        Städtebau. Im Auftrage des Bundesministeriums
        für Wohnungswesen und Städtebau. Bear. von
        Wolfgang Triebel et al. Hanover, 1966.
        97p. (Die Demonstrativbauvorhaben des
        Bundesministeriums für Wohnungswesen.
        Städtebau. Informationen Nr. 11)

                        (Cont'd on next card)

711.3
(43)   Institut für Bauforschung. Wirtschaftliche...
157   1966.   (Card 2)
no.11
          1. Regional planning - Germany.
        2. Housing - Germany. I. Triebel, Wolfgang.
        (Series: Germany Bundesministerium für
        Wohnungswesen, Städtebau und Raumordnung.
        Informationen Nr. 10)

711.3
(43)   Triebel, Wolfgang.
157   Institut für Bauforschung.
no. 12,13   Wohnungen in Demonstrativbauvorhaben.
        Eine Grundrisssammlung. Teil I:
        Mehrfamilienhäuser. Teil II: Einfamilien-
        häuser. Im Auftrag des Bundesministeriums
        für Wohnungswesen und Städtebau. Von
        Wolfgang Triebel et al. Bad Godesberg,
        1967.
        2v. (Die Demonstrativbauvorhaben des
        Bundesministeriums für Wohnungswesen und
        Städtebau. Informationen Nr. 12,13)
          1. Regional planning - Germany.
        2. Housing - Germany.
                        (Cont'd on next card)

711.3
(43)   Institut für Bauforschung.
157   Wohnungen.. 1967.   (Card 2)
no. 12,13
          I. Triebel, Wolfgang. (Series: Germany.
        Bundesministerium für Wohnungswesen.
        Städtebau und Raumordnung. Informationen
        Nr. 12,13)

690.015
157   International Council for Research, Studies
no. 22 and Documentation.
        The mechanization of building in Western
        Germany, by Wolfgang Triebel and Alvin
        Marsch at the Building Research Institute,
        Hanover; prepared on behalf of the Federal
        Ministry for Housing construction (Western
        Germany). Geneva, 1953.
        28p.   (CIB/22)
        At head of title: General Assembly.
        (Palais des Nations, Geneva, 25 to 30
        June inclusive).
          1. Building research.   I. Triebel, Wolfgang.
        II. Marsch, Alvin.

711.3
(43)   Triebel, Wolfgang.
157   Institut für Bauforschung.
no. 9   Nutzung von Hausarbeitsräumen in der Praxis.
        Erhebungen in den Demonstrativbauvorhaben
        Nürnberg-Zollhaus und München-Fürstenried.
        Im Auftrage des Bundesministeriums für
        Wohnungswesen, Städtebau und Raumordnung.
        Bear. von Wolfgang Triebel. Von Karl
        Richard Kräntzer, et al. Hanover, 1967.
        27p. (Die Demonstrativbauvorhaben des
        Bundesministeriums für Wohnungswesen.
        Städtebau und Raumordnung. Informationen
        Nr. 9)

                        (Cont'd on next card)

711.3
(43)   Institut für Bauforschung. Nutzung von
157   Hausarbeiten...1967.   (Card 2)
no. 9
          1. Regional planning - Germany.
        I. Triebel, Wolfgang. II. Krantzer,
        Karl Richard. (Series: Germany.
        Bundesministerium für Wohnungswesen,
        Städtebau und Raumordnung. Informationen
        Nr. 9)

690.022
(43)   Triebel, Wolfgang.
T74   Rationalisierung im Hoch- und Wohnungsbau;
Ger.   Aufgaben - Mitte - Erfolge, 1946-1966.
        Bericht über Arbeiten und Ergebnisse des
        Instituts für Bauforschung aus 20 jähriger
        Tätigkeit. Wiesbaden, Bauverlag GMBH, 1966.
        180p.

          Bibliography: p. 173-180.

          1. Prefabricated construction. I. Institut
        für Bauforschung. II. Title.

690.022
(43)
T74
Eng.

Triebel, Wolfgang.
Rationalization in building and housing projects; tasks - methods - achievements, 1946-1966. Report on functions and results of the Institute for Building Research during 20 years of activity. Wiesbaden, Bauverlag GMBH, 1966.
180p.
Bibliography: p. 173-181.
1. Prefabricated construction. I. Institut fur Bafors   chung. II. Title.

690
(43)
I57

Triebel, Wolfgang.

Institut für Bauforschung.
Wirtschaftlich bauen! Aber wie? Bearbeitet von Wolfgang Triebel und Karl Richard Kräntzer. Hannover, 1955.
30p.

1. Building construction - Germany. I. Triebel, Wolfgang. II. Kräntzer, Karl Richard.

711.3
(43)
I57
no. 10

Triebel, Wolfgang.
Institut für Bauforschung.
Wirtschaftliche Planung und Rationelle Ausführung von Einfamilienhäusern. Querschnittsbericht über Untersuchungen und Versuchs- und Vergleichsbauten des Bundesministeriums für Wohnungswesen, Städtebau und Raumordnung. Im Auftrage des Bundesministeriums für Wohnungswesen, Städtebau und Raumordnung. Bear. von Wolfgang Triebel. Von Karl Richard Krantzer und Engelbert Janik. Hanover, 1967.
98p. (Die Demonstrativbauvorhaben des
(Cont'd on next card)

711.3
(43)
I57
no. 10

Institut für Bauforschung.
Wirtschaftliche...1967.   (Card 2)

Bundesministeriums für Wohnungswesen, Städtebau und Raumordnung. Informationen Nr. 10)
1. Regional planning - Germany.
2. Housing - Germany. I. Triebel, Wolfgang. II. Krantzer, Karl Richard. (Series: Germany Bundesministerium für Wohnungswesen, Städtebau und Raumordnung. Informationen Nr. 10)

VF
711.4
T74

Trieschmann, G   V
Pattern and behavior in the constructed environment, a comparative study. Athens, Greece, Athens Technological Organisation, Athens Center of Ekistics, 1968.
3p. (Athens Center of Ekistics. Research discussions document B, no. 5)
At head of title: The 1968 Athens Ekistics month.
Partial contents.-Design for living; form and pattern, by F.S.C. Northrop.
1. City   planning.
(Cont'd on next card)

VF
711.4
T74

Trieschmann, G   V   Pattern...1968.
(Card2)

2. Men - Influence of environment. I. Athens Center of Ekistics, Athens, Greece. II. Title.

690
P34

Trigg, Earnest T.

Philadelphia Conference on the Construction Industries, Philadelphia, Feb. 1921.
Proceedings of the Philadelphia and National Conferences on the Construction Industries... under the auspices of the Industrial Relations Committee of the Philadelphia Chamber of Commerce [and] the National Federation of Construction Industries, Philadelphia, Pa. Philadelphia, April 1921.
254 p. graphs
National Conference held in Chicago on March 2 and 3, 1921.
Chairman both   conferences: Earnest T. Trigg.
(see card 2)

690
P34

Philadelphia Conference on the Construction Industries, Philadelphia, Feb. 1921.
Proceedings... April 1921. (card 2)

1. Building industry - Congresses.
I. National Conference on the Construction Industries, Chicago, March 1921.
II. Trigg, Earnest T.

510
P27

TRIGONOMETRIC FUNCTIONS.
PETERS, JEAN, 1869-1941.
EIGHT-PLACE TABLE OF TRIGONOMETRIC FUNCTIONS FOR EVERY SEXAGESIMAL SECOND OF THE QUADRANT. BERLIN, REICHSAMT FUR LANDESAUFNAHME, 1939. ANN ARBOR, EDWARDS BROTHERS, 1943.
901P.

TITLE ALSO IN TERMAN.

1. MATHEMATICS.   I. GERMANY. REICHSAMT FUR LANDESAUFNAHME.   II. TITLE.
III. TITLE: TRIGONOMETRIC FUNCTIONS.

728.1
:362.6
T74

TRILLIN, CALVIN.
WAKE UP AND LIVE. NEW YORK, 1964.
120P.

REPORTER AT LARGE FEATURE CLIPPED FROM NEW YORKER MAGAZINE, APRIL 4, 1964.

1. HOUSING FOR THE AGED.   2. NEW TOWNS - SUN CITY, ARIZ.   I. TITLE.

333.32
K67

TRIMBLE, HAROLD G   JR.
KORB, IRVING.
REAL ESTATE SALE-LEASEBACK--A BASIC ANALYSIS, BY IRVING KORB AND HAROLD G. TRIMBLE, JR. WASHINGTON, SOCIETY OF INDUSTRIAL REALTORS, 1966.
16P.

BIBLIOGRAPHY: P.13-16.
FIRST PUBLISHED IN TWO PARTS IN THE JANUARY AND FEBRUARY, 1966, ISSUES OF THE NEWSLETTER OF THE SOCIETY OF INDUSTRIAL REALTORS.

1. LEASES.   2. REAL ESTATE
(CONTINUED ON NEXT CARD)

333.32
K67

KORB, IRVING. REAL ESTATE SALE-LEASEBACK--A ...1966.   (CARD 2)

BUSINESS.   I. TRIMBLE, HAROLD G., JR. II. SOCIETY OF INDUSTRIAL REALTORS.
III. TITLE.

371.7
(76843)
T25

Trimble, Otis M
Tennessee. State Planning Commission.
A recreation plan for Lewis County, Tennessee, by Otis M. Trimble. Nashville, 1958.
67p. illus., maps.

1. Recreation - Lewis Co., Tenn.
I. Trimble, Otis M.

711.3
(76812)
T25

Trimble, Otis M
Tennessee. State Planning Commission.
Reelfoot, plan for comprehensive development, by Otis M. Trimble and Walter L. Criley. Nashville, 1958.
85p. illus., maps. (Its Publication no. 291)

1. Regional planning - Reelfoot Lake Area.
I. Trimble, Otis M. II. Criley, Walter L.
III. Title.

LAW
T
R227r

Trimble, Robert jt. au.

Rector, Milton G
The role of private agencies in correction, by Milton G. Rector and Robert Trimble. [Report] submitted by the President's Commission on Law Enforcement and Administration of Justice. [Washington, D.C.] 1967.
22p.

1. Law enforcement. I. Trimble, Robert, jt. au. II. U.S. President's Commission on Law Enforcement and Administration of Justice. III. Title.

728.1
(7298)
T74hc

Trinidad. Central Statistical Office.
Housing 1957-1958; a preliminary report on the housing census. Trinidad, 1960.
17p.

1. Housing - Trinidad and Tobago.

083.41
(7298)
T74

Trinidad. Central Statistical Office.
Statistical digest, no. 6-1956-
Port of Spain, Govt. Print. Off., 1958- v. annual.

For complete information see shelf list.

1. Statistics - Trinidad. 2. Statistics - Tobago.

VF
728.1
(7298)
T74h

Trinidad. Ministry of Housing and Local Government.
[Housing] Trinidad, [1961?]
[30]p.

1. Housing - Trinidad.

VF
711
:728.1
(729)
T74

Trinidad. Ministry of Labour and Social Affairs.
Planning and housing in the West Indies; a summary of activities Port-of-Spain,
v.

For complete information see shelflist.

1. Planning - West Indies. 2. Housing - West Indies.

728.1
(7298)
T74

Trinidad. Planning and Housing Commission.
Report for the year Trinidad,
v.

1. Housing - Trinidad. 2. Housing - Tobago.

330
(7298)
T74

Trinidad. Office of Premier.
Trinidad and Tobago 1956-1959. Trinidad, 1960.
75p.

1. Economic conditions - Trinidad and Tobago.

Trinidad and Tobago.
see Trinidad.

388
(41)
T74
TRIPP, HERBERT ALKER, 1883•
TOWN PLANNING AND ROAD TRAFFIC, BY H.
ALKER TRIPP. FOREWORD BY PATRICK
ABERCROMBIE••• LONDON, ARNOLD, 1943•
118P.

1• TRAFFIC - U.K.   2• CITY PLANNING -
U.K.

386
T74   Tri-State Transportation Commission.
(Connecticut-New Jersey-New York)
The changing harborfront; a report of prospects for new development of released lands.
Report financed in part through the Dept.
of Commerce, Bureau of Public Roads. New York,
1966.
21p.
U.S. Dept. of Housing, and Urban Development. UPAP.

(Cont'd on next card)

358
TRINIDAD, COLO. PLANNING COMMISSION.
CAPITAL IMPROVEMENT PLAN. FINAL
PROPOSED. DENVER, SAM L. HUDDLESTON,
1963.
107-118P. (ITS COMPREHENSIVE PLAN FOR
TRINIDAD, COLORADO. PT.3: PLAN FOR
ACTION) HUD 701 REPORT)

1. CAPITAL IMPROVEMENT PROGRAMS -
TRINIDAD, COLO.   I• HUDDLESTON, SAM L.
II• HUD. 701. TRINIDAD, COLO.

312•1
T74•   TRIPP, THOMAS ALFRED.
RURAL AMERICANS ON THE MOVE. NEW
YORK, FRIENDSHIP PRESS, 1945.
24P.

1. POPULATION SHIFTS.   I• TITLE.

386
T74   Tri-State Transportation Commission.
(Connecticut-New Jersey-New York) The changing harborfront: a report of prospects for
new development of released lands...1966.
(Card 2)

1. Harbors - Connecticut-New Jersey-New York.
2. Recreation-Connecticut-New Jersey-New York.
I. U.S. Bureau of Public Roads. II. U.S.
HUD-UPAP. Connecticut-New Jersey-New York.
III. Title.

Trinidad, Colo. Planning Commission.
711.4
(78896)   Huddleston, Sam L
T74   City of Trinidad, Colorado, comprehensive
master plan. Prepared for Trinidad Planning Commission Denver, 1962.
103p.

U.S. Urban Renewal Adm. UPAP.

1. Master plan - Trinidad, Colo.
I. Trinidad, Colo. Planning Commission.
II. U.S. URA-UPAP. Trinidad, Colo.

711.14
:538.56   Tri-State Conference on a Comprehensive,
T74   Unified Land Data System (CULDATA)
1966   Cincinnati, 1966.
Proceedings. Edited by Robert N. Cook,
James L. Kennedy, Jr. Sponsored by
University of Cincinnati with support from
the Economic Research Service, U.S. Dept.
of Agriculture, Cincinnati, College of Law,
University of Cincinnati, 1967.
253p.
1. Land use - Automation. 2. Land titles.
I. Cook, Robert N., ed. II. Kennedy, James
ed. III. Cincinnati. University. College
of Law. IV. U   S. Economic Research
Service.

1769
TRI-STATE TRANSPORTATION COMMISSION.
(CONNECTICUT - NEW JERSEY - NEW YORK)
COMPLETION REPORT 1969-70 YEAR
CONTINUING COMPREHENSIVE PLANNING PROGRAM.
NEW YORK, 1970.
27L. (HUD 701 REPORT)

1. REGIONAL PLANNING - CONN. - N.J. -
N.Y.   I• HUD. 701. CONN. - N.J. - N.Y.

728.1
(81)   Trindade, Mario.
T74   Housing and urban development. Remarks presented by the president of the National Housing
Bank of Brazil to the 9th Interamerican Conference on Savings and Loans, Panama, Jan., 1971.
Rio de Janeiro, Banco Nacional da Habitacao,
1971.
58p.

1. Housing - Brazil. 2. City planning -
Brazil. I. Banco Nacional da Habitacao, Rio de
Janeiro, II. Title.

388
(746)   Tri-State Regional Planning Commission
T74te   (Connecticut-New Jersey-New York)
Test of fare restructuring in a multicarrier,
multizone bus transportation system.
Final report. New York, 1972.
17p.

1. Transportation - Conn. - N.J. - N.Y.
I. Title.

1759
TRI-STATE TRANSPORTATION COMMISSION.
(CONNECTICUT - NEW JERSEY - NEW YORK)
COMPLETION REPORT, PROJECT 3810,
COORDINATION WITH STATE AND LOCAL PLANS.
NEW YORK, 1970.
1 V. (HUD 701 REPORT)

1. TRANSPORTATION - CONN. - N.J. - N.Y.
I• HUD. 701. CONN. - N.J. - N.Y.

Trip characteristics and traffic assignment.
388
:331   Highway Research Board.
H43   Meeting. 41st, Washington, D.C., 1962.
Trip characteristics and traffic assignment. Washington, National Academy of
Sciences, National Research Council, 1962.
318p. (Highway Research Board. Bulletin
347)

National Research Council. Publication
1042.

1. Journey to work.   I. Title.

308
:728.1 Tri-State Survey Committee, Inc., New York.
(78199)   A preliminary report on living, working
T74   and health conditions in the tri-state mining
area (Missouri,Oklahoma and Kansas)   New
York, 1939.
82 p., 35 p.   illus.

1.Housing surveys - Cherokee Co., Kan.
2.Housing surveys - Jasper Co., Mo. 3. Housing
surveys - Ottawa Co., Okla. 4.Housing and
Health.

388
T74c   Tri-State Transportation Committee
(Connecticut, New Jersey, and New York)
A consultant's report to the Tri-State
Transportation Committee on a reconnaissance
of the Tri-State Region and some ideas for a
development plan. New Haven, 1963.
48p.
U.S. Urban Renewal Adm. UPAP.

1. Transportation - Connecticut-New Jersey-
New York. I. Title.   II. U.S. URA-UPAP.
Connecticut-New   Jersey-New York.

384
(751)   Tripact.
P25   Pennsylvania/New Jersey/Delaware Committee
on Regional Development.
Tripact; a report to the three governors on
the need for a tri-state authority to administer air-related transportation in the
Delaware Valley. Philadelphia, 1971.
49p.

1. Air transportation - Delaware River and
Valley. I. Title.

Tri-State Transportation Commission.   1966
(formerly the Tri-State Transportation Committee)
Connecticut-New Jersey-New York.

388
T74co   Tri-State Transportation Commission.
(Connecticut-New Jersey-New York)
Coordinated bus-rail service; Rockland
County-Westchester County, New York City.
A final report on the Mass Transportation
Demonstration Project, Sept. 17, 1963-
3c   June 25, 1965. [Prepared in cooperation
with the] U.S. Dept. of Housing and Urban
Development and others. New York, 1967.
47p.
U.S. Dept. of Housing and Urban Development. Mass Transportation Demonstration
Grant Program.
(Cont'd on next card)

658.564   THE TRIPLE REVOLUTION.
A23   THE AD HOC COMMITTEE ON THE TRIPLE
REVOLUTION.
THE TRIPLE REVOLUTION.   SANTA
BARBARA, CALIF., 1964.
15P.

1. AUTOMATION.   2. SOCIAL
CONDITIONS.   I. TITLE.

Tri-State Transportation Commission.
(Connecticut-New Jersey-New York)
Annual regional report.

see

Its Report. annual

388
T74co   Tri-State Transportation Commission.
(Connecticut-New Jersey-New York) Coordinated bus-rail service; Rockland County-
Westchester County New York City...1967.
(Card 2)

1. Transportation - Connecticut-New Jersey-
New York. 2. Journey to work. I. Title.
II. Title: Bus rail service. III. U.S.
Dept. of Housing and Urban Development. Mass
Transportation Demonstration Grant Program.

388
T74d   Tri-State Transportation Committee
     (Connecticut, New Jersey, and New York)
     Designs for growth; a report on the Tri-
     State Transportation Committee, 1961-1966.
     [New York] 1967.
     [30] p.
     U.S. Dept. of Housing and Urban Develop-
     ment. UPAP.

       1. Transportation - Connecticut—New Jersey
     —New York. I. Title. II. U.S. Dept. of
     Housing and Urban Development. UPAP.
     Connecticut—New   Jersey—New York.

711.14
(746)
T74   Tri-State Transportation Commission.
     (Connecticut-New Jersey-New York)
     Interim 1985 land use maps (completion
     report) New York, 1966.
     55p. (Its Interim technical report
     4051-8321)

     Bibliography: p. 49-55.

       1. Land use - Conn.-N.J.-N.Y.
     2. Maps and mapping - Conn.-N.J.-N.Y.
     I. Title.

388
(746)
T74   Tri-State Transportation Commission.
     (Connecticut-New Jersey-New York)
     Measure of a region. New York, 1967.
     32p.

       1. Transportation - Connecticut-New Jersey-
     New York. 2. Journey to work. 3. Land use -
     Connecticut-New Jersey-New York. I. Title.

388
:308
T74   Tri-State Transportation Commission.
     (Connecticut-New Jersey-New York)
     Direct traffic estimation method; systematic
     inputs and method of computation. New York,
     1967.
     20p. (Its Interim technical report
     4075-7111)

       1. Traffic surveys. 2. Transportation.
     3. Journey to work. I. Title.

388
T74   Tri-State Transportation Committee. (Connecticut,
     Interim report   new jersey, new york)

     [New York,
     v.

     For complete information see shelflist.

       1. Transportation - Connecticut.
     2. Transportation - New Jersey. 3. Transporta-
     tion - New York.

534.83
T74   Tri-State Transportation Commission.
     (Connecticut-New Jersey-New York)
     Metropolitan aircraft noise abatement
     policy study, John F. Kennedy International
     Airport, N.Y. New York, 1970.
     124p.
     Research conducted pursuant to contract with
     U.S. Dept. of Housing and Urban Development.
     PB 199 723
     1. Noise. 2. Airports. I. U.S. Dept. of
     Housing and Urban Development. II. Title.

1765
     TRI-STATE TRANSPORTATION COMMISSION.
     (CONNECTICUT - NEW JERSEY - NEW YORK)
     THE DUTCHESS-ORANGE-PUTNAM SUBREGION.
     NEW YORK, 1970.
     1 V. (HUD 701 REPORT)

       1. POPULATION - CONN. - N.J. - N.Y.
     I. HUD. 701. CONN. - N.J. - N.Y.

1760-
1764   TRI-STATE TRANSPORTATION COMMISSION.
     (CONNECTICUT - NEW JERSEY - NEW YORK)
     INTERIM TECHNICAL REPORT: 1, LOCAL
     TRANSIT TRIP; 2, VEHICLE REGISTRATION
     FORECASTS; 3, VEHICLE TRIP PROJECTIONS,
     1985, 2000; 4, VEHICLE TRIP PROJECTIONS
     1990; 5, PARKING ANALYSIS. NEW YORK,
     1969-70.
     5 V. (HUD 701 REPORT)

       1. TRANSPORTATION - CONN. - N.J. - N.Y.
     I. HUD. 701. CONN. - N.J. - N.Y.

1754
     TRI-STATE TRANSPORTATION COMMISSION.
     (CONNECTICUT - NEW JERSEY - NEW YORK)
     MONITORING OPEN SPACE ACTION. NEW
     YORK, 1970.
     1 V. (HUD 701 REPORT)

       1. TRANSPORTATION - CONN. - N.J. - N.Y.
     I. HUD. 701. CONN. - N.J. - N.Y.

388
(7472)
T74   Tri-State Transportation Commission.
     (Connecticut-New Jersey-New York)
     Findings of the taxi survey. New York,
     1968.
     12p. (Its Technical bulletin, vol. IV,
     no. 3, April, 1968)

       1. Transportation - New York
     metropolitan area. 2. Traffic surveys -
     New York metropolitan area. I. Title:
     Taxi survey.

1755
1756   TRI-STATE TRANSPORTATION COMMISSION.
     LAND DEVELOPMENT DIVISION.
     (CONNECTICUT - NEW JERSEY - NEW YORK)
     INTERIM TECHNICAL REPORT: PLAN
     EVALUATION SERIES: 4, LAND AREA CHANGES;
     5, LAND AREA FLOOR SPACE, POPULATION,
     EMPLOYMENT. NEW YORK, 1970.
     2 V. (HUD 701 REPORT)

       1. LAND USE - CONN. - N.J. - N.Y.
     I. HUD. 701. CONN. - N.J. - N.Y.

388
T74o   Tri-State Transportation Committee.
     (Connecticut, New Jersey, and New York)
     Origin-destination survey. Park 'n ride
     station and service at New Brunswick, New
     Jersey on Pennsylvania Railroad. New York,
     1963.
     50p.
     Participating agencies: New Jersey State
     Highway Dept., Div. of Railroad Transportation,
     Middlesex County, City of New Brunswick,
     Pennsylvania Railroad.

             (Continued on next card)

3708
     TRI-STATE TRANSPORTATION COMMITTEE.
     FOR URBAN PLANNING GRANT COVERING THE
     IMMEDIATE ACTION STUDY PROGRAM:
     APPLICATION NO. 2 FOR THE STATE OF NEW
     JERSEY. NEW YORK, 1963.
     1 V. (HUD 701 REPORT)

       1. STATE PLANNING - NEW JERSEY.
     I. HUD. 701. NEW JERSEY.

388
T74i   Tri-State Transportation Commission.
     (Connecticut-New Jersey-New York)
     The intermodal transportation of van-size
     containers. New York, 1967.
     32p. (Its Interim technical report 4055-8081)

       1. Transportation. 2. Highways.
     3. Railroads. 4. Air transportation.
     I. Title.

388
T74o   Tri-State Transportation Committee.
     (Connecticut, New Jersey, and New York)
     Origin-destination survey...1963. (Card 2)

     Submitted by Research Data Processing Corp.,
     Traffic Research Corp., R.L.M. Associates.
     U.S. Housing and Home Finance Agency Mass
     Transportation Demonstration Grant Program.

     1. Journey to work. 2. Transportation-- Connecticut-
     New Jersey-New York. I. U.S. Housing and Home Finance
     Agency. Mass Transportation Demonstration Grant
     Program.

1758
     TRI-STATE TRANSPORTATION COMMISSION.
     (CONNECTICUT - NEW JERSEY - NEW YORK)
     GATEWAY NATIONAL RECREATION AREA
     PROPOSAL. NEW YORK, CA. 1970.
     6L. (HUD 701 REPORT)

       1. RECREATION - CONN. - N.J. - N.Y.
     I. HUD. 701. CONN. - N.J. - N.Y.

711.14
T74   Tri-State Transportation Committee.
     (Connecticut, New Jersey, New York)
     Land use inventory: organization, a staff.
     report. [Prepared] in cooperation with:
     U.S. Dept. of Commerce, Bureau of Public
     Roads: U.S. Housing and Home Finance
     Agency. [New York] 1963.
     1v.

       1. Land use - Conn. 2. Land use - New
     Jersey. 3. Land use - New York. I. U.S.
     Housing and Home   Finance Agency.

5717
     TRI-STATE TRANSPORTATION COMMISSION
     (CONNECTICUT, NEW JERSEY, NEW YORK)
     OUTDOOR RECREATION IN A CROWDED REGION.
     NEW YORK, 1969.
     19P. (HUD 701 REPORT)

       1. RECREATION - CONNECTICUT-NEW
     JERSEY-NEW YORK. I. HUD. 701.
     CONNECTICUT-NEW JERSEY-NEW YORK.

4531
     TRI-STATE TRANSPORTATION COMMISSION, NEW
     YORK.
     IMPROVING ACCESS TO NEWARK AIRPORT.
     NEWARK, 1969.
     20P. (HUD 701 REPORT)

       1. AIRPORTS. I. HUD. 701. NEWARK,
     N.J.

1753
     TRI-STATE TRANSPORTATION COMMISSION.
     (CONNECTICUT-NEW JERSEY-NEW YORK)
     LAND USE UPDATE - OUTSIDE MAJOR CITIES.
     NEW YORK, 1970.
     1 V. (HUD 701 REPORT)

       1. TRANSPORTATION - CONN.-N.J.-N.Y.
     I. HUD. 701. CONN., N.J., N.Y.

388
T74ps   Tri-State Transportation Commission.
     (Connecticut-New Jersey-New York)
     Park'n ride rail service: New Brunswick,
     Newark, New York City: a final report on
     the Mass Transportation Demonstration
     Project October 27, 1963-April 24, 1965.
     New York, 1967.
     39p.
     U.S. Dept. of Housing and Urban
     Development. Mass Transportation Demon-
     stration Grant Program.

          (Cont'd on next card)

388
T74pe Tri-State Transportation Commission.
(Connecticut-New Jersey-New York) Park'n
ride rail service: New Brunswick, Newark,
New York...1967.   (Card 2)

1. Transportation - Conn. 2. Parking -
Conn.-N.J.-N.Y. 3. Railroads - Conn.-N.J.-
N.Y. I. U.S. Dept. of Housing and Urban
Development. Mass Transportation Demon-
stration   Grant Program.
II. Title.

385
T74 Tri-State Transportation Committee.
Railroad suburban equipment study, status
report. New York, 1963.
46p.

1. Railroads - Connecticut-New Jersey-New York.

711.73
T74 Tri-State Transportation Committee.
(Connecticut, New Jersey, and New York)
Regional highways status report. In
coordination with: Connecticut State Highway
Department, New Jersey State Highway Depart-
ment, New York State Department of Public
Works; in cooperation with: United States
Department of Commerce, Bureau of Public
Roads. New York, 1962.
1v.

1. Highways.

388
T74pe
1968 Tri-State Transportation Commission.
(Connecticut-New Jersey-New York)
People, transportation, jobs: public
transport services to non-CBD employment
concentration. Prepared in cooperation with
U.S. Dept. of Housing and Urban Development.
New York, 1968.
21p. (Progress report no. 2. 2046-5620-
6C; INT-MTD 13)
1. Transportation - Connecticut-New Jersey-
New York. 2. Journey to work. 3. Employment -
Connecticut-New Jersey-New York. I. Title.
II. U.S. Dept.   of Housing and Urban
Development.

1752 TRI-STATE TRANSPORTATION COMMISSION.
(CONNECTICUT - NEW JERSEY - NEW YORK)
RECREATION ASPECTS OF THE PASSAIC RIVER
WATER DEVELOPMENT AND FLOOD CONTROL
PROPOSAL OF THE CORPS OF ENGINEERS. NEW
YORK, 1970.
5L. (HUD 701 REPORT)

1. TRANSPORTATION - CONN. - N.J. - N.Y.
I. HUD. 701. CONN. - N.J. - N.Y.

1757 TRI-STATE TRANSPORTATION COMMISSION.
(CONNECTICUT - NEW JERSEY - NEW YORK)
REGIONAL PLANNING AND IMPLICATIONS FOR
THE ELDERLY. NEW YORK, 1970.
19P. (HUD 701 REPORT)

1. REGIONAL PLANNING - CONN. - N.J. -
N.Y. I. HUD. 701. CONN. - N.J. - N.Y.

388
(747245)
T74 Tri-State Transportation Commission.
(Connecticut-New Jersey-New York)
People, transportation, jobs; public trans-
port services to non-CBD employment concen-
trations. Participating agencies: Tri-State
Transportation Commission, U.S. Department of
Transportation, State of New York, Dept. of
Transportation. New York, 1969.
36p. (Nassau and Suffolk Counties Progress
report no. 3)
INT-MTD 13.
U.S. Dept of Housing and Urban Develop-
ment. Mass   Transportation Demonstra-
tion Grant   (Cont'd on next card)

388
(746)
T74r Tri-State Transportation Committee.
(Connecticut-New Jersey-New York)
A region on the move: travel choices
depend on destinations. New York, 1966.
20p. (Its Technical bulletin, vol.
11, no. 1, Feb., 1966)
U.S. Mass Transportation Demonstration
Grant Program.
1. Transportation - Conn.-N.J.-N.Y.
2. Journey to work. 3. Highways -
Conn.-N.J.-N.Y. I. U.S. Mass
Transportation Demonstration Grant
Program.   II. Title.

711.14
T74r Tri-State Transportation Commission.
(Connecticut-New Jersey-New York)
Regional profile, floor space and travel,
New York, 1966.
4p. (v. 1, no. 2)

U.S. Dept of Housing and Urban Development. UPAP.

1. Land use - Connecticut-New Jersey -
New York. 2. Journey to work. I. Title.
II. U.S. HUD-UPAP. Connecticut-New Jersey-
New York.

388
(747245)
T74 Tri-State Transportation Commission.
(Connecticut-New Jersey-New York)
People, transportation, jobs...1969.
(Card 2)

Program.

1. Transportation - Nassau Co., N.Y.
2. Transportation - Suffolk Co., N.Y.
3. Journey to work. I. Title. II. U.S. HUD.
Mass Transportation Demonstration Grant
Program.

Folio
388   Tri-State Transportation Committee (Connecti-
E28   Edwards and Kelcey cut-New Jersey-New York)
Region-wide passenger potential study, 1963.
[Prepared] for the Tri-State Transportation
Committee (Connecticut-New Jersey-New York)
New York, 1963.
1v.
Prepared in cooperation with U.S. Dept. of
Commerce, Bureau of Public Roads and the Hous-
ing and Home Finance Agency.
1. Transportation - Conn.-N.J.-N.Y. I. Tri-
State Transporta-   tion Committee

(Continued on   next card)

1791
1792 TRI-STATE TRANSPORTATION COMMISSION.
(CONNECTICUT - NEW JERSEY - NEW YORK)
REGIONAL PROFILE: 12, HIGHWAY PROGRESS
AND HIGHWAY STATUS MAP; 13, COUNTY TRAVEL
PATTERNS. NEW YORK; 1969.
2 V. (HUD 701 REPORT)

1. TRANSPORTATION - CONN. - N.J. - N.Y.
I. HUD. 701. CONN. - N.J. - N.Y.

388
T74pr Tri-State Transportation Commission
Projecting vehicle miles of travel in a
metropolitan region. New York, 1967.
25p. (Interim technical report 4070-8078)

1. Transportation. 2. Traffic. I. Title.

Folio
388   Edwards and Kelcey. Region-wide passenger
E28   potential study, 1963...1963. (Card 2)

(Connecticut-New Jersey-New York) II. Title:
Passenger potential study. III. U.S. Housing and Home Finance Agency.

339.5
T74 Tri-State Transportation Commission.
(Connecticut-New Jersey-New York)
Regional profiles: power, fuel and land use.
New York, 1968.
8p. (v.1, no.9)

1. Power resources. 2. Fuel. 3. Land use.
I. Title.

388
T74p Tri-State Transportation Committee. (Connec-
Prospectus. New York, 1962. ticut
51p.   New Jersey and
"The Tri-State Metropolitan Region, consists New York)
of portions of the states of Connecticut, New
Jersey and New York."

1. Transportation - Connecticut.
2. Transportation - New Jersey. 3. Transportation - New York.

711.3
T74 Tri-State Transportation Commission.
(Connecticut-New Jersey-New York)
Regional development alternates. [Prepared
in cooperation with U.S. Bureau of Public Roads]
New York, 1967.
31p.
U.S. Dept. of Housing and Urban Development.
UPAP.

1. Regional planning - Connecticut-New Jersey-
New York. 2. Transportation - Connecticut-
New Jersey-New York. I. U.S. Bureau of Public
Roads. II. Title.   III. U.S. HUD-UPAP.
Connecticut-New   Jersey-New York.

388
T74re Tri-State Transportation Commission.
(Connecticut-New Jersey-New York)
Regional profile, transit strike highlights.
New York, 1967.
8p. (v.1, no. 4)
U.S. Housing and Urban Development. UPAP.

1. Transportation - Connecticut-New Jersey-
New York. 2. Journey to work. I. Title.
II. U.S. HUD-UPAP. Connecticut-New Jersey-
New York.

388
T74pu Tri-State Transportation Commission.
(Connecticut-New Jersey-New York)
Public transport services to non-CBD
employment concentrations. New York, 1967.
26p. (Progress report no. 1. 2044-5620-
5C)
U.S. Dept. of Housing and Urban Develop-
ment. Mass Transportation Demonstration
Project.
1. Transportation - Conn.-N.J.-N.Y.
2. Journey to work. 3. Employment - Conn.-
N.J.-N.Y. I. Title. II. U.S. Dept. of
Housing and Ur   ban Development.
Mass Transporta   tion Demonstration
Project.

1768 TRI-STATE TRANSPORTATION COMMISSION.
(CONNECTICUT - NEW JERSEY - NEW YORK)
REGIONAL DEVELOPMENT GUIDE. NEW YORK;
1969.
53P. (HUD 701 REPORT)

1. REGIONAL PLANNING - CONN. - N.J. -
N.Y. I. HUD. 701. CONN. - N.J. - N.Y.

388
T74rep Tri-State Transportation Commission.
(Connecticut-New Jersey-New York)
Report, 1967; 69-71

New York, 1967-
4v.   annual.

U.S. Dept. of Housing and Urban Development.
UPAP.
For Library holdings see main entry.

1. Transportation - Connecticut-New Jersey-
New York. I. U.S. HUD-UPAP.
Connecticut-   New Jersey-New York.

388
T74s Tri-State Transportation Commission.
(Connecticut-New Jersey-New York)
Station fare collection; Kew Gardens-Forest
Hills, Queens County, New York; a final report
on the Mass Transportation Demonstration Pro-
ject, July 1, 1964-June 30, 1965. New York,
1966.
32p.
U.S. Dept. of Housing and Urban Develop-
ment. Mass Transportation Demonstration
Grant Program.

(Cont'd on next card)

388
T74s Tri-State Transportation Commission. (Connecticut-New Jersey-New York) Station fare
collection...1966. (Card 2)

1. Transportation - Connecticut-New Jersey-
New York. I. U.S. Dept. of Housing and
Urban Development. Mass Transportation
Demonstration Grant Program. II. Title.

388
T74rep Tri-State Transportation Commission.
(Connecticut-New Jersey-New York)
Report, 1967-68.

New York, 1967-68.
2v. annual.

For complete information see main card.
U.S. Dept. of Housing and Urban Development.
UPAP.

1. Transportation - Connecticut-New Jersey-
New York. I. U.S. HUD-UPAP.
Connecticut- New Jersey-New York.

388
T74su Tri-State Transportation Commission.
(Connecticut-New Jersey-New York)
Suburban service adjustment experiment; a
summary, Harlem Division, New York Central
Railroad, Westchester and Putnam Counties;
a final report on the Mass Transportation
Demonstration Grant Project. New York,
1967.
8p.
U.S. Dept. of Housing and Urban Develop-
ment. Mass Transportation Demonstration
Grant Program.

(Continued on next card)

388
T74su Tri-State Transportation Commission.
(Connecticut-New Jersey-New York)
Suburban service adjustment...1967.
(Card 2)

1. Transportation - Conn.-N.J.-N.Y.
2. Journey to work. I. Title. II. U.S.
Dept. of Housing and Urban Development.
Mass Transportation Demonstration Grant
Program.

388
T74te Tri-State Transportation Commission
(Connecticut-New Jersey-New York)
Test of gas turbine rail car; a summary
report on part one of the mass transportation
demonstration grant project. Long Island
Railroad; July 1967-May 1968. New York, 1969.
14p.
INT-MTD 12.
U.S. Dept. of Housing and Urban Develop-
ment. Mass Transportation Demonstration Grant
Program.
1. Transportation - Conn.-N.J.-N.Y. area.
2. Journey to work. 3. Railroads -
Conn.-N.J.-N.Y. I. Title. II. Title:
Gas turbine rail car.
(Cont'd on next card)

388
T74te Tri-State Transportation Commission
(Connecticut-New Jersey-New York) Test
of gas turbine...1969. (Card 2)

III. U.S. HUD Mass Transportation
Demonstration Grant Program.

388
T74t Tri-State Transportation Commission
(Connecticut-New Jersey-New York)
Tri-State transportation 1985; an interim
plan. New York, 1966.
39p.

U.S. Urban Renewal Adm. UPAP.

1. Transportation - Connecticut- New Jersey-
New York. I. Title. II. U.S. URA-UPAP.

Tri-State Transportation Committee.
(Connecticut-New Jersey-New York)
388
(746) Ronan, William J
R65 Tri-State transportation planning, by
Chairman, Tri-State Transportation Committee,
New York. In Newark commerce (Newark
Association of Commerce and Industry) vol. 7,
no. 4, September 1962. p. 18-20, 42-43.

1. Transportation - Connecticut-New Jersey-
New York. I. Newark commerce. II. Tri-State
Transportation Committee.
(Connecticut- New Jersey-New
York)

388
(746) Tri-State Transportation Commission.
T74t (Connecticut-New Jersey-New York)
Truck transportation. New York, 1968.
4p. (Its Regional profile, vol. 1, no. 8,
Jan., 1968)

U.S. Mass Transportation Demonstration Grant
Program.

1. Transportation - Conn.-N.J.-N.Y.
2. Highways - Conn.-N.J.-N.Y. I. U.S. Mass
Transportation Demonstration Grant Program.
II. Title.

388
(746) Tri-State Transportation Commission.
T74u (Connecticut-New Jersey-New York)
Urban corridor demonstration program. Interim report, Oct. 1970 - March 1971. New York,
1971.
45p.

1. Transportation - Conn.-N.J.-N.Y.
2. Highways. I. Title.

Triton City: a prototype floating community.
711.417
T74 Triton Foundation.
A study of a prototype floating community.
Prepared for the Dept. of Housing and Urban
Development. Cambridge, Mass., 1968.
1v.
Cover title: Triton City: a prototype
floating community.
U.S. Dept. of Housing and Urban Development.
Urban Planning Research and Demonstration
Project. (Mass. PD-6)
CFSTI PB180051.
Bibliography: p. A-104 - A-105.
(Cont'd on next card)

711.417
T74 Triton Foundation. A study...1968.
(Card 2)

1. New towns. 2. Harbors. I. Title.
II. Title: Triton City: a prototype floating
community. III. Title: Floating community.
IV. U.S. HUD—UPRDP.

711.417
T74 Triton Foundation.
A study of a prototype floating community.
Prepared for the Dept. of Housing and Urban
Development. Cambridge, Mass., 1968.
1v.
Cover title: Triton City: a prototype
floating community.
U.S. Dept. of Housing and Urban Development.
Urban Planning Research and Demonstration
Project. (Mass. PD-6)
CFSTI PB180051.
Bibliography: p. A-104 - A-105.
(Cont'd on next card)

711.417
T74 Triton Foundation. A study...1968.
(Card 2)

1. New towns. 2. Harbors. I. Title.
II. Title: Triton City: a prototype floating
community. III. Title: Floating community.
IV. U.S. HUD—UPRDP.

370
:325 Damerell, Reginald G
D15 Triumph in a white suburb.
Triumph in a white suburb; the dramatic
story of Teaneck, N.J., the first town in
the nation to vote for integrated schools.
New York, William Morrow, 1968.
351p.
1. Education - Negroes. 2. Schools -
Teaneck, N.J. 3. Minority groups - Teaneck,
N.J. I. Title.

VF
711.6 Triumphing over the gridiron plan.
N172 National Housing Association.
Triumphing over the gridiron plan, by
Lawrence Veiller. New York, Dec. 1918.
[10] p. plans (Its Publication no. 52)

Reprinted from Architectural Record, July
1918.

1. Subdivision design. I. Veiller, Lawrence. II. Title.

621.9
:690 Trivino, F
T74por Tecnica general de análisis por espectro-
grafía de rayos con equipos Philips tipo
PW-1540, by F. Trivino y J. L. Segrera.
Madrid, Consejo Superior de Investigaciones
Cientificas, Patronato Juan de la Cierva de
Investigacion Tecnica, 1966.
[57]p. (Spain. Instituto Eduardo
Torroja de la Construcción y del Cemento.
Monografias n. 251)
English summary.

(Cont'd on next card)

621.9
:690 Trivino, F. Tecnica general de análisis
T74 por espectrografía de rayos con equipos
Philips tipo PW-1540...1966.
(Card 2)

1. Building equipment. 2. Cement
I. Segrera, J. L., jt. au. I. Spain.
Consejo Superior de Investigaciones
Cientificas. Instituto Technico de la
Construccion y del Cemento.

500.15
T76 Troan, John.
An adventure in knowledge; the story of the
Chemical Abstracts Service. Washington,
American Chemical Society [1963?]
24p.

1. Scientific research. I. American
Chemical Society. II. Title: Chemical
Abstracts Service.

720
T76 Troedsson, Carl Birger.
Architecture, urbanism and socio-political
developments in our Western civilization.
Göteborg, Scandinavian University Books, 1964.
313p. (Chalmers University of Technology,
Gothenburg, Sweden. Transactions no. 283;
Avd. Arkitektur 6. 1964)
1. Architecture. 2. City planning - Europe.
3. Art. 4. Public buildings - Europe.
I. Chalmers University of Technology, Gothen-
burg, Sweden. II. Title.

388
T76
TROEDSSON, CARL B
THE CITY, THE AUTOMOBILE AND MAN.
STOCKHOLM, FLANDERS, 1957.
50P. ILLUS.

NA 9108 .T7

1. TRAFFIC. I. TITLE.

362.6
P47
Tronozo, Alfred L
Pittsburgh. Housing Authority.
A statement presented to the Subcommittee
on Problems of the Aged and Aging of the United
States Senate Committee on Labor and Public
Welfare, by Alfred L. Tronzo, Administrator,
Housing Authority of the City of Pittsburgh.
Pittsburgh, 1959.
11p.

1. Old age. 2. Housing for the aged.
I. Tronzo, Alfred L.

VF
312
:383
C31
Troedsson, Carl Birger.
Chalmers University of Technology, Gothenburg,
Sweden.
Transportation and city-building, by
Carl Birger Troedsson. Gothenburg, Sweden,
Elanders Boktryckeri Aktiebolag, 1954.
30 p. illus., charts. (Its transac-
tion no. 146 [Avd. Arkitektur 2])

1. City growth. 2. Transportation. I. Troedsson, Carl
Birger.

330
(60)
K45
Tropical Africa.
Kimble, George H   T
Tropical Africa. Vol. I. Land and
livelihood. Vol. II. Society and
polity. New York, Twentieth Century
Fund, 1960.
2v.   illus., maps, tables.

1. Economic conditions - Africa.
2. Economic geography. 3. Political science -
Africa. I. Title.

360
L25t
The troubled American.
Lemon, Richard.
The troubled American. New York, Simon
and Schuster, 1970.
256p.

1. Social conditions. 2. Political
science. 3. Public opinion polls.
I. Title.

658
T76
1970
TROELSTRUP, ARCHIE WILLIAM.
THE CONSUMER IN AMERICAN SOCIETY,
PERSONAL AND FAMILY FINANCE. 4TH ED.
NEW YORK, MCGRAW-HILL, 1970.
668P.
FIRST ED. PUBLISHED IN 1952 UNDER
TITLE: CONSUMER PROBLEMS; 2D-3D EDS.
PUBLISHED UNDER TITLE: CONSUMER PROBLEMS
AND PERSONAL FINANCE.

1. BUYING. 2. FAMILY INCOME AND
EXPENDITURE. I. TITLE.

VF
728
:551.5
A723
Tropical architecture by British architects.
Architectural Design, part I, Oct. 1953; part II,
Jan. 1954, entire issues.   illus., plans.
Partial contents.-An introduction to tropical
building design, G. A. Atkinson.-Town planning in
Kuwait.-Flats in French West Africa.-Commercial and
domestic building in West Indies.-Hostel and houses
in French West Africa.-Prefabrication in Barbados.
1. Architecture and climate. 2. City planning-Kuwait.
3. Housing in the tropics. 4. Prefabricated
construction-Barbados. Atkinson, G. A.

711.4
U71t
The troubled environment.
Urban America.
The troubled environment: business examines
social and economic barriers to improving our
cities. Sponsored by the Action Council for
Better Cities. New York, 1966.
202p.
The record of a National Symposium conducted
Dec. 8-10, 1965... published by Urban America,
Inc., and the Action Council for Better
Cities.
Partial contents:-Cities in crisis, an ad-
dress, by the Hon. R.C. Weaver, Secretary,
Dept. of Housing   and Urban Development.

(Continued on   next card)

658
T76
1965
TROELSTRUP, ARCHIE WILLIAM.
CONSUMER PROBLEMS AND PERSONAL FINANCE
[BY] ARCH W. TROELSTRUP. 3D ED. NEW
YORK, MCGRAW-HILL, 1965.
611P.
FIRST ED. PUBLISHED IN 1952 UNDER
TITLE: CONSUMER PROBLEMS.

1. BUYING. 2. FAMILY INCOME AND
EXPENDITURE. I. TITLE.

690.37
F79TR
TROPICAL ARCHITECTURE IN THE DRY AND
HUMID ZONES.
FRY, MAXWELL.
TROPICAL ARCHITECTURE IN THE DRY AND
HUMID ZONES, BY MAXWELL FRY AND JANE
DREW. NEW YORK, REINHOLD, 1964.
264P.

1. ARCHITECTURE, DOMESTIC - TROPICS.
2. HOUSING IN THE TROPICS. I. DREW,
JANE, JT. AU. II. TITLE.

711.4
U71t
Urban America. The troubled environment:
business examines social and economic bar-
riers to improving our cities...1966.
(Card 2)

1. City planning - Social aspects.
2. Social welfare. 3. Race relations.
I. Weaver, Robert Clifton. Cities in crisis.
II. Action Council for Better Cities.
III. Title.

728.1
(07)
T76
TROELSTRUP, ARCHIE WILLIAM.
HOUSING IN THE UNITED STATES.
PREPARED FOR THE COMMITTEE ON
EXPERIMENTAL UNITS OF THE NORTH CENTRAL
ASSOCIATION OF COLLEGES AND SECONDARY
SCHOOLS. BOSTON, GINN, 1941.
79P. (UNIT STUDIES IN AMERICAN
PROBLEMS)

1. HOUSING - STUDY AND TEACHING.
I. NORTH CENTRAL ASSOCIATION OF COLLEGES
AND SECONDARY SCHOOLS.

690.37
F79t
Tropical architecture in the humid zone.
Fry, Edwin Maxwell.
Tropical architecture in the humid zone,
by Maxwell Fry and Jane Drew. New York,
Reinhold, 1956.
320 p. illus., charts, tables, diagrs.

1. Architecture - Tropics. 2. Housing in
the tropics. I. Title. II. Drew, Jane,
jt. author.

697.9
E52
Troubleshooters' handbook for mechanical systems.
Emerick, Robert Henderson.
Troubleshooters' handbook for mechanical
systems. New York, McGraw-Hill, 1969.
510p.
Bibliography: p. 497-499.

1. Ventilation. 2. Air conditioning.
3. Heating. 4. Engineering. I. Title.

720
(07)
T76
Trogler, George E
Beginning experiences in architecture: a
guide for the elementary school teacher.
Photographs by Marjorie Pickens. New York,
Van Nostrand Reinhold, 1972.
143p.

1. Architecture - Study and teaching.
I. Title.

VF
728
:551.5
N171
Tropical building design and construction,
Scientific principles and their application
in.
Narayana, S   K
Scientific principles and their application
in tropical building design and construction: a
review [by] S. K. Narayana, S. K. Chopra and
B. C. Raychoudhuri. Reprinted from the Journal
of Scientific and Industrial Research, 1953,
v. 12A.
4 p.

1. Architecture and climate. I. Chopra, S. K.
II. Raychoudhuri, B. C. III. Title: Tropical
building design and construction, Scientific
principles and their application in.

3684
TROUTDALE, OR. CITY PLANNING COMMISSION.
COMPREHENSIVE PLAN. TROUTDALE, OR.,
1970.
33P. (HUD 701 REPORT)

1. MASTER PLAN - TROUTDALE, OR.
I. HUD 701. TROUTDALE, OR.

624.131
T75
TROLL, CARL.
STRUCTURE SOILS, SOLIFLUCTION, AND
FROST CLIMATES OF THE EARTH
(STRUKTURBÖDEN, SOLIFLUKTION, UND
FROSTKLIMATE DER ERDE). WILMETTE,
ILL., U.S. ARMY SNOW, ICE AND
PERMAFROST RESEARCH ESTABLISHMENT,
1958.
121P. (U.S. ARMY. CORPS OF
ENGINEERS. TRANSLATION 43)

1. FROZEN GROUND. 2. SOILS.
I. U.S. ARMY. SNOW, ICE AND
PERMAFROST RESEARCH ESTABLISHMENT.

690.37
O14
TROPICAL HOUSES.
OAKLEY, DAVID.
TROPICAL HOUSES, A GUIDE TO THEIR
DESIGN. LONDON, B.T. BATSFORD, 1961.
272P.

1. ARCHITECTURE, DOMESTIC - TROPICS.
2. HOUSING IN THE TROPICS. I. TITLE.

694.1
C152
TROXELL, GEORGE EARL.
CALIFORNIA. UNIVERSITY. INSTITUTE OF
ENGINEERING RESEARCH.
ACTION OF TIMBER STRUCTURES SUBJECTED
TO LATERAL LOADS. REPORT TO DIVISION OF
ARCHITECTURE, STATE DEPARTMENT OF PUBLIC
WORKS, SACRAMENTO, CALIFORNIA, BY G.E.
TROXELL AND V. BERTERO. BERKELEY,
CALIF., 1959.
19P.

1. WOOD CONSTRUCTION. 2. STRUCTURAL
ENGINEERING. I. TROXELL, GEORGE EARL.
II. BERTERO, V.
III. CALIFORNIA. DEPT. OF PUBLIC
(CONTINUED ON NEXT CARD)

694.1
C152
CALIFORNIA. UNIVERSITY. INSTITUTE OF ENGINEERING RESEARCH. ACTION OF TIMBER ...1959. (CARD 2)

WORKS. (DIVISION OF ARCHITECTURE)
~~IV. TITLE.~~ IV. TITLE: TIMBER STRUCTURES.

728.1
(85)
T76
Troy, Robert D
Lima, Peru; a study of housing in an arid coastal region, 1967-1968. Sponsored by the American Institute of Architects and the Texas Architectural Foundation. [Lubock, Tex.] 1969.
55p. (International Center for Arid and Semi-arid Land Studies. Special report no. 13)
1. Housing - Peru. 2. Housing in the tropics. I. American Institute of Architects. II. Texas Architectural Foundation. III. International Center for Arid and Semi-arid Land Studies. IV. Title.

628.515
T78
phase 1
Truax-Traer Coal Co.
Control of mine drainage from coal mine mineral wastes. Phase I, hydrology and related experiments. Prepared for the Environmental Protection Agency. Pinckneyville, Ill., 1971.
148p. (Water pollution control research series)
1. Water pollution. I. U.S. Environmental Protection Agency. II. Title.

691.32
T76
Troxell, George Earl.
Composition and properties of concrete, by George Earl Troxell and others. 2d ed. New York, McGraw-Hill, 1968.
529p. (McGraw-Hill civil engineering series)
Bibliography: p. 475-513.
1. Concrete. I. Title.

352.6
(76135)
T76
Troy, Ala. City Planning Commission.
Troy, Alabama: community facilities plan. [Prepared for] Alabama State Planning and Industrial Development Board. Troy, 1961.
23p.
U.S. Urban Renewal Adm. UPAP.
1. Community facilities - Troy, Ala. I. U.S. URA-UPAP. Troy, Ala.

623
T78
Trubert, Marc R P
Response of elastic structures to statistically correlated multiple random excitations. Gainesville, Fla., University of Florida, Florida Engineering and Industrial Experiment Station, 1963.
15p. (Florida. University. Engineering and Industrial Experiment Station. Technical paper series no. 268)
Engineering progress at the University of Florida, v. 17, no. 8, Aug. 1963.
(Cont'd. on next card)

691.11
T76
Troxell, H E
Solar lumber drying in the Central Rocky Mountain region, by H.E. Troxell and L.A. Mueller. Presented at the 20th annual meeting of the Forest Products Research Society, July 21, 1968, Minneapolis, Minn. Madison, Wis., Forest Products Research Society, 1968.
19-24p.
Reprinted from Forest Products Journal, Jan., 1968.
(Cont'd on next card)

711.74
(76135)
T76
Troy, Ala. City Planning Commission.
Troy, Alabama: major street plan. [Prepared for] Alabama State Planning and Industrial Development Board. Troy, 1960.
25p.
U.S. Urban Renewal Adm. UPAP.
1. Street planning - Troy, Ala. I. U.S. URA-UPAP. Troy, Ala.

623
T78
Trubert, Marc R P Response to elastic structures to...(Card 2)

Reprinted, from the Journal of Acoustical Society of America, vol. 35, no. 7, July, 1963, p. 1009-1022.
1. Structural engineering. 2. Loads. I. Florida. University. Engineering and Industrial Experiment Station.

691.11
T76
Troxell, H E Solar lumber.... 1968. (Card 2)
1. Wood. I. Mueller, L.A ., jt. au. II. Forest Products Research Society. Meeting, 20th Minneapolis, 1967. III. Title.

711.4
(76135)
T76
Troy, Ala. City Planning Commission.
Troy, Alabama: public improvements program. [Prepared in cooperation with] Alabama State Planning and Industrial Development Board. Troy, 1962.
18p.
U.S. Urban Renewal Adm. UPAP.
1. Capital improvement programs - Troy, Ala. I. U.S. URA-UPAP. Troy, Ala.

388
(775)
S68t
Truck and taxi survey.
Southeastern Wisconsin Regional Planning Commission.
Truck and taxi survey. Land use-transportation study. Rev. Waukesha, Wis., 1964.
49p. (Its Procedural manual no. 3)
Prepared in cooperation with State Highway Commission of Wisconsin, the U.S. Dept. of Commerce, Bureau of Public Roads.
U.S. Urban Renewal Adm. UPAP.
1. Transportation - Wis. 2. Traffic surveys - Wis. I. Title. II. U.S. URA-UPAP. Wis.

059
:650
T76
1972
Troy, Leo
Almanac of business and industrial financial ratios, 1972 edition. Englewood Cliffs, N.J., 1971.
169p.
1. Business - Almanacs. 2. Business-Statistics. 3. Industry - Statistics. I. Title.

352.6
(76135)
T76p
Troy, Ala. City Planning Commission.
Troy, Alabama: public utilities plan. [Prepared in cooperation with] Alabama State Planning and Industrial Development Board. Troy, 1962.
31p.
U.S. Urban Renewal Adm. UPAP.
1. Public utilities - Troy, Ala. I. U.S. URA-UPAP. Troy, Ala.

388
:308
C25c
v.2
Truck inventory and use survey.
U.S. Bureau of the Census.
1963 census of transportation. Vol. 2. Truck inventory and use survey. Wash., U.S. Dept. of Commerce, Bureau of the Census, 1965.
698p.
"Publication graphics and design developed by Stuart Freeman."
1. Transportation - Surveys. 2. Census - Transportation. I. Freeman, Stuart. II. Title. III. Title: Truck inventory and use survey.

330.15
N17o
no.56
Troy, Leo.
Distribution of union membership among the states, 1939 and 1953. New York, 1957.
32 p. illus. (National Bureau of Economic Research. Occasional paper 56).
1. Trade - unions. I. Title. II. National Bureau of Economic Research. Occasional paper, no. 56.

691.328.2
T76
Troyano, Leonardo Fernandez.
Cálculo del pretensado en puentes. Madrid, Consejo Superior de Investigaciones Cientificas, Patronato Juan de la Cierva de Investigacion Tecnica, 1964.
80p. (Spain. Instituto Eduardo Torroja de la Construcción y del Cemento. Monografias no. 243)
English summary.
1. Concrete, Prestressed. I. Spain. Consejo Superior de Investigaciones Cientificas. Instituto Eduardo de la Construccion y del Cemento.

388
:308
1967
C25c
v.2
Truck inventory and use survey.
U.S. Bureau of the Census.
1967 census of transportation. Vol. 2. Truck inventory and use survey. Wash., 1967.
693p.
1. Transportation - Surveys. 2. Census - Transportation. I. Title. II. Title: Truck inventory and use survey.

330.15
N17o
no.92
Troy, Leo.
Trade union membership, 1897-1962. New York, 1965.
21,65 p. (National Bureau of Economic Research. Occasional paper 92).
1. Trade-unions. I. Title. II. National Bureau of Economic Research. Occasional paper, no. 92.

VF
691.018.44
F67
D1760
Truax, T R
U.S. Forest Service. Forest Products Laboratory, Madison, Wis.
Making wood fire retardant, by T. R. Truax. Madison, Wis., Mar. 1950.
8 p. (Its D1760)
Bibliography: p. 8.
Mimeographed.
1. Building materials-Fire resistance. 2. Wood. I. Truax, T. R. II. Title.

388
(746)
T74t
Truck transportation.
Tri-State Transportation Commission. (Connecticut-New Jersey-New York)
Truck transportation. New York, 1968.
4p. (Its Regional profile, vol. 1, no. 8, Jan., 1968)
U.S. Mass Transportation Demonstration Grant Program.
1. Transportation - Conn.-N.J.-N.Y. 2. Highways - Conn.-N.J.-N.Y. I. U.S. Mass Transportation Demonstration Grant Program. II. Title.

388
C87

A trucker looks at rapid transit.
Currey, Neil J
A trucker looks at rapid transit. Presented before the 4th Annual Meeting, Institute for Rapid Transit, May 19, 1965, Washington, D.C. [n.p.] 1965.
9p.

1. Transportation. 2. Journey to work. 3. Highways. I. Institute for Rapid Transit. Meeting, 4th, Washington, 1965. II. Title.

624.131
I55SO

TRUESDALE, W B
ILLINOIS INSTITUTE OF TECHNOLOGY. RESEARCH INSTITUTE.
SOIL STRAIN GAGE INSTRUMENTATION BY W.B. TRUESDALE AND OTHERS. SPRINGFIELD, VA., CLEARINGHOUSE FOR FEDERAL SCIENTIFIC AND TECHNICAL INFORMATION, 1966.
92P.

1. SOILS - TESTING. I. TRUESDALE, W.B. II. TITLE.

328.368
T78

Truman, David Bicknell, 1913-
The governmental process; political interests and public opinion. New York, Knopf, 1951.
544p. (Borzoi books in political science)
Bibliography: p. 537-544.

1. Lobbying. 2. Political science. I. Title.

388
S54m

Trucks.
Smith (Wilbur) and Associates.
Motor trucks in the metropolis. Prepared under commission from the Automobile Manufacturers Association. New Haven, 1969.
208p.
Bibliography: p. 195-199.

1. Traffic. 2. Transportation. I. Title. II. Title: Trucks.

312
C25
P-23
no.1

Truesdell, Leon E
U.S. Bureau of the Census.
Current population reports: population characteristics. The development of the urban-rural classification in the United States: 1874 to 1949, by Leon E. Truesdell. Washington, Govt. Print. Off., 1949.
16 p. tables. (Its P-23, no. 1)

Processed.

1.Census. I.Truesdell, Leon E. II.Title. III.Title: Urban-Rur...

320
W27

Truman, David B
Westin, Alan F ed.
Politics and government in the United States; National, State and local edition, by Alan F. Westin and others. Alan F. Westin, coordinating editor. New York, Harcourt, 1965.
1004p.
Contents:-pt.1. Democracy and the American way.-pt.2. The political process, by A. Hacker.-pt.3. The President, Congress, and the Executive Branch, by D. Truman -pt.4. Liberty, justice, and law, by A. Westin.-pt.5. Government in action, by E. Redford and R. Wood.-

(Continued on next card)

728.1
I336.18
T78

TRUCKSESS, ELIZABETH.
POSITIVE RESULTS OF PUBLIC HOUSING AS OF JUNE 28, 1944. WASHINGTON, 1944.
1 V.

1. PUBLIC HOUSING. I. TITLE.

312
C25t
no.3

Truesdell, Leon E
U.S. Bureau of the Census.
Farm population 1880 to 1950, by Leon E. Truesdell. Washington, 1960.
31p. (Its Technical paper no. 3)

1. Population shifts. I. Truesdell, Leon E. II. Title.

320
W27

Westin, Alan F ed. Politics and government in the United States...1965. (Card 2)

pt.6. The States and communities, by R. Wood.

1. Political science. 2. History. 3. Intergovernmental relations. 4. Democracy. I. Hacker, Andrew. II. Truman, David B. III. Redford, Emmette S. IV. Wood, Robert C. V. Title.

VF
330
T78

True Story Women's Group.
America today; the new potential at mid century. New York, Macfadden, 1950.
24p.

1. Economic conditions. I. Title.

628.44
T78

Truitt, Marcus M
Mathematical modeling of solid waste collection policies, by Marcus M. Truitt and others. [Wash.] U.S. Public Health Service, Environmental Health Service, Bureau of Solid Waste Management, 1970.
2v. in 1 (U.S. Public Health Service. Publication no. 2030)
Final report under research grant to John Hopkins University.
Bibliography: p. 217-220.

1. Refuse and refuse disposal. (Cont'd on next card)

728.1
D18

Truman, Harry S. Pres., U.S., 1884-
Davies, Richard O
Housing reform during the Truman administration. Columbia, University of Missouri Press, 1966.
197p.

Bibliography: p. 174-185.

1. Housing. 2. Public housing. 3. Rent control. 4. Slum clearance. 5. Truman, Harry S. Pres., U.S., 1884- I. Title.

711.4
(8)
R11

Trueblood, Felicity M jt. ed.
Rabinovitz, Francine F ed.
Latin American urban research, by Francine F. Rabinovitz and Felicity M. Trueblood. Beverly Hills, Calif., Sage Publications, 1971.
v. (Latin American urban research)

1. City planning - Latin America. I. Trueblood, Felicity M., jt. ed. II. Title.

628.44
T78

Truitt, Marcus M Mathematical... 1970. (Card 2)

2. Mathematics. I. John Hopkins University II. U.S. Public Health Service. III. Title.

632.95
T78

TRUMAN, LEE C
SCIENTIFIC GUIDE TO PEST CONTROL OPERATIONS, 2D ED. BY LEE C. TRUMAN AND WILLIAM L. BUTTS. CLEVELAND, PEST CONTROL MAGAZINE, 1967.
187P.

1. PESTICIDES. I. TITLE. II. TITLE: PEST CONTROL OPERATIONS.

657
T78
2c.

TRUEBLOOD, ROBERT M
SAMPLING TECHNIQUES IN ACCOUNTING, BY ROBERT M. TRUEBLOOD AND RICHARD M. CYERT. ENGLEWOOD CLIFFS, N.J., PRENTICE-HALL, 1957.
211P.

1. ACCOUNTING. 2. SAMPLING (STATISTICS) I. CYERT, RICHARD MICHAEL, JT. AU. II. TITLE.

312.1
(81)
825

Trujillo Ferrari, Alfonso.
Seminario Sobre Problemas de Urbanizacion en America Latina, Santiago de Chile, 1959.
Movimentos migratorios internos y problemas de acomodacion del immigrante nacional en Sao Paulo (Brasil); estudio preliminar, por Alfonso Trujillo Ferrari. [n.p.] 1959.
86p. (General E/CN.12/URB/12; UNESCO/SS/URB/La/12)

1. Population shifts - Brazil. I. Trujillo Ferrari, Alfonso. II. United Nations. (Economic and Social Council)

728.1
1940.42
(749)
T78

TRUMAN COMMITTEE EXPOSES HOUSING MESS. NEW YORK ? 1942.
45-52P.
EXTRACTED FROM LIFE, NOV. 30, 1942.

1. DEFENSE HOUSING - NEW JERSEY.

624.131
I55S

TRUESDALE, W B
ILLINOIS INSTITUTE OF TECHNOLOGY. RESEARCH INSTITUTE.
SOIL STRAIN GAGE INSTRUMENTATION, BY W.B. TRUESDALE AND OTHERS. KIRTLAND AIR FORCE BASE, N.M. AIR FORCE WEAPONS LABORATORY. RESEARCH AND TECHNOLOGY DIVISION, 1966.
92P.

1. SOILS - TESTING. I. TRUESDALE, W.B. II. U.S. AIR FORCE WEAPONS LABORATORY, NEW MEXICO. III. TITLE.

972.93
T78h

Trujillo Molina, Rafael Leonidas.
Hicks, Albert C
Blood in the streets; the life and rule of Trujillo. Introd. by Quentin Reynolds. New York, Creative Age Press [c1946]
230 p.

1.Trujillo Molina, Rafael Leonidas. 2.Dominican Republic. I.Title.

333.38
(76796)
A74a

Trumann, Ark. City Planning Commission.
Arkansas. University. City Planning Div.
Administrative guide, subdivision regulations. Prepared for City Planning Commission, Trumann, Arkansas. Fayetteville, Ark., 1963.
12p. (Document no. 3D-3)

U.S. Urban Renewal Adm. UPAP.

1. Subdivision regulation - Trumann, Ark. I. Trumann, Ark. City Planning Commission. II. U.S. URA-UPAP. Trumann, Ark.

711.5
(76796
:347)
A74a

Trumann, Ark. City Planning Commission.
Arkansas. University. City Planning Div.
Administrative guide, zoning ordinance.
Prepared for City Planning Commission
Trumann, Arkansas. Fayetteville, 1963.
7p. (Document no. 3D-2)

U.S. Urban Renewal Adm. UPAP.

1. Zoning legislation - Trumann, Ark.
I. Trumann, Ark. City Planning Commission.
II. U.S. URA-UPAP. Trumann, Ark.

711.729
(76796)
A74

Trumann, Ark. City Planning Commission.
Arkansas. University. City Planning Div.
A parking study for the Trumann Central
business district. Prepared for City
Planning Commission. Fayetteville, Ark.,
1963.
(18)p. (Document no. 3D-1)

U.S. Urban Renewal Adm. UPAP.

1. Parking - Trumann, Ark. 2. Business districts -
Trumann, Ark. I. Trumann, Ark. City Planning
Commission. II. U.S. URA-UPAP. Trumann,
Ark.

711.4
(76796)
A74p

Trumann, Ark. City Planning Commission.
Arkansas. University. City Planning
Div.
A planning report for Trumann,
Arkansas. Prepared for City Planning
Commission, Trumann, Arkansas.
Fayetteville, Ark., 1963.
1v. (Report no. 3R-1)

U.S. Urban Renewal Adm. UPAP.

1. City planning - Trumann, Ark.
I. Trumann, Ark. City Planning
Commis-   sion. II. U.S.
URA-UPAP.   Trumann, Ark.

333.38
(76796)
A74

Trumann, Ark. City Planning Commission.
Arkansas. University. City Planning
Div.
Subdivision regulations, Trumann,
Arkansas. Ordinance no. 152. Prepared
for City Planning Commission, Trumann,
Arkansas. Fayetteville, Ark., 1963.
[12]p.

U.S. Urban Renewal Adm. UPAP.

1. Subdivision regulation - Trumann, Ark.
I. Trumann, Ark. City Planning
Commission. II. U.S. URA-UPAP. Trumann,
Ark.

711.5
(76796
:347)
A74

Trumann, Ark. City Planning Commission.
Arkansas. University. City Planning
Div.
Zoning ordinance Trumann, Arkansas;
ordinance no. 153. Prepared for City
Planning Commission, Trumann, Ark.
Fayetteville, Ark., 1963.
26p.

U.S. Urban Renewal Adm. UPAP.

1. Zoning legislation - Trumann, Ark. I. Trumann,
Ark. City Planning Commission. II. U.S. URA-
UPAP. Trumann, Ark.

711.4
(77138)
W17

Trumbull County, Ohio. Regional Planning
Commission.
The general plan for Warren, Ohio; sum-
mary and project completion report. [Pre-
pared for Warren City Planning Commission]
[Trumbull Co., Ohio] 1961.
1v.
U.S. URban Renewal Adm. UPAP.

1. Master plan - Warren, Ohio.
I. Warren, Ohio. City Planning Commission.
II. U.S. URA-UPAP. Warren, Ohio.

711.333
(77138)
T78

Trumbull Co., Ohio. Regional Planning
Commission.
Organization plan and program. Warren,
Ohio, 1958.
1v. diagrs.

1. County planning - Trumbull Co.,
Ohio.

FOLIO
711.333
(77138)
T78t

Trumbull County, Ohio. Regional Planning
Commission.
Trumbull County, Ohio: comprehensive regional plan. Warren, Ohio, 1960.
2 pts.
Contents:-pt. 1. Summary and project completion report.-pt. 2. Historical establishment of Trumbull Co., Ohio.
U.S. Urban Renewal Adm. UPAP.

(Continued on
next card)

FOLIO
711.333
(77138)
T78t

Trumbull County, Ohio. Regional Planning
Commission. Trumbull County...(Card 2)

1. Master plan - Trumbull Co., Ohio.
2. County planning - Trumbull Co., Ohio.
3. Economic base studies - Trumbull Co.,
Ohio. I. U.S. URA-UPAP. Trumbull Co.,
Ohio.

VF
728.1
:336.18
B92

Trump, Clarence A

Byer, Herman B
Labor and unit costs in PWA low-rent
housing, by Herman B. Byer and Clarence A.
Trump. From the Monthly Labor Review
(Sept. 1939) of the Bureau of Labor
Statistics, United States Dept. of Labor)
p. 1-9.

(Serial no. R. 998)

1. Public housing. I. Trump, Clarence A. II. U.S.
Public Works Administration. III. Title.

VF
711.14
T78

Trumper, R W
The function of the professions in the
use and development of land. Reproduced
from the Chartered surveyor, August 1962.
p. 64-69.

1. Land use. I. Title. II. Chartered
surveyor.

325.2
K45t

The trumpet of conscience.
King, Martin Luther, Jr.
The trumpet of conscience. New York, Harper,
1968.
78p.

1. Race relations. 2. Negroes. 3. Civil
rights. I. Title.

DATE OF REQUEST 10/10/ OCT 24 1952   L.C. CARD NO.

Mintz

AUTHOR
Truscon Laboratories, Detroit, Mich.

TITLE
How to paint concrete and plaster successfully.

SERIES

EDITION   PUB. DATE [1952]   PAGING 48 p.

PUBLISHER
same

RECOMMENDED BY   REVIEWED IN
         Bldg Supply News 10/52 p.174

ORDER RECORD

330
(7291)
I57

International Bank for Reconstruction and Development.
Report on Cuba. Findings and recommendations
of an economic and technical mission organized
by the International Bank for Reconstruction
and Development in collaboration with the government of Cuba in 1950. Baltimore, Johns Hopkins
Press, 1951.
1049p. tables.

(Continued on next card)

330
(7291)
I57

International Bank for Reconstruction and Development. Report on Cuba. . . .(Card 2)

Francis Adams Truslow, Chief of Mission.

1. Economic conditions - Cuba.
I. Truslow, Francis Adams.

33
(7291)
I57
summary

Truslow, Francis Adams
International Bank for Reconstruction and
Development.
Summary of report on Cuba. Findings and
recommendations of an economic and technical
mission organized ... in collaboration with
the government of Cuba in 1950. Washington,
1951.
30 p.

Francis Adams Truslow, chairman of mission.

1.Cuba-Econ. condit. I.Truslow, Francis Adams.

691.8
N17T

TRUSS-CORE SANDWICH CYLINDER.
U.S. NATIONAL AERONAUTICS AND SPACE
ADMINISTRATION.
TEST OF A TRUSS-CORE SANDWICH CYLINDER
LOADED TO FAILURE IN BENDING, BY JAMES
P. PETERSON AND JAMES KENT ANDERSON.
WASHINGTON, 1965.
28P. (ITS NASA TECHNICAL NOTE D-3157)

1. PANELS. I. PETERSON, JAMES P.
II. ANDERSON, JAMES KENT. III. TITLE:
TRUSS-CORE SANDWICH CYLINDER.

VF
690.2
N17
no.2

Trussed rafter construction as used by NAHB
members.
National Association of Home Builders. Research
Institute.
Trussed rafter construction as used by NAHB
members. Washington, Mar. 1953.
8 l. illus. (Operation trade secrets,
report no. 2)

Lee Frankl, consultant.
Processed.

1.Trusses. I.Frankl, Lee. II.Title. III.Ser.

691.11
F67MO

TRUSSED RAFTER JOINTS.
U.S. FOREST PRODUCTS LABORATORY,
MADISON, WIS.
MOISTURE CYCLING OF TRUSSED RAFTER
JOINTS, BY THOMAS LEE WILKINSON.
MADISON, WIS., 1966.
38P. (U.S. FOREST SERVICE RESEARCH
PAPER FPL 67)

1. WOOD. 2. TRUSSES. 3. MOISTURE.
I. WILKINSON, THOMAS LEE.
II. TITLE: TRUSSED RAFTER JOINTS.

690.24
B72

Trussed rafters.
Stern, E George.
Trussed rafters. Wash., Society of American
Military Engineers, 1960.
114-116p.

Reprinted from The Military engineer,
March - April, 1960.

1. Roofs and roofing. 2. Trusses.
I. Military engineer. II. Title.

690.248
A53

TRUSSES.
ANGLETON, HUGH D
CHOOSING A ROOF TRUSS SYSTEM. FINAL
PAPER. BUILDING RESEARCH INSTITUTE
CONFERENCE NOVEMBER 19-21, 1963.
WASHINGTON, BRI, 1963.
18L.

1. TRUSSES. 2. ROOFS AND ROOFING.
I. BUILDING RESEARCH INSTITUTE.

690.248
H18

TRUSSES.
BAUM, GUNTER.
BASIC VALUES ON SINGLE SPAN BEAMS;
TABLES FOR CALCULATING CONTINUOUS
BEAMS AND FRAME CONSTRUCTIONS
INCLUDING PRESTRESSED BEAMS. NEW
YORK, SPRINGER-VERLAG, 1966.
113P. TABLES.

1. TRUSSES. 2. STRAINS AND
STRESSES. 3. STRENGTH OF MATERIALS.
I. TITLE.

690.248
H15

TRUSSES.
HANSEN, CARL C.
DESIGN WITH STEEL CONNECTOR PLATES.
PRESENTED AT THE BUILDING RESEARCH
INSTITUTE CONFERENCE ON SIGNIFICANCE
OF MECHANICAL FASTENERS IN RESIDENTIAL
FRAME CONSTRUCTION. NOVEMBER 19-21,
1963. WASHINGTON, BRI, 1963.
6L.

1. TRUSSES. I. BUILDING RESEARCH
INSTITUTE.

690.248
I55

Trusses.
Illinois. University. Small Homes Council.
Clear-span framing for 1-1/2 story houses.
[Urbana, Ill., 1953?]
1 v. (various pagings) diagrs., illus.

Prepared under Research project no. I-T-
118, Housing and Home Finance Agency.
Project director: James T. Lendrum.
Staff technician: Philip A. Randall.

Processed.
(over)

690.248
B71

TRUSSES.
BRANSON, DAN EARLE.
INSTANTANEOUS AND TIME-DEPENDENT
DEFLECTIONS OF SIMPLE AND CONTINUOUS
REINFORCED CONCRETE BEAMS. PART1 BY
DAN E. BRANSON, PART2 BY GENE ALAN
METZ. SPONSORED BY ALABAMA HIGHWAY
DEPARTMENT IN COOPERATION WITH U.S.
DEPT. OF COMMERCE, BUREAU OF PUBLIC
ROADS. AUBURN, ALA., AUBURN
UNIVERSITY, DEPT. OF CIVIL
ENGINEERING, 1963-64.
2PTS. IN 1 V. (ALABAMA. STATE
HIGHWAY DEPAR TMENT. BUREAU OF
RESEARCH AND DEVELOPMENT. HPR
(CONTINUED ON NEXT CARD)

690.015
H68
H

Trusses.
Housing Research. No. 1 - 7. Washington, Govt.
Print. Off., Fall 1951 - Apr. 1954.
7 nos. illus., diagrs., graphs, maps, plans,
tables.

Publication of U.S. Housing and Home Finance
Agency, Office of the Administrator, Division of
Housing Research.

694.54
I55

Trusses.
Illinois. University. Small Homes Council.
Structural analyses and calculations for (A)
systems of wood framing for dwellings and (B)
1-1/2 story roof truss 2' - 0" O.C., contained in
Housing research paper no. 33 resulting from
Project no. 1-T-118 under contract with the
University of Illinois Small Homes Council and
Housing and Home Finance Agency. [Urbana, Ill.
1953]
112, 48 l. plates.

Project director, James T. Lendrum; staff
technician, Philip A. Randall.
Processed.

690.248
B71

BRANSON, DAN EARLE. INSTANTANEOUS AND
TIME-DEPENDENT ...3-64. (CARD 2)

REPORT NO. 7)

1. TRUSSES. 2. CONCRETE
CONSTRUCTION. I. METZ, GENE ALAN,
JT. AU. II. ALABAMA. STATE HIGHWAY
DEPT.

691.328.2
I55B

TRUSSES.
ILLINOIS. UNIVERSITY. DEPT. OF
CIVIL ENGINEERING.
BEHAVIOR AND STRENGTH IN COMBINED
BENDING AND SHEAR OF TWO-SPAN
CONTINUOUS PRESTRESSED CONCRETE
BEAMS, BY NEIL M. HAWKINS AND
OTHERS. URBANA, 1963.
58P.

1. CONCRETE, PRESTRESSED.
2. TRUSSES. I. HAWKINS, NEIL M.

690.248
I52

Trusses.
Independent Nail and Packing Co.
New ideas for using all-nailed king-post
trussed rafters. Bridgewater, Mass., 1960.
23p. diagrs.

1. Trusses.

691.32
B72r

TRUSSES.
BREEN, JOHN E.
THE RESTRAINED LONG CONCRETE
COLUMN AS PART OF A RECTANGULAR
FRAME; PARTS 1 AND 2, BY JOHN E.
BREEN AND PHIL M. FERGUSON.
URBANA, ILL., 1964.
25P. (BULLETIN 16, REINFORCED
CONCRETE RESEARCH COUNCIL, AMERICAN
SOCIETY OF CIVIL ENGINEERS)

"REPRINTED FROM MATERIAL OF THE
AMERICAN CONCRETE INSTITUTE."

1. CONCRETE
(CONTINUED ON NEXT CARD)

691.328.2
I55

TRUSSES.
ILLINOIS. UNIVERSITY. DEPT. OF
CIVIL ENGINEERING.
STRENGTH AND BEHAVIOR OF TWO-SPAN
CONTINUOUS PRESTRESSED CONCRETE
BEAMS, BY N.M. HAWKINS AND OTHERS.
ISSUED AS A PART OF THE TENTH
PROGRESS REPORT OF THE INVESTIGATION
OF PRESTRESSED REINFORCED CONCRETE
FOR HIGHWAY BRIDGES. URBANA, ILL.,
1961.
1 V. (VARIOUS PAGINGS) (ITS
CIVIL ENGINEERING STUDIES)
STRUCTURAL RESEARCH SERIES NO.
225)
(CONTINUED ON NEXT CARD).

690.248
I52d

Trusses.
Indiana. Agricultural Experiment Station.
(Wood Research Laboratory)
Determination of member stresses in
wood trusses with rigid joints, by Stanley
K. Suddarth. Lafayette, 1961.
15p. (Its Research bulletin no. 714)

1. Trusses. I. Suddarth, Stanley K.

691.32
B72r

BREEN, JOHN E THE RESTRAINED LONG
...1964. (CARD 2)

2. TRUSSES. I. FERGUSON, PHIL M.
II. AMERICAN SOCIETY OF CIVIL
ENGINEERS. REINFORCED CONCRETE
RESEARCH COUNCIL. III. AMERICAN
CONCRETE INSTITUTE.

691.328.2
I55

ILLINOIS. UNIVERSITY. DEPT. OF
CIVIL ENGINEERING. STRENGTH AND
BEHAVIOR ...1961. (CARD 2)
1. CONCRETE, PRESTRESSED.
2. TRUSSES. 3. BRIDGES.
I. HAWKINS, NEIL M. II. TITLE.

690.248
I77

Trusses.
Israel. Institute of Technology. (Building Research Station)
Precast reinforced concrete roof trusses for
public housing schemes, by A. Alweyl and others.
Haifa, 1957.
1v. illus., diagrs., tables. (Its Research
paper no. 5)

English and Hebrew.

1. Trusses. 2. Reinforced concrete construction. I. Alweyl, A.

624
B76

TRUSSES.
BROWNE, J S C
BASIC THEORY OF STRUCTURES. NEW YORK,
PERGAMON PRESS, 1966.
243P.

1. STRUCTURAL ENGINEERING. 2. STRAINS
AND STRESSES. 3. TRUSSES. I. TITLE.

VF
694.54
I551

Trusses.
Illinois. University. Small Homes Council.
Identification of materials and labor
savings in wood framing for dwellings; to
be presented at the Eighth Annual Short
Course for Contractors and Builders.
[Urbana, Ill.] 1953.
33 l. / diagrs.

Iterim report, research contract No.
1-T-118, Housing and Home Finance Agency.

(see card 2)

690.248
I84

TRUSSES.
Iwinski, T
Theory of beams; the application of the
Laplace transformation method to engineering
problems. Translated from the Polish by
E.P. Bernat. New York, Pergamon Press,
1958.
85p. (International series of monographs
on electronics and instrumentation)

1. Trusses. 2. Structural engineering.
3. Strains and stresses. I. Title.
II. Title: Laplace transformation.

690.248
F25

TRUSSES.
FELTON, KENNETH E
EFFECTIVENESS OF PUNCHED TRUSS
PLATES, BY K.E. FELTON AND HOWARD D.
BARTLETT. BUILDING RESEARCH INSTITUTE
CONFERENCE, NOVEMBER 19-21, 1963,
WASHINGTON, BRI, 1963.
6P.

1. TRUSSES. I. BUILDING RESEARCH
INSTITUTE.

690
694.54
I551

Illinois. University. Small Homes Council.
Identification of materials... 1953.
(card 2)

Project director: James T. Lendrum;
staff technician: Philip A. Randall.

1. Wood framing. 2. Trussess. 3. Housing
research contracts. I. Lendrum, James T.
II. Randall, Philip A. III. Housing and
Home Finance Agency, Office of the
Administrator, Div. of Housing Research.
IV. Title.

691.32
J82

TRUSSES.
JUDD, THAYNE HANSEN.
STRENGTH OF LAPPED SPLICES IN
CONCRETE BEAMS USING HOOKS. BOULDER,
COLO., 1965.
87P.

THESIS (M.S.) - UNIVERSITY OF
COLORADO.

1. CONCRETE. 2. TRUSSES.
I. COLORADO. UNIVERSITY. DEPT. OF
CIVIL ENGINEERING. II. TITLE.

624.043
M14
TRUSSES.
Maier, G
The unstable flexural behaviour of inflexible elasto-plastic beams, Garston, Eng., Building Research Station, 1971.
[25]p. (Library communication no. 1618)
Translated from the Italian.

1. Strains and stresses. 2. Trusses. I. U.K. Building Research Station. II. Title. (Series)

Trusses.
690.248
R12
Radcliffe, Byron M
Effect of variables on performance of trussed rafters, by Byron M. Radcliffe and Alan Sliker. Research project was co-sponsored by the National Lumber Manufacturers Association. East Lansing, Mich., Michigan State University, Agricultural Experiment Station, 1963.
19p.

1. Trusses. I, Sliker, Alan., jt. au. I. Michigan. Agricultural Experiment Station II. National Lumber Manufacturers Association.

690.24
U54C
TRUSSES.
UNION CARBIDE NUCLEAR COMPANY.
A COMPARISON OF FLAT AND GABLED ROOF BUILDINGS SUPPORTED BY RIGID STEEL FRAMES, BY C.J. WILLIAMS. OAK RIDGE, TENN., 1963.
137L. (ITS REPORT Y-1418)

1. ROOFS AND ROOFING. 2. TRUSSES. I. WILLIAMS C.J.

Trusses.
690.248
M19
Mayeda, R
Minimum-weight design of beams for multiple loading, by R. Mayeda and W. Praeger. Prepared for Office of Naval Research as Technical rept. no. 8. San Diego, University of California, Dept. of Aerospace and Mechanical Engineering Sciences, 1967.
21p. (U.S. Defense Documentation Center. Defense Supply Agency [Document] AD 650 194)
Distributed by U.S. Clearinghouse for Federal Scientific and Technical Information.

(Continued on next card)

690.248
S68
TRUSSES.
SOUTH AFRICAN COUNCIL FOR SCIENTIFIC AND INDUSTRIAL RESEARCH.
THE MECHANICAL PROPERTIES OF S.A. TIMBER FOR USE IN STRUCTURES WITH SPECIAL REFERENCE TO ROOF TRUSSES, BY P.A.V. BRYANT. PRETORIA, 1964.
14P. (ITS CSIR REFERENCE NO. RU 1.26)

1. TRUSSES. 2. ROOFS AND ROOFING. I. BRYANT, P.A.V.

690
(41)
B84S
PT.2
TRUSSES.
U.K. DEPT. OF SCIENTIFIC AND INDUSTRIAL RESEARCH.
STUDIES IN COMPOSITE CONSTRUCTION. PT. II. THE INTERACTION OF FLOORS AND BEAMS IN MULTI-STORY BUILDINGS, BY R.H. WOOD. LONDON, H.M. STAT. OFF., 1955.
124P. (ITS NATIONAL BUILDING STUDIES. RESEARCH PAPER NO. 22)

1. FLOORS AND FLOORING. 2. TRUSSES. I. WOOD, R.H.

690.248
M19
Mayeda, R Minimum-weight design of beams for multiple loading...1967. (Card 2)

1. Trusses. 2. Structural engineering. 3. Loads. I. California. University. II. U.S. Defense Documentation Center. Defense Supply Agency. III. U.S. Clearinghouse for Federal Scientific and Technical Information. IV. Praeger, W., jt. au. V. U.S. Office of Naval Research. VI. Title.

690.248
S720
Laf.
Trusses.
Steel Joist Institute.
Open web steel joists, load and spacing tables; standard J and H series. Washington, 1964.
27p.
A.I.A. File no. 13G.

1. Trusses. 2. Standardization. I. Title.

690.248
F67
TRUSSES.
U.S. FOREST PRODUCTS LABORATORY, MADISON, WIS.
FLEXURAL BEHAVIOR OF LARGE GLUED-LAMINATED BEAMS. BY BILLY BOHANNAN. MADISON, 1966.
16P. (ITS RESEARCH PAPER FPL 72)

1. TRUSSES. 2. STRAINS AND STRESSES. I. BOHANNAN, BILLY. II. TITLE.

690.248
M44
Trusses.
Mikkola, Martti.
Lateral buckling of I beams beyond the limit of proportionality. Helsinki, State Institute for Technical Research, 1968.
25p. (Finland. State Institute for Technical Research. Julkaisu 131 publication)

1. Trusses. 2. Strains and stresses. I. Finland. State Institute for Technical Research. II. Title.

690.248
S72
Laf.
Trusses.
Steel Joist Institute.
Standard specifications and load tables; open web steel joists: J-series, H-series; longspan steel joists: LJ-series, LH-series. Washington, 1967.
31p.
A.I.A. File no. 13G.

1. Trusses. 2. Stnadardization. I. Title.

690.248
F67L
TRUSSES.
U.S. FOREST PRODUCTS LABORATORY, MADISON, WIS.
LIGHT WOOD TRUSSES, BY R.F. LUXFORD. MADISON 1958.
50P. (ITS PUBLICATION 2113)

1. TRUSSES. I. LUXFORD, R.F. II. TITLE.

VF
690.2
N17
no.3
Trusses.
National Association of Home Builders. Research Institute.
Small Homes Council 1-1/2 story truss for spans from 22'-8" to 28'-8". Washington, June 1953.
2 l. illus. (Operation trade secrets, report no. 3)

Lee Frankl, consultant. Processed.

1.Trusses. 2.Illinois. University. Small Homes Council. I.Frankl, Lee. II.Title. III.Ser.

690.24
S72
Trusses.
Stern, E George.
Trussed rafters. Wash., Society of American Military Engineers, 1960.
114-116p.

Reprinted from The Military engineer, March - April, 1960.

1. Roofs and roofing. 2. Trusses. I. Military engineer. II. Title.

691.11
F67MO
TRUSSES.
U.S. FOREST PRODUCTS LABORATORY, MADISON, WIS.
MOISTURE CYCLING OF TRUSSED RAFTER JOINTS, BY THOMAS LEE WILKINSON. MADISON, WIS., 1966.
38P. (U.S. FOREST SERVICE RESEARCH PAPER FPL 67)

1. WOOD. 2. TRUSSES. 3. MOISTURE. I. WILKINSON, THOMAS LEE. II. TITLE: TRUSSED RAFTER JOINTS.

VF
690.2
N17
no.2
Trusses.
National Association of Home Builders. Research Institute.
Trussed rafter construction as used by NAHB members. Washington, Mar. 1953.
8 l. illus. (Operation trade secrets, report no. 2)

Lee Frankl, consultant. Processed.

1.Trusses. I.Frankl, Lee. II.Title. III.Ser.

VF
690.248
S77
Trusses.
Structural Engineers Association of Southern California.
Horizontal bracing systems in buildings having masonry or concrete walls. [Los Angeles, Calif.] 1949.
[3] p. graph. (Its Technical bulletin no.1)

At head of title: Report of Special Committee.

1.Trusses. I.Title.

690.248
K18
Laf.
Trusses.
U.S. Naval Civil Engineering Laboratory, Port Hueneme, Calif.
Dynamic shear strength of reinforced concrete beams, by William A. Keenan and Richard H. Seabold. Port Hueneme, Calif., 1965, 1967.
2pts. (Its Technical report R 395 and R 502)
U.S. Defense Documentation Center. Defense Supply Agency [Documents] AD 627 661 and AD 644 823.
Distributed by U.S. Clearinghouse for Scientific and Technical Information.

(Cont'd on next card)

690.248
075
Trusses.
Oslo. Norges Byggforskningsinstitutt.
Frittbaerende tretakstoler [Wooden roof trusses] av Rolf Schjødt. Oslo, 1958.
75p. diagrs., tables. (Its Rapport nr. 25)

English summary: p. 74-75.

1. Trusses. I. Schjødt, Rolf. (Series)

658.564
S82
TRUSSES.
SUDDARTH, STANLEY K
A DIGITAL COMPUTER PROGRAM FOR ANALYSIS OF MEMBER STRESSES IN SYMMETRIC W TRUSSES, BY STANLEY K. SUDDARTH AND OTHERS. LAFAYETTE, IND., AGRICULTURAL EXPERIMENT STATION, 1964.
23P. (WOOD RESEARCH LABORATORY RESEARCH BULLETIN NO. 783)

1. AUTOMATION. 2. TRUSSES.

690.248
K18
U.S. Naval Civil Engineering Laboratory, Port Hueneme, Calif. Dynamic shear strength of reinforced concrete beams...1967. (Card 2)

1. Trusses. 2. Strength of materials. 3. Concrete, Reinforced. I. U.S. Defense Documentation Center. Defense Supply Agency. II. U.S. Clearinghouse for Federal Scientific and Technical Information. III. Keenan, William A. IV. Seabold, Richard H. V. Title.

691.328.2
W17
TRUSSES.
U.S. WATERWAYS EXPERIMENT STATION,
VICKSBURG, MISS.
DURABILITY AND BEHAVIOR OF
PRESTRESSED CONCRETE BEAMS,
PRETENSIONED CONCRETE INVESTIGATION,
PROGRESS TO JULY 1960. VICKSBURG,
MISS., 1961.
V. (ITS TECHNICAL REPORT NO.
6-570)
For Library holdings see main entry
BIBLIOGRAPHY: V. 1, P. 25.

1. CONCRETE, PRESTRESSED.
2. TRUSSES.

352.6
(76178)
T78
Trussville, Ala. City Planning Commission.
Trussville, Alabama: community facilities
plan. [Prepared for] Alabama State Planning
and Industrial Development Board. Trussville,
1961.
23p.

U.S. Urban Renewal Adm. UPAP.

1. Community facilities - Trussville, Ala.
I. U.S. URA-UPAP. Trussville, Ala.

332
A52tr
Trust business.
American Institute of Banking.
Trust business. New York [1946].
466p.

690.248
W17
TRUSSES.
U.S. WATERWAYS EXPERIMENT STATION,
VICKSBURG, MISS.
REVIEW OF THE LITERATURE PERTAINING
TO THE ANALYSIS OF DEEP BEAMS, BY G.E.
ALBRITTON. VICKSBURG, MISS., 1965.
80P. (ITS TECHNICAL REPORT NO.
1-701)

1. TRUSSES. 2. CONCRETE.
3. CONCRETE - BIBLIOGRAPHY.
I. ALBRITTON, G.E. II. U.S. DEFENSE
ATOMIC SUPPORT AGENCY. III. TITLE.

333.38
(76178)
T78
Trussville, Ala. City Planning Commission.
Trussville, Alabama: land subdivision regu-
lations. [In cooperation with] Alabama
State Planning and Industrial Development
Board. Trussville, 1959.
10p.

U.S. Urban Renewal Administration, Urban Planning
Assistance Program.

1. Subdivision regulation - Trussville, Ala. I. U.S.
URA-UPAP. Trussville, Ala.

332
(52)
T78
Trust Companies Association of Japan.
Trust banks in Japan. [Tokyo] [1969?]
20p.

..... Questionnaire; trust and banking
business, study team VII. [n.p.] 1969.
40p.

1. Banks and banking - Japan. 2. Trusts
and trustees - Japan I. Title.

624
:69
U76
Trusses.
Urquhart, Leonard Church
Civil engineering handbook. 3d ed. New
York, McGraw-Hill, 1950.
x, 1002 p. illus., diagrs., graphs, tables.

Bibliographies at end of chapters.

1.Strength of materials. 2.Trusses. 3.Cement.
4.Concrete construction. 5.Foundations. 6.Steel
construction. 7.Sewerage and sewage disposal.
8.Soils. 9.Water supply. 10.Airports. 11.Highways.
I.Title.

711.14
(76178)
T78
Trussville, Ala. City Planning Commission.
Trussville, Alabama: long range land use
plan. [In cooperation with] Alabama State
Planning and Industrial Development Board.
Trussville, 1959.
32p. maps.

U.S. Urban Renewal Administration, Urban Planning
Assistance Program.

1. Land use - Trussville, Ala. I. U.S. URA-
UPAP. Trussville, Ala.

332
A52t
Trust department services.
American Institute of Banking.
Trust department services. New York [1954].
486p.

690.248
V47
Trusses.
Virginia Polytechnic Institute. Wood
Research Laboratory.
All-nailed king-post trussed rafters of
18-40-ft. span. Blacksburg, Va. [1959?]
[14]p. diagrs.

1. Trusses.

711.74
(76178)
T78
Trussville, Ala. City Planning Commission.
Trussville, Alabama: major street plan.
[Prepared for] Alabama State Planning and
Industrial Development Board. Trussville,
1960.
25p.

U.S. Urban Renewal Adm. UPAP.

1. Street planning - Trussville, Ala.
I. U.S. URA-UPAP. Trussville, Ala.

LAW
Trust indenture act of 1939 and general rules and
regulations thereunder as in effect
August 1, 1958.
U.S. Securities and Exchange Commission.
Trust indenture act of 1939 and general
rules and regulations thereunder as in
effect August 1, 1958. Washington, Govt.
Print. Off., 1958.
35p.

1. Securities. I. Title.

624.043
V51
TRUSSES.
VLASOV, VASILII ZAKHAROVICH.
BEAMS, PLATES AND SHELLS ON ELASTIC
FOUNDATIONS, BY V.Z. VLASOV AND N.N.
LEONT'EV. TRANSLATED FROM THE RUSSIAN
BY A. BAROUCH. JERUSALEM, ISRAEL
PROGRAM FOR SCIENTIFIC TRANSLATIONS,
1966.
357P.

PUBLISHED FOR THE NATIONAL
AERONAUTICS AND SPACE
ADMINISTRATION... AND THE NATIONAL
SCIENCE FOUNDATION.
BIBLIOGRAPHY: P. 347-353.
(CONTINUED ON NEXT CARD)

351.712
(76178)
T78
Trussville, Ala. City Planning Commission.
Trussville, Alabama: public works program.
[Prepared for] Alabama State Planning and
Industrial Development Board. Trussville,
1961.
15p.

U.S. Urban Renewal Adm. UPAP.

1. Public works - Trussville, Ala.
I. U.S. URA-UPAP. Trussville, Ala.

Trust Territory of the Pacific Islands.

see

Pacific Islands (Ter.)

624.043
V51
VLASOV, VASILII ZAKHAROVICH. BEAMS...
1966.
(CARD 2)

1. STRAINS AND STRESSES.
2. TRUSSES. 3. STRUCTURAL
ENGINEERING. I. TITLE.
II. LEONT'EV, N.N.

711.5
(76178
:347)
T78
Trussville, Ala. City Planning Commission.
Trussville, Alabama: zoning ordinance.
[In cooperation with] Alabama State Planning
and Industrial Development Board. Trussville, 1959.
22p. map.

U.S. Urban Renewal Administration, Urban Planning
Assistance Program.

1. Zoning legislation - Trussville, Ala. I. U.S.
URA-UPAP. Trussville, Ala.

327
UN
Trusteeship Council.

United Nations. (Trusteeship Council)
Rules of procedure of the Trusteeship Council
(as amended up to and during its twenty-second
session) New York, 1958.
20p. (T/1Rev.5)

1. Trusteeship Council.

690.248
W45
TRUSSES.
Wilkinson, Thomas Lee.
Longtime performance of trussed rafters:
initial evaluation. Madison, Wis., Forest
Products Laboratory, 1968.
12p. (U.S. Forest Service. Research
paper FPL 93)

1. Trusses. 2. Loads. I. U.S. Forest
Products Laboratory, Madison, Wis. II. Title.

332
(52)
T78
Trust banks in Japan.
Trust Companies Association of Japan.
Trust banks in Japan. [Tokyo] [1969?]
20p.

..... Questionnaire; trust and banking
business, study team VII. [n.p.] 1969.
40p.

1. Banks and banking - Japan. 2. Trusts
and trustees - Japan. I. Title.

362.6
T78
U. S. Board of Trustees of the Federal
Old-Age and Survivors Insurance Trust
Fund.
Report of the Board of Trustees of the
Federal Old-Age and Survivors Insurance
Trust Fund and the Federal Disability
Insurance Trust Fund, 18-22,25
Washington, Govt. Print. Off., 1958-62,65
6 v. annual (85th Cong. 2d session.
House. Doc. no. 401-   )

(Continued on next card)

362.6
T78
U.S. Board of Trustees of the Federal Old-Age
and Survivors Insurance Trust Fund.   Report
of the Board of Trustees ... (Card 2)

For complete information see shelf list.

1. Old age. 2. Social security. I.Title:
Disability Insurance Trust Fund. II. U.S. Congress. House. Committee on Ways and Means.

351.1
J25
Trusted leaders; perceptions of appointed
    Federal officials.
Jennings, M Kent.
    Trusted leaders: perceptions of appointed
Federal officials , by M.K. Jennings and
others. Washington, Brookings Institution,
1967.
    368-384p.   (Brookings Institution.
Reprint no. 126)
    Reprinted from the Public opinion quarterly,
v. 30, Fall 1966.

    1. Federal civil service. 2. Political
science. I. Brookings Institution, Washington,
D.C. II. Title.   III. Title. Appointed
Federal   officials.

LAW
T
A52
L184re
TRUSTS AND TRUSTEES - U.S.
American law institute.
    Restatement of the law of restitution : quasi contracts and
constructive trusts, as adopted and promulgated by the
American law institute at Washington, D. C., May 8, 1936.
St. Paul, American law institute publishers, 1937.
    xxv, 1033 p.   23½ cm.
    W. A. Seavey, reporter for pt. I, A. W. Scott, reporter for pt. II.
    "Notes" inserted in pocket on inside of back cover.
    CONTENTS.—pt. I. The right to restitution (quasi contractual and
kindred equitable relief)—pt. II. Constructive trusts and analogous
equitable remedies.

    (Continued on next card)
    38—6448
    [50g1]

LAW
T
A52
L184re
TRUSTS AND TRUSTEES - U.S.
American law institute.   Restatement of the law of resti-
tution ... 1937. (Card 2)
  —— Notes on certain important sections of Restatement of
restitution, by the reporters Warren A. Seavey and Austin
W. Scott. St. Paul, American law institute publishers, 1937.
    ix, 208 p.   22½ cm.

    1. Quasi contracts—U. S. 2. Trusts and trustees—U. S. 3. Unjust
enrichment—U. S. 4. Equitable remedies—U. S.   I. Seavey, Warren
Abner, 1880–   II. Scott, Austin Wakeman, 1884–   III. Title.
IV. Title: Restitution, Restatement of the law of.

    38—6448
Library of Congress   [50g1]

LAW
T
A52
L184TR
2D
TRUSTS AND TRUSTEES.
AMERICAN LAW INSTITUTE.
    RESTATEMENT OF THE LAW, SECOND:
TRUSTS 2D, AS ADOPTED AND PROMULGATED
BY THE AMERICAN LAW INSTITUTE AT
WASHINGTON, D.C., MAY 23, 1957. ST.
PAUL, 1959.
    3 V.

    1. TRUSTS AND TRUSTEES.

LAW
T
A52
L184tr
TRUSTS AND TRUSTEES - U.S.
American law institute.
    Restatement of the law of trusts, as adopted and promul-
gated by the American law institute at Washington, D. C.,
May 11, 1935 ... St. Paul, American law institute publishers, 1935.
    2 v.   23½ cm.
    Paged continuously.
    To the end that the bench and bar of each state may be apprised
of any local variations, the state bar associations, with the assistance
of members of local school faculties and other experts, are producing
state annotations for their respective states in the various subjects
undertaken for restatement. cf. Introd.

    1. Trusts and trustees—U. S.   I. Title.

    35—30986
Library of Congress   [49m1]

TRUSTS AND TRUSTEES - U.S.
Bogert, George Gleason, 1884–
    The law of trusts and trustees; a treatise covering the law
relating to trusts and allied subjects affecting trust creation
and administration, with forms, by George Gleason Bogert ... Kansas City, Mo., Vernon law book company; St.
Paul, Minn., West publishing co. [*1935–49]
    8 v. [*25 cm.
    Vols. 1 to 6 paged continuously.
    Kept up to date by pocket supplements.

    1. Trusts and trustees—U. S. 2. Trusts and trustees—Gt. Brit.
3. Forms (Law)—U. S.

    35—6016
Library of Congress   [48m1]

LAW
T
B63
1959–66
TRUSTS AND TRUSTEES.
BOGERT, GEORGE GLEASON.
    THE LAW OF TRUSTS AND TRUSTEES; A
TREATISE COVERING THE LAW RELATING TO
TRUSTS AND ALLIED SUBJECTS AFFECTING
TRUST CREATION AND ADMINISTRATION,
WITH FORMS, BY GEORGE C. BOGERT AND
GEORGE T. BOGERT. 2D ED. KANSAS
CITY, MO., VERNON LAW BOOK CO.,
1959–66.
    16 V.

    1. TRUSTS AND TRUSTEES.   I. BOGERT,
GEORGE TAYLOR, JT. AU.

LAW
T
C165LA
TRUSTS AND TRUSTEES.
CAPLAN, OSCAR S
    THE LAW OF LAND TRUSTS. 2D ED.
MIAMI, FLA., CENTRAL BANK AND TRUST
CO., 1958.
    111P.

    1. TRUSTS AND TRUSTEES.   I. TITLE:
LAND TRUSTS.

360
N17t
Trusts and trustees.
National Foundation of Health, Welfare and
Pension Plans.
    Textbook for welfare, pension trustees, and
administrators; eleventh annual conference, San
Francisco, 1965. Elm Grove, Wis., 1965.
    593p.   (vol. 7)

    1. Social welfare. 2. Insurance. 3. Public
health. 4. Pensions. 5. Trusts and trustees.
I. Title.

LAW
T
S267LA
TRUSTS AND TRUSTEES.
SCOTT, AUSTIN WAKEMAN, 1884–.
    THE LAW OF TRUSTS. 3D ED. BOSTON,
LITTLE, BROWN, 1967.
    6 V.

    1. TRUSTS AND TRUSTEES.

LAW
U.S.
Trusts and trustees — U.S.
U.S. Library of Congress. Legislative Reference Service.
    Congress and the monopoly problem, fifty-six
years of antitrust development, 1900-1956.
History of Congressional action in the antitrust field since 1900, prepared at the in-
stance and under the direction of the Chairman
of the Select Committee on Small Business,
House of Representatives, Eighty-fourth Congress pursuant to H. Res. 114. Washington,
Govt. Print. Off., 1957.
    662p.

    (Continued on next
    card)

LAW
U.S.
U.S. Library of Congress. Legislative Ref-
erence Service. Congress...1957.
    (Card 2)

    At head of title: 85th Cong., 1st sess.
House. Document no. 240.

    1. Trusts and trustees - U.S.   I. Title.

TRUSTS AND TRUSTEES - GT.BRIT.
Bogert, George Gleason, 1884–
    The law of trusts and trustees; a treatise covering the law
relating to trusts and allied subjects affecting trust creation
and administration, with forms, by George Gleason Bogert ... Kansas City, Mo., Vernon law book company; St.
Paul, Minn., West publishing co. [*1935–49]
    8 v. [*25 cm.
    Vols. 1 to 6 paged continuously.
    Kept up to date by pocket supplements.

    1. Trusts and trustees—U. S. 2. Trusts and trustees—Gt. Brit.
3. Forms (Law)—U. S.

    35—6016
Library of Congress   [48m1]

332
(52)
T78
TRUSTS AND TRUSTEES - JAPAN.
Trust Companies Association of Japan.
    Trust banks in Japan. [Tokyo] [1969?]
20p.

    ... ... Questionnaire; trust and banking
business, study team VII. [n.p.] 1969.
40p.

    1. Banks and banking - Japan. 2. Trusts
and trustees - Japan. I. Title.

332.3
C657
1968
H-R
Truth in lending act.
U.S. Congress. House. Committee of
Conference.
    Consumer credit protection act; conference
report to accompany S.5. Washington, Govt.
Print. Off., 1968.
    32p. (90th Cong., 2d sess. House. Report
no. 1458)
    Short title: Truth in lending act.

    1. Credit. 2. Installment finance.
I. Title: Truth in lending act. II. Title.

336
C65t
1962
S-H
Truth in lending, 1962.
U.S. Congress. Senate. Committee on Banking
and Currency.
    Truth in lending, 1962. Hearings before a
subcommittee of the Committee on Banking and
Currency, United States Senate, Eighty-seventh
Congress, second session on S. 1740, a bill to
assist in the promotion of economic stabiliza-
tion by requiring the disclosure of finance
charges in connection with extensions of credit.
Washington, Govt. Print. Off., 1962.
    416p.
    Hearings held May 8-18, 1962.

    1. Finance. 2. Credit.   I. Title.

336
C65t
1963/64
S-H
Truth in lending, 1963-64.
U.S. Congress. Senate. Committee on
Banking and Currency.
    Truth in lending, 1963-64. Hearings be-
fore a subcommittee of the Committee on
Banking and Currency, United States
Senate, Eighty-eighth Congress, first
and second sessions on S. 750, a bill to
assist in the promotion of economic stabi-
lization by requiring the disclosure of
finance charges in connection with exten-
sions of credit. Washington, Govt. Print.
Off., 1964.
    2pts.   (Continued on
    next card)

336
C65t
1963/64
S-H
U.S. Congress. Senate. Committee on
Banking and Currency. Truth in lending,
1963-64. Hearings...1964. (Card 2)

    Financing charges and fees; a compila-
tion of material on consumer and housing
credit. p. 1195-1253.

    1. Finance. 2. Credit. I. U.S. Hous-
ing and Home   Finance Agency.
II. Title.   III. Title: Financing charges   and fees.

336
C65t
1967
S-H
Truth in lending - 1967.
U.S. Congress. Senate. Committee on
Banking and Currency.
    Truth in lending - 1967. Hearings before
the Subcommittee on Financial Institutions
of the Committee on Banking and Currency,
United States Senate, Ninetieth Congress,
first session, on S. 5, a bill to assist
in the promotion of economic stabilization
by requiring the disclosure of finance
charges in connection with extension of
credit. Wash., Govt. Print. Off., 1967.
    766p.
    Hearings held   April 13-May 10, 1967.
    1. Finance.   2. Credit. I. Title.

336
C65t
1961
S-H
Truth in lending bill.
U.S. Congress. Senate. Committee on Banking
and Currency.
    Truth in lending bill. Hearings before a
subcommittee of the Committee on Banking and
Currency, United States Senate, Eighty-seventh
Congress, first session on S. 1740 a bill to
assist in the promotion of economic stabiliza-
tion by requiring the disclosure of finance
charges in connection with extensions of credit.
Wash., Govt. Print. Off., 1961.
    1388p.
    Hearings held   July 17-27, 1961.

    1. Finance. 2. Credit.   I. Title.

333.33
A17

Truth in real estate lending.
Abraham, Joseph L
   Truth in real estate lending. New York,
Commerce Clearing House, 1970.
   299 p.

   1. Real estate business. 2. Consumer
protection. I. Title.

711.4
(74795)
O52
no. 1

Tryon and Schwartz and Associates.
   A preliminary report on land use and pop-
ulation, City of Olean, N.Y... For the City
Planning Board. Buffalo, 1958.
   50p. maps, tables. (Olean, N.Y. City Plan-
ning Board. Master plan report no. 1)
   U.S. Urban Renewal Administration, Urban
Planning Assistance Program.
   1. Master plan - Olean, N.Y. 2. Land use -
Olean, N.Y. 3. Population - Olean, N.Y.
I. Olean, N.Y.   City Planning Board.
II. U.S.   URA-UPAP.

711.552
(74736)
T79

Tryon and Schwartz and Associates.
   Proposed administrative (R-B) business
district. Supplementary report to the
future development plan, Village of Sidney,
N.Y. Prepared for the New York State Dept.
of Commerce. East Aurora, N.Y., 1960.
   [3]p.
   U.S. Urban Renewal Adm. UPAP.
   1. Business districts - Sidney, N.Y.
I. U.S. URA-UPAP. Sidney, N.Y.

362.6
H21pa
no. 10

Tryon, Arthur H
   A senior citizens service center. Washington, Dept. of Health, Education, and
Welfare, Special Staff on Aging, 1961.
   18p. (U.S. Dept. of Health, Education,
and Welfare. Special Staff on Aging.
Patterns for progress in aging. Case study
no. 10)

   1. Old age. 2. Recreation. I. U.S. Dept. of Health,
Education, and Welfare. (Special Staff on Aging)
(Series)

711.4
(74796)
L15
no. 1

Tryon and Schwartz and Associates.
   A preliminary report on land use and
population, Town of Lancaster, N.Y.
Prepared for the Town Planning Board.
Buffalo, 1959.
   39p. (Lancaster master plan report
no. 1)
   U.S. Urban Renewal Adm. UPAP.

   1. Master plan - Lancaster, N.Y. 2. Land use -
Lancaster, N.Y. 3. Population - Lancaster, N.Y.
I. Lancaster, N.Y.   Town Planning
Board. II. U.S.   URA-UPAP.
Lancaster, N.Y.

711.4
(74788)
T79

Tryon and Schwartz and Associates.
   Proposed comprehensive development plan.
Town of Perinton, N.Y. Prepared in coopera-
tion with the Town Planning Board. Buffalo,
1959.
   1v. diagrs., maps.
   U.S. Urban Renewal Administration, Urban
Planning Assistance Program.
   1. City planning - Perinton, N.Y.
I. Perinton, N.Y. Town Planning Board.
II. U.S. URA-UPAP.

33
(73)
L28
v.2

Tryon, Frederick Gale, 1892 - 1940, jt. au.
Nourse, Edwin Griswold, 1883-
   America's capacity to produce, by Edwin G. Nourse and
associates, Frederick G. Tryon, Horace B. Drury, Maurice
Leven, Harold G. Moulton, Cleona Lewis. Washington,
D. C., The Brookings institution, 1934.
   xiii, 608 p. diagrs. 21½ cm. (Half-title: The Institute of eco-
nomics of the Brookings institution ... Publication no. 55)
   Vol. 1 of "The distribution of wealth and income in relation to
economic progress." cf. Foreword.
   1. U. S.—Econ. condit.—1918-   2. Natural resources—U. S. 3.
U. S.—Indus. 4. Agriculture—U. S. 5. U. S.—Govt.   I. Tryon,
Frederick Gale, 1882-1940, joint author. II. Drury, Horace B—
joint author. III. Leven, Maurice, joint author. IV.
Moulton, Harold Glenn, 1883- joint author. V. Lewis, Cleona,
joint author. VI. Title. VII. Brookings Institution.
                       34—20234
   Library of Congress   HC106.3.D55 vol. 1
                [a51w7]   330.973

711.4
(74796)
L15
no. 3

Tryon and Schwartz and Associates.
   A preliminary report on schools and
recreation, Town of Lancaster, N.Y.
Prepared for the Town Planning Board.
Buffalo, 1959.
   32p. (Lancaster master plan report
no. 3)
   U.S. Urban Renewal Adm. UPAP.

   1. Master plan - Lancaster, N.Y. 2. Schools -
Lancaster, N.Y. 3. Recreation - Lancaster, N.Y.
I. Lancaster, N.Y.   Town Planning
Board. II. U.S.   URA-UPAP.
Lancaster, N.Y.

711.4
(74783)
T79

Tryon and Schwartz and Associates.
   Proposed development plan, City of Hornell,
N.Y. Prepared for City Planning Board.
Buffalo, 1958.
   39p. diagrs., maps, tables.
   U.S. Urban Renewal Administration, Urban
Planning Assistance Program.
   1. City planning - Hornell, N.Y.
I. Hornell, N.Y. City Planning Board.
II. U.S. URA-UPAP.

2525

TRYON AND SCHWARTZ AND ASSOCIATES.
JAMESTOWN, N.Y. PLANNING COMMISSION.
COMPREHENSIVE PLAN. BY TRYON AND
SCHWARTZ AND ASSOCIATES AND OTHERS.
JAMESTOWN, N.Y., 1967.
   1 V. (HUD 701 REPORT)

   1. MASTER PLAN - JAMESTOWN, N.Y.
I. TRYON AND SCHWARTZ AND ASSOCIATES.
II. HUD. 701. JAMESTOWN, N.Y.

711.4
(74795)
O52
no. 2

Tryon and Schwartz and Associates.
   A preliminary report on traffic and park-
ing, City of Olean, N.Y. For the City
Planning Board. Buffalo, N.Y., 1959.
   52p. diagrs., maps. (Olean, N.Y. City
Planning Board. Master plan rept. no. 2)
   U.S. Urban Renewal Administration, Urban
Planning Assistance Program.
   1. Master plan - Olean, N.Y. 2. Transporta-
tion - Olean, N.Y. I. Olean, N.Y. City
Planning Board.   II. U.S. URA-UPAP.

711.4
(74795)
O52p

Tryon and Schwartz and Associates.
   Proposed development plan, City of
Olean, N.Y. Prepared for City Planning
Board. East Aurora N.Y., 1959.
   1v.
   U.S. Urban Renewal Adm. UPAP.
   1. Master plan - Olean, N.Y. I. Olean,
N.Y. City Planning Board. II. U.S.
URA-UPAP. Olean, N.Y.

711.4
(74857)
B71

Tryon and Schwartz and Associates.
   Comprehensive plan study. [Prepared
in cooperation with] Harland Bartholomew
and Associates, City Planning Commission
of Bradford, Township of Bradford, [and]
Township of Foster, Pa. East Aurora,
N.Y., 1963.
   1v.
   U.S. Urban Renewal Adm. UPAP.
   1. Master plan - Bradford, Pa. 2. Master plan -
Foster, Pa.   I. Bradford, Pa.
City Planning   Commission.
II. Bartholomew and   Associates. III. U.S.
URA-UPAP. Bradford,   Pa.

711.4
(74796)
L15
no. 2

Tryon and Schwartz and Associates.
   A preliminary report on trafficways,
Town of Lancaster, N.Y. Prepared for the
Town Planning Board. Buffalo, 1959.
   27p. (Lancaster master plan report
no. 2)
   U.S. Urban Renewal Adm. UPAP.

   1. Master plan - Lancaster, N.Y. 2. Traffic -
Lancaster, N.Y. I. Lancaster, N.Y. Town Planning
Board. II. U.S.   URA-UPAP.
Lancaster, N.Y.

5376

TRYON AND SCHWARTZ AND ASSOCIATES.
WELLSVILLE, N.Y. TOWN PLANNING BOARD.
PROPOSED DEVELOPMENT PLAN, TOWN AND
VILLAGE OF WELLSVILLE, N.Y. PREPARED BY
TRYON AND SCHWARTZ AND ASSOCIATES, INC.
EAST AURORA, N.Y., 1962.
   88P. (HUD 701 REPORT)

   1. CITY PLANNING - WELLSVILLE, N.Y.
I. WELLSVILLE, N.Y. VILLAGE PLANNING
COMMISSION. II. TRYON AND SCHWARTZ AND
ASSOCIATES. III. HUD. 701.
WELLSVILLE, N.Y.

330
(74736)
T79

Tryon and Schwartz and Associates.
   Economy of the area. Supplementary
report to the future development plan,
Village and Town of Sidney, N.Y.
East Aurora, N.Y., 1960.
   16p.
   Prepared for the New York State Dept.
of Commerce.
   U.S. Urban Renewal Adm. UPAP.
   1. Economic conditions - Sidney, N.Y. I. U.S.
URA-UPAP. Sidney, N.Y.

711.4
(74751)
T79

Tryon and Schwartz and Associates.
   Preliminary reports on: basic studies,
traffic circulation and major street plan,
recreation plan, proposed development plans,
Village of Lake George and Town of Caldwell,
N.Y. Prepared for the Joint Planning Boards,
Village of Lake George, Town of Caldwell.
Buffalo, 1958.
   62p. diagrs., maps, tables. (Master plan
reports no. 1, 2, 3, and 4)

               (Continued on next card)

711.4
(74796)
T79

Tryon and Schwartz and Associates.
   Proposed development plan, Town of Eden,
N.Y. Prepared for Town Planning Board.
Buffalo, 1958.
   33p. diagrs., maps.
   U.S. Urban Renewal Administration, Urban
Planning Assistance Program.

   1. City planning - Eden, N.Y. I. Eden, N.Y. Town
Planning Board. II.   U.S. URA-UPAP. Eden,
N.Y.

711.4
(74736)
T79

Tryon and Schwartz and Associates.
   A joint planning program, Village and Town
of Sidney, New York. Prepared for the joint
planning boards, Village and Town of Sidney,
New York. Buffalo, N.Y., 1959.
   1v. diagrs., maps, tables.
   U.S. Urban Renewal Administration, Urban
Planning Assistance Program.
   1. City planning - Sidney, N.Y. I. Sidney,
N.Y. Planning Board. II. U.S. URA-UPAP.

711.4
(74751)
T79

Tryon and Schwartz and Associates. Prelimi-
nary reports ... 1958. (Card 2)
   U.S. Urban Renewal Administration, Urban
Planning Assistance Program.

   1. City planning - Lake George, N. Y.
   2. City planning - Caldwell, N. Y.
I. Joint Planning Boards, Lake George and
Caldwell. N. Y. II. U.S. URA-UPAP.

711.4
(74796)
T79pr

Tryon and Schwartz and Associates.
   Proposed development plan, Town of
Lancaster, N.Y. Prepared for Town Plan-
ning Board. Buffalo, 1959.
   113p.
   U.S. Urban Renewal Adm. UPAP.
   1. City planning - Lancaster, N.Y.
I. Lancaster, N.Y. Town Planning Board.
II. U.S. URA-UPAP. Lancaster, N.Y.

711.4
(74798)
T79
    Tryon and Schwartz and Associates.
      Proposed development plan, Town of Levis-
ton, New York. Prepared for Town Planning
Board. Buffalo, 1959.
      1v. diagrs., maps.
      U.S. Urban Renewal Administration, Urban
Planning Assistance Program.
      1. City planning - Leviston, N.Y.
I. Leviston, N. Y. Town Planning Board.
II. U.S. URA-UPAP.

333.38
(74794)
T79
    Tryon and Schwartz and Associates.
      Proposed subdivision regulations, Village
of Govanda, N.Y. Prepared for Village Planning Board. Buffalo, 1958.
      24p.

      Addendum to proposed development plan.
      U.S. Urban Renewal Administration, Urban
Planning Assistance Program.

      1. Subdivision regulation - Govanda, N.Y. I. Govanda,
N.Y. Village Planning Board. II. U.S. URA-UPAP.
Govanda, N.Y.

058.7
(794)
T79
    Trzyna, Thaddeus C   ed.
      The California handbook; a comprehensive
guide to sources of current information
and action, with selected background
material, and compiled and edited by
Thaddeus C. Trzyna and William Shank.
Claremont, Center for California Public
Affairs, 1969.
      300p.

      1. Directories - Calif. 2. Bibliography -
Calif. I. Shank, William, jt. ed.
II. Center for   California Public
Affairs,   Claremont, Calif.
III. Title.

711.4
(74796)
E17
no.4
    Tryon and Schwartz and Associates.
      Proposed development plan, Village of East
Aurora, N.Y. Buffalo, N.Y., 1959.
      86p. diagrs., maps, tables. ([East Auro-
ra, N. Y. Village Planning Commission]
Master plan rept. no. 4)
      U.S. Urban Renewal Administration, Urban
Planning Assistance Program.
      1. Master plan - East Aurora, N. Y. I.
East Aurora, N.Y. Village Planning Commis-
sion. II. U.S. URA-UPAP.

5377
    TRYON AND SCHWARTZ AND ASSOCIATES.
WELLSVILLE, N.Y. TOWN PLANNING BOARD.
PROPOSED ZONING ORDINANCE. PREPARED BY
TRYON AND SCHWARTZ AND ASSOCIATES, INC.
EAST AURORA, N.Y., CA. 1963.
      1 V. (HUD 701 REPORT)

      1. ZONING LEGISLATION - WELLSVILLE, N.Y.
I. TRYON AND SCHWARTZ AND ASSOCIATES.
II. HUD. 701. WELLSVILLE, N.Y.

670
(79454)
T71
    Tsagris, B   E
      Changing pattern of industrialization,
land use, and values: Sacramento metropolitan
area, 1950-1961, by B.E. Tsagris and Robert
K. Coe. [Sacramento] California Division of
Real Estate, 1962.
      174p.

      1. Industry - Sacramento metropolitan area.
2. Land use - Sacramento metropolitan area.
I. Coe, Robert K.   II. California.
Division of   Real Estate.

711.4
(74794)
T79
    Tryon and Schwartz and Associates.
      Proposed development plan, Village of
Govanda, N.Y. Prepared for Village
Planning Board. Buffalo, 1958.
      44p. maps.

      U.S. Urban Renewal Administration, Urban
Planning Assistance Program.

      1. City planning - Govanda, N.Y. I. Govanda, N.Y.
Village Planning Board. II. U.S. URA-UPAP. Govanda,
N.Y.

333.38
(74834)
T79
    Tryon and Schwartz & Associates.
      Subdivision regulations, Township of
Foster, Pennsylvania. Preliminary report.
[Prepared in cooperation with] Harland
Bartholomew and Associates. [n.p., 1963?]
      19p.
      U.S. Urban Renewal Adm. UPAP.

      1. Subdivision regulation - Foster, Pa. I. Foster,
Pa. Ordinances, etc. II. Bartholomew (Harland)
and Associates. III. U.S. URA-UPAP. Foster,
Pa.

308
:728.1
(79454)
T71
    Tsagris, B   E
      Housing market analysis, Sacramento
metropolitan area, 1962-1965, by B.E.
Tsagris and others. Sacramento, Calif.,
Real Estate Research Bureau, Sacramento
State College, 1963.
      175p.

      1. Housing market analysis - San
Francisco metropolitan area. I. California.
State College,   Sacramento.
Real Estate   Research Bureau.

711.4
(74751)
T79p
    Tryon and Schwartz and Associates.
      Proposed development plan, Village of
Lake George and Town of Caldwell, N.Y. For
the Joint Planning Boards, Village of Lake
George, Town of Caldwell. Buffalo, N.Y.,
1959.
      61p. maps, tables.

      U.S. Urban Renewal Administration, Urban
Planning Assistance Program.
      1. City planning - Lake George, N.Y. 2.
City planning - Caldwell, N.Y. I. Joint
planning   Boards, Lake George and
Caldwell, N.Y. II. U.S. URA-UPAP.

711.4
(74796)
E81
    Tryon and Schwartz and Associates.
      Town of Evans, N.Y. comprehensive plan
study. [Prepared for the New York State
Department of Commerce and Evans Planning
Board] East Aurora, N.Y., 1963.
      1v.
      Cover title.
      U.S. Urban Renewal Adm. UPAP.

      1. Master plan - Evans, N.Y. I. Evans,
N.Y. Planning Board. II. U.S. URA-UPAP.
Evans, N.Y.

711.4
T71
    Tsagris, B   E
      Urban growth and development; an urban econo-
mist's viewpoint. Fullerton, California State
College, School of Business Administration and
Economics, 1971.
      150p.

      Bibliography: p. 147-150.

      1. City growth. 2. Urban renewal. 3. City
planning. I. California. State College,
Fullerton. II. Title.

333.38
(74783)
T79
    Tryon and Schwartz and Associates.
      Proposed subdivision regulations, City of
Hornell, New York. Prepared for City Planning Board. Buffalo, 1958.
      24p.

Addendum to proposed development plan.
U.S. Urban Renewal Administration, Urban Planning
Assistance Program.

      1. Subdivision regulation - Hornell, N.Y. I. Hor-
nell, N.Y. City Planning Board. II. U.S. URA-UPAP.
Hornell, N.Y.

711.5
(74834)
T79
    Tryon and Schwartz and Associates.
      Zoning. Preliminary report. [Prepared
in cooperation with] Harland Bartholomew
and Associates and Pennsylvania Bureau of
Community Development. East Aurora, N.Y.,
1962.
      [90]p. (Rept. no. 6)
      U.S. Urban Renewal Adm. UPAP.

      1. Zoning - Foster, Pa.
I. Bartholomew (Harland) and Associates.
II. U.S. URA-UPAP. Foster, Pa.

711.5
(791)
F18
    Tsaguris, John S.
    Faure, Andre M
      The nature of zoning as an instrument of
planning and orderly development; a summary
of the history, changing conditions, emerging
patterns, and features of good zoning with
special reference to its application in
Arizona. Compiled and edited by Andre M.
Faure and John S. Tsaguris. [1960]
      30p.

      1. Zoning - Ariz. I. Tsaguris, John S.
II. Title.

333.38
(74796)
T79
    Tryon and Schwartz and Associates.
      Proposed subdivision regulations, Town
of Eden, N.Y. Prepared for Town Planning
Board. Buffalo, 1958.
      26p.

      Addendum to proposed development plan.
      U.S. Urban Renewal Administration, Urban
Planning Assistance Program.

      1. Subdivision regulation - Eden, N.Y. I. Eden,
N.Y. Town Planning Board. II. U.S. URA-UPAP.
Eden, N.Y.

699.81
N17R
1962
    Tryson, George H   ed.
    National Fire Protection Association.
      Fire protection handbook, edited by
George H. Tryson. 12th ed. Boston,
1962.
      1v.

      1. Fire prevention. I. Tryson, George H.,
ed.

728.1
(529)
T71
    Tsai, Ten-pi.
      Possible means for improvement of housing
condition in Taiwan. [Washington] Agency
for International Development, 1962.
      58p.
      Program planning: Office of International
Housing, Housing and Home Finance Agency, U.S.A.

      1. Housing - Taiwan. I. U.S. Agency for
International Development. II. U.S. Housing
and Home Finance Agency, Office of the Adminis-
tor, Office of   International Housing.

711.4
(74796)
E17
no. 4
addend.
    Tryon and Schwartz and Associates.
      Proposed subdivision regulations, Village
of East Aurora, N.Y. Buffalo, N. Y., 1959.
      24p. (East Aurora, N.Y. Village Plan-
ning Commission. Master plan rept. no. 4,
addendum)
Addendum to proposed development plan.
U.S. Urban Renewal Administration, Urban
Planning Assistance Program.
      1. Master plan - East Aurora, N. Y. 2. Subdivision
regulation - East Aurora   N. Y. I. East Aurora,
N.Y. Village Planning   Commission. II. U.S.
URA-UPAP.

699.81
N17h
1969
    Tryson, George H   ed.
    National Fire Protection Association.
      Fire protection handbook. Edited by
George H. Tryson. 13th ed. Boston, 1969.
      1v.

      1. Fire prevention. I. Tryson, George H.,
ed. II. Title.

VF
711.583
(764)
T71
    Tsanoff, Corrinne S
      How the residents of a housing project
in Houston have been roused into working
together for neighborhood improvement.
Washington, Govt. Print. Off., 1964.
      179-182p.
      Reproduced by the U.S. Dept. of Health,
Education, and Welfare, Welfare Administration, Children's Bureau, from Children.
Sept.-Oct. 1964.

      1. Neighborhood planning - Houston. 2. Com-
munity de-   velopment - Citizen
participation.

VF
029
T25

Tschantre, Maurice Albert.
[Tennessee Valley Authority. (*Office of Chief Conservation Engineer. Division of Chemical Engineering*)
Preparation of research and engineering reports, by M. A. Tschantre [chief, Administrative Section] Wilson Dam, Ala., 1950.

33 l. illus. 28 cm.

Bibliography: leaf 22-23.

Report
1. Technical writing. I. Tschantre, Maurice Albert. II. Title.
2. Engineering research.
T11.T37   651.78   51-60422
Library of Congress   [2]

728.1
(758231)
T72

Tschappat, Carl J
Housing the underhoused in Atlanta, Georgia, by Carl J. Tschappat and Joe M. Lee, III. Prepared for Housing, Real Estate, and Urban Land Studies Program, Graduate School of Business Administration, University of California, Los Angeles. Sponsored by Life Insurance Association of America. Atlanta, Dept. of Real Estate and Urban Affairs, School of Business Administration, Georgia State University, 1970.
261p.

(Cont'd on next card)

728.1
(758231)
T72

Tschappat, Carl J   Housing the...1970.
(Card 2)

Bibliography: p. 259-261.

1. Housing – Atlanta. 2. Housing market – Atlanta. I. Georgia. State University, Atlanta. Dept. of Real Estate and Urban Affairs. II. Lee, Joe M., jt. au. III. Title.

624.131
T72

TSCHEBOTARIOFF, GREGORY P
SOIL MECHANICS, FOUNDATIONS, AND EARTH STRUCTURES; AN INTRODUCTION TO THE THEORY AND PRACTICE OF DESIGN AND CONSTRUCTION. NEW YORK, MCGRAW-HILL, 1957.
655P.

2c

1. SOILS. 2. FOUNDATIONS (BUILDING) I. TITLE.

VF
352
(51)
T78

Tsung-huang, Li.
Local government in the Republic of China. Taipei, Taiwan (Formosa) Local Government Association of the Republic of China, 1961.
50p.
Participant in attendance at World Conference on Local Governments in Wash., D. C., 1961.

1. Local government – China. 2. Local Government Association of the Republic of China. I. World Conference of Local Governments, Washington, D. C., 1961.

388
E28b

Tube Transit Corp.
Edwards, L   K
Baseline system definition: urban gravity-vacuum-transit, by L.K. Edwards and R.E. Skov, Tube Transit Corporation. Silver Spring Md., Applied Physics Laboratory, Johns Hopkins University, 1968.
1v. (Johns Hopkins University. Applied Physics Laboratory. Contractor report. BFM-097)
1. Transportation. 2. Transportation – Research. I. Johns Hopkins University. Applied Physics Laboratory. II. Tube Transit Corp. III. Skov, R.E., jt. au. IV. Title.

388
T81

Tube Transit, inc.
Gravity-vacuum transit system as presented at EXPO '67. Palo Alto, Calif., 1967.
1v.

1. Transportation. 2. Journey to work. I. Title.

388
T81t

Tube Transit, inc.
Tube Transit, inc. presents gravity-vacuum transportation (GVT) [n.p.] 1965.
51p.

1. Transportation. 2. Journey to work. I. Title: Gravity-vacuum transportation (GVT)

VF
711.4
(41)
T81

Tubbs, Ralph
Living in cities. Harmondshire, Middlesex, Eng., Penguin Books, 1942.
51 p. illus., plans.

A sequel to the exhibition "Living in Cities" which the author designed for the 1940 Council and the British Institute of Adult Education.

1. City planning – United Kingdom.

614
K25

TUBERCULOSIS.
KENDRICK, MILDRED A
THE RELATIONSHIP OF HOUSING TO TUBERCULOSIS IN MUSCOGEE COUNTY, GEORGIA. ABSTRACT OF A DISSERTATION...CATHOLIC UNIVERSITY OF AMERICA. WASHINGTON, CATHOLIC UNIVERSITY OF AMERICA PRESS, 1957.
33P. TABLES. (CU STUDIES IN SOCIOLOGY, ABSTRACT SERIES V. 4)

1. TUBERCULOSIS. 2. HOUSING AND HEALTH. I. TITLE.

614
P6lar

Tuberculosis.
U.S. Public Health Service.
Areawide planning of facilities for tuberculosis services. Report of the Joint Committee of the National Tuberculosis Association, Public Health Service. Wash., U.S. Dept. of Health, Education, and Welfare, Public Health Service, 1963.
46p. (Its Publication no. 930-B-4)
Bibliography: p. 45-46.

1. Tuberculosis. 2. Public health. I. National Tuberculosis Association.

711.4
(74727)
T82

Tuckahoe, N. Y. Planning Board.
Brown and Anthony.
Tuckahoe, New York master plan. Submitted to the Dept. of Commerce of the State of New York and the Village of Tuckahoe Planning Board. New York, 1960.
87p. maps, tables.

U.S. Urban Renewal Administration, Urban Planning Assistance Program.

1. Master plan – Tuckahoe, N. Y. I. Tuckahoe, N. Y. Planning Board. II. U.S. URA-UPAP. Tuckahoe, N. Y.

728.2
N17G

TUCKER, CHARLES.
NATIONAL ASSOCIATION OF HOME BUILDERS.
GUIDE LINES TO SUCCESSFUL ADVERTISING AND PROMOTION IN MULTIFAMILY HOUSING, BY CHARLES TUCKER. WASHINGTON, 1968.
43P.

A PUBLICATION OF THE COMPENDIUM OF MULTIFAMILY HOUSING.

1. APARTMENT HOUSES. 2. RENTAL HOUSING. I. TUCKER, CHARLES. II. TITLE.

659
T82

Tucker, Charles.
Guidelines to successful advertising and promotion in multifamily housing. A publication of the compendium of multifamily housing. Rev. Wash., National Association of Home Builders, 1970.
60p.

1. Advertising. 2. Apartment houses. 3. Rental housing. I. National Association of Home Builders. II. Title.

711
(016)
C65
no.42

Tucker, Dorothy.
Computers and information systems in planning and related governmental functions. [Nashville] Tennessee State Planning Commission, 1968.
21p. (Council of Planning Librarians. Exchange bibliography no. 42)

1. Planning – Bibl. 2. Planning – Automation – Bibl. 3. Automation – Bibl. I. Tennessee. State Planning Commission. II. Title. (Series: Council of Planning Librarians. Exchange bibliography no. 42)

628.4
T25

Tucker, Dorothy.
Tennessee. State Planning Commission.
Sanitary services in Tennessee, by Dorothy Tucker. Nashville, 1963.
66p. (Its Publication no. 326)

1. Sanitation. 2. Sewerage and sewage disposal – Tennessee. 3. Water-supply – Tennessee. I. Tucker, Dorothy.

628.4
T25
1965

Tucker, Dorothy.
Tennessee. State Planning Commission.
Sanitary services in Tennessee, by Dorothy Tucker. Nashville, 1965.
70p. (Its Publication no. 339)

1. Sanitation. 2. Sewerage and sewage disposal – Tennessee. 3. Water-supply – Tennessee. I. Tucker, Dorothy.

362.6
(797)
T82

TUCKER, ELIZABETH LAMBERTY.
PERSONNEL TIME IN NURSING HOMES OF WASHINGTON STATE, BY ELIZABETH L. TUCKER AND MILDRED A. SNYDER. WASHINGTON, GOVT. PRINT. OFF., 1958.
85-95P.

REPRINT OF ARTICLE IN PUBLIC HEALTH SERVICE, PUBLIC HEALTH REPORTS, JANUARY 1958.

1. NURSING HOMES – WASHINGTON (STATE) I. TITLE.

711.585
(74811)
T82

Tucker, George J
Philadelphia Community Renewal Program. Phase 1, months 1-30 progress report. Philadelphia, Community Renewal Program, 1965.
40p. (Community Renewal Program. Technical report no. 15)
U.S. Urban Renewal Adm. CRP.

2c

1. Urban renewal – Philadelphia. 2. Economic base studies – Philadelphia. I. Philadelphia. Community Renewal Program. II. U.S. URA-CRP. Philadelphia. [ ]

352.1
(747)
T82

Tucker, Gilbert M
The self-supporting city. New York, Robert Schalkenbach Foundation, c1946.
108 p.

1. Municipal finance – New York. I. Robert Schalkenbach Foundation. II. Title.

Tucker, J. Oliver, 1891- ed.
Alaska (Ter.) *Laws, statutes, etc.*
Compiled laws of Alaska, 1949, containing the general laws of the Territory of Alaska, annotated with decisions of the district courts of Alaska, the Circuit Court of Appeals and the Supreme Court of the United States. Pub. under authority of ch. 28, SLA, 1947. Ralph J. Rivers, Frank A. Boyle [and] Norman C. Banfield, Alaska Law Compilation Commission. J. Oliver Tucker, editor in chief. San Francisco, Bancroft-Whitney Co., 1948]
2 v. (clv, 2759 p.) 25 cm.
To be kept up to date by pocket supplements.
1. Alaska (Ter.) Law Compilation Commission. II. Tucker, J. Oliver, 1891- ed.

49-14253*

Library of Congress   [2]

628.2
A52t
no.8

Tucker, L.S.
American Society of Civil Engineers.
    Availability of rainfall runoff data
for sewered drainage catchments, by L.S.
Tucker. New York, 1969.
    43p. (ASCE Urban Water Resources Research
Program. Technical memo. no. 8)

    1. Drainage. I. Tucker, L.S.
II. Title.

325.2
T82

C.1, E.O.

Tucker, Sterling.
    Black reflections on white power. Grand
Rapids, Mich., William B. Eerdmans, 1969.
151p.

    1. Race relations. I. Title.

727
(791)
T82

Tucson, Ariz. City-County Planning Dept.
    Flowing Wells District 8, school plan,
1964-68. Tucson, Ariz., 1964.
    26p.

    1. Schools - Tucson, Ariz. 2. School
management and organization. I. Title.

628.2
T82

Tucker, L S
    Availability of rainfall-runoff data for
several drainage catchments. New York,
American Society of Civil Engineers, 1969.
    43p. (ASCE urban water resources research
program. Technical memorandum no. [3?]

    CFSTI. PB 184 703.

    1. Drainage. I. American Society of Civil
Engineers. II. Title.

Tucson, Ariz.

VF:
Industrial location - Ariz.
Economic conditions-Ariz.
Industrial Location-Ariz.

027
(791)
T82

Tucson, Ariz. City-County Planning Dept.
    1970 library plan; prepared by the City-
County Planning Department in cooperation
with the Tucson Public Library. Tucson,
Ariz., 1964.
    61p.

    Bibliography: p. 60-61.

    1. Libraries - Tucson, Ariz. I. Tucson,
Ariz. Public Library. II. Title.

628.2
A52t
no.9

Tucker, L.S.
American Society of Civil Engineers.
    Raingage networks in the largest cities,
by L.S. Tucker. New York, 1969.
    90p. (ASCE Urban Water Resources
Research Program. Technical memo. no.
9)

    1. Drainage. I. Tucker, L.S.
II. Title.

712
(791)
T82
1967

Tucson, Ariz. City-County Planning Dept.
    Population study, 1967; Tucson standard
metropolitan statistical area. Tucson, Ariz.,
1967.
    30p.

    1. Population - Tucson, Ariz. 2. Pop-
ulation - Pima Co., Ariz. I. Title.

Tucson, Ariz. Office of the Mayor.
    Action program, 1st
1970-

    see Its

City of Tucson Model Cities Program, pt. 2.

628.2
A52t
no.10

Tucker, L.S.
American Society of Civil Engineers
    Sewered drainage catchments in major
cities, by L.S. Tucker. New York, 1969.
    72p. (ASCE Urban Water Resources
Research Program. Technical memo. no.
10)

    1. Drainage. I. Tucker, L.S.
II. Title.

711.4
(791)
T82r

Tucson, Ariz. City-County Planning Dept.
    Report; planning achievements in 19 60
Tucson, Ariz., 1961

    / v. annual.

    For complete information see main card.

    1. City planning - Tucson, Ariz.
    2. County planning - Pima Co., Ariz.

711.585.1
(791)
T 82

Tucson, Ariz. Office of the Mayor.
    City of Tucson Model Cities Program,
comprehensive city demonstration program.
Tucson, Ariz., 1970.
    210p.
    U.S. Dept. of Housing and Urban
Development. Model Cities Program.

    1. Model cities - Tucson, Ariz.
    2. Master plan - Tucson, Ariz.
    I. U.S. HUD. Model Cities Program.

711.585
(77866)
T82

Tucker, Minnie H
    Community resources, how to use them. A
manual for volunteer community leaders, collected and comp. by Minnie H. Tucker.
St. Louis, Urban League, 1958.
    33p.

    1. Neighborhood planning - St. Louis. 2. Com-
munity development - Citizen participation.
3. Neighborhood rehabilitation - Citizen
participation.

727.1
(791)
T82

Tucson, Ariz. City-County Planning Dept.
    School building plan, 1957-1960.
Tucson District No. 1. Tucson, 1957.
    [20] p. charts, plans.

    1. Schools - Arizona. I. Title.

711.585.1
(791)
T82m

Tucson, Ariz. Office of the Mayor.
    Mid-planning statement, 1970-
Tucson, Ariz., 1970-
    v.
    U.S. Dept. of Housing and Urban
Development. Model Cities Program.

    1. Model Cities - Tucson, Ariz.
    I. U.S. HUD. Model Cities Program.

711.585
T82

TUCKER, ROSS F
    PLANNING FOR HOUSING. A PAPER
PRESENTED AT THE 21ST ANNUAL
CONFERENCE, MASSACHUSETTS FEDERATION
OF PLANNING BOARDS. CAMBRIDGE, 1934.
15P.

    1. SLUMS. 2. HOUSING.

727.1
(791)
T82

Tucson, Ariz. City-County Planning Dept.
    Tucson public schools (District no. 1)
a plan for school locations; proposed part
of the master plan for the city of Tucson
and Pima County, Arizona. Tucson, 1955.
    20 p. illus., tables.

    1. Schools - Tucson, Ariz. 2. Schools -
Pima County, Ariz.

711.585
(791)
T82w

Tucson, Ariz. Office of the Mayor.
    A workable program for urban renewal
in the City of Tucson, Arizona, December
1958-59. Tucson, 1958.
    33p.

    1. Workable program - Tucson, Ariz.

325
T82b

Tucker, Sterling.
    Beyond the burning: life and death of the
ghetto. New York, Association Press, 1968.
    160p.

c.1, E.O.

    1. Negroes. 2. Minority groups - Housing.
I. Title.

712.21
(791)
P45

Tucson, Ariz. City Planning Division.
    Pima County, Ariz. Planning Dept.
    Concept, sketch plan; regional parks plan.
Tucson, Ariz., 1967.
    18p.

    1. Parks - Tucson, Ariz. I. Tucson, Ariz.
City Planning Div.

027
(791)
T82

Tucson, Ariz. Public Library.
    Tucson, Ariz. City-County Planning Dept.
    1970 library plan; prepared by the City-
County Planning Department in cooperation
with the Tucson Public Library. Tucson,
Ariz., 1964.
    61p.

    Bibliography: p. 60-61.

    1. Libraries - Tucson, Ariz. I. Tucson,
Ariz. Public Library. II. Title.

711.585
(791) Tucson, Ariz. Urban Renewal Staff.
T82   History of slum clearance and redevelopment programs in the City of Tucson,
Arizona, Old Pueblo District, Project no.
Ariz. R-6. Tucson, 1959.
22p.

1. Urban renewal - Tucson, Ariz.
2. Slum clearance - Tucson, Ariz.

711.552.1   TUCSON SHOPPING CENTER STUDY.
F47T   FIRST NATIONAL BANK OF ARIZONA.
TUCSON SHOPPING CENTER STUDY; A
SURVEY OF SHOPPING CENTER
DEVELOPMENTS AND THE CENTRAL
BUSINESS DISTRICT OF GREATER TUCSON.
PHOENIX, 1963.
52P.

1. SHOPPING CENTERS.   I. TITLE.

330
(58)   Tudor Engineering Co.
T82   Development of Helmand Valley, Afghanistan.
Washington, 1956.
203p. maps.

Prepared for International Cooperation
Administration.

1. Economic development - Afghanistan.
2. Irrigation. I. U.S. International
Cooperation Administration.

388
(791)   Tucson Area Transportation Planning Agency.
T82   Tucson Area Transportation Study: Vol. 1.
Inventory and analysis of existing conditions,
1960. Vol.2. Forecasts and the plan 1965.
Sponsoring agencies, City of Tucson, County
of Pima, State of Arizona in cooperation
with U.S. Dept. of Commerce, Bureau of Public
Roads. Tucson, Ariz., 1965.
2v.
Cover title on v.2. Forecasts and plans,
1980.

(Cont'd on next card)

979.1   Tucson, sunshine city in the desert.
A74   Arizona Highways.
Tucson, sunshine city in the desert.
Phoenix, 1958.
[40] p. illus.

Arizona Highways, February 1958.

1.City growth - Tucson, Ariz.
I.Title.

711.73
(75281)   Tuemmler (Fred W.) and Associates.
T82   Access control study; new U.S.
Columbia Pike [Route] 29. [Prepared
in cooperation with the] Maryland State
Roads Commission, and Howard County,
Maryland, Planning Commission.
Hyattsville, Md., 1960.
37p.
Cover title.

1. Highways - Howard Co., Md. 2. Highways -
Maryland. I. Howard Co., Md. Planning
Commission.

388
(791)   Tucson Area Transportation Planning Agency.
T82   Tucson Area Transportation Study...1965.
(Card 2)

1. Transportation - Tucson, Ariz. 2. Trans-
portation - Research. 3. Highways - Tucson,
Ariz. 4. Land use - Tucson, Ariz. I. U.S.
Bureau of Public Roads. II. Title.

711
(016)   Tudor, Dean.
C65   Planning-programming-budgeting
no.121   systems. [Toronto] Ontario Dept.
of Revenue, 1970.
19p. (Council of Planning Librarians.
Exchange bibliography no. 121)

1. Planning - Bibl. 2. Management -
Bibl. 3. Budget - Bibl. 4. Public
administration - Bibl. I. Ontario. Dept.
of Revenue. II. Title. (Series: Council
of Planning Librarians. Exchange
bibliography   no. 121)

711.4
(74755)   Tuemmler (Fred W.) and Associates.
A57   Economic factors for planning in the Altamont-
no. 1   Tupper Lake, N.Y. region. [In cooperation with
the] Altamont-Tupper Lake, New York, Regional
Planning Board [and] New York (State) Dept. of
Commerce. College Park, Md., 1962.
37p. (Comprehensive plan rept. no. 1)
U.S. Urban Renewal Adm. UPAP.

1. Master plan - Altamont-Tupper Lake, N.Y.
I. Altamont-Tupper Lake, N.Y. Regional Planning
Board. II. U.S.   URA-UPAP.
Altamont - Tupper   Lake, N.Y.

388
(791)   Tucson Area Transportation Study.
T82   Tucson Area Transportation Planning Agency.
Tucson Area Transportation Study: Vol. 1.
Inventory and analysis of existing conditions,
1960. Vol.2. Forecasts and the plan 1965.
Sponsoring agencies, City of Tucson, County
of Pima, State of Arizona in cooperation
with U.S. Dept. of Commerce, Bureau of Public
Roads. Tucson, Ariz., 1965.
2v.
Cover title on v.2. Forecasts and plans,
1980.

(Cont'd on next card)

711
(016)   Tudor, Dean.
C65   Planning-programming-budgeting systems (A
no.183   supplement to Exchange Bibliography No. 121 of
March 1970) [Toronto] Ontario Dept. of Revenue,
1971.
5p. (Council of Planning Librarians. Exchange
bibliography no. 183)

1. Planning - Bibl. 2. Management - Bibl.
3. Budget - Bibl. 4. Public administration -
Bibl. I. Ontario. Dept. of Revenue. II. Title.
(Series: Council of Planning Librarians. Exchange bibliography no. 183)

711.4
(75291)   Washington County, Md. Planning and Zoning
W17   Commission.
no. 2   Economic survey, Washington County Maryland. Hagerstown, Md., 1960.
77p. maps, tables. (Its Master plan
report no. 2)

Prepared by Fred W. Tuemmler and Associates.
1. Master plan - Washington Co., Md. 2. Economic
base studies - Washington Co., Md. I. Tuemmler
(Fred W.) and Associates.

Tuemmler (Fred W) and Associates.

388
(791)   Tucson Area Transportation Planning Agency.
T82   Tucson Area Transportation Study...1965.
(Card 2)

1. Transportation - Tucson, Ariz. 2. Trans-
portation - Research. 3. Highways - Tucson,
Ariz. 4. Land use - Tucson, Ariz. I. U.S.
Bureau of Public Roads. II. Title.

711
(016)   Tudor, Dean   comp.
C65   Provincial-municipal relations in
no. 112   Canada. [Toronto] Ontario Dept. of
Revenue, 1970.
5p. (Council of Planning Librarians
Exchange bibliography no. 112)

1. Planning - Bibl. 2. Intergovernmental
relations - Canada - Bibl. 3. Municipal
government - Canada - Bibl. 4. State
government - Canada - Bibl. I. Ontario.
Dept. of Revenue. II. Title. (Series:
Council of   Planning Librarians.
(Cont'd on next card)

711.4
(75291)   Washington County, Md. Planning and Zon-
W17   ing Commission.
no.1   Population, past present, future, Washington County, Maryland. Hagerstown, Md.,
1959.
52p. diagrs., maps, tables. (Its Master
plan report no. 1)

Prepared by Fred W. Tuemmler and Associates.

1. Master plan - Washington Co., Md. 2. Population - Washington Co., Md. I. Tuemmler (Fred W.)
and Associates.

Tuemmler (Fred W) and Associates.

301.15   Tucson community goals.
(791)   Citizens' Committee on Community Goals,
C47   Tucson.
Tucson community goals. Tucson, 1966.
96p.

1. Community development - Tucson, Ariz.
I. Title.

711
(016)   Tudor, Dean   comp.   Provincial...
C65   1970. (Card 2)
no. 112

Exchange bibliography no. 112)

711.4
(75284)   Tuemmler (Fred W.) and Associates.
T82   Preliminary master plan for the Rock
Creek planning area. A plan for stream
valley protection and development. A proposed amendment to the general plan for the
physical development of the Maryland-
Washington Regional District. Prepared in
cooperation with Maryland-National Capital
Park and Planning Commission and Montgomery
County Planning Board. College Park, Md.,
1956.
80p.

(Cont'd on next card)

VP
711.585   Tucson Regional Plan, Inc.
(791)   Segoe, Ladislas
S23   Rehabilitation of blighted areas; conservation of sound neighborhoods. Prepared for the
Tucson Regional Plan, Inc., Ladislas Segoe,
Planning consultant, Andre M. Faure, Resident
planner. [Tucson?] 1942.
45 p.   tables.

Processed.
1.Neighborhood rehabilitation. I.Tucson Regional
Plan, Inc. II.Faure, Andre M. III.Title.

711
(016)   Tudor, Dean.
C65   Regional development and regional government
no.157   in Ontario. [Toronto] Ontario Dept. of Revenue
Library, 1970.
53p. (Council of Planning Libraries.
Exchange bibliography no. 157)

1. Planning - Bibl. 2. Economic development -
Ontario, Can. - Bibl. 3. Economic planning -
Ontario, Can. - Bibl. I. Ontario. Dept. of
Revenue. Library. II. Title. (Series: Council
of Planning Librarians. Exchange biblio-
graphy no. 157)

711.4
(75284)   Tuemmler (Fred W.) and Associates. Pre-
T82   liminary master plan for the Rock Creek
planning area.. 1966.
(Card 2)

1. Master plan - Maryland-Washington
Regional District 2. Regional planning -
Maryland-Washington Regional District.
I. Maryland. Maryland-National Capital
Park and Planning Commission. II. Mont-
gomery Co. Md. Planning Board
III. Title.

711.4
(75291)
W17
no.3

Tuemmler (Fred W.) and Associates.
Washington County, Md. Planning and
Zoning Commission.
Sanitary district study, Washington
County, Maryland. Hagerstown, Md.,
1961.
38p. (Its Master plan report no.
3)
Prepared in cooperation with Fred
W. Tuemmler and Associates.
1. Master plan - Washington Co., Md. 2. Sewerage
and sewage disposal - Washington Co., Md.
3. County planning -   Washington Co., Md.
I. Tuemmler (Fred W.)   and Associates.

711.73
(76335)
A52

Tulane University of Louisiana. School of
Architecture.
American Institute of Architects. (New
Orleans Chapter)
Study of the proposed riverfront and
Elysian Fields Expressway and an alternate
proposal, New Orleans. Conducted by the
School of Architecture, Tulane University,
New Orleans. Sponsored by the New Orleans
Chapter of the American Institute of
Architects and the WDSU Foundation. New
Orleans, Published under the sponsorship
of Urban America, inc., 1965.
25p.   (Continued on
next card)

728.1
:336.18
(79486)
T85
1949

TULARE COUNTY, CALIF. HOUSING
AUTHORITY.
ANNUAL REPORT, 1949-   VISALIA,
1949-
1 v.

FIRST REPORT ENTITLED CONSOLIDATED
ANNUAL REPORT, COVERS 1945-49.

1. PUBLIC HOUSING - TULARE COUNTY,
CALIF.

300.15
T83

Tufte, Edward R   ed.
The quantitative analysis of social
problems. Reading, Mass., Addison-Wesley,
1970.
449p. (Addison-Wesley series in
behavioral science: quantitative methods)

1. Social science research.
2. Statistics. I. Title.

711.73
(76335)
A52

American Institute of Architects. (New
Orleans Chapter) Study of the proposed
riverfront and Elysian fields expressway...1965.   (Card 2)

1. Highways - New Orleans.
2. Recreation - New Orleans. I. Tulane
University of Louisiana. School of
Architecture.

VF
333.38
T85
1949

Tulare County, Calif. Planning Commission.
Community subdivision practices, Tulare
County, California. Tulare Co., Calif., July
1949.
8 p.

1. Subdivision.

159.9
:62
T83

Tufts College. Institute for Applied Experimental
Psychology.
Handbook of human engineering data for design
engineers...prepared by Handbook Staff, Tufts
College, in cooperation with Technical Publications
Division, Jackson & Moreland, Engineers, for the
Special Services Center. Port Washington, N.Y.
U.S. Office of Naval Research, c1949.
1 v. (loose-leaf) diagrs., tables. (U.S.
Office of Naval Research. Technical report
no. SDC 199-1-1)

(Continued on next card)

720
(76335)
L25

Tulane University of Louisiana. School of
Architecture.
Lemann, Bernard.
The Vieux Carré; a general statement.
With a foreword by John W. Lawrence.
New Orleans, Tulane University, School of
Architecture, 1966.
91p.

1. Architecture - New Orleans. 2. Architecture - Conservation and restoration.
I. Lawrence, John W. II. Tulane University
of Louisiana. School of Architecture.
II. Title.

Ph file
DATE OF REQUEST March 9, 1951   MAR 26 1951   L.C. CARD NO.
AUTHOR Calif.
Tulare County Planning Commission.
TITLE
Planning Commission activities, 1949-50.
SERIES Visalia, Calif
EDITION   PUB. DATE 1950   PAGING 16
PUBLISHER same
RECOMMENDED BY   REVIEWED IN ASPO Newsltr. 1/51 pg.6
ORDER RECORD

Tufts College. Institute for Applied Experimental
Psychology. Handbook of human engineering
data for design engineers... c1949 (Card 2)

Bibliographies included.

1. Experimental psychology. I. U.S.Office of Naval
Research.Special Devices Center.Human Engineering
Branch. II. Jackson & Moreland, Engineers. Technical
Publications Bureau. III. Title: Human engineering
data for design engineers.

711.3
(76335
H17

Tulane University of Louisiana. Urban
Studies Center.
Harter, Carl L
Metropolitan New Orleans urban affairs bib-
liography, by Carl L. Harter and others.
New Orleans, Urban Studies Center, Tulane
University, 1969.
103p.

1. Metropolitan areas - New Orleans - Bibl.
I. Tulane University of Louisiana. Urban
Studies Center. II. Title.

DATE OF REQUEST 3/17/52   MAR 30 1952   C. CARD NO.
AUTHOR Tulare County, California. Planning Commission.
TITLE Preliminary population estimate for Tulare County,
California. 1950 -1980.
SERIES
EDITION   PUB. DATE 1952   PAGING 10 p.
PUBLISHER Same, 221 East Center St., Visalia, California.
RECOMMENDED BY   REVIEWED IN ASPO Newsletter 3/53, p. 24.
ORDER RECORD

Tufts University.
728.1
:336.18
(74461)
Y15

Yankelovich (Daniel) inc.
The Columbia Point Housing Project.
Description of a public housing population
in the urban North. Prepared for Dept.
of Preventive Medicine, Tufts University
School of Medicine. [Boston] 1966.
68p.

1. Public housing - Boston. 2. Population - Boston. 3. Housing - Social aspects.
I. Tufts University. II. Title.

711
(016)
C65
no.246

Tulane University of Louisiana. Urban Studies
Center.
Booher, David E
Poverty in an urban society: a bibliography
New Orleans, Tulane University, Urban Studies
Center, 1971.
32p. (Council of Planning Librarians. Ex-
change bibliography no. 246)
1. Poverty - Bibl. I. Tulane University of
Louisiana. Urban Studies Center. II. Title.
(Series: Council of Planning Librarians. Ex-
change bibliography no. 246)

House numbering
DATE OF REQUEST 3/17/52   APR 3 1952   L.C. CARD NO.
AUTHOR Tulare County, Calif. Planning Commission.
TITLE Road and house numbering system.
SERIES
EDITION   PUB. DATE 12/51   PAGING 9 p. map,
PUBLISHER   plans, charts.
same
RECOMMENDED BY   REVIEWED IN ASPO Newsltr 2/52 p. 16
ORDER RECORD

711
(7295)
T83

Tugwell, Rexford G
The place of planning in society. 2d ed.
Seven lectures on the place of planning in
society with special reference to Puerto
Rico. San Juan, Puerto Rico, 1958.
88p. (Puerto Rico Planning Board.
Technical paper 7)

1. Planning - Puerto Rico. I. Puerto
Rico. Planning Board.

Tulare, Calif.

VF
Parking.
House numbering.

711.4
(764)
T85
no.6

Tulia, Tex. City Planning Commission.
Koch & Fowler and Grafe, inc.
Tulia administrative regulations. [Pre-
pared for Texas State Department of Health
and Tulia City Planning Commission] Dallas,
1961.
62 p. (Its Comprehensive plan report 6)

U.S. Urban Renewal Adm. UPAP.

1. Master plan - Tulia, Tex. 2. Subdivision regulation - Tulia, Tex. 3. Zoning
legislation - Tulia, Tex. I. Tulia, Tex.
City Planning   Commission. II. U.S.
URA-UPAP.   Tulia, Tex.

720
(76335)
T85

Tulane University of Louisiana. School of
Architecture.
The mint. [New Orleans] 1971.
1v.

1. Architecture - New Orleans. I. Title.

Tulare County, Calif.

VF:
Population - Calif.

711.4
(764)
T85
no.5

Tulia, Tex. City Planning Commission.
Koch & Fowler and Grafe, inc.
Tulia capital improvement. [Prepared for
Texas State Department of Health and Tulia
City Planning Commission] [Dallas?] 1961.
23p. (Its Comprehensive plan report 5)

U.S. Urban Renewal Adm. UPAP.

1. Master plan - Tulia, Tex. 2. Capital
improvement programs - Tulia, Tex.
I. Tulia, Tex. City Planning Commission.
II. U.S. URA-   UPAP. Tulia, Tex.

711.4
(764)
T85
Summary

Tulia, Tex. City Planning Commission.
Koch & Fowler and Grafe, inc.
Tulia comprehensive plan 1980. [Summary
report. Prepared in cooperation with]
Texas State Department of Health.
[Prepared for Tulia City Planning Com-
mission] Dallas, 1961.
43p.

U.S. Urban Renewal Adm. UPAP.

1. Master plan - Tulia, Tex. I. Tulia,
Tex. City Planning Commission.
II. U.S. URA-UPAP. Tulia,
Tex.

330
(76864)
T85

Tullahoma, Tenn. Planning Commission. Economic survey of Tullahoma, ... (Card 2)

1. Economic base studies - Tullahoma,
Tenn. I. Tennessee. State Planning Commission. II. U.S. Urban Renewal Administration. Urban Planning Assistance
Program.

728.6
T85

TULLER, MARGARET H.
A FARMHOUSE TO FIT YOUR SITE.
CORVALLIS, COOPERATIVE EXTENSION WORK IN
AGRICULTURE AND HOME ECONOMICS, N.D.
6 L. (HE-7-303)

1. FARM HOUSING.

711.4
(764)
T85
no.4

Tulia, Tex. City Planning Commission.
Koch & Fowler and Grafe, inc.
Tulia facilities. [Prepared for Texas
State Department of Health and Tulia City
Planning Commission] Dallas, 1961.
27p. (Its Comprehensive plan report 4)

U.S. Urban Renewal Adm. UPAP.

1. Master plan - Tulia, Tex. 2. Community
facilities - Tulia, Tex. I. Tulia, Tex.
City Planning Commission. II. U.S. URA-
UPAP. Tulia, Tex.

711.14
(76864)
T85

Tullahoma, Tenn. Planning Commission.
Land use analysis of Tullahoma, Tennessee. Prepared by Tennessee State Planning Commission, Middle Tennessee Office.
Tullahoma, 1957.
12p. maps, tables. (MTO publication
no. 57-42)

U.S. Urban Renewal Administration,

(Continued on next card)

728.6
T851

TULLER, MARGARET H.
IS THIS A GOOD FARMHOUSE? CORVALLIS,
COOPERATIVE EXTENSION WORK IN
AGRICULTURE AND HOME ECONOMICS, N.D.
12L. (HE-302)

1. FARM HOUSING. I. OREGON. STATE
COLLEGE, CORVALLIS.

711.4
(764)
T85
no.2

Tulia, Tex. City Planning Commission.
Koch & Fowler and Grafe, inc.
Tulia land use. [Prepared for Texas State
Department of Health and Tulia City Planning
Commission] Dallas, 1960.
26p. (Its Comprehensive plan report 2)

U.S. Urban Renewal Adm. UPAP.

1. Master plan - Tulia, Tex. 2. Land use -
Tulia, Tex. I. Tulia, Tex. City Planning
Commission. II. U.S. URA-UPAP. Tulia, Tex.

711.14
(76864)
T85

Tullahoma, Tenn. Planning Commission.
Land use analysis of ... (Card 2)

Urban Planning Assistance Program.

1. Land use - Tullahoma, Tenn. I. Tennessee. State Planning Commission. II. U.S.
Urban Renewal Administration. Urban Planning Assistance Program.

728.1
T85Y

TULLER, MARGARET H.
YOUR FAMILY'S HOUSING NEEDS.
CORVALLIS, OREGON STATE COLLEGE AND U.S.
DEPT. OF AGRICULTURE, N.D.
9L. (HE7-302)

1. HOUSING. 2. FARM HOUSING.
I. OREGON. STATE COLLEGE, CORVALLIS.

711.4
(764)
T85
no.1

Tulia, Tex. City Planning Commission.
Koch & Fowler and Grafe, inc.
Tulia population. [Prepared for Texas
State Department of Health and Tulia City
Planning Commission] Dallas, 1960.
44p. (Its Comprehensive plan report 1)

U.S. Urban Renewal Adm. UPAP.

1. Master plan - Tulia, Tex. 2. Popula-
tion - Tulia, Tex. I. Tulia, Tex. City
Planning Commission. II. U.S. URA-UPAP.
Tulia, Tex.

711.581
(76864)
T85

Tullahoma, Tenn. Planning Commission.
Neighborhood analysis of Tullahoma,
Tennessee. Tullahoma, 1958.
56p. maps, tables.

U.S. Urban Renewal Administration, Urban
Planning Assistance Program.

1. Neighborhood planning - Tullahoma,
Tenn. I. U.S. URA-UPAP. Tullahoma,
Tenn.

330
T85

3c

Tullock, Gordon.
Private wants, public means; an economic
analysis of the desirable scope of government.
New York, Basic Books, 1970.
262p.

1. Economics. 2. Political science.
3. Municipal services. I. Title.

711.4
(764)
T85
no.3

Tulia, Tex. City Planning Commission.
Koch & Fowler and Grafe, inc.
Tulia thorofare. [Prepared for Texas State
Department of Health and Tulia City Planning
Commission] Dallas, 1961.
1v. (Its Comprehensive plan report 3)

U.S. Urban Renewal Adm. UPAP.

1. Master plan - Tulia, Tex. 2. Streets -
Tulia, Tex. 3. Highways - Tulia, Tex.
I. Tulia, Tex. City Planning Commission.
II. U.S. URA-UPAP. Tulia,
Tex.

352.1
(76864)
T85

Tullahoma, Tenn. Planning Commission.
Public improvements for Tullahoma, Ten-
nessee. Prepared by the Tennessee State
Planning Commission, Middle Tennessee Of-
fice. Tullahoma, 1957.
14p. tables. (MTO publication no. 57-46)
U.S. Urban Renewal Administration, Urban
Planning Assistance Program.

1. Capital improvement programs - Tullahoma,
(Continued on next card)

362.6
(771)
034

TULLY, JAMES K.
OHIO. LEGISLATIVE SERVICE COMMISSION.
NURSING HOME REGULATION, BY JAMES K.
TULLY. COLUMBUS, OHIO, 1965.
44P. (STAFF RESEARCH REPORT NO. 68)

1. NURSING HOMES - OHIO. 2. NURSING
HOMES - LAW AND LEGISLATION. I. TULLY,
JAMES K. II. TITLE.

711.4
(76864)
T85

Tullahoma, Tenn. Planning Commission.
Comprehensive plan. Tullahoma, Tenn.,
1957.
36p. maps, diagrs. (MTO Publication
no. 57-5)

"Assisted by Tennessee State Planning
Commission, Middle Tennessee Office."

1. Master plan - Tullahoma, Tenn.
I. Tennessee. State Planning Commission.

352.1
(76864)
T85

Tullahoma, Tenn. Planning Commission.
Public improvements ... (Card 2)

Tenn. 2. Municipal finance - Tullahoma,
Tenn. I. Tennessee. State Planning Commission. II. U.S. Urban Renewal Administration. Urban Planning Assistance
Program.

90
AUTHOR: *Tulsa (Okla.) Chamber of Commerce*
Library: OA-Hsg-U.S.-Okla.
TITLE: *1949 Tulsa housing survey.*
PLACE: *Tulsa*   PUBLISHER:
DATE: *5/49*   EDITION: PAGING: *12p. + 6 Tables*
DESCRIPTIVE NOTE AND SERIES: *Mimeo.*
ANNOTATION:
(OA-196)

330
(76864)
T85

Tullahoma, Tenn. Planning Commission.
Economic survey of Tullahoma, Tennessee.
Prepared by the Tennessee State Planning
Commission, Middle Tennessee Office. Tullahoma, 1957.
19p. diagrs., tables. (MTO publication
no. 57-47)

U.S. Urban Renewal Administration, Urban
Planning Assistance Program.
(Continued on next card)

Class No. Arch.-Dept Author (surname first) Tuller, Margaret H.
Des + plans -
Single family

Accession No.

Ordered
2/4/50
Source
Ltr
Received
APR 2 5 1950

Purchase Order No.

Date

L. C. No.

Title Corvallis, Extension Service -
Templates to test your house plan
Place Corvallis, Ore. Publisher Ore. State College
Address

Date 1950 Paging 13 p List Price Est. Cost gratus
Edition or Series

Recommended by

Reviewed in Check List of State Pub. March 50

VF
336.2
T85

Tulsa, Okla. Chamber of Commerce.
1966 survey of comparative tax rates of
141 American cities. Final report. Tulsa,
Okla., Dept. of Business Research, Chamber
of Commerce, 1966.
17p.

1. Taxation. 2. Municipal finance.
I. Title.

711.585.1
(766861)
T85
Tulsa, Okla. Office of the Mayor.
Application to the Department of
Housing and Urban Development for a grant
to plan a comprehensive city demonstration
program. Tulsa, Okla., 1967.
1v.
Selected to receive the first HUD Model
Cities Program planning grants.
1. Model cities - Tulsa, Okla. I. U.S.
HUD - Model Cities Program first planning
grants.

711.14
(766861)
T85L
2c
Tulsa, Okla. Metropolitan Area
Planning Commission.
Land use; a procedural manual for
collection, storage, and retrieval of
data. Tulsa, 1965.
1 v.
U.S. Urban Renewal Adm. UPAP.

1. Land use - Tulsa, Okla.
2. Automation. I. U.S. URA-UPAP.
Tulsa, Okla.

629.136
T85
Tulsa, Okla. Metropolitan Area Planning Commission.
1975 metropolitan Tulsa airports and their
relationship with surrounding land use. Tulsa,
1960.
36p. diagrs., tables.

1. Airports. 2. Land use - Tulsa, Okla.

711.73
:330
(766861)
R21
Tulsa, Okla. Metropolitan Area Planning Commission.
Real Estate Research Corp.
Analysis of economic effects of proposed
expressway system on business thoroughfares.
Prepared for Tulsa Metropolitan Area Planning Commission. Tulsa, 1957.
50p.

1. Highways - Economic effect - Tulsa,
Okla. I. Tulsa, Okla. Metropolitan Area
Planning Commission.

352.1
(766861)
T85L
Tulsa, Okla. Metropolitan Area Planning
Commission.
Legal basis of revenue for local govern-
ment. A supplement to 1975 metropolitan
Tulsa public financial capacity. Tulsa,
1961.
1v.

1. Municipal finance - Tulsa, Okla.
2. Taxation - Oklahoma. 3. Metropolitan
areas - Tulsa, Okla. I. Title.

711.552
(766861)
T85
Tulsa, Okla. Metropolitan Area
Planning Commission.
1975 metropolitan Tulsa commercial
land needs. Tulsa, Okla., 1959.
101p.

U.S. Urban Renewal Adm. UPAP.

1. Business districts - Tulsa, Okla.
2. Shopping centers. I. U.S. URA-UPAP.
Tulsa, Okla.

711.4
(76686)
815
Tulsa, Okla. Metropolitan Area Planning
Commission.
A comprehensive plan for the city of Sand
Springs, Oklahoma. [Prepared for Sand
Springs City Planning Commission] Tulsa,
Okla., 1964.
36p.
Prepared for Oklahoma Dept. of Commerce
and Industry.
U.S. Urban Renewal Adm. UPAP.

1. Master plan - Sand Springs, Okla.
I. Sand Springs, Okla.
City Planning Commission. II. U.S.
URA-UPAP. Sand Springs, Okla.

711.3
:538.56
M27m
Tulsa, Okla. Metropolitan Area Planning
Commission.
Metropolitan Data Center Project, Tulsa,
Okla.
Metropolitan Data Center Project. Tulsa,
1966.
112p.
Cooperating agencies: Tulsa Metropolitan
Area Planning Commission and others.
U.S. Urban Renewal Adm. Demonstration
Grant Program.

1. Metropolitan area planning - Automation.
I. U.S. Urban Renewal Adm. Demonstration
Grant Program. II. Tulsa, Okla.
Metropolitan Area Planning Commission.

711.4
(766861)
T85
Tulsa, Okla. Metropolitan Area Planning
Commission.
1975 metropolitan Tulsa effectuation of
the comprehensive plan. Tulsa, Okla.,
1960.
21p.
U.S. Urban Renewal Adm. UPAP.

1. Master plan - Tulsa, Okla. metropolitan area I. Title. II. U.S. URA-
UPAP. Tulsa, Okla.

711.4
(76625)
S44
Tulsa, Okla. Metropolitan Area Planning
Commission.
A comprehensive plan for the city of
Skiatook, Oklahoma. [Prepared in cooperation
with Skiatook City Planning Commission and
Oklahoma Department of Commerce and Industry,
the Tulsa County Commission] Tulsa, Okla.,
1964.
25p.
U.S. Urban Renewal Adm. UPAP.

1. Master plan - Skiatook, Okla. I. Skiatook, Okla.
City Planning Commission.
II. U.S. URA-UPAP. Skiatook, Okla.

711.3
(766861)
T85
Tulsa, Okla. Metropolitan Area Planning
Commission.
Metropolitan Tulsa, goals for growth.
Tulsa, 1958.
8p. illus.

1. Metropolitan area planning -
Tulsa, Okla.

711.14
(766861)
T85m
Tulsa, Okla. Metropolitan Area Planning
Commission.
1975 metropolitan Tulsa; industrial
land needs. Tulsa, 1958.
71p.

1. Land use - Tulsa, Okla.
2. Industrial districts - Tulsa, Okla.

711.3
(766861)
T85c
Tulsa, Okla. Metropolitan Area Planning
Commission.
Comprehensive plan, Tulsa metropolitan
area. Tulsa, 1960.
1v.
U.S. Urban Renewal Adm. UPAP.

1. Master plan - Tulsa, Okla. I. U.S.
URA-UPAP. Tulsa, Okla.

711.585
(766861)
T85
Tulsa, Okla. Metropolitan Area Planning
Commission.
Metropolitan Tulsa program for community
renewal. General development plan.
Tulsa, Okla., 1963.
[183]p.

1. Urban renewal - Tulsa, Okla.
2. Economic conditions - Tulsa, Okla.
3. Housing market - Tulsa, Okla.
4. Industrial location - Tulsa, Okla.
I. Title.

711.14
(766861)
T85
Tulsa, Okla. Metropolitan Area Planning
Commission.
1975 metropolitan Tulsa preliminary land
use plan. Tulsa, Okla., 1959.
folder. diagrs., maps.

1. Land use - Tulsa, Okla.

711.14
(766861)
T85i
Tulsa, Okla. Metropolitan Area Planning
Commission.
Industrial land use. Requirements and
site development standards in the Tulsa
metropolitan area, by Sherman Griselle.
A preliminary report. Tulsa, Okla.,
1958.
1v.
U.S. Urban Renewal Adm. UPAP.

1. Land use - Tulsa, Okla. 2. Industrial location -
Tulsa, Okla. I. Griselle,
Sherman. I. U.S. URA-UPAP. Tulsa,
Okla.

711.3
(766861)
T85m
Tulsa, Okla. Metropolitan Area Planning
Commission.
Metropolitan Tulsa residential land
needs. Statistical supplement, 1975.
Tulsa, Okla., 1960.
26p.
U.S. Urban Renewal Adm. UPAP.

1. Metropolitan area planning - Tulsa, Okla.
2. Land use - Tulsa, Okla. I. U.S.
URA-UPAP. Tulsa, Okla.

712.25
(766861)
T85
Tulsa, Okla. Metropolitan Area Planning
Commission.
1975 Metropolitan Tulsa; public
recreation land needs. Tulsa, 1960.
40p.

U.S. Urban Renewal Adm. UPAP.

1. Recreation - Tulsa, Okla. 2. Parks
- Tulsa, Okla. I. U.S. URA-UPAP. Tulsa,
Okla.

3944
TULSA, OKLA. METROPOLITAN AREA PLANNING
COMMISSION.
LAND DEVELOPMENT PROCEDURES. TULSA,
OKLA., 1965.
1 V. (HUD 701 REPORT)

1. LAND USE - TULSA METROPOLITAN AREA.
I. HUD 701. TULSA METROPOLITAN AREA.

627.4
(766861)
T85
Tulsa, Okla. Metropolitan Area Planning
Commission.
Metropolitan Tulsa; summary of flood
control studies and recommendations.
Prepared by Louis Levy, and Don Venhaus.
Tulsa, Okla., 1963.
30p.

U.S. Urban Renewal Adm. UPAP.

1. Flood control - Tulsa, Okla.
I. Levy, Louis.
II. Venhaus, Don. III. U.S.
URA-UPAP. Tulsa, Okla.

727.1
(766861)
T85
Tulsa, Okla. Metropolitan Area Planning
Commission.
1975 metropolitan Tulsa public school
needs. Tulsa, Okla., 1960.
48p.

1. Schools - Tulsa, Okla. 2. Land use -
Tulsa, Okla. metropolitan area.

711.3
(766861)
T85n

Tulsa, Okla. Metropolitan Area Planning
Commission.
1975 metropolitan Tulsa residential
land needs. Tulsa, Okla., 1959.
53p.

U.S. Urban Renewal Adm. UPAP.

1. Metropolitan area planning - Tulsa, Okla.
2. Land use - Tulsa, Okla. 3. Residential
areas. I. U.S. URA-UPAP. Tulsa, Okla.

690.091.82.
1613.5
(766861)
T85

TULSA, OKLA. ORDINANCES, ETC.
MINIMUM HOUSING CODE. TITLE 55
OF THE TULSA REVISED ORDINANCES.
AMENDED THROUGH MAY 1, 1964.
TULSA, OKLA., 1964.
1 V.

1. HOUSING CODES - TULSA, OKLA.

510
T85

Tuma, Jan J
Engineering mathematics handbook; definitions,
theorems, formulas, tables. New York, McGraw-
Hill, 1970.
334p.

Bibliography: p. 324-326.

1. Mathematics. 2. Engineering. I. Title.

352.1
(766861)
T85

Tulsa, Okla. Metropolitan Area Planning
Commission.
1975 Tulsa public financial capacity.
Tulsa, 1960.
192p.

U.S. Urban Renewal Adm. UPAP.

1. Municipal finance - Tulsa, Okla.
2. Metropolitan areas - Tulsa, Okla.
3. Local government - Tulsa, Okla.

Tulsa, Okla. Urban Renewal Authority.

711.552
(766861)
E75

Erling Helland Associates.
Downtown Tulsa; General neighborhood
renewal plan. [Prepared in cooperation
with] Tulsa Urban Renewal Authority.
Tulsa, Okla., 1964.
1v.

U.S. Urban Renewal Adm. GNRP.
1. Business districts - Tulsa, Okla.
2. Neighborhood rehabilitation - Tulsa,
Okla. I. Tulsa, Okla. Urban Renewal
Authority. II. U.S. URA-GNRP. Tulsa,
Okla.

624
T85

Tuma, Jan J
Schaum's outline of theory and problems
of structural analysis; with an introduction to transport, flexibility and stiffness matrices and their applications.
New York, McGraw-Hill, 1969.
292p. (Schaum's outline series)

Bibliography: p. 277-283.

1. Structural engineering. I. Title.

5742

TULSA, OKLA. METROPOLITAN AREA PLANNING
COMMISSION.
PROGRAM FOR ACTION, 1965-1975. TULSA,
OKLA., 1965.
1 V. (HUD 701 REPORT)

1. CITY PLANNING - TULSA, OKLA.
I. HUD 701. TULSA, OKLA.

711.585
(766861)
T85R

TULSA, OKLA. URBAN RENEWAL AUTHORITY.
REPORT 4?. 1963/64
TULSA.
1 V. ANNUAL

1. URBAN RENEWAL - TULSA, OKLA.

PC3/64

323.25
M85

Tumin, Melvin M   jt. au.
Mulvihill, Donald J
Crimes of violence a staff report submitted
to the National Commission on the Causes and
Prevention of Violence, by Donald J. Mulvihill
and Melvin M. Tumin. Wash., Govt. Print.
Off., 1969.
1597p. in 3pts. (v.11-13) (U.S. National
Commission on the Causes and Prevention of
Violence. Task force reports)
Numbers 11-13 on spine.
Report of the Task Force on Individual
Acts of Violence.

(Cont'd on next card)

711.3
(766861)
045

Tulsa, Okla. Metropolitan Area Planning
Commission.
Oklahoma. University. Institute of
Community Development.
A program for automatic tabulation of
basic data for the Tulsa metropolitan
area. Prepared for the Tulsa Metropolitan Area Planning Commission. Program
prepared by J. L. Rodgers, senior planner.
Norman, Okla., 1958.
25p.

1. Metropolitan area planning - Tulsa, Okla.
2. Automation.   I. Tulsa, Okla.
Metropolitan Area   Planning
Commission.

DATE OF REQUEST 1/2/53 JAN 28 1953   L. C. CARD NO.
AUTHOR Tulsa Co., Okla. Planning Commission.
TITLE Population. Its growth and distribution in Tulsa
County, (Report no. 2 [Basic data for Tulsa master
SERIES plan) 1907-1950.
EDITION | PUB. DATE 1952 SEPT. | PAGING 25 p.
PUBLISHER   graphs, tables.
same, 1212 South Frisco, Tulsa, Okla.   Processed.
RECOMMENDED BY   REVIEWED IN
                        TPO Newsltr 12/52 p.102
                    ORDER RECORD

323.25
M85

Mulvihill, Donald J   Crimes...1969.
                        (Card 2)

1. Civil disorders. 2. Law enforcement.
I. Tumin, Melvin M., jt. au. II. U.S.
National Commission on the Causes and
Prevention of Violence. Task Force on
Individual Acts of Violence. III. Title.

711.73
(766861)
W47

Tulsa, Okla. Metropolitan Area Planning
Commission.
Wise (Harold F.) Associates.
Sketch plan for Tulsa and five-mile
perimeter area. Report to the Tulsa
Metropolitan Area Planning Commission.
A part of Expressway Location Studies.
[Prepared] with the assistance of
Pate Engineering. Tulsa, Okla., 1956.
50p.

1. Highways - Tulsa metropolitan area.
I. Tulsa, Okla. Metropolitan Area Planning   Commission.

Class No.
VF
Population
-Okla.
Accession No.
Ordered
Source
Received
1-29-53
Cost
Purchase Order No.
Date
L. C. No.

Author (surname first)
Tulsa County, Okla. Planning
Commission.
Title
Population, its growth and
Place   Publisher
Address
Date 11/52 Paging 5p. Processed
                    List Price   Est. Cost
Edition or Series Planning Bulletin No. 8
Recommended by
Reviewed in
Distribution. Prepd on Report no. 1:
Basic Data for the Tulsa

H-305 (2-50) HOUSING AND HOME FINANCE AGENCY: Office of the Administrator 16-61197-1 GPO

301
T85
1965

TUMIN, MELVIN M   ED.
RESEARCH ANNUAL ON INTERGROUP RELATIONS
- 1965. PREPARED BY THE ANTI-DEFAMATION
LEAGUE OF B'NAI B'RITH. NEW YORK,
FREDERICK A. PRAEGER, 1966.
176P.

1. SOCIOLOGY. 2. MINORITY GROUPS.
3. RACE RELATIONS. I. ANTI-DEFAMATION
LEAGUE OF B'NAI B'RITH. II. TITLE.

711.3
(766861)
T85t

Tulsa, Okla. Metropolitan Area Planning
Commission.
Tulsa tomorrow. Tulsa, 1957.
8p. illus.

1. Metropolitan area planning -
Tulsa, Okla.

VF
690.43
T85

Tuma, Ing Jan
Wind stress analysis of one story bents by
new distribution factor. [Stillwater, Okla.]
Oklahoma Agricultural and Mechanical College,
May 1951.
71 p.   (Oklahoma Engineering Experiment
Station publication no. 80)

Processed.

1. Wind stress. I. Series.

301
T85
1966

Tumin, Melvin M ed.
Research annual on intergroup relations,
edited by Melvin M. Tumin and Cathy S. Green-
blat. A research study of the Anti-Defamation
League of B'nai B'rith. New York, Frederick A.
Praeger, 1966.
338p.
1. Sociology. 2. Minority groups. 3. Race
relations. 4. International relations. I. Green-
blat, Cathy S., jt. ed. II. Anti-Defamation
League of B'nai B'rith. III. Title.

690.091.82.
(766861)
T85

TULSA, OKLA. ORDINANCES, ETC.
BUILDING CODE, CITY OF TULSA,
OKLAHOMA. TULSA, OKLA., 1961.
1 V.

1. BUILDING CODES - TULSA, OKLA.

DATE OF REQUEST 12/29/54   L. C. CARD NO.
AUTHOR Tuma, Jan J. and Mervin T. Anderson.
TITLE Analysis of continuous beams by infinite series.
SERIES Anderson Steel research ser., report 3.
Publication #91.
EDITION | PUB. DATE 1954 | PAGING 117p. illus
PUBLISHER
RECOMMENDED BY   REVIEWED IN Mo. Checklist of
                    I'm1 State Pub., 12/54, p.410
                    ORDER RECORD

301
T85
1970

Tumin, Melvin M ed.
Research annual on intergroup relations -
1970. Chicago, Quadrangle Books, 1970.
310p.

c.1,Ref.

1. Sociology. 2. Minority groups. 3. Race
relations. I. Anti-Defamation League of B'nai
B'rith. II. Title.

301.15
(7295)
T85

Tumin, Melvin M
Social class and social change in Puerto Rico, by Melvin M. Tumin and Arnold S. Feldman. 2d ed. Indianapolis, Bobbs-Merrill, 1961.
549p.
Social Science Research Center Study, College of Social Sciences, University of Puerto Rico.
1. Community structure - Puerto Rico. 2. Social change. I. Puerto Rico. University. Social Science Research Center. II. Feldman, Arnold S., jr. III. Title.

711.73
(016)
T85

2c.

Tummins, Marvin.
Forecasting and estimating; a selected annotated bibliography with special emphasis on methodology (supplemented by a section of unannotated entries), by Marvin Tummins and William R. Trenor. Charlottesville, Va. Virginia Council of Highway Investigation and Research. In cooperation with the U.S. Bureau of Public Roads, 1961.
96p.
1. Highways - Bibliography. I. Trenor, William R., jt. au. II. Virginia   Council of Highway Investigation and   Research. III. U.S. Bureau of Public   Roads.

330
(611)
897

Tunisia.
Systems Research Corp.
Area handbook for the Republic of Tunisia, by Howard C. Reese and others. Prepared for the American University [Foreign Area Studies] Wash., Govt. Print. Off., 1970.
415p.
Bibliography: p. 381-401.
1. Economic conditions - Tunisia. I. Reese, Howard C. II. American University. Foreign Area Studies. III. Title. IV. Title: Tunisia.

VF
912
(611)
F71

Tunisia.
France. Office du Tourisme et de l'Expansion Commerciale.
Tunisie, par Magdelaine Farisot. [Paris] 1955.
217p.   maps.   (Les Guides bleus)
Le present ouvrage est un extrait du volume Algerie-Tunisie publie dans la collection Les Guides bleus.
1. Travel - Tunisia 2. Tunisia. I. Farisot, Magdelaine.

711.4
(861)
T85

Tunja, Colombia.
Plan piloto, Tunja 1958-1985. Prepared by Eduardo Mejia T., César Garces V., Alberto Mendoza M. [of the] Arquitectos Urbanistas Asociados. Bogota, Colombia, 1958.
81p.
1. City planning - Colombia. I. Arquitectos Urbanistas Asociados, Bogota, Colombia. II. Inter-American Housing and Planning Center. III. Title.

VF
711.585
(74811)
T85

Tunley, Roul.
Comeback of a shabby city. Old Philadelphia has been on a ten-year, $2,000,000,000 binge, restoring, rebuilding and generally recapturing the spirit of its elegant and dynamic youth. Detached from the Saturday Evening Post, Dec. 3, 1959. p. 32-35, 76-78.
1. Urban renewal - Philadelphia.

711.585
(74461)
T85

TUNLEY, ROUL.
TRAGEDY OF A VERTICAL SLUM. PHILADELPHIA, CURTIS PUB. CO., 1963.
5P.
REPRODUCED FROM THE SATURDAY EVENING POST, JUNE 29-JULY 6, 1963, P.89-93.
1. SLUMS - BOSTON. 2. PUBLIC HOUSING - BOSTON. I. TITLE.

301.15
T85a

2C

Tunnard, Christopher.
American skyline; the growth and form of our cities and towns, by Christopher Tunnard and Henry Hope Reed. New York, New American Library, 1956.
224p.   (Mentor MQ764)
1. City growth. 2. City planning - History. I. Reed, Henry Hope, jt. au. II. Title.

VF
301.15
T85

2c

Tunnard, Christopher
America's super-cities. Detached from Harper's Magazine, August 1958, p. 59-65.
1. City growth. I. Title. II. Harper's Magazine.

711.4
T85

2C

Tunnard, Christopher.
The city of man. 2d ed. New York, Scribner's, 1970.
424p.
Bibliography: p. 403-409.
1. City planning. 2. City planning - History. I. Title.

711.3
T85i

TUNNARD, CHRISTOPHER.
IMPROVING COMMUNITY APPEARANCE. NEW YORK, REGIONAL PLAN ASSOCIATION, 1962.
9L.
PAPER PRESENTED AT THE 17TH REGIONAL PLAN CONFERENCE, ROOSEVELT HOTEL, NEW YORK CITY, OCTOBER 10, 1962.
1. REGIONAL PLANNING.   2. CITY PLANNING.   I. REGIONAL PLAN ASSOCIATION.

711.3
T85

5C

Tunnard, Christopher.
Man-made America: chaos or control? An inquiry into selected problems of design in the urbanized landscape, by Christopher Tunnard and Boris Pushkarev. In association with Geoffrey Baker and others. With drawings by Philip Lin and Vladimir Pozharsky, and photographs by John Reed and Charles R. Schulze. New Haven, Yale University Press, 1963.
479p.   Keep all copies
Bibliography: p. 452-460.
(Cont'd. on next card)

711.3
T85

Tunnard, Christopher. Man-made America: chaos or control? An inquiry into selected problems...1963   (Card 2)
1. Regional planning. 2. City planning. 3. Landscape architecture. I. Pushkarev, Boris, jt. au.   II. Title.

711.3
T85m

3C.

Tunnard, Christopher.
The modern American city. Princeton, N.J., Van Nostrand, 1968.
191p.   (An anvil original)
Bibliography: p. 185-186.
1. City growth. 2. Architecture - History. I. Title.

624.043
B18

Tunnel.
Baudendistel, M
The effect of discontinuities on the stresses and strains in the ground behind a tunnel wall, by M. Baudendistel and others. Garston, Eng., Building Research Station, 197
[31]p. (Library communication no. 1603)
Translated from the German and reprinted from Rock Mechanics, 1970, (2), 17-40.
1. Strains and stresses. 2. Soils. I. U.K. Building Research Station. II. Title: Tunnel III. Title. (Series)

691.421
W17y

Tunnel.
Ward, W   H
Yielding of the ground and the structural behaviour of linings of different flexibility in a tunnel in London clay. Garston, Eng., Building Research Station, 1970.
[8]p. (U.K. Building Research Station. Current paper CP 34/70)
Reprinted from: Proceedings of the 7th International Conference on Soil Mechanics and Foundation Engineering, Mexico, 1969, Vol. III, pp. 320-325.
1. Clay. I. U.K. Building Research Station. II. Title: Tunnel. III. Title.

699.85
B62

Tunnel blast shelter.
Boegly, W   J
Conceptual design of a dual-use utility tunnel blast shelter for White Plains, N.Y., by W.J. Boegly, Jr. and others. Oak Ridge, Tenn., Oak Ridge National Laboratory, 1969.
67p. (ORNL-4362. UC-41-Health and Safety)
Prepared according to agreement between Office of Civil Defense and U.S. Atomic Energy Commission.
1. Protective construction. 2. Civilian defense. I. U.S. National Laboratory, Oak Ridge, Tenn. II. Title. III. Title: Tunnel blast shelter.

690
P17

Tunnel-driving methods.
Parker, Albert T
Planning and estimating underground construction. New York, McGraw-Hill, 1970.
300p.
Partial contents.-Conventional tunnel-driving methods and equipment.
1. Building industry. 2. Building construction - Estimates. I. Title. II. Title: Underground construction. III. Title: Tunnel-driving methods.

623
T36

Tunnel linings.
Thomas, H   S   H
The measurement of strain in tunnel linings using the vibrating-wire technique. Garston, Eng., Building Research Station, Ministry of Technology, 1966.
8p.   (U.K. Building Research Station. Building research current papers. Engineering series 34)
Reprinted from: Strain, 1966, vol. 2(July), p. 16-21.
1. Structural engineering. I. U.K. Building Research Station. II. Title. III. Title: Tunnel linings.

690.015
(485)
S82
R45
1970

Tunnel sealing.
Bergman, Sten G   A
Tunneltätning. Injekteringsmedels inträngning i sand och smala spalter (Tunnel sealing. Penetration of injection compound into sand and narrow cracks) av Sten G.A. Bergman et al. Stockholm, Statens Institut för Byggnadsforskning, 1970.
65p. (Rapport R45:1970)
English summary.
1. Building research - Sweden. 2. Adhesives. 3. Waterproofing. I. Stockholm. Statens Institut för Byggnadsforskning. II. Title: Tunnel sealing.

690.015
(485)
S82
R45
1970

Tunnel sealing. Penetration of injection compound into soil and narrow cracks.
Bergman, Sten G   A
Tunneltätning. Injekteringsmedel-inträngning i sand och smala spalter (Tunnel sealing. Penetration of injection compound into sand and narrow cracks, av Sten G.A. Bergman et al. Stockholm, Statens Institut för Byggnadsforskning, 1970.
65p. (Stockholm. Statens Institut för Byggnadsforskning. (Rapport R45:1970)
English summary.
1. Building research - Sweden. 2. Adhesives.
(Con't on next card)

690.015
(485)
S82
R45
1970

Bergman, Sten G A Tunneltätning...1970.
(Card 2)

3. Waterproofing. I. Stockholm. Statens
Institut för Byggnadsforskning. II. Title:
Tunnel sealing. Penetration of injection
compound into soil and narrow cracks.

620.1
T86

Tuomola, T
Koekuutioiden valmistus-, säilytys-ja
koetusteven sekä vesipitoisuuden veikutus
kevytbetonien lujuusarvoihin (The effect of
the test cube preparing, keeping and testing
procedure and of the cubes water content on
the strength values of light-weight concretes),
av T. Tuomola and S. Rønnikko. Helsinki,
State Institute for Technical Research, 1966.
119p. (Finland. State Institute for
Technical Research. Julkaisu 106 publication)
English summary.

(Cont'd on next card)

628.44
T87

Turbiville, Jack.
Garbage collection practices and financing
in Georgia municipalities, 1963. Atlanta,
1963.
39p. (Georgia Municipal Association. GMA
study number 63-1)

1. Refuse and refuse disposal. 2. Municipal
finance - Georgia. I. Title.

690
(016)
C74

Tunneling.
Cristy, G A
Tunneling: an annotated bibliography with
permuted-title and key-word index, by G.A.
Cristy and C.B. Brooks. Oak Ridge, Tenn.,
Director's Div., Civil Defense Research
Project, Oak Ridge National Laboratory, 1970.
269p. (ORNL-HUD-17; UC-38-engineering and
equipment)
Work supported by the Dept. of Housing and
Urban Development and the U.S. Atomic Energy
Commission under interagency agreement no.
IAA-H-2-69 AEC 40-155A-68.
Bibliography: p. 1-137.
(Cont'd on next card)

620.1
T86

Tuomola, T. Koekuutioiden valmistus-, säilytys-
je koetusteven sekä vesipitoisuuden veikutus
kevytbetonien lujuusarvoihin...1966.
(Card 2)

1. Strength of materials. 2. Concrete.
I. Finland. State Institute for Technical
Research. II. Rønnikko, S., jt.au.
III. Finland. State Institute for Technical
Research.

339.5
(79)
T87

Turck (F. B.) & Co.
A study of non-ferrous metal refining
opportunities in the Four Corners States
(Utah, Colorado, Arizona and New Mexico).
Prepared for U.S. Area Redevelopment Admin-
istration. Washington, U.S. Dept. of
Commerce, Area Redevelopment Administration,
For sale by the Supt. of Documents, Govt.
Print. Off., 1965.
246p.
1. Natural resources - Western States.
2. Industrial location - Western States.
I. U.S. Area Redevelopment
Administration.

690
(016)
C74

Cristy, G A Tunneling...1970.
(Card 2)

1. Building construction - Bibl. I. Brooks,
C.B., jt. au. II. U.S. Oak Ridge National
Laboratory. III. U.S. Dept. of Housing and
Urban Development. IV. Title.

728.1
1308
(762935)
T86

TUPELO, MISS. HOUSING AUTHORITY.
TUPELO HOUSING SURVEY, 1941.
TUPELO, MISS., HOUSING AUTHORITY,
1941.
29P.

1. HOUSING MARKET - TUPELO, MISS.

657
T87

Ture, Norman B
Accelerated depreciation in the United
States, 1954-60. New York, National Bureau
of Economic Research; distributed by
Columbia University Press, 1967.
238p. (National Bureau of Economic
Research. Fiscal studies 9)

1. Accounting. 2. Taxation. 3. Business.
I. National Bureau of Economic Research.
II. Title.

388
M19

Tunneling; the state of the art.
Mayo (Robert S.) and Associates.
Tunneling; the state of the art; a review
and evaluation of current tunneling techniques
and costs, with emphasis on their application
to urban rapid-transit systems in the U.S.A.;
prepared for the U.S. Dept. of Housing and
Urban Development. Lancaster, Pa., 1968.
263p.
Distributed by U.S. Clearinghouse for Federal
Scientific and Technical Information as document PB 178 036.
1. Transportation. 2. Building methods.
3. Soils. I. U.S. Dept. of Housing and
Urban Development. II. Title.

712.25
T86

Tupper, Margo.
No place to play. [Foreword by Stewart L.
Udall, Secretary of the Interior]
Philadelphia, Chilton Books, 1966.
293p.
Bibliography: p. 261-275.
Points out failures to provide adequate
recreational facilities in urban areas for
both children and their elders.

1. Recreation. 2. Natural resources. 3. Open
space land. 4. Water pollution. 5. Air
pollution. 6. Satel- lite cities. 7. City
planning. I. Udall, Stewart L. II. Title.

69
T87

Turek, Charles Busch, 1919-
How to save up to $3000 on your new home, by Kenneth
Lee [pseud.] and James Hogan [pseud.] St. Louis, Murek
[1960]
127 p. diagrs. 22 cm. (A Money saver book)

1. Building construction. 2. Home ownership.
1. Building & Dwellings. I. Murphy, Paul Henry, 1922-
joint author. II. Title.

TH148.T78 690 50-13942
Library of Congress [3]

69
T86

Tuomey, Douglas, 1893-
How to build your own house; illus. by Charles J. Spiess,
Jr. New York, Grosset & Dunlap [1949]
223 p. illus. 26 cm.

1. Building construction. 2. Owner-built houses.
3. Building & Dwellings. I. Title. 3. House plans.

TH148.T75 690 49—3223*
Library of Congress [50q7]

R
029
T87

Turabian, Kate L
A manual for writers of term papers, theses
and dissertations. Rev. Chicago, U. of
Chicago Press, 1958.
82p. tables.

1. Style Manuals. 2. Theses. I. Title

VF
690.591
B27d

Turek, William J
Better Homes and Gardens.
Do-it-yourself ideas for gates and
fences, comp. and ed. by William J. Turek.
Des Moines, Meredith Pub. Co., 1954.
[52]p. illus.

1. Houses - Maintenance and modernization.
2. Fences. I. Turek, William J

690.015
(485)
S82
R75

Tuominen, Teuvo, jt. au.
Brown, Gösta.
Solar position at various hours, dates and
latitudes, ta les. Solens läge på himlen vid
olika klockslag, årstider och latituder,
tabeller, by Gösta Brown and Teuvo Tuominen.
Stockholm, Statens Råd för Byggnadsforskning,
1962.
44p. (Sweden. Statens Kommitté för
Byggnadsforskning. Rapport 75)

1. Solar radiation. I. Sweden. Statens Kommitté
för Byggnadsforskning. II. Tuominen, Teuvo,
jt. au.

029
T87
1960

TURABIAN, KATE L
A MANUAL FOR WRITERS OF TERM PAPERS,
THESES AND DISSERTATIONS. CHICAGO,
UNIVERSITY OF CHICAGO PRESS, 1960.
110P. (A PHOENIX BOOKS PAPERBACK
SERIES)

1. STYLE MANUALS. I. TITLE.

VF
728.9
B27

Turek, William J comp.
Better Homes and Gardens.
Do-it-yourself ideas for your garage,
comp. and ed by William J. Turek. Des Moines,
Meredity Pub. Co., 1954.
[52]p.

1. Garages. I. Turek, William J., comp.

693.5
H97

Tuomioja, Mauri, jt. au.
Hyttinen, Esko.
Dome action in reinforced concrete slabs, by
Esko Hyttinen and Mauri Tuomioja. Helsinki,
State Institute for Technical Research, 1971.
67p. (Finland. State Institute for Technical
Research. Julkaisu 160 publication)

1. Concrete construction. 2. Concrete,
Reinforced. I. Finland. State Institute for
Technical Research. II. Title. III. Tuomioja,
Mauri, jt. au.

Ref.
029
T87
1967

Turabian, Kate L
A manual for writers of term papers, theses,
and dissertations. 3d ed rev. Chicago,
University of Chicago Press, 1967.
164p. (Phoenix books)

1. Style manuals. 2. Theses. I. Title.

712.25
M87

TURF MANAGEMENT.
MUSSER, H BURTON.
TURF MANAGEMENT; A PUBLICATION OF THE
UNITED STATES GOLF ASSOCIATION.
FORWORD BY JAMES D. STANDISH JR. NEW
YORK, MCGRAW-HILL, 1950.
354P.

1. RECREATION. I. UNITED STATES
GOLF ASSOCIATION. II. TITLE.

058.7
:690
U54

Turin, D   A
U.K. Ministry of Public Building and Works.
Directory of construction statistics. A report prepared for the Ministry of Public Building and Works by Cynthie Cockburn and Michael Verstage under the supervision of D.A. Turin, London Master Builders' Professor of Building, University of London. London, H.M.S.O., 1968.
98p. (R. & D. bulletin. SfB As2)
1. Building construction - Direct. I. Cockburn, Cynthia. II. Verstage, Michael. II. Turin, D.A. IV.   Title.

Türkiye Emlak Bankası
see
Credit Foncier de Turquie

658
U74t

The turned-on executive.
Uris, Auren.
The turned-on executive; building your skills for the management revolution ¡by¡ Auren Uris ¡and¡ Marjorie Noppel. New York, McGraw-Hill ¡1970¡.
xiv, 236 p. illus. 24 cm.
Includes bibliographical references.

1. Management.
I. Executive ability. I. Noppel, Marjorie, joint author. II. Title.

HF5500.2.U7   658.42   76-111998
MARC
Library of Congress   70 ¡10-2¡

711.4
(7291)
L66

Turismo y urbanismo.
Lopez Lima, Reinaldo
Turismo y urbanismo. [Habana, P. Fernandez, 1950?]
125 p. illus., maps (part fold.)

1.City planning-Cuba. I.Title.

691.7
1620.19
B14

TURKOVSKAYA, A   V   , JT. AU.
BAKHVALOV, G   T
CORROSION AND PROTECTION OF METALS, BY G.T. BAKHVALOV AND A.V. TURKOVSKAYA. TRANSLATED AND EDITED BY G. ISSERLIS. OXFORD, NEW YORK, PERGAMON PRESS, 1965.
322P.

1. CORROSION.   2. METALS.
I. TURKOVSKAYA, A.V., JT. AU.
II. TITLE: PROTECTION OF METALS.

711.73
T87

Turner, A   Keith.
Computer-aided regional highway location studies, by A. Keith Turner and Robert D. Miles. Lafayette, Ind., Purdue Univ., 1969.
39p. (Joint Highway Research Project, Purdue University. Technical paper no. 12)
Prepared in cooperation with the Indiana State Highway Commission and the U.S. Bureau of Public Roads.
Paper presented at National Conference of the AASHO Committee on Electronics, Seattle, 1969.
Bibliography: p. 37-39.
(Cont'd on next card)

625.7
A75r

Turk, David Milan, jt. au.
Arman, Ara
A revaluation of triaxial testing of remolded soils and pavement design methods, by Ara Arman and David Milan Turk. Baton Rouge, Louisiana State University and Agricultural and Mechanical College, 1967.
159p. (Louisiana State University and Agricultural and Mechanical College. Div. of Engineering Research. Engineering research bulletin no. 94)
Research conducted for Louisiana Dept.
(Cont'd on next card)

711.585
(74)
F22

Turley, Joseph F
Federal Reserve Bank of Boston.
Goals in urban renewal for New England, by Joseph F. Turley. Research report. Boston, 1959.
51p. tables. (Its Research report: 1970 projection no. 6)

1. Urban renewal - New England. I. Turley, Joseph F.

711.73
T87

Turner, A   Keith.   Computer-aided regional...1969.   (Card 2)

1. Highways. I. Miles, Robert D., jt. au. II. Joint Highway Research Project, Purdue University. III. Title. IV. Title: Highway location study.

625.7
A75r

Arman, Ara. A revaluation...1967.
(Card 2)
of Highways in cooperation with U.S. Bureau of Public Roads.
Bibliography: p. 79-81.

1. Road construction. 2. Soils.
I. Turk, David Milan, jt. au.
II. Louisiana. State University and Agricultural and Mechanical College. Div. of Engineering Research. III. Title.

330
(7441)
H68

Turley, Joseph F
Architects Collaborative.
Houlton town plan, Houlton, Maine: economic base study, by Joseph F. Turley and Richard H. Doherty. Cambridge, Mass. 1959.
67p. tables.
U.S. Urban Renewal Administration, Urban Planning Assistance Program.
1. Economic base studies - Houlton, Me. I. Turley, Joseph F. II. Doherty, Richard H. III. Title. IV. U.S. URA-UPAP. Houlton, Me.

711.73
T87c

Turner, A   K   F
Computer-assisted procedures to generate and evaluate regional highway alternatives. Final report (Part I) Lafayette, Ind., Joint Highway Research Project, Purdue University, 1968.
281p. (Joint Highway Research Project no. 32)

Bibliography: p. 268-279.
1. Highways. I. Joint Highway Research Project, Purdue University and Indiana State Highway   Commission.
II. Title.

LAW

Turkey - Laws, Statutes, etc.
Turkey. Ministry of Reconstruction and Resettlement.
Law for the foundation and duties of the Ministry of Reconstruction and Resettlement. Ankara, Turkey, 1958.
1v. (Law no. 7116)

Attached: Reconstruction law. Date of passing: 9 July 1956. Date of issue in Official Gazette: 16 July 1956. No. 9359. Law no. 6785.

I.Turkey - Laws, Statutes, etc.

336.18
T87

Turnbull, H   Rutherford, III.
Federal revenue sharing: a Maryland case study. Chapel Hill, Distributed by the Institute of Government, The University of North Carolina, 1969.
123p.

1. Grants-in-aid. 2. State finance - Md.
3. Municipal finance. 4. Intergovernmental relations. I. Title.

058.7
:360
(771)
034

Turner, Alberta B., ed.
Ohio. Youth Commission.
Directory of schools, agencies and institutions for children with special needs. Editor: Alberta B. Turner. 2d. ed. Columbus, 1968.
383p.

1. Social welfare - Ohio - Direct.
2. Schools - Ohio - Direct. I. Turner, Alberta B., ed. II. Title: Schools, agencies and institutions for children with special   needs.

LAW

Turkey. Ministry of Reconstruction and Resettlement.
Law for the foundation and duties of the Ministry of Reconstruction and Resettlement. Ankara, Turkey, 1958.
1v. (Law no. 7116)

Attached: Reconstruction law. Date of passing: 9 July 1956. Date of issue in Official Gazette: 16 July 1956. No. 9359. Law no. 6785.

I.Turkey - Laws, Statutes, etc.

FOLIO
711.4
(79751)
T87

Suppl.

Turnbull (J. Gordon) Inc.
Master plan for Richland, Washington. Cleveland [Nov. 1948]
74 p. maps, tables.
Prepared for General Electric Company, Nucleonics Department, Hanford Works, and U.S. Atomic Energy Commission, Hanford Operations Office, Study GES 22.
1.Master plan-Richland, Wash. 2.City planning-Richland, Wash. I.General Electric Company. II.U.S. Atomic Energy Commission.

388
T87

Turner, Daniel L
The fundamentals of transit planning for cities. [New York] National Conference on City Planning, 1922.
20p.

1. Transportation. I. Title.

711.585
(77178)
C45t

Turkey Ridge area general redevelopment plan.
Cincinnati. City Planning Commission.
Turkey Ridge area general redevelopment plan. Cincinnati, 1961.
36p.

1. Urban renewal - Cincinnati.
I. Title.

503
(016)
T87

Turnbull, William R
Scientific and technical dictionaries; an annotated bibliography, by William R. Turnbull, Jr. San Bernardino, Calif., Bibliothek Press, 1966-
v. 23 cm.
CONTENTS.—v. 1. Physical science and engineering.

1. Science — Dictionaries — Bibl. 2. Technology — Dictionaries — Bibl. I. Title.

Z7401.T8   503   67-25830
(016500
737
Library of Congress

711.4
(7471)
R23
v.4

Turner, Daniel L.
Lewis, Harold MacLean
Transit and transportation, and a study of port and industrial areas and their relation to transportation. By Harold M. Lewis... with supplementary reports by William J. Wilgus and Daniel L. Turner... New York, Regional plan of New York and its environs, 1928.
226p. (Regional plan of New York and its environs. Survey volumes. v.4)
1.Transportation-New York, N.Y. I.Wilgus, William J. II.Turner, Daniel L.

351.1
T87
Turner, David R
Clerk, GS 1 through GS 4. A complete and intensive examination study guide for beginning and intermediate clerical positions in the Federal civil service. New York, Arco Publishing Co., 1963.
1v.

1. Federal civil service. 2. Federal government. I. Title.

351.1
T87
1965
Turner, David R
Clerk GS-1 through GS-4. Complete study guide to pass high on your civil service test. New York, Arco, 1965.
1v.

1. Federal civil service. 2. Occupations. I. Title. II. Arco.

Ref.
351.1
T87
1967
Turner, David R
Clerk, GS-1 through GS-4; office aide-office assistant. The complete study guide for scoring high. Previous test questions, practice examinations--understandable yet authoritative text. 8th ed. New York, Arco Publishing Co., 1967.
288p. (Arco civil service test tutor)

1. Federal civil service. 2. Occupations. 3. Employment. I. Title. II. Arco Publishing Co.

351.1
T87f
latest ed. R.J.
Turner, David Reuben.
Federal service entrance examinations; the complete guide for scoring high. 7th ed. New York, ARCO, 1968.
448p.

1968

1. Federal civil service. I. Arco Publishing Co. II. Title.

DATE OF REQUEST MAR 30 1951   3-21-51   L. C. CARD NO.
AUTHOR Turner, Donald
TITLE *the development of a* Mortgage Lending Policy *Based on Experience* for *a country bank*
SERIES *Submitted in partial fulfillment of the requirement*
EDITION   PUB. DATE   PAGING
PUBLISHER *of the Graduate School of Banking conducted by the American Bankers Association at*
RECOMMENDED BY *Rutgers University,* 1vt. *over*
REVIEWED IN *New Brunswick, September 1948.*

352
T87
Turner, Glen R
Intergovernmental cooperation; an address by Director, Tulsa Metropolitan Areas Planning Commission, at the Region V, Housing and Home Finance Agency, 701 Administrators' Conference, April 13-14, 1961, Fort Worth, Texas. [n.p.] 1961.
11p.

1. Intergovernmental relations - Addresses. I. U.S. Housing and Home Finance Agency. II. Administrators' Conference, Fort Worth, Texas, 1961.

691.32
L68 1
TURNER, HUMPHREYS T
LOUISIANA. STATE UNIVERSITY AND AGRICULTURAL AND MECHANICAL COLLEGE. DIVISION OF ENGINEERING RESEARCH. INVESTIGATION OF PROPERTIES OF LIGHTWEIGHT CONCRETE, BY DEAN C. MCKEE AND HUMPHREYS T. TURNER. BATON ROUGE, LA., 1964.
70P. (ITS ENGINEERING RESEARCH BULLETIN NO. 74)

BIBLIOGRAPHY: P. 65-67.

1. CONCRETE
(CONTINUED ON NEXT CARD)

691.32
L68 1
LOUISIANA. STATE UNIVERSITY AND AGRICULTURAL AND MECHANICAL COLLEGE. DIVISION OF ENGINEERING RESEARCH. INVESTIGATION OF PROPERTIES ....1964. (CARD 2)

2. CONCRETE AGGREGATES. I. MCKEE, DEAN C. II. TURNER, HUMPHREYS T. III. TITLE: LIGHTWEIGHT CONCRETE.

691.328.2
T87
Turner, Humphreys T
Stability of slender prestressed concrete piling, by Humphreys T. Turner and others. Research was conducted by Louisiana State University, Division of Engineering Research for Louisiana Dept. of Highways in cooperation with U.S. Dept. of Transportation, Federal Highway Administration, Bureau of Public Roads. Baton Rouge, Louisiana State University and Agricultural and Mechanical College, Div. of Engineering Research, 1968.
64p. (Louisiana. State University and Agricultural and Mechanical College. Div. of Engineering research; Engineering research bulletin no. 96)
(Cont'd on next card)

691.328.2
T87
Turner, Humphreys T   Stability...1968. (Card 2)

1. Concrete, Prestressed. 2. Road construction. I. Louisiana. State University and Agricultural and Mechanical College. Div. of Engineering Research. II. Title.

360
N24
Turner, John B., ed.
Neighborhood organization for community action. John B. Turner, editor. New York, National Association of Social Workers, 1968.
220p.
Report of the conference on "citizen self-help organizations: relevance and problems," held in Cleveland, Mar. 15-17, 1967, as a part of the Project on Neighborhood Organization for Community Action.

(Cont'd on next card)

360
N24
Neighborhood organization for community action...1968. (Card 2)

1. Social service. 2. Community development - Citizen participation. I. Turner, John B., ed. II. National Association of Social Workers. III. Project on Neighborhood Organization for Community Action.

690
H68
IME
no.66
Turner. John F.C., jt. au.
U.S. Dept. of Housing and Urban Development.
Industrialized housing, by Ian Donald Terner and John F.C. Turner. In conjunction with OSTI, the Organization for Social and Technical Innovation, Cambridge, Massachusetts. Prepared for the U.S. Agency for International Development. Wash., U.S. Dept. of Housing and Urban Development, Office of International Affairs, 1972.
1v. (Ideas and methods exchange no. 66)

Bibliography: p. A-7 - A-12.

(Cont'd on next card)

690
H68
IME
no.66
U.S. Dept. of Housing and Urban Development.
Industrialized...1972. (Card 2)

1. Prefabricated construction. I. Turner, John F.C., jt. au. II. Organization for Social and Technical Innovation. III. U.S. Agency for International Development. IV. Terner, Ian Donald. V. Title.

711.73
(016)
T87
Turner, Laura R
Highway safety, 1960-1965; an annotated bibliography, by Laura R. Turner and Louise Philpot. Charlottesville, Virginia Highway Research Council, 1966
82p.
Sponsored jointly by the Virginia Dept. of Highways and the University of Virginia.

1. Highways - Bibl. 2. Traffic safety - Bibl. I. Philpot, Louise, jt. au. II. Virginia. Dept. of Highways. III. Title. IV. Virginia Highway Research Council.

Turner, Leigh Cilley, 1879-   joint ed.
Kentucky. *Laws, statutes, etc.*
Notes and annotations to the Kentucky Revised statutes. 1944. Embracing complete legislative history of the Kentucky Revised statutes as enacted in 1942, full explanatory notes by the reviser and annotations through v. 294 of the Kentucky reports (v. 172 of Southwestern reporter, 2d ser.) Ed. by Robert K. Cullen [and] L. C. Turner. [Frankfort] Kentucky Statute Revision Commission [1944]
cclxxviii, 1958 p. 27 cm.
This work constitutes a permanent volume; current annotations will be published in the statute volumes, or by the issuance of a supplement. Current pocket annotation service may be published in the intervals between the republication of statute volumes.
(Continued on next card)
[19-48g]   44-42670*

Turner, Leigh Cilley, 1870-   joint ed.
Kentucky. Laws, statutes, etc. Notes and annotations [1944] (Card 2)
——— Cumulative supplement ... 19
[Frankfort, Kentucky, Statute Revision Commission,
19- v. 27cm.   *See main entry*

332
H45
TURNER, MARION, JT. AU.
HILL, RICHARD WILLIAM, 1878-1947.
FIFTY YEARS OF BANKING EDUCATION; HISTORY OF THE AMERICAN INSTITUTE OF BANKING, BY RICHARD W. HILL AND MARION TURNER. 1ST ED. NEW YORK, AMERICAN INSTITUTE OF BANKING, SECTION AMERICAN BANKERS ASSOCIATION, 1950.
696P.

1. BANKS AND BANKING - U.S.
2. AMERICAN INSTITUTE OF BANKING.
I. TURNER, MARION, JT. AU. II. TITLE.

920
C51w
Turner, Nat, 1800? - 1831. The confessions of Nat Turner.
Clarke, John Henrik, ed.
William Styron's Nat Turner; ten black writers respond. Boston, Beacon Press, 1968.
120p.
Appendix (p. [93]-117): The text of the Confessions of Nat Turner.

1. Styron, William. The confessions of Nat Turner. I. Turner, Nat, 1800? - 1831. The confessions of Nat Turner. II. Title.

Class No. *Termites*   Author (Surname first) *Turner, Neely*   Agricultural Experiment Station   NOT RUSH
Accession No.   Title Control of termites in buildings, by Neely Turner.
Ordered 2/6/50 ltr.   (Circular 172)
Of   New Haven, Conn.
Received FEB 13 1950   Edition or Series   Place   Publisher
Cost   Date 1949   Vols.   List Price 8 p.   Est. Cost
Charged to   Recommended by
Date of bill   Address   Library of Congress Checklist of Publications.
L. C. No.   Reviewed In   p.4

VF
666.3
G72
Turner, P.P., jt. au.
Greaves-Walker, A
The development of a structural clay products industry using Florida clays. Pt.1. Development of the Jacksonville area, by A.F. Greaves-Walker, P.P. Turner and R.S. Hagerman. Gainesville, Fla., Florida Engineering and Industrial Experiment Station, Dec. 1949.
48 p. illus., diagrs., maps, tables.
(Florida. University. Engineering and Industrial Experiment Station. Bulletin no. 30)
1. Clay. I. Turner, P.P., jt. au. II. Hagerman, R.S., jt. au. III. Series.

330
(772)
I52

Turner, Robert C.
Indiana. University. School of Business.
An economic portrait of Indiana in 1970.
Bloomington, Ind., Jan. 1956.
1 v. graphs

Summary of the 14 volume study: Indiana's
economic resources and potential. Prepared by
Robert C. Turner, with the assistance of
William B. O'Connell.

1. Economic conditions - Indiana. I. Turner,
Robert C. II. Indiana. University. School
of Business. Indiana's economic
resources and potential.

711.4
(54)
T87

Turner, Roy, ed.
India's urban future. Selected studies from
an international conference, sponsored by
Kingsley Davis and others. Berkeley,
University of California Press, 1962.
470p.
Supported by the Ford Foundation.

1. City planning - India. 2. City growth -
India. I. Seminar on Urbanization in India,
Berkeley, Calif., 1960. II. Title.

351.74
T87

Turner, William W
The police establishment. New York, Putnam,
1968.
319p.

2C

1. Police. 2. Law enforcement. I. Title.

628.1
(016)
A37

TURNEY, JACK R
U.S. DEPT. OF AGRICULTURE.
STATE WATER-RIGHTS LAWS AND RELATED
SUBJECTS; A BIBLIOGRAPHY. COMPILED BY
JACK R. TURNEY AND HAROLD H. ELLIS.
WASHINGTON, GOVT. PRINT. OFF., 1962.
199P. (ITS MISCELLANEOUS PUBLICATION
NO. 921)

1. WATER-SUPPLY - LAW AND LEGISLATION.
I. TURNEY, JACK R. II. ELLIS, HAROLD
H. III. TITLE.

360
U71t

The turning point.
Urban America, inc.
The turning point. Washington, [1968?]
15p.

1. Social welfare. 2. Social conditions.
3. Economic conditions. 4. Minority groups.
I. Title.

338
A97

Turning points in business cycles.
Ayres, Leonard P
Turning points in business cycles. New York,
Macmillan, 1939.
214 p.

1. Business cycles. I. Title.

330
E26t

Turning the tide.
U.S. Economic Development Administration.
Turning the tide; how communities are creating
jobs to boost lagging economies. Wash., 1970.
74p.

1. Economic development. 2. Community
development. 3. Employment. I. Title.

690.022
(492)
I57

Turnkey.
Internationale Bouw Compagnie.
80 jaar IBC; evolutie naar turnkey (80 years
IBC; evolution to turnkey) Best, 1969.
86p.

1. Prefabricated construction - Netherlands.
I. Title: Turnkey.

690.022
(778)
M49

Turn-key construction.
Bauman, Richard A
Financing housing construction. Mizzou
Housing Project; application of turn-key
construction to industrialized urban housing
in Missouri. A report. Columbia, University
of Missouri, 1970.
51p.
Bibliography: p. 37-44.
Thesis (M.S.) University of Missouri.
1. Prefabricated construction - Missouri.
2. Construction loans. I. Mizzou Housing
Project. II. Title. III. Title: Turn-key
construction. IV. Title: Industrialized
urban housing.

690.022
(778)
M49p

Turn-key construction.
Vogel, John Karl.
Performance specifications for industrialized urban housing in Missouri. Mizzou
Housing Project; application of turn-key
construction to industrialized urban housing
in Missouri. Summary report. Columbia,
University of Missouri, 1970.
88p.
Bibliography: p. 83-88.
Thesis (M.S.) University of Missouri.
1. Prefabricated construction - Missouri.
2. Building methods. I. Mizzou Housing Project.
II. Title. III. Title: Turn-key
construction. IV. Title: Industrialized
urban housing.

690.022
(778)
M49pe

Turn-key construction.
Long, Joseph John.
Performance specifications for residential
land planning for urban housing in Missouri.
Mizzou Housing Project; application of turnkey construction to industrialized urban
housing in Missouri. Columbia, University
of Missouri, 1970.
132p.
Bibliography: p. 84-92.
Thesis (M.S.) University of Missouri.
1. Prefabricated construction - Missouri.
2. Land use - Missouri. 3. Residential areas
- Missouri. I. Mizzou Housing Project.
II. Title. III. Title: Turn-key
construction.

728.1
:336.18
(79466)
O14

Turnkey housing.
Oakland, Calif. City Planning Commission.
Oakland's turnkey housing: its impact
on the community. Oakland, 1970.
21p. (Its OCPD 210)

1. Public housing - Oakland, Calif.
I. Title. II. Title: Turnkey housing.

728.1
:336.18
(79466)
G74

Turnkey program.
Griffin, Jill
View from the inside; an assessment of
the new turnkey program in Oakland as
seen by turnkey residents. Oakland,
Calif., Oakland City Planning Dept., 1969.
20p. (OCPD 207)

1. Public housing - Oakland, Calif.
I. Oakland, Calif. City Planning Dept.
II. Title: Turnkey program.
III. Title.

728.1
:336.18
H68g

Turnkey method of public housing construction.
U.S. Dept. of Housing and Urban Development. Housing Assistance Administration.
A guide to the "turnkey" method of
public housing construction. Washington,
1967.
20p. (U.S. Dept. of Housing and Urban
Development HUD PG-6)

1. Public housing. 2. Construction
loans. 3. Federal housing programs.
I. Title. II. Title: Turnkey method of
public housing construction.

058.7
:728.1
:336.18
H68t

Turnkey programs.
U.S. Housing Production and Mortgage
Credit-FHA. Div. of Research and Statistics.
Turnkey programs; development progress
directory.
Washington, 19
v. (Special report)
At head of title: Housing act of 1949.
For Library holdings see main entry.
1. Local housing authorities - Direct.
2. Mortgage finance - Direct. 3. Nonprofit
housing organizations - Direct. I. Title.

728
:333
(76212)
U71

Turnkey III.
Urban America. Nonprofit Housing Center.
Turnkey III: a case study of the pilot program of homeownership under public housing in
North Gulfport, Mississippi. Wash., 1969.
1v.
1. Home ownership - Gulfport, Miss.
2. Public housing - Gulfport, Miss. 3. Non-
profit housing organizations. I. Title.

330
V15

Turnpike theorem.
Vanek, Jaroslav.
Maximal economic growth; a geometric
approach to Von Neumann's growth theory
and the turnpike theorem. Ithaca, N.Y.,
Cornell University Press, 1968.
122p.

1. Economic development. 2. Von Neumann,
John, 1903-1957. I. Title: Turnpike
theorem. II. Title.

690.022
(016)
C25

TURRELL, VIRGINIA.
CENTRAL HOUSING COMMITTEE
(SUB-COMMITTEE ON RESEARCH AND
STATISTICS. LIBRARY SECTION.)
SOME RECENT REFERENCES ON
PREFABRICATED HOUSING, COMPILED BY
VIRGINIA TURRELL. WASHINGTON, 1936.
9L.

1. PREFABRICATED CONSTRUCTION -
BIBLIOGRAPHY. I. TURRELL, VIRGINIA.

620.015
T87

Turunen, W   A
The General Motors research GT-309
gas turbine engine, by W.A. Turunen
and others. Prepared for presentation
at SAE Combined National Transportation
and Power Plant Meeting, Cleveland, Ohio
Oct. 18-21, 1965. Warren, Mich.,
Research Laboratories, General Motors
Corp., 1965.
43p. (General Motors Corp. Research
Laboratories. Research publication
GMR-495)

(Cont'd on next card)

620.015
T87

Turunen, W   A
The General...1965.   (Card 2)

1. Engineering research. I. General
Motors Corp. II. Society of Automotive
Engineers Combined National Transportation and Power Plant Meeting, Cleveland
1965. III. Title: Gas turbine engine.

3858-
3863

TUSCARAWAS CO., OHIO. REGIONAL PLANNING
COMMISSION.
PLANNING FOR THE FUTURE: 1,
ORGANIZATIONAL PROSPECTUS; 2, BACKGROUND
FOR PLANNING; 3, DEVELOPMENT GOALS AND
PROPOSALS; 4, PLANNING ADMINISTRATION
AND IMPLEMENTATION; 5,
POTENTIAL INDUSTRIAL SITES; 6, MODEL
SUBDIVISION REGULATIONS. BY CARROLL
HILL AND ASSOCIATES. NEW PHILADELPHIA,
OHIO, 1967-69.
6 V. (HUD 701 REPORT)

1. COUNTY PLANNING - TUSCARAWAS
(CONTINUED ON NEXT CARD)

3858- 3863 TUSCARAWAS CO., OHIO. REGIONAL PLANNING COMMISSION. PLANNING FOR THE ...7-69. (CARD 2) CO., OHIO. I. HILL (CARROLL V.) AND ASSOCIATES. II. HUD. 701. TUSCARAWAS CO., OHIO.	711.4 (761915) T87 Tuscumbia, Ala. City Planning Commission. Tuscumbia, Alabama: public ... (Card 2) Planning Assistance Program. 1. City planning - Tuscumbia, Ala. 2. Public works - Tuscumbia, Ala. 3. Capital improvement programs - Tuscumbia, Ala. I. Alabama. State Planning and Industrial De- velopment Board. II. U.S. Urban Renewal Administration. Urban Planning Assistance Program.	VF 693.5 :691.8 T87 Tuskegee Normal and Industrial Institute. (*Rural Life Council.*) Low cash cost housing. Tuskegee Institute, Ala., 1950. 26 p. illus. 23 cm. (Rural life information series, bull. no. 2) Cover title. "A progress report on experimentation at Tuskegee Institute. George Williams and Royal Dunham, technical advisers, by Ernest E. Neal." -p. 5. 1. Concrete blocks. 2. Dwellings. I. Title. II.(Series) 3. Building research. 4. Farm housing. II. Neal, Ernest E TH1421.T8 693.5 51-24890 Library of Congress [1]
225- 229 TUSCALOOSA AREA COUNCIL OF LOCAL GOVERNMENT. PLANNING PROGRAM: 1. INITIAL HOUSING ELEMENT; 2. INVENTORY OF COMMUNITY FACILITIES; 3. RECREATION PLAN; 4. SOLID WASTE MANAGEMENT: STUDY AND PLAN; 5. A SUPPLEMENT TO THE USE OF LAND. TUSCALOOSA, ALA., 1969-70. 5 V. (HUD 701 REPORT) 1. METROPOLITAN AREA PLANNING - TUSCALOOSA, ALA. I. HUD. 701. TUSCALOOSA, ALA.	711.74 (76195) T87 Tuscumbia, Ala. City Planning Commission. Tuscumbia, Alabama: street naming and block numbering system. [Prepared in cooperation with] Alabama State Planning and Industrial Development Board. Tuscum- bia, 1962. 14p. U.S. Urban Renewal Adm. UPAP. 1. Streets - Tuscumbia, Ala. I. U.S. URA-UPAP. Tuscumbia, Ala.	VF 690 336.18 T87 Tuskegee Institute. Organization and direction of family labor for self-help house construction. [Tuskegee, Ala.] Oct. 1952. 71 l. illus., forms, plans, tables. Bibliography: p. 69-71. At head of title: Low cash cost housing. Final report, Research Project no. O-T-42, Housing and Home Finance Agency. (Continued on next card)
4834 4835 TUSCOLA CO., MICH. PLANNING COMMISSION. TECHNICAL MEMORANDUM: 1. POPULATION AND EXISTING LAND USE; 2. HOUSING CONDITION ANALYSIS AND PHYSICAL FEATURES. PREPARED BY VILICAN-LEMAN AND ASSOCIATES, INC. SOUTHFIELD, MICH., 1969. 2 V. (HUD 701 REPORT) 1. COUNTY PLANNING - TUSCOLA CO., MICH. I. VILICAN-LEMAN AND ASSOCIATES. II. HUD. 701. TUSCOLA CO., MICH.	711.14 (76149) T87 Tuskegee, Ala. City Planning Commission. Land use map of Tuskegee, Alabama. [Prepared in cooperation with] Alabama State Planning and Industrial Develop- ment Board. Tuskegee, 1963. [2]p. U.S. Urban Renewal Adm. UPAP. 1. Land use - Tuskegee, Ala. I. U.S. URA-UPAP. Tuskegee, Ala.	Tuskegee Institute. Organization ... Oct. 1952 (Card 2) Project director, F. D. Patterson; staff technician, William A. Russell. Typewritten. 1. Owner-built houses. 2. Building construction. 3. Housing research contracts. I. Patterson, F. D. II. Russell, William A. III. U.S. Housing and Home Finance Agency. O.A. Division of Housing Research. IV. Title. V. Title: Self-help house construction. VI. Title: Low cash cost housing.
711.4 (761915) T87c Tuscumbia, Ala. City Planning Commission. Tuscumbia, Alabama: community facilities plan. [In cooperation with Alabama State Planning and Industrial Development Board] Tuscumbia, 1957. 44p. map. U.S. Urban Renewal Administration, (Continued on next card)	711.585.1 (76149) T87 Tuskegee, Ala. Office of the Mayor. Application to the Department of Housing and Urban Development for a grant to plan a comprehensive city demonstration program. Tuskegee, Ala., 1967. 1v. Selected to receive the first HUD Model Cities Program planning grants. 1. Model cities - Tuskegee, Ala. I. U.S. HUD - Model Cities Program first planning grants.	Tuskegee Institute. (Department of Records and Research) Pamphlets. VF 325 (016) G89 1950 no. 2. Civil rights and the Negro; a list of references relating to present day discussions. 1950.
711.4 (761915) T87c Tuscumbia, Ala. City Planning Commission, Tuscumbia, Alabama: community ... (Card 2) Urban Planning Assistance Program. 1. Master plan - Tuscumbia, Ala. 2. Community facilities - Tuscumbia, Ala. I. Alabama. State Planning and Indus- trial Development Board. II. U.S. Urban Renewal Administration. Urban Planning Assistance Program.	711.585.1 (76149) T87c Tuskegee, Ala. Office of the Mayor. Tuskegee, Model Cities Program, comprehensive plan. Tuskegee, Ala., 1970. 1v. U.S. Dept. of Housing and Urban Development. Model Cities Program. 1. Model cities - Tuskegee, Ala. 2. Master plan - Tuskegee, Ala. I. U.S. HUD. Model Cities Program.	325.2 T87 Tuskegee Institute. Race relations in the South, 1962; 49th annual report to the American people on developments on race relations, by the Dept. of Records and Research, Tuskegee Institute, Ala., 1963. 24p. At head of title: A Tuskegee Institute report. 1. Race relations.
711.4 (761915) T87c Tuscumbia, Ala. City Planning Commission. Tuscumbia, Alabama: long range land use plan; population, housing, neighborhoods, schools, streets. [In cooperation with Alabama State Planning and Industrial De- velopment Board] Tuscumbia, 1956. 1v. diagrs., map. U.S. Urban Renewal Administration, Urban (Continued on next card)	VF 690 :336.18 T871 Tuskegee Concrete Block Construction. Tuskegee Institute. Instruction manual, Tuskegee concrete block construction. [Tuskegee, Alabama, 1952?] 1 v. (various pagings) diagrs., plans, tables. Prepared under Research Project No. O-T-42, Housing and Home Finance Agency. Project director: F. D. Patterson; Staff technician: William A. Russell. Processed.	378 T87 Tuskegee Institute. Report of the President. Tuskegee Institute, Ala. v. annual Issued also as Bulletin of Tuskegee Institute. For complete information see shelflist. 1. Universities and colleges.
711.4 (761915) T87 Tuscumbia, Ala. City Planning Commission. Tuscumbia, Alabama: public works program. [In cooperation with Alabama State Planning and Industrial Development Board] Tuscumbia, 1957. 21p. diagrs., tables. U.S. Urban Renewal Administration, Urban (Continued on next card)	VF 690 :336.18 T871 Tuskegee Institute. Instruction manual, Tuskegee concrete block construction. [Tuskegee, Alabama, 1952?] 1 v. (various pagings) diagrs., plans, tables. Prepared under Research Project No. O-T-42, Housing and Home Finance Agency. Project director: F. D. Patterson; Staff technician: William A. Russell. Processed.	Tuskegee Normal and Industrial Institute. see Tuskegee Institute.

FOLIO
728.1
(71)
T87
TUTHILL, JOHN W
HOUSING IN CANADA. OTTAWA, 1942.
31L.

1. HOUSING - CANADA.

323.25
(77311)
T87
Tuttle, William M   Jr.
Race riot; Chicago in the Red Summer of 1919.
New York, Atheneum, 1970.
305p. (Studies in American Negro life)

c.1, E.D.

Bibliography: p. 269-289.

1. Civil disorders - Chicago. 2. Negroes
- Chicago. I. Title.

690.22
T82
Tveit, Annanias.
Klimaets og utførelsens innflytelse på
varmegjennomgangen i lettbetongvegger
[Influence of climate and workmanship
on the thermal transmittance of light-weight
concrete walls] Oslo, 1961.
7p.   (Oslo. Norges Byggforskningsinstitutt. Saertrykk nr. 52)
Saertrykk av BYGG, nr. 1, 1961.

1. Walls. 2. Concrete construction.
I. Oslo. Norges Byggforskningsinstitutt.

711.??
(??4)
H21
Tutt, Paul R., jt. au.
Heathington, Kenneth W
Traffic volume analysis of urban free-
ways, by Kenneth W. Heathington and Paul R.
Tutt. [Prepared] in cooperation with the
U.S. Dept. of Commerce, Bureau of Public
Roads. [Austin, Texas] Texas Highway Dept.
1966.
56p. (Texas. Highway Dept. Departmental
Research. Report no. SS 5.0)
1. Highways - Texas. 2. Traffic surveys -
Texas. 3. Transportation - Statistics. I. Tutt,
Paul R., jt. au. II. Texas. Highway Dept.
IV. Title.

728.1
(47)
T87
Tutuchenko, Semyon.
Housing in the U.S.S.R.; notes of an
architect. Moscow, Foreign Languages
Publishing House, 1960.
135p.   illus.

1. Housing - U.S.S.R.

691
(481)
T82
Tveit, Annanias.
Measurements of moisture sorption and
moisture permeability of porous materials.
Oslo, Norwegian Building Research Institute.
1966.
39p.   (Oslo. Norges Byggforskningsinstitutt. Rapport 45)

1. Building materials - Norway.
2. Moisture condensation. I. Oslo. Norges
Byggforskningsinstitutt. II. Title.

LAW
T
F722tr
Tuttle, Edward William, 1877-   ed.
Freeman, Abraham Clark, 1843-1911.
A treatise of the law of judgments; including all final de-
terminations of the rights of parties in actions or proceedings
at law or in equity, by A. C. Freeman. 5th ed., rev. and
greatly enl., by Edward W. Tuttle ... San Francisco, Bancroft-Whitney company, 1925.
3 v. 25 cm.

1. Judgments—U. S.   i. Tuttle, Edward William, 1877-   ed.

25—8381

Library of Congress   (4911)

VF
699.82
T24
Tveit, Annanias.
Factors effecting the moisture permeability of porous materials and the calculation of moisture transport and condensation hazard in building structures. Oslo,
Norwegian Building Research Institute, 1966.
[8]p.   (Oslo. Norwegian Building
Research Institute. Reprint 118)

Reprint from the Proceedings of the RILEM/
CIB Symposium on Moisture Problems in Build-
ings, Helsinki, Aug. 16-19, 1965.
(Cont'd on next card)

690.22
T82u
Tveit, Annanias.
Undersøkelse av varmegjennomgang i vegger
[Investigation of heat transmission in walls]
Oslo, 1959.
8p.   (Oslo. Norges Byggforsknings-
institutt. Saertrykk nr. 38)
Saertryk av tidsskriftet VARME, nr. 4/1959.

1. Walls. 2. Heat transmission. I. Oslo.
Norges Byggforskningsinstitutt.

666.293
B84
Tuttle, E   X
Building Research Institute.
Porcelain enamel in the building industry,
November 12 and 13, 1953, sponsored by the
Building Research Advisory Board and the Porcelain
Enamel Institute.   Washington, Mar. 1954.
146 p.   illus., diagrs., graphs, tables.

Contains bibliographies.
At head of title: Research conference report
no. 6.
Partial contents.-Physical characteristics of
(Continued on next card)

VF
699.82
T24
Tveit, Annanias.   Factors effecting the
moisture...1965   (Card 2)

1. Moisture condensation. 2. Humidity.
I. Oslo. Norges Byggforskningsinstitutt.
II. Title.

362.5
T82
Tweeten, Luther G
Rural poverty; incidence, causes and
cures. [Stillwater, Okla.] Oklahoma State
University Experiment Station, 1968.
105 p. (Oklahoma. Agricultural Experiment
Station. Processed series P-590R)
Bibliography: p. 99-105.

1. Poverty. I. Oklahoma. Agricultural
Experiment Station, Stillwater. II. Title.

Building Research Institute.   Porcelain enamel
... Mar. 1954.   (Card 2)

porcelain enamel, by E. E. Howe.-Weather resistance
of porcelain enameled structural units, by Dwight
G. Moore.-The design, manufacture, and erection of
architectural porcelain metal parts, by Benjamin B.
Loring.-Porcelain enamel curtain walls and their
utilization in the building industry, by E. X.
Tuttle.-Creative uses of porcelain enamel, by
Richard W. Hamilton.-Engineering properties of
porcelain enamel, by Forrest R. Nagley.-Porcelain
(Continued on next card)

691
T82
Tveit, Annanias.
Fukt og fukttransport i porøse materialer.
Oslo, Norges Byggforskningsinstitutt, 1964.
19p.   (Oslo. Norges Byggforskningsins-
titutt. Rapport 39)

1. Building materials. 2. Building
research. I. Oslo. Norges Byggforskningsinstitutt.   (Series)

331
E56T
1934
TWELVE AND ONE-HALF MILLION REGISTERED
FOR WORK.
U.S. EMPLOYMENT SERVICE.
TWELVE AND ONE-HALF MILLION REGISTERED
FOR WORK, 1934. PREPARED BY DIVISION OF
STANDARDS AND RESEARCH, WILLIAM H.
STEAD, ASSOCIATE DIRECTOR. WASHINGTON,
GOVT. PRINT. OFF., 1935.
98P.

1. EMPLOYMENT.   I. STEAD, WILLIAM
HENRY.   II. TITLE.

Building Research Institute.   Porcelain enamel
... Mar. 1954.   (Card 3)

enameled aluminum, by B. C. Bricker.-The use of
porcelain enamel for houses, by Wentworth W.
Lobdell.
1. Building materials. I. Building Research Advisory
Board. II. Porcelain Enamel Institute. III. Howe, E.
E. IV. Moore, Dwight G. V. Loring, Benjamin B.
VI. Tuttle, E. X. VII. Hamilton, Richard W.
VIII. Nagley, Forrest R. IX. Bricker, B. C
X. Lobdell, Wentworth W. XI. Title.

697.133
T82
Tveit, Annanias.
Heat transmission through test walls of
autoclaved cellular concrete. Oslo, 1960.
381-403p. (Oslo. Norges
Byggforskninginstitutt, Reprint no. 68)

1. Heat transmission. I. Oslo. Norges
Byggforskninginstitutt.

658
H17
TWELVE BUSINESS PROBLEMS ANALYZED.
HARVARD BUSINESS REVIEW.
TWELVE BUSINESS PROBLEMS ANALYZED.
BOSTON, PRESIDENT AND FELLOWS OF HARVARD
COLLEGE,
V. ANNUAL.
For Library holdings see main entry
1. MANAGEMENT. 2. PUBLIC RELATIONS.
3. INDUSTRIAL MANAGEMENT. 4. LABOR
RELATIONS. I. TITLE.

720
T87
Tuttle, Edward X
With benefit of architect; a manual for
those about to build. New York, Macmillan,
1968.
277p.

1. Architecture - Designs and plans.
2. Contracts. 3. Contract documents.
I. Title.

693.5
:691.8
075
Tveit, Annanias.
Oslo. Norges Byggforskningsinstitutt.
Klimaets innflytelse på betonghulstein-
veggers varmeisolasjon, [Influence of the
climate on the thermal resistance of hollow
concrete block walls] av Annanias Tveit.
Oslo, 1959.
52p. illus., diagrs., tables. (Its
Rapport nr. 30)

English summary: p. 51-52.
1. Concrete blocks. 2. Walls. I. Tveit,
Annanias. (Series)

711.3
G85
Twelve cities.
Gunther, John, 1901-
Twelve cities. 1st ed. New York, Harper
& Row, 1969.
370p.

1. Metropolitan areas. 2. Sociology, Urban.
I. Title.

658
R62t

The twelve hats of a company President.
Rockwell, Willard F Jr.
The twelve hats of a company President; what
it takes to run a company. Englewood Cliffs,
N.J., 1971.
244p.

1. Industrial management. I. Title.

301.15
S77

The Twentieth Century city.
Strong, Josiah.
The Twentieth Century city. New York,
Arno Press & The New York Times, 1970, 1898.
186p. (The rise of urban America)

1. Community structure. 2. Social conditions.
I. Title. (Series: The rise of urban America)

330
(5)
M97

Twentieth Century Fund.
Myrdal, Gunnar.
Asian drama; an inquiry into the poverty
of nations. A Twentieth Century Fund Study
New York, Pantheon, 196=.
3v.

1. Economic conditions - Asia.
2. Asia - Economic conditions. I. Twentieth
Centruy Fund. II. Title.

728.1
:308
(41)
T82

TWELVE IN SEARCH OF A HOUSE; A
SYMPOSIUM. LONDON, J.M. DENT, 1944.
39P. (CO-OPERATIVE PERMANENT
BUILDING SOCIETY. DESIGN FOR BRITAIN,
2D SER., BOOKLET NO. 37)

1. HOUSING MARKET - U.K.
I. COOPERATIVE PERMANENT BUILDING
SOCIETY.

330
(75)
M12

Twentieth Century Fund.
Maddox, James G
The advancing South; manpower prospects and
problems, by James G. Maddox and others. New
York, Twentieth Century Fund, 1967.
276p. (A Twentieth Century Fund report)
1. Minority groups - Southern states.
2. Economic conditions - Southern states.
3. Employment - Minority groups. I. Twentieth
Century Fund. II. Title.

330
(41)
L28

Twentieth Century Fund
Lewis, Ben W
British planning and nationalization.
New York, The Twentieth Century Fund, 1952.
313p.

Bibliography: p. 286-301.

1. Economic planning - U.K. 2. Planning - U.K.
I. Twentieth Century Fund. I. Title.

FILM
12M

Jespersen (industrialised building) (Motion
picture) London, John Laing and Son, ltd.,
1966.

16mm., 630 ft., sd., color, 17min.

Cost: $100.00

1. Films. 2. Prefabricated construction.
I. Laing (John) and Son, London.

33(73)
T82
1950

Twentieth Century Fund. (America's needs and
resources.)
Hartley, Robert W 1911-
America's capital requirements; estimates for
1946-1960. By Robert W. Hartley, with the
collaboration of Eleanor Wolkind, and assisted by
Maynard Hufschmidt and Sidney Jaffe. New York,
Twentieth Century Fund, 1950.
xviii, 244 p.

"A technical supplement to ... America's needs
and resources ... published in 1947."

50-14725

338.8
S76

Twentieth Century Fund. (Committee on
Cartels and Monopoly).
Stocking, George W
Cartels in action; case studies in inter-
national business diplomacy, by George W.
Stocking and Myron W. Watkins. New York,
The Twentieth Century Fund, 1946.
533 p. tables.

A Twentieth Century Fund Survey.

1.Monopolies. I.Watkins, Myron W., jt. author.
II.Twentieth Century Fund. (Committee on Cartels and
Monopoly) III.Title.

711.4
:670
(798)
J63

Twenhofel, W S , jt. au.
Johnson, Arthur.
Potential industrial sites in the
Lynn Canal area, Alaska, by Arthur
Johnson and W.S. Twenhofel. Washington,
U.S. Dept. of the Interior, Geological
Survey, 1953.
17p. (U.S. Geological Survey. Circular
280)

1. Industrial location - Alaska.
I. Twenhofel, W.S., jt. au. II. U.S.
Geological Survey.

33
(73)
T82
1955

Twentieth Century Fund.
America's needs and resources; a new survey,
by J. Frederic Dewhurst and Associates.
New York, 1955.
xxix, 1148 p. graphs, tables.

2c.

1. U. S. - Econ. Condit. I. Dewhurst, James
Frederick. II. Title.

332
T82

TWENTIETH CENTURY FUND.
DEBTS AND RECOVERY. A STUDY OF CHANGES
IN THE INTERNAL DEBT STRUCTURE FROM 1929
TO 1937 AND A PROGRAM FOR THE FUTURE. THE
FACTUAL FINDINGS BY ALBERT GAILORD HART.
NEW YORK, 1938.
366P.

1. FINANCE. I. HART, ALBERT GAILORD.
II. TITLE.

331
065tw

Twentieth anniversary of the Employment act of
1946; an economic symposium.
U.S. Cong. Joint Economic Committee.
Twentieth anniversary of the Employment
act of 1946; an economic symposium. Supple-
ment to Hearing before the Joint Economic
Committee, Congress of the United States,
Eighty-ninth Congress, second session. In-
vited comments on directions for the future.
Wash., For sale by Supt. of Doc., Govt.
Print. Off., 1966.
192p.

1. Employment. 2. Economic development.
I. Title.

33(73)
T82
1947

Twentieth century fund.
America's needs and resources, a Twentieth century fund
survey which includes estimates for 1950 and 1960. By J.
Frederic Dewhurst and associates. New York, The Twentieth century fund, 1947.
xxviii, 812 p. incl. tables, diagrs. 26 cm.

3c.

1. U. S.—Econ. condit.—1945- I. Dewhurst, James Frederic,
1895- II. Title.

HC106.5.T9   330.973   47—8562
Library of Congress   [40b⁵30]

330
:355.8
H17

Twentieth Century Fund (Committee on
Economic Stabilization.)
Hart, Albert W
Defense without inflation; with
recommendations of the Committee on
Economic Stabilization. New York,
The Twentieth Century Fund, 1951.
186 p.

1.Economic policy 2.National defense I.Twentieth Century
Fund. Committee on Economic Stabilization. II.Title.

720.36
J12

TWENTIETH-CENTURY ARCHITECTURE.
JACOBUS, JOHN M
TWENTIETH-CENTURY ARCHITECTURE; THE
MIDDLE YEARS, 1940-65. NEW YORK,
FREDERICK A. PRAEGER, 1966.
215P. (BOOKS THAT MATTER SERIES)

1. ARCHITECTURE, MODERN.
2. ARCHITECTS. I. TITLE.

728.1
T82
1944

Twentieth Century Fund. (The Housing Committee.)
American housing; problems and prospects.
The factual findings by Miles L. Colean. The
program by the Housing Committee. New York,
1944.
466 p. graphs.

5c.

1.Housing. 2.Building industry. 3.Housing market.
I.Colean, Miles L.

711.4
G67

The Twentieth Century Fund.
Gottmann, Jean.
Economics, esthetics, and ethics in modern
urbanization. New York, Twentieth Century
Fund, 1962.
37p.

1. City planning. 2. Sociology, Urban.
I. The Twentieth Century Fund. II. Title.

655
L28

The Twentieth century book.
Lewis, John.
The Twentieth century book; its illustration and design. New York, Reinhold,
1967.
272p.

1. Printing. 2. Art. I.Title.

728.1
T82
1949

TWENTIETH CENTURY FUND. (THE HOUSING
COMMITTEE)
AMERICAN HOUSING; PROBLEMS AND
PROSPECTS. THE FACTUAL FINDINGS BY
MILES L. COLEAN. THE PROGRAM BY THE
HOUSING COMMITTEE. NEW YORK, 1949.
466P.

1. HOUSING. 2. BUILDING INDUSTRY.
3. HOUSING MARKET. I. COLEAN, MILES L.

FILM

Twentieth Century Fund.
Encyclopaedia Britannica Films. The living
city. [1953]
16 mm., black and white, sound, 24 min.
Produced in cooperation with the
Twentieth Century Fund; collaborator,
Miles Colean.

Cost: $100

1. Urban renewal. 2. Films. II.
Twentieth Century Fund. II. Colean, Miles
III. Title.

336.2
T82   TWENTIETH CENTURY FUND.
     FACING THE TAX PROBLEM. A SURVEY OF
     TAXATION IN THE UNITED STATES AND A
     PROGRAM FOR THE FUTURE. NEW YORK, 1937.
     606P.

       1. TAXATION. I. TITLE.

360
H22   Twentieth Century Fund.
     Heckscher, August.
       The individual and the mass. New York,
   Twentieth Century Fund, 1965.
     29p.

       1. Social conditions. I. Twentieth Century
   Fund. II. Title.

362.5
075P   TWENTIETH CENTURY FUND.
     ORNATI, OSCAR.
     POVERTY AMID AFFLUENCE; A REPORT ON A
   RESEARCH PROJECT CARRIED OUT AT THE NEW
   SCHOOL FOR SOCIAL RESEARCH. NEW YORK,
   TWENTIETH CENTURY FUND, 1966.
     208P.

       1. POVERTY. 2. LOW INCOME HOUSING.
   I. TITLE. II. NEW YORK (CITY) NEW
   SCHOOL FOR SOCIAL RESEARCH.
   III. TWENTIETH CENTURY FUND.

630
H43   TWENTIETH CENTURY FUND.
     HIGBEE, EDWARD.
     FARMS AND FARMERS IN AN URBAN AGE. NEW
   YORK, TWENTIETH CENTURY FUND, 1963.
     183P.
     BIBLIOGRAPHY: P. 145-151.

       1. AGRICULTURE. 2. LAND USE.
   I. TITLE. II. TWENTIETH CENTURY FUND.

332
C51   Twentieth century fund.
     Clark, Evans, 1888-   ed.
       The internal debts of the United States, edited by Evans
   Clark ... assisted by George B. Galloway. New York, Pub.
   for Twentieth century fund, inc., The Macmillan company,
   1933.
     xx, 430 p. diagrs. 24½ᵐ.
     "Sources of data on public utilities": p. 415-423.

     1. U. S.—Econ. condit.—1918-   2. Debts, Public—U. S.   I. Gal-
loway, George Barnes, 1806-   Joint author. II. Twentieth century
fund. III. Title.
                                      33—14111
   Library of Congress   HG181.C6
                   [45u²]   332.0973

LAW
T
M242rs   Twentieth Century Fund.
     McKay, Robert B
       Reapportionment reappraised; a report by Robert
   B. McKay on the one man, one vote principle in
   practice. New York, Twentieth Century Fund,
   1968.
     36p.

       1. Apportionment. 2. Voting. I. Twentieth
   Century Fund. II. Title.

330
H65   Twentieth Century Fund.
     Homan, Paul T   , ed.
       Financing American prosperity; a symposium
   of economists; editors: Paul T. Homan [and]
   Fritz Machlup. New York, The Twentieth
   Century Fund, 1945.
     508 p.

2C.   Contributors: Benjamin M. Anderson; John
   Maurice Clark; Howard S. Ellis; Alvin H. Hansen;
   Sumner H. Slichter; John H. Williams.

     1. Economic policy. I. Machlup, Fritz, jt. ed. II.
   Twentieth Century Fund. III. Title.

327
L18   Twentieth Century Fund.
     Laufer, Leopold.
       Israel and the developing countries: new
   approaches to cooperation. New York, Twentieth Century Fund, 1967.
     298p.

       1. International relations. 2. Technical
   assistance programs (Israel) 3. Underdeveloped countries. I. Twentieth Century Fund.
   II. Title.

330
B82   Twentieth Century Fund. (Committee on Foreign
       and Economic Relations)
     Buchanan, Norman S
       Rebuilding the world economy; America's
   role in foreign trade and investment; by
   Norman S. Buchanan and Friedrich A. Lutz;
   with the report and recommendations of the
   Committee on Foreign Economic Relations.
   New York, The Twentieth Century Fund, 1947.
     434 p. charts, tables.

       Bibliography: p. 415-421.

     1. Economic policy. 2. Economic conditions. I. Lutz,
   Friedrich A., jt. author. II. Twentieth Century Fund.
   (Committee on Foreign and   Economic Relations)
   III. Title.

330
:355.8
H17f   Twentieth Century Fund. (Committee on Economic
                Stabilization.)
     Hart, Albert G
       Financing defense; federal tax and
   expenditure policies [by] Albert G. Hart
   [and] E. Cary Brown, assisted by H. F. Rasmussen;
   with policy recommendations by the Committee on
   Economic Stabilization.
     161 p.

     1. Economic policy. 2. National defense. 3. Federal
   taxation. I. Brown, E   Cary, jt. author.
   II. Twentieth Century Fund. Committee on Economic
   Stabilization. III. Title.

331
T82   TWENTIETH CENTURY FUND. LABOR COMMITTEE.
     LABOR AND NATIONAL DEFENSE, A SURVEY OF
   THE SPECIAL LABOR PROBLEMS ARISING FROM
   AMERICA'S DEFENSE ACTIVITIES AND A PROGRAM
   FOR ACTION; THE FACTUAL FINDINGS BY LLOYD
   G. REYNOLDS, THE PROGRAM BY THE LABOR
2C.   COMMITTEE. NEW YORK, 1941.
     130P.

       1. LABOR SUPPLY. 2. NATIONAL DEFENSE.
   I. REYNOLDS, LLOYD GEORGE. II. TITLE.

711.585
C652   Twentieth Century Fund.
     Colean, Miles L
       Renewing our cities. New York, Twentieth
   Century Fund, 1953.
     x, 181 p. plates.

       Bibliographical footnotes.

     1. Urban redevelopment. I. Twentieth Century Fund.
   II. Title.

728.1
:940.42
T82   Twentieth Century Fund. (The Housing Committee.)
       Housing for defense, a review of the role of
   housing in relation to America's defense and a
   program for action. The factual findings, by
3c.   Miles L. Colean; The program, by the Housing
   Committee. New York, N.Y., 1940.
     xx, 198 p. tables.

       Bibliographical footnotes.

     1. Housing—Wartime. I. Colean, Miles L.

338.8
876m   Twentieth Century Fund. (Committee on Cartels
                and Monopoly).
     Stocking, George W
       Monopoly and free enterprise, by George W.
   Stocking and Myron W. Watkins; with the report
   and recommendations of the Committee on Cartels
   and Monopoly. New York, The Twentieth Century
   Fund, 1951.
     596 p.

     1. Monopolies. I. Twentieth Century Fund. (Committee
   on Cartels and Monopoly). II. Watkins, Myron W.,
   jt. author.

330
T82   Twentieth Century Fund.
     Report, 1958-66   67, 68
     1971-2C   New York, 1959-1971
       Ov. illus., tables. annual.

       For complete information see shelf list.

728.1
:711.585   Twentieth Century Fund. (Survey of Postwar Needs
T82   and Resources.)
       Housing requirements and urban redevelopment,
   [by] Lawrence N. Bloomberg, Howard G. Brunsman
   [and] A. B. Handler. Washington [May 1944]
     98 l. tables.
       Bibliographical footnotes.
       "Preliminary and confidential".
       Processed.
     1. Housing. 2. Housing market. 3. Family living
   requirements. 4. Urban redevelopment. 5. Neighborhood rehabilitation. I. Bloomberg, Lawrence N.
   II. Brunsman, Howard G. III. Handler, A. B.
   IV. Title.

352
T82   Twentieth Century Fund.
       Pickets at city hall; report and recommenda-
   tions of the Twentieth Century Fund Task Force
   on Labor Disputes in Public Employment.
   New York, 1970.
     38p.

       1. Municipal government. 2. Labor relations.
   I. Title.

330
B17u   Twentieth Century Fund.
     Barach, Arnold B
       U.S.A. and its economic future. Graphics by
   Rudolf Modley. New York, Macmillan, 1964.
     148 p. (A Twentieth Century Fund survey)

       1. Econ. condit. 2. Housing. I. Title.
   II. Twentieth Century Fund.

VF
728.100.15   Twentieth Century Fund.
H62   Housing Research Conference.
       Housing research survey. Washington, D.C.
   [1948]
     xvi, 89 p.
       William H. Scheick, chairman.
       Duplicated and distributed by the Producers
   Council, Inc., and the American Institute of
   Architects.
       Prepared for the Building Research Advisory
   Board.
       Processed.

300.2
L67   Twentieth Century Fund.
     Lorwin, Lewis Levitski, 1883 -
       Postwar plans of the United Nations, by
   Lewis L. Lorwin. New York, The Twentieth
   century fund, 1943.
     xii, 307 p.

       Bibliographical foot-notes.

330
(73)
T82u   Twentieth Century Fund.
       USA in new dimensions; the measure
   and promise of America's resources, by
   Thomas R. Carskadon and George Soule.
   Graphics by Rudolf Modley. Macmillan,
   New York, 1957.
     124 p. illus.

       "Based on America's needs and resources:
   a new survey, by J. Frederic Dewhurst and
   Associates."
           (Card No. 2)

330
(73)
T82u
Twentieth Century Fund. USA in new dimensions.
1957. (Card No. 2)

1.Economic conditions. 2.Family income and
expenditures - Housing. I.Carskadon, Thomas R
II.Soule, George. III.Title.

709.2
H68
21 HUD employees honored at annual awards
ceremony.
U.S. Dept. of Housing and Urban Development.
21 HUD employees honored at annual awards
ceremony. Washington, 1970.
3p. (HUD news. HUD-no. 70-359)

1. Awards. I. Title.

711.585
M47
Twenty years of urban renewal.
Mister, Melvin A
Twenty years of urban renewal.
Statement by Melvin A. Mister, District
of Columbia Redevelopment Land Agency at
the meeting of the Potomac Chapter,
National Association of Housing and
Redevelopment Officials. Jan. 8, 1970.
[n.p.] 1970.
12p.
1. Urban renewal – District of Columbia.
I. Title.

VF
33(73)
T82
1949
Twentieth Century Fund.
U. S. A., measure of a nation; a graphic presentation of
America's needs and resources, by Thomas R. Carskadon
and Rudolf Modley. Prepared by the Twentieth Century
Fund. New York, Macmillan Co., 1949.
101 p. illus. (part col.) 28 cm.
"Based on ... America's needs and resources, by J. Frederic Dewhurst and associates, published by the Twentieth Century Fund in
1947." 2.Family income and expenditures-Housing.
1. U. S.—Econ. condit.—1945-   I. Carskadon, Thomas Reyn-
olds, 1900-   II. Modley, Rudolf. III. Title.
HC106.5.T93   330.973   49—5268*
Library of Congress   [49v^30]

Ref.
808.8
F96
2500 anecdotes for all occasions: a new classified collection of the best anecdotes...
Fuller, Edmund
2500 anecdotes for all occasions: a new
classified collection of the best anecdotes
from ancient times to the present day.
Garden City, N. Y., Doubleday, 1943.
495 p.

Originally published as Thesaurus of anecdotes.

1.Quotations. I. Title. II. Title:...Thesaurus
of quotations.

VF
728.1
:613.5
A52
Twichell, Allan.
American Public Health Association. Committee
on the Hygiene of Housing.
An appraisal method for measuring the quality
of housing: A yardstick for health officers,
housing officials and planners. New York, N.Y.,
1945-1950.
3 v. in 5 pts. diagrs.,forms, maps, tables.

Parts 1 and 2 prepared by Allan Twichell; Part
3 prepared by Anatole A. Solow, Allan Twichell and
Emil A. Tiboni.
Contents.-Pt.1. Nature and uses of the method.
1945.-Pt.2.Appraisal : dwelling conditions:
(Continued on next card)

940.42
T82
Twentieth Century Fund.
Wartime facts and postwar problems, a study
and discussion manual. Ed. Evans Clark.
New York, N.Y., 1943.
vii, 136 p.

Bibliography: p.120-136.
Housing, Section 8, p.90-96, Urban redevelopment, Section 7, p.82-89.
1.Housing-Wartime. 2.Urban redevelopment-
Wartime. I.Clark, Evans, ed. II.Title.

030.2
L27
20,000 words for stenographers, students,
authors and proofreaders.
Leslie, Louis A   comp
20,000 words for stenographers, students,
authors and proofreaders. New York, Gregg
Div., McGraw-Hill Book, 1959.
250p.

1. English language - Dict. 2. English
language - Grammar. I. Title.

American Public Health Association. Commission
on the Hygiene of Housing. An appraisal
method for measuring the quality of housing
1945-1950. (Card 2).

Contents cont'd.-v.A.Survey director's manual.1946.
v.B.Field procedures.1946.v.C.Office procedures.
1946.-Pt.3.Appraisal of neighborhood environment:
Manual of survey procedures. 1950.

1.Building inspection-Handbooks,manuals, etc.
2.Neighborhood surveys-Handbooks, manuals, etc.
I.Twichell, Allan. II.Solow, Anatole A. III.Tiboni,
Emil A. IV.Title.

330
C31
Twentieth Century Fund.
Chase, Stuart
When the war ends; guide lines to America's
future as reported to the Twentieth Century Fund.
New York, Twentieth Century Fund, 1942-1946.
6 v.

Contents.-v.1. The road we are travelling,
1914-1942.-v.2.Goals for America: A budget of
our needs and resources.-v.3.Where's the money
coming from? Problems of postwar finance.-v.4.
Democracy under pressure: Special interests
vs. the public welfare.-v.5.Tomorrow's trade;
problems of our foreign commerce.-v.6. For this
we fought.

711.585
(7471)
U71
Twenty-four hundred Negro families in Harlem.
Urban League of New York.
Twenty-four hundred Negro families in
Harlem; an interpretation of the living
conditions of small wage earners. New
York, 1927.
32p.

1. Slums - New York (City) 2. Minority
groups - New York (City) 3. Housing -
New York (City) I. Title.

728.1
:613.5
H68
Twichell, Allen
Housing for health; papers presented under the
auspices of the Committee on the Hygiene of
Housing of the American Public Health
Association. Lancaster, Pa., Science Press
Print. Co., 1941.
221 p.

Contents.-Health and housing, C.-E.A.
Winslow.-Enforcement and subsidy in the control
of slums, L.M. Graves and A.H. Fletcher.-An
experiment in housing survey and inspection
procedures for health departments, G.C. Ruhland.-
(Continued on next card)

301.15
T82
Twentieth Century Fund. Task Force on
Community Development Corporations.
CDC's: new hope for the inner city. Report
of the Twentieth Century Fund Task Force on
Community Development Corporations. Background paper by Geoffrey Faux. New York,
1971.
121p.
1. Community development. 2. Economic
development. I. Title. II. Faux, Geoffrey.
III. Title: Community Development Corporations.

VF
061.6
A51
Twenty years of business research, 1930-1950.
Alabama. University. Bureau of Business Research.
Twenty years of business research, 1930-1950.
Tuscaloosa. [1951]
43 p. illus., table. (Its Printed series
no. 11)

"Publication of the Bureau of Business
Research, University of Alabama":p. 36-38.

1.Economic research. I.Title. II.Series.

Housing for health...194?. (Card 2)

Contents continued.
Housing codes, M.G. Lloyd.-Health centers and
health services in housing projects, A.A.
Twichell.-Heating and ventilation of the home,
C.-E.A. Winslow.-New possibilities in low-cost
home construction, R.L. Davison.-Planning for
recreation, F.J. Adams.-Family life as the basis
for home planning, S.H. Riemer.-Social effects of
good housing, F.S. Chapin.-Certain characteristics
of urban housing and their relation to illness and
(Continued on next card)

711.417
T82
Twentieth Century Fund. Task Force on
Governance of New Towns.
New towns: laboratories for democracy.
Report of the Twentieth Century Fund Task
Force on Governance of New Towns. Background
paper by Royce Hanson. New York, 1971.
73p.

1. New towns. I. Hanson, Royce. II. Title.

Class No. 84
Urban rel. 45
Accession
No.Y.
1949
Or
1949
Cost
Date 6/15/49 Vols.
Charged to
Date of bill
L. C. No.

Author (Surname first)
Urban Land Inst.
Title
A block plan for business in a
typical area
Edition or Series   Place   Publisher
N.Y.
List Price   Est. Cost
Recommended by   Plans table
Address
Reviewed in
Planning 10/2/49

NOT RUSH

Housing for health...194?. (Card 3)

Contents continued.
accidents, R.H. Britten, J.E. Brown, and
I. Altman.-Basic principles of healthful housing.-
Organization of research subcommittees, Committee
on the Hygiene of Housing, A.P.H.A.
1.Housing and health. 2.Housing codes. 3.Public
housing-Social effect. I.American Public Health
Association. Committee on the Hygiene of Housing.
II.Winslow, Charles-Edward A. III.Twichell, Allen.
IV.Riemer, Svend H. V.Chapin, F. Stuart.

711.4
(74886)
L81
Twentieth Century Pittsburgh.
Lubove, Roy
Twentieth Century Pittsburgh; government,
business, and environmental change.
New York, John Wiley & Sons, 1969.
189p. (New dimensions in history.
Historical cities)

1. City planning - Pittsburgh.
2. Urban renewal - Pittsburgh. 3. Social
conditions - Pittsburgh. I. Title.

85
AUTHOR: Twenty-third Street Association, Inc
TITLE: A block plan for residence in a
typical area suitable for new residential
development
PLACE: N.Y.
PUBLISHER:
DATE: 6/15/49 EDITION: PAGING: Folder
DESCRIPTIVE NOTE AND SERIES: Plans, Table
ANNOTATION:

175 - 5th Ave N.Y. 10   (OA-198)

711.585
T84
Twichell, Allan
Measuring the need for redevelopment,
blighted area surveys as a basis for local
programs. Chicago, Urban Redevelopment Study,
1949.
1 v. (various pagings)

Preliminary draft. Not for publication.

(See Card No. 2)

711.585
T84
Twichell, Allan. Measuring the need for redevelopment. 1949. (Card No. 2)

1.Urban redevelopment. 2.Housing. 3.Federal Housing programs. I.Title: Blighted area survey as a basis for local programs.

301.15
G87   Gutkind, Erwin Anton, 1886-
The twilight of cities.
The twilight of cities. New York, Free Press of Glencoe, 1962.
201p.

1. Sociology, Urban. 2. City planning. I. Title.

711.14
(77135)   Twinsburg, Ohio. Planning Commission.
T74   Tri-County Regional Planning Commission. (Medina, Summit, Portage, Ohio)
Land use and thoroughfare plan, Twinsburg, Ohio. Akron, Ohio, Tri-County Regional Planning Commission, Community Assistance Division, 1963.
57p.   (Its Planning report no. 3)
Prepared in cooperation with Twinsburg Planning Commission.
U.S. Urban Renewal Adm. UPAP.

1. Land use - Twinsburg, Ohio. 2. Highways - Twinsburg, Ohio. I. Twins-   burg, Ohio. Planning
Commission. II. U.S.   URA-UPAP. Twinsburg,
Ohio.   Ohio.

728.1
T84   TWICHELL, ALLAN A
A NEW METHOD FOR MEASURING THE QUALITY OF URBAN HOUSING; A TECHNIC OF THE COMMITTEE ON THE HYGIENE OF HOUSING. NEW YORK, AMERICAN PUBLIC HEALTH ASSOCIATION, 1943.
729-740P.

REPRINTED FROM AMERICAN JOURNAL OF PUBLIC HEALTH, V. 33, NO. 6, JUNE 1943. ADAPTED FROM PAPER PRESENTED ... AT MEETING OF AMERICAN PUBLIC HEALTH ASSOCIATION, ST . LOUIS, MO., OCT. 28, 1942.
(CONTINUED ON NEXT CARD)

711.3
(77657)   Twin cities area metropolitan development guide...
M45t   Minneapolis-St. Paul Metropolitan Council.
Twin cities area metropolitan development guide; the joint program. Minneapolis, 1968.
72p. (Its Report no. 5)
U.S. Dept. of Housing and Urban Development. UPAP.

1. Metropolitan area planning - Minneapolis-St. Paul. I. Title. II. U.S. HUD-UPAP. Minneapolis-St. Paul.

728.3
R28   Twitchell, Ralph S
Revere Quality House Institute.
Revere quality houses. [1-8]
New York [1948-1949?]
9 pts. illus.

Houses built in Houston, Tex., Sarasota, Fla., Springfield, N.J., Boston, Mass., South Bend Ind., Cleveland, Ohio, Seattle, Wash., San Francisco, Calif.

728.1   TWICHELL, ALLAN A   A NEW METHOD ...1943.
T84   (CARD 2)
1. HOUSING STANDARDS. 2. SLUM CLEARANCE. I. AMERICAN PUBLIC HEALTH ASSOCIATION. II. TITLE.

Twin Cities Area Metropolitan Transit Commission

see

Minneapolis-St. Paul Metropolitan Transit Commission

333
T84   Twitty, Siewright & Mills.
Legal study of the nonfuel mineral resources. Prepared under contract with the Public Land Law Review Commission. Phoenix, 1969.
5v.

Summary -- --- Summary 1969.
29p.
1. Public lands. 2. Natural resources. I. U.S. Public Land Law Review Commission. II. Title.

711.585
W66   Twichell, Allan A
Woodbury, Coleman, ed.
Urban redevelopment: problems and practices, by Charles S. Ascher and others.   Chicago, University of Chicago Press [1953]
xvi, 525 p. illus., map.

"This volume and its companion, The future of cities and urban redevelopment, are the chief products of the Urban Redevelopment Study."
Includes bibliographies.
(Continued on next card)

388
(77657)   Minnesota. Dept. of Highways.
M45t   Twin Cities area transportation study.
v.1   Volume 1, Study findings. In cooperation with U.S. Dept. of Commerce, Bureau of Public Roads. [St. Paul] 1962.
99p.

1. Transportation - Minneapolis-St. Paul. 2. Metropolitan area planning - Minneapolis-St. Paul. I. Title.

VF
370   Ford Foundation.
(60)   Two African patterns. [The newly inde-
F67   pendent countries of Africa below the Sahara]
New York, 1966.
47p.

1. Education - Africa. 2. Political science. I. Title.

Woodbury, Coleman, ed.   Urban redevelopment ...
[1953]   (Card 2)

Contents.-Measuring the quality of housing in planning for urban redevelopment, Allan A. Twichell.-Urban densities and their costs: an exploration into the economics of population densities and urban patterns, William H. Ludlow.-Private covenants in urban redevelopment, Charles S. Ascher.-Urban redevelopment short of clearance: rehabilitation, reconditioning, conservation and code enforcement, in local programs, William L.
(Continued on next card)

1521   TWIN CITIES METROPOLITAN COUNCIL. METROPOLITAN SEWER PLAN; A PRELIMINARY CONCEPT PLAN. ST. PAUL, 1968.
36P. (HUD 701 REPORT)

1. SEWERAGE AND SEWAGE DISPOSAL - MINNEAPOLIS - ST. PAUL. I. HUD. 701. MINNEAPOLIS - ST. PAUL.

658.3   Two approaches to the politics of personnel policy.
T36   Thompson, Frank J
Two approaches to the politics of personnel policy. Wash., Urban Institute, 1970.
81p. (Workings paper no. 107-14)

Research conducted through contract with University of California, Oakland Project. Draft.

1. Personnel management. I. Urban Institute. II. California. University. Oakland Project. III. Title.

Woodbury, Coleman, ed.   Urban redevelopment ...
[1953]   (Card 3)

Slayton.-Relocation of families displaced in urban redevelopment: experience in Chicago, Jack Meltzer [and] Sheilah Orloff.-Eminent domain in acquiring subdivision and open land in redevelopment programs: a question of public use, Ira S. Robbins and Marian Perry Yankauer.

Twin Cities Metropolitan Planning Commission

see

Minneapolis-St. Paul Metropolitan Planning Commission.

333.332
(07)   2 CASE STUDY COURSES IN REAL ESTATE APPRAISAL OFFERED BY THE AMERICAN
A52T   AMERICAN INSTITUTE OF REAL ESTATE APPRAISERS.
2 CASE STUDY COURSES IN REAL ESTATE APPRAISAL OFFERED BY THE AMERICAN INSTITUTE OF REAL ESTATE APPRAISERS AT THE UNIVERSITY OF SOUTHERN CALIFORNIA, SUMMER OF 1940. LOS ANGELES, 1940.
11P.

1. APPRAISAL - STUDY AND TEACHING. I. TITLE.

550
T84   Twidale, C R
Structural landforms; landforms associated with granitic rocks, faults, and folded strata. Cambridge, Mass., MIT Press, 1971.
247p. (An introduction to systematic geomorphology, vol. 5)

Bibliography: p. 219-231.

1. Geology. I. Title.

336.2
(77657)   Litterer, Oscar F
L47   Twin Cities metropolitan tax study.
Twin Cities metropolitan tax study. Minneapolis, Upper Midwest Research and Development Council, 1966.
166p.

1. Taxation - Minneapolis-St. Paul metropolitan area. I. Upper Midwest Research and Development Council. II. Title.

720
E17   Eaton, Leonard K
Two Chicago architects and their clients.
Two Chicago architects and their clients, Frank Lloyd Wright and Howard Van Doren Shaw. With an appendix by Elizabeth M Douvan. Cambridge, MIT Press, 1969.
259p.

Bibliography: p. 237-242.

1. Architecture. 2. Architecture - Chicago. 3. Wright, Frank Lloyd. 4. Shaw, Howard Van Doren. I. Title.

711.4
(77311)
M87
TWO CITIES.
MUSEUM OF MODERN ART.
TWO CITIES; PLANNING IN NORTH AND
SOUTH AMERICA. NEW YORK, 1947.
19P. (THE MUSEUM OF MODERN ART
BULLETIN, V. 14, NO. 3)

1. CITY PLANNING - CHICAGO.
2. CITY PLANNING - BRAZIL. I. TITLE.

320
S23t
Two hundred million Americans in search of
a government.
Schattschneider, E E
Two hundred million Americans in search of
a government. New York, Holt, Rinehart and
Winston, 1969.
133p.

1. Political science. 2. Democracy. I. Title.

308
(5)
N17
Two sides of one world.
U.S. National Commission for the United
Nations Educational, Scientific and
Cultural Organization.
Two sides of one world; a report on an inter-
national discussion of human values in social
change in South and Southeast Asia and in the
United States; implications for Asian-
American cooperation, April 19-May 19, 1956,
by Arthur Goodfriend. Co-sponsored by ...
and UNESCO. Washington, 1957.
79p. illus.

(Continued on next card)

691
F22
UM-4
Two-coat paint systems for exterior use.
U.S. Federal Housing Administration.
Two-coat paint systems for exterior use.
In Its Use of materials bulletin UM-4.
Washington, May 1948. 5 p.

Supersedes Technical circular no. 6, rev.
Sept. 1, 1942.
Processed.

728.3
P65t
201 HOMES FOR EVERY BUDGET.
POLLMAN, RICHARD B
201 HOMES FOR EVERY BUDGET. DETROIT,
HOME PLANNERS INC, 1962.
90P. (HOME PLANNERS, INC, DESIGNS
FOR CONVENIENT LIVING, BOOK NO. 22)

1. ARCHITECTURE, DOMESTIC - DESIGNS
AND PLANS. I. TITLE.

308
(5)
N17
U.S. National Commission for the United
Nations Educational, Scientific and Cul-
tural Organization. Two sides ... (Card 2)

1. Social conditions - Asia. 2. International relations. I. Goodfriend, Arthur.
II. Title.

698
F67
R1259
The two-coat system of house painting.
U.S. Forest Service. Forest Products Laboratory.
Madison, Wis.
The two-coat system of house painting, by
F. L. Browne. Rev. Madison, Wis., Nov. 1950.
21 p. plates, tables. (Its R1259)

Bibliography: p. 18-20.
Processed.

1.Paints and painting. I.Browne, F. L. II.Title.

728.3
H65t
203 homes; split-level, contemporary, ranch,
low-cost, hillside, traditional.
Home Planners, inc.
203 homes; split-level, contemporary, ranch,
low-cost, hillside, traditional, custom-deluxe,
frame-brick, 1 1/2 and 2 story. New York,
Universal Pub. and Distributing Corp. for Home
Planners, 1961.
96p. (Its designs for convenient living.
Book no. 34. Library series no. 3)

Richard B. Pollman, designer.

1. Architecture, Domestic - Designs and
plans. 2. House plans. I. Title. II. Pollman,
Richard B.

728.1
S77t
1952
Two-thirds of a nation.
Straus, Nathan, 1889-
Two-thirds of a nation; a housing program.
1st ed. New York, Knopf, 1952.
291p.

1. Housing. I. Title.

362.6
S81t
TWO DOZEN TRADITIONAL MISTAKES MADE BY
WOMEN'S BOARDS OF HOMES.
SWAIM, WILLIAM T
TWO DOZEN TRADITIONAL MISTAKES MADE BY
WOMEN'S BOARDS OF HOMES FOR THE AGING.
DILLSBURG, PRESBYTERIAN HOME OF CENTRAL
PENNSYLVANIA, 1963.
7P. (TOPIC NO. 20, 1963 SHORT
COURSE...)

1. OLD AGE. I. TITLE.
II. PRESBYTERIAN HOMES OF CENTRAL
PENNSYLVANIA.

711.552
(7471)
D68
250 best ideas from Downtown Idea Exchange.
Downtown Idea Exchange, New York.
250 best ideas from Downtown Idea
Exchange. New York, 1958.
22p.

1. Business districts - New York (City)
2. Shopping centers. I. Title.

VF
341.1
:338
P81
no.2
Two-thirds of the world.
Public Affairs Institute.
Two-thirds of the world; problems of a new
approach to the peoples of Asia, Africa, and
Latin America, by Harold R. Issacs. Washington
[1950]
64 p. maps. (Bold new program series,
no. 2)
"The series was made possible through funds
granted ... by the Foundation for World Government" - p.[2]
1.Technical assistance programs. I.Issacs, Harold
R. II.Foundation for World Government. III.Title.
IV.Series.

320
C25t
Two faces of Federalism; an outline of an
argument about pluralism, unity and law.
Center for the Study of Democratic Institu-
tions.
Two faces of Federalism; an outline of an
argument about pluralism, unity and law, by
Robert M. Hutchins. Followed by a discussion.
Santa Barbara, Calif., 1961.
126p.

On cover: A contribution to the discussion
of the free society.

1. Political science. I. Hutchins, Robert M.
II. Title.

301.15
(52)
C67
Two Japanese villages.
Cornell, John Bilheimer, 1921-
Two Japanese villages: Matsunagi, a
Japanese mountain community by J.B. Cornell;
Kurusu, a Japanese agricultural community,
by Robert J. Smith. New York, Greenwood
Press, 1969.
232p. (Michigan. University. Center for
Japanese Studies. Occasional papers no. 5)

1. Community structure - Japan. I. Smith,
Robert J., jt. au. II. Michigan. University.
Center for Japanese Studies. III. Title.

301.15
I53
Two views of urban dynamics.
Ingram, Gregory K
Two views of urban dynamics, by Gregory K.
Ingram and John F. Kain. Cambridge, Mass.,
Program on Regional and Urban Economics,
Harvard University, 1970.
15p. (Program on regional and urban
economics. Discussion paper no. 71)

1. Community structure. I. Harvard University.
Program on Regional and Urban Economics.
II. Kain, John F., jt. au. III. Title.

330.148
K25
Two-factor theory.
Kelso, Louis O
Two-factor theory: the economics of
reality, by Louis O. Kelso and Patricia
Hetter. How to turn eighty million
workers into capitalists on borrowed
money and other proposals. New York,
Vintage Books, 1967.
202p.

1. Capitalism. I. Hetter, Patricia,
jt. au. II. Title.

658
E28t
Two lessons in group dynamics.
Educator's Washington Dispatch.
Two lessons in group dynamics; so you
appointed a committee when you run a
conference. Washington, D.C., 1948.
12p.

1. Management. I. Title.

388
(7471)
N28t
Two-way radio communication.
New York (City) Transit Authority.
Two-way radio communication; Mass Trans-
portation Demonstration Project. Final report
New York, 1966.
92p. (Project NY-MTD-8)

U.S. Dept. of Housing and Urban Development
Mass Transportation Demonstration Grant Program.
1. Transportation - New York (City)
2. Communication systems. I. U.S. HUD-Mass
Transportation Demonstration Grant Program.
II. Title.

312
C25tw
200 million Americans.
U.S. Bureau of the Census.
200 million Americans. Washington, For sale
by Supt. of Doc., U.S. Govt. Print. Off.,
1967.
75p.

1. Population. 2. Social conditions.
I. Title.

711.585.1
(79466)
M19
Two model cities.
May, Judith V
Two model cities: political development on
the local level. Wash., Urban Institute,,
1969.
65p. (Working paper no. 107-11)
Research conducted through contract with
University of California, Oakland Project.
Prepared for a meeting of the American
Political Science Association, New York City,
Sept. 2-6, 1969.
1. Model cities - Oakland, Calif. I. Urban
Institute. II. California. University.
Oakland Project. III. Title.

VF
711.585
F22t
221 relocation housing.
U.S. Federal Housing Administration.
221 relocation housing. Washington,
Dec. 1956.
Leaflet.

1.Relocation. 2.Mortgage insurance. I.Title.

VF
711.585
F22t
1958
221 relocation housing.
U.S. Federal Housing Administration.
221 relocation housing. Washington,
1958.
leaflet.

1. Relocation. 2. Mortgage insurance.
I. Title.

628.515
T92
Tyco Laboratories.
Basic salinogen ion-exchange resins for
selective nitrate removal from potable and
effluent waters, by A.L. Walitt and H.L. Jones.
Cincinnati, U.S. Advanced Waste Treatment
Research Laboratory, 1969?
88p. (U.S. Federal Water Quality Administra-
tration. Water pollution control research
series)
1. Water pollution. I. Jones, H.L., jt. au.
II. Walitt, A.L. III. U.S. Federal Water
Quality Administration. IV. U.S. Advanced
Waste Treatment Research Laboratory.
V. Title.

Tyler, R G. jt. au.
691.54
H38
pt. 1
Hughes, J
Concrete strengths in West Africa. 1.
Ghana Coastal region, by J. Hughes and R. G.
Tyler. Accra, Ghana, West African Building
Research Institute, 1962.
15p. (West African Building Research
Institute. Note no. 12)

1. Cement. 2. Concrete. I. Tyler, R. C.,
jt. au. II. West African Building Research
Institute.

VF
711.585
F22t
1959
221 relocation housing.
U.S. Federal Housing Administration.
221 relocation housing. Washington,
1959.
leaflet.

1. Relocation. 2. Mortgage insurance. I. Title.

628.515
T92e
Tyco Laboratories.
Electrochemical treatment of acid mine
waters. [Wash.] Environmental Protection
Agency, 1972.
81p. (Water pollution control research
series)

1. Water pollution. I. U.S. Environmental
Protection Agency. II. Title.

693.5
:691.8
T95
Tyler, R G
Sandcrete blocks. Accra, Ghana, West
African Building Research Institute, 1961.
6p. (West African Building Research
Institute. Note no. 4)

1. Concrete blocks. 1. West African
Building Research Institute.

711.585
H68e
221 relocation housing programs.
U.S. Housing and Home Finance Agency. Office of the Administrator.
An evaluation of the Section 221 relocation
housing program. A report to the Housing Administrator. Prepared under the supervision
of Albert Thompson. Washington, 1959.
48p.
Cover-title.

1. Relocation. I. Thompson, Albert.
2. Mortgage finance. II. Title: 221 relocation
housing programs.

628.515
T92s
Tyco Laboratories, inc.
Silicate treatment for acid mine drainage
prevention; silicate and alumina/silica gel
treatment of coal refuse for the prevention
of acid mine drainage. [Prepared] for the
Environmental Protection Agency, Water Quality
Office. Waltham, Mass., 1971.
94p. (Water pollution control research
series)
1. Water pollution. I. U.S. Environmental
Protection Agency. II. Title.

691
(60)
T95
Tyler, R G
The structural properties of West African
timbers. Accra, Ghana, West African Building
Research Institute, 1962.
30p. (Note n.3)
References: p. 16-17.

1. Building materials - Africa.
2. Lumber industry. I. West African
Building Research Institute.

VF
711.585
M27
221, the program nobody knows.
Metropolitan Association of General Improvement Contractors.
221, the program nobody knows; housing rehabilitation and relocation housing under
Section 221 of the National Housing Act of
1959, by John H. Haas. Washington, 1959.
23p.
1. Relocation. 2. Mortgage finance.
I. Title. I. Haas, John H.

691.421
T95
1935
Tyler, Paul M
Clay. Rev. Washington, Dept. of
the Interior, U.S. Bureau of Mines,
1935.
66p. (U.S. Bureau of Mines.
[Information circular] I. C. 6155)
Bibliography: p. 57-66.
1. Clay. I. U.S. Bureau of Mines.

378
T95
Tyler, Ralph W
Report on cooperative education; summary of
the two-year national study of cooperative
education made possible by a grant from the Fund
for the Advancement of Education, by Ralph W.
Tyler and Annice L. Mills. New York, Thomas
Alva Edison Foundation, 1961.
32p.

1. Education. 2. Universities and colleges.
I. Mills, Annice L., jt. au. II. Title:
Cooperative education.

332.72
(73
[347]
C65
1963
S-R
NO.304
TWO-YEAR EXTENSION OF FHA SECTION 22
MORTGAGE INSURANCE AUTHORITY.
U.S. CONGRESS. SENATE. COMMITTEE ON
BANKING AND CURRENCY.
TWO-YEAR EXTENSION OF FHA SECTION 221
MORTGAGE INSURANCE AUTHORITY. REPORT
TO ACCOMPANY H.J. RES. 467.
WASHINGTON, GOVT. PRINT. OFF., 1963.
3P. (88TH CONGRESS, 1ST SESSION.
SENATE. REPORT NO. 304)

1. MORTGAGE FINANCE LEGISLATION.
I. TITLE. II. TITLE: FHA SECTION
221 MORTGAGE INSURANCE.

728.1
T95
2c.
Tyler, Poyntz, ed.
City and suburban housing. New York,
H. W. Wilson, 1957.
190p.
Bibliography: p. 181-190.
Partial contents: -What the aged need in their
homes, by Albert M. Cole. (Reprint from New York
Times Magazine, p. 11, Aug. 4, 1957) -The dreary
deadlock of public housing, by Catherine Bauer.
(Continued on next card)

711.4
(764)
T95
Tyler, Tex. City Plan Commission.
Koch & Fowler, Dallas.
Tyler city plan, 1945. Dallas, 1945.
70 p. maps (fold.)

1.Master plan-Tyler, Tex. I.Tyler, Tex. City
Plan Commission.

500.15
(71)
C15
no.8
Tyas, J P I
Scientific and technical information in
Canada. Prepared for the Science Council of
Canada, by J.P.I. Tyas and others. Ottawa,
Queen's Printer, 1969.
2pts. in 8 v. (Canada. Science Secretariat.
Special study report no.8)
Contents: -pt.1. pt.2. chap.1. Government
depts. and agencies. chap.2. Industry. chap.3.
Universities. chap.4. International organiza-
tions and foreign countries. chap.5. Techniques
and sources. chap.6. Libraries. chap.7.
Economics.
(Cont'd. on next card)

728.1
T95
Tyler, Poyntz, ed. City and suburban housing.
1957. ... (Card 2)
(Reprint from Architectural Forum. 106:140-
2, May 1957)
1. Housing. 2. Public housing. 3. Slum
clearance. 4. Housing for the aged. I.
Cole, Albert M. II. Bauer, Catherine.

388
(764)
T29t
v.1
Tyler urban transportation study.
Texas. Highway Dept.
Tyler urban transportation study. Vol. 1.
Origin-destination survey. Sponsoring
agencies: City of Tyler, County of Smith
[and] Texas Highway Dept. in cooperation
with U.S. Dept. of Commerce, Bureau of
Public Roads. [Austin?] 1964.
1 v.

1. Transportation - Tyler, Tex.
2. Journey to work. 3. Transportation -
Statistics. I. U.S. Bureau of
Public Roads. II. Title.

500.15
(71)
C15
no.8
Tyas, J P I Scientific...1969.
(Card 2)

1. Scientific research - Canada. I. Science
Council of Canada. II. Title. (Series: Canada.
Science Secretariat. Special study report no.8)

690.24
T95
Tyler, R G
Allowable spans for timber rafters and
purlins, by R. G. Tyler and J. Hughes.
Accra, Ghana, West African Building
Research Institute, 1962.
22p. (West African Building Research
Institute. Note N.5)

1. Roofs and roofing. I. Hughes, J., jt. au.
II. West African Building Research Institute.

690.015
(485)
S82
R101
Tynelius, Sven.
Förnyelse av det äldre villabeståndet;
en modellundersökning i eskilstuna
(Modernization of old detached houses; a
pattern survey) Stockholm, Statens råd
för Byggnadsforskning, 1964.
36p. (Sweden. Statens Kommitté för
Byggnadsforskning. Rapport no. 101)
English summary.
1. Building research - Sweden. 2. Houses -
Maintenance and modernization. I. Sweden. Statens
Kommitté för Byggnadsforskning.

690.015
(435)
S82
R29-
1966

Tynelius, Sven.
Förnyelse av det gamla låghusbeståndet i stadskärnan; en modellundersökning i Lund (Renewal of old, small houses in the town centre. A model investigation in Lund) Stockholm, 1966.
55p. (Sweden. Statens Kommitté för Byggnadsforskning. Rapport 29:1966)
English summary.

1. Building research - Sweden. 2. Houses - Maintenance and modernization. I. Sweden. Statens Kommitté for   Byggnadsforskning.

336.18
E52

TYPES OF ASSISTANCE AVAILABLE TO ALASKA FROM FEDERAL DEPARTMENTS.
U.S. OFFICE OF EMERGENCY PLANNING.
TYPES OF ASSISTANCE AVAILABLE TO ALASKA FROM FEDERAL DEPARTMENTS AND AGENCIES. PREPARED FOR FEDERAL RECONSTRUCTION AND DEVELOPMENT PLANNING COMMISSION. WASHINGTON, 1964.
27L.

1. GRANTS-IN-AID. I. U.S. FEDERAL RECONSTRUCTION AND DEVELOPMENT PLANNING COMMISSION. II. TITLE.

551.5
N18

TYPHOON KAREN.
U.S. NAVAL CIVIL ENGINEERING LABORATORY, PORT HUENEME, CALIF.
STUDY AND ANALYSIS OF DAMAGE BY TYPHOON KAREN ON GUAM BY R.M. WEBB AND OTHERS. PORT HUENEME, 1963.
205P. (ITS TECHNICAL NOTE, 497)

1. STORMS. I. WEBB, R.M.
II. TITLE: DAMAGE BY TYPHOON KAREN ON GUAM. III. TYPHOON KAREN.

690.015
(485)
S82
R30
1966

Tynelius, Sven.
Fri sikt i gathörn (Clear view at street corners), av Sven Tynelius and Carl-Olof Berglund. Stockholm, Statens Institut för Byggnadsforskning, 1966.
99p. (Sweden. Statens Kommitté för Byggnadsforskning. Rapport 30: 1966)
English summary.

1. Building research - Sweden.
2. Traffic safety. I. Berglund, Carl-Olof, jt.au. II. Sweden. Statens Kommitté för Byggnadsforskning.

728.1
(7527l)
B15t
1964

Types of families living in Baltimore's low-rent projects, 1951-1964.
Baltimore. Urban Renewal and Housing Agency.
Types of families living in Baltimore's low-rent projects, 1951-1964, by Sara S. Hartman and Joseph F. Kish. Baltimore, 1965.
32p.

1. Low income housing - Baltimore.
2. Rental housing - Baltimore. 3. Family income and expenditure - Housing - Baltimore. 4. Housing statistics - Baltimore.   I. Title.
II. Hartman, Sara S. III. Kish, Joseph F.

VF
623
U54
AE7C

Typical design analyses for water supply systems.
U.S. Army. Corps of Engineers.
Water supply: Typical design analyses for water supply systems. Washington, D.C., Govt. Print. Off., Feb. 1946.
8 p. (Its Engineering manual for War Department construction. Pt. VII, Appendix C)

1. Water supply engineering. I. Title: Typical design analyses for water supply systems. II. Series: Engineering manual for War Department construction.

691.161
F56p

Tyner, M
Florida. University. Engineering and Industrial Experiment Station.
Properties of Florida asphalt-filler mixtures, by H. E. Schveyer and M. Tyner. Gainesville, Fla., 1959.
19p. diagrs., tables. (Its Bulletin series no. 103)
Engineering progress at the University of Florida, vol. XIII, no. 11, Nov. 1959.
1. Building materials. I. Schveyer, H.E. II. Tyner, M. (Series)

312
(7526
:083.41)
B15

Types of families living in Baltimore's low-rent projects, 1968.
Baltimore. Dept. of Housing and Community Development.
Types of families living in Baltimore's low-rent projects, 1968. Baltimore, 1968.
31p.

1. Population - Baltimore - Statistics.
2. Low-income housing - Baltimore - Statistics.
3. Public housing - Baltimore - Statistics.
I. Title.

VF
697.3
:621.415
D15

Typical design problems on the residential heat pump.
Dana, Homer Jackson, 1890-
Typical design problems on the residential heat pump. Pullman, State College of Washington [1949]
36 p. illus. 23 cm. (Washington (State) State College, Pullman. Engineering Experiment Station. Bulletin no. 73)

"Engineering bulletins:" p. 32-36.

1. Heat pump. I. Title. II. Series: Washington (State) State College, Pullman. Engineering Experiment Station. Engineering bulletin no. 73.

[TA7.W27 no. 73]   (620.72)   A 49-10529*

Washington. State Coll.   Pullman. Library
for Library of Congress   [3]

655
R67

Type and typography.
Rosen, Ben.
Type and typography; the designers type book. New York, Van Nostrand Reinhold, 1963.
406p.

1. Printing. 2. Visual aids. I. Title.

614
N17t
1957/61

Types of injuries incidence and associated disability.
U.S. National Center for Health Statistics.
Types of injuries incidence and associated disability, United States, July 1957-June 1961. Wash., U.S. Dept. of Health, Education, and Welfare, Public Health Service, 1964.
47p. (Its Vital and health statistics. Series 10: Data from the National Health Survey, no. 8)
U.S. Public Health Service. Publication no. 1000, series 10, no. 8.
1. Health. 2. Health - Statistics. I. Title.

VF
694.1
T45

Typical designs of timber structures.
Timber Engineering Company.
Typical designs of timber structures; a reference for use of architects and engineers. 1949 ed. Washington [1948]
114 p. illus. 23 x 35 cm.

Wood construction.
1. Building, Wooden. I. Title.

TH1101.T5   694.1   49-2734*

Library of Congress   [5]

720
(4391)
I57

Type designing in Hungary.
Institute of Building Types Design, Budapest.
Type designing in Hungary. Budapest, 1964.
1v.

1. Architecture - Hungary. 2. Architecture - Designs and plans. I. Title.

614
N17t

Types of injuries, incidence and associated disability.
U.S. National Health Survey.
Types of injuries, incidence and associated disability, United States, July 1958-June 1959. Washington, Public Health Service, Div. of Public Health Methods, 1960.
36p. (Its Health statistics, ser. B 16)
Public Health Service. Publication no. 584, B 16.

1. Health. 2. Sick. I. Title.

VF
728
:392
U54
Jan.1951

Typical dwellings in 14 European countries.
United Nations. Economic and Social Council. Economic Commission for Europe. Industry and Materials Committee.
Typical dwellings in 14 European countries, a comparative study of the utilisation of space. [Geneva, Switzerland] Jan. 1951.
33 p. plans, tables (one fold) (Its IM/HOU/25)
Abstract: p. 1.
Definitions: p. 8-9.
Restricted.
Mimeographed.

(Continued on next card)

VF
693.5
N17

Types and sizes of forms for one-way concrete joist construction.
U.S. National Bureau of Standards.
Types and sizes of forms for one-way concrete joist construction. [Wash.] 1969.
6p. (NBS voluntary product standard PS 16-69)

1. Concrete construction. I. Title.

658.564
G74

TYPEWRITER FONTS FOR AUTOMATIC READING.
U.S. GRIFFIS AIR FORCE BASE, ROME, N.Y.
STANDARDIZATION OF TYPEWRITER FONTS FOR AUTOMATIC READING, BY JAMES F. GREENLY. ROME, N.Y., 1966.
49P.

1. AUTOMATION. I. GREENLY, JAMES F. II. TITLE. III. TITLE: TYPEWRITER FONTS FOR AUTOMATIC READING.

United Nations. Economic and Social Council. Economic Commission for Europe. Industry and Materials Committee. Typical dwellings in 14 European countries...1951. (Card 2)

1. Space considerations. 2. Family living requirements. 3. House plans. I. Blackshaw, Maurice B. II. Title.

627.4
B87t

Types of agricultural occupance of flood plains in the United States.
Burton, Ian.
Types of agricultural occupance of flood plains in the United States. Chicago, 1962.
167p. (University of Chicago. Dept. of Geography. Research paper no. 75)
Bibliography: p. 163-167.

1. Flood control. 2. Agriculture.
I. Chicago. University. (Dept. of Geography) II. Title: Agricultural occupance of flood plains in the United States. III. Title.

691
P67
E81-
1960

Typewriting.
Portugal. Laboratório Nacional de Engenharia Civil.
Regras de dactilografia (Rules of typewriting) Lisboa, 1961.
11p. (Its Especificações E81-1960)

English summary.

1. Title: Typewriting.

621.3
F22

Typical electric bills.
U.S. Federal Power Commission.
Typical electric bills. Typical net monthly bills for residential, commercial, and industrial services. Wash., Govt. Print. Off.,
v. (FPC R-)
For Library holdings see main entry.

1. Electricity. 2. Public utilities. I. Title.

711.6
C25T
TYPICAL LOT AND BLOCK GRADING FOR
SINGLE UNIT PROJECTS.
CENTRAL MORTGAGE AND HOUSING CORPORATION.
TYPICAL LOT AND BLOCK GRADING FOR
SINGLE UNIT PROJECTS. OTTAWA, CANADA,
1959.
14P. ILLUS.

1. SITE PLANNING. I. TITLE.

711.4
(016)
T97
Tyrwhitt, Jacqueline.
Urban design bibliography. [Cambridge,
Mass.] Harvard University Graduate School
of Design, 1962.
26p.

1. City planning - Bibl. 2. Landscape
architecture - Bibl. I. Harvard
University. Graduate School of Design.
II. Title.

LAW
T
U548L

2 c
U.C.L.A. law review.
Land planning and the law emerging policies
and techniques. Los Angeles, University of
California, 1965.
1011p. (Entire issue March 1965)
Partial contents:-National land policies,
historic and emergent, by Robert C. Weaver.
c.3. Reprint, p. 719-733.

1. Land use. 2. open space land. 3. Land
economics. I. Weaver, Robert Clifton.
National land   policies, historic
and emergent.   II. Title.

651.4
R24
1959
TYPING.
REIGNER, CHARLES G
ROWE COLLEGE TYPING. 2D ED.
CHICAGO, H.M. ROWE CO., 1959.
148P.

1. OFFICE PROCEDURES. I. TITLE.
II. TITLE: COLLEGE TYPING.
III. TITLE: TYPING.

711.4
3662
TYSEN, FRANK J
GOODALL, MERRILL, ED.
SUBURBAN PLANNING; THREE STUDIES.
CLAREMONT, CALIF., CLAREMONT
ADMINISTRATIVE STUDIES, 1962.
63P.

CONTENTS.- PT.1. THE CLAREMONT
PLANNING COMMISSION, BY ENIO HART
DOUGLASS.- PT.2. THE ELECTION CASE BY
FRANK J. TYSEN.- PT.3. RECREATION
PLANNING, BY DAVID STERN.

1. CITY PLANNING. I. TITLE.
II. DOUGLASS, ENIO HART.
(CONTINUED ON NEXT CARD)

LAW
T
C178La

2c
UCLA law review.
Carter, Lisle C   Jr.
Law and the urban crisis. Ithaca, N.Y.,
Center for Housing and Environmental Studies,
Div. of Urban Studies, Cornell University,
1968.
[18] p. (Cornell University. Center for
Housing and Environmental Studies. Article
28, reprints)
Reprinted from: UCLA law review, June 1968,
p. 1135-1152.
1. Poor. 2. Public assistance. I. Cornell
University. Center for Housing and Environ-
mental Studies. II. UCLA law review.
III. Title.

655
G68t
1963
Typography and design.
U.S. Government Printing Office.
Typography and design. Rev.
Washington, For sale by Supt. of
Documents, Govt. Print. Off., 1963.
107p. (Its Training series)

1. Printing and publishing.
I. Title.

711.4
G662
GOODALL, MERRILL, ED. SUBURBAN PLANNING.
...1962.   (CARD 2)

III. TYSEN, FRANK J. IV. STERN, DAVID.

711.4
(79471)
S22
UCSC environs development.
Sedway/Cooke.
UCSC environs development; needs and
methods for intergovernmental action; a
summary report. Prepared for the Office
of Physical Planning and Construction,
University of California, Santa Cruz. San
Francisco, 1968.
37p.
1. City planning - Santa Cruz, Calif.
2. Intergovernmental relations - Santa Cruz,
Calif. I. California. University, Santa
Cruz. Office of Physical Planning and
Construction. II. Title.

534.83
B17t
The tyranny of noise.
Baron, Robert Alex.
The tyranny of noise. New York, St. Martin's
Press, 1970.
294p.

Bibliography: p. 279-284.

1. Noise. I. Title.

388
T97
Tyson, David O
A close look at the transit crisis.
[Trenton, 1961?]
9p.
Reprinted by: Bureau of Public Information,
New Jersey State Highway Department, Trenton,
New Jersey.

1. Transportation - New York.
2. Transportation - New Jersey.

711.552
(77434)
D27d
UDA Research Project.
Detroit Edison Co.
Detroit critical area; guidelines for
future development. Detroit, 1969.
57p. (UDA Research Project. Document
DOX-USA-DT 21)
A project of the Detroit Edison Co., Wayne
State University and Doxiadis Associates.

1. Business districts - Detroit.
I. UDA Research Project. II. Title.

360
(016)
A52
The tyranny of poverty; a selected bibliography of books, pamphlets, articles and...
American Jewish Committee.
The tyranny of poverty; a selected
bibliography of books, pamphlets, articles
and memoranda on government and community
action, employment, education, legal and
social services [and] economic and social
problems. New York, American Jewish
Committee, Institute of Human Relations,
1966.
18p.

1. Social wel-   fare - Bibl.
2. Social   service - Bibl.
I. Title.

UAW-CIO

see

International Union, United Automobile,
Aircraft and Agricultural Implement Workers
of America (UAW-CIO).

388
(77434)
D27e
UDA Research Project.
Detroit Edison Co.
Elaboration of the land transportation
system of UDA [Urban Detroit Area] Detroit,
1969.
66p. (UDA Research Project. Document
DOX-USA-A 70)
A project of the Detroit Edison Co., Wayne
State University and Doxiadis Associates.

1. Transportation - Detroit. 2. Land use -
Detroit. I. UDA Research Project. II. Title.

6228-
6237
TYRONZA, ARK. CITY PLANNING COMMISSION.
PLANNING: 1, ADMINISTRATIVE GUIDE,
SUBDIVISION REGULATIONS; 2, PROPOSED
SUBDIVISION REGULATIONS; 3, PROPOSED
ZONING ORDINANCE; 4, ADMINISTRATIVE
GUIDE, ZONING ORDINANCE; 5, GENERAL PLAN
FOR LAND USE, PROPOSED; 6, SEWERAGE
SYSTEM (MAP); 7, PLANNING AREA MAP; 8,
DETAILED LAND USE (MAP); 9, LAND USE
COVERAGE (MAP); 10, PAVING TYPES AND TRAFFIC
DEVICES. TYRONZA, ARK., 1963.
10 V. (HUD 701 REPORT)
1. CITY PLANNING - TYRONZA, ARK.
I. HUD. 701. TYRONZA, ARK.

711.3
(77434)
D27e
UDA Research Project.
Detroit Edison Co.
Elaboration of the selected alternative.
Detroit, 1969.
78p. (UDA Research Project. Document DOX-
USA-A 71)
A project of the Detroit Edison Co., Wayne
State University and Doxiadis Associates.

1. Metropolitan area planning - Detroit.
2. City growth - Detroit. I. UDA Research
Project. II. Title.

711(41)
A77
Tyrwhitt, Jacqueline, editor.

Association for Planning and Regional Reconstruction.

Basic surveys for planning; an attempt by specialists in
conference with Kent County officers to outline a scheme
for surveys satisfying the requirements of the 1947 Town
planning act, edited by Jacqueline Tyrwhitt and W. L.
Waide. London, Published for the Architect & Building
News by G. Wood; distributed by Iliffe [1949]
42 p. fold. maps. 23 cm.

1. City planning-Gt. Brit.

1.Cities and towns—Planning—Gt. Brit. 2. Regional planning—
Gt. Brit. I. Tyrwhitt, Jacqueline. ed. II. Waide, W. L. ed. III.
Title. 3. City planning—Surveys.

NA9185.A8   711   49-54130*

Library of Congress   [1]

352
(79471)
S22
UC Santa Cruz environs development.
Sedway Cooke, San Francisco.
UC Santa Cruz environs development, needs
and methods for intergovernmental action; a
summary report. Prepared for the Office of
Physical Planning and Construction, University
of California, Santa Cruz. San Francisco,
1968.
37p.

1. Intergovernmental relations - Santa Cruz,
Calif. 2. Universities and colleges -
Research services to neighboring communities.
I. California. University, Santa Cruz.
II. Title.

711.3
(77434)
D27u
UDA Research Project.
Detroit Edison Co.
[Urban Detroit Area]; the development plan.
Preliminary concept for the year 2000.
[Detroit] 1969.
136p. (UDA Research Project. Document DOX-
USA-A 72)
A project of the Detroit Edison Co., Wayne
State University, Doxiadis Associates.

1. Metropolitan area planning - Detroit.
2. City growth - Detroit. I. UDA Research
Project. II. Title.

388
(762)
M47urb

UMT [urban mass transportation] program
planning requirements...
Mississippi-Arkansas-Tennessee Council
of Governments.
UMT [urban mass transportation] program
planning requirements; supplemental documentation MATCOG. Regular program planning
requirements. Memphis, 1968.
13p.
U.S. Dept. of Housing and Urban Development. Mass Transportation Demonstration
Grant Program.
1. Transportation - Mississippi.
2. Transportation - Arkansas. 3. Transportation
- Tennessee. 4. Journey to work.

(Continued on next card)

388
(762)
M47urb

Mississippi-Arkansas-Tennessee Council of
Governments. UMT...1968.

(Card 2)

I. U.S. Dept. of Housing and Urban Develop-
ment. Mass Transportation Demonstration
Grant Program Miss.-Ark.-Tenn.
II. Title.

058.7
:370
U54u

Unesco handbook of international exchanges.
United Nations Educational, Scientific and
Cultural Organization.
Unesco handbook of international exchanges.
Paris, 1965.
861p.
At head of title: I 1965.

1. Educational exchanges - Direct.
2. International organizations - Direct.
I. Title: Handbook of international exchanges.
II. Title.

UNICEF   (United Nations International
Children's Emergency Fund)

301.158
U54
1964

UNICEF Conference on Planning for the Needs
of Children in Developing Countries,
Bellagio, Italy, 1964.
United States experience in planning for
the needs of children and youth. Washington
U.S. Dept. of Health, Education, and Welfare,
1964.
68p.

1. Youth - Congresses. 2. Children -
Congresses.   I. U.S. Dept.
of Health,   Education and
Welfare.

The UNICOM method of house construction.

693.068
:389.6
N17

National Lumber Manufacturers Association.
(UNICOM - Technical Services Division)
A brief description of the UNICOM method
of house construction. Washington, 1962.
11p.

1. Modular coordination. 2. Coordinated components.
I. Title: The UNICOM method of house construction.

Folio
693.068
:389.6
N17d

UNICOM method of house construction.
National Lumber Manufacturers
Association.
Design principles; the UNICOM method
of house construction. Washington, D.C.,
1962.
122p.   (Its Manual no. 1)

1. Modular coordination. 2. Coordinated
components. I. Title: UNICOM method of
house con-   struction.

FILM

UNICOM [Uniform components] method of house
construction.
Wilding, inc.
UNICOM [Uniform components] method of
house construction. Chicago, 1963.
16mm., sound and color film, 32 1/2 min.

Released by National Lumber Manufacturers
Association.
Cost: $195.82

1. Films. 2. Prefabricated construction.
3. Coordinated   components.
I. National   Lumber Manufacturers
Association.   II. Title.

693.068
:389.6
H65

UNICOM modular components.
Home Planners, inc.
Moduler component design file, and
merchandising program. Detroit, 1964.
3v. (36 pieces)

Partial contents:-v. 1. Home planners
designs for convenient living, 50
suburban homes edition.-Modular component
vacation homes.-Designs for convenient
living, portfolio no. 13.-v. 2. A brief
description of the UNICOM method of house
construction.-v. 3. UNICOM modular components: Home planner
designs for   convenient living,
(Cont'd. on next card)

693.968
:389.6
H65

Home Planners, inc.   Modular component
design file ...   (Card 2)

102 plans for every need.-Construction
blue prints.-Using UNICOM.

1. Modular coordination. 2. House plans.
I. Title. II. Title: UNICOM modular
components.

002
UNu
1971

UNISIST.
United Nations Educational, Scientific and
Cultural Organization.
UNISIST. Intergovernmental Confernece for
the Establishment of a World Science Infor-
mation System, Paris, 4-8 October 1971.
Final report. Paris, 1971.
60 p.
Appx.   Report and remarks of the U.S. Delegation
to the Conference, prepared by Andrew A. Aines.
1. Documentation. 2. Library science.
I. Aines, Andrew A. II. Intergovernmental
Conference for the Establishment of a World
Science Informa-   tion System. Paris,
1971.   III. Title.

002
A81

UNISTAR (User Network for Information Storage,
Transfer, Acquisition, and Retrieval)
Auburn University.
UNISTAR (User Network for Information Storage,
Transfer, Acquisition, and Retrieval) Final
report prepared under contract [with] National
Aeronautics and Space Administration, with the
cooperation of the American Society for Engineer-
ing Education... Auburn, Ala., 1970.
1v.

1. Documentation. 2. Scientific research.
I. Title.

UOP

see

Universal Oil Products Co.

002
N28

URBANDOC input index cumulation...
New York. City University of New York
(Project URBANDOC)
URBANDOC input index cumulation, a publication
of Project URBANDOC at the City University of
New York. New York, 1968.
3v.

1. Documentation. 2. Library science -
Automation. I. Title.

699.81
S71
no. 8

URS Research Co.
Staackmann, Milton.
Damage to and analysis of fire department
capabilities, city of Albuquerque. Final report. Burlingame, Calif., URS Research Co.,
1969.
1v. (URS 697-8)
For Office of Civil Defense through U.S.
Naval Radiological Defense Laboratory.

1. Fire protection (Municipal) 2. Civilian
defense - Albuquerque, N.M. I. URS Research
Co. II. Title.

699.81
S71
no. 5

URS Research Co.
Staackmann, Milton.
Damage to and analysis of fire department
capabilities, city of Detroit. Final report,
March 1969. Burlingame, Calif., URS Research
Co., 1969.
1v. (URS 697-5)
For Office of Civil Defense through U.S.
Naval Radiological Defense Laboratory.

1. Fire protection (Municipal) 2. Civilian
defense - De   troit. I. URS Research
Co. II. Title.

699.81
S71
no. 6

URS Research Co.
Staackmann, Milton.
Damage to and analysis of fire department
capabilities, city of New Orleans. Final report. Burlingame, Calif., URS Research Co.,
1969.
1v. (URS 697-6)
For Office of Civil Defense through U.S.
Naval Radiological Defense Laboratory.

1. Fire protection (Municipal) 2. Civilian
defense - New Orleans. I. URS Research Co.
II. Title.

699.81
S71
no. 9

URS Research Co.
Staackmann, Milton.
Damage to and analysis of fire department
capabilities, city of Providence. Final report. Burlingame, Calif., URS Research Co.,
1969.
1v. (URS 697-9)
For Office of Civil Defense through U.S.
Naval Radiological Defense Laboratory.

1. Fire protection (Municipal) 2. Civilian
defense - Pro   vidence. I. URS Research
Co. II. Title.

699.81
S71
no. 7

URS Research Co.
Staackmann, Milton.
Damage to and analysis of fire department
capabilities, city of San Jose. Final report.
Burlingame, Calif., URS Research Co., 1969.
1v. (URS 697-7)
For Office of Civil Defense through U.S.
Naval Radiological Defense Laboratory.
1. Fire protection (Municipal) 2. Civilian
defense - San Jose, Calif. I. URS Research
Co. II. Title.

699.81
B51d

URS Research Co.
Black, R
Developing a blast-resistant carbon-smoke
generator for civil defense, by R. Black and
M. Staackmann. Final report, Burlingame,
Calif., URS Research Co., 1969.
1v. (URS 701-4)
For Office of Civil Defense.
1. Fire prevention. 2. Civilian defense.
I. Staackmann, M., jt. au. II. URS Research
Co. III. Title: Smoke generator.
IV. Title.

699.81
M17d

URS Research Co.
Martin, Stanley.
Development and application of an interim
fire-behavior model, by Stanley Martin and
others. Final report for Office of Civil
Defense through U.S. Naval Radiological Defense
Laboratory. Burlingame, Calif., URS Research
Co., 1968.
1v. (URS Research Co. URS 674-3)

Bibliography: p. 6-1 - 6-3.

1. Fire prevention. I. URS Research Co.
II. U.S. Office   of Civil Defense.
III. Title.

355.58
B51

URS Research Co.

Black, Robert H

Development of procedures for assessment of local industrial productive capacity following nuclear attack; final report, by Robert H. Black and William H. Van Horn. San Mateo, Calif., URS Research Co., 1970. 58p. (URS Research Co. URS 753-6)

Bibliography: p. 57-58.

1. Atomic bomb. 2. Industry. I. Van Horn, William H., jt. au. II. URS Research Co. III. Title.

699.81
M17e

URS Research Co.

Martin, S B

Effects of air blast on urban fire response, by S.B. Martin and others. Final report for Office of Civil Defense. Burlingame, Calif., URS Research, Co., 1969. 1v. (URS Research Co. URS 705-5)

1. Fire prevention. 2. Atomic bomb. I. URS Research Co. II. U.S. Office of Civil Defense. III. Title.

621.9
:690
U77

URS Research Co.

Evaluation of selected earthmoving equipment for the restoration of oil-contaminated beaches. [Prepared] for the Federal Water Quality Administration. San Mateo, Calif., 1970. 169p. (Water pollution control research series 15080EOS 10/70-1)

1. Building equipment. 2. Soils. I. Title. II. U.S. Federal Water Control Administration.

699.81
M17
Appx.D

URS Research Company.

Martin, Stanley.

Fire damage to New Orleans in the five-city attack, appendix D to Development and application of an interim fire-behavior model, by Stanley Martin and others. Final report, Burlingame, Calif., URS Research Co., 1968. 1v. (URS 674-3; NRDL-TRC-68-29) For Office of Civil Defense through U.S. Naval Radiological Defense Laboratory.

1. Fire prevention. 2. Civilian defense - New Orleans. I. URS Research Company. II. Title.

699.81
M17
Appx. C

URS Research Co.

Martin, Stanley.

Fire damage to San Jose in the five-city attack; appendix C to Development and application of an interim fire-behavior model, by Stanley Martin and others. Final report. Burlingame, Calif., URS Research Company, 1968. 1v. (URS 674-3; NRDL-TRC-68-29) For Office of Civil Defense through U.S. Naval Radiological Defense Laboratory.

1. Fire prevention. 2. Civilian defense - San Jose, Calif. I. URS Research Co. II. Title.

628.44
U77

URS Research Co.

Methods of predicting solid waste characteristics, by Gail B. Boyd and Myron B. Hawkins. [Wash.] U.S. Environmental Protection Agency, 1971. 28p. (SW-23c)

1. Refuse and refuse disposal. I. Boyd, Gail B. II. Hawkins, Myron B. III. U.S. Environmental Protection Agency. IV. Title.

697
:662.6
066

URS Systems Corp.

Goodale, Thomas.

Improvement of the performance of carbon smoke generators by the choice of fuels and fuel additives. Final report. For Office of Civil Defense through U.S. Naval Radiological Defense Laboratory. Burlingame, Calif., URS Systems Corp., 1968. 1v. (URS Systems Corp. URS 678-4)

1. Fuel. 2. Thermal radiation. I. URS Systems Corp. II. U.S. Office of Civil Defense. III. U.S. Naval Radiological Defense Laboratory. IV. Title.

330
B17u

U.S.A. and its economic future.

Barach, Arnold B

U.S.A. and its economic future. Graphics by Rudolf Modley. New York, Macmillan, 1964. 148 p. (A Twentieth Century Fund survey)

1. Econ. condit. 2. Housing. I. Title. II. Twentieth Century Fund.

728.1
H68us

USA-1966; a challenge for housing and urban development.

U.S. Dept. of Housing and Urban Development. USA-1966; a challenge for housing and urban development. Wash., 1966. 118p.

Draft for comment, May 1966.

1. U.S. Dept. of Housing and Urban Development. 2. Federal housing programs. I. Title.

624.131
(016)
A75U

USA SIPRE LIST OF PUBLICATIONS.

U.S. ARMY. CORPS OF ENGINEERS. SNOW, ICE AND PERMAFROST RESEARCH ESTABLISHMENT. USA SIPRE LIST OF PUBLICATIONS. WASHINGTON, GOVT. PRINT. OFF., V. IRREGULAR. For Library holdings see main entry 1. FROZEN GROUND - BIBLIOGRAPHY. 2. ICE - BIBLIOGRAPHY. I. TITLE.

029
U54

USA Standard basic criteria for indexes.

United States of America Standards Institute. USA Standard basic criteria for indexes. New York 1969. 12p. (USAS Z39.4-1968) Sponsor; Council of National Library Association Revision of Z39.4-1959.

1. Indexing-Standards and specifications. I. Council of National Library Associations. II. Title.

658.564
B87

USA standard: COBOL.

Business Equipment Manufacturers Association. USA standard: COBOL [Computer program language] New York, United States of America Standards Institute, 1969. 1v. (USAS X3.23-1968)

1. Automation. I. Title: COBOL [Computer program language] II. United States of America Standards Institute. III. Title.

658.564
U54u

USA standard character set for optical character recognition.

United States of America Standards Institute. USA standard character set for optical character recognition. Sponsor: Business Equipment Manufacturers Association. New York, 1966. 43p. At head of title: USAS X3.17-1966.

1. Automation. 2. Lettering. I. Business Equipment Manufacturers Association. II. Title.

658.564
U54

USA standard code for information interchange.

United States of America Standards Institute. USA standard code for information interchange. Sponsor: Business Equipment Manufacturers Association. New York, 1968. 15p. At head of title: USAS X3.4-1968.

1. Automation. 2. Communication systems. I. Business Equipment Manufacturers Association. II. Title.

621.6
A52

USA standard code for pressure piping.

American Society of Mechanical Engineers. Liquid petroleum transportation piping systems. New York, American Society of Mechanical Engineers, United Engineering Center, 1966. 60p. (USAS B31.4-1966) At head of title: USA standard code for pressure piping.

1. Pipes. 2. Petroleum industry and trade. I. Title: USA standard code for pressure piping. II. Title.

658.564
U54n

USA standard eleven-sixteenths inch perforated paper tape.

United States of America Standards Institute. USA standard eleven-sixteenths inch perforated paper tape. Sponsor: Business Equipment Manufacturers Association. New York, 1967. 7p. At head of title: X3.19-1967.

1. Automation. 2. Tapes. I. Business Equipment Manufacturers Association. II. Title.

658.564
U54s

USA standard flowchart symbols and their usage in information processing.

United States of America Standards Institute. USA standard flowchart symbols and their usage in information processing. Sponsor: Business Equipment Manufacturers Association. New York, 1968. 16p. At head of title: USAS X3.5-1968. Revision of X3.5-1966.

1. Automation. I. Business Equipment Manufacturers Association. II. Title.

658.564
U54i

USA standard for bit sequencing of the USA standard code for information interchange...

United States of America Standards Institute. USA standard for bit sequencing of the USA standard code for information interchange in serial-by-bit data transmission. Sponsor: Business Equipment Manufacturers Association. New York, 1966. 7p. At head of title: USAS X3.15.

1. Automation. I. Business Equipment Manufacturers Association. II. Title. III. Title: Data transmission.

696.2
U54

USA standard for domestic gas ranges.

United States of America Standards Institute. USA standard for domestic gas ranges. Vol. 1, free standing units (Formerly USA standard approval requirements for domestic gas ranges, vol. I, free standing units) New York, 1967. 61p. USAS Z21.2.2-1967. Sponsor: American Gas Association.

1. Gas apparatus and appliances - Standards and specifications. I. American Gas Association. II. Title.

696.1
N17u

USA standard for gel-coated glass-fiber reinforced polyester resin bathtub units.

NAHB Research Foundation. USA standard for gel-coated glass-fiber reinforced polyester resin bathtub units. Approved April 5, 1967, United States of America Standards Institute, 1967. 12p. (USAS Z124.1-1967)

1. Plumbing - Standards and specifications. 2. Bathrooms - Standards and specifications. I. Title. II. United States of America Standards Institute.

027
(083.41)
C68

USA standard for library statistics.

Council of National Library Associations. USA standard for library statistics. [New York] United States of America Standards Institute, 1969. 31p. (USAS Z39.7-1968)

1. Libraries - Statistics. I. United States of America Standards Institute. II. Title.

658.564
U54un
	USA standard FORTRAN.
	United States of America Standards Institute.
	USA standard FORTRAN. Approved March 7,
	1966. Sponsor: Business Equipment Manufac-
	turer's Association. New York, 1966.
	  36p.
	  ASA X3.9-1966.
	
	  1. FORTRAN (Computer program language)
	2. Automation. I. Business Equipment Manu-
	facturers Association. II. Title.
		658.564
		U54re
			**USA standard rectangular holes in twelve-
			row punched cards.**
			United States of America Standards Institute.
			USA standard rectangular holes in twelve-row
			punched cards. Approved October 27, 1967.
			Sponsor: Business Equipment Manufacturers
			Association. New York, 1967.
			  8p.
			  USAS X3.21-1967.
			
			  1. Automation. I. Business Equipment
			Manufacturers Association. II. Title.
				693.068.32 **USA standard specifications for: glazed**
				T45U Tile Council of America, inc. ceramic wall tile.
				  USA standard specifications for: glazed
				ceramic wall tile installed with portland
				cement mortar A108.1-1967; ceramic mosaic tile
				installed with portland cement mortar A108.2-
				1967; quarry tile and paver tile installed with
				portland cement mortar A108.2-1967;quarry tile
				and paver tile installed with portland cement
				mortar A108.3-1967. Approved [by] United States
				of America Standards Institute, with suggested
				guide outline form for specifiers. New York,
				1967.
				  20p.
				  1. Tile construc tion - Standards and
				specifications. (Cont'd on next card)

690.281
S72u
	**USA standard nomenclature for steel doors
	and steel door frames.**
	Steel Door Institute.
	  USA standard nomenclature for steel doors
	and steel door frames. Cleveland, Ohio, 1967.
	  13p.
	  At head of title: USAS A123.1-1967.
	  Approved October 4, 1967, United States of
	America Standards Institute.
	  1. Doors - Standards and specifications.
	I. United States of America Standards
	Institute. II. Title.
		658.564
		U54r
			**USA standard signaling speeds for data
			transmission.**
			United States of America Standards Institute.
			  USA standard signaling speeds for data
			transmission. Sponsor: Business Equipment
			Manufacturers Association. New York, 1962.
			  5p.
			
			  At head of title: X3.1-1962.
			  Approved August 8, 1962.
			
			  1. Automation. I. Business Equipment
			Manufacturers Association. II. Title.
				693.068.32
				T45u Tile Council of America, inc. USA
				  Standard...1967. (Card 2)
				
				  2. Walls. 3. Portland cement. I. Title.

658.564
U54o
	**USA standard one-inch perforated paper tape
	for information interchange.**
	United States of America Standards Institute.
	  USA standard one-inch perforated paper tape
	for information interchange. Sponsor: Busi-
	ness Equipment Manufacturers Association.
	New York, 1967.
	  6p.
	  At head of title: USAS X3.18-1967.
	
	  1. Automation. 2. Tapes. I. Business
	Equipment Manufacturers Association.
	II. Title.
		690.281
		A72
			**USA standard specifications for aluminum
			sliding glass doors.**
			Architectural Aluminum Manufacturers Associa-
			tion.
			  USA standard specifications for aluminum
			sliding glass doors. Chicago, 1968.
			  16p.
			  At head of title: AAMA 402.6, Jan. 1968;
			USAS A134.2-1968.
			
			  1. Doors - Standards and specifications.
			I. United States of America Standards
			Institute. II. Title.
				690.013
				A52ame
				1967
					**USA standard specifications for interior
					lathing and furring.**
					United States of America Standards Institute.
					  USA standard specifications for interior
					lathing and furring. Sponsor: American
					Society for Testing and Materials. New Yor.
					1967.
					  10p.
					
					  1. Building materials - Standards and
					specifications. 2. Plaster and plastering -
					Standards and specifications. I. American
					Society for Testing and Materials.
					II. Title. III. Title: Lathing and furring.

658.564
U54t
	**USA standard perforated tape code for
	information interchange.**
	United States of America Standards Institute.
	  USA standard perforated tape code for
	information interchange. Sponsor: Business
	Equipment Manufacturers Association.
	New York, 1965.
	  7p.
	  At head of title: USAS X3.6-1965.
	
	  1. Automation. 2. Tapes. I. Business
	Equipment Manufacturers Association.
	II. Title.
		690.282
		U54u
			**USA standard specifications for aluminum
			windows.**
			United States of America Standards Institute.
			  USA standard specifications for aluminum
			windows. New York, 1968.
			  49p.
			  AAMA 302.6, Jan. 1968; USAS A134.1-1968.
			  Sponsor: Architectural Aluminum Manufacturers
			Association.
			
			  1. Windows - Standards and specifications.
			2. Aluminum. I. Architectural Aluminum
			Manufacturers Association. II. Title.
				658.564
				U54a
					**USA standard take-up reels for one-inch
					perforated tape for information interchange.**
					United States of America Standards Institute.
					  USA standard take-up reels for one-inch
					perforated tape for information interchange.
					Sponsor: Business Equipment Manufacturers
					Association. New York, 1967.
					  12p.
					  At head of title: USAS X3.20-1967.
					
					  1. Automation. 2. Tapes. I. Business
					Equipment Manufacturers Association.
					II. Title.

691.6
N17
	USA standard performance specifications.
	National Safety Council.
	  USA standard performance specifications and
	methods of test for transparent safety glazing
	material used in buildings. New York, United
	States of America Standards Institute, 1967.
	  15p. (USAS Z97.1-1968)
	  1. Glass - Standards and specifications.
	2. Plastics - Standards and specifications.
	3. Accidents. I. United States of America
	Standards Institute. II. Title: Glazing
	material used in buildings. III. Title.
		693.068.32
		U54
			**USA standard specification for ceramic tile
			approved June 7, 1967.**
			United States of America Standards Institute.
			  USA standard specification for ceramic
			tile approved June 7, 1967, United States
			of America Standards Institute. Sponsor:
			Tile Council of America. New York, 1967.
			  10p.
			
			  1. Tile construction - Standards and
			specifications. I. Tile Council of America.
			II. Title. III. Title: Ceramic tile.
				R
				538.56
				(03)
				N28
					**USA standard vocabulary for information
					processing.**
					Newsweek.
					  Words of the computer age. An abridged
					glossary of terms used in modern informa-
					tion processing. Excerpted by Newsweek
					from the USA standard vocabulary for infor-
					mation processing. Published by the United
					States of America Standards Institute, and
					sponsored by the Business Equipment Manu-
					facturers Association. New York, 1966.
					  [32]p.
					
					  1. Automation - Dict. I. Business Equip-
					ment Manu- facturers Association.
					II. USA standard vocabulary
					for informa- tion processing.

658.564
U54m
	**USA standard print specifications for
	magnetic ink character recognition.**
	United States of America Standards Institute.
	  USA standard print specifications for
	magnetic ink character recognition. Sponsor:
	Business Equipment Manufacturers Association.
	New York, 1963.
	  17p.
	
	  At head of title: USAS X3.2-1963.
	  Approved November 7, 1963.
	
	  1. Automation. I. Business Equipment
	Manufacturers Association. II. Title.
		693.068.32
		T45uni
			**USA standard specifications for: ceramic tile
			installed with dry-set portland cement.**
			Tile Council of America, inc.
			  USA standard specifications for: ceramic
			tile installed with dry-set portland cement
			mortar A108.5-1967; dry-set portland cement
			mortar A118.1-1967. Approved [by] United
			States of America Standards Institute, with
			suggested guide outline form for specifiers.
			New York, 1968.
			  16p.
			  On cover: 9 tile work.
			  1. Tile construction - Standards and
			specifications. 2. Portland cement.
			I. Title. II. Title: Ceramic tile
			installed with dry-set portland cement
			mortar.
				666.81
				G96u
					**USA standard specifications for reinforced
					gypsum concrete.**
					Gypsum Association.
					  USA standard specifications for reinforced
					gypsum concrete. Sponsors: Building Officials
					Conference of America and the Gypsum Associa-
					tion. Approved as USA standard March 22, 1968
					Chicago, 1968.
					  6p.
					
					  1. Gypsum - Standards and specifications.
					2. Concrete, Reinforced. I. Building
					Officials Conference of America. II. United
					States of America Standards Institute.
					III. Title.

658.564
U54d
	**USA standard recorded magnetic tape for
	information interchange (800 CPI, MRZI)**
	United States of America Standards Institute.
	  USA standard recorded magnetic tape for
	information interchange (800 CPI, MRZI)
	Sponsor: Business Equipment Manufacturers
	Association. New York, 1967.
	  16p.
	
	  1. Automation. 2. Tapes. I. Business
	Equipment Manufacturers Association.
	II. Title.
		693.068.32
		T45un
			**USA standard specifications for: ceramic tile
			installed with water.**
			Tile Council of America, inc.
			  USA standard specifications for ceramic
			tile installed with water resistant organic
			adhesives A108.4-1968. Approved Feb. 14,
			1968, United States of America Standards
			Institute. Including related standard: USA
			standard for organic adhesives for installa-
			tion of ceramic tiles USAS A136.1-1967 with
			suggested guide outline form for specifiers.
			New York, 1968.
			  24p.
			  On cover: 9 tile work. USAS A108.4-1968.
			  1. Tile con struction - Standards
			and specifica tions. 2. Adhesives.
			3. Waterproof ing. I. Title.
				728.1
				I336.18
				S72
					U.S.A., THE MAGAZINE OF AMERICAN
					  AFFAIRS.
					STEWART, CHARLES T
					  PUBLIC HOUSING, WRONG WAY PROGRAM
					  (IN U.S.A., THE MAGAZINE OF AMERICAN
					  AFFAIRS, JUNE 1952, P.91-98)
					
					  1. PUBLIC HOUSING. I. U.S.A., THE
					MAGAZINE OF AMERICAN AFFAIRS.

USAC

SEE

U.S. Urban Information Systems Inter-Agency Committee.

630
:770
(016)
A37u
1963

USDA films for television.
U.S. Dept. of Agriculture. (Office of Information. Motion Picture Service)
USDA films for television. Rev. Washington, For sale by the Supt. of Documents, Govt. Print. Off., 1963.
50p. (Its Miscellaneous publication no. 942)

Publication supersedes Agriculture handbook no. 131, Television film catalog of the U.S. Dept. of Agriculture.

1. Agri-   cultural films -
Bibl.   2. Films - Bibl.
I. Title.

690.091.82
U54S
FEB.1940

USHA-AIDED PROJECTS.
U.S. HOUSING AUTHORITY.
SUMMARY OF STANDARDS AND REQUIREMENTS FOR USHA-AIDED PROJECTS. WASHINGTON, D.C., 1940.
35P.

1. BUILDING STANDARDS.
I. TITLE: USHA-AIDED PROJECTS.

690.091.82
U54S
JULY 1940

USHA-AIDED PROJECTS.
U.S. HOUSING AUTHORITY.
SUMMARY OF STANDARDS AND REQUIREMENTS FOR USHA-AIDED PROJECTS. WASHINGTON, 1940.
42P.

1. BUILDING STANDARDS.
I. TITLE: USHA-AIDED PROJECTS.

388
L85

The UTU [United Transportation Union] handbook of transportation in America.
Luna, Charles.
The UTU [United Transportation Union] handbook of transportation in America.
New York, Popular Library, 1971.
282p.

Bibliography: p. 236-276.

1. Transportation. 2. Federal government.
I. United Transportation Union. II. Title.

334.1
(54)
U13

Ubhayaker, N   G
A primer of cooperative housing. Bombay, Bombay Cooperative Housing Federation, Ltd. [1953]
116 p. forms.

1. Cooperative housing - India. I. Bombay. Cooperative Housing Federation, Ltd. II. Title.

339.5
U21

Udall, Stewart L
1976: agenda for tomorrow. New York, Harcourt, Brace & World, inc., 1968.
173p.

1. Natural resources. 2. Social conditions. I. Title.

712.25
T86

Udall, Stewart L
Tupper, Margo.
No place to play. [Foreword by Stewart L. Udall, Secretary of the Interior]
Philadelphia, Chilton Books, 1966.
293p.
Bibliography: p. 261-275.
Points out failures to provide adequate recreational facilities in urban areas for both children and their elders.

1. Recreation. 2. Natural resources. 3. Open space land. 4. Water   pollution. 5. Air pollution. 6. Satel-   lite cities. 7. City planning. I. Udall,   Stewart L. II. Title.

LAW
US

Udell, Gilman G   comp.
U.S. Laws, statutes, etc.
Antitrust laws with amendments, 1890-1970.
Compiled by Gilman G. Udell. Wash., Govt. Print. Off., 1971.
144p.

1. Monopolies. I. Udell, Gilman G., comp. II. Title.

LAW
T
N125LA

UDELL, GILMAN G   : BANKRUPTCY LAW OF THE UNITED STATES.
NADLER, CHARLES ELIHU.
THE LAW OF BANKRUPTCY. ATLANTA, HARRISON, 1968.
1022P.

BOUND AT BACK: BANKRUPTCY LAW OF THE UNITED STATES, COMPILED BY GILMAN G. UDELL.

1. BANKRUPTCY. I. UDELL, GILMAN G.: BANKRUPTCY LAW OF THE UNITED STATES.

LAW
U.S.

Udell, Gilman G   comp.
U.S. Laws, statutes, etc.
Civil service preference retirement, and salary classification laws. Comp. by Gilman G. Udell. Wash., Govt. Print. Off., 1971.
336p.

Cover title: Laws relating to civil service retirement.

1. Federal government - Salaries.
2. Federal civil service. I. Udell, Gilman G., comp. II. Title: Civil service retirement.

LAW
U.S.

Udell, Gilman G   comp.
U.S. Laws, statutes, etc.
Federal farm loan act with amendments and farm mortgage and farm credit acts, comp. by Gilman G. Udell. Wash., Govt. Print. Off., 1971.
375p.

1. Agricultural laws and legislation.
2. Farm mortgages. 3. Housing legislation.
I. Udell, Gilman G., comp. II. Title.

LAW
T

Udell, Gilman G   comp.
U.S. Laws, statutes, etc.
Federal reserve act of 1913 with amendments and laws relating to banking, compiled by Gilman G. Udell. Wash., Govt. Print. Off., 1971.
745p.

1. Banks and banking - Law and legislation. I. Udell, Gilman G., comp. II. Title.

LAW
T
L187L

Udell, Gilman G   comp.
U.S. Laws, statutes, etc.
Laws relating to civil service salary classification, civil service preference, etc.
Washington, U.S. Govt. Print. Off., 19
v.

Compiler:19   Gilman G. Udell.

For complete information see main card.

1. Federal civil service -Laws and legislation. 2. Social security. 3. Pension funds.
I. Udell, Gilman   G., comp. II. Title.

LAW
T
L187La

Udell, Gilman G   comp.
U.S. Laws, statutes, etc.
Laws relating to Federal aid in construction of roads, comp. by Gilman G. Udell. Wash., Govt. Print. Off., 1971.
447p.

1. Highways - Finance. I. Udell, Gilman G., comp. II. Title.

LAW
U.S.

Udell, Gilman G   comp.
U.S. Laws, statutes, etc.
Public building act of 1926 with amendments. Condemnation laws with amendments, comp. by Gilman G. Udell. Public works and construction laws. Wash., Govt. Print. Off., 1971.
682p.

1. Public buildings - Law and legislation.
2. Eminent domain. 3. Community facilities.
I. Udell, Gilman G., comp. II. Title.

694.1
N174

Uebelhack, Howard J.
National Plan Service, Inc.
National handbook of plan reading and material listing for lumber and building material dealers, contractors, estimators and designers; containing useful information and data pertaining especially to frame dwelling construction, by Martin F. White, Frank Z. Smith and Howard J. Uebelhack. [4th ed] Chicago [1953]

158 p. illus., tables.

Definitions of building terms: p. 18-34.

(continue on next card)

National Plan Service, Inc. National handbook of plan...1953 (Card 2)

1. Wood framing. 2. Building construction-Glossary. I. White, Martin F. II. Smith, Frank Z. III. Uebelhack, Howard J. IV. Title: Plan reading and material listing, National handbook of.

728.1
(6761)
U31

Uganda. African Housing Department.
Report,
Entebbe,
v. tables. annual.

Report year ends 30th June.

For complete information see shelflist.

1. Housing - Uganda.

301.15
(6761)
U31

Uganda. Dept. of Community Development.
Report
Entebbe,
v. illus., tables. annual.

For complete information see shelflist.

1. Community development - Uganda.

690.015
(485)
S82
1971
R36

Ugander, Mikael.
Transporter av byggelement; hanterings-och förflyttningskostnader för systemtransporter med lastbil (Transport of industrialized building units; handling and haulage costs relating to transport system by road of units in. industrialized building systems) Stockholm, Statens Institut för Byggnadsforskning, 1971.
174p. (Rapport R36:1971)
Bibliography: p. 142-147.

(Cont'd on next card)

690.015
(485)
S82
1971
Ugander, Mikael. Transporter av...1971.
(Card 2)
1. Prefabricated construction.
2. Transportation. I. Stockholm. Statens
Institut för Byggnadsforskning. II. Title:
Transport of industrialised building units.

624.131
U43
UKHOV, S   B
USING SALT IN TREATING CLAYEY SOILS
FOR CONSTRUCTION IN THE WINTER TIME.
CONSTRUCTION AND ARCHITECTURE, NO. 1.
MINISTRY FOR HIGHER EDUCATION, USSR,
1959.
17L.

TRANSLATED FROM THE RUSSIAN BY D.L.
KASSELL, DEPT. OF THE ARMY, OFF. OF
CHIEF OF STAFF FOR INTELLIGENCE,
WASH., D.C. INTELLIGENCE TRANSLATION
NO. H-6330. DISTRIBUTED BY U.S.
OTS.
(CONTINUED ON NEXT CARD)

720
(47)
U47
The Ukraine; the architecture of towns
and villages. Kiev, 1959.
342p. illus.

Text in Russian, English, French and
German.

1. Architecture - USSR.

333.63
(7471)
N28RE
UHL, CHARLES F
NEW YORK (CITY) HOUSING AUTHORITY.
RENT TABLES FOR COMPUTING NET MONTHLY
RENT PER ROOM, FROM GIVEN CAPITAL
COSTS, SUBSIDIES, INTEREST RATES, AND
AMORTIZATION PERIODS... WITH
ILLUSTRATIVE CHARTS, BY CHARLES F.
UHL. NEW YORK, 1937.
1 V. (U.S. WORKS PROGRESS
ADMINISTRATION PROJECT 65-97-201)

1. RENTS - NEW YORK (CITY) I. UHL,
CHARLES F. II. U.S. WORKS PROGRESS
ADMINISTRATION.

624.131
U43
UKHOV, S   B   USING SALT IN ...1959.
(CARD 2)

1. SOILS. I. TITLE. II. TITLE:
CONSTRUCTION AND ARCHITECTURE.

651.5
N17P
NO.92
ULASEK, HENRY T   COMP.
U.S. NATIONAL ARCHIVES AND RECORDS
SERVICE.
PRELIMINARY INVENTORY OF THE RECORDS
OF THE OFFICE OF EMERGENCY MANAGEMENT
(RECORD GROUP 214) COMPILED BY HENRY T.
ULASEK. WASHINGTON, 1956.
20P. (ITS PUBLICATION NO. 56-11.
PRELIMINARY INVENTORIES, NO. 92)

1. DEFENSE HOUSING. 2. U.S. OFFICE
OF EMERGENCY MANAGEMENT. I. ULASEK,
HENRY T., COMP.

628.1
(77266)
I52
Uhl, John E
Indiana. Dept. of Natural Resources.
Water resources of Randolph County, with
emphasis on ground-water availability, by
John E. Uhl. [Indianapolis] 1969.
map (with text)

1. Water resources - Randolph Co., Ind.
I. Uhl, John E. II. Title.

336.2
(772)
M67
Ukockis, James R., jt. au.
Mott, Charles F
Financing local government in Indiana: a study
of property tax rate limits and alternative local
nonproperty revenue sources, by Charles F. Mott
and James R. Ukockis. Indianapolis, Institute of
Public Administration, Indiana University, 1966.
85p.
Bibliography: 86-89.
1. Taxation - Indiana. 2. Local government -
Finance. I. Ukockis, James R. jt. au. II.
Indiana. University. Institute of Public Adminis-
tration. III. Indiana. Commission State Tax and
Financing Policy. IV. Title.

625.7
U51
Ulbricht, Edgar P
A method for comparing alternate
pavement designs. Final report. Lafayette
Ind., Purdue University, 1967.
149p. (Purdue University. Joint
Highway Research Project. No. 28)
Bibliography: p. 131-132.

1. Road construction. I. Purdue
University. Joint Highway Research Project.
II. Title.

920
:020
B46
1970
Uhlendorf, B   A   jt. ed.
A Biographical directory of librarians in the
United States and Canada. 5th ed. Lee Ash,
editor and B.A. Uhlendorf, associated editor.
Chicago, American Library Association, 1970.
1250p.
Sponsored by the Council of National Library
Associations.
Formerly Who's who in library service.
1. Librarians - Biography. I. Ash, Lee, ed.
II. Uhlendorf, B.A., jt. ed. III. American
Library Association. IV. Council of National
Library Associations. V. Title: Who's who in
library service. VI. Title: Directory of
librarians in the United States and Canada.

690
(47)
G65
Ukraina budivnicha.
Golovko, L   N   ed.
Ukraina budivnicha. Kiev, Budivelnik,
1967.
176p.

1. Building construction - U.S.S.R.
I. Title.

711.4
A521
Nov. 1945
Ullman, Edward L
American Academy of Political and Social Science.
Building the future city, ed. by Robert B.
Mitchell. Philadelphia, 1945.
215 p. (Its Annals, v. 242)

Partial contents.-The nature of cities, Chauncy
D. Harris and Edward L. Ullman.-Population trends
and city growth, Abram J. Jaffe.-Industrial
expansion and location, Glenn E. McLaughlin.-
Municipal land policy and control, Myres S.
McDougal.-City building and renewal, Joseph D.
McGoldrick.-Citizen participation in city
(Continued on next card)

728
: 333
(43)
U35
Uhlig, Klaus.
Mehr Wohneigentum durch neue finanzierungs-
methoden. Köln-Mülheim, Deutschen Verbandes
für Wohnungswesen, Städtebau und Raumplanung,
1970.
44p. (Deutschen Verbandes für Wohnungswesen
Städtebau und Raumplanung. Kleine schriften
dv 26)

1. Home ownership - Germany. 2. Building
methods. I. Deutschen Verbandes für
Wohnungswesen Städtebau und Raumplanung.

620
U47
Ukraine.
Zilishchno-grashdanskoe stroitelstvo v
Ukrainskoe SSR. (Civil engineering in the
Ukrainian SSR) Kiev, 1968.
15p.
Text in Russian, English, French.

1. Engineering. I. Title: Civil
engineering in the Ukrainian SSR.

American Academy of Political and Social Science.
Building the future city ... 1945. (Card 2)
Partial contents continued
planning, Tracy B. Augur.-Good neighborhoods,
Catherine Bauer.-Changing city patterns, Martin
D. Meyerson and Robert B. Mitchell.
1.City planning. I.Mitchell, Robert B., ed.
II.Augur, Tracy B. III.Bauer, Catherine.
IV.Harris, Chauncy D. V.Jaffe, Abram J.
VI.McDougal, Myres S. VII.McGoldrick, Joseph D.
VIII.McLaughlin, Glenn E. IX.Meyerson, Martin D.
X.Ullman, Edward L. XI.Title.

711.585
U35
Uhlmann, Frank W
Report on skid row, by Frank W.
Uhlmann, Wayne State University.
[n.p.] 1959.
13p.

1. Slums - Detroit. 2. Slums - Social
effect.

670
(47)
U47
Ukraine. Komitet po pechati.
Norodnoe khozeiaistvo Ukraina. Kiev, 1967.
30p.

1. Industry - U.S.S.R. 2. U.S.S.R. -
Industry.

330
U55e
Ullman, Edward L
The economic base of American cities:
profiles for the 101 metropolitan areas
over 250,000 population based on minimum
requirements for 1960, by Edward L. Ullman
and others. Seattle, University of
Washington Press, 1969.
112p. Washington. University. Center
for Urban and Regional Research.
Monograph no. 1)
1. Economic base studies. 2. Metropolitan
areas. I. Washington (State)
University. Center for Urban and
Regional Research. II. Title.

711.5
U42
Ukeles, Jacob B
The consequences of municipal zoning.
A research study, prepared under a grant
from the J.C. Nichols Foundation of
Urban Land Institute to the University of
Pennsylvania. Washington, Urban Land
Institute, 1964.
68p.
Bibliography: p. 65-68.

1. Zoning. I. Nichols
(J.C.) Foundation.
II. Urban Land Institute. III. Title.

914
(47)
U47
Ukraine. Komitet po pechati.
Sovetskaia Ukraina. Kiev, 1967.
38p.

1. Travel - U.S.S.R. 2. U.S.S.R. -
Travel.

DATE OF REQUEST   VF   L.C. CARD NO.
10/12/51   11/2/57
AUTHOR
Ullman, Edward L.
TITLE
Population map of metropolitan Boston.
SERIES
EDITION | PUB DATE 1/8/50 | PAGING
PUBLISHER
Harvard University.
RECOMMENDED BY   RLM | REVIEWED IN
ORDER RECORD

16

Ullman, Morris B
330.015
C65g Conference on Research in Income and
Wealth.
The geographic area in regional economic
research, by Morris B. Ullman and Robert C.
Klove. Princeton, Princeton Univ.
Press, 1957.
87-111p.
A report of the National Bureau of
Economic Research.
A reprint from Regional income, studies
in income and wealth, volume twenty-one.
1. Economic research.   I. Ullman, Morris B.
II. Klove, Robert C.   III. National Bureau
of Economic Research.

690.015
P87
v.1   Ulmer, C   Paul.
no.14-15   Purdue University. Better Homes in America.
Description and cost analysis of a wood
frame and stucco house, by C. Paul Ulmer.
Lafayette, Ind., 1936.
44p. (Home information Bulletin no. 14-15)

In looseleaf binder with other numbers in
the series.

1. Housing. 2. Building cost. I. Ulmer,
C. Paul. II. Title.

330
U55w   Ulmer, Melville Jack.
The welfare state: U.S.A.; an exploration in
and beyond the new economics. Boston, Houghton,
1969.
203p.

1. Economic policy. I. Title.

334
(75)
U55   Ulmer, Al.
Cooperatives and poor people in the
South. Atlanta, Southern Regional
Council, 1969.
31p.

At head of title: Special report.

1. Cooperatives - Southeastern states.
2. Buying. I. Southern Regional Council.
II. Title.

690.015
P87r
Ulmer, C   Paul
Description and cost analysis of a wood
frame and stucco house; House no. 1, Purdue
Housing Research Project.   Lafayette, Ind.
[July-Aug. 1936]
45 p.   illus., diagrs., tables.   (Purdue
Univ. Better Homes in America. Home information,
v.1, no.14-15)

In looseleaf binder with Dept. of Housing
Research Report and proposal to the Rockefeller
Research Foundation.

(Continued on next card)

690
(03)
U57   Ulrey, Harry F
Builders encyclopedia. Indianapolis,
Theodore Audel & Co., 1970.
593p.

C.1, Ref.

1. Building construction - Dictionaries.
I. Ulrey, Harry F.

690.015
P87
v.1   Ulmer, C   Paul.
no.23-24   Description and cost analysis of a house
built of reinforced concrete; House no. 3.
Purdue Housing Research Project.   Lafayette,
Ind. [Dec.1936]
50 p.   illus., diagrs., tables.   (Purdue
Univ. Better Homes in America. Home information,
v.1, no.23-24.)

In looseleaf binder with other numbers
in the series. Another copy in looseleaf binder
with Housing Research Dept. Report and proposal

(Continued on next card)

Ulmer, C   Paul.   Description and cost
analysis of a wood frame and stucco house...
[July-Aug. 1936]   (Card 2)

1.Wood construction. 2.Stucco. 3.Building costs.
I.Purdue Housing Research Project. II.Ser.

720
U57b   Ulrey, Harry F
Building construction and design (revision of
Architects and builders guide) 2d ed.
Indianapolis, Theodore Audel, 1970.
390p.

1. Architecture - Designs and plans.
2. Building construction. I. Title.

Ulmer, C   Paul.   Description and cost
analysis of a house built of reinforced
concrete...[Dec. 1936]   (Card 2)

to the Rockefeller Research Foundation, 690.015
P87r.

1.Reinforced concrete construction. 2.Building costs
3.Experimental houses-Lafayette, Ind. I.Purdue
Housing Research Project. II.Ser.

690.015
P87
v.1   Ulmer, C   Paul
no.17-18   Description and cost analysis of an all-
wood house; House no.5, Purdue Housing Research
Project.   Lafayette, Ind. [Sept. 1936]
42 p.   illus., diagrs., tables.   (Purdue
Univ. Better Homes in America. Home information,
v.1, no. 17-18)

In looseleaf binder with other numbers in
the series. Another copy in looseleaf binder
with Housing Research Dept. Report and
proposal to the Rockefeller Foundation, 690.015,
P87r.

(Continued on next card)

331.26
(016)
H14   Ulrich, B. Elizabeth, jt. au.
Haigh, Robert.
Guaranteed income: family allowances and
the negative income tax; a bibliography,
by Robert Haigh and B. Elizabeth Ulrich.
Harrisburg, Pa., Governor's Council for
Human Services, 1969.
4p.
1. Guaranteed annual income - Bibl.
I. Ulrich, B. Elizabeth, jt. au.
II. Pennsylvania. Governor's Council for
Human Services. III. Title.

690.015
P87
v.1   Ulmer, C   Paul.
no.10-11   Purdue University. Better Homes in America.
Description and cost analysis of a steel
house, by C. Paul Ulmer. Lafayette, Ind.,
1936.
37p. (Home information Bulletin no. 10-11)

In looseleaf binder with other numbers
in the series.

1. Steel construction. 2. Building cost.
I. Ulmer, C. Paul. II. Title.

Ulmer, C   Paul   Description and cost analysis
of an all-wood house...[Sept. 1936]   (Card 2)

1.Wood construction. 2.Building costs. 3.Experi-
mental houses-Lafayette, Ind. I.Purdue Housing
Research Project. II.Ser.

Ulrich's periodicals directory...

see

R
058.7   Ulrich's international periodicals directory...
(05)
U57

690.015
P87r
Ulmer, C   Paul
Description and cost analysis of a steel
house; House no. 4, Purdue Housing Research
Project.   Lafayette, Ind. [May-June 1936]
38 p.   illus., diagrs., tables.   (Purdue
Univ. Better Homes in America. Home information,
v.1, no.10-11)

In looseleaf binder with Dept. of Housing
Research Report and proposal to the Rockefeller
Research Foundation.

(Continued on next card)

330.15
N17o
no.43   Ulmer, Melville Jack
Trends and cycles in capital formation
by United States railroads, 1870-1950.
New York, 1954.
70 p. illus., diagrs., tables. (National Bureau of Economic
Research. Occasional paper 43).
Studies in capital formation and financing.
1. Railroads. 2. Finance. I. Title.
II. Capital formation. III. National
Bureau of Economic Research. Occasional
paper, no. 43. IV. Studies in capital
formation and financing.

058.7
(05)
U57   Ulrich's international periodicals
directory: a classified guide to a selected list of current periodicals,
foreign and domestic, ed. 13th-14th,
[9/65-71/72]
New York, R. R. Bowker,
v. Keep 3 years, latest ed. in Ref.
Title varies: 1951-1963; Ulrich's
periodicals directory.
Editor: 1951-   Eileen C. Graves; ed.
1967/68-12-2c
1969/70-13th 2c
1971/72-14th 2c   Contents: v.1. Scientific
(Continued   on next card)

Ulmer, C   Paul.   Description and cost
analysis of a steel house... [May-June 1936]
(Card 2)

1.Steel construction2.Building costs. 3.Experimental
house-Lafayette, Ind. I.Purdue Housing Research
Project. II.Ser.

338.53
L11WA   ULMER, MELVILLE J
U.S. BUREAU OF LABOR STATISTICS.
WARTIME PRICES.   PART 1. AUGUST
1939 TO PEARL HARBOR, BY JOHN M. BLAIR
AND MELVILLE J. ULMER. WASHINGTON,
GOVT. PRINT. OFF., 1944.
272P. (ITS BULLETIN NO. 749)

1. PRICES.   I. BLAIR, JOHN M.
II. ULMER, MELVILLE J.   III. TITLE.

058.7
(05)
U57   Ulrich's international periodicals
directory: a classified guide to a selected list of current periodicals,
foreign and domestic...19   (Card 2)
technical and medical. v.2. Arts, humanities.

058.7
(05)
U57   For complete information see main card.
suppl.   1972 supplement, 1st- 3d;   1 v. annual
1. Periodicals - Direct. I. Graves,
Eileen C., ed.
1966 suppl.3c   1969-2c
1967 suppl. 2c
1969 suppl 2c
1970 suppl.2c

3132
3133 ULSTER CO., N.Y. PLANNING BOARD.
ULSTER COUNTY: 1. DEVELOPMENT FACTORS:
THE SUPPLY OF HOUSING, AND SCHOOL GROWTH
COSTS: 2. HOUSING STUDY: ATTITUDES
TOWARD ENVIRONMENT. BY ECONOMIC
CONSULTANTS ORGANIZATION. KINGSTON,
N.Y., 1969.
2 V. (HUD 701 REPORT)

1. COUNTY PLANNING - ULSTER CO., N.Y.
I. ECONOMIC CONSULTANTS ORGANIZATION.
II. HUD. 701. ULSTER CO., N.Y.

Ultimate torque of reinforced rectangular
beams.
691.328
H78 Hsu, Thomas T   C
Ultimate torque of reinforced rectangular
beams. Skokie, Ill., Portland Cement
Association, Research and Development Labora-
tories, 1968.
485-510p. (Portland Cement Association.
Research and Development Laboratories.
Development Dept. Bulletin D127)
Reprinted from Journal of the Structural
Division, Proceedings of the American Society
of Civil Engineers, Feb., 1968.
1. Concrete, Reinforced. 2. Strength of
materials. I. Portland Cement Association.
III. American Society of Civil Engineers.
III. Title.

693.5 ULTRASOUND IN THE PRODUCTION AND
U57 INSPECTION OF CONCRETE. AUTHORIZED
TRANSLATION FROM THE RUSSIAN BY JAMES
S. WOOD. NEW YORK, CONSULTANTS
BUREAU, 1965.

2PTS.

CONTENTS.-- PT.1. PRODUCTION
APPLICATIONS, BY YU. E. KORNILOVICH AND
V.I. BELOKHVOSTIKOVA.--PT.2. INSPECTION
IN HYDRAULIC CONSTRUCTION, BY A.K.
TRETYAKOV AND A. M. FILONIDOV.
1. CONCRETE CONSTRUCTION.

628.3 Ultimate disposal of phosphate from waste
D85 water.
Dunseth, Maria G
Ultimate disposal of phosphate from waste
water by recovery as fertilizer, by Maria
G. Dunseth and others. Chicago, Dearborn
Chemical Div., W.R. Grace & Co., 1970.
74p. (U.S. Federal Water Quality
Administration. Water Pollution Control
research series 17070 ESJ 01/70)
1. Severage and sewage disposal. I. Grace
(W.R.) & Co. II. U.S. Federal Water Quality
Administration. III. Title. IV. Title:
Phosphate from waste water by recovery as
fertilizer.

628.515 Ultrafiltrative dewatering of spent powdered
A54 carbon.
Amicon Corp.
Ultrafiltrative dewatering of spent powdered
carbon, by C.W. Desaulniers and R.W. Hausslein.
Lexington, Mass., 1970.
68p. (U.S. Federal Water Quality Administration. Water pollution control research
series)

1. Water pollution. I. Desaulniers, C.W.
II. Hausslein, R.W. III. U.S. Federal Water
Quality Administration. IV. Title.

628.515 Ultrathin membranes for treating metal...
N67 North Star Research and Development Institute
Ultrathin membranes for treating metal
finishing effluents by reverse osmosis, by
North Star Research and Development Institute
through the State of Minnesota Pollution
Control Agency for the Environmental Protection Agency. Minneapolis, 1971.
92p. (Water pollution control research
series)
Bibliography: p. 69-70.
1. Water pollution. I. Minnesota. Pollution Control Agency. II. U.S. Environmental
Protection Agency. III. Title.

720.112 The ultimate highrise.
(79461) Brugmann, Bruce, ed.
B78 The ultimate highrise: San Francisco's mad
rush toward the sky, edited by Bruce Brugmann
and Greggar Sletteland. San Francisco
San Francisco Bay Guardian Books, 1971.
255p.

1. Tall buildings - San Francisco.
2. Apartment houses - San Francisco.
I. Sletteland, Greggar, jt. ed. II. Title.

628.3 Ultrasonic filtration of combined sewer
A52u overflows.
American Process Equipment Corp.
Ultrasonic filtration of combined sewer
overflows. [Prepared] for the Environmental
Protection Agency, Water Quality Office.
Hawthorne, Calif., 1970.
49p. (Water pollution control research
series)

1. Sewerage and sewage disposal. I. U.S.
Environmental Protection Agency. II. Title.

711.4 Ulysses, N.Y. Planning Board.
(74771) Sargent, Webster, Crenshaw and Folley.
S17 Planning report, Town of Ulysses, New
York; including proposed zoning ordinance,
land subdivision regulations and trailer
park ordinance, by Thomas W. Mackesey.
[Prepared for] Town of Ulysses Planning
Board. Syracuse, N.Y., [1959]
1v.

U.S. Urban Renewal Adm. UPAP.

1. City planning - Ulysses, N.Y. 2. Zoning legis-
lation - Ulysses, N.Y.   I. Mackesey, Thomas W.
II. Ulysses, N.Y. Planning Board.
III. U.S. URA-UPAP. Ulysses, N.Y.

624.042 Ultimate load tests of slabs designed by
A75 the strip method.
Armer G   S   T
Ultimate load tests of slabs designed
by the strip method. Garston, Eng., Build-
ing Research Station, 1968.
12p. (U.K. Building Research Station.
Current paper CP 83/68)

Reprinted from Proceedings of the
Institution of Civil Engineers, 1968, Vol. 41
(October), pp. 313-331.

1. Loads. I. U.K. Building Research
Station. II. Title.

Ultrasonic methods of testing materials.
620.1 Filipczynski, Leszek.
F45 Ultrasonic methods of testing materials [by] Prof. Dr.
inz. Leszek Filipczynski, Dr. inz. Zdzislaw Pawlowski and
Dr. inz. Jerzy Wehr; translated [from the Polish] by K. R.
Schlachter and edited by J. Blitz. London, Butterworths,
1966.
xii, 280 p. illus. tables, diagrs. 24 cm. 84/-
Ref.   (B 67-791)
Originally published as Ultradźwiękowe metody badania mate-
rialów. Warsaw, Wydawnictwa, 1959.
Bibliography: p. 274-277.   1. Strength of materials.
1. Ultrasonic testing.   I. Pawlowski, Zdzislaw, joint author.
II. Wehr, Jerzy, joint author.   III. Title.   jt. su.
TA417.4.F513   620.3287   67-73632
Library of Congress   [3]

Umatilla County, Oregon.

Housing-U.S.-Oregon.

691.328.2 Ultimate strain and ultimate moment of pre-
M23 stressed concrete beams.
Mehto, Lauri
Taivutetun jännebetonipalkin
murtopuristumasta ja murtomomentista (Ultimate
strain and ultimate moment of prestressed concrete beams) Helsinki, State Institute for
Technical Research, 1969.
38p. (Finland. State Institute for Technical Research. Tiedotus. Sarja 3 - Rakennus
134)
English summary.
1. Concrete, Prestressed. 2. Strains and
stresses. 3.   Loads. I. Finland. State
Institute for   Technical Research.
II. Title: (Cont'd on next card)

534.83 Ultrasonic testing literature.
(016) Merhib, Charles.
M27 A report guide to ultrasonic testing lit-
erature, by Charles P. Merhib and Ernest E.
Rodgers. Watertown, Mass., U.S. Army Mater-
ials Research Agency, Materials Technology
Division, 1966-67.
Ref. 4v. (U.S. Defense Documentation Center.
Defense Supply Agency. [Documents] AD 630
652, AD 648 905, AD 638 749, AD 650 279)
Distributed by U.S. Clearinghouse for Federal
Scientific and Technical Information.

(Cont'd on next card)

691.328.2
M23 Mehto, Lauri.   Taivutetun...1969. (Card 2)

Ultimate strain and ultimate moment of prestressed concrete beams.

534.83 Merhib, Charles.   A report guide to
(016) ultrasonic testing literature...1966-67.
M27   (Card 2)

1. Noise - Bibl. 2. Architectural
acoustics - Bibl. I. Rodgers, Ernest E., jt.
au. II. U.S. Defense Documentation Center.
Defense Supply Agency. III. U.S. Clearinghouse for Federal Scientific and Technical
Information. IV. Title. V. Title: Ultrasonic
testing literature.

VF Ultimate strength of slender prestressed
691.328.2 concrete columns.
F56 Florida. University. Engineering
and Industrial Experiment Station.
Ultimate strength of slender prestressed
concrete columns, by Paul Zung-Teh Zia.
Gainesville, Fla., 1957.
16 p. graphs. (Its technical paper series
no. 131)

"Engineering Progress at the University of
Florida, vol. xi, no. 7, July 1957."

1. Concrete, Prestressed. I. Zia, Paul Zung-Teh
II. Title.

---

674 Ultrasonics.
M12 McDonald, Kent A
Locating lumber defects by ultrasonics,
by Kent A. McDonald and Erwin H. Bulgrin.
Madison, Wis., U.S. Forest Products
Laboratory, 1969.
12p. (U.S. Forest Service. Research
paper FPL 120)

1. Lumber industry. I. Bulgrin, Erwin
H., jt. au. II. U.S. Forest Products
Laboratory, Madison, Wis. III. Title.
IV. Title: Ultrasonics.

711.4 Umbau der Städte.
S24 Seidensticker, Wilhelm.
Umbau der Städte. Essen, Vulkan-Verlag,
1959.
106p.

Bibliography: p. 104-105.

1. City planning. I. Title.

728.1
(4)
I57e
Umrath, H
International Confederation of Free Trade
Unions. (European Regional Organisation)
European labour movement and housing, by
H. Umrath. Brussels, 1953.
102p. illus.

Bibliography: p. 101-102.

1. Housing - Europe. 2. Cooperative housing - Europe. 3. Public housing - Europe.
I. Umrath, H.

325
C34
Unbought and unbossed.
Chisholm, Shirley.
Unbought and unbossed. Boston, Houghton
Mifflin, 1970.
177p.

1. Negroes - Biography. I. Title.

Under 65; the older worker over 40.
LAW
T
N28
S713un
New York (State) Commission for Human Rights.
Under 65; the older worker over 40. Rulings
interpretive of the age provisions of the law
against discrimination. Albany, 1963.
11p.

1. Employment - New York (State)
2. Minority groups - New York (State) I. Title:
Rulings interpretive of the age provisions of the
law against discri-   mination.
II. Title.

728.1
:333.63
(4)
I57e
2 c.
Umrath, H
International Confederation of Free
Trade Unions. (European Regional
Organization)
European rent policy, by H. Umrath.
Amsterdam, 1953.
33p. diagrs., tables.

1. Rental housing - Europe. I.
Umrath, H.

LAW
T
0677un
"Uncle Sam" as a landlord under the Federal
tort claims act.
Gottlieb, Irvin M
"Uncle Sam" as a landlord under the Federal
tort claims act, by Irvin M. Gottlieb and
Paul H. Gantt. Vienna, Va., Coiner Publications,
ltd., 1967.
145p.
At head of title: A special report.

1. Public lands. 2. Public buildings.
3. Real property. 4. Torts. I. Gantt, Paul
H., jt. au. II. Title.

LAW
T
C315u
Under the dome; how our Congress works.
Chamber of Commerce of the United States.
Under the dome; how our Congress works.
Washington, D.C., Chamber of Commerce of the
United States, Legislative Dept., 1955.
18p.

1. Federal government. 2. U.S. Congress.
I. Title.

728
:333
(4)
U57
UMRATH, HEINE.
THE PROBLEM OF OWNERSHIP IN WORKERS'
HOUSING POLICY IN WESTERN EUROPE.
GENEVA, INTERNATIONAL LABOR OFFICE, 1955.
REPRINTED FROM THE INTERNATIONAL LABOR
REVIEW, V. 71, NO. 2, 1955.

1. HOME OWNERSHIP - EUROPE. 2. LOW
INCOME HOUSING - EUROPE. I. TITLE.
II. TITLE: WORKERS' HOUSING POLICY IN
WESTERN EUROPE.

728.1
:336.18
M22
UNCLE SAM AS LANDLORD.
MCCLOY, WILLIAM C
UNCLE SAM AS LANDLORD: HOW THE
HOUSING PROGRAM IS ACTUALLY WORKING
OUT. WASHINGTON, U.S. PUBLIC WORKS
ADMINISTRATION, HOUSING DIVISION, 1936.
22L.

1. PUBLIC HOUSING. I. TITLE.

VF
330
A25
Under-developed countries.
Adler, John H
The underdeveloped areas: their industrializa-
tion. New Haven, Conn., Yale Institute of Inter-
national Studies, Mar. 1949.
30L. (Yale Institute of International Studies
Memorandum no. 31)

VF
690
U51
Umrath, H
The social framework of new developments
in the building and construction industry.
Amsterdam, Elsevier Pub. Co., 1960.
72-77p.

Reprinted from Innovation in building,
edited by C.I.B.

1. Building industry.

320
B87u
Uncommon sense.
Burns, James MacGregor.
Uncommon sense. New York, Harper and Row,
1972.
196p.

1. Political science. 2. Social conditions.
I. Title.

658.3
A32a
Underdeveloped countries.
U.S. Agency for International Development.
A.I.D. participant training program. The
transfer and use of development skills. An
evaluation study of U.S. technical training
programs for participants from underdeveloped
areas. Washington, U.S. Dept. of State, Agency
for International Development, 1966.
286p.
Bibliography: p.284-286.
1. Personnel management - Study and teaching.
2. Technical assistance programs. 3. Underdeveloped countries. I. Title.

020
:658.564
U57a
Umstead, Charles R
Automated library control systems, by
Charles R. Umstead and Fred E. Croxton.
Detroit, American Data Processing, inc.,
1968.
168p. (Library automation monograph
series)

1. Library science - Automation.
I. Title. II. Croxton, Fred E., jt. au.
III. American Data Processing, inc.

624.131.3
S64
The unconfined compression test of cohesive
soils.
Soiltest, Inc.
The unconfined compression test of
cohesive soils; apparatus, test procedures,
interpretation, use of test results.
Chicago, Ill., 1957.
56 p. illus. (Its testing series, v. 1
no. 1)

1.Soils - testing. I.Title.

728.1
:061.3
A51
Under-developed countries.
Albert Farwell Bemis Foundation.
Housing and economic development; the report
of a conference sponsored at the Massachusetts
Institute of Technology...on April 30 and May 1
and 2, 1953. Edited by Burnham Kelly. [Cam-
bridge, Mass., School of Architecture and Planning,
Massachusetts Institute of Technology] Jan. 1955
161 p.

Processed.

Partial contents. - The economist's view of
the role of   housing, Max F.
(continued on next card)

020
:538.56
U57
Umstead, Charles R
Compatible automated library circulation
control systems, by Charles R. Umstead and
Fred E. Croxton. Processed for U.S.
Defense Documentation Center, Defense
Supply Agency. Redstone, Ala., Redstone
Arsenal, 1967.
174p.

1. Library science - Automation.
I. Croxton, Fred E. II. U.S. Redstone
Arsenal. III. Title.

388
H62
Unconventional heat engines for urban
vehicles.
Hoess, J A
Unconventional heat engines for urban
vehicles. Columbus, Ohio, Battelle
Memorial Institute, Columbus Laboratories,
1967.
8p. (Battelle Memorial Institute.
Columbus Laboratories, Monograph no. 16)
Prepared for New Systems Study Project,
Urban Transportation Administration, Dept.
of Housing and Urban Development.
U.S. Mass Transportation Demonstration
Grant Program. Contract no. H-778.
(Cont'd on next card)

Albert Farwell Bemis Foundation. Housing and
economic...1955 (card 2)

Milliken. - Possibilities of international
financing of housing, Leo Grebler. - The dilem-
mas of housing, Paul A. Samuelson. - The case for
regional planning and urban dispersal, Catherine
Bauer. - The importance of housing and planning
in Latin America, Anatole A. Solov. - Importance
of physical planning in economic development,
Ernest Weissmann. - Measuring housing needs in
underdeveloped countries, Lloyd Rodwin. - Land
(continued on next card)

330
G25u
Unauthorized assistance to seemingly non-
depressed areas under the public works...
U.S. General Accounting Office.
Unauthorized assistance to seemingly non-
depressed areas under the Public works
acceleration act and the Area redevelopment
act, Area Redevelopment Administration,
Department of Commerce. Report to the Congress of the United States, by the Comptroller General of the United States. Washington, 1964.
19p.

1. Economic development.   2. Community facilities. 3. U.S. Area   Redevelopment Administration. I. Public   works acceleration act
of 1962. II. Title.

388
H62
Unconventional heat engines for urban
vehicles.
Hoess, J A   Unconventional
heat...1967.   (Card 2)

1. Transportation. 2. Journey to work.
3. Highways. 4. Air pollution.
5. Engineering. I. Battelle Memorial
Institute. (Columbus Laboratories).
II. U.S. Dept. of Housing and Urban
Development. Urban Transportation
Administration. III. U.S. Mass
Transportation Demonstration Grant
Program. IV.   Title.

Albert Farwell Bemis Foundation. Housing and
economic...1955 (card 3)

Policies and their effect on development poss-
ibilities, Charles Abrams. - Housing in a village
of India, Robert E. Alexander. - Design, José Luis
Sert. - Housing experience of the Standard Oil
Company, K.H. Quick. - A study of permanent housing
in overseas mining development, David M. Hansen. -
Redevelopment in El Salvador, George A. Dudley. -
Operational and statistical research in building,
J. Bronowski. - The role of the U.S. Government,

Albert Farwell Bemis Foundation. Housing and
economic...1955 (card 4)

Jacob L. Crane. - Opportunities for training,
Howard T. Fisher.
1. Housing-Congresses. 2.Economic planning.
3. Technical assistance programs. 4. Under-
developed countries. I. Kelly, Burnham. II. Grebler,
Leo. III. Bauer, Catherine IV. Solow, Anatole A.
V. Weissmann, Ernest. VI. Rodwin, Lloyd. VII.
Abrams, Charles. VIII. Sert, José Luis. IX. Dudley,
George A. X. Crane, Jacob L. XI. Fisher, Howard T.
XII. Title.

Underdeveloped countries.

728.1
A17m   Abrams, Charles.
Men's struggle for shelter in an urbanizing world. Cambridge, Mass., M.I.T. Press,
1964.
307p.

Published for The Joint Center for Urban
Studies of the Massachusetts Institute of
Technology and Harvard University.
1. Housing. 2. Land use. 3. Low income housing.
4. Underdeveloped countries. 5. Public housing.
I. Title. II. Joint   Center for Urban
Studies.

330
B17   UNDERDEVELOPED COUNTRIES.
Baranson, Jack.
Industrial technologies for developing coun-
tries. Introduction by Walter A. Chudson.
New York, Frederick A. Praeger, 1969.
168p. (Praeger special studies in inter-
national economics and development)
Bibliography: p. 145-168.

1. Economic development. 2. Technical assistance programs. 3. Underdeveloped countries.
I. Title.

Underdeveloped countries.

332.6
B87   Burkhard, Paul L
Investment trust certificates; suggested
ways and means of implementing the foreign
aid programs with respect to housing in underdeveloped nations through utilization of private investment funds. Glendale, Calif.,
International Housing Associates, [1963?]
[45]p.

1. Investments. 2. Mortgage finance. 3. Under-
developed countries.   4. Housing -
Guatemala.   I. International
Housing Associates,   Glendale, Calif.

728.1
B87ho   Burns, Leland S
Housing and development; two excerpts.
Los Angeles, International Housing Productiv-
ity Study, Housing, Real Estate, and Urban
Land Studies Program, Graduate School of
Business Administration, University of
California, 1966.
57p. (Reprint no. IHPS-5)
Reprinted from Development digest, Vol.
IV, no. 1. Prepared by the National Planning
Association for the Agency for International
Development, Dept. of State, April, 1966.
Contents: Economic analysis of
housing programs   for developing countries.
(Cont'd on next card)

728.1
B87ho   Burns, Leland S   Housing and development...
1966.   (Card 2)

Cost-benefit analysis of a housing project.

1. Housing.   2. Underdeveloped countries. I. California. University. University at Los Angeles. International Housing Productivity Study.
II. National Planning Association. III. Burns,
Leland S. Economic analysis of housing programs for developing countries. IV. Burns,
Leland S. Cost-   benefit analysis of a
housing project.   V. Title.

728.1
C17   UNDERDEVELOPED COUNTRIES.
Carlson, Eric.
The administration of housing programs and
housing institutions in developing countries.
[n.p.] [1965?]
1v.
Treatise submitted under Contract no. AID/
csd-764.

1. Housing. 2. Underdeveloped countries.
I. Title.

301.15
C17   UNDERDEVELOPED COUNTRIES.
Carnegie review.
The role of the university [in urban devel-
opment particularly in underdeveloped nations]
Pittsburgh, Carnegie Institute of Technology,
1966.
31p.

Carnegie review, no. 9, Oct., 1966.

1. City growth. 2. Underdeveloped countries.
3. Universities and colleges. I. Title.

332.6
(60)   Underdeveloped countries.
061   Coates, Austin.
Portuguese roots in Africa. Johannesburg,
S. Africa, 1965.
16p.

Reprinted from Optima.

1. Investments - Africa. 2. Underdeveloped countries. I. Title.

341.1
:338   UNDEVELOPED COUNTRIES.
(6668)   Colwell, Robert C
C65   Ivory Coast Republic, Africa: pre-investment
survey, February 10 - March 8, 1971, Abidjan,
Ivory Coast, by Robert C. Colwell and others.
Wash., Agency for International Development,
1971.
51p.
At head of title: Report to the Office of
Housing, Agency for International Development.
Author is Director, Planning-Programming-
Budgeting Staff, Dept. of Housing and Urban
Development.
(Cont'd on next card)

341.1
:338   Colwell, Robert C   Ivory Coast...1971.
(6668)   (Card 2)
C65
1. Technical assistance programs - Ivory
Coast. 2. Underdeveloped countries.
I. U.S. Agency for International Development.
II. Title.

338
C65pa   UNDERDEVELOPED COUNTRIES.
Commission on International Development.
Partners in development. New York,
Praeger, 1969.
399p. (Praeger paperbacks)

Lester B. Pearson, Chairman.

1. Business cycles. 2. Economic
development. 3. Technical assistance
programs. 4. Underdeveloped countries.
I. Pearson, Lester B. II. Title.

330
C65as   UNDERDEVELOPED COUNTRIES.
Committee for Economic Development. (Research
and Policy Committee)
Assisting development in low-income countries:
priorities for U.S. Government policy. A state-
ment of National policy by the Research and
Policy Committee of the Committee for Economic
Development. New York, 1969.
81p.

1. Economic development. 2. Technical
assistance programs. 3. Underdeveloped
countries.   I. Title.

330
C655   Underdeveloped countries.
Committee for Economic Development. (Research
and Policy Committee.
Economic development abroad and the role of
American foreign investment; a statement on
national policy. [New York] Feb. 1956.

1. Underdeveloped countries. 2 Economic
policy.

330
C65h   Underdeveloped countries.
Committee for Economic Development.
How low income countries can advance their
own growth: the lessons of experience. A
statement on national policy by the Research
and Policy Committee of the Committee for
economic Development. Including a statement
on economic development of Latin America by
the Inter-American Council for Commerce and
Production. New York, 1966.

1. Economic development. 2. Economic
development -   Latin America.
3. Under-   developed countries.
I. Title.

341.1
:338   Underdeveloped countries.
C65n   Committee for Economic Development.
The new role of the Soviets in the world
economy. A supplementary paper of the Committee
for Economic Development, by Michael Sapir.
Washington, 1958.
64p., illus., tables. (Its Supplementary
paper no. 5)

1.Technical assistance programs (USSR)
2.Underdeveloped countries. I.Sapir, Michael.
(Series)

330
C655o   Underdeveloped countries.
Committee for Economic Development.
Our stake in economic development abroad;
an address by J. D. Zellerbach ... to the
Overseas Writers, Washington, D. C., Feb. 16,
1956. [New York, Feb. 1956]
10 p.

1.Underdeveloped countries. 2.Economic
policy. I.Zellerbach, J   D

330
C655p   Under-developed countries.
Committee for Economic Development.
Problems of United States economic
development. New York, 1958.
2v.

Papers on economic problems to be
faced by the United States in the next
twenty years.

1. Economic development. 2. Underdeveloped countries. 3. International
relations. 4. Metropolitan areas.
5. Inflation.

330
C655a   Under-developed countries.
Committee for Economic Development.
Soviet progress vs. American enterprise.
Report of a confidential briefing session
held at the Fifteenth Anniversary Meeting
of the Committee for Economic Development,
on Nov. 21, 1957, in Washington, D. C.
Garden City, N. Y., Doubleday, 1958.
125p.

"Prepared for the Committee for Economic
Development by Clarence B. Randall and others."

1.Economic   development. 2.Under-
developed   countries. I.Title.
II.Randall,   Clarence B

332.6
C65e   UNDERDEVELOPED COUNTRIES.
Compagnie Financiere pour l'Outre-Mer.
Exercice, rapport annuel. 19

Paris, 19

v.

For Library holdings see main entry.

1. Investments. 2. Underdeveloped
countries.

330
C65reg   UNDERDEVELOPED COUNTRIES.
1960   Conference on Regional Economic Planning,
Bellagio, Italy, 1960.
Regional economic planning: techniques of
analysis for less developed areas. Papers and
proceedings of the first study conference on
problems of economic development organised by
the European Productivity Agency. Edited by
Walter Isard and John H. Cumberland. Paris,
European Productivity Agency of the Organisation for European Economic Co-operation, 1960.
450p.
1. Economic policy. 2. Underdeveloped countries. 3. Regional planning. I. Isard,
Walter, ed. II. Organisation for European
Economic Co-op   eration. III. Cumberland,
John H., jt. ed. IV. Title.

330
D28a

UNDERDEVELOPED COUNTRIES.
Deutsche Stiftung fur Entwicklungslander.
Almanach, 19

Berlin, 19

v.
English summary.
For Library holdings see main entry.

1. Economic development. 2. Underdeveloped
countries.

341.1
:338
(8)
G71

Underdeveloped countries.
Grace, J Peter.
It is not too late in Latin America: pro-
posals for action now. [n.p. 1962?]
74p.
Bibliography: p. 69-74.

1. Technical assistance programs - Latin
America. 2. Economic conditions - Latin
America. 3. Underdeveloped countries.
I. Title.

341.1
:338
H63

Underdeveloped countries.
Hoffman, Michael L
Development needs the business man. [Wash-
ington, D.C.]   1963.
12p.

Reprinted from Lloyds bank review, April,
1963.

1. Technical assistance programs. 2. Underdeveloped countries. I. Lloyds bank review.

332.72
F65h

UNDERDEVELOPED COUNTRIES.
Fonseca, Jose.
Housing finance in developing countries.
Paper presented to the 30th World Congress
of IFHP, Barcelona, Spain in May, 1970. The
Hague, 1971.
88p. (Housing and planning conference
papers, no. 3)
1. Mortgage finance. 2. Underdeveloped
countries. I. International Federation for
Housing and Planning. 30th Congress,
Barcelona, 1970. II. Title.

728.1
G72ho

Long.

Underdeveloped countries.
Grebler, Leo.
Housing and community facilities as
factors in human development. Los Angeles,
International Housing Productivity Study,
Real Estate Research Program, Graduate
School of Business Administration, Div. of
Research, University of California, 1962.
65-72p. (Reprint no. IHPS no. 1)
Reprinted from Social problems of develop-
ment and urbanization, vol. 7 of Science
and technology, and development, United
States papers. Prepared for the United
States   Conference on the

(Cont'd on next card)

354
I52

UNDERDEVELOPED COUNTRIES.
Ilchman, Warren F
The unproductive study of productivity: public
administration in developing nations. New York,
Southeast Asia Development Advisory Group, Asia
Society, 1967.
21p. (SEADAG papers on problems of development
in Southeast Asia. No. 40)
Paper presented at a meeting of the SEADAG
Development Administration Seminar, Carmel,
Calif., Nov. 24-25, 1967.
1. Public administration. 2. Underdeveloped
countries. I. Southeast Asia Development
Advisory Group.   II. Title.

330
F671

UNDERDEVELOPED COUNTRIES.
Forum International.
International Action Corps. [San Francisco,
1969]
13p.

1. Underdeveloped countries. 2. International Action Corps.

728.1
G72ho

Grebler, Leo.   Housing and community
facilities....1962.   (Card 2)

Application of Science and Technology for
the Benefit of the Less Developed Areas.
Washington, D.C. U.S. Govt. Print. Off.,
1962.

International Housing Productivity Study is
a project supported by contract with the
Agency for International Development, Dept.
of State and the University of Calif.

(Cont'd on next card)

711
(5694)
I57

UNDERDEVELOPED COUNTRIES.
Institute for Planning and Development, Tel
Aviv.
Comprehensive planning in Israel; a selection
of interdisciplinary studies and projects for
Israel and developing countries. Tel Aviv,
[1969?]
47p.

1. Planning - Israel. 2. Underdeveloped
countries. I. Title.

334.1
F68

Underdeveloped countries.
Foundation for Cooperative Housing, Wash., D.C.
A program of assistance for cooperative
housing in less developed countries. Prepared
by the Foundation for Cooperative Housing for
the Agency for International Development.
Wash., 1962.
1 v.

1. Cooperative housing. 2. Underdeveloped
countries. 3. Technical assistance programs.
I. U.S. Agency for International Development.
II. Title.

728.1
G72ho

Grebler, Leo.   Housing and community
facilities...1962.   (Card 3)

1. Housing. 2. Economic development.
3. Underdeveloped countries. 4. Community
facilities. 5. Community development.
I. California. University. University at
Los Angeles. International Housing Productivity Study. II. Title.

711.3
(5694)
I57

UNDERDEVELOPED COUNTRIES.
Institute for Planning and Development, Tel
Aviv.
Rural-urban integration; an approach for
developing countries based on Israeli experience. Tel Aviv, Institute for Planning and
Development, Center for Agricultural Cooperation with Developing Countries, 1969.
97p.
1. Regional planning - Israel. 2. Economic
development - Israel. 3. Underdeveloped
countries. I. Israel. Center for Agricultural
Cooperation with Developing Countries.
II. Title.

341.1
:338
F71

Underdeveloped countries.
France. Embassy. U.S. (Press and
Information Div.)
France aid and cooperation. New York,
1962.
56p.

1. Technical assistance programs (France)
2. Underdeveloped countries.

330
(728)
H15

Underdeveloped countries.
Hansen, Roger D
Central America; regional integration and
economic development. Washington, National
Planning Association, 1967.
106p. (National Planning Association.
Studies in development progress, no. 1)

1. Economic development - Central America.
2. Underdeveloped countries. I. National
Planning Association. II. Title.

332
(8)
I57an

Underdeveloped countries.
Inter-American Development Bank.
Anales; Novena Reunion de la Asamblea de
Gobernadores, Bogota, D.E., Abril 1968.
Wash., 1968.
229p.
Partial contents.-Expositores que
participaron en la mesa redonda sobre las
inversiones multinacionales, publicas y
privadas, en el desarrollo y la integracion
de America Latin.
1. Banks and banking - Latin America.
2. Latin America - Banks and banking. 3. Economic development   - Latin America. 4. Underdeveloped count   ries.

728.1
:308
(8)
F71

UNDERDEVELOPED COUNTRIES.
Frankenhoff, Carlos A
Investimento em habitação (Housing invest-
ment and housing market in developing economy)
Rio de Janeiro, Centro Nacional de Pesquisas
Habitacionais, 1969.
29p. (Brazil. Centro Nacional de Pesquisas
Habitacionais. Cadernos 4)
1. Housing market - Latin America. 2. Under-
developed countries. I. Brazil. Centro
Nacional de Pesquisas Habitacionais.
II. Title: Housing investment and housing
market in de   veloping economy.

332
(8)
H27

Underdeveloped countries.
Herrera, Felipe.
Ocho anos de labor. Wash., Banco
Interamericano de Desarrollo, 1968.
62p.
Discursos de Felipe Herrera, Presidente del
Banco Interamericano de Desarrollo, en la
Novena Reunion Anual de la Asamblea de
Gobernadores, celebrada en la ciudad de Bogota
entre el 22 y 26 de abril de 1968.
1. Banks and banking - Latin America. 2. Latin
America - Banks and banking. 3. Economic
development - Latin America. 4. Latin America -
Economic develop   ment. 5. Underdeveloped
countries. I.   Inter-American Develop-
ment Bank.

728.1
(8)
I57g

Underdeveloped countries.
Inter-American Housing and Planning Center.
Guia para la vivienda de bajo costo en
paises sub-desarrollados, por Robert L.
Davison. Bogota, Colombia, 1956.
18p. (Its Informes tecnicos no. 1)

1. Housing - Latin America. 2. Underdeveloped countries. I. Davison, Robert L

630
F72

Underdeveloped countries.
Freeman, Orville L
World without hunger. New York, Frederick
A. Praeger, 1968.
190p.
Bibliography: p. 181-185.

1. Agriculture. 2. Underdeveloped countries.
I. Title.

330
H47

Underdeveloped countries.
Hirschman, Albert O
The strategy of economic development.
New Haven, Yale University Press, 1958.
217p.

1. Economic development. 2. Underdeveloped
countries. I. Title.

352
I57d

Underdeveloped countries.
International Union of Local Authorities.
Decentralization in a developing nation.
A joint report by the participants of the
course in comparative local government,
"Decentralization for development," Sept.
7th to November 6th, 1964. The Hague, 1965.
[63]p.

1. Decentralization. 2. Local government.
3. Underdeveloped countries.

711.4
I57ur
Underdeveloped countries.
International Union of Local Authorities.
Urbanization in developing countries; report of a symposium held in Dec. 1967, at Noordwijk, Netherlands. The Hague, Martinus Nijhoff, 1968.
177p. (no.93)

1. City planning. 2. City growth.
3. Regional planning. 4. Underdeveloped countries. I. Title.

330
L28d
Underdeveloped countries.
Lewis, W Arthur.
Development planning; the essentials of economic policy. New York, Harper & Row, 1966.
278p.

1. Economic development. 2. Economic planning. 3. Underdeveloped countries. I. Title.

330
N87p
Underdeveloped countries.
Nurkse, Ragnar.
Problems of capital formation in underdeveloped countries. New York, Oxford University Press, 1953.
163p.

1. Underdeveloped countries. 2. Investments. I. Title.

669
I57
UNDERDEVELOPED COUNTRIES.
Interregional Symposium on Metalworking Industries in Developing Countries, Moscow, 1966.
Report. Vienna, United Nations Industrial Development Organization, 1968.
97p. (United Nations Industrial Development Organization. ID/8)
Bibliography: p. 95-97.
1. Metal-work. 2. Underdeveloped countries. 3. Industrial development. I. United Nations Industrial Development Organization. II. Title: Metalworking in dustries in developing countries.

325
M17l
UNDERDEVELOPED COUNTRIES.
Markovitz, Irving Leonard.
Leopold Sedar Senghor and the politics of negritude. New York, Atheneum, 1969.
300p.

Bibliography: p. 241-289.

1. Negroes. 2. Underdeveloped countries. 3. Senghor, Leopold Sedar. I. Title.

330
N87
Underdeveloped countries.
Nurkse, Ragnar.
Some aspects of capital accumulation in underdeveloped countries; National Bank of Egypt, Fiftieth anniversary commemoration lectures. Cairo, Egypt [N.B.E. printing press] 1952.
65 p.

Contents.-Investment incentives and balanced growth. - Population and capital supply. - Standards of living and the capacity to save. - External and internal sources of capital formation.

330
(60)
J12
1962
Underdeveloped countries.
Jackson, E F ed.
Economic development in Africa. Papers presented to the Nyasaland Economic Symposium held in Blantyre, July 18-28, 1962. Oxford, Basil Blackwell, 1965.
368p.

1. Economic development - Africa.
2. Underdeveloped countries. I. Nyasaland Economic Symposium, Blantyre, 1962. Papers. II. Title.

691.16
M42
Underdeveloped countries.
Michigan. University. Architectural Research Laboratory.
Architectural research on structural potential of foam plastics for housing in underdeveloped areas. Research conducted and reported by Project director, S.C.A. Paraskevopoulos and others. Sponsored by Agency for International Development, U.S. Dept. of State. Ann Arbor, 1966.
1 v.

1. Plastics. 2. Building research. 3. Underdeveloped countries. I. Paraskevopoulos, Stephens C.A. II. U.S. Agency for International Development. III. Title.

330
N87
Underdeveloped countries.
Nurkse, Ragnar.
Some aspects of capital accumulation in underdeveloped countries. 1952 (Card 2)

"Lectures delivered at the Société Fouad Ier d'Economie Politique, de Statistique et de Legislation, Cairo ... April 1952."

1. Underdeveloped countries. 2. Economic development. I. National Bank of Egypt. II. Title.

330
J18
Underdeveloped countries.
Javits, Benjamin A
The Peace by Investment Corporation, to build people-to-people economic relations, by Benjamin A. Javits and Leon H. Keyserling. Washington, International Committee for Peace by Investment, 1961.
63p.

1. Underdeveloped countries. 2. Technical assistance programs. I. Keyserling, Leon H. II. Title.

33
M97
Under-developed countries.
Myrdal, Gunnar
An international economy; problems and prospects. New York, Harper, [1956].
381 p.

Bibliography: p. 367-373.

691.16
P17
Underdeveloped countries.
Paraskevopoulos, Stephen C A
A preliminary investigation of the potential use of foam plastics for housing in underdeveloped areas. Research conducted and reported by Stephen C.A. Paraskevopoulos and others. Sponsor: Agency for International Development, U.S. Dept. of State. Ann Arbor, Architectural Research Laboratory, University of Michigan, 1963.
1v. (CRA Research Project 05215)

1. Plastics. 2. Underdeveloped countries. 3. Housing. I. U.S. Agency for International Development. II. Michigan. University. Architectural Research Laboratory.

341.1
:338
K67
Underdeveloped countries.
Kotschnig, Walter M
Social action: an instrument of foreign policy. Speech delivered at the 85th Annual Forum, National Conference on Social Welfare. Chicago, May 1958. [Washington, Office of International Economic and Social Affairs] 1958.
17p.

1. Technical assistance programs. 2. Underdeveloped countries. I. U.S. Dept. of State.

341.1
:338
N17
1963
Underdeveloped countries.
National Conference on International Economic and Social Development, Washington, D.C., 1963.
Yardsticks for international development. Highlights of the tenth annual meeting. Washington, 1963.
35p.

1. Technical assistance programs - Congresses. 2. Underdeveloped countries.

330
(73)
P27
Underdeveloped countries.
Petersen, Howard C.
Needed: a new foreign aid policy; based on a statement on national policy issued by the Research and Policy Committee of the Committee for Economic Development. New York, Committee for Economic Development, Apr. 1957.
28 p. illus., map, diagrs.

1. Economic development. 2. Underdeveloped countries. I. Committee for Economic Development. II. Title.

670
L17
Laf.
Underdeveloped countries.
Lary, Hal B
Imports of manufactures from less developed countries. New York, National Bureau of Economic Research; distributed by Columbia University Press, 1968.
286p. (National Bureau of Economic Research. Studies in international economic relations, 4)

1. Manufacturers. 2. International relations. 3. Industry. 4. Underdeveloped countries. I. National Bureau of Economic Research. II. Title.

341.1
:338
(60)
N17
Underdeveloped countries.
National Research Council.
Recommendations for strengthening science and technology in selected areas of Africa, south of the Sahara. Prepared for the International Cooperation Administration. Wash., National Academy of Sciences, National Research Council, 1959.
[159]p.

1. Technical assistance programs - Africa. 2. Underdeveloped countries. 3. Natural resources - Africa. I. Title. II. U.S. International Cooperation Administration.

341.1
F83
Underdeveloped countries.
Puerto Rico. Planning Board.
A program of technical assistance to economically underdeveloped countries. Puerto Rico's participation. Rev. [San Juan] 1950.
48 p.

1. Technical assistance programs.
2. Underdeveloped countries.

327
L18
Underdeveloped countries.
Laufer, Leopold.
Israel and the developing countries: new approaches to cooperation. New York, Twentieth Century Fund, 1967.
298p.

1. International relations. 2. Technical assistance programs (Israel) 3. Underdeveloped countries. I. Twentieth Century Fund. II. Title.

330
N25m
UNDERDEVELOPED COUNTRIES.
Nelson, Joan M
Migrants, urban poverty and instability in developing nations. [Cambridge, Mass.] Center for International Affairs, Harvard University, 1969.
81p. (Harvard University. Center for International Affairs. Occasional papers in international affairs no. 22)

1. Underdeveloped countries. 2. Population shifts. 3. Poverty. I. Harvard University. Center for International Affairs. II. Title.

370
R67e
Underdeveloped countries.
Rosen, Martha O
Education and economic growth. An analysis of the economic effects of investments in education and a study of the major research which has been done in the field. Cambridge, Mass., ABT Associates, inc., [1964?]
[44]p.

Bibliography: p. [40-44]

1. Education. 2. Economic development. 3. Underdeveloped countries. I. Title.

Underdeveloped countries.

320
R87 Rustow, Dankwart A
    A world of nations: problems of political
modernization. Washington, Brookings Institution, 1967.
    306p.

    1. Democracy. 2. Political science. 3. Com-
munism. 4. Underdeveloped countries. 5. Federal
government. I. Brookings Institution, Washington, D.C. II. Title. III. Title: Problems
of political modernization.

728.1   Underdeveloped countries.
(8)   Seminario Tecnico Administracion de
S25   Programas Habitacionales, (Control-Inspec-
1968 cion-Vigilancia) 1st, Wash., 1968.
    Primer Seminario Tecnico Administracion de
Programas Habitacionales, Wash., D.C., Junio,
1968. Wash., Inter-American Development Bank,
1968.
    1v.
    At head of title: Banco Interamericano de
Desarrollo. Agencia para el Desarrollo
Internacional.
    1. Housing - Latin America. 2. Latin America -
Housing. 3. Und   erdeveloped countries.
I. Inter-Americ   an Development Bank.
II. U.S. Agency   for International Develop-
ment.

330
S31 UNDERDEVELOPED COUNTRIES.
    Shaw, Carroll K
    Outline of researchable questions on development
administration of particular interest to the
Agency for International Development. Research
on development administration, by Fred W. Riggs.
New York, Southeast Asia Development Advisory
Group, 1967.
    13p. (SEADAG papers on problems of development
in Southeast Asia. No. 15)
    1. Economic development. 2. Underdeveloped
countries. I. Southeast Asia Development Advisory
Group. II. Title.

332.72   UNDERDEVELOPED COUNTRIES.
S541   Smith, Halbert C
    Interregional mortgage placement; lenders'
policies, practices and characteristics.
Storrs, Conn., Center for Real Estate and Urban
Economic Studies, School of Business Adminis-
tration, University of Connecticut, 1969.
    48p. (Real estate reports: no. 5)
    1. Mortgage finance. 2. Economic
development. 3. Underdeveloped countries.
I. Title. II. Connecticut. University.
Center for Real Estate and Urban Economic
Studies.

728.100.15 Underdeveloped countries.
(44)   Spira, Ephraim.
S64   Selective examination and assessment of re-
search in France, Israel and in the United
Kingdom in the field of housing and building,
applicable in developing countries. A report
prepared by Ephraim Spira and Jan de Geus. Pre-
pared for UNESCO. Rotterdam, International
Council for Building Research Studies and
Documentation, 1966.
    48p.
    1. Housing research - France. 2. France -
Housing research.   3. Housing research -
Israel. 4. Israel   - Housing research.
5. Housing rese   arch - U.K. 6. U.K. -
Housing research.   (Cont'd on next card)

728.100.15 Spira, Ephraim.   Selective examination...
(44) 1966.   (Card 2)
S64
    7. Building research - France. 8. France -
Building research. 9. Building research -
Israel. 10. Israel - Building research.
11. Building research - U.K. 12. U.K. - Building research. 13. Underdeveloped countries.
I. Geus, Jan de, jt. au. II. United Nations.
(Economic and Social Council) III. International Council for Building Research Studies
and Documentation.

728.100.15 Spria, Ephraim. Selec...1966 (Card 3)
(44)
S64
    I. Geus, Jan de, jt. au. II. United
Nations. (economic and Social Council)
III. International Council for Building
Research Studies and Documentation.

690.015 Underdeveloped countries.
(485)
882   Sweden. Statens Kommitté för
R28   Byggnadsforskning.
1967   Building and planning in developing
countries; a partially annotated bibliography.
Stockholm, 1967.
    71p. (Its Rapport 28:1967)

    1. Building research - Sweden. 2. Building
construction - Bibl. 3. Planning - Bibl.
4. Underdeveloped countries. I. Title.

339.5   Underdeveloped countries.
T24   Teitelbaum, Perry D
    Energy cost comparisons; theoretical and
practical problems in comparing nuclear and
conventional energy costs, with particular
reference to less developed areas. Washington,
Resources for the Future, inc., 1963.
    222p. (Resources for the Future, inc.
Reprint number 38)
    Reprinted from Science, technology, and
development - United States papers prepared for
the United Nations Conference on the Application
of Science and Technology for the Benefit of the
Less Developed Areas,   Vol. I, Natural resources - Energy,   water, and river basin
               (Continued on next card)

339.5   Teitelbaum, Perry D
T24   Energy...1963.   (Card 2)

    development (Washington: U.S. Government
Printing Office, 1963)

    1. Power resources. 2. Atomic energy.
3. Underdeveloped countries. 4. Technical
assistance programs. I. Resources for the
Future, inc. II. Title.

341.1   Underdeveloped countries.
:338
(5487) U. K. British Information Services.
U54   The Colombo plan. I. Britain's part.
pt. 1 London [1962]
    32p.

    1. Technical assistance programs (U. K.)
- South and Southeast Asia. 2. Underdeveloped
countries. I. Title.

341.1   Underdeveloped countries.
:338
U54r U.K. British Information Services.
no.4 (Economics Div.)
    The Colombo plan for South and South
East Asia. Facts on Britain's aid to less
developed countries, no. 4. New York, 1963.
    5p.   (Reference paper no. 4; ID1446-4)

    1. Technical assistance programs (U.K) -
South and South East Asia. 2. Underdeveloped
countries. I. Title.

---

330   Underdeveloped countries.
U54br U.K. British Information Services.
    (Reference Division)
    Britain and economic development over-
seas. New York, 1960.
    32p. (I.D. 1349)

    1. Technical assistance programs (U.K.) 2. Under-
developed countries.

325.3   Underdeveloped Countries.
(41)
U54   U. K. British Information Services. (Refer-
    ences Div.)
    Community development in the United King-
dom dependencies. New York, 1958.
    20p.

    1. Community development - U.K. 2. Under-
developed Countries.

Underdeveloped countries

341.1
:338 U.K. British Information Services.
U54i   Investment in progress, Britain's
1958 contribution to overseas development,
by Duncan Crow. London, 1958.
    40p.

    Partial contents: the Columbo plan.

    1. Technical assistance programs (U.K.) 2. Under-
developed countries. I. Crow, Duncan. II. Title:
The Columbo plan.

Under-developed countries.

341.1
:338 U.K. British Information Services.
U54i   Investment in progress, Britain's contri-
1960 bution to overseas development, by Duncan
    Crow. London, 1960.
    40p. illus.

    Partial contents:- The Columbo plan.

    1. Technical assistance programs (U.K.) 2. Under-
developed countries. I. Crow, Duncan. II. Title:
The Columbo plan.

341.1   Underdeveloped countries.
:338
(41)   U.K. British Information Services. (Refer-
U54p   ence Division)
    Political development in the United Kingdom
dependencies. New York, 1958.
    28p. map.

    1. Technical assistance programs (UK)
2. Underdeveloped countries.

341.1   Underdeveloped countries.
:338
(41)   U.K. British Information Services.
U54p   (Reference Division)
1959   Political development in the United
    Kingdom dependencies. Rev. New York, 1959.
    28p. (I.D. 1286)

    1. Technical assistance programs (U.K.) 2. Under-
developed countries.

341.1   Underdeveloped countries.
:338 U.K. British Information Services. (Reference
(41) Div.)
U54p   Political development in the United Kingdom
1961 dependencies. Rev. New York, 1961.
    26p. (I.D. 1286 (rev.))

    1. Technical assistance programs (U.K.)
2. Underdeveloped countries.

---

360   Underdeveloped countries.
(41) U.K. British Information Services. (Refer-
U54   ence Div.)
    Social welfare in the United Kingdom de-
pendencies. New York, 1960.
    38p. (Its I.D. 1347)

    1. Social welfare - U.K. 2. Community develop-
ment - U.K. 3. Underdeveloped countries.

341.1   Underdeveloped countries.
:338 U.K. British Information Services. (Economics
U54r Div.)
no.3   Technical assistance. Facts on Britain's
aid to less developed countries, no. 3. New
York, 1963.
    9p.   (Reference papers no. 3; ID 1446-3)

    1. Technical assistance programs (U.K.)
2. Underdeveloped countries.

330
U54u
1960

Underdeveloped countries.

U.K. British Information Services.
(Reference Division)
The U.K. colonial development and
welfare acts. Rev. New York, 1960.
28p. tables. (I.D. 892 (rev))

1. Economic development. 2. Underdeveloped
countries. I. Title.

332.72
UNF
1966

UNDERDEVELOPED COUNTRIES.
UNITED NATIONS. ECONOMIC AND SOCIAL
COUNCIL.
FINANCE FOR HOUSING AND COMMUNITY
FACILITIES IN DEVELOPING COUNTRIES.
NEW YORK 1966.
132P. (UNITED NATIONS PUBLICATION
NO. E C.6 32 REV.1)

1. MORTGAGE FINANCE. 2. COMMUNITY
FACILITIES. 3. UNDERDEVELOPED
COUNTRIES. I. TITLE.

341.1
:338
UNu

Under-developed countries.

United Nations. (Economic and Social Council)
United States of America: report of experience in the field of social development of
potential assistance to under-developed
countries. Information furnished in response
to Resolution 731 C (XXVII) of the Economic
and Social Council. New York 1960.
226p.

Bibliography: p. I-IX.

1. Technical assistance programs. 2. Under-developed
countries.

VF
330
U54b

Underdeveloped countries.

U.K. Central Office of Information.
British colonial policy today, by
Alan Lennox-Boyd, British Secretary of
State for the Colonies. Prepared by the
Central Office of Information. London,
1957.
8 p. map.

1.Underdeveloped countries. I.Lennox-Boyd,
Alan. II.Title.

332.72
UNf

UNDERDEVELOPED COUNTRIES.
United Nations. (Dept. of Economic and
Social Affairs)
Finance for housing and community facilities in developing countries. New York, 1968.
67p. (United Nations. [Document] ST/SOA/
79)

1. Mortgage finance. 2. Community facilities. 3. Underdeveloped countries. I. Title.

341.1
:338
C65f
1966
H-H

Underdeveloped countries.

U.S. Congress. House. Committee on
Appropriations.
Foreign assistance and related agencies
appropriations for 1966. Hearings before a
subcommittee of the Committee on Appropriations, House of Representatives, Eighty-
ninth Congress, first session. Washington,
Govt. Print. Off., 1965.
1719p.

1. Technical assistance programs.
2. Underdeveloped countries.

341.1
:338
U54c

Underdeveloped countries.

U.K. Central Office of Information.
Reference Div.
Community development. London, H.M.S.O.,
1966.
40p. (U.K. Central Office of Information
Reference pamphlet 76)
At head of title: Britain and the develop-
ing countries.
Bibliography: p. 40.

1. Technical assistance programs (U.K.)
2. Underdeveloped countries. I. Title.
II. Title: Britain and the developing
countries.

332
U54
1949

Underdeveloped countries.

United Nations. (Secretary-General, 1946-   Lie)
Methods of increasing domestic savings and of
insuring their most advantageous use for the
purpose of economic development. [Lake Success,
New York] Economic and Social Council, 1949.
354 p. (General E/1562, 16 Dec. 1949)

Tenth session, Economic development of underdeveloped countries, methods of financing economic
development of under-developed countries.
Mimeographed.

341.1
:338
C65f
1972

UNDERDEVELOPED COUNTRIES.

U.S. Congress. House. Committee on
Appropriations.
Foreign assistance and related agencies
appropriations for 1972. Hearings before a
Subcommittee of the Committee on Appropriations,
House of Representatives, Ninety-second Congress,
first session. Washington, Govt. Print. Off.,
1971.
pts.

1. Technical assistance programs.
2. Underdeveloped countries. I. Title.

330
U54u

Underdeveloped countries.

U.K. Central Office of Information.
(Reference Division)
The United Kingdom colonial development
and welfare acts. London, 1956.
28p. tables.

1.Economic development. 2.Underdeveloped
countries. I.Title.

339.3
U54
1951

Under-developed countries.

United Nations. (Secretariat. Dept. of Economic
Affairs.)
National income and its distribution in under-
developed countries. New York, 1951.
35 p. tables. ([U.N. Document]
ST/STAT/SER.E/3, 9 Oct. 1951; Sales no.: 1951.
XVII.3)

Bibliography: p. 34-35.

1.National income. 2.Under-developed countries.
I.Title. II.Series: United Nations. Statistical
papers.

341.1
:338
C65e

Underdeveloped countries.

U.S. Congress. Joint Economic Committee.
Economic policies toward less developed
countries, by Raymond F. Mikesell and Robert
Loring Allen. Subcommittee on Foreign Economic
Policy of the Joint Economic Committee, Congress
of the United States. Washington, Govt. Print.
Off., 1961.
96p.
At head of title: 87th Cong., 1st sess.

1. Technical assistance programs. 2. Underdeveloped
countries. I. Mikesell, Raymond F. II. Allen,
Robert Loring.

330
U54u
1957

Underdeveloped countries.

U.K. Central Office of Information
(Reference Division)
The United Kingdom colonial development
and welfare acts; April 1, 1956 to March 31,
1957. London, 1957.
10p. tables.

1. Economic development. 2. Underdeveloped
countries. I. Title.

VF
332.72
(60)
UNa

UNDERDEVELOPED COUNTRIES.

United Nations. (Economic Commission for
Africa.
New methods and machinery to increase the
flow of capital to housing. [New York]
United Nations, Economic and Social Council,
1968.
15p. (United Nations. [Document] E/
CN.14/HOU/33)
At head of title: United Nations
Economic and Social Council, Economic
Commission for Africa and German Foundation
for Developing Countries Meeting on
Technical   and Social Problems
(Cont'd on next card)

341.1
:338
C65f
S-H

UNDERDEVELOPED COUNTRIES.

U.S. Congress. Senate. Committee on
Appropriations.
Foreign assistance and related programs
appropriations. Hearings: 19
Wash., Govt. Print. Off., 19
v.
For Library holdings see main entry.
1. Technical assistance programs.
2. Underdeveloped countries. I. Title.

330
(56)
UN

Underdeveloped countries.

United Nations. (Conciliation Commission for
Palestine)
An approach to economic development in the
Middle East. Final report of the United Na-
tions Economic Survey Mission for the Middle
East. Lake Success, N.Y., 1949.
2 pts. tables. (AAC.25/6)

Contents: Part I. The final report and appendices.-Part II. The technical supplement.

1. Economic de-   velopment - Middle East.
2. Underdeveloped   countries.

VF
332.72
(60)
UNa

United Nations. (Economic Commission for
Africa.) New...1968   (Card 2)

of Urbanization (With Emphasis on
Financing of Housing) Addis Ababa, 8-23
Jan. 1969.

1. Mortgage finance - Africa. 2. Under-
developed countries. I. United Nations.
(Economic and Social Council. Economic
Commission for Africa) II. Deutsche
Stiftung für Entwicklungsländer.
III. Title.

VF
341.1
:338
I572

Under-developed countries.

U.S. International Development Advisory Board.
Conclusions and recommendations of the International Development Advisory Board; report to
Harold E. Stassen, Director of Foreign Operations,
regarding the United States participation in
technical cooperation programs for underdeveloped
countries. [Washington] Dec. 1953.
27 p.

Processed.
1.Technical assistance programs. 2.Under-developed
countries. I.U.S. Foreign Operations Administration.

330
UNes

UNDERDEVELOPED COUNTRIES.

United Nations. (Industrial Development Organization)
The establishment of the brick and tile
industry in developing countries, by H.W.H. West.
New York, United Nations, 1969.
122p. (United Nations. [Document] ID/15)

1. Underdeveloped countries. 2. Brick
industry. 3. Tile. I. West, H.W.H. II. Title.

330
UNra

Underdeveloped countries.

United Nations. (Dept. of Economic and
Social Affairs)
Rapport sur une politique coordonnée en
matière de niveaux de vie familiaux. New
York, 1957.
82p. (Its [Document] ST/SOA/34)

1. Underdeveloped countries. 2. Social
conditions.

330
N17ma

Under-developed countries.

U.S. National Advisory Council on the
Proposed International Development
Association.
Message from the President of the United
States relative to a special report of the
National Advisory Council on the Proposed
International Development Association.
Washington, Govt. Print. Off., 1960.
50p.

At head of title: 86th Cong., 2d sess.
House. Document no. 345.
1. Under-   developed countries.

327
P72u

Under-developed countries.

U.S. President.
U.S. participation in the U.N.

Washington, Govt. Print. Off.
v. annual (U.S. Dept. of State.
Publication)

Issued also as International Organization
and conference series.

For complete information see shelflist.

(Continued on Card No. 2)

327
P72u

U.S. President. U.S. participation in the U.N.
(Card No. 2)

1. International relations. 2. Non-self
governing territories. 3. Under-developed
countries. 4. United Nations. I. U.S. Dept.
of State. II. Title.

341.1
:338
S71a

Underdeveloped countries.

U.S. Dept. of State. Bureau of Public
Affairs.
An act for international development;
a program for the decade of development.
Summary presentation. Washington, 1961.
189p. (U.S. Dept. of State. General
foreign policy series 169)

U.S. Dept. of State. Publication 7205)

1. Technical assistance programs.
2. Underdeveloped   countries.

341.1
:338
S71e

Underdeveloped countries.

U.S. Dept. of State.
Economic development of underdeveloped
countries. Washington, Govt. Print. Off.,
1958.
15p.

1. Technical assistance programs. 2. Underdeveloped countries.

341.1
:338
S71

Underdeveloped countries.

U.S. Dept. of State.
Point four; cooperative program for aid in
the development of economically under-developed
areas [prepared by the Dept. of State with
assistance of an Interdepartmental Advisory
Committee on Technical Assistance and of the
staff of the National Advisory Council]
[Washington, 1949]
157 p.
Cover title.
1. Technical assistance programs. 2. Underdeveloped countries.

341.1
:338
S71s

Underdeveloped countries.

U.S. Dept. of State.
The Sino-Soviet economic offensive in the less
developed countries. Washington, Govt. Print.
Off., 1958.
111p. illus., tables. (Its Publication no.6632)
(European and British Commonwealth series 51)

1. Technical assistance programs (USSR)
2. Underdeveloped countries. I. Title.

VF
341.1
:338
S71n

Underdeveloped countries.

U.S. Dept. of State. Bureau of Public
Affairs.
A new program for a decade of development
for underdeveloped areas of the world.
Washington, 1961.
40p. (U.S. Dept. of State. General
foreign policy series 165)

U.S. Dept. of State. Publication 7190.

1. Technical assistance programs.
2. Underdeveloped   countries.

330
W67e

Underdeveloped countries.

World Coffee Information Center.
Economic impact of coffee; how the Inter-
national Coffee Agreement contributes to the
progress of the developing countries and the
United States. Washington, World Coffee
Information Center (an agency of the Pan-
American Coffee Bureau) 1968.
50p.

1. Economic development. 2. Underdeveloped
countries. I. Title.

330
(60)
W85

Underdeveloped countries.

Wülker, Gabriele.
Togo- tradition und Entwicklung. Stuttgart,
Ger., Ernst Klett Verlag, 1966.
159p. (Wissenschaftliche Schriftenreihe des
Bundesministeriums für wirtschaftliche
Zusammenarbeit. Band 6)

1. Economic development - Africa (Togo)
2. Africa (Togo) - Economic development.
3. Underdeveloped countries. I. Germany.
(Federal Republic, 1949-   )
Bundesministerium für wirtschaftliche
Zusammenarbeit.

330
(016)
B17
1967

UNDERDEVELOPED COUNTRIES - BIBLIOGRAPHY.

Bärensen, Jack
Technology for underdeveloped areas; an
annotated bibliography, 1st. ed. Oxford,
New York, Pergamon Press, 1967.
81p. (International series of monographs
in library and information science, v.6)

1. Underdeveloped countries - Bibl.
2. Technical assistance programs - Bibl.
I. Title.

330
(016)
D28

UNDERDEVELOPED COUNTRIES - BIBLIOGRAPHY.

Deutsche Stiftung für Entwicklungslander.
Entwicklungslander-studien; Bibliographie der Entwicklungslander-Forschung.
Bonn, 1966.
v.
-- --- Register. 1958-64. Bonn, 1966.
v.
1. Underdeveloped countries - Bibl.
2. Economic development - Bibl.

330
(016)
E57

UNDERDEVELOPED COUNTRIES - BIBLIOGRAPHY.

Entwicklungsländer-Studien. Bd. 1-
Bonn, Deutsche Stiftung für Entwicklungslander, 1966-
v.

INDEXES:
Vols. 1-3, 1966. ov.

1. Economic development - Bibl.
2. Underdeveloped countries - Bibl.
3. Technical assistance programs (Germany)
I. Deutsche Stiftung für Entwicklungslander.

330
(016)
868

Underdeveloped countries - Bibliography.

South Pacific Commission.
Annotated select bibliography on urbanization in the South Pacific. Noumea, New
Caledonia, South Pacific Commission, Urbanization Research Information Centre, 1965.
152p.

1. Underdeveloped countries - Bibl.
I. Title: Urbanization in the South
Pacific.

711.4
:670
(54)
S71

UNDERDEVELOPED COUNTRIES - INDIA.

Stanford Research Institute.
Costs of urban infrastructure for industry
as related to city size in developing countries. India case study. Menlo Park, Calif.,
1968.
435p.
Prepared in cooperation with School of Planning and Architecture, New Delhi, Small Industry Extension Training Institute, Hyderabad.
Bibliography: p. 401-435.
1. Industrial development - India. 2. Underdeveloped countries - India. I. Title.

330
(678)
U54t

Underdeveloped countries - Tanganyika.

U.K. British Information Services.
Tanganyika; a story of progress. New
York, 1961.
[40]p.

1. Economic development - Tanganyika.
2. Underdeveloped countries - Tanganyika.

696.63
B84

Underfloor duct distribution systems.

Building Research Advisory Board.
Underfloor duct distribution systems,
by James R. Smith. Washington, 1959.
23p. tables. (Federal Construction,
Council. Survey of practice report no. 1)

1. Electric wiring. I. Smith, James R. II. Federal
Construction Council. III. Title.

690
P17

Underground construction.

Parker, Albert D
Planning and estimating underground construction. New York, McGraw-Hill, 1970.
300p.

Partial contents.-Conventional tunnel-
driving methods and equipment.

1. Building industry. 2. Building construction - Estimates. I. Title. II. Title:
Underground construction. III. Title: Tunnel-
driving methods.

690
M67

Underground facilities.

Mostkov, Vladimir Mikhaylovich.
Construction of large underground facilities.
Wash., U.S. Dept. of Commerce, Office of Tech-
nical Services, Joint Publications Research
Service, 1964.
343p.
Translation of Stroitel'stvo podzemnykh
sooruzheniy bol'shogo secheniya.
Bibliography: p. 337-343.
1. Building construction. I. U.S. Joint
Publications Research Service. II. Title.
III. Title: Underground facilities.

711.73
H63

Underground highways.

Hoffman, George A
Urban underground highways and parking
facilities. Santa Monica, Calif., Rand
Corp., 1963.
47p. (Rand Corp Memo RM-3680-RC)

1. Highways. 2. Parking. 3. Road con-
struction. 4. Protective construction.
I. Rand Corporation. II. Title. III. Title:
Underground highways.

VF
690.015
F22
R27

Underground insulated piping systems.

Building Research Advisory Board.
Underground insulated piping systems (excluding walk-in tunnels), by Task Group T-24
under contract CST 263 between National
Academy of Sciences and National Bureau of
Standards, prepared and edited by F. A. Govan
Washington, 1957.
34p. (Federal Construction Council Techni
cal report no. 27)

(Continued on Card No. 2

VF
690.015
F22
R27

621.643
B84

Building Research Advisory Board. Underground insulated piping systems. 1957.
(Card No. 2)

Issued also as Building Research Institute
Technical reprint no. 15. 1958.

1. Pipes. I. Building Research Institute.
II. Federal Construction Council. III. Title.

Underground insulated piping systems
(excluding walk-in tunnels)
VF
690.015 Building Research Advisory Board.
F22   Underground insulated piping systems
R27   (excluding walk-in tunnels) by Task Group
1963   T-24. Washington, National Academy of
        Sciences, National Research Council,
        1963.
          33p. (Federal Construction Council.
        Technical report no. 27)
          National Research Council. Publication
        no. 1073.

          1. Pipes.   2. Insulation.
        I. Federal   Construction
        Council.   II. Title.

728.1   ..   ...
(768191) Cartee, P   Charles. The underhoused...
C17   1970.   (Card 2)

          Memphis. I. California. University.
        University at Los Angeles. Housing, Real
        Estate, and Urban Land Studies Program.
        II. Tennessee. State University, Memphis.
        Bureau of Business and Economic Research.
        III. Title.

          Understanding other cultures.
300
P17 Parker, William A   ed.
          Understanding other cultures. Washington,
        D.C., American Council of Learned Societies,
        91p.

          Bibliography: p. [84-92]

          1. Social sciences. 2. Political science.
        I. American Council of Learned Societies.
        II. Title.

711.4   UNDERGROUND PLANNING.
1573A INTERNATIONAL FEDERATION FOR HOUSING AND
       TOWN PLANNING. 16TH CONGRESS.
       MEXICO, 1938.
       L'AMENAGEMENT SOUTERRAIN.
       UNDERGROUND PLANNING. BRUXELLES, 1938.
       1 V. (VARIOUS PAGINGS)

       TEXT IN FRENCH, ENGLISH AND GERMAN.

       1. CITY PLANNING. I. TITLE:
       UNDERGROUND PLANNING.

          The undersized house: a municipal
                  problem.
VF
690.091.82 McCloy, Robert
M12   The undersized house: a municipal prob-
          lem. Chicago-Kent Law Review, Mar. 1949.
          4p
          Reprint.

          1. Building codes. 2. Room sizes.
        I. Title.

---

370   Understanding school desegregation.
:325   U.S. Commission on Civil Rights.
C65u   Understanding school desegregation. Wash.,
       1971.
          [16]p. (Clearinghouse publication no. 27)

          1. Education - Minority groups. I. Title.

.352.6   UNDERGROUND RESIDENTIAL DISTRIBUTION.
N175   NATIONAL ASSOCIATION OF HOME BUILDERS.
       TRANSCRIPT OF THE CONFERENCE ON
       UNDERGROUND RESIDENTIAL DISTRIBUTION.
       WASHINGTON, 1966.
       1 V. (VARIOUS PAGINGS)

       1. CITY PLANNING. I. TITLE.

       1. PUBLIC UTILITIES. I. TITLE: UNDERGROUND
       RESIDENTIAL DISTRIBUTION.

---

328   Understanding Congress.
E84   Evins, Joe Landon.
          Understanding Congress. New York,
       Clarkson N. Potter, 1963.
          304p.

          1. U.S. Congress. 2. Political science.
       I. Title.

---

392   Understanding the multi-problem family.
G24   Geismar, Ludwig L
          Understanding the multi-problem family:
       a conceptual analysis and exploration in
       early identification, by L.L. Geismar and
       Michael A. La Sorte. New York, Association
       Press, 1964.
          224p.

          1. Family. 2. Health. I. La Sorte,
       Michael A., jt. au. II. Title.

624.043   Underground structure.
K68   Kovari, K
          The design of underground structures: the
       secondary stress and strain state of an
       inhomogeneous elastic-ideally plastic
       material near a lined underground cavity.
       Garston, Eng., Building Research Station,
       1970.
          [33]p. (Library communication no. 1578)
          Translated from the German and reprinted
       from Schweizerische Bauzeitung, 1969, 87
       (37), 687-97.
          1. Strains and stresses. I. U.K. Building
       Research Station. II. Title: Underground
       structures. III. Title. (Series)

301.15   Understanding environmental education.
E28   U.S. Office of Education.
          Understanding environmental education; a
       collection of readings in environmental aware-
       ness. Wash., 1970.
          69p.
          Partial contents.-Ecology notebooks. Poems
       and other expressions of environmental concern,
       by Morton Leeds, Director, Plans, Program
       Evaluation Staff, HUD.

          1. Man - Influence of environment. I. Title.
       II. Leeds, Morton. Ecology notebook.

628.3   Underwater storage of combined sewer overflows.
R63   Rohrer (Karl R.) Associates, inc.
          Underwater storage of combined sewer
       overflows. Wash., Environmental Protection
       Agency, 1971.
          170p. (Water pollution control research
       series)
          Bibliography: p. 135-138.

          1. Sewerage and sewage disposal. 2. Water
       pollution. I. U.S. Environmental Protection
       Agency. II. Title.

          Underground tunnels.
697
B84 U.K. Building Research Station.
          Heat transfer in deep underground tunnels,
       by A.W. Pratt and L. F. Davs. London, H.M.
       Stat. Off., 1958.
          37p. illus., graphs, tables. (National
       building studies research paper no. 26)

          1. Heat transmission. I. Pratt, A W
       II. Davs, L F   III. Title: Under-
       ground tunnels.

628.515   Understanding environmental pollution.
S77   Strobbe, Maurice A   ed.
          Understanding environmental pollution.
       Saint Louis, C.V. Mosby, 1971.
          357p.

          Bibliography: p. 336-342.

          1. Water pollution. 2. Air pollution.
       3. Natural resources. I. Title.

690.031
U52

       Underwood, George, 1880-
          House construction costs. 1st ed. New York, McGraw-
       Hill, 1950.
          ix, 814 p. illus. 24 cm.

          1. Building costs-Estimates. I. Title.

       TH435.U57   692.5   50-9423

       Library of Congress   [20]

---

325   Underhill, Jack.
U52   The Italian immigrants and the American Negro
       in the urban north: comparisons of group
       adjustment. Cambridge, Mass., Harvard Univer-
       sity, Kennedy School of Government, 1968.
          96p.
          Bibliography: p. 90-96.
          1. Minority groups. 2. Sociology, Urban.
       I. Harvard University. Kennedy School of
       Government. II. Title.

---

658   Understanding linear programming.
:538.56 Fourre, James P
F68   Understanding linear programming.
       New York, American Management Associa-
       tion, General Management Div., 1967.
          23p.   (American Management Associa-
       tion. AMA management bulletin no. 94)

          1. Management - Automation. 2. Busi-
       ness. I. American Management Associa-
       tion. II. Title. (Series)

621.9 Underwriters' Laboratories, inc.
1690   Accident, automotive, and burglary protection
U52a   equipment lists. Chicago, 1959-
          v. annual.

          KEEP ONLY LATEST ISSUE. SEE SERIAL RECORD.

          1. Title.

728.1   The underhoused of Memphis.
(768191) Cartee, P   Charles.
C17   The underhoused of Memphis, by P. C. Cartee
       and others. Prepared for Housing, Real
       Estate, and Urban Land Studies Program, Gradu-
       ate School of Business Administration, Univer-
       sity of California, Los Angeles. Sponsored
       by Life Insurance Association of America.
       Memphis, Bureau of Business and Economic
       Research, Div. of Urban and Regional Studies,
       Memphis State University, 1970.
          86p.
          1. Housing - Memphis. 2. Housing market -

          (Cont'd on next card)

621.39 Understanding media.
M12   McLuhan, Herbert Marshall.
          Understanding media; the extensions of man.
       1st ed. New York, McGraw-Hill, 1964.
          359p.
          Bibliography: p. [391]-365.

          1. Communication systems. 2. Education.
       3. Transportation. 4. Automation.
       I. Title. II. Title: The extensions of
       man.

621.9 Underwriters' Laboratories, Inc.
1690   Bi-monthly supplement to lists of....
U52   Chicago, 1957-
          v. Bi-monthly.

621.9
r690
U52b Underwriters' Laboratories, inc.
    Building materials list. Chicago, 1960-
    3 v. annual.

    KEEP ONLY LATEST ISSUE. SEE SERIAL RECORD.

            I. Title.

621.9
r690
U52f Underwriters' Laboratories, inc.
    Fire protection equipment list. Chicago, 1960-
    v. annual.

    KEEP ONLY LATEST ISSUE. SEE SERIAL RECORD.

        I. Title.

VF
691.018.44
U52 Underwriters' Laboratories, Inc.
    Standard for fire tests of building construction
and materials. 6th ed. [Chicago] Jan. 1955.
    22p. illus., tables.

    1.Building materials-Fire resistance. I.Title: Fire
tests of building construction and materials.

691.015
A77 UNDERWRITERS' LABORATORIES, INC.
    ASSOCIATED FACTORY MUTUAL FIRE
      INSURANCE COMPANIES.
      FIRE TESTS OF BUILDING COLUMNS BY
    ASSOCIATED FACTORY MUTUAL FIRE
    INSURANCE COMPANIES, THE NATIONAL
    BOARD OF FIRE UNDERWRITERS, AND THE
    BUREAU OF STANDARDS, DEPARTMENT OF
    COMMERCE. JOINTLY CONDUCTED AT
    UNDERWRITERS' LABORATORIES, CHICAGO,
    ILLINOIS, 1917-1919. CHICAGO, 1919.
    389P.

    1. BUILDING   MATERIALS, FIREPROOF.
  2. FIREPROOF CONSTRUCTION.
          (CONTINUED ON NEXT CARD)

691.018.44
U52 Underwriters' Laboratories, inc.
1950 Standard test method for
    fire hazard classification of
    building materials. 1st. ed.
    [n.p.] 1950.
    13p. (Subject 723)

    1. Building materials - Fire
resistance. 2. Fire prevention.

621.9
r690
U52el Underwriters' Laboratories, inc.
    Electrical appliance and utilization equipment
list. Chicago, 1956-
    v. annual.

    KEEP ONLY LATEST ISSUE. SEE SERIAL RECORD.

    .. I. Title.

691.015
A77 ASSOCIATED FACTORY MUTUAL FIRE
    INSURANCE COMPANIES. FIRE TESTS OF
    ...1919.   (CARD 2)

    I. NATIONAL BOARD OF FIRE UNDERWRITERS.
  II. U.S. NATIONAL BUREAU OF
  STANDARDS.   III. UNDERWRITERS
  LABORATORIES, INC. IV. TITLE.

691.018.44
U52 Underwriters' Laboratories, inc.
1960 Standards for safety; test method
    for fire hazard classification of
    building materials. 3rd ed.
    Chicago, 1960.
    19p. (UL 723)

    1. Building materials - Fire
resistance. 2. Fire prevention.

621.9
r690
U52 e Underwriters' Laboratories, inc.
    Electrical construction materials list. Chicago,
1956-
    v. annual.

    KEEP ONLY LATEST ISSUE. SEE SERIAL RECORD.

    1. Building equipment. I. Title.

621.9
r690
U52g Underwriters' Laboratories, inc.
    Gas and oil equipment list. Chicago, 1959-
    v. annual.

    KEEP ONLY LATEST ISSUE. SEE SERIAL RECORD.

    . I. Title.

691.018.44   Underwriters' Laboratories, inc.
D83 Dufour, R E
    Survey of available information on the toxi-
    city of the combustion and thermal decomposition
    products of certain building materials under
    fire conditions. Chicago, Underwriters' Labora-
    tories, inc., 1963.
Laf.   66p. (Underwriters' Laboratories, Research
    bulletin no. 53)
    Bibliography: p. 53-66.
    1. Building materials - Fire resistance.
  2. Fire prevention. I. Underwriters' Laboratories, inc. II. Title.

697.4
U52F UNDERWRITERS' LABORATORIES, INC.
    FACT-FINDING REPORT ON MASONRY
    FIREPLACES, JUNE 29, 1962. CHICAGO,
    1962.
    1 V. (VARIOUS PAGINGS)

    RESEARCH PERFORMED FOR THE FEDERAL
    HOUSING ADMINISTRATION.

    1. FIREPLACES. I. U.S. FEDERAL
  HOUSING ADMINISTRATION. II. TITLE:
  MASONRY FIREPLACES.

621.9
r690
U52 h Underwriters' Laboratories, inc.
    Hazardous location equipment list. Chicago,
1955-
    v. annual.

    KEEP ONLY LATEST ISSUE. SEE SERIAL RECORD.

    1. Title.

        Underwriting manual.
728.1 U.S. Federal Housing Administration.
HUD   FHA manual. Washington, 1966-
FHA   v. (looseleaf)

    Contents:-v.1. National housing act.
  v.2. Regulations and rulings. v.3. Organization.
  v.4. Personnel. v.5. Book 1-2: Transmittal.
  Services. v.6. Book 1-2. Administrative.
  Multifamily mortgages. Pt. B. Home mortgages.
  v.7. Book ;-3. Underwriting manual. Reports and
  forms. v.8. Property disposition. v.9. Title 1.
  v.10. Mortgagee's handbook. v.11. Authorized
  agent's handbook certified Agency program.

           (Cont'd on next card)

697.8
U52FA UNDERWRITERS' LABORATORIES, INC.
    FACT-FINDING REPORT ON MASONRY
    FIREPLACES, OCT. 18, 1962. CHICAGO,
    1962.
    39P.

    RESEARCH SPONSORED BY THE FEDERAL
    HOUSING ADMINISTRATION. SUPPLEMENTS
    REPORT OF JUNE 29, 1962.

    1. FIREPLACES. I. U.S. FEDERAL
  HOUSING ADMINISTRATION. II. TITLE:
  MASONRY FIREPLACES.

551.59
U52 Underwriters' Laboratories, inc.
    Master labeled lightning protection systems.
    7th ed. Chicago, 1960.
    47p. (Its UL 96A)

    At head of title: Installation requirements.

    1. Lightning. I. Title.

728.1 U.S. Federal Housing Administration. FHA
HUD   manual...   (Card 2)
FHA
    v. 12. Table of contents.

    1. Housing. 2. Mortgage finance.
  3. Construction loans. I. Title. II. Title:
  National housing act. III. Title: Multifamily
  mortgages. IV. Title: Home mortgages.
  V. Title: Underwriting manual. VI. Title:
  Property disposition. VIII. Title: Mortgagee's
  handbook.

691.018.44
U52f Underwriters' Laboratories, inc.
    Fire hazard classification of
    building materials. Sept., 1944.
    34p. (Its Bulletin of Research
    no. 32)

    1. Building materials - Fire
resistance. 2. Fire prevention.

614.8
U52 Underwriters' Laboratories, inc.
    Report, 1967.

    [Chicago] 19

    v. annual.

    For Library holdings see main entry.

    1. Accidents.

728.1 UNDERWRITING MANUAL.
HUD   U.S. FEDERAL HOUSING ADMINISTRATION.
FHA   UNDERWRITING MANUAL. REV. WASHINGTON,
1935   1935.
    1 V. (UNPAGED)

    1. MORTGAGE FINANCE. I. TITLE.

728.1 HUD FHA 1936	UNDERWRITING MANUAL. U.S. FEDERAL HOUSING ADMINISTRATION. UNDERWRITING MANUAL. REV. WASHINGTON, 1936. 1 V. (UNPAGED) 1. MORTGAGE FINANCE. I. TITLE.

728.1 HUD FHA 1955	UNDERWRITING MANUAL. U.S. FEDERAL HOUSING ADMINISTRATION. UNDERWRITING MANUAL. REV. WASHINGTON, 1955. 1 V. (UNPAGED) 1. MORTGAGE FINANCE. I. TITLE.

332.72 G25u	U.S. General Accounting Office. Undue increases in the maximum Federal con- tributions ... (Card 2) 1. Mortgage finance. 2. Low-income housing. 3. U.S. Public Housing Administration. 4. Community facilities. I. Title. II. Title: Financing off-site community facilities for low-rent housing projects.

728.1 HUD FHA 1938	UNDERWRITING MANUAL. U.S. FEDERAL HOUSING ADMINISTRATION. UNDERWRITING MANUAL. REV. WASHINGTON, 1938. 1 V. (UNPAGED) 1. MORTGAGE FINANCE. I. TITLE.

728.1 HUD FHA 1934	UNDERWRITING MANUAL. U.S. FEDERAL HOUSING ADMINISTRATION. UNDERWRITING MANUAL. WASHINGTON, 1934. 1 V. (UNPAGED) 1. MORTGAGE FINANCE. I. TITLE.

300.15 L96	The uneasy partnership. Lyons, Gene M The uneasy partnership; social science and the Federal government in the twentieth century. New York, Russell Sage Foundation, 1969. 394p. 1. Social science research. 2. Governmental research. 3. Grants-in-aid. I. Title.

728.1 HUD FHA 1940	UNDERWRITING MANUAL. U.S. FEDERAL HOUSING ADMINISTRATION. UNDERWRITING MANUAL. REV. WASHINGTON, 1940. 1 V. (UNPAGED) 1. MORTGAGE FINANCE. I. TITLE.

728.1 HUD FHA 1960	UNDERWRITING MANUAL, SUPERSEDED PAGES. U.S. FEDERAL HOUSING ADMINISTRATION. UNDERWRITING MANUAL. SUPERSEDED PAGES DATED NOVEMBER 1, 1947 - FEBRUARY 11, 1960. WASHINGTON, 1960. 1 V. (UNPAGED) 1. MORTGAGE FINANCE. I. TITLE: UNDERWRITING MANUAL, SUPERSEDED PAGES.

	Unemployment see Employment Public assistance

728.1 HUD FHA 1947	UNDERWRITING MANUAL. U.S. FEDERAL HOUSING ADMINISTRATION. UNDERWRITING MANUAL. REV. WASHINGTON, 1947. 1 V. (UNPAGED) 1. MORTGAGE FINANCE. I. TITLE.

368 N17s	UNDERWRITING PROFIT OR LOSS. NATIONAL ASSOCIATION OF INSURANCE COMMISSIONERS. SECOND REPORT OF THE SPECIAL SUB-COMMITTEE OF THE FIRE AND MARINE COMMITTEE ... RE UNDERWRITING PROFIT OR LOSS AND THE COMMISSIONERS' 1921 STANDARD PROFIT FORMULA. CHICAGO, 1947. 106P. 1. INSURANCE. I. TITLE: UNDERWRITING PROFIT OR LOSS. II. TITLE: THE COMMISSIONERS' 1921 STANDARD PROFIT FORMULA.

331 F27U	UNEMPLOYMENT. FERGUSON, ROBERT H UNEMPLOYMENT: ITS SCOPE, MEASUREMENT, AND EFFECT ON POVERTY. ITHACA, N.Y., NEW YORK STATE SCHOOL OF INDUSTRIAL AND LABOR RELATIONS, CORNELL UNIVERSITY, 1965. 76 P. (BULLETIN 53-2) SECOND IN THE SERIES: THE DIMENSIONS OF POVERTY AND ITS REMEDIES. 1. EMPLOYMENT. 2. POVERTY. I. TITLE. II. NEW YORK STATE SCHOOL OF INDUSTRIAL AND LABOR RELATIONS.

728.1 HUD FHA 1947-58	UNDERWRITING MANUAL. U.S. FEDERAL HOUSING ADMINISTRATION. UNDERWRITING MANUAL. REV. WASHINGTON, 1947. 1 V. (UNPAGED) 1. MORTGAGE FINANCE. I. TITLE.

332.72 (07) F22	UNDERWRITING TRAINING HANDBOOK. U.S. FEDERAL HOUSING ADMINISTRATION. UNDERWRITING TRAINING HANDBOOK. WASHINGTON, 19 V. 1. MORTGAGE FINANCE--STUDY AND TEACHING. I. TITLE.

331 C657U 1961	UNEMPLOYMENT. U.S. CONGRESS. JOINT ECONOMIC COMMITTEE. UNEMPLOYMENT: TERMINOLOGY, MEASUREMENT, AND ANALYSIS BEFORE THE SUBCOMMITTEE ON ECONOMIC STATISTICS. WASHINGTON, GOVT. PRINT. OFF., 1961. 113P. AT HEAD OF TITLE: 87TH CONGRESS, 1ST SESSION, JOINT COMMITTEE PRINT. 1. EMPLOYMENT. I. TITLE.

728.1 HUD FHA 1948-59	UNDERWRITING MANUAL. U.S. FEDERAL HOUSING ADMINISTRATION. UNDERWRITING MANUAL. REV. WASHINGTON, 1948. 1 V. (UNPAGED) 1. MORTGAGE FINANCE. I. TITLE.

691.41 R22 Suppl.	Undisturbed sampling of earth materials. U.S. Bureau of Reclamation. Undisturbed sampling of earth materials: a supplement to the Earth manual. Denver, Aug. 1954. 10 p. plates. 1. Earth wall construction. I. Title. II. Title: Earth manual.

362.6 C657um 1971 S-H	Unemployment among older workers. U.S. Congress. Senate. Special Committee on Aging. Unemployment among older workers. Hearings before the Subcommittee on Employment and Retirement Incomes of the Special Committee on Aging, United States Senate, Ninety-second Congress, first session. Wash., Govt. Print. Off. 1971. pts. Hearings held June 4. 1. Old age - Employment. I. Title.

728.1 HUD FHA 1952	UNDERWRITING MANUAL. U.S. FEDERAL HOUSING ADMINISTRATION. UNDERWRITING MANUAL. REV. WASHINGTON, 1952. 1 V. (UNPAGED) 1. MORTGAGE FINANCE. I. TITLE.

332.72 G25u	Undue increases in maximum federal contri- butions resulting from method of financing off-site community facilities for low-rent housing projects ... U.S. General Accounting Office. Undue increases in maximum Federal contributions resulting from method of financing off-site community facilities for low-rent housing projects: Public Housing Administration, Housing and Home Finance Agency; report to the Congress of the United States by the Comptroller General of the United States. [Washington] 1963. 31p. (Cont'd. on next card)

368 U64	Unemployment and income security. Upjohn Institute for Employment Research. Unemployment and income security; goals for 1970's. Kalamazoo, Mich., 1969. 27p. (Studies in unemployment insurance) A report of the Committee on Unemployment Insurance Objectives sponsored by the Institute. 1. Insurance. 2. Employment. I. Title.

331
W24

UNEMPLOYMENT AND INCREASING PRODUCTIVITY.
WEINTRAUB, DAVID.
UNEMPLOYMENT AND INCREASING PRODUCTIVITY,
BY DAVID WEINTRAUB ASSISTED BY HAROLD L.
POSNER. PREPARED FOR THE NATIONAL
RESOURCES COMMITTEE, REPORT ON
TECHNOLOGICAL TRENDS AND THEIR SOCIAL
IMPLICATIONS. PHILADELPHIA, WORKS
PROGRESS ADMINISTRATION, 1937.
75L.

1. EMPLOYMENT. 2. LABOR PRODUCTIVITY.
3. SOCIAL CONDITIONS. I. POSNER, HAROLD
L., JT. AU. II. WORKS PROGRESS
ADMINISTRATION. III. TITLE.

331
C65TEMP
1959
H-R
MAR.25

UNEMPLOYMENT COMPENSATION.
U.S. CONGRESS. CONFERENCE
COMMITTEES, 1959.
TEMPORARY UNEMPLOYMENT COMPENSATION.
CONFERENCE REPORT TO ACCOMPANY H.R.
5640. WASHINGTON, GOVT. PRINT. OFF.,
1959.
3P. (86TH CONGRESS, 1ST SESSION.
HOUSE. REPORT NO. 257)

1. EMPLOYMENT. I. TITLE.
II. TITLE: UNEMPLOYMENT COMPENSATION.

331
C65u
1970
S-H

Unemployment compensation.
U.S. Congress. Senate. Committee
on Finance.
Unemployment compensation. Hearings
before the Committee on Finance, United
States Senate, Ninety-first Congress,
second session on H.R. 14705, to extend
and improve the Federal-State unemployment
compensation program. Wash., Govt.
Print. Off., 1970.
368p.
Hearings held Feb. 5-18, 1970.
1. Employment. I. Title.

331
C65WE
1938
S-H

UNEMPLOYMENT AND RELIEF.
U.S. CONGRESS. SENATE. SPECIAL
COMMITTEE TO INVESTIGATE UNEMPLOYMENT
AND RELIEF.
UNEMPLOYMENT AND RELIEF. HEARINGS,
SEVENTY-FIFTH CONGRESS, THIRD SESSION,
PURSUANT TO S. RES. 36, FEBRUARY 28 TO
APRIL 8, 1938. WASHINGTON, GOVT. PRINT.
OFF., 1938.
V.

1. EMPLOYMENT. I. TITLE.

331
C65TEMP
1959
H-R
MAR.13

UNEMPLOYMENT COMPENSATION.
U.S. CONGRESS. HOUSE. COMMITTEE ON
WAYS AND MEANS.
TEMPORARY UNEMPLOYMENT
COMPENSATION... REPORT TO ACCOMPANY
H.R. 5640. WASHINGTON, GOVT. PRINT.
OFF., MARCH 13, 1959.
7P. (86TH CONGRESS, 1ST SESSION.
HOUSE. REPORT NO. 212)

1. EMPLOYMENT. I. TITLE.
II. TITLE: UNEMPLOYMENT COMPENSATION.

331
C65TEMP
1958
S-R

UNEMPLOYMENT COMPENSATION, 1958.
U.S. CONGRESS. SENATE. COMMITTEE ON
FINANCE.
TEMPORARY UNEMPLOYMENT COMPENSATION
ACT OF 1958... REPORT TO ACCOMPANY HR
12065. WASHINGTON, GOVT. PRINT. OFF.,
1958.
2PTS. IN 1 V. (85TH CONGRESS, 2D
SESSION. SENATE. REPORT NO. 1625)
CONTENTS.--IPT.II

1. EMPLOYMENT. I. TITLE.
II. TITLE: UNEMPLOYMENT COMPENSATION,
1958.

331
G56

Unemployment and the central city.
Gloster, Jesse E
Unemployment and the central city; a
research project, by Jesse E. Gloster,
[n.p.] 1968.
43p.
1. Employment. 2. Employment - Negroes.
3. Employment - Houston. I. Texas
Southern University. II. Title.

331
C65U
1959
H-H

UNEMPLOYMENT COMPENSATION.
U.S. CONGRESS. HOUSE. COMMITTEE ON
WAYS AND MEANS.
UNEMPLOYMENT COMPENSATION. HEARINGS
BEFORE THE COMMITTEE ON WAYS AND MEANS,
HOUSE OF REPRESENTATIVES, EIGHTY-SIXTH
CONGRESS, FIRST SESSION ON THE SUBJECT OF
PROPOSED AMENDMENTS TO THE FEDERAL LAWS
ON UNEMPLOYMENT COMPENSATION, APRIL 7-10,
13-16, 1959. WASHINGTON, GOVT. PRINT.
OFF., 1959.
1167P.

1. EMPLOYMENT.
I. TITLE.

331
C65TEMP
1958
H-R

UNEMPLOYMENT COMPENSATION ACT.
U.S. CONGRESS. HOUSE. COMMITTEE ON
WAYS AND MEANS.
TEMPORARY UNEMPLOYMENT COMPENSATION
ACT OF 1958. REPORT TO ACCOMPANY
H.R. 12065. WASHINGTON, GOVT. PRINT.
OFF., 1958.
38P. (85TH CONGRESS, 2D SESSION.
HOUSE. REPORT NO. 1656)

1. EMPLOYMENT. I. TITLE.
II. TITLE: UNEMPLOYMENT COMPENSATION
ACT.

368
M12

Unemployment benefits.
Mackin, Paul J
Extended unemployment benefits. Kalamazoo,
Mich., W. E. Upjohn Institute for Employment
Research, 1965.
41p. (Studies in employment and unemployment)
1. Insurance. 2. Workmen's compensation.
3. Employment. I. Upjohn Institute for Employment Research. II. Title: Unemployment
benefits.

331
C65U
1965
H-H

UNEMPLOYMENT COMPENSATION.
U.S. CONGRESS. HOUSE. COMMITTEE ON
WAYS AND MEANS.
UNEMPLOYMENT COMPENSATION. HEARINGS,
EIGHTY-NINTH CONGRESS, FIRST SESSION, ON
H.R. 8282... WASHINGTON, GOVT. PRINT.
OFF., 1965.
V.

1. EMPLOYMENT. I. TITLE. II. TITLE:
EMPLOYMENT SECURITY AMENDMENTS OF 1965.

331
C6593
1961
H-R

UNEMPLOYMENT COMPENSATION ACT OF 1961.
U.S. CONGRESS. CONFERENCE COMMITTEES,
1961.
TEMPORARY EXTENDED UNEMPLOYMENT
COMPENSATION ACT OF 1961... CONFERENCE
REPORT TO ACCOMPANY H.R. 4806.
WASHINGTON, GOVT. PRINT. OFF., 1961.
6P. (87TH CONGRESS, 1ST SESSION.
HOUSE. REPORT NO. 183)

1. EMPLOYMENT. I. TITLE.
II. TITLE: UNEMPLOYMENT COMPENSATION
ACT OF 1961.

331
(083.41)
A25

UNEMPLOYMENT CENSUS, 1937.
U.S. OFFICE OF ADMINISTRATOR OF THE
CENSUS OF PARTIAL EMPLOYMENT,
UNEMPLOYMENT, AND OCCUPATIONS.
PRELIMINARY REPORT ON TOTAL AND
PARTIAL UNEMPLOYMENT. UNITED STATES
SUMMARY BY STATES, COUNTIES, AND
CITIES OF 10,000 OR MORE POPULATION
AS OF NOVEMBER 16-20, 1937.
WASHINGTON, GOVT. PRINT. OFF., 1938.
99P.

RUNNING TITLE: UNEMPLOYMENT
CENSUS, 1937
(CONTINUED ON NEXT CARD)

331
C65TEMP
1959
S-H

UNEMPLOYMENT COMPENSATION.
U.S. CONGRESS. SENATE. COMMITTEE ON
FINANCE.
TEMPORARY UNEMPLOYMENT COMPENSATION.
HEARING ... EIGHTY-SIXTH CONGRESS,
FIRST SESSION, ON H.R. 5640, AN ACT
TO EXTEND THE TIME DURING WHICH
CERTAIN INDIVIDUALS MAY CONTINUE TO
RECEIVE TEMPORARY UNEMPLOYMENT
COMPENSATION. WASHINGTON, GOVT.
PRINT. OFF., 1959.
81P.
1. EMPLOYMENT. I. TITLE.
II. TITLE: UNEMPLOYMENT
COMPENSATION.

331
C65T
1961
S-R
NO.27

UNEMPLOYMENT COMPENSATION ACT OF 1961.
U.S. CONGRESS. SENATE. COMMITTEE ON
FINANCE.
TEMPORARY EXTENDED UNEMPLOYMENT
COMPENSATION ACT OF 1961... REPORT...
TO ACCOMPANY H.R. 4806. WASHINGTON,
GOVT. PRINT. OFF., 1961.
27P. (87TH CONGRESS, 1ST SESSION.
SENATE. REPORT NO. 69)

1. EMPLOYMENT. I. TITLE.
II. TITLE: UNEMPLOYMENT COMPENSATION
ACT OF 1961.

331
(083.41)
A25

U.S. OFFICE OF ADMINISTRATOR OF THE
CENSUS OF PARTIAL EMPLOYMENT,
UNEMPLOYMENT, AND OCCUPATIONS.
PRELIMINARY REPORT ...1938. (CARD 2)

1. EMPLOYMENT - STATISTICS.
I. TITLE: UNEMPLOYMENT CENSUS, 1937.

331
C65TEMP
1959
S-R

UNEMPLOYMENT COMPENSATION.
U.S. CONGRESS. SENATE. COMMITTEE ON
FINANCE.
TEMPORARY UNEMPLOYMENT COMPENSATION.
REPORT TOGETHER WITH SUPPLEMENTAL
VIEWS TO ACCOMPANY H.R. 5640.
WASHINGTON, GOVT. PRINT. OFF., 1959.
13P. (86TH CONGRESS, 1ST SESSION.
SENATE. REPORT NO. 135)

1. EMPLOYMENT. I. TITLE.
II. TITLE: UNEMPLOYMENT COMPENSATION.

331
C657TEM
1961
H-H

UNEMPLOYMENT COMPENSATION AND AID TO
DEPENDENT CHILDREN.
U.S. CONGRESS. HOUSE. COMMITTEE ON
WAYS AND MEANS.
TEMPORARY UNEMPLOYMENT COMPENSATION
AND AID, TO DEPENDENT CHILDREN OF
UNEMPLOYED PARENTS. HEARINGS,
EIGHTY-SEVENTH CONGRESS, FIRST
SESSION, ON H.R. 3864... AND H.R.
3865. WASHINGTON, GOVT. PRINT. OFF.,
1961.
423P.
HEARINGS HELD FEB. 15-17, 1961.

1. EMPLOYMENT. I. TITLE.
II. TITLE: U-NEMPLOYMENT
(CONTINUED ON NEXT CARD)

368
(759)
P15

UNEMPLOYMENT COMPENSATION.
PAN AMERICAN CONSULTING CORP., MIAMI,
FLA.
UNEMPLOYMENT COMPENSATION; A SURVEY OF
BENEFIT ADEQUACY, 1956-1957. MIAMI
1957.
70P.

SURVEY MADE IN COOPERATION WITH
FLORIDA INDUSTRIAL COMMISSION AND U.S.
BUREAU OF EMPLOYMENT SECURITY.
1. INSURANCE. 2. EMPLOYMENT -
FLORIDA. I. FLORIDA. INDUSTRIAL
COMMISSION. I. I. U.S. BUREAU OF
EMPLOYMENT SECURITY. III. TITLE.

331
C65U
1961
S-H

UNEMPLOYMENT COMPENSATION.
U.S. CONGRESS. SENATE. COMMITTEE ON
FINANCE.
UNEMPLOYMENT COMPENSATION. HEARINGS,
EIGHTY-SEVENTH CONGRESS, FIRST SESSION ON
H.R. 4806... WASHINGTON, GOVT. PRINT.
OFF., 1961.
186P.
HEARINGS HELD: MARCH 8-10, 1961.

1. EMPLOYMENT. I. TITLE.

331
C657TEM
1961
H-H

U.S. CONGRESS. HOUSE. COMMITTEE ON
WAYS AND MEANS. TEMPORARY
UNEMPLOYMENT COMPENSATION ...1961
(CARD 2)

COMPENSATION AND AID TO DEPENDENT
CHILDREN.

UNEMPLOYMENT COMPENSATION LAW IN
LABOR DISPUTES.
LAW
T   LEWIS, WILLARD A
L285UN   UNEMPLOYMENT COMPENSATION LAW IN
LABOR DISPUTES. MICHIGAN COMPARED WITH
SEVEN SELECTED STATES, 1936-1964.
KALAMAZOO, MICH., THE W.E. UPJOHN
INSTITUTE FOR EMPLOYMENT RESEARCH, 1964.
63P.

1. EMPLOYMENT.   I. TITLE.

Unemployment compensation beneficiaries.
368
D86   Duquesne University.
A digest of the survey of unemployment compensation beneficiaries in Pittsburgh, Pennsylvania. Study conducted by Duquesne University and U.S. Dept. of Labor, Bureau of
Employment Security. Pittsburgh, 1955.
13p.   tables.

1. Insurance. I. U.S. Bureau of Employment
Security.   II. Title: Unemployment compensation
beneficiaries.

Unemployment rate in Washington Cardozo area.
VF
331   [District of Columbia. Board of Education]
(753)   Unemployment rate in Washington Cardozo
D47   area... Washington, 1966.
4p.

1. Employment - District of Columbia.
2. Employment - Negroes. I. Title.

UNEMPLOYMENT INDEMNITY AND ACCIDENT AND
SICKNESS INDEMNITY.
368
C653   CONTINENTAL CASUALTY COMPANY.
UNEMPLOYMENT INDEMNITY AND ACCIDENT AND
SICKNESS INDEMNITY FOR MORTGAGE
PAYMENTS. CHICAGO, 1961.
4L.

1. INSURANCE.   I. TITLE.   II. TITLE:
ACCIDENT AND SICKNESS INDEMNITY FOR
MORTGAGE PAYMENTS.

Unemployment compensation beneficiaries.
368
E56   U.S. Bureau of Employment Security.
Proposed method for a survey of unemployment compensation beneficiaries.
Washington, 1956.
6p.

1. Insurance I. Title: Unemployment compensation
beneficiaries.

Unemployment rates in larger cities.
VF
331   U.S. Area Redevelopment Administration.
A72u   Unemployment rates in larger cities.
Prepared by Robert S. Ray. Wash., U.S. Dept.
of Commerce, Area Redevelopment Administration, Office of Planning and Research, for
sale by the Dept. of Commerce, 1964.
3p.   (Area staff study)

1. Employment. I. Ray, Robert S.
II. Title.

UNEMPLOYMENT INSURANCE: COSTS OF THE ABC
CORPORATION.
331
M12U   MCKEAN, EUGENE C
UNEMPLOYMENT INSURANCE: COSTS OF THE ABC
CORPORATION IN MICHIGAN AND NEARBY
STATES. KALAMAZOO, MICH., UPJOHN
INSTITUTE FOR EMPLOYMENT RESEARCH, 1962.
64P. (STUDIES IN THE MICHIGAN ECONOMY)

1. EMPLOYMENT.   2. INSURANCE.
I. UPJOHN INSTITUTE FOR EMPLOYMENT
RESEARCH.   II. TITLE.

Unemployment, idle capacity, and the evaluation
of public expenditures.
331
H18   Haveman, Robert H
Unemployment, idle capacity, and the
evaluation of public expenditures; national
and regional analyses, by Robert H. Haveman
and others. Published for Resources for the
Future, inc. Baltimore, Johns Hopkins Press,
1968.
159p.

1. Employment. 2. U.S. Appropriations and
expenditures. I. Johns Hopkins University.
II. Resources for the Future. III. Title.

UNEMPLOYMENT STATISTICS.
331
C65EMPL   U.S. CONGRESS. JOINT COMMITTEE ON
1955   THE ECONOMIC REPORT.
EMPLOYMENT AND UNEMPLOYMENT
STATISTICS.   HEARINGS BEFORE THE
SUBCOMMITTEE ON ECONOMIC STATISTICS,
EIGHTY-FOURTH CONGRESS, FIRST SESSION,
PURSUANT TO SEC. 5(A) OF PUBLIC LAW
304, 79TH CONGRESS. WASHINGTON, GOVT.
PRINT. OFF., 1955.
167P.
HEARINGS HELD NOVEMBER 7 AND 8, 1955.

1. EMPLOYMENT.   I. TITLE.
II. TITLE   UNEMPLOYMENT STATISTICS.

UNEMPLOYMENT INSURANCE AMENDMENTS OF
1966.
368
C65U   U.S. CONGRESS. HOUSE. COMMITTEE ON
1966   WAYS AND MEANS.
H-R   UNEMPLOYMENT INSURANCE AMENDMENTS OF
1966. REPORT ... TO ACCOMPANY H.R.
15119... WASHINGTON, GOVT. PRINT. OFF.,
1966.
83P. (89TH CONGRESS, 2D SESSION.
HOUSE. REPORT NO. 1636)

1. INSURANCE.   2. EMPLOYMENT.
I. TITLE.

Unemployment insurance financing.
331
M12   McKean, Eugene C
The taxable wage base in unemployment
insurance financing. Kalamazoo, Mich., W. E.
Upjohn Institute for Community Research, 1965.
96p.   (W. E. Upjohn Institute for
Employment Research. Unemployment insurance
monograph)

1. Employment. 2. Taxation. I. Upjohn
Institute for Employment Research. II. Title:
Unemployment insurance financing.

THE UNEVEN DISTRIBUTION OF LEISURE.
712*25
W45   WILENSKY, HAROLD L
THE UNEVEN DISTRIBUTION OF LEISURE;
THE IMPACT OF ECONOMIC GROWTH ON FREE
TIME.   ANN ARBOR, 1961.
27P. (INSTITUTE OF LABOR AND
INDUSTRIAL RELATIONS. REPRINT SERIES
20)

REPRINTED FROM SOCIAL PROBLEMS, V. 9,
NO. 1, SUMMER, 1961, P. 32-56.
1. RECREATION.   2. ECONOMIC
DEVELOPMENT.   I. INSTITUTE OF LABOR
AND INDUSTRIAL   RELATIONS.
II. TITLE.

UNEMPLOYMENT INSURANCE AMENDMENTS OF
1966.
368
C65U   U.S. CONGRESS. SENATE. COMMITTEE ON
1966   FINANCE.
S-H   UNEMPLOYMENT INSURANCE AMENDMENTS OF
1966. HEARINGS...EIGHTY-NINTH CONGRESS,
ON H.R. 15119. WASHINGTON, GOVT.
PRINT. OFF., 1966.
827P.
HEARINGS HELD JULY 13-16, 1966.

1. INSURANCE.   2. EMPLOYMENT.
I. TITLE.

Unemployment insurance in Michigan.
368
M42   Michigan. Employment Security Commission.
Financing of unemployment insurance in
Michigan 1959-'60. An analysis of the
Michigan economy in 1959 and 1960 with pro-
jections as to the short-range aspects of
unemployment insurance benefit financing in
Michigan. Lansing, 1959.
54p. diagrs., tables.

1. Insurance.   I. Title: Unemployment insurance in Michigan.

Unfilled orders, price changes, and business
fluctuations.
330.15
N17o   Zarnowitz, Victor, 1919-
no.84   Unfilled orders, price changes, and business
fluctuations. [New York] 1962.
28 p. (National Bureau of Economic
Research. Occasional paper 84)

1. Manufacturers. 2. Prices. I. Title. II.
Title: Business fluctuations. III. National
Bureau of Economic Research. Occasional paper,
no. 84.

UNEMPLOYMENT INSURANCE AMENDMENTS OF
1966.
368
C65U   U.S. CONGRESS. SENATE. COMMITTEE ON
1966   FINANCE.
S-R   UNEMPLOYMENT INSURANCE AMENDMENTS OF
1966. REPORT...TOGETHER WITH MINORITY
VIEWS TO ACCOMPANY H.R. 15119...
WASHINGTON, GOVT. PRINT. OFF., 1966.
92P. (89TH CONGRESS, 2D SESSION.
SENATE. REPORT NO. 1425)

1. INSURANCE.   2. EMPLOYMENT.
I. TITLE.

Unemployment insurance objectives and issues.
368
B5lu   Blaustein, Saul J
Unemployment insurance objectives and issues;
an agenda for research and evaluation.
Kalamazoo, Mich., W.E. Upjohn Institute for
Employment Research, 1968.
64p. (Upjohn Institute for Employment
Research. Studies in unemployment insurance)

1. Insurance. I. Upjohn Institute for
Employment Research. II. Title.

Unfinished business in Puerto Rico.
VF
33
(7295)   Perloff, Harvey S
P27   Unfinished business in Puerto Rico.
[San Juan, P.R. American Society for Public
Administration, Puerto Rico Chapter [1951]
13 1.
Address delivered before the Society on
May 29, 1951.
Processed.

1. Puerto Rico-Econ. condit. I. American Society
for Public Administration. Puerto Rico Chapter.
II. Title.

UNEMPLOYMENT SITUATION AND OUTLOOK.
331
C65UN   U.S. CONGRESS. SENATE. COMMITTEE ON
1961   LABOR AND PUBLIC WELFARE.
S-H   UNEMPLOYMENT SITUATION AND OUTLOOK,
HEARINGS, EIGHTY-SEVENTH CONGRESS, FIRST
SESSION. WASHINGTON, GOVT. PRINT. OFF.,
1961.
528P.
HEARINGS HELD FEB. 22, 23, 27, MARCH
2, 3, AND 9, 1961.
BIBLIOGRAPHY: P.516-528.

1. EMPLOYMENT - BIBLIOGRAPHY.
I. TITLE.

UNEMPLOYMENT PROBLEMS.
331
C65UNE   U.S. CONGRESS. SENATE. SPECIAL
1959-60   COMMITTEE ON UNEMPLOYMENT PROBLEMS.
S-H   UNEMPLOYMENT PROBLEMS. HEARINGS...
EIGHTY-SIXTH CONGRESS, FIRST [
-SECOND] SESSION[S] PURSUANT TO S.
RES. 196. WASHINGTON, GOVT. PRINT.
OFF., 1959-60.
9 V.
HEARINGS HELD OCT. 5, 1959-JAN. 11,
1960.

1. EMPLOYMENT.   I. TITLE.

The unfinished but habitable home.
728.1
S32   Shenkel, William M
The unfinished but habitable home. Prepared
for the Housing and Home Finance Agency.
Contracted with the Bureau of Economic and
Business Research, College of Business
Administration, University of Florida,
Gainesville. Wash., Govt. Print. Off., 1965.
86p.

1. Housing. 2. Family living requirements.
3. Mortgage finance. 4. Owner-built houses.
I. Florida. University.   Bureau of Economic
and Business Research.   II. U.S. Housing
and Home Finance   Agency. III. Title.

370
:325
C65un

The unfinished education.
U.S. Commission on Civil Rights.
The unfinished education; outcomes for minorities in the five southwestern states. Wash., 1971.
101p. (Mexican American educational series report no. 2)

1. Education - Minority groups. 2. Mexican Americans. I. Title.

Unfolding of the American tradition.

323.4
P72u

U.S. President's Commission for the Observance of Human Rights Year.
Unfolding of the American tradition. Wash., Govt. Print. Off., 1968.
127p. (U.S. Dept. of State. Publication 8403)

1. Civil rights. 2. History. I. United Nations. II. Title: Unfolding of the American tradition.

624.131
A52s
1966

Unger, David G
ASPO National Planning Conference, Philadelphia, 1966.
Soils and land-use planning. Papers presented at the ASPO National Planning Conference, Philadelphia, Pennsylvania, April 17-21, 1966, by David G. Unger and others. Chicago, 1966.
44p.

1. Soils. 2. Land use. 3. Natural resources. I. Unger, David G. II. American Society of Planning Officials. III. Title.

301.15
G65

Unger, Elizabeth L   jt. au.
Goldsmith, Harold F
Differentiation of urban subareas: a re-examination of social area dimensions, by Harold F. Goldsmith and Elizabeth L. Unger. [Bethesda, Md.] Mental Health Study Center, National Institute of Mental Health, 1970.
49p. (Laboratory paper no. 35)
Bibliography: p. 44-49.
1. Community structure. I. Unger, Elizabeth L., jt. au. II. U.S. National Institute of Mental Health. III. Title.

333.33
U53

Unger, Maurice A
Real estate, principles and practices. Ed. 3. Cincinnati, South-Western Pub. Co., 1964.
758p.

1. Real property. 2. Real estate business. I. Title.

2c.

333.33
U53
1969

Unger, Maurice A
Real estate principles and practices. 4th ed. Cincinnati, South-Western Pub. Co., 1969.
754p.

1. Real property. 2. Real estate business. I. Title.

728.1
1336.18
U53

UNGER, PAUL A
THE GUS JOHNSONS IN A HOUSING PROJECT. WASHINGTON, UNITED STATES HOUSING AUTHORITY, TENANT RELATIONS DIVISION, 1941.
15L.

2c

1. PUBLIC HOUSING - SOCIAL EFFECT. I. U.S. HOUSING AUTHORITY. II. TITLE.

711.417
(747)
U53

Ungers, O M
Lysander, new city; a project of fourth and fifth year students, by O.M. Ungers and Tilman Heyde. Ithaca, N.Y., Dept. of Architecture, College of Architecture, Art, and Planning, 1970.
225p.

1. New towns - New York (State) I. Heyde, Tilman, jt. au. II. Cornell University. College of Architecture. Art and Planning. III. Title.

625.85
H43u

Ungraded aggregated in bituminous mixes.
Highway Research Board.
Ungraded aggregated in bituminous mixes, presented at the thirty-fourth annual meeting January 11-14, 1955. Washington, 1955.
49 p. illus., tables, diagrs. (Its Bulletin 109)

National Research Council. Publication 361.

1. Road construction. I. Title.

301.15
B15

The unheavenly city.
Banfield, Edward C
The unheavenly city; the nature and future of our urban crisis. Boston, Little, Brown and Company, 1970.
308p.

1. City growth. 2. Metropolitan areas. I. Title.

693.068
1389.6
N17
1964

THE UNICOM METHOD OF HOUSE CONSTRUCTION.
NATIONAL LUMBER MANUFACTURERS ASSOCIATION.
A BRIEF DESCRIPTION OF THE UNICOM METHOD OF HOUSE CONSTRUCTION. WASHINGTON, 1964.
23P.

1. MODULAR COORDINATION. I. TITLE. I. TITLE: THE UNICOM METHOD OF HOUSE CONSTRUCTION.

693.5
F67

Unified design of reinforced concrete...
Forsyth, Benjamin.
Unified design of reinforced concrete members. New York, McGraw-Hill, 1971.
528p.

1. Concrete construction. 2. Concrete, Reinforced. I. Title.

651.4
B68u

Unified issuances system.
U.S. Dept. of Housing and Urban Development.
Unified issuances system. A HUD handbook. Washington, 1967.
1v.

1. Office procedures. I. Title. II. Title: A HUD handbook.

728.1
I57u

A unified planning requirements system.
U.S. Interdepartmental Planning Requirements Task Group.
A unified planning requirements system; recommendations to improve the management and effectiveness of Federal planning requirements. Wash., 1969.
129p.
For administrative use only.

1. Federal housing programs. 2. City planning. I. Title.

352
I57u

A unified response to urbanism.
International City Managers' Association.
A unified response to urbanism; council-manager plan. Wash., 1966.
15p.

1. City manager government. I. Title: Council-manager plan. II. Title.

624.131
W17

THE UNIFIED SOIL CLASSIFICATION SYSTEM.
U.S. WATERWAYS EXPERIMENT STATION, VICKSBURG, MISS.
THE UNIFIED SOIL CLASSIFICATION SYSTEM. VICKSBURG, 1953-
V. (CORPS OF ENGINEERS, U.S. ARMY. TECHNICAL MEMORANDUM NO. 3-357)
For Library holdings see main entry

VOLS. 2 CALLED ALSO APPENDIX A WITH TITLE: CHARACTERISTICS OF SOIL GROUPS PERTAINING TO EMBANKMENTS AND FOUNDATIONS. APPENDIX B (REV. 1957) HAS TITLE: CHARACTERISTICS OF SOIL GROUPS PERTAINING TO ROADS AND AIRFIELDS.
(CONTINUED ON NEXT CARD)

624.131
W17

U.S. WATERWAYS EXPERIMENT STATION, VICKSBURG, MISS. THE UNIFIED SOIL ...1953-   (CARD 2)

1. SOILS. 1. TITLE.

388.015
B68

Unified theory of transport and transfer systems.
Bouladon, Gabriel A
Unified theory of transport and transfer systems. Translation of an exposé given on April 4, 1966 at Round Table on Transport, under the auspices of the Délégation Générale à la Recherche Scientifique et Technique, Paris. [Geneva, Switzerland. Battelle Memorial Institute, 1967?]
21p.
illus. -- --- Illustrations. 10p. [1967?]
1. Transportation - Research. 2. Journey to work. I. Battelle Memorial Institute. Geneva, Switzerland. II. Title.

388
B27u

Uniflow; a mass transit system concept.
Berggren Transportation System Co.
Uniflow; a mass transit system concept, by Lloyd E. Berggren. Minneapolis, 1966.
28p.

1. Transportation. 2. Journey to work. 3. Railroads. 4. Automation. I. Title.

690.091.82
(94)
A87
1970

Uniform building code.
Australia. Dept. of Housing.
Tentative uniform home building code. Canberra, 1970.
61p.

1. Building codes - Australia. I. Title. II. Title: Uniform building code.

690.091.82
I57

Uniform building code.
International Conference of Building Officials.
Uniform building code. 1958:V.1,3; 1961;V.1,3. Los Angeles, 1958-   1964:V.1,3
v.
analysis of revisions, 1970 ed.
For earlier editions, see Pacific Coast Building Officials Conference.

For complete information see shelflist.

1. Building codes. I. Title.

690.091.82
I57um International Conference of Building
Officials.
Uniform building code. Standards, 1967
Pasadena, Calif., 1967-
/ v.

For complete information see main card.

1. Building standards. 2. Building
materials - Standards and specifications.
I. Title.

VF
690.091.82
U543

Uniform Building Code Association.
Adopting the uniform building code. Los
Angeles [n.d.]
6 p.

1. Building codes. I. Title.

711.585 UNIFORM COMPENSATION FOR RELOCATION.
C657 U.S. CONGRESS. SENATE. COMMITTEE ON
1965 GOVERNMENT OPERATIONS.
S-H (SUBCOMMITTEE ON INTERGOVERNMENTAL
RELATIONS.)
UNIFORM COMPENSATION FOR RELOCATION.
HEARINGS... EIGHTY-NINTH CONGRESS,
FIRST SESSION ON S. 1201... AND S.
1681... JUNE AND JULY 1965.
WASHINGTON, 1965.
323P.

1. RELOCATION. I. TITLE.

690.091.82
I57u International Conference of Building
1967 Officials.
Uniform building code. Short form, based
on Uniform building code, 1967 ed., volume I.
Pasadena, Calif., 1967.
140p.

1. Building codes. I. Title.

690.091.82
C45
A uniform building permit application
system utilizing computer technology.
Cincinnati. University. Urban Information
Systems.
A uniform building permit application
system utilizing computer technology.
Cincinnati, 1970.
20p.

1. Building permits. 2. Building industry.
I. Title.

LAW Uniform crime reports for the United States.
T U.S. Federal Bureau of Investigation.
F222 Uniform crime reports for the United States.
I582u 19
Washington, U.S. Dept. of Justice, Federal
Bureau of Investigation, 19
v. annual.
19_.   issued by John Edgar Hoover.
For complete information see main card.

1. Law enforcement. 2. Municipal services.
3. Juvenile delinquency. I. Hoover, John Edgar.
II. Title.

690.091.82 Uniform building code.
I57u International Conference of Building
1970 Officials.
Uniform building code. Short form,
based on Uniform building code, 1970 ed.,
vol. I. Pasadena, Calif., 1970.
150p.

1. Building codes. I. Title.

690.091.82 The uniform building permit reporting
H65u system.
Homer Hoyt Institute.
The uniform building permit reporting
system: a demonstration in the Washing-
ton, D.C. SMSA. The final report of a
Homer Hoyt Institute project conducted
under the direction of Michael Sumichrast
and Maury Seldin. Wash., 1970.
135p.
Prepared under contract H-1020 for the
Dept. of Housing and Urban Development.
1. Building permits. I. Sumichrast,
Michael. II. Seldin, Maury. III. U.S.
Dept. of   Housing and Urban Develop-
ment.   IV. Title.

699.81 Uniform fire code.
I57u International Conference of Building
Officials
Uniform fire code. Pasadena, Calif.,
International Conference of Building
Officials; San Leandro, Calif., Western
Fire Chiefs Association, 1971-
/ v.

For Library holdings see main entry.

1. Fire prevention. I. Western Fire
Chiefs Association. II. Title.

Uniform building code.
690.091.82
P12 Pacific Coast Building Officials Conference.
Uniform building code. 1940, 43, 46, 49,
52, 55. Los Angeles.
6 nos. in 8 v.

Later editions are issued by the International Conference of Building Officials.

1. Building codes. I. Title.

690.091.82 Uniform building regulations in South
(68) Africa.
M67 Morris, S S
Uniform building regulations in South
Africa. A paper presented to the
Building Research Congress of the National
Building Research Institute, Pretoria,
South Africa, 28-31st July, 1964. Cape
Town, S.A., 1964.
28p.
Cover title.

1. Building codes - South Africa.
I. Building   Research Congress,
Pretoria,   South Africa, 1964.
II. Title.

690.091.82
:613.5
I57 Uniform housing code,
International Conference of Building
Officials
Uniform housing code, 1955, 61, 64
Los Angeles, 1957-
v. tables.

For complete information see shelflist.

1. Housing codes. I. Title.

Uniform building code. Short form.
690.091.82
I57u International Conference of Building
1961 Officials.
Uniform building code. Short form,
based on Uniform building code, 1961
ed., volume I. Los Angeles, 1961.
92p.

Earlier editions are issued by Pacific
Coast Building Officials Conference.

1. Building codes. I. Title.

---

657 Uniform CPA examination questions and unoffi-
A52 cial answers,
American Institute of Certified Public Accountants.
Uniform CPA examination questions and unofficial answers,   A supplement to the Journal of accountancy [n.p.]
v.

For complete information see main card.

1. Accounting. I. Journal of accountancy.
II. Title.

LAW
T UNIFORM LAW ANNOTATED. BROOKLYN, N.Y.,
U543L EDWARD THOMPSON, 1922-65
10 v. in 1.

SOME VOLUMES OF ORIGINAL EDITION
REPLACED BY REV. ED.

1. LAW.

690.091.82 Uniform building code. Short form,
I57u based on Uniform building code, 1964.
1964 International Conference of Building
Officials.
Uniform building code. Short form,
based on Uniform building code, 1964
ed., volume I. Pasadena, Calif., 1964.
136p.

1. Building codes. I. Title.

333.65 UNIFORM CLASSIFICATION OF ACCOUNTS
C25U FOR LARGE SCALE HOUSING PROJECTS.
U.S. CENTRAL HOUSING COMMITTEE.
UNIFORM CLASSIFICATION OF ACCOUNTS
FOR LARGE SCALE HOUSING PROJECTS.
WASHINGTON, D.C., N.D.
9L.

1. HOUSING MANAGEMENT.   I. TITLE.

Uniform law commissioners' revised model state
LAW administrative procedure act.
T National Conference of Commissioners on
N17 Uniform State Laws. St. Louis, Mo., 1961.
C651m Uniform law commissioners' revised model
state administrative procedure act. Drafted
by the National Conference of Commissioners on
Uniform State Laws, and by it approved at its
annual conference meeting in its 17th year at
St. Louis, Mo., July 31-August 5, 1961, with
prefatory note and comments. Chicago, 1961.
27p. (American Society for Public
Administration. Reprint service)

(Cont'd. on next card)

Uniform building code. Short form.
690.091.82
P12u Pacific Coast Building Officials Conference.
Uniform building code. Short form. 1949, 52.
Los Angeles.
2v.

"Excerpts from the parent document."
Later editions are issued by the International
Conference of Building Officials.

1. Building codes. I. Title.

711.14 A uniform coding system for land use.
B17 Barton-Aschman Associates.
A uniform coding system for land use. A
technical guide prepared for the Housing
and Home Finance Agency, Office of the
Administrator. Evanston, Ill., 1963.
159p.
Draft.
Bibliography: p. 149-159.

1. Land use. I. U.S. Housing and Home Finance
Agency, Office of the Administrator. II. Title.

LAW
T National Conference of Commissioners on
N17 Uniform State Laws. St. Louis Mo., 1961.
C651u Uniform law commissioners'... (Card 2)

1. Administrative law - Congresses.
I. American Society for Public Administration.
Reprint service,   II. Title.

FILM

Uniform plumbing code..
U. S. Housing and Home Finance Agency. Office of the Administrator. Division of Housing Research.
Toward a uniform plumbing code. [1948?]

Prepared with National Bureau of Standards.

1. Films. I. U.S. National Bureau of Standards.
II. Title: Uniform Plumbing Code..

696.1
:690.091.82
I57

Uniform plumbing code.
International Association of Plumbing and Mechanical Officials.
Uniform plumbing code. 11th ed.
Los Angeles, 1967.
201p.
Adopted at the thirty-seventh annual conference, October 1966.

1. Plumbing codes. 2. Building standards. I. Title.

696.1
:690.091.82
I57
1970

Uniform plumbing code.
International Association of Plumbing and Mechanical Officials.
Uniform plumbing code. 12th ed.
Los Angeles, 1970.
206p.

1. Plumbing codes. 2. Building standards. I. Title.

VF
696.1
:690.091.82
C66
1949
3c

Uniform Plumbing Code Committee.
Report. Issued jointly by U.S. Dept. of Commerce, Office of Domestic Commerce, Construction Division [and] Housing and Home Finance Agency, Office of the Administrator, Division of Standardized Building Codes and Materials. Washington, Govt. Print. Off., July 1949.
83 p. diagrs., graphs, tables.
At head of title: Uniform plumbing code.
1.Plumbing codes I. U.S.Bur.of For.and Domes. Commerce.Office of Domes.Commerce II.U.S. Hsg.and Home Finance Agency.O.A.Div.of Stand.Bldg. Codes and Materials.

VF
696.1
:690.091.82
C66
1948

Uniform Plumbing Code Committee.
[Report of comments and suggestions on U.S. Housing and Home Finance Agency, Office of Administrator, Technical Staff's Technical paper no. 6, The uniform plumbing code for housing, dated February 1948.] [Washington] U.S. Dept. of Commerce, Sept. 1948.
107 p.

Processed.

1.Plumbing codes. J . Housing and Home Finance Agency. O.A. Techni Staff. II.U.S. Bureau of Foreign and Domestic Commerce. Office of Domestic Commerce.

690.015
H68
T6

The uniform plumbing code for housing.
U.S. Housing and Home Finance Agency. Office of the Administrator. Technical Office.
The uniform plumbing code for housing. Washington, D.C., Feb. 1948.
iv, 83 p. diagrs., graphs, tables. (Its Technical paper no. 6)

Processed.

1.Plumbing codes. I.Title.

Office of
General
Counsel

Uniform real estate mortgage act.
National Conference of Commissioners on Uniform State Laws.
Uniform real estate mortgage act, drafted by the National Conference of Commissioners on Uniform State Laws, and by it approved and recommended for enactment in all the states at its conference at Buffalo, N. Y., with introductory statement and notes approved by the American Bar Association at its meeting at Buffalo, N. Y. [Chicago] 1927.
67p.

1. Mortgage finance legislation. I. Title.

LAW
U.S.

Uniform real estate mortgage and foreclosure act.
Central Housing Committee.
Uniform real estate mortgage and foreclosure act. Prepared by the Sub-Committee on Law and Legislation of the Central Housing Committee. [Washington] 1936.
[34] p.

1. Mortgage foreclosure - Procedures.
I. Title.

711.585
C657
1966
S-R

UNIFORM RELOCATION ACT OF 1966.
U.S. CONGRESS. SENATE. COMMITTEE ON GOVERNMENT AFFAIRS.
UNIFORM RELOCATION ACT OF 1966.
REPORT TO ACCOMPANY S. 1681.
WASHINGTON, 1966.
43P. (89TH CONGRESS, 2D SESSION.
SENATE. REPORT NO. 1378.

1. RELOCATION. 2. RELOCATION - LAW AND LEGISLATION. I. TITLE.

LAW
T
A52
B171uni

Uniform relocation assistance and land acquisition policies.
American Bar Association. National Institute.
Uniform relocation assistance and land acquisition policies. Proceedings, May 20-21, 1971, Houston, Tex. Sponsored by the Section of Local Government Law of the American Bar Association in cooperation with the Section of Real Property Probate and Trust Law. Chicago, 1971.
1v.

1. Relocation. 2. Land acquisition.
I. Title.

711.585
C657

Uniform relocation assistance and land acquisition policy.
U.S. Congress. House. Committee on Public Works.
Uniform relocation assistance and land acquisition policy. Hearings before the Committee on Public Works, House of Representatives, Ninetieth Congress, second session on H.R. 386 and related bills to provide uniform, fair, and equitable treatment of persons, businesses, or farms displaced by Federal and Federally assisted programs. Wash., Govt. Print. Off., 1968.
615p.
Hearings held Sept. 11-24, 1968.
1. Relocation. 2. Land acquisition.
3. Eminent domain. I. Title.

711.585
C657
S-H
1969

Uniform relocation assistance and land acquisition policies act of 1969.
U.S. Congress. Senate. Committee on Government Operations.
Uniform relocation assistance and land acquisition policies act of 1969. Hearings before the Subcommittee on Intergovernmental Relations of the Committee on Government Operations, United States Senate, Ninety-First Congress, first session, on S. 1, to provide for uniform and equitable treatment of persons displaced from their homes, businesses, or farms by Fede ral and Federally assisted programs. Wash., Govt. Print. Off., 1969. (Cont'd on next card)

711.585
C657
S-H
1969

U.S. Congress. Senate. Committee on Government Operations. Uniform relocation assistance...1969. (Card 2)
306p.

Hearings held Feb. 19-27, 1969.

1. Relocation. 2. Land acquisition.
3. Eminent domain. I. Title.

711.585
C65uni
1970
H-H

Uniform relocation assistance and land acquisition policies - 1970.
U.S. Congress. House. Committee on Public Works.
Uniform relocation assistance and land acquisition policies - 1970. Hearings before the Committee on Public Works, House of Representatives, Ninety-first Congress, first and second sessions on H.R. 14898, H.R. 14899, S. 1, and related bills to establish uniform relocation assistance and land acquisition policies applicable to Federal programs and Federal grant-in-aid programs. Wash., Govt. Print. Off., 1970.
1118p.

(Cont'd on next card)

711.585
C65uni
1970
H-H

U.S. Congress. House. Committee on Public Works. Uniform...1970. (Card 2)

Hearings held Dec. 2, 1969 - March 19, 1970.

1. Relocation. 2. Land acquisition.
3. Eminent domain. I. Title.

LAW
T

Uniform rules of procedure for Government Agency Boards of Contract Appeals.
Federal Publications, inc., Wash. D.C.
Proposed uniform rules of procedure for Government Agency Boards of Contract Appeals. Washington, D.C., 1967.
28p. (A Public service paper no. 1)

1. Federal contracts. 2. Federal government. I. Title. II. Title: Uniform rules of procedure for Government Agency Boards of Contract Appeals.

691
A52u

Uniform system for construction specifications.
American Institute of Architects.
Uniform system for construction specifications, data filing and cost accounting; title one buildings. [Washington] 1966.
1v.

Co-publishers: Associated General Contractors of America, inc.; Construction Specifications Institute, inc.; Council of Mechanical Specialty Contracting Industries, inc.
1. Building materials - Standards and specifications. 2. Building methods. 3. Building construction - Standa rds and specifications. 4. Building industry. 5. Accounting.
IV. Title.

657
:333.65
F22U

UNIFORM SYSTEM OF ACCOUNTS.
U.S. FEDERAL HOUSING ADMINISTRATION.
UNIFORM SYSTEM OF ACCOUNTS FOR LARGE SCALE HOUSING PROJECTS. WASHINGTON, GOVT. PRINT. OFF., 1936.
37P.

1. ACCOUNTING. 2. HOUSING MANAGEMENT. I. TITLE: UNIFORM SYSTEM OF ACCOUNTS.

657
:333.65
F22
1938

UNIFORM SYSTEM OF ACCOUNTS.
U.S. FEDERAL HOUSING ADMINISTRATION.
UNIFORM SYSTEM OF ACCOUNTS FOR MULTI-FAMILY AND GROUP HOUSING PROJECTS INSURED UNDER THE NATIONAL HOUSING ACT. WASHINGTON, GOVT. PRINT. OFF., 1938.
36P.

1. ACCOUNTING. 2. HOUSING MANAGEMENT. I. TITLE: UNIFORM SYSTEM OF ACCOUNTS.

657
:333.65
F22
1942

UNIFORM SYSTEM OF ACCOUNTS.
U.S. FEDERAL HOUSING ADMINISTRATION.
UNIFORM SYSTEM OF ACCOUNTS FOR MULTI-FAMILY AND GROUP HOUSING PROJECTS INSURED UNDER THE NATIONAL HOUSING ACT. WASHINGTON, 1942.
37P.

1. ACCOUNTING. 2. HOUSING MANAGEMENT. I. TITLE: UNIFORM SYSTEM OF ACCOUNTS.

333.65
F22U

UNIFORM SYSTEM OF ACCOUNTS FOR LARGE SCALE HOUSING PROJECTS.
U.S. FEDERAL HOUSING ADMINISTRATION.
UNIFORM SYSTEM OF ACCOUNTS FOR LARGE SCALE HOUSING PROJECTS. JUNE 15, 1936. WASHINGTON, 1937.
37P.

1. HOUSING MANAGEMENT - ACCOUNTING. 2. PUBLIC HOUSING - FINANCE. I. TITLE.

657
N28U
UNIFORM SYSTEM OF ACCOUNTS FOR LIMITED
DIVIDEND HOUSING COMPANIES.
NEW YORK (STATE) STATE BOARD OF HOUSING.
UNIFORM SYSTEM OF ACCOUNTS FOR LIMITED
DIVIDEND HOUSING COMPANIES, PRESCRIBED BY
THE BOARD OF HOUSING, DIVISION OF
ARCHITECTURE, DEPARTMENT OF PUBLIC WORKS,
STATE OF NEW YORK. ALBANY, 1929.
22P.

1. ACCOUNTING. 2. LIMITED DIVIDEND
HOUSING - ASSOCIATIONS. I. TITLE.

628.515
U54c
Union Carbide Corp.
Continued evaluation of oxygen use in
conventional activated sludge processing.
[Prepared] for the Office of Research and
Monitoring, Environmental Protection Agency.
Wash., For sale by Supt. of Docs., U.S.
Govt. Print. Off., 1972.
164p. (Water pollution control research
series)
1. Water pollution. I. U.S. Environ-
mental Protection Agency. II. Title.
III. Title: Activated sludge processing.

728.1
:336.18
(76813)
U54
1953/54
UNION CITY, TENN. HOUSING AUTHORITY.
REPORT, 1953/54.
UNION CITY.
/V. ANNUAL.

1. PUBLIC HOUSING - UNION CITY, TENN.

657
:333.65
F22
1947
Uniform system of accounts for multi-family
and group housing projects.
U.S. Federal Housing Administration.
Uniform system of accounts for multi-family
and group housing projects insured under the
National Housing Act. Washington, May 1947.
37 p.

Processed.

1. Apartment houses-Accounting. 2. Housing
management. I. Title: Uniform system of accounts
for multi-family and group housing projects.

355.58
B62
Union Carbide Corp.
Boegly, W J Jr.
A survey of underground utility tunnel
practice, by W.J. Boegly, Jr. and W.L.
Griffith. Oak Ridge, Tenn., Oak Ridge
National Laboratory operated by Union
Carbide Corporation for the U.S. Atomic
Energy Commission, 1967.
115p. (ORNL-TM-1714)
Bibliography: p. 109-110.
1. Civilian defense. 2. Public utilities.
I. Griffith, W.L., jt. au. II. U.S. National Labora-
tory, Oak Ridge, Tenn. III. Union Carbide Corp.
V. Title.

711.552
(76813)
U54
Union City, Tenn. Regional Planning Com-
mission.
Central business district, Union City,
Tennessee. With the assistance of the
Tennessee State Planning Commission,
West Tennessee Office. Union City,
1957.
35p. illus., maps, tables.

U.S. Urban Renewal Administration,
(Continued on next card)

LAW
T
A uniform system of citation.
Harvard Law Review Association.
A uniform system of citation; forms of
citation and abbreviation. Cambridge, Mass.,
1967.
117p.

Copyright, 1967 by: Columbia law review,
Harvard law review, University of Pennsylvania
law review, Yale law journal.

1. Annotations and citations (Law) I. Title.

711.4
(79465)
U54
Union City, Calif. City Council.
Ruth and Krushkhov.
1960 general plan, Union City,
California. [Prepared for Union City
City Council] Berkeley, Calif., 1963.
51p.

U.S. Urban Renewal Adm. UPAP.

1. Master plan - Union City, Calif.
I. Union City, Calif. City Council.
II. U.S. URA-UPAP. Union City, Calif.

711.552
(76813)
U54
Union City, Tenn. Regional Planning Commission. Central business ... (Card 2)

Urban Planning Assistance Program.

1. Business districts - Union City,
Tenn. I. Tennessee. State Planning Commission. II. U.S. Urban Renewal Administration. Urban Planning Assistance
Program.

LAW
R
1958:67
A Uniform system of citation; forms of citation
and abbreviations, 10th ed. rev.
Cambridge, Harvard Law Review Assn.,
1958.
2v.

For complete information see main card.

1. Annotations and citations (Law)
2. Law - Abbreviations.

1958 - 2c

711.585.1
(79465)
U54
Union City, Calif. Office of the City
Manager.
Application to the Department of Housing
and Urban Development for a grant to plan
a comprehensive model cities program.
Union City, Calif., 1968.
1v.

1. Model cities - Union City, Calif.
I. U.S. HUD. Model Cities Program.

330
(76813)
U54
Union City, Tenn. Regional Planning Commission.
Economic base study for Union City. Assisted
by the Tennessee State Planning Commission,
West Tennessee Office. Union City, 1956.
28p. tables.

U.S. Urban Renewal Administration, Urban
Planning Assistance Program.
1. Economic base studies - Union City, Tenn.
I. Tennessee. State Planning Commission. II.
U.S. Urban Planning Assistance Program. Urban
Planning Assistance Program.

711.4
(79493)
P17u
Unincorporated urban area study.
Pasadena, Calif. [Planning Commission]
Unincorporated urban area study; a co-
operative study of interlying unincorporated
areas by the cities of Pasadena and Arcadia.
[Pasadena, Calif.] 1966.
126p.

1. City planning - Pasadena, Calif.
2. City planning - Arcadia, Calif.
3. Annexation. I. Title.

694
UNION CITY, CALIF. PLANNING COMMISSION.
GENERAL PLAN PROGRAM. BY KAPLAN
(MARSHALL), GANS AND KAHN. UNION CITY,
CALIF., 1970.
233L. (HUD 701 REPORT)

1. MASTER PLAN - UNION CITY, CALIF.
I. KAPLAN (MARSHALL), GANS AND KAHN.
II. HUD. 701. UNION CITY, CALIF.

711.585
(76813)
U54
Union City, Tenn. Regional Planning Com-
mission.
General community renewal plan, Union
City, Tennessee. Prepared by Tennessee
State Planning Commission, West Tennessee
Office. Union City, 1958.
44p. illus., maps, tables.
U.S. Urban Renewal Administration, Urban Planning
Assistance Program.
1. Urban renewal - Union City, Tenn. I. Tennessee.
State Planning Commis-
sion. II. U.S. URA-
UPAP. Union City,
Tenn.

711.4
(7467)
U54
Union and New Haven Trust Company.
Guide to city planning in New
Haven, 1955. Journal of the Union
and New Haven Trust Co., vol. 20, no. 5,
June 1955.
folder.

1. City planning - New Haven, Conn.
I. Title.

693
UNION CITY, CALIF. PLANNING COMMISSION.
INITIAL SUMMARY REPORT. BY KAPLAN
(MARSHALL), GANS AND KAHN. UNION CITY,
CALIF., 1968.
212L. (HUD 701 REPORT)

1. MASTER PLAN - UNION CITY, CALIF.
I. KAPLAN (MARSHALL), GANS AND KAHN.
II. HUD. 701. UNION CITY, CALIF.

690.091.82
:613.5
(75813)
U54
Union City, Tenn. Regional Planning Commission.
Housing code for Union City, Tennessee.
With the assistance of the Tennessee State
Planning Commission, West Tennessee Office. Union City, 1957.
30p.

U.S. Urban Renewal Administration,
(Continued on next card)

658
B69
UNION CARBIDE CORP.
BOYD, J H
AN APPLICATION OF CRITICAL PATH
SCHEDULING TO DESIGN ENGINEERING (SANS
COMPUTER), BY J.H. BOYD. OAK RIDGE,
TENNESSEE, MARCH 1, 1965.
94L. ILLUS. (UNION CARBIDE
CORPORATION. REPORT NO. Y-1480)

BIBLIOGRAPHY: P. 92-94.

1. INDUSTRIAL MANAGEMENT. I. UNION
CARBIDE CORP. II. TITLE: CRITICAL PATH
SCHEDULING. III. TITLE: DESIGN
ENGINEERING.

4526
UNION CITY, S.C. CITY PLANNING
COMMISSION.
COMMUNITY FACILITIES PLAN, PUBLIC
IMPROVEMENTS PROGRAM, CAPITAL
IMPROVEMENTS BUDGET. UNION CITY, 1970.
78P. (HUD 701 REPORT)

1. CITY PLANNING - UNION CITY, S.C.
I. HUD. 701. UNION CITY, S.C.

690.091.82
:613.5
(76813)
U54
Union City, Tenn. Regional Planning Commission. Housing code ... (Card 2)

Urban Planning Assistance Program.

1. Housing codes - Union City, Tenn.
I. Tennessee. State Planning Commission.
II. U.S. Urban Renewal Administration.
Urban Planning Assistance Program.

728.1
(76813)
U54   Union City, Tenn. Regional Planning Commission.
     Housing survey and analysis, Union City,
Tennessee. With the assistance of the Tennessee State Planning Commission, West Tennessee Office. Union City, 1957
     51p. maps, tables.

     U.S. Urban Renewal Administration, Urban

             (Continued on next card)

728.1
(76813)
U54   Union City, Tenn. Regional Planning Commission. Housing survey ... (Card 2)

   Planning Assistance Program.

     1. Housing surveys - Union City, Tenn.
I. Tennessee. State Planning Commission.
II. U.S. Urban Renewal Administration.
Urban Planning Assistance Program.

711.14
(76813)
U54   Union City, Tenn. Regional Planning Commission.
     Land use plan for Union City, Tennessee. With
the assistance of the Tennessee State Planning
Commission. Union City, 1956.
     31p. maps, tables.

     U.S. Urban Renewal Administration, Urban
Planning Assistance Program.

     1. Land use - Union City, Tenn. I. Tenn-
essee. State Planning Commission. II. U.S.
Urban Renewal   Administration. Urban
Planning Assist-   ance Program.

312
(76813)
U54   Union City, Tenn. Regional Planning Commission.
     Population study for Union City. Assisted
by the Tennessee State Planning Commission,
West Tennessee Office. Union City, 1956,
     16p. tables.

     U.S. Urban Renewal Administration, Urban
Planning Assistance Program.

     1. Population - Union City, Tenn. I. Tenn-
essee. State Planning Commission. II. U.S.
Urban Renewal Administration. Urban Planning Assistance   Program.

371.7
(76813)
U54   Union City, Tenn. Regional Planning Commission.
     Recreation study for Union City. Assisted
by the Tennessee State Planning Commission.
Union City, 1956.
     52p. illus., maps.

     U.S. Urban Renewal Administration, Urban
Planning Assistance Program.

     1. Recreation - Union City, Tenn. I.
Tennessee. State Planning Commission.

727.1
(76813)
U54   Union City, Tenn. Regional Planning Commission.
     School study for Union City, Tennessee.
With the assistance of Tennessee State
Planning Commission, West Tennessee Office. Union City, 1957.
     29p. diagrs., maps, tables.

     U.S. Urban Renewal Administration,

        (Cont'd. on next card)

727.1
(76813)
U54   Union City, Tenn. Regional Planning Commission. School study... (Card 2)

   Urban Planning Assistance Program.

     1. Schools - Union City, Tenn. I. Tenn-
essee. State Planning Commission. II. U.S.
Urban Renewal Administration. Urban Planning Assistance Program.

711.74
(76813)
U54   Union City, Tenn. Regional Planning Commission.
     Street classification and improvement
program, Union City, Tennessee. With the
assistance of the Tennessee State Planning
Commission. Union City 1956.
     30p. maps.

   U.S. Urban Renewal Administration, Urban Planning
Assistance Program.

     1. Street planning - Union City, Tenn. I. Tennes-
see. State Planning Com-   mission. II. U.S.
Urban Renewal Adminis-   tration. Urban Planning Assistance Pro-   gram.

711.4
(76813)
U54t   Union City, Tenn. Regional Planning Commission.
     Thinking of tomorrow, a comprehensive plan
for the development and redevelopment of
Union City, Tennessee. Assisted by Tennessee State Planning Commission, West Tennessee Office. Union City, 1959.
     12p. illus., diagrs., maps.

   U.S. Urban Renewal Administration, Urban Planning
Assistance Program.

   1. Master plan - Union City, Tenn. I. U.S. URA-
UPAP. Union City,   Tenn.

711.4
(76813)
U54   Union City, Tenn. Regional Planning Commission.
     Union City capital budget improvement pro-
gram, a study. With the assistance of the
Tennessee State Planning Commission. Union
City, 1956.
     23p. tables.

     U.S. Urban Renewal Administration, Urban
Planning Assistance Program.

     1. Capitol improvement programs - Union
City, Tenn. I. Tennessee. State Planning
Commission. II. U.S. Urban Renewal Ad-
ministration. U n Planning Assistance
Program.

352.6
(76813)
U54   Union City, Tenn. Regional Planning Commis-
sion.
     Utilities survey, Union City, Tennessee.
With the assistance of the Tennessee State
Planning Commission. Union City, 1957.
     7p. maps.

     U.S. Urban Renewal Administration, Urban
Planning Assistance Program.

     1. Public utilities - Union City, Tenn. I.
Tennessee. State Planning Commission. II.U.S.
Urban Renewal Administration. Urban Planning
Assistance Pro-   gram.

5658
5659
5660
5661
5662   UNION CITY JOINT PLANNING COMMISSION.
COMPREHENSIVE PLANNING: 1. THE
COMPREHENSIVE PLAN; 2. BACKGROUND FOR
PLANNING; 3. GUIDE FOR ACTION; 4. ZONING
ORDINANCE; 5. SUBDIVISION CONTROL
ORDINANCE. UNION CITY, IND., 1966.
     5 V. (HUD 701 REPORT)

     1. MASTER PLAN - UNION CITY, IND.
2. MASTER PLAN - UNION CITY, OHIO.
I. HUD. 701. UNION CITY, IND.
II. HUD. 701. UNION CITY, OHIO.

331.881
L11   Union constitution provisions.
     U.S. Bureau of Labor Statistics.
     Union constitution provisions: election and
tenure of national and international union
officers, 1958. Qualifications for office,
nominating and election procedures, term of
office, presidential salaries, removal procedures, by Harry P. Cohany and Irving P.
Phillips. Washington, Govt. Print. Off.,
1958.

        (Continued on next card)

331.881
L11   U.S. Bureau of Labor Statistics.   Union
constitution provisions:...(Card 2)

     37p. (Its Bulletin no. 1239)

     85th Cong., 2d sess. House document
no. 446.
     1. Labor relations. 2. Trade unions.
I. Phillips, Irving Philip. II. Title.
III. Title: Election and tenure of national
and international union officers, 1958.

331.1
F85   Union constitutions.
     Fund for the Republic.
     Union constitutions, by Leo Bromwich. A
report to the Fund for the Republic.
New York, 1959.
     43p.

     1. Labor relations. I. Bromwich, Leo.
II. Title.

5671   UNION CO., IND. AREA PLAN COMMISSION.
COMPREHENSIVE AREA PLAN. BY JAMES H.
NEIDIGH AND ASSOCIATES. LIBERTY, IND.,
1969.
     105P. (HUD 701 REPORT)

     1. MASTER PLAN - UNION CO., IND.
I. NEIDIGH, (JAMES H.) AND ASSOCIATES.
II. HUD. 701. UNION CO., IND.

3257-
3264   UNION CO., N.J. PLANNING BOARD.
MASTER PLAN PROGRAM: 1. PLANNING
PROPOSALS AND FUTURE LAND USE
ALTERNATIVES; 2. OPEN SPACE AND
RECREATION; 3. A MASTER WATER PLAN; 4.
COUNTY FACILITY STUDY, SECOND YEAR
REPORT; 5. A MASTER SEWERAGE PLAN; 6.
PRELIMINARY REPORT UPON STORM DRAINAGE
FACILITIES; 7. SANITARY FACILITIES. BY
ELSON T. KILLAM ASSOCIATES. ELIZABETH,
N.J., 1969-70.
     7 V. (HUD 701 REPORT)

     1. COUNTY PLA NNING - UNION CO., N.J.
            (CONTINUED ON NEXT CARD)

3257-
3264   UNION CO., N.J. PLANNING BOARD. MASTER
PLAN ...9-70.   (CARD 2)

     I. KILLAM (ELSON T.) ASSOCIATES.
II. HUD. 701. UNION CO., N.J.

3279   UNION CO., N.J. PLANNING BOARD.
MASTER PLAN PROGRAM: TRANSPORTATION
STUDY, INTERIM REPORT. PREPARED BY JAMES
P. PURCELL ASSOCIATES. N.P., 1970.
     91L. (HUD 701 REPORT)

     1. COUNTY PLANNING - UNION CO., N.J.
I. PURCELL (JAMES P.) ASSOCIATES.
II. HUD. 701. UNION CO., N.J.

2647   UNION CO., N.J. PLANNING BOARD.
REPORT UPON WATER SUPPLIES AND WATER
FACILITIES IN UNION COUNTY. BY ELSON T.
KILLAM ASSOCIATES. ELIZABETH, N.J., 1969.
     39L. (HUD 701 REPORT)

     1. WATER SUPPLY - UNION CO., N.J.
I. KILLAM (ELSON T.) ASSOCIATES.
II. HUD. 701. UNION CO., N.J.

VF
647.7
U54   Union de Banques Suisses.
     L'hotellerie suisse: hier, aujourd'hui,
demain. Bern, 1958.
     32p. (American Embassy, Bern. Foreign
service dispatch no. 108, 1958, enclosure
no. 1)

     1. Hotels - Switzerland. I Series: American
Embassy, Bern. Foreign service dispatch no.
108, 1958, enclosure no. 1.

728.1
(493)
U54
Union Européenne des Constructeurs de
Logements. (Secteur Privé)
Comment devenir propriétaire de son
logement. Bruxelles, 1960.
1v.

1. Housing - Belgium.

LAW
Union list of legislative histories.
Law Librarians' Society of Washington, D.C.
Union list of legislative histories. 47th
Congress, 1883 - 85th Congress, 1958. 2d ed.
Albany, N. Y., Matthew Bender & Co., 1959.
202p.
——— Kept up to date by supplements.
"Second edition compiles the 1950 edition
and 1954 supplement into one list and contin-
ues the list through the 85th Congress (1958)"
I. Title. II. Title: Legislative histories.

058.7
(05)
J64
UNION LIST OF SERIALS IN THE LIBRARIES OF THE
UNITED STATES AND CANADA. 3d ed.
Joint Committee on the Union List of Serials.
Final report on the third edition of the
Union list of serials. Submitted by Howard
Rovelstad, chairman. Washington, Council on
Library Resources, 1966.
viii, 52 p. illus., facsims.

"Prepared by the Union List of Serials Project at the Library of Congress."

1. Union list of serials in the libraries of the
United States and Canada. 3d ed. I. Rovelstad,
(continued on next card)

728.1
(4)
U54re
Union Europeenne des Constructeurs de
Logements.
Les réalisations, le financement, les
caractéristiques de la construction de
logements en France, Hollande, Allemagne
Federale, Belgique. Bruxelles [1960]
1v.

1. Housing - France. 2. Housing - Holland.
3. Housing - Germany (Federal Republic)
4. Housing - Belgium.

LAW
R
Union list of legislative histories.
Law Librarians' Society of Washington, D.C.
(Legislative History Committee)
Union list of legislative histories, 47th
Congress, 1883- 89th Congress, 1966. Com-
piled by Legislative History Committee, Law
Librarians' Society of the District of
Columbia. Vienna, Va., Coiner Publications,
ltd., 1967.
329p.
1. Law - Period. I. Title.

058.7
(05)
J64
Joint Committee on the Union List of Serials.
Final report on the third edition of the
Union list of serials. (card 2)

Howard. II. U.S. Library of Congress.
III. Council on Library Resources. IV. Title.

rds

711.73
(7291)
U54
Union Interamericana del Caribe.
Cuba y la Carretera Panamericana.
La Habana, 1957.
24 p.

1. Highways - Cuba.

R
058.7
(05)
U54
A Union list of serials in the libraries of
the consortium of universities of the
Metropolitan Washington area. Martha Toms,
editor and Joseph T. Popecki, general
editor. Washington, D.C., Distributed by
Catholic University of America Press, 1967.
370p.

1. Periodicals - Direct. 2. Libraries -
District of Columbia. I. Catholic University
of America. II. Toms, Martha, ed.
III. Popecki, Joseph T. ed. IV. Title.

332.72
(44)
L85
L'Union Nationale des Associations Familiales.
Pour un authentique financement du logement
familial. Publication mensuelle. [Paris,
1953?]
103p. (Compte rendu des Journees du
Logement Familial. Deuxieme partie.)
Numéro spécial.

1. Mortgage finance - France.

A Union list of serials in the libraries ...

R
058.7
(05)
U54
A Union list of serials in the libraries of
the consortium of universities of the
Metropolitan Washington area. Martha Toms,
editor and Joseph T. Popecki, general
editor. Washington, D.C., Distributed by
Catholic University of America Press, 1967.
370p.

1. Periodicals - Direct. 2. Libraries -
District of Columbia. I. Catholic University
of America. II. Toms, Martha, ed.
III. Popecki, Joseph T. ed. IV. Title.

Union Internationale des Architectes

see

International Union of Architects

R
058.7
:341.1
A55
Union of International Associations.
Annuaire des organisations internationales. Yearbook of
international organizations. 1st ed.; 1948 /1951/52-
[Genève]
v. 24 cm.

Editors: 1948- Marcel Henchoz, R.H. Wüst.

1. International organizations Yearbooks. I. Henchoz, Marcel,
ed.

JX1904.A49   341.1058   49—22132*
Library of Congress   [51y10]

Union Internationale des Organismes Familiaux.

see

International Union of Family Organizations.

R
058.7
:05
U54
Union list of serials in libraries of the United
States and Canada; edited by Winifred
Gregory. 2d ed. New York, Wilson, 1943.
3065 p.

Lists serials which began publication through
December 30, 1940.

——— Supplement, January 1, 1941, -
December 30, 1943; edited by Gabrielle E.
Malikoff. 1945.
1123 p.

(see card 2)

341.1
(016)
Y21
Union of International Associations.
Yearbook of international congress proceedings

Brussels, Union of International Associations.
v. (Union of International Associations.
Publication)
"Bibliography of reports arising out of
meetings held by international organizations."
On spine, 1960/67- : International meeting
reports.
1. International organizations - Bibl.
I. Union of International Associations.
II. Title: International meeting reports.

016
:07
(8)
P15
Union list of Latin American newspapers in
libraries in the United States.
Pan American Union. Columbus Memorial
Library.
Union list of Latin American newspapers in
libraries in the United States, comp. by
Arthur E. Gropp. Washington, Dept. of Cultural Affairs, 1953.
235p. (Its Bibliographic series 39)

1. Newspapers - Directories. 2. Newspapers - Latin America. I. Gropp, Arthur E.,
comp. II. Title.

R
058.7
:05
U54
suppl.
Union list of serials... 2d ed. 1943. (card 2)

1944/49

——— Supplement, Jan. 1944-Dec. 1949; edited
by Marga Franck. 1953.
1365p.

Kept up-to-date by New serial titles:
R 058.7:05 U54a
1. Periodicals - Direct. I. Gregory,
Winifred, ed. II. Malikoff, Gabrielle E., ed.
III. Franck, Marga, ed.

Ref.
058.7
:341.7
Y21
Union of International Associations.
Yearbook of international organizations;
the encyclopaedic dictionary of international organizations, their officers,
their abbreviations, 68/69-

Brussels, Union of International
Associations.
v.
For Library holdings see main entry.

1. International organizations - Direct.
I. Union of International
Associations

Union list of legal periodicals, District of
Columbia area.
LAW
R
LAW Librarians' Society of Washington, D.C.
(Committee on Legal Periodicals)
Union list of legal periodicals, District of
Columbia area. Compiled by Committee on Legal
Periodicals of the Law Librarians' Society of
Washington, D.C., Chapter of the American
Association of Law Libraries. Fairfax, Va.,
Coiner Publications, 1963.
136p.

1. Law - Period. II. Title.

058.7
:05
U54
1965
Union List of Serials in Libraries of the
United States and Canada, edited by
Edna Brown Titus. 3rd ed. New York,
H.W. Wilson, 1965
5 v.

Contents:-v.1 A-B. -v.2. C-G. -v.3.
H-M. -v.4. N-R. -v.5. S-Z.

1. Periodicals - Directories. I. Titus, Edna
Brown

Union of South Africa.

see also

West African Building Research Institute.

690.015 Union of South Africa.
(68 South African Council for Scientific and
:016) Industrial Research. National Building
S68 Research Institute.
NBRI publications. Pretoria, 1968.
40p. (CSIR bibliography A7)

1. Building research - Union of South Africa - Bibl. 2. Union of South Africa. National Building Research Institute - Publications. I. Title.

---

720 Union of South Africa - Architecture.
(68) Fairbairn, D G
F14 Architectural research on the planning of buildings. Pretoria, National Building Research Institute, South African Council for Scientific & Industrial Research, 1968.
[3]p. (South African Council for Scientific and Industrial Research. CSIR reference no. R/BOU 259)
Reprinted from Public works, roads, and transport, May, 1968.

1. Architecture - Union of South Africa. 2. Union of South Africa - Architecture. I. Title. II. South African Council

(Cont'd on next card)

720
(68) Fairbairn, D G Architectural research
F14 ...1968. (Card 2)

for Scientific and Industrial Research. National Building Research Institute.

690.031 Union of South Africa - Building costs.
(68) Miners, T W
M45 Cost planning as a tool for management. Pretoria, National Building Research Institute, South African Council for Scientific and Industrial Research, 1967.
4p. (South African Council for Scientific and Industrial Research. CSIR reference no. R/Bou 225)
Reprinted from Proceedings of the Third Australian Building Research Congress, Melbourne, 1967.
1. Building costs - Union of South Africa. 2. Building industry - Union of South Africa.

(Cont'd on next card)

690.031
(68) Miners, T W Cost planning...1967.
M45

3. Union of South Africa - Building costs. 4. Union of South Africa - Building industry. I. Title. II. South African Council for Scientific and Industrial Research.

690.031 Union of South Africa - Building industry.
(68) Miners, T W
M45 Cost planning as a tool for management. Pretoria, National Building Research Institute, South African Council for Scientific and Industrial Research, 1967.
4p. (South African Council for Scientific and Industrial Research. CSIR reference no. R/Bou 225)
Reprinted from Proceedings of the Third Australian Building Research Congress, Melbourne, 1967.
1. Building costs - Union of South Africa. 2. Building industry - Union of South Africa.

(Cont'd on next card)

690.031
(68) Miners, T W Cost planning...1967.
M45

3. Union of South Africa - Building costs. 4. Union of South Africa - Building industry. I. Title. II. South African Council for Scientific and Industrial Research.

Union of South Africa - Building research.
711.4
:670 South African Council for Scientific and
(68) Industrial Research. National Building Re-
S68 search Institute.
South Africa: improving the climate for industry. Pretoria, South African Council for Scientific and Industrial Research, National Building Research Institute, 1967.
4p. (C.S.I.R. reference no. R/Bou 246)
Reprinted from Interbuild-arena, Nov., 1967.

1. Industrial location - Union of South Africa. 2. Union of South Africa - Building research.

(Cont'd on next card)

711.4
:670 South African Council for Scientific and
(68) Industrial Research. National Building Re-
S68 search Institute. South Africa...1967. (Card 2)

I. Interbuild-arena. II. Title

Union of South Africa - Housing for the aged.
728.1
:362.6 South African Council for Scientific and
(68) Industrial Research. National Building
S68 Research Institute.
A guide to special housing for the aged people. Pretoria, 1967.
54p. (Its Bulletin no. 43; C.S.I.R. Research report no. 245)

1. Housing for the aged - Union of South Africa. 2. Union of South Africa - Housing for the aged. I. Title.

South Africa. *Cape Town Forshore Joint Technical Committee.*
The Cape Town forshore plan. Final report, June 1947. [Pretoria, Govt. Printer of the Union of South Africa, 1948.
xi, 125 p. illus. (part col.) plans (1 col., 2 fold. in pocket) 26 cm.
J. W. B. Carter, chairman.
"Errata" slip mounted on front lining paper.

1. Cities and towns—Planning—Cape Town. I. Title.
NA9278.C3A5 1947 711.0968 50-16963

Library of Congress [1]
454[ ] February 1950

Marge - Do we have
yes

620.1
(68)
U54 Union of South Africa. Council of South African
Rept. Bureau of Standards.
Report (Jaarverslag), [Pretoria]

v. annual

Eleventh report covers the period from January 1, 1956 - August 16, 1956.
Includes reports of the activities of the Bureau of Standards.

(see card 2)

620.1
(68)
U54 Union of South Africa. Council of South African
Rept. Bureau of Standards. Report (Jaarverslag) 1956. (card 2)

1. Testing laboratories - Union of South Africa. I. Union of South Africa. Bureau of Standards.

058.7
:690.08 Union of South Africa. National Federation
(68) of Building Trade Employers.
U54 Building and allied trades official handbook, 1958/59. Official handbook of: the National Federation of Building Trade Employers in South Africa and affiliated organizations: Master Builders' and Allied Trades' Associations, Electrical Contractors' Association (South Africa. Johannesburg,

(Continued on Card 2)

058.7
:690.08 Union of South Africa. National Federation
(68) of Building Trade Employers. Build-
U54 ing and allied trades ... (Card 2)

The South African Builder, 1958.
324p.
1. Building trades - Directories - Union of South Africa. I. Master Builders' and Allied Traded' Associations. II. Electrical Contractors' Association (South Africa) III. Master Masons' and Quarry Owners' association (South Africa)

VF
728
:392 Union of South Africa. National Housing and
(68) Planning Commission.
U54 Minimum standards of housing accommodation for non-Europeans. Minimum standaarde van wonings vir nie-blankes. Pretoria, July 1951.
1 v. (various pagings) illus., plans (fold.), tables.

Text in English and Dutch.
Processed.

1. Family living requirements. 2. Housing-Union of South Africa. I. Title.

VF
711.4
(68) ~~Union of~~ South Africa. National Housing and
U54 Planning Commission.
'N leidraad vir die beplanning van nie-blanke dorpsgebiede. A guide to the planning of non-European townships. Pretoria, July 1951.
39 l. /9 plates. tables.

Text in English only.
Processed.

1. City planning-Union of South Africa. 2. Land use. I. Title: A guide to the planning of non-European townships.

728.1
(68) Union of South Africa. South African
U541 Information Service.
In the Republic of South Africa, each a roof of his own. Johannesburg, Voortrekkerpers, Ltd. [1962]
48p.

1. Housing - Union of South Africa.

694.1
(68) Union of South Africa. Bureau of
U54 Standards.
Code of practice for the construction of timber buildings. Section 5. Approved by the Council of the South African Bureau of Standards. Pretoria, 1962.
54p. (SABS 082-1962)

1. Wood construction - Union of South Africa.

690.091.82
(68) Union of South Africa. Bureau of Standards.
U54c Comprehensive model building regulations.
pt. 12 Chapter 12. Drainage and water supply. Pretoria, South Africa, Cape Times, 1953.
112p.

English and Afrikaanse.

1. Building codes - Union of South Africa. 2. Water-supply - Union of South Africa. 3. Drainage.

VF
690.091.82 Union of South Africa. Council of South
(68) African Bureau of Standards.
U54c Comprehensive model building regula-
pt. 13 tions. Ch. 13. Ventilation. Johannesburg, 1958.
18p.
"A guide to building by-laws for local authority.
English and Afrikaans.
1. Building codes - Union of South Africa. 2. Ventilation.

620.1
(68)
U541
Union of South Africa. Bureau of Standards.
Inspection and testing services for industry. Pretoria [1965]
[32]p.

1. Testing laboratories - Union of South Africa. 2. Industrial research - Union of South Africa. I. Title.

VF
914
U54
U.S.S.R.
Guide to the map of Kiev. Kiev, State Publishing House for Literature on Building and Architecture Ukranian SSR, 1958.
86p.

1. Travel - U.S.S.R. 3. Maps and mapping - U.S.S.R.

914
(47)
U54
U.S.S.R.
Leningrad. Moscow, Intourist [1965?]
[28] p. (no. 1730)

1. Travel - U.S.S.R. I. Intourist, Moscow, U.S.S.R. II. Title.

620.1
(68)
U54
Rept.
Union of South Africa. Bureau of Standards.

Union of South Africa. Council of South African Bureau of Standards. Report (Jaarverslag),
[Pretoria]

v. annual

Eleventh report covers the period from January 1, 1956 - August 16, 1956.
Includes reports of the activities of the Bureau of Standards.
(see card 2)

VF
693.002.22
(47)
U54
U.S.S.R.
House-building-factory in Polustrovo, Glavleningradstroy, Leningrad. Leningrad, 1959.
folder.
English, Russian and French.

1. Prefabricated construction - U.S.S.R. I. Title.

690
(47)
U54p
U.S.S.R.
Progressive building materials for housing construction. Moscow, 1963.
54p.

Russian, English, French, Spanish.

1. Building industry - U.S.S.R. 2. Building materials - U.S.S.R. I. Title.

620.1
(68)
U54
Rept.
Union of South Africa. Council of South African Bureau of Standards. Report (Jaarverslag) 1956. (card 2)

1. Testing laboratories - Union of South Africa. I. Union of South Africa. Bureau of Standards.

690
(47)
U54
U.S.S.R.
Housing construction in the U.S.S.R., Moscow, Leningrad, Kiev. Moscow, 1963.
137p.

Russian, English, French and Spanish.

1. Building industry - U.S.S.R. 2. Prefabricated construction - U.S.S.R.

691
UN
U.S.S.R.
United Nations.
Report of the Workshop on Organizational and Technical Measures for the Development of Building Materials. New York, 1970.
130p. (United Nations [document] ST/TAO/SER.C/123)

1. Building materials. 2. Building industry. I. U.S.S.R. II. Workshop on Organizational and Technical Measures for the Development of Building Materials, Moscow, 1968.

VF
690.013
(68)
U54
Union of South Africa. Council of South African Bureau of Standards. Standard specification for concrete roofing tiles. Johannesburg, 1956.
[24] p. (Its S.A.B.S. 542-1956)

English and Dutch.

1. Building standards - Union of South Africa. 2. Tile construction. 3. Roofs and roofing. I. Title.

728.1
(47)
U54
U.S.S.R.
[Housing in the USSR] Moscow, 1964.
kit. (11 pieces)
Partial contents:-no. 9. Site in New Cheryomushki.-nos. 37 and 38. Sites in Moscow's southwest.-no. 69. Site of Filimozilovo.-Housing construction in the U.S.S.R., Moscow, Leningrad, Kiev.-Vibro-rolling installation ... for manufacturing of large sized reinforced concrete members.
(Continued on next card)

947
U41
U.S.S.R.
[U.S.S.R.] [n.p.] 1962, 1964.
Kit. (25 pieces)

1. Travel - U.S.S.R.

690.013
(68)
U54st
Union of South Africa. Council of South African Bureau of Standards. Standard specification for glazed ceramic wall tiles and fittings. Johannesburg, 1956.
[20] p. illus., tables. (Its S.A.B.S. 22-1956)
English and Dutch.

1. Building standards - Union of South Africa. 2. Tile construction. 3. Walls.

728.1
(47)
U54
U.S.S.R. [Housing in the USSR]...1964.
(Card 2)

1. Housing - U.S.S.R. 2. Apartment houses - U.S.S.R. 3. Building materials - U.S.S.R. 4. Prefabricated construction - U.S.S.R.

947
S32
U.S.S.R.
Shcherbakov, D   ed.
Views of the USSR. Moscow, Foreign Language Publishing House, [1959?]
271p. illus.

"Compiled from Nature of Our Motherland, Moscow, 1955."

1. U.S.S.R.

690.013
(68)
U54
no.
523-1957
Union of South Africa. Bureau of Standards. Standard specification for limes for use in building. Pretoria [1957]
1v. illus., tables, diagrs. (Its S.A.B.S. 523-1957)

English and Dutch.

1. Building materials - Lime. 2. Building standards - Union of South Africa.

720
(47)
U54
U.S.S.R.
Illustrations to the Report on rural housing of the Ukrainian SSR. [Kiev] 1960.
Kit.
In Russian. Subtitles in English.

1. Architecture - U.S.S.R. 2. Farm housing - U.S.S.R.

720
(47)
G67
U.S.S.R. - Architecture.
Gosudarstvennoe izdatel'stvo izobrazitelnogo iskusstva, Moscow. Leningrad vidutoroda [Leningrad; town's views] Mockba, 1963.
1v.
Bibliography: p. 83-86.

1. Architecture - U.S.S.R. 2. U.S.S.R. - Architecture. I. Title: Leningrad; town's views.

S
Union of South Africa Scientific Liaison Office.
British Commonwealth Scientific Office (North America)
List of documents received from British Commonwealth sources   List B.
Washington, D.C.

For full information see Periodical kardex file.

1. Building construction-Bibl. 2. Engineering-Bibl. I. United Kingdom Scientific Mission. II. Canadian N.R.C. Scientific Liaison Office. III. Australian Scientific Liaison Office. IV. New Zealand Scientific Liaison Office. V. Union of South Africa Scientific Liaison Office.

693.002.22
(47)
U541
U.S.S.R.
Industrialised techniques in housing. Moscow, 1963.
84p.

English, Russian, French and Spanish.

1. Prefabricated construction - U.S.S.R. I. Title.

720
(47)
K17
U.S.S.R. - architecture.
Kasumov, Imran.
Baku. Izdanie otdela kultury bakinskogo gorddskogo soveta, 1965?
1v.

1. Architecture - U.S.S.R. 2. U.S.S.R. - Architecture. I. Baku. Izdanie otdela kultury bakinskogo soveta.

720
(47)
N68
U.S.S.R. - Architecture.
Novosibirsk. Novosibirsk, 1960.
175p.

1. Architecture - U.S.S.R. 2. U.S.S.R. -
Architecture.

711.4
(47)
A41p
no.10
U.S.S.R. - City planning.
Akademiia stroitel'stva i arkhitektury SSSR.
Institut gradostroitelstva i raionnoi
planirovki.
Gorodskoe dvizhenie i transport. Moskva,
Gosudarstvennoe izdatelstvo literaturi po
stroitelstvu, arkhitekture i stroitelnim
materialam, 1963.
144p. (Problemi sovetskogo gradostroitelstva no. 10)

1. City planning - U.S.S.R. 2. Transportation - U.S.S.R. 3. U.S.S.R. - Transportation.
4. U.S.S.R. - City planning.

711.4
(47)
(109)
E36
U.S.S.R. - City planning - History.
Egorov, Iurii Alekseevich.
The architectural planning of St. Petersburg;
its development in the 18th and 19th centuries.
Athens, Ohio University Press, 1969.
237p.
Translation by Eric Dluhosch from the
Russian: Ansambl V gradostroitelstve SSSR.
1. City planning - U.S.S.R. - History.
2. U.S.S.R. - City planning - History.
3. Architecture - Designs and plans.
4. U.S.S.R. - Architecture - History.
I. Title.

720
(47)
S38
U.S.S.R. - Architecture.
Shulkevich, M M
Kiev istoriko-arkhitekturnyi ocherk. Kiev,
Iedatelstvo Budivelnik, 1968.
393p. (Kievskaia knizhnaia tipografiya
no. 6)

1. Architecture - U.S.S.R. 2. City planning
U.S.S.R. 3. City growth - U.S.S.R. 4. U.S.S.R.
Architecture. 5. U.S.S.R. - City planning.
6. U.S.S.R. - City growth.

711.4
1670
(47)
D18
U.S.S.R. - City planning.
Davidovich, V G
Town planning in industrial districts
(engineering and economics). Edited by I.V.
Bordukov. Translated from Russian by A.
Skotnicki. Published pursuant to an agreement
with the National Science Foundation.
Jerusalem, Israel Program for Scientific
Translation, 1968.
314p. (National Science Foundation. TT
67-51378)
On title page: Gosudarstvennoe Izdatel'stvo
Literatury po Stroitel'stvu, Arkhitekture i
Stroitel'nym Mat erialam, Moskva 1960.

(Cont'd on next card)

711.4
(47)
A41p
no.12
U.S.S.R. - Community facilities.
Akademiia stroitel'stva i arkhitektury SSSR.
Institut gradostroitelstva i raionnoi
planirovki.
Ceti kulturno-bitovogo obslushivaniya.
Moskva, Gosudarstvennoe izdatelstvo
literaturi po stroitelstvu, arkhitekture i
stroitelnim materialam, 1962.
133p. (Problemi sovetskogo gradostroites-
stva no. 12)

1. City planning - U.S.S.R. 2. U.S.S.R. -
City planning. 3. Community facilities -
U.S.S.R. 4. U.S. S.R. - Community
facilities.

711.4
1(47
109)
E36
U.S.S.R. - Architecture - History.
Egorov, Iurii Alekseevich.
The architectural planning of St. Petersburg;
its development in the 18th and 19th centuries.
Athens, Ohio University Press, 1969.
237p.
Translation by Eric Dluhosch from the
Russian: Ansambl V gradostroitelstve SSSR.
1. City planning - U.S.S.R. - History.
2. U.S.S.R. - City planning - History.
3. Architecture - Designs and plans.
4. U.S.S.R. - Architecture - History.
I. Title.

711.4
1670
(47)
D18
Davidovich, V G   Town planning...1968.
(Card 2)

Distributed by U.S. Clearinghouse for
Federal Scientific and Technical Information.
Bibliography: p. 298-314.

1. Industrial districts - U.S.S.R. 2. New
towns - U.S.S.R. 3. City planning - U.S.S.R.
4. U.S.S.R. - Industrial districts.
5. U.S.S.R. - New towns. 6. U.S.S.R. - City
planning. I. Gosudarstvennoe Izadel'stvo
Literatury po Str oitel'stvu, Arkhitekture i Stroitel' nym Materialam,
Moscow. (Cont'd on next card)

728.1
(47)
U54
U.S.S.R. - Housing.
U.S.S.R. Gosudarstvennyi komitet po
grazhdanskomu stroitelstvu i arkhitekture
pri gosstroe.
Zhilishchnaya politika v SSSR. Moskva,
1965.
28p.

1. Housing - U.S.S.R. 2. U.S.S.R. -
Housing. 3. Building industry - U.S.S.R.
4. U.S.S.R. - Building industry.

728.1
(47)
U54
U.S.S.R. - Building industry
U.S.S.R. Gosudarstvennyi komitet po
grazhdanskomu stroitelstvu i arkhitekture
pri gosstroe.
Zhilishchnaya politika v SSSR. Moskva,
1965.
28p.

1. Housing - U.S.S.R. 2. U.S.S.R. -
Housing. 3. Building industry - U.S.S.R.
4. U.S.S.R. - Building industry.

711.4
1670
(47)
D18
Davidovich, V G   Town planning...1968.
(Card 3)

II. U.S. National Science Foundation.
IV. Title.

711.4
1670
(47)
D18
U.S.S.R. - Industrial districts.
Davidovich, V G
Town planning in industrial districts
(engineering and economics). Edited by I.V.
Bordukov. Translated from Russian by A.
Skotnicki. Published pursuant to an agreement
with the National Science Foundation.
Jerusalem, Israel Program for Scientific
Translation, 1968.
314p. (National Science Foundation. TT
67-51378)
On title page: Gosudarstvennoe Izdatel'stvo
Literatury po Stroitel'stvu, Arkhitekture i
Stroitel'nym Mat erialam, Moskva 1960.

(Cont'd on next card)

691
(47)
R28
U.S.S.R. - Building materials.
Reutov, Oleg Aleksandrovich.
Novye sinteticheskie materiali. Moskva,
Znanie, 1958.
30p. (Vsesoiuznoe obshchestvo po
rasprostraneniiu politicheskikh i nauchnykh
znanii. Seriya IV, no. 13)

1. Building materials - U.S.S.R.
2. U.S.S.R. - Building materials.
I. Vsesoiuznoe obshchestvo po
rasprostraneniiu politicheskikh i nauchnykh
znanii.

711.4
1(47)
M45
Union of Soviet Socialist Republics - City
planning.
Minsk. Instytut stroitelstva i arkhitektur
gosstroia BSSR.
Gradostroitelstvo v Belourusskoi SSR;
kratkii obzor. (Town planning in the
Byelorussian SSR, brief review) Minsk, 1968.
53p.
Text in Russian, English, and French.

1. City planning - USSR. 2. Union of Soviet
Socialist Republics - City planning. I. Title.

711.4
1670
(47)
D18
Davidovich, V G   Town planning...1968.
(Card 2)

Distributed by U.S. Clearinghouse for
Federal Scientific and Technical Information.
Bibliography: p. 298-314.

1. Industrial districts - U.S.S.R. 2. New
towns - U.S.S.R. 3. City planning - U.S.S.R.
4. U.S.S.R. - Industrial districts.
5. U.S.S.R. - New towns. 6. U.S.S.R. - City
planning. I. Gosudarstvennoe Izadel'stvo
Literatury po Str oitel'stvu, Arkhitekture i Stroitel' nym Materialam,
Moscow. (Cont'd on next card)

720
(47)
S38
U.S.S.R. - City growth.
Shulkevich, M M
Kiev istoriko-arkhitekturnyi ocherk. Kiev,
Iedatelstvo Budivelnik, 1968.
393p. (Kievskaia knizhnaia tipografiya
no. 6)

1. Architecture - U.S.S.R. 2. City planning
U.S.S.R. 3. City growth - U.S.S.R. 4. U.S.S.R.
Architecture. 5. U.S.S.R. - City planning.
6. U.S.S.R. - City growth.

711.4
1(47)
U54
U.S.S.R. - City planning.
U.S.S.R. Izdatelstvo literaturi po
stroitelstvu.
Minsk; poslevoennyi opyt rekonstruktsii i
rasvitiya. Moskva, 1966.
178p.

1. City planning - U.S.S.R. 2. Reconstruction
- U.S.S.R. 3. U.S.S.R. - City planning.
4. U.S.S.R. - Reconstruction.

711.4
1670
(47)
D18
Davidovich, V G   Town planning...1968.
(Card 3)

II. U.S. National Science Foundation.
IV. Title.

711.4
(47)
A41p
no.12
U.S.S.R. - City planning.
Akademiia stroitel'stva i arkhitektury SSR.
Institut gradostroitelstva i raionnoi
planirovki.
Ceti kulturno-bitovogo obslushivaniya.
Moskva, Gosudarstvennoe izdatelstvo
literaturi po stroitelstvu, arkhitekture i
stroitelnim materialam, 1962.
133p. (Problemi sovetskogo gradostroites-
stva no. 12)

1. City planning - U.S.S.R. 2. U.S.S.R. -
City planning. 3. Community facilities -
U.S.S.R. 4. U.S. S.R. - Community
facilities.

720
(47)
S38
U.S.S.R. - City planning.
Shulkevich, M M
Kiev istoriko-arkhitekturnyi ocherk. Kiev,
Iedatelstvo Budivelnik, 1968.
393p. (Kievskaia knizhnaia tipografiya
no. 6)

1. Architecture - U.S.S.R. 2. City planning
U.S.S.R. 3. City growth - U.S.S.R. 4. U.S.S.R.
Architecture. 5. U.S.S.R. - City planning.
6. U.S.S.R. - City growth.

670
(47)
U47
U.S.S.R. - Industry.
Ukraine. Komitet po pechati.
Norodnoe khoeiaistvo Ukraina. Kiev, 1967.
30p.

1. Industry - U.S.S.R. 2. U.S.S.R. -
Industry.

711.4
:670
(47)
D18
U.S.S.R. - New towns.
Davidovich, V G
Town planning in industrial districts
(engineering and economics). Edited by I.V.
Bordukov. Translated from Russian by A.
Skotnicki. Published pursuant to an agreement
with the National Science Foundation.
Jerusalem, Israel Program for Scientific
Translation, 1968.
314p. (National Science Foundation. TT
67-51378)
On title page: Gosudarstvennoe Izdatel'stvo
Literatury po Stroitel'stvu, Arkhitekture i
Stroitel'nym Mat   erialam, Moskva 1960.

(Cont'd on next card)

711.4
:670
(47)
D18
Davidovich, V G   Town planning...1968.
(Card 2)

Distributed by U.S. Clearinghouse for
Federal Scientific and Technical Information.
Bibliography: p. 298-314.

1. Industrial districts - U.S.S.R. 2. New
towns - U.S.S.R. 3. City planning - U.S.S.R.
4. U.S.S.R. - Industrial districts.
5. U.S.S.R. - New towns. 6. U.S.S.R. - City
planning. I. Gosudarstvennoe Izadel'stvo
Literatury po Str   oitel'stvu, Arkhitekture i Stroitel'   nym Materialam,
Moscow.   (Cont'd on next card)

711.4
:670
(47)
D18
Davidovich, V G   Town planning...1968.
(Card 3)

II. U.S. National Science Foundation.
IV. Title.

VF
711.417
(47)
K42
U.S.S.R - New towns.
Kiev. Nauchno-issledovatel'skii i
proektnyi institut gradostroitel'stva.
Building for the village of Kodaky.
Kiev, [1967?]
[6]p. (Its Publication no. 213)

1. New towns - U.S.S.R. 2. U.S.S.R. -
New towns. I. Title.

711.4
(47)
U54
U.S.S.R. - Reconstruction.
U.S.S.R. Izdatelstvo literaturi po
stroitelstvu.
Minsk; poslevoennyi opyt rekonstruktsii i
razvitiya. Moskva, 1966.
178p.

1. City planning - U.S.S.R. 2. Reconstruction
- U.S.S.R. 3. U.S.S.R. - City planning.
4. U.S.S.R. - Reconstruction.

331.252
(47)
L94
U.S.S.R. - Social security.
Lykova, Lydia.
Social security in the USSR. [Moscow]
Novosty Press Agency, 1963.
46p.

1. Social security - U.S.S.R. 2. U.S.S.R. -
Social security. I. Title.

711.4
(47)
A41p
no.10
U.S.S.R. - Transportation.
Akademiia stroitel'stva i arkhitektury SSSR.
Institut gradostroitelstva i raionnoi
planirovki.
Gorodskoe dvizhenie i transport. Moskva,
Gosudarstvennoe izdatelstvo literaturi po
stroitelstvu, arkhitekture i stroitelnim
materialam, 1963.
144p. (Problemi sovetskogo gradostroitelstva no. 10)
1. City planning - U.S.S.R. 2. Transportation - U.S.S.R. 3. U.S.S.R. - Transportation.
4. U.S.S.R. -   City planning.

914
(47)
R21
U.S.S.R. - Travel.
Redro, P
Zaporizhzhia. Kiev, Vidavnitstvo
Mistetstvo, 1965.
81p.

1. Travel - U.S.S.R. 2. U.S.S.R. - Travel.

914
(47)
U47
U.S.S.R. - Travel.
Ukraine. Komitet po pechati.
Sovetskaia Ukraina. Kiev, 1967.
38p.

1. Travel - U.S.S.R. 2. U.S.S.R. -
Travel.

691.7
P74
U.S.S.R. Akademiia Nauk SSSR. Institut
Metallurgii imeni A.A. Baikova.
Pridantsev, M V ed.
Structure and properties of heat-
resistant metals and alloys. Jerusalem,
Israel Program for Scientific Translations,
1970.
371p. (NASA TT-F-557; TT 69-55020)
At head of title: Akademiya Nauk SSSR.
Institut Metallurgii imeni A.A. Baikova.
Translated from Russian.
Published pursuant to agreement with
National Aeronautics and Space Administra-
tion and   National Science
(Cont'd on next card)

691.7
P74
Pridantsev, M V ed.   Structure
and properties...1970.   (Card 2)

Foundation.

1. Metals. I. U.S.S.R. Akademiia Nauk
SSSR. Institut Metallurgii imeni A.A.
Baikova. II. U.S. National Aeronautics
and Space Administration. III. Title.

711.4
(47)
U54p
U.S.S.R. Gosudarstvennyi komitet po delam
stroitel'stva.
Pravila i normy planirovki i zastroiki
gorodov (Regulations and norms for the
planning and building of cities) Moscow,
Gosstroiizdat, 1959.
178p.
Item 41 in Frolic's draft, bibliography.
Paragraph 305, Frolic's article related
to English version.

1. City planning - U.S.S.R. 2. Housing -
U.S.S.R.

690.091.82
(47)
U54
U.S.S.R. Gosudarstvennyi komitet po delam
stroitel'stva.
Stroitelnie normiipravila, shast II,
razdel K. Glava 3. Ulitsi, dorogi i
ploshchadi naselennikh mest. Normi
proektirovanira. SNiP II-K.3-62.
Moskva, 1963.
32p.
"Izdanie ofitsialnoe."
1. Building standards - U.S.S.R.

690.022
(47)
U54
U.S.S.R. Gosudarstvennyi komitet po
grazhdanskomu stroitel'stvu i
arkhitekture.
Industrializatsiya zhilishchnogo
stroitelstva i SSSR. Moskva, 1965.
31p.

1. Prefabricated construction - USSR.

711.14
(47)
U54
U.S.S.R. Gosudarstvennyi Komitet po
Grazhdanskomu Stroitel'stvu i Arkhitekture.
Ispolzovanie territorii zhilykh raionov
krupnykh gorodov (Utilization of the land of
residential areas of large cities) Moskva,
1968.
45p.

1. Land use - U.S.S.R.

711.3
(47)
U54
U.S.S.R. Gosudarstvennyi komitet po
grazhdanskomu stroitel'stvu i arkhitekture.
Rekommendatsii po planirovke i zastroike
sel'skikh naselennykh mest. Mockbe, 1964.
163p.

1. Metropolitan area planning - U.S.S.R.
I. Smirnov, Nikolai Semenovich.

690.022
(47)
U54t
U.S.S.R. Gosudarstvennyi Komitet po Grazhdanskomu Stroitel'stvu i Arkhitekture.
Tekhnologiia proizvodstva elementov krup-
noianejnykh domov (The technology of producing
the elements of buildings prefabricated from
large panels) Moskva, 1968.
23p.

1. Prefabricated construction - U.S.S.R.

728.1
(47)
U54
U.S.S.R. Gosudarstvennyi komitet po
grazhdanskomu stroitelstvu i arkhitekture
pri Gosstroe.
Zhilishchnaya politika v SSSR. Moskva,
1965.
28p.

1. Housing - U.S.S.R. 2. U.S.S.R. -
Housing. 3. Building industry - U.S.S.R.
4. U.S.S.R. - Building industry.

690
(47)
R62
U.S.S.R. Gosudarstvennyi Komitet po
Grazhdanskomu Stroitelstvu i Arkhitekture.
Rodin, Iurii Mikhailovich, ed.
Zhilishchno-grazhdanskoe stroitelstvo SSSR.
[Moscow] Gosudarstvennyi Komitet po
Grazhdanskomu Stroitelstvu i Arkhitekture pri
Gosstroe SSSR, Tsentr Nauchno-Tekhnicheskoi
Informatsii po Grazhdanskomu Stroitelstvu i
Arkhitekture, [1968?]
[51] p.

1. Building construction - U.S.S.R.
I. U.S.S.R. Gosudarstvennyi Komitet po
Grazhdanskomu   Stroitelstvu i
Arkhitekture.

690
(47)
U54z
U.S.S.R. Gosudarstvennii Komitet po
Grazhdanskomu Stroitel'stvu i Arkhitekture.
Zhilishchnskoe stroitelstvo SSSR, 1917-1967.
Moskva, 1967.
[50]p.

1. Building construction - U.S.S.R.

699.841
U54
U.S.S.R. Gosudarstvennyi komitet soveta
ministrov.
Construction in earthquake regions: design
code SN & P II-A.12-69. Garston, Eng.,
Building Research Station, 1970.
[39]p. (Library communication no. 1587)
Translated from the Russian and reprinted
from Stroitel'nye normy i pravila, Chast' II,
razdel A, glava 12.
1. Earthquake resistant construction.
I. U.K. Building Research Station. II. Title.
(Series)

711.4
1(47)
U54

U.S.S.R. Izdatelstvo literaturi po stroitelstvu.
Minsk; poslevoennyi opyt rekonstruktsii i rasvitiya. Moskva, 1966.
178p.

1. City planning - U.S.S.R. 2. Reconstruction - U.S.S.R. 3. U.S.S.R. - City planning. 4. U.S.S.R. - Reconstruction.

690.24
U54C

UNION CARBIDE NUCLEAR COMPANY.
A COMPARISON OF FLAT AND GABLED ROOF BUILDINGS SUPPORTED BY RIGID STEEL FRAMES, BY C.J. WILLIAMS. OAK RIDGE, TENN., 1963.
137L. (ITS REPORT Y-1418)

1. ROOFS AND ROOFING. 2. TRUSSES. I. WILLIAMS C.J.

711.4
(76148)
U54

Union Springs, Ala. City Planning Commission.
Union Springs, Alabama: community facilities plan. [Prepared in cooperation with] Alabama State Planning and Industrial Development Board. Union Springs, 1961.
28p.

U.S. Urban Renewal Adm. UPAP.

1. Master plan - Union Springs, Ala. 2. Community facilities - Union Springs, Ala. I. U.S. URA-UPAP. Union Springs, Ala.

690.013
(47)
U546

U.S.S.R. People's Commissariat for Construction
Tipovye detali zdanii [Standard details of construction] Moskva, 1939.
9 v. diagrs., plans
Contents.-v.1. Grazhdanskie zdaniya [Public buildings] -v.2-6. Promyshlennye zdaniya [Industrial buildings] -v.7. Ventilyatsiya. Otoplenie. Komnatnye pechi i ochagi. Teplove seti. [Ventilation. Heating. Room stoves and hearths. [Heating systems] -v.8. Vnutrennie vodoprovod, kanalizatsiya, vodostoki,

(see card 2)

331.881
065

Union powers and union functions: toward a better balance.
Committee for Economic Development.
Union powers and union functions: toward a better balance. A statement on national policy. New York, 1964.
43p.

1. Trade-unions. 2. Labor relations. I. Title.

711.4
(76148)
U54m

Union Springs, Ala. City Planning Commission.
Union Springs, Alabama: major thorough-fare plan. [Prepared in cooperation with] Alabama State Planning and Industrial Development Board. Union Springs, 1961.
[48]p.

U.S. Urban Renewal Adm. UPAP.

1. Master plan - Union Springs, Ala. 2. Streets - Union Springs, Ala. I. U.S. URA-UPAP. Union Springs, Ala.

690.013
(47)
U546

U.S.S.R. People's Commissariat for Construction
Tipovye detali zdanii . Moskva, 1939.
(card 2)

gazoprovod i Goryachee vodosna'zhenie [Interior water-pipes, severage, drains, gas pipes and hot water supply] v. 9. Naruzhnyi vodoprovod. Naruzhnaya kanalizatsiya [Exterior water-pipes and drainage.]

1. Building standards - U.S.S.R.

351.11
C650
S=H

UNION RECOGNITION.
U.S. CONGRESS. SENATE. COMMITTEE ON POST OFFICE AND CIVIL SERVICE.
UNION RECOGNITION. HEARINGS... EIGHTY-FOURTH CONGRESS, SECOND SESSION ON S. 3593... MAY 15, 24, AND JUNE 14, 1956. WASHINGTON, 1956.
371P.

1. FEDERAL CIVIL SERVICE. I. TITLE.

352.6
(76148)
U54

Union Springs, Ala. City Planning Commission.
Union Springs, Alabama: public improve-ments program. [Prepared in cooperation with] Alabama State Planning and Industrial Development Board. Union Springs, 1962.
21p.

U.S. Urban Renewal Adm. UPAP.

1. Capital improvement programs - Union Springs, Ala. I. U.S. URA-UPAP. Union Springs, Ala.

500.15
(47)
U54

U.S.S.R. Sibriskoe Otdelenie Akademii Nauk Soiuza.
Novosibirskii Nauchnyi Tsentr. Novosibirsk, 1963.
[22]p.

1. Scientific research - U.S.S.R.

331.2
L11U

UNION SCALES OF WAGES AND HOURS IN THE BUILDING TRADES IN 70 CITIES.
U.S. BUREAU OF LABOR STATISTICS.
UNION SCALES OF WAGES AND HOURS IN THE BUILDING TRADES IN 70 CITIES. MAY 15, 1937. PREPARED BY INDUSTRIAL RELATIONS DIVISION. WASHINGTON, GOVT. PRINT. OFF., 1938.
67P. (ITS BULLETIN NO. 657)

1. WAGES AND SALARIES. 2. BUILDING TRADES. 3. TRADE UNIONS. I. TITLE.

711.5
(76148
:347)
U54

Union Springs, Ala. City Planning Commission.
Union Springs, Alabama: zoning ordinance. [Prepared for] Alabama State Planning and Industrial Development Board. Union Springs, 1961.
23p.

U.S. Urban Renewal Adm. UPAP.

1. Zoning legislation - Union Springs, Ala. I. U.S. URA-UPAP. Union Springs, Ala.

691.54
(03)
U54

U.S.S.R. State Publishing Office for Literature on Building, Architecture and Building Materials.
English-Russian dictionary on cement and concrete, by J. B. Khaikin. Moscow, 1959.
283p.

1. Cement - Dictionaries. 2. Concrete - Dictionaries. I. Khaikin, J. B. II. Title.

230.
234

UNION SPRING, ALA. CITY PLANNING COMMISSION.
PLANNING PROGRAM: 1. LAND USE SURVEY AND ANALYSIS; 2. COMPREHENSIVE PLAN; 3. SUBDIVISION REGULATIONS; 4. ZONING ORDINANCE; 5. POPULATION AND ECONOMY. BY ALABAMA DEVELOPMENT OFFICE. UNION SPRING, ALA., 1970.
5 v. (HUD 701 REPORT)

1. CITY PLANNING - UNION SPRING, ALA. I. ALABAMA DEVELOPMENT OFFICE. II. HUD. 701. UNION SPRING, ALA.

330
(79498)
U54

Union-Tribune Publishing Co., San Diego, Calif.
The annual review of San Diego business activity, San Diego, v.
Prepared in cooperation with Copley International Corporation.
For complete information see main card.

1. Economic development - Calif. 2. Economic conditions - Calif - Statistics. I. Copley International Corp. II. Title. III. Title: San Diego business activity, 1967.

69
(47)
C68
A3

The U.S.S.R. construction industry.
Council for Economic and Industry Research, Inc.
The U.S.S.R. construction industry, by Joseph S. Berliner. [Washington] 1955.
185 l. tables. (Its Report no. A-3)
Bibliography: p. 172-181.

1. Building industry - U.S.S.R. I. Berliner, Joseph S. II. Title.

711.14
(76148)
U54

Union Springs, Ala. City Planning Commission.
Union Springs, Alabama: long range land use plan. [Prepared for] Alabama State Planning and Industrial Development Board. Union Springs, 1961.
26p.

U.S. Urban Renewal Adm. UPAP.

1. Land use - Union Springs, Ala. I. U.S. URA-UPAP. Union Springs, Ala.

33
(45)
U54

Unione italiana delle camere di commercio, industria e agricoltura.
Economic survey of Italy. Roma, 1951.
90 p. illus. col. maps. 24 cm.

1. Economic conditions-Italy.
~~1. Italy - Econ. condit. 1945~~ ~~2. Title~~

HC305.U48   330.945   59-65519
Library of Congress   [2]

330
(49)
U54

USSR today and tomorrow, facts, figures, pictures. Moscow, Foreign Languages Publishing House, 1959.
326p. illus., diagrs.

1. Economic conditions - U.S.S.R. 2. Political science - U.S.S.R.

333.38
(76148)
U54

Union Springs, Ala. City Planning Commission.
Union Springs, Alabama: subdivision regula-tions. [Prepared for] Alabama State Planning and Industrial Development Board. Union Springs, 1960.
36p.

U.S. Urban Renewal Adm. UPAP.

1. Subdivision regulation - Union Springs, Ala. I. U.S. URA-UPAP. Union Springs, Ala.

331
W25u

The unions and the cities.
Wellington, Harry H
The unions and the cities, by Harry H. Wellington and Ralph K. Winter, Jr. Wash., Brookings Institution, 1971.
226p. (Studies of unionism in government)
Partial contents: Collective bargaining and the role of government.
1. Labor relations. 2. Management. I. Winter, Ralph K., 1935- jt. au. II. Brookings Institution, Wash., D.C. III. Title. IV. Title: Collective bargaining and the role of government.

658.3
S62U
UNIONS ARE HERE TO STAY.
SOCIETY FOR PERSONNEL ADMINISTRATION.
UNIONS ARE HERE TO STAY; A GUIDE FOR
EMPLOYEE-MANAGEMENT REALTIONS IN THE
FEDERAL SERVICE, BY ANN HOLLAND.
WASHINGTON, 1962.
41P. (ITS PAMPHLET NO. 17)

1. PERSONNEL MANAGEMENT. 2. FEDERAL
CIVIL SERVICE. I. HOLLAND ANN.
II. TITLE.

330
(76144)
U54
Uniontown, Ala. Town Planning Commission.
Uniontown, Alabama: population and economic study. [In cooperation with] Alabama State Planning and Industrial Development Board. Uniontown, 1958.
34p. maps, diagrs., tables.

U.S. Urban Renewal Administration, Urban Planning
Assistance Program.

1. Economic base studies - Uniontown, Ala. 2. Population - Uniontown, Ala. I. U.S. URA-UPAP.
Uniontown, Ala.

697.8
F82
UNIROYAL, inc.
Fuest, Ronald W
Development of regenerable fibers for removal
of sulfur dioxide from waste gases, by Ronald
W. Fuest and Merlin P. Harvey. Technical
report covering the period January 1 to June 30,
1968. Prepared for National Center for Air
Pollution Control. Wayne, N.J., UNIROYAL, inc.,
1968.
49p.
CFSTI. PB 185 093.

1. Air pollution. I. Harvey, Merlin P.,
jt. au. II. UNIROYAL, inc. III. Title.

237
UNIONTOWN, ALA. PLANNING COMMISSION.
COMMUNITY DEVELOPMENT PLAN, BY ALABAMA
DEVELOPMENT OFFICE. UNIONTOWN, ALA., 1970.
77P. (HUD 701 REPORT)

1. COMMUNITY DEVELOPMENT - UNIONTOWN,
ALA. I. ALABAMA, DEVELOPMENT OFFICE.
II. HUD. 701. UNIONTOWN, ALA.

351.712
(76144)
U54
Uniontown, Ala. City Planning Commission.
Uniontown, Alabama: public works program.
[In cooperation with] Alabama State Planning
and Industrial Development Board. Uniontown,
1961.
13p.

U.S. Urban Renewal Adm. UPAP.

1. Public works - Uniontown, Ala. I. U.S.
URA-UPAP. Uniontown, Ala.

628.515
U54
Uniroyal inc.
Feasibility study of regenerative fibers
for water pollution control. [Wash.]
Environmental Protection Agency, 1970.
74p. Water pollution control research
series)

1. Water pollution. I. U.S. Environmental
Protection Agency. II. Title.

236
UNIONTOWN, ALA. PLANNING COMMISSION.
INITIAL MINIMUM HOUSING ELEMENT, BY
ALABAMA DEVELOPMENT OFFICE. UNIONTOWN,
ALA., 1970.
25P. (HUD 701 REPORT)

1. HOUSING - UNIONTOWN, ALA.
I. ALABAMA. DEVELOPMENT OFFICE.
II. HUD. 701. UNIONTOWN, ALA.

711.4
(74844)
U54
Uniontown, Pa. City Planning and Zoning
Commission.
Metropolitan Planners, Indianapolis.
Comprehensive plan report, 1957. Prepared
for the Uniontown City Planning and Zoning
Commission, under ... Program of the Bureau
of Community Development, Pennsylvania Dept.
of Commerce. Indianapolis, 1957.
73p. maps, tables.

U.S. Urban Renewal Administration, Urban Planning
Assistance Program.

1. Master plan - Uniontown, Pa. I. Uniontown, Pa.
City Planning and Zoning Commission.
II. U.S. URA-UPAP. Uniontown, Pa.

IF-UK-Prefab.contr.-Uni-Sco

DATE OF REQUEST 6/12/53   L C CARD NO.
SEP 18 1953
AUTHOR
Uni-Seco Limited.
TITLE
Design in 'Seco'.
SERIES

EDITION | PUB. DATE | PAGING 66p.
PUBLISHER
11 Upper Brook St., Park Lane, London W.1, England.
RECOMMENDED BY | REVIEWED IN
Arch. Jrnl. 7/23/53 p. xlv
ORDER RECORD

235
UNIONTOWN, ALA. PLANNING COMMISSION.
SUBDIVISION REGULATIONS, BY ALABAMA
DEVELOPMENT OFFICE. UNIONTOWN, ALA., 1970.
30P. (HUD 701 REPORT)

1. SUBDIVISION REGULATION - UNIONTOWN,
ALA. I. ALABAMA, DEVELOPMENT OFFICE.
II. HUD. 701. UNIONTOWN, ALA.

333.38
(74844)
U54
Uniontown, Pa. Ordinances, etc.
Uniontown, Pa.: sub-division ordinance.
Uniontown, 1957.
24p. diagrs.

U.S. Urban Renewal Administration, Urban Planning
Assistance Program.

1. Subdivision regulation - Uniontown, Pa.
I. U.S. URA-UPAP. Uniontown, Pa.

002
UNu
Unisist.
United Nations Educational, Scientific and
Cultural Organization.
Unisist. Synopsis of the feasibility study
on a world science information system. Paris,
Unesco, 1971.
92p.

1. Documentation. 2. Scientific research.
3. Cataloging. I. Title.

352.6
(76144)
U54
Uniontown, Ala. Town Planning Commission.
Uniontown, Alabama: community facilities
plan. [In cooperation with] Alabama State
Planning and Industrial Development Board.
Uniontown, 1961.
23p.

U.S. Urban Renewal Adm. UPAP.

1. Community facilities - Uniontown, Ala.
I. U.S. URA-UPAP. Uniontown, Ala.

711.5
(74844
:347)
U54
Uniontown, Pa. Ordinances, etc.
Zoning ordinance for the City of Uniontown, Pennsylvania. Uniontown, 1957.
44p.

U.S. Urban Renewal Administration, Urban Planning
Assistance Program.

1. Zoning legislation - Uniontown, Pa. I. U.S.
URA-UPAP. Uniontown, Pa.

DATE OF REQUEST 1/9/52 JAN 18 1952   L. C. CARD NO.
AUTHOR
Unistrut.
TITLE
Unistrut - world's most flexible all purpose
metal framing
SERIES
EDITION | PUB. DATE | PAGING 78 p.
PUBLISHER
Unistrut Products Company.
RECOMMENDED BY | REVIEWED IN
Prog. Arch. 10/51 p. 102
ORDER RECORD

333.38
(76144)
U54
Uniontown, Ala. Town Planning Commission.
Uniontown, Alabama: land subdivision regulations and manual. [In cooperation with]
Alabama State Planning and Industrial Development Board. Uniontown, 1958.
23p. diagrs.

U.S. Urban Renewal Administration, Urban Planning
Assistance Program.
1. Subdivision regulation - Uniontown, Ala. I. U.S.
URA-UPAP.

3137
3138
3139
UNIONVILLE, N.Y. PLANNING BOARD.
VILLAGE OF UNIONVILLE: 1,
COMPREHENSIVE DEVELOPMENT PLAN; 2,
PROPOSED ZONING ORDINANCE; 3, SUBDIVISION
REGULATIONS. RAYMOND AND MAY ASSOCIATES.
UNIONVILLE, N.Y., 1967-69.
3 V. (HUD 701 REPORT)

1. MASTER PLAN - UNIONVILLE, N.Y.
I. RAYMOND AND MAY ASSOCIATES. II. HUD.
701. UNIONVILLE, N.Y.

332
J15
UNIT BANKS.
JAMISON, CHARLES LASELLE.
MANAGEMENT OF UNIT BANKS. ANN ARBOR,
UNIVERSITY OF MICHIGAN, BUREAU OF BUSINESS
RESEARCH, 193 .
217-279P. MICHIGAN. UNIVERSITY.
BUREAU OF BUSINESS RESEARCH, MICHIGAN
BUSINESS STUDIES. VOL. III, NO. 2)

1. BANKS AND BANKING. I. TITLE.
II. TITLE: UNIT BANKS.

711.74
(76144)
U54
Uniontown, Ala. City Planning Commission.
Uniontown, Alabama: major street plan. [In
cooperation with] Alabama State Planning and
Industrial Development Board. Uniontown, 1960.
25p.

U.S. Urban Renewal Adm. UPAP.

1. Street planning - Uniontown, Ala. I. U.S.
URA-UPAP. Uniontown, Ala.

R
058.7
U68
The unique 3-in-1 research & development direct
Government Data Publications, Washington,
D.C.
The unique 3-in-1 research & development
directory, 1967;
Washington, 1967-
1v.

For complete information see main card.

1. Research - Direct. 2. Scientific research - Direct. I. Title.

VF
728.1
:362.6
U54
Unitarian Universalist Association.
Living all our years. Boston, 1965.
31p.

Bibliography: p.27-31.

1. Housing for the aged. 2. Church and
social problems. I. Title.

VF
697.9
A47u

The unitary method of meeting air-
conditioning needs in apartment buildings.
Air-Conditioning and Refrigeration Institute.
The unitary method of meeting air-
conditioning needs in apartment
buildings.
Arlington, Va., [1970?]
folder.

1. Air-conditioning. 2. Apartment
houses. I. Title.

331.2
S62

United Church of Christ.
Social action.
Guaranteed income; how? New York, Council
for Christian Social Action of the United
Church of Christ, 1967.
56p.
Bibliography: p. 54-55.
Entire issue: Nov. 1967.

1. Wages and salaries - Annual wages.
2. Poor. 3. Public assistance. I. Title.
II. United Church of Christ.

725.83
(74661)
U54

United Community Services, Boston.
Evaluation report of the Community
Services Center, 1st-
1960/61
A service program of United South End settle-
ments, in cooperation with the Boston Housing
Authority. [Boston, 1961-
v.
For complete information see shelflist.

1. Community centers - Boston. I. Boston. Housing
Authority.

72
J21u

L'unité d'habitation de Marseille.
Jeanneret-Gris, Charles Edouard
L'unité d'habitation de Marseille. [Toulouse,
France] Le Point, Nov. 1950.
58 p. illus., diagrs.

Special issue.

I. Le Point. II. Title.

Class No. Arch.- Domes
-Desplo.-
Accession No. Single fam
Ordered DEC 29 1950
Source Phone
Received JAN 3 1951
Cost
Purchase Order No.
Date
L. C. No.

Author (surname first) The United Clay Products
Company
Title Photoplan 50-6 "Popular
Homes Hilltp Home and Workshop
Place Wash., D.C. Publisher
Address Investment Bldg.
Date Paging List Price 10¢ Est. Cost
Edition or Series
Recommended by No. 6
Reviewed in Popu(Home Autumn 1950

H-305 (2-50) HOUSING AND HOME FINANCE AGENCY: Office of the Administrator 16—61167-1 GPO

360
(77595)
U54

United Community Services of Greater
Milwaukee.
Social services in community renewal as
part of the Community Renewal Program.
[Milwaukee] 1964.
6p.

1. Social welfare - Milwaukee. I. Title.
II. Milwaukee. Community Renewal Program.

United Aircraft Corp.

629.13
C52

Cleary, R E
Properties of high emittance materials, by
R.E. Cleary and others. Prepared by United
Aircraft Corp., East Hartford, Conn., for Lewis
Research Center, National Aeronautics and Space
Administration, Wash., National Aeronautics and
Space Administration, 1969.
120p. (NASA CR-1278)
CFSTI
1. Aircraft construction. 2. Metals. I. Title.
II. United Aircraft Corp. III. U.S. National
Aeronautics and Space Administration.

Hsa - Wartime
Class No. VF Defense
housing
Accession No.
Ordered
Source
Received 2-17-53
Cost
Purchase Order No.
Date
L. C. No.

Author (surname first) United Community Defense Service
Title Defense Town, USA

Place Publisher
Address 129 E. 52nd St. New York 22,
n.y.
Date n.d. Paging folde List Price Est. Cost
(1952?)
Edition or Series
Recommended by
Reviewed in

H-305 (2-50) HOUSING AND HOME FINANCE AGENCY: Office of the Administrator 16—61167-1 GPO

312
(74461)
U54

c.1,E.0.

United Community Services of Metropolitan
Boston.
Black and white in Boston; a report based
on the Community Research Project. [Boston]
1968.
44p.

1. Population - Boston. 2. Negroes - Boston.
I. Title.

301.15
M19m

United Automobile, Aerospace and
Agricultural Implement Workers of America.
May, Richard, Jr.
Major trends in world urbanization and their
environmental implications: Symposium on the
Impact of Urbanization on Man's Environment,
Onaway, Mich., 14-20 June 1970. Working paper
no. 1, Agenda item 1. New York, United
Nations, 1970.
54p.
Sponsored by the United Nations in co-
operation with the International Trade Union
of the United Automobile, Aerospace and
Agricultural Implement Workers of America.

(Cont'd on next card)

360
G72p
1967

United Community Funds and Councils of
America.
Great Lakes Institute. Williams Bay, Wis.,
Proceedings of the Great Lakes Institute.
Manpower and money: how can we use them
better. Jointly sponsored by United
Community Funds and Council of America, inc.,
and the National Assembly for Social Policy
and Development, inc. Williams Bay, Wis.,
1967.
70p.
1. Social welfare. 2. Employment.
I. Title: Manpower and money: how can we use
them better. II. United Community Funds and
Councils of America.

728.1
:362.6
(7446)
U54
1959

United Community Services of Metropolitan
Boston.
Housing preferences of older people.
Study no. 2. Boston, 1959.
68p.

1. Housing for the aged - Boston.

301.15
M19m

May, Richard, Jr. Major...1970. (Card 2)

Bibliography: p. 53-54.

1. City growth. I. Symposium on the Impact
of Urbanization on Man's Environment, Onaway,
Mich., 1970. II. United Automobile,
Aerospace and Agricultural Implement Workers
of America. III. Title. IV. Title: Impact
of Urbanization on man's environment.
V. United Nations.

711.4
U54c

United Community Funds and Councils of
America Southeast Regional Conference,
Jacksonville, Fla., 1959.
Coordination of physical and social
planning, by Gerald Gimre. Jacksonville,
Fla., 1959.
12p.

1. City planning. I. Gimre, Gerald.

728.1
:362.6
(7446)
U54
1962
2 c

United Community Services of Metropolitan
Boston.
Housing preferences of older people.
Follow up study no. 2. West end couples.
Boston, 1962.
91p.

1. Housing for the aged - Boston.

728.1
:362.6
U54o
30.

United Church Board for Homeland Ministries.
(Div. of Health and Welfare Services)
Older hotels and older Americans; a survey
report. New York, 1960.
23p.

1. Housing for the aged. 2. Hotels.

058.7
:360
U54

United Community Funds and Councils of
America.
Directory, 1966;

New York, 1966-
1v.

For complete information see main card.

1. Social welfare - Direct. 2. Social
service - Direct.

DATE OF REQUEST 6/15/55   L. C. CARD NO.
Place - Wash - Detroit
AUTHOR United Community Services of Metropolitan Detroit.
TITLE Maps of population characteristics and social
conditions in Detroit and neighboring communities.
SERIES
EDITION   PUB. DATE 19   PAGING
PUBLISHER
RECOMMENDED BY   REVIEWED IN
   Ref., 4/55, p.7.
ORDER RECORD

331.2
N42

United Church of Christ.
Nicol, Helen O
Alternative methods to income maintenance:
children's allowances and public assistance.
Presented at the Consultation on Guaranteed
Income, Anti-Poverty Task Force, Council for
Christian Social Action, United Church of
Christ, New York, New York. New York, [1967?]
11p.
1. Wages and salaries - Annual wages.
2. Children. 3. Public assistance. I. Title.
II. Consultation on Guaranteed Income, New
York, III. United Church of Christ.

VF
614
U54g

United Community Funds and Councils of
America.
Government and the voluntary sector in
health and welfare: a statement of con-
sensus. New York, 1966.
3p.

1. Public health. 2. Social welfare.
I. Title.

362.6
L68t

United Community Services of Metropolitan
Lowy, Louis. Boston.
Training manual for human service tech-
nicians working with older people. Developed
under the auspices of United Community
Services of Metropolitan Boston and Boston
University, School of Social Work. Boston,
Boston University Bookstores, 1968.
2 pts.
1. Old age. 2. Social service. I. United
Community Services of Metropolitan Boston.
II. Boston University. School of Social
Work. III. Title.

VF
728.1
(753)
C65
United Community Services of Washington.
Community Research Associates, Inc.
A report on: Citizens housing associations with special reference to the Washington Housing Association ... Washington, Dec. 1952.
24 p.

Prepared for United Community Services of Washington.
Thomas Devine, Survey director.
Processed.
1.Housing-Assoc. 2.Washington Housing Association. 3.Housing-D.C. I.United Community Services of Washington.

FILM
United Community Services of Metropolitan Boston.
You and your neighborhood (Motion picture)
Dekko Films, inc., 1954.

12 min., sd., color, 16mm.
Cost: $100.00

On cover: United Community Service.

1. Community development - Films.
2. Community development - Citizen perticipation. 3. Films. I. Dekko Films.
II. United Community Services of Metropoliten Boston. 4. Neighborhood rehabilitation.

711.4
(4)
M45
United Europe.
Miller, J Marshall.
Leke Europa; a new capital for a United Europe. New York, Books International, 1963.
114p.

Bibliography: p. 106-108.

1. City planning - Europe. 2. International organizations. 3. New towns - Europe. I. Title: United Europe. II. Title.

338
N17
United Fruit Company in Latin America.
National Planning Association.
The United Fruit Company in Latin America, by Stacy May and Galo Plaza. Washington, 1958.
263p. charts, illus. (Seventh case study on United States business performance abroad)

1. United Fruit Company in Latin America.
2. Economic policy. I. May, Stacy. II. Plaza, Galo.

058.7
:614
(761)
S68
United Fund and Community Chest and Council, Mobile, Ala.
South Alabama Regional Planning Commission.
A guide to services in health, education, welfare and recreation in Baldwin, Escambria and Mobile Counties, Alabama. Mobile, The United Fund and Community Chest and Council of Mobile, 1970.
62p.
U.S. Dept. of Housing and Urban Development. UPAP.
1. Health - Ala. - Direct. 2. Education - Ala. - Direct. 3. Social welfare - Ala. - Direct. I. United Fund and Community Chest and Council, Mobile, Ala. II. Title. III. U.S. HUD- UPAP. Ala.

VF
728.1
(74885)
U54
United Housing Council.
Newsletter; a review of 1949 and prospects for 1950, progress and developments in housing in Pittsburgh and Alleghany county. Pittsburgh, Jan. 1950.
7 p.

Processed.

1.Housing-Pittsburgh, Pa. 2.Housing-Alleghany Co., Pa.

334.1
U54c
3 c
United Housing Foundation.
Cooperative housing; a primer of self help. New York, 1959.
[28]p.

1. Cooperative housing.

334.1
(7471)
U54
UNITED HOUSING FOUNDATION.
THE STORY OF THE ILGWU COOPERATIVE HOUSES. NEW YORK, 1963
34P.

1. COOPERATIVE HOUSING - NEW YORK (CITY) I. TITLE.

334.1
U54u
3 c
United Housing Foundation.
United Housing Foundation, a federation of non-profit organizations established to promote better housing through self-help: purpose, program, principles, progress, plans. New York, James Peter Warbasse Memorial Library, 1960.
15p. illus.

1. Cooperative housing. 2. Aided self-help housing.

VF
334.1
U54
United Housing Foundation.
What every cooperator should know: a guide to cooperative housing. New York [1953?]
32 p. illus.

1.Cooperative housing.

728.1
(41)
U54d
U.K. - Apartment houses.
U.K. Ministry of Public Building and Works.
Decisions affecting design of five point blocks; a study carried out by the Architecture Research Unit, Dept. of Architecture, University of Edinburgh. London, Ministry of Public Building and Works, Directorate of Research and Information, 1968.
68p. (Its R & D paper C1/SfB 815 Alf)
1. Low-income housing - U.K. 2. U.K. - Low-income housing. 3. Apartment houses - U.K. 4. U.K - Apartment houses. 5. Architecture, Domestic - Designs and plans. I. Edinburgh, Scot. University. Dept. of Architecture. II. Title.

061.3
(41)
M45
U.K. - ASSOCIATIONS.
Millard, Patricia, ed.
Trade associations and professional bodies of the United Kingdom. 3d ed. Oxford, Eng., Pergamon, 1966.
372p.

1. Associations - U.K. 2. U.K. - Associations. I. Title.

Ref.
016
W34
U.K. - Bibliography
Whitaker's five-year cumulative book list, 19 the complete list of all books published in the United Kingdom in the years 19 giving details as to author, title, subtitle, size, number of pages, price, date, classification and publisher of every book. London, J. Whitaker & Sons, ltd., 19
v annual.

1. Catalogs, Publishers'. 2. Bibliography. 3. U.K. - Bibliography

---

690.091.82
(41)
H18
U.K. - Building codes.
Hawkes, Dean.
Building bulk legislation: a description and analysis. Cambridge, Eng., Centre for Land Use and Built Form Studies, University of Cambridge, [1969?]
45p. (Cambridge, Eng. Centre for Land Use and Built Form Studies. Working paper 4)
Prepared under the sponsorship of the Ministry of Public Building and Works.
Bibliography: p. 43-45.
1. Building codes - U.K. 2. U.K. - Building codes. 3. Office buildings. 4. Site planning. I. Cambridge, Eng. University. Dept. of Architecture. II. Cambridge, Eng. University. Centre for (Cont'd on next card)

690.091.82
(41)
H18
Hawkes, Dean. Building...1969. (Card 2)

Land Use and Built Form Studies. IV. Title.

690.091.82
(41)
U54
U.K. - Building codes.
U.K. Ministry of Public Building and Works.
Guide to the building regulations, 1965 Public health act, 1961. London, H.M.S.O., 1965.
18p.

1. Building codes - U.K. 2. U.K. - Building codes. 3. Building standards - U.K. 4. U.K. - Building standards.

690.031
.G22
U.K. - Building costs.
Geddes, Spence.
Building and public works administration, estimating and costing for the use of civil engineers, surveyors, and building contractors. Rev. by G. Chrystal-Smith. 6th ed. London, George Newnes, ltd., 1967.
296p.

1. Building costs - Estimates. 2. Building costs - U.K. 3. U.K. - Building costs. I. Title. II. Chrystal-Smith, G.

690.031
(41)
S46
U.K. - Building costs.
Skoyles, E R
Introducing bills of quantities (operational format). Garston, Eng., Building Research Station, Ministry of Public Building and Works, 1968.
139-146p. (U.K. Building Research Station. Building research current paper 62/68)
Reprinted from: Quantity surveyor, May and June, 1968.
1. Building costs - U.K. 2. U.K. - Building costs. I. U.K. Building Research Station. II. Title.

690
(41)
B47
U.K.-Building industry.
Bishop, D
The background to management studies by BRS. Garston, Eng., Building Research Station, Ministry of Public Building and Works, 1968.
11p. (U.K. Building Research Station. Current papers 60/68)
Bibliography: p. 10-11.
1. Building industry - U.K. 2. U.K. - Building industry. 3. Industrial management. I. Title. II. U.K. Building Research Station.

690
(41)
G45
U.K. - BUILDING INDUSTRY.
Gilchrist, A
A study of coding and data co-ordination for the construction industry: information systems relating to the construction industry, by A. Gilchrist and Kathleen Gaster. Garston, Eng., Building Research Station, Ministry of Public Works, 1969.
65p. (U.K. Building Research Station. Current paper 11/69)
Bibliography: p. 57-64.
1. Building industry - U.K. 2. U.K. - Building industry. (Cont'd on next card)

690
(41)
G45
Gilchrist, A A study of coding...1969. (Card 2)

3. Building industry - Automation. I. U.K. Building Research Station. II. Gaster, Kathleen, jt. au. III. Title.

690
(41)
H43

U.K. - Building industry.
Higgin, Gurth.
Communications in the building industry;
the report of a pilot study, by Gurth Higgin
and Neil Jessop. London, Tavistock
Publications, 1965.
125p.
Bibliography: p. 112-117.

1. Building industry - U.K. 2. U.K. -
Building industry. I. Title. II. Jessop,
Neil, jt. au.

690
(41)
J63

U.K. - BUILDING INDUSTRY.
Johnston, H P
A study of coding and data co-ordination for
the construction industry: electrical design
and contracting. Garston, Eng., Building Research Station, Ministry of Public Building
and Works, 1969.
70p. (U.K. Building Research Station.
Current paper 7/69)

1. Building industry - U.K. 2. U.K. - Building industry. 3. Building industry - Automation. 4.   Electrical wiring.
I. U.K. Buil   ding Research Station.
II. Title.

690
(41)
N25

U.K. - BUILDING INDUSTRY.
Nelson, J I'a
A study of coding and data co-ordination for
the construction industry: instructions to
operatives. Garston, Eng., Building Research
Station, 1969.
30p. (U.K. Building Research Station.
Current paper 10/69)

1. Building industry - U.K. 2. U.K. - Building industry. 3. Building industry - Automation. I. U.K. Building Research Station.
II. Title.

728.100.15
(41)
U54

U.K. - Building industry.
U.K. Building Research Station.
BRS. Garston, Eng., 1967.
16p.

1. U.K. Building Research Station.
2. Housing research - U.K. 3. U.K. - Housing
research. 4. Building industry - U.K.
5. U.K. - Building industry.

690
(41)
W45

U.K. - Building industry.
Wilson, W L
Engineering and building; presidential
address. [London] Ministry of Public Building
and Works, 1968.
[5]p.
Reprinted from: Electrical supervisor, Dec.,
1968.
1. Building industry - U.K. 2. U.K. -
Building industry. I. U.K. Ministry of
Public Building and Works. II. Title.

728.100.15
(44)
S64

U.K. - Building research.
Spira, Ephraim.
Selective examination and assessment of re-
search in France, Israel and in the United
Kingdom in the field of housing and building,
applicable in developing countries. A report
prepared by Ephraim Spira and Jan de Geus. Pre-
pared for UNESCO. Rotterdam, International
Council for Building Research Studies and
Documentation, 1966.
48p.
1. Housing research - France. 2. France -
Housing research. 3. Housing research -
Israel. 4. Israel - Housing research.
5. Housing rese   arch - U.K. 6. U.K. -
Housing research.   (Cont'd on next card)

728.100.15
(44)
S64

Spira, Ephraim.   Selective examination...
1966.   (Card 2)
7. Building research - France. 8. France -
Building research. 9. Building research -
Israel. 10. Israel - Building research.
11. Building research - U.K. 12. U.K. - Building research. 13. Underdeveloped countries.
I. Geus, Jan de, jt. au. II. United Nations.
(Economic and Social Council) III. International Council for Building Research Studies
and Documentation.

728.100.15
(44)
S64

Spira, Ephraim. Selec...1966 (Card 3)

I. Geus, Jan de, jt. au. II. United
Nations. (economic and Social Council)
III. International Council for Building
Research Studies and Documentation.

690.091.82
(41)
U54

U.K. - Building standards.
U.K. Ministry of Public Building and
Works.
Guide to the building regulations, 1965
Public health act, 1961. London, H.M.S.O.,
1965.
18p.

1. Building codes - U.K. 2. U.K. - Building
codes. 3. Building standards - U.K. 4. U.K. -
Building standards.

711.3
(41)
A73

U.K. - CITY PLANNING.
Ash, Maurice.
Regions of tomorrow; towards the open city.
New York, Schocken Books, 1969.
99p.
Bibliography: p. 95-97.
1. Regional planning - U.K. 2. U.K. -
Regional planning. 3. City planning - U.K.
4. U.K. - City planning. 5. New towns - U.K.
6. U.K. - New towns. I. Title.

301.15
(41)
R61

U.K. - COMMUNITY STRUCTURE.
Robson, B T
Urban analysis; a study of city structure
with special reference to Sunderland.
Cambridge, Eng., Cambridge University Press,
1969.
301p. (Cambridge geographical studies
no. 1)
Bibliography: p. 278-294.

1. Community structure - U.K. 2. U.K. -
Community structure. 3. Education - U.K.
4. U.K. - Education. I. Cambridge.
University.   II. Title.

301.15
(41)
R61

U.K. - EDUCATION.
Robson, B T
Urban analysis; a study of city structure
with special reference to Sunderland.
Cambridge, Eng., Cambridge University Press,
1969.
301p. (Cambridge geographical studies
no. 1)
Bibliography: p. 278-294.

1. Community structure - U.K. 2. U.K. -
Community structure. 3. Education - U.K.
4. U.K. - Education. I. Cambridge.
University.   II. Title.

331
(41)
U54

U.K. - Employment.
U.K. Royal Commission on Trade Unions and
Employers' Associations.
Two studies in industrial relations. 1.
The position of women in industry, by Nancy
Seear. 2. Changing wage payment systems, by
Robert B. McKersie. London, H.M.S.O., 1968.
66p. (Its Research papers 11)
1. Employment - U.K. 2. U.K. - Employment.
3. Wage incentives - U.K. 4. U.K. - Wage in-
centives. 5. Labor relations - U.K. 6. U.K. -
Labor relations. I. Title: Women in industry.
II. Seear, Nancy,   jt. au. III. McKersie,
Robert B., jt.   au.

332
(41)
P21

U.K. - Finance.
Peacock, Alan T
The growth of public expenditure in the
United Kingdom, by Alan T. Peacock and Jack
Wiseman. Princeton, N.J., Princeton University
Press, 1961.
213p. (National Bureau of Economic Research.
General series no. 72)

1. Finance - U.K. 2. U.K. - Finance.
3. Budget. I. Wiseman, Jack, jt. au.
II. National Bureau of Economic Research.
III. Title.

711.417
(41)
O71g

U.K. - GARDEN CITIES.
Osborn, Frederic J
Green-belt cities. New York, Schocken
Books, 1969.
203p.

Bibliography: p. 195-198.

1. Garden cities - U.K. 2. U.K. - Garden
cities. I. Title.

711.417
(41)
U54g

U.K. - Garden cities.
U.K. Ministry of Housing and Local
Government.
The green belts. London, H.M.S.O.,
1962.
30p.

1. Garden cities - U.K. . U.K. -
Garden cities. 3. Open space land.
I. Title.

728
.333
(41)
U54b

U.K. - Home ownership.
U.K. Ministry of Housing and Local Government.
Buying your own home: your guide to the
option mortgage scheme. London, H.M.S.O.,
1967.
18p.

1. Home ownership - U K. 2. Mortgage
finance - U.K. 3. U.K. - Home ownership.
4. U.K. - Mortgage finance. I. Title.

728.100.15
(41)
A55

U.K. - Housing.
Allen, Phyllis.
Hotel user study: 1. Living accomodations
for young people. 2. Storage fitments and
furniture. Garston, Eng., Building Research
Station, Ministry of Technology, 1968.
847-914p. (U.K. Building Research Station.
Current paper 50/68)
Reprinted from the Architects' journal,
April, 1968.
1. Housing research - U.K. 2. U.K. -
Housing research. 3. Housing - U.K. 4. U.K. -
Housing. 5. Youth. 6. Family living require-
ments. I. U.K.   Building research
Station. II.   Title.

728.1
(41)
T36

U.K. - HOUSING.
Thompson, W
The housing handbook. London, National
Housing Reform Council, 1903.
101p.
A practical manual for the use of officers,
members, and committees of local authorities,
ministers of religion, members of Parliament,
and all social or municipal reformers interested in the housing of the working classes.

1. Housing - U.K. 2. U.K. - Housing.
3. Company housing. I. National Housing
Reform Coun   cil, London. II. Title.

690.591
U54ol

U. K. - Housing.
U.K. Ministry of Housing and Local
Government. (Welsh Office)
Old houses into new homes. Presented to
Parliament by the Minister of Housing and
Local Government and the Secretary of State
for Wales by command of Her Majesty, London,
H.M.S.O., 1968.
29p. (Papers by Command (Cmnd. 3602)

1. Houses - Maintenance and modernization. 2. Housing - U.K. 3. U.K. - Housing.
I. Title.

728.100.15
(41)
A55

U.K. - Housing research.
Allen, Phyllis.
Hotel user study: 1. Living accomodations
for young people. 2. Storage fitments and
furniture. Garston, Eng., Building Research
Station, Ministry of Technology, 1968.
847-914p. (U.K. Building Research Station.
Current paper 50/68)
Reprinted from the Architects' journal,
April, 1968.
1. Housing research - U.K. 2. U.K. -
Housing research. 3. Housing - U.K. 4. U.K. -
Housing. 5. Youth. 6. Family living require-
ments. I. U.K.   Building research
Station. II.   Title.

728.100.15
(41)
B47

U.K. - Housing research.
Birmingham, Eng. University Centre for Urban and Regional Studies.
The work of the Centre, incorporating the Centre's second annual report, 1967-68. Birmingham, 1969.
104p. (Its Occasional paper no. 4)

1. Housing research - U.K. 2. U.K. - Housing research. I. Birmingham, Eng. University. Centre for Urban and Regional Studies. Annual report; 2d. 1967/68 II. Title.

728.100.15
(44)
S64

U.K. - Housing research.
Spira, Ephraim.
Selective examination and assessment of research in France, Israel and in the United Kingdom in the field of housing and building, applicable in developing countries. A report prepared by Ephraim Spira and Jan de Geus. Prepared for UNESCO. Rotterdam, International Council for Building Research Studies and Documentation, 1966.
48p.
1. Housing research - France. 2. France - Housing research. 3. Housing research - Israel. 4. Israel - Housing research. 5. Housing research - U.K. 6. U.K. - Housing research. (Cont'd on next card)

728.100.15
(44)
S64

Spira, Ephraim.   Selective examination...
1966.   (Card 2)

7. Building research - France. 8. France - Building research. 9. Building research - Israel. 10. Israel - Building research. 11. Building research - U.K. 12. U.K. - Building research. 13. Underdeveloped countries. I. Geus, Jan de, jt. au. II. United Nations. (Economic and Social Council) III. International Council for Building Research Studies and Documentation.

728.100.15
(44)
S64

Spria, Ephraim. Selec...1966 (Card 3)

I. Geus, Jan de, jt. au. II. United Nations. (economic and Social Council) III. International Council for Building Research Studies and Documentation.

728.100.15
(41)
U54

U.K. - Housing research.
U.K. Building Research Station.
BRS. Garston, Eng., 1967.
16p.

1. U.K. Building Research Station. 2. Housing research - U.K. 3. U.K. - Housing research. 4. Building industry - U.K. 5. U.K. - Building industry.

711.4
:670
(41)
C15

U.K.-Industrial location.
Cameron, G   C
Industrial movement and the regional problem, by G.C. Cameron and B.D. Clark. Edinburgh, Oliver & Boyd, 1966.
220p. (Glasgow. University. Social and economic studies occasional papers no. 5)

1. Industrial location - U.K. 2. U.K. - Industrial location. I. Clark, B.D., jt. au. II. Glasgow. University. III. Title.

711.4
:670
(016)
T68

U.K. - Industrial location - Bibliography.
Townroe, P   M
Industrial location and regional economic policy; a selected bibliography. Birmingham, Eng., Centre for Urban and Regional Studies, University of Birmingham, 1968.
43p. (Birmingham, Eng. University. Centre for Urban and Regional Studies. Occasional paper no. 2)
1. Industrial location - Bibl. 2. Industrial location - U.K. - Bibl. 3. U.K. - Industrial location - Bibl. I. Birmingham, Eng. University. Centre for Urban and Regional Studies. II. Title.

331
(41)
U54

U.K. - Labor relations.
U.K. Royal Commission on Trade Unions and Employers' Associations.
Two studies in industrial relations. 1. The position of women in industry, by Nancy Seear. 2. Changing wage payment systems, by Robert B. McKersie. London, H.M.S.O., 1968.
66p. (Its Research papers 11)

1. Employment - U.K. 2. U.K. - Employment. 3. Wage incentives - U.K. 4. U.K. - Wage incentives. 5. Labor relations - U.K. 6. U.K. - Labor relations. I. Title: Women in industry. II. Seear, Nancy,   jt. au. III. McKersie, Robert B., jt.   au.

711.14
(41)
C15

U.K. - Land use.
Cambridge, Eng. University. School of Architecture.
Land use and built form studies, lent term, 1969. Directory of research. Cambridge, 1969.
11p.
Bibliography: p. 11-12.

1. Land use - U.K. 2. Architecture - Designs and plans. 3. U.K. - Land use. I. Title.

728.1
(41)
S71

U.K. - Low-income housing.
Stack, Unity.
The development of a housing association; the experience of the Hanover Housing Association, 1963-67. Birmingham, Eng., Centre for Urban and Regional Studies, University of Birmingham, 1968.
64p. (Birmingham, Eng. University. Centre for Urban and Regional Studies. Occasional paper no. 1)
1. Housing - Associations   2. Low-income housing - U.K. 3. U.K. - Low-income housing. I. Title: Hanover Housing Association. II. Birmingham, Eng. University. Center for Urban and Regional Studies. III. Title.

728.1
(41)
U54d

U.K. - Low-income housing.
U.K. Ministry of Public Building and Works.
Decisions affecting design of five point blocks; a study carried out by the Architecture Research Unit, Dept. of Architecture, University of Edinburgh. London, Ministry of Public Building and Works, Directorate of Research and Information, 1968.
68p. (Its R & D paper Cl/SfB 815 Alf)
1. Low-income housing - U.K. 2. U.K. - Low-income housing. 3. Apartment houses - U.K. 4. U.K. - Apartment houses. 5. Architecture, Domestic - Designs and plans. I. Edinburgh, Scot. University.   Dept. of Architecture. II. Title.

711.3
(41)
P51

U.K. - METROPOLITAN AREA PLANNING.
Planning and Transport Research and Computation Co.
Planning in the city region I; proceedings of a PTRC Seminar, Feb., 1968, London. London, 1968.
103p.

1. Metropolitan area planning - U.K. 2. U.K. - Metropolitan area planning. I. Title.

728
:333
(41)
U54b

U.K. - Mortgage finance.
U.K. Ministry of Housing and Local Government.
Buying your own home: your guide to the option mortgage scheme. London, H.M.S.O., 1967.
18p.

1. Home ownership - U.K. 2. Mortgage finance - U.K. 3. U.K. - Home ownership. 4. U.K. - Mortgage finance. I. Title.

339.5
A78

U.K. - Natural resources.
Arvill, Robert.
Man and environment; crisis and the strategy of choice. Harmondsworth, Penguin, 1967.
332p. (Pelican books A889) 8/6
Bibliography: p. 314-318.

1. Natural resources - U.K. 2. Man - Influence of environment. 3. U.K. - Natural resources. I. Title.

711.3
(41)
A73

U.K. - NEW TOWNS.
Ash, Maurice.
Regions of tomorrow; towards the open city. New York, Schocken Books, 1969.
99p.
Bibliography: p. 95-97.
1. Regional planning - U.K. 2. U.K. - Regional planning. 3. City planning - U.K. 4. U.K. - City planning. 5. New towns - U.K. 6. U.K. - New towns. I. Title.

711.417
.(41)
O34

U.K. - New towns.
Ogilvy, Audrey A
The self-contained new town. Garston, Eng., Building Research Station, Ministry of Technology, 1968.
38-54p. (U.K. Building Research Station. Current paper 56/68)
Reprinted from: Town Planning review, Apr., 1968.

1. New towns - U.K. 2. U.K. - New towns. I. U.K. Building Research Station. II. Title.

711.417
(41)
U54ne
1969

U.K. - New towns.
U.K. Central Office of Information.
The new towns of Britain. New York, British Information Services, 1969.
26p.

1. New towns - U.K. 2. U.K. - New towns.

711
(41)
U54
1967

U.K. - Planning.
U.K. Central Office of Information.
(Reference Div.)
Town and country planning in Britain, 1967. London, H.M.S.O., 1968.
31p. (Its Reference pamphlet 9)
Bibliography: p. 31-32.
Prepared for U.K. British Information Services.

1. Planning - U.K. 2. U.K. - Planning. I. U.K. British Information Services. II. Title.

693.002.22
(41)
T19

U.K. - Prefabricated construction.
Taylor Woodrow-Anglian.
Industrialized building. Ealing, Eng., 1968.
[12]p.
SfB (2) Gf2

1. Prefabricated construction - U.K. 2. U.K. - Prefabricated construction. I. Title. II. Larsen and Nielsen, Copenhagen.

693.5
U54a

U.K. - Prefabricated construction.
U.K. Ministry of Public Building and Works.
Accuracy in precast concrete panel construction. London, Ministry of Public Building and Works, Directorate of Research and Information, 1968.
45p. (R & D paper Cl/SfB (2-) GF)

1. Concrete construction. 2. Prefabricated construction - U.K. 3. U.K. - Prefabricated construction. 4. Panels. I. Title.

728.1
:336.1B
(41)
U54

U.K. - Public housing.
U.K. Ministry of Housing and Local Government. (Welsh Office)
Housing subsidies manual; Housing subsidies act of 1967. London, H.M.S.O., 1968.
92p.

1. Public housing - U.K. 2. U.K. - Public housing. I. Title.

VF
016
(354:41)
U54

U.K. - Publications.
U.K. H.M. Stationery Office.
    Government publications: official indexes, lists, guides, catalogues. London, 1955.
    13 p.

    1. U.K. - Publications.

696
(U54)

U.K. - Wage incentives.
U.K. Ministry of Public Building and Works.
    An introduction to incentive schemes in building maintenance. London, 1969.
    52p. (Its R & D paper Cl/SfB (w))

    1. Building maintenance. 2. Wage incentives - U.K. 3. U.K. - Wage incentives. 4. Job analysis. I. Title.

690
(016)
871

Stannett, Annette. Bibliography...1968.
    (Card 2)

    I. Title: Application of computers in the construction industry, 1962-1967. II. U.K. Ministry of Public Building and Works. III. U.K. Committee on the Application of Computers in the Construction Industry.

388
S31

U.K. - Railroads.
Sharp, Clifford.
    Problems of urban passenger transport; with special reference to Leicester. Leicester, Eng., Leicester University Press, 1967.
    118p.

    1. Transportation - U.K. 2. U.K. - Transportation. 3. Journey to work. 4. Railroads - U.K. 5. U.K. - Railroads. I. Title.

331
(41)
U54

U.K. - Wage incentives.
U.K. Royal Commission on Trade Unions and Employers' Associations.
    Two studies in industrial relations. 1. The position of women in industry, by Nancy Seear. 2. Changing wage payment systems, by Robert B. McKersie. London, H.M.S.O., 1968.
    66p. (Its Research papers 11)

    1. Employment - U.K. 2. U.K. - Employment. 3. Wage incentives - U.K. 4. U.K. - Wage incentives. 5. Labor relations - U.K. 6. U.K. - Labor relations. I. Title: Women in industry. II. Seear, Nancy, jt. au. III. McKersie, Robert B., jt. au.

690
(016)
S71
Suppl.

U.K. Committee on the Application of Computers in the Construction Industry.
Stannett, Annette.
    Bibliography on the application of computers in the construction industry, 1962-1967. Supplement, 1st-3rd. Jan.-June, 1968-Jan.-June 1969
    Prepared on behalf of the Committee on the Application of Computers in the Construction Industry. London, H.M.S.O., 1969-70
    2v. (R & D bulletin)
    At head of title: Ministry of Public Building and Works.

    (Cont'd on next card)

712.015
B87

U.K. - Recreation.
Burton, Thomas L
    Recreation research methods; a review of recent studies, by Thomas L. Burton and P.A. Noad. Birmingham, Eng., Centre for Urban and Regional Studies, University of Birmingham, 1968.
    78p. (Birmingham, Eng. Centre for Urban and Regional Studies. Occasional paper no. 3)
    Bibliography: p. 73-78.
    1. Recreation research. 2. Recreation - U.K. 3. U.K. - Recreation. I. Noad, P.A., jt. au. II. Birmingham, Eng. Center for Urban and Regional Studies. III. Title.

711.3
(41)
U54R

U.K. ADVISORY COMMITTEE FOR LONDON REGIONAL PLANNING.
    REPORT TO THE MINISTER OF TOWN AND COUNTRY PLANNING AND REPORT OF THE TECHNICAL SUBCOMMITTEE. LONDON, H.M. STAT. OFF., 1946.
    39P.

    BOUND IN BACK: GREATER LONDON PLAN; REPORT OF LONDON REGIONAL PLANNING ADVISORY COMMITTEE, BY E.M. HODGKINSON. LONDON, 1947. 7L.

    1. METROPOLIT... AN AREA PLANNING ...
    (CONTINUED ON NEXT CARD)

690
(016)
S71
Suppl.

Stannett, Annette. Bibliography on...1969-
    (Card 2)

    1. Building construction - Automation - Bibl. I. U.K. Ministry of Public Building and Works. II. Committee on the Application of Computers in the Construction Industry. III. Title: Application of computers in the construction industry, 1962-1967. Supplement.

711.3
(41)
A73

U.K. - REGIONAL PLANNING.
Ash, Maurice.
    Regions of tomorrow; towards the open city. New York, Schocken Books, 1969.
    99p.
    Bibliography: p. 95-97.
    1. Regional planning - U.K. 2. U.K. - Regional planning. 3. City planning - U.K. 4. U.K. - City planning. 5. New towns - U.K. 6. U.K. - New towns. I. Title.

711.3
(41)
U54R

U.K. ADVISORY COMMITTEE FOR LONDON REGIONAL PLANNING. REPORT TO THE ...
    1946. (CARD 2)

    U.K. - LONDON. I. HODGKINSON, E.M. II. TITLE: LONDON PLAN.

690
(41:07)
U54

U.K. Board of Building Education.
    Education in Great Britain with particular reference to the building industry. Prepared by a Committee of Study. [London, 1958]
    [72]p.

    1. Building industry - Study and teaching - U. K.

711.6
U54c

U.K. - Traffic.
U.K. Ministry of Housing and Local Government.
    Cars in housing 1; some medium density layouts. London, H.M.S.O., 1966.
    52p. (Its Design bulletin 10)

    1. Site planning. 2. Traffic - U.K. 3. U.K. - Traffic. I. Title.

728.6
U54

U.K. BOARD OF AGRICULTURE AND FISHERIES. REPORT OF THE COMMITTEE APPOINTED... TO CONSIDER AND ADVISE THE BOARD ON PLANS, MODELS, SPECIFICATIONS, AND METHODS OF CONSTRUCTION FOR RURAL COTTAGES AND OUTBUILDINGS; WITH APPENDICES AND REDUCED PLANS. LONDON, H.M. STAT. OFF., 1914.
    96P.

    AT HEAD OF TITLE PAGE: ADVISORY COMMITTEE ON RURAL COTTAGES.
    1. FARM HOUSING. I. TITLE: RURAL COTTAGES AND OUTBUILDINGS.

VF
727.1
(41)
U54b

U.K. British Council.
    Britain's new schools, by D. H. Morrell and A. Pott. London, Longmans, Green, 1960.
    31p. illus.

    1. Schools - U.K. I. Morrell, D. H. II. Pott, A.

388
S31

U.K. - Transportation.
Sharp, Clifford.
    Problems of urban passenger transport; with special reference to Leicester. Leicester, Eng., Leicester University Press, 1967.
    118p.

    1. Transportation - U.K. 2. U.K. - Transportation. 3. Journey to work. 4. Railroads - U.K. 5. U.K. - Railroads. I. Title.

M
Gt.Brit.

Gt. Brit. Ministry of Agriculture and Fisheries Wales. Welsh Plant Breeding Station.
    Vegetation, grasslands of England and Wales. Southampton, Gt. Brit. Ordnance Survey, 1945.
    2 sheets col.

    1. Agriculture-England-Maps. 2. Agriculture-Wales-Maps. I. Gt. Brit. Ministry of Agriculture and Fisheries.

U.K. British Information Services
see also
U.K. Central Office of Information

388
:331
S78

U.K. - Transportation.
Sturt, Alan R
    The relationship between distance and commuting to central London, 1951-1961. London, London School of Economics and Political Science, Graduate Geography Dept., 1968.
    12p. (London School of Economics and Political Science. Graduate School of Economics and Political Science. Discussion paper no. 25)

    1. Journey to work. 2. Transportation - U.K. 3. U.K. - Transportation. I. London School of Economics and Political Science. Graduate School of ... Geography. II. Title.

690
(016)
871

U.K. Committee on the Application of Computers in the Construction Industry.
Stannett, Annette.
    Bibliography on the application of computers in the construction industry, 1962-1967. Prepared on behalf of the Committee on the Application of Computers in the Construction Industry. London, H.M.S.O., 1968.
    87p. (R & D bulletin)
    List of periodicals cited: p. 74-82.
    At head of title: Ministry of Public Building and Works, Directorate of Research and Information.
    1. Building construction - Automation - Bibl.

    (Cont'd on next card)

330
(729)
U54

U.K. British Information Services.
U.K. Central Office of Information.
    Barbados. Prepared for British Information Services. New York, British Information Services, 1966.
    26p.

    1. Economic conditions - Barbados, W.I. I. U.K. British Information Services. II. Title.

330
(68)
U54

U.K. British Information Services.

U.K. Central Office of Information.
Bechuanaland. Prepared for U.K.-British
Information Services. London, H.M. Stat.
Off., 1966.
[14]p.

1. Economic conditions - Bechuanaland, S.
Africa. 2. Agriculture - Bechuanaland, S.
Africa. 3. Planning - Bechuanaland, S.
Africa. I. U.K. British Information
Services. II. Title.

972.82
B74

U.K. British Information Services. (Reference Division)
British Honduras. New York, 1959.
26p. maps. (Its I. D. 1319)

1. British Honduras. 2. Economic conditions - British Honduras.

VF
320
(41)
U54
1961

U.K. British Information Services. (Reference Div.)
The central government of Britain. London, 1961.
36p. (I.D. 1367 (Rev.))

1. Political science - U.K.

728.1
(41
:016)
U54B
1946

U.K. BRITISH INFORMATION SERVICES.
A BIBLIOGRAPHY OF HOUSING AND TOWN AND
COUNTRY PLANNING IN BRITAIN; BEING A
HANDLIST OF BOOKS, PAMPHLETS, DOCUMENTS
AND PERIODICALS IN THE LIBRARIES OF
BRITISH INFORMATION SERVICES, NEW YORK,
AND ITS BRANCHES AT CHICAGO, SAN
FRANCISCO AND WASHINGTON. 2D ED. WITH
SUPPLEMENT. NEW YORK, 1946.
28, 4P.

1. HOUSING - U.K. - BIBLIOGRAPHY.
2. CITY PLANNING - U.K. -
BIBLIOGRAPHY.

972.82
B74
1961

U.K. British Information Services.
(Reference Div.)
British Honduras. Rev. New York, 1961.
30p. (Its I.D. 1319 rev.)

1. British Honduras. 2. Economic
conditions - British Honduras.

VF
320
(41)
U54
1963

U.K. British Information Services.
(Reference Div.)
The central government of Britain. London, 1963.
38p. (I.D. 1367 (Rev.))

1. Political science - U.K.

330
U54br

U.K. British Information Services.
(Reference Division)
Britain and economic development overseas. New York, 1960.
32p. (I.D. 1349)

1. Technical assistance programs (U.K.) 2. Underdeveloped countries.

320
(41)
U54b

U.K. British Information Services.
(Reference Division)
The British Parliament. Rev. New York, 1961.
26p. (I.D. 952 (rev.))

1. Political science - U.K.

VF
320
(41)
U54
1965

U.K. British Information Services.
(Reference Div.)
The central government of Britain.
London, 1965.
35p.

1. Political science - U.K.

351.7
:325.3
(41)
U54b

U.K. British Information Services.
Britain and the United Nations. New York, 1962.
79p. (Its I.D. 1308 (Revised) March 1962)

1. British Commonwealth of Nations.
2. United Nations.

320
(41)
U54b
1962

U.K. British Information Services.
(Reference Div.)
The British Parliament. Rev. New York, 1962.
40p. (Its I.D. 952 (Rev.))

1. Political science - U.K.

649
U54

U.K. British Information Services.
(Reference Div.)
Children in Britain. New York, 1962.
51p. (Its I.D. 1395, April 1962)

Bibliography: p. 47-51.

1. Children.

VF
351.1
(41:016)
U54

U.K. British Information Services. (Reference Division)
The British Civil Service: a select bibliography. New York, 1957.
8 p. (Its ID 884, (revised))

I.Title.

320
(41)
U54b
1963

U.K. British Information Services.
(Reference Div.)
The British Parliament. Rev. New York, 1963.
38p. (Its I.D. 953 (rev.))

1. Political science - U.K.

649
U54
1964

U.K. British Information Services.
(Reference Div.)
Children in Britain. Rev. New York, 1964.
54p.

1. Children. 2. Social service.

VF
341.1
:338
(60)
U54

U.K. British Information Services.
(Reference Division)
British colonial policy and achievement in Africa. New York, 1959.
12p. (Its I.D. 1321)

1. Technical assistance programs (U.K.) - Africa. I. Title.

720
(41)
U542

U.K. BRITISH INFORMATION SERVICES.
BUILDINGS OF BRITAIN, YESTERDAY, TODAY
AND TOMORROW. LONDON, 1943.
84P.

1. ARCHITECTURE - U.K. I. TITLE.

341.1
:338
(5487)
U54
pt. 1

U. K. British Information Services.
The Colombo plan. I. Britain's part.
London [1962]
32p.

1. Technical assistance programs (U. K.) - South and Southeast Asia. 2. Underdeveloped countries. I. Title.

330
(881)
U54

U.K. British Information Services.
British Guiana. New York, 1959.
30p. (Its I.D. 1323)

1. British Guiana. 2. Economic conditions - British Guiana.

VF
320
(41)
U54

U.K. British Information Services.
(Reference Div.)
The central government of the United Kingdom. London, 1960.
36p. (I.D. 1367)

1. Political science - U.K.

341.1
:338
U54r
no.4

U.K. British Information Services.
(Economics Div.)
The Colombo plan for South and South East Asia. Facts on Britain's aid to less developed countries, no. 4. New York, 1963.
5p. (Reference paper no. 4; ID1446-4)

1. Technical assistance programs (U.K.) - South and South East Asia. 2. Underdeveloped countries. I. Title.

351.7
:325.3
(41)
U54
    U.K. British Information Services.
       The Commonwealth Association in brief.
London, Fosh & Cross, 1957.
      36p. map.

       1. British Commonwealth of Nations.
    I. Title.

VF
330
(5643)
U54
    U.K. British Information Services.
      Cyprus looks forward. New York, 1959.
      15p. illus.

   1. Economic development - Cyprus.

354
(41)
U54
1958
    U.K. British Information Services. (Refer-
      ence Division)
      Government and administration of the United
Kingdom. Rev. New York, 1958.
      84p. (Its I.D. 1233)

      1. Public Administration - U. K.

351.7
:325.3
(41)
U54
1958
    U.K. British Information Services.
      The Commonwealth Association in brief.
New York, 1958.
      40p. map, tables.

      1. British Commonwealth of Nations.
    I. Title.

330
U54e
    U.K. British Information Services.
      (Reference Division)
      Economic development in the United King-
dom dependencies. Rev. New York, 1959.
      48p. (I.D. 1243 rev.)

   1. Economic development. 2. Technical assistance
programs (U.K.)

354
(41)
U54
1960
    U.K. British Information Services. (Refer-
      ence Div.)
      Government and administration of the United
Kingdom. Rev. New York, 1960.
      84p. (Its I.D. 1233 (Rev.))

      1. Public administration - U.K.

351.7
:325.3
(41)
U54
1959
    U. K. British Information Services.
      The Commonwealth Association in
brief. Rev. New York, 1959.
      42p.

    1. British Commonwealth of Nations. I. Title.

370
(41)
U54
1960
    U.K. British Information Services.
      Education in Great Britain; an outline
of the educational system. Rev. New
York, 1960.
      45p. (I.D. 606(Rev.))

    1. Education - U.K.

330
(881)
U54
1966
    U.K. British Information Services.
    U.K. Central Office of Information.
      (Reference Div.)
      Guyana. London, H.M. Stat. Off., 1966.
      46p.

      Prepared for U.K. British Information
Services.

      1. Economic conditions - Guyana. 2. Social
conditions - Guyana. 3. Political science.
I. U.K. British Information Services.
II. Title.

VF
351.7
:325.3
(41)
U54
1965
    U.K. British Information Services.
    U.K. Central Office of Information.
      (Reference Division)
      The Commonwealth in brief. Prepared
for British Information Services. New
York, British Information Services,
1965.
      52p.
      1. British Commonwealth of Nations.
I. Title. II. U.K. British Information Services.

VF
351.7
:325.3
(41)
U54e
    U.K. British Information Services.
      Evolving commonwealth, a reference
map. New York, 1961.
      folder.

      1. British Commonwealth of Nations.

614
(41)
U54
    U.K. British Information Services. (Refer-
      ence Div.)
      Health services in Britain. New York,
1960.
      54p.

      1. Public health - U.K.

325.3
(41)
U54
    U. K. British Information Services. (Refer-
      ences Div.)
      Community development in the United King-
dom dependencies. New York, 1958.
      20p.

      1. Community development - U.K. 2. Under-
developed Countries.

VF
341.1
:338
U54fa
    U.K. British Information Services.
      Fact sheets on the Colombo plan. New
York, 1958—
      v.

      For complete information see shelflist.

      1. Technical assistance programs (U.K.)
I. Title: The Colombo plan.

728.1
(41)
U54
1960
    U.K. British Information
      Services.
      Housing in Britain. Rev. London,
British Information Services, Reference
Division, 1960.
      48p.
    3c.

      1. Housing - U.K.

711.583
(41)
U54
    U.K. British Information Services.
      (Reference Div.)
      Community development: the British
contribution. New York, 1962.
      37p. (Its I.D. 1397, May 1962)

      1. Community development - U.K.

330
(595)
U54f
    U.K. British Information Services.
      The Federation of Malaysia. New York,
1963.
      75p. (I.D. 1417)

      1. Economic conditions - Malaysia.

728.1
(41)
U54
1970
    U.K. British Information Services.
      Housing in Britain. Prepared by Reference
Div., Central Office of Information for British
Information Services. London, H.M.S.O., 1970.
      19p. (Central Office of Information reference
pamphlet 41)

      Bibliography: p. 19 - [20]

      1. Housing - U.K. I. U.K. Central Office
of Information.

330
(5643)
U54e
    U.K. British Information Services.
      Cyprus. New York, 1960.
      28p. map. (I. D. 1340)

   1. Economic conditions - Cyprus.

354
(41)
U54
    U.K. British Information Services.
      (Reference Division)
      Government and administration of the
United Kingdom. Rev. London, Cox and
Sharland, 1957.
      81p. tables.

    1. Public administration - U.K.

341.1
:338
U54i
1958
    U.K. British Information Services.
      Investment in progress, Britain's
contribution to overseas development,
by Duncan Crow. London, 1958.
      40p.

      Partial contents: the Columbo plan.

      1. Technical assistance programs (U.K.) 2. Under-
developed countries. I. Crow, Duncan. II. Title:
The Columbo plan.

341.1
:338
U541
1960
U.K. British Information Services.
Investment in progress, Britain's contribution to overseas development, by Duncan Crow. London, 1960.
40p. illus.

Partial contents:- The Colombo plan.

1. Technical assistance programs (U.K.) 2. Underdeveloped countries. I. Crow, Duncan. II. Title: The Colombo plan.

352
(41)
U54
U.K. British Information Services. (Reference Div.)
Local government in Britain. New York, 1968.
41p.

1. Local government - U.K. I. Title.

330
(669)
U54
U.K. British Information Services. (Reference Division)
Nigeria: the making of a nation. New York, 1960.
66p. illus., maps, tables.
(I. D. 1355)

1. Economic development - Nigeria.

330
(7292)
U54
U.K. British Information Services.
Jamaica, Island in the sun. New York, [1962?]
[16]p.

1. Economic conditions - Jamaica.

330
(6897)
U54m
U.K. British Information Services.
Malawi. New York, 1964.
33p. (I.D. 1485)

1. Economic conditions-Malawi.

341.1
:338
(41)
U54p
U.K. British Information Services. (Reference Division)
Political development in the United Kingdom dependencies. New York, 1958.
28p. map.

1. Technical assistance programs (UK)
2. Underdeveloped countries.

330
(7292)
U54j
U.K. British Information Services. (Reference Div.)
Jamaica: the making of a nation. New York, 1962.
36p. (Its I.D. 1403)

1. Economic conditions - Jamaica.
I. Title.

330
(458)
U54
U.K. British Information Services. (Reference Div.)
Malta. New York, 1964.
29p. (I.D. 1447 (rev.) RF.P. 5568/64)

330
(458)
U54
Suppl.
--- --- Malta: Independence constitution 1964. Supplement to Malta, RF.P. 5568/64. New York, 1964. 4p.

1. Economic conditions - Malta. 2. Social conditions - Malta. 3. Political science - Malta. I. Title.

341.1
:338
(41)
U54p
1959
U.K. British Information Services. (Reference Division)
Political development in the United Kingdom dependencies. Rev. New York, 1959.
28p. (I.D. 1286)

1. Technical assistance programs (U.K.) 2. Underdeveloped countries.

339.5
U54
U.K. British Information Services.
The Kariba hydro-electric scheme. New York, 1959.
8p. (Its I.D. 1338)

1. Power resources. I. Title.

330
(458)
U54m
U.K. British Information Services.
U.K. Central Office of Information.
Malta; one of the smallest nations in the world, with one of the longest histories. Prepared for British Information Services. New York, 1964.
[14]p.

1. Economic conditions - Malta.
I. U.K. British Information Services.

341.1
:338
(41)
U54p
1961
U.K. British Information Services. (Reference Div.)
Political development in the United Kingdom dependencies. Rev. New York, 1961.
26p. (I.D 1286 (rev.))

1. Technical assistance programs (U.K.)
2. Underdeveloped countries.

330
(676)
U54k
U.K. British Information Services.
U.K. Central Office of Information.
Kenya. Prepared for British Information Services. New York, 1963.
35p.

1. Economic conditions - Kenya.
I. U.K. British Information Services.

VF
330
(595)
U54m
U.K. British Information Services.
U.K. Central Office of Information.
The meaning of Malaysia. New York, British Information Services, 1963.
15p.

1. Economic development - Malaya, Federation of. I. U.K. British Information Services.

711
(41)
U541
U.K. BRITISH INFORMATION SERVICES.
POST-WAR PLANNING IN BRITAIN. UNOFFICIAL POST-WAR PLANNING, 1939-1943. NEW YORK, BRITISH INFORMATION SERVICES, 1944.
80P.
BIBLIOGRAPHY: P.68-80.

1. PLANNING - U.K. I. TITLE.

330
(676)
U54
U.K. British Information Services. (Reference Division)
Kenya; progress and problems. New York, 1958.
25p. map. (Its I.D. 1293)

1. Economic conditions - Kenya.

330
(56)
U54
U.K. British Information Services. (Reference Division)
Middle East background. New York, 1959.
44p. (Its I.D. 1318)

1. Economic conditions - Middle East.
I. Title.

727.1
(41)
U54p
U.K. British Information Services. (Reference Div.)
Primary and secondary schools in Britain. New York, 1960.
13p. (I.D. 1299 rev.)

1. Schools - U.K.

330
(676)
U54
1960
U.K. British Information Services.
Kenya: progress and problems. Rev. New York, 1960.
28p. (I.D. 1293)

1. Economic conditions - Kenya.

711.417
(41)
U54ne
1969
U.K. British Information Services. (Reference Div.)
The new towns of Britain. New York, 1969.
26p.

1. New towns - U.K. I. Title.

727.1
(41)
U54p
1962
U.K. British Information Services. (Reference Div.)
Primary and secondary schools in Britain. Rev. New York, 1962.
13p. (I.D. 1299, rev.)

1. Schools - U.K.

727.1
(41)   U.K. British Information Services.
U54p   (Ref. Div.)
1964   Primary and secondary schools in
        Britain. Rev. New York, 1964.
        13p.   (I.D. 1299 rev.)

        1. Schools - U.K.

330
(595) U.K. British Information Services. (Reference
U54   Div.)
1961   The state of Singapore. New York, 1961.
        17p.   (Its ID 1320. Rev. Oct. 1961)

        1. Economic conditions - Singapore.

711.4
(41)   U.K. British Information Services.
U54   (Reference Div.)
1949   Town and country planning in Britain;
        the main problems, Barlow, Scott, and
2 c.   Uthwatt reports, the Planning acts, 1947,
        replanning in action, new towns. New
        York, 1949.
        43p.   (I.D. 920)

        1. City planning - U.K. I. Title.

341.1
:338   U.K. British Information Services.
(60)   Regional co-operation in British East
U54r   Africa. New York, 1959.
        13p. map, tables. (Its I.D. 1337)

        1. Technical assistance programs (U.K.) -
        Africa.   I. Title.

330
(678) U.K. British Information Services.
U54t   Tanganyika; a story of progress. New
        York, 1961.
        [40]p.

        1. Economic development - Tanganyika.
        2. Underdeveloped countries - Tanganyika.

330
(72 98) U.K. British Information Services.
U54   (Reference Division)
        Trinidad and Tobago. New York, .
        1960.
        26p. map, table. (I.D. 1356)

        1. Economic conditions - Trinidad. 2. Economic
        conditions - Tobago.

330
(664) U.K. British Information Services.
U54   Sierra Leone: a nation is born.
        New York [1961]
        [40]p.

        1. Economic conditions - Sierra Leone.

330
(678) U.K. British Information Services.
U54   (Reference Division)
        Tanganyika; the making of a nation.
        New York, 1961.
        44p.   (Its I.D. 1385)

        1. Economic conditions - Tanganyika.

330
(7298) U.K. British Information Services.
U54   Trinidad and Tobago. New York, 1962.
1962   9p.

        1. Economic conditions - Trinidad.
        2. Economic conditions - Tobago.

330
(664) U.K. British Information Services.
U54s   (Reference Div.)
        Sierra Leone: the making of a nation.
        New York, 1960.
        39p.   (Its I.D. 1371)

        1. Economic conditions - Sierra Leone.

341.1
:338   U.K. British Information Services. (Economics
U54r   Div.)
no.3   Technical assistance. Facts on Britain's
        aid to less developed countries, no. 3. New
        York, 1963.
        9p.   (Reference papers no. 3; ID 1446-3)

        1. Technical assistance programs (U.K.)
        2. Underdeveloped countries.

330
(7298) U.K. British Information Services.
U54   (Reference Division)
1962   Trinidad and Tobago: the making of a
        nation. New York, 1962.
        46p.   (I.D. 1356, July 1962)

        1. Economic conditions - Trinidad.
        2. Economic conditions - Tobago.

        U.K. British Information Services.
        (Reference Div.)
360
U54s   U.K. Central Office of Information. (Ref-
        erence Div.)
        Social services in Britain. New York,
        Reference Div., British Information Ser-
        vices,

        v.
        For complete information see main card.

        1. Social service. 2. Housing - Social
        aspects. 3. Housing - U.K. I. U.K. British
        Information Services. (Reference Div.)

711.4
(41)   U.K. British Information Services.
U54   (Reference Div.)
1951   Town and country planning. New York, 1951.
        31p.   (I.D. 920, rev.)

        1. City planning - U.K. I. Title.

330
(6761) U.K. British Information Services.
U54   (Reference Division)
        Uganda. New York, 1962.
        40p.   (I.D. 1400 January, 1962)

        Housing: p. 30-31.

        1. Economic development - Uganda.
        2. Political science - Uganda.

360
(41)   U.K. British Information Services. (Refer-
U54   ence Div.)
        Social welfare in the United Kingdom de-
        pendencies. New York, 1960.
        38p.   (Its I.D. 1347)

        1. Social welfare - U.K. 2. Community develop-
        ment - U. K. 3. Underdeveloped countries.

        U.K. British Information Services.
711
(41)   U.K. Central Office of Information.
U54   (Reference Div.)
1967   Town and country planning in Britain, 1967
        London, H.M.S.O., 1968.
        31p.   (Its Reference pamphlet 9)
        Bibliography: p. 31-32.
        Prepared for U.K. British Information
        Services.

        1. Planning - U.K. 2. U.K. - Planning.
        I. U.K. British Information Services.
        II. Title.

330
(667) U.K. British Information Services.
U54   (Reference Div.)
        Uganda: the making of a Nation.
        New York, 1962.
        50p.   (Its I.D. 1413, July 1962)

        1. Economic conditions - Uganda.

330
(595) U.K. British Information Services. (Refer-
U54   ence Division)
1959   The State of Singapore. New York, 1959.
        15p. map. (Its ID 1320)

        1. Economic conditions - Singapore.

        U.K. British Information Services. (Reference
711   Div.)
(41)   U.K. Central Office of Information.
U54   (Reference Div.)
1968   Town and country planning in Britain. Rev.
        New York, 1968.
        32p.

        Bibliography: p. 31-32.
        Prepared for U.K. British Information
        Services.
        1. Planning - U.K. I. U.K. British
        Information Services. (Reference Div.)
        II. Title.

VF
341.1
:338   U.K. British Information Services.
(60)   United Kingdom aid to Africa. New York,
U54u   1959.
        7p. tables.

        1. Technical assistance programs (U.K.) -
        Africa.

330
U54u
1960
U.K. British Information Services.
(Reference Division)
The U.K. colonial development and
welfare acts. Rev. New York, 1960.
28p. tables. (I.D. 892 (rev))

1. Economic development. 2. Underdeveloped
countries. I. Title.

VF
341.1
U54w
1960
U.K. British Information Services.
Western co-operation in brief. [rev.]
New York, 1960.
39p.

1. International organisations.

690
:331.86
(41)
U54
U.K. Building Apprenticeship and
Training Council.
Final report. London, H. M. Stationery
Off., 1957.
94 p. tables.

1. Building trades - U.K. 2. Apprenticeship

320
(41)
U54u
U.K. British Information Services.
The United Kingdom constitution, some
selected quotations. New York [1960]
36p.

1. Political science - U.K.

VF
341.1
U54w
1962
U.K. British Information Services.
Western co-operation in brief. Rev.
London, 1962.
36p.

1. International organizations.

331.86
B84
1943
U.K. BUILDING APPRENTICESHIP AND
TRAINING COUNCIL.
REPORT. 1ST-
LONDON, H.M. STAT. OFF., 1944-
V.

1. APPRENTICESHIP.

341.1
:338
(41)
U54uni
U.K. British Information Services.
The United Kingdom dependencies 1957-58
Swindon, Eng., 1958-
nos. tables.

For complete information see shelflist.

1. Technical assistance programs (U.K.)
2. British Commonwealth of Nations.

351.7
:325.3
(41)
U54w
U.K. British Information Services.
(Reference Division)
What is the Commonwealth? New York, 1962.
12p. (I.D. 1379. Feb. 1962)

1. British Commonwealth of Nations.
I. Title.

690
(41)
U54ra
U.K. Building Centre.
Report, 1967/68 - 68/69;
London, 1968 -
2 v. annual.

For Library holdings see main entry.

1. Building industry - U.K.

341.1
:338
(41)
U54un
U.K. British Information Services.
The U.K. dependencies in brief. Rev.
New York,
v. map, tables.

For complete information see shelflist.

1. Technical assistance programs (U.K.) 2. British
Commonwealth of Nations.

351.7
:325.3
(41)
U54w
1963
U.K. British Information Services.
(Reference Division)
What is the Commonwealth? New York, 1963.
11p. (I.D. 1379 (Revised) March, 1962.
(With addendum October, 1963))

1. British Commonwealth of Nations.

690.59
U54pr
U.K. Committee on Building Maintenance.
U.K. Ministry of Public Building and Works.
Profitable building maintenance; conference
papers, London, 1967. London, 1969.
338p. (R & D paper)

Jointly sponsored by Ministry of Public
Building and Works and the Mercury House
Journal, Maintenance Engineering.

1. Building maintenance. I. U.K. Committee
on Building Maintenance. II. Title.

VF
300.2
(41)
U54
U.K. British Information Services. (Information Division)
Wartime planning for physical reconstruction in Great Britain. New York, 1944.
24p. (Its ID 569)

1. Reconstruction - U.K.

330
(6781)
U54
U.K. British Information Services.
(Reference Div.)
Zanzibar. New York, 1963.
38p. (I.D. 1474)

1. Economic conditions - Zanzibar.

621.32
U54Li
U.K. BUILDING RESEARCH BOARD.
THE LIGHTING OF BUILDINGS. LONDON,
H.M. STAT. OFF., 1944.
163P. (U.K. MINISTRY OF WORKS.
POST-WAR BUILDING STUDIES NO. 12)

1. LIGHTING.

972.9
U54
U.K. British Information Services.
(Reference Division)
The West Indies; a nation in the
making. London, Cox and Sharland, 1957.
55p. maps, tables.

1. West Indies. 2. Economic conditions -
West Indies. I. Title.

330
(6781)
U54z
U.K. British Information Services.
U.K. Central Office of Information.
Zanzibar; Isle of Cloves. New York,
British Information Services, 1963.
[15]p.

1. Economic conditions - Zanzibar.
I. U.K. British Information Services.

696.1
U54P
U.K. BUILDING RESEARCH BOARD.
PLUMBING. LONDON, H.M. STAT. OFF.,
1944.
42P. (U.K. MINISTRY OF WORKS.
POST-WAR BUILDING STUDIES NO. 4)

1. PLUMBING.

VF
341.1
U54w
U.K. British Information Services.
Western co-operation in brief.
London, 1959.
40p.

1. International organizations.

VF
728.1
(41
:016)
U54b
U.K. British Information Services. Library.
A bibliography of housing and town and
country planning in Britain, being a handlist of books, pamphlets, documents and periodicals in the libraries of British Information Services, New York, and its branches at
Chicago, San Francisco and Washington. New
York, 1944.
20p. (ID 584)
1. Housing - Bibliography - U.K. 2. City
Planning - Bibliography - U.K.

699.844
U54S
U.K. BUILDING RESEARCH BOARD.
SOUND INSULATION AND ACOUSTICS.
LONDON, H.M. STAT. OFF., 1944.
79P. (U.K. MINISTRY OF WORKS.
POST-WAR BUILDING STUDIES, NO. 14)

1. ARCHITECTURAL ACOUSTICS.
2. SOUNDPROOFING.

534.83
K24   U.K. Building Research Station.
     Keighley, E   C
     Acceptability criteria for noise in large
offices. [Garston, Eng] Building Research
Station, 1970.
     [9]p.
     Reprinted from: Journal of sound and
vibration, 1970, 11(1) January pp. 83-93.

     1. Noise. 2. Office buildings. I. U.K.
Building Research Station. II. Title.

362
(41)
B76   U.K. Building Research Station.
     Stone, P   A
     Administration and costs of hospital
maintenance. Garston, Eng., Building
Research Station, Dept. of Scientific
and Industrial Research, 1964.
     [10]p. (U.K. Building Research
Station. Building research current
papers. Design series 28)
     Reprinted from: The Hospital, 1964,
vol. 60 (7), p. 411-5; (8) p. 479-84.

     1. Hospitals - U.K.   I. U.K. Building
Research Station.   II. Title.

691.54
D65   U.K. Building Research Station.
     Doleszai, K
     Applicability of the autoclave test for
evaluating the magnesia swelling of cements,
by K. Doleszai and L. Szatura. Garston, Eng.,
Building Research Station, 1971.
     [9]p. (Library communication no. 1613)
     Translated from the Hungarian and reprinted
from Epitoanyag, 1970, 22(b), 208-12.

     1. Cement. 2. Strength of materials.
I. Szatura, L., jt. au. II. U.K. Building
Research Station. III. Title. (Series)

690
G74   U.K. Building Research Station.
     Griffiths, T   J
     Accuracy in building. Garston, Eng.,
Building Research Station, Ministry of
Technology, 1966
     7-10p. (U.K. Building Research Station.
Building research current papers. Construction
series 23)

     Reprinted from: Building technology and
management, Jan., 1966.

     1. Building industry. I. U.K. Building
Research Station.   II. Title.

690
(41)
B74a   U.K. Building Research Station.
     Britten, J   R
     The advantages of time-scaled networks and
planning frames. Garston, Eng., Building
Research Station, Ministry of Technology,
1967.
     234-240p. (U.K. Building Research Station.
Building research current papers. Construction papers 41)
     Reprinted from: The National Builder, April,
1967.
     1. Building research - U.K. I. U.K. Building Research Station. II. Title.

690.072
B47a   U.K. Building Research Station.
     Bishop, D
     Architects and productivity. Garston, Eng.,
Building Research Station, Ministry of Technology, 1966.
     [13]p. (U.K. Building Research Station.
Building research current papers. Design
series 57)
     Reprinted from RIBA journal, 1966, vol. 73
(November) p. 513-18.

     1. Building construction - Labor requirements. I. U.K. Building Research Station.
II. Title.

693
M45   U.K. Building Research Station.
     Milner, R   M
     Accuracy of measurement with steel tapes.
Garston, Eng., Building Research Station,
1969.
     [3]p. (U.K. Building Research Station.
Current paper 51/69)

     Reprinted from: Building, 1969, Sept. 19,
pp. 38/139-140, 142.

     1. Building methods. I. U.K. Building
Research Station. II. Title. III. Title:
Measurement.

691.54
Z14   U.K. Building Research Station.
     Zakharov, L   A
     Aluminous-belite cement. Garston, Eng.,
Building Research Station, 1970.
     [71]p. (Library communication no. 1579)
     Translated from the Russian.

     1. Cement. I. U.K. Building Research
Station. II. Title. (Series)

621.32
U54AR   U.K. BUILDING RESEARCH STATION.
     ARCHITECTURAL PHYSICS: LIGHTING, BY
R.G. HOPKINSON. LONDON, H.M. STAT.
OFF., 1963.
     360P.

     INCLUDES BIBLIOGRAPHIES.
ERRATUM SLIP INSERTED.

     1. LIGHTING. I. HOPKINSON, RALPH
GALBRAITH. II. TITLE.

693
S72a   U.K. Building Research Station.
     Stevens, A   J
     Activity sampling on building sites.
Garston, Eng., Building Research Station,
Ministry of Public Building and Works, 1969.
     [5]p. (U.K. Building Research Station.
Current paper 16/69)
     Reprinted from: Work study, 1969, Vol. 18
(2), Feb., p. 27-33.

     1. Building methods. 2. Sampling
(Statistics) I. U.K. Building Research
Station. II. Title.

691.542
F52   U.K. Building Research Station.
     Fletcher, K   E
     The analysis of belite in Portland cement
clinker by means of an elcetron-probe microanalyser. Garston, Eng., Building Research
Station, 1969.
     167-170p. (U.K. Building Research Station.
Current paper 13/69)
     Reprinted from: Magazine of concrete research, Sept., 1968, pp. 167-170.
     1. Portland cement. I. U.K. Building
Research Station. II. Title.

699.844
P17   U.K. Building Research Station.
     Parkin, P   H
     Assisted resonance in the Royal Festival
Hall, London: 1965-1969, by P.H. Parkin and
K. Morgan. Garston, Eng., Building Research
Station, 1971.
     [11]p. (Current paper no. 17/71)
     Reprinted from: Journal of the Acoustical
Society of America, Nov. 1970; Journal of
sound and vibration, vol. 15, no. 1, 1971.

     1. Architectural acoustics. I. Morgan, K.,
jt. au. II. U.K. Building Research Station.
III. Title.

693
S72   U.K. Building Research Station.
     Stevens, A   J
     Activity sampling studies aided by
the use of an optical reader. Garston, Eng.,
Building Research Station, Ministry of
Technology, 1967.
     [9]p. (U.K. Building Research Station.
Building research current papers. Construction series no. 38)
     Reprinted from: Work study, 1967, vol. 16
(Jan.) p. 21-9.

     1. Building methods. 2. Automation. I. U.K.
Building Research Station. II. Title.

693.5
690.24
U54   United Kingdom. Building Research Station.
     Analysis of symmetric cylindrical shells;
its application to civil engineering design,
by John McNamee. London, H.M. Stat. Off.,
1955.
     84 p.

     Bibliographies.

     1.Concrete construction. 2.Roofs and roofing.
I.McNamee, John. I.Title: Symmetric cylindrical
shells.

621.9
:690
(41)
C51   U.K. Building Research Station.
     Clapp, Margaret A
     Automatic recording of crane movements.
Garston, Eng., Building Research Station,
Ministry of Technology, 1966.
     [466-8]p. (U.K. Building Research
Station. Building research current papers.
Engineering series 30)
     Reprinted from: The Engineer, 1966, vol.
221 (March 25th), pp. [466-8]

     1. Building equipment - U.K. I. U.K.
Building Research Station.
II. Title.

690.015
L21   U.K. Building Research Station.
     Lea, F   M
     Address [discussing the effects of
industrialized building on the manufacturers
of materials] to the National Council of
Building Materials Producers, Dec. 20, 1962.
[London] Building Research Station, Dept. of
Scientific and Industrial Research, 1962.
     5p.
     Cover title: Building research current
papers, Supplements 1

     1. Building research - U.K.
Building Research   I. U.K.
     Station.

690.24
K69   U.K. Building Research Station.
     Kozhinov, I   A
     Analytical study of the thermal resistance
of ventilated cavity roofs, by I.A. Kozhinov
and Yu. A. Tabunshchikov. Garston, Eng.,
Building Research Station, 1971.
     [5]p. (Library communication no. 1629)
     Translated from the Russian.

     1. Roofs and roofing. 2. Ventilation.
I. Tabunshchikov, Yu. A., jt. au. II. U.K.
Building Research Station. III. Title.
(Series)

728.100.15
(41)
U54   U.K. Building Research Station.
     BRS. Garston, Eng., 1967.
     16p.

     1. U.K. Building Research Station.
2. Housing research - U.K. 3. U.K. - Housing
research. 4. Building industry - U.K.
5. U.K. - Building industry.

691
E527   U.K. Building Research Station.
     Eldridge, H   J
     Adjustable fixings for curtain walling: a
B.R.S. survey, by H. J. Eldridge and R. B.
Bonshor. Garston, Eng., Building Research
Station, Dept. of Scientific and Industrial
Research, 1964.
     [4]p. (U.K. Building Research Station.
Building research current papers. Design
series 29)
     Reprinted from: The Builder, vol. 207
(6329), p. 493-6, 1964.
     1. Building materials.   2. Walls. I. U.K.
Building Research   Station.
     II. Title.

691
M14   U.K. Building Research Station.
     Majumdar, A   J
     Application of scanning electron
microscopy of building materials, by
A.J. Majumdar and others. Garston,
Eng., Building Research Station, 1969.
     9p. (U.K. Building Research
Station. Current paper 48/69)

     1. Building materials. I. U.K.
Building Research Station. II. Title.

728.100.15
(41)
U54   U.K. Building Research Station.
     BRS. Garston, Eng., 1967.
     16p.

     1. U.K. Building Research Station.
2. Housing research - U.K. 3. U.K. - Housing
research. 4. Building industry - U.K.
5. U.K. - Building industry.

621.32
165   U.K. Building Research Station.
    Longmore, J
      BRS daylight protractors. London H.M.S.O.,
    1968.
      25p.

      At head of title: Ministry of Public Build-
    ing and Works, Building Research Station.

      1. Lighting. I. U.K. Building Research
    Station. II. Title: Daylight protractors.

691.542
S71   U.K. Building Research Station.
    Stahel, A
      The behaviour of magnesium in clinker under
    different cooling conditions, by A. Stahel
    and W. Schramli. Garston, Eng., Building
    Research Station, 1970.
      [13]p. (Library communication no. 1593)
    Translated from the German and reprinted
    from Zement-Kalk-Gips, 1969, 22 (9), 407-13.

      1. Portland cement. I. Schramli, W., jt. au.
    II. U.K. Building Research Station.
    III. Title. (Series)

690.091.82
H68bri   U.K. Building Research Station.
    Howel, B   F
      British and continental standards com-
    pared for domestic fittings and equipment.
    Garston, Eng., Building Research Station,
    Ministry of Technology, 1968.
      201-205p. (U.K. Building Research
    Station. Current paper 34/68)
      Reprinted from: Building, Feb., 1968.
      1. Building standards. 2. Building
    materials - Standards and specifications.
    I. U.K. Building Research Station.
    II. Title.

690
(41)
B47   U.K. Building Research Station.
    Bishop, D
      The background to management studies by
    BRS. Garston, Eng., Building Research
    Station, Ministry of Public Building and
    Works, 1968.
      11p. (U.K. Building Research Station.
    Current papers 60/68)
      Bibliography: p. 10-11.
      1. Building industry - U.K. 2. U.K. -
    Building industry. 3. Industrial management.
    I. Title. II. U.K. Building Research
    Station.

690.22
S45b   U.K. Building Research Station.
    Simms, L   G
      The behavior of no-fines concrete panels as
    the infill in reinforced concrete frames.
    Garston, Eng., Building Research Station,
    Ministry of Public Building and Works, 1968.
      8p. (U.K. Building Research Station.
    Current paper 22/68)
      Reprinted from Civil engineering and public
    works review, Nov., 1967.
      1. Walls. 2. Concrete, Reinforced. I. U.K.
    Building Research Station. II. Civil
    engineering and public works review.
    III. Title.

728
551.5
S29   U.K. Building Research Station.
    Sexton, D   E
      Building aerodynamics. Garston, Eng.,
    Building Research Station, Ministry of
    Public Building and Works, 1968.
      16-21p. (U.K. Building Research Station.
    Current paper 64 68)
      Reprinted from: Proceedings of the CIB
    Symposium on Weathertight Joints for Walls,
    held in Oslo, September 25-28, 1967.
      Bibliography: p. 20-21.
      1. Architecture and climate. 2. Buildings -
    Wind stresses. I. U.K. Building Re-
    search Station. II. Title. III. Title:
    Aerodynamics.

614.8
:690
T36   U.K. Building Research Station.
    Thomas, F   G
      Basic parameters and terminology in the
    consideration of structural safety.
    Garston, Eng., Building Research Station,
    Dept. of Scientific and Industrial Research,
    1964.
      7p. (U.K. Building Research Station.
    Building research current papers.
    Engineering series 20)
      Reprinted from: C.I.B. Bulletin, 1964
    (3), pp. 4-12.

                (Continued on next card)

690.015
(41
:016)
U541
no.
219   U.K. Building Research Station.
      Belt conveyors for concrete. Garston, Eng.,
    Building Research Station, 1969.
      3p. (Its Library bibliography 219)

      1. Concrete construction - Bibl. I. U.K.
    Building Research Station. II. Title.

690.091.82
(494)
C41   U.K. Building Research Station.
    Cibula, Evelyn.
      Building control in Switzerland.
    Garston, Eng., Building Research Station,
    1970.
      10p. (U.K. Building Research Station.
    Current paper CP 21/70)

      1. Building codes - Switzerland.
    I. U.K. Building Research Station.
    II. Title.

614.8
:690
T36   Thomas, F   G   Basic parameters
    and terminology...1964.   (Card 2)

      1. Building construction - Accidents.
    I. U.K. Building Research Station.

Mrs. Landis
690.015
(41:016)
U541
no. 133   Gt. Brit. Building Research Station.
      A bibliography of native housing in Africa
    (prepared by G.A. Atkinson) Garston, Eng.,
    Nov. 1948.
      4 l. (Its Library bibliography no. 133)

      Annotated.
      Processed.

    1.Housing-Africa. 2.Housing in the tropics-Bibl.
    I.Atkinson, G.A. II.Series.

690.091.82
(43)
C41   U.K. Building Research Station.
    Cibula, Evelyn.
      Building control in West Germany.
    Garston, Eng., Building Research Station,
    1970.
      39p. (U.K. Building Research Station.
    Current paper CP10/70)
      Bibliography: p. 24-26.

      1. Building codes - Germany. I. U.K.
    Building Research Station. II. Title.

VF
690.37
F71   Great Britain Building Research Station.
TApr.1950   Atkinson, G   Anthony
      Bâtir sous les tropiques. [Paris, France]
    Centre Scientifique et Technique du Bâtiment,
    Service de l'Habitat Intertropical [Apr. 1950]
      34 l. graphs. (France. Centre Scientifique
    et Technique du Bâtiment. Service de l'Habitat
    Intertropical. Traductions.)
      English title: Research into housing in tropical
    countries, especially in the Commonwealth.
      Bibliographical footnotes.
      Mimeographed.
    1.Housing in the tropics. I.Gt. Brit. Building Re-
    search Station. II.Series.

691.32
C34   U.K. Building Research Station.
    Chigerovich, M   I
      Bitumening concrete to increase its
    corrosion resistance, by M.I. Chigerovich
    et al. Garston, Eng., Building Research
    Station, 1971.
      5p. (Library communication no. 1639)
    Translated from the German.

      1. Concrete. I. U.K. Building Research
    Station. II. Title. (Series)

690.015
(41
:016)
U541
no.239   U.K. Building Research Station.
      Building in warm climates. London, 1970.
      18p. (Its Library bibliography no. 239)

      1. Housing in the tropics - Bibl.
    I. Title.

691.8
C71   U.K. Building Research Station.
    Craig, C   N
      Battery-cast cladding panels. Garston, Eng.,
    Building Research Station, Ministry of Tech-
    nology, 1968.
      171-174p. (U.K. Building Research Station
    current paper 36/68)
      Reprinted from Building, Nov., 1967.

      1. Panels. 2. Building methods. I. U.K.
    Building Research Station. II. Title.

690.282
M14   U.K. Building Research Station.
    Mainstone, R   J
      The breakage of glass windows by gas
    explosions. Garston, Eng., Building Re-
    search Station, 1971.
      [17]p. (U.K. Building Research Station.
    Current paper CP 26/71)

      1. Windows. 2. Glass. I. U.K. Building
    Research station. II. Title.

690.091.82
(4)
A74   U.K. Building Research Station.
    Atkinson, G   A
      Building law in Western Europe: how
    responsibility for safety and good per-
    formance is shared. Garston, Eng.,
    Building Research Station, 1971.
      [17]p. (U.K. Building Research Station.
    Current paper 6/71)

      1. Building codes - Europe.
    I. U.K. Building Research Station.
    II. Title.

693.5
H27   U.K. Building Research Station.
    Herbert, M   R   M
      Battery casting in concrete moulds: selection
    of mould oils. Garston, Eng., Building
    Research Station, Ministry of Technology, 1966.
      [4p.] (U.K. Building Research Station.
    Building research current papers. Construction
    series 24)
      Reprinted from: Contract Journal, Feb., 1966,
    vol. 209 p. 698-700.

      1. Concrete construction. I. U.K. Building
    Research Station. II. Title.

720
072   U.K. Building Research Station.
    O'Reilly, J   J   N
      Briefing and design - a case study.
    Garston, Eng. Building Research Station,
    Ministry of Public Building and Works, 1969.
      [7]p. (U.K. Building Research Station.
    Current paper 34/69)
      Reprinted from: Architects' journal,
    June 18, 1969, pp. 1637-1643.
      1. Architecture - Designs and plans.
    I. U.K. Building Research Station.
    II. Title.

690.015
(41
:016)
U541
no.230   U.K. Building Research Station.
    Atkinson, G   A
      Building legislation in Scandinavia;
    sources of information, by G.A. Atkinson
    and Miriam K. Gray. Garston, Eng.,
    Building Research Station, 1969.
      16p. (U.K. Building Research Station.
    Library bibliography 230)

      1. Building codes - Scandinavia - Bibl.
    I. U.K. Building Research Station.
    II. Gray, Miriam K., jt. au. III. Title.

590.015
(41)
U54bu
U.K. BUILDING RESEARCH STATION.
U.K. Building Research Station.
Building Research Station, 1968.
H.M.S.O., 1969-
v.

1. Building research - U.K. 2. U.K.
Building Research Station.

690.015
(41)
U54bu

2C-68
U.K. Building Research Station.
Building Research Station, 1968r
H.M.S.O., 1969-
v.

1. Building research - U.K. 2. U.K.
Building Research Station.

690.015
U54
U.K. Building Research Station.
U.K. Dept. of Scientific and Industrial
Research.
The Building Research Station, its history,
organisation and work, by F. M. Lea. London,
1959.
12p. illus.

"Originally published in The Financial Times,
Supplement on the Building Industry, 14th July,
1958.

1. Building research - U.K. 2. U.K. Building Research Station. I. Lea, F. M.

S
Gt. Brit. Building Research Station.
Building Research Station digest no. 1-
Dec. 1948- London, H.M. Stationery
Office, 1948-
v. illus.

Indexes: nos. 1-12 in no. 13.
For full information see Periodical Kardex
file.

1. Building research-Gt. Brit. I.Gt. Brit. Building Research Station.

699.844
W47
U.K. Building Research Station.
Wise, A F E
Buildings in noisy areas: interaction
of acoustic and thermal design. Garston,
Eng., Building Research Station, 1969.
7p. (U.K. Building Research Station.
Current paper 43/69)

Paper presented to the Institution
of Heating and Ventilating Engineers'
Symposium on Engineering in the Home, London,
4 March 1969, pp. 20-24.

1. Sound proofing.
(cont'd on next card)

699.844
W47
Wise, A F E
Buildings...1969 (Card 2)

I. U.K. Building Research Station.
II. Title.

691
E52
U.K. Building Research Station.
Eldridge, H J
The CIB master list of properties: an out-
line of its scope and limitations. Garston,
Eng., Building Research Station, Ministry of
Public Building and Works, 1968.
155-157p. (U.K. Building Research Station.
Current paper 68/68)
Reprinted from: Building, 1968, June 14th,
pp. 155-6, 158)
1. Building materials. I. U.K. Building
Research Station. II. Title.

691.54
K71
U.K. Building Research Station.
Kravchenko, I V
Calcining clinker in a fluidized bed, by
I.V. Kravchenko and others. Garston, Eng.,
Building Research Station, 1969.
[13]p. (U.K. Building Research Station.
Library communication no. 1529)
Translated from the Russian. Tr. Gos.
Vses Nauchno-Issled. Inst. Tsem. Prom., 1967,
(22) 63-83.

1. Cement. I. U.K. Building Research
Station. II. Title. (Series)

621.9
W15
U.K. Building Research Station.
Wander, R
Cartridge-operated fixing tools: some safe-
ty considerations. Garston, Eng., Building
Research Station, Ministry of Technology,
1967.
7p. (U.K. Building Research Station.
Building research current papers. Construc-
tion series 36)
Reprinted from: The Illustrated carpenter
and builder, 1967, vol. 156 (Jan. 27) p. 194-6.

1. Tools. 2. Building construction - Accidents.
I. U.K. Building Research Station.
II. Title.

691.32
S36
U.K. Building Research Station.
Short, A
The CEB recommendations and the structural
use of lightweight concrete. Garston, Eng.,
Building Research Station, Ministry of Public
Building and Works, 1968.
284p. (U.K. Building Research Station.
Currenty paper SfB Gf4)

1. Concrete. I. U.K. Building Research
Station. II. Title.

691.328
S36
U.K. Building Research Station.
Short A
The CEB recommendations and the structural
use of lightweight concrete. Garston, Eng.,
1968.
281-284p. (U.K. Building Research Station.
Current paper 9/68)

1. Concrete, Reinforced. I. U.K. Building
Research Station. II. Title.

693.5
M25c
U.K. Building Research Station.
Menzies, J B
CP 117 and shear connectors in steel-
concrete composite beams made with normal
density light-weight concrete. Garston,
Eng., Building Research Station [1971]
[17]p. (U.K. Building Research Station.
Current paper no. 22/71)
Reprinted from: The structural engineer,
vol. 49, no. 3, March 1971, pp. 137-153.
1. Concrete construction. 2. Adhesives.
I. U.K. Building Research Station.
II. Title.

691.54
S23c
U.K. Building Research Station.
Scholze, H
Carbonate-containing and sulphate-containing
compounds in cement manufacture, by H. Scholze
and U. Hildebrandt. Garston, Eng., Building
Research Station, 1971.
[15]p. (Library communication no. 1617)
Bibliography: p. 10-12.
Translated from the German.
1. Cement. I. Hildebrandt, U., jr. au.
II. U.K. Building Research Station.
III. Title. (Series)

691.328
N67c
U.K. Building Research Station.
Nosenko, N E
The centralization of the manufacture of
reinforcement for concrete; a task for the
immediate future, by N.E. Nosenko and A.I.
Pichugin. Garston, Eng., Building Research
Station, 1970.
5p. (U.K. Building Research Station.
Library communication no. 1559)
Translated from the Russian [and reprinted
from] Beton i zhelezobeton, 1969, (8), 33-36.
1. Concrete, Reinforced. I. Pichugin, A.I.,
jt. au. II. U.K. Building Research Station.
III. Title. (Series)

693
U54
U.K. Building Research Station.
Changing appearance of buildings. London,
H.M.S.O., 1967.
64p.

1. Building methods. 2. Architecture - Design.
3. Building materials - Climatic effects.
I. Title.

620.1
U72
U.K. Building Research Station.
Ur'ev, N B
Characteristics of the mechanism of failure
of glass fibre on formation of new crystals,
by N.B. Ur'ev and others. Garston, Eng.,
Building Research Station, 1968.
[5]p. (Library communication no. 1425)
Translated from the Russian and reprinted
from Doklady Akademii Nauk SSSR, 1967, 177 (6),
1404-6.
1. Strength of materials. I. U.K. Building
Research Station. II. Title: Failure of glass
fibre. III. Title. (Series)

712.25
(41)
H65ch
U.K. Building Research Station.
Hole, W V
Children's play on housing estates: a
summary of two B.R.S. studies, by W.V. Hole
and A. Miller. Garston, Eng., Building
Research Station, Ministry of Technology,
1966.
[8]p. (U.K. Building Research Station.
Building research current papers. Design
series 46)
Reprinted from Architects' journal, June,
1966, p. 1529-33; 1535-6.

1. Recreation - U.K. 2. Children.
I. U.K. Building Research Station.
II. Miller, A., jt.au. III. Title.

712.25
(41)
H65
U.K. Building Research Station.
Hole, Vere.
Children's play on housing estates.
London, H.M.S. Stat. Off., 1966.
40p. (U.K. Building Research
Station. National building studies. Re-
seach paper 39)

1. Recreation - U.K. 2. Children.
I. U.K. Building Research Station.
II. Title.

691.328
S56
U.K. Building Research Station.
Snowdon, L C
Classifying reinforcing bars for bond
strength. Garston, Eng., Building Research
Station, 1970.
[22]p. (Current paper 36/70)

Edited version of paper no. 223/70 prepared
for the Building Research Station seminar
Deformed Bars in Concrete.

1. Concrete, Reinforced. I. U.K. Building
Research Station. II. Title.

S
United Kingdom. Building Research Station.
Colonial Liaison Officer.
Colonial building notes, no. 1-
June 1950- Prepared by the
Colonial Liaison Officer. Garston, Eng.,
Building Research Station, 1951-

For full information see Periodical Kardex file

1. Building research-U.K. I.U.K. Building Research
Station. Colonial Liaison Officer.

690.015
(41
:016)
U541
no. 232
U.K. Building Research Station.
Colour in buildings. Garston,
Eng., 1969.
14p. (Its Library bibliography
232)

1. Color - Bibl. I. Title.

690.072
K45

U.K. Building Research Station.
Kinniburgh, W
A comparison of times required to build walls in building units of various sizes. Garston, Eng., Building Research Station, 1968.
4p. (U.K. Building Research Station. Current paper CP 77/68)
Reprinted from: Building, Oct. 11, 1968, pp. 151-152, 155-156.
1. Building construction - Labor requirements. 2. Walls. I. U.K. Building Research Station. II. Title.

690.015
(47)
M44

U.K. Building Research Station.
Mikhailov, K V
The Concrete and Reinforced Concrete Research Institute (NIIZhB) of the USSR Gosstroi (NIIZhB Gosstroya SSSR) Garston, Eng., Building Research Station, 1970.
6p. (U.K. Building Research Station. Library communication no. 1564)
Translated from the Russian [and reprinted from] Beton i zhelezobeton, 1970, 16(4), 4-6.
1. Building research - U.S.S.R. 2. Concrete construction - U.S.S.R. I. U.K. Building Research Station. II. Title. (Series)

699.841
U54

U.K. Building Research Station.
U.S.S.R. Gosudarstvennyi komitet soveta ministrov.
Construction in earthquake regions: design code SN & P II-A.12-69. Garston, Eng., Building Research Station, 1970.
[39]p. (Library communication no. 1587)
Translated from the Russian and reprinted from Stroitel'nye normy i pravila, Chast' II, razdel A, glava 12.
1. Earthquake resistant construction. I. U.K. Building Research Station. II. Title. (Series)

693.2
B87

U.K. Building Research Station.
Burhouse, P
Composite action between brick panel walls and their supporting beams. Garston, Eng., Building Research Station, 1970.
[30]p.
Reprinted from: Proceeding of the Institution of Civil Engineers, June, 1969. p. 175-194.
1. Brick construction. 2. Walls. I. U.K. Building Research Station. II. Title.

690.022
L18

U.K. Building Research Station.
Laursen, F B
Concrete elements: dimensional deviations. Garston, Eng., Building Research Station, 1970.
6p. (U.K. Building Research Station. Library communication no. 1563)
Translated from the Danish [and reprinted from] Byggeindustrien, 1970, 21 (4), 132-4.
1. Prefabricated construction. 2. Concrete construction. I. U.K. Building Research Station. II. Title. (Series)

534.83
S23

U.K. Building Research Station.
Schneider, P
A contribution to the question of system noises. Garston, Eng., Building Research Station, 1968.
3p. (U.K. Building Research Station. Library Communication 1440)
Translated and reprinted from: Proceedings 3rd International Congress on Acoustics.
1. Noise. 2. Plumbing. I. U.K. Building Research Station. II. Title. (Series)

691.54
M42

U.K. Building Research Station.
Midgley, H G
The composition and possible structure of the quaternary phase in high-alumina cement and its relation to other phases in the system CaO-MgO-Al_2-Al_2O_3. Garston, Eng., Building Research Station, Ministry of Public Building and Works, 1968.
[7]p. (U.K. Building Research Station. Current paper 75/68)
Reprinted from: Transactions of the British Ceramic Society, Jan., 1968. pp. 1-14.
1. Cement. I. U.K. Building Research Station. II. Title.

690.25
E527

U.K. Building Research Station.
Eldridge, H J
Concrete floors on shale hardcore. Garston, Eng., Building Research Station, Dept. of Scientific and Industrial Research, 1964.
[2]p. (U.K. Building Research Station. Building research current papers. Design series 30)
Reprinted from: The Municipal journal, vol. 72(3734)1964, p. 2893-4, 2896
1. Floors and flooring. 2. Concrete floors. I. U.K. Building Research Station.

691.54
G63

U.K. Building Research Station.
Goggi, G
Contribution to the study of the soundness of cements. Garston, Eng., Building Research Station, 1971.
[19]p. (Library communication no. 1609)
Translated from the German.
1. Cement. I. U.K. Building Research Station. II. Title. (Series)

691.542
M42

U.K. Building Research Station.
Midgley, H G
The composition of alite (tricalcium silicate) in a portland cement clinker. Garston, Eng., 1968.
44p. (U.K. Building Research Station. Current paper 7/68)
Reprinted from: Magazine of concrete research, Mar., 1968. pp. 41-44.
1. Portland cement. I. Title. II. U.K. Building Research Station.

693.002.22
(437)
S29
N.c.1
Laf.c.2

U.K. Building Research Station.
Seymour-Walker, K J
Concrete panel production in Czechoslovakia. Garston, Eng., Building Research Station, Ministry of Technology, 1967.
11p. (U.K. Building Research Station current papers. Construction series 37)
First published in Interbuild, 1967, vol. 14 (Feb.) pp. 16-19.
1. Prefabricated construction - Czechoslovakia. 2. Panels. 3. Concrete construction. I. U.K. Building Research Station. II. Title.

691.542
T26

U.K. Building Research Station.
Teoreanu, I
Correlations between the mineralizing effect of substances on Portland cement clinker formation and the periodic system of the elements, by I. Teoreanu and Tran van Huynh. Garston, Eng., Building Research Station, 1971.
[11]p. (Library communication no. 1650)
Translated from the German.
1. Portland cement. I. Tran van Huynh, jt. au. II. U.K. Building Research Station. III. Title. (Series)

690
(41)
B74

U.K. Building Research Station.
Britten, J R
Computerising resource needs. Garston, Eng., Building Research Station, Ministry of Technology, 1967.
[4]p. (U.K. Building Research Station. Building research current papers. Construction series 39)
Reprinted from: Building, 1967, Feb. 17, p. 125, 6, 9, 130.
1. Building research - U.K. 2. Automation. I. U.K. Building Research Station. II. Title.

699.82
B15

U.K. Building Research Station.
Ball, E F
Condensation in large panel construction: avoidance in buildings investigated at B.R.S. Garston, Eng., Building Research Station, Dept. of Scientific and Industrial Research, 1964.
5p. (U.K. Building Research Station. Building research current papers. Design series 24)
Reprinted from: Builder, vol. 206 (6314), 1964, pp. 1093-7.
1. Moisture condensation. 2. Panels. I. U.K. Building Research Station.

691.7
:620.19
R69

U.K. Building Research Station.
Rozenfel'd, I L
Corrosion and coating of metals. Garston, Eng., Building Research Station, 1967.
8p. (U.K. Building Research Station. Library communication no. 1567)
Translated from the Russian.
1. Corrosion. 2. Metals. I. U.K. Building Research Station. II. Title. (Series)

690.015
(41
:016)
U541
no.238

U.K. Building Research Station.
Concerning methods of calculating for depreciation of buildings. London, 1970.
6p. (Its Library bibliography no. 238)
1. Depreciation and obsolescence (Building) - Bibl. I. Title.

699.82
P71

U.K. BUILDING RESEARCH STATION.
PRATT, A W
CONDENSATION IN SHEETED ROOFS. LONDON, H.M. STAT. OFF., 1958.
40P. ILLUS. (U.K. BUILDING RESEARCH STATION. NATIONAL BUILDING STUDIES RESEARCH PAPER NO. 23)
1. MOISTURE CONDENSATION. 2. ROOFS AND ROOFING. I. U.K. BUILDING RESEARCH STATION. II. TITLE.

690.282
P22

U.K. Building Research Station.
Pedder-Smith, D W
Cost benefits from variety reduction in standard steel windows. Garston, Eng., Building Research Station, 1971.
10p. (U.K. Building Research Station. Current paper CP 39/71)
1. Windows. 2. Building materials - Prices. I. U.K. Building Research Station. II. Title.

690.015
(41
:016)
U541
no.235

U.K. Building Research Station.
Concerning the application of damp-proof courses to existing buildings. Garston, Eng., 1970.
13p. (Its Library bibliography no. 235)
1. Waterproofing - Bibl. I. Title: The application of damp-proof courses to existing buildings. (Series)

693.5
B87

U.K. Building Research Station.
Burhouse, P
Connexions (joints) in structural concrete. Garston, Eng., Building Research Station, Ministry of Public Building and Works, 1967.
16p. (U.K. Building Research Station. Building research current papers. Engineering series 46)
Reprinted from: Proceedings of the British Concrete Federations Fifth International Congress, London, 1966.
1. Concrete construction. 2. Building methods. 3. Panels. I. U.K. Building Research Station. II. Title.

690.512.2
(41)
N87c

U.K. Building Research Station.
Nuttall, J F
Critical path method applied to building site control by J. F. Nuttall and E. E. Amos. Garston, Eng., Building Research Station, Dept. of Scientific and Industrial Research, 1964.
[12]p. (U.K. Building Research Station. Building research current papers. Construction series 12)
Reprinted from: Builder, vol. 207 (6327), 1964, p. 381-92.
1. Site selection - U.K. 2. Building industry - U.K. I. Amos, E. E., jt. au. II. U.K. Building Research Station.

U.K. Building Research Station.

691.322
G87   Gutt, W
Crystallisation of merwinite from melilite compositions. Garston, Eng., Building Research Station, Ministry of Public Building and Works, 1968.
840-841p. (U.K. Building Research Station. Current paper CP 80/68)
1. Concrete aggregates. I. Title. II. U.K. Building Research Station.

U.K. Building Research Station.

711
(41)
S76   Stone, P A
Decision techniques for town development. Garston, Eng., Building Research Station, Ministry of Technology, 1964.
16p. (U.K. Building Research Station. Building research current papers. Design series 37)
Reprinted from Operational research quarterly, September, 1964, p. 185-205.
1. Planning - U.K. 2. City planning - U.K. I. U.K. Building Research Station. II. Title.

Mrs. Landis
690.015
(41:016)
U541
no. 142   Gt. Brit. Building Research Station.
The design of buildings for warm climates. Garston, Feb. 1950.
17 l. (Its Library bibliography no. 142)
Processed.
1. Architecture, Domestic-Tropics. 2. Housing in the tropics-Bibl. I. Title. II. Series.

699.83
E17d   U.K. Building Research Station.
Eaton, K J
Damage due to tornadoes in SE England 25 January 1971. Garston, Eng., Building Research Station, 1971.
8p. (U.K. Building Research Station. Current paper no. 27/71)
1. Buildings - Wind stresses. I. U.K. Building Research Station. II. Title.

691.421
B87   U.K. Building Research Station.
Burland, J B
Deformation of soft clay beneath loaded areas. Garston, Eng., Building Research Station, 1970.
10p. (U.K. Building Research Station. Current paper CP 5/70)
Reprinted from: Proceedings of the 7th International Conference on Soil Mechanics and Foundation Engineering, Mexico, 1969, pp. 55-63.
1. Clay. 2. Strains and stresses. I. U.K. Building Research Station. II. Title.

U.K. Building Research Station.

690.22
H15d
Engl.   Hallquist, Age.
Design of masonry walls subject to wind forces, by A. Hallquist and G. Grandheim. Garston, Eng., Building Research Station, 1971.
15p. (Library communication no. 1627)
Translated from the Norwegian.
1. Walls. 2. Buildings - Wind stresses. I. Granheim, G., jt. au. II. U.K. Building Research Station. III. Title. (Series)

699.82
R65   U.K. Building Research Station.
Rönning, Mats.
Damp and water insulation. Garston, Eng., Building Research Station, 1968.
6p. (Library communication no. 1430)
Translated from the Swedish and reprinted from Byggmästaren, 1968, 47 (March), 27-30.
1. Waterproofing. 2. Moisture condensation. I. U.K. Building Research Station. II. Title. (Series)

U.K. Building Research Station.

691
(41)
M12   Mack, G W
Demands on rubbers in building. Garston, Eng., Building Research Station, Ministry of Technology, 1964.
9p. (U.K. Building Research Station. Building research current papers. Design series 36)
Reprinted from Institution of the Rubber Industry Transactions and proceedings, 1964. Oct., 1964. p. 134-44.
1. Building materials - Building Research. U.K. I. U.K. Building Research Station. II. Title.

624.043
K68   U.K. BUILDING RESEARCH STATION.
Kovari, K
The design of underground structures: the secondary stress and strain state of an inhomogeneous elastic-ideally plastic material near a lined underground cavity. Garston, Eng., Building Research Station, 1970.
[33]p. (Library communication no. 1578)
Translated from the German and reprinted from Schweizerische Bauzeitung, 1969, 87 (37), 687-97.
1. Strains and stresses. I. U.K. Building Research Station. II. Title: Underground structures. III. Title. (Series)

VF
690.22
B84   U.K. Building Research Station.
Damp-proof course insertion. London, H.M. Stat. Off., 1958.
[6]p. illus. (Its Digest 107)
1. Walls. I. Title.

U.K. Building Research Station.

727.1
(485)
H65   Holmberg, I
The dependence of performance in school on classroom temperature, by I. Holmberg and D. Wyon, Translated from the Swedish by P.J. Elvin. Garston, Eng., Building Research Station, Ministry of Technology, 1968.
16p. (U.K. Building Research Station. Library communication 1417)
Report no. 55 of the Pedagogisk-psykologiska Institutionen, Lärarhögskolan Fack, Malmo, 23 October 1967.
(Cont'd on next card)

534.83
S23d   U.K. Building Research Station.
Scholes, W E
Designing against noise from road traffic, by W.E. Scholes and J.W. Sargent. Garston, Eng., Building Research Station, 1971.
22p. (Current paper 20/71)
1. Noise. 2. Traffic. I. Sargent, J.W., jt. au. II. U.K. Building Research Station. III. Title.

U.K. Building Research Station.

696.92
H66   Hopkinson, R G
Daylight as a cause of glare. Garston, Eng., Building Research Station, Dept. of Scientific and Industrial Research, 1964.
[5]p. (U.K. Building Research Station, Dept. of Scientific and Industrial Research. Building research current papers. Design series 27)
Reprinted from: Light and lighting, vol. 56(11) p. 322-6, 1964.
1. Daylight. 2. Lighting. I. U.K. Building Research Station.

727.1
(485)
H65   Holmberg, I
The dependence...1968. (Card 2)
1. Schools - Sweden. 2. Ventilation. 3. Heating - Sweden. I. Wyon, D., jt. au. II. U.K. Building Research Station. III. Title.

621.32
M17   U.K. Building Research Station.
Matveev, A B
Determining luminosity in terms of threshold increments, by A.B. Matveev and I.L. Tokhadze. Garston, Eng., Building Research Station, 1968.
[7]p. (Library communication no. 1428)
Translated from the Russian and reprinted from Svetotekhnika, 1965, 11 (12), 10-14.
1. Lighting. I. Tokhadze, I.L., jt. au. II. U.K. Building Research Station. III. Title. (Series)

621.32
G87   U.K. Building Research Station.
Gusev, N M
The daylighting of buildings. Garston, Eng., Building Research Station, 1970.
5p. (U.K. Building Research Station. Library communication no. 1554)
Translated from the Russian [and reprinted from] Svetotekhnika, 1967, 13 (9), 1-5.
1. Lighting. I. U.K. Building Research Station. II. Title. (Series)

624.131
T36   U.K. Building Research Station.
Thomas, H S H
The design, construction and performance of a vibrating-wire earth pressure cell, by H.S.H. Thomas and W.H. Ward. Garston, Eng., Building Research Station, 1969.
[16]p. (U.K. Building Research Station. Current paper 13/69)
Reprinted from: Geotechnique, Mar. 1969, p. 39-51.
1. Soils. 2. Strains and stresses. I. Ward, W.H., jt. au. II. U.K. Building Research Station. III. Title.

691.54
S23   U.K. Building Research Station.
Schwiete, H -E.
Determining the open porosity of hardened cement paste, by H.-E. Schwiete and U. Ludwig. Garston, Eng., Building Research Station, 1971.
[35]p. (Library communication no. 1626)
Translated from the German.
Bibliography: p. 13-14.
1. Cement. I. Ludwig, U., jt. au. II. U.K. Building Research Station. III. Title. (Series)

U.K. Building Research Station.

711.4
(41)
L28   Levin, P H
Decision making in urban design. (Text of a talk given to a meeting of the Design Research Society on April 27th, 1966, London) Garston, Eng., Building Research Station, Ministry of Technology, 1966.
12p. (U.K. Building Research Station. Building research current papers. Design series 49)
1. City planning - U.K. 2. Landscape architecture. I. U.K. Building Research Station. III. Title.

U.K. Building Research Station.

352
(41)
S76d   Stone, P A
Design evaluation for a hospital building. Garston, Eng., Building Research Station, Dept. of Scientific and Industrial Research, 1964.
[6]p. (U.K. Building Research Station. Building research current papers. Design series 31)
Reprinted from: The Architects' Journal, vol. 140(10) 1964, p. 553-8.
1. Hospitals - U.K. I. U.K. Building Research Station.

621.643
C51d   U.K. Building Research Station.
Clarke, N W B
The development and use of modern flexible joints for underground pipelines. Garston, Eng., Building Research Station, Dept. of Scientific and Industrial Research, 1964.
[28]p. (U.K. Building Research Station. Building Research. Current papers. Engineering series 13)
Reprinted from: Institution of Public Health Engineers Journal, 1964, vol. 63 (2) 1964. p. 108-32.
(Cont'd. on next card)

621.643
C51d   Clarke, N W B   The develop-
            ment and use of modern flexible joints
            for underground pipelines ... (Card 2)

            1. Pipes. 2. Engineering.
       I. U.K. Building Research Station.
       II. Title.

Building Research Station digest no. 1-
    Dec. 1948-   London, H.M. Stationery
    Office, 1948-
       v.   illus.

    Indexes: nos. 1-12 in no. 13.
    For full information see Periodical Kardex
file.

    1. Building research-Gt. Brit. I.Gt. Brit. Build-
ing Research Station.

693.97   U.K. Building Research Station.
M45   Milner, R M
            Dimensional variations in light steel
            frames. Garston, Eng. Building Research
            Station, 1969.
            5p. @U.K. Building Research Station.
       Current paper CP 18/69)
            Reprinted from: Building, Feb. 21, 1968,
       vol. 216 (6562), pp. 8/155-8/156, 8/159-
       6/160.
            1. Steel construction. 2. Schools.
       I. U.K. Building Research Station.
       II. Title.

691.54   U.K. Building Research Station.
K18   Kawert, K
            Development of a shrinkage; compensated
       cement. Garston, Eng., Building Research
       Station. Library communication no. 1555)
       Translated from German [and reprinted from]
       Zement-Kalk-Gips, 1969, 22 (10), 457-61.

            1. Cement. I. U.K. Building Research
       Station. II. Title. (Series)

693.97   U.K. Building Research Station.
B12   Baehre, R
            The dimensional accuracy of steel structures.
       Garston, Eng., Building Research Station, 1970.
       [15]p. (Library communication no. 1592)

            Translated from the Swedish and reprinted
       from Byggmastaren, 1970, 49 (5), 22-26.

            1. Steel construction. 2. Quality control.
       I. U.K. Building Research Station. II. Title.
       (Series)

621.32   U.K. Building Research Station.
K65   Konig, O
            A direct reading daylight factor meter, by
       O. Konig and J. Krochmann. Garston, Eng.,
       Building Research Station, 1970.
            4p. (U.K. Building Research Station.
       Library communication no. 1569)
            Translated from the German [and reprinted
       from] Lichttechnik, 1970, 22 (4), 183-5.

            1. Lighting. I. Krochman, J., jt. au.
       II. U.K. Building Research Station.
       III. Title. (Series)

621.9   U.K. Building Research Station.
:590 Webb, J   T
W21   Development of an experimental press for
       large concrete units. Garston, Eng., Build-
       ing Research Station, Ministry of Technology
       [1966?]
            5p. (U.K. Building Research Station.
       Building research current papers. Construc-
       tion series 27)

            1. Building equipment. 2. Concrete.
       I. U.K. Building Research Station.
       II. Title.

690.091.82   U.K. Building Research Station.
A37   Agri, O
            Dimensional control; an end in itself?
       Garston, Eng., Building Research Station,
       1971.
            [9]p. (Library communication no. 1620)
       Translated from the Swedish.

            1. Building standards. I. U.K.
       Building Research Station. II. Title.
       (Series)

697
(41)   U.K. Building Research Station.
L15   Langdon, F J
            Discomfort in schools from overheating in
       summer, by F.J. Langdon and A.G. Loudon.
       [Garston, Eng.] Building Research Station,
       1970.
            [10]p. (U K. Building Research Station.
       Current paper 19/70)
            Reprinted from: The Journal of the Institution
       of Heating and Ventilating Engineers, 1970,
       vol. 37, March, pp. 265-274.
            1. Heating - U.K. 2. School management and
       organization I. Loudon, A.G., jt. au. II. U.K.
       Building Research Station. III. Title.

693.5   U.K. Building Research Station.
S29d Seymour-Walker, K J
            Development of pressed concrete panels, by
       K.J. Seymour-Walker and D.J.T. Webb. Garston,
       Eng., Building Research Station, Ministry of
       Public Building and Works, 1969.
            31-37p. (U.K. Building Research Station.
       Current paper CP2/69)
            Reprinted from: Build International, Dec.,
       1968.
            1. Concrete construction. 2. Panels.
       I. Webb, D.J.T., jt. au. II. U.K. Building
       Research Station. III. Title.

693.2   U.K. Building Research Station.
F67d Forbes, W S
            Dimensional disciplines and the output of
       bricklayers: a case study. Garston, Eng.,
       Building Research Station, 1971.
            4p. (U.K. Building Research Station.
       Current paper CP 34/71)
       Reprinted from: Building, v. 221, no. 6693,
       27 Aug. 1971, pp. 78-84.

            1. Bricklaying. I. U.K. Building Research
       Station. II. Title.

690.015
(41:016)
U541   United Kingdom. Building Research
No. 55N   Station. (Library)
            District heating. 4th rev. ed.
       Garston, England, Oct. 1947.
            22 p. (Its Library bibliography no. 55N)

            1. District heating - Bibliographies.
       (Series)

VF
002   U.K. Building Research Station.
:690 Eliasson, Goran
E54   Development of techiques for the design
       process. Translated from the Swedish, by
       P.J. Elvin. Garston, Eng., Building Research
       Station, 1969.
            6p. (U.K. Building Research Station.
       Library communication no. 1454)

            Translated from the Swedish and reprinted
       from: Byggmastaren 1968, 47 (9), 10-5.

            1. Building documentation. I. U.K. Building
       Research Station. II. Title. (Series)

693.068   U.K. Building Research Station.
:389.6   Denmark. Statens Byggeforskningsinstitutt.
D25   Dimensional standarisation. Preferred
       dimensions. Garston, Eng., Building Research
       Station, 1968.
            86p. (U.K. Building Research Station.
       Library communication 1434)
            Translation of: SBI rapport 56, 1966.

            1. Coordinated components. I. U.K. Building
       Research Station. II. Title. (Series)

534.83   U.K. Building Research Station.
B78   Bruckmayer, F
            Disturbance by traffic noise in classrooms,
       by F. Bruckmayer and J. Lang. Garston, Eng.,
       Building Research Station, 1968.
            [8]p. (Library communication no. 1433)
            Translated from the German and reprinted
       from Osterreichische Ingenieur-Zeitschrift,
       1968, 11 (3), 73-77.

            1. Noise. I. Lang, J., jt. au.
       II. U.K. Building Research Station. III. Title.
       (Series)

691.32   U.K. Building Research Station.
S29   Seymour-Walker, K   J
            Developments in production of concrete panels.
       Garston, Eng., Building Research Station, Min-
       istry of Public Building and Works, 1968.
            12p. (U.K. Building Research Station.
       Building research current papers. Current
       paper 14/68)
            Reprinted from: The Public Works and
       Municipal Services Congress, held at Olympia,
       Nov. 17, 1966.
            1. Concrete. 2. Prefabricated construction.
       3. Panels. I. U.K. Building Research Station.
       II. Title.

693.068   U.K. Building Research Station.
:389.6
(41)   Bishop, D
B47   Dimensional tolerances and the develop-
       ment of building systems. Garston, Eng.,
       Building Research Station, Dept. of
       Scientific and Industrial Research, 1963.
            [5]p. (U.K. Building Research Station.
       Building Research. Current papers.
       Construction series 8)
            Version of this paper was presented to
       the Modular-Coordination Conference, at
       the 1963 International Building Exhibition.
       1. Modular coordination -   - U.K.
       2. Building con-   struction - U.K.
       I. U.K. Building   Research Station.
       II. Title.

690.37
U54d U.K. Building Research Station.
            The diurnal variation of warmth and
       discomfort in some buildings in Singapore,
       by C. G. Webb. Garston, Eng., 1960.
            11p. (Its Note no. E 1024)

            "A talk given at a joint meeting of the
       British Occupational Hygiene and the Ergo-
       nomics Research Societies, at the London
       School of Hygiene and Tropical Medicine
       on June 24 1960."

            1. Housing   in the tropics.
            2. Architecture   and climate.

---

624   U.K. Building Research Station.
K54   Klingberg, L
            Deviations in the horizontal dimensions of
       structures. Garston, Eng., Building Research
       Station, 1970.
            5p. (U.K. Building Research Station.
       Library communication 1570)
            Translated from the Swedish [and reprinted
       from] Byggmastaren, 1970, (5), 13-17.

            1. Structural engineering. I. U.K. Building
       Research Station. II. Title. (Series)

---

720   U.K. Building Research Station.
H17   Hardwick, T   R
            Dimensional variations in framed structures,
       by T.R. Hardwick and R.M. Milner. Garston,
       Eng., Building Research Station, Ministry of
       Public Building and Works, 1967.
            745-748p. (U.K. Building Research Station.
       Building research current paper. 8/68)
            Reprinted from: Architects' journal, Sept.
       20, 1967.
            1. Architecture - Designs and plans.
       2. Building research - U.K. I. Milner, R
       M., jt. au. II. U.K. Building Research
       Station.   III. Title.

697
G72   Great Britain. Building Research Station.
       Gt. Brit. Ministry of Fuel and Power.
            Domestic heating in America; a study of
       heating, cooking and hot water supply in small
       houses in U. S. A. and Canada. Report of a
       Joint Party from the Ministry of Fuel and Power
       and the Department of Scientific and Industrial
       Research. London, H. M. Stationery Off., 1946.
            x, 152 p. illus., diagrs., graphs, tables.

            Bibliography: p. 126-148.
            Committee composed of J. C. Pritchard,
       Ministry of Fuel and Power; C. C. Handisyde,
       Building Research Station; R. H. Rowse, Fuel
       Research Station.   (Continued on next card)

Gt. Brit. Ministry of Fuel and Power.
Domestic heating in America ... 1946. (Card 2)

Description of research at sixteen
laboratories: p. 83-94.

1.Heating. 2.Heating-Canada. 3.Heating research.
I.Gt. Brit. Building Research Station. II.Gt.
Brit. Dept. of Scientific and Industrial.Research.
III.Title.

693.97   U.K. BUILDING RESEARCH STATION.
W66   WOOD, R   H
     AN ECONOMICAL DESIGN OF RIGID STEEL
FRAMES FOR MULTI-STOREY BUILDINGS.
LONDON, H.M. STATIONERY OFFICE, 1951.
120P. (U.K. BUILDING RESEARCH
STATION. NATIONAL BUILDING STUDIES
RESEARCH PAPER NO. 10)

    1. STEEL CONSTRUCTION.
2. STRUCTURAL ENGINEERING.   I. U.K.
BUILDING RESEARCH STATION.

693.55
U54e   U.K. Building Research Station.
     The effect of impact loading on
prestressed and ordinary reinforced
concrete beams, by S.C.C. Bate. London,
Her Majesty's Stat. Off., 1961.
[52]p. (National building studies
research paper 35)

2c   1. Reinforced concrete construction.
2. Concrete, Prestressed. I. Bate, S.C.C.

VF
693.55
U54d   U.K. Building Research Station.
     The durability of reinforced concrete in
buildings; a report on a survey undertaken
in 1954 jointly by the Building Research
Station and the Cement and Concrete Association. London, H.M. Stat. Off., 1956.
     27 p. illus., tables (Its National
Building Studies. Special report no. 25)
2C   Survey made by S.B. Hamilton of the
Building Research Station and A.G. Bray of
the Cement and Concrete Association.

           (see card 2)

690.031
(41)   U.K. Building Research Station.
U54ec   The economics of building design, by
P. A. Stone. Garston, Eng., 1960.
     1v. diagrs., tables. (Its Note
no. E984)

1. Building costs - U. K.   I. Title.
II. Stone, P. A.

691.54
V54   U.K. Building Research Station.
     V'lkov, V
     The effect of P205 on clinker formation and
the quality of the cement, by V. V'lkov and
N. Tabakova. Garston, Eng., Building Research
Station, 1971.
     [11]p. (Library communication no. 1602)
     Bibliography: p. 5-6.
     Translated from the Bulgarian and reprinted
from Stroitelni materiali i silikatna promish-
lenost, 1967, 8 (9), 6-10.
     1. Cement. I. Tabakova, N., jt. au.
II. U.K. Building Research Station.
III. Title. (Series)

VF
693.55
U54d   U.K. Building Research Station.
     The durability... 1956. (card 2)

     1. Reinforced concrete construction.
I. Cement and Concrete Association, London.
II. Title.

728.1
U54e   U.K. Building Research Station.
     The economics of housing and urban
development, by P. A. Stone. [Garston,
Eng.] 1959.
     [66]p. (Its Note no. E895)

     1. Housing - Economic effect. 2. Building
costs - U.K. 3. Land use - U.K. I. Stone,
P. A.

534.83
H62   U.K. Building Research Station.
     Hoch, R
     Effect of reflection on sound-pressure
spectra of jets, by R. Hoch and P. Thomas.
Garston, Eng., Building Research Station, 1969.
     [11]p. (U.K. Building Research Station.
Library communication no. 1523)
     Translated from the French and reprinted
from: Revue d'acoustique, 1969, (5), 47-54.

     1. Noise. I. Thomas, P., jt. au.
II. U.K. Building Research Station.
III. Title. (Series)

691.328
U54   U.K. Building Research Station.
     The durability of reinforced concrete in
sea water, by F. M. Lea and C. M. Watkins.
Twentieth report of the Sea Action Committee of the Institution of Civil Engineers. London, 1960.
     42p. illus., diagrs. (Its National
2c   building studies research paper no. 30)

1. Reinforced concrete. I. Lea, F. M. II.
Watkins, C. M.

693.002.22   U.K. Building Research Station.
(41)
B47   Bishop, D
     The economics of industrialised building.
Garston, Eng., Building Research Station,
Ministry of Technology, 1966.
     [10]p. (U.K. Building Research Station.
Building research current papers. Design
series 54)
     Reprinted from Chartered surveyor, 1966,
vol. 99, no. 4, p. 196-205.

     1. Prefabricated construction - U.K.
2. Building methods. 3. Building costs - U.K.
I. U.K. Build-   ing Research Station.

621.32   U.K. Building Research Station.
H17e   Hartman, E
     The effect of size of surround on perception
of detail. Garston, Eng., Ministry of Public
Building and Works, Building Research Station,
1968.
     4p. (U.K. Building Research Station.
Library communication 1436)
     Reprinted and translated from: Lichttechnik,
1966, 18 (7), 79A-81A.

     1. Lighting. I. Title. II. U.K. Building
Research Stat   ion. (Series)

693.55   U.K. Building Research Station.
G74   Grimer, F   J
     The durability of steel embedded in light-
weight concrete. Garston, Eng., Building Research Station, Ministry of Technology, 1966.
     17p. (U.K. Building Research Station. Build-
ing research current papers. Engineering series
49)
     An abridged version appears in Concrete, 1967,
vol. 1, April, pp. 125-31.
     1. Concrete, Reinforced. 2. Concrete aggregates.
I. U.K. Building Research Station. II. Title.

691.542   U.K. Building Research Station.
R61   Roberts, M   H
     Effect of admixtures on the composition of
the liquid phase and the early hydration re-
actions in Portland cement pastes. Garston,
Eng., Building Research Station, Ministry of
Public Building and Works, 1968.
     12p. (U.K. Building Research Station.
Building research current paper 61/68)
     Bibliography: p. 11-12.
     Paper presented at the RILEM Symposium on
Admixtures for Mortar and Concrete, Brussels,
Aug. 30-Sept. 1, 1967.
     1. Portland ce   ment. I. U.K. Build-
ing Research Sta   tion. II. Title.

691.328.2   U.K. Building Research Station.
B17   Bate, S   C   C
     The effect of temperature on prestressing
wires, by S.C.C. Bate and R.H. Corson.
Garston, Eng., Building Research Station,
Ministry of Technology, 1967.
     [4]p. (U.K. Building Research Station.
Current papers. Engineering series 41)
     Reprinted from Proceedings of the I.C.E.
Conference on Prestressed Concrete Pressure
Vessels, March 13th and 17th, 1967, p.21-24.

     1. Concrete, Prestressed. I. U.K. Building
Research Station   II. Corson, R.H.,
jt. au.   III. Title.

629.136   U.K. Building Research Station.
M14d   Mainstone, R   J
     Dynamic measurements on an experimental
helicopter platform and on the Moat Street fly-
over, Coventry, by R.J. Mainstone and others.
Garston, Eng., Building Research Station,
Ministry of Technology, 1967.
     [13]p. (U.K. Building Research Station.
Building research current papers. Engineering
series 40)
     Reprinted from: The Conference on Stresses in
Service arranged by the Institution of Civil
Engineers, March 1966, paper 9, p. 21-33.

          (Cont'd on next card)

---

728   U.K. Building Research Station.
1551.5
C51   Clapp, M   A
     The effect of adverse weather conditions
on productivity on five building sites.
Garston, Eng., Building Research Station,
Ministry of Technology, 1966.
     [6]p. (U.K. Building Research Sta-
tion. Building research current papers.
Construction series 32)
     Reprinted from Building, 1966, vol. 211,
no. 6439, p. 171, 2, 5, 6, 9, 180.

     1. Architecture and climate. I. U.K.
Building   Research Station.
II. Title.

691.328   U.K. Building Research Station.
M65   Mommens, A
     Effect of the initial curing conditions of
concrete and the thickness of cover on the
corrosion of the reinforcement in concrete.
Garston, Eng., Building Research Station,
1969.
     [17]p. (U.K. Building Research Station.
Library communication no. 1528)
     Translated from the French and reprinted
from proceedings of: RILEM symposium on the
durability of concrete, Prague, Sept. 2-5,
1969.
     1. Concrete, Reinforced. I. U.K.
Building Research Station. II. Title.
(Series)

629.136
M14d   Mainstone, R   J   Dynamic measurements
     on an experimental helicopter platform and
on the Moat Street flyover, Coventry...1967.
          (Card 2)

     1. Heliports. 2. Loads. I. U.K. Building
Research Station. II. Title.

624.043   U.K. Building Research Station.
B18   Baudendistel, M
     The effect of discontinuities on the
stresses and strains in the ground behind a
tunnel wall, by M. Baudendistel and others.
Garston, Eng., Building Research Station, 197
     [31]p. (Library communication no. 1603)
     Translated from the German and reprinted
from Rock Mechanics, 1970, (2), 17-40.
     1. Strains and stresses. 2. Soils. I. U.K
Building Research Station. II. Title: Tunnel
III. Title. (Series)

697.9   U.K. Building Research Station.
H25   Held, E   F   M   van der
     The effect of turbulence on ventilation.
Garston, Eng., Building Research Station, 1971.
     [11]p. (Library communication no. 1632)

     Translated from the German.

     1. Ventilation. I. U.K. Building Research
Station. II. Title. (Series)

728.3
H65ef
U.K. Building Research Station.
Hole, W V
The effects of current and future social changes on house design. Garston, Eng., Building Research Station, 1971.
[8]p. (U.K. Building Research Station. Current paper 8/71)

1. Architecture, Domestic - Designs and plans. 2. Housing - Social aspects. I. U.K. Building Reseach Station. II. Title.

691.51
F71
U.K. Building Research Station.
Franz, D
Electron probe microanalysis of deposits in lime shaft kiln overflow channels, by D. Franz and D. Merz. Garston, Eng., Building Research Station, 1971.
[13]p. (Library communication no. 1636)
Translated from the German by G.L. Cairns.

1. Lime. I. Merz, D., jt. au. II. U.K. Building Research Station. III. Title. (Series)

697.9
B51
U.K. Building Research Station.
Black, Flora A
Experience of air-conditioning in offices, by Flora A. Black and Elizabeth A. Milroy. Garston, Eng., Building Research Station, Ministry of Technology, 1966.
[9]p. (U.K. Building Research Station. Building research current papers. Design series 51)
Reprinted from Journal of the Institution of Heating and Ventilating Engineers, 1966, vol. 34 (September) p. 188-96.

1. Air conditioning. I. Milroy, Elizabeth A., jt. au. II. U.K. Building Research Station. III. Title.

699.82
L68
U.K. Building Research Station.
Loudon, A G
The effects of ventilation and building design factors on the risk of condensation and mould growth in dwellings. Garston, Eng., Building Research Station, 1971.
11p. (U.K. Building Research Station. Current paper CP 31/71)
Reprinted from: Architects' Journal, May 1971, pp. 1149-1159.
1. Moisture condensation. 2. Ventilation. I. U.K. Building Research Station. II. Title.

711.417
(41)
O34e
U.K. Building Research Station.
Ogilvy, A A
Employment expansion and the development of New Town hinterlands, 1961-1966. Garston, Eng., Building Research Station, 1971.
[15]p. (U.K. Building Research Station. Current paper CP 10/71)

1. New towns - U.K. 2. Employment. 3. Journey to work. I. U.K. Building Research Station. II. Title.

690
(41)
W34
U.K. Building Research Station.
Whitaker, T
Experiences with the constant rate of penetration test for piles. Garston, Eng., Building Research Station, Ministry of Technology, 1967.
6p. (U.K. Building Research Station. Building research current papers. Engineering series 48)

1. Building research - U.K. 2. Building methods. I. U.K. Building Research Station. II. Title.

691.421
G41
U.K. Building Research Station.
Gibson, R E
The efficiency of horizontal drainage layers for accelerating consolidation of clay embankments, by R.E. Gibson and Gilliane C. Shefford. Garston, Eng., Building Research Station, 1968.
[9]p. (U.K. Building Research Station. Current paper 24/69)
Reprinted from: Geotechnique, Sept. 1968, p. 327-335.
1. Clay. 2. Foundations (Building) I. Shefford, Gilliane C., jt. au. II. U.K. Building Research Station. III. Title.

690
(41)
S72
U.K. Building Research Station.
Stevens, R F
Encased stanchions. Garston, Eng., Building Research Station, Ministry of Technology, 1965.
[8]p. (U.K. Building Research Station. Building research current papers. Engineering series 22)
Reprinted from: The Structural engineer, Feb., 1965. p. 59-66.

1. Building construction - U.K. I. U.K. Building Research Station. II. Structural engineer. III. Title.

VF
697.001.5
D42
Gt. Brit. Building Research Station.
Dick, J B
Experimental studies in natural ventilation of houses. Garston, Eng., Building Research Station, 1950?
49p. diagrs.
Reprinted from the Journal of the Institute of Heating and Ventilating Engineers, Dec. 1949.
1. Ventilation-Research. 2. Experimental houses-Eng.-Abbots Langley, I. Gt. Brit. Building Research Station.

VF
697.001.5
W27e
Gt. Brit. Building Research Station.
Weston, J C
The efficiency of house heating. Journal of the Institute of Fuel, p. 133-139, Feb. 1949.

Reprint.

1. Heating research. 2. Experimental houses-Eng.-Abbots Langley. I. Title. II. Gt. Brit. Building Research Station.

697.9
M45e
U.K. Building Research Station.
Milbank, N O
Estimation of air conditioning loads, by N.O. Milbank and J. Harrington-Lynn. [Garston, Eng.] Building Research Station, 1970.
[17]p. (U.K. Building Research Station. Current paper 13/70)
Reprinted from: The Proceedings of the Joint Conference held at the University of Nottingham, 26-27th March, 1969, organised by the Dept. of Architecture and Civil Planning, Building Science Laboratories...Proceedings published as Air conditioning system design for buildings, 1969, p. 41-71, Elsevier Pub. Co.
(Cont'd on next card)

693.2
S42
U.K. Building Research Station.
Skeen, J W
Experiments on the rain penetration of brickwork: the effect of mortar type. Garston, Eng., Building Research Station, 1971.
[6]p. (U.K. Building Research Station. Current paper CP 33/71)
Reprinted from: Transactions of the British Ceramic Society, vol. 70, no. 1, January 1971, pp. 27-30.
1. Bricklaying. 2. Waterproofing. I. U.K. Building Research Station. II. Title.

691
S23
U.K. Building Research Station.
Segalova, E E
Elasto-plastic properties of calcium stearate oleogels (Uprugo-plasticheskie svoistva oleogelei stearata kal'tsiya), by E.E. Segalova and others. Garston, Eng., Building Research Station, Ministry of Public Building and Works, 1968.
10p. (U.K. Building Research Station. Library communication no. 1448)
Translated from the Russian and reprinted from: Kolloidnyi zhurnal, 1951, 13 (6), 461-72.
1. Building materials. I. U.K. Building Research Station. II. Title: Calcium stearate oleogels. III. Title.

697.9
M45e
Milbank, N O Estimation...1970.
(Card 2)

1. Air conditioning. I. Harrington-Lynn, J., jt. au. II. U.K. Building Research Station. III. Title.

691.55
B47
U.K. Building Research Station.
Bishop, D
Experiments with pumped screeds, by D. Bishop and E. Kempster. Garston, Eng., Building Research Station, Dept. of Scientific and Industrial Research, 1964.
4p. (U.K. Building Research Station. Building research current papers. Construction series 10)
Reprinted from: Builder, vol. 206(6319), 1964, pp. 1361-4.
1. Plaster and plastering. I. U.K. Building Research Station. II. Kempster, E., jt. au.

621.3
C74
U.K. Building Research Station.
Crisp, J
Electrical supplies for construction sites. Garston, Eng., Building Research Station, Ministry of Technology, 1966.
[24]p. (U.K. Building Research Station. Building research current papers. Construction series 40)
Reprinted from Electronics and power, Jan. 1966, p. 20-23.

1. Electricity. 2. Electric wiring. I. U.K. Building Research Station. II. Title.

VF
623
U54e
U.K. Building Research Station.
An exhibition of work on structural engineering and soil mechanics. [London] 1955.
36p. illus.

"Selected bibliography:" p. 31-35.

1. Structural engineering. 2. Soils.

691
R92
U.K. Building Research Station.
Ryder, J F
The extent and rate of joint movements in modern buildings, by J.F. Ryder and T.A. Baker. Garston, Eng., Building Research Station, 1971.
19p. (U.K. Building Research Station. Current paper 2/71)
Paper presented at the Symposium Joint Movement, Design and Materials, Brighton, 1970.
1. Building materials. I. Baker, T.A., jt. au. II. U.K. Building Research Station. III. Title.

699.86
W34
U.K. Building Research Station.
Whiteley, P
Electron probe analysis in the investigation of surface coating problems, by P. Whiteley and others. [Garston, Eng.] Building Research Station, 1969.
[4]p. (U.K. Building Research Station. Current paper 44/69)
Reprinted from: Journal of the Oil and Colour Chemists' Association, May, 1969, pp. 410-417.
1. Insulating materials. 2. Paints and painting. I. U.K. Building Research Station. II. Title.

699.83
H25
U.K. Building Research Station.
Hellers, B G
Experience in storm damage incidents in 1967 and 1969, by B.G. Hellers and G. Johansson. Garston, Eng., Building Research Station, 1971.
[11]p. (Library communication no. 1611)
Translated from the Swedish.
1. Buildings - Wind stresses. 2. Storms. I. Johansson, G., jt. au. II. U.K. Building Research Station. III. Title. (Series)

690.22
075fa
U.K. Building Research Station.
Oslo. Norges Byggforskningsinstitutt.
Facade cladding; asbestos cement sheets as ventilated cladding on an insulated external wall. Garston, Eng., Building Research Institute, 1968.
2p. (U.K. Building Research Institute. Library communication no. 1443)
Translation of: NBI (41) 211.
1. Walls. 2. Ventilation. I. U.K. Building Research Station. II. Title: Asbestos. III. Title. (Series)

690.22
075f   U.K. Building Research Station.
     Oslo. Norges Byggforskningsinstitutt.
     Facade cladding - ventilated claddings.
Garston, Eng., Building Research Station.
     5p. (U.K. Building Research Station. Library
communication 1442)
     Norges Byggforskningsinstitutt NBI (41) 201.

     1. Walls. 2. Ventilation. 3. Building materi-
als - Weather effects. I. U.K. Building Research Station. II. Title: Cladding. III. Title.

690.22
F671   U.K. Building Research Station.
     Forbes, W   S
     The first operational assessment of
V-bricks, by W.S. Forbes and A.J. Stevens.
Garston, Eng., Building Research Station,
Ministry of Technology, 1965.
     23-30p. (U.K. Building Research
Station. Building research current papers.
Construction series no. 22)
     Reprinted from: PACE, 1965

     1. Walls. 2. Bricklaying. I. U.K.
Building   Research Station.
II. Title.   III. Stevens, A.J.

720
F82   U.K. Building Research Station.
     Fueg, Franz.
     The Foundation for Architectural Research.
Zoning in modular construction. Garston, Eng.,
Ministry of Public Building and Works, Building
Research Station, 1968.
     13p. (U.K. Building Research Station.
Library communication no. 1432)
     Reprinted and translated from: Bauen u.
Wohnen, 1968, 22 (5), 165-70.
     1. Architecture - Designs and plans. 2. Pre-
fabricated construction. 3. Modular coordina-
tion. I. Tit   le. II. Title: Zoning in
modular con   (Cont'd on next card)

690.015
(41
:016)
U541
no.240   U.K. Building Research Station.
     Factory building design. London, 1970.
     7p. (Its Library bibliography no. 240)

     1. Industrial buildings - Bibl.
2. Architects - Designs and plans - Bibl.
I. Title.

690.25
M47   U.K. Building Research Station.
     Mitchell, G   R
     Floor loadings in office buildings: the
results of a survey, by G.R. Mitchell and
R.W. Woodgate. Garston, Eng., Building Research
Station, 1971.
     [30]p. (Current paper 3/71)

     1. Floors and flooring. 2. Loads. 3. Office
buildings. I. U.K. Building Research Station.
II. Woodgate, R.W., jt. au. III. Title.

720
F82   Fueg, Franz.   The Foundation...1968.
                   (Card 2)

struction. III. U.K. Building Research
Station. (Series)

691.328
M25   U.K. Building Research Station.
     Menzies, J   B
     The fatigue strength of steel reinforcement
in concrete. Garston, Eng., Building Research
Station, 1971.
     [11]p. (Current paper no. 16/71)

     1. Concrete, Reinforced. I. U.K. Building
Research Station. II. Title.

690.25
M47f   U.K. Building Research Station.
     Mitchell, G   R
     Floor loadings in retail premises: the results
of a survey, by G.R. Mitchell and R.W. Woodgate.
Garston, Eng., Building Research Station, 1971.
     37p. (U.K. Building Research Station.
Current paper CP 25/71)

     1. Floors and flooring. 2. Loads.
3. Retail stores. I. U.K. Building Research
Station. II. Woodgate, R.W., jt. au.
III. Title.

690.21
B87   U.K. Building Research Station.
     Burland, J   B
     Foundations of buildings in clay. Garston,
Eng., Building Research Station, 1970.
     [3]p. (U.K. Building Research Station.
Current paper CP 22/70)
     Reprinted from Proceedings of the 7th
International Conference on Soil Mechanics
and Foundation Engineering, Mexico, 1969,
pp. 248-250.
     1. Foundations (Building) 2. Clay.
I. U.K. Building Research Station. II. Title.

699.844
U54f   U.K. Building Research Station.
     Field measurements of sound insulation
between dwellings, by P. H. Parkin and
others. London, H. M. Stat. Off., 1960.
     571p. (Its National building studies
research paper no. 33)

     1. Soundproofing. I. Parkin, P. H.
II. Title.

697.9
829   U.K. Building Research Station.
     Sexton, D   E
     A flow meter for field tests of
ventilation systems. Garston, Eng.,
Building Research Station, Dept. of
Scientific and Industrial Research, 1964.
     [3]p. (U.K. Building Research Station.
Building research current papers. Engineering series 21)
     Reprinted from: Heating and ventilating
engineer, vol. 38 (448) 1964, p. 245-7.

     1. Ventilation. I. U.K.   Building Research
Station. II. Title.

690
(41)
A57   U.K. Building Research Station.
     Alsop, K
     Frameless large-panel systems of construc-
tion-assessment of technical performance for
use in dwellings, by K. Alsop and R. B.
Bonshor. Garston, Eng., Building Research
Station, Ministry of Technology, 1965.
     13p. (U.K. Building Research Station.
Building research current papers. Design
series 35)
     Reprinted, with additions, from the Builder,
Feb. 5, 1965, p. 307-10.

                (Continued on
                next card)

690
:770   U.K. Building Research Station.
(016)   Film list. [London] 1959.
U54   7p.

     1. Building construction films - Bibliography.

VF
697.8
S67   U.K. Building Research Station.
     Sprung, S
     Fluorine balance and fluorine emission from
cement kilns, by S. Sprung and H.M. von Seebach.
Garston, Eng., Building Research Station, 1968.
     20p. (U.K. Building Research Station.
Library communication 1450)
     Translated from the German and reprinted
from: Zement-Kalk-Gips, 1968, 21 (1), 1-8.

     1. Air pollution. I. Von Seebach, H.M.,
jt. au. II. U.K. Building Research Station.
III. Title. (Series)

690
(41)
A57   Alsop, K   Frameless large-panel systems
of construction-assessment of technical
performance for use in dwellings...1965.
                (Card 2)

     1. Building materials - U.K. 2. Panels.
1. Bonshor, R. B., jt. au. II. U.K.
Building Research Station. III. Builder.
IV. Title.

U.K. Building Research Station.
699.81
M15   Malhotra, H   L
     Fire resistance of encased steel
stanchions, by H.L. Malhotra and R.F.
Stevens. Garston, Eng., Building Research
Station, Dept. of Scientific and Industrial
Research, 1964.
     17p. (U.K. Building Research Station.
Building Research. Current papers.
Engineering series 10)

          (Cont'd. on next card)

690.25   U.K. Building Research Station.
H17   Harper, F   C
     The forces applied to the floor by the foot
in walking: I. Walking on a level surface.
II. Walking on a slope. III. Walking on stairs,
by F.C. Harper and others. London, H.M.S.O.,
1967.
     2v. (U.K. Building Research Station.
National Building Studies, research paper 32)

     1. Floors and flooring. I. Title.
II. U.K. Building Research Station.

U.K. Building Research Station.
624.131
P25f   Penman, Arthur Douglas MacNaughton.
     Foundations for storage tanks on reclaimed
land at Teesmouth, by A.D.M. Penman and G.H.
Watson. Garston, Eng., Building Research
Station, Ministry of Public Building and
Works, 1967.
     19-42p. (U.K. Building Research Station.
Building research current papers. Current
paper 29/68)
     Originally published in: The Institution of
Civil Engineers Proceedings, 1967, Vol. 37
(May) pp. 19-42.
     1. Soils. I.   Watson, George Hamilton.
II. U.K. Build   ing Research Station.
III. Title.

699.81
M15   Malhotra, H   L   Fire resistance of
     encased steel stanchions ... (Card 2)

     Reprinted from: Institution of Civil
Engineers Proceedings, 1964. vol.
27 (January) 77-98.

     1. Fireproof construction. 2. Building materials -
Fire resistance. 3. Steel. I. Stevens, R.R., jt.
au. II. U.K. Building Research Station.
III. Title.

691.542
H24   U.K. Building Research Station.
     Heimann, R
     Formation of calcium silicates in the system
$CaO-SiO_2-CaF_2$, by R. Heimann and W. Franke,
Garston, Eng., Building Research Station,
1970.
     [7]p. (Library communication no. 1586)
     Translated from the German and reprinted
from Berichte der Deutschen Keram. Ges., 1970,
47 (3), 165-8.

     1. Portland cement. I. Franke, W., jt. au.
II. U.K. Building Research Station.
III. Title. (Series)

624.131
H87   U.K. Building Research Station.
     Hutchinson, J   N
     The free degradation of London clay cliffs.
Garston, Eng., Building Research Station,
Ministry of Public Building and Works, 1968.
     113-118p. (U.K. Building Research Station.
Current paper 54/68)
     Reprinted from: Vol. 1 of the Proceedings
of the Geotechnical Conference, Oslo, 1967.

     1. Soils. I. Title. II. U.K. Building
Research Station.

712
C66

U.K. Building Research Station.
Cook, J A
Gardens on housing estates: a survey of user attitudes and behaviour on seven layouts. Garston, Eng., Building Research Station, 1969.
[16]p. (U.K. Building Research Station. Current paper 42/69)
Published in: Town planning review, Oct., 1968. pp. 217-234.

1. Landscape architecture. 2. Housing - Social aspects. I. U.K. Building Research Station. II. Title.

697.2
M45

U.K. Building Research Station.
Milroy, Elizabeth A
Heating for high density housing: a guide to modern methods in use, by E. A. Milroy and G. A. Atkinson. Garston, Eng., Building Research Station, Dept. of Scientific and Industrial Research, 1964.
14p. (U.K. Building Research Station. Building research current papers. Design series no. 26)

1. Heating, Central. I. U.K. Building Research Station.

691.32
Y68

U.K. Building Research Station.
Young, O C
High-strength beddings for unreinforced concrete and clayware pipes. London, H.M.S.O., 1967.
35p. (U.K. Building Research Station. National Building studies. Special report 38)

1. Concrete. 2. Concrete, Reinforced. 3. Pipes. I. U.K. Building Research Station. II. Title.

699.83
W45

U.K. Building Research Station.
Wilson, P H
Glasgow wind damage: design and construction facets. Garston, Eng., Building Research Station, 1968.
49p. (U.K. Building Research Station. Current paper 76/68)
Reprinted from: Construction technology, July, 1968, pp. 45-7, 49.

1. Buildings - Wind stresses. 2. Architecture - Designs and plans. I. Title. II. U.K. Building Research Station.

697.27
B51

U.K. Building Research Station.
Black, Flora W
Heating for old people: some conclusions based on their experience of electric floor-warming. Garston, Eng., Building Research Station, Dept. of Scientific and Industrial Research, 1962.
14p. (Building research. Current papers. Design series 19)

1. Heating, Electric. 2. Old age. 3. Floors and flooring. I. U.K. Building Research Station.

362
(41)
A74

2 C

U.K. Building Research Station.
Atkinson, G A
Hospital design: factors influencing the choice of shape, by G.A. Atkinson and R.J. Phillips. Garston, Eng., Building Research Station, Dept. of Scientific and Industrial Research, 1964.
[5]p. (Building research. Current papers. Design series 20)
Reprinted from The Architects' Journal, vol. 139(16), pp. 851-5.

1. Hospitals - U.K. Phillips, R.J., jt. au. II. U.K. Building Research Station.

691.54
M14

U.K. Building Research Station.
Majumdar, A J
Glass fibre reinforcement of cement products, by A.J. Majumdar and J.F. Ryder. Garston, Eng., Building Research Station, Ministry of Public Building and Works, 1968.
78-84p. (U.K. Building Research Station. Current paper 67/68)
Reprinted from: Glass technology, 1968, Vol. 9 (3), June, pp. 78-84.

1. Cement. 2. Glass. I. Ryder, J.F., jt. au. II. U.K. Building Research Station. III. Title.

VF
697.001.5
W27

Gt. Brit. Building Research Station.
Weston, John C.
Heating research in houses. Institution of Heating and Ventilating Engineers, p. 235-267.
Reprint.

1. Heating research. 21 Experimental houses-Eng.- Abbots Langley. I.Gt. Brit. Building Research Station.

728.100.15
(41)
A55

U.K. Building research station.
Allen, Phyllis.
Hotel user study: 1. Living accomodations for young people. 2. Storage fitments and furniture. Garston, Eng., Building Research Station, Ministry of Technology, 1968.
847-914p. (U.K. Building Research Station. Current paper 50/68)
Reprinted from the Architects' journal, April, 1968.
1. Housing research - U.K. 2. U.K. - Housing research. 3. Housing - U.K. 4. U.K. - Housing. 5. Youth. 6. Family living requirements. I. U.K. Building research Station. II. Title.

691.55
M14

U.K. Building Research Station.
Majumdar, A J
Glass fibre reinforced cement and gypsum products. Garston, Eng., Building Research Station, 1970.
7p. (Current paper 12/71)
Presented to the Royal Society meeting Strong fibrous solids, 29 Jan. 1970 and published in the Proceedings A, vol. 319, 1970. pp. 69-78.

1. Plaster and plastering. 2. Cement. 3. Gypsum. I. U.K. Building Research Station. II. Title.

VF
697.001.5
G72

Great Britain. Building Research Station.
Heating studies in open plan houses at B.R.S. Garston, Eng., Apr. 1950.
6 l. illus., graphs, plans, tables(fold.)
(Its Note no. C 154)
Restricted.
B.R.S./A.48C/13/1.
Mimeographed.
1.Experimental houses-Eng.-Abbots Langley. 2.Heating research. I.Title. II.Series.

338
S34

U.K. Building Research Station.
Shippam, Roberta.
House-building productivity in USA. Garston, Eng., Building Research Station, Ministry of Public Building and Works, 1968.
127-132p. (U.K. Building Research Station. Building research current papers. Current paper 28/68)
Reprinted from: Building, Dec. 15, 1967.

1. Labor productivity. 2. Building industry. I. U.K. Building Research Station. II. Title.

697
A52he

U.K. Building Research Station.
Andersen, Ib.
Health considerations and the thermal environment, by Ib Andersen and G.R. Lundqvist. Garston, Eng., Building Research Station, 1969.
10p. (U.K. Building Research Station. Library communication 1467)
Translated from the Danish, V.V.S. 1968 (10) 487-8, 490-2, 495-6, 505-6.

1. Heating. 2. Health. I. U.K. Building Research Station. II. Lundqvist, G.R., jt. au. III. Title. (Series)

VF
691.32
U54h

U.K. Building Research Station.
Heavy concrete. Method of determining frost resistance. Garston, 1968.
5p. (Its Library communication no. 1449)
GOST 10060-62 (USSR standard)
Translated from the Russian, by D.R. Gray.

1. Concrete. 2. Building materials - Climatic effects. I. Title. (Series)

728.1
(41)
H65

U.K. BUILDING RESEARCH STATION.
HOLE, W VERE.
HOUSES AND PEOPLE: A REVIEW OF USER STUDIES AT THE BUILDING RESEARCH STATION, BY W.V. HOLE AND J.J. ATTENBURROW. LONDON, H.M. STATIONERY OFF., 1966.
69P.
AT HEAD OF TITLE: MINISTRY OF TECHNOLOGY BUILDING RESEARCH STATION.
BIBLIOGRAPHY: P.64-69.
1. HOUSING - U.K. I. U.K. BUILDING RESEARCH STATION. II. ATTENBURROW, J.J., JT. AU. III. TITLE.

697
B84

U.K. Building Research Station.
Heat transfer in deep underground tunnels, by A.W. Pratt and L. F. Daws. London, H.M. Stat. Off., 1958.
37p. illus., graphs, tables. (National building studies research paper no. 26)

1. Heat transmission. I. Pratt, A W II. Daws, L F III. Title: Underground tunnels.

691.542
R23h
1970

U.K. Building Research Station.
Rehsi, S S
High-magnesia portland cements: studies on cements prepared with reagent-grade chemicals, by S.S. Rehsi and A.J. Majumdar. Garston, Eng., Building Research Station, 1970.
[11]p. (U.K. Building Research Station. Current paper no. 12/70)
Reprinted from: The Magazine of concrete research, 1969, vol. 21(67) June pp. 67-78.
1. Portland cement. I. Majumdar, A.J., jt. au. II. U.K. Building Research Station. III. Title.

Mrs. Landis
690.015
(41:016)
U541
no. 149

Gt. Brit. Building Research Station.
Housing and town planning in British Colonial territories other than Africa and West Indies. Garston, Eng., Nov. 1948.
3 l. (Its Library bibliography no. 135)
Annotated.
Processed.

1.Housing in the tropics-Bibl. I.Series.

697.133
L68

U.K. Building Research Station.
Loudon, A G
Heating effect of sunshine, by A.G. Loudon, and P. Petherbridge. Garston, Eng., Building Research Station, Ministry of Technology, 1966.
138-43p. (U.K. Building Research Station. Building research current papers. Design series 40)
Reprinted from: the Architects' journal, Jan 12, 1966.

1. Heat transmission. 2. Heating, Solar. 3. Architecture and climate. I. Petherbridge, P., jt. au. II. U.K. Building Research Station. III. Title.

691.542
R23

U.K. Building Research Station.
Rehsi, S S
High magnesia portland cements: study of cement prepared with commercial raw materials, by S.S. Rehsi and A.J. Majumdar. Garston, Eng., Building Research Station, 1969.
221-226p. (U.K. Building Research Station. Current paper 39/69)
Reprinted from: The Indian concrete journal, June, 1969, pp. 221-226.
1. Portland cement. I. Majumdar, A.J., jt. au. II. U.K. Building Research Station. III. Title.

Mrs. Landis
690.015
(41:016)
U541
no. 134

Gt. Brit. Building Research Station.
Housing and town planning in the West Indies. Garston, Eng., Nov. 1948.
7 l. (Its Library bibliography no. 134)
Includes British Guiana, British Honduras, Bermuda, Puerto Rico and the Virgin Islands.
Annotated.
Processed.

1.Housing in the tropics-Bibl. I.Series.

690.22
M13

U.K. Building Research Station.
Magdalinski, J
How to design brick walls for wind
pressures. Garston, Eng., Building Research
Station, 1972.
[27]p. (Library communication no. 1660)
Translated from the Swedish.

1. Walls. 2. Brick construction. I. U.K.
Building Research Station. II. Title.
(Series)

693.002.22
B47

U.K. Building Research Station.
Bishop, D
Industrialised building, with special
reference to formwork. Garston, Eng., Building
Research Station, Ministry of Technology, 1968.
13-37p. (U.K. Building Research Station.
Current paper 45/68)
"Originally contributed under the title
Formwork for precast concrete - with special
reference to industrialised building.
Reprinted from the Proceedings (published by
the Concrete Society), pp. 13-37.
1. Prefabricated construction. 2. Concrete.
I. U.K. Building   Research Station.
II. Title.

699.83
E17

U.K. Building Research Station.
Eaton, K   J
Instrumentation and analysis of full-
scale wind pressure measurements, by K.J.
Eaton and J.R. Mayne. London, Building
Research Station, Ministry of Public
Building and Works, 1969.
11p. (U.K. Building Research Station.
Current paper CP1/69)
Reprinted from: Proceedings of the
National Physical Laboratory Symposium on
Instrumentation and Data Processing for
Industrial   Aerodynamics, Teddington,
Middlesex,   Nov. 21-22, 1968.
(Cont'd on next card)

690.016
(41
:016)
U541
no.224

U.K. Building Research Station.
Human factors in the building process: some
recent references in six parts. Garston, Eng.,
1969.
1v. in 6 pts. (Its Library bibliography
no. 224)

1. Building industry - Bibl. I. Title.
(Series)

691.542
B87

U.K. Building Research Station.
Butt, Yu   M
The influence of fluoride mineralizers on
the crystal structure of portland cement
clinker, by Yu. M. Butt and others. Garston,
Eng., Building Research Station, 1969.
5p. (U.K. Building Research Station.
Library communication no. 1501)
Translated from the Russian and reprinted
from Neorganicheskie materialy, 1969, 5 (6),
1116-20.
1. Portland cement. I. U.K. Building
Research Station. II. Title. (Series)

699.83
E17

Eaton, K   J   Instrumentation
...1969.   (Card 2)

1. Buildings - Wind stresses.
I. Mayne, J.R., jt. au. II. U.K.
Building Research Station. III. Title.

620
H47

U.K. Building Research Station.
Hirn, H
Hydraulic linear reciprocating motor as
vibratory drive. Garston, Eng., Building
Research Station, 1970.
6p. (U.K. Building Research Station.
Library communication no. 1560)
Translated from the German [and reprinted from]
Fördern und Heben, 1970, 20 (4), 175-8.

1. Engineering. I. U.K. Building Research
Station. II. Title. (Series)

691.421.015
S23

U.K. Building Research Station.
Schwiete, H   E
The influence of the clay minerals on dust
formation in the burning of clinker.
Garston, Eng., Building Research Station,
1970.
[15]p. (Library communication no. 1589)
translated from the German and reprinted
from Zement-Kalk-Gips, 1959, 9 (8), 351-7.

1. Clay - Research. 2. Cement.
I. U.K. Building Research Station. II. Title.

628.1
P251

U.K. Building Research Station.
Penman, A   D   M
Instrumentation for earth and
rockfill dams. Garston, Eng.,
Building Research Station, 1969.
6p. (U.K. Building Research
Station. Current paper 35/69)
Reprinted from: BNCOLD news and
views, May 1969, pp. 7-10.

1. Water supply. I. U.K Building
Research Station. II. Title.

624
S47

U.K. Building Research Station.
Sittig, J
Improved quality brings reduced costs.
Garston, Eng., Building Research Station, 1968.
4p. (U.K. Building Research Station.
Library communication 1441)
Reprinted and translated from: Bouw, 1966,
39, 1500-1501.

1. Structural engineering. 2. Building costs.
I. U.K. Building Research Station. II. Title.
(Series)

002
:690
D25

U.K. Building Research Station.
Delany, D   P
Information retrieval at the Building Re-
search Station, 1969.
6-9p. (U.K. Building Research Station.
Current paper 28/69)

Reprinted from: Build international, May
1969, pp. 6-9.

1. Building documentation. I. Neville, H.
H., jt. au. II. U.K. Building Research Station. III.   Title.

362
B51

U.K. BUILDING RESEARCH STATION.
BLACK, FLORA W
INTERDEPARTMENTAL TRAFFIC IN
NON-TEACHING ACUTE GENERAL HOSPITALS.
GARSTON, HERTS, 1966.
15P. (BUILDING RESEARCH CURRENT PAPERS,
DESIGN SERIES 43)

REPRINTED FROM THE ARCHITECTS' JOURNAL,
VOL. 143, 1966.

1. HOSPITALS. I. U.K. BUILDING
RESEARCH STATION. II. TITLE.

690
(41)
E57

U.K. Building Research Station.
Entwistle, Alison.
Incentives in the building industry, by
Alison Entwistle and W. J. Reiners. London,
H. M. Stat. Off., 1958.
43p. (National building studies. Special
report no. 28)
At head of title: Dept. of Scientific and
Industrial Research.   Building Research
Station
1. Building industry - U.K. I. Reiners,
W. J., jt. au.   II. U.K. Building
Research   Station.

691.71
T72

U.K. Building Research Station.
Treadaway, K   W   J
Inhibition of the corrosion of steel in
concrete, by K.W.J. Treadaway and A.D. Russell.
Garston, Eng., Building Research Station,
Ministry of Public Building and Works, 1968.
5p. (U.K. Building Research Station.
Current paper CP 82/68)
Reprinted from: Highways and public works,
Aug., 1968. pp. 19-21; Sept., 1968. pp. 41-41.
1. Steel. 2. Concrete. 3. Corrosion. I. Title.
II. Russell, A.D., jt. au. III. U.K. Building
Research Station.

690.031
U541

U.K. Building Research Station.
International comparison of building costs
with particular reference to U.S.A. and
Great Britain, by P. A. Stone. Garston, Eng.,
1960.
16p. tables. (Its Note no. E968)
c. 2. Reproduced from the Bulletin of the
Oxford University Institute of Statistics,
vol. 22, no. 2, May 1960. p. 105-115.

1. Building costs.   I. Stone, P.A.

693.2
B47

U.K. Building Research Station.
Bishop, D
Industrialisation and the brick. Garston,
Eng., Building Research Station, Dept. of
Scientific and Industrial Research, 1964.
[4]p. (U.K. Dept. of Scientific and
Industrial Research. Building Research
Station. Construction series 11)
Reprinted from The Builder, vol. 207(6322),
p. 131-4, 1964.
1. Brick construction. I. U.K. Building Research
Station. II. Title.

628.1
(41)
P25

U.K. Building Research Station.
Penman, A   D   M
Initial behaviour of Scammonden Dam, by
A.D.M. Penman and P.B. Mitchell. Garston, Eng.
Building Research Station, 1970.
[20]p. (U.K. Building Research Station.
Current paper 20/70)
Reprinted from: Proceedings of the 10th
Conference of the International Commission on
Large Dams, Montreal 1970, pp. 723-747.
1. Water resources - U.K. I. Mitchell,
P.B., jt. au. II. U.K. Building Research
Station. III. Title.

690.091.82
H65

U.K. Building Research Station.
Honey, C   R
International comparison of building
regulations: the content and arrangement
of regulating documents. Garston, Eng.,
Building Research Station, 1970.
38p. (U.K. Building Research Station.
Current paper CP 37/70)

1. Building codes. I. U.K. Building
Research Station. II. Title.

690.015
(41
:016)
U541
no. 236

U.K. Building Research Station.
Industrialised building in relation to
low-cost housing. Garston, Eng., 1971.
10p. (Its Library bibliography no. 236)

1. Prefabricated construction - Bibl.
2. Aided self-help housing - Bibl.
3. Low-income housing - Bibl. I. Title.
(Series)

628.1
(41)
U54

U.K. BUILDING RESEARCH STATION.
AN INQUIRY INTO DOMESTIC HOT WATER
SUPPLY IN GREAT BRITAIN. LONDON, H.M.
STATIONERY OFF., 1952.
2PTS. (NATIONAL BUILDING STUDIES
SPECIAL REPORT NO. 8, 14)

PART 1 PREPARED BY THE CHIEF
SCIENTIFIC ADVISOR'S DIVISION OF THE
MINISTRY OF WORKS, 1950.
1. WATER SUPPLY - U.K. 2. HEATING,
HOT WATER. I. U.K. MINISTRY OF WORKS.
II. TITLE: DOMESTIC HOT WATER SUPPLY.

690.091.82
C411

U.K. Building Research Station.
Cibula, Evelyn.
International comparison of building
regulations: loading requirements.
Garston, Eng., Building Research Station,
1970.
[30]p. (U.K. Building Research Station.
Current paper CP 38/70)

1. Building codes. 2. Loads. I. U.K.
Building Research Station. II. Title.

690.091.82
C41in

U.K. Building Research Station.
Cibula, Evelyn.
International comparison of building regulations: thermal insulation.
Garston, Eng., Building Research Station, 1970.
32p. (U.K. Building Research Station. Current paper CP 33/70)

1. Building codes. 2. Insulation. I. U.K. Building Research Station. II. Title.

691
B74

Briner, E   investigation...1968
(card 2)

1. Building materials. I. U.K. Building Research Station. II. Title. (Series)

VF
696.1
G67

U.K. Building Research Station.
Gösele, K
Laboratory measurement of the noise behaviour of water fittings for draft standard DIN 52218, by K. Gösele and C.A. Voigtsberger. Garston, Eng., Building Research Station, 1968.
8p. (U.K. Building Research Station. Library communication no. 1445)
Translated from the German and reprinted from: Heiz.-Luft.-Haustechnik, 1967, 18 (6), 230-5.
1. Plumbing. 2. Noise. I. Voigtsberger, C.A., jt. au. II U.K. Building Research Station. III. Title. (Series)

690.031
(41)
S46

U.K. Building Research Station.
Skoyles, E   R
Introducing bills of quantities (operational format). Garston, Eng., Building Research Station, Ministry of Public Building and Works, 1968.
139-146p. (U.K. Building Research Station. Building research current paper 62/68)
Reprinted from: Quantity surveyor, May and June, 1968.
1. Building costs - U.K. 2. U.K. - Building costs. I. U.K. Building Research Station. II. Title.

691.421
W34

U.K. Building Research Station.
Whitaker, T
An investigation of the shaft and base resistances of large bored piles in London clay, by T. Whitaker and R. W. Cooke, Garston, Eng., Building Research Station, Ministry of Technology, 1966.
49p. (U.K. Building Research Station Building research current papers. Engineering series 31)
Reprint of paper presented at the Symposium on Large Bored Piles, Institution of Civil Engineers, London, Feb. 1966.

(Cond't on next card)

624
W22

U.K. Building Research Station.
Weeks, G   A
Laboratory testing of large structures. Garston, Eng., Building Research Station, 1969.
6p. (U.K. Building Research Station. Current paper 22/69)
To be presented at the RILEM International Symposium on Testing Methodology and Technique of Full-Scale Structures under Static and Dynamic Loads, Bucharest, Sept., 1969.
1. Structural engineering. 2. Loads. I. U.K. Building Research Station. II. Title.

691.55
F671

U.K. Building Research Station.
Forbes, W   S
The introduction of mechanical plastering, by W. S. Forbes and H. G. Cooper. Garston, Eng., Building Research Station, Ministry of Technology, 1965.
[6]p. (U.K. Building Research Station. Building research current papers. Construction series 16)
Reprinted from the National builder April, 1965.

1. Plaster and plaster-   ing. I. Cooper, H. G., jt. au. II. U.K.   Building Research Station. III. Title.

691.421
W34

Whitaker, T. An investigation of the shaft and base resistances of large bored piles in London clay...1966.   (Card 2)

1. Clay. I. U.K. Building Research Station. II. Cooke, R. W. jt. au. III. Title.

VF
696.1
U54la

U.K. Building Research Station.
Laboratory testing of the noise behaviour of fittings and equipment for water supply installations; provisional German standard DIN 52218. Garston, Eng., 1968.
7p. (Its Library communication no. 1438)

Translation from the German by T.R. Gray.

1. Plumbing. 2. Noise. I. Title. (Series)

690.031
S46

U.K. Building Research Station.
Skoyles, E   R
Introduction to operational bills. Garston, Eng., Building Research Station, Dept. of Scientific and Industrial Research, 1964.
6p. (U.K. Building Research Station. Building research current papers. Design series 32)
Reprinted from the Quantity surveyor, 1964, vol. 21 (2) pp. 27-32.

1. Building costs - Estimates. 2. Land use. I. U.K. Building   Research Station.

534.83
B76

U.K. Building Research Station.
Brockmeyer, H
Investigations of aerodynamic noise in duct system components for high-velocity plant. Garston, Eng., Building Research Station, 1969.
[19]p. (U.K. Building Research Station. Library communication no. 1526)
Translated from the German.
Bibliography: p. 9-10.

1. Noise. 2. Air conditioning - Research. I. U.K. Building Research Station. II. Title. (Series)

690.072
C51l

U.K. Building Research Station.
Clapp, Margaret A
Labour requirements for conventional houses. Garston, Eng., Building Research Station, Ministry of Technology, 1965.
11p. (U.K. Building Research Station. Building research current papers. Construction series 17)

1. Building construction - Labor requirements. 2. Housing - U.K. I. U.K. Building Research Station. II. Title.

600.15
N171

U.K. Building Research Station.
Náray-Szabó, I
Investigation of chemical reactions in the lime treatment of red mud, by I. Náray-Szabó and others. Garston, Eng., Building Research Station, 1969.
5p. (U.K. Building Research Station. Library communication no. 1502)
Translated from the German and reprinted from: Acta chimica academiae scientiarum Hungaricae, 1968, 57 (4), 377-83.
1. Industrial research. I. U.K. Building Research Station. II. Title. (Series)

690
G78

U.K. Building Research Station.
Grün, W
Jointing technique. Garston, Eng., Building Research Station, 1970.
[19]p. (Library communication no. 1595)

Translated from the German and reprinted from Deutsche Bauzeitschrift, 1968, 102 (5), 763-76.

1. Building construction. I. U.K. Building Research Station. II. Title. (Series)

690.072
B47l

U.K. Building Research Station.
Bishop, D
Labour requirements for house building. Advantages of continuity of work and experience. Garston, Eng., Building Research Station, Ministry of Technology, 1965.
5p. (U.K. Building Research Station. Building research current papers. Construction series 18)
[Reprinted from] Builder, July 16, 1965, p. 150-151.

1. Building construc-   tion - Labor require-ments. I. U.K. Build-   ing Research Station. II. Title.

725.23
M45

U.K. Building Research Station.
Milbank, N   O
Investigation of maintenance and energy costs for services in office buildings, by N.O. Milbank and others. Garston, Eng., Building Research Station, 1971.
[12]p. (U.K. Building Research Station. Current paper CP 38/71)
Reprinted from Journal of the Institution of Heating and Ventilating Engineers, Oct. 1971, pp. 145-154.
1. Office buildings. 2. Heating. 3. Lighting. 4. Air conditioning. I. U.K. Building Research   Station. II. Title.

691
(41)
H17

U.K. Building Research Station.
Harrison, H   W
Joints and component interchange. Garston, Eng., Building Research Station, Ministry of Technology, 1966.
8p. (U.K. Building Research Station. Building research current papers. Design series 56)
Reprinted from Building, 1966, vol. 211, no. 6443, p. 145, 6, 9, 150, 3, 4, 7, 8.

1. Building materials - U.K. 2. Coordinated components. I. U.K. Building Research Station.

691.8
B47

U.K. Building Research Station.
Bishop, D
Large panel construction. Garston, Eng. Building Research Station, Dept. of Scientific and Industrial Research 1964.
[233-238p.]
Building Research Station. Current papers. Design series 17)
Reprinted from : The Architect and building news, 1964, vol. 225(6), pp. 233-8; (7), pp. 277-280.

1. Panels. 2. Structural engineering. I. U.K. Building Research   Station.

691
B74

U.K. Building Research Station.
Briner, E
Investigation of the equilibrium of dissociation of calcium, potassium and sodium sulphates, both alone and in the presence of additives, by E. Briner and others. Garston, Eng., Ministry of Building and Works, Building Research Station, 1968.
12 p. (U.K. Building Research Station. Library communication]435)
Reprinted from: Helvetica chimica acta, 1948,   31(7), 2220-2235.
(Cont'd on next card)

691
E22

U.K. Building Research Station.
Eden, J   F
Joints in the context of an assembly process, by J.F. Eden and K. Seymour-Walker. Garston, Eng., Building Research Station, 1971.
[5]p. (U.K. Building Research Station. Current paper 1/71)
Reprinted from: Building, vol. 219, no. 6648, 16 October 1970, pp. 155-163. Proceedings of the Conference on Joints in Structure at Sheffield University, 8-10 July 1970, session C, paper3.
1. Building materials. I. Seymour-Walker, K., jt. au. II. U.K. Building Research Station. III. Title.

690.372
B47

U.K. Building Research Station.
Bishop, D
Large panel construction: production methods. Garston, Eng., Building Research Station, Dept. of Scientific and Industrial Research, 1964.
9p. (U.K. Building Research Station. Building research current papers. Construction series 9)
Reprinted from: Architect and building news, vol. 226 (1), 1964, pp.23-8; pp. 86-88.
1. Building construction - Labor requirements. 2. Panels.   I. U.K. Building Research Station.

16

693.5
S36
U.K. Building Research Station.
Short, A
Large-panel structures; notes on the draft
addendum 1 to CP 116 (1965), by A. Short and
J.R. Miles. Garston, Eng., Building Research
Station, 1969.
12p. (U.K. Building Research Station.
Current paper 30/69)
Reprinted from: The Concrete Society,
Technical paper PCS 47, May 12, 1969.

1. Concrete construction. 2. Panels.
I. Miles, J.R., jt. au. II. U.K. Building
Research Station. III. Title.

690.015
(41
:016)
U541
U.K. Building Research Station.
Library bibliographies.

no.227 U.K. Building Research Station. Concerning
methods of calculating for depreciation of buildings
1970

no.228 U.K. Building Research Station.
Photography in building. 1969.

no.229 U.K. Building Research Station.
Safety. 1969.

U.K. Building Research Station.
Library communications.

620.1
U72
no.
1425
Ur'ev, N.B. Characteristics of the
mechanism of failure of glass fibre
on formation of new crystals. 1968.

690.015
(41
:016)
U541
U.K. Building Research Station.
Library bibliography; 1968 list.
[Garston, Eng.] Building Research
Station, Ministry of Public Building and
Works, 1968.
[4]p.

1. Building research – U.K. – Bibl.
2. Building construction – U.K. – Bibl.
I. Title.

690.015
(41
:016)
U541
U.K. Building Research Station.
Library bibliographies.

no.
230
Atkinson, G.A. Building
legislation in Scandinavia.
1969.

no.231 U.K. Building Research Station
Weather, and its effect on building operations and costs. 1969

no.
232
U.K. Building Research Station.
Colour in building Research
Station. 1969

U.K. Building Research Station.
Library communications.

624.043
IA1
no.
1427
Libert, Y. Stress corrosion of
high strength steel wires.
1968.

690.015
(41:016)
U541
Gt.Brit. Building Research Station. Library
bibliographies.
no.
133. A bibliography of native housing in Africa.
Nov. 1948.
134. Housing and town planning in the West Indies.
Nov. 1948.
135. Housing and town planning in British Colonial
territories other than Africa and West Indies.
Nov. 1948.
142. Design of buildings for warm climates. Feb.1950
128 Some references on solar heating. Nov. 1946

690.015
(41
:016)
U541
U.K. Building Research Station.
Library bibliographies.

no. 233 U.K. Building Research Station.
Plastics in central heating and hot water
systems. 1970.

no. 234 U.K. Building Research Station.
Tendering documents with a production bias.
1970.

no. 235 U.K. Building Research Station.
Concerning the application of damp-proof
courses to existing buildings. 1970.

U.K. Building Research Station.
Library communications.

621.32
M17
no.
1428
Matveev, A.B. Determining luminosity
in terms of threshold increments.
1968.

Mrs. Landis.
690.015
(41:016)
U541
Gt.Brit. Building Research Station. Library
bibliographies.
no.
149. Low cost housing and town planning in colonial
territories. July 1950.
no.
166
Selection of books on building. Feb., 1969.

no. References on housing for old people.
176R 1959.

690.015
(41
:016)
U541
U.K. Building Research Station.
Library bibliographies.

no. 236 U.K. Building Research Station.
Industrialised building in relation to low-
cost housing. 1970.

no. 237 U.K. Building Research Station.
Modernising old dwellings. 1970.

no. 238 U.K. Building Research Station.
Concerning methods of calculating for
depreciation of buildings. 1970.

U.K. Building Research Station.
Library communications.

690.091.82
(485)
E77
no.
1429
Essunger, Gunnar. Swedish
building standards 67. 1968.

690.015
(41:016)
U541
no. 176R
U.K. Building Research Station. Library
bibliography no. 176R.
U.K. Building Research Station.
References on housing for old people.
Garston, England, 1959.
17p. (Library bibliography no. 176R)

Superseding Bibliography no. 176.

1. Housing for the aged - Bibliography. (Series:
U.K. Building Research Station. Library bibliography
no. 176R)

690.015
(41
:016)
U541
U.K. Building Research Station.
Library bibliographies.

no. 239 U.K. Building Research Station.
Building in warm climates. 1970.

no. 240 U.K. Building Research Station.
Factory building design. 1970.

U.K. Building Research Station.
Library communications.

699.82
R65
no.
1430
Rönning, Mats. Damp and water
insulation. 1968.

690.015
(41
:016)
U541
U.K. Building Research Station.
Library bibliographies.

no.
221
U.K. Building Research Station.

no.
222
U.S. Building Research Station.
The building industry in Britain.

nos.
226

U. K. Building Research Station. Library
Communications.

VF
697.133
F68
482
Fournel, A. Relation between heat-losses
and various climatological factors ...
May 1951.

U.K. Building Research Station.
Library communications.

697.9
R25
no.
1431
Rengholt, Ulf. Ventilation. 1968.

690.015
(41
:016)
U541
U.K. Building Research Station.
Library bibliographies.

no. 224 U.K. Building Research Station.
Human factors in the building process; some
recent references in six parts. 1969.

Contents.-pt. A. The labourer on the site.-
pt. B. Site management.-pt. C. Contractor
management problems.-pt. D. Relationship
between members of the team.-pt. E. Planning.-pt. F. Firms and their goals.

U.K. Building Research Station.
Library communications.

691.328
D87
no.
1317
Dutron, R. Research on the corrosion
behaviour of reinforcement in
reinforced concrete. 1965.

U.K. Building Research Station.
Library communications.

534.83
B78
no.
1433
Bruckmayer, F. Disturbance by
traffic noise in classrooms.
1968.

U.K. Building Research Station. Library communications.

693.068 no. Denmark. Statens Byggeforskningsinstitut.
:389.6 1434 Dimensional standardisation.
D25 Preferred dimensions. 1968.

U.K. Building Research Station. Library communications.

690.22 no. Oslo. Norges Byggforskningsinstitutt.
075.fa 1443 Facade cladding - asbestos cement sheets as ventilated cladding on an insulated external wall. 1968.

U.K. Building Research Station. Library Communications.

697.9 no. Denmark. Arbejds- og Boligministeriet.
D25 1466 Ventilation. March, 1969.

U.K. Building Research Station. Library Communications.

691 no. Briner, E Investigation of
B74 1435 the equilibrium of dissociation of calcium, potassium and sodium sulphates...1968.

U.K. Building Research Station. Library communications.

690.22 no. Christensen, Georg. The properties of
C37 1444 non-loadbearing internal walls as determined by functional requirements. 1968.

U.K. Building Research Station. Library Communications.

691.542 no. Butt, Yu. M. The influence of fluoride
B87 1501 mineralizers on the crystal structure.. 1969.

U.K. Building Research Station. Library communications.

699.844 no. Westphal, W The propagation of
W27 1437 structure-borne sound in buildings. 1968.

U.K. Building Research Station. Library Communications.

VF
691.32 no. U.K. Building Research Station. Heavy
U54h 1449 concrete. Method of determining frost resistance. 1968.

U.K. Building Research Station. Library Communications.

600.15 no. Náray-Szabó, I. Investigation of chemical
N171 1502 reactions in the lime treatment of red mud 1969.

U.K. Building Research Station. Library Communications.

VF
696.1 no. U.K. Building Research Station.
U54a 1438 Laboratory testing of the noise behaviour of fittings and equipment for water supply installations; provisional German standard DIN 52218. 1968.

U.K. Building Research Station. Library communication ....

VF
697.8 no. Sprung, S Fluorine balance and fluorine
S67 1450 emission from cement kilns. 1968.

U.K. Building Research Station. Library Communications.

691.32 no. Rüsch, H. Statistical analysis of the
R87s 1504 strength of concrete. 1969.

U.K. Building Research Station. Library communications.

534.83 no. Schneider, P A contribution to
S23 1440 the question of system noises. 1968.

U.K. Building Research Station. Library Communications.

VF
002 no. Eliasson, Goran. Development of techniques
:690 1454 for the design process. 1969.
554

U.K. Building Research Station. Library Communications.

691.32 no. Ernst, K. Moisture measurement for
E75 1506 concrete production. 1969.

U.K. Building Research Station. Library Communications.

624 no. Sittig, J. Improved quality brings
S47 1441 reduced costs. 1968.

U.K. Building Research Station. Library Communications.

VF
:690 no. Joss, H. The standard library of descriptions
J67 1455 (CRB) 1969.

U.K. Building Research Station. Library Communications.

691.54 no. Bombled, J.P. Test apparatus for auto-
B65 1507 matically measuring the setting time... 1969.

U.K. Building Research Station. Library communications.

690.22 no. Oslo. Norges Byggforsknings-
075 1442 institutt. Facade cladding. 1968.

U.K. Building Research Station. Library Communications.

VF
691.32 no. Rusch, Hubert. Statistical quality control
R87 1456 of concrete. 1969.

U.K. Building Research Station. Library Communications.

691.542 no. Method for increasing the strength of
M27 1509 cement formed as a by-product of the... 1969.

U.K. Building Research Station. Library communications. 301.36 no. Carlstein, T. The urbanisation C17 1513 process: 17 individuals' 24- hour movements in some types of families.	U.K. Building Research Station. Library Communications. 621.32 no. Gusev, N.M. The daylighting of buildings. G87 1554 1970.	U.K. Building Research Station. Library Communications. 690.022 no. Laursen, F.B. Concrete elements. 1970. L18 1563
U.K. Building Research Station. Library Communications. 534.83 no. Hoch, R. Effect of reflection on sound- H62 1523 pressure spectra of jets. 1969.	U.K. Building Research Station. Library Communications. 691.54 no. Kawert, K. Development of a shrinkage K18 1555 compensated cement. 1970.	U.K. Building Research Station. Library Communications. 690.015 no. Mikhailov, K.V. The Concrete and Rein- (47) 1564 forced Concrete Research Institute... M44 1970.
U.K. Building Research Station. Library Communications. 534.83 no. Brockmeyer, H. Investigations of B76 1526 aerodynamic noise in duct system... 1969.	U.K. Building Research Station. Library Communications. 691 no. Kjaer, A. Should property specification be (489) 1558 introduced in Denmark? K41	U.K. Building Research Station. Library Communications. 691.542 no. Goria, C. On the possibility of estimating G67 1566 chemically the pozzolanic activity...1970
U.K. Building Research Station. Library Communications. 629.136 no. Jørgen, Gunnar Ø. Residential areas in J67 1527 the vicinity of an airport. 1969. Eng.	U.K. Building Research Station. Library Communications. 691.328 no. Nosenko, N.E. The centralization of the N67c 1559 manufacture...1970.	U.K. Building Research Station. Library Communications. 691.7 no. Rozenfel'd, I.L. Corrosion and coating :620.19 1567 of metals. 1967. R69
U.K. Building Research Station. Library Communications. 691.328 no. Mommens, A. Effect of the initial M65 1528 curing conditions of concrete and ... 1969.	U.K. Building Research Station. Library Communications. 620 no. Hirn, H. Hydraulic linear reciprocating H47 1560 motor as vibratory drive. 1970.	U.K. Building Research Station. Library Communications. 621.32 no. Konig, O. A direct reading daylight factor K62 1569 meter. 1970.
U.K. Building Research Station. Library Communications. 691.54 no. Kravchenko, I.V. Calcining clinker in a K71 1529 fluidized bed. 1969.	U.K. Building Research Station. Library Communications. 696.1 no. Association Nationale des Services d'Eau. A77 1561 Regulations on the construction and testing of non-return valves ...1970.	U.K. Building Research Station. Library Communications. 624 no. Klingberg, L. Deviations in the horizontal K54 1570 Dimensions of structures. 1970.
U.K. Building Research Station. Library Communications. 624.043 no. Longchal, M. The natural weathering L65 1530 of composite materials subjected to.. 1969.	U.K. Building Research Station. Library Communications. 725.4 no. Vyzhigin, G.V. New designs of multi-storey V99 1562 factory buildings for seismic regions. 1970.	U.K. Building Research Station. Library Communications. 628.1 no. Deyagin, B.V. The thermal stability of D27 1572 modified water. 1970.

U.K. Building Research Station. Library Communications.

693.97 no. Von Essen, W. Standards for steel
V65 1574 structures. 1970.

U.K. Building Research Station.
Library communications.

691.542 no. Matouschek, F. The lime saturation
M17 1588 value of Portland cement clinker
relative to the raw material
analysis, the burning of the
clinker, and the mortar strengths.
1970.

U.K. Building Research Station.
Library communications.

534.83 no. Méry, J. Physiological studies -
M27 1597 introductory survey (part 2)
1971.

U.K. Building Research Station
Library communications.

624.043 no. Kovári, K. The design of under-
K68 1578 ground structures: the secondary
stress and strain state of an
inhomogeneous elastic-ideally
plastic material near a lined
underground cavity. 1970.

U.K. Building Research Station.
Library communications.

691.421.015 no. Schwiete, H.E. The influence of
823 1589 the clay minerals on dust
formation in the burning c'
clinker. 1970.

U.K. Building Research Station.
Library communications.

621.9 no. U.K. Building Research Station.
:690 1601 Tower cranes for building. 1971.
(47)
U54

U.K. Building Research Station.
Library communications.

691.54 no. Zakharov, L.A. Aluminous-belite
Z14 1579 cement. 1970.

U.K. Building Research Station.
Library communications.

600.15 no. Lapin, V.V. The varying nature of
L16 1591 the precipitation of dicalcium
silicate in blast-furnace slags.
1970.

U.K. Building Research Station.
Library communications.

691.54 no. V'lkov, V. The effect of P_2O_5
V54 1602 on clinker formation and the
quality of the cement. 1971.

U.K. Building Research Station.
Library communications.

693.2 no. Künzel, H. Research into moisture
K85 1583 movements in renderings and rendered
walls. 1970.

U.K. Building Research Station.
Library communications.

693.97 no. Baehre, R. The dimensional accuracy
B12 1592 of steel structures. 1970.

U.K. Building Research Station.
Library communications.

624.043 no. Baumendistel, M. The effect of discon-
B18 1603 tinuities on the stresses and strains
in the ground behind a tunnel wall.
1971.

U.K. Building Research Station.
Library communications.

621.32 no. Haubner, P. Study of psychological
H18 1584 glare in interiors. 1970.

U.K. Building Research Station.
Library communications.

691.542 no. Stahel, A. The behaviour of
S71 1593 magnesium in clinker under different cooling conditions. 1970.

U.K. Building Research Station.
Library communications.

699.83 no. Holmer, B. Properties of wind in
H65 1604 built-up areas. 1971.

U.K. Building Research Station.
Library communications.

691.542 no. Heimann, R. Formation of calcium
H24 1586 silicates in the system
$CaO-SiO_2-CaF_2$. 1970.

U.K. Building Research Station.
Library communications.

691.54 no. Pfrunder, V.R. Some tests on the
P37 1594 effect of chemical composition and
grinding on the sintering of cement
raw mixes. 1970.

U.K. Building Research Station.
Library communications.

620.1 no. Ur'ev, N.B. The mechanism of failure
U72m 1605 of reinforcing glass fibre in harden-
ing cement paste, by N.B. Ur'ev and
N.V. Mikhailov. 1971.

U.K. Building Research Station.
Library communications.

699.841 no. U.S.S.R. Gosudarstvennyi komitet
U54 1587 soveta ministrov. Construction
in earthquake regions: design
code SN & P II-A.12-69. 1970.

U.K. Building Research Station.
Library communications.

690 no. Grün, W. Jointing technique. 1970.
G78 1595

U.K. Building Research Station.
Library communications.

690.015 no. Wiren, Bengt. Wind tunnel investiga-
(485) 1606 tion of the pressure distribution
S82 on a flat roof with different edge
R35 profiles. 1971.
1970
Engl.

U.K. Building Research Station.
Library communications.

621.32   no.   Fischer, D. Study and measurements of
F47   1607   the luminance distribution of
              fluorescent lamps. 1971.

U.K. Building Research Station.
Library communications.

691.542   no.   Rio, Arturo. The role and reaction
R46   1616   mechanism of celestine ($SrSO_4$) in
              the manufacture of Portland cement
              in absence and in presence of a
              fluxing agent (CaF_2). 1971.

U.K. Building Research Station.
Library communications.

621.6   no.   Dezheni, I. Vacuum testing of concrete
D29   1623   pipes for watertightness. 1971.

U.K. Building Research Station.
Library communications.

691.54   no.   Goggi, G. Contribution to the study
C63   1609   of the soundness of cements. 1971.

U.K. Building Research Station.
Library communications.

691.54   no.   Scholze, H. Carbonate-containing
S23c   1617   and sulphate-containing compounds
              in cement manufacture, by H.
              Scholze and U. Hildebrandt. 1971.

U.K. Building Research Station.
Library communications.

690.22   no.   Hallquist, Å. Design of masonry
H15d   1627   walls subjected to wind forces,
Engl.   by Å. Hallquist and G. Granheim.
              1971.

U.K. Building Research Station.
Library communications.

600.15   no.   Elstner, I. Research into the di-
E57   1610   calcium silicate falling of blast
              furnace slags, by I. Elstner et al.
              1971.

U.K. Building Research Station.
Library communications.

624.043   no.   Maier, G. The unstable flexural
M14   1618   behaviour of inflexible elasto-
              plastic beams. 1971.

U.K. Building Research Station.
Library communications.

621.32   no.   Gusev, N.M. A method of calculating
G87m   1628   the reflected light in side-lighted
              factory bays, by N.M. Gusev and
              V.A. Simonov. 1971.

U.K. Building Research Station.
Library communications.

699.83   no.   Hellers, B.G. Experience in storm
H25   1611   damage incidents in 1967 and 1969,
              by B.G. Hellers and G. Johansson.
              1971.

U.K. Building Research Station.
Library communications.

690.013   no.   U.K. Building Research Station.
U54   1619   Specifications for structures of
              large wall and floor panels: May
              1970 edition. 1971.

U.K. Building Research Station.
Library communications.

690.24   no.   Kozhinov, I.A. Analytical study of
K69   1629   the thermal resistance of ventilated
              cavity roofs, by I.A. Kozhinov and
              Yu.A. Tabunshchikov. 1971.

U.K. Building Research Station.
Library communications.

699.83   no.   Carlsson, A. Measures to prevent
C17   1612   storm damage: some reflections.
              1971.

U.K. Building Research Station.
Library communications.

690.091.82   no.   Agri, O. Dimensional control;
A37   1620   an end in itself? 1971.

621.32   U.K. Building Research Station.
N22

Ne'eman, E
    The lighting of compact plan hospitals,
by E. Ne'eman and others. Garston, Eng.,
Building Research Station, Ministry of
Technology, 1966.
    58p.   (U.K. Building Research Station.
Building research current papers. Design
series 48)
    Reprinted from Transactions, Illuminating
Engineering Society (London) Apr., 1966,
p. 37-58.

    1. Light-   ing. 2. Hospitals -
U.K. I. U.K.   Building Research
Station.   I. Title.

U.K. Building Research Station.
Library communications.

691.54   no.   Doleszai, K. Applicability of the
D65   1613   autoclave test for evaluating the
              magnesia swelling of cements, by
              K. Doleszai and L. Szatura. 1971.

U.K. Building Research Station.
Library communications.

693.5   no.   Suu, V. Tolerance measurements in
(485)   1621   precast concrete construction at
S88   Norrköping. 1971.

U.K. Building Research Station.
Library communications.

691.32   no.   Bauer, Hermann. Pumping concrete
B18   1630   through small bore pipelines.
              1971.

U.K. Building Research Station.
Library communications.

699.83   no.   Lethenström, B. Storm damage and
L27   1615   insurance cover. 1971.

U.K. Building Research Station.
Library communications.

691.542   no.   Danyushevskii, S.I. Technical
D15   1622   properties of cements containing
              free calcium oxide, by S.I.
              Danyushevskii et al. 1971.

U.K. Building Research Station.
Library communications.

697.9   no.   Held, E.F.M. van der. The effect of
H25   1632   turbulence on ventilation. 1971.

U.K. Building Research Station.
Library communications.

691.542 no. Nudel'man, B.I. Portland cement
N82 1633 manufacturing process. 1971.

U.K. Building Research Station.
Library communications.

691.54 no. U.K. Building Research Station.
U54r 1645 Refractory calcium-magnesium-
alumina cements. 1971.

693.5 U.K. Building Research Station.
R61 Roberts, E H
Load-carrying capacity of slab-strips
restrained against longitudinal expansion.
Garston, Eng., Building Research Station, 1970.
[10]p. (U.K. Building Research Station.
Current paper CP 4/70)
Reprinted from: Concrete, Sept. 1969,
pp. 369-378.

1. Concrete construction. 2. Loads.
I. U.K. Building Research Station. II. Title.

U.K. Building Research Station.
Library communications.

691.54 no. Rackwitz, R. Variability of concrete
R12 1634 cube crushing strength. 1971.

U.K. Building Research Station.
Library communications.

691.16 no. Berndtsson, B.S. Long-term strength
B27l 1646 of reinforced plastics under
static loading. 1971.

U.K. Building Research Station.
690.237
W34 Whitaker, T
Load cells for measuring the base
loads in bored piles and cylinder
foundations. Garston, Eng., Building
Research Station, Dept. of Scientific and
Industrial Research, 1954.
9p (U.K. Building Research Station.
Building Research current papers.
Engineering series 11)

1. Loads. 2. Foundations (Building) I. U.K.
Building Research Station.

U.K. Building Research Station.
Library communications.

658.562 no. Blaut, H. Recommendations for quality
B51 1635 control by the manufacturer. 1971.

U.K. Building Research Station.
Library communications.

691.542 no. Teoreanu, I. Correlations between
T26 1650 the mineralizing effect of substances on Portland cement clinker
formation and the periodic system
of the elements, by I. Teoreanu
and Tran van Huynh. 1971.

624.131 U.K. Building Research Station.
B87 Burland, J B
The load-deformation behaviour of middle chalk
at Mundford, Norfolk: a comparison between full-
scale performance and in situ and laboratory
measurements, by J.B. Burland and J.A. Lord.
[Garston, Eng.] Building Research Station,
1970.
10p. (U.K. Building Research Station.
Current paper 6/70)
Reprinted from: The proceedings of the
Conference on In Situ Investigations in Soils
and Rock, British Geographical Society
Institution of Civil Engineers
(Cont'd on next card)

U.K. Building Research Station.
Library communications.

691.51 no. Franz, D. Electron probe microanalysis
F71 1636 of deposits in lime shaft kiln over-
flow channels, by D. Franz and D.
Merz. 1971.

U.K. Building Research Station.
Library communications.

690.22 no. Magdalinski, J. How to design brick
M13 1660 walls for wind pressures. 1972.

624.131
B87 Burland, J B The load...1970.
(Card 2)

Conference. London, 13-15 May, 1969.

1. Soils 2. Loads. I. U.K. Building
Research Station. II. Lord, J.A., jt. au.
III. Title

U.K. Building Research Station.
Library communications.

691.32 no. Chigerovich, M.I. Bitumening concrete
C34 1639 to increase its corrosion resistance,
by M.I. Chigerovich et al. 1971.

691.322 U.K. Building Research Station.
T29l Teychenne, D C
Lightweight aggregates: their properties
and use in concrete in the U.K. Garston,
Eng., Building Research Station, Ministry
of Public Building and Works, 1968.
15p. (U.K. Building Research Station.
Current paper 73/68)
Bibliography: p. 14-15.
Reprint from: Volume I of the Proceedings
of the International Congress of Lightweight
Concrete, London, May 27-29, 1968, pp. 23-27.
1. Concrete aggregates. I. U.K. Building
Research Station. II. Title.

U.K. Building Research Station.
690.237
S451 Simms, L C
Loading tests on a three-storey structure.
Garston, Eng., Building Research Station,
Ministry of Technology, 1967.
10p. (U.K. Building Research Station.
Building research current papers. Engineering
papers 44)
Reprinted from: Institute of Structural
Engineers Conference 1966, 19th May.
1. Loads. 2. Steel construction. 3. Strength
of materials. I. U.K. Building Research
Station. II. Title.

U.K. Building Research Station.
Library communications.

691.542 no. U.K. Building Research Station.
U54 1642 Process for burning cement clinker
with simultaneous production of
sulphuric acid from raw materials
containing calcium sulphate in a
shaft kiln. 1971.

691.542 U.K. Building Research Station.
M17 Matouschek, F
The lime saturation value of Portland cement
clinker relative to the raw material analysis,
the burning of the clinker, and the mortar
strengths. Garston, Eng., Building Research
Station, 1970.
[27]p. (Library communication no. 1588)
Translated from the German and reprinted
from Zement-Kalk-Gips, 1970, 23 (2), 80-87.
1. Portland cement. 2. Strength of materials.
I. U.K. Building Research Station. II. Title:
(Series)

624.042 U.K. Building Research Station.
M47 Mitchel, G R
Loadings on buildings - a review paper.
Garston Eng., Building Research Station,
1969.
9p. U.K. Building Research Station.
Current paper 50/69)

Paper written for IABSE Symposium on
Concepts of Safety of Structures and
Methods of Design, London, Sept. 1969.
1. Loads. I. U.K. Building Research
Station. II. Title.

U.K. Building Research Station.
Library communications.

691.542 no. U.K. Building Research Station.
U54p 1644 Process for manufacture of low-
fluorine cement clinker from
phosphoric-acid-waste gypsum.
1971.

690.015
(41:016)
U541 United Kingdom. Building Research Station.
No. 117/1 (Library)
A list of bibliographies compiled in the
BRS Library from September, 1932 to Dec.,
1948, together with bibliographies included
in other BRS publications, and a subject index
to the whole. Garston, England, Dec. 1948.
11 p. (Its Library bibliography no.
117/1)

1. Building research - Bibliographies.

727.1 U. K. Building Research Station.
L28 Levin, P H
The location of primary schools: some
planning implications, by P.H. Levin and A.J.
Bruce. Garston, Eng., Building Research Sta-
tion, Ministry of Public Building and Works,
1968.
56-66p. U.K. Building Research Station.
Building research current papers. Current
paper 39/68)
Reprinted from: Journal of the Town
Planning Institute, Feb. 1968.
1. Schools. 2. City planning. I. U.K.
Building Research Station. II. Bruce,
A.J., jt. au III. Title.

534.83
P17   U.K. Building Research Station.
Parkin, P H
London noise survey by P.H. Parkin and others. London, Building Research Station, Ministry of Public Building and Works, H.M.S.O. 1968.
60p.

1. Noise. I. U.K. Building Research Station. II. Title.

691.542
G87m   U.K. Building Research Station.
Gutt, W
Manufacture of portland cement from phosphatic raw materials. Garston, Eng., Building Research Station, Ministry of Public Building and Works, 1968.
22p. (U.K. Building Research Station. Current paper CP 90/68)
Bibliography: p. 21-22.
To be published in the Proceedings of the fifth International Symposium on the Chemistry of Cement, Tokyo Oct. 1968.
1. Portland cement. I. Title. II. U.K. Building Research Station.

620.1
U72m   U.K. Building Research Station.
Ur'ev, N B
The mechanism of failure of reinforcing glass fibre in hardening cement paste, by N.B. Ur'ev and N.V. Mikhailov. Garston, Eng., Building Research Station, 1971.
5p. (Library communication no. 1605)
Translated from the Russian and reprinted from Neorganicheskie Materialy, 1969, 5 (8), 1451-5.

1. Strength of materials. I. Mikhailov, N.V., jt. au. II. U.K. Building Research Station. III. Title. (Series)

691.16
B27L   U.K. Building Research Station.
Berndtsson, B S
Long-term strength of reinforced plastics under static loading. Garston, Eng., Building Research Station, 1971.
27p. (Library communication no. 1646)
Translated from the Swedish.

1. Plastics. 2. Strength of materials. I. U.K. Building Research Station. II. Title. (Series)

691
(41)   U.K. Building Research Station.
C85   Cullen, B D
Materials usage in new buildings. Garston, Eng., Building Research Station, Ministry of Technology, 1967.
7p. (U.K. Building Research Station. Building research current papers. Design series 58)
Reprinted from Building, 1967, vol. 212, January 27, p. 115-116, 119-20, 123-24, 127.

1. Building materials - U.K. 2. Materials handling. I. U.K. Building Research Station. II. Title.

691.542
M14   U.K. Building Research Station.
Majumdar, A J
Mechanism of stabilization of high-magnesia portland cements by reactive silica under autoclave conditions, by A. J. Majumdar and S.S. Rehsi. Garston, Eng., Building Research Station, 1970.
[10]p. (U.K. Building Research Station. Current paper 9/70)

Bibliography: p. 149-150.

Reprinted from: The Magazine of
(Cont'd on next card)

690.015
(41:016)   Gt. Brit. Building Research Station.
U541   Low cost housing and town planning in colonial
no. 149   territories; some selected references. Garston, Eng., July 1950.
6 p. (Its Library bibliography no. 149)
Annotated.
Processed.

1.Housing in the tropics-Bibl. I.Series.

623
T36   U.K. Building Research Station.
Thomas, H S H
The measurement of strain in tunnel linings using the vibrating-wire technique. Garston, Eng., Building Research Station, Ministry of Technology, 1966.
8p. (U.K. Building Research Station. Building research current papers. Engineering series 34)
Reprinted from: Strain, 1966, vol. 2(July), p. 16-21.

1. Structural engineering. I. U.K. Building Research Station. II. Title. III. Title: Tunnel linings.

691.542
M14   Majumdar, A J   Mechanism...1970.
(Card 2)

concrete research, Sept. 1969, pp. 141-150.

1. Portland cement. I. Rehsi, S.S., jt. au. II. U.K. Building Research Station. III. Title.

693.002.22
(41)   U.K. Building Research Station.
S29   Seymour-Walker, K J
L-shaped well units. Garston, Eng., Building Research Station, Ministry of Technology, 1966.
4p. (U.K. Building Research Station. Building research current papers. Design series 47)
Reprinted from Architect and building news, 1966, vol. 230/4 (July 27th), p. 159-62.

1. Prefabricated construction - U.K. 2. Wells. I. U.K. Building Research Station. II. Title.

699.83
C17   U.K. Building Research Station.
Carlsson, A
Measures to prevent storm damage: some reflections. Garston, Eng., Building Research Station, 1971.
[11]p. (Library communication no. 1612)
Translated from the Swedish.

1. Buildings - Wind stresses. 2. Storms. I. U.K. Building Research Station. II. Title. (Series)

691.542
M27   U.K. Building Research Station.
Method for increasing the strength of cement formed as a by-product of the manufacture of sulphuric acid from calcium sulphate. Garston, Eng., Building Research Station, 1969.
3p. (U.K. Building Research Station. Library communication no. 1509)
Translated from the German. East German patent 63318.

1. Portland cement. 2. Strength of materials. I. U.K. Building Research Station. (Series)

727.1
C51   U.K. Building Research Station.
Clapp, Margaret A
The maintenance and running costs of school building, by Margaret A. Clapp and B.D. Cullen. Garston, Eng., Building Research Station, 1968.
552-560p. (U.K. Building Research Station. Current paper 72/68)
Reprinted from: Chartered surveyor, May 1968, pp. 552-560.

1. Schools. 2. Building maintenance. I. Cullen, B.D., jt. au. II. U.K. Building Research Station. III. Title.

526
P25   U.K. Building Research Station.
Penman, A D M
Measuring movements of engineering structures, by A.D.M. Penman and J.A. Charles. Garston, Eng., Building Research Station, 1971.
16p. (U.K. Building Research Station. Current paper CP 32/71)
Reprinted from: Proceedings of the 13th International Congress of Surveyors, Wiesbaden, 1971, Commission 6, Paper 605.4.
1. Surveying. I. Charles, J.A., jt. au. II. U.K. Building Research Station. III. Title.

621.32
G87m   U.K. Building Research Station.
Gusev, N M
A method of calculating the reflected light in side-lighted factory bays, by N.M. Gusev and V.A. Simonov. Garston, Eng., Building Research Station, 1971.
[11]p. (Library communication no. 1628)
Translated from the Russian.

1. Lighting. 2. Daylight. I. Simonov, V.A., jt. au. II. U.K. Building Research Station. III. Title. (Series)

721.9
690   U.K. Building Research Station.
V15   Vellings, H G
Making concrete panels for industrialized building by pressing. Garston, Eng., Building Research Station, Ministry of Technology [1966?]
6p. (U.K. Building Research Station. Building research current papers. Construction series 25)

1. Building equipment. 2. Panels. 3. Concrete. I. U.K. Building Research Station. II. Title.

691.32
K25m   U.K. Building Research Station.
Kempster, E
Measuring void content: new apparatus for aggregates, sands and fillers. Garston, Eng., Building Research Station, 1969.
[3]p. (U.K. Building Research Station. Current paper 19/69)
Reprinted form: Contract journal, March 27, 1969. pp. 409-410.

1. Concrete. I. U.K. Building Research Station. II. Title.

693.002.22
E22   U.K. Building Research Station.
Eden, J F
Metrology and the module. Garston, Eng., Building Research Station, Ministry of Technology, 1968.
8p. (U.K. Building Research Station. Current paper 31/68)
Abridged version of this paper appeared in Architectural design, March, 1967. p. 148-150.
1. Prefabricated construction. 2. Modular coordination. I. U.K. Building Research Station. II. Title.

691.54
G87m   U.K. Building Research Station.
Gutt, W
Manufacture of cement from industrial by-products. Garston, Eng., Building Research Station, 1971.
[9]p. (Current paper no. 19/71)

Reprinted from: Chemistry and industry, 13 Feb. 1971, pp. 189-197.

1. Cement. I. U.K. Building Research Station. II. Title. III. Title: Industrial by-products.

666.81
A54   U.K. Building Research Station.
Ali, M A
Mechanical properties of glass fibre-reinforced gypsum, by M.A. Ali and F.J. Grimer. Garston, Eng., Building Research Station, 1969.
[7]p. (U.K. Building Research Station. Current paper 33/69)
Reprinted from: Journal of materials science, May 1969, pp. 389-395.
1. Gypsum. 2. Glass. I. Grimer, F.J., jt. au. II. U.K. Building Research Station. III. Title.

620.1
(014)   U.K. Building Research Station.
H15   Hansagi, I
Mining method of determining the strength of rock in the mass and of classifying rock (Bergmännisches Verfahren der Gebirgsfestigkeitsbestimmung und der Gebirgsklassifizierung) Garston, Eng., Building Research Station, Ministry of Public Building and Works, 1968.
6p. (U.K. Building Research Station. Library communication 1446)
Translated from the German and reprinted from: Proc. 1st Congress of the International Society of Rock
(Cont'd on next card)

620.1
(014)
H15

Hansagi, I   Mining...1968.   (Card 2)

Mechanics, Lisbon. 1966, Vol. I, pp. 179-83.

1. Strength of materials - Testing.
I. U.K. Building Research Station.

696.1
861b

U.K. Building Research Station.
Sobolev, A
The modified flushing efficiency test for
WC pans of the wash down type. Garston, Eng.,
Building Research Station, Ministry of Tech-
nology, 1967.
4p.   (U.K. Building Research Station.
Building research current papers. Engineer-
ing series 38)
Reprinted form Journal of the Institution
of Water Engineers, vol. 20, no. 7, p. 490-
494.

1. Plumbing.   I. U.K. Building
Research Sta-   tion. II. Title.

690
(41)
J21

U.K. Building Research Station.
Jesnes, R E
Network diagrams: some notes on alternative
presentations, by R.E. Jesnes and J.R.
Britten. Garston, Eng., Building Research
Station, Ministry of Technology, 1966.
102-6p.   (U.K. Building Research Sta-
tion. Building research current papers.
Construction series 29)
Reprinted from: Building, 1966, vol. 210
(10th June), pp. 102-6.

1. Building research - U.K. I. Britten,
J.R., jt. au.   II. U.K. Building
Research   Station.

690
U54m

U.K. Building Research Station.
Mobile tower cranes for two- and three-
story building, by H.F. Broughton and others.
London, H. M. Stat. Off., 1960.
36p. illus., diagrs. (Its National building studies. Special report no. 31)

1. Building construction. I. Broughton, H. F.

691.32
E75

U.K. Building Research Station.
Ernst, K
Moisture measurement for concrete produc-
tion. Garston, Eng., Building Research
Station, 1969.
[15]p. (U.K. Building Research Station.
Library communication no. 1506)
Translated from the German and reprinted
from: Betonstein-Zeitung, 1969, 35 (2), 74-80.

1. Concrete. 2. Concrete aggregates.
I. U.K. Building Research Station. II. Title.
(Series)

623
B17

U.K. Building Research Station.
Bate, S C C
New design and research on structural use
of concrete. Garston, Eng., Building Research
Station, Ministry of Technology, 1966.
[3]p.   U.K. Building Research Station.
Building research current papers. Engineering
series 36)
Reprinted from Municipal engineering, vol.
143, no. 35, 1966, p. 1739, 41, 43.

1. Structural engineering. 2. Concrete
construction I. U.K. Building Research
Station.   II. Title.

720
B87

U.K. Building Research Station.
Butler, A J
Model design techniques. Garston, Eng.,
Building Research Station, Dept. of
Scientific and Industrial Research, 1964.
10p. (U.K. Building Research Station.
Building research current papers. Design
series 21)
Part 1 is reprinted from the Institution
of Heating and Ventilating Engineers
Journal, 1964, vol. 31 (February) pp. 401-6.

1. Architecture - Design. 2. Heating.
3. Ventilation.   I. U.K. Building
Research   Station.
I. Title.

728.2
(41)
C71

U.K. Building Research Station.
Craig, C N
Multi-story flats: design, building
methods and costs. London, H.M. Stat.
Off., 1963.
80p.   (U.K. Building Research Station.
National building studies special
report 34)

1. Apartment houses - U.K. 2. Building methods -
U.K. 3. Building costs - U.K. I. U.K. Building
Research Station. II. Title.

725.4
V99

U.K. Building Research Station.
Vyzhigin, G V
New designs of multi-storey factory buildings
for seismic regions, by G.V. Vyzhigin and others.
Garston, Eng., Building Research Station, 1970.
4p. (U.K. Building Research Station.
Library communication no. 1562)
Translated from the Russian and reprinted
from Promyshlennoe Stroitel'stvo, 1970, (1),
25-9.
1. Industrial buildings. 2. Architecture
- Designs and plans. I. U.K. Building
Research Station. II. Title. (Series)

691.32
L22

U.K. Building Research Station.
Lee, C R
Model studies of concrete reactor shields
under temperature loading, by C.R. Lee and
others. Garston, Eng., Building Research
Station, Ministry of Public Building and
Works, 1968.
85-93p.   (U.K. Building Research
Station. Current paper 43/68)
"Originally published as paper 46"
Proceedings of Conference on Prestressed
Concrete Pressure Vessels, Institution of
Civil Engineering, London, 1967.

(Cont'd on next card)

693.5
F79

U.K. BUILDING RESEARCH STATION. NATIONAL BUILDING
STUDIES SPECIAL REPORT NO. 23.
FRYER, K G H
A STUDY OF CONCRETING METHODS ON
HOUSING SITES, BY K.G.H. FRYER AND J.F.
EDEN. LONDON, H.M. STAT. OFF., 1954.
46P. (U.S. BUILDING RESEARCH
STATION. NATIONAL BUILDING STUDIES
SPECIAL REPORT NO. 23)

1. CONCRETE CONSTRUCTION - RESEARCH.
I. EDEN, J.F., JT. AU. (SERIES)

691.32
C67

U.K. Building Research Station.
Corson, R H
A new gauge for the measurement of internal
strains in concrete. Garston, [Eng.], Building Research Station. Ministry of Technology,
1966.
[10]p.   (U.K. Building Research Station.
Building research current papers. Engineering
series 29)
Reprinted from: Concrete and Constructional
Engineering, 1965, vol. 60 (December), pp.437-
43.

(Cont'd on next card)

691.32
L22

Lee, C   R   Model studies...1968
(Card 2)

1. Concrete. 2. Walls. 3. Protective
construction. I. U.K. Building Research
Station. II. Title.

691.320.15
868

U.K. BUILDING RESEARCH STATION. NATIONAL
BUILDING STUDIES TECHNICAL PAPER NO. 8.
BOWDEN, S R
THE ANALYSIS OF CONCRETES, BY
S.R. BOWDEN AND E.W. GREEN.
LONDON, H.M. STAT. OFF., 1950.
16P. (U.K. BUILDING RESEARCH
STATION. NATIONAL BUILDING STUDIES
TECHNICAL PAPER NO. 8)

BIBLIOGRAPHY: P. 16.

1. CONCRETE - RESEARCH.
I. GREEN, E.W., JT. AU.
II. TITLE. (SERIES)

691.32
C67

Corson, R.H. A new gauge for the measurement
of internal strains in concrete...1966.
(Card 2)

1. Concrete. 2. Building methods. I. U.K.
Building Research Station. II. Concrete and
constructional engineering. III. Title.

725.23
(41)
U54

U.K. BUILDING RESEARCH STATION,
GARSTON, HERTS.
MODERN OFFICES: A USER SURVEY, BY
F.J. LANGDON. LONDON, H.M.
STATIONERY OFFICE, 1966.
61P. (ITS NATIONAL BUILDING
STUDIES, RESEARCH PAPER 41)

1. OFFICE BUILDINGS. 2. OFFICE
BUILDINGS - U.K. I. LANGDON, F.J.
II. TITLE.

624.043
L65

U.K. Building Research Station.
Longchal, M
The natural weathering of composite materi-
als subjected to torsional stress. Garston,
Eng., Building Research Station, 1969.
[17]p. (U.K. Building Research Station.
Library communication no. 1530)
Translated from the French and reprinted
from: Revue generale du caoutchouc et des
plastiques, Plastiques, 1968, 5 (4), 235-42.

1. Strains and stresses. 2. Building
materials - Climatic effects. I. U.K.
Building Research Station. II. Title.
(Series)

690.015
(41)
L21n

U.K. Building Research Station.
Lea, F M
New paths in building. Garston, Eng.,
Building Research Station, Ministry of
Technology, 1965.
7p.   (U.K. Building Research Station.
Building research current papers.
Supplements no. 6)
Reprinted from: National provincial
bank review, Nov., 1965, p. 8-14.

1. Building research - U.K. I. U.K.
Building Research   Station. II. Title.

690.015
(41
:016)
U541
no.237

U.K. Building Research Station.
Modernising old dwellings. Garston, Eng.,
1970.
20p. (It Library bibliography no. 237)

1. Houses - Maintenance and modernization -
Bibl. I. Title. (Series)

699.83
N28

U.K. Building Research Station.
Newberry, C W
The nature of gust loading on tall build-
ings, by C.W. Newberry and others. Paper
presented at the International Seminar on Wind
Effects on Buildings and Structures, Ottawa,
Sept., 1967. Garston, Eng., Building
Research Station, Ministry of Public Building
and Works, 1968.
11p. (U.K. Building Research Station.
Building research current paper 66/68)

1. Buildings - Wind stresses. 2. Loads.
I. U.K. Building   Research Station.
II. Title.

534.83
(41)
U54

UNITED KINGDOM. BUILDING RESEARCH
STATION, GARSTON, HERTS.
NOISE IN THE HOME. GARSTON, HERTS.,
1961.
4L.

FROM BUILDING RESEARCH STATION
DIGEST, 2D SERIES, 7.

1. NOISE. 2. ARCHITECTURAL
ACOUSTICS. I. TITLE.

699.844
U54
U.K. Building Research Station.
Noise in three groups of flats with different floor insulations, by P. G. Gray and others. London, H.M. Stat. Off., 1959.
61p. diagrs., tables. (Its National building studies research paper no. 27)

1. Soundproofing. 2. Insulation. 3. Floors and flooring.

693.5
L22
U.K. Building Research Station.
Lee, C R
Observations on the massive concrete structures of the 7 geV proton synchrotron ('NIMROD'). Garston Eng. Building Research Station, Ministry of Technology, 1966.
29p. (U.K. Building Research Station. Building research current papers. Engineering series 33)
Reprinted from: Conference on Stresses in Service, London, March 1966, p. 17-29.

1. Concrete construction. 2. Concrete.
I. U.K. Building Research Station.
II. Title.

693.2 U.K. Building Research Station.
F67 Forbes, W S
The output of bricklayers, by W.S. Forbes and J. F. Mayer. Garston, Eng., Building Research Station, Ministry of Public Building and Works, 1968.
146p. (U.K. Building Research Station. Building research current papers. Current paper 32/68)
Reprinted from: Building, Jan. 26, 1968.

1. Bricklaying. I. Mayer, J.F., jt. au.
II. U.K. Building Research Station. III. Title.

VF
693.55
U54
U.K. Building Research Station.
A note on the history of reinforced concrete in buildings, by S. B. Hamilton. London, H.M. Stat. Off., 1956.
30 p. illus. (Its National Building Studies. Special report no. 24)

1. Reinforced concrete construction.
I. Hamilton, S B

624.131
P25o
U.K. Building Research Station.
Penman, A D M
Observed and predicted deformations in a large embankment dam during construction, by A.D.M. Penman and others. Garston, Eng., Building Research Station, 1971.
19p. (U.K. Building Research Station. Current paper 18/71)
Paper published in the Proceedings of the Institution of Civil Engineers, vol. 49, May, 1971, pp. 1-21.
Bibliography: p. 13-14.
1. Soils. 2. Strains and stresses. I. U.K. Building Research Station. II. Title.

691.328
W66p
U.K. Building Research Station.
Wood, R H
A partial failure of limit analysis for slabs, and the consequences for future research. Garston, Eng., Building Research Station, 1970.
[12]p. (U.K. Building Research Station. Current paper 11/70)

Bibliography: p. 89-90.

Reprinted from: The Magazine of concrete
(Cont'd on next card)

VF
690.091.82
(6)
G72
D75
Great Britain. Building Research Station. Notes
no. Space and accommodation standards for low-cost housing in colonial territories. May 1949.

697.001.5 Heating studies in open plan houses at B.R.S.
G72
C154 Garston, Eng. 1950.

690.21 Atkinson, G.A. Note on the design of
A74
D116 foundations in unstable soils in Africa. Sept. 1950

690
:331.86
U54
U.K. Building Research Station.
The occupational structure and the training of operatives for the building industry, by J. I'a Nelson and others. Garston, Eng., 1968.
18p. (Its Current paper 25/68)

1. Building trades. 2. Building industry.
I. Nelson, J. I'a. II. Title.

691.328
W66p
Wood, R H A partial...1970.
(Card 2)

research. June. 1969. pp. 79-90.

1. Concrete, Reinforced. 2. Structural engineering. I. U.K. Building Research Station. II. Title.

VF
691
D18
Gt. Brit. Building Research Station. Notes.

no.
E190 Davey, N. Building materials in antiquity. Oct. 1949.

VF
690.015 C166 Atkinson, G.A. Report on a visit ...
(6)   to Africa. Oct. 1950.
A74

693
C71
U.K. Building Research Station.
Craig, C N
On-site battery casting. Garston, Eng., Building Research Station, Ministry of Technology, 1966.
[7]p. (U.K. Building Research Station. Building research current papers. Construction series 34)
Reprinted from the Architect and building news, 14th December 1966, p. 1051-57.

1. Building methods. I. U.K. Building Research Station.

690.22
B87
U.K. Building Research Station.
Burgess, R A
Partitioning, an operational study. Garston, Eng., Building Research Station, Ministry of Technology [1967?]
25p. (U.K. Building Research Station. Building research current papers. Construction series 31)

1. Walls. 2. Panels. I. U.K. Building Research Station. II. Title.

VF
711.4
(60)
A74
Gt. Brit. Building Research Station. Notes.

E 843 Atkinson, G.A. Urbanization and town growth in Africa. Problems of mass housing and techniques assisting towards their solution. 1958.

691.542
G67
U.K. Building Research Station.
Goria, C
On the possibility of estimating chemically the pozzolanic activity of a material added to portland cement. Proposal to the Technical Committee ISO/74. Garston, Eng., Building Research Station, 1970.
8p. (U.K. Building Research Station. Library communication no. 1566)
Translated from the Italian [and reprinted from] L'Industria Italiana del cemento, 1963, 33 (7), 491-8.
1. Portland cement. I. U.K. Building Research Station. II. Negro, A., jt. au. III. Title. (Series)

690.015
(41)
L21
U.K. Building Research Station.
Lea, F M
The pattern of building research. Garston, Eng., Dept. of Scientific and Industrial Research, Building Research Station, 1963.
[4]p. (Building Research current papers. Supplements 2)

1. Building research - U.K. I. U.K. Building Research Station.

690.37
327
U.K. Building Research Station. Notes.

E 394 Atkinson, G. A. Building in warm climates... [1952]

690.031
B47o
U.K. Building Research Station.
Bishop, D
Operational bills and cost communication. Garston, Eng., Building Research Station, Ministry of Technology, 1966.
[4]p. (U.K. Building Research Station. Building research current papers. Design series 55)
Reprinted from: Architects journal, vol. 139, no. 828, p. 158, 160, 2.

1. Building costs. I. U.K. Building Research Station. II. Title.

211.58
M45
U.K. Building Research Station.
Miller, A
Pedestrians and vehicles on housing estates: a user study, by A. Miller and J.A. Cook. Garston, Eng., Building Research Station, Ministry of Public Building and Works, 1968.
1075-1082p. (U.K. Building Research Station. Current paper 23/68)
Originally published in The Architects' journal, Nov., 1967.
1. Residential areas. 2. Housing - Social aspects. 3. Architecture - Designs and plans 4. Streets - U.K. 5. Sidewalks - U.K. I. Cook, J.A. II. U.K. Building Research Station. III. Architects' journal. IV. Title.

696
U54
U.K. Building Research Station.
Notes on the repair and renovation of flood-damaged buildings. Prepared in collaboration with the Forest Products Research Laboratory. Garston, Eng., Building Research Station, Dept. of Scientific and Industrial Research, 1964.
5p. (Its Building research current papers. Construction series no. 13)
1. Building maintenance. 2. Flood control.

690.031
F47
U.K. Building Research Station.
Firmstone, C J
Operational drawings and bills: report of their use on a live project, by C. J. Firmstone and E. R. Skoyles. Garston, Eng., Ministry of Public Works, 1967.
47p. (U.K. Building Research Station current papers, Design series 63)
Reprinted from Architect's journal, 1967.
B.c.1 vol. 45, (May 31), pp. 1279-1282.
Lcf.c.2
1. Building costs - Estimates. 2. Building costs - U.K. I. Skoyles, E.R. II. U.K. Building Research Station. III. Title.

690.091.82
A74
U.K. Building Research Station.
Atkinson G A
The performance concept in building: the international theme. Garston, Eng., Building Research Station, 1971.
[5]p. (U.K. Building Research Station. Current paper no. 11/71)
Prepared for the Royal Institute of British Architects' conference, Why performance specifications? 18 Feb. 1971.
1. Building standards. I. U.K. Building Research Station. II. Title.

690.091.82
M14
U.K. Building Research Station.
Mainstone, R J
Performance parameters and performance specification in architectural design, by R.J. Mainstone and others. Garston, Eng., Building Research Station, 1969.
125-133p. (U.K. Building Research Station. Current paper 23/69)
Reprinted from: Building science, 1969, vol. 3(3), Jan., pp. 125-133.

1. Building standards. 2. Architecture - Designs and plans. I. U.K. Building Research Station.   II. Title.

534.83
M27
U.K. Building Research Station.
Máry, J
Physiological studies - introductory survey (part 2) Garston, Eng., Building Research Station, 1971.
16p. (Library communication no. 1597)

Bibliography: p. 14-16.
Translated from the French and reprinted from Revue d'Acoustique, 1970 (10), 113-22.

1. Noise. 2. Hearing. I. U.K. Building Research Station. II. Title. (Series)

690.031
(41)
U54p
pt.2
U.K. Building Research Station.
Skoyles, E R
Practical application of operational bills. Part 2: Use of bill when employment of main contractor is determined, by E.R. Skoyles and R.F. Lear. Garston, Eng., Building Research Station, Ministry of Public Building and Works, 1968.
70-76p. (U.K. Building Research Station. Current paper 74/68)
Reprinted from: The chartered surveyor, August, 1968 pp.70-76.
1. Building costs - U.K. 2. Building methods.

(Cont'd on next card)

690.091.82
(41)
H17
U.K. Building Research Station.
Harrison, H   W
Performance specifications for building components. Garston, Eng., Building Research Station, 1969.
[10]p. (U.K. Building Research Station. Current paper 37/69)
Reprinted from: The Architects journal, June 25, 1969, pp. 1705-1714.
1. Building standards - U.K. I. U.K. Building Research Station. II. Title.

2C

678.7
C51
U.K. Building Research Station.
Clarke, N W B
Pipe laying principles; notes on construction methods for underground pipelines designed by the computed load method. London, H.M. Stat. Off., 1964.
23p. (U.K. Building Research Station. National building studies. Special report 35)
At head of title: Dept. of Scientific and Industrial Research. Building Research Station.
1. Pipes. 2. Loads.   I. Title.
II. U.K. Building   Research
Station.

690.031
(41)
U54p
pt.2
Skoyles, E R   Practical application...
1968.   (Card 2)

I. U.K. Building Research Station.
II. Lear, R.F., jt. au. III. Title.

621.32
C62
U.K. Building Research Station.
Cockram, A H
Permanent supplementary artificial lighting of deep hospital wards with an estimate of costs in use, by A.H. Cockram and others. Garston, Eng., Building Research Station, 1970.
[19]p. (U.K. Building Research Station. Current paper 30/70)

1. Lighting. 2. Hospitals.
I. U.K. Building Research Station.
II. Title.

621.6
Y58
U.K. Building Research Station.
Young, O C
Pipeline design: the relationship between structural theory and laying practice. Garston, Eng., Building Research Station, Ministry of Technology, 1964.
17p. (U.K. Building Research Station. Building research current papers. Engineering series 23)
Reprinted from Public Works and Municipal Services Congress and Exhibition. Final report, 1964, p. 264-73.

1. Pipes. 2. Struc-   tural engineering.
I. U.K. Building Re-   search Station.
III. Title.

690.015
(41
:016)
U541
no.
216
U.K. Building Research Station.
Precast concrete units. Garston, Eng., Building Research Station, 1969.
6p. (Its Library bibliography 216)

1. Concrete construction - Bibl. 2. Prefabricated construction - Bibl. I. Title.

VF
621.32
U54
U.K. Building Research Station.
The permanent supplementary artificial lighting of interiors (PSALI) Garston, Eng., 1960.
7p. illus.

Building Research Station Digest no. 135, June 1960.

1. Lighting.

690.015
(41
:016)
U541
no. 233
U.K. Building Research Station.
Plastics in central heating and hot water systems. Garston, Eng., 1970.
3p. (Its Library bibliography 233)

1. Plastics - Bibl. 2. Heating, Central - Bibl. I. Title.

VF
690.37
F71
TMar.1949
Gt. Brit. Building Research Station.
Préfabrication et construction coloniale. [Paris, France] Centre Scientifique et Technique du Bâtiment, Service de l'Habitat Intertropical [Mar. 1949]
15, vi l. (France. Centre Scientifique et Technique du Bâtiment. Service de l'Habitat Intertropical. Traductions.)

English title: Prefabrication and colonial building.
Building Research Station Note no. D66.
Mimeographed.

(Continued on next card)

691.542
N87
U.K. Building Research Station.
Nurse, R W
Phase equilibria and formation of portland cement minerals. Garston, Eng., Building Research Station, 1969.
21p. (U.K. Building Research Station. Current paper CP 21/69)
To be published in the Proceedings of the Fifth International Symposium on the Chemistry of Cement, held in Tokyo, Oct., 1968.

1. Portland cement. I. U.K. Building Research Station.   II. Title.

691.542
N82
U.K. Building Research Station.
Nudel'man, B I
Portland cement manufacturing process. Garston, Eng., Building Research Station, 1971.
2p. (Library communication no. 1633)

Translated from the Russian.

1. Portland cement. I. U.K. Building Research Station. II. Title. (Series)

Gt. Brit. Building Research Station. Préfabrication et construction coloniale...1949. (Card 2)

1.Prefabricated construction-Africa. 2.Housing in the tropics. I.Ser.

691.16
V14
U.K. Building Research Station.
Vaiman, E Ya
The photodegradation of PVC fibres (O fotodestriktsii polivinilkhloridnykh volokon), by E. Ya. Vaiman and others. Garston, Eng., Building Research Station, Ministry of Public Building and Works, 1968.
4p. (U.K. Building Research Station. Library communication no. 1439)
Translated from the Russian and reprinted from: Zhurnal prikladnoi khimii, 1968, 41 (21),   362-5.
(Cont'd on next card)

697.9
L68
U.K. Building Research Station.
Loudon, A G
Possible economies in air-conditioning by accepting temperature swings, by A.G. Loudon and P. Petherbridge. Garston, Eng., Building Research Station, Ministry of Technology, 1968.
7p. (U.K. Building Research Station. Current paper 48/68)
Paper presented at the IHVE/BRS Symposium "Thermal environment in modern buildings - aspects affecting the design team", Feb. 29, 1968.
1. Air conditioning. I. Petherbridge, P., jt. au. II. U.K. Building Research Station. III.   Title.

690.512.2
(41)
S76
U.K. Building Research Station.
Stone, P A
The price of sites for residential building. Garston, Eng., Building Research Station, Dept. of Scientific and Industrial Research, 1964.
[12]p. (U.K. Building Research Station. Building Research. Current papers. Design series 23)
Reprinted from: The Estates gazette, vol. 189 (5138) 1964. p. 85-91.
1. Site selection - U.K. 2. Residential areas.
3. Building costs.   I. U.K. Building Research Station.   II. Title.

691.16
V14
Vaiman, E Ya The...1968. (Card 2)

1. Plastics. I. U.K. Building Research Station. II. Title: PVC fibres. III. Title.

690.031
(41)
U54p
pt.1
U.K. Building Research Station.
Forbes, W S
A practical application of operational bills. Part 1: Preparation and tendering stages, by W.S. Forbes and E.R. Skoyles. Garston, Eng., Building Research Station, Ministry of Technology, 1966.
[5]p. (U.K. Building Research Station. Building research current papers. Construction series 35)
Reprinted from Chartered surveyor, 1966, vol. 98, no. 9. p. 489-493.
1. Building costs -   U.K. 2. Building
methods. I. U.K.   Building Research
Station. II. Skoyles, E.R., jt.au. III. Title.

697.133
P27
U.K. Building Research Station.
Petherbridge, P
Principles of sun control. Garston, Eng., Building Research Station, Ministry of Technology, 1966.
143-149p. (U.K. Building Research Station. Building research current papers. Design series 41)

Reprinted from the Architects' journal, Jan. 12, 1966.

1. Heat trans-   mission. 2. Heating,
Solar. 3. Archi-   tecture and climate.
I. U.K. Building   Research Station.
II. Title.

624
B17

U.K. Building Research Station.
Bate, S C C
Priorities in structural engineering research. Garston, Eng., Building Research Station, 1969.
15-27p. (U.K. Building Research Station. Current paper 12/69)
Reprinted from: Structural engineer, 1969, vol. 47(1), Jan., pp. 15-27.

1. Structural engineering. 2. Engineering research. I. U.K. Building Research Station. II. Title.

690.22
K25

U. K. Building Research Station.
Kempster, E
Producing building components by spray techniques, E. Kempster and R. Wander. Garston, Eng., Building Research Station, Ministry of Public Building and Works, 1967.
445-8, 451p. (U.K. Building Research Station. Building research current papers. Current paper 5/68)
Reprinted from the National builder, July 1967

1. Walls. 2. Prefabricated construction - U.K. 3. Concrete. I. Wander, R., jt. au. II. U.S. Building Research Station. III. Title.

691.328
B22

U.K. Building Research Station.
Beeby, A W
Proposals for the control of deflection in the new unified code for structural concrete, by A.W. Beeby and J.R. Miles. Garston, Eng., Building Research Station, Ministry of Public Building and Works, 1969.
[13]p. (U.K. Building Research Station. Current paper 17/69)
Reprinted from: Concrete, 1968, Vol. 2(12), Dec., pp. 511-513; 1969, Vol. 3(3) March, pp. 101-110.

1. Concrete, Reinforced. 2. Concrete construction. I. Miles, J.R., jt. au. II. U.K. Building Research Station. III. Title.

690.015
C65
1950

Gt. Brit. Building Research Station.
Conference on Building Research, Geneva, Nov. 13-18, 1950.
Proceedings. Geneva, United Nations Economic Commission for Europe, Industry and Materials Committee, Housing Sub-committee, Dec. 1950.
285 p. (General E/ECE/122;E/ECE/IM/HOU/BR/2)

Partial contents.-Transition from research to industrial application, Ir J.P.Mazure, J.Aitken,p. 116-136.-The application of statistical techniques to building research, J.Bronowski,p.137-151.-

(Continued on next card)

699.844
W27

U.K. Building Research Station.
Westphal, W
The propagation of structure-borne sound in buildings. Garston, Eng., Building Research Station, 1968.
11p. (U.K. Building Research Station. Library communication no. 1437)

Reprinted and translated from: Acustica, 1957, 7, 335-348.

1. Architectural acoustics. I. U.K. Building Research Station. II. Title. (Series)

691.8
D28

U.K. Building Research Station.
Deutscher Ausschuss fur Stahlbeton.
Provisional directives for buildings of large floor and wall panels, July 1963 edition. Garston, Eng., Building Research Station, Ministry of Public Building and Works, 1968.
8p. (U.K. Building Research Station. Library communication no. 1426)
Reprinted and translated from: Beton-u. Stahlbetonbau, 1963, 58(10), 245-7.

1. Panels. 2. Floors and flooring. 3. Walls. I. Title. II. U.K. Building Research Station. (Series)

Conference on Building Research, Geneva, Nov.13-18, 1950. Proceedings...Dec. 1950. (Card 2

The application of building research in the building industry, C.L.a'Court,p.152-167.-
The development of winter construction techniques as a contribution to the reduction of seasonal unemployment in the construction industry, the Secretariat of the International Labour Office, p.168-189.-Housing and health, J.M.Mackintosh, p.190-202.-Transition from research to industrial

(Continued on next card)

690.22
C37

U.K. Building Research Station.
Christensen, Georg
The properties of non-loadbearing internal walls as determined from functional requirements, by Georg Christensen and Klaus Blach. Garston, Eng., Building Research Station, 1968.
14p. (U.K. Building Research Station. Library communication 1444)
Reprinted and translated from: Byggeindustrien 1967, 18 (8), 306-10, 313.
1. Walls. I. Blach, Klaus, jt. au. II. U.K. Building Research Station. III. Title. (Series)

690.015
(41:016)
U541pu

U.K. Building Research Station.
Publications of the Building Research Station as available October 1959. [Garston, Eng.] 1959.
34p.

1. Building research - Bibliography.

Conference on Building Research, Geneva, Nov.13-18, 1950. Proceedings...Dec. 1950. (Card 3

application, Building Research Station (U.K.) p. 203-215.-Operational research in building,Building Research Station (U.K.)p.216-238.-Application of research in the building industry,J.H.Orendorff, p.239-275.

1.Building research. 2.Research application. 3.Building construction-Winter. 4.Housing and health. I.United Nations. Economic Commission for

(Continued on next card)

699.8
S62

U.K. Building Research Station.
Speakman, K
The properties of compacted synthetic kilchoanite material. Garston, Eng., Building Research Station, Ministry of Public Building and Works, 1968.
[6]p. (U.K. Building Research Station. Current papers 70/68)
Reprinted from: Transactions of the British Ceramic Society, June, 1968. pp. 233-242.
1. Insulation. 2. Refuse and refuse disposal. I. U.K. Building Research Station. II. Title.

VF
690.015
(41:016)
U541p

United Kingdom. Building Research Station.
Publications other than those issued through H.M.S.O., 1st January, 1937 - 31st December, 1945. Garston, England, Dec., 1945.
10 p.

1. Building research - Bibliographies.

Conference on Building Research, Geneva, Nov.13-18, 1950. Proceedings...Dec. 1950. (Card 4

Europe. Industry and Materials Committee. II.Orendorff, Joseph H. III.Gt. Brit. Building Research Station. IV.International Labour Office.

691.322
E28

U.K. Building Research Station.
Edwards, A G
Properties of concrete made with Scottish crushed rock aggregates. Garston, Eng., Building Research Station, Ministry of Public Building and Works, 1966.
[12]p. (U.K. Building Research Station. Building research current papers. Engineering papers 42)
Reprinted from: Journal of the British Granite and Whinstone Federation, Autumn 1966.
1. Concrete aggregates. I. U.K. Building Research Station. II. Title.

691.32
K25p

U.K. Building Research Station.
Kempster, E
Pumpable concrete. Garston, Eng., Building Research Station, 1969.
8p. (U.K. Building Research Station. Current paper 29/69)
Version of paper published in: Contract journal, 1969, June 5, pp. 605-607 and June 12, pp. 740-741, 744.
1. Concrete. I. U.K. Building Research Station. II. Title.

691.542
U54

U.K. Building Research Station.
Process for burning cement clinker with simultaneous production of sulfuric acid from raw materials containing calcium sulphate in a shaft kiln. Garstone, Eng., 1971.
[4]p. (Library communication no. 1642)
Translated from the German.

1. Portland cement. I. Title. (Series)

691.421
W17

U.K. Building Research Station.
Ward, W H
Properties of the London clay at the Ashford Common shaft: in-situ and undrained strength tests. Garston, Eng., Building Research Station, Ministry of Technology, 1966.
[321-44]p. (U.K. Building Research Station. Building research current papers. Engineering series 28)
Reprinted from: Géotechnique, 1965, vol. 15 (December), pp. 321-44.

1. Clay. I. U.K. Building Research Station. II. Title.

691.32
K25

U.K. Building Research Station.
Kempster, E
Pumpability of mortars. Garston, Eng., Building Research Station, Ministry of Public Building and Works, 1967.
28-30p. (U.K. Building Research Station. Building research current papers. Current paper 10/68)
Reprinted from: Contract journal May 4, 1967.

1. Concrete. 2. Plaster and plastering. I. U.K. Building Research Station. II. Title.

691.542
U54p

U.K. Building Research Station.
Process for manufacture of low-fluorine cement clinker from phosphoric-acid-waste gypsum. Garstone, Eng., 1971.
4p. (Library communication no. 1644)
Translated from the German.

1. Portland cement. 2. Gypsum. I. Title. (Series)

699.83
H65

U.K. Building Research Station.
Holmer, B
Properties of wind in built-up areas. Garston, Eng., Building Research Station, 1971.
[9]p. (Library communication no. 1604)
Translated from the Swedish.

1. Buildings - Wind stresses. I. U.K. Building Research Station. II. Title. (Series)

691.32
B18

U.K. Building Research Station.
Bauer, Hermann.
Pumping concrete through small bore pipelines. Garston, Eng., Building Research Station, 1971.
[11]p. (Library communication no. 1630)
Translated from the German.

1. Concrete. 2. Building equipment. I. U.K. Building Research Station. II. Title. (Series)

U.K. Building Research Station.

691.55
K25
Kempster, E
Pumping mortar and plasters. Garston, Eng., Building Research Station, Ministry of Technology, 1965.
[2]p. (U.K. Building Research Station. Building research current papers. Construction series 15)
Reprinted from the National builder. March 1965, p. 256-8.

1. Plaster and plastering. I. U.K. Building Research Station. II. National builder. III. Title.

658.562
B51
U.K. Building Research Station.
Blaut, H
Recommendations for quality control by the manufacturer. Garston, Eng., Building Research Station, 1971.
[19]p. (Library communication no. 1635)
Translated from the German and reprinted from CEB/CIB/FIP/RILEM Joint Committee WG II April 1971.

1. Quality control. I. U.K. Building Research Station. II. Title. (Series)

693.068
:389.6
B65
U.K. Building Research Station.
Bonshor, R   B
The relationship between component size and joint dimension, by R.B. Bonshor and H.W. Harrison. Garston, Eng., Building Research Station, 1971.
[6]p. (U.K. Building Research Station. Current paper 5/71)
Reprinted from: Building, 13 Nov. 1970, pp. 141-150.
1. Coordinated components. 2. Building materials - Standards and specifications. I. Harrison, H.W., jt. au. II. U.K. Building Research Station. III. Title.

690.015
(41)
W34
U.K. BUILDING RESEARCH STATION.
WHITE, RALPH BARTON.
QUALITATIVE STUDIES OF BUILDINGS: THE DE LA WARR PAVILION, BEXHILL-ON-SEA AND THE GILBEY BUILDING, OVAL ROAD, LONDON, N.W. LONDON, H.M. STAT. OFF., 1966.
59p. (U.K. BUILDING RESEARCH STATION. NATIONAL BUILDING STUDIES. SPECIAL REPORT NO. 39)

1. BUILDING RESEARCH - U.K.
I. U.K. BUILDING RESEARCH STATION.
I. TITLE: DE LA WARR PAVILION.
II. TITLE: GILBEY BUILDING.

690.015
(41:016)
U541
no. 176R
U.K. Building Research Station.
References on housing for old people. Garston, England, 1959.
17p. (Library bibliography no. 176R)

Superseding Bibliography no. 176.

1. Housing for the aged - Bibliography. (Series: U.K. Building Research Station. Library bibliography no. 176R)

690.592
U54
United Kingdom. Building Research Station.
Repair of damaged buildings. Notes. 1 - Garston, Eng., 1944 -
1 v. (loose-leaf)   illus.

For full information see shelf list card.

1. Houses-Maintenance and modernization. I. Title.

U.K. Building Research Station.

711.74
(74921)
M45
U.K. Building Research Station.
Miller, A
Radburn and its validity today. Garston, Eng., Building Research Station, 1969.
14p. (U.K. Building Research Station. Current paper 36/69)
Reprinted from: The Architect and building news, 1969, Mar. 13, pp. 40-47; 1969, Mar. 27, pp. 30-35.
1. Streets - Radburn, N.J. 2. Traffic - Radburn, N.J. I. U.K. Building Research Station. II.   Title.

690.015
(41:016)
U541
No. 63
United Kingdom. Building Research Station. (Library)
References on prefabrication.
[Garston, Herts, England, Dec. 1941]
8 p. (Its Library Bibliography no. 63)

1. Prefabricated construction - Bibliographies. (Series)

690.015
(41)
G72
Gt. Brit. Building Research Station.
Gt. Brit. Dept. of Scientific and Industrial Research. Building Research Station.
Report of the Building Research Board, with the report of the Director of Building Research for the years 19
London, H.M. Stationery Office, 19
v.   illus.

Cover title: Building research.
Includes lists of publications.
For full information see shelf list card.

1. Building research-Gt. Brit. I.Gt. Brit. Building Research Station.

691.322
U54r
U.K. Building Research Station.
Reactions between aggregates and cement. London, H. M. Stat. Off., 1952
v. illus., graphs, tables. (Its National building studies research paper no.

For complete information see shelf list.

1. Concrete aggregate. 2. Cement.

691.54
U54r
U.K. Building Research Station.
Refractory calcium-magnesium-alumina cements. Garston, Eng., 1971.
4p. (Library communication no. 1645)
Translated from the German.

1. Cement. I. Title.

690.015
(41)
L21r
U.K. Building Research Station.
Lea, F   M
Research for a changing industry. Garston, Eng., Building Research Station, Dept. of Scientific and Industrial Research, 1964.
[8] p. U.K. Building Research Station. Building research current papers. Supplements 4)
Reprinted from: Proceedings of the Building Research Congress, Pretoria, July 1964, vol.1.
1. Building research - U.K. 2. Prefabricated construction - U.K. 3. Building industry - U.K. I. U.K. Building Research Station. II. Building Research Congress, Pretoria, 1964. Proceedings.

691.7
:620.19
E82
U.K. Building Research Station.
Everett, L H
Recognition of corrosion hazards to metals in building, by L. H. Everett and R. D. J. Tarleton. Garston, Eng., Building Research Station, Ministry of Technology, 1967.
[4] p. (U.K. Building Research Station current papers. Design series 62)
Reprinted from British Corrosion Journal, 1967, vol.2 (March) pp. 61-64.

N.c.1
Laf.c.2

(Cont'd on next card)

696.1
A77
U.K. Building Research Station.
Association Nationale des Services d'Eau.
Regulations on the construction and testing of non-return valves for use in water supply systems in buildings. Garston, Eng., Building Research Station, 1970.
6p. (U.K. Building Research Station. Library communication no. 1561)

1. Plumbing. I. U.K. Building Research Station. II. Title. (Series)

693.2
K85
U.K. Building Research Station.
Kunzel, H
Research into moisture movements in renderings and rendered walls. Garston, Eng., Building Research Station, 1970.
[91]p. (Library communication no. 1583)
Translated from the German.
Thesis - Technische Hochschule, Stuttgart.

1. Brick construction. 2. Walls. I. U.K. Building Research Station. II. Title: Moisture movements in renderings and rendered walls. III. Title: Rendered walls. (Series)

691.7
:620.19
E82
Everett, L H   Recognition of corrosion hazards to metals in building...(Card 2)

1. Corrosion. 2. Metal construction. I. Tarleton, R. D. J., jt. au. II. U.K. Building Research Station. III. Title.

691.55
M14r
U.K. Building Research Station.
Majumdar, A   J
Reinforcement of cements and gypsum plaster by glass fibres, by A.J. Majumdar and J.F. Ryder. Garston, Eng., Building Research Station, 1970.
[11]p. (Current paper 40/70)

Reprinted from: Science of ceramics, vol. 5, 1970, pp. 539-564.

1. Plaster and plastering. 2. Cement. 3. Gypsum. I. U.K. Building Research Station. II. Ryder, J.F., jt. au. III. Title.

600.15
E57
U.K. Building Research Station.
Elstner, I
Research into the dicalcium silicate falling of blast furnace slags, by I. Elstner et al. Garston, Eng., Building Research Station, 1971.
[35]p. (Library communication no 1610)
Bibliography: p. 17-18.
Translated from the German.
1. Industrial research. I. U.K. Building Research Station. II. Title: Slags. III. Title. (Series)

U.K. Building Research Station.

698
W34
Whiteley, P
Recommendations for painting in tropical climates. London, H.M. Stat. Off., 1962.
36p. (U.K. Dept. of Scientific and Industrial Research. Building Research Station. Tropical building studies no. 4)

1. Paints and painting. I. U.K. Building Research Station.

691.328
W66
U.K. Building Research Station.
Wood, R   H
The reinforcement of slabs in accordance with a pre-determined field of moments. Garston, Eng., Building Research Station, Ministry of Public Building and Works, 1968.
69-76p. (U.K. Building Research Station. Building research current papers. Current paper 44/68)
Reprinted from: Concrete, 1968.
1. Concrete, Reinforced. 2. Loads. I. U.K. Building Research Station. II. Title.

620.015
(41)
W47
U.K. Building Research Station.
Wise, A   F   E
Research on engineering services for buildings; a review of work at the Building Research Station. Garston, Eng., Building Research Station, Department of Scientific and Industrial Research, [1947]
4p. U.K. Building Research Station. Building research current papers. Engineering series 7)

1. Engineering research - U.K. 2. U.K. Building Research Station. I. U.K. Building Research Station.

691.328
D87
U.K. Building Research Station.
Dutron, R
Research on the corrosion behaviour of reinforcement in reinforced concrete. Garston, Eng., Building Research Station, 1965.
61p. (Library communication no. 1317)
Translated from the French by L.M.L. Booth.

1. Concrete, Reinforced. I. U.K. Building Research Station. II. Title: Corrosion behaviour of reinforcement in reinforced concrete. (Series)

625.7
P25r
U.K. Building Research Station.
Penman, A   D   M
Rockfill. Garston, Eng., Building Research Station, 1971.
10p. (Current paper 15/71)

Bibliography: p. 91-10.

1. Road construction. I. U.K. Building Research Station. II. Title.

628.4
(41)
W48
U.K. Building Research Station.
Wise, A   F   E
Sanitary services for modern housing, by A.F.E. Wise and others. Garston, Eng., Building Research Station, Ministry of Technology, [1967?]
7p. (U.K. Building Research Station. Building research current papers. Design series 60)
Reprinted from: The Public Works and Municipal Services Congress, 17th November 1966.

1. Sanitation - U.K. 2. Drainage. 3. Housing and health. I. U.K. Building Research Station. II. Title.

620.015
(41)
W47
U.K. Building Research Station.
Wise, A   F   E
Research on engineering services for buildings; a review of work at the Building Research Station. Garston, Eng., Building Research Station, Department of Scientific and Industrial Research, [1964?]
4p. (U.K. Building Research Station. Building research current papers. Engineering series 7)

1. Engineering research - U.K. 2. U.K. Building Research Station. I. U.K. Building Research Station.

691.542
R46
U.K. Building Research Station.
Rio, Arturo.
The role and reaction mechanism of celestine ($SrSO_4$) in the manufacture of Portland cement in absence and in presence of a fluxing agent (CaF_2), by A. Rio and others. Garston, Eng., Building Research Station, 1971.
[14]p. (Library communication no. 1616)
Translated from the Italian.
1. Portland cement. I. U.K. Building Research Station. II. Title. (Series)

691.322
E28s
U.K. Building Research Station.
Edwards, A   G
Scottish aggregates: their suitability for concrete with regard to rock constituents. Garston, Eng., Building Research Station, 1970.
[10]p. (U.K. Building Research Station. Current paper 28/70)

1. Concrete aggregates. I. U.K. Building Research Station. II. Title.

629.136
J67
Eng.
U.K. Building Research Station.
Jørgen, Gunnar Ø
Residential areas in the vicinity of an airport. Garston, Eng., Building Research Station, 1969.
[11]p. (U.K. Building Research Station. Library communication no. 1527)
Translated from the Norwegian and reprinted from: Norges Byggforskningsinstitutt, Saertrykk 161.
1. Airports. 2. Noise. I. U.K. Building Research Station. II. Title. (Series)

725.5
(41)
C85
U.K. Building Research Station.
Cullen, B   D
Running costs of hospital buildings; an analysis of published information, by B.D. Cullen and Iris M. Jeffery. Garston, Eng., Building Research Station, Ministry of Public Building and Works, 1967.
6p. (U.K. Building Research Station. Design papers 65)
Reprinted from: The Hospital, June 1967, p. 234-8.
1. Hospitals - U.K. I. U.K. Building Research Station. I. Title. II. Jeffery, Iris M.

690.015
(41
:016)
U541
no.
166
U.K. Building Research Station.
Selection of books on building. Garston, Eng., Building Research Station, 1969.
16p. (Its Library bibliography 166)

1. Building industry - Bibl. 2. Architecture - Designs and plans - Bibl. I. Title.

690
N87
U.K. Building Research Station.
Nuttall, J   F
Resource scheduling: coping with labour problems as they occur on site. Garston, Eng., Building Research Station, Ministry of Technology, 1966.
311-316p. (U.K. Building Research Station. Building research current papers. Construction series 25)
Reprinted from: The Builder, Feb., 1966.

1. Building construction. 2. Building construction - Labor requirements. I. U.K. Building Research Station. II. Title.

690
(41)
F45s
U.K. Building Research Station.
Fine, B
Safety nets for urban planners, by B. Fine and J.B. Britten. Garston [Eng.] Building Research Station, Ministry of Technology, 1966.
1 v. (U.K. Building Research Station. Building research current papers. Design series 50)
Reprinted from: Journal of the Town Planning Institute, 1966, vol. 52 (May).

1. Building research - U.K. 2. City planning - U.K. I. U.K. Building Research Station. II. Title.

333.323
U54
U.K. Ministry of Housing and Local Government.
U.K. Central Housing Advisory Committee.
Selection of tenants and transfers and exchanges. Third report of the Housing Management Sub-Committee of the Central Housing Advisory Committee. Issued by the Ministry of Housing and Local Government. London, H.M.S.O., 1949.
28p.

1. Tenant selection. I. U.K. Ministry of Housing and Local Government. II. Title.

VF
690.091.82
(489)
K42
U.K. Building Research Station.
Kjeldsen, M
Revisions in the 1966 edition of the building regulations. Garston, Eng., Building Research Station, 1968.
7p. (U.K. Building Research Station. Library communication no. 1452)
Translated from the Danish and reprinted from: Byggeindustrien, 1966, 17 (19), 768-72.

1. Building codes - Denmark. I. U.K. Building Research Station. II. Title. (Series)

691.42
U54SA
U.K. BUILDING RESEARCH STATION.
SAND-LIME BRICKS, BY G.E. BESSEY. LONDON, H.M. STAT' OFF., 1948.
58P. (ITS NATIONAL BUILDING STUDIES SPECIAL REPORT NO. 3)

1. BRICKS. I. BESSEY, G.E. II. TITLE.

711.417
(41)
O34
U.K. Building Research Station.
Ogilvy, Audrey A
The self-contained new town. Garston, Eng., Building Research Station, Ministry of Technology, 1968.
38-54p. (U.K. Building Research Station. Current paper 56/68)
Reprinted from: Town Planning review, Apr., 1968.

1. New towns - U.K. 2. U.K. - New towns. I. U.K. Building Research Station. II. Title.

699.83
(016)
J65
U.K., Eng., Building Research Station.
Jones, M   E
A review of the literature on the structure of wind turbulence, with special regard to its effect on buildings. Garston, Eng., Building Research Station, Ministry of Public Building and Works, 1968.
50p. (U.K. Building Research Station. Current paper CP 85/68)
Cover title: Wind turbulence and buildings: a literature review.
Reprinted from: Building science, 1968, Vol. 3(1) August. 41-50.
(Cont'd on next card)

691.55
U54
U.K. BUILDING RESEARCH STATION.
SANDS FOR PLASTERS, MORTARS AND EXTERNAL RENDERINGS, BY A.D. COWPER. LONDON, H.M. STAT' OFF., 1950.
19P. (ITS NATIONAL BUILDING STUDIES BULLETIN NO. 7)

1. PLASTER AND PLASTERING. 2. BUILDING MATERIALS - U.K. I. COWPER, A.D. II. TITLE.

690.015
D15
U.K. Building Research Station.
Daldy, A   F
Setting up a national building research station, by A.F. Daldy and R. Sperling. Garston, Eng., Building Research Station, 1970.
4p. (U.K. Building Research Station. Current paper 32/70)
Reprinted from: Build International, July/Aug. 1970, pp. 211-214.

1. Building research. I. Sperling, R., jt. au. II. U.K. Building Research Station. III. Title.

699.83
(016)
J65
Jones, M   E   A review...1968.
(Card 2)

1. Buildings - Wind stresses - Bibl. I. Title: Wind turbulence and buildings: a literature review. II. Garston, Eng., Building Research Station. III. Title.

696.1
(41)
W84
U.K. Building Research Station.
Wise, A   F   E
Sanitary services for hospitals; a review of current faults, by A. F. E. Wise and R. Payne. Garston, Eng., Building Research Station, Ministry of Technology, 1965.
[4]p. (U.K. Building Research Station. Building research current papers. Design series 39)
Reprinted from: The Architects' Journal, July 21, 1965, vol. 142, p. 153-6.

1. Sanitation - U.K. I. Payne, R., jt. au. II. U.K. Building Research Station. III. Title.

690.237
P25
U.K. Building Research Station.
Penman, A   D   M
Settlement observations on an oil tank, by A.D. M. Penman and G.H. Watson. Garston, Eng., Building Research Station, Dept. of Scientific and Industrial Research, 1964.
[9]p. (U.K. Building Research Station. Building research current papers. Engineering series 19)
Reprinted from: Proceedings of the European Conference on Soil Mechanics, Oct. 1963. v. 1, p. 163-71.

(Continued on next card)

690.237
P25 Penman, A D M Settlement
observations on an oil tank...1964. (Card 2)

1. Loads. 2. Foundations (Building)
I. Watson, G. H., jt. au. II. European
Conference on Soil Mechanics, Proceedings, 1963.
III. U.K. Building Research Station.

691
(489)
K41 U.K. Building Research Station.
Kjaer, A
Should property specification be introduced
in Denmark? Garston, Eng., Building Research
Station, 1970.
9p. (U.K. Building Research Station.
Library communication no. 1558)
Translated from the Danish [and reprinted from]
Byggeindustrien, 1969, (20), 802-8.

1. Building materials - Denmark. I. U.K.
Building Research Station. II. Title. (Series)

623
872 U.K. Building Research Station.
Steffens, R J
Some aspects of structural vibration.
Garston, Eng., Building Research Station,
Ministry of Technology, 1966.
30p. (U.K. Building Research Station.
Building research current papers. Engineering
series 37)
Reprinted from Vibration in civil engineer-
ing; proceedings of a symposium organized by
the British National Section of the Interna-
tional Association for Earthquake Engineering.
Bibliography: p. 25-30.

(Cont'd on next card)

U.K. Building Research Station.
693.5
M14 Mainstone, R J
Shear connectors in steel concrete composite
beams for bridges and the new C.P. 117.
Part 2. Garston, Eng., Building Research
Station, Ministry of Public Building and Works,
1968.
1v. (U.K. Building Research Station.
Building research current papers. Current
paper 21/68)
Reprinted from: Proceedings of the Institution of Civil Engineers, September, 1967;
February, 1968.
1. Concrete construction - Standards and specifi cations.

(Cont'd on next card)

699.83
N28s U.K. Building Research Station.
Newberry, C W
Significant features of wind loading in
relation to the design of structures.
Garston, Eng., Building Research Station,
1969.
6p. (U.K. Building Research Station.
Current paper 49/69)
Paper presented at a Symposium on Concepts
of Safety of Structures and Methods of
Design, held by the International Associ-
ation for Bridge and Structural Engineering
in London, Sept., 1969.
1. Buildings - Wind stresses.
I. U.K. Building Research Station
II. Title.

623
872 Steffens, R.J. Some aspects of structural
vibration...1966. (Card 2)

1. Structural engineering. 2. Vibration.
3. Earthquake resistant construction.
I. U.K. Building Research Station. II. Title.

693.5
M14 Mainstone, R J Shear connectors...
1968. (Card 2)

2. Steel construction - Standards and
specifications. 3. Loads - Standards and
specifications. 4. Bridges - Standards and
specifications. I. U.K. Building Research
Station. II. Title.

691.551.5
H17 U.K. Building Research Station.
Harris, P B
A simple ultra-violet sensor and integrating
recorder for long-term field operation. Garston,
Eng., Building Research Station, Ministry of
Public Building and Works, 1968.
1007-1010p. (U.K. Building Research Station.
Current paper CP86/68)
Reprinted from: Journal of scientific instru-
ments, 1968, Vol. 1 (Series 2), October, pp.
1007-1010.
1. Building materials - Climatic effects.
2. Building research. I. Title. II. U.K.
Building Research Station.

338
P67 U.K. Building Research Station.
Forbes, W S
Some aspects of the measurement of productivity in the building industry. Garston,
[Eng.] Building Research Station, Ministry
of Technology, 1966.
13-16p. (U.K. Building Research Station.
Building research current papers. Construction series 28)
Reprinted from: PACE 1966, vol. 1 (April),
pp. 13-16.
1. Labor productivity. 2. Industrial
management. I. U.K. Building Research Station. II. Title: Productivity in the building industry.

624.2
M14 U.K. Building Research Station.
Mainstone, R J
Shear connectors in steel-concrete composite
beams for bridges, by R.J. Mainstone and J.B.
Menzies. Garston, Eng., Building Research
Station, Ministry of Public Building and Works,
1968.
291-358p. (U.K. Building Research Station.
Building research current papers. Current paper
20/68)
Reprinted from: Concrete, 1967, Vol. 1(9)
pp. 291-302; 1967, Vol. 1(10), pp. 351-58.
1. Bridges. 2. Concrete. 3. Steel.
I. U.K. Building Research Station.
II. Title.

699.83
S29 U.K. Building Research Station.
Sexton, D E
A simple wind tunnel for studying air-flow
round buildings. Garston, Eng., Building Research Station, Ministry of Public Building
and Works, 1968.
983-985p. (U.K. Building Research Station.
Current paper 69/68)
Reprinted from: Architect and building
news, 1968, June 26th, pp. 983-985.
1. Buildings - Wind stresses. I. U.K.
Building Research Station. II. Title.

693.2
B6b U.K. BUILDING RESEARCH STATION.
BONNELL, DAVID GLYNWYN ROBERT.
SOME COMMON DEFECTS IN BRICKWORK, BY
D.G.R. BONNELL AND W.R. PIPPARD.
LONDON, H.M. STAT. OFF., 1950.
22P. (U.K. BUILDING RESEARCH
STATION. NATIONAL BUILDING STUDIES
BULLETIN NO. 9)

1. BRICK CONSTRUCTION. I. PIPPARD,
W.R., JT. AU. II. U.K. BUILDING
RESEARCH STATION. III. TITLE.

690.22
S45 U.K. Building Research Station.
Simms, L G
The shear strength of some storey-height
brickwork and blockwork walls. Garston,
Eng., Building Research Station, Dept. of
Scientific and Industrial Research,
1964.
[4]p. (U.K. Building Research Station.
Building research current papers.
Engineering series 14)
Reprinted from the Chartered municipal
engineer, vol. 91(1) 1964. pp. 87-91.
1. Walls. 2. Brick
construction. I. U.K.
Building Research Station. II. Title.

621.6
C51 U.K. Building Research Station.
Clarke, N W B
Simplified tables of external loads on
buried pipelines. London, H.M. Stat. Off.,
1962.
12p. (U.K. Building Research Station.
National building studies special report 32)

1. Pipes. I. U.K. Building Research
Station.

693.55
T19 U.K. Building Research Station.
Taylor, R
Some fatigue tests on reinforced concrete
beams. Garston, Eng., Building Research
Station, Dept. of Scientific and Industrial
Research, 1964.
[8]p. (U.K. Building Research Station.
Building research current papers.
Engineering series 16)
Reprinted from: Magazine of concrete research,
vol. 16(46) 1964. p. 31-8.
1. Concrete, Reinforced. I. U.K. Building
Research Station.

691.421
M17s U.K. Building Research Station.
Marsland, A
The shear strength of still fissured clays.
Garston, Eng., Building Research Station, 1971.
8p. (U.K. Building Research Station.
Current paper CP 21/71)
Reprinted from: Proceedings of the Roscoe
Memorial Symposium, Cambridge University
Engineering Dept., 1971.
1. Clay. 2. Strains and stresses.
I. U.K. Building Research Station.
II. Title.

534.83
U54s U.K. Building Research Station.
Simulated sonic boom tests on greenhouses
at Efford Experimental Horticulture Station,
Lymington, Hants, October 20-24 1969. Garston,
Eng., 1971.
25p. (Its Current paper 9/71)

1. Noise. I. Title.

711.6
W17s U.K. Building Research Station.
Ward, W H
Some field techniques for improving site
investigation and engineering design. Garston,
Eng., Building Research Station, 1971.
6p. (U.K. Building Research Station.
Current paper CP 30/71)
Reprinted from: Proceedings of the Roscoe
Memorial Symposium, Cambridge, March 29-31, 1971.

1. Site planning. I. U.K. Building Research
Station. II. Title.

699.81
U54 U.K. Building Research Station.
A short history of the structural fire protection of buildings particularly in England,
by S. B. Hamilton. London, H.M. Stat. Off.,
1958.
73p. illus. (Its National building studies
special report no. 27)
1. Fire prevention. 2. Building
materials - Fire resistance. I. Hamilton,
S B

301.36
L15 U.K. Building Research Station.
Langdon, F J
The social and physical environment: a
social scientist's view. Garston, England,
Building Research Station, Ministry of Technology, 1966.
10p. (U.K. Building Research Station Current
papers. Design series 61)

Abridged version of this paper appeared in
R. I. B. A. Journal, 1966, vol. 73 (Oct.) pp.
460-464.
No.1
Laf.c.2 1. Sociology, Urban. I. U.K. Building Re-
search Station. II. Title.

728.1
:308
(41)
A77 U.K. Building Research Station.
Attenburrow, J J
Some impressions of the private sector of
the housing market. Garston, Eng., Building
Research Station, Ministry of Public Building
and Works, 1968.
8-12p. U.K. Building Research Station.
Current paper 57/68)
1. Housing market - U.K. 2. Architecture
- Designs and plans. 3. Building industry -
U.K. 4. Family living requirements.
I. U.K. Building Research Station.
II. Title.

389.1
M17
U.K. Building Research Station.
Harrison, H W
Some observations on metric practice. Garston [Eng.], Building Research Station, Ministry of Technology, 1966.
102p. (U.K. Building Research Station. Building research current papers. Design series 44)
Reprinted from: Building, 1966, vol. 210, Part I, (April 22) pp. 87-90; Part II, (April 29) pp. 99-102.

1. Standardization. I. Building. II. U.K. Building Research Station.
III. Title.

534.83
W66
U.K. Building Research Station.
Woolley, R M
Sound insulation of windows. Garston, Eng., Building Research Station, Ministry of Technology, 1967.
6p. (U.K. Building Research Station. Building research current papers. Design papers 64)
Reprinted from Glass age, May, 1967. p. 44,6, 8.
1. Noise. 2. Insulation. 3. Windows. I. U.K. Building Research Station. II. Title.

693.5
G74s
Griffiths, T J Standardization...1968.
(Card 2)

2. Coordinated components. I. U.K. Building Research Station. II. Title: Precast concrete construction.

690.015
(41:016)
U541
no. 128N
United Kingdom. Building Research Station. Library.
Some references on solar heating. Garston, England, Nov., 1946.
4 p. (Its Library bibliography) no. 128N).

1. Heating - Solar - Bibliography. (Series.)

690.091.82
(6)
G72
Gt. Brit. Building Research Station.
Space and accommodation standards for low-cost housing in colonial territories. Garston, Eng., May 1949.
8 [3] l. tables. (Its Note no.D75)

Bibliography: p. 8.
Not available for publication.

1.Space considerations. 2.Building codes-Africa. 3.Housing in the tropics. I.Title. II.Series.

691.328
S56s
U.K. Building Research Station.
Snowdon, L C
The static and fatigue performance of concrete beams with high strength deformed bars. Garston, Eng., Building Research Station, 1971.
31p. (Current paper 7/71)

1. Concrete, Reinforced. I. U.K. Building Research Station. II. Title.

691.42
B27
U.K. Building Research Station.
Bessey, G E
Some results of exposure tests on durability of calcium silicate bricks, by G.E. Bessey and W.H. Harrison. [Garston, Eng] Building Research Station, 1970.
[14]p. (U.K. Building Research Station. Current paper 24/70)
Reprinted from: Building science, 1969, vol. 4, pp. 63-76)
1. Bricks. 2. Building materials - Climatic effects. I. Harrison, W.H., jt. au. II. U.K. Building Research Station. III. Title. IV. Title: Calcium silicate bricks.

691.32
T29sp
U.K. Building Research Station.
Teychenne, D C
Specification of concrete with special reference to the proposed unified code. Garston, Eng., Building Research Station, 1968.
[9]p. (Current paper no. 58/68)
Reprinted from: The Structural engineer, 1968, vol. 46 (5), May, p. 131-139.

1. Concrete - Standards and specifications. I. U.K. Building Research Station. II. Title.

691.32
R87s
U.K. Building Research Station.
Rüsch, Hubert.
Statistical analysis of the strength of concrete, by H. Rüsch and others. Garston, Eng., Building Research Station, 1969.
[50]p. (U.K. Building Research Station. Library communication no. 1504)
Translated from the German.
Bibliography: p. 27-28.

1. Concrete. 2. Strength of materials. I. U.K. Building Research Station. II. Title. (Series)

701.8
M17
U.K. Building Research Station.
Matveev, A B
Some rules on harmonic colour combinations (O nekotorykh zakonomernostyakh garmonichnikh tsvetovykh sochetanii), by A.B. Matveev and V.M. Petrov. Garston, Eng., building Research Station, Ministry of Public Building and Works, 1968.
4p. (U.K. Building Research Station. Library communication 1451)
Translated from the Russian and reprinted from: Svetotekhnika, 1968, 14
(Cont'd on next card)

690.013
U54
U.K. Building Research Station.
Specifications for structures of large wall and floor panels: May 1970 ed. Garston, Eng., 1971.
9p. (Library communication no. 1619)

Translated from the German.

1. Building construction - Contracts and specifications. 2. Walls. 3. Panels. 4. Floors and flooring. I. Title. (Series)

VF
691.32
R87
U.K. Building Research Station.
Rusch, Hubert.
Statistical quality control of concrete. Garston, Eng., Building Research Station, 1969.
14p. (U.K. Building Research Station. Library communication no. 1456)

Translated from the German and reprinted from: Materialprufung, 1964, 6 (11), 387-94.

1. Concrete. 2. Quality control. I. U.K. Building Research Station. II. Title. (Series)

701.8
M17
Matveev, A B Some...1968. (Card 2)

(5), 7-11.

1. Color. I. U.K. Building Research Station. II. Petrov, V.M., jt. au. III. Title.

VF
002
:690
J67
U.K. Building Research Station.
Joss, H
The standard library of descriptions (CRB) Garston, Eng., Building Research Station, 1969.
3p. (U.K. Building Research Station. Library communication 1455)
Translated from the German and reprinted from: Schweizerische Bauzeitung, 1967, 85 (11), 183-5.

1. Building documentation. I. U.K. Building Research Station. II. Title. (Series)

699.83
L27
U.K. Building Research Station.
Lethenström, B
Storm damage and insurance cover. Garston, Eng., Building Research Station, 1971.
[11]p. (Library communication no. 1615)
Translated from the Swedish.

1. Buildings - Wind stresses. 2. Insurance. I. U.K. Building Research Station. II. Title. (Series)

691.32
T19
U.K. Building Research Station.
Taylor, R
Some shear tests on reinforced concrete beams with stirrups. Garston, Eng., Building Research Station, Ministry of Public Building and Works, 1967.
10p. (U.K. Building Research Station. Building research current papers. Engineering series 47)

1. Concrete, Reinforced. 2. Building methods. I. U.K. Building Research Station. II. Title.

693.97
V65
U.K. Building Research Station.
Von Essen, W
Standards for steel structures. Garston, Eng., Building Research Station, 1970.
5p. (U.K. Building Research Station. Library communication no. 1574)
Translated from the Swedish [and reprinted from] Byggmastaren, 1969, (9), 37-9.

1. Steel construction. I. U.K. Building Research Station. II. Title. (Series)

690.015
(485)
S 82
R44
1970
U.K. Building Research Station.
Falk, Hans.
Stormskador i Stockholmsområdet (Storm damage in the Stockholm area) av Hans Falk et al. Stockholm, 1970.
82p. (Stockholm. Statens Institut for Byggnadsforskning. Rapport R44:1970)
English summary.
1. Building research - Sweden. 2. Storms. 3. Buildings - Wind stresses. I. U.K. Building Research Station. II. Title: Storm damage in the Stockholm area.

691.54
P37
U.K. Building Research Station.
Pfrunder, V R
Some tests on the effect of chemical composition and grinding on the sintering of cement raw mixes, by V.R. Pfrunder and H. Wickert. Garston, Eng., Building Research Station, 1970.
[9]p. (Library communication no. 1594)
Translated from the German and reprinted from Zement-Kalk-Gips, 1970, 23 (4), 147-51.

1. Cement. 2. Clay - Research. I. Wickert, R., jt. au. II. U.K. Building Research Station. III. Title. (Series)

693.5
G74s
U.K. Building Research Station.
Griffiths, T J
Standardization and tolerances in precast concrete construction. Garston, Eng., Building Research Station, 1968.
175-179p. (U.K. Building Research Station. Current paper CP 88/68)
Reprinted from: Symposium of the International Association for Bridge and Structural Engineering, "Design philosophy and its application to precast concrete structures," London.
1. Concrete construction - Standards and specifications.
(Cont'd on next card)

699.83
E17s
U.K. Building Research Station.
Eaton, K J
Strain measurements at the GPO Tower, London, by K.J. Eaton and J.R. Mayne. Garston, Eng., Building Research Station, 1971.
[8]p. (U.K. Building Research Station. Current paper CP 29/71)
Reprinted from: Strain, vol. 7, no. 3, July 1971, pp. 103-109.
1. Buildings - Wind stresses. 2. Strains and stresses. I. Mayne, J.R., jt. au. II. U.K. Building Research Station. III. Title.

U.K. Building Research Station.
691.328.2
S72 Stevens, R   F
Strains in some prestressed concrete structures, by R.F. Stevens and R.H. Corson. Garston, Eng., Building Research Station, Ministry of Technology, 1966.
[10]p. (U.K. Building Research Station. Building research current papers. Engineering series 39)
Reprinted from: Conference on Stresses in Service, arranged by the Institution of Civil Engineers, March 1966, paper 2, p. 13-22.

(Cont'd on next card).

691.328.2
S72 Stevens, R   F Strains in some prestressed concrete structures...1966. (Card 2)

1. Concrete, Prestressed. 2. Strength of materials. I. U.K. Building Research Station. II. Corson, R.H., jt. au. III. Title.

U.K. Building Research Station.
691.421
M17 Marsland, A
Strength measurements on stiff fissured Barton Clay from Fawley (Hampshire), by A. Marsland and M.E. Butler. Garston, Eng., Building Research Station, Ministry of Public Building and Works, 1967.
[8]p. (U.K. Building Research Station. Building research current papers. Current paper 30/68)
Reprinted from: Proceedings of the Geotechnical Conference, Oslo, 1967.
1. Clay. 2. Strains and stresses. I. Butler, M.E. II. U.K. Building Research Station. III. Title.

693.97
U54 U.K. BUILDING RESEARCH STATION.
THE STRENGTH OF ENCASED STANCHIONS, BY R.F. STEVENS. LONDON, H.M.S.O., 1965.
38P. (ITS NATIONAL BUILDING STUDIES RESEARCH PAPER NO. 38)

1. STEEL CONSTRUCTION. 2. STRENGTH OF MATERIALS. I. STEVENS, R.F. II. TITLE: ENCASED STANCIONS.

691.421
S45 U.K. Building Research Station.
Simms, L   G
The strength of walls built in the laboratory with some types of clay bricks and blocks. Garston, Eng., Building Research Station, Ministry of Technology, 1965.
11p. (U.K. Building Research Station. Building research current papers. Engineering series no. 24)
Reprinted from Transactions of the British Ceramic Society, July 1965, p. 81-92.

(Continued on next card)

691.421
S45 Simms, L   G   The strength of walls built in the laboratory...1965. (Card 2)

1. Clay. 2. Tile construction. 3. Walls. I. U.K. Building Research Station. II. Title.

691.54
G74 U. K. Building Research Station.
Grimer, F   J
The strengths of cements reinforced with glass fibres, by F. J. Grimer and M.A. Ali. Garston, Eng., Building Research Station, 1969.
[8]p. (U.K. Building Research Station. Current paper 40/69)
Reprinted from: Magazine of concrete research, March, 1969. pp. 23-30.

1. Cement. 2. Concrete, Reinforced. I. Ali, M.A., Jt. au. II. U.K. Building Research sta-   tion. III. Title.

624.043
L41 U.K. Building Research Station.
Libert, Y
Stress corrosion of high strength steel wires, by Y. Libert and A. Hache. Garston, Eng., Building Research Station, 1968.
16p. (U.K. Building Research Station. Library communication no. 1427)

Translated from the French and reprinted from VIIIe Colloque de Metallurgie, Cadarache, 1964.
1. Strains and stresses. 2. Concrete, Prestressed. I. Hache, A., jt. au. II. U.K. Building Research Station. III. Title.   (Series)

691.421
L28 U.K. Building Research Station.
Lewin, P   I
Stress-probe experiments on saturated normally consolidated clay, by P.I. Lewin and J.B. Burland. Garston, Eng., Building Research Station, 1970.
56p. (U.K. Building Research Station. Current paper CP 18/70)
Reprinted from: Geotechnique, 1970, Vol. 20 (1), March pp. 38-56.
1. Clay. 2. Strains and stresses. I. Burland, J.B., jt. au. II. U.K. Building Research Station. III. Title.

691.328
A75 U.K. Building Research Station.
Armer, G   S   T
The strip method: a new approach to the design of slabs. Garston Eng., Building Research Station, Ministry of Public Building and Works, 1968.
[6]p. (U.K. Building Research Station. Current paper CP 81/68)
Reprinted from: Concrete, 1968, Vol. 2 (9), September, pp. 358-363.

1. Concrete, Reinforced. I. Title. II. U.K. Building Research Station.

693.5
W66s U.K. Building Research Station.
Wood, R   H
The strip method for designing slabs, by R.H. Wood and G.S.T. Armer. Garston, Eng., Building Research Station, 1970.
53p. (U.K. Building Research Station. Current paper 39/70)

1. Concrete construction. 2. Concrete, Reinforced. I. Armer, G.S.T., jt. au. II. U.K. Building Research Station. III. Title.

624.2
M25 U.K. Building Research Station.
Menzies, J   B
Structural behaviour of the Moat Street flyover, Coventry. Garston, Eng., Building Research Station, Ministry of Public Building and Works, 1968.
967-971p. (U.K. Building Research Station. Current paper CP 78/68)
Reprinted from: Civil engineering and public works review, Sept., 1968. pp. 967-971.
1. Bridges. 2. Strains and stresses. 3. Road construction. I. Title. II. U.K. Building Research Station.

691.322
T29 U.K. Building Research Station.
Teychenne, D   C
Structural concrete made with lightweight aggregates. Garston, Eng., Building Research Station, Ministry of Public Building and Works, 1967.
111-122p. (U.K. Building Research Station. Building research current papers. Engineering papers 48)
Reprinted from: Concrete, April 1967.
1. Concrete aggregates. 2. Concrete construction. .I. U.K. Building Research Station. II. Title.

VF
690
(41)
U54st U.K. Building Research Station.
Structural loading in factories, by H. V. Apcar. London, H.M. Stat. Off., 1960.
21p. illus., tables. (Factory building studies no. 4)

1. Building construction - U.K. I. Apcar, H.V.

629.136
M14 U.K. Building Research Station.
Mainstone, R   J
Structural tests on an experimental helicopter platform. Garston, Eng., Building Research Station, Ministry of Technology, 1966.
65-91p. (U.K. Building Research Station. Building research current papers. Engineering series no. 26)
Reprinted from Institution of civil engineers, Proceedings, Jan., 1966.

1. Heliports.   2. Loads. I. U.K. Building   Research Station. II. Title.

691.421
S27 U.K. Building Research Station.
Serb-Serbina, N   N
Structure-formation in aqueous suspensions of bentonite clay (Strukturoobrazovanie v vodnykh suspenziyakh bentonitovykh glin), by N.N. Serb-Serbina and P.A. Rebinder. Garston, Eng., Building Research Station, Ministry of Public Building and Works, 1968.
8p. (U.K. Building Research Station. Library Communication 1447)
Translated from the Russian and reprinted from: Kolloidnyi zhurnal, 1947, 9   (5), 381-91.
1. Clay   (Cont'd on next card)

691.421
S27 Serb-Serbina, N   N Structure...
(Card 2)

I. U.K. Building Research Station.
II. Rebinder, P.A., jt. au.
III. Title: Bentonite clay.
IV. Title.

690.091.82
C41s U.K. Building Research Station.
Cibula, Evelyn.
The structure of building control: an international comparison. Garston, Eng., Building Research Station, 1971.
21p. (U.K. Building Research Station. Current paper CP 28/71)

1. Building codes. 2. Building standards. I. U.K. Building Research Station. II. Title

---

690.22
C65 U.K. Building Research Station.
Colbourne, J   R
Studies in composite construction: an elastic analysis of wall-beam structures. Garston, Eng., Building Research Station, 1969.
11p. (U.K. Building Research Station. Current paper CP15/69)

1. Walls. I. U.K. Building Research Station. II. Title.

690
(41)
B84s U.K. Building Research Station.
pt.3 Studies in composite construction. Part III. Tests on the new government offices, Whitehall Gardens, by R. J. Mainstone. London, H. M. Stat. Off., 1960.
54p. illus., diagrs. (National Building studies. Research paper no. 28)

1. Building construction - U.K. I. Mainstone, R.J.

728
551.5
W47 U.K. Building Research Station.
Wise, A   F   E
Studies of air flow round buildings, by A. F. E. Wise and others. Garston, Eng., Building Research Station, Ministry of Technology, 1965.
[5]p. (U.K. Building Research Station. Building research current papers. Design series)
Reprinted from: The Architects' Journal, vol. 141, May 1965. p. 1185-9.

1. Architecture and climate. 2. Wind resistance. I. U.K. Building   Research Station. II. Title: Air flow   round buildings.

691.542 U.K. Building Research Station.
G87 Gutt, W
   Studies of the role of calcium sulphate in the manufacture of portland cement clinker, by W. Gutt and M.A. Smith. Garston, Eng., Building Research Station, Ministry of Public Building and Works, 1968.
   489-509p. (U.K. Building Research Station. Current papers CP 89/68)
   Bibliography: p. 508-509.
   Reprinted from: Transactions of the British Ceramic Society, Oct., 1968, pp. 487-509.
   1. Portland cement. I. Title. II. Smith, M.A., jt. au. III. U.K. Building Research Station.

VF
625.7 U.K. Building Research Station.
U54s   Studies on bridge-deck systems. II.
pt. 2   Bending moments in a plate-and-girder system, by C. C. Ritchie. London, H.M. Stat. Off., 1960.
   67p. diagrs., tables. (National building studies. Research paper no. 31)
   1. Bridges. I. Ritchie, C. C.

        U.K. Building Research Station.
625.7
U54s Short, A
pt.3   Studies on bridge-deck systems. III. Tests on model slab-and-girder bridge-deck systems, by A. Short and F.G. Thomas. London, H.M. Stationery Office, 1963.
   70p. (U.K. Building Research Station. National Building Studies. Research paper 37)
   1. Bridges. 2. Building methods. I. Thomas, F.G., jt. au. I. U.K. Building Research Station

        U.K. Building Research Station.
621.32
F47 Fischer, D
   Study and measurements of the luminance distribution of fluorescent lamps. Garston, Eng., Building Research Station, 1971.
   [11]p. (Library communication no. 1607) Translated from the German, by P.A. Ross.
   1. Lighting. I. U.K. Building Research Station. II. Title. (Series)

690 U.K. Building Research Station.
(41)   A study of alternative methods of house
U54s construction, by H. F. Broughton and W. J. Reiners. London, H. M. Stat. Off., 1959.
   93p. illus., diagrs., tables. (Its National building studies. Special report no. 30)
   1. Building construction - U.K. I. Broughton, H.F. II. Reiners, W.J.

720 U.K. Building Research Station.
H65 Honey, C R
   A study of coding and data co-ordination for the construction industry: architectural design. Garston, Eng., Building Research Station, Ministry of Public Building and Works, 1969.
   29p. (U.K. Building Research Station. Current paper 4/69)
   1. Architecture - Designs and plans. 2. Building documentation. 3. Building construction - U.K. 4. U.K. - Building construction. I. U.K. Building Research Station. II. Title.

002 U.K. Building Research Station.
:690 Britten, John R
B74   A study of coding and data co-ordination for the construction industry: contractors' management. Garston, Eng., Building Research Station, 1969.
   46p. (U.K. Building Research Station. Current paper 9/69)
   1. Building documentation. 2. Building industry - U.K. 3. U.K. - Building industry. 4. Contractors (Building industry) I. U.K. Building Research Station. II. Title.

---

690 U.K. Building Research Station.
(41) Johnston, H P
J63   A study of coding and data co-ordination for the construction industry: electrical design and contracting. Garston, Eng., Building Research Station, Ministry of Public Building and Works, 1969.
   70p. (U.K. Building Research Station. Current paper 7/69)
   1. Building industry - U.K. 2. U.K. - Building industry. 3. Building industry - Automation. 4.   Electrical wiring. I. U.K. Building Research Station. II. Title.

690 U.K. Building Research Station.
(41) Gilchrist, A
G45   A study of coding and data co-ordination for the construction industry: information systems relating to the construction industry, by A. Gilchrist and Kathleen Gaster. Garston, Eng., Building Research Station, Ministry of Public Works, 1969.
   65p. (U.K. Building Research Station. Current paper 11/69)
   Bibliography: p. 57-64.
   1. Building   industry - U.K. 2. U.K. -   Building industry. (Cont'd on next card)

690 Gilchrist, A   A study of coding...1969.
(41)   (Card 2)
G45   3. Building industry - Automation. I. U.K. Building Research Station. II. Gaster, Kathleen, jt. au. III. Title.

690 U.K. Building Research Station.
(41) Nelson, J I'a
N25   A study of coding and data co-ordination for the construction industry: instructions to operatives. Garston, Eng., Building Research Station, 1969.
   30p. (U.K. Building Research Station. Current paper 10/69)
   1. Building industry - U.K. 2. U.K. - Building industry. 3. Building industry - Automation. I. U.K. Building Research Station. II. Title.

002 U.K. Building Research Station.
:690 Foster, A G
F67   A study of coding and data co-ordination for the construction industry: mechanical engineering services, by A.G. Foster and others. Garston, Eng., Building Research Station, Ministry of Public Building and Works, 1969.
   81p. (U.K. Building Research Station. Current paper 6/69)
   1. Building documentation. 2. Building industry. 3. Architecture - Designs and plans. 4. Civil engineering. I. U.K. Building   Research Station. II. Title.

002 U.K. Building Research Station.
:690 Stevens, R F
S72   A study of coding and data co-ordination for the construction industry: structural engineering design, by R.F. Stevens and L. Monument. Garston, Eng., Building Research Station, 1969.
   32p. (U.K. Building Research Station. Current paper 5/69)
   1. Building documentation. 2. Structural engineering. I. Monument, L., jt. au. II. U.K. Building Research Station. III. Title.

690.512.2 U.K. Building Research Station.
N87 Nuttall, J F
   A study of decision rules for site control: guidance for foremen when programmes change. Garston, Eng., Building Research Station, Ministry of Technology, 1965.
   [3]p. (U.K. Building Research Station. Building research current papers. Construction series 19)
   Reprinted from: Builder, Aug., 1965, p. 407-9.
   1. Site planning. I.   U.K. Building Research Station. II.   Title.

---

331 U.K. Building Research Station.
(41) Jesnes, R E
J21   Study of operative skills: a guide to the first report. Garston, Eng., Building Research Station, Ministry of Technology, 1966.
   6p. (U.K. Building Research Station. Building research current paper. Construction series 30)
   1. Labor supply - U.K. 2. Building industry - U.K. I. U.K. Building Research Station. II. Title.

621.32 U.K. Building Research Station.
H18 Haubner, P
   Study of psychological glare in interiors, by P. Haubner and H. Johanni. Garston, Eng., Building Research Station, 1970.
   [13]p. (Library communication no. 1584)
   Translated from the German and reprinted from Lichttechnik, 1970, 22 (6), 304-6; (7) 345-7.
   1. Lighting. I. Johanni, H., jt. au. II. U.K. Building Research Station. III. Title: Glare. IV. Title.

697.4 U.K. Building Research Station.
U54   A study of space and water heating in local-authority flats, 1956-59, by J. B. Dick and others. London, H. M. Stat. Off., 1961.
   110p. (Its National building studies research paper no. 34)
   1. Hot-water heating. I. Dick, J. B.

621.32 U.K. Building Research Station.
C62s Cockram, A H
   A study of user preferences for fluorescent lamp colours for daytime and night-time lighting, by A.H. Cockram and others. Garston, Eng., Building Research Station, 1971.
   [8]p. (Current paper no. 13/71)
   Reprinted from: Lighting research and technology, vol. 2, no. 4, 1970, pp. 249-256.
   1. Lighting. I. U.K. Building Research Station. II. Title.

693.5 U.K. Building Research Station.
N14 Nakano, Kiyoshi.
   Study on load-deflection characteristics of prestressed concrete structures. Tokyo, Building Research Institute, Ministry of Construction, Japanese Government, 1965.
   33p. (Japan. Building Research Institute. BRI occasional report no. 24)
   1. Concrete construction. 2. Concrete, Prestressed. I. U.K. Building Research Station. II. Title.

691.32 U.K. Building Rearch Station.
T29s Teychenne, D C
   A survey of crushed stone sands for concrete. Garston, Eng., Ministry of Public Building and Works, Building Research Station, 1968.
   5p. (Building Research Station. Current paper 11)
   Reprinted from: British Granite and Whinstone Federation Journal, 1967, p. 53-60.
   1. Concrete. I. U.K. Building Research Station. II. Title.

728.1 U.K. Building Research Station.
:362.6 Hole, W V
(41)   A survey of housing for old people, by W.
H65 V. Hole and P. G. Allen. Garston, Eng., Building Research Station, Dept. of Scientific and Industrial Research [1965?]
   [20]p. (U.K. Building Research Station. Building research current papers. Design series 33)
   Reprinted from: The Architects' Journal, 1962, vol. 135, p. 1017-24, 1026. 1964, vol. 139 (2) p. 75-82.
   1. Housing for the   aged - U.K. 2. Old age. I. Allen, P. G., jt. au. II. U.K. Building Research   Station. III. Title.

690.072
F67

U.K. Building Research Station.
Forbes, W S
A survey of progress in house building.
Garston, Eng., Building Research Station,
1969.
88-91p. (U.K. Building Research Station.
Current paper 25/69)
Reprinted from: Building technology and
management, Apr., 1969, pp. 88-91.

1. Building construction - Labor requirements. I. U.K. Building Research Station.
II. Title.

690.015
(41)
B47

U.K. Building Research Station.
Bishop, D
Systems of construction; assessment of
economic performance. Gerston, Eng.,
Building Research Station, Department of
Scientific and Industrial Research, [1964?]
15p. (U.K. Building Research Station.
Building research current papers.
Construction series 7)

1. Building research - U.K. 2. Building
construction - U.K. I. U.K.
Building Research Station.

696
P17

U.K. Building Research Station.
Parker, T W
The technology of maintenance. Gerston, Eng.,
Building Research Station, Ministry of Tech-
nology, 1966.
4p. (U.K. Building Research Station.
Building research current papers. Design
series 53.
A paper given at the Conference on the Main-
tenance of Buildings held in Edinburgh, June 1966.
Reprinted from Building, 1966, vol. 211,
no. 6434, p. 171, 2, 5,6.

1. Building maintenance. I. U.K.
Building Research Station.

690.5
:551.5
W45

U.K. Building Research Station.
Wilson, P H
Surveys of winter working practices in
Scotland. Gerston, Eng., Building
Research Station, Ministry of Technology,
1965.
5p. (U.K. Building Research
Station. Building research current papers.
Construction series 20)

1. Winter construction. 2. Labor
productivity. I. U.K. Building Research
Station. II. Title.

691
(41)
N28

U.K. Building Research Station.
Newman, A J
A technical and historical review of the
sand grading requirements in British
Standard 882 by A. J. Newman and D. C.
Teychenne. Garston, Eng., Building Research
Station, Dept. of Scientific and Industrial
Research, 1964.
[3]p. (U.K. Building Research Station.
Building research current papers. Engineering
series 18)
Reprinted from: Cement, lime and gravel,
vol. 39 (10), p. 336-8.

(Continued on next card)

693.5
H27t

U.K. Building Research Station.
Herbert, M R M
Temperatures within battery moulds during
curing. Garston, Eng., Building Research
Station, Ministry of Technology, 1967.
[3]p. (U.K. Building Research Station
Building research current papers. Construction series 33)
Reprinted from: Industrialised building
systems and components, 1966, vol. 3, no. 11,
p. 44, 45, 47.

1. Concrete construc-   tion. 2. Coordinated
components.   II. Title.
I. U.K. Building   Research Station.

690.091.82
(485)
E77

U.K. Building Research Station.
Essunger, Gunnar.
Swedish building standards 67. Garston,
Eng., Building Research Station, 1968.
10p. (Library communication no. 1429)
Translated from the Swedish and reprinted
from Byggmastaren, 1968, 47 (March), 4-10.

1. Building standards - Sweden.
I. U.K. Building Research Station.
II. Title. (Series)

691
(41)
N28

Newman, A J   A technical and
historical review of the sand grading
requirements in British Standard
882...1964.   (Card 2)

1. Building materials - U.K. 2. Building
standards - U.K. I. Teychenne, D. C., jt. au.
II. U.K. Building   Research Station.

690.015
(41
:016)
U541
no.234

U.K. Building Research Station.
Tendering documents with a production bias.
Garston, Eng., 1970.
3p. (Its Library bibliography no. 234)

1. Building costs - Bibl. I. Title.
(Series)

693.002.22
(4)
B47

U.K. Building Research Station.
Bishop, D
System building in Europe. Gerston, Eng.,
Building Research Station, Ministry of
Technology, 1966.
[4]p. (U.K. Building Research Station,
Building research current papers. Design
series 59)
Reprinted from System building and design,
1966, November, p. 32-4, 6.

1. Prefabricated construction - Europe.
I. U.K. Building Research Station.

699.86
P71

U.K. Building Research Station.
Pratt, A W
Technical aspects of thermal insulation in
buildings. Gerston, Eng., Building Research
Station, Dept. of Scientific and Industrial
Research, 1964.
[10]p. (U.K. Building Research Station,
Building research current papers.
Engineering series 17)
Paper given to the Insulation Convention,
London, 25th-28th, February 1964.

1. Insulating materials.   2. Heat transmission.
I. U.K. Building   Research Station.

690.22
W65

U.K. Building Research Station.
Wood, R H
A tentative design method for the composite
action of heavily loaded brick panel walls
supported on reinforced concrete beams, by
R.H. Wood and L.G. Simms. Garston, Eng.,
Building Research Station, 1969.
6p. (U.K. Building Research Station.
Current paper CP 26/69)
1. Walls. 2. Brick construction. 3. Con-
crete, Reinforced. I. Simms, L.G., jt. au.
II. U.K. Building Research Station.
III. Title.

690
H65

U.K. Building Research Station.
Honey, C R
System building: sponsorship and disciplines.
Gerston, Eng., Building Research Station,
Ministry of Technology, 1966.
11p. (U.K. Building Research Station.
Building research current papers. Design
series 52)
Reprinted from: Architectural review,
June, September 1966. p. 48-6; 241-8.

1. Building industry. 2. Architectural
details. 3. Building methods. I. U.K.
Building   Research Station.
II. Title.

691.542
D15

U.K. Building Research Station.
Danyushevskii, S I
Technical properties of cements containing
free calcium oxide, by S.I. Danyushevskii
et al. Garston, Eng., Building Research
Station, 1971.
5p. (Library communication no. 1622)
Translated from the Russian and reprinted
from Tsement, 1970, (7), 15-17.
1. Portland cement. I. U.K. Building
Research Station. II. Title. (Series)

691.54
B65

U.K. Building Research Station.
Bombled, J P
Test apparatus for automatically measuring
the setting time of cement. Garston, Eng.,
Building Research Station, 1969.
[6]p. (U.K. Building Research Station.
Library communication no. 1507)

Translated from the German.

1. Cement. I. U.K. Building Research
Station. II. Title. (Series)

691.54
G87

U.K. Building Research Station.
Gutt, W
The system CaO-2CaO.SiO2-CaF2, by W. Gutt and
G.J. Osborne. [Garston, Eng.] Building Re-
search Station, 1970.
[5]p. (U.K. Building Research Station.
Current paper 27/70)
Reprinted from Transactions of the British
Ceramic Society, May 1970. p. 125-129.
1. Cement. I. Osborne, G.J., jt. au.
II. U.K. Building Research Station.
III. Title.

693.5
S29

U.K. Building Research Station.
Seymour-Walker, K J
Techniques for making large concrete units-
a survey, and some development work at the
Building Research Station. Gerston, Eng.,
Building Research Station, Ministry of
Technology, 1965.
17p. (U.K. Building Research
Station. Building research current papers.
Construction series 21)

1. Concrete construction. 2. Pipes. I. U.K.
Building Research Station. II. Title.

691.71
W66

U.K. Building Research Station.
Wood, R H
Test of a multi-storey rigid steel frame,
by R.H. Wood and others. Garston, Eng.,
Building Research Station, Ministry of Public
Building and Works, 1968.
107-119p. (U.K. Building Research Station.
Building research current paper 53/68)
Reprinted from: The structural engineer,
April, 1968.

1. Steel. 2. Structural engineering.
I. U.K. Building Research Station. II. Title.

690.091.82
C41

U.K. Building Research Station.
Cibula, Evelyn.
Systems of building control. Garston,
Eng., Building Research Station, 1970.
[7]p. (U.K. Building Research Station.
Current paper CP 31/70)

1. Building codes. I. U.K. Building
Research Station. II. Title.

690.015
(41
:016)
U541
no.
218

U.K. Building Research Station.
Technological forecasting and project
evaluation. Garston, Eng., 1969.
7p. (Its Library bibliography 218)

1. Building industry - Bibl. 2. Building
costs - Bibl. I. Title.

699.8
W34

U.K. Building Research Station.
Whiting, R W
A test rig for establishing the dimensional
needs of weatherproof joints. Garston, Eng.,
Building Research Station, 1970.
4p. (U.K. Building Research Station.
Current paper 26/70)

1. Insulation. I. U.K. Building Research
Station. II. Title.

693.5
1691.8
U54

U.K. BUILDING RESEARCH STATION.
   TEST WALLS FOR ASSESSING CONSTRUCTION
TIMES WITH NEW BUILDING BLOCKS, BY W.
KINNIBURGH. LONDON, H.M. STAT. OFF.,
1950.
   8P. (ITS NATIONAL BUILDING STUDIES
TECHNICAL PAPER NO. 9)

   1. CONCRETE BLOCKS.   I. KINNIBURGH,
W.

691.32
L68

U.K. Building Research Station.
Loudon, A   G
   The thermal and acoustic properties of light-
weight concretes, by A.G. Ludon and E.F. Stacy.
Garston, Eng., Building Research Station,
Ministry of Technology, 1966.
   10p.   (U.K. Building Research Station.
Building research current papers. Design
series 45)
   Reprinted from: Structural concrete, March/
April 1966. pp. 58-76.

   1. Concrete.   I. U.K.   Building Research
Station. II. Title.

711.4
L28t

U.K. Building Research Station.
Levin, P   H
   Toward decision-making rules for urban
planners. Garston, Eng., Building Research
Station, Ministry of Public Building and
Works, 1968.
   437-442p. (U.K. Building Research Station.
Building research current papers. Current
paper 41/68)
   Reprinted from the Journal of the Town
Planning Institute, December, 1967.
   1. City planning. I. U.K. Building
Research Station. II. Title.

693.97
R61

U.K. Building Research Station.
Roberts, E   H
   Tests of a full-scale rigid-jointed multi-
storey steel frame in high-yield steel
(BS 4360, Grade 50), by E.H. Roberts and
R.F. Smith. Garston, Eng., Building
Research Station, 1971.
   56p. (U.K. Building Research Station.
Current paper CP 36/71)

   1. Steel construction. 2. Strains and
stresses. I. Smith, R.F., jt. au. II. U.K.
Building Research Station. III. Title.

691.42
A75

U.K. Building Research Station.
Arnold, Pamela J
   Thermal conductivity of masonry materials.
Garston, Eng., Building Research Station, 1970.
   [8]p. (U.K. Building Research Station.
Current paper 1/70)
   Reprinted from: The Journal of the Institution
of Heating and Ventilating Engineers, 1969,
vol. 37 (August), pp. 101-108 and 117.

   1. Bricks. 2. Concrete. 3. Heat transmission. I. U.K. Building Research Station.
II. Title.

362
(41)
W47
2 L

U.K. Building Research Station.
Wise, A   F   E
   Towards economic design of water and sanitary services for hospitals. Garston, Eng.,
Building Research Station Ministry of Technology, 1966.
   12p.   (U.K. Building Research Station.
Building research current papers. Engineering series 25)
   Paper presented to the Hospital Engineering
Service Symposium of the I.H.V.E., January,
1966.
   1. Hospitals - U.K.   2. Water-supply.
   3. Sanitation.   I. U.K. Building
Research Station.   II. Title.

693.5
865

U.K. Building Research Station.
Somerville, G
   Tests on joints between precast concrete
members, by G. Somerville and P. Burhouse.
Garston, Eng., Building Research Station, Ministry
of Public Building and Works, 1966.
   18p. (U.K. Building Research Station. Building research current papers. Engineering papers
45)
   Reprinted from Proceedings of the Institution
of Structural Engineers' Conference, 1966.
   1. Concrete construction. 2. Prefabricated construction. I. Burhouse, P., jt. au. II. U.K.
Building Research   Station. III. Title.

691.32
86b

U.K. BUILDING RESEARCH STATION.
BONNELL, DAVID GLYNWYN ROBERT.
   THE THERMAL EXPANSION OF CONCRETE, BY
D.G.R. BONNELL AND F.C. HARPER.
LONDON, H.M. STAT. OFF., 1951.
   24P. (U.K. BUILDING RESEARCH
STATION. NATIONAL BUILDING STUDIES.
TECHNICAL PAPER NO. 7)

   1. CONCRETE.   I. HARPER, F.C., JT.
AU.   II. U.K. BUILDING RESEARCH
STATION.   III. TITLE.

628.2
L45

U.K. Building Research Station.
Lillywhite, M   S   T
   Towards general method for the design of
drainage systems in large buildings, by
M.S.T. Lillywhite and A.F.E. Wise.
Garston, Eng., Building Research Station,
1969.
   22p. (U.K. Building Research Station.
Current paper 27/69)
   Paper presented at a meeting of the
Institution of Public Health Engineers,
Caxton Hall, Westminster, London, 6th
Feb. 1969.
   1. Drainage.   I. Wise, A.F.E., jt. au.
         (Cont'd on next card)

593.5
G74

U.K. Building Research Station.
Grimer, F   J
   Tests on lightweight concrete columns.
Garston, Eng., Building Research Station,
Ministry of Technology [1966?]
   [18p.]   (U.K. Building Research
Station. Building research current papers.
Engineering Series 27)
   Reprinted from: Structural concrete, Nov/Dec.
1965. p. 503-20.

   1. Concrete construction. 2. Concrete
aggregates. I. U.K. Building Research
Station.   II. Title.

628.1
D27

U.K. Building Research Station.
Deryagin, B   V
   The thermal stability of modified water, by
B.V. Deryagin and others. Garston, Eng.,
Building Research Station, 1970.
   4p. (U.K. Building Research Station.
Library communication no. 1572)
   Translated from the Russian [and reprinted
from] Doklady Akademii Nauk SSSR, 1970, 191 (4),
859-61.
   1. Water-supply. I. U.K. Building Research
Station. II. Title. (Series)

628.2
L45

Lillywhite, M   S   T   Towards
     general...1969.   (Card 2)

   II. U.K. Building Research Station.
   III. Title.

691.328.2
S72t

U.K. Building Research Station.
Stevens, R   F
   Tests on prestressed reinforced concrete
beams. Garston, Eng., Building Research
Station, 1970.
   [6]p. (U.K. Building Research Station.
Current paper CP 8/70)
   Reprinted from: Concrete, Nov., 1969.
p. 457-462.
   1. Concrete, Prestressed. 2. Concrete,
Reinforced. I. U.K. Building Research
Station. II. Title.

691.11
A74

U.K. Building Research Station.
Atkinson, J   E
   Timber content of two-storey houses, by
J.E. Atkinson and C.R. Honey. Garston, Eng.,
Building Research Station, Ministry of Public
Building and Works, 1968.
   26-27, 29-30, 33p. (U.K. Building Research
Station. Building research current papers.
Current paper 6/68)
   Reprinted from: Industrialized building.
July 1967.
   1. Wood. 2. Housing. 3. Architecture.
Domestic - Designs and plans.
I. Honey, C   R., jt. au. II. U.K.
Building Research   Station. III. Title.

621.9
:690
(47)
U54

U.K. Building Research Station.
   Tower cranes for building. Garstone, Eng.,
1971.
   [57]p. (Library communication no. 1601)

   Translated from the Russian.

   1. Building equipment - U.S.S.R. I. Title.
(Series)

697
H85

U.K. Building Research Station.
Humphreys, M   A
   Theoretical and practical aspects of thermal
comfort, by M.A. Humphreys and J.F. Nicol.
Garston, Eng., Building Research Station, 1971.
   [13]p. (Current paper no. 14/71)

   1. Heating. I. U.K. Building Research
Station. II. Nicol, J.F., jt. au. III. Title.

694.1
B46

U.K. Building Research Station.
Bjork, S   O
   Timber structures (Träkonstruktioner)
Garston, Eng., Building Research Station,
Ministry of Public Building and Works, 1969.
   5p. (U.K. Building Research Station.
Library communication 1479)
   Translated from the Swedish Byggmastaren,
1968, (3), 23-26.

   1. Wood construction. I. U.K. Building
Research Station. II. Title.

711.4
C41

U.K. Building Research Station.
Ciborowski, A
   Town planning problems in the reconstruct-
ion of badly damaged towns. Translated
from the German by D.R. Gray. Garston, Eng.,
Ministry of Public Building and Works,
Building Research Station, 1968.
   5p. (Library communication no. 1422)

   1. City planning. 2. Reconstruction.
I. U.K. Building Research Station.
II. Title.

691.328
W66t

U.K. Building Research Station.
Wood, R   H
   The theory of the strip method for design of
slabs, by R.H. Wood and G.S.T. Armer. Garston,
Eng., Building Research Station, 1968.
   311p. (U.K. Building Research Station.
Current paper CP84/68)
   Reprinted from: Proceedings of the Institution
of Civil Engineers, 1968, Vol. 41 (October),
pp. 285-311.
   1. Concrete, Reinforced. 2. Loads. I. Armer,
G.S.T., jt. au.   II. U.K. Building Research Station.   III. Title.

693.5
(485)
S88

U.K. Building Research Station.
Suu, V
   Tolerance measurements in precast concrete
construction at Norrköping. Garston, Eng.,
Building Research Station, 1971.
   [9]p. (Library communication no. 1621)
   Translated from the Swedish.

   1. Concrete construction - Sweden.
I. U.K. Building Research Station.
II. Title. (Series)

690.031
B47

U.K. Building Research Station.
Bishop, D
   Traditional building costs; the target for
system building. Garston, Eng., Building
Research Station, Ministry of Technology,
1966.
   34-37p.   (U.K. Building Research
Station. Building research current papers.
Design series no. 42)

   Reprinted from the National builder,
Jan., 1966.

   1. Building   costs. 2. Building
research.   I. U.K. Building
Research Sta-   tion. II. Title.

534.83
S23t
United Kingdom Building Research Station.
Scholes, W E
Traffic noise criteria. [Garston, Eng.] Building Research Station, 1969.
9p. (U.K. Building Research Station. Current paper 38/69)

1. Noise. 2. Traffic. I. U.K. Building Research Station. II. Title.

711.4
(60)
A74
U.K. Building Research Station.
Atkinson, G A
Urbanization and town growth in Africa. Problems of mass housing and techniques assisting towards their solution. Paper for the Inter-African Conference on Housing and Urbanization, Nairobi, 19th to 30th, January, 1959. Garston, Eng., Building Research Station, 1958.
18p. (U.K. Building Research Station. Note no. E 843)

(Cont'd on next card)

690.015
(41)
L214
U.K. Building Research Station.
Lea, F M
The users of building research. Garston, Eng., Dept. of Scientific and Industrial Research, Building Research Station, 1963.
3p. (U.K. Building research current papers. Supplements 5)

Preface to the report of the Director of Building Research for 1963.

1. Building research - U.K. I. U.K. Building Research Station.

534.83
L15
U.K. Building Research Station.
Langdon, F J
The traffic noise index: a method of controlling noise nuisance, by F.J. Langdon and W.E. Scholes. Garston, Eng., Building Research Station, Ministry of Public Building and Works, 1968.
8p. (U.K. Building Research Station. Building research current papers, Current paper 38/68)
Version of this paper in the Architects' journal, April 1968.
1. Noise. 2. Traffic. 3. Highways - Social effect. I. Scholes, W.E. jt. au. II. U.K. Building Research Station. III. Title.

711.4
(60)
A74
Atkinson, G.A. Urbanization and town growth in Africa...1958.
(Card 2)

1. City planning - Africa. 2. Housing - Africa. 3. Housing in the tropics. 4. Family living requirements. I. U.K. Building Research Station. II. Inter-African Conference on Housing and Urbanization, Nairobi, 1959. III. Title. (Series)

690.015
(41
:016)
U541
no.
220
U.K. Building Research Station.
The utilisation of solar energy. Garston, Eng., 1968.
5p. (Its Library bibliography 220)

1. Heating, Solar - Bibl. I. Title.

699.844
S31
U.K. Building Research Station.
Sharp, B H S
The transmission loss of multi-layer structures, by B.H.S. Sharp and J.W. Beauchamp. Garston, Eng., Building Research Station, 1969.
383-392p. (U.K. Building Research Station. Current paper 31/69)
Reprinted from: Journal of sound and vibration, May, 1969, pp. 383-392.
1. Architectural acoustics. 2. Panels. I. Beauchamp, J.W., jt. au. II. U.K. Building Research Station. III. Title.

301.36
C17
U.K. Building Research Station.
Carlstein, T
The urbanisation process: 17 individuals' 24-hour movements in some types of families, by T. Carlstein and others. Garston, Eng., Building Research Station, 1969.
[66]p. (Library communication no. 1513)

Translated from the Swedish.

1. Sociology, Urban. 2. Social science research. I. U.K. Building Research Station. II. Title. (Series)

697.3
L68
U.K. Building Research Station.
Loudon, A G
U-values in the 1970 guide. Garston, Eng., Building Research Station, Ministry of Public Building and Works, 1968.
167-174p. (U.K. Building Research Station. Current paper CP 79/68)
Reprinted from: Journal of the Institution of Heating and Ventilating Engineers, Sept., 1968 pp. 167-174.
1. Thermal radiation. 2. Walls. 3. Roofs and roofing. I. Title. II. U.K. Building Research Station.

534.83
P97
U.K. Building Research Station.
Purkis, H J
Transport noise and town planning. Garston, Eng., Building Research Station, Dept. of Scientific and Industrial Research, 1964.
13p. (U.K. Building Research Station. Building research current papers. Design series 25)
Reprinted from: Journal of sound and vibration, vol. (3) 1964, pp. 323-34.

1. Noise. 2. City planning. I. U.K. Building Research Station. II. Title.

621.9
:690
B87
U.K. Building Research Station.
Butler, A J ed.
The use of cranes on low-rise high density industrialised housing; report of a working party. Garston, Eng., Building Research Station, 1970.
54p. (U.K. Building Research Station. Current paper 25/70)

1. Building equipment. 2. Prefabricated construction. I. U.K. Building Research Station. II. Title.

621.6
D29
U.K. Building Research Station.
Dezheni, I
Vacuum testing of concrete pipes for water-tightness. Garston, Eng., Building Research Station, 1971.
19p. (Library communication no. 1623)
Translated from the Russian.

1. Pipes - Testing. I. U.K. Building Research Station. II. Title. (Series)

621.643
C76
U.K. Building Research Station.
Crowder, J R
Trial of plastics pipes for hot water services, by J.R. Crowder and A. Rixon. Garston, Eng., Building Research Station, Ministry of Public Building and Works, 1968.
[4]p. (U.S. Building Research Station. Building research current papers. Current paper 7/68)
Reprinted from: British plastics, July, 1967.

1. Pipes. 2. Plastics. I. Rixon, A., jt. au. II. U.K. Building Research Station. III. Title.

691.328
E82
U.K. Building Research Station.
Everett, L H
The use of galvanized steel reinforcement in building, by L.H. Everett and K.W.J. Treadaway. Garston, Eng., Building Research Station, 1970.
5p.
Paper first published in the Proceedings of the 8th International Conference on Hot Dip Galvanising held in London, June 1967, by the Zinc Development Association.
1. Concrete, Reinforced. I. Treadaway, K.W.J., jt. au. II. U.K. Building Research Station. III. Title.

691.54
R12
U.K. Building Research Station.
Rackwitz, R
Variability of concrete cube crushing strength. Garston, Eng., Building Research Station, 1971.
[14]p. (Library communication no. 1634)

Translated from the German.

1. Cement. 2. Strength of materials. I. U.K. Building Research Station. II. Title. (Series)

624.042
A75
U.K. Building Research Station.
Armer, G S T
Ultimate load tests of slabs designed by the strip method. Garston, Eng., Building Research Station, 1968.
12p. (U.K. Building Research Station. Current paper CP 83/68)

Reprinted from Proceedings of the Institution of Civil Engineers, 1968, Vol. 41 (October), pp. 313-331.

1. Loads. I. U.K. Building Research Station. II. Title.

725.13
L15
U.K. Building Research Station.
Langdon, F J
User research in office design, by F.J. Langdon and E. C. Keighley. Garston, England, Building Research Station, Dept. of Scientific and Industrial Research, 1964.
[7]p. (U.K. Building Research Station. Current papers. Design series 18)
Reprinted from: Architects' journal, 1964, vol. 139 (6), pp. 333-9.

(Cont'd. on next card)

691.32
T29
U.K. Building Research Station.
Teychenne, D C
The variability of the strength of concrete and its treatment in codes of practice. Garston, [Eng.] Building Research Station, Ministry of Technology, 1966.
13p. (U.K. Building Research Station. Building research current papers. Engineering series 32)
Reprinted from: Structural Concrete, 1966, vol. 3 (January/February), pp. 3047.

1. Concrete. 2. Concrete, Reinforced. I. U.K. Building Research Station. II. Title.

624.043
M14
U.K. Building Research Station.
Maier, G
The unstable flexural behaviour of inflexible elasto-plastic beams. Garston, Eng., Building Research Station, 1971.
[25]p. (Library communication no. 1618)
Translated from the Italian.

1. Strains and stresses. 2. Trusses. I. U.K. Building Research Station. II. Title. (Series)

725.13
L15
Langdon, F J User research in office design... (Card 2)

1. Public buildings. 2. Architecture - Design. I. Title. II. U.K. Building Research Station.

690.281
L62
U.K. Building Research Station.
Lockwood, A J
Variety reduction in doormaking, by A.J. Lockwood and D.W. Pedder-Smith. Garston, Eng., Building Research Station, 1969.
7p. (U.K. Building Research Station. Current paper 32/69)
Reprinted from: Building, June 13, 1969, pp. 161-166.
1. Doors. I. Pedder-Smith, D.W., jt. au. II. U.K. Building Research Station. III. Title.

600.15
L16
U.K. Building Research Station.
Lapin, V V
The varying nature of the precipitation of dicalcium silicate in blast-furnace slags, by V.V. Lapin and I.P. Solovova. Garston, Eng., Building Research Station, 1970.
[7]p. (Library communication no. 1591)
Translated from the Russian and reprinted from proceedings of: Ural petrographic conference, 2d. Petrografiya ogneuporov, shlakov i sinteticheskikh mineralov, 1968, (7), 84-8.
1. Industrial research. 2. Glass.

(Cont'd on next card)

600.15
L16
Lapin, V V   The varying...1970.
(Card 2)

I. Solovova, I.P., jt. au. II. U.K. Building Research Station. III. Title: Blast-furnace slags. IV. Title: Slags. V. Title. (Series)

697.9
D25
U.K. Building Research Station.
Denmark. Arbejds- og Boligministeriet.
Ventilation. Garston, Eng., Building Research Station, 1969.
6p. (U.K. Building Research Station. Library communication 1466)

Translated from the Danish, Bygningsreglement for kobstaederne og landet, chapt. 11, pp. 108-15.

1. Ventilation. I. U.K. Building Research Station. II. Title.

697.9
R25
U.K. Building Research Station.
Rengholt, Ulf.
Ventilation. Garston, Eng., Building Research Station, 1968.
5p. (Library communication no. 1431)
Translated from the Swedish and reprinted from Byggmastarem, 1968, 47 (March), 41-43.

1. Ventilation. I. U.K. Building Research Station. II. Title. (Series)

693.002.22
S29
U.K. Building Research Station.
Seymour-Walker, K J
Vertically cast L-shaped panels. Garston, Eng., Building Research Station, Ministry of Public Building and Works, 1968.
4p. (U.K. Building Research Station. Building research current papers. Current paper 16/68)

1. Prefabricated construction. 2. Concrete. 3. Panels. I. U.K. Building Research Station. II. Title.

697.9
W47
U.K. Building Research Station.
Wise, A F E
Ventilation of internal bathrooms and water closets. Garston, Eng., Building Research Station, Department of Scientific and Industrial Research, [1964?]
14p. (U.K. Building Research Station. Building research current papers. Engineering series 9)

1. Ventilation. 2. Bathrooms.
I. U.K.   Building Research Station.

690.015
(41
:016)
U541
no. 231
U.K. Building Research Station.
Weather, and its effect on building operations and costs.
Garston, Eng., 1969.
9p. (Its Library bibliography 231)

1. Winter construction - Bibl.
2. Architecture and climate - Bibl.
I. Title.

699.8
H17w
U.K. Building Research Station.
Harrison, H W
Weatherproofing of joints: a systematic approach to design, by H.W. Harrison and R.B. Bonshor. Garston, Eng., Building Research Station, 1970.
11p. (U.K. Building Research Station. Current paper 29/70)
Reprinted from: Proceedings of the Conference on Joints in Structures held at the University of Sheffield, 8-10 July 1970, session D, paper 3.
1. Insulation. I. Bonshor, R.B., jt. au.
II. U.K. Building Research Station.
III. Title.

691.328
B17
U.K. Building Research Station.
Bate, S C C
Why limit state design? Garston, Eng., Building Research Station, Ministry of Public Building and Works, 1968.
103-108p. (U.K. Building Research Station. Current paper 52)
Reprinted from Concrete, Mar. 1968.

1. Concrete, Reinforced. 2. Concrete, Prestressed. I. U.K. Building Research Station.

699.83
M25
U.K. Building Research Station.
Menzies, J B
Wind damage to buildings in the United Kingdom 1962-1969. Garston, Eng., Building Research Station, 1971.
9p. (U.K. Building Research Station. Current paper CP 35/71)
Reprinted from: Building, v. 221, no. 6693, 27 Aug. 1971, pp. 67-76.

1. Buildings - Wind stresses. I. U.K. Building Research Station. II. Title.

699.83
W47w
U.K. Building Research Station.
Wise, A F E
Wind effects due to groups of buildings. Garston, Eng., Building Research Station, 1970.
8p. (U.K. Building Research Station. Current paper no. 23/70)
Paper presented at the Royal Society Symposium Architectural Aerodynamics Session 3(iii) Effect of buildings on the local wind, London, 1970.
1. Buildings - Wind stresses. I. U.K. Building Research Station. II. Title.

699.83
U54
U.K. Building Research Station.
Wind loading on buildings - 3. Garston, Eng., 1969.
104-105p. (Building Research Station. Digest 105)

1. Buildings - Wind stresses. I. Title.

699.83
N28w
U.K. Building Research Station.
Newberry, C W
Wind loading on Vickers Tower, Millbank, by C.W. Newberry and others. Garston, Eng., Building Research Station, 1970.
[8]p. (U.K. Building Research Station. Current paper CP 35/70)

Reprinted from: Building, Vol. 219, No. 6639, 14 August 1970, pp. 53-56.

1. Buildings - Wind stresses. I. U.K. Building Research Station. II. Title.

699.83
N28wi
U.K. Building Research Station.
Newberry, C W
Wind pressures on the Post Office Tower, London, by C.W. Newberry and others. Garston, Eng., Building Research Station, 1971.
12p. (U.K. Building Research Station. Current paper CP 37/71)
Reprinted from: Proceedings of the 3d International Conference on Wind Effects on Buildings and Structures, Tokyo, Sept. 1971.
1. Buildings - Wind stresses. I. U.K. Building Research Station. II. Title.

699.83
M19
U.K. Building Research Station.
Mayne, J R
A wind-pressure transducer. Garston, Eng., Building Research Station, 1970.
[3]p. (U.K. Building Research Station. Current paper 17/70)
Reprinted from: Journal of physics E: Scientific instruments 1970, vol. 3, pp. 248-250.

1. Buildings - Wind stresses. I. U.K. Building Research Station. II. Title.

690.015
(485)
S82
R35
1970
Engl.
U.K. Building Research Station.
Wiren, Bengt.
Wind tunnel investigation of the pressure distribution on a flat roof with different edge profiles. Garston, Eng., Building Research Station, 1971.
[73]p. (Library communication no. 1606)

Translated from the Swedish.

1. Building research - Sweden. 2. Roofs and roofing. 3. Buildings - Wind stresses.
I. U.K. Building Research Station.
II. Title. (Series)

699.83
W47
U.K. Building Research Station.
Wise, A F E
Wind studies at the Building Research Station, by A.F.E. Wise and D.E. Sexton. Garston, Eng., Building Research Station, Dept. of Scientific and Industrial Research, 1963.
7p. (U.K. Building Research Station. Building research current papers. Engineering series 15)

1. Wind resistance. 2. Ventilation. I. Sexton, D.E. II. U.K. Building Research Station.

690.282
L68
U.K. Building Research Station.
Loudon, A G
Window design criteria to avoid overheating by excessive solar heat gains. Garston, Eng., Building Research Station, Ministry of Public Building and Works, 1967.
95-102p. (U.K. Building Research Station. Building Research current papers. CP4/68)
Reprinted from: Sunlight in buildings, Proceedings of C.I.E. Intersessional Conference on Sunlighting in Buildings, April, 1965.
1. Windows. 2. Heating, Solar.
I. U.K. Building Research Station.
II. Title.

690
(41)
E22
U.K. Building Research Station.
Eden, J F
The work of the Building Research Station on the development of mechanical plant for building. Garston, Eng., Building Research Station, Dept. of Scientific and Industrial Research, 1964.
[21]p. (U.K. Building Research Station. Building research current papers. Construction series 14)

Reprinted from: Preprint of paper and discussion presented to the Public Works and
(Continued on next card)

690
(41)
E22
Eden, J.F. The work of the ... (Card 2)

Municipal Services Congress, 1964.

1. Building construction - U.K. I. U.K. Building Research Station.
2. Building methods - U.K.

693.5
1691.8
U54W
U.K. BUILDING RESEARCH STATION.
A WORK STUDY OF BLOCKLAYING, BY W. KINNIBURGH AND L.S. VALLANCE. LONDON, H.M. STAT. OFF., 1948.
34P. (ITS NATIONAL BUILDING STUDIES TECHNICAL PAPER NO. 1)

1. CONCRETE BLOCKS. I. KINNIBURGH, W. II. VALLANCE, L.S.

691.421
W17y
U.K. Building Research Station.
Ward, W H
Yielding of the ground and the structural behaviour of linings of different flexibility in a tunnel in London clay. Garston, Eng., Building Research Station, 1970.
[8]p. (U.K. Building Research Station. Current paper CP 34/70)
Reprinted from: Proceedings of the 7th International Conference on Soil Mechanics and Foundation Engineering, Mexico, 1969, Vol. III, pp. 320-325.
1. Clay. I. U. K. Building Research Station. II. Title: Tunnel. III. Title.

628.1
Y68
U.K. Building Research Station.
Young, O C
The use underground of flexible pipes for water supply with special reference to plastic pipes, by O.C. Young and J.H. Smith. Garston, Eng., Building Research Station, Ministry of Technology, 1966.
3p. (U.K. Building Research Station. Building research current papers. Engineering series 35)
Reprinted from Civil engineering and public works review, 1966, vol. 61, no. 717(August) p. 467-9.

(Cont'd on next card)

628.1
Y68
Young, O.C. The use underground of flexible pipes for water supply with special reference to plastic pipes...1966. (Card 2)

1. Water supply - U.K. 2. Pipes. I. Smith, J.H., jt.au. II. U.K. Building Research Station. III. Title.

312
(41)
U54
U.K. CENSUS OFFICE.
CENSUS OF ENGLAND AND WALES, 1931. HOUSING. REPORT AND TABLES. LONDON, H.M. STAT. OFF., 1935.
89p.

1. CENSUS - HOUSING - U.K.

362.4
U54
U.K. Central Council for the Disabled.
Planning for disabled people in the urban environment. London, 1969.
64p.

Bibliography: p. 63-64.

1. Handicapped. I. Title.

728.1
(41)
U54c
U.K. Central Housing Advisory Committee. (Housing Management Sub-Committee)
U.K. Ministry of Housing and Local Government. (Welsh Office)
Council housing purposes, procedures and priorities. Ninth report of the Housing Management Sub-Committee of the Central Housing Advisory Committee. London, H.M.S.O., 1969.
183p.

1. Housing - U.K. 2. Public housing - U.K. I. U.K. Central Housing Advisory Committee. (Housing Management Sub-Committee) II. Title.

VF
711.585
U54c
U.K. Central Housing Advisory Committee. (Housing Management Sub-Committee)
Councils and their houses; management of estates; eighth report ... London, H. M. Stat. Off., 1959.
39p.
At head of title: Ministry of Housing and Local Government.

1. Relocation - U.K. 2. Housing management. I. U.K. Ministry of Housing and Local Government.

728.2
U54
U.K. Central Housing Advisory Committee. (Flats Sub-Committee)
Living in flats. London, H. M. Stat. Off., 1952.
39p.

1. Apartment houses. 2. Architecture - Design. I. Title.

VF
711.585
U54
U.K. Central Housing Advisory Committee. (Housing Management Sub-Committee)
Moving from the slums; seventh report... London, H.M. Stat. off., 1956.
24 p.

1. Relocation - U.K. I. Title.

728.1
(41)
U54op
U.K. Central Housing Advisory Committee.
The operations of housing associations; report of the House Management and Housing Associations Sub-committee. London, H.M. Stat. Off., 1939.
17 p.
At head of title: Ministry of Health.

1. Housing -

728.6
(41)
U54R
U.K. CENTRAL HOUSING ADVISORY COMMITTEE. RURAL HOUSING COMMITTEE. RURAL HOUSING. 3D - REPORT. LONDON, H.M. STATIONERY OFF., 1944-
V.

1. FARM HOUSING - U.K. I. TITLE.

333.323
U54
U.K. Central Housing Advisory Committee.
Selection of tenants and transfers and exchanges. Third report of the Housing Management Sub-Committee of the Central Housing Advisory Committee. Issued by the Ministry of Housing and Local Government. London, H.M.S.O., 1949.
28p.

1. Tenant selection. I. U.K. Ministry of Housing and Local Government. II. Title.

333.323
U54u
1955
U.K. Central Housing Advisory Committee. (Housing Management Sub-Committee)
Unsatisfactory tenants. London, H. M. Stat. Off., 1955.
32p.

1. Landlord and tenant.
2. Tenant selection.

333.323
U54u
U.K. Central Housing Advisory Committee. (Housing Management Sub-Committee)
Unsatisfactory tenants. Sixth report of the Housing Management Sub-Committee of the Central Housing Advisory Committee. London, H.M.S.O., 1968.
31p.

1. Landlord and tenant. I. Title.

VF
333
(41)
U54
U.K. Central Land Board.
Report
London, H.M. Stat. Off.,
v. tables. annual.
Report year ends March 31.
For complete information see shelflist.

1. Real property - U.K. 2. Regional planning - U.K. 3. City planning - U.K.

U.K. Central Office of Information

see also

U.K. British Information Services

330
(729)
U54
U.K. Central Office of Information.
Barbados. Prepared for British Information Services. New York, British Information Services, 1966.
26p.

1. Economic conditions - Barbados, W.I. I. U.K. British Information Services. II. Title.

330
(68)
U54
U.K. Central Office of Information.
Bechuanaland. Prepared for U.K.-British Information Services. London, H.M. Stat. Off., 1966.
[14]p.

1. Economic conditions - Bechuanaland, S. Africa. 2. Agriculture - Bechuanaland, S. Africa. 3. Planning - Bechuanaland, S. Africa. I. U.K. British Information Services. II. Title.

Folio
711.3
(41)
U54
Pictures
U.K. Central Office of Information.
Before we build -- a plan on behalf of the Ministry of Town and Country Planning. London, n.d.
12 pictures.

1. Regional planning - U.K. I. Title.

330
(41)
U54
U.K. Central Office of Information.
Britain, an official handbook.
London,
v. illus., maps, tables. annual.
For complete information see shelf list.
Earlier editions titled: Britain, a reference handbook.

1. Economic conditions - U. K.

VF
330
U54b
U.K. Central Office of Information.
British colonial policy today, by Alan Lennox-Boyd, British Secretary of State for the Colonies. Prepared by the Central Office of Information. London, 1957.
3 p. map.

1. Underdeveloped countries. I. Lennox-Boyd, Alan. II. Title.

VF
341.1
:338
W45

U.K. Central Office of Information.
    (Reference Division)
Wilson, G   M
    The Colombo plan. London, Central Office of
Information, 1957.
    9p.

    Lecture delivered in Rome at the invitation of
the Societa Italiana per L'Organizzazione
Internazionale, June 1957.

    1.Technical assistance programs. I.Title.
II.U.K. Central Office of Information. (Reference
Division)

058.7
:3411
U547

United Kingdom. Central Office of
    Information, London. (Reference Division)
    Guide to international organizations.
London [November 1953]
    2 v. (looseleaf)

    Contents. - v.1.Governmental organizations.
v.2. Non-governmental organizations.
    1.International organizations - Directories.

330
(676)
U54k

U.K. Central Office of Information.
    Kenya. Prepared for British Information
Services. New York, 1963.
    35p.

    1. Economic conditions - Kenya.
I. U.K. British Information Services.

VF
351.7
:325.3
(41)
U54
1965

U.K. Central Office of Information.
    (Reference Division)
    The Commonwealth in brief. Prepared
for British Information Services. New
York, British Information Services,
1965.
    52p.

    1. British Commonwealth of Nations.
I. Title. II. U.K. British Information Services.

330
(881)
U54
1966

U.K. Central Office of Information.
    (Reference Div.)
    Guyana. London, H.M. Stat. Off., 1966.
    46p.

    Prepared for U.K. British Information
Services.

    1. Economic conditions - Guyana. 2. Social
conditions - Guyana. 3. Political science.
I. U.K. British Information Services.
II. Title.

330
(458)
U54m

U.K. Central Office of Information.
    Malta; one of the smallest nations in
the world, with one of the longest
histories. Prepared for British Information
Services. New York, 1964.
    [14]p.

    1. Economic conditions - Malta.
I. U.K. British Information Services.

351.7
:325.3
(41)
U54c

U.K. Central Office of Information.
    Commonwealth or colonialism? London,
1957.
    13p.

    "Based on a lecture delivered by Sir
Ashley Clarke, British Ambassador in
Rome, at Florence on 21st May, 1957."

    1. British Commonwealth of Nations.
I. Clarke, Sir Ashley.

614
(41)
U54h

U.K. Central Office of Information.
    (Reference Division)
    Health in the United Kingdom dependen-
cies. Rev. London, 1960.
    37p. illus., tables.

    1. Public health - U.K.

VF
330
(595)
U54m

U.K. Central Office of Information.
    The meaning of Malaysia. New York, British
Information Services, 1963.
    15p.

    1. Economic development - Malaya, Federation
of. I. U.K. British Information Services.

341.1
:338
U54c

U.K. Central Office of Information.
    Reference Div.
    Community development. London, H.M.S.O.,
1966.
    40p. (U.K. Central Office of Information
Reference pamphlet 76)
    At head of title: Britain and the develop-
ing countries.
    Bibliography: p. 40.

    1. Technical assistance programs (U.K.)
2. Underdeveloped countries. I. Title.
II. Title: Brit   ain and the developing
countries.

614
(41)
U54
1964

U.K. Central Office of Information.
    (Reference Div.)
    Health services in Britain. Rev. New
York, 1964.
    68p.
    Bibliography: p. 57-62.

    1. Public health - U.K. I. Title.

351.7
:325.3
(41)
U54m

U.K. Central Office of Information.
    The modern Commonwealth, by Duncan
Sandys. [London, H.M. Stationery Off.,
1962]
    28p.

    "Prepared for the Commonwealth Relations
Office by the Central Office of Information."

    1. British Commonwealth of Nations.
I. Sandys, Duncan.

697
(41)
U54

U.K. Central Office of Information.
    Domestic heating, by P. G. Gray. An in-
quiry made for the Building Research Station
in 1955. London, 1955.
    41p. forms, tables.

    1. Heating - U. K.   I. Gray, P. G.

VF
728.1
(41)
U54

U.K. Central Office of Information. (Reference Division)
    Housing in Britain. London [1961]
    42 p. 25 cm.

    1. Housing - U.K.
HD7333.A3A54 1951   331.833   53-16892 ‡

711.417
(41)
U54ne

U.K. Central Office of Information.
    New towns in Britain. New York,
[1960?]
    1v.   illus.

    1. New towns - U.K.

630
(41)
D82

U.K. Central Office of Information.

Duckham, A   N
    Farming, Britain. London, Central Office
of Information, 1957.
    48 p. illus., map.

    1. Agriculture - U.K. I. U.K. Central
Office of Information. II. Title.

728.1
(41)
U547ho

U.K. Central Office of Information.
    (Reference Div)
    Housing in Britain: a short account.
Rev. New York, Reference Div., British
Information Service, 1967.
    8p.

    1. Housing - U.K. I. Title.

711.417
(41)
U54ne
1961

U.K. Central Office of Information.
    The new towns of Britain. London,
H. M. Stat. Off., 1961.
    20p.

    1. New towns - U.K.

VF
320
(41)
U54f

U.K. Central Office of Information.
    Freedom in a democracy. London [1961?]
    62p. (Modern world series)

    1. Democracy - U.K. - Collections.

728.1
(41)
U54
1970

U.K. Central Office of Information.
U.K. British Information Services.
    Housing in Britain. Prepared by Reference
Div., Central Office of Information for British
Information Services. London, H.M.S.O., 1970.
    19p. (Central Office of Information reference
pamphlet 41)

    Bibliography: p. 19 - [20]

    1. Housing - U.K. I. U.K. Central Office
of Information.

711.417
(41)
U54ne
1964

U.K. CENTRAL OFFICE OF INFORMATION.
    THE NEW TOWNS OF BRITAIN. LONDON,
H.M. STAT. OFF., 1964.
    19P. (ITS REFERENCE PAMPHLETS 44)

    1. NEW TOWNS - U.K.

711.417
[(41)
U54ne   U.K. Central Office of Information.
1969   The new towns of Britain. New York,
British Information Services, 1969.
26p.

    1. New towns - U.K. 2. U.K. - New towns.

711
(41)
U54   U.K. Central Office of Information.
1967   (Reference Div.)
Town and country planning in Britain, 1967.
London, H.M.S.O., 1968.
31p. (Its Reference pamphlet 9)
Bibliography: p. 31-32.
Prepared for U.K. British Information
Services.

    1. Planning - U.K. 2. U.K. - Planning.
I. U.K. British Information Services.
II. Title.

711.4
(41)
U54hu   U.K. Central Unit for Environmental Planning.
Humberside: a feasibility study. London,
H.M.S.O., 1969.
142p.

    1. City planning - U.K. I. Title.

330
(669)
U54n   U.K. Central Office of Information.
Nigeria today. London, 1960.
56p. illus., maps.

    1. Economic conditions - Nigeria.

711
(41)
U54   U.K. Central Office of Information.
1968   (Reference Div.)
Town and country planning in Britain. Rev.
New York, 1968.
32p.

    Bibliography: p. 31-32.
Prepared for U.K. British Information
Services.
    1. Planning - U.K. I. U.K. British
Information Services. (Reference Div.)
II. Title.

VF
691.545
V17   U.K. Colonial Geological Surveys. Mineral
Resources Division. Report.
no.1 Varley, E.R. Vermiculite. 1952.

330
(911)
U54   U.K. Central Office of Information.
North Borneo and Sarawak. Prepared for
British Information Services. New York,
H.M. Stat. Office, 1963.
32p.

    1. Economic conditions - North Borneo.
    2. Economic conditions - Sarawak.

330
(6761)
U54u   U.K. Central Office of Information.
Uganda. New York, 1962.
35p.

    1. Economic conditions - Uganda.
    2. Political science - Uganda.

VF
728.1
(6)
U54   U.K. Colonial Office.
Housing in British African territories.
London, H. M. Stationery Off., 1954.
39 p.

    Bibliography: p. 34-39.

    1.Housing-Africa. I.Title.

330
(6897)
U54   U.K. Central Office of Information.
Nyasaland. Prepared for British
Information Services. New York, 1964.
15p.

    1. Economic conditions - Nyasaland.
I. Title.

330
U54u   U.K. Central Office of Information.
(Reference Division)
The United Kingdom colonial development
and welfare acts. London, 1956.
28p. tables.

    1.Economic development. 2.Underdeveloped
countries. I.Title.

711.417
(41)
U54r   U.K. Commission for the New Towns.
Report 1969; 1970
London, H.M. Stat. Off.,
v. annual. 1965
At head of title: New towns act, 1959.
Report year ends 21st March.
Report to the Minister of Housing and Local
Government.
    1. New towns - U.K. I. U.K. Ministry of Housing and
Local Government. II. Title: New
towns act, 1959.

360
U54s   U.K. Central Office of Information. (Ref-
erence Div.)
Social services in Britain. New York,
Reference Div., British Information Ser-
vices, 1959, 61, 66

    3 v.
For complete information see main card.

    1. Social service. 2. Housing - Social
aspects. 3. Housing - U.K. I. U.K. British
Information Services. (Reference Div.)

330
U54u   U.K. Central Office of Information
1957   (Reference Division)
The United Kingdom colonial development
and welfare acts; April 1, 1956 to March 31,
1957. London, 1957.
10p. tables.

    1. Economic development. 2. Underdeveloped
countries. I. Title.

370
:325
C65equ   U.S. Commission on Civil Rights.
Equal educational opportunities for the
Spanish-speaking child. Bilingual and bicul-
tural educational programs. Wash., 1970.
[17]p. (Clearinghouse publication no. 27)

    1. Education - Minority groups.
    2. Spanish - Americans. I. Title.

    Great Britain. Central Office of Information.
The social survey, new series.
308   no.
(421)   88 Hutchinson, B.A. Willesden and the new towns.
H87   1947.

FF DATE OF REQUEST 11/16/51   L.C. CARD NO.
British Colonial Empire - Grants in aid
AUTHOR Gt. Brit. Central Office of Information.
TITLE UK financial aid to the colonies, 1920-1950.
SERIES
London, June 5,
EDITION   PUB. DATE 1951   PAGING 13 p.
PUBLISHER same
RECOMMENDED BY   REVIEWED IN Dept. of State. Wkly Access.
List no. 33 8/17/51 p.1
ORDER RECORD

690.015
(41)
U54d   U.K. Construction Development Co-Ordination
Committee.
Departmental programmes for development
projects, July 1969. London, Ministry of
Public Building and Works, 1969.
40p.

    1. Building research - U.K. 2. Building
industry - U.K. I. U.K. Ministry of
Public Building and Works. II. Title.

FF DATE OF REQUEST 11/16/51   L.C. CARD NO.
Brit. Colonial Empire - Tech. Assistance
AUTHOR U.K.
Gt. Brit. Central Office of Information.
TITLE Technical assistance to South and South-East Asia,
the contribution of the United Kingdom.
SERIES
London, May 16,
EDITION   PUB. DATE 1951   PAGING 13 p.
PUBLISHER same
RECOMMENDED BY   REVIEWED IN Dept. of State. Wkly Access.
List no. 33 8/17/51 p.5
ORDER RECORD

330
(6781)
U54z   U.K. Central Office of Information.
Zanzibar; Isle of Cloves. New York,
British Information Services, 1963.
[15]p.

    1. Economic conditions - Zanzibar.
I. U.K. British Information Services.

VF
690.031
(41)
U54   U.K. Committee on the Cost of House-Building.
U.K. Ministry of Housing and Local Government.
The cost of house-building; third report of
the committee of inquiry. London, H.M.
Stationery Off., 1952.
25 p. tables.

    Committee on the Cost of House-Building, J. G.
Girdwood, Chairman.
    1.Building costs-U.K. I.U.K. Committee on the Cost
of House-Building. II.Girdwood, J. G. III.Title.

VP
690.591
U54   U.K. Committee on the Cost of House-Building.
U.K. Ministry of Housing and Local Government.
      The cost of house maintenance; report of the
      committee of inquiry.   London, H.M. Stationery
      Off., 1953.
        23 p.   tables.

        Committee on the Cost of House-Building, J. G.
      Girdwood, Chairman.
      1.Houses-Maintenance and modernization. I.U.K.
      Committee on the Cost of House-Building.
      II.Girdwood, J. G. III.Title.

      U.K. Departmental Committee on Garden Cities
      and Satellite Towns

            see

      U.K. Ministry of Health. Committee on Garden
      Cities and Satellite Towns.

725.83
U54
      U.K. Board of Education. Juvenile Organisations
      Committee.
        Report on the need for youth community centres
      on new housing estates. London, H.M. Stat. Off.,
      1936.
        14 p.   plans

        1. Community centers. 2. Public housing
      projects.

640
U54   U.K. COUNCIL FOR ART AND INDUSTRY.
       THE WORKING CLASS HOME; ITS FURNISHINGS
       AND EQUIPMENT. LONDON, H.M. STAT. OFF.,
       1937.
         63P.

         1. INTERIOR DECORATION.   I. TITLE.

526.8
R69   U.K. Dept. of Economic Affairs.
       Royal College of Art, London. Experimental
       Cartography Unit.
         Automatic cartography and planning. Commis-
       sioned by the former Dept. of Economic Affairs.
       London, Architectural Press, 1971.
         32p.

         1. Maps and mapping - Automation. I. U.K.
       Dept. of Economic Affairs. II. Title.

727.1   U.K. Ministry of Education.
(41)   The story of CLASP [Construction of Local
U54s   Authorities Special Programme] London, H.M.
         Stat. Off., 1961.
           81p.   (Its Building bulletin 19)

           1. Schools - U.K. 2. Architecture - U.K -
         Design. I. Title.

      U.K. Council for Codes of Practice.
         see
      U.K. Ministry of Works. Council for Codes of Practice
      for Buildings.

      U.K. Dept. of Economic Affairs. Central Unit
      for Environmental Planning.

            see

      U.K. Central Unit for Environmental Planning.

727.1
(41)
U54   U.K. Ministry of Education.
         The story of post-war school building.
       London, H.M. Stationery Off., 1957.
         71 p. illus., tables. (Its Pamphlet
       no. 33)

         1.Schools - U.K. 2.Building construction -
       U.K. I.Title: Post-war school building.

378
(41)
U54   U.K. Council for Scientific Policy.
         Report of the Working Party on Liaison
       Between Universities and Government Research
       Establishments. London, H.M.S.O., 1967.
         203p. (Gt. Brit. Parliament. Papers by
       command 3222)
         1. Universities and colleges - U.K. 2. U.K. -
       Universities and colleges. 3. Governmental
       research - U.K. 4. U.K. - Governmental re-
       search. I. Title: Working Party on Liaison
       Between Universities and Government Research
       Establishments. II. Title.

      U.K. Ministry of Education.

         see also

      U.K. Dept. of Education and Science

701.8
U54   U.K. Dept. of Education and Science.
         Colour in school buildings. 4th ed.
       [London] 1969.
         67p. (Its Building bulletin no. 9)

         Bibliography: p. 66-67.

         1. Color. 2. Schools. I. Title.

711.333
(41)
U54   U.K. County Borough of East Ham. (County
1956   Council)
         Development plan; (prepared in accordance
       with Section 5 of the Town and Country
       Planning Act, 1947) written statement.
       Essex, Eng., 1956.
         [15]p. tables.

         Plan submitted to the Minister of Housing
       and Local Government.

               (See Card No. 2)

DATE OF REQUEST 4/14/52   L. C. CARD NO.

AUTHOR
   Great Britain. Ministry of Education.

TITLE
   Acquisition and designation of sites for educational
   purposes and planning consent under the Town and
SERIES Country Planning Act, 1947.
   Circular no. 188 and Circular 243
EDITION   PUB. DATE 1948 PAGING 6 p.
PUBLISHER   1952   5 p.
   same

RECOMMENDED BY   REVIEWED IN
                        L #77 p. 8
         ORDER RECORD

727.1
(41)
U54n   U.K. Dept. of Education and Science.
         New problems in school design: comprehensive
       schools from existing buildings. London,
       H.M.S.O., 1967.
         139p. (Its Building bulletin no. 40)

         1. Schools - U.K. 2. Architecture - Designs
       and plans. I. Title.

711.333
(41)
U54   U.K. County Borough of East Ham. (County
1956   Council) Development plan. 1956. (Card No.2)

711.333   With this is issued: 3 maps: - 1. Designa-
(41)   tion area no. 1. - 2. Town map. - 3. Programme
U54   map.
1956
map
         1.County planning - U.K. 2.Town and Country
       Planning Act, 1947 (U.K.)

690
(41)
U54B   U.K. MINISTRY OF EDUCATION.
        BUILDING CRAFTS. LONDON, H.M. STAT.
        OFF., 1945.
          73P. (ITS PAMPHLET NO. 4)

          1. BUILDING CONSTRUCTION - U.K.
        I. TITLE.

027
(41)
U54   U.K. Dept. of Education and Science.
         Principal documentary evidence submitted
       to the National Libraries Committee. London,
       H.M.S.O., 1969.
         2v.

         1. Libraries - U.K. I. U.K. National
       Libraries Committee. II. Title.

711.333
(41)
U54   U.K. County Borough of East Ham. (Engineer
1952   and Surveyor's Department)
         Town and Country Planning Act of 1947.
       Development plan, 1952: written analysis, an
       analysis of the planning problems in the
       county borough. [Essex, Eng.] 1952.
         1 v. maps, tables.

         1.County planning - U.K. 2.Town and Country
       Planning Act, 1947. (U.K.)

725.83
(41)
U54   U.K. MINISTRY OF EDUCATION.
        COMMUNITY CENTRES. LONDON, H.M.
        STAT. OFF., 1945.
          40P.

          1. COMMUNITY CENTERS - U.K.

647.1
(41)
U54   U.K. Dept. of Employment and Productivity.
1967   Family expenditure survey; report for 1967.
       London, H.M.S.O., 1968.
         132p.

         1. Family income and expenditure - U.K.
       I. Title.

614.8
:690
U54
1971

U.K. Dept. of the Environment.
　　Building without accidents. 2d ed. London,
H.M.S.O., 1971.
　　folder. (Advisory leaflet no. 67)

　　　1. Building construction – Accidents.
I. Title.

696.63
U54

U.K. Dept. of the Environment.
　　Electric ring and radial circuits. London,
H.M.S.O., 1971.
　　folder. (Advisory leaflet no. 81)

　　　1. Electric wiring. I. Title.

621.6
U54ℓa

U.K. Dept. of the Environment.
　　Laying rigid drain and small sewer pipes. 2d
ed. London, H.M.S.O., 1971.
　　folder. (Advisory leaflet no. 24)

　　　1. Pipes. 2. Sewers. I. Title.

711.729
(41)
U54c

U.K. Dept. of the Environment.
　　Cars in housing/2. I. Dimensions. II.
Multi-storey parking garages. Metric edition.
London, H.M.S.O., 1971.
　　27p. (U.K. Ministry of Housing and Local
Government. Design bulletin no. 12)

　　　Bibliography: p. 24-25.

　　　1. Parking – U.K. 2. Garages. I. U.K
Ministry of Housing and Local Government.
II. Title.

621.3
U54

U.K. Dept. of the Environment.
　　Electricity on building sites. 2d ed.
London, H.M.S.O., 1971.
　　folder. (Advisory leaflet no. 59)

　　　1. Electricity. 2. Building construction.
I. Title.

691.32
U54ℓ
1971

U.K. Dept. of the Environment.
　　Lightweight concrete. 3d ed. London,
H.M.S.O., 1971.
　　folder. (Advisory leaflet no. 38)

　　　1. Concrete. I. Title.

621.9
U54c

U.K. Dept. of the Environment.
　　Care of small plant and hand tools. 3d ed.
London, H.M.S.O., 1971.
　　folder. (Advisory leaflet no. 22)

　　　1. Tools. I. Title.

728.1
(41)
U54fai

U.K. Dept. of the Environment.
　　Fair deal for housing. London, H.M.S.O.,
1971.
　　36p.

　　　1. Housing – U.K. I. Title.

691.32
U54m

U.K. Dept. of the Environment.
　　Making concrete on site. 3d ed. London,
H.M.S.O., 1971.
　　folder. (Advisory leaflet no. 26)

　　　1. Concrete. 2. Portland cement. I. Title.

691.32
U54c
1971

U.K. Dept. of the Environment.
　　Concreting in cold weather. 3d ed.
London, H.M.S.O., 1971.
　　folder (Advisory leaflet no. 7)

　　　1. Concrete. 2. Building materials – Climatic
effects. I. Title.

699.81
U54fi
1970

U.K. Dept. of the Environment.
　　Fire research 1970. Report of the Fire
Research Steering Committee with the report of
the Director of Fire Research. London, H.M.S.O.,
1971.
　　120p.

　　　At head of title: Dept. of the Environment
and Fire Offices' Committee, Joint Fire Research
Organization.
　　　Bibliography: p. 94-103.

　　　1. Fire preventi — on. I. U.K. Joint Fire
Research Organiza — tion. II. Title.

728.1
:303
(41)
U54n

U.K. Dept. of the Environment.
　　New housing in a cleared area; a study of
St. Mary's Oldham. London, H.M.S.O., 1971.
　　77p. (Design bulletin no. 22)

2c

　　　1. Housing surveys – U.K. 2. Housing projects
– U.K. I. Title.

699.82
U54c

U.K. Dept. of the Environment.
　　Condensation. 2d ed. London, H.M.S.O., 1970.
　　folder. (Advisory leaflet no. 61)

　　　1. Moisture condensation. I. Title.

614
U54h

U.K. Dept. of the Environment.
　　Health risks in construction. London, H.M.S.O.,
1971.
　　folder. (Advisory leaflet no. 80)

　　　1. Health. 2. Building construction.
I. Title.

698
U54p

U.K. Dept. of the Environment.
　　Painting woodwork. 4th ed. London, H.M.S.O.,
1971.
　　folder. (Advisory leaflet no. 25)

　　　1. Paints and painting. I. Title.

697.34
H17di

U.K. Department of the Environment.
　Haseler, Ernest.
　　District heating and the builder. London,
Dept. of the Environment, 1971.
　　[6]p.
　　Reprinted from Building trades journal,
1971, p. 14-8; 36-7.
　　Reprints of articles by staff of the
Department selected by the Library Service.
　　1. Heating, District. I. U.K. Dept. of
the Environment. II. Title.

728.54
U54h

2c

U.K. Dept. of the Environment.
　　Housing single people: 1: how they live at
present. London, H.M.S.O., 1971.
　　62p. (Its Design bulletin 23)

　　　1. Housing for single persons. I. Title.

621.9
U54po

U.K. Dept. of the Environment.
　　Powered hand tools: electric tools. 2d ed.
rev. London, H.M.S.O., 1971.
　　folder. (Advisory leaflet no. 18)

　　　1. Tools. 2. Electric apparatus and appliances. I. Title.

691.11
:620.193.82
U54d

U.K. Dept. of the Environment.
　　Dry rot and wet rot. 4th dd.
London, H.M.S.O., 1971.
　　folder. (Advisory leaflet no. 10)

　　　1. Dry rot. 2. Ventilation.
I. Title.

696.1
U54ℓag

U.K. Dept. of the Environment.
　　Lagging hot and cold water systems. 3d ed.
London, H.M.S.O., 1971.
　　folder. (Advisory leaflet no. 3)

　　　1. Plumbing. 2. Insulation. I. Title.

621.9
U54p
1971

U.K. Dept. of the Environment.
　　Powered hand tools 3; safety and maintenance.
2d ed. rev. London, H.M.S.O., 1971.
　　folder. (Advisory leaflet no. 20)

　　　1. Tools. 2. Building construction –
Accidents. I. Title.

690.22
U54r   U.K.   Dept. of the Environment.
Rendering outside walls. 3d ed. London,
H.M.S.O., 1971.
folder. (Advisory leaflet no. 27)

1. Walls.   I. Title.

674
U54w   U.K.   Dept. of the Environment.
Woodworking machinery for builders. 2d ed.
London, H.M.S.O., 1971.
folder. (Advisory leaflet no. 54)

1. Lumber industry.   I. Title.

674
U54   U.K.   Forest Products Research Laboratory.
Forest products research, 1969/70;

report of the Forest Products Research Laboratory
Steering Committee with the report of the direc-
tor of Forest Products Research. London,
Ministry of Technology, 19

|v.
For Library holdings see main entry.
1. Lumber industry.   I. Title.

614.8
:643
U54   U.K.   Dept. of the Environment.
1971   Safety in the home, by Anne S. Acland.
Metric ed. London, H.M.S.O., 1971.
32p. (Its Design bulletin 13)

2C

1. Home accidents. 2. Architecture, Domestic
- Designs and plans - U.K.   I. Acland, Anne S.
II. Title.

624
U54   U.K.   Dept. of the Environment, Research and
Development.
GENESYS; a computer system for structural
engineers and others. A report by the Committee
on the Application of Computers in the Construction Industry; with a note by the director of
the GENESYS Centre. London, 1971.
21p. (R & D paper)

Publication originally prepared under the
Ministry of Public Building and Works.
1. Structural engineering. 2. Building
industry - Automation. I. U.K. Ministry of
Public Building   and Works. II. Title.

634.9
C87   U.K.   Forest Products Research Laboratory.
Curry, W   T
Grade stresses for structural laminated timber.
2d ed. London, H.M. Stat. Off., 1967.
Laf.   20p. (U.K. Ministry of Technology. Forest
Products Research. Special report no. 15)

1. Forests and forestry. 2. Strains and stresses
I. U.K. Forest Products Research Laboratory.
II. Title.

691.55
U54s   U.K.   Dept. of the Environment.
Sands for plasters, mortars and renderings.
3d ed. London, H.M.S.O., 1971.
folder. (Advisory leaflet no. 15)

1. Plaster and plastering. 2. Bricklaying.
I. Title.

U.K.   Expert Committe on Compensation and
Betterment.

see

U.K.   Ministry of Works and Planning. Expert
Committee on Compensation and Betterment.

611.110.15
U54   U.K.   FOREST PRODUCTS RESEARCH
LABORATORY.
THE MOVEMENT OF TIMBERS.
LONDON, H.M. STATIONERY OFF., 1965.
7P. (ITS LEAFLET NO. 47, REV.)

1. WOOD - RESEARCH.   I. TITLE.

691.54
U54   U.K.   Dept. of the Environment.
1971   Special cements. 3d ed. London, H.M.S.O.,
1971.
folder. (Advisory leaflet no. 39)

1. Cement.   I. Title.

711
(41)
U54F   U.K.   EXPERT COMMITTEE ON COMPENSATION
AND BETTERMENT.
FINAL REPORT PRESENTED BY THE MINISTER
OF WORKS AND PLANNING TO PARLIAMENT BY
COMMAND OF HIS MAJESTY, SEPTEMBER, 1942.
LONDON, H.M. STATIONERY OFF., 1942.
180P. (GT. BRIT. PARLIAMENT. PAPERS
BY COMMAND. CMD. 6386)

AT HEAD OF TITLE: MINISTRY OF WORKS
AND PLANNING. EXPERT COMMITTEE ON
COMPENSATION AND BETTERMENT.

1. PLANNING -   U.K.   2. EMINENT
(CONTINUED ON NEXT CARD)

674
U54r   U.K.   Forest Products Research Laboratory.
Research programme, 1970/71;

London, Ministry of Technology, 19

|v. (Timberlab papers)

For Library holdings see main entry.

1. Lumber industry.   I. Title.

690.031   U.K.   Dept. of the Environment.
(41)   Mitchell, Robert.
M47   A tender-based building price index. London,
Dept. of the Environment, 1971.
[3]p.

Reprints of articles by staff of the Department selected by the Library Service.

Reprinted for the Dept. of the Environment
from the Chartered surveyor, vol. 104, no. 1,
July 1971, pp. 34-6.

(Cont'd on next card)

711
(41)
U54F   U.K.   EXPERT COMMITTEE ON COMPENSATION
AND BETTERMENT. FINAL REPORT PRESENTED
...1942.   (CARD 2)

DOMAIN - U.K.   3. REAL PROPERTY -
TAXATION - U.K.

VP
691.116
U54   U.K.   Forest Products Research Laboratory.
The strength properties of plywood.   London,
H.M. Stationery Off., 1953.
pts.   graphs, plates, tables.
(Forest Products Research bulletin no. 29)

N.C.1   Pt.1.Comparison of 3-ply woods of a standard
Lf.c.2   thickness, by W. T. Curry.

1.Plywood. I.Curry   T. II.Series.

699.86
U54w   U.K.   Dept. of the Environment.
1971   Warmth without waste. Rev. ed. London,
H.M.S.O., 1971.
folder. (Advisory leaflet no. 45)

1. Insulating materials.   I. Title.

691.11
:620.193.82   U.K.   FOREST PRODUCTS RESEARCH
U54   LABORATORY.
DRY ROT IN BUILDINGS;
RECOGNITION, PREVENTION AND CURE.
LONDON, H.M. STATIONERY OFF.,
1964.
12P. (ITS LEAFLET NO. 6)

1. DRY ROT.   I. TITLE.

634.9
U54   U.K.   Forest Products Research Laboratory.
Timber decay and its control. London,
H.M.S.O., 1962.
12p. (Its Leaflet no. 39)

1. Forests and forestry. 2. Lumber industry.
I. Title.

699.82
U54w   U.K.   Dept. of the Environment.
pt.2   Watertight basements. Part 2. 2d ed.
London, H.M.S.O., 1971.
folder. (Advisory leaflet no. 52)

1. Waterproofing. 2. Basements.   I. Title.

Great Britain. Forest Products Research bulletins.
VP
691.11 no.24 MacGregor, W.D. The protection of buildings
:690.193.82   and timber against termites.
M12

691.11
:620.197   U.K.   Forest Products Research Laboratory.
C62   Cockcroft, R
Timber preservatives and methods of
treatment. Princes Risborough, Eng.,
Forest Products Research Laboratory, 1971.
6p. (Timberlab papers no. 46, 1971)

1. Wood preservation. I. U.K. Forest
Products Research Laboratory. II. Title.

697.34
U54
ac

U.K. MINISTRY OF FUEL AND POWER.
DISTRICT HEATING IN AMERICAN HOUSING,
THE REPORT OF A MISSION TO THE UNITED
STATES OF AMERICA, FEBRUARY-APRIL 1947.
LONDON, H.M. STAT. OFF., 1949.
191P. (NATIONAL BUILDING STUDIES.
SEPCIAL REPORT NO. 7)

1. HEATING, DISTRICT.

M
Gt.Brit.

Gt. Brit. Geological Survey.
Geological map of Scotland, England, and Wales.
Southampton, 1948.
2 sheets col.

1.Geology-Gt. Brit.-Maps.

728.1
1613.5
U54H
1944

U.K. MINISTRY OF HEALTH.
HOUSE CONSTRUCTION, BY AN
INTERDEPARTMENTAL COMMITTEE APPOINTED
BY THE MINISTER OF HEALTH, THE
SECRETARY OF STATE FOR SCOTLAND, AND
THE MINISTER OF WORKS. LONDON, H.M.
STAT. OFF., 1944.
151P. U.K. MINISTRY OF WORKS.
POST-WAR BUILDING STUDIES NO. 1)

1. HOUSING AND HEALTH.

697
072
ac.

Gt. Brit. Ministry of Fuel and Power.
Domestic heating in America; a study of
heating, cooking and hot water supply in small
houses in U. S. A. and Canada. Report of a
Joint Party from the Ministry of Fuel and Power
and the Department of Scientific and Industrial
Research. London, H. M. Stationery.Off., 1946.
x, 152 p.   illus., diagrs., graphs, tables.

Bibliography: p. 126-148.
Committee composed of J. C. Pritchard,
Ministry of Fuel and Power; C. C. Handisyde,
Building Research Station; R. H. Rowse, Fuel
Research Station.   (Continued on next card)

728.1
(41)
U541A
2C

U.K. MINISTRY OF HEALTH.
ABOUT HOUSING. LONDON, H.M.
STATIONERY OFF., 1939.
24P.

1. HOUSING - U.K.   I. TITLE.

728.1
1613.5
U54H
1946

U.K. MINISTRY OF HEALTH.
HOUSE CONSTRUCTION, SECOND REPORT, BY
AN INTERDEPARTMENTAL COMMITTEE
APPOINTED BY THE MINISTER OF HEALTH,
THE SECRETARY OF STATE FOR SCOTLAND,
AND THE MINISTER OF WORKS. LONDON,
H.M. STAT. OFF., 1946.
67, 1P. (U.K. MINISTRY OF WORKS.
POST-WAR BUILDING STUDIES NO. 23)

1. HOUSING AND HEALTH.

Gt. Brit. Ministry of Fuel and Power.
Domestic heating in America ... 1946.   (Card 2)

Description of research at sixteen
laboratories: p. 83-94.

1.Heating. 2.Heating-Canada. 3.Heating research.
I.Gt. Brit. Building Research Station. II.Gt.
Brit. Dept. of Scientific and Industrial.Research.
III.Title.

728.1
(41)
U54C

U.K. MINISTRY OF HEALTH.
CONSTRUCTION OF FLATS FOR THE WORKING
CLASSES. FINAL REPORT OF THE
DEPARTMENTAL COMMITTEE. LONDON, H.M.
STAT. OFF., 1937.
55P.

1. APARTMENTS - U.K.   I. TITLE.

728.3
(41)
U54h
ac.

U. K. Ministry of Health.
Houses we live in. London, H. M. Stationery Off., 1939.
1v. illus.

1. Architecture, Domestic - Design.
2. Architecture, Domestic - U. K.

697
1662.6
U54

U.K. MINISTRY OF FUEL AND POWER. (FUEL
EFFICIENCY COMMITTEE)
THE EFFICIENT USE OF FUEL. PREPARED
UNDER THE DIRECTION OF THE EDUCATION
SUB-COMMITTEE. WITH FOREWORD FOR THE
AMERICAN EDITION BY JOHN C. OLSEN ...
BROOKLYN, CHEMICAL PUBLISHING CO.,
INC., 1945.
807P.

1. FUEL.   2. HEATING.   3. FURNACES.

690.013
(41)
U54

U.K. MINISTRY OF HEALTH.
THE COST OF HOUSE-BUILDING, SECOND
REPORT OF THE COMMITTEE OF INQUIRY
APPOINTED BY THE MINISTER OF HEALTH.
LONDON, 1950.
35P.

1. BUILDING COSTS - U.K.

728.1
(41)
U541H
ac.ad

U.K. MINISTRY OF HEALTH.
HOUSING. HOUSE PRODUCTION, SLUM
CLEARANCE, ETC., ENGLAND AND WALES.
STATEMENT SHOWING FOR THE PERIOD UP TO
30TH SEPTEMBER, 1934-35 - 31 Mar, 1937
LONDON, H.M. STATIONERY OFF., 1934-1935
IV. SEMIANNUAL.

1. HOUSING - U.K.   2. COMMUNITY
FACILITIES - U.K.   3. SLUM CLEARANCE -
U.K.   I. TITLE: HOUSE PRODUCTION, SLUM
CLEARANCE, ETC., ENGLAND AND WALES.

M
Gt.Brit.

Gt. Brit. Ministry of Fuel and Power.
Gas act 1948, areas of gas boards superimposed
on map of administrative areas.   Southampton,
Gt. Brit. Ordnance Survey, 1948.
2 sheets col.

1.Public utilities-Gt. Brit.-Maps.

690.596
(41)
U54

U.K. MINISTRY OF HEALTH.
THE DEMOLITION OF INDIVIDUAL UNFIT
HOUSES IN RURAL AREAS. REPORT OF THE
DEMOLITION PROCEDURE SUB-COMMITTEE OF
THE CENTRAL HOUSING ADVISORY
COMMITTEE. LONDON, H.M. STAT. OFF.,
1939.
16P.

1. DEMOLITION - U.K.

332.72
(41)
U54

U.K. MINISTRY OF HEALTH.
HOUSING ACCOUNTS. ASSISTED SCHEMES
OF LOCAL AUTHORITIES. NOTES AND
EXEMPLIFICATIONS. LONDON, H.M. STAT.
OFF., 1921.
150P.

1. MORTGAGE FINANCE - U.K.   I. TITLE.

U.K. Committee on Garden Cities and Satellite
Towns

see

U.K. Ministry of Health. Committee on Garden
Cities and Satellite Towns.

728.3
(41)
U54

U.K. MINISTRY OF HEALTH.
DESIGN OF DWELLINGS. REPORT OF THE
DESIGN OF DWELLINGS SUB-COMMITTEE ON THE
CENTRAL HOUSING ADVISORY COMMITTEE
APPOINTED BY THE MINISTER OF HEALTH, AND
REPORT OF A STUDY GROUP OF THE MINISTRY
OF TOWN AND COUNTRY PLANNING ON SITE
PLANNING AND LAYOUT IN RELATION TO
HOUSING. LONDON, H.M. STAT. OFF., 1944.
75P.
1. ARCHITECTURE, DOMESTIC - DESIGNS
AND PLANS - U.K.   2. SITE PLANNING.
I. U.K. MINISTRY OF TOWN AND COUNTRY
PLANNING.

728.1
(41)
1347)
U54
ch.ap.
M.A. co'

U.K. MINISTRY OF HEALTH.
HOUSING ACT, 1935. MEMORANDUM A - E
... LONDON, H.M. STAT. OFF., 1935.
5 V.

1. HOUSING LEGISLATION - U.K.
I. TITLE.

308
:728.1
(41)
U54

U.K. General Register Office.
Census 1951, England and Wales: Housing
report. London, H.M. Stat. Off., 1956.
150 p.

1. Census - Housing - U.K. 2. Housing
surveys - U.K.

728.1
:613.5
U54h

U.K. Ministry of Health.
House construction. Third report by an
Interdepartmental Committee appointed by
the Minister of Health, Secretary of State
for Scotland and the Minister of Works.
London, H. M. Stat. Off., 1948.
73p.   (Post-war building studies no. 25)

1. Housing and health. 2. Building
construction -   U.K.

728.1
(41)
U542

U.K. MINISTRY OF HEALTH.
HOUSING (FINANCIAL PROVISIONS) ACT,
1938. RURAL HOUSING MANUAL. LONDON,
H.M. STAT. OFF., 1938.
54P.

1. HOUSING - U.K.   I. TITLE: RURAL
HOUSING MANUAL.

69 (41)
G72
1944   Great Britain. Ministry of Health.
        Housing manual, 1944.   London, Eng., H.M.
   Stationery Off. [1944]
        103 p.   illus., diagrs., plans, tables.
   3c
        Bibliographical footnotes.

Suppl. --------Technical appendices, 1944.   London,
   Eng., H.M. Stationery Off. [1944]
        92 p.   diagrs., tables.
   3c
        1.Building construction-U.K. 2.Housing-U.K.
   I.Gt. Brit. Ministry of Works.

728.1
(41)
U54NE   U.K.   MINISTRY OF HEALTH.
      NEW HOMES FOR OLD.   LONDON, FOSH AND
   CROSS, 1938.
      13P.

      1. HOUSING - U.K.   I. TITLE.

333.63
(41)
U54   U.K.   MINISTRY OF HEALTH.
      REPORTS OF THE INTER-DEPARTMENTAL
   COMMITTEE ON THE RENT RESTRICTIONS ACTS.
   PRESENTED BY THE MINISTER OF HEALTH TO
   PARLIAMENT BY COMMAND... DECEMBER,
   1937. LONDON, H.M. STATIONERY OFF.,
   1937.
      58P.   (CMD. 5621)

      1. RENT CONTROL - U.K.   2. RENTAL
   HOUSING - U.K.   I. TITLE: RENT
   RESTRICTIONS ACTS.

---

69 (41)
G72
1949   Great Britain. Ministry of Health.
        Housing manual, 1949.   London, Eng., H.M.
   Stationery Off. [1949]
        150 p.   illus., diagrs., plans, tables.
   3c
        Bibliographical footnotes.

        1.Building construction-U.K. 2.Housing-U.K.

333.63
(41)
U54RE   U.K.   MINISTRY OF HEALTH.
      RENT CONTROL IN ENGLAND AND WALES.
   LONDON, H.M. STATIONERY OFF., 1946.
      15P.

      1. RENT CONTROL - U.K.

728.1
(41)
U54RU   U.K.   MINISTRY OF HEALTH.
      RURAL HOUSING; REPORT OF THE RURAL
   HOUSING SUB-COMMITTEE OF THE CENTRAL
   HOUSING ADVISORY COMMITTEE.   LONDON,
   H.M. STAT. OFF., 1936-44
      3V.

      1. HOUSING - U.K.   I. TITLE.

690
(41)
U542
1927   U.K.   MINISTRY OF HEALTH.
      HOUSING MANUAL ON THE DESIGN,
   CONSTRUCTION AND REPAIR OF DWELLINGS.
   LONDON, H.M. STATIONERY OFF., 1927.
      42P.

      1. BUILDING CONSTRUCTION - U.K.
   2. HOUSING - U.K.   I. TITLE.

333.63
(41)
U54REN   U.K.   MINISTRY OF HEALTH.
      RENTS OF HOUSES AND FLATS OWNED BY
   LOCAL AUTHORITIES: ENGLAND AND WALES.
   LONDON, H.M. STATIONERY OFF., 1937.
      24P.   (CMD. 5527)

      1. RENTS - U.K.   2. PUBLIC HOUSING -
   U.K.   I. TITLE.

728.6
(41)
U542   U.K.   MINISTRY OF HEALTH.
      RURAL HOUSING MANUAL; HOUSING
   (FINANCIAL PROVISIONS) ACT 1938.
   LONDON, H.M. STATIONERY OFF., 1938.
      54P.

      1. FARM HOUSING - U.K.   2. SITE
   PLANNING.   I. TITLE.

728.1
(41)
U541HO   U.K.   MINISTRY OF HEALTH.
      HOUSING PROGRAMME FOR 1947 ...
   LONDON, H.M. STATIONERY OFF., 1947.
      12P.   (CMD. 7021)
   AT HEAD OF TITLE: MINISTRY OF HEALTH
   AND DEPT. OF HEALTH FOR SCOTLAND.

      1. HOUSING - U.K.   I. SCOTLAND.
   DEPT. OF HEALTH.

VF
728.1   U.K. Ministry of Health.
:613.5   Report of the Departmental Committee on
U54   Housing. London, H. M. Stat. Off., 1933.
      68p. table. (Cmd. 4397)

   3 c.

      1. Housing and health - U.K.

728.1
1613.5   U.K.   MINISTRY OF HEALTH   (UNHEALTHY
U54R   AREAS COMMITTEE)
NO.2   SECOND AND FINAL REPORT OF THE
   COMMITTEE APPOINTED BY THE MINISTER OF
   HEALTH TO CONSIDER AND ADVISE ON THE
   PRINCIPLES TO BE FOLLOWED IN DEALING
   WITH UNHEALTHY AREAS. LONDON, H.M.
   STAT. OFF., 1928.
      24P.

      1. HOUSING AND HEALTH.   2. SLUM
   CLEARANCE - U.K.

728.1
(41)
U541   U.K.   MINISTRY OF HEALTH.
      HOUSING PROGRESS; DESCRIPTION OF
   EXHIBIT AND IDEAL HOME EXHIBITION,
   OLYMPIA, 1948. LONDON, H.M. STATIONERY
   OFFICE, 1948.
      12P.

      1. HOUSING - U.K.   I. TITLE.

333.63
(41)
U54R   U.K.   MINISTRY OF HEALTH.
      REPORT OF THE INTER-DEPARTMENTAL
   COMMITTEE ON RENT CONTROL.   PRESENTED
   BY THE MINISTER OF HEALTH AND THE
   SECRETARY OF STATE FOR SCOTLAND TO
   PARLIAMENT BY COMMAND ... APRIL 1945.
   LONDON, H.M. STATIONERY OFF., 1945.
      63P.   (CMD. 6621)

      1. RENT CONTROL - U.K.   2. RENTAL
   HOUSING - U.K.

728.1
(41)
U541T   U.K.   MINISTRY OF HEALTH.
      TEMPORARY ACCOMMODATION. MEMORANDUM
   FOR THE GUIDANCE OF LOCAL AUTHORITIES.
   LONDON, H.M. STAT. OFF., 1944.
      32P.

      AT HEAD OF TITLE: MINISTRY OF HEALTH,
   MINISTRY OF WORKS.

      1. HOUSING - U.K.   I. U.K. MINISTRY
   OF WORKS.   II. TITLE.

3

   Gt. Brit. *Ministry of Health.*
      Housing summary.   July 1948-

   London, H. M. Stationery Off.
      v. in   25 cm. ((Gt. Brit. Parliament. Papers by command; cmd.
     At head of title: Ministry of Health (and) Dept. of Health for Scotland.

     For full information see Periodical Kardex file.
      1. Housing—Gt. Brit.   I. Scotland. Dept. of Health.   (Series)

     HD7333.A3A47   331.833   49-48379*
     Library of Congress   (2)

VF
728.3   U. K. Ministry of Health.
:333   Report of the Inter-Departmental
UK   Committee on the selling price of houses.
   London, H. M. Stat. Off., 1945.
      31p. tables. (Cmd. 6670)

     At head of title: Ministry of Health, Dept.
   of Health for Scotland.

      1. Houses - Sales price. I. Scotland,
   Dept. of Health.

728.1
1336.18   U.K.   MINISTRY OF HEALTH. CENTRAL
(41)   HOUSING ADVISORY COMMITTEE.
U541A   THE APPEARANCE OF HOUSING ESTATES;
   REPORT OF THE SUBCOMMITTEE ON THE
   MEANS OF IMPROVING THE APPEARANCE OF
   LOCAL AUTHORITY HOUSING ESTATES.
   LONDON, H.M. STATIONERY OFFICE., 1948.
      27P.

      1. PUBLIC HOUSING - U.K.
   2. HOUSING MANAGEMENT.   I. TITLE.
   II. TITLE: HOUSING ESTATES.

728
1392   U.K.   MINISTRY OF HEALTH.
S71   STANDING JOINT COMMITTEE OF WORKING
   WOMEN'S ORGANISATIONS.
      MEMORANDUM SUBMITTED TO CENTRAL HOUSING
   ADVISORY COMMITTEE TO MINISTRY OF HEALTH,
   SUBCOMMITTEE ON DESIGN OF DWELLINGS.
   LONDON 1943. 14L.

      TYPESCRIPT.

      1. FAMILY LIVING REQUIREMENTS.
   I. U.K. MINISTRY OF HEALTH.

FOLIO
728.1
(41)
U541R   U.K.   MINISTRY OF HEALTH.
      REPORT ON THE OVERCROWDING SURVEY IN
   ENGLAND AND WALES, 1936. HOUSING ACT,
   1935. LONDON, H.M. STATIONERY OFFICE,
   1936.
      157P.

      1. HOUSING - U.K.   I. TITLE:
   OVERCROWDING SURVEY IN ENGLAND AND WALES.

VF
590.591
G72

   Gt. Brit. *Ministry of Health. Central Housing Advisory Committee.*
     The care and maintenance of fittings and equipment in the modern house, report of a sub-committee of the Central Housing Advisory Committee. London, H. M. Stationery Off., 1950.
      60 p. 25 cm.

     Houses—Maintenance & modernization.
     1. Building—Repair and reconstruction. 2. Building fittings.
   I. Title: Fittings and equipment in the modern house.
   2. Household equipment.
     TH8901.G7 1950   643   51-35318
     Library of Congress   (1)

690.591
U54C
U.K. MINISTRY OF HEALTH. CENTRAL
HOUSING ADVISORY COMMITTEE.
CONVERSION OF EXISTING HOUSES;
REPORT OF THE SUBCOMMITTEE OF THE
CENTRAL HOUSING ADVISORY COMMITTEE.
LONDON, H.M. STATIONERY OFF., 1945.
52P.

1. HOUSES - MAINTENANCE AND
MODERNIZATION. 2. HOUSING - U.K.
I. TITLE.

U.K. Ministry of Health. Departmental Committee on Garden Cities and Satellite
Towns

see

U.K. Ministry of Health. Committee on Garden
Cities and Satellite Towns.

United Kingdom. Ministry of Housing and Local
Government.
Name changed, Nov. 1951, from:
Gt. Brit. Ministry of Local Government and
Planning
changed, Jan. 1951, from:
Gt. Brit. Ministry of Town and Country Planning

728.1
:336.18
(41)
U541M
2c
U.K. MINISTRY OF HEALTH. CENTRAL
HOUSING ADVISORY COMMITTEE.
THE MANAGEMENT OF MUNICIPAL HOUSING
ESTATES; REPORT OF THE HOUSE
MANAGEMENT AND HOUSING ASSOCIATIONS
SUBCOMMITTEE. LONDON, H.M.
STATIONERY OFF., 1938.
44P.

1. PUBLIC HOUSING - U.K.
2. HOUSING MANAGEMENT. I. TITLE.

U.K.-apartments
DATE OF REQUEST 12/23/52 | L.C. CARD NO.
AUTHOR U.K. Ministry of Health. Library.
TITLE References on the needs and problems of flat dwellers
SERIES
EDITION | PUB. DATE [1951] | PAGING 2 p.
PUBLISHER
RECOMMENDED BY MML | REVIEWED IN
HLD Accns List 11-12/52 p.11
ORDER RECORD
Typewritten.

United Kingdom. Ministry of Housing and Local
Government.
see also
Gt. Brit. Ministry of Town and Country
Planning.
Gt. Brit. Ministry of Local Government and
Planning.

728.1
:336.18
(41)
U541M
1945
2c
U.K. MINISTRY OF HEALTH. CENTRAL
HOUSING ADVISORY COMMITTEE.
MANAGEMENT OF MUNICIPAL HOUSING
ESTATES. SECOND REPORT OF THE
HOUSING MANAGEMENT SUBCOMMITTEE.
LONDON, H.M. STATIONERY OFF., 1945.
31P.
COVER TITLE: HOUSING MANAGEMENT.

1. PUBLIC HOUSING - U.K.
2. HOUSING MANAGEMENT.

U.K. Dept. of Health for Scotland.

see

Scotland. Dept. of Health.

711.5
(41)
U54
no. 11
U.K. Ministry of Housing and Local Government.
(Welsh Office)
Amusement centres. London, H.M.S.O., 1969.
[2]p. (Its Development control policy note,
11)

1. Zoning - U.K. 2. Recreation - U.K.
I. Title

728.1
(41)
U541P
U.K. MINISTRY OF HEALTH. CENTRAL
HOUSING ADVISORY COMMITTEE.
PRIVATE ENTERPRISE HOUSING; REPORT OF
THE PRIVATE ENTERPRISE SUB-COMMITTEE OF
THE CENTRAL HOUSING ADVISORY COMMITTEE.
LONDON, H.M. STATIONERY OFF., 1944.
55P.

1. HOUSING - U.K. I. TITLE.

728
(41)
U54
U.K. Historic Buildings Council for Eng-
land.
Report, 4th-

London, H. M. Stationery Off.
v. annual.

1. Architecture, Domestic - U.K.
2. Public buildings - U.K.

720.2
B82
U.K. Ministry of Housing and Local
Government.
Buchanan (Colin) and Partners.
Bath; a study in conservation. Report
to the Minister of Housing and Local
Government and Bath City Council. London,
H.M.S.O., 1968.
14p.
1. Architecture - Conservation and
restoration. I. U.K. Ministry of Housing
and Local Government. II. Title.

728.1
(41)
U54C0
U.K. MINISTRY OF HEALTH. COMMITTEE ON
CONSTRUCTION OF FLATS FOR THE WORKING
CLASSES.
CONSTRUCTION OF FLATS FOR THE WORKING
CLASSES. INTERIM REPORT. LONDON, H.M.
STAT. OFF., 1935.
39P.

1. APARTMENT HOUSES - U.K. I. TITLE.

U.K. His (Her) Majesty's Stationery Office.

see

U.K. His (Her) Majesty's Stationery Office.

728
:333
U54
U.K. Ministry of Housing and Local Government.
Bigger loans to help home ownership. Improve
your house with a grant. House purchase and
housing act, 1959. London, 1959.
3v. in 1. (American Embassy, London. Foreign
service dispatch no. 26, 1959, encl. no. 2,
3, and 4)

1. Home ownership - U.K. 2. Housing legislation -
U.K. (Series: American Embassy, London. Foreign
service dispatch no. 26, 1959, encl. no. 2, 3,
and 4)

Crane
Gt. Brit. *Ministry of Health. Committee on House-Building Costs.*
The cost of house-building. First report of the committee of inquiry appointed by the Minister of Health. London, H. M. Stationery Off., 1948.
vi, 65 p. 25 cm.
J. G. Girdwood, chairman.

1. Building trades—Gt. Brit.
HD9715.G715A52 1948   690.942   49-48855*

Library of Congress   [2]

355.58:
(41)
U54
UNITED KINGDOM. HOME OFFICE. SCOTTISH
HOME DEPT.
NUCLEAR WEAPONS. LONDON, H.M.
STATIONERY OFF., 1956.
55P. (MANUAL OF CIVIL DEFENSE. VOL.
I. PAMPHLET NO. 1)

1. CIVILIAN DEFENSE - SCOTLAND.

728
:333
(41)
U54b
U.K. Ministry of Housing and Local Government
Buying your own home: your guide to the
option mortgage scheme. London, H.M.S.O.,
1967.
18p.

1. Home ownership - U.K. 2. Mortgage
finance - U.K. 3. U.K. - Home ownership.
4. U.K. - Mortgage finance. I. Title.

711.417
(41)
U54GA
U.K. MINISTRY OF HEALTH. COMMITTEE
ON GARDEN CITIES AND SATELLITE TOWNS.
GARDEN CITIES AND SATELLITE TOWNS;
REPORT. LONDON, H.M. STAT. OFF.,
1935.
31P.

1. GARDEN CITIES - U.K.
2. SATELLITE CITIES - U.K.

69
(41)
U54
U.K. Committee on House Interiors.
Quicker completion of house interiors;
report ... presented to the Minister of Housing
and Local Government and the Secretary of State
for Scotland. London, H.M. Stationery Off.,
1953.
63 p. illus., plans, tables.
Sir Donald C. Bailey, chairman.
1.Building industry-U.K. 2.Architecture, Domestic-
U.K. 3.Modular coordination. I.U.K. Ministry of
Housing and Local Government. II.Bailey, Donald C.
III.Title. IV.Title: House interiors, Quicker
completion of.

728.9
U54
U.K. Ministry of Housing and Local Govern-
ment.
Cars in housing. London, H.M.S.O.
2 pts. (Its Design bulletin 12)

1. Garages - Designs and plans. 2. Architecture, Domestic. I. Title.

711.6
U54c

U.K. Ministry of Housing and Local Government.
   Cars in housing 1; some medium density layouts. London, H.M.S.O., 1966.
   52p. (Its Design bulletin 10)

   1. Site planning. 2. Traffic - U.K. 3. U.K. - Traffic. I. Title.

VF
690.031
(41)
U54

3 c.

U.K. Ministry of Housing and Local Government.
   The cost of house-building; third report of the committee of inquiry. London, H.M. Stationery Off., 1952.
   25 p. tables.
   Committee on the Cost of House-Building, J. G. Girdwood, Chairman.
   1.Building costs-U.K. I.U.K. Committee on the Cost of House-Building. II.Girdwood, J. G. III.Title.

711.5
(41)
U54.::
no.10

U.K. Ministry of Housing and Local Government.
   (Welsh Office)
   Design. London, H.M.S.O., 1969.
   [2]p. (Its Development control policy note, 10)

   1. Zoning - U.K. 2. Architectural control. 3. Landscape architecture. I. Title.

711.729
(41)
U54c

U.K. Ministry of Housing and Local Government.
U.K. Dept. of the Environment.
   Cars in housing/2. I. Dimensions. II. Multi-storey parking garages. Metric edition. London, H.M.S.O., 1971.
   27p. (U.K. Ministry of Housing and Local Government. Design bulletin no. 12)

   Bibliography: p. 24-25.

   1. Parking - U.K. 2. Garages. I. U.K Ministry of Housing and Local Government. II. Title.

VF
690.591
U54

U.K. Ministry of Housing and Local Government.
   The cost of house maintenance; report of the committee of inquiry. London, H.M. Stationery Off., 1953.
   23 p. tables.
   Committee on the Cost of House-Building, J. G. Girdwood, Chairman.
   1.Houses-Maintenance and modernization. I.U.K. Committee on the Cost of House-Building. II.Girdwood, J. G. III.Title.

711.4
(41)
U54

U.K. Ministry of Housing and Local Government.
   Design in town and village. London, H. M. Stationery Off., 1953.
   120 p. illus.
   Contents.-pt.1.The English village, by Thomas Sharp.-pt.2.The design of residential areas, by Frederick Gibberd.-pt.3.Design in city centres, by W. G. Holford.
   1.City planning-U.K. 2.Neighborhood planning-U.K. 3.Subdivision design. I.Sharp, Thomas. II.Gibberd, Frederick. III.Holford, William Graham. IV.Title.

711.5
(41)
U54
no. 8

U.K. Ministry of Housing and Local Government.
   (Welsh Office)
   Caravan sites. London, H.M.S.O., 1969.
   [3]p. (Its Development control policy note, 8)

   1. Zoning - U.K. 2. Trailers and trailer courts. I. Title.

728.1
(41)
U54c

U.K. Ministry of Housing and Local Government.
   (Welsh Office)
   Council housing purposes, procedures and priorities. Ninth report of the Housing Management Sub-Committee of the Central Housing Advisory Committee. London, H.M.S.O., 1969.
   183p.
   1. Housing - U.K. 2. Public housing - U.K. I. U.K. Central Housing Advisory Committee. (Housing Management Sub-Committee) II. Title.

690.022
(41)
U54

U.K. Ministry of Housing and Local Government.
   Designing a low-rise housing system; how the 5M system was evolved; the pilot project at Sheffield. London, H.M.S.O., 1970.
   55p. (Its Design bulletin 18)
   Bibliography: p. 53-54.

   1. Prefabricated construction - U.K. 2. Public housing projects. 3. Architecture - Designs and plans. I. Title.

711.417
(41)
M45

U.K. Ministry of Housing and Local Government.
   Central Lancashire, study for a city; consultants' proposals for designation. London, H.M.S.O., 1967.
   99p.

   1. New towns - U.K. I. Title.

VF
711.585
U54c

U.K. Ministry of Housing and Local Government.
U.K. Central Housing Advisory Committee. (Housing Management Sub-Committee)
   Councils and their houses; management of estates; eighth report ... London, H. M. Stat. Off., 1959.
   39p.
   At head of title: Ministry of Housing and Local Government.
   1. Relocation - U.K. 2. Housing management. I. U.K. Ministry of Housing and Local Government.

711.5
(41)
U54
no. 2

U.K. Ministry of Housing and Local Government.
   (Welsh Office)
   Development in residential areas. London, H.M.S.O., 1969.
   [4]p. (Its Development control policy note, 2)

   1. Zoning - U.K. 2. Residential areas. I. Title.

720.2
I57

U.K. Ministry of Housing and Local Government.
Insall (Donald W.) and Associates.
   Chester; a study in conservation. Report to the Minister of Housing and Local Government and the city and county of the City of Chester. London, H.M.S.O., 1968.
   257p. (Theory of business finance. Advanced readings)

   1. Architecture - Conservation and restoration. I. U.K. Ministry of Housing and Local Government. II. Title.

026
W34

U.K. Ministry of Housing and Local Government.
White, Brenda.
   Current use of information in planning. [London, Ministry of Housing and Local Government, Library] [1969?]
   17p.
   Paper given to C.E.S. Conference on Information and Urban Planning, London, 1969.
   1. Planning libraries. 2. Planning documentation. I. U.K. Ministry of Housing and Local Government. II. Title.

711.5
(41)
U54
no. 4

U.K. Ministry of Housing and Local Government.
   (Welsh Office)
   Development in rural areas. London, H.M.S.O., 1969.
   [4]p. (Its Development control policy note, 4)

   1. Zoning - U.K. 2. Rural planning - U.K. I. Title.

728
.333
(41)
U54

U.K. Ministry of Housing and Local Government.
   Choosing your house. London, H.M.S.O., 1968.
   44p.

   1. Home ownership - U.K. I. Title.

711.585
:308
U54

U.K. Ministry of Housing and Local Government.
   The Deeplish study; improvement possibilities in a district of Rochdale. London, H.M.S.O., 1966.
   74p.

   1. Urban renewal - Surveys. 2. Urban renewal - U.K. I. Title.

711.5
(41)
U54
no. 5

U.K. Ministry of Housing and Local Government.
   (Welsh Office)
   Development in town centres. London, H.M.S.O., 1969.
   [2]p. (Its Development control policy note, 5)

   1. Zoning - U.K. 2. Business districts - U.K. I. Title.

693.068
:389.6
U54c

U.K. Ministry of Housing and Local Government.
   Co-ordination of components in housing; metric dimensional framework. London, H.M.S.O., 1968.
   43p. (Its design bulletin 16)

   1. Coordinated components. I. Title.

711.15
(41)
U54

2c.

U.K. Ministry of Housing and Local Government.
   The density of residential areas. London, H. M. Stationery Off., 1952.
   71 p. illus., graphs, tables(part fold.)

   1.Population density. 2.Housing-U.K. 3.Subdivision design. I.Title.

526.8
(41)
U54

U.K. Ministry of Housing and Local Government.
   Development plan maps. Part 1. Continuous revision. Part 2. The addition of colour. London, H.M. Stat. Off., 1964.
   7p. (Its Planning bulletin 6)
   At head of title: Town and country planning act, 1962.

   1. Maps and mapping - U.K. 2. Color.

711
(41)
U54d

U.K. Ministry of Housing and Local Government.
(Welsh Office)
Development plans; a manual on form and content. London, H.M.S.O., 1970.
104p.

1. Planning – U.K. I. Title.

728.3
(41)
U54f

U.K. Ministry of Housing and Local Government.
Family houses at West Ham: an account of the project with an appraisal. London, H.M.S.O., 1969.
120p. (Its Design bulletin 15)

1. Architecture, Domestic – Designs and plans – U.K. 2. Family living requirements. 3. Housing – U.K. I. Title.

VF
728.1
+711.4
(41:016)
U54
1956

U.K. Ministry of Housing and Local Government.
United Kingdom (H.M.) Stationery Office.
Government publications: Ministry of Housing and Local Government. Rev. [London] June, 1956.
19 p. (Its Sectional list no. 5)

Have also earlier ed., 31 August 1954.   26 p.

1. Housing – United Kingdom – Bibliographies.
2. City planning – United Kingdom – Bibliographies.
3. Municipal services – United Kingdom – Bibliographies. I. United Kingdom. Ministry of Housing and Local Government.

693.068
:389.6
U54d

U.K. Ministry of Housing and Local Government.
Dimensions and components for housing with special reference to industrialised building. London, H.M. Stat. Off., 1963.
52p. (Its Design bulletin 8)

1. Coordinated components. 2. Industrial buildings.

728
:392
U54f

U.K. Ministry of Housing and Local Government.
The first hundred families: a guide to the community services and facilities which should be available for the first families arriving in an expanding town. London, H.M. Stat. Off., 1965.
18p.

1. Family living requirements. 2. Community facilities. 3. Community relations. 4. New towns-   U.K. I. Title.

VF
728.1
+711.4
(41:016)
U54
1962

U.K. Ministry of Housing and Local Government.
U.K. (H.M.) Stationery Office.
Government publications: Ministry of Housing and Local Government. Rev. [London] 1962.
22p. (Its Sectional list no. 5, rev. to 31st Dec. 1962)

1. Housing – U.K. – Bibliography.
2. City planning – U.K. – Bibliography.
3. Municipal services – U.K. – Bibliography. I. U.K. Ministry of Housing and Local Government.

728.1
(41)
U54fam

U.K. Ministry of Housing and Local Government.
Families living a high density. [London] 1964.
87p.

1. Housing projects – U.K.
2. Family living requirements.

728.1
:362.6
(41)
U54

U.K. Ministry of Housing and Local Government.
Flatlets for old people. London, H.M. Stat. Off., 1958.
20p. illus., plans.

1. Housing for the aged – U. K.

VF
728.1
+711.4
(41:016)
U54
1961

United Kingdom. Ministry of Housing and Local Government.
U.K. (H.M.) Stationery Office.
Government publications: Ministry of Housing and Local Government. Rev. [London 1961.
17p. (Its Sectional list no. 5 Rev. to March, 1961)

1. Housing – U.K. – Bibl. 2. City planning – U.K. – Bibl. 3. Municipal services – U.K. – Bibl. I. United Kingdom. Ministry of Housing and Local Government.

728.1
:308
(41)
U54

U.K. Ministry of Housing and Local Government.
Families living at high density; a study of estates in Leeds, Liverpool and London. London, H.M.S.O., 1970.
68p. (Its Design bulletin 21)

1. Housing surveys – U.K. 2. Housing – Social aspects. I. Title.

728
(41)
U54f

U.K. Ministry of Housing and Local Government.
Flats and houses, 1958, design and economy. London, H. M. Stat. Off., 1958.
1v. illus., plans, tables. (American Embassy, London. Foreign service dispatch no. 1506, 1958. Encl. no. 1)

Bound with American Embassy, London. Foreign service dispatch no. 1506, 1958,

(Continued on next card)

VF
728.1
(41:016)
U54
1964

U.K. MINISTRY OF HOUSING AND LOCAL GOVERNMENT.
U.K. H.M. STATIONERY OFFICE.
GOVERNMENT PUBLICATIONS: MINISTRY OF HOUSING AND LOCAL GOVERNMENT.
REV. LONDON 1964.
25p. (ITS SECTIONAL LIST NO. 5, REV. TO 29TH FEBRUARY, 1964)

1. HOUSING – U.K. – BIBLIOGRAPHY.
2. CITY PLANNING – U.K. – BIBLIOGRAPHY. I. U.K. MINISTRY OF HOUSING AND LOCAL GOVERNMENT.

728.1
(41)
U54f

U.K. Ministry of Housing and Local Government. (Sociological Research Section)
The family at home, Sheffield. [London] 1963?]
54p.

1. Housing projects – U.K. 2. Family living requirements. I. Title.

728
(41)
U54f

U.K. Ministry of Housing and Local Government.
Flats and houses ... (Card 2)

Encl. no. 2. U.K. Ministry of Housing and Local Government. Circular no. 6, 1958. 2p.

1. Architecture, Domestic – U.K. 2. Family living requirements. I. Title. II. Series: American Embassy, London. Foreign service dispatch no. 1506, 1958.

711.417
(41)
U54g

U.K. Ministry of Housing and Local Government.
The green belts. London, H.M.S.O., 1962.
30p.

1. Garden cities – U.K. . U.K. – Garden cities. 3. Open space land. I. Title.

728.1
(41)
U54f
1969

U.K. Ministry of Housing and Local Government.
The family at home; a study of households in Sheffield. London, H.M.S.O., 1969.
53p. (Its Design bulletin 17)

1. Housing projects – U.K. 2. Family living requirements. I. Title.

711.4
(41)
U54f

U.K. Ministry of Housing and Local Government.
The future of development plans; a report by the Planning Advisory Group. London, H.M. Stat. Off., 1965.
62p.

1. City planning – U.K. 2. County planning – U.K. I. Title.

728.1
:362.6
(41)
U54g

U.K. Ministry of Housing and Local Government.
Grouped flatlets for old people; a sociological study. London, H.M. Stationery Office, 1962.
38p. (Design bulletin 2)

1. Housing for the aged – U.K. I. Title.

728.1
(41)
U54fa

U.K. Ministry of Housing and Local Government. (Sociological Research Section)
The family at home, West Ham. [London] 1961.
18p.

1. Housing projects – U.K. 2. Family living requirements. I. Title.

711.5
(41)
U54
no.1

U.K. Ministry of Housing and Local Government. (Welsh Office)
General principles. London, H.M.S.O., 1969.
[4]p. (Its Development control policy note, 1)

1. Zoning – U.K.

325
(41)
U54

U.K. Ministry of Housing and Local Government. (Welsh Office)
Gypsies and other travellers; a report of a study carried out in 1965 and 1966 by a sociological research section of the Ministry of Housing and Local Government. London, H.M.S.O., 1967.
86p.
1. Minority groups – U.K. 2. Population – U.K. 3. Housing – U.K. 4. Mobile homes. 5. U.K. – Minority groups. 6. U.K. – Population. 7. U.K. – Housing.   I. Title.

310
(41)
U54

U.K. Ministry of Housing and Local Government.
Handbook of statistics, 1965-70

London, H. M. Stationery Off., 1966-71
6 v.

For complete information see main card.

1. Statistics - U.K. 2. Housing - U.K.
3. Planning-U.K. 4. Local government - U.K.
I. Title.

69
(41)
G72
1949
Suppl.3

U.K. Ministry of Housing and Local Government.
Houses 1953; third supplement to the Housing manual, 1949. London, H.M. Stationery Off., 1953.
64 p. illus., plans.

1.Architecture, Domestic-Design. 2.Subdivision design. I.Title. II.Title: The housing manual, 1949.

728.1
:362.6
(41)
U54H

U.K. MINISTRY OF HOUSING AND LOCAL GOVERNMENT.
HOUSING OF OLD PEOPLE. LONDON, HER MAJESTY'S STATIONERY OFFICE, 1957.
4P. (ITS CIRCULAR NO. 18/57)

1. HOUSING FOR THE AGED - U.K.
I. TITLE.

711.4
(41)
U54h

U.K. Ministry of Housing and Local Government.
Historic towns: preservation and change.
London, H.M.S.O., 1967.
49p.

1. City planning - U.K. 2. Architecture - Conservation and restoration. I. Title.

VF
728.1
(41)
U54H

U.K. Ministry of Housing and Local Government.
Houses, the next step. London, H.M. Stationery Off., 1953.
19 p. tables. (Cmd. 8996)

1.Housing-U.K. 2.Slum clearance-U.K. 3.Neighborhood rehabilitation. I.Title.

728.1
B25h

U.K. Ministry of Housing and Local Government.
Bellamy, Alec A
Housing in large cities in the U.S.A.
London, Ministry of Housing and Local Government, 1958.
28p. illus., plans.

1. Housing. 2. Public housing. 3. Housing projects. I. U.K. Ministry of Housing and Local Government.

728
(41)
U54h

U.K. Ministry of Housing and Local Government.
Homes for today and tomorrow. London, H. M. Stat. Off., 1961.
91p.

1. Architecture, Domestic - U.K.
2. Family living requirements.

728.1
(41)
U54hou

U.K. Ministry of Housing and Local Government.
Housing. Presented by the Ministry of Housing and Local Government and Minister for Welsh Affairs, and the Secretary of State for Scotland to Parliament by Command of Her Majesty. London, H.M. Stationery, 1963.
16p. (Cmnd. 2050)

1. Housing - U.K.

728.1
(41)
T67

U.K. Ministry of Housing and Local Government.
Toronto. Metropolitan Housing Authority.
Housing in the United Kingdom. [Prepared in cooperation with] Ontario Association of Housing Authorities, and the British Ministr of Housing and Local Government. Toronto, 1962.
81p.

1. Housing - U.K. I. Ontario Association of Housing Authorities II. U.K. Ministry of Housing and Local Government.

728
:392
U54h

U.K. Ministry of Housing and Local Government.
House planning; a guide to user needs with a checklist. London, H.M.S.O., 1968.
40p. (Its design bulletin 14)

1. Family living requirements. 2. Architecture; Domestic - Designs and plans.
3. Interior decoration. I. Title.

334.1
U54h

U.K. Ministry of Housing and Local Government.
Housing associations and self-help groups contribution to local housing needs. London, 1952.
3p. (Its Circular no. 44/52)

1. Cooperative housing.

728.1
(41)
U547h

U.K. Ministry of Housing and Local Government. (Welsh Office)
The housing programme, 1965 to 1970.
London, H.M. Stat. Off., 1965.
[22]p. (Papers by Cmnd. 2838)

1. Housing - U.K.

728
:333
(41)
U54H

U.K. MINISTRY OF HOUSING AND LOCAL GOVERNMENT.
HOUSE PURCHASE, PROPOSED GOVERNMENT SCHEME. PRESENTED TO PARLIAMENT BY THE MINISTER OF HOUSING AND LOCAL GOVERNMENT AND MINISTER FOR WELSH AFFAIRS AND THE SECRETARY OF STATE FOR SCOTLAND... NOVEMBER 1958. LONDON, H.M. STATIONERY OFF., 1958.
7P. (CMND. 571)

1. HOME OWNERSHIP - U.K. I. TITLE.

728.1
:308
(41)
U54h

U.K. Ministry of Housing and Local Government. (Sociological Research Section)
Housing at Coventry; a user reaction study. London, 1967.
20p. (Its Living in houses, vol. 30, no. 12, 1961)

Reprinted from: Official architecture and planning, vol. 30, no. 12, 1967.

1. Housing surveys - U.K. I. Title.

728.100.15
(41)
U54h

U.K. Ministry of Housing and Local Government.
Housing research and development. London, 1966.
[24]p.

Architectural design, Aug., 1966.

1. Housing research - U.K. I. Title.

690
U54h

U.K. Ministry of Housing and Local Government.
Housebuilding in the USA; a study of rationalisation and its implications. London, H.M. Stat. Off., 1966.
71p.

1. Building industry. 2. Housing market.
3. Prefabricated construction. I. Title.

728.1
(41)
U54hous

U.K. Ministry of Housing and Local Government.
Housing cost yardstick for schemes at medium and high densities. London, H.M. Stationery Off., 1963.
13p. (Its Design bulletin 7)

1. Housing costs - U.K. 2. Population density - U.K. 3. Residential areas.

728.1
:336.18
(41)
U54

U.K. Ministry of Housing and Local Government. (Welsh Office)
Housing subsidies manual; Housing subsidies act of 1967. London, H.M.S.O., 1968.
92p.

1. Public housing - U.K. 2. U.K. - Public housing. I. Title.

69
(41)
G72
1949
Suppl.2

U. K. Ministry of Housing and Local Government.
Houses 1952; second supplement to The housing manual, 1949. London, H. M. Stationery Off., 1952.
15 p. illus., plans.

1.Architecture, Domestic-Design. 2.Family living requirements. I.Title. II.Title: The housing manual, 1949.

728.1
(41)
U54ho

U.K. Ministry of Housing and Local Government.
Housing in England and Wales. Presented to Parliament by the Minister of Housing and Local Government and Minister for Welsh Affairs by Command of Her Majesty. London, H. M. Stat. Off., 1961.
15p. (Cmnd. 1290)

1. Housing - U.K.

728.1
(083.41
:41)
U54

U.K. MINISTRY OF HOUSING AND LOCAL GOVERNMENT.
HOUSING SUMMARY, 30TH APRIL, 1965...
LONDON, H.M. STATIONERY OFF., 1965.
2P. (CMND. 2671)

1. HOUSING STATISTICS - U.K.

711.5
(41)
U54
no.3
U.K. Ministry of Housing and Local Government. (Welsh Office)
Industrial and commercial development. London, H.M.S.O., 1969.
[3]p. (Development control policy note 3)

1. Industrial development - U.K. I. Title.

711.585
(41)
U54li
U.K. Ministry of Housing and Local Government.
Living in a slum; a study of St. Mary's Oldham. London, H.M.S.O., 1970.
45p. (Its Design bulletin 19)

2c.

Bibliography: p. 45-[46]

1. Urban renewal - U.K. - Oldham.
2. Slums - U.K. I. Title.

711.417
(41)
W22
U.K. Ministry of Housing and Local Government.
Weeks (Llewelyn-Davies) and Partners.
A new city. A study of urban development in an area including Newbury, Swindon and Didcot. [Prepared for Ministry of Housing and Local Government] London, H. M. S. O., 1966.
99p.
Bibliography: p. 92-97.

1. New towns - U.K. I. U.K. Ministry of Housing and Local Government. II. Title.

693.002.22
(41)
U541
U.K. Ministry of Housing and Local Government.
Industrialised building; four case studies of the selection of a main contractor. London, H.M.S.O., 1966.
28p. (Its R. & D. bulletin. SfB Ba6;Ba7)

2c

1. Prefabricated construction - U.K. I. Title.

VF
628.3
:728.1
U54
U.K. Ministry of Housing and Local Government.
Memorandum on principles of design for small domestic sewage treatment works. London, H.M. Stationery Off., 1953.
21 p. diagrs.

1.Sewerage and sewage disposal. 2.Septic tanks.
I.Title: Small domestic sewage treatment works.

690.591
U54n
U. K. Ministry of Housing and Local Government.
New homes for old; improvements and conversions. London, H. M. Stationery Off., 1954.
67 p. illus., plans.

1. Houses - Maintenance and modernization.
2. House conversion. I. Title.

693.002.22
(41)
U54
U.K. Ministry of Housing and Local Government.
Industrialised housebuilding. London, 1965.
8p. (Its Circular no. 76/65)

1. Prefabricated construction - U.K. I. Title.

728.1
(41)
S31
U.K. MINISTRY OF HOUSING AND LOCAL GOVERNMENT.
Sharp, Evelyn.
The Ministry of Housing and Local Government. London, Allen & Unwin, 1969.
253p. (U.K. Ministry of Housing and Local Government. New Whitehall series no. 14)

1. U.K. Ministry of Housing and Local Government. I. Title.

711.417
(016)
U54
U.K. Ministry of Housing and Local Government. (Library)
New towns, 1898-1955.

London, 1955

1v. (looseleaf) (Its Bibliography no. 65)
Supplemented by appendices, 1955-67.
For Library holdings see main entry.

1. New towns - Bibl. 2. New towns - U.K. - bibl. (Series)

628.3
(41)
U54
U.K. MINISTRY OF HOUSING AND LOCAL GOVERNMENT. (TECHNICAL COMMITTEE ON STORM OVERFLOWS AND THE DISPOSAL OF STORM SEWAGE)
INTERIM REPORT. LONDON, H.M. STAT. OFF., 1963.
15P.

1. SEWERAGE AND SEWAGE DISPOSAL - U.K.

FF-UK- Building codes
DATE OF REQUEST 12/5/52 L.C. CARD NO.
JAN 13 1953
AUTHOR U.K. Ministry of Housing and Local Government.
TITLE Model building byelaws.
SERIES Model byelaws, series 4, buildings.
EDITION | PUB. DATE 1952 | PAGING 26 p.
PUBLISHER
London, HMSO
RECOMMENDED BY | REVIEWED IN TPA Info. Bul. 11/18/52 p.2
ORDER RECORD

711.417
(41)
U54new
U.K. Ministry of Housing and Local Government.
The new towns. London, H.M.S.O., 1969.
44p.

1. New towns - U.K. I. Title.

712
U54
U.K. Ministry of Housing and Local Government.
Landscaping for flats; the treatment of ground space on high density housing estates. London, H.M. Stationery Off., 1963.
67p. (Design bulletin 5)

1. Landscape architecture.

728.1
:362.6
(41)
U54
1960
U.K. Ministry of Housing and Local Government.
More flatlets for old people. London, H.M. Stat. Off., 1960.
20p.

2c.

1. Housing for the aged - U.K. I. Title.

711.417
(41)
U54a
United Kingdom. Ministry of Housing and Local Government.
New towns acts; accounts 1947/50-1951/52
London, England, Her Majesty's Stationery Office,
v.

"In continuation of House of Common Papers."

1.New Towns Act, 1946 (United Kingdom) 2.New Towns Act, 1955 (United Kingdom) 3.New Towns - United Kingdom. I.United Kingdom. House of Commons.

712
U54
1967
U.K. Ministry of Housing and Local Government.
Landscaping for flats; the treatment of ground space on high density housing estates. 2d ed. London, H.M. Stat. Off., 1967.
67p. (Its Design bulletin 5)

3-

1. Landscape architecture. 2. Land use - U.K.

711.585
(41)
U54m
U.K. Ministry of Housing and Local Government.
Moving out of a slum; a study of people moving from St. Mary's, Oldham. London, H.M.S.O., 1970.
70p. (Its Design bulletin 20)

2c.

Bibliography: p. 67-70.

1. Relocation - U.K. I. Title.

711.417
(41)
U54AC
U.K. MINISTRY OF HOUSING AND LOCAL GOVERNMENT.
NEW TOWNS ACTS 1946 TO 1964;
ACCOUNTS 1963-64. LONDON, H.M. STAT. OFF., 1964.
13P.

1. NEW TOWNS - U.K. I. TITLE.

711.585
(41)
U54l
U.K. Ministry of Housing and Local Government.
Living in a slum; a study of people in a central slum clearance area in Oldham. [London] 1963.
59p.

1. Slums - U.K.

301.15
(41)
U54
U.K. Ministry of Housing and Local Government. (Welsh Office)
The needs of new communities; a report on social provision in new and expanding communities. Prepared by a sub-committee of the Central Housing Advisory Committee. London, H.M. Stat. Off., 1967.
123p.

2c

1. City growth - U.K. 2. Social service. 3. Community development - U.K. 4. Community development - Citizen participation. I. Title.

690.591
U54ol
U.K. Ministry of Housing and Local Government. (Welsh Office)
Old houses into new homes. Presented to Parliament by the Minister of Housing and Local Government and the Secretary of State for Wales by command of Her Majesty, London, H.M.S.O., 1968.
29p. (Papers by Command (Cmnd. 3602)

1. Houses - Maintenance and modernization. 2. Housing - U.K. 3. U.K. - Housing. I. Title.

728.1
:362.6 U.K. Ministry of Housing and Local Govern-
(41)   ment.
U540   Old people's flatlets at Stevenage; an
account of the project with an appraisal.
London, H.M. Stationery Off., 1966.
2c   63p.

1. Housing for the aged - U.K.
2. Architectural details. I. Title.

DATE OF REQUEST 12/18/53   L C CARD NO.

AUTHOR
U.K. Ministry of Housing and Local Government.

TITLE
The people's house, 1953.

SERIES

EDITION   PUB. DATE [1953]   PAGING 4 p.
PUBLISHER

RECOMMENDED BY H&L   REVIEWED IN Child Lib Ass List no. 87
~5/53 p.18
ORDER RECORD

711.5   U.K. Ministry of Housing and Local
(41)   Government. (Welsh Office)
U54   Preservation of historic buildings and
no.7   areas. London, H.M.S.O., 1969.
[2]p. (Development control policy note 7)

1. Architecture - Conservation and
restoration. I. Title.

VF
728.1
(41)   U.K. Ministry of Housing and Local Government.
U54h   Operation rescue; a summary of the government
S   white paper, "Houses, the next step". London,
H.M. Stationery Off. [1953]
14 p.   illus., tables.

1.Housing-U.K. 2.Slum clearance-U.K. 3.Neighbor-
hood rehabilitation. I.Title. II.Title: Houses,
the next step.

711.5   U.K. Ministry of Housing and Local
(41)   Government. (Welsh Office)
U54   Petrol filling stations and motels.
no.9   London, H.M.S.O., 1969.
[2]p. (Development control policy note 9)

1. Zoning - U.K. 2. Tourist courts.
I. Title.

---

69   U.K. Ministry of Housing and Local Government.
(41)   U.K. Committee on House Interiors.
U54   Quicker completion of house interiors;
report ... presented to the Minister of Housing
and Local Government and the Secretary of State
for Scotland.   London, H.M. Stationery Off.,
1953.
63 p.   illus., plans, tables.
Sir Donald C. Bailey, chairman.
1.Building industry-U.K. 2.Architecture, Domestic-
U.K. 3.Modular coordination. I.U.K. Ministry of
Housing and Local Government. II.Bailey, Donald C.
III.Title. IV.Title: House interiors, Quicker
completion of.

728.1   U.K. MINISTRY OF HOUSING AND LOCAL
(41)   GOVERNMENT.
U540U   OUR OLDER HOMES: A CALL FOR ACTION.
REPORT OF THE SUBCOMMITTEE ON STANDARDS
2C   OF HOUSING FITNESS. LONDON, H.M. STAT.
OFF., 1966.
57P.

1. HOUSING - U.K. 2. HOUSING -
STANDARDS. I. TITLE.

711.417   U.K. Ministry of Housing and Local Government.
(41)   Llewelyn-Davies Weeks Forestier-Walker & Bor.
L52   The plan for Milton Keynes. Presented by
the Milton Keynes Development Corporation to
the Minister of Housing and Local Government.
London, 1970.
v.
Contents.-vols. 1-2: The plan for Milton
Keynes.-Technical supplement no.

no.2, Household survey.-no. 3, Public reaction
to the interim report.-no. 4, Notes on
monitoring and evaluation.-no. 5, Demographic

(Cont'd on next card)

VF
352.1   United Kingdom. Ministry of Housing and Local
(41)   Government.
U54   Rates and rateable values in England and
Wales, 1955-56. London, H.M. Stat. Off. 1956.
— Supplement, showing rateable values and
number of hereditaments in the new valuation lists
... 1st April 1956.
Enclosures 5 & 6 to dispatch 2012, 2/14/57,
American Embassy, London.
For complete information see shelflist card.
1.Municipal finance - U. K. 2.Taxation - U. K. I.Title.

333.65   U.K. Ministry of Housing and Local
C85   Government.
Cullingworth, J   B
The ownership and management of housing in
the new towns. Report submitted to the
Minister of Housing and Local Government, by
J.B. Cullingworth and V.A. Karn, Centre for
Urban and Regional Studies, The University
of Birmingham. London, H.M.S.O., 1968.
198p.

1. Housing management. 2. Home ownership - U.K. 3. New towns - U.K. I. Karn,
V.A., jt. au. II. Birmingham, Eng. University.   Centre for Urban
and Re-   gional Studies.
(Cont'd on next card)

711.417
(41)   Llewelyn-Davies Weeks Forestier-Walker & Bor.
L52   The plan...1970.   (Card 2)

base studies.-no. 6, Economic studies.-no. 7,
vol. 1, Transportation.-no. 7, vol. 2,
Transportation.-no. 8, Preservanda and
conservanda in Milton Keynes.-no. 9, Agriculture in Milton Keynes.-no. 10, vol. 1, Sewerage
and sewage disposal.-no. 10, vol. 2, Surface
water drainage.
1. New towns - U.K. I. Milton Keynes
Development Corporation. II. U.K. Ministry
of Housing and Lo   cal Government.
III. Title.

VF
336.211
(41)   U.K. Ministry of Housing and Local Government.
U54   (Scottish Home Department.)
The rating of site values. Report of the
Committee of Enquiry.   London, H. M. Stationery
Off., 1952.
133 p.

Erskine Simes, chairman.

1.Real property-Taxation-U.K. I.Title.

333.65
C85   Cullingworth, J   B
The ownership...1968   (Card 2)

III. U.K. Ministry of Housing and Local
Government. IV. Title.

712
U54p U.K. Ministry of Housing and Local Govern-
ment. (Welsh Office)
Planning control of signs and posters.
London, H.M. Stat. Off., 1966.
2c   90p.

1. Landscape architecture. 2. Architectural
control. 3. Highways - U.K. Control of signs
and posters. I. Title. II. Title: Control of
signs.

628.44
U54 U.K. Ministry of Housing and Local Government.
Refuse storage and collection; report of the
Working Party on refuse collection. London,
H.M.S.O., 1967.
165p.

1. Refuse and refuse disposal. I. Title.

711.729
(41)   U.K. Ministry of Housing and Local
U54   Government.
Parking in town centers. London,
H.M. Stat. Off., 1965.
46p.   (Its Design bulletin no. 7)
At head of title: Ministry of Housing
and Local Government. Ministry of
Transport, Scottish Development Dept.
The Welsh Off.

1. Parking - U.K. 2. Traffic surveys.

696.92   U.K. Ministry of Housing and Local
U54p   Government.
Planning for daylight and sunlight.
2c   London, H.M. Stat. Off., 1964.
35p.   (Its Planning bulletin 5)

1. Daylight. 2. Lighting.

U.K. Ministry of Housing and Local
Government.
728.1   Toronto. Metropolitan Housing Authority.
:336.18   Relating public housing abroad to
(71)   Canadian public housing. [Prepared in
T67   cooperation with] Ontario Association of
Housing Authorities and the British
Ministry of Housing and Local Government.
Toronto, 1962.
46p.

1. Public housing - Canada. 2. Housing - U.K.
3. Housing - Sweden. 4. Mortgage finance -
Canada. I. Ontario Association of Housing
Authorities. II. U.K.   Ministry of Housing
and Local Government.

711.4
(41)   U.K. Ministry of Housing and Local Government.
U54p   (Welsh Office)
People and planning; report of the Committee
3C   on Public Participation in Planning. [A.M.
Skeffington, Chairman] London, H.M.S.O., 1969.
71p.

1. City planning - U.K. 2. City planning -
Citizen participation. I. Skeffington, A.M.
II. Title.

728.1
(41)   U.K. Ministry of Housing and Local Government.
U54p   Postwar housing in the United Kingdom;
2c   Prepared for the Housing Committee of the
Economic Commission for Europe. London,
H. M. Stat. Off., 1962.
1v.

1. Housing - U.K. 2. Architecture,
Domestic - U.K. I. United Nations.
(Economic Commission for Europe. Housing
Committee)

VF
333.63
U54r U.K. Ministry of Housing and Local Govern-
ment.
Rent Act, 1957. The Rent Act and you.
Questions and answers for landlord and tenant.
London, H. M. Stat. Off., 1957.
23p.

1. Rent control. 2. Rental housing -
U.K.

333.63
(41)
U541   U.K. MINISTRY OF HOUSING AND LOCAL
GOVERNMENT.
RENTS AND SECURITY OF TENURE: THE
RENT BILL. LONDON, H.M. STATIONERY
OFF., 1965.
8p. (CMND. 2622)

1. RENT CONTROL - U.K.   2. RENTS -
U.K. I. TITLE.

711.417
(41)   U.K. Ministry of Housing and Local Government.
U54   Reports of the East Kilbride and Glenrothes
development corporations for the year ended 31st
March, 1950- ?/
Edinburgh, H. M. Stationery Off.,
v.   maps, plates, tables.
At head of title, 1950-   : New towns act,
1946; (8
Ordered by the House of Commons to be printed
For full information see shelf list card.
1.New towns-U.K. 2.New Towns Act, 1946 (U.K.).
I.U.K. House of Commons.

696.1
U54s   U.K. Ministry of Housing and Local
Government.
Service cores in high flats; sanitary
plumbing. London, H. M. Stationery Office,
1962.
31p. (Its Design bulletin 3, pt. 1)

1. Plumbing.   2. Sanitation - U.K.

711.417
(41)   U.K. Ministry of Housing and Local
U54r   Government.
U.K. Commission for the New Towns.
Report 1963-64
London, H.M. Stat. Off., 1963-
5 v.   annual.
At head of title: New towns act, 1959.
Report year ends 31st March.
Report to the Minister of Housing and Local
Government.
1. New towns - U.K. I. U.K. Ministry of Housing and
Local Government.   II. Title: New
towns act, 1959.

711.4
U54r   U.K. Ministry of Housing and Local
Government.
Residential areas; higher densities.
London, H. M. Stat. Off., 1962.
12p. (Its Planning bulletin 2)

1. Residential areas.   2. Population
density - U.K.

690.26
U54s   U.K. Ministry of Housing and Local
Government.
Service cores in high flats; the
selection and planning of passenger
lifts. London, H.M. Stat. Off., 1962.
8p. (Design bulletin 3, pt. 2)

1. Elevators.

728.1
(41)
U54r   United Kingdom. Ministry of Housing and
Local Government.
Report for 1950/51-54; 1956, 1958, 60-65, 8/71
London., H.M. Stationery Off.
15 v.
Issued in the parliamentary series as
Papers by command.
1. Housing - U.K.   2. Local government -
U.K.
1963 Cmnd-2338-
1964 -   -2c.
-2605
1966 Cmnd. 3282 - 3c.

711.5
(41)
U54   U.K. Ministry of Housing and Local
no.6   Government. (Welsh Office)
Road safety and traffic requirements.
London, H.M.S.O., 1969.
[4]p. (Development control policy note 6)

1. Highways - U.K.   I. Title.

711.3
(41)   U.K. Ministry of Housing and Local Government.
U54   (Welsh Office)
Settlement in the countryside; a planning
method. London, H.M.S.O., 1965.
Laf.   12p. (Its Planning bulletin 8)
c.1
N.c.2   1. Rural planning - United Kingdom. I. Title.

690.24
U54r   U.K. Ministry of Housing and Local Government.
Report of local inquiry into the causes of
damage to houses at Hatfield New Town, by
Michael Edward Rowe. London, H.M. Stat. Off.,
1958.
19p.

1. Roofs and roofing.   I. Rowe, Michael
Edward.

614.8
:643   U.K. Ministry of Housing and Local
U54   Government.
Safety in the home, by Anne S. Acland.
London, H.M. Stat. Off., 1967.
32p.   (Its Design bulletin 13)

1. Home accidents.   2. Architecture,
Domestic - Design - U.K. I. Acland, Anne S.
II. Title.

728.1
:362.6   U.K. Ministry of Housing and Local
(41)   Government.
U54s   Some aspects of designing for old people.
London, H.M. Stat. Off., 1962.
14p. (Its Design bulletin 1)

1. Housing for the aged.   2. Architecture
- Design - U.K. 3. Space considerations.

728.1
(41)   U.K. MINISTRY OF HOUSING AND LOCAL
U54RE   GOVERNMENT.
REPORT OF THE COMMITTEE ON HOUSING IN
GREATER LONDON. LONDON, H.M.
STATIONERY OFF., 1965.
450p. (CMD. 2605)

1. HOUSING - U.K. - LONDON.
I. TITLE: HOUSING IN GREATER LONDON.

352.6
U54   U.K. Ministry of Housing and Local
Government.
Service cores in high flats. Part 4.
G.P.O. telephone installations. Part 5.
Aerial installations for sound and tele-
vision reception. London, H.M. Stat. Off.,
1964.
7p.   (Its Design bulletin 3, pts. 4
and 5)

1. Public utilities.

711.4
(41)   U.K. Ministry of Housing and Local Government.
U54s   The South East Study, 1961-1981. London,
H.M.S.O., 1964.
144p.

1. City planning - U.K. 2. City growth -
U.K. 3. New towns - U.K. 4. Economic conditions -
U.K. I. Title.

711.417
(41)   Gt. Brit. Ministry of Local Government and
U54   Planning.
Reports of the Aycliffe, Basildon, Crawley,
Harlow, Hatfield, Hemel Hempstead, Peterlee,
Stevenage & Welwyn Garden City development
corporations. 1945-1955; 1963-1964,
London, H. M. Stationery Off. 1949-
11 v.   illus., maps (part fold.)
At head of title, 1947-   : New towns act,
19

(Continued on next card)

696.1
U54s   U.K. Ministry of Housing and Local Government.
Service cores in high flats; cold water
services. London, H.M. Stat. Off., 1965.
40p.   (Its Design bulletin 3, pt. 6)

1. Plumbing. I. Title: Cold water
services.

728
:392   U.K. Ministry of Housing and Local
U54s   Government.
Space in the home. London, H.M. Stat.
Off., 1963.
38p.   (Its Design bulletin 6)

1. Family living requirements.   2. Space
considerations. 3. Architecture, Domestic -
Design - U.K.

Gt. Brit. Ministry of Local Government and
Planning.   Reports of the Aycliffe ...
(Card 2)

Issued in the series of Reports and papers of
the House of Commons of Parliament.

For full information see shelf list card.
1.New towns-U.K. 2.New Towns Act, 1946 (U.K.).
I.U.K. House of Commons.

697.9
U54   U.K. Ministry of Housing and Local
Government.
Service cores in high flats; mechanical
ventilation of inner rooms. London, H.M.
Stat. Off., 1963.
14p. (Its Design bulletin 3, pt. 3)

1. Ventilation. I. Title: Mechanical
ventilation of inner rooms.

728
:392   U.K. Ministry of Housing and Local Govern-
U54s   ment.
1968   Space in the home. Metric ed. London, H.
M. S. O., 1968.
37p.   (Its design bulletin 6)

1. Family living requirements.   2. Space
considerations. 3. Architecture, Domestic
- Designs and plans.

712.25
(41)
U54
1965

U.K. Ministry of Housing and Local
Government.
Swimming both costs with some notes on
design. London, H.M. Stat. Off., 1965.
12p. (Its Design bulletin 9)

1. Recreation - U.K. I. Title.

300.2
(41)
U54P

U.K. MINISTRY OF INFORMATION.
POST-WAR RECONSTRUCTION IN BRITAIN; A
RECORD OF PROGRESS, JANUARY, 1941 -
NOVEMBER, 1944. LONDON, 1944.
223P.

1. RECONSTRUCTION - U.K. I. TITLE.

699.81
(016)
U54

U.K. Joint Fire Research Organization.
Fire research notes; a list of fire research
notes issued by the Joint Fire Research Organization (1957-1967) [n.p.] 1968.
24p.

Suppl.

... ... Suppl. 1- 4, 196...
1. Fire prevention - Bibl. 2. U.K. Joint
Fire Research Organization - Publications.
I. Title.

712.25
(41)
U54

U.K. Ministry of Housing and Local Government.
Swimming pools. London, H.M. Stat. Off.,
1962.
16p. (Design bulletin 4)

1. Recreation - U.K. I. Title.

69
(41)
U54
P25

Gt. Brit. *Interdepartmental Committee on House Construction.*
House construction, third report. London, Published for
the Ministry of Works by H. M. Stationery Off., 1948.
73 p. illus. 25 cm. (Post-war building studies, no. 25)

Cover title.
George M. Burt, chairman.

1. Prefabricated construction-U.K.
1. Building-Gt. Brit. (Series: Gt. Brit. Ministry of Works.
Post-war building studies, no. 25)

TH57.A253 no. 25   690.942   50-25365

Library of Congress   [1]

699.81
C31f

U.K. Joint Fire Research Organization.
Chandler, S   E
Fires in hotels. London, H.M.S.O., 1969.
13p. (U.K. Joint Fire Research Organization. Fire research technical paper no. 23)

At head of title: Ministry of Technology
and Fire Offices' Committee, Joint Fire
Research Organization.

1. Fire prevention. 2. Hotels.
I. U.K. Joint Fire Research Organization.
II. Title.

711.
(41)
U54t
1958

U. K. Ministry of Housing and Local
Government. (Scottish Office)
Town and country planning bill. Ex-
planatory memorandum. London, H.M.
Stat. Off., 1958.
77p. (American Embassy. London.
Foreign Service dispatch no. 1058,
encl. no. 2)

1. City planning - U.K. 2. Regional
planning - U.K. 3. Land use - U. K.
(Series)

331.252
Q72
1942

2c.

Gt. Brit. *Inter-departmental committee on social insurance
and allied services.*
Social insurance and allied services, report by Sir William
Beveridge. American ed. Reproduced photographically
from the English edition and published by arrangement with
His Majesty's Stationery office. New York, The Macmillan
company, 1942.
1 p. l., 299, [2] p. incl. tables. 23½ cm.
On cover: "The Beveridge report."
Report of the Inter-departmental committee on social insurance
and allied services, consisting of opinions and recommendations only.
1. Insurance, State and compulsory-Gt. Brit. 1. Beveridge, Sir
William Henry, 1879-   II. Title: The Beveridge report.
1. Social security-U.K.   42-36424
Library of Congress   HD7165.A7 1942a
       [49e²3]   331.2544

699.81
(016)
U54ℓ
1958/68

U.K. Joint Fire Research Organization.
List of reports, etc. published by H.M.
Stationery Office and in technical journals
(1958-March, 1968) London, H.M.S.O., 1968.
20p.
At head of title: Ministry of Technology
and Fire Offices' Committee, Joint Fire Research Organization.

1. Fire prevention - Bibl.

711.585
(41)
U54

3 c

U.K. Ministry of Housing and Local
Government.
Town centres; approach to renewal.
[In cooperation with] Ministry of
Transport. London, H.M. Stat.
Office, 1962.
21p. (Its Planning bulletin 1)

1. Urban renewal - U.K. I. Title.
II. U.K. Ministry of Transport.

690.22
U54

U.K. Interdepartmental Sub-Committee for
Component Co-Ordination.
Performance requirements for opaque, non
load-bearing partitions. London, 1970.
21p. Technical note no.3)

1. Walls. 2. Panels. 3. Strength of
materials. I. Title.

699.81
U54m

U.K. Joint Fire Research Organization.
U.K. Dept. of Trade and Industry.
Movement of smoke on escape routes in
buildings. Proceedings of the Symposium held
at Watford College of Technology, Watford,
Herts, 9th and 10th April, 1969. London, H.M.-
S.O., 1971.
125p. (Symposium no. 4)
At head of title: Dept. of Trade and Industry
and Fire Offices' Committee Joint Fire Research
Organization.
1. Fire prevention. I. U.K. Joint Fire
Research Organization. II. Title.
III. Title: Smoke.

711.552
(41)
U54

U.K. Ministry of Housing and Local
Government.
Town centres; cost and control of re-
development. [Prepared in cooperation with]
Ministry of Transport. London, H.M.
Stationery Off., 1963.
12p. (Its Planning bulletin 3)

1. Business districts - U.K.
I. Title.

690.282
U54

U.K. Interdepartmental Sub-Committee for
Component Coordination.
Performance requirements for windows.
[London] Ministry of Public Building and
Works, Directorate of Research and Information,
1970.
43p. (Its Technical note no. 1)

1. Windows. I. Title.

699.81
C31

U.K. Joint Fire Research Organization.
Chandler, S   E
Multiple death fires. London, H.M.S.O.,
1969.
19p. (U.K. Joint Fire Research Organization. Fire research technical paper no. 22)

1. Fire prevention. I. U.K. Joint Fire
Research Organization. II. Title.

711.552
(41)
U54t

U.K. Ministry of Housing and Local
Government.
Town centres; current practice.
[Prepared in cooperation with] the
Ministry of Transport. London, H.M.
Stationery Off., 1963.
1v. (Its Planning bulletin 4)

1. Business districts - U.K. 2. City planning - U.K.
3. Urban renewal - U.K.   I. U.K. Ministry
of Transport.   II. Title.

691
(41)
M15

U.K. Joint Fire Research Organization.
Malhotra, H   L
Expanded polystyrene linings for domestic
buildings. London, H.M.S.O., 1971.
7p. (U.K. Joint Fire Research Organization.
Fire note no. 12)
At head of title: Dept. of the Environment
and Fire Offices Committee. Joint Fire
Research Organization.
1. Building materials - U.K. I. U.K.
Joint Fire Research Organization. II. Title.

699.81
U54un

U.K. Joint Fire Research Organization.
United Kingdom fire and loss statistics, 19
London, H.M.S.O., 19

1 v.

For Library holdings see main entry.

1. Fire prevention. I. Title.

352
(41)
U54w

U.K. MINISTRY OF HOUSING AND LOCAL GOVERNMENT.
U.K. Royal Commission on Local Government in
England.
Written evidence of the Ministry of Housing
and Local Government. London, H.M.S.O., 1967.
88p. (S.O. code no. 73-44-5)

1. Local government - U.K. 2. Municipal
services - U.K. 3. U.K. Ministry of Housing
and Local Government. I. Title.

699.81
U54fi
1970

U.K. Joint Fire Research Organization.
U.K. Dept. of the Environment.
Fire research 1970. Report of the Fire
Research Steering Committee with the report of
the Director of Fire Research. London, H.M.S.O.,
1971.
120p.

At head of title: Dept. of the Environment
and Fire Offices' Committee, Joint Fire Research
Organization.
Bibliography: p. 94-103.

1. Fire prevention. I. U.K. Joint Fire
Research Organization. II. Title.

690.24
M15

U.K. Joint Fire Research Organization.
Malhotra, H   L
Weathering properties of fire-retardant
plastics rooflights, by H.L. Malhotra and
J. Crowder. London, H.M.S.O., 1969.
4p. (U.K. Joint Fire Research Organization. Fire note no. 11)
1. Roofs and roofing. 2. Building materials.
Fireproof. 3. Plastics. I. Crowder, J., jt.
au. II. U.K. Joint Fire Research Organization. III. Title.

699.81
(016)
U54

U.K. JOINT FIRE RESEARCH ORGANIZATION -
PUBLICATIONS.
U.K. Joint Fire Research Organization.
Fire research notes; a list of fire research
notes issued by the Joint Fire Research Organization (1957-1967) [n.p.] 1968.
24p.

Suppl. ...... Suppl.
1. Fire prevention - Bibl. 2. U.K. Joint
Fire Research Organization - Publications.
I. Title.

728.1
(41
:347)
H25

U.K. LAWS, STATUTES, ETC.
HENDERSON, ARTHUR, 1893-
HENDERSON AND MADDOCK'S HOUSING ACTS,
1925 AND 1930. LONDON, EYRE AND
SPOTTISWOODE, 1930.
514P.

1. HOUSING LEGISLATION - U.K.
I. MADDOCK, LESLIE, JT. AU. II. U.K.
LAWS, STATUTES, ETC. III. TITLE:
HOUSING ACTS.

333.63
(41)
S13

U.K. LAWS, STATUTES, ETC.
SAFFORD, ARCHIBALD, 1892- ED.
THE RENT AND MORTGAGE INTEREST
RESTRICTIONS ACTS, 1920 TO 1933, WITH
INTRODUCTION, NOTES, RULES AND FORMS
AND THE TEXT OF THE REPEALED ACTS, BY
ARCHIBALD SAFFORD ... 7TH ED. LONDON,
SWEET AND MAXWELL, 1933.
270P.

1. RENT CONTROL - U.K. 2. MORTGAGE
FINANCE - U.K. I. U.K. LAWS,
STATUTES, ETC. II. TITLE.

VF
690.24
U54s

U.K. Ministry of Labour and National
Service.
Safety in building operations, roofing. London, H.M. Stat. Off., 1958.
12p. diagrs. (Its Safety, health
and welfare booklets. New series no. 6B)

1. Roofs and roofing. 2. Building construction - Accidents.

LAW
T
H252he

U.K. LAWS, STATUTES, ETC.
HENDERSON, ARTHUR.
HENDERSON AND MADDOCK'S HOUSING ACTS,
1925 AND 1930, A TREATISE ON THE HOUSING
ACT, 1930, INCLUDING THE COMPLETE TEXT OF
THE ACT, ANNOTATED AND EXPLAINED, AND IN
ADDITION THE PRINCIPAL ACT, THE HOUSING
ACT, 1925, AS AMENDED, TOGETHER WITH OTHER
HOUSING LEGISLATION UNREPEALED ... BY
ARTHUR HENDERSON AND LESLIE MADDOCK.
LONDON, EYRE AND SPOTTISWOODE, 1930.
514P.
1. HOUSING - U.K. I. MADDOCK, LESLIE,
JT. AU. II. U.K. LAWS, STATUTES, ETC.
III. TITLE: HOUSING ACTS.

368
:347
U54

U.K. LAWS, STATUTES, ETC.
WAR DAMAGE ACT, 1941. 45 GEO. 6, CH.
12. LONDON, 1941.
96P.

1. INSURANCE - LAW AND LEGISLATION.

614.8
:690
U54s

U.K. Ministry of Labour.
Safety in construction work scaffolding.
London, H.M.S.O., 1968.
30p. (New series no. 6D)

At head of title: Safety, health
and welfare.

1. Building construction - Accidents.
I. Title.

728
:333
U54h

U. K. Laws, statutes, etc.

U.K. Parliament.
House purchase and housing act, 1959.
London, H.M. Stat. Off., 1959.
24p. (7 & 8 Eliz. 2, ch. 33) (American
Embassy, London. Foreign service dispatch
no. 26, 1959, encl. no. 1)

Attached: American Embassy, London. Foreign
service dispatch no. 26, 1959.

1. Home ownership - U.K. 2. Housing legislation -
U. K. I. U.K. Laws, statutes, etc.
(Series: American Embassy London. Foreign service
dispatch no. 26, 1959, encl. no. 1)

Gt. Brit. Ministry of Local Government and
Planning.

Name changed, January 1951, from:

Gt. Brit. Ministry of Town and Country
Planning.

Name changed, Nov. 1951, to:
United Kingdom. Ministry of Housing and Local
Government.

333.332
U54

U.K. Ministry of Labour and National
Service.
Surveying. London, H.M. Stat. Off.,
1958.
55p. illus., diagrs. (Choice of
careers 87)

1. Appraisal. I. Title.

728.1
(41
:347)
S66

U.K. LAWS, STATUTES, ETC.
SOPHIAN, THEODORE JOHN, ED.
THE HOUSING ACT, 1935. LONDON, I.
PITMAN AND SONS, 1935.
217P.

1. HOUSING LEGISLATION - U.K.
I. U.K. LAWS, STATUTES, ETC.
II. TITLE.

Gt. Brit. Ministry of Local Government and
Planning.

see also

Gt. Brit. Ministry of Town and Country Planning.
United Kingdom. Ministry of Housing and Local
Government.

VF
711.4
(41)
U54to

U.K. Labour Publications Dept.
Town and country planning. London,
Labour Party, Transport House, 1947.
16p.

1. City planning - U.K. I. Title.

728.1
(41
:347)
M12

U.K. LAWS, STATUTES, ETC.
MADDOCK, HERBERT LESLIE, ED.
THE HOUSING ACT 1936, WITH INDEX
TOGETHER WITH A COMPARATIVE TABLE
SHOWING THE CORRESPONDENCE BETWEEN THE
SECTIONS OF THE HOUSING ACT 1936 AND THE
SECTIONS OF THE PREVIOUS HOUSING ACTS.
LONDON, EYRE AND SPOTTISWOODE, 1936.
172, 42P.

1. HOUSING LEGISLATION - U.K.
I. U.K. LAWS, STATUTES, ETC.
II. TITLE.

69(41)
G72
1949
Suppl.1

United Kingdom. Ministry of Local Government and
Planning.
Housing for special purposes; supplement to
the housing manual, 1949. Report of the Housing
manual sub-committee of the Central housing
advisory committee under extended terms of reference. London, Eng., H.M. Stationery Off., 1951.
43 p. illus., plans.

(Continued on next card)

333.34
U54

U.K. Land Registry.
Registration of title to land. London,
H.M.S.O., 1968.
19p.

At head of title: Land registration
acts, 1925 to 1966.

1. Land titles. I. Title.

728.1
(41
:347)
A55

U.K. LAWS, STATUTES, ETC.
ALLAN, CHARLES EDWARD, 1861- ED.
THE HOUSING OF THE WORKING CLASSES
ACTS, 1890-1909, AND TOWN PLANNING,
ANNOTATED AND EXPLAINED, TOGETHER WITH
THE STATUTORY RULES AND FORMS. BY
CHARLES E. ALLAN, ASSISTED BY FRANCIS
J. ALLAN ... 3D ED. LONDON,
BUTTERWORTH, 1911.
372P.
1. HOUSING LEGISLATION - U.K.
2. CITY PLANNING - U.K. I. ALLAN,
FRANCIS JOHN, 1858- , JT. AU.
II. U.K. LAWS, STATUTES, ETC.
III. TITLE.

United Kingdom. Ministry of Local Government and
Planning. Housing for special purposes...
1951. (Card 2)

Contents.-Housing of old people.-Housing needs
of single workers, students and apprentices.-
Dwellings for disabled persons.-Housing needs of
district nurses and midwives.-Houses for higher
income groups.-Summary of recommendations.

1.Housing for the aged. I.Title. II.Title: The
housing manual, 1949.

728.1
(41
:347)
H45

U.K. LAWS, STATUTES, ETC.
HILL, HAROLD ARTHUR.
THE COMPLETE LAW OF HOUSING. 3D ED.
BY H.A. HILL ASSISTED BY A.W.
NICHOLLS. LONDON, BUTTERWORTH, 1938.
719P.

1. HOUSING LEGISLATION - U.K.
I. NICHOLLS, ARTHUR WILLIAM. II. U.K.
LAWS, STATUTES, ETC. III. TITLE.

728.1
(41
:347)
J25

U.K. LAWS, STATUTES, ETC.
JENNINGS, WILLIAM IVOR, ED.
THE LAW OF HOUSING, BY W. IVOR
JENNINGS, WITH A CHAPTER ON HOUSING
FINANCE AND ACCOUNTS AND FINANCIAL NOTES
BY FRANK E. PRICE. LONDON, C. KNIGHT,
1935.
654P.

1. HOUSING LEGISLATION - U.K.
I. PRICE, FRANK EDWARD. II. U.K.
LAWS, STATUTES, ETC.

69(41)
G72
1949

United Kingdom. Ministry of Local Government
and Planning.
United Kingdom. Ministry of Works.
Housing manual 1949; technical appendices.
London, H.M. Stationery Off., 1951.
87 p. diagrs., tables.

List of British standard codes of practice
and British standards: p. 70-78.
Bibliography: p. 79-82.
1.Building construction-U.K. 2.Housing-U.K.
3.Building standards-U.K.-Bibl. I.U.K. Ministry
of Local Government and Planning.

728.1
A- 352
(41)
U54
R1943-51
United Kingdom. Ministry of Local Government and Planning.
Town and country planning, 1943-1951; progress report by the Minister of Local Government and Planning on the work of the Ministry of Town and Country Planning.   London, H.M. Stationery Off. 1951.
vii, 215 p.   maps (Part fold.), tables.
Bibliographical footnotes.
1.Gt. Brit. Ministry of Town and Country Planning. 2.New towns-U.K.

027
(41)
U54
U.K. National Libraries Committee.
U.K. Dept. of Education and Science.
Principal documentary evidence submitted to the National Libraries Committee. London, H.M.S.O., 1969.
2v.

1. Libraries - U.K. I. U.K. National Libraries Committee. II. Title.

711.417
(41)
U54n
1958
U.K. Parliament. House of Commons.
New Towns bill. Explanatory and financial memorandum. London, H.M. Stat. Off., 1958.
18p. (Its Bill 33)

Bound with American Embassy. London. Foreign service dispatch no. 1248, 1958. New Towns bill; change of policy respecting ownership, summary. 9p.
1. New towns - U.K. I. American Embassy, London. Foreign Service dispatch no. 1248, 1958.

690
(41)
U54REP
U.K. LOCAL GOVERNMENT BOARD.
REPORT OF THE COMMITTEE APPOINTED BY THE PRESIDENT OF THE LOCAL GOVERNMENT BOARD AND THE SECRETARY FOR SCOTLAND TO CONSIDER QUESTIONS OF BUILDING CONSTRUCTION IN CONNECTION WITH THE PROVISIONS OF DWELLINGS FOR THE WORKING CLASSES IN ENGLAND AND WALES AND SCOTLAND, AND REPORT UPON METHODS OF SECURING ECONOMY AND DESPATCH IN THE PROVISION OF SUCH DWELLINGS. LONDON, H.M. STAT. OFF., 1918. 97P. (PAPERS BY COMMAND, CD. 9191)
(CONTINUED ON NEXT CARD)

711.417
(41)
U54RE
NO.3
U.K. NEW TOWNS COMMITTEE.
FINAL REPORT OF THE NEW TOWNS COMMITTEE ... LONDON, H.M. STAT. OFF., 1946.
83P. (U.K. PARLIAMENT. PAPERS BY COMMAND. CMD. 6876)

LIST OF GOVERNMENT PUBLICATIONS OF INTEREST IN THE DEVELOPMENT OF NEW TOWNS : P. 72-74.
1. NEW TOWNS - U.K. I. U.K. MINISTRY OF TOWN AND COUNTRY PLANNING. II. SCOTLAND. DEPT. OF HEALTH.

711.417
(41)
U54
U.K. House of Commons.
Gt. Brit. Ministry of Local Government and Planning.
Reports of the Aycliffe, Basildon, Crawley, Harlow, Hatfield, Hemel Hempstead, Peterlee, Stevenage & Welwyn Garden City development corporations.
London, H. M. Stationery Off.
v.   illus., maps (part fold.)
At head of title, 19   :New towns act, 19
(Continued on next card)

690
(41)
U54REP
U.K. LOCAL GOVERNMENT BOARD. REPORT OF ... 9191)   (CARD 2)
1. BUILDING CONSTRUCTION - U.K.
2. BUILDING INDUSTRY - U.K.   3. PUBLIC HOUSING - U.K.

711.417
(41)
U54RE
NO.1
U.K. NEW TOWNS COMMITTEE.
INTERIM REPORT OF THE NEW TOWNS COMMITTEE ... LONDON, H.M. STAT. OFF., 1946.
21P. (U.K. PARLIAMENT. PAPERS BY COMMAND. CMD. 6759)

1. NEW TOWNS - U.K. I. U.K. MINISTRY OF TOWN AND COUNTRY PLANNING. II. SCOTLAND. DEPT. OF HEALTH.

Gt. Brit. Ministry of Local Government and Planning.   Reports of the Aycliffe ... (Card 2)
Issued in the series of Reports and papers of the House of Commons of Parliament.

For full information see shelf list card.
1.New towns-U.K. 2.New Towns Act, 1946 (U.K.). I.U.K. House of Commons.

711.585
(41)
U54S
U.K. LOCAL GOVERNMENT BOARD.
SLUM CLEARANCE AND HOUSING, 1889-1919. LONDON, H.M. STAT. OFF., 1919.
1 V. (VARIOUS PAGINGS)

BINDER'S TITLE.
EXCERPTS FROM THE BOARD'S ANNUAL REPORTS, 1889-1919, ISSUED IN THE SERIES OF PAPERS BY COMMAND.
1. SLUM CLEARANCE - U.K.

711.417
(41)
U54RE
NO.2
U.K. NEW TOWNS COMMITTEE.
SECOND INTERIM REPORT OF THE NEW TOWNS COMMITTEE ... LONDON, H.M. STAT. OFF., 1946.
25P. (U.K. PARLIAMENT. PAPERS BY COMMAND. CMD. 6794)

1. NEW TOWNS - U.K. I. U.K. MINISTRY OF TOWN AND COUNTRY PLANNING. III. SCOTLAND. DEPT. OF HEALTH.

711.417
(411)
U54
U.K. House of Commons.
U.K. Ministry of Housing and Local Government.
Reports of the East Kilbride and Glenrothes development corporations for the year ended 31st March,
Edinburgh, H. M. Stationery Off.,
v.   maps, plates, tables.
At head of title, 19   : New towns act, 19
Ordered by the House of Commons to be printed
For full information see shelf list card.
1.New towns-U.K. 2.New Towns Act, 1946 (U.K.). I.U.K. House of Commons.

U.K. Local Government Commission for England.
see
U.K. Royal Commission on Local Government in England.

341.1
:338
(41)
U54
U.K. Ministry of Overseas Development.
Overseas development: the work of the new Ministry. London, H.M. Stat. Off., 1965.
74p.   (Cmnd. 2736)

1. Technical assistance programs (U.K.) I. Title.

711
(41)
U54T
UNITED KINGDOM. PARLIAMENT.
TOWN AND COUNTRY PLANNING (SCOTLAND) BILL. ORDERED BY THE HOUSE OF COMMONS TO BE PRINTED. 26, JANUARY, 1945. LONDON, H.M. STAT. OFF., 1945.
99P.

1. PLANNING - SCOTLAND.

711.14
U54t
U.K. National Coal Board.
Topographical planning design processes: first special process. [n.p.] [1970?]
1v.
Cover title: Planning the design of settled topographies; means of thinking creatively about realities as features of localities.
1. Land use. 2. Landscape architecture. I. Title.

728
:333
U54h
U.K. Parliament.
House purchase and housing act, 1959. London, H.M. Stat. Off., 1959.
24p. (7 & 8 Eliz. 2, ch. 33) (American Embassy, London. Foreign service dispatch no. 26, 1959, encl. no. 1)
Attached: American Embassy, London. Foreign service dispatch no. 26, 1959.
1. Home ownership - U.K. 2. Housing legislation - U.K. I. U.K. Laws, statutes, etc.
(Series: American Embassy, London. Foreign service dispatch no. 26, 1959,   encl. no. 1)

711
(41)
U54TS
U.K. PARLIAMENT.
TOWN AND COUNTRY PLANNING (SCOTLAND) BILL, AND FINANCIAL MEMORANDUM. ORDERED PRINTED BY THE HOUSE OF COMMONS, FEB. 5, 1947. LONDON, H.M. STATIONERY OFF., 1947.
135P.

1. PLANNING - SCOTLAND.

728.1
:325
(41)
U54
U.K. National Committee for Commonwealth Immigrants.
The housing of Commonwealth immigrants. London, 1968.
20p.

1. Minority groups - Housing - U.K. I. Title.

711.417
(41)
U54a
United Kingdom. House of Commons.
United Kingdom. Ministry of Housing and Local Government.
New towns acts; accounts 1949/50-1951/52 and 1954/55
London, England, Her Majesty's Stationery Office, 1953/54-7v.
"In continuation of House of Common Papers."
1.New Towns Act, 1946 (United Kingdom) 2.New Towns Act, 1955 (United Kingdom) 3.New Towns - United Kingdom. I.United Kingdom. House of Commons.

534.83
U54
U.K. Committee on the Problem of Noise.
Noise; final report. Presented to Parliament by the Lord President of the Council and Minister for Science by Command of Her Majesty. London, H.M. Stat. Off., 1964.
235p. (CMnd. 2056)

1. Noise.

693.5
[U54a] U.K. Ministry of Public Building and Works.
Accuracy in precast concrete panel construction. London, Ministry of Public Building and Works, Directorate of Research and Information, 1968.
45p. (R & D paper Cl/SfB (2-) GF)

1. Concrete construction. 2. Prefabricated construction - U.K. 3. U.K. - Prefabricated construction. 4. Panels. I. Title.

690
(016)
S71
Suppl.
Stannett, Annette. Bibliography on...1969-
(Card 2)

1. Building construction - Automation - Bibl. I. U.K. Ministry of Public Building and Works. II. U.K. Committee on the Application of Computers in the Construction Industry. III. Title: Application of computers in the construction industry, 1962-1967. Supplement.

690.59
[U54b] U.K. Ministry of Public Building and Works.
Building maintenance; the interim report of a committee appointed by the Minister of Public Building and Works. London, H.M.S.O., 1969.
23p. (R & D bulletin)
Cl/SfB.

1. Building maintenance.

697.9
K54 U.K. Ministry of Public Building and Works.
Knight, J C
Acoustic problems and the lighting load in air conditioning design. London, Ministry of Public Building and Works, 1968.
15p.
Reprinted from the Institution of Heating and Ventilating Engineers Journal, April 1968.
1. Air conditioning. 2. Lighting. 3. Soundproofing. I. U.K. Ministry of Public Building and Works. II. Institution of Heating and Ventilating Engineers Journal. III. Title.

VF
693.2
U54
U.K. Ministry of Public Building and Works.
Bricklaying in cold weather. 3d ed. London, 1968.
folder. (Advisory leaflet no. 8)

1. Bricklaying. 2. Winter construction.

693
U54b U.K. Ministry of Public Building and Works.
The building process; a case study from Marks and Spencer, ltd. London, H.M.S.O., 1970.
60p. (R & D bulletin)

1. Building methods. 2. Building industry - U.K. I. Title.

VF
668.3
U54 U.K. Ministry of Public Building and Works.
Adhesives used in building. London, H.M.S.O., 1969.
folder. (Its Advisory leaflet no. 77)

1. Adhesives.

690.091.82
(41)
U54b
U.K. Ministry of Public Building and Works.
Building and buildings; the building regulations, 1965. London, H.M.S. Office, 1968.
168p. (1965 no. 1373)
Reprinted in 1968.

1. Building standards - U.K. I. Title.

614.8
:690
U54
U.K. Ministry of Public Building and Works.
Building without accidents. London, H.M. Sta., Off., 1967.
[4]p. (Advisory leaflet no. 67)

1. Building construction - Accidents. 2. Accidents. I. Title.

621.32
H17 U.K. Ministry of Public Building and Works.
Harris, J B
Artificial lighting in government buildings. [n.p.] 1965.
150-161p.

Reprinted from Light and lighting, May 1965, for Ministry of Public Building and Works.

1. Lighting. I. U.K. Ministry of Public Building and Works. II. Title.

690.015
(41)
U54b
U.K. Ministry of Public Building and Works.
Building for expansion; a short account of the aims and objectives of the Directorate General of Research and Development of the Ministry of Public Building and Works. Rev. London, 1968.
7p.

1. Building research - U.K. I. Title.

VF
691.42
U54c
U.K. Ministry of Public Building and Works.
Calcium silicate bricks and how to use them. 2d ed. London, H.M.S.O., 1970.
folder. (Advisory leaflet no. 65)

1. Bricks. I. Title.

690
(016)
S71
U.K. Ministry of Public Building and Works.
Stannett, Annette.
Bibliography on the application of computers in the construction industry, 1962-1967. Prepared on behalf of the Committee on the Application of Computers in the Construction Industry. London, H.M.S.O., 1968.
87p. (R & D bulletin)
List of periodicals cited: p. 74-82.
At head of title: Ministry of Public Building and Works, Directorate of Research and Information.
1. Building construction - Automation - Bibl.

(Cont'd on next card)

690
(47)
K54
U.K. Ministry of Public Building and Works.
Knight, J C
The building industry in the U.S.S.R.; as seen by a services engineer. London, Ministry of Public Building Works, 1968.
12p.
Reprinted from Instn. Heat. vent. engnrs. J., July, 1968. p.99-110.
1. Building industry - U.S.S.R. I. U.K. Ministry of Public Building and Works. II. Title.

691.11
U54
U.K. Ministry of Public Building and Works.
Care in the use of timber. 3d ed. London, H.M.S.O., 1970.
folder. (Advisory leaflet no. 29)

1. Wood. I. Title: Timber. II. Title.

690
(016)
S71
Stannett, Annette. Bibliography...1968.
(Card 2)

I. Title: Application of computers in the construction industry, 1962-1967.
II. U.K. Ministry of Public Building and Works. III. U.K. Committee on the Application of Computers in the Construction Industry.

690.59
U54
U.K. Ministry of Public Building and Works.
Building maintenance conference papers. London, Ministry of Public Building and Works, Directorate of Research and Information, 1969.
215p. (R & D paper Cl/SfB (W))

1. Building maintenance.

VF
690
U54ca
U.K. Ministry of Public Building and Works.
Care of builders' machines. London, 1969.
folder. (Its Advisory leaflet 33)

1. Building construction. 2. Tools. I. Title.

690
(016)
S71
Suppl.
U.K. Ministry of Public Building and Works.
Stannett, Annette.
Bibliography on the application of computers in the construction industry, 1962-1967. Supplement, 1st-
Jan.-June, 1968-
Prepared on behalf of the Committee on the Application of Computers in the Construction Industry. London, H.M.S.O., 1969-
2v. (R & D bulletin)
At head of title: Ministry of Public Building and Works.

(Cont'd on next card)

690.59
U54bu
U.K. Ministry of Public Building and Works.
Building maintenance statistics; a report of a working group of the Committee on Building Maintenance. London, 1970.
78p. (R & D paper)

1. Building maintenance. I. Title.

624
G52
U.K. Ministry of Public Building and Works.
Glenn, W J
Civil engineering in the Ministry of Public Building and Works. [London] Ministry of Public Buildings and Works, 1968.
[5]p.
Reprinted from Proc. Instn. Civ. Engrs., 40 (July) N8-N12.

1. Civil engineering. I. U.K. Ministry of Public Building and Works. II. Title.

389.6
U54c

U.K. Ministry of Public Building and Works.
A commodity identification code for the construction industry. London, H.M.S.O., 1970. 34p. (R & D paper)

1. Commodity classification. 2. Building industry - U.K. I. Title.

690.031
I57

U.K. Ministry of Public Building and Works.
International Tutor Machines.
Cost control in building design; a programmed text in two parts. Part I: The principles of cost control. Part II: techniques of cost control. Written by the Programme Division of International Tutor Machines, ltd. in conjunction with the Directorate of Building Management, Ministry of Public Building and Works. London, H.M. S.O., 1968.
419p. (R&D. Building management handbook 4)
1. Building costs. 2. Building industry. I. U.K. Ministry of Public Building and Works. II. Title.

693.068
:389.6
U54di

U.K. Ministry of Public Building and Works.
Dimensional co-ordination for building; recommended dimensions of spaces allocated for selected components and assemblies used in educational, health, housing and office buildings. London, H.M.S.O., 1968.
16p. (Its D.C.8)

1. Coordinated components. I. Title.

720
U54

U.K. Ministry of Public Building and Works.
Computer-aided architectural design.
Pt.1: Reports of three working groups.
Pt.2: Some case histories. London, 1969. 2v. (R & D paper)

1. Architecture - Designs and plans. I. Title.

699.82
U54

U.K. Ministry of Public Buildings and Works.
Dampness in buildings. London, H.M. Stat. Off., 1967.
[4]p. (Advisory leaflet no. 47)

1. Moisture condensation. 2. Waterproofing. I. Title.

058.7
:690
U54

U.K. Ministry of Public Building and Works.
Directory of construction statistics. A report prepared for the Ministry of Public Building and Works by Cynthia Cockburn and Michael Verstage under the supervision of D.A. Turin, London Master Builders' Professor of Building, University of London. London, H.M.S.O., 1968.
98p. (R. & D. bulletin. SfB Ae2)
1. Building construction - Direct. I. Cockburn, Cynthia. II. Verstage, Michael. II. Turin, D.A. IV. Title.

690
U54co

U.K. Ministry of Public Building and Works.
Computers for contractors in the building industry. First report of the Sub-Committee on Computer Uses in the Construction of Buildings to the Committee on the Application of Computers in the Construction Industry. London, 1969.
99p. (R & D paper)
1. Building industry - Automation. I. Title.

VF
699.82
U54d

U.K. Ministry of Public Building and Works.
Damp-proof courses. 2d ed. London, H.M.S.O., 1970.
folder. (Advisory leaflet no. 23)

1. Waterproofing. I. Title.

VF
697.34
H17

U.K. Ministry of Public Building and Works
Haseler, A E
District heating development. London, Ministry of Public Building and Works, 1965.
[5]p.

Reprinted from Interbuild, June 1965.

1. Heating, District. 2. Heating, Central. I. U.K. Ministry of Public Building and Works. II. Title.

690
(41)
U54co

U.K. Ministry of Public Building and Works.
Computers in the construction industry. Conference papers. London, 1968.
158p. (R & D paper)

1. Building industry - Automation - U.K.
2. Building construction - Automation - U.K. I. Title.

728.1
(41)
U54d

U.K. Ministry of Public Building and Works.
Decisions affecting design of five point blocks; a study carried out by the Architecture Research Unit, Dept. of Architecture, University of Edinburgh. London, Ministry of Public Building and Works, Directorate of Research and Information, 1968.
68p. (Its R & D paper C1/SfB 815 Alf)
1. Low-income housing - U.K. 2. U.K. - Low-income housing. 3. Apartment houses - U.K. 4. U.K. - Apartment houses. 5. Architecture, Domestic - Designs and plans. I. Edinburgh, Scot. University. Dept. of Architecture. II. Title.

697.34
H17d

U.K. Ministry of Public Building and Works.
Haseler, Ernest.
District heating in Denmark. A paper presented at the Institution's Summer Conference aboard the S.S. Orsova on 21st May, 1968. [London] Ministry of Public Building and Works, 1968.
26p.
Reprinted from Sept. and Oct., 1968 issues I.H.V.E. journal, Ministry of Public Building and Works Library.

1. Heating, District. I. U.K. Ministry of Public Building and Works. II. Title.

691.32
U54c

U.K. Ministry of Public Building and Works.
Concreting in cold weather. 2d ed. London, H.M.S.O., 1968.
folder. (Advisory leaflet no. 7)

1. Concrete. 2. Winter construction.
3. Building methods. I. Title.

690.015
(41)
U54d

U.K. Ministry of Public Building and Works.
U.K. Construction Development Co-Ordination Committee.
Departmental programmes for development projects, July 1969. London, Ministry of Public Building and Works, 1969.
40p.

1. Building research - U.K. 2. Building industry - U.K. I. U.K. Ministry of Public Building and Works. II. Title.

697.34
H17

U.K. Ministry of Public Building and Works.
Haseler, A E
District heating in new cities. Reprinted for U.K. Ministry of Public Building and Works, from the I.H.V.E. journal, September, 1965, p. 3-19.

1. Heating, District. 2. Heating, Central.
3. New towns. I. U.K. Ministry of Public Building and Works.

690
(41)
U54c

U.K. Ministry of Public Building and Works.
Construction, education and the computer; conference report: Cambridge: 1968. London, Ministry of Public Building and Works, Directorate of Research and Information, 1969.
33p. (R & D paper C1/SfB (Ango))
Sponsored by the Ministry of Public Building and Works on behalf of the Committee on the Applications of Computers in the Construction Industry, Churchill College, Cambridge. 15-17 Sept. 1968.
1. Building industry - U.K.
2. Building industry - Automation. I. Title.

696
K25

U.K. Ministry of Public Building and Works.
Kemp, James.
Design, maintenance and operation. London, H.M.S.O., 1966.
16p.
At head of title: Ministry of Public Building and Works.

1. Building maintenance. I. U.K. Ministry of Public Building and Works. II. Title.

VF
691.42
U54

U.K. Ministry of Public Building and Works.
Efflorescence and stains on brickwork. London, H.M.S.O., 1969.
folder. (Its Advisory leaflet no. 75)

1. Bricks. 2. Building materials - Climatic effects. I. Title: Stains on brickwork. II. Title.

690.59
U54c

U.K. Ministry of Public Building and Works.
Contractual policies and techniques for maintenance work [a description of methods used by the Ministry of Public Building and Works] London, 1969.
15p. (R & D paper)

1. Building maintenance. I. Title.

693.068
:389.6
U54dim

U.K. Ministry of Public Building and Works.
Dimensional co-ordination for building: recommended dimensions of basic spaces for selected building components and assemblies used in educational, health, housing and office buildings. London, 1968.
84p.

1. Coordinated components. I. Title.

690
(41)
W45

U.K. Ministry of Public Building and Works.
Wilson, W L
Engineering and building; presidential address. [London] Ministry of Public Building and Works, 1968.
[5]p.
Reprinted from: Electrical supervisor, Dec., 1968.

1. Building industry - U.K. 2. U.K. - Building industry. I. U.K. Ministry of Public Building and Works. II. Title.

720
R22e
U.K. Ministry of Public Building and Works.
Redpath, J   T
The environmental design of buildings.
[London] Ministry of Public Building and Works, 1968.
11p.
Reprinted from: Transactions of the Illuminating Engineering Society, Vol. 33, No. 4, 1968, pp. 141-149.
1. Architecture - Designs and plans.
2. Office buildings. I. Title. II. U.K. Ministry of Public Building and Works.

690.091.82
(41)
U54
U.K. Ministry of Public Building and Works.
Guide to the building regulations, 1965
Public health act, 1961. London, H.M.S.O., 1965.
18p.
1. Building codes - U.K. 2. U.K. - Building codes. 3. Building standards - U.K. 4. U.K. - Building standards.

691.51
U54
U.K. Ministry of Public Building and Works
Limes for building. 2d ed. London, 1968.
folder. (Its Advisory leaflet no. 6)
1. Lime. 2. Plaster and plastering.

VF
699.81
U54fir
U.K. Ministry of Public Building and Works.
Fire risks on building sites. 2d ed.
London, H.M.S.O., 1970.
folder. (Its Advisory leaflet no. 63)
1. Fire prevention. 2. Building construction. I. Title.

VF
693
U54h
U.K. Ministry of Public Building and Works.
Heating and drying out. London, 1969.
folder. (Its Advisory leaflet no. 78)
1. Building methods. 2. Heating.
I. Title.

691.51
U54
1970
U.K. Ministry of Public Building and Works.
Limes for building. 3d ed. London, H.M.S.O., 1970.
folder. (Advisory leaflet no. 6)
1. Lime. I. Title.

629.136
U54f
U.K. Ministry of Public Building and Works.
Floating aerodromes; a report on the possibility of building aerodromes in offshore locations. London, 1969.
34p. (Its R & D paper)
1. Airports. I. Title.

690.59
IU54i
U.K. Ministry of Public Building and Works.
Incentive schemes applied to building maintenance by small firms; a report on a survey carried out by Advisory Service for the Building Industry. London, Ministry of Public Building and Works, Directorate of Research and Information, 1969.
57p. (R & D paper Cl/SfB (w))
1. Building maintenance. 2. Wage incentives - U.K. 3. U.K. - Wage incentives. I. Title.

050
U54l
U.K. Ministry of Public Building & Works.
List of current periodicals, M.E.
London 1965-
1v. (Library communication no. 478)
For complete information see main card.
1. Periodicals - Bibl.

VF
621.6
U54f
U.K. Ministry of Public Building and Works.
Frost precautions. 2d ed. London, H.M.S.O., 1970.
folder. (Advisory leaflet no. 41)
1. Pipes. 2. Frozen ground. I. Title.

690.022
(41)
U54i
U.K. Ministry of Public Building and Works.
Industrialised building; four case studies of the selection of a main contractor. London, H.M. Stationery Off., 1966.
28p. (R&D bulletin)
1. Prefabricated construction - U.K.
I. Title.

690.59
U54m
U.K. Ministry of Public Building and Works.
Maintenance by design, report of a Seminar on Maintenance Considerations in the Design of Building Components. London, 1969.
83p. (R. & D. paper)
Sponsored on behalf of the Committee on Building Maintenance.
1. Building maintenance. 2. Building methods. I.   Title.

624
U54
U.K. Ministry of Public Building and Works.
U.K. Dept. of the Environment, Research and Development.
GENESYS; a computer system for structural engineers and others. A report by the Committee on the Application of Computers in the Construction Industry; with a note by the director of the GENESYS Centre. London, 1971.
21p. (R & D paper)
Publication originally prepared under the Ministry of Public Building and Works.
1. Structural engineering. 2. Building industry - Automa   tion. I. U.K. Ministry of Public Building   and Works. II. Title.

696
IU54i
U.K. Ministry of Public Building and Works.
An introduction to incentive schemes in building maintenance. London, 1969.
52p. (Its R & D paper Cl/SfB (w))
1. Building maintenance. 2. Wage incentives - U.K. 3. U.K. - Wage incentives. 4. Job analysis. I. Title.

690
(41)
U54m
U.K. Ministry of Public Building and Works.
Management innovation in the construction industry; a case study on the introduction of programming: Lindsey (Lincs) County Architects Department. London, H.M.S.O., 1970.
19p. (R & D paper)
1. Building industry - U.K. 2. Industrial management - U.K. I. Title.

690
(41)
U54g
pt.1
U.K. Ministry of Public Building and Works.
Going metric in the construction industry.
1. Why and when. London, H.M.S.O., 1967.
15p.
1. Building industry - U.K. 2. Metric system. 3. Architecture - Designs and plans.
I. Title.

VF
690.25
U54
U.K. Ministry of Public Building and Works.
Laying floor screeds. 5th ed. London, H.M.S.O., 1969.
folder. (Its Research and development advisory leaflet 5)
1. Floors and flooring. 2. Building methods. I. Title.

VF
691.7
U54
U.K. Ministry of Public Building and Works.
Metal scaffolding. 3d ed. London, H.M.S.O., 1969.
folder. (Its Research and development advisory leaflet 36)
1. Metal construction. 2. Building methods. I. Title.

690
(41)
U54g
pt.2
2c
U.K. Ministry of Public Building and Works.
Going metric in the construction industry.
2. Dimensional co-ordination. London, H.M.S.O., 1968.
47p.
Prepared in consultation with the British Standards Institution.
1. Building industry - U.K. 2. Metric system. 3. Coordinated components. 4. U.K. - Building industry. I. Title.

VF
691.32
U54l
U.K. Ministry of Public Building and Works.
Lightweight concrete. London, 1969.
folder. (Its Advisory leaflet no. 38)
1. Concrete. I. Title.

690
S78
U.K. Ministry of Public Building and Works.
Stuart Malcolm.
Metric controlling dimensions demonstration building. London, Ministry of Public Building and Works, 1969.
[5]p
Reprinted from: Industrialised building systems and components, 1969, 6(5) May, p. 38-46.
1. Building industry - U.K. 2. Coordinated components. I. U.K. Ministry of Public Building and Works. II. Title.

389.1
U54m

U.K. Ministry of Public Buildings and Works.
Metrication in the construction industry no.
3. Craftsmen's pocket book. London H.M.S.O.,
1970.
80p.

1. Metric system. 2. Building methods.
3. Building industry - U.K. I. Title.

697
(41)
D63

U.K. Ministry of Public Building and Works.
Doherty, C H
Practices in the domestic field. London,
Ministry of Public Building and Works, 1968.
107-112p.
Reprinted from the Proceedings of the
Institution of Mechanical Engineers, 1967-68,
Part 3E.

1. Heating - U.K. I. U.K. Ministry of
Public Building and Works. II. Institution
of Mechanical Engineers, 1967/68. Proceedings. III. Title.

720
U54r

U.K. Ministry of Public Building and Works.
The relationship between design and building
maintenance. Report of a Sub-committee of the
Committee on Building Maintenance. London,
1970.
64p. (R & D paper)

1. Architecture - Designs and plans.
2. Building maintenance. I. Title.

690.59
N17p

U.K. Ministry of Public Building and Works.
National Building Maintenance Conference. 2d,
London, 1969.
Papers. Sponsored jointly by the Ministry of
Public Building and Works and the Journal
Building maintenance. London, Ministry of
Public Building and Works, 1970.
248p. (R & D paper)

1. Building maintenance. I. U.K. Ministry
of Public Building and Works.

690.59
U54pr

U.K. Ministry of Public Building and Works.
Profitable building maintenance; conference
papers, London, 1967. London, 1969.
338p. (R & D paper)

Jointly sponsored by Ministry of Public
Building and Works and the Mercury House
jor
journal

690.59
U54r

U.K. Ministry of Public Building and Works.
The relationship of capital maintenance
and running costs; a case study of two Crown
office buildings. London, 1970.
12p. (R & D paper)

1. Building maintenance. I. Title.

690
(41)
U54mo

U.K. Ministry of Public Building and Works.
Modernization of the construction
industry. London, 1968.
27p. (R&D paper)

1. Building industry - U.K. I. Title.

690.59
U54pr

U.K. Ministry of Public Building and Works.
Profitable building maintenance; conference
papers, London, 1967. London, 1969.
338p. (R & D paper)

Jointly sponsored by Ministry of Public
Building and Works and the Mercury House
journal, Maintenance Engineering.

1. Building maintenance. I. U.K. Committee
on Building Maintenance. II. Title.

690
(41)
U54r

U.K. Ministry of Public Building and Works.
Review of the structure, activities and
new developments in the building industry.
National monograph: United Kingdom. Prepared
for the Working Party on the Building Industry of the Economic Commission for Europe by
the Directorate General of Research and Development, Ministry of Public Building and Works.
London, Directorate General of Research and
Development, Ministry of Public Building and
Works, 1966.
21p. (R&D paper)

1. Building industry -   U.K. 2. Automation.
3. Community facili-   ties - U.K. I. Title.

VF
621.6
U54

U.K. Ministry of Public Buildings and Works.
Plastics pipes for cold water supply.
London, H.M.S.O., 1969.
folder. (Its Research and development
advisory leaflet 76)

1. Pipes. 2. Plastics. I. Title.

693
U54p

U.K. Ministry of Public Building and
Works.
Programming and progressing in the design
of buildings. London, H.M.S.O., 1969.
68p. (Its R & D building management
handbook 6)

1. Building methods. I. Title.

690.08
U54

U.K. Ministry of Public Building and Works.
Serial tendering; a case study from
Hampshire County Council. London, H.M.S.O.,
1969.
24p. (R & D bulletin)

SfB Ba7. SBN 11 670215 X.

1. Contractors (Building industry)
I. Title.

621.9
U54

U.K. Ministry of Public Buildings and Works.
Pneumatic tools; powered hand tools 2. 2d ed.
London, H.M.S.O., 1969.
folder. (Its Advisory leaflet no. 19)

1. Tools. I. Title: Powered hand tools
II. Title.

621.9
:690
U54

U.K. Ministry of Public Building and Works.
Protective screens and enclosures. London,
H.M.S.O., 1969.
folder. (Advisory leaflet no. 74)

1. Building equipment. 2. Weather. I. Title.

VF
693
U54s

U.K. Ministry of Public Building and Works.
Setting out on site. 2d ed. London,
1969.
folder. (Its Advisory leaflet no. 48)

1. Building methods. I. Title.

621.9
U54p

U.K. Ministry of Public Building and Works.
Powered hand tools 3; safety and maintenance.
2d ed. London, H.M.S.O., 1970.
folder. (Advisory leaflet no. 20)

1. Tools. 2. Building construction -
Accidents. I. Title.

658.562
U54

U.K. Ministry of Public Building and Works.
Quality control; conference papers; two-
day conference sponsored by the Ministry of
Public Building and Works and held during
the International Building Exhibition at
Olympia in 1969. London, 1970.
82p. (R. & D. paper)
Cover title.
1. Quality control. I. International
Building Exhibition.

696.1
U54si

U.K. Ministry of Public Building and Works.
Single stack plumbing. London, H.M.S.O.,
1968.
folder. (Advisory leaflet no. 73)

1. Plumbing. I. Title.

690.59
U54p

U.K. Ministry of Public Building and Works.
Practice in property maintenance management;
a review. London, H.M.S.O., 1970.
38p. (R & D bulletin)

Bibliography: p. 37-38.

1. Building maintenance. I. Title.

697
(41)
H17

U.K. Ministry of Public Building and
Works.
Haseler, A E
Rationalised heat supply. London,
Ministry of Public Building and Works, 1969.
933-938p. (London. Ministry of Public
Building and Works. Technical study:
heating and ventilating services 1)
Reprinted from: Archits. J., April
2, 1969.

1. Heating - U.K. I. U.K. Ministry
of Public Building and Works.
II. Title.

VF
697.8
U54s

U.K. Ministry of Public Building and
Works.
Smoky chimneys. 2d ed. London, H.M.S.O.,
1968.
folder. (Its Advisory leaflet no. 44)

1. Chimneys. 2. Air pollution. I. Title.

691.54
U54
    U.K. Ministry of Public Building and Works.
      Special cements. 2d. ed. London, H.M.S.O.,
    1968.
      folder. (Advisory leaflet no. 39)

      1. Cement. I. Title.

699.86
U54w
    U.K. Ministry of Public Building and
    Works.
      Warmth without waste. London, H.M.S.O.,
    1967.
      Folder (Advisory leaflet no. 45)
            materials.
      1. Insulating/ 2. Heating. I. Title.

352
(41)
U54lo
    U.K. Royal Commission on Local Government
    in England.
      Local government reform; short version of
    the report of the Royal Commission on Local
    Government in England. London, H.M.S.O.,
    1969.
      21p.
      Chairman: The Rt. Hon. Lord Redcliffe-Maud.

      1. Local government - U.K. I. Redcliffe-
    Maud, John Primatt. II. Title.

690.015
(41)
U54s
    U.K. Ministry of Public Building and
    Works.
      Survey of research and development for the
    construction industry. London, H.M.S.O.,
    1968.
      177p. (U.K. Ministry of Public Building
    and Works. Directorate of Research and
    Information. R & D bulletin no. SfB Aa2)
      1. Building research - U.K. 2. U.K. -
    Building research. 3. Building industry - U.K.
    4. U.K. - Building industry. I. Title.

699.82
U54w
pt.1
    U.K. Ministry of Public Building and Works.
      Watertight basements. Part 1. 2d ed.
    London, H.M.S.O., 1970.
      folder. (Advisory leaflet no. 51)

      1. Waterproofing. 2. Basements. I. Title.

352
(41)
U54
    U.K. Royal Commission on Local Government
    in England.
      Report, 1966-1969. London, H.M. Stationery
    Off., 1959.
      3v. in 6.
      (U.K. Parliament. Papers by command,
    cmnd. 4040)

      1. Local government - U.K.

VF
691.32
U54t
    U.K. Ministry of Public Building and Works.
      Testing concrete. 2d ed. London, H.M.S.O.,
    1970.
      folder. (Its Advisory leaflet no. 43)

      1. Concrete. I. Title.

VF
551.5
U54
    U.K. Ministry of Public Building and Works.
      Weather and the builder. 5th ed. London,
    H.M.S.O., 1970.
      folder. (Advisory leaflet no. 40)

      1. Weather. 2. Architecture and climate.
    I. Title.

352
(41)
U54w
    U.K. Royal Commission on Local Government in
    England.
      Written evidence of the Ministry of Housing
    and Local Government. London, H.M.S.O., 1967.
      80p. (S.O. code no. 73-44-5)

      1. Local government - U.K. 2. Municipal
    services - U.K. 3. U.K. Ministry of Housing
    and Local Government. I. Title.

699.86
U54
    U.K. Ministry of Public Building and Works.
      Thermal insulation. London, H.M.S.O., 1968.
      folder. (Its Advisory leaflet 34)

      1. Insulating materials. I. Title.

721.4
(41)
M17
    U.K. Ministry of Public Buildings and Works.

Laf.
    Martin, Leslie.
      Whitehall; a plan for the national and
    government centre, by Leslie Martin. Accom-
    panied by a report on traffic, by Colin
    Buchanan. London, H.M.S.O., 1965.
      171p.
      At head of title: Ministry of Public Build-
    ing and Works.
      1. City planning - U.K. 2. Public build-
    ings - U.K. I. Buchanan, Colin. A report on
    traffic. II. U.K. Ministry of Public Build-
    ing and Works. III. Title.

670
(41)
W67
    U.K. Royal Commission on the Geographical
      Distribution of the Industrial Population.
    U.S. Works Progress Administration.
      Planning - localisation of industry -
    depressed areas - housing - unemployment -
    financing - government - planning. Royal Com-
    mission on the Geographical Distribution of the
    Industrial Population. Minutes of Evidence,
    1937-1938, a summary. Wash., 1938.
      53p. (Its Research library abstracts. Item
    554 foreign.
      1. Industry - U.K. 2. Industrial location -
    U.K. 3. Economic conditions - U.K. 4. Housing -
    U.K. 5. Planning - U.K. 6. New towns - U.K.
    I. U.K. Royal Commission on the Geograph-
    ical Distribution of the Industrial
    Population. II. Title.

389.1
U54
    U.K. Ministry of Public Building and Works.
      Think metric. London, H.M.S.O., 1969.
      [6] p.
      Cl/SfB (F7)
      Leaflet suggests guide lines for learning
    and appreciating metric units of measurements.

      1. Metric system. 2. Building industry -
    U.K. I. Title.

VF
595.7
U54
    U.K. Ministry of Public Building and Works.
      Woodworm. 3d ed. London, H.M.S.O., 1970.
      folder. (Advisory leaflet no. 42)

      1. Insects. 2. Wood preservation.
    I. Title.

331
(41)
U54
    U.K. Royal Commission on Trade Unions and
      Employers' Associations.
      Two studies in industrial relations. 1.
    The position of women in industry, by Nancy
    Seear. 2. Changing wage payment systems, by
    Robert B. McKersie. London, H.M.S.O., 1968.
      66p. (Its Research papers 11)

      1. Employment - U.K. 2. U.K. - Employment.
    3. Wage incentives - U.K. 4. U.K. - Wage in-
    centives. 5. Labor relations - U.K. 6. U.K. -
    Labor relations. I. Title: Women in industry.
    II. Seear, Nancy, jt. au. III. McKersie,
    Robert B., jt. au.

VF
694.1
U54t
    U.K. Ministry of Public Building and Works.
      Timber sizes for small buildings; part two.
    2d ed. London, H.M.S.O., 1970.
      folder. (Its Advisory leaflet no. 56)

      1. Wood construction. I. Title.

    U.K. Ministry of Public Building and Works.
    Committee on the Application of Computers in
    the Construction Industry.

        see

    U.K. Ministry of Public Building and Works.

VF
720
(41)
U54
    U.K. Royal Fine Art Commission.
      Report,
    London, H.M. Stat. Off.,
      v. (Gt. Brit. Parliament. Papers by
    command)
      Irregular.

      For complete information see shelf list.

      1. Architecture - U.K. 2. Public works -
    U.K.

002
(1690
U54
    U.K. Ministry of Public Building and Works.
      The use of information in the construction
    industry; a study of twenty five firms.
    London, Ministry of Public Building and Works,
    Directorate of Research and Information,
    1968.
      47p. (R & D paper Cl/Sfb (Algm))

      1. Building documentation. I. Title.

VF
325.2
U54
    U.K. Race Relations Board.
      Discrimination and you. London, 1967.
      folder.

      1. Race relations. I. Title.

690.591
U54b
    U.K. Dept. of Scientific and
      Industrial Research.
      Building research; repair of damaged
    buildings notes. London, 1945-1946.
      v.

      1. Houses - maintenance and
    modernization. I. Title.

690.015
U54   U.K. Dept. of Scientific and Industrial
    Research.
      The Building Research Station, its history,
  organisation and work, by F. M. Lea. London,
  1959.
    12p.   illus.

    "Originally published in The Financial Times,
  Supplement on the Building Industry, 14th July,
  1958.

  1. Building research - U.K.   2. U.K. Building Research Station.   I. Lea, F. M.

624.2
U54D   UNITED KINGDOM. DEPT. OF SCIENTIFIC AND
    INDUSTRIAL RESEARCH.
    DYNAMIC STRESSES IN CAST IRON GIRDER
  BRIDGES, BY C.R. MITCHELL. LONDON, H.M.
  STATIONERY OFF., 1954.
    58P.   (ITS NATIONAL BUILDING STUDIES
  RESEARCH PAPER NO. 19)

    1. BRIDGES.   2. STRAINS AND STRESSES.
  I. MITCHELL, C.R.   II. TITLE.

VF
690   U.K. Dept. of Scientific and Industrial Re-
(41)   search.
U541   Incentives in building; how target bonus
  schemes operate. London, 1959.
    16p.   diagrs.

  1. Building industry - U.K.   2. Labor productivity.

691.42
U54CL   U.K. DEPT. OF SCIENTIFIC AND
    INDUSTRIAL RESEARCH.
    CLAY BUILDING BRICKS; THEIR
  MANUFACTURE, PROPERTIES AND TESTING
  WITH NOTES ON EFFICIENCY OF BRICKWORK,
  BY B. BUTTERWORTH. LONDON, H.M.
  STATIONERY OFF., 1948.
    24P.   (ITS NATIONAL BUILDING STUDIES
  BULLETIN NO. 1)

    1. BRICKS.   2. CLAY.
  I. BUTTERWORTH, B.

699.81
U54e   U.K. Dept. of Scientific and Industrial
    Research.
    Effect of draughts on the burning of
  portable oil heaters. London, H.M. Stat.
  Off., 1960.
    12p.   illus., diagrs., tables.

    Attached: Articles from London
  Times, Mar. 9, 10, 11, 1960.

  1. Fire prevention.

691.018.44
U54   U.K. DEPT. OF SCIENTIFIC AND
    INDUSTRIAL RESEARCH.
    INVESTIGATIONS ON BUILDING FIRES.
  LONDON, H.M. STATIONERY OFF., 1951.
  4 PTS. IN 3 V.   (ITS NATIONAL
  BUILDING STUDIES TECHNICAL PAPER
  NOS. 4, 5, 6)

    1. BUILDING MATERIALS, FIREPROOF.

VF
690.37   Great Britain. Department of Scientific and
F71   Industrial Research.
T1949   Gt. Brit. Ministry of Supply.
    Conservation des matériaux en zones tropicales.
  [Paris, France] Centre Scientifique et Technique du
  Bâtiment, Service de l'Habitat Intertropical, 1949.
    58 l.   (France. Centre Scientifique et Tech-
  rique du Bâtiment. Service de l'Habitat Intertropi-
  cal. Traductions.)

    English title: Tropic proofing.
    Mimeographed.
  1.Building materials-Tropics. 2.Termites. I.Gt. Brit
  Dept. of Scientific and Industrial Research. II.Ser

691.771
U54   U.K. DEPT. OF SCIENTIFIC AND
    INDUSTRIAL RESEARCH.
    EFFECT OF EMBEDDING ALUMINUM AND
  ALUMINUM ALLOYS IN BUILDING MATERIALS,
  BY F.E. JONES AND R.D. TARLETON.
  LONDON, H.M. STAT. OFF., 1963.
    62P.   (ITS NATIONAL BUILDING
  STUDIES, RESEARCH PAPER NO. 36)

    1. ALUMINUM.   I. JONES, F.E.
  II. TARLETON, R.D., JT. AU.

624.131
D85I   U.K. DEPT. OF SCIENTIFIC AND
    INDUSTRIAL RESEARCH.
    DUMBLETON, M J
    INVESTIGATIONS TO ASSESS THE
  POTENTIALITIES OF LIME FOR SOIL
  STABILIZATION IN THE UNITED KINGDOM.
  LONDON, H.M. STATIONERY OFF., 1962.
    76P.   (DEPT. OF SCIENTIFIC AND
  INDUSTRIAL RESEARCH. ROAD RESEARCH
  LABORATORY. ROAD RESEARCH TECHNICAL
  PAPER NO. 64)

    1. SOILS.   I. U.K. DEPT. OF
  SCIENTIFIC AND INDUSTRIAL RESEARCH.
  II. TITLE: L IME FOR SOIL
  STABILIZATION .

691.7
:620.19   U.K. DEPT. OF SCIENTIFIC AND
U54   INDUSTRIAL RESEARCH.
    THE CORROSION OF STEEL IN STEEL
  HOUSES; AN EXAMINATION OF THE
  CORROSION OF STEELWORK IN STEEL-CLAD
  AND STEEL-FRAMED HOUSES. LONDON, H.M.
  STAT. OFF., 1951.
    29P.   (ITS NATIONAL BUILDING STUDIES
  SPECIAL REPORT NO. 16)

    1. CORROSION.   2. STEEL
  CONSTRUCTION.

690.22
U54E   U.K. DEPT. OF SCIENTIFIC AND
    INDUSTRIAL RESEARCH.
    EXTERNAL RENDERED FINISHES FOR WALLS
  BY G.F. BESSEY. LONDON, H.M.
  STATIONERY OFF., 1951.
    24P.   (ITS NATIONAL BUILDING STUDIES
  BULLETIN NO. 10)

    1. WALLS.   I. BESSEY, G.F.

621.32
U54l   U.K. Dept. of Scientific and Industrial Re-
    search.
    Lighting of dwellings; an inquiry carried out
  for the Committee on the Lighting of Buildings
  of the Dept. of Scientific and Industrial Research, by Dennis Chapman. [London] 1943.
    48p.   (New series no. 24)
    At head of title: Wartime social survey.

  1. Lighting. I. Chapman, Dennis. II. Title.

697
G72   Great Britain. Department of Scientific and
    Industrial Research.
  Gt. Brit. Ministry of Fuel and Power.
    Domestic heating in America; a study of
  heating, cooking and hot water supply in small
  houses in U. S. A. and Canada. Report of a
  Joint Party from the Ministry of Fuel and Power
  and the Department of Scientific and Industrial
  Research. London, H. M. Stationery Off., 1946.
    x, 152 p.   illus., diagrs., graphs, tables.

    Bibliography: p. 126-148.
    Committee composed of J. C. Pritchard,
  Ministry of Fuel and Power; C. C. Handisyde,
  Building Research Station; R. H. Rowse, Fuel
  Research Station.   (Continued on next card)

690.25
U54F   U.K. DEPT. OF SCIENTIFIC AND
    INDUSTRIAL RESEARCH.
    FLOOR FINISHES FOR HOUSES AND OTHER
  NON-INDUSTRIAL BUILDINGS, BY H.M.
  LLEWELLYN AND F.C. HARPER. LONDON,
  H.M. STAT. OFF., 1950.
    25P.   (ITS NATIONAL BUILDING STUDIES
  BULLETIN NO. 11)

    1. FLOORS AND FLOORING.
  I. LLEWELLYN, H.M.   II. HARPER, F.C.

691.322
L21   U.K. DEPT. OF SCIENTIFIC AND
    INDUSTRIAL RESEARCH.
    LEA, F M
    LIGHTWEIGHT CONCRETE AGGREGATES.
  REV. ED. LONDON, H.M. STAT. OFF.,
  1944.
    13P.   (U.K. DEPT. OF SCIENTIFIC
  AND INDUSTRIAL RESEARCH. BUILDING
  RESEARCH BULLETIN NO. 15)

    1. CONCRETE AGGREGATES.   I. U.K.
  DEPT. OF SCIENTIFIC AND INDUSTRIAL
  RESEARCH.   II. TITLE.

    Gt. Brit. Ministry of Fuel and Power.
    Domestic heating in America ... 1946.   (Card 2)

    Description of research at sixteen
  laboratories: p. 83-94.

  1.Heating. 2.Heating-Canada. 3.Heating research.
  I.Gt. Brit. Building Research Station. II.Gt.
  Brit. Dept. of Scientific and Industrial Research.
  III.Title.

DATE OF REQUEST 12/18/53   L. C. CARD NO.

AUTHOR   U.K. Dept. of Scientific and Industrial Research.
    Forest Products Research.
TITLE   Dry rot in buildings: recognition, prevention and
    cure.

SERIES   Leaflet no. 6.

| EDITION | PUB. DATE [1947] | PAGING 8 p. |
| PUBLISHER | | |

| RECOMMENDED BY | REVIEWED IN Ohio Lib Acc List no. 87 |
| | ~5/53 p. 25 |
    ORDER RECORD

(handwritten order card)

Class No.   Author (Surname first)   NOT RUSH
    Gt. Britain. Dept of Sci + Indus Res.
Accession No.   Title   List of publications of the Depart
    ment of Scientific and Indus-
Ordered 6-1-49   trial Research.
Of   Write to SalesDept., British Info Serv
Received 6-9-49   Edition or Series   Place   Publisher

600.15
(41)   U.K. Dept. of Scientific and Industrial Research.
U54co   Combining for research, the work of the
  grant-aided industrial research organizations. London, H. M. Stationery Office
  [1962?]
    31p.

    1. Industrial research - U.K.
    2. Cooperative research.

VF
690.015   U.K. Dept. of Scientific and Industrial
(41:016)   Research.
U542   Government publications. Rev. London,
1964   H.M. Stationery Office, 1964.
    1v.   (Its Sectional list no. 3, rev.)

    1. Building research - U.K. - Bibl.
    2. Scientific research - U.K. - Bibl.
    3. Industrial research - U.K. - Bibl.

691.54
U541   U.K. SCIENTIFIC AND INDUSTRIAL
    RESEARCH DEPARTMENT.
    MORTAR FOR BRICKWORK, BLOCK
  CONSTRUCTION AND MASONRY, BY H.
  ANDREWS. LONDON, H.M. STATIONERY
  OFF., 1950.
    12P.   (ITS NATIONAL BUILDING STUDIES
  BULLETIN NO. 8)

    1. CEMENT.   I. TITLE.   II. ANDREWS,
  H.

690.512.2
(4)
U54

UNITED KINGDOM. DEPT. OF SCIENTIFIC
AND INDUSTRIAL RESEARCH.
ORGANIZATION OF BUILDING SITES
(EUROPEAN PRODUCTIVITY AGENCY
PROJECT NO. 302-1) BY R.C. SANSOM.
LONDON, H.M. STATIONERY OFF., 1960,
I.E., 1959.
186P. (ITS NATIONAL BUILDING AND
STUDIES SPECIAL REPORT NO. 29)

1. SITE SELECTION - EUROPE.
2. BUILDING INDUSTRY - EUROPE.
I. SANSOM, R.C.

VF
690.015
(41)
G72

Gt. Brit. Dept. of Scientific and Industrial
Research. Building Research Board.
Report of the Building Research Board, with
the report of the Director of Building Research
for the years 1939-6769
London, H.M. Stationery Office, 19
29. illus.
Cover title: Building research.
Includes lists of publications.
For full information see shelf list card.
1.Building research-Gt. Brit. I.Gt. Brit. Building
Research Station.

690
(41)
B34S
PT.1

U.K. DEPT. OF SCIENTIFIC AND INDUSTRIAL
RESEARCH.
STUDIES IN COMPOSITE CONSTRUCTION. PT.
I. THE COMPOSITE ACTION OF BRICK PANEL
WALLS SUPPORTED ON REINFORCED CONCRETE
BEAMS, BY R.H. WOOD. LONDON, H.M.
STAT. OFF., 1952.
25P. (ITS NATIONAL BUILDING STUDIES.
RESEARCH PAPER NO. 13)

1. WALLS. 2. BRICK CONSTRUCTION.
3. CONCRETE, REINFORCED. I. WOOD, R.H.
II. TITLE: BRICK PANEL WALLS.

690.22
U54P

U.K. DEPT. OF SCIENTIFIC AND
INDUSTRIAL RESEARCH.
PARTY WALLS BETWEEN HOUSES; THEIR
FIRE RESISTANCE AND SOUND INSULATION,
BY R.C. BEVAN AND W.A. ALLEN.
LONDON, H.M. STATIONERY OFF., 1949.
53P. (ITS NATIONAL BUILDING STUDIES
SPECIAL REPORT NO. 5)

1. WALLS. 2. SOUNDPROOFING.
3. FIRE PROTECTION. I. BEVAN, R.C.
II. ALLEN, W.A., JT. AU. III. TITLE.

691.328
U54R

U.K. DEPT. OF SCIENTIFIC AND
INDUSTRIAL RESEARCH.
RESISTANCE OF REINFORCED CONCRETE
STRUCTURES TO AIR ATTACK. LONDON,
H.M. STATIONERY OFF., 1941.
9P. (BUILDING RESEARCH. WARTIME
BUILDING BULLETIN NO. 17)

1. CONCRETE, REINFORCED.
2. PROTECTIVE CONSTRUCTION. I. TITLE.

690
(41)
B34S
PT.2

U.K. DEPT. OF SCIENTIFIC AND INDUSTRIAL
RESEARCH.
STUDIES IN COMPOSITE CONSTRUCTION. PT.
II. THE INTERACTION OF FLOORS AND BEAMS
IN MULTI-STORY BUILDINGS, BY R.H. WOOD.
LONDON, H.M. STAT. OFF., 1955.
124P. (ITS NATIONAL BUILDING STUDIES.
RESEARCH PAPER NO. 22)

1. FLOORS AND FLOORING. 2. TRUSSES.
I. WOOD, R.H.

691.328.2
U542

U.K. DEPT. OF SCIENTIFIC AND
INDUSTRIAL RESEARCH.
PLANT FOR PRESTRESSING CONCRETE.
LONDON, H.M. STATIONERY OFF., 1951.
7P. (NATIONAL BUILDING STUDIES
BULLETIN NO. 12)

1. CONCRETE, PRESTRESSED.
I. TITLE.

691.42
U548

UNITED KINGDOM. DEPT. OF SCIENTIFIC
AND INDUSTRIAL RESEARCH.
SAND-LIME AND CONCRETE BRICKS, BY
G.E. BESSEY. LONDON, H.M. STATIONERY
OFF., 1948.
12P. (ITS NATIONAL BUILDING STUDIES
BULLETIN NO. 4)

1. BRICKS. 2. CONCRETE.
I. BESSEY, G.E. II. TITLE.

624.2
U54

UNITED KINGDOM. DEPT. OF SCIENTIFIC AND
INDUSTRIAL RESEARCH.
STUDIES ON BRIDGE-DECK SYSTEMS. I.
TESTS ON A MODEL JACK-ARCH SLAB, BY A.
SHORT AND R.I. LEWIS, LONDON, H.M.
STATIONERY OFF., 1955.
70P. (ITS NATIONAL BUILDING STUDIES
RESEARCH PAPER NO. 21)

1. BRIDGES. 2. STRAINS AND STRESSES.
I. SHORT, A. II. LEWIS, R.

690
(41)
U54PR

UNITED KINGDOM. DEPT. OF SCIENTIFIC AND
INDUSTRIAL RESEARCH.
PRINCIPLES OF MODERN BUILDING.
LONDON, H.M. STATIONERY OFF., 1961-62.
2 V.

VOL. 1, 3D ED., 1959 (1962 REPRINT);
V. 2, 1ST ED., 1961.

1. BUILDING CONSTRUCTION - UNITED
KINGDOM. I. TITLE.

500.15
U54sc

U.K. Dept. of Scientific and Industrial Research
Scientific research in British universities,
1951-52. London, H. M. Stationery Off., 1953.
485 p.

1.Research-U.K. I.Title.

690.031
(41)
U54S

U.K. DEPT. OF SCIENTIFIC AND
INDUSTRIAL RESEARCH.
A STUDY OF ALTERNATIVE METHODS OF
HOUSE CONSTRUCTION. LONDON, H.M.
STATIONERY OFF., 1959.
92P. (NATIONAL BUILDING STUDIES.
SPECIAL REPORT NO. 30)

1. BUILDING COSTS - U.K.
2. PREFABRICATED CONSTRUCTION - U.K.
3. BUILDING CONSTRUCTION - U.K.

690
(41)
U54PRO

U.K. DEPT. OF SCIENTIFIC AND
INDUSTRIAL RESEARCH.
PRODUCTIVITY IN HOUSE-BUILDING.
SECOND REPORT, BY W.J. REINERS AND
H.F. BROUGHTON. LONDON, H.M.
STATIONERY OFF., 1953.
37P. (ITS NATIONAL BUILDING STUDIES
SPECIAL REPORT NO. 21)

1. BUILDING CONSTRUCTION - U.K.
2. BUILDING COSTS - U.K. I. REINERS,
W.J. II. BROUGHTON, H.F.

696.92
U54

U.K. Dept. of Scientific and Industrial
Research.
Simplified daylight tables (tables for the
quick estimating of direct and indirect daylight in buildings lit by vertically glazed
windows) by R. G. Hopkinson and others.
London, 1958.
24p. tables, diagrs. (Its National building
studies special report no. 26)

1.Daylight. I.Hopkinson, R. G. II.Graham, A
Murray.

624
U54S

UNITED KINGDOM. DEPT. OF SCIENTIFIC AND
INDUSTRIAL RESEARCH.
A STUDY OF THE VOUSSOIR ARCH, BY A.J.
SUTTON PIPPARD AND LETITIA CHITTY.
LONDON, H.M. STATIONERY OFF., 1951.
52P. (ITS NATIONAL BUILDING STUDIES
RESEARCH PAPER NO. 11)

1. STRUCTURAL ENGINEERING.
I. PIPPARD, A.J. SUTTON. II. CHITTY,
LETITIA. III. TITLE: VOUSSOIR ARCH.

691
(41)
U54Q

U.K. DEPT. OF SCIENTIFIC AND INDUSTRIAL
RESEARCH.
A QUALITATIVE STUDY OF SOME BUILDIN-
IN THE LONDON AREA, BY S.B. HAMILTON AND
OTHERS. LONDON, H.M. STATIONERY OFF.,
1964.
165P. (ITS NATIONAL BUILDING STUDIES
SPECIAL REPORT 33)

1. BUILDING MATERIALS - U.K. - LONDON.
2. BUILDING CONSTRUCTION - U.K. - LONDON.
I. HAMILTON, S.B. II. TITLE.

699.844
F37

U.K. Department of Scientific and Industrial
Research.
Fitzmaurice, R
Sound transmission in buildings; practical
notes for architects and builders, by R. Fitz-
maurice and William Allen. London, H. M.
Stationery Off., 1939.
48 p. illus., diagrs.
At head of title: Department of Scientific
and Industrial Research.
1.Soundproofing. I.Allen, William, jt. au. II.U.K.
Dept. of Scientific and Industrial Research.
III.Title.

534.83
C31

U.K. DEPT. OF SCIENTIFIC AND
INDUSTRIAL RESEARCH.
CHAPMAN, DENNIS.
A SURVEY OF NOISE IN BRITISH HOMES.
LONDON, H.M. STATIONERY OFF., 1948.
34P. (DEPT. OF SCIENTIFIC AND
INDUSTRIAL RESEARCH. NATIONAL BUILDING
STUDIES TECHNICAL PAPER NO. 2)

1. NOISE. I. U.K. DEPT. OF
SCIENTIFIC AND INDUSTRIAL RESEARCH.

500.15
U54
R

U.K. Dept. of Scientific and Industrial
Research.
Report for the year
London, H.M. Stationery Off.,
v. (Cmd.

1. Research - U.K.

690
(41)
U54STU

UNITED KINGDOM. DEPT. OF SCIENTIFIC
AND INDUSTRIAL RESEARCH.
STRUCTURAL REQUIREMENTS FOR HOUSES,
BY F.G. THOMAS. LONDON, H.M.
STATIONERY OFF., 1948.
8P. (ITS NATIONAL BUILDING STUDIES
SPECIAL REPORT NO. 1)

1. BUILDING CONSTRUCTION - UNITED
KINGDOM. 2. STRUCTURAL ENGINEERING.
I. THOMAS, F.G. II. TITLE.

624.2
U54T

UNITED KINGDOM. DEPT. OF SCIENTIFIC AND
INDUSTRIAL RESEARCH.
TEST ON ROAD BRIDGES, BY NORMAN DAVEY.
LONDON, H.M. STATIONERY OFF., 1953.
34P. (ITS NATIONAL BUILDING STUDIES
RESEARCH PAPER NO. 16)

1. BRIDGES. I. DAVEY, NORMAN.
II. TITLE: ROAD BRIDGES.

16

674
U54T   U.K. DEPT. OF SCIENTIFIC AND INDUSTRIAL
     RESEARCH.
     TESTING OF STRUCTURAL TIMBERS, POLES AND
     PIT-PROPS, BY J.G. SUNLEY. LONDON, H.M.
     STAT. OFF., 1963.
     4P. (ITS FOREST PRODUCTS RESEARCH
     SPECIAL REPORT NO. 19)

     1. LUMBER INDUSTRY.   I. SUNLEY, J.G.
     II. TITLE: STRUCTURE TIMBER

600.15
(41)
E28   United Kingdom. Department of Scientific
       and Industrial Research.
    Edwards, Ronald Stanley.
     Co-operative industrial research; a study of the economic
   aspects of the research associations grant-aided by the Department of Scientific and Industrial Research. London,
   Pitman [1950]
     xiv, 285 p. 23 cm.   tables

     1. Research, Industrial. 2. Gt. Brit. Dept. of Scientific and Indus-
   trial Research.   I. Title.

     T177.G7E3   607   50—33533

     Library of Congress   [51c1]

     U.K. Dept. of Scientific and Industrial
     Research. Building Research Station.

     see

     U.K. Building Research Station.

     Gt. Brit. Department of Scientific and Indus-
     trial Research. Forest Products Research
     Laboratory.

     see

     Gt. Brit. Forest Products Research Laboratory.

     U.K. Secretary of State for Scotland.

     see

     Scotland. Secretary of State.

330
(41)
U54s   U.K. South East Economic Planning Council.
     A strategy for the South East. A first
     report. London, H.M.S.O., 1967.
     100p. (Maps on verso of back cover)

     1. City planning - U.K. 2. Metropolitan area
     planning - U.K. 3. Population - U.K.
     4. Employment - U.K. I. Title.

VF
728.1
(41:016)   U.K. H.M. STATIONERY OFFICE.
U54   GOVERNMENT PUBLICATIONS: MINISTRY
1964   OF HOUSING AND LOCAL GOVERNMENT.
     REV. LONDON 1964.
     25P. (ITS SECTIONAL LIST NO. 5,
     REV. TO 29TH FEBRUARY, 1964)

     1. HOUSING - U.K. - BIBLIOGRAPHY.
     2. CITY PLANNING - U.K. -
     BIBLIOGRAPHY. I. U.K. MINISTRY OF
     HOUSING AND LOCAL GOVERNMENT.

VF
016
(354:41)   U.K. H.M. Stationery Office.
U54   Government publications: official indexes,
     lists, guides, catalogues. London, 1955.
     13 p.

     1. U.K. - Publications.

711.3
(41)
U54s   U.K. H.M. Stationery Office.
     South East England. Presented to
     Parliament by the Secretary of State for
     Industry, Trade and Regional Development,
     and the Minister of Housing and Local
     Government and Minister for Welsh Affairs
     by Command of Her Majesty. London, 1964.
     7p. (Cmnd. 2308)

     1. Regional planning - U.K.
     2. Transportation - U.K.

VF
690.37
F71
T1949   Gt. Brit. Ministry of Supply.
     Conservation des matériaux en zones tropicales.
     [Paris, France] Centre Scientifique et Technique du
     Bâtiment, Service de l'Habitat Intertropical, 1949.
     58 l. (France. Centre Scientifique et Tech-
     nique du Bâtiment. Service de l'Habitat Intertropi-
     cal. Traductions.)
     English title: Tropic proofing.
     Mimeographed.
     1.Building materials-Tropics. 2.Termites. I.Gt. Brit
     Dept. of Scientific and Industrial Research. II.Ser

697
(43)
L65   Great Britain. Technical Information and
    Longworth, A   Leslie   Documents Unit.
     Heating, ventilating, & district heating in
     Germany.   London, Technical Information &
     Documents Unit [1947?]
     243 p.   illus., diagrs. (part fold.), tables
     (B.I.O.S. Final report no. 1820, item no. 33)

     1.Heating-Germany. 2.District heating. 3.Air
     conditioning-Germany. I.Gt. Brit. Technical
     Information & Documents Unit.

621.6
U54L   U.K. MINISTRY OF TECHNOLOGY.
     LOADING CHARTS FOR THE DESIGN OF
     BURIED RIGID PIPES, BY N.W.B. CLARKE.
     LONDON, H.M. STAT. OFF., 1966.
     33P. (ITS NATIONAL BUILDING STUDIES,
     SPECIAL REPORT NO. 37)

     1. PIPES.   I. CLARKE, N.W.B.

699.81
U54u   U.K. Ministry of Technology.
     United Kingdom fire statistics 1966-68;
     Statistical analysis of reports of fires
     attended by fire brigades in the United
     Kingdom during 1966-68
     London, H.M.S.O., 1968-1970.
     4 v.
     1. Fire protection. 2. Fire prevention -
     U.K. - Statistics. I. Title: Fire statistics.

672
U54
1967   U.K. Ministry of Technology and Fire Offices'
     Committee Joint Fire Research Organization.
     Behaviour of structural steel in fire.
     Proceedings of the symposium held at the Fire
     Research Station, Herts on 24th January, 1967.
     London, H.M.S.O., 1968.
     135p. (Its Symposium no. 2)

     1. Steel. 2. Building materials, Fire proof.
     I. Symposium on the Behaviour of Structural
     Steel in Fire, Herts, 1967. II. Title.

699.81
U54f   U.K. Ministry of Technology and Fire
     Offices' Committee. Joint Fire Research
     Organization.
     Fire and structural use of timber in
     buildings. Proceedings of the Symposium
     held at the Fire Research Station, Boreham
     Wood, Herts on 25th October, 1967. London,
     H.M.S.O., 1970.
     96p. (Symposium no. 3)

     1. Fire prevention. 2. Wood construction.
     I. Title.

699.81
U54fi   U.K. Ministry of Technology and Fire Offices
     Committee. Joint Fire Research Organization.
     Fire research: report of the Fire Research
     Steering Committee with report of the
     Director of Fire Research, 1969

     London, H.M.S.O., 19
     1 v.

     1. Fire prevention. I. Title.

699.81
R63   U.K. Ministry of Technology and Fire Offices'
     Committee. Joint Fire Research Organiza-
     tion.
    Rogowski, Barbara F   W
     The fire propagation test: its development
     and application. London, H.M.S.O., 1970.
     9p. (U.K. Ministry of Technology and Fire
     Offices' Committee. Joint Fire Research
     Organization. Fire research technical paper
     no. 25)

     1. Fire prevention. I. U.K. Ministry of
     Technology and Fire Offices' Committee. Joint
     Fire Research Organization. II. Title.

699.81
(016)
U54r   U.K. Ministry of Technology and Fire Offices'
     Committee. Joint Fire Research Organization.
     References to scientific literature on
     fire. Boreham Wood, Eng., Fire Research
     Station, 1963/4, '65-69.
     2v. (U.K. Ministry of Technology and
     Fire Offices' Committee. Joint Fire Research
     Organization. Library bibliography no. 5/Parts
     XV-XVI   XVIII-XIX, XX.)
     1.   prevention - Bibl. 2. Fireproof
     construction - Bibl.
     II. Title.

     U.K. Ministry of Technology and Fire Offices'
     Committee. Joint Fire Research Organization.
     United Kingdom fire and loss statistics, 19

     see

     U.K. Ministry of Technology.
     United Kingdom fire statistics, 19

     Gt. Brit. Ministry of Town and Country Planning.

     Name changed, January 1951, to:

     Gt. Brit. Ministry of Local Government and
     Planning.

     Name changed again, Nov. 1951, to:
     United Kingdom. Ministry of Housing and Local
         Government

     Gt. Brit. Ministry of Town and Country
     Planning.

     see also

     Gt. Brit. Ministry of Local Government and
     Planning.
     United Kingdom. Ministry of Housing and Local
         Government.

711.585
(41)
G72
1947
Gt. Brit. Ministry of Town and Country Planning.
Advisory handbook on the redevelopment of central areas.   London, H. M. Stationery Off., 1947.
99 p.   illus.

Cover title: The redevelopment of central areas.
Bibliography: leaf at the end.

1.Urban redevelopment-U.K. I.Title: Redevelopment of central areas.

711.417
(41)
U54RE
N8.1
U.K. MINISTRY OF TOWN AND COUNTRY PLANNING.
U.K. NEW TOWNS COMMITTEE.
INTERIM REPORT OF THE NEW TOWNS COMMITTEE ... LONDON, H.M. STAT. OFF., 1946.
21P. (U.K. PARLIAMENT. PAPERS BY COMMAND. CMD. 6759)

1. NEW TOWNS = U.K. I. U.K. MINISTRY OF TOWN AND COUNTRY PLANNING. II. SCOTLAND. DEPT. OF HEALTH.

711.417
(41)
U54RE
N8.2
U.K. MINISTRY OF TOWN AND COUNTRY PLANNING.
U.K. NEW TOWNS COMMITTEE.
SECOND INTERIM REPORT OF THE NEW TOWNS COMMITTEE ... LONDON, H.M. STAT. OFF., 1946.
25P. (U.K. PARLIAMENT. PAPERS BY COMMAND. CMD. 6794)

1. NEW TOWNS = U.K. I. U.K. MINISTRY OF TOWN AND COUNTRY PLANNING. III. SCOTLAND. DEPT. OF HEALTH.

728.3
(41)
U54
U.K. MINISTRY OF TOWN AND COUNTRY PLANNING.
U.K. MINISTRY OF HEALTH.
DESIGN OF DWELLINGS. REPORT OF THE DESIGN OF DWELLINGS SUB-COMMITTEE ON THE CENTRAL HOUSING ADVISORY COMMITTEE APPOINTED BY THE MINISTER OF HEALTH, AND REPORT OF A STUDY GROUP OF THE MINISTRY OF TOWN AND COUNTRY PLANNING ON SITE PLANNING AND LAYOUT IN RELATION TO HOUSING. LONDON, H.M. STAT. OFF., 1944.
75P.
1. ARCHITECTURE, DOMESTIC = DESIGNS AND PLANS = U.K. 2. SITE PLANNING. I. U.K. MINISTRY OF TOWN AND COUNTRY PLANNING.

M
Gt.Brit.
Gt. Brit. Ministry of Town and Country Planning.
Population, total changes 1921-1931.   Southampton, Gt. Brit. Ordnance Survey, 1949.
2 sheets col.

1.Population-Gt. Brit.-Maps. I.Scotland. Dept. of Health.

711.4
(41)
U54t
1947
U.K. Ministry of Town and Country Planning.
Town and country planning bill, explanatory memorandum, 1947. London, H.M. Stat. Off., 1947.
22p. (Cmd. 7006)

1. City planning - U.K. 2. Regional planning - U.K. I. Title.

M
Gt.Brit.
Gt. Brit. Ministry of Town and Country Planning.
Electricity, statutory supply areas.   Southampton, Gt. Brit. Ordnance Survey, 1946.
2 sheets col.

1.Public utilities-Gt. Brit.-Maps. I.Scotland. Dept. of Health.

M
Gt.Brit.
Gt. Brit. Ministry of Town and Country Planning.
Population change by migration: Scotland 1931-38; England and Wales 1931-39.   Southampton, Gt. Brit. Ordnance Survey, 1949.
2 sheets col.

1.Population-Gt. Brit.-Maps. I.Scotland. Dept. of Health.

308
(421)
H87
Great Britain. Ministry of Town and Country Planning.
Hutchinson, Bertram A
Willesden and the new towns; an inquiry carried out for the Ministry of Town and Country Planning in the winter of 1946-1947, to obtain social data relevant to the establishment of new towns and to the replanning of the borough of Willesden. [London?] 1947.
ii, 126 p. maps, diagrs. 33 cm. (The social survey, n. s. 88)
Cover title.
1. Willesden, Eng.—Soc. condit. 2. Cities and towns—Planning—Gt. Brit. i. Gt. Brit. Ministry of Town and Country Planning. (Series: Gt. Brit. Central Office of Information. Social Survey Division. The social survey, new ser. 88)

HN398.W55H8   51-35862

Library of Congress   [3]

711.417
(41)
U54RE
N8.3
U.K. MINISTRY OF TOWN AND COUNTRY PLANNING.
U.K. NEW TOWNS COMMITTEE.
FINAL REPORT OF THE NEW TOWNS COMMITTEE ... LONDON, H.M. STAT. OFF., 1946.
83P. (U.K. PARLIAMENT. PAPERS BY COMMAND. CMD. 6876)

LIST OF GOVERNMENT PUBLICATIONS OF INTEREST IN THE DEVELOPMENT OF NEW TOWNS : P. 72-74.
1. NEW TOWNS = U.K. I. U.K. MINISTRY OF TOWN AND COUNTRY PLANNING. II. SCOTLAND. DEPT. OF HEALTH.

M
Gt.Brit.
Gt. Brit. Ministry of Town and Country Planning.
Population changes by migration, 1921-31. Southampton, Gt. Brit. Ordnance Survey, 1949.
2 sheets col.

1.Population-Gt. Brit.-Maps. I.Scotland. Dept. of Health.

728.1
+352
(41)
U54
R1943-51
Gt. Brit. Ministry of Town and Country Planning.
United Kingdom. Ministry of Local Government and Planning.
Town and country planning, 1943-1951; progress report by the Minister of Local Government and Planning on the work of the Ministry of Town and Country Planning. London, H.M.Stationery Off., 1951.
vii, 215 p. maps (part fold.), tables.
Bibliographical footnotes.
1.Gt. Brit. Ministry of Town and Country Planning. 2.New towns-U.K.

711.3
(421)
A12
1944
U.K. MINISTRY OF TOWN AND COUNTRY PLANNING.
ABERCROMBIE, PATRICK.
GREATER LONDON PLAN 1944. A REPORT PREPARED ON BEHALF OF THE STANDING CONFERENCE ON LONDON REGIONAL PLANNING BY PROFESSOR ABERCROMBIE AT THE REQUEST OF THE MINISTER OF TOWN AND COUNTRY PLANNING. PRELIM. ED. LONDON, H.M. STAT. OFF., 1944.
217P.

1. CITY PLANNING = U.K. = LONDON.
1. REGIONAL PLANNING = U.K.
I. STANDING CONFERENCE ON LONDON REGIONAL PLANNING. II. U.K.
(CONTINUED ON NEXT CARD)

M
Gt.Brit.
Gt. Brit. Ministry of Town and Country Planning.
Population of urban areas.   Southampton, Gt. Brit. Ordnance Survey, 1945.
2 sheets col.

1.Population-Gt. Brit.-Maps.

FOLIO
647.1
U547
U.K. BOARD OF TRADE.
COST OF LIVING IN AMERICAN TOWNS: REPORT OF AN INQUIRY BY THE BOARD OF TRADE INTO WORKING CLASS RENTS, HOUSING AND RETAIL PRICES, TOGETHER WITH THE RATES OF WAGES IN CERTAIN OCCUPATIONS IN THE PRINCIPAL INDUSTRIAL TOWNS OF THE UNITED STATES OF AMERICA ... LONDON, H.M. STAT. OFF., 1911.
533P. (U.K. PARLIMENT. PAPERS BY COMMAND. CD. 5609)

1. COST AND STANDARD OF LIVING.
2. WAGES AND SALARIES.

711.3
(421)
A12
1944
ABERCROMBIE, PATRICK. GREATER LONDON PLAN ... 1944.   (CARD 2)
MINISTRY OF TOWN AND COUNTRY PLANNING.
III. TITLE.

M
Gt.Brit.
Gt. Brit. Ministry of Town and Country Planning.
Railways.   Southampton, Gt. Brit. Ordnance Survey, 1946.
2 sheets col.

1.Railroads-Gt. Brit.-Maps. I.Scotland. Dept. of Health.

699.81
U54m
U.K. Dept. of Trade and Industry.
Movement of smoke on escape routes in buildings. Proceedings of the Symposium held at Watford College of Technology, Watford, Herts, 9th and 10th April, 1969. London, H.M.S.O., 1971.
125p. (Symposium no. 4)
At head of title: Dept. of Trade and Industry and Fire Offices' Committee Joint Fire Research Organization.
1. Fire prevention. I. U.K. Joint Fire Research Organization. II. Title. III. Title: Smoke.

Gt. Brit. Ministry of town and country planning
Abercrombie, Patrick, 1879–
Greater London plan 1944, by Patrick Abercrombie ... A report prepared on behalf of the Standing conference on London regional planning by Professor Abercrombie at the request of the minister of town and country planning. London, H. M. Stationery off., 1945.
x, 220, [1] p. incl. illus., tables, plates (part col.) maps (part fold.) plans (part col. part fold.) diagrs. 32]".
Two colored folded plans in pocket.
A continuation of County of London plan, prepared for the London County council by J. H. Forshaw and Patrick Abercrombie, 1943.
1. Cities and towns—Planning—London. 2. Regional planning—London. i. Standing conference on London regional planning. ii. Gt. Brit. Ministry of town and country planning. iii. Title.
[Full name: Leslie Patrick Abercrombie]
Harvard univ. Library   A 45-5284
for Library of Congress   NA9188.L7A6
[7]   711.0942

M
Gt. Brit.
Gt. Brit. Ministry of Town and Country Planning.
Roads. Southampton, Gt. Brit. Ordnance Survey, 1946.
2 sheets col.

1.Highways-U.K. - Maps.

368
(41)
U54a
U.K. Ministry of Transport. (Scottish Development Dept.)
Advisory memorandum on urban traffic engineering techniques. London, H.M.S.O., 1965.
92p.
Reprinted 1966.

1. Traffic - U.K. 2. Traffic safety. I. Title. II. Title: Traffic engineering techniques.

388
(41)
U54b

U.K. Ministry of Transport.
Better use of town roads: the report of a study of the means of restraint of traffic on urban roads. London, H.M.S.O., 1967.
50p.

1. Traffic - U.K. 2. Highways - U.K.
I. Title.

711.585
(41)
U54

U.K. Ministry of Transport.
U.K. Ministry of Housing and Local Government.
Town centres approach to renewal. [In cooperation with] Ministry of Transport. London, H.M. Stat. Office, 1962.
21p. (Its Planning bulletin 1)

1. Urban renewal - U.K. I. Title.
II. U.K. Ministry of Transport.

354
(41)
C25
no.2

Laf.

U.K. Treasury.
Lewis, B N
Flow charts, logical trees and algorithms for rules and regulations, by B. N. Lewis and others. [Prepared in cooperation with] H.M. Treasury. London, H.M.S.O., 1967.
27p. (CAS (Centre for Administrative Studies) occasional paper no.2)
1. Public administration - U.K. 2. Office procedures. 3. Management - Automation. I. U.K. Treasury. II. Title.

388
(41)
U54c

U.K. Ministry of Transport.
Cars for cities. A study of trends in the design of vehicles with particular reference to their use in towns. Reports of the Steering Group and Working Group appointed by the Minister of Transport. London, H.M.S.O., 1967.
107p.

1. Transportation - U.K. 2. Traffic.
3. Air pollution. I. Title.

711.552
(41)
U54t

U.K. Ministry of Transport.
U.K. Ministry of Housing and Local Government.
Town centres; current practice. [Prepared in cooperation with] the Ministry of Transport. London, H.M. Stationery Off., 1963.
1v. (Its Planning bulletin 4)

1. Business districts - U.K. 2. City planning - U.K. 3. Urban renewal - U.K. I. U.K. Ministry of Transport. II. Title.

354
(41)
C25
no.4

Laf.

U.K. Treasury.
Williams, Alan.
Output budgeting and the contribution of micro-economics to efficiency in government. [Prepared in cooperation with] H.M. Treasury. London, H.M.S.O., 1967.
18p. (CAS(Center for Administrative Studies) occasional paper no. 4)

1. Public administration - U.K. 2. Finance - U.K. I. U.K. Treasury. II. Title.

711.729
(41)
U54P

U.K. Ministry of Transport.
Parking, the next stage. A new look by the Ministry of Transport at London's parking problem: July 1963. London, H.M.S.O., 1963.
47p.

1. Parking - U.K. 2. Traffic regulations - U.K. I. Title.

388
(41)
U54

U.K. Ministry of Transport.
Traffic in towns; a study of the long term problems of traffic in urban areas. Report of the Steering Group and Working Group appointed by the Minister of Transport. London, H.M. Stat. Off., 1963.
223p.

Report of Working Group in the Ministry is led by Colin D. Buchanan.

1. Traffic - U.K. 2. Parking - U.K. 3. Transportation - U.K. 4. Journey to work. I. Buchanan (Colin D.) Report.

333.32
(41)
T36

U.K. WELSH LAND COMMISSION.
THOMAS, D LLEUFER
THE WELSH LAND COMMISSION: A DIGEST OF ITS REPORT, BY D. LLEUFER THOMAS... LONDON, WHITTAKER, 1896.
465P.

1. LAND TENURE - U.K. 2. U.K. WELSH LAND COMMISSION.

711.73
:336
(41)
U54

U.K. Ministry of Transport.
Road pricing: the economic and technical possibilities. Report of a panel set up by the Ministry of Transport. London, H.M.S.O., 1964.
60p.

1. Highways - Finance - U.K. I. Title.

388
(41)
U54t

U.K. Ministry of Transport.
Transport policy. Presented to Parliament by the Minister of Transport, by Command of Her Majesty. London, H.M. Stat. Off., 1966.
36p. ([U.K. Parliament. Papers by command] cmnd. 3057)

1. Transportation - U.K. 2. Railroads - U.K. I. Title.

690.5
:551.5
U54

U.K. Committee on Winter Building.
Winter building; an interim review by the Committee on Winter Building. London, H.M.S.O., 1963.
33p.

1. Winter construction. I. Title.

711.73
(41)
U54r

U.K. Ministry of Transport.
Roads for the future; a new inter-urban plan. London, H.M.S.O., 1969.
10p.

1. Highways - U.K. I. Title.

U.K. Ministry of Transport. Scottish Development Dept., Welsh Office.
See
U.K. Ministry of Transport. (Welsh Office)

690.015
(41)
U54

United Kingdom. Ministry of Works.
Advisory leaflets. No. 1 -
[London] 1949 -
pts. illus., tables.

For full information see shelf list card.

1. Building research-U.K. I.Title.
selected analytics: 4, 7, 8, 13-14.

712
W45r

U.K. Ministry of Transport.
Williams-Ellis, Clough. 1883-
Roads in the landscape. London, H.M.S.O., 1967.
22p.

At head of title: Ministry of Transport.

1. Landscape architecture. 2. Highways.
I. U.K. Ministry of Transport. II. Title.

538.56
R61d

Laf.

U.K. Treasury.
Robertson, James H
The design of information-processing systems for government. London, H.M.S.O., 1967.
9p. (CAS Occasional paper, no. 1)
At head of title: HM Treasury.

1. Automation. 2. Documentation. I. U.K. Treasury. II. Title. III. Title: Information-processing systems for government.

69(03)
G72
Oct.
1950

Gt. Brit. Ministry of Works.
Alphabetical list of terms defined in British standard codes of practice. [London, Eng.] Oct. 1950.
90 p. (Its Technical notes and papers. Technical paper no. 19)

Mimeographed.

1.Building construction-Dict. I.British standard code of practice.

711.73
(41)
U54

U.K. Ministry of Transport. (Welsh Office)
Roads in urban areas. London, H.M.S. Stat. Off., 1966.
95p.

1. Highways - U.K. I. Title.

354
(41)
C25
no.3

Laf.

U.K. Treasury.
Ryan, W S
Network analysis in forming a new organization. [Prepared in cooperation with] H.M. Treasury. London, H.M.S.O., 1967.
8p. (CAS (Centre for Administrative Studies) occasional paper no. 3)

1. Public administration - U.K. 2. Operations research. 3. Management - Automation. I. U.K. Treasury. II. Title.

69
(03)
G72

Gt. Brit. Ministry of Works.
Alphabetical list of terms defined in British standard codes of practice. [London, Eng.] June 1950.
2 pts. in 1 v. (Its Technical notes and papers. Technical note no.98, 99)

"For internal circulation only."
Mimeographed.
1.Building construction-Dict. I.British standard code of practice.

VF
690.015
(41)
U54
no. 8
United Kingdom. Ministry of Works.
Bricklaying in cold weather. *In Its*
Advisory leaflet series. London, 1950. 5 p.,
folder.

1.Winter construction. 2.Bricklaying.

VF
690
(41:016)
U54b
U.K. Ministry of Works.
United Kingdom (H.M.) Stationery Office.
Government publications: Building; a list,
compiled by the Ministry of Works, of books,
pamphlets and leaflets issued by government
departments. Rev. [London] Dec. 1953.
24 p. (Its Sectional list no. 61)

1.Building construction - Bibliographies. 2.Building
research - United Kingdom - Bibliographies. I.United
Kingdom. Ministry of Works.

VF
690.015
(41)
U54t
no.3
U.K. Ministry of Works.
The importance of thermal insulation
in building, by A. G. Sutton. London,
H.M. Stationery Off., 1957.
11 p. (Its Technical notes no. 3)

1. Insulation. I. Sutton, A. G.
II. Title: Thermal insulation in
Building. (Series)

VF
690.015
(41)
U54
no. 4
United Kingdom. Ministry of Works.
Cavity party wall construction for sound-
insulation. *In Its* Advisory leaflet series,
London, 1949. [4] p.

1.Soundproofing. I.Title.

VF
690
(41:016)
U54
U.K. Ministry of Works.
United Kingdom. (H.M.) Stationery Office.
Government publications: Ministry of Works.
Rev. [London] July 1953.
12 p. (Its Sectional list No. 30)

1.Building construction - United Kingdom - Bibliographies. 2.Building research - United Kingdom -
Bibliographies. I.United Kingdom. Ministry of
Works.

648
U54
U.K. MINISTRY OF WORKS.
AN INQUIRY INTO COMMUNAL LAUNDRY
FACILITIES, BY JANET C. WILSON. LONDON,
H.M. STAT. OFF., 1949.
35P. (ITS NATIONAL BUILDING STUDIES
SPECIAL REPORT NO. 9)

1. LAUNDRIES. I. WILSON, JANET C.

VF
690.015
(41)
U54
no. 7
United Kingdom. Ministry of Works.
Concreting in cold weather. *In Its*
Advisory leaflet series. London, 1950.

1.Winter construction. 2.Concrete construction.

69(41:016)
P25
Gt. Brit. Ministry of Works.
Penn, Colin Troughton.
A guide to official publications on buildings, with a foreword
by J. D. Bernal. London, Pub. for the Royal Institute of British Architects by the Architectural Press [1946]
120 p. 19 cm.

1.Building construction-Bibl.
1. Building. Bibl. 2 Gt. Brit. Government publications Bibl.
I.Gt. Brit. Ministry of Works.
Z5941.P4   016.69   47-28622*
Library of Congress   [1]

628.1
(41)
U54
U.K. MINISTRY OF WORKS.
U.K. BUILDING RESEARCH STATION.
AN INQUIRY INTO DOMESTIC HOT WATER
SUPPLY IN GREAT BRITAIN. LONDON, H.M.
STATIONERY OFF., 1952.
2PTS. (NATIONAL BUILDING STUDIES
SPECIAL REPORT NO. 8, 14)

PART 1 PREPARED BY THE CHIEF
SCIENTIFIC ADVISOR'S DIVISION OF THE
MINISTRY OF WORKS, 1950.
1. WATER SUPPLY - U.K. 2. HEATING,
HOT WATER. I. U.K. MINISTRY OF WORKS.
II. TITLE: DOMESTIC HOT WATER SUPPLY.

728.1
(41)
U54DE
U.K. MINISTRY OF WORKS.
DEMONSTRATION HOUSES; A SHORT ACCOUNT
OF THE DEMONSTRATION HOUSES & FLATS
ERECTED AT NORTHOLT. LONDON, H.M. STAT.
OFF., 1944.
75P.

1. HOUSING - U.K. I. TITLE:
NORTHOLT.

VF
690.015
(41)
U54
no.32
United Kingdom. Ministry of Works.
Handling concrete on housing sites.
In Its Advisory leaflet series. London, 1953.

1.Concrete construction. I.Title.

VF
690
U54
U. K. Ministry of Works.
Methods of building in the U.S.A.; the report
of a mission. London, H. M. Stationery Off.,
1944.
20 p.

2c

1.Building industry. I.Title.

VF
691
(41)
U54
U.K. Ministry of Works.
Economy of building materials; report by the
heads of the works directorates of the service
departments and the Ministry of Works; Charles
J. Mole [and others] London, H.M. Stationery
Off., 1952.
64 p.

1.Building materials. I.Mole, Charles J.
II.Title.

VF
690.015
(41)
U54
no.34
U.K. Ministry of Works.
House insulation. *In Its* Advisory leaflet
series. London, 1953.

1.Insulation.

VF
690.015
(41)
U54t
no.6
U.K. Ministry of Works.
Mix design for vibrated concrete,
by R. Cameron. London, 1957.
11 p. (Its Technical notes no. 6)

1.Concrete construction. I.Cameron, R

690.091.82
(41)
U542
1946
U.K. MINISTRY OF WORKS.
FURTHER USES OF STANDARDS IN
BUILDING: SECOND PROGRESS REPORT
OF THE STANDARDS COMMITTEE.
LONDON, H.M. STAT. OFF., 1946.
24P.

1. BUILDING STANDARDS - U.K.

69(41)
G72
1944
3c.
Great Britain. Ministry of Works.
Great Britain. Ministry of Health.
Housing manual, 1944. London, Eng., H.M.
Stationery Off. [1944]
103 p. illus., diagrs., plans, tables.
Bibliographical footnotes.

Suppl. --------Technical appendices, 1944. London,
Eng., H.M. Stationery Off. [1944]
3c.   92 p. diagrs., tables.

1.Building construction-U.K. 2.Housing-U.K.
I.Gt. Brit. Ministry of Works.

VF
690.015
(41)
U54
no.1314
United Kingdom. Ministry of Works.
Modern site organisation. *In Its*
Advisory leaflet series. London, 1950.
2 pts., folders.

Contents.-pt.1.Introduction to site costing
for builders.-pt.2.Introduction to programming
and progressing for builders.

1.Building costs-Estimates. I.Title.

VF
690
(41:016)
U54
1958
U.K. Ministry of Works.
U.K. (H.M.) Stationery Office.
Government publications: Rev. London,
1958.
7p. (Its Sectional list no. 30)

1. Building construction - U.K. -
Bibliography. 2. Building research - U.K.
- Bibliography. I. U.K. Ministry of
Works.

69(41)
G72
1949
United Kingdom. Ministry of Works.
Housing manual 1949; technical appendices.
Appendices.London, H.M. Stationery Off., 1951.
87 p. diagrs., tables.
List of British standard codes of practice
and British standards: p. 70-78.
Bibliography: p. 79-82.
3c. 1.Building construction-U.K. 2.Housing-U.K.
3.Building standards-U.K.-Bibl. I.U.K. Ministry
of Local Government and Planning.

691.015
(41)
U54
U.K. MINISTRY OF WORKS.
NEW METHODS OF HOUSE CONSTRUCTION.
LONDON, H.M. STAT. OFF., 1948.
35P. (ITS NATIONAL BUILDING
STUDIES SPECIAL REPORT NO. 4)

1. BUILDING RESEARCH - U.K.

690.031
(41)
U54N
U.K. MINISTRY OF WORKS.
NEW METHODS OF HOUSE CONSTRUCTION;
REPORT. LONDON, H.M. STATIONERY
OFF., 1949.
21P. (ITS NATIONAL BUILDING
STUDIES SPECIAL REPORT NO. 10)

SUPPLEMENT TO SPECIAL REPORT NO. 4.

1. BUILDING CONSTRUCTION - U.K.
2. BUILDING COSTS - U.K. I. TITLE.

727.1
(41)
U54SC
U.K. MINISTRY OF WORKS.
SCHOOL FURNITURE AND EQUIPMENT.
LONDON, H.M. STAT. OFF., 1946.
27P. (U.K. MINISTRY OF WORKS.
POST-WAR BUILDING STUDIES NO. 24)

1. SCHOOLS. I. TITLE.

728.1
(41)
U541T
U.K. MINISTRY OF HEALTH.
TEMPORARY ACCOMMODATION. MEMORANDUM
FOR THE GUIDANCE OF LOCAL AUTHORITIES.
LONDON, H.M. STAT. OFF., 1944.
32P.

AT HEAD OF TITLE: MINISTRY OF HEALTH,
MINISTRY OF WORKS.

1. HOUSING - U.K. I. U.K. MINISTRY
OF WORKS. II. TITLE.

690
(41)
U54P
U.K. MINISTRY OF WORKS.
THE PLACING AND MANAGEMENT OF BUILDING
CONTRACTS. REPORT OF THE CENTRAL
COUNCIL FOR WORKS AND BUILDINGS. LONDON,
H.M. STATIONERY OFF., 1944.
72P.

1. BUILDING CONSTRUCTION - U.K. -
CONTRACTS AND SPECIFICATIONS. I. TITLE.

VF
690.015
(41)
U54
no. 1
U.K. Ministry of Works.
Simplified plumbing. London, H.M. Stat. Off.
[1957]
11 p. (Its Technical notes no. 1)

1. Plumbing. (Series)

690.091.82
(41)
J542
1944
U.K. MINISTRY OF WORKS.
THE USE OF STANDARDS IN BUILDING;
FIRST PROGRESS REPORT OF THE
STANDARDS COMMITTEE. LONDON, H.M.
STAT. OFF., 1944.
25P.

1. BUILDING STANDARDS - U.K.

VF
690.015
(42)
U54t
no. 2
U.K. Ministry of Works.
Polythene tubes for cold water services.
London, H.M. Stat. Off. [1957]
7 p. (Its Technical notes no. 2)

1. Pipes. I. Title. (Series)

VF
690.031
U541
United Kingdom. Ministry of Works.
Site records for builders, pts. 1-
London, H.M. Stat. Off., 1952-
v. charts.
Contents.-pt. 1 Programming and progressing
for traditional house building.

1. Building costs. I. Title. 2. Building construction -
Labor requirements.

VF
690.015
(41)
U54t
no. 5
U.K. Ministry of Works.
Vibrated concrete in building, by
R. Cameron. London, 1957.
11 p., illus., tables. (Its Technical
notes no. 5)

1. Concrete construction. I. Cameron, R.
(series)

VF
690.015
(41)
U54
no. 35
U.K. Ministry of Works.
Prestressed concrete. _In Its Advisory leaflet
series._ London, 1953.

1. Concrete-Prestressed.

VF
690.013
(41)
G72
CP
draft
2/5/58
U.K. Ministry of Works. Council for Codes
of Practice for Buildings.
Storage and removal of refuse from residential
property. London, British Standards Institution, 1958.
[14]p. illus. (British standard code of
practice)
CP (BLCP) 3653
Issued for comment only.

1. Sewerage and sewage disposal.

Cat.
DATE OF REQUEST 12/18/53   L. C. CARD NO.
                          JAN 21 1954
AUTHOR U.K. Ministry of Works. Advisory Council on
          Building Research and Development.
TITLE 2nd report. [Gater report].

SERIES

EDITION | PUB. DATE 1953 | PAGING 33 p.
PUBLISHER

RECOMMENDED BY   M&L   REVIEWED IN
                             UHLD Lib Acc List no. 88
                             7/53 p. 26
                  ORDER RECORD

VF
690.015
(41)
U54t
no. 7
U.K. Ministry of Works.
Prestressed concrete, by F. Walley.
London, 1957.
10 p., illus. (Its technical notes no. 7)

1. Concrete, Prestressed. I. Walley, F.
(Series)

690
(41)
U54SU
U.K. MINISTRY OF WORKS.
SUMMARY REPORT FOR THE PERIOD, 1ST
JANUARY 1947 TO 31ST DECEMBER 1947...
LONDON, H.M. STATIONERY OFF., 1948.
35P. (CMD. 7541)

1. BUILDING CONSTRUCTION - U.K.

U.K. Ministry of Works. Building Apprenticeship
and Training Council.
see
U.K. Building Apprenticeship and Training Council.

VF
711.14
(41)
U54
U.K. Ministry of Works.
Report of the Committee on Land Utilisation in Rural Areas. London, H. M.
Stat. Off., 1942.
138p. (Cmd. 6378)

1. Land use - U.K.

Library: Crane
AUTHOR: (Great Britain) Ministry of Works

TITLE: A survey of prefabrication.

PLACE: London, England   PUBLISHER: The Ministry

DATE: 3/45   EDITION: PAGING: 72p. plus
                                       xxxvi and 300 Case sheets.
DESCRIPTIVE NOTE AND SERIES: processed.

ANNOTATION: The survey was undertaken to find out the
scope and range of prefabrication in the building industry in other countries besides Britain, and to have
available a comparative analysis of the movement (over)

VF
691(41)
G72
Gt. Brit. *Ministry of Works. Committee of Enquiry into
the Distribution of Building Materials and Components.*
The distribution of building materials and components,
report. London, H. M. Stationery Off., 1948.
144 p. 25 cm.
Simon of Wythenshawe, chairman.

1. Building materials. I. Simon, Franz Eugen Simon, baron,
1893- II. Title.
HD9715.G715A5 1948   338.47691   48-23987*

Library of Congress   [1]

VF
690.015
(41)
U54t
no.4
U.K. Ministry of Works.
Ring circuit; electrical installations
for housing, by C. A. Farr. London, 1957.
11 p. (Its Technical notes no. 4)

1. Electric apparatus and appliances.
I. Title. II. Farr, C. A.

VF
690.015
(41)
U54t
U.K. Ministry of Works.
Technical notes no. 1-
London, H.M. Stat. Off., 1957-
v.
For complete information see shelflist card.
Contents.-no. 1. Simplified plumbing.-no.2.
Polythene tubes for cold water services.

1. Building construction - U.K.

analyzed

Gt. Brit. Ministry of Works. Codes of
Practice Committee for Civil Engineering.
Public Works and Building

Filed under

Gt. Brit. Ministry of Works. Council for Codes
of Practice for Buildings.

VF
691(41)
G72

Gt. Brit. *Ministry of Works. Committee of Enquiry into the Distribution of Building Materials and Components.*
The distribution of building materials and components, report. London, H. M. Stationery Off., 1948.

144 p. 25 cm.

Simon of Wythenshawe, chairman.

1. Building materials. u.к. i. Simon, Franz Eugen Simon, baron, 1893- II. Title.
HD9715.G715A5 1948   338.47691   48-23987*

Library of Congress ₁₁₎

690.013
(41)
G72
CP3.3
1960

U.K. MINISTRY OF WORKS. COUNCIL FOR CODES OF PRACTICE.
CODE OF BASIC DATA FOR THE DESIGN OF BUILDINGS: CHAPTER III---SOUND INSULATION AND NOISE REDUCTION.
LONDON, BRITISH STANDARDS INSTITUTE, 1960.
113P.

1: BUILDING CODES - U.K.
2. SOUNDPROOFING. I. BRITISH STANDARDS INSTITUTE.

690.013(41)
G72
CP3.7

Gt. Brit. Ministry of Works. Council for Codes of Practice for Buildings.
Code of functional requirements of buildings: ch. 7, Engineering and utility services.
London, British Standards Institution, 1950.
35 p. (British standard code of practice. CP 3, ch. 7, 1950)

1.Public utilities. 2.Building standards-Gt. Brit. I.Ser.

U.K. Ministry of Works. Council for Codes of Practice.
see
U.K. Ministry of Works. Council for Codes of Practice for Buildings.

VF
690.013
(41)
G72
CP5

Gt. Brit. Ministry of Works. Council for Codes of Practice for Buildings.
Code of functional requirements of buildings: Ch. 1(B) Sunlight, houses, flats and schools only.
London, British Standards Institution, 1945.
6 p. diagrs. (British standard code of practice. CP 5, 1945)

1.Lighting. 2.Building standards-Gt. Brit. I.Ser.

VF
690.013
(41)
G72
CP7

Gt. Brit. Ministry of Works. Council for Codes of Practice for Buildings.
Code of functional requirements of buildings: Ch. 7 (F) Provision of artificial light (houses, flats and schools only) London, British Standards Institution, 1945.
13 p. chart, tables. (British standard code of practice. CP 7, 1945)

1.Lighting. 2.Building standards-Gt. Brit. I.Ser.

VF
690.013
(41)
G72
CP
draft
4/24/61

U.K. Ministry of Works. Council for Codes of Practice for Buildings.
Asbestos cement sheet roof coverings. London, British Standards Institution, 1961.
14p. (British draft code of practice; revision of C.P. 143. 201:1951)

AA (BLCP) 9261.

1. Roofs and roofing. I. British Standards Institution.

VF
690.013(41)
G72
CP3.1(C)

Gt. Brit. Ministry of Works. Council for Codes of Practice for Buildings.
Code of functional requirements of buildings: ch.1(C) Ventilation. London, British Standards Institution, 1950.
22 p. tables. (British standard code of practice. CP3,ch.1(C) 1950)

1.Ventilation. 2.Building standards-Gt.Brit. I.Series.

VF
690.013(41)
G72
CP3.10

Gt. Brit. Ministry of Works. Council for Codes of Practice for Buildings.
Code of functional requirements of buildings: ch. 10, Precautions against vermin and dirt. London, British Standards Institution, 1950.
9 p. (British standard code of practice. CP 3, ch. 10, 1950)

1.Insects. 2.Building standards-Gt. Brit. I.Ser.

VF
690.013
(41)
G72
CP
draft
8/1/60

U.K. Ministry of works. Council for Codes of Practice for Buildings. London, British Standards Institution, 1960.
Bitumen felt roof coverings. 13p. diagrs., tables. (British draft code of practice; Revision of C.P. 144.101:1952)

A (BLCP) 9498. Supersedes A(NLCP) 7454.
Issued for comment only.

1. Roofs and roofing. I. British Standards Institution.

VF
690.013
(41)
G72
CP6

Gt. Brit. Ministry of Works. Council for Codes of Practice for Buildings.
Code of functional requirements of buildings: ch. 1 (C) Ventilation, houses and flats. London, British Standards Institution, 1945.
4 p. (British standard code of practice. CP 6, 1945)

1.Ventilation. 2.Building standards-Gt. Brit. I.Ser.

VF
690.013(41)
G72
CP3.9

Gt. Brit. Ministry of Works. Council for Codes of Practice.
Code of functional requirements of buildings: ch.IX, Durability. London, British Standards Institution, 1950.
35 p. tables. (British standard code of practice. CP 3, ch.9, 1950)

1.Building standards-Gt.Brit. I.Title. II.Series.

VF
690.013
(41)
G72
CP
draft
11/15/61

U.K. Ministry of Works. Council for Codes of Practice for Buildings.
Brickwork and blockwork. London, British Standards Institution, 1961.
36p. (British draft code of practice revision of C.P. 121.101)

AB (BLCP) 5961.
Issued for comment only.

1. Brick construction. I. British Standards Institution.

VF
690.013
(41)
G72
CP3.4

Gt. Brit. Ministry of Works. Council for Codes of Practice for Buildings.
Code of functional requirements of buildings: ch. 4 Precautions against fire (houses and flats of not more than two storeys) London, British Standards Institution, 1948.
11 p. table. (British standard code of practice. CP 3, ch. 4, 1944)

1.Fire prevention. 2.Building standards-Gt. Brit. I.Ser.
/c:

VF
690.013
(41)
G72
CP
Drafts

Gt. Brit. Ministry of Works. Codes of Practice Committee for Civil Engineering, Public Works and Building.
₍Codes of practice₎ drafts for comment, subject to revision. London, British Standards Institution, 1944-1950.
pts. (British standard code of practice)
For volumes in library see:
Gt. Brit. Ministry of Works. Council for codes of Practice for Buildings. List of codes in the scheme showing those available.

1.Building standards-Gt. Brit. I.Ser.

VF
690.013
(41)
G72
CP
draft
10/5/61

U.K. Ministry of Works. Council for Codes of Practice for Buildings.
Care and maintenance of floor surfaces. Part I: Timber floor surfaces. London, British Standards Institution, 1961.
13p. (British draft code of practice)

AB (BLCP) 4716.
Issued for comment only.

1. Floors and flooring. I. British Standards Institution.

VF
690.013
(41)
G72
CP3.3

Gt. Brit. Ministry of Works. Council for Codes of Practice for Buildings.
Code of functional requirements of buildings: Ch. 3, Sound insulation (houses, flats and schools) London, British Standards Institution, 1948.
31 p. diagr., graph, plans. (British standard code of practice. CP 3, ch. 3, 1948)

1.Noise. 2.Building standards-Gt. Brit. I.Ser.

VF
690.013
(41)
G72
CP
draft
6/8/59

U.K. Ministry of Works. Council for Codes of Practice for Buildings.
Copper roof coverings (CP 143) - sheet roof coverings. Part 4: copper roof coverings. (Revision of C.P. 143: 104:1951)
London, British Standards Institution, 1959.
14p. diagrs., tables.

CZ (BLCP) 5712.
Issued for comment only.
1. Roofs and roofing. 2. Copper. I. British Standards Institution.

VF
690.013
(41)
G72
draft
CP
5/10/60

U.K. Ministry of Works. Council for Codes of Practice for Buildings.
Climate proofing of electrical equipment. London, British Standards Institution, 1960.
28p. tables. (British draft code of practice)

A (ELCP) 6512.
Issued for comment only.

1. Electrical codes - U.K.

VF
690.013
(41)
G72
CP3.5

U.K. Ministry of Works. Council for Codes of Practice for Buildings.
Code of functional requirements of buildings: ch. 5, Loading. London ₍British Standards Institution₎ 1952.
33 p. diagrs. (British standard code of practice. CP 3, ch. 5, 1952)

1.Loads. 2.Building standards-U.K. I.Series.

VF
690.013
(41)
G72
CP
draft
7/25/61

U.K. Ministry of Works. Council for Codes of Practice for Buildings.
Daylight. London, British Standards Institution, 1961.
46p. (British draft code of practice; revision of C.P.3 Chapter 1A)

AB (BLCP) 2200.
Issued for comment only.

1. Lighting. I. British Standards Institution.

VF 690.013 (41) G72 CP draft 10/14/57

U.K. Ministry of Works. Council for
Codes of Practice for Buildings.
The design and construction of reinforced
concrete structures for the storage of
liquids. London, British Standards Institution, 1957.
35p. illus.

CX (CVCP 7507)
Issued for comment only.

1.Reinforced concrete construction.
I.British Standards Institution.

VF 690.013 (41) G72 CP draft 5/25/60

U.K. Ministry of Works. Council for Codes
of Practice for Buildings.
Galvanized corrugated steel sheet roofing
and siding for buildings. London, British
Standards Institution, 1959.
21p. diagrs., tables. (British standard
code of practice)

A (BLCP) 7609.
Issued for comment only.

1. Roofs and roofing. I. British Standards
Institution.

VF 690.013 (41) G72 CP342

Gt. Brit. Ministry of Works. Council for Codes
of Practice for Buildings.
General series: Centralized domestic hot water
supply. London, British Standards Institution,
1950.
89 p. tables. (British standard code of
practice. CP 342)

Definitions: p. 13-18.
Relevant British standard: p. 21, 37-38, 50,
60-61, 75.

(Continued on next card)

VF 690.013 (41) G72 CP draft 5/4/60

U.K. Ministry of Works. Council for Codes
of Practice for Buildings.
Domestic space heating by means of independent gas appliances. London, British
Standards Institution, 1960.
32p. diagrs., tables. (British draft
code of practice; Revision of C.P. 332.
301:1947)

A (MECP) 8240.
Issued for comment only.

1. Heating, Gas. I. British Standards Institution.

VF 690.013 (41) G72 CP 113.102

United Kingdom. Ministry of Works. Council for
Codes of Practice for Buildings.
General series: Arc welded construction.
London [British Standards Institution] 1951.
32 p. diagrs. (British standard code of
practice. CP 113.102, 1951)

1.Welding. 2.Building standards-U.K. I.Title.
II.Series.

Gt. Brit. Ministry of Works. Council for Codes
of Practice for Buildings. General series
Centralized domestic hot water supply...1950.
(Card 2)

Contents.-Code 342. Centralized domestic hot
water supply.-Sub-code 342.101. Boilers.-Sub-code
342.102. Calorifiers.-Sub-code 342.103. Storage
vessels.-Sub-code 342.104. Pipework installation.-
Sub-code 342.105. Electrically driven circulators.-
Sub-code 342.106. Thermal insulation.

1.Hot water. 2.Building standards-Gt. Brit. I.Ser.

VF 690.013 (41) G72 CP draft 6/19/59

U.K. Ministry of Works. Council for Codes
of Practice for Buildings.
Electrical installations. (Revision of
C.P. 321 Electrical installations, and C.P.
321.101 Electrical wiring system) London,
British Standards Institution, 1959.
35p. tables.

CZ (ELCP) 6605.
Issued for comment only.
1. Electrical apparatus and appliances.
I. British Standards Institution.

VF 690.013 (41) G72 CP327.401

United Kingdom. Ministry of Works. Council for
Codes of Practice for Buildings.
General series: Bell and call systems.
London [British Standards Institution] 1952.
35 p. (British standard code of practice.
CP 327.401, 1952)

1.Building standards-U.K. I.Title. II.Series.

VF 690.013 (41) G72 CP143.104

United Kingdom. Ministry of Works. Council for
Codes of Practice for Buildings.
General series: Copper coverings for roofs.
London [British Standards Institution] 1951.
34 p. diagrs. (British standard code of
practice. CP 143.104, 1951)

1.Roofs and roofing. 2.Building standards-U.K.
I.Title. II.Series.

VF 690.013 (41) G72 CP draft 7/28/60

U.K. Ministry of Works. Council for
Codes of Practice for Buildings.
Fire precautions in flats and maisonettes.
London, British Standards Institution, 1960.
22p. diagrs. (British draft code of
practice)

A (BLCP) 9303.
Issued for comment only.

1. Fire prevention. I. British Standards Institution.

VF 690.013 (41) G72 CP144.101

United Kingdom. Ministry of Works. Council for
Codes of Practice for Buildings.
General series: Bitumen felt roof coverings.
London [British Standards Institution] 1952.
32 p. diagrs. (British standard code of
practice. CP 144.101, 1952)

1.Roofs and roofing. 2.Building standards-U.K.
I.Title. II.Series.

VF 690.013 (41) G72 CP123.101

United Kingdom. Ministry of Works. Council for
Codes of Practice for Buildings.
General series: Dense concrete walls.
London [British Standards Institution] 1951.
47 p. diagrs. (British standard code of
practice. CP 123.101, 1951)

1.Walls. 2.Concrete construction. I.Title.
II.Series.

VF 690.013 (41) G72 Rep.no.1

Gt. Brit. Ministry of Works. Codes of Practice
Committee for Civil Engineering Public Works,
Building and Constructional Work.
First Report. London, H. M. Stationery Off.,
1943.
20 p.

List of codes: p. 13-16.
"Outline of the main codes:" p. 17-20.

1. Building standards - Gt. Brit.

VF 690.013 (41) G72 CP121.101

United Kingdom. Ministry of Works. Council for
Codes of Practice for Buildings.
General series: Brickwork. London [British
Standards Institution] 1951.
57 p. diagrs., tables. (British standard
code of practice. CP 121.101, 1951)

Definitions: p. 9-11.

1.Brick construction. 2.Building standards-U.K.
I.Title. II.Series.

VF 690.013 (41) G72 CP413

Building standards - United Kingdom
United Kingdom. Ministry of Works. Council
for Codes of Practice for Buildings.
General series: Design and construction
of ducts for services. London, British
Standards Institution, 1951.
25 p. diagrs. (British standard
code of practice. CP413, 1951)

1.Building standards-U.K. I.Title:Ducts for
services. II.Series.

VF 690.013 (41) G72 CP draft 7/11/60

U.K. Ministry of Works. Council for Codes
of Practice for Buildings.
Flues for gas appliances. London, British
Standards Institution, 1960.
30p. diagrs. (British draft code of
practice; Revision of C.P. 331.104:1947)

A (MECP) 8992.
Issued for comment only.

1. Gas apparatus and appliances. I. British Standards Institution. II. Title.

VF 690.013 (41) G72 CP327.201

United Kingdom. Ministry of Works. Council for
Codes of Practice for Buildings.
General series: Broadcast receptions, sound
and television by radio. London [British
Standards Institution] 1951.
56 p. (British standard code of practice.
CP 327.201, 1951)

1.Building standards-U.K. I.Title. II.Series.

VF 690.013 (41) G72 CP324.202

U.K. Ministry of Works. Council for Codes of
Practice for Buildings.
General series: Domestic electric water-
heating installations. London [British
Standards Institution] 1951.
36 p. diagrs., tables. (British
standard code of practice. CP 324.202, 1951)

1.Hot water. 2.Building standards-U.K. I.Title.
II.Series.

VF 690.013 (41) G72 Rep.no.4

Gt. Brit. Ministry of Works. Council for Codes of
Practice for Buildings, Construction and
Engineering Services.
Fourth report. Jan. 1947 to Dec. 1949.
London, H.M. Stationery Off., 1950.
45 p.

1.Building standards-Gt. Brit.

VF 690.013 (41) G72 CP301

Gt. Brit. Ministry of Works. Council for Codes
of Practice for Buildings.
General series: Building drainage. London,
British Standards Institution, 1950.
77 p. diagrs., tables. (British standard code of practice. CP 301)

Definitions: p. 7-13.
Relevant British standard: p. 21.
1.Drainage. 2.Building standards-Gt. Brit. I.Ser.

VF 690.013 (41) G72 CP332.201

Gt. Brit. Ministry of Works. Council for Codes
of Practice for Buildings.
General series: Domestic hot water supply by
gas, single family dwellings. London, British
Standards Institution, 1947.
40 p. diagrs., tables. (part fold.)
(British standard code of practice. CP 332.201,
1947)

Definitions: p. 7-8.
Relevant British Standards: p. 10-11.

(Continued on next card)

Gt. Brit. Ministry of Works. Council for Codes of Practice for Buildings. General series: Domestic hot water supply by gas ... 1947. (Card 2)

1.Hot water. 2.Gas apparatus and appliances. 3.Building standards-Gt. Brit. I.Ser.

VF
690.013
(41)
G72
CP131.101

U.K. Ministry of Works. Council for Codes of Practice for Buildings.
General series: Flues for domestic appliances burning solid fuel. London [British Standards Institution] 1951.
68 p. diagrs. (British standard code of practice. CP 131.101, 1951)

Definitions: p. 11-13.

1.Building standards-U.K. I.Title. II.Series.

VF
690.013
(41)
G72
CP332.501

Gt. Brit. Ministry of Works. Council for Codes of Practice for Buildings.
General series: Gas operated refrigerators. London, British Standards Institution, 1947.
11 p. table. (British standard code of practice. CP 332.501, 1947)

Definitions: p. 5.
Relevant British Standards: p. 6.

1.Refrigerators-Gas. 2.Building standards-Gt. Brit. I.Ser.

VF
690.013
(41)
G72
CP321.101

Gt. Brit. Ministry of Works. Codes of Practice Committee for Civil Engineering, Public Works and Building.
General series: Electric wiring systems (for power, lighting, and heating circuits) in buildings. London, British Standards Institution, 1949.
38 p. tables. (British standard code of practice, CP321.101,1949)

Definitions: p.8-10.
1.Electric wiring. 2.Building standards-Gt.Brit. I.Ser.

VF
690.013
(41)
G72
CP331.104

Gt. Brit. Ministry of Works. Council for Codes of Practice for Buildings.
General series: Flues for gas appliances. London, British Standards Institution, 1947.
31 p. diagrs., tables. (British standard code of practice. CP 331.104, 1947)

Definitions: p. 7-8.
Relevant British Standards: p. 9.
1.Gas apparatus and appliances. 2.Building standards-Gt. Brit. I.Ser.

VF
690.013
(41)
G72
CP331.101

Gt. Brit. Ministry of Works. Council for Codes of Practice for Buildings.
General series: Gas service pipes. London, British Standards Institution, 1947.
14 p. tables. (British standard code of practice. CP 331.101, 1947)

Definitions: p. 5.
Relevant British Standards: p. 6.
1.Gas apparatus and appliances. 2.Building standards-Gt.Brit. I.Ser.

VF
690.013
(41)
G72
CP327.404/
402.501

United Kingdom. Ministry of Works. Council for Codes of Practice for Buildings.
General series: Electrical fire alarms. London [British Standards Institution] 1951.
49 p. (British standard code of practice. CP 327.404/402.501, 1951)

1.Building standards-U.K. I.Title. II.Series.

VF
690.013
(41)
G72
CP101

Gt. Brit. Ministry of Works. Council for Codes of Practice for Buildings.
General series: Foundations and substructures. London, British Standards Institution, 1948.
26 p. table. (British standard code of practice. C P 101, 1948)

"List of revelant British Standards:" p.25-26.

1.Foundations. 2.Building standards-Gt. Brit. I.Ser.

VF
690.013
(41)
G72
672
CP407.301

Gt. Brit. Ministry of Works. Council for Codes of Practice for Buildings.
General series: Hand-power lifts for passengers, goods, and service. London, British Standards Institution, 1951.
26 p. diagrs., tables. (British standard code of practice. CP407.301)

Definitions: p.7-9.

1.Elevators. 2.Building standards-Gt.Brit. I.Series.

VF
690.013(41)
G72
CP321

Gt. Brit. Ministry of Works. Codes of Practice Committee for Civil Engineering, Public Works and Building.
General series: Electrical installations, general. London, British Standards Institution, 1948.
71 p. (British standard code of practice. CP 321, 1948)

Definitions: p.8-10.
Relevant British Standards: p.11-14.

(Continued on next card)

VF
690.013
(41)
G72
CP332.401

Gt. Brit. Ministry of Works. Council for Codes of Practice for Buildings.
General series: Gas cooking installations, single family dwellings. London, British Standards Institution, 1947.
11 p. diagrs., table. (British standard code of practice. CP 332.401, 1947)

Definitions: p. 5.
Relevant British Standards: p.6-7.
1.Gas apparatus and appliances. 2.Building standards-Gt. Brit. I.Ser.

VF
690.013
(41)
G72
CP402.101

United Kingdom. Ministry of Works. Council for Codes of Practice for Buildings.
General series: Hydrant systems. London [British Standards Institution] 1952.
22 p. (British standard code of practice. CP 402.101, 1952)

1.Building standards-U.K. I.Title. II.Series.

Gt. Brit. Ministry of Works. Codes of Practice Committee for Civil Engineering, Public Works and Building. General series: Electrical installations, general...1948. (Card 2)

1.Electric apparatus and appliances. 2.Building standards-Gt. Brit. I.Ser.

VF
690.013
(41)
G72
CP331.103

Gt. Brit. Ministry of Works. Council for Codes of Practice for Buildings.
General series: Gas installation pipes. London, British Standards Institution, 1947.
19 p. tables. (British standard code of practice. CP 331.103, 1947)

Definitions: p. 6-8.
Relevant British Standards: p. 9-10.
1.Gas apparatus and appliances. 2.Building standards-Gt. Brit. I.Ser.

VF
650.013
(41)
G72
CP327.403

United Kingdom. Ministry of Works. Council for Codes of Practice for Buildings.
General series: Impulse clock and timing systems. London [British Standards Institution] 1952.
35 p. (British standard code of practice. CP 327.403, 1952)

1.Building standards-U.K. I.Title. II.Series.

VF
690.013(41)
G72
CP322.102

Gt. Brit. Ministry of Works. Codes of Practice Committee for Civil Engineering, Public Works and Building.
General series: Electricity supply intake arrangements for flats and other multi-occupier buildings. London, British Standards Institution, 1948.
14 p. (British standard code of practice, CP 322.102, 1948)

Definitions: p.6.
Relevant British standards: p.7-8.

(Continued on next card)

VF
690.013(41)
G72
CP332.101

Gt. Brit. Ministry of Works. Codes of Practice Committee for Civil Engineering, Public Works and Building.
General series: Gas lighting, single family dwellings. London, British Standards Institution, 1947.
19 p. tables. (British standard code of practice. CP 332.101, 1947)

Definitions: p. 6-7.

1.Lighting. 2.Building standards-Gt. Brit. I.Ser.

VF
690.013
(41)
G72
CP204

U.K. Ministry of Works. Council for Codes of Practice for Buildings.
General series: In-situ flooring. London [British Standards Institution] 1951.
82 p. (British standard code of practice. CP 204, 1951)

1.Floors and flooring. 2.Building standards-U.K. I.Title. II.Series.

Gt. Brit. Ministry of Works. Codes of Practice Committee for Civil Engineering, Public Works and Building. General series: Electricity supply intake arrangements for flats and other multi-occupier buildings. 1948.. (Card 2)

1.Electric apparatus and appliances. 2.Building standards-Gt.Brit. I.Ser.

VF
690.013
(41)
G72
CP331.102

Gt. Brit. Ministry of Works. Council for Codes of Practice for Buildings.
General series: Gas metering and consumers control. Longon, British Standards Institution, 1947.
11 p. diagrs. (British standard code of practice. CP 331.102, 1947)

Definitions: p.5-6.
Relevant British Standards: p.6-7.
1.Gas apparatus and applicances. 2.Building standards-Gt.Brit. I.Ser.

VF
690.013
(41)
G72
CP321.102

Gt. Brit. Ministry of Works. Council for Codes of Practice for Buildings.
General series: Installation & maintenance of electrical machines, transformers, rectifiers, capacitors and associated equipment. London, British Standards Institution, 1950.
31 p. tables. (British standard code of practice. CP 321.102)

Definitions: p. 6.
Relevant British standard: p. 7-8.
1.Electric apparatus and appliances. 2.Building standards-Gt. Brit. I.Ser.

VF
690.013
(41)
G72
CP322.103   Gt. Brit. Ministry of Works. Council for Codes of Practice for Buildings.
General series: Installation of consumers' electricity supply controls for small dwellings (for A.C. systems)   London, British Standards Institution, 1948.
9 p.   (British standard code of practice. CP 322.103, 1948)

Definitions: p.6.
1.Electric apparatus and appliances. 2.Building standards-Gt.Brit. I.Ser.

Gt. Brit. Ministry of Works. Council for Codes of Practice for Buildings.   General series: Internal plastering...1949.   (Card 2)

Contents.-Code 211. Internal plastering.-
Sub-code 211.101. Backgrounds for internal plastering.-Sub-code 211.201. Internal lime plastering.-Sub-code 211.202. Internal gypsum and anhydrite plastering.-Sub-code 211.203. Internal cement plastering.

1.Plaster and plastering. 2.Building standards-Gt. Brit. I.Ser.

VF
690.013
G72
CP324.101   Gt. Brit. Ministry of Works. Council for Codes of Practice for Buildings.
General series: The provision of electric lighting in dwellings.   London, British Standards Institution, 1948.
18 p.   graph, tables.   (British standard code of practice. CP 324.101, 1948)

Bibliography (definitions): p. 6-7.
Relevant British Standards: p. 7-8.

1.Lighting. 2.Building standards-Gt.Brit. I.Ser.

VF
690.013(41)
G72
CP324.201   Gt. Brit. Ministry of Works. Codes of Practice Committee for Civil Engineering, Public Works and Building.
General series: Installation of domestic electric space heating equipment. London, British Standards Institution, 1948.
19 p.   (British standard code of practice. CP 324.201, 1948)

Definitions: p. 7-8.

1.Heating-Electric. 2.Building standards-Gt. Brit. I.Ser.

VF
690.013
(41)
G72
CP406   U.K. Ministry of Works. Council for Codes of Practice in Buildings.
General series: Mechanical refrigeration. London [British Standards Institution] 1952.
50 p.   graphs(fold.), tables(part.fold.) (British standard code of practice. CP406)

1.Refrigeration. 2.Insulation. I.Ser.

VF
690.013
(41)
G72
CP324.102   Gt. Brit. Ministry of Works. Council for Codes of Practice for Buildings.
General series: Provision of electric lighting in schools. London, British Standards Institution, 1948.
19 p.   diagr., tables.   (British standard code of practice. CP 324.102, 1948)

Bibliography (definitions): p. 7.
Relevant British Standards: p. 9.

1.Lighting. 2.Building standards-Gt.Brit. I.Ser.

VF
690.013
(41)
G72
CP332.303   United Kingdom. Ministry of Works. Council for Codes of Practice for Buildings.
General series: installation of gas fired boilers for central heating by hot water. London, British Standards Institution, 1951.
28 p.   diagrs.   (British standard code of practice. CP 332.303, 1951)

1.Gas apparatus and appliances. 2.Building standards-U.K. I.Series.

VF
690.013
(41)
G72
CP145.101   United Kingdom. Ministry of Works. Council for Codes of Practice for Buildings.
General series: Patent glazing.   London, British Standards Institution, 1951.
19 p.   (British standard code of practice. CP145.101, 1951)

Definitions: p. 8.

1.Title. II.Series.

VF
690.013
(41)
G72
CP322.101   Gt. Brit. Ministry of Works. Council for Codes of Practice for Buildings.
General series: Provision of electricity service cables for small houses. London, British Standards Institution, 1947.
11 p.   diagrs.   (British standard code of practice. CP 322.101, 1947)

Definitions: p. 5.

1.Electric apparatus and appliances. 2.Building standards-Gt.Brit. I.Ser.

VF
690.013
(41)
G72
CP332.601   Gt. Brit. Ministry of Works. Council for Codes of Practice for Buildings.
General series: Installation of gas heated appliances for laundering and ancillary domestic purposes. London, British Standards Institution, 1947.
22 p.   diagrs., tables.   (British standard code of practice. CP 332.601, 1947)

(Continued on next card)

VF
690.013
(41)
G72
CP402.401   United Kingdom. Ministry of Works. Council for Codes of Practice for Buildings.
General series: Portable fire extinguishers. London [British Standards Institution] 1951.
14 p.   (British standard code of practice. CP 402.401, 1951)

1.Building standards-U.K. I.Title. II.Series.

VF
690.013
(41)
G72
CP305   U.K. Ministry of Works. Council for Codes of Practice for Buildings.
General series: Sanitary appliances. London [British Standards Institution] 1952.
28 p.   (British standard code of practice. CP 305, 1952)

1.Building standards-U.K. I.Title: Sanitary appliances. II.Series.

Gt. Brit. Ministry of Works. Council for Codes of Practice for Buildings.   General series: Installation of gas heated appliances ... 1947.   (Card 2)

Definitions: p. 6-7.
Relevant British Standards: p. 8-9.

1.Laundry. 2.Gas apparatus and appliances. 3.Building standards-Gt.Brit. I.Ser.

VF
690.013
(41)
G72
CP323   Gt. Brit. Ministry of Works. Council for Codes of Practice for Buildings.
General series: Private electric generating plant. London, British Standards Institution, 1948.
23 p.   (British standard code of practice, CP 323, 1948)

Definitions of terms used are in B. S. 205 "Glossary of terms used in electrical engineering" p.6.

(Continued on next card)

VF
690.013
(41)
G72
CP324.301   Gt. Brit. Ministry of Works. Council for Codes of Practice for Buildings.
General series: Selection and installation of domestic electric cookers. London, British Standards Institution, 1948.
11 p.   tables.   (British standard code of practice. CP 324.301, 1948)

Definitions: p.6.
Relevant British Standards: p.7.
1.Electric apparatus and appliances. 2.Building standards-Gt.Brit. I.Ser.

VF
690.013
(41)
G72
CP324.403   Gt. Brit. Ministry of Works. Council for Codes of Practice for Building.s
General series: Installation of vapour compression type domestic electric refrigerators. London, British Standards Institution, 1948.
13 p.   diagrs.   (British standard code of practice. CP 324.403, 1948)

Definitions: p. 7.
Relevant British Standards: p. 8.
1.Refrigerators-Electric. 2.Building standards-Gt.Brit. I.Ser.

Gt. Brit. Ministry of Works. Council for Codes of Practice for Buildings.   General series: Private electric generating plant... 1948. (Card 2)

1.Electric apparatus and appliances. 2.Building standards-Gt. Brit. I.Ser.

VF
690.013
(41)
G72
CP203   United Kingdom. Ministry of Works. Council for Codes of Practice for Buildings.
General series: Sheet and similar floorings. London, British Standards Institution, 1951.
25 p.   (British standard code of practice. CP203, 1951)

1.Floors and flooring. 2.Building standards-U.K. I.Title. II.Series.

VF
690.013
(41)
G72
CP211   Gt. Brit. Ministry of Works. Council for Codes of Practice for Buildings.
General series: Internal plastering. London, British Standards Institution, 1949.
120 p.   charts, tables.   (British standard codes of practice. CP 211, 1949)

Definitions: p. 12-31.
Bibliography: p. 60, 79.

(Continued on next card)

VF
690.013
(41)
G72
CP326.101   Gt. Brit. Ministry of Works. Council for Codes of Practice for Buildings.
General series: Protection of structures against lightning. London, British Standards Institution, 1948.
38 p.   diagrs., table.   (British standard code of practice. CP 326.101, 1948)

Definitions: p. 8-9.

1.Lightning. 2.Building standards-Gt. Brit. I.Ser.

VF
690.013
(41)
G72
CP142   United Kingdom. Ministry of Works. Council for Codes of Practice for Buildings.
General series: Slating and tiling. London [British Standards Institution] 1951.
63 p.   (British standard code of practice. CP142, 1951)

1.Roofs and roofing. I.Title: Slating and tiling. II.Ser.

Row 1

VF
690.013
(41)
G72
CP403.101
U.K. Ministry of Works. Council for Codes of
Practice for Buildings.
General series: Small boiler systems using
solid fuel. London [British Standards
Institution] 1952.
32 p. diagrs. (British standard code
of practice. CP 403.101, 1952)

Definitions: p. 10-11.

1.Boilers. 2.Building standards-U.K. I.Series.

VF
690.013
(41)
G72
CP113.201
United Kingdom. Ministry of Works. Council
for Codes of Practice for Buildings.
General series: The structural use of
steel tubes in buildings. London
[British Standards Institution] 1953.
26 p. diagrs., tables. (British
standard code of practice. CP113.201, 1953)

1.Steel construction. I.Ser.

VF
690.013
(41)
G72
CP202
United Kingdom. Ministry of Works. Council for
Codes of Practice for Buildings.
General series: Tile flooring and slab
flooring. London, British Standards Institution,
1951.
28 p. tables. (British standard code of
practice. CP 202)

1.Floors and flooring. 2.Building standards-U.K.
I.Title. II.Series. 3.Concrete floors.

Row 2

VF
690.013
(41)
G72
CP327.300
United Kingdom. Ministry of Works. Council for
Codes of Practice for Buildings.
General series: Sound distribution systems.
London [British Standards Institution] 1952.
54 p. (British standard code of practice.
CP 327.300, 1952)

1.Building standards-U.K. I.Title. II.Series.

VF
690.013
(41)
G72
CP112
U.K. Ministry of Works. Council for Codes of
Practice for Buildings.
General series: The structural use of timber
in buildings (incorporating CP112.100 - Preserva-
tive treatments for timber used in buildings).
London [British Standards Institution] 1952.
83 p. illus., tables. (British standard
code of practice. CP112)
1.Wood construction. 2.Wood-Testing. 3.Wood
preservation. I.Title: The structural use of
timber in buildings. II.Ser.

VF
690.013
(41)
G72
CP122
U.K. Ministry of Works. Council for Codes of
Practice for Buildings.
General series: Walls and partitions of
blocks and of slabs. London [British Standards
Institution] 1952.
108 p. illus. (British standard code of
practice. CP122)
1.Walls. 2.Concrete blocks. 3.Gypsum. 4.Plaster
and plastering. 5.Glass. 6.Clay. 7.Wood construction. I.Ser.

Row 3

VF
690.013
(41)
G72
CP332.301
Gt. Brit. Ministry of Works. Council for Codes
of Codes of Practice for Buildings.
General series: Space heating by means of
independent gas appliances (single family dwellings
London, British Standards Institution, 1947.
17 p. diagrs., tables. (British standard
code of practice. CP 332.301, 1947)

Definitions: p. 5-6.
Relevant British Standards: p. 7.

1.Heating-Gas. 2.Building standards-Gt. Brit.
I.Ser.

VF
690.013
(41)
G72
CP303
United Kingdom. Ministry of Works. Council for
Codes of Practice for Buildings.
General series: Surface water and subsoil
drainage. London [British Standards Institution]
1952.
15 p. (British standard code of practice.
CP 303, 1952)

1.Drainage. 2.Building standards-U.K. I.Title.
II.Series.

VF
690.013
(41)
G72
CP310
U.K. Ministry of Works. Council for Codes of
Practice for Buildings.
General series: Water supply. London
[British Standards Institution] 1952.
68 p. tables. (British standard code
of practice. CP310)

1.Water supply. I.Ser.

Row 4

VF
690.013
(41)
G72
CP402.201
United Kingdom. Ministry of Works. Council for
Codes of Practice for Buildings.
General series: sprinkler systems. London
[British Standards Institution] 1952.
26 p. (British standard code of practice.
CP 402.201, 1952)

1.Building standards-U.K. I.Title. II.Series.

VF
690.013
(41)
G72
CP114
.100-5
Gt. Brit. Ministry of Works. Council for Codes
of Practice for Buildings.
General series: Suspended concrete floors and
roofs (including stairs) London, British Standards Institution, 1950.
66 p. diagrs., tables. (British
standard code of practice. CP 114.100-114.105)

Definitions: p. 47-48, 55, 59, 63.
Contents.-Sub-code 114.100. Suspended concrete
floors and roofs.-Sub-code 114.101. Floors and
roofs of solid slab construction.-Sub-code 114.102.

(Continued on next card)

VF
690.013
(41)
G72
CP
draft
12/18/58
U.K. Ministry of Works. Council for Codes
of Practice for Buildings.
Installation and maintenance of flame-
proof and intrinsically-safe electrical
equipment for industries other than coal
mining. London, British Standards Institution, 1958.
24p. tables
CZ (ELCP) 377. (Revision of C.P. 1003:
1948) (Continued on next card)

Row 5

VF
690.013
(41)
G72
CP327.402
U.K. Ministry of Works. Council for Codes of
Practice for Buildings.
General series: Staff location systems.
London [British Standards Institution] 1951.
33 p. (British standard code of practice.
CP 327.402, 1951)

1.Building standards-U.K. I.Title. II.Series.

VF
690.013
(41)
G72
CP114
.100-5
Gt. Brit. Ministry of Works. Council for Codes
of Practice for Buildings. General series:
Suspended concrete floors and roofs (including
stairs)...1950. (Card 2)

Floors and roofs of flat slab construction.-Sub-
code 114.103. Floors and roofs of ribbed construction.-Sub-code 114.104. Floors and roofs of
pre-cast construction.-Sub-code 114.105. Floors
and roofs of filler joist construction.

1.Roofs and roofing. 2.Floors. 3.Stairs. 4.Building
standards-Gt. Brit. I. er. flooring
5.Concrete floors.

VF
690.013
(41)
G72
CP
draft
12/18/58
U.K. Ministry of Works. Council for Codes
of Practice for Buildings. Installation
and maintenance ... (Card 2)

Issued for comment only.

1. Electrical apparatus and appliances.
I. British Standards Institution.

Row 6

VF
690.013
(41)
G72
CP114
Gt. Brit. Ministry of Works. Council for Codes
of Practice for Buildings.
General series: The structural use of normal
reinforced concrete in buildings. London,
British Standards Institute, 1948.
77 p. diagrs., tables. (British
standard code of practice. CP 114, 1948)

Definitions: p.7-8.
"Schedule of symbols:" p.53-54.

1.Reinforced concrete construction. 2.Building
standards-Gt. Brit. I.Ser.

VF
690.013
(41)
G72
CP327.102
U.K. Ministry of Works. Council for Codes of
Practice for Buildings.
General series: Telephones and telegraphs,
private services. London [British Standards
Institution] 1952.
62 p. (British standard code of practice
CP327.102)

1.Public utilities. I.Ser.

VF
690.013
(41)
G72
CP
draft
1/22/57
U.K. Ministry of Works. Council for Codes
of Practice for Buildings.
Installation of gas appliances for laundering and ancillary domestic purposes. London,
British Standards Institution, 1957.
11p. diagrs. (British draft code of practice; Revision of C.P. 332.601:1947)

CX (HECP) 103.

Issued for comment only.

1. Laundries. 2. Gas apparatus and appliances.
I. British Standards Institution.

Row 7

VF
690.013
(41)
G72
CP113
Gt. Brit. Ministry of Works. Council for Codes
of Practice for Buildings.
General series: The structural use of steel
in buildings. London, British Standards
Institute, 1948.
77 p. diagrs., tables. (British standard
code of practice. CP 113, 1948)

1.Steel construction. 2.Building standards-Gt.
Brit. I.Ser.

VF
690.013
(41)
G72
CP327.101
U.K. Ministry of Works. Council for Codes of
Practice for Buildings.
General series: Telephones and telegraphs,
public services. London [British Standards
Institution] 1952.
54 p. illus. (British standard code
of practice. CP327.101)

1.Public utilities. I.Ser.

VF
690.013
(41)
G72
CP
draft
6/5/59
U.K. Ministry of Works. Council for Codes
of Practice for Buildings.
Lead roof coverings (CP 143 - sheet roof
coverings, Part 3: lead roof coverings).
London, British Standards Institution,
1959.
11p. diagrs., tables.

CZ (BLCP) 5713.
Issued for comment only.

1. Roofs and roofing. 2. Lead. I.
British Standards Institution.

VF
690.013
(41:016)
G72   Gt. Brit. Ministry of Works. Council for Codes
         of Practice for Buildings.
         List of codes in the scheme showing those
         available.   London, 1949.
         23 p.

         Mimeographed.
         OA Library holdings checked; additions written
         in.

         1.Building standards-Gt. Brit.-Bibl.

VF
690.013
(41)
G72   U.K. Ministry of Works. Council for Codes
CP   of Practice for Buildings.
draft   Selection and installation of domestic gas
7/8/60   cooking appliances. London, British Stand-
         ards Institution, 1960.
         9p. diagrs. (British draft code of prac-
         tice; Revision of C.P. 332.401:1947)

         A (MECP) 8991

         "Issued for comment only."

         1. Gas apparatus and appliances. I. British Stand-
         ards Institution.

693.002.22 Great Britain. Ministry of Works.
H17   Directorate of Post War Building.
Harrison, D Dex
         A survey of prefabrication [by] D. Dex
         Harrison, J. M. Albery, [and] M.W. Whiting.
         [London?] Ministry of Works, Mar. 1945.
         1 v. illus., diagrs., plans.

         "This survey ... may be regarded as
         supplementing the Report of the Interdepart-
         mental Committee on House Construction."-t.-p.
         Bibliography: p. xxxvi-xxxix.
         Index of systems: p.i-xxxi.
         Processed.
                        (Continued on next card)

VF
690.013
(41)
G72   U.K. Ministry of Works. Council for Codes
CP   of Practice for Buildings.
draft   The maintenance of insulating oils for
9/27/57 transformers and switchgear. London,
         British Standards Institution, 1957.
         [20]p. illus.

         CX (ELCP) 7411
         Issued for comment only.

         1.Electric appratus and appliances.
         I.British Standard Institution.

VF
690.013
(41)
G72   U.K. Ministry of Works. Council for Codes
CP   of Practice for Buildings.
draft   Sheet and similar flooring. London,
12/13/60 British Standards Institution, 1960.
         12p. tables. (British draft code of
         practice; Revision of C.P. 203:1951)
         AA (BLCP) 4614.
         Issued for comment only.

         1. Floors and flooring.
         I. British Standards Institution.

Harrison, D Dex.   A survey of
prefabrication ... Mar. 1945. (Card 2)

         1.Prefabricated construction. I.Albery, J.M.,
         jt. au. II.Whiting, M. W., jt. au. III.Gt. Brit.
         Ministry of Works. Directorate of Post War
         Building.

VF
690.013
(41)
G72   U.K. Ministry of Works. Council for Codes of
CP   Practice for Buildings.
draft   Oil firing. Part I. Installations burning
1/9/59   class D and C.T.F. 50 fuels. London, British
         Standards Institution, 1959.
         28p. diagrs., tables.

         CZ (MECP) 1169.
         Issued for comment only.

         1. Fuel. 2. British standards - U.K.

VF
690.013
(41)
G72   U.K. Ministry of Works. Council for Codes
CP   of Practice for Buildings.
draft   Sound insulation and noise reduction. (Re-
5/20/59 vision of chapter III of C.P.3) London,
         British Standards Institution, 1959.
         85p. diagrs., tables.
         CZ(BLCP)4399.
         Issued for comment only.

         1. Soundproofing. 2. Insulation.
         I. British Standards Institution.

711.14
(41)
U54F   U.K. MINISTRY OF WORKS AND PLANNING.
         EXPERT COMMITTEE ON COMPENSATION AND
         BETTERMENT.
         FINAL REPORT. LONDON, H.M.
         STATIONERY OFF., 1942.
         180 P. (H.M. STATIONERY OFFICE.
         CMD.6386)
         THE HON. MR. JUSTICE UTHWATT,
         CHAIRMAN.
         COPY 2 --- --- REPRODUCED COPY.

         1. LAND USE - U.K. 2. EMINENT DOMAIN.
         I. UTHWATT, SIR AUGUSTUS ANDREWES.
         II. TITLE.

VF
690.013
(41)
G72   U.K. Ministry of Works. Council for
CP   Codes of Practice for Buildings.
draft   Oil firing. Part 2: Vaporizing oil.
11/23/61 London, British Standards Institution,
         1961. 21p. (British draft code of practice)
         AB (MECP) 6141.
         Issued for comment only.

         1. Heating. I. British Standards
         Institution.

VF
690.013
(41)
G72   U.K. Ministry of Works. Council for
CP   Codes of Practice for Buildings.
draft   Street lighting. (Revision of C.P.
11/8/61 1004-parts I and II) London, British
         Standards Institution, 1961.
         39p. (British draft code of practice;
         revision of C.P. 1004-parts I and II)
         AB (ILCP) 6042.
         Issued for comment only.

         1. Lighting. 2. Streets. I. British Standards
         Institution.

KARDEX

         U.K. Ministry of Works. Library
         Consolidated building references to
         articles in periodicals, no. 1-
         London, Jan. 1946-
         v. (Its Communication no. 18)

         nos. 1-4 called: Building references.
         For its list of book and pamphlet
         accessions see: U.K. Ministry of Works.
         Library. Consolidated accessions list
         (Periodical shelf)
                        (see card 2)

VF
690.013
(41)
G72   U.K. Ministry of Works. Council for
CP   Codes of Practice for Buildings.
draft   Painting. London, British Standards
12/1/61 Institution, 1961.
         80p. (British draft code of practice,
         revision of C.P. 231)
         AB (BLCP) 6607.
         Issued for comment only.

         1. Paints and painting. I. British
         Standards Institution.

VF
690.013
(41)
G72   Gt. Brit. Ministry of Works. Codes of Practice
Rep.no.3 Committee for Civil Engineering Public Works,
         Building and Constructional Work.
         Third Report...to Dec., 1946. London,
         H. M. Stationery Off., 1948.
         35 p.

         1. Building standards - Gt. Brit.

KARDEX

         U.K. Ministry of Works. Library
         Consolidated building references to
         articles in periodicals, no. 1-
         Jan. 1946-   (card 2)

         1. Building industry - Bibliography.
         2. Building construction - Bibliography.
         I. Title. II. Title: Building references.

VF
690.013
(41)
G72   U.K. Ministry of Works. Council for Codes
CP   of Practice for Buildings.
draft   Protection of buildings against water
5/17/61 from the ground. London, British Standards
         Institution, 1961.
         36p. (British draft code of practice)

         AB (BLCP) 183.
         Issued for comment only.

         1. Building construction - U.K.
         I. British   Standards
         Institution.

VF
690.013
(41)
G72   U.K. Ministry of Works. Council for Codes
CP   of Practice for Buildings.
draft   Tile flooring and slab flooring. London,
8/14/58 British Standards Institution, 1958.
         12p.

         CY (BLCP) 6621. (Revision of C.P. 202 :1951)
         VF690.013(41)G72 CP202.
         Issued for comment only.

         1. Floors and flooring. 2. Building stand-
         ards - U.K. I.British Standards Institution.
         II.Title.

728.1
(016)
U54H   UNITED KINGDOM. MINISTRY OF WORKS.
         LIBRARY.
         HOUSING; SELECTED LIST OF REFERENCES
         TO HOUSING AND HOUSE CONSTRUCTION.
         LONDON, 1947.
         37P. (BIBLIOGRAPHY NO. 19, JUNE 1947)
2C.
         1. HOUSING - BIBLIOGRAPHY.
         2. BUILDING CONSTRUCTION - BIBLIOGRAPHY.

VF
690.013
(41)
G72   Gt. Brit. Ministry of Works. Codes of Practice
Rep.no.2 Committee for Civil Engineering Public Works,
         Building and Constructional Work.
         Second Report, Sept. 1943. London, H. M.
         Stationery Off., 1943.
         16 p.

         Bibliography: p. 12-16.

         1. Building standards - Gt. Brit.

VF
690.013
(41)
G72   U.K. Ministry of Works. Council for
CP   Codes of Practice for Buildings.
draft   Wall tiling. Part I: Internal wall
10/23/61 tiling under normal conditions. London,
         British Standards Institution, 1961.
         16p. (British draft code of practice)
         AB (BLCP) 5005.
         Issued for comment only.
         1. Tile construction. 2. Walls.
         I. British Standards Institution.

728.1
(41:016)
U54   United Kingdom. Ministry of Works. Library.
         Housing; selected list of references to
         housing and house construction. London, June
         1947-Oct. 1949.
         2 pts. (Its bibliography No. 19 & 19A)

         1.Housing - United Kingdom - Bibliographies.
         2.Building construction - United Kingdom -
         Bibliographies. 3.Household equipment - Biblio-
         graphies.

VF
693.57
(016)
U54
United Kingdom. Ministry of Works. Library.
Prestressed concrete; some references to
the literature. London, Eng., Sept. 1950.
12 p. (Its Bibliography no. 87A)

1.Concrete - Prestressed - Bibliography.

U.K. Ministry of Works and Planning.

see

U. K. Ministry of Works

362.6
U54
United Mine Workers of America.
United Mine Workers of America welfare and
retirement fund; report. Wash., 1968-
1 v.

For complete information see main card.

1. Old age. 2. Social welfare. I. Title:
Welfare and retirement fund.

VF
691
(016)
U54
U.K. Ministry of Works. Library.
Some references to economy in the use of
building materials. London, Dec. 1951.
3 p. (Its Bibliography no. 100)

Mimeographed.

1.Building materials-Bibl. I.Title: Economy in the
use of building materials.

690.091.82
(41)
U54U
U.K. MINISTRY OF WORKS STANDARDS
COMMITTEE.
THE USE OF STANDARDS IN BUILDING.
FIRST PROGRESS REPORT. LONDON,
H.M. STATIONERY OFF., 1944.
26P.

1. BUILDING STANDARDS - U.K.
I. TITLE.

354
UN
United Nations. (Dept. of Economic and Social
Affairs)
The administration of organization and methods
series. New York, 1969.
121p. (United Nations Document ST/TAO/M/44)
Bibliography: p. 117-121.

1. Public administration. I. Title.

VF
643.3
(016)
U54
United Kingdom. Ministry of Works. Library.
Some references to kitchen design and
equipment. [London] Jan. 1948.
4 p. (Its Bibliography no. 4C)

1. Kitchens - Bibliographies.

330
U54u
The United Kingdom colonial development
and welfare acts.
U.K. Central Office of Information.
(Reference Division)
The United Kingdom colonial development
and welfare acts. London, 1956.
28p. tables.

1.Economic development. 2.Underdeveloped
countries. I.Title.

711.4
UN
1970
United Nations. (Dept. of Economic and Social
Affairs)
Administrative aspects of urbanization.
New York, 1970.
228p. ([Document] ST/TAO/M/51)
Bibliography: p. 219-228.

1. City planning. 2. City growth.
3. Public administration. 4. International
relations. I. Title.

UR-Bldg industry
DATE OF REQUEST 12/10/53   1954 C. CARD NO.
            FEB 1
AUTHOR:
U.K. Ministry of Works. Library.
TITLE: Some references to productivity in house building.

SERIES   Bibliography no. 109.

EDITION   PUB. DATE [1952]   PAGING   2 p.
PUBLISHER

RECOMMENDED BY   REVIEWED IN
                ML   World lib Acc List no. 87
                       4-5/53 p. 18
                    ORDER RECORD

330
U54u
1957
The United Kingdom colonial development and
welfare acts.
U.K. Central Office of Information
(Reference Division)
The United Kingdom colonial development
and welfare acts; April 1, 1956 to March 31,
1957. London, 1957.
10p. tables.

1. Economic development. 2. Underdeveloped
countries. I. Title.

341.1
:338
(56)
UN
United Nations. (Dept. of Economic and
Social Affairs. Div. for Public
Administration)
Administrative problems of rapid urban
growth in the Arab States. Report of a
United Nations workshop held at Beirut,
Lebanon 11 to 22 March 1963. New York,
United Nations, 1964.
153p. (United Nations [Document]
ST/TAO/M/21)

(Cont'd. on next card)

VF
697
:551.5
(016)
U54
U.K. Ministry of Works. Library.
Some references to solar heating: 1950-52.
London, April, 1952.
4 p. (Its Bibliography no. 102)

1. Heating - Solar - Bibliography.

330
U54u
1960
The U.K. colonial development and welfare acts
U.K. British Information Services.
(Reference Division)
The U.K. colonial development and
welfare acts. Rev. New York, 1960.
28p. tables. (I.D. 892 (rev))

1. Economic development. 2. Underdeveloped
countries. I. Title.

341.1
:338
(56)
UN
United Nations. (Dept. of Economic and
Social Affairs. Div. for Public
Administration)   Administrative
problems ...   (Card 2)

At head of title: United Nations
Technical Assistance Programme.

1. Technical assistance programs -
Middle East. 2. City growth - Middle
East. I. Title.

VF
614.8
:643
G72
Gt. Brit. Ministry of Works. Scientific
Advisory Committee.
An inquiry into accidents in the home.
[London, Eng.] M.O.W. Chief Scientific
Adviser's Division, Jan. 1950.
59 p. tables.

Bibliography: p.51-55.
Mimeographed.
"Issued for the benefit of research workers
and students and is not for general publication."
1.Accidents in the home.

699.81
U54un
United Kingdom fire and loss statistics, 19
U.K. Joint Fire Research Organization.
United Kingdom fire and loss statistics, 19
London, H.M.S.O., 19

v.

For Library holdings see main entry.

1. Fire prevention. I. Title.

672
UN
United Nations. (Economic Commission for
Europe)
Advances in steel technology in 1956.
Geneva, 1958.
107p. diagrs. (CE/ECE/305;E/ECE/STEEL/119)

1.Steel.

Library:
AUTHOR: Gt. Brit. Ministry of Works.
Working Party on Building Operations.
TITLE: Building. Working Party report.

PLACE: London   PUBLISHER: H.M.Sta.Off.

DATE: 1950   EDITION:
                     PAGING: 89 p.

DESCRIPTIVE NOTE AND SERIES:
ANNOTATION: Report with recommendations
on the organization and efficiency
of building operations, including those of the
specialist and subcontracting trades; the position
                    (OA-196)

S
United Kingdom Scientific Mission.
British Commonwealth Scientific Office (North
America)
List of documents received from British
Commonwealth sources   List B-
Washington, D.C.

For full information see Periodical kardex file.

1.Building construction-Bibl. 2.Engineering-Bibl.
I.United Kingdom Scientific Mission. II.Canadian
N.R.C. Scientific Liaison Office. III.Australian
Scientific Liaison Office. IV.New Zealand Sci-
entific Liaison Office. V.Union of South Africa
Scientific Liaison Office.

728.1
(4)
UNag
United Nations. (Economic and Social Council.
Economic Commission for Europe)
[Agenda items and miscellaneous publications]
Geneva.
nos. in folder. (E/ECE/)   E/ECE/SR

1. Housing - United Nations. 2. Housing -
Europe.

362.6
(083.41)
UN   UNITED NATIONS. DEPT. OF ECONOMIC
          AND SOCIAL AFFAIRS.
          THE AGING OF POPULATIONS AND ITS
          ECONOMIC AND SOCIAL IMPLICATIONS.
          NEW YORK, 1956.
          168P.

          1. OLD AGE - STATISTICS.
          2. POPULATION - STATISTICS.
          I. TITLE.

312
U54   United Nations. (Secretariat. Dept. of Social
P9   Affairs.)
          Application of international standards to
          census data on the economically active population.
          New York, Dept. of Social Affairs, Population Div.
          [and] Dept. of Economic Affairs, Statistical
          Office [1951]
          139 p.   tables (part fold.)   ([U.N.
          Document] ST/SOA/Series A. Population studies,
          no. 9; Sales no.: 1951.XIII.2)

(Continued on next page)

690.24
UN   United Nations. (Economic Commission for
1967   Asia and the Far East)
          Asphaltic roofing sheets. New York, 1967.
          9p. ([Document] L&NR/BM/12)

          At head of title: Seminar on the Development
          of Building Materials, 8-15 Jan. 1968,
          Bangkok, Thailand.

          1. Roofs and roofing. I. Title.

          United Nations. (Economic and Social Council)
330
(81)   Seminario Sobre Problemas de Urbanizacion
S25   en America Latina, Santiago de Chile, 1959.
          Algunas caracteristicas de la urbanizacion
          en Rio de Janeiro, por Andrew Pearse. [n.p.]
          United Nations, Economic and Social Council,
          1959.
          18p.   (General E/CN.12/URB/17;
          UNESCO/SS/URB/LA/17)

          1. Economic conditions - Brazil. I. Pearse,
          Andrew. II. United Nations. (Economic and
          Social Council)

          United Nations. (Secretariat. Dept. of Social
          Affairs.)   Application of international
          standards to census data ... 1951.   (Card 2)

          Prepared with the collaboration of the
          International Labour Office.
          Bibliography: p. 139.

          1.Census. I.International Labour Office. II.Title.
          III.Series: United Nations. Population studies.

691
B42   United Nations. (Economic Commission for Asia
          and the Far East)
          Bietry, J
          Assessment of the suitability for use of
          building materials and components. New York,
          United Nations, Economic Commission for Asia
          and the Far East, 1967.
          8p. (United Nations. [Document] I&NR/BM/20)
          At head of title: Seminar on the Development
          of Building Materials, 8-15 Jan. 1968,
          Bangkok, Thailand.
          1. Building materials. I. United Nations.
          (Economic Commission for Asia and the Far East)
          II. Title.

330
(8)   United Nations. (Dept. of Economic and
UN   Social Affairs.)
          Analyses and projections of economic
          development: I.An introduction to the
          technique of programming, a study prepared
          by the Economic Commission for Latin America.
          New York, 1955-
          52 p. Graphs, tables. (E/cn. 12/363-)

          Contents.-v.I. An introduction to the
          technique of programming.

          1.Economic forecasting. 2.   Economic planning -
          Latin America. I.Title.

330
(56)   United Nations. (Conciliation Commission for
UN   Palestine)
          An approach to economic development in the
          Middle East. Final report of the United Na-
          tions Economic Survey Mission for the Middle
          East. Lake Success, N.Y., 1949.
          2 pts. tables. (AAC.25/6)

          Contents: Part I. The final report and appen-
          dices.-Part II. The technical supplement.

          1. Economic de-   velopment - Middle East.
          2. Underdeveloped   countries.

690.013
UN   UNITED NATIONS. (ECONOMIC AND SOCIAL
          COUNCIL. ECONOMIC COMMISSION FOR
          EUROPE.)
          AN ATTEMPT TO COMPARE THE
          CONSTRUCTION COST OF A WORKING CLASS
          DWELLING UNIT IN DIFFERENT COUNTRIES.
          N.P., 1952.
          14P.

          1. BUILDING COSTS.

961.2
U54   United Nations. (General Assembly.)
A1950   Annual report of the United Nations
          Commissioner in Libya, prepared in consultation
          with the Council for Libya.   Lake Success,
          New York, 1950.
          110 p.   map (fold.), tables.   (Its
          Official records: 5th sess., suppl. no. 15
          (A/1340)

          Supplement, General A/1405, 28 Sept. 1950,
          mimeographed, attached.
          1.Libya.

711
:308   United Nations.
UN   Approaches to community development in urban
          areas; notes on recent experience in twenty-
          four countries and territories. New York,
          1959.
          19p. (Its series on community development)
          (ST/SOA/SER.O/32; ST/TAO/SER.D/32)

          1. Community development.

332.72
(436)   United Nations. (Economic Commission for
UN   Europe. Committee on Housing, Building,
          and Planning)
          Austria's contribution toward a study on
          housing construction finance. New York, 1969.
          14p.

          1. Mortgage finance - Austria. I. Title.

          United Nations.
          Annual survey of European housing.

728.1
(4)   1952-1955
UNe   =

728.1
(4)   1956-
UNeu

728.1
(5)   United Nations. (Technical Assistance Program)
UNa.   Asia and the Far East Seminar on Housing
          through Non-profit Organizations, Copenhagen,
          31 July - 27 August, 1956. New York, 1958.
          86p. tables. (ST/TAA/Ser.C/29,ILO/TAP/
          INT/R.1)

          1.Housing - Asia. 2.Technical assistance
          programs - Asia. I.International Labour
          Organization.

312
UN   United Nations. (Economic and Social
          Council. Population Commission.)
          Background facts on world population
          and population trends. [New York] Feb. 1957.
          56 p. (E/CN.9/139)

          Population Commission, 9th session,
          item 12 of the provisional agenda.

          1.Population.

711
:308   United Nations. (Economic and Social
UNa   Council. Social Commission)
          The applicability of community develop-
          ment to urban areas; report by the Secre-
          tary-General. [New York] 1961.
          53p. (E/CN.5/356)

          At head of title: Thirteenth session, item
          4 (b) of the provisional agenda.

          1. Community development.

312
(5)   United Nations. (Economic Commission for Asia
UNa   and the Far East)
          Asian recommendations for the 1970 housing
          censuses. New York, 1966.
          43p. (Its Document no. E/CN.11/772)

          1. Census - Housing - Asia. I. Title.

          United Nations.
711.417 Round Table Conference on the Planning and
R68   Development of New Towns, Moscow, 1964.
1964   Background paper, no. 1-15. Organized
          by the United Nations Bureau of Technical
          Assistance Operations [and others] and in
          cooperation with the Government of the Union
          of Soviet Socialist Republics. [New York]
          1964.
          15 nos.

          Contents:-no.1. The processes of world
          urbanization, by B. Ward.-no.2. Urbanization
          and urban   development in
          South-East   Asia, by the
(Cont'd. on next card).

658.564
UN   United Nations. (Dept. of Economic and
          Social Affairs)
          The application of computer technology for
          development. New York, 1971.
          122p. (United Nations publication E/4800;
          ST/ECA/136)

          1. Automation. 2. Economic development -
          Automation. I. Title.

          United Nations. (Economic and Social Council)
312
(8)   Seminario Sobre Problemas de Urbanizacion
S25   en America Latina, Santiago de Chile, 1959.
          Aspectos demograficos de la urbanizacion
          en la America Latina, por la Departamento
          de Asuntos Sociales, Naciones Unidas. [n.p.]
          United Nations, Economic and Social Council,
          1959.
          65p. (General E/CN.12/URB/18;
          UNESCO/SS/URB/LA/18)

          1. Population - Latin America. I. United
          Nations. (Economic and Social Council)

711.417 Round Table Conference on the Planning and
R68   Development of New Towns, Moscow, 1964.
1964   Background paper ...   (Card 2)

          Demographic Training and Research Centre,
          Bombay.-no.3. Urban-rural pattern of
          population distribution in Latin America
          and changes in this pattern during the
          last few decades, by Latin American
          Demographic Centre, Santiago.-
(Cont'd. on next card)

711.417
R68
1964
Round Table Conference on the Planning and
Development of New Towns, Moscow, 1964.
Background paper ...   (Card 3)

no.4. Economic problems in developing
new towns and expanded towns (with emphasis
on industrial planning and development)
by L. Rodwin.-no.5. Economic considerations
in the planning and development of new
towns, by P.B. Desai and Ashish Bose.-no.6.
Regional economic planning for the develop-
                              (Cont'd. on next card)

711.417
R68
1964
Round Table Conference on the Planning and
Development of New Towns, Moscow, 1964.
Background paper ...   (Card 4)

ment of new towns, by A.R. Kuklinski.-
no.7. Financing the construction of new
towns, by P.A. Stone.-no.8. The social
factors involved in the planning and
development of new towns, by L.E. White.-
no.9. Physical planning for the development of new towns, by B. Malisz.-

                    (Cont'd. on next card)

711.417
R68
1964
Round Table Conference on the Planning and
Development of New Towns, Moscow. 1964.
Background paper ...   (Card 5)

no.10. Physical planning for the development
of satellite and new towns, by C.A. Doxiadis.-
no.11. Building new towns, by N.V. Baranov.-
no.12. Health and sanitation factors in the
planning and development of new towns, by
World Health Organization.-no.13. Public
administration   problems of new

                    (Cont'd. on next card)

711.417
R68
1964
Round Table Conference on the Planning and
Development of New Towns, Moscow, 1964.
Background paper ...   (Card 6)

and rapidly growing towns in Asia, Report
of the Regional Seminar on Public
Administration Problems of New and Rapidly
Growing Towns in Asia.-no.14. The planning
of new capital cities, by J.E. Hardoy.-no.
15. New towns and workers' housing: action
of the ILO, by International Labour Organization.   (Cont'd. on next card)

711.417
R68
1964
Round Table Conference on the Planning and
Development of New Towns, Moscow, 1964.
Background paper ...   (Card 7)

1. New towns - Congresses. 2. Company
housing - Congresses. I. Ward, Barbara.
The processes of world urbanization.
II. Demographic Training and Research
Centre, Bombay. Urbanization and urban
development in South-East Asia. III. Latin
American Demographic Centre, Santiago.
                    (Cont'd. on next card)

711.417
R68
1964
Round Table Conference on the Planning and
Development of New Towns, Moscow, 1964.
Background paper ...   (Card 8)

IV. Rodwin, Lloyd. Economic problems in
developing new towns and expanded towns.
V. Desai, P.B. Economic considerations in
the planning and development of new towns.
VI. Kuklinski, Antoni R. Regional economic
planning for the development of new towns.
VII. Stone, P.A. Financing the con-
                    (Cont'd. on next card)

711.417
R68
1964
Round Table Conference on the Planning and
Development of New Towns, Moscow, 1964.
Background paper ...   (Card 9)

struction of new towns. VIII. White, Lesley
E. The social factors involved in the
planning and development of new towns.
IX. Malisz, Boleslaw. Physical planning
for the development of new towns.
X. Doxiadis, C.A. Physical planning for the
development of satellite and new towns.
                    (Cont'd. on next card)

711.417
R68
1964
Round Table Conference on the Planning and
Development of New Towns, Moscow, 1964.
Background paper ...   (Card 10)

XI. Baranov, N.V. Building new towns.
XII. World Health Organization. Health
and sanitation factors in the planning and
development of new towns. XIII. Regional
Seminar on Public Administration Problems
of New and Rapidly Growing Towns in Asia.
XIV. Hardoy, Jorge E. The planning of
                    (Cont'd. on next card)

711.417
R68
1964
Round Table Conference on the Planning and
Development of New Towns, Moscow, 1964.
Background paper ...   (Card 11)

new capital cities. XV. International
Labour Organization. New towns and workers'
housing. XVI. United Nations.

333.65
UNB
United Nations. (Dept. of Economic and
Social Affairs)
Basics of housing management. New York,
1969.
    80p. (Its Document ST/SOA/92)

2 c

    1. Housing management.

310
(016)
UN
United Nations. (Economic and Social Council.
Economic Commission for Africa)
Bibliography of African statistical
publications. [New York] 1962.
    206p. (United Nations [Document]
E/CN. 14/112)
    At head of title: 4th session,
Addis-Abeba, Feb.-Mar. 1962.

    1. Statistics - Africa - Bibl.

341.12
(016)
UN
United Nations. (Economic Commission for Asia
and the Far East)
Bibliography of reports issued by the United
Nations Economic Commission for Asia and the
Far East (ECAFE) July 1948-March 1957.
New York, 1958.
    129p. (UNEC D-39/58)

    1. United Nations - Publications.

691.161
UN
United Nations. (Economic and Social
Council. Economic Commission for
Asia and the Far East)
Bituminous construction terminology.
[n.p.] 1957.
    35p. tables. (E/CN.11/TRANS/Sub. 2/28)

    1.Building materials - Terminology.

---

cat.
DATE OF REQUEST 10/19/54   L. C. CARD NO.
AUTHOR United Nations.
TITLE Budget management; report of the workshop on
problems of budgetary classification and management.
SERIES
EDITION   PUB. DATE 1954   PAGING 47p.
PUBLISHER
RECOMMENDED BY   REVIEWED IN
    MML   4, 9/4/54, p.876.
          ORDER RECORD

728.1
/ 711.4
UN
No. 8
United Nations (Department of) Social Affairs.
Building and housing research. [New York]
1953.
    111 p. (Its Housing and town and country
planning bulletin 8)

    1.Building research. 2.Housing research.

691.51
UN
1968
United Nations (Economic Commission for
Asia and the Far East)
Building lime. New York, 1968.
    24p. (Its ISNR/EM/23)
    At head of title: Seminar on the Develop-
ment of Building Materials, 8-15 Jan. 1968,
Bangkok, Thailand.

    1. Lime. I. Title.

690
:331.86
(4971)
I57
United Nations.
International Labour Office.
Building trades training centre, Skopje,
Yugoslavia. Final report prepared for the
Government of Yugoslavia by the International
Labour Organisation. Geneva, United Nations,
Development Programme, 1969.
    65p.

    1. Building trades - Yugoslavia. I. United
Nations. II. Title.

728
:690
(4)
UN
United Nations (Economic Commission for
Europe)
Bulletin of housing and building statis-
tics for Europe, 1957-68-70
Geneva, 1958-64, 67, 69
    v. tables. annual.
    English and French.
    For complete information see shelf list.

1966-2C
1965-5C
1970-2C
1961-2C
1962-2C
1963-1C
1964-2C
1970-2C

    1. Housing - Europe. 2. Building construc-
tion - Europe - Statistics.

690
(4)
UNc
United Nations. (Economic Commission for
Europe. Committee on Housing)
La capacite familiale d'occupation des
logements. Note de l'Union Internationale
des Organismes Familiaux. [Geneva] 1957.
    6p.
    At head of title: Commission Economique
pour l'Europe, Comité de l'Habitat. 14ème
session - 29-31 mai 1957.

    1. Building industry - Europe.
    I. International   Union of Family
Organizations.   Family Housing
Commission.

728.1
(4)
UN.
HOU/WP
no. 100
United Nations. (Economic Commission for
Europe. Housing Committee)
Capital funds for housing. New York,
1959.
    3p. (HOU/Working paper no. 100)
    "Item 11 (ii) (a) of the provisional
agenda of the eighteenth session."

    1. Mortgage finance - Europe.

341.12
U54
C
United Nations.
Catalogue of economic and social projects.
Lake Success, N.Y.
    v. (Its Publications)

    For full information see shelf list card.

    1.City planning-Research. 2.Economic research.
3.Housing research. 4.Population. I.Title.
5.Technical assistance programs.

691.54
UNc United Nations. (Economic Commission for
Asia and the Far East).
Cement and cement products. New York,
1967.
30p. (Its I&NR/BM/13)
At head of title: Seminar on the Development of Buildings Materials, 8-15 Jan.
1968, Bangkok, Thailand.

1. Cement. 2. Concrete. 3. Building
industry - Asia. I. Title.

711.583
(5) United Nations.
UN Community development and economic
development. Bangkok, 1960.
3v. (E/CN.11/540, E/CN.11/541;
E/CN.11/542)

Contents:-pt.1. A study of the contribution of
rural community development programmes to national
economic development in Asia and the Far East.-
pt.2A. A case study of the Ghosi community
development block, Uttar Pradesh, India.-pt. 2B. A
study of farmer's associations in Taiwan.

1. Community   development -
Asia. 2. Economic   development -
Asia.

711.417
(54) United Nations. (Technical Assistance
UN Administration).
Community planning and housing for the
Pallikkaranai project, Madras, India; a
demonstration project of "the rural city": report
and recommendations of a United Nations expert
[Robert E. Alexander] New York, 1952.
143 p. illus., map, plans, tables.
(ST/TAA/K/India/1)
1.Housing-India. 2.New towns-India-Pallikkaranai.
3.Villages. I.Alexander, Robert E. II.Title.
III.Title: The Palli nai project, Community
planning and housing IV.Title: The rural
city, A demonstration project of.

711.3
T67a United Nations.
Toronto. Bureau of Municipal Research.
The centennial study and training programme
on metropolitan problems. Toronto, 1968.
[8]p.
Prepared with the co-operation of the
United Nations Public Administration Branch.

1. City growth. 2. Metropolitan areas.
I. United Nations. II. Title.

301.15
UNco United Nations. (Dept. of Economic and
1963 Social Affairs)
Community development and national
development. Report by an ad hoc Group of
Experts appointed by the Secretary-General
of the United Nations. New York, 1963.
78p. (United Nations. [Document]
E/CN.5/379/Rev.1)

1. Community development. 2. Economic
development. 3. Technical assistance
programs.

VF
728
:392 United Nations. (Economic and Social Council.
U54 Economic Commission for Europe. Industry
June 1951 and Materials Committee.
A comparative study of the utilisation of
space in current types of dwellings in 14
European countries (1948-1949) Prepared by
Maurice B. Blackshaw for the Housing Sub-
Committee. [Geneva, Switzerland] June 1951.
47 p. plans, tables (one fold.) (Its
IM/HOU/25/Rev.1)

(Continued on next card)

711.4
(84) Seminario Sobre Problemas de Urbanizacion
S25 en America Latina, Santiago de Chile, 1959.
La ciudad de Cochabamba, por Ricardo Anaya.
[n.p.] United Nations, Economic and Social
Council, 1959.
176p. (General E/CN.12/URB/16;
UNESCO/SS/URB/LA/16)

1. City planning - Bolivia. I. Anaya,
Ricardo. II. United Nations. (Economic
and Social Council)

United Nations. (Economic and Social Council)

301.15
UNc United Nations. (Economic and Social Council)
Community development and related services.
[New York] 1956.
23p.
"Twentieth report of the Administrative Com-
mittee on Co-ordination to the Economic and
Social Council, Annex III."

1. Community development. 2. Technical
assistance programs.

United Nations. Economic and Social Council.
Economic Commission for Europe. Industry
and Materials Committee. A comparative
study of the utilisation of space...1951.
(Card 2)

Abstract: p. 1.
Definitions: p. 7-8.
Mimeographed.

1.Space considerations. 2.Family living
requirements. 3.House ns. I.Blackshaw,
Maurice B. II.Title: The utilisation of space.

VF
002
:690 United Nations.
UN Classification for building documentation, by
Ellen Schoendorff. Paper presented at a conference on building documentation sponsored by the
Building Research Advisory Board, Washington,
1953.
19p.

1. Building documentation. I. Schoendorff,
Ellen.

711.583
(6) United Nations. (Economic and Social
UN Council. Economic Commission for Africa)
Community development in Africa; report of
a United Nations study tour in Ghana, Nigeria,
Tanganyika and United Arab Republic (15 October
- 3 December 1960) [New York] 1960.
26p. (E/CN.14/80)

1. Community development - Africa.

711.3
UN United Nations. (Economic and Social Council.
Economic Commission for Asia and the Far East)
The concept of a planning region; the evolution
of an idea in the United States, by John Friedmann. Tokyo, 1958.
24p.

Reproduced from Land Economics, vol. XXXII,
no. 1.
United Nations Seminar on Regional Planning.
28 July - 8 August 1958, Tokyo, Japan.
1. Regional planning I. Friedmann, John

VF
728
UN United Nations. (Economic Commission for
Europe)
Classified report of the United States dele-
gation to the Economic Commission for Europe,
Housing Committee, 19th session, Geneva,
Switzerland, December 10-11, 1959.
3p.
OFFICIAL USE ONLY
Supplements Foreign Service despatch no. 6-97,
Dec. 12, 1959 from U.S. Resident Delegation...
Geneva.
1. Housing.

711.583
UNC UNITED NATIONS. SECRETARY-GENERAL,
1953-1961 (HAMMARSKJOLD)
COMMUNITY DEVELOPMENT IN URBAN AREAS;
REPORT. NEW YORK, UNITED NATIONS,
DEPT. OF ECONOMICS AND SOCIAL AFFAIRS,
1961.
44P.

1. COMMUNITY DEVELOPMENT.

United Nations. Economic and Social Council.
Economic Commission for Europe. Industrial
and Materials Committee.)
002.69
C65 Conference on Building Documentation, Geneva,
1949 Oct. 6 - 15, 1949.
Proceedings. [Geneva] United Nations
Economic Commission for Europe [1949]
iv, 225 p. chart, tables. (E/ECE/111,
E/ECE/HOU/BD/2)

Includes papers.
Mimeographed.
Robert Fitzmaurice, chairman, Housing Sub-
Committee, also chairman of the conference.

728.1
(5) United Nations. (Economic Commission
UNc for Asia and the Far East)
Classified report of the United States
delegation to the sixth session of the
Working Party on Housing and Building
Materials of the Economic Commission for
Asia and the Far East, Bangkok, Thailand,
Nov. 21-29, 1960, by J. Robert Dodge.
[Washington] 1961.
4p.

OFFICIAL USE ONLY.

1. Housing -   Asia. 2. Building
materials - Asia.   I. Dodge, J. Robert.

UN file - Community development
DATE OF REQUEST 6/2/55   L. C/CARD NO.
AUTHOR United Nations. (Gen. assembly. Com. on informa-
tion from non-self-governing territories.)
TITLE Community development policy and administration in
non-self-governing territories.
SERIES A/AC.35/L.188. (1955)
EDITION   PUB. DATE 1955   PAGING 54p.
PUBLISHER
RECOMMENDED BY   REVIEWED IN
MWL   AIS, 5/21/55, p.4.
ORDER RECORD

690.015
C65 United Nations (Economic Commission for Europe,
1950 Industry and Materials Committee.)
Conference on Building Research, Geneva, Nov. 13-
18, 1950.
Proceedings. Geneva, United Nations Economic
Commission for Europe, Industry and Materials
Committee, Housing Sub-committee, Dec. 1950.
285 p. (General E/ECE/122;E/ECE/IM/HOU/BR/2)

Partial contents.-Transition from research to
industrial application, Ir J.P.Mazure, J.Aitken,p.
116-136.-The application of statistical techniques
to building research, J.Bronowski, p.137-151.-

(Continued on next card)

352.6
UNc United Nations. (Economic Commission for
Europe)
Committee on Electric Power, tenth
anniversary. Geneva, 1957.
1v. tables. (E/ECE/301;E/ECE/EP/191

1.Public utilities - United Nations.

728.1
/ 711.4 United Nations. (Dept. of Social Affairs.)
UN Community facilities and services. [New
No. 5 York] 1951.
113 p. (Its Housing and town and
country planning. Bulletin 5)
Bibliography: p. 58-79.

Bibliography (Building, housing and
physical planning in the USSR) p. 94-112.

1.Community facilities. 2.Community facilities - Israel.
3.Community facilities - Sweden. 4.Community facilities -
United Kingdom. 5.Housing - USSR.

Conference on Building Research, Geneva, Nov.13-
18, 1950. Proceedings...Dec. 1950. (Card 2

The application of building research in the
building industry, C.L.a'Court,p.152-167.-
The development of winter construction techniques
as a contribution to the reduction of seasonal
unemployment in the construction industry, the
Secretariat of the International Labour Office,
p.168-189.-Housing and health, J.M.Mackintosh,
p.190-202.-Transition from research to industrial

(Continued on next card)

Conference on Building Research, Geneva, Nov.13-18, 1950. Proceedings...Dec. 1950. (Card 3

application, Building Research Station (U.K.) p. 203-215.-Operational research in building,Building Research Station (U.K.)p.216-238.-Application of research in the building industry,J.H.Orendorff, p.239-275.

1.Building research. 2.Research application. 3.Building construction-Winter. 4.Housing and health. I.United Nations. Economic Commission for

(Continued on next card)

Conference on Building Research, Geneva, Nov.13-18, 1950. Proceedings...Dec. 1950. (Card 4

Europe. Industry and Materials Committee. II.Orendorff, Joseph H. III.Gt. Brit. Building Research Station. IV.International Labour Office.

341.1
:338
UN
United Nations. (Economic and Social Council)
Consideration of the establishment of an economic commission for Africa; certain questions related to the establishment and development of regional economic commissions. [Geneva] 1958.
1 v. (E/3052)

1.Technical assistance programs.

334.1
H24
UNITED NATIONS. (ECONOMIC AND SOCIAL COUNCIL, ECONOMIC COMMISSION FOR AFRICA).
Heinen, B
The contribution of cooperative housing societies to the solution of technical and social problems of urbanization. [New York] 1969.
12p. (United Nations. [Document] E/CN.14/HOU/37)
At head of title: United Nations Economic and Social Council, Economic Commission for Africa and German Foundation for Developing Countries Meeting on Technical and Social Problems of Urbanization (With
(Cont'd on next card)

334.1
H24
Heinen, B   The Contribution...1969
(Card 2)

Emphasis on financing of housing) Addis Ababa 8-23 Jan. 1969.

1. Cooperative housing. I. Title. II. United Nations. (Economic and Social Council, Economic Commission for Africa)

334.1
UN
United Nations. (Department of Social Affairs. Housing and Town and Country Planning Section)
Cooperative housing; an approach towards solving world shelter needs, prepared by Eric Carlson. [n.p., n.d.]
200 p. illus., tables.

Draft, for comments only

Bibliography: p. 183-200.

1.Cooperative housing. I.Carlson, Eric.

/F
690.031
U54c
3c.
United Nations. (Economic Commission for Europe.)
The cost of house construction; a preliminary study of measures to reduce housing costs and of the development of the building industry, prepared by the Industry Division, Economic Commission for Europe, in collaboration with Mr. A. Marini and Mr. P. Arctander. [Geneva] May 1953.
42 p. (E/ECE/165, IM/HOU/51 Rev.1)
Bibliographical footnotes.
Processed.
1.Building costs. 2.Building industry. 3.Prefabricated construction. 4.Building standards.
I.Marini, A. II.Arctander, P. III.Title.

690.031
(4)
UN
United Nations. (Economic Commission for Europe)
Cost, repetition, maintenance; related aspects of building prices. Geneva, 1963.
165p. ([Document] ST/ECE/HOU/7)

Issued also in Swedish as Statens Institut för Byggnadsforskning. Rapport R2-1965.

1. Building costs - Europe. 2. Building maintenance.   3. Building materials - Europe.

728.1
:362.6
(4)
U41
United Nations. (Economic Commission for Europe. Committee on Housing, Building and Planning)
Country monographs prepared for the general report on housing for the elderly. [n.p.] 1968.
226p. (United Nations. Document ST/ECE/HOU/22)

1. Housing for the aged - Europe.
2. Europe - Housing for the aged. I. Title.

690.031
(4)
UN
1963
FrenchEurope
United Nations. (Economic Commission for Europe)
Le coût de la construction de logements en Europe. Préparé par le Secrétariat de la Commission Economique pour l'Europe. Geneva, 1963.
1v. (United Nations. [Document] ST/ECE/HOU/8)

1. Building costs - Europe.

690.015
(485)
S82
R2-1965
United Nations. Cost, repetition, maintenance... ([U.N. Document] ST/ECE/HOU/7]
Sweden. Statens Kommitté för Byggnadsforskning.
.. Underhåll av bostadsfastigheter. Oversettning ur ECE-rapporten:(Cost, repetition, maintenance, related aspects of building prices) Stockholm, 1965.
72p. (Its Rapport R2-1965)
Issued also in English as U.N. Document ST/ECE/HOU/7.

1. Building research - Sweden. 2. Building costs - Europe. 3. Building maintenance - Europe. 4. Building materials - Europe. I. United Nations. Cost, repetition, maintenance... ([U.N. Document] ST/ECE/HOU/7)

331
(8)
825
United Nations.(Economic and Social Council)
Seminario Sobre Problemas de Urbanizacion en America Latina, Santiago de Chile, 1959. Creacion de oportunidades de empleo en relacion con la mano de obra disponible. [n.p.] United Nations, Economic and Social Council, 1959.
42p. (General E/CN.12/URB/19; UNESCO/SS/URB/LA/19)

1. Employment - Latin America. I. United Nations. (Economic and Social Council)

711.3
UNc
United Nations. (Economic Commission for Asia and the Far East)
A critical analysis of urban and regional planning practice in the countries of the ECAFE region. Paper prepared [for] Seminar on Planning for Urban and Regional Development, including metropolitan areas, new towns and land policies; sponsored by the United Nations and the Government of Japan, 10-20 October 1966, Nagoya, Japan. [n.p.] 1966.
67p. (Its E/CN.11/I&NR/PURD/L1)
1. Metropolitan area planning. 2. New towns. I. Title.

728.1
(016)
UN
United Nations. (Bureau of Social Affairs)
Cumulative list of documents and publications of the United Nations, its regional economic commissions and the specialized agencies in the field of housing, building and planning. New York,
v. (List no.
1957-   compiled by M. Monasterial.
For complete information see shelflist.

1. Housing - Bibl. 2. Building construction - Bibl. 3. Planning - Bibl. I. Monasterial, M., comp. 4. United Nations - Publications.

728.1
(016)
U54
United Nations. (Centre for Housing, Building and Planning
Cumulative list of United Nations documents and publications related to the field of housing, building and planning. New York, United Nations, Centre for Housing, Building and Planning Research, Training and Information Section, 1968.
49p.

1. Housing - Bibl. 2. Building construction - Bibl. 3. Planning - Bibl. 4. United Nations - Publications.

341.1
:338
UNc
No. 1
United Nations. (Bureau of Social Affairs)
Current activities of the United Nations, its regional economic commissions and the specialized agencies in the fields of housing, building and planning. First report... Geneva, 1957.
[44]p.

1. Technical assistance programs (UN)
2. Housing.

728.1
(083.41)
UN
United Nations. (Economic and Social Council)
Current housing statistics (Memorandum by the Secretary-General). [New York] 1960.
5p. (E/CN.3/275)

At head of title: Statistical Commission, eleventh session, item 11 of the provisional agenda.

1. Housing   statistics.

711.14
U54
1952
pt.2
United Nations. (Secretariat. Dept. of Social Affairs.)
Current information on urban land policies; a preliminary report. New York. Apr. 1952.
263 p. (General ST/SOA/9, 15 April 1952)

Includes bibliographies.
Contents.-Urban land problems and policies: preliminary analysis [Charles Abrams]-Belgium [Victor Bure]-France [Yves Salaun]-Netherlands [Th. Gundlach]-Sweden [Sven Markelius]-United States [Charles Haar and Lloyd Rodwin]-
(Continued on next card)

United Nations. (Secretariat. Dept. of Social Affairs.) Current information on urban land policies ... 1952. (Card 2)
Contents continued
United Kingdom [Gordon Stephenson]-Latin America [Francis Violich]-Less developed areas: Costa Rica; India; Israel; Singapore.-Timing of a housing scheme: case studies: Yugoslavia, Celje; United Kingdom, Liverpool; U.S., New York City; Singapore.
Processed.

(Continued on next card)

United Nations. (Secretariat. Dept. of Social Affairs.) Current information on urban land policies ... 1952. (Card 3)

1.Land use-Belgium   6.Land use-Latin America
2. "   "   -Costa Rica 7. "   " -Netherlands
3. "   "   -France   8. "   " -Singapore
4. "   "   -India   9. "   " -U.S.S.R.
5. "   "   -Israel   10. "   " -United Kingdom
I.Abrams, Charles. II.Haar, Charles. III.Markelius, Sven. IV.Rodwin, Lloyd. V.Salaun, Yves VI.Stephenson, Gordon VII.Violich, Francis VIII.Title

---

711.14
U54
1952
pt.1
United Nations. (Economic and Social Council. Social Commission)
Current information on urban land policies; interim report by the Secretary-General. New York, Apr. 1952.
10 p. (General E/EC.5/264, 3 April 1952)

Processed.

1.Land use. I.Title.

728.1
(44)
U54

3C

United Nations. (Economic Commission for
Europe. Committee on Housing, Building and
Planning)
Current trends and policies in the field of
housing, building and planning. [New York]
1969.
28p. (National monograph of France)
At head of title: Republique Francaise,
Ministere de l'Equipement et du Logement.
1. Housing - France. 2. Building construction - France. 3. City planning - France.
I. France. Min   istere de l'Equipement
et du Logement.   II. Title.

500.15
A83

United Nations.

Auger, Pierre.
Current trends in scientific research;
survey of the main trends of inquiry in
the field of natural sciences, the dissemination of scientific knowledge, and
the application of such knowledge for
peaceful ends. New York, United Nations,
1961.
245p.
In cooperation with UNESCO.

1. Scientific research.   I. United Nations.
II. United Nations   Educational,
Scientific and   Cultural Organi-
zation.

711.4
(4)
UN
1962

United Nations. (Economic Commission for
Europe)
Cycle d'etude sur la politique et la plan-
ification du développement urbain en
Europe, Varsovie, Pologne, 19-29 Septembre
1962. Rapport. Genéve, 1962.
224p. (Its [Document] SOA/ESWP/1962/1,
ST/ECE/HOU/9)
Cover title.

1. City planning - Europe.

728.1
(44)
UN

United Nations.
Cycle d'etudes europeen sur les aspects
sociaux de l'habitat, Servres, Paris, 7-16
octobre 1957. Organise par le Bureau europeen de l'Administration de l'Assistance
Technique des Nations Unies, en collaboration avec le Ministere, francais de la Sante
Publique et de la Population et l'Ecole Nationale de la Sante Publique en France.
Geneve, 1958.
173p. (UN/TAA/SEM/1957/rep.2)

1. Housing - Fra   - Social aspects.

312
U54
P8

United Nations. (Secretariat. Dept. of Social
Affairs.)
Data on urban and rural population in recent
censuses. Lake Success, New York, Dept. of
Social Affairs, Population Div. [and] Dept. of
Economic Affairs, Statistical Office, July 1950.
27 p. tables. ([U.N. Documents]
ST/SOA/Series A. Population studies, no. 8;
Sales no.: 1950.XIII.4)
(Continued on next card)

United Nations. (Secretariat. Dept. of Social
Affairs.) Data on urban and rural
population ... 1950. (Card 2)

Prepared by the Food and Agriculture
Organization of the United Nations in
collaboration with the Population Division and
the Statistical Office.
1.Census. I.Food and Agriculture Organization of
the United Nations. II.Title. III.Series: United
Nations. Population studies.

312
UNd

United Nations.
Declaracion de los jefes de estado sobre
el problema de poblacion. Presentado en
las Naciones Unidas el dia de los derechos
humanos, Diciembre, 1967. [New York] 1967.
15p.

1. Population.

312
UNde

dC

United Nations. (Economic and Social Council)
Demographic and housing statistics; principles
and recommendations for a vital statistics
system; report of the Secretary-General.
[New York] 1969.
184p. (U.N. [Document] E/CN.3/411)
At head of title: Statistical Commission,
Sixteenth session, Item 15(a) of the provisional
agenda.

1. Population. 2. Housing statistics.
I. Title.

058.7:312
D25

United Nations. (Secretariat. Statistical
Office.)
Demographic yearbook. 1948-
Lake Success.
/ v. 30 cm.
Yearbooks for 1948-   issued with the United Nations publica-
tions sales no.: 1949.XIII.1;
Prepared 1948-   by the Statistical Office of the United Nations
in collaboration with the Dept. of Social Affairs.
English and French.

Bibliography: v.1, p. 549-596.

1. Population—Yearbooks.   I. United Nations. Secretariat, Statistical Office.

HA17.D45   312.058   50—641
Library of Congress   [50t20]

330
R27

United Nations. (Economic and Social Council)

Resources for the Future.
Design for a worldwide study of regional
development. A report to the United Nations
on a proposed research-training program. A
Resources for the Future staff study.
Baltimore, Distributed by the Johns Hopkins
Press, 1966.
82p.

1. Economic development. 2. Social
conditions. 3. International organizations.
I. United Nations.   (Economic and Social
Council)   II. Title.

728
:551.5
UN
v.1

2C

United Nations. (Dept. of Economic and Social
Affairs)
Design of low-cost housing and community
facilities. V.1. Climate and house design.
New York, 1971.
93p.

1. Architecture and climate. I. Title.
II. Title: Climate and house design.

727.1
(595)
UN

[United Nations]
Design of low cost school buildings.
Federation of Malaya, Working Party on
Housing and Building Materials, sixth
session, Bangkok, Thailand. Provisional
agenda item 7. [n.p., 1960?]
[13]p.

1. Schools - Malaya.

312
U54
P17

United Nations. (Dept. of Economic and Social
Affairs).
The determinants and consequences of population
trends. A summary of the findings of studies on
the relationships between population changes and
economic and social conditions. New York, United
Nations, 1953.
404 p. (United Nations. Dept. of Social
Affairs, Ser. A: Population studies, 17)
Bibliography: p. 319-369.
ST/SOA/Series A/17
1. Population. 2. Population - Bibl. 3. Econ.
condit. 4. Social condit. I. Title.

691.54
UN
1967

United Nations. (Economic Commission for Asia
and the Far East)
Development of asbestos cement products in
the ECAFE region. New York] 1967.
17p. (Its I&NR/BM/4)

At head of title: Seminar on the Development
of Building Materials, 8-15 Jan. 1968,
Bangkok, Thailand.

1. Cement. 2. Roofs and roofing. I. Title.

666.81
K15

United Nations. (Economic Commission for
Asia and the Far East)
Kamimura, Katsuro.
Development of gypsum and gypsum products
in the ECAFE region. New York, United Nations,
Economic Commission for Asia and the Far East,
1968.
18p. (United Nations. [Document]
(L&NR/BM/27)
At head of title: Seminar on the Development
of Building Materials, 8-15, Jan. 1968, Bangkok,
Thailand.

1. Gypsum. I. United Nations. (Economic
Commission for   Asia and the Far East)
II. Title.

691.322
UN
1967

7C

United Nations. (Economic Commission for
Asia and the Far East)
Development of lightweight aggregate industry
in the ECAFE region.
1967.
37p.   (Its I&NR/BM/10)

At head of title: Seminar on the Development
of Building Materials, 8-15 Jan. 1968,
Bangkok, Thailand.

1. Concrete aggregates. I. Title.

VF
327
UNd

United Nations. (Economic and Social Council.
Economic Commission for Europe)
The development of contacts between countries
of eastern and western Europe. Report by the
executive secretary on the results achieved pursuant to resolutions 1 (X) and 4 (XI). Geneva,
1957.
1v. (E/ECE/271)

Twelfth session. Provisional agenda item no. 8.

1. International relations.

360
UN

United Nations. (Dept. of Economic and
Social Affairs)
The development of national social
service programmes; report by the group
of experts appointed by the Secretary-
General of the United Nations. New
York, 1959.
70p. (ST/SOA/40)

1. Social service.

691.338
UN
1967

United Nations.(Economic Commission for Asia
and the Far East)
Development of the fibreboard and particle
board industry in the ECAFE region. [New York]
1967.
34p. (Its I&NR/BM/3)
At head of title: Seminar on the Development
of Building Materials, 8-15 Jan. 1968, Bangkok,
Thailand.

1. Wallboard. I. Title: Fibreboard and
particle board industry in the ECAFE region.
II. Title.

Ref
058.7
:690
UN
1968

3C

United Nations. (Economic and Social
Council. Economic Commission for Europe.
Committee on Housing, Building and
Planning.)
Directory of authorities and principal
organization related to the building
industry. Geneva, 1968.
77p. ([United Nations. Document]
ST/ECE/HOU/35; United Nations Publication,
sales number: E.69.II.E.9)
1. Building industry - Direct.
2. Building   industry - Europe -
Direct.   I. Title.

Ref
058.7
:690.015
(4)
U54
1951

2C

United Nations. (Economic and Social Council.
Economic Commission for Europe.)
Directory of building research and development
organizations in Europe. Geneva, published
jointly with the Housing and Town and Country
Planning Section of the Department of Social
Affairs, 1951.
114 p. ([United Nations. Document]
ST/SOA/SER.H/4, Sept. 1951; United Nations
Publications, sales number: 1951.IV.5)

(Continued on next card)

United Nations. Economic and Social Council.
Economic Commission for Europe. Directory
of building research and development
organizations in Europe...1951.   (Card 2)

UN series: Organizations concerned with
building, housing and town and country planning.

1. Building research-Europe-Direct. I. United
Nations. Secretariat. Dept. of Social Affairs.
2. Research-Direct.

308
:728.1
H68e

United Nations. (Economic Commission
for Europe)
U.S. Housing and Home Finance Agency.
Office of the Administrator. Office
of International Housing.
ECE seminar on the preparation of
housing surveys and housing programs;
a memorandum and publications submitted
by the United States of America (Office
of International Housing, Housing and
Home Finance Agency) [Washington] 1961.
5p.

1. Housing surveys. I. United Nations.
(Economic   Commission for
Europe)

VF
330
(8)
UNe

United Nations (Department of Public
Information)
The economic growth of twenty republics;
the work of the Economic Commission for
Latin America. 3d rev. ed. New York [1956]
34 p.

1. Economic conditions - Latin America.

058.7
:690.015
(4)
U54
1950

United Nations. (Economic Commission for
Europe. Industry and Materials Committee. Housing Sub-Committee)
Directory of building research organizations in Europe. Geneva, 1950.
108p. ([United Nations. Document]
General E/ECE/121, IM/HOU/BR/3)

1. Building research - Europe - Direct.

330
(4)
UNe

United Nations. (Economic and Social Council.
Economic Commission for Europe)
ECE, the first ten years, 1947-1957. Geneva,
1957.
1v. charts. (E/ECE/291)

Housing: Chapter VI.

1. Economic development - Europe. 2. Housing -
Europe.

361
U54

United Nations. (Secretariat. Dept. of Social
Affairs.)
Economic measures in favour of the family; a
survey of laws and administrative regulations
providing for economic measures in favour of the
family in various countries.   New York, 1952.
175 p.   (United Nations. [Document] ST/SOA/8.
31 Mar. 1952; Sales no.: 1952.IV.6)

Housing: p. 75-114.
1. Public assistance. Family income and
expenditure. I. Title.

058.7
:711.400.15
Un

United Nations. (Economic Commission for
Europe. Committee on Housing, Building
and Planning)
Directory of national bodies concerned
with urban and regional research. Second
provisional version. New York, 1968.
3v. (Its HOU/CONF.URB.Research/B.1)
At head of title: Conference of Senior
Officials of National Bodies Concerned
with Urban and Regional Research,
Stockholm, 24 April - 1 May 1968.
1. City planning - Research - Direct.
2. Regional planning - Research -
Direct. I.   Title.

728.1
(485)
UN

United Nations. (Economic Commission for
Europe. Housing Committee)
ECE's Housing Committees study-trip in
Sweden, June 19-22, 1960. [Stockholm]
1960.
kit. (19 pieces)

1. Housing - Sweden. 2. Cooperative
housing - Sweden. 3. Economic development -
Sweden.

330
(60)
UN

United Nations. (Dept. of Economic and
Social Affairs)
Economic survey of Africa since 1950. New
York, 1959.
248p. tables. (E/CN.14/28)

1. Economic conditions - Africa.

058.7
:711.400.15
UNd

United Nations.
Directory of national bodies concerned
with urban and regional research. [New
York] 1968.
134p. (Its [Document] ST/ECE/HOU/34)

3c.
c.1, Ref.

1. City planning - Research - Direct.
2. Regional planning - Research - Direct.
3. Associations - Direct. I. Title:
National bodies concerned with urban and
regional research.

330
(8)
P15

United Nations. (Economic Commission for
Latin America)
Pan American Union.
Economic and social survey of Latin America,
1961. Prepared jointly by the Secretariats of
the Organization of American States (OAS)
and the Economic Commission for Latin America
(ECLA) under the direction of the OAS.
Washington, 1961.
2v.
At head of title: Provisional.
1. Economic conditions- Latin America.
2. Social conditions - Latin America. I. United
Nations. (Economic Commission for Latin America)
II. Title.

33
(5)
U54

United Nations. (Economic and Social Council.
Economic Commission for Asia and the Far East.
Economic survey of Asia and the Far East.
194 -   New York, 19
v. tables. (United Nations.
[Document] E/CN ...)

For full information see shelf list card.

1. Econ. condit.-Asia. I.Title.

058.7
:061.6
U54

United Nations. (Economic and Social Council.
Economic Commission for Asia and the Far East.
Sub-Committee on Iron and Steel.)
Directory of research and technical facilities
relating to the iron and steel industry.   New
York, Nov. 1951.
64 p.   (E/CN.11/I&S/29, 8 Nov. 1951)
Reproduced from original issued at Bangkok,
on 4th session, 15-17 Jan. 1952, Rangoon, Burma.
Processed.
1. Industrial research-Direct.

VF
33(8)
U54
1950

United Nations. (*Economic and Social Council. Economic
Commission for Latin America.*)
The economic development of Latin America and its prin-
cipal problems. Lake Success, United Nations Dept. of Eco-
nomic Affairs, 1950.
v, 59 p. diagrs. 28 cm. (United Nations. [Document] E/CN.12/
89/rev. 1. 27 Apr. 1950)
"United Nations publications. Sales no.: 1950. II. G. 2."
1. Econ. condit.-Latin America.
1. Spanish-American—Econ. condit.—1918—   (Series)
JX1977.A2 E/CN.12/89/rev.1   330.98   50-9828
— Copy 2.   HC161.U523
I. United Nation: Secretariat. Dept of
Economic Affairs.
Library of Congress   [5]

33(4)
U54

United Nations. Economic and Social Council.
Economic Commission for Europe. Research
and Planning Division.)
Economic survey of Europe in 1950 -
Geneva, United Nations Dept. of Economic Affairs,
1951 -
v. tables. (United Nations.
[Document] E/ECE/ ...)

For full information see shelf list card.
1951 survey also issued as v.3, no.3 of the
Economic Bulletin for Europe.
(Continued on next card)

R
058.7
:711.4
H58

United Nations.
U.S. Dept. of Housing and Urban Development.
Div. of International Affairs
A directory of urban and regional planning
research agencies of national scope in the
USA for the United Nations, Economic Com-
mission for Europe. Washington, 1967.
28p.

1. City planning - Direct. 2. Regional
planning - Direct. I. United Nations.
(Economic Commission for Europe) II. Title.

VF
330
(4)
UN

United Nations. (Economic and Social Council.
Economic Commission for Europe)
Economic development of Southern Europe. Note
by the executive secretary on action taken pursuant to resolution 7 (XI). Geneva, 1957.
3p. (E/ECE/274)

Twelfth session. Provisional agenda item
no. 11.

1. Economic development - Europe.

United Nations. Economic and Social Council.
Economic Commission for Europe. Research
and Planning Division. Economic survey
of Europe in 1950 - ... 1951. (Card 2)

1. Economic conditions-Europe. I.Title:Economic
survey of Europe.

338
UN

United Nations. (Economic and Social
Council. Statistical Commission)
Draft revised international standard
industrial classification of all
economic activities. [Geneva] 1958.
1 v. (E/CN.3/243)

1. Manufacturers. I.Title: International
standard industrial classification of all
economic   activities.

330
(8)
UNeco

United Nations. (Economic and Social Council.
Economic Commission for Latin America)
Economic development, planning and international co-operation. [New York] 1961.
76p. (E/CN.12/582)

At head of title: Economic and Social Council
Economic Commission for Latin America, ninth
session, Caracas, May 1961.

1. Economic development - Latin America.

33(8)
U54
1951

United Nations. (Economic and Social Council.
Economic Commission for Latin America)
Economic survey of Latin America 1950, general
introduction: Recent developments and trends in
the economy of Latin America. New York, Apr.
1951.
205 p. graphs. (United Nations.
[Document] E/CN.12/217. 16 April 1951)

Item 4 of agenda of fourth session, Mexico
City, May 28, 1951.
"Reproduced in New York from the original
issued at Mexico City." processed.
(Continued on next card)

United Nations. Economic and Social Council.
Economic Commission for Latin America.
Economic survey of Latin America 1950...1951.
(Card 2)

1.Econ. condit.-Latin America. I.Title.

647.1
U54
1951
United Nations. (Secretariat. Dept. of Social
Affairs.)
Enquiries into household standards of living
in less-developed areas; a survey of the organization and geographic and demographic range of
field investigations of the income, expenditure,
and food consumption of selected households in
Africa, Asia, the Caribbean, Latin America, and
the Pacific (1940-1950)   New York, 1951.
191 p.   (ST/SOA/1, 6 July 1950; Sales no.:
1950.IV.7)

(Continued on next card)

711.4
(8
:016)
UN
United Nations. (Economic and Social Council)
Ensayo bibliografico sobre urbanizacion en
America Latina. [n.p.] 1959.
88p.   (E/CN.12/URB/14; UNESCO/SS/URB/LA/
14)

At head of title: Seminario sobre Problems de
Urbanizacion en America Latina, Santiago, Chile,
1959.

1. City planning - Latin America - Bibliography.

694.1
UN
United Nations. (Economic and Social Council)
Economic Commission for Europe. Timber
Comm.)
Economy in the use of timber for housing
purposes. [New York] March 1951.
16, 10 p. diagrs., tables. (Its
Publication E/ECE/124, E/ECE/TIM/36)

Report by Evert Strokirk, submitted to
the Working Party on More Rational
Utilisation of Wood, July 1950.
1.Wood construction. 2.Building costs.
I.Strokirk,   Evert.

United Nations. (Secretariat. Dept. of Social
Affairs.)   Enquiries ... 1951.   (Card 2)

"Descriptions of the enquiries with bibliographical references:" p. 63-182.

1.Family income and expenditure. I.Title.

330
UNes
United Nations. (Industrial Development Organi-
zation)
The establishment of the brick and tile
industry in developing countries, by H.W.H. West.
New York, United Nations, 1969.
122p. (United Nations. [Document] ID/15)

1. Underdeveloped countries. 2. Brick
industry. 3. Tile. I. West, H.W.H. II. Title.

728.1
(4)
UN
HOU/WP
no.87
United Nations. (Economic Commission for
Europe. Housing Committee)
Effect of government measures designed to
promote the technological development of the
building industry and reduce housing costs.
New York, 1958.
132p. diagrs., tables. (HOU/Working
paper no. 87)

1. Housing - Europe. 2. Building industry - Europe.
3. Housing costs - Europe.

301.15
(6761)
UN
United Nations. (Economic and Social
Council. Economic Commission for
Africa)
An enquiry into community development
in Uganda, by V. L. Griffith. New York.
1960.
86p.   ([Document] E/CN.14/81)

Third session. Provisional agenda item
10(c)

1. Community development - Uganda. I. Griffith,
V. L.

711.73
UNe
United Nations. (Economic Commission for
Europe. Inland Transport Committee)
European agreement on road markings done
at Geneva on 13 December 1957. [Geneva]
7p. (E/ECE/303; E/ECE/TRANS/501)

English and French.

1.Traffic safety. I.Title: Road markings.

728.1
(4)
UN
HOU/WP
no. 97
United Nations. (Economic and Social Council.
Economic Commission for Europe. Housing
Committee)
Effect of government measures designed to
promote the technological development of the
building industry and reduce housing costs.
New York, 1959.
31 pts. in 1 v. (HOU/Working paper no. 97)
"Item 11 (ii) (a) of the provisional
agenda of the eighteenth session."
1. Housing - Europe. 2. Housing costs -
Europe. 3. Building industry - Europe.

728
:392
UN
1951
UNITED NATIONS. ECONOMIC COMMISSION FOR
EUROPE. HOUSING COMMITTEE.
A COMPARATIVE STUDY OF THE UTILISATION
OF SPACE IN CURRENT TYPES OF DWELLINGS
IN 14 EUROPEAN COUNTRIES (1948-1949).
PREPARED BY MAURICE B. BLACKSHAW. NEW
YORK, 1951.
1 V.

1. SPACE CONSIDERATIONS.
I. BLACKSHAW, MAURICE B.   II. TITLE.

728.1
:711.4
UN
United Nations. (Economic Commission for
Europe)
European governments agree on main lines
of co-operation in the fields of housing,
building and town planning. Geneva, 1961.
2p. (Press release no. ECE/HOU/69)

1. Housing. 2. Planning.

690
(4)
UN
UNITED NATIONS. ECONOMIC COMMISSION FOR
EUROPE.
EFFECT OF REPETITION ON BUILDING
OPERATIONS AND PROCESSES ON SITE. REPORT
OF AN ENQUIRY UNDERTAKEN BY THE COMMITTEE
ON HOUSING, BUILDING AND PLANNING. NEW
YORK, 1965.
140P.

1. BUILDING CONSTRUCTION - EUROPE.
2. BUILDING COSTS - EUROPE. 3. BUILDING
INDUSTRY - EUROPE.

333.332
U71
2c.
United Nations. (Economic Commission for
Europe. Housing Committee)
U.S. Urban Renewal Administration.
Enquiry into techniques of appraising the
quality of neighbourhood units, housing
areas and individual dwellings. [Prepared]
for Economic Commission for Europe Housing
Committee. [Wash.] 1964.
66p.

1. Appraisal. 2. Real property -
Valuation. 3. Urban renewal. I. Title.
II. United Nations. (Economic Commission
for Europe.   Housing Committee)
III. U.S. Hous-   ing and Home Finance
Agency.

728.1
(4)
UNEURO
UNITED NATIONS. (ECONOMIC COMMISSION
FOR EUROPE. INDUSTRY DIVISION.)
THE EUROPEAN HOUSING DEVELOPMENT AND
POLICIES IN 1954. GENEVA, 1955.
61P. (E/ECE/209; E/ECE/HOU/54)

1. HOUSING - EUROPE. I. TITLE.

690
UNe
1965
United Nations. (Economic Commission for
Europe)
Effect of repetition on building operations
and processes on site. Report of an enquiry
undertaken by the Committee on Housing,
Building and Planning. New York, 1965.
140p. (United Nations. [Document]
ST/ECE/HOU/14)

1. Building industry. 2. Building
construction. 2. Building costs. I. Title:
Building operations   and processes on
site.

728.1
(4)
UNen
United Nations. (Economic Commission for
Europe. Housing Committee)
Enquiry into the economic and technical
aspects of the lifetime of a house. [New
York] 1960-62.
Kit. (18 pieces)

Partial contents: List of participants.-
Comparative costs of wooden and steel standard
windows.-Depreciation on multi-family houses.-
Annual costs of different types of constructions.-Country memoranda: Austria, Netherlands,

(Cont'd on next card)

728.1
(4)
UNeur
1949

3 c.
United Nations. (*Economic and Social Council. Economic Commission for Europe. Industry and Materials Committee.*)
The European housing problem; a preliminary review [by]
United Nations Economic Commission for Europe, Industry
and Materials Committee, Housing Sub-committee. Geneva,
1949.
1 v. (various pagings) 33 cm. (United Nations. [Document]
E/ECE/110. 1 Oct 1949)
See card 2 for subjects 2-19.
1. Housing—Europe.   I. Title.
JX1977.A2 E/ECE/110   331.833   50-997
—— Copy 2.   HD7332.U45
                                                (Continued on next card)
Library of Congress   [3]

728.1
(4)
UNenc
United Nations. (Economic Commission for
Europe. Housing Committee)
Encuentros Mediterraneos. Barcelona,
Spain, 1961.
154p.

1. Housing - Europe - Congresses.

728.1
(4)
UNen
United Nations. (Economic Commission for
Europe. Housing Committee) Enquiry...
(Card 2)

Denmark.-Monographies nationales: Italie.

1. Housing - Europe. 2. Building costs -
Europe. I. Title: Economic and technical
aspects of the lifetime of a house.

United Nations. Economic and Social Council.
Economic Commission for Europe. Industry and
Materials Committee. The European housing
problem...1949.   (Card 2)

2.Housing-Austria. 3.Housing-Belgium. 4.Housing-
Czechoslovakia. 5.Housing-Denmark. 6.Housing-Finland.
7.Housing-France. 8.Housing-Great Britain. 9.Housing-
Greece. 10.Housing-Hungary. 11.Housing-Ireland.
12.Housing-Italy. 13.Housing-Luxembourg. 14.Housing-
Netherlands. 15.Housing-Norway. 16.Housing-Poland.
17.Housing-Sweden. 18.Housing-Switzerland. 19.Housing-
Union of Soviet Socialistic Republics.

728.1
(4)
UNe
United Nations (Economic Commission for
Europe. Industry and Materials Committee.
Housing Subcommittee)
European housing progress and policies in
1952 - Geneva, 1953 -
v. tables.
1953 has also: Preliminary report;
Appendix (Country reports) with addendum
(translation of foreign language reports)
Processed.

1. Housing - Europe. I. Title.

338
:672
U54e
1954
United Nations. (Economic Commission for
Europe.)
The European steel market, 1954-55-
Geneva, 1955-56-
v. tables (Its [Document] E/ECE/.
E/ECE/Steel/)

1. Steel industry - Europe. I. Title.
(Series)

312
(5
:016)
UNf
United Nations. (Economic Commission for
Asia and the Far East)
Family planning, internal migration and
urbanization in ECAFR countries. A bibliography of available materials. Part one:
Family planning. Part two: Internal
migration and urbanization. New York, 1968.
66p. (Asian population studies series
no. 2. E/CN.11/807)

1. Population - Asia - Bibl. 2. Population
shifts - Asia - Bibl. 3. City growth - Asia -
Bibl. 4. Asia - Population - Bibl.
5. Asia - Population shifts - Bibl.
6. Asia - City growth - Bibl. I. Title.

728.1
(4)
UNh
1956
United Nations. (Economic Commission for Europe)
The European housing situation. Geneva,
January 1956. tables. (E/ECE/221;E/ECE/
HOU/57)

1. Housing - Europe. I. Title.

341.1
1338
UNe
United Nations. (Economic and Social Council. Technical assistance Committee)
Expanded programme of technical assistance. New York,
v. tables. (E/TAC/--)

For complete information see shelf list.

1. Technical assistance programs (U.N.)

332.72
UNF
1966
UNITED NATIONS. ECONOMIC AND SOCIAL
COUNCIL.
FINANCE FOR HOUSING AND COMMUNITY
FACILITIES IN DEVELOPING COUNTRIES.
NEW YORK 1966.
132P. (UNITED NATIONS PUBLICATION
NO. E C.6 32 REV.1)

1. MORTGAGE FINANCE. 2. COMMUNITY
FACILITIES. 3. UNDERDEVELOPED
COUNTRIES. I. TITLE.

728.1
(4)
UNh
United Nations. (Economic Commission
for Europe. Housing Committee)
The European housing situation.
[New York] Sept. 1955.
104 p. appendices. tables (part
fold.) (HOU/WP. 1/23)

Mimeographed.

1. Housing - Europe.

728.1
711.585 United Nations. (Housing and Town and Country
UN Planning Section.)
The experience of national governments in pre-
paring programmes for housing and community
improvement; a preliminary report by Jacob L.
Crane, consultant. [New York] United Nations
Technical Assistance Administration, Dec. 1953.
42 l.
Preliminary background paper for the United
Nations Regional Seminar for Asia and the Far East
on Housing and Community Improvement, New Delhi,
21 January - 17 February 1954.
Processed.
1. Housing. 2. Urban redevelopment. I. Crane,
Jacob L. II. Title.

332.72
UNf
1968
United Nations. (Dept. of Economics and
Social Affairs)
Finance for housing and community
facilities in developing countries. New
York, 1968.
67p. (United Nations. [Document]
ST/SOA/79)

1. Mortgage finance. 2. Community
facilities. I. Title.

728.1
(4)
UNeu
United Nations. (Economic and Social Council.
Economic Commission for Europe)
European housing trends and policies in 1956-
Geneva, 1957-
v. tables. (Its Document E/ECE/.
1957-2c E/ECE/HOU/...
1960-2c
1961/62-2c For complete information see shelf list.

1. Housing - Europe. I. Title.

DATE OF REQUEST 10/7/53 L.C. CARD NO.

Cat. OCT 13 1953

AUTHOR U.N. (Economic Commission for Latin America.)

TITLE 5th Session, Rio de Janeiro, Brasil, 9 April, 1953;
preliminary study of the technique of programming
economic development.

SERIES E/CN.12/292

EDITION | PUB. DATE May. 1953 | PAGING 305 p.

PUBLISHER

RECOMMENDED BY MWL REVIEWED IN LJ 8/8/53 p.7

ORDER RECORD

332.72
UNf
United Nations. (Dept. of Economic and
Social Affairs)
Finance for housing and community facilities in developing countries. New York, 1968.
67p. (United Nations. Document ST/SOA/
79)
4c.
1. Mortgage finance. 2. Community facilities. 3. Underdeveloped countries. I. Title.

312
(4)
UN
1970
United Nations. (Statistical Commission and
Economic Commission for Europe)
European recommendations for the 1970 population
censuses; regional variant of parts V and VI of
the world recommendations for the 1970 population
censuses. New York, 1969.
97p. (Conference of European Statisticians.
Statistical standards and studies no. 13; United
Nations. [Document] ST/CES/13)
1. Population - Europe. 2. Census - Population
- Europe. I. Conference of European Statisticians.
II. Title.

711.4
P17f
United Nations. (Economic Commission for Europe.
Committee on Housing, Building and Planning)
Perfait, F
Factors influencing the future pattern and
forms of urban settlements. Demographic,
economic and social factors. [n.p.] 1966.
8p. (United Nations. [Document] HOU/
URB/SETT.SEM/C.1)
At head of title: [United Nations] Economic
Commission for Europe. Committee on Housing,
Building and Planning. Seminar on the Future
Pattern and Forms of Urban Settlements,
Amsterdam, 25 Sept.-7 Oct. 1966.

(Cont'd on next card)

332.72
(60)
T74
United Nations. (Economic Commission for
Africa)
Tribe, M
The finance of housing in the public and
private sectors. [New York] United Nations,
Economic and Social Council, 1968.
21p. (United Nations. [Document] E/CN.14
HOU/31)
At head of title: United Nations Economic
and Social Council, Economic Commission for
Africa and German Foundation for Developing
Countries Meeting on Technical and Social
Problems of Urbanization (With Emphasis on
Financing of Housing) Addis Ababa,
(Cont'd on next card)

VF
333.63
(4)
U54
United Nations. (Economic Commission for Europe.)
European rent policies. [Geneva] Aug. 1953.
62 p. (E/ECE/170, E/ECE/IM/HOU/44)

1. Rent control 2. Family income and expenditure-
Housing. I. Title.

711.4
P17f
Perfait, F. Factors influencing the future
pattern and forms of urban settlements 1966.
(Card 2)

1. City planning. 2. Land use. 3. Population. 4. Housing. I. United Nations. Economic Commission for Europe. Committee on
Housing, Building and Planning. II. Title.

332.72
(60)
T74
Tribe, M The finance...1968. (Card 2)

8-23 Jan. 1969.

1. Mortgage finance - Africa. I. United
Nations. (Economic Commission for
Africa) II. Title.

691.71
U54
United Nations. (Economic Commission for
Europe.)
European steel exports and steel demand in
non-European countries. Geneva, 1953.
242, 14 p. maps, tables. (E/ECE/163,
E/ECE/Steel/75)

1. Steel.

312
(5:016)
UN
United Nations. (Economic and Social
Council. Economic Commission for Asia
and the Far East)
Family planning in Asia: a draft
bibliography. Bangkok, Thailand, 1967.
57p. (Its Asian population studies
series no. 2; United Nations Document
E/CN.11/797)

1. Population - Asia - Bibl. I. Title.

VF
332.72
(8)
UN
Spanish
United Nations. (Technical Assistance
Adm.)
Financiamiento de los programas de
construccion de viviendas y de mejoramiento de la communidad en America Latina,
por Carlos L. Acevedo, Eric Carlso, Jorge
A Videla. Nueva York, 1956.
93p. (TAA/LAT/7, rev. 1)

1. Mortgage finance - Latin America.
2. Housing - Latin America. I. Acevedo,
Carlos L.

Card 1 (row 1, col 1)

728.1
:33
UN

United Nations. (Economic and Social Council.
Social Commission.)
Financing of housing and community improvement programmes. [New York?] March 1955.
100 p. (E/CN. 5/307)

Bibliographical footnotes.

1. Housing. 2. Housing - Asia. 3. Housing -
Latin America. 4. Housing - Europe. 5. Housing -
Canada. 6. Cooperative housing. 7. Mortgage
finance. 8. Housing costs. I. Title.

Card (row 1, col 2)

VF
312
U54f
1950

United Nations. (Economic and Social Council.
Population Commission.)
Findings of studies on the relationships
between population trends and economic and
social factors (report submitted by the
Secretariat) [Lake Success, N.Y., April -
May 1950]
3 pts. (UN [Document] E/CN. 9/55, E/CN.9/
55 Add. 1, E/CN. 9/55/Add.2)

Bibliographical footnotes.
Housing: pt. 2, p. 17-20.
Mimeographed.
1.Population. 2. Housing. I.United Nations.
Secretariat.

Card (row 1, col 3)

711.3
1(4)
S25

United Nations.
Seminar on the Future Pattern and Forms of
Urban Settlements.
The future pattern and forms of urban
settlements; proceedings of the seminar, the
Netherlands, 25 Sept. - 7 Oct., 1966. New
York, 1968.
2v. (United Nations [Document] ST/ECE/
HOU/28)

1. City growth - Europe. 2. New towns -
Europe. 3. Europe - City growth. 4. Europe -
New towns. I. Title. II. United Nations.

Card (row 2, col 1)

728.1
:330
UN
1957

United Nations. (Dept. of Economic and
Social Affairs.)
Financing of housing and community improvement programmes. New York, 1957.
61p.

1. Housing. 2. Housing - Africa. 3. Housing
- Latin America. 4. Housing - Europe.
5. Housing - Asia. 6. Housing - North America.
7. Mortgage finance.

Card (row 2, col 2)

33
(8)
UNf

United Nations. (Department of Economic and
Social Affairs.)
Foreign capital in Latin America.
New York, 1955.
164 p. tables. (E/CN.12/360,ST/ECA/28)

1. Economic conditions - Latin America. I. Title

Card (row 2, col 3)

690.072
UNg

United Nations. (Economic and Social
Council. Committee on Housing, Building
and Planning)
General activities of the Centre for
Housing, Building and Planning; training of
skilled manpower in the field of housing,
building and planning. Report of the
International Labour Organisation.
[New York] 1969.
123p. (Its [Document] E/C.6/95)
At head of title: Committee on Housing,
Building and Planning, Sixth Session, 2 to
12 Sept. 1969, item 8 (d) of the
provisional agenda.
(Cont'd on next card)

Card (row 3, col 1)

332.72
UN
1957

United Nations. (Social Commission)
Financing of housing and community
improvement programmes; draft position
paper. New York, 1957.
5p. (Agenda Item 5)

11th session.

1. Mortgage finance.

Card (row 3, col 2)

728.1
/711.4
UNf
no. 11

United Nations. (Dept. of Economic and Social
Affairs)
Formacion de personal para la planificacion
urbana y rural. Seminario sobre formacion de
personal para la planificacion urbana y rural.
Puerto Rico, marzo de 1956. New York, 1957.
129p. illus., charts. (ST/SOA/Ser.C/11;
Vivienda, construccion y planificacion no. 11)

Issued also in English.

1. Housing. 2. City planning.

Card (row 3, col 3)

690.072
UNg

United Nations. (Economic and Social
Council) General activities...1969.
(Card 2)

1. Building construction - Labor
requirements. I. International Labour
Organisation. II. Title.

Card (row 4, col 1)

VF
332.72
(8)
UN

United Nations. (Technical Assistance Administration)
Financing of housing and community improvement
programmes in Latin America; prepared by Carlos L.
Acevedo, Eric Carlson, Jorge A. Videla. New York,
October 1956.
87 p. (Its TAA/LAT/7)

1.Mortgage finance - Latin America. 2.Housing -
Latin America. I.Acevedo, Carlos L. II.Title.

Card (row 4, col 2)

341.1
:338
U54f

United Nations. (Secretariat. Technical Assistance
Administration.)
Formulation and economic appraisal of
development projects ... lectures delivered at the
Asian Centre on Agricultural and Allied Projects,
Lahore, Pakistan, Oct. - Dec. 1950. [Lahore?]
Technical Assistance Administration Training
Institute on Economic Appraisal of Development
Projects [1951]
2 v.

1.Technical assistance programs.I.Asian Centre
on Agricultural and Allied Projects. II.Title.

Card (row 4, col 3)

690.015
(061.3)
UN

United Nations (Economic and Social
Council. Economic Commission for
Europe. Industry and Materials Committee)
General Assembly of the International
Council for Building; to be held in the
Palais des Nations, Geneva, from 25 to
30 June 1953 inclusive. [Geneva] 1953.
4p. (Document E/ECE/161/, E/ECE/IM/HOU/
CIB/1)

At head of title: United Nations. Economic
and Social Council. Economic Commission for
Europe. (Cont'd on next card)

Card (row 5, col 1)

332.72
(4)
UN

United Nations. (Economic Commission for
Europe. Housing Committee)
Financing of housing in Europe. Geneva,
1958.
86p. tables.

1. Housing - Europe. 2.Mortgage finance -
Europe.

Card (row 5, col 2)

711.585
(44)
UN

[United Nations] (Economic Commission for
Europe. Housing Committee)
France. Documents photographiques sur des
operations de renovation urbaine. Geneve,
1961.
[16]p.

1. Urban renewal - France.

Card (row 5, col 3)

690.015
(061.3)
UN

United Nations ... General Assembly of
the International Council...1953. (Card 2)

Industry and Materials Committee. Housing
Sub-Committee.

1. Building research - Congresses.
2. International Council for Building
Research Studies and Documentation.

Card (row 6, col 1)

728.1
(4)
UN
HOU/wp
no. 66/add 5

United Nations. (Economic Commission
for Europe. Housing Committee)
Financing of housing in Europe. Chapter V. Summary of conclusions [n.p.]
1957.
21p. tables. (Its HOU/working paper
no. 66/Add 5)

"Item 2 of the provisional agenda of the fifteenth
session."

1. Mortgage finance - Europe. 2. Housing - Europe.

Card (row 6, col 2)

DATE OF REQUEST   FEB 24 1953   L. C. CARD NO. 52-2343

AUTHOR U. N. (Relief and Works Agency for Palestine
Refugees in the Near East.)
TITLE From camps to homes,
SERIES United Nations publication. 1951.I.16.
EDITION | PUB. DATE [1951] | PAGING unpaged.
PUBLISHER New York, U.N. Dept. of Public Information.
RECOMMENDED BY MML | REVIEWED IN
ORDER RECORD

Card (row 6, col 3)

647.1
UNg

United Nations. (Economic and Social Council)
General conclusions concerning statistical
aspects of international definition and measurement of levels of living. Prepared by the
Secretary - General. [n.p.] 1956.
19p. (E/CN.3/2 14)

1. Cost and standard of living.

Card (row 7, col 1)

VF
312
U54f
1951

United Nations. (Economic and Social Council.
Population Commission.)
Findings of studies on relationships between
population trends and economic and social factors
(provisional revised report submitted by the
Secretariat) New York, N.Y., Mar. 1951-
pts.
For full information see shelf listcards
Includes bibliographies.
Mimeographed.

1.Population. I.United Nations. Secretariat.

Card (row 7, col 2)

330
(6678)
UN

United Nations. (General Assembly)
The future of Togoland under French
administration. [n.p.] 1957.
86p. (A/3677)

Previously T/1336 and Corr.1, T/1336/
Add.1 and Corr.1 and T/1336/Add.2.

1.Economic conditions - Togoland, French.

Card (row 7, col 3)

33
(612)
L45

United Nations. (Technical Assistance Adminis-
tration.
Lindberg, John
A general economic appraisal of Libya.
New York, United Nations, Technical Assistance
Administration, 1952.
55 p. tables. (ST/TAA/K/Libya/1)

1.Econ. condit.-Libya. 2.Population-Libya.
I.United Nations. (Technical Assistance Administration.) II.Title.

UN file - Social welfare
DATE OF REQUEST April 20, 1953 L. C. CARD NO.
AUTHOR
United Nations
TITLE General policies and major problems of social
development (U.N. Secretariat)
SERIES A/AC.35/L.24
EDITION | PUB. DATE Aug. 1952 | PAGING 36 p.
PUBLISHER
RECOMMENDED BY | REVIEWED IN
ORDER RECORD

United Nations. (Economic Commission
for Africa)
332.72
(667) Koenigsberger, O   H
K62   The Ghana roof loan scheme. [New York]
United Nations, Economic and Social Council,
1969.
10p. (United Nations. [Document]
E/CN.14/HOU/32, 10 Jan. 1969)
At head of title: United Nations Economic
and Social Council Economic Commission for
Africa and German Foundation for Developing
Countries Meeting on Technical and Social
Problems of Urbanization (With Emphasis on
Financing of Housing) Addis Ababa, 8-23 Jan.
1969.   (Cont'd on next card)

647.1
UNh   United Nations. (Statistical Office)
1965   Handbook of household surveys; a practical
guide for inquiries on levels of living.
Provisional ed. New York, 1954.
172p.   (Its Studies in methods, ser.
F, no. 10)
United Nations. [Document]
ST/Stat/ser.F/10.
Bibliography: p. 165-169.

1. Cost and standard of living. I. Title.

312
:728.1 United Nations. (Statistical Office)
UN   General principles for a housing census
1st   (first draft) New York, 1956.
draft   27p. ([Document] ST/STAT/P/L/22)

1. Census - Housing.

690.031
UNg   United Nations. (Economic Commission for
Europe)
Government policies and the cost of build-
3 c   ing. Geneva, 1959.
1v. diagrs., tables. (E/ECE/364;
E/ECE/HOU/86)

1. Building costs. 2. Building industry.
I. Title.

312
UNh   United Nations. (Statistical Office)
Handbook of population census methods.
New York,
v. tables. (Its Studies in methods,
ser. F, no. 5, rev. 1)
United Nations. Document. ST/STAT/Ser. F/
5/rev. 1.
Provisional edition published in 1949 under
title: Population census handbook.

(Continued on next card)

312
:728.1   United Nations. (Economic and Social
UN   Council)
2d draft   General principles for a housing census.
(second draft) New York, 1957.
34p. (E/CN.3/240/Add.1,ST/STAT/P/L.22/
Rev.1)

1.Census - Housing.

312
UNg   United Nations. (Dept. of Economic and Social
Affairs)
Growth of the world's urban and rural popula-
tion, 1920-2000. New York, 1969.
124p. (Its Population studies no. 44;
[Document] ST/SOA/series A/44)

1. Population. I. Title.

312
UNh   United Nations. (Statistical Office) Handbook of population census ... (Card 2)

Contents: -v. 1. General aspects of a
population census. -v. 2. Economic characteristics of the population.

1. Census - Population. I. Title.

312
:728.1   United Nations. (Statistical Office)
UN   General principles for a housing census.
1958   New York, 1958.
14p. (Its Statistical papers series M,
no. 28, ST/STAT/Ser. M/28)

1. Census - Housing.

711.585
UN   United Nations. (Dept. of Economic and Social
Affairs)
Improvement of slums and uncontrolled
settlements. Report of the Interregional
Seminar on the Improvement of Slums and
Uncontrolled Settlements, Medellin, Colombia,
15 Feb. - 1 March 1970. New York, 1971.
203p. (United Nations [document] ST/TAO/
SER.C/124)
Bibliography: p. 184-189.
1. Slums. 2. City growth. I. Interregional
Seminar on the Improvement of Slums and
(Cont'd on next card)

United Nations. (Economic Commission for Asia
691.11   and the Far East)
I52   India. National Buildings Organisation.
Hardboards. New Delhi, National Buildings
Organisation and U.N. Regional Housing Centre
ECAFE, 1968.
10p. (Its Technical information series 29)

1. Wood. I. United Nations. (Economic
Commission for Asia and the Far East) II. Title.

67
(41)   United Nations. (Economic and Social Council.
U54   Economic Commission for Europe. Industry and
Materials Committee.)
A general survey of the European engineering
industry. Geneva, Apr. 1951.
228 p. tables (part fold.) (General
E/ECE/125, E/ECE/IM/56, 18 April 1951)

Mimeographed.

1.Industry-Europe. I.Title.

711.585
UN   United Nations. (Dept. of Economic and Social
Affairs) Improvement...1971. (Card 2)

Uncontrolled Settlements, Medellin,
Colombia, 1970. II. Title.

VF
691.41   United Nations.(West Indian Conference, 1950.)
C51   Crane, Jacob L
Homes of earth. [New York, United Nations
1951?]
12 p.

Issued as separate document for 1950 West
Indian Conference.
Processed.

United Nations. (Economic Commission for
332.72   Africa).
(43)   Lehmann, Werner.
L23   The German saving-for-building system -
a pattern for the encouragement of private
home financing. [New York] United Nations,
Economic and Social Council, 1968.
19p. (United Nations. [Document] E/CN.14
HOU/36, 19 Dec. 1968)
At head of title: United Nations Economic
and Social Council, Economic Commission for
Africa and German Foundation for Developing
Countries Meeting on Technical and Social
Problems of Urbanization (With Emphasis on
(Cont'd on next card)

058.7
:670   United Nations. (Economic Commission for
UN   Africa)
A guide to manufacturers of small-scale
machinery in the Federal Republic of
Germany, France, Japan, and India. [New York]
1969.
114p. (Its [Document] E/CN.14/INR.151)

1. Manufacturers - Direct. I. Title.

690
UN   United Nations. (Social Commission)
1963   Housing, building, and planning. 15th
session, position paper. [New York]
1963.
6p. (Document E/CN.5/36)
Unclassified; SD/E.CN/5/145. Apr. 11, 1963

1. Building construction. 2. Housing.
3. City planning.

332.72
(43)   Lehmann, Werner. The German...1968.
L23   (Card 2)

Financing of Housing) Addis Ababa, 8-23 Jan.
1969.

1. Mortgage finance - Germany. I. United
Nations. (Economic Commission for Africa)
II. Title.

728.1
(4)   United Nations. (Economic Commission for
UNho   Europe. Housing Committee)
HOU/Conf. Room documents. New
New York,
nos. in 1v. (looseleaf)

1. Housing - Europe.

690.031
(5)   United Nations. (Economic Commission for Asia
UN   and the Far East)
Housing and building materials. New York,
1958.
16p. (Its Industrial development series.
ST/ECAFE/SER.M/11)

1.Building costs - Asia. 2. Mortgage finance -
Philippine Islands

691
:338
(8)
UN

United Nations. (Economic Commission for Latin America)
Housing and building materials industry, Central American economic integration programme. New York, 1960.
96p. tables. (ST/SOA/41)

1. Building materials industry - Latin America.

330
:728.1
UN

United Nations. (Economic Commission for Europe. Housing Committee)
Housing and economic development, by D. V. Stefanovic. [New York] 1961.
28p. (Housing Seminar/7)
Seminar on problems that arise in the preparation of housing surveys and the drawing up of housing programmes, with special reference to countries in the course of industrialization.
1. Economic development.   2. Housing.
I. Stefanovic, D. V.

728.1
:362.6
(485)
UNh

United Nations.
Housing and social services for old people. Introductory talk by the Director of the Social Welfare Office, Helge Dahlström, before the European Section of the United Nations Conference at Wegimont, Belgium. [n.p.] 1955.

1. Housing for the aged - Sweden.
I. Dahlström, Helge.

728.1
711.4
UN

United Nations. (Dept. of Social Affairs)
Housing and town and country planning, bulletin no. 1 - Lake Success, N.Y. [etc.] 1948 -
v. (ST/SOA/SER.C/3-)

Title varies: no. 9 - Housing, Building and Planning.
1. Housing. 2. City planning. I. Title.
II. Title: Housing, building and planning.

VF
728.1
711.4
U54

United Nations. (*Secretary-General, 1946- (Lie*)
Housing and town and country planning; report prepared in consultation with the interested specialized agencies through the Administrative Committee on Co-ordination. [Lake Success, 1949]
50 p. 32 cm. (United Nations. [Document] E 1343. 8 June 1949)
Caption title.
At head of title: United Nations Economic and Social Council. 9th sess., item 6 of the provisional agenda.
1. Housing. 2. Cities and towns—Planning. I. United Nations. Economic and Social Council. (Series)
JX1977.A2 E/1343   331.833   50–13534
——— Copy 2.   HD7287.U47

Library of Congress   [3]

728.1
711
UN

United Nations. (Dept. of Social Affairs)
Housing and town and country planning organizations. New York, 1949, 50
New York,
(Its Miscellany no. 1 -
——— Alphabetical index.

For complete information see shelf list.
1. Housing. 2. City planning. I. Title.

728.1
711.4
(729)
W66

United Nations. (Social and Economic Council.)
Woodhouse, W M
Housing and town planning in tropical areas. Barbados, Development and Welfare in the West Indies, July 1949.
59 l.

United Nations, Social and Economic Council, Resolution 122 (VI); report requested by Secretary-General Oct. 13, 1948 (SOA 14/01/CHF).

728.1
H68hou

United Nations. (Economic Commission for Europe)
U.S. Housing and Home Finance Agency.
Housing and urban development - U.S.A. A current review. [Washington, D.C.?] 1964.
96p.
Prepared for the Committee on Housing, Building and Planning of the United Nations Economic Commission for Europe.
English, French and Russian.
1. Housing. 2. Mortgage finance. 3. Community development. 4. City planning.
I. United Nations. (Economic Commission for Europe)

728.1
:77
UN

United Nations. (Department of Economic and Social Affairs)
Housing, Building, Planning; an international film catalogue. New York [May 1956]
246 p. (Its ST/SOA/Ser. E/5)

1. Housing films.

United Nations.

Housing, building and planning bulletin.

see its

Housing and town and country planning bulletin.

341.1
:338
UNc
no. 2

United Nations. (Bureau of Social Affairs)
Housing, building and planning; current activities of the United Nations, its regional economic commissions and the specialized agencies. Bangkok, Thailand, 1958.
[41]p. (E/CN.11/I&NR/HBWP.5/L.6)

Economic Commission for Asia and the Far East. Working paper no. 2.
Second report on Current activities in housing, building and planning of the United Nations.

1. Technical assistance programs (UN) 2. Housing.

VF
312
(489)
D25

United Nations.
Denmark. Boligministeriet.
Housing censuses in Denmark. Copenhagen, 1966.
13p. (Working paper no. 30)
Prepared by the Statistical Dept., Denmark.
At head of title: United Nations Seminar on Housing Statistics and Programmes.

1. Census - Housing - Denmark. 2. Housing - Denmark. I. Title. II. United Nations.

690
(47)
UN

[United Nations. (Economic Commission for Asia and the Far East)]
Housing construction in the USSR. Documents for the VIth session of the Working Party on Housing and Building Materials of the Committee on Industry and Natural Resources of the ECAFE. Moscow, 1960.
19p.

1. Building construction - U.S.S.R.

690.031
(4)
UNh
1963

United Nations. [Economic Commission for Europe]
Housing costs in European countries. Geneva, 1963.
78p. (United Nations. [Document] ST/ECE/HOU/8)

1. Building costs - Europe.

VF
728.1
W67

United Nations.
World Veterans Federation.
Housing for the disabled. Preliminary report prepared for the Housing Committee of the Economic Commission for Europe by the World Veterans Federation as rapporteur. Paris, 1958.
33p. (WVF-DOC/1004)

1. Housing for the handicapped. I. United Nations. (Economic Commission for Housing Committee)

728.1
:362.6
UN
1965

United Nations. (Economic Commission for Europe. Committee on Housing, Building and Planning)
Housing for the elderly. Proceedings of the Colloquim, held in Belgium and the Netherlands, 4-15 October, 1965. New York, 1966.
2v. (Its [Document] ST/ECE/HOU/19)
1. Housing for the aged. 2. Old age.
3. Nursing homes. 4. Mortgage finance.
I. Title.

728.1
(60)
UNho

United Nations.
Housing in Africa. New York, 1965.
221p. (United Nations publication E/CN/14HOU/7/Rev.)

1. Housing - Africa. 2. Economic conditions - Africa. I. Title.

728.1
(481)
N67h

United Nations. (Economic Commission for Europe).
Norway. Boligdirektoratet.
Housing in Bergen and Fana, Voss, Oslo and Baerum (Documentation material for ECE's study trip 1960) Oslo, 1960.
1v.

1. Housing - Norway. 2. Norway - Housing. I. United Nations. (Economic Commission for Europe). II. Title.

728.1
(667)
UNh

United Nations. (Technical Assistance Housing Mission to Ghana)
Housing in Ghana. New York, 1957.
220p. (ST/TAA/K/GHANA/1)

1. Housing - Ghana.

728.1
(4391)
U54

United Nations. (Economic Commission for Europe. Committee on Housing, Planning and Town Planning in Hungary)
Housing in Hungary. [Geneva] 1965.
110p.

1. Housing - Hungary. I. Title.

VF
728.1
(497+56)
UN

United Nations. (Economic Commission for Europe. Housing Committee)
Housing in the less industrialized countries of Europe. Geneva, July 1956.
58 p. tables. (E/ECE/HOU/61)

Contents. - Pt. 1. Mission to Yugoslavia. - Pt.2. Mission to Turkey.

Processed.

1. Housing - Turkey. 2. Housing - Yugoslavia. I. Title.

728.1
/711.4
UN
no. 6

United Nations. Dept. of Social Affairs.
Housing and Town and Country Planning
Section.
Housing in the tropics. [New York, Jan.
1952]
148 p. illus. (Its Housing and town and
country planning. Bulletin 6)
Bibliography: p. 100-140.
Partial contents.-Economics of rural
tropical housing, by Roy J. Burroughs.
-A manual for developing an aided self-help
housing   programme, prepared by

(see card 2)

728.1
/711.4
UN
no.10

United Nations (Dept. of Economic and
Social Affairs.) Housing through
non-profit organizations. (Card 2)

"Bibliography on non-profit housing":
p.119-121.

1.Housing. 2.Aided-self-help housing.
3.Cooperative housing.

728.6
UN1

United Nations. (Economic Commission for
Europe. Housing Committee)
Inquiry on rural housing in the United
States of America, by Roy J. Burroughs and
J. Robert Dodge of the International Housing
Service, Housing and Home Finance Agency.
Washington, 1958.
41p.
"Preliminary draft for review."
---- --- Appendix by J. Robert Dodge.
Rev. 1960. 14p.
1. Farm housing.   I. Burroughs, Roy J.
II. Dodge, J. Robert.   III. U.S. Housing
and Home Finance Agency.   Office of the
Administrator. Inter-   national Housing Service

728.1
/711.4
UN
no. 6

United Nations. Dept. of Social Affairs.
Housing and Town... Jan. 1952. (card 2)

the Housing and Home Finance Agency.

1. Housing in the tropics. 2 Aided
self-help housing. 3. Sanitation. I.
Burroughs, Roy J   II. U.S. Housing and
Home Finance Agency.

711.585
UN

United Nations. (Dept. of Economic and Social
Affairs)
Improvement of slums and uncontrolled
settlements. Report of the Interregional
Seminar on the Improvement of Slums and
Uncontrolled Settlements, Medellin, Colombia,
15 Feb. - 1 March 1970. New York, 1971.
203p. (United Nations document ST/TAO/
SER.C/124)
Bibliography: p. 184-189.

1. Slums. 2. City growth. I. Interregional
Seminar on the Improvement of Slums and

(Cont'd on next card)

United Nations.
332.72
(8)
B82

Buelink, J   H
Instituciones de ahorro y prestamo para la
vivienda. Trabajo realizado para la Seccion
de Vivienda y Planeamiento Urbano y Rural de
las Naciones Unidas, por encargo del Grupo de
Estudio de la mencionada Organizacion sobre
el Financiamiento de la Vivienda y Desarrollo
Comunal. Mexico, 1955.
53p. diagrs., tables.

1. Savings and loan associations - Latin
America. I. United Nations.

728.1
(51)
UN
1967

2C

United Nations. (Economic and Social
Council. Committee for Housing, Build-
ing and Planning)
Housing management: Hong-Kong Housing
Society. Prepared in compliance with
Resolution 1168 (XLI) Economic and Social
Council on Social Aspects of Housing and
Urban Development. New York, Center for
Housing, Building and Planning, United
Nations, 1967.
[14]p.   (Case report no.1)

1. Housing - Hong-   Kong. 2. Housing
management. 3. Build-   ing societies.
I. Hong-Kong Housing   Society. II. Title.

711.585
UN

United Nations. (Dept. of Economic and Social
Affairs) Improvement...1971.

Uncontrolled Settlements, Medellin, Colombia,
1970. II. Title.

058.7
:3
U54
1950

United Nations. (Economic and Social Council.)
Inter-governmental organizations; list of
inter-governmental organizations in the economic
and social fields. [Lake Success, N.Y.] May
1950.
59 p.   (General E/1687, 23 May 1950)

Processed.

1.Associations-Directory. I.Title.

728.1
:362.6
(485)
UN

United Nations.
The housing needs of elderly people, by
Hjalmar Mehr, Mayor for Social Affairs,
Stockholm. Wegimont, Belgium, European
Office of the United Nations, 1955.
21p.

1. Housing for the aged - Sweden.
I. Mehr, Hjalmar.

728.1
(083.41)
UNs
Spanish

United Nations. (Dept. of Economic and
Social Affairs. Statistical Office of
the United Nations)
Indicadores estadisticos de las condi-
ciones de habitacion. Naciones Unidas,
1962.
33p.   (Its Informes estadisticos serie
M no. 37)

1. Housing statistics.

728.1
/711.4
UN
No. 9

United Nations. (Dept. of) Social Affairs.
International action in Asia and the
Far East. [New York] 1955.
131 p. (Its Housing, building and
planning no. 9)

Contents.-pt. 1 - United Nations
programme in housing, building and planning. -
pt. 2 - United Nations Seminar on housing and
community improvement: papers and reports.

728.1
(4)
UNh
1968

United Nations. (Economic Commission for
Europe)
The housing situation and perspectives for
long-term housing requirements in European
countries. Geneva, 1968.
116p. (Its Documents ST/ECE/HOU/32)

1. Housing - Europe. 2. Housing statistics -
Europe. 3. Europe - Housing. 5. Europe -
Housing statistics. I. Title.

330
(60)
UN1

United Nations. (Economic Commission for
Africa)
Industrial growth in Africa. New York, 1963.
100p.   (United Nations. [Document]
E/CN.14/ONR/1/Rev.1)

1. Economic development - Africa.
2. Technical assistance programs - Africa.
I. Title.

354.
(016)
UN

UNITED NATIONS (TECHNICAL ASSISTANCE
PROGRAMME)
INTERNATIONAL BIBLIOGRAPHY OF PUBLIC
ADMINISTRATION. NEW YORK, 1957.
101P.

TITLE PAGE, INTRODUCTION, AND CAPTIONS
IN ENGLISH, FRENCH, AND SPANISH.
ENTRIES IN THE LANGUAGE OF THE
ORIGINAL WORK.

1. PUBLIC ADMINISTRATION -
BIBLIOGRAPHY.

728.1
(436)
UN

United Nations. (Economic and Social Council.
Economic Commission for Europe. Housing
Committee)
Housing study trip to Austria. [n.p.] 1957.
Kit.

Material in English, German, French.

1.Housing - Austria. 2.Building materials -
Austria. I.Title.

FF-UN-Special OCT 30 1951;   DATE OF REQUEST   yet agencies   L. C. CARD NO.
10/25/51
AUTHOR
U.N. (Secretary General.)
TITLE Information on regional co-ordination of programmes
of the United Nations and specialized agencies.
SERIES
E/1884
EDITION   PUB. DATE Nov. 10,   PAGING 48 p.
PUBLISHER Lake Success, N.Y.   1950
U.N. Economic and Social Council,
RECOMMENDED BY | REVIEWED IN
                        ORDER RECORD

UN-Technical assistance   DATE OF REQUEST   C CARD NO.
April 20, 1953   MR 24 1953
AUTHOR
United Nations
TITLE International collaboration in regard to economic,
social and educational conditions (U.N. Secretariat)
SERIES
A/AC.35/L.95
EDITION   PUB. DATE Aug 1952   PAGING 34 p.
PUBLISHER
RECOMMENDED BY | REVIEWED IN
            MWL   UN
                        ORDER RECORD

728.1
/711.4
UN
no.10

3C

United Nations (Dept. of Economic and
Social Affairs.)
Housing through non-profit organizations.
Seminar sponsored by the United Nations
and the Government of Denmark, in collaboration with the Organization of American
countries, Copenhagen, Sept.-Oct. 1954.
New York, 1956.
121p. illus. (Its Housing, building
and planning no. 10; ST/SOA/SER.C/10).

(Continued on Card 2)

690
UN
1952

United Nations.
Information on United Nations activities
in the fields of building, housing, and
town and country planning. New York, 1952.
17p.

1. Building construction. 2. Housing.
3. City planning.

551.015
U54

2C

UNITED NATIONS. ECONOMIC AND SOCIAL
COUNCIL.
INTERNATIONAL CO-OPERATION IN THE
FIELD OF SEISMOLOGICAL RESEARCH,
SEISMOLOGY AND EARTHQUAKE ENGINEERING.
NEW YORK, 1962.
37P. (ITS 34TH SESSION, AGENDA
ITEM 14(C))

1. EARTHQUAKES - RESEARCH.
I. TITLE.

690.015
UN
1953
United Nations. (Economic Commission for
Europe)
International Council for Building
Research and Documentation, structure and
programme of work. Geneva, 1953.
6p. (Its Press release no. ECE/HOU/
15)
At head of title: Information Centre,
European Office of the United Nations,
Geneva. Economic Commission for Europe.

1. Building research - Europe.
2. International Council
for Building   Research, Studies and
Documentation.

690.015
I572c
United Nations.
International Council for Building Research,
Studies and Documentation.
[The Council] set up. (CIB). Geneva,
1953.
3p. (Press release no. ECE/HOU/14)

At head of title: United Nations Centre.
European Office of the United Nations,
Geneva.

1. Building research. 2. Building
documentation. I. United
Nations.

647.1
Un1
United Nations. (Economic and Social
Council)
International definition and measurement
of levels of living, progress report by the
Secretary-General. New York, 1960.
32p. (E/CN.3/270)

1. Cost and standard of living.
2. Family living requirements. I. Title.

647.1
UN
United Nations. (Economic and Social Council)
International definition and measurement of
standards and levels of living, by Sir Andrew
Davidson. [n.p.] 1955.
18p. (E/CN.5/302/ add. 3)

1. Cost and standard of living. I. Davidson,
Sir Andrew.

058.7
:362
U54
United Nations. (Department of Social Affairs.)
International directory of nation-wide
organizations concerned with family, youth and
child-welfare. [New York] Dec. 1952.
289 p. (ST/SOA/14)

1.Social welfare. I.Title.

551
U54
United Nations. (Governing Council)
International Institute of Seismology and
Earthquake Engineering, Phase II (JPN 2)
New York, 1968.
7p. (United Nations. [Document] DP/SF/R.6/
Add. 20)
At head of title: United Nations Develop-
ment Programme (special fund) Recommendation
of the Administrator. Japan.
Governing Council, sixth session, 11-28
June 1968. Agenda item 3.
1. Earthquakes. I. I. Title.

VF
658
UN
U.N. (Statistical Office)
International standard industrial classification of all economic activities. New York,
1958.
27p. tables. (Its ST/STAT/SER.M/4/Rev.1)

--- Indexes. New York, 1959. 359p.

I. Title: Industrial classification of all
economic activities.

308
UN
United Nations. (Economic and Social
Council. Bureau of Social Affairs.)
International survey of programmes of
social development. Prepared by the
Bureau of Social Affairs, United Nations
Secretariat, in cooperation with the
International Labour Office, the Food and
Agricultural Organization, the United
Nations Educational, Scientific and Cultural
Organization and the World Health Organiza-
tion. [n.p.] 1955.
591p. (Document E/CN.5/301)

1.Social   conditions. 2.Housing.

308
UN
rev.
United Nations. (Secretariat. Bureau of
Social Affairs)
International survey of programmes of social
development. Prepared in cooperation with the
International Labor Office, the Food and Agriculture Organization, the United Nations Educational, Scientific and Cultural Organization
and the World Health Organization. Rev. ed.
New York, 1955.
219p. (E/CN.5/301/Rev.1; ST/SOA/21)
1. Social conditions. 2. Housing.
3. Planning.

308
UN
1959
United Nations.
International survey of programmes of
social development, prepared by the Bureau
of Social Affairs, United Nations Secretariat
in cooperation with the International Labour
Office, the Food and Agricultural Organization
of the United Nations, the United Nations
Educational Scientific and Cultural Organization and the World Health Organization. New
York, 1959.
190p. (E/CN.5/332; ST/SOA/39)

1. Social   conditions.
2. Housing.   3. Planning.

669
I57
United Nations. (Industrial Development Organi-
zation)
Interregional Symposium on Metalworking In-
dustries in Developing Countries, Moscow,
1966.
Report. Vienna, United Nations Industrial
Development Organization, 1968.
97p. (United Nations Industrial Development
Organization. ID/8)
Bibliography: p. 95-97.
1. Metal-work. 2. Underdeveloped countries.
3. Industrial development. I. United Nations
(Industrial Development Organization) II. Title:
Metalworking in   dustries in developing
countries.

69
(4)
U54
1951
United Nations. (Economic and Social Council.
Economic Commission for Europe. Industry
and Materials Committee.)
Investment in housing and building in
selected European countries; a preliminary
review, prepared by Yves Salaün. [New York]
Economic Commission for Europe, Industry and
Materials Committee, Housing Sub-committee,
Working Party on Programmes and Resources, Oct.
1951.
60 p. charts, tables. (IM/HOU/WP.1/10,
9 Oct. 1951)
(continued on next card)

United Nations ...   Investment in housing and
building ... Oct. 1951.   (Card 2)

Restricted.
Processed.

1.Building industry-Europe. I.Salaün, Yves.
II.Title.

333.65
M22m
1964
Spanish
United Nations.-.(Bureau of Social Affairs)
Meeting of Group of Experts on Housing Management and Tenant Education, Wellington, N.Z.,
1964.
Junta de un grupo de expertos en administracion de viviendas y en educacion de
inquilinos. Bajo los auspicios de la Direccion
de Ayuda Tecnica y la Direccion de Asuntos
Sociales y la cooperacion del Gobierno de
Nueva Zelandia. New York, Naciones Unidas,
1964, 1968.
79p.
1. Housing management. 2. Tenant selection.
I. United Nations   (Bureau of Social
Affairs)

711.14
UN
U.N. (Economic Commission for Europe.
Committee on Housing, Building and Planning)
Land planning,
[New York] 1964
/ nos. (Its HOU/LAND no. 15-1720)
Title varies.
At head of title: Preparatory group for the
Seminar on the Supply and Allocation of Land
for Housing and related purposes.
For complete information see shelf list.
1. Land use.
planning.
government.
    2. City
    3. Local

711.14
(415)
I72
United Nations
Ireland (Eire) National Institute for
Physical Planning and Construction Research.
Land use and building condition surveys.
Dublin, [1968?]
27p.
At head of title: Specimen development
plan manual; a project of the Government of
Ireland assisted by the United Nations Special
Fund and the United Nations.

1. Land use - Ireland. 2. Housing surveys -
Ireland. I. United Nations. II. Title.

728.1
(8)
L17
1962
United Nations.
Latin American Seminar on Housing Statistics and
Programmes, Copenhagen and Stockholm, 1962.
Report. New York, United Nations, 1963.
87p. (United Nations. [Document] E/CN.12/647/
rev.1)
Sponsored by the United Nations and the
Government of Denmark.
Bibliography: p. 83-84.

1. Housing - Latin America. I. United Nations.
II. Denmark. (Series)

VF
728.1
UN1i
United Nations. (Economic and Social Council.
Economic Commission for Europe. Housing
Committee)
List of delegates,   session,
    Geneva,
    (HOU/WP/3/)

Library keeps latest list only.

1. Housing - Congresses.

341.1
(016)
UN 2
United Nations. (Economic Commission for
Europe)
List of documents in the HOU series and
HOU subseries. Geneva, 1955-
nos. (Its HOU/--)

1. United Nations - Publications.

690.37
U54
1951
United Nations. (Secretariat. Dept. of Social
Affairs.)
A list of institutions connected with
building research or testing of building
materials in India. In Its Low cost housing
in south and south-east Asia. New York, N.Y.,
Mar. - Apr. 1951, v.2, App. E, 2 p.

1.Building research-India.

712.23
UN
United Nations. (Economic and Social Council)
List of national parks and equivalent re-
serves; report by the Secretary-General.
[New York] 1961.
301p. ([Document] E/3436)

Thirty-first session, agenda item 12.

1. National parks and reserves.

690
(03-4)
UN

United Nations. (Department of Conferences
and General Services)
List of terms relating to building
construction and town planning. Liste de
termes concernant les questions de construction et d'urbanisme. [New York, n.d.]
10 L. (Its terminology bulletin no. 55)

English - French

1. Building construction - Dictionaries.
2. City   planning - Dictionaries.

United Nations. Secretariat. Dept. of Social
Affairs.   Low cost housing...1951   (Card 2)

1.Housing in the tropics. 2.Housing-Asia.
3.Housing-India. 4.Housing-Indonesia. 5.Housing-
Malaya, Federation of. 6.Housing-Pakistan.
7.Housing-Philippines. 8.Housing-Siam. 9.Housing-
Singapore. I.United-Nations-Tropical-Housing
Mission. II.Crane, Jacob L. III.Title.

336.211
U54

United Nations. (Dept. of Economic and Social
Affairs)
Manual of land tax administration; including
valuation of urban and rural land and improvements. New York, 1968.
176p. (United Nations [Document] ST/ECA/103)

1. Real property - Taxation. 2. Real property - Valuation. I. Title.

DATE OF REQUEST 7/2/53   L. C. CARD NO.
Technical assistance   JUL 13 1953
AUTHOR U.N. (ECOSOC)
TITLE Local costs to be borne by governments under the
expanded programme of technical assistance, report of
the working party of the Technical Assistance Committee
SERIES   E/TAC/4
EDITION   PUB. DATE Mar. 1953   PAGING   26 p.
PUBLISHER
RECOMMENDED BY   REVIEWED IN
                    TCP 5/4/53 p.8
            ORDER RECORD

647.1
UNm

United Nations. (Economic and Social Council)
Maintenance of family levels of living;
social policy relating to social insurance,
social assistance and related social services.
Report by the Secretary-General. [New York]
1957.
87p. (E/CN.5/321)
At head of title: Social Commission, eleventh
session, agenda item 6.

1. Family income and expenditure. I. Title:
Family levels of   living.

690
:336.18
UN

United Nations. (Dept. of Economic and
Social Affairs)
Manual on self-help housing. New York,
1964.
114p. (United Nations. [Document]
ST/SOA/53)

1. Aided self-help housing.

711.583
UN

United Nations. (Social Development Div.)
Local participation in development planning;
a preliminary study of the relationship of
community development to national planning.
New York, 1967.
64p. (United Nations [Document] ST/SOA/77)

1. Community development. I. Title.

728-1
(4)
UNM

UNITED NATIONS. ECONOMIC COMMISSION FOR
EUROPE.
MAJOR LONG-TERM PROBLEMS OF GOVERNMENT
HOUSING AND RELATED POLICIES.   NEW
YORK, 1966.
2 V. (ST/ECE/HOU/20.)

1. HOUSING - EUROPE.   I. TITLE.

690
021

United Nations. Dept. of Economic and Social
Affairs. Manual on self-help housing.
Oceana Publications, inc.
Self help housing; a handbook for village
workers, prepared by the staff of Oceana
Publications in cooperation with the Housing
Building and Planning Branch of the United
Nations Secretariat. Dobbs Ferry, N.Y., 1964.
59p.
"Based on... Manual on self-help housing,
published by the United Nations Secretariat/as
document ST/SOA/53, 1964."

1. Owner-built houses.   2. Aided self-help
housing. I. United   Nations. Dept. of
Economic and Social   Affairs. Manual on
self-help housing.   II. Title.

728.1
(4)
UN
HOU/wp
no. 99

United Nations. (Economic and Social Council. Economic Commission for Europe.
Housing Committee)
Long-range program of concerted international action in the field of low-cost
housing and related community facilities.
New York, 1959.
27p. (HOU/Working paper no. 99; E/CN.5/339.
"Item 10(1) of the provisional agenda of the
eighteenth session."

I. Housing. 2. Community facilities. I. Title:
Low-cost housing and related community facilities.

301.15
M19m

United Nations.
May, Richard, Jr.
Major trends in world urbanization and their
environmental implications; Symposium on the
Impact of Urbanization on Man's Environment,
Onaway, Mich., 14-20 June 1970. Working paper
no. 1, Agenda item 1. New York, United
Nations, 1970.
54p.
Sponsored by the United Nations in co-
operation with the International Trade Union
of the United Automobile, Aerospace and
Agricultural Implement Workers of America.

(Cont'd on next card)

691.41
UN

United Nations. (Technical Assistance Programme)
Manual on stabilized soil construction for
housing, by Robert Fitzmaurice. New York,
1958.
125p. illus., tables. (ST/TAA/K2)

1. Earth wall construction. I. Fitzmaurice,
Robert.

690.37
U54
1951
Rev.

United Nations. (Secretariat. Dept. of Social
Affairs.)
Low cost housing in south and south-east Asia;
report of Mission of experts, 22 November 1950 -
23 January 1951. New York, July 1951.
211 p. (U.N. General ST/SOA/3/Rev. 1,
16 July 1951)

U.N. Tropical Housing Mission, Jacob L. Crane,
chairman.
Bibliography: App. K, p. 205-208.

(Continued on next card)

301.15
M19m

May, Richard, Jr. Major...1970. (Card 2)

Bibliography: p. 53-54.

1. City growth. I. Symposium on the Impact
of Urbanization on Man's Environment, Onaway,
Mich., 1970. II. United Automobile,
Aerospace and Agricultural Implement Workers
of America. III. Title. IV. Title: Impact
of Urbanization on man's environment.
V. United Nations.

333.65
M22m
1963

United Nations. (Bureau of Social Affairs)
Meeting of Group of Experts on Housing
Management and Tenant Education,
Wellington, New Zealand, 1963.
Meeting...under the sponsorship of the
Bureau of Technical Assistance Operations
and the Bureau of Social Affairs in coopera-
tion with the Government of New Zealand.
New York, United Nations, 1964.
155p. (United Nations. [Document]
ST/TAO/SER.C/61)
Bibliography: p. 148-155.

1. Housing manage-   ment - Congresses.
2. Tenant selec-   tion. I. United
Nations. (Bureau   of Social Affairs)

United Nations. Secretariat. Dept. of Social
Affairs. Low cost housing in south and
south-east Asia...July 1951.   (Card 2)

1.Housing in the tropics. 2.Housing-Asia.
3.Housing-India. 4.Housing-Indonesia.
5.Housing-Malaya, Federation of. 6.Housing-
Pakistan. 7.Housing-Philippines. 8.Housing-
Siam. 9.Housing-Singapore. I.United Nations
Tropical Housing Mission. II.Crane, Jacob L.
III.Title.

330
(016)
UN
1967

United Nations. (Economic and Social Council. Economic Commission for Africa)
Manpower and training problems in economic
and social development; selected bibliography.
(Problemes de main-d'oeuvre et de formation
dans le developpement economique et social;
choix de bibliographie) [n.p.] 1967.
45p. (E/CN.14/LIB/ Ser. C/3)
Issue in English and French.

1. Economic development - Bibl. 2. Planning - Bibl. I. Title.

333.65
UN

UNITED NATIONS. BUREAU OF TECHNICAL
ASSISTANCE OPERATIONS.
MEETING OF GROUP OF EXPERTS ON
HOUSING MANAGEMENT AND TENANT EDUCATION,
WELLINGTON, NEW ZEALAND, 9 TO 23 MARCH
1963. NEW YORK, UNITED NATIONS, 1964.
155P. (ST/TAO/SER. C/61)

BIBLIOGRAPHY: P.148-155.

1. HOUSING MANAGEMENT.   2. PUBLIC
HOUSING. I. TITLE: TENANT EDUCATION.

690.37
U54
1951

United Nations. (Secretariat. Dept. of Social
Affairs.)
Low cost housing in south and south-east
Asia; report of Mission of experts, 22 Nov.
1950 - 23 Jan. 1951. New York, N.Y., Mar.
1951 - Apr. 1951.
2 pts. (continuous paging)   (U.N. General
ST/SOA/3, 12 Mar. 1951; ST/SOA/3/Add. 1, 9 Apr.
1951)

UN Tropical Housing Mission, Jacob L. Crane,
chairman.
Bibliography: App.
(Continued on next card)

336
UN
1965

United Nations. (Dept. of Economic and
Social Affairs)
A manual for programme and performance
budgeting. New York, United Nations, 1965.
103p. (United Nations. [Document]
ST/ECA/89. ST/TAO/ser. C/75)

1. Budget. 2. Management. I. Title.

058.7
UN

United Nations.
Members of the United Nations and the
main organs of the United Nations, 1958.
[n.p.] 1958.
3p. (SD/GEN/74/Rev.4)

1.United Nations - Directories.

Column 1, Card 1

728.1
(4)
U54
1952

3c

United Nations. (Economic and Social Council.
Economic Commission for Europe. Industry
and Materials Committee.)
Methods and techniques of financing housing
in Europe. Prepared by the Industry and Materials
Division. [Geneva, United Nations Economic
Commission for Europe, Mar. 1952]
275 p. tables (part fold.) (E/ECE/IM/
HOU/38; IM/HOU/WP.1/11 Rev.1, 11 Feb. 1952)

(Continued on next card)

Column 1, Card 2

United Nations. (Economic and Social Council.
Economic Commission for Europe. Industry and
Materials Committee.) Methods and techniques
of financing housing ... 1952. (Card 2)
Prepared by Y. Salaün, A. Johansson, G. Pepe,
and A. Wirz, of the Housing Sub-committee.
Includes chapters on Western Germany, Austria,
Belgium, Denmark, Finland, France, Italy, Norway,
Netherlands, United Kingdom, Sweden, Switzerland,
Union of Soviet Socialist Republics.
Mimeographed.

Column 1, Card 3

United Nations. Economic and Social Council.
Economic Commission for Europe. Industry and
Materials Committee.) Methods and techniques
of financing housing ... 1952. (Card 3)

1.Housing-Austria. 2.Housing-Belgium. 3.Housing-
Denmark. 4.Housing-Finland. 5.Housing-France.
6.Housing-Germany. 7.Housing-Italy. 8.Housing-
Netherlands. 9.Housing-Norway. 10.Housing-Sweden.
11.Housing-Switzerland. 12.Housing-U.S.S.R.
13.Housing-U.K. I.Salaün, Y. II.Title.
14.Housing-Europe. 15.Mortgage finance-Europe.
III.Title: Financing housing in Europe, Methods
and techniques of.

Column 1, Card 4

728.1
(4)
U54
1951

United Nations.(Economic and Social Council.
Economic Commission for Europe. Industry
and Materials Committee.)
Methods and techniques of financing housing
in various European countries. [Prepared by]
Y. Salaün ... assisted by Mr. Johansson, Mr. Pepe
and Mr. Wirz. [Geneva?] Economic Commission for
Europe, Industry and Materials Committee, Housing
Sub-committee, Working Party on Programmes and
Resources, Oct. 1951.
323 p. tables. (IM/HOU/WP.1/11, 12 Oct.
1951)
(continued on next card)

Column 1, Card 5

United Nations. Economic and Social Council.
Economic Commission for Europe. Industry and
Materials Committee. Methods and techniques
of financing housing ... 1951. (Card 2)
Prepared for the third session, 17-19 December
1951.
Includes sections on West Germany, Austria,
Belgium, Denmark, Finland, France, Italy, Norway,
Netherlands, United Kingdom, Sweden, Switzerland,
Union of Soviet Socialist Republics.
Mimeographed.

Column 1, Card 6

United Nations. Economic and Social Council.
Economic Commission for Europe. Industry and
Materials Committee. Methods and techniques
of financing housing ... 1951. (Card 3)

1.Housing-Austria. 2.Housing-Belgium. 3.Housing-
Denmark. 4.Housing-France. 5.Housing-Finland.
6.Housing-Germany. 7.Housing-Italy. 8.Housing-
Netherlands. 9.Housing-Norway. 10.Housing-Sweden.
11.Housing-Switzerland. 12.Housing-U.S.S.R.
13.Housing-U.K. I.Salaün, Y. II.Title.

Column 1, Card 7

728.1
UNm

3c

United Nations. (Dept. of Economic and Social
Affairs)
Methods for establishing targets and standards
for housing and environmental development. New
York, 1958.
59p. (Its Document ST/SOA/76)

1. Housing. 2. Man - Influence of environment.
I. Title.

Column 2, Card 1

728.1
:308
UNm
1967

United Nations. (Statistical Office)
Methods of estimating housing needs. New
York, United Nations, 1967.
99p. (Its Studies in methods, ser. F,
no. 12. United Nations. Document.
N.c.1 ST/STAT/ser.F/12)
Laf.c.2 Bibliography: p.87-90.

1. Housing surveys. 2. Family living
requirements. I. Title.

Column 2, Card 2

DATE OF REQUEST 7/20/53   L.C. CARD NO. 53-10067

AUTHOR [U.N.]

TITLE Methods of estimating total population for current
dates.

SERIES Population studies, no. 10; Manuals on methods of
estimating population, manual No. 1.

EDITION | PUB. DATE [1952] | PAGING 52 p.
PUBLISHER

RECOMMENDED BY   NBL   Periodically 6/13/53 p.2516

ORDER WORD

Column 2, Card 3

341.1
:338
U54
1949

United Nations. (Secretariat. Department of
Economic Affairs.)
Methods of financing economic development
in under-developed countries. Lake Success,
N.Y., 1949.
vii, 163 p. (UN publications sales no.:
1949.II.B.4)

1.Technical assistance programs.

Column 2, Card 4

352.6
UN

United Nations. (Economic Commission for
Europe)
Methods of forecasting gas demand.
Geneva, 1957.
[28]p. tables. (E/ECE/298; E/ECE/GAS/11)

1.Public utilities.

Column 2, Card 5

332
U54
1949

United Nations. (Secretary-General, 1946- Lie)
Methods of increasing domestic savings and of
insuring their most advantageous use for the
purpose of economic development. [Lake Success,
New York] Economic and Social Council, 1949.
354 p. (General E/1562, 16 Dec. 1949)
Tenth session, Economic development of underdeveloped countries, methods of financing economic
development of under-developed countries.
Mimeographed.
1.Finance.2.Banks and banking.3.Saving and thrift.
4.Underdeveloped countries. I.Title.

Column 2, Card 6

36
U54

United Nations. (Secretariat. Dept. of Social
Affairs.)
Methods of social welfare administration.
New York, 1950.
299 p. (E/CN.5/224, 25 Oct. 1950; Sales no.:
1950.IV.10; Add. 1, 23 May 1951; Add. 2, 30 July
1951)

Addenda mimeographed.

1.Social welfare. I.Title.

Column 2, Card 7

VF
690.091.82
U54

United Nations.(Economic and Social Council.)
Minimum standards of occupancy and fitness for
habitation of urban dwellings enforceable under
penalty; interim reports of the Secretary-General.
[1]- [Lake Success, N.Y.?] Mar. 1950-
3 pts. tables. (General E/CN.5/207)
Processed.
For full information see main entry.

1.Building codes-Brazil. 2.Building codes-Chile.
3.Building codes-Cuba. 4.Building codes-Czecho-
slovakia.
(continued on next card)

Column 3, Card 1

United Nations. Economic and Social Commission.
Minimum standards of occupancy and fitness...
Mar. 1950- (Card 2)
5.Building codes-Ecuador. 6.Building codes-Egypt.
7.Building codes-France. 8.Building codes-India.
9.Building codes-New Zealand. 10.Building codes-
Nigeria. 11.Building codes-Norway. 12.Building
codes-Philippines. 13.Building codes-Poland.
14.Building codes-Southern Rhodesia. 15.Building
codes-Sweden. 16.Building codes-Syria. 17.Building
codes-Tanganyika. 18.Building codes-Thailand.

(Continued on next card)

Column 3, Card 2

United Nations. Economic and Social Commission.
Minimum standards of occupancy and fitness...
Mar. 1950- (Card 3)

19.Building codes-Union of South Africa.
20.Building codes-United Kingdom. 21.Building
codes-U.S. 22.Building codes-Zanzibar. I.Title.

Column 3, Card 3

VF
690.37
U54m
1951

United Nations. (Secretary-General, 1946- Lie)
Mission of experts on tropical housing
(south and south-east Asia, November, December
1950 and January 1951) Report of the secretary-
general. [New York] United Nations Economic and
Social Council, Mar. 1951.
11 p. (E/CN.5/251, 1 March 1951)

Social Commission, seventh session, item 7(b)
of the provisional agenda.
Processed.

(Continued on next card)

Column 3, Card 4

United Nations. Secretary-General, 1946-
Mission of Experts on tropical housing...1950.
(Card 2)

1.Housing in the tropics. I.United Nations Tropical
Housing Mission. II.United Nations. Economic and
Social Council. Social Commission.

Column 3, Card 5

972.94
U54

United Nations.(Mission of Technical Assistance
to the Republic of Haiti.)
Mission to Haiti; report. Lake Success, N.Y.,
July 1949.
xvii, 327 p. illus., maps (2 col. fold. in
pocket) graphs, tables. (U.N. Publications. 1949.
IIB. 2;)

1.Haiti-Econ. condit. 2.Technical assistance pro-
grams-Haiti. I.Title.

Column 3, Card 6

693.068
:389.6
UNm
1966

7c

United Nations. (Dept. of Economic and
Social Affairs)
Modular co-ordination in building; Asia,
Europe and the Americas. New York, 1966.
67p. ([Document] ST/SOA/62 E/c.6/
36/Add.9, Rev. 1)

1. Modular coordination. 2. Prefabricated construction. I. Title.

Column 3, Card 7

693.068
:389.6
(8)
UNm

3c

United Nations. (Economic Commission for
Latin America)
Modular coordination in low cost housing,
by Alvaro Ortega, expert of the United
Nations Technical Assistance Operations
Board assigned to the Central American
Economic Cooperation Committee. San
Salvador, El Salvador Economic Commission
for Latin America, Central American Economic
Cooperation Committee, Central American
Housing Subcommittee, Central Housing Sub-
committee, 1961.
(Cont'd. on next card)

693.068
:389.6
(8)
UNm
United Nations. (Economic Commission for Latin America) Modular coordination in low cost housing...(Card 2)

114p. (United Nations. [Document] E/CN 12/CCE/SC.4/9/ TAO/LAT/35)

1. Modular coordination - Latin America. 2. Housing - Latin America. I. Ortega, Alvaro.

058.7
:341.1
United Nations. (Economic and Social Council.) Non-governmental organizations in consultative status. Information ... compiled by the Secretariat. New York, Aug. 1949. 353 p. (E/C.2/224, 31 Aug. 1949)

I.Title.

711.585
(4)
UNo
United Nations. (Economic Commission for Europe. Housing Committee) Outline of possible work on urban renewal and town planning aspects of housing. [Geneva?] 1962. 20p. (Hou/WP/urb/2)

At head of title: Working Party on Urban Renewal and Town Planning aspects of Housing (11 to 14 March 1963)

1. Urban renewal - Europe. 2. Housing - Europe.

693.068
:389.6
UNmo
United Nations. (Dept. of Economic and Social Affairs) Modular co-ordination of low-cost housing. New York, 1970.

220p. (Its [Document] ST/SOA/90)

1. Modular coordination. I. Title.

341.12
U54
N
United Nations. (Secretary-General.) Non-self-governing territories; summaries and analysis of information transmitted during New York, v. tables.

Only v.2, Summaries of information, in OA Library. For full information see shelf list card.

1.Non-self-governing territories.

392
UN
United Nations. (Commission on the Status of Women) Parental rights and duties, including guardianship (report submitted by the Secretary-General) New York, 1968. 114p. (United Nations Document E/CN.6/474/ Rev. 1) United Nations Publication. Sales no. : E.68.IV.3. Bibliography: p. 111-114. 1. Family. 2. Children. I. Title.

United Nations. (Economic and Social Council)

312.1
(81)
S25
Seminario Sobre Problemas de Urbanizacion en America Latina, Santiago de Chile, 1959. Movimentos migratorios internos y problemas de acomodacion del inmigrante nacional en Sao Paulo (Brasil); estudio preliminar, por Alfonso Trujillo Ferrari. [n.p.] 1959. 86p. (General E/CN.12/URB/12; UNESCO/SS/URB/La/12)

1. Population shifts - Brazil. I. Trujillo Ferrari, Alfonso. II. United Nations. (Economic and Social Council)

VF
002
:728
UN
United Nations. Note on documentation techniques in housing, building and planning: United Nations and other systems of classification and indexing. New York, 1957. 8p.

1. Housing documentation. 2. Building documentation. 3. Planning documentation.

711.4
(4)
UNp
United Nations. (Dept. of Economic and Social Affairs) The physical planning of industrial estates. New York, 1962. 54p. (United Nations [Document] ST/SOA/45)

1. City planning - Europe. I. Title.

339.3
U54
1951
United Nations. (Secretariat. Dept. of Economic Affairs.) National income and its distribution in under-developed countries. New York, 1951. 35 p. tables. ([U.N. Document] ST/STAT/SER.E/3, 9 Oct. 1951; Sales no.: 1951. XVII.3)

Bibliography: p. 34-35.

1.National income. 2.Under-developed countries. I.Title. II.Series: United Nations. Statistical papers.

690
(4)
UN
United Nations (Economic Commission for Europe. Housing Committee) La notion de capacite familiale d'occupation du logement. Note de la Commission du Logement de l'Union Internationale des Organismes Familiaux. [Geneva] 1956. 8p.

At head of title: Groupe de travail des statistiques de logement et de la construction (Sixième Session, 14-16 mai 1956)

1. Building industry - Europe. I. International Union of Family Or- ganizations. Family Housing Commission.

712.25
(4)
UN
United Nations. (Economic Commission for Europe) Planning and development of recreational areas including the development of the natural environment. Proceedings of the seminar organized by the Committee on Housing, Building and Planning of the United Nations Economic Commission for Europe and held in France and Luxembourg, 27 April—10 May 1969. New York, 1969. 2v. (Its [Document] ST/ECE/HOU/40) 1. Recreation Europe. I. Title.

VF
332.72
(60)
UNn
United Nations. (Economic Commission for Africa.) New methods and machinery to increase the flow of capital to housing. [New York] United Nations, Economic and Social Council, 1968. 15p. (United Nations. [Document] E/ CN.14/HOU/33) At head of title: United Nations Economic and Social Council, Economic Commission for Africa and German Foundation for Developing Countries Meeting on Technical and Social Problems (Cont'd on next card)

691
(60)
B51
United Nations. (Economic Commission for Asia and the Far East). Blachere, G Observations on the development prospects of the building materials industry in Africa. New York, United Nations, Economic Commission for Asia and the Far East, 1967. 8p. ([United Nations.] [Document] I&NR/BM/21) At head of title: Seminar on the Development of Building Materials, 8-15 January 1968, Bangkok, Thailand. 1. Building materials - Africa. I. United Nations. (Economic Commission for Asia and the Far East) II. Title

---

711.333
(415)
I72
United Nations.

Ireland (Eire) National Institute for Physical Planning and Construction Research. Planning for amenity and tourism; illustrated by excerpts from the model amenity - tourism study of County Donegal. Dublin, 1966. 110p. (Its Specimen development plan manual 2-3) A project of the Government of Ireland assisted by the United Nations Special Fund and the United Nations. 1. County planning - Ireland. 2. Travel - Ireland. 3. Ireland - County planning. 4. Ireland - Tr avel. I. United Nations. II. Title.

VF
332.72
(60)
UNn
United Nations. (Economic Commission for Africa.) New...1968 (Card 2)

of Urbanization (With Emphasis on Financing of Housing) Addis Ababa, 8-23 Jan. 1969.

1. Mortgage finance - Africa. 2. Under-developed countries. I. United Nations. (Economic and Social Council. Economic Commission for Africa) II. Deutsche Stiftung für Entwicklungslander. III. Title.

330
D65o
United Nations. (Centre for Economic and Social Information). Domenach, Jean-Marie. Our moral involvement in development. New York, United Nations Center for Economic and Social Information, 1971. 36p.

1. Economic development. I. United Nations. (Center for Economic and Social Information) II. Title.

728.1
(728)
J67
United Nations (Technical Assistance Administration) Jordan, Ricardo. La planificacion del desarrollo y las programacion de la vivienda. Santiago, Chile, Universidad Catolica de Chile, Comite Interdisciplinario de Desarrollo Urbano, 1967. 37p. 1. Housing - Central America. 2. Economic planning - Central America. 3. Economic development - Central America. I. Universidad Catolica de Chile, Santiago. II. United Nations (Technical Assistance Administration)

312
UNn
United Nations. (Economic and Social Council) 1960 world population census programme: Principles and recommendations for national population censuses. [n.p.] 1958. 63p. (E/CN.3/236/Add.1; ST/STAT/P/1.1/ rev. 2)

1.Census - Population.

370
(6)
C65
United Nations. Conference of African States on the Develop-ment of Education in Africa, Addis Ababa, 1961. Outline of a plan for African educational development. [New York] United Nations Economic Commission for Africa, United Nations Educational, Scientific and Cultural Organi-zation, 1961. 27p.

1. Education - Africa. I. United Nations. II. United Nations Educational, Scientific and Cultural Organization.

728.1
UN
1962
United Nations. (Economic and Social Council. Committee on Housing, Building and Planning) Planning and implementation of pilot projects in housing, building and planning. Report by the Secretary-General. [Geneva] 1962. 35p. (Its [Document] E/C/6/5)

First session, Agenda item 6.

1. Housing. 2. Building construction.

711.417
UNp
1967
3 c
United Nations. (Dept. of Economic and
Social Affairs)
Planning of metropolitan areas and new
towns. Meeting of the United Nations,
Group of Experts on Metropolitan Planning and
Development, Stockholm, 14-30. September
1961 (and United Nations Symposium on the
Planning and Development of New Towns,
Moscow, 24 August-7 September 1964. New
York, 1967.
255p. (Its Document) ST/SOA/65)
1. Metropolitan area planning. 2. New

(Continued on next card)

711.417
UNp
1967
United Nations. (Dept. of Economic and
Social Affairs) Planning of metropolitan
areas...1967.
(Card 2)

towns. I. United Nations Meeting of the
Group of Experts on Metropolitan Planning and
Development, Stockholm, 1961. II. United
Nations Symposium on the Planning and Develop-
ment of New Towns, Moscow, 1964. III. Title.

691.116
UN
UNITED NATIONS. FOOD AND AGRICULTURE
ORGANIZATION.
PLYWOOD AND OTHER WOOD-BASED PANELS;
TECHNICAL PAPERS SUBMITTED TO THE
INTERNATIONAL CONSULTATION ON PLYWOOD
AND OTHER WOOD-BASED PANEL PRODUCTS,
ROME, 1963. ROME, 1965.
5 V.

1. PLYWOOD. 2. PANELS. I. TITLE.

312
066
United Nations. (Office of Public Information)
Cook, Robert C
Population and food supply. [New York]
United Nations, Office of Public Information,
1962.
49p. (Freedom from Hunger Campaign.
Basic study no. 7)

Sponsored by the Food and Agricultural
Organization of the United Nations.
1. Population. 2. Population forecasting.
3. Agriculture. I. United Nations. Office of
Public Information. (Series: Freedom
from Hunger Campaign. Basic
study no. 7)

312
U54
P4
United Nations. (Secretariat. Dept. of Social
Affairs.)
Population census methods. Lake Success,
New York, Dept. of Social Affairs, Population Div.
[and] Dept. of Economic Affairs, Statistical
Office, Nov. 1949.
197 p. tables. ([U.N. Document]
ST/SOA/Series A. Population studies, no. 4;
Sales no.: 1949.XIII.4)
Prepared in collaboration with the Food and
Agriculture Organization and the International
Labour Office. (Continued on next card)

United Nations. (Secretariat. Dept. of Social
Affairs.) Population Census methods...
Nov. 1949. (Card 2)

1. Census. I. Food and Agriculture Organization
of the United Nations. II. International Labour
Office. III. Title. IV. Series: United Nations.
Population studies.

312
(5)
UN
United Nations. (Economic and Social
Council)
Population projections needed for planning
and policy-making, by K. C. Zachariah.
Bombay, India, 1960.
37p. (E/CN.9/CONF.2/L.15)

United Nations Seminar on Evaluation and
Utilization of Population Census Data in
Asia and the Far East, 20 June - 8 July 1960

1. Population - Asia. I. Zachariah, K.C.

312
(4)
UN
1966
United Nations. (Economic Commission for
Europe)
Population structure in European countries
tables and pyramids showing the distribution
of population by sex, age and marital status.
New York, 1966.
115p. ([U.N. Document] ST/ECE/HOU/21)

1. Population - Europe. 2. Population -
~~~~~. I. Title.

312
U54
P
United Nations. Population studies.
no.
3 World population trends, 1920-1947. Dec.1949

4 Population census methods. Nov. 1949.

8 Data on urban and rural population in recent
censuses. July 1950.

9 Application of international standards to
census data on the economically active
population. [1951]

728.1
(41)
U54p
United Nations. (Economic Commission for
Europe. Housing Committee)
U.K. Ministry of Housing and Local Government.
Postwar housing in the United Kingdom;
Prepared for the Housing Committee of the
Economic Commission for Europe. London,
H. M. Stat. Off., 1962.
1v.

1. Housing - U.K. 2. Architecture,
Domestic - U.K. I. United Nations.
(Economic Commission for Europe. Housing
Committee)

VF
693.002.22
(485)
U54
United Nations. (Economic and Social Council.
Economic Commission for Europe. Industry
and Materials Committee.)
Prefabrication of housing in Sweden. Prepared
by Lennart Bergvall. [New York] Economic
Commission for Europe, Industry and Materials
Committee, Housing Sub-committee, Working Party on
Technical Problems, Sept. 1951.
5 p. (IM/HOU/WP.2/11, 7 Sept. 1951)
Restricted.
Mimeographed.
1. Prefabricated construction-Sweden. I. Bergvall,
Lennart.

690
S25
1964
United Nations. (Economic Commission for
Europe)
Seminar on Changes in the Structure of the
Building Industry, Prague, 1964.
Principal issues concerning the structure
and the development of the building industry.
Introductory report by the Secretariat. [n.
p.] 1964.
33p. ([United Nations. Document]
HOU. Industry/B.1)
At head of title: Economic Commission for
Europe.
1. Building industry - Congresses.
2. Housing - Con- gresses. I. United
Nations. (Economic Commission for Europe)

312
UNp
1966
United Nations. (Economic and Social Council)
Principles and recommendations for a population census: draft recommendations for the
1970 censuses. Report by the Secretary-General
[New York] 1966.
122p. (Its [Document] E/CN/S/342/ July
1966)
At head of title: Statistical Commission
14th session. Item 4 (b) of the provisional
agenda.

1. Census - Population. I. Title.

312
UNp
United Nations.
Principles and recommendations for national
population censuses. New York, 1958.
29p. (ST/STAT/SER.M/27; Statistical papers
series M, no. 27)

1. Census - Population.

728.1
:308
UNp
1967
United Nations. Statistical Office.
Principles and recommendations for the
1970 housing censuses. New York, United
Nations, 1967.
140p. (Its Statistical papers, ser. M,
no. 45. United Nations. Document ST/Stat/
ser.M/45)

1. Housing surveys. I. Title.

N.c.1
Lef.c.2

301.15
UN
United Nations. (Economic and Social Council)
Principles of community development; social
progress through local action. Report by the
Secretary General. [n.p.] 1955.
156p. (E/CN.5303)

1. Community development.

728.1
(5)
UNp
United Nations. (Economic Commission for
Asia and the Far East)
Problem of high housing costs in the
countries of ECAFE region. New York, 1958.
16p (Industrial development series.
Housing and building materials
ST/ECAFE/SER.M/11)

1. Housing costs - Asia. 2. Mortgage
finance - Asia.

728.1
(861)
S15
United Nations.
Salaun, Yves.
El problema de la vivienda en Colombia.
New York, United Nations, 1956.
81p. ([United Nations. Document]
TAA 173/13/06, TAA/col/1.)

At head of title: Programa de Asistencia
Tecnica.

1. Housing - Colombia. 2. Technical
assistance programs - Colombia. I. United
Nations.

312.1
(86)
S25
United Nations. (Economic and Social Council)
Seminario Sobre Problemas de Urbanizacion
en America Latina, Santiago de Chile, 1959.
Problemas economico-sociales sobre migracion
y urbanizacion en la Ciudad de Esmeraldas,
Republica del Ecuador. [n.p.] United Nations,
Economic and Social Council, 1959.
84p. (General E/CN.12/URB/LA/20)

1. Population shifts - Ecuador. I. United
Nations. (Economic and Social Council)

697.8
UN
United Nations. (Economic Commission for
Europe)
Problems of air and water pollution arising
in the iron and steel industry. New York, 1970.
86p. (Its Publication no. ST/ECE/STEEL/32)

1. Air pollution. 2. Water pollution.
3. Industry. I. Title.

728.1
(4)
UN
HOU/WP
no. 89
United Nations. (Economic Commission for
Europe. Housing Committee)
Problems of building documentation. New
York, 1958.
11p. (HOU/Working paper no. 89)

1. Building documentation.

VF
690.072
U54p
United Nations. Educational, Scientific
and Cultural Organization.
Problems of education and training in
the construction industry. [New York]
1970.
15p. (HBP/Build/Sem.3/C.2)
At head of title: Economic Commission
for Europe, Committee on Housing, Building
and Planning, Third Seminar on the
Building Industry, Moscow, 5-17 October
1970.

1. Building   construction - Labor
(Cont'd on next card)

VF
690.072
U54p
United Nations Educational, Scientific
and Cultural Organization.
Problems...1970.   (Card 2)

requirements. I. United Nations.
(Economic Commission for Europe.
Committee on Housing, Building and
Planning) II. Title.

VF
728.1
(81)
L26
United Nations. (Technical Assistance Adminis-
tration.)
Leonard, Olen E
Problems of rural housing in Eastern
Pernambuco; prepared for the Government of Brazil.
[New York] United Nations, Technical Assistance
Administration [1952]
60 p. (ST/TAA/K/Brazil/1)
C1 has Appendix number 1 (plates) [i.e.
photographs]
Processed.
Bibliographical footnotes.
1.Housing-Brazil. 2.Farm housing-Brazil. I.United
Nations. (Technical Assistance Administration.)
II.Title.

301.15
UNp
United Nations. (Economic and Social
Council)
Problems of the human environment: report
of the Secretary-General. [New York] 1969.
66p. United Nations. [Document] E/4667)
Forty-seventh session, agenda item 10.

1. Man - Influence of environment.
I. Title.

352.6
(5694)
UN
United Nations. (Economic Commission for
Asia and the Far East)
Problems relating to the development of
services. Report prepared for the sixth
session of the Working Party on Housing
and Building Materials of the Economic
Commission for Asia and the Far East [by]
Government of Israel, Ministry of Labour,
Housing Div. [n.p.] 1960.
4p.

1. Municipal   services -
Israel.   I. Israel.
Ministry of   Labor.
(Housing Div.)

United Nations.
330
(415)
S25
Seminar on Industrial Development and the
Development Plan, Dublin, 1966.
Proceedings. Dublin, National Institute
for Physical Planning and Construction Research, 1967.
52p.
A project of the Government of Ireland
assisted by the United Nations Special Fund
and the United Nations.
1. Economic development - Ireland. 2. Industrial development - Ireland. 3. Ireland - Economic development. 4. Ireland - Industrial
districts.
(Cont'd on next card)

330
(415)
S25
Seminar on Industrial Development and the
Development Plan, Dublin, 1966.
Proceedings...1967.   (Card 2)

I. United Nations. II. Ireland (Eire)
National Institute for Physical Planning and
Construction Research.

693.068
:389.6
UN
United Nations.
Proceedings of the Ad Hoc meeting on
standardization and modular co-ordination
in building. Geneva, 1959.
1v. (E/ECE/361; E/ECE/HOU/85)

1. Modular coordination.

690
UNp
1955
United Nations. (Economic Commission for
Europe. Committee on Housing, Building
and Planning)
Proceedings of the Seminar on Changes in
the Structure of the Building Industry
Necessary to Improve Its Efficiency and to
Increase Its Output, Prague, Czechoslovakia,
19-30 April 1964. New York, 1965.
3v. ([Document] ST/ECE/HOU/L3)

1. Building industry. 2. Building
materials.

691.542
G17p
United Nations. (Commission for Asia and
the Far East).
Gaskin, A
The production and utilization of
asbestos-cement products in Australia.
[New York] United Nations, Economic
Commission for Asia and the Far East, 1967.
15p. (United Nations. [Document]
I&NR/BM/18)
At head of title: Seminar on the Develop-
ment of Building Materials, 8-15 Jan. 1968,
Bangkok, Thailand.
1. Portland cement. I. United Nations.
(Commission for Asia and the Far East)
II. Title.

728.1
(489)
UN
United Nations. (Economic Commission for
Europe. Housing Committee)
Programme for the visit in Denmark,
June 22 - 26, 1960. [Copenhagen]
Ministry of Housing, 1960.
kit. (12 pieces)

Partial contents.-Denmark Ministry of housing. Explanation of some special Danish
housing and building terms.
1. Housing - Denmark. 2. Cooperative housing -
Denmark. I. Denmark.   Ministry of
Housing.

333.32
UN
United Nations.
Progress in land reform   5 th report
1970
Prepared jointly by the United Nations, the
Food and Agriculture Organization of the
United Nations, and the International
Labour Organisation. New York, 19
/ v. (E/4769; ST/SOA/94)

Bibliography: [1970]: p. 358-367.

1. Land tenure. I. Title.

728.1
UNp
United Nations. (Economic and Social Council)
Progress made by the United Nations in the
social field during the period 1 January 1955
- 31 December 1958 and proposals for the programme of work 1957-1961. Report by the
Secretary-General. [New York] 1957, 1959.
2v. (E/CN.5/326; 334)
Partial contents:-Chapter IV. Housing,
building and planning.

1. Housing. 2. Planning.

963.5
U54
1951
United Nations. (General Assembly.)
Progress report of the United Nations
Commissioner in Eritrea during the year 1951.
[New York?] 1951.
182 p. (General. A/1959, 16 Nov. 1951)

Mimeographed.

1.Eritrea.

312
:728.1
UN
1960
United Nations. (Economic and Social
Council)
Progress report on housing census ac-
tivities and plans (report by the Secretary
-General) [New York] 1960.
10p. (E/CN.3/272)

At head of title: Statistical Commission,
eleventh session, item 12 of the provisional
agenda.
1. Census -   Housing.

693
UN
United Nations. (Economic Commission for
Europe)
Progressive methods of design, organization
and management in building. Report on the
proceedings of the Third ECE Seminar on the
Building Industry. Prepared by the ECE Sec-
retariat. Moscow, USSR 5-10 October 1970.
New York, 1971.
2v. (ST/ECE/HBp/42)

1. Building methods. 2. Prefabricated
construction. I. Seminar on the Building
Industry. 3d,   Moscow, 1970. II. Title.

728.100.15
UN
1962
United Nations. (Economic and Social Council.
Committee on Housing, Building and
Planning)
The promotion of research and of the ex-
change and dissemination of experience and
information on housing building and planning.
Report by the Secretary-General. [Geneva]
1962.
22p. (Its [Document] E/C/6/4)
First session, Item 5 of the provisional
agenda.

1. Housing   research.

332.72
UNp
United Nations. (Economic and Social
Council. Committee on Housing, Building
and Planning)
Proposals for action on finance for housing
building and planning. Report of the
Secretary-General, New York, 1970.
97p. (United Nations [Document]
E/C.6/106/Rev.1).
Bibliography: p. 85-89.

1. Mortgage finance. I. Title.

711.4
UNp
draft
United Nations. (Social Commission)
Proposals for concerted international
action in the field of urbanization.
United Nations Social Commission, thirteenth session, position paper (Agenda item
no. 4(a) Doc. no. E/CN.5/351).
[Washington] 1961.
5p.

Draft: OIH:HHFA, March 24, 1961.

1. City planning.   I. U.S. Housing
and Home Finance   Agency. Office
of the Administrator.   Office of International Housing.   II. Title: Urbanization.

711.4
UNp
United Nations. (Economic and Social Council.
Social Commission)
Proposals for concerted international
action in the field of urbanization; memorandum by the Secretary-General. [New York]
1961.
13p. (E/CN.5/351)

Thirteenth session, item 4 (a) of the
provisional agenda.

1. City planning.   I. Title:
Urbanization.

308
:728.1
UN
United Nations. (Economic and Social
Council)
Proposed methods of estimating housing
needs; note by the Statistical Office.
[New York] 1960.
42p. (E/CN.3/27-)
Statistical Commission, eleventh
session, Item 11 of the provisional
agenda.

1. Housing market analysis.

2c.

330
(4)
UNp
United Nations. (Economic Commission for Europe)
Provisional agenda for the eleventh session of the Economic Commission for Europe. [Geneva, 1956?]
1v.

1. Economic development - Europe. I. Title.

690.015
(485)
S82
R27
1967
United Nations.
Sweden. Statens Kommitté fur Byggnadsforskning.
Quality of dwellings and housing areas; published in agreement with the United Nations. Stockholm, 1967.
149p. (Sweden. Statens Kommitté for Byggnadsforskning. Rapport 27)
1. Housing - Sweden. 2. Housing - Social aspects. 3. Housing and health. I. United Nations. II. Title.

330
UNrs
United Nations. (Dept. of Economic and Social Affairs)
Rapport sur une politique coordonnée en matière de niveaux de vie familieux. New York, 1957.
82p. (Its [Document] ST/SOA/34)

1. Underdeveloped countries. 2. Social conditions.

VF
728.1
Unpr
United Nations. (Economic and Social Council. Committee on Housing, Building, and Planning)
Provisional annotated agenda. (United Nations Headquarters, 21 January-1 February, 1963) First session. [n.p.] 1962.
5p ([U.N. Document] E/C.6/1)

1. Housing. 2. City planning.

33
UNe
1953-54
Suppl.
United Nations. (Department of Economic and Social Affairs.)
The quest for freer trade. New York 1955.
55 p (E/2737, ST/ECA/31).

"Supplement to the World economic report, 1953-54".-p.iii

1. Economic conditions. I. Title. II. Title: World economic report, 1953-54.

728.1
/711.4
(016)
UN
United Nations. Housing and Town and Country Planning Reference Centre.
Recent accessions; selected references, no. 1 - 6, Mar. 1, 1954 - May 15, 1954. [New York, N. Y.] 1954.
6 Nos. bi-weekly.

1.Housing - Bibliographies. 2.Building industry - Bibliographies. 3.City planning - Bibliographies.

728.1
(8)
UNp
United Nations. (Economic and Social Council. Economic Commission for Latin America)
Provisional report of the Latin American Seminar on Housing Statistics and Programmes. [Geneva] 1963.
233p. (United Nations. [Document] E/CN.12/647. February 1963)
"Preliminary report..."
At head of title: Tenth session, Mar del Plata, Argentina, May 1963.
1. Housing - Latin America. 2. Housing statistics - Latin America.
I. Latin Ameri- ___ an Seminar on Housing Statistics and Programmes. Mar del Plata, 1963.

061.6
U54
United Nations. (Secretariat. Department of Social Affairs.)
The question of establishing United Nations research laboratories. Lake Success, Dec. 1948.
289 p. (UN Publications. Sales no.:1949.IV. 1)
Includes pertinent correspondence.
Emphasis on scientific research; only a brief mention of building and housing on p. 18.
1.Research. 2.Housing research. 3.Building research. I.Title.

728.1
(41)
UN
June
1962
United Nations. (Economic Commission for Europe. Housing Committee)
Redevelopment in the city of Glasgow.
Visit of Housing Committee of the United Nations Economic Commission for Europe, 15th June, 1962. Glasgow, Scotland, 1962.
6 pieces. (AGJ/JRB 1 June 1962)

Contents:-Station Point 1.-Architects: Hutchescontown/Gorbals - Building area, C. 20-storey maisonettes.-Station Point C.4.-Contractors: Hutchescontown/Gorbals - Building
(Cont'd. on next card)

341.1
:338
UNp
United Nations. (Technical Assistance Programs)
Public administration aspects of community development programmes. New York, 1959.
107p. (ST/TAO/M/14)

1. Technical assistance programs. 2. Public administration.

UN file - minority groups 1953
DATE OF REQUEST April 20, 1953 * | L.C. CARD NO.
AUTHOR United Nations
TITLE Race Relations in Non-Self-Governing Territories (U.N. Secretariat)
SERIES A/AC.35/L.87
EDITION | PUB. DATE June 1952 | PAGING 60 p.
PUBLISHER
RECOMMENDED BY | REVIEWED IN
ORDER RECORD

728.1
(41)
UN
June
1962
United Nations. (Economic Commission for Europe. Housing Committee)
Redevelopment in the city of Glasgow...
(Card 2)

Area C. 20-storey maisonettes.-Station 1. Hutchescontown/Gorbals building area B.-Station 2. Hutchescontown/Gorbals building area B.-Station 3. Hutchescontown/Gorbals building area B.-The Corporation of Glasgow Clerk of Works.-
(Cont'd. on next card)

VF
728.1
(016)
UNp
United Nations. (Economic Commission for Europe. Housing, Building and Planning Committee)
Publications, 1965,

Geneve, Switzerland, 1965
/v.

For complete information see main card.

1. Housing - Bibl. 2. Building industry - Bibl. 3. Planning - Bibl. 4. United Nations - Publications.

691.71
UN
United Nations. (Economic Commission for Europe)
Railways and steel. Geneva, 1957.
63p. tables. (E/EC/E296, E/ECE/Steel/115)

1.Steel. 2.Railroads.

728.1
(41)
UN
June
1962
United Nations. (Economic Commission for Europe. Housing Committee)
Redevelopment in the city of Glasgow...
(Card 3)

1. Housing - Glasgow, Scotland. 2. Building construction - Glasgow, Scotland.

711.417
R23
1960
United Nations.
Regional Seminar on Public Administration Problems of New and Rapidly Growing Towns in Asia, New Delhi, India, 1960.
Public administration problems of new and rapidly growing towns in Asia. Co-sponsored by the United Nations [and others] with the co-operation of the Indian Institute of Public Administration. New York, United Nations, 1962.
90p. (United Nations. [Document] ST/TAO/M/181)
(Cont'd on next card)

728.1
/711.4
UN
No. 4
United Nations. (Dept. of Social Affairs.)
[Rammed earth construction.] New York, October 1950.
121 p. (Its Housing and town and country planning. Bulletin no. 4)

Bibliography: p. 60-67.

1. Earth wall construction.

United Nations (Economic Commission for Asia and the Far East)
330
(861)
M67
Morcillo-Dosman, Pedro Pablo.
The regional autonomous Corporation of the Cauca. Cali, Colombia, 1958.
35p. map. (United Nations. Working paper no. 50, E/CN. 11/RP/L.7)

1. Economic conditions - Colombia. I. United Nations (Economic Commission for Asia and the Far East) II. Title: Corporation of the Cauca.

711.417
R23
1960
Regional Seminar on Public Administration Problems of New and Rapidly Growing Towns in Asia, New Delhi, India, 1960. Public administration...
(Card 2)

At head of title: United Nations technical assistance programme.

1. New towns - Congresses. 2. Technical assistance programs (UN) - Asia. 3. Community development - Asia. I. United Nations. II. Indian Institute of Public Administration.

711.585
(4)
UN
1962
French
United Nations. (Economic Commission for Europe)
Rapport sur le cycle d'etude sur la renovation urbaine, organise a Geneve en Juin 1961, par le Comite de l'Habitat de la Commission Economique pour l'Europe. Geneve, 1962.
98p. (ST/ECE/HOU/4)

1. Urban renewal - Europe - Congresses. I. Urban Renewal Symposium, Geneva, 1961.

728.100.15
(5)
UN
United Nations. (Economic and Social Council. Economic Commission for Asia and the Far East)
Regional housing research centers in Asia and the Far East, by United Nations Dept. of Economic and Social Affairs. [New York] 1955.
15p.

Third session of Inter-Secretariat Working Party on Housing and Building in Asia and the Far East.

1. Housing research - Asia.

711.3
(4)
UN
1966
United Nations. (Economic Commission for
Europe)
Regional physical planning. New York,
1966.
72p.   (Its [Document] ST/ECE/HOU/24)

1. Regional planning - Europe.
2. Economic policy. I. Title.

690
823
1964
Schechter, Henry B   Relationship
between house building and the National
level of economic activity ... (Card 2)

1. Building industry-Economic effect.I.United
Nations. (Economic Commission for Europe.
Committee on Housing, Building and Planning)
II. U.S. Housing and Home Finance Agency.

728.1
(4)
U54r
1948
United Nations. (Economic and Social Council.
Economic Commission for Europe. Panel on
Housing Problems.)
Report no. 1 - 3.   [Geneva, Apr. 1948]
4 pts. in l. tables(part fold.)   (E/ECE/HOU/
15-17, April 1948)
Restricted.
Countries included: Austria, Belgium,
Czechoslovakia, Denmark, Eire, Finland, France,
Greece, Italy, Netherlands, Norway, Sweden,
Switzerland, England, Wales, Northern Ireland.
(continued on next card)

VF
711.3
(676)
C17
United Nations. (Economic Commission
for Africa)
Carvalho, E   F   C
Regional physical planning in Kenya; a
case study. [New York] United Nations,
Economic and Social Council, 1969.
10p. (United Nations. [Document] E/CN.
14/HOU/35, 8 Jan. 1969)
At head of title: United Nations, Economi
and Social Council, Economic Commission for
Africa and German Foundation for Developing
Countries Meeting on Technical and Social
Problems of Urbanization (With Emphasis on
Financing of Housing) Addis Ababa, 8-23
Jan. 1969.   (Cont'd on next card)

711.585
(498)
UN
United Nations. (Economic Commission for
Europe. Committee on Housing)
La rénovation urbaine dans la République
Populaire Roumaine. Genève, 1961.
17p.

At head of title: La Délégation de la
Republique Populaire Roumain X-e Session.

1. Urban renewal - Rumania.

United Nations. (Economic and Social Council.
Economic Commission for Europe. Panel on
Housing Problems. Report no. 1 - 3...
April 1948.   (Card 2)
Questionnaire (E/ECE/HOU/12, 29 Nov. 1947)
attached.
Contents.-1.Housing needs and programmes [by]
C.A. Doxiades.-2.Needs in building materials [by]
H.G. van Beusekom.-3.Economies in scarce materials
[by] A. Johansson.
Mimeographed.

VF
711.3
(676)
C17
United Nations. (Economic Commission
for Africa).
Carvalho, E   F   C Regional. . .1969.
(Card 2)

1. Regional planning - Kenya. I. United
Nations. (Economic Commission for Africa).
II. Title.

691.71
UNr
United Nations. (Economic Commission for
Europe)
Repertoire des organisations nationales
d'Europe et des Etats-Unis d'Amerique et des
organisations internationales s'occupant
de siderugie. Geneva, 1957.
104p.

1.Steel.   2.Iron.

United Nations. Economic and Social Council.
Economic Commission for Europe. Panel on
Housing Problems.   Report no. 1 - 3 ...
April 1948.   (Card 3)

1.Housing-Europe. 2.Building materials-Austria.
3.Building materials-Belgium. 4.Building materials-
Czechoslovakia. 5.Building materials-Denmark.
6.Building materials-Eire. 7.Building materials-
Eng. 8.Building materials-Finland. 9.Building
materials-France. 10.Building materials-Greece.
11.Building materials-Italy. 12.Building materials-
Netherlands.   (Continued on next card.)

728.1
(711.4
UN
nos.
12 & 13
United Nations. (Dept. of Economic and
Social Affairs)
Regional planning. Seminar on Regional
Planning, Tokyo, 28 July to 8 August 1958.
New York, 1959.
220p. illus., maps. (ST/SOA/SER.C/ 12
and 13; Housing and town and country planning bulletin nos. 12 and 13)

1. Regional planning.   2. Housing.

711.4
(061.3)
E87
1962
United Nations.
European Seminar on Urban Development
Policy and Planning, Warsaw, 1962.
Report. Genèva United Nations,
1962.
193p.   (SOA/ESWP/1962/1. st/ECE/HOU/9)

1. Home ownership.   2. Housing market.
3. Mortgage finance.   4. Building industry.
I. United Nations.

United Nations. Economic and Social Council.
Economic Commission for Europe. Panel on
Housing Problems.   Report no. 1 - 3 ...
April 1948.   (Card 4)

13.Building materials-Northern Ireland. 14.Building
materials-Sweden. 15.Building materials-Norway.
16.Building materials-Switzerland. 17.Building
materials-Wales. I.van Beusekom, H.G. II.Doxiades,
C.A. III.Johansson, A. IV.Title: Housing needs
and programmes. V.Title: Needs in building material
VI.Title: Economies in scarce materials.

690
S23
United Nations. (Economic Commission for
Europe. Housing Committee)
Schechter, Henry B
Relationship between house building and
the National level of economic activity,
by Director, Div. of Housing Analysis,
Housing and Home Finance Agency, United
States. [n.p] 1963.
5p. (HOU. Demand/14)
At head of title: Economic Commission for
Europe. Housing Committee. Third meeting
of the group of rapporteurs on effective
housing demand.
(Cont'd. on next card)

330
(4)
UNrep
United Nations. (Economic and Social Council.
Economic Commission for Europe)
Report,
New York,
v. annual. (Official records, --- session.
Supplement no....)

For complete information see shelf list.

1. Economic conditions - Europe.   2. Housing -
Europe.

691.542
I57r
1964
United Nations.
Interregional Seminar on the Cement
Industry, Humlebaek, Denmark, 1964.
Report of the Interregional Seminar on
the Cement Industry, Denmark, 2-16 May 1964.
New York, United Nations, 1965.
134p. ([U.N. Document] ST/TAO/SER.C/71)

Bibliography: p. 131-134.

1. Portland cement - Congresses.
2. Industrial location. I. United Nations.

690
S23
Schechter, Henry B   Relationship
between house building and the National
level...   (Card 2)

1. Building industry - Economic effect.
I. United Nations. (Economic Commission for
Europe. Housing Committee) II. U.S.
Housing and Home   Finance Agency.

728.1
(60)
S25
1966
United Nations.
Seminar on Housing Statistics and Programmes for
Africa, Copenhagen, 1966.
Report. New York, 1968.
71p. (United Nations. [Document]
E/CN.14/CAS.5/16/R1.c.1)

1. Housing - Africa. I. United Nations.

711.4
UNre
United Nations.
Report of the United Nations Interregional
Seminar on Development Policies and Planning
in Relation to Urbanization, Pittsburgh, Pa.,
24 Oct. - 4 Nov., 1965. New York, 1967.
74p. (Its [Document] ST/TAO/SER.C/97)

1. City growth. 2. Economic planning.
3. Population. 4. Planning.

690
S23
1964
United Nations. (Economic Commission for Europe.
Committee on Housing, Building and Planning)
Schechter, Henry B
Relationship between house building and
the National level of economic activity.
Paper prepared by Director, Div., of Housing
Analysis, U.S. Housing and Home Finance
Agency. [New York, United Nations] Economic
Commission for Europe, Committee on Housing,
Building, and Planning, Group of Rapporteurs
on Housing Demand, 1964.
7p. ([United Nations Document] HOU: Demand/
14 Rev. 1)
(Cont'd. on next card)

728.1
(5)
S25
1965
United Nations.
Seminar on Housing Statistics and Programmes for
Asia and the Far East, Copenhagen, 1963.
Report. New York, United Nations, 1965.
73p. (United Nations. [Document] E/CN11/
677/rev.1)

1. Housing - Asia. I. United Nations.

728.1
M66r
United Nations.(Economic and Social Council.
Committee on Housing, Building and Planning)
Moore, James A
Report of the United States Delegation to the
Committee on Housing, Building and Planning
of the United Nations Economic and Social
Council, 4th session, Geneva, Switzerland,
Sept. 5-16, 1966. Prepared by James A. Moore
and Stanley E. Smigel. [n.p.] 1966.
12p.

1. Housing. 2. Planning. 3. International
organizations. I. Smigel, Stanley E., jt.su.
II. United Nations Economic and Social Council. (Committee   on Housing, Building and Plan-   ing)

711.4
(52)
UN
1965
United Nations.
Report of the United Nations Team on Urbanization and Regional Planning in Japan (1964) Chubu region. Nagoya, Japan, 1965. [38]p.

1. City planning - Japan. 2. Regional planning - Japan. 3. Economic development - Japan.

728.1
UNrep
Suppl.
no.7
1958
United Nations. (Economic and Social Council. Committee on Housing, Building and Planning)
Report of the fifth session (16-27 October 1957) New York, 1958. 69p. (Official records; 44th session. Suppl. no. 7. [Document] E/4440,E/C.6/85) Meeting held at Geneva.

1. Housing. 2. Planning. 3. International organizations. I. Title.

330
(8)
Unl
United Nations. (Economic and Social Council. Economic Commission for Latin America)
Report of the Latin American Seminar on Planning. [Geneva] 1963. 128p. (United Nations. [Document] E/CN.12/644. 14 February 1963)
At head of title: Economic Commission for Latin America, Tenth session Mar del Plata, Argentina, May 1963.

1. Economic policy - Latin America. I. Latin American Seminar on Planning, Santiago, Chile, 1963.

728.1
(5)
UNr
1965
United Nations. (Economic Commission for Asia and the Far East)
Report of the United States Delegation to the Working Party on Housing and Building Materials, Committee on Industry and Natural Resources Economic Commission for Asia and the Far East, Bangkok, Thailand, June 24 to July 2, 1965. Prepared by J. Robert Dodge. [Washington] 1965. 6p.
Official use only.

1. Housing - Asia.   2. Building materials. I. Dodge, J Robert.

728.1
UN rep
Suppl.
no.13
1963
United Nations. (Economic and Social Council. Committee on Housing, Building and Planning)
Report of the first session, 21 January-1 February 1963. New York, 1963. 31p. ([Document] E. 3719/Rev. 1, E/C. 6/9/ Rev. 1)

Official records: Thirty-sixth session suppl. no. 13.

1. Housing. 2. Building construction.

728.1
(60)
UN
United Nations. (Economic and Social Council. Economic Commission for Africa)
Report of the meeting of experts on housing problems in Africa (Addis Ababa, Ethiopia, 9-17 January 1963) [New York] 1963. 29p. [Document] E/CN.14/191, E/CN.14/HOU/1

At head of title: "Fifth session, Leopoldville, February-March 1963, Item 7 of the provisional agenda."

1. Housing - Africa. 2. Mortgage finance - Africa.

728.1
UNr
1962
United Nations. (Dept. of Economic and Social Affairs)
Report of the ad hoc group of experts on housing and urban development. New York, 1962. 76p ([Document] ST/SOA/50/E/CN.5/367/rev. 1)

1. Housing. 2. City planning. 3. Urban renewal.

DATE OF REQUEST 7/8/53   JUL 18 1958   CARD NO.
AUTHOR U.N. (ECOSOC. Economic Commission for Asia and the Far East. Committee on Industry and Trade.)
TITLE Report of the first session of the inter-secretariat working party on housing and building materials to the Fifth session of the Committee on Industry and Trade.
SERIES E/CN.11/IMT/77
EDITION   PUB. DATE Dec. 1952   PAGING 25 p.
PUBLISHER
RECOMMENDED BY   REVIEWED IN 5/4/53 p.3
ORDER RECORD

DATE OF REQUEST 7/20/54   1954   CARD NO.
AUTHOR United Nations. Technical Assistance Administration.
TITLE Report of the mission on community organization and development in South and Southeast Asia. Report [by] Horace Belshaw and J. B. Grant.
SERIES ST/SOA/Ser.O/10   ST/TAA/Ser. D/10
EDITION   PUB. DATE 1953   PAGING 167 p.
PUBLISHER
RECOMMENDED BY NML   REVIEWED IN PAIS 2/20/54 p. 95
ORDER RECORD

728.1
UNr
United Nations. (Economic and Social Council. Social Commission)
Report of the Ad Hoc group of experts on housing and urban development. [n.p.] 1962. 1v. ([Document] E/CN.5/367)

--- Appendix. 1962. 42p. ([Document] E/CN.5/367/Add.1)

1. Housing. 2. Urban renewal.

728.1
(5)
Unr
1957
United Nations. (Economic Commission for Asia and the Far East)
Report of the fourth meeting of the Working Party on Housing and Building Materials (30 July-August 1956, Bangkok, Thailand) ninth session 7-15 March 1957, Bangkok. [Washington] 1957. 43p.

1. Housing - Asia. 2. Building materials.

312
(8)
UN
United Nations.
Report of the Regional Census Training Centre for Latin America, Lima, Peru, 11 August to 21 November 1958. Sponsored and organized by: The Food and Agriculture Organization of the United Nations, The United Nations Statistical Office and Technical Assistance Administration, The Inter American Statistical Institute, The Government of Peru. New York, 1959.
(Continued on next card)

693.068
:389.6
UNr
United Nations. (Economic Commission for Europe. Housing Committee)
Report of the Ad Hoc meeting [and] Provisional agenda of the Symposium on Preferred Dimensions of Large Components. Geneva, 1959. 2v. [7]p. in 1v. (HOU/105, 106)

1. Modular coordination.

341.12
UNr
1946
United Nations. (Headquarters Commission)
Report of the Headquarters Commission to the second part of the first session of the General Assembly of the United Nations. New York, 1946. 143p.

1. United Nations. I. Title.

312
(8)
UN
United Nations. Report of the Regional Census Training Centre for Latin ... (Card 2)

38p. (Its Statistical papers, series M, no. 33; ST/TAO/SER.C/40)

1. Census - Latin America.

VF
630
UN
United Nations. (Economic and Social Council. Economic Commission for Europe)
Report of the Committee on Agricultural Problems to the Economic Commission for Europe. Geneva, 1956. 1v. (E/ECE/226-A to J)

Eleventh session. Agenda item no. 3.

1. Agriculture.

VF
728.1
(4)
UNr
United Nations. (Economic and Social Council. Economic Commission for Europe. Housing Committee)
Report of the Housing Committee to the Economic Commission for Europe. Geneva, nos. (E/ECE/ 265-D, 307 D)

Provisional agenda items

For complete information see shelf list.

1. Housing - Europe.

VF
690.072
U54
1952
United Nations. (Economic and Social Council. Economic Commission for Europe. Industry and Materials Committee.)
Report of the Secretariat on a Pilot study of the consumption of man-hours on site in house building in 9 European countries, carried out by R. Fitzmaurice and H. F. Broughton. [New York?] 1952. 24 p. appendixes. (IM/HOU/WP.2/12, 3 Jan. 1952)
(Continued on next card)

VF
330
(4)
UNre
United Nations. (Economic and Social Council. Economic Commission for Europe)
Report of the expert group on the economic development of Southern Europe. Geneva, 1956. 1v. (E/ECE/233, Add.1. Eleventh session. Agenda item no. 7)

1. Economic development - Europe.

728.6
I157r
United Nations.
Interregional Seminar on Rural Housing and Community Facilities.
Report of the Interregional Seminar on Rural Housing and Community Facilities, Maracay, Venezuela, 2-19 April 1967. New York, United Nations, 1968. 213p. (United Nations Document ST/TAO/Ser. C/103)
1. Farm housing. 2. Community facilities. 3. Economic development. I. Title: Rural housing and community facilities. II. United Nations.

United Nations. (Economic and Social Council. Economic Commission for Europe. Industry and Materials Committee.) Report of the Secretariat ... 1952. (Card 2)

Housing Sub-committee, Working Party on Technical Problems, third sess., 28-30 Jan. 1952; item 3 of the Provisional agenda.

1. Building construction-Labor requirements. I. Fitzmaurice, R. II. Broughton, H. F.

VF
693.002.22
U54
United Nations. (Economic Commission for
Europe)
Report of the Secretariat on the
study of non-traditional building.
[n.p.] Economic Commission for Europe,
Industry and Materials Committee, Housing
Sub-committee, Working Party on Technical
Problems, 1951.
4 p.

Third session, 28-30 Jan., 1951.

1. Prefabricated construction.

---

cat.
DATE OF REQUEST 8/5/54   L. C. CARD NO.
AUTHOR
United Nations. AUG 11 1954
TITLE Report of the United Nations Commission on the
Racial Situation in the Union of South Africa.
SERIES (U.N. General Assembly, official records 8th session,
suppl. no. 16)
EDITION   PUB. DATE [1954]   PAGING 177 p.
PUBLISHER

RECOMMENDED BY   REVIEWED IN
MHL   PW 7/17/54 p. 222
ORDER RECORD

728.1
(5)
UNr
United Nations. (Economic Commission
for Asia and the Far East)
Report of the United States delegation
to the sixth session of the Working Party
on Housing and Building Materials of the
Economic Commission for Asia and the
Far East, Bangkok, Thailand, Nov. 21-29,
1960. [Washington] 1961.
12p.

1. Housing - Asia. 2. Building
materials - Asia. I. Dodge, J. Robert.

711.73
UN
United Nations. (Economic Commission
for Asia and the Far East. Inland
Transport Committee)
Report of the Seminar on Engineering
and Traffic Aspects of Highway Safety
held in Tokyo, Japan, 13-23, May 1957.
[n.p.] 1957.
152p. illus., tables. (E/CN. 11/
TRANS/Sub. 2/29)

1. Highways.

355.58
UN
United Nations. (General Assembly)
Report of the United Nations Scientific
Committee on the effects of atomic radiation.
New York, 1962.
442p.

Official records: Seventeenth Session,
Supplement no. 16 (A/5216)

1. Thermal radiation. 2. Civilian defense.

728.6
UN
United Nations. (Economic Commission for
Europe. Housing Committee)
Report of the United States Rapporteur
to the meeting of rural housing rapporteurs,
Housing Committee, Economic Commission for
Europe, Geneva, Switzerland, Dec. 8-9, 1960,
by J. Robert Dodge. [Washington] 1960.
4p.

1. Farm housing. I. Dodge, J. Robert.

691
(5)
UN
United Nations. (Economic and Social
Council. Economic Commission for Asia
and the Far East)
Report of the Seminar on the Development of
Building Materials, 8-15 Jan. 1968, Bangkok,
Thailand. New York, 1968.
57p. (Its E/CN.11/I&NR/BM/L.3)

1. Building materials - Asia.
2. Building industry - Asia.

966
U54
1950
United Nations. (Trusteeship Council.)
Report of the United Nations Visiting Mission
to Trust Territories in West Africa and related
documents. New York, 1951.
138 p. map.

Official records of the Seventh session
(1 June - 21 July 1950) Suppl. no. 2(T/798)

1. Cameroons. 2. Togoland.

VF
728
UNr
United Nations. (Economic Commission for
Europe)
Report of the United States delegation to
the Economic Commission for Europe Housing
Committee, 19th session, Geneva, Switzer-
land, Dec. 10-11, 1959, by J. Robert Dodge.
Washington, 1960.
11p.
Author is with Office of International Housing,
Housing and Home Finance Agency.

1. Housing. I. Dodge, J. Robert.

728.1
(4)
UNre
United Nations. (Economic and Social Council.
Economic Commission for Europe. Housing
Committee)
Report of the ... session. Geneva,
nos. in 1v. (E/ECE/HOU 58, 59, 63-67,
71, 73, 74, 78-
Includes Press releases.

For complete information see shelf list.

1. Housing - Europe.

388
(52)
UN
1963
United Nations. (Economic Commission for
Asia and the Far East)
Report of the United States Delegation to
the United Nations Economic Commission for
Asia and the Far East. Study week of the
New Tokaido Line, Tokyo, Japan (April 11 to
April 18, 1963 inclusive) Submitted to the
Secretary of State. [n.p.] 1963.
108p.
Laurence K. Walrath, Chairman.

1. Transportation -   Japan. I. Walrath,
Laurence K.

VF
728.1
(5)
UNr
United Nations. (Economic and Social Council.
Economic Commission for Asia and the Far East)
Report of the working party on housing and
building materials (fifth session) to the Committee on Industry and Natural Resources
(eleventh session). New York, 1958.
39p. (E/CN.11/I& NR/10)

1. Housing - Asia. 2. Building materials -
Asia.

360
UNs
United Nations. (Economic and Social Council)
Report of the Social Commission on on its
twelfth session, held in New York, from
27 April to 15 May 1959. [New York] 1959.
84p. (E/3265; E/CN.5/343)
"The present document is a preliminary limited
edition of the report which will be issued in
printed form in Supplement no. 11 of the
Official records of the twenty-eighth session
of the Economic and Social Council."

1. Social conditions.   2. Housing -
Social aspects.

728
B87
United Nations. (Economic Commission for
Europe. Committee on Housing, Building and
Planning)
Burroughs, Roy J
Report of the United States Delegation
to the Economic Commission for Europe,
Committee on Housing, Building, and
Planning, Washington, D.C., June 2-5, 1964.
Submitted to the Secretary of State.
Robert Clifton Weaver, Chairman of the
Delegation. Washington, 1964.
6p.

(Cont'd on next Card)

691
UN
United Nations.
Report of the Workshop on Organizational and
Technical Measures for the Development of Build-
ing Materials. New York, 1970.
130p. (United Nations [document] ST/TAO/SER.C/
123)

1. Building materials. 2. Building industry.
I. U.S.S.R. II. Workshop on Organizational and
Technical Measures for the Development of
Building Materials, Moscow, 1968.

VF
672
UNr
United Nations. (Economic and Social Council.
Economic Commission for Europe)
Report of the Steel Committee to the
Economic Commission for Europe. [Geneva]
1957.
5p. (E/ECE/265-G)

Twelfth session. (Provisional agenda
item no. 3)

1. Steel industry. 2. Statistics.

728
B87
Burroughs, Roy J   Report of the
United States... (Card 2)

1. Housing. I. Weaver, Robert Clifton.
II. United Nations. (Economic Commission
for Europe. Committe on Housing, Building
and Planning)

711.4
UNr
United Nations. (Economic and Social Council)
Report on concepts and principles of community development and recommendations on
further practical measures to be taken by
international organizations. Report by the
Secretary-General. [New York] 1957.
160p. (E/CN.5/325)
At head of title: Social Commission,
eleventh session, agenda item 4.

1. Community development. 2. International
organizations.

VF-UN-Technical assistance programs
DATE OF REQUEST
10/8/51   L. C. CARD NO.
AUTHOR
U.N. Economic & Social Council.
TITLE
2nd Report of the Technical Assistance Board.
SERIES
U.N. document E/1911.
EDITION   PUB. DATE Jan. 24, 1951   PAGING 82
PUBLISHER

RECOMMENDED BY   REVIEWED IN
ORDER RECORD

711.585
W31w
United Nations. (Economic Commission for Europe
Committee on Housing, Building and Planning)
Wharton, Howard J
Report of the United States Delegation
to the Economic Commission for Europe,
Committee on Housing, Building and
Planning, Working Party on Urban Renewal
and Planning. [New York?] 1964.
10p.
Submitted to the Deputy Commissioner, URA
and the Secretary of State by Howard J.
Wharton, Chairman of the United States
Delegation.
1. Urban renewal. 2. Population forecasting.
3. Planning. I. United   Nations. (Economic
Commission for Europe   Committee on
Housing, Building and   Planning)

728.1
(667)
UN
United Nations. (Technical Assistance
Administration)
Report on housing in the Gold Coast;
prepared for the government of the Gold Coast
by Otto H. G. Koenigsberger. New York,
Nov. 1956.
50 p. (TAA/GOC/1, add. 1)

Annex: Report to the Council of Kumasi
College of Technology, Gold Coast, on
professional education in subjects (See No. 2)
(See Card No. 2)

728.1
(667)
UN
United Nations. Technical Assistance
Administration. Report on housing in
the Gold Coast...Nov. 1956. (Card No. 2)

allied to building, by R. Gardner-Medwin
and J.A.L. Matheson. p. 19-50.

1. Housing - Ghana. 2. Building construction - Study and teaching.

DATE OF REQUEST 7/20/54   C. CARD NO.

AUTHOR   United Nations. Technical Assistance Administration.

TITLE Report on the mission on community organization and
development in selected Arab countries of the Middle
East [by] Oswald Allen and others.

SERIES ST/SOA/Ser.O/229   ST/TAA/Ser.D/9

EDITION   PUB. DATE 1953   PAGING 60 p.

PUBLISHER

RECOMMENDED BY   REVIEWED IN PAIS 2/20/54 p. 95

ORDER-RECORD

301.15
UNr
United Nations. (Economic Commission for
Africa)
Report on the workshop on planning and
administration of national programmes of
community development, Addis Ababa,
Ethiopia, 14 - 25 September 1959. New
York, 1959.
1v. (E/CN.14/24; E/CN.14/A.C.1/6)

1. Community development. 2. Technical
assistance programs.

VF
331
(4)
UN
United Nations. (Economic and Social Council.
Economic Commission for Europe)
Report on manpower problems in Europe, trans-
mitted by the International Labor Office.
Geneva, 1957.
13p. (E/ECE/266)

Twelfth session. Provisional agenda
item no. 3.

1. Labor supply - Europe.

332.72
(60)
UN
United Nations. (Economic Commission for
Africa)
Report on the Regional Meeting on Technical
and Social Problems of Urbanization with
Emphasis on Financing of Housing, Addis Ababa,
8-23 Jan. 1969. [New York] 1969.
64p.
At head of title: Economic Commission for
Africa and German Foundation for Developing
Countries.
DOK 465 A-F 1/69.
1. Mortgage   finance - Africa.
2. City grow   th - Africa.
(Cont'd on next card)

360
UNr
United Nations. (Economic and Social Council)
Report on the world social situation. In
cooperation with the International Labour
Office, the Food and Agriculture Organiza-
tion, the United Nations Educational, Scien-
tific and Cultural Organization and the
World Health Organization. [New York] 1957.
2 pts. (E/CN.5/324 and E/CN.5/324/Add.1)
Social Commission. Eleventh session.
Agenda item 3.

1. Social   conditions.

711.585
(47)
UN
United Nations. (Economic Commission for
Europe. Housing Committee)
Report on policy and program of town
redevelopment on the questionnaire plan of
the UN EEC Housing Committee. Kiev, 1960.
36p.

At head of title: Ukrainian SSR.
Bibliography: p. 32-36.

1. Urban renewal - U.S.S.R. 2. Housing -
U.S.S.R.

332.72
(60)
UN
United Nations. (Economic Commission for
Africa)   Report...1969.   (Card 2)

I. Title: Technical and social problems of
urbanization with emphasis on financing of
housing.

330
(4971)
UN
United Nations. (Economic and Social Council)
Report on the world social situation: planning for balanced social and economic development in Yugoslavia. [New York] 1962.
79p. (E/CN.5/346/Add.8)
At head of title: Social Commission,
fourteenth session, item 3 of the provisional
agenda.

1. Economic development - Yugoslavia.
2. International organizations.

728.1
UNre
United Nations. (General Assembly)
Report on promotion of refugee housing
and its financing. Submitted by the High
Commissioner. [New York] United Nations,
1962.
9p. ([United Nations Document] A/AC96/182)
At head of title: Executive Committee of
the High Commissioners Programme. 8th session.

1. Housing. 2. Mortgage finance.

308
:728.1
(4)
UN
1961
United Nations. (Economic Commission for
Europe)
Report on the Seminar on Housing Surveys
and Programmes with particular reference to
problems in the developing countries, held
at Zagreb, Yugoslavia, in Oct. 1961.
Geneva, 1962.
170p. (ST/ECE/HOU/5)

1. Housing surveys - Europe - Congresses. I. Seminar
on Housing Surveys and Programmes. Zagreb,
Yugoslavia, 1961.

360
UNre
United Nations. (Economic and Social
Council)
Report on the world social situation, note
by the Secretary-General. Conclusions and
recommendations. New York, 1961.
10p. (E/CN.5/361)
Social Commission, thirteenth session.
Item 3(a) of provisional agenda.

1. Social conditions. 2. Economic
development.

691.42
152
United Nations. (Economic Commission for Asia
and the Far East)
India. National Buildings Organisation.
Report on strength of brick masonry in relation to strength and mix proportion of
mortars. New Delhi, National Buildings
Organisation and U.N. Regional Housing Centre
ECAFE, 1968.
30p.
1. Bricks. 2. Strength of materials. I. United
Nations. (Economic Commission for Asia and the
Far East) II. Title: Strength of brick masonry
in relation to strength and mix proportion of
mortars.

330
(8)
UNec
United Nations. (Economic Commission
for Latin America)
Report on the third extraordinary session
of the Committee of the Whole, 28-30 June
1960. New York, 1960.
7p. (E/3402; E/CN.12/AC/46/4)

Economic and Social Council. Official
records: thirtieth session. Supplement
no. 4A.

1. Economic conditions - Latin America.

360
UNrep
United Nations. (Economic and Social Council)
Report on the world social situation, with
special reference to the problem of balanced
social and economic development. New York,
1961.
229p. (E/CN.5/346)
Social Commission, thirteenth session.
Item 3(a) of the provisional agenda.
Housing: p. 91-105.
1. Social conditions. 2. Housing - Social aspects.
3. Economic development.

VF
690.031
UNr
United Nations. (Economic Commission for
Europe. Housing Committee)
Report on the enquiry on the planning and
cost of new residential areas in selected
countries. Note by the Secretariat.
[Geneva] 1962. [U.N.] [Document]
3p. (HOU/WP/URB/3)

At head of title: Working Party on Urban
Renewal and Town Planning Aspects of
Housing.

1. Building costs.   2. Residential areas.

351.1
U54
United Nations. (Secretariat.)
Report on the United Nations Seminar on Public
Personnel Management (United Nations Headquarters,
New York City, 30 Oct. 1950 to 30 Jan. 1951)
New York, 1952.
236 p. (General ST/TAA/CONF.1/1, 31 Jan.
1951)

Mimeographed.

1. Personnel management.

301.15
UNre
United Nations.
Asian Seminar on Planning and Administration
of National Community Development Programmes,
Bangkok, 1961.
Report; organized by the United Nations in
cooperation with the Government of Thailand.
New York, United Nations, 1962.
153p. (ST/TAO/SER.C/54 ST/SOA/SER.T/3)

1. Community development - Congresses.
2. Technical assistance programs. I. United
Nations.

312
:728.1
UN
United Nations. (Economic and Social Council)
Report on the development of general
principles for housing census. [n.p.] 1957.
3p. (E/CN.3/240)

1. Census - Housing.

711.585
(4)
UN
1961
United Nations. (Economic Commission for
Europe)
Report on the Urban Renewal Symposium
organized by the Housing Committee of the
United Nations Economic Commission for Europe
and held in Geneva in June 1961. Geneva,
1961.
80p. (ST/ECE/HOU/4)

1. Urban renewal - Europe - Congresses.
I. Urban Renewal   Symposium,
Geneva,   1961.

693.002.22
(5)
S25
United Nations. (Economic Commission for
Asia and the Far East)
Seminar on the Industrialization of Housing
for Asia and the Far East, Copenhagen,
1968.
Report sponsored by the United Nations
Economic Commission for Asia and the Far
East and the United Nations Office of
Technical Co-operation in co-operation with
the Government of Denmark [Ministry of Housing]
26 Aug. - 14 Sept., 1968, Copenhagen, Denmark.
New York United Nations Economic and Social
Council, 1968.
74p. (E/CN.11/I&NR/IH/L.1)

(Cont'd on next card)

693.002.22
(5)
S25 Seminar on the Industrialization of Housing
for Asia and the Far East, Copenhagen, 1968.
Report...1968. (Card 2)

1. Prefabricated construction - Asia.
2. Asia - Prefabricated construction.
I. United Nations. (Economic Commission for
Asia and the Far East) II. Denmark. Ministry
of Housing.

711.417 United Nations. (Secretariat)
R68c Round Table Conference on the Planning
1964 and Development of New Towns, Moscow,
1964.
Comprehensive report on the planning and
the development of new towns. Prepared by
the United Nations, Secretariat, New York.
Organized by the United Nations Bureau of
Technical Assistance Operations and others.
New York, 1964.
99p. (United Nations. Secretariat.
Conference document no. 3)

1. New towns - Congresses.
I. United Nations. Secretariat.
II. Title.

FF-UN-Pacific Islands
DATE OF REQUEST 12/31/52 JAN 13 1953. CARD NO. 52-3288
AUTHOR
United Nations. (Library.)
TITLE
Select bibliography and catalogue of publications and
maps relating to trust territories in the Pacific
SERIES available in the United Nations Library at Headquarters.
U.N. Doc. T/INF/25. 29 Feb. 1952.
EDITION | PUB. DATE 1952 | PAGING 11 p.
PUBLISHER
same
RECOMMENDED BY | REVIEWED IN
ORDER RECORD

330
(8)
U54r United Nations. (Economic Commission for
Latin America)
Report to the Economic and Social Council,
1956/57-
La Paz, Bolivia [etc.] 1957-
v. annual (Its [Document] E/. E/CN)

1. Economic conditions - Latin America.

330
UNr United Nations. (Economic and Social
Council)
Rules of procedure of the Economic
and Social Council. New York, 1958.
29p. (E/3063)

1. United Nations. (Economic and
Social Council)

312
(016)
UN United Nations. (Economic and Social
Council)
Selected bibliography on methods of projecting the school-age population, the
economically active population, the urban
and rural populations and the number and
size of households. Bombay, India, 1960.
21p. (E/CN.9/CONF.2/L.11 English)

United Nations Seminar on evaluation and
utilization of population census data in
Asia and the Far East, 20 June-8 July 1960.

1. Population fore-   casting - Bibliography.

728.1
(595)
UN United Nations. (Economic and Social Council)
The Republic of Singapore. Written statement
for the 5th session of the Committee on Housing,
Building and Planning. [New York, 1967]
11p.

1. Housing - Singapore. 2. City planning -
Singapore. I. United Nations. Committee on
Housing, Building and Planning, 5th sess. 1967.

327
UN United Nations. (Trusteeship Council)
Rules of procedure of the Trusteeship Council
(as amended up to and during its twenty-second
session) New York, 1958.
20p. (T/1Rev.5)

1. Trusteeship Council.

728.100.15 United Nations. (Economic and Social Council
(44)
S64 Spira, Ephraim.
Selective examination and assessment of research in France, Israel and in the United
Kingdom in the field of housing and building,
applicable in developing countries. A report
prepared by Ephraim Spira and Jan de Geus. Prepared for UNESCO. Rotterdam, International
Council for Building Research Studies and
Documentation, 1966.
48p.
1. Housing research - France. 2. France -
Housing research. 3. Housing research -
Israel. 4. Israel - Housing research.
5. Housing rese   arch - U.K. 6. U.K. -
Housing research.   (Cont'd on next card)

FOLIO United Nations.
728.1 Philippine Islands. Special Housing Research
(914) Team of the People's Homesite and Housing
P34r Corporation.
Republic of the Philippines; preliminary
report on housing needs, metropolitan Manila.
Prepared in collaboration with United Nations
Planning and Housing Expert. Manila, 1963.
1v.

1. Housing - Philippine Islands. 2. Urban
renewal - Philippine Islands. I. United
Nations.

728.6
UNr United Nations. (Dept. of Economic and Social
Affairs)
Rural housing; a review of world conditions.
New York, 1969.
186p. (Its [Document] ST/SOA/87)

2c.
1. Farm housing. 2. Housing. 3. Rural
planning. I. Title.

728.100.15
(44) Spira, Ephraim. Selective examination...
S64 1966. (Card 2)
7. Building research - France. 8. France -
Building research. 9. Building research -
Israel. 10. Israel - Building research.
11. Building research - U.K. 12. U.K. - Building research. 13. Underdeveloped countries.
I. Geus, Jan de, jt. au. II. United Nations.
(Economic and Social Council) III. International Council for Building Research Studies
and Documentation.

VF
330
(4)
UNr United Nations. (Economic and Social Council.
Economic Commission for Europe)
Resolutions adopted by the Economic and Social
Council during its twenty-first and twenty-second
sessions and by the General Assembly during its
eleventh session of concern to the Commission.
Note by the executive secretary. Geneva, 1957.
7p. (E/ECE/277)

Twelfth session. Provisional agenda
item no. 13.
1. Economic development - Europe.

728.6
(4)
UN United Nations. (Economic Commission for
Europe)
The rural housing situation in Europe.
Geneva, 1962.
76p. (United Nations. [Document] ST/ECE/
HOU/3)

1. Farm housing - Europe. 2. Housing
statistics - Europe.

728.100.15
(44) Spria, Ephraim. Selec...1966 (Card 3)
S64

I. Geus, Jan de, jt. su. II. United
Nations. (economic and Social Council)
III. International Council for Building
Research Studies and Documentation.

United Nations. (Economic Commission for
728.1 Asia and the Far East)
(54) India. Ministry of Works, Housing and
I52re Supply.
A review of the housing situation in
India. Prepared ... for the sixth meeting of the ECAFE Working Party on Housing
and Building Materials, Bangkok, 22nd to
29th Nov. 1960. New Delhi, 1960.
24p.

1. Housing - India. I. United Nations.
(Economic Commission for Asia and the Far
East)

728.1
(4)
UN United Nations. (Economic Commission for
Hou/WP Europe. Housing Committee)
no. 116 The rural housing situation; provisional
report by the Secretariat. New York,
1960.
56p. tables. (Hou/Working paper
no. 116)

1. Housing - Europe. 2. Farm housing.

United Nations.
690
S25p Seminar on Changes in the Structure of the
1964 Building Industry, Prague, 1964.
Proceedings. [n.p.] 1965.
3v. ([United Nations] Document
ST/ECE/HOU/13)

1. Building industry. 2. Housing.
I. United Nations.

691
(5)
UNr United Nations. (Economic Commission for
1967 Asia and the Far East)
Role of building centres in the development
of the building materials industry and
popularizing the use of new materials.
[New York] 1967.
14p. (United Nations. [Document] L&NR/BM/9)
At head of title: Seminar on the Development of Building Materials, 8-15 Jan. 1968,
Bangkok, Thailand.
1. Building materials - Asia. I. Title.

727.1
(47)
UN United Nations. (Economic Commission for
Asia and the Far East)
School building in the U.S.S.R. For the
report at the Sixth Session of the Working
Party on Housing and Building Materials of
the Committee on Industry and Natural Resources of ECAF, [Bangkok] Moscow, 1960.
13p.

1. Schools - U.S.S.R.

728.1 United Nations. (Economic Commission for Asia
(5)   and the Far East)
S25 Seminar on Housing Statistics and Programmes
1963 for Asia and the Far East, Copenhagen, 1963.
Report. [New York] 1964.
177p. ([United Nations. Document]
E/CN.11/677)
At head of title: United Nations, Economic
and Social Council, Economic Commission for
Asia and the Far East.
"Circulated as a document for the sixth
session of the Conference of Asian Statisti-
cians under the number E/CN.11/ASTAT/HSP/
L.54 [i.e. L.34]"

(Continued on next card)

728.1
(5)
S25
1963

Seminar on Housing Statistics and Programmes
for Asia and the Far East, Copenhagen, 1963.
Report...1964   (Card 2)

"Sponsored by the United Nations and the
Government of Denmark."

1. Housing - Asia. I. United Nations.
(Economic Commission for Asia and the Far
East)

728.1
(4)
UN
HOU/WP
no. 96

United Nations. (Economic and Social
Council. Economic Commission for Europe)
Slum clearance policies and programs.
New York, 1959.
12p. (HOU/Working paper no. 96)

"Item 5 of the provisional agenda
for the eighteenth session."

1. Slum clearance - Europe.

339.3
UN

United Nations. (Dept. of Economic and Social
Affairs)
Social policy and the distribution of income
in the Nation. New York, 1969.
175p. (United Nations [Document] ST/SOA/88)

1. Income. I. Title. II. Title: Distribution
of income.

728.1
(5)
S25
1963
Agenda

United Nations. (Economic Commission for Asia
and the Far East)
Seminar on Housing Statistics and Programmes
for Asia and the Far East, Copenhagen,
1963.
Report. New York 1964.
11p. (United Nations. Document
E/CN.11/651)
At head of title: United Nations, Economic
and Social Council, Economic Commission for
Asia and the Far East. 20th sess. 2-17
March 1964, Teheran, Iran.
(Agenda item 5c (ii))

1. Housing -   Asia. I. United
Nations. (Eco-   nomic Commission for
Asia and the   Far East)

728.1
UNs
1967

AC.

Nsel1
2
daf-9-3
Long.
8.4

United Nations. (Dept. of Economic and Social
Affairs)
Social aspects of housing and urban development. New York, 1967.
58p. (United Nations [Document] ST/SOA/71)
United Nations Publication. Sales no.:
67.IV.12.

1. Housing - Social aspects. 2. Urban renewal -
Social effect. I. Title.

308
UNs

United Nations.
Social programmes and measures relating
to urbanization; major trends and developments
since 1955. Material for UN Second International
Survey of Programmes of Social Development.
[New York] 1958.
46p.

At head of title: United States of America.

1. Social conditions. 2. Housing.

333.65
S25

United Nations. (Economic Commission for
Europe)
Seminar on Management, Maintenance and
Modernization of Housing, Warsaw, 1968.
Proceedings. Organized by the Committee on
Housing, Building and Planning of the United
Nations Economic Commission for Europe. New
York, United Nations, 1969.
2v. (United Nations [Document] ST/ECE/HOU/
38)
1. Housing management. 2. Houses - Maintenance
and modernization. I. United Nations. (Economic
Commission for Europe)

728.1
UNso

United Nations. (Dept. of Economic and
Social Affairs)
Social aspects and management of housing
projects; selected case studies. New York,
1970.
104p. (Its [Document] no. ST/SOA/98)

1. Housing projects. 2. Housing - Social
aspects. I. Title.

728.1
U54s

United Nations. (Dept. of Economic and Social
Affairs)
Social programming of housing in urban areas.
Report of the Ad Hoc Group of Experts on Social
Programming of Housing in Urban Areas, New York,
17-28 August 1970. New York, 1971.
81p. (United Nations. [Document]
ST/SOA/109)

1. Housing - Social aspects. I. Title.

711.14
S25

United Nations. (Economic Commission
for Europe)
Seminar on the Supply, Development and
Allocation of Land for Housing and
Related Purposes, Paris, 1965.
Proceedings. New York, United Nations,
1965.
2v. (U.N. Document ST/ECE/HOU/15)

At head of title: Economic Commission
for Europe.

1. Land use. 2. Housing. I. United
Nations.   (Economic Commission
for Europe)

728.1
UNs
1965

United Nations. (Economic and Social Council)
Social aspects of housing and urban development. Note by the Secretary-General. New
York, 1965.
84p. ([Document] E/CN.5/392)
At head of title: Social Commission, 16th
sess. item 5(b) of the provisional agenda.
1. Housing - Social aspects. 2. City planning. 3. Community development. I. Title.

301.15
UNs

United Nations. (Dept. of Economic and
Social Affairs)
Social service in community development.
New York, 1960.
64p. illus. (ST/SOA/Ser.Q/6)

International Social Service Review
no. 6, Mar. 1960.

1. Community development. I. Title.

691.6
UN

United Nations. (Economic and Social Council.
Economic Commission for Asia and the Far East)
Sheet glass for glazing. (New York) 1968.
12p. (Its E/CN.11/I&NR/BM/L.2)
At head of title: Seminar on the Development
of Building Materials, 8-15 Jan. 1968,
Bangkok, Thailand.

1. Glass. I. Title.

728.1
(016)
S76

United Nations. (Centre for Housing, Building
and Planning.)
Stockholm. Statens Institut for Byggnadsforskning.
Social aspects of housing and urban development; a bibliography. Stockholm, 1969.
173p. (Its Document no. 3)
Compiled and published in agreement with the
United Nations Centre for Housing, Building
and Planning; Dept. of Economic and Social
Affairs, New York.
1. Housing - Social aspects - Bibl. I. United Nations. Centre for Housing, Building and
Planning. II.   Title.

624.131
I57s

United Nations. (Dept. of Economic and
Social Affairs)
Inter-American Housing and Planning Center.
Soil-cement, its use in building. New
York, United Nations, 1964.
87p. ([U.N. Document] ST/SOA/54)

1. Soil-cement. 2. Earth wall
construction. I. United Nations.
(Dept. of Economic and Social Affairs)

311.2
U54

United Nations. (Statistical Office.)
A short manual on sampling. Vol. 1, Elements
of sample survey theory. New York, 1960.
214 p. (Studies in methods, series F, no. 9).

1. Sampling (Statistics). I. Title: Elements
of sample survey theory. II. Title: A short
manual on sampling.

711.4
UN

United Nations. (Secretariat)
Social aspects of urban development; report.
[New York] 1961.
150p. (A/AC.35/L.335)

1. City planning - Social aspects.
2. Community development.

VF
728.1
(41)
B87

United Nations (Economic Commission for Europe.
Housing Committee)
Burroughs, Roy J
Some aspects of housing and planning in
British Isles worthy of U.S. consideration.
Based on observations made on a study tour
conducted by the Housing Committee of the
United Nations Economic Commission for Europe
- June 1962. Washington, Housing and Home
Finance Agency, Office of International
Housing, 1962.
3p.
1. Housing - U.K. I. United Nations Economic Com-
mission for Europe.   Housing Committee.
II. U.S. Housing and   Home Finance Agency.
Office of the   Administrator.
Office of International   Housing.

711.4
(4971)
UN

United Nations.
Skopje resurgent; the story of a United
Nations special fund; town planning project.
New York, 1970.
383p. (United Nations [document] no. DP/
SF/UN/17 Yugoslavia)
At head of title: United Nations Development
Program.
Bibliography: p. 381-383.
1. City planning - Yugoslavia.
2. Earthquakes - Yugoslavia. 3. Urban renewal
- Yugoslavia. I. Title.

330
P14

United Nations. (Centre for Economic and
Social Information)
Pajestka, Josef.
Social dimensions of development. [Prepared]
for the United Nations Centre for Economic and
Social Information. New York, United Nations,
1970.
36p. (Executive briefing paper no. 3)

1. Economic development. I. United Nations.
(Centre for Economic and Social Information)
II. Title.

711.3
L47
United Nations. (Economic Commission for
Asia and the Far East)
Litchfield Whiting Panero Associates.
Special report on United Nations Seminar
on regional planning, Tokyo, Japan,
28 July - 8 August 1958. Bangkok, Thai-
land, 1958.
6p.

1. Regional planning. I. United Nations.
(Economic Commission for Asia and the Far East)

VF
33
(73)
C68s
United Nations. (Secretary General.)
U.S. Council of Economic Advisers.
Statements by the United States Government
submitted to the Secretary General of the United
Nations pursuant to ECOSOC resolution 483(XVI).
[Washington, U.S. Dept. of State] Mar. 1954.
45, 2 l.   tables.

Contents.-Recent experience of the United
States in dealing with inflationary pressures
under conditions of high levels of economic
activity.-Measures to prevent foreseeable adverse
(Continued on next card)

728.1
(8)
L17
Latin American Seminar on Housing,
Statistics and Programmes, Copenhagen,
1962. [Papers]...1962. (Card 2)

-Current housing statistics.

1. Housing - Latin America.
2. Housing statistics - Latin
America. I. United Nations. (Economic
and Social Council)

341.12
UN
United Nations.
Special study on social conditions in non-
self-governing territories; analyses of
information transmitted to the Secretary-
General (1957-1958) New York, 1958.
239p. tables. (ST/TRI/SER.A/14)

Partial contents: -Workers' housing problems, p. 75-93.
1. Company housing. 2. Non-self governing
territories.

U.S. Council of Economic Advisers.   Statements
... Mar. 1954.   (Card 2)

effects on the United States economy arising from
reductions in defense expenditures.
Processed.

1.Economic conditions-U.S. 2.Inflation. 3.Rent
control. I.United Nations. Secretary General.

728.1
(8)
M47
United Nations.
Mitchell, Neal B   Jr.
Squatter housing: criteria for development,
directions for policy, by Neal B. Mitchell,
Jr. and Ian Donald Terner. [New York]
United Nations, 1967.
26p. (United Nations. Information Document
no. 10)
At head of title: United Nations Seminar on
Prefabrication of Houses for Latin America.
1. Housing - Latin America. 2. Prefabricated
construction. 3. Housing in the tropics.
I. Terner, Ian   Donald, jt. au.
II. United Nation   s. III. Title.

728.1
(083.41)
UNs
United Nations. (Dept. of Economic and
Social Affairs. Statistical Office of
the United Nations)
Statistical indicators of housing
conditions. New York, 1962.
21p. (Its Statistical papers,
series M, no. 37)

1. Housing statistics. I. Title.

614.8
(083.41
:4)
UN
United Nations. (Economic Commission
for Europe)
Statistics of road traffic accidents in
Europe, 1956,
Statistiques des accidents de la circula-
tion routière en Europe, 1956-
Geneva, 1958
v. (E/ECE/327, (393;ECE/TRANS-
506,(516)
For complete information see shelflist.

1. Accidents - Statistics.-2. Traffic safety.

382
U54
United Nations. (Secretariat. Dept. of Economic
Affairs.)
Standard international trade classification.
2d ed.   New York, June 1951.
150 p.   tables. ([U.N. Document] ST/STAT/
Ser. M/10/Rev.1, 7 May 1951; Sales no.:
1951.XVII.1)

1.Commodity classification. 2.Building materials.
I.Title. II.Series: United Nations. Statistical
papers.

United Nations. Statistical papers.
no.
339.3 E/3 National income and its distribution in
U54   under-developed countries.   1951.
1951

382 M/10Standard international trade classification.
U54   June 1951.

United Nations. (Economic and Social
Council. Economic Commission for Europe)
728.1 Rutland, E   H
(4)   Statistics on housing finance.
UN [Geneva] 1962.
HOU/WP.3 42p. (United Nations. (Economic
no. 41   and Social Council. Economic Commission
1962   for Europe. Housing Committee/HOU/WP.3
        working paper no. 41)
3c.   Item 4(d) of the provisional agenda for
        the first joint meeting)

1. Mortgage finance. 2. Housing statistics.
I. United Nations.   (Economic and Social
Council. Economic   Commission for
Europe)

728.1
(083.41
:4)
UN
United Nations. (Economic Commission for
Europe)
A statistical survey of the housing
situation in European countries around
1960. New York, 1965.
3c.   75p. (United Nations. [Document]
ST/ECE/HOU.12)
English, French, Russian.
1. Housing statistics - Europe.
I. Title.

728.1
(4)
UN
HOU/WP.3
no.3
United Nations. (Economic and Social Council.
Economic Commission for Europe)
Fey, W
Statistics on the financing of housing.
[Geneva] 1963.
9p. (United Nations. Economic and
Social Council. Economic Commission for
Europe. Housing Committee HOU/WP.3
working paper no. 50)

1. Mortgage finance. 2. Housing
statistics. I. United Nations. (Economic
and Social   Council.
Economic   Commission for
Europe)

696.6
UN
United Nations.
The state of rural electrification in
Europe in 1956. Geneva, 1958.
43p. tables. (E/ECE/320;E/ECE/EP/193)

1. Electric apparatus and appliances.
I. Title: Rural electrification in
Europe.

083.41
UNs
United Nations. (Statistical Office.)
Statistical yearbook, 1948 '70
1st   issue.
Lake Success, N. Y., 1949
v.   tables.

For full information see shelflist.

1. Statistics - Yearbooks.

1967 suppl.

691.421
UN
United Nations. (Economic Commission for
Asia and the Far East)
Structural clay products. New York,
1967.
30p. ([Document] I7NR/BM/22)
At head of title: Seminar on the
Development of Building Materials, 8-15
January 1968, Bangkok, Thailand.

1. Clay. 2. Bricks. I. Title.

728.1
(5)
UNs
United Nations. (Economic Commission for Asia
and the Far East)
Statement on Item 5 of the agenda Review of
the development in the field of housing, by
Max Spandau. ECAF Working Party on Housing and
Building Materials, Sixth session, 21-29
Nov. 1960. Bangkok, 1960.
6p.

1. Housing - Asia. I. Spandau, Max.

728.1
(8)
L17
United Nations. (Economic and Social Council)
Latin American Seminar on Housing,
Statistics and Programmes, Copenhagen,
1962.
[Papers] [n.p.]
4 nos. in 1 v. ([U.N. Document]
ST/ECIA/CONF.9/L.12;L.18/L.20;/28)

Contents: Demographic information required
for housing programs with special reference
to Latin America.-Basic features of the
housing plan for Chile, with special reference
to financing by means of a system of adjust-
able savings   and credits.-The
housing situa-   tion in Europe and
recent trends.   (Cont'd. on next card)

728.1
:308
UN
United Nations. (Economic Commission for
Europe)
Studies of effective demand for housing.
3c. New York, 1963.
96p. ([U.N. Document] ST/ECE/HOU/10)
Partial contents: United States of America:
Estimating National housing demand; Local
housing market analysis by M. Schussheim.

1. Housing market . I. Schussheim, Morton.
Estimating National housing demand.
II. Schussheim,   Morton. Local
housing analysis.

690.031
(5694)
UN
United Nations. (Economic Commission
for Asia and the Far East)
A study of building costs in Israel.
Report prepared for the sixth session of
the Working Party on Housing and Building
Materials of the Economic Commission for
Asia and the Far East [by] Government of
Israel, Ministry of Labour, Housing Division.
[n.p.] 1960.
6p.

1. Building costs - Israel. I. Israel.
Ministry of Labor. (Housing
Div.)

728.1
(5)
UN
United Nations. (Economic Commission for Asia and
the Far East.)
Survey of housing and building materials in
Asia and the Far East, 1956. Bangkok, 1956.
116 p. illus. (E/CN.11/432)

"List of reference documents": p.113-114.

1.Housing - Asia. 2.Building materials - Asia.
3.Building construction - Asia.

UN file -
Technical assistance
DATE OF REQUEST 7/2/53 L.C. CARD NO.

AUTHOR
U.E. (ECOSOC. Economic Commission for Asia and the Far
TITLE East)
Technical assistance activities in the ECAFE region.

SERIES
E/CN.11/343

EDITION | PUB. DATE Jun. 1953 | PAGING 33 p.

PUBLISHER

RECOMMENDED BY | REVIEWED IN
UCP 5/4/53 p.8

ORDER RECORD

360
S11
United Nations.
Saario, Vieno Voitto.
Study of discrimination against persons born
out of wedlock. New York, Sub-Commission on
Prevention of Discrimination and Protection of
Minorities, United Nations, 1967.
227p. (United Nations [Document] E/CN.4/Sub.
2/265/Rev.1)
United Nations Publication. Sales no.: E.
68.XIV.3.
1. Social conditions. 2. Family. I. United
Nations. II. Title.

VP
690.37
U54
1950
2c
United Nations. (Secretariat. Department of
Social Affairs)
Survey of problems of low cost rural housing
in tropical areas; a preliminary report with
special reference to the Caribbean area. New
York, N.Y., Nov. 1950.
93 p. (UN General ST/SOA/2 17 Nov. 1950)
Bibliography: p. 71-93.
1.Housing in the tropics. 2.Building materials-
Tropics. I.Title. II.Title: Low cost rural
housing in tropical areas.

UN - Technical assistance
DATE OF REQUEST 11/17/52 JV 24 1952 L.C. CARD NO.

AUTHOR U.N. ECOSOC. Economic Commission for Asia and the
TITLE Far East.
Technical assistance activities in the ECAFE region.

SERIES
E/CN.11/313

EDITION | PUB. DATE 2/4/52 | PAGING 59 p.

PUBLISHER
same

RECOMMENDED BY | REVIEWED IN
UCP 11/3/52 p.6

ORDER RECORD

690.031
UN
United Nations. (Economic and Social Council)
Economic Commission for Asia and the Far East)
Study on building costs and measures for re-
ducing them. Bangkok, Thailand, 1958.
13p. (E/CN.11/IANR/HBWP.5/L.3)

1. Building costs.

711.3
(62)
UN
United Nations. (Relief and Works Agency for
Palestine Refugees in the Near East.)
Survey report, Northwest Sinai Project,
Republic of Egypt; prepared by the United
Nations Relief and Works Agency for Palestine
Refugees in the Near East and the Permanent
Council for the Development of National
Production of the Republic of Egypt. Cairo,
Northwest Sinai Project Investigation Staff,
July 1955.
342 L. Graphs, maps.
(See Card No. 2)

UN - Technical assistance
DATE OF REQUEST 3/2/54 L.C. CARD NO.

AUTHOR
U.N. (Economic and Social Council.)
TITLE
Report by the Technical Assistance Administration on
Technical assistance activities in the ECLA region.

SERIES
Document E/CN.12/AC.24/4.

EDITION | PUB. DATE 1954 | PAGING

PUBLISHER

RECOMMENDED BY
NBL | REVIEWED IN

ORDER RECORD

690.031
(5)
UNs
United Nations. (Economic Commission for
Asia and the Far East)
Study on building costs in Asia and the
Far East. Bangkok, 1961.
42p. (United Nations. [Document]
E/CN 11/568)

1. Building costs - Asia.

711.3
(62)
UN
United Nations. Relief and Works Agency for
Palestine Refugees in the Near East.
Survey report...July 1955. (Card No. 2)

1.Rural planning - Egypt. 2.Displaced
persons. I.Egypt. Permanent Council for
the Development of National Production.

341.1
:338
U54t
United Nations.
Technical assistance for economic development;
plan for an expanded co-operative programme through
the United Nations and the specialized agencies.
Report prepared by the Secretary-General in consultation with the executive heads of the interested
agencies through the Administrative Committee on
Co-ordination pursuant to resolution 180 (VIII) of
the Economic and Social Council. Lake Success,
N.Y., May 1949.
viii, 328 p. tables. (UN Publications.
Sales no.:1949.11.B.1)
Errata sheet inside front cover.
1.Technical as- sistance programs.

728.1
UN
United Nations. (Dept. of Social Affairs)
Study on methods of preparing national
programmes for housing and community
development. First draft of preliminary
report. [New York] 1951.
36p.

1. Housing. 2. Community development.

332.72
1 (54)
S95
United Nations. (Economic Commission for Asia
and the Far East. Regional Housing Center.
Symposium on Housing Finance, New Delhi, 1965.
Selected papers from Symposium on Housing
Finance (held in New Delhi on 1-3 Feb. 1965)
New Delhi, National Buildings Organisation
and U.N. Regional Housing Centre (ESCAFE) 1966.
18p.
1. Mortgage finance - India. I. India.
National Buildings Organization. II. United
Nations. (Economic Commission for Asia and
the Far East. Regional Housing Center. New
Delhi)

UN file
DATE OF REQUEST 7/2/53 L.C. CARD NO.
Technical assistance
AUTHOR
U.N. (ECOSOC)

TITLE Technical assistance for economic development provided
under General Assembly resolution 200 (III).

SERIES
E/2373

EDITION | PUB. DATE Feb. 1953 | PAGING 8 p.

PUBLISHER

RECOMMENDED BY | REVIEWED IN
UCP 5/4/53 p.8

ORDER RECORD

690
(47)
UNs
United Nations. (European Economic Commission.
Housing Committee)
Study tour of the U.S.S.R. Moscow,
1959.
136p.

Issue in Russian, English and French.

1. Building industry - U.S.S.R.
2. Housing - U.S.S.R.

UN file - Non-self-governing territories
DATE OF REQUEST 9/25/53 OCT 12 1953 L.C. CARD NO.

AUTHOR
U.N.

TITLE Tanganyika, its present and its future; ann account of
the Trusteeship Council's review of the administering
authority's annual report.

SERIES

EDITION | PUB. DATE [1952] | PAGING 26 p.
PUBLISHER

RECOMMENDED BY
NBL | REVIEWED IN
8/22/53 p.719

ORDER RECORD

UN file - Tech. assistance
DATE OF REQUEST April 20, 1953 APR 24 1953 L.C. CARD NO.

AUTHOR
United Nations

TITLE Technical assistance in Non-Self-Governing
Territories (U.N. Secretariat)

SERIES
A/AC.35/L.96

EDITION | PUB. DATE Aug. 20, 1952 | PAGING 15 p.
PUBLISHER

RECOMMENDED BY | REVIEWED IN

ORDER RECORD

728.1
:308
UNs
1964
United Nations. (Economic Commission for
Europe. Committee on Housing, Building and
Planning)
Study tour of the United States of America,
June 6-18, 1964. [New York] 1964.
38p. (United Nations. [Document] HOU/118)
Summary of final "Round Up" prepared by the
U.S. Housing and Home Finance Agency.

1. Housing market. I. U.S. Housing and
Home Finance Agency. II. Title.

UN file - Research
DATE OF REQUEST 6/4/53 JUN 25 1953 L.C. CARD NO.
AUTHOR United Nations. (ECAFE.)

TITLE Technical and Marketing Research as an Aid to
Trade.

SERIES E/CN.11/TP/7 & Teen.

EDITION | PUB. DATE Nov.1952 | PAGING 17 p.
PUBLISHER

RECOMMENDED BY | REVIEWED IN

ORDER RECORD

690
(415)
S95
United Nations.
Symposium on Technical Documentation
for the Building Industry, Dublin, 1967.
Technical documentation for the
building industry, sponsored by An
Foras Forbartha Teoranta, the National
Institute for Physical Planning and
Construction Research. Edited by: Pierce
T. Pigott and Lindsay N. Johnston. Dublin,
National Institute for Physical Planning
and Construction Research, 1967.
306p.
A project for the Government of Ireland
assisted by the United Nations
Special Fund and the United Nations.
(Cont'd on next card)

690
(415)
S95

Symposium on Technical Documentation for
the Building Industry, Dublin, 1967.
Technical...1967.   (Card 2)

1. Building industry - Ireland.
2. Building documentation. I. Pigott,
Pierce T., ed. II. Ireland (Eire)
National Institute for Physical
Planning and Construction Research.
III. United Nations. IV. Title.

UN-Population
DATE OF REQUEST 7/23/54   L. C. CARD NO.
AUG 6 1954

AUTHOR United Nations.

TITLE Training in techniques of demographic analysis.

SERIES

EDITION   PUB. DATE [1953]   PAGING   21 p.
PUBLISHER

RECOMMENDED BY   PW 3/6/54 p. 1371
MWL   REVIEWED IN

ORDER RECORD

United Nations. Economic and Social Council.
Economic Commission for Europe. Industry
and Materials Committee.   Typical dwellings
in 14 European countries...1951.   (Card 2)

1.Space considerations. 2.Family living
requirements. 3.House plans. I.Blackshaw,
Maurice B. II.Title.

334.1
I57t

United Nations. (Center for Housing,
Building, and Planning)
International Cooperative Housing Development
Association.
Techniques of financing cooperative and
non-profit housing developments in selected
countries. Wash., 1967.
1v.
Prepared under contract with the United
Nations, Centre for Housing, Building, and
Planning.

1. Cooperative housing. 2. Mortgage fi-
nance. I. United Nations. (Center for
Housing,   Building, and Planning)
II. Title.

690.022
UN
3o.

bc.

United Nations. (Dept. of Economic and Social
Affairs)
Trends in the industrialization of building.
New York, 1970.
58p. (United Nations [Document] ST/SOA/102)

1. Prefabricated construction. I. Title.

341.1
:338
UNr

United Nations. (Economic and Social
Council)
United Nations Conference on the Application
of Science and Technology for the Benefit
of the Less Developed Areas,
Report of the Secretary-General, 19

Geneva, 19
v. (United Nations. [Document]

At head of title: United Nations. Economic
and Social Council. Session   Agenda
item

For complete   information see shelflist.   (Cont'd. on next card)

308
:728.1
UNt
3 c

United Nations.
Techniques of surveying a country's
housing situation, including estimating
of current and future housing requirements.
Geneva, 1962.
1v.   ([U.N. Document] ST/ECE/HOU/6)

1. Housing surveys.

694.1
F66

United Nations. (Economic Commission for Europe)
Food and Agriculture Organization of the United
Nations.
Trends in utilization of wood and its products
in housing; a study prepared jointly by the
secretariats of the Food and Agriculture Organization of the United Nations and the United Nations
Economic Commission for Europe. Geneva, 1957.
49p. tables.

1.Wood construction. I.United Nations.
(Economic Commission for Europe)

341.1
:338
UNr

United Nations Conference on the Application
of Science and Technology... (Card 2)

1. Technical assistance programs (UN)
I. United Nations. (Economic and Social
Council)

728.1
(44)
F71

United Nations.
France. Ministere de l'Equipement et
du Logement.
Tendances et politiques actuelles dans le
domaine de l'Habitation de la construction
et de la planification. [Paris] 1969.
32p. (Monographie nationale de la
France)
On cover: Nationas Unies, Commission
Economique pour l'Europe, Comite de
l'Habitation de la Construction et de
la Planification.
1. Housing - France. 2. Building
construction -   France. I. United
Nations.

694.1
F66

United Nations. (Economic Commission for
Europe. Timber Committee)
Trends in the utilization of wood and its
products (item 6 of the provisional agenda)
Geneva, 1956.
1 v. (TIM/107 (b)

1. Wood construction.

341.1
:338
UNun

United Nations. (Economic and Social Council)
United Nations development decade: activities of the United Nations and related
agencies in the immediate future. Note by
the Secretary-General. [Geneva] 1963.
189p. (United Nations [Document] E/3776)
At head of title: Thirty-sixth session
agenda item 6(a)

1. Technical assistance programs (UN)
2. United Nations.

VF
341.12
UNt

United Nations.
Terms of reference and rules of procedure
of the Economic Commission for Latin
America. New York, 1960.
15p.   ([Document] E/CN.12/544)

1. United Nations. (Economic and Social
Council. Economic Commission for Latin
America)

694.1
F66t

United Nations (Economic Commission for
Europe. Timber Committee)
Trends in the utilization of wood and its
products (Item 6 of the provisional agenda)
Geneva, 1956.
1v.   (TIM/107 and TIM/107a)
14th session, Geneva 20 - 25 October 1956.

1. Wood construction.

002
UN

United Nations.
United Nations documents symbols.
[New York] 1954.
53p. (Its SD/Adm/3rev.19)

1. Documentation.

728.1
(07)
UN

United Nations. (Economic and Social Council.
Committee on Housing, Building, and Planning)
Training and educational facilities in
housing, building and planning. [n.p.] 1962.
11p.   ([U.N. Document] E/C.6/7)

At head of title: First session; Agenda
item 8.

1. Housing - Study and teaching.

728.1
(43)
397

United Nations. (Economic Commission for
Europe. Housing Committee)
Burroughs, Roy J
Trip report for Germany, by U.S. delegates
June 15-24, 1961, by Roy J. Burrough, Office of
International Housing. [Washington, Housing and
Home Finance Agency, 1961]
6p.
At head of title: Economic Commission for
Europe, Housing Committee.
1. Housing - Germany. I. United Nations.
(Economic Commission for Europe. Housing
Committee. II. U.S. Housing and Home
Finance Agency.   Office of
International   Housing.

VF
332.72
:331.252
UN

United Nations (General Assembly.)
United Nations Joint Staff Pension Fund;
Use of pension fund capital for housing loans
to staff. [New York, N.Y.] November 1956.
10 p. (Its A/C. 5/L. 395)

Letter from Director-General of the
International Labour Organization, and
reply of Secretary-General.

1.Pension funds.

728.1
+711.4
UN

United Nations. (Dept. of Economic and Social
Affairs.
no. 11 Training for town and country planning.
Seminar on training for town and country planning, Puerto Rico, March 1956. New York, 1957.
119p. charts, illus. (ST/SOA/SER.C11) Housing
and town and country planning [bulletin] no. 11)

Issued also in Spanish.

1. Housing. 2. City planning.

VF
728
:392
U54
Jan.1951

United Nations. (Economic and Social Council.
Economic Commission for Europe. Industry
and Materials Committee.)
Typical dwellings in 14 European countries,
a comparative study of the utilisation of space.
[Geneva, Switzerland] Jan. 1951.
33 p.   plans, tables (one fold)   (Its
IM/HOU/25)
Abstract: p. 1.
Definitions: p. 8-9.
Restricted.
Mimeographed.
(Continued on next card)

UN-Technical assistance
DATE OF REQUEST 2/11/53   L. C. CARD NO. 53-353
FEB 18 1953
AUTHOR
U.N. (Secretariat. Dept. of Public Information.)
TITLE
United Nations programs for technical assistance.

SERIES   U.N. Publications. 1952.1.24

EDITION 3d   PUB. DATE 1952   PAGING 56 p.
PUBLISHER
New York.

RECOMMENDED BY   REVIEWED IN

ORDER RECORD

728.1
(62)
UN

United Nations.
United Nations Seminar on Financing of Housing
and Related Community Facilities for the
Arab States, Cairo, United Arab Republic,
1963.
Report. New York, United Nations, 1965.
125p. (U.N. [Document] ST/TAO/SER.C.72)
Bibliography: p. 106-114.
1. Housing - Egypt. 2. Housing - Congresses.
3. Mortgage finance - Egypt. I. United Nations.

332.6
:336.2
U54

United Nations. (Dept. of Economic Affairs.)
United States income taxation of private
United States investment in Latin America.
(A description of the United States system and
some of its limitations.) New York, Jan. 1953.
viii, 80 p.   graphs, tables (part fold. in
back)   (ST/ECA/18)

1.Federal taxation. 2.Investments. I.Title: Income
taxation of private United States investment in
Latin America.

388
UN
1970

United Nations. (Economic Commission for Asia
and the Far East)
Urban transportation in the renewal of
American cities; an information paper. Workshop
on Urban Traffic and Transportation, Bangkok,
Thailand, December 8-17, 1970. Presented by
the Dept. of Housing and Urban Development.
Washington, D.C., 1970.
14p.
1. Transportation. 2. Traffic. I. Workshop
on Urban Traffic and Transportation, Bangkok,
1970. II. U.S. Dept. of Housing and Urban
Development. III. Title.

323.4
P72u

United Nations.
U.S. President's Commission for the
Observance of Human Rights Year.
Unfolding of the American tradition. Wash.,
Govt. Print. Off., 1968.
127p. (U.S. Dept. of State. Publication
8403)

1. Civil rights. 2. History. I. United
Nations. II. Title: Unfolding of the American
tradition.

341.1
:338
UNu

United Nations. (Economic and Social Council)
United States of America: report of experience in the field of social development of
potential assistance to under-developed
countries. Information furnished in response
to Resolution 731 C (XXVII) of the Economic
and Social Council. New York 1960.
226p.

Bibliography: p. I-IX.

1. Technical assistance programs. 2. Under-developed
countries.

301.15
U54

United Nations. (Dept. of Economic and
Social Affairs)
Urbanization: development policies and
planning. New York, 1968.
130p. (Its [Document] ST/SOA/Ser.X/1)
International social development review,
no. 1.

Bibliography: p. 128-130.

1. City growth. I. Title.

728.1
(5)
UNu

United Nations. (Technical Assistance
Program)
United Nations Seminar on Housing and
Community Improvement in Asia and the Far
East, New Delhi, India, 21 January - 17
February, 1954. [n.p.] 1954.
73p. (TAA/NS/AFE/1)

1.Housing - Asia. 2.Building materials.
3.Community development - Asia.

728.1
711.4
UN
No. 7

United Nations. (Dept. of Social Affairs.)
Urban land problems and policies.
New York, 1953.
182 p.   (Its Housing and town and
country planning bulletin 7)

Bibliography: p. 140-172.

Edited by Charles Abrams.

1.Land use. 2.Land acquisition. 3.Land tenure.
I.Abrams, Charles. II.Title.

301.15
(5)
J64

United Nations.
Joint UN/UNESCO Seminar on Urbanization in the
ECAFE Region, Bangkok, 1956.
Urbanization in Asia and the Far East; proceedings, ed. by Philip M. Hauser. Calcutta,
UNESCO Research Centre on the Social Implications of Industrialization in Southern Asia,
1957.
286p. diagrs., tables. (Tensions and technology series)

1. City growth - Asia. I. Hauser, Philip
M   ed. II. United Nations.   III. Title.

360
(56)
UN

United Nations.
United Nations social welfare seminar for
Arab states in the Middle East. Beirut, 15
August to 8 September 1949. [Lake Success, N.Y.
July 1950]
68 p.   (Its Technical Assistance for social
progress no. 3)

1. Social welfare - Middle East.

United Nations.

711.585
(415)
I72

Ireland (Eire) National Institute for
Physical Planning and Construction Research.
Urban redevelopment, New Ross. Dublin
[1966?]
16p.

A project of the Government of Ireland
assisted by the United Nations Special Fund
and the United Nations.

1. Urban renewal - Ireland. 2. Ireland
(Eire) - Urban renewal. I. United Nations.
II. Title.

711.4
(8)
UN
1963

United Nations. (Economic and Social
Council. Economic Commission for Latin
America.)
Urbanization in Latin America; results
of a field survey of living conditions in an
urban sector. [Geneva] 1963.
35p. ([Document] E/CN.12/662)

At head of title: Tenth session, Mar de
Plata, Argentina, May, 1963.

1. City planning - Latin America. 2. Economic
conditions - Latin   America.
I. Title.

967.57
U54
1950

United Nations. (Trusteeship Council.)
United Nations Visiting Mission to East
Africa: report on Ruanda-Urundi and related
documents.   Lake Success, New York [1950]
114 p.   (T/217 & T/217/Add.1, T/361/Add.1,
T/376, 1 Sept. 1950)

Trusteeship Council Official records Fourth
session, suppl. no. 2.
French and English.

1.Ruanda-Urundi.

711.400.15
G27

United Nations. (Economic Commission for
Europe. Committee on Housing,...)
Germany (Federal Republic, 1949-   )
Bundesministerium fur Wohnungswesen
und Stadtebau.
Urban and regional research in the
Federal Republic of Germany. A selective
review prepared for the United Nations
Economic Commission for Europe, Committee
on Housing, Building and Planning, Group
of Experts on Urban and Regional Research,
Palais des Nations, Geneva, Switzerland.
Bonn, 1971.
36p.

(Cont'd on next card)

711.4
UNu

United Nations. (Dept. of Economic and
Social Affairs)
Urbanization in the second United Nations
development decade. New York, 1970.
39p. (Its [Document] ST/ECA/132)

1. City growth. I. Title.

967.8
U54
1948

United Nations. (Trusteeship Council.)
United Nations Visiting Mission to East Africa
report on Tanganyika and related documents.
Lake Success, New York [1948]
315 p.   tables.   (T/218 & T/218/Add.1,
T/333, T/376, 13 Nov. 1948)

Trusteeship Council Official records Fourth
session, suppl. no. 3
French and English.

1.Tanganyika.

711.400.15
G27

Germany (Federal Republic, 1949-   )
Bundesministerium für Wohnungswesen
und Städtebau. Urban and...1971.
(Card 2)

Bibliography: p. 13-15.
1. City planning - Research. I. United
Nations. (Economic Commission for
Europe. Committee on Housing, Building
and Planning) II. Title.

711.4
W247

United Nations. (Bureau of Social Affairs)
Weissmann, Ernest.
Urbanization in the world. Remarks by Ernest
Weissmann, Bureau of Social Affairs, United
Nations. Presented to the Board of Directors
of ACTION, Inc., May 24, 1961. New York, ACTION,
Inc., The National Council for Good Cities,
1961.
9p.

1. City growth. I. American Council to
Improve Our Neighborhoods. II. United Nations.
(Bureau of Social   Affairs)

728.1
(5)
UN
1965

United Nations. (Economic Commission for Asia
and the Far East)
United States delegation to the Working
Party on Housing and Building Materials,
Committee on Industry and Natural Resources,
Economic Commission for Asia and the Far
East, Bangkok, Thailand, June 24 to July
2, 1955. Prepared by J. Robert Dodge.
[n.p.] 1965.

1. Housing - Asia. 2. Building materials.
I. Dodge, J.   Robert.

711.585
I55

United Nations. (Economic Commission for Europe
Housing Committee)
Innes, John W
Urban renewal policies and programs in the
U.S.A. For use of Housing Committee, United
Nations Economic Commission for Europe.
Washington, Housing and Home Finance Agency,
Office of the Administrator, Office of Inter-
national Housing, 1961.
42p.
Provisional draft.
1. Urban renewal. I. United Nations. (Economic
Commission for Europe. Housing Committee. II. U.S.
Housing and Home   Finance Agency.
Office of the Admin-   istrator. Office
of International   Housing.

666.81
RA2u

United Nations. (Economic Commission for
Asia and the Far East)
Ridge, M J
The use of gypsum in building in Australia.
New York, Economic Commission for Asia and the
Far East, 1967.
16p. (United Nations (Document) I&NR/BM/7)
At head of title: Seminar on the Development
of Building Materials, 8-15, Jan. 1968,
Bangkok, Thailand.
1. Gypsum. 2. Building materials - Australia.
I. United Nations. (Economic Commission for
Asia and the Far East) II. Title.

672
UNu
1964
United Nations. (Economic Commission for
Europe)
The use of steel in construction. New
York, 1964.
177p. (United Nations. [Document]
ST/ECE/Steel/10)

1. Steel. 2. Steel construction.

728.1
(44)
F71
United Nations. (Economic and Social Council,
Economic Commission for Europe. Comm. on Hsg)
France. Ministere de la Reconstruction.
Voyage des 15. 16 et 17 Novembre 1957 a
Grenoble. Programme des visites. [Paris,
1957]
1 v. map.

1. Housing - France. I. United Nations.
(Economic and Social Council, Economic Commission for Europe. Committee on Housing)

728.1
(4)
HOU/WP.1
United Nations. (Economic and Social
Council. Economic Commission for Europe.
Housing Committee)
Working Party on Development of Housing
Policies. Series HOU/WP.1/ Working paper
no. 1-
Geneva, 1956-
nos.

For complete information see shelflist.
1. Housing - Europe.

691
(05)
UNu
United Nations. (Economic Commission for
Asia and the Far East)
Utilization of industrial wastes in the
building materials industry. New York,
1967.
51p. (United Nations. [Document]
LAND/BM/11)
At head of title: Seminar on the Development of Building materials, 8-15 Jan. 1968,
Bangkok, Thailand.
1. Building materials - Asia. 2. Refuse
and refuse disposal. I. Title.

697.2
UN
United Nations. (Economic Commission
for Europe)
Ways of improving the flexibility of
the gas industry. Geneva, 1958.
50p. diagrs., tables. (E/ECE/331;
E/ECE/GAS/15)

1. Gas industry.

728.1
(4)
HOU/WP.3
United Nations. (Economic and Social Council.
Economic Commission for Europe. Housing
Committee)
Working Party on Housing and Building
Statistics. Series HOU/WP.3/ Working
paper no. 1-
Geneva, 1956-
nos.
Partially analyzed.
For complete information see shelflist.
1. Housing - Europe.

728
:392
UN
United Nations. (Economic and Social Council)
Utilization of space in dwellings, by
M. B. Blackshaw and others. New York, 1959.
1v. diagrs., tables. (E/ECE/350;
E/ECE/HOU/82)

1. Space considerations. 2. Family living requirements. I. Blackshaw, M. B.

312
UNwo
United Nations. (Statistical Commission)
Working group on censuses of population
and housing.
Geneva,
folder. (Conference of European Statisticians/
WG.6/ ...) .

For complete information see shelf list.

1. Census - Population. 2. Census - Housing.

33
UNe
1953-54
United Nations. (Department of Economic and
Social Affairs.)
World economic report, 1953-54.
New York, 1955.
163 p (E/2729, ST/ECA/30)

1. Economic conditions. I. Title

728
:392
UN
prov.
3c
United Nations. (Economic Commission for Europe.
Housing Committee)
Utilization of space in dwellings, by M. B.
Blackshaw and others. New York, 1959.
1v. diagrs., tables. (HOU/Working paper
no. 98)
Item 8 of the provisional agenda for the
eighteenth session.
1. Space considerations. 2. Family living
requirements. I. Blackshaw, M. B.

711.4
UNw
1966
United Nations. (Economic Commission for
Europe. Committee on Housing, Building
and Planning)
Working Group for the Promotion of International Co-operation between National Bodies
Concerned with Urban and Regional Research.
Report of the first meeting. [New York?]
1966.
[16]p. (United Nations. [Document]
HOU/SUB-C/URB/2)
1. City planning. 2. Regional planning.
3. Urban   renewal.

330
U54w
United Nations. (Dept. of Economic and
Social Affairs)
World economic survey, 1956-
New York, 1957-
v. (Its [Document] E/. ST/ECA)
Title varies.

For complete information see shelflist.

1. Economic conditions. I. Title.

551
I57
United Nations. (Technical Assistance Team)
Institute for Planning and Development, Tel Aviv.
Village planning and reconstruction of the
earthquake zone in the Ghazvin area-Iran.
[New York?] United Nations Technical Assistance
(U.N.T.A.) Team, 1968.
70p.

1. Earthquakes. 2. City planning - Iran.
I. United Nations. (Technical Assistance Team)
II. Title.

728.1
(4)
UN
HOU/WP
United Nations. (Economic and Social Council.
Economic Commission for Europe. Housing
Committee)
Working papers,
Geneva,
nos.

For complete information see shelflist.

1. Housing - Europe.

728.1
UNw
1964
United Nations. (Economic and Social
Council)
World housing conditions and estimated
housing requirements. Paper prepared by the
Secretariat. [New York] 1963.
65p. ([Document] E/c.6/13)

At head of title: Committee on Housing,
Building and Planning. Second session,
New York, 22 January 4-February 1964. Item
3 of the provisional agenda.
(Cont'd. on next card)

910
(415)
UN
1962
United Nations. (Economic Commission for
Europe. Housing Committee)
Visit to Northern Ireland. Belfast,
H.M. Stat. Off., 1962.
1v.

1. Travel - Ireland.

728.1
UN
GRO/WP
UNITED NATIONS (GROUP OF EXPERTS OF
HOUSING AND URBAN DEVELOPMENT)
WORKING PAPER[S] NO. 1-10, FOR
MEETING OF GROUP OF EXPERTS ON HOUSING
AND URBAN DEVELOPMENT, NEW YORK, FEB.
7-21, 1962. NEW YORK, 1962.
1 V.

1. HOUSING.   2. URBAN RENEWAL.

728.1
UNw
1964
United Nations. (Economic and Social
Council) World housing ...   (Card 2)

1. Housing. 2. Community facilities.
I. United Nations. Committee on Housing,
Building and Planning, 2d sess. New York,
1964. II. Title.

728.1
(8)
UN
United Nations.
La vivienda en el desarrollo economico de
la America Latina. Informe preparado para el
Seminario de la Union Panamericana sobre
Financiamiento de la Vivienda y Servicios
Publicos en la America Latina. New York,
1959.
28p. tables.

1. Housing - Latin America. 2. Mortgage
finance - Latin America.

728.1
(4)
UN
HOU/WP.2
United Nations. (Economic and Social
Council. Economic Commission for
Europe. Housing Committee)
Working Party on Cost of Building. Series
HOU/WP.2. Working paper no. 1-
Geneva, 1956-
nos.

For complete information see shelflist.
1. Housing - Europe.

728.1
UNw
1965
United Nations. (Dept. of Economic and
Social Affairs)
World housing conditions and estimated
housing requirements. New York, 1965.
58p.

1. Housing. 2. Housing market.

312
UNw

United Nations. (Economic and Social
Council)
World population census programme.
Progress report. 1960-
[Geneva]
v. tables. (E/CN,
ST/STAT/P/L

For complete information see shelflist.

1. Census - Population.

341.12
A52
July 1946

United Nations.
American Academy of Political and Social Science.
Making the United Nations work, ed. by Ernest
Minor Patterson. Philadelphia, 1946.
183 p. (Its Annals, v. 246)

1.United Nations. I.Patterson, Ernest M., ed.
II.Title.

United Nations.

327
C65

Commission to Study the Organization of Peace.
Strengthening the United Nations. Arthur
N. Holcombe, Chairman. New York, Harper, 1957.
276p.

1.International relations. 2.United Nations.
I.Holcombe, Arthur N II.Title.

312
U54wo

United Nations. (Dept. of Economic and
Social Affairs)
World population prospects as assessed in
1963. New York, 1966.
149p. (Its Population studies no. 41.
ST/SOA/Series A.41)

1. Population. I. Title.

341.12
A52
July 1947

United Nations.
American Academy of Political and Social Science.
Progress and prospects of the United Nations,
ed. by Ernest Minor Patterson. Philadelphia,
1947.
183 p. (Its Annals, v. 252)

1.United Nations. I.Patterson, Ernest M., ed.
II.Title.

United Nations.

351.7
:325.3
(41)
U54b

U.K. British Information Services.
Britain and the United Nations. New
York, 1962.
79p. (Its I.D. 1308 (Revised) March
1962)

1. British Commonwealth of Nations.
2. United Nations.

312
U54
P3

United Nations. (Secretariat. Dept. of Social
Affairs.)
World population trends, 1920-1947. [Lake
Success, New York] Dec. 1949.
16 p. tables. ([U.N. Document]
ST/SOA/Series A. Population studies, no. 3; Sales
no.: 1949.XIII.3)

1.Population. I.Title. II.Series: United Nations.
Population studies.

300.2
L67

United Nations.
Lorwin, Lewis Levitzki, 1883-
Postwar plans of the United nations, by Lewis L. Lorwin.
New York, The Twentieth century fund, 1943.
xii, 307 p. 24 cm.
Bibliographical foot-notes.

1. Reconstruction (1989-) I. Title.
[Name originally: Louis Levitzki, later Louis Levine]

Illinois. Univ. Library   A 44—256
for Library of Congress   D825.L67
[50o7]   940.53144

United Nations.

341.12
UNr
1946

United Nations. (Headquarters Commission)
Report of the Headquarters Commission to
the second part of the first session of the
General Assembly of the United Nations. New
York, 1946.
143p.

1. United Nations. I. Title.

647.1
UNw

United Nations. (Economic and Social Council)
World social situation; international definition and measurement of standards and
levels of living. Comments on the report of
the Committee of Experts on International
Definition and Measurement of Standards and
Levels of Living. [n.p.] 1955.
11p. (E/2747)

1. Cost and standard of living. I. Committee of Experts on International Definition
and Measurement of Standards and Levels of
Living.

327
M12

United Nations.
McKitterick, Nathaniel M
U.S. diplomacy in the development agencies
of the United Nations. Washington, National
Planning Association, 1965.
67p. (National Planning Association.
Planning pamphlet 122)

1. International relations. 2. Economic
policy. 3. United Nations. I. National
Planning Association. II. Title.

United Nations. (Economic and Social Council.
Economic Commission for Latin America)

VF
341.12
UNt

United Nations.
Terms of reference and rules of procedure
of the Economic Commission for Latin
America. New York, 1960.
15p. ([Document]E/CN.12/544)

1. United Nations. (Economic and Social
Council. Economic Commission for Latin
America)

389.6
UN
1966

UNITED NATIONS. (STATISTICAL OFFICE)
WORLD WEIGHTS AND MEASURES; HANDBOOK
FOR STATISTICIANS. REV. ED. NEW YORK,
1966.
138P. (STATISTICAL PAPERS, SER. M,
NO. 21, REV. 1)

1. STANDARDIZATION. I. TITLE.

VF
33
N17
P50

United Nations. (Economic and Social Council)
National Planning Association.
International economic collaboration; role of
the Economic and Social Council on the United
Nations Organization; a report by the NPA
Committee on International Policy. [Washington]
Feb. 1946.
26 p. (Planning pamphlets, no. 50)

1.U.N. Economic and Social Council. I.Title.
II.Series.

United Nations.

341.1
:338
UNun

United Nations. (Economic and Social Council)
United Nations development decade: activities of the United Nations and related
agencies in the immediate future. Note by
the Secretary-General. [Geneva] 1963.
189p. (United Nations [Document] E/3776)
At head of title: Thirty-sixth session
agenda item 6(a)

1. Technical assistance programs (UN)
2. United Nations.

910
(03)
W67

UNITED NATIONS.
Worldmark encyclopedia of the nations; a
practical guide to the geographic,
historical, political, social and economic
status of all nations, their international
relationships, and the United States
system. Editor and publisher: Moshe Y.
Sachs. New York, Worldmark Press [1965]
5v.

1. Geography - Dict. 2. History - Dict.
3. United Nations. I. Sachs, Moshe Y., ed.

323.4
8238

United Nations.
Schwelb, Egon.
Human rights and the international
community; the roots and growth of the
universal declaration of human rights,
1948-1963. Chicago, Quadrangle Books,
published for the B'nai B'rith, International
Council, Anti-Defamation League of B'nai
B'rith, and the United States Committee for
the United Nations, 1964.
96p.

1. Civil rights. 2. United
Nations. I. Title.

VF
341.1
L65

United Nations.
U. S. *Congress. House. Committee on Foreign Affairs.*
International organizations and movements. Hearings
before the Subcommittee on International Organizations and
Movements of the Committee on Foreign Affairs, House of
Representatives, Eighty-third Congress, first session ...
Washington, U. S. Govt. Print. Off., 1953.
vi, 299 p. illus. 24 cm.

Chester B. Merrow, chairman of subcommittee.
Hearings held Mar. 27-July 29, 1953.

1. International agencies. 2. United Nations—U. S. 3. Title.

JX1977.2.U5A52   *341.11   53—63368
Library of Congress   [53c8]

910
(03)
W67
1971

United Nations.
Worldmark encyclopedia of the nations; a
practical guide to the geographic, historical,
political, social and economic status of
all nations, their international relationships, and the United States system. Editor
and publisher: Moshe Y. Sachs. New York,
Worldmark Press, 1971.
v.
Contents: v.1. United Nations.-v.2.Africa.
-v.3. Americas.-v.4. Asia and Australasia.-
v.5. Europe.
1. Geography - Dict. 2. History - Dict.
3. United Nations. I. Sachs,
Moshe Y., ed.

330
UNr

United Nations. (Economic and Social Council)
United Nations. (Economic and Social
Council)
Rules of procedure of the Economic
and Social Council. New York, 1958.
29p. (E/3063)

1.United Nations. (Economic and
Social Council)

United Nations. (Economic Commission for
Europe. Housing Committee)

VF
728.1
H68b

U.S. Housing and Home Finance Agency.
Background paper concerning the Housing
Committee, Economic Commission for Europe;
prepared for officials and delegates of
U.S.A. Rev. [Washington] 1960.
8p.

1. Housing - Congresses. 2. United Nations. (Economic Commission for Europe. Housing Committee)

United Nations.
341.12
P72   U.S. President, 1953-   (Eisenhower)
       Text of the address by the President of the
United States, Dwight D. Eisenhower at the
Fifteenth General Assembly of the United Na-
tions, September 22, 1960. Washington, U.S.
Dept. of State, 1960.
       12p. (Dept. of State publication 7086;
International organization and conference
series 17)

1. United Nations. 2. U.S. President - Messages.
I. U.S. Dept. of State.

United Nations.
VF
341.12   U.S. Dept. of State. Bureau of Public
S71u   Affairs.
1960   The UN, meeting place of nations. Rev.
          Washington, Govt. Print. Off., 1960.
          folder. (International organization and
          conference series 15)

          U.S. Dept. of State Publication 7074.

1. United Nations. (Series)

United Nations. (Economic Commission for
711.585   Europe. Housing Committee)
W31   Wharton, Howard J
       Report on the Working Party on Urban
Renewal and Town Planning Aspects of
Housing; Housing Committee, Economic
Commission for Europe, Geneva, Switzerland,
March 11-14, 1963. [Washington] Urban
Renewal Administration, 1963.
       5p.

       1. Urban renewal. 2. Housing.
3. United Nations. (Economic Commission
for Europe.   Housing Committee)
I. U.S.   Urban Renewal
Administra-   tion.

---

327   United Nations.
P72u
       U.S. President.
       U.S. participation in the U.N.

Washington, Govt. Print. Off.
       v. annual (U.S. Dept. of State.
Publication)

       Issued also as International Organization
and conference series.

       For complete information see shelflist.

                 (Continued on Card No. 2)

United Nations.
VF
341.12   U.S. Dept. of State. Bureau of Public
S71u   Affairs.
1961   The UN, meeting place of nations. Rev.
          Washington, Govt. Print. Off., 1961.
          folder. (U.S. Dept. of State. Inter-
national organization and conference series 21)

          U.S. Dept. of State. Publication 7247.

          1. United Nations.

058.7   United Nations - Directories.
UN
       United Nations.
       Members of the United Nations and the
main organs of the United Nations, 1958.
[n.p.] 1958.
       3p. (SD/GEN/74/Rev.4)

                 1. United Nations - Directories.

---

327   U.S. President. U.S. participation in the U.N.
P72u   (Card No. 2)

       1. International relations. 2. Non-self
governing territories. 3. Under-developed
countries. 4. United Nations. I. U.S. Dept.
of State. II. Title.

United Nations.
VF
341.12   U.S. Dept. of State. Bureau of Public
S71u   Affairs.
1962   The UN, meeting place of nations. Rev.
          Washington, Govt. Print. Off., 1962.
          folder. (U.S. Dept. of State.
International organization and conference
series 32)

          U.S. Dept. of State. Publication 7407.

          1. United Nations.   (Series)

. United Nations - Publications.
341.12
(016)   United Nations. (Economic Commission for Asia
UN   and the Far East)
       Bibliography of reports issued by the United
Nations Economic Commission for Asia and the
Far East (ECAFE) July 1948-March 1957.
New York, 1958.
       129p. (UNEC D-39/58)

       1. United Nations - Publications.

United Nations.
VF
341.12   U.S. Dept. of State. Bureau of Public
S71unit   Affairs.
       The UN action agency for peace and
progress. Washington, Govt. Print. Off.,
1963.
       folder. (U.S. Dept. of State. Inter-
national organization and conference series
44)
       U.S. Dept. of State. Publication 7576.

       1. United Nations.

United Nations.
341.12
S71un   U.S. Dept. of State.
       The U.S. in the U.N. Washington, 1960.
       8p. (International organization and
conference series 16)

       U.S. Dept. of State. Publication 7080.

1. United Nations.

United Nations - Publications.
R
728.1   United Nations. (Bureau of Social Affairs)
(016)   Cumulative list of documents and publications
UN   of the United Nations, its regional economic
       commissions and the specialized agencies in
       the field of housing, building and planning.
New York,
       v. (List no.
1957-   compiled by M. Monasterial.
       For complete information see shelflist.

       1. Housing - Bibl. 2. Building
construction - Bibl. 3. Planning - Bibl.
4. United Nations - Publications.
I. Monasterial -   Publications.

VF   United Nations.
341.12   U.S. Dept. of State. Bureau of Public
S71unit   Affairs.
1965   The UN action agency for peace and
progress. Rev. Wash., Govt. Print. Off.,
1965.
       folder. (U.S. Dept. of State.
International organization and conference
series 55)
       U.S. Dept. of State Publication 7733.

       1. United Nations. I. Title.

United Nations.
VF
341.12   U.S. Dept. of State. Bureau of Public Affairs.
S71   You and the United Nations, 1958-59;
Henry Cabot Lodge, U.S. Representative to the
UN, answers your questions. Rev. Washington,
Govt. Print. Off., 1958.
       48p. (Its Publication 6692) (International
Organization and Conference Series III, 131)

       1. United Nations.

728.1   United Nations - Publications.
(016)   United Nations. (Centre for Housing,
U54   Building and Planning)
       Cumulative list of United Nations documents
and publications related to the field of
housing, building and planning. New York,
United Nations, Centre for Housing, Building
and Planning Research, Training and Information Section, 1968.
       49p.

       1. Housing - Bibl. 2. Building construction -
Bibl. 3. Planning - Bibl. 4. United Nations -
Publications.

United Nations.
341.12
S71uni   U.S. Dept. of State. Bureau of Public
       Affairs.
       United Nations, guardian of peace.
Washington, Govt. Print. Off., 1961.
       45p. (U.S. Dept. of State. Inter-
national organization and conference series
20; Publication 7225)

       1. United Nations.

United Nations.
VF
341.12   U.S. Dept. of State. Bureau of Public Affairs.
871   You and the United Nations, 1959-60;
1959/60   Henry Cabot Lodge, U.S. representative to the
UN answers your questions. Washington, Govt.
Print. Off., 1959.
       46p. (Its Publication 6872) (International
organization and conference series 6)

       1. United Nations.   I. Lodge, Henry
Cabot.

341.1   United Nations - Publications.
(016)
UN 2   United Nations. (Economic Commission for
       Europe)
       List of documents in the HOU series and
HOU subseries. Geneva, 1955-
       nos. (Its HOU/--)

       1. United Nations - Publications.

United Nations.
VF
341.12   U.S. Dept. of State. Bureau of Public
S71u   Affairs.
       The U.N., meeting place of nations. Wash-
ington, Govt. Print. Off., 1959.
       folder. (International organization and
conference series 7)

       1. United Nations

United Nations.
VF
341.12   U.S. Dept. of State. Bureau of Public
871   Affairs.
1962   You and the United Nations. Rev.
Washington, Govt. Print. Off., 1962.
       55p. (U.S. Dept. of State. International
organization and conference series 35;
Publication 77442)

       1. United Nations.

341.12   United Nations - Yearbooks.
:06   Annual review of United Nations affairs. 1949-
U54   New York, New York University Press.
       v. 24 cm.

       Issued by the New York University Graduate Program of Studies
in United Nations and World Affairs in co-operation with the Dept.
of Public Information of the United Nations.
       Editor: 1949-   C. Eagleton.
       Contains the proceedings of the 1st-   Institute for Annual
Review of United Nations Affairs, New York University 1949-
       For full information see shelf list card.
       1. United Nations—Yearbooks. I. Eagleton, Clyde, 1891-   ed.
II. New York University. Graduate Program of Studies in United
Nations and World Affairs. III. Institute for Annual Review of
United Nations Affairs, New York University.

JX1977.A1A5   341.13058   50—548

Library of Congress   [50k50]

VF
728.1
(016)
UNp
United Nations. (Economic Commission for
Europe. Housing, Building and Planning
Committee)
Publications,

Geneva, Switzerland, 19
v.

For complete information see main card.

1. Housing - Bibl. 2. Building industry
- Bibl. 3. Planning - Bibl. 4. United
Nations -   Publications.

341.123   UNITED NATIONS - YEARBOOKS
(058)   Yearbook of the United Nations, 1964.
Y21   Published by Columbia University Press in
cooperation with the United Nations. New
York, /1965?/
710 p.

Includes bibliographies.

1. United Nations - Yearbooks.

728.1   United Nations. Committee on Housing,
(595)   Building and Planning, 5th sess. 1967.
UN   United Nations. (Economic and Social Council)
The Republic of Singapore. Written statement
for the 5th session of the Committee on Housing,
Building and Planning. [New York, 1967]
11p.

1. Housing - Singapore. 2. City planning -
Singapore. I. United Nations. Committee on
Housing, Building and Planning, 5th sess. 1967.

728.1   United Nations. Committee on Housing,
UNv   Building and Planning, 2d sess. New York,
1964   1964.
United Nations. (Economic and Social
Council)
World housing conditions and estimated
housing requirements. Paper prepared by the
Secretariat. [New York] 1963.
65p. ([Document] E/c.6/13)

At head of title: Committee on Housing,
Building and Planning. Second session,
New York, 22 January 4-February 1964. Item
3 of the provisional agenda.
(Cont'd. on next card)

728.1   United Nations. (Economic and Social
UNv   Council) World housing ...   (Card 2)
1964
1. Housing. 2. Community facilities.
I. United Nations. Committee on Housing,
Building and Planning, 2d sess. New York,
1964. II. Title.

VF   The UN action agency for peace and progress.
341.12   U.S. Dept. of State. Bureau of Public
S71unit   Affairs.
1965   The UN action agency for peace and
progress. Rev. Wash., Govt. Print. Off.,
1965.
folder.   (U.S. Dept. of State.
International organization and conference
series 55)
U.S. Dept. of State Publication 7733.

1. United Nations. I. Title.

---

327   United Nations Association of the United States
U54   of America.
The United Nations in the 1970's. A strategy
for a unique era in the affairs of nations.
A report of a National Policy Panel. New York,
1971.
88p.

1. International relations. I. Title.

---

312   United Nations Association of the
U54w   United States of America.
World population; a challenge to the
United Nations and its system of
agencies. A report of a National Policy
Panel. New York, 1969.
57p.

1. Population. I. Title.

341.1
:338   United Nations Conference on the Application
UNr   of Science and Technology for the Benefit
of the Less Developed Areas,
Report of the Secretary-General, 19

Geneva, 19
v. (United Nations. [Document]

At head of title: United Nations. Economic
and Social Council. Session   Agenda
item

For complete   information see shelflist.   (Cont'd. on next card)

341.1
:338   United Nations Conference on the Application
UNr   of Science and Technology...   (Card 2)

1. Technical assistance programs (UN)
I. United Nations. (Economic and Social
Council)

341.1
:338 United Nations Conference on the Application
UNs   of Science and Technology for the Benefit
of the Less Developed Areas, Geneva, 1962.
Science, technology, and development,
United States papers prepared for the United
Nations... Geneva, 1962.
13 v.
Contents:-v. 1. Natural resources; energy, water and
river basin development.-v. 2. Natural resources;
minerals and mining, mapping and geodetic control.-
v. 3. Agriculture.-v. 4. Industrial development.-
v. 5. Transportation.-   v. 6. Health and
nutrition.-v. 7.   Social problems of
(Continued on next card)

341.1
:338 United Nations Conference on the Application
UNs   of Science and Technology for the Benefit
of the Less Developed Areas, Geneva, 1962.
Science, technology, and development...1962.
(Card 2)
development and urbanization.-v. 8. Organizations,
planning, and programming for economic development.-
v. 9. Scientific and technological policy, planning
and organization.-v. 10. International cooperation
and problems of transfer and adaptation.-v. 11.
Human resources. Training of scientific and
technical personnel.-v. 12. Communications.
(Continued on next card)

341.1
:338 United Nations Conference on the Application
UNs   of Science and Technology for the Benefit
of the Less Developed Areas, Geneva, 1962.
Science, technology, and development...1962
(Card 3)
v.13   A selected list of U.S. readings on
development.

1. Technical assistance programs - Congresses.
2. Sociology, Urban. 3. Community development.
4. Transportation. I. Title: Social problems
of development and   urbanization.
I. Title.

341.1   United Nations Conference on the Application
:338   of Science and Technology for the Benefit
(016)   of the Less Developed Areas, Geneva, 1962.
K17   Katz, Saul M
A selected list of U.S. readings on
development. Prepared for the United Nations
Conference on the Application of Science and
Technology for the Benefit of the Less
Developed Areas, by Saul M. Katz and Frank
McGowan. Washington, Agency for International
Development, 1963.
363p.

1. Technical assistance programs - Bibl. I. McGowan,
Frank, jt. au. II. U.S. Agency for International
Development.   III. United Nations
Conference on the   Application of Science and
Technology for the   Benefit of the Less
Developed Areas, Geneva,   1962.

United Nations Educational, Scientific and
Cultural Organization.

see also

U.S. National Commission for UNESCO.

---

370   United Nations Educational, Scientific and
I57a   Cultural Organization.
International Bureau of Education, Geneva.
Annuaire international de l'education, 19

Paris, UNESCO, 19

v. (Publication no.

For Library holdings see main entry.
1. Education. 2. Universities and colleges.
I. United Nations Educational, Scientific and
Cultural Organization. II. Title.

---

370   United Nations Educational, Scientific
(083.41)   and Cultural Organization.
UN   Basic facts and figures; international
statistics relating to education, culture
and mass communication. Faits et chiffres;
statistiques internationales relatives a
l'education, a la culture et a l'information,

Paris,
v. tables.   annual. (UNESCO/SS)

For complete information see shelflist.
English   and French.

1. Education   -   Statistics.

R   United Nations Educational, Scientific
010   and Cultural Organization.
L42   U.S. Library of Congress.
v.1   Bibliographical services; their present
state and possibilities of improvement;
report prepared as a working paper for an
international conference on bibliography.
Washington, 1950.
67 p. (UNESCO/Library of Congress bibliographical survey, v. 1)
"References": p. 61-67.

(See Card No. 2)

R   U.S. Library of Congress. Bibliographical
010   services...1950. (Card No. 2)
L42
v.1   Appendix: Notes on the development of the
concept of current complete national
bibliography, by Katherine Oliver Murra. 42 p.
"References": p. 31-42.

1.Bibliography. I.United National
Educational, Scientific and Cultural Organization. II.Murra, Katherine Oliver. III.
UNESCO/Library of Congress bibliographical survey.

United Nations Educational, Scientific and
Cultural Organization.
(03:016) Holmstrom, J   E
H65   Bibliography of interlingual scientific and
technical dictionaries.   Paris, UNESCO, 1951.
220 p.   tables.

English and French.

1.Architecture-Dict.-Bibl. 2.Building construction-
Dict.-Bibl. I.United Nations Educational,
Scientific and Cultural Organization. II.Title.
III.Title: Scientific and technical dictionaries.

---

34   United Nations Educational, Scientific and
(016)   Cultural Organization. (International
U54   Committee of Comparative Law)
Catalogue des sources de documentation
juridique dans le monde ... A register of legal
documentation in the world, prepared by the
International Committee of Comparative Law with the
support of the International Committee for Social
Science Documentation.   [Paris, 1953]
362 p. (Documentations in the social
sciences)

1.Law-Bibl. I.Title: documentation in the
world, A register of

711.4
:67
S26
United Nations. [Educational, Scientific and Cultural Organization.]
Scott, Jerome F
The community factor in modern technology; an international study of the "sense of belonging" in industry, by Jerome F. Scott and R. P. Lynton. [Paris] United Nations Educational, Scientific and Cultural Organization [1952]
169 p. (Tensions and technology series)
Bibliographical footnotes.
1.Industrial communities. 2.Community development. I.Lynton, R. P. II.United Nations Educational, Scientific and Cultural Organization. III.Title.

300.15
H18
United Nations Educational, Scientific and Cultural Organization.
Heuser, Philip M ed.
Handbook for social research in urban areas. New York, United Nations Educational, Scientific and Cultural Organization, 1965.
214p. (Technology and society series)

1. Social science research. 2. Sociology, Urban. I. United Nations Educational, Scientific and Cultural Organization. II. Title.

VF
025.3
UN
U.N.E.S.C.O. (Dept. of Mass Communication. Clearing House)
International rules for cataloguing of educational, scientific and cultural films and filmstrips. Prelim. ed. Paris, May 1956.
53 p. (Its Reports and papers on mass communication no. 17)

1.Cataloging - Films. I.Title.

370
(6)
C65
United Nations Educational, Scientific and Cultural Organization.
Conference of African States on the Development of Education in Africa, Addis Ababa, 1961.
Outline of a plan for African educational development. [New York] United Nations Economic Commission for Africa, United Nations Educational, Scientific and Cultural Organization, 1961.
27p.

1. Education - Africa. I. United Nations. II. United Nations Educational, Scientific and Cultural Organization.

744
UN
United Nations Educational, Scientific and Cultural Organization.
The healthy village; an experiment in visual education in West China. Paris [1951]
119 p. illus. (Its Monographs on fundamental education, no. 5)

1.Visual aids. 2.Public health - China. I.Title.

010
L42
v.1
UNESCO/Library of Congress bibliographical survey.
U.S. Library of Congress.
Bibliographical services; their present state and possibilities of improvement; report prepared as a working paper for an international conference on bibliography. Washington, 1950.
67 p. (UNESCO/Library of Congress bibliographical survey, v. 1)
"References": p. 61-67.

(See Card No. 2)

500.15
A83
United Nations Educational, Scientific and Cultural Organization.
Auger, Pierre.
Current trends in scientific research; survey of the main trends of inquiry in the field of natural sciences, the dissemination of scientific knowledge, and the application of such knowledge for peaceful ends. New York, United Nations, 1961.
245p.
In cooperation with UNESCO.

1. Scientific research. I. United Nations. II. United Nations Educational, Scientific and Cultural Organization.

FF International - Tech.assistance
DATE OF REQUEST 12/7/53   L C. CARD NO.
AUTHOR   JAN ?? 1954
UNESCO.
TITLE Human problems in technical assistance: guidance for American understanding and overseas service, by John W. Provinse.
SERIES   (EC IV/EM.II/1)
EDITION   PUB. DATE   PAGING
PUBLISHER
RECOMMENDED BY   REVIEWED IN
              W.L.
        ORDER RECORD

010
L42
v.1
U.S. Library of Congress. Bibliographical services...1950. (Card No. 2)
Appendix: Notes on the development of the concept of current complete national bibliography, by Katherine Oliver Murra. 42 p.
"References": p. 31-42.

1.Bibliography. I.United National Educational, Scientific and Cultural Organization. II.Murra, Katherine Oliver. III. UNESCO/Library of Congress bibliographical survey.

R
300
(03)
G68
United Nations Educational, Scientific, and Cultural Organization.
Gould, Julius, ed.
A dictionary of the social sciences, edited by Julius Gould and William L. Kolb. Compiled under the auspices of the United Nations Educational, Scientific and Cultural Organization. New York, Free Press, 1964.
761p.

1. Social sciences - Dictionaries. I. Kolb, William L., jt. ed. II. United Nations Educational, Scientific and Cultural Organization. III. Title.

339.5
I57f
United Nations Educational, Scientific, and Cultural Organization.
Intergovernmental Conference of Experts on the Scientific Basis for Rational Use and Conservation of the Resources of the Biosphere, Paris, 1968.
Final report. Paris, United Nations Educational, Scientific, and Cultural Organization, 1968.
35p. (SC/MD/9)
1. Natural resources. 2. Man - Influence of environment. I. United Nations Educational, Scientific, and Cultural Organization. II. Title: Scientific basis for rational use and conservation of the resources of the biosphere.

010
L42
v.2
UNESCO/Library of Congress bibliographical survey
United Nations Educational, Scientific and Cultural Organization.
National development and international planning of bibliographical services. Paris, 1950.
59 p. (Unesco/Library of Congress bibliographical survey, v. II; UNESCO/CUA/1)

1.Bibliography. I.U.S. Library of Congress Bibliographical survey.

R
058.7
:500.15 UNESCO
U54
1950
Directory of international scientific organizations. Paris [1950]
224 p.

Engineering: p. 102-123.

1.Scientific research-Direct. 2.Engineering research-Direct. I.Title: International scientific organizations.

058.7
:370
U54
United Nations Educational, Scientific and Cultural Organization.
An international directory of education associations. Paris, 1959.
91p. (Its Educational studies and documents no. 34)

1. Education - Directories.

331
G65mae
United Nations Educational, Scientific and Cultural Organization.
Goldstein, Harold.
Methods of long-term projection of requirements for and supply of qualified manpower, by Harold Goldstein and Sol Swerdloff. [New York] United Nations Educational, Scientific and Cultural Organization, 1967.
48p. (United Nations Educational, Scientific and Cultural Organization. Statistical reports and studies. ST/S/12)
Bibliography: p. 47-48.
1. Labor supply. 2. Employment. 3. Occupations. I. United Nations Educational, Scientific. II. Title.

628.1
UNE
UNITED NATIONS EDUCATIONAL, SCIENTIFIC, AND CULTURAL ORGANIZATION.
EVAPORATION REDUCTION; PHYSICAL AND CHEMICAL PRINCIPLES AND REVIEW OF EXPERIMENTS, BY J. FRENKIEL. PARIS, 1965.
79P. (ITS ARID ZONE RESEARCH NO. 27)

BIBLIOGRAPHY: 69-79.

1. WATER SUPPLY. I. FRENKIEL, J. II. TITLE.

058.7
:300
UN
United Nations Educational, Scientific, and Cultural Organization.
International organizations in the social sciences; a summary description of the structure and activities of non-governmental organizations in consultative relationship with UNESCO and specialized in the social sciences. Rev. and aug. ed. with an introduction by Jean Meynaud. Paris, 1961.
145p. (Its Reports and papers in the social sciences no. 13)

1. Social science - Directories. I. Title.

R
010
L42
v.2
United Nations Educational, Scientific and Cultural Organization.
National development and international planning of bibliographical services. Paris, 1950.
59 p. (Unesco/Library of Congress bibliographical survey, v. II; UNESCO/CUA/1)

1.Bibliography. I.U.S. Library of Congress Bibliographical survey. II.UNESCO/Library of Congress bibliographical survey.

770
UN
United Nations Educational, Scientific and Cultural Organization.
Film-making on a low budget; the Unesco-UNRWA pilot project, by Myrtle Winter and Norman F. Spurr. Paris, 1960.
31p. (Reports and papers on mass communication no. 29)

1. Films. 2. Visual aids. I. Winter, Myrtle. II. Spurr, Norman F.

058.7
:002
:3
U54
United Nations Educational, Scientific and Cultural Organization.
International repertory of social science documentation centres. [Paris, 1952]
42 p.

1.Documentation. 2.Social sciences. 3.Associations-Direct. I.Title.

FF UNESCO
DATE OF REQUEST 12/10/51 DEC 17 19?? CARD NO.
AUTHOR
U.N Educational, scientific, and cultural organization.
TITLE National administration and international organization
SERIES
EDITION   PUB. DATE 1951   PAGING 78 p.
PUBLISHER
same
RECOMMENDED BY   REVIEWED IN
              PAIS 10/27/51 p. 10
        ORDER RECORD

362.6
I57o
United Nations Educational Scientific and Cultural Organizations.
International social science journal. Old age. Paris, UNESCO. (vol. 15, no. 3, 1963, p. 339-514)

Entire issue.

1. Old age. I. United Nations Educational Scientific and Cultural Organizations.

VF
690.37
UN
U.N.E.S.C.O., Science Cooperation Office for South Asia. Regional symposium... 1952. (card 2)

1. Housing in the tropics. 2. Building materials - Tropics. I. National Institute of Sciences of India. II. Title.

058.7
:378
UN
United Nations Educational, Scientific and Cultural Organization.
Study abroad; international handbook, fellowships, scholarships, educational exchange. 10th ed. Paris, 1958.
779p.

English, French, and Spanish.

1. Universities and colleges - Directories.
2. Educational exchange. I. Title.

025.3
I57
1961
United Nations Educational, Scientific and Cultural Organization.
International Conference on Cataloging Principles, Paris, 1961.
Preliminary official report. Sponsored by International Federation of Library Associations, with the aid of a grant from the Council on Library Resources. Paris, 1962.
p. 53-63. (UNESCO bulletin for libraries. vol. 16, no. 2, March-April 1962)

1. Cataloging - Congresses. I. International Federation of Library Associations. II. Council on Library Resources. III. United Nations Educational, Scientific and Cultural Organization.

058.7
:300.15
I57
United Nations Educational, Scientific, and Cultural Organization.
International Committee for Social Sciences Documentation.
Repertoire international des centres de recherche sociologique en dehors des Etats-Unis d'Amerique (International repertory of sociological research centres outside the USA) Paris, United Nations Educational, Scientific, and Cultural Organization, 1961.
125p. (United Nations Educational, Scientific, and Cultural Organization. Reports and papers in the social sciences. No. 20)

(Cont'd on next card)

United Nations Educational, Scientific and Cultural Organization.
025.3
:744
L22
Ledoux, Jacques.
Study of the establishment of national centres for cataloguing of films and television programmes. Paris, United Nations Educational, Scientific and Cultural Organization, 1963.
34p. (Reports and papers on mass communication, no. 40)
Bibliography: p. 33-34.

1. Cataloging - Films. 2. Indexing. I. United Nations Educational, Scientific and Cultural Organization.

VF
690.072
U54p
United Nations Educational, Scientific and Cultural Organization.
Problems of education and training in the construction industry. New York 1970.
16p. (HBP/Build/Sem.3/C.2)
At head of title: Economic Commission for Europe, Committee on Housing, Building and Planning, Third Seminar on the Building Industry, Moscow, 5-17 October 1970.

2c

1. Building construction-Labor requirements. I. United Nations. (Economic Commission for

---

058.7
:300.15
I57
International Committee for Social Sciences Documentation. Repertoire international ...1961. (Card 2)

1. Social science research - Direct. I. United Nations Educational, Scientific, and Cultural Organization. II. Title: International repertory of sociological research centres outside the USA.

VF
341.1
:338
S38
United Nations Educational, Scientific and Cultural Organizations.
Shuster, George N
The task of peaceful cooperation. Remarks by chairman of the U.S. delegation before the 55th meeting of the Executive Board of the United Nations Educational, Scientific and Cultural Organization. [Washington] 1959.
3p.
Reprinted from the Dept. of State Bulletin, Jan. 1960.

1. Technical assistance programs (U.N.) I. United Nations Educational, Scientific and Cultural Organizations.

VF
690.072
U54p
United Nations Education, Scientific and Cultural Organization. Problems...1970. (Card 2)

Europe. Committee on Housing, Building and Planning) II. Title.

301.15
(8)
UN
United Nations Educational, Scientific and Cultural Organization.
Report by the Director-General of the Joint UN/UNESCO Seminar on Urbanization in Latin America (Santiago, Chile, 6-18 July 1959) Paris, 1960.
27p. (UNESCO/SS/28)

1. City growth - Latin America.

330
(07)
E55
United Nations, Educational, Scientific and Cultural Organization.
Ellis, Howard S
The teaching of economics in Latin America. Report submitted to the United Nations Educational, Scientific, and Cultural Organization (UNESCO), [and others] by Howard S. Ellis and others. Washington, Pan American Union, General Secretariat, Organization of American States, 1961.
100p. (Pan American Union. Studies and monographs, 1)

1. Economics - Study and teaching. I. Organization of American States. II. United Nations Educational, Scientific and Cultural Organization.

370
R212
United Nations Educational Scientific and Cultural Organisation.
Readings in the economics of education; a selection of articles, essays and texts from the works of economists, past and present, on the relationships between economics and education. Textes choisis sur l'économie de l'éducation: articles, essais et autres textes tirés des oeuvres anciennes ou récentes, d'économistes qui traite des rapports entre économie et éducation. Editorial advisory committee: Mary Jean Bowman and others. Paris, Unesco, 1968.
945p.

(Cont'd on next card)

R
6
(03:004.1)
H65
United Nations Educational, Scientific and Cultural Organization.
Holmstrom, J E
Report on interlingual scientific and technical dictionaries. Paris, UNESCO, 1951.
33 p. tables. (UNESCO publication 884)

Includes bibliography.

I. United Nations Educational, Scientific and Cultural Organization. II. Title. III. Title: Scientific and technical dictionaries.

058.7
:370
U54u
United Nations Educational, Scientific and Cultural Organization.
Unesco handbook of international exchanges. Paris, 1965.
861p.
At head of title: I 1965.

1. Educational exchanges - Direct.
2. International organizations - Direct.
I. Title: Handbook of international exchanges.
II. Title.

370
R212
Readings in the...1968. (Card 2)

English and/ or French.

1. Education - Economic effect. I. Bowman, Mary Jean. ed. II. United Nations Educational Scientific and Cultural Organisation. III. Title: Textes choisis sur l'économie de l'éducation.

002
U54
UNITED NATIONS, EDUCATIONAL, SCIENTIFIC, AND CULTURAL ORGANIZATION.
SCIENTIFIC AND TECHNICAL DOCUMENTATION CENTRES; UNESCO'S CONTRIBUTION TO THEIR DEVELOPMENT. PARIS, 1965.
55P.

1. DOCUMENTATION. 2. LIBRARIES. I. TITLE.

002
UNu
1971
United Nations Educational, Scientific and Cultural Organization.
UNISIST. Intergovernmental Conference for the Establishment of a World Science Information System, Paris, 4-8 October 1971. Final report. Paris, 1971.
60 p.
Appx. Report and remarks of the U.S. Delegation to the Conference, prepared by Andrew A. Aines.
1. Documentation. 2. Library science. I. Aines, Andrew A. II. Intergovernmental Conference for the Establishment of a World Science Information System. Paris, 1971. III. Title.

VF
690.37
UN
U.N.E.S.C.O., (Science Cooperation Office for South Asia)
Regional symposium on "Scientific principles and their application in tropical building design and construction", Dec. 21st-25th, 1952; programme, abstracts of papers. New Delhi, National Institute of Science of India, [1952]
v.
Co-sponsored by National Institute of Sciences of India.

(see card 2)

058.7
:378
UN
1960
United Nations Educational, Scientific and Cultural Organization.
Study abroad. International handbook, fellowships, scholarships, educational exchange. 12th ed. Paris, 1960.
766p.

English, French and Spanish.

1. Universities and colleges - Directories. 2. Educational exchanges. I. Title.

002
UNu
United Nations Educational, Scientific and Cultural Organization.
Unisist. Synopsis of the feasibility study on a world science information system. Paris, Unesco, 1971.
92p.

2c.

1. Documentation. 2. Scientific research. 3. Cataloging. I. Title.

301.15
(8)
S25
United Nations Educational Scientific and
Cultural Organization.
Seminario Sobre Problemas de Urbanizacion en
America Latina, Santiago de Chile, 1959.
La urbanizacion en America Latina; documentos
del Seminario Sobre Problemas de Urbanizacion
en America Latina, patrocinado conjuntamente
por la ONU, la CEPAL y la Unesco, con la co-
operacion de la OIT y la OEA, Santiago de Chile,
del 6 al 18 de julio de 1959. Preparada por
Philip M. Hauser. New York, United Nations
Educational Scientific and Cultural Organization, 1962.
340p. (Tecnologia y sociedad)
Bibliography: p. 338-340.
1. City growth - Latin America.
(Cont'd on next card)

058.7
:500
UN
1969
United Nations Educational Scientific and
Cultural Organization.
World guide to technical information and
documentation services. New York, 1969.
287p.

1. Science - Direct. 2. Documentation -
Direct. 3. Technology - Direct. I. Title.

330
UNre
United Nations Interregional Seminar on
Development Policies and Planning in Relation
to Urbanization.
Report of the United Nations Interregional
Seminar on Development Policies and Planning
in Relation to Urbanization, Pittsburgh, Pa.,
24 Oct. - 4 Nov. 1966. New York, United
Nations, 1967.
74p. (United Nations Document ST/TAO/Ser.
C/97)
1. Economic development. 2. City growth.
3. Planning. 4. Population.

301.15
(8)
S25
Seminario Sobre Problemas de Urbanización en
América Latina, Santiago de Chile, 1959.
La urbanización...1962   (Card 2)

2. Latin America - City growth. I. Hauser,
Philip M., ed. II. United Nations Educational
Scientific and Cultural Organization.

341.1
F56
United Nations Educational, Scientific, and
Cultural Organization.
Florida. University. [School of] Inter-
American Studies.
Latin America and UNESCO, the first five
years, by Frederick Elvyn Kidder.
Gainesville, Fla., 1960.
38p. (Latin American monograph no. 12)

1. United Nations Educational, Scientific,
and Cultural Organization. I. Kidder,
Frederick Elvyn.

330
UNrep
1969
United Nations Interregional Seminar on
Physical Planning, for Urban, Regional and
National Development, Bucharest, Romania,
1969.
Report. New York, United Nations, 1971.
43p. (United Nations. [Document]
ST/TAO/SER.C/132)

1. Economic planning. 2. United Nations.

300.15
(7295)
U51
United Nations Educational, Scientific and
Cultural Organization.
The use of social research in a community
education programme. [New York] [1954?]
50p. (Its Educational studies and docu-
ments no. 10)
"Prepared by the Analysis Unit of the
Division of Community Education, Dept. of
Education, San Juan, Puerto Rico, and the
Survey Research Centre of the University
of Michigan."
Bibliography: p. 47-49.
(Cont'd on next card)

327
U54
The United Nations in the 1970's.
United Nations Association of the United States
of America.
The United Nations in the 1970's. A strategy
for a unique era in the affairs of nations.
A report of a National Policy Panel. New York,
1971.
88p.

1. International relations. I. Title.

United Nations International Children's
Emergency Fund.

see

UNICEF.

300.15
(7295)
U51
United Nations Educational, Scientific and
Cultural Organization.   The use of
social research...1954.   (Card 2)

1. Social science research - Puerto Rico.
2. Education - Puerto Rico. I. Puerto Rico.
Dept. of Education. (Division of Community
Education) II. Michigan. University. Survey
Research Center. III. Title.

711.4
:670
(016)
UN
United Nations Industrial Development
Organization, Vienna.
Industrial location and regional
development; an annotated bibliography.
New York, 1970.
165p. (ID/43)

1. Industrial location - Bibliography.
2. Economic development - Bibliography.
I. Title.

711.417
UNp
1967
United Nations Meeting of the Group of Experts on
Metropolitan Planning and Development, Stockholm,
1961.
United Nations. (Dept. of Economic and
Social Affairs)
Planning of metropolitan areas and new
towns. Meeting of the United Nations,
Group of Experts on Metropolitan Planning and
Development, Stockholm, 14-30, September
1961 [and United Nations Symposium on the
Planning and Development of New Towns,
Moscow, 24 August-7 September 1964. New
York, 1967.
255p. (Its Document) ST/SOA/65)
1. Metropolitan area planning. 2. New
(Continued on next card)

712.25
V12
United Nations Educational, Scientific and
Cultural Organization.
Vacations abroad; courses, study tours,
work camps, 1
19
Paris, United Nations Educational, Scientific
and Cultural Organization, 19
v.
English, French and Spanish.
For complete information see shelflist.
1. Recreation.   2. Universities and
colleges.   I. United Nations
Educational,   Scientific and
Cultural Organi-   zation.

690.022
(4)
UN
United Nations Industrial Development
Organization, Vienna.
Production of prefabricated wooden houses.
New York, United Nations, 1971.
94p. (United Nations. ID/61 ID/WG.45/5
rev. 1)

1. Prefabricated construction - Europe.
I. Title.

711.417
UNp
1967
United Nations. (Dept. of Economic and
Social Affairs) Planning of metropolitan
areas...1967.   (Card 2)

towns. I. United Nations Meeting of the
Group of Experts on Metropolitan Planning and
Development, Stockholm, 1961. II. United
Nations Symposium on the Planning and Develop-
ment of New Towns, Moscow, 1964. III. Title.

711.417
(016)
UN
United Nations Educational, Scientific and
Cultural Organization.
Les villes nouvelles; eléments d'une bibliographie annotée réunis. New towns; a
selected annotated bibliography, comp. by
Jean Viet. Paris, 1960.
82p. (Reports and papers in the social
sciences no. 12, 1960)

1. New towns - Bibliography. I. Viet, Jean, comp.

FOLIO
300.2
(016)
UNR
UNITED NATIONS INFORMATION OFFICE, NEW
YORK.
RESEARCH AND POSTWAR PLANNING;
BIBILIOGRAPHY. PT. 1=6,10-18   NEW
YORK, 1942=
15v.
1. RECONSTRUCTION - BIBLIOGRAPHY.
2. PLANNING - BIBLIOGRAPHY.   I. TITLE.
II. TITLE: POSTWAR PLANNING.

728.1
(676)
B56
United Nations Mission to Kenya on Housing.
Bloomberg, Lawrence Nelson, 1909-
United Nations Mission to Kenya on Housing
[report] prepared for the Government of Kenya by
Lawrence N. Bloomberg and Charles Abrams,
appointed under the United Nations Programme of
Technical Assistance. [Nairobi] United Nations,
Commissioner for Technical Assistance, Dept. of
Economic and Social Affairs, 1964.
79p.
1. Housing - Kenya. I. Abrams, Charles,
1901-   jt. au. II. Title.

058.7
:500
U54
United Nations. Educational, Scientific, and
Cultural Organization.
World guide to science information and docu-
mentation services. Paris, 1965.
211 p.

Text in English and French.

1. Science - Direct. I. Title.

691.16
L42
United Nations Inter-regional Conference, Petro-
chemical Industries in Developing Countries,
Tehran, 1964.
Lien, Arthur P
Plastics as construction materials for de-
veloping countries. A paper presented at the
Inter-Regional Conference, Petrochemical In-
dustries in Developing Countries, United Na-
tions, Tehran, Iran, November 22, 1964.
Columbus, Ohio, Battelle Memorial Institute,
1964.
40p.

1. Plastics. 2. Building materials.
I. Battelle Memorial Institute.   (over)

728.1
/711.4
UN
No. 9
United Nations Regional Seminar on Housing
and Community Development, New Delhi, 1954.
United Nations. (Dept. of) Social Affairs.
International action in Asia and the
Far East. [New York] 1955.
131 p. (Its Housing, building and
planning no. 9)

Contents.-pt. 1 - United Nations
programme in housing, building and planning. -
pt. 2 - United Nations Seminar on housing and
community improvement: papers and reports.

330 (83) B64 v.2	United Nations Research Institute for Social Development. Boisier, Sergio. Case studies of information systems for regional development. v.2. Chile. Geneva, United Nations Research Institute for Social Development, 1970. 76p. (United Nations Research Institute for Social Development. Report no. 70.9) Bibliography: p. 77-78. 1. Economic development - Chile. 2. Automation I. United Nations Research Institute for Social Development. I. Title: Informational systems for regional deve lopment.

341.1 :361 G67	United Nations Research Institute for Social Development. Gosselin, G Le changement social et les institutions du development dans une population refugiee. Geneva, United Nations Research Institute for Social Development, 1970. 78p. (United Nations Research Institute for Social Development. Report no. 70.17) 1. Displaced persons. 2. Social change. I. United Nations Research Institute for Social Development. II. Title.

334 (5) UN	United Nations Research Institute for Social Development. Cooperatives and planned change in Asian rural communities: case studies and diaries. Ed. by Inayatullah. Geneva, 1970. 349p. (Rural institutions and planned change, vol. VI) 1. Cooperatives - Asia. I. Inayatullah, ed. II. Title. (Series: Rural institutions and planned change, vol. 6)

334 (8) B67	United Nations Research Institute for Social Development. Borda, Orlando Fals. Cooperatives and rural development in Latin America; an analytic report. Geneva, United Nations Research Institute for Social Development, 1971. 147p. (Rural institutions and planned change, vol. 3; report no. 71.1; (UNRISD/71/C.2)) 1. Cooperatives - Latin America. 2. Rural planning - Latin America. I. United Nations Research Institute for Social Development. II. Title.

658.564 M12co	United Nations Research Institute for Social Development. McGranahan, D V Contents and measurement of socio-economic development; an empirical enquiry, by D.V. McGranahan and others. Geneva, United Nations Research Institute for Social Development, 1970. 162p. (United Nations Research Institute for Social Development. Report no. 70.10) 1. Automation - Social effect. 2. Economic development. I. United Nations Research Institute for Social Development. II. Title.

360 H271	United Nations Research Institute for Social Development. Hermansen, Tormod. Interregional allocation of investments for social and economic development; an elementary model approach to analysis. Geneva, United Nations Research Institute for Social Development, 1970. 61p. (United Nations Research Institute for Social Development. Report no. 70.4) Bibliography: p. 55-61. 1. Social conditions. 2. Economic development. I. United Nations Research Institute for Social Development. II. Title.

658.564 C65e pt.1	United Nations Research Institute for Social Development. Collette, J M Etude sur les systemes de decision. Premiere partie. Geneva, United Nations Research Institute for Social Development, 1970. 220p. (United Nations Research Institute for Social Development. Report no. 70.11/1) 1. Automation - Social effect. I. United Nations Research Institute for Social Development.

330 (4972) B27 v.3	United Nations Research Institute for Social Development. Bernard, Philippe. Growth poles and growth centres in regional development. v.3. Growth poles and growth centres as instruments of regional development and modernization with special reference to Bulgaria and France. Geneva, United Nations Research Institute for Social Development, 1970. 97p. (United Nations Research Institute for Social Development. Report no. 70.14) 1. Economic development - Bulgaria. 2. Economic development - France. I. United Nations Research Institute for Social Development. II. Title.

330 (669) M11	United Nations Research Institute for Social Development. Mabogunje, Akin L Growth poles and growth centres in the regional development of Nigeria. Geneva, United Nations Research Institute for Social Development, 1971. 81p. (Report no. 71.3) At head of title: United Nations Research Institute for Social Development. Nueva Universidad Autonoma de Madrid. Bibliography: p. 80-81. 1. Economic development - Nigeria. I. United Nations Research Institute for Social Develop- ment. II. Title.

333.32 P15	United Nations Research Institute for Social Development. Palmier, L H Organization of land redistribution Geneva, United Nations Research Institute for Social Development, 1970. 80p. (United Nations Research Institute for Social Development. Report no. 70.1) 1. Land tenure. 2. Land economics. 3. Agriculture. I. United Nations Research Institute for Social Development. II. Title: Land redistributio III. Title.

334 (60) UN	United Nations Research Institute for Social Development. Rural cooperatives and planned change in Africa: case materials, ed. by Raymond Apthorpe. Geneva, 1970. 361p. (Rural institutions and planned change, vol. IV) 1. Cooperatives - Africa. I. Apthorpe, Raymond, ed. II. Title. (Series: Rural institutions and planned change, vol. 4)

711.3 (6761) T71	United Nations Research Institute for Social Development. Trappe, P Social change and development institutions in a refugee population (Development from below as an alternative: the case of the Nakapiripirit Settlement Scheme in Urganda) Prepared for the Institute and the Office of the High Commissioner by P. Trappe. Geneva, United Nations Research Institute for Social Development, 1971. 102p. (Report no. 71.2) Bibliography: p. 93-95. 1. Rural planning - Uganda. I. United Nations Research Institute for Social Development. II. Title.

360 (82) G27	United Nations Research Institute for Social Development. Germani, Gino. Social modernization and economic development in Argentina. Geneva, United Nations Research Institute for Social Development, 1970. 75p. (United Nations Research Institute for Social Development. Report no. 70.6) Bibliography: p. 72-75. 1. Social conditions - Argentina. 2. Economic development - Argentina. I. United Nations Research Institute for Social Development. II. Title.

300.15 B18	United Nations Research Institute for Social Development. Baudot, Jacques. Social prognosis. Geneva, United Nations Research Institute for Social Development, 1970. 41p. (United Nations Research Institute for Social Development. Report no. 70.19) 1. Social science research. I. United Nations Research Institute for Social Development. II. Title.

647.1 D72	United Nations Research Institute for Social Development. Drewnowski, Jan. Studies in the measurement of levels of living and welfare. Geneva, United Nations Research Institute for Social Development, 1970. 103p. (United Nations Research Institute for Social Development. Report no. 70.3) 1. Cost and standard of living. 2. Family income and expenditure. 3. Social welfare. I. United Nations Research Institute for Social Development.

360 D72	United Nations Research Institute for Social Development. Drewnowski, Jan. Studies in the methodology of social planning, by Jan Drewnowski and Muthu Subramanian with the cooperation of Claude Richard-Proust. Geneva, United Nations Research Institute for Social Development, 1970. 127p. (United Nations Research Institute for Social Development. Report no. 70.5) 1. Social conditions. 2. Automation - Social effect. I. Subramanian, Muthu, jt. au. II. United Nations Research Institute for Social Development. III. Title: Social planning.

630 D85	United Nations Research Institute for Social Development. Dumont, Rene. Notes sur les implications sociales de la revolution verte dans quelques pays d'Afrique. New York, Institut de Recherche des Nations Unies pour le Development Social, 1971. 166p. (Report no. 17.5) 1. Agriculture. I. United Nations Research Institute for Social Development.

330 (76193) 832	United Nations Scientific Conference on the Conservation and Utilization of Resources, Shelton, Barrett. Lake Success, New York, 1949. The Decatur story: an address, United Nations Scientific Conference on the Conservation and Utilization of Resources, Lake Success, New York, September 5, 1949. [n.p.] Tennessee Valley Authority, 1949. 11 p. 1. Economic base studies - Decatur, Ala. 2. Tennessee Valley Authority. I. United Nations Scientific Conference on the Conservation and Utilization of Resources, Lake Success, New York, 1949. II. Title.

728.1 (62) UN 3 C	United Nations Seminar on Financing of Housing and Related Community Facilities for the Arab States, Cairo, United Arab Republic, 1963. Report. New York, United Nations, 1965. 125p. (U.N. [Document] ST/TAO/SER.C.72) Bibliography: p. 106-114. 1. Housing - Egypt. 2. Housing - Congresses. 3. Mortgage finance - Egypt. I. United Nations.

341.1 UNi 1969	United Nations Institute for Training and Research. Report of the Executive Director of the United Nations Institute for Training and Research. New York, 1969. 71p. General Assembly. Official records: twenty-fourth session, supplement no. 15 (A/7615) 1. International organizations.

728.1 (62) UN	United Nations Seminar on Financing of Housing and Related Community Facilities for the Arab States, Cairo, United Arab Republic, 1963. Report. New York, United Nations, 1965. 125p. (U.N. [Document] ST/TAO/SER.C.72) Bibliography: p. 106-114. 1. Housing - Egypt. 2. Housing - Congresses. 3. Mortgage finance - Egypt. I. United Nations.

728.1
(489)
D25ℓ
United Nations Seminar on Housing Statistics and Programmes for Africa.
Denmark. Ministry of Housing.
Le logement au Danemark. Copenhague, 1966.
51p.

At head of title: United Nations Seminar on Housing Statistics and Programmes for Africa.

1. Housing - Denmark. I. United Nations Seminar on Housing Statistics and Programmes for Africa.

327
S71u
UN, U.S. participation in the.
U.S. Dept. of State.
US participation in the UN; report by the President to the Congress for the year 1952. [Washington, Govt. Print. Off., 1953]
285 p.   charts, tables.   (Its Publication 5034)

At head of title: 83d Congress, 1st session, House document no. 222.

1. International relations. 2. Non-self governing territories. 3. Under-developed countries. I. U.S. President. II. Title.   Title: UN, U. participation in the.

728.1
(7531)
F45
United Planning Organization.
Finkelstein, V R
Housing inventory for the District of Columbia and the UPO target area as of December, 1966. [Wash., United Planning Organization] 1968.
29p.

1. Low-income housing - District of Columbia. 2. Housing surveys - District of Columbia metropolitan area. I. Title. II. United Planning Organization.

711.417
UNt
United Nations Seminar on Physical Planning Techniques for the Construction of New Towns, Moscow, 1968.
Report. New York, 1968.
52p. (United Nations document ST/TAO/SER.C/127)

1. New towns. 2. City planning. 3. Community development.

728.1
1336.18
(7471)
J25
UNITED NEIGHBORHOOD HOUSES OF NEW YORK.
JENKINS, SUSAN.
COMMUNITY RELATIONS IN PUBLIC HOUSING AREAS, CONTAINING A REPORT ON RECREATIONAL AND COMMUNITY FACILITIES IN NEW YORK CITY'S PUBLIC HOUSING PROJECTS PREPARED BY THE HOUSING COMMITTEE OF THE UNITED NEIGHBORHOOD HOUSES, AND HIGHLIGHTS OF A CONFERENCE IN FEBRUARY 1946 ... NEW YORK, UNITED NEIGHBORHOOD HOUSES OF NEW YORK, INC., 1946.
1 V. (UNPAGED)

1. PUBLIC HOUSING - SOCIAL EFFECT
(CONTINUED ON NEXT CARD)

728.1
(753)
H68
United Planning Organization.
Housing Development Corp., Wash., D.C.
Housing proposal for the National Capital Area submitted by Housing Development Corp. through the United Planning Organization. Amended program. Wash., 1966.
39p.

1. Housing projects - District of Columbia. 2. Nonprofit housing organizations. I. United Planning Organization. II. Title.

711.3
UNu
United Nations Seminar on Regional Planning, Tokyo, 1958.
United Nations Seminar on Regional Planning, Tokyo, 28 July to 8 August 1958. New York, 1958.
51p. (ST/TAA,ser.C/35)

1. Regional planning - Congresses.

728.1
1336.18
(7471)
J25
JENKINS, SUSAN. COMMUNITY RELATIONS IN ...1946.   (CARD 2)

- NEW YORK (CITY) I. UNITED NEIGHBORHOOD HOUSES OF NEW YORK. II. TITLE.

330
U546
UNITED PLANNING ORGANIZATION.
PROGRAM SUMMARIES. WASHINGTON, 1965.
16P.

"DRAFT, NOT FOR PUBLICATION."

1. ECONOMIC CONDITIONS - DISTRICT OF COLUMBIA. 2. HOUSING - DISTRICT OF COLUMBIA. 3. EMPLOYMENT.

711.417
UNp
1967
United Nations Symposium on the Planning and Development of New Towns, Moscow, 1964.
United Nations. (Dept. of Economic and Social Affairs)
Planning of metropolitan areas and new towns. Meeting of the United Nations, Group of Experts on Metropolitan Planning and Development, Stockholm, 14-30, September 1961 [and] United Nations Symposium on the Planning and Development of New Towns, Moscow, 24 August-7 September 1964. New York, 1967.
255p. (Its Document ST/SOA/65)
1. Metropolitan area planning. 2. New

(continued on next card)

301.158
B76
United Planning Organization.
Brooks, Ed
Analysis of the allocation of youth program funds among the twenty neighborhood planning council areas. [Wash.] 1969.
24p.
1. Youth. 2. Family income and expenditure - District of Columbia. 3. Poverty. I. Title. II. United Planning Organization.

711.585
(753)
U54
United Planning Organization.
Social function plan. A plan of social action for community renewal in the District of Columbia. Prepared for District of Columbia Community Renewal Program. [Wash.] 1965.
114p.
U.S. Dept. of Housing and Urban Development. Community Renewal Program.
1. Urban renewal - District of Columbia. 2. Social conditions - District of Columbia. I. District of Columbia - Community Renewal Program. II. Title. III. U.S. HUD-CRP, District of Columbia.

711.417
UNp
1967
United Nations. (Dept. of Economic and Social Affairs) Planning of metropolitan areas...1967.   (Card 2)

towns. I. United Nations Meeting of the Group of Experts on Metropolitan Planning and Development, Stockholm, 1961. II. United Nations Symposium on the Planning and Development of New Towns, Moscow, 1964. III. Title.

5574
UNITED PLANNING ORGANIZATION, WASHINGTON, D.C.
SOCIAL FUNCTION STUDY, A GEOGRAPHIC ANALYSIS OF SOCIAL PATTERNS IN THE DISTRICT OF COLUMBIA. WASHINGTON, 1965.
50F. (HUD 701 REPORT)

1. SOCIAL CONDITIONS - DISTRICT OF COLUMBIA. I. HUD. 701. DISTRICT OF COLUMBIA.

361
C65e
United Planning Organization.
U.S. Congress. House. Committee on Education and Labor.
Antipoverty in the District of Columbia. Hearing before the Task Force on Antipoverty in the District of Columbia of the Committee on Education and Labor, House of Representatives, Eighty-ninth Congress, second session on investigation of the United Planning Organization in the District of Columbia and its relation to poverty. Wash., Govt. Print. Off., 1966.
105p.

(Cont'd on next card)

711.417
UN
United Nations Symposium on the Planning and Development of New Towns, Moscow, USSR, 1964.
Report. New York, United Nations, 1966.
48p. ([U.N. Document] ST/TAO/SER.C/79)

1. New towns. I. United Nations.

301.158
B76y
United Planning Organization, Wash., D.C.
Brooks, Ed.
Youth program fund allocations revisited. [Wash.] Research Div., United Planning Organization, 1969.
12p.

2. Poverty. 1. Youth. I. United Planning Organization, Wash., D.C. II. Title.

361
C65e
U.S. Congress. House. Committee on Education and Labor. Antipoverty in the District of Columbia... 1966   (Card 2)

Hearing held March 14, 1966.

1. Public assistance. 2. Social welfare. 3. U.S. United Planning Organization.

628.1
UN
UNITED NATIONS. WATER RESOURCES DEVELOPMENT CENTRE.
LARGE-SCALE GROUND-WATER DEVELOPMENT. NEW YORK, 1960.
84P.

1. WATER RESOURCES. I. TITLE.

330
(7531)
U54
UNITED PLANNING ORGANIZATION.
FACTS; UNITED PLANNING ORGANIZATION OF THE NATIONAL CAPITAL AREA. WASHINGTON, D.C., 1965.
8P.

1. ECONOMIC CONDITIONS - DISTRICT OF COLUMBIA METROPOLITAN AREA. 2. HOUSING - DISTRICT OF COLUMBIA METROPOLITAN AREA.

728.2
U54c
UNITED PRESBYTERIAN CHURCH IN THE U.S.A.
THE CHURCH AND THE APARTMENT HOUSE. PRELIMINARY FINDINGS FOR DISCUSSION IN SYNODS AND PRESBYTERIES AND FURTHER TESTING IN LOCAL PARISHES. NEW YORK, DIVISION OF EVANGELISM AND DEPT. OF THE URBAN CHURCH, UNITED PRESBYTERIAN CHURCH IN THE U.S.A., 1963.
32P.

1. APARTMENT HOUSES. 2. CHURCH AND SOCIAL PROBLEMS. I. TITLE.

301
U54   United Presbyterian Church.
     Residential desegregation; the church's
new frontier. Philadelphia, 1958.
     39p.

     At head of title: A social progress
reprint.

     1. Church and social problems.
     2. Minority groups - Housing.

728.1
U54ho   United Presbyterian Church in the U.S.A.
     Housing and the Church. New York, 1967.
     6p. (Up to date, no. 11)

     1. Low income housing. 2. Housing and the
Church. I. Up to date. II. Title.

728.1
U54m   United Presbyterian Church in the U.S.A.
     Mission through housing. Guidelines,
case studies, resources. New York, United
Presbyterian Church in the U.S. A., Office
of Church and Housing, 1967.
     63p.

     1. Low income housing. 2. Church and
social problems. I. Title.

     United Presbyterian Church in the U.S.A.
711.4
(8) Rycroft, W   Stanley.
R92   A study of urbanization in Latin America,
by W. Stanley Rycroft and Myrtle M. Clemmer.
New York, Office for Research, Commission on
Ecumenical Mission and Relations, United
Presbyterian Church in the U.S.A., 1962.
     130p.

     1. City planning - Latin America.
     2. Economic development - Latin America.
I. Clemmer, Myrtle M., jt. au. II. United
Presbyterian   Church in the
U.S.A.   III. Title: Urbani-
zation in Latin   America.

VF
330
(678)
U54p   United Republic of Tanzania. Ministry of
     Economic Affairs and Development
     Planning.
     Progress report on the implementation of
the five-year development plan (Public
sector) 1st-   1964/65-

     Dar es Salaam, 1965-
        v.
     Report year ends June 30.
     For complete information see main card.

     1. Economic   conditions -
Tanzania.

388
N67fu   United Research, Inc.
     Norling, A   H
     Future transportation needs. Cambridge,
Mass., United Research, inc., 1963.
     1v.

     Distributed by U.S. Clearinghouse for
Federal Scientific and Technical Information as N 64 25006.

     1. Transportation. 2. Journey to work.
I. United Research, inc. II. Title.

388
:657   United Research, inc.
U54   Responsibility accounting system and work
measurement for the motor carrier industry.
Prepared for Office of Transportation
Research, Office of the Under Secretary for
Transportation, U.S. Dept. of Commerce, Wash.,
D.C. Cambridge, Mass., 1966.
     1v.
     CFSTI PB 173202-2

     1. Transportation - Accounting. I. U.S.
Dept. of Transportation. II. Title.